SUSAN THERAN
Publisher & Editorial Director

KATHERYN ACERBO
Editor

LEONARD'S

ANNUAL PRICE INDEX OF

PRINTS • POSTERS

& PHOTOGRAPHS

Volume 2
July 1, 1992 – June 30, 1993

AUCTION INDEX, INC.
Newton, MA

Editorial staff:

Joyce Annanian
Sarah Betzer
Linda Bellamy
Fabia Bird
Kristin Dalton
Edward DeLeon
Andrea DesJardins
Allison Goldberg
Jennifer Hays
Paula Jacoff
Margaret McDonald
Lauren Muckian
Jennifer Shafer
Faye Stark
Trudy Weinstein
Shirley Yee

Circulation manager: Kristin Dalton
German translations: Christina Lanzel
Print consultant: Norma Steinberg

Published by Auction Index, Inc.
30 Valentine Park, Newton, Massachusetts 02165

Subscriptions may be obtained from Auction Index, Inc.,
or from booksellers and subscription agents. Back issues
of Volume #1 are available for $195.

Library of Congress Catalog Card Number: NE85.L46
International Standard Special Number: 1064-0452
International Standard Book Number: 0-918819-32-6

From the Publisher
by Susan Theran

Each year Auction Index compiles a statistical report from over 40,000 print and photography lots. The top lots each season are sold at many of the same houses. The list below is comprised of the top lots at each of these houses. Refer to the specific citation for each lot for further information on date of sale and catalogue raisonné.

Christie-London	Pablo Picasso	*The Vollard Suite*	$998,910*
Sotheby-NY	Rembrandt	*Jan Six*	$618,500*
Christie-NY	Edward S. Curtis	*North American Indian, 20 Vol*	$396,000*
Sotheby-London	Giovanni Battista Piranesi	*Vedute Di Roma; 19 Vol*	$297,654*
Kornfeld	Erich Heckel	*Brucke Mappe 1911*	$235,860*
Hauswedell/Nolte	Edvard Munch	*Melancholie*	$155,367*
Sotheby-Japan	Pablo Picasso	*Le Repas Frugal*	$122,542*
Grisebach	Wassily Kandinsky	*Der Spiegel*	$116,848*
Lempertz	Otto Dix	*Der Krieg*	$109,249*
Loudmer	Francisco de Goya	*Los Caprichos*	$59,936*
Picard	Pierre Auguste Renoir	*L'Enfant Au Biscuit*	$57,540*
Finarte S.A.	Giorgio Morandi	*Natura Morta Con Oggetti Bianchi Su Fondo Scuro, 1931*	$55,539*
Butterfield	Edward S. Curtis	*North American Indian, 20 Vol*	$55,539*
Karl/Faber	Otto Dix	*Leonie*	$53,393*
Christie-East	Anonymous	*Poster:The Devil is a Woman, 1935*	$46,200*
Swann	Mathew Brady	*Sample Book from Brady's National Photographic Art Gallery*	$41,800*
Ader Tajan	Pierre Auguste Renoir	*Le Chapeau Epingle*	$39,307*
Bassenge	Edvard Munch	*Eifersucht*	$36,885*
Winterberg	Rembrandt	*Die Windmuhle*	$34,451*
Julia	Anonymous	*E & J Burke Ale Poster, c. 1881*	$33,000*
Phillips-London	Giovanni Battista Piranesi	*Carceri D'Invenzione: Sixteen*	$31,664*
Camden	Anonymous	*City Lights, 1931 -Movie Poster*	$30,800*
Finarte-Milan	Giorgio Morandi	*Natura Morta Con La Tazzina Biancia A Sinistra, 1930*	$30,296*
Skinner	Odilon Redon	*Arbre, 1982*	$26.400*
Doyle	John James Audubon	*American Flamingo, 1838*	$25,300*
Germann	Erich Heckel	*Weisse Pferde*	$24,704*
AB Stockholm	David Hockney	*Hotel Acatlan: Two Weeks Later*	$23,725*
Hindman	Paul Cezanne	*Les Baigneurs*	$22,000*
Dunning	John Lennon	*Bag One, 1970:Fourteen*	$22,000*
Granier	Henri de Toulouse-Lautrec	*Mademoisell Marcelle Lender, En Buste, 1895*	$21,722*
Hartung	Francisco de Goya	*Los Caprichos, c 1855:Eighty*	$20,338*

*includes buyer premium

Explanatory Notes

Auction Index, Inc. has compiled in *Leonard's ANNUAL Price Index of Prints, Posters, & Photographs* a complete listing of the prices realized at auctions worldwide. Great care has been taken to include both minor and major sales; there is *no* price cutoff for sales reported. Miscellaneous offerings are not included; sets or pairs and portfolios and some books are listed in this index.

The data has been organized alphabetically by artist, and under each artist alphabetically by title. Anonymous prints and photographs are listed under "Anonymous Prints" and "Anonymous Photographs". Posters that are not attributed to an artist are listed under "Anonymous Posters"; there is also a separate heading titled "Anonymous Poster - Movie."

The title field (in italics) also includes a catalogue raisonné citation if given and the date of a vintage print. In many print catalogues the full name of the author of a catalogue raisonné is given in the first lot cited and abbreviated to a letter in subsequent citations. The citations in this book are drawn directly from auction catalogues which may vary in their format; the information in our database reflects these variables. The field of photography technically has no catalogue raisonnés, but auction house experts frequently cite a well-known book or journal where the image has appeared. Following our bibliography is a list of photography monographs frequently cited. The term "vintage print" refers to a print or photograph that has been printed at the time it was executed. These dates appear in the title field. Oftentimes a print or photograph may have been printed later, either by the artist, or by another hand. This information follows the title field and appears as "1953 p. 1989" or "1953 p.l." (printed later).

The listings of some artists and their life dates may differ from one auction house to another. In recording the names of artists it is the policy of *Leonard's ANNUAL Price Index of Prints, Posters, & Photographs* to add life dates, nationalities, and full names whenever possible to provide as much information as we can about each artist as well as to facilitate the reading of each listing. Any name modifier such as "attributed to", "circle of," etc. will result in separate listings. When there is any doubt whatsoever as to the exact identity of an artist, the names and life dates as quoted in the catalogue have been left untouched. Whenever possible we have added nationalities and life dates. Listings for some artists, such as Eugene Atget or Diane Arbus, may vary in style. These artists had a large number of their works printed posthumously. We have listed these works exactly as they appear in the auction catalogue. In some catalogues, works by Diane Arbus printed by Neal Selkirk appear just under the name "ARBUS, Diane"; in others they are listed as "ARBUS, Diane and Neil SELKIRK." We have not attempted to merge these entries but have listed them exactly as they appear in each catalogue.

All prices reported include the buyer's premium. Taxes are not included. Premiums vary, refer to our list of sale dates to find the premium charged at each house. Works of art offered for sale at auction usually have a "reserve," a minimum that the owner will accept for the lot. Some European auction houses list their reserve; in the United States and elsewhere the reserve is usually a percentage of the estimate. If a lot does not reach reserve, it is bought-in. For these lots "BI" will appear instead of a price and the estimate or reserve will be listed. Sometimes a piece will not sell at auction but a sale price will be negotiated afterwards. If reported, these lots are listed with a price and "sold after sale."

All prices are reported in the currency in which they sold as well as the five major world currencies — the American dollar, British pound, French franc, German mark, and Japanese yen. Prices for lira are reported in the thousands. The price to the left of each title is always the price in U.S. dollars; the last information listed on each entry is the conversion to other currencies. If the native currency is other than the stated five it is also listed. Our programs report each price in the currency of the country of origin. If the price reported is in French francs, our conversion tables convert francs to dollars and then to marks, yen and pounds.

Most auction catalogues give a condition report for prints. Be aware that condition reports are somewhat subjective; what may be *good* condition in one expert's estimation might be only *fair* when described by another. Some auction houses state condition with a proviso when it affects the image. If a print is listed as "image in good condition" this does not mean the print is in good condition. All pertinent information has been recorded. All signatures, abbreviated as "s.," are in pencil unless otherwise stated.

The glossaries in this book have been compiled from terms found in auction catalogues and are comprehensive within the parameters cited. Additional definitions may be added with subsequent editions.

Leonard's ANNUAL Price Index of Prints, Posters, & Photographs is compiled from catalogues, price lists, and other information supplied by the auction houses listed. Great care has been taken to extract information accurately, but Auction Index, Inc. cannot be held responsible for errors accidentally made, or for unknowingly reproducing information subsequently found to be incorrect.

Glossary
by Norma S. Steinberg

General Terms on Condition, Papers, and Collecting

4to
: A paper size. See *quarto*.

8vo
: A paper size. See *octavo*.

AAA
: An abbreviation for the Associated American Artists, a gallery and publisher of fine art prints.

A.P.
: See *artist's proof*.

after letters
: An edition of a print pulled in its final *state* after the addition of the complete text or engraved inscription.

after
: When referring to prints *after* has several meanings which convey varying degrees of authenticity. The correct meaning of *after* refers to a *print* based on another artist's painting, drawing, or watercolor. The engraver or lithographer who executed the print may become as well–known as the original artist. The first edition of Audubon prints were engraved and colored mainly by Havell, a significant artist in his own right. All of the Audubon prints are *afters*, but they may be catalogued in different ways. *After* is also used incorrectly to mean a *restrike*. *After* is sometimes used as a catch–all term.

annotated
: Information handwritten by the artist, someone representing the estate, a collector, or someone else.

artist's proof
: An impression of a work different from the stated edition. Pulled during the creative process as an example of a stage in development, it may be called a *trial proof, proof, artist's proof* (A.P.), *edition proof, bon à tirer, hors commerce* (H.C..), or *épreuve d'artiste*. There is often a cachet to these prints, which may be numbered with Roman numerals or annotated. See *state*.

as issued
: This phrase indicates that the condition of the print, such as mounting to cardboard, which would ordinarily lower the print's value, is one the artist or publisher accepted or authorized.

attributed
: When a work is catalogued as attributed to an artist, this means there is a lesser degree of certainty as to its authenticity.

B.I.
: See *bought in*.

bears date
: Has a date which, in the opinion of the auction house, has been *inscribed* or written on the print by someone other than the artist.

bears signature
: Has a signature which, in the opinion of the auction house, has been added to the print in a hand other than the artist's.

before letters	That portion of a *run* pulled before the addition of the engraved text, titles, or inscriptions. Sometimes this is designated as *hors texte*.
blindstamp	An embossed stamp without color, outside the image, used to identify the publisher, printer, photographer, printmaking studio, collector, or, less often, the artist. The stamp may be a symbol, initials, or the full name and address. *Drystamp* and *chop* are synonyms.
bon à tirer	See *edition proof, artist's proof*.
bought-in	If a lot does not achieve its *reserve*, it is said to be bought-in by the auction house and will be returned to the consignor or offered at a later sale. It is increasingly common that, after the sale, the auction house will accept bids on a lot that has been bought-in. Also referred to as *BI*. See *sold after sale*.
buyer's premium	A surcharge that is added to the hammer price of each lot. Usually 10% in the United States, it varies elsewhere. A sales tax or VAT is charged on the total.
canceled	A plate or stone that was defaced after the edition to ensure that no reprinting would be possible. Sometimes the canceled prints are marketed, as with Picasso or Degas, or the marks are removed and the prints sold as if pre-cancellation.
catalogue raisonné	A published, systematic list of prints (or paintings) of an artist with titles, dates, sizes, states, editions, reprintings, and conditions of known prints.
chine-collé	An impression printed on a thin sheet of China or Japan paper that is adhered to a sheet of heavier artist backing paper and printed at the same time. It may be an intaglio or planographic print. *Chine-appliqué* is a synonym.
chop	See *blindstamp*.
collector's mark	A handwritten annotation, ink stamp or *drystamp* by the owner(s) of the work. This mark does not indicate authenticity but a work with a *provenance* from an important collection might indicate high quality.
colophon	When a group of works is presented as a whole (as in a portfolio or book), the *colophon* is the statement that presents the pertinent information for the work — the artist's signature, the *edition* size and *number*, publisher, and date. The *colophon* is most often on the last page, but sometimes the frontispiece serves as a *colophon*.
copyright	An inscription or mark under a print indicating protection by government acts. The *copyright* usually includes the date since copyrights are in effect for a specific number of years.
counterproof	A counterproof is made by running the print, before the ink has dried, through the press against another sheet. The resulting image is in reverse of the print, but in the same direction as the plate. Artists often make counterproofs during the printmaking process to facilitate corrections. See *offset*.

dated	Printed on that date, either as indicated in the plate or stone, by the hand of the artist, or as annotated or attested to by the *catalogue raisonné*.
deckle edge	The soft, naturally ragged edge of a handmade piece of paper, produced by small amounts of the paper pulp slipping beneath the sides of the frame (deckle) that holds the paper pulp on the screen.
dedicated	An annotation designating the recipient and/or donor of a gift or presentation print.
drystamp	See *blindstamp*.
E.A.	See *épreuve d'artiste*.
edition	A limited run of numbered impressions pulled by (or under the supervision of) the artist. This term is relevant only for works printed since about 1880, when artists like Whistler began to limit the number of *impressions* and to cancel the plate. Prints issued in various states are often considered different editions — e.g. *before letters*, *after letters*, or in different colors. See also *limited edition*, *numbered*.
edition proof	The specific impression used by the artist or designated to the printer as the standard against which every impression in the edition is to be judged. Also *bon à tirer*, literally "good to pull."
épreuve d'artiste	An *artist's proof*. Abbreviated *E.A.*
estate stamp	A stamp affixed to an impression by the family of an artist, or the executor of the artist's estate, which attests to the authenticity of the work. This was usually done when the work was found in the artist's studio after his or her death.
estimate	The price range within which an auction house expects to sell a particular *lot*. The estimate is frequently included in a printed catalogue.
folio	A paper size at least 12 inches in height. When used for books, it refers to a sheet folded in half to make four pages or two leaves. For prints it refers to size only.
foxing	Brown or pale patches of discoloration or stains on a sheet of paper. Foxing is caused either by impurities in the paper or by molds. It can be treated with conservation methods.
full margins	A phrase indicating that the margins have not been trimmed since the print was issued. Some cataloguers will use the phrase to mean only that the margins are wide.
gum arabic	This natural gum of the acacia tree is a main ingredient in lithographic etching materials. It was also used as a glaze on the surface of some hand–colored prints (e.g. Currier and Ives) to produce a darker tone in certain areas.
H.C.	See *hors commerce*.
hand-colored	A phrase indicating that watercolor, ink, or other colored medium has been applied to the print after printing.

hinge	The paper or tape used to affix a print to a backing.
hors commerce	A term refering to an *impression* outside the limits of the edition. The phrase originally meant "not for sale." Since these prints have a cachet, artists often produce a large number of *H.C.* prints. See *artist's proof, proof, bon à tirer*.
hors texte	See *before letters*.
identified	Information supplied by a label or collector's annotations.
impression	A print that is part of the stated edition or artist's proofs. Sometimes the term refers to the quality of the image.
initials	Letters of an artist's name rather than the full signature.
inscribed	The word *inscribed* has different meanings when used for paintings and prints. For prints it refers to the information (title, date, copyright, publisher, etc.) supplied in letterpress or engraving outside the image of the print. When the information is handwritten, the correct term is *annotated*.
laid down	A condition in which a print has been affixed to a mount to give it greater strength, to repair minor tears, or to prepare it for presentation. A paper conservator may be required to remove the backing. "Laid to cardboard as issued" means that the artist or publisher intended the use of a support. See *mounted*.
laid paper	Paper showing the pattern of vertical wire–marks and horizontal chain-lines produced by the papermaker's mould during its manufacture.
light staining	When a print has been exposed to strong or prolonged light, the discoloration (light or dark) is referred to as *light staining* or light toning.
limited edition	An annotation indicating that the edition is of a specific size without stating the number of prints in the edition.
losses	A general term for such changes to the pristine condition of a print as tears, skinning, rubbing, punctures, pin holes, and shavings. Remargined and reinforced refer to repairs of losses.
lot	An individual work or group of works offered for sale at one time.
margins	See *full margins* and *thread margins*.
mat staining	Discoloration of a print due to its contact with an acid-bearing mount, support surface or facing.
matrix	A term used to refer to the image when the printmaking process is uncertain, or to refer to the base on which the image to be printed is prepared, such as wood, linoleum, copper and so on.

mounted	Attached to a support or backing. Photographs are often affixed to mounts by the artist's studio to give them greater strength. Photography authentication stamps are often on the back of the mount. Both prints and photographs can be mounted. See *laid down* and *as issued*.
multiples	This refers to any art object that can be reproduced in quantity from a single original matrix. Prints were the first multiples, but many sculptures and pottery are now classed as multiples.
numbered	When a print is numbered, the numbering is usually handwritten below the image as a fraction. The top number is that of the particular *impression*, and the bottom number is the size of the *edition*. Since there may be *A.P.* prints in addition to the total *edition*, the denominator may be slightly below the number of *impressions* in the complete *run*. The print number is for cataloguing identification only and does not indicate the order of printing. No individual prints were numbered before the beginning of the twentieth century.
octavo	A sheet of paper about 9 x 6 inches. The size (and thus the term) results when a full sheet of about 18 x 24 inches is folded in eighths. This size is often used for botanical and scientific prints. Abbreviated *8vo*.
offset	A method of printing in which the inked image is transferred to an intermediary support, such as the rubber cylinders of an offset press, and from that to the sheet of paper. This term most often designates a print reproduced commercially in fairly large runs, or one that is photomechanically reproduced.
plate	A sheet of metal used for *intaglio* prints. The size of a print is sometimes measured by the area within visible plate marks.
portfolio	This term refers to both the group of prints presented together and the case that holds and protects the group of prints.
posthumous edition	The edition printed from the artist's plates after the artist has died. These prints might be authorized by the artist's estate but are not necessarily marked as posthumous printings, e.g. Rembrandt's.
printed later	*Impressions* printed after the regular edition, with or without the artist's knowledge or supervision.
printer's proof	A proof retained by the printer, sometimes the same as the *edition proof*.
proof	See *impression* and *artist's proof*.
provenance	The ownership history of a work of art. Most often this history is not known for a print, unless there is a *collector's mark*. Ex-collection indicates that the named person was a recent owner.
publisher	The association responsible for overseeing the printing and distribution of a print or series of prints.

pull	Each separate print that is placed in the press and removed as a finished print.
quarto	A sheet of paper about 9 x 12 inches. The size (and thus the term) results when a full sheet of about 18 x 24 inches is folded in fourths. Abbreviated *4to*.
recto	The side of the paper with the image.
registration	Prints that use more than one plate, such as multicolor prints, need a way of aligning the paper with the plates. These marks, called the registration, may be pinholes or symbols on the paper or plates, but most are not visible in the finished print.
reserve	The lowest price that a consignor will accept for a lot at auction. Reserves vary, but a useful guideline is that the reserve is about two-thirds of the low estimate.
restrike	This term has numerous meanings. Most commonly it refers to a reprint of a plate, without a hand signature or numbering, printed without the artist's supervision or knowledge. It may also refer to a reworked plate such as a posthumous edition of Rembrandt's prints. Improperly used, it refers to *photomechanical reproductions*.
run	The complete *edition*, including the stated edition, *proofs*, and *H.C.* prints.
series	Prints, in separate editions, that belong together because of related imagery, content, or style, or that the artist or publisher has designated as a series or set.
sheet	The measurement that records the dimensions of the entire sheet of paper. The image may fill the sheet, or it may be irregular, or the sheet may have been trimmed to the image.
sight	An approximate measure of the visible image generally recorded through the protective glass of the frame.
signed in pencil	Has a handwritten signature which, in the opinion of the auction house, is the artist's signature.
sold after sale	If a lot has been *bought-in* but purchased from the auction house after the sale, it is *sold after sale*.
state	One stage in the progress toward completion of the plate. Any impression that shows additional work on the plate is another state. Some artists (Rembrandt and Degas, for example) produced numerous states, each of which can stand on its own.
thread margins	Margins that are so narrow they can only be described as the width of a thread, less than one millimeter.
time staining	A condition that indicates evidence of dust and handling.
trial proof	A proof made during the creative process by the artist to check on the progress of the work. See *proof, artist's proof, edition proof*.

trimmed to subject	A phrase refering to a print with no margin, with not even a thread of paper remaining beyond the image. This is usually considered detrimental to the print, for it cannot be repaired adequately.
verso	The back of a sheet of paper.
water staining	Damage to a print from seeping water. It can be treated by a conservator.
watermark	A translucent identifying mark on a sheet of paper made during its manufacture by variations in pulp thickness. It may be a symbol (e.g., fool's cap or crown), a monogram, or company name that has been formed in wire on the papermaker's mould. Whatman paper often has the date of manufacture included in the watermark. Watermarks are usually read from the image side of the paper.
wove paper	Paper manufactured on a screen of brass wires all of the same weight that have been woven to produce an even, smooth surface. The paper itself is smooth and free of visible marks from the wires. See *laid paper*.

Print Media and Techniques

aquatint	An *intaglio* process. Particles of powdered resin are adhered to a metal plate with heat, either before or after *etching* the lines. When the plate is treated with acid, the acid corrodes it, leaving tiny depressions around each granule that retain ink when the plate is wiped. Treating (*stopping out*) some areas with varnish may vary the effect. Aquatints have broad tonal values and are thought to resemble ink or watercolor washes.
block print	A phrase used to describe certain woodcuts, particularly Japanese ukiyo–e prints, but sometimes also Provincetown or other Arts and Crafts relief prints. See *woodblock* and *woodcut*.
burin	A steel rod with a sharp beveled point that forms an incised V-shaped line in a metal plate. See *burr*.
burnished aquatint	A method by which the granular surface of an aquatint is partially polished with a scraper and burnisher to produce lighter areas or highlights.
burr	The ridge of metal raised on either side of a line incised by a *burin* or *drypoint* needle. The rough surface on a mezzotint is also called a burr. See *steel facing*.
carborundum	An abrasive powdered mixture, primarily silicon carbide, used to produce a dotted or tonal effect when the plate is passed through a press. Similar to a *sandpaper ground*.
chromolith-ograph	A color lithograph, specifically those of the nineteenth and early twentieth centuries, e.g., Louis Prang. Modern colored lithographs are usually catalogued as "printed in colors." In lithographs, each color requires a separate stone or plate.

cliché verre	See *photographic processes*.
collagraph	A relief plate formed by adding materials like found objects or textured materials to a solid base such as cardboard, metal, masonite, or plastic.
collotype	A *photomechanical* process. The preparation of a plate by coating a metal surface with light-sensitive gelatin. A photographic negative is placed on the surface and the two are exposed to light. The gelatin dries and hardens in proportion to the strength of the light transmitted through the negative. Collotypes are primarily lithographs and are especially good for reproducing watercolors, lithographs, drawings, and photographs.
copperplate	See *intaglio*.
crayon manner	An *intaglio* method. When a *roulette*, or other stippling tool, is used to prepare a *grounded* plate, the marks have a soft effect that resembles the crumbly look of a chalk, pastel, or crayon drawing. *Pastel–manner* prints use the same methodology, but separate plates are prepared for each color. See *ground*.
drypoint	An *intaglio* process by which the marks are scratched directly into the copper, zinc, or steel plate with a sharp steel point. The *burr* that is thrown up on either side of the line catches and holds extra ink, which produces a rich tone. The plate usually produces only twenty or thirty good impressions, for the *burr* is fragile The printer's skill is an important component in the quality of the print. See *steel facing*.
electrotyping	An electrolytic casting process used to copy a block or plate into a metal facsimile. Wood engravings made for book illustration in the late nineteenth century were printed mainly from electrotypes rather than the original wood, which might have deteriorated over the run.
embossed print	A print with an impression in high relief, that is, with all or part of the image higher than the unmarked areas. Some embossed prints have no color other than that of the paper.
engraving	Metal plates that have been engraved (incised) with a *burin*. The oldest form of *intaglio* prints, the word is sometimes used incorrectly to refer to all *intaglio* prints.
etching	An *intaglio* method in which the lines are bitten by acid. The plate is coated with an acid-resistant material (*ground*) through which the artist draws lines that expose the metal. The plate is immersed in acid until the lines are bitten into the plate. The ground is removed before the plate is inked for printing. See *ground*.
ground	The surface applied to an etching plate that is impervious to acid.
half-tone block	A photomechanical process that reproduces all gradations of black through white on a relief metal plate. The process produces thousands of black and white dots of varying sizes that give the illusion of a range of values. There are procedures for making half–tone blocks in all of the classes of printmaking (*intaglio, relief, planographic, stencil*). See *photogravure*.

heliogravure	See *photogravure*.
intaglio	One of the four major classes of printmaking. After a metal plate has been incised, ink is dabbed into the lines, the surface is cleaned by *wiping*, and dampened paper is placed onto the plate. The two are passed through a roller press, which lifts the ink up onto the paper. *Engraving, etching, aquatint, stipple, drypoint,* and *photogravure* are forms of intaglio prints. Intaglio is sometimes called *copperplate*.
letterpress	Printing of text from *relief* type, especially of pre–twentieth century broadsides and books. Since the advent of laser printing, phototypesetting, and offset lithograpy in the past twenty years, little is printed by letterpress.
lift ground	See *sugarlift process*.
line–block	A photomechanical process, similar to electrotyping, that reproduces a line drawing. Modern methods of line block use electronic scanners and automatic etching machines. Line-block facsimiles of woodcuts and wood engravings may be difficult to discern from the originals except that the lines in the reproductions are more consistent in tonality. *Photoengraving* is a synonym.
linocut	An abbreviation for linoleum cut, a popular relief process due to the soft, pliable nature of linoleum. Multicolor linocuts usually use separate blocks for each color.
lithograph	The *planographic* method, invented in 1792 by Aloïs Senefelder, based on the natural antipathy of water and grease. Greasy crayon or fluids are applied to a stone (or zinc or linoleum) matrix. Water is washed across the matrix and then ink is applied and adheres to the greasy crayon creating the image. Stone and paper are then passed together through a flat–bed scraper press. See *planography*.
metalcuts	A metal plate made in the fifteenth century by punching designs and dots into the surface of the metal and then printing the relief surfaces. Often called "dotted–manner" prints.
mezzotint	An *intaglio* process. The plate is prepared by completely roughening (grounding) the plate with a spiked tool (rocker) that produces an overall *burr*. The artist develops the image by scraping and burnishing to produce gradations of dark through light. This technique was used widely in 18th century England for the reproduction of portraits.
monoprint	A unique printmaking technique. The artist paints an image in printing ink on a sheet of metal, plexiglas, or other flat nonabsorbent surface and then runs it and a piece of paper through a press. Only one good impression can be made. Monotype is a synonym.
monotype	See *monoprint*.
multilevel color intaglio printing	A color print technique first developed by Stanley Hayter in the late 1920s. Various depths of etched lines retain the separate inks based on their individual viscosities. *Simultaneous color printing* and *viscosity printing* are synonyms.

Northeast Auctions tel: (603) 926-9800 *10% buyer's premium*
Ronald Bourgeault Auctioneer fax: (603) 926-3545
694 Lafayette Road
Hampton, New Hampshire 03842

August 1-2, 1992 - New Hampshire Auction, Important Americana and Folk Art
November 7, 1992 - New Hampshire Auction, Marine Paintings, Nautical Antiques, and American Furniture from the Marblehead Estate of Albert Goodhue, Jr.
November 8, 1992 - New Hampshire Auction, American and European Furniture, Clocks, Paintings, Decorative Arts and Oriental Carpets
March 20-21, 1993 - New Hampshire Auction, Important Americana, European Funiture, Clocks, Paintings, Decorative Arts and Oriental Rugs
May 29, 1993 - New Hampshire Auction, The Collection of John Howland Ricketson III
May 29-30, 1993 - New Hampshire Auction, Memorial Day Weekend Auction

Pescheteau-Badin-Ferrien tel: (1) 47 70 88 38 *Premiums: 12.67% up to 15,000FF*
16, rue de la Grange-Bateliere fax: (1) 48 01 04 45 *8.23% 15,001 to 40,000FF*
75009 Paris *6.15% 40,001 to 300,000FF*
France *4.96% 300,001 and over*

October 18, 1992 - Affiches d'Exposition Ouvrages de Documentation Livres Illustres, Estampes Modernes
January 28, 1993 - Affices D'Exposition Ouvrages de Documentation, Livres Illustres, Estampes Modernes
March 22, 1993 - Estampes Anciennes, Dessins et Tableaux Anciens, Estampes Modernes, Dessins et Tableaux Modernes, Armes, Militaria, Souvenirs Historiques, Objets Russes, Objets D'Art, Instruments de Musique, Mobilier Ancien et de Style, Tapisserie
April 4-5, 1993 - Tableaux Modernes, Sculptures XXe Siecle, Livres Illustres, Estampes Modernes et Multiples, L'Art du Verre, Dinanderie Contemporaine, Ceramiques XXe Siecle

Auction Phila Srl tel: (2) 54 66 506 *15% buyer's premium*
Corso di Porta Romana, 132 fax: (2) 54 57 912 *(includes V.A.T.)*
20122 Milan
Italy

May 18, 1993 - Auction (#67)

Phillips, Son and Neale tel: (71) 629 6602 *10% buyer's premium*
11 New Bond Street fax: (71) 629 8876 *(some include V.A.T.)*
London W1Y 0AS
England

October 13, 1992 - Twentieth Century Posters, To include a Collection from the Archives of Shell U.K. Ltd. (#29,088)
October 27, 1992 - Old Master, Modern, Decorative and Topographical Prints (#29,100)
November 30, 1992 - Old Master, Nineteenth and Twentieth Century and Contemporary Prints (#29,133)

John Moran Auctioneers, Inc.
3202 East Foothill Blvd.
Pasadena, California 91107

tel: (818) 793-1833
fax: (818) 798-2079

10% buyer's premium

November 10, 1992 - California and American Paintings
February 16, 1993 - California and American Paintings
June 15, 1993 - California and American Paintings

Jean Morelle-Pascale Marchandet
50, rue Sainte-Anne
75002 Paris
France

tel: 42 96 69 22
fax: 40 20 09 96

Premiums: 12.67 % up to 15,000FF
8.23% 15,001 to 40,000FF
6.15% 40,001 to 300,000FF
4.96% 300,001 and over

January 31, 1993 - La Danse et Les Arts du Spectacle
February 13, 1993 - Objets de Pub, Affiches de Pub

Kunsthaus am Museum
Drususgasse 1-5
5000 Koln 1
Germany

tel: (2 21) 25 20 57
fax: (2 21) 23 60 77

15% buyer's premium

November 13-14, 1992 - Moderne Kunst (#144)
April 24, 1993 - Moderne Kunst (#147)

Myers, Antiques &
Auction Gallery
1600 4th Street North
St. Petersburg, Florida 33704

tel: (813) 823-3249
fax: (813) 823-3247

10% buyer's premium

March 7, 1993 - Auction

Mystic Fine Arts
47 Holmes Street
Mystic, Connecticut 06355-2623

tel: (203) 572-8873

10% buyer's premium

September 24, 1992 - Auction of American and European Prints, Paintings, Watercolors and Sculpture
December 17, 1992 - Auction of American and European Prints, Paintings, Watercolors and Sculpture

Neal Auction Company
4038 Magazine Street
New Orleans, Louisiana 70115

tel: (504) 899-5329
fax: (504) 897-3808

10% buyer's premium

October 16-18, 1992 - Auction of the Grove's Painting Collection with Selected Other Property
December 5-6, 1992 - Auction
December 6, 1992 - Auction
February 13-14, 1993 - Auction
February 13-14, 1993 - Estates Auction
May 22-23, 1993 - Auction

November 22, 1992 - Auction
December 12, 1992 - Auction
January 2, 1993 - Auction

Loudmer,
Commissaires Prieurs S.C.P   tel: (1) 44 79 50 50   *premiums: 10.67% up to 14,999FF*
7, rue Rossini   fax: (1) 44 79 50 51   *6.23% from 15,000 to 39,99FF*
75009 Paris   *4.15% from 40,000 to 299,999FF*
France   *2.96% over 300,000FF*

May 15, 1993 - Collection du Docteur Gachet
June 28, 1993 - Estampes Anciennes, Modernes et Contemporaines, Livres Illustres,
Estampes Japonaises

Louisiana Auction Exchange, Inc.   tel: (504) 924-1803   *10% buyer's premium*
2031 Government Street
Baton Rouge, Louisiana 70806

September 12, 1992 - Fine Art Auction, American and European Paintings
March 6, 1993 - Fine Art Auction, American and European Paintings
June 5, 1993 - Fine Art AUction, American and European Paintings

Rudolf Mangisch   tel: (1) 422 50 33   *premiums: 15% up to 29,999SF*
Muhle Tiefenbrunnen   fax: (1) 422 36 41   *12% 30,000 to 99,999SF*
Seefeldstrasse 233   *10% over 100,000SF*
8008 Zurich
Switzerland

Decmber 5, 1992 - Zeitgenossische Kunst

Maynard's Antiques & Fine Arts   tel: (604) 876-6787   *6% buyer's premium*
415 West 2nd Avenue   fax: (604) 876-2678
Vancouver, B.C.
V5Y 1E3 Canada

October 21-22, 1992 - Auction
March 10-11, 1993 - Antique, Art and Collectibles Auction
May 12-13, 1993 - Antique and Art Auction

Millon et Robert   tel: (1) 48 00 99 44   *Premiums: 12.67 up to 15,000FF*
19, Rue de la Grange-Bateliere   fax: (1) 48 00 98 58   *8.23% 15,001 to 40,000FF*
75009 Paris   *6.15% 40,001 to 300,000FF*
France   *4.96% 300,000 and over*

January 31, 1993 - VI/L'Ecole de Paris, Michonze-Pascin-Pressmane...
March 15, 1993 - Estampes, Lithographies, Eaux-Fortes, Serigraphies, Bardonne-
Duvernay-Tsigal

Galerie Kornfeld-Bern
Laupenstrasse 41
Postfach 6265
3001 Bern
Switzerland

tel: (31) 25 46 73
fax: (31) 26 18 91

Retail: 15% buyer's premium
Dealer: 10% buyer's premium

June 23, 1993 - Graphik und Handzeichnungen Alter Meister (#210)
June 23-25, 1993 - Kunst des 19. und 20. Jahrhunderts, Part II (#211)
June 25, 1993 - Kunst Des 19. und 20. Jahrhunderts, Teil I (#211)

Kunsthallen Kunstaauktioner
Gothersgade 9
1123 Kobenhavn K
Copenhagen
Denmark

tel: (33) 32 52 00
fax: (33) 32 46 70

15% buyer's premium

September 30, 1992 - Moderne Grafik (#417)
December 2-3, 1992 - Nutidskunst (#422)
March 24, 1993 - Moderne Grafik (#425)
April 21-22, 1993 - Klassisk Modernisme (#426)
June 3, 1993 - Nutidskunst (#428)

Laurin-Guilloux-
Buffetaud-Tailleur
12, rue Drouot
75009 Paris
France

tel: (1) 42 46 61 16
fax: (1) 47 70 12 51

premiums : 12.67% up to 15,000FF
8.23% from 15,001 to 40,000FF
6.15% from 40,001 to 300,000FF
4.96% from 300,001 and up

March 13, 1993 - Affices D'Outre-Mer IV
May 6, 1993 - Estampes Modernes, Tableaux, Dessins, Modernes

Kunsthaus Lempertz
Neumarkt 3
50667 Koln
Germany

tel: (221) 925 72 90
fax: (221) 925 72 96

15% buyer's premium

November 12, 1992 - Photographie and Photoarbeiten (#682)
November 20, 1992 - Zeitgenossische Kunst (#683)
November 21, 1992 - Moderne Kunst (#684)
May 26, 1993 - Moderne Kunst (#691)
May 27, 1993 - Zeitgenossische Kunst (#692)

Litchfield Auction Gallery
P.O. Box 1337
425 Phantom Road
Litchfield, Connecticut 06759

tel: (203) 567-3126
fax: (203) 567-3266

10% buyer's premium

August 8, 1992 - Auction
October 10, 1992 - Auction
October 31, 1992 - Auction

Joyner Auctioneers & Appraisers   tel: (416) 323-0909   *10% buyer's premium*
222 Gerrard Street East   fax: (416) 323-0249
Toronto, Ontario M5A 2E8
Canada

      November 24, 1992 - Canadian Art
          May 18, 1993 - Canadian Art

James D. Julia Inc.   tel: (207) 453-7125   *10% buyer's premium*
Post Office Box 830
Route 201, Skowhegan Road
Fairfield, Maine 04937

      July 25-26, 1992 - Important Antique and Country Store Auction
    February 6-7, 1993 - Important Americana, Orientalia and Continental Furnishings at
                       Auction
      March 27, 1993 - Fine 19th and 20th Century Furniture and Accessories at Auction

Karl & Faber   tel: (89) 22 18 65   *15% buyer's premium*
Amiraplatz 3   fax: (89) 228 33 50
8000 Munich 2
Germany

    December 1-2, 1992 - Kunst, Alter und Neuer Meister (#184)
      June 8-9, 1993 - Kunst, Alter und Neuer Meister (#185)

G.A. Key Fine Art Auctioneers   tel: (263) 733195   *10% buyer's premium*
8 Market Place Aylsham   fax: (263) 732140   *(includes V.A.T.)*
Norwich Norfolk NR11 6EH
England

      August 14, 1992 - English and Continental Oil and Watercolour Paintings and Prints
                     (#388)
      October 9, 1992 - English and Continental Oil and Watercolour Paintings and Prints
                     (#393)
    December 11, 1992 - English and Continental Oil and Watercolour Paintings and Prints
                     (#398)
    February 5, 1993 - English and Continental Oil and Watercolour Paintings and Prints
                     (#402)
      April 16, 1993 - English and Continental Oil and Watercolour Paintings and Prints
                     (#407)
      June 11, 1993 - English and Continental Oil and Watercolour Paintings and Prints
                     (#412)

Gallerie Koller Zurich   tel: (1) 273 01 01   *premiums: 16% up to 30,000SF*
Hardturmstrasse 102   fax: (1) 273 19 6611   *15% from 30,001 to 100,000SF*
CH-8031 Zurich   *12% 100,001SF and up*
Switzerland

    November 13-14, 1992 - Impressionisten und Gemalde des 20. JH., Aquarelle, Zeichnungen
                       und Moderne Graphik, Skulpturen, Bucher des 16 bis 19. JH. (#85/2)

March 14-17, 1993 - Old Master, 19th and 20th Century Paintings, Drawings, Prints and Sculpture, English, American and Continental Furniture and Decorative Arts, 20th Century American and European Design Furniture and Decorative Arts, including Arts and Crafts, Art Nouveau and Art Deco, Oriental Works of Art, Rugs and Jewelry

April 18-21, 1993 - The Ruth K. Flower Collection

May 16-18, 1993 - Old Master, 19th and 20th Century Paintings, Drawings and Prints, Sculpture and Photographs, English, American and Continental Furniture and Decorative Arts, Oriental Works of Art, Books and Manuscripts, Rugs and Jewelry

June 13-15, 1993 - English, American and Continental Furniture and Decorative Arts, 19th and 20th Century Paintings, Drawings, Prints and Sculpture, Oriental Works of Art, Jade, Glass and Rugs

Hodgins Art Auctions Ltd.   tel: (403) 243-0866   *10% buyer's premium*
#100, 437-36th Avenue S.E.   fax: (403) 243-0856
Calgary, Alberta
T2G 1W5 Canada

November 16-17, 1992 - Fine Paintings, Watercolours, Prints and Sculpture
May 10-11, 1993 - Fine Paintings, Watercolours, Prints and Sculpture

Hollywood Poster Art   tel: (201) 488-6333   *10% buyer's premium*
65 Hudson Street
Hackensack, New Jersey 07601

December 12, 1992 - Hollywood Poster Art Auction

Jackson's Auction Gallery   tel: (317) 255-7563   *10% buyer's premium*
5330 Pendleton Avenue
Anderson, Indiana 46013

September 20, 1992 - Auction

Arthur James Galleries   tel: (407) 278-2373   *10% buyer's premium*
615 East Atlantic Avenue
Delray Beach, Florida 33483

November 12-14, 1992 - Estate Auction
December 12-13, 1992 - Estate Auction
January 21-23, 1993 - Estate Auction
March 25-17, 1993 - Estate Auction

Leonard Joel   tel: (3) 822 1040   *10% buyer's premium*
1195 High Street   fax: (3) 822 8573
Armadale, 3143
Victoria, Australia

August 11-12, 1992 - Australian and European Paintings

Gary Guyette/Frank Schmidt Inc. tel: (207) 778-6266
P.O. Box 522   fax: (207) 778-6501
West Farmington, Maine 04992

    October 2-3, 1992 - North American Decoys Auction
    April 22-23, 1993 - Important Waterfowl Decoys and Bird Carvings at Auction

Hanzel Galleries, Inc.   tel: (312) 922-6234   *10% buyer's premium*
1120 South Michigan Avenue fax: (312) 922-6972
Chicago, Illinois 60605

    October 11-14, 1992 - Fine Antiques at Auction
    November 1, 1992 - Fine Art at Auction
    February 14-16, 1993 - Fine Art and Antiques Auction
    May 16-18, 1993 - Auction (#4903)

Hartung & Hartung   tel: (89) 28 40 34   *15% buyer's premium*
Karolinenplatz 5a   fax: (89) 28 55 69
8000 Munich
Germany

    November 3-6, 1992 - Wertvolle Bucher, Manuskripte, Autographen, Graphik (#70)
    April 27-29, 1993 - Wertvolle Bucher, Manuskripte, Autographen, Graphik (#71)

Hauswedell & Nolte   tel: (40) 44 83 66   *15% buyer's premium*
Poeseldorfer Weg 1   fax: (40) 410 41 98
2000 Hamburg 13
Germany

    June 10, 1993 - Gemalde, Zeichnungen und Graphik des 15. bis 19. Jahrhunderts
                (#299)
    June 10-11, 1993 - Moderne Kunst (#300)
    June 12, 1993 - Kunst Nach 1945 (#301)

Leslie Hindman Auctioneers tel: (312) 670-0010   *10% buyer's premium*
215 West Ohio Street   fax: (312) 670-4248
Chicago, Illinois 60610

    September 20-22, 1992 - English, American and Continental Furniture and Decorative Arts,
                Old Master, 19th and 20th Century Paintings, Drawings, Prints
                Sculpture, 20th Century American Design Furniture and Decorative
                Arts, including Arts and Crafts, Art Nouveau and Art Deco, Books,
                Manuscripts, Silver and Rugs
    October 18-20, 1992 - English, American and Continental Furniture and Decorative Arts,
                Oriental Works of Art, Rugs and Tapestries, Old Master, 19th and
                20th Century Paintings, Drawings, Prints and Sculpture, Jewelry and
                20th Century Crime Memorabilia
    December 13-15, 1992 - Old Master, 19th and 20th Century Paintings, Drawings, Prints and
                Sculpture, Oriental Works of Art, English, American and Continental
                Furniture and Decorative Arts, African Tribal Art, American and
                European Cut Glass, Art Glass, Jewelry, Rugs and Tapestries

May 21-22, 1993 - Antiques Auction, Early American Furniture and Accessories, Pewter, Ohio Pottery and Firearms and Accessories (#11, #12)
June 17-18, 1993 - American, English, Continental and Oriental Furniture and Accessories Plus Indian Jewelry, Silver and Oriental Rugs (#13, #14)

Germann Auktionshaus
Zeltweg 67
8032 Zurich
Switzerland

tel: (1) 251 83 58
fax: (1) 261 53 87

Premiums: 18% up to 999SF
15% over 1,000SF

October 14-16, 1992 - Gemalde, Druckgrafik, Skulpturen, Grafik
December 4-5, 1992 - Gemalde, Druckgrafik, Skulpturen, Grafik
April 21-23, 1993 - Gemalde, Druckgrafik, Skulpturen, Grafik
June 24-26, 1993 - Gemalde, Druckgrafik, Skulpturen, Grafik

Morton M. Goldberg
Auction Galleries, Inc.
547 Baronne Street
New Orleans, Louisiana 70113

tel: (504) 592-2300
fax: (504) 592-2311

10% buyer's premium

August 29-30, 1992 - Two-Session Important Estates Auction
October 10, 1992 - Autumn Estates Auction
October 31, 1992 - At Auction, Wilds and Canon, Antiques and Interiors
November 21-22, 1992 - The Eleventh Annual Louisiana Purchase Auction
December 12-13, 1992 - December Estates Auction
January 23-24, 1993 - Winter Estates Auction
March 12-14, 1993 - Spring Estates Auction
May 7-8, 1993 - Estates Auction

Granier Auktionshaus
Welle 9
Postfach 101287
4800 Bielefeld 1
Germany

tel: (521) 571 48
fax: (521) 671 46

15% buyer's premium

September 25-26, 1992 - Wertvolle Bucher, Graphik, Alte und Moderne Kunst (#33)

Grogan & Company
890 Commonwealth Avenue
Boston, Massachusetts 02215

tel: (617) 566-4100
fax: (617) 566-7715

10% buyer's premium

October 5-8, 1992 - The October Auction (#42)
December 9-10, and 15, 1992 - The December Auction (#43)
March 24-25 and 30, 1993 - The March Auction (#46)
May 24-25 and 27, 1993 - The May Auction (#48)

Finarte S.A.
via Pasteur, 1
6830 Chiasso
Italy

fax: (4191) 430012   *15% buyer's premium*

    October 10, 1992 - Arte Moderna e Contemporanea

Galerie Fischer Luzern
Haldenstrasse 19
6006 Luzern
Switzerland

tel: (41) 51 57 72   *premiums: 20% up to 29,999SF*
fax: (41) 51 25 64   *15% 30,000 to 99,999SF*
                                      10% over 100,000SF

    November 3-4, 1992 - Mobel, Porzelian, Skulpturen, Schmuck, Silber, Kugendstil,
                           Aussereuropaische Kunst

Freeman\Fine Arts of
Philadelphia, Inc.
1808 Chestnut Street
Philadelphia, Pennsylvania 19103

tel: (215) 563-9275   *10% buyer's premium*
fax: (215) 563-8236

    November 12, 1992 - Fine Prints and Drawings (#513)
      April 22-24, 1993 - Auction (#542)
         June 11, 1993 - American and European Prints (#550)

Garth's Auction, Inc.
2690 Stratford Road, P.O. Box 369
Delaware, Ohio 43105

tel: (614) 362-4771   *10% buyer's premium*
fax: (614) 363-0164

    September 4-5, 1992 - Antiques Auction, Country Furniture and Accessories (#19, #20)
       October 3, 1992 - Antiques Auction, American, English, Continental and Oriental
                           Furniture and Accessories (#21)
    October 23-24, 1992 - Auction, Fine Early American Furniture and Accessories, Quilts,
                           Glass, Samplers and Staffordshire, The Collection of Jean Crutcher
                           (#22, #23)
  November 13-14, 1992 - Antiques Auction, Early American Furniture and Accessories (#24,
                           #25)
  November 27-28, 1992 - Fine Early American Furniture and Accessories, Toys, Banks, Folk
                           Art and Historic American Indian Material (#26, #27)
  December 10-11, 1992 - Antiques Auction, English, American, Continental and Oriental
                           Furniture and Accessories and Clocks (#28, #29)
      January 8-9, 1993 - Antiques Auction, Fine Early American Furniture and Accessories
                           from the Collection of Dr. and Mrs. W.E. Kettelkamp, Cast Iron
                           Banks from the Collection of Peter Markoff and Historical Indian
                           Material (#1, #2)
    February 5-6, 1993 - Antiques Auction, Country Furniture and Accessories (#3, #4)
   February 19-20, 1993 - Antiques Auction, English, American, Continental and Oriental
                           Furniture and Accessories and Oriental Rugs (#5, #6)
       March 13, 1993 - Antiques Auction, Early American Furniture and Accessories,
                           Lusterware and Quilts (#7)
         April 2, 1993 - Antiques Auction, American, English and Continental Furniture and
                           Accessories (#8)
   April 30-May 1, 1993 - Antiques Auction, Early American Furniture and Accessories, Gaudy
                           Welsh, Coverlets, Quilts and Historic Indian Material (#9, #10)

Hotel des Encans de Montreal   tel: (514) 344-4081   *11% buyer's premium*
2825 rue Bates   fax: (514) 344-4125
Montreal H3S 1B3
Canada

August 18-20, 1992 -	Venete Aux Encheres Publique
September 15-17, 1992 -	Vente aux Encheres Publique
October 20-21, 1992 -	Venete aux Encheres Publique
November 17-19, 1992 -	Vente aux Encheres Publique Provenant de Diverses Successions, Collections Privees et Par Ordre de Trusts et Syndic
February 16-18, 1993 -	Vente aux Encheres Publique Provenant de Diverses Successions et de Collections Privees
March 16-18, 1993 -	Vente aux Encheres Publique Provenant de Diverses Successions et de Collections Privees
April 20-22, 1993 -	Vente aux Encheres Publique Provenant de Diverses Successions et de Collections Privees
May 18-20, 1993 -	Vente aux Encheres Publique Provenant de la Succession de M. Janos Lukacs et de Diverses Collections Privees et Successions
June 15-17, 1993 -	Vente aux Encheres Publique Provenant de Diverses Collections Privees et Successions
July 14-16, 1993 -	Vente aux Encheres Publique d'une Collection de Tableaux au Profit de OXFAM Quebec et de Biens et de Collections Provenant de Divers

Falkkloo's Auktioner   tel: (40) 11 86 95   *10% buyer's premium*
Hamngatan 2   fax: (40) 30 37 62
211 22 Malmo
Switzerland

November 7, 1992 -	Hostauktionen 1922 (#23)
April 17, 1993 -	Varauktionen (#24)

Carte Casa D'Aste   tel: (2) 877 041   *15% buyer's premium*
Via dei Bossi 2   fax: (2) 867 318
Milano 20121
Italy

November 9, 1992 -	Opere D'Arte Moderna e Contemporanea, Dipinti, Disegni, Grafica (#839)
December 15, 1992 -	Opere D'Arte Moderna e Contemporanea, Dipinti, Disegni, Grafica (#847)
May 20, 1993 -	Disegni e Grafica Contemporanea (#861)

Finarte Casa D'Aste   tel: (6) 320 76 79   *15% buyer's premium*
via Margutta 54   fax: (6) 320 76 38
Roma 00187
Italy

March 25, 1993 -	Opere D'Arte Moderna e Contemporanea (#853)
May 20, 1993 -	Desegni e Grafica Contemporanea (#861)

Du Mouchelle Art Galleries   tel: (313) 963-6255   *10% buyer's premium*
409 East Jefferson Avenue   fax: (313) 963-8199
Detroit, Michigan 48226

July 17-16, 1992   - Auction
August 14-16, 1992   - Auction
September 18-20, 1992 - Auction
October 16-18, 1992   - Auction
October 24, 1992   - Rare Autograph and Book Auction, Featuring the Collection of Pierre
                         Belmoor
November 13-15, 1992 - Auction
December 11-13, 1992 - Auction
January 15-17, 1993   - Auction
February 12-14, 1993 - Auction
March 12-14, 1993   - Auction
April 16-18, 1993   - Auction
May 14-16, 1993   - Auction
June 11-13, 1993   - Auction

Dunning's Auction Service, Inc.   tel: (708) 741-3483   *10% buyer's premium*
P.O. Box 866   fax: (708) 741-3589
755 Church Road
Elgin, Illinois 60123

September 12-13, 1992 - Paper Collectibles/Ephemera Auction
October 10-11, 1992   - Fine Decorative Arts and Furniture
October 24-25, 1992   - American Indian Art Auction
November 28-29, 1992 - Auction
February 27-28, 1993 - Fine Art, Decorative Arts and Furniture
May 15-16, 1993   - Fine Art

Fernando Duran   tel: (1) 575 39 11   *15% buyer's premium*
Substa De Arte   fax: (1) 577 51 44   *(includes V.A.T.)*
Conde de Aranda, 23
(Semiesquina a Velazquez)
28001 Madrid
Spain

October 15-16, 1992   - Gran Subasta de Inauguracion de Temporada
December 17-18, 1992 - Extraordinaria Subasta de Navidad
February 3-5, 1993   - Gran Subasta de Ocasion
March 17-18, 1993   - Extraordinaria Subasta de Primavera

Robert C. Eldred Co., Inc.   tel: (508) 385-3116   *10% buyer's premium*
1483 Route 6A, Box 796   fax: (508) 385-7201
East Dennis, Massachusetts 02641

November 20-21, 1992 - Americana and Marine Art at Auction
December 4-5, 1992   - Oriental Art at Auction
December 11-12, 1992 - Fine and Decorative Art at Auction
April 2-3, 1993   - American at Auction
May 20-21, 1993   - Fine, Decorative and Oriental Art at Auction

William Doyle Galleries
175 East 87th Street
New York, New York 10128

tel: (212) 427-2730
fax: (212) 369-0892

15% first $50,000
10% over $50,000
(as of August 1, 1993)

June 3, 1992 -	Belle Epoque, 19th and 20th Century Decorative Arts
June 24, 1992 -	Fine English and Continental Furniture, Decorations and Paintings, including French Empire, Provincial and Regency Furniture, Porcelain, Silver and Rugs
September 9, 1992 -	Belle Epoque, 19th and 20th Century Decorative Arts
September 30, 1992 -	Property from the Estate of James Cagney
October 14, 1992 -	Fine English and Continental Furniture, Decorations and Paintings, including French Empire, Provincial and Regency Furniture, Porcelain, Silver and Rugs
October 28, 1992 -	Important 17th and 18th Century English and Continental Furniture and Decorations, including Old Master Paintings, Georgian Silver, Tapestries and Rugs
December 4, 1992 -	Old Master, Modern and Contemporary Prints and Books, Maps and Autographs
December 10, 1992 -	Fine English and Continental Furniture, Decorations and Paintings, including French Empire, Provincial and Regency Furniture, Porcelain, Silver and Rugs
January 6, 1993 -	Belle Epoque, 19th and 20th Century Decorative Arts
February 3, 1993 -	Fine English and Continental Furniture, Decorations and Paintings, including French Empire, Provincial and Regency Furniture, Porcelain, Silver and Rugs
February 17, 1993 -	Fine English and Continental Furniture, Decorations and Paintings, including French Empire, Provincial and Regency Furniture, Porcelain, Silver and Rugs
March 3, 1993 -	Fine English and Continental Furniture, Decorations and Paintings, including French Empire, Provincial and Regency Furniture, Porcelain, Silver and Rugs
March 24, 1993 -	Fine English and Continental Furniture, Decorations and Paintings, including French Empire, Provincial and Regency Furniture, Porcelain, Silver and Rugs
April 28, 1993 -	Belle Epoque
May 19, 1993 -	Important 17th and 18th Century English and Continental Furniture and Decorations
June 2, 1993 -	Americana, including Furniture, Paintings, Porcelain, Silver, Decoys and Rugs
June 11, 1993 -	Old Master, Modern and Contemporary Prints, Books, Maps and Autographs
June 23, 1993 -	Fine English and Continental Furniture, Decorations and Paintings, including French Empire, Provincial and Regency Furniture, Porcelain and Silver

Hotel Drouot
9 rue Drouot
75009 Paris
France

tel: (1) 48 00 20 20
fax: (1) 48 00 20 38

*See individual houses

Cleveland Print Auction phone and fax: (216) 791-6663 *10% buyer's premium*
12803 Larchmere Blvd.
Shaker Heights, Ohio 44120

    October 31, 1992 - Prints and Drawings at Auction
    May 15, 1993 - Prints and Drawings at Auction

Collins Galleries tel: (207) 967-5004 *10% buyer's premium*
35 Western Avenue
Kennebunk, Maine 04043

    October 24, 1993 - Fine American and European Paintings and Prints
    February 13, 1993 - Sporting Art Auction
    May 22, 1993 - Fine American and European Paintings and Prints

Dobiaschofsky Auktionen Ag tel: (31) 25 23 72 *premiums: 20% up to 4,999SF*
Monbijoustrasse 30 fax: (31) 25 23 74 *15% over 5,000SF*
CH-3001 Berne *12% over 100,000SF*
Switzerland

    October 21-24, 1992 - Kunstauktionen (#75)
    May 5-8, 1993 - Kunstauktionen (#76)

F. Dorling tel: (40) 364 670 *15% buyer's premium*
Neuer Wall 40 fax: (40) 362 358
2000 Hamburg 36
Germany

    December 2, 1992 - Alte und Moderne Kunst (#145)
    May 26, 1993 - Alte und Moderne Kunst (#147)

Dorotheum Kunstabteilung tel: (222) 515 60 0 *12% buyer's premium*
Dorotheergasse 17 fax: (222) 515 60 474
1010 Vienna - Wien
Austria

    November 11, 1992 - Aquarelle, Miniaturen, Alte Meisterzeichnungen und Druckgraphik
        bis 1900
    November 25, 1992 - Kunst 20. Jahrhunderts Olgemalde, Skupturen, Aquarelle,
        Mischtechniken, Zeichnungen, Druckgraphik
    April 21, 1993 - Kunst Des 20. Kahrhunderts
    April 27, 1993 - Asiatika
    May 19, 1993 - Klassische Moderne
    June 4, 1993 - Kunst des 20. Jahrhunderts

Douglas Auctioneers tel: (413) 655-2877 *10% buyer's premium*
Route 5
South Deerfield, Massachusetts 01373

    March 26, 1993 - Auction

February 22, 1993 - Modern and Contemporary Paintings, Drawings and Sculpture (Penny #7407; Filene #7409)
March 25, 1993 - 20th Century Decorative Arts (#7411)
April 27, 1993 - English and Continental Furniture, Decorative Objects, European and American Paintings, and Old Master Paintings and Drawings (#7423)
May 4, 1993 - American Paintings, Drawings, Watercolors and Sculpture (Robert #7415)
May 19, 1993 - Engagement, Wedding Gifts and Furnishings for the New Home (#7429)
June 1, 1993 - Chinese, Japanese, Southeast Asian and Tribal Works of Art, European Furniture and Objects of Art, and Rugs (#7433)
June 8, 1993 - 20th Century Decorative Arts, including Arts and Crafts (#7437)

Christie, Manson & Woods Ltd.   tel: (71) 839 9060   *15% first 30,000 BP*
8 King Street, St. James's   fax: (71) 839 1611   *10% over 30,000 BP*
London SW1Y 6QT   *(as of March 1, 1993)*
England

October 29, 1992 - 19th and 20th Century Photographs, including Soviet Photography 1925-1965 (Prism #4832)
December 1-2, 1992 - Important Old Master, Modern and Contemporary Prints (Rosso #4890)
May 6, 1993 - Photographs (Pylon #4963)
May 20, 1993 - German and Austrian Art, Part II (Teutonic II #5023)

Christie's South Kensington   tel: (71) 581 7611   *10% buyer's premium*
85 Old Brompton Road   fax: (71) 321 3321
London SW7 3LD
England

October 7, 1992 - Decorative, Topographical, Sporting and Modern Prints (PRT #4789)
December 10, 1992 - The Works of Felicien Rops and Associated Material (AND #4867)
December 17, 1992 - Film and Entertainment, including the Private Collection of John Kobal (Eph #4875)
February 4, 1993 - 19th and 20th Century Posters (And #6008)
May 7, 1993 - Photographic Posters and Ephemera, The James L. Bikoff Collection, Part II (MCA #6103)

Christie's International S.A.   tel: (22) 311 1766   *13% buyer's premium*
8, Place de la Taconnerie   fax: (22) 311 5559
1204 Geneva
Switzerland

November 15, 1992 - Twentieth Century Decorative Arts and Modern Illustrated Books (Jocelyne #1121-1122)

**Clearing House Auction
Galleries Inc.**   tel: (203) 529-3344   *10% buyer's premium*
207 Church Street
Wethersfield, Connecticut 06109

November 27, 1992 - Important Estate Auction
April 23, 1993 - Important Evening Auction

Camden House Auctioneers, Inc. tel: (310) 246-1212   *10% buyer's premium*
427 N. Canon Drive   fax: (310) 246-0416
Beverly Hills, California 90210

    November 7-8, 1992 - Vintage Film Posters and Hollywood Memorabilia
      June 5-6, 1993 - Hollywood Posters, Autographs and Memorabilia

Cheval-Robert   tel: (1) 47 70 56 26   *premiums: 12.67% up to 15,000F*
33, rue de Faubourg Montmatre   fax: (1) 42 46 79 56   *8.23% from 15,001 to 40,000FF*
75009 Paris
France

    February 12, 1993 - Affiches Anciennes et Vieux Papiers

Christie's   tel: (212) 546-1000   *premiums: 15% first $50,000*
502 Park Avenue   fax: (212) 980-8163   *10% over $50,000*
New York, New York 10022   *(as of March 1, 1993)*

      October 8, 1992 - 19th and 20th Century Photographs (Rasa #7510)
   November 9, 1992 - American, Modern and Contemporary Prints and Illustrated Books
                (Henriette #7536)
  November 19, 1992 - Contemporary Art, Part II (Jimmy #7570)
November 24-25, 1992 - Important Latin American Paintings, Drawings and Sculpture (Vivian
                #7538)
   December 12, 1992 - Important 20th Century Decorative Arts (Cheuret #7550)
 January 22-23, 1993 - Important American Furniture, Silver, Prints, Folk Art and Decorative
                Arts (Hicks #7604)
  February 24, 1993 - Contemporary Art (Joshua #7622)
    March 27, 1993 - Important 20th Century Decorative Arts (Pacyderm #7636)
     April 8, 1993 - 19th and 20th Century Photographs (Relume #7646)
      May 5, 1993 - Contemporary Art, Part II (Candace #7666)
   May 11-12, 1993 - Old Master, American, Modern and Contemporary Prints and
                Illustrated Books (Albion #7670)
   May 17-18, 1993 - Important Latin American Painting, Drawings, Sculpture and Prints
                (America #7676)
      June 5, 1993 - Sporting Paintings and Memorabilia from the Collection of Anthony
                N.B. Garvan (Garvan #7696)
    June 12, 1993 - Important 20th Century Decorative Arts, including works by the
                Tiffany Studios, American Arts and Crafts and Architectural Designs
                (A & M #7702)

Christie's East   tel: (212) 606-0400   *premiums: 15% first $50,000*
219 East 67th Street   fax: (212) 737-6076   *10% over $50,000*
New York, New York 10021   *(as of March 1, 1993)*

    August 23, 1992 - Christie's At Pebble Beach, Exceptional Motor Cars (Pebble #7283)
September 19, 1992 - American Prints 1900-1990 (Andiamo #7343)
  October 13, 1992 - English and Continental Furniture, Decorative Objects, Paintings and
                Old Master Paintings (#7347)
November 17, 1992 - Contemporary Paintings, Drawings and Sculpture (Andrew #7367)
 December 2, 1992 - American Paintings, Drawings and Watercolors, including an
                Important Collection of Civil War Paintings (Rocco #7369)
December 14, 1992 - Hollywood Posters III (Bagdad #7375)

Francis Briest
24, avenue Matignon
75008 Paris
France

tel: (1) 41 68 11 30
fax: (1) 42 68 12 67

premiums: 10.67% up to 15,000FF
6.23% from 15,001 to 40,000FF
4.15% from 40,001 to 300,000FF
2.96% from 300,001 and up

November 16, 1992 - Estampes Modernes et Contemporaines Livres Illustres
March 31, 1993 - Estampes, Livres Illustres, Art Abstrait et Contemporain, Tableaux
May 27, 1993 - Estampes, Livres Illustres

Robert S. Brunk
Auction Services
Post Office Box 2135
Asheville, North Carolina 28802

tel: (704) 254-7919

10% buyer's premium

January 2, 1993 - Auction, Fine Antiques and Accessories

Bubb Kuyper
Jansweg 39
2011 KM Haarlem
The Netherlands

tel: (31 23) 32 39 86
fax: (31 23) 32 38 93

20% buyer's premium

November 18-19, 1992 - Auction Sale of Books and Prints
June 9-10, 1993 - Auction Sale of Books and Prints

Bukowskis
Aktieselskabet Bukowski Danmark
Kongens Nytorv 20-22
1050 Kobenhavn K
Denmark

tel: (33) 33 01 05
fax: (33) 33 01 07

15% buyer's premium

November 14, 1992 - International Kunstauktion (#8)
April 29, 1993 - International Kunstauktion (#9)

Butterfield & Butterfield
220 San Bruno Avenue

tel: (415) 861-7500
fax: (415) 861-8951

10% buyer's premium
15% premium as of March 1, 1993

San Francisco, California 94103

September 21-22, 1992 - Fine Art Nouveau, Art Deco and Arts and Crafts, including Prints,
Posters and 20th Century Design (#5060N, #5065K)
October 28, 1992 - Fine American, European and Contemporary Prints (#5118K,
#5121L)
November 16, 1992 - Fine Photographs (#5245M)
February 24, 1993 - Fine American, European and Contemporary Prints (#5366K,
#5367L)
March 30-31, 1993 - Fine Art Nouveau, Art Deco and Arts and Crafts in Los Angeles
(#5481K, #5482N)
May 19, 1993 - Fine American, European and Contemporary Prints (#5486K,
#5487L)
May 23, 1993 - Fine Photographs (#5522M)

Bonham's Chelsea
65-69 Lots Road
London SW10 0RN
England

tel: (71) 351 7111
fax: (71) 351 7754

10% buyer's premium
(V.A.T. included on
designated lots only)

July 16, 1992 - Decorative and Modern Prints (#25539)
August 20, 1992 - Decorative and Modern Prints (#25568)
September 17, 1992 - Decorative and Modern prints, including a Collection of Drypoint Etchings by Winifred Austen, R.E. (#25592)
October 15, 1992 - Old Master, Decorative and Modern Prints (#25622)
October 29, 1992 - Sporting Sale (#25637)
November 12, 1992 - A Collection of Decorative and Sporting Prints, including Original Copper Plates Etched by George Belcher, R.A. (#25653)
November 19, 1992 - Old Master, Decorative and Modern Prints (#25665)
December 10, 1992 - Decorative and Modern Prints and English and Continental Watercolours (#25690)
January 21, 1993 - Old Master, Decorative and Modern Prints (#25716)
February 17, 1993 - Decorative and Modern Prints (#25738)
March 3, 1993 - Sporting Sale (#25754)
March 17, 1993 - Decorative and Modern Prints (#25768)
April 22, 1993 - Decorative and Modern Prints (#25810)
May 20, 1993 - Decorative and Modern prints (#25835)
May 26, 1993 - Flower and Garden Oil Paintings, Watercolours and Prints (#25840)
June 16, 1993 - Old Master and Decorative Prints (#25861)
June 30, 1993 - Sporting Sale (#25877)

Frank H. Boos Gallery, Inc.
420 Enterprise Court
Bloomfield Hills, Michigan 48302

tel: (313) 332-1500
fax: (313) 332-6370

10% buyer's premium

August 5-6, 1992 - Paintings, Sculpture, Furniture and Decorative Arts (#167-Vonnoh)
October 8-9, 1992 - Paintings, Furniture and Decorative Arts, including The Fell Collection of 20th Century Art (#168-Fell)
December 2-4, 1992 - Paintings, Furniture, Jewelry and Decorative Arts (#169-Holiday)
February 11-12, 1993 - Paintings, Furniture, Clocks and Decorative Arts (#170-February, 1993)
March 25-26, 1993 - Paintings, Furniture and 20th Century Decorative Arts (#171-March, 1993)
May 20-21, 1993 - Paintings, Furniture and Decorative Arts (#172-May, 1993)
June 24-25, 1993 - Paintings, Furniture, Jewelry and Decorative Arts (#174-June, 1993)

Richard A. Bourne Co., Inc.   tel: (508) 775-0797   *10% buyer's premium*
Corporation Road-Hyannis, MA 02601
Mail: P.O. Box 141
Hyannis Port, Massachusetts 02647

October 27, 1992 - Public Auction of Americana, Rare Paintings, Etc.
January 5, 1993 - Public Auction of Americana and Accessories, Oriental Rugs, Paintings, Etc.
February 13, 1993 - Winter Marine Auction
April 13, 1993 - Americana, Paintings, Folk Art and Glass

James R. Bakker Antiques, Inc. tel: (617) 864-7067 *10% buyer's premium*
370 Broadway fax: (617) 864-6626
Cambridge, Massachusetts 02139

July 19, 1992	- Paintings, Watercolors and Prints
September 27, 1992	- Paintings, Prints and Sculpture
November 21, 1992	- American and European Works on Paper, Paintings, Sculpture and Objects d'Art
February 7, 1993	- Paintings, Watercolors and Prints
March 28, 1993	- Paintings, Prints and Sculpture
April 25, 1993	- American and European Paintings, Prints and Sculpture, Candace Lovely: Selections from the Fenway Studio

Barridoff Galleries tel: (207) 772-5011 *10% buyer's premium*
P.O. Box 9715 fax: (207) 772-5049
Portland, Maine 04104

February 10, 1993 - American and European Art Public Auction

Galerie Gerda Bassenge tel: (30) 892 90 13 *15% buyer's premium*
Erdenerstrasse 5a fax: (30) 891 80 25
D-1000 Berlin 33
Germany

December 4, 1993	- Kunst Und Buchauktionen
December 5, 1992	- Kunst Und Buchauktionen
December 12, 1992	- Kunst Und Buchauktionen
June 4, 1993	- Kunst Und Buchauktionen
June 5, 1993	- Kunst Und Buchauktionen

Claude Boisgirard tel: (1) 47 70 81 36 *premiums: 12.67% up to 15,000FF*
2, rue de Provence fax: (1) 42 47 05 84 *8.23& from 15,001 to 40,000FF*
75009 Paris *6.15% from 40,001 to 300,000FF*
France *4.96% from 300,001 and up*

March 16, 1993	- Affiches de Collection
June 11, 1993	- Affiches 1900, Collection B. de L.

Bonham's tel: (71) 584 9161 *10% buyer's premium*
Montpelior Street fax: (71) 589 4072
Knightsbridge
London SW7 1HH, England

August 12-13, 1992	- Marine Paintings and Works of Art (#25573, #25563, #25564)
October 10, 1992	- Hollywood Sale, Marilyn Monroe and Hollywood Glamour Photographs (#25615)
October 17, 1992	- Sir William Russell Flint, R.A., P.R.W.S., Watercolours, Drawings, Prints and Books (#25623)
January 14, 1993	- Marine Paintings and Works of Art (#25707, #25708)
January 18, 1993	- Dogs and Cats in Art (#25710)
May 22, 1993	- Sir William Russell Flint, R.A., P.R.W.S., Watercolours, Drawings, Prints and Books (#25836)

Auction houses and sale dates cited

AB Stockholm Auktionsvert   tel: (8) 14 24 48   *12% buyer's premium*
Gallerian/T-Baneplanet   fax: (8) 10 28 45
Kungstragarden, Box 16256
103 25 Stockholm, Sweden
Sweden

    December 1-4, 1992 - Internationella, Moderna, Grafik
    May 10-12, 1993 - Internationella, Moderna, Grafik
    May 25, 1993 - Grafik

Ader Tajan   tel: (1) 42 61 80 07   *premiums: 12.67% up to 15,000FF*
12, rue Favart   fax: (1) 42 61 39 57   *8.23% from 15,001 to 40,000FF*
75002 Paris   *6.15% from 40,001 to 300,000FF*
France   *4.96% from 300,001 and up*

    February 3, 1993 - Estampes
    March 11, 1993 - Judaica
    June 16, 1993 - Estampes

U.S. Representative: tel: (212) 737-3597
Ketty Maisonrouge & Co., Inc.   fax: (212)861-1434

    September 24, 1991 - Estampes
    February 21, 1992 - Estampes
    March 19, 1992 - Tableaux Modernes, Tableaux Contemporains
    June 16, 1992 - Estampes

Alderfer Auction Company   tel: (215) 368-5477   *no premium charged*
501 Fairgrounds Road   fax: (215) 368-9055
Hatfield, Pennsylvania 19440

    September 24, 1992 - Art, Antiques, Decorative Accessories and Works on Paper
    March 4, 1993 - Antiques, Art, Oriental Rugs and Decorative Accessories
    May 20, 1993 - Antiques, Art, Oriental Rugs and Decorative Accessories

Auktionhaus Arnold   tel: (69) 28 27 79   *18% buyer's premium*
Bleichstrasse 42   fax: (69) 2 97 79 29
6000 Frankfurt am Main 1
Germany

    September 5, 1992 - Kunst-Auktion
    November 21, 1992 - Kunst-Auktion

Adam Clark Vroman

Webb, William and Robert A. Weinstein. *Dwellers at the Source: Southwestern Indian Photographs of A.C. Vroman, 1895-1904.* New York: Grossman Pub., 1973.

Carleton E. Watkins

Alinder, James, ed. *Carleton E. Watkins: Photographs of the Columbia River and Oregon.* The Friends of Photography: Weston Gallery, Carmel, Calif., 1979.

Palmquist, Peter E. *Carleton E. Watkins: Photographer of the American West.* Albuquerque, N.M.: University of New Mexico Press, 1983.

Weegee

Naked City. New York: Essential Books, 1945.

Stettner, Louis, ed. *Weegee.* New York: Knopf, 1977.

Weegee's Creative Camera. Garden City, N.Y.: Hanover House, 1959.

Weegee's New York: 335 Photographien 1935-60. Munich: Schirmer/Mosel, 1982.

Weegee's People. New York: DaCapo Press, 1975.

William Wegman

Kunz, Martin, ed. *William Wegman: Paintings, Drawings, Photographs, Video Tapes.* New York: Abrams, 1990.

Brett Weston

Cravens, R.H. *Brett Weston: Photographs From Five Decades.* Millerton, New York: Aperture, 1980.

Brett Weston: Master Photographer. Carmel, CA: Photography West Graphics, 1989.

Voyage of the Eye. Millerton, New York: Aperture, 1975.

Edward Weston

Conger, Amy. *Edward Weston in Mexico 1923-1926.* Albuquerque: Univ. of New Mexico Press, 1983.

Maddow, Ben. *Edward Weston: Fifty Years.* Millerton, New York: Aperture, Inc., 1973.

Newhall, Beaumont. *Supreme Instants: The Photography of Edward Weston.* Boston: Little, Brown, 1986.

Newhall, Nancy, ed. *Edward Weston: The Flame of Recognition.* Millerton, N.Y.: Grossman, 1971.

_____. *The Daybooks of Edward Weston, Volume I. Mexico and Volume II. California.* Rochester, N.Y.: George Eastman House, 1961-66.

Stebbins, Theodore E., Jr. *Weston's Westons: Portraits and Nudes.* Boston: Museum of Fine Arts, 1989.

Weston, Edward. *Edward Weston Nudes, His Photographs accompanied by Excerpts from the Daybooks and Letters.* New York: Aperture, 1977.

Clarence H. White

Clarence H. White. Millerton, N.Y.: Aperture, 1979.

Barnes, Lucinda, ed. *A Collective Vision: Clarence H. White and His Students.* Long Beach, Calif.: The Museum, 1985.

Minor White

Bunnell, Peter C. *Minor White, The Eye That Shapes.* Princeton: Art Museum, Princeton University, 1989.

Minor White: Rites and Passages. Essay by James Baker Hall. Millerton, New York: Aperture, 1969.

White, Minor. *Mirrors, Messages, Manifestations.* Millerton, New York: Aperture, 1969.

Gary Winogrand

Szarkowski, John. *Winogrand: Figments from the Real World.* Exhibition catalogue. Museum of Modern Art, New York. New York: Museum of Modern Art, 1988.

Winogrand, Gary. *Women are Beautiful.* Essay by Helen Gary Bishop. New York: Farrar, Straus and Giroux, 'Light Gallery Book', 1975.

Joel Peter Witkin

Coke, Van Deren. *Joel Peter Witkin: Forty Photographs.* San Francisco: San Francisco Museum of Modern Art, 1985.

Joel-Peter Witkin: Photographs. Pasadena, California: Twelvetrees Press, 1985.

Max Yavno

Maddow, Ben and Max Yavno. *The Photography of Max Yavno.* Berkeley, CA.: Univ. of CA Press, 1981.

Ralph Steiner

Steiner, Ralph. *A Point of View*. Middletown, CT: Wesleyan University Press, 1978.

Alfred Stieglitz

Bry, Doris. *Alfred Stieglitz: Photographer*. Boston: Museum of Fine Arts, 1965.

Greenough, Sarah and Juan Hamilton. *Alfred Stieglitz: Photographs and Writings*. Washington, D.C.: National Gallery of Art, 1983.

Homer, William Innes. *Alfred Stieglitz and the Photo-Secession*. Boston: Little, Brown, 1983.

Naef, Weston. *The Collection of Alfred Stieglitz: Fifty Pioneers of Modern Photography*. New York: Metropolitan Museum of Art, 1978.

Norman, Dorothy. *Alfred Stieglitz: An American Seer*. New York: Random House, 1973.

Paul Strand

Greenough, Sarah. *Paul Strand, An American Vision*. Exhibition catalog. Washington, D.C.: National Gallery of Art, 1990.

Paul Strand: Sixty Years of Photographs. Excerpts from correspondence, interviews and other documents. Millerton, N.Y.: Aperture, 1976.

A Retrospective Monograph. Millerton, N.Y.: Aperture, 1971.

Karl Struss

Harvith, Susan and John. *Karl Struss, Man with a Camera*. Exhibition catalog, Cranbrook Academy of Art. Bloomfield Hills, Mich.: The Museum, 1976.

Roy Emerson Stryker

Plattner, Steven W. *Roy Stryker, U.S.A., 1943-1950, The Standard Oil (New Jersey) Photography Project*. Austin, Tx.: The University of Texas Press, 1983.

Josef Sudek

Bullaty, Sonya. *Sudek*. New York: Clarkson N. Potter, Inc., 1978.

Frank Meadow Sutcliffe

Sutcliffe, Frank. *Frank Meadow Sutcliffe*. Millerton, N.Y.: Aperture, 1979.

William Henry Fox Talbot

Arnold, H. J. P. *William Henry Fox Talbot: Pioneer of Photography and Man of Science*. London: Hutchinson Benhan, 1977.

Buckland, Gail. *Fox Talbot and the Invention of Photography*. Boston: David R. Godine, 1980.

Lassam, Robert. *Fox Talbot, Photographer*. Tisbury, England: Compton Press, 1979.

John Thomson

White, Stephen. *John Thomson: a Window to the Orient*. New York: Thames and Hudson, 1985.

George A. Tice

Urban Landscapes: A New Jersey Portrait. New Brunswick, N.J.: Rutgers University Press, 1975.

Deborah Turbeville

Unseen Versailles. Garden City, N.Y.: Doubleday & Co., Inc., 1981.

Jerry N. Uelsmann

Jerry N. Uelsmann. Introduction by Peter C. Bunnell. Exhibition catalog, Alfred Stieglitz Center of the Philadelphia Museum of Art. New York: Aperture, 1970.

Doris Ulmann

The Darkness and The Light. Preface by William Clift. Millerton, N.Y.: Aperture, 1974.

Roman Vishniac

A Vanished World/ Roman Vishniac. New York: Farrar, Straus & Giroux, 1983.

Vishniac, Roman. *Polish Jews, A Pictorial Record*. Essay by Abraham Joshua Heschel. New York: Schocken Books, 1947.

Jacob August Riis

Alland, Alexander, Sr. *Jacob A. Riis: Photographer and Citizen.* Millerton, N.Y.: Aperture, 1974.

Riis, Jacob A. *How the Other Half Lives.* New York: Dover Publications, 1971.

Alexander Rodchenko

Elliot, David, ed. *Rodchenko and the Arts of Revolutionary Russia.* New York: Pantheon Books, 1979.

Khan-Magomedov, Selim O. *Rodchenko, The Complete Work.* Cambridge, Mass.: MIT Press, 1986.

Lavrentjev, Alexander. *Rodchenko Photography.* New York: Rizzoli, 1982.

Sebastiao Salgado

An Uncertain Grace, Photographs by Sebastiao Salgado. New York: Aperture, 1990.

August Sander

August Sander, Antlitz der Zeit: 60 Aufnahmen dt. Menschen d. 20. Jh. Preface by Alfred Doblin. Munich: Schirmer/Mosel, 1976.

August Sander: Photographs of an Epoch, 1904-1959. Millerton, N.Y.: Aperture, 1980.

David Seymour

Capa, Cornell and Bhupendra Karia, eds. *David Seymour-"Chim": 1911-1956.* (ICP Library of Photographers), New York: Grossman Publishers, 1974.

Charles Sheeler

Lucic, Karen. *Charles Sheeler and the Cult of the Machine.* Cambridge, Mass.: Harvard University Press, 1991.

Stebbins, Theodore and Norman Keyes, Jr. *Charles Sheeler, The Photographs.* Exhibition catalog, Museum of Fine Arts, Boston. Boston: Little, Brown, 1987.

Cindy Sherman

Cindy Sherman. New York: Pantheon Books, 1984.

Cindy Sherman. New York: Whitney Museum of American Art, 1987.

Jeanloup Sieff

Jeanloup Sieff. Englewood Cliffs, N.J.: Prentice-Hall, 1982.

Aaron Siskind

Aaron Siskind Photographer. Rochester, New York: George Eastman House, 1965.

Chiarenza, Carl. *Aaron Siskind: Pleasures & Terrors.* Boston: Little, Brown in assoc. with Center for Creative Photography, 1982.

Places: Aaron Siskind Photographs. Introduction by Thomas B. Hess. New York: Light Gallery and Farrar, Straus and Giroux, 1976.

Siskind, Arron. *Harlem: Photographs 1932-1940.* Washington, D.C.: National Museum of American Art, Smithsonian Institute, 1990.

W. Eugene Smith

Hughes, Jim. *W. Eugene Smith: Shadow and Substance, the Life and Work of an American Photographer.* New York: McGraw-Hill Publishing, 1989.

Johnson, William S, ed. *W. Eugene Smith, Master of the Photographic Essay.* Millerton, N.Y.: Aperture, 1981.

Frederick Sommer

Sommer at Seventy-Five: A Retrospective. Long Beach, Calif.: Long Beach Art Museum and Galleries, California State University, 1980.

Eve Sonneman

Real Time: Eve Sonneman 1968-1974. New York: Printed Matter, 1976.

Edward Steichen

Longwell, Dennis. *Steichen: The Master Prints, 1895-1914: The Symbolist Period.* New York: Museum of Modern Art, 1978.

Steichen, Edward. *The Family of Man.* New York: Simon and Schuster for the Museum of Modern Art, 1955.

Tina Modotti

Constantine, Mildred. *Tina Modotti: A Fragile Life: An Illustrated Biography.* New York: Rizzoli, 1983.

Laszlo Moholy-Nagy

Haus, Andreas. *Moholy-Nagy: Photographs and Photograms.* New York: Pantheon Books, 1980.
Moholy-Nagy, Laszlo. *Vision in Motion.* Chicago: Paul Theobald & Co., 1947.

Barbara Morgan

Barbara Morgan. Hasting-on-Hudson, N.Y.: Morgan & Morgan, 1972.

Wright Morris

Morris, Wright. *God's Country and My People.* New York: Harper & Row, 1968.
Morris, Wright. *Photographs & Words.* Carmel, Calif.: The Friends of Photography, 1982.

Nickolas Murry

The Revealing Eye, Personalities of the 1920's in Photographs. New York: Atheneum Press, 1967.

Eadweard Muybridge

Naef, Weston J. *Era of Exploration.* Buffalo, N. Y.: Albright-Knox Gallery, 1975.
Wolf, Daniel, ed. *The American Space: Meaning in Nineteenth-Century Landscape Photography.* Middletown, Conn.: Wesleyan University Press, 1983.

Arnold Newman

Arnold Newman: Five Decades. San Diego, Calif.: Harcourt Brace Jovanovich, 1986.

Ruth Orkin

A Photo Journal. New York: Viking Press, 1981.

Timothy O'Sullivan

Horan, James D. *Timothy O'Sullivan, America's Forgotten Photographer.* Garden City, N.Y.: Doubleday, 1976.
Snyder, Joel. *American Frontiers: The Photographs of Timothy H. O'Sullivan, 1867-1874.* Millerton, N.Y.: Aperture, 1981.

Paul Outerbridge Jr.

Dines, Elaine and Graham Howe, eds. *Paul Outerbridge: A Singular Aesthetic: Photographs and Drawings 1921-1941: Catalogue raisonne.* Santa Barbara, Calif.: Arabesque Books, 1981.
Howe, Graham and G. Ray Hawkins, eds. *Paul Outerbridge Jr: Photographs.* New York: Rizzoli, 1980.

Olivia Parker

Under the Looking Glass. Boston: Little, Brown, 1983.

Irving Penn

Passage: A Work Record. New York: Knopf, 1991.
Szarkowski, John. *Irving Penn.* New York: Museum of Modern Art, 1984.
Worlds in a Small Room. New York: Viking, 1980.

John Pfahl

Altered Landscapes: The Photographs of John Pfahl. Introduction by Peter C. Bunnell. Carmel, Calif.: The Friends of Photography, 1981.

Herbert Ponting

Arnold, H.J.P. *Photographer of the World: the Biography of Herbert Ponting.* Rutherford, N.J.: Fairleigh Dickinson University Press, 1971.
Ponting, Herbert G. *The Great White South.* London: G. Duckworth & Co., 1923.
Savours, A., ed. *Scott's Last Voyage.* New York: Praeger Pub., 1975.

Hans Richter

Hans Richter. New York: Holt, Rinehart &Winston, Inc., 1971.

O. Winston Link

Hensley, Tim. *Steam Steel & Stars: The Last Days of Steam Railroad in America, Photographs by O. Winston Link.* New York: Harry N. Abrams, Inc., 1985.

El Lissitzky

El Lissitzky, 1890-1941. Cambridge, Mass.: Harvard University Art Museums: Busch-Reisinger Museum, 1987.

Herbert List

Metken, Gunter. *Herbert List: Photographs, 1930-1970.* New York: Rizzoli, 1981.

George Platt Lynes

Woody, Jack. *George Platt Lynes Photographs, 1931-1955.* Pasadena, Calif.: Twelvetrees Press, 1983.

Hippolyte Malegue

Goldschmidt, Lucien and Weston J. Naef. *The Truthful Lens.* New York: The Grolier Club, 1980.

Man Ray

Baum, Timothy. *Man Ray's Paris Portraits 1921-1939.* Washington, DC: Middendorf Gallery, 1989.

Foresta, Merry, et al. *Perpetual Motif: The Art of Man Ray.* Washington D.C., National Museum of American Art, Smithsonian Institution; New York: Abbeville Press, 1988.

Man Ray Photographs: With 347 Duotone Plates. New York: Thames and Hudson, 1982.

Man Ray, The Photographic Image. Woodbury, N. Y.: Barron's, 1980.

Photographs by Man Ray: 105 Works, 1920-1934. Reprint of 1934 edition. New York: Dover Pub., 1979.

Self Portrait. Boston: Little, Brown, 1963.

Schwarz, Arturo. *Man Ray: The Rigour of Imagination.* New York: Rizzoli, 1977.

Robert Mapplethorpe

Kardon, Janet. *Robert Mapplethorpe: The Perfect Moment.* Exhibition catalog. Philadelphia, Pa.: Institute of Contemporary Art, 1988.

Marshall, Richard. *Robert Mapplethorpe.* New York: Whitney Museum of American Art, 1988.

Black Book/ Photographs by Robert Mapplethorpe. Forward by Ntozake Shange. New York: St. Martin's Press, 1986.

Mapplethorpe, Robert. *Certain People: A Book of Portraits.* Preface by Susan Sontag. Pasadena, Calif.: Twelve Trees Press, 1985.

Charles Marville

Marville, Charles. *Etudes de Cies.* Paris: Galerie Octant, 1978.

Ralph Eugene Meatyard

James Baker Hall, ed. *Ralph Eugene Meatyard.* Millerton, N.Y.: Aperture, 1974.

Ray Metzker

Tucker, Anne Wilkes. *Unknown Territory: Photographs by Ray K. Metzker.* Millerton, N.Y.: Aperture/Houston: Museum of Fine Arts, 1984.

Joel Meyerowitz

Cape Light: Color Photographs. Boston: Museum of Fine Arts, 1978.

Duane Michals

Real Dreams: Photo Stories. Danbury, N. H.: Addison House, 1976.

Richard Misrach

Richard Misrach. San Francisco: Grapestake Gallery, 1979.

Lisette Model

Thomas, Ann. *Lisette Model.* Exhibition catalog. Ottawa: National Gallery of Canada, 1990.

Lisette Model. Millerton, N.Y.: Aperture, 1979.

Kenneth Josephson

Kenneth Josephson. Exhibition catalog, Museum of Contemporary Art, Chicago. Chicago, Ill.: The Museum, 1983.

Guillermo Kahlo

Herrera, Hayden. Frida, A Biography of Frida Kahlo. New York: Harper & Row, 1983.

Yousuf Karsh

Karsh Canadians. Toronto; Buffalo: University of Toronto Press, 1978.

Karsh: A Fifty-Year Retrospective. Boston: Little, Brown, 1983.

Karsh Portraits. Boston: New York Graphic Society, 1976.

Karsh: The Art of the Portrait, Ottawa: National Gallery of Canada, 1989.

Gertrude Kasebier

Homer, William Innes. Pictorial Heritage: The Photographs of Gertrude Kasebier. Exhibition catalog. Delaware: Delaware Art Museum, 1979.

Gyorgy Kepes

Gyorgy Kepes, Light Graphics May 31-July 8, 1984. New York: International Center of Photography, 1984.

Andre Kertesz

Ducrot, Nicolas. Andre Kertesz, Sixty Years of Photography. New York: Penguin Books, 1978.

Ducrot, Nicolas, ed. J'aime Paris: Photographs Since the Twenties. New York, Grossman Publishers, 1974.

_____. Portraits. New York: Mayflower Books, 1979.

Harder, Susan, ed. Andre Kertesz, Diary of Light 1912-1985. New York: Aperture, 1987.

Hungarian Memories. Introduction by Hilton Kramer. Boston: Little, Brown, 1982.

Phillips, Sandra S., David Travis, and Weston J. Naef. Andre Kertesz: Of Paris and New York. Chicago: Art Institute of Chicago, 1985.

Gustave Klucis

Gassner, Hubertus and Roland Nachtigaeller, eds. Gustav Klucis Retrospektive. Stuttgart: Verlag Gerd Hatje, 1991.

Josef Koudelka

Gypsies: Photographs. Millerton, N.Y.: Aperture, 1975.

Dorothea Lange

Dorothea Lange. Introduction by George P. Elliott. New York: Museum of Modern Art, 1966.

Jacques Henri Lartigue

Avendon, Richard, ed. Diary of a Century. New York: Viking Press, 1970.

Bonjour Monsieur Lartigue. Paris: Association des Amis de J.H. Lartigue, 1980.

Jacques-Henri Lartigue. Millerton, N. Y.: Aperture, 1976.

Jacques-Henri Lartigue. New York: Pantheon Books, 1986.

Clarence John Laughlin

Clarence John Laughlin, The Personal Eye. Millerton, N. Y.: Aperture, 1973.

Davis, Keith F. Clarence John Laughlin: Visionary Photographer. Kansas City, Mo.: Hallmark Cards, 1990.

Alma Lavenson

Ehrens, Susan. Alma Lavenson Photographs. Berkeley, Calif.: Wildwood Arts, 1990.

Nathan Lerner

Nathan Lerner: Fifty Years of Inquiry. Exhibition catalog, Chicago Public Library Cultural Center. Chicago, Ill.: Columbia College, 1984.

Helen Levitt

Levitt, Helen. A Way of Seeing. Essay by James Agee. New York: Horizon Press, 1981.

Emmet Gowin

Emmet Gowin--Photographs. Exhibition catalog. Philadelphia: Philadelphia Museum of Art, 1990.
Emmet Gowin, Photographs. New York: Knopf, 1976.

Philippe Halsman

Halsman at Work: Philippe Halsman and Yvonne Halsman. Introduction by Yvonne Halsman. New York: Harry N. Abrams, Inc., 1989.
Eliot, Alexander. *Sight and Insight.* New York: McDowell, 1959.

David Octavius Hill and Robert Adamson

Ford, Colin, ed. *An Early Victorian Album: the Photographic Masterpieces (1843-1847) of David Octavius Hill and Robert Adamson.* New York: Knopf, 1976.
Stevenson, S. *David Octavius Hill and Robert Adamson: Catalogue of their Callotypes taken between 1843 and 1847.* Edinburgh: National Galleries of Scotland, 1981.

Lewis Hine

Gutman, Judith Mara. *Lewis W. Hine 1874-1940: Two Perspectives.* (ICP Library of Photographers), New York: Grossman Publishers, 1974.
Hine, Lewis. *Men at Work: Photographic Studies of Modern Men and Machines.* New York: Dover Publications, 1977.
Rosenblum, Walter and Naomi. *America & Lewis Hine: Photographs 1904-1940.* Millerton, New York: Aperture, 1977.

David Hockney

David Hockney: A Retrospective. Los Angeles: Los Angeles County Museum of Art; New York: Harry N. Abrams, 1988.
David Hockney, Photographs. Pompidou, New York: Petersburg Press, 1982.

Horst P. Horst

Lawford, Valentine. *Horst: His Work and His World.* New York: Knopf, 1984.
Salute to the Thirties: Horst. New York: Viking Press, 1971.

Eikoh Hosoe

Eikoh Hosoe: Photographs 1960-1980. Rochester, N.Y.: Dark Sun, 1982.

L. A. Huffman

Brown, Mark Herbert and W.R. Felton. *Before Barbed Wire.* New York: Henry Holt and Company, 1956.

Georges Hugnet

Jaguer, Edouard. *Les Mysteres de la Chambre Noire: Le Surrealisme et la Photographie.* Paris: Flammarion, 1981.
Kraus, Rosalind E. and Jane Livingston. *L'Amour Fou.* New York: Abbeville Press, 1985.

Frank Hurley

Herbert Ponting and Frank Hurley. *1910-1916 Antarctic Photographs: Scott, Mawson, and Shackleton Expeditions.* New York: St. Martin's Press, 1979.

George Hurrell

Stine, Whitney. *The Hurrell Style: 50 Years of Photographing Hollywood.* New York: John Day Company, 1976.

William Henry Jackson

Newhall, Beaumont and Diana E. Edkins. *William H. Jackson.* Dobbs Ferry, N.Y.: Morgan & Morgan, 1974.

Lotte Jacobi

Wise, Kelly, ed. *Lotte Jacobi.* Danbury, N. H.: Addison House Inc., 1978.
Lotte Jacobi. Beverly Hills, Calif.: Stephen White Gallery of Photography, 1986.
Theater and Dance Photographs. (Introduction by Cornell Capa). Woodstock, VT: Country Press, 1982.

Elliott Erwitt

Personal Exposures. New York: W.W. Norton & Co., 1988.

Frederick H. Evans

Newhall, B. *Frederick H. Evans: Photographer of the Majesty, Light, and Space of the Medieval Cathedrals of England and France.* Millerton, N. Y.: Aperture, 1973.

Walker Evans

Agee, James and Walker Evans. *Let Us Now Praise Famous Men.* Boston: Houghton Mifflin, 1969.

Evans, Walker. *American Photographs.* 50th anniversary edit. New York: Museum of Modern Art, 1988.

Greenough, Sarah. *Walker Evans, Subways and Streets.* Exhibition catalog. Washington, D.C.: National Gallery of Art, 1991.

Walker Evans. Introduction by John Szarkowski. New York: The Museum of Modern Art, 1971.

Walker Evans at Work. Essay by Jerry L. Thompson. New York: Harper & Row, 1982.

Walker Evans, First and Last. New York: Harper & Row, 1978.

Walker Evans: Photographs for the Farm Security Administration, 1935-1938. New York: Da Capo Press, Inc, 1973.

Roger Fenton

Hannavy, John. *Roger Fenton of Crimble Hall.* Boston: D.R. Godine, 1975.

Lloyd, Valerie. *Roger Fenton, Photographer of the 1850's.* London: South Bank Board and Yale University Press, 1988.

Robert Frank

The Americans. Introduction by Jack Kerouac. Millerton, N. Y.: Aperture, 1978.

Robert Frank. Millerton, N. Y.: Aperture, 1976.

Tucker, Anne and Philip Brookman, eds. *Robert Frank: New York to Nova Scotia.* Boston: Little & Brown; Houston: Museum of Fine Arts, 1986.

Lee Friedlander

The American Monument. New York: Eakins Press Foundation, 1976.

Lee Friedlander Portraits. Boston: Little, Brown, 1985.

Slemmons, Rod. *Like a One-Eyed Cat: Photographs by Lee Friedlander, 1956-1987.* New York: Harry N. Abrams Inc., 1989.

Arnold Genthe

As I Remember. New York: Reynal & Hitchcock, 1936.

Gisele Freund

Gisele Freund, Photographer. New York: Harry N. Abrams, 1985.

Alexander Gardner

Goldschmidt, Lucien and Weston J. Naef. *The Truthful Lens.* New York: The Grolier Club, 1980.

Hamilton, Charles. *Lincoln in Photographs: An Album of Every Known Pose.* Norman: University of Oklahoma Press, 1963.

Mellon, James ed. *The Face of Lincoln.* New York: Viking Press, 1979.

Stephane Geoffray

Jammes, Andre and Eugenia Parry Janis. *The Art of French Calotype.* Princeton: Princeton University Press, 1983.

Mario Giacomelli

Mario Giacomelli. Introduction by Stephen Brigidi and Claire V.C. Peeps. Carmel, Calif.: Friends of Photography, 1983.

Ralph Gibson

Days at Sea. New York: Lustrum Press, 1974.

Imogen Cunningham

Cunningham, Imogen. *Photographs.* Seattle: University of Washington Press, 1970.

Imogen! Imogen Cunningham Photographs 1910-1973. Introduction by Margery Mann. Seattle: University of Washington Press, 1974.

Edward S. Curtis

Andrews, Ralph W. *Curtis' Western Indians.* Seattle: Superior Pub. Co., 1962.

Portraits from North American Indian Life. Introductions by A.D. Colman and T.C. McLuhan. New York: A & W Visual Library, 1972.

Davis, Barbara A. *Edward S. Curtis: The Life and Times of a Shadow Catcher.* San Francisco, Calif.: Chronicle Books, 1985.

Fleming, Paula Richardson and Judith Luskey. *The North American Indians in Early Photographs.* New York: Harper and Row, 1986.

Graybill, Florence Curtis and Victor Boeson. *Edward Sheriff Curtis: Visions of a Vanishing Race.* New York: Crowell, 1976.

Hodge, Frederick Webb, ed. *The North American Indian, Edward S. Curtis.* Forward by Theodore Roosevelt.

Field research conducted under the patronage of J. Pierpont Morgan. New York: Johnson Reprint Corp., 1970, (c)1907-1930.

Louise Dahl-Wolfe

Louise Dahl-Wolfe: A Photographer's Scrapbook. New York: St. Martin's/Marek Press, 1984.

Judy Dater

Comar, Carolyn, ed. *Body and Soul, Ten American Women.* Boston: Hill & Co., 1988.

Enyeart, James L. *Judy Dater: Twenty Years.* Tuscon, Ariz.: University of Arizona Press, 1986.

J. Daziaro

Buerger, Janet E. *French Daguerreotypes.* Chicago: University of Chicago Press, 1989.

Baron Adolf De Meyer

Brandau, Robert, ed. *De Meyer.* New York: Knopf, 1976.

Robert Doisneau

Three Seconds from Eternity: Photographs. Boston: New York Graphic Society, 1980.

Marcel Duchamp

Schwartz, Arturo. *The Complete Work of Marcel Duchamp.* New York: Harry N. Abrams Inc., 1969.

Harold Edgerton

Edgerton, Harold Eugene and James Killian, Jr. *Moments of Vision: The Stroboscopic Revolution in Photography.* Cambridge: MIT Press, 1979.

Jussim, Estelle. *Stopping Time: the Photographs of Harold Edgerton.* New York: Harry N. Abrams, 1987.

William Eggleston

William Eggleston's Guide. Exhibition catalog. Essay by John Szarkowski. New York: Museum of Modern Art, 1976.

Eauclaire, Sally. *The New Color Photography.* New York: Abbeville Press, 1981.

Rudolf Eickemeyer, Jr.

Naef, Weston J. *The Collection of Alfred Stieglitz: Fifty Pioneers of Modern Photography.* New York: Metropolitan Museum of Modern Art, 1978.

Panzer, Mary. *In My Studio: Rudolf Eickemeyer Jr. and the Art of the Camera, 1885-1930.* Yonkers: Hudson River Museum, 1986.

Peter Henry Emerson

Goldschmidt, Lucien and Weston J. Naef. *The Truthful Lens.* New York: The Grolier Club, 1980.

Newhall, Nancy. *P.H. Emerson: the Fight for Photography as a Fine Art.* Millerton, N.Y.: Aperture, 1975.

Turner, Peter and Richard Wood. *P.H. Emerson: Photographer of Norfolk.* Boston: D.R. Godine, 1974.

Wynn Bullock

Bullock, Barbara. *Wynn Bullock.* San Francisco: Scrimshaw Press, 1971.

Bullock-Wilson, Barbara. *Wynn Bullock, Photography: A Way of Life.* Dobbs Ferry, N. Y.: Morgan & Morgan, 1973.

Dilley, Clyde H. *The Photography and Philosophy of Wynn Bullock.* Philadelphia: Art Alliance Press, 1984.

Wynn Bullock. Millerton, N.Y.: Aperture, 1976.

Harry Callahan

Davis, Keith F. *Harry Callahan, New Color: Photographs 1978-1987.* Kansas City, Mo.: Hallmark Cards, 1988.

Callahan, Harry M. *Eleanor.* New York: Callaway Editions, 1984.

Callahan, Harry. *Photographs.* Santa Barbara, CA: El Mochelo Gallery and Van Riper and Thompson, 1964.

Harry Callahan. New York: Museum of Modern Art, 1967.

Harry Callahan, Color 1941-1980. Providence: Matrix Publications, 1980.

Szarkowski, John, ed. *Harry Callahan.* Exhibition Catalog, Museum of Modern Art. Millerton, N.Y.: Aperture, 1976.

Julia Margaret Cameron

Ford, Colin. *The Cameron Collection.* New York: Van Nostrand Reinhold, 1975.

Weaver, Mike. *Julia Margaret Cameron, 1815-1879.* Boston: Little, Brown, 1984.

Robert Capa

Capa, Cornell and Richard Whelan, ed. *Robert Capa Photographs.* New York: Knopf, 1985.

Paul Caponigro

Landscape. New York: McGraw Hill Book Co., 1975.

Paul Caponigro. New York: Grossman, 1967.

The Wise Silence: Photographs. Boston: New York Graphic Society, 1983.

Lewis Carroll

Gernshiem, Helmut. *Lewis Carroll Photographer.* New York: Dover Publications Inc., 1969.

Henri Cartier-Bresson

Galassi, Peter. *Henri Cartier-Bresson: The Early Work.* New York: The Museum of Modern Art, 1987.

Henri Cartier-Bresson: Photographer. Boston: New York Graphic Society, 1979.

Photoportraits. New York: Thames and Hudson, 1985.

The World of Henri Cartier-Bresson. New York: Viking Press, 1968.

Larry Clark

Tulsa. New York: Lustrum Press, 1971.

Alvin Langdon Coburn

Coburn, Alvin Langdon. *Alvin Langdon Coburn, Photographer: An Autobiography.* New York: Dover Pub., 1978.

Weaver, Mike. *Alvin Langdon Coburn, Symbolist Photographer, 1882-1966: Beyond the Craft.* New York: Aperture Foundation, 1986.

Howard Coster

Pepper, Terence. *Howard Coster's Celebrity Portraits.* London: National Portrait Gallery; New York: Dover Publications Inc., 1985.

Konrad Cramer

Wolf, Tom and Franklin Riehlman. *Konrad Cramer: A Retrospective.* Annandale-on-Hudson, N. Y.: Bard College Center, 1981.

Cecil Beaton

Danziger, James. *Beaton.* New York: Viking Press, 1980.

Strong, Roy C. *Cecil Beaton: The Royal Portraits.* New York: Simon & Schuster, 1988.

Bernd and Hilla Becher

Becher, Bernd and Hilla. *Water Towers.* Cambridge: MIT Press, 1988.

E.J. Bellocq

Szarkowski, John, ed. *E.J. Bellocq: Storyville Portraits.* New York: Museum of Modern Art, 1970.

Erwin Blumenfeld

Blumenfeld, Erwin. *My One Hundred Best Photos.* New York: Rizzoli, 1981.

A. Aubrey Bodine

Ewing, Kathleen M. H. *A. Aubrey Bodine, Baltimore Pictorialist, 1906-1970.* Baltimore: Johns Hopkins University Press, 1985.

Edouard Boubat

George, Bernard. *Edouard Boubat.* New York: Macmillan, 1973.

Margaret Bourke-White

Callahan, Sean, ed. *The Photographs of Margaret Bourke-White.* Greenwich, Conn.: New York Graphic Sociey, 1972.

Goldberg, Vicki. *Margaret Bourke-White, A Biography.* New York: Harper & Row, 1986.

Margaret Bourke-White. *Portrait of Myself.* New York: Simon and Schuster, 1963.

Silverman, Johnathan. *For The World To See, The Life of Margaret Bourke-White.* Callahan, Dean, ed. New York: Viking Press, 1983.

Mathew Brady and Brady Studio

Horan, James David. *Mathew Brady, Historian with a Camera.* New York: Crown Publishers, 1955.

Kunhardt, Dorothy Meserve. *Mathew Brady and His World.* Alexandria: Time-Life Books, 1977.

Lossing, Benson John. *Mathew Brady's Illustrated History of the Civil War.* New York: Fairfax Press, 1912.

Constantin Brancusi

Brancusi: Photographer. New York: Agrinde Pub., 1979.

Tabart, Marielle and Isabelle Monod-Fontaine, ed. *Brancusi, Photographe.* Paris: Musee National d'art Modern, 1979.

Bill Brandt

Mellor, David. *Bill Brandt: Behind the Camera.* New York: Aperture, 1985.

Nudes: 1945-1980. Boston: New York Graphic, 1980.

Perspective of Nudes. New York: Amphoto, 1961.

Shadow of Light: A Collection of Photographs from 1931 to the Present. New York: Viking Press, 1966.

Brassai

Brassai. Paris: Editions Neuf, 1952.

Brassai. New York: Museum of Modern Art, 1968.

Paris de Nuit. Paris: Arts et Metiers Graphique, 1933.

The Secret Paris of the 30s. New York: Pantheon Books, 1976.

Manuel Alvarez Bravo

Livingston, Jane. *M. Alvarez Bravo.* Washington D.C.: Corcoran Gallery of Art, 1978.

Manuel Alvarez Bravo. New York: Aperture Foundation, 1978.

A Selected Bibliography of Photographer's Monographs

Berenice Abbott

Berenice Abbott: Documentary Photographs of the 1930's. Cleveland: Gallery, 1980.

McCausland, Elizabeth. *New York in the Thirties.* New York: Dover Publications, 1973.

O'Neal, Hank. *Berenice Abbott, American Photographer.* New York: McGraw Hill, 1982.

Ansel Adams

Adams, Adams and Nancy Newhall. *This is the American Earth.* San Francisco: Sierra Club, 1960.

Alinder, Mary Street, ed. *Ansel Adams: An Autobiography.* Boston: Little, Brown and Company, 1985.

Ansel Adams: Letters and Images, 1916-1984. Boston: Little, Brown and Company, 1988.

De Cock, Liliane, ed. *Ansel Adams.* Hastings-on-Hudson: Morgan & Morgan, 1972.

Hill, Tim, ed. *The Portfolios of Ansel Adams.* Boston: New York Graphic Society, 1977.

Newhall, Nancy Wynne. *Ansel Adams.* San Francisco: Sierra Club, 1963.

Singular Images 1923-1974. Dobbs Ferry, N.Y.: Morgan & Morgan, 1974.

Yosemite and the Range of Graphic Light. Boston: New York Graphic Society, 1979.

Max Alpert

Shudakov, Grigory, Olga Suslova, and Lilya Ukntonskaya. *Pioneers of Soviet Photography.* New York: Thames and Hudson, 1983.

Diane Arbus

Diane Arbus. Millerton, N.Y.: Aperture, 1972.

Diane Arbus: Magazine Work. Millerton, N.Y.: Aperture, 1984.

Eugene Atget

Szarkowski, John. *The Work of Atget, Volume I, Old France.* New York: Museum of Modern Art, 1981.

_____. *The Work of Atget, Volume II, The Art of Old Paris.* New York: Museum of Modern Art, 1982.

_____. *The Work of Atget, Volume III, The Ancien Regime.* New York: Museum of Modern Art, 1983.

_____. *The Work of Atget, Volume IV, Modern Times.* New York: Museum of Modern Art, 1985.

Richard Avedon

In The American West, 1979-1984. New York: Harry N. Abrams, 1985.

Portraits, Richard Avedon. New York: Farrar, Staus and Giroux, 1976.

George N. Barnard

Barnard, George N. *Photographic Views of Sherman's Campaign.* New York: Dover Publications, Inc., 1977.

Davis, Keith F. *George N. Barnard, Photographer of Sherman's Campaign.* Kansas City: Hallmark Cards, 1990.

Goldschmidt, Lucien, and Weston J. Naef. *The Truthful Lens.* New York: The Grolier Club, 1980.

Herbert Bayer

Cohen, Arthur Allen. *Herbert Bayer: The Complete Work.* Cambridge: MIT Press, 1984.

Herbert Bayer: Photographic Works. Exhibition catalog. Los Angeles: Arco Center for Visual Art, 1977.

Felice Beato

Pare, Richard, ed. *Photography and Architecture: 1839-1939.* Montreal: Centre Canadien d'Architecture/Canadian Center for Architecture, 1982.

Worswick, Clark, ed. *Japan Photographs 1854-1905.* New York: Knopf, 1979.

Andy Warhol

>Brown, Andreas. *Andy Warhol: His Early Work 1947-1959*. New York: Gotham Book Mart Gallery, 1971.

>Wünsche, Hermann. *Andy Warhol, das graphische werk, 1962-1980*. Köln: Bonner Universität Buchruckerei, 1980.

Anthonie Waterloo

>Bartsch, Adam. *Anton Waterloo's Kupferstiche ausführlich beschreiben*. Vienna: A. Blumauer, 1795.

>Dutuit, Eugène. *Manuel de l'amateur d'estampes*, Vol. VI. Paris: A. Lévy, 1884-1885.

Max Weber

>Rubenstein, Daryl R. *Max Weber: A Catalogue Raisonné of His Graphic Work*. Chicago: University of Chicago Press, 1980.

Stow Wengenroth

>Stuckey, R. and J. *The Lithographs of Stow Wengenroth*. Massachusetts: Barre Publishers, 1973.

James Abbott McNeill Whistler

>Kennedy, Edward G. *The Etched Work of Whistler*. New York: Grolier Club, 1910.

>Levy, Mervyn. *Whistler Lithographs: An Illustrated Catalogue Raisonné*. London: Jupiter, 1975.

>Mansfield, Howard. *A Descriptive Catalogue of the Etchings and Drypoints of James Abbott McNeill Whistler*. Chicago: Caxton Club, 1909.

Grant Wood

>Garwood, Darrell. *Artist in Iowa: A Life of Grant Wood*. New York: W.W. Norton and Co., 1944.

Paul Wunderlich

>Brusberg, Dieter. *Paul Wunderlich: Werk-verzeichnis der Lithographien von 1949-1965*. Hanover: Verlag der Galerie Dieter Brusberg, 1966.

Zao-Wou-Ki

>Jacometti, N. *Catalogue raisonné de l'oeuvre gravé et lithographie 1949-1954*. Berne: Gütekunst V. Klipstein, 1955.

Anders Zorn

>Asplund, Karl. *Anders Zorn, his life and work*. London: The Studio, 1921.

>Delteil, Loys. *Le peintre-graveur illustré*, Vol. IV. Paris: Loys Delteil, 1906-1926.

>Hjert, Svenolof and Bertil Hjert. *Zorn: Engravings/etsningar; a complete catalog/en komplett katalog*. Uppsala: Hjert and Hjert, 1980.

Antonio Tapies

Galfetti, M. and C. Vogel. *Antonio Tápies: Obra Grafica, 1947-1972*. New York: Wittenborn and Co., 1973.

Wayne Thiebaud

Coplas, John. *Wayne Thiebaud: Graphics*. California: Pasadena Art Museum, 1968.

Giovanni Battista Tiepolo

Rizzi, Aldo. *L'Opera Grafica dei Tiepolo: Le Acqueforti*. Venice: Electa Editrice, 1971.

Vesme, Alessandro Baudi de. *Le Peintre-graveur Italien*. Milan: U. Hoepli, 1906.

Giovanni Domenico Tiepolo

Rizzi, Aldo. *L'Opera Grafica dei Tiepolo: Le Acqueforti*. Venice: Electa Editrice, 1971.

Vesme, Alessandro Baudi de. *Le Peintre-graveur Italien*. Milan: U. Hoepli, 1906.

James Jacques Tissot

Wentworth, M. *James Jacques Joseph Tissot: A Retrospective Exhibition*. Rhode Island: Rhode Island School of Design and Ontario: The Art Gallery of Ontario, 1968.

Henri de Toulouse-Lautrec

Adhémar, Jean. *Toulouse-Lautrec: His Complete Lithographs and Drypoints*. New York: Abrams, 1965.

Adriani, Götz. *Toulouse-Lautrec: des gesamte graphische werk*. Köln: DuMont, 1976.

Delteil, Loys. *Le peintre-graveur illustré: Toulouse Lautrec*, Vol. X, XI. Paris: Loys Delteil, 1920.

Wolf Traut

Geisberg, Max. *Der deutsche Einblatt-Holzschnitt in der ersten Halfte des 16 Jahrhunderts*. Munich: Hugo Schmidt Verlag, 1923-1931.

Maurice Utrillo

Fabris, Jean. *Utrillo: sa vie, son oeuvre*. Paris: Birr, 1982.

Pétridès, Paul. *L'Oeuvre Complet de Maurice Utrillo*. Paris: Pétridès, 1959-1974.

Suzanne Valadon

Pétridès, Paul. *L'Oeuvre Complet de Suzanne Valadon*. Paris: Compagnie Française des Arts Graphiques, 1971.

Roger-Marx, Claude. *Dix-huit planches originales de Suzanne Valadon (1895-1910) avec un essai de catalogue*. Paris: Daragnes, 1932.

Felix Vallotton

Stein, Donna and Donald Karshan. *L'Estampe Originale: A Catalogue Raisonné*. New York: The Museum of Graphic Art, 1970.

Vallotton, Maxime and Charles Georg. *Félix Vallotton, catalogue raisonné de l'oeuvre gravé et lithographie*. Genève: Bonvent, 1972.

Jacques Villon

Ginestet, Colette de et Catherine Pouillon. *Jacques Villon: les estampes et les illustrations; catalogue raisonné*. Paris: Arts et Métiers Graphiques, 1979.

Maurice de Vlaminck

Fels, Florent. *Vlaminck*. Paris: Seheur, 1928.

Walterskirchen, Katalin von. *Maurice de Vlaminck: Verzeichnis des graphischen werkes*. Bern: Benteli, 1974.

Edouard Vuillard

Johnson, Una E. *Ambroise Vollard, Éditeur*. New York: Wittenborn and Co., 1944.

Roger-Marx, Claude. *L'Oeuvre gravé de Vuillard*. Monte Carlo: Sauret, 1948.

Martin Schongauer

Bartsch, Adam. *Le Peintre Graveur,* Vol. VI. Vienna: J.V. Degen, 1803-1821.

Lehrs, Max. *Geschichte un Kritscher Katalog des deutschen, niederländischen und Französischen Kupferstichs im XV. Jahrhundert,* Vol. V. Vienna: Gesellschaft für vervielfaltigende Kunst, 1908-1934.

Armand Seguin

Stein, Donna, and Donald Karshan. *L'Estampe Originale: A Catalogue Raisonné.* New York: The Museum of Graphic Art, 1970.

Gino Severini

Wingler, H.M. *Graphic Work from The Bauhaus.* Connecticut: New York Graphic Society, 1965.

Sir Francis Seymour-Haden

Harrington, H. Nazeby. *The Engraved Work of Sir Francis Seymour-Haden, P.R.E., An Illustrated and Descriptive Catalogue.* Liverpool: Henry Young and Sons, 1910.

Salaman, Malcom C. *The Etchings of Sir Francis Seymour-Haden, P.R.E.* London: Halton and Truscott Smith, Ltd., 1923.

Ben Shahn

Prescott, Kenneth W. *The Complete Graphic Works of Ben Shahn.* New York: Quadrangle, 1973.

Paul Signac

Johnson, Una E. *Ambroise Vollard, Éditeur.* New York: Wittenborn and Co., 1944.

Kornfeld, E.W. and P.A. Wick. *Catalogue raisonné de l'oeuvre gravé et lithographie de Paul Signac.* Berne: Kornfeld et Klipstein, 1974.

Alfred Sisley

Delteil, Loys. *Le peintre-graveur illustré,* Vol. XVII. Paris: Loys Delteil, 1906-1926.

Leymarie, Jean and Michel Melot. *The Graphic Works of the Impressionists: The Complete Prints of Manet, Pissarro, Renoir, Cézanne, and Sisley.* New York: Abrams, 1972.

John Sloan

Morse, Peter. *John Sloan's Prints: a catalogue raisonné of the etchings, lithographs, and posters.* New Haven/London: Yale University Press, 1969.

Pierre Soulages

Duby, Georges, et al. *Soulages: Eaux-fortes, lithographies, 1952-1973.* Paris: Arts et Métiers Graphiques, 1974.

Juin, H. *Soulages.* Paris: Musée de Poche, 1958.

Raphael Soyer

Cole, Sylvan, Jr. *Raphael Soyer; fifty years of print-making.* New York: Da Capo Press, 1967.

Theophile Alexandre Steinlen

Crauzat, Ernest de. *L'Oeuvre gravé et lithographie de Steinlen.* Paris: Societé de Propagation des Livres d'Art, 1913.

Frank Stella

Kunsthalle Bielefeld. *Frank Stella: Werke 1958-1976.* Bielefeld: Kunsthalle Bielefeld, 1977.

Rubin, William S. *Frank Stella.* New York: Museum of Modern Art, 1970.

George Stubbs

Taylor, Basil. *Stubbs.* London: Phaidon, 1975.

Taylor, Basil. *The Prints of George Stubbs.* London: The Paul Mellon Foundation for British Art, 1969.

Graham Sutherland

Tassi, Roberto. *Graham Sutherland: Complete Graphic Work.* New York: Rizzoli, 1978.

Yves Tanguy

Wolfgang Wittrock Kunsthandel. *Yves Tanguy, das druckgraphische werk: Ausstellung April-Mai 1976.* Düsseldorf: Wolfgang Wittrock Kunsthandel, 1976.

Pierre Auguste Renoir

    Delteil, Loys. *Le peintre-graveur illustré*, Vol. XVII. Paris: Loys Delteil, 1906-1926.

    Johnson, Una E. *Ambroise Vollard, Éditeur*. New York: Wittenborn and Co., 1944.

    Roger-Marx, Claude. *Renoir*. Paris: Floury, 1937.

    Stella, Joseph G. *The Graphic Work of Renoir, catalogue raisonné*. London: Humphries, 1975.

    Vollard, Ambroise. *Renoir, an intimate record*. New York: Knopf, 1925.

Jusepe de Ribera

    Bartsch, Adam. *Le Peintre Graveur*, Vol. XV. Vienna: J.V. Degen, 1803-1821.

Gerhard Richter

    Block, René, and Karl Vogel. *Graphik des Kapitalistischen Realismus: Werkverzeichnisse bis 1971*. Berlin: Edition René Block, 1971.

    Museum Foldwang, Essen. *Gerhard Richter, Graphik 1965-1970*. Essen, 1970.

Larry Rivers

    Hunter, Sam. *Larry Rivers*. New York: Harry N. Abrams, 1970.

Auguste Rodin

    Delteil, Loys. *Le peintre-graveur illustré*, Vol. VI. Paris: Loys Delteil, 1906-1926.

    Thorson, Victoria. *Rodin Graphics: A Catalogue Raisonné of Drypoints and Book Illustrations*. San Francisco: Fine Arts Museum of San Francisco, 1975.

Christian Rohlfs

    Vogt, Paul. *Christian Rohlfs*. Köln: DuMont Schauberg, 1967.

    Vogt, Paul. *Christian Rohlfs: das graphische werk*. Recklinghausen: A. Borgers, 1960.

Felicien, Rops

    Exsteems, Maurice. *L'Oeuvre Gravé et Lithographie de Félicien Rops*. Paris: Editions Pellet, 1928.

    Ramiro, Evasténe. *Catalogue descriptif et analytique de l'oeuvre gravé de Félicien Rops*. Brussels: Daman and Paris, Conquet, 1887.

Georges Rouault

    Chapon, François. *Rouault: oeuvre gravé*, 2v. Monte Carlo: Sauret, 1978/79.

    Wofsy, Alan. *Georges Rouault, The Graphic Work*. London: Secker and Warburg, 1976.

Ker Xavier Roussel

    Johnson, Una E. *Ambroise Vollard, Éditeur*. New York: Wittenborn and Co., 1944.

    Salomon, Jacques. *Ker Xavier Roussel*. Paris: La Bibliotèque des Arts, 1967.

Ed Ruscha

    Auckland City Art Gallery. *Graphic Works of Edward Ruscha*. Auckland: Auckland City Art Gallery, 1978.

    Minneapolis Institute of Arts. *Edward Ruscha*. Minneapolis, 1972.

Augustin de Saint-Aubin

    Bocher, Emmanuel. *Augustin de Saint-Aubin*. Paris: Morgand et Fatout, 1879.

    Lawrence, H.W., and Basil Lewis Dighton. *French Line Engravings of the Late Eighteenth Century*. London: Lawrence and Jellicoe Ltd., 1910.

Egon Schiele

    Kallir, Otto. *Egon Schiele, The Graphic Work*. New York: Crown, 1970.

Karl Schmidt-Rottluff

    Rathenau, Ernst. *Karl Schmidt-Rottluffs: das graphische werk nach 1928*. Hamburg, 1964.

    Schapire, Rosa. *Karl Schmidt-Rottluffs graphisches werk bis 1923*. Berlin: Euphorion-Verlag, 1924.

Adriaen van Ostade

    Bartsch, Adam. *Le Peintre Graveur*, Vol. I. Vienna: J.V. Degen, 1803-1821.

    Godefroy, Louis. *L'Oeuvre gravé de Adriaen van Ostade*. Paris: Louis Godefroy, 1930.

    Hollstein, F.W.H., et al. *Dutch and Flemish Etchings, Engravings and Woodcuts, ca. 1450-1700*, Vol. XV. Amsterdam: Menno Hertzberger, 1949-1969.

Jules Pascin

    Georges, Waldemar. *Pascin Retrospective: 1885-1930: Peintures, Aquarelles, Dessins, Graveurs*. Paris: Galeries Jean Marc Vidal, 1945.

Philip Pearlstein

    Dückers, Alexander. *Philip Pearlstein: Drawings and Prints 1946-1972*. Berlin: Staatliche Museum, 1973.

Max Pechstein

    Fechter, Paul. *Das Graphische Werk: Max Pechstein*. Berlin, 1921.

Georg Pencz

    Bartsch, Adam. *Le Peintre Graveur*, Vol. VIII. Vienna: J.V. Degen, 1802-1821.

Joseph Pennell

    Wuerth, Louis A. *Catalogue of the Etchings of Joseph Pennell*. Boston: Little Brown, 1928.

Pablo Picasso

    Bloch, Georges. *Pablo Picasso*. Berne: Kornfeld and Klipstein, 1968-1979.

    Czwiklitzer, Christopher. *Picasso's Posters*. New York: Random House, 1971.

    Geiser, Bernhard. *Picasso, peintre-graveur*, 2v. Berne: Geiser, 1933/1963.

    Mourlot, Fernand. *Picasso Lithographe*, 4v. Monte Carlo: Sauret, 1949-1964.

Giovanni Piranesi

    Focillon, Henri. *G.B. Piranesi/Giovanni Battista Piranesi, essai de catalogue raisonné de son oeuvre*, 2v. Paris: Laurens, 1918.

    Hind, Arthur M. *Giovanni Battista Piranesi: A Critical Study with A List of His Published Works and Detailed Catalogues of The Prisons and the Views of Rome*. London: Cotswold Gallery, 1922.

Camille Pissarro

    Delteil, Loys. *Le peintre-graveur illustré*, Vol. XVII. Paris: Loys Delteil, 1906-1926.

Serge Poliakoff

    Ragon, M. *Poliakoff*. Paris: Musée de Poche, 1956.

Maurice Prendergast

    Rhys, Hedley Howell. *Maurice Prendergast, 1859-1924*. Massachusetts: Harvard University Press, 1960.

Robert Rauschenberg

    Adriani, Gotz. *Robert Rauschenberg: Zeichnungen, Gouachen, Collagen 1949 bis 1979*. München/Zürich: Piper, 1979.

    Forge, Andres. *Rauschenberg*. New York: Abrams, 1969.

Man Ray

    Bramly, Serge. *Man Ray*. Paris: Belfond, 1980.

    Penrose, Roland. *Man Ray*. London: Thames and Hudson, 1975.

    Ribemont-Dessaignes, Georges. *Man Ray*. Paris: Gallimard, 1924.

Odilon Redon

    Mellerio, André. *Odilon Redon*. Paris: Société pour l'Etude de la Gravure Française, 1913.

    Mellerio, André. *Odilon Redon: peintre, dessinateur et graveur*. Paris: Floury, 1923.

Benedetto Montagna

    Bartsch, Adam. *Le Peintre Graveur*, Vol. XIII. Vienna: J.V. Degen, 1803-1821.

    Hind, Arthur M. *Early Halan Engraving: A Critical Catalogue with Complete Reproduction of All the Prints Described*, Vol. V. London: Bernard Quaritch Ltd., 1938-1948.

Henry Moore

    Galerie Gérald Cramer, Geneva. *Henry Moore: oeuvre gravé et lithographie 1939-1967*. Geneva, 1968.

    Gallery Cramer. *Henry Moore: Catalogue of Graphic Work 1931-1972*. Geneva: 1973.

Thomas Moran

    Kochler, Sylvester R. "The Works of the American Etchers, V: Thomas Moran," *American Art Review* 1 (1880).

Giorgio Morandi

    Vitali, Lamberto. *L'opera grafica di Giorgio Morandi*. Turin: Einaudi, 1964.

Jean Michel Moreau

    Boucher, Emmanuel. *Jean Michel Moreau le jeune*. Paris: Morgand et Fatout, 1882.

Robert Motherwell

    Terenzio, Stephanie. *The Painter and The Printer: Robert Motherwell's Graphics, 1943-1980*. New York: American Federation of Arts, 1980.

Alphonse Mucha

    Bridges, Ann, ed. *Alphonse Mucha, the Complete Graphic Work*. New York: Harmony, 1980.

Otto Mueller

    Karsch, Florian and L.G. Buchheim. *Otto Müller: Leben und werk: with a list of Graphic Work*. Feldafing, 1963.

Edvard Munch

    Schiefler, Gustav. *Verzeichnis des Graphische Werk Edvard Munch bis 1960*. Berlin: Cassirer, 1907.

    Schiefler, Gustav. *Edvard Munch das Graphische Werk 1906-1926*. Berlin: Euphorion, 1928.

    Willoch, Sigurd. *Edvard Munch: Etchings*. Oslo: G. Tanum, 1950.

Antonio Zoran Music

    Schmicking, Rolf. *Music; Das graphische werk 1947 bis 1962*. Brunswick: Verlag Galerie Schmucking, 1962.

Louise Nevelson

    Glimcher, Arnold B. *Louise Nevelson*. New York: Dutton, 1976.

Barnett Newman

    Baltimore Museum of Art. *Barnett Newman: The Complete Drawings, 1944-1969*. Baltimore: Museum of Art, 1979.

Kenneth Noland

    Waldman, Diane. *Kenneth Noland, a retrospective*. New York: Guggenheim Foundation Collaboration with Abrams, 1977.

Emil Nolde

    Schiefler, Gustav. *Emil Nolde: das graphische werk*. Köln: Dumont Schauberg, 1966-1967.

    Schiefler, Gustav, and Christel Mosel. *Emil Nolde; das graphische werk . . . neu bear beitet, ergänzt und mit Abbildungen versehen*. Cologne: Verlag M. DuMont Schauberg, 1966.

Claes Oldenburg

    Baro, Gene. *Claes Oldenburg Drawings and Prints*. London and New York: Chelsea House Publishers, 1969.

Emil Orlik

    Pauli, Friedrich W. *Emil Orlik; Wege eines Zeichners und Graphikers*. Darmstadt: Blaschke, 1972.

Andrea Mantegna

Bartsch, Adam. *Le Peintre Graveur*, Vol. XIII. Vienna: J.V. Degen, 1803-1821.

Hind, Arthur M. *Early Italian Engraving; A Critical Catalogue with Complete Reproduction of All the Prints Described*, Vol. V. London: Bernard Quaritch Ltd., 1938-1948.

Franz Marc

Lankheit, Klaus. *Franz Marc: Katalog der Werke*. Cologne: Dumont Schauberg, 1970.

Gerhard Marcks

Rieth, Adolph. *Gerhard Marcks*. Recklinghausen: Bongers, 1959.

John Marin

Zigrosser, Carl. *The Complete Etchings of John Marin: Catalogue Raisonné*. Philadelphia: Philadelphia Museum of Art, 1969.

Marino Marini

Philadelphia Museum of Art. *Marino Marini; Graphics and Related Works*. Philadelphia, 1969.

Reginald Marsh

Sasowsky, Norman. *Reginald Marsh; Etchings, Engravings, Lithographs*. New York: Praeger, 1956.

Andre Masson

Museum of Modern Art (New York). *André Masson*. New York: Museum of Modern Art, 1976.

Henri Matisse

Guichard-Meili, J. and F. Woimant. *Matisse: l'oeuvre gravé*. Paris: Biblioteque Nationale, 1970.

Lieberman, William S. *Matisse, 50 Years of His Graphic Art*. New York: Braziller, 1956.

Roberto Matta

Silkeborg Museum. *Matta; kataloget over en naesten komplet samling af Mattas grafiske arbejder*. Silkeborg: Silkeborg Museum, 1969.

Israhel van Meckenem

Bartsch, Adam. *Le Peintre Graveur*, Vol. VI. Vienna: J.V. Degen, 1803-1821.

Lehrs, Max. *Geschichte und Kritischer Katalog das deutschen, niederlandischen und Franzosischen Kupferstichs im XV. Jahrhundert*, Vol. III. Vienna: Gesellschraft für vervielfaltigen de kunst, 1908-1934.

Charles Meryon

Delteil, Loys. *Le peintre-graveur illustré: Meryon*, Vol. 2. Paris: Loys Delteil, 1907.

Wright, Harold J.L., ed. *Catalogue Raisonné of the Etchings of Charles Meryon, by Loys Delteil*. London and New York, 1924.

Jean Mignon

Bartsch, Adam. *Le Peintre Graveur*, Vol. XVI. Vienna: J.V. Degen, 1803-1821.

Herbet, Felix. "Les Graveurs de l'ecole de Fontainebleau", *Annales 18*. Fontainebleau: Maurice Bourges, 1896-1902.

Zerner, Henri. *École de Fontainebleau, graveurs*, no. 3. Paris: Arts et Metiers Graphiques, 1969.

Jean Francois Millet

Deteil, Loys. *Le peintre-graveur illustré*, Vol. I. Paris: Loys Delteil, 1906-1926.

Joan Miro

Corredor-Matheos, José. *Los carteles de Miró*. Barcelona: Poligrafa, 1980.

Hunter, Sam. *Joan Miro: L'oeuvre gravé*. Paris: Calmann-Lévy, 1958.

Mourlot, Fernand. *Joan Miro Lithographe, I*. New York: Tudor Publishing Co., 1972.

Paula Modersohn-Becker

Werner, Wolfgang. *Paula Modersohn-Becker, 1876-1907, Oeuvreverzeichnis der Graphik*. Bemen: Graphisches Kabinett, 1972.

BUSINESS REPLY MAIL
FIRST CLASS MAIL   PERMIT NO. 843   BOSTON, MASS.

POSTAGE WILL BE PAID BY ADDRESSEE

AUCTION INDEX INC.
30 VALENTINE PARK
NEWTON, MA 02165-9921

BUSINESS REPLY MAIL
FIRST CLASS MAIL   PERMIT NO. 843   BOSTON, MASS.

POSTAGE WILL BE PAID BY ADDRESSEE

AUCTION INDEX INC.
30 VALENTINE PARK
NEWTON, MA 02165-9921

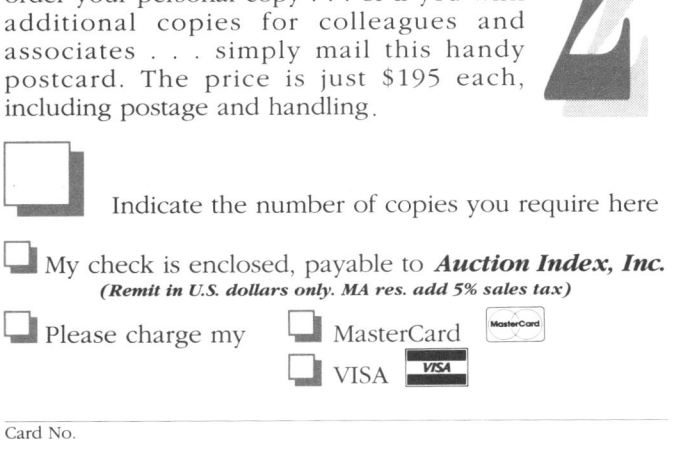 

Oskar Kokoschka

Wingler, H.M. *Kokoschka: Das Graphische Werk*. Munich, 1971.

Kathe Kollowitz

Klipstein, August. *Käthe Kollwitz: Verzeichnis des graphischen werkes*. Berne: Kornfeld and Klipstein, 1955.

Yasuo Kuniyoshi

Davis, Richard A. "The Graphic Work of Yasuo Kuniyoshi 1893-1953." *Archives of American Art 5*, no. 3 (1965).

Marie Laurencin

Allard, Roger. *Marie Laurencin*. Paris: Editions de la Nouvelle Revue Française, 1921.

Henri Laurens

Arts Council of Great Britain. *Henri Laurens, 1895-1954*. London: Arts Council, 1971.

Fernand Leger

Saphire, Lawrence. *Fernand Léger, the Complete Graphic Work*. New York: Blue Moon Press, 1978.

Alphonse Legros

Wright, H.J.C. *Catalogue Raisonné of the Works of Alphonse Legros*, 1929.

Martin Lewis

McCarron, Paul. *Martin Lewis: The Graphic Work*. New York: Kennedy Galleries, 1973.

Sol Lewitt

Museum of Modern Art. *Sol Lewitt*. New York: Museum of Modern Art, 1978.

Lucas van Leyden

Bartsch, Adam. *Le Peintre Graveur*, Vol. VII. Vienna: J.V. Degen, 1803-1821.

Hollstein, F.W.H. et al. *Dutch and Flemish Etchings, Engravings and Woodcuts, ca. 1450-1700*, Vol. X. Amsterdam: Menno Hertzberger, 1949-1969.

Roy Lichtenstein

Bianchini, Paul. *Roy Lichtenstein: Drawings and Prints*. New York: Chelsea House, 1970.

Max Liebermann

Schiefler, G. *Das Graphische Werk von Max Liebermann*, Vol. 1-2. Berlin, 1902,1914.

Claude Lorrain (Claude Gellée)

Blum, André. *Les eaux-fortes de Claude Gellée dit le Lorrain*. Paris: Editions Albert Morancé, 1923.

Louis Lozowick

Robert Hull Fleming Museum. *Paintings, Drawings and Lithographs of Louis Lozowick*. Vermont: University of Vermont, 1971.

Rene Magritte

Passeron, René and Jean Saucet. *René Magritte*. Chicago: O'Hara, 1972.

Aristide Maillol

Guérin, Marcel. *Catalogue raisonné de l'oeuvre gravé et lithographie de Aristide Maillol*, 2v. Geneva: Cailler, 1965-1967.

Kazimir Malevich

Karshan, Donald. *Malevich: the Graphic Work 1913-1930*. Jerusalem: Israel Museum, 1975.

Edouard Manet

Beraldi, Henri. *Les graveurs du XIXe Siècle, guide de l'amateur d'estampes modernes*, Vol. IX. Paris: Libraire L. Conquet, 1885-1892.

Guérin, Marcel. *L'oeuvre Gravé de Manet*. Paris, 1944.

Harris, Jean. *Édouard Manet: Graphic Works: A Definitive Catalogue Raisonné*. New York: Collector's Editions, 1976.

William Hogarth

Paulson, Ronald. *Hogarth's Graphic Works; first complete edition.* New Haven: Yale University Press, 1965.

Winslow Homer

Gelman, Barbara. *The Wood Engravings of Winslow Homer.* New York: Bounty Books, 1969.

Edward Hopper

Levin, Gail. *Edward Hopper as Illustrator.* New York: Norton/Whitney Museum of American Art, 1979.

Zigrosser, Carl. *The Complete Graphic Work of Edward Hopper: Catalogue of the Exhibition.* Philadelphia: Philadelphia Museum of Art, 1962.

Friedensreich Hundertwasser

Kestner-Gesellschaft. *Hundertwasser; vollständiger oeuvre-katalog mit 100 farbigen reproduktionen.* Hannover: Kestner-Gesellschaft, 1964.

William Holman Hunt

Schleinitz, Otto von. *William Holman Hunt.* Bielefeld/Leipzig, Velhagen and Klasing, 1907.

Louis Icart

Schnessel, S.M. *A Collector's Guide to Louis Icart.* New Jersey: The Exhumation, 1973.

Robert Indiana

McCoubrey, John W. *Robert Indiana.* Pennsylvania: Institute of Contemporary Art, 1968.

Jean Francois Janinet

Beraldi, Henri. *Les graveurs du XIXe Siècle, guide de l'amateur d'estampes modernes*, Vol. VIII. Paris: Librairie L. Conquet, 1885-1892.

Jasper Johns

Field, Richard S. *Jasper Johns: Prints 1960-1970.* New York: Praeger and Philadelphia: Philadelphia Museum of Art, 1970.

Asger Jorn

Dotremont, C. *Asger Jorn.* Copenhagen, 1950.

Wassily Kandinsky

Roethel, Hans Konrad. *Kandinsky, des graphische werk.* Schauberg: Verlag M. DuMont, 1970.

Ellsworth Kelly

Waldman, Diane. *Ellsworth Kelly: Drawings, Collages, Prints.* Connecticut: New York Graphic Society, 1972.

Rockwell Kent

Jones, Dan B. *The Prints of Rockwell Kent, a Catalogue Raisonné.* Chicago/London: University of Chicago Press, 1975.

Ernst Ludwig Kirchner

Dube, Annemarie, and Wolf-Dieter Dube. *E.L. Kirchner; das graphische werk.* Munich: Prestel-Verlag, 1967.

Schiefler, Gustav. *Die Graphik Ernst Ludwig Kirchners; Band II 1917-1927.* Berlin-Charlottenburg: Euphorion-Verlag, 1927-1931.

Paul Klee

Kornfeld, Eberhard W. *Verzeichnis des graphischen werkes von Paul Klee.* Bern: Verlag Kornfeld und Klipstein, 1963.

Max Klinger

Singer, Hans W. *Max Klingers Radierungen, Stiche und Steindrucke; Wissenschaftliches Verzeichnis.* Berlin: Amsier und Ruthardt, 1909.

Laura Knight

Salaman, Malcolm C. *Laura Johnson Knight.* Modern Masters of Etching Series No. 29. London: The Studio Ltd., 1932.

Theodore Gericault

Delteil, Loys. *Le peintre-graveur illustré*, Vol. XVIII. Paris: Loys Delteil, 1906-1926.

Alberto Giacometti

Lust, Herbert C. *Giacometti; the Complete Graphics*. New York: Tudor Publishing Co., 1970.

Luca Giordano

Bartsch, Adam. *Le Peintre Graveur*, Vol. XXI. Vienna: J.V. Degen, 1803-1821.

Hendrik Goltzius

Bartsch, Adam. *Le Peintre Graveur*, Vol. III. Vienna: J.V. Degen, 1803-1821.

Hirschmann, Otto. *Verzeichnis des graphischen werks von Hendrick Goltzius (1558-1617) mit Benutzung der durch E.W. Moest Ninterlassenen notizen zusarnmengestellt*. Leipzig: Verlag von Klinkhardt und Biermann, 1921.

Hollstein, F.W.H. et al. *Dutch and Flemish Etchings, Engravings and Woodcuts ca. 1450-1700*, Vol. VIII. Amsterdam: Menno Hertzberger, 1949-1969.

Nataliia Sergeevna Goncharova

Wingler, H.M. *Graphic Work from The Bauhaus*. Connecticut: New York Graphic Society, 1965.

Francisco de Goya

Delteil, Loys. *Le peintre-graveur illustré*, Vol. XIV-XV. Paris: Loys Delteil, 1906-1926.

Harris, Thomás. *Goya; Engravings and Lithographs*. Oxford: Bruno Cassirer, 1964.

H. A. P. Grieshaber

Fuerst, Margot. *Hap Grieshaber der Holzschneider*. Stuttgart: Verlag Gerd Hatje, 1964.

Frederick Landseer Maur Griggs

Comstock, Francis Adams. *A Gothic Vision; F.L. Griggs and His Work*. Boston: Boston Public Library and Oxford: Ashmolean Museum, 1966.

Giovanni Francesco Grimaldi

Bartsch, Adam. *Le Peintre Graveur*, Vol. XIX. Vienna: J.V. Degen, 1803-1821.

George Grosz

Dückers, Alexander. *George Grosz: Frühe Druckgraphik, Sammelwerke Illustrierte Büher 1914-1923*. Berlin: Berlin-Dahlem Museum, 1971.

Yozo Hamaguchi

Krzhshnik, Z. *Catalogue of the Biennale of Graphic Art in Ljublana*. Ljublana, Yugoslavia, 1961.

Nantenshi Gallery. *Hamaguchi: Graphic Works*. New York: Wittenborn and Co., 1973.

Richard Hamilton

Davidson Art Center. *The Prints of Richard Hamilton*. Connecticut: Wesleyan University, 1973.

Childe Hassam

Griffith, Fuller. *The Lithographs of Childe Hassam*. Washington: Smithsonian Institution, 1962.

Leonard Clayton Gallery. *Handbook of the Complete Set of Etchings and Drypoints, with 25 Illustrations of Childe Hassam*. New York: Leonard Clayton Gallery, 1933.

Stanley William Hayter

Corcoran Gallery of Art. *Stanley William Hayter: Paintings, Drawings and Prints 1922-1950*. Washington, D.C.: Corcoran Gallery of Art, 1973.

Erich Heckel

Dube, Annemarie and Wolf-Dieter Dube. *Erich Heckel – das graphische Werke*. New York: Ernest Ratherau, 1964.

Jan van der Heyden

Hollstein, F.W.H. et al. *Dutch and Flemish Etchings, Engravings and Woodcuts, ca. 1450-1700*, Vol. IX. Amsterdam: Menno Hertzberger, 1949-1969.

David Hockney

M. Knoedler and Co. *David Hockney: Print Retrospective*. New York, 1973.

Marcel Duchamp

Schwarz, Arturo. *The Complete Works of Marcel Duchamp*. New York: Harry N. Abrams, 1969.

Albrecht Durer

Bartsch, Adam. *Le Peintre Graveur*, Vol. VII. Vienna: J.V. Degen, 1803-1821.

Hollstein, F.W.H. et al. *German Engravings, Etchings and Woodcuts ca. 1400-1700*, Vol. VII. Amsterdam: Menno Hertzberger, 1954-1968.

Meder, Joseph. *Dürer-Katalog*. Vienna: Verlag Gilhofer un Ranschburg, 1932.

Cornelis Dusart

Bartsch, Adam. *Le Peintre Graveur*, Vol. V. Vienna: J.V. Degen, 1803-1821.

Dutuit, Eugène. *Manuel de l'amateur d'estampes*, Vol. IV. Paris: A. Levy, 1884-1885.

Hollstein, F.W.H. et al. *Dutch and Flemish Etchings, Engravings and Woodcuts ca. 1450-1700*, Vol. VI. Amsterdam: Menno Hertzberger, 1949-1969.

Jean Duvet

Bartsch, Adam. *Le Peintre Graveur*, Vol. VII. Vienna: J.V. Degen, 1803-1821.

James Ensor

Delteil, Loys. *Le peintre-graveur illustré*, Vol. XIX. Paris: Loys Delteil, 1906-1926.

Croquez, Albert. *L'Oeuvre gravé de James Ensor, catalogue raisonné*. Paris: Maurice le Garrec, 1935.

Max Ernst

Galerie Brusberg. *Max Ernst*. Hanover: Galerie Brusberg, 1972.

Maurits Cornelis Escher

Locher, J.L. et al. *De Werelden van M.C. Escher*. Amsterdam: Meulenhoff, 1971.

Maurice Esteve

Muller, J.E. *Maurice Estève*. Paris: Hazan, 1961.

Antonio Fantuzzi

Bartsch, Adam. *Le Peintre Graveur*, Vol. XVI. Vienna: J.V. Degen, 1803-1821.

Herbert, Felix. *Catalogue de l'oeuvre de Fantuzi*. Fonainebleau: Maurice Bourges, 1899.

Zerner, Henri. *Ecole de Fontainebleau, graveurs*. Paris: Arts et Metiers Graphiques, 1969.

Lyonel Feininger

Prasse, Leona E. *Lyonel Feininger*. Berlin: Gebrüder Mann Verlag, 1972.

Conrad Felixmuller

Boettger, Fritz. *Felixmüller; Katalog Seiner Holzschnitte, Lithographien, Radierungen*. Dresden: Verlag Emil Richter, 1919.

Tsuguharu Foujita

Bauer, Gerard. *Foujita, l'homme et le peintre*. Paris: Les Presses Artistiques, 1958.

Sam Francis

Klipstein and Kornfeld. *Sam Francis Ausstellung*. Berne: Klipstein and Kornfeld, 1957.

San Francisco Museum of Art. *Sam Francis: Exhibition of Drawings and Lithographs*. San Francisco, 1967.

Helen Frankenthaler

Krens, Thomas. *Helen Frankenthaler, Prints, 1961-1979*. New York: Harper and Row, 1980.

Johnny Friedländer

Schmücking, Rolf. *Johnny Friedländer*. Brunswick: Städtisches Museum, 1960.

Henry Fuseli

Kunsthaus Zürich. *Johann Heinrich Füssli, 1741-1825; Gemälde und Zeichnungen*. Zürich: Kunsthaus Zürich, 1969.

Paul Gauguin

Guérin, Marcel. *L'Oeuvre gravé de Gaugin*. Paris: H. Floury, 1927.

Currier and Ives, Publishers

Conningham, Frederick Arthur. *An Alphabetical List of 5735 of N. Currier and Currier and Ives Prints, with Dates of Publication, Sizes and Recent Auction Prices.* New York: F.A. and M.B. Conningham, 1930.

Peters, Harry T. *Currier and Ives: Printmakers to the American People.* Garden City: Doubleday, 1929, 1931.

John Steuart Curry

Cole, Sylvan. *The Lithographs of John Steuart Curry: A Catalogue Raisonné.* New York: Associated American Artists, 1976.

Czestochowski, Joseph H. *John Steuart Curry and Grant Wood: A Portrait of Rural America.* Missouri: University of Missouri Press, 1981.

Salvador Dali

Centre Georges Pompidou (Paris). *Salvador Dali: Rétrospective 1920-1980.* Paris: Centre Georges Pompidou, 1979.

Charles Francois Daubigny

Delteil, Loys. *Le peintre-graveur illustré*, Vol. VIII. Paris: Loys Delteil, 1906-1926.

Honore Daumier

Delteil, Loys. *Le peintre-graveur illustré*, Vol. XX-XXIX. Paris: Loys Delteil, 1906-1926.

Dimier, Louis. *Physionomies et Physiologies; quatre-vingt-une graveurs sur bois d'après Daumier exécutées par Eugene Dété, avec une préface et un catalogue de l'oeuvre gravé sur bois de Daumier.* Paris: Emile Nourry, 1930.

Willem DeKooning

Gaugh, Harry F. *Willem de Kooning.* New York: Abbeville Press, 1983.

Philibert Louis Debucourt

Fenaille, Maurice. *L'Oeuvre gravé de P.L. Debucourt (1755-1832).* Paris: Libraire Damascène Morgand, 1899.

Edgar Degas

Delteil, Loys. *Le peintre-graveur illustré*, Vol. IX. Paris: Loys Delteil, 1906-1926.

Janis, Eugenia Parry. *Degas Monotypes: Essay, Catalogue and Checklist.* Cambridge: Fogg Art Museum, 1968.

Adhémar, Jean and Francoise Cachin. *Degas, graveures et monotypes.* Paris: Arts et Metiers Graphiques, 1975.

Robert Delaunay

Dorival, Bernard. *Robert Delaunay 1885-1941.* Paris/Bruxelles: Jacques Damase Gallery, 1975.

Paul Delvaux

Nadeau, Maurice, *Les dessins de Paul Delvaux.* Paris: Denoël, 1967.

Gilles Demarteau

Leymarie, L. de. *L'Oeuvre de Gilles Demarteau l'ainé graveur du roi, catalogue descriptif.* Paris: Georges Rapilly, 1896.

Maurice Denis

Cailler, Pierre. *Catalogue raisonné de l'oeuvre gravé et lithographie de Maurice Denis.* Geneva: Editions Pierre Cailler, 1968.

Jim Dine

Galerie Mikro, Berlin. *Jim Dine Complete Graphics.* Berlin: Galerie Mikro, 1970.

Otto Dix

Karsch, Florian. *Otto Dix; das graphische werk.* Hannover: Fackelträger-Verlag Schmidt-Küster, 1970.

Jean Dubuffet

Loreau, Max. *Catalogue des travaux de Jean Dubuffet; Fascicule XVI; Les Phénomènes.* Paris: Jean-Jacques Pauvert, 1964.

Paul Cezanne

Gachet, Paul. *Cézanne d'Auvers; Cézanne graveur*. Paris: Les Beaux Arts, Editions d'etudes et de documents, 1952.

Venturi, Lionello. *Cézanne, son art - son oeuvre*. Paris: Paul Rosenberg, 1936.

Marc Chagall

Cramer, Gerald. *Marc Chagall Monotypes, 1961-1965*. Geneva: Gerald Cramer, 1966.

Mourlot, Fernand. *Chagall Lithographie*. Monte Carlo: Andre Sauvet, 1960.

Sorlier, Charles. *Les Affiches de Marc Chagall*. Paris: Draeger-Vilo, 1975.

Eduardo Chillida

Man, Felix H., ed. *Europäische Graphik*, Vol. 6. Munich: Galerie Wolfgang Ketterer, 1969.

Giorgio de Chirico

Ciranna, Alfonso. *Giorgio de Chirco: Catalogo delle opere grafichi [incisioni e litografie] 1921-1969*. Milan: Alfonso Ciranna, 1969.

Christo

Houdenakk, Pei and Jorg Schellman. *Christo: The Complete Editions, 1964-1982*. New York: New York University Press, 1982.

Antonio Clave

Weintraub Gallery. *Clavé: Paintings, Sculpture, Graphics*. New York: 1974.

Hieronymous Cock (Publisher)

Riggs, Timothy A. "Hieronymus Cock (1510-1570), Printmaker and Publisher in Antwerp at the Sign of the Four Winds." Yale Unversity (Thesis), 1971.

Hollstein, F.W.H. et al. *Dutch and Flemish Etchings, Engravings and Woodcuts, ca. 1450-1700,,* Vol. IV. Amsterdam: Menno Hertzberger, 1949-1969.

Lovis Corinth

Muller, Heinrich. *Die Späte Graphik von Lovis Corinth*. Hamburg: Lichtwarkstiftung, 1960.

Schwarz, Karl. *Das Graphische Werk von Lovis Corinth*. Berlin: Verlag von Fritz Gurlitt, 1917, 1922.

Corneille

Robert-Dumesnil, A.P.F. *Le Peintre-Graveur Français, ou Catalogue Raisonné des Estampes Gravées par les Peintres et les dessinateurs de l'ecole Française, ouvrage faisant suite au peintre-graveur de M. Bartsch*. Paris: Gabriel Waree, 1835-1871.

Jean Baptiste Camille Corot

Delteil, Loys. *Le peintre-graveur illustré*, Vol. V. Paris: Delteil Loys, 1906-1926.

Cornelis Cort

Bierens de Haan, J.C.J. *L'Oeuvre gravé de Cornelis Cort, graveur hollandais*. The Hague: Martinus Nijhoff, 1948.

Hollstein, F.W.H. et al. *Dutch and Flemish Etchings, Engravings and Woodcuts, ca. 1450-1700,* Vol. V. Amsterdam: Menno Hertzberger, 1949-1969.

Pierre-Francois Courtois

Lawrence, H.W., and Basil Lewis Dighton. *French Line Engravings of the Late 18th Century*. London: Lawrence and Jellicoe Ltd., 1910.

Lucas Cranach

Bartsch, Adam. *Le Peintre Graveur*, Vol. VII. Vienna: J.V. Degen, 1803-1821.

Hollstein, F.W.H. et al. *German Engravings, Etchings and Woodcuts, ca. 1400-1700*, Vol. VI. Amsterdam: Menno Hertzberger, 1954-1968.

Lucas Cranach, the Elder

Bartsch, Adam. *Le Peintre Graveur*, Vol. VII. Vienna: J.V. Degen, 1803-1821.

Hollstein, F.W.H. et al. *German Engravings, Etchings and Woodcuts ca. 1400-1700*, Vol. VI. Amsterdam: Menno Hertzberger, 1954-1968.

Louis Marin Bonnet

   Herold, Jacques. *Louis-Marin Bonnet (1756-1793) Catalogue de l'oeuvre gravé*. Paris: Société pour l'etude de la gravure française, 1935.

Georges Braque

   Mourlot, Fernand. *Braque Lithographe*. Monte Carlo: André Sauret, 1963.

Gerald Brockhurst

   Wright, Harold J.L. "Catalogue of the Etchings of G.L. Brockhurst, A.R.A., R.E." *Print Collector's Quarterly*, 22 (1935).

Pieter Brueghel, the Elder

   Bastelaer, René van. *Les Estampes de Peter Bruegel l'ancien*. Brussels: G. van Oest et Cie, 1908.

   Hollstein, F.W.H. et al. *Dutch and Flemish Etchings, Engravings and Woodcuts, ca. 1450-1700*, Vol. III. Amsterdam: Menno Hertzberger, 1949-1969.

   Lebeer, Louis. *Catalogue raisonné des estampes de Bruegel l'ancien*. Bruxelles, 1969.

Bernard Buffet

   Mourlot, Fernand. *Bernard Buffet; Lithographs 1952-1966*. New York: Tudor Publishing Co., 1968.

   Sorlier, Charles. *Bernard Buffet Lithographe*. Paris: Draeger Trinckvel, 1980.

Felix Buhot

   Beraldi, Henri. *Les Graveurs du XIXe Siècle, Guide de l'amateur d'estampes modernes*, Vol. IV. Paris: Librairie L. Conguet, 1885-1892.

   Bourcard, Gustav. *Felix Buhot . . . Catalogue descriptif de son oeuvre gravé*. Paris: H. Floury, 1899.

Edward Coley Burne-Jones

   Hayward Gallery, London. *Burne-Jones: The Paintings, Graphic and Decorative Work of Sir Edward Burne-Jones, 1833-1898*. London: Arts Council of Great Britain, 1975.

Paul Cadmus

   Johnson, Una E., and J. Miller. *Paul Cadmus: Prints and Drawings 1922-1967*. Brooklyn: Brooklyn Museum, 1968.

Jacques Callot

   Lievre, J. *Jacques Callot*. Paris: Editions de la Gazette des Beaux-Arts, 1924-1927.

   Meaume, Edouard. *Recherches sur la vie et les ouvrages de Jacques Callot*. Paris: VVe Jules Renouard, 1860.

Canaletto

   Meyer, Rudolph. *Die beiden Canaletto, Antonio Canale und Bernardo Belotto, Versuch einer Monographie der radierten Werke beider Meister*. Dresden: Rudolph Meyer, 1878.

Agostino Carracci

   Bartsch, Adam. *Le Peintre Graveur*, Vol. XVIII. Vienna: J.V. Degen, 1803-1821.

Eugene Carriere

   Delteil, Loys. *Le peintre — graveur illustré*, Vol. VII. Paris: Loys Delteil, 1906-1926.

Mary Cassatt

   Breeskin, Adelyn D. *The Graphic Work of Mary Cassatt; A Catalogue Raisonné*. New York: H. Bittner and Co., 1948.

Giovanni Benedetto Castiglione

   Bartsch, Adam. *Le Peintre Graveur*, Vol. XXI. Vienna: J.V. Degen, 1803-1821.

   Percy, Ann. *Giovanni Benedetto Castiglione: Master Draughtsman of the Italian Baroque*. Philadelphia: Philadelphia Museum of Art, 1971.

Karel Appel

  Claus, Hugo. *Karel Appel, Painter.* Amsterdam: A.J.G. Strengholt, 1962.

Alexander Archipenko

  Karshan, Donald. *Alexander Archipenko – A Memorial Exhibition 1967-1969.* California: UCLA Art Galleries, 1967.

Arman

  Hahn, Otto. *Arman.* Paris: Hazan, 1972.

Jean (Hans) Arp

  Arntz, Wilhelm F. *Hans (Jean) Arp: das graphische Werk – L'Oeuvre gravé – The Graphic Work, 1912-1966.* Haag: Arntz - Winter, 1980.

Milton Avery

  Brooklyn Museum. *Milton Avery, Prints and Drawings 1930-1964.* New York: Shorewood Publishers, 1966.

Leonard Baskin

  Roylance, Dale. *Leonard Baskin: The Graphic Work 1950-1970.* New York: FAR Gallery, 1970.

Max Beckmann

  Gallwitz, Klaus. *Max Beckmann: Katalog der Druckgraphik: Radierungen, Lithographien, Holzschnitte, 1901-1948.* Karlswhe: Badischer Kunstverein, 1962.

  Glaser, Curt et al. *Max Beckmann.* Munich: R. Piper and Co., 1924.

Hans Sebald Beham

  Bartsch, Adam. *Le Peintre Graveur*, Vol. VIII. Vienna: J.V. Degen, 1803-1821.

  Hollstein, F.W. et al. *German Engravings, Etchings and Woodcuts ca. 1400-1700,* Vol. III. Amsterdam: Menno Hertzberger, 1954-1968.

  Pauli, Gustav. *Itans Sebald Beham: ein Kritisches Verzeichniss Seiner Kupferstiche, Radierungen und Holzschnitte.* Strasbourg: J.H. Ed. Heitz, 1901.

George Bellows

  Bellows, Emma S. et al. *George W. Bellows; His Lithographs.* New York: Alfred A. Knopf, 1927.

Frank W. Benson

  Paff, Adam E.M., and Arthur William Heintzelman. *Etchings and Drypoints by Frank W. Benson; An Illustrated and Descriptive Catalogue.* Boston: Houghton Mifflin Co., 1917-1959.

Thomas Hart Benton

  Fath, Creekmore. *The Lithographs of Thomas Hart Benton.* Austin: University of Texas Press, 1969.

George Caleb Bingham

  Bloch, E. Maurice. *George Caleb Bingham; A Catalogue Raisonné.* Berkeley and Los Angeles: University of California Press, 1967.

Isabel Bishop

  Brooklyn Museum. *Isabel Bishop: Prints and Drawings, 1925-1964.* New York: Shorewood Publishers, 1964.

William Blake

  Binyon, Laurence. *The Engraved Designs of William Blake.* London: Ernest Benn Ltd., 1926.

Hans Bol

  Hollstein, F.W.H. et al. *Dutch and Flemish Etchings, Engravings and Woodcuts, ca. 1450-1700,* Vol. III. Amsterdam: Menno Hertzberger, 1949-1969.

Pierre Bonnard

  Roger-Marx, Claude. *Pierre Bonnard.* Paris: Henry Babov, 1931.

  Roger-Marx, Claude. *Bonnard Lithographe.* Monte Carlo: André Sauret, 1952.

Catalogue Raisonné

Josef Albers

Miller, J. *Josef Albers Prints:* 1915-1970. New York, 1973.

Ivan LeLorraine Albright

Grayson, Gael (comp.). *Graven Image; The Prints of Ivan Albright 1931-1977.* Lake Forest, Illinois, 1978.

Hans Aldegrever

Bartsch, Adam. *Le Peintre Graveur,* Vol. VIII. Vienna: J.V. Degen, 1803-1821.

Hollstein, F.W.H. et al. *German Engravings, Etchings and Woodcuts ca. 1400-1700,* Vol. I. Amsterdam: Menno Hertzberger, 1954-1968.

Heinrich Aldegrever

Zschelletzschky, Herbert. *Das Graphische Werk Heinrich Aldegrevers.*, Strassburg: Heitz, 1933.

Pierre Alechinsky

Arntz, Wilhelm F., ed. *Arntz-Bulletin; Dokumentation der Kunst des 20. Jahrhunderts,* Vol. I. West Germany: Haasg/Oberbayern, 1968-1972.

Galerie van de Loo. *Pierre Alechinsky; 20 Jahre Impressionen; Oeuvrekatalog Druckgraphik.* Munich, 1967.

Riviere, Y. *Pierre Alechinsky: Les Estampes de 1946 a 1972.* Paris, 1973.

Pierre Michel Alix

Beraldi, Henri. *Les Graveurs du XIXe Siécle, Guide de l'amateur d'estampes modernes,* Vol. I. Paris: Librairie L. Conquet, 1885-1892.

Meyer, Julius et al. *Allgemeines Künstler-Lexikon, unter mitwirkung der namhaftesten Fach Gelehrten des In-und Auslandes,* Vol. I. Leipzig: Wilhelm Engelmann, 1872-1885.

Henry Alken

Meyer, Julius et al. *Allgemeines Künstler-Lexikon, unter mitwirkung der namhaftesten Fach Gelehrten des In-und Auslandes,* Vol. I. Leipzig: Wilhelm Engelmann, 1872-1885.

Siltzer, Captain Frank. *The Story of British Sporting Prints.* London: Hutchingson and Company, 1925.

Albrecht Altdorfer

Bartsch, Adam. *Le Peintre Graveur,* Vol. VIII. Vienna: J.V. Degen, 1803-1821.

Hollstein, F.W.H. et al. *German Engravings, Etchings and Woodcuts ca. 1400-1700,* Vol. I. Amsterdam: Menno Hertzberger, 1954-1968.

Winzinger, Franz. *Albrecht Altdorfer, Graphik: Itolzschnitte, Kupferstiche, Radierungen.* Munich: R. Piper and Co, 1963.

Cuno Amiet

Mandach, Conrad De. *Cuno Amiet: Vollstandiges Verzeichnis der Druckgraphik des Kunstlers.* Bern, 1939.

Jost Amman

Andresen, Andreas. *Der deutsche Peintre-graveur,* Vol. I. Leipzig: Rudolph Weigel, 1864-1878.

Becker, Carl. *Jost Amman; Zeichnerund Formschneider, Kupferdtzer und Stecher.* Leipzig: Rudolph Weigel, 1854.

Hollstein, F.W.H. et al. *German Engravings, Etchings and Woodcuts ca. 1400-1700,* Vol. II. Amsterdam: Menno Hertzberger, 1954-1968.

Andrea Andreani

Bartsch, Adam. *Le Peintre Graveur,* Vol. XII. Vienna: J.V. Degen, 1803-1821.

Krantz, Les, Ed. *American Artists, An Illustrated Survey of Leading Contemporary American,* New York, Facts on File, 1985.

MacDonald, Colin S. *A Dictionary of Canadian Artists,* Ottawa, Canadian Paperbacks, 1972.

Mallet, Daniel Trowbridge. *Mallett's Index of Artists.* New York, Bowker, 1935, Supplement, 1940.

Meyer, George H., Ed. *Folk Artists Biographical Index,* Detroit, Gale Research Co., 1987.

Naylor, Colin, and Genesis P-Orridge. *Contemporary Artists.* New York, St. Martin's Press, 1977.

Osborne, Harold, ed. *The Oxford Companion to Twentieth-Century Art,* Oxford, Oxford University Press, 1981.

Paviere, Sydney H. *A Dictionary of British Sporting Painter,* Leigh-on-Sea, England, F. Lewis, Publisher, Ltd., 1965.

Pettys, Chris. *Dictionary of Women Artists, An International Dictionary of Women Artists Born Before 1900,* Boston, G.K. Hall & Co., 1985.

Rubinstein, Charlotte Streifer. *American Women Artists: Early Indian Times to the Present,* Boston, G.K. Hall & Co., 1982.

Samuels, Peggy and Harold. *The Illustrated Biographical Encyclopedia of Artists of the American West.* Garden City, N.Y., Doubleday, 1976.

Samuels, Peggy and Harold. *Contemporary Western Artists,* Southwest Art Publishing, 1982.

Strickland, Walter George. *A Dictionary of Irish Artists,* Shannon, Ireland, Irish University Press, 1969.

Tannock, Michael. *Portuguese 20th Century Artists, A Biographical Dictionary,* Chichester, West Sussex, England, Philimore & Co. Ltd., 1978.

Thieme, Ulrich, and Felix Becker. *Allgemeines Lexikon der bildenden Kunstler von der Antike bis zur Gegenwart; unter Mitwirkung von 300 Fachgelehrten des In-und Auslandes.* Leipzig, Seemann, 1907-50.

Vollmer, Hans. *Allgemeines Lexikon der biblenden Kunstler des XX. Jahrhunderts.* Leipzig; E.A. Seemann, 1953-62.

Walker, John A. *Glossary of Art, Architecture and Design Since 1945: terms and labels describing movements, styles, and groups derived from the vocabulary of artists and critics.* London, England, Clive Bingley Ltd., revised 1977.

Waters, Grant M. *Dictionary of British Artists Working 1900-1955.* Eastbourne Fine Art, Eastbourne, England, 1975.

Who's Who in American Art. New York, Jacques Cattell Press, 1953, 1982, 1987.

Witt Library. *A Checklist of Painters C. 1200-1976 Represented in the Witt Library,* Courtauld Institute of Art, London, Mansell Information Publishing, 1978.

Wood, Lieut. Colonel J.C., *A Dictionary of British Animal Painters,* Leigh-on-Sea, England, F. Lewis, Publisher, Ltd., 1973.

Young, William, ed. *A Dictionary of American Artists, Sculptors, and Engraver: From the Beginnings to the Turn of the 20th Century,* Cambridge, Massachusetts, William Young and Co., 1968.

Bibliography

American Art Annual Volume XXV(1928), copyright 1929, American Federation of Arts, Washington, D.C.

Archives of American Art. *The Card Catalog of the Manuscript Collection of the Archives of American Art,* Wilmington, Delaware, Scholarly Resources Inc., 1980.

Art In America Annual Guide 1991-1992. New York, Art In America Magazine, August 1992.

Baigell, Matthew. *Dictionary of American Art,* New York, Harper & Row, 1979.

Benezit, Emmanuel. *Dictionnaire Critique et Documentaire des Peintres, Sculpteurs, Dessinateurs et Graveurs.* 3rd ed., Paris, Grund, 1976, 2nd ed., 1948-1955.

Boston Art Information Files (unpublished artists files), Boston Public Library, Fine Arts Department.

Castagno, John. *Artists as Illustrators,* Metuchen, N.J., The Scarecrow Press, 1989.

Cederholm, Theresa Dickason, *Afro-American Artists: A Biobibliographical Dictionary.* Boston, Trustees of the Boston Public Library, 1973.

Cummings, Paul. *Dictionary of Contemporary American Artists, New York,* St. Martin's Press, 1982.

Dictionnaire Biographique des Artistes Belges de 1830 a 1970, Bruxelles, Arto, 1978.

Encyclopedia of New Orleans Artists 1718-1918. New Orleans, The Historic New Orleans Collection, 1987.

Falk, Peter Hastings. *Who Was Who in American Art,* Madison, CN, Soundview Press 1985.

Fielding, Mantle. *Dictionary of American Painters, Sculptors & Engravers,* Poughkeepsie, Apollo Press, 1984, 2nd printing.

Groce, George C. and Wallace, David H. *The New York Historical Society's Dictionary of Artists in America, 1564-1860,* New Haven and London, Yale University Press, 1957.

Guide to Exhibited Artists, Vols. 1-5, Santa Barbara, CA, Clio Press, 1985.

Harper, J. Russell. *Early Painters and Engravers in Canada,* University of Toronto Press, 1970.

Havlice, Patricia Pate. *Index to Artistic Biography,* Metuchen, N.J., The Scarecrow Press, 1973, Supplement 1981.

Hughes, Edan Milton. *Artists in California, 1786-1940, Volume II,* San Francisco, Hughes Publishing Co., 1989.

Johnson, J. and Greutzner, A. *Dictionary of British Artists, 1880-1940: An Antique Collector's Club Research Project Listing 41,000 Artists.* Baron Publishing, Woodbridge, England, Antique Collectors Club, 1976.

I   =   image size
S   =   sheet size
P   =   measurements taken from platemark
L   =   measurement taken from borderline

How to read an entry

All works of art have been listed by artist in alphabetical sequence, and under each artist alphabetically by title.

> **CASSATT, Mary**   American 1844-1926
> $104,500* *Gathering Fruit (Breeskin 157; Mathews/Shapiro 15)* (c)
> 1893, 11th (final state), full margins, good cond., mat/
> light staining, glue, horizontal folds, lit, ex-coll, (10-31-
> 91, Sotheby-NY, #19 illus.), 16⁵/₈ x 11⁵/₈ in., (423 x 295
> mm.) drypoint, softground etching and aquatint p. in
> colors on laid paper. (BP 181,725, DM 62,522, FF 18,287,
> Y 799).

CASSATT	artist's name
Mary	artist's forename
American	nationality
1844-1926	lifedates
$104,500	price in dollars
*	buyer's premium has been added
Gathering Fruit	title
(Breeskin 157; Mathews/Shapiro 15)	catalogue raisonne
c. 1893	year work printed
good cond.	good condition as stated in auction catalog
mat/light staining	qualifications of condition
lit.	cited in a reference source
ex-coll.	cited former owner
10-31-91	date of auction, October 31, 1991
Sotheby-New York	auction house
#19	catalog lot number
illus.	illustrated
16 5/8 x 11 5/8 in., 423 x 295 mm.	measurements in inches and millimeters
drypoint, softground etching and aquatint p. in colors on laid paper	media and type of paper
BP 181,725, DM 62,522 FF 18,287, Y 799	conversion of $ price into other major currencies

Abbreviations

As few abbreviations as possible have been used to facilitate reading the text.

*	=	includes buyer's premium
ac.	=	active
annot.	=	annotated
attrib.	=	attributed
b/w	=	black/white
bears sig.	=	bears signature
c.	=	circa
(c)	=	copyright
cent.	=	century
d.	=	dated
ded.	=	dedicated
ed.	=	editor
edit.	=	edition
exec.	=	executed in _____ where the date of the work of art is known even though it does not bear a date
ex-coll.	=	ex-collection
exhib.	=	exhibited
i.	=	inscribed
ident.	=	identified
info.	=	information
inits.	=	initials
insig.	=	insignia
just.	=	justification
illus.	=	illustrated
lit.	=	literature
mono.	=	monogram
neg.	=	negative
num.	=	numbered
pencil s.	=	signed in pencil
prop.	=	property
prov.	=	provenance
p.l.	=	printed later
p.	=	printed
pub.	=	publisher
reprod.	=	reproduced as in an illustration
s.	=	signed
sig.	=	signature
t.	=	titled
verso	=	on the reverse

photogravure   A photomechanical printing process to reproduce photographs. First developed in 1879, the process is based on the traditional printmaking technique of *intaglio*. Most of the reproductions in Steiglitz's *Camera Work* were photogravures, for the process produces prints (gravures) of high quality. Under magnification, the black areas may look like a fine mesh pattern rather than the dots of a *halftone* reproduction. Also referred to as *heliogravure*.

photomontage   A composite image made by bringing together different photographs or parts of photographs to form a blended whole, which is often photographed.

platinum print   First developed in 1873, platinum coated papers were commercially available until 1937, when the cost of platinum made the process prohibitively expensive. For a short while the platinum was replaced with the less costly palladium. The process is based on the light sensitivity of paper that has been treated with iron salts and a platinum compound and then developed in potassium oxalate. Platinum prints were popular because of their permanency and their wide range of soft gray tonalities. Some modern photographers such as Irving Penn still use this process by hand-sensitizing their own papers.

printing-out paper   A paper treated with sodium chloride and silver nitrate (forming silver chloride) that becomes light-sensitized and darkens when exposed to direct sunlight or daylight. (No chemical treatment is required to make the image visible.)

rayograph   The name the artist Man Ray gave to his *photograms*.

salt print   A *contact print* made from a *calotype* or *collodion* negative. A sheet of paper that has been treated with light-sensitive silver chloride salts is placed into a frame in contact with the negative and exposed to sunlight. Salt prints are reddish-brown with a matte surface. The color may be a purplish-brown if it has been toned or a gold-brown if it has faded. The resolution is not as sharp as in albumen prints. Invented in 1840, salt prints were the earliest form of positive prints; they were in use until about 1860 when they were replaced by the albumen print.

schadograph   The name Christian Schad gave to his *photograms*.

silver print   See *gelatin silver print*.

stereograph   A cardboard mount holding two photographs of the same subject, each from a slightly different point of view. When viewed with binocular vision, a stereoscopic effect, 3-D (depth of field) is achieved.

talbotype   See *calotype*.

Type-C print   Kodak's old designation (before Kodacolor, 1941) for a color print made from a color negative or color transparency. See *chromogenic color print*.

wet-collodion print   See *collodion process*.

negative or positive, depending on the angle and light from which it is viewed. Daguerreotypes are light-sensitive and fragile and are usually stored in cases for protection.

dry-collodion print
See *collodion process*.

dye-transfer print
The most permanent of color prints, this complex method is based on the earliest *carbro print* method. The subject is photographed three times, using a different color filter each time. After several steps, the three, or more, separate gelatin negatives dyed cyan, magenta, and yellow are transferred one at a time in daylight in registration to form a positive color image. Also called a dye imbibition print.

Ektachrome print
A brand name. See *chromogenic color print*.

gelatin silver print
A photograph printed on paper that has been coated with gelatin containing light-sensitive silver halides. First introduced in 1872, gelatin silver prints are the standard black-and-white prints in use today.

gum bichromate print
A photograph printed on paper that has been coated with an emulsion of gum arabic, potassium bichromate, and pigment. The emulsion hardens in relation to the amount of light it receives, and the emulsion is then washed away. Introduced in 1894, popular into the 1920s, and occasionally used today; the gum bichromate process is valued for the artistic control it gives the photographer; gum bichromate prints have broad tones and often resemble crayon or charcoal drawings. Also called a gum print.

half tone
A photomechanical process to transfer a photographic image to a relief plate that can be printed on the same press as type. The continuous tones of the photograph are converted into a pattern of tiny dots (larger and closer together in the dark areas) that are visible under magnification. In duotone printing, two passes of the press are used. The process was first used commercially in 1880.

heliogravure
See *photogravure*.

jetgraph
The color-print process in which cyan, magenta, yellow, and black are controlled by a computer and a digital scanning system.

orotone print
Using a negative, an image is printed on a glass plate that has been covered with a gelatin silver emulsion. After the image has been developed, the back of the plate is painted gold. Orotones were popularized by Edward S. Curtis in the early 20th century.

palladium print
See *platinum print*.

photogram
A photograph made without a camera by laying objects on a light sensitive surface. The images are negative silhouettes. See *rayograph*.

carbro print	A permanently colored (less often monochrome) photographic print popular about 1920-1930. It is produced like the carbon print, but with three bromide transfer prints stacked in registration to produce a single colored image. The color negatives are made by photographing through a red, a green, and a blue filter. About 5 or 6 images may be made from the original negative. The name carbro comes from *car*bon and *bro*mide. See *dye-transfer*.
carte-de-visite	A stiff piece of card measuring about 4 1/2 x 2 1/2 inches, the size of a formal visiting card of the 1860s, with an attached photograph, usually a full-length studio portrait, of nearly the same size. Sometimes the subject matter was a tourist attraction or a work of art. Cartes-de-visite were most popular during the 1860s and were often collected in albums.
chromogenic color print	A subtractive color print process developed about 1930. The developer contains dye couplers which compound with silver in three layers of emulsion. Each layer is sensitive to one of the primary colors in light–blue, green, and red. Colors in these prints are not as stable as those in *dye-transfer prints*.
Cibachrome print	A brand name. See *chromogenic color print*.
collodion positive	See *ambrotype*.
collodion process	Collodion (a derivative of gun cotton that has been dissolved in alcohol and ether and then mixed with potassium iodide and potassium bromide) is a viscous fluid that forms a transparent film when the solvents evaporate. The wet-collodion process, in use from about 1851 to 1855, used a glass plate coated with wet collodion and sensitized with silver nitrate. The plate was placed in the camera while still wet and immediately exposed. After being exposed, the plate had to be developed before it dried, generally within the hour. This process was valued for its resolution of detail and because exposure times were shorter than for *daguerreotypes* or *colotypes*. The dry-collodion process, in use from the mid-1850s to the mid-1860s, was a variant of the wet-collodion process, but the exposure time was almost six times as long and dry-collodion plates never became widely popular. Multiple prints could be made from the collodion process.
contact print	A print made by placing light-sensitive paper in direct contact with a negative. Most 19th century prints were contact prints; most modern-day prints are enlargements.
cyanotype	Cyanotypes are produced by placing a negative, plant specimen, or drawing on a sheet of paper treated with iron salt and potassium ferricyanide. When the sheet is placed in direct sunlight, an impression will form that eventually turns bright blue (cyan) where it has been exposed to light and white and where the sunlight was blocked. Although the process was first invented in 1841, most cyanotypes were produced from the late 1880s to 1920. One common use was for architectural drawings in blueprints.
daguerreotype	The first practical photographic process, popular from the early 1840s until the late 1850s. A daguerreotype is a unique image on metal produced by treating a copper plate with a light-sensitized surface coating of silver iodide. A daguerreotype is distinctive for its highly polished silver support and its quality of appearing either as a

Photography Media

albumen print   A *contact print* on paper usually made from a *collodion* negative. The paper, which has been treated with a solution of albumen (egg white) and salt, is sensitized with silver nitrate. The print is made by placing the paper in contact with the negative and exposing it to the sun. The prints are often brown with gold highlights, but they may be reddish or purple-brown. The most popular kind of print of the 19th century, albumen prints were used mainly from 1850-1890.

ambrotype   A *collodion* wet-plate negative on glass that appears as a positive image when backed with an opaque coating like black-lacquer. Ambrotypes are sometimes confused with *daguerreotypes* because both are fragile and presented in cases. A good way to differentiate the two is to hold the image at an angle; unlike *daguerreotypes,* ambrotypes will appear positive no matter what the angle of view. Named after James Ambrose Cutting, they were in vogue from the 1850s to the mid 1860s.

autochrome   A colored, transparent image on glass meant to be viewed by being held up to the light or projected onto a surface. The process, which was invented in 1904, involves coating a glass plate with grains of starch dyed red, green, and blue-violet, a varnish, and then a bromide emulsion solution that acts as a light filter. The result is a unique positive transparency.

bichromate   See *gum bichromate print.*

bromoil print   A print based on a gelatin silver-bromide *contact print* or enlargement that has been treated with a potassium bichromate solution. After the print has been chemically altered, it will selectively accept an oil pigment in proportion to the amount of silver in the original image. Different colored oil pigments may be used. The resulting image may be dried as is or transferred to another matrix while wet under pressure. This process originated in England in 1907 and was popular into the 1930s.

C-print   See *Type-C print.*

calotype   The first successful negative to positive process and thus the first to produce multiple photographic images. The paper negative was used to produce a *salt print* positive. Calotypes were popular from their invention in 1841 until the early 1850s; the process was revived about 1900 by the Pictorialist photographers. Characteristics of calotypes are a lack of sharp detail and an overall subtle mottling of tones. They are sometimes called *talbotypes* after their inventor William Henry Fox Talbot.

carbon print   Significant as the first permanent photographic process, carbon prints were most popular between 1870 and 1910, although they remained in use until the 1940s. Unlike other photographic processes that use silver, which deteriorates over time, carbon prints use a paper that has been treated with potassium bichromate and a pigment (usually carbon black). The print is made by a contact process in daylight; the gelatin hardens in proportion to the light that is exposed through the negative, and the excess gelatin is washed away. Characteristics are visible paper fibers in the lighter areas and sometimes cracks in the thicker layers of gelatin.

stencil	One of the four major classes of printmaking, this method involves the application of ink onto the paper's surface through previously cut stencils. This is the one printmaking method which does not reverse the image. Examples are *screenprint* and *pochoir*.
stipple engraving	A method of modeling areas of a plate by using the tip of the *burin* to make dashes rather than full lines where a lighter tone is required. Stipple engraving is often used in conjunction with *crayon manner* or regular *engraving*.
stopping out	The method of protecting with varnish any part of a metal plate that is not to be etched during the biting process. Differential stopping out provides the opportunity for *etching* various of parts of the plate to different depths. See *multilevel color intaglio printing*.
sugar lift process	An *intaglio* method. The artist draws on a plate with a fluid saturated with sugar. After drying, *stopping-out* varnish is applied to the whole plate, and the plate is immersed in water. This causes the sugar to lift the stopping-out varnish off the plate and expose the metal. The plate is then etched and printed in the usual way. An *aquatint* base may have been applied first, so that the etched portions carry an aquatint tone. *Lift ground* is a synonym for this process.
viscosity printing	See *multilevel color intaglio printing*.
wiping	A part of the inking process in intaglio printmaking. To remove surface ink, the printer uses several muslin or tarlatan pads. The wiping motion is circular and the printer may accidentally leave scratches or circular deposits of ink on the plate. A final step uses the palm of the hand or a piece of tissue. See *plate tone* and *retroussage*.
woodblock	This term, used interchangeably with *woodcut* but more often for Japanese ukiyo-e prints and the woodcuts of Provincetown or Arts and Crafts printmakers, also refers to the block of wood that forms the basis of this relief process. Soft wood is cut lengthwise along the grain, seasoned to prevent warping, and planed smooth. See *woodcut*. and *block print*.
woodcut	A *relief* printmaking method. The design is cut with a knife or v–shaped gouge into plank wood with the grain. Chisels and gouges are used to remove large areas of background and ink is then applied to the raised surfaces. Historically the oldest printmaking method. See *woodblock, linocut,* and *block print*.
wood engraving	A *relief* print made from end–grain wood. Boxwood or other hard fruitwoods were usually selected for its fine grain. Since boughs of such wood have a small diameter, small squares of wood are clamped together to make up the block. *Burins* are used for carving into the wood. What distinguishes wood engravings from *woodcuts* is the grain of the wood, the tool used, and the fine details of the image.

relief	One of the four major classes of printmaking, a relief print is one in which the printed mark is created by the raised areas of the matrix. Examples are *metalcuts*, *woodcut*, *wood engraving*, *linocut*, *line–block*, *half-tone block*, and *cliché verre*. Ink is rolled onto the raised areas, and when paper is pressed against the block, either with a press or various hand tools, the ink is transferred to the paper.
relief etching	A *relief* method first used by Blake for producing illuminated books printed in 1788-1820. Text and image were transferred to the metal so that they formed the acid–resistant element and the background was etched away. The prints were either printed in colors or handcolored after printing, or in some cases both kinds of coloration were used.
remarque	A scribbled sketch by an artist outside the main design that might serve as a trade-mark but is often removed before the final edition is pulled.
retroussage	A technique sometimes used in the final wiping of intaglio plates. A fine muslin is dragged along the inked lines to soften their definition and give a richer, almost *drypoint* effect.
roulette	A multispiked wheel that produces a series of *intaglio* dots with *burr*. It is used for *crayon–manner* prints and to repair *mezzotint* plates.
sandpaper ground	A background prepared by running the plate and a sheet of sandpaper together through the press. This produces an overall grey in the final print for each of the resulting dots holds a small quantity of ink.
screenprint	A *stencil* process in which the stencil is placed on a screen. Ink is forced through the screen onto paper, fabric, or metal, forming a distinct layer of pigment on the surface. The terms serigraph, screenprint, and silkscreen are synonymous.
serigraph	A term used to indicate a fine art *screenprint*.
silkscreen print	The original support for stencils in *screenprinting* was fine silk.
simultaneous color printing	See *multilevel color intaglio printing*.
soft ground etching	An *intaglio* method in which the lines are bitten by the acid. The *etching* plate is covered with an acid–resistant material (the soft ground) through which the artist draws lines to expose the metal. Because the ground is highly sensitive, it can be marked by hand or any tool, such as a pencil. Fabrics and other soft materials may be applied and then removed, leaving a textured surface.
steel facing	Copper plates are commonly used for *engravings* because they are receptive to the artist's touch, but they have a limited run because they wear down easily. Steel facing, a process patented in 1857, lengthens the life of the plate by depositing through electrolysis a fine layer of steel on its surface. Some connoisseurs believe that steel facing decreases the richness of the *burr* in *drypoints*.

nature print	A color impression from a printing plate based on actual plants. Plants are embossed into a soft lead plate under pressure, and this is transformed into a printing plate by *electrotyping*. The final *intaglio* plate is printed *à la poupée*. This method was popular in the late nineteenth century.
pastel manner	See *crayon manner.*
photo-engraving	See *line–block.*
photogravure	A photomechanical process that reproduces all gradations of black through white on an *intaglio* metal plate. The process produces a finer image than *half–tone block* and *photoengraving*. Stieglitz used photogravure to reproduce the facsimile photographs for *Camera Work*. Photogravures are sometimes referred to as heliogravures.
photographic processes	Photographic processes can be used to transfer a positive or negative image to any *matrix* (wood, metal, or silkscreen) that has been light–sensitized beforehand. Words beginning with the prefix "photo" or "process" (photoetching, photolithography, photosilk-screen, or process lithography) and other terms like *line block, half-tone block, collotype,* and *photogravure* all indicate that a photographic process is involved. When a print has been reproduced with a photographic process *after* a work in another medium, it is not considered an original print. When the photo-graphic process is a part of the artist's working method, then it is authentic. *Cliché-verre* (literally "printing from glass") is an example of an original photographic process. E.g., Frenchmen Corot, Millet, Rousseau, and Daubigny, and Americans Thomas Moran and Eastman Johnson.
photomechanical	Any of several processes that combine photographic (rather than an artist's hand methods) with printmaking techniques. See *photographic processes.*
photomontage	A photographic print of a montage or assemblage of disparate images which may be photographs themselves, engravings, collage elements, and so on.
planography	One of the four major classes of printmaking. Unlike *intaglio* and *relief* matrices, there is no difference in level between the inked surface and the non-inked surface. Planography usually refers to *lithographs,* but it also includes zincographs, aluminographs (algraphs), and *photolithographs.*
plate tone	The gray or other light tone that may be left on the surface of the plate during the *wiping* process. It is transferred to the paper during printing. It may be an overall tone or differentially wiped, in which parts of the background seem to be brighter than others.
pochoir	A method of applying color to a print. Color is applied through stencils (pochoirs) after the print has been pulled. Characteristics of this method are crisp edges and flat color. See *à la poupée* for another way to add color.
à la poupée	A method of adding color to an *intaglio* plate. Tightly rolled cloth (called a dabber or poupée) is dipped into colored ink and applied to the plate. Small areas of mixed color are a sign that this method has been used.

Jean-Louis Picard
5, rue Drouot
75009 Paris
France

tel: (1) 47 70 77 22
fax: (1) 47 70 77 49

premiums: 12.67% up to 15,000FF
8.23% from 15,001 to 40,000FF
6.15% from 40,001 to 300,001FF
4.96% from 300,001 and up

February 24, 1993 - Estampes XIXe et XXe Siecles
April 2, 1993 - Estampes
June 11, 1993 - Estampes Modernes, Quatrieme vente Henri M. Petiet

Bruun Rasmussen Kunstauktioner
Bredgade 33
1260 Copenhagen K
Denmark

tel: (33) 13 69 11
fax: (33) 32 49 20

15% buyer's premium

September 29-October 1, 1992 - Modern Art (#577)
October 20-29, 1992 - Paintings, Works of Art, Weapons and Toys (#579)

Riba Auctions, Inc.
Historical Emphemera
P.O. Box 53
South Glastonbury, Connecticut 06073

tel: (203) 633-3076

10% buyer's premium

October 31, 1992 - Auction

Dominique Ribeyre et
Florence Baron
5, rue de Provence
75009 Paris
France

tel: (1) 42 46 00 77
fax: (1) 45 23 22 92

Premiums: 12.67% up to 15,000FF
8.23% 15,001 to 40,000FF
6.15% 40,001 to 300,000FF
4.96% 300,001 and over

November 19, 1992 - Affiches Art Deco et Modernes
January 23, 1993 - Le Tour de France en Affiches

D & J Ritchie Inc.
Auctioneers and Appraisers
288 King Street East
Toronto, Ontario
M5A 1K4 Canada

tel: (416) 364-1864
fax: (416) 364-0704

10% buyer's premium

November 30, 1992 - Canadian Art Auction (#324)
December 1, 1992 - European and American Art Auction (#325)
June 7, 1993 - Canadian Art Auction (#342)
June 8, 1993 - European and American Art Auction (#343)

Hugo Ruef
Gabelsbergstrasse 28
D-8000 Munich 2
Germany

tel: (89) 52 40 84
fax: (89) 523 69 36

15% buyer's premium

November 11-13, 1992 - Alte und Moderne Kunst (#455)
December 10-11, 1992 - Alte und Moderne Kunst (#456)

March 24-26, 1993 - Alte und Moderne Kunst (#457)

Kunstauktionshaus Schloss Ahlden tel: (5164) 575   *15% buyer's premium*
3031 Ahlden/Aller   fax: (5164) 522
Germany

September 18-19, 1992 - Schmuck, Dosen/Miniaturen, Porzellan, Gemalde, Mobel/Teppiche,
                          Uhren, Skulpturen, Graphik, Keramik/Fayence, Zinn/Metalle,
                          Spielzeug, Silber, Glas, Jugendstil, Art Deco, Modern Art (#77, #78)
November 20-21, 1992 - Schmuck, Dosen/Miniaturen, Porzellan, Silber, Glas,
                          Keramik/Fayence, Zinn, Gemalde, Mobel/Teppiche, Uhren,
                          Skulpturen, Graphik, Speilzeug, Militaria, Jugendstil, ARt Deco,
                          Modern Art (#79, #80)
May 8-15, 1993 - Schmuck, Dosen/Minituren, Porzellan, Silber, Glas, Keramik/Fayence,
                    Zinn, Gemalde/Graphik, Mobel/Teppiche, Uhren, Skulpturen,
                    Gartenplastiken, Jagdtrophaen, Militaria, Judendstil, Art Deco,
                    Modern Art (#81, #82)

Schoppmann & Partner   tel: (211) 32 58 58   *15% buyer's premium*
Benrather Strasse 11   fax: (211) 32 50 05
4000 Dusseldorf 1
Germany

November 28, 1992 - Bucher und Kunst der Moderne (#16)
June 5, 1993 - Bucher und Kunst der Moderne (#17)

Philippe Schuler Versteigerungen tel: (1) 482 47 48   *15% buyer's premium*
Seestrasse 341   fax: (1) 482 48 07
8038 Zurich
Switzerland

March 16-19, 1993 - Schuler Auktionen (#50)
June 15-18, 1993 - Schuler Auktionen (#51)

Selkirk Galleries   tel: (314) 533-1700   *10% buyer's premium*
4166 Olive Street   fax: (314) 533-1704
St. Louis, Missouri 63108

September 21-24, 1992 - Autumn Gallery Auction 1992
November 30-December 3, 1992 - Winter Gallery Auction 1992
February 8-10, 1993 - February Gallery Auction 1993
April 26-29, 1993 - Spring Gallery Auction 1993

Skinner, Inc., Auctioneers   tel: (508) 779-6241   *10% buyer's premium*
357 Main Street   fax: (508) 779-5144
Bolton, Massachusetts 01740

July 10, 1992 - Toys and Dolls and Specialty Collections (#1455)
August 21, 1992 - Americana (#1459)
September 11, 1992 - American and European Paintings and Prints (#1462)
October 9, 1992 - Arts and Crafts, Art Deco and Modernism, Art Glass and Lamps
                     (#1466)
October 16-17, 1992 - Fine Silver, Fine English and Continental Furniture and Decorations

(#1468-1469)
October 31, 1992 - Americana (#1472)
November 20, 1992 - Oriental Works of Art (#1477)
December 4, 1992 - English and Continental Furniture and Decorations and Silver (#1478)
January 2, 1993 - Arts and Crafts, Art Deco and Modernism, Art Glass and Lamps (#1486)
January 9, 1993 - American Indian Art at Auction (#1487)
January 16, 1993 - Americana (#1488)
March 12, 1993 - American and European Paintings and Prints (#1495)
March 19, 1993 - Victorian and Continental Furniture and Decorative Arts (#1497)
March 27, 1993 - Americana (#1499)
April 23, 1993 - European Furniture and Decorations, including Silver and Russian Works of Art (#1500)
May 1, 1993 - Books and Manuscripts (#1505)
May 22, 1993 - Art Glass and Lamps, Arts and Crafts, and 20th Century Design (#1509)
June 5, 1993 - Fine Americana (#1512)
June 25, 1993 - European and Oriental Furniture and Decorations (#1515)
June 26, 1993 - American Indian Art (#1519)

C.G. Sloan & Company, Inc.   tel: (301) 468-4911   *10% buyer's premium*
4920 Wyaconda Road   fax: (301) 468-9182
North Bethesda, Maryland 20852

July 3-6, 1992 - Estate Auction (#831)
September 17-20, 1992 - Fine Jewelry Estate Auction (#832)
October 30-November 1, 1992 - Estate Auction (#833)
December 10-13, 1992 - Fine Jewelry, Estate Auction (#834)
February 4-7, 1993 - Fine Jewelry, Estate Auction (#835)
April 2-4, 1993 - Estate Auction (#836)
May 27-30, 1993 - Fine Jewelry, Estate Auction (#837)

Sotheby's   tel: (212) 606-7000   *premiums: 15% first $50,000*
1334 York Avenue   fax: (212) 606-7027   *10% over $50,000*
New York, New York 10021   *(as of January 1, 1993)*

September 12, 1992 - The Stanley Caidin Collection (#6333 Caidin)
September 26, 1992 - French and Continental Furniture and Decorations (#6337 Sayonara)
September 30, 1992 - Comic Books and Comic Art (#6338 Monster)
October 6, 1992 - Contemporary Art (#6342 Tea)
October 15-16, 1992 - Photographs (#6344 Modern)
October 24, 1992 - Important English Furniture, Decorations and Carpets (#6349 Tweed)
November 5-6, 1992 - 19th and 20th Century Prints (#6356 Stinger)
November 7, 1992 - Contemporary Prints (#6385 Scorpion)
November 7, 1992 - 20th Century Decorative Arts (#6357 Star)
November 17, 1992 - Contemporary Art, Part I (#6363 Sahara)
November 18, 1992 - Contemporary Art, Part II (#6364 Once Over)
November 19, 1992 - 20th Century Design, The Collection of Barry Friedman, Ltd. (#6365 Friedman)
November 23-24, 1992 - Latin American Paintings, Drawings, Sculpture and Prints (#6367 Virreinato)
December 16, 1992 - Fine Manuscript and Printed Americana, including The Charles Goddard Slack Collection (#6339 Union)
December 17, 1992 - Fine Books and Manuscripts, including the Collection of Dr. Morton McMichael (#6381 Rejoice)

January 28-31, 1993 - Fine Americana (#6392 Tassel)
February 11-12, 1993 - 19th and 20th Century and Contemporary Prints (#6395 Seabreeze)
February 23-25, 1993 - Impressionist, Modern and Contemporary Art (#6397 Torse)
March 19-20, 1993 - 20th Century Decorative Arts (#6404 Wolves)
April 6, 1993 - Photographs (#6407 Solstice)
April 16-17, 1993 - English Furniture, Decorations and Ceramics, including Property from a Private Long Island Collection (#6409 Toby)
May 4, 1993 - Contemporary Art, Part II (#6414 Rondine)
May 13, 1993 - The Dr. Otto Schafer Collection of Rembrandt Etchings (#6453 Rembrandt)
May 13-14, 1993 - Old Master, 19th and 20th Century Prints (#6418 Negroni)
May 15, 1993 - Contemporary Prints (#6419 Manhattan)
May 18-19, 1993 - Latin American Paintings, Drawings, Sculpture and Prints (#6421 Nopal)
May 21, 1993 - Fine Manuscript and Printed Americana, including A Manuscript on Slavery from The Lincoln Carpetbag (#6424 Triumph)
May 27, 1993 - American Paintings, Drawings and Sculpture (#6429 Hassam)
June 10-11, 1993 - 20th Century Decorative Arts, including Property from the Collection of the Fifty/50 Gallery (#6429 Posy)
June 14-15, 1993 - Fine Books and Manuscripts (#6438 Troll)
June 23, 1993 - Collectors' Carrousel, including Dolls, Toys, Mechanical Banks, Hollywood and Rock 'n' Roll Memorabilia (#6443 Witch)
May 13-14, 1993 - Old Master, 19th and 20th Century Prints (#6418 Negroni)

Sotheby's Arcade Auctions
1334 York Avenue
New York, New York 10021

tel: (212) 606-7409
fax: (212) 606-7027

premiums: 15% first $50,000
10% over $50,000
(as of January 1, 1993)

September 23, 1992 - Decorations, French and Continental Furniture, Rugs and Carpets (#1409)
October 9, 1992 - Modern and Contemporary Paintings, Drawings and Sculpture (#1411)
November 6, 1992 - 20th Century Decorative Works of Art (#1414)
February 18, 1993 - Decorations, Furniture, Rugs and Carpets (#1422)
March 3, 1993 - Decorations, Furniture, Rugs and Carpets (#1424)
March 24, 1993 - Decorations, French and Continental Furniture (#1425)
March 31, 1993 - American Paintings, Drawings and Sculpture (#1426)
April 7, 1993 - Decorations and Furniture (#1428)
June 9-10, 1993 - 20th Century Decorative Works of Art (#1428)

Sotheby's Amsterdam
Rokin 102
1012 K2 Amsterdam
Netherlands

tel: (20) 627 56 56
fax: (20) 620 10 57

15% buyer's premium

December 9, 1992 - Modern and Contemporary Art (#573)
May 27-28, 1993 - Modern and Contemporary Art (#578)

Sotheby's Japan Ltd.
Imperial Hotel
1-1-1 Uchisaiwaicho, Chiyoda-ku
Tokyo 100
Japan

tel: (3) 3503 2944
fax: (3) 3503 2839

10% buyer's premium

October 14, 1992 -	19th and 20th Century Prints, Contemporary Prints and Paintings by Japanese Artists (#9210J8)	

Sotheby's London
34-35 New Bond Street
London W1A 2AA
England

tel: (71) 493-3080
fax: (71) 409-3100

premium: 15% first 30,000 BP
10% over 30,000 BP
(as of January 1, 1993)

October 15, 1992 -	The Contents of the Nigel Greenwood Gallery (Greenwood)
December 3-4, 1992 -	Old Master, 19th and 20th Century and Contemporary Prints (Vincent)
May 7, 1993 -	Photographic Images and Related Material (Milton)
June 10, 1993 -	Japanese Works of Art, Paintings and Prints (Neko)
June 11, 1993 -	Kabuki in Japanese Prints from the Collection of the Late Prof. H.R.W. Kuhne (Kabuki)
June 29, 1993 -	Old Master Prints, A Private European Collection (Colmar)
June 29-30, 1993 -	Old Master, 19th and 20th Century and Contemporary Prints (Charlie)

Sotheby's Milan
Via Broggi, 19
20129 Milano
Italy

tel: (2) 295001
fax: (2) 29518595

10% buyer's premium
13% premium as of July 1, 1993

November 24, 1992 -	Arte Moderna e Contemporanea (Tobia)

Swann Galleries, Inc.
104 East 25th Street
New York, New York 10010

tel: (212) 254-4710
fax: (212) 979-1017

10% buyer's premium

August 6, 1992 -	Posters (#1599)
September 17, 1992 -	Autographs, Letters, Documents, Photographs, Collections, Signed and Inscribed Books, Signed Portraits, Caricatures (#1601)
September 24, 1992 -	History of Printing, Printing Manuels, Type Specimen, Press Books, Bodini, Kelmscott, Doves (#1602)
October 14, 1992 -	Photographs (#1604)
November 12, 1992 -	Rare Books (#1608)
December 8, 1992 -	Works of Art on Paper (#1611)
January 28, 1993 -	Autographs, Letters, Documents, Photographs, Collections, Early Royal Documents, Signed and Inscribed Books (#1615)
March 18, 1993 -	Movie Posters, including The Wolffe Nadoolman Collection of Fantasy, Science Fiction and Horror (#1621)
April 7, 1993 -	Photographs (#1623)
April 29, 1993 -	Ephemera (#1625)
May 27, 1993 -	Works of Art on Paper (#1627)

Kenneth Van Blarcom
63 Eliot Street
South Natick, Massachusetts 01760

tel: (508) 653-7017

10% buyer's premium

June 6, 1993 -	Auction

Venator & Hanstein
Caecilienstrasse 48
50667 Koln
Germany

tel: (221) 257 5419
fax: (221) 257 5526

15% buyer's premium

September 14-15, 1992 - Bibliothek Schloss Dick (#66)
March 24-27, 1993 - Der Furstlichen Schlossbibliothek II. Teil (#67)

Villa Grisebach Auktionen
Fasanenstrasse 25
D-1000 Berlin 15
Germany

tel: (30) 882 68 11
fax: (30) 885 40 95

15% buyer's premium

U.S. Representative:
Renee Price
900 Park Avenue
New York, New York 10021

November 27, 1992 - Ausgewahlte Werke (#27)
November 28, 1992 - Kunst des 19. und 20, Jahrhunderts (#28)
November 28, 1992 - Kunst des 19. und 20. Jahrhunderts (#29)
June 4, 1993 - Kunst des 19. und 20. Jahrhunderts (#30)
June 4, 1993 - Ausgewahlte Werke (#31)
June 5, 1993 - Kunst des 19. und 20. Jahrhunderts (#32)
June 5, 1993 - Versteigerung: Samstag (#33)

Henner Wachholtz
Mittelweg 43
2000 Hamburg 13
Germany

tel: (40) 44 04 14
fax: (40) 410 76 87

15% buyer's premium

September 19, 1992 - Alte und Moderne Kunst, Seitgenossische Kunst, Werkverzeichnisse, Photographien (#13)
December 12, 1992 - Alte und Moderne Kunst, Zeitgenossische Kunst, Plakate, Fotografien, Werkverzeichnisse (#15)
June 19, 1993 - Moderne Kunst, Zeitgenossische Kunst, Plakate, Photographien (#18)

Weschler's
909 East Street, N.W.
Washington, D.C. 20004

tel: (202) 628-1281
fax: (202) 628-2366

10% buyer's premium

September 19, 1992 - Twentieth Century Works of Art (#1080)
October 17, 1992 - English and Continental Furniture and Decorations (#1083)
December 12, 1992 - American and European Paintings, Prints, Drawings and Sculpture (#1085)
January 16, 1993 - American Furniture and Decorations (#1087)
January 30, 1993 - English and Continental Furniture and Decorations (#1088)
March 13, 1993 - American and European Paintings, Drawings and Sculpture (#1090)
March 13, 1993 - Twentieth Century Decorative Works of Art (#1091)
April 2, 1993 - Oriental Works of Art (#1092)
May 22, 1993 - American and European Paintings, Prints and Drawings (#1094)
June 11, 1993 - English and Continental Furniture and Decorations (#1095)

Arno Winterberg
Blumenstrasse 15
Postfach 105927
6900 Heidelberg 1
Germany

tel: (0 62 21) 22 631   *15% buyer's premium*
fax: (0 62 21) 16 46 31

October 9-10, 1993 - Landkarten, Stadtansichten, Dekorative Graphik Kunst des 15. bis 20. Jahrhunderts, Gemalde, Aquarelle, Zeichnungen, Graphik (#45)

Wolf's Auction Gallery
1239 West 6th Street
Cleveland, Ohio 44113

tel: (216) 575-9653   *10% buyer's premium*
fax: (216) 621-8011

September 25, 1992 - Prints, Drawings, Modern and Contemporary Paintings, a Collection of R. Lalique Glass, Photographs, Books and Jewelry
December 12, 1992 - 18th, 19th and 20th Century Fine Art, Decorations, Furniture and Jewelry
March 6, 1993 - 18th and 19th Century Decorations, Furniture, Paintings and Orientalia
April 17, 1993 - Fine Art, Decorations, Furniture and Jewelry
May 15, 1993 - 18th, 19th and 20th Century Decorative and Fine Arts, Featuring the Collection of Freda Frazier of Columbus, Ohio and Art of the Cleveland School
June 26, 1993 - 18th, 19th and 20th Century Paintings, Prints and Drawings, Continental and Arts and Crafts Furniture and Decorative Arts at Auction

Young Fine Arts Gallery, Inc.
P.O. Box 313
North Berwick, Maine 03906

tel: (207) 676-3104   *10% buyer's premium*
fax: (207) 676-3105

August 29, 1992 - Fine Paintings, Watercolors, Drawings and Prints
November 28, 1992 - Fine Paintings, Watercolors, Drawings and Prints
February 27, 1993 - Fine Paintings, Watercolors, Drawings and Prints
May 8, 1993 - Fine Paintings, Watercolors, Drawings and Prints

Auktionshaus Michael Zeller
Bindergasse 7
Postfach 1867
D-8990 Lindau (B)
Germany

tel: (83 82) 93 020   *15% buyer's premium*
fax: (83 82) 265 35

October 6-10, 1992 - 48. Internationale Bodensee-Kunstauktion
November 27-28, 1992 - Weihnachtsauktion
May 4-8, 1993 - 49. Internationale Bodensee-Kunstauktion

AACHEN, Johann von   1552-1615
$528* *Mariae Verkundigung(Hollstein Bd. 17, 3),* tears, (03-24-93, Venator/Hansten, #2474), approx. 10⁷⁄₁₆ x 7½ in., (26.5 x 19 cm.), engraving (BP 358, DM 862, FR 2935, Y 62,037).

ABBE
$927* *Rudolph Valentino,* autograph?, prov., (10-10-92, Bonhams, #80, illus.), 10 x 8 in., (25.4 x 20.3 cm.), photograph (BP 550, DM 1377, FR 4623, Y 112,856).

ABBE, Salomon von
$102* *"J'Accuse",* s., i., margins, (12-10-92, Bonhams-Chelsea, #73), plate 10½ x 10⅜ in., (26.7 x 26.4 cm.), etching (BP 66, DM 161, FR 551, Y 12,618).

ABBE, William P.   American 20th cent.
BI *"Edgartown Waterfront",* s. William P. Abbe, num. 8/30, very good cond., est. $1/200, (11-21-92, Bakker, #74), image 8¼ x 14¾ in., (21 x 37.5 cm.), lithograph.

ABBENSETH, William H.
BI *Car And Victorian House, San Francisco, c. 1935,* est. $2/2,500, (04-06-93, Sotheby-NY, #181, illus.), 9⅝ x 7⅜ in., photograph.
BI *Sculpture At The De Young Museum, San Francisco, c. 1936,* est. $2/3,000, (04-06-93, Sotheby-NY, #182, illus.), 9½ x 7⅝ in., photograph.

ABBEY, E.A. (after)
$34* *The Coronation Of Edward VII,* d. 1903-4, s. by both artists, pub. Thomas Agnew & Sons, 1907, blindstamp, margins, staining, (05-20-93, Bonhams-Chelsea, #124), plate 26¾ x 40½ in., (67.9 x 102.9 cm.), engraving (BP 22, DM 55, FR 185, Y 3754).

ABBO, Jussuf   1888-1953
BI *Portrait,* s., #I/V, margins, good cond., minor soiling at edges of sheet, handling creases, paper discoloration, Late Gerhard Brauer Coll., est. Dfl. 2/400, (05-27-93, Sotheby-Amstrdm, #709), 6⁹⁄₁₆ x 4¹⁵⁄₁₆ in., (166 x 125 mm.), etching on Japan.
$295* *Preludes,* s., t., artist's proof, (12-05-92, Bassenge, #6989), 10⅝ x 8¹⁄₁₆ in., (27 x 20.5 cm.), lithograph on Japan (BP 185, DM 460, FR 1567, Y 36,551).
$1064* *"Versunkene", "Mannlicher Kopf", "Ferne", "Liegende", "Visionare Landschaft", "Das Lied", "Frauenkopf", "Ruckenakt"* and *"Madchen Vom Grunen Weg", 1923:* Ten, s., num., (06-05-93, Bassenge, #5848), each approx. 20⅞ x 16⅛ in., (53 x 41 cm.), lithograph on hand-made China (BP 700, DM 1725, FR 5814, Y 114,139).

ABBOTT, Berenice   American 1898-1991
$1045* *Arch At Washington Square,* photog.'s sig., notations, handstamp, 1930s, (04-07-93, Swann, #374, illus.), 9½ x 7½ in., photograph, silver print (BP 691, DM 1690, FR 5720, Y 118,723).
$1725* *"El At Battery",* 1932, p.l., s., photog.'s stamp, illus., (05-23-93, Butterfield, #3258, illus.), 15½ x 19⅝ in., photograph, gelatin silver print (BP 1123, DM 2820, FR 9494, Y 190,671).
BI *"Berenice Abbott's New York II":* Twelve, Parasol Press, each mounted, s. and #32/60 by photog., portfolio stamp, 1930's, p. c. 1979, est. $6/8,000, (04-06-93, Sotheby-NY, #117, illus.), 19½ x 15½ in., photograph.
$5750* *"Berenice Abbott's New York III":* Twelve, Parasol Press, each mounted, s. and #32/60 by photog., portfolio stamp, 1930's, p. c. 1979, (04-06-93, Sotheby-NY, #118, illus.), 19½ x 15½ in., photograph (BP 3798, DM 9264, FR 31,369, Y 655,794).
BI *"Berenice Abbott's New York IV",* Parasol Press, portfolio; each mounted, s., #32/60 by photog.; portfolio stamp, 1930s, p. c. 1979, est. $6/8,000, (04-06-93, Sotheby-NY, #119, illus.), 19½ x 15½ in., photograph.
$2185* *Blossom Restaurant,* 1930s, from New York Portfolio, pub. Parasol Press Ltd., 1979, s., #38/60, portfolio stamp, lit., (04-08-93, Christie-NY, #247, illus.), 18 x 23¼ in., (45.7 x 59.1 cm.), photograph, gelatin silver print (BP 1433, DM 3510, FR 11,881, Y 247,957).
$6600* *Blossom Restaurant, 103 Bowery-Manhattan, 1935, (New York in the Thirties, pl. 31),* t., d., annot. by photog., stamps, (10-15-92, Sotheby-NY, #149, illus.), 7⅝ x 9⅝ in., (19.4 x 24.4 cm.), photograph, gelatin silver print (BP 4039, DM 9824, FR 33,317, Y 791,842).

$605* *Boston, Back Bay,* inits., handstamp, 1930s, p.l., (04-07-93, Swann, #375), 9½ x 7¼ in., photograph, silver print (BP 400, DM 978, FR 3311, Y 68,734).
$8800* *Bread Store, 259 Bleeker Street, Manhattan (New York In The Thirties,pl. 37), 1937,* t., d., annot. by photog., stamp, (10-15-92, Sotheby-NY, #150, illus.), 9⅝ x 7⅝ in., (24.4 x 19.4 cm.), photograph, gelatin silver print (BP 5385, DM 13,099, FR 44,422, Y 1,055,789).
$2750* *Brownstone And Skyscraper, 4 East 78th Street, 1938,* t. in ink w/Federal Art Project stamp, (10-13-92, Christie-NY, #87, illus.), 9¾ x 7¾ in., (24.8 x 19.7 cm.), photograph, gelatin silver print (BP 1602, DM 4029, FR 13,688, Y 333,455).
BI *Buddy Gilmore (O'Neal, p. 73), 1927,* s. by photog., name stamp, est. $7/9,000, (10-15-92, Sotheby-NY, #146, illus.), 4⅜ x 3¼ in., (11.1 x 8.3 cm.), photograph, gelatin silver print.
$1035* *"Central House, Eaton, Ohio", 1935,* s., t., d., photog.'s stamp, (05-23-93, Butterfield, #3253, illus.), 4¾ x 6¾ in., photograph, gelatin silver print (BP 674, DM 1692, FR 5696, Y 114,403).
$4313* *"Chicken Market, 55 Hester Street, Manhattan" (New York in the Thirties, pl. 30), 1937,* t., d., annot. by photog., (04-06-93, Sotheby-NY, #103, illus.), 9⅝ x 7⅝ in., photograph (BP 2849, DM 6949, FR 23,530, Y 491,902).
$138* *Children's Blocks,* stamp, (03-27-93, Julia, #320, illus.), 8 x 10 in., photograph, silvertone (BP 93, DM 225, FR 762, Y 16,121).
$1430* *"Christopher Street Shop",* 1930's/later, s. on mount; photog. Maine stamp verso of mount, lit., (11-16-92, Butterfield, #5811, illus.), 93⅞ x 76⅜ in., (238.5 x 194 mm.), photograph, gelatin silver print (BP 942, DM 2280, FR 7680, Y 177,839).
$935* *"Church Of God",* 1930's/1979, s., edit. 25/60 on mount; photog. New York portfolio and Parasol Press stamps verso of mount, (11-16-92, Butterfield, #5809, illus.), 152¾ x 190⅜ in., (388 x 483.5 mm.), photograph, gelatin silver print (BP 616, DM 1491, FR 5021, Y 116,279).
$575* *"Columbus Circle", 1936, p. 1979,* s., #38/60, photog.'s stamps, illus., (05-23-93, Butterfield, #3262, illus.), 15½ x 19½ in., photograph, gelatin silver print (BP 374, DM 940, FR 3165, Y 63,557).
BI *"Consolidated Edison Power House, 666 First Avenue" (O'Neal, p. 138), 1930's,* mounted, s. by photog., studio stamp, est. $1/2,000, (04-06-93, Sotheby-NY, #109, illus.), 9¾ x 7 in., photograph.
$990* *"Courtyard Of Early Model Tenement, East Seventies", 1936/1979,* s., edit. 25/60 on mount; photog. New York portfolio and Parasol Press stamps verso, lit., (11-16-92, Butterfield, #5807, illus.), 189⅛ x 154 in., (480.3 x 391.2 mm.), photograph, gelatin silver print (BP 652, DM 1578, FR 5317, Y 123,119).
$1925* *Custom House Statue (New York in the Thirties, pl. 40), 1936,* t., d., annot. by photog., stamp, (10-15-92, Sotheby-NY, #151, illus.), 7⅝ x 9⅝ in., (19.4 x 24.4 cm.), photograph, gelatin silver print (BP 1178, DM 2865, FR 9717, Y 230,954).
$1495* *Dead Person,* 1930s, s., t. Commerce Street stamp, (04-08-93, Christie-NY, #235, illus.), 4 x 3 in., (10.2 x 7.6 cm.), photograph, gelatin silver print (BP 980, DM 2402, FR 8129, Y 169,655).
$1980* *Department Of Docks And Police Station, Pier A, North River,* (1936), 1936-45, s., stamp, t., d., (10-13-92, Christie-NY, #83, illus.), 7⅝ x 9½ in., (19.4 x 24.1 cm.), photograph, gelatin silver print (BP 1153, DM 2901, FR 9856, Y 240,087).
BI *Department Of Docks And Police, Pier A, North River (1936),* from portfolio New York Portfolio, pub. Parasol Press Ltd., 1979, s., #38/60, portfolio stamp, lit., est. $1,5/2,000, (04-08-93, Christie-NY, #246, illus.), 15⅝ x 19½ in., (39.7 x 49.5 cm.), photograph, gelatin silver print.
$1100* *Designer's Window, Bleecker Street, New York,* 1947, p.l., s. on mount, Maine Stamp, lit., (10-13-92, Christie-NY, #89, illus.), 9½ x 7½ in., (24.1 x 19.1 cm.), photograph, gelatin silver print (BP 641, DM 1611, FR 5475, Y 133,382).
$1210* *Display Window With Reindeer,* photog.'s sig. and handstamp, 1930s, p.l., (04-07-93, Swann, #376, illus.), 9½ x

7½ in., photograph, silver print (BP 800, DM 1957, FR 6623, Y 137,469).

$1100* *"Dixie Loan, Charleston, South Carolina", 1934,* s. on mount, t., annot. "Vintage print mounted in 1980"; photog. Maine stamp verso of mount, (11-16-92, Butterfield, #5801, illus.), 62⅝ x 80³⁄₁₆ in., (159 x 203.6 mm.), photograph, gelatin silver print (BP 724, DM 1754, FR 5908, Y 136,799).

$2070* *Doorway: 16-18 Charles Street, Manhattan, 1938,* s., t., d., Federal Art Project stamp, (04-08-93, Christie-NY, #240, illus.), 9¾ x 7¾ in., (24.8 x 19.7 cm.), photograph, gelatin silver print (BP 1357, DM 3325, FR 11,256, Y 234,907).

$2875* *"Drug Store: Whelan's, 44th Street And Eighth Avenue, Manhattan", 1936,* s., t., d., annot. by photog. stamp, (04-06-93, Sotheby-NY, #99, illus.), 7½ x 9⅝ in., photograph (BP 1899, DM 4632, FR 15,685, Y 327,897).

BI *"Druggists Exchange Building, Philadelphia", 1934,* s. on mount, t., d., annot "Vintage print mounted 1980"; photog. Maine stamp verso of mount, est. $2/3,000, (11-16-92, Butterfield, #5802, illus.), 70⅛ x 88⅞ in., (178.1 x 225.8 mm.), photograph, toned gelatin silver print.

$2475* *EL, Second And Third Avenue Lines, 250 Pearl Street (O'Neal, p. 119),1930's,* mounted, s. by photog., studio stamp, (10-15-92, Sotheby-NY, #157, illus.), 13½ x 10¼ in., (34.3 x 26 cm.), photograph, gelatin silver print (BP 1515, DM 3684, FR 12,494, Y 296,941).

BI *Edna St. Vincent Millay (Photographs, p. 55),* mounted., s. by photog., studio stamp, c. 1930, p.l., est. $1/1,500, (10-15-92, Sotheby-NY, #554, illus.), 13¼ x 10¼ in., (33.7 x 26 cm.), photograph, gelatin silver print.

$880* *Edward Hopper In His Studio,* notations, sig., 1950's, (10-14-92, Swann, #363, illus.), 10 x 8 in., (25.4 x 20.3 cm.), photograph, silver print (BP 517, DM 1288, FR 4367, Y 106,641).

$935* *"Edward Hopper",* 1947/later, s.; photog. Commerce Street stamp verso, lit., (11-16-92, Butterfield, #5812, illus.), 137¾ x 105⁹⁄₁₆ in., (349.9 x 267.2 mm.), photograph, gelatin silver print (BP 616, DM 1491, FR 5021, Y 116,279).

BI *"El" 9th Avenue Line, Christopher Street Station, 1936,* s., t., d., stamp, lit, est. $3/5,000, (10-13-92, Christie-NY, #86, illus.), 9⅝ x 7⅝ in., (24.4 x 19.4 cm.), photograph, gelatin silver print.

$3220* *The Empire State Building,* 1930s, s., Commerce Street stamp twice verso mount, flush-mounted, (04-08-93, Christie-NY, #233, illus.), 8⅜ x 5½ in., (21.3 x 14 cm.), photograph, gelatin silver print (BP 2111, DM 5173, FR 17,510, Y 365,411).

BI *Entrance And Lobby, Former Whitney Museum, c. 1934,* s., t., Commerce Street stamp, est. $2/2,500, (04-08-93, Christie-NY, #236, illus.), 9½ x 7½ in., (24.1 x 19.1 cm.), photograph, gelatin silver print.

$715* *Eugene Atget (Modern Vision, pl. 4; O'Neal, p. 64),* mounted, s. by photog., studio stamp, 1927, p.l., (10-15-92, Sotheby-NY, #144, illus.), 13¼ x 10¼ in., (33.7 x 26 cm.), photograph, gelatin silver print (BP 438, DM 1064, FR 3609, Y 85,783).

$8050* *"Exchange Place" (O'Neal, p. 130), 1930's,* backed w/ heavy card, s. by photog., studio stamp, (04-06-93, Sotheby-NY, #98A, illus.), 16¾ x 3⅞ in., photograph (BP 5317, DM 12,969, FR 43,917, Y 918,111).

$605* *Facade Of Brownstone At 4 East 78 Street, Manhattan, And Sky Scraper, 1938,* photog.'s handstamp, t., d., neg. num., (04-07-93, Swann, #378, illus.), 9 x 7½ in., photograph, silver print (BP 400, DM 978, FR 3311, Y 68,734).

$4400* *Faces Of The 20's,* Parasol Press, 1981, mounted, each s., #42/60 by photog., stamp, 1920's, p.c. 1981, (10-15-92, Sotheby-NY, #145, illus.), each approx. 13½ x 10½ in., (34.3 x 26.7 cm.), photograph, porfolio of 12 (BP 2692, DM 6550, FR 22,211, Y 527,894).

BI *"Faces Of The 20's": Twelve,* Parasol Press, portfolio; each mounted, s., #53/60 by photog.; portfolio stamp, 1920's, p.c. 1981, est. $4/6,000, (04-06-93, Sotheby-NY, #119A, illus.), each approx. 13½ x 10½ in., photograph.

$6900* *"Father Duffy, Times Square, Manhattan" (O'Neal, p. 135), 1937,* t., d., annot. by photog., stamp, (04-06-93, Sotheby-NY, #104, illus.), 9⅜ x 7⅝ in., photograph (BP 4557, DM 11,116, FR 37,643, Y 786,953).

$2860* *Federal Reserve Building, Liberty Street,* (c. 1935), 1940s, t. in ink, stamp, lit., (10-13-92, Christie-NY, #81, illus.), 7⅜ x 9½ in., (18.7 x 24.1 cm.), photograph, gelatin silver print (BP 1666, DM 4190, FR 14,236, Y 346,793).

$1320* *Fifth Avenue, Nos. 4, 6, And 8. Built For Mary Wetherbee, Mrs. Rhinelander Stewart And Mrs. J. Herbert Johnson,* (1936), p.l., s. Abbott on mount, Maine stamp, lit., (10-13-92, Christie-NY, #93, illus.), 10¾ x 13½ in., (27.3 x 34.3 cm.), photograph, gelatin silver print (BP 769, DM 1934, FR 6570, Y 160,058).

$2070* *"Flat Iron Building",* 1938, p.l., s., photog.'s stamp, illus., (05-23-93, Butterfield, #3257, illus.), 13½ x 10½ in., photograph, gelatin silver print (BP 1348, DM 3385, FR 11,392, Y 228,805).

$1980* *Flatiron Building, Broadway And Fifth Avenue,* (1938), p.l., s. Abbott, Maine stamp, lit., (10-13-92, Christie-NY, #92, illus.), 13¼ x 10⅛ in., (33.7 x 25.7 cm.), photograph, gelatin silver print (BP 1153, DM 2901, FR 9856, Y 240,087).

$2070* *Fortieth Street Between Sixth And Seventh Avenues: Looking SouthwestFrom 42nd Street, 1935,* s., t., d. in ink, Federal Art Project stamp, (04-08-93, Christie-NY, #237, illus.), 9½ x 7⅞ in., (24.1 x 20 cm.), photograph, gelatin silver print (BP 1357, DM 3325, FR 11,256, Y 234,907).

$575* *"Foujita",* 1920s, p.l., s., photog.'s stamp, (05-23-93, Butterfield, #3264, illus.), 13½ x 10⅝ in., photograph, gelatin silver print (BP 374, DM 940, FR 3165, Y 63,557).

$2300* *Gunsmith And Police Department (1937), 1979,* from New York Portfolio, pub. Parasol Press Ltd., s., #38/60, portfolio, lit., (04-08-93, Christie-NY, #245, illus.), 15½ x 19½ in., (39.4 x 49.5 cm.), photograph, gelatin silver print (BP 1508, DM 3695, FR 12,507, Y 261,008).

$5500* *Gunsmith, Centre Market Place (O'Neal, p. 106, variant), c. 1937,* mounted, s. by photog., label, s. Berenice Abbott, Supervisor, t., i.by photog., studio stamp, exhib. label, (10-15-92, Sotheby-NY, #154, illus.), 9⅜ x 7¼ in., (23.8 x 18.4 cm.), photograph, gelatin silver print (BP 3366, DM 8187, FR 27,764, Y 659,868).

$4600* *"Harlem Street, 422-424 Lenox Avenue, Manhattan", 1938,* s., t., d., annot. by photog., (04-06-93, Sotheby-NY, #100, illus.), 7½ x 9½ in., photograph (BP 3038, DM 7411, FR 25,095, Y 524,635).

$1320* *Holland Transportation Company,* photog.'s sig., unident. notations, 1930s, (04-07-93, Swann, #379, illus.), 7½ x 9 in., photograph, silver print (BP 872, DM 2135, FR 7225, Y 149,966).

$2300* *Java-China Trading Company, 1930s,* s. by photog., studio stamp, (04-06-93, Sotheby-NY, #108, illus.), 9½ x 7½ in., photograph (BP 1519, DM 3705, FR 12,548, Y 262,318).

BI *"Jean Guerin", 1925,* s., t., d., photog.'s stamp, est. $1/1,500, (05-23-93, Butterfield, #3255, illus.), 3⅛ x 2⅜ in., photograph, gelatin silver print.

BI *Jean Prevost (Atelier Man Ray, p. 17), 1927,* s., t., d. by photog., name stamp, est. $3/5,000, (10-15-92, Sotheby-NY, #147, illus.), 3¼ x 2½ in., (8.3 x 6.4 cm.), photograph, gelatin silver print.

$978* *"Lebanon Restaurant",* 1935, p. 1979, s., #25/60, photog.'s stamps, (05-23-93, Butterfield, #3260, illus.), 19½ x 15½ in., photograph, gelatin silver print (BP 637, DM 1599, FR 5382, Y 108,102).

BI *"Lescaze House, Brownstone Front", 1938,* t., d., neg. num.; photog. Federal Art Project, "Changing New York",release agreement stamps verso, lit., est. $1,0/1,500, (11-16-92, Butterfield, #5805, illus.), 93⅞ x 76⅜ in., (238.5 x 194 mm.), photograph, gelatin silver print.

$2300* *Lower East Side, New York,* 1930s, s., t. West 67th Street stamp, (04-08-93, Christie-NY, #234, illus.), 6¾ x 4⅛ in., (17.1 x 10.5 cm.), photograph, gelatin silver print (BP 1508, DM 3695, FR 12,507, Y 261,008).

$690* *"Lyric Theatre",* 1936, p.l., s., t., photog.'s stamp, illus.(05-23-93, Butterfield, #3263, illus.), 10¼ x 13¼ in., photograph, gelatin silver print (BP 449, DM 1128, FR 3797, Y 76,268).

$3680* *Manhattan Bridge, 1938,* t., d., Commerce Street stamp, (04-08-93, Christie-NY, #241, illus.), 9¼ x 7⅜ in., (23.5 x 18.7 cm.), photograph, gelatin silver print (BP 2413, DM 5912, FR 20,011, Y 417,612).

$5225* *Manhattan Bridge; Looking Up (New York in the Thirties, pl. 10), 1936,* t., d., annot. by photog., stamp, (10-15-92, Sotheby-NY, #148, illus.), 9⅝ x 7⅝ in., (24.4 x 19.4 cm.), photograph, gelatin silver print (BP 3197, DM 7778, FR 26,376, Y 626,875).

$13,800* *"Murray Hill Hotel, 112 Park Avenue" (O'Neal, p. 107), 1930's,* mounted on cardboard, s. by photog., photog. stamp, (04-06-93, Sotheby-NY, #102, illus.), 9⅜ x 7⅜ in., photograph (BP 9115, DM 22,233, FR 75,286, Y 1,573,905).

$4025* *New York At Night,* 1932, p.l., s., lit., (04-08-93, Christie-NY, #244, illus.), 13⅝ x 10½ in., (34.6 x 26.7 cm.), photograph, gelatin silver print (BP 2639, DM 6466, FR 21,887, Y 456,764).

$3850* *New York At Night,* (1932), p.l., s. on mount, stamp, lit., (10-13-92, Christie-NY, #80, illus.), 13¾ x 10½ in., (34.9 x 26.7 cm.), photograph, gelatin silver print (BP 2242, DM 5640, FR 19,164, Y 466,836).

$2200* *New York At Night,* sig., handstamp, 1932, p.l., (10-14-92, Swann, #364, illus.), 13¾ x 10½ in., (34.9 x 26.7 cm.), photograph, silver print (BP 1291, DM 3220, FR 10,918, Y 266,602).

$2750* *New York At Night (O'Neal frontispiece),* s. by photog., 1932, probably p. in the 1950's or 1960's, (10-15-92, Sotheby-NY, #158, illus.), 13¾ x 10¾ in., (34.9 x 27.3 cm.), photograph, gelatin silver print (BP 1683, DM 4093, FR 13,882, Y 329,934).

$5225* *New York At Night (O'Neal, frontispiece),* s. by photog., 1932, p.l., (10-15-92, Sotheby-NY, #159, illus.), 22 x 17⅜ in., (55.9 x 44.1 cm.), photograph, gelatin silver print (BP 3197, DM 7778, FR 26,376, Y 626,875).

$2750* *"New York At Night",* 1932/later, s. verso, lit., (11-16-92, Butterfield, #5803, illus.), 137¾ x 107¹¹⁄₁₆ in., (349.9 x 273.5 mm.), photograph, gelatin silver print (BP 1811, DM 4385, FR 14,769, Y 341,997).

$3450* *"New York At Night",* 1932, p.l., s., photog.'s stamp, illus., (05-23-93, Butterfield, #3251, illus.), 13⅝ x 10⅝ in., photograph, gelatin silver print (BP 2247, DM 5641, FR 18,987, Y 381,342).

$1540* *"New York At Night",* t., stamp, (03-27-93, Julia, #319, illus.), 11 x 14 in., photograph, silvertone (BP 1034, DM 2507, FR 8508, Y 179,907).

$4600* *"New York At Night" (O'Neal, frontispiece), 1932,* each mounted, s. by photog., studio stamp, p. 1979, (04-06-93, Sotheby-NY, #114, illus.), 23⅛ x 18⅛ in., photograph (BP 3038, DM 7411, FR 25,095, Y 524,635).

$2750* *New York Stock Exchange, New York (Commerce Graphics, unpaginated variant),* studio stamp, s., c. 1934, p.l., (10-15-92, Sotheby-NY, #161, illus.), 9½ x 7½ in., (24.1 x 19.1 cm.), photograph, gelatin silver print (BP 1683, DM 4093, FR 13,882, Y 329,934).

$920* *New York: "Edward Hopper" and "Designer's Window, Bleeker Street" (O'Neal, pp. 191 and 192): Two,* plates from Berenice Abbott Retrospective portfolio, Parasol Press, each mounted, s., #4/40 by photog., stamp, 1947, p.l., (04-06-93, Sotheby-NY, #115, illus.), photograph (BP 608, DM 1482, FR 5019, Y 104,927).

BI *New York: "Gunsmith And Police Department, 6 Centre Market Place And240 Centre Street" and "Chicken Market, 55 Hester Street, Manhattan" (O'Neal, p. 106; New York in the Thirties, pl. 30): Two,* each mounted, t. by photog., photog. studio stamp, 1930's, p.l., est. $2/3,000, (04-06-93, Sotheby-NY, #116A, illus.), one 7½ x 9½ in., other 13⅜ x 10⅜ in., photograph.

$1610* *New York: "Manhattan Bridge, Looking Up" and "Consolidated Edison Power House, 666 First Avenue" (O'Neal, pp. 138 and 169): Two,* each mounted, s. by photog., studio stamp, 1936 and 1938, p.l., (04-06-93, Sotheby-NY, #116, illus.), each approx. 9¾ x 7⅛ in., photograph (BP 1063, DM 2594, FR 8783, Y 183,622).

BI *New York: "Rector Street, Italian Festival" and "East Side Portrait"O'Neal, p. 180): Two,* plates from Berenice Abbott Retrospective portfolio, Parasol Press, each mounted, s., #4/40, stamp, 1930's and 1938, p.l., est. $1,5/2,500, (04-06-93, Sotheby-NY, #110, illus.), each 23 x 18½ in., photograph.

$1150* *New York: "Yuban Warehouse, Water And Dock Streets, Brooklyn", "Hardware Store, 316-318 Bowery" and "Billboards" (O'Neal, pp. 126 and 137-38): Three,* plates from Berenice Abbott Retrospective portfolio, Parasol Press, each mounted, s., #4/40 by photog., stamp, 1938 and 1930s p.l., (04-06-93, Sotheby-NY, #112, illus.), each 18⅓ x 23⅛ in., photograph (BP 760, DM 1853, FR 6274, Y 131,159).

BI *New York: Two,* Parasol Press Ltd., 1979, s., num. 47/60 on mount, ltd. edit. of 60 plus 5, brown linen portfolio box, est. $7/9,000, (10-13-92, Christie-NY, #94, illus.), each 11 x 14 in., (27.9 x 35.6 cm.), photograph, gelatin silver prints.

$6325* *"Newsstand, 32nd St. and 3rd Avenue, Manhattan" (New York in the Thirties, pl. 52), 1935,* t., d, annot. by photog., stamp, (04-06-93, Sotheby-NY, #105, illus.), 7⅝ x 9⅝ in., photograph (BP 4178, DM 10,190, FR 34,506, Y 721,373).

$1035* *"Old Drug Store, Market St., Interior", 1931,* t., d., photog.'s stamp, (05-23-93, Butterfield, #3254, illus.), 9⅜ x 7 in., photograph, gelatin silver print (BP 674, DM 1692, FR 5696, Y 114,403).

BI *"The Old Saloon",* 1930s, s., t., photog.'s stamp, est. $1/1,500, (05-23-93, Butterfield, #3256, illus.), 7⅝ x 9½ in., photograph, gelatin silver print.

$3080* *Pawn Shop, 48 Third Avenue, 1937,* Federal Art Project, lit., (10-13-92, Christie-NY, #84, illus.), 7⅝ x 9½ in., (19.4 x 24.1 cm.), photograph, gelatin silver print (BP 1794, DM 4512, FR 15,331, Y 373,469).

$1870* *Pennsylvania Station Interior,* (1936), p.l., s. on mount, Maine stamp, lit., (10-13-92, Christie-NY, #90, illus.), 12⅞ x 10⅝ in., (32.7 x 27 cm.), photograph, gelatin silver print (BP 1089, DM 2740, FR 9308, Y 226,749).

BI *"Pingpank Barber Shop",* 1935, p. 1979, s., #25/60, photog.'s stamps, est. BP 1/1,500, (05-23-93, Butterfield, #3259, illus.), 19½ x 15½ in., photograph, gelatin silver print.

BI *Portrait Of Adrienne Monnier,* photog.'s sig., notations, handstamp, 1930s, est. $1,5/2,500, (04-07-93, Swann, #380, illus.), 9½ x 6¾ in., photograph, silver print.

BI *Portrait Of Eugene Atget,* 1927, p. 1960s, s., Commerce Street stamp, lit., est. $3/4,000, (04-08-93, Christie-NY, #243, illus.), 9½ x 7⅜ in., (24.1 x 18.7 cm.), photograph, gelatin silver print.

$990* *Portrait Of Leadbelly,* photog.'s sig., handstamp, 1930s, (04-07-93, Swann, #381, illus.), 13¼ x 11 in., photograph, silver print (BP 654, DM 1601, FR 5419, Y 112,474).

$605* *Portrait Of Lewis Hine,* photog.'s sig., handstamp, 1930s, p.l., (04-07-93, Swann, #382, illus.), 9½ x 7½ in., photograph, silver print (BP 400, DM 978, FR 3311, Y 68,734).

$8050* *Portraits In Palladium: Paris-New York (1926-1929): Eleven,* Commerce Graphics w/Lunn, LTD., 1989, p. to photog.'s specificationsby Jim Frank, each s., num. w/ photog.'s inits. embossed, num., t. w/credit stamp, 1st in edit., Abbott's personal copy, only copy in edit. to have each prints., Berenice Abbott Estate, (04-08-93, Christie-NY, #242, illus.), each approx. 4½ x 3½ in., (11.4 x 8.9 cm.), photograph, palladium print, hand-coated on Strathmore Bristol (BP 5279, DM 12,932, FR 43,774, Y 913,527).

$935* *"Poultry Shop, East 7th Street, New York",* 1935/1979, s., #25/60 on mount; photog. New York portfolio and Parasol Press stamps verso of mount, lit., (11-16-92, Butterfield, #5810, illus.), 195⅜ x 155¼ in., (496.2 x 394.4 mm.), photograph, gelatin silver print (BP 616, DM 1491, FR 5021, Y 116,279).

$3300* *Rector Street, New York,* late 1930s-early 1940s, s. in ink, credit, stamps, (10-13-92, Christie-NY, #85, illus.), 9⅜ x 3 in., (23.8 x 7.6 cm.), photograph, gelatin silver print (BP 1922, DM 4834, FR 16,426, Y 400,146).

$3450* *Rockefeller Center And St. Nicolas' Chruch, 1936,* s., t., d., Federal Art Project stamp w/t. and d., (04-08-93, Christie-NY, #238, illus.), 9½ x 7½ in., (24.1 x 19.1 cm.), photograph, gelatin silver print (BP 2262, DM 5542, FR 18,760, Y 391,512).

BI *"Rockefeller Center With Collegiate Church Of St. Nicholas In Foreground", 1936,* t., d., neg. num; photog. Federal Art Project, "Changing New York" stamp verso, lit., est. $1,5/2,000, (11-16-92, Butterfield, #5804, illus.), 96⁷⁄₁₆ x 76⅜ in., (244.9 x 194 mm.), photograph, toned gelatin silver print.

$8050* *"Saints For Sale" (O'Neal, p. 92), 1930's*, s. by photog., (04-06-93, Sotheby-NY, #101, illus.), 7½ x 9B, in., photograph (BP 5317, DM 12,969, FR 43,917, Y 918,111).

$1150* *Selected Images: "Transformation Of Energy" and "Designer's Window, Bleecker Street" (O'Neal, pp. 192 and 220): Two*, each mounted, s. by photog., studio stamp, 1947 and 1939, p.l., (04-06-93, Sotheby-NY, #113, illus.), one 10½ x 13½ in., other 9½ x 7½ in., photograph (BP 760, DM 1853, FR 6274, Y 131,159).

$770* *Sidney Place And Joralemon Street, Brooklyn Heights, 1936*, handstamp, (10-14-92, Swann, #365, illus.), 9½ x 7½ in., (24.1 x 19.1 cm.), photograph, silver print (BP 452, DM 1127, FR 3821, Y 93,311).

$1035* *Skyscraper, 1930s*, s., (05-23-93, Butterfield, #3252, illus.), 8¼ x 2½ in., photograph, gelatin silver print (BP 674, DM 1692, FR 5696, Y 114,403).

$4400* *Sleeping Vagrant, 1930s*, s., (10-13-92, Christie-NY, #88, illus.), 7B, x 9¾ in., (19.4 x 24.8 cm.), photograph, gelatin silver print (BP 2563, DM 6446, FR 21,901, Y 533,527).

$935* *"Snuff Shop", 1938/1979*, s., edit. 25/60 on mount; photog. New York portfolio and Parasol Press stamps verso, lit., (11-16-92, Butterfield, #5808, illus.), 195C, x 155¼ in., (496.2 x 394.4 mm.), photograph, gelatin silver print (BP 616, DM 1491, FR 5021, Y 116,279).

BI   *"Snuff Shop, 113 Division Street', "Hardware Store, 316-318 Bowery",and "Corcoran Wind Mill Factory" (O'Neal, pp. 126 and 144): Three*, each mounted, init. by photog., stamp, 1932 and 1938, each p. in the1950's, est. $2/3,000, (10-15-92, Sotheby-NY, #160, illus.), each approx. 9½ x 7½ in., (24.1 x 19.1 cm.), photograph, gelatin silver prints.

$1925* *St Mark's Church, Statue In Courtyard, 1937*, s., t., d., annot. by photog., stamp, (10-15-92, Sotheby-NY, #153, illus.), 9M, x 7M, in., (25.1 x 20 cm.), photograph, gelatin silver print (BP 1178, DM 2865, FR 9717, Y 230,954).

BI   *Starrett Lehigh Building II, 601 West 26th Street, Manhattan, 1938*, t., d., Federal Art Project stamp, est. $2/3,000, (04-08-93, Christie-NY, #239, illus.), 7¾ x 9B, in., (19.7 x 24.4 cm.), photograph, gelatin silver print.

$880* *"Stevens House, Vernon Boulevard And 30 Road, Astoria, Long Island City, New York", 1937*, t., d., neg. num.; photog. Federal Art Project "Changing New York" and Commerce St. stamps, (11-16-92, Butterfield, #5806, illus.), 75Z, x 95Cn in., (190.8 x 241.7 mm.), photograph, toned gelatin silver print (BP 579, DM 1403, FR 4726, Y 109,439).

$605* *Street Scene*, inits., handstamp 1930s, p.l., (04-07-93, Swann, #383), 7¼ x 9¼ in., photograph, silver print (BP 400, DM 978, FR 3311, Y 68,734).

$220* *Street Scene, Baltimore*, inits., handstamp, 1930's, p.l., (10-14-92, Swann, #366), 9½ x 7½ in., (24.1 x 19.1 cm.), photograph, silver print (BP 129, DM 322, FR 1092, Y 26,660).

$4400* *Sunlight And Bark, c. 1947*, mounted, s. by photog., (c) stamp, studio stamp,, (10-15-92, Sotheby-NY, #163A, illus.), 15M, x 15¼ in., (40.3 x 38.7 cm.), photograph, gelatin silver print (BP 2692, DM 6550, FR 22,211, Y 527,894).

$1320* *Talman Street, Between Jay And Bridge Streets, Brooklyn (cf. New Yorkin the Thirties, pl. 89), 1936*, s. by photog., stamp, (10-15-92, Sotheby-NY, #156, illus.), 7B x 9B, in., (19.4 x 24.4 cm.), photograph, gelatin silver print (BP 808, DM 1965, FR 6663, Y 158,368).

BI   *"Townhouses Off East 57th St., New York City", 1930's*, s., on mount, t., annot. "Vintage print from 1930's, mounted 1980"; photog. Maine stamp verso of mount, est. $2/3,000, (11-16-92, Butterfield, #5800, illus.), 75Z x 95Cn in., (190.8 x 241.7 mm.), photograph, gelatin silver print.

$2420* *Trinity Church, 1930s*, s. on mount, stamp, lit., (10-13-92, Christie-NY, #82, illus.), 9½ x 7B, in., (24.1 x 19.4 cm.), photograph, gelatin silver print (BP 1409, DM 3545, FR 12,046, Y 293,440).

$3575* *Wall Street From The Irving Trust Co. Building, 1938*, t., d. by photog., stamp, (10-15-92, Sotheby-NY, #155, illus.), 10 x 7C, in., (25.4 x 18.7 cm.), photograph, gelatin silver print (BP 2188, DM 5322, FR 18,046, Y 428,914).

BI   *Warehouse, Lower Manhattan*, (1936), p.l., s. on mount, Maine stamp, lit., est. $2,5/3,500, (10-13-92, Christie-NY, #91, illus.), 10½ x 13½ in., (26.7 x 34.3 cm.), photograph, gelatin silver print.

$7188* *"Warehouse, Water And Dock Streets, Brooklyn" (New York in the Thirties, pl. 94), 1936*, t., d., annot. by photog., stamp, (04-06-93, Sotheby-NY, #106, illus.), 7B, x 9B, in., photograph (BP 4748, DM 11,580, FR 39,214, Y 819,799).

$3163* *"Warehouse, Water And Dock Streets, Brooklyn", 1936*, t., d., neg. num., photog.'s stamp, illus., (05-23-93, Butterfield, #3250, illus.), 8 x 10 in., photograph, gelatin silver print (BP 2060, DM 5172, FR 17,408, Y 349,619).

$3450* *"Watuppa", Pier 5, East River, 1936*, t., d., annot. by photog., studio stamps, (04-06-93, Sotheby-NY, #107, illus.), 9C, x 7B, in., photograph (BP 2279, DM 5558, FR 18,822, Y 393,476).

$978* *"West Street", 1935*, p. 1979, s., #25/60, photog.'s stamps, illus., (05-23-93, Butterfield, #3261, illus.), 15½ x 19½ in., photograph, gelatin silver print (BP 637, DM 1599, FR 5382, Y 108,102).

$247* *Woman Walking, Back Bay Area, Boston*, inits., handstamp, 1930's, p.l., (10-14-92, Swann, #367), 7 x 9½ in., (17.8 x 24.1 cm.), photograph, silver print (BP 145, DM 361, FR 1226, Y 29,932).

$1100* *Yuban Warehouse, Water And Dock Streets, Brooklyn (O'Neal, pp. 136-137)*, mounted, s. by photog., studio stamp, 1936, p.l., (10-15-92, Sotheby-NY, #163, illus.), 13B, x 10½ in., (34.6 x 26.7 cm.), photograph, gelatin silver print (BP 673, DM 1637, FR 5553, Y 131,974).

$4675* *Zito's Bakery (cf. New York in the Thirties, pl. 37), c. 1939*, s. by photog., mistakenly stamped w/Eugene Atget photograph p. by Berenice Abbott stamp, (10-15-92, Sotheby-NY, #152, illus.), 9½ x 7½ in., (24.1 x 19.1 cm.), photograph, gelatin silver print (BP 2861, DM 6959, FR 23,599, Y 560,888).

ABBOTT, L.F.

$107 *"To The Society Of Golfers At Blackheath"*, (04-16-93, G.A. Key, #32), 15 x 11 in., (38.1 x 27.9 cm.), colored print (BP 70, DM 173, FR 584, Y 12,032).

ABBOTT, L.F. (after)

BI   *"To The Society Of Goffers At Blackheath"*, modern, (12-11-92, G.A. Key, #35), 15 x 11 in., (38.1 x 27.9 cm.), colored print.

BI   *"To The Society Of Golfers At Blackheath", 1790*, s., d. in matrix, ident. in i., est. $4/600, (07-10-92, Skinner, #372), sight 26¾ x 18 in., (67.9 x 45.7 cm.), engraving, hand coloring.

ABEILLE, Jack

$217* *Lina Munte Prochaine Tournee*, (01-31-93, Morelle/Marchan, #220), 39C, x 62Bn in., (100 x 160 cm.), poster (BP 146, DM 350, FR 1182, Y 27,071).

ABELES, Sigmund   American b.1934

$72* *Self-Portrait With Cat*, s., i. AP, (11-12-92, Freemn/Fine Art, #1), 12 x 17½ in., (30.5 x 44.5 cm.), etching (BP 47, DM 114, FR 385, Y 8927).

ABERLI, Johann Ludwig   Swiss 1723-1786

$764* *La Vallee D'Oberhasli (Geiser 104), 1769*, watermark, (06-23-93, Kornfeld, #1), handcolored etching (BP 519, DM 1293, FR 4348, Y 83,233, SF 1150).

ABRAHAM, Syd

$400* *Shell Motor Oil, Silverstone Success, 1952*, ref. P 17A, cond. 3, (10-13-92, Phillips-London, #168), 29Bzn x 39C, in., (76 x 100 cm.), color lithograph (BP 233, DM 586, FR 1991, Y 48,502).

ABRAHAMS, Ivor

BI   *Femme Du Midi, 1979: Six*, s., d., num. from edit. full margins, good cond., creasing, est. BP 6/700, (06-30-93, Sotheby-London, #725, illus.), each sh 27½ x 22½ in., (699 x 572 mm.), color aquatint on Arches.

$938* *Summer Sundial, 1975*, s., d., #17/95, good cond., (12-03-92, Sotheby-London, #600, illus.), 39½ x 47¼ in., (100.3 x 120 cm.), silkscreen in colors w/collage and flocking (BP 605, DM 1475, FR 5035, Y 116,710).

$32* *Up The Garden Path*, artist's proof, s., d. '71, (03-17-93, Bonhams-Chelsea, #321), image 22 x 30 in., (55.9 x

76.2 cm.), collage in screenprint (BP 22, DM 53, FR 181, Y 3753).

ABRAHAMS, R., Publisher
$84 *"The Fleet Has Assembled At Spithead For The Coronation Review, June1902",* (10-09-92, G.A. Key, #25), 17 x 28 in., (43.2 x 71.1 cm.), colored lithograph (BP 50, DM 125, FR 424, Y 10,244).

ACCONCI, Vito   American b. 1940
$8800* *Directions (2-Hr. Activity Performed During Showing Of Films, Video Tapes, Providence, Rhode Island, Dec. 1, 1971),* s., i., d. Dec, 1 1971, prov., exhib., Sylvio Perlstein Coll., (11-18-92, Sotheby-NY, #197, illus.), 30 x 40 in., (76.2 x 101.6 cm.), crayon and photographs mounted on black paper (BP 5794, DM 14,031, FR 47,261, Y 1,094,391).
BI *Fitting Room I & II,* s., t., i., prov., exhib., Sylvio Perlstein Coll., est. $15/20,000, (11-18-92, Sotheby-NY, #198, illus.), each sheet 30 x 40 in., (76.2 x 101.6 cm.), ink and photographs mounted on four sheets of paper.

ACCONI, Vito   American b. 1940
$1870* *Crash, 1984: Two,* s., d., t., #14/30, full margins, good cond., image dent, surface soiling, creases, (10-28-92, Butterfield, #2871), each sheet 20⅞, x 25½ in., (511 x 648 mm.), color aquatint w/silkscreen and embossing on 2 sheets cream wove (BP 1191, DM 2888, FR 9806, Y 229,448).
BI *Wav(er)ing Flag, 1990,* complete portfolio, d., #18/35, pub. Landfall Press, Inc., good cond., est. $1,5/2,000, (11-07-92, Sotheby-NY, #502), each sheet approx. 18 x 24 in., (457 x 610 mm.), six lithographs p. in colors.

ACHENBACH, Andreas   German 1815-1910
$437* *Erftlandschaft" Mit Wassermuhle (Boetticher Bd. 1, 128), 1866,* trimmed, (03-24-93, Venator/Hansten, #2589), image approx. 16⅞, x 22⅛, in., (41 x 57.5 cm.), etching (BP 296, DM 714, FR 2429, Y 51,345).

ACKERMAN, Arthur   English 19th cent.
$132* *"The Tumbletown Steeple-Chase, No. 2 - The Start. Ten To One On Bobby",* artist: Phiz, pub. Ackerman, (12-05-92, Neal, #150), image 8 x 13 in., (20.3 x 33 cm.), hand-colored graphotype (BP 83, DM 206, FR 701, Y 16,355).
$39* *"The Tumbletown Steeple-Chase, No. 3 - Too Hot To Last",* artist: Phiz, pub. Ackerman, (12-05-92, Neal, #148), image 7½ x 11 in., (19.1 x 27.9 cm.), hand-colored graphotype (BP 24, DM 61, FR 207, Y 4832).
$39* *"The Tumbletown Steeple-Chase, No. 6 - The Brook. In For A Penny And More Than A Pound!",* artist: Phiz, pub. Ackerman, (12-05-92, Neal, #149), image 8 x 13 in., (20.3 x 33 cm.), hand-colored graphotype (BP 24, DM 61, FR 207, Y 4832).

ACKERMANN
$330* *"Banquette", "A Mona Marble Chimney Piece", "Fashionable Furniture",and "Drawing Room Chairs": Four Empire Interiors,* 4to., (12-10-92, Sloan, #2092), hand colored antique engraved plates (BP 213, DM 522, FR 1783, Y 40,821).
$690* *Caricatures, c. 1830: Eight,* (03-03-93, Sotheby-Arcade, #122), sight 5¼ x 7½ in., (13.3 x 19.1 cm.), hand-colored aquatint (BP 476, DM 1136, FR 3855, Y 80,626).

ACKERMANN, Max   1887-1975
$605* *Blue Serenade, 1964,* s., d., num. 72/100, margins, good cond., surface soiling, (02-24-93, Butterfield, #3170), 19 x 13¼ in., (483 x 337 mm.), silkscreen in colors on heavy paper (BP 422, DM 982, FR 3330, Y 70,993).
$1135* *"Capriccio", 1953,* s., d., num., (06-05-93, Grisebach, #501, illus.), 18¾ x 9⅞n in., (47.6 x 24 cm.), color serigraph on copper print hand-made (BP 747, DM 1840, FR 6202, Y 121,755).
$581* *Komposition Mit Blau, 1973,* s., d., E.A., (12-01-92, Karl/Faber, #300), 18⅞n x 12Cꭐn in., (47.5 x 31 cm.), colored serigraph on wove (BP 384, DM 926, FR 3156, Y 72,336).
$880* *Komposition, 1958,* #35/100, d., s., (04-24-93, Kunsthaus, #450), 19⅞, x 12Ꭿ, in., (48.5 x 31.4 cm.), color lithograph on wove (BP 555, DM 1379, FR 4659, Y 97,109).
$247* *Untitled Abstract Composition, 1956,* trimmed bottom margin, d., num., s., (05-27-93, Swann, #2), 17¾ x 14

in., (45.1 x 35.6 cm.), color lithograph on Murillo cream (BP 158, DM 396, FR 1336, Y 26,479).
$236* *Untitled, 1972,* s., num., (12-05-92, Bassenge, #6990), 12¾ x 19⅛, in., (32.4 x 49.8 cm.), color screenprint on copper print paper (BP 148, DM 368, FR 1254, Y 29,240).
$496* *Zwei Figuren, (19)47,* s., d., num., (06-08-93, Karl/Faber, #473), approx. 12⅞ꭐn x 10⅞n in., (32.5 x 25.5 cm.), lithograph on cream machine paper (BP 326, DM 805, FR 2710, Y 52,682).

ACKERMANN, Peter   b. 1943
$244* *Architekturcapriccio, 1973,* s., num., (12-05-92, Bassenge, #6992), 21¼ x 23⅞ꭐn in., (54 x 58.5 cm.), etching (BP 153, DM 380, FR 1296, Y 30,232).
$258* *Marx In Seiner Familie (Hering 55), 1966,* s., num., (12-05-92, Bassenge, #6991), 17⅜ꭐn x 19⅜ꭐn in., (44.6 x 49.7 cm.), etching on Japan (BP 162, DM 402, FR 1371, Y 31,966).
$251* *Ruinenlandschaft, 1974,* s., epreuve d'artiste, i., (12-05-92, Bassenge, #6994), 15⅜ꭐn x 17¾ in., (39.5 x 45.1 cm.), etching on wove (BP 157, DM 391, FR 1334, Y 31,099).

ACKERMANN, R., Publisher
$522* *A History Of The University Of Oxford And Cambridge (Abbey Life 79 and 278): Sixteen,* pub. 1814, full margins, 7 badly trimmed, time stained, (10-27-92, Phillips-London, #124), plate 9Ꭿ, x 11¾ in., (251 x 298 mm.), aquatint w/hand-coloring (BP 330, DM 800, FR 2715, Y 63,853).

ACKERMANN and Co., Publisher
$128* *The History Of Charter House: Five,* bound volume, w/ text, pub. 1816, (09-17-92, Bonhams-Chelsea, #85D), hand-colored aquatint (BP 72, DM 190, FR 650, Y 15,936).
$138* *"The Naval Review At Spithead",* pub. Ackermann 1853, label verso, (05-15-93, Dunning, #104A, illus.), 15¾ x 33½ in., (40 x 85.1 cm.), color lithograph (BP 90, DM 222, FR 746, Y 15,298).
$161* *The Trial Of Bill Burn, Under Martin's Act,* by Charles Hunt, (08-20-92, Bonhams-Chelsea, #7), image 16¼ x 22 in., (41.3 x 55.9 cm.), aquatint w/hand-coloring (BP 83, DM 233, FR 791, Y 20,331).

ACKROYD, Norman   England b. 1938
$39* *Loch,* s., t., d. 1975, The Print Club of Cleveland pub. no. 54, 1976, (07-03-92, Sloan, #322), 7⅛, x 7⅞, in., (19.4 x 18.1 cm.), aquatint (BP 20, DM 59, FR 199, Y 4862).

ADAL
$920* *"The Evidence Of Things Not Seen": Ten,* 1974, p. 1976, Foto Gallery, each ink t.; s., t., d., including p. t. sheet, colophon s., t., d., #8/10, intro., s., d., i., lit., (04-08-93, Christie-NY, #462, illus.), each approx. 7¼ x 6½ in., (18.4 x 16.5 cm.), photograph, gelatin silver print (BP 603, DM 1478, FR 5003, Y 104,403).

ADAM, Henri Georges
BI *"Aout" and "Vigie", 1952, 1959: Two,* s., d., t., #14/120, #28/125, blindstamp publisher, George Goodstadt, margins, good cond.?, est. $2/400, (05-19-93, Butterfield, #2031), one 23 x 14¾ in., (584 x 375 mm.), the other 28 x 20 in., (584 x 375 mm.), etching (one w/aquatint) on Rives BFK.

ADAM, V*
BI *Chevaux Du Haut Poiton,* by Becquet Bros., est. BP 6/ 80, (06-30-93, Bonhams-Chelsea, #16), image 12 x 17½ in., (30.5 x 44.5 cm.), lithograph w/hand-coloring.

ADAM, Victor   French 1801-1866
$110* *Bull Fight Prints: Twelve,* complete set, (12-13-92, Hindman, #260), each 11¼ x 14¼ in., hand-colored lithograph (BP 70, DM 173, FR 589, Y 13,609).

ADAMI, Valerio   Italian b. 1935
BI *Adami-Ausstellung Hamburg, 1973,* s., #48/50, est. DM 300, (09-18-92, Schloss Ahlden, #973), 28⅞ꭐn x 18⅞, in., (73.5 x 46 cm.), color screen print.
$428* *"Angelus" and "L'Enlevement D'Europe", 1982 and 1985: Two,* s., #47/100, 25/75, p. and pub. Galerie Maeght-Lelong, full margins,good cond., (06-30-93, Sotheby-London, #726, illus.), one 30 x 22⅞, in., (762 x 562 mm.),

the other 29C, x 22C, in., (762 x 562 mm.), color lithograph, etching and aquatint in color on Arches (BP 287, DM 730, FR 2463, Y 45,859).

BI *Le Baiser Et Les Violinistes: Two,* s., #117/180, #107/160, est. FF1,800/2,000, (05-27-93, Briest, #3), one 22¼ x 29B\n in., (56.5 x 76 cm.), other 29Azn x 22zn in., (56.5 x 76 cm.), color lithographs.

BI *"Le Baiser" and "Les Violonistes": Two,* #117/180, 107/160, est. FF2,000/2,500, (03-31-93, Briest, #E1), one 22¼ x 29B\n in., (56.5 x 76 cm.), other 29Azn x 22zn in., (56.5 x 76 cm.), color lithographs.

$461* *"Calamus" and "Sans Titre": Two,* s., #12/100 and 30/100, ed. Studio Marconi, (11-16-92, Briest, #3), one 27zn x 39C, in., (70 x 100 cm.), other 39C, x 25Zn in., (70 x 100 cm.), lithographs in 12 and 9 colors (BP 303, DM 735, FR 2477, Y 57,532).

BI *Composition,* s. E.A., est. DK 800, (09-30-92, Kunsthallen, #1), color lithograph.

$189* *Femme Accoudee, 1990,* epreuve d'artiste, s., (11-16-92, Briest, #4), 22zn x 29Bzn in., (56 x 76 cm.), serigraph in colors (BP 124, DM 301, FR 1016, Y 23,587).

BI *Heart and "Rainbow",* s., AP, num., est. DM 800, (12-01-92, Karl/Faber, #301), 26C, x 16Azn in., (67 x 43 cm.), colored serigraph on wove.

BI *Homme A La Pipe,* regular edition, s., est. FF800/1,000, (05-27-93, Briest, #4), 29Azn x 15B\n in., (76 x 40.5 cm.), color lithograph.

$84* *"M. Untel",* #24/75, s., (01-28-93, Pescheteau, #57), 20M, x 29Azn in., (53 x 76 cm.), color lithograph on wove (BP 55, DM 133, FR 450, Y 10,430).

$120* *"Moments Musicaux", 1975,* num. 1/150, s., (04-04-93, Pescheteau, #152), 27zn x 20M, in., (70 x 53 cm.), color lithograph on wove (BP 79, DM 193, FR 655, Y 13,663).

BI *"Olympische Spiele Munchen 1972",* s. twice, num., est. DM 600, (12-01-92, Karl/Faber, #302), 34¼ x 21¼ in., (87 x 54 cm.), poster, colored serigraph on cardboard.

BI *Ottiero Ottieri,* s., annot., #100/150, large margins, (05-06-93, Laurin, #1), color lithograph.

BI *"Petit Odeon",* #1/125, s., est. FF4/600, (04-04-93, Pescheteau, #153), 19Z, x 15Czn in., (48.5 x 38.5 cm.), lithograph on wove.

BI *"Petit Odeon",* #1/125, s., (01-28-93, Pescheteau, #56), 19Z, x 15Czn in., (48.5 x 38.5 cm.), lithograph on wove.

$263* *Tramonto, 1991,* artist's proof, s., (05-27-93, Briest, #5), 47¼ x 62Azn in., (120 x 160 cm.), color serigraph (BP 168, DM 422, FR 1422, Y 28,195).

ADAMS, Ansel American 1902-1984

$2875* *"Alders, Prairie Creek Beach, Northern California",* 1949, p. 1974, s., #13/100, t., Portfolio VI label, (05-23-93, Butterfield, #3273, illus.), 15½ x 19½ in., photograph, gelatin silver print (BP 1872, DM 4701, FR 15,823, Y 317,785).

BI *Alfred Stieglitz At An American Place, New York, New York, c. 1939 (Letters and Images. p. 53),* s. by photog., studio stamp, p. 1978, est. $2,5/3,500, (10-15-92, Sotheby-NY, #240, illus.), 12B, x 8M, in., (32.1 x 22.5 cm.), photograph, gelatin silver print.

$2475* *"Alfred Stieglitz",* 1939/1970's, s. mount, t.; photog. Carmel 93921 stamp verso mount, (11-16-92, Butterfield, #5832, illus.), 13¼ x 8¾ in., (337.2 x 222.6 mm.), photograph, gelatin silver print (BP 1630, DM 3946, FR 13,292, Y 307,798).

$5225* *The American West: "Milestone Mountain-Sierra Nevada" and "Grand Canon, Arizona": Two,* each s. by photog., t., num. 1497 & 1496, label, 1920's, (10-15-92, Sotheby-NY, #235, illus.), each approx. 5¾ x 7¾ in., (14.6 x 19.7 cm.), photograph, parmelian prints (BP 3197, DM 7778, FR 26,376, Y 626,875).

$7700* *The American West: "Mt. Clark and Echo Ridge-Yosemite, California", "Cockscomb Crest, Yosemite", "Cliffs near Big Bird Lake-Sierra Nevada", "BannerPeak-Sierra Nevada Range" and "In Cliff Creek Canyon-Sierra Nevada": Five,* each s. Ansel E. Adams by photog., t., num. 1490, 1495, 1494, & 1493,label, 1920's, (10-15-92, Sotheby-NY, #234, illus.), each approx. 5¾ x 7¾ in., (14.6 x 19.7 cm.), photograph, parmelian prints (BP 4712, DM 11,462, FR 38,869, Y 923,815).

BI *Arches, North Court, Mission San Xavier Del Bac, Tucson, Arizona, 1968,* mounted, s. by photog., studio stamp, p. 1970's, est. $3/5,000, (10-15-92, Sotheby-NY, #256A, illus.), 15¼ x 19½ in., (38.7 x 49.5 cm.), photograph, gelatin silver print.

$11,000* *Aspens, New Mexico, 1958 (Portfolios, p. 116),* mounted on Hi-Art Illustration Board, s. by photog., studio stamp, p.early 1960's, (10-15-92, Sotheby-NY, #252, illus.), 14M, x 19Z, in., (37.8 x 48.6 cm.), photograph, gelatin silver print (BP 6731, DM 16,374, FR 55,528, Y 1,319,736).

$4950* *"Aspens, Northern New Mexico",* 1958/1970's, s. mount, t., d. photog. Carmel 93921 stamp verso mount, lit., (11-16-92, Butterfield, #5820, illus.), 15 x 19Zzn in., (381.7 x 483.5 mm.), photograph, gelatin silver print (BP 3259, DM 7892, FR 26,584, Y 615,595).

$11,500* *"Aspens, Northern New Mexico" (Letters and Images, p. 314),* s. by photog., t., studio stamp, 1958, p. c. 1960, (04-06-93, Sotheby-NY, #208, illus.), 15½ x 19B, in., photograph, mounted on Crescent Illustration Board (BP 7596, DM 18,527, FR 62,739, Y 1,311,588).

$5500* *"Banner Peak, Thousand Island Lake, High Sierras",* 1923/1927, from Parmelian Portfolio, s., t. p. margin, lit., (11-16-92, Butterfield, #5818, illus.), 5M, x 8 in., (149.5 x 203.6 mm.), photograph, gelatin silver print (BP 3621, DM 8769, FR 29,538, Y 683,995).

BI *Big Tree, Winter, Mariposa Grove, Yosemite National Park, 1935-40,* s. on mount, lit., est. $9/12,000, (10-13-92, Christie-NY, #102, illus.), 19 x 14 in., (48.3 x 35.6 cm.), photograph, gelatin silver print.

$1955* *"The Black And The Red Kaweahs From Little Five Lakes",* 1920s, s., t., (05-23-93, Butterfield, #3276, illus.), 6½ x 9 in., photograph, gelatin silver print (BP 1273, DM 3197, FR 10,759, Y 216,094).

$3163* *"Branches In Snow" and "Grass And Pool" (Portfolios, pp. 45 and 51):Two,* plates 5 and 11 from Portfolio III, Sierra Club, mounted, each s. byphotog., portfolio stamp, c. 1932 and 1935, p. 1959, num. 8 and 11, (04-06-93, Sotheby-NY, #200, illus.), one 8½ x 6½ in., photograph (BP 2089, DM 5096, FR 17,256, Y 360,744).

$1955* *"Bridal Veil Fall",* 1952, p. 1960, s., Portfolio Three, Yosemite Valley portfolio stamp, (05-23-93, Butterfield, #3282, illus.), 11 x 7¾ in., photograph, gelatin silver print (BP 1273, DM 3197, FR 10,759, Y 216,094).

$3450* *"El Capitan, Yosemite Valley", 1940's,* backed w/card, mounted, s. by photog., t., (04-06-93, Sotheby-NY, #198, illus.), 7C, x 9½ in., photograph (BP 2279, DM 5558, FR 18,822, Y 393,476).

BI *El Capitan, c. 1930,* s., offset-printed t., est. $5/7,000, (10-13-92, Christie-NY, #97, illus.), 7¼ x 5B, in., (18.4 x 14.3 cm.), photograph, parmelian print.

$1925* *Cathedral Peak And Lake, Yosemite National Park, California, c. 1960(Portfolios, p. 65),* plate 5 from Portfolio IV, Sierra Club, mounted, s. by photog. in ink, label, p. 1963, #83/260 ed., (10-15-92, Sotheby-NY, #250, illus.), 7 x 9C, in., photograph, gelatin silver print (BP 1178, DM 2865, FR 9717, Y 230,954).

$2200* *"Cemetery Point, Timber Cove" and "At Timber Cove", c. 1960: Two,* each ink s. mount, each t., neg. num.; photog. Carmel Route I stamp verso mount, (11-16-92, Butterfield, #5824, illus.), one 15¼ x 19zn in., (388 x 483.5 mm.), other 15½ x 19zn in., (388 x 483.5 mm.), photograph, gelatin silver print (BP 1449, DM 3508, FR 11,815, Y 273,598).

$8800* *Church At Ranchos De Taos-New Mexico (An Autobiography, p. 95),* s. "Ansel E. Adam"s by photog., t., num. 1492, label, 1920s, (10-15-92, Sotheby-NY, #232, illus.), 5½ x 7B, in., (14 x 19.4 cm.), photograph, parmelian prints (BP 5385, DM 13,099, FR 44,422, Y 1,055,789).

$11,500* *"Clearing Winter Storm, Yosemite National Park" (Morgan and Morgan, pl. 71), 1944,* mounted, s. Ansel E. Adams by photog., (04-06-93, Sotheby-NY, #204, illus.), 7 x 9Z, in., photograph (BP 7596, DM 18,527, FR 62,739, Y 1,311,588).

$9900* *Clearing Winter Storm, Yosemite National Park, California, 1944 (Morgan & Morgan, pl. 71),* mounted, s. by photog., studio stamp, p. 1978, (10-15-92, Sotheby-NY, #243, illus.), 15½ x 19 in., (39.4 x 48.3 cm.), photograph, gelatin silver print (BP 6058, DM 14,737, FR 49,975, Y 1,187,762).

$14,950* *Clearing Winter Storm, Yosemite Valley,* 1944, p. early 1960s, ink s., stamp, lit., (04-08-93, Christie-NY, #365, illus.), 15½ x 19½ in., (39.4 x 49.5 cm.), photograph, gelatin silver print (BP 9803, DM 24,016, FR 81,294, Y 1,696,550).

$6600* *"Clearing Winter Storm, Yosemite Valley",* 1944/early 1960's, ink s. on Crescent Board mount, t. "Winterstorm, Gates of the Valley, Yosemite Valley"; photog. Carmel 93921 stamp verso on mount, lit., (11-16-92, Butterfield, #5815, illus.), 10¾ x 13C, in., (273.5 x 340.3 mm.), photograph, gelatin silver print (BP 4346, DM 10,523, FR 35,446, Y 820,793).

BI *Courthouse, Mariposa, California, c. 1935 (An American Place, pl. 15),* s. by photog., studio stamp, p.l., est. $2/3,000, (10-15-92, Sotheby-NY, #242, illus.), 10 x 12½ in., (25.4 x 31.8 cm.), photograph, gelatin silver print.

$4400* *Cypress, Carmel,* 1950s, s., stamp, (10-13-92, Christie-NY, #406, illus.), 15C, x 19¼ in., (39.1 x 48.9 cm.), photograph, gelatin silver print (BP 2563, DM 6446, FR 21,901, Y 533,527).

$2530* *Dawn, Autumn Forest, Great Smokey Mountains National Park, Tennessee,* 1948, from Portfolio Two: The National Parks and Monuments, 1950, s., num., portfolio and limitation stamps, lit., (04-08-93, Christie-NY, #369, illus.), 12 x 8B, in., (30.5 x 21.9 cm.), photograph, gelatin silver print (BP 1659, DM 4064, FR 13,757, Y 287,108).

$3300* *Dawn, Autumn, Dolores River Canyon, Colorado, 1937 (An Autobiography,p. 234),* mounted, s. by photog., studio stamp, p. 1978, (10-15-92, Sotheby-NY, #242A, illus.), 9¼ x 13½ in., (23.5 x 34.3 cm.), photograph, gelatin silver print (BP 2019, DM 4912, FR 16,658, Y 395,921).

$4400* *"Dawn, Autumn, Great Smoky Mountains National Park, Tennessee",* 1948/c. 1980, s., d., i. on mount, lit., (11-16-92, Butterfield, #5828, illus.), 19½zn x 14B, in., (496.2 x 372.1 mm.), photograph, gelatin silver print (BP 2897, DM 7015, FR 23,631, Y 547,196).

$633* *"Donald Tressider", 1940,* s., (05-23-93, Butterfield, #3295, illus.), 7B, x 7 in., photograph, gelatin silver print (BP 412, DM 1035, FR 3484, Y 69,968).

$1725* *Downhill Skier, 1935,* mounted, s., d. by photog., i., (04-06-93, Sotheby-NY, #193, illus.), 6 x 8¾ in., photograph (BP 1139, DM 2779, FR 9411, Y 196,738).

$4125* *Eagle Dance-Tesuque Pueblo, New Mexico (Morgan & Morgan, pl. 14),* s. Ansel E. Adams by photog., t., num. 1499, label, 1920s, (10-15-92, Sotheby-NY, #228, illus.), 5½ x 7B, in., (14 x 19.4 cm.), photograph, parmelian print (BP 2524, DM 6140, FR 20,823, Y 494,901).

$3575* *"Edward Weston, Carmel Highlands, California",* 1945/1974, s., edit. VI-I 90/110 mount, t., d.; Portfolio VI stamp verso mount, lit., (11-16-92, Butterfield, #5825, illus.), 19½zn x 14½ in., (496.2 x 369 mm.), photograph, gelatin silver print (BP 2354, DM 5700, FR 19,200, Y 444,596).

$3300* *Edward Weston, Tenaya Lake, 1937,* prov., lit., (10-13-92, Christie-NY, #101, illus.), 9½ x 7¼ in., (24.1 x 18.4 cm.), photograph, gelatin silver print (BP 1922, DM 4834, FR 16,426, Y 400,146).

$379* *Eiche Nach Schneesturm,* 50's, 1982, s., #54/85, (11-12-92, Lempertz, #1, illus.), 9Mzn x 7½ in., (24 x 19 cm.), photograph, gelatin silver print (BP 242, DM 596, FR 2030, Y 46,889).

$2200* *"Emerald Bay, Lake Tahoe, California", 1940,* t., d., annot. Mounted 1978; photog. Carmel 93923 stamp verso mount, (11-16-92, Butterfield, #5830, illus.), 15C\ x 18Zzn in., (391.2 x 477.1 mm.), photograph, gelatin silver print (BP 1449, DM 3508, FR 11,815, Y 273,598).

$1093* *"Falls, Palisade Creek, Sierra Nevada",* 1927, p. c. 1954, s., t., d., photog.'s stamp, (05-23-93, Butterfield, #3292, illus.), 15¾ x 10 in., photograph, gelatin silver print (BP 712, DM 1787, FR 6015, Y 120,814).

$2070* *"Fern Spring, Yosemite Valley, California",* 1961, p. 1974, s., t., d., photog.'s stamp, (05-23-93, Butterfield, #3293, illus.), 12¼ x 9 in., photograph, gelatin silver print (BP 1348, DM 3385, FR 11,392, Y 228,805).

BI *Fern Spring, Yosemite Valley, California, 1961,* s. in ink, t., lit., est. $4/6,000, (10-13-92, Christie-NY, #409, illus.), 13½ x 10 in., (34.3 x 25.4 cm.), photograph, gelatin silver print.

$2875* *"Forest Floor, Yosemite Valley, California" (Yosemite and the Range of Light, pl. 11), c. 1950,* mounted, s., #37/50 by photog., label, p. 1979, orig. includ. w/deluxe edit., (04-06-93, Sotheby-NY, #207, illus.), 15 x 19¼ in., photograph (BP 1899, DM 4632, FR 15,685, Y 327,897).

$1380* *"Forest, Early Morning, Mt. Ranier", 1950,* s., photog.'s Portfolio Two stamp, (05-23-93, Butterfield, #3284, illus.), 9½ x 7¼ in., photograph, gelatin silver print (BP 899, DM 2256, FR 7595, Y 152,537).

$1955* *"From Moose Pass, Telephotograph, Jasper National Park, Canada",* 1928, p. 1970s, s., d., t., photog.'s stamp, (05-23-93, Butterfield, #3280, illus.), 7¾ x 9¾ in., photograph, gelatin silver print (BP 1273, DM 3197, FR 10,759, Y 216,094).

$7475* *Frozen Lake And Cliffs, Sierra Nevada, California,* 1932, p. 1979, s., stamp w/t., and d. in ink, lit., (04-08-93, Christie-NY, #361, illus.), 14B, x 17C, in., (37.1 x 44.1 cm.), photograph, gelatin silver print (BP 4902, DM 12,008, FR 40,647, Y 848,275).

BI *"Glacial Cirque, Milestone Ridge, Sequoia National Park" and "CanyonView" (Morgan and Morgan, pl. 7): Two,* each s. by photog., labels, num. 1318 and 1320, 1920's, est. $4/6,000, (04-06-93, Sotheby-NY, #192, illus.), each approx. 5¾ x 7¾ in., photograph.

$2070* *The Great White Throne, Zion National Park, Utah,* 1942, p. mid 1950s-early 1960s, ink s., stamp, (04-08-93, Christie-NY, #364, illus.), 15Z, x 19Z, in., (38.4 x 48.6 cm.), photograph, gelatin silver print (BP 1357, DM 3325, FR 11,256, Y 234,907).

$1430* *"Group Riding Horses, Yosemite" and "Mountains And River, Yosemite": Two,* photog.'s handstamp, 1940s(?), (04-07-93, Swann, #387, illus.), one 7 x 9 in., other 9 x 7 in., photograph, silver print (BP 945, DM 2313, FR 7827, Y 162,463).

$3080* *"Half Dome And Moon" and "Oaktree, Snowstorm": Two Photographs Of Yosemite,* photog.'s inits., handstamp, 1960s, (04-07-93, Swann, #384, illus.), each approx. 10 x 7½ in., photograph, silver print (BP 2035, DM 4981, FR 16,858, Y 349,920).

$5225* *Half Dome Blowing Snow, Yosemite National Park, California, c. 1955 (Portfolios, p. 119),* mounted, s. by photog., studio stamp, p.l., (10-15-92, Sotheby-NY, #251, illus.), 15C, x 19Z, in., (39.1 x 48.6 cm.), photograph, gelatin silver print (BP 3197, DM 7778, FR 26,376, Y 626,875).

BI *Half Dome, Blowing Snow, Yosemite National Park, California,* c. 1955, from Portfolio VII, 1976, s., #23/115, portfolio stamp, lit., est. $5/7,000, (04-08-93, Christie-NY, #374, illus.), 15½ x 19½ in., (39.4 x 49.5 cm.), photograph, gelatin silver print.

$6900* *"Half Dome, Blowing Snow, Yosemite National Park, California",* 1955, p.l., t., d., photog.'s stamp, illus., (05-23-93, Butterfield, #3270, illus.), 15 x 19 in., photograph, gelatin silver print (BP 4494, DM 11,282, FR 37,975, Y 762,684).

$6900* *"Half Dome, Blowing Snow, Yosemite National Park, California" (Portfolios, p. 119),* mounted, s. by photog., studio stamp, c. 1955, p.l., (04-06-93, Sotheby-NY, #200A, illus.), 15½ x 19½ in., photograph (BP 4557, DM 11,116, FR 37,643, Y 786,953).

BI *Hands Of Annette Rosenshine, San Francisco, Ca.,* (c. 1932), 1970s, s. on mount, t. in ink, Carmel stamp, est. $2,5/3,500, (10-13-92, Christie-NY, #100, illus.), 10M, x 13M, in., (27.6 x 35.2 cm.), photograph, gelatin silver print.

$385* *Head Of A Nisei Girl, Manzanar, California (Born Free And Equal, plate 11),* 1940s, p.l., (04-07-93, Swann, #282, illus.), 9 x 7 in., photograph, silver print (BP 254, DM 623, FR 2107, Y 43,740).

BI *Highway Sign, Near Wenden, Utah,* (1942), late 1960s, s. on mount, Carmel stamp w/t., d. in ink, est. 2,5/3,500, (10-13-92, Christie-NY, #105, illus.), 15C, x 19Z, in., (39.1 x 48.6 cm.), photograph, gelatin silver print.

$1725* *"Images 1923-1974",* New York Graphic Society, deluxe edit. w/orig. photo, book illus. w/115 reprod. of Adams's photos, s. by photog., num. in unident. hand, oblong folio, w/photo, "Fern Spring, Dusk, Yosemite Valley", s. by pub., label num. 91, c. 1961, p. 1974, (04-06-93, Sotheby-NY, #214, illus.), photo 12¼ x 9 in., photograph (BP 1139, DM 2779, FR 9411, Y 196,738).

$3163* *"Interior, Santuario De Chimayo, New Mexico"*, 1960, p. c. 1976, s., t., d., photog.'s stamp, (05-23-93, Butterfield, #3286, illus.), 10½ x 12 in., photograph, gelatin silver print (BP 2060, DM 5172, FR 17,408, Y 349,619).

$3300* *"Juan Pancho-Peublo de Cochiti, New Mexico (Pueblo Indian Type)" and"Buffalo Dancers and Singing Chorus, Tesuque Pueblo, New Mexico", Pueblo Indians, 1920s: Two*, s. "Ansel E.Adams" by photog., t., num. 1500 & 150l, label, (10-15-92, Sotheby-NY, #229, illus.), approx. 7¾ x 5¾ in., (19.7 x 14.6 cm.), photograph, parmelian print (BP 2019, DM 4912, FR 16,658, Y 395,921).

$1980* *Lake Tenaya*, s., prov., (05-16-93, Hindman, #329, illus.), 9½ x 7¾ in., photograph, silver print (BP 1292, DM 3195, FR 10,761, Y 220,490).

$6325* *"Lake Tenaya, Yosemite National Park, California" (Yosemite and the Range of Light, pl. 75)*, s., t. by photog.; studio stamp, 1960's, (04-06-93, Sotheby-NY, #202A, illus.), 10½ x 13½ in., photograph, mounted on Hi-Art Illustration Board (BP 4178, DM 10,190, FR 34,506, Y 721,373).

$2588* *"Leaves, Mt. Rainier National Park, Washington"*, 1942, p. 1978, s., t., d., photog.'s stamp, illus., (05-23-93, Butterfield, #3275, illus.), 14½ x 19½ in., photograph, gelatin silver print (BP 1685, DM 4232, FR 14,243, Y 286,062).

$2750* *Leaves-Mt. Rainier National Park, c. 1960*, mounted on Crescent Illustration Board, s. by photog. in ink, t., studio stamp, (10-15-92, Sotheby-NY, #254, illus.), 15½ x 19℃, in., (39.4 x 49.2 cm.), photograph, gelatin silver print (BP 1683, DM 4093, FR 13,882, Y 329,934).

$3300* *Lower Yosemite Falls, 1959*, photog.'s sig., Portfolio Three handstamp, (04-07-93, Swann, #385, illus.), 9½ x 7½ in., photograph, silver print (BP 2181, DM 5337, FR 18,062, Y 374,915).

$330* *Madrone Park, 1980*, from the Presidential Portfolio, s., d., i., #39/150, reprod. by Pacific Lithograph Co., good cond.?, (12-12-92, Weschler, #97), image 18 x 13 in., (45.7 x 33 cm.), photolithograph (BP 212, DM 520, FR 1782, Y 40,837).

$8800* *"Mirror Lake, Yosemite", c. 1928*, s., t., d., i. 1937 on mount, (11-16-92, Butterfield, #5817, illus.), 7½ x 9½ in., (190.8 x 241.7 mm.), photograph, gelatin silver print (BP 5794, DM 14,031, FR 47,261, Y 1,094,391).

BI   *Mono Lake*, (1950), 1956-61, s., i. in ink, lit., est. $15/ 18,000, (10-13-92, Christie-NY, #407, illus.), 20 x 26½ in., (50.8 x 67.3 cm.), photograph, gelatin silver print.

$3163* *"Monolith, Face Of Half Dome" (Morgan and Morgan, pl. 8), 1927*, s. Ansel E. Adams by photog., (04-06-93, Sotheby-NY, #196, illus.), 8 x 6 in., photograph, silver gelatin on Dassonville paper (BP 2089, DM 5096, FR 17,256, Y 360,744).

$5750* *"Monolith, The Face Of Half Dome"*, 1927, p. 1970s, s., t., d., photog.'s stamp, (05-23-93, Butterfield, #3267, illus.), 19 x 14¼ in., photograph, gelatin silver print (BP 3745, DM 9402, FR 31,646, Y 635,570).

$5225* *Monolith, The Face Of Half Dome, 1927 (Morgan & Morgan, pl. 8)*, mounted, s. by photog., t., i., d. in ink, p. before 1938, (10-15-92, Sotheby-NY, #239, illus.), 7M, x 6 in., (20 x 15.2 cm.), photograph, gelatin silver print (BP 3197, DM 7778, FR 26,376, Y 626,875).

$8800* *Monolith, The Face Of Half Dome, Yosemite National Park, Ca.*, (c. 1927), 1970s, s., t., d. in ink, Carmel stamp, lit., (10-13-92, Christie-NY, #99, illus.), 19 x 14¼ in., (48.3 x 36.2 cm.), photograph, gelatin silver print (BP 5125, DM 12,892, FR 43,803, Y 1,067,055).

$4125* *Monolith-The Face Of Half Dome-Yosemite, California, 1927 (An Autobiography, p. 76)*, s. Ansel E. Adams by photog., t., num. 1486, label, (10-15-92, Sotheby-NY, #236, illus.), 7M, x 5M, in., (20 x 14.9 cm.), photograph, parmelian print (BP 2524, DM 6140, FR 20,823, Y 494,901).

BI   *Monolith: The Face Of Half Dome*, (c. 1927), s., t., p. in margin, est. 7/9,000, (10-13-92, Christie-NY, #98, illus.), 8 x 6 in., (20.3 x 15.2 cm.), photograph, parmelian print.

$3680* *Monument Valley, Utah*, 1958, p. 1970s, s.; stamp w/ink, (04-08-93, Christie-NY, #375, illus.), 15½ x 19¼ in., (39.4 x 48.9 cm.), photograph, gelatin silver print (BP 2413, DM 5912, FR 20,011, Y 417,612).

$10,350* *"Moon And Half Dome, Yosemite National Park, CA." (Yosemite and the Range of Light, pl. 115)*, mounted, s. by photog., studio stamp, 1960, p.l., (04-06-93, Sotheby-NY, #213, illus.), 19 x 14B, in., photograph (BP 6836, DM 16,675, FR 56,465, Y 1,180,429).

$4125* *"Moon And Half Dome, Yosemite Valley", 1960's print*, ink s. mount; photog. Carmel Route I stamp, ink t. verso mount, lit., (11-16-92, Butterfield, #5826, illus.), 13½ x 10ℤ, in., (343.5 x 257.6 mm.), photograph, gelatin silver print (BP 2716, DM 6577, FR 22,154, Y 512,996).

$11,000* *Moonrise Over Hernandez, New Mexico*, (1941), p.l., s. on mount, Carmel stamp, (10-13-92, Christie-NY, #103, illus.), 15½ x 19½ in., (39.4 x 49.5 cm.), photograph, gelatin silver print (BP 6407, DM 16,115, FR 54,754, Y 1,333,818).

$12,650* *Moonrise, Hernandez, New Mexico*, 1941, p.l., s.; ink t., d., stamp, (04-08-93, Christie-NY, #363, illus.), 15½ x 19½ in., (39.4 x 49.5 cm.), photograph, gelatin silver print (BP 8295, DM 20,321, FR 68,787, Y 1,435,542).

$13,200* *Moonrise, Hernandez, New Mexico*, s. by photog., photog.'s handstamp, notations, 1941, p.l., (04-07-93, Swann, #386, illus.), 15¼ x 18½ in., photograph, silver print (BP 8723, DM 21,349, FR 72,250, Y 1,499,659).

$6050* *"Moonrise, Hernandez, New Mexico"*, 1941/1970's, s. on mount, t., d.; photog. Carmel 93921 stamp verso of mount, lit., (11-16-92, Butterfield, #5814, illus.), 15½ x 19Bзn in., (394.4 x 489.8 mm.), photograph, gelatin silver print (BP 3983, DM 9646, FR 32,492, Y 752,394).

$6900* *"Moonrise, Hernandez, New Mexico"*, 1941, p. 1978, s., t., d., photog.'s stamp, illus., (05-23-93, Butterfield, #3265, illus.), 15¼ x 19 in., photograph, gelatin silver print (BP 4494, DM 11,282, FR 37,975, Y 762,684).

$10,925* *"Moonrise, Hernandez, New Mexico" (Morgan and Morgan, p. 63)*, mounted, s. by photog., studio stamp, 1941, p.l., (04-06-93, Sotheby-NY, #202, illus.), 15 x 19¼ in., photograph (BP 7216, DM 17,601, FR 59,602, Y 1,246,008).

$12,100* *Moonrise, Hernandez, New Mexico, c. 1941 (Morgan & Morgan, pl. 63)*, s. by photog., studio stamp, p. 1978, (10-15-92, Sotheby-NY, #244, illus.), 15¼ x 19¼ in., (38.7 x 48.9 cm.), photograph, gelatin silver print (BP 7404, DM 18,011, FR 61,080, Y 1,451,710).

$4675* *"Mount Williamson, Sierra Nevada From Manzanar, California", 1944/1970's*, s. mount, t., d.; photog. Carmel 93921 stamp verso mount, lit., (11-16-92, Butterfield, #5819, illus.), 15B, x 18ℤ'n in., (397.6 x 473.9 mm.), photograph, gelatin silver print (BP 3078, DM 7454, FR 25,107, Y 581,395).

$2200* *Mt. Clark*, plate from "Parmelian Prints of the High Sierras" portfolio, Jean Chambers Moore, 1927, s. by photog., t., 1920's. p. c. 1927, (10-15-92, Sotheby-NY, #238A, illus.), 8 x 6 in., (20.3 x 15.2 cm.), photograph, parmelian print (BP 1346, DM 3275, FR 11,106, Y 263,947).

$1650* *Mt. Le Conte, Great Smoky Mts. Nat. Park, c. 1960*, mounted on Crescent Illustration Board, s. by photog. in ink, t., studio stamp, (10-15-92, Sotheby-NY, #255, illus.), 15 x 19½ in., (38.1 x 49.5 cm.), photograph, gelatin silver print (BP 1010, DM 2456, FR 8329, Y 197,960).

$8050* *Mt. McKinley And Wonder Lake, Denali National Park, Alaska*, 1947, p. 1960s, ink s., lit., (04-08-93, Christie-NY, #368, illus.), 15℃, x 19½ in., (39.1 x 49.5 cm.), photograph, gelatin silver print (BP 5279, DM 12,932, FR 43,774, Y 913,527).

$5463* *"Mt. Williamson, Sierra Nevada From Owens Valley, California"*, 1944, p. 1978, s., t., d., photog.'s stamp, (05-23-93, Butterfield, #3272, illus.), 14 xℤin., photograph, gelatin silver print (BP 3558, DM 8932, FR 30,066, Y 603,847).

$6325* *Mt. Williamson, Sierra Nevada, From Manzanar, California*, 1944, p. 1978, s.; ink t., d., stamp, sold after sale, (04-08-93, Christie-NY, #366, illus.), 15B, x 18B, in., (39.7 x 47.3 cm.), photograph, gelatin silver print (BP 4148, DM 10,161, FR 34,394, Y 717,771).

$10,350* *"Mt. Williamson, The Sierra Nevada From Manzanar, California" (Yosemite and the Range of Light, pl. 46), 1944*, mounted, s. by photog., photog. studio stamp, 1948, p. 1978, (04-06-93, Sotheby-NY, #210, illus.), 19¾ x 14M, in., photograph (BP 6836, DM 16,675, FR 56,465, Y 1,180,429).

$1320* *Near Sunrise Mountain,* s. by photog., 1920s, (10-15-92, Sotheby-NY, #238, illus.), 5M, x 7M, in., (14.9 x 20 cm.), photograph, parmelian print (BP 808, DM 1965, FR 6663, Y 158,368).

$3163* *"Nevada Fall, Rainbow" (Portfolios, p. 52),* plate 12 from Portfolio III, Sierra Club, mounted, s. by photog., portfolio stamp, c. 1947, p. c. 1960, num. 193, (04-06-93, Sotheby-NY, #209, illus.), 9½ x 7¼ in., photograph (BP 2089, DM 5096, FR 17,256, Y 360,744).

$3850* *Nevada Fall, Yosemite National Park, California, c. 1947 (Portfolios,p. 52),* mounted, s. by photog., t., d. in unidentified hand, studio stamp, p.l., (10-15-92, Sotheby-NY, #246A, illus.), 18¾ x 14½ in., (47.6 x 36.8 cm.), photograph, gelatin silver print (BP 2356, DM 5731, FR 19,435, Y 461,908).

$2588* *"The New Church, Taos Pueblo",* mounted, s. by photog., studio stamp, c. 1930, p. 1977, (04-06-93, Sotheby-NY, #197, illus.), 8½ x 10Z, in., photograph (BP 1709, DM 4169, FR 14,119, Y 295,164).

$5500* *"Oak Tree, Snowstorm, Yosemite National Park, California",* 1948/1970's, s. mount, t., d.; photog. Carmel 93921 stamp verso mount, lit., (11-16-92, Butterfield, #5821, illus.), 19½zn x 15½ in., (496.2 x 394.4 mm.), photograph, gelatin silver print (BP 3621, DM 8769, FR 29,538, Y 683,995).

$6600* *Oak Tree, Snowstorm, Yosemite Valley, California, 1948 (Morgan * Morgan, pl. 72),* mounted, s. by photog., studio stamp, p. 1978, (10-15-92, Sotheby-NY, #247, illus.), 19¼ x 15¼ in., (48.9 x 38.7 cm.), photograph, gelatin silver print (BP 4039, DM 9824, FR 33,317, Y 791,842).

$2875* *"Oak Tree, Sunset City, Sierra Foothills, California",* 1962, p. 1963, s., t., label, (05-23-93, Butterfield, #3278, illus.), 7¼ x 8½ in., photograph, gelatin silver print (BP 1872, DM 4701, FR 15,823, Y 317,785).

$1650* *Old Faithful Geyser, Late Evening, Yellowstone National Park, Wyoming, 1942 (Morgan & Morgan, pl. 50),* plate 13 from Portfolio II, Grabhorn Press, 1950, mounted, s. by photog., stamp, p. 1950, #70/105 ed., (10-15-92, Sotheby-NY, #245A, illus.), 9½ x 7Z, in., (24.1 x 18.1 cm.), photograph, gelatin silver print (BP 1010, DM 2456, FR 8329, Y 197,960).

$1955* *"Orchard, Early Spring, Near Stanford University, California",* 1940, p. 1963, s., t., What Majestic Word Portfolio IV label, (05-23-93, Butterfield, #3288, illus.), 10 x 12¾ in., photograph, gelatin silver print (BP 1273, DM 3197, FR 10,759, Y 216,094).

$1955* *"Orchard, Portola Valley, California",* 1940, p. 1978, s., t., d., photog.'s stamp, illus., (05-23-93, Butterfield, #3287, illus.), 15½ x 19½ in., photograph, gelatin silver print (BP 1273, DM 3197, FR 10,759, Y 216,094).

$3450* *"Pine Forest In Snow, Yosemite National Park, California",* 1933, p. 1978, s., t., d., photog.'s stamp, illus., (05-23-93, Butterfield, #3279, illus.), 13 x 10½ in., photograph, gelatin silver print (BP 2247, DM 5641, FR 18,987, Y 381,342).

$3738* *"Pinnacles, Alabama Hills, Owens Valley, California" (Portfolios, p.81),* plate from Portfolio V, Parasol Press, mounted, s., #61/110 by photog., portfolio stamp, p. c. 1971, num. 61, (04-06-93, Sotheby-NY, #205, illus.), photograph (BP 2469, DM 6022, FR 20,393, Y 426,323).

$24,200* *Portfolio Three, Yosemite Valley: Ten, 1960,* Sierra Club, each s. in ink, stamp, num., #149/208, images include: Monolith, The Face Of Half Dome, (1927); Lower Yosemit Fall, c. 1946; Trees AndSnow, 1933; Branches In Snow, c. 1932, (10-13-92, Christie-NY, #408, illus.), each 11¼ x 8¼ in., (28.6 x 21 cm.), photograph, gelatin silver prints (BP 14,094, DM 35,453, FR 120,458, Y 2,934,400).

$23,000* *"Portfolio VII", 1976: Twelve,* Parasol Press, portfolio, each mounted, s., #G/115 by photog., Portfolio VII stamp, 1932-1968, p. c. 1976, ded. page i., d. by Ansel Adams, (04-06-93, Sotheby-NY, #212, illus.), various sizes to 18 x 22½ in., photograph (BP 15,192, DM 37,055, FR 125,477, Y 2,623,175).

$2588* *Portraits: The Westons: Two,* 1950s, s., photog.'s stamp, (05-23-93, Butterfield, #3290, illus.), 9½ x 7½ in., photograph, gelatin silver print (BP 1685, DM 4232, FR 14,243, Y 286,062).

$3850* *Pueblo De Taos New Mexico: Two (An Autobiography, p. 92),* t., s. "Ansel E. Adams" by photog., num. 1483 & 1502, label, 1920s, (10-15-92, Sotheby-NY, #231, illus.), each approx. 7¾ x 5¾ in., (19.7 x 14.6 cm.), photograph, parmelian prints (BP 2356, DM 5731, FR 19,435, Y 461,908).

$2760* *Rails And Jet Trails, Roseville, California,* c. 1953, p. 1960s, ink s., Hasselblad Photograph/San Francisco stamp, lit., (04-08-93, Christie-NY, #373, illus.), 13½ x 10 in., (34.3 x 25.4 cm.), photograph, gelatin silver print (BP 1810, DM 4434, FR 15,008, Y 313,209).

$2200* *A Rainy Day, New York City, New York, 1933,* mounted, s. by photog., studio stamp, p. 1982, (10-15-92, Sotheby-NY, #239A, illus.), 13¼ x 9Z, in., (33.7 x 23.2 cm.), photograph, gelatin silver print (BP 1346, DM 3275, FR 11,106, Y 263,947).

$4600* *"Roaring River Falls, High Sierra",* 1923, p. c. 1927, from Parmelian Portfoliom s., t., (05-23-93, Butterfield, #3269, illus.), 8 x 6 in., photograph, gelatin silver print on Dassonville paper (BP 2996, DM 7521, FR 25,316, Y 508,456).

BI *Rock And Grass, Moraine Lake, Sequoia National Park, c. 1932,* mounted, s. by photog., studio stamp, p. 1974, est. $3/5,000, (10-15-92, Sotheby-NY, #241, illus.), 14½ x 17M, in., (36.8 x 45.4 cm.), photograph, gelatin silver print.

$3163* *"Rocks And Clouds, Sierra Nevada Foothill, California",* 1938, p. 1979, s., t., d., photog.'s stamp, (05-23-93, Butterfield, #3281, illus.), 10½ x 13½ in., photograph, gelatin silver print (BP 2060, DM 5172, FR 17,408, Y 349,619).

$2990* *Sand Dunes, Oceano, California,* c. 1950, p. 1970s, s.; ink stamp w/t., d., (04-08-93, Christie-NY, #371, illus.), 19¼ x 14¾ in., (48.9 x 37.5 cm.), photograph, gelatin silver print (BP 1961, DM 4803, FR 16,259, Y 339,310).

$5175* *"Sand Dunes, Sunrise, Death Valley National Monument, CA." (Morgan and Morgan, pl. 52),* mounted, s. by photog., photog. studio stamp, 1948, p. 1978, (04-06-93, Sotheby-NY, #211, illus.), photograph (BP 3418, DM 8337, FR 28,232, Y 590,214).

$5750* *Sand Dunes, Sunrise, Death Valley National Monument, California,* c. 1948, p. 1977, s.; ink stamp w/t., d., lit., (04-08-93, Christie-NY, #370, illus.), 19½ x 15 in., (49.5 x 38.1 cm.), photograph, gelatin silver print (BP 3770, DM 9237, FR 31,267, Y 652,519).

BI *Sea Cliff, Path, San Francisco, California,* (1919), 1970s, s. on mount, t., d. in ink, Carmel stamp, est. 2/2,500, (10-13-92, Christie-NY, #95, illus.), 10 x 7B, in., (25.4 x 19.4 cm.), photograph, gelatin silver print.

$1610* *Selected Works: Three,* 1950s, s., photog.'s stamp, (05-23-93, Butterfield, #3291, illus.), from 13 x 10½ in., to 10½ x 10¼ in., photograph, gelatin silver print (BP 1049, DM 2632, FR 8861, Y 177,960).

BI *"Sequoia Roots, Mariposa Grove, Yosemite National Park, California",* 1950, p. 1963, s., What Majestic Word Portfolio IV label, est. $2/3,000, (05-23-93, Butterfield, #3283, illus.), 9½ x 7½ in., photograph, gelatin silver print.

BI *Sequoia Roots, Mariposa Grove, Yosemite National Park, California, c.1950 (Portfolios, p. 62),* plate 2 from Portfolio IV, Sierra Club, mounted, s. by photog. in ink, label, p. 1963, #83/260 ed., est. $2/3,000, (10-15-92, Sotheby-NY, #248, illus.), 9½ x 7C, in., (24.1 x 18.7 cm.), photograph, gelatin silver print.

BI *"Shore, South Of Timber Cove" and "Rock, Surf, Timber Cove", c. 1960: Two,* each ink s. on mount, each t., neg. num., photog. Carmel Route I stamp verso mount, est. $3/5,000, (11-16-92, Butterfield, #5823, illus.), one 13½ x 19½zn in., (343.5 x 496.2 mm.), other 19Zn x 15 in., (343.5 x 496.2 mm.), photograph, gelatin silver print.

$2300* *"The Sierra Nevada West Of Manzanar, California",* 1943, p. 1950, s., t., d., photog.'s stamp, (05-23-93, Butterfield, #3285, illus.), 7½ x 9½ in., photograph, gelatin silver print (BP 1498, DM 3761, FR 12,658, Y 254,228).

$2185* *"Sierra Nevada, Winter Evening, From The Owens Valley, California",* 1962, p. 1963, s., t., label, (05-23-93, Butterfield, #3277, illus.), 11½ x 9 in., photograph, gelatin silver print (BP 1423, DM 3573, FR 12,025, Y 241,517).

$8050* *"Sierra Nevada, Winter From Owens Valley, California",* 1944, p. 1978, s., t., d., photog.'s stamp, (05-23-93, Butterfield, #3271, illus.), 14¾ x 19¼ in., photograph, gelatin silver print (BP 5243, DM 13,162, FR 44,304, Y 889,798).

$3025* *Silverton, Colorado, 1951 (Portfolios, p. 100),* plate 4 from Portfolio VI, Parasol Press, mounted, s. by photog., num. VI-4 38/110 in unidentified hand, portfolio stamp, p. 1974, #38/110 ed., (10-15-92, Sotheby-NY, #249, illus.), 15¼ x 19C\ in., (38.7 x 49.2 cm.), photograph, gelatin silver print (BP 1851, DM 4503, FR 15,270, Y 362,927).

$2475* *"Singing Dancers-Sun and Moon Dance, San Ildefonso Pueblo, New Mexico" and Buffalo Dancers Before the Church at Tesuque Pueblo, New Mexico", PuebloIndians, 1920s: Two,* s. "Ansel E. Adams" by photog., t., num. 1500 & 1501, label, (10-15-92, Sotheby-NY, #230, illus.), each approx. 5¾ x 7¾ in., (14.6 x 19.7 cm.), photograph, parmelian prints (BP 1515, DM 3684, FR 12,494, Y 296,941).

$3850* *Sonoma County Hills, c. 1960,* mounted on Crescent Illustration Board, s. by photog. in ink, t., studio stamp, (10-15-92, Sotheby-NY, #256, illus.), 15B, x 19C in., (39.7 x 49.2 cm.), photograph, gelatin silver print (BP 2356, DM 5731, FR 19,435, Y 461,908).

$4600* *"Stream, Sea, Clouds, Rodeo Lagoon, Marin County, California",* 1962, p.l., s., t., d., photog.'s stamp, (05-23-93, Butterfield, #3274, illus.), 19½ x 15½ in., photograph, gelatin silver print (BP 2996, DM 7521, FR 25,316, Y 508,456).

$2875* *"Sunrise, Mount Tom, Sierra Nevada" (Portfolios, p. 121),* s. by photog., t., studio stamp, label, 1948, p. early 1960's, (04-06-93, Sotheby-NY, #203, illus.), photograph, mounted on Crescent Illustration Board (BP 1899, DM 4632, FR 15,685, Y 327,897).

$9200* *"The Teton Range And The Snake River, Grand Teton National Park, Wyoming (Morgan and Morgan, pl. 56), 1942,* mounted, s., t., i. by photog., photog. stamp, (04-06-93, Sotheby-NY, #199, illus.), 7½ x 9½ in., photograph (BP 6077, DM 14,822, FR 50,191, Y 1,049,270).

$7700* *"The Tetons And Snake River, Grand Teton National Park, Wyoming",* 1942/1970's, s. mount, t., d.; photog. Carmel 93921 stamp verso mount, lit., (11-16-92, Butterfield, #5822, illus.), 15 x 19Zzn in., (381.7 x 483.5 mm.), photograph, gelatin silver print (BP 5070, DM 12,277, FR 41,353, Y 957,592).

$10,350* *"The Tetons And The Snake River, Grand Teton National Park, Wyo." (Morgan and Morgan, pl. 56),* mounted, s. by photog., studio stamp, 1942, p.l., (04-06-93, Sotheby-NY, #201, illus.), 15 x 18¾ in., photograph (BP 6836, DM 16,675, FR 56,465, Y 1,180,429).

$8800* *The Tetons And The Snake River, Grand Teton National Park, Wyoming, 1942 (Morgan & Morgan, pl. 56),* mounted, s. by photog., studio stamp, p. 1980, (10-15-92, Sotheby-NY, #245, illus.), 15¼ x 19 in., (38.7 x 48.3 cm.), photograph, gelatin silver print (BP 5385, DM 13,099, FR 44,422, Y 1,055,789).

$2875* *"Thousand Island Lake And Banner Peak At Sunset", 1923,* image init., s.; ink s., t., d., i., (05-23-93, Butterfield, #3268, illus.), 5¾ x 7¾ in., photograph, gelatin silver print on heavy textured paper (BP 1872, DM 4701, FR 15,823, Y 317,785).

$3575* *Thunder-Storm Over The Great Plains Near Cimarron, New Mexico, 1958,* mounted on Hi-Art Illustration board, s. by photog. in ink, t., d., studio stamp, p. early 1960's, (10-15-92, Sotheby-NY, #253, illus.), 14½ x 19¼ in., (36.8 x 48.9 cm.), photograph, gelatin silver print (BP 2188, DM 5322, FR 18,046, Y 428,914).

$2750* *"Tony Lujan, Taos Pueblo, New Mexico", 1930,* s., t. Tony Lujan in margin; t., d. verso, (11-16-92, Butterfield, #5829, illus.), 7M, x 5M, in., (200.4 x 149.5 mm.), photograph, gelatin silver print on Dassonville paper (BP 1811, DM 4385, FR 14,769, Y 341,997).

$2200* *"Tuolumne Meadows, Yosemite National Park",* 1947/1963, ink s. mount, ink num.; Portfolio Four label verso mount,lit., (11-16-92, Butterfield, #5827, illus.), 9Z, x 7¼ in., (232.2 x 184.5 mm.), photograph, gelatin silver print (BP 1449, DM 3508, FR 11,815, Y 273,598).

$2185* *Upper Yosemite Falls, Spring,* c. 1950, p. 1960s, ink s.; t. Special Edition of Fine Prints stamp, (04-08-93,

Christie-NY, #372, illus.), 9½ x 8¼ in., (24.1 x 21 cm.), photograph, gelatin silver print (BP 1433, DM 3510, FR 11,881, Y 247,957).

BI *"Walbridge Ranch, Healdsburg, CA", 1930,* s., photog.'s stamp, est. $1/1,500, (05-23-93, Butterfield, #3294, illus.), 9 x 13½ in., photograph, gelatin silver print.

$1760* *"Walbridge Ranch, Healdsburg, California",* 1939/later, s., t. on mount; photog. Carmel 93923 stamp verso mount, (11-16-92, Butterfield, #5834, illus.), 10C, x 13½ in., (264 x 343.5 mm.), photograph, gelatin silver print (BP 1159, DM 2806, FR 9452, Y 218,878).

$3163* *"Water And Foam" and "Rushing Water, Merced River" (Portfolios, pp. 48 and 55): Two,* plates 8 and 13 from Portfolio III, s. by photog., portfolio stamp, c. 1955, p. 1959, (04-06-93, Sotheby-NY, #206, illus.), one 7Z, x 6B, in., photograph (BP 2089, DM 5096, FR 17,256, Y 360,744).

$1610* *Waterfall, 1925,* mounted, s. by photog., d., i., (04-06-93, Sotheby-NY, #194, illus.), 7¾ x 5¾ in., photograph (BP 1063, DM 2594, FR 8783, Y 183,622).

$3450* *"Wind", 1928,* s., d., num. 487, illus., (05-23-93, Butterfield, #3289, illus.), 6 x 7¾ in., photograph, gelatin silver print on Dassonville paper (BP 2247, DM 5641, FR 18,987, Y 381,342).

$8800* *Winter Storm, Yosemite, California,* (1947), 1960s, s. in ink, t., stamp, lit., (10-13-92, Christie-NY, #405, illus.), 10B, x 13¼ in., (27 x 33.7 cm.), photograph, gelatin silver print (BP 5125, DM 12,892, FR 43,803, Y 1,067,055).

BI *Winter Sunrise, Sierra Nevada From Lone Pine,* c. 1944, p.l., s.; ink t., d., stamp, est. $7/9,000, (04-08-93, Christie-NY, #367, illus.), 15 x 19¼ in., (38.1 x 48.9 cm.), photograph, gelatin silver print.

$6900* *"Winter Sunrise, Sierra Nevada From Lone Pine, California",* 1944, p. 1978, s., t., d., photog.'s stamp, illus., (05-23-93, Butterfield, #3266, illus.), 14½ x 19½ in., photograph, gelatin silver print (BP 4494, DM 11,282, FR 37,975, Y 762,684).

$7700* *Winter Sunrise, Sierra Nevada From Lone Pine, c. 1944 (Yosemite and the Range of Light, pl. 99),* mounted on Hi-Art Illustration board, s. by photog. in ink, partiallyt., studio stamp, p. early 1960's, (10-15-92, Sotheby-NY, #246, illus.), 15½ x 19¼ in., (39.4 x 48.9 cm.), photograph, gelatin silver print (BP 4712, DM 11,462, FR 38,869, Y 923,815).

$7700* *"Winter Sunrise, The Sierra Nevada From Lone Pine, California",* 1944/c. 1955, typed t., ink s. on label, (11-16-92, Butterfield, #5813, illus.), 182Zzn x 290½ in., (464.4 x 737.9 mm.), photograph, gelatin silver print mounted on Masonite w/black ink edges (BP 5070, DM 12,277, FR 41,353, Y 957,592).

$9350* *"Winter Sunrise, The Sierra Nevada From Lone Pine, California",* 1944/1970's, s. mount, t.; photog. Carmel 93921 stamp verso mount, lit., (11-16-92, Butterfield, #5816, illus.), 15½ x 19Bzn in., (394.4 x 489.8 mm.), photograph, gelatin silver print (BP 6156, DM 14,908, FR 50,215, Y 1,162,791).

$6325* *"Winter, Yosemite Valley" (Autobiography, p. 188), mid-1930's,* mounted, s. by photog., label, num. 16, (04-06-93, Sotheby-NY, #195, illus.), 7 x 9 in., photograph (BP 4178, DM 10,190, FR 34,506, Y 721,373).

$1650* *Wooden Crosses, Los Trampas, N.M.,* (1927), late 1960s, s. on mount, Carmel stamp w/t. in ink, (10-13-92, Christie-NY, #104, illus.), 19C, x 15¼ in., (49.2 x 38.7 cm.), photograph, gelatin silver print (BP 961, DM 2417, FR 8213, Y 200,073).

BI *"Yosemite Valley From Inspiration Point" and "Winter, Yosemite National Park",* (c. 1940): Two, mounted together, c. 1955, lit., est. $15/25,000, (04-08-93, Christie-NY, #362, illus.), 72 x 96 in., (182.9 x 243.8 cm.), photograph, toned, mural-sized gelatin silver print.

$2475* *Yosemite, c. 1929,* s. in margin; annot. Landscape 7-B verso, (11-16-92, Butterfield, #5831, illus.), 5M, x 8 in., (149.5 x 203.6 mm.), photograph, gelatin silver print on Dassonville paper (BP 1630, DM 3946, FR 13,292, Y 307,798).

BI *Yosemite, c. 1929,* s., est. $2/3,000, (10-13-92, Christie-NY, #96, illus.), 5M, x 8 in., (14.9 x 20.3 cm.), photograph, dassonville print.

$4950* *Yosemite: Four:* "Cathedral Rocks-Detail-Yosemite", "Crag Near CastleCliffs, Yosemite", "Eagle Peak-Yosemite", and "Unicorn Peak, Yosemite", each s. "Ansel E. Adams" by photog., t., num. 1489, 1488, 1487, & 150label, 1920's, (10-15-92, Sotheby-NY, #233, illus.), each approx. 7¾ x 5¾ in., (19.7 x 14.6 cm.), photograph, parmelian prints (BP 3029, DM 7368, FR 24,987, Y 593,881).

ADAMS, Douglas (after)

$135 *"The Drive", "A Difficult Bunker" and "The Putting Green": Three,* pub. H. Graves and Co., (10-09-92, G.A. Key, #53), 14 x 23 in., (35.6 x 58.4 cm.), colored lithograph (BP 80, DM 201, FR 682, Y 16,463).

ADAMS, Eddie   American contemporary

$1430* *Execution In The Streets Of Saigon, 1968,* handstamp, (10-14-92, Swann, #276, illus.), 8 x 10 in., (20.3 x 25.4 cm.), photograph, silver print (BP 839, DM 2093, FR 7097, Y 173,291).

$3520* *"Prisoner Being Lead Along The Street", "Police Executing Prisoner" and "Police Holstering Pistol", 1968: Three,* (04-07-93, Swann, #283, illus.), 11Ҳ, x 14 in., photograph, silver print (BP 2326, DM 5693, FR 19,267, Y 399,909).

ADAMS, Kenneth

BI *Taos Indian,* s., t., full margins, good cond., surface soiling, est. $3/400, (10-28-92, Butterfield, #2722), 12M, x 9¾ in., (327 x 248 mm.), lithograph on wove.

ADAMS, Mark

$633* *Handkerchief, 1979,* s., annot. Presque BAT, margins, good cond., soiling, mat staining, stray printing ink, (05-19-93, Butterfield, #2103), 13¾ x 16¾ in., (349 x 425 mm.), aquatint and etching in colorsw/hand-coloring on wove (BP 411, DM 1029, FR 3467, Y 70,076).

$288* *Water Jar (State II), 1984,* s., d., t., #1/100, full margins, very good cond., stain, (05-19-93, Butterfield, #2104), 16Mҳn x 16M, in., (418 x 429 mm.), aquatint in oranges on wove (BP 187, DM 468, FR 1577, Y 31,883).

ADAMSON, J.

$41* *Melbourne From The South Side Of The Yarra Yarra 1839,* (08-11-92, L. Joel, #189G), 13Ҳ, x 15ҳn in., (34 x 39.5 cm.), color reproduction lithograph (BP 21, DM 60, FR 204, Y 5250, A$ 55).

ADDAMS, Charles   American 20th cent.

BI *The Addams Family--This Little Piggy,* pub. 1945, New Yorker Magazine, est. $300/350, (09-17-92, Sloan, #1994), 15 x 10¾ in., (38.1 x 27.3 cm.), lithograph.

ADOLPHE, Joseph Antoine (after)

$200* *His Royal Highness The Prince Of Wales, 1755,* by B. Baron, watermark, full margins, holes, repairs, (11-30-92, Phillips-London, #98), plate 25Ҳ, x 18M, in., (638 x 479 mm.), engraving on laid (BP 132, DM 319, FR 1082, Y 24,891).

ADVENTURAS DE JUAN

$43* *Esparraguito O El Nino Casi Legumbre,* album, illus., damage, (07-16-92, Bonhams-Chelsea, #513), album size 15¾ x 11½ in., (40 x 29.2 cm.), colored woodcut (BP 22, DM 64, FR 214, Y 5386).

ADZAK, Roy

BI *Visage Negatif,* s., est. FF3/400, (06-28-93, Loudmer, #2), 24Ҳzn x 17Bҳn in., (630 x 455 mm.), sh 24Ҳzn x 18Ҳzn in., (630 x 455 mm.), 2-color serigraph on Arches wove.

AEPPLI, Eva

$5231* *Untitled, Heart,* #13/150, s., from portfolio "Kulturguterwagen der Galerie Klaus Littmann, Basel, (12-05-92, Mangisch, #501, illus.), 22Ҳn x 29Ҳzn in., (56 x 76 cm.), color serigraph (BP 3276, DM 8156, FR 27,795, Y 648,123, SF 7475).

AES, Eric

$504* *Enrade, Au Theatre Du Vieux Colombier, 1927,* fold marks, tears, creases, (02-04-93, Christie-S. Ken, #94, illus.), 47 x 32 in., (119.4 x 81.3 cm.), color lithograph (BP 352, DM 830, FR 2814, Y 62,694).

AFRO (Afro BASALDELLA)   Italian 1912-1976

BI *Charles Baudelaire, 1975: Ten,* complete portfolio, s., #57/80, num. on colophon, blindstamp of publisher, 2RC Editions, full margins, very good cond., original portfolio, est. $4/6,000, (05-19-93, Butterfield, #2105, illus.), 7M

x 9Ҳzn in., (200 x 252 mm.), aquatint in colors on Fabriano.

$825* *La Chiave,* s., #29/89, prov., (05-16-93, Hindman, #585), 19 x 27¼ in., (48.3 x 69.2 cm.), color etching and aquatint (BP 536, DM 1327, FR 4459, Y 91,453).

$11,054* *Grande Grigio, 1973,* #XIII/XV, s., (12-15-92, Finarte-Milan, #49, illus.), 34B, x 77Ҳzn in., (88 x 197 cm.), etching and aquatint (BP 7052, DM 17,326, FR 59,207, Y 1,370,954, L 15,525).

$532* *Komposition In Schwarz, Gelb Und Grun,* s., num., blindstamp, (06-08-93, Karl/Faber, #480), approx. 22¼ x 30Ҳ, in., (56.5 x 76.5 cm.), color lithograph on BFK Rives wove (BP 350, DM 863, FR 2907, Y 56,506).

$543* *Nero II (Bettini 45), 1969,* 6/VII, P.S., s., (10-14-92, Germann, #202), 19Ҳzn x 25Ҵ, in., (500 x 645 mm.), aquatint/etching on zinc (BP 319, DM 795, FR 2695, Y 65,802, SF 708).

$588* *Nero V (Bettini 48), 1969,* 32/40, s., (10-14-92, Germann, #201), 13Ҳzn x 19B, in., (355 x 498 mm.), etching on zinc (BP 345, DM 861, FR 2918, Y 71,255, SF 767).

AGAM, Jacob   Israeli 1928-1953

$385* *Magic Rainbow 4, 1980,* s. in crayon, num. 3/37, (11-12-92, Freemn/Fine Art, #3), 22 x 25 in., (55.9 x 63.5 cm.), screenprint (BP 253, DM 610, FR 2058, Y 47,737).

AGAM, Yaacov   Israeli b. 1928

$1185* *5 Kompositionen,* A.P., s., (04-21-93, Germann, #203), 22Ҳn x 38Ҳzn in., (570 x 980 mm.), color serigraph (BP 769, DM 1894, FR 6405, Y 131,186, SF 1725).

$468* *AG-2,* s. ink, #24/200, prov., (05-16-93, Hindman, #582), 28 x 29½ in., (71.1 x 74.9 cm.), color serigraph (BP 304, DM 753, FR 2530, Y 51,879).

$248* *Abstract Composition,* s., #60/90, (05-20-93, Boos, #534, illus.), sight 25Ҵ, x 37Ҵ, in., (645 x 950 mm.), silkscreen in colors (BP 159, DM 400, FR 1348, Y 27,385).

$648* *Big Bang, 1989: Album Of Six,* artist's proof, s., (05-27-93, Briest, #7), serigraphs on Arches in 32 colors (BP 415, DM 1040, FR 3505, Y 69,468).

BI *Composition,* artist's proof, est. FF1,500/2,000, (03-31-93, Briest, #E3), 22Ҳzn x 29Ҳzn in., (58 x 76 cm.), color serigraph.

$304* *Composition,* s., #7/90, (05-27-93, Briest, #8), 40Bҳn x 8Ҳzn in., (104 x 22 cm.), color serigraph (BP 195, DM 488, FR 1644, Y 32,590).

$273* *Composition,* epreuve d'artiste, s., (11-16-92, Briest, #5), 30½ x 37Ҳzn in., (77.5 x 96 cm.), serigraph in colors (BP 179, DM 435, FR 1467, Y 34,070).

$199* *Composition Cinetique,* epreuve d'artiste, s., (11-16-92, Briest, #257), 29Ҳzn x 31½ in., (76 x 80 cm.), serigraph in colors on Arches (BP 131, DM 317, FR 1069, Y 24,835).

$131* *"Composition Cinetique", c. 1975,* #136/144, s. Agam, (06-16-93, Encans, #118), 23B, x 17Ҳzn in., (60 x 45 cm.), color lithograph (BP 87, DM 217, FR 730, Y 13,972, C$ 167).

BI *Composition, 1986,* epreuve d'artiste, s., num., est. FF 5/6,000, (11-16-92, Briest, #253), 31½ x 25Ҳzn in., (80 x 65.5 cm.), serigraph in colors on plaque d'acier.

$3080* *Haggadah: Fifty-Eight,* each s., book, (12-13-92, Hindman, #330, illus.), overall 15½ x 18¾ in., color serigraph (BP 1969, DM 4840, FR 16,497, Y 381,047).

$1659* *Hommage A G.B., 1973: Five,* portfolio, #108/200, s., (09-04-92, Germann, #201, illus.), each 25Ҳzn x 35Mҳn in., (637 x 900 mm.), color serigraph (BP 831, DM 2325, FR 7915, Y 204,210, SF 2070).

$474* *Komposition,* E.A., s., (04-21-93, Germann, #205), 19M, x 24Ҳzn in., (505 x 630 mm.), color serigraph (BP 308, DM 758, FR 2562, Y 52,474, SF 690).

$395* *Komposition,* E.A., s., (04-21-93, Germann, #202), 23Ҳzn x 32Ҳzn in., (585 x 830 mm.), color serigraph (BP 256, DM 631, FR 2135, Y 43,729, SF 575).

$1185* *Komposition,* E.A. #1/9, s., 750mm x 1001mm, (04-21-93, Germann, #204), color serigraph (BP 769, DM 1894, FR 6405, Y 131,186, SF 1725).

$440* *"Metamorphosis",* s., edit. #61/180, (10-16-92, DuMouchelle, #2128), 8½ x 12¾ in., (21.6 x 32.4 cm.), color lithograph (BP 267, DM 650, FR 2208, Y 52,537).

$132* *"Nine x Three x Five XII"*, (03-06-93, Wolf, #185), 11 x 13 in., (27.9 x 33 cm.), seriograph (BP 91, DM 220, FR 742, Y 15,515).

$176* *Optigram,* s. Agam, #144/200, (03-06-93, Wolf, #184), image 17½ x 18 in., (44.5 x 45.7 cm.), seriograph (BP 121, DM 293, FR 989, Y 20,686).

$440* *Petit Secret,* s. in white ink, num. 139/200, apparently good cond., (02-24-93, Butterfield, #3171), 28¼ x 34½ in., (718 x 876 mm.), silkscreen in colors on wove (BP 307, DM 714, FR 2422, Y 51,631).

$107* *"Positives And Negatives" and "Geometric Shapes On Black And Orange": Two,* each crayon s., first #53/99, (12-01-92, Ritchie, #83), 20½ x 24¾ in., (52.1 x 62.9 cm.), color serigraph (BP 71, DM 171, FR 581, Y 13,322, C$ 138).

BI *Sans Titre, 1972,* artist proof, s., d., creases, est. FF1,500/1,800, (06-28-93, Loudmer, #3), 19Zn x 17Zn in., (500 x 452 mm.), sh 26Cn x 23Mn in., (500 x 452 mm.), color serigraph on cardboard.

BI *Slow Jazz, c. 1975,* s., full margins, est. $4/600, (12-08-92, Swann, #1), 24 x 24 in., (61 x 61 cm.), color serigraph.

BI *Tour Guggenheim, 1980,* epreuve d'artiste, s., #2/2, est. FF 8/10,000, (11-16-92, Briest, #254, illus.), serigraph in colors.

$990* *"Triple Galaxy B",* ink s. Agam, annot. 12/25 H.C.; ident. verso, very good cond., (10-09-92, Skinner, #249, illus.), 20½ x 19½ in., (52.1 x 49.5 cm.), mixed media (BP 588, DM 1475, FR 5000, Y 120,732).

$193* *Union III: La Femme,* s., 71/235, (06-28-93, Loudmer, #181), 33Zn x 28¾ in., (840 x 730 mm.), color serigraph on Arches wove (BP 129, DM 328, FR 1105, Y 20,477).

$220* *"Untitled",* s., #131/180, margins, very good cond.?, (10-28-92, Butterfield, #2873), 17¾ x 28C, in., (451 x 721 mm.), color silkscreen on wove (BP 140, DM 340, FR 1154, Y 26,994).

$935* *"Untitled": Two,* s., #67/180, margins, good cond.?, (10-28-92, Butterfield, #2872), each 20 x 7½ in., (508 x 191 mm.), color silkscreen on wove (BP 596, DM 1444, FR 4903, Y 114,724).

$248* *Untitled-Split Diamonds,* s. Agam, num. A.P. 6/18, very good cond., (09-11-92, Skinner, #110A), 27B, x 29Cc in., (70.2 x 73.7 cm.), color screenprint on wove (BP 128, DM 357, FR 1213, Y 30,727).

AGASSE, J.L. (after)

$40 *"The Last Stage On The Portsmouth Road", 1930,* engraved by Robert Houston, (02-05-93, G.A. Key, #18), 15 x 21 in., (38.1 x 53.3 cm.), colored aquatint (BP 28, DM 66, FR 224, Y 4978).

AGHA, Dr. M.F.

BI *Positive-Negative Study, 1930's,* Estate stamp, est. $2/3,000, (04-06-93, Sotheby-NY, #376A, illus.), 9B, x 7B in., photograph.

AGHA, Dr. M.F. 1896-1978

BI *Mask, 1943,* lit., est. $1,8/2,200, (10-13-92, Christie-NY, #106, illus.), 9¾ x 7¾ in., (24.8 x 19.7 cm.), photograph, gelatin silver print.

AGOSTINI, Tony Italian b. 1916

$39* *The Guitar Player,* s., #185/275, (10-30-92, Sloan, #837), 14¾ x 15 in., (37.5 x 38.1 cm.), color lithograph (BP 25, DM 60, FR 204, Y 4831).

$39* *Still Life Of Grapes, Apples And Watermelon,* s., #44/275, (10-30-92, Sloan, #838), 21½ x 16 in., (54.6 x 40.6 cm.), color lithograph (BP 25, DM 60, FR 204, Y 4831).

$28* *Still Life With Guitar,* s., #9/275, (10-30-92, Sloan, #836), 14½ x 17½ in., (36.8 x 44.5 cm.), color lithograph (BP 18, DM 43, FR 146, Y 3468).

AGRICOLA, Karl J.A. 1779-1852

$140* *Portrait Eines Alteren Mannes Mit Bart,* plate s., stained, wear, (09-25-92, Granier, #2604), plate 6M, x 4M, in., (17.4 x 12.4 cm.), sheet 7Zn x 5Z in., (17.4 x 12.4 cm.), etching (BP 82, DM 208, FR 702, Y 16,898).

AHRENS, Carl Henry von

$107* *"Beech Trees" and "In The Woods/Tree Roots" (Watson No.'s 19 and 20): Two,* each s., lit., (11-30-92, Ritchie, #15), each approx. 7Z, x 5½ in., (18.1 x 14 cm.), etching and aquatint (BP 71, DM 170, FR 579, Y 13,317, C$ 138).

$128* *"In The Woods" and "In The Woods/Tree Roots" (Watson No.'s 17 and 20): Two,* s., t., d. 1932 and 1934, lit., (11-30-92, Ritchie, #14), one 4Z x 3M, in., (10.5 x 9.8 cm.), other 7 x 5¼ in., (10.5 x 9.8 cm.), etching and aquatint (BP 84, DM 204, FR 692, Y 15,930, C$ 165).

$150* *Landscape With Wild Turkeys (Watson No. 16),* s., d. 1934, lit., (11-30-92, Ritchie, #13, illus.), 10 x 7M, in., (25.4 x 20 cm.), etching, aquatint and drypoint (BP 99, DM 239, FR 811, Y 18,668, C$ 193).

$434* *Tree Studies: Twelve,* each s., (05-18-93, Joyner, #312), 11 engravings and 1 aquatint (BP 283, DM 704, FR 2378, Y 48,367, C$ 550).

$434* *Tree Studies: Twelve,* each s., (05-18-93, Joyner, #311), engravings (BP 283, DM 704, FR 2378, Y 48,367, C$ 550).

AIGNER, Lucien Czech b. 1901

BI *"Einstein Facing The Universe" and "The Duke And Duchess Of Windsor Visiting The Austrian Pavilion At The Paris Expo": Two,* 1930s, p.l., s., t., second phtog.'s stamp, est. $1/1,500, (05-23-93, Butterfield, #3296, illus.), each approx. 14 x 11 in., photograph, gelatin silver print.

$805* *"Gare St Lazare Avant Le Depart", St Lazare Station Before Departureand "London": Two,* 1935, p.l., second s.; each t., photog.'s stamp, (05-23-93, Butterfield, #3297, illus.), one 16 x 19M, in., other 9C, x 13C, in., photograph, gelatin silver print (BP 524, DM 1316, FR 4430, Y 88,980).

$1100* *Marlene Dietrich: Two, c. 1940,* p.l., each s., 2nd w/ reprod. limit. stamps, (10-13-92, Christie-NY, #107, illus.), 5¾ x 6M, in., (14.6 x 17.5 cm.), 9 x 12 in., (14.6 x 17.5 cm.), photograph, gelatin silver prints (BP 641, DM 1611, FR 5475, Y 133,382).

AILLAUD, J.-P.-M.

$642* *Le Cafe Du Bresil Est Le Meilleur Du Monde, c. 1900,* cond. B+, (06-11-93, Boisgirard, #38), 33Mn x 39C, in., (85 x 100 cm.), poster (BP 422, DM 1043, FR 3518, Y 68,117).

AIZPIRI, Paul French b. 1919

$399* *"Bouquet Dans Un Pot",* E.A., s., (01-28-93, Pescheteau, #59), 29Zn x 22Zn in., (76 x 56 cm.), color lithograph on Arches (BP 263, DM 632, FR 2139, Y 49,541).

BI *Chess Pieces,* #41/50, s., est. BP 150/250, (03-17-93, Bonhams-Chelsea, #431), image 18¾ x 25½ in., (47.6 x 64.8 cm.), lithograph in colors.

$112* *Chess Pieces,* #41/50, s., (05-20-93, Bonhams-Chelsea, #107), image 18¾ x 25½ in., (47.6 x 64.8 cm.), lithograph in colors (BP 72, DM 181, FR 609, Y 12,367).

$193* *Deux Personnages,* artist proof, s., (06-28-93, Loudmer, #4), 19Zn x 26C, in., (500 x 670 mm.), color lithograph on wove (BP 129, DM 328, FR 1105, Y 20,477).

$110* *Figure With Birds,* s., #5/90, (06-11-93, Freemn/Fine Art, #1), 24½ x 16 in., (62.2 x 40.6 cm.), screenprint (BP 72, DM 179, FR 603, Y 11,671).

$259* *Flowers In Pot,* s., #14/130, margins, good cond.?, (05-19-93, Butterfield, #2034), 19½ x 13 in., (495 x 330 mm.), lithograph in colors on wove (BP 168, DM 421, FR 1418, Y 28,673).

$337* *"Les Musiciens",* epreuve d'artiste, s., (10-18-92, Pescheteau, #65), 22Zn x 29Zn in., (56 x 76 cm.), lithograph in colors on Japan (BP 204, DM 498, FR 1691, Y 40,239).

$168* *"Petit Bouquet",* #44/200, s., drystamp, (10-18-92, Pescheteau, #67), 12B, x 9Zn in., (32 x 25 cm.), lithograph in colors (BP 102, DM 248, FR 843, Y 20,060).

$176* *Still Life,* s., #64/220, (03-14-93, Hindman, #293), 19¼ x 12¾ in., (48.9 x 32.4 cm.), color lithograph (BP 123, DM 293, FR 996, Y 20,742).

$288* *Still Life With Mandolin And Pitcher,* s., annot. Epreuve d'artiste XXIX/XXX, margins, good cond., (05-19-93, Butterfield, #2035), 17½ x 23¾ in., (445 x 603 mm.), lithograph in colors on wove (BP 187, DM 468, FR 1577, Y 31,883).

$495* *Untitled (Flowers),* s., annot. Arches HC 11/12, pub. Editions Romanet, full margins, goodcond., light-staining, masking tape, water staining, surface soiling, old hingeremains, (02-24-93, Butterfield, #3172), 21 x 16¾ in., (533 x 425 mm.), lithograph in colors on Arches (BP 345, DM 804, FR 2724, Y 58,085).

$256* *Woman Playing Cards,* s., num. H.C. 26/40, (12-01-92, Ritchie, #25, illus.), 22 x 18½ in., (55.9 x 47 cm.), color lithograph (BP 169, DM 408, FR 1391, Y 31,873, C$ 330).

AKREL, Carl Frederick

BI *Swedish Country Houses: Twenty,* from the series, defects, water staining, est. BP 3/350, (10-27-92, Phillips-London, #138), plate 12 x 16 in., (305 x 406 mm.), aquatint on wove.

ALANIZ, Arnold

$88* *"Cattails" and "Winter Wonderland": Two,* artist's proofs, both s., t., annot. below image, (08-05-92, Boos, #734), color print (BP 46, DM 130, FR 439, Y 11,207).

BI *"Winter Woods" and "Autumn Woods": Two,* each s., t., #209/250, 202/250, prov., est. C$ 2/300, (12-01-92, Ritchie, #45), each 23B, x 17M, in., (60 x 45.4 cm.), color lithograph.

ALASBORATI

BI *A Timber Bridge Across A Continental River,* #80/100, s., d. 1920, margins, est. BP 40/60, (11-19-92, Bonhams-Chelsea, #25), plate 6 x 16 in., (15.2 x 40.6 cm.), etching.

$17* *A Timber Bridge Across A Continental River,* num. 80/100, s., d. 1920, margins, (01-21-93, Bonhams-Chelsea, #165), plate 6 x 16 in., (15.2 x 40.6 cm.), etching (BP 11, DM 27, FR 91, Y 2128).

ALBEE, Grace American 1890-1985

BI *"Residual",* s., t., annot., excell. cond., est. $150/200, (10-31-92, Cleveland, #55), 7½ x 5 in., (19.1 x 12.7 cm.), wood engraving.

BI *"Touro Synagogue, New Port, RI", 1966,* good cond., est. $2/300, (10-31-92, Cleveland, #56), 7ZBzn x 9Zzn in., (20.2 x 24.9 cm.), wood engraving.

$275* *"Under The Chinaberry Tree", "Manhattan Backwash", and "In For A Landing", 1938, 1947, 1970: Three,* each s., d., t., num. Ed. 20, Ed. 100, and Ed. 20; margins, good cond., pencil notations, (02-24-93, Butterfield, #2800), smallest 5Zzn x 5 in., (129 x 127 mm.), largest 6B\ x 8zn in., (129 x 127 mm.), wood engraving on thin paper (BP 192, DM 446, FR 1513, Y 32,269).

ALBERS, Josef American 1888-1976

BI *Duo E, 1959,* s., d., t., #9/25, margins, old glue, good cond.?, prop. Woodward Foundation, est. $4/600, (12-12-92, Weschler, #98), 24 x 16½ in., (61 x 41.9 cm.), embossed print.

$385* *Embossed Linear Construction (G. 141), 1969,* s., d., t., #6/100, blindstamp pub. Gemini G.E.L., full margins, very good cond.?, (10-28-92, Butterfield, #2876), 20Z, x 26zn in., (511 x 662 mm.), embossing on Arches watercolor paper (BP 245, DM 595, FR 2019, Y 47,239).

$2070* *Fenced (Millers 69), 1944,* s., d., t., #10/30, p. Biltmore Press, large margins, good cond., presure mark, soiling, (05-15-93, Sotheby-NY, #900, illus.), 9M, x 12¼ in., (25.1 x 31.1 cm.), linoleum cut (BP 1346, DM 3330, FR 11,189, Y 229,465).

$1100* *Formulation: Articulation, 1972,* complete two volume set, s., #887, pub. Harry N. Abrams/Ives-Sillman, good cond., original folders and slipcases, (11-07-92, Sotheby-NY, #504), 127 silkscreens p. in colors (BP 719, DM 1756, FR 5936, Y 135,769).

$1955* *Formulation: Articulation, 1972: One Hundred And Twenty-Seven,* complete two volume set, s. felt tip pen, copy #964, co-pub. Harry N. Abrams and Ives-Sillman Inc., good cond., in original folders, (05-15-93, Sotheby-NY, #901), silkscreen in colors (BP 1271, DM 3145, FR 10,568, Y 216,717).

$495* *Homage To A Red Square, 1968,* inits. A'68, i. DRa, (11-12-92, Freemn/Fine Art, #6), 23½ x 23½ in., (59.7 x 59.7 cm.), color silkscreen (BP 325, DM 784, FR 2646, Y 61,376).

$495* *Homage To A Square,* inits., d. '68, num. 51/100, i. DRa, (11-12-92, Freemn/Fine Art, #5), 23½ x 23½ in., (59.7 x 59.7 cm.), color silkscreen (BP 325, DM 784, FR 2646, Y 61,376).

$440* *Homage To A Square,* s., d. '71, num. I-S LXXI and 105/125, (09-20-92, Hindman, #710), 15 x 15 in., (38.1 x 38.1 cm.), color serigraph (BP 258, DM 653, FR 2234, Y 54,381).

$330* *Homage To Square ISL XXIA,* s., d. 71, t., #109/125, prov., (05-16-93, Hindman, #570, illus.), 15 x 15 in., (38.1 x 38.1 cm.), color serigraph (BP 215, DM 531, FR 1784, Y 36,581).

$1650* *Homage To The Square, 1962,* complete portfolio, #150/250, pub. Ives-Sillman, full margins, good cond., crease, scuffs, foxing, soiling, original portfolio, (11-07-92, Sotheby-NY, #503), each sheet 16M, x 16M, in., (430 x 430 mm.), 10 silkscreens p. in colors (BP 1079, DM 2635, FR 8904, Y 203,653).

$1298* *Homage To The Square: I-S E. 1970,* #34/125, pencil i., mono., d., (11-20-92, Lempertz, #427), sh 21¼ x 21¼ in., (54 x 54 cm.), color serigraph on Velin (BP 855, DM 2070, FR 6971, Y 161,423).

$2420* *"Homage To The Square: MMA-1", "Homage To The Square: MMA-2" and "Variant: MMA-3", 1970: Three,* each s., t., d., num. 34/100, Metropolitan Museum of Art blindstamps, full margins, excell. cond., (09-19-92, Christie-E, #74), screenprint in colors on wove (BP 1392, DM 3624, FR 12,410, Y 301,520).

$523* *Hommage To The Square I-S LXX b, 1970,* s., d., t., num. 85/125, blindstamp of pub. Ives-Sillman, full margins, apparently good cond., surface scuff in image, (02-24-93, Butterfield, #3173), 12 x 12 in., (305 x 305 mm.), silkscreen in yellows on wove (BP 365, DM 849, FR 2878, Y 61,371).

$385* *I-S Va 1,* s., d. 69, t., #71/150, prov., (05-16-93, Hindman, #569), 22½ x 26 in., (57.2 x 66 cm.), color serigraph (BP 250, DM 619, FR 2081, Y 42,678).

$1320* *I-S Varient 4, 1969,* s., t., d., #42/150, pub. Ives-Sillman, very good cond.?, (12-12-92, Weschler, #99, illus.), 14¾ x 29¾ in., (37.5 x 75.6 cm.), silkscreen on BFK Rives (BP 846, DM 2080, FR 7127, Y 163,346).

$660* *Interaction Of Color: Eighty, 1963,* (09-25-92, Wolf, #30, illus.), colored silkscreen (BP 385, DM 978, FR 3308, Y 79,662).

$374* *Komposition, (19)66,* s., d., num., Jahresgabe der Kestner-Gesellschaft, light-stained, (12-01-92, Karl/Faber, #303), 11 x 11 in., (28 x 28 cm.), serigraph on thin cardboard (BP 247, DM 596, FR 2032, Y 46,564).

$610* *Komposition, (19)70,* mono., d., num., i., (06-08-93, Karl/Faber, #482), approx. 13¾ x 13¾ in., (35 x 35 cm.), serigraph on wove (BP 401, DM 990, FR 3333, Y 64,790).

$9350* *Never Before (Tyler 58-69), 1976: Set Of Twelve,* each s., t., num. 32/46, Tyler Graphics and artist's blindstamps, full margins, staining, (09-19-92, Christie-E, #75, illus.), each sheet 19 x 20 in., (483 x 508 mm.), screenprint in colors on Arches (BP 5378, DM 14,001, FR 47,949, Y 1,164,964).

BI *"Olympische Spiele, Munchen 1972", (19)70,* s., d., num., signs of wear, est. DM 900, (12-01-92, Karl/Faber, #304), 32M, x 24 in., (83.5 x 61 cm.), poster, colored serigraph on wove/cardboard.

BI *"Portfolio II Folder 22",* pub. Harry Abrams, Inc. and Ives-Sillman, Inc., s., scuffing, est. $3/500, (05-15-93, Cleveland, #444, illus.), 13 x 15 in., (33 x 38.1 cm.), color silkscreen.

BI *"Porto Negra",* from "Soft Edge-Hard Edge", s., d. '65, est. $5/800, (01-15-93, DuMouchelle, #2023), 11 x 11 in., (27.9 x 27.9 cm.), color silkscreen.

$715* *"Porto Negra" From "Soft Edge-Hard Edge",* s., d. '65, (03-12-93, DuMouchelle, #2327), 11 x 11 in., (27.9 x 27.9 cm.), color silkscreen (BP 499, DM 1190, FR 4046, Y 84,266).

$2860* *"Ten Variants" Portfolio Of Ten, 1967,* each init., d. A. '66, t., num. 107/200, (09-25-92, Wolf, #29), each 8½ x 13 in., (21.6 x 33 cm.), colored silkscreen (BP 1670, DM 4240, FR 14,336, Y 345,202).

$330* *"Variant VIII",* mono. sig., d. '66, t., #43/200, bears blindstamp, prov., (12-02-92, Boos, #514), sight 10Bzn x 11Zzn in., (279 x 300 mm.), color serigraph (BP 213, DM 519, FR 1771, Y 41,060).

BI *Weg VII, 1971,* 44/125, mono., d., t., signs of wear, est. SF 5/700, (10-14-92, Germann, #203, illus.), 26Czn x 20zn in., (665 x 510 mm.), lithograph w/embossing.

$332* *Weg VII, 1971,* #44/125, mono., d., t., staining, (09-04-92, Germann, #202), 26Czn x 20zn in., (665 x 510 mm.), lithograph w/embossing (BP 166, DM 465, FR 1584, Y 40,867, SF 414).

BI *Weg VIII, 1971,* 44/125, mono., d., t., est. SF 4/600, (10-14-92, Germann, #204), 26Czn x 20Zzn in., (665 x 510 mm.), lithograph w/embossing.

$313* *Weg VIII, 1971,* #44/125, mono., d., t., tear, (09-04-92, Germann, #203), 26Czn x 20Zzn in., (665 x 510 mm.), lithograph w/embossing (BP 157, DM 439, FR 1493, Y 38,528, SF 391).

$272* *Weg X, 1971,* 44/125, mono., d., signs of wear, (10-14-92, Germann, #205), 26Czn x 20¼ in., (665 x 515 mm.), lithograph w/embossing (BP 160, DM 398, FR 1350, Y 32,962, SF 354).

$230* *White Embossing On Grey III (G. 322), 1971,* init., d., t., #40/125, blindstamp publisher, Gemini G.E.L., p. LloydBaggs, full margins, good cond.?, (05-19-93, Butterfield, #2107), 23 x 15½ in., (584 x 394 mm.), line cut embossing on Roleaf (BP 149, DM 374, FR 1260, Y 25,462).

$440* *White Line Square IV (G. 5), 1966,* s., t., d., #110/125, blindstamp pub. Gemini G.E.L., full margins, good cond.?, (10-28-92, Butterfield, #2874), 15¾ x 15¾ in., (400 x 400 mm.), color lithograph on Arches (BP 280, DM 680, FR 2307, Y 53,988).

$715* *White Line Square IV, Red And Umber, 1966,* s., d., t., #16/125, pub. Gemini G.E.L., full margins, good cond., wear to margin edges; toning verso, (12-12-92, Weschler, #100), sheet 21 x 21 in., (53.3 x 53.3 cm.), color lithograph on Arches (BP 458, DM 1127, FR 3861, Y 88,479).

$690* *White Line Square VI (G.7), 1966,* s., d., t., #15-125, blindstamp publisher Gemini G.E.L., very good cond.?, (05-19-93, Butterfield, #2106), 15¾ x 15¾ in., (400 x 400 mm.), lithograph in colors on Arches (BP 448, DM 1122, FR 3779, Y 76,387).

$303* *Yellow Square,* mono., d. '72, very good cond.?, (11-21-92, Bakker, #87), image 13¾ x 13¾ in., (34.9 x 34.9 cm.), screen print (BP 199, DM 483, FR 1627, Y 37,682).

ALBERTI, Cherubino 1553-1615

$133* *Madonna Mit Dem Christuskind Und Der Lilie Auf Den Wolken (B. 27),* (12-01-92, Karl/Faber, #1), engraving (BP 88, DM 212, FR 722, Y 16,559).

$118* *La Sainte Vierge (Bartsch, T 17, 27),* small margins, (06-16-93, Ader Tajan, #1), 6 x 5Czn in., (15.3 x 13.2 cm.), copper engraving (BP 79, DM 196, FR 657, Y 12,585).

ALBERTI, Pietro Francesco 1584-1638

$1841* *Die Malerschule (B. XVII, 313, 1),* watermark, (06-04-93, Bassenge, #5001, illus.), 15Zzn x 20Mzn in., (40.2 x 51.9 cm.), etching (BP 1218, DM 2990, FR 10,077, Y 198,555).

ALBERTINI

$169* *Air Atlas Maroc,* good cond., (03-13-93, Laurin, #86), 39C, x 23B, in., (100 x 60 cm.), (BP 118, DM 281, FR 956, Y 19,918).

ALBIN, Eleazar 1713-1759

$110* *"Magpie", "Jay", "Turkey", and "Unidentified Bird": Four,* from "Natural History of Birds", London 1731-1738, (07-03-92, Sloan, #319), hand colored etching (BP 57, DM 166, FR 561, Y 13,712).

ALBIN, Eleazer (after) British d. 1740

$880* *The Natural History Of Insects: Eight,* s. E Albin del w/ in matrix, good cond., (04-23-93, Skinner, #182), sight 10½ x 8 in., (26.7 x 20.3 cm.), hand-colored engraving (BP 559, DM 1392, FR 4701, Y 97,195).

ALBIN, James

$555* *Lillian Gish, Autographed Portrait,* 1923, ink s., photog.'s credit/blindstamp, mounted, lit., (12-17-92, Christie-S. Ken, #76, illus.), 9Z, x 6Z, in., (23.2 x 15.6 cm.), photograph, gelatin silver print (BP 352, DM 867, FR 2960, Y 68,207).

ALBIN-GUILLOT, Laure

BI *The Model 'Mado' In Jean Patou, 1925,* photog. credit stamp, caption labels, est. $1,5/2,500, (04-06-93, Sotheby-NY, #244A, illus.), 8½ x 6Z, in., photograph.

ALBRIGHT, Adam Emory American 1862-1957

$235* *Couple In Landscape, 1936,* s., d., glue stains, crease, image scuff, (05-15-93, Cleveland, #50), 5Z, x 4Z, in., (13 x 10.5 cm.), monoprint (BP 153, DM 378, FR 1270, Y 26,050).

$225* *Untitled, 1936,* s., d., glue stains, light struck, pencil line, (05-15-93, Cleveland, #51), 5Z, x 4Z, in., (13 x 10.5 cm.), monoprint (BP 146, DM 362, FR 1216, Y 24,942).

ALBRIGHT, Ivan Le Lorraine American 1897-1983

$880* *Fleeting Time Thou Hast Left Me Old (G. II), 1945,* s., t., pub. AA, full margins, very good cond., soiling, pencil mark, (10-28-92, Butterfield, #2500), 13Zzn x 9Zzn in., (348 x 246 mm.), lithograph on cream wove (BP 561, DM 1359, FR 4615, Y 107,975).

$1150* *Fleeting Time, Thou Hast Left Me Old (G. II), 1945,* s., t., full margins, taped, good cond., mat and light-staining, (05-19-93, Butterfield, #1750, illus.), 13¾ x 9B, in., (349 x 244 mm.), lithograph on wove (BP 747, DM 1869, FR 6298, Y 127,311).

$578* *Follow Me (Grayson 14), 1948,* s., t., pub. AAA, (05-16-93, Hindman, #554), 13M, x 9 in., (35.2 x 22.9 cm.), lithograph (BP 376, DM 930, FR 3124, Y 64,073).

$2200* *"Heavy The Oar To Him Who Is Tired, Heavy The Coat, Heavy The Sea", Circa 1939, (Grayson #6),* s. stone, annot., num., s., limited edit. 10 prints, (02-27-93, Dunning, #1164, illus.), sh 19½ x 12 in., (49.5 x 30.5 cm.), pl 16¾ x 10½ in., (49.5 x 30.5 cm.), lithograph (BP 1547, DM 3617, FR 12,291, Y 259,710).

$1430* *Self Portrait At 55 East Division Street (Grayson 13), 1947,* s., full margins, good cond., mat/light stain, discoloration, foxing, (11-05-92, Sotheby-NY, #1), 14¼ x 10Z, in., (361 x 258 mm.), lithograph (BP 930, DM 2262, FR 7651, Y 175,439).

BI *"Self Portrait, Division St.",* pub. AAA, s. Ivan Le Lorraine Albright, good cond., mount staining, tape residue, est. $15/2500, (09-11-92, Skinner, #29, illus.), 14Z, x 10¼ in., (35.9 x 26 cm.), lithograph on off-white wove.

BI *Self-Portrait At 55 East Division Street (Grayson 13), 1947,* s., pub. AAA, est. $1/1,500, (03-14-93, Hindman, #320), 14Z, x 10Z, in., (35.9 x 25.7 cm.), lithograph on wove.

ALBRIGHT, Malvin Marr American b. 1897

BI *Lobster Man's Wharf, Maine,* s., pseudonym Zissly, AAA label, est. $2/300, (03-24-93, Grogan, #85), 9¾ x 13 in., (24.8 x 33 cm.), lithograph.

$165* *"Victoria", 1947,* pub. AAA, s. Z. Sissly and in stone, t., good cond., staining verso,tape residue, (09-11-92, Skinner, #32, illus.), 8B, x 12M, in., (21.9 x 32.7 cm.), lithograph on cream wove (BP 85, DM 238, FR 807, Y 20,444).

ALBUISSON

$12* *"Le Vezir" and "L'Alan": Two,* s., t., first #18/50, second #27/50, (06-28-93, Loudmer, #5), both 7Zzn x 5Zzn in., (195 x 145 mm.), both sh 14Zzn x 11Z, in., (195 x 145 mm.), black aquatint on BFK Rives wove, second on wove (BP 8, DM 20, FR 69, Y 1273).

ALCORLO, Manuel

BI *"Puppa",* s., t., d. 74, #12/30, reserve P18,000, (02-03-93, Duran, #228), 19Zzn x 14Zzn in., (50 x 38 cm.), etching.

ALDEGREVER, Hans

BI *Ornament With Leaves (Holl. 289),* only state, small to thread margins, discoloration, good cond., ex-coll., est. BP 3/400, (12-03-92, Sotheby-London, #5), 2 x 2¾ in., (51 x 70 mm.), engraving.

$3993* *The Standard Bearer In A Landscape (B., Holl. 177), 1540,* inky plate edges, narrow to thread margins, trimmed, paper thin, losses, foxing, surface dirt, ex. coll. P. Mariette (L. 1788 d. 1682); Friedrich Kale (L. 1021); P. Davidsohn (L. 654), (06-29-93, Sotheby-London, #1, illus.), 4¾ x 3 in., (12.1 x 7.6 cm.), engraving (BP 2645, DM 6743, FR 22,726, Y 425,059).

ALDEGREVER, Heinrich German 1502-1555/61

BI *Absalom Totet Ammon (Hollstein Bd. 1, 27),* sheet 6 from Ammon und Tamar, mono., d. AG 1540, trimmed, 2nd state,est. DM 300-, (03-24-93, Venator/Hansten,

#2475), approx. 4Zēn x 3Zn in., (11.9 x 7.7 cm.), engraving.

BI *Amnon Wird Von Absalom Getotet (B. 27), 1540,* num., trimmed, glue stained, est. DM 1800, (12-01-92, Karl/ Faber, #4), engraving.

$1725* *"Apollo", "Mars", "Mercury", "Jupiter" and "Saturn" (B., Holl. 74, 76-8, 80), 1533: Five,* from The Gods Who Preside Over the Seven Planets, thread margins or trimmed to platemark, B. 76 printing creases across center, repaired tears, laid down, defects, prov., (05-11-93, Christie-NY, #1, illus.), each plate 3¾ x 2½ in., (95 x 64 mm.), engraving on laid (BP 1101, DM 2717, FR 9156, Y 189,748).

$532* *Aufsteigendes Ornament Mit Zwei Delphinen (B. und Hollst. 233), 1529,* (06-08-93, Karl/Faber, #2), engraving (BP 350, DM 863, FR 2907, Y 56,506).

$658* *Die Erschaffung Evas (Bartsch 1; Hollstein S. 6), 1540,* sheet 1 of series Die Geschichte Des Ersten Menschen, mono., d. in plate, (10-09-92, Winterberg, #710), 3Mēn x 2>ēn in., (8.8 x 6.5 cm.), engraving (BP 390, DM 977, FR 3282, Y 80,107).

$361* *Der Gute Samariter Liefert Den Kranken An Einem Gasthaus Ab (B. 43; Hollstein 43), 1554,* from series Der Gute Samariter, prov., (12-04-92, Bassenge, #6004), 2ZBēn x 4Cēn in., (7.4 x 10.7 cm.), engraving (BP 232, DM 575, FR 1950, Y 45,069).

$649* *Herkules Erwurgt Die Schlange (Hollstein 83), 1550,* sheet 1 of series: Die Taten des Herkules, (06-23-93, Kornfeld, #2), engraving (BP 441, DM 1098, FR 3694, Y 70,705, SF 978).

$465* *Judith Mit Dem Haupt Des Holofernes (Bartsch 34; Hollstein, S. 18), 1528,* plate mono., d., slight foxing, (09-25-92, Granier, #2605), plate 3¼ x 2¼ in., (8.2 x 5.7 cm.), sheet 3Bēn x 2Bēn in., (8.2 x 5.7 cm.), copper engraving (BP 272, DM 689, FR 2331, Y 56,126).

$2672* *Die Jungfrau, Das Kind Saugend (B. 56, Hollstein 56 I), 1527,* very rare, (12-04-92, Bassenge, #6005, illus.), 2¾ x 1Aēn in., (7 x 4.9 cm.), engraving (BP 1714, DM 4255, FR 14,435, Y 333,583).

$449* *Lot Und Seine Familie Verlassen Sodom (Hollstein Bd. 1, 16),* mono., d. AG 1555, (09-14-92, Venator/Hansten, #1458), 4Mēn x 3Z, in., (11.3 x 8 cm.), engraving (BP 237, DM 667, FR 2262, Y 55,832).

$850* *Loth Und Seine Familie Verlassen Sodom (B. 16, Hollstein 16), 1555,* (06-04-93, Bassenge, #5002), 4C, x 3Zēn in., (11.1 x 7.7 cm.), engraving (BP 562, DM 1380, FR 4652, Y 91,674).

$650* *Loth Und Seine Tochter (B. 17; Hollstein), 1555,* thin spots, (12-04-92, Bassenge, #6002), 4Mēn x 3Z, in., (11.3 x 8 cm.), engraving (BP 417, DM 1035, FR 3512, Y 81,149).

$493* *Medea Und Jason (Bartsch Und Hollstein 65), 1529,* mono., watermark, (05-26-93, Dorling, #2187), 4B\ x 2ZBēn in., (11.7 x 7.4 cm.), engraving (BP 319, DM 804, FR 2707, Y 53,564).

BI *Medea Und Jason (Bartsch and Hollstein 65), 1529,* est. DM 1,000, (06-10-93, Hauswedell/Nolt, #5), engraving.

$614* *Die Nachstenliebe (B. 118; Hollstein 118), 1552,* Viribus, from series Die sieben Tugenden, foxed, (12-04-92, Bassenge, #6008), 3Zēn x 2C, in., (10.1 x 6 cm.), engraving (BP 394, DM 978, FR 3317, Y 76,654).

$155* *Die Nachstenliebe (Hollstein 118),* sheet 2 from series 7 Tugenden, mono., d. AG 1552, trimmed, worm hole, (03-24-93, Venator/Hansten, #2477), sheet 3B, x 2Mēn in., (9.2 x 6.2 cm.), engraving (BP 105, DM 253, FR 862, Y 18,212).

$709* *Ornament Mit Allegorischen Figuren Und Einer Trophae (B. und Hollst.281), 1550,* prov., (06-08-93, Karl/Faber, #3), engraving (BP 466, DM 1150, FR 3874, Y 75,305).

BI *Portrait Of A Nobleman,* est. $4/600, (11-01-92, Hanzel, #243), 11M, x 8½ in., (30.2 x 21.6 cm.), engraving.

$317* *Rauber Uberfallen Und Berauben Einen Mann (Hollstein 40),* sheet 1 from barmherzigen Samariter, mono., d. AG 1554, trimmed, (03-24-93, Venator/Hansten, #2478), sh 2B\ēn x 4Cēn in., (7.5 x 10.7 cm.), engraving (BP 215, DM 518, FR 1762, Y 37,246).

$211* *Der Reiche Mann Und Der Teufel (Hollstein 46),* sheet 3 from Man und Lazarus, mono., d. AG 1554, trimmed, (03-24-93, Venator/Hansten, #2479), sh 2Aēn x 4Cēn in., (7.5 x 10.7 cm.), engraving (BP 143, DM 345, FR 1173, Y 24,791).

$991* *Sechs Putten Um Eine Tafel Mit Dem Lateinischen Alphabet (B. 250; Hollst., S. 117), 1535,* mono., d. in plate, trimmed, prov., (10-09-92, Winterberg, #719), 3Zēn x 4ZCēn in., (7.7 x 12.2 cm.), engraving (BP 588, DM 1472, FR 4943, Y 120,648).

$929* *Sich Kussendes Tanzpaar (B. 167; Hollst., S. 70), 1538,* sheet 8 of large series Hochzeitstanzer, mono., d., num. in plate, trimmed, (10-09-92, Winterberg, #718), 4B\ x 3Zēn in., (11.8 x 7.8 cm.), engraving (BP 551, DM 1380, FR 4633, Y 113,100).

$1165* *The Story Of The First Men (B., Holl. 2-6), 1540: Five,* thread margins or trimmed, corner made-up, creases, mounting, prov., (12-01-92, Christie-London, #165), averaging sheet 3Mēn x 2½ in., (87 x 64 mm.), engraving (BP 770, DM 1857, FR 6328, Y 145,045).

$316* *Tamar Wird Von Amnon Verstoben (B. 24), 1540,* num. 3 from series Die Geschichte von Amnon und Tamar, trimmed, prov., (12-01-92, Karl/Faber, #3), engraving (BP 209, DM 504, FR 1716, Y 39,343).

$141* *Der Zorn (Hollstein 126),* sheet 3 from series 7 Laster, mono., d. AG 1552, trimmed, (03-24-93, Venator/Hansten, #2476), sheet 3>ēn x 2C, in., (9.1 x 6.1 cm.), engraving (BP 95, DM 230, FR 784, Y 16,567).

ALDIN, Cecil English 1870-1930

$1045* *"The Breakfast At The Three Pigeon", "Breaking Cover" and "The Death", 1900: Three,* from The Fallowfield Hunt, s., d., ident., good cond.?, toning, (01-02-93, Skinner, #144, illus.), sheet, sight 18½ x 27½ in., (47 x 69.9 cm.), color lithograph on paper (BP 697, DM 1712, FR 5845, Y 131,018).

$385* *The Fallowfield Hunt, 1900: Three,* each s., d. in matrix, good cond., trimmed, toning, losses, (05-22-93, Skinner, #102), 11¼ x 18½ in., (28.6 x 47 cm.), color lithograph on paper (BP 249, DM 626, FR 2106, Y 42,448).

$257* *The Oxford Coach, 1830,* plate s., (06-08-93, Ritchie, #9, illus.), plate 9½ x 19 in., (24.1 x 48.3 cm.), color chromolithograph (BP 169, DM 417, FR 1404, Y 27,297, C$ 330).

$1179* *Repose,* num. 56/100, s., margins, (01-18-93, Bonhams, #66, illus.), plate 7C, x 9B, in., (18.7 x 24.4 cm.), drypoint etching (BP 770, DM 1928, FR 6429, Y 148,620).

$219* *A Sealyham Puppy,* (01-18-93, Bonhams, #65), 6 x 7½ in., (15.2 x 19.1 cm.), print w/hand coloring on ivorine (BP 143, DM 358, FR 1194, Y 27,606).

$943* *A Temporary Partnership,* num. 38/150, s., t., margins, (01-18-93, Bonhams, #67), plate 5¾ x 8¼ in., (14.6 x 21 cm.), drypoint etching (BP 616, DM 1542, FR 5142, Y 118,871).

$358* *"Unlucky At Cards" and "A Bit More Breakfast": Two,* mono. sig. Cecil Aldin, good cond., (10-09-92, Skinner, #169, illus.), sight 14 x 23 in., (35.6 x 58.4 cm.), chromolithograph on paper (BP 212, DM 533, FR 1808, Y 43,659).

$707* *A Well Earned Rest,* num. 91/150. s., margins, (01-18-93, Bonhams, #68), plate 8¼ x 11¼ in., (21 x 28.6 cm.), drypoint etching (BP 462, DM 1156, FR 3855, Y 89,121).

ALDIN, Cecil (after)

$78* *Attempting The Hedge,* (10-29-92, Bonhams-Chelsea, #118), image 17 x 29½ in., (43.2 x 74.9 cm.), reproduction in colors (BP 50, DM 120, FR 407, Y 9662).

BI *The Bluemarket Races,* surface defects, est. BP 50/70, (03-03-93, Bonhams-Chelsea, #176), image 14¾ x 23½ in., (37.5 x 59.7 cm.), chromolithograph.

BI *The Bluemarket Races,* surface defects, est. BP 5/70, (06-30-93, Bonhams-Chelsea, #191), image 14¾ x 23½ in., (37.5 x 59.7 cm.), chromolithograph.

$91* *The Bluemarket Races, Homewards,* pub. Lawrence and Bullen Ltd., 1902, full margins, (06-30-93, Bonhams-Chelsea, #190), image 14¾ x 23½ in., (37.5 x 59.7 cm.), chromolithograph (BP 61, DM 155, FR 524, Y 9750).

$578* *"Brains" and "Quality": A Pair,* (05-28-93, Sloan, #1606, illus.), each sight 14¼ x 14B\ in., (36.2 x 37.1 cm.), chromolithograph (BP 370, DM 917, FR 3099, Y 61,977).

$123   *"The Christmas Coach"*, 1909: Two, (02-05-93, G.A. Key, #89), 13 x 22 in., (33 x 55.9 cm.), colored lithograph (BP 85, DM 204, FR 689, Y 15,306).

$518* *Coming From Market Harboro'*, c. 1900, s., plate, defects, Anthony N. B. Garvan Coll., (06-05-93, Christie-NY, #74), sh 14¾ x 39¾ in., (37.5 x 101 cm.), chromolithograph on wove (BP 341, DM 840, FR 2831, Y 55,567).

$112* *A Cropper*, finished by hand, (03-03-93, Bonhams-Chelsea, #114), image 17¼ x 29½ in., (43.8 x 74.9 cm.), chromolithograph (BP 77, DM 184, FR 626, Y 13,087).

$175* *Dinner-Time*, by J.M. Kronheim & Co., s., pub. William Sands, 1901, margins, (03-03-93, Bonhams-Chelsea, #52), image 13¼ x 19¼ in., (33.7 x 48.9 cm.), chromolithograph (BP 121, DM 288, FR 978, Y 20,449).

$80   *Dogs: Four*, (02-05-93, G.A. Key, #54), colored print (BP 55, DM 133, FR 448, Y 9955).

$190   *"Drawn Blank"*, pub. 1900, (04-16-93, G.A. Key, #143), 15 x 27 in., (38.1 x 68.6 cm.), chromolithograph (BP 125, DM 307, FR 1037, Y 21,365).

$345* *Every Dog Has His Day, 1897*, margins, foxed, minor defects, Anthony N. B. Garvan Coll., (06-05-93, Christie-NY, #72), sh 22¾ x 19B, in., (578 x 498 mm.), chromolithograph on wove (BP 227, DM 559, FR 1885, Y 37,009).

$73   *"The George Inn, Salisbury" and "The Kings Head Inn, Aylesbury": Two*, (04-16-93, G.A. Key, #88), 7 x 6 in., (17.8 x 15.2 cm.), colored lithograph (BP 48, DM 118, FR 398, Y 8209).

$255* *Goldie Locks And The Three Bears*, from The "A.L." Fairy Tale Fictures, margins, (03-17-93, Bonhams-Chelsea, #386), image 31½ x 21¾ in., (80 x 55.2 cm.), chromolithograph (BP 176, DM 424, FR 1442, Y 29,909).

$460* *The Hunt Breakfast, 1900*, s., plate, laid down on board, minor defects, Anthony N. B. Garvan Coll., (06-05-93, Christie-NY, #73), sh 11½ x 18¾ in., (292 x 476 mm.), chromolithograph on wove (BP 303, DM 746, FR 2514, Y 49,346).

$478* *"The Hunt Dinner"*, bears sig., (03-03-93, Bonhams-Chelsea, #115), image 15 x 24 in., (38.1 x 61 cm.), color reproduction (BP 330, DM 787, FR 2670, Y 55,854).

$190   *"A Hunting Morning"*, pub. 1899, (04-16-93, G.A. Key, #142), 15 x 27 in., (38.1 x 68.6 cm.), chromolithograph (BP 125, DM 307, FR 1037, Y 21,365).

$16*   *Snowed Up On Christmas Eve*, margins, (06-30-93, Bonhams-Chelsea, #242), image 14 x 19½ in., (35.6 x 49.5 cm.), chromolithograph (BP 11, DM 27, FR 92, Y 1714).

$198   *"Snowed Up On Christmas Eve"*, (04-16-93, G.A. Key, #35), 15 x 19 in., (38.1 x 48.3 cm.), chromolithograph (BP 130, DM 320, FR 1081, Y 22,265).

$32*   *The Sweetest Music In All The World*, faded, (03-03-93, Bonhams-Chelsea, #116), image 15¼ x 12¼ in., (38.7 x 31.1 cm.), color reproduction (BP 22, DM 53, FR 179, Y 3739).

$401* *"A Toast To The Huntsman"*, s., (11-19-92, Bonhams-Chelsea, #109), image 15¼ x 24¼ in., (38.7 x 61.6 cm.), chromolithograph (BP 264, DM 639, FR 2154, Y 49,869).

ALECHINSKY, Pierre   Belgian b. 1927

BI   *Administration Communale De Saint-Gilles, Avis*, s., num., est. DM 750, (12-05-92, Bassenge, #7000), 18M, x 13C, in., (48 x 34 cm.), color lithograph on Arches.

$309* *Ailleurs, 1977*, t., s., d. 1977, #16/120, (03-31-93, Briest, #E7), 39C, x 24Mzn in., (100 x 62 cm.), color lithograph (BP 204, DM 497, FR 1689, Y 35,534).

$275* *Arene, (Riviere 599), 1972*, 23/100, (03-24-93, Kunsthallen, #5), color lithograph (BP 186, DM 449, FR 1529, Y 32,311, DK 1725).

$248* *Astres Et Desastres VI*, s., #26/99, (05-16-93, Hindman, #581), 15¼ x 19 in., (38.7 x 48.3 cm.), color aquatint (BP 161, DM 399, FR 1341, Y 27,491).

$1373* *Les Ateliers Du Marais, "Foret", "Serpent Soleil", "Profil", "Tete" and "Saint Michel Terrasse Par Le Dragon" (See Riviere 70-73 and 75), 1951: SetOf Five*, s., t., #9/99, p. and pub. 1979 by Maeght, good cond., discoloration, (06-30-93, Sotheby-London, #727, illus.), photo-etching on wove (BP 920, DM 2342, FR 7900, Y 147,112).

BI   *"Avignon", 1983*, HC XVI/XXX, t., d., s., est. FF 2,5/3,000, (10-18-92, Pescheteau, #70), 30Zzn x 22Zzn in., (78 x 58 cm.), lithograph and etching in black on wove.

$252* *"Avignon-1983"*, H.C. XVI/XXX, t., d., s., (01-28-93, Pescheteau, #60), 30Zzn x 22Zzn in., (78 x 58 cm.), black etching and lithograph on wove (BP 166, DM 399, FR 1351, Y 31,289).

$385* *"Bouef Gros Sel"*, good cond., (10-31-92, Cleveland, #354, illus.), 17¼ x 12Z, in., (43.8 x 30.8 cm.), color lithograph (BP 247, DM 592, FR 2009, Y 47,690).

$369* *Central Park NY, #116/175*, s., (11-13-92, Koller, #5230, illus.), 18Bzn x 25Czn in., (46.5 x 64 cm.), lithograph on wove (BP 238, DM 579, FR 1953, Y 45,799, SF 522).

BI   *"Central Park, NY", 1976*, pub. Transworld Art, s., num. XXXIII/L Alechinsky, t. on stone, pub.dry stamp, good cond., handling crease, est. $4/600, (09-11-92, Skinner, #98C), sheet 19¾ x 26Zzn in., (50.2 x 66.2 cm.), lithograph in nine colors on wove.

$211* *Charmante Soiree, (Riviere 223), 1964*, s. Alechinsky, 11/50, (09-30-92, Kunsthallen, #8), lithograph (BP 119, DM 299, FR 1012, Y 25,321, DK 1150).

$717* *Chute Blanche*, s., e.a. XXV/XXX, (05-27-93, Lempertz, #546), 23B, x 34Z, in., (60 x 86.7 cm.), color lithograph on Arches wove (BP 459, DM 1151, FR 3878, Y 76,865).

$165* *Comme des Chiens, (Riviere 143), 1962*, (03-24-93, Kunsthallen, #3), color lithograph (BP 112, DM 269, FR 917, Y 19,387, DK 1035).

BI   *Composition*, s. Alechinsky, 73/99, est. DK 1,800, (09-30-92, Kunsthallen, #2), color lithograph and etching.

$969* *Composition*, s. Alechinsky 1978, 30/60, (09-30-92, Kunsthallen, #9), color lithograph and etching in colors (BP 547, DM 1374, FR 4647, Y 116,285, DK 5290).

$184* *Composition*, s. Alechinsky, IX/XX, (03-24-93, Kunsthallen, #4), color lithograph (BP 125, DM 301, FR 1023, Y 21,619, DK 1150).

$239* *Composition*, s. Alechinsky, 171/500, (03-24-93, Kunsthallen, #6), color lithograph (BP 162, DM 390, FR 1329, Y 28,081, DK 1495).

$358* *Composition*, from Gnomes et Gnose, s. Alechinsky, 71/150, (09-30-92, Kunsthallen, #7), color lithograph (BP 202, DM 508, FR 1717, Y 42,962, DK 1955).

$337* *Composition*, s. Alechinsky, 119/150, (09-30-92, Kunsthallen, #17), color lithograph (BP 190, DM 478, FR 1616, Y 40,442, DK 1840).

$295* *Composition*, s. Alechinsky, 119/150, (09-30-92, Kunsthallen, #16), color lithograph (BP 166, DM 418, FR 1415, Y 35,401, DK 1610).

$387* *Composition*, s. 96/150, (04-17-93, Falkkloos, #8, illus.), 29½ x 21¼ in., (75 x 54 cm.), color serigraph (BP 251, DM 619, FR 2091, Y 43,033, SK 2860).

$293* *Composition*, s., #23/100, (11-16-92, Briest, #7), 18M, x 26¾ in., (48 x 68 cm.), lithograph and aquatint in colors (BP 193, DM 467, FR 1574, Y 36,566).

$210* *"Composition"*, E.A. XI/XX, (01-28-93, Pescheteau, #61), 33Zzn x 22Mzn in., (84 x 57 cm.), color lithograph on wove (BP 139, DM 333, FR 1126, Y 26,074).

$358* *Composition, 1974*, from Gnomes and Gnose, s. Alechinsky, 71/150, (09-30-92, Kunsthallen, #3), color lithograph (BP 202, DM 508, FR 1717, Y 42,962, DK 1955).

$400* *Composition, 1974*, from Gnomes and Gnose, s. Alechinsky, 71/150, (09-30-92, Kunsthallen, #4), color lithograph (BP 226, DM 567, FR 1918, Y 48,002, DK 2185).

$337* *Composition, 1974*, from Gnomes and Gnose, s. Alechinsky, 71/150, (09-30-92, Kunsthallen, #6), color lithograph (BP 190, DM 478, FR 1616, Y 40,442, DK 1840).

$358* *Composition, 1974*, from Gnomes et Gnose, s. Alechinsky, 71/150, (09-30-92, Kunsthallen, #5), color lithograph (BP 202, DM 508, FR 1717, Y 42,962, DK 1955).

$295* *Composition, 1974*, s. Alechinksy 13-9-74, E.A., (09-30-92, Kunsthallen, #15), color lithograph (BP 166, DM 418, FR 1415, Y 35,401, DK 1610).

$1286* *Composition, 1977*, s., d., #19/60, i. barde fou, good cond., handling creases, (06-30-93, Sotheby-London, #729, illus.), sh 38½ x 23C, in., (978 x 594 mm.), color etching on thin Japan (BP 862, DM 2193, FR 7399, Y 137,791).

$480* *Composition, c. 1980,* s., #28/300, full margins, good cond., handling creases, mount-staining, (06-30-93, Sotheby-London, #731, illus.), 15Z, x 20¾ in., (384 x 527 mm.), color lithograph on Arches (BP 322, DM 819, FR 2762, Y 51,430).

$466* *Darmstadt,* s., t., #98/100, (05-27-93, Lempertz, #545), 30Zzn x 22Czn in., (78 x 56.3 cm.), etching on China bordered w/color lithograph (BP 298, DM 748, FR 2520, Y 49,957).

$717* *Devidoir (Riviere 516), 1972,* s., t., #45/50, from folio Devidoirs, (05-27-93, Lempertz, #540), 22Zzn x 17½ in., (56 x 44.5 cm.), color etching on Arches wove (BP 459, DM 1151, FR 3878, Y 76,865).

$248* *"Digitales",* good cond., (10-31-92, Cleveland, #355, illus.), 17¼ x 12Z, in., (43.8 x 30.8 cm.), color lithograph (BP 159, DM 382, FR 1294, Y 30,720).

$208* *Double Vue,* s., H(ors) C(ommerce), (12-01-92, Karl/Faber, #308), approx. 19Z\ x 25Czn in., (48.5 x 64 cm.), color lithograph on Arches wove (BP 137, DM 332, FR 1130, Y 25,896).

$1791* *Fenetre, 1977: Four,* s., t., d., #6/99, full sheet, good cond., (05-27-93, Sotheby-Amstrdm, #530), each sh 40Czn x 26ZBzn in., (102 x 68.4 cm.), lithograph and etching p. in colors on wove (BP 1147, DM 2874, FR 9686, Y 192,003, G 3220).

$184* *Festival D'Automne, (Riviere 524), 1972,* s. Alechinsky, (03-24-93, Kunsthallen, #2), color lithograph (BP 125, DM 301, FR 1023, Y 21,619, DK 1150).

$369* *Florale Komposition,* s., num., blindstamp, (12-05-92, Bassenge, #6997), 23½ x 19C\n in., (59.7 x 50.3 cm.), woodcut on Arches (BP 231, DM 575, FR 1961, Y 45,719).

BI *Le Genou De La Grande Robe, 1981,* s., d. 1981, #53/60, est. FF4/5,000, (05-27-93, Briest, #10), 62ZBzn x 46Mzn in., (160 x 118 cm.), color lithograph.

$1285* *Gnomes Et Gnose, 1974,* s. 58/150, p. Clot, Bramsen et Georges, portfolio, (03-24-93, Kunsthallen, #7), color lithographs (BP 870, DM 2099, FR 7143, Y 150,981, DK 8050).

$3170* *Honore De Balzac, Traite Des Excitants Modernes: Portfolio,* s., 91/125, ed. Yves Riviere, #91, (05-25-93, AB Stockholm, #1), etching in colors (BP 2054, DM 5163, FR 17,379, Y 346,486, SK 4620).

$209* *"Honore",* S., 48/99, (09-29-92, B. Rasmussen, #265), lithograph in colors (BP 117, DM 295, FR 1007, Y 24,949, DK 1150).

$312* *Illusion D'Optique, (Riviere 345), 1967,* s. Alechinsky, IX/XV e.a., (03-24-93, Kunsthallen, #1), color lithograph (BP 211, DM 510, FR 1734, Y 36,658, DK 1955).

$326* *Je Ne Sais Pas (Riviere 114), 1961,* s., proof, margins, good cond., soiling, creases, tears, (12-09-92, Sotheby-Amstrdm, #456), 16≯zn x 22Zzn in., (420 x 580 mm.), color lithograph (BP 208, DM 512, FR 1746, Y 40,422, G 575).

$532* *Komposition,* num., s., (06-08-93, Karl/Faber, #485), sh approx. 19Zzn x 25ZAzn in., (50 x 66 cm.), color lithograph on wove (BP 350, DM 863, FR 2907, Y 56,506).

$603* *Komposition,* s., num., (06-08-93, Karl/Faber, #484), sh approx. 33¼ x 23B, in., (84.5 x 60 cm.), color lithograph on wove (BP 396, DM 978, FR 3295, Y 64,047).

$516* *Komposition Mit Runder Scheibe,* s., num., (12-05-92, Bassenge, #6998), 28≯zn x 20M, in., (72.5 x 53 cm.), color lithograph with aquatint (BP 323, DM 804, FR 2742, Y 63,933).

$295* *Komposition Mit Spirale Und Knopf,* h.c., s., (12-05-92, Bassenge, #6996), 19½ x 13ZAzn in., woodcut on Arches (BP 185, DM 460, FR 1567, Y 36,551).

BI *Krach Portfolio, 1973: Five,* complete portfolio, s., annot. I/P, crayon s., annot. i/p, pub. YvesRiviere, full margins, good cond., buckling, printing creases, stains, orig. portfolio, est. $2/4,000, (10-28-92, Butterfield, #2877, illus.), each sheet 30 x 22¼ in., (762 x 565 mm.), color aquatint w/collage on Japon nacre.

$959* *L'Inconditionnement Humain (Riviere 437), 1970,* s., #116/300, pub. Atelier Clot, p. by Clot, Bramsen et Georges, margins, good cond., (05-27-93, Sotheby-Amstrdm, #529, illus.), 24Mzn x 38≯zn in., (620 x 980 mm.), colored lithograph on Arches (BP 614, DM 1539, FR 5187, Y 102,809, G 1725).

BI *Labyrinthe D"Apparat, (Riviere 601), 1972,* s. Alechinsky, 19/100, est. DK 2,000, (09-30-92, Kunsthallen, #11), color lithograph.

BI *Labyrinthe D'Apparat, (Riviere 597), 1972,* s. Alechinsky, 19/100, est. DK 2,000, (09-30-92, Kunsthallen, #10), color lithograph.

$427* *"La Liberte C'Est D'Etre Inegal", 1974,* #66/150, s., (10-18-92, Pescheteau, #68), 33M, x 24 in., (86 x 61 cm.), lithograph in colors on wove (BP 259, DM 631, FR 2142, Y 50,985).

$190* *Lino-Litho, Planche V. 1970, (Riviere 467),* s. Alechinsky, 5/99, (09-30-92, Kunsthallen, #18), linocut and color lithograph (BP 107, DM 269, FR 911, Y 22,801, DK 1035).

$253* *Louisiana, (Riviere 371), 1969,* s. Alechinsky, 101/300, (09-30-92, Kunsthallen, #14), color lithograph (BP 143, DM 359, FR 1213, Y 30,361, DK 1380).

$1879* *Mat,* s. Alechinsky 1975, 33/50, (06-03-93, Kunsthallen, #186, illus.), 62ZBzn x 46Zzn in., (160 x 117 cm.), lithograph in colors and etching (BP 1218, DM 3007, FR 10,135, Y 201,523, DK 11,500).

$480* *Das Meer Mit Verdunkelter Sonne,* s., num., (12-05-92, Bassenge, #6999), 28≯zn x 21Zzn in., (72.5 x 53.5 cm.), color lithograph (BP 301, DM 748, FR 2550, Y 59,472).

$295* *Milan, (Riviere 435), 1970,* s. Alechinsky, 58/100, (09-30-92, Kunsthallen, #13), color lithograph (BP 166, DM 418, FR 1415, Y 35,401, DK 1610).

BI *Ou Etes-Vous, 1988,* s., t., d., #55/70, blindstamp, full margins, good cond., creases, sheet 1872 x 943 mm, est. G 5/7,000, (12-09-92, Sotheby-Amstrdm, #458, illus.), hand-colored etching on Japan.

$232* *Rad,* s., num., (12-01-92, Karl/Faber, #310), approx. 19Zzn x 10¼ in., (50 x 26 cm.), woodcut on Arches France wove (BP 153, DM 370, FR 1260, Y 28,884).

$907* *La Reine Des Murs: Seven,* original edit., s., #40/65, one 39/65, 75 impressions, num. 45, (03-31-93, Briest, #E134), lithographs (BP 600, DM 1459, FR 4956, Y 104,301).

BI *Remarques Au Pinceau, 1974: Five,* booklet, s., #305/405, pub. Yves Riviere, good cond., est. G 6/900, (12-09-92, Sotheby-Amstrdm, #454), each sheet 12C, x 19≯zn in., (315 x 497 mm.), color offset print on verge de Hollande.

$573* *Roue Sans Jante (Riviere 561), 1972,* s., from Hommage a Picasso, pub. Propylaen, (05-27-93, Lempertz, #541), 29¾ x 22Zzn in., (75.5 x 56 cm.), color etching on Arches wove (BP 367, DM 919, FR 3099, Y 61,428).

$247* *"Rue Serpente", 1981,* t., d., s., (10-18-92, Pescheteau, #71), 32Zzn x 23B, in., (83 x 60 cm.), lithograph on wove (BP 150, DM 365, FR 1239, Y 29,493).

BI *"Sud-Ouest. B-", 1989,* #30/99, d., s., est. FF 2,5/3,000, (10-18-92, Pescheteau, #69), 26C, x 40Czn in., (67 x 102 cm.), etching on map.

$2372* *"Sur Femth Volanie",* s. 1990, Yves Riviere, (05-12-93, AB Stockholm, #7001, illus.), 25≯zn x 49B, in., (65 x 126 cm.), hand-colored etching w/linoleum print (BP 1549, DM 3827, FR 12,891, Y 264,821, SK 17,600).

$2280* *Sur L'Ecorce, 1989: Seven,* complete, s., d., #41/99, full margins, good cond., (12-09-92, Sotheby-Amstrdm, #457, illus.), each approx. 23¼ x 35Zzn in., (590 x 910 mm.), color aquatint (BP 1455, DM 3579, FR 12,212, Y 282,703, G 4025).

$435* *Untitled,* s., #111/190, sheet p. to edges, good cond., (05-27-93, Sotheby-Amstrdm, #381, illus.), sh 29Mzn x 20Zzn in., (747 x 528 mm.), colored lithograph on wove (BP 279, DM 698, FR 2353, Y 46,634, G 782).

BI *Untitled,* s., #57/99, est. DM 1,000-, (05-27-93, Lempertz, #544), 15¾ x 19Zzn in., (40 x 50 cm.), etching in green laid down on 1 p. sheet on Japon nacre.

$248* *Untitled,* s., #102/400, good cond., discoloration, (12-09-92, Sotheby-Amstrdm, #453), sheet 20M, x 29¾ in., (530 x 755 mm.), color lithograph on wove (BP 158, DM 389, FR 1328, Y 30,750, G 437).

$435* *Untitled,* s., sheet p. to edges, good cond., (05-27-93, Sotheby-Amstrdm, #382), sh 29Mzn x 20Zzn in., (747 x 528 mm.), colored lithograph on wove (BP 279, DM 698, FR 2353, Y 46,634, G 782).

$25* *Untitled,* s., scuffs, smudges, marks throughout image, (05-15-93, Cleveland, #445), 25 x 35 in., (63.5 x 88.9 cm.), silkscreen (BP 16, DM 40, FR 135, Y 2771).

$3942* *Untitled, 1975,* s., d., (05-27-93, Lempertz, #542, illus.), 42Æzn x 23ªzn in., (109 x 59.8 cm.), etching and watercolor on thin Japan (BP 2524, DM 6325, FR 21,320, Y 422,599).

BI *Volcan Depeint (Riviere 501), 1971,* s., 233/300, est. FF1,000/1,500, (06-28-93, Loudmer, #182), 24B, x 17Æzn in., (625 x 450 mm.), sh 25ªzn x 19½ in., (625 x 450 mm.), color lithograph on Arches wove.

BI *Le Volturno, (Blaise Cenrars), 1989,* s., 54/99, Atelier Clot, est. DK est. 15,000, (03-24-93, Kunsthallen, #8), portfolio, inc. 3 lithographs.

$1449* *Yves Bonnefoy.Par Experience: Portfolio,* each s., #48/75, w/t. and poems in facsimile, s. by author and artist, num. 48, p. Arte, pub. Editions F.B., 1976, good cond., handling marks, orig.box, (12-03-92, Sotheby-London, #599, illus.), overall size 16½ x 12C, in., (418 x 312 mm.), three hand-colored collotypes on Richard de Bas wove (BP 935, DM 2279, FR 7778, Y 180,291).

ALECHINSKY, Pierre and Christian DOTREMONT

$438* *Brassee Sismographique (Riviere 513), 1972,* s., #433/500, Maeght, (06-12-93, Hauswedell/Nolt, #1), 28ªzn x 21¼ in., (72.5 x 54 cm.), color lithograph on Arches (BP 287, DM 713, FR 2396, Y 46,091).

ALEJANDRO

$19* *Sans Titre: Two,* s., from 50 impressions, (06-28-93, Loudmer, #6), approx. 7M, x 5M, in., (200 x 150 mm.), sh 14Æzn x 11Z, in., (200 x 150 mm.), black etchings and drypoint on wove (BP 13, DM 32, FR 109, Y 2016).

ALEXANDER, Peter American b. 1939

$715* *Riccoso, 1987: Diptych,* inits., d., t., #30/40, blindstamp pub. Cirrus, very good cond.?, (10-28-92, Butterfield, #2879), each sheet 31 x 33 in., (787 x 838 mm.), color lithograph on wove (BP 456, DM 1104, FR 3749, Y 87,730).

ALEXANDER, William English 1767-1816

$303* *From G. Staunton's "An Authentic Account: China": Six,* G. Nicol, pub. London 1796, (12-10-92, Sloan, #1015), each, sheet 16¼ x 21¾ in., (41.3 x 55.2 cm.), engravings (BP 195, DM 479, FR 1637, Y 37,481).

ALEXANDER, William (after) English 1767-1816

$88* *Chinese Barges Of The Embassy Preparing To Pass Under A Bridge,* by William Byrne, pub. London, (07-03-92, Sloan, #331), 13½ x 19 in., (34.3 x 48.3 cm.), engraving (BP 46, DM 133, FR 449, Y 10,970).

ALI, Muhammad

$880* *"Sting Like A Bee", "Under The Sun", "Guiding Light", and "Mosque II", c. 1979: Four,* s., full margins, (05-27-93, Swann, #198, illus.), approx. 18 x 24 in., (45.7 x 61 cm.), color serigraphs (BP 564, DM 1412, FR 4759, Y 94,340).

ALIKNOK, Peter b. 1928

BI *W2-494 Holman Island. Spearing Fishes,* s., t., d. Western Arctic 1969, #47/50, est. C$250/400, (06-07-93, Ritchie, #73, illus.), 23Æzn x 17B\n in., (60.9 x 45.7 cm.), color stone cut.

ALINARI, Fratelli

$550* *"Firenze, Palazzo Pitti" and "Firenze, Campanile Del Duomo": Two,* each ink t.; photog. blindstamp mount, (11-16-92, Butterfield, #5835, illus.), each approx. 13½ x 10½ in., (343.5 x 267.2 mm.), xin., (343.5 x 267.2 mm.), photograph, albumen prints (BP 362, DM 877, FR 2954, Y 68,399).

$935* *"Gates Of Paradise, Baptistery By Ghiberti", "Loggia Dei Lanzi With Sculptures (Including Rape Of The Sabine Woman)", Palazzo Vecchio" and "Sculptur Of Caine, Uffizi Gallery": Four,* photog. num. in neg., blindstamp, 1870s, (04-07-93, Swann, #221, illus.), photograph, albumen print (BP 618, DM 1512, FR 5118, Y 106,226).

ALIX, Pierre Michel 1762-1817

$633* *Les Consuls, Camberceres, Bonaparte, Lebrun, Beneath The Portraits AScene (P. and B., I, p. 22, no. 11; Inventaire 18e Siecle, I, p. 114, no. 176), c. 1803,* after Henri Nicolas van Gorp, etched by Jean Duplessis-Bertaux, pub.Levachez, Mousseaux and Blaisot, margins, foxing, repaired tear, (12-01-92, Christie-London, #281), plate 15½ x 10¾ in., (393 x 273 mm.), etching w/engraving in colors (BP 418, DM 1009, FR 3438, Y 78,810).

ALKEN, H.

$220* *"Full Cry",* full margins, pub. 1828, (01-15-93, DuMouchelle, #117), 14 x 21 in., (35.6 x 53.3 cm.), hand colored print (BP 144, DM 360, FR 1216, Y 27,736).

$165* *"Pigeon Match", "Fishing", "Racing" and "Fox Hunting": Four,* pub. T. McLean, c. 1820, (11-13-92, DuMouchelle, #367), 7 x 11 in., (17.8 x 27.9 cm.), prints (BP 107, DM 259, FR 873, Y 20,479).

$55* *"Something Slap",* Lewis Printsellers, (02-27-93, Dunning, #138), 10½ x 15 in., (26.7 x 38.1 cm.), color print (BP 39, DM 90, FR 307, Y 6493).

ALKEN, Henry

$132* *The Death, 1818,* full margins, (02-13-93, Collins, #18, illus.), 9¼ x 12½ in., (23.5 x 31.8 cm.), hand-colored aquatint (BP 93, DM 219, FR 741, Y 15,919).

$44* *Doing It Furiously, 1818,* full margins, (02-13-93, Collins, #9), 6¼ x 8¾ in., (15.9 x 22.2 cm.), hand-colored aquatint (BP 31, DM 73, FR 247, Y 5306).

$286* *Doing It No How, 1818,* full margins, (02-13-93, Collins, #4, illus.), 6 x 8¾ in., (15.2 x 22.2 cm.), hand-colored aquatint (BP 201, DM 474, FR 1605, Y 34,491).

$83* *Doing It Somehow, 1818,* full margins, (02-13-93, Collins, #6, illus.), 6 x 8¾ in., (15.2 x 22.2 cm.), hand-colored aquatint (BP 58, DM 138, FR 466, Y 10,010).

$83* *Doing The Down Leap, 1818,* full margins, (02-13-93, Collins, #7, illus.), 6¼ x 8¾ in., (15.9 x 22.2 cm.), hand-colored aquatint (BP 58, DM 138, FR 466, Y 10,010).

$83* *Doing The Thing Well, 1818,* full margins, (02-13-93, Collins, #5, illus.), 6¼ x 8¾ in., (15.9 x 22.2 cm.), hand-colored aquatint (BP 58, DM 138, FR 466, Y 10,010).

$44* *The Down Leap Done, 1818,* full margins, (02-13-93, Collins, #8, illus.), 6¼ x 8¾ in., (15.9 x 22.2 cm.), hand-colored aquatint (BP 31, DM 73, FR 247, Y 5306).

$127* *Drawing A Cover, 1818,* full margins, (02-13-93, Collins, #15, illus.), 9¼ x 12C, in., (23.5 x 31.4 cm.), hand-colored aquatint (BP 89, DM 211, FR 713, Y 15,316).

BI *Driving Discoveries, 1817: Four,* stone s., pub. S. & J. Fuller, margins, laid down, mat staining, foxing, scuffs/staining image, est. $800/1,000, (10-28-92, Butterfield, #2780), 7C, x 10C, in., (187 x 264 mm.), hand-colored lithograph on laid paper.

BI *Epsom Races-The Derby Day (Abbey Life 472), 1819,* continuous strip in orig. round wooden holder (varnished), pub. S. &J. Fuller, good cond., tears, rubbed, est. BP 200/250, (11-30-92, Phillips-London, #261), sheet (panorama) 2C, x 180 in., (6 x 457.2 cm.), hand-colored aquatint.

$358* *"The First Steeple Chase On Record", Plate I And Plate II: Two,* s. J. Harris, Engr., Pub. March 1, 1839 Ben Brooks, (02-27-93, Dunning, #1127), sight 13 x 15½ in., (33 x 39.4 cm.), etching (BP 252, DM 589, FR 2000, Y 42,262).

$275* *"The First Steeple Chase On Record", Plate III and "The Last Field Near Nacton Heath", Plate IV: Two,* (02-27-93, Dunning, #1128), sight 13 x 15½ in., (33 x 39.4 cm.), etching (BP 193, DM 452, FR 1536, Y 32,464).

$66* *The First Steeple-Chase On Record. Ipswich, The Wateringplace BehindThe Barracks. Plate 1, 1839,* full margins, (02-13-93, Collins, #31), 10¾ x 14B\ in., (27.3 x 37.1 cm.), hand-colored aquatint (BP 46, DM 109, FR 370, Y 7959).

$66* *The First Steeple-Chase On Record. Nacton Church And Village.Plate 4, 1839,* full margins, (02-13-93, Collins, #34), 10B, x 14½ in., (27 x 36.8 cm.), hand-colored aquatint (BP 46, DM 109, FR 370, Y 7959).

$66* *The First Steeple-Chase On Record. The Large Field Near Bile'sCorner. Plate 2, 1839,* full margins, (02-13-93, Collins, #32), 10¾ x 14B, in., (27.3 x 37.1 cm.), hand-colored aquatint (BP 46, DM 109, FR 370, Y 7959).

$198* *The First Steeple-Chase On Record. The Last Field Near Nacton Heath.Plate 3, 1839,* full margins, (02-13-93, Collins, #33), 10ᴮ, x 14½ in., (27 x 36.8 cm.), hand-colored aquatint (BP 139, DM 328, FR 1111, Y 23,878).

$44* *Flacker Shooting, 1820,* margins, (02-13-93, Collins, #29), 8 x 12 in., (20.3 x 30.5 cm.), hand-colored aquatint (BP 31, DM 73, FR 247, Y 5306).

$132* *Full Cry, 1818,* full margins, (02-13-93, Collins, #17, illus.), 9¼ x 12ᶜ, in., (23.5 x 31.4 cm.), hand-colored aquatint (BP 93, DM 219, FR 741, Y 15,919).

$165* *Gone Away, 1818,* full margins, (02-13-93, Collins, #14, illus.), 9¼ x 12ᶜ, in., (23.5 x 31.4 cm.), hand-colored aquatint (BP 116, DM 274, FR 926, Y 19,899).

$88* *Keepers On The Look Out, 1828,* margins, (02-13-93, Collins, #29A), 10 x 8 in., (25.4 x 20.3 cm.), hand-colored aquatint (BP 62, DM 146, FR 494, Y 10,613).

$121* *The Leap, 1818,* full margins, (02-13-93, Collins, #16, illus.), 9¾ x 12ᶜ, in., (24.8 x 31.4 cm.), hand-colored aquatint (BP 85, DM 201, FR 679, Y 14,592).

$9200* *The National Sports Of Great Britain (Mellon/Podeschi 111; Schwerdt I:19; Siltzer 70; Tooley 41), 1821,* Thomas McLean, folio, after Alken by I. Clark, pencil marks, inner hinges renewed, first ed., prov., (06-14-93, Sotheby-NY, #358, illus.), 18¾ x 12¼ in., (47.6 x 31.1 cm.), hand-colored extra illus. t., t. and text, 50 hand-colored aquatints (BP 6022, DM 14,974, FR 50,328, Y 968,115).

$88* *The Poachers Detected, 1828,* margins, (02-13-93, Collins, #29B), 10 x 8 in., (25.4 x 20.3 cm.), hand-colored aquatint (BP 62, DM 146, FR 494, Y 10,613).

$3738* *R. Ackermann's Steeple Chase Scraps (Siltzer 67), 1850,* Rudoloph Ackermann, by J. Harris, w/out letterpress, 1st ed., prov., (06-14-93, Sotheby-NY, #362, illus.), each 7¾ x 10ᶻ, in., (19.7 x 25.7 cm.), 4 hand-colored aquatints (BP 2447, DM 6084, FR 20,449, Y 393,349).

$121* *The Refreshment, 1818,* full margins, (02-13-93, Collins, #13, illus.), 9ᶜ, x 12ᶜ, in., (23.8 x 31.4 cm.), hand-colored aquatint (BP 85, DM 201, FR 679, Y 14,592).

$5463* *The Roadster's Album, 1845,* Messer. Fores, soiling, blindstamp, wear, (06-14-93, Sotheby-NY, #368), 14ᴹ, x 10¾ in., (37.8 x 27.3 cm.), handcolored engraving, title-page by Alken, 16 hand-colored aquatints by Newhouse (BP 3576, DM 8892, FR 29,885, Y 574,871).

$1380* *Scraps From Sketch-Book (Schwerdt I:21), 1821,* Thomas McLean, 4to, by Alken, soiling, FIRST ED., (06-14-93, Sotheby-NY, #359), 10ᶜ, x 8¼ in., (26.4 x 21 cm.), 24 hand-colored softground etchings (BP 903, DM 2246, FR 7549, Y 145,217).

$3220* *Shooting, Or One Day's Sport Of Three Real Good Ones (Schwerdt I, 21-22; Tooley 49), 1823: Six,* Thomas McLean, stains, soiling, Anthony N. B. Garvan Coll., (06-05-93, Christie-NY, #3, illus.), hand-colored plate of crayon-manner engraving (BP 2120, DM 5220, FR 17,596, Y 345,419).

$1840* *Sporting Notions (SChwerdt I:24), 1831-33,* Thomas M'Lean, folio, 1st ed., prov., (06-14-93, Sotheby-NY, #360), 14¼ x 10 in., (36.2 x 25.4 cm.), 36 hand-colored aquatints (BP 1204, DM 2995, FR 10,066, Y 193,623).

$1380* *Sporting Scrab Book (Mellon/Podeschi 120; Schwerdt I:24), 1824,* Thomas McLean, 8vo, original boards, 1st ed.,, (06-14-93, Sotheby-NY, #361), 10¼ x 7 in., (26 x 17.8 cm.), 50 hand-colored softground etchings (BP 903, DM 2246, FR 7549, Y 145,217).

$69* *Spree At Melton Mowbray, Plates 20 and 21: Two,* margins, staining, other defects, (10-29-92, Bonhams-Chelsea, #124), 12 x 15¾ in., (30.5 x 40 cm.), aquatint w/hand coloring (BP 44, DM 106, FR 360, Y 8547).

$176* *The Toast, 1818,* full margins, (02-13-93, Collins, #19, illus.), 9ᶻ, x 12ᶜ, in., (23.2 x 31.4 cm.), hand-colored aquatint (BP 124, DM 292, FR 988, Y 21,225).

$345* *"Tutor's Assistant", "Involuntary Thoughts" and "New Symptoms" (Tooley 59), 1823-4: Three,* Thomas McLean, soiling, staining, (06-14-93, Sotheby-NY, #363), sheet 10ᶜ, x 14½ in., (26.4 x 36.8 cm.), 3 sets comprising 26 softground etchings (BP 226, DM 562, FR 1887, Y 36,304).

BI *"Water Hen Shooting", "Badger Catching", "Pheasant Shooting", "Spaniels" and "Flacker Shooting": Five,* The National Sports of Great Britain folio, pub. T. McLean, 1820, est. C$ 4/600, (12-01-92, Ritchie, #4), each 10ᴮ, x 14¼ in., (27 x 36.2 cm.), hand-colored aquatint.

$43* *"Wattle Fence With A Deep Drop", Plate 2 and "In And Out Of The Lane" Plate 3: Two,* from Fore's Steeple

Chase Scenes, by John Harris, pub. Messrs. Fores, April 24th, 1848, later impression, (06-08-93, Ritchie, #7), plate 13¼ x 17¼ in., (33.7 x 43.8 cm.), hand-colored aquatint (BP 28, DM 70, FR 235, Y 4567, C$ 55).

ALKEN, Henry (Sr.) (after)   English 1784-1850

$165* *The Right And Wrong Sort: Two,* by John Harris, from Fore's "Hunting Sketches", (10-30-92, Sloan, #898), each 14ᶻ, x 17¾ in., (35.9 x 45.1 cm.), color aquatints (BP 106, DM 254, FR 861, Y 20,438).

$110* *"Swishing A Rasper" and "Going Along A Slapping Pace": Two,* by John Harris, from Fore's "Hunting Accomplishments", (10-30-92, Sloan, #889), each 10ᶻᵃⁿ x 13 in., (27.8 x 33 cm.), color aquatint (BP 70, DM 169, FR 574, Y 13,626).

BI *"Swishing A Rasper" and "Going Along A Slapping Pace": Two,* by John Harris, from Fore's Hunting Accomplishments, est. $300/400, (09-17-92, Sloan, #1448), each 10ᴮᶻⁿ x 13 in., (26.2 x 33 cm.), color aquatints.

ALKEN, Henry (after)

$193* *Away,* pub. R. Ackerman, from Fox Hunting Series #2, (11-12-92, Freemn/Fine Art, #9), 16½ x 24½ in., (41.9 x 62.2 cm.), colored engraving (BP 127, DM 306, FR 1032, Y 23,931).

$330* *"Breaking Cover" and "Full Cry": A Pair,* (12-13-92, Hindman, #257), 12 x 28 in., hand-colored aquatint (BP 211, DM 519, FR 1768, Y 40,826).

$64 *"Crab",* by J. Clark, (06-11-93, G.A. Key, #58), 6 x 8 in., (15.2 x 20.3 cm.), colored aquatint (BP 42, DM 104, FR 351, Y 6790).

BI *"Drawing The Cover", "Getting Away", "The Full Cry" and "The Death":Four,* by R.G. Reeve, pub. Messrs Brall and Sons, margins, est. BP 3/400, (06-30-93, Bonhams-Chelsea, #107), plate 13ᴹ, x 17ᴮ, in., (35.2 x 44.8 cm.), aquatint w/hand-coloring.

$213* *The First Steeple Chase On Record, Plate I-IV: Four,* by J. Harris, pub. Ben Brooks, 1839, (06-30-93, Bonhams-Chelsea, #193), image 10½ x 14ᶜ, in., (26.7 x 36.5 cm.), aquatint w/hand-coloring (BP 143, DM 363, FR 1226, Y 22,822).

BI *The First Steeple Chase On Record, Plate II, Whoop! And Away!,* by J. Harris, pub. Ben Brooks, 1839, trimmed, est. BP 30/50, (03-03-93, Bonhams-Chelsea, #177), image 10¾ x 14½ in., (27.3 x 36.8 cm.), hand-colored aquatint.

$275* *"The First Steeple-Chase On Record", 1839: A Set Of Four,* by J. Harris, margins, pub. Ben Brooks, (10-29-92, Bonhams-Chelsea, #154), plate 13¼ x 16 in., (33.7 x 40.6 cm.), aquatint w/hand coloring (BP 176, DM 423, FR 1435, Y 34,064).

$152 *"The First Steeple-Chase On Record", 1839: Four,* by J. Harris, (06-11-93, G.A. Key, #73), 10 x 14 in., (25.4 x 35.6 cm.), colored aquatint (BP 100, DM 247, FR 833, Y 16,127).

$213* *"The First Steeple-Chase On Record": Four,* by J. Harris, pub. Ben Brooks, 1839, margins, foxing, (06-30-93, Bonhams-Chelsea, #192), plate 14½ x 16½ in., (36.8 x 41.9 cm.), aquatint w/hand-coloring (BP 143, DM 363, FR 1226, Y 22,822).

$277* *The First Steeplechase On Record: Plates I-IV,* by J. Harris, foxed, (07-16-92, Bonhams-Chelsea, #535), image 10ᴮ, x 14½ in., (27 x 36.8 cm.), aquatint w/hand coloring (BP 143, DM 409, FR 1382, Y 34,699).

$110* *"Flaker Shooting" and "Salmon Fishing": Two, 1820,* by I. Clark, (12-13-92, Hindman, #258), each 9 x 12¾ in., hand-colored aquatint (BP 70, DM 173, FR 589, Y 13,609).

$848* *Fore's Hunting Scraps, Plates 1-6 (S. 74),* by J. Harris, pub. Messrs. Fores, margins, discoloration, staining onimage and platemark, foxing, laid, (10-07-92, Christie-S. Ken, #51), pl 14¼ x 18 in., (36.2 x 45.7 cm.), colored aquatint (BP 495, DM 1227, FR 4161, Y 101,984).

$51 *"Fox Hunting": Two,* engraved by T. Sutherland, (02-05-93, G.A. Key, #65), 7 x 12 in., (17.8 x 30.5 cm.), colored stipple engraving (BP 35, DM 85, FR 286, Y 6346).

$64* *"Full Cry" and "The Death": Two,* (07-16-92, Bonhams-Chelsea, #522), image 4 x 17½ in., (10.2 x 44.5 cm.), reproduction w/hand coloring (BP 33, DM 95, FR 319, Y 8017).

$5328* *Grand Leicestershire Steeple Chase, On The 12th Of March, 1829 (S.p. 61; L., II, p. 17), 1830: Set Of Eight,* by Charles Bentley, watermark, pub. R. Ackermann, small margins, light-staining, very good cond., (12-01-92, Christie-London, #296, illus.), averaging plate 14⌀n x 17⅞⌀n in., (360 x 450 mm.), colored aquatint (BP 3520, DM 8492, FR 28,941, Y 663,347).

$550* *"The Hunt At Milton": Set of Twelve,* (06-03-92, Doyle, #3), 3 x 21¾ in., (7.6 x 55.2 cm.), color lithographs (BP 303, DM 882, FR 2970, Y 70,252).

$151* *Hunting, Or Six Hours Sport, By Three Real Good Ones From The East End, And Without Seeing A Hound, Plates 1-4 (S. 71): Four,* pub. T.McLean, margins, discoloration, dirt, laid, (10-07-92, Christie-S. Ken, #50), pl 9¾ x 10¾ in., (24.8 x 27.3 cm.), colored etching (BP 88, DM 218, FR 741, Y 18,160).

$220* *In And Out,* (11-12-92, Freemn/Fine Art, #10), plate 15½ x 23 in., (39.4 x 58.4 cm.), hand colored engraving (BP 144, DM 349, FR 1176, Y 27,278).

$101 *"Ipswich-Weighing", "Newmarket-Training", "Epsom-Running" and "AscotHeath-Preparing To Start": A Set Of Four,* engraved T. Sutherland, (10-09-92, G.A. Key, #147), 8¼ x 25 in., (21 x 63.5 cm.), colored print (BP 60, DM 150, FR 510, Y 12,317).

$4662* *The Leicestershire Covers (S.p. 60; L., II, p. 44), 1824: Set Of Four,* by Thomas Sutherland, pub. S. and J. Fuller, trimmed, nicks, staining, defects, (12-01-92, Christie-London, #297), averaging sheet 10⌀n x 29⌀n in., (274 x 742 mm.), colored aquatint partly p. in colors (BP 3080, DM 7431, FR 25,323, Y 580,428).

$246* *"The Leicestershire Covers", "The Meeting", "Breaking Cover", "Full Cry" and "The Death": Four,* by T. Sutherland, pub. S. and J. Fuller, 1824, margins, (06-30-93, Bonhams-Chelsea, #109), plate 10½ x 29 in., (26.7 x 73.7 cm.), hand-colored etching (BP 165, DM 420, FR 1415, Y 26,358).

$38* *"A Match At The Badger" and "Drawing The Badger": Two,* by Clark, staining, (03-03-93, Bonhams-Chelsea, #42), image 6½ x 9 in., (16.5 x 22.9 cm.), hand-colored etching (BP 26, DM 63, FR 212, Y 4440).

$2261* *"Newmarket, Training", "Ipswich, Weighing", "Epsom, Running" and "Ascot, Preparing To Start" (S.p. 58): Four,* by T. Sutherland, pub R. Ackermann, margins, spotting on image, foxing, good cond., (10-07-92, Christie-S. Ken, #56, illus.), pl 10½ x 28 in., (26.7 x 71.1 cm.), colored aquatint part p. in color (BP 1320, DM 3272, FR 11,094, Y 271,918).

$248* *Perfect Pink and A Jonquill: Two,* by J. Harris, from series One of the Flowers of our Hunt, plates 2 and 5, (11-12-92, Freemn/Fine Art, #7), each 11 x 15 in., (27.9 x 38.1 cm.), engraved, hand colored (BP 163, DM 393, FR 1325, Y 30,750).

$263* *"Pheasant Shooting", "Grouse Shooting", "Wood-Cock Shooting" and "Parridge Shooting": Four,* by James Pollard, pub. I.W. Laird, 1841, margins, time-staining, (06-30-93, Bonhams-Chelsea, #52), plate 8⅞, x 11⅞, in., (22.5 x 30.2 cm.), aquatint (BP 176, DM 449, FR 1513, Y 28,180).

$1760* *"Preparing To Start", "Whoop And Away", "Accomplished Smashers" and "The Finish", 1836: Set Of Four,* first edit., engraved J. Harris, pub. R. Ackerman, (02-12-93, DuMouchelle, #2117, illus.), engraving (BP 1239, DM 2919, FR 9877, Y 212,253).

$103* *A Promising Field,* engraving by George Hunt, (10-29-92, Bonhams-Chelsea, #123), image 16½ x 24¾ in., (41.9 x 62.9 cm.), hand colored reproduction (BP 66, DM 158, FR 538, Y 12,759).

$472 *"The Quorn Hunt", 1835: Four,* by F.C. Lewis, (06-11-93, G.A. Key, #10, illus.), 12 x 20 in., (30.5 x 50.8 cm.), hand-colored aquatint (BP 310, DM 767, FR 2586, Y 50,080).

$165* *The Right And Wrong Sort,* Fores's Hunting Sketches, (11-12-92, Freemn/Fine Art, #8), 10½ x 15½ in., (26.7 x 39.4 cm.), hand colored engravings (BP 108, DM 261, FR 882, Y 20,459).

$137 *"The Right And Wrong Sorts": Two,* engraved by J Harris, plates 2 and 5 from Fores's Hunting Sketches, (04-

16-93, G.A. Key, #87), 10 x 14 in., (25.4 x 35.6 cm.), colored aquatint (BP 90, DM 221, FR 748, Y 15,405).

$148* *"The Right Sort" and "The Wrong Sort": A Pair,* by E. Duncan, pub. R. Ackermann, 1835, (06-30-93, Bonhams-Chelsea, #111), image 15¾ x 19 in., (40 x 48.3 cm.), aquatint w/hand-coloring (BP 99, DM 252, FR 852, Y 15,858).

BI *Tattenham Corner,* est. BP 50/70, (03-03-93, Bonhams-Chelsea, #179), image 15¾ x 27¼ in., (40 x 69.2 cm.), hand-colored reproduction.

ALKEN, Henry (after)   British 1785-1851

$330* *"Fox Hunting," "Spaniels" and "Owling": Three,* by I. Clark, (10-18-92, Hindman, #508), larger 9¾ x 13½ in., (24.8 x 34.3 cm.), hand colored aquatints (BP 202, DM 491, FR 1666, Y 39,592).

$275* *The High Mettled Racer, 1821: Two,* engraved Alken and T. Sutherland, plates 3 and 5 of a set of six, (05-16-93, Hindman, #435), each 13½ x 16 in., (34.3 x 40.6 cm.), hand-colored aquatints (BP 179, DM 442, FR 1486, Y 30,484).

$358* *Untitled: Three,* from the Series Ideas, (10-18-92, Hindman, #507), each 10 x 8 in., (25.4 x 20.3 cm.), hand colored lithographs (BP 219, DM 533, FR 1807, Y 42,951).

ALKEN, Henry (after)   English 1784-1871

$330* *Tattenham Corner,* aquatint by W. Sumers, pub. 1871, (05-28-93, Sloan, #1594, illus.), (42.9 x 73.7 cm.), aquatint (BP 211, DM 523, FR 1769, Y 35,385).

ALLAN, David (after)

$1023* *"The Horse Race At Rome During The Carnival", "The Winner Conducted In Triumph", "The Opening Of The Carnival At Rome" and "The Romans Polite To Strangers": Four,* by Paul Sandby, trimmed, laid down, repaired tears, (06-16-93, Bonhams-Chelsea, #367, illus.), 13½ x 20½ in., (34.3 x 52.1 cm.), aquatint p. in sepia (BP 682, DM 1698, FR 5699, Y 109,108).

ALLAN, Ted   b. 1910

BI *Cary Grant,* 1936, p. 1981, s., d., num. AP2/10, est. BP 250/300, (12-17-92, Christie-S. Ken, #36, illus.), 13 x 10⌀, in., (33 x 26.4 cm.), photograph, gelatin silver print.

$953* *A Day At The Races,* 1937, p.l., white ink s. recto, (12-17-92, Christie-S. Ken, #34, illus.), 26 x 44 in., (66 x 111.8 cm.), photograph, gelatin silver print (BP 605, DM 1488, FR 5083, Y 117,119).

BI *Douglas Fairbanks Jnr.,* c. 1937, p.l., white ink s., est. BP 3/500, (12-17-92, Christie-S. Ken, #40, illus.), 37 x 26 in., (94 x 66 cm.), photograph, gelatin silver print on textured paper.

$659* *Groucho Marx,* 1935, p.l., white ink s. recto, (12-17-92, Christie-S. Ken, #32, illus.), 10 x 13 in., (25.4 x 33 cm.), photograph, matt gelatin silver print (BP 418, DM 1029, FR 3515, Y 80,988).

$780* *Groucho Marx,* 1935, p.l., white ink s. recto, (12-17-92, Christie-S. Ken, #33, illus.), 15¼ x 19½ in., (38.7 x 49.5 cm.), photograph, matt gelatin silver print (BP 495, DM 1218, FR 4160, Y 95,858).

$193* *Groucho Marx,* s., #100/325, (04-26-93, Selkirk, #530), 21½ x 16 in., (54.6 x 40.6 cm.), b/w photograph, litho print (BP 122, DM 303, FR 1022, Y 21,298).

$742* *Groucho Marx, Lying On Sofa, Eyes Closed Smoking A Cigar,* s., #100/325, (10-10-92, Bonhams, #21, illus.), 18 x 23 in., (45.7 x 58.4 cm.), photograph (BP 440, DM 1102, FR 3701, Y 90,334).

BI *James Stewart,* 1936, p.l., white ink s., d., est. BP 250/300, (12-17-92, Christie-S. Ken, #38, illus.), 19½ x 15⌀, in., (49.5 x 39.1 cm.), photograph, matt gelatin silver print.

BI *James Stewart,* 1936, p. 1981, s., d., num. AP2/10, est. BP 250/300, (12-17-92, Christie-S. Ken, #37, illus.), 12¾ x 10½ in., (32.4 x 26.7 cm.), photograph, gelatin silver print.

BI *Jean Harlow,* 1937, p. 1981, t., s., d., num. AP1/10, est. BP 250/300, (12-17-92, Christie-S. Ken, #41, illus.), 12¾ x 10½ in., (32.4 x 26.7 cm.), photograph, gelatin silver print.

BI *Robert Taylor,* 1936, p.l., white ink s., est. BP 250/300, (12-17-92, Christie-S. Ken, #39, illus.), 13¼ x 10¼ in., (33.7 x 26 cm.), photograph, gelatin silver print.

$433* *Spencer Tracy,* 1936, p. 1981, t., s., d. Ted Allan '81, num. AP1/10, (12-17-92, Christie-S. Ken, #35, illus.), 12¾ x 10½ in., (32.4 x 26.7 cm.), photograph, gelatin silver print (BP 275, DM 676, FR 2309, Y 53,214).

ALLARD, G.

$248* *Les Chaussons Rouges (The Red Shoes), 1948,* (01-31-93, Morelle/Marchan, #56), 47¼ x 62Æzn in., (120 x 160 cm.), poster (BP 167, DM 400, FR 1351, Y 30,938).

ALLBOK, John

$220* *King On His Throne,* photog.'s sig., t., handstamp, 1930s, (04-07-93, Swann, #391), 10½ x 11 in., photograph, silver print (BP 145, DM 356, FR 1204, Y 24,994).

ALLEN, Albert Arthur

BI *Nudes: 18 Studies,* from Allen's series "The Human Figure", 1920's, est. $350/450, (10-14-92, Swann, #528, illus.), 6 x 4 in., (15.2 x 10.2 cm.), photograph, silver prints.

ALLEN, James E. American 1894-1964

$805* *Big Bend (R. 5), 1937,* s., num. Ed 10, full margins, good cond., staining, (05-19-93, Butterfield, #1751), 11Z, x 14Mzn in., (283 x 367 mm.), lithograph on wove (BP 523, DM 1309, FR 4409, Y 89,118).

$1380* *Brazilian Builders (R. 59), 1933,* s., margins, good cond., mat stain, tape stains, glue remains, discolored, (05-13-93, Sotheby-NY, #401, illus.), 16M, x 8 in., (428 x 203 mm.), sh 19¼ x 11¼ in., (428 x 203 mm.), etching (BP 906, DM 2228, FR 7516, Y 154,069).

$2070* *The Builders (R. 62), 1933,* s., margins, good cond., mat stain, scotch tape, masking tape, (05-13-93, Sotheby-NY, #402, illus.), 9M, x 11¾ in., (252 x 300 mm.), sh 12 x 13M, in., (252 x 300 mm.), etching (BP 1359, DM 3342, FR 11,275, Y 231,104).

$100* *"The Burning Galleon" (Ryan 81),* s., very good cond., (05-15-93, Cleveland, #52), 7M\ x 15M, in., (20 x 40.3 cm.), etching (BP 65, DM 161, FR 541, Y 11,085).

$193* *"Mailboat Panama",* s., d. 37, very good cond.?, (02-07-93, Bakker, #4), plate 8¾ x 11¾ in., (22.2 x 29.8 cm.), etching (BP 134, DM 320, FR 1082, Y 24,017).

BI *Steel Workers,* s., margins, mat burn, light staining, repaired tear, surface scuffs, toning/backboard stain, tape, est. $7/900, (12-12-92, Weschler, #101), 12 x 10 in., (30.5 x 25.4 cm.), drypoint etching.

ALLOM, T. (after)

$64 *"Port Of London",* engraved by F J Havell, (04-16-93, G.A. Key, #31), 8 x 15 in., (20.3 x 38.1 cm.), hand-colored b/w engraving (BP 42, DM 103, FR 349, Y 7197).

ALLOM, Thomas (after) English 1804-1872

$66* *"Grand Temple At Poo-Too, Chusan Island" and "An Itinerant Doctor AtTien-Sing, China": Two,* (05-28-93, Sloan, #1019, illus.), each 5 x 7½ in., (12.7 x 19.1 cm.), hand colored engraving (BP 42, DM 105, FR 354, Y 7077).

ALMA-TADEMA, Sir Lawrence English 1836-1912

$143* *Classical Courtship, 1876,* s. by engraver and by Alma-Tadema, pub. Printsellers Association, (10-18-92, Hindman, #519), 18¼ x 14 in., (46.4 x 35.6 cm.), etching (BP 88, DM 213, FR 722, Y 17,157).

$110* *Isle Of Lesbos,* s., pub. 1892, (04-02-93, Sloan, #807), 17 x 32½ in., (432 x 826 mm.), chromolithograph (BP 72, DM 177, FR 600, Y 12,524).

ALMA-TADEMA, Sir Lawrence (after)

$101* *The Ill Favorite, 1986,* by Charles O. Cummings, pub. Virtue and Co. Ltd., foxing, (01-21-93, Bonhams-Chelsea, #146), image 20½ x 13¼ in., (52.1 x 33.7 cm.), etching (BP 66, DM 161, FR 543, Y 12,641).

$222* *The Ill Favourite, 1896,* by Charles O. Cummings, s. by both artists, pub. Virtue and Co. Ltd., (12-10-92, Bonhams-Chelsea, #53), image 20½ x 13¼ in., (52.1 x 33.7 cm.), etching (BP 143, DM 351, FR 1199, Y 27,462).

$118* *"The Scattering Of Flowers", 1902,* s., pub. Berlin Photographic Co., foxing, scuffing to image, (09-17-92, Bonhams-Chelsea, #175), image 12 x 19¾ in., (30.5 x 50.2 cm.), photogravure (BP 66, DM 175, FR 600, Y 14,691).

BI *The Scattering Of Flowers, 1902,* s., pub. Berlin Photographic Co., foxing, scuffing, est. BP 150/200, (07-16-92, Bonhams-Chelsea, #538), image 12 x 19¾ in., (30.5 x 50.2 cm.), photogravure.

$187* *Spring,* pub. Berlin Photographic Company, blindstamp, (04-22-93, Bonhams-Chelsea, #65), plate 39 x 19 in., photogravure (BP 121, DM 300, FR 1014, Y 20,561).

ALMAREZ, Carlos American b. Mexico 1951

BI *Bathers, 1984,* s., d., #7/25, blindstamp p. Woolf Studios, full margins, very good cond., est. $800/1,000, (10-28-92, Butterfield, #2880), 10 x 4M, in., (254 x 124 mm.), etching and aquatint on wove.

BI *Bathers, 1984,* s., d., #7/25, blindstamp printer, Woolf Studios, full margins, verygood cond., est. $8/1,000, (05-19-93, Butterfield, #2108), 10 x 4M, in., (254 x 124 mm.), etching and aquatint on wove.

$1540* *Car Crash, 1990,* s., d., num. 33/140, margins, apparently very good cond., (02-24-93, Butterfield, #2990, illus.), 18½ x 55¼ in., (47 x 140.3 cm.), lithograph in colors on wove (BP 1074, DM 2500, FR 8476, Y 180,709).

BI *The Clock Struck Three, 1989,* s., d., num. 75/120, pub. Future Perfect, apparently very good cond.,est. $2/3,000, (02-24-93, Butterfield, #2988, illus.), 36¾ x 47¼ in., (93.3 x 120 cm.), silkscreen in colors on wove.

$2750* *The Clock Struck Three, 1989,* s., d., #68/120, pub. Future Perfect, very good cond.?, (10-28-92, Butterfield, #2883, illus.), 36¾ x 47¼ in., (93.3 x 120 cm.), color silkscreen on wove (BP 1752, DM 4247, FR 14,421, Y 337,423).

BI *"Composition",* s. Almaraz, d. '86, #50/90, prov., est. $1/1,500, (12-12-92, A. James, #363), 44 x 30 in., (111.8 x 76.2 cm.), lithograph.

$1980* *Echo Park Lake,* s., annot. H/C 2/5, margins, apparently good cond., (02-24-93, Butterfield, #2989, illus.), 38 x 38 in., (965 x 965 mm.), silkscreen in colors on wove (BP 1381, DM 3214, FR 10,897, Y 232,340).

$2200* *Fool's Paradise, 1986,* s., d., #80/90, pub. Richard Duardo, Future Perfect, good cond.?, creases, (10-28-92, Butterfield, #2881), 30 x 45 in., (76.2 x 114.3 cm.), color silkscreen on wove (BP 1402, DM 3398, FR 11,536, Y 269,939).

$2200* *The Southwest Song, 1988,* s., d., #46/120, pub. Richard Duardo, Future Perfect, very good cond.?, (10-28-92, Butterfield, #2882), 34B, x 48 in., (87.9 x 121.9 cm.), color silkscreen on wove (BP 1402, DM 3398, FR 11,536, Y 269,939).

$1540* *The Struggle Of Mankind, 1989,* s., #2/80, blindstamp p. Multiples, very good cond.?, (10-28-92, Butterfield, #2884), 28½ x 37B, in., (724 x 956 mm.), color silkscreen on wove (BP 981, DM 2378, FR 8076, Y 188,957).

$1955* *Tree Of Life, 1989,* s., d., #57/90, pub. Future Perfect, very good cond.?, (05-19-93, Butterfield, #2109), 48 x 38B, in., (121.9 x 98.1 cm.), silkscreen in colors on wove (BP 1269, DM 3178, FR 10,706, Y 216,429).

ALMELOVEN, Jan van b.c. 1652, ac. 1678-83

$939* *Ansichten Von Hollandischen Ortschaften Bei Utrecht (B. 1-9, 11,12; Hollstein 1-9, 11, 12): Ten,* (12-04-92, Bassenge, #6009, illus.), etching (BP 602, DM 1495, FR 5073, Y 117,228).

ALO

$189* *Ch. De Fer De L'Etat: La Bretagne Pittoresque, "Camaret, Les Tas De Pois", c. 1934,* excell. cond., (01-23-93, Ribeyre/Baron, #49), 39Czn x 24Mzn in., (99.5 x 62 cm.), poster (BP 124, DM 301, FR 1017, Y 23,655).

$335* *Ch. De Fer Du Nord: Senlis, "Centre Unique D'Excursions Forestieres,Son Musee De La Verrerie", 1935,* excell. cond., (01-23-93, Ribeyre/Baron, #19), 39C, x 24Mzn in., (100 x 62 cm.), poster (BP 219, DM 533, FR 1802, Y 41,927).

$294* *Chemins De Fer D'Alsace Et De Lorraine: Kaysersberg,* p. Cornille & Serre, good cond., 104 x 7599 cm, (11-19-92, Ribeyre/Baron, #84), poster (BP 194, DM 469, FR 1579, Y 36,563).

$147* *P.O.: Aurillac "Les Bords De La Jordanne", 1928,* p. L. Serre, fair cond., (11-19-92, Ribeyre/Baron, #83), 62Æzn x 47¼ in., (160 x 120 cm.), poster (BP 97, DM 234, FR 789, Y 18,281).

$1038* *PLM. Chamonix Mont-Blanc. "Toutes Les Installations De Sports D'Hiver",* very good cond., (03-15-93, Arcole, #72, illus.), 41Bzn x 29Azn in., (105 x 76 cm.), (BP 723, DM 1724, FR 5861, Y 122,957).

$557* *PLM: Cie De Navigation Mixte Touache. Formentor. Ile De Majorque. Les Baleares Par Marseille, c. 1930,* very good cond., (03-13-93, Laurin, #150), 39C, x 24Mzn in., (100 x 62 cm.), (BP 389, DM 927, FR 3152, Y 65,645).

$272* *PLM: Gien, "Son Chateau, Sa Plage, Ses Vieilles Maisons", 1937,* excell. cond., (01-23-93, Ribeyre/Baron, #21), 39C, x 24Mzn in., (100 x 62 cm.), poster (BP 178, DM 433, FR 1463, Y 34,043).

$84* *Pont-Audemer Et La Basse Risle, "La Venise Normande", c. 1924,* good cond., (01-23-93, Ribeyre/Baron, #48), 41Bzn x 29½ in., (105 x 75 cm.), poster (BP 55, DM 134, FR 452, Y 10,513).

ALOE, Carlo b. 1939

BI *Quotidien, 1988,* 26/30, s., d., est. SF 150/180, (10-14-92, Germann, #476), 22¼ x 29Azn in., (565 x 760 mm.), color lithograph.

ALPERT, Max 1899-1980

$1725* *Magnitogorsk Steel Foundry, 1956,* s., t., d. by photog., (04-06-93, Sotheby-NY, #321, illus.), 19½ x 16¼ in., photograph (BP 1139, DM 2779, FR 9411, Y 196,738).

$997* *"Zaporozhie Steel Works Blast Furnace",* 1930s, s., t., num. 17, annots., t., num., (05-06-93, Christie-London, #174, illus.), 6 x 8¾ in., photograph, toned gelatin silver print (BP 632, DM 1570, FR 5286, Y 109,693).

ALSTYNE, Thelma Salina Aylma Van

BI *Rainbow Series,* s., t., d. 72, #1/25, est. C$100/150, (06-07-93, Ritchie, #50), 30 x 22 in., (76.2 x 55.9 cm.), color serigraph.

ALTARS, Meister H.L. Des Breisacher

$2214* *Der Heilige Georg Als Sieger Uber Den Drachen (Lossnitzer 13/III; Hollstein 15/III),* before 1533, (06-23-93, Kornfeld, #69, illus.), engraving (BP 1504, DM 3746, FR 12,601, Y 241,203, SF 3335).

ALTDORFER, Albrecht German c. 1480-1538

$6491* *Die "Schone Maria" Auf Dem Thron (Winz. 137/a (vc); Hollst 14), c. 191520),* early print, (06-23-93, Kornfeld, #4, illus.), engraving (BP 4410, DM 10,983, FR 36,944, Y 707,158, SF 9775).

BI *The Ascension Of Christ (B. 47; Holl. 49; W. 20),* trimmed on/within border, discoloration, est. BP 1,5/2,000, (12-03-92, Sotheby-London, #4), 8¾ x 7 in., (222 x 178 mm.), woodcut.

$455* *Beweinung (B. 32; Winzinger 57),* from the series "Sundenfall und Erlosung des Menschengeschlechtes", prov., (12-01-92, Karl/Faber, #5), woodcut (BP 301, DM 725, FR 2471, Y 56,648).

$847* *Christus Am Kreuz (Bartsch and Hollstein 30; Winzinger 55), c. 1513,* (06-10-93, Hauswedell/Nolt, #9), wood cut (BP 554, DM 1379, FR 4644, Y 89,906).

$709* *Christus In Der Vorholle (B. 34; Winz 59), 1515,* (06-08-93, Karl/Faber, #10), woodcut (BP 466, DM 1150, FR 3874, Y 75,305).

$495* *Gleiehnis Vom Barmherzigen Samariter, 1554,* (10-30-92, Sloan, #2799, illus.), 3Z, x 4ZBzn in., (7.9 x 12.5 cm.), engraving (BP 317, DM 762, FR 2584, Y 61,315).

BI *Mucius Scaevola Burning His Hand (Holl. 49; W. 157), c. 1520-1526,* 2nd final state, narrow margins, good cond., est. BP 800/1,000, (06-30-93, Sotheby-London, #70), 2½ x 1½ in., (64 x 38 mm.), engraving.

$9379* *Portrait Of Martin Luther (Holl. 80; W. 171),* c. 15mm margins, good cond., (12-03-92, Sotheby-London, #3, illus.), 2½ x 1B, in., (64 x 41 mm.), engraving (BP 6050, DM 14,749, FR 50,344, Y 1,166,978).

$6491* *Sundenfall Und Erlosung Des Menschengeschlechtes (Winzinger 25-64; Hollstein 1-40), c. 1513: Forty,* (06-23-93, Kornfeld, #3, illus.), woodcut (BP 4410, DM 10,983, FR 36,944, Y 707,158, SF 9775).

$5457* *Triton And Nereid (Holl. 46; W. 165),* narrow margins, rubbed area, good cond., ex-coll., (12-03-92, Sotheby-London, #2, illus.), 2C, x 1B\ in., (60 x 41 mm.), engraving (BP 3520, DM 8582, FR 29,291, Y 678,985).

$452* *Die Verklarung Christi (Bartsch and Hollstein 15; Winzinger 40), c. 1513,* (06-10-93, Hauswedell/Nolt, #8), woodcut (BP 296, DM 736, FR 2478, Y 47,978).

$7844* *The Virgin On The Crescent (Holl. 12; Winzinger 119),* scratches, thread margins, thin spot, good cond., (12-03-92, Sotheby-London, #1, illus.), 2¼ x 1C, in., (57 x 35 mm.), engraving (BP 5060, DM 12,335, FR 42,104, Y 975,986).

$1373* *The Virgin With The Child In A Landscape (Holl. 19; Winzinger 122),* Winzinger B impression, trimmed, restoration, edges thin, foxing, good cond., (06-30-93, Sotheby-London, #69), 6½ x 4½ in., (165 x 114 mm.), engraving (BP 920, DM 2342, FR 7900, Y 147,112).

BI *The Virgin With The Child On An Altar (B. 13; Holl. 14; Winzinger 137), 1520,* narrow margins, trimmed irregularly, paper disturbance, ex. coll. Dr. F. Winzinger (Lugt 2600a), est. BP 2/3,000, (06-29-93, Sotheby-London, #2, illus.), 2¼ x 1½ in., (5.7 x 3.8 cm.), engraving.

ALTENBOURG, Gerhard 1926-1989

$1862* *Ariadne, 1973,* s., d., t., num. light-staining, (09-25-92, Granier, #2735), 16≽zn x 27Czn in., (42 x 69.1 cm.), sheet 22Mzn x 30¼ in., (42 x 69.1 cm.), color woodcut on wove Arches (BP 1087, DM 2760, FR 9333, Y 224,744).

$619* *"Aufschweigender Grund, Voller Gnaden", 1980,* blindstamp, s., mono. Altenbourg GA, i., d. #20/20, ded., (09-14-92, Venator/Hansten, #2431), plate 8Zzn x 10Mzn in., (20.5 x 26.5 cm.), chalk lithograph on paper (BP 327, DM 920, FR 3118, Y 76,971).

$1372* *Der Barmherzige Samariter, 1949,* autograph, t., mono., d., (11-28-92, Schoppmann, #351), 13≽zn x 14≽zn in., (34.5 x 37 cm.), lithograph on framed handmade (BP 906, DM 2186, FR 7420, Y 170,753).

$1328* *Berge, 1962,* s., t., artist's proof, d., artist's proof, (12-05-92, Bassenge, #7007), 5M, x 15ZZzn in., (15 x 39.8 cm.), lithograph watercolored in blue on wove (BP 832, DM 2070, FR 7056, Y 164,540).

$738* *Dort Oben Der Kleine Jesaja, 1967,* t., s., num., (12-05-92, Bassenge, #7010), 14>zn x 9Mzn in., (37 x 24 cm.), lithograph (BP 462, DM 1151, FR 3921, Y 91,438).

$1561* *Ei, Ei Es War Am Siebten Mai, 1978,* s., mono., t., d., num., (06-05-93, Bassenge, #5862), 10¼ x 12B, in., (26 x 32 cm.), woodcut on hand-made (BP 1028, DM 2531, FR 8530, Y 167,453).

$1277* *Erloste Landschaft, 1976,* s., t., d., num., blindstamp, (06-05-93, Bassenge, #5861), 9Zzn x 24ZZzn in., (23 x 63 cm.), woodcut on strong hand-made (BP 841, DM 2070, FR 6978, Y 136,988).

$1033* *Erzgebirgiges, 1968,* artist's proof, t., s., num., (12-05-92, Bassenge, #7011), 7M, x 11Mzn in., (20 x 29 cm.), lithograph on tan (red color) handmade (BP 647, DM 1611, FR 5489, Y 127,989).

$582* *Flocken, Minuten: Aufdammern Der Nacht, 1970,* s., d., t., num., (09-25-92, Granier, #2734), 14B\zn x 14ZZzn in., (37.9 x 37.3 cm.), color woodcut on wove (BP 340, DM 863, FR 2917, Y 70,247).

$1254* *Geschnabelt Waren Sie, 1973,* t., s., num., artist's blindstamp, (12-05-92, Bassenge, #7006), 8¼ x 14Gzn in., (21 x 36 cm.), color woodcut on Fabriano (BP 785, DM 1955, FR 6663, Y 155,371).

$1106* *Das Gesicht Der Dammerung, 1965,* t., s., num., (12-05-92, Bassenge, #7009), 7M, x 11 in., (20 x 28 cm.), lithograph on thin cardboard (BP 693, DM 1724, FR 5877, Y 137,034).

$310* *Grafik Ausstellung Schloss Hinterglauchau, 1976,* s., d., mono., wear, (09-25-92, Granier, #2736), 13Mzn x 21¾ in., (34.2 x 55.3 cm.), sheet 31ZBzn x 22B, in., (34.2 x 55.3 cm.), color offset print (BP 181, DM 460, FR 1554, Y 37,417).

$1135* *Heraufgeholt Aus Dem Garsblickenden Schweigen Des Pilgrims, 1982,* s., i., d., num., blindstamp, (06-05-93, Bassenge, #5863, illus.), 9≽zn x 7≽zn in., (24.3 x 19.2 cm.), etching on copper print (BP 747, DM 1840, FR 6202, Y 121,755).

$738* *Herr Brummbaeer In Seelisches Leid Verstrickt, 1970,* t., s., num., artist's blindstamp, (12-05-92, Bassenge, #7012), 16Z, x 11Mzn in., (41 x 29 cm.), lithograph (BP 462, DM 1151, FR 3921, Y 91,438).

$1623* *Im Zauberkreis Der Circe, 1970,* t., s., num., (12-05-92, Bassenge, #7005), 15Zzn x 7½ in., (38.2 x 19 cm.), woodcut on handmade (BP 1016, DM 2530, FR 8624, Y 201,090).

$853* *Komm Albertine, 1970,* s., d., t., num., traces mounting, (09-25-92, Granier, #2733), 14Zzn x 10B, in., (37.6 x 27 cm.), woodcut on grey-green machine hand-made (BP 498, DM 1264, FR 4276, Y 102,957).

$659* *"Lobpreis Von Wanderung Erfullt", 1970,* blindstamp, #70/100, t., d., s., (11-13-92, Kunsthaus, #354), 14Mzn x 7M in., (36.6 x 20 cm.), color woodcut on werkdruckpapier (BP 426, DM 1035, FR 3489, Y 81,792).

$1038* *"Lobpreis: Von Wunderung Erfullt", 1970,* s., d., t., (12-01-92, Karl/Faber, #312), 13Zzn x 8Zzn in., (35.5 x 20.5 cm.), color woodcut on hand-made (BP 686, DM 1654, FR 5638, Y 129,233).

$1770* *Nicht Doch Meerlinchen, 1969,* t., d., num., s., from the portfolio Schulz, Leipzig, (12-05-92, Bassenge, #7004, illus.), 8Zzn x 16zn in., (22 x 42 cm.), color woodcut (BP 1108, DM 2760, FR 9405, Y 219,304).

$885* *Sieh An: Die Grosse Pappel Da , 1985,* t., s., num., artist's blindstamp, (12-05-92, Bassenge, #7013), 10B, x 14Zzn in., (27 x 38 cm.), lithograph on copper print paper (BP 554, DM 1380, FR 4702, Y 109,652).

$1612* *"Das Sind Die Wege Wurzelentlang", 1974,* blindstamp, #6/206, t., d., s., (11-13-92, Kunsthaus, #356), 16Zzn x 27C, in., (43 x 69.5 cm.), woodcut on handmade board (BP 1042, DM 2531, FR 8534, Y 200,074).

$851* *Unaussprechlich, 1963,* s., t., num., blindstamp, (06-05-93, Bassenge, #5866), 12C, x 8¼ in., (31.5 x 21 cm.), lithograph on hand-made (BP 560, DM 1380, FR 4650, Y 91,289).

BI *"Von Erinnerung Zu Erinnerung, Ach Servilia", 1967,* blindstamp, #101/150, t., d., s., est. DM 800, (11-13-92, Kunsthaus, #353), 12 x 8Zzn in., (30.5 x 22 cm.), color lithograph on werkdruckbutten.

$1254* *Waldiges, 1962,* t., s., num., artist's blindstamp, (12-05-92, Bassenge, #7008), 11Mzn x 18Z, in., (29 x 46 cm.), lithograph on smooth (BP 785, DM 1955, FR 6663, Y 155,371).

$1475* *Du Willst Es Wagen?, 1959,* s., t., d., num., artist's blindstamp, (12-05-92, Bassenge, #7003), 18½ x 5½ in., (47 x 14 cm.), woodcut on handmade (BP 924, DM 2300, FR 7837, Y 182,753).

$346* *Wurzel - Melencolia, 1971,* s., d., num., t., blindstamp, (05-26-93, Dorling, #2513), 17Zzn x 13zn in., (45 x 34.5 cm.), color lithograph on handmade von (by) "Ingres Cover-Fabriano" (BP 224, DM 565, FR 1900, Y 37,592).

$645* *Wurzel-Melencolia, 1971,* s., d., t., blindstamp, #7/150, (05-27-93, Lempertz, #555), 25zn x 19Zzn in., (65 x 50 cm.), lithograph on wove (BP 413, DM 1035, FR 3488, Y 69,147).

ALTMAN, Harold American b. 1924

$198* *Afternoon Shadows, 1983,* s., #24/285, (05-16-93, Hindman, #653, illus.), 25¼ x 18 in., (64.1 x 45.7 cm.), color lithograph (BP 129, DM 318, FR 1070, Y 21,949).

$39* *Monceau,* s., #162/185, (06-11-93, Freemn/Fine Art, #2), 6¾ x 10¾ in., (17.1 x 27.3 cm.), color lithograph (BP 26, DM 63, FR 214, Y 4138).

$358* *Rue Mouffetard, 1984 II, 1984,* s., t., i., artist's proof, blindstamp, good cond., (05-22-93, Weschler, #161, illus.), 9¼ x 13½ in., (23.5 x 34.3 cm.), lithograph in colors on Arches (BP 232, DM 582, FR 1958, Y 39,471).

$330* *September 1982,* s., t., num. 106/285, (05-22-93, Weschler, #162), 12½ x 9¼ in., (31.8 x 23.5 cm.), lithograph in colors on Arches (BP 214, DM 537, FR 1805, Y 36,384).

$165* *"Walking Man",* annot., s., #144/150, s. Altman, (05-15-93, Dunning, #215), 19 x 25 in., (48.3 x 63.5 cm.), aquatint and etching in color (BP 107, DM 265, FR 892, Y 18,291).

ALTOBELLI, Gioacchino and Pompeo MOLINS

BI *"Pyramid Of Cestius", "View From The Monte Pincio", "The Forum", "The Chruch Of Trinita Dei Monti With The Spanish Steps": Four,* 1860s, mounted on card, ink credit stamp, t., lit., est. BP 6/800, (05-06-93, Christie-London, #51, illus.), photograph, albumen print.

ALTOON, John American 1925-1969

$55* *2183,* s., d. 68, #13/20, prov., (05-16-93, Hindman, #614), 22 x 30 in., (55.9 x 76.2 cm.), color lithograph (BP 36, DM 88, FR 297, Y 6097).

ALTZENBACH, Gerhard b. 1609

$1558* *Die Vier Elemente: Four,* (06-04-93, Bassenge, #5008), each approx. 4 x 5Czn in., (10.2 x 13.2 cm.), engraving in oval (BP 1031, DM 2530, FR 8528, Y 168,033).

ALVA 1901-1973

BI *"Six Lithographs", 1949: Six,* s., frontispiece num., London, St. George's Gallery, 1949, est. DM 3/400, (11-28-92, Grisebach, #403, illus.), 21zn x 14¾ in., (53.5 x 37.5 cm.), lithograph on slightly grey cardboard.

ALVAR 20th cent.

$138* *Woman With Bird And Fruit,* s., #94/200, (06-11-93, Freemn/Fine Art, #3), 25¾ x 20 in., (65.4 x 50.8 cm.), lithograph (BP 91, DM 224, FR 756, Y 14,642).

ALVAR, Sunol Spanish b. 1935

$275* *"Barcelona Suite",* edit. #89/185, (09-18-92, DuMouchelle, #2306), 24½ x 18 in., (62.2 x 45.7 cm.), color lithograph (BP 158, DM 412, FR 1410, Y 34,264).

$303* *"Musica De Tempo",* s., edit. #106/150, (09-18-92, DuMouchelle, #2305), 19¼ x 28½ in., (48.9 x 45.7 cm.), color lithograph (BP 174, DM 454, FR 1554, Y 37,752).

ALVAREZ American 20th cent.

$5* *Untitled,* (05-15-93, Cleveland, #446), etching in colors w/embossing (BP 3, DM 8, FR 27, Y 554).

ALVAREZ, Mabel American 1891-1985

$138* s., d. 1931, (11-10-92, Moran, #157), sight 7½ x 10 in., (19.1 x 25.4 cm.), lithograph on paper (BP 91, DM 221, FR 748, Y 17,177).

$193* *"Nudes Above The Sea",* s. Mabel Alvarez, edit. of 20, (11-10-92, Moran, #156), sight 13 x 11 in., (33 x 27.9 cm.), lithograph on paper (BP 128, DM 309, FR 1046, Y 24,023).

AMAN-JEAN, Edmond

$748* *Femme A La Rose, 1900,* stone s., margins, good cond., foxing, mat staining, tape remains, surface soiling, creases, (05-19-93, Butterfield, #1875), 9 x 13Zzn in., (229 x 348 mm.), lithograph on Chine colle (BP 486, DM 1216, FR 4096, Y 82,807).

BI *Mme. Moreno, 1900,* s., margins, good cond., foxing, surface soiling, buckling, hinge remains, skinned/thinned area in image, est. $6/800, (05-19-93, Butterfield, #1877), 13½ x 15 in., (343 x 381 mm.), lithograph in colors on Japan colle.

$805* *La Rieuse, 1900,* s., #13/90, margins, good cond., foxing, surface soiling, (05-19-93, Butterfield, #1876, illus.), 17¼ x 14¼ in., (438 x 362 mm.), lithograph in colors on heavy wove (BP 523, DM 1309, FR 4409, Y 89,118).

AMAN-JEAN, Edmond French 1860-1935

BI *Head Of A Woman, 1900,* s. Aman Jean; d. label verso, good cond.?, est. $1/1500, (09-11-92, Skinner, #17, illus.), sight 15 x 18C in., (38.1 x 46.7 cm.), lithograph in color on paper.

AMANO, K. Japanese 20th cent.

$110* *Birds,* s., also in image, d. 1962-12, i. in Japanese, num. (u) 3/50, (09-20-92, Hindman, #734), 22¾ x 14 in., (53.3 x 38.1 cm.), color woodcut (BP 64, DM 163, FR 558, Y 13,595).

AMANO, Kunihiro Japanese b. 1929

BI *Flying Cranes,* s., est. $2/400, (05-16-93, Hindman, #396), 13 x 23 in., (33 x 58.4 cm.), color woodcut.

AMARTRO-VALERIO

$85* *In The Space,* (12-10-92, Christie-S. Ken, #77), sheet 9Bzn x 11Mzn in., (237 x 291 mm.), wood engraving (BP 55, DM 134, FR 459, Y 10,515).

AMBRAS, Victor

BI *Wandsworth Bridge,* s., t., d. 1960, est. BP 30/50, (07-16-92, Bonhams-Chelsea, #408), image 16 x 23 in., (40.6 x 58.4 cm.), lithograph in colors.

AMBROGIANI, Pierre French 1907-1985

$124* *"Paysage De Provence - Le Faucheur",* #30/170, s., (10-18-92, Pescheteau, #73), 14Zzn x 11 in., (38 x 28 cm.), lithograph on wove (BP 75, DM 183, FR 622, Y 14,806).

AMELIN, Albin Swedish 1902-1975
$2340* *Blomsterstilleben,* s., #199/200, 1965-1981, (05-25-93, AB Stockholm, #2), 33Yzn x 23B, in., (84 x 60 cm.), lithograph in colors (BP 1517, DM 3811, FR 12,829, Y 255,766, SK 3410).
$584* *Blomsterstilleben,* s. 1954, 7/360, (12-04-92, AB Stockholm, #7001), 27⅜n x 20M, in., (70 x 53 cm.), lithograph in colors (BP 375, DM 930, FR 3155, Y 72,909, SK 3960).
$584* *Blomsterstilleben, 1954,* s., 7/360, (12-04-92, AB Stockholm, #7001), 70 x 53 in., (177.8 x 134.6 cm.), color lithograph (BP 375, DM 930, FR 3155, Y 72,909, SK 3960).

AMEN, Irving American b. 1918
$110* *Portrait,* s., d. 1965, very good cond.?, (02-07-93, Bakker, #217), image 21 x 16 in., (53.3 x 40.6 cm.), color woodcut (BP 76, DM 182, FR 617, Y 13,688).

AMENOFF, Gregory American b. 1948
$154* *Final Hours, 1986,* s., t., d., num. 39/40, pub. Diane Cillani Editions, full sheet, excell. cond., (09-19-92, Christie-E, #76), sheet 37 x 38¼ in., (940 x 972 mm.), lithograph in colors on wove (BP 89, DM 231, FR 790, Y 19,188).
$605* *"In The Fifth Season", 1983,* pub. Diane Villani Editions, s., t., d. Amenoff 83, num. p.o. 1/3, very good cond., (09-11-92, Skinner, #114, illus.), sight 36C, x 32 in., (92.4 x 81.3 cm.), color woodcut on Sekishu paper (BP 313, DM 871, FR 2960, Y 74,960).
$220* *El Santuario De Chimayo, 1986,* s., t., d., num. 39/40, pub. Diane Villani Editions, full sheet, excell. cond., (09-19-92, Christie-E, #77, illus.), sheet 37 x 38¼ in., (940 x 972 mm.), lithograph in colors on wove (BP 127, DM 329, FR 1128, Y 27,411).

AMERICAN SCHOOL, 19TH CENTURY
BI *"The Late Fire In Duane Street, New York",* t., i. Worcester & Co. w/in matrix, good cond.?, puncture w/in image, creasing, est. $3/500, (03-27-93, Skinner, #209A), sight 8¾ x 6 in., (22.2 x 15.2 cm.), hand-colored wood engraving on paper.
BI *"Pump And Fire Engine Works Of Rumsey & Co., Seneca Falls, N.Y., U.S.A.",* s. Ferguson, ident. w/in matrix, good cond.?, fox marks, creasing, est. $3/500, (03-27-93, Skinner, #210), sight, sheet 23½ x 17 in., (59.7 x 43.2 cm.), wood engraving and letter press on paper.

AMERO, Emilio
BI *Where,* s., full margins, good cond., surface soiling, creases, est. $4/500, (02-24-93, Butterfield, #2661), 12C x 10¼ in., (314 x 260 mm.), lithograph on cream wove.

AMICI, Domenico
$522* *Views Of Rome And The Surroundings, 1835/36: Thirty-Three Plates,* from the series, watermarked, full margins, defects, time stained, foxed, (10-27-92, Phillips-London, #2), 8B, x 11C, in., (219 x 289 mm.), etching w/engraving on wove (BP 330, DM 800, FR 2715, Y 63,853).

AMIEL, Leon, Publisher
$150* *Homage To Wassily Kandinsky (Du Mont 106, 124, 146, 203), 1975: Four,* book, special issue of Vingtieme Siecle Review, covers slightly warped, staining, very good cond., (11-30-92, Phillips-London, #440), sheet 12¼ x 9½ in., (311 x 241 mm.), woodcut on wove, one in color (BP 99, DM 239, FR 811, Y 18,668).

AMIET, Cuno Swiss 1868-1961
$709* *Bahnhof Buffet, Basel, 1921,* tears, creases, losses, lit., (02-04-93, Christie-S. Ken, #41, illus.), 50 x 35½ in., (127 x 90.2 cm.), color lithograph (BP 495, DM 1167, FR 3959, Y 88,195).
$5858* *Giovanni Giacometti Beim Lesen (Von Mandach 25), 1907,* s. C. Amiet, (06-25-93, Kornfeld, #19, illus.), image 10B, x 9¼ in., (27 x 23.5 cm.), sheet size 20C, x 14⅜n in., (27 x 23.5 cm.), woodcut on Japan (BP 3962, DM 9973, FR 33,589, Y 620,946, SF 8855).
BI *Haslital (Mandach 81), 1927,* 154/300, s., d., est. SF 180/250, (10-14-92, Germann, #478), 12Zzn x 16⅜n in., (323 x 420 mm.), lithograph.
BI *Im Hinterstock (Mandach 84), 1927,* 154/300, s., d., est. SF 180/250, (10-14-92, Germann, #479), 12Zzn x 16⅜n in., (323 x 420 mm.), lithograph.
$993* *Die Kunst (Mandach 50), 1912,* s., d., (06-23-93, Kornfeld, #162), color lithograph (BP 675, DM 1680, FR 5652, Y 108,182, SF 1495).
$1451* *Kunsthaus Zurich 9. Marz - 9. April 1922 (Mand 117), 1922,* poster, (06-23-93, Kornfeld, #164), 50C, x 35Mn in., (128 x 90 cm.), color lithograph (BP 986, DM 2455, FR 8258, Y 158,078, SF 2185).

AMKER, Lufv 20th cent.
$53* *Untitled,* E.A. VII/X, s., (01-28-93, Pescheteau, #193), 24Mzn x 17Z⅛n in., (62 x 45 cm.), lithograph on wove (BP 35, DM 84, FR 284, Y 6581).

AMMAN, Jost 1539-1591
$1165* *Wenzel Jamnitzer, Goldsmith And Mathematician In His Study, (Andr., Holl. 6), c. 1570,* trimmed, foxmarks, good cond., (12-01-92, Christie-London, #193), S. 6¾ x 10Yzn in., (171 x 256 mm.), etching (BP 770, DM 1857, FR 6328, Y 145,045).

ANCELIN, Charles (after)
$358* *Horse Racing: Ten,* pub. Galerie Lutetia, surface dirt, good cond., (10-07-92, Christie-S. Ken, #55), subject 11¾ x 19 in., (29.8 x 48.3 cm.), pochoir process (BP 209, DM 518, FR 1757, Y 43,055).

ANCOURT, Edward
$281* *Manege Grouls and Cie. Lecons, Pension, Dressage, c. 1890,* Paris, Lith. F. Appel, cond. B+, (06-11-93, Boisgirard, #39), 35Yzn x 25 in., (89 x 63.5 cm.), poster (BP 185, DM 457, FR 1540, Y 29,814).

ANDERSEN, Mogens
$202* *Komposition,* s. M.A., 79/120, (03-24-93, Kunsthallen, #10), color lithograph (BP 137, DM 330, FR 1123, Y 23,734, DK 1265).
$147* *Komposition,* s. M.A., 14/135, (03-24-93, Kunsthallen, #11), color lithograph (BP 100, DM 240, FR 817, Y 17,272, DK 920).
$128* *Komposition, 1961,* s. Mogens Andersen 61, 224/300, (03-24-93, Kunsthallen, #9), color lithograph (BP 87, DM 209, FR 712, Y 15,039, DK 805).
$209* *Untitled,* s. 76, 17/200, (09-29-92, B. Rasmussen, #266), lithograph in colors (BP 117, DM 295, FR 1007, Y 24,949, DK 1150).
$293* *Untitled,* s., 20/100, (09-29-92, B. Rasmussen, #267), lithograph in colors (BP 165, DM 414, FR 1412, Y 34,977, DK 1610).

ANDERSON, Clarence William American 1891-1972
$130* *"Citation" and "Early Speed": Two,* both s., t., pub. AAA, taped to mats, mat stains, (05-15-93, Cleveland, #53), lithograph (BP 85, DM 209, FR 703, Y 14,411).
$55* *"New England Night",* s. C.W. Anderson, very good/good cond., (11-21-92, Bakker, #131), 9M, x 13C, in., (25.1 x 34 cm.), lithograph (BP 36, DM 88, FR 295, Y 6840).

ANDERSON, Domenico 1854-1939
BI *Castel Sant'Angelo, Rome,* photog. bindstamp, 1860s, est. $800/1,200, (04-07-93, Swann, #223), 15½ x 21 in., photograph, albumen print.
$1725* *"Photographs Of Rome": Thirty-Six,* album of mammoth-plate studies, mounted, some t., num. in neg., (04-06-93, Sotheby-NY, #54, illus.), 16 x 21½ in., photograph, albumen print (BP 1139, DM 2779, FR 9411, Y 196,738).

ANDERSON, J.S.
$2998* *Motorists Prefer Shell, 1935,* p. Waterlow and Sons, ref. #430, cond. 1, creased, (10-13-92, Phillips-London, #96, illus.), 29Bzn x 45⅜n in., (76 x 114.4 cm.), color lithograph (BP 1746, DM 4392, FR 14,923, Y 363,526).
$555* *To Visit Britain's Landmarks, Bond's Folly, Dorset, 1937,* ref. #480, cond. 1, (10-13-92, Phillips-London, #119), 29Bzn x 45 in., (76 x 114.3 cm.), color lithograph (BP 323, DM 813, FR 2763, Y 67,297).

ANDERSON, John Corbet
$515* *Caffyn, Born At Reigate, Surrey, Feb. 2nd, 1828,* p. R. Black, margins, foxing, surface dirt, (10-29-92, Bonhams-Chelsea, #15), image 11B, x 7M, in., (29.5 x 20 cm.), lithograph w/hand coloring (BP 330, DM 792, FR 2688, Y 63,793).

ANDERSON, Katharine M.
$660* *Mighty Lak'A Rose, c. 1927,* s. on mount, s., t., exhib. data, (10-13-92, Christie-NY, #110, illus.), 6 x 7¾ in., (15.2 x 19.7 cm.), photograph, platinum print (BP 384, DM 967, FR 3285, Y 80,029).

ANDERSON, Laurie American b. 1947
BI *"Hello", 1983,* s. Hello from Laurie Anderson in red felt pen w/in image, num. 113 in red, very good cond., est. $150/250, (09-11-92, Skinner, #123, illus.), approx. sight 10¼ x 16 in., (26 x 40.6 cm.), silkscreen on paper.

ANDERSON, Marian American 20th cent.
$77* *"Mountain Man With Game Birds",* s., #745/750, (02-27-93, Dunning, #22), 24½ x 16¾ in., (62.2 x 42.5 cm.), offset lithograph (BP 54, DM 127, FR 430, Y 9090).

ANDERSON, Morgens b. 1906
$32* *"Composition 1960",* s., (01-28-93, Pescheteau, #63), lithograph on wove (BP 21, DM 51, FR 172, Y 3973).

ANDERSON, P. Douglas 1887-1964
$2875* *Calla Lily, early 1930's,* mounted, s., i. A.R.P.S. by photog., studio stamps, labels, stamps, (04-06-93, Sotheby-NY, #187, illus.), 12Z, x 10Z, in., photograph (BP 1899, DM 4632, FR 15,685, Y 327,897).
$330* *Chinatown, San Francisco Street Towers, c. 1926,* photog.'s sig., notations, (04-07-93, Swann, #392, illus.), 11¼ x 7¼ in., photograph, Platinum print (BP 218, DM 534, FR 1806, Y 37,491).
BI *Marbles, mid-1930's,* mounted, s., i. A.R.P.S. by photog., studio stamps, labels, stamps, est. $2/3,000, (04-06-93, Sotheby-NY, #186, illus.), photograph.
BI *Towers Of Finance, San Francisco, c. 1926,* s. on overmat, t., est. $2/3,000, (10-13-92, Christie-NY, #109, illus.), 13C, x 8C, in., (34 x 21.3 cm.), photograph, gelatin silver print.
BI *Water Gully Formations, California, c. 1933,* s. on mount w/penciled border, t., exhib. stamps and labels, lit., est. $2/3,000, (10-13-92, Christie-NY, #108, illus.), 9¾ x 7½ in., (24.8 x 19.1 cm.), photograph, toned gelatin silver print.

ANDERSON, Stanley English b. 1884
$279* *Le Marche Falaise,* s., t. in pen and ink, i. Edition 60 proofs, full margins, good cond., (10-27-92, Phillips-London, #229), plate 7½ x 10½ in., (191 x 267 mm.), drypoint on wove (BP 176, DM 428, FR 1451, Y 34,128).
$330* *Untitled: A Pair,* s., ed. 60, ed. 50, very good cond.?, (03-28-93, Bakker, #135), one 8¼ x 6 in., (21 x 15.2 cm.), other 7¾ x 6 in., (21 x 15.2 cm.), wood engraving (BP 222, DM 538, FR 1830, Y 38,408).

ANDERSON, William (after)
$471* *A View Of Waterloo Bridge, 1811,* by W. Dubourg, pub. W. Anderson, trimmed, tear, defects, (01-21-93, Bonhams-Chelsea, #144), image 17 x 32 in., (43.2 x 81.3 cm.), aquatint w/handcoloring (BP 308, DM 749, FR 2534, Y 58,949).

ANDO HIROSHIGE Japanese 1797-1858
BI *Ichikawa Danjuro VII,* Chuban, aizuri-e, s. Hiroshige hitsu, d. Bunsei 11 (1828)? or early Tempo period (c. 1828-1836)?, trimmed, top corners repaired, laid down, Prof. H.R.W. Kuhne Coll., est. BP 4/500, (06-11-93, Sotheby-London, #425), 9 x 6B, in., (22.9 x 16.8 cm.), woodblock.
BI *The Theatre Model Decorations At The Front Of Shibai-chaya,* from the series Toto Meisho, s. Hiroshige ga, d. c. Kaei 1-2 (1849-50), pub. Sanoya Kihei, censor's seals, center fold mark, margin trimmed, renewed, Prof. H.R.W. Kuhne Coll., est. BP 5/700, (06-11-93, Sotheby-London, #420, illus.), woodblock.
BI *The Theatre Streets Of Edo: Two,* 1 from the series Toto Meisho; 2nd from the series Edo Meisho; both s. Hiroshige ga, pub.'s mark Kikakudo (Sanoya Kihei), & Marujin (cut off), d. Tenpo 3-10 (1833-39) & Kaei 6-Ansei 1 (1853-54), soiled, rubbed, margins, trimmed, Prof. H.R.W. Kuhne Coll., est. BP 700/1,000, (06-11-93, Sotheby-London, #426), one 10 x 14½ in., (25.4 x 36.8 cm.), other 9 x 14 in., (25.4 x 36.8 cm.), woodblock.
$840* *Upstairs Room Of A Shibai-chaya Overlooking The Theatres In Sarawakamachi,* from the series Edo Meisho, Oban yoko-e, s. Hiroshige ga, pub. Yamadaya Shojiro, d.

Ansei 5 (1858), Prof. H.R.W. Kuhne Coll., (06-11-93, Sotheby-London, #419, illus.), 9M, x 14B, in., (25.1 x 37.1 cm.), woodblock (BP 552, DM 1365, FR 4603, Y 89,125).
$665* *View Of The Saruwakacho Street At Night,* from the series Meisho Edo Hyakkei, Oban tate-e, s. Hiroshige ga, pub. Uoya Eikichi, d. Ansei 3 (1856), late edit., trimmed, browned, laid down, Prof. H.R.W. Kuhne Coll., (06-11-93, Sotheby-London, #424), 13¾ x 9Z, in., (34.9 x 23.2 cm.), woodblock (BP 437, DM 1081, FR 3644, Y 70,557).

ANDRADE, Edna American 20th cent.
$72* *Abstract Design In Silver And Black,* s., d. '75, num. 31/200, (11-12-92, Freemn/Fine Art, #13), 25 x 25 in., (63.5 x 63.5 cm.), screen print (BP 47, DM 114, FR 385, Y 8927).

ANDRE, Rogi (Rosa Klein) 1905-1970
$3300* *Pablo Picasso, c. 1935,* s.; s, i, by Picasso, credit & reprod. limit., lit., (10-13-92, Christie-NY, #254, illus.), 15B, x 11½ in., (39.7 x 29.2 cm.), photograph, gelatin silver print (BP 1922, DM 4834, FR 16,426, Y 400,146).

ANDREANI, Andrea c. 1546-1623
BI *Christus Zu Tisch Bei Simon, Dem Pharisaer (Bartsch XII 40, 17 II), 1609,* after Raphael, est. DM 4,500, (06-10-93, Hauswedell/Nolt, #10, illus.), chiaro scuro woodcut in 3 blocks.
$2833* *La Femme En Meditation (B. XII, 148, 14; Meyer, Allgem. Kunstler-Lexikon, I, 35), 1591,* after Alessandro Casolano, watermark, (06-04-93, Bassenge, #5010, illus.), 11¼ x 8Bn in., (28.5 x 21.1 cm.), chiaroscuro woodcut on 4 blocks (BP 1874, DM 4601, FR 15,506, Y 305,544).
$9437* *The Triumph Of Julius Caesar (B. XII, 11 (1-9)): Set Of Nine,* complete, after Andrea Mantegna, strong embossing, trimmed, repairedtear, hole, stained, rubbed, Ex. coll. Brentano-Birckenstock, (06-30-93, Sotheby-London, #71), chiaroscuro woodcut, p. from 4 blocks in black, mushroom and ochre (BP 6325, DM 16,096, FR 54,298, Y 1,011,143).

ANDREINI, J.
$154* *Nitidor, 1900,* Armanino, B cond., fold marks, fraying, creasing, scuffing, color loss, (08-06-92, Swann, #37, illus.), 39¼ x 27 in., (99.7 x 68.6 cm.), (BP 80, DM 228, FR 768, Y 19,643).

ANDRESON, Carlos
$22* *"Home Port",* AAA, s., t., (02-11-93, Boos, #405), 9Zn x 12Zn in., (250 x 325 mm.), lithograph (BP 16, DM 36, FR 123, Y 2652).

ANDREW-POWER
$2203* *Wimbledon, 1933,* p. Waterlow and Sons, good cond., lit., (11-19-92, Ribeyre/Baron, #126), 39>n x 24Zn in., (100.5 x 63 cm.), poster (BP 1450, DM 3512, FR 11,831, Y 273,971).

ANDREWS, Benny
$412* *"Moving On" and "Black Bird", 1980: Two,* s., creases, (05-27-93, Swann, #14), 30 x 22 in., (76.2 x 55.9 cm.), color lithograph (BP 264, DM 661, FR 2228, Y 44,168).

ANDREWS, Sybil b. 1898
$3410* *Bringing In The Boat (Redfern Gallery Catalogue 10), c. 1933,* s., t., #44/60, margins, good cond., tape at tips, creasing, taped tomount, (12-03-92, Sotheby-London, #167, illus.), sheet 14B\ x 12 in., (371 x 305 mm.), linocut in colors on fine Japan (BP 2200, DM 5362, FR 18,304, Y 424,288).
BI *Christ's College, Cambridge,* s., t., prov., est. C$4/600, (05-10-93, Hodgins, #315), 9 x 6 in., (22.9 x 15.2 cm.), etching on paper.
$260* *Christ's College, Cambridge,* s., t., prov., (05-10-93, Hodgins, #123, illus.), 9 x 6 in., (22.9 x 15.2 cm.), etching on paper (BP 170, DM 418, FR 1409, Y 29,054, C$ 330).
BI *Christ's College, Cambridge,* s., t., prov., est. C$4/600, (11-16-92, Hodgins, #350), 8Zn x 5Bn in., (22.9 x 15.2 cm.), etching on paper.
$303* *King Henry VII's Chapel, West Minster Abbey,* #30/40, s., t., prov., (11-16-92, Hodgins, #49), 12 x 7Zn in., (30.5

x 20.3 cm.), etching on paper (BP 199, DM 483, FR 1628, Y 37,814, C$ 385).

$303* *King's School Ely*, s., t., prov., (11-16-92, Hodgins, #289), 8⅞n x 5⅞n in., (22.9 x 15.2 cm.), etching on paper (BP 199, DM 483, FR 1628, Y 37,814, C$ 385).

$304* *Manoir De Formeville, Lisieux*, #40/40, t., (05-10-93, Hodgins, #261, illus.), 9 x 11¾ in., (22.9 x 29.8 cm.), etching on paper (BP 198, DM 488, FR 1648, Y 33,970, C$ 385).

$260* *The Old Steelyard, Woodbridge*, s., t., prov., (11-16-92, Hodgins, #227), 8⅞n x 5⅞n in., (22.9 x 15.2 cm.), etching on paper (BP 171, DM 415, FR 1397, Y 32,447, C$ 330).

$1299* *Rock*, #16/60, s., t., prov., (11-16-92, Hodgins, #132, illus.), 8½ x 9½ in., (21.6 x 24.1 cm.), 4 color linocut on paper (BP 854, DM 2072, FR 6980, Y 162,112, C$ 1650).

BI *Rue Malpalu, Rouen*, #60/60, s., t., est. C$4/600, (05-10-93, Hodgins, #167, illus.), 10 x 8 in., (25.4 x 20.3 cm.), etching on paper.

$390* *Rue Malpalu, Rouen*, #59/60, s., t., prov., (11-16-92, Hodgins, #154), 10 x 7⅞n in., (25.4 x 20.3 cm.), etching on paper (BP 256, DM 622, FR 2096, Y 48,671, C$ 495).

$295* *Scholar's Lane, Stratford On Avon*, T/P Edition of 13 s., t., i. "No. 1 T.P", prov., (05-10-93, Hodgins, #39), 10 x 8 in., (25.4 x 20.3 cm.), etching on paper (BP 192, DM 474, FR 1599, Y 32,965, C$ 374).

$1415* *Tumulus (W. 36), 1936*, s., t., #27/60, margins, excellent cond., (12-01-92, Christie-London, #301), L. 13¾ x 9⅝n in., (350 x 240 mm.), linocut in colors on cream Japan (BP 935, DM 2255, FR 7686, Y 176,170).

$260* *Untitled*, prov., (11-16-92, Hodgins, #168), 9 x 5⅜n in., (22.9 x 15.2 cm.), etching on paper (BP 171, DM 415, FR 1397, Y 32,447, C$ 330).

ANDRIESSE, Emmy   1914-1953
$1100* *Foto '37, 1937*, lit., (10-13-92, Christie-NY, #277, illus.), 32¾ x 23½ in., (83.2 x 59.7 cm.), photograph, photo-offset lithography (BP 641, DM 1611, FR 5475, Y 133,382).

ANDRIESSE, Eric
$192* *Flowers*, s., #6/50, full sheet p. to edges, good cond., (05-27-93, Sotheby-Amstrdm, #531), sh 19½ x 25ℂ in., (495 x 645 mm.), colored silkscreen on wove (BP 123, DM 308, FR 1038, Y 20,583, G 345).

ANDRY-FARCY
$273* *Exposition Internationale Grenoble. Houille, Blanche Et Tourisme, 1925*, p. Generale, creases, good cond., (11-19-92, Ribeyre/Baron, #127), 45⅞n x 31ℤ in., (116 x 79 cm.), poster (BP 180, DM 435, FR 1466, Y 33,951).

ANGELL, Lydia Becker
$39* *"Through The Arches, Madame John's Legacy"*, s., t., num., plate mark, Groves' Coll., (10-16-92, Neal, #38), 5 x 6𝕄 in., (12.7 x 17.5 cm.), etching (BP 24, DM 58, FR 196, Y 4657).

ANGOSAGLO, Luke   b. 1895
$440* *"Boy"*, s. in syllabics, num., d., ident. 35/44, 1970, Angasaglo Amarook, blindstamped, Baker Lake (Sanavik) cooperative symbol, very good cond., creases, foxing, prov., (06-26-93, Skinner, #60, illus.), 25½ x 19¾ in., (64.8 x 50.2 cm.), black stone cut (BP 295, DM 748, FR 2519, Y 46,684).

$550* *"Woman"*, t., num., d., s. 4/43, 1972 Angerhadlug Tavinig, blindstamped, BakerLake (Sanavik) Cooperative symbol, very good cond., prov., (06-26-93, Skinner, #72, illus.), 32 x 25 in., (81.3 x 63.5 cm.), stone cut and stencil in yellow, red and black (BP 368, DM 935, FR 3148, Y 58,355).

ANGUETIN
$4169* *Photographie Des Couleurs*, p. Camis, creases, repairs, defects, backed on linen, (05-07-93, Christie-S. Ken, #132, illus.), 74 x 48¾ in., (188 x 123.8 cm.), color lithograph (BP 2640, DM 6591, FR 22,211, Y 459,040).

ANIKEEFF, Sybil
$2300* *Selected Images: Group Of Thirty-Seven*, s. by photog., (04-06-93, Sotheby-NY, #174, illus.), various sizes to

9¾ x 7¾ in., photograph (BP 1519, DM 3705, FR 12,548, Y 262,318).

ANINGRNIQ, Phillipa   b. 1944
$385* *"Spirit With Animals"*, #44/50, s. in syllabics, d. 1963, blindstamped, good cond., stained,soiling, prov., (06-26-93, Skinner, #84, illus.), 12½ x 17½ in., (31.8 x 44.5 cm.), black stonecut (BP 258, DM 654, FR 2204, Y 40,849).

ANNAN, James Craig   1864-1946
$748* *"Old Gitana, Granada"*, 1870, s., t., (05-23-93, Butterfield, #3298, illus.), 7¾ x 5ℂ, in., photograph, photogravure (BP 487, DM 1223, FR 4117, Y 82,679).

$2575* *"A Snake Charmer, Tangier"*, *"Blind Musician, Granada"*, *"Scene On A Mountain Road, Outside A Posada"* and *"Old City Walls, Toledo"*, Early 1900s: Four, each s., t., (10-29-92, Christie-London, #86, illus.), image, smallest 4½ x 7 in., (11.4 x 17.8 cm.), image, largest 8 x 4¾ in., (11.4 x 17.8 cm.), photograph, photogravures on tissue, mounted in paper folders (BP 1650, DM 3962, FR 13,439, Y 318,964).

ANNAN, Thomas   Scottish 1829-1877
BI *Broad Close, No. 167 High Street*, 1872, est. $800/1,200, (04-07-93, Swann, #103, illus.), 11 x 9 in., (27.9 x 22.9 cm.), photograph, carbon print.

BI *"The Fountain At Hamilton Palace"*, n.d., 1860s, ink i. w/p. t. on mount, est. BP 2/300, (10-29-92, Christie-London, #32), 13½ x 16¼ in., (34.3 x 41.3 cm.), photograph, albumen print mounted on card.

$1271* *"Old Closes And Streets Of Glasgow"*, including *"2. Trongate, From Tron Steeple"*, *"3. High Street, From The Cross"*, *"5. Close, No. 37 High Street"*, *"11. Close, No. 115 High Street"* and Three Others, 1868-77: Seven Plates, mounted on card, between 275 x 225mm and 300 x 460mm, (05-07-93, Sotheby-London, #91), photograph, albumen print (BP 805, DM 2009, FR 6771, Y 139,947).

ANON PHOTOS
$2588* *2nd U.S. Colored Light Artillery Regiment, Battery A* (Images of War III, p. 237), 1864, mounted, (04-06-93, Sotheby-NY, #8, illus.), 5¼ x 7¼ in., photograph, oval albumen print (BP 1709, DM 4169, FR 14,119, Y 295,164).

$605* *Across The Atlantic Via Zeppelin Movie Still*, c. 1925, typed legend, (10-13-92, Christie-NY, #326, illus.), 7¼ x 9½ in., (18.4 x 24.1 cm.), photograph, gelatin silver print (BP 352, DM 886, FR 3011, Y 73,360).

$660* *Advertising Photographs For The Cruise Ships Vulcania And Saturnia: Twenty-Three*, photog.'s credit, 1930's, (10-14-92, Swann, #371, illus.), 10½ x 13½ in., (26.7 x 34.3 cm.), photograph, silver prints mounted on linen (BP 387, DM 966, FR 3275, Y 79,981).

$99* *Arturo Toscanini*, (01-15-93, DuMouchelle, #1551), photograph (BP 65, DM 162, FR 547, Y 12,481).

$770* *Asian Woman*, modern seal, 1850s, (04-07-93, Swann, #146, illus.), photograph, sixth-plate daguerrotype, hand-tinted, leather case (BP 509, DM 1245, FR 4215, Y 87,480).

$1870* *Assassination Of Martin Luther King*, 1968, notations, (10-14-92, Swann, #299, illus.), 5½ x 8½ in., (14 x 21.6 cm.), photograph, silver print (BP 1098, DM 2737, FR 9280, Y 226,612).

$165* *Astrid, Queen Of Belgium (1934-35)*, (09-17-92, Swann, #21), 3½ x 5½ in., (8.9 x 14 cm.), photograph, sepia (BP 93, DM 245, FR 838, Y 20,543).

$730* *Austellung Fur Amateur-Photographie, Interlaken 1908*, p. Wassermann & Schaublin Basel, fold, B.M., (05-07-93, Christie-S. Ken, #84, illus.), 28 x 71 in., (71.1 x 180.3 cm.), color lithograph (BP 462, DM 1154, FR 3889, Y 80,379).

$330* *Babe Ruth With Fans*, news agency handstamp, 1935, p.l., (04-07-93, Swann, #288, illus.), 7½ x 9 in., photograph, silver print (BP 218, DM 534, FR 1806, Y 37,491).

$550* *Baden-Powell, Robert, 1st Baron, Wearing Scout Uniform With Hat And All His General's Service Ribbons*, s. Baden Powell of Gilwell/Chief Scout, (09-17-92, Swann, #39), 3ℂ, x 5 in., (8.6 x 12.7 cm.), photograph, sepia (BP 309, DM 817, FR 2795, Y 68,476).

$1320* *Beatles After "Capture" of Buckingham, 1965,* label, (10-14-92, Swann, #283, illus.), 8 x 10 in., (20.3 x 25.4 cm.), photograph, silver print (BP 775, DM 1932, FR 6551, Y 159,961).

$1725* *Beatles Autographed Photograph, Sgt. Pepper's Lonely Hearts Club Band, c. 1967,* autographs, (06-23-93, Sotheby-NY, #377, illus.), 15 x 16 in., photograph (BP 1172, DM 2919, FR 9818, Y 187,929).

$330* *Ben-Gurion, David, late 1960's,* s. in Hebrew, (09-17-92, Swann, #35), oblong 4to image 7 x 8½ in., (17.8 x 21.6 cm.), photograph (BP 185, DM 490, FR 1677, Y 41,086).

$660* *Bespactacled, Goateed, Eutopean Gentleman, Holding His Watch Chain InOne Hand And A Journal Or Pamphlet In The Other,* late 1850s, (04-07-93, Swann, #151, illus.), photograph, half-plate daguerrotype (BP 436, DM 1067, FR 3612, Y 74,983).

$935* *Boy And His Dog,* 1850s, (04-07-93, Swann, #128, illus.), photograph, 6th plate daguerreotype (BP 618, DM 1512, FR 5118, Y 106,226).

$660* *Boy On Crutches,* 1860s, (04-07-93, Swann, #133, illus.), photograph, 6th plate daguerreotype (BP 436, DM 1067, FR 3612, Y 74,983).

$1540* *Brooklyn Bridge,* calligraphic t. in red ink, 1880's, (10-14-92, Swann, #213, illus.), 10 x 13½ in., (25.4 x 34.3 cm.), photograph, albumen print (BP 904, DM 2254, FR 7643, Y 186,621).

$308* *C. Early 1860s Street Scene From Martin's Gallery Views In Minnesota, "Red-River Dog Train",* label, yellowing, soiling, surface abrasion, excell. cond., (10-31-92, Riba, #56, illus.), 5¾ x 8 in., (14.6 x 20.3 cm.), albumen photograph (BP 201, DM 484, FR 1637, Y 38,081).

$660* *Chaplin, Charles, 1936,* i., tear, creases, (09-17-92, Swann, #59, illus.), approx. 7¾ x 9¾ in., (19.7 x 24.8 cm.), photograph (BP 371, DM 980, FR 3354, Y 82,171).

$835* *China, An Album Of One Hundred And Fifty Four, c. 1900,* each t., each approx. 150 x 200mm, (05-07-93, Sotheby-London, #37), photograph, gelatin silver print (BP 529, DM 1320, FR 4449, Y 91,940).

BI *Chinese Street Scene, 1880's,* est. $6/800, (11-16-92, Butterfield, #5836, illus.), 10½ x 7B, in., (267.2 x 194 mm.), photograph, albumen print.

$2090* *Churchill, Roosevelt, And Stalin At Yalta, 1945,* (10-14-92, Swann, #358, illus.), 8 x 10 in., (20.3 x 25.4 cm.), photograph, silver print (BP 1227, DM 3059, FR 10,372, Y 253,272).

$6050* *Clemens, Samuel (Mark Twain),* s., i. twice, surface rubbing, (10-31-92, Riba, #197, illus.), overall 10½ x 8 in., (26.7 x 20.3 cm.), photograph (BP 3956, DM 9498, FR 32,164, Y 748,022).

$770* *Close-Up Image Of Standing Zouave With Rifle,* surface abrasions, excell. cond., (10-31-92, Riba, #92, illus.), photograph, 1/4 plate tintype (BP 503, DM 1209, FR 4094, Y 95,203).

$385* *Close-Up Of Seated Confederate Soldier,* tarnish, scratches, excell. cond., (10-31-92, Riba, #82, illus.), photograph, 1/2 plate tintype (BP 252, DM 604, FR 2047, Y 47,601).

$330* *Close-Up Scene Of Pvt. William Wright On His Horse,* excell. cond., (10-31-92, Riba, #91, illus.), photograph, 1/4 plate tintype (BP 216, DM 518, FR 1754, Y 40,801).

$275* *Confederate Soldier With Sword,* (11-21-92, Goldberg, #621, illus.), photograph, tintype (BP 181, DM 438, FR 1477, Y 34,200).

$2750* *Confederate Spy, Rose O'Neal Greenhow, Outdoor View Og "The Wild Rose", Greenhow Standing Outside A White Clapboard House With Her Daughter And Other Family Members,* label verso, image w.lacquer loss, (10-31-92, Riba, #64, illus.), photograph, 1/2 plate ambrotype (BP 1798, DM 4317, FR 14,620, Y 340,010).

$550* *Confederate Va. Vol. With Pistol Tucked In His Belt, Sword, Dragoon Equipment, Etc.,* tarnish, excell. cond., (10-31-92, Riba, #77, illus.), photograph, 1/6 plate ambrotype (BP 360, DM 863, FR 2924, Y 68,002).

$581* *Country Scene With Trees Masking Building, And Five-Bar Gate, 1850s,* 246 x 289mm, (05-07-93, Sotheby-London, #55), photograph, waxed paper neg. (BP 368, DM 919, FR 3095, Y 63,973).

$121* *Cross-Eyed Gentleman,* thermoplastic case, 1850s, (04-07-93, Swann, #148), photograph, quarter-plate ambrotype, hand-tinted (BP 80, DM 196, FR 662, Y 13,747).

$605* *Cross-Eyed Woman,* 1850s, (04-07-93, Swann, #134, illus.), photograph, 6th plate daguerreotype (BP 400, DM 978, FR 3311, Y 68,734).

$247* *Crystal Palace (?) Interior,* 1860s, (04-07-93, Swann, #127), photograph, 6th plate daguerreotype (BP 163, DM 399, FR 1352, Y 28,062).

$275* *D.W. Griffiths,* s. by sitter, d. 1/11/1922, (10-24-92, DuMouchelle, #3010), approx. 8 x 10 in., (20.3 x 25.4 cm.), photograph, b/w (BP 174, DM 424, FR 1438, Y 33,606).

$605* *Dapper Young Boy Holding An Accordion,* 1850s, (04-07-93, Swann, #136, illus.), photograph, 6th plate daguerreotype, hand-tinted (BP 400, DM 978, FR 3311, Y 68,734).

$4400* *David Bronson, Cigar-Peddler, In Vermont, c. 1850,* quarter-plate, (10-15-92, Sotheby-NY, #1, illus.), photograph, quarter plate daguerreotype (BP 2692, DM 6550, FR 22,211, Y 527,894).

$7700* *Dentist Extracting Tooth,* minor tarnish, sealed, (10-31-92, Riba, #1, illus.), photograph, 1/4 plate daguerreotype (BP 5034, DM 12,088, FR 40,936, Y 952,028).

BI *Detention Room, Ellis Island,* handstamps, label, c. 1920's, est. $3/500, (10-14-92, Swann, #337), 7¾ x 9½ in., (19.7 x 24.1 cm.), photograph, silver print.

$9* *Dick Powell,* s. by sitter, (10-24-92, DuMouchelle, #3013), approx. 8 x 10 in., (20.3 x 25.4 cm.), photograph, b/w (BP 6, DM 14, FR 47, Y 1100).

$22* *Dick Powell,* s. by sitter, head shot, (10-24-92, DuMouchelle, #3023), approx. 11 x 14 in., (27.9 x 35.6 cm.), photograph, b/w (BP 14, DM 34, FR 115, Y 2689).

$1320* *Double Image Of Man Photographed From Shoulders Up By A Camera Equipped With A Rotary Plate Holder,* minor tarnish, sealed, (10-31-92, Riba, #3, illus.), photograph, 1/6 plate daguerreotype (BP 863, DM 2072, FR 7018, Y 163,205).

$138* *Douglas Fairbanks,* s. by sitter, d. 1920, 3/4 shot, (10-24-92, DuMouchelle, #3019), approx. 13½ x 10½ in., (34.3 x 26.7 cm.), photograph, b/w (BP 88, DM 213, FR 722, Y 16,864).

BI *Dr. Goebbels, At Geneva Conference For Disarmament, With Herr Von Keler And The Minister Of Propaganda, 1933,* news agency's caption, est. $4/600, (04-07-93, Swann, #339, illus.), 6½ x 8½ in., photograph, silver print.

$635* *Early AIrplanes, c. 1915-1920: Forty-Three,* album, t., each approx. 158 x 193mm, (05-07-93, Sotheby-London, #207, illus.), photograph, silver print (BP 402, DM 1004, FR 3383, Y 69,919).

$412* *Edward VIII, King Of England, 1940,* s. Wallis Windsor, Edward/Duke Of Windsor/1940, d., (09-17-92, Swann, #95), 4 x 5M, in., (10.2 x 14.9 cm.), photograph (BP 231, DM 612, FR 2093, Y 51,295).

$308* *Eisenhower, Dwight D., 1953,* s., soiling, excell. cond., (10-31-92, Riba, #151), 10 x 8 in., (25.4 x 20.3 cm.), photograph, silver print (BP 201, DM 484, FR 1637, Y 38,081).

$1045* *Engineer Corps, 12th N.Y.S.M., Camp Anderson, 1860s,* handwritten caption on orig. mount recto, (04-07-93, Swann, #170, illus.), 11 x 14 in., photograph, Albumen print (BP 691, DM 1690, FR 5720, Y 118,723).

BI *The Erection Of A Dry Dock Along An Indian River, 1870-1872: Forty-Four,* album, notations on mount recto, est. $1/1,500, (04-07-93, Swann, #218), 9 x 11½ in., photograph, albumen print.

$302* *European Scenes Including Animals, Bathers, Games, Scenic Views, Ports, Venice, Marie Antoinette's Bedroom, And Classical Ruins In Athens: Twenty-Nine,* pinholes and/or hand-colored, 1860s, (04-07-93, Swann, #262), photograph, stereograph (BP 200, DM 488, FR 1653, Y 34,310).

$429* *"Execution At Kowloon", 1891: Two,* negs. t., d., (10-29-92, Christie-London, #57), each 7¾ x 10C\ in., (19.7 x 26.4 cm.), photograph, albumen prints mounted on card (BP 275, DM 660, FR 2239, Y 53,140).

BI *Family Of Four Posed On A Rustic Settee, With Niagara Falls In Background,* emulsion loss or scratching, est. $4/

600, (10-31-92, Riba, #23, illus.), photograph, whole plate ambrotype.

$990* *Female Nudes: Forty-Seven,* studio insignias, numerical notations in neg., 1890s, (04-07-93, Swann, #243), 3¼ x 5¼ in., photographic postcards, silver prints and printing-out pa (BP 654, DM 1601, FR 5419, Y 112,474).

$357* *First Communion Portrait Of A Girl In Her Confirmation Dress HoldingThe Bible, And Her Younger Sister, Who Is Also Dressed In White And Standing Next To A Large Candlestick Decorated With Flowers,* 1870s, (04-07-93, Swann, #269), approx. 2½ x 1½ in., photograph, tintype (BP 236, DM 577, FR 1954, Y 40,559).

$715* *"First Congregational Church, Harwich, Massachusetts",* (07-10-92, Skinner, #340, illus.), photograph, half plate ambrotype (BP 371, DM 1069, FR 3598, Y 88,875).

$660* *Floridian Landscape With Cypress And Palm Trees, c. 1900,* Haberle-tones label, (10-14-92, Swann, #219, illus.), 10 x 11½ in., (25.4 x 29.2 cm.), photograph, oro-tone (BP 387, DM 966, FR 3275, Y 79,981).

$453* *Four Modernist Studies, Skater From High Vantage Point, Hand Cracking A Walnut, And Two Studies Of Machinery,* 1930s, largest 299 x 231mm, smallest 247 x 195mm, (05-07-93, Sotheby-London, #226, illus.), photograph, silver print (BP 287, DM 716, FR 2413, Y 49,879).

$20,900* *Frederick Douglass,* remnants of orig. seal and additional vintage seal, Douglass clippedsig. attached to red velvet lining, late 1840s, (04-07-93, Swann, #129, illus.), photograph, 6th plate daguerreotype (BP 13,812, DM 33,802, FR 114,395, Y 2,374,460).

$660* *Frost, Robert, October 1961,* i., (09-17-92, Swann, #117, illus.), image 6℃, x 9℃, in., (16.2 x 23.8 cm.), photograph (BP 371, DM 980, FR 3354, Y 82,171).

$418* *Full-Length Standing Confederate SC Soldier, Sword At Side,* orig. paper label under coverglass, Wearn & His Artists, Columbia, SC, scattered spots, excell. cond., (10-31-92, Riba, #80, illus.), photograph, 1/4 plate tintype (BP 273, DM 656, FR 2222, Y 51,682).

$357* *Gandhi, Mohandas K. ("Mahatma"), c. 1930,* s. M.K. Gandhi, (01-28-93, Swann, #108, illus.), 4 x 3 in., (10.2 x 7.6 cm.), photograph (BP 236, DM 566, FR 1914, Y 44,326).

$4355* *The Gardens Of The Villa Albani,* 1850s, t. in French in later hand, lit., (05-06-93, Christie-London, #48, illus.), 9M, x 7¾ in., photograph, light albumen print from paper neg. (BP 2760, DM 6859, FR 23,091, Y 479,151).

$17* *Gene Autry, Cowboy,* s. by sitter, trimmed, (10-24-92, DuMouchelle, #3022), approx. 14 x 10 in., (35.6 x 25.4 cm.), photograph, b/w (BP 11, DM 26, FR 89, Y 2077).

$357* *General MacArthur Signing Terms Of Japanese Surrender, 1945,* handstamps, label, (10-14-92, Swann, #359, illus.), 8 x 10 in., (20.3 x 25.4 cm.), photograph, silver print (BP 210, DM 522, FR 1772, Y 43,262).

$330* *General View Of Gymnastics In Czechoslovakia,* handstamp, notations, 1930's, (10-14-92, Swann, #303, illus.), 7 x 5 in., (17.8 x 12.7 cm.), photograph, silver print (BP 194, DM 483, FR 1638, Y 39,990).

$3300* *Gershwin, George, c. 1929,* i., creasing, (09-17-92, Swann, #126), oblong 4to 8 x 10 in., (20.3 x 25.4 cm.), photograph, silver print (BP 1853, DM 4899, FR 16,768, Y 410,857).

$1045* *Girl Standing Beside Chair, Holding Large French Doll,* hand-tinted, sealed, oxidized around mat, (10-31-92, Riba, #4, illus.), photograph, 1/4 plate daguerreotype (BP 683, DM 1641, FR 5556, Y 129,204).

$1180* *"Graf Zeppelin", 1929: Thirty-Four,* in card wallet, each 165 x 120mm, (05-07-93, Sotheby-London, #230, illus.), photograph, silver print (BP 747, DM 1866, FR 6287, Y 129,927).

$495* *Group Of Nurnberg Firemen With Extension Ladders, 1869,* label, (04-07-93, Swann, #208, illus.), 13½ x 17 in., photograph, albumenized salt print(?) (BP 327, DM 801, FR 2709, Y 56,237).

$76* *Group Of Seven Exhibition, 1920: Two,* i. in Thoreau MacDonald's hand, d. 1920, prov., (06-07-93, Ritchie, #5, illus.), 8 x 10 in., black and white photographs (BP 50, DM 123, FR 415, Y 8153, C$ 97).

$302* *Groves, Major General Leslie R., c. 1945-46,* s., (09-17-92, Swann, #22), approx. 4½ x 5℞, in., (11.4 x 14.3

cm.), photograph (BP 170, DM 448, FR 1535, Y 37,600).

$121* *"Harry Truman Takes Oath Of Office As President Of The United States"and "President Truman At His Desk", 1945: Two,* news agency's caption, (04-07-93, Swann, #363), each 4½ x 6½ in., photograph, silver print (BP 80, DM 196, FR 662, Y 13,747).

$935* *Heavily Armed Georgia Soldier With Pistols, Bowie Knife, Bayonet, And A Captured Yankee Battle Flag Worn In Turban Style On His Head,* tarnish, scratches, excell. cond., in Albaugh's More Confederate Faces, Fig. 329, (10-31-92, Riba, #74, illus.), photograph, 1/6 plate ambrotype (BP 611, DM 1468, FR 4971, Y 115,603).

$495* *Helen Keller,* d. 8/9/1913, (01-15-93, DuMouchelle, #1142, illus.), approx. 10 x 8 in., (25.4 x 20.3 cm.), photograph (BP 324, DM 809, FR 2736, Y 62,405).

$2420* *Hitler And Goebbels, 1947,* handstamp, label, (10-14-92, Swann, #360, illus.), 9 x 7 in., (22.9 x 17.8 cm.), photograph, silver copy print (BP 1420, DM 3542, FR 12,010, Y 293,262).

$6600* *Horse With Man Holding Reins, Carriage On Side, Barn In Background,* sealed, (10-31-92, Riba, #2, illus.), photograph, 1/4 plate daguerreotype (BP 4315, DM 10,361, FR 35,088, Y 816,024).

$4620* *Horse-Drawn American Express Wagon,* 1850s, (04-07-93, Swann, #141, illus.), photograph, quarter-plate daguerreotype, case (BP 3053, DM 7472, FR 25,287, Y 524,881).

$581* *"Hoyningen-Huene Photographiant Au Studio Vogue",* 1930s, s., 225 x 164mm, (05-07-93, Sotheby-London, #325, illus.), photograph, silver print (BP 368, DM 919, FR 3095, Y 63,973).

BI *Hunter Wearing A Straw Hat And Neckerchief Posing With His Dog And ADouble-Barreled Shotgun,* modern seal, 1850s, est. $7/10,000, (04-07-93, Swann, #131, illus.), photograph, half-plate daguerreotype.

$1210* *Igor Stravinsky, 1948,* (01-28-93, Swann, #230), 10 x 8 in., (25.4 x 20.3 cm.), photograph (BP 799, DM 1917, FR 6488, Y 150,236).

$1090* *India: Sixty-Two,* album, 1850s, neg. num., each approx. 190 x 240mm, (05-07-93, Sotheby-London, #32, illus.), photograph, albumen print (BP 690, DM 1723, FR 5807, Y 120,018).

$1633* *Indian Survey Album: Sixty-Nine,* possibly J. Mackenzie, majority mounted one-per-page, s. in negs., t., lit., (05-06-93, Christie-London, #78, illus.), majority approx. 8 x 6 in., three approx. 8 x 11½ in., photograph, albumen print (BP 1035, DM 2572, FR 8659, Y 179,668).

$302* *Individual Portraits, Two Of Women: Three,* 1860s, (04-07-93, Swann, #272), photograph, tintype, hand-painted whole-plate (BP 200, DM 488, FR 1653, Y 34,310).

$550* *Industrial And Scenic Views In And Around Woonsocket, Rhode Island, 1899-1903: Sixty-Four,* (04-07-93, Swann, #193, illus.), largest 4¾ x 7½ in., photograph, cyanotypes (BP 363, DM 890, FR 3010, Y 62,486).

$770* *J.P. Morgan Striking A Papparazzi,* 1920s, stamp, paper label, (10-13-92, Christie-NY, #111, illus.), 6℞, x 8℞, in., (16.8 x 20.6 cm.), photograph, gelatin silver print (BP 448, DM 1128, FR 3833, Y 93,367).

$220* *James Cagney As A Clown Leaning Up Against A Theatrical Trunk,* presumably done for "Man of a Thousand Faces", James Cagney Estate, (09-30-92, Doyle, #385, illus.), color photograph (BP 124, DM 312, FR 1055, Y 26,401).

$330* *James Cagney As A Young Boy Posing On A Stoop,* James Cagney Estate, (09-30-92, Doyle, #496), oversized 13¼ x 10½ in., (33.7 x 26.7 cm.), photograph (BP 186, DM 468, FR 1583, Y 39,602).

$1053* *Japan, An Album Of Fifty, 1880s,* t., num., each approx. 200 x 260mm, (05-07-93, Sotheby-London, #40, illus.), photograph, hand-colored albumen print (BP 667, DM 1665, FR 5610, Y 115,944).

$690* *Japan, An Album Of Fifty, 1880s,* num., t., each approx. 220 x 270mm, (05-07-93, Sotheby-London, #39), photograph, hand-colored albumen print (BP 437, DM 1091, FR 3676, Y 75,974).

$816* *Japanese Landscape, Townscape And Costume Portraits: Fifty,* 1880s-90s, album, all but 3 num., t. in negs., (05-06-93, Christie-London, #87), each approx. 8 x 10½ in., photograph, hand-tinted albumen print (BP 517, DM 1285, FR 4327, Y 89,779).

$467* *Jascha Heifetz, 1924,* i., s., d., (01-28-93, Swann, #128), 9 x 6½ in., (22.9 x 16.5 cm.), photograph (BP 308, DM 740, FR 2504, Y 57,984).

$825* *Jazz and Be-Bop Musicians, Composers, And Vocalists,* 1950s-70s, (04-07-93, Swann, #390), 10 x 8 in., photograph, 129 publicity stills, silver and vintage copy prints (BP 545, DM 1334, FR 4516, Y 93,729).

$1150* *Jimi Hendrix Photographs From Grona Lund, Stockholm, 1970: Six,* s., d., (06-23-93, Sotheby-NY, #468, illus.), each 15 x 17 in., b/w photograph (BP 781, DM 1946, FR 6545, Y 125,286).

$330* *Joe Dimaggio And Marilyn Monroe,* from wrinkled neg. damaged by Monroe, (04-26-93, Selkirk, #546), 11 x 14 in., (27.9 x 35.6 cm.), b/w photograph (BP 208, DM 517, FR 1747, Y 36,416).

$880* *Joe Lewis Boxing Max Schmeling, 1938,* 9 images on 3 sheets, (10-15-92, Sotheby-NY, #207, illus.), each image 4¼ x 5¼ in., (10.8 x 13.3 cm.), photograph, gelatin silver print (BP 538, DM 1310, FR 4442, Y 105,579).

BI *John Marin, 1946,* backed w/heavy board, s., i. by John Marin, est. $1,5/2,500, (04-06-93, Sotheby-NY, #390, illus.), 10½ x 13 in., photograph.

$715* *John Brown,* 1850s, (10-14-92, Swann, #117, illus.), photograph, ninth-plate ambrotype (BP 420, DM 1046, FR 3548, Y 86,646).

$220* *Johnson, Lyndon B., c. 1965-67,* i., (09-17-92, Swann, #157), image 6¾ x 8 in., (17.1 x 20.3 cm.), photograph (BP 124, DM 327, FR 1118, Y 27,390).

$358* *Judy Garland,* s. by sitter, (10-24-92, DuMouchelle, #3008, illus.), approx. 9 x 8 in., (22.9 x 20.3 cm.), photograph, b/w (BP 227, DM 552, FR 1872, Y 43,749).

$605* *K.K.K.'ers Loading Guns,* news agency handstamp, notations, 1930s, (04-07-93, Swann, #325, illus.), 6½ x 6 in., photograph, silver print (BP 400, DM 978, FR 3311, Y 68,734).

$440* *Klan Leader With Klan Tyke, 1948,* handstamp, label, (10-14-92, Swann, #326, illus.), 9 x 7 in., (22.9 x 17.8 cm.), photograph, silver print (BP 258, DM 644, FR 2184, Y 53,320).

$330* *Klan March On Washington, 1925,* handstamps, label, (10-14-92, Swann, #327, illus.), 8 x 10 in., (20.3 x 25.4 cm.), photograph, silver print (BP 194, DM 483, FR 1638, Y 39,990).

$715* *Knee-Up Confederate Soldier Holding A Pepper-Box Pistol And A Knife,* surface abrasions, excell. cond., (10-31-92, Riba, #81, illus.), photograph, 1/4 plate ambrotype (BP 467, DM 1122, FR 3801, Y 88,403).

$660* *Knee-Up Standing View Of Gen. Burnside With Sword And Gloves,* tarnish, excell. cond., (10-31-92, Riba, #89, illus.), photograph, 1/6 plate ambrotype (BP 432, DM 1036, FR 3509, Y 81,602).

$17,600* *The Liberty Bell Cross-Country Tour, 1915,* album of Journey Made by the Liberty Bell from Philadelphia to the Panama-Pacific Exposition in San Francisco and Back; some t. in unidentified hand, est. $2/3,000, (10-15-92, Sotheby-NY, #68, illus.), average 4½ x 6½ in., (11.4 x 16.5 cm.), photograph, gelatin silver prints (BP 10,770, DM 26,198, FR 88,844, Y 2,111,578).

$825* *Little Girl Sitting On Table, With Stuffed Dog Pull-Toy On Chair,* lightly tinted, sealed, light oxidizing, (10-31-92, Riba, #12, illus.), photograph, 1/6 plate daguerreotype (BP 539, DM 1295, FR 4386, Y 102,003).

$825* *Lizzie And Andrew Borden-From Life, c. 1890,* cabinet card format, mint condition, (10-14-92, Swann, #101, illus.), photograph, album w/34 portraits of denizens of Fall River, printing-out paper & silver prints (BP 484, DM 1207, FR 4094, Y 99,976).

$1100* *"The Lone Teepe",* t. verso, (01-09-93, Skinner, #240, illus.), image, sight 14¼ x 24½ in., (36.2 x 62.2 cm.), photograph, sepia toned (BP 708, DM 1795, FR 6098, Y 137,517).

$2640* *"Lou Gehrig And Babe Ruth, Home Run Kings", "Babe Ruth Waiting To Bat"* and *"Frank Nekala Holding A Baseball", 1929-30s: Three,* news agency's caption, (04-07-93, Swann, #289, illus.), each approx. 6 x 8 in., photograph, silver print (BP 1745, DM 4270, FR 14,450, Y 299,932).

$748* *Lucille Ball,* autographed, i., (06-23-93, Sotheby-NY, #306, illus.), 24 x 36 in., color photograph (BP 508, DM 1266, FR 4257, Y 81,490).

$660* *Lyndon Baines Johnson Being Sworn In As President,* notations, handstamp, 1963, p.l, (10-14-92, Swann, #323, illus.), 6½ x 9½ in., (16.5 x 24.1 cm.), photograph, silver print (BP 387, DM 966, FR 3275, Y 79,981).

$222* *Mae Murray, Dressed As U.S. Marshall, Holding Pistol,* (10-10-92, Bonhams, #78, illus.), 10 x 8 in., (25.4 x 20.3 cm.), mounted photograph (BP 132, DM 330, FR 1107, Y 27,027).

$77* *Mae West, As Playbill, "Sextet",* 7/18/1961, (10-24-92, DuMouchelle, #3007), photograph, (BP 49, DM 119, FR 403, Y 9410).

$880* *Man And Woman Posing With A Keyboard Instrument,* 1850s, (04-07-93, Swann, #137, illus.), photograph, 6th plate daguerreotype (BP 582, DM 1423, FR 4817, Y 99,977).

BI *Man And Woman With Board Game, 1855,* label, i. in unidentified hand, est. $10/15,000, (10-15-92, Sotheby-NY, #78, illus.), 4½ x 6 in., (11.4 x 15.2 cm.), photograph, whole plate daguerreotype.

$192* *Man With Eerily Light Eyes Posing With A Trophy,* orig. seal., 1840s, (04-07-93, Swann, #153), photograph, quarter-plate daguerreotype, leather case (BP 127, DM 311, FR 1051, Y 21,813).

$7700* *Man With Gun And Dog (Rinhart 29),* full plate, (10-15-92, Sotheby-NY, #3, illus.), photograph, full plate daguerreotype (BP 4712, DM 11,462, FR 38,869, Y 923,815).

$74* *Marge And Gower Champion With Elephants, 1955,* a still from "Jupiter's Darling", prov., (10-10-92, Bonhams, #10, illus.), 9 x 13 in., (22.9 x 33 cm.), photograph (BP 44, DM 110, FR 369, Y 9009).

BI *"Marilyn Monroe And Clark Gable On The Set Of "The Misfits""* and *"Fouteen Bottles Of Pills Were Found On A Table Near Monroe's Bed": Two,* handstamps, 1960's, p.l., 1962, est. $3/400, (10-14-92, Swann, #334), each, approx. 7½ x 8½ in., (19.1 x 21.6 cm.), photograph, silver prints.

$408* *Marilyn Monroe And Jane Russell About To Make Hand And Foot Prints Outside Grauman's Chinese Theatre,* (10-10-92, Bonhams, #158, illus.), 11 x 14 in., (27.9 x 35.6 cm.), photograph (BP 242, DM 606, FR 2035, Y 49,671).

BI *Marilyn Monroe Autographed Junior High School Class Photograph, 1941,* s. Norma Jeane Baker, i., est. $3/4,000, (06-23-93, Sotheby-NY, #294, illus.), 8 x 24¾ in., photograph.

$371* *Marilyn Monroe Boarding Aircraft, Waving,* (10-10-92, Bonhams, #155, illus.), 20 x 16 in., (50.8 x 40.6 cm.), photograph (BP 220, DM 551, FR 1850, Y 45,167).

$371* *Marilyn Monroe Emerging From Army Tank In Korea Surrounded By Thousands Of GIs Armed With Cameras,* (10-10-92, Bonhams, #157, illus.), 11 x 14 in., (27.9 x 35.6 cm.), photograph (BP 220, DM 551, FR 1850, Y 45,167).

$352* *Marilyn Monroe Leaning On Elbow In Window,* "The Seven Year Itch", (10-10-92, Bonhams, #151, illus.), 14 x 11 in., (35.6 x 27.9 cm.), photograph (BP 209, DM 523, FR 1756, Y 42,854).

$352* *Marilyn Monroe Singing At Microphone,* (10-10-92, Bonhams, #156, illus.), 11 x 14 in., (27.9 x 35.6 cm.), photograph (BP 209, DM 523, FR 1756, Y 42,854).

$371* *Marilyn Monroe Together With An Escort,* (10-10-92, Bonhams, #159, illus.), 11 x 14 in., (27.9 x 35.6 cm.), photograph (BP 220, DM 551, FR 1850, Y 45,167).

$715* *Marilyn Monroe, 1968,* rare full sheet uncut, Artist's Proof, s., images from The Last Sitting, Bel Air Hotel, 1962, (04-26-93, Selkirk, #553), 35 x 45½ in., (88.9 x 115.6 cm.), color mixed media photograph (BP 451, DM 1121, FR 3785, Y 78,901).

$165* *Marilyn Monroe, Under The Boardwalk,* blind embossed Edward Weston Coll. sig., (04-26-93, Selkirk, #540), 14 x 11 in., (35.6 x 27.9 cm.), b/w photograph (BP 104, DM 259, FR 873, Y 18,208).

BI *Marion Davies, Portrait In Feathered Hat,* autograph?, est. BP 2/300, (10-10-92, Bonhams, #86, illus.), 10 x 8 in., (25.4 x 20.3 cm.), photograph.

$779* *Marlene Dietrich,* still from "Seven Sinners", autograph, prov., (10-10-92, Bonhams, #5, illus.), 10 x 8 in., (25.4 x 20.3 cm.), photograph (BP 462, DM 1157, FR 3885, Y 94,838).

$220* *"Medford Ladder #1", c. 1912,* (07-10-92, Skinner, #343), photograph (BP 114, DM 329, FR 1107, Y 27,346).

$3450* *Member Of The 54th Massachusetts Infantry Regiment, Company I, c. 1863-1864,* half-case, quarter-plate, (04-06-93, Sotheby-NY, #7, illus.), photograph, quarter-plate ambrotype (BP 2279, DM 5558, FR 18,822, Y 393,476).

$278* *Merle Oberon, Portrait, Seated,* autograph, (10-10-92, Bonhams, #87, illus.), 10 x 8 in., (25.4 x 20.3 cm.), photograph (BP 165, DM 413, FR 1387, Y 33,845).

$357* *Mikhail Gorbachev,* (01-28-93, Swann, #113), 5½ x 4 in., (14 x 10.2 cm.), color photograph (BP 236, DM 566, FR 1914, Y 44,326).

$412* *Miller, Glenn, c. 1930's,* s. in ink, (09-17-92, Swann, #186), 4¼ x 6C, in., (10.8 x 16.2 cm.), photograph (BP 231, DM 612, FR 2093, Y 51,295).

BI *"Mining Scene; River Valley", "Thunderbolt Mine U.S.V.", "Petroglyphs", "Southwest Scene", "Wall Placque", "Sheep Farmer", "Prairie Scene", and "Jordan Marsh": Nine,* 1940's, handstamps, est. $2/3,000, (10-14-92, Swann, #568, illus.), each, approx. 3½ x 5½ in., (8.9 x 14 cm.), photograph, silver prints.

$2200* *"Moon Mosaic" (Survey Of Apollo Moon Landing), 1966-68,* 52 num. images, orig. mount reads "Day 018, Survey L, Sectors 19 and20" example of machine-made, relay-photographs taken on unmanned flight to themoon, (04-07-93, Swann, #523, illus.), overall 11 x 12 in., photograph, silver print (BP 1454, DM 3558, FR 12,042, Y 249,943).

$165* *"The Nation's Leading Exponent Of The 'Swing Trombone', c. 1938,* s., Glenn Miller, (01-28-93, Swann, #167), 5 x 7¼ in., (12.7 x 18.4 cm.), sepia photograph (BP 109, DM 261, FR 885, Y 20,487).

BI *Nearly Naked Man Sitting In A Chair,* orig. seal, 1840s, est. $1,5/2,500, (04-07-93, Swann, #154, illus.), photograph, quarter-plate daguerreotype, hand-tinted, leather case.

$770* *Neil Armstrong,* N.A.S.A., s., i., (01-28-93, Swann, #13), 8 x 10 in., (20.3 x 25.4 cm.), color photograph (BP 508, DM 1220, FR 4129, Y 95,605).

BI *Novel Subway Station In The Bronx, With D.W. Griffith Poster,* 1920's, est. $4/600, (10-14-92, Swann, #338), 6½ x 8 in., (16.5 x 20.3 cm.), photograph, silver print.

$247* *Nudes, 1925: Seventeen,* edited by Dr. Peter Landow, handstamps, notations, (10-14-92, Swann, #530), 8 x 6 in., (20.3 x 15.2 cm.), 17 photogravures after photographs (BP 145, DM 361, FR 1226, Y 29,932).

BI *"Old Peter" (Images of War I, p. 42), c. 1850-60,* resealed, cased, paper label, 6th plate, est. $3,5/5,000, (04-06-93, Sotheby-NY, #6, illus.), photograph, 6th-plate daguerreotype.

$660* *Olivier, Laurence; and Leigh, Vivien,* s. L. Olivier, Vivien Leigh, (09-17-92, Swann, #1), 8 x 10 in., (20.3 x 25.4 cm.), photograph (BP 371, DM 980, FR 3354, Y 82,171).

$1210* *Outdoor Scene Of Union Cavalry Sgt., June 1862, Full-Standing View With Horse,* spotting, lacquer loss, excell. cond., (10-31-92, Riba, #90, illus.), photograph, 1/2 plate ambrotype (BP 791, DM 1900, FR 6433, Y 149,604).

$247* *Paderewski, I.J.,* i., (09-17-92, Swann, #220), approx. 8 x 9½ in., (20.3 x 24.1 cm.), sepia photogravure (BP 139, DM 367, FR 1255, Y 30,752).

BI *Panorama Of The Roman Forum,* 1880s, est. BP 2/250, (05-06-93, Christie-London, #52), total size approx. 20¼ x 45½ in., photograph, three-part albumen print panorama.

$7475* *"Panoramic View Of Washington City", c. 1880,* 5-plate Panorama, hinges broken, orig. folio, (04-06-93, Sotheby-NY, #5, illus.), each panel 16 x 22 in., photograph, albumen print mounted on heavy board (BP 4937, DM 12,043, FR 40,780, Y 852,532).

$2760* *Pennsylvania Station, c. 1910,* (04-08-93, Christie-NY, #64, illus.), 10C, x 13½ in., (26.4 x 34.3 cm.), gelatin silver print (BP 1810, DM 4434, FR 15,008, Y 313,209).

$385* *Petain, Henri Philippe, 15 May 1936,* i. in French, d., s., (09-17-92, Swann, #225), approx. 5 x 9½ in., (12.7 x 24.1 cm.), photograph (BP 216, DM 572, FR 1956, Y 47,933).

$1430* *Photographer, Posing Alongside His Camera, 1850,* (04-07-93, Swann, #142, illus.), photograph, lightly tinted 6th plate ambrotype, case (BP 945, DM 2313, FR 7827, Y 162,463).

$605* *"Photographic Souveniers Of San Francisco", The Earthquake And Its Aftermath, 1906: Forty-One,* album, ident., oblong 4to, dampstaining, (04-07-93, Swann, #543), largest 7½ x 6 in., photograph, silver print (BP 400, DM 978, FR 3311, Y 68,734).

$330* *"Photographs Of Ceylon",* album, pub. W.L.H. Skeen & Co., num., credit in negative, most captioned on mount recto, large 4to, 1880s, (04-07-93, Swann, #168), photograph, 34 albumen prints (BP 218, DM 534, FR 1806, Y 37,491).

$6896* *Piazza Barberini,* c. 1847, lit., (05-06-93, Christie-London, #38, illus.), 7C, x 9B, in., photograph, non-matt salt print from paper neg. (BP 4370, DM 10,862, FR 36,564, Y 758,719).

$1307* *Portrait And View Album: Forty-Eight,* c. 1850 and later, i., lit., (05-06-93, Christie-London, #34, illus.), smallest 7½ x 4B, in., largest 8½ x 10B, in., photograph, 1 paper neg., 7 salt prints, 3 uncut albumen print stereos and 37 albumen prints (BP 828, DM 2059, FR 6930, Y 143,800).

$247* *Portrait Of 9-Year-Old,* 1860s, (04-07-93, Swann, #143), photograph, quarter-plate ambrotype, leather case (BP 163, DM 399, FR 1352, Y 28,062).

$1452* *Portrait Of A Black Woman,* late 1850s, (05-06-93, Christie-London, #1), sixth-plate daguerreotype, hand-tinted, gilt highlights, gilt surround w/embossed scroll design (BP 920, DM 2287, FR 7699, Y 159,754).

$363* *Portrait Of A Lady,* 1850s, trimmed corners, (05-06-93, Christie-London, #33, illus.), 6¾ x 5 in., photograph, salt print (BP 230, DM 572, FR 1925, Y 39,938).

BI *Portrait Of A Lady In Riding Habit With Hat And Crop, c. 1845,* half-plate, paper, folding morocco case, est. BP 5/700, (10-29-92, Christie-London, #2), photograph, daguerreotype.

$220* *Portrait Of A Large Family Group Including 3 Sullen Looking Children, A Smiling Matron, And A Serious Looking Gentleman In An Enormous Stove-Pipe Hat, c. 1850,* (04-07-93, Swann, #155), photograph, quarter-plate daguerreotype, hand-tinted (BP 145, DM 356, FR 1204, Y 24,994).

$247* *Portrait Of A Little Girl Wearing A Very Large Scarf On Her Head,* in thermoplastic case, 1860s, (04-07-93, Swann, #147), photograph, nine-plate ambrotypes, hand-tinted (BP 163, DM 399, FR 1352, Y 28,062).

$302* *"Portrait Of Benjamin Hill Hammaford" and "Portrait Of David O. Hammaord": Two,* 1850s, (04-07-93, Swann, #213), each approx. 11 x 9 in., photograph, oval ivorytypes, tinted in warm, amber tones (BP 200, DM 488, FR 1653, Y 34,310).

BI *Portrait Of Brevet General George V. Stannard of Vermont, c. 1864,* est. $6/900, (10-14-92, Swann, #165, illus.), photograph, salt print.

$1375* *Portrait Of Den Tillotson, Stagecoach Driver For The Bradford And Montpelier, Vermont Stage Line,* image is 1/6 plate, seals intact, label, split case in two halves, image in excellent cond., spotting, (03-27-93, Julia, #324, illus.), photograph, daguerreotype (BP 923, DM 2238, FR 7597, Y 160,631).

$357* *"Portrait Of Man With Beard", "Portrait Of Man With Sideburns" and "Portrait Of Young Man": Three,* 1850s, (04-07-93, Swann, #253), approx. 10 x 8 in., photograph, salt print, heavily tinted w/watercolor (BP 236, DM 577, FR 1954, Y 40,559).

$3190* *Portrait Of Maungwudaus, Chief, Of The Ojibway Tribe Of Pennsylvania,* 1/6 plate, excellent image, (03-27-93, Julia, #323, illus.), photograph, ambrotype (BP 2141, DM 5193, FR 17,624, Y 372,664).

$467* *Portrait Of The Graduating Class Of Rutgers Institute, c. 1850,* (04-07-93, Swann, #144, illus.), photograph, half-plate (BP 309, DM 755, FR 2556, Y 53,056).

$220* *Portraits, c. 1875: Four,* (04-07-93, Swann, #271), photograph, tintype, 2 hand-painted whole-plate (BP 145, DM 356, FR 1204, Y 24,994).

$220* *Post-Mortem Image Of Young Woman, Large Scar On Her Forehead,* surface scratches, resealed, (10-31-92, Riba, #13, illus.), photograph, 1/4 plate daguerreotype (BP 144, DM 345, FR 1170, Y 27,201).

$385* *Post-Mortem Of A Mother Cradling Her Baby,* 1860s, (04-07-93, Swann, #163), photograph, sixth-plate daguerreotype (BP 254, DM 623, FR 2107, Y 43,740).

$192* *Post-Mortem Of A Very Little Girl With A Peaceful Expression On Her Face, Holding a Delicate Wreath With Leaves And Flowers,* 1860s, (04-07-93, Swann, #162, illus.), photograph, quarter-plate ambrotype, half case (BP 127, DM 311, FR 1051, Y 21,813).

$495* *Post-Mortem Of Mother And Baby, Lying Together,* cased, excell. cond., (10-31-92, Riba, #26, illus.), photograph, 1/4 plate ambrotype (BP 324, DM 777, FR 2632, Y 61,202).

$165* *Press Photograph Of The Vanderbilts, Drexels, And Goulds: Eighteen,* news agency's handstamp, typewritten caption, 1920s, (04-07-93, Swann, #342), each approx. 6½ x 8½ in., photograph, silver print (BP 109, DM 267, FR 903, Y 18,746).

BI *Press Photographs Of John F. Kennedy, As U.S. Senator, Presidential Candidate, And President, 1953-1963: Eighteen,* handstamp, est. $2/3,000, (10-14-92, Swann, #321, illus.), 8 x 10 in., (20.3 x 25.4 cm.), photograph, silver prints.

$715* *Railroad Engineers With The Boston And Lowell Locomotive, c. 1889,* handstamp, (10-14-92, Swann, #206, illus.), 13 x 16 in., (33 x 40.6 cm.), photograph, albumen print (BP 420, DM 1046, FR 3548, Y 86,646).

$47* *Ramon Navarro,* tear, prov., (10-10-92, Bonhams, #79, illus.), 14 x 10½ in., (35.6 x 26.7 cm.), photograph (BP 28, DM 70, FR 234, Y 5722).

$440* *The Reichstag In Ruins, c. 1933,* handstamps, label, (10-14-92, Swann, #356, illus.), 8 x 10 in., (20.3 x 25.4 cm.), photograph, silver print (BP 258, DM 644, FR 2184, Y 53,320).

BI *"Rex Theatre For Colored People", "This Part Of Bus For Colored Race"and "How A Negro Travels In The Southland": Three,* F.S.A., photog.'s and/or agency's handstamps, 1930s, est. $1,5/2,500, (04-07-93, Swann, #304, illus.), largest 10 x 8 in., photograph, silver prints.

$121* *Robert F. Kennedy Autographed Photo,* s. ink, (03-14-93, Hindman, #410), 8 x 10 in., photograph (BP 84, DM 201, FR 683, Y 14,333).

BI *Ronald Colman,* still showing him at "Scene Of The Crime", est. BP 120/180, (10-10-92, Bonhams, #91A, illus.), 14 x 11 in., (35.6 x 27.9 cm.), photograph.

$167* *Ronald Colman And Vilma Banky In An Embrace,* prov., (10-10-92, Bonhams, #91, illus.), 11 x 14 in., (27.9 x 35.6 cm.), photograph (BP 99, DM 248, FR 833, Y 20,331).

$660* *Ruby-Glass Image Of A Seated Miss. Soldier With Pistol Tucked In HisBelt,* tarnish, excell. cond., (10-31-92, Riba, #78, illus.), photograph, 1/6 plate ambrotype (BP 432, DM 1036, FR 3509, Y 81,602).

$715* *Ruby-Glass Image Of Confederate Seated Cavalryman With Canteen,* in Albaugh's Confederate Faces, Fig. 391, surface abrasions, excell.cond., (10-31-92, Riba, #73, illus.), photograph, 1/6 plate ambrotype (BP 467, DM 1122, FR 3801, Y 88,403).

$715* *Rudolph Valentino,* s. by sitter, i. in green ink, (10-24-92, DuMouchelle, #3015, illus.), approx. 9 x 7 in., (22.9 x 17.8 cm.), photograph, b/w (BP 454, DM 1103, FR 3740, Y 87,376).

$357* *Russian Revolution Of 1917 And Its Aftermath, 1917-20: Fourteen,* orig. mounts, (04-07-93, Swann, #354), 6 x 8 in., photograph, silver print (BP 236, DM 577, FR 1954, Y 40,559).

BI *Russian Soldiers On A Tank, c. 1936,* reprod. limit. stamp, est. $1,5/2,500, (10-15-92, Sotheby-NY, #369, illus.), 5¾ x 7M, in., (14.6 x 20 cm.), photograph, gelatin silver print.

BI *Russian Soldiers On A Tank, c. 1936,* reprod. limit. stamp, est. $1,5/2,500, (10-15-92, Sotheby-NY, #360, illus.), 5¾ x 7M, in., (14.6 x 20 cm.), photograph,.

$549* *Sample Case Of Daguerreotypes, 1845,* rare hinged wooden sample case containing 16 9th-plate portraits, lit., (10-29-92, Christie-London, #1), photograph, daguerreotype (BP 352, DM 845, FR 2865, Y 68,004).

$2640* *Scenic, Genre, Topographic, And Architectural Views In Moscow: Twenty,* caption in Russian and French in neg., 1860s, (04-07-93, Swann, #252, illus.), each approx. 8½

x 10½ in., photograph, albumen print (BP 1745, DM 4270, FR 14,450, Y 299,932).

$522* *Schooner At Dock,* 1860s, (04-07-93, Swann, #274), photograph, tintype, hand-colored whole-plate (BP 345, DM 844, FR 2857, Y 59,305).

BI *Scottish Military Gentleman In Full Uniform, c. 1860,* est. BP 250/350, (05-07-93, Sotheby-London, #3, illus.), photograph, quarter plate ambrotype.

$440* *Seated Confederate Cavalryman Cradling A Pistol In His Lap,* excell. cond., (10-31-92, Riba, #75, illus.), photograph, 1/9 plate ambrotype (BP 288, DM 691, FR 2339, Y 54,402).

$1320* *Seated Confederate Soldiers With Rifle, Bowie Knife, Dagger, Shot Pouch, Etc.,* (10-31-92, Riba, #79, illus.), photograph, 1/6 plate ambrotype (BP 863, DM 2072, FR 7018, Y 163,205).

$495* *Seated Man Holding Violin And Bow,* (10-31-92, Riba, #7, illus.), photograph, 1/4 plate daguerreotype (BP 324, DM 777, FR 2632, Y 61,202).

$440* *Seated Man With Cornet,* tarnished, cased, (10-31-92, Riba, #8, illus.), photograph, 1/6 plate daguerreotype (BP 288, DM 691, FR 2339, Y 54,402).

$825* *Seated Uniformed Fireman With Brass Fire Horn And Helmut, "Co. X, Atlantic Foreman",* lightly hand-colored, tarnished at mat opening, sealed, (10-31-92, Riba, #5, illus.), photograph, 1/6 plate daguerreotype (BP 539, DM 1295, FR 4386, Y 102,003).

$275* *Seated Uniformed Fireman With Helmet And Belt, "D.D. Tompkin," Co. VIII,* hand-tinted, (10-31-92, Riba, #25, illus.), photograph, 1/6 plate ambrotype (BP 180, DM 432, FR 1462, Y 34,001).

BI *Shakespeare's House,* 1850s, possibly from paper neg., est. BP 4/600, (05-06-93, Christie-London, #35, illus.), 8C\ x 11 in., photograph, light albumen print.

$2722* *"Shop Windows And Interiors Bullocks Wilshire, Los Angeles Also Other Shops At Los Angeles, Hollywood, Beverly Hills And Westwood, August, 1936": Ninety-Two,* album, t., d., (05-06-93, Christie-London, #182, illus.), each approx. 7¼ x 9 in., photograph, gelatin silver print (BP 1725, DM 4287, FR 14,433, Y 299,483).

$165* *Sir Lawrence Olivier as "Henry IV",* s. by sitter, (10-24-92, DuMouchelle, #3065, illus.), photograph, b/w (BP 105, DM 254, FR 863, Y 20,164).

$330* *Sitters Are Posed With Books: Nine,* 1860s, (04-07-93, Swann, #273), photograph, tintype (BP 218, DM 534, FR 1806, Y 37,491).

BI *"Smithsonian Institute",* late 1850's, t., caption in German, unident. hand, est. $1/2,000, (04-06-93, Sotheby-NY, #3, illus.), photograph, salt print.

$352* *Soldier Assuming The "Texas" Style Sharpshooting Position With A 4570 Springfield Model Rifle, c. 1870s,* surface scratches, excell. cond., rare, (10-31-92, Riba, #107, illus.), photograph, 1/6 plate tintype (BP 230, DM 553, FR 1871, Y 43,521).

$880* *Solid-Looking Young Man Enjoying A Cigar And A Bottle Of Liquor,* modern seal, thermoplastic case, 1850s, (04-07-93, Swann, #150, illus.), photograph, sixth-plate daguerrotype, hand-tinted (BP 582, DM 1423, FR 4817, Y 99,977).

$2090* *Standing Identified Rebel Soldier, R.N. Reed, Tiller's Co., Light Artillery, Ga.,* Albaugh's More Confederate Faces, Fig. 271, excell. cond., (10-31-92, Riba, #66, illus.), photograph, 1/4 plate ambrotype (BP 1366, DM 3281, FR 11,111, Y 258,408).

BI *Starved Prisoners, At Concentration Camps At Evensee, Autstria, 1945,* est. $4/600, (04-07-93, Swann, #369, illus.), 7½ x 9½ in., photograph, silver print.

$345* *Stevie Ray Vaughan Autographed Promotional Photo, 1989,* autographs by Stevie Ray Vaughan and Double Trouble, Tommy Shannon, Chris Layton and Reese Wynans, obtained on 1989 tour, (06-23-93, Sotheby-NY, #475, illus.), 11 x 8 in., photograph (BP 234, DM 584, FR 1964, Y 37,586).

BI *Study Of A Church, c. 1850,* half plate, est. $3,5/5,000, (10-15-92, Sotheby-NY, #2, illus.), photograph, half plate daguerreotype.

BI *Summer Portrait Of A Young Girl Wearing A Lace Dress,* 1900(?), est. $1/1,500, (04-07-93, Swann, #212), 26½ x 21½ in., photograph, hand-colored silver print.

BI *Three Gentlemen Engaged In A Lively Discussion, Seated At A Very Small, Ornate Table, Two Of Them Smoking Long Clay Pipes,* 1850s, est. $6/900, (04-07-93, Swann, #165, illus.), photograph, quarter-plate ambrotype, hand-colored.

$544* *Tintern Abbey Detail,* 1850s, lit., (05-06-93, Christie-London, #36, illus.), 7B, x 6 in., photograph, salt print (BP 345, DM 857, FR 2884, Y 59,853).

$74* *Tom Mix, Standing With Clenched Fists,* (10-10-92, Bonhams, #78A, illus.), 10 x 8 in., (25.4 x 20.3 cm.), photograph (BP 44, DM 110, FR 369, Y 9009).

$660* *Tonkin, Tetes De Prisonniers, c. 1900(?),* handwritten t., (04-07-93, Swann, #301, illus.), 6½ x 4¼ in., photograph, cyanotype (BP 436, DM 1067, FR 3612, Y 74,983).

$1100* *Travel: Burma And India, 1860's,* leather album, landscapes, genre scenes, portraits of Sikkim royalty, (11-16-92, Butterfield, #6200, illus.), from 2½ x 3½ in., (63.6 x 89.1 mm.), to 8½ x 11¼ in., (63.6 x 89.1 mm.), photograph, 106 albumen prints (BP 724, DM 1754, FR 5908, Y 136,799).

$1373* *Turkoman Gentleman With Tall Hat, n.d., c. 1850,* quarter-plate, paper-taped, (10-29-92, Christie-London, #3, illus.), photograph, daguerreotype (BP 880, DM 2112, FR 7166, Y 170,073).

BI *Turkoman Lady In Decorative Costume, n.d., c. 1850,* quarter-plate, paper-taped, est. BP 8/1,200, (10-29-92, Christie-London, #4, illus.), photograph, daguerreotype.

$1210* *Two Black Men Polishing A Stove, c. 1870(?),* (10-15-92, Sotheby-NY, #13, illus.), 14Z, x 11Z, in., (35.9 x 28.3 cm.), photograph, albumen print (BP 740, DM 1801, FR 6108, Y 145,171).

BI *Two Gentlemen, 1850s,* half-plate, lightly hand-tinted, arched-top, est. BP 2/400, (10-29-92, Christie-London, #7), photograph, daguerreotype.

$3520* *Two Seated Gamblers Wearing High Hats And Smoking Stogies, One Player Holds 4 Aces And A Queen, The Other Holds 5 Face Cards, 4 Of Which Appear To Be Kings, He Also Holds A Derringer Pointed At The Other Player,* featured in History of Photography, An International Quarterly, July1978, excell. cond., (10-31-92, Riba, #22, illus.), photograph, 1/2 plate ambrotype (BP 2301, DM 5526, FR 18,713, Y 435,213).

$1760* *Two Seated Virginia Militiamen, One With Rifle, Bowie Knife, Etc.,* tarnished, excell. cond., (10-31-92, Riba, #72, illus.), photograph, 1/6 plate tintype (BP 1151, DM 2763, FR 9357, Y 217,606).

$770* *Two Seated Young Ladies, One Strums An Inlaid Mother-Of-Pearl Guitar,* sealed, excell. cond., (10-31-92, Riba, #10, illus.), photograph, 1/4 plate daguerreotype (BP 503, DM 1209, FR 4094, Y 95,203).

$275* *Two Young Men Sitting At A Small Table, One, Smoking A Cigar, Is Pointing A Pistol At His Friend, Who Is Cross-Eyed,* cased, excell. cond., (10-31-92, Riba, #24, illus.), photograph, 1/4 plate ambrotype (BP 180, DM 432, FR 1462, Y 34,001).

$825* *Uniformed Naval Engineer Casually Leaning Against A Floral Chair, c.1860,* surface scratches, rubbing, resealed, fine cond., (10-31-92, Riba, #108, illus.), photograph, 1/2 plate daguerreotype (BP 539, DM 1295, FR 4386, Y 102,003).

BI *"Vidy Mugdena I Pekina 1902" (Views Of Muckden And Peking): Fifty-Three,* possibly Aleksandr Vasil'Evich Vereshchagin, 1855-1909, mounts ink t., prov., est. BP 1/1,500, (10-29-92, Christie-London, #56, illus.), each approx. 4 x 6 in., (10.2 x 15.2 cm.), photograph, gelatin silver prints.

BI *View Of Two Panamanian Laborers Standing By A Railroad Track And Operating A Rock-Cutting Instrument,* 1870s, est. $2/300, (04-07-93, Swann, #219), approx. 8 x 10 in., photograph, albumen print.

$11,260* *Views In Lyon In: Five,* 1840s, (05-07-93, Sotheby-London, #104, illus.), photograph, whole plate daguerrotypes in daguerreotype plate box (BP 7130, DM 17,802, FR 59,989, Y 1,239,815).

BI *Vilma Banky, Portrait In Evening Dress And Fur Stole,* prov., est. BP 120/180, (10-10-92, Bonhams, #91B, illus.), 14 x 11 in., (35.6 x 27.9 cm.), photograph.

$495* *W.C. Fields,* s. by sitter, tear, trimmed, (10-24-92, DuMouchelle, #3006, illus.), approx. 7 x 9 in., (17.8 x 22.9 cm.), photograph, b/w (BP 314, DM 763, FR 2589, Y 60,491).

$660* *W.C. Handy, June 1956,* s. William C. Handy, d., (01-28-93, Swann, #124), 10 x 8 in., (25.4 x 20.3 cm.), photograph (BP 436, DM 1046, FR 3539, Y 81,947).

$247* *Wedding Album Of Tiny Tim's Marriage To Miss Vicky On N.B.C.'s The Johnny Carson Show, December 18, 1969: Twelve,* ident., (04-07-93, Swann, #343, illus.), photograph, chromagenic print (BP 163, DM 399, FR 1352, Y 28,062).

$550* *Well-Dressed Child Cradling A Doll In Her Right Arm And Holding A Book On Her Lap,* tarnished at mat opening, excell. cond., (10-31-92, Riba, #11, illus.), photograph, 1/6 plate daguerreotype (BP 360, DM 863, FR 2924, Y 68,002).

$578* *Wilbur Wright In Grant Park, 1911, Expecting Airplanes,* stamped Frederic H. Wagner verso, (09-12-92, Dunning, #220, illus.), approx. 8 x 10 in., (20.3 x 25.4 cm.), photograph (BP 299, DM 832, FR 2828, Y 71,614).

$247* *Wilson, Woodrow,* s., (09-17-92, Swann, #316), 3C, x 5C, in., (8.6 x 13.7 cm.), photograph, sepia (BP 139, DM 367, FR 1255, Y 30,752).

$467* *Winston Churchill, F.D.R., And Joseph Stalin At The Yalta Conference,1945,* U.S. Signal Corps's credit and num., Pictures for Democracy handstamp and caption, (04-07-93, Swann, #370, illus.), 7½ x 9 in., photograph, silver print (BP 309, DM 755, FR 2556, Y 53,056).

$385* *Wm. T. Sampson,* s. on image W.T. Sampson/U.S.N., (01-28-93, Swann, #214), cabinet photograph (BP 254, DM 610, FR 2064, Y 47,802).

$247* *Woman Wearing A Bonnet Wih Flowers, 1858,* (04-07-93, Swann, #152, illus.), photograph, sixth-plate daguerreotype, hand-tinted, leather case (BP 163, DM 399, FR 1352, Y 28,062).

BI *Woman With Roses, c. 1900,* est. $1/2,000, (04-06-93, Sotheby-NY, #72A, illus.), 14 x 11 in., photograph, on heavy wove.

$412* *World War I, France, 1917-1919: 250,* several ink/pencil captions, (10-29-92, Christie-London, #96), 2½ x 4¼ in., (6.4 x 10.8 cm.), and 3¼ x 4½ in., (6.4 x 10.8 cm.), photograph, gelatin silver print (BP 264, DM 634, FR 2150, Y 51,034).

$1980* *"Young Black Men At Lincoln Memorial", "James Edwards, Migratory Laboer", "Feggen Jones Resting On A Plow", "Family Vacating House" and "Negro Children Going Home From School": Five,* F.S.A., news agency's or photog.'s handstamps, 1940s, (04-07-93, Swann, #305, illus.), each approx. 7 x 9 in., photograph, silver print (BP 1308, DM 3202, FR 10,837, Y 224,949).

$660* *Young Man With Rifle And Powderhorn, Wears Wide-Brimmed Hat With Attached Flowers,* (10-31-92, Riba, #14, illus.), photograph, 1/6 plate daguerreotype (BP 432, DM 1036, FR 3509, Y 81,602).

$825* *Young Nude Woman Touching Her Left Breast,* 1850s, (04-07-93, Swann, #138), photograph, stereo daguerreotype (BP 545, DM 1334, FR 4516, Y 93,729).

$55* *A Young Woman Seated On A Gothic Chair,* (11-21-92, Goldberg, #623, illus.), photograph, daguerrotype (BP 36, DM 88, FR 295, Y 6840).

$523* *"Yuma Indians, Arizona" (Male) and "Yuma Indians, Arizona" (Female):Two,* t., ident., mounted, (01-09-93, Skinner, #54), 7¼ x 4¾ in., (18.4 x 12.1 cm.), photograph, sepia tone portraits in studio setting (BP 337, DM 853, FR 2899, Y 65,383).

$16,500* *Zachary Taylor And William W.S. Bliss (Facing The Light, pl. 21), c.1847,* half plate, (10-15-92, Sotheby-NY, #4, illus.), photograph, half plate dauguerreotype (BP 10,097, DM 24,561, FR 83,291, Y 1,979,604).

ANON PRINTS

$28* *Acrobats On Horses: Two,* (03-12-93, DuMouchelle, #2440), 7 x 8 in., (17.8 x 20.3 cm.), 7 x 6½ in., (17.8 x 20.3 cm.), b/w lithograph (BP 20, DM 47, FR 158, Y 3300).

$77* *"The Alexandrian Cioutat Grape" and "The Elton Pear": Pair,* (12-10-92, Sloan, #931), each, sight 10B, x 8½ in., (27 x 21.6 cm.), colored engravings (BP 50, DM 122, FR 416, Y 9525).

$110* *Allegory Of Time,* (03-20-93, Northeast, #220), print (BP 74, DM 180, FR 612, Y 12,760).

$83* *American Eagle, Ship, British Lion, American Flag And Other Symbols,* wear, damage, (05-21-93, Garth, #341, illus.), 5B, x 9B, in., (14.3 x 24.4 cm.), black and white copper engraving (BP 54, DM 135, FR 454, Y 9151).

$33* *Antique Bird Prints: A Pair,* (06-24-93, Boos, #349), sight 10 x 7 in., (254 x 178 mm.), hand-colored print (BP 22, DM 56, FR 190, Y 3599).

$61* *"Ass And Pigs",* pub. Edward Orme, 1804, (02-19-93, Garth, #331, illus.), 22¼ x 26¼ in., (56.5 x 66.7 cm.), handcolored engraving (BP 42, DM 100, FR 338, Y 7238).

$275* *Battle Of Gettysburg,* (11-27-92, Clearing House, #306), 17½ x 37½ in., (44.5 x 95.3 cm.), lithograph (BP 181, DM 439, FR 1492, Y 34,225).

$132* *Birds: Two,* not matching, (01-08-93, Garth, #516, illus.), one 15 x 13 in., (38.1 x 33 cm.), (38.1 x 33 cm.), handcolored engravings (BP 86, DM 217, FR 737, Y 16,546).

$110* *"Blenheim", 1793,* pub. J & J Boydell, (02-12-93, DuMouchelle, #1304, illus.), 8 x 13 in., (20.3 x 33 cm.), colored engraving (BP 77, DM 182, FR 617, Y 13,266).

$77* *Botanical,* (03-13-93, Garth, #386, illus.), 16¼ x 14¼ in., (41.3 x 36.2 cm.), hand-colored lithograph (BP 54, DM 128, FR 436, Y 9075).

$330* *"British Fleet In An Attack At The Bassein River On February 26, 1925,* from painting by G. Webster, pub. 1826, very good cond., foxing, (02-13-93, Bourne, #200, illus.), image 10 x 14B, in., (25.4 x 37.1 cm.), aquatint engraving (BP 232, DM 547, FR 1852, Y 39,797).

$193* *"Buffons Skua", "Hearing Gull", "Trochilus Anais" and "Hen": Four,* (02-27-93, Dunning, #105), largest 5¼ x 9 in., (13.3 x 22.9 cm.), smallest 3¾ x 6 in., (13.3 x 22.9 cm.), print (BP 136, DM 317, FR 1078, Y 22,784).

$962* *Bust-Portraits Of Nine Actors In Fans,* Hosoban, urushi-e, d. c. Kyoho 15 (1730), pub. Igaya, rubbed, soiled,wormage restored, Prof. H.R.W. Kuhne Coll., Torii School, (06-11-93, Sotheby-London, #10), 12 x 6 in., (30.5 x 15.2 cm.), hand-colored woodblock (BP 632, DM 1563, FR 5271, Y 102,069).

$288* *Buster Keaton In "L'Horloger Amoureus",* (03-25-93, Christie-E, #194), 31½ x 23¾ in., (80 x 60.3 cm.), color lithograph (BP 196, DM 473, FR 1609, Y 33,739).

$2185* *"Cabinet Of Natural History" and "Rural Sports With Illustrations" (Bnnett 35; Henderson 40; Howes D433), 1830-31: Two,* J. & T. Doughty, 3 vols. in 2, foxing, browning, offsetting, first ed., (06-14-93, Sotheby-NY, #376, illus.), 11Z, x 9Z, in., (28.3 x 23.2 cm.), 53 hand-colored and 2 uncolored engraved plates, one woodcut plate, 2 engraved portraits, 3 engraved t. p., 17 woodcuts (BP 1430, DM 3556, FR 11,953, Y 229,927).

$110* *Caterpillars And Moths,* stains, (03-13-93, Garth, #326, illus.), 16¾ x 13¾ in., (42.5 x 34.9 cm.), hand-colored lithograph (BP 77, DM 183, FR 623, Y 12,964).

$110* *"The Child Lost",* stains, margin damaged, (02-05-93, Garth, #32, illus.), 9 x 7 in., (22.9 x 17.8 cm.), hand-colored print (BP 76, DM 182, FR 617, Y 13,688).

$330* *"A Chipewa Widow", c. 1850,* octavo edit., by Bowen, (02-13-93, Neal, #752), hand colored lithograph (BP 232, DM 547, FR 1852, Y 39,797).

$94* *Coaching Print,* s. Dovico, (12-11-92, DuMouchelle, #1256, illus.), approx. 19½ x 11¾ in., (49.5 x 29.8 cm.), hand colored print (BP 60, DM 148, FR 508, Y 11,632).

$33* *The Coat Of Arms Of Edward Howard, Duke Of Norfolk,* (02-12-93, DuMouchelle, #357), 17½ x 10¼ in., (44.5 x 26 cm.), engraving on paper (BP 23, DM 55, FR 185, Y 3980).

$83* *"Cock Robin": Four,* from children's book, stains, edge damage, (01-08-93, Garth, #183, illus.), 7½ x 4½ in., (19.1 x 11.4 cm.), four pages, handcolored block printed (BP 54, DM 136, FR 464, Y 10,404).

$116* *Contemporary Portrait,* Ezekiel 40/100, David Hunter, (02-19-93, Garth, #84), 12½ x 10½ in., (31.8 x 26.7 cm.), b/w etching (BP 80, DM 190, FR 643, Y 13,764).

$7425* *The Continents: Set of Four,* (08-01-92, Northeast, #548), hand-colored mezzotint engravings (BP 3872, DM 11,015, FR 37,312, Y 947,671).

$22* *"Coracopsis Barklyi",* (11-13-92, Garth, #52, illus.), 15 x 12 in., (38.1 x 30.5 cm.), handcolored print (BP 14, DM 35, FR 116, Y 2731).

$55* *Courtesan By Tree,* Japanese, 19th cent., (04-02-93, Sloan, #1880), 12 x 7¾ in., (305 x 197 mm.), color woodcut (BP 36, DM 88, FR 300, Y 6262).

BI *Custer's Last Fight, 1896,* pub. Anheuser Busch Brewing Assoc., water/foxing damage, image ink loss, paper loss, discoloration, laid down on board, est. $2/2,500, (12-04-92, Doyle, #10, illus.), largest area 3 x 8 in., (76 x 203 mm.), chromolithograph.

$577* *Dans Le Ciel Mediterraneen, 1965,* s., d., (11-28-92, Schoppmann, #474B), 18Zzn x 16Z, in., (47.5 x 41 cm.), color lithograph on Arches (BP 381, DM 919, FR 3121, Y 71,811).

BI *"Dedia A L. Monsero, Le Duc D'Orleans": Pair,* est. $2/250, (12-11-92, DuMouchelle, #1283), aquatints.

$17* *"Dendrocygna Autumnalis",* from "United States & Mexican Boundary Birds, (11-13-92, Garth, #451, illus.), 16½ x 13¾ in., (41.9 x 34.9 cm.), handcolored lithograph (BP 11, DM 27, FR 90, Y 2110).

$383* *Diane Et Atteon Transforme En Cerf,* thin margins, fold verso, good cond., (05-15-93, Loudmer, #19, illus.), 7M x 9Zzn in., (200 x 250 mm.), copper engraving on laid (BP 249, DM 616, FR 2070, Y 42,456).

$66* *Duck Prints: A Pair,* (06-24-93, Boos, #351), sight each 10½ x 14 in., (267 x 356 mm.), colored print (BP 45, DM 113, FR 380, Y 7199).

$11* *Eight Moths,* (02-19-93, Garth, #399), 12½ x 11Z, in., (31.8 x 28.3 cm.), handcolored engraving (BP 8, DM 18, FR 61, Y 1305).

$22* *"Esther",* from a 1716 history of the Bible by John Sturt, (02-19-93, Garth, #85), 10½ x 8½ in., (26.7 x 21.6 cm.), copper plate engraving (BP 15, DM 36, FR 122, Y 2610).

$107* *Exotic Birds: Three,* (03-13-93, Garth, #16, illus.), 8 x 4½ in., (20.3 x 11.4 cm.), hand-colored engravings (BP 75, DM 178, FR 606, Y 12,610).

$440* *"Falcon" and "White-Faced Honey Eater": Two,* p. J. Gould and W. Hart, (04-16-93, DuMouchelle, #164, illus.), approx. 19 x 13 in., (48.3 x 33 cm.), hand-colored lithograph (BP 289, DM 711, FR 2402, Y 49,477).

$4620* *Feuilles Eparses, 1965: Set Of Eight,* Rene Crevel, s., copy 70 of 150, very good cond., includ. works by Arp; Bellmer; Bryen; Dominguez; Ernst (S. and L. 70); Giacometti (L. 186); Hayter' Hugo; Lam; Masson; Miro (Cramer 99, D. 119); and Wols, (11-09-92, Christie-NY, #192A, illus.), 9Azn x 8Czn in., (252 x 208 mm.), 8 color etchings, 4 b/w etching, 2 colored lithograph on BFK Rives (BP 3055, DM 7375, FR 24,919, Y 573,343).

$220* *"The First Battle Between Iron Ships Of War",* 19th cent., foxing, stains, fold, (11-21-92, Goldberg, #705, illus.), 12½ x 18 in., (31.8 x 45.7 cm.), color lithograph (BP 145, DM 351, FR 1182, Y 27,360).

$468* *Fox Hunting Scenes, "Breaking Cover" Plate 3, "Full Cry" Plate 4, "The Death" Plate 5 and "The Toast" Plate 6 : Set Of Four,* subtitle 'Bachelor's Hall' on each, full margins, pub. mid 1800's, (02-13-93, Collins, #23, illus.), each 10½ x 13¾ in., (26.7 x 34.9 cm.), (BP 330, DM 776, FR 2626, Y 56,440).

$77* *Genre Scenes: Two,* inits. G.P., (03-25-93, Boos, #644), each sight 13 x 31½ in., (33 x 80 cm.), illustration print (BP 52, DM 126, FR 430, Y 9021).

$39* *"George Washington" and "Dance Lessons": Two,* (02-27-93, Dunning, #150F), first 23¾ x 19½ in., (60.3 x 49.5 cm.), second 13¼ x 19¼ in., (60.3 x 49.5 cm.), print (BP 27, DM 64, FR 218, Y 4604).

$28* *"Girl At Well",* SURIMONO, margins laid down matt, fading, soiling, (05-07-93, Goldberg, #1408), woodblock (BP 18, DM 44, FR 149, Y 3083).

$77* *Golf Subjects: Two,* d. 1955, (03-12-93, DuMouchelle, #2448), 12 x 8 in., (30.5 x 20.3 cm.), print (BP 54, DM 128, FR 436, Y 9075).

$445* *Gossipers Le Castelet,* #413/850, blindstamp, (02-17-93, Bonhams-Chelsea, #311), image 19½ x 26¼ in., (49.5 x 66.7 cm.), color reproduction (BP 308, DM 723, FR 2448, Y 53,153).

$413* *Group Of Idlers (Gardner and Clark 90), 1967,* s., blindstamp, pub. Medici Society, (02-17-93, Bonhams-Chelsea, #312), image 19¼ x 26½ in., (48.9 x 67.3 cm.), sepia reproduction (BP 286, DM 671, FR 2272, Y 49,331).

$187* *"Hard Hit"*, (11-27-92, Clearing House, #95), 20¼ x 28¾ in., (51.4 x 73 cm.), lithograph (BP 123, DM 299, FR 1015, Y 23,273).

$86* *A Harvest Scene,* hole, (11-18-92, Bubb Kuyper, #1585), 10⅞n x 15C, in., (25.5 x 39 cm.), woodblock print (BP 57, DM 137, FR 462, Y 10,695, G 156).

$253* *Der Hl. Hieronymus In Der Hohle (Nagler Mon. IV, 860, 14; Hollstein XIII; S. 72, 21),* mono., prov., watermark, (12-04-92, Bassenge, #6315), 7⅞zn x 5Bzn in., (19.2 x 13.5 cm.), engraving (BP 162, DM 403, FR 1367, Y 31,586).

$46 *Hunting Prints: Six,* from Punch, 1897, (04-16-93, G.A. Key, #121), 4 x 6 in., (10.2 x 15.2 cm.), hand-colored prints (BP 30, DM 74, FR 251, Y 5173).

$1400* *Ichikawa Danjuro II As Soga Juro And Ichikawa Monnosuke As The Courtesan Oiso No Tora In The Play Wakai Midoriiki Soga,* Hosoban, sumizuri-e, d. Kyoho 3 (1718), extensively restored, laid down, Prof. H.R.W. Kuhne Coll., (06-11-93, Sotheby-London, #16, illus.), 13½ x 6¼ in., (34.3 x 15.9 cm.), hand-colored woodblock (BP 920, DM 2275, FR 7671, Y 148,541).

$5055* *Illustriss Et Excellentiss Domino Michaeli Peretto Marchioni Incisae, c. 1585,* mono. GG, stained, on 3 sheets, watermark, (12-04-92, Bassenge, #6313, illus.), each approx. 18¾ x 15Zzn in., (47.6 x 38.2 cm.), etching (BP 3242, DM 8051, FR 27,310, Y 631,086).

$187* *"Innocence"*, large folio, (11-13-92, Garth, #123, illus.), 28½ x 22¾ in., (72.4 x 57.8 cm.), colored lithograph (BP 121, DM 294, FR 990, Y 23,210).

$495* *"Ki-On-Twog-Ky (Cornplanter), A Seneca Chief", c. 1850,* octavo edit., by Bowen, (02-13-93, Neal, #751), hand colored lithograph (BP 349, DM 821, FR 2778, Y 59,696).

$176* *"L'Enfance De Paul Et Virginie" and "L'Adolescene De Paul Et Virginie": A Pair,* (12-10-92, Sloan, #2086), each, approx. 6½ x 8¾ in., (16.5 x 22.2 cm.), colored engraving (BP 113, DM 278, FR 951, Y 21,771).

$83* *Landscape Scenes: Two,* (02-12-93, DuMouchelle, #1325), 24 x 19½ in., (61 x 49.5 cm.), print (BP 58, DM 138, FR 466, Y 10,010).

$83* *Landscapes: Six,* edit. by Nicolas, Kostia, Hahn, Desclaux, and Menojisky, (02-19-93, Garth, #447), colored lithographs (BP 57, DM 136, FR 460, Y 9848).

$83* *London,* English, 19th cent., (02-12-93, DuMouchelle, #361), 10 x 23 in., (25.4 x 58.4 cm.), hand colored engraving (BP 58, DM 138, FR 466, Y 10,010).

$440* *"Ma-Ka-Tai-Me-She-Kia-Kiah (Black Hawk), A Saukie Brave", c. 1850,* octavo edit., by Bowen, (02-13-93, Neal, #750), hand colored lithograph (BP 310, DM 730, FR 2469, Y 53,063).

BI *"Mayflower"*, from painting by Gordon Grant, excell. cond., est. $2/300, (02-13-93, Bourne, #168), 13½ x 19 in., (34.3 x 48.3 cm.), print.

$770* *"Middle Lake" and "Artulley Bridge": A Pair,* eglomise mat, (05-29-93, Northeast, #626), 12½ x 17 in., (31.8 x 43.2 cm.), polychromed engravings (BP 493, DM 1221, FR 4129, Y 82,565).

$165* *"Mirage"*, restrike, toning, foxing, (02-13-93, Bourne, #174), lithograph (BP 116, DM 274, FR 926, Y 19,899).

$198* *"Mode De Paris": Six,* from Petit Courrier des Dames, pub. 1826, (12-10-92, Garth, #378, illus.), 8 x 5 in., (20.3 x 12.7 cm.), hand-colored engraving (BP 128, DM 313, FR 1070, Y 24,493).

$28* *"Modes De Paris": Ten,* six frontis sheets, pub. date 1826, stains, (02-19-93, Garth, #349, illus.), 8 x 5 in., (20.3 x 12.7 cm.), handcolored engravings (BP 19, DM 46, FR 155, Y 3322).

$160* *"Moses" and "Le Grand Pretre Aaron": A Pair,* (12-10-92, Sloan, #950), each, sight 24 x 19¼ in., (61 x 48.9 cm.), color lithograph (BP 103, DM 253, FR 864, Y 19,792).

$193* *"Nea-Math-La, A Seminole Chief", c. 1850,* octavo edit., by Bowen, (02-13-93, Neal, #753), hand colored lithograph (BP 136, DM 320, FR 1083, Y 23,275).

$83* *Nelson,* proof before letters, wide borders, trimmed to plate, c. 1800, (11-30-92, Phillips-London, #229), sheet 8 x 6¼ in., (203 x 159 mm.), stipple engraving (BP 55, DM 132, FR 449, Y 10,330).

$28* *Nudes: Six,* edit. w/works by: Alan, Heine, Desclaux, Beneton, Castaneda, and Bady, (02-19-93, Garth, #446), colored lithograph (BP 19, DM 46, FR 155, Y 3322).

$198* *"Oche-Finceco", c. 1850,* octavo edit., Bowen, (02-13-93, Neal, #747), hand colored lithograph (BP 139, DM 328, FR 1111, Y 23,878).

$330* *"Old Squaw Drake", "Pintail Drake", "Northern Loon" and "Great Crested Grebe": Set Of Four,* fading, overall good cond., (04-22-93, Guyette, #850, illus.), image 5 x 7 in., (12.7 x 17.8 cm.), framed 8¾ x 10¼ in., (12.7 x 17.8 cm.), hand-colored prints (BP 213, DM 530, FR 1789, Y 36,284).

$332* *Op De Waag-Schaal, 1618,* rare proof-state, (11-18-92, Bubb Kuyper, #1822, illus.), 12B\zn x 12Zzn in., (33 x 32.2 cm.), engraving on very thin paper, watermark (BP 219, DM 529, FR 1783, Y 41,288, G 600).

$413* *"The Oracle",* t., ident., #20/50, s. in syllabics and Anergua, d. 1965, 20th cent., (01-09-93, Skinner, #284), sight 16 x 22½ in., (40.6 x 57.2 cm.), stone cut and stencil (BP 269, DM 679, FR 2307, Y 51,767).

$39* *Orange Orchids,* foxing, (03-13-93, Garth, #391), 15½ x 12½ in., (39.4 x 31.8 cm.), hand-colored engraving (BP 27, DM 65, FR 221, Y 4596).

$275* *Paderewski, I.J.,* s. I.J. Paderewski, (09-17-92, Swann, #219), approx. 6¼ x 7 in., (15.9 x 17.8 cm.), sepia etching (BP 154, DM 408, FR 1397, Y 34,238).

$199* *Palais Des Sports Bruxelles, Courses de Levries/ Sportpaleis Brussel,Windhondenkoersen, c. 1930,* (11-18-92, Bubb Kuyper, #1518), approx. 30Zzn x 23B\ in., (78 x 60 cm.), color lithograph (BP 131, DM 317, FR 1069, Y 24,748, G 360).

$110* *"Peony", "Double Stock" and "Cineroria": Three,* (02-27-93, Dunning, #103), each 6¾ x 4½ in., (17.1 x 11.4 cm.), hand colored print (BP 77, DM 181, FR 615, Y 12,985).

$138* *"Plantations On The Mississippi River From Natchez To New Orleans 1858",* (11-21-92, Goldberg, #721), 50 x 30 in., (127 x 76.2 cm.), lithograph (BP 91, DM 220, FR 741, Y 17,162).

$165* *"Pont Neuf" and "La Bastille": A Pair,* restrikes, (12-10-92, Garth, #501, illus.), 14 x 22½ in., (35.6 x 57.2 cm.), hand-colored French engraving (BP 106, DM 261, FR 891, Y 20,411).

$77* *Portrait Of A Gentleman,* English, (04-02-93, Sloan, #2272), 17M, x 11½ in., (454 x 292 mm.), mezzotint (BP 51, DM 124, FR 420, Y 8767).

$38 *Portrait Of A Young Child With Hat,* indistinctly s., (04-16-93, G.A. Key, #14), 9 x 6 in., (22.9 x 15.2 cm.), etching (BP 25, DM 61, FR 207, Y 4273).

$40* *Portrait Of A Young Woman,* (03-10-93, Maynard, #647), 11¾ x 9¼ in., (29.8 x 23.5 cm.), mezzotint (BP 28, DM 67, FR 226, Y 4726, C$ 50).

$77* *"Portrait of A Young Lady" and "Portrait Of A Lady Wearing A Cape": Two,* (02-27-93, Dunning, #119), first 13 x 10½ in., (33 x 26.7 cm.), second 13 x 10 in., (33 x 26.7 cm.), print (BP 54, DM 127, FR 430, Y 9090).

$220* *"Les Preludes Des Bach",* engraved Paul Allais, Paris-Bulla pub., foxing, full margins, 19th cent., (03-12-93, Goldberg, #904, illus.), 31 x 41 in., (78.7 x 104.1 cm.), engraving (BP 153, DM 366, FR 1245, Y 25,928).

$220* *Queen Victoria As A Young Woman,* small portrait of old queen in margin, artist sig., (02-19-93, Garth, #159, illus.), 10 x 7¼ in., (25.4 x 18.4 cm.), handcolored mezzotint (BP 151, DM 360, FR 1220, Y 26,103).

$484* *"Red Bird, A Winnebago", c. 1850,* octavo edit., (02-13-93, Neal, #748), hand colored lithograph (BP 341, DM 803, FR 2716, Y 58,370).

$55* *Red Camellia,* foxing, (03-13-93, Garth, #222, illus.), 11½ x 8½ in., (29.2 x 21.6 cm.), hand-colored lithograph (BP 38, DM 92, FR 311, Y 6482).

$12,486* *Revue Verve, Vols. I-X, Nos. 1-38, Teriade Editeur, Paris, 1937-60,* complete set of illus. w/text in 26 albums, p. by draeger and Mourlot, very good cond., (12-01-92, Christie-London, #509), overall sheet 14Zzn x 10½ in., (357 x 267 mm.), lithograph in color and in black, reproductions and photographs (BP 8250, DM 19,901, FR 67,822, Y 1,554,532).

$88* *"The Room In The McLean House", 1867,* margin tears, (09-12-92, Dunning, #1180), 21½ x 31 in., (54.6 x 78.7 cm.), engraving (BP 46, DM 127, FR 431, Y 10,903).

$50* *Rural Meeting Hall With Horse And Buggy,* (11-13-92, Garth, #426, illus.), 9½ x 9½ in., (24.1 x 24.1 cm.), handcolored engraving (BP 32, DM 78, FR 265, Y 6206).

$1705* *The Saint Veronica Cloth (Schreiber II, 761),* margins, worm holes, worm-track, other defects, margins annot., ex-coll., Swiss or German School, (12-03-92, Sotheby-London, #60, illus.), 5½ x 3½ in., (138 x 90 mm.), hand-colored woodcut (BP 1100, DM 2681, FR 9152, Y 212,144).

$116* *"Scenes Of Old Man And Woman Dining 'Darby & Joan'": Three,* (12-10-92, Garth, #408), two 24 x 20 in., (61 x 50.8 cm.), one 24 x 29 in., (61 x 50.8 cm.), hand-colored engraving (BP 75, DM 183, FR 627, Y 14,349).

$100 *Second Liberty Loan Of 1917,* American Lithographic Co. N.Y. No. 7, fold marks, (09-24-92, Alderfer, #235), 36 x 48 in., (91.4 x 121.9 cm.), lithograph (BP 59, DM 148, FR 503, Y 12,029).

$385* *"Seils - Sterling" and "Carta & Mirtziana": Two,* American, 20th cent., (02-14-93, Hanzel, #713), 39½ x 26½ in., (100.3 x 67.3 cm.), 35½ x 25½ in., (100.3 x 67.3 cm.), color lithographic poster (BP 271, DM 638, FR 2160, Y 46,430).

$28* *Several Cormorants,* stains, (03-13-93, Garth, #60), 11 x 13¾ in., (27.9 x 34.9 cm.), hand-colored lithograph (BP 20, DM 47, FR 158, Y 3300).

$110* *"Small Hopes And Lady Mack",* by Pheonix Lithography Co., t., old restoration, Theresa Patenn Estate, (02-06-93, Julia, #326), 17½ x 22½ in., (44.5 x 57.2 cm.), hand-colored lithograph (BP 76, DM 182, FR 617, Y 13,688).

$4901* *Table/Plan Of The Sugoroku Game,* t., Dai-oban, sumi-zuri-e, pub.'s mark, d. c. Horeki 3 (1753), soiled,rubbed, trimmed, repaired, Prof. H.R.W. Kuhne Coll., Japanese Kabuki, close toKiyohiro, (06-11-93, Sotheby-London, #35, illus.), 11¼ x 15M, in., (28.6 x 40.3 cm.), woodblock (BP 3220, DM 7965, FR 26,855, Y 520,000).

$847* *Titelholzschnitt Zum Terenz (Schramm II, S. 4 and Abb. 338; Muther I,533), 1496,* title woodcut from Terentius cum Directorio vocabularum of 2 edit., Joh. Gruninger, late 15th cent., prov., (06-10-93, Hauswedell/Nolt, #41, illus.), partially colored woodcut (BP 554, DM 1379, FR 4644, Y 89,906).

$66* *"To Calais", 1835,* pub. Tho. McLean, (02-12-93, DuMouchelle, #1305, illus.), 6 x 8½ in., (15.2 x 21.6 cm.), color engraving (BP 46, DM 109, FR 370, Y 7959).

$100* *"Veduta Dell' Eroe Combattente, Detto Comunemente Il Gladiatore Di Borghese, Scultura Greca D'Agasia Efesino", c. 1750,* waterstain, (11-18-92, Bubb Kuyper, #1823), 12Œn x 10Mœn in., (31 x 26.5 cm.), copper engraving (BP 66, DM 159, FR 537, Y 12,436, G 180).

$330* *A View Of High St., Birmingham,* (05-29-93, Northeast, #625), colored engraving (BP 211, DM 523, FR 1769, Y 35,385).

$132* *View Of Marcelus Theatre, Rome,* (12-10-92, Sloan, #588), sight 10¾ x 16¾ in., (27.3 x 42.5 cm.), color engraving (BP 85, DM 209, FR 713, Y 16,329).

$3178* *Vom Weyerberg, 1895: Ten,* partially plate s., mono., (06-10-93, Hauswedell/Nolt, #985), sh 20¾ x 13Zœn in., (52.7 x 35.4 cm.), etching on copper print (BP 2079, DM 5175, FR 17,423, Y 337,331).

$55* *"Vu Du Port De Brest Prise Du Cote Du Bureau General",* (02-27-93, Dunning, #137), 8½ x 15 in., (21.6 x 38.1 cm.), hand colored engraving (BP 39, DM 90, FR 307, Y 6493).

$275* *Washington And His Generals,* (11-27-92, Clearing House, #418), 28½ x 39½ in., (72.4 x 100.3 cm.), colored lithograph (BP 181, DM 439, FR 1492, Y 34,225).

$165* *Weapons For Liberty, Keep Him Free: Two,* American, 20th cent., (02-14-93, Hanzel, #703), each 30 x 20 in., (76.2 x 50.8 cm.), color lithographic poster (BP 116, DM 274, FR 926, Y 19,899).

$143* *"Women Reading",* 19th cent., (05-15-93, Dunning, #162), 21 x 27¾ in., (53.3 x 70.5 cm.), chromolithograph (BP 93, DM 230, FR 773, Y 15,852).

$220* *"Women With Paint Pallet" and "Women With Pen And Paper": A Pair,* (02-27-93, Dunning, #100), each 9½ x 11 in., (24.1 x 27.9 cm.), print (BP 155, DM 362, FR 1229, Y 25,971).

$575* *Women's Fashion, c. 1930: Eight,* (04-07-93, Sotheby-Arcade, #155), sight 13½ x 10½ in., (34.3 x 26.7 cm.), hand-colored lithograph (BP 380, DM 930, FR 3147, Y 65,326).

$6600* *The Works In Architecture Of Robert And James Adam, Esquires, 1779,* p. for the authors, two volumes folio, decent cond., scattered lightbrowning or foxing, tears, Alice C. Backus Estate, (10-24-92, Sotheby-NY, #10), 26 x 19¼ in., (66 x 48.9 cm.), 80 engraved plates (BP 4080, DM 10,092, FR 34,215, Y 804,878).

ANON POSTERS

$770* *24 Heures Du Mans: Three,* original posters from 1967 to 1969, (08-23-92, Christie-E, #18), each 23B, x 15¾ in., (60 x 40 cm.), color posters (BP 395, DM 1103, FR 3743, Y 96,868).

$27* *25 Aniversario Del Ballet Nacional De Cuba, 1974,* (01-31-93, Morelle/Marchan, #11), 27Œn x 39Œ, in., (70 x 100 cm.), poster (BP 18, DM 43, FR 147, Y 3368).

$70* *2eme Foire De Paris. Grand Palais, 1905,* Imp. Courmont, good cond., (02-12-93, Cheval/Robert, #126), 47¼ x 31Z, in., (120 x 79 cm.), poster (BP 49, DM 116, FR 393, Y 8442).

$385* *A.P.I. Voghera,* Guintoli, Milan, A- cond., marginal creasing, (08-06-92, Swann, #1, illus.), 19¼ x 13½ in., (48.9 x 34.3 cm.), (BP 201, DM 569, FR 1921, Y 49,107).

$1045* *Aero Show, 4 Days Starting May 30, 2 To 6 P.M. Daily, Cicero Field Of The Aero Club Of Illinois,* (09-12-92, Dunning, #212, illus.), approx. 20M, x 14 in., (53 x 35.6 cm.), poster (BP 540, DM 1504, FR 5113, Y 129,476).

$159* *Air France: "Afrique Occidentale Francaise, Afrique Equatoriale Francaise",* fairly good cond., (03-13-93, Laurin, #127), 39Œ, x 24 in., (100 x 61 cm.), (BP 111, DM 265, FR 900, Y 18,739).

$130* *Aladin,* cond. A, (03-16-93, Boisgirard, #40), 88Œn x 39¾ in., (224 x 101 cm.), (BP 90, DM 216, FR 734, Y 15,201).

$165* *Alexander, "The Man Who Knows",* A cond., chartexbacked, (08-06-92, Swann, #182, illus.), 42 x 28 in., (106.7 x 71.1 cm.), (BP 86, DM 244, FR 823, Y 21,046).

$186* *Un Americain A Paris (An American In Paris), De V. Minelli, Avec L. Caron (French), 1951,* (01-31-93, Morelle/Marchan, #115), 23B, x 31½ in., (60 x 80 cm.), poster (BP 125, DM 300, FR 1013, Y 23,204).

$1303* *American Entertainment Co.,* repaired tears, backed on linen, (05-07-93, Christie-S. Ken, #71, illus.), 41½ x 28 in., (105.4 x 71.1 cm.), color lithograph (BP 825, DM 2060, FR 6942, Y 143,471).

$134* *Amica, Opera De Pietro Mascagni, 1905,* (01-31-93, Morelle/Marchan, #156), 17Zœn x 27Œn in., (45 x 70 cm.), poster (BP 90, DM 216, FR 730, Y 16,717).

$385* *Anisetta De Giorgi,* Prager and Lojda, init. E.B., A-cond., creasing, (08-06-92, Swann, #38, illus.), 20¼ x 15½ in., (51.4 x 39.4 cm.), (BP 201, DM 569, FR 1921, Y 49,107).

$124* *Anna Pavlova Avec Laurent Novikoff. Theatre Des Champs Elysees,* (01-31-93, Morelle/Marchan, #6), 31½ x 23B, in., (80 x 60 cm.), poster (BP 83, DM 200, FR 675, Y 15,469).

$1182* *Antibes, Cotes D'Azur. PLM., c. 1920,* minor defects, (02-04-93, Christie-S. Ken, #98, illus.), 42 x 30 in., (106.7 x 76.2 cm.), color lithograph backed on linen (BP 825, DM 1946, FR 6600, Y 147,033).

$120* *Arenes Bayonnaises,* c. 1890?, Paris, Imp. Camis, cond. B, ink spot, (06-11-93, Boisgirard, #10), 21Mœn x 28Œ in., (54.5 x 72 cm.), poster (BP 79, DM 195, FR 658, Y 12,732).

$486* *Articulos Para Fotografia Y Pintura,* p. Font Lithografia, (05-07-93, Christie-S. Ken, #82, illus.), sight 20 x 14 in., (50.8 x 35.6 cm.), color lithograph (BP 308, DM 768, FR 2589, Y 53,512).

$371* *Au Bon Marche. Specialite De Gants, Dentelles,* Imp. Chaix, good cond., (02-12-93, Cheval/Robert, #43), (BP 261, DM 615, FR 2082, Y 44,742).

$602* *Automobile Club De France. 2eme Exposition Internationale D'Automobiles Au Jardin Des Tuileries, 1899,* Paris, Imp. J. Barreau, cond. B+, (06-11-93, Boisgirard, #23), 51Œn x 37Œn in., (130 x 94.5 cm.), poster (BP 396, DM 978, FR 3299, Y 63,873).

$281* *Ba-Ta-Clan. Revue Le Avarietes De L'Annee, c. 1895,* Paris, Imp. G. Bataille, cond. A-, (06-11-93, Boisgirard, #30), 51Œzn x 37 in., (130 x 94 cm.), poster (BP 185, DM 457, FR 1540, Y 29,814).

$160 *Back Our Girls Over There,* YWCA, cracking, (09-24-92, Alderfer, #261), 28¼ x 21¼ in., (71.8 x 54 cm.), (BP 94, DM 237, FR 805, Y 19,247).

$83* *"Bal" (Couples Et Musiciens Jazz), c. 1930,* (01-31-93, Morelle/Marchan, #13), 15¾ x 22ÆŒzn in., (40 x 58 cm.), poster (BP 56, DM 134, FR 452, Y 10,354).

$120* *La Bande A Fifi, c. 1900,* cond. C, text repainted, (03-16-93, Boisgirard, #41), 49Czn x 35Æzn in., (125 x 89 cm.), (BP 83, DM 200, FR 678, Y 14,032).

$935* *The Barnum & Bailey Greatest Show On Earth: Three,* American, 20th cent., (02-14-93, Hanzel, #716), each approx. 73 x 26 in., (185.4 x 66 cm.), color lithographic poster (BP 658, DM 1551, FR 5247, Y 112,759).

$798* *The Barnum & Bailey The Greatest Show On Earth: Three,* American, 20th cent., (02-14-93, Hanzel, #715), each approx. 28 x 40 in., (71.1 x 101.6 cm.), color lithographic poster (BP 562, DM 1323, FR 4478, Y 96,237).

$1540* *Barnum & Bailey The Greatest Show On Earth: Three,* American, 20th cent., (02-14-93, Hanzel, #717), each approx. 73 x 26½ in., (185.4 x 67.3 cm.), lithographic poster (BP 1085, DM 2554, FR 8642, Y 185,721).

$345* *The Barnum & Bailey Greatest Show On Earth,* (03-03-93, Sotheby-Arcade, #64), 30½ x 38 in., (77.5 x 96.5 cm.), poster (BP 238, DM 568, FR 1927, Y 40,313).

$605* *Barnum And Bailey, Oriental India, 1896,* Strobridge Litho. Co., A cond., (08-06-92, Swann, #92, illus.), 30 x 37½ in., (76.2 x 95.3 cm.), (BP 316, DM 894, FR 3019, Y 77,168).

$556* *Bebe Chez Le Pharmacien,* p. Gaumont, folds, defects, backed on linen, laid on board, (05-07-93, Christie-S. Ken, #103, illus.), color lithograph (BP 352, DM 879, FR 2962, Y 61,220).

$201* *Belle Irene. Veritable Femme Tatouee, c. 1895,* Paris, Affiches Americaines Ch. Levy, cond. B+, (06-11-93, Boisgirard, #31), 48ÆŒzn x 35Mzn in., (124 x 90 cm.), poster (BP 132, DM 327, FR 1101, Y 21,326).

$171* *La Belle Villageoise. Confections. "Medaille D'Argent 1888",* Imp. H. Laas, good cond., (02-12-93, Cheval/Robert, #42), 47¼ x 62ÆŒzn in., (120 x 160 cm.), (BP 120, DM 284, FR 960, Y 20,622).

$361* *Biere De La Meuse,* Imp. Lemercier, fairly good cond., loss, (02-12-93, Cheval/Robert, #32), 50E⅓n x 38>⅓n in., (129 x 98 cm.), (BP 254, DM 599, FR 2026, Y 43,536).

$80* *Biere Du Lion,* Imp. Pichot, very good cond., (02-12-93, Cheval/Robert, #33), 31Bzn x 22ÆŒzn in., (79.5 x 58 cm.), (BP 56, DM 133, FR 449, Y 9648).

$392* *"Biere Saint-Germain" and "Brasserie Diekirch. Bieres Fines": Two,* first, creases, loss; second, Imp. V. Rose, good cond., (02-12-93, Cheval/Robert, #34), first 39C, x 27⅜n in., (100 x 70 cm.), second 28C, x 22Æzn in., (100 x 70 cm.), second on thick paper (BP 276, DM 650, FR 2200, Y 47,274).

$141* *Blanche Lescaut, c. 1895,* Paris, Affiches Americaines Ch. Levy, cond. B+, (06-11-93, Boisgirard, #32), 62B, x 24 in., (159 x 61 cm.), poster (BP 93, DM 229, FR 773, Y 14,960).

$630* *"Blue Star" and "Blue Star Line, Mediterranean Cruises": Two,* creasing, excell. cond., (02-04-93, Christie-S. Ken, #21), 39½ x 25 in., (100.3 x 63.5 cm.), color lithograph (BP 440, DM 1037, FR 3518, Y 78,368).

$880* *Bonnie Togs-For Rugged Action Wear, 1930s,* surface wear, small tear, (04-29-93, Swann, #110), 22 x 17 in., (55.9 x 43.2 cm.), poster (BP 560, DM 1392, FR 4691, Y 97,897).

$80* *Brasserie De Sochaux, c. 1900,* cond. B, (03-16-93, Boisgirard, #14), 23B, x 32Ææzn in., (60 x 83 cm.), (BP 55, DM 133, FR 452, Y 9355).

$869* *Bring Your Selo Films Here (C. 34),* 1930s, fold marks, laid on board, (05-07-93, Christie-S. Ken, #64, illus.), 20 x 76 in., (50.8 x 193 cm.), color lithograph (BP 550, DM 1374, FR 4630, Y 95,684).

$191* *British Columbia,* p. Colonist Litho Victoria BC, creases, laid on board, (05-07-93, Christie-S. Ken, #67, illus.), 24 x 36 in., (61 x 91.4 cm.), color lithograph (BP 121, DM 302, FR 1018, Y 21,031).

$100* *Broadhurst's (...) What Happened To Jones, c. 1900,* Cincinatti, Russel Morgan Print, cond. A-, (06-11-93, Boisgirard, #25), 27Ææzn x 19Bzn in., (71 x 49 cm.), poster (BP 66, DM 163, FR 548, Y 10,610).

$1870* *Buffalo Bill, Actual Scenes In Moving Pictures,* A- cond., blemishing, well-repaired closed tear, (08-06-92, Swann, #93, illus.), 42 x 28 in., (106.7 x 71.1 cm.), (BP 977, DM 2763, FR 9331, Y 238,520).

BI *"Bus Stop",* 20th Century Fox movie poster, est. C$3/350, (10-21-92, Maynard, #327), poster.

$165* *Busch, Panther,* B cond., closed tear, fold mark, by Hanno Coldan, (08-06-92, Swann, #94, illus.), 46 x 33 in., (116.8 x 83.8 cm.), (BP 86, DM 244, FR 823, Y 21,046).

$357* *Bust Portrait Of Queen Wilhelmina,* A cond., (08-06-92, Swann, #50, illus.), 15 x 14 in., (38.1 x 35.6 cm.), (BP 186, DM 527, FR 1781, Y 45,536).

$670* *C.I.W.L. Et Cie Des Ch. De Fer Du P.L.M.: Les Wagons-Lits De 2eme Classe "Paris Vers L'Italie, La Suisse, La Cote D'Azur,* good cond., (01-23-93, Ribeyre/Baron, #2, illus.), 39C, x 25⅓n in., (100 x 65 cm.), poster (BP 438, DM 1065, FR 3604, Y 83,855).

$502* *Cacao Van Houten, Le Meilleur Chocolat A Consommer Liquide, c. 1900,* Imp. F. Champenois, Paris, cond. B+, (06-11-93, Boisgirard, #3), 60Mzn x 40⅜n in., (153.5 x 103 cm.), poster (BP 330, DM 816, FR 2751, Y 53,263).

$181* *Cafes Gilbert,* (02-13-93, Morelle/Marchan, #24), 39C, x 59Żzn in., (100 x 150 cm.), poster (BP 127, DM 300, FR 1016, Y 21,828).

$605* *Calvert Litho. Co. 1895,* A cond., (08-06-92, Swann, #2, illus.), 27½ x 20½ in., (69.9 x 52.1 cm.), (BP 316, DM 894, FR 3019, Y 77,168).

$867* *"Canadian Pacific, Empress Of Britain" and "To The Far East, Canadian Pacific", c. 1930: Two,* p. Great Britain, nicks, creases, (02-04-93, Christie-S. Ken, #19, illus.), 40 x 25 in., (101.6 x 63.5 cm.), color lithograph (BP 605, DM 1428, FR 4841, Y 107,849).

$662* *Cantando Sotto La Pioggia (Singin' In The Rain), De G. Kelly Et S. Donen, Avec Gene Kelly Et Debbie Reynolds (Italian), 1952,* (01-31-93, Morelle/Marchan, #112), 39C, x 55Ż, in., (100 x 140 cm.), poster (BP 445, DM 1067, FR 3606, Y 82,585).

$412* *Carl Hagenbeck, Wallace Circus,* Erie Litho. Co., A- cond., (08-06-92, Swann, #96, illus.), 39½ x 25½ in., (100.3 x 64.8 cm.), (BP 215, DM 609, FR 2056, Y 52,551).

$275* *Carter The Great, A Baffling Chinese Mystery, c. 1930,* fold/creasing/damage/repair, (09-12-92, Dunning, #321, illus.), 79 x 41 in., (200.7 x 104.1 cm.), poster laid on cloth, 3 sheets (BP 142, DM 396, FR 1345, Y 34,073).

$495* *Carter The Great, The Modern Priestess Of Delphi, "Your Mind Is An Open Book To Her", c. 1930,* fold/creasing/damage/repair, (09-12-92, Dunning, #322, illus.), 77½ x 41 in., (196.9 x 104.1 cm.), poster, 3 sheets, laid on cloth (BP 256, DM 713, FR 2422, Y 61,331).

$220* *Central Plaza And Buildings At The Fair, 1929,* Exposition-Barcelona 1929, linen-backed, (04-29-93, Swann, #138), 20½ x 27½ in., (52.1 x 69.9 cm.), lithograph (BP 140, DM 348, FR 1173, Y 24,474).

$372* *Chantons Sous La Pluie (Singin' In The Rain) (Belgian),* (01-31-93, Morelle/Marchan, #117, illus.), 14Czn x 18½ in., (36 x 47 cm.), poster (BP 250, DM 599, FR 2026, Y 46,407).

$124* *Chantons Sous La Pluie (Singin' In The Rain), De S. Donen, Avec D. Reynolds (French), 1952,* (01-31-93, Morelle/Marchan, #110), 23B, x 31½ in., (60 x 80 cm.), poster (BP 83, DM 200, FR 675, Y 15,469).

$440* *"Charnay Aperitif",* pub. Vercasson, (11-13-92, DuMouchelle, #181, illus.), 77 x 49 in., (195.6 x 124.5 cm.), poster (BP 284, DM 691, FR 2329, Y 54,611).

$100* *Charrues Barjac. La Grande Marque Francaise, c. 1935,* cond. A, (03-16-93, Boisgirard, #27), 41⅜n x 29½ in., (105.5 x 75 cm.), (BP 69, DM 166, FR 565, Y 11,693).

BI *Chase And Bachelder's American Museum Of Art, c. 1880-1885,* Stafford and Co., A- cond., creasing, surface soiling, est. $1/1,500, (08-06-92, Swann, #3, illus.), 36¾ x 28 in., (93.3 x 71.1 cm.), .

$192* *Chateau D'Amboise, 1935,* Chaix, B cond., fraying, surface soiling, s. A.T.O., (08-06-92, Swann, #270, illus.), 39 x 24½ in., (99.1 x 62.2 cm.), (BP 100, DM 284, FR 958, Y 24,490).

$272* *Chatel-Guyon, "A 6 Heures De Paris, Splendides Excursions", c. 1900,* excell. cond., (01-23-93, Ribeyre/Baron, #72), 41Bzn x 29½ in., (105 x 75 cm.), poster (BP 178, DM 433, FR 1463, Y 34,043).

$165* *Les Chaussons Rouges (Belgian), 1948,* (01-31-93, Morelle/Marchan, #79), 14Azn x 22Zzn in., (38 x 58 cm.), poster (BP 111, DM 266, FR 899, Y 20,584).

$201* *Chemin De Fer D'Orleans (...) Luchon, La Reine Des Pyrenees. Eaux Sulfureuses, c. 1895,* Nimes, Montpellier, Imp. J. Navatel, cond. A-, (06-11-93, Boisgirard, #13), 51Czn x 35Mzn in., (130 x 90 cm.), poster (BP 132, DM 327, FR 1101, Y 21,326).

$341* *Chemin De Fer Du Nord. Treport Mers. Ete 1890,* Paris, Lith. F. Appel, cond. B, (06-11-93, Boisgirard, #15), 57M x 38Czn in., (147 x 97 cm.), poster (BP 224, DM 554, FR 1868, Y 36,180).

$241* *Chemin De Fer P.L.M. Saint-Honore Les Bains (Nievre), c. 1895,* Chatelles, Imp. L. Geissler, cond. B+, (06-11-93, Boisgirard, #12), 42½ x 29Bzn in., (108 x 76 cm.), poster (BP 158, DM 392, FR 1321, Y 25,570).

$210* *Chemins De Fer D'Alasace Lorraine: Strasbourg, c. 1925,* excell. cond., (01-23-93, Ribeyre/Baron, #145), 41¾ x 28¾ in., (106 x 73 cm.), poster (BP 137, DM 334, FR 1130, Y 26,283).

$315* *Chemins De Fer D'Alsace Et De Lorraine: Strasbourg, c. 1925,* p. Alsacienne, good cond., (11-19-92, Ribeyre/Baron, #82), 42Z, x 29¾ in., (107 x 75.5 cm.), poster (BP 207, DM 502, FR 1692, Y 39,174).

$221* *Chemins De Fer D'Orleans, De L'Etat Et Du Midi. Arachon, Bains De Mer(...) Casino Municipal, c. 1898,* Paris, Imp. Pichot, cond. B+, (06-11-93, Boisgirard, #14), 62Bzn x 47¼ in., (160 x 120 cm.), poster (BP 145, DM 359, FR 1211, Y 23,448).

$335* *Chemins De Fer Du Nord: Saint-Amand Thermal, c. 1900,* excell. cond., (01-23-93, Ribeyre/Baron, #16), 41¾ x 29½ in., (106 x 75 cm.), poster (BP 219, DM 533, FR 1802, Y 41,927).

$2780* *Chikanobu, Study Of A Lady,* (05-07-93, Christie-S. Ken, #65, illus.), 9 x 13½ in., (22.9 x 34.3 cm.), color woodblock print (BP 1760, DM 4395, FR 14,811, Y 306,100).

$495* *Christy Bros. Wild Animal Show,* excell. cond., chipping, dry mounted on heavy backing, (07-25-92, Julia, #376, illus.), 42 x 28 in., (106.7 x 71.1 cm.), poster (BP 261, DM 745, FR 2514, Y 63,114).

$348* *Cie De Navigation Sud-Atlantique: Brodeaux Bresil Plata. "Paquebots Lutetia Et Massilia", c. 1930,* very good cond., (03-13-93, Laurin, #151), 40>zn x 28¾ in., (103 x 73 cm.), (BP 243, DM 579, FR 1969, Y 41,014).

$241* *Cie Franco-Americaine Machines A Coudre Elias Howe,* excell. cond., (02-13-93, Morelle/Marchan, #34), 23¼ x 32Bzn in., (59 x 82 cm.), lithograph (BP 170, DM 400, FR 1352, Y 29,064).

$225* *Cie Gle De Boites-Lumieere, 27 Rue Desrenaudes-Paris, c. 1920,* artwork by Vany d'Aroche, (12-17-92, Christie-S. Ken, #186), 60 x 40 in., (152.4 x 101.6 cm.), lithograph (BP 143, DM 351, FR 1200, Y 27,651).

$261* *"Cie Le Regulateur Incandescent. Systeme Francais" and "Triomphe De L'Olympienne": Two,* first, Affiches Camis, good cond.; second bad cond., (02-12-93, Cheval/Robert, #37), first 57Zzn x 35Mzn in., (145 x 90 cm.), (BP 184, DM 433, FR 1465, Y 31,476).

$90* *Cigarettes Alba,* very good cond., (03-13-93, Laurin, #3), 46M, x 31½ in., (119 x 80 cm.), (BP 63, DM 150, FR 509, Y 10,607)

$413* *Circus Posters: Three,* American, 20th cent., (02-14-93, Hanzel, #708), each approx. 19 x 25½ in., (48.3 x 64.8 cm.), color lithographic poster (BP 291, DM 685, FR 2318, Y 49,807).

$220* *Clausen Beer,* good/very good cond., bottom cropped, trimmed, staining, overall soiling, (07-25-92, Julia, #247, illus.), 17¾ x 22 in., (45.1 x 55.9 cm.), paper poster (BP 116, DM 331, FR 1117, Y 28,050).

$462* *Consolation Des Enfants Avec Les Gaufrettes Et Biscuits Edmond Guillot, c. 1900,* Paris, Soc. Generale De L'Imprimerie, cond. B+, (06-11-93, Boisgirard, #37), 47¼ x 32Zzn in., (120 x 83 cm.), poster (BP 304, DM 751, FR 2532, Y 49,019).

$301* *Cycles Desaix, Cycles Favor, Clermont-Ferrand, c. 1905,* Paris, Affiches Camis, cond. A, (06-11-93, Boisgirard, #20), 62Azn x 45Z\n in., (159.5 x 116 cm.), poster (BP 198, DM 489, FR 1649, Y 31,936).

$499* *Cycles Gladiator, c. 1900,* cond. C, S. E.B., (03-16-93, Boisgirard, #100), 36¼ x 50>zn in., (92 x 128.5 cm.), poster (BP 345, DM 830, FR 2819, Y 58,349).

$2090* *Cycles Jules Du Bois,* Dupuy & Fils, B+ cond., fold marks, closed tears, minor repainting, (08-06-92, Swann, #7, illus.), 88¼ x 40½ in., (224.2 x 102.9 cm.), (BP 1092, DM 3088, FR 10,429, Y 266,582).

$50* *Cycles The Vulcain. "Toujours Le Sourire",* Imp. Romand, good cond., (02-12-93, Cheval/Robert, #78), 31Azn x 23B, in., (80.5 x 60 cm.), (BP 35, DM 83, FR 281, Y 6030).

$181* *D'Jelmako. Le Metis Canadien, c. 1895,* Paris, Affiches Americaines Ch. Levy, cond. B+, (06-11-93, Boisgirard, #33), 49Czn x 35B, in., (125 x 90.5 cm.), poster (BP 119, DM 294, FR 992, Y 19,204).

BI *Les Deux Lions, Veritable Vieux Systeme,* La Lithographie Artistique, A- cond., scuffing, est. $2/300, (08-06-92, Swann, #8, illus.), 23 x 15½ in., (58.4 x 39.4 cm.), .

$41* *Doublepatte And Patachon Vedettes (Belgian), 1920,* (01-31-93, Morelle/Marchan, #76), 23B, x 31½ in., (60 x 80 cm.), poster (BP 28, DM 66, FR 223, Y 5115).

$605* *Dunlap's Seeds,* litho. J. Ottmann, very good/excell. cond., tear, creasing, wrinkling, (07-25-92, Julia, #246, illus.), 16 x 23½ in., (40.6 x 59.7 cm.), paper poster (BP 319, DM 910, FR 3073, Y 77,139).

$33,000* *E & J Burke Ale Paper Sign, c. 1881,* image of Chicago and NY World Series teams' captains toasting each other, 1 of 2 known, good cond., wood/water staining, overall soiling, (07-25-92, Julia, #168, illus.), approx. 20 x 26 in., (50.8 x 66 cm.), poster (BP 17,423, DM 49,639, FR 167,598, Y 4,207,574).

$247* *E.C. Simmons Fine Fishing Tackle,* A cond., (08-06-92, Swann, #24, illus.), 18 x 36 in., (45.7 x 91.4 cm.), (BP 129, DM 365, FR 1233, Y 31,505).

$103* *Ecole Pour La Danse Isadora Duncan Et Elisabeth Duncan,c. 1920,* (01-31-93, Morelle/Marchan, #8), 23B, x 31½ in., (60 x 80 cm.), poster (BP 69, DM 166, FR 561, Y 12,849).

$660* *Emil Wunsche, Dresden,* p. Aktiengesellschaft fur Kunstdruck, repaired tears, creases, backed on linen, (05-07-93, Christie-S. Ken, #78, illus.), 18 x 46 in., (45.7 x 116.8 cm.), color lithograph (BP 418, DM 1043, FR 3516, Y 72,671).

$502* *En Vente Partout, Reglisse Zan, 1902,* Imp. H. Laas, Paris, cond. B+, (06-11-93, Boisgirard, #5), 47¼ x 31½ in., (120 x 80 cm.), poster (BP 330, DM 816, FR 2751, Y 53,263).

$302* *The English Opera Co., "Madame Butterfly", 1910,* Enquirer Litho. Co., B+ cond., marginal restoration, closed tears, (08-06-92, Swann, #216, illus.), 42 x 28 in., (106.7 x 71.1 cm.), (BP 158, DM 446, FR 1507, Y 38,520).

$220* *Esclarmonde,* Lith. F. Appel, A cond., (08-06-92, Swann, #9, illus.), 46½ x 32 in., (118.1 x 81.3 cm.), (BP 115, DM 325, FR 1098, Y 28,061).

$11,000* *Exhibition Poster For FILM UND FOTO, Stuttgart, 1929,* exhib., lit., catalog cover lot, (10-13-92, Christie-NY, #279, illus.), 33 x 23Z, in., (83.8 x 58.7 cm.), photo-offset lithography (BP 6407, DM 16,115, FR 54,754, Y 1,333,818).

$221* *Exposition De 1900. Paris En 1400. La Tour Des Miracles, 1899,* Marseille, Imp. Marseillaise, cond. B+, (06-11-93, Boisgirard, #29), 51Czn x 35B\ in., (130 x 90.5 cm.), poster (BP 145, DM 359, FR 1211, Y 23,448).

$839* *Exposition Des Voitures Citroen,* p. Chaix, very good cond., (11-19-92, Ribeyre/Baron, #54), 31Bzn x 47B, in., (79.5 x 121 cm.), poster (BP 552, DM 1338, FR 4506, Y 104,340).

$339* *Exposition Des Voitures Citroen, 1925,* cond. B, (03-16-93, Boisgirard, #24), 31Bzn x 47¼ in., (79.5 x 120 cm.), (BP 234, DM 564, FR 1915, Y 39,640).

$161* *Exposition Internationale, Universelle Et Coloniale De Lyon, 1894,* fairly good cond., (02-12-93, Cheval/Robert, #127), 50℃, x 39℃, in., (128 x 100 cm.), poster (BP 113, DM 267, FR 903, Y 19,416).

$1911* *Exposition Russe, Grand Ballon Captif,* p. Emile Levy, defects, creasing, laid on linen, (05-07-93, Christie-S. Ken, #131, illus.), 36 x 50 in., (91.4 x 127 cm.), color lithograph (BP 1210, DM 3021, FR 10,181, Y 210,416).

$165* *Fak-Hongs, Hooded Man,* Adolph Friedlander, B cond., fold marks, creasing, scuffing, (08-06-92, Swann, #185, illus.), 37 x 28 in., (94 x 71.1 cm.), (BP 86, DM 244, FR 823, Y 21,046).

$880* *Farmers And Workers, You Must Replace The Men Who Went To War, 1902,* Nikolaev, "Ukrosta", B cond., portion missing center, (08-06-92, Swann, #248, illus.), 37 x 24½ in., (94 x 62.2 cm.), b/w woodcut (BP 460, DM 1300, FR 4391, Y 112,245).

$72* *Feerie De Broadway (There's No Business Like Show Business), De W. Lang, Avec Marilyn Monroe (Belgian), 1955,* (01-31-93, Morelle/Marchan, #89), 21℃, x 14℃n in., (55 x 38 cm.), poster (BP 48, DM 116, FR 392, Y 8982).

$660* *Ferrovia Elettrica Stresamottarone, c. 1908,* Richter, B cond., marginal restoration, (08-06-92, Swann, #14, illus.), 39 x 26½ in., (99.1 x 67.3 cm.), (BP 345, DM 975, FR 3293, Y 84,184).

$130* *Folies Bergere: Constantin. "Le Plus Grand Geant Du Monde 2,59 m",* Imp. Chaix, fairly good cond., (02-12-93, Cheval/Robert, #143), 48℃n x 33℃, in., (124 x 86 cm.), poster (BP 92, DM 216, FR 730, Y 15,678).

$385* *For Peace And Freedom, 1940,* World's Fair of 1940, linen-backed, New York: Polygraphic Company, 1940, w/ two lithographed railway placards, (04-29-93, Swann, #212), 30 x 20 in., (76.2 x 50.8 cm.), color lithograph poster (BP 245, DM 609, FR 2052, Y 42,830).

$440* *Fourepaugh & Sells Brothers, Circus: Two,* American, 20th cent., (02-14-93, Hanzel, #710), each 27 x 37 in., (68.6 x 94 cm.), color lithographic poster (BP 310, DM 730, FR 2469, Y 53,063).

$145* *Fuocco Nella Stiva (Fire Down Bellow), 1957, De R. Parrish Avec RitaHayworth, Robert Mitchum (Italian),* (01-31-93, Morelle/Marchan, #67), 39℃, x 55℃, in., (100 x 140 cm.), poster (BP 98, DM 234, FR 790, Y 18,089).

$382* *GD. Bazar Parisien & Nouvelles Galeries,* creases, edges torn, repairs, backed on canvas, laid on board, (05-07-93, Christie-S. Ken, #99, illus.), 45 x 63 in., (114.3 x 160 cm.), color lithograph (BP 242, DM 604, FR 2035, Y 42,061).

$100* *Gds Magasins De La Samaritaine,* fair cond., (02-13-93, Morelle/Marchan, #49), 47¼ x 62℃n in., (120 x 160 cm.), poster (BP 70, DM 166, FR 561, Y 12,060).

$357* *George, Master Of Magic,* Otis Litho. Co., A cond., chartex-backed, (08-06-92, Swann, #191, illus.), 40½ x 26½ in., (102.9 x 67.3 cm.), (BP 186, DM 527, FR 1781, Y 45,536).

$165* *George, The Supreme Master Of Magic,* Otis Litho. Co., A cond., (08-06-92, Swann, #190, illus.), 26½ x 20 in., (67.3 x 50.8 cm.), (BP 86, DM 244, FR 823, Y 21,046).

$248* *"George, The Supreme Master Of Magic",* the Otis Lithograph Co., (08-05-92, Boos, #584), 40½ x 26 in., (102.9 x 66 cm.), color lithograph (BP 130, DM 366, FR 1238, Y 31,584).

$660* *Gilets D'Ete Du Docteur Rasurel, 1913,* Affiches-Frossard-Courbet, B+ cond., fold marks, cracking, repairs, (08-06-92, Swann, #12, illus.), 61 x 45½ in., (154.9 x 115.6 cm.), (BP 345, DM 975, FR 3293, Y 84,184).

$165* *Girl Of My Dreams, c. 1930(?),* (04-29-93, Swann, #311), 25 x 17 in., (63.5 x 43.2 cm.), color poster on canvas (BP 105, DM 261, FR 880, Y 18,356).

$990* *Gold Soap,* fair/good cond., trimmed, overall soiling, wrinkling, tears, (07-25-92, Julia, #212, illus.), approx. 22 x 17¾ in., (55.9 x 45.1 cm.), paper poster (BP 523, DM 1489, FR 5028, Y 126,227).

$330* *Gorton's,* good/very good cond., crease borders trimmed, tears, wear, (07-25-92, Julia, #243, illus.), 26½ x 20¼ in., (67.3 x 51.4 cm.), paper poster (BP 174, DM 496, FR 1676, Y 42,076).

$110* *Grands Vins De Champagne C. Gauthier & Cie. Chateau Des Archers, Epernay. Maison Fondee En 1858,* good cond., (02-12-93, Cheval/Robert, #7), sight 19℃, x 8M, in., (48.5 x 22.5 cm.), (BP 77, DM 182, FR 617, Y 13,266).

BI *The Great Kar-Mi Troupe,* The Donaldson-Litho. Co., A- cond., est. $3/400, (08-06-92, Swann, #184, illus.), 42 x 48 in., (106.7 x 121.9 cm.), .

$1760* *The Greater 1913 Williamson County Fair, Marion, ILL. Aug. 9 To 13, Aviation - Roy Francis And "Shy High" Irving,* fold/creasing, Francis Aero Collection, (09-12-92, Dunning, #208, illus.), approx. 42 x 14¼ in., (106.7 x 36.2 cm.), poster (BP 910, DM 2533, FR 8611, Y 218,065).

$479* *Guerre Russo-Japonaise, 1904,* cond. B, (03-16-93, Boisgirard, #3), 25℃n x 33℃n in., (65 x 85 cm.), lithograph poster (BP 331, DM 796, FR 2706, Y 56,010).

$110* *Guion Line,* advertisement by Hatch Litho. Co., fair cond., wrinkling, image loss, center fold, trimmed, (07-25-92, Julia, #120, illus.), 31 x 21 in., (78.7 x 53.3 cm.), poster (BP 58, DM 165, FR 559, Y 14,025).

$495* *Hagenbeck, Wallace Circus, 1933,* Central PTg., Illinois Litho. Co., A- cond., closed tears, stamps w/d., (08-06-92, Swann, #95, illus.), 28 x 41½ in., (71.1 x 105.4 cm.), (BP 259, DM 731, FR 2470, Y 63,138).

$608* *Harrogate. "Greenup", c. 1930,* pub. London and North Eastern, very good cond., (11-19-92, Ribeyre/Baron, #80, illus.), 39℃n x 24℃n in., (101.5 x 63 cm.), poster (BP 400, DM 969, FR 3265, Y 75,612).

$440* *"He Did His Duty, U.S. Marines", "Treed", "Capturing Paris", An Appeal" and "Enlist In The Navy": Group Of Five,* cond. varies, (08-06-92, Swann, #298, illus.), (BP 230, DM 650, FR 2196, Y 56,122).

$330* *"Headquarters For The Best In Kosher Wines. Enjoy A Fine Rich Wine","The Best In Kosher Wines" and "Schapiro's Kosher Wine's, The Wine You Can Almost Cut With A Knife": Three,* discoloration, damages, (06-24-93, Swann, #336), largest 27℃n x 22℃n in., (700 x 560 mm.), smallest 10℃n x 21℃n in., (700 x 560 mm.), (BP 225, DM 564, FR 1898, Y 35,995).

$1445* *Holland-America Line (…) Rotterdam, Boulogne s/ mer, New York, c. 1905,* Bruxelles, Affiches O. de Rycker and Mendel, cond. A, (06-11-93, Boisgirard, #17), 38>℃n x 58℃n in., (98 x 147.5 cm.), poster (BP 949, DM 2348, FR 7918, Y 153,316).

$220* *Hooded Man,* Lith. Adolph Friedlander, B+ cond., creasing, marginal chipping, (08-06-92, Swann, #186, illus.), 37¼ x 28 in., (94.6 x 71.1 cm.), (BP 115, DM 325, FR 1098, Y 28,061).

$10 *Horse Race,* folds, rips, (03-04-93, Alderfer, #279), 26 x 37 in., (66 x 94 cm.), poster (BP 7, DM 16, FR 56, Y 1164).

$330* *Horse, Super Cigarettes,* B+ cond., closed tears, marginal tears, (08-06-92, Swann, #13, illus.), 49½ x 35 in., (125.7 x 88.9 cm.), (BP 172, DM 488, FR 1647, Y 42,092).

$1100* *Horsman's,* rare, good cond., trimmed to border image, tears, wrinkling, soiling, (07-25-92, Julia, #214, illus.), approx. 17½ x 22¼ in., (44.5 x 56.5 cm.), paper poster (BP 581, DM 1655, FR 5587, Y 140,252).

$378* *IIIeme Exposition Internationale Aeronautique De Prague, 1924,* p. Pacold & Cie, fair cond., (11-19-92, Ribeyre/Baron, #53), 37℃n x 24M℃n in., (96 x 62 cm.), poster (BP 249, DM 603, FR 2030, Y 47,009).

$159* *Il Arrive Bien Cremeux…Babybel,* cond. B, (03-16-93, Boisgirard, #18), 55℃, x 86℃, in., (140 x 220 cm.), (BP 110, DM 264, FR 898, Y 18,592).

$302* *Infant King On Horseback, 1929,* Exposition-Barcelona 1929, linen-backed, (04-29-93, Swann, #141), 25½ x 18 in., (64.8 x 45.7 cm.), color lithograph poster (BP 192, DM 478, FR 1610, Y 33,597).

$4620* *International Great Lakes Flying Boat Cruise, Chicago's 1913 GreaterAviation, Grant Park, July 5th To 8th,* margin dirty, (09-12-92, Dunning, #210, illus.), approx. 28¼ x 21 in., (71.8 x 53.3 cm.), poster (BP 2389, DM 6650, FR 22,603, Y 572,420).

$414* *Invitation A La Dance (Invitation To The Dance), De G. Kelly, Avec T. Toumanova (Belgian), 1956,* (01-31-93, Morelle/Marchan, #111), 14℃n x 20½ in., (36 x 52 cm.), poster (BP 278, DM 667, FR 2255, Y 51,647).

$110* *"Iolanthe", "A Girl Of The Mountains" and "The Girl He Couldn't Buy": Group Of Three,* A- cond., (08-06-92, Swann, #267, illus.), approx. 36 x 25 in., (91.4 x 63.5 cm.), (BP 57, DM 163, FR 549, Y 14,031).

$181* *Irradiateur A Gaz. Incandescence Sans Manchon! Sans Verre!,* Imp. Lemercier, good cond., (02-12-93, Cheval/ Robert, #38), 53Z, x 43Bzn in., (135 x 110 cm.), (BP 127, DM 300, FR 1016, Y 21,828).

$468* *James Gordon Bennett Aviation Trophy, Other Chicago Aviation Events In 1912, Season Subscription Membership Certificate And Identification Coupon Entitling Holder To All 1912 Events,* (09-12-92, Dunning, #213, illus.), approx. 22 x 28 in., (55.9 x 71.1 cm.), poster (BP 242, DM 674, FR 2290, Y 57,985).

$100* *Je Ne Fume Que Le Nil, c. 1895,* Bordeaux, Imp. Nouvelle F. Pech and Cie, cond. B, (06-11-93, Boisgirard, #9), 31M, x 24 in., (81 x 61 cm.), poster (BP 66, DM 163, FR 548, Y 10,610).

$303* *"Je Ne Fumekque Le Nil",* p. Vercasson, (08-05-92, Boos, #589), 44½ x 63¼ in., (113 x 160.7 cm.), color lithograph (BP 158, DM 448, FR 1512, Y 38,589).

$103* *Je Suis De La Revue Avec Fernandel, S. Delair, Louis Armstrong, Katherine Dunham...,* (01-31-93, Morelle/ Marchan, #205), 47¼ x 62B\n in., (120 x 160 cm.), poster (BP 69, DM 166, FR 561, Y 12,849).

$1035* *Jimi Hendrix Experience Autographed Poster, 1967,* i., (06-23-93, Sotheby-NY, #467, illus.), 18 x 24 in., (45.7 x 61 cm.), (BP 703, DM 1751, FR 5891, Y 112,757).

$440* *John Robinson's Circus,* Erie Litho. Co., B+ cond., repair, closed tear, (08-06-92, Swann, #101, illus.), 40½ x 26 in., (102.9 x 66 cm.), (BP 230, DM 650, FR 2196, Y 56,122).

$110* *John Sanger & Sons. "Le Plus Grand Cirque Du Monde",* good cond., (02-12-93, Cheval/Robert, #146), 43Bzn x 106Bzn in., (110 x 270 cm.), poster (BP 77, DM 182, FR 617, Y 13,266).

$550 *Join The Air Service,* W.Z., Forbes, Boston, minor edge loss, (09-24-92, Alderfer, #281), 30 x 20 in., (76.2 x 50.8 cm.), (BP 322, DM 815, FR 2768, Y 66,161).

$83* *Kaline Dans Son Numero Lumineux,* (01-31-93, Morelle/ Marchan, #218), 30Bzn x 46Zzn in., (77 x 117 cm.), poster (BP 56, DM 134, FR 452, Y 10,354).

$80* *Kalodont. "Le Meilleur Dentifrice Americain", c. 1910,* Imp. Charles Verneau, good cond., (02-12-93, Cheval/ Robert, #30), 22¼ x 14¾ in., (56.5 x 37.5 cm.), (BP 56, DM 133, FR 449, Y 9648).

$410* *Kandersteg, c. 1930,* p. Kunstanstalt Brugger Meiringen, excell. cond., (02-04-93, Christie-S. Ken, #1, illus.), 39 x 24½ in., (99.1 x 62.2 cm.), color lithograph backed on japan (BP 286, DM 675, FR 2289, Y 51,001).

$550* *Kansas City Automobile Show, 1908,* Tingle-Titus Printing Co., B+ cond., closed tears, creasing, (08-06-92, Swann, #15, illus.), 22 x 15 in., (55.9 x 38.1 cm.), (BP 287, DM 813, FR 2745, Y 70,153).

$495* *Keep It Under Your Stetson: Two,* issued by Stetson Hat Co., B- cond., chartex-backed, borders trimmed, (08-06-92, Swann, #32, illus.), 29 x 39 in., (73.7 x 99.1 cm.), (BP 259, DM 731, FR 2470, Y 63,138).

$5907* *Kodak No. 1 Diodak Shutter,* folds, color repaired, backed on linen, front cover illus., (05-07-93, Christie-S. Ken, #60, illus.), 23 x 31½ in., (58.4 x 80 cm.), color lithograph (BP 3740, DM 9339, FR 31,470, Y 650,407).

$608* *Kodak, Velox,* creases, defects, backed on linen, (05-07-93, Christie-S. Ken, #59, illus.), 29¾ x 45½ in., (75.6 x 115.6 cm.), color lithograph (BP 385, DM 961, FR 3239, Y 66,946).

$99* *Kranebet Liquore, 1946,* Arti Grafiche Votta, A cond., (08-06-92, Swann, #17, illus.), 40 x 28¼ in., (101.6 x 71.8 cm.), (BP 52, DM 146, FR 494, Y 12,628).

$40* *L'Aube Rouge. Drame Lyrique (...) Musique De Camille Erlanger, c. 1905,* cond. A, (03-16-93, Boisgirard, #39), 32Bzn x 23B, in., (82 x 60 cm.), (BP 28, DM 67, FR 226, Y 4677).

$2750* *L'Excursionniste,* Edw. Ancourt and Co., B+ cond., bleed through of tape on closed tear, (08-06-92, Swann, #10, illus.), 47 x 35 in., (119.4 x 88.9 cm.), (BP 1436, DM 4063, FR 13,723, Y 350,765).

$110* *"L'Instant Taittinger",* pub. Publicis, (08-05-92, Boos, #591), 66 x 47½ in., (167.6 x 120.7 cm.), color poster (BP 58, DM 162, FR 549, Y 14,009).

$161* *Lavix, Une Fidele Servante,* creased, (02-13-93, Morelle/ Marchan, #5), 47¼ x 62Azn in., (120 x 160 cm.), poster (BP 113, DM 267, FR 903, Y 19,416).

$115* *Led Zeppelin Ampex Poster, 1969,* (06-23-93, Sotheby-NY, #411), 36 x 24 in., (91.4 x 61 cm.), (BP 78, DM 195, FR 655, Y 12,529).

$40 *Liberty Bond,* Edwards and Deutsch, No. 10, minor edge damage, (09-24-92, Alderfer, #310), (BP 23, DM 59, FR 201, Y 4812).

BI *Liqueur Du Pere Kermann. F. Cazanove, Bordeaux,* Imp. Prouteaux et Chaubin, good cond., (02-12-93, Cheval/ Robert, #35), 45Zzn x 33Mzn in., (116 x 85 cm.), .

$605* *Liquore Del Reno, c. 1920's,* A cond., (08-06-92, Swann, #16, illus.), 21 x 13½ in., (53.3 x 34.3 cm.), (BP 316, DM 894, FR 3019, Y 77,168).

$120* *Londres, Paris, Madrid, Lisbonne (Sud-Express), c. 1900,* cond. B, (03-16-93, Boisgirard, #34), 44Zzn x 33Bzn in., (113.5 x 84 cm.), (BP 83, DM 200, FR 678, Y 14,032).

$825* *Lugano-Grand Palace Hotel,* Trueb, A- cond., (08-06-92, Swann, #18, illus.), 27½ x 39½ in., (69.9 x 100.3 cm.), (BP 431, DM 1219, FR 4117, Y 105,230).

$1154* *Maison Bremer, Tennis,* good cond., (11-19-92, Ribeyre/ Baron, #6, illus.), 39C, x 24Mzn in., (100 x 62 cm.), gouache maquette (BP 760, DM 1840, FR 6198, Y 143,514).

$2200* *Make Your Flying Contract With Aviation's Big Concern - The Curtiss-Wright - Bleriot Aviators,* fold, creasing, Francis Aero Coll., (09-12-92, Dunning, #207, illus.), approx. 42 x 28¼ in., (106.7 x 71.8 cm.), poster (BP 1138, DM 3167, FR 10,763, Y 272,581).

$550* *Manifesto, Power To The Rich, Whips For The Poor, 1920,* B cond., portion missing, (08-06-92, Swann, #249, illus.), 27¼ x 20¼ in., (69.2 x 51.4 cm.), (BP 287, DM 813, FR 2745, Y 70,153).

$62* *Mariage Royal (Royal Wedding), De S. Donen, Avec J. Powell (French),1951,* (01-31-93, Morelle/Marchan, #107), 23B, x 31½ in., (60 x 80 cm.), poster (BP 42, DM 100, FR 338, Y 7735).

$289* *Marokko. Freitag In Rabat. 1957,* good cond., (03-13-93, Laurin, #85), 39C, x 24Czn in., (100 x 61.5 cm.), (BP 202, DM 481, FR 1636, Y 34,060).

BI *Marseille, Porte De L'Afrique Du Nord,* very good cond., (03-13-93, Laurin, #152), 39C, x 24Mzn in., (100 x 62 cm.), .

$72* *Mason Et Mason (Comiques Americains) Avalanche Of Fun, c. 1900,* (01-31-93, Morelle/Marchan, #217), 43Bzn x 38Czn in., (110 x 97 cm.), poster (BP 48, DM 116, FR 392, Y 8982).

$442* *Le Mauvais Hote. Film Gaumont. Avec le Mime Wague, c. 1910,* Imp. des Ets Gaumont, good cond., (02-12-93, Cheval/Robert, #197), 58¼ x 43Bzn in., (148 x 110 cm.), poster (BP 311, DM 733, FR 2480, Y 53,304).

$350 *Men Wanted For The Army,* form No. 404AGO, folds, edge damage, (09-24-92, Alderfer, #318), 41 x 30 in., (104.1 x 76.2 cm.), (BP 205, DM 519, FR 1761, Y 42,103).

$83* *Meryac - Combe Duettistes - Bouffes - Parodistes,* (01-31-93, Morelle/Marchan, #230), 23¼ x 31½ in., (59 x 80 cm.), poster (BP 56, DM 134, FR 452, Y 10,354).

$723* *Messieurs!! Voulez-vous Conquerir Les Coeurs, Offrez Du Champagne DeLa Jarretiere, c. 1900,* Aff. Art. Vercasson, Paris, cond. B-, restored, (06-11-93, Boisgirard, #2), 62Azn x 44M, in., (160 x 114 cm.), poster (BP 475, DM 1175, FR 3962, Y 76,711).

$46* *Mister Swing (Mister Big), De C. Lamont, Avec D. O'Connor, Gloria Jean (Belgian), 1943,* (01-31-93, Morelle/Marchan, #91), 11E\n x 15¾ in., (30 x 40 cm.), poster (BP 31, DM 74, FR 251, Y 5739).

$88* *Musee National D'Art Moderne - Le Cubisme, 1907-1914,* exhibition poster, (06-11-93, Freemn/Fine Art, #133), 28 x 20 in., (71.1 x 50.8 cm.), lithograph (BP 58, DM 143, FR 482, Y 9337).

BI *"My Lady Molly", c. 1900,* est. $150/250, (01-15-93, DuMouchelle, #1304), 30 x 20 in., (76.2 x 50.8 cm.), poster.

$5940* *The Nation, State And City Welcome The World's Greatest Aviators, Dayton, Ohio, June 17-18, 1909,* creasing, tears, pin holes, (09-12-92, Dunning, #211, illus.), 30½ x

21 in., (77.5 x 53.3 cm.), poster (BP 3072, DM 8550, FR 29,061, Y 735,968).

$247* *Nederlandsche Spoorwegen, 1939,* Druk Mes and Bronkhorst, B+ cond., creasing, repairs, (08-06-92, Swann, #19, illus.), 39 x 24 in., (99.1 x 61 cm.), (BP 129, DM 365, FR 1233, Y 31,505).

$642* *Nestle's Milk, c. 1900,* cond. B+, (06-11-93, Boisgirard, #35), 59Ɀzn x 39Ȼ, in., (150 x 100 cm.), poster (BP 422, DM 1043, FR 3518, Y 68,117).

$210* *Netherland. La Hollande. "Visitez Les Champs De Fleurs",* p. L. Van Leer & Co., very good cond., (11-19-92, Ribeyre/Baron, #79), 39Ȼzn x 24Mzn in., (99.5 x 62 cm.), poster (BP 138, DM 335, FR 1128, Y 26,116).

$275* *The New York Circus, 1872,* few chips and tears, (04-29-93, Swann, #80, illus.), 24 x 8½ in., (61 x 21.6 cm.), poster w/8 wood-engraved vignettes (BP 175, DM 435, FR 1466, Y 30,593).

$165* *New York Life Insurance Company,* good cond., creasing, fading, (07-25-92, Julia, #77R, illus.), 15¼ x 20¾ in., (38.7 x 52.7 cm.), paper poster (BP 87, DM 248, FR 838, Y 21,038).

$310* *A Night At The Opera, De S. Wood Avec Les Marx Brothers, 1935,* (01-31-93, Morelle/Marchan, #152), poster (BP 208, DM 499, FR 1688, Y 38,673).

$114* *Nijinsky, Clown De Dieu,* (01-31-93, Morelle/Marchan, #3), 31½ x 23B\ in., (80 x 60 cm.), poster (BP 77, DM 184, FR 621, Y 14,222).

$3850* *Norumbega Park,* excell. cond., tears, (07-25-92, Julia, #213, illus.), 22 x 28 in., (55.9 x 71.1 cm.), paper poster (BP 2033, DM 5791, FR 19,553, Y 490,884).

$100* *Nouvelle Machine A Coudre A Navette Circulaire H. Vigneron, c. 1898,* cond. B+, (06-11-93, Boisgirard, #21), 29Bzn x 23¼ in., (74.5 x 59 cm.), poster (BP 66, DM 163, FR 548, Y 10,610).

$55* *"La Nouvelle Rente Francaise-Defense Nationale" and "Jeanne D'Arc": Two,* frayed margins, tears, (06-11-93, Freemn/Fine Art, #72A), 23¼ x 15¼ in., (59.1 x 38.7 cm.), lithographic poster (BP 36, DM 89, FR 301, Y 5836).

$31* *Une Nuit A Rio (That Night In Rio), De I. Cummings, Avec A. Faye Et C. Miranda (Belgian), 1941,* (01-31-93, Morelle/Marchan, #90), 11Ȥzn x 14\zn in., (30 x 37 cm.), poster (BP 21, DM 50, FR 169, Y 3867).

$389* *O.N.T. Predeal. Scoala Nationale De Ski, c. 1935,* cond. B, (03-16-93, Boisgirard, #31), 39¾ x 27\zn in., (101 x 70 cm.), (BP 269, DM 647, FR 2198, Y 45,486).

$221* *Olympia. Looping The Loop, Seul Createur Americain, Diavolo, c. 1900,* Paris, Imp. Delanchy, cond. A-, (06-11-93, Boisgirard, #34), 49Ȼzn x 35Mzn in., (125 x 90 cm.), poster (BP 145, DM 359, FR 1211, Y 23,448).

$275 *Order Coal Now,* Edwards and Deutsch Litho. Co., Chicago, No. 2, very good cond., (09-24-92, Alderfer, #239, illus.), 29½ x 20 in., (74.9 x 50.8 cm.), (BP 161, DM 408, FR 1384, Y 33,081).

BI *Ordre De Mobilisation Generale Du 2 Aout 1914,* good cond., (02-12-93, Cheval/Robert, #105), 35Ȼ\zn x 26ȤBzn in., (91 x 68.5 cm.), poster.

$80* *The Original Brothers Onzella,* good cond., (02-12-93, Cheval/Robert, #144), 32½ x 23B, in., (82.5 x 60 cm.), poster (BP 56, DM 133, FR 449, Y 9648).

$199* *Original Victoria. Machines A Coudre. Guiton Horloger-Bijoutier(...)Riom, Puy-de-Dome, c. 1900,* cond. B, (03-16-93, Boisgirard, #28), 39Ȼzn x 26ȤBzn in., (99.5 x 68.5 cm.), (BP 137, DM 331, FR 1124, Y 23,269).

$174* *The Orpheum Show, 1900,* p. U.S. Printing Co. Russell-Morgan Print, creases, (05-07-93, Christie-S. Ken, #69), sight 39 x 26 in., (99.1 x 66 cm.), color lithograph (BP 110, DM 275, FR 927, Y 19,159).

$120* *Osborne (...) Mailloles, Perpignan (Pyrenees Orientales), c. 1900,* Paris, Imp. Henon, cond. A, (06-11-93, Boisgirard, #18), 30Ȥzn x 23¼ in., (78 x 59 cm.), poster (BP 79, DM 195, FR 658, Y 12,732).

$788* *Overhead Railway, Liverpool, c. 1920: Two,* fold marks, tears, losses, (02-04-93, Christie-S. Ken, #79, illus.), 39½ x 25 in., (100.3 x 63.5 cm.), color lithograph (BP 550, DM 1298, FR 4400, Y 98,022).

$550* *"Overtake And Surpass", c. 1936,* B cond., restoration, closed tears, yellowing, (08-06-92, Swann, #247, illus.), 42½ x 27½ in., (108 x 69.9 cm.), (BP 287, DM 813, FR 2745, Y 70,153).

$330* *P. Sescau Photographe,* (05-07-93, Christie-S. Ken, #118, illus.), 11 x 8½ in., (27.9 x 21.6 cm.), color lithograph (BP 209, DM 522, FR 1758, Y 36,336).

$161* *P.L.M. Brides-Les-Bains. Salins-Moustiers, c. 1895,* Paris, Imp. Lemercier, cond. A, (06-11-93, Boisgirard, #16), 41\zn x 29½ in., (105.5 x 75 cm.), poster (BP 106, DM 262, FR 882, Y 17,082).

$231* *P.L.M.-C.I.W.L. Et De Grands Express Europeens. Services De La Mediterranee. Hiver 1901-1902,* Paris, Lith. G. Bataille, cond. B+, (06-11-93, Boisgirard, #11), 41¾ x 29Ȥzn in., (106 x 76 cm.), poster (BP 152, DM 375, FR 1266, Y 24,509).

$121* *P.T. Barnum's Broadside, Multiple Images Of Various People And Circus Animals,* good cond., creasing, paper loss, (07-25-92, Julia, #83, illus.), 14½ x 21½ in., (36.8 x 54.6 cm.), poster (BP 64, DM 182, FR 615, Y 15,428).

$597* *PLM: L'Algerie Et La Tunisie Pa La Cie Generale Transatlantique,* very good cond., (03-13-93, Laurin, #76, illus.), 41Ɀ, x 28Ȼ, in., (104.5 x 72 cm.), (BP 416, DM 994, FR 3379, Y 70,359).

$159* *Palai Du Velodrome D'Hiver. Champ De Mars. "Le Sahara A Paris",* good cond., (03-13-93, Laurin, #19), 46¼ x 25ȤBzn in., (117.5 x 66 cm.), (BP 111, DM 265, FR 900, Y 18,739).

$730* *Panama And The Canal From An Aeroplane,* Schmidt Litho S.F., creases, tear, (05-07-93, Christie-S. Ken, #68, illus.), 26½ x 41 in., (67.3 x 104.1 cm.), color lithograph (BP 462, DM 1154, FR 3889, Y 80,379).

$181* *Papier A Cigarettes Abadie,* creased, (02-13-93, Morelle/Marchan, #7), 62B\zn x 47¼ in., (160 x 120 cm.), poster (BP 127, DM 300, FR 1016, Y 21,828).

$361* *Paris Mai 1903. Concours Internationale De Photographie Sur Les Papiers Et Tissus Artistiques Luna, Vielle and Cie, Lausanne,* Lausanne, Corbaz and Cie, cond. A-, (06-11-93, Boisgirard, #24, illus.), 45½ x 28\zn in., (115.5 x 72.5 cm.), photolithographic poster (BP 237, DM 587, FR 1978, Y 38,302).

$566* *Pates "La Lune" Bozon-Verduraz, c. 1935,* p. Damour, good cond., (11-19-92, Ribeyre/Baron, #3), 61 x 44½ in., (155 x 113 cm.), poster (BP 373, DM 902, FR 3040, Y 70,389).

$201* *Pates Alimentaires Ceres, Nice. Fabrication A L'Italienne,* Pub. Dumas, fairly good cond., (02-12-93, Cheval/Robert, #28), 62Ȥzn x 47¼ in., (160 x 120 cm.), (BP 142, DM 333, FR 1128, Y 24,240).

$315* *Pedras Salgadas. "Deliciosas Ferias De Cura",* p. Bolhao, good cond., (11-19-92, Ribeyre/Baron, #77), 56Ȥn x 42Bzn in., (144 x 107.5 cm.), poster (BP 207, DM 502, FR 1692, Y 39,174).

$100* *Petrole Des Salons, Luciline En Bidons De 5 Litres, c. 1900,* Paris, Imp. Camis, cond. B+, (06-11-93, Boisgirard, #8), 20½ x 16Ɀ, in., (52 x 41 cm.), poster (BP 66, DM 163, FR 548, Y 10,610).

$1390* *Photographie Abel, Tours,* p. Raymond Pitrou, creases, ink stamp, backed on linen, (05-07-93, Christie-S. Ken, #113, illus.), 49½ x 38¾ in., (125.7 x 98.4 cm.), color lithograph (BP 880, DM 2198, FR 7405, Y 153,050).

$1320* *Pianos Daude,* Pag, A cond., (08-06-92, Swann, #20, illus.), 62½ x 46½ in., (158.8 x 118.1 cm.), (BP 689, DM 1950, FR 6587, Y 168,367).

$110* *A Pictorial Map Of Southern Rhodesia, 1938,* Litho. Press for the Department of Publicity, B+ cond., creasing, peeling, (08-06-92, Swann, #271, illus.), 37 x 24½ in., (94 x 62.2 cm.), (BP 57, DM 163, FR 549, Y 14,031).

$385* *Picturing The King, Queen, And Joker From A Deck Of Cards,* Universal Exposition-Paris 1900, various colors, linen-backed, (04-29-93, Swann, #133), 23½ x 16 in., (59.7 x 40.6 cm.), color lithographed poster (BP 245, DM 609, FR 2052, Y 42,830).

$602* *Pierrot Et Colombine A Bicyclette,* before letters, Paris, Imp. Camis, (06-11-93, Boisgirard, #36), 51Ȼzn x 39Ȼ, in., (130 x 100 cm.), poster (BP 396, DM 978, FR 3299, Y 63,873).

BI *"Pirates Of Penzance", c. 1900,* English, est. $150/250, (10-16-92, DuMouchelle, #1307, illus.), 30 x 20 in., (76.2 x 50.8 cm.), poster.

BI *"Pirates Of Penzance", c. 1900,* est. $150/250, (01-15-93, DuMouchelle, #1305), 30 x 20 in., (76.2 x 50.8 cm.), poster.

$944* *Pneu Michelin, Le Seul S'Adaptant A La Roue De La Fortune, c. 1896,* Paris, Imp. Moderne De Brunoff, cond. B+, (06-11-93, Boisgirard, #19), 592zn x 43½ in., (150 x 110.5 cm.), poster (BP 620, DM 1534, FR 5173, Y 100,159).

$1103* *Polo Wettspiele, Berlin Frohnau, 1927,* indistinctly s., yellowing, creasing, tears, (02-04-93, Christie-S. Ken, #154, illus.), 37½ x 28 in., (95.3 x 71.1 cm.), color lithograph (BP 770, DM 1816, FR 6159, Y 137,206).

$275* *"Pour La Liberte DuMonde",* Banque Nationale de Credit, Visa No. 8735 Devambez IMP Paris, restored, (09-12-92, Dunning, #313, illus.), 41 x 62 in., (104.1 x 157.5 cm.), poster laid on cloth (BP 142, DM 396, FR 1345, Y 34,073).

$52* *Pour Moi Et Ma Mie (For Me And My Gall), De B. Berkeley, Avec J. Garland (Belgian), 1942,* (01-31-93, Morelle/Marchan, #116), 23B, x 31½ in., (36 x 55 cm.), poster (BP 35, DM 84, FR 283, Y 6487).

$440* *"Pourle Dropeau Pourla Victoire", 1917,* Devambeg IMP Paris, Visa No. 9498, restored, (09-12-92, Dunning, #314, illus.), 47 x 62 in., (119.4 x 157.5 cm.), poster laid on cloth (BP 228, DM 633, FR 2153, Y 54,516).

$730* *Premier Exposition De Photographie,* Affiches-Camis, creases, defects, repairs to edges, backed on linen, (05-07-93, Christie-S. Ken, #128, illus.), 38¾ x 51½ in., (98.4 x 130.8 cm.), color lithograph (BP 462, DM 1154, FR 3889, Y 80,379).

$330* *Public Warning: The Public Are Advised To Familiarize Themselves With The Appearance Of British And German Airships And Aeroplanes, 1915,* (04-29-93, Swann, #313), 35 x 23 in., (88.9 x 58.4 cm.), poster in black and red (BP 210, DM 522, FR 1759, Y 36,712).

$275* *Railroad, 1925,* A cond., Japanese lettering, (08-06-92, Swann, #156, illus.), 41½ x 30 in., (105.4 x 76.2 cm.), (BP 144, DM 406, FR 1372, Y 35,077).

$120* *Rasoir Star,* good cond., (02-13-93, Morelle/Marchan, #40), 31½ x 47¼ in., (80 x 120 cm.), poster (BP 85, DM 199, FR 673, Y 14,472).

$90* *"Reconciliation. Par Le Chateau Cognac" and "Moutarde Mavoisine": Two,* first, Ch. Verneau, good cond.; second, Lith. Appel, bad cond., (02-12-93, Cheval/Robert, #36), first 54Bzn x 37C, in., (139.5 x 95 cm.), second 592zn x 39C, in., (139.5 x 95 cm.), (BP 63, DM 149, FR 505, Y 10,854).

$30 *"Remember The Flag",* rip, (03-04-93, Alderfer, #277), 30 x 20 in., (76.2 x 50.8 cm.), poster (BP 21, DM 49, FR 167, Y 3493).

$221* *Representation De Bienfaisance Au Benefice Des Sinistres De La Martinique, 1902,* Paris, Imp. Chales Verneau, cond. A-, (06-11-93, Boisgirard, #28), 47¼ x 30Z, in., (120 x 76.5 cm.), poster (BP 145, DM 359, FR 1211, Y 23,448).

$1045* *Rice's Seeds "The True Early Winning Stadt",* p. Cosack & Co., excell. cond., (07-25-92, Julia, #244, illus.), approx. 20 x 27 in., (50.8 x 68.6 cm.), paper poster (BP 552, DM 1572, FR 5307, Y 133,240).

$1430* *Ringling Bros. And Barnum And Bailey,* Strobridge Litho. Co., B+ cond., fold mark, closed tear, back cover illus., (08-06-92, Swann, #98, illus.), 41½ x 28 in., (105.4 x 71.1 cm.), (BP 747, DM 2113, FR 7136, Y 182,398).

$605* *Ringling Bros. And Barnum And Bailey,* The Strobridge Litho. Co., B+ cond., closed tear, marginal tearing, (08-06-92, Swann, #100, illus.), 42 x 28½ in., (106.7 x 72.4 cm.), (BP 316, DM 894, FR 3019, Y 77,168).

$688* *"Ringling Bros. And Barnum And Bailey Circus - Giraffe-neck Woman From Burma",* creasing, tears, (09-12-92, Dunning, #37, illus.), 28 x 42 in., (71.1 x 106.7 cm.), poster (BP 356, DM 990, FR 3366, Y 85,243).

$121* *Ringling Bros. And Barnum And Bailey Circus; The Great Yacopi Troupe; Argentine Acrobatic Marvels Without Equal,* steamer traces, (04-29-93, Swann, #81), 28 x 42 in., (71.1 x 106.7 cm.), color lithographed posters (BP 77, DM 191, FR 645, Y 13,461).

BI *Ringling Bros. And Barnum And Bailey Circus; The Marvelous MarcellusTroupe; Living Art Creations In Bronze,* est. $2/300, (04-29-93, Swann, #82), 28 x 21 in., (71.1 x 53.3 cm.), color lithographed poster.

$715* *Root Beer,* excell. cond., (07-25-92, Julia, #77S, illus.), 10¼ x 14½ in., (26 x 36.8 cm.), paper poster (BP 378, DM 1076, FR 3631, Y 91,164).

$272* *SNCF: Font-Romeu, "Hiver Comme Ete, La Sante", 1937,* excell. cond., (01-23-93, Ribeyre/Baron, #98), 39>zn x 24Nzn in., (100.5 x 62 cm.), poster (BP 178, DM 433, FR 1463, Y 34,043).

$168* *SNCF: Vichy, La Ville D'Eau Eternelle. Saison Mai-Octobre. "Tous LesBienfaits D'Une Cure, Toutes Les Joies Des Vacances", 1938,* very good cond., (11-19-92, Ribeyre/Baron, #81), 38Czn x 24Czn in., (97 x 61.5 cm.), poster (BP 111, DM 268, FR 902, Y 20,893).

$525* *Saint-Raphael Quinquina. "Rouge Et Blanc, Dans Tous Les Cafes", c. 1935,* very good cond., lit., (11-19-92, Ribeyre/Baron, #4), 54Bzn x 39>zn in., (139.5 x 100.5 cm.), poster (BP 346, DM 837, FR 2820, Y 65,290).

$126* *Salon D'Automne. Palais Des Beaux-Arts De la Ville De Paris, 1942,* p. Art et Tourisme, good cond., (11-19-92, Ribeyre/Baron, #125), 62Bzn x 47¼ in., (160 x 120 cm.), poster (BP 83, DM 201, FR 677, Y 15,670).

$1129* *Salon De Photographie, Paris 1897,* p. Chaix, fold marks, repairs, backed on linen, (05-07-93, Christie-S. Ken, #129, illus.), 46¾ x 32½ in., (118.7 x 82.6 cm.), color lithograph (BP 715, DM 1785, FR 6015, Y 124,312).

$482* *San Sebastian "A 18 Km De La France",* fair cond., (11-19-92, Ribeyre/Baron, #78), 39C, x 27Czn in., (100 x 69 cm.), poster (BP 317, DM 768, FR 2589, Y 59,943).

$3575* *Sanford's Ginger,* very good/excell. cond., edge tear, water staining, p. Forbes Co., (07-25-92, Julia, #215, illus.), 21½ x 28½ in., (54.6 x 72.4 cm.), paper poster (BP 1888, DM 5378, FR 18,156, Y 455,820).

$161* *Saponite. Produit Antiseptique Francais (...) Pour Lessive Et Blanchissage, c. 1900,* Paris, Imp. Bourgerie and Cie, A. Mansion lith., cond. B+, (06-11-93, Boisgirard, #7), 54Bzn x 39C, in., (139.5 x 100 cm.), poster (BP 106, DM 262, FR 882, Y 17,082).

$330* *Scotland And Ireland, Burns-Laird Line,* B- cond., fold marks, chipping, repairs, (08-06-92, Swann, #22, illus.), 40 x 25 in., (101.6 x 63.5 cm.), (BP 172, DM 488, FR 1647, Y 42,092).

$220* *"Scribner's", "An Engagement", "Penny Magazine", "Glass Of Fashion" and "St. Nicholas": Group Of Five,* cond. varies, (08-06-92, Swann, #176, illus.), approx. 24 x 10 in., (61 x 25.4 cm.), (BP 115, DM 325, FR 1098, Y 28,061).

$385* *Seal Of North Carolina Tobacco "The Honorable Bardwell Slote",* excell. cond., borders trimmed, (07-25-92, Julia, #252, illus.), 8¼ x 20¼ in., (21 x 51.4 cm.), (BP 203, DM 579, FR 1955, Y 49,088).

$85 *Second Liberty Loan Of 1917,* Sackette and Wilhelms Corp., No. 9, small tears, (09-24-92, Alderfer, #265), 30 x 20 in., (76.2 x 50.8 cm.), (BP 50, DM 126, FR 428, Y 10,225).

BI *Seils Sterling Circus; The Show Of A Thousand Wonders,* Mason City: Central Show Printing, est. $2/300, (04-29-93, Swann, #83), 14 x 41 in., (35.6 x 104.1 cm.), color lithographed poster.

$660* *Sells Bros., Grand Spectacular Pageant, 1893,* Strobridge Litho. Co., A- cond., crack, (08-06-92, Swann, #102, illus.), 29½ x 40 in., (74.9 x 101.6 cm.), (BP 345, DM 975, FR 3293, Y 84,184).

BI *Seme Bachi,* Barabino and Graeve, A- cond., creasing, open tears, est. $3/400, (08-06-92, Swann, #23, illus.), 39½ x 27½ in., (100.3 x 69.9 cm.), .

$503* *Sevres, "Le Musee Ceramique, Les Bois, La Manufacture Nationale De Porcelaine",* fair cond., (01-23-93, Ribeyre/Baron, #15), 46M, x 31½ in., (119 x 80 cm.), poster (BP 329, DM 800, FR 2706, Y 62,954).

$192* *Shipping Exhibition, Olympia, 1919,* Hill Siffken, inits. E.J.K., B+ cond., marginal closed tears, edge loss, (08-06-92, Swann, #160, illus.), 39½ x 24 in., (100.3 x 61 cm.), (BP 100, DM 284, FR 958, Y 24,490).

$80* *"The Sisters Levy" and "Eden Theatre: Viviane": Two,* first, Lith. F. Appel, fairly good cond., creases; second. Imp. Em. Levy, fairly good cond., (02-12-93, Cheval/Robert, #176), first 46M, x 32Z\n in., (119 x 83 cm.), second 50Zzn x 38Czn in., (119 x 83 cm.), (BP 56, DM 133, FR 449, Y 9648).

$229* *Societe Des Bons Commerciaux. Tout A Credit (...) Nantes, c. 1900,* cond. B, (03-16-93, Boisgirard, #30), 50 x 36Mn in., (127 x 92.5 cm.), (BP 158, DM 381, FR 1294, Y 26,777).

$281* *St Raphael (Les 2 Serveurs),* (02-13-93, Morelle/Marchan, #14), 47¼ x 62Ān in., (120 x 160 cm.), poster on zinc (BP 198, DM 466, FR 1577, Y 33,888).

$319* *The St. George's Engineering C New Rapid Cycles, c. 1900,* cond. B, (03-16-93, Boisgirard, #22), 54Z, x 37Ān in., (137.5 x 96.5 cm.), (BP 220, DM 530, FR 1802, Y 37,301).

$783* *Succes!! Regeneration De La Chevelure Par La Lotion Americaine Du DrMackay, c. 1900,* Paris, Imp. E. Barret and Cie, cond. A-, (06-11-93, Boisgirard, #6), 51Cn x 37 in., (130 x 94 cm.), poster (BP 514, DM 1273, FR 4290, Y 83,077).

$221* *Suchard Milka "Pure Creme De Cacao Et Sucre",* good cond., (02-12-93, Cheval/Robert, #27), 57M, x 39C, in., (147 x 100 cm.), (BP 156, DM 367, FR 1240, Y 26,652).

$2793* *Suivons La Flotte (Follow The Fleet), De M. Sandrich, Avec G. Rogers(Belgian), 1936,* (01-31-93, Morelle/ Marchan, #100, illus.), 23B, x 31½ in., (60 x 80 cm.), poster (BP 1878, DM 4500, FR 15,212, Y 348,428).

$120* *Super Film Paris: Les Sept Perles: Two,* good cond. and fairly good cond., (02-12-93, Cheval/Robert, #201), 62Ān x 47¼ in., (160 x 120 cm.), poster (BP 85, DM 199, FR 673, Y 14,472).

$1241* *Symphonie En Blanc Serge Lifar, 1943,* ed. de Champrosay, (01-31-93, Morelle/Marchan, #9), 37C, x 56Ān in., (95 x 144 cm.), poster (BP 835, DM 1999, FR 6759, Y 154,815).

$440* *Teddy-Ted, 1930,* Andre B., Imp. Naboulet, B cond., chipping, yellowing, (08-06-92, Swann, #36, illus.), 46½ x 31 in., (118.1 x 78.7 cm.), (BP 230, DM 650, FR 2196, Y 56,122).

$440* *Terminus Absinthe,* Affiches-Camis, B cond., fold marks, closed tears, (08-06-92, Swann, #26, illus.), 49 x 38 in., (124.5 x 96.5 cm.), (BP 230, DM 650, FR 2196, Y 56,122).

$70* *Theatre Cluny. Le Papa De Francine (...),* cond. A, (03-16-93, Boisgirard, #42), 31½ x 23Mn in., (80 x 59.5 cm.), (BP 48, DM 116, FR 395, Y 8185).

$1004* *Theatre De L'Opera, c. 1900,* before letters, Paris, Affiches Camis, cond. A-, (06-11-93, Boisgirard, #27, illus.), 51>n x 39C, in., (131 x 100 cm.), poster (BP 660, DM 1632, FR 5501, Y 106,525).

$191* *Theatre De La Gaite: La Fille Du Tambour Major,* Imp. Em. Levy, fairly good cond., (02-12-93, Cheval/Robert, #161), 49Cn x 37Ān in., (125 x 96 cm.), poster (BP 135, DM 317, FR 1072, Y 23,034).

$221* *Theatre Sarah Bernhardt, Francesca Di Rimini, c. 1900,* Paris, Imp. Champenois, cond. A-, (06-11-93, Boisgirard, #26), 47Zn x 35Mn in., (121.5 x 90 cm.), poster (BP 145, DM 359, FR 1211, Y 23,448).

$1760* *"Theodor Herzl", "The Shekel" and "Gatherings Of The Zionist CongressIncluding The First Following The Establishment Of The State Of Israel": Seven,* (06-24-93, Swann, #337, illus.), largest 39C, x 27>n in., (100 x 70 cm.), (BP 1198, DM 3006, FR 10,121, Y 191,972).

$220* *"There It Goes",* A- cond., cracking, (08-06-92, Swann, #27, illus.), 40½ x 33½ in., (102.9 x 85.1 cm.), (BP 115, DM 325, FR 1098, Y 28,061).

$20 *They Give Their Lives,* Sackette and Wilhelms Corp., edge loss, (09-24-92, Alderfer, #267), 30 x 20 in., (76.2 x 50.8 cm.), (BP 12, DM 30, FR 101, Y 2406).

$100 *Three Horses,* inits. F.R., J. Weiner, No. 242, edge damage, stains, (09-24-92, Alderfer, #315), 25 x 37½ in., (63.5 x 95.3 cm.), (BP 59, DM 148, FR 503, Y 12,029).

$550* *Three Horses In Equipage, c. 1880,* Camille-Paris, (04-29-93, Swann, #310), 50 x 22 in., (127 x 55.9 cm.), color lithograph poster (BP 350, DM 870, FR 2932, Y 61,186).

$52* *Three Little Words, De R. Thorpe, Avec Vera Ellen (United States), 1950,* (01-31-93, Morelle/Marchan, #104), poster (BP 35, DM 84, FR 283, Y 6487).

$1303* *Three Men With A Camera,* p. Kossuth, creases, backed on linen, (05-07-93, Christie-S. Ken, #95, illus.), 47½ x 56 in., (120.7 x 142.2 cm.), color lithograph (BP 825, DM 2060, FR 6942, Y 143,471).

$275* *"Tom Mix Circus, 1936" and "Ringling Brothers, 1944": Two,* B cond., (08-06-92, Swann, #105, illus.), one 20½ x 28 in., (52.1 x 71.1 cm.), the other 39½ x 27¾ in., (52.1 x 71.1 cm.), (BP 144, DM 406, FR 1372, Y 35,077).

$31* *Tous En Scene (The Band Wagon), De V. Minelli, Avec C. Charisse (French), 1953,* (01-31-93, Morelle/Marchan, #106), 23B, x 31½ in., (60 x 80 cm.), poster (BP 21, DM 50, FR 169, Y 3867).

$660* *Tretorn, 1937,* Vastsvenska Kartonnage, inits. O.H., B+ cond., numerous closed tears, image scratches, (08-06-92, Swann, #152, illus.), 48 x 34 in., (121.9 x 86.4 cm.), (BP 345, DM 975, FR 3293, Y 84,184).

$55* *Triners Bitter Wine,* very good cond., (07-25-92, Julia, #77Q, illus.), 13 x 18 in., (33 x 45.7 cm.), paper poster (BP 29, DM 83, FR 279, Y 7013).

$495* *Triple Sec Allary,* F. Javanaud-Angouleme, A- cond., chipping, creasing, (08-06-92, Swann, #28, illus.), 60½ x 45 in., (153.7 x 114.3 cm.), (BP 259, DM 731, FR 2470, Y 63,138).

BI *Tripoli, c. 1935,* good cond., (03-13-93, Laurin, #109), 39>n x 24Cn in., (100.5 x 61.5 cm.), .

$302* *Tuxedoed Magician With Red Devils, Doves, And A Female Figure RisingFrom A Spirit Pot On A Multi-Colored Background, 1932,* Donaldson Litho. Co., B+ cond., chipping, marginal closed tears, (08-06-92, Swann, #189, illus.), 36½ x 27½ in., (92.7 x 69.9 cm.), (BP 158, DM 446, FR 1507, Y 38,520).

$220* *Unlettered Poster,* minor chipping, Milwaukee and Chicago: Riverside Print Co., (04-29-93, Swann, #85), 41 x 27 in., (104.1 x 68.6 cm.), color lithographed poster (BP 140, DM 348, FR 1173, Y 24,474).

$220* *Untitled: Group Of Four,* pub. during American occupation of Japan, B+ cond., (08-06-92, Swann, #158, illus.), (BP 115, DM 325, FR 1098, Y 28,061).

$165* *Urania, Zurich Bier Und Speise Restaurant, c. 1950,* J.C. Muller, A- cond., (08-06-92, Swann, #29, illus.), 50 x 35 in., (127 x 88.9 cm.), (BP 86, DM 244, FR 823, Y 21,046).

$259* *Vichy-Gazeux "Sparkling Vichy", c. 1900,* cond. B, (03-16-93, Boisgirard, #15), 37C, x 25>n in., (95 x 65 cm.), (BP 179, DM 431, FR 1463, Y 30,285).

$579* *Ville De Bayonne, Aida,* (01-31-93, Morelle/Marchan, #153), 39C, x 54Bn in., (100 x 138 cm.), poster (BP 389, DM 933, FR 3154, Y 72,231).

$605* *Virginia Brights Cigarattes, Pirates Of The Spanish Main,* Geo. F. Harris and Sons, B cond., closed tears, creasing, (08-06-92, Swann, #30, illus.), 22 x 31 in., (55.9 x 78.7 cm.), (BP 316, DM 894, FR 3019, Y 77,168).

$70* *Vitraux Francais. Imitation De Vitraux Anciens,* Imp. Verneau, good cond., (02-12-93, Cheval/Robert, #39), 45Ān x 31½ in., (116 x 80 cm.), (BP 49, DM 116, FR 393, Y 8442).

$83* *Vive Las Vegas, De Rowland, Avec Cyd Charisse (French), 1956,* (01-31-93, Morelle/Marchan, #86), 23B, x 31½ in., (60 x 80 cm.), poster (BP 56, DM 134, FR 452, Y 10,354).

$559* *Voulez-Vous Danser Avec Moi,* (01-31-93, Morelle/ Marchan, #65, illus.), 14Cn x 22Zn in., (36 x 56 cm.), poster (BP 376, DM 901, FR 3045, Y 69,736).

$155* *Voulez-Vous Danser Avec Moi, 1959,* (01-31-93, Morelle/ Marchan, #64), 47¼ x 62Ān in., (120 x 160 cm.), poster (BP 104, DM 250, FR 844, Y 19,336).

$40* *W. Jackson and Co.: Old Superior Rum Kingston. Jamaica,* fairly good cond., (03-13-93, Laurin, #1), 31Bn x 24Mn in., (79.5 x 62 cm.), (BP 28, DM 67, FR 226, Y 4714).

$207* *Les Walton's Leurs Celebres Marionnettes (J. Baker, M. Chevalier, Charlot...),* (01-31-93, Morelle/Marchan, #219, illus.), 47¼ x 62Ān in., (120 x 160 cm.), poster (BP 139, DM 333, FR 1127, Y 25,823).

$110* *Week End Impermeabili,* Ind. Graf. C. Re and C, A- cond., yellowing, creasing, (08-06-92, Swann, #31, illus.), 39½ x 27½ in., (100.3 x 69.9 cm.), (BP 57, DM 163, FR 549, Y 14,031).

$65 *Welcome Home, Uncle Sam And Soldier,* top damaged, (09-24-92, Alderfer, #311, illus.), 33 x 18¼ in., (83.8 x 46.4 cm.), (BP 38, DM 96, FR 327, Y 7819).

$72* *West Side Story, De R. Wise, Avec N. Wood, G. Chakiris (French), 1961,* (01-31-93, Morelle/Marchan, #81), 47¼ x 62Æzn in., (120 x 160 cm.), poster (BP 48, DM 116, FR 392, Y 8982).

$120* *White Machines A Coudre, Toujours Les Meilleures, c. 1900,* London, Liverpool, Grafton Works, Cond. A-, (06-11-93, Boisgirard, #22), 34Mzn x 22Zzn in., (87.5 x 56 cm.), poster (BP 79, DM 195, FR 658, Y 12,732).

$121* *Wild West Show, c. 1910,* Milwaukee: Riverside Printing, (04-29-93, Swann, #86), 28 x 41 in., (71.1 x 104.1 cm.), color lithographed poster (BP 77, DM 191, FR 645, Y 13,461).

$990* *Williams Aviation Meet Cicero September 12-15, Hydroaeroplanes GrantPark, September 16-21, Gordon Bennett World's Championship Race, September 9, Clearing Ill.,* fold/creasing/tears/damage, (09-12-92, Dunning, #303), approx. 106 x 158 in., (269.2 x 401.3 cm.), 16 sheet poster (BP 512, DM 1425, FR 4843, Y 122,661).

$880* *Williams Aviation Meet Cicero, September 12-15, Hydroaeroplanes, Grant Park September 16-21, Gordon Bennett World's Championship Race September 9, Clearing Ill.,* fold/creasing/tears/damage, (09-12-92, Dunning, #302), approx. 106 x 158 in., (269.2 x 401.3 cm.), 16 sheet poster (BP 455, DM 1267, FR 4305, Y 109,032).

$695* *Willie Sparks Edouin's,* p. H.A. Thomas, crease, defects, (05-07-93, Christie-S. Ken, #66), 25 x 19½ in., (63.5 x 49.5 cm.), color lithograph (BP 440, DM 1099, FR 3703, Y 76,525).

BI *The Witches' Caldron,* The National, B cond., cracking throughout, est. $3/400, (08-06-92, Swann, #192, illus.), 41 x 28 in., (104.1 x 71.1 cm.), .

BI *Woman In Ethnic Costume, 1929,* Exposition-Barcelona 1929, linen-backed, s., est. $4/600, (04-29-93, Swann, #139, illus.), 41 x 29 in., (104.1 x 73.7 cm.), color lithograph poster in red and black.

$1042* *Women On Steps,* p. Foulon Freres & M. Peuchet, backed on linen, (05-07-93, Christie-S. Ken, #112, illus.), 30¾ x 46 in., (78.1 x 116.8 cm.), color lithograph (BP 660, DM 1647, FR 5551, Y 114,732).

BI *XIX Mille Miglia, Brescia, 3-4 Maggio 1952,* est. $4/6000, (08-23-92, Christie-E, #17, illus.), 38*zn x 26Bzn in., (98 x 68.5 cm.), lithograph in colors.

$1540* *XXI Mille Miglia, 1-2 Maggio 1954,* (08-23-92, Christie-E, #20), 26Czn x 26Czn in., (66.5 x 66.5 cm.), lithograph in colors (BP 789, DM 2207, FR 7487, Y 193,735).

$299* *Your New Year Will Be What You Make It, 1929,* cond. A, (03-16-93, Boisgirard, #37), 43½ x 35Zzn in., (110.5 x 91 cm.), litho-offset (BP 206, DM 497, FR 1689, Y 34,963).

$402* *Zan Chasse Le Rhume, c. 1895,* Imp. H. Lass, Paris, cond. B+, (06-11-93, Boisgirard, #4), 47¼ x 31½ in., (120 x 80 cm.), poster (BP 264, DM 653, FR 2203, Y 42,653).

$473* *Zoologischer Garten, Basle, c. 1935,* p. Wassermann, fold mark, excell. cond., (02-04-93, Christie-S. Ken, #42, illus.), 50 x 35½ in., (127 x 90.2 cm.), color lithograph (BP 330, DM 779, FR 2641, Y 58,838).

ANON MOVIE PO

BI *20 Million Sweethearts, First National, 1934,* insert, very fine cond., Stanley Caidin Coll., est. $6/900, (09-12-92, Sotheby-NY, #148, illus.), 36 x 14 in., (91.4 x 35.6 cm.),

$1100* *"2001: A Space Odyssey", 1968,* MGM, one-sheet, cond. B, (11-07-92, Camden, #221, illus.), 41 x 27 in., (104.1 x 68.6 cm.), restored on linen (BP 719, DM 1756, FR 5936, Y 135,769).

$440* *2001: A Space Odyssey, 1968,* Spanish, cond. A, linen backed, (03-18-93, Swann, #221, illus.), 82 x 39 in., (208.3 x 99.1 cm.), (BP 297, DM 723, FR 2465, Y 51,204).

$3080* *3 On A Match, First National, 1932,* one-sheet, cond. A, paper backed, (12-14-92, Christie-E, #109, illus.), 41 x 27 in., (104.1 x 68.6 cm.), (BP 1969, DM 4840, FR 16,497, Y 381,047).

$1430* *3 Wise Girls, Columbia, 1931,* one-sheet, cond. A, linen backed, (12-14-92, Christie-E, #297, illus.), 41 x 27 in., (104.1 x 68.6 cm.), (BP 914, DM 2247, FR 7659, Y 176,915).

$14,300* *The 39 Steps, Gaumont British, 1935,* one-sheet, cond. A, paper backed, (12-14-92, Christie-E, #59, illus.), 41 x 27 in., (104.1 x 68.6 cm.), (BP 9143, DM 22,474, FR 76,593, Y 1,769,145).

$440* *The 400 Blows, 1959,* fine cond., (12-12-92, Hollywd Poster, #196, illus.), (BP 282, DM 693, FR 2376, Y 54,449).

$550* *42nd Street, Warner Brothers, 1933,* lobby card, fine cond., Stanley Caidin Coll., (09-12-92, Sotheby-NY, #6, illus.), 11 x 14 in., (27.9 x 35.6 cm.), (BP 291, DM 818, FR 2771, Y 68,391).

$1760* *42nd Street, Warner Brothers, 1933,* window card, fine cond., Stanley Caidin Coll., (09-12-92, Sotheby-NY, #5, illus.), 17 x 14 in., (43.2 x 35.6 cm.), linen backed (BP 931, DM 2616, FR 8866, Y 218,851).

$4620* *Adventures Of Captain Marvel, Republic, 1941,* six-sheet, cond. A, linen backed, (12-14-92, Christie-E, #37, illus.), 81 x 81 in., (205.7 x 205.7 cm.), (BP 2954, DM 7261, FR 24,746, Y 571,570).

$990* *The Adventures Of Robin Hood, 1938,* near mint cond., (12-12-92, Hollywd Poster, #224, illus.), lobby card (BP 635, DM 1560, FR 5346, Y 122,510).

$990* *The Adventures Of Robin Hood, Warner Brothers, 1938,* title lobby card, fine cond., Stanley Caidin Coll., (09-12-92, Sotheby-NY, #225, illus.), 11 x 14 in., (27.9 x 35.6 cm.), (BP 524, DM 1472, FR 4987, Y 123,104).

$2420* *The Adventures Of Robin Hood, Warner Brothers, 1953,* Italian, cond. A, linen backed, (12-14-92, Christie-E, #94, illus.), 55 x 39 in., (139.7 x 99.1 cm.), (BP 1547, DM 3803, FR 12,962, Y 299,394).

$605* *Adventures Of Sherlock Holmes, 1939,* fine cond., (12-12-92, Hollywd Poster, #264, illus.), lobby card (BP 388, DM 953, FR 3267, Y 74,867).

$1540* *"Adventures Of Tarzan", 1921,* Weiss Bros./Numa Pictures, window card, cond. B, (11-07-92, Camden, #151, illus.), 22 x 14 in., (55.9 x 35.6 cm.), restored on linen (BP 1007, DM 2459, FR 8311, Y 190,077).

$440* *Africa Speaks, 1930,* near mint cond., (linen), (12-12-92, Hollywd Poster, #42, illus.), (BP 282, DM 693, FR 2376, Y 54,449).

$935* *The African Queen, 1952,* three sheet, near mint cond., (linen), (12-12-92, Hollywd Poster, #171, illus.), (BP 600, DM 1473, FR 5049, Y 115,704).

$1320* *After Office Hours, MGM, 1935,* one-sheet, cond. A, paper backed, (12-14-92, Christie-E, #301, illus.), 41 x 27 in., (104.1 x 68.6 cm.), (BP 844, DM 2074, FR 7070, Y 163,306).

$770* *After The Ball, 1933,* near mint cond., (paper), (12-12-92, Hollywd Poster, #231, illus.), (BP 494, DM 1213, FR 4158, Y 95,285).

$1100* *After Your Own Heart, 1921,* fine cond. (linen), (12-12-92, Hollywd Poster, #81, illus.), (BP 705, DM 1733, FR 5940, Y 136,122).

$330* *The Alamo, United Artists, 1960,* one-sheet, cond. B+, (03-18-93, Swann, #1, illus.), (BP 223, DM 542, FR 1849, Y 38,403).

$440* *Alexander's Ragtime Band, 1938,* near mint cond., (12-12-92, Hollywd Poster, #326, illus.), mini w/c (BP 282, DM 693, FR 2376, Y 54,449).

$2750* *Alexander's Ragtime Band, 20th Century Fox, 1938,* one-sheet, very good cond., Stanley Caidin Coll., (09-12-92, Sotheby-NY, #275, illus.), 41 x 27 in., (104.1 x 68.6 cm.), linen backed (BP 1454, DM 4088, FR 13,854, Y 341,955).

$462* *Alias The Night Wind, Fox, 1923,* one-sheet, cond. A, linen backed, (12-14-92, Christie-E, #1, illus.), 41 x 27 in., (104.1 x 68.6 cm.), (BP 295, DM 726, FR 2475, Y 57,157).

$248* *Alice Brady, 1918,* near mint cond., (12-12-92, Hollywd Poster, #60, illus.), (BP 159, DM 391, FR 1339, Y 30,689).

$1100* *Alice In Wonderland, 1933,* fine cond., (linen), (12-12-92, Hollywd Poster, #90, illus.), (BP 705, DM 1733, FR 5940, Y 136,122).

$605* *Alkali Ike's Misfortunes, Essanay, 1913,* one-sheet, cond. A, linen backed, (12-14-92, Christie-E, #196, illus.), 41 x 27 in., (104.1 x 68.6 cm.), (BP 387, DM 951, FR 3240, Y 74,848).

$770* *All About Eve, 1950,* near mint cond., (12-12-92, Hollywd Poster, #256, illus.), lobby card (BP 494, DM 1213, FR 4158, Y 95,285).

$1760* *All Of A Sudden Norma, 1919,* three-sheet, very fine cond., Stanley Caidin Coll., (09-12-92, Sotheby-NY, #35, illus.), 81 x 41 in., (205.7 x 104.1 cm.), linen backed (BP 931, DM 2616, FR 8866, Y 218,851).

$935* *All This, And Heaven Too, 1940,* near mint cond., (linen), (12-12-92, Hollywd Poster, #296, illus.), (BP 600, DM 1473, FR 5049, Y 115,704).

$412* *All Through The Night (Echec A La Gestapo), 1942,* French, cond. A-, linen backed, (03-18-93, Swann, #134, illus.), 63 x 47 in., (160 x 119.4 cm.), (BP 278, DM 677, FR 2308, Y 47,946).

$275* *All Through The Night, 1942,* fine cond., (12-12-92, Hollywd Poster, #132, illus.), window card (BP 176, DM 433, FR 1485, Y 34,030).

$1320* *American Entertainment Co., c. 1900,* good cond., Stanley Caidin Coll., one-sheet, (09-12-92, Sotheby-NY, #27, illus.), 27 x 41 in., (68.6 x 104.1 cm.), linen backed (BP 698, DM 1962, FR 6650, Y 164,138).

$1100* *American Entertainment Company, circa 1900,* very good cond., (linen), (12-12-92, Hollywd Poster, #298, illus.), (BP 705, DM 1733, FR 5940, Y 136,122).

$825* *An American In Paris (Un Americain A Paris), 1951,* French, cond. B+, linen backed, (03-18-93, Swann, #7, illus.), 63 x 47 in., (160 x 119.4 cm.), (BP 556, DM 1356, FR 4622, Y 96,008).

$660* *An American In Paris, 1951,* near mint cond., (12-12-92, Hollywd Poster, #93, illus.), (BP 423, DM 1040, FR 3564, Y 81,673).

$605* *"Amour Et Salut", c. 1910,* French, American-Kinema, cond. C, (06-05-93, Camden, #280, illus.), 62 x 47 in., (157.5 x 119.4 cm.), linen, attached to wood (BP 398, DM 981, FR 3306, Y 64,900).

$192* *Anatomy Of A Murder, Columbia, 1959,* one-sheet, cond. A-, linen backed, (03-18-93, Swann, #2, illus.), (BP 129, DM 316, FR 1076, Y 22,344).

$495* *And Then There Were None, 20th Century, 1945,* one-sheet, cond. B+, linen backed, (03-18-93, Swann, #3, illus.), (BP 334, DM 813, FR 2773, Y 57,605).

$303* *Angels With Dirty Faces, 1938,* very good cond., (12-12-92, Hollywd Poster, #272, illus.), lobby card (BP 194, DM 477, FR 1636, Y 37,495).

$440* *Animal Crackers, 1930,* near mint cond., (12-12-92, Hollywd Poster, #17, illus.), lobby card (BP 282, DM 693, FR 2376, Y 54,449).

$1210* *Animal Crackers, Paramount, 1930,* lobby card, near mint cond., Stanley Caidin Coll., (09-12-92, Sotheby-NY, #98, illus.), 11 x 14 in., (27.9 x 35.6 cm.), (BP 640, DM 1799, FR 6096, Y 150,460).

$1100* *Animal Crackers, Paramount, 1930,* jumbo lobby card, cond. A, (12-14-92, Christie-E, #288, illus.), 17 x 14 in., (43.2 x 35.6 cm.), (BP 703, DM 1729, FR 5892, Y 136,088).

$220* *Anna And The King of Siam, 1946; White Cliffs Of Dover, 1944: Two,* one-sheets, (03-18-93, Swann, #4, illus.), (BP 148, DM 362, FR 1232, Y 25,602).

$660* *Anna Christie, MGM, 1930,* lobby card, fine cond., Stanley Caidin Coll., (09-12-92, Sotheby-NY, #174, illus.), 11 x 14 in., (27.9 x 35.6 cm.), (BP 349, DM 981, FR 3325, Y 82,069).

$7150* *Any Wife, William Fox, 1922,* one-sheet, very fine cond., Stanley Caidin Coll., (09-12-92, Sotheby-NY, #251, illus.), 41 x 27 in., (104.1 x 68.6 cm.), linen backed (BP 3781, DM 10,629, FR 36,020, Y 889,082).

$467* *The Ape, Monogram, 1940,* one-sheet, cond. B+, linen backed, (03-18-93, Swann, #76, illus.), (BP 315, DM 767, FR 2616, Y 54,347).

$275* *Aping Hollywood, 1920(?),* one-sheet, cond. A, linen backed, (03-18-93, Swann, #18, illus.), (BP 185, DM 452, FR 1541, Y 32,003).

$605* *Ariane, 1930,* German, cond. C+, linen backed, (03-18-93, Swann, #120, illus.), 83 x 37 in., (210.8 x 94 cm.), (BP 408, DM 994, FR 3389, Y 70,406).

$3300* *Arrowsmith, United Artists, 1932,* one-sheet, cond. A, linen backed, (12-14-92, Christie-E, #146, illus.), 41 x 27 in., (104.1 x 68.6 cm.), (BP 2110, DM 5186, FR 17,675, Y 408,264).

$2090* *The Aryan, Triangle, 1916,* one-sheet, cond. A, linen backed, (12-14-92, Christie-E, #46, illus.), 41 x 27 in., (104.1 x 68.6 cm.), (BP 1336, DM 3285, FR 11,194, Y 258,567).

$6050* *"As You Desire Me", 1932,* MGM, one-sheet, cond. A, (11-07-92, Camden, #223, illus.), 41 x 27 in., (104.1 x 68.6 cm.), on linen (BP 3956, DM 9660, FR 32,650, Y 746,729).

$715* *Ashes Of Vengeance, First National Pictures, 1923,* one-sheet, very fine cond., Stanley Caidin Coll., (09-12-92, Sotheby-NY, #168, illus.), 41 x 27 in., (104.1 x 68.6 cm.), linen backed (BP 378, DM 1063, FR 3602, Y 88,908).

$275* *The Asphalt Jungle, 1950,* near mint cond., (12-12-92, Hollywd Poster, #212, illus.), title card (BP 176, DM 433, FR 1485, Y 34,030).

$385* *The Astounding She Monster, 1958,* near mint cond., (linen), (12-12-92, Hollywd Poster, #149, illus.), (BP 247, DM 607, FR 2079, Y 47,643).

$990* *At The Circus, 1939,* insert, good cond., Stanley Caiden Coll., (09-12-92, Sotheby-NY, #99, illus.), 36 x 14 in., (91.4 x 35.6 cm.), linen backed (BP 524, DM 1472, FR 4987, Y 123,104).

$7700* *"Atom Man Vs. Superman", 1950,* Columbia, six-sheet, cond. B, (06-05-93, Camden, #318, illus.), 81 x 81 in., (205.7 x 205.7 cm.), on linen (BP 5069, DM 12,484, FR 42,077, Y 826,003).

$1430* *"Attack Of The 50 Ft. Woman", 1958,* Allied Artists, one-sheet, cond. B, (06-05-93, Camden, #33, illus.), 41 x 27 in., (104.1 x 68.6 cm.), on linen (BP 941, DM 2318, FR 7814, Y 153,401).

$1760* *"Attack Of The 50 Ft. Woman", 1958,* Allied Artists, insert, cond. A, (06-05-93, Camden, #69, illus.), 36 x 14 in., (91.4 x 35.6 cm.), on linen (BP 1159, DM 2853, FR 9617, Y 188,801).

$990* *"Attack Of The 50 Ft. Woman", 1958,* Allied Artists, half-sheet, cond. B, (06-05-93, Camden, #292, illus.), 22 x 28 in., (55.9 x 71.1 cm.), on paper (BP 652, DM 1605, FR 5410, Y 106,200).

$1760* *"Attack Of The 50 Ft. Woman", 1958,* Allied Artists, one-sheet, cond. A, (11-07-92, Camden, #209, illus.), 41 x 27 in., (104.1 x 68.6 cm.), (BP 1151, DM 2810, FR 9498, Y 217,230).

$2090* *Attack Of The 50 Ft. Woman, Allied Artists, 1958,* one-sheet, cond. A, linen backed, (12-14-92, Christie-E, #193, illus.), 41 x 27 in., (104.1 x 68.6 cm.), (BP 1336, DM 3285, FR 11,194, Y 258,567).

$550* *"Attack Of The Crab Monsters", 1957,* Allied Artists, insert, cond. B, (06-05-93, Camden, #72, illus.), 36 x 14 in., (91.4 x 35.6 cm.), on linen (BP 362, DM 892, FR 3005, Y 59,000).

$485* *Audrey Hepburn, Breakfast At Tiffany's, Paramount, 1961,* British Quad., cond. A, linen-backed, (12-17-92, Christie-S. Ken, #401), 30 x 40 in., (76.2 x 101.6 cm.), poster (BP 308, DM 757, FR 2587, Y 59,604).

$1760* *The Avenging Conscience, Mutual Film Corporation, 1914,* one-sheet, very fine cond., Stanley Caidin Coll., (09-12-92, Sotheby-NY, #34, illus.), 41 x 27 in., (104.1 x 68.6 cm.), linen backed (BP 931, DM 2616, FR 8866, Y 218,851).

$550* *Bab's Burglar, Paramount, 1917,* one-sheet, good cond., Stanley Caidin Coll., (09-12-92, Sotheby-NY, #38, illus.), 41 x 27 in., (104.1 x 68.6 cm.), linen backed (BP 291, DM 818, FR 2771, Y 68,391).

$3740* *Babe Comes Home, First National, 1927,* lobby card, cond. A, (12-14-92, Christie-E, #76, illus.), 11 x 14 in., (27.9 x 35.6 cm.), (BP 2391, DM 5878, FR 20,032, Y 462,699).

$1320* *"Babes In Toyland", 1934,* MGM, lobby card, cond. A, (11-07-92, Camden, #248, illus.), 11 x 14 in., (27.9 x 35.6 cm.), (BP 863, DM 2108, FR 7124, Y 162,923).

$770* *Babes In Toyland, Hal Roach, 1934,* lobby card, fine cond., Stanley Caidin Coll., (09-12-92, Sotheby-NY, #164, illus.), 11 x 14 in., (27.9 x 35.6 cm.), (BP 407, DM 1145, FR 3879, Y 95,747).

$1100* *Babes On Broadway, MGM, 1941,* one-sheet, very fine cond., Stanley Caidin Coll., (09-12-92, Sotheby-NY, #279, illus.), 41 x 27 in., (104.1 x 68.6 cm.), linen backed (BP 582, DM 1635, FR 5542, Y 136,782).

$3520* *Back Street, Universal, 1932,* one-sheet, cond. A, linen backed, (12-14-92, Christie-E, #151, illus.), 41 x 27 in., (104.1 x 68.6 cm.), (BP 2251, DM 5532, FR 18,854, Y 435,482).

$550* *Back To God's Country, Universal Pictures, 1919,* one-sheet, very fine cond., (09-12-92, Sotheby-NY, #49, illus.), 41 x 27 in., (104.1 x 68.6 cm.), linen backed (BP 291, DM 818, FR 2771, Y 68,391).

$715* *Bad Girl, 1931,* near mint cond., (linen), (12-12-92, Hollywd Poster, #309, illus.), (BP 458, DM 1127, FR 3861, Y 88,479).

$2420* *Bad Girl, Fox, 1931,* one-sheet, cond. A, linen backed, (12-14-92, Christie-E, #9, illus.), 41 x 27 in., (104.1 x 68.6 cm.), (BP 1547, DM 3803, FR 12,962, Y 299,394).

$302* *Le Bal, 1931,* French, linen backed, cond. B, (03-18-93, Swann, #8, illus.), 56 x 82 in., (142.2 x 208.3 cm.), (BP 204, DM 496, FR 1692, Y 35,145).

$605* *Ball Of Fire, 1941,* near mint cond., (linen), (12-12-92, Hollywd Poster, #34, illus.), (BP 388, DM 953, FR 3267, Y 74,867).

$385* *Bambi, 1942,* insert, fine cond., (12-12-92, Hollywd Poster, #71, illus.), (BP 247, DM 607, FR 2079, Y 47,643).

$1320* *Bambi, 1943,* three sheet, fine cond., (linen), (12-12-92, Hollywd Poster, #164, illus.), (BP 846, DM 2080, FR 7127, Y 163,346).

$193* *Barbara Stanwyck,* French, near mint cond., (12-12-92, Hollywd Poster, #59, illus.), (BP 124, DM 304, FR 1042, Y 23,883).

$770* *"The Barkley's Of Broadway", 1949,* MGM, three-sheet, cond. B, (06-05-93, Camden, #118, illus.), 81 x 41 in., (205.7 x 104.1 cm.), restored on linen after catalogue photography (BP 507, DM 1248, FR 4208, Y 82,600).

$770* *Barney Bear's Victory Garden, MGM, 1942,* one-sheet, cond. A, linen backed, (12-14-92, Christie-E, #274, illus.), 41 x 27 in., (104.1 x 68.6 cm.), (BP 492, DM 1210, FR 4124, Y 95,262).

$156* *Batman, 20th Century Fox, 1966,* British Quad., cond. A., (12-17-92, Christie-S. Ken, #397), 30 x 40 in., (76.2 x 101.6 cm.), poster (BP 99, DM 244, FR 832, Y 19,172).

$495* *Battling Butler, 1926,* fine cond., (12-12-92, Hollywd Poster, #120, illus.), lobby card (BP 317, DM 780, FR 2673, Y 61,255).

$550* *The Bear And The Beavers, Barney Bear, 1942,* fine cond., (linen), (12-12-92, Hollywd Poster, #111, illus.), (BP 353, DM 867, FR 2970, Y 68,061).

$381* *The Beatles, A Hard Day's Night, United Artists, 1964,* British Quad., cond. A, (12-17-92, Christie-S. Ken, #428), 30 x 40 in., (76.2 x 101.6 cm.), poster (BP 242, DM 595, FR 2032, Y 46,823).

$312* *The Beatles, Help!, United Artists, 1965,* British Quad., cond. A, (12-17-92, Christie-S. Ken, #429), 30 x 40 in., (76.2 x 101.6 cm.), poster (BP 198, DM 487, FR 1664, Y 38,343).

$3190* *Beau Geste, 1939,* fine cond., (linen), (12-12-92, Hollywd Poster, #48, illus.), (BP 2046, DM 5026, FR 17,225, Y 394,753).

$3850* *Beau Geste, Paramount, 1939,* one-sheet, good cond., Stanley Caidin Coll., (09-12-92, Sotheby-NY, #90, illus.), 41 x 27 in., (104.1 x 68.6 cm.), linen backed (BP 2036, DM 5723, FR 19,395, Y 478,737).

$9900* *Beau Hunks, MGM, 1931,* one-sheet, very fine cond., Stanley Caidin Coll., (09-12-92, Sotheby-NY, #160, illus.), 41 x 27 in., (104.1 x 68.6 cm.), linen backed (BP 5235, DM 14,717, FR 49,874, Y 1,231,037).

$660* *Beau Hunks, MGM, 1931: Two,* lobby cards, very fine cond., Stanley Caidin Coll., (09-12-92, Sotheby-NY, #161, illus.), 11 x 14 in., (27.9 x 35.6 cm.), (BP 349, DM 981, FR 3325, Y 82,069).

$11,000* *"Beauty And The Beast", 1946,* French, Discina, two-panel, cond. A, (11-07-92, Camden, #283, illus.), 62 x 91½ in., (157.5 x 232.4 cm.), on linen (BP 7192, DM 17,563, FR 59,363, Y 1,357,689).

$5225* *"Beauty And The Beast", 1946,* French, Discina, cond. A, (11-07-92, Camden, #336, illus.), 63 x 47 in., (160 x 119.4 cm.), on linen (BP 3416, DM 8343, FR 28,198, Y 644,902).

BI *"Beauty And The Beast", 1946,* French, Discina, cond. B, est. $1,5/2,500, (06-05-93, Camden, #159, illus.), 31 x 24 in., (78.7 x 61 cm.), on linen.

$4400* *"Beauty And The Beast", 1946,* Discina, cond. A, (06-05-93, Camden, #313, illus.), 63 x 47 in., (160 x 119.4 cm.), on linen (BP 2896, DM 7134, FR 24,044, Y 472,002).

$193* *Bedtime For Bonzo, 1951,* fine cond., (12-12-92, Hollywd Poster, #232, illus.), (BP 124, DM 304, FR 1042, Y 23,883).

$1320* *A Bedtime Story, Paramount, 1933,* insert, near mint cond., Stanley Caidin Coll., (09-12-92, Sotheby-NY, #124, illus.), 36 x 14 in., (91.4 x 35.6 cm.), linen backed (BP 698, DM 1962, FR 6650, Y 164,138).

$1210* *"Beggars Of Life", 1928,* Paramount, lobby card, cond. B, (11-07-92, Camden, #342, illus.), 11 x 14 in., (27.9 x 35.6 cm.), (BP 791, DM 1932, FR 6530, Y 149,346).

$715* *Beggars Of Life, 1928,* near mint cond., (12-12-92, Hollywd Poster, #127, illus.), lobby card (BP 458, DM 1127, FR 3861, Y 88,479).

$192* *Behave Yourself!, RKO, 1951,* one-sheet, cond. A-, linen backed, (03-18-93, Swann, #6, illus.), (BP 129, DM 316, FR 1076, Y 22,344).

$1870* *La Belle Et La Bete, Paulve, 1946,* orig. French poster, cond. A, linen backed, (12-14-92, Christie-E, #262, illus.), 33 x 24 in., (83.8 x 61 cm.), (BP 1196, DM 2939, FR 10,016, Y 231,350).

$357* *The Belle Of New York, MGM, 1951,* 3-sheet, cond. A, linen backed, (03-18-93, Swann, #9, illus.), (BP 241, DM 587, FR 2000, Y 41,545).

$770* *Belle Of The 90's (It Ain't No Sin), Paramount, 1934,* insert, good cond., Stanley Caidin Coll., (09-12-92, Sotheby-NY, #139, illus.), 36 x 14 in., (91.4 x 35.6 cm.), linen backed (BP 407, DM 1145, FR 3879, Y 95,747).

$248* *"Belle Of The Nineties", 1934,* Paramount, window card, cond. B, (06-05-93, Camden, #106, illus.), 22 x 14 in., (55.9 x 35.6 cm.), on linen (BP 163, DM 402, FR 1355, Y 26,604).

$4620* *La Belle Russe, Fox, 1919,* one-sheet, cond. B, linen backed, (12-14-92, Christie-E, #197, illus.), 41 x 27 in., (104.1 x 68.6 cm.), (BP 2954, DM 7261, FR 24,746, Y 571,570).

$1430* *Ben-Hur, MGM, 1926,* window card, very fine cond., Stanley Caidin Coll., (09-12-92, Sotheby-NY, #47, illus.), 22 x 14 in., (55.9 x 35.6 cm.), linen backed (BP 756, DM 2126, FR 7204, Y 177,816).

$248* *"The Best Years Of Our Lives", 1947,* RKO, titled card and six lobby cards, cond. A, (06-05-93, Camden, #185, illus.), each 11 x 14 in., (27.9 x 35.6 cm.), (BP 163, DM 402, FR 1355, Y 26,604).

BI *Bette Davis, That Certain Woman, 1937,* cond. C, three-sheet, linen-backed, est. BP 150/250, (12-17-92, Christie-S. Ken, #364), 81 x 41 in., (205.7 x 104.1 cm.), poster.

$330* *Betty Grable,* French, near mint cond., (12-12-92, Hollywd Poster, #57, illus.), (BP 212, DM 520, FR 1782, Y 40,837).

$990* *Beware Of Bachelors, Warner Brothers, 1928,* one-sheet, cond. A, linen backed, (12-14-92, Christie-E, #57, illus.), 41 x 27 in., (104.1 x 68.6 cm.), (BP 633, DM 1556, FR 5303, Y 122,479).

$2420* *The Big Game, RKO, 1936,* one-sheet, cond. A, linen backed, (12-14-92, Christie-E, #75, illus.), 41 x 27 in., (104.1 x 68.6 cm.), (BP 1547, DM 3803, FR 12,962, Y 299,394).

$770* *The Big Pond, Paramount, 1930,* one-sheet, cond. A, linen backed, (12-14-92, Christie-E, #302, illus.), 41 x 27 in., (104.1 x 68.6 cm.), (BP 492, DM 1210, FR 4124, Y 95,262).

$247* *The Big Sleep (Le Grand Sommeil), 1946,* Belgian, cond. A, linen backed, (03-18-93, Swann, #44, illus.), 32 x 14 in., (81.3 x 35.6 cm.), (BP 167, DM 406, FR 1384, Y 28,744).

$495* *The Big Store, 1941,* insert, near mint cond., (12-12-92, Hollywd Poster, #300, illus.), (BP 317, DM 780, FR 2673, Y 61,255).

$1210* *Bird Of Paradise (L'Oiseau De Paradis), RKO, 1932,* very fine cond., Stanley Caidin Coll., (09-12-92, Sotheby-NY, #121, illus.), 33 x 24 in., (83.8 x 61 cm.), linen backed (BP 640, DM 1799, FR 6096, Y 150,460).

$357* *The Birds (Les Oiseaux), 1963,* French, cond. A-, (03-18-93, Swann, #11, illus.), (BP 241, DM 587, FR 2000, Y 41,545).

$330* *The Birds, 1963,* fine cond., (12-12-92, Hollywd Poster, #45, illus.), (BP 212, DM 520, FR 1782, Y 40,837).

$49,500* *Birth Of A Nation, Epoch, 1916,* one-sheet, very fine cond., Stanley Caidin Coll., (09-12-92, Sotheby-NY, #31, illus.), 41 x 27 in., (104.1 x 68.6 cm.), linen backed (BP 26,177, DM 73,584, FR 249,370, Y 6,155,185).

$2420* *The Black Camel, Fox, 1931,* one-sheet, cond. A, linen backed, (12-14-92, Christie-E, #64, illus.), 41 x 27 in., (104.1 x 68.6 cm.), (BP 1547, DM 3803, FR 12,962, Y 299,394).

$4400* *Black Friday, Universal, 1940,* one-sheet, cond. A, linen backed, (12-14-92, Christie-E, #308, illus.), 41 x 27 in., (104.1 x 68.6 cm.), (BP 2813, DM 6915, FR 23,567, Y 544,352).

$412* *Black Orpheus (Orfeu Negro), 1958,* French, cond. B+, (03-18-93, Swann, #12, illus.), (BP 278, DM 677, FR 2308, Y 47,946).

$11,000* *The Black Pirate, United Artists, 1926,* one-sheet, fine cond., Stanley Caidin Coll., (09-12-92, Sotheby-NY, #109, illus.), 41 x 27 in., (104.1 x 68.6 cm.), linen backed (BP 5817, DM 16,352, FR 55,416, Y 1,367,819).

$1320* *"The Black Swan", 1942,* Italian, Fox, cond. B, (06-05-93, Camden, #177, illus.), 78 x 55 in., (198.1 x 139.7 cm.), on linen (BP 869, DM 2140, FR 7213, Y 141,601).

$27,500* *Der Blaue Engel (The Blue Angel), UFA, 1929,* very fine cond., original German poster, Stanley Caidin Coll., (09-12-92, Sotheby-NY, #70, illus.), 85 x 38 in., (215.9 x 96.5 cm.), linen backed (BP 14,543, DM 40,880, FR 138,539, Y 3,419,547).

$3300* *A Blind Bargain, Goldwyn Picture, 1922,* one-sheet, fine cond., Stanely Caidin Coll., (09-12-92, Sotheby-NY, #186, illus.), 41 x 27 in., (104.1 x 68.6 cm.), linen backed (BP 1745, DM 4906, FR 16,625, Y 410,346).

$550* *The Blob, 1958: Three,* half-sheet, insert, Belgian, (03-18-93, Swann, #32, illus.), 22 x 14 in., (55.9 x 35.6 cm.), (BP 371, DM 904, FR 3081, Y 64,006).

$550* *Blockade, Walter Wanger, 1938,* one-sheet, very fine cond., Stanley Caidin Coll., (09-12-92, Sotheby-NY, #269, illus.), 41 x 27 in., (104.1 x 68.6 cm.), linen backed (BP 291, DM 818, FR 2771, Y 68,391).

$2750* *Blond Venus (Blonda Venus), Paramount, 1932,* one-sheet, very good cond., Swedish poster, Stanley Caidin Coll., (09-12-92, Sotheby-NY, #76, illus.), 41 x 27 in., (104.1 x 68.6 cm.), linen backed (BP 1454, DM 4088, FR 13,854, Y 341,955).

$1650* *Blonde Venus, 1932,* very good cond., (12-12-92, Hollywd Poster, #24, illus.), lobby card (BP 1058, DM 2600, FR 8909, Y 204,183).

$2420* *Blondie, Columbia, 1938,* one-sheet, cond. A, linen backed, (12-14-92, Christie-E, #40, illus.), 41 x 27 in., (104.1 x 68.6 cm.), (BP 1547, DM 3803, FR 12,962, Y 299,394).

$357* *Blood For Dracula (Du Sang Pour Dracula), 1975,* French, cond. A-, linen backed, (03-18-93, Swann, #33, illus.), 63 x 47 in., (160 x 119.4 cm.), (BP 241, DM 587, FR 2000, Y 41,545).

$2420* *The Blue Dahlia, 1946,* near mint cond., (linen), (12-12-92, Hollywd Poster, #182, illus.), (BP 1552, DM 3813, FR 13,067, Y 299,468).

$192* *Boccaccio '70, 1962: Two,* orig. Italian, paper backed, (03-18-93, Swann, #27, illus.), 19 x 27 in., (48.3 x 68.6 cm.), (BP 129, DM 316, FR 1076, Y 22,344).

$6600* *Bolero, Paramount, 1934,* one-sheet, cond. A, paper backed, (12-14-92, Christie-E, #148, illus.), 41 x 27 in., (104.1 x 68.6 cm.), (BP 4220, DM 10,372, FR 35,351, Y 816,529).

$247* *Boniface Somnambule,* orig. French, cond. B+, linen backed, (03-18-93, Swann, #21, illus.), 63 x 47 in., (160 x 119.4 cm.), (BP 167, DM 406, FR 1384, Y 28,744).

$660* *Bonnie Scotland, 1935,* Austrian, near mint cond., (linen), (12-12-92, Hollywd Poster, #200, illus.), (BP 423, DM 1040, FR 3564, Y 81,673).

$3740* *The Border Wireless, Artcraft, 1918,* one-sheet, cond. A, linen backed, (12-14-92, Christie-E, #47, illus.), 41 x 27 in., (104.1 x 68.6 cm.), (BP 2391, DM 5878, FR 20,032, Y 462,699).

$8800* *Bordertown, Warner Brothers, 1934,* one-sheet, cond. B, paper backed, (12-14-92, Christie-E, #110, illus.), 41 x 27 in., (104.1 x 68.6 cm.), (BP 5627, DM 13,830, FR 47,134, Y 1,088,705).

$3300* *Bordertown, Warner Brothers, 1935,* half-sheet, fine cond., only known copy of this style, Stanley Caidin Coll., (09-12-92, Sotheby-NY, #209, illus.), 22 x 28 in., (55.9 x 71.1 cm.), linen backed (BP 1745, DM 4906, FR 16,625, Y 410,346).

$3986* *Boris Karloff, The Mummy (La Momia), Universal, 1932,* Argentinian, cond. A-, one-sheet, linen-backed, (12-17-92, Christie-S. Ken, #258, illus.), approx. 41 x 27 in., (104.1 x 68.6 cm.), poster (BP 2530, DM 6223, FR 21,259, Y 489,861).

$2080* *Boris Karloff, The Walking Dead, Warner,* re-issue 1937, cond. B, one-sheet, (12-17-92, Christie-S. Ken, #257), 41 x 27 in., (104.1 x 68.6 cm.), poster (BP 1320, DM 3247, FR 11,093, Y 255,622).

$2640* *Born To Be Bad, 20th Century, 1934,* one-sheet, cond. A, linen backed, (12-14-92, Christie-E, #10, illus.), 41 x 27 in., (104.1 x 68.6 cm.), (BP 1688, DM 4149, FR 14,140, Y 326,611).

$220* *"Born To Kill", 1946,* RKO, one sheet, cond. B, (06-05-93, Camden, #28, illus.), 41 x 27 in., (104.1 x 68.6 cm.), (BP 145, DM 357, FR 1202, Y 23,600).

$303* *Born To Kill, 1946,* very good cond., (12-12-92, Hollywd Poster, #7, illus.), (BP 194, DM 477, FR 1636, Y 37,495).

$605* *Borneo, 20th Century Fox, 1937,* one-sheet, cond. A, paper backed, (12-14-92, Christie-E, #208, illus.), 41 x 27 in., (104.1 x 68.6 cm.), (BP 387, DM 951, FR 3240, Y 74,848).

$550* *Bottoms Up, Fox, 1934,* one-sheet, very fine cond., Stanley Caidin Coll., (09-12-92, Sotheby-NY, #185, illus.), 41 x 27 in., (104.1 x 68.6 cm.), linen backed (BP 291, DM 818, FR 2771, Y 68,391).

$550* *A Bout De Souffle, 1960,* orig. French, cond. B, linen backed, (03-18-93, Swann, #28, illus.), 63 x 47 in., (160 x 119.4 cm.), (BP 371, DM 904, FR 3081, Y 64,006).

$1540* *The Bowery, 20th Century Fox, 1933,* one-sheet, fine cond., Stanley Caidin Coll., (09-12-92, Sotheby-NY, #9, illus.), 41 x 27 in., (104.1 x 68.6 cm.), linen backed (BP 814, DM 2289, FR 7758, Y 191,495).

$440* *The Brasher Doubloon, 1946,* near mint cond., (linen), (12-12-92, Hollywd Poster, #4, illus.), (BP 282, DM 693, FR 2376, Y 54,449).

$2090* *The Brat, Fox, 1931,* one-sheet, cond. A, linen backed, (12-14-92, Christie-E, #12, illus.), 41 x 27 in., (104.1 x 68.6 cm.), (BP 1336, DM 3285, FR 11,194, Y 258,567).

$1045* *"Break Of Hearts", 1935,* RKO, window card, cond. B, (06-05-93, Camden, #250, illus.), 22 x 14 in., (55.9 x 35.6 cm.), on paper (BP 688, DM 1694, FR 5710, Y 112,100).

$495* *Breakfast At Tiffany's, 1961,* fine cond., (12-12-92, Hollywd Poster, #279, illus.), (BP 317, DM 780, FR 2673, Y 61,255).

$8800* *The Bride Of Frankenstein (La Novia De Frankenstein), 1935,* Spanish, (03-18-93, Swann, #100, illus.), 39 x 27 in., (99.1 x 68.6 cm.), (BP 5935, DM 14,462, FR 49,300, Y 1,024,089).

BI *Brides Of Dracula (Les Maitresses De Dracula), 1960,* French, cond. B, linen backed, est. $6/900, (03-18-93, Swann, #34, illus.), 63 x 47 in., (160 x 119.4 cm.), .

BI *Bright Eyes, 20th Century Fox, 1934,* one sheet, very fine cond., Stanley Caidin Coll., est. $2/3,000, (09-12-92, Sotheby-NY, #286, illus.), 41 x 27 in., (104.1 x 68.6 cm.), linen backed.

$330* *Broadcasting, 1920(?),* one-sheet, cond. A, linen backed, (03-18-93, Swann, #19, illus.), (BP 223, DM 542, FR 1849, Y 38,403).

$193* *Broadway Big Shot, 1942,* near mint cond., (12-12-92, Hollywd Poster, #233, illus.), (BP 124, DM 304, FR 1042, Y 23,883).

$1100* *"Broadway Bill", 1934,* Columbia, one sheet, cond. A, (06-05-93, Camden, #236, illus.), 41 x 27 in., (104.1 x 68.6 cm.), on linen (BP 724, DM 1783, FR 6011, Y 118,000).

$2750* *The Broadway Melody, MGM, 1929,* window card, near mint cond., Stanley Caidin Coll., (09-12-92, Sotheby-

NY, #7, illus.), 14 x 22 in., (35.6 x 55.9 cm.), (BP 1454, DM 4088, FR 13,854, Y 341,955).

$660* *The Broadway Melody, MGM, 1929,* lobby card, near mint cond., Stanley Caidin Coll., (09-12-92, Sotheby-NY, #8, illus.), 11 x 14 in., (27.9 x 35.6 cm.), (BP 349, DM 981, FR 3325, Y 82,069).

$550* *Brothers, Columbia, 1930,* one-sheet, cond. A, linen backed, (12-14-92, Christie-E, #212, illus.), 41 x 27 in., (104.1 x 68.6 cm.), (BP 352, DM 864, FR 2946, Y 68,044).

$2200* *The Bull Dogger, Norman Film Co., 1923,* one-sheet, cond. A, (03-18-93, Swann, #20, illus.), (BP 1484, DM 3615, FR 12,325, Y 256,022).

$440* *Bulldog Drummond At Bay, 1937; Ellery Queen And The Murder Ring, 1941: Two,* one-sheets, linen backed, (03-18-93, Swann, #29, illus.), (BP 297, DM 723, FR 2465, Y 51,204).

$416* *Burt Lancaster And Ava Gardner, The Killers, Universal International, 1946,* cond. A, one-sheet, (12-17-92, Christie-S. Ken, #279, illus.), 41 x 27 in., (104.1 x 68.6 cm.), poster (BP 264, DM 649, FR 2219, Y 51,124).

$385* *Bus Stop, 1956,* fine cond., (12-12-92, Hollywd Poster, #234, illus.), (BP 247, DM 607, FR 2079, Y 47,643).

$385* *The Busher,* very good cond., (12-12-92, Hollywd Poster, #121, illus.), lobby card (BP 247, DM 607, FR 2079, Y 47,643).

$495* *Cabaret, Allied Artists, 1972,* orig. Polish poster, cond. A, (12-14-92, Christie-E, #257, illus.), 33 x 23 in., (83.8 x 58.4 cm.), (BP 316, DM 778, FR 2651, Y 61,240).

$1430* *"Cabin In The Sky", 1943,* MGM, complete set of eight lobby cards, conds. A to C, (11-07-92, Camden, #249, illus.), each 11 x 14 in., (27.9 x 35.6 cm.), (BP 935, DM 2283, FR 7717, Y 176,500).

$3575* *"Cabin In The Sky", 1943,* MGM, one-sheet, cond. A, (11-07-92, Camden, #141, illus.), 41 x 27 in., (104.1 x 68.6 cm.), restored on linen (BP 2337, DM 5708, FR 19,293, Y 441,249).

$3850* *Cabin In The Sky, MGM, 1943,* one-sheet, very fine cond., created by Al Hirschfeld, Stanley CaidinColl., (09-12-92, Sotheby-NY, #276, illus.), 41 x 27 in., (104.1 x 68.6 cm.), linen backed (BP 2036, DM 5723, FR 19,395, Y 478,737).

$1100* *Cabin In The Sky, MGM, 1943: Set Of Eight,* lobby cards, very fine cond., created by Al Hirschfeld, Stanley Caidin Coll., (09-12-92, Sotheby-NY, #277, illus.), 11 x 14 in., (104.1 x 68.6 cm.), (BP 582, DM 1635, FR 5542, Y 136,782).

$247* *Caesar Film-Roma,* orig. Italian, cond. A, linen backed, (03-18-93, Swann, #30, illus.), 39 x 27 in., (99.1 x 68.6 cm.), (BP 167, DM 406, FR 1384, Y 28,744).

$247* *The Caine Mutiny, Columbia, 1954,* three-sheet, cond. A, linen backed, (03-18-93, Swann, #45, illus.), (BP 167, DM 406, FR 1384, Y 28,744).

$1045* *The Calgary Stampede, Universal, 1925,* one-sheet, cond. A, linen backed, (12-14-92, Christie-E, #49, illus.), 41 x 27 in., (104.1 x 68.6 cm.), (BP 668, DM 1642, FR 5597, Y 129,284).

$880* *California Straight Ahead, Universal Pictures, 1937,* half-sheet, near mint cond., Stanley Caidin Coll., (09-12-92, Sotheby-NY, #257, illus.), 22 x 28 in., (55.9 x 71.1 cm.), (BP 465, DM 1308, FR 4433, Y 109,426).

$1210* *Call Her Savage, Fox, 1932,* one-sheet, cond. A, linen backed, (12-14-92, Christie-E, #29, illus.), 41 x 27 in., (104.1 x 68.6 cm.), (BP 774, DM 1902, FR 6481, Y 149,697).

$220* *Call Northside 777, 1948,* very good cond., (12-12-92, Hollywd Poster, #180), (BP 141, DM 347, FR 1188, Y 27,224).

$2200* *"Call Of The Wild", 1935,* United Artists, one-sheet, cond. D, (11-07-92, Camden, #386, illus.), 41 x 27 in., (104.1 x 68.6 cm.), on linen (BP 1438, DM 3513, FR 11,873, Y 271,538).

$3850* *The Call Of The Wild, Pathe, 1923,* one-sheet, cond. A, linen backed, (12-14-92, Christie-E, #182, illus.), 41 x 27 in., (104.1 x 68.6 cm.), (BP 2462, DM 6051, FR 20,621, Y 476,308).

$935* *Camille (Le Roman De Marguerite Gautier, 1946,* orig. French, cond. A, linen backed, (03-18-93, Swann, #36, illus.), 63 x 47 in., (160 x 119.4 cm.), (BP 631, DM 1537, FR 5238, Y 108,809).

$3025* *"Camille", 1912,* three-sheet, cond. D, (11-07-92, Camden, #295, illus.), 77½ x 38 in., (196.9 x 96.5 cm.), on linen stretched over a wooden frame (BP 1978, DM 4830, FR 16,325, Y 373,365).

$440* *Camille, First National Picture, 1927,* insert, fine cond., Stanley Caidin Coll., (09-12-92, Sotheby-NY, #169, illus.), 36 x 14 in., (91.4 x 35.6 cm.), (BP 233, DM 654, FR 2217, Y 54,713).

$2750* *Camille, MGM, 1936,* one-sheet, cond. A, linen backed, (12-14-92, Christie-E, #172, illus.), 41 x 27 in., (104.1 x 68.6 cm.), (BP 1758, DM 4322, FR 14,730, Y 340,220).

$660* *Camille, Metro Pictures, 1921,* half-sheet, very fine cond., Stanley Caidin Coll., (09-12-92, Sotheby-NY, #171, illus.), 22 x 28 in., (55.9 x 71.1 cm.), (BP 349, DM 981, FR 3325, Y 82,069).

$28,600* *The Canary Murder Case, Paramount, 1929,* one-sheet, cond. A, paper backed, (12-14-92, Christie-E, #31, illus.), 41 x 27 in., (104.1 x 68.6 cm.), (BP 18,286, DM 44,947, FR 153,187, Y 3,538,290).

$6820* *Captain Blood, Warner Brothers, 1935,* one-sheet, cond. A, (12-14-92, Christie-E, #91, illus.), 41 x 27 in., (104.1 x 68.6 cm.), (BP 4361, DM 10,718, FR 36,529, Y 843,746).

$1210* *Captain Blood, Warner Brothers, 1935: Three,* lobby cards, very fine cond., Stanley Caidin Coll., (09-12-92, Sotheby-NY, #226, illus.), 11 x 14 in., (27.9 x 35.6 cm.), (BP 640, DM 1799, FR 6096, Y 150,460).

$2750* *"Captain January", 1936,* Fox, three-sheet, cond. A, (11-07-92, Camden, #199, illus.), 81 x 41 in., (205.7 x 104.1 cm.), on linen (BP 1798, DM 4391, FR 14,841, Y 339,422).

$880* *Captain Kidd, Jr., Artcraft Pictures, 1919,* one-sheet, good cond., Stanley Caidin Coll., (09-12-92, Sotheby-NY, #107, illus.), 41 x 27 in., (104.1 x 68.6 cm.), linen backed (BP 465, DM 1308, FR 4433, Y 109,426).

$193* *Captains Of The Clouds, 1942,* very good cond., (linen), (12-12-92, Hollywd Poster, #158, illus.), (BP 124, DM 304, FR 1042, Y 23,883).

$1870* *The Captive God, Triangle, 1916,* one-sheet, cond. B, linen backed, (12-14-92, Christie-E, #45, illus.), 41 x 27 in., (104.1 x 68.6 cm.), (BP 1196, DM 2939, FR 10,016, Y 231,350).

BI *Carl Dreyer, Vredens Dag (Day Of Wrath), Palladium, 1943,* Dutch, cond. A, linen-backed, est. BP 2/300, (12-17-92, Christie-S. Ken, #245, illus.), approx. 32 x 24 in., (81.3 x 61 cm.), poster.

$1650* *"Carmen", 1918,* German, artwork by Fenneker, cond. A, (06-05-93, Camden, #157, illus.), 35½ x 23 in., (90.2 x 58.4 cm.), (BP 1086, DM 2675, FR 9016, Y 177,001).

BI *Carol Baker, Baby Doll, Warner Brothers, 1956,* cond. A, one-sheet, est. BP 2/300, (12-17-92, Christie-S. Ken, #411A, illus.), 41 x 27 in., (104.1 x 68.6 cm.), poster.

$440* *Carrying Mail, William Pizor, c. 1930,* one-sheet, near mint cond., Stanley Caidin Coll., (09-12-92, Sotheby-NY, #242, illus.), 41 x 27 in., (104.1 x 68.6 cm.), linen backed (BP 233, DM 654, FR 2217, Y 54,713).

$6050* *"Casablanca", 1942,* Warner Bros., one sheet, cond. A, (06-05-93, Camden, #306, illus.), 41 x 27 in., (104.1 x 68.6 cm.), on linen (BP 3983, DM 9809, FR 33,060, Y 649,002).

$4400* *Casablanca, 1942,* near mint cond., (linen), (12-12-92, Hollywd Poster, #35, illus.), (BP 2821, DM 6932, FR 23,758, Y 544,487).

$18,700* *Casablanca, 1946,* French, linen backed, catalog cover illus., (03-18-93, Swann, #41, illus.), 63 x 94 in., (160 x 238.8 cm.), (BP 12,611, DM 30,731, FR 104,762, Y 2,176,190).

$7700* *Casablanca, Warner Brothers, 1943,* insert, cond. B, folded, (12-14-92, Christie-E, #174, illus.), 36 x 14 in., (91.4 x 35.6 cm.), (BP 4923, DM 12,101, FR 41,243, Y 952,617).

$19,800* *Casablanca, Warner Brothers, 1946,* orig. French poster, cond. A, linen backed, (12-14-92, Christie-E, #254, illus.), 63 x 47 in., (160 x 119.4 cm.), (BP 12,660, DM 31,117, FR 106,052, Y 2,449,586).

$2860* *Casablanca, Warner, 1943,* one-sheet, cond. B, linen backed, (03-18-93, Swann, #42, illus.), (BP 1929, DM 4700, FR 16,022, Y 332,829).

$248* *Casey At The Bat, 1927,* fine cond., (12-12-92, Hollywd Poster, #129, illus.), window card (BP 159, DM 391, FR 1339, Y 30,689).

$440* *Casey Bats Again, Walt Disney, 1954,* near mint cond., (12-12-92, Hollywd Poster, #108, illus.), (BP 282, DM 693, FR 2376, Y 54,449).

$1210* *The Cat And The Canary, Paramount, 1939,* one-sheet, cond. B, linen backed, (12-14-92, Christie-E, #69, illus.), 41 x 27 in., (104.1 x 68.6 cm.), (BP 774, DM 1902, FR 6481, Y 149,697).

$220* *The Cat Creeps, 1946,* one-sheet, cond. A, linen backed, (03-18-93, Swann, #26, illus.), (BP 148, DM 362, FR 1232, Y 25,602).

$413* *"Cat People", 1952* reissue, RKO, one-sheet, cond. B, (06-05-93, Camden, #32, illus.), 41 x 27 in., (104.1 x 68.6 cm.), (BP 272, DM 670, FR 2257, Y 44,304).

$880* *Cat People, 1952,* fine cond., (linen), (12-12-92, Hollywd Poster, #150, illus.), (BP 564, DM 1386, FR 4752, Y 108,897).

$138* *Catnip Capers, Terry Toon's, 1939,* fine cond., (12-12-92, Hollywd Poster, #97, illus.), (BP 88, DM 217, FR 745, Y 17,077).

$660* *The Cattle Thief's Escape, Selig, 1913,* one-sheet, cond. A, linen backed, (12-14-92, Christie-E, #198, illus.), 41 x 27 in., (104.1 x 68.6 cm.), (BP 422, DM 1037, FR 3535, Y 81,653).

$381* *Cecil B. De Mille, Le Signe De La Croix/The Sign Of The Cross, Paramount, 1932,* French, artwork by Rene Peron, cond. B+, double-panel, linen-backed, (12-17-92, Christie-S. Ken, #367, illus.), 94 x 63 in., (238.8 x 160 cm.), poster (BP 242, DM 595, FR 2032, Y 46,823).

$248* *"Cette Sacree Gamine...Mademoiselle Pigalle", 1956,* French, Sofradis, cond. B, (06-05-93, Camden, #314, illus.), 63 x 47 in., (160 x 119.4 cm.), restored on linen after catalogue photography (BP 163, DM 402, FR 1355, Y 26,604).

$440* *The Champ, MGM, 1931,* insert, very fine cond., Stanley Caidin Coll., (09-12-92, Sotheby-NY, #266, illus.), 36 x 14 in., (91.4 x 35.6 cm.), (BP 233, DM 654, FR 2217, Y 54,713).

$1980* *"The Champeen", 1922,* Pathe, one-sheet, cond. B, (06-05-93, Camden, #207, illus.), 41 x 27 in., (104.1 x 68.6 cm.), restored on linen after catalogue photography (BP 1303, DM 3210, FR 10,820, Y 212,401).

$247* *Charle Chaplin, "The Gold Rush",* Stafford and Co., B cond., creasing, bubbling, closed tears, (08-06-92, Swann, #129, illus.), 59 x 20¼ in., (149.9 x 51.4 cm.), (BP 129, DM 365, FR 1233, Y 31,505).

$1100* *Charlie Chan At Monte Carlo, 20th Century Fox, 1937,* one-sheet, cond. A, linen backed, (12-14-92, Christie-E, #66, illus.), 41 x 27 in., (104.1 x 68.6 cm.), (BP 703, DM 1729, FR 5892, Y 136,088).

$3080* *Charlie Chan At The Circus, 20th Century Fox, 1936,* one-sheet, cond. A, paper backed, (12-14-92, Christie-E, #65, illus.), 41 x 27 in., (104.1 x 68.6 cm.), (BP 1969, DM 4840, FR 16,497, Y 381,047).

$193* *Charlie Chan In Shanghai, 1935,* fine cond., (12-12-92, Hollywd Poster, #131, illus.), window card (BP 124, DM 304, FR 1042, Y 23,883).

$1210* *Charlie Chan On Broadway, 20th Century Fox, 1937,* three-sheet, cond. A, linen backed, (12-14-92, Christie-E, #14, illus.), 81 x 41 in., (205.7 x 104.1 cm.), (BP 774, DM 1902, FR 6481, Y 149,697).

$1100* *Charlie Chan's Courage, 20th Century Fox, 1934,* one-sheet, fine cond., Stanley Caidin Coll., (09-12-92, Sotheby-NY, #59, illus.), 41 x 27 in., (104.1 x 68.6 cm.), linen backed (BP 582, DM 1635, FR 5542, Y 136,782).

$1980* *Charlot En Bombe, Himalaya, 1916,* orig. French poster, cond. A, (12-14-92, Christie-E, #267, illus.), 63 x 47 in., (160 x 119.4 cm.), (BP 1266, DM 3112, FR 10,605, Y 244,959).

$2420* *Check And Double Check, RKO, 1930,* window card, cond. A, (12-14-92, Christie-E, #133, illus.), 22 x 14 in., (55.9 x 35.6 cm.), (BP 1547, DM 3803, FR 12,962, Y 299,394).

$275* *"Children Of Divorce", 1927,* Paramount, window card, cond. B, (06-05-93, Camden, #107, illus.), 22 x 14 in., (55.9 x 35.6 cm.), (BP 181, DM 446, FR 1503, Y 29,500).

$385* *Children Of Divorce, 1927,* very good cond., (12-12-92, Hollywd Poster, #142, illus.), window card (BP 247, DM 607, FR 2079, Y 47,643).

$2200* *"The Chimp", 1932,* MGM, one-sheet, cond. A, (11-07-92, Camden, #132, illus.), 41 x 27 in., (104.1 x 68.6 cm.), on linen (BP 1438, DM 3513, FR 11,873, Y 271,538).

$110* *China Seas, 1935,* very good cond., (12-12-92, Hollywd Poster, #329, illus.), lobby card (BP 71, DM 173, FR 594, Y 13,612).

$550* *China Seas, MGM, 1935: Two,* lobby cards, very fine cond. Stanley Caidin Coll., (09-12-92, Sotheby-NY, #180, illus.), 11 x 14 in., (27.9 x 35.6 cm.), (BP 291, DM 818, FR 2771, Y 68,391).

$247* *Chinatown, 1974,* German, cond. A, paper backed, (03-18-93, Swann, #50, illus.), (BP 167, DM 406, FR 1384, Y 28,744).

$220* *Chinatown, 1974,* three sheet, fine cond., (12-12-92, Hollywd Poster, #167, illus.), (BP 141, DM 347, FR 1188, Y 27,224).

$770* *Christmas In July, Paramount, 1940,* one-sheet, good cond., Stanley Caidin Coll., (09-12-92, Sotheby-NY, #135, illus.), 41 x 27 in., (104.1 x 68.6 cm.), linen backed (BP 407, DM 1145, FR 3879, Y 95,747).

$660* *Christmas In July, Paramount, 1940,* one-sheet, cond. B, linen backed, (12-14-92, Christie-E, #140, illus.), 41 x 27 in., (104.1 x 68.6 cm.), (BP 422, DM 1037, FR 3535, Y 81,653).

$248* *Christopher Strong, 1933,* fine cond., (12-12-92, Hollywd Poster, #25, illus.), lobby card (BP 159, DM 391, FR 1339, Y 30,689).

$220* *Chu Chin Chow, 1933,* near mint cond., (linen), (12-12-92, Hollywd Poster, #295, illus.), (BP 141, DM 347, FR 1188, Y 27,224).

$6500* *Cimarron, RKO, 1931,* one-sheet, cond. B, linen backed, (12-14-92, Christie-E, #240, illus.), 41 x 27 in., (104.1 x 68.6 cm.), (BP 4156, DM 10,215, FR 34,815, Y 804,157).

$440* *Cinderella, Walt Disney, 1950,* fine cond., (12-12-92, Hollywd Poster, #98, illus.), (BP 282, DM 693, FR 2376, Y 54,449).

$3300* *Cinema Pathe, Pathe, c. 1898,* orig. French poster, cond. A, linen backed, (12-14-92, Christie-E, #264, illus.), 47 x 63 in., (119.4 x 160 cm.), (BP 2110, DM 5186, FR 17,675, Y 408,264).

$770* *The Circus Queen Murder, Columbia, 1933,* one-sheet, cond. A, linen backed, (12-14-92, Christie-E, #67, illus.), 41 x 27 in., (104.1 x 68.6 cm.), (BP 492, DM 1210, FR 4124, Y 95,262).

$18,700* *The Circus, United Artists, 1928,* one-sheet, cond. A, linen backed, (12-14-92, Christie-E, #118, illus.), 41 x 27 in., (104.1 x 68.6 cm.), (BP 11,957, DM 29,389, FR 100,161, Y 2,313,497).

$412* *Citizen Kane, 1948,* Polish, cond. A, (03-18-93, Swann, #52, illus.), 34 x 24 in., (86.4 x 61 cm.), (BP 278, DM 677, FR 2308, Y 47,946).

$8250* *Citizen Kane, RKO, 1941,* one-sheet, cond. B, linen backed, (12-14-92, Christie-E, #216, illus.), 41 x 27 in., (104.1 x 68.6 cm.), (BP 5275, DM 12,966, FR 44,189, Y 1,020,661).

$22,000* *Citizen Kane, RKO, 1941,* six-sheet, cond. B, linen backed, (12-14-92, Christie-E, #215, illus.), 81 x 81 in., (205.7 x 205.7 cm.), (BP 14,066, DM 34,575, FR 117,836, Y 2,721,762).

$880* *Citizen Kane, RKO, 1941: Two,* lobby cards, very fine cond., Stanley Caidin Coll., (09-12-92, Sotheby-NY, #305, illus.), 11 x 14 in., (27.9 x 35.6 cm.), (BP 465, DM 1308, FR 4433, Y 109,426).

$770* *City For Conquest, 1940,* insert, fine cond., (linen), (12-12-92, Hollywd Poster, #80, illus.), (BP 494, DM 1213, FR 4158, Y 95,285).

$30,800* *"City Lights", 1931,* United Artists, one-sheet, cond. A, (11-07-92, Camden, #140, illus.), 41 x 27 in., (104.1 x 68.6 cm.), on linen (BP 20,137, DM 49,178, FR 166,217, Y 3,801,530).

$660* *City Lights, United Artists, 1931,* lobby card, fine cond., (09-12-92, Sotheby-NY, #105, illus.), 11 x 14 in., (27.9 x 35.6 cm.), (BP 349, DM 981, FR 3325, Y 82,069).

$3813* *Clark Gable And Vivien Leigh, Gone With The Wind, M.G.M./David O. Selznick, 1939,* three-sheet, linen-backed, cond. A+, lit., (12-17-92, Christie-S. Ken, #333), 81 x 41 in., (205.7 x 104.1 cm.), (BP 2420, DM 5953, FR 20,336, Y 468,600).

$555* *Clark Gable And Vivien Leigh, Gone With The Wind, M.G.M./David O. Selznick, 1939*, Argentinian, cond. A, one-sheet, linen-backed, (12-17-92, Christie-S. Ken, #334, illus.), 41 x 27 in., (104.1 x 68.6 cm.), poster (BP 352, DM 867, FR 2960, Y 68,207).

$555* *Clark Gable And Vivien Leigh, Gone With The Wind, M.G.M./David O. Selznick, 1939: Two*, Argentinian, cond. B & B-, one-sheets, (12-17-92, Christie-S. Ken, #282), both 41 x 27 in., (104.1 x 68.6 cm.), poster (BP 352, DM 867, FR 2960, Y 68,207).

$1650* *Classified, First National Pictures, 1925*, one-sheet, very fine cond., Stanley Caidin Coll., (09-12-92, Sotheby-NY, #306, illus.), 41 x 27 in., (104.1 x 68.6 cm.), linen backed (BP 873, DM 2453, FR 8312, Y 205,173).

$462* *Claws, Sun Pictures, c. 1923*, one-sheet, cond. A, linen backed, (12-14-92, Christie-E, #183, illus.), 41 x 27 in., (104.1 x 68.6 cm.), (BP 295, DM 726, FR 2475, Y 57,157).

$2640* *Clive Of India, 20th Century, 1935*, one-sheet, cond. A, linen backed, (12-14-92, Christie-E, #28, illus.), 41 x 27 in., (104.1 x 68.6 cm.), (BP 1688, DM 4149, FR 14,140, Y 326,611).

$440* *The Clock, 1945*, near mint cond., (linen), (12-12-92, Hollywd Poster, #235, illus.), (BP 282, DM 693, FR 2376, Y 54,449).

$385* *A Clockwork Orange, 1971*, three sheet, near mint cond., (12-12-92, Hollywd Poster, #161, illus.), (BP 247, DM 607, FR 2079, Y 47,643).

$3575* *College, United Artists, 1927*, insert, near mint cond., created by Hap Hadley, Stanley Caidin Coll., (09-12-92, Sotheby-NY, #261, illus.), 36 x 14 in., (91.4 x 35.6 cm.), (BP 1891, DM 5314, FR 18,010, Y 444,541).

$1045* *Coming Out Party, 1934*, near mint cond., (paper), (12-12-92, Hollywd Poster, #185, illus.), (BP 670, DM 1646, FR 5643, Y 129,316).

$1980* *The Conquerors, 1932*, near mint cond., (paper), (12-12-92, Hollywd Poster, #157, illus.), (BP 1270, DM 3120, FR 10,691, Y 245,019).

$1300* *Constance Bennett, Moulin Rouge, 20th Century Fox, 1934*, cond. B-, mounted on board, borders trimmed, one-sheet, (12-17-92, Christie-S. Ken, #360), 41 x 27 in., (104.1 x 68.6 cm.), poster (BP 825, DM 2030, FR 6933, Y 159,764).

$550* *A Cottage Garden, Kelley, c. 1924*, one-sheet, cond. A, linen backed, (12-14-92, Christie-E, #199, illus.), 41 x 27 in., (104.1 x 68.6 cm.), (BP 352, DM 864, FR 2946, Y 68,044).

$138* *The Country Doctor, 1936*, fine cond., (12-12-92, Hollywd Poster, #308, illus.), (BP 88, DM 217, FR 745, Y 17,077).

$440* *The Covered Wagon, Paramount, 1923*, half-sheet, fine cond., Stanley Caidin Coll., (09-12-92, Sotheby-NY, #238, illus.), 22 x 28 in., (55.9 x 71.1 cm.), (BP 233, DM 654, FR 2217, Y 54,713).

$1100* *The Covered Wagon, Paramount, 1923*, one-sheet, very fine cond., Stanley Caidin Coll., (09-12-92, Sotheby-NY, #237, illus.), 41 x 27 in., (104.1 x 68.6 cm.), linen backed (BP 582, DM 1635, FR 5542, Y 136,782).

$605* *Creature From The Black Lagoon (L'Etrange Creature Du Lac Noir), Universal, 1954*, French, cond. B+, linen backed, (03-18-93, Swann, #86, illus.), 63 x 47 in., (160 x 119.4 cm.), (BP 408, DM 994, FR 3389, Y 70,406).

$1210* *Creature From The Black Lagoon, 1954*, insert, (03-18-93, Swann, #201, illus.), (BP 816, DM 1988, FR 6779, Y 140,812).

$2090* *Creature From The Black Lagoon, 1954*, one-sheet, cond. B, linen backed, (03-18-93, Swann, #200, illus.), (BP 1409, DM 3435, FR 11,709, Y 243,221).

$440* *Creature From The Black Lagoon, 1954*, French, cond. A-, linen backed, (03-18-93, Swann, #87, illus.), 31 x 23 in., (78.7 x 58.4 cm.), (BP 297, DM 723, FR 2465, Y 51,204).

$440* *Creature From The Black Lagoon, 1954*, top trimmed, very good cond., (12-12-92, Hollywd Poster, #136, illus.), window card (BP 282, DM 693, FR 2376, Y 54,449).

$1980* *Creature From The Black Lagoon, Universal, 1954*, half-sheet, cond. A, (12-14-92, Christie-E, #187, illus.), 22 x 28 in., (55.9 x 71.1 cm.), (BP 1266, DM 3112, FR 10,605, Y 244,959).

$247* *Creature Walks Among Us, Universal, 1956: Two*, lobby, insert, Belgian, (03-18-93, Swann, #35, illus.), 18 x 14 in., (45.7 x 35.6 cm.), (BP 167, DM 406, FR 1384, Y 28,744).

$2750* *Crime And Punishment, Columbia, 1935*, orig. Swedish poster, cond. A, (12-14-92, Christie-E, #259, illus.), 40 x 27 in., (101.6 x 68.6 cm.), (BP 1758, DM 4322, FR 14,730, Y 340,220).

$248* *Criss Cross, 1949*, near mint cond., (12-12-92, Hollywd Poster, #179, illus.), (BP 159, DM 391, FR 1339, Y 30,689).

$440* *Cruise Cat, Tom & Jerry, 1952*, near mint cond., (linen), (12-12-92, Hollywd Poster, #99, illus.), (BP 282, DM 693, FR 2376, Y 54,449).

$121* *Cuban Rebel Girls, UA, 1959*, one-sheet, cond. B+, (03-18-93, Swann, #55, illus.), (BP 82, DM 199, FR 678, Y 14,081).

$1430* *Curly Top, Fox, 1935*, one-sheet, cond. B, linen backed, (12-14-92, Christie-E, #159, illus.), 41 x 27 in., (104.1 x 68.6 cm.), (BP 914, DM 2247, FR 7659, Y 176,915).

$880* *The Curse Of The Cat People, RKO, 1944*, one-sheet, fine cond., Stanley Caidin Coll., (09-12-92, Sotheby-NY, #298, illus.), 41 x 27 in., (104.1 x 68.6 cm.), linen backed (BP 465, DM 1308, FR 4433, Y 109,426).

$138* *The Curse Of The Werewolf, 1961*, fine cond., (12-12-92, Hollywd Poster, #297, illus.), (BP 88, DM 217, FR 745, Y 17,077).

$550* *Custer's Last Stand, Weiss, 1936*, one-sheet, fine cond., Stanley Caidin Coll., (09-12-92, Sotheby-NY, #250, illus.), 41 x 27 in., (104.1 x 68.6 cm.), linen backed (BP 291, DM 818, FR 2771, Y 68,391).

$1210* *Dad For A Day, MGM, 1939*, one-sheet, very fine cond., Stanley Caidin Coll., (09-12-92, Sotheby-NY, #285, illus.), 41 x 27 in., (104.1 x 68.6 cm.), linen backed (BP 640, DM 1799, FR 6096, Y 150,460).

$495* *Dancers In The Dark, 1932*, near mint cond., (linen), (12-12-92, Hollywd Poster, #184, illus.), (BP 317, DM 780, FR 2673, Y 61,255).

$2090* *Dancing Lady, MGM, 1933*, one-sheet, cond. A, (12-14-92, Christie-E, #116, illus.), 41 x 27 in., (104.1 x 68.6 cm.), (BP 1336, DM 3285, FR 11,194, Y 258,567).

$715* *Dancing Mothers, Paramount, 1926*, insert, very fine cond., Stanley Caidin Coll., (09-12-92, Sotheby-NY, #20, illus.), 36 x 14 in., (91.4 x 35.6 cm.), (BP 378, DM 1063, FR 3602, Y 88,908).

$156* *Danny Kaye, Hans Christian Anderson, Samuel Goldwyn, 1952*, British, cond. B+, twenty four-sheet, (12-17-92, Christie-S. Ken, #421), 108 x 240 in., (274.3 x 609.6 cm.), poster (BP 99, DM 244, FR 832, Y 19,172).

$4180* *Dante's Inferno, 1921*, near mint cond., (linen), (12-12-92, Hollywd Poster, #189, illus.), (BP 2680, DM 6586, FR 22,570, Y 517,263).

$357* *Daredevils Of The Red Circle, Republic Serial, 1939: Two: Chapter 4,Sabotage, and Chapter 5, The Ray Of Death*, one-sheets, cond. A-, (03-18-93, Swann, #56, illus.), (BP 241, DM 587, FR 2000, Y 41,545).

$303* *The Dark Corner, 1946*, rolled, half sheet, near mint cond., (12-12-92, Hollywd Poster, #250, illus.), (BP 194, DM 477, FR 1636, Y 37,495).

$385* *Dark Victory, 1938*, near mint cond., (12-12-92, Hollywd Poster, #26, illus.), lobby card (BP 247, DM 607, FR 2079, Y 47,643).

$193* *Daughter Of The Dragon, 1929*, fine cond., (12-12-92, Hollywd Poster, #134, illus.), window card (BP 124, DM 304, FR 1042, Y 23,883).

$1870* *David Copperfield, MGM, 1935*, one-sheet, fine cond., Stanley Caidin Coll., (09-12-92, Sotheby-NY, #300, illus.), 41 x 27 in., (104.1 x 68.6 cm.), linen backed (BP 989, DM 2780, FR 9421, Y 232,529).

$1650* *David Copperfield, MGM, 1935*, one-sheet, cond. A, linen backed, (12-14-92, Christie-E, #122, illus.), 41 x 27 in., (104.1 x 68.6 cm.), (BP 1055, DM 2593, FR 8838, Y 204,132).

$248* *The Dawn Maker, 1916*, near mint cond., (12-12-92, Hollywd Poster, #262, illus.), lobby card (BP 159, DM 391, FR 1339, Y 30,689).

$3025* *The Dawn Patrol, Warner Brothers, 1938*, jumbo window card, fine cond., Stanley Caidin Coll., (09-12-92,

Sotheby-NY, #16, illus.), 28 x 22 in., (71.1 x 55.9 cm.), (BP 1600, DM 4497, FR 15,239, Y 376,150).

$2420* *The Dawn Patrol, Warner Brothers, 1938,* one-sheet, cond. A, linen backed, (12-14-92, Christie-E, #92, illus.), 41 x 27 in., (104.1 x 68.6 cm.), (BP 1547, DM 3803, FR 12,962, Y 299,394).

$5500* *"A Day At The Races", 1937,* MGM, one-sheet, cond. A, (11-07-92, Camden, #134, illus.), 41 x 27 in., (104.1 x 68.6 cm.), on linen (BP 3596, DM 8782, FR 29,682, Y 678,845).

$3850* *A Day At The Races, MGM, 1937,* one-sheet, good cond., Stanley Caidin Coll., (09-12-92, Sotheby-NY, #94, illus.), 41 x 27 in., (104.1 x 68.6 cm.), linen backed (BP 2036, DM 5723, FR 19,395, Y 478,737).

$220* *The Day Of The Triffids, 1963,* French, near mint cond., (linen), (12-12-92, Hollywd Poster, #193, illus.), (BP 141, DM 347, FR 1188, Y 27,224).

$605* *The Day Of The Triffids, Allied Artists, 1962: Two,* one-sheet, (03-18-93, Swann, #57, illus.), 30 x 40 in., (76.2 x 101.6 cm.), (BP 408, DM 994, FR 3389, Y 70,406).

$1045* *The Day The Earth Stood Still (Le Jour Ou La Terre S'Arreta), 1951,* French, cond. A-, linen backed, (03-18-93, Swann, #81, illus.), 63 x 47 in., (160 x 119.4 cm.), (BP 705, DM 1717, FR 5854, Y 121,611).

$302* *The Day The Earth Stood Still (Le Jour Ou La Terre S'Arreta), 1951,* French, cond. A, linen backed, (03-18-93, Swann, #83, illus.), 31 x 24 in., (78.7 x 61 cm.), (BP 204, DM 496, FR 1692, Y 35,145).

$1320* *The Day The Earth Stood Still, 1951,* one-sheet, (03-18-93, Swann, #80, illus.), (BP 890, DM 2169, FR 7395, Y 153,613).

$605* *The Day The Earth Stood Still, 1951,* jumbo lobby card, (03-18-93, Swann, #85, illus.), (BP 408, DM 994, FR 3389, Y 70,406).

$4400* *The Day The Earth Stood Still, 20th Century Fox, 1951,* three-sheet, (03-18-93, Swann, #82, illus.), (BP 2967, DM 7231, FR 24,650, Y 512,045).

$3520* *The Day The Earth Stood Still, 20th Century Fox, 1951,* lobby standee, cond. A, (12-14-92, Christie-E, #191, illus.), 60 x 32 in., (152.4 x 81.3 cm.), (BP 2251, DM 5532, FR 18,854, Y 435,482).

$275* *The Day With Jack Dempsey, 1921,* fine cond., (12-12-92, Hollywd Poster, #126, illus.), lobby card (BP 176, DM 433, FR 1485, Y 34,030).

$110* *Day-Time Wife, 1939,* insert, fine cond., (paper), (12-12-92, Hollywd Poster, #67, illus.), (BP 71, DM 173, FR 594, Y 13,612).

$935* *Dead Of Night, 1946,* near mint cond., (linen), (12-12-92, Hollywd Poster, #151, illus.), (BP 600, DM 1473, FR 5049, Y 115,704).

$110* *Deadline At Dawn, 1946,* fine cond., (12-12-92, Hollywd Poster, #5, illus.), (BP 71, DM 173, FR 594, Y 13,612).

$880* *Desire, 1936,* near mint cond., (12-12-92, Hollywd Poster, #27, illus.), lobby card (BP 564, DM 1386, FR 4752, Y 108,897).

$121* *Desperate Hours, Paramount, 1955,* one-sheet, cond. C+, (03-18-93, Swann, #46, illus.), (BP 82, DM 199, FR 678, Y 14,081).

$467* *Destination Moon, Eagle Lion, 1950,* one-sheet, cond. B, linen backed, (03-18-93, Swann, #114, illus.), (BP 315, DM 767, FR 2616, Y 54,347).

$2750* *Detour, P.R.C., 1945,* one-sheet, cond. A, linen backed, (12-14-92, Christie-E, #180, illus.), 41 x 27 in., (104.1 x 68.6 cm.), (BP 1758, DM 4322, FR 14,730, Y 340,220).

$440* *Devil Doll, MGM, 1936: Three,* lobby cards, very fine cond., Stanley Caidin Coll., (09-12-92, Sotheby-NY, #200, illus.), 11 x 14 in., (27.9 x 35.6 cm.), (BP 233, DM 654, FR 2217, Y 54,713).

$1045* *Devil Girl From Mars, 1955,* three sheet, near mint cond., (linen), (12-12-92, Hollywd Poster, #162, illus.), (BP 670, DM 1646, FR 5643, Y 129,316).

$1210* *Devil Girl From Mars, London Films, 1956,* one-sheet, cond. A, linen backed, (12-14-92, Christie-E, #192, illus.), 41 x 27 in., (104.1 x 68.6 cm.), (BP 774, DM 1902, FR 6481, Y 149,697).

BI *Devil Girl From Mars, Spartan, 1955,* insert, est. $4/600, (03-18-93, Swann, #60, illus.), .

$1100* *"The Devil Is A Woman", 1935,* Paramount, window card, cond. C, (06-05-93, Camden, #103, illus.), 22 x 14 in., (55.9 x 35.6 cm.), on paper (BP 724, DM 1783, FR 6011, Y 118,000).

$770* *The Devil Is A Woman, 1935,* restored, fine cond., (12-12-92, Hollywd Poster, #139, illus.), window card (BP 494, DM 1213, FR 4158, Y 95,285).

$495* *The Devil Is A Woman, Paramount, 1935,* lobby card, very fine cond., Stanley Caidin Coll., (09-12-92, Sotheby-NY, #72, illus.), 11 x 14 in., (27.9 x 35.6 cm.), (BP 262, DM 736, FR 2494, Y 61,552).

$46,200* *The Devil Is A Woman, Paramount, 1935,* one-sheet, cond. A, (12-14-92, Christie-E, #250, illus.), 41 x 27 in., (104.1 x 68.6 cm.), (BP 29,540, DM 72,607, FR 247,456, Y 5,715,700).

$2640* *The Devil's Double, Triangle, 1916,* one-sheet, cond. A, linen backed, (12-14-92, Christie-E, #44, illus.), 41 x 27 in., (104.1 x 68.6 cm.), (BP 1688, DM 4149, FR 14,140, Y 326,611).

$605* *"Dial M For Murder", 1954,* Italian, Warner Bros., cond. B, (06-05-93, Camden, #277, illus.), 55 x 39 in., (139.7 x 99.1 cm.), on linen (BP 398, DM 981, FR 3306, Y 64,900).

$440* *The Diamond Queen, Universal Serial, 1921,* one-sheet, very fine cond., Stanley Caidin Coll., (09-12-92, Sotheby-NY, #252, illus.), 41 x 27 in., (104.1 x 68.6 cm.), linen backed (BP 233, DM 654, FR 2217, Y 54,713).

$693* *Dick Tracy, R.K.O., 1945,* cond. A, one-sheet, linen-backed, (12-17-92, Christie-S. Ken, #396, illus.), 41 x 27 in., (104.1 x 68.6 cm.), poster (BP 440, DM 1082, FR 3696, Y 85,167).

$605* *Dig Up, Pathe, 1922,* one-sheet, very fine cond., Stanley Caidin Coll., (09-12-92, Sotheby-NY, #10, illus.), 41 x 27 in., (104.1 x 68.6 cm.), linen backed (BP 320, DM 899, FR 3048, Y 75,230).

$1320* *Dinner At 8, MGM, 1933,* jumbo window card, very fine cond., extremely rare, Stanley Caidin Coll., (09-12-92, Sotheby-NY, #179, illus.), 28 x 22 in., (71.1 x 55.9 cm.), (BP 698, DM 1962, FR 6650, Y 164,138).

$1760* *Dishonored, 1931,* fine cond., (12-12-92, Hollywd Poster, #324, illus.), jumbo lobby (BP 1129, DM 2773, FR 9503, Y 217,795).

$132* *Disputed Passage, Paramount, 1939,* one-sheet, cond. B, (03-18-93, Swann, #59, illus.), (BP 89, DM 217, FR 739, Y 15,361).

$3520* *The Dissatisfied Cobbler, Pathe, 1922,* one-sheet, cond. A, linen backed, (12-14-92, Christie-E, #269, illus.), 41 x 27 in., (104.1 x 68.6 cm.), (BP 2251, DM 5532, FR 18,854, Y 435,482).

$1540* *Doctor Cyclops, 1940,* near mint cond., (linen), (12-12-92, Hollywd Poster, #148, illus.), (BP 987, DM 2426, FR 8315, Y 190,570).

$880* *Dodge City, Warner Brothers, 1939,* lobby card, very fine cond., Stanley Caidin Coll., (09-12-92, Sotheby-NY, #228, illus.), 11 x 14 in., (27.9 x 35.6 cm.), (BP 465, DM 1308, FR 4433, Y 109,426).

$605* *Dodsworth, 1936,* half sheet, very good cond., (paper), (12-12-92, Hollywd Poster, #252, illus.), (BP 388, DM 953, FR 3267, Y 74,867).

$550* *"A Dog's Life", c. 1920's,* reissue Pathe, half-sheet, cond. B, (06-05-93, Camden, #121, illus.), 22 x 28 in., (55.9 x 71.1 cm.), (BP 362, DM 892, FR 3005, Y 59,000).

$770* *Doin' Their Bit, MGM, 1942,* one-sheet, cond. A, linen backed, (12-14-92, Christie-E, #157, illus.), 41 x 27 in., (104.1 x 68.6 cm.), (BP 492, DM 1210, FR 4124, Y 95,262).

$4675* *"La Dolce Vita", 1960,* Italian, Cineriz, cond. A, (06-05-93, Camden, #312, illus.), 78 x 55 in., (198.1 x 139.7 cm.), restored on linen after catalogue photography (BP 3077, DM 7579, FR 25,546, Y 501,502).

$385* *La Dolce Vita, 1960,* Argentinian, linen backed, cond. A, (03-18-93, Swann, #65, illus.), 43 x 28 in., (109.2 x 71.1 cm.), (BP 260, DM 633, FR 2157, Y 44,804).

$990* *La Dolce Vita, 1964,* fine cond., (linen), (12-12-92, Hollywd Poster, #55, illus.), (BP 635, DM 1560, FR 5346, Y 122,510).

$193* *La Dolce Vita, 1964,* Original Italian release, fine cond., (linen), (12-12-92, Hollywd Poster, #202, illus.), (BP 124, DM 304, FR 1042, Y 23,883).

$935* *La Dolce Vita, Riama And Pathe, 1961,* orig. Italian poster, cond. A, linen backed, (12-14-92, Christie-E, #98, illus.), 55 x 39 in., (139.7 x 99.1 cm.), (BP 598, DM 1469, FR 5008, Y 115,675).

$7150* *Don Juan, Warner Brothers, 1926,* one-sheet, very fine cond., Stanley Caidin Coll., (09-12-92, Sotheby-NY, #77, illus.), 41 x 27 in., (104.1 x 68.6 cm.), linen backed (BP 3781, DM 10,629, FR 36,020, Y 889,082).

$330* *"Don Q Son Of Zorro", 1925,* Elton Corp., half-sheet, cond. C, (06-05-93, Camden, #123, illus.), 22 x 28 in., (55.9 x 71.1 cm.), (BP 217, DM 535, FR 1803, Y 35,400).

$330* *"Don Q Son Of Zorro", 1925,* Elton Corp., half-sheet, cond. C, (06-05-93, Camden, #124, illus.), 22 x 28 in., (55.9 x 71.1 cm.), (BP 217, DM 535, FR 1803, Y 35,400).

$225* *Don Quixote, 1947,* Mexican, cond. A-, one-sheet, linen-backed, (12-17-92, Christie-S. Ken, #243, illus.), approx. 24 x 33 in., (61 x 83.8 cm.), poster (BP 143, DM 351, FR 1200, Y 27,651).

$1100* *"Don't Bother To Knock", 1952,* Fox, three-sheet, cond. C, (06-05-93, Camden, #113, illus.), 81 x 41 in., (205.7 x 104.1 cm.), dry mounted on foamcore (BP 724, DM 1783, FR 6011, Y 118,000).

$275* *Don't Bother To Knock, 1952,* half sheet, fine cond., (12-12-92, Hollywd Poster, #251, illus.), (BP 176, DM 433, FR 1485, Y 34,030).

$1100* *Don't Bother To Knock, 20th Century Fox, 1952,* one-sheet, cond. A, linen backed, (12-14-92, Christie-E, #235, illus.), 41 x 27 in., (104.1 x 68.6 cm.), (BP 703, DM 1729, FR 5892, Y 136,088).

$193* *Don't Knock The Rock, 1957,* near mint cond., (12-12-92, Hollywd Poster, #317, illus.), (BP 124, DM 304, FR 1042, Y 23,883).

$1210* *"Donald Duck", "Looney Tunes" and Two "Tom And Jerry": Four,* Andy Warhol Estate, (04-16-93, DuMouchelle, #2535), 41 x 27 in., (104.1 x 68.6 cm.), poster (BP 794, DM 1954, FR 6605, Y 136,062).

$303* *Doomed To Die, 1940,* near mint cond., (linen), (12-12-92, Hollywd Poster, #152, illus.), (BP 194, DM 477, FR 1636, Y 37,495).

$385* *Dorothy Gish, circa 1920,* fine cond., (linen), (12-12-92, Hollywd Poster, #206, illus.), (BP 247, DM 607, FR 2079, Y 47,643).

$1760* *Dorothy Vernon Of Haddon Hall, Marshall Neilan Production, 1924,* one-sheet, fine cond., Stanley Caidin Coll., (09-12-92, Sotheby-NY, #106, illus.), 41 x 27 in., (104.1 x 68.6 cm.), linen backed (BP 931, DM 2616, FR 8866, Y 218,851).

$3850* *Dorothy Vernon Of Haddon Hall, United Artists, 1924,* one-sheet, cond. A, paper backed, (12-14-92, Christie-E, #87, illus.), 41 x 27 in., (104.1 x 68.6 cm.), (BP 2462, DM 6051, FR 20,621, Y 476,308).

$1760* *Double Indemnity, 1944,* fine cond., (linen), (12-12-92, Hollywd Poster, #6, illus.), (BP 1129, DM 2773, FR 9503, Y 217,795).

$550* *Double Indemnity, Paramount, 1944,* half-sheet, very fine cond., Stanley Caidin Coll., (09-12-92, Sotheby-NY, #236, illus.), 22 x 28 in., (55.9 x 71.1 cm.), (BP 291, DM 818, FR 2771, Y 68,391).

$880* *Double Indemnity, Paramount, 1944: Set Of Eight,* lobby cards, very fine cond., Stanley Caidin Coll., (09-12-92, Sotheby-NY, #235, illus.), 11 x 14 in., (27.9 x 35.6 cm.), (BP 465, DM 1308, FR 4433, Y 109,426).

$935* *Down Argentine Way, 20th Century Fox, 1940,* one-sheet, cond. A, linen backed, (12-14-92, Christie-E, #231, illus.), 41 x 27 in., (104.1 x 68.6 cm.), (BP 598, DM 1469, FR 5008, Y 115,675).

$605* *Dr. Cyclops, 1940,* Italian, linen backed, (03-18-93, Swann, #77, illus.), 55 x 39 in., (139.7 x 99.1 cm.), (BP 408, DM 994, FR 3389, Y 70,406).

$312* *Dr. Cyclops, Paramount, 1939,* cond. C, British Quad. linen-backed, (12-17-92, Christie-S. Ken, #231, illus.), 40 x 30 in., (101.6 x 76.2 cm.), poster (BP 198, DM 487, FR 1664, Y 38,343).

$1387* *Dr. Cyclops, Paramount, 1940,* cond. B+, one-sheet, linen-backed, (12-17-92, Christie-S. Ken, #232, illus.), 41 x 27 in., (104.1 x 68.6 cm.), poster (BP 880, DM 2165, FR 7397, Y 170,456).

$2420* *Dr. Jekyll And Mr. Hyde, 1932,* Swedish, cond. A, (03-18-93, Swann, #135, illus.), 39 x 27 in., (99.1 x 68.6 cm.), (BP 1632, DM 3977, FR 13,557, Y 281,625).

$7700* *Dr. Jekyll And Mr. Hyde, Paramount, 1931,* insert, good cond., Stanley Caidin Coll., (09-12-92, Sotheby-NY, #127, illus.), 36 x 14 in., (91.4 x 35.6 cm.), (BP 4072, DM 11,446, FR 38,791, Y 957,473).

$770* *Dr. Jekyll And Mr. Hyde, Paramount, 1931,* jumbo lobby card, good cond., Stanley Caidin Coll., (09-12-92, Sotheby-NY, #130, illus.), 17 x 14 in., (43.2 x 35.6 cm.), linen backed (BP 407, DM 1145, FR 3879, Y 95,747).

$4840* *Dr. Jekyll And Mr. Hyde, Paramount, 1932,* lobby card, cond. A, (12-14-92, Christie-E, #80, illus.), 11 x 14 in., (27.9 x 35.6 cm.), (BP 3095, DM 7606, FR 25,924, Y 598,788).

$440* *Dr. No, 1962,* French, linen backed, cond. B+, (03-18-93, Swann, #62, illus.), 63 x 47 in., (160 x 119.4 cm.), (BP 297, DM 723, FR 2465, Y 51,204).

$220* *Dr. No, 1962,* near mint cond., (linen), (12-12-92, Hollywd Poster, #53, illus.), (BP 141, DM 347, FR 1188, Y 27,224).

$550* *Dr. Syn, Gaumont, 1937,* one-sheet, very fine cond., Stanley Caidin Coll., (09-12-92, Sotheby-NY, #62, illus.), 41 x 27 in., (104.1 x 68.6 cm.), linen backed (BP 291, DM 818, FR 2771, Y 68,391).

$1100* *Dracula's Daughter, Universal Pictures, 1936,* pressbook, very fine cond., Stanley Caidin Coll., (09-12-92, Sotheby-NY, #197, illus.), (BP 582, DM 1635, FR 5542, Y 136,782).

$5500* *Dracula, Universal Pictures, 1931,* pressbook, very fine cond., Stanley Caidin Coll., (09-12-92, Sotheby-NY, #196, illus.), (BP 2909, DM 8176, FR 27,708, Y 683,909).

$1210* *Drums Along The Mohawk, 20th Century Fox, 1939,* one-sheet, good cond., Stanley Caidin Coll., (09-12-92, Sotheby-NY, #271, illus.), 41 x 27 in., (104.1 x 68.6 cm.), linen backed (BP 640, DM 1799, FR 6096, Y 150,460).

$1980* *Duck Soup, 1933,* very good cond., (12-12-92, Hollywd Poster, #141, illus.), window card (BP 1270, DM 3120, FR 10,691, Y 245,019).

$2475* *"Dumbo", 1941,* Disney, complete set of eight lobby cards, cond. A, (11-07-92, Camden, #241, illus.), each 11 x 14 in., (27.9 x 35.6 cm.), (BP 1618, DM 3952, FR 13,357, Y 305,480).

$19,800* *Dumbo, Disney, 1941,* three-sheet, cond. A, linen backed, (12-14-92, Christie-E, #102, illus.), 81 x 41 in., (205.7 x 104.1 cm.), (BP 12,660, DM 31,117, FR 106,052, Y 2,449,586).

$440* *E.T. and Star Wars: Four,* one-sheet and insert for each, cond. A-, (03-18-93, Swann, #63, illus.), (BP 297, DM 723, FR 2465, Y 51,204).

$825* *The Early Bird, Pathe, 1928,* one-sheet, cond. B, linen backed, (12-14-92, Christie-E, #270, illus.), 41 x 27 in., (104.1 x 68.6 cm.), (BP 527, DM 1297, FR 4419, Y 102,066).

$385* *Early Magniscope Poster,* Rolled, fine cond., (linen), (12-12-92, Hollywd Poster, #207, illus.), (BP 247, DM 607, FR 2079, Y 47,643).

$275* *East Of Eden, 1955,* near mint cond., (12-12-92, Hollywd Poster, #33, illus.), (BP 176, DM 433, FR 1485, Y 34,030).

$302* *East Of Eden, Warner Bros., 1955,* one-sheet, cond. A-, linen backed, (03-18-93, Swann, #64, illus.), (BP 204, DM 496, FR 1692, Y 35,145).

$1210* *"Easter Parade", 1948,* MGM, three-sheet, cond. B, (11-07-92, Camden, #185, illus.), 81 x 41 in., (205.7 x 104.1 cm.), on linen (BP 791, DM 1932, FR 6530, Y 149,346).

$660* *Easter Parade, 1948,* near mint cond., (12-12-92, Hollywd Poster, #92, illus.), (BP 423, DM 1040, FR 3564, Y 81,673).

$8800* *Emperor Jones, United Artists, 1933,* one-sheet, very fine cond., Stanley Caidin Coll., (09-12-92, Sotheby-NY, #113, illus.), 41 x 27 in., (104.1 x 68.6 cm.), linen backed (BP 4654, DM 13,082, FR 44,332, Y 1,094,255).

$3850* *Emperor Jones, United Artists, 1933: Set Of Eight,* lobby cards, very fine cond., Stanley Caidin Coll., (09-12-92, Sotheby-NY, #114, illus.), 11 x 14 in., (27.9 x 35.6 cm.), (BP 2036, DM 5723, FR 19,395, Y 478,737).

$880* *Employees' Entrance, First National Pictures, 1933*, one-sheet, very fine cond., Stanley Caidin Coll., (09-12-92, Sotheby-NY, #220, illus.), 41 x 27 in., (104.1 x 68.6 cm.), linen backed (BP 465, DM 1308, FR 4433, Y 109,426).

$550* *Eternal Love, 1929*, half sheet, fine cond., (paper), (12-12-92, Hollywd Poster, #245, illus.), (BP 353, DM 867, FR 2970, Y 68,061).

$770* *Eternal Love, United Artists, 1929*, insert, near mint cond., Stanley Caidin Coll., (09-12-92, Sotheby-NY, #65, illus.), 36 x 14 in., (91.4 x 35.6 cm.), (BP 407, DM 1145, FR 3879, Y 95,747).

$2200* *"Every Day's A Holiday", 1938*, Paramount, half-sheet, cond. B, (06-05-93, Camden, #127, illus.), 22 x 28 in., (55.9 x 71.1 cm.), on linen (BP 1448, DM 3567, FR 12,022, Y 236,001).

$2090* *Every Day's A Holiday, Paramount, 1937*, one-sheet, fine cond., Stanley Caidin Coll., (09-12-92, Sotheby-NY, #136, illus.), 41 x 27 in., (104.1 x 68.6 cm.), linen backed (BP 1105, DM 3107, FR 10,529, Y 259,886).

$2200* *Every Day's A Holiday, Paramount, 1938*, one-sheet, cond. A, linen backed, (12-14-92, Christie-E, #51, illus.), 41 x 27 in., (104.1 x 68.6 cm.), (BP 1407, DM 3457, FR 11,784, Y 272,176).

$440* *The Exiles, 1923*, fine cond., (linen), (12-12-92, Hollywd Poster, #82, illus.), (BP 282, DM 693, FR 2376, Y 54,449).

$192* *Exodus, United Artists, 1966*, one-sheet, cond. A-, linen backed, (03-18-93, Swann, #70, illus.), (BP 129, DM 316, FR 1076, Y 22,344).

$770* *Eye For Eye, Metro, 1918*, one-sheet, cond. B, linen backed, (12-14-92, Christie-E, #277, illus.), 41 x 27 in., (104.1 x 68.6 cm.), (BP 492, DM 1210, FR 4124, Y 95,262).

$440* *The Eyes Of The World, 1919*, fine cond., (linen), (12-12-92, Hollywd Poster, #9, illus.), (BP 282, DM 693, FR 2376, Y 54,449).

$3025* *Faithless, MGM, 1932*, insert, fine cond., Stanley Caidin Coll., (09-12-92, Sotheby-NY, #43, illus.), 36 x 14 in., (91.4 x 35.6 cm.), (BP 1600, DM 4497, FR 15,239, Y 376,150).

$275* *The Fallen Idol, 1949*, near mint cond., (12-12-92, Hollywd Poster, #3, illus.), (BP 176, DM 433, FR 1485, Y 34,030).

$1320* *Falling Hare, Warner Brothers, 1941/42*, one-sheet, cond. A, linen backed, (12-14-92, Christie-E, #107, illus.), 41 x 27 in., (104.1 x 68.6 cm.), (BP 844, DM 2074, FR 7070, Y 163,306).

$1650* *Fantasia, 1941*, insert, fine cond., (12-12-92, Hollywd Poster, #70, illus.), (BP 1058, DM 2600, FR 8909, Y 204,183).

$6600* *Fantasia, Disney, 1941*, one-sheet, cond. A, linen backed, (12-14-92, Christie-E, #103, illus.), 41 x 27 in., (104.1 x 68.6 cm.), (BP 4220, DM 10,372, FR 35,351, Y 816,529).

$2090* *Fantasia, Disney, 1942*, orig. Swedish poster, cond. A, linen backed, (12-14-92, Christie-E, #258, illus.), 40 x 27 in., (101.6 x 68.6 cm.), (BP 1336, DM 3285, FR 11,194, Y 258,567).

$1045* *Fantasia, RKO-Disney, 1940*, Argentinian, linen backed, (03-18-93, Swann, #185, illus.), 44 x 29 in., (111.8 x 73.7 cm.), (BP 705, DM 1717, FR 5854, Y 121,611).

$192* *Fantasie Di Charlot, 1957: Three*, Italian, paper backed, (03-18-93, Swann, #71, illus.), each 19 x 27 in., (48.3 x 68.6 cm.), (BP 129, DM 316, FR 1076, Y 22,344).

$3080* *Fantomas, 1932*, Belgian, cond. A, linen backed, (03-18-93, Swann, #121, illus.), 31 x 24 in., (78.7 x 61 cm.), (BP 2077, DM 5062, FR 17,255, Y 358,431).

$440* *Faster Pussycat! Kill! Kill!, 1966*, near mint cond., (linen), (12-12-92, Hollywd Poster, #319, illus.), (BP 282, DM 693, FR 2376, Y 54,449).

$2090* *"Faust", 1926*, MGM, insert, cond. A, unfolded, (06-05-93, Camden, #67, illus.), 36 x 14 in., (91.4 x 35.6 cm.), (BP 1376, DM 3388, FR 11,421, Y 224,201).

$555* *Federico Fellini, La Dolce Vita, Riama/Pathe Consortium, 1960*, British Quad., cond. A, linen-backed, (12-17-92, Christie-S. Ken, #400, illus.), 30 x 40 in., (76.2 x 101.6 cm.), poster (BP 352, DM 867, FR 2960, Y 68,207).

$1100* *"The Female", 1959*, French, Pathe Consortium, cond. C, (11-07-92, Camden, #410, illus.), 63 x 47 in., (160 x 119.4 cm.), restored on linen (BP 719, DM 1756, FR 5936, Y 135,769).

$467* *La Femme Et Le Pantin, 1958*, orig. French, cond. B, linen backed, (03-18-93, Swann, #67, illus.), 63 x 47 in., (160 x 119.4 cm.), (BP 315, DM 767, FR 2616, Y 54,347).

$192* *La Femme Nue, Sigma, 1949*, orig. French, linen backed, (03-18-93, Swann, #68, illus.), 63 x 47 in., (160 x 119.4 cm.), (BP 129, DM 316, FR 1076, Y 22,344).

$825* *Fifth Avenue Girl, RKO, 1939*, one-sheet, cond. A, linen backed, (12-14-92, Christie-E, #16, illus.), 41 x 27 in., (104.1 x 68.6 cm.), (BP 527, DM 1297, FR 4419, Y 102,066).

$330* *The Fight Never Ends*, very good cond., (12-12-92, Hollywd Poster, #285, illus.), (BP 212, DM 520, FR 1782, Y 40,837).

$220* *The Fighting 69th, 1940*, fine cond., (linen), (12-12-92, Hollywd Poster, #284, illus.), (BP 141, DM 347, FR 1188, Y 27,224).

$990* *The Fighting Fool, 1931*, near mint cond., (linen), (12-12-92, Hollywd Poster, #83, illus.), (BP 635, DM 1560, FR 5346, Y 122,510).

$715* *The Fighting Marine, Pathe, 1926*, one-sheet, cond. A, linen backed, (12-14-92, Christie-E, #74, illus.), 41 x 27 in., (104.1 x 68.6 cm.), (BP 457, DM 1124, FR 3830, Y 88,457).

$330* *The Firefly, MGM, 1937*, insert, near mint cond., Stanley Caidin Coll., (09-12-92, Sotheby-NY, #154, illus.), 36 x 14 in., (91.4 x 35.6 cm.), (BP 175, DM 491, FR 1662, Y 41,035).

$385* *First National Pictures, 1924*, fine cond., (12-12-92, Hollywd Poster, #10, illus.), (BP 247, DM 607, FR 2079, Y 47,643).

$110* *The First Year, 1932*, fine cond., (12-12-92, Hollywd Poster, #310, illus.), (BP 71, DM 173, FR 594, Y 13,612).

$2200* *Five And Ten, MGM, 1931*, one-sheet, cond. B, linen backed, (12-14-92, Christie-E, #318, illus.), 41 x 27 in., (104.1 x 68.6 cm.), (BP 1407, DM 3457, FR 11,784, Y 272,176).

$8250* *Flash Gordon Conquers The Universe, Universal, 1940*, one-sheet, cond. A, linen backed, (12-14-92, Christie-E, #227, illus.), 41 x 27 in., (104.1 x 68.6 cm.), (BP 5275, DM 12,966, FR 44,189, Y 1,020,661).

$935* *The Fleets's In, Paramount, 1928*, insert, very fine cond., artwork created by William J. Hanneman, Stanley Caidin Coll., (09-12-92, Sotheby-NY, #21, illus.), 36 x 14 in., (66 x 35.6 cm.), (BP 494, DM 1390, FR 4710, Y 116,265).

$3300* *Flesh And The Devil, MGM, 1927: Set Of Eight*, lobby cards, cond. A, (12-14-92, Christie-E, #169, illus.), each 11 x 14 in., (27.9 x 35.6 cm.), (BP 2110, DM 5186, FR 17,675, Y 408,264).

$4180* *Flip The Frog, MGM, 1933*, one-sheet, cond. A, linen backed, (12-14-92, Christie-E, #106, illus.), 41 x 27 in., (104.1 x 68.6 cm.), (BP 2673, DM 6569, FR 22,389, Y 517,135).

$1760* *"Flirting With Love", 1924*, First National, one-sheet, cond. B, (06-05-93, Camden, #85, illus.), 41 x 27 in., (104.1 x 68.6 cm.), on linen (BP 1159, DM 2853, FR 9617, Y 188,801).

$121* *The Fly, 1958; Return Of The Fly, 1959: Two*, one-sheet, half sheet, (03-18-93, Swann, #72, illus.), (BP 82, DM 199, FR 678, Y 14,081).

$3740* *Flying Down To Rio, 1933*, very good cond., (12-12-92, Hollywd Poster, #221, illus.), title card (BP 2398, DM 5893, FR 20,194, Y 462,814).

$330* *"Fog Over Frisco", 1934*, First National, window card, cond. B, (06-05-93, Camden, #248, illus.), 22 x 14 in., (55.9 x 35.6 cm.), on paper (BP 217, DM 535, FR 1803, Y 35,400).

$330* *"Fool's First", 1922*, First National, one-sheet, cond. B, (06-05-93, Camden, #87, illus.), 41 x 27 in., (104.1 x 68.6 cm.), restored on linen after catalogue photography (BP 217, DM 535, FR 1803, Y 35,400).

$1650* *For A Few Dollars More, PEA, 1967*, orig. Italian poster, cond. B, paper backed, (12-14-92, Christie-E, #99, illus.), 39 x 27½ in., (99.1 x 69.9 cm.), (BP 1055, DM 2593, FR 8838, Y 204,132).

$110* *For Heaven's Sake, 1926,* fine cond., (12-12-92, Hollywd Poster, #119, illus.), title card (BP 71, DM 173, FR 594, Y 13,612).

$330* *For Whom The Bells Toll, 1943,* very good cond., (12-12-92, Hollywd Poster, #156, illus.), (BP 212, DM 520, FR 1782, Y 40,837).

$1320* *Forbidden Planet,* English, cond. A-, linen backed, (03-18-93, Swann, #202, illus.), 30 x 40 in., (76.2 x 101.6 cm.), (BP 890, DM 2169, FR 7395, Y 153,613).

$1650* *Forbidden Planet (Planete Interdit), 1956,* French, cond. A-, linen backed, (03-18-93, Swann, #203, illus.), 63 x 47 in., (160 x 119.4 cm.), (BP 1113, DM 2712, FR 9244, Y 192,017).

$193* *"Forbidden Planet", 1956,* Italian, MGM, fotobusta, cond. B, (06-05-93, Camden, #291, illus.), 19 x 26½ in., (48.3 x 67.3 cm.), (BP 127, DM 313, FR 1055, Y 20,704).

$1320* *"Forbidden Planet", 1956,* MGM, half-sheet, cond. B, (06-05-93, Camden, #290, illus.), 22 x 28 in., (55.9 x 71.1 cm.), (BP 869, DM 2140, FR 7213, Y 141,601).

$3575* *"Forbidden Planet", 1956,* MGM, cond. B, (11-07-92, Camden, #204, illus.), 41 x 27 in., (104.1 x 68.6 cm.), on linen (BP 2337, DM 5708, FR 19,293, Y 441,249).

$1210* *"Forbidden Planet", 1956,* MGM, half-sheet, cond. A, (11-07-92, Camden, #163, illus.), 22 x 28 in., (55.9 x 71.1 cm.), on paper (BP 791, DM 1932, FR 6530, Y 149,346).

$3080* *Forbidden Planet, 1956,* near mint cond., (linen), (12-12-92, Hollywd Poster, #52, illus.), (BP 1975, DM 4853, FR 16,631, Y 381,141).

$193* *Forbidden Planet, 1956,* fine cond., (12-12-92, Hollywd Poster, #327, illus.), lobby card (BP 124, DM 304, FR 1042, Y 23,883).

$1540* *Forbidden Planet, 1956: Set Of Eight,* lobby cards, (03-18-93, Swann, #89, illus.), (BP 1039, DM 2531, FR 8627, Y 179,216).

$165* *Forbidden Planet, 1956: Two,* Belgian, (03-18-93, Swann, #90, illus.), one 14 x 22 in., (35.6 x 55.9 cm.), other 22 x 12 in., (35.6 x 55.9 cm.), (BP 111, DM 271, FR 924, Y 19,202).

$2420* *Forbidden Planet, MGM, 1956,* one-sheet, cond. B+, linen backed, (03-18-93, Swann, #88, illus.), (BP 1632, DM 3977, FR 13,557, Y 281,625).

$2750* *Forbidden Planet, MGM, 1956,* cond. A, (12-14-92, Christie-E, #190, illus.), 40 x 30 in., (101.6 x 76.2 cm.), (BP 1758, DM 4322, FR 14,730, Y 340,220).

$715* *Forbidden Trails, 1941,* near mint cond., (linen), (12-12-92, Hollywd Poster, #288, illus.), (BP 458, DM 1127, FR 3861, Y 88,479).

$330* *"A Foreign Affair", 1948,* Paramount, one-sheet, cond. B, (06-05-93, Camden, #311, illus.), 41 x 27 in., (104.1 x 68.6 cm.), (BP 217, DM 535, FR 1803, Y 35,400).

$2750* *Foreign Correspondent, United Artists, 1940,* one-sheet, fine cond., Stanley Caidin Coll., (09-12-92, Sotheby-NY, #230, illus.), 41 x 27 in., (104.1 x 68.6 cm.), linen backed (BP 1454, DM 4088, FR 13,854, Y 341,955).

$1760* *Forsaking All Others, MGM, 1934,* one-sheet, cond. A, paper backed, (12-14-92, Christie-E, #114, illus.), 41 x 27 in., (104.1 x 68.6 cm.), (BP 1125, DM 2766, FR 9427, Y 217,741).

$1045* *Forty Second Street, 1933,* near mint cond., (12-12-92, Hollywd Poster, #219, illus.), lobby card (BP 670, DM 1646, FR 5643, Y 129,316).

$660* *The Fountainhead, Warner Brothers, 1949,* one-sheet, cond. A, linen backed, (12-14-92, Christie-E, #143, illus.), 41 x 27 in., (104.1 x 68.6 cm.), (BP 422, DM 1037, FR 3535, Y 81,653).

$1760* *Frank Duck Brings 'Em Back Alive, Walt Disney Productions, 1946,* one-sheet, very fine cond., Stanley Caidin Coll., (09-12-92, Sotheby-NY, #290, illus.), 41 x 27 in., (104.1 x 68.6 cm.), linen backed (BP 931, DM 2616, FR 8866, Y 218,851).

$5500* *Frankenstein Meets The Wolf Man, Universal, 1943,* three-sheet, cond. A, linen backed, (12-14-92, Christie-E, #310, illus.), 81 x 41 in., (205.7 x 104.1 cm.), (BP 3517, DM 8644, FR 29,459, Y 680,440).

$2750* *"Frankenstein", 1931,* Universal, lobby card, cond. B, (11-07-92, Camden, #92, illus.), 11 x 14 in., (27.9 x 35.6 cm.), on paper (BP 1798, DM 4391, FR 14,841, Y 339,422).

$4125* *"Frankenstein", 1931,* Universal, lobby card, cond. B, (11-07-92, Camden, #91, illus.), 11 x 14 in., (27.9 x 35.6 cm.), on paper (BP 2697, DM 6586, FR 22,261, Y 509,134).

$3575* *"Frankenstein", 1931,* Universal, lobby card, cond. B, (11-07-92, Camden, #90, illus.), 11 x 14 in., (27.9 x 35.6 cm.), (BP 2337, DM 5708, FR 19,293, Y 441,249).

$2200* *"Frankenstein", 1931,* Swedish, cond. A, unfolded, (11-07-92, Camden, #104, illus.), 39 x 27 in., (99.1 x 68.6 cm.), on linen (BP 1438, DM 3513, FR 11,873, Y 271,538).

$1210* *"Frankenstein", c. 1950,* German, reissue, cond. A, (11-07-92, Camden, #105, illus.), 33 x 23 in., (83.8 x 58.4 cm.), (BP 791, DM 1932, FR 6530, Y 149,346).

$8250* *Frankenstein, 1931,* Argentinian, cond. A, (03-18-93, Swann, #101, illus.), 44 x 29 in., (111.8 x 73.7 cm.), $17,000**Frankenstein, Universal, 1931,* orig. Spanish poster, cond. A, (12-14-92, Christie-E, #304, illus.), 41 x 27 in., (104.1 x 68.6 cm.), (BP 10,870, DM 26,717, FR 91,055, Y 2,103,180).

$2200* *Frankenstein, Universal, 1931: Set Of Twelve,* special mini-lobby card set, cond. A, (12-14-92, Christie-E, #305, illus.), each 5½ x 4¼ in., (14 x 10.8 cm.), (BP 1407, DM 3457, FR 11,784, Y 272,176).

$385* *From Russia With Love, 1963,* French, cond. A-, linen backed, (03-18-93, Swann, #75, illus.), 63 x 47 in., (160 x 119.4 cm.), (BP 260, DM 633, FR 2157, Y 44,804).

$220* *From Russia With Love, 1963,* near mint cond., (12-12-92, Hollywd Poster, #54, illus.), (BP 141, DM 347, FR 1188, Y 27,224).

$660* *From The Manger To The Cross, Kalem Co., 1913,* one-sheet, very fine cond., Stanley Caidin Coll., (09-12-92, Sotheby-NY, #48, illus.), 41 x 27 in., (104.1 x 68.6 cm.), linen backed (BP 349, DM 981, FR 3325, Y 82,069).

$18,700* *G-Men, First National, 1935,* three-sheet, cond. A, linen backed, (12-14-92, Christie-E, #41, illus.), 81 x 41 in., (205.7 x 104.1 cm.), (BP 11,957, DM 29,389, FR 100,161, Y 2,313,497).

$440* *"The GReat Dictator", 1940,* United Artists, half-sheet, cond. C, (06-05-93, Camden, #122, illus.), 22 x 28 in., (55.9 x 71.1 cm.), on linen (BP 290, DM 713, FR 2404, Y 47,200).

$990* *Gambling Ship, 1933,* near mint cond., (linen), (12-12-92, Hollywd Poster, #43, illus.), (BP 635, DM 1560, FR 5346, Y 122,510).

$440* *Gang Busters, 1941,* near mint cond., (12-12-92, Hollywd Poster, #321, illus.), (BP 282, DM 693, FR 2376, Y 54,449).

$220* *Garden of Allah, 1936,* near mint cond., (12-12-92, Hollywd Poster, #28, illus.), lobby card (BP 141, DM 347, FR 1188, Y 27,224).

$2750* *"Gaslight", 1944,* MGM, six-sheet, cond. A, (11-07-92, Camden, #277, illus.), 81 x 81 in., (205.7 x 205.7 cm.), on linen (BP 1798, DM 4391, FR 14,841, Y 339,422).

$550* *Gaslight, 1944,* fine cond., (12-12-92, Hollywd Poster, #286, illus.), (BP 353, DM 867, FR 2970, Y 68,061).

$1980* *The Gaucho, United Artists, 1928,* half-sheet, fine cond., Stanley Caidin Coll., (09-12-92, Sotheby-NY, #111, illus.), 22 x 28 in., (55.9 x 71.1 cm.), (BP 1047, DM 2943, FR 9975, Y 246,207).

$3300* *A Gem Of A Jam, Columbia, 1943,* one-sheet, cond. A, linen backed, (12-14-92, Christie-E, #290, illus.), 41 x 27 in., (104.1 x 68.6 cm.), (BP 2110, DM 5186, FR 17,675, Y 408,264).

$1540* *General Crack, Warner Brothers, 1929,* one-sheet, cond. A, paper backed, (12-14-92, Christie-E, #280, illus.), 41 x 27 in., (104.1 x 68.6 cm.), (BP 985, DM 2420, FR 8249, Y 190,523).

$165* *General Spanky, 1937,* half sheet, fine cond., (paper), (12-12-92, Hollywd Poster, #244, illus.), (BP 106, DM 260, FR 891, Y 20,418).

$13,200* *The General, United Artists, 1926,* half-sheet, cond. A, (12-14-92, Christie-E, #121, illus.), 22 x 28 in., (55.9 x 71.1 cm.), (BP 8440, DM 20,745, FR 70,702, Y 1,633,057).

$5500* *Gentlemen Prefer Blondes, 20th Century Fox, 1953,* cond. A, (12-14-92, Christie-E, #233, illus.), 60 x 40 in., (152.4 x 101.6 cm.), (BP 3517, DM 8644, FR 29,459, Y 680,440).

$1045* *Geraldine, Pathe, 1929,* one-sheet, fine cond., Stanley Caidin Coll., (09-12-92, Sotheby-NY, #41, illus.), 41 x 27 in., (104.1 x 68.6 cm.), linen backed (BP 553, DM 1553, FR 5264, Y 129,943).

$1320* *The Ghost Breakers, Paramount, 1940,* three-sheet, very fine cond., Stanley Caidin Coll., (09-12-92, Sotheby-NY, #131, illus.), 81 x 41 in., (205.7 x 104.1 cm.), linen backed (BP 698, DM 1962, FR 6650, Y 164,138).

$1980* *The Ghost Breakers, Paramount, 1940,* one-sheet, cond. A, linen backed, (12-14-92, Christie-E, #68, illus.), 41 x 27 in., (104.1 x 68.6 cm.), (BP 1266, DM 3112, FR 10,605, Y 244,959).

$10,450* *The Ghost Of Frankenstein, Universal, 1942,* one-sheet, cond. A, linen backed, (12-14-92, Christie-E, #307, illus.), 41 x 27 in., (104.1 x 68.6 cm.), (BP 6682, DM 16,423, FR 55,972, Y 1,292,837).

$522* *Giant (Geant), 1963,* French, cond. A-, linen backed, (03-18-93, Swann, #92, illus.), 63 x 47 in., (160 x 119.4 cm.), (BP 352, DM 858, FR 2924, Y 60,747).

$248* *Giant, 1956,* fine cond., (12-12-92, Hollywd Poster, #330, illus.), lobby card (BP 159, DM 391, FR 1339, Y 30,689).

$7700* *Gilda, Columbia, 1946,* one-sheet, cond. A, linen backed, (12-14-92, Christie-E, #217, illus.), 41 x 27 in., (104.1 x 68.6 cm.), (BP 4923, DM 12,101, FR 41,243, Y 952,617).

$220* *The Girl Can't Help It, 1956,* near mint cond., (linen), (12-12-92, Hollywd Poster, #278, illus.), (BP 141, DM 347, FR 1188, Y 27,224).

$770* *Girl Crazy, MGM, 1943,* one-sheet, very fine cond., Stanley Caidin Coll., (09-12-92, Sotheby-NY, #281, illus.), 41 x 27 in., (104.1 x 68.6 cm.), linen backed (BP 407, DM 1145, FR 3879, Y 95,747).

$2750* *"The Girl From 10th Avenue", 1935,* First National, window card, cond. C, (06-05-93, Camden, #247, illus.), 22 x 14 in., (55.9 x 35.6 cm.), on linen (BP 1810, DM 4458, FR 15,027, Y 295,001).

$17,600* *The Girl From 10th Avenue, First National, 1935,* half-sheet, cond. A, (12-14-92, Christie-E, #108, illus.), 22 x 28 in., (55.9 x 71.1 cm.), (BP 11,253, DM 27,660, FR 94,269, Y 2,177,409).

$6600* *The Girl From Missouri, MGM, 1934,* one-sheet, cond. A, paper backed, (12-14-92, Christie-E, #295, illus.), 41 x 27 in., (104.1 x 68.6 cm.), (BP 4220, DM 10,372, FR 35,351, Y 816,529).

$358* *"The Glass Key", 1942,* French, Paramount, cond. A, (06-05-93, Camden, #278, illus.), 63 x 47 in., (160 x 119.4 cm.), on linen (BP 236, DM 580, FR 1956, Y 38,404).

$555* *Gloria Swanson/Erich Von Stroheim, Sunset Boulevard, Paramount, 1950,* cond. A., one-sheet, linen-backed, (12-17-92, Christie-S. Ken, #399, illus.), 41 x 27 in., (104.1 x 68.6 cm.), poster (BP 352, DM 867, FR 2960, Y 68,207).

$495* *"The Glorious Fool", 1921,* Goldwyn, one-sheet, cond. B, (06-05-93, Camden, #88, illus.), 41 x 27 in., (104.1 x 68.6 cm.), restored on linen after catalogue photography (BP 326, DM 803, FR 2705, Y 53,100).

$357* *Go Into Your Dance (Entrez Dans La Dance), 1935,* Belgian, cond. A, linen backed, (03-18-93, Swann, #180, illus.), (BP 241, DM 587, FR 2000, Y 41,545).

$880* *Go Into Your Dance, Warner Brothers, 1935,* insert, very fine cond., Stanley Caidin Coll., (09-12-92, Sotheby-NY, #144, illus.), 36 x 14 in., (91.4 x 35.6 cm.), (BP 465, DM 1308, FR 4433, Y 109,426).

$2640* *Go West, 1926,* French, very good cond., (linen), (12-12-92, Hollywd Poster, #198, illus.), (BP 1693, DM 4159, FR 14,255, Y 326,692).

$2200* *Go West, MGM, 1940,* one-sheet, fine cond., Stanley Caidin Coll., (09-12-92, Sotheby-NY, #100, illus.), 41 x 27 in., (104.1 x 68.6 cm.), linen backed (BP 1163, DM 3270, FR 11,083, Y 273,564).

$660* *Godzilla V. Mosura,* Japanese, linen backed, (03-18-93, Swann, #93, illus.), 70 x 47 in., (177.8 x 119.4 cm.), (BP 445, DM 1085, FR 3697, Y 76,807).

$660* *"Godzilla", 1956,* Toho, insert, cond. B, (06-05-93, Camden, #71, illus.), 36 x 14 in., (91.4 x 35.6 cm.), (BP 434, DM 1070, FR 3607, Y 70,800).

$605* *Godzilla, 1956,* French, (03-18-93, Swann, #94, illus.), 31 x 23 in., (78.7 x 58.4 cm.), (BP 408, DM 994, FR 3389, Y 70,406).

$1430* *Godzilla, 1956,* French, cond. B, linen backed, (03-18-93, Swann, #96, illus.), 63 x 47 in., (160 x 119.4 cm.), (BP 964, DM 2350, FR 8011, Y 166,415).

$1320* *Godzilla, Toho, 1956,* Italian, cond. A, linen backed, (12-14-92, Christie-E, #97, illus.), 55 x 39 in., (139.7 x 99.1 cm.), (BP 844, DM 2074, FR 7070, Y 163,306).

$143* *Going My Way, Paramount, 1944,* one-sheet, cond. A-, linen backed, (03-18-93, Swann, #103, illus.), (BP 96, DM 235, FR 801, Y 16,641).

$1430* *Going! Going! Gone!!, Pathe, 1918,* one-sheet, cond. B, linen backed, (12-14-92, Christie-E, #293, illus.), 41 x 27 in., (104.1 x 68.6 cm.), (BP 914, DM 2247, FR 7659, Y 176,915).

$6600* *Gold Diggers Of 1933, Warner Brothers, 1933,* one-sheet, cond. A, paper backed, (12-14-92, Christie-E, #230, illus.), 41 x 27 in., (104.1 x 68.6 cm.), (BP 4220, DM 10,372, FR 35,351, Y 816,529).

$1430* *The Gold Rush, United Artists, 1925,* lobby card, very fine cond., Stanley Caidin Coll., (09-12-92, Sotheby-NY, #104, illus.), 11 x 14 in., (27.9 x 35.6 cm.), (BP 756, DM 2126, FR 7204, Y 177,816).

$4950* *Golden Arrow, First National Picture, 1936,* one-sheet, very fine cond., Stanley Caidin Coll., (09-12-92, Sotheby-NY, #214, illus.), 41 x 27 in., (104.1 x 68.6 cm.), linen backed (BP 2618, DM 7358, FR 24,937, Y 615,519).

$1045* *Golden Boy, Columbia, 1939,* one-sheet, cond. B, linen backed, (12-14-92, Christie-E, #27, illus.), 41 x 27 in., (104.1 x 68.6 cm.), (BP 668, DM 1642, FR 5597, Y 129,284).

$385* *Gone With The Wind,* near mint cond., (linen), (12-12-92, Hollywd Poster, #201, illus.), (BP 247, DM 607, FR 2079, Y 47,643).

$825* *Gone With The Wind (Autant En Emporte Le Vent), 1939,* Belgian, linen backed, (03-18-93, Swann, #37, illus.), 31 x 23 in., (78.7 x 58.4 cm.), (BP 556, DM 1356, FR 4622, Y 96,008).

$880* *Gone With The Wind (Prezeminelo Z Wiatrem), c. 1955,* Polish, (03-18-93, Swann, #105, illus.), 26 x 38 in., (66 x 96.5 cm.), (BP 593, DM 1446, FR 4930, Y 102,409).

$3850* *"Gone With The Wind", 1939,* Selznick/MGM, insert, cond. C, (11-07-92, Camden, #372, illus.), 36 x 14 in., (91.4 x 35.6 cm.), on paper (BP 2517, DM 6147, FR 20,777, Y 475,191).

$330* *Gone With The Wind, 1947,* one-sheet, paper backed, (03-18-93, Swann, #75A, illus.), (BP 223, DM 542, FR 1849, Y 38,403).

$220* *Gone With The Wind, 1947,* fine cond., (linen), (12-12-92, Hollywd Poster, #91, illus.), (BP 141, DM 347, FR 1188, Y 27,224).

$1100* *Gone With The Wind, 1954,* one-sheet, linen backed, (03-18-93, Swann, #104, illus.), (BP 742, DM 1808, FR 6162, Y 128,011).

$4950* *Gone With The Wind, MGM, 1939,* insert, very fine cond., Stanley Caidin Coll., (09-12-92, Sotheby-NY, #184, illus.), 36 x 14 in., (91.4 x 35.6 cm.), (BP 2618, DM 7358, FR 24,937, Y 615,519).

$462* *The Good Earth, MGM, 1937,* one-sheet, cond. A, linen backed, (12-14-92, Christie-E, #241, illus.), 41 x 27 in., (104.1 x 68.6 cm.), (BP 295, DM 726, FR 2475, Y 57,157).

$385* *The Good, The Bad And The Ugly, 1966,* near mint cond., Italian, (12-12-92, Hollywd Poster, #50, illus.), (BP 247, DM 607, FR 2079, Y 47,643).

$385* *"Goodbye Mr. Chips", 1939,* MGM, one-sheet, cond. C, (06-05-93, Camden, #30, illus.), 41 x 27 in., (104.1 x 68.6 cm.), (BP 253, DM 624, FR 2104, Y 41,300).

$1100* *Grand Biorama, Lumiere, c. 1900,* orig. French poster, cond. A, paper backed, (12-14-92, Christie-E, #265, illus.), 27 x 41 in., (68.6 x 104.1 cm.), (BP 703, DM 1729, FR 5892, Y 136,088).

$1540* *Grand Hotel, MGM, 1932,* lobby card, cond. A, (12-14-92, Christie-E, #171, illus.), 11 x 14 in., (27.9 x 35.6 cm.), (BP 985, DM 2420, FR 8249, Y 190,523).

$715* *Grand Slam, 1933,* near mint cond., (linen), (12-12-92, Hollywd Poster, #312, illus.), (BP 458, DM 1127, FR 3861, Y 88,479).

$1733* *Grausige Nachte (Horrible Nights), 1920,* German, cond. A, linen-backed, (12-17-92, Christie-S. Ken, #252, illus.), 37 x 55 in., (94 x 139.7 cm.), poster (BP 1100, DM 2706, FR 9243, Y 212,978).

$605* *The Great Gamble, Pathe, 1919,* one-sheet, cond. B, linen backed, (12-14-92, Christie-E, #223, illus.), 41 x 27 in., (104.1 x 68.6 cm.), (BP 387, DM 951, FR 3240, Y 74,848).

$1320* *The Great Love, Artcraft, 1918,* one-sheet, cond. A, linen backed, (12-14-92, Christie-E, #200, illus.), 41 x 27 in., (104.1 x 68.6 cm.), (BP 844, DM 2074, FR 7070, Y 163,306).

$110* *The Great Ziegfeld, 1936,* near mint cond., (12-12-92, Hollywd Poster, #218, illus.), lobby card (BP 71, DM 173, FR 594, Y 13,612).

$2200* *"The Green Eyed Monster", c. 1920s,* Norman, one-sheet, cond. A, (11-07-92, Camden, #216, illus.), 42 x 28 in., (106.7 x 71.1 cm.), on linen (BP 1438, DM 3513, FR 11,873, Y 271,538).

$243* *Greta Garbo, Camille (Le Roman De Marguerite Gautier), M.G.M., 1945,* French, re-issue, artwork by Roger Soubie, cond. B-, linen-backed, (12-17-92, Christie-S. Ken, #213, illus.), 63 x 47 in., (160 x 119.4 cm.), poster (BP 154, DM 379, FR 1296, Y 29,864).

$522* *Greta Garbo, MGM, c. 1937,* French, cond. C, linen backed, (03-18-93, Swann, #38, illus.), 63 x 47 in., (160 x 119.4 cm.), (BP 352, DM 858, FR 2924, Y 60,747).

$2420* *Greta Garbo, MGM, c. 193?,* special promotional poster, cond. A, (12-14-92, Christie-E, #173, illus.), 28 x 22 in., (71.1 x 55.9 cm.), (BP 1547, DM 3803, FR 12,962, Y 299,394).

$312* *Greta Garbo, Two Faced Woman, M.G.M., 1941,* cond. B, one-sheet, style C, linen-backed, (12-17-92, Christie-S. Ken, #211, illus.), 47 x 21 in., (119.4 x 53.3 cm.), poster (BP 198, DM 487, FR 1664, Y 38,343).

$3080* *The Grim Game, Paramount-Artcraft, 1919: Four,* lobby cards, cond. A, (12-14-92, Christie-E, #77, illus.), each 11 x 14 in., (27.9 x 35.6 cm.), (BP 1969, DM 4840, FR 16,497, Y 381,047).

$242* *Guadalcanal Diary, 20th Century Fox, 1943,* one-sheet, cond. A, paper backed, (12-14-92, Christie-E, #156, illus.), 41 x 27 in., (104.1 x 68.6 cm.), (BP 155, DM 380, FR 1296, Y 29,939).

$1760* *Gulliver's Travels, Paramount, 1939,* one-sheet, good cond., Stanley Caidin Coll., (09-12-92, Sotheby-NY, #293, illus.), 41 x 27 in., (104.1 x 68.6 cm.), linen backed (BP 931, DM 2616, FR 8866, Y 218,851).

$2640* *Gun Crazy, 1950,* near mint cond., (12-12-92, Hollywd Poster, #181, illus.), (BP 1693, DM 4159, FR 14,255, Y 326,692).

$3080* *Gun Crazy, United Artists, 1950,* one-sheet, cond. A, linen backed, (12-14-92, Christie-E, #179, illus.), 41 x 27 in., (104.1 x 68.6 cm.), (BP 1969, DM 4840, FR 16,497, Y 381,047).

$550* *The Half Way Girl, First National Picture, 1925,* one-sheet, very fine cond., Stanley Caidin Coll., (09-12-92, Sotheby-NY, #309, illus.), 41 x 27 in., (104.1 x 68.6 cm.), (BP 291, DM 818, FR 2771, Y 68,391).

$660* *Hallelujah, I'm A Bum, United Artists, 1933,* insert, very fine cond., Stanley Caidin Coll., (09-12-92, Sotheby-NY, #145, illus.), 36 x 14 in., (91.4 x 35.6 cm.), (BP 349, DM 981, FR 3325, Y 82,069).

$330* *Halloween Hilarities, Walt Disney, 1953,* fine cond., (12-12-92, Hollywd Poster, #100, illus.), (BP 212, DM 520, FR 1782, Y 40,837).

$440* *The Hands Of Nara, Metro, 1922,* one-sheet, cond. A, linen backed, (12-14-92, Christie-E, #278, illus.), 41 x 27 in., (104.1 x 68.6 cm.), (BP 281, DM 691, FR 2357, Y 54,435).

$248* *A Hard Days Night, 1964,* near mint cond., (12-12-92, Hollywd Poster, #316, illus.), (BP 159, DM 391, FR 1339, Y 30,689).

$275* *Harold Teen, 1928,* fine cond., (linen), (12-12-92, Hollywd Poster, #159, illus.), (BP 176, DM 433, FR 1485, Y 34,030).

$660* *Harvey, 1950,* very good cond., (12-12-92, Hollywd Poster, #277, illus.), (BP 423, DM 1040, FR 3564, Y 81,673).

$770* *The Hatchet Man, First National Pictures, 1932,* one-sheet, very fine cond., Stanley Caidin Coll., (09-12-92, Sotheby-NY, #216, illus.), 41 x 27 in., (104.1 x 68.6 cm.), linen backed (BP 407, DM 1145, FR 3879, Y 95,747).

$715* *Headin' Home, 1920,* fine cond., (12-12-92, Hollywd Poster, #125, illus.), lobby card (BP 458, DM 1127, FR 3861, Y 88,479).

$660* *The Headline Woman, Mascot, 1935,* one-sheet, cond. A, linen backed, (12-14-92, Christie-E, #89, illus.), 41 x 27 in., (104.1 x 68.6 cm.), (BP 422, DM 1037, FR 3535, Y 81,653).

$715* *The Heart Specialist, Realart, 1922,* one-sheet, cond. A, linen backed, (12-14-92, Christie-E, #283, illus.), 41 x 27 in., (104.1 x 68.6 cm.), (BP 457, DM 1124, FR 3830, Y 88,457).

$110* *Heaven Can Wait, 1943,* near mint cond., (12-12-92, Hollywd Poster, #301, illus.), (BP 71, DM 173, FR 594, Y 13,612).

$248* *Heidi, 1937,* very good cond., (12-12-92, Hollywd Poster, #323, illus.), jumbo lobby (BP 159, DM 391, FR 1339, Y 30,689).

$110* *Hell Divers,* Belgian, fine cond., (12-12-92, Hollywd Poster, #199, illus.), (BP 71, DM 173, FR 594, Y 13,612).

$440* *Hell's Angels, Howard Hughes, 1930,* lobby card, very fine cond., Stanley Caidin Coll., (09-12-92, Sotheby-NY, #182, illus.), 11 x 14 in., (27.9 x 35.6 cm.), (BP 233, DM 654, FR 2217, Y 54,713).

$440* *Hell's Kitchen, 1939,* very good cond., (linen), (12-12-92, Hollywd Poster, #283, illus.), (BP 282, DM 693, FR 2376, Y 54,449).

BI *Her Gilded Cage, Paramount, 1922,* insert, very fine cond., Stanley Caidin Coll., est. $7/1,000, (09-12-92, Sotheby-NY, #26, illus.), 36 x 14 in., (91.4 x 35.6 cm.),

$193* *Heres To Good Old Jail, Terry Toon's, 1937,* fine cond., (12-12-92, Hollywd Poster, #101, illus.), (BP 124, DM 304, FR 1042, Y 23,883).

$880* *Heroes For Sale, First National Pictures, 1933,* one-sheet, very fine cond., Stanley Caidin Coll., (09-12-92, Sotheby-NY, #222, illus.), 41 x 27 in., (104.1 x 68.6 cm.), linen backed (BP 465, DM 1308, FR 4433, Y 109,426).

$825* *Heroes For Sale, First National, 1933,* one-sheet, cond. A, paper backed, (12-14-92, Christie-E, #25, illus.), 41 x 27 in., (104.1 x 68.6 cm.), (BP 527, DM 1297, FR 4419, Y 102,066).

$1760* *Hi De Ho, 1947,* near mint cond., (12-12-92, Hollywd Poster, #315, illus.), (BP 1129, DM 2773, FR 9503, Y 217,795).

$385* *High Noon, 1952,* fine cond., (12-12-92, Hollywd Poster, #293, illus.), (BP 247, DM 607, FR 2079, Y 47,643).

$990* *High Sierra, Warner Brothers, 1941: Two,* lobby cards, very fine cond., Stanley Caidin Coll., (09-12-92, Sotheby-NY, #207, illus.), 11 x 14 in., (27.9 x 35.6 cm.), (BP 524, DM 1472, FR 4987, Y 123,104).

$1210* *"His Girl Friday", 1939,* Columbia, one-sheet, cond. B, (11-07-92, Camden, #271, illus.), 41 x 27 in., (104.1 x 68.6 cm.), restored on linen (BP 791, DM 1932, FR 6530, Y 149,346).

$605* *"Hollywood Party", 1934,* MGM, window card, cond. C, (06-05-93, Camden, #252, illus.), 22 x 14 in., (55.9 x 35.6 cm.), on paper (BP 398, DM 981, FR 3306, Y 64,900).

$1760* *Homer's Odyssey, Monopol Film, 1909,* orig. U.S. poster, cond. A, linen backed, (12-14-92, Christie-E, #261, illus.), 20 x 28 in., (50.8 x 71.1 cm.), (BP 1125, DM 2766, FR 9427, Y 217,741).

$990* *The Honor Of His House, Paramount, 1918,* one-sheet, cond. A, linen backed, (12-14-92, Christie-E, #282, illus.), 41 x 27 in., (104.1 x 68.6 cm.), (BP 633, DM 1556, FR 5303, Y 122,479).

$5280* *Hopalong Cassidy, Paramount, 1935,* three-sheet, cond. A, linen backed, (12-14-92, Christie-E, #248, illus.), 81 x 41 in., (205.7 x 104.1 cm.), (BP 3376, DM 8298, FR 28,281, Y 653,223).

$1100* *"Horse Feathers", 1932,* Paramount, lobby card, cond. A, (11-07-92, Camden, #247, illus.), 11 x 14 in., (27.9 x 35.6 cm.), (BP 719, DM 1756, FR 5936, Y 135,769).

$660* *Horse Feathers, Paramount, 1932,* lobby card, very fine cond., Stanley Caidin Coll., (09-12-92, Sotheby-NY, #97, illus.), 11 x 14 in., (27.9 x 35.6 cm.), (BP 349, DM 981, FR 3325, Y 82,069).

$220* *"The Horse Soldiers", 1959,* Italian, United Artists, cond. B, (06-05-93, Camden, #180, illus.), 55 x 59 in., (139.7 x 149.9 cm.), on linen (BP 145, DM 357, FR 1202, Y 23,600).

$495* *Hot Spot, 1941,* rolled, half sheet, very good cond., (12-12-92, Hollywd Poster, #253, illus.), (BP 317, DM 780, FR 2673, Y 61,255).

$770* *Hotel Imperial, 1939,* near mint cond., (linen), (12-12-92, Hollywd Poster, #95, illus.), (BP 494, DM 1213, FR 4158, Y 95,285).

$220* *The Hottentot, 1922,* very good cond., (12-12-92, Hollywd Poster, #11, illus.), (BP 141, DM 347, FR 1188, Y 27,224).

$330* *Hound Hunters, Tex Avery, 1947,* fine cond., (12-12-92, Hollywd Poster, #102, illus.), (BP 212, DM 520, FR 1782, Y 40,837).

$412* *House Of Wax, Warner Brothers, 1953,* three-sheet, cond. B+, linen backed, (03-18-93, Swann, #109, illus.), 81 x 41 in., (205.7 x 104.1 cm.), (BP 278, DM 677, FR 2308, Y 47,946).

$440* *Housewife, Warner Brothers, 1934,* insert, good cond., Stanley Caidin Coll., (09-12-92, Sotheby-NY, #218, illus.), 36 x 14 in., (91.4 x 35.6 cm.), (BP 233, DM 654, FR 2217, Y 54,713).

BI *How Molly Made Good,* three-sheet, unbacked separate sheets, cond. B, est. $4/600, (03-18-93, Swann, #110, illus.), .

$248* *How To Marry A Millionaire, 1953,* half sheet, fine cond., (12-12-92, Hollywd Poster, #254, illus.), (BP 159, DM 391, FR 1339, Y 30,689).

$693* *Humphrey Bogart And Ingrid Bergman, Casablanca, Warner,* Belgian, cond. A+, linen-backed, (12-17-92, Christie-S. Ken, #405, illus.), 14½ x 10¼ in., (36.8 x 26 cm.), poster (BP 440, DM 1082, FR 3696, Y 85,167).

$520* *Humphrey Bogart, Dark Passage, Warner, 1947,* cond. A, half-sheet, (12-17-92, Christie-S. Ken, #402), 22 x 28 in., (55.9 x 71.1 cm.), poster (BP 330, DM 812, FR 2773, Y 63,906).

$312* *Humphrey Bogart, In A Lonely Place/Le Violent, Columbia, 1950,* cond. B, linen-backed, (12-17-92, Christie-S. Ken, #403), 63 x 47 in., (160 x 119.4 cm.), poster (BP 198, DM 487, FR 1664, Y 38,343).

$780* *Humphrey Bogart, The African Queen, IFD/Romulus/Sam Spiegal, 1951,* French release, cond. A, linen-backed, (12-17-92, Christie-S. Ken, #404, illus.), 62½ x 47 in., (158.8 x 119.4 cm.), poster (BP 495, DM 1218, FR 4160, Y 95,858).

$5280* *The Hunchback Of Notre Dame, RKO, 1939,* three-sheet, cond. A, linen backed, (12-14-92, Christie-E, #138, illus.), 81 x 41 in., (205.7 x 104.1 cm.), (BP 3376, DM 8298, FR 28,281, Y 653,223).

$1650* *The Hunchback Of Notre Dame, Universal, 1923,* lobby card, good cond., Stanley Caidin Coll., (09-12-92, Sotheby-NY, #189, illus.), 11 x 14 in., (27.9 x 35.6 cm.), (BP 873, DM 2453, FR 8312, Y 205,173).

$2200* *"The Hurricane Express", 1932,* Mascot, one-sheet, cond. A, (11-07-92, Camden, #129, illus.), 41 x 27 in., (104.1 x 68.6 cm.), on linen (BP 1438, DM 3513, FR 11,873, Y 271,538).

$1320* *The Hurricane Express, Mascot, 1932,* one-sheet, good cond., Stanley Caidin Coll., (09-12-92, Sotheby-NY, #254, illus.), 41 x 27 in., (104.1 x 68.6 cm.), linen backed (BP 698, DM 1962, FR 6650, Y 164,138).

$1760* *The Hurricane, United Artists, 1939,* one-sheet, very fine cond., Stanley Caidin Coll., (09-12-92, Sotheby-NY, #120, illus.), 41 x 27 in., (104.1 x 68.6 cm.), linen backed (BP 931, DM 2616, FR 8866, Y 218,851).

$330* *I Confess, Warner, 1953,* one-sheet, cond. B+, linen backed, (03-18-93, Swann, #106, illus.), (BP 223, DM 542, FR 1849, Y 38,403).

BI *I Married A Monster From Outer Space, Paramount, 1958: Three,* one-sheet, lobby card, and insert, est. $5/750, (03-18-93, Swann, #95, illus.), .

$121* *I Married A Witch (Min Kone Er En Heks),* Danish, cond. B, (03-18-93, Swann, #111, illus.), 33 x 24 in., (83.8 x 61 cm.), (BP 82, DM 199, FR 678, Y 14,081).

$1320* *"I Married A Witch", 1942,* United Artists, three-sheet, cond. B, (11-07-92, Camden, #304, illus.), 81 x 41 in., (205.7 x 104.1 cm.), on linen (BP 863, DM 2108, FR 7124, Y 162,923).

$660* *I Married A Witch, 1942,* half sheet, fine cond., (12-12-92, Hollywd Poster, #243, illus.), (BP 423, DM 1040, FR 3564, Y 81,673).

$1100* *I Married A Witch, United Artists, 1942,* three-sheet, very fine cond., Stanley Caidin Coll., (09-12-92, Sotheby-NY, #128, illus.), 81 x 41 in., (205.7 x 104.1 cm.), linen backed (BP 582, DM 1635, FR 5542, Y 136,782).

$193* *"I Met Him In Paris", "Police Call", "We Have Our Moments", "Cabin In The Sky", "A Tragedy At Midnight" and "Rudyard Kipling's Jungle Book": Six,* Andy Warhol Estate, (04-16-93, DuMouchelle, #2534), 41 x 27 in., (104.1 x 68.6 cm.), poster (BP 127, DM 312, FR 1053, Y 21,702).

$3025* *I Was A Spy, Fox, 1933,* one-sheet, very fine cond., Stanley Caidin Coll., (09-12-92, Sotheby-NY, #267, illus.), 41 x 27 in., (104.1 x 68.6 cm.), linen backed (BP 1600, DM 4497, FR 15,239, Y 376,150).

$880* *"I'll Take Romance", 1938,* Columbia, three-sheet, cond. B, (06-05-93, Camden, #117, illus.), 81 x 41 in., (205.7 x 104.1 cm.), restored on linen after catalogue photography (BP 579, DM 1427, FR 4809, Y 94,400).

BI *The Ice Follies Of 1939, MGM, 1939,* insert, near mint cond., Stanley Caidin Coll., est. $6/900, (09-12-92, Sotheby-NY, #84, illus.), 36 x 14 in., (91.4 x 35.6 cm.),

$2750* *Idol Of The Crowds, Universal Pictures, 1937,* one-sheet, very good cond., Stanley Caidin Coll., (09-12-92, Sotheby-NY, #259, illus.), 41 x 27 in., (104.1 x 68.6 cm.), linen backed (BP 1454, DM 4088, FR 13,854, Y 341,955).

$55* *If I Were King, 1938,* near mint cond., (12-12-92, Hollywd Poster, #325, illus.), jumbo lobby (BP 35, DM 87, FR 297, Y 6806).

$660* *If I Were King, Paramount, 1938,* insert, fine cond., Stanley Caidin Coll., (09-12-92, Sotheby-NY, #53, illus.), 36 x 14 in., (91.4 x 35.6 cm.), (BP 349, DM 981, FR 3325, Y 82,069).

BI *Il Bidone, 1955,* French, linen backed, est. $3/400, (03-18-93, Swann, #10, illus.), 22 x 16 in., (55.9 x 40.6 cm.), .

$302* *Il Conformista, 1971,* orig. Italian, cond. A, linen backed, (03-18-93, Swann, #53, illus.), 55 x 39 in., (139.7 x 99.1 cm.), (BP 204, DM 496, FR 1692, Y 35,145).

$1320* *In Love With Love, Fox, 1924,* one-sheet, cond. A, linen backed, (12-14-92, Christie-E, #5, illus.), 41 x 27 in., (104.1 x 68.6 cm.), (BP 844, DM 2074, FR 7070, Y 163,306).

$1320* *"Incaders From Mars", 1953,* Fox, one-sheet, w/censor stamp, cond. B, (06-05-93, Camden, #36, illus.), 41 x 27 in., (104.1 x 68.6 cm.), (BP 869, DM 2140, FR 7213, Y 141,601).

BI *The Incredible Shrinking Man, 1957: Three,* jumbo window card, window card, half sheet, est. $4/600, (03-18-93, Swann, #112, illus.), .

BI *The Incredible Shrinking Man, Universal International, 1957,* six-sheet, est. $1,2/1,800, (03-18-93, Swann, #97, illus.), .

$6600* *The Informer, RKO, 1935,* three-sheet, very fine cond., Stanley Caidin Coll., (09-12-92, Sotheby-NY, #202, illus.), 81 x 41 in., (205.7 x 104.1 cm.), linen backed (BP 3490, DM 9811, FR 33,249, Y 820,691).

$14,300* *The Informer, RKO, 1935,* three-sheet, cond. A, linen backed, (12-14-92, Christie-E, #145, illus.), 81 x 41 in., (205.7 x 104.1 cm.), (BP 9143, DM 22,474, FR 76,593, Y 1,769,145).

$2420* *Ingagi, 1930,* three sheet, fine cond., (linen), (12-12-92, Hollywd Poster, #172, illus.), (BP 1552, DM 3813, FR 13,067, Y 299,468).

$277* *Ingrid Bergman, Gaslight, M.G.M., 1944,* cond. B, one-sheet, linen-backed, (12-17-92, Christie-S. Ken, #361), 41 x 27 in., (104.1 x 68.6 cm.), poster (BP 176, DM 432, FR 1477, Y 34,042).

$935* *Intermezzo, United Artists, 1939,* one-sheet, cond. B, linen backed, (12-14-92, Christie-E, #23, illus.), 41 x 27 in., (104.1 x 68.6 cm.), (BP 598, DM 1469, FR 5008, Y 115,675).

$303* *Internes Can't Take Money, 1937,* near mint cond., (linen), (12-12-92, Hollywd Poster, #183, illus.), (BP 194, DM 477, FR 1636, Y 37,495).

$4400* *Intolerance (Mother And The Law), D.W. Griffith, reissue 1919,* one-sheet, very fine cond., Stanley Caidin Coll., (09-12-92, Sotheby-NY, #33, illus.), 41 x 27 in., (104.1 x 68.6 cm.), linen backed (BP 2327, DM 6541, FR 22,166, Y 547,128).

$467* *Invaders From Mars, 20th Century Fox, 1953:* Two, insert, Belgian, (03-18-93, Swann, #113, illus.), 18 x 14 in., (45.7 x 35.6 cm.), (BP 315, DM 767, FR 2616, Y 54,347).

$2750* *"Invasion Of The Body Snatchers", 1956,* Allied Artists, half-sheet, cond. A, (06-05-93, Camden, #288, illus.), 22 x 28 in., (55.9 x 71.1 cm.), (BP 1810, DM 4458, FR 15,027, Y 295,001).

$935* *Invasion Of The Body Snatchers, 1956,* one-sheet, cond. A-, linen backed, (03-18-93, Swann, #125, illus.), (BP 631, DM 1537, FR 5238, Y 108,809).

$825* *Invasion Of The Body Snatchers, 1956,* three sheet, fine cond., (linen), (12-12-92, Hollywd Poster, #163, illus.), (BP 529, DM 1300, FR 4455, Y 102,091).

$1760* *Invasion Of The Body Snatchers, Allied Artists, 1956,* Six-sheet, (03-18-93, Swann, #99, illus.), (BP 1187, DM 2892, FR 9860, Y 204,818).

$825* *"Invasion Of The Saucer Men", 1957,* A.I.P., half-sheet, cond. B, (06-05-93, Camden, #289, illus.), 22 x 28 in., (55.9 x 71.1 cm.), on linen (BP 543, DM 1338, FR 4508, Y 88,500).

$770* *Invasion Of The Saucer Men, 1957,* half-sheet, (03-18-93, Swann, #130, illus.), (BP 519, DM 1265, FR 4314, Y 89,608).

$1100* *"Invasion Of The Saucer-Men", 1957,* A.I.P., insert, cond. A, (06-05-93, Camden, #70, illus.), 36 x 14 in., (91.4 x 35.6 cm.), (BP 724, DM 1783, FR 6011, Y 118,000).

$1430* *"Invasion Of The Saucer-Men", 1957,* one-sheet, cond. A, on linen, (11-07-92, Camden, #211, illus.), 41 x 27 in., (104.1 x 68.6 cm.), on linen (BP 935, DM 2283, FR 7717, Y 176,500).

$3850* *Invasion Of The Saucer-Men, A.I.P., 1957,* three-sheet, cond. A, linen backed, (12-14-92, Christie-E, #189, illus.), 81 x 41 in., (205.7 x 104.1 cm.), (BP 2462, DM 6051, FR 20,621, Y 476,308).

$385* *The Invisible Boy, 1957,* three sheet, cond. A, linen backed, (03-18-93, Swann, #126, illus.), (BP 260, DM 633, FR 2157, Y 44,804).

$220* *The Invisible Boy, 1957,* fine cond., (12-12-92, Hollywd Poster, #147, illus.), (BP 141, DM 347, FR 1188, Y 27,224).

$277* *The Invisible Boy, M.G.M., 1957,* cond. A, one-sheet, (12-17-92, Christie-S. Ken, #229, illus.), 41 x 27 in., (104.1 x 68.6 cm.), poster (BP 176, DM 432, FR 1477, Y 34,042).

$330* *The Invisible Man Returns,* Original French, fine cond., (12-12-92, Hollywd Poster, #195, illus.), (BP 212, DM 520, FR 1782, Y 40,837).

$660* *The Invisible Man Returns (El Hombre Invisible Vuelve), 1939,* Spanish, (03-18-93, Swann, #116, illus.), 41 x 27 in., (104.1 x 68.6 cm.), (BP 445, DM 1085, FR 3697, Y 76,807).

$4620* *The Invisible Man Returns, Universal, 1939,* one-sheet, cond. A, linen backed, (03-18-93, Swann, #115, illus.), (BP 3116, DM 7592, FR 25,882, Y 537,647).

$357* *The Invisible Man's Revenge, Universal, 1944,* one-sheet (linen backed), half sheet, cond. B, (03-18-93, Swann, #128, illus.), (BP 241, DM 587, FR 2000, Y 41,545).

$715* *The Invisible Man, 1951; The Invisible Ray; Things To Come, 1947:* Three, inserts, (03-18-93, Swann, #127, illus.), (BP 482, DM 1175, FR 4006, Y 83,207).

$5060* *The Invisible Man, Universal, 1933,* window card, cond. A, folded, trimmed, (12-14-92, Christie-E, #81, illus.), 21 x 14 in., (53.3 x 35.6 cm.), (BP 3235, DM 7952, FR 27,102, Y 626,005).

$192* *Invisible Stripes, Warner Bros., 1939,* one-sheet, (03-18-93, Swann, #47, illus.), (BP 129, DM 316, FR 1076, Y 22,344).

$495* *The Irish In Us, 1934,* restored, very good cond., (12-12-92, Hollywd Poster, #140, illus.), window card (BP 317, DM 780, FR 2673, Y 61,255).

$330* *The Iron Mask, 1929,* fine cond., (12-12-92, Hollywd Poster, #130, illus.), window card (BP 212, DM 520, FR 1782, Y 40,837).

$1100* *The Iron Mask, United Artists, 1929,* insert, very fine cond., Stanley Caidin Coll., (09-12-92, Sotheby-NY, #112, illus.), 36 x 14 in., (91.4 x 35.6 cm.), (BP 582, DM 1635, FR 5542, Y 136,782).

BI *The Ironman, Universal Pictures, 1931,* one-sheet, near mint cond., Stanley Caidin Coll., est. $2,5/3,000, (09-12-92, Sotheby-NY, #181, illus.), 41 x 27 in., (104.1 x 68.6 cm.), linen backed.

BI *It Came From Outer Space (Le Meteore De La Nuit), 1953,* French, cond. B, linen backed, est. $6/900, (03-18-93, Swann, #129, illus.), 63 x 47 in., (160 x 119.4 cm.),

$522* *It Came From Outer Space, 1953,* half-sheet, insert, cond. B, (03-18-93, Swann, #131, illus.), (BP 352, DM 858, FR 2924, Y 60,747).

$2475* *"It's A Wonderful Life", 1946,* RKO, complete set of eight lobby cards, cond. A, (06-05-93, Camden, #184, illus.), each 11 x 14 in., (27.9 x 35.6 cm.), (BP 1629, DM 4013, FR 13,525, Y 265,501).

$6600* *"It's A Wonderful Life", 1946,* RKO, one-sheet, cond. A, (06-05-93, Camden, #235, illus.), 41 x 27 in., (104.1 x 68.6 cm.), on linen (BP 4345, DM 10,700, FR 36,066, Y 708,003).

$1870* *"It's A Wonderful Life", 1946:* Eight, RKO, lobby cards, cond. A, (11-07-92, Camden, #96, illus.), each 11 x 14 in., (27.9 x 35.6 cm.), (BP 1223, DM 2986, FR 10,092, Y 230,807).

$330* *It's A Wonderful Life, 1946,* fine cond., (12-12-92, Hollywd Poster, #258, illus.), title card (BP 212, DM 520, FR 1782, Y 40,837).

$8800* *It's A Wonderful Life, Liberty Films, 1946,* one-sheet, cond. A, linen backed, (12-14-92, Christie-E, #204, illus.), 41 x 27 in., (104.1 x 68.6 cm.), (BP 5627, DM 13,830, FR 47,134, Y 1,088,705).

$2860* *It's A Wonderful Life, Liberty, 1947,* half-sheet, cond. B+, linen backed, (03-18-93, Swann, #107, illus.), 63 x 47 in., (160 x 119.4 cm.), (BP 1929, DM 4700, FR 16,022, Y 332,829).

$825* *It's The Old Army Game, Paramount, 1926,* window card, cond. A, (12-14-92, Christie-E, #124, illus.), 22 x 14 in., (55.9 x 35.6 cm.), (BP 527, DM 1297, FR 4419, Y 102,066).

$780* *Jacques Tati, Mon Uncle,* French, cond. A, linen-backed, lit., (12-17-92, Christie-S. Ken, #417, illus.), 63 x 47 in., (160 x 119.4 cm.), poster (BP 495, DM 1218, FR 4160, Y 95,858).

$1320* *"Jailhouse Rock", 1957,* MGM, three-sheet, cond. B, (06-05-93, Camden, #119, illus.), 81 x 41 in., (205.7 x 104.1 cm.), on linen (BP 869, DM 2140, FR 7213, Y 141,601).

$1045* *Jailhouse Rock, 1957,* near mint cond., (12-12-92, Hollywd Poster, #318, illus.), (BP 670, DM 1646, FR 5643, Y 129,316).

$1320* *Jailhouse Rock, MGM, 1957,* one-sheet, cond. A, linen backed, (12-14-92, Christie-E, #238, illus.), 41 x 27 in., (104.1 x 68.6 cm.), (BP 844, DM 2074, FR 7070, Y 163,306).

$451* *James Bond, From Russia With Love, United Artists, 1963,* British Quad., cond. B+, linen-backed, (12-17-92, Christie-S. Ken, #415A, illus.), 30 x 40 in., (76.2 x 101.6 cm.), poster (BP 286, DM 704, FR 2405, Y 55,426).

$1870* *James Cagney Is Red Hot In 'White Heat'... Co-Starring Virginia Mayo, Warner Bros.,* d. 1949, num. 49/457, James Cagney Estate, (09-30-92, Doyle, #464), 36 x 14 in., (91.4 x 35.6 cm.), (BP 1055, DM 2652, FR 8969, Y 224,409).

$381* *James Cagney, White Heat, Warner, 1949,* cond. A-, one-sheet, (12-17-92, Christie-S. Ken, #280), 41 x 27 in., (104.1 x 68.6 cm.), poster (BP 242, DM 595, FR 2032, Y 46,823).

$192* *The James Dean Story, 1957,* Australian, (03-18-93, Swann, #132, illus.), 41 x 27 in., (104.1 x 68.6 cm.), (BP 129, DM 316, FR 1076, Y 22,344).

$550* *James Dean Story, 1957,* six sheet, fine cond., (linen), (12-12-92, Hollywd Poster, #333, illus.), (BP 353, DM 867, FR 2970, Y 68,061).

$302* *Jayne Mansfield Door Poster, c. 1960,* cond. B+, linen backed, (03-18-93, Swann, #133, illus.), 62 x 21 in., (157.5 x 53.3 cm.), (BP 204, DM 496, FR 1692, Y 35,145).

$1906* *Jean Harlow And William Powell, Reckless, M.G.M., 1935,* cond. B, mounted on board, borders trimmed, one-sheet, lit., (12-17-92, Christie-S. Ken, #303, illus.), 41 x 27 in., (104.1 x 68.6 cm.), poster (BP 1210, DM 2976, FR 10,165, Y 234,239).

$1650* *Jean Harlow, MGM, c. 1933,* special promotional poster, cond. A, (12-14-92, Christie-E, #296, illus.), 28 x 22 in., (71.1 x 55.9 cm.), (BP 1055, DM 2593, FR 8838, Y 204,132).

$990* *Jesse James,* near mint cond., (linen), British, (12-12-92, Hollywd Poster, #56, illus.), (BP 635, DM 1560, FR 5346, Y 122,510).

$550* *Jezebel, Warner Brothers, 1938,* lobby card, fine cond., Stanley Caidin Coll., (09-12-92, Sotheby-NY, #215, illus.), 11 x 14 in., (27.9 x 35.6 cm.), (BP 291, DM 818, FR 2771, Y 68,391).

$3300* *Jezebel, Warner Brothers, 1938,* other co. one-sheet, cond. A, linen backed, (12-14-92, Christie-E, #111, illus.), 41 x 27 in., (104.1 x 68.6 cm.), (BP 2110, DM 5186, FR 17,675, Y 408,264).

$495* *Joan Crawford Portrait, MGM, 1930s,* very fine cond., Stanley Caidin Coll., (09-12-92, Sotheby-NY, #83, illus.), 28 x 22 in., (71.1 x 55.9 cm.), (BP 262, DM 736, FR 2494, Y 61,552).

$990* *Joan Crawford, MGM, c. 1936,* special promotional poster, cond. A, (12-14-92, Christie-E, #117, illus.), 28 x 22 in., (71.1 x 55.9 cm.), (BP 633, DM 1556, FR 5303, Y 122,479).

$770* *Joan Of Arc, RKO, 1948,* one-sheet, cond. A, linen backed, (12-14-92, Christie-E, #26, illus.), 41 x 27 in., (104.1 x 68.6 cm.), (BP 492, DM 1210, FR 4124, Y 95,262).

$4180* *Johanna Enlists, Artcraft, 1918,* one-sheet, cond. B, linen backed, (12-14-92, Christie-E, #86, illus.), 41 x 27 in., (104.1 x 68.6 cm.), (BP 2673, DM 6569, FR 22,389, Y 517,135).

$1760* *"Johnny Come Lately" and "The Public Enemy": Two,* each image s. by Cagney, James Cagney Estate, (09-30-92, Doyle, #481), each 11 x 14 in., (27.9 x 35.6 cm.), (BP 993, DM 2496, FR 8441, Y 211,208).

$3850* *"Joining The Tanks", c. late 1910s,* Wm. Fox, cond. B, one-sheet, (11-07-92, Camden, #16, illus.), 42 x 28 in., (106.7 x 71.1 cm.), on paper (BP 2517, DM 6147, FR 20,777, Y 475,191).

$1320* *Juarez, Warner Brothers, 1939,* one-sheet, very good cond., Stanley Caidin Coll., (09-12-92, Sotheby-NY, #210, illus.), 41 x 27 in., (104.1 x 68.6 cm.), linen backed (BP 698, DM 1962, FR 6650, Y 164,138).

$1210* *Juke Girl, Warner Brothers, 1942,* three-sheet, cond. A, linen backed, (12-14-92, Christie-E, #220, illus.), 81 x 41 in., (205.7 x 104.1 cm.), (BP 774, DM 1902, FR 6481, Y 149,697).

$715* *Kentucky Days, 1923,* fine cond., (linen), (12-12-92, Hollywd Poster, #12, illus.), (BP 458, DM 1127, FR 3861, Y 88,479).

$770* *The Key, Warner Brothers, 1934,* one-sheet, cond. A, paper backed, (12-14-92, Christie-E, #72, illus.), 41 x 27 in., (104.1 x 68.6 cm.), (BP 492, DM 1210, FR 4124, Y 95,262).

$1650* *Kid Galahad, Warner Brothers, 1937,* title lobby card, near mint cond., Stanley Caidin Coll., (09-12-92, Sotheby-NY, #217, illus.), 11 x 14 in., (27.9 x 35.6 cm.), (BP 873, DM 2453, FR 8312, Y 205,173).

$27,500* *The Kid, First National Attraction, 1921,* one-sheet, very fine cond., Stanley Caidin Coll., (09-12-92, Sotheby-NY, #101, illus.), 41 x 27 in., (104.1 x 68.6 cm.), linen backed (BP 14,543, DM 40,880, FR 138,539, Y 3,419,547).

$6600* *The Kid, First National, 1921,* three-sheet, cond. A, linen backed, (12-14-92, Christie-E, #120, illus.), 81 x 41 in., (205.7 x 104.1 cm.), (BP 4220, DM 10,372, FR 35,351, Y 816,529).

$4675* *"Kill Or Cure", 1923,* Pathe, cond. B, (06-05-93, Camden, #205, illus.), 41 x 27 in., (104.1 x 68.6 cm.), restored on linen after catalogue photography (BP 3077, DM 7579, FR 25,546, Y 501,502).

$330* *King Kong,* Belgian, cond. A-, linen backed, (03-18-93, Swann, #145, illus.), 22 x 14 in., (55.9 x 35.6 cm.), (BP 223, DM 542, FR 1849, Y 38,403).

$1650* *"King Kong", c. 1940s,* Argentine, cond. B, (11-07-92, Camden, #107, illus.), 44 x 29 in., (111.8 x 73.7 cm.), on linen (BP 1079, DM 2635, FR 8904, Y 203,653).

$5280* *King Kong, 1933,* French, cond. C+, linen backed, (03-18-93, Swann, #140, illus.), 63 x 47 in., (160 x 119.4 cm.), (BP 3561, DM 8677, FR 29,580, Y 614,454).

$715* *King Kong, 1933,* Spanish, cond. C+, linen backed, (03-18-93, Swann, #141, illus.), 43 x 29 in., (109.2 x 73.7 cm.), (BP 482, DM 1175, FR 4006, Y 83,207).

BI *King Kong, 1933,* French, cond. C, linen backed, est. $1,5/2,000, (03-18-93, Swann, #142, illus.), 63 x 47 in., (160 x 119.4 cm.),

$7700* *King Kong, 1933,* French, cond. B, linen backed, (03-18-93, Swann, #139, illus.), 63 x 47 in., (160 x 119.4 cm.), (BP 5193, DM 12,654, FR 43,137, Y 896,078).

$7700* *King Kong, 1933,* French, near mint cond., (linen), (12-12-92, Hollywd Poster, #194, illus.), (BP 4937, DM 12,132, FR 41,577, Y 952,852).

$605* *King Kong, 1933,* Frenchl, near mint cond., (12-12-92, Hollywd Poster, #204, illus.), (BP 388, DM 953, FR 3267, Y 74,867).

$247* *King Kong, 1952,* one-sheet, cond. C+, linen backed, (03-18-93, Swann, #144, illus.), (BP 167, DM 406, FR 1384, Y 28,744).

$14,300* *King Kong, RKO, 1933,* orig. French poster, cond. A, linen backed, (12-14-92, Christie-E, #263, illus.), 63 x 47 in., (160 x 119.4 cm.), (BP 9143, DM 22,474, FR 76,593, Y 1,769,145).

$4950* *King Kong, RKO, 1933,* lobby standee made by local theater, cond. B, mounted on board, (12-14-92, Christie-E, #306, illus.), 37 x 26 in., (94 x 66 cm.), (BP 3165, DM 7779, FR 26,513, Y 612,396).

$1540* *"King Of The Rocket Men", 1949,* Republic, one-sheet, cond. A, (11-07-92, Camden, #122, illus.), 41 x 27 in., (104.1 x 68.6 cm.), on linen (BP 1007, DM 2459, FR 8311, Y 190,077).

$880* *King Of The Rocket Men, Republic, 1949,* one-sheet, cond. B, linen backed, (12-14-92, Christie-E, #229, illus.), 41 x 27 in., (104.1 x 68.6 cm.), (BP 563, DM 1383, FR 4713, Y 108,870).

$440* *King Solomon's Mines, 1937,* fine cond., (linen), (12-12-92, Hollywd Poster, #41, illus.), (BP 282, DM 693, FR 2376, Y 54,449).

$825* *"Kiss Me Deadly", 1955,* United Artists, three-sheet, cond. B, (06-05-93, Camden, #115, illus.), 81 x 41 in., (205.7 x 104.1 cm.), restored on linen after catalogue photography (BP 543, DM 1338, FR 4508, Y 88,500).

$330* *"Klondike Annie", 1936,* Paramount, window card, cond. B, (06-05-93, Camden, #105, illus.), 22 x 14 in., (55.9 x 35.6 cm.), on linen (BP 217, DM 535, FR 1803, Y 35,400).

$770* *The Knickerbocker Buckaroo, 1919,* fine cond., (linen), (12-12-92, Hollywd Poster, #237, illus.), (BP 494, DM 1213, FR 4158, Y 95,285).

$605* *Knockout, National Film, 1935,* orig. Swedish poster, cond. A, (12-14-92, Christie-E, #260, illus.), 40 x 27 in., (101.6 x 68.6 cm.), (BP 387, DM 951, FR 3240, Y 74,848).

$330* *Konigin Der Arena, c. 1955,* orig. Austrian, cond. B, (03-18-93, Swann, #146, illus.), 46 x 33 in., (116.8 x 83.8 cm.), (BP 223, DM 542, FR 1849, Y 38,403).

$1210* *"Krazy Kat", c. 1930s,* Columbia, cond. B, one-sheet, (11-07-92, Camden, #10, illus.), 41 x 27 in., (104.1 x 68.6 cm.), on linen (BP 791, DM 1932, FR 6530, Y 149,346).

$3080* *The Lady Eve, Paramount, 1941,* one-sheet, cond. A, linen backed, (12-14-92, Christie-E, #139, illus.), 41 x 27 in., (104.1 x 68.6 cm.), (BP 1969, DM 4840, FR 16,497, Y 381,047).

$1870* *"The Lady From Shanghai", 1947,* Columbia, one-sheet, cond. B, (06-05-93, Camden, #26, illus.), 41 x 27 in., (104.1 x 68.6 cm.), (BP 1231, DM 3032, FR 10,219, Y 200,601).

$2090* *"The Lady From Shanghai", 1948,* Columbia, one-sheet, cond. A, (11-07-92, Camden, #43, illus.), 41 x 27 in., (104.1 x 68.6 cm.), on linen (BP 1366, DM 3337, FR 11,279, Y 257,961).

$1320* *The Lady Lies, Paramount, 1929,* one-sheet, fine cond., Stanley Caidin Coll., (09-12-92, Sotheby-NY, #91, illus.), 41 x 27 in., (104.1 x 68.6 cm.), linen backed (BP 698, DM 1962, FR 6650, Y 164,138).

$9350* *The Lady Vanishes, Gaumont British, 1938,* one-sheet, cond. A, linen backed, (12-14-92, Christie-E, #60, illus.), 41 x 27 in., (104.1 x 68.6 cm.), (BP 5978, DM 14,694, FR 50,080, Y 1,156,749).

$495* *The Last Command, 1928,* near mint cond., (12-12-92, Hollywd Poster, #144, illus.), window card (BP 317, DM 780, FR 2673, Y 61,255).

$825* *The Last Command, Paramount, 1928,* insert, very fine cond., Stanley Caidin Coll., (09-12-92, Sotheby-NY, #68, illus.), 36 x 14 in., (91.4 x 35.6 cm.), (BP 436, DM 1226, FR 4156, Y 102,586).

$660* *The Last Flight, First National, 1931,* one-sheet, cond. A, linen backed, (12-14-92, Christie-E, #154, illus.), 41 x 27 in., (104.1 x 68.6 cm.), (BP 422, DM 1037, FR 3535, Y 81,653).

$990* *The Last Gangster, MGM, 1937,* one-sheet, very fine cond., Stanley Caidin Coll., (09-12-92, Sotheby-NY, #219, illus.), 41 x 27 in., (104.1 x 68.6 cm.), linen backed (BP 524, DM 1472, FR 4987, Y 123,104).

$550* *The Last Of The Mohicans, Reliance, 1936,* one-sheet, fine cond., Stanley Caidin Coll., (09-12-92, Sotheby-NY, #247, illus.), 41 x 27 in., (104.1 x 68.6 cm.), linen backed (BP 291, DM 818, FR 2771, Y 68,391).

$192* *Last Tango In Paris, UA, 1973,* English, cond. A-, linen backed, (03-18-93, Swann, #194, illus.), 27 x 41 in., (68.6 x 104.1 cm.), (BP 129, DM 316, FR 1076, Y 22,344).

$1320* *Laughing Sinners, MGM, 1931,* one-sheet, cond. A, linen backed, (12-14-92, Christie-E, #115, illus.), 41 x 27 in., (104.1 x 68.6 cm.), (BP 844, DM 2074, FR 7070, Y 163,306).

$2475* *"Laura", 1944,* Fox, one-sheet, cond. B, (11-07-92, Camden, #317, illus.), 41 x 27 in., (104.1 x 68.6 cm.), on linen (BP 1618, DM 3952, FR 13,357, Y 305,480).

$173* *Laurel And Hardy, The Flying Deuces, Borris Morros, 1939,* cond. B-, insert, linen-backed, (12-17-92, Christie-S. Ken, #419), 36 x 14 in., (91.4 x 35.6 cm.), poster (BP 110, DM 270, FR 923, Y 21,261).

$1210* *Law And Order, Pathe, 1932,* one-sheet, very fine cond., Stanley Caidin Coll., (09-12-92, Sotheby-NY, #11, illus.), 41 x 27 in., (104.1 x 68.6 cm.), linen backed (BP 640, DM 1799, FR 6096, Y 150,460).

$550* *Lawrence Of Arabia, 1962: Two,* Italian, paper backed, (03-18-93, Swann, #147, illus.), 27 x 19 in., (68.6 x 48.3 cm.), (BP 371, DM 904, FR 3081, Y 64,006).

$220* *Leave Her To Heaven, 1945,* insert, fine cond., (12-12-92, Hollywd Poster, #77, illus.), (BP 141, DM 347, FR 1188, Y 27,224).

BI *The Leopard (Le Guepard), 1963,* French, cond. A, est. $4/600, (03-18-93, Swann, #150, illus.), 63 x 47 in., (160 x 119.4 cm.), .

$605* *Let's Fall In Love, Columbia, 1933,* one-sheet, cond. A, paper backed, (12-14-92, Christie-E, #317, illus.), 41 x 27 in., (104.1 x 68.6 cm.), (BP 387, DM 951, FR 3240, Y 74,848).

$440* *Let's Make Love, 1960,* three sheet, fine cond., (12-12-92, Hollywd Poster, #166, illus.), (BP 282, DM 693, FR 2376, Y 54,449).

$660* *Life Begins For Andy Hardy, MGM, 1941,* one-sheet, good cond., Stanley Caidin Coll., (09-12-92, Sotheby-NY, #282, illus.), 41 x 27 in., (104.1 x 68.6 cm.), linen backed (BP 349, DM 981, FR 3325, Y 82,069).

$660* *Life Of Emile Zola, Warner Brothers, 1937,* half-sheet, very fine cond., Stanley Caidin Coll., (09-12-92, Sotheby-NY, #211, illus.), 22 x 28 in., (55.9 x 71.1 cm.), (BP 349, DM 981, FR 3325, Y 82,069).

$495* *The Life Of The Party, Warner Brothers, 1937,* one-sheet, very fine cond., Stanley Caidin Coll., (09-12-92, Sotheby-NY, #42, illus.), 41 x 27 in., (104.1 x 68.6 cm.), linen backed (BP 262, DM 736, FR 2494, Y 61,552).

$1760* *"Lifeboat", 1943,* Fox, one-sheet, cond. B, (11-07-92, Camden, #292, illus.), 41 x 27 in., (104.1 x 68.6 cm.), (BP 1151, DM 2810, FR 9498, Y 217,230).

$1650* *"Lifeboat", 1943,* Fox, one-sheet, cond. B, (06-05-93, Camden, #307, illus.), 41 x 27 in., (104.1 x 68.6 cm.), (BP 1086, DM 2675, FR 9016, Y 177,001).

$935* *Lifeboat, 1943,* insert, fine cond., (12-12-92, Hollywd Poster, #73, illus.), (BP 600, DM 1473, FR 5049, Y 115,704).

$1980* *Lifeboat, 20th Century Fox, 1943,* one-sheet, cond. B, linen backed, (12-14-92, Christie-E, #61, illus.), 41 x 27 in., (104.1 x 68.6 cm.), (BP 1266, DM 3112, FR 10,605, Y 244,959).

$715* *The Light In The Dark, First National, 1922,* one-sheet, cond. A, linen backed, (12-14-92, Christie-E, #88, illus.), 41 x 27 in., (104.1 x 68.6 cm.), (BP 457, DM 1124, FR 3830, Y 88,457).

$1045* *Lights Of Old Broadway, MGM, 1925,* one-sheet, cond. A, linen backed, (12-14-92, Christie-E, #18, illus.), 41 x 27 in., (104.1 x 68.6 cm.), (BP 668, DM 1642, FR 5597, Y 129,284).

BI *"The Lion In Winter, 1968", "Boxcar Bertha, 1972", "The Love Machine, 1971", "Butch Cassidy And The Sundance Kid, 1969", "Airport, 1970", "The French Connection, 1971", "The Andromeda Strain, 1971" and Four Others,* creasing, some tears, est. $4/500, (03-03-93, Sotheby-Arcade, #176), sheets 41 x 27 in., (104.1 x 68.6 cm.), poster.

$6820* *Little Black Sambo, Celebrity Productions, 1933,* one-sheet, cond. A, paper backed, (12-14-92, Christie-E, #134, illus.), 41 x 27 in., (104.1 x 68.6 cm.), (BP 4361, DM 10,718, FR 36,529, Y 843,746).

$4125* *"The Little Foxes", 1941,* RKO, three-sheet, cond. A, (11-07-92, Camden, #180, illus.), 81 x 41 in., (205.7 x 104.1 cm.), on linen (BP 2697, DM 6586, FR 22,261, Y 509,134).

$825* *Little Lord Fauntleroy, United Artists, 1936,* one-sheet, cond. A, linen backed, (12-14-92, Christie-E, #161, illus.), 41 x 27 in., (104.1 x 68.6 cm.), (BP 527, DM 1297, FR 4419, Y 102,066).

$880* *The Little Minister, RKO, 1934,* insert, very fine cond., Stanley Caidin Coll., (09-12-92, Sotheby-NY, #203, illus.), 36 x 14 in., (91.4 x 35.6 cm.), (BP 465, DM 1308, FR 4433, Y 109,426).

$550* *Little Miss Broadway, 1938,* fine cond., (linen), (12-12-92, Hollywd Poster, #236, illus.), (BP 353, DM 867, FR 2970, Y 68,061).

$110* *Little Miss Marker, 1934,* rolled, fine cond., (12-12-92, Hollywd Poster, #242, illus.), (BP 71, DM 173, FR 594, Y 13,612).

$440* *Little Robinson Corkscrew, 1926,* fine cond., (linen), (12-12-92, Hollywd Poster, #188, illus.), (BP 282, DM 693, FR 2376, Y 54,449).

BI *"Little Women", 1949; "A Date With Judy", 1948: Two,* one-sheets, est. $3/400, (03-18-93, Swann, #151, illus.), .

$385* *Little Women, 1933,* fine cond., (12-12-92, Hollywd Poster, #29, illus.), title card (BP 247, DM 607, FR 2079, Y 47,643).

$3850* *The Littlest Rebel, 20th Century Fox, 1935,* one-sheet, very fine cond., Stanley Caidin Coll., (09-12-92, Sotheby-NY, #288, illus.), 41 x 27 in., (104.1 x 68.6 cm.), linen backed (BP 2036, DM 5723, FR 19,395, Y 478,737).

$1430* *The Littlest Rebel, 20th Century Fox, 1935,* special one-sheet, cond. A, (12-14-92, Christie-E, #160, illus.), 41 x 27 in., (104.1 x 68.6 cm.), (BP 914, DM 2247, FR 7659, Y 176,915).

$935* *Lolita, 1962,* French, cond. A, linen backed, (03-18-93, Swann, #22, illus.), 63 x 47 in., (160 x 119.4 cm.), (BP 631, DM 1537, FR 5238, Y 108,809).

$2426* *Lolita, M.G.M., 1962,* French, artwork by Subie, cond. A+, linen-backed, (12-17-92, Christie-S. Ken, #411, illus.), 63 x 47 in., (160 x 119.4 cm.), poster (BP 1540, DM 3788, FR 12,939, Y 298,144).

$1430* *"The Lone Chance", 1924,* Wm. Fox, one-sheet, cond. A, (11-07-92, Camden, #56, illus.), 41 x 27 in., (104.1 x 68.6 cm.), on linen (BP 935, DM 2283, FR 7717, Y 176,500).

$1320* *"The Lone Ranger Rides Again", 1939,* Republic, one-sheet, cond. A, (11-07-92, Camden, #125, illus.), 41 x 27 in., (104.1 x 68.6 cm.), restored on linen (BP 863, DM 2108, FR 7124, Y 162,923).

$1210* *The Lone Ranger, Republic, 1938,* one-sheet, cond. B, linen backed, (12-14-92, Christie-E, #246, illus.), 41 x 27 in., (104.1 x 68.6 cm.), (BP 774, DM 1902, FR 6481, Y 149,697).

$1540* *Look Out Below, Pathe, 1928,* one-sheet, good cond., Stanley Caidin Coll., (09-12-92, Sotheby-NY, #295, illus.), 41 x 27 in., (104.1 x 68.6 cm.), linen backed (BP 814, DM 2289, FR 7758, Y 191,495).

$303* *Lord Byron Of Broadway, 1929,* near mint cond., (12-12-92, Hollywd Poster, #191, illus.), (BP 194, DM 477, FR 1636, Y 37,495).

$275* *The Lost Jungle, 1934,* near mint cond., (linen), (12-12-92, Hollywd Poster, #40, illus.), (BP 176, DM 433, FR 1485, Y 34,030).

$2860* *The Lost Squadron, RKO, 1932,* one-sheet, cond. A, linen backed, (12-14-92, Christie-E, #155, illus.), 41 x 27 in., (104.1 x 68.6 cm.), (BP 1829, DM 4495, FR 15,319, Y 353,829).

$1045* *The Lottery Man, Paramount-Artcraft, 1919,* three-sheet, cond. A, linen backed, (12-14-92, Christie-E, #281, illus.), 81 x 41 in., (205.7 x 104.1 cm.), (BP 668, DM 1642, FR 5597, Y 129,284).

$138* *Love And Hisses, 1937,* fine cond., (12-12-92, Hollywd Poster, #96, illus.), stone litho (BP 88, DM 217, FR 745, Y 17,077).

$5500* *Love Before Breakfast, Universal, 1936,* one-sheet, cond. A, linen backed, (12-14-92, Christie-E, #150, illus.), 41 x 27 in., (104.1 x 68.6 cm.), (BP 3517, DM 8644, FR 29,459, Y 680,440).

$248* *"Love Letters", 1945,* Paramount, one-sheet, cond. A, (06-05-93, Camden, #239, illus.), 41 x 27 in., (104.1 x 68.6 cm.), on linen (BP 163, DM 402, FR 1355, Y 26,604).

$935* *Love Letters, 1924,* fine cond., (linen), (12-12-92, Hollywd Poster, #307, illus.), (BP 600, DM 1473, FR 5049, Y 115,704).

$440* *Love Or Hate,* near mint cond., (linen), (12-12-92, Hollywd Poster, #225, illus.), (BP 282, DM 693, FR 2376, Y 54,449).

$550* *Lucretia Lombard, Warner Brothers, 1923,* one-sheet, fine cond., Stanley Caidin Coll., (09-12-92, Sotheby-NY, #37, illus.), 41 x 27 in., (104.1 x 68.6 cm.), linen backed (BP 291, DM 818, FR 2771, Y 68,391).

$550* *Lure Of The Circus (The Knockout), Universal Pictures, 1918,* one-sheet, very fine cond., Stanley Caidin Coll., (09-12-92, Sotheby-NY, #265, illus.), 41 x 27 in., (104.1 x 68.6 cm.), linen backed (BP 291, DM 818, FR 2771, Y 68,391).

$5500* *"M", 1931,* German, Nero Film, cond. B, (06-05-93, Camden, #276, illus.), 56 x 36 in., (142.2 x 91.4 cm.), on linen (BP 3621, DM 8917, FR 30,055, Y 590,002).

$143* *Madame Bovary, MGM, 1949,* 2 half-sheets, (03-18-93, Swann, #148, illus.), (BP 96, DM 235, FR 801, Y 16,641).

$550* *Madame Butterfly, Paramount, 1932,* insert, very fine cond., Stanley Caidin Coll., (09-12-92, Sotheby-NY, #60, illus.), 36 x 14 in., (91.4 x 35.6 cm.), (BP 291, DM 818, FR 2771, Y 68,391).

$1320* *Madame Sans-Gene, Paramount, 1926,* orig. Austrian poster, cond. A, linen backed, (12-14-92, Christie-E, #256, illus.), 55 x 37 in., (139.7 x 94 cm.), (BP 844, DM 2074, FR 7070, Y 163,306).

BI *The Magic Flame, United Artists, 1927,* insert, near mint cond., Stanley Caidin Coll., est. $6/900, (09-12-92, Sotheby-NY, #52, illus.), 36 x 14 in., (91.4 x 35.6 cm.),

BI *La Maison Du Silence, 1920,* orig. French, cond. B, linen backed, est. $7/1,000, (03-18-93, Swann, #153, illus.), 63 x 47 in., (160 x 119.4 cm.), .

$990* *Make Me A Star, Paramount, 1932,* one-sheet, very fine cond., Stanley Caidin Coll., (09-12-92, Sotheby-NY, #12, illus.), 41 x 27 in., (104.1 x 68.6 cm.), linen backed (BP 524, DM 1472, FR 4987, Y 123,104).

BI *The Making Of O'Malley, First National Picture, 1925,* one-sheet, very fine cond., Stanley Caidin Coll., est. $7/900, (09-12-92, Sotheby-NY, #82, illus.), 41 x 27 in., (104.1 x 68.6 cm.), linen backed.

$2860* *The Maltese Falcon, Warner Bros., 1941,* insert, (03-18-93, Swann, #43, illus.), (BP 1929, DM 4700, FR 16,022, Y 332,829).

$6600* *The Maltese Falcon, Warner Brothers, 1941,* three-sheet, fine cond., Stanley Caidin Coll., (09-12-92, Sotheby-NY, #205, illus.), 81 x 41 in., (205.7 x 104.1 cm.), (BP 3490, DM 9811, FR 33,249, Y 820,691).

$4950* *The Maltese Falcon, Warner Brothers, 1941,* three-sheet, cond. A, linen backed, (12-14-92, Christie-E, #175, illus.), 81 x 41 in., (205.7 x 104.1 cm.), (BP 3165, DM 7779, FR 26,513, Y 612,396).

$2475* *Mammy, Warner Brothers, 1930,* one-sheet, very fine cond., Stanley Caidin Coll., (09-12-92, Sotheby-NY, #143, illus.), 41 x 27 in., (104.1 x 68.6 cm.), linen backed (BP 1309, DM 3679, FR 12,469, Y 307,759).

$770* *Mammy, Warner Brothers, 1930,* window card, cond. C, backed on board, (12-14-92, Christie-E, #132, illus.), 22 x 14 in., (55.9 x 35.6 cm.), (BP 492, DM 1210, FR 4124, Y 95,262).

$2200* *"The Man From Planet X", 1951,* United Artists, one sheet, cond. B, (06-05-93, Camden, #35, illus.), 41 x 27 in., (104.1 x 68.6 cm.), on linen (BP 1448, DM 3567, FR 12,022, Y 236,001).

$990* *The Man From Planet X, 1951,* insert, (03-18-93, Swann, #205, illus.), (BP 668, DM 1627, FR 5546, Y 115,210).

$1320* *The Man From Planet X, 1951,* fine cond., (12-12-92, Hollywd Poster, #322, illus.), (BP 846, DM 2080, FR 7127, Y 163,346).

$2640* *The Man From Planet X, United Artists, 1951,* one-sheet, cond. B, linen backed, (03-18-93, Swann, #204, illus.), (BP 1780, DM 4339, FR 14,790, Y 307,227).

BI *The Man From Utah, Lone Star Western, 1934,* one-sheet, very fine cond., Stanley Caidin Coll., est. $2/3,000, (09-12-92, Sotheby-NY, #258, illus.), 41 x 27 in., (104.1 x 68.6 cm.), linen backed.

$193* *Man In The Iron Mask, 1939,* very good cond., (12-12-92, Hollywd Poster, #46, illus.), (BP 124, DM 304, FR 1042, Y 23,883).

$935* *The Man Who Lived Again, Gaumont British, 1936,* one-sheet, cond. A, paper backed, (12-14-92, Christie-E, #311, illus.), 41 x 27 in., (104.1 x 68.6 cm.), (BP 598, DM 1469, FR 5008, Y 115,675).

$440* *The Man With Nine Lives, 1940,* fine cond., (12-12-92, Hollywd Poster, #153, illus.), (BP 282, DM 693, FR 2376, Y 54,449).

$550* *"Man's Castle", 1933,* Columbia, half-sheet, cond. B, (06-05-93, Camden, #128, illus.), 22 x 28 in., (55.9 x 71.1 cm.), on linen (BP 362, DM 892, FR 3005, Y 59,000).

$1320* *Mandrake, The Magician, Columbia, 1939,* one-sheet, cond. A, linen backed, (12-14-92, Christie-E, #226, illus.), 41 x 27 in., (104.1 x 68.6 cm.), (BP 844, DM 2074, FR 7070, Y 163,306).

$1760* *Manhattan Cocktail, Paramount, 1928,* one-sheet, good cond., Stanley Caidin Coll., (09-12-92, Sotheby-NY, #4, illus.), 41 x 27 in., (104.1 x 68.6 cm.), linen backed (BP 931, DM 2616, FR 8866, Y 218,851).

$715* *Manhattan Melodrama, 1934,* near mint cond., (12-12-92, Hollywd Poster, #290, illus.), title card (BP 458, DM 1127, FR 3861, Y 88,479).

$2420* *Manhattan Melodrama, MGM, 1934,* insert, cond. A, (12-14-92, Christie-E, #298, illus.), 36 x 14 in., (91.4 x 35.6 cm.), (BP 1547, DM 3803, FR 12,962, Y 299,394).

$247* *Manon Des Sources, 1952,* orig. French, cond. C+, linen backed, (03-18-93, Swann, #154, illus.), 63 x 47 in., (160 x 119.4 cm.), (BP 167, DM 406, FR 1384, Y 28,744).

$193* *March Of The Wooden Soldiers, 1950,* fine cond., (linen), (12-12-92, Hollywd Poster, #238, illus.), (BP 124, DM 304, FR 1042, Y 23,883).

$87* *Margaret Lockwood, Jassy, G.F.D./Gainsborough, 1947,* British, cond. B, three-sheet, linen-backed, (12-17-92, Christie-S. Ken, #363, illus.), 81 x 41 in., (205.7 x 104.1 cm.), poster (BP 55, DM 136, FR 464, Y 10,692).

$440* *Marihuana, 1936,* very good cond., (12-12-92, Hollywd Poster, #320, illus.), (BP 282, DM 693, FR 2376, Y 54,449).

$312* *Marilyn Monroe, Bus Stop, 20th Century Fox, 1956,* cond. A, one-sheet, (12-17-92, Christie-S. Ken, #225), 41 x 27 in., (104.1 x 68.6 cm.), poster (BP 198, DM 487, FR 1664, Y 38,343).

$277* *Marilyn Monroe, Bus Stop, 20th Century Fox, 1956,* cond. A, insert, (12-17-92, Christie-S. Ken, #407, illus.), 36 x 14 in., (91.4 x 35.6 cm.), poster (BP 176, DM 432, FR 1477, Y 34,042).

$3120* *Marilyn Monroe, Don't Bother To Knock, 20th Century Fox, 1952,* cond. A+ to near mint, three-sheet, linen-backed, back cover illus., (12-17-92, Christie-S. Ken,

#226, illus.), 81 x 41 in., (205.7 x 104.1 cm.), poster (BP 1980, DM 4871, FR 16,640, Y 383,434).

BI   *Marilyn Monroe, Love Nest, 20th Century Fox, 1951,* cond. A, one-sheet, linen-backed, est. BP 3/500, (12-17-92, Christie-S. Ken, #408, illus.), 41 x 27 in., (104.1 x 68.6 cm.), poster.

BI   *Marilyn Monroe, Love Nest, 20th Century Fox, 1951,* cond. C, tape, three-sheet, est. BP 1/200, (12-17-92, Christie-S. Ken, #223), 81 x 41 in., (205.7 x 104.1 cm.), poster.

$440*   *Marked Woman, 1937,* fine cond., (12-12-92, Hollywd Poster, #30, illus.), lobby card (BP 282, DM 693, FR 2376, Y 54,449).

$2773*   *Marlene Dietrich And Herbert Marshall, Angel, Paramount, 1937,* cond. B, mounted on board, borders trimmed, one-sheet, lit., (12-17-92, Christie-S. Ken, #302, illus.), 41 x 27 in., (104.1 x 68.6 cm.), poster (BP 1760, DM 4329, FR 14,789, Y 340,789).

BI   *Mary Of Scotland, RKO, 1936,* insert, good cond., Stanley Caidin Coll., est. $1,2/1,800, (09-12-92, Sotheby-NY, #204, illus.), 36 x 14 in., (91.4 x 35.6 cm.), .

$605*   *Masked Emotions, Fox, 1929,* one-sheet, cond. A, linen backed, (12-14-92, Christie-E, #4, illus.), 41 x 27 in., (104.1 x 68.6 cm.), (BP 387, DM 951, FR 3240, Y 74,848).

$50*   *"The Masquerader",* Andy Warhol Estate, (04-16-93, DuMouchelle, #2537), 54 x 41 in., (137.2 x 104.1 cm.), poster (BP 33, DM 81, FR 273, Y 5622).

$5500*   *Mati Hari, MGM, 1931,* insert, very fine cond., Stanley Caidin Coll., (09-12-92, Sotheby-NY, #172, illus.), 36 x 14 in., (91.4 x 35.6 cm.), (BP 2909, DM 8176, FR 27,708, Y 683,909).

$2475*   *Mati Hari, MGM, 1931,* lobby card, fine cond., Stanley Caidin Coll., (09-12-92, Sotheby-NY, #173, illus.), 11 x 14 in., (27.9 x 35.6 cm.), (BP 1309, DM 3679, FR 12,469, Y 307,759).

$440*   *Matrimonio All' Italiana, 1964,* orig. Italian, cond. A-, paper backed, (03-18-93, Swann, #162, illus.), 39 x 27 in., (99.1 x 68.6 cm.), (BP 297, DM 723, FR 2465, Y 51,204).

$605*   *Maytime, MGM, 1937,* insert, near mint cond., Stanley Caidin Coll., (09-12-92, Sotheby-NY, #152, illus.), 36 x 14 in., (91.4 x 35.6 cm.), (BP 320, DM 899, FR 3048, Y 75,230).

$660*   *Meet Me In St. Louis, MGM, 1944,* insert, very fine cond., Stanley Caidin Coll., (09-12-92, Sotheby-NY, #283, illus.), 36 x 14 in., (91.4 x 35.6 cm.), (BP 349, DM 981, FR 3325, Y 82,069).

$3575*   *Melody Cruise, RKO, 1933,* one sheet, very fine cond., Stanley Caidin Coll., (09-12-92, Sotheby-NY, #133, illus.), 41 x 27 in., (104.1 x 68.6 cm.), linen backed (BP 1891, DM 5314, FR 18,010, Y 444,541).

$880*   *Men In White, 1934,* near mint cond., (paper), (12-12-92, Hollywd Poster, #227, illus.), (BP 564, DM 1386, FR 4752, Y 108,897).

$660*   *Merely Mary Ann, Fox Picture, 1931,* insert, very fine cond., Stanley Caidin Coll., (09-12-92, Sotheby-NY, #150, illus.), 36 x 14 in., (91.4 x 35.6 cm.), (BP 349, DM 981, FR 3325, Y 82,069).

$1430*   *Merry Go Round, 1922,* fine cond., (12-12-92, Hollywd Poster, #15, illus.), (BP 917, DM 2253, FR 7721, Y 176,958).

$3300*   *Merry Xmas And A Happy New Year, Fox, 1934,* special promotional one-sheet, cond. A, (12-14-92, Christie-E, #203, illus.), 41 x 27 in., (104.1 x 68.6 cm.), (BP 2110, DM 5186, FR 17,675, Y 408,264).

$220*   *Metropolis, 1984: Two,* Italian, paper backed, (03-18-93, Swann, #149, illus.), 19 x 26 in., (48.3 x 66 cm.), (BP 148, DM 362, FR 1232, Y 25,602).

$33,000*   *Metropolis, Paramount, 1926,* insert, very fine cond., Stanley Caidin Coll., (09-12-92, Sotheby-NY, #303, illus.), 36 x 14 in., (91.4 x 35.6 cm.), (BP 17,451, DM 49,056, FR 166,247, Y 4,103,457).

$4675*   *Metropolis, Paramount, 1926,* lobby card, very fine cond., Stanley Caidin Coll., (09-12-92, Sotheby-NY, #304, illus.), 11 x 14 in., (27.9 x 35.6 cm.), linen backed (BP 2472, DM 6950, FR 23,552, Y 581,323).

$26,400*   *Metropolis, Paramount, 1927,* window card, cond. A, (12-14-92, Christie-E, #79, illus.), 22 x 14 in., (55.9 x

35.6 cm.), (BP 16,880, DM 41,490, FR 141,403, Y 3,266,114).

$770*   *Michael Strogoff, Universal Pictures, 1926,* one-sheet, very fine cond., Stanley Caidin Coll., (09-12-92, Sotheby-NY, #63, illus.), 41 x 27 in., (104.1 x 68.6 cm.), linen backed (BP 407, DM 1145, FR 3879, Y 95,747).

$605*   *Mickey's Bargain, RKO, 1930,* one-sheet, cond. A, linen backed, (12-14-92, Christie-E, #163, illus.), 41 x 27 in., (104.1 x 68.6 cm.), (BP 387, DM 951, FR 3240, Y 74,848).

$935*   *Mickey's Stampede, RKO, 1931,* one-sheet, cond. A, linen backed, (12-14-92, Christie-E, #162, illus.), 41 x 27 in., (104.1 x 68.6 cm.), (BP 598, DM 1469, FR 5008, Y 115,675).

$1650*   *The Midnight Man, Universal, 1919,* three-sheet, cond. B, linen backed, (12-14-92, Christie-E, #73, illus.), 81 x 41 in., (205.7 x 104.1 cm.), (BP 1055, DM 2593, FR 8838, Y 204,132).

$2475*   *A Midsummer Night's Dream, Warner Brothers, 1935,* one-sheet, good cond., Stanley Caidin Coll., (09-12-92, Sotheby-NY, #302, illus.), 41 x 27 in., (104.1 x 68.6 cm.), linen backed (BP 1309, DM 3679, FR 12,469, Y 307,759).

$495*   *Million Dollar Legs, 1932,* near mint cond., (12-12-92, Hollywd Poster, #18, illus.), lobby card (BP 317, DM 780, FR 2673, Y 61,255).

$357*   *Ministry Of Fear, Paramount, 1944,* one-sheet, cond. B+, linen backed, (03-18-93, Swann, #155, illus.), (BP 241, DM 587, FR 2000, Y 41,545).

$2750*   *The Miracle Man, Paramount, 1932,* one-sheet, cond. A, paper backed, (12-14-92, Christie-E, #213, illus.), 41 x 27 in., (104.1 x 68.6 cm.), (BP 1758, DM 4322, FR 14,730, Y 340,220).

$770*   *The Miracle Of Manhattan, Selznick, 1921,* one-sheet, cond. B, linen backed, (12-14-92, Christie-E, #13, illus.), 41 x 27 in., (104.1 x 68.6 cm.), (BP 492, DM 1210, FR 4124, Y 95,262).

$550*   *The Miracle Of Morgan's Creek, 1943,* fine cond., (linen), (12-12-92, Hollywd Poster, #276, illus.), (BP 353, DM 867, FR 2970, Y 68,061).

$248*   *Miracle On 34th Street, 1947,* fine cond., (12-12-92, Hollywd Poster, #257, illus.), title card (BP 159, DM 391, FR 1339, Y 30,689).

$220*   *Miracle On 34th Street, 1947,* insert, near mint cond., (12-12-92, Hollywd Poster, #302, illus.), (BP 141, DM 347, FR 1188, Y 27,224).

$1650*   *Miracle On 34th Street, 20th Century Fox, 1947,* three-sheet, cond. A, linen backed, (12-14-92, Christie-E, #205, illus.), 81 x 41 in., (205.7 x 104.1 cm.), (BP 1055, DM 2593, FR 8838, Y 204,132).

$110*   *The Misfits, 1961,* insert, fine cond., (12-12-92, Hollywd Poster, #65, illus.), (BP 71, DM 173, FR 594, Y 13,612).

$495*   *The Misfits, 1961,* three sheet, near mint cond., (linen), (12-12-92, Hollywd Poster, #165, illus.), (BP 317, DM 780, FR 2673, Y 61,255).

BI   *Miss Sadie Thompson (La Belle Du Pacifique), 1953,* French, cond. A-, linen backed, est. $5/750, (03-18-93, Swann, #136, illus.), 63 x 47 in., (160 x 119.4 cm.), .

BI   *Missile To The Moon, Astor, 1959: Two,* three-sheet and insert, est. $4/600, (03-18-93, Swann, #118, illus.), .

$2750*   *Mississippi, Paramount, 1935,* one-sheet, very fine cond., Stanley Caidin Coll., (09-12-92, Sotheby-NY, #134, illus.), 41 x 27 in., (104.1 x 68.6 cm.), paper backed (BP 1454, DM 4088, FR 13,854, Y 341,955).

BI   *Modern Times, 1972,* re-issue, one-sheet, cond A-, linen backed, est. $3/400, (03-18-93, Swann, #157, illus.), .

$191*   *Modern Times, Charles Chaplin,* re-issue 1952, British, cond. A, half-sheet, (12-17-92, Christie-S. Ken, #265, illus.), 22 x 28 in., (55.9 x 71.1 cm.), poster (BP 121, DM 298, FR 1019, Y 23,473).

$7700*   *Modern Times, United Artists, 1936,* insert. good cond., Stanley Caidin Coll., (09-12-92, Sotheby-NY, #103, illus.), 36 x 14 in., (91.4 x 35.6 cm.), (BP 4072, DM 11,446, FR 38,791, Y 957,473).

$1540*   *Modern Times, United Artists, 1936,* window card, cond. A, trimmed, (12-14-92, Christie-E, #119, illus.), 20 x 14 in., (50.8 x 35.6 cm.), (BP 985, DM 2420, FR 8249, Y 190,523).

$192* *The Mole People, Universal, 1956: Two,* insert, lobby card, (03-18-93, Swann, #158, illus.), (BP 129, DM 316, FR 1076, Y 22,344).

$1650* *Monkey Business, Paramount, 1931,* window card, very fine cond., Stanley Caidin Coll., (09-12-92, Sotheby-NY, #95, illus.), 22 x 14 in., (55.9 x 35.6 cm.), (BP 873, DM 2453, FR 8312, Y 205,173).

$880* *Monsieur Beaucaire, 1924,* near mint cond., (12-12-92, Hollywd Poster, #123, illus.), title card (BP 564, DM 1386, FR 4752, Y 108,897).

$1100* *Monsieur Beaucaire, Paramount, 1924,* insert, very fine cond., Stanley Caidin Coll., (09-12-92, Sotheby-NY, #56, illus.), 36 x 14 in., (91.4 x 35.6 cm.), (BP 582, DM 1635, FR 5542, Y 136,782).

$4620* *Monsieur Beaucaire, Paramount, 1924,* one-sheet, cond. A, linen backed, (12-14-92, Christie-E, #276, illus.), 41 x 27 in., (104.1 x 68.6 cm.), (BP 2954, DM 7261, FR 24,746, Y 571,570).

$1100* *Moon Over Miami, 20th Century Fox, 1941,* jumbo window card, cond. A, (12-14-92, Christie-E, #218, illus.), 28 x 22 in., (71.1 x 55.9 cm.), (BP 703, DM 1729, FR 5892, Y 136,088).

BI *Morocco (Marocko), 1930,* Swedish, est. $2,5/3,500, (03-18-93, Swann, #137, illus.), 39 x 27 in., (99.1 x 68.6 cm.), .

$3520* *Morocco, Paramount, 1930,* jumbo lobby card, cond. A, (12-14-92, Christie-E, #252, illus.), 17 x 14 in., (43.2 x 35.6 cm.), (BP 2251, DM 5532, FR 18,854, Y 435,482).

$715* *Motor Mania, Walt Disney, 1950,* fine cond., (linen), (12-12-92, Hollywd Poster, #103, illus.), (BP 458, DM 1127, FR 3861, Y 88,479).

$522* *Moulin Rouge, 1953,* French, cond. A-, linen backed, (03-18-93, Swann, #108, illus.), 63 x 47 in., (160 x 119.4 cm.), (BP 352, DM 858, FR 2924, Y 60,747).

$330* *Moulin Rouge, 1953,* Italian, cond. A-, paper backed, (03-18-93, Swann, #163, illus.), 28 x 13 in., (71.1 x 33 cm.), (BP 223, DM 542, FR 1849, Y 38,403).

$550* *Moulin Rouge, 1953,* French, near mint cond., (linen), (12-12-92, Hollywd Poster, #205, illus.), (BP 353, DM 867, FR 2970, Y 68,061).

$1045* *The Mountain Woman, Fox, 1921,* one-sheet, cond. A, linen backed, (12-14-92, Christie-E, #285, illus.), 41 x 27 in., (104.1 x 68.6 cm.), (BP 668, DM 1642, FR 5597, Y 129,284).

$495* *Mr. Bug Goes To Town, 1941,* fine cond., (linen), (12-12-92, Hollywd Poster, #104, illus.), (BP 317, DM 780, FR 2673, Y 61,255).

$2200* *"Mr. Deeds Goes To Town", 1936,* Columbia, six-sheet, cond. B, (11-07-92, Camden, #275, illus.), trimmed to 75 x 76 in., (190.5 x 193 cm.), restored on linen (BP 1438, DM 3513, FR 11,873, Y 271,538).

$358* *"Mr. Hulot's Holiday", 1953,* French, Disci Film, cond. B, (06-05-93, Camden, #160, illus.), 32 x 23 in., (81.3 x 58.4 cm.), on linen (BP 236, DM 580, FR 1956, Y 38,404).

$660* *Mr. Lucky, RKO, 1943,* one-sheet, cond. A, (12-14-92, Christie-E, #303, illus.), 41 x 27 in., (104.1 x 68.6 cm.), (BP 422, DM 1037, FR 3535, Y 81,653).

$605* *"Mr. Moto's Gamble", 1938,* Fox, one-sheet, cond. C, (06-05-93, Camden, #27, illus.), 41 x 27 in., (104.1 x 68.6 cm.), (BP 398, DM 981, FR 3306, Y 64,900).

$3575* *"Mr. Smith Goes To Washington", 1939,* Columbia, three-sheet, cond. C, (06-05-93, Camden, #109, illus.), 81 x 41 in., (205.7 x 104.1 cm.), on linen (BP 2353, DM 5796, FR 19,536, Y 383,501).

$990* *Mr. Smith Goes To Washington, 1939,* fine cond., (12-12-92, Hollywd Poster, #292, illus.), title card (BP 635, DM 1560, FR 5346, Y 122,510).

$605* *Mr. Smith Goes To Washington, 1939,* restored, fine cond., (12-12-92, Hollywd Poster, #133, illus.), window card (BP 388, DM 953, FR 3267, Y 74,867).

$6050* *Mr. Smith Goes To Washington, Columbia, 1939,* one-sheet, cond. B, linen backed, (12-14-92, Christie-E, #239, illus.), 41 x 27 in., (104.1 x 68.6 cm.), (BP 3868, DM 9508, FR 32,405, Y 748,484).

$193* *Mr. Washington Goes To Town,* very good cond., (linen), (12-12-92, Hollywd Poster, #314, illus.), (BP 124, DM 304, FR 1042, Y 23,883).

$303* *Mrs. Wiggs Of The Cabbage Patch, 1934,* near mint cond., (12-12-92, Hollywd Poster, #19, illus.), lobby card (BP 194, DM 477, FR 1636, Y 37,495).

$1980* *"The Mummy's Curse", 1944,* Universal, one-sheet, cond. B, (06-05-93, Camden, #31, illus.), 41 x 27 in., (104.1 x 68.6 cm.), on linen (BP 1303, DM 3210, FR 10,820, Y 212,401).

$1100* *The Mummy's Ghost, Universal, 1944,* half-sheet, cond. C, linen backed, (03-18-93, Swann, #164, illus.), (BP 742, DM 1808, FR 6162, Y 128,011).

$5280* *Murder By Television, Cameo Pictures, 1935,* one-sheet, cond. A, linen backed, (12-14-92, Christie-E, #309, illus.), 41 x 27 in., (104.1 x 68.6 cm.), (BP 3376, DM 8298, FR 28,281, Y 653,223).

$715* *Murder In Greenwich Village, Columbia, 1937,* one-sheet, cond. A, linen backed, (12-14-92, Christie-E, #15, illus.), 41 x 27 in., (104.1 x 68.6 cm.), (BP 457, DM 1124, FR 3830, Y 88,457).

$1760* *Murder, My Sweet, RKO, 1944,* one-sheet, cond. A, linen backed, (12-14-92, Christie-E, #178, illus.), 41 x 27 in., (104.1 x 68.6 cm.), (BP 1125, DM 2766, FR 9427, Y 217,741).

$990* *Mutiny On The Bounty, MGM, 1935,* insert, very fine cond., Stanley Caidin Coll., (09-12-92, Sotheby-NY, #183, illus.), 36 x 14 in., (91.4 x 35.6 cm.), (BP 524, DM 1472, FR 4987, Y 123,104).

$1210* *My Darling Clementine, 20th Century Fox, 1946,* one-sheet, cond. B, linen backed, (12-14-92, Christie-E, #141, illus.), 41 x 27 in., (104.1 x 68.6 cm.), (BP 774, DM 1902, FR 6481, Y 149,697).

$116* *"My Foolish Heart" and "Ship Of Wanted Men": Two,* Andy Warhol Estate, (04-16-93, DuMouchelle, #2536), 41 x 27 in., (104.1 x 68.6 cm.), posters (BP 76, DM 187, FR 633, Y 13,044).

$3025* *"My Little Chickadee", 1940,* Universal, three-sheet, cond. B, (11-07-92, Camden, #196, illus.), 81 x 41 in., (205.7 x 104.1 cm.), on linen (BP 1978, DM 4830, FR 16,325, Y 373,365).

$4125* *My Little Chickadee, Universal Studios, 1939,* one-sheet, very fine cond., Stanley CAidin Coll., (09-12-92, Sotheby-NY, #140, illus.), 41 x 27 in., (104.1 x 68.6 cm.), one-sheet (BP 2181, DM 6132, FR 20,781, Y 512,932).

$2200* *My Man Godfrey, 1936,* near mint cond., (12-12-92, Hollywd Poster, #20), lobby card (BP 1411, DM 3466, FR 11,879, Y 272,244).

$990* *My Man Godfrey, Universal Pictures, 1936,* window card, good cond., Stanley Caidin Coll., (09-12-92, Sotheby-NY, #141, illus.), 22 x 14 in., (55.9 x 35.6 cm.), linen backed (BP 524, DM 1472, FR 4987, Y 123,104).

$7150* *My Man Godfrey, Universal, 1936,* one-sheet, cond. A, paper backed, (12-14-92, Christie-E, #149, illus.), 41 x 27 in., (104.1 x 68.6 cm.), (BP 4572, DM 11,237, FR 38,297, Y 884,573).

$2200* *My Pal, The King, Universal, 1932,* one-sheet, cond. A, linen backed, (12-14-92, Christie-E, #164, illus.), 41 x 27 in., (104.1 x 68.6 cm.), (BP 1407, DM 3457, FR 11,784, Y 272,176).

$4400* *Les Mysteres Du Ciel, 1907,* orig. French, cond. B+, linen backed, (03-18-93, Swann, #78, illus.), 63 x 47 in., (160 x 119.4 cm.), (BP 2967, DM 7231, FR 24,650, Y 512,045).

$6050* *Nanook Of The North, Pathe, 1921,* one-sheet, very fine cond., Stanley Caidin Coll., (09-12-92, Sotheby-NY, #64, illus.), 41 x 27 in., (104.1 x 68.6 cm.), linen backed (BP 3199, DM 8994, FR 30,479, Y 752,300).

BI *Nanook, United Artists,* Mexican, cond. A, one-sheet, linen-backed, est. BP 150/250, (12-17-92, Christie-S. Ken, #244, illus.), 23 x 33 in., (58.4 x 83.8 cm.), poster.

$1100* *Naughty Marietta, MGM, 1935,* three-sheet, very fine cond., Stanley Caidin Coll., (09-12-92, Sotheby-NY, #151, illus.), 81 x 41 in., (205.7 x 104.1 cm.), linen backed (BP 582, DM 1635, FR 5542, Y 136,782).

$1980* *Navy Blues, 1930,* fine cond., (paper), (12-12-92, Hollywd Poster, #160, illus.), (BP 1270, DM 3120, FR 10,691, Y 245,019).

$770* *Nevada, Paramount, 1935,* one-sheet, cond. A, linen backed, (12-14-92, Christie-E, #247, illus.), 41 x 27 in., (104.1 x 68.6 cm.), (BP 492, DM 1210, FR 4124, Y 95,262).

$385* *Never Give A Sucker An Even Break, Universal, 1941,* jumbo window card, (03-18-93, Swann, #160, illus.), (BP 260, DM 633, FR 2157, Y 44,804).

$605* *The New Neighbor, Donald Duck, 1953,* fine cond., (12-12-92, Hollywd Poster, #112, illus.), (BP 388, DM 953, FR 3267, Y 74,867).

$110* *New York, New York, United Artists, 1976,* one-sheet, cond. A-, linen backed, (03-18-93, Swann, #161, illus.), (BP 74, DM 181, FR 616, Y 12,801).

$1100* *New York, Paramount, 1927,* one-sheet, very fine cond., Stanley Caidin Coll., (09-12-92, Sotheby-NY, #2, illus.), 41 x 27 in., (104.1 x 68.6 cm.), linen backed (BP 582, DM 1635, FR 5542, Y 136,782).

$660* *New York-By Heck!, Nestor Comedy, 1918,* one-sheet, good cond., Stanley Caidin Coll., (09-12-92, Sotheby-NY, #3, illus.), 41 x 27 in., (104.1 x 68.6 cm.), linen backed (BP 349, DM 981, FR 3325, Y 82,069).

$440* *Niagara, 1952,* insert, fine cond., (12-12-92, Hollywd Poster, #78, illus.), (BP 282, DM 693, FR 2376, Y 54,449).

$4400* *Night After Night, Paramount, 1932,* one-sheet, very fine cond., Stanley Caidin Coll., (09-12-92, Sotheby-NY, #138, illus.), 41 x 27 in., (104.1 x 68.6 cm.), linen backed (BP 2327, DM 6541, FR 22,166, Y 547,128).

$7700* *A Night At The Opera, MGM, 1935,* one-sheet, cond. B, linen backed, (12-14-92, Christie-E, #286, illus.), 41 x 27 in., (104.1 x 68.6 cm.), (BP 4923, DM 12,101, FR 41,243, Y 952,617).

$1870* *A Night At The Opera, MGM, 1935: Two,* lobby cards, very fine cond., Stanley Caidin Coll., (09-12-92, Sotheby-NY, #96, illus.), 11 x 14 in., (27.9 x 35.6 cm.), (BP 989, DM 2780, FR 9421, Y 232,529).

$6050* *A Night In The Show, Perfection Pictures, 1915,* one-sheet, good cond., Stanley Caidin Coll., (09-12-92, Sotheby-NY, #102, illus.), 41 x 27 in., (104.1 x 68.6 cm.), linen backed (BP 3199, DM 8994, FR 30,479, Y 752,300).

$1210* *Night Monster, Universal, 1942,* one-sheet, cond. A, (12-14-92, Christie-E, #312, illus.), 41 x 27 in., (104.1 x 68.6 cm.), (BP 774, DM 1902, FR 6481, Y 149,697).

$165* *"The Night Rose", 1921,* Goldwyn, one-sheet, cond. C, (06-05-93, Camden, #89, illus.), 41 x 27 in., (104.1 x 68.6 cm.), restored on linen after catalogue photography (BP 109, DM 268, FR 902, Y 17,700).

$467* *Nightmare Alley, 20th Century, 1947,* one-sheet, cond. B+, (03-18-93, Swann, #165, illus.), (BP 315, DM 767, FR 2616, Y 54,347).

BI *Ninotchka (Ninoska), 1939,* Spanish, cond. B+, linen backed, est. $4/600, (03-18-93, Swann, #39, illus.), .

$330* *"Ninotchka", 1939,* Australian, cond. C, (06-05-93, Camden, #238, illus.), 40 x 27 in., (101.6 x 68.6 cm.), (BP 217, DM 535, FR 1803, Y 35,400).

$1870* *Non-Stop New York, Gaumont British, 1937,* half-sheet, cond. B, folded, (12-14-92, Christie-E, #17, illus.), 22 x 28 in., (55.9 x 71.1 cm.), (BP 1196, DM 2939, FR 10,016, Y 231,350).

$550* *Northwest Passage, MGM, 1940,* one-sheet, very fine cond., Stanley Caidin Coll., (09-12-92, Sotheby-NY, #245, illus.), 41 x 27 in., (104.1 x 68.6 cm.), linen backed (BP 291, DM 818, FR 2771, Y 68,391).

$605* *Notorious!, 1946,* Belgian, cond. A, linen backed, (03-18-93, Swann, #119, illus.), 32 x 14 in., (81.3 x 35.6 cm.), (BP 408, DM 994, FR 3389, Y 70,406).

$770* *Notorious!, RKO, 1946,* insert, very fine cond., Stanley Caidin Coll., (09-12-92, Sotheby-NY, #232, illus.), 36 x 14 in., (91.4 x 35.6 cm.), (BP 407, DM 1145, FR 3879, Y 95,747).

$1980* *Notorious!, RKO, 1946,* one-sheet, cond. A, linen backed, (12-14-92, Christie-E, #62, illus.), 41 x 27 in., (104.1 x 68.6 cm.), (BP 1266, DM 3112, FR 10,605, Y 244,959).

$4950* *A Nous La Liberte, Tobis, 1931,* orig. French poster, cond. B, linen backed, (12-14-92, Christie-E, #266, illus.), 63 x 94 in., (160 x 238.8 cm.), (BP 3165, DM 7779, FR 26,513, Y 612,396).

BI *Now Or Never, Pathe, 1921,* half-sheet, very fine cond., Stanley Caidin Coll., est. $6/900, (09-12-92, Sotheby-NY, #296, illus.), 22 x 28 in., (55.9 x 71.1 cm.), .

BI *The Nth Commandment, Paramount, 1923,* half-sheet, very fine cond., Stanley Caidin Coll., est. $6/900, (09-12-

92, Sotheby-NY, #30, illus.), 22 x 28 in., (55.9 x 71.1 cm.), half-sheet.

$1100* *Nursing A Viper, Biograph, 1909,* one-sheet, cond. A, linen backed, (12-14-92, Christie-E, #201, illus.), 41 x 27 in., (104.1 x 68.6 cm.), (BP 703, DM 1729, FR 5892, Y 136,088).

$770* *October (10 Dagen Die De Wereld Deden Wankelen), 1928,* Dutch, linen backed, (03-18-93, Swann, #124, illus.), 42 x 25 in., (106.7 x 63.5 cm.), (BP 519, DM 1265, FR 4314, Y 89,608).

$330* *October (10 Jours Qui Ebranierent Le Monde), 1928,* French, cond. A, linen backed, (03-18-93, Swann, #122, illus.), 44 x 28 in., (111.8 x 71.1 cm.), (BP 223, DM 542, FR 1849, Y 38,403).

$165* *"Of Mice And Men", 1939,* French, Hal Roach, cond. B, (06-05-93, Camden, #176, illus.), 63 x 47 in., (160 x 119.4 cm.), (BP 109, DM 268, FR 902, Y 17,700).

$770* *Of Mice And Men, Hal Roach, 1939,* one sheet, very fine cond., Stanley Caidin Coll., (09-12-92, Sotheby-NY, #299, illus.), 41 x 27 in., (104.1 x 68.6 cm.), linen backed (BP 407, DM 1145, FR 3879, Y 95,747).

$1980* *Office Girl, RKO, 1932,* insert, very fine cond., Stanley Caidin Coll., (09-12-92, Sotheby-NY, #307, illus.), 36 x 14 in., (91.4 x 35.6 cm.), (BP 1047, DM 2943, FR 9975, Y 246,207).

$4180* *Officer Duck, Disney, 1939,* one-sheet, cond. B, linen backed, (12-14-92, Christie-E, #105, illus.), 41 x 27 in., (104.1 x 68.6 cm.), (BP 2673, DM 6569, FR 22,389, Y 517,135).

$1760* *Oh, For A Man!, Fox, 1930,* one-sheet, cond. A, linen backed, (12-14-92, Christie-E, #313, illus.), 41 x 27 in., (104.1 x 68.6 cm.), (BP 1125, DM 2766, FR 9427, Y 217,741).

$550* *The Oklahoma Kid, 1939,* near mint cond., (12-12-92, Hollywd Poster, #261, illus.), lobby card (BP 353, DM 867, FR 2970, Y 68,061).

$2200* *The Oklahoma Kid, Warner Brothers, 1939,* insert, good cond., Stanley Caidin Coll., (09-12-92, Sotheby-NY, #243, illus.), 36 x 14 in., (91.4 x 35.6 cm.), linen backed (BP 1163, DM 3270, FR 11,083, Y 273,564).

$1980* *The Oklahoma Kid, Warner Brothers, 1939,* one-sheet, cond. A, linen backed, (12-14-92, Christie-E, #43, illus.), 41 x 27 in., (104.1 x 68.6 cm.), (BP 1266, DM 3112, FR 10,605, Y 244,959).

$12,100* *The Old Dark House, Universal, 1932: Set Of Eight,* lobby cards, cond. A, (12-14-92, Christie-E, #21, illus.), each 11 x 14 in., (27.9 x 35.6 cm.), (BP 7737, DM 19,016, FR 64,810, Y 1,496,969).

$1100* *Olympic Games, Pathe, 1927,* one-sheet, cond. A, linen backed, (12-14-92, Christie-E, #130, illus.), 41 x 27 in., (104.1 x 68.6 cm.), (BP 703, DM 1729, FR 5892, Y 136,088).

$247* *On The Town, MGM, 1949: Three,* one-sheet, 2 lobby cards, (03-18-93, Swann, #166, illus.), (BP 167, DM 406, FR 1384, Y 28,744).

$220* *On The Waterfront, 1954,* rolled, half sheet, near mint cond., (12-12-92, Hollywd Poster, #248, illus.), (BP 141, DM 347, FR 1188, Y 27,224).

$495* *On The Waterfront, Columbia, 1954,* one-sheet, linen backed, (03-18-93, Swann, #168, illus.), (BP 334, DM 813, FR 2773, Y 57,605).

$495* *On The Waterfront, Columbia, 1960,* Italian, cond. A, linen backed, (12-14-92, Christie-E, #95, illus.), 55 x 39 in., (139.7 x 99.1 cm.), (BP 316, DM 778, FR 2651, Y 61,240).

$2750* *"One Good Turn", 1931,* MGM, one-sheet, cond. B, (11-07-92, Camden, #131, illus.), 41 x 27 in., (104.1 x 68.6 cm.), on linen (BP 1798, DM 4391, FR 14,841, Y 339,422).

$1100* *Only Yesterday, Universal, 1933,* one-sheet, cond. A, linen backed, (12-14-92, Christie-E, #316, illus.), 41 x 27 in., (104.1 x 68.6 cm.), (BP 703, DM 1729, FR 5892, Y 136,088).

$440* *Orient Express, 1933,* near mint cond., (linen), (12-12-92, Hollywd Poster, #192, illus.), (BP 282, DM 693, FR 2376, Y 54,449).

$385* *Orphans Of The Storm, 1922,* rolled, half sheet, fine cond., (12-12-92, Hollywd Poster, #249, illus.), (BP 247, DM 607, FR 2079, Y 47,643).

$467* *Orphee, 1950,* orig. French, cond. B+, linen backed, (03-18-93, Swann, #169, illus.), 63 x 47 in., (160 x 119.4 cm.), (BP 315, DM 767, FR 2616, Y 54,347).

$990* *Our Blushing Brides, MGM, 1930,* one-sheet, cond. A, linen backed, (12-14-92, Christie-E, #113, illus.), 41 x 27 in., (104.1 x 68.6 cm.), (BP 633, DM 1556, FR 5303, Y 122,479).

$3575* *"Our Gang", 1922,* Pathe, one-sheet, cond. B, (11-07-92, Camden, #137, illus.), 41 x 27 in., (104.1 x 68.6 cm.), on linen (BP 2337, DM 5708, FR 19,293, Y 441,249).

$495* *Our Relations, 1936,* fine cond., (12-12-92, Hollywd Poster, #21, illus.), title card (BP 317, DM 780, FR 2673, Y 61,255).

$550* *Our Relations, MGM, 1936: Two,* lobby cards, very fine cond., Stanley Caidin Coll., (09-12-92, Sotheby-NY, #167, illus.), 11 x 14 in., (27.9 x 35.6 cm.), (BP 291, DM 818, FR 2771, Y 68,391).

$385* *Out Of The Past,* French Reissue, near mint cond., (12-12-92, Hollywd Poster, #51, illus.), (BP 247, DM 607, FR 2079, Y 47,643).

$2475* *"Out Of The Past", 1947,* RKO, one-sheet, cond. A, (11-07-92, Camden, #42, illus.), 41 x 27 in., (104.1 x 68.6 cm.), (BP 1618, DM 3952, FR 13,357, Y 305,480).

$3300* *Out Of The Past, RKO, 1947,* one-sheet, cond. A, linen backed, (12-14-92, Christie-E, #177, illus.), 41 x 27 in., (104.1 x 68.6 cm.), (BP 2110, DM 5186, FR 17,675, Y 408,264).

$8800* *The Outlaw, Howard Hughes, 1942,* one-sheet, very fine cond., rare poster, Stanley Caidin Coll., (09-12-92, Sotheby-NY, #274, illus.), 41 x 27 in., (104.1 x 68.6 cm.), linen backed (BP 4654, DM 13,082, FR 44,332, Y 1,094,255).

$825* *Over The Top, Vitagraph, 1918,* one-sheet, cond. A, linen backed, (12-14-92, Christie-E, #78, illus.), 41 x 27 in., (104.1 x 68.6 cm.), (BP 527, DM 1297, FR 4419, Y 102,066).

$5720* *The Painted Lady, Fox, 1924,* one-sheet, cond. A, linen backed, (12-14-92, Christie-E, #3, illus.), 41 x 27 in., (104.1 x 68.6 cm.), (BP 3657, DM 8989, FR 30,637, Y 707,658).

$1320* *The Painted Veil, MGM, 1934,* insert, very fine cond., Stanley Caidin Coll., (09-12-92, Sotheby-NY, #176, illus.), 36 x 14 in., (91.4 x 35.6 cm.), (BP 698, DM 1962, FR 6650, Y 164,138).

$11,000* *The Painted Veil, MGM, 1934,* six-sheet, cond. A, linen backed, (12-14-92, Christie-E, #168, illus.), 81 x 81 in., (205.7 x 205.7 cm.), (BP 7033, DM 17,287, FR 58,918, Y 1,360,881).

$193* *The Paleface, 1948,* very good cond., (linen), (12-12-92, Hollywd Poster, #275, illus.), (BP 124, DM 304, FR 1042, Y 23,883).

$1210* *The Palm Beach Story, Paramount, 1942,* one-sheet, very fine cond., Stanley Caidin Coll., (09-12-92, Sotheby-NY, #92, illus.), 41 x 27 in., (104.1 x 68.6 cm.), linen backed (BP 640, DM 1799, FR 6096, Y 150,460).

$495* *Parachute Jumper, 1932,* near mint cond., (12-12-92, Hollywd Poster, #269, illus.), lobby card (BP 317, DM 780, FR 2673, Y 61,255).

$880* *"Le Paradis Des Pilotes Perdus", 1948,* French, Midi Cine, cond. B, (06-05-93, Camden, #281, illus.), 63 x 47 in., (160 x 119.4 cm.), attached to wood doweling on linen (BP 579, DM 1427, FR 4809, Y 94,400).

$770* *Paradise Canyon, Monogram Pictures, 1935,* half-sheet, near mint cond., Stanley Caidin Coll., (09-12-92, Sotheby-NY, #256, illus.), 22 x 28 in., (55.9 x 71.1 cm.), (BP 407, DM 1145, FR 3879, Y 95,747).

$4400* *Paradise Canyon, Monogram, 1935,* one-sheet, cond. A, paper backed, (12-14-92, Christie-E, #244, illus.), 41 x 27 in., (104.1 x 68.6 cm.), (BP 2813, DM 6915, FR 23,567, Y 544,352).

$1870* *Paradise Canyon, Monogram, 1935,* one-sheet, cond. A, linen backed, (12-14-92, Christie-E, #245, illus.), 41 x 27 in., (104.1 x 68.6 cm.), (BP 1196, DM 2939, FR 10,016, Y 231,350).

$495* *Paris, First National Pictures, 1929,* insert, very fine cond., Stanley Caidin Coll., (09-12-92, Sotheby-NY, #125, illus.), 36 x 14 in., (91.4 x 35.6 cm.), (BP 262, DM 736, FR 2494, Y 61,552).

$357* *Paris-Champagne, c. 1960,* French, linen backed, (03-18-93, Swann, #170, illus.), (BP 241, DM 587, FR 2000, Y 41,545).

$660* *Pat And Mike, MGM, 1952,* one-sheet, set of 8 lobby cards, (03-18-93, Swann, #171, illus.), (BP 445, DM 1085, FR 3697, Y 76,807).

$660* *The Patriot, Paramount, 1928,* one-sheet, very fine cond., Stanley Caidin Coll., (09-12-92, Sotheby-NY, #66, illus.), 41 x 27 in., (104.1 x 68.6 cm.), linen backed (BP 349, DM 981, FR 3325, Y 82,069).

$825* *"Peacock Alley", 1922,* Metro, one-sheet, cond. B, (06-05-93, Camden, #86, illus.), 41 x 27 in., (104.1 x 68.6 cm.), (BP 543, DM 1338, FR 4508, Y 88,500).

$440* *Penny Serenade, 1941,* fine cond., (linen), (12-12-92, Hollywd Poster, #187, illus.), (BP 282, DM 693, FR 2376, Y 54,449).

$6050* *The Perils Of Pauline, Eclectic Film Co., 1914,* one-sheet, very fine cond., Stanley Caidin Coll., (09-12-92, Sotheby-NY, #249, illus.), 41 x 27 in., (104.1 x 68.6 cm.), linen backed (BP 3199, DM 8994, FR 30,479, Y 752,300).

$6600* *The Perils Of Pauline, Eclectic Film, 1914,* one-sheet, cond. A, linen backed, (12-14-92, Christie-E, #221, illus.), 41 x 27 in., (104.1 x 68.6 cm.), (BP 4220, DM 10,372, FR 35,351, Y 816,529).

$715* *Personal Property, 1937,* fine cond., (12-12-92, Hollywd Poster, #31, illus.), title card (BP 458, DM 1127, FR 3861, Y 88,479).

$13,200* *The Petrified Forest, Warner Brothers, 1936,* three-sheet, fine cond., only three-sheet known to exist, Stanley Caidin Coll., (09-12-92, Sotheby-NY, #213, illus.), 81 x 41 in., (205.7 x 104.1 cm.), (BP 6980, DM 19,622, FR 66,499, Y 1,641,383).

$1870* *The Phantom Empire, Mascot, 1935,* three-sheet, cond. B, linen backed, (12-14-92, Christie-E, #225, illus.), 81 x 41 in., (205.7 x 104.1 cm.), (BP 1196, DM 2939, FR 10,016, Y 231,350).

$3850* *"The Phantom Of The Opera", 1925,* Universal, lobby card, cond. B, (11-07-92, Camden, #94, illus.), 11 x 14 in., (27.9 x 35.6 cm.), (BP 2517, DM 6147, FR 20,777, Y 475,191).

BI *The Phantom Of The Opera, Universal Pictures, 1925,* lobby card, very fine cond., Stanley Caidin Coll., est. $1/2,000, (09-12-92, Sotheby-NY, #195, illus.), 11 x 14 in., (27.9 x 35.6 cm.), .

$3850* *The Phantom Of The Opera, Universal Pictures, 1925,* title lobby card, very fine cond., Stanley Caidin Coll., (09-12-92, Sotheby-NY, #191, illus.), 11 x 14 in., (27.9 x 35.6 cm.), (BP 2036, DM 5723, FR 19,395, Y 478,737).

$1540* *The Phantom Of The Opera, Universal Pictures, 1925,* lobby card, very fine cond., Stanley Caidin Coll., (09-12-92, Sotheby-NY, #193, illus.), 11 x 14 in., (27.9 x 35.6 cm.), (BP 814, DM 2289, FR 7758, Y 191,495).

BI *The Phantom Of The Opera, Universal Pictures, 1925,* lobby card, very fine cond., Stanley Caidin Coll., est. $1/2,000, (09-12-92, Sotheby-NY, #194, illus.), 11 x 14 in., (27.9 x 35.6 cm.), .

$1320* *The Phantom Of The Opera, Universal Pictures, 1925,* lobby card, very fine cond., Stanley Caidin Coll., (09-12-92, Sotheby-NY, #192, illus.), 11 x 14 in., (27.9 x 35.6 cm.), (BP 698, DM 1962, FR 6650, Y 164,138).

$7700* *The Phantom Of The Opera, Universal, 1925: Set Of Eight,* lobby cards, cond. A, (12-14-92, Christie-E, #137, illus.), each 11 x 14 in., (27.9 x 35.6 cm.), (BP 4923, DM 12,101, FR 41,243, Y 952,617).

$330* *Phantom Of The Opera, Universal, 1943,* French, linen backed, (03-18-93, Swann, #167, illus.), 31 x 23 in., (78.7 x 58.4 cm.), (BP 223, DM 542, FR 1849, Y 38,403).

$550* *The Phantom President, Paramount, 1932,* insert, very fine cond., Stanley Caidin Coll., (09-12-92, Sotheby-NY, #93, illus.), 36 x 14 in., (91.4 x 35.6 cm.), (BP 291, DM 818, FR 2771, Y 68,391).

$770* *"Pick And Shovel", 1923,* Pathe, one-sheet, cond. B, (06-05-93, Camden, #206, illus.), 41 x 27 in., (104.1 x 68.6 cm.), restored on linen after catalogue photography (BP 507, DM 1248, FR 4208, Y 82,600).

$1760* *Picking Peaches, Pathe, 1924,* one-sheet, cond. A, linen backed, (12-14-92, Christie-E, #292, illus.), 41 x 27 in.,

(104.1 x 68.6 cm.), (BP 1125, DM 2766, FR 9427, Y 217,741).

$715* *The Pied Piper Of Hamelin, Thomas A. Edison, 1917,* one-sheet, good cond., Stanley Caidin Coll., (09-12-92, Sotheby-NY, #28, illus.), 41 x 27 in., (104.1 x 68.6 cm.), one-sheet, linen backed (BP 378, DM 1063, FR 3602, Y 88,908).

$1650* *The Pig's Curly Tail, Bray, 1926,* one-sheet, cond. A, linen backed, (12-14-92, Christie-E, #271, illus.), 41 x 27 in., (104.1 x 68.6 cm.), (BP 1055, DM 2593, FR 8838, Y 204,132).

$138* *The Pilgrim, 1923,* near mint cond., (12-12-92, Hollywd Poster, #328, illus.), lobby card (BP 88, DM 217, FR 745, Y 17,077).

$193* *"Pillow Talk", 1959,* Universal, three-sheet, cond. A, (06-05-93, Camden, #120, illus.), 81 x 41 in., (205.7 x 104.1 cm.), (BP 127, DM 313, FR 1055, Y 20,704).

$3300* *"Pinocchio", 1940,* Disney, half-sheet, cond. B, (11-07-92, Camden, #159, illus.), 22 x 28 in., (55.9 x 71.1 cm.), on paper (BP 2158, DM 5269, FR 17,809, Y 407,307).

$3025* *"Pinocchio", 1940,* Disney/RKO, five lobby cards, cond. A, (11-07-92, Camden, #242, illus.), each 11 x 14 in., (27.9 x 35.6 cm.), (BP 1978, DM 4830, FR 16,325, Y 373,365).

$1430* *"Pinocchio", Danish, 1940,* Disney/RKO, cond. A, (11-07-92, Camden, #263, illus.), 33 x 24 in., (83.8 x 61 cm.), on linen (BP 935, DM 2283, FR 7717, Y 176,500).

$880* *Pinocchio, 1939,* fine cond., (12-12-92, Hollywd Poster, #137, illus.), window card (BP 564, DM 1386, FR 4752, Y 108,897).

$6050* *Pinocchio, Disney, 1940,* one-sheet, cond. A, linen backed, (12-14-92, Christie-E, #100, illus.), 41 x 27 in., (104.1 x 68.6 cm.), (BP 3868, DM 9508, FR 32,405, Y 748,484).

$6380* *Pinocchio, Disney, 1940,* half-sheet, cond. A, (12-14-92, Christie-E, #101, illus.), 22 x 28 in., (55.9 x 71.1 cm.), (BP 4079, DM 10,027, FR 34,172, Y 789,311).

$5280* *Pinocchio, RKO-Disney, 1940,* one-sheet, cond. A, linen backed, (03-18-93, Swann, #186, illus.), (BP 3561, DM 8677, FR 29,580, Y 614,454).

$247* *The Pirate, 1948: Three,* one-sheet, 2 lobby cards, (03-18-93, Swann, #172, illus.), (BP 167, DM 406, FR 1384, Y 28,744).

$770* *A Place In The Sun (Une Place Au Soleil), Paramount, 1951,* French, linen backed, (03-18-93, Swann, #173, illus.), 63 x 47 in., (160 x 119.4 cm.), (BP 519, DM 1265, FR 4314, Y 89,608).

$2200* *The Plainsman, Paramount, 1936,* one-sheet, fine cond., (09-12-92, Sotheby-NY, #89, illus.), 41 x 27 in., (104.1 x 68.6 cm.), linen backed (BP 1163, DM 3270, FR 11,083, Y 273,564).

$1650* *"Plan 9 From Outer Space", 1958,* DCA, one-sheet, cond. A, (11-07-92, Camden, #207, illus.), 41 x 27 in., (104.1 x 68.6 cm.), on linen (BP 1079, DM 2635, FR 8904, Y 203,653).

$1100* *Playboy Of Paris, Paramount, 1930,* one-sheet, fine cond., Stanley Caidin Coll., (09-12-92, Sotheby-NY, #126, illus.), 41 x 27 in., (104.1 x 68.6 cm.), linen-backed (BP 582, DM 1635, FR 5542, Y 136,782).

$1387* *Pluto's Christmas Tree, Walt Disney, 1952,* cond. A+, one-sheet, (12-17-92, Christie-S. Ken, #393, illus.), 41 x 27 in., (104.1 x 68.6 cm.), poster (BP 880, DM 2165, FR 7397, Y 170,456).

$550* *Polly Of The Storm Country, First National, 1920,* one-sheet, cond. A, linen backed, (12-14-92, Christie-E, #279, illus.), 41 x 27 in., (104.1 x 68.6 cm.), (BP 352, DM 864, FR 2946, Y 68,044).

$495* *Popeye,* fine cond., (linen), (12-12-92, Hollywd Poster, #110, illus.), (BP 317, DM 780, FR 2673, Y 61,255).

$193* *Poppy, 1936,* near mint cond., (12-12-92, Hollywd Poster, #22, illus.), lobby card (BP 124, DM 304, FR 1042, Y 23,883).

$1100* *Poppy, Paramount, 1936,* one-sheet, cond. B, mounted on Kraft, (03-18-93, Swann, #159, illus.), (BP 742, DM 1808, FR 6162, Y 128,011).

$1760* *Poppy, Paramount, 1936,* one-sheet, very fine cond., Stanley Caidin Coll., (09-12-92, Sotheby-NY, #142, illus.), 41 x 27 in., (104.1 x 68.6 cm.), linen backed (BP 931, DM 2616, FR 8866, Y 218,851).

$467* *Porgy And Bess, 1959,* one-sheet, (03-18-93, Swann, #174, illus.), (BP 315, DM 767, FR 2616, Y 54,347).

$330* *Ports of Call, 1925,* very good cond., (12-12-92, Hollywd Poster, #16, illus.), (BP 212, DM 520, FR 1782, Y 40,837).

$1320* *Possessed,* near mint cond., (linen), Original Belgian Release, (12-12-92, Hollywd Poster, #62, illus.), (BP 846, DM 2080, FR 7127, Y 163,346).

$1980* *The Postman Always Rings Twice, 1946,* near mint cond., (linen), (12-12-92, Hollywd Poster, #178, illus.), (BP 1270, DM 3120, FR 10,691, Y 245,019).

$3575* *The Postman Always Rings Twice, MGM, 1946,* one-sheet, very fine cond., Stanley Caidin Coll., (09-12-92, Sotheby-NY, #234, illus.), 41 x 27 in., (104.1 x 68.6 cm.), linen backed (BP 1891, DM 5314, FR 18,010, Y 444,541).

$2200* *The Postman Always Rings Twice, MGM, 1946,* one-sheet, cond. A, linen backed, (12-14-92, Christie-E, #181, illus.), 41 x 27 in., (104.1 x 68.6 cm.), (BP 1407, DM 3457, FR 11,784, Y 272,176).

$660* *The Pride Of New York, Fox, 1917,* one-sheet, cond. A, linen backed, (12-14-92, Christie-E, #153, illus.), 41 x 27 in., (104.1 x 68.6 cm.), (BP 422, DM 1037, FR 3535, Y 81,653).

$110* *Pride Of The Yankees, 1946,* Australian, (03-18-93, Swann, #175, illus.), 30 x 13 in., (76.2 x 33 cm.), (BP 74, DM 181, FR 616, Y 12,801).

$770* *Primitive Man, Kalem, 1913,* one-sheet, very fine cond., Stanley Caidin Coll., (09-12-92, Sotheby-NY, #29, illus.), 41 x 27 in., (104.1 x 68.6 cm.), one-sheet, linen backed (BP 407, DM 1145, FR 3879, Y 95,747).

BI *The Prince And The Pauper (Le Prince Et Le Pauvre), Warner, 1937,* French, cond. A-, linen backed, est. $1,5/2,500, (03-18-93, Swann, #23, illus.), 63 x 47 in., (160 x 119.4 cm.), .

$1430* *"The Prince And The Pauper",* Italian, d. 1952, Warner Bros., original release, cond. A, (06-05-93, Camden, #178, illus.), 55 x 39 in., (139.7 x 99.1 cm.), restored on linen after catalogue photography (BP 941, DM 2318, FR 7814, Y 153,401).

$385* *The Prince And The Showgirl, 1957,* near mint cond., (12-12-92, Hollywd Poster, #274, illus.), (BP 247, DM 607, FR 2079, Y 47,643).

$2200* *The Prince And The Showgirl, Warner Bros., 1957,* three-sheet, cond. A, linen backed, (12-14-92, Christie-E, #236, illus.), 81 x 41 in., (205.7 x 104.1 cm.), (BP 1407, DM 3457, FR 11,784, Y 272,176).

$5500* *The Prisoner Of Zenda, United Artists, 1937,* one-sheet, cond. A, linen backed, (12-14-92, Christie-E, #33, illus.), 41 x 27 in., (104.1 x 68.6 cm.), (BP 3517, DM 8644, FR 29,459, Y 680,440).

$3300* *The Private Lives Of Elizabeth And Essex, Warner Brothers, 1939,* insert, very fine cond., Stanley Caidin Coll., (09-12-92, Sotheby-NY, #224, illus.), 36 x 14 in., (91.4 x 35.6 cm.), (BP 1745, DM 4906, FR 16,625, Y 410,346).

$330* *The Prizefighter And The Lady, MGM, 1933,* insert, near mint cond., Stanley Caidin Coll., (09-12-92, Sotheby-NY, #263, illus.), 36 x 14 in., (91.4 x 35.6 cm.), (BP 175, DM 491, FR 1662, Y 41,035).

$990* *Prodigal Daughters, Paramount, 1922,* half-sheet, very fine cond., Stanley Caidin Coll., (09-12-92, Sotheby-NY, #23, illus.), 22 x 28 in., (55.9 x 71.1 cm.), half-sheet, linen backed (BP 524, DM 1472, FR 4987, Y 123,104).

$880* *Professional Sweetheart, RKO, 1933,* one-sheet, cond. A, linen backed, (12-14-92, Christie-E, #315, illus.), 41 x 27 in., (104.1 x 68.6 cm.), (BP 563, DM 1383, FR 4713, Y 108,870).

$385* *Psycho, 1960,* near mint cond., (12-12-92, Hollywd Poster, #154, illus.), (BP 247, DM 607, FR 2079, Y 47,643).

$347* *Puttin' On The Ritz, United Artists/Joseph M. Schneck, 1930,* cond. B, tape, three-sheet, linen-backed, (12-17-92, Christie-S. Ken, #203, illus.), 81 x 41 in., (205.7 x 104.1 cm.), poster (BP 220, DM 542, FR 1851, Y 42,645).

$2200* *Pygmalion, MGM, 1938,* one-sheet, very fine cond., portrait of George Shaw, created by Al Hirschfeld, Stanley Caidin Coll., (09-12-92, Sotheby-NY, #278, illus.), 41 x

27 in., (104.1 x 68.6 cm.), linen backed (BP 1163, DM 3270, FR 11,083, Y 273,564).

$467* *Les Quatre Cents Coup, 1959,* orig. French, cond. C+, linen backed, (03-18-93, Swann, #176, illus.), 63 x 47 in., (160 x 119.4 cm.), (BP 315, DM 767, FR 2616, Y 54,347).

$5280* *Queen Christina, MGM, 1934,* one-sheet, cond. A, linen backed, (12-14-92, Christie-E, #170, illus.), 41 x 27 in., (104.1 x 68.6 cm.), (BP 3376, DM 8298, FR 28,281, Y 653,223).

$550* *Querelle, 1984,* orig. French, cond. A, linen backed, (03-18-93, Swann, #193, illus.), 63 x 47 in., (160 x 119.4 cm.), (BP 371, DM 904, FR 3081, Y 64,006).

$550* *Racket Busters, Warner Brothers, 1938,* one-sheet, good cond., Stanley Caidin Coll., (09-12-92, Sotheby-NY, #208, illus.), 41 x 27 in., (104.1 x 68.6 cm.), linen backed (BP 291, DM 818, FR 2771, Y 68,391).

$660* *A Railroad Conspiracy, Kalem, c. 1912,* one-sheet, very fine cond., Stanley Caidin Coll., (09-12-92, Sotheby-NY, #253, illus.), 41 x 27 in., (104.1 x 68.6 cm.), linen backed (BP 349, DM 981, FR 3325, Y 82,069).

$1760* *Rain, Atlantic Picture, reissue c. 1937,* one-sheet, fine cond., Stanley Caidin Coll., (09-12-92, Sotheby-NY, #86, illus.), 41 x 27 in., (104.1 x 68.6 cm.), linen backed (BP 931, DM 2616, FR 8866, Y 218,851).

$605* *Rainbow Trail, 1931,* fine cond., (linen), (12-12-92, Hollywd Poster, #86, illus.), (BP 388, DM 953, FR 3267, Y 74,867).

$3575* *Randy Rides Alone, Lone Star Productions, 1934,* one-sheet, fine cond., Stanley Caidin Coll., (09-12-92, Sotheby-NY, #255, illus.), 41 x 27 in., (104.1 x 68.6 cm.), linen backed (BP 1891, DM 5314, FR 18,010, Y 444,541).

BI *Rango, 1931,* German, cond. A, linen backed, est. $1,5/2,000, (03-18-93, Swann, #79, illus.), 55 x 37 in., (139.7 x 94 cm.), .

$5225* *"The Raven", 1935,* Universal, lobby card, cond. B, (11-07-92, Camden, #88, illus.), 11 x 14 in., (27.9 x 35.6 cm.), (BP 3416, DM 8343, FR 28,198, Y 644,902).

$3575* *"The Raven", 1935,* Universal/Liberty, lobby card, cond. B, (11-07-92, Camden, #89, illus.), 11 x 14 in., (27.9 x 35.6 cm.), (BP 2337, DM 5708, FR 19,293, Y 441,249).

$1100* *The Raven, 1935,* near mint cond., (12-12-92, Hollywd Poster, #124, illus.), lobby card (BP 705, DM 1733, FR 5940, Y 136,122).

$880* *"Rear Window", 1954,* Paramount, three-sheet, cond. B, (06-05-93, Camden, #110, illus.), 81 x 41 in., (205.7 x 104.1 cm.), (BP 579, DM 1427, FR 4809, Y 94,400).

$3300* *"Rebecca", 1939,* United Artists, one-sheet, cond. B, (11-07-92, Camden, #311, illus.), 41 x 27 in., (104.1 x 68.6 cm.), on paper (BP 2158, DM 5269, FR 17,809, Y 407,307).

$1320* *"Rebecca", 1939,* United Artists, half-sheet, cond. B, (06-05-93, Camden, #129, illus.), 22 x 28 in., (55.9 x 71.1 cm.), (BP 869, DM 2140, FR 7213, Y 141,601).

BI *Rebecca, 1940,* French, cond. B, linen backed, (03-18-93, Swann, #40, illus.), .

$2090* *Rebecca, United Artists, 1940,* insert, very fine cond., Stanley Caidin Coll., (09-12-92, Sotheby-NY, #231, illus.), 36 x 14 in., (91.4 x 35.6 cm.), (BP 1105, DM 3107, FR 10,529, Y 259,886).

BI *Rebel Without A Cause, 1955,* Australian, cond. A, est. $6/900, (03-18-93, Swann, #177, illus.), 41 x 27 in., (104.1 x 68.6 cm.), .

$1980* *Rebel Without A Cause, 1955,* three sheet, near mint cond., (linen), (12-12-92, Hollywd Poster, #168, illus.), (BP 1270, DM 3120, FR 10,691, Y 245,019).

$1430* *Rebel Without A Cause, Warner Brothers, 1955,* one-sheet, cond. A, linen backed, (12-14-92, Christie-E, #237, illus.), 41 x 27 in., (104.1 x 68.6 cm.), (BP 914, DM 2247, FR 7659, Y 176,915).

$495* *Rebel Without A Cause, Warner Brothers, 1960,* Italian, cond. A, linen backed, (12-14-92, Christie-E, #96, illus.), 55 x 39 in., (139.7 x 99.1 cm.), (BP 316, DM 778, FR 2651, Y 61,240).

$55* *Recaptured Love, 1931,* fine cond., (12-12-92, Hollywd Poster, #311, illus.), (BP 35, DM 87, FR 297, Y 6806).

$138* *Reckless, 1935,* fine cond., (12-12-92, Hollywd Poster, #32, illus.), lobby card (BP 88, DM 217, FR 745, Y 17,077).

BI *"Red Pony", 1949 and "Rachel And The Stranger", 1948: Two,* half-sheets, est. $2/300, (03-18-93, Swann, #178, illus.), .

$330* *"Red River Valley" and "Sunset On The Desert": Two,* one-sheets, (03-18-93, Swann, #192, illus.), (BP 223, DM 542, FR 1849, Y 38,403).

$330* *Redskin, Paramount, 1929,* insert, very fine cond., created by W. Hanneman, Stanley Caidin Coll., (09-12-92, Sotheby-NY, #246, illus.), 36 x 14 in., (91.4 x 35.6 cm.), (BP 175, DM 491, FR 1662, Y 41,035).

$303* *The Reluctant Dragon, 1941,* insert, fine cond., (12-12-92, Hollywd Poster, #69, illus.), (BP 194, DM 477, FR 1636, Y 37,495).

$4620* *Rembrandt, United Artists, 1936,* one-sheet, cond. A, (12-14-92, Christie-E, #243, illus.), 41 x 27 in., (104.1 x 68.6 cm.), (BP 2954, DM 7261, FR 24,746, Y 571,570).

BI *The Rescue, United Artists, 1929,* insert, very fine cond., Stanley Caidin Coll., est. $6/900, (09-12-92, Sotheby-NY, #50, illus.), 36 x 14 in., (91.4 x 35.6 cm.),

$495* *The Return Of Chandu, 1935,* fine cond., (linen), (12-12-92, Hollywd Poster, #39, illus.), (BP 317, DM 780, FR 2673, Y 61,255).

$880* *The Return Of Frank James, 20th Century Fox, 1940,* one-sheet, very fine cond., Stanley Caidin Coll., (09-12-92, Sotheby-NY, #272, illus.), 41 x 27 in., (104.1 x 68.6 cm.), linen backed (BP 465, DM 1308, FR 4433, Y 109,426).

$1980* *Revenge Of The Creature, Universal, 1955,* three-sheet, cond. A, linen backed, (12-14-92, Christie-E, #184, illus.), 81 x 41 in., (205.7 x 104.1 cm.), (BP 1266, DM 3112, FR 10,605, Y 244,959).

$1540* *Revenge, United Artists, 1928,* one-sheet, cond. B, linen backed, (12-14-92, Christie-E, #90, illus.), 41 x 27 in., (104.1 x 68.6 cm.), (BP 985, DM 2420, FR 8249, Y 190,523).

$880* *Rhodes, Gaumont, 1936,* one-sheet, very fine cond, Stanley Caidin Coll., (09-12-92, Sotheby-NY, #122, illus.), 41 x 27 in., (104.1 x 68.6 cm.), linen backed (BP 465, DM 1308, FR 4433, Y 109,426).

$825* *Rhythm On The Range, Paramount, 1936,* one-sheet, good cond., Stanley Caidin Coll., (09-12-92, Sotheby-NY, #132, illus.), 41 x 27 in., (104.1 x 68.6 cm.), linen backed (BP 436, DM 1226, FR 4156, Y 102,586).

$330* *Ringling Bros. Barnum And Bailey Two Panel Poster,* Andy Warhol Estate, (04-16-93, DuMouchelle, #2538), each panel 79½ x 58¼ in., (201.9 x 148 cm.), poster (BP 217, DM 533, FR 1801, Y 37,108).

$550* *Rinty Of The Desert, Warner Brothers, 1928,* one-sheet, cond. A, linen backed, (12-14-92, Christie-E, #185, illus.), 41 x 27 in., (104.1 x 68.6 cm.), (BP 352, DM 864, FR 2946, Y 68,044).

$220* *Rita Hayworth,* fine cond., (linen), German, (12-12-92, Hollywd Poster, #58, illus.), (BP 141, DM 347, FR 1188, Y 27,224).

$381* *Rita Hayworth, My Gal Sal, 20th Century Fox, 1942,* cond. B, three-sheet, linen-backed, (12-17-92, Christie-S. Ken, #210, illus.), 81 x 41 in., (205.7 x 104.1 cm.), poster (BP 242, DM 595, FR 2032, Y 46,823).

$220* *Road House, 1948,* fine cond., (paper), (12-12-92, Hollywd Poster, #1, illus.), (BP 141, DM 347, FR 1188, Y 27,224).

$935* *Robbers' Roost, 1932,* near mint cond., (linen), (12-12-92, Hollywd Poster, #87, illus.), (BP 600, DM 1473, FR 5049, Y 115,704).

BI *"Roberta", 1935,* RKO, window card, cond. A, est. $1/1,500, (06-05-93, Camden, #251, illus.), 22 x 14 in., (55.9 x 35.6 cm.), on linen.

$440* *Roberta, 1935,* restored, very good cond., (12-12-92, Hollywd Poster, #138, illus.), window card (BP 282, DM 693, FR 2376, Y 54,449).

$1760* *Roberta, RKO, 1935,* half-sheet, very fine cond., Stanley Caidin Coll., (09-12-92, Sotheby-NY, #159, illus.), 22 x 28 in., (55.9 x 71.1 cm.), linen backed (BP 931, DM 2616, FR 8866, Y 218,851).

$1210* *Roberta, RKO, 1935: Two,* lobby cards, very fine cond., Stanley Caidin Coll., (09-12-92, Sotheby-NY, #158, illus.), 11 x 14 in., (27.9 x 35.6 cm.), (BP 640, DM 1799, FR 6096, Y 150,460).

$1760* *"Robot Monster", 1953,* Astor Pictures, one-sheet, cond. A, (06-05-93, Camden, #34, illus.), 41 x 27 in., (104.1 x 68.6 cm.), on linen (BP 1159, DM 2853, FR 9617, Y 188,801).

$1320* *Rockabye, RKO, 1932,* one-sheet, cond. A, paper backed, (12-14-92, Christie-E, #314, illus.), 41 x 27 in., (104.1 x 68.6 cm.), (BP 844, DM 2074, FR 7070, Y 163,306).

BI *Rocket Ship X-M, Lippert, 1951,* one-sheet, cond. B+, linen backed, est. $800/1,200, (03-18-93, Swann, #189, illus.), .

BI *Rocky Horror Picture Show, 20th Century Fox, 1975,* cond. A, one-sheet, est BP 150/200, (12-17-92, Christie-S. Ken, #422, illus.), poster.

$880* *Roman Scandals, United Artists, 1933,* insert, fine cond., Stanley Caidin Coll., (09-12-92, Sotheby-NY, #147, illus.), 36 x 14 in., (91.4 x 35.6 cm.), (BP 465, DM 1308, FR 4433, Y 109,426).

$660* *Romance And Riches, Grand National, 1937,* one-sheet, very fine cond., Stanley Caidin Coll., (09-12-92, Sotheby-NY, #61, illus.), 41 x 27 in., (104.1 x 68.6 cm.), linen backed (BP 349, DM 981, FR 3325, Y 82,069).

$2420* *Romance In Manhattan, RKO, 1934,* one-sheet, cond. A, linen backed, (12-14-92, Christie-E, #71, illus.), 41 x 27 in., (104.1 x 68.6 cm.), (BP 1547, DM 3803, FR 12,962, Y 299,394).

$247* *Romeo And Juliet, 1936,* Argentinian, cond. A-, linen backed, (03-18-93, Swann, #179, illus.), 43 x 29 in., (109.2 x 73.7 cm.), (BP 167, DM 406, FR 1384, Y 28,744).

$330* *Romeo And Juliet, MGM, 1936,* jumbo window card, very fine cond., Stanley Caidin Coll., (09-12-92, Sotheby-NY, #301, illus.), 28 x 22 in., (71.1 x 55.9 cm.), (BP 175, DM 491, FR 1662, Y 41,035).

$1540* *Romeo And Juliet, MGM, 1936,* one-sheet, cond. A, linen backed, (12-14-92, Christie-E, #35, illus.), 41 x 27 in., (104.1 x 68.6 cm.), (BP 985, DM 2420, FR 8249, Y 190,523).

$1100* *Romeo And Juliet, MGM, 1936,* insert, cond. A, folded, (12-14-92, Christie-E, #36, illus.), 36 x 14 in., (91.4 x 35.6 cm.), (BP 703, DM 1729, FR 5892, Y 136,088).

BI *Ronald Coleman, Clive Of India, Twentieth Century, 1935,* cond. A-, one-sheet, linen-backed, est. BP 8/1,200, (12-17-92, Christie-S. Ken, #312, illus.), 41 x 27 in., (104.1 x 68.6 cm.), poster.

$467* *Room Service (Panik I Hotellet), RKO, 1939,* Danish, cond. B+, linen backed, (03-18-93, Swann, #182, illus.), 32½ x 24½ in., (82.6 x 62.2 cm.), (BP 315, DM 767, FR 2616, Y 54,347).

$1100* *Room Service, RKO, 1938,* one-sheet, cond. B, linen backed, (12-14-92, Christie-E, #287, illus.), 41 x 27 in., (104.1 x 68.6 cm.), (BP 703, DM 1729, FR 5892, Y 136,088).

$248* *Rope, 1956,* original French release, fine cond., (12-12-92, Hollywd Poster, #49, illus.), (BP 159, DM 391, FR 1339, Y 30,689).

$440* *"Rose O' The Sea", 1922,* First National, one-sheet, cond. B, (06-05-93, Camden, #90, illus.), 41 x 27 in., (104.1 x 68.6 cm.), (BP 290, DM 713, FR 2404, Y 47,200).

$1045* *The Roughneck, 1925,* near mint cond., (linen), (12-12-92, Hollywd Poster, #14, illus.), (BP 670, DM 1646, FR 5643, Y 129,316).

$1100* *Ruggles Of Red Gap, Paramount, 1935,* one-sheet, very fine cond., Stanley Caidin Coll., (09-12-92, Sotheby-NY, #137, illus.), 41 x 27 in., (104.1 x 68.6 cm.), linen backed (BP 582, DM 1635, FR 5542, Y 136,782).

$770* *The Ruling Voice, First National Picture, 1931,* one-sheet, very fine cond., Stanley Caidin Coll., (09-12-92, Sotheby-NY, #223, illus.), 41 x 27 in., (104.1 x 68.6 cm.), linen backed (BP 407, DM 1145, FR 3879, Y 95,747).

$495* *Runaway Girls, Columbia, 1928,* one-sheet, cond. A, linen backed, (12-14-92, Christie-E, #54, illus.), 41 x 27 in., (104.1 x 68.6 cm.), (BP 316, DM 778, FR 2651, Y 61,240).

$1540* *The Runway, Paramount, 1926,* one-sheet, cond. A, linen backed, (12-14-92, Christie-E, #30, illus.), 41 x 27

in., (104.1 x 68.6 cm.), (BP 985, DM 2420, FR 8249, Y 190,523).

$605* *Rusty Rides Alone, Columbia, 1933,* one-sheet, cond. B, linen backed, (12-14-92, Christie-E, #249, illus.), 41 x 27 in., (104.1 x 68.6 cm.), (BP 387, DM 951, FR 3240, Y 74,848).

$770* *Saboteur, Universal Pictures, 1942,* one-sheet, very fine cond., Stanley Caidin Coll., (09-12-92, Sotheby-NY, #233, illus.), 41 x 27 in., (104.1 x 68.6 cm.), linen backed (BP 407, DM 1145, FR 3879, Y 95,747).

$1210* *Sabrina, 1954,* one-sheet, linen backed, (03-18-93, Swann, #48, illus.), (BP 816, DM 1988, FR 6779, Y 140,812).

$5280* *Sadie Thompson, United Artists, 1928,* one-sheet, cond. A, linen backed, (12-14-92, Christie-E, #275, illus.), 41 x 27 in., (104.1 x 68.6 cm.), (BP 3376, DM 8298, FR 28,281, Y 653,223).

$8250* *A Sainted Devil, Paramount, 1924,* one-sheet, very fine cond., Stanley Caidin Coll., (09-12-92, Sotheby-NY, #51, illus.), 41 x 27 in., (104.1 x 68.6 cm.), linen backed (BP 4363, DM 12,264, FR 41,562, Y 1,025,864).

$990* *Sally, First National, 1925,* one-sheet, very fine cond., Stanley Caidin Coll., (09-12-92, Sotheby-NY, #36, illus.), 41 x 27 in., (104.1 x 68.6 cm.), linen backed (BP 524, DM 1472, FR 4987, Y 123,104).

$1540* *Sally, First National, 1925,* one-sheet, cond. A, linen backed, (12-14-92, Christie-E, #85, illus.), 41 x 27 in., (104.1 x 68.6 cm.), (BP 985, DM 2420, FR 8249, Y 190,523).

$4400* *Salome, Allied Producers, 1922,* one-sheet, cond. A, linen backed, (12-14-92, Christie-E, #32, illus.), 41 x 27 in., (104.1 x 68.6 cm.), (BP 2813, DM 6915, FR 23,567, Y 544,352).

$1100* *Saludos Amigos, RKO, 1943,* one-sheet, good cond., Stanley Caidin Coll., (09-12-92, Sotheby-NY, #292, illus.), 41 x 27 in., (104.1 x 68.6 cm.), linen backed (BP 582, DM 1635, FR 5542, Y 136,782).

BI *Salute, Fox, 1929,* insert, near mint cond., Stanley Caidin Coll., est. $6/900, (09-12-92, Sotheby-NY, #260, illus.), 36 x 14 in., (91.4 x 35.6 cm.), .

$303* *San Francisco, 1936,* near mint cond., (12-12-92, Hollywd Poster, #291, illus.), lobby card (BP 194, DM 477, FR 1636, Y 37,495).

$660* *Sanders Of The River, United Artists, 1935,* insert, near mint cond., Stanley Caidin Coll., (09-12-92, Sotheby-NY, #115, illus.), 36 x 14 in., (91.4 x 35.6 cm.), (BP 349, DM 981, FR 3325, Y 82,069).

$770* *Sands Of Iwo Jima, Republic, 1950,* one-sheet, cond. A, paper backed, (12-14-92, Christie-E, #158, illus.), 41 x 27 in., (104.1 x 68.6 cm.), (BP 492, DM 1210, FR 4124, Y 95,262).

$550* *Santa Fe Trail, Warner Brothers, 1940,* title lobby card, good cond., Stanley Caidin Coll., (09-12-92, Sotheby-NY, #229, illus.), 11 x 14 in., (27.9 x 35.6 cm.), (BP 291, DM 818, FR 2771, Y 68,391).

$247* *Santo Y Blue Demon Contra Los Monstruos, 1968,* orig. Mexican, cond. A-, linen backed, (03-18-93, Swann, #195, illus.), 40 x 28 in., (101.6 x 71.1 cm.), (BP 167, DM 406, FR 1384, Y 28,744).

$550* *"Saratoga", 1937,* MGM, one-sheet, cond. B, (06-05-93, Camden, #237, illus.), 41 x 27 in., (104.1 x 68.6 cm.), on linen (BP 362, DM 892, FR 3005, Y 59,000).

$880* *Savage Girl, 1932,* six sheet, fine cond., (linen), (12-12-92, Hollywd Poster, #176, illus.), (BP 564, DM 1386, FR 4752, Y 108,897).

$1870* *Scar-Face, Warner Brothers, 1932,* title lobby card, very fine cond., Stanley Caidin Coll., (09-12-92, Sotheby-NY, #212, illus.), 11 x 14 in., (27.9 x 35.6 cm.), (BP 989, DM 2780, FR 9421, Y 232,529).

$660* *The Scarlet Clue, 1945,* three sheet, near mint cond., (linen), (12-12-92, Hollywd Poster, #170, illus.), (BP 423, DM 1040, FR 3564, Y 81,673).

$6050* *The Scarlet Empress, Paramount, 1934,* half-sheet, very fine cond., Stanley Caidin Coll., (09-12-92, Sotheby-NY, #69, illus.), 22 x 28 in., (55.9 x 71.1 cm.), linen backed (BP 3199, DM 8994, FR 30,479, Y 752,300).

$7700* *The Scarlet Empress, Paramount, 1934,* orig. French poster, cond. A, linen backed, (12-14-92, Christie-E, #253, illus.), 63 x 47 in., (160 x 119.4 cm.), (BP 4923, DM 12,101, FR 41,243, Y 952,617).

$3850* *The Scarlet Empress, Paramount, 1934,* jumbo window card, cond. B, (12-14-92, Christie-E, #251, illus.), 28 x 22 in., (71.1 x 55.9 cm.), (BP 2462, DM 6051, FR 20,621, Y 476,308).

$2860* *The Scarlet Letter, MGM, 1926: Set Of Eight,* lobby cards, cond. A, (12-14-92, Christie-E, #84, illus.), each 11 x 14 in., (27.9 x 35.6 cm.), (BP 1829, DM 4495, FR 15,319, Y 353,829).

$385* *Scarlet Street, 1945,* fine cond., (linen), (12-12-92, Hollywd Poster, #2, illus.), (BP 247, DM 607, FR 2079, Y 47,643).

BI *"The Scarlett Empress", 1934,* Paramount, window card, cond. C, est. $2/3,000, (06-05-93, Camden, #104, illus.), 22 x 14 in., (55.9 x 35.6 cm.), on linen.

$3520* *The Sea Hawk, 1940,* fine cond., (12-12-92, Hollywd Poster, #44, illus.), (BP 2257, DM 5546, FR 19,006, Y 435,590).

$4400* *The Sea Hawk, Warner Brothers, 1940,* three-sheet, cond. B, linen backed, (12-14-92, Christie-E, #93, illus.), 81 x 41 in., (205.7 x 104.1 cm.), (BP 2813, DM 6915, FR 23,567, Y 544,352).

$6600* *Sea Scouts, Disney, 1939,* one-sheet, cond. A, linen backed, (12-14-92, Christie-E, #104, illus.), 41 x 27 in., (104.1 x 68.6 cm.), (BP 4220, DM 10,372, FR 35,351, Y 816,529).

$330* *"The Sea Wolf", 1941,* Warner Bros., one-sheet, cond. C, (06-05-93, Camden, #308, illus.), 41 x 27 in., (104.1 x 68.6 cm.), (BP 217, DM 535, FR 1803, Y 35,400).

$550* *The Searchers, 1956,* insert, fine cond., (12-12-92, Hollywd Poster, #304, illus.), (BP 353, DM 867, FR 2970, Y 68,061).

$880* *The Second Floor Mystery, Warner Brothers, 1930,* one-sheet, very fine cond., Stanely Caidin Coll., (09-12-92, Sotheby-NY, #221, illus.), 41 x 27 in., (104.1 x 68.6 cm.), linen backed (BP 465, DM 1308, FR 4433, Y 109,426).

$303* *Secret Agent, 1936,* near mint cond., (12-12-92, Hollywd Poster, #222, illus.), lobby card (BP 194, DM 477, FR 1636, Y 37,495).

$1320* *Secret Agent, Gaumont British, 1936,* half-sheet, cond. B, folded, (12-14-92, Christie-E, #63, illus.), 22 x 28 in., (55.9 x 71.1 cm.), (BP 844, DM 2074, FR 7070, Y 163,306).

$138* *Secret Valley, 1936,* near mint cond., (paper), (12-12-92, Hollywd Poster, #85, illus.), stone litho (BP 88, DM 217, FR 745, Y 17,077).

$1210* *Senor Daredevil, First National Picture, 1926,* one-sheet, very fine cond., Stanley Caidin Coll., (09-12-92, Sotheby-NY, #244, illus.), 41 x 27 in., (104.1 x 68.6 cm.), linen backed (BP 640, DM 1799, FR 6096, Y 150,460).

$1650* *Senor Droopy, Tex Avery, 1948,* near mint cond., (linen), (12-12-92, Hollywd Poster, #105, illus.), (BP 1058, DM 2600, FR 8909, Y 204,183).

$440* *"Sergeant York", 1941,* Warner Bros., one-sheet, cond. B, (06-05-93, Camden, #309, illus.), 41 x 27 in., (104.1 x 68.6 cm.), (BP 290, DM 713, FR 2404, Y 47,200).

$715* *Seven Keys To Baldpate, 1929,* fine cond., (linen), (12-12-92, Hollywd Poster, #47, illus.), (BP 458, DM 1127, FR 3861, Y 88,479).

$605* *The Seven Year Itch, 1955,* fine cond., (linen), (12-12-92, Hollywd Poster, #239, illus.), (BP 388, DM 953, FR 3267, Y 74,867).

$1540* *The Seven Year Itch, 1955,* fine cond., (linen), (12-12-92, Hollywd Poster, #197, illus.), (BP 987, DM 2426, FR 8315, Y 190,570).

$1870* *The Seven Year Itch, 20th Century Fox, 1955,* one-sheet, very fine cond., Stanley Caidin Coll., (09-12-92, Sotheby-NY, #310, illus.), 41 x 27 in., (104.1 x 68.6 cm.), linen backed (BP 989, DM 2780, FR 9421, Y 232,529).

$2750* *The Seven Year Itch, 20th Century Fox, 1955,* three-sheet, cond. A, linen backed, (12-14-92, Christie-E, #234, illus.), 81 x 41 in., (205.7 x 104.1 cm.), (BP 1758, DM 4322, FR 14,730, Y 340,220).

$990* *The Seven Year Itch, 20th Century Fox, 1955: Set Of Eight,* lobby cards, very fine cond., Stanley Caidin Coll., (09-12-92, Sotheby-NY, #311, illus.), 11 x 14 in., (27.9 x 35.6 cm.), (BP 524, DM 1472, FR 4987, Y 123,104).

BI *Sexy Al Neon, c. 1960,* orig. Italian, cond. B+, linen backed, est. $4/600, (03-18-93, Swann, #196, illus.), 55 x 39 in., (139.7 x 99.1 cm.), .

$605* *The Shadow Laughs, Trojan Pictures, 1933,* one-sheet, very fine cond., Stanley Caidin Coll., (09-12-92, Sotheby-NY, #80, illus.), 41 x 27 in., (104.1 x 68.6 cm.), linen backed (BP 320, DM 899, FR 3048, Y 75,230).

$825* *Shadows Of Paris, Paramount, 1924,* one-sheet, cond. A, linen backed, (12-14-92, Christie-E, #284, illus.), 41 x 27 in., (104.1 x 68.6 cm.), (BP 527, DM 1297, FR 4419, Y 102,066).

$440* *Shall We Dance, 1937,* fine cond., (12-12-92, Hollywd Poster, #216, illus.), lobby card (BP 282, DM 693, FR 2376, Y 54,449).

$825* *Shall We Dance, 1937,* fine cond., (12-12-92, Hollywd Poster, #331, illus.), jumbo w/c (BP 529, DM 1300, FR 4455, Y 102,091).

BI *Shanghai Empress, Paramount, 1932,* jumbo lobby card, fine cond., Stanley Caidin Coll., est. $2/3,000, (09-12-92, Sotheby-NY, #71, illus.), 17 x 14 in., (43.2 x 35.6 cm.), linen backed.

$770* *Shanghai Express, 1931,* restored, very good cond., (12-12-92, Hollywd Poster, #135, illus.), window card (BP 494, DM 1213, FR 4158, Y 95,285).

$5775* *She Done Him Wrong, 1933,* fine cond., (linen), (12-12-92, Hollywd Poster, #273, illus.), (BP 3703, DM 9099, FR 31,183, Y 714,639).

$4620* *She Done Him Wrong, Paramount, 1933,* three-sheet, cond. A, linen backed, (12-14-92, Christie-E, #50, illus.), 81 x 41 in., (205.7 x 104.1 cm.), (BP 2954, DM 7261, FR 24,746, Y 571,570).

$605* *She Made Her Bed, Paramount , 1934,* one-sheet, cond. A, linen backed, (12-14-92, Christie-E, #8, illus.), 41 x 27 in., (104.1 x 68.6 cm.), (BP 387, DM 951, FR 3240, Y 74,848).

$1320* *She Wore A Yellow Ribbon, RKO, 1949,* one-sheet, cond. A, paper backed, (12-14-92, Christie-E, #147, illus.), 41 x 27 in., (104.1 x 68.6 cm.), (BP 844, DM 2074, FR 7070, Y 163,306).

$1650* *She, RKO, 1935,* three-sheet, fine cond., Stanley Caidin Coll., (09-12-92, Sotheby-NY, #297, illus.), 81 x 41 in., (205.7 x 104.1 cm.), (BP 873, DM 2453, FR 8312, Y 205,173).

$825* *The Sheik, 1922,* near mint cond., (12-12-92, Hollywd Poster, #117, illus.), lobby card (BP 529, DM 1300, FR 4455, Y 102,091).

$1320* *The Sheik, 1922,* near mint cond., (12-12-92, Hollywd Poster, #118, illus.), lobby card (BP 846, DM 2080, FR 7127, Y 163,346).

$3080* *The Sheik, 1922,* near mint cond., (12-12-92, Hollywd Poster, #116, illus.), title card (BP 1975, DM 4853, FR 16,631, Y 381,141).

$935* *The Shepherd King, Fox, 1923,* one-sheet, cond. A, linen backed, (12-14-92, Christie-E, #6, illus.), 41 x 27 in., (104.1 x 68.6 cm.), (BP 598, DM 1469, FR 5008, Y 115,675).

$1650* *"Sherlock Holmes And The Voice Of Terror", 1942,* Universal, three-sheet, cond. B, (06-05-93, Camden, #112, illus.), 81 x 41 in., (205.7 x 104.1 cm.), on linen (BP 1086, DM 2675, FR 9016, Y 177,001).

$605* *Sherlock Holmes, 1922,* near mint cond., (12-12-92, Hollywd Poster, #289, illus.), title card (BP 388, DM 953, FR 3267, Y 74,867).

$3300* *Sherlock Holmes, 1939,* French, cond. B, linen backed, (03-18-93, Swann, #138, illus.), 63 x 47 in., (160 x 119.4 cm.), (BP 2226, DM 5423, FR 18,487, Y 384,034).

$605* *Sherlock Holmes/Voice Of Terror, 1942,* Kraft paper backed, three sheet, fine cond., (paper), (12-12-92, Hollywd Poster, #173, illus.), (BP 388, DM 953, FR 3267, Y 74,867).

$659* *The Shooting Of Dan McGoo, M.G.M., 1944,* cond. A, one-sheet, linen-backed, (12-17-92, Christie-S. Ken, #391, illus.), 41 x 27 in., (104.1 x 68.6 cm.), poster (BP 418, DM 1029, FR 3515, Y 80,988).

$1045* *The Shooting Of Dan McGoo, MGM, 1944,* one-sheet, cond. A, linen backed, (12-14-92, Christie-E, #273, illus.), 41 x 27 in., (104.1 x 68.6 cm.), (BP 668, DM 1642, FR 5597, Y 129,284).

$660* *The Shopworn Angel, Paramount, 1928,* insert, very fine cond., Stanley Caidin Coll., (09-12-92, Sotheby-NY, #88, illus.), 36 x 14 in., (91.4 x 35.6 cm.), (BP 349, DM 981, FR 3325, Y 82,069).

$605* *A Short Life And A Merry One, Edison, 1913,* one-sheet, cond. A, linen backed, (12-14-92, Christie-E, #195, illus.), 41 x 27 in., (104.1 x 68.6 cm.), (BP 387, DM 951, FR 3240, Y 74,848).

BI *Showboat (Teater Baten), 1936,* Swedish, linen backed, est. $2/3,000, (03-18-93, Swann, #183, illus.), 39 x 27 in., (99.1 x 68.6 cm.), .

BI *Side Show, Warner, 1931,* one-sheet, cond. A-, est. $4/700, (03-18-93, Swann, #184, illus.), .

$1100* *Sidewalks Of New York, MGM, 1931,* one-sheet, fine cond., Stanley Caidin Coll., (09-12-92, Sotheby-NY, #262, illus.), 41 x 27 in., (104.1 x 68.6 cm.), linen backed (BP 582, DM 1635, FR 5542, Y 136,782).

$715* *The Silent Witness, Fox, 1931,* one-sheet, cond. A, linen backed, (12-14-92, Christie-E, #210, illus.), 41 x 27 in., (104.1 x 68.6 cm.), (BP 457, DM 1124, FR 3830, Y 88,457).

$385* *Silk Stockings, MGM, 1957: Three,* one-sheet, 2 different lobby cards, (03-18-93, Swann, #190, illus.), (BP 260, DM 633, FR 2157, Y 44,804).

$935* *"Silver Blaze", 1937,* British, Associated British, three-sheet, cond. B, (06-05-93, Camden, #111, illus.), 87 x 40 in., (221 x 101.6 cm.), restored on linen after catalogue photography (BP 615, DM 1516, FR 5109, Y 100,300).

BI *The Sin Of Madelon Claudet (La Faute), MGM, 1931,* very fine cond., Belgian poster, Stanley Caidin Coll., est. $6/900, (09-12-92, Sotheby-NY, #45, illus.), 33 x 24 in., (83.8 x 61 cm.), linen backed.

$19,800* *The Sin Of Nora Moran, Majestic Pictures, 1933,* one-sheet, cond. B, linen backed, (12-14-92, Christie-E, #7, illus.), 41 x 27 in., (104.1 x 68.6 cm.), (BP 12,660, DM 31,117, FR 106,052, Y 2,449,586).

$1430* *"Singin' In The Rain", 1952,* MGM, three-sheet, cond. B, (11-07-92, Camden, #184, illus.), 81 x 41 in., (205.7 x 104.1 cm.), restored on linen (BP 935, DM 2283, FR 7717, Y 176,500).

$1320* *Singin' In The Rain, MGM, 1952,* one-sheet, cond. A, linen backed, (12-14-92, Christie-E, #232, illus.), 41 x 27 in., (104.1 x 68.6 cm.), (BP 844, DM 2074, FR 7070, Y 163,306).

$1100* *Sinners In The Sun, Paramount, 1932,* half-sheet, fine cond., Stanley Caidin Coll., (09-12-92, Sotheby-NY, #44, illus.), 22 x 28 in., (55.9 x 71.1 cm.), linen backed (BP 582, DM 1635, FR 5542, Y 136,782).

$495* *Sins Of Man, 20th Century Fox, 1936,* one-sheet, cond. A, linen backed, (12-14-92, Christie-E, #58, illus.), 41 x 27 in., (104.1 x 68.6 cm.), (BP 316, DM 778, FR 2651, Y 61,240).

$605* *The Slacker, Bad Girl From Hell, 1917,* very good cond., (linen), (12-12-92, Hollywd Poster, #306, illus.), (BP 388, DM 953, FR 3267, Y 74,867).

$1210* *Sleeping Beauty, Walt Disney, 1959,* near mint cond., (paper), (12-12-92, Hollywd Poster, #107, illus.), (BP 776, DM 1906, FR 6533, Y 149,734).

$440* *Sleepy Time Tom, Tom & Jerry, 1950,* near mint cond., (linen), (12-12-92, Hollywd Poster, #109, illus.), (BP 282, DM 693, FR 2376, Y 54,449).

$3300* *Sleepy-Time Donald, Walt Disney Productions, 1947,* one-sheet, fine cond., Stanley Caidin Coll., (09-12-92, Sotheby-NY, #291, illus.), 41 x 27 in., (104.1 x 68.6 cm.), linen backed (BP 1745, DM 4906, FR 16,625, Y 410,346).

$248* *Smash-Up, 1947,* British, fine cond., (linen), (12-12-92, Hollywd Poster, #203, illus.), (BP 159, DM 391, FR 1339, Y 30,689).

$770* *Smash-Up, Universal, 1946,* one-sheet, cond. A, linen backed, (12-14-92, Christie-E, #219, illus.), 41 x 27 in., (104.1 x 68.6 cm.), (BP 492, DM 1210, FR 4124, Y 95,262).

$1100* *"Smitten Kitten", 1951,* MGM, cond. A, one-sheet, (11-07-92, Camden, #25, illus.), 41 x 27 in., (104.1 x 68.6 cm.), on linen (BP 719, DM 1756, FR 5936, Y 135,769).

$1870* *Snow White And The Seven Dwarfs, 1937,* one-sheet, cond. C+, linen backed, (03-18-93, Swann, #188, illus.), (BP 1261, DM 3073, FR 10,476, Y 217,619).

$9350* *Snow White And The Seven Dwarfs, RKO-Disney, 1937,* insert, (03-18-93, Swann, #187, illus.), (BP 6306, DM 15,366, FR 52,381, Y 1,088,095).

$9350* *Snow White And The Seven Dwarfs, Walt Disney Productions, 1937,* insert, very fine cond., Stanley Caidin Coll., (09-12-92, Sotheby-NY, #289, illus.), 36 x 14 in., (91.4 x 35.6 cm.), (BP 4944, DM 13,899, FR 47,103, Y 1,162,646).

BI *"Snows Of Kilimanjaro", 1952 and "The Macomber Affair", 1947: Two,* one-sheets, est. $3/400, (03-18-93, Swann, #191, illus.), .

$248* *"So Ends Our Night", "Mannequin", "Sing You Sinners", and "Goodbye Mr. Chips": Four,* Andy Warhol Estate, (04-16-93, DuMouchelle, #2531), 41 x 27 in., (104.1 x 68.6 cm.), posters (BP 163, DM 401, FR 1354, Y 27,887).

$2200* *"Some Like It Hot", 1959,* United Artists, cond. A, restored on linen, (11-07-92, Camden, #408, illus.), 77 x 58 in., (195.6 x 147.3 cm.), restored on linen (BP 1438, DM 3513, FR 11,873, Y 271,538).

$550* *Some Like It Hot, 1959,* fine cond., (linen), (12-12-92, Hollywd Poster, #240, illus.), (BP 353, DM 867, FR 2970, Y 68,061).

$880* *Some Like It Hot, United Artists, 1959,* one-sheet, very fine cond., Stanley Caidin Coll., (09-12-92, Sotheby-NY, #312, illus.), 41 x 27 in., (104.1 x 68.6 cm.), linen backed (BP 465, DM 1308, FR 4433, Y 109,426).

$4400* *Son Of Frankenstein, 1938,* three-sheet, cond. C+, linen backed, (03-18-93, Swann, #102, illus.), 81 x 41 in., (205.7 x 104.1 cm.), (BP 2967, DM 7231, FR 24,650, Y 512,045).

$11,000* *Son Of Frankenstein, Universal, 1939,* three-sheet, cond. A, linen backed, (12-14-92, Christie-E, #22, illus.), 81 x 41 in., (205.7 x 104.1 cm.), (BP 7033, DM 17,287, FR 58,918, Y 1,360,881).

$1540* *The Son Of Tarzan, The National Film Co., 1920,* one-sheet, very fine cond., Stanley Caidin Coll., (09-12-92, Sotheby-NY, #118, illus.), 41 x 27 in., (104.1 x 68.6 cm.), linen backed (BP 814, DM 2289, FR 7758, Y 191,495).

$2860* *The Son Of The Sheik, 1926,* insert, fine cond., (12-12-92, Hollywd Poster, #76, illus.), (BP 1834, DM 4506, FR 15,443, Y 353,917).

$13,200* *The Son Of The Sheik, United Artists, 1926,* one-sheet, very fine cond., Stanley Caidin Coll., (09-12-92, Sotheby-NY, #54, illus.), 41 x 27 in., (104.1 x 68.6 cm.), linen backed (BP 6980, DM 19,622, FR 66,499, Y 1,641,383).

$1650* *Son Of The Sheik, United Artists, 1926: Six,* lobby cards, fine cond., Stanley Caidin Coll., (09-12-92, Sotheby-NY, #55, illus.), 11 x 14 in., (27.9 x 35.6 cm.), (BP 873, DM 2453, FR 8312, Y 205,173).

$110* *The Song Of Life, 1922,* fine cond., (12-12-92, Hollywd Poster, #229, illus.), (BP 71, DM 173, FR 594, Y 13,612).

$6600* *The Song Of Songs, Paramount, 1933,* insert, very fine cond., Stanley Caidin Coll., (09-12-92, Sotheby-NY, #78, illus.), 36 x 14 in., (91.4 x 35.6 cm.), (BP 3490, DM 9811, FR 33,249, Y 820,691).

$275* *Song Of The Thin Man, Loews, 1947,* half-sheet, cond. A, paper backed, (03-18-93, Swann, #197, illus.), (BP 185, DM 452, FR 1541, Y 32,003).

$990* *Sons Of The Desert, Hal Roach, 1933,* lobby card, very fine cond., Stanley Caidin Coll., (09-12-92, Sotheby-NY, #163, illus.), 11 x 14 in., (27.9 x 35.6 cm.), (BP 524, DM 1472, FR 4987, Y 123,104).

$2475* *Sons Of The Desert, Hal Roach, 1933,* lobby card, very fine cond., Stanley Caidin Coll., (09-12-92, Sotheby-NY, #162, illus.), 11 x 14 in., (27.9 x 35.6 cm.), (BP 1309, DM 3679, FR 12,469, Y 307,759).

$2090* *Sons Of The Desert, MGM, 1933,* lobby card, cond. A, (12-14-92, Christie-E, #291, illus.), 11 x 14 in., (27.9 x 35.6 cm.), (BP 1336, DM 3285, FR 11,194, Y 258,567).

$220* *Soul Of The Slums,* near mint cond., (12-12-92, Hollywd Poster, #226, illus.), (BP 141, DM 347, FR 1188, Y 27,224).

$440* *Sparrows, 1926,* rolled, half sheet, fine cond., (12-12-92, Hollywd Poster, #241, illus.), (BP 282, DM 693, FR 2376, Y 54,449).

$825* *Speed, Pathe, 1922,* one-sheet, cond. A, linen backed, (12-14-92, Christie-E, #222, illus.), 41 x 27 in., (104.1 x 68.6 cm.), (BP 527, DM 1297, FR 4419, Y 102,066).

$3080* *Speedy, Paramount, 1928,* three-sheet, cond. A, linen backed, (12-14-92, Christie-E, #294, illus.), 81 x 41 in., (205.7 x 104.1 cm.), (BP 1969, DM 4840, FR 16,497, Y 381,047).

$468* *"Spellbound", 1945,* Untied Artists, half-sheet, cond. B, (06-05-93, Camden, #131, illus.), 22 x 28 in., (55.9 x 71.1 cm.), (BP 308, DM 759, FR 2557, Y 50,204).

$193* *Spellbound, 1945,* fine cond., (12-12-92, Hollywd Poster, #267, illus.), title card (BP 124, DM 304, FR 1042, Y 23,883).

BI *"Spitfire", 1934,* RKO, window card, cond. B, est. $4/700, (06-05-93, Camden, #249, illus.), 22 x 14 in., (55.9 x 35.6 cm.), on linen.

$660* *The Splendid Road, First National Picture, 1925,* one-sheet, very fine cond., Stanley Caidin Coll., (09-12-92, Sotheby-NY, #240, illus.), 41 x 27 in., (104.1 x 68.6 cm.), linen backed (BP 349, DM 981, FR 3325, Y 82,069).

$550* *Sporting Youth, Universal, 1924,* one-sheet, cond. A, linen backed, (12-14-92, Christie-E, #211, illus.), 41 x 27 in., (104.1 x 68.6 cm.), (BP 352, DM 864, FR 2946, Y 68,044).

$660* *Springtime For Tom, Tom & Jerry, 1946,* fine cond., (linen), (12-12-92, Hollywd Poster, #313, illus.), (BP 423, DM 1040, FR 3564, Y 81,673).

$1100* *Spy Smasher, Republic, 1942,* one-sheet, linen backed, (12-14-92, Christie-E, #228, illus.), 41 x 27 in., (104.1 x 68.6 cm.), (BP 703, DM 1729, FR 5892, Y 136,088).

$3080* *The St. Louis Kid, Warner Brothers, 1934,* one-sheet, cond. A, linen backed, (12-14-92, Christie-E, #42, illus.), 41 x 27 in., (104.1 x 68.6 cm.), (BP 1969, DM 4840, FR 16,497, Y 381,047).

$1650* *Stagecoach, 1939,* fine cond., (12-12-92, Hollywd Poster, #260, illus.), lobby card (BP 1058, DM 2600, FR 8909, Y 204,183).

$880* *Stand Up And Cheer, 1934,* near mint cond., (linen), (12-12-92, Hollywd Poster, #230, illus.), (BP 564, DM 1386, FR 4752, Y 108,897).

$13,200* *Star Of Midnight, RKO, 1935,* three-sheet, cond. A, linen backed, (12-14-92, Christie-E, #70, illus.), 81 x 41 in., (205.7 x 104.1 cm.), (BP 8440, DM 20,745, FR 70,702, Y 1,633,057).

$248* *"State Of The Union", 1948,* MGM, one-sheet, cond. A, (06-05-93, Camden, #240, illus.), 41 x 27 in., (104.1 x 68.6 cm.), on linen (BP 163, DM 402, FR 1355, Y 26,604).

$660* *State's Attorney, RKO, 1932,* insert, near mint cond., Stanley Caidin Coll., (09-12-92, Sotheby-NY, #75, illus.), 36 x 14 in., (91.4 x 35.6 cm.), (BP 349, DM 981, FR 3325, Y 82,069).

$1210* *Stella Dallas, United Artists, 1937,* one-sheet, cond. A, linen backed, (12-14-92, Christie-E, #24, illus.), 41 x 27 in., (104.1 x 68.6 cm.), (BP 774, DM 1902, FR 6481, Y 149,697).

$715* *The Stigma, Essanay Film, c. 1914,* one sheet, very fine cond., Stanley Caidin Coll., (09-12-92, Sotheby-NY, #22, illus.), 41 x 27 in., (104.1 x 68.6 cm.), linen backed (BP 378, DM 1063, FR 3602, Y 88,908).

$495* *Stolen Holiday, 1937,* fine cond., (linen), (12-12-92, Hollywd Poster, #88, illus.), (BP 317, DM 780, FR 2673, Y 61,255).

$1210* *Stormy Weather, 20th Century Fox, 1943,* Italian, cond. A, linen backed, (12-14-92, Christie-E, #131, illus.), 39 x 28 in., (99.1 x 71.1 cm.), (BP 774, DM 1902, FR 6481, Y 149,697).

$550* *The Story Of Vernon And Irene Castle, RKO, 1939,* title lobby card, very fine cond., Stanley Caidin Coll., (09-12-92, Sotheby-NY, #157, illus.), 11 x 14 in., (27.9 x 35.6 cm.), (BP 291, DM 818, FR 2771, Y 68,391).

$193* *Strangers On A Train, 1951,* half sheet, near mint cond., (12-12-92, Hollywd Poster, #247, illus.), (BP 124, DM 304, FR 1042, Y 23,883).

$330* *Street Of Chance, 1942,* near mint cond., (paper), (12-12-92, Hollywd Poster, #177, illus.), (BP 212, DM 520, FR 1782, Y 40,837).

$1100* *Street Scene, United Artists, 1931,* one-sheet, cond. A, linen backed, (12-14-92, Christie-E, #142, illus.), 41 x 27 in., (104.1 x 68.6 cm.), (BP 703, DM 1729, FR 5892, Y 136,088).

$550* *Strike Up The Band, MGM, 1940,* one-sheet, very good cond., Stanley Caidin Coll., (09-12-92, Sotheby-NY, #280, illus.), 41 x 27 in., (104.1 x 68.6 cm.), linen backed (BP 291, DM 818, FR 2771, Y 68,391).

$385* *Suddenly, Last Summer, Columbia, 1959,* three-sheet, cond. B+, linen backed, (03-18-93, Swann, #198, illus.), (BP 260, DM 633, FR 2157, Y 44,804).

$116* *"Sullivan's Travels", "Campus Confessions", "Small Town Girl", and "Always Goodbye": Four,* Andy Warhol Estate, (04-16-93, DuMouchelle, #2530), 41 x 27 in., (104.1 x 68.6 cm.), posters (BP 76, DM 187, FR 633, Y 13,044).

$2475* *"Sullivan's Travels", 1941,* Paramount, one-sheet, cond. B, (11-07-92, Camden, #314, illus.), 41 x 27 in., (104.1 x 68.6 cm.), restored on linen (BP 1618, DM 3952, FR 13,357, Y 305,480).

$1045* *Sullivan's Travels, 1941,* very good cond., (linen), (12-12-92, Hollywd Poster, #299, illus.), (BP 670, DM 1646, FR 5643, Y 129,316).

$192* *Sundown (Cuando Muere El Dia), 1941,* Argentinian, linen backed, (03-18-93, Swann, #199, illus.), 43 x 29 in., (109.2 x 73.7 cm.), (BP 129, DM 316, FR 1076, Y 22,344).

$83* *"Sunny", "Prairie Law", "Where Are Your Children" and "The Southern": Four,* Andy Warhol Estate, (04-16-93, DuMouchelle, #2533), 41 x 27 in., (104.1 x 68.6 cm.), poster (BP 54, DM 134, FR 453, Y 9333).

$1210* *Sunrise, Fox, 1927,* orig. German poster, cond. A, linen backed, (12-14-92, Christie-E, #255, illus.), 55 x 37 in., (139.7 x 94 cm.), (BP 774, DM 1902, FR 6481, Y 149,697).

$3850* *"Sunset Boulevard", 1950,* Paramount, one-sheet, cond. A, (11-07-92, Camden, #323, illus.), 41 x 27 in., (104.1 x 68.6 cm.), on linen (BP 2517, DM 6147, FR 20,777, Y 475,191).

$660* *Sunset Boulevard, Paramount, 1950,* jumbo window card, (03-18-93, Swann, #210, illus.), (BP 445, DM 1085, FR 3697, Y 76,807).

$990* *Sunset Boulevard, Paramount, 1950,* half-sheet, fine cond., Stanley Caidin Coll., (09-12-92, Sotheby-NY, #24, illus.), 22 x 28 in., (55.9 x 71.1 cm.), half-sheet, linen backed (BP 524, DM 1472, FR 4987, Y 123,104).

$3300* *Superman And The Mole Men, Lippert Pictures, 1951,* one-sheet, cond. A, linen backed, (12-14-92, Christie-E, #39, illus.), 41 x 27 in., (104.1 x 68.6 cm.), (BP 2110, DM 5186, FR 17,675, Y 408,264).

$1045* *Superman, Columbia, 1948,* one-sheet, cond. A, linen backed, (12-14-92, Christie-E, #38, illus.), 41 x 27 in., (104.1 x 68.6 cm.), (BP 668, DM 1642, FR 5597, Y 129,284).

BI *Svengali, Warner Brothers, 1931,* very fine cond., Spanish poster, Stanley Caidin Coll., est. $2/3,000, (09-12-92, Sotheby-NY, #74, illus.), 39 x 27 in., (99.1 x 68.6 cm.), linen backed.

$330* *Swanee River, 1939,* insert, near mint cond., (12-12-92, Hollywd Poster, #72, illus.), (BP 212, DM 520, FR 1782, Y 40,837).

$248* *Sweet Rose O'Grady, 1943,* near mint cond., (linen), (12-12-92, Hollywd Poster, #294, illus.), (BP 159, DM 391, FR 1339, Y 30,689).

$440* *Sweethearts, MGM, 1938,* insert, very fine cond., Stanley Caidin Coll., (09-12-92, Sotheby-NY, #153, illus.), 36 x 14 in., (91.4 x 35.6 cm.), (BP 233, DM 654, FR 2217, Y 54,713).

$385* *Swing Time, 1936,* near mint cond., (12-12-92, Hollywd Poster, #215, illus.), lobby card (BP 247, DM 607, FR 2079, Y 47,643).

$990* *Swing Time, 1936,* fine cond., (12-12-92, Hollywd Poster, #214, illus.), title card (BP 635, DM 1560, FR 5346, Y 122,510).

$1320* *Swing Time, RKO, 1936,* window card, very fine cond., Stanley Caidin Coll., (09-12-92, Sotheby-NY, #156, illus.), 22 x 14 in., (55.9 x 35.6 cm.), linen backed (BP 698, DM 1962, FR 6650, Y 164,138).

BI *Swing Your Lady, Warner, 1938,* one-sheet, cond. B, est. $2/300, (03-18-93, Swann, #49, illus.), .

$83* *The Sword In The Stone, 1963,* near mint cond., (linen), Walt Disney, Danish, (12-12-92, Hollywd Poster, #61, illus.), (BP 53, DM 131, FR 448, Y 10,271).

$990* *A Tale Of Two Cities, 1935,* insert, fine cond., (12-12-92, Hollywd Poster, #74, illus.), (BP 635, DM 1560, FR 5346, Y 122,510).

$330* *Tales Of Manhattan, 1942,* near mint cond., (12-12-92, Hollywd Poster, #303, illus.), (BP 212, DM 520, FR 1782, Y 40,837).

$1430* *"The Talk Of The Town", 1942,* Columbia, one-sheet, cond. B, (11-07-92, Camden, #270, illus.), 41 x 27 in., (104.1 x 68.6 cm.), on linen (BP 935, DM 2283, FR 7717, Y 176,500).

BI *Taming Of The Shrew, United Artists, 1929,* insert, very fine cond., Stanley Caidin Coll., est. $1/1,500, (09-12-92, Sotheby-NY, #108, illus.), 36 x 14 in., (91.4 x 35.6 cm.), .

$6050* *Tarzan And His Mate, MGM, 1934,* one-sheet, very fine cond., Stanley Caidin Coll., (09-12-92, Sotheby-NY, #117, illus.), 41 x 27 in., (104.1 x 68.6 cm.), linen backed (BP 3199, DM 8994, FR 30,479, Y 752,300).

BI *Tarzan Escapes (Tarzan S'Evade), 1936,* French, cond. B, linen backed, est. $4/600, (03-18-93, Swann, #215, illus.), 28 x 22 in., (71.1 x 55.9 cm.), .

$550* *Tarzan Escapes, 1936,* near mint cond., (12-12-92, Hollywd Poster, #265, illus.), lobby card (BP 353, DM 867, FR 2970, Y 68,061).

$770* *Tarzan Escapes, MGM, 1936,* jumbo window card, fine cond., Stanley Caidin Coll., (09-12-92, Sotheby-NY, #119, illus.), 28 x 22 in., (71.1 x 55.9 cm.), (BP 407, DM FR 3879, Y 95,747).

$30,800* *Tarzan Of The Apes, First National, 1918,* one-sheet, cond. A, linen backed, (12-14-92, Christie-E, #206, illus.), 41 x 27 in., (104.1 x 68.6 cm.), (BP 19,693, DM 48,405, FR 164,971, Y 3,810,466).

$3575* *Tarzan, The Ape Man, MGM, 1932: Four,* lobby cards, very fine cond., Stanley Caidin Coll., (09-12-92, Sotheby-NY, #116, illus.), 11 x 14 in., (27.9 x 35.6 cm.), (BP 1891, DM 5314, FR 18,010, Y 444,541).

$1100* *Tea With A Kick, Associate Exhibitors, 1923,* one-sheet, good cond., Stanley Caidin Coll., (09-12-92, Sotheby-NY, #1, illus.), 41 x 27 in., (104.1 x 68.6 cm.), linen backed (BP 582, DM 1635, FR 5542, Y 136,782).

$440* *The Telephone Girl, Paramount, 1927,* insert, very fine cond., Stanley Caidin Coll., (09-12-92, Sotheby-NY, #308, illus.), 36 x 14 in., (91.4 x 35.6 cm.), (BP 233, DM 654, FR 2217, Y 54,713).

BI *The Tempest, United Artists, 1928,* insert, near mint cond., Stanley Caidin Coll., est. 9/1,200, (09-12-92, Sotheby-NY, #73, illus.), 36 x 14 in., (91.4 x 35.6 cm.), .

$880* *The Temple Of Venus, Fox, 1923,* one-sheet, cond. B, linen backed, (12-14-92, Christie-E, #2, illus.), 41 x 27 in., (104.1 x 68.6 cm.), (BP 563, DM 1383, FR 4713, Y 108,870).

$1045* *Temptation, Micheaux Pictures, 1923,* one-sheet, cond. A, linen backed, (12-14-92, Christie-E, #129, illus.), 41 x 27 in., (104.1 x 68.6 cm.), (BP 668, DM 1642, FR 5597, Y 129,284).

$1100* *"The Ten Commandments", 1923,* Paramount, half-sheet, cond. C, (11-07-92, Camden, #176, illus.), 22 x 28 in., (55.9 x 71.1 cm.), (BP 719, DM 1756, FR 5936, Y 135,769).

$990* *Ten Modern Commandments, Paramount, 1927,* one-sheet, cond. A, linen backed, (12-14-92, Christie-E, #56, illus.), 41 x 27 in., (104.1 x 68.6 cm.), (BP 633, DM 1556, FR 5303, Y 122,479).

$770* *Ten Of Diamonds, Triangle Plays, 1917,* one-sheet, very fine cond., Stanley Caidin Coll., (09-12-92, Sotheby-NY, #79, illus.), 41 x 27 in., (104.1 x 68.6 cm.), linen backed (BP 407, DM 1145, FR 3879, Y 95,747).

$2475* *The Terror, William Fox, 1920,* one-sheet, good cond., Stanley Caidin Coll., (09-12-92, Sotheby-NY, #241, illus.), 29 x 41 in., (73.7 x 104.1 cm.), linen backed (BP 1309, DM 3679, FR 12,469, Y 307,759).

$1650* *"Tess Of The Storm Country", 1922,* Mary Pickford, one-sheet, cond. B, (11-07-92, Camden, #58, illus.), 41 x 27 in., (104.1 x 68.6 cm.), on paper (BP 1079, DM 2635, FR 8904, Y 203,653).

BI *"Test Pilot", 1938,* MGM, half-sheet, cond. B, est. $5/700, (06-05-93, Camden, #130, illus.), 22 x 18 in., (55.9 x 45.7 cm.), on linen.

$715* *Test Pilot, MGM, 1938,* insert, fine cond., Stanley Caidin Coll., (09-12-92, Sotheby-NY, #17, illus.), 36 x 14 in., (91.4 x 35.6 cm.), (BP 378, DM 1063, FR 3602, Y 88,908).

$1210* *Testament D'Orphee, 1960,* orig. French, cond. A, linen backed, (03-18-93, Swann, #24, illus.), 63 x 47 in., (160 x 119.4 cm.), (BP 816, DM 1988, FR 6779, Y 140,812).

$385* *Them, 1954,* fine cond., (12-12-92, Hollywd Poster, #146, illus.), (BP 247, DM 607, FR 2079, Y 47,643).

$990* *Them, Warner Bros., 1954,* insert, (03-18-93, Swann, #216, illus.), (BP 668, DM 1627, FR 5546, Y 115,210).

$990* *Theodora Goes Wild, Columbia, 1936,* one-sheet, cond. A, (12-14-92, Christie-E, #152, illus.), 41 x 27 in., (104.1 x 68.6 cm.), (BP 633, DM 1556, FR 5303, Y 122,479).

$330* *There's No Business Like Show Biz, 1954,* three sheet, fine cond., (linen), (12-12-92, Hollywd Poster, #169, illus.), (BP 212, DM 520, FR 1782, Y 40,837).

$4400* *They Died With Their Boots On (La Charge Fantastique), Warner Brothers, 1941,* very fine cond., Stanely Caidin Coll., (09-12-92, Sotheby-NY, #227, illus.), 63 x 94 in., (160 x 238.8 cm.), French 2-panel, linen backed (BP 2327, DM 6541, FR 22,166, Y 547,128).

$2200* *"Thicker Than Water", 1935,* MGM, one-sheet, cond. B, (11-07-92, Camden, #133, illus.), 41 x 27 in., (104.1 x 68.6 cm.), on paper (BP 1438, DM 3513, FR 11,873, Y 271,538).

BI *The Thief Of Bagdad, United Artists, 1924,* window card, good cond., Stanley Caidin Coll. est. $2/3,000, (09-12-92, Sotheby-NY, #110, illus.), 22 x 14 in., (55.9 x 35.6 cm.), linen backed.

$30,800* *The Thief Of Bagdad, United Artists, 1924,* one-sheet, cond. B, paper backed, (12-14-92, Christie-E, #135, illus.), 41 x 27 in., (104.1 x 68.6 cm.), (BP 19,693, DM 48,405, FR 164,971, Y 3,810,466).

$1100* *The Thief Of Bagdad, United Artists, 1940,* one-sheet, cond. A, linen backed, (12-14-92, Christie-E, #136, illus.), 41 x 27 in., (104.1 x 68.6 cm.), (BP 703, DM 1729, FR 5892, Y 136,088).

$550* *The Thing From Another World, RKO, 1951: Three,* one-sheet, half sheet, and Belgian, (03-18-93, Swann, #217, illus.), third 18 x 14 in., (45.7 x 35.6 cm.), (BP 371, DM 904, FR 3081, Y 64,006).

$22,000* *Things To Come, United Artists, 1936,* six-sheet, cond. A, linen backed, (12-14-92, Christie-E, #82, illus.), 81 x 81 in., (205.7 x 205.7 cm.), (BP 14,066, DM 34,575, FR 117,836, Y 2,721,762).

$660* *Think Fast, Mr. Moto, 1937,* fine cond., (linen), (12-12-92, Hollywd Poster, #281, illus.), (BP 423, DM 1040, FR 3564, Y 81,673).

$6050* *"This Gun For Hire", 1942,* Paramount, one-sheet, cond. B, (06-05-93, Camden, #25, illus.), 41 x 27 in., (104.1 x 68.6 cm.), (BP 3983, DM 9809, FR 33,060, Y 649,002).

BI *This Island Earth (Truslen Fra Verdensrummet), Universal, 1953,* Dutch, est. $700/1,000, (03-18-93, Swann, #218, illus.), 33 x 25 in., (83.8 x 63.5 cm.), .

$522* *This Island Earth, 1955: Two,* insert, (03-18-93, Swann, #35A, illus.), 24 x 82 in., (61 x 208.3 cm.), (BP 352, DM 858, FR 2924, Y 60,747).

$1213* *This Island Earth, Universal International, 1954,* cond. A, one-sheet, linen-backed, (12-17-92, Christie-S. Ken, #236, illus.), 41 x 27 in., (104.1 x 68.6 cm.), poster (BP 770, DM 1894, FR 6469, Y 149,072).

$2090* *This Island Earth, Universal, 1955,* cond. A, (12-14-92, Christie-E, #188, illus.), 60 x 40 in., (152.4 x 101.6 cm.), (BP 1336, DM 3285, FR 11,194, Y 258,567).

$412* *Thousands Cheer, MGM, 1943,* three-sheet, cond. C, linen backed, (03-18-93, Swann, #211, illus.), (BP 278, DM 677, FR 2308, Y 47,946).

$330* *The Three Caballeros, Walt Disney, 1944,* fine cond., (12-12-92, Hollywd Poster, #106, illus.), (BP 212, DM 520, FR 1782, Y 40,837).

BI *"The Three Musketeers", 1948 and "Lady In The Iron Mask", 1952: Two,* one-sheets, est. $3/400, (03-18-93, Swann, #212, illus.), .

$1320* *The Three Musketeers, Mascot, 1933,* one-sheet, cond. A, linen backed, (12-14-92, Christie-E, #224, illus.), 41 x 27 in., (104.1 x 68.6 cm.), (BP 844, DM 2074, FR 7070, Y 163,306).

$154* *Three On A Weekend, 20th Century, 1938,* cond. B+, one-sheet, linen backed, (03-18-93, Swann, #213, illus.), (BP 104, DM 253, FR 863, Y 17,922).

$220* *Thunderbirds, 1942,* near mint cond., (12-12-92, Hollywd Poster, #186, illus.), (BP 141, DM 347, FR 1188, Y 27,224).

$1210* *Thunderbolt, Paramount, 1929,* one-sheet, cond. B, linen backed, (12-14-92, Christie-E, #214, illus.), 41 x 27 in., (104.1 x 68.6 cm.), (BP 774, DM 1902, FR 6481, Y 149,697).

$248* *Tillie And Gus, 1933,* restored, very good cond., (12-12-92, Hollywd Poster, #143, illus.), window card (BP 159, DM 391, FR 1339, Y 30,689).

BI *The Time Machine, MGM, 1960,* one-sheet, autographed by Director George Pal, est. $4/600, (03-18-93, Swann, #219, illus.), .

$660* *Titanic, 20th Century Fox, 1953,* one-sheet & set of 8 lobby cards, (03-18-93, Swann, #214, illus.), (BP 445, DM 1085, FR 3697, Y 76,807).

$550* *To Love And Cherish, Lubin, 1910-1916,* one-sheet, very fine cond., Stanley Caidin Coll., (09-12-92, Sotheby-NY, #46, illus.), 41 x 27 in., (104.1 x 68.6 cm.), linen backed (BP 291, DM 818, FR 2771, Y 68,391).

$880* *To-Day We Live, MGM, 1933,* insert, near mint cond., Stanley Caidin Coll., (09-12-92, Sotheby-NY, #85, illus.), 36 x 14 in., (91.4 x 35.6 cm.), (BP 465, DM 1308, FR 4433, Y 109,426).

$715* *The Toast Of New York, RKO, 1937,* one-sheet, cond. A, linen backed, (12-14-92, Christie-E, #300, illus.), 41 x 27 in., (104.1 x 68.6 cm.), (BP 457, DM 1124, FR 3830, Y 88,457).

$825* *Tobacco Road, 20th Century Fox, 1941,* one-sheet, cond. A, paper backed, (12-14-92, Christie-E, #144, illus.), 41 x 27 in., (104.1 x 68.6 cm.), (BP 527, DM 1297, FR 4419, Y 102,066).

$605* *"Tobor The Great", 1954,* Republic, half-sheet, cond. A, unfolded, (06-05-93, Camden, #293, illus.), 22 x 28 in., (55.9 x 71.1 cm.), (BP 398, DM 981, FR 3306, Y 64,900).

$302* *Tobor The Great, Republic, 1954,* insert, (03-18-93, Swann, #220, illus.), (BP 204, DM 496, FR 1692, Y 35,145).

$277* *Tobor The Great, Republic, 1954,* British Quad., cond. A, linen-backed, (12-17-92, Christie-S. Ken, #394, illus.), 30 x 40 in., (76.2 x 101.6 cm.), poster (BP 176, DM 432, FR 1477, Y 34,042).

$1760* *Tol'Able David, First National Attraction, 1921,* one-sheet, very fine cond., Stanley Caidin Coll., (09-12-92, Sotheby-NY, #270, illus.), 41 x 27 in., (104.1 x 68.6 cm.), linen backed (BP 931, DM 2616, FR 8866, Y 218,851).

$2200* *Tom And Jerry In The Hollywood Bowl, MGM, 1950,* one-sheet, very fine cond., Stanley Caidin Coll., (09-12-92, Sotheby-NY, #294, illus.), 41 x 27 in., (104.1 x 68.6 cm.), linen backed (BP 1163, DM 3270, FR 11,083, Y 273,564).

$550* *Tony, Fox, c. 1925,* one-sheet, cond. A, linen backed, (12-14-92, Christie-E, #186, illus.), 41 x 27 in., (104.1 x 68.6 cm.), (BP 352, DM 864, FR 2946, Y 68,044).

BI *Top Hat, RKO, 1935,* half-sheet, good cond., Stanley Caidin Coll., est. $3/4,000, (09-12-92, Sotheby-NY, #155, illus.), 22 x 28 in., (55.9 x 71.1 cm.), linen backed.

$770* *Topper, 1937,* near mint cond., (linen), (12-12-92, Hollywd Poster, #280, illus.), (BP 494, DM 1213, FR 4158, Y 95,285).

$880* *Topsy And Eva, United Artists, 1927,* one-sheet, cond. B, linen backed, (12-14-92, Christie-E, #127, illus.), 41 x 27 in., (104.1 x 68.6 cm.), (BP 563, DM 1383, FR 4713, Y 108,870).

$248* *Tortilla Flat, 1942,* fine cond., (linen), (12-12-92, Hollywd Poster, #37, illus.), (BP 159, DM 391, FR 1339, Y 30,689).

$1650* *"La Tosca", 1911,* cond. D, missing bottom panel, (11-07-92, Camden, #296, illus.), 60 x 39 in., (152.4 x 99.1 cm.), on linen stretched over a wooden frame (BP 1079, DM 2635, FR 8904, Y 203,653).

$1320* *"Tower Of London", 1939,* Universal, six-sheet, cond. B, (11-07-92, Camden, #276, illus.), 81 x 81 in., (205.7 x

205.7 cm.), on linen (BP 863, DM 2108, FR 7124, Y 162,923).

$440* *The Tower Of London, 1939,* fine cond., (linen), (12-12-92, Hollywd Poster, #155, illus.), (BP 282, DM 693, FR 2376, Y 54,449).

$715* *Traffic In Souls, 1913,* near mint cond., (linen), (12-12-92, Hollywd Poster, #8, illus.), (BP 458, DM 1127, FR 3861, Y 88,479).

$1100* *The Trail Of The Lonesome Pine, Paramount, 1936,* insert, very fine cond., Stanley Caidin Coll., (09-12-92, Sotheby-NY, #273, illus.), 36 x 14 in., (91.4 x 35.6 cm.), (BP 582, DM 1635, FR 5542, Y 136,782).

$385* *Transatlantic Tunnel, 1935,* rolled, half sheet, near mint cond., (12-12-92, Hollywd Poster, #246, illus.), (BP 247, DM 607, FR 2079, Y 47,643).

$3520* *A Trap For Santa Claus, Biograph, 1909,* one-sheet, cond. A, paper backed, (12-14-92, Christie-E, #202, illus.), 41 x 27 in., (104.1 x 68.6 cm.), (BP 2251, DM 5532, FR 18,854, Y 435,482).

$302* *Travolti Da Un Insolito Destino Nell' Azzuro Mare D'Agosto (Swept Away), 1975,* orig. Italian, cond. A-, linen backed, (03-18-93, Swann, #227, illus.), 55 x 39 in., (139.7 x 99.1 cm.), (BP 204, DM 496, FR 1692, Y 35,145).

$660* *"Treasure Of The Sierra Madre",* French, c. 1950's, reissue Warner Bros., cond. A, (06-05-93, Camden, #179, illus.), 63 x 47 in., (160 x 119.4 cm.), on linen (BP 434, DM 1070, FR 3607, Y 70,800).

$990* *The Treasure Of The Sierra Madre, 1948,* fine cond., (linen), (12-12-92, Hollywd Poster, #38, illus.), (BP 635, DM 1560, FR 5346, Y 122,510).

$1100* *The Treasure Of The Sierra Madre, Warner Brothers, 1948,* one-sheet, very fine cond., Stanley Caidin Coll., (09-12-92, Sotheby-NY, #206, illus.), 41 x 27 in., (104.1 x 68.6 cm.), linen backed (BP 582, DM 1635, FR 5542, Y 136,782).

BI *"True To The Navy", 1930,* French, Paramount, est. $4/600, (06-05-93, Camden, #158, illus.), 32 x 24 in., (81.3 x 61 cm.), on linen.

$358* *"The Truth Juggler", 1922,* Pathe, one-sheet, cond. B, (06-05-93, Camden, #209, illus.), 41 x 27 in., (104.1 x 68.6 cm.), restored on linen after catalogue photography (BP 236, DM 580, FR 1956, Y 38,404).

$770* *Tugboat Annie, MGM, 1933,* one-sheet, very good cond., Stanley Caidin Coll., (09-12-92, Sotheby-NY, #177, illus.), 41 x 27 in., (104.1 x 68.6 cm.), linen backed (BP 407, DM 1145, FR 3879, Y 95,747).

$693* *Turned Out Nice Again, A.T.P., 1941,* British, cond. B-, three-sheet, linen-backed, (12-17-92, Christie-S. Ken, #314, illus.), 81 x 41 in., (205.7 x 104.1 cm.), poster (BP 440, DM 1082, FR 3696, Y 85,167).

$413* *"Twelve Crowded Hours", 1939,* RKO, three-sheet, cond. A, (06-05-93, Camden, #114, illus.), 81 x 41 in., (205.7 x 104.1 cm.), restored on linen after catalogue photography (BP 272, DM 670, FR 2257, Y 44,304).

$495* *Twinkletoes, First National Picture, 1926,* one-sheet, fine cond, Stanley Caidin Coll., (09-12-92, Sotheby-NY, #39, illus.), 41 x 27 in., (104.1 x 68.6 cm.), linen backed (BP 262, DM 736, FR 2494, Y 61,552).

$247* *Two English Girls (Le Due Inglesi), 1971,* Italian, cond. B, linen backed, (03-18-93, Swann, #228, illus.), 55 x 39 in., (139.7 x 99.1 cm.), (BP 167, DM 406, FR 1384, Y 28,744).

$385* *Two-Faced Woman, 1941,* insert, fine cond., (12-12-92, Hollywd Poster, #66, illus.), (BP 247, DM 607, FR 2079, Y 47,643).

$1100* *Two-Faced Woman, MGM, 1941,* one-sheet, very fine cond., Stanley Caidin Coll., (09-12-92, Sotheby-NY, #175, illus.), 41 x 27 in., (104.1 x 68.6 cm.), linen backed (BP 582, DM 1635, FR 5542, Y 136,782).

BI *Tyrone Power, Lloyds Of London, 20th Century Fox, 1936,* cond. A, one-sheet, linen-backed, est. BP 2/4,000, (12-17-92, Christie-S. Ken, #413, illus.), 41 x 27 in., (104.1 x 68.6 cm.), poster.

$825* *Uncle Tom's Cabin, Universal, 1927,* one-sheet, cond. A, linen backed, (12-14-92, Christie-E, #126, illus.), 41 x 27 in., (104.1 x 68.6 cm.), (BP 527, DM 1297, FR 4419, Y 102,066).

$4950* *Uncle Tom's Cabin, Universal, 1927,* six-sheet, cond. A, linen backed, (12-14-92, Christie-E, #125, illus.), 81 x 81 in., (205.7 x 205.7 cm.), (BP 3165, DM 7779, FR 26,513, Y 612,396).

$495* *Uncle Tom's Caboose, Universal, 1920,* one-sheet, cond. A, linen backed, (12-14-92, Christie-E, #128, illus.), 41 x 27 in., (104.1 x 68.6 cm.), (BP 316, DM 778, FR 2651, Y 61,240).

$605* *"The Uncovered WAgon", 1923,* Pathe, one-sheet, cond. C, (06-05-93, Camden, #208, illus.), 41 x 27 in., (104.1 x 68.6 cm.), restored on linen after catalogue photography (BP 398, DM 981, FR 3306, Y 64,900).

$3850* *The Unholy Three, MGM, 1930,* one-sheet, very fine cond., Stanley Caidin Coll., (09-12-92, Sotheby-NY, #187, illus.), 41 x 27 in., (104.1 x 68.6 cm.), linen backed (BP 2036, DM 5723, FR 19,395, Y 478,737).

$440* *The Uninvited, 1944,* fine cond., (12-12-92, Hollywd Poster, #145, illus.), (BP 282, DM 693, FR 2376, Y 54,449).

$3080* *The Unknown, MGM, 1927,* insert, cond. B, paper backed, folded once, (12-14-92, Christie-E, #112, illus.), 36 x 14 in., (91.4 x 35.6 cm.), (BP 1969, DM 4840, FR 16,497, Y 381,047).

$1650* *The Vampire Bat, 1933,* six sheet, fine cond., (linen), (12-12-92, Hollywd Poster, #175, illus.), (BP 1058, DM 2600, FR 8909, Y 204,183).

$5280* *The Vanishing American, Paramount, 1926,* three-sheet, cond. A, linen backed, (12-14-92, Christie-E, #48, illus.), 81 x 41 in., (205.7 x 104.1 cm.), (BP 3376, DM 8298, FR 28,281, Y 653,223).

$440* *Venus Of Venice, First National Picture, 1927,* insert, very fine cond., Stanley Caidin Coll., (09-12-92, Sotheby-NY, #170, illus.), 36 x 14 in., (91.4 x 35.6 cm.), (BP 233, DM 654, FR 2217, Y 54,713).

$715* *The Vermilion Pencil, R.C. Pictures, 1922,* one-sheet, near mint cond., Stanley Caidin Coll., (09-12-92, Sotheby-NY, #58, illus.), 41 x 27 in., (104.1 x 68.6 cm.), linen backed (BP 378, DM 1063, FR 3602, Y 88,908).

$1647* *Veronica Lake, Sullivan's Travels, Paramount, 1941,* cond. B+, one-sheet, linen-backed, lit., (12-17-92, Christie-S. Ken, #366, illus.), 41 x 27 in., (104.1 x 68.6 cm.), poster (BP 1045, DM 2571, FR 8784, Y 202,409).

$1210* *Vertigo, Paramount, 1958,* three-sheet, cond. B+, linen backed, (03-18-93, Swann, #229, illus.), (BP 816, DM 1988, FR 6779, Y 140,812).

$3575* *Les Vieux Marcheurs, Pathe, c. 1900,* French, very fine cond., created by Farla, Stanley Caidin Coll., (09-12-92, Sotheby-NY, #123, illus.), 46 x 63 in., (116.8 x 160 cm.), (BP 1891, DM 5314, FR 18,010, Y 444,541).

$715* *Virginia City, 1940,* fine cond., (12-12-92, Hollywd Poster, #84, illus.), (BP 458, DM 1127, FR 3861, Y 88,479).

$9350* *The Virginian, Paramount, 1929,* one-sheet, very fine cond., Stanley Caidin Coll., (09-12-92, Sotheby-NY, #87, illus.), 41 x 27 in., (104.1 x 68.6 cm.), linen backed (BP 4944, DM 13,899, FR 47,103, Y 1,162,646).

$1100* *Viva Villa!, MGM, 1934,* very fine cond., Stanley Caidin Coll., (09-12-92, Sotheby-NY, #178, illus.), 33 x 24 in., (83.8 x 61 cm.), linen backed (BP 582, DM 1635, FR 5542, Y 136,782).

$225* *Vivien Leigh And Claude Rains, Caesar And Cleopatra, Rank, 1945,* cond. B, three-sheet, (12-17-92, Christie-S. Ken, #365, illus.), 81 x 41 in., (205.7 x 104.1 cm.), poster (BP 143, DM 351, FR 1200, Y 27,651).

$385* *"The WAtch Dog", 1923,* Pathe, one-sheet, cond. B, (06-05-93, Camden, #210, illus.), 41 x 27 in., (104.1 x 68.6 cm.), restored on linen after catalogue photography (BP 253, DM 624, FR 2104, Y 41,300).

BI *"Wabash Avenue", 1950 and "How To Be Very, Very Popular", 1955: Two,* one-sheets, est. $3/400, (03-18-93, Swann, #230, illus.), .

$660* *Waifs, Biograph, 1914,* one-sheet, cond. A, linen backed, (12-14-92, Christie-E, #194, illus.), 41 x 27 in., (104.1 x 68.6 cm.), (BP 422, DM 1037, FR 3535, Y 81,653).

$3520* *The Walking Dead, Warner Brothers, 1936,* half-sheet, cond. B, (12-14-92, Christie-E, #20, illus.), 22 x 28 in., (55.9 x 71.1 cm.), (BP 2251, DM 5532, FR 18,854, Y 435,482).

$28,600* *The Walking Dead, Warner Brothers, 1936,* six-sheet, cond. A, linen backed, (12-14-92, Christie-E, #19, illus.), 81 x 81 in., (205.7 x 205.7 cm.), (BP 18,286, DM 44,947, FR 153,187, Y 3,538,290).

BI *The War Of The Worlds (La Guerre Des Mondes), 1953,* French, cond. C+, linen backed, est. $1,5/2,000, (03-18-93, Swann, #208, illus.), 63 x 47 in., (160 x 119.4 cm.), .

$825* *The War Of The Worlds, 1953,* one-sheet, cond. B, linen backed, (03-18-93, Swann, #209, illus.), (BP 556, DM 1356, FR 4622, Y 96,008).

$495* *The War Of The Worlds, 1953,* insert, (03-18-93, Swann, #223, illus.), (BP 334, DM 813, FR 2773, Y 57,605).

$3740* *The War Of The Worlds, Paramount, 1953,* half-sheet, cond. C, (03-18-93, Swann, #222, illus.), (BP 2522, DM 6146, FR 20,952, Y 435,238).

$2750* *A Warrior's Faith, Bison Film, 1912,* one-sheet, very fine cond., Stanley Caidin Coll., (09-12-92, Sotheby-NY, #248, illus.), 41 x 27 in., (104.1 x 68.6 cm.), linen backed (BP 1454, DM 4088, FR 13,854, Y 341,955).

$1045* *Washington Merry-Go-Round, Columbia, 1932,* one-sheet, cond. A, linen backed, (12-14-92, Christie-E, #209, illus.), 41 x 27 in., (104.1 x 68.6 cm.), (BP 668, DM 1642, FR 5597, Y 129,284).

$605* *Waterloo Bridge, MGM, 1940,* Danish, cond. B+, (03-18-93, Swann, #231, illus.), (BP 408, DM 994, FR 3389, Y 70,406).

$440* *Way Down East, 1935,* near mint cond., (paper), (12-12-92, Hollywd Poster, #36, illus.), (BP 282, DM 693, FR 2376, Y 54,449).

$440* *Way Down East, 20th Century Fox, 1935,* one-sheet, fine cond., Stanley Caidin Coll., (09-12-92, Sotheby-NY, #268, illus.), 41 x 27 in., (104.1 x 68.6 cm.), linen backed (BP 233, DM 654, FR 2217, Y 54,713).

$2090* *Way Out West, Hal Roach, 1937: Two,* lobby cards, very fine cond., Stanley Caidin Coll., (09-12-92, Sotheby-NY, #166, illus.), 11 x 14 in., (27.9 x 35.6 cm.), (BP 1105, DM 3107, FR 10,529, Y 259,886).

$1045* *The Way To Love, Paramount, 1933,* one-sheet, cond. A, linen backed, (12-14-92, Christie-E, #299, illus.), 41 x 27 in., (104.1 x 68.6 cm.), (BP 668, DM 1642, FR 5597, Y 129,284).

$2200* *We Live Again, United Artists, 1934,* one-sheet, cond. A, linen backed, (12-14-92, Christie-E, #34, illus.), 41 x 27 in., (104.1 x 68.6 cm.), (BP 1407, DM 3457, FR 11,784, Y 272,176).

$6600* *The Wedding March, Paramount, 1928,* one-sheet, fine cond., Stanley Caidin Coll., (09-12-92, Sotheby-NY, #67, illus.), 41 x 27 in., (104.1 x 68.6 cm.), linen backed (BP 3490, DM 9811, FR 33,249, Y 820,691).

$1210* *Wedding Worries, MGM, 1941,* one-sheet, very fine cond., Stanley Caidin Coll., (09-12-92, Sotheby-NY, #284, illus.), 41 x 27 in., (104.1 x 68.6 cm.), linen backed (BP 640, DM 1799, FR 6096, Y 150,460).

$220* *Week End Millionare, 1936,* near mint cond., (paper), (12-12-92, Hollywd Poster, #228, illus.), (BP 141, DM 347, FR 1188, Y 27,224).

$192* *Les Week-ends De Neron, 1956,* French, cond. B+, (03-18-93, Swann, #69, illus.), 78 x 23 in., (198.1 x 58.4 cm.), (BP 129, DM 316, FR 1076, Y 22,344).

$330* *Wells Fargo, Paramount, 1937,* insert, very fine cond., Stanley Caidin Coll., (09-12-92, Sotheby-NY, #239, illus.), 36 x 14 in., (91.4 x 35.6 cm.), (BP 175, DM 491, FR 1662, Y 41,035).

$770* *Werewolf Of London, Universal Pictures, 1935: Two,* lobby cards, very fine cond., Stanley Caidin Coll., (09-12-92, Sotheby-NY, #199, illus.), 11 x 14 in., (27.9 x 35.6 cm.), (BP 407, DM 1145, FR 3879, Y 95,747).

BI *West Side Story, UA, 1961,* one-sheet, cond. B+, paper backed, est. $3/500, (03-18-93, Swann, #233, illus.), .

$825* *What A Widow!, United Artists, 1930,* half-sheet, cond. A, (12-14-92, Christie-E, #53, illus.), 22 x 28 in., (55.9 x 71.1 cm.), (BP 527, DM 1297, FR 4419, Y 102,066).

$825* *What Every Girl Should Know, Warner Brothers, 1927,* one-sheet, cond. A, linen backed, (12-14-92, Christie-E, #55, illus.), 41 x 27 in., (104.1 x 68.6 cm.), (BP 527, DM 1297, FR 4419, Y 102,066).

$2750* *What's The Matador, Columbia, 1942,* one-sheet, cond. A, linen backed, (12-14-92, Christie-E, #289, illus.), 41 x 27 in., (104.1 x 68.6 cm.), (BP 1758, DM 4322, FR 14,730, Y 340,220).

BI *When Tomorrow Comes (Stormnatten), Universal, 1939,* Danish, cond. B+, linen-backed, est. $3/400, (03-18-93, Swann, #234, illus.), 33 x 24 in., (83.8 x 61 cm.), .

$302* *When Worlds Collide (Choc Des Mondes), 1951,* French, cond. B+, linen backed, (03-18-93, Swann, #224, illus.), 63 x 47 in., (160 x 119.4 cm.), (BP 204, DM 496, FR 1692, Y 35,145).

BI *When Worlds Collide, 1951,* insert, est. $6/900, (03-18-93, Swann, #225, illus.), .

$715* *When Worlds Collide, Paramount, 1951,* one-sheet, cond. B+, linen backed, (03-18-93, Swann, #207, illus.), (BP 482, DM 1175, FR 4006, Y 83,207).

BI *Where East Is East, MGM, 1929,* half-sheet, very fine cond., Stanley Caidin Coll., est. $1,2/1,800, (09-12-92, Sotheby-NY, #188, illus.), 22 x 28 in., (55.9 x 71.1 cm.),

$193* *White Cargo, 1942,* fine cond., (12-12-92, Hollywd Poster, #305, illus.), (BP 124, DM 304, FR 1042, Y 23,883).

$440* *White Christmas, 1954,* three sheet, fine cond., (12-12-92, Hollywd Poster, #174, illus.), (BP 282, DM 693, FR 2376, Y 54,449).

$248* *White Hear, 1949,* near mint cond., (12-12-92, Hollywd Poster, #282, illus.), (BP 159, DM 391, FR 1339, Y 30,689).

$495* *White Heat, 1949,* insert, near mint cond., (12-12-92, Hollywd Poster, #79, illus.), (BP 317, DM 780, FR 2673, Y 61,255).

$220* *The White Sister, 1933,* fine cond., (linen), (12-12-92, Hollywd Poster, #63, illus.), (BP 141, DM 347, FR 1188, Y 27,224).

$8250* *The White Sister, Metro, 1923,* three-sheet, cond. B, linen backed, (12-14-92, Christie-E, #83, illus.), 81 x 41 in., (205.7 x 104.1 cm.), (BP 5275, DM 12,966, FR 44,189, Y 1,020,661).

$770* *White Zombie, United Artists, 1932,* lobby card, very fine cond., Stanley Caidin Coll., (09-12-92, Sotheby-NY, #198, illus.), 11 x 14 in., (27.9 x 35.6 cm.), (BP 407, DM 1145, FR 3879, Y 95,747).

$880* *Who Are My Parents, William Fox, 1922,* one-sheet, very fine cond., Stanley Caidin Coll., (09-12-92, Sotheby-NY, #25, illus.), 41 x 27 in., (104.1 x 68.6 cm.), linen backed (BP 465, DM 1308, FR 4433, Y 109,426).

$1760* *Why Men Work, Pathe, 1924,* one-sheet, very fine cond., Stanley Caidin Coll., (09-12-92, Sotheby-NY, #13, illus.), 41 x 27 in., (104.1 x 68.6 cm.), linen backed (BP 931, DM 2616, FR 8866, Y 218,851).

$2750* *Wild And Woolfy, MGM, 1945,* one-sheet, cond. A, linen backed, (12-14-92, Christie-E, #272, illus.), 41 x 27 in., (104.1 x 68.6 cm.), (BP 1758, DM 4322, FR 14,730, Y 340,220).

BI *"Wild And Woolly", 1917,* Artcraft Pictures, half-sheet, cond. C, est. $3/500, (06-05-93, Camden, #125, illus.), 22 x 28 in., (55.9 x 71.1 cm.), .

$110* *Wild Brian Kent, 1936,* near mint cond., (paper), (12-12-92, Hollywd Poster, #287, illus.), stone litho (BP 71, DM 173, FR 594, Y 13,612).

$660* *Wild Cargo, RKO, 1934,* one-sheet, cond. A, linen backed, (12-14-92, Christie-E, #207, illus.), 41 x 27 in., (104.1 x 68.6 cm.), (BP 422, DM 1037, FR 3535, Y 81,653).

$468* *"The Window", 1949,* RKO, three sheet, cond. B, (06-05-93, Camden, #116, illus.), 81 x 41 in., (205.7 x 104.1 cm.), on linen (BP 308, DM 759, FR 2557, Y 50,204).

$2200* *"Wings", 1927,* Paramount, window card, cond. A, (11-07-92, Camden, #150, illus.), 22 x 14 in., (55.9 x 35.6 cm.), (BP 1438, DM 3513, FR 11,873, Y 271,538).

$385* *Wings, 1927,* fine cond., (12-12-92, Hollywd Poster, #114, illus.), lobby card (BP 247, DM 607, FR 2079, Y 47,643).

$4950* *Wings, Paramount, 1927,* one-sheet, very fine cond., (09-12-92, Sotheby-NY, #14, illus.), 41 x 27 in., (104.1 x 68.6 cm.), linen backed (BP 2618, DM 7358, FR 24,937, Y 615,519).

BI *Wings, Paramount, 1927:Two,* lobby cards, very fine cond., Stanley Caidin Coll., est. $3/4,000, (09-12-92, Sotheby-NY, #15, illus.), 11 x 14 in., (27.9 x 35.6 cm.),

$3300* *Winsor McCay, Vitagraph, 1911,* orig. French poster, cond. A, linen backed, (12-14-92, Christie-E, #268, illus.), 63 x 47 in., (160 x 119.4 cm.), (BP 2110, DM 5186, FR 17,675, Y 408,264).

$550* *The Wiser Sex, Paramount, 1932,* one-sheet, cond. A, linen backed, (12-14-92, Christie-E, #52, illus.), 41 x 27 in., (104.1 x 68.6 cm.), (BP 352, DM 864, FR 2946, Y 68,044).

$3300* *"The Wizard Of Oz", 1939,* MGM, lobby card, cond. B, (06-05-93, Camden, #181, illus.), 11 x 14 in., (27.9 x 35.6 cm.), (BP 2172, DM 5350, FR 18,033, Y 354,001).

$12,100* *"The Wizard Of Oz", 1939,* MGM, half-sheet, cond. B, (11-07-92, Camden, #175, illus.), 22 x 28 in., (55.9 x 71.1 cm.), on paper (BP 7911, DM 19,320, FR 65,300, Y 1,493,458).

$1100* *The Wizard Of Oz, 1949,* Rolled, insert, near mint cond., (12-12-92, Hollywd Poster, #68, illus.), (BP 705, DM 1733, FR 5940, Y 136,122).

$19,800* *The Wizard Of Oz, MGM, 1939,* half-sheet, cond. A, paper backed, (12-14-92, Christie-E, #165, illus.), 22 x 28 in., (55.9 x 71.1 cm.), (BP 12,660, DM 31,117, FR 106,052, Y 2,449,586).

$4620* *The Wizard Of Oz, MGM, 1939,* one-sheet, cond. A, linen backed, (12-14-92, Christie-E, #166, illus.), 41 x 27 in., (104.1 x 68.6 cm.), (BP 2954, DM 7261, FR 24,746, Y 571,570).

$3850* *The Wizard Of Oz, MGM, 1939,* lobby card, cond. A, (12-14-92, Christie-E, #167, illus.), 11 x 14 in., (27.9 x 35.6 cm.), (BP 2462, DM 6051, FR 20,621, Y 476,308).

$1210* *"The Wizrd Of Oz", 1939,* MGM, lobby card, cond. B, (06-05-93, Camden, #183, illus.), 11 x 14 in., (27.9 x 35.6 cm.), (BP 797, DM 1962, FR 6612, Y 129,800).

$3025* *"The Wizrd Of Oz", 1939,* MGM, lobby card, cond. B, (06-05-93, Camden, #182, illus.), 11 x 14 in., (27.9 x 35.6 cm.), (BP 1991, DM 4904, FR 16,530, Y 324,501).

$9900* *The Wolf Man, Universal, 1941,* one-sheet, cond. B+, linen backed, (03-18-93, Swann, #206, illus.), (BP 6677, DM 16,270, FR 55,462, Y 1,152,101).

$9350* *"The Wolfman", 1941,* Universal, one-sheet, cond. B, (11-07-92, Camden, #213, illus.), 41 x 27 in., (104.1 x 68.6 cm.), on linen (BP 6113, DM 14,929, FR 50,459, Y 1,154,036).

$1650* *"The Woman Alone", 1936,* Gaumont-British, insert, cond. A, (06-05-93, Camden, #68, illus.), 36 x 14 in., (91.4 x 35.6 cm.), on paper (BP 1086, DM 2675, FR 9016, Y 177,001).

$330* *The Woman In Green, 1945,* insert, fine cond., (12-12-92, Hollywd Poster, #75, illus.), (BP 212, DM 520, FR 1782, Y 40,837).

$302* *A Woman's Face, MGM, 1941,* one-sheet, cond. A-, linen backed, (03-18-93, Swann, #235, illus.), (BP 204, DM 496, FR 1692, Y 35,145).

$990* *Wonder Bar, Warner Brothers, 1934,* insert, fine cond., Stanley Caidin Coll., (09-12-92, Sotheby-NY, #146, illus.), 36 x 14 in., (91.4 x 35.6 cm.), (BP 524, DM 1472, FR 4987, Y 123,104).

$247* *World Without End, 1956: Three,* one-sheet, lobby card, and Belgian, (03-18-93, Swann, #226, illus.), 22 x 14 in., (55.9 x 35.6 cm.), (BP 167, DM 406, FR 1384, Y 28,744).

$550* *The Worst Woman In Paris?, Fox, 1933,* one-sheet, cond. A, linen backed, (12-14-92, Christie-E, #11, illus.), 41 x 27 in., (104.1 x 68.6 cm.), (BP 352, DM 864, FR 2946, Y 68,044).

$660* *"Wuthering Heights", 1939,* Belgian, United Artists, cond. B, (06-05-93, Camden, #161, illus.), 31 x 23 in., (78.7 x 58.4 cm.), on linen (BP 434, DM 1070, FR 3607, Y 70,800).

$165* *"Wuthering Heights", 1939,* French, Goldwyn, cond. C, (06-05-93, Camden, #175, illus.), 60 x 44 in., (152.4 x 111.8 cm.), on linen (BP 109, DM 268, FR 902, Y 17,700).

$1045* *Wuthering Heights, United Artists, 1939,* one-sheet, cond. A, linen backed, (12-14-92, Christie-E, #242, illus.), 41 x 27 in., (104.1 x 68.6 cm.), (BP 668, DM 1642, FR 5597, Y 129,284).

BI *A Yank In The R.A.F., 20th Century Fox, 1941,* one-sheet, good cond., Stanley Caidin Coll., est. $6/900, (09-12-92, Sotheby-NY, #18, illus.), 41 x 27 in., (104.1 x 68.6 cm.), linen backed.

$248* *The Yankee Don,* fine cond., (linen), (12-12-92, Hollywd Poster, #94, illus.), (BP 159, DM 391, FR 1339, Y 30,689).

$412* *Yellow Submarine, 1968,* cond. B+, (03-18-93, Swann, #236, illus.), (101.6 x 152.4 cm.), (BP 278, DM 677, FR 2308, Y 47,946).

$440* *You Can't Cheat An Honest Man, 1939,* fine cond., (12-12-92, Hollywd Poster, #332, illus.), jumbo w/c (BP 282, DM 693, FR 2376, Y 54,449).

$3300* *You Can't Cheat An Honest Man, Universal, 1939,* one-sheet, cond. A, linen backed, (12-14-92, Christie-E, #123, illus.), 41 x 27 in., (104.1 x 68.6 cm.), (BP 2110, DM 5186, FR 17,675, Y 408,264).

$2750* *You Can't Get Away With Murder, Warner Bros., 1939,* one-sheet, cond. A, linen backed, (12-14-92, Christie-E, #176, illus.), 41 x 27 in., (104.1 x 68.6 cm.), (BP 1758, DM 4322, FR 14,730, Y 340,220).

$275* *You'll Never Get Rich (Nunca Tendras Un Centavo), 1942,* Argentinian, linen backed, (03-18-93, Swann, #237, illus.), 43 x 29 in., (109.2 x 73.7 cm.), (BP 185, DM 452, FR 1541, Y 32,003).

$330* *Young Donovan's Kid, Radio Pictures, 1931,* one-sheet, very fine cond., created by Cardiff, Stanley Caidin Coll., (09-12-92, Sotheby-NY, #264, illus.), 41 x 27 in., (104.1 x 68.6 cm.), linen backed (BP 175, DM 491, FR 1662, Y 41,035).

BI *The Young Rajah, Paramount, 1922,* half-sheet, good cond., Stanley Caidin Coll., est. $1,2/1,800, (09-12-92, Sotheby-NY, #57, illus.), 22 x 28 in., (55.9 x 71.1 cm.), linen backed.

$302* *Youth Aflame, c. 1947,* one-sheet, cond. B, linen backed, (03-18-93, Swann, #238, illus.), (BP 204, DM 496, FR 1692, Y 35,145).

$385* *Youth to Youth, 1922,* fine cond., (12-12-92, Hollywd Poster, #13, illus.), (BP 247, DM 607, FR 2079, Y 47,643).

$1045* *Zero De Conduite, 1933/1945,* French, cond. A-, linen backed, (03-18-93, Swann, #25, illus.), 63 x 47 in., (160 x 119.4 cm.), (BP 705, DM 1717, FR 5854, Y 121,611).

$1100* *"Ziegfeld Follies", 1946,* MGM, three-sheet, cond. C, (11-07-92, Camden, #181, illus.), 81 x 41 in., (205.7 x 104.1 cm.), on linen (BP 719, DM 1756, FR 5936, Y 135,769).

ANQUENTIN, Louis

BI *La Course,* w/out margin, (02-24-93, Picard, #9), color lithograph on thin chine.

ANSDELL, Richard (after)

$171* *Coursing On The Heath,* by S.W. Reynolds, trimmed, repaired image tears, laid down, (12-10-92, Bonhams-Chelsea, #21), image 17¾ x 39¼ in., (45.1 x 99.7 cm.), hand colored engraving (BP 110, DM 270, FR 924, Y 21,153).

$43* *The Wounded Hound, 1872,* by Robert Bowyer Parkes, pub. J. Dickinson and Co., slight staining, (01-18-93, Bonhams, #70), image 11C\ x 18 in., (28.9 x 45.7 cm.), mezzotint (BP 28, DM 70, FR 234, Y 5420).

ANSELMO

$901* *Lato Destro, 1970,* #31/50, s., d., (12-15-92, Finarte-Milan, #12), 12B, x 8M, in., (32 x 22.5 cm.), color photograph (BP 575, DM 1412, FR 4826, Y 111,745, L 1265).

ANSTEY, Richard

BI *"Three Angels", 1981,* #5/300, lim. edit., est. $100/150, (05-12-93, Maynard, #275), color print.

ANTES, Horst German b. 1936

$435* *Bepackte Figur (Lutze 340), 1965,* #100/100, s., (04-21-93, Germann, #216, illus.), 13⅍n x 11Bzn in., (344 x 288 mm.), color lithograph (BP 282, DM 695, FR 2351, Y 48,157, SF 633).

BI *Bildnis Des Fursten Putjatin (Lutze 555), 1967,* s., d., est. DM 300/400, (06-24-93, Germann, #201), 25⅍n x 19Zzn in., (650 x 500 mm.), color lithograph.

$1471* *Euler, Walter; On My Way Now (L. 458-465), 1966: Eight,* #95/100, s., (10-09-92, Winterberg, #1677), smallest 11 x 10B, in., (28 x 27 cm.), largest 11Mzn x 11Z in., (28 x 27 cm.), color serigraph on wove (BP 873, DM 2185, FR 7337, Y 179,084).

$513* *Figur (Oflingen), 1971,* s., num., (12-01-92, Karl/Faber, #319), 23¼ x 16Bzn in., (59 x 41.5 cm.), color lithograph on cardboard (BP 339, DM 818, FR 2787, Y 63,870).

$367* *Figur Beautiful (Lutze 648), 1970/71,* s., #653/999, (06-12-93, Hauswedell/Nolt, #21), 37C, x 25Zzn in., (95 x 65.5 cm.), color lithograph on BFK Rives (BP 240, DM 597, FR 2008, Y 38,619).

$397* *"Figur Fur Hannover" (Lutze 308a), 1964,* s., num., (11-28-92, Grisebach, #404, illus.), 24Czn x 17B, in., (61.5 x 44.8 cm.), colored lithograph on handmade (BP 262, DM 632, FR 2147, Y 49,409).

$636* *Figur Mit Landschaft (Lutze 571), 1968,* s., i., artist's proof, (06-12-93, Hauswedell/Nolt, #16), 18¼ x 16Z in., (46.3 x 41 cm.), color lithograph (BP 416, DM 1035, FR 3479, Y 66,926).

$577* *"Figur Mit Zwei Wunden" (Lutze 647), 1970,* s., num., (11-28-92, Grisebach, #405, illus.), 24¾ x 17Z\n in., (62.8 x 45 cm.), colored lithograph on wove (BP 381, DM 919, FR 3121, Y 71,811).

$139* *Gefleckte Figur Mit Reif,* s., lit., (09-04-92, Germann, #210), 16⅍n x 11Zzn in., (420 x 300 mm.), color lithograph (BP 70, DM 195, FR 663, Y 17,110, SF 173).

$325* *Grosses Stilleben Mit Kopf, 1965,* s., #114/125, (06-12-93, Hauswedell/Nolt, #15), 16B, x 22¼ in., (42.2 x 56.5 cm.), color lithograph on BFK Rives (BP 213, DM 529, FR 1778, Y 34,200).

$155* *Mann Mit Grun-Weissem Reifen Nach Rechts Mit Kleinem Orangen Mann Links,* s., E.A., (09-25-92, Granier, #2742), 16Z, x 11½ in., (41 x 29.2 cm.), sheet 16⅍n x 11Zzn in., (41 x 29.2 cm.), color lithograph on wove (BP 91, DM 230, FR 777, Y 18,709).

$542* *Mannliche Figur Im Glaskasten (Lutze 666), 1971,* s., (11-28-92, Schoppmann, #353), 26Czn x 19M, in., (66.5 x 50.5 cm.), color lithograph on BFK Rives (BP 358, DM 863, FR 2931, Y 67,455).

$514* *Mannliche Figur Im Kasten (Lutze Nr. 554), 1967,* s., d., state proof, ded., (04-21-93, Germann, #218), 25⅍n x 19Zzn in., (650 x 500 mm.), color lithograph (BP 334, DM 822, FR 2778, Y 56,902, SF 748).

$268* *Mannliche Figur Vor Schwarz,* s., #71/105, (06-12-93, Hauswedell/Nolt, #11), 9B, x 5ZCzn in., (24.4 x 14.7 cm.), etching on thick wove (BP 175, DM 436, FR 1466, Y 28,202).

$367* *Paar (Interieur) (Lutze 307), 1965,* s., d., proof, i., (06-12-93, Hauswedell/Nolt, #13), 16Z, xin., (41 x cm.), color offset on offset board (BP 240, DM 597, FR 2008, Y 38,619).

$84* *Rote Figur,* s. Antes, (09-30-92, Kunsthallen, #19), color lithograph (BP 47, DM 119, FR 403, Y 10,080, DK 460).

BI *Schlangenwesen,* from Der Engel der Geschichte, center crease, est. DM 150-, (09-25-92, Granier, #2741), 16ZCzn x 23M\ in., (42.7 x 60.7 cm.), woodcut on beige wove.

$353* *Stilleben Mit Leiter, Kugel Und Rohr, 1970,* s., #22/90, (06-12-93, Hauswedell/Nolt, #19), 15M, x 20B, in., (40.3 x 52.4 cm.), color lithograph (BP 231, DM 575, FR 1931, Y 37,146).

$228* *Untitled,* s., #94/190, pub. Prent 190, good cond., staining, (12-09-92, Sotheby-Amstrdm, #461), sheet 30¼ x 22¼ in., (768 x 565 mm.), color lithograph on wove (BP 146, DM 358, FR 1221, Y 28,270, G 403).

BI *Untitled,* s., margins, good cond., est. Dfl. 4/600, (05-27-93, Sotheby-Amstrdm, #532), 16B\n x 21⅍n in., (430 x 535 mm.), colored lithograph on wove.

$293* *Untitled: Two,* s., e.a., 58/100, (09-29-92, B. Rasmussen, #274), lithograph in colors (BP 165, DM 414, FR 1412, Y 34,977, DK 1610).

$430* *Vielfarbiger Kopf Nach Links,* s. Antes 6, #67/85, (03-24-93, Venator/Hansten, #4466), image 13M, x 11Zzn in., (35.2 x 30 cm.), color lithograph (BP 291, DM 702, FR 2390, Y 50,523).

$212* *Weibliche Figur Vor Schwarz, 1966,* s., num., #28/35, (06-12-93, Hauswedell/Nolt, #10), 9¾ x 8Czn in., (24.7 x 20.8 cm.), etching on thick wove (BP 139, DM 345, FR 1160, Y 22,309).

$239* *Zurcher Kopf,* i., s., (11-28-92, Schoppmann, #354), 4ZBn x 7Bzn in., (12.5 x 18.5 cm.), etching on wove (BP 158, DM 381, FR 1293, Y 29,745).

ANTON, O.

$119* *Hamburg Amerika Linie Croisieres Aux Iles Atlantiques Par Le Vapeur De Plaisance "Oceana",* good cond., (03-13-93, Laurin, #153), 33¼ x 23½ in., (84.5 x 59.5 cm.), (BP 83, DM 198, FR 673, Y 14,025).

ANTONIO

BI *"Diana Vreeland", 1970: Nine,* t., Jocelyn Kargere Coll., est. BP 8/1,200, (10-29-92, Christie-London, #180, illus.), each 4½ x 3½ in., (11.4 x 8.9 cm.), photograph, polaroid coulour prints mounted together on card.

BI *"Regine", 1970: Nine,* t., Jocelyn Kargere Coll., est. BP 8/1,200, (10-29-92, Christie-London, #179, illus.), each 4½ x 3½ in., (11.4 x 8.9 cm.), photograph, polaroid colour prints mounted together on card.

ANTREASIAN, Garo

$330* *"Untitled", "Untitled", and "Untitled", 1971; 1975: Three,* 1st 2 s., d., num. 4/5 & Artist's Proof, 1st w/blindstamp of pub. Tamarind Institute, 2nd w/blindstamp on pub. Origins Press, margins, good cond., surface soiling, (02-24-93, Butterfield, #3174), from 27 x 19 in., (68.6 x 48.3 cm.), to 40 x 23⅛ in., (68.6 x 48.3 cm.), lithograph in colors on wove (BP 230, DM 536, FR 1816, Y 38,723).

ANUSZKIEWICZ, Richard   American b. 1930

BI *6 Seritypien, Galerie Der Spiegel, Cologne, 1965: Set Of Six,* t., just., s., num. 32, creasing, defects, scuffing, splits, est. BP3/400, (12-01-92, Christie-London, #558, illus.), overall S. 25 x 24⅞ in., (635 x 630 mm.), screenprints in colors on firm wove.

BI *Blue And Red, 1979,* 10/95, s., d., est. SF 24/280, (10-14-92, Germann, #207), 31⅞ x 30⅞ in., (790 x 770 mm.), color etching.

$121* *"Diamond Chroma",* s., #41/200, d. 1965, prov., (12-02-92, Boos, #512), sight 20⅞ x 14⅞ in., (510 x 380 mm.), serigraph (BP 78, DM 190, FR 649, Y 15,055).

$88* *"Double Square",* s., #73/200, d. 1969, prov., (12-02-92, Boos, #509), sight 23⅞ x 24 in., (605 x 610 mm.), serigraph (BP 57, DM 138, FR 472, Y 10,949).

$39* *"From The Inward Eye",* (05-14-93, DuMouchelle, #2534), 26 x 20 in., (66 x 50.8 cm.), serigraph (BP 25, DM 63, FR 211, Y 4323).

BI *Green And Silver, 1979,* AP 2/15, s., d., crease, est. SF 24/280, (10-14-92, Germann, #208), 31⅞ x 30⅞ in., (795 x 770 mm.), color etching.

$83* *"Inward Eye 10",* w/orig. portfolio, prov., (12-02-92, Boos, #471), sight 25⅜ x 19⅞ in., (650 x 50 mm.), serigraph (BP 54, DM 131, FR 446, Y 10,327).

$83* *"Inward Eye 3",* w/orig. portfolio, prov., (12-02-92, Boos, #469), sight 25⅜ x 19⅞ in., (650 x 500 mm.), serigraph (BP 54, DM 131, FR 446, Y 10,327).

$83* *"Inward Eye 5",* w/orig. portfolio, prov., (12-02-92, Boos, #468), sight 25⅜ x 19⅞ in., (650 x 500 mm.), serigraph (BP 54, DM 131, FR 446, Y 10,327).

$83* *"Inward Eye 7",* w/orig. portfolio, prov., (12-02-92, Boos, #470), sight 25⅜ x 19⅞ in., (650 x 500 mm.), serigraph (BP 54, DM 131, FR 446, Y 10,327).

$66* *"New York City Opera",* s., #115/144, d. 1968, prov., (12-02-92, Boos, #507), sight 33⅞ x 23¼ in., (850 x 590 mm.), serigraph (BP 43, DM 104, FR 354, Y 8212).

BI *Red And Blue, 1979,* 14/95, s., d., est. SF 24/280, (10-14-92, Germann, #206), 31⅞ x 30⅞ in., (795 x 770 mm.), color etching.

$34* *Sequential,* s., d. 1972, num. II, 55/200; t. label verso, prov., (12-01-92, Ritchie, #52), 28 x 21 in., (71.1 x 53.3 cm.), color serigraph (BP 22, DM 54, FR 185, Y 4233, C$ 44).

$138* *"Sequential",* s., #82/200, d. 1972, i. III, prov., (12-02-92, Boos, #511), sight 25⅞ x 18⅞ in., (660 x 482 mm.), serigraph (BP 89, DM 217, FR 741, Y 17,171).

$132* *"Sequential",* s., #82/200, d. 1972, i. VII, prov., (12-02-92, Boos, #510), sight 25⅝ x 19⅞ in., (645 x 485 mm.), serigraph (BP 85, DM 208, FR 709, Y 16,424).

$187* *"Spectral Cadmius",* s., d. 1968, #69/125, prov., (12-02-92, Boos, #506), sight 27¾ x 27¾ in., (705 x 705 mm.), serigraph (BP 121, DM 294, FR 1004, Y 23,267).

$209* *Untitled,* s., #78/200, d. 1969, prov., (12-02-92, Boos, #508), sight 24 x 35⅞ in., (610 x 910 mm.), serigraph (BP 135, DM 329, FR 1122, Y 26,005).

$209* *"Zonal",* incised sig., d. '68, #38/50, prov., (02-92, Boos, #516), 35⅞ x 36 in., (910 x 915 mm.), graph on plexiglas (BP 135, DM 329, FR 1122, Y).

APGER, Virgil

$275* *Ava Gardner,* (04-26-93, Selkirk, #538), 11 in., (27.9 x 35.6 cm.), b/w photograph (BP 17 431, FR 1456, Y 30,347).

$204* *Ava Gardner, Portrait For "Bwohani Junc rov.,* (10-10-92, Bonhams, #19, illus.), 8 x 10 25.4 cm.), photograph (BP 121, DM 303, Y 24,836).

$297* *Ava Gardner, Reclining On Sofa, Right Arm ish-net Stockings,* prov., (10-10-92, Bonhams, us.), 11 x 14 in., (27.9 x 35.6 cm.), photograph (B DM 441, FR 1481, Y 36,158).

$248* *Marlon Brando,* from Julius Caesar, (04-26-9 rk, #539), 14 x 11 in., (35.6 x 27.9 cm.), b/w ph (BP 157, DM 389, FR 1313, Y 27,367).

$371* *Marlon Brando As Marc Anthony In "Julius ",* sepia, prov., (10-10-92, Bonhams, #18, illus.), in., (35.6 x 27.9 cm.), photograph (BP 220, DM R 1850, Y 45,167).

APPAREILS and PELLICULES

$556* *Splendide,* marks, (05-07-93, Christie-S. Ken, illus.), 14½ x 19½ in., (36.8 x 49.5 cm.), colo graph (BP 352, DM 879, FR 2962, Y 61,220).

APPEL

$288* *Untitled Figure,* #20/99, s., d. 1967, (03-10-93, Ma d, #635), 26¾ x 20 in., (67.9 x 50.8 cm.), silkscreen BP 201, DM 479, FR 1627, Y 34,026, C$ 358).

APPEL, Karel   Dutch/American b. 1921

BI *Komposition, c. 1955/60* s., num., est. DM 1,4/1,800 (11-28-92, Grisebach, #407, illus.), 19⅞ x 19⅞ in., (50 x 50 cm.), colored lithograph on handmade.

$550* *Abstract Composition,* #15/160, (08-29-92, Young, #32, illus.), 29 x 21 in., (73.7 x 53.3 cm.), color lithograph (BP 277, DM 774, FR 2638, Y 67,818).

$165* *"Abstract Face", 1969,* s., d. Appel 69; ident. on label verso, good cond., tear, abrasion into image, (05-22-93, Skinner, #308, illus.), 25¼ x 19¼ in., (64.1 x 48.9 cm.), color lithograph on wove (BP 107, DM 268, FR 903, Y 18,192).

BI *"Abstract Face", 1969,* s., d. Appel 69, #103/200, ident. on label, good cond., tear into image, est. $4/600, (03-12-93, Skinner, #95, illus.), sight 25¼ x 19¼ in., (64.1 x 48.9 cm.), lithograph in colors on wove.

$523* *Abstract Figures,* s., d. 1970, #31/100, prov., (05-16-93, Hindman, #579), 26 x 39¾ in., (66 x 101 cm.), color lithograph (BP 340, DM 841, FR 2827, Y 57,976).

$303* *Abstractions: Two,* inits. ka, #131/300 and 171/300, good cond., staining, (05-22-93, Skinner, #309, illus.), 12½ x 9 in., (31.8 x 22.9 cm.), lithograph on paper (BP 196, DM 493, FR 1658, Y 33,407).

BI *Abstractions: Two,* init. ka, #131/300 and 171/300, good cond., mount staining, est. $8/1,200, (03-12-93, Skinner, #96, illus.), sight 12½ x 9 in., (31.8 x 22.9 cm.), lithographs on paper.

$715* *"Animal Fantastique", 1976,* s., d. Appel 76 in white paint, num. 95/110, good cond., rippling, (09-11-92, Skinner, #99, illus.), sight 28⅞ x 34½ in., (73.3 x 87.6 cm.), lithograph in colors on handmade paper (BP 370, DM 1029, FR 3498, Y 88,589).

$1422* *Animal Fantastique, 1976,* #95/100, s., d., (04-21-93, Germann, #17, illus.), 28¾ x 34¼ in., (730 x 870 mm.), color etching w/embossing on handmade (BP 923, DM 2273, FR 7686, Y 157,423, SF 2070).

$419* *Ansigt,* s., 79, 121/130, (09-29-92, B. Rasmussen, #272), lithograph and etching in colors (BP 236, DM 592, FR 2019, Y 50,018, DK 2300).

$837* *Ansigt,* s. 79, 121/130, (09-29-92, B. Rasmussen, #268), lithograph and etching in colors (BP 470, DM 1182, FR 4034, Y 99,916, DK 4600).

$2166* *Bewegte Formen, 1957,* s., d., Ep(reuve) d'Artiste, (11-28-92, Grisebach, #408, illus.), 21⅞ x 27⅞ in., (53.5 x 71 cm.), colored lithograph on wove (BP 1430, DM 3451, FR 11,714, Y 269,571).

BI *Cat,* s., i. epreuve d'artiste, margins, good cond., est. G 6/900, (12-09-92, Sotheby-Amstrdm, #474), sheet 24B, x 32Bzn in., (625 x 820 mm.), color lithograph on wove.

$313* *Cat,* s., #118/175, margins, good cond., (12-09-92, Sotheby-Amstrdm, #476), sheet 24Czn x 31Bzn in., (615 x 812 mm.), color lithograph on wove (BP 200, DM 491, FR 1676, Y 38,810, G 552).

$352* *Cat,* s., i. Epreuve d'Atelier, full margins, good cond., (05-27-93, Sotheby-Amstrdm, #546), 22Czn x 30Zzn in., (564 x 763 mm.), colored lithograph on wove (BP 225, DM 565, FR 1904, Y 37,736, G 633).

$320* *Cat With Guitar, 1977,* s., #66/100, pub. London Arts, full margins, good cond., minor defects, margins, handling creases, (05-27-93, Sotheby-Amstrdm, #542), 37Bzn x 26Zzn in., (964 x 662 mm.), colored silkscreen on BFK Rives (BP 205, DM 513, FR 1731, Y 34,305, G 575).

$4885* *Cats, 1978: Seventeen,* complete, each plate s., #124/125, pub. London Arts, Inc., good cond., (12-09-92, Sotheby-Amstrdm, #473), each sheet 24Zzn x 32Bzn in., (630 x 820 mm.), color lithograph on wove (BP 3117, DM 7668, FR 26,165, Y 605,704, G 8625).

$6396* *Cats, 1978: Seventeen,* each plate s., #125/125, w/list of plates and just., pub. London Arts, Inc., full sheets, good cond., (05-27-93, Sotheby-Amstrdm, #543), each sheet 24Zzn x 32Bzn in., (630 x 820 mm.), lithograph on wove (BP 4096, DM 10,263, FR 34,592, Y 685,678, G 11,500).

$8050* *Circus (Volume I and III), 1978: Thirteen,* s. in crayon, #55/130, pub. ABCD Editions, full sheets, good cond., soiling, (02-11-93, Sotheby-NY, #301), each sheet approx. 30 x 22¼ in., (762 x 565 mm.), color woodcut (BP 5680, DM 13,334, FR 45,123, Y 970,464).

$5463* *Circus (Volume II), 1978: Eight,* from suite of 10, each s. in crayon, #55/130, pub. ABCD Editions, full sheets, p., good cond., soiling, (02-11-93, Sotheby-NY, #302), each sheet approx. 30 x 22¼ in., (762 x 565 mm.), color woodcuts (BP 3855, DM 9049, FR 30,622, Y 658,590).

$9900* *Circus, 1978: Set Of Ten,* Vol. 1, ABCD, s., num., #65/130, excell. cond., (11-09-92, Christie-NY, #237, illus.), 30 x 22¼ in., (762 x 565 mm.), colored wood engraving on wove (BP 6545, DM 15,805, FR 53,398, Y 1,228,593).

$1694* *Composition,* s., i. epreuve d'artiste, margins, good cond., creasing, (12-09-92, Sotheby-Amstrdm, #471, illus.), sheet 33M, x 24Bzn in., (860 x 633 mm.), color lithograph on Rives (BP 1081, DM 2659, FR 9073, Y 210,043, G 2990).

BI *Composition,* s., #69/160, full margins, good cond., est. G 7/900, (12-09-92, Sotheby-Amstrdm, #479), sheet 24¼ x 32 in., (616 x 813 mm.), color lithograph on wove.

$456* *Composition,* s., #25/160, good cond., (12-09-92, Sotheby-Amstrdm, #463), sheet 21B, x 29½ in., (550 x 750 mm.), color lithograph on wove (BP 291, DM 716, FR 2442, Y 56,541, G 805).

$294* *Composition,* s. Appel, 34/75, (03-24-93, Kunsthallen, #12), color lithograph (BP 199, DM 480, FR 1634, Y 34,544, DK 1840).

$239* *Composition,* s. Appel, E.A., (03-24-93, Kunsthallen, #15), color lithograph (BP 162, DM 390, FR 1329, Y 28,081, DK 1495).

$404* *Composition,* s. Appel, 121/160, (03-24-93, Kunsthallen, #17), color lithograph (BP 274, DM 660, FR 2246, Y 47,468, DK 2530).

$147* *Composition,* s. Appel, 43/75, (03-24-93, Kunsthallen, #16), color lithograph (BP 100, DM 240, FR 817, Y 17,272, DK 920).

BI *(Composition With Figure), c. 1976,* crayon s., #101/110, good cond., est. BP 1/1,500, (12-03-92, Sotheby-London, #601, illus.), 34 x 28¼ in., (862 x 720 mm.), aquatint and carborundum in colors.

BI *Composition With Figure, c. 1963,* s., #86/120, pub. L'Oeuvre Gravee, blindstamp, full margins, scuffs,light/mount-staining, est. BP 6/800, (06-30-93, Sotheby-London, #732), 25Z, x 19B, in., (638 x 498 mm.), color lithograph on Arches.

$413* *(Composition), 1957,* s., d., num. 49/50, full margins, good cond., creases, surface soiling, foxing, mat staining, Thomas Milbrook estate, (02-24-93, Butterfield, #3175), sheet 22C, x 30Z, in., (568 x 765 mm.), lithograph in colors on Arches wove (BP 288, DM 670, FR 2273, Y 48,463).

$339* *Composition, 1958,* s., d., #90/100, (06-12-93, Hauswedell/Nolt, #23), 22Mzn x 20¼ in., (57 x 51.5 cm.), color lithograph on Arches (BP 222, DM 552, FR 1854, Y 35,673).

$514* *Composition, 1969,* s. Appel 69, epreuve d'artiste, (03-24-93, Kunsthallen, #13), color lithograph (BP 348, DM 839, FR 2857, Y 60,392, DK 3220).

BI *Composition, 1969,* s. Appel 69, Epreuve d'artiste, est. DK 2,500, (09-30-92, Kunsthallen, #21), color lithograph.

$283* *Composition, 1969,* s., d., #38/85, (06-12-93, Hauswedell/Nolt, #24), 25Czn x 19Zzn in., (64 x 50 cm.), color lithograph on Arches (BP 185, DM 461, FR 1548, Y 29,780).

$506* *Composition, 1971,* s. Appel 71, 47/225, (09-30-92, Kunsthallen, #20), color lithograph (BP 285, DM 718, FR 2427, Y 60,722, DK 2760).

$367* *Composition, 1973,* s. Appel 73, 47/100, (03-24-93, Kunsthallen, #18), color lithograph (BP 249, DM 599, FR 2040, Y 43,121, DK 2300).

$295* *Composition, 1976,* s. Appel 76, 41/100, from Pour Jorn portfolio, (09-30-92, Kunsthallen, #23), color lithograph (BP 166, DM 418, FR 1415, Y 35,401, DK 1610).

$352* *Composition, 1976,* s., d., i. E.A., full margins, good cond., (05-27-93, Sotheby-Amstrdm, #540), 20Bzn x 14M in., colored silkscreen on wove (BP 225, DM 565, FR 1904, Y 37,736, G 633).

$367* *Composition, 1977,* s. Appel, 236/300, (03-24-93, Kunsthallen, #14), color lithograph (BP 249, DM 599, FR 2040, Y 43,121, DK 2300).

$480* *Composition, 1979,* s., #73/160, pub. Martin Rosen, full margins, good cond., (05-27-93, Sotheby-Amstrdm, #536), 21zn x 29Z, in., (547 x 740 mm.), colored lithograph on wove (BP 307, DM 770, FR 2596, Y 51,458, G 863).

$1421* *Dog And Clown,* 55/130, s., (06-24-93, Germann, #218, illus.), 22Mzn x 30Czn in., (570 x 767 mm.), color woodcut w/embossing (BP 935, DM 2304, FR 7765, Y 152,435, SF 2070).

$605* *"Dream Colored Head",* HC, s., (06-11-93, DuMouchelle, #2098), 26 x 40 in., (66 x 101.6 cm.), lithograph (BP 398, DM 983, FR 3315, Y 64,191).

$468* *Elephant, 1978,* s. white pencil, num. 20/130, from the series Circus, (09-20-92, Hindman, #820), 30 x 22¼ in., (76.2 x 56.5 cm.), embossed color woodcut (BP 274, DM 694, FR 2376, Y 57,842).

$463* *Fabeldyr, 1973,* s. Appel 73, E.A., (09-30-92, Kunsthallen, #25), color lithograph (BP 261, DM 657, FR 2221, Y 55,562, DK 2530).

$715* *"La Famille" and "Figure With Bird", 1969: Two,* s., d., num. 66/120, 18/75, La Famille w/L'Oeuvre Gravee blindstamp,each w/full margins, good cond., creases, surface soiling, mat-staining, FigureWith Bird w/rubbed areas, hinge removal, surface abrasions in image, prop. Thomas Milbrook estate, (02-24-93, Butterfield, #2991), 19B, x 25¼ in., (498 x 641 mm.), 19¾ x 25¼ in., (498 x 641 mm.), lithograph in colors on wove (BP 499, DM 1161, FR 3935, Y 83,900).

BI *Figur Mit Grossen Ohren, (19)76,* s., d., E a, est. DM 700, (12-01-92, Karl/Faber, #321), 12Bzn x 11 in., (33 x 28 cm.), color lithograph on wove.

BI *Figur, (19)70,* s., d., E.A., est. DM 700, (12-01-92, Karl/Faber, #320), 12C, x 9Bzn in., (31.5 x 23 cm.), color lithograph on wove.

$358* *Figural Abstraction,* s., d. 1970, #97/100. prov., (05-16-93, Hindman, #580), 26 x 20 in., (66 x 50.8 cm.), color serigraph (BP 233, DM 576, FR 1935, Y 39,685).

$1716* *Figurative Composition, 1975,* s., d., #26/50, margins, good cond., (06-30-93, Sotheby-London, #733, illus.), 22B, x 28Z, in., (575 x 714 mm.), aquatint w/carborundum in color (BP 1150, DM 2927, FR 9873, Y 183,864).

BI *Figure,* s., #53/175, good cond., creasing, est. G 7/900, (12-09-92, Sotheby-Amstrdm, #472), sheet 29Bzn x 21¼ in., (744 x 540 mm.), color lithograph on wove.

$220* *Figure,* edit. #159/300, inits., (09-18-92, DuMouchelle, #2401), image 12¼ x 9¼ in., (31.8 x 26 cm.), color lithograph (BP 127, DM 329, FR 1128, Y 27,411).

$220* *Figure,* edit. #110/300, inits., (09-18-92, DuMouchelle, #2402), image 12½ x 10¼ in., (31.8 x 26 cm.), color lithograph (BP 127, DM 329, FR 1128, Y 27,411).

BI *Figure,* s., #42/120, full margins, good cond., occasional handling creases, est. Dfl. 7/1,000, (05-27-93, Sotheby-Amstrdm, #545), 28Z, x 20Zzn in., (715 x 525 mm.), colored silkscreen on wove.

$440* *Figure,* s., d. 75, annot. E.A., (05-16-93, Hindman, #506), 40 x 26 in., (101.6 x 66 cm.), color lithograph (BP 286, DM 708, FR 2378, Y 48,775).

BI *Figure, 1979,* s., d., #69/120, margins, good cond., est. G 7/900, (12-09-92, Sotheby-Amstrdm, #478), sheet 21M, x 29Zzn in., (555 x 758 mm.), color lithograph on Arches.

$521* *Figures,* s., #84/90, full margins, good cond., hinges, (12-09-92, Sotheby-Amstrdm, #475), sheet 14¾ x 20C\ in., (375 x 518 mm.), color lithograph on wove (BP 332, DM 818, FR 2791, Y 64,600, G 920).

BI *Figures,* s., #8/120, full margins, good cond., est. Dfl. 7/900, (05-27-93, Sotheby-Amstrdm, #551), 18M, x 26Zn in., colored lithograph on wove.

BI *Figures, 1973,* s., d., #74/120, full margins, good cond., est. Dfl. 700/1,000, (05-27-93, Sotheby-Amstrdm, #539), 20zn x 26Z, in., (522 x 663 mm.), colored silkscreen on BFK Rives.

BI *Figures, 1977,* s., d., i. E.A., full margins, good cond., occasional handling creases, est. Dfl. 7/1,000, (05-27-93, Sotheby-Amstrdm, #538), 26C, x 20zn in., (670 x 523 mm.), colored silkscreen on wove.

$463* *Figurkomposition, 1974,* s. Appel, 32/110, (09-30-92, Kunsthallen, #22), color lithograph (BP 261, DM 657, FR 2221, Y 55,562, DK 2530).

$275* *Floating Flower Passion, 1978,* s., annot. E.A., inkstamp pub. London Arts, Inc., blindstamp p. Editions Press, good cond., creases, few in image, (10-28-92, Butterfield, #2888), 26 x 38 in., (660 x 965 mm.), color silkscreen on white wove (BP 175, DM 425, FR 1442, Y 33,742).

$935* *Flying Hat Meets Sleeping Dog (E.P. 312), 1974,* s., d., annot. E.P.A.P., blindstamps of Editions Press, full margins,good cond., creases, Thomas Milbrook Estate, (02-24-93, Butterfield, #3181), 22½ x 30½ in., (572 x 775 mm.), lithograph in colors on wove w/gold foil adhesive (BP 652, DM 1518, FR 5146, Y 109,716).

$645* *Happy Battle,* #43/160, s., (09-04-92, Germann, #214, illus.), 21Mzn x 29Zzn in., (545 x 758 mm.), color lithograph (BP 323, DM 904, FR 3077, Y 79,394, SF 805).

$248* *Head,* inits., num. 168/300, margins, good cond., minor surface scuffing, creases, mat staining, light-staining, taped to mat, (02-24-93, Butterfield, #3183), sheet 15 x 11 in., (381 x 279 mm.), lithograph in colors on wove (BP 173, DM 403, FR 1365, Y 29,101).

$193* *Head,* inits., num. 218/300, margins, good cond., mat & light-staining, (02-24-93, Butterfield, #3182), sheet 14¾ x 11Z, in., (375 x 283 mm.), lithograph in colors on wove (BP 135, DM 313, FR 1062, Y 22,647).

BI *Head,* 147/160, s., est. SF 1,4/1,800, (10-14-92, Germann, #209), 21Mzn x 29½ in., (545 x 750 mm.), color lithograph.

$921* *Head,* #147/160, s., (09-04-92, Germann, #212), 21Mzn x 29½ in., (545 x 750 mm.), color lithograph (BP 462, DM 1291, FR 4394, Y 113,368, SF 1150).

$239* *Head Study,* #37/75, s., d. '69, (03-17-93, Bonhams-Chelsea, #324), subject 22¼ x 30 in., (56.5 x 76.2 cm.), lithograph in colors on Arches (BP 165, DM 398, FR 1352, Y 28,032).

BI *"Head Study",* num. 37/75, s., d. '69, est. BP2/300, (01-21-93, Bonhams-Chelsea, #107), 22¼ x 30 in., (56.5 x 76.2 cm.), lithograph in colors on Arches.

$275* *Head, c. 1972,* full margins, num., s., (05-27-93, Swann, #15), 26 x 20C, in., (66 x 51.8 cm.), color serigraph (BP 176, DM 441, FR 1487, Y 29,481).

$716* *Kat Met Guitaar,* s., #46/100, full margins, good cond., 1040 x 750 mm, (12-09-92, Sotheby-Amstrdm, #480, illus.), color silkscreen on wove (BP 457, DM 1124, FR 3835, Y 88,779, G 1265).

$565* *Klovn,* s. 79, 121/130, (09-29-92, B. Rasmussen, #271), lithograph and etching in colors (BP 318, DM 798, FR 2723, Y 67,447, DK 3105).

$737* *Komposition,* E.A., s., light-stain, staining, (09-04-92, Germann, #211), 24Zzn x 32M, in., (627 x 835 mm.), color lithograph (BP 369, DM 1033, FR 3516, Y 90,719, SF 920).

$474* *Komposition,* H.C., s., (06-24-93, Germann, #205), 21C, x 29½ in., (543 x 750 mm.), color lithograph (BP 312, DM 768, FR 2590, Y 50,847, SF 690).

BI *Komposition Blau-Rot-Gelb, c. 1965,* s., est. DM 6/800, (11-28-92, Grisebach, #409, illus.), 10B, x 8Zzn in., (27 x 22 cm.), colored lithograph on wove.

$1106* *L'Homme A La Guitare,* #8/120, s., (04-21-93, Germann, #219), 42½ x 29Z, in., (108 x 74 cm.), color lithograph (BP 718, DM 1768, FR 5978, Y 122,440, SF 1610).

$2475* *Laughing Frog And All His Friends, 1979,* s., d., annot. E.P.A.P., blindstamp of pub. Editions Press, apparently good cond., scuffing, prop. Thomas Milbrook estate, (02-24-93, Butterfield, #2992), 40½ x 72 in., (102.9 x 182.9 cm.), silkscreen in colors on Arches (BP 1726, DM 4018, FR 13,621, Y 290,425).

$2750* *Laughing Frog And All His Friends, 1979,* s., d., annot. E.P.A.P., blindstamp pub. Editions Press, good cond.?, scuffing, Thomas Milbrook Estate, (10-28-92, Butterfield, #2889), 40½ x 72 in., (102.9 x 182.9 cm.), color silkscreen on Arches (BP 1752, DM 4247, FR 14,421, Y 337,423).

$496* *Meeting The Sun, (19)74,* s., d., num., (06-08-93, Karl/Faber, #496), approx. 20½ x 27Zzn in., (52 x 71 cm.), color lithograph on Arches wove (BP 326, DM 805, FR 2710, Y 52,682).

$793* *Meeting The Sun, 1974,* #32/120, pencil s., d., (11-20-92, Lempertz, #431), sh 22zn x 29Zzn in., (56 x 76 cm.), color lithograph on Arches-Velin (BP 522, DM 1264, FR 4259, Y 98,620).

$1006* *Meeting The Sun, 1978,* #78/120, s., d., stained, (10-09-92, Winterberg, #1680, illus.), 20Zzn x 28Z, in., (52.5 x 71.5 cm.), color lithograph on Arches wove (BP 597, DM 1494, FR 5017, Y 122,474).

$1342* *Monkey,* #55/130, s., (06-24-93, Germann, #212, illus.), 30Z, x 22Mzn in., (765 x 570 mm.), color woodcut w/embossing (BP 883, DM 2176, FR 7333, Y 143,961, SF 1955).

$554* *Morning Face And Blue Sea, 1979,* s., #50/175, good cond.?, (12-09-92, Sotheby-Amstrdm, #469), 21B, x 25zn in., (550 x 650 mm.), color lithograph on wove (BP 354, DM 870, FR 2967, Y 68,692, G 978).

$431* *Mother And Little Boy, 1979: Two,* s., #51/160, #52/160, very good cond., (05-19-93, Butterfield, #2110), each 21C, x 29½ in., (543 x 749 mm.), lithograph in colors on Arches (BP 280, DM 701, FR 2360, Y 47,714).

$715* *Mother and Little Boy, 1970: Two,* s., num. 49/160 and 50/160, very good cond., Nathaniel R. Dumont estate, (02-24-93, Butterfield, #3178), each 21C\ x 29½ in., (543 x 749 mm.), lithograph in colors on Arches (BP 499, DM 1161, FR 3935, Y 83,900).

$330* *"Mother" and "Little Boy", 1970: Two,* s., #47/160, 48/160, very good cond., (10-28-92, Butterfield, #2886), each 21C, x 29½ in., (543 x 749 mm.), color lithograph on Arches (BP 210, DM 510, FR 1730, Y 40,491).

BI *Personnage,* 93/160, s., est. SF1,4/1,800, (10-14-92, Germann, #210, illus.), 21Mzn x 29½ in., (545 x 750 mm.), color lithograph.

$1106* *Personnage,* #93/160, s., (09-04-92, Germann, #50, illus.), 21Mzn x 29½ in., (545 x 750 mm.), color lithograph (BP 554, DM 1550, FR 5277, Y 136,140, SF 1380).

BI *Personnage,* H.C., s., est. SF 800/1,000, (04-21-93, Germann, #221), 21zn x 29½ in., (547 x 750 mm.), color lithograph.

$435* *Personnage,* H.C., s., (06-24-93, Germann, #206), 21zn x 29½ in., (547 x 750 mm.), color lithograph (BP 286, DM 705, FR 2377, Y 46,664, SF 633).

$316* *Personnages,* 35/120, s., tear, (06-24-93, Germann, #213), 25zn x 35¼ in., (650 x 896 mm.), color lithograph (BP 208, DM 512, FR 1727, Y 33,898, SF 460).

$316* *Personnages, 1971,* #14/100, s., d., (06-24-93, Germann, #211), 39C, x 25zn in., (100 x 65 cm.), color lithograph (BP 208, DM 512, FR 1727, Y 33,898, SF 460).

$593* *Personnages, 1973,* #10/120, s., d., (06-24-93, Germann, #210), 24Mzn x 35Mzn in., (620 x 900 mm.), color lithograph (BP 390, DM 961, FR 3240, Y 63,613, SF 863).

$578* *The Philosopher,* s., d. '77, num. 63/100, (11-12-92, Freemn/Fine Art, #21), 25½ x 19½ in., (64.8 x 49.5 cm.), etching (BP 380, DM 916, FR 3089, Y 71,668).

BI *Portrait, 1974,* #15/100, pencil s., d., (11-20-92, Lempertz, #432), sh 31 x 23⅜zn in., (78.8 x 59.9 cm.), color lithograph on Velin.

$337* *"Putting Green Kiss", 1978,* #72/100, s., (10-18-92, Pescheteau, #75), serigraph in colors (BP 204, DM 498, FR 1691, Y 40,239).

$468* *Rearing Horse, 1978,* s. white pencil, num. 20/130, from the series Circus, (09-20-92, Hindman, #819), 30 x 22¼ in., (76.2 x 56.5 cm.), embossed color woodcut (BP 274, DM 694, FR 2376, Y 57,842).

$576* *Recontre Au Soleil, 1974,* s., d., #49/100, pub. L'Oeuvre Gravee, w/their blindstamp, full margis, good cond., (05-27-93, Sotheby-Amstrdm, #537), 20Œzn x 26Œzn in., (513 x 665 mm.), colored silkscreen on wove (BP 369, DM 924, FR 3115, Y 61,750, G 1035).

$569* *Sans Titre, 1969,* artist proof, s. Appel, (05-18-93, Encans, #167), 24Ⱬzn x 34¼ in., (63 x 87 cm.), color lithograph on Arches (BP 371, DM 923, FR 3118, Y 63,412, C$ 722).

BI *Sans Titre, c. 1977,* s., 55/100, est. FF1,500/2,000, (06-28-93, Loudmer, #183), 37Ⱬzn x 25Ⱬzn in., (965 x 660 mm.), color serigraph on wove.

$770* *She Is Back Again, 1974,* s., d., num. 107/120, blindstamp of pub. Editions Press, full margins, apparently good cond., buckling, (02-24-93, Butterfield, #3180), 22 x 30 in., (559 x 762 mm.), silkscreen in colors w/ embossing on wove (BP 537, DM 1250, FR 4238, Y 90,354).

BI *Summerlife,* s., i. e.a. 9/25, est. $2/4,000, (02-14-93, Hanzel, #662), 25½ x 22 in., (64.8 x 55.9 cm.), color lithograph.

BI *Summerlife,* s., i. E.A. 9/25, est. $3/500, (11-01-92, Hanzel, #280), 25½ x 20 in., (64.8 x 50.8 cm.), color lithograph.

$456* *Tete, 1974,* s., d., #58/100, margins, good cond., (12-09-92, Sotheby-Amstrdm, #466), sheet 31Mzn x 23½ in., (798 x 597 mm.), color lithograph on wove (BP 291, DM 716, FR 2442, Y 56,541, G 805).

$489* *Tete, 1976,* s., d., #96/99, good cond., creases, soiling, (12-09-92, Sotheby-Amstrdm, #465), sheet 31½ x 24Ⱬzn in., (800 x 627 mm.), color silkscreen on stiff wove (BP 312, DM 768, FR 2619, Y 60,632, G 863).

$770* *Three Figures,* HC, s., prov., (06-11-93, DuMouchelle, #2099), 26 x 40 in., (66 x 101.6 cm.), lithograph (BP 506, DM 1251, FR 4219, Y 81,698).

BI *Toi Et Moi,* s., #41/200, t., est. DM 1,600, (05-08-93, Schloss Ahlden, #2833), 25Ⱬzn x 19M, in., (65.5 x 50.5 cm.), color lithograph on Arches-handmade.

$499* *Two Faces,* s., #85/100, full margins, good cond., (05-27-93, Sotheby-Amstrdm, #550), 20C, x 26Mzn in., (517 x 672 mm.), colored screenprint on Arches (BP 320, DM 801, FR 2699, Y 53,495, G 897).

$416* *Two Figures,* s., #74/100, full margins, good cond., minor handling creases, (05-27-93, Sotheby-Amstrdm, #548, illus.), 26Ⱬzn x 37Ⱬzn in., (662 x 964 mm.), colored silkscreen on wove (BP 266, DM 668, FR 2250, Y 44,597, G 748).

$1151* *Two Figures, 1964,* s., d., i. Epreuve divinitif 1/1, margins, good cond., minor paper dicoloration, (05-27-93, Sotheby-Amstrdm, #534, illus.), 19B, x 25Ⱬzn in., colored lithograph on wove (BP 737, DM 1847, FR 6225, Y 123,392, G 2070).

$416* *Two Figures, 1977,* s., #III/XXV, pub. London Arts, full margins, good cond., minor handling creases, (05-27-93, Sotheby-Amstrdm, #535), 25Ⱬzn x 37Ⱬzn in., (660 x 963 mm.), colored silkscreen on BFK Rives (BP 266, DM 668, FR 2250, Y 44,597, G 748).

$416* *Two Figures, 1977,* s., #91/100, pub. London Arts, full margins, good cond., minor handling creases, (05-27-93, Sotheby-Amstrdm, #541), 25M, x 37Ⱬzn in., (657 x 963 mm.), colored silkscreen on wove (BP 266, DM 668, FR 2250, Y 44,597, G 748).

$935* *Two Heads,* #90/100, s., (06-11-93, DuMouchelle, #2097), 26 x 40 in., (66 x 101.6 cm.), lithograph (BP 614, DM 1520, FR 5123, Y 99,204).

$385* *Two People, Autumn Like, c. 1970s,* s., #2/160, (12-08-92, Swann, #11), 22 x 30 in., (55.9 x 76.2 cm.), color lithograph (BP 241, DM 599, FR 2044, Y 47,719).

$605* *Untitled,* s., num. 151/175, (09-20-92, Hindman, #818), 29½ x 21 in., (74.9 x 53.3 cm.), print (BP 354, DM 898, FR 3071, Y 74,774).

$391* *Untitled,* s., i. E.A., good cond., discoloration, rubbing, (12-09-92, Sotheby-Amstrdm, #477), 11Ⱬ, x 8Ⱬzn in., (282 x 228 mm.), color lithograph on wove (BP 250, DM 614, FR 2094, Y 48,481, G 690).

$586* *Untitled,* s., #68/115, pub. l'OEuvre Gravee, blindstamp, discoloration, foxing, tape, (12-09-92, Sotheby-Amstrdm, #464), sheet 19Ⱬzn x 19Ⱬzn in., (503 x 504 mm.), color lithograph on wove (BP 374, DM 920, FR 3139, Y 72,660, G 1035).

$651* *Untitled,* s., #7/100, margins, good cond., light staining, (12-09-92, Sotheby-Amstrdm, #462), sheet 33Ⱬzn x 24Ⱬzn in., (840 x 630 mm.), color lithograph on wove (BP 415, DM 1022, FR 3487, Y 80,719, G 1150).

BI *Untitled,* s., i. E.A., full margins, good cond., est. Dfl. 6/700, (05-27-93, Sotheby-Amstrdm, #547), 12½ x 20C in., (317 x 518 mm.), colored lithograph on wove.

$1663* *Untitled,* s., #4/50, i. bleu, margins, good cond., (05-27-93, Sotheby-Amstrdm, #533, illus.), 19M, x 25C\zn in., (505 x 655 mm.), colored lithograph on wove (BP 1065, DM 2668, FR 8994, Y 178,280, G 2990).

$330* *Untitled,* s., #96/100, d. '71, (11-30-92, Selkirk, #711), paper 25 x 35 in., (63.5 x 88.9 cm.), lithograph in colors (BP 218, DM 526, FR 1785, Y 41,070).

$419* *Untitled,* s. 73, 69/120, (09-29-92, B. Rasmussen, #270), lithograph in colors (BP 236, DM 592, FR 2019, Y 50,018, DK 2300).

$293* *Untitled,* s. 39/175, (09-29-92, B. Rasmussen, #269), lithograph in colors (BP 165, DM 414, FR 1412, Y 34,977, DK 1610).

$419* *Untitled,* s., 59/175, (09-29-92, B. Rasmussen, #273), lithograph in colors (BP 236, DM 592, FR 2019, Y 50,018, DK 2300).

$413* *Untitled,* s., d. 1971, #83/100, (05-16-93, Hindman, #640A), 23 x 33 in., (58.4 x 83.8 cm.), color lithograph (BP 269, DM 664, FR 2232, Y 45,782).

$33* *Untitled,* (12-02-92, Boos, #342), 25¾ x 19 in., (65.4 x 48.3 cm.), color serigraphic poster (BP 21, DM 52, FR 177, Y 4106).

$456* *Untitled,* s., #26/100, full margins, good cond., sheet 1040 x 750 mm, (12-09-92, Sotheby-Amstrdm, #481), color silkscreen on wove (BP 291, DM 716, FR 2442, Y 56,541, G 805).

$489* *Untitled,* s., #68/100, full margins, good cond., sheet 1040 x 750 mm, (12-09-92, Sotheby-Amstrdm, #482), color silkscreen on wove (BP 312, DM 768, FR 2619, Y 60,632, G 863).

$544* *Untitled,* s., i. E.A., margins, good cond., occasional minor defects, (05-27-93, Sotheby-Amstrdm, #544), 24Mzn x 28½ in., (620 x 724 mm.), colored silkscreen and gouache on Fabriano wove (BP 348, DM 873, FR 2942, Y 58,319, G 978).

$320* *Untitled,* s., #23/75, full sheet, good cond., minor handling creases, (05-27-93, Sotheby-Amstrdm, #549), sh 29Ⱬzn x 22Ⱬzn in., (758 x 560 mm.), colored screenprint on wove (BP 205, DM 513, FR 1731, Y 34,305, G 575).

$880* *Untitled Face,* d. 1970, #88/100, (10-16-92, DuMouchelle, #2404, illus.), 26 x 20 in., (66 x 50.8 cm.), colored lithograph (BP 533, DM 1300, FR 4415, Y 105,075).

$330* *Untitled Paturages, 1961,* s., annot. H.C., full margins, good cond., creases, surface soiling,tears, rubbed area, pencil notations, Thomas Milbrook estate, (02-24-93, Butterfield, #3176), sheet 22½ x 30 in., (572 x 762 mm.), lithograph in colors on Rives BFK (BP 230, DM 536, FR 1816, Y 38,723).

$275* *"Untitled",* crayon s., #10/50, good cond., pressure mark, (10-28-92, Butterfield, #2890), 21½ x 29B, in., (546 x 752 mm.), color lithograph on Somerset paper (BP 175, DM 425, FR 1442, Y 33,742).

$303* *(Untitled), 1971,* s., d., num. 27/100, blindstamp of pub., margins, apparently good cond., light-staining, Thomas Milbrook estate, (02-24-93, Butterfield, #3179), 26¼ x 40 in., (66.7 x 101.6 cm.), silkscreen in colors on wove (BP 211, DM 492, FR 1668, Y 35,555).

$693* *Untitled, 1965,* #57/200, s., d., ref., est. C$ 1,2/1,500, (11-16-92, Hodgins, #120), 20Ⱬzn x 28½ in., (53.3 x

72.4 cm.), serigraph on paper (BP 455, DM 1105, FR 3724, Y 86,484, C$ 880).

$619* *Untitled, 1971,* s., d., #99/125, full margins, good cond., (12-09-92, Sotheby-Amstrdm, #470), 26Czn x 20Zzn in., (665 x 510 mm.), color silkscreen on Arches (BP 395, DM 972, FR 3315, Y 76,751, G 1093).

$1265* *Untitled, 1974,* s., d., #81/120, blindstamp publisher, Editions Press, margins, goodcond.?, stains, (05-19-93, Butterfield, #2111), 22¾ x 30B, in., (578 x 778 mm.), silkscreen in colors w/metallic silver collage on wove (BP 821, DM 2056, FR 6928, Y 140,042).

BI *Untitled, 1975,* #29/125, s., d., prov., est. C$ 1,2/1,500, (11-16-92, Hodgins, #317, illus.), 23½ x 17Bzn in., (59.7 x 45.7 cm.), serigraph on paper.

BI *Untitled, 1977,* from portfolio Seven Summer Days, s., d., #66/100, full margins, good cond., est. G 6/800, (12-09-92, Sotheby-Amstrdm, #467), 29Bzn x 22Bzn in., (745 x 583 mm.), color screenprint on Economos-Etching paper.

BI *Untitled, 1977,* from portfolio Seven Summer Days, s., d., #66/100, full margins, good cond.?, est. G 6/800, (12-09-92, Sotheby-Amstrdm, #468), 29Mzn x 23zn in., (748 x 598 mm.), color screenprint on Economos-Etching paper.

$880* *Untitled, Face, 1969,* s., d., annot. E.A., full margins, mat staining, (10-28-92, Butterfield, #2885), 19¾ x 25¼ in., (502 x 641 mm.), color lithograph on Arches (BP 561, DM 1359, FR 4615, Y 107,975).

BI *Visage, 1969,* s. Appel 69, 7/85, est. DK 2,500, (03-24-93, Kunsthallen, #19), color lithograph.

BI *Visage, 1969,* s. Appel 69, 7/85, est. DK 3,000, (09-30-92, Kunsthallen, #24), color lithograph.

$737* *Walking With My Bird,* #23/160, s., (09-04-92, Germann, #213), 21Mzn x 29Mzn in., (545 x 748 mm.), color lithograph (BP 369, DM 1033, FR 3516, Y 90,719, SF 920).

BI *Walking With My Bird,* s., num., est. DM 800, (12-01-92, Karl/Faber, #322), 21¼ x 29Bzn in., (54 x 74.5 cm.), color lithogrph on Arches wove.

BI *Walking With My Bird, c. 1979,* num., s., est. $5/750, (05-27-93, Swann, #16), sh 21½ x 29½ in., (54.6 x 74.9 cm.), color serigraph.

$770* *"What Are They Waiting For?",* d. 1970, #88/100, (10-16-92, DuMouchelle, #2403, illus.), image 20 x 26 in., (50.8 x 66 cm.), colored lithograph (BP 467, DM 1137, FR 3864, Y 91,940).

$358* *Woman And Fish, 1966,* s., d., num. 113/200, full margins, good cond., surface soiling, rubbed area, mat-staining, (02-24-93, Butterfield, #3177), 25¼ x 19¾ in., (641 x 502 mm.), lithograph in colors on Rives BFK (BP 250, DM 581, FR 1970, Y 42,009).

$770* *"Woman With Bird", 1975,* s., d. Appel 75, #74/100, ident. on label, very good cond., wrinkling, (03-12-93, Skinner, #94, illus.), sight 39¼ x 26 in., (99.7 x 66 cm.), color screenprint on wove (BP 537, DM 1282, FR 4358, Y 90,748).

APPEL, Karel (after)

$264* *Birds In Flight,* s., #8/9, p. Chiron Press, good cond., (10-07-92, Christie-S. Ken, #136), 25¼ x 38¾ in., (64.1 x 98.4 cm.), lithograph p. in color (BP 154, DM 382, FR 1295, Y 31,750).

APPIAN, Adolphe French 1819-1898

$560* *"Le Champ De Ble", 1863 and "Une Mare", 1867 (A. Curtis et P. Proute2 et 23): Two,* first, first state of four, creases; second, first state of three, large margins, collector's stamps, (06-11-93, Picard, #1), one 3Czn x 7C, in., (97 x 187 mm.), other 9Czn x 6Mzn in., (97 x 187 mm.), etchings on laid (BP 368, DM 910, FR 3068, Y 59,416).

BI *"Marais De La Burbanche (Ain)" (Jennings 23, Curtis/ Proute 26 iii/iv), 1868,* pub. Hammerton's Etchings and Etchers, 3rd edit., 1880, good cond.,est. $75-125, (10-31-92, Cleveland, #242), 5C, x 9¼ in., (13.7 x 23.5 cm.), etching.

APPLEBY, Leonard

$579* *A Friend To The Farmer, Shell Tractor Oil, The Greater Spotted Woodpecker, 1952,* p. Waterlow and Sons, ref. P 28, cond. 3, (10-13-92, Phillips-London, #172), 29Bzn x 39¾ in., (76 x 101 cm.), color lithograph (BP 337, DM 848, FR 2882, Y 70,207).

APPLETON and CO.

$303* *Portrait Of John Ruskin, 1863,* Ruskin's sig. p. in margin, (11-16-92, Butterfield, #5837, illus.), 5M, x 4¼ in., (149.5 x 108.1 mm.), photograph, photogravure (BP 199, DM 483, FR 1627, Y 37,682).

ARAKAWA, Shusaku Japanese b. 1936

$1029* *By Or In Surd,* s., #1/24, good cond., (06-30-93, Sotheby-London, #734, illus.), sh c. 30M, x 59M, in., (78.4 x 152.1 cm.), color lithograph (BP 690, DM 1755, FR 5921, Y 110,254).

$1650* *Dear Picasso..., 1973,* s., d., bears 2nd sig., p. to 2 sides, good cond., (02-24-93, Butterfield, #2996), 21Czn x 30 in., (538 x 762 mm.), offset lithograph & silkscreen on Arches (BP 1151, DM 2679, FR 9081, Y 193,617).

$1210* *Evening On Which,* s., t., d., pub. Multiples, Inc., full sheet, excell. cond., (09-19-92, Christie-E, #78, illus.), sheet 31Z, x 62Z, in., (79.1 x 157.8 cm.), lithograph and screenprint in colors w/embossing on wove (BP 696, DM 1812, FR 6205, Y 150,760).

$990* *I See The Ceiling From My Bed,* s., t., d., num. 48/60, pub. Marion Goodman, blindstamp of printer Styria Studio, apparently good cond., creases, est. $1/2,000, (02-24-93, Butterfield, #2995), 30 x 42 in., (76.2 x 106.7 cm.), lithograph & silkscreen w/embossing on wove (BP 690, DM 1607, FR 5449, Y 116,170).

BI *If Possible, Please Fold Along The Dotted Line Once Folded, Please Think Of What Is Inside, 1969,* s. in ink, d., num. 20/95, apparently good cond., est. $800/1,000, (02-24-93, Butterfield, #2993), 26 x 40 in., (66 x 101.6 cm.), silkscreen in colors on silver mylar.

BI *If Possible, Please Fold Along The Dotted Line Once Folded, Please Think Of What Is Inside, 1969,* s., d., #20/95, good cond.?, est. $7/900, (05-19-93, Butterfield, #2112), 26 x 40 in., (66 x 101.6 cm.), silkscreen in colors on silver mylar.

$690* *Landscape, 1990,* s., d., t., #4/75, good cond.?, light surface scuffing, (05-19-93, Butterfield, #2113), 35 x 45 in., (88.9 x 114.3 cm.), silkscreen in colors on silver mylar (BP 448, DM 1122, FR 3779, Y 76,387).

$1100* *Next To The Last, 1969-71,* s., d., annot. P.P., full margins, good cond., staining, creases, (02-24-93, Butterfield, #2994), 21½ x 41M, in., (54.6 x 106.4 cm.), silkscreen in colors on wove (BP 767, DM 1786, FR 6054, Y 129,078).

BI *The Old Story (Explosion), 1967,* s., #8/100, margins, good cond.?, est. G 1,5/2,000, (12-09-92, Sotheby-Amstrdm, #483, illus.), 32Bzn x 24Czn in., (820 x 615 mm.), color silkscreen on wove.

$1760* *Or Detail/Of The Model/Hypartatizing Distance And/Or Embodying Weight/The Call Of..., 1980,* s., d., t., annot., num. 19/48, blindstamps of pub. & p., full margins, apparently good cond., creases(02-24-93, Butterfield, #2997), 34 x 63 in., (86.4 x 160 cm.), lithograph in colors on wove (BP 1227, DM 2857, FR 9686, Y 206,524).

$1201* *"Outside Blanket" and "For Aime", 1982 and 1984: Two,* each s., d., t., #35/100 and 10/80, i., good cond., (06-30-93, Sotheby-London, #735, illus.), one 15 x 21M, in., (381 x 556 mm.), the other 21¼ x 28 in., (381 x 556 mm.), etching w/lithograph in black/grey, and color lithograph (BP 805, DM 2048, FR 6910, Y 128,683).

$1218* *Redolence, 1974,* s., d., t., #26/60, (05-27-93, Lempertz, #568), 29Zzn x 41M, in., (75.8 x 106.3 cm.), color lithograph w/serigraph and blind embossing (BP 780, DM 1954, FR 6587, Y 130,575).

ARAKI, Jypo Japanese 20th cent.

$11* *Beribboned Flower,* pencil s., #25/75, (04-02-93, Sloan, #1873), 11B, x 9¼ in., (295 x 235 mm.), color etching and aquatint (BP 7, DM 18, FR 60, Y 1252).

ARAUJO, Emanoel

$107* *"Blue And Black Angles" and "Green And Brown Angles": Two,* each s., d. 74 and 75, #2/12 and 6/10, prov., exhib., (12-01-92, Ritchie, #88), each approx. 27½ x 40½ in., (69.9 x 102.9 cm.), woodcut (BP 71, DM 171, FR 581, Y 13,322, C$ 138).

ARBEIT, Mark

$429* *"The Chrysler Building, NYC", 1988,* s., t. Harpers Bazaar Australia October 1988 in pencil, (10-29-92, Christie-London, #201, illus.), image, approx. 20 x 16 in., (50.8 x 40.6 cm.), photograph, toned gelatin silver print (BP 275, DM 660, FR 2239, Y 53,140).

ARBUS, Diane American 1923-1971

$825* *Bishop By The Sea, L.A., Ca.,* p. later by Neil Selkirk, stamp, s., t., d., num. 5/75 in ink, reprod. limit. stamp, lit., (1964), (10-13-92, Christie-NY, #516, illus.), 14½ x 15 in., (36.8 x 38.1 cm.), photograph, gelatin silver print (BP 480, DM 1209, FR 4107, Y 100,036).

$863* *Bishop Ethel Predonzan By Sea,* 1964, p. 1985 by Neil Selkirk, stamped A Diane Arbus Photograph, inks. by Doon Arbus, t., d., #15/75, reprod. limitation stamp, lit., (04-08-93, Christie-NY, #465, illus.), 14Z, x 14Z, in., (35.9 x 35.9 cm.), photograph, gelatin silver print (BP 566, DM 1386, FR 4693, Y 97,935).

$770* *Charles Atlas,* (1969), p. 1984 by Neil Selkirk, stamped, s., t., d., num. 3/75 in ink by Doon Arbus, (c) & reprod. limit. stamps, lit., (10-13-92, Christie-NY, #519, illus.), 14½ x 14½ in., (36.8 x 36.8 cm.), photograph, gelatin silver print (BP 448, DM 1128, FR 3833, Y 93,367).

$6900* *Child With A Toy Hand Grenade In Central Park, NYC,* 1962, p.l. by Neil Selkirk, stamped a Diane Arbus photograph, s. by Doon Arbus, ink t., d., edit. #53/75, (c) and reprod. limitation stamps, lit., (04-08-93, Christie-NY, #464, illus.), 14¾ x 14B\ in., (37.5 x 37.1 cm.), photograph, gelatin silver print (BP 4525, DM 11,084, FR 37,520, Y 783,023).

$2090* *A Flower Girl At A Wedding, Conn.,* p. later by Neil Selkirk, stamped, s., t., d. in ink, reprod. limit.stamp, lit., (1964), (10-13-92, Christie-NY, #517, illus.), 14C, x 14½ in., (36.5 x 36.8 cm.), photograph, gelatin silver print (BP 1217, DM 3062, FR 10,403, Y 253,425).

$1725* *Four People At A Gallery Opening, New York City,* 1968, p.l. by Neil Selkirk, stamped A Diane Arbus photograph, ink s., t., d., #19/75 by Doon Arbus, reprod. limitation stamp, lit., (04-08-93, Christie-NY, #468, illus.), 14M, x 14¾ in., (37.8 x 37.5 cm.), photograph, gelatin silver print (BP 1131, DM 2771, FR 9380, Y 195,756).

$2640* *The King And Queen Of A Senior Citizens Dance, N.Y.C.,* (1970), from A Box Of Ten Photographs Portfolio, p. 1970 by Neil Selkirk, stamped, s., t., d., num. 34/50 in ink, reprod. limit. stamps, lit., (10-13-92, Christie-NY, #520, illus.), 14¾ x 14½ in., (37.5 x 36.8 cm.), photograph, gelatin silver print (BP 1538, DM 3868, FR 13,141, Y 320,116).

$1760* *Mae West,* (1965), p. 1985 by Neil Selkirk, stamped, s. Doon Arbus, t., d., edit. num. 5/75 in ink, (c) & reprod. limit. stamps, lit., (10-13-92, Christie-NY, #518, illus.), 14½ x 14½ in., (36.8 x 36.8 cm.), photograph, gelatin silver print (BP 1025, DM 2578, FR 8761, Y 213,411).

$1840* *Masked Man At A Ball, N.Y.C.,* 1967, p.l. by Neil Selkirk, stamped A Diane Arbus Photograph, ink s., t., d., #10/75 by Doon Arbus, reprod. limitation and (c) stamps, lit., (04-08-93, Christie-NY, #466, illus.), 14C, x 14C, in., (36.5 x 36.5 cm.), photograph, gelatin silver print (BP 1207, DM 2956, FR 10,005, Y 208,806).

$1373* *"Teenage Couple On Hudson Street, N.Y.C.", 1963,* p.l., stamped , s., t., d., (10-29-92, Christie-London, #196, illus.), image 15 x 14¾ in., (38.1 x 37.5 cm.), photograph, gelatin silver print (BP 880, DM 2112, FR 7166, Y 170,073).

$2200* *"Two Ladies At The Automat",* 1966/1980, s. Doon Arbus, t., d., edit. 26/75; photog. A Diane Arbusphotograph printed by Neil Selkirk and estate stamps verso, Dixon Collection, (11-16-92, Butterfield, #5838, illus.), 14C, x 14½ in., (365.8 x 369 mm.), photograph, gelatin silver print (BP 1449, DM 3508, FR 11,815, Y 273,598).

$1760* *Untitled (6),* (1970-71), p.l. by Neil Selkirk, stamped, s., t., d., num. 60/75 in imk, reprod. limit. & (c) stamps, lit., (10-13-92, Christie-NY, #521, illus.), 14¾ x 4¾ in., (37.5 x 12.1 cm.), photograph, gelatin silver print (BP 1025, DM 2578, FR 8761, Y 213,411).

$1100* *Untitled (Psychiatric Patients),* p. Neil Selkirk, stamped A Diane Arbus Photograph, w/ Doon Arbus's sig., 1970-71, p.l., (04-07-93, Swann, #393, illus.), 19¾ x 15¾ in., photograph, silver print (BP 727, DM 1779, FR 6021, Y 124,972).

$5500* *Waitress, Nudist Camp, New Jersey, 1963,* s. twice, t., d., reprod limit., i. in ink, (10-13-92, Christie-NY, #522, illus.), 2¾ x 2¾ in., (7 x 7 cm.), photograph, gelatin silver print (BP 3203, DM 8057, FR 27,377, Y 666,909).

$1955* *A Young Man And His Pregnant Wife In Washington Square Park, N.Y.C.,* 1965, p.l. by Neil Selkirk, stamped A Diane Arbus photograph, ink s., t., d., #9/75 by Doon Arbus, reprod. limitation and (c) stamps, lit., (04-08-93, Christie-NY, #463, illus.), 14½ x 14¾ in., (36.8 x 37.5 cm.), photograph, gelatin silver print (BP 1282, DM 3141, FR 10,631, Y 221,857).

ARBUS, Diane and Neil SELKIRK

$805* *"Feminist Group", 1969,* s., t., d. #2/75 by photog. daughter, Doon Arbus, Diane Arbus Estate's t., (c), reprod. lim. stamps, p. 1985 by Neil Selkirk from neg. by Diane Arbus, (04-06-93, Sotheby-NY, #473, illus.), photograph (BP 532, DM 1297, FR 4392, Y 91,811).

$1725* *"A Flower Girl At A Wedding, Connecticut" (MoMA, unpaginated), 1964,* s., t., d. by photog. daughter, Doon Arbus, reprod. lim. stamp, p.l.by Neil Selkirk from neg. by Diane Arbus, (04-06-93, Sotheby-NY, #475, illus.), 14½ x 14¼ in., photograph (BP 1139, DM 2779, FR 9411, Y 196,738).

$1725* *"Girl In A Shiny Dress, N.Y.C" (MoMA, unpaginated), 1967,* s., t., d., #25/75 by photog. daughter, Doon Arbus, Diane Arbus Estate's t., (c), all rights reserved stamps, p. after 1972 by Neil Selkirk from neg. by Diane Arbus, (04-06-93, Sotheby-NY, #472, illus.), photograph (BP 1139, DM 2779, FR 9411, Y 196,738).

$990* *Lady At A Masked Ball With Two Roses On Her Dress, N.Y.C., (MoMA, unpaginated),* s., t., d., num. 32/75 by photog.'s daughter, t., (c) stamps, 1967, p. l. by NEIL SELKIRK from neg., #32/75 ed., (10-15-92, Sotheby-NY, #566, illus.), photograph, gelatin silver print (BP 606, DM 1474, FR 4997, Y 118,776).

$1610* *"Man At A Parade On Fifth Avenue, NYC",* 1969, p.l., s. Neil Selkirk and Doon Arbus, #17/75, photog.'s Diane Arbus and estate stamps, illus., (05-23-93, Butterfield, #3301, illus.), 14½ x 14½ in., photograph, gelatin silver print (BP 1049, DM 2632, FR 8861, Y 177,960).

$1100* *Masked Woman In A Wheelchair, Pa.,* s. by photog.'s daughter, num. 29/75 in ink, t., (c), reprod. limit.stamps, 1970, p.l. by NEIL SELKIRK from neg., #29/75 ed., (10-15-92, Sotheby-NY, #567, illus.), 15Z, x 14½ in., (38.4 x 36.8 cm.), photograph, gelatin silver print (BP 673, DM 1637, FR 5553, Y 131,974).

$1100* *A Naked Man Being A Woman, N.Y.C. (MoMA, unpaginated),* s., t., d., num. 10/75 by photog.'s daughter, t., (c) stamps, 1968, p. l. by NEIL SELKIRK from neg., #10/75 ed., (10-15-92, Sotheby-NY, #564, illus.), 14¼ x 14½ in., (36.2 x 36.8 cm.), photograph, gelatin silver print (BP 673, DM 1637, FR 5553, Y 131,974).

$1495* *"Russian Midget Friends In A Living Room On 100th Street, N.Y.C.",* 1963, p.l., s. Neil Selkirk and Doon Arbus, t., photog.'s Diane Arbus stamp, illus., (05-23-93, Butterfield, #3302, illus.), 14½ x 14½ in., photograph, gelatin silver print (BP 974, DM 2444, FR 8228, Y 165,248).

$1610* *"Two Ladies At The Automat, N.Y.C." (MoMA, unpaginated), 1966,* s., t., d., #30/75 by photog. daughter, Doon Arbus, Diane Arbus Estate t., (c), all rights reserved stamps, p.l. by Neil Selkirk from neg. by DianeArbus, (04-06-93, Sotheby-NY, #474, illus.), photograph (BP 1063, DM 2594, FR 8783, Y 183,622).

$880* *Two Men Dancing At A Drag Ball, N.Y.C. (MoMA, unpaginated),* s., t., d., num. 15/75 by photog.'s daughter, t., (c) stamps, 1970, p. l. by NEIL SELKIRK from neg., #15/75 ed., (10-15-92, Sotheby-NY, #565, illus.), 14½ x 14¾ in., (36.8 x 37.5 cm.), photograph, gelatin silver print (BP 538, DM 1310, FR 4442, Y 105,579).

$1495* *"Woman With A Veil On Fifth Avenue, N.Y.C." (MoMA, unpaginated), 1968,* s., t., d., #38/75 by photog. daughter, Doon Arbus, Diane Arbus Estate's t., (c), all rights reserved stamps, p. after 1972 by Neil Selkirk from neg. by Diane Arbus, (04-06-93, Sotheby-NY, #471, illus.), photograph (BP 987, DM 2409, FR 8156, Y 170,506).

$3450* *"A Young Brooklyn Family Going For A Sunday Outing",* 1966, p. 1973, s. Doon Arbus, #12/50, portfolio stamp, t., d. on label, t., from Box of Ten portfolio, illus., (05-23-93, Butterfield, #3299, illus.), 15¼ x 14¾ in., photograph, gelatin silver print (BP 2247, DM 5641, FR 18,987, Y 381,342).

$1840* *"A Young Man In Curlers At Home On West 20th Street", 1966,* p. 1973, s. Doon Arbus, #12/50, portfolio stamp, t., d. on label, from Box of Ten portfolio, illus., (05-23-93, Butterfield, #3300, illus.), 15 x 14¼ in., photograph, gelatin silver print (BP 1198, DM 3009, FR 10,127, Y 203,382).

ARCHAMBAULT, Luc Canadian b. 1954

$18* *"L'Homme De Florence",* #44/125, t., s., (02-16-93, Encans, #1), 21Z, x 24Z, in., (53.7 x 61.2 cm.), lithograph (BP 12, DM 29, FR 100, Y 2156, C$ 22).

$235* *"Le Sacre Du Printemps-Nijinsky",* #83/185, s. Archambault, (06-16-93, Encans, #1), 21B, x 30Zn in., (55 x 76.3 cm.), serigraph (BP 157, DM 390, FR 1309, Y 25,064, C$ 300).

$347* *"Trilogie Des Elements: Eau, Air, Feu": Three,* #83/150, s. Archambault, (06-16-93, Encans, #4), 22Zn x 29Zn in., (56 x 76 cm.), serigraph (BP 231, DM 576, FR 1933, Y 37,009, C$ 444).

ARCHER, Fred R.

BI *Myrna Loy, In Exotic Pose,* autograph, est. BP 180/250, (10-10-92, Bonhams, #85, illus.), 10 x 8 in., (25.4 x 20.3 cm.), photograph.

$805* *Shahrazad,* 1920s, s., t., (04-08-93, Christie-NY, #226, illus.), 13C, x 10C, in., (34 x 26.4 cm.), photograph, gelatin silver print (BP 528, DM 1293, FR 4377, Y 91,353).

ARCHIPENKO, Alexander Russian/American 1887-1964

$1540* *"Coquette" (Karshan 78), 1950,* s., pub. AAA, light stain, (10-31-92, Cleveland, #57, illus.), 14 x 10 in., (35.6 x 25.4 cm.), lithograph (BP 987, DM 2369, FR 8038, Y 190,759).

$1011* *Coronation Of Forms (Karshan 49), 1963,* s., blindstamp Erker Presse, est. DM 2,200, (11-28-92, Schoppmann, #357), 24Mn x 16Zn in., (62 x 43 cm.), lithograph on BFK Rives (BP 667, DM 1611, FR 5468, Y 125,825).

$3547* *"Les Formes Vivantes" (Karshan 97-106), 1963: Ten,* s., ded., num., blindstamp Erker Presse, (06-05-93, Grisebach, #372, illus.), each plate 30Z, x 22¼ in., (76.5 x 56.5 cm.), lithograph on wove (BP 2335, DM 5751, FR 19,383, Y 380,498).

$345* *Les Formes Vivantes: Les Amoreux, La Danse Noir, and Le Group (Karshan 44, 45 and 46), 1963: Three,* from portfolio Les Formes Vivantes, s., two #62/75, last #52/75, pub. blindstamp, Ersker-Presse, full sheets, good cond., creases, first w/foxing, (02-18-93, Sotheby-Arcade, #85), each sheet 30 x 22¼ in., (76.2 x 56.5 cm.), lithograph (BP 238, DM 563, FR 1905, Y 41,101).

BI *Le Groupe (Karshan 99), 1963,* #68/75, s., blindstamp, est. SF 1/1,500, (04-21-93, Germann, #228), 30Z, x 22¼ in., (765 x 565 mm.), lithograph.

$666* *La Luminosita Delle Forme (D. Karshan 51), 1963,* #13/75, s., from Les Formes Vivantes Erker-Presse, 1963, (05-20-93, Finarte-Milan, #1), 26Zn x 17½ in., (67.5 x 44.4 cm.), lithograph (BP 427, DM 1075, FR 3620, Y 73,542, L 978).

$1011* *The Mannikins (Karshan 47), 1963,* s., blindstamp Erker Presse, est. DM 2200, (11-28-92, Schoppmann, #356), 24Zn x 17Zn in., (63 x 45 cm.), lithograph on BFK Rives (BP 667, DM 1611, FR 5468, Y 125,825).

$2166* *"Stilleben" (Karshan 28 and 65; Jahn/Berger 82), 1921,* in "Die Schaffenden", III. Jg. 1. Mappe 1921, (11-28-92, Grisebach, #410, illus.), 11Zn x 15Cn in., (29.4 x 38.5 cm.), lithograph on beige Japan (BP 1430, DM 3451, FR 11,714, Y 269,571).

BI *Two Figures (Karshan 8), 1920-21,* s., i. I, margins, good cond., creases, discoloration, est. BP 3,5/4,500, (12-03-92, Sotheby-London, #184, illus.), sheet 22M, x 16¾ in., (581 x 425 mm.), lithograph on cream wove.

$354* *Weibliche Akte (Karshan 29 c), 1923,* from the series Dritten Jahresmappe des Kreises graphischer Kunstlerund Sammler, (06-08-93, Karl/Faber, #498), approx. 12Zn x 10¼ in., (32.5 x 26 cm.), lithograph on wove (BP 233, DM 574, FR 1934, Y 37,600).

$1419* *Weibliche Akte (Karshan 29), 1923,* s., in portfolio Dritte Jahresgabe des Kreises graphischer Kunstler und Sammler, (06-05-93, Bassenge, #5872, illus.), 12Zn x 10¼ in., (33 x 26 cm.), lithograph on hand-made (BP 934, DM 2301, FR 7754, Y 152,221).

ARDINE, Sir William 1800-1874

$99* *"Maneless Lion" and "Brit Mus": Two,* from "The Naturalist's Library", Edinborough, 1833-43, (07-03-92, Sloan, #324), hand colored engraving (BP 52, DM 150, FR 505, Y 12,341).

ARDISSON, Yolande

$33* *Marina And Houses,* (12-11-92, DuMouchelle, #1469), 23 x 16½ in., (58.4 x 41.9 cm.), lithograph (BP 21, DM 52, FR 178, Y 4084).

ARDIZZONE, Edward

$226* *On The Beach,* watermarked 1948, s., t., #1/50, light staining, good cond., (10-27-92, Phillips-London, #230), (191 x 225 mm.), black lithograph on J. Whatman (BP 143, DM 346, FR 1175, Y 27,645).

ARDIZZONE, Edward b. 1900

$1377* *These Men Use Shell, Lifeboatmen, 1938,* p. Waterlow and Sons, ref. #509, cond. 1, creasing, (10-13-92, Phillips-London, #133), 29Zn x 44M, in., (76 x 114 cm.), color lithograph (BP 802, DM 2017, FR 6854, Y 166,970).

ARENDSEN, Arentine H. (after)

$1741* *Album Van Eeden, Haarlem's Flora: Ninety-Eight,* by G. Severeyns, from the series pub. A.C. Van Eeden and C. Wagenberg, (10-27-92, Phillips-London, #172), sheet 13¾ x 10C, in., (349 x 264 mm.), colored chromolithograph on wove (BP 1100, DM 2668, FR 9054, Y 212,966).

ARENTZ, Dick

$345* *"River Garry, Scotland", 1981,* s., t., d., #8/50, photog.'s blindstamp, (05-23-93, Butterfield, #3303, illus.), 7½ x 9½ in., photograph, platinum print (BP 225, DM 564, FR 1899, Y 38,134).

BI *"Sunrise, Goblin Valley, Utah", 1986,* s., t., d., edit. 16/50; photog. blindstamp margin, est. $800/1,000, (11-16-92, Butterfield, #5839, illus.), 11¾ x 19Zn in., (299 x 496.2 mm.), photograph, platinum print.

ARESSY, Emile

$486* *Produits Appareils Pour La Photographie, 1901,* p. Charite-Montpellier, crease, repaired creases, (05-07-93, Christie-S. Ken, #120, illus.), 32½ x 24 in., (82.6 x 61 cm.), color lithograph (BP 308, DM 768, FR 2589, Y 53,512).

ARLINGTON, L.C.

$28* *"The Chinese Drama", 1930,* autographed, 1st edit., printed cover, end papers, (09-17-92, Sloan, #2661), 115 color plates (BP 16, DM 42, FR 142, Y 3486).

ARMAN (Armand FERNANDEZ) French b. 1928

BI *Accords A Cordes (Otmezguine and Moreau 252), 1989: Three,* Edition GKM, #52/200, s., est. DM 1,800-, (05-27-93, Lempertz, #572), 26C, x 20Zn in., (67 x 52.5 cm.), color serigraph on thick Japan.

$722* *Auslaufende Tuben,* s., num., (11-28-92, Grisebach, #413, illus.), 17Zn x 11Zn in., (44 x 30 cm.), serigraph on foil (BP 477, DM 1150, FR 3905, Y 89,857).

$361* *Bonjour Max Ernst (Otmezguine/Moreau 26), 1976,* s., est. DM 750, (11-28-92, Schoppmann, #358), 19½ x 14¾ in., (49.5 x 37.5 cm.), color etching on handmade (BP 238, DM 575, FR 1952, Y 44,928).

$451* *Bonjour Max Ernst (Otmezguine/Moreau 267), 1976,* #68/100, s., (11-13-92, Koller, #5236), 19½ x 14¾ in., (49.5 x 37.5 cm.), color etching on Arches (BP 291, DM 708, FR 2388, Y 55,976, SF 638).

$1227* *"Brushing Aside" (Otmezguine/Moreau 244a), 1970,* s., sheet 1 of series Paint Box, (11-28-92, Grisebach, #411, illus.), 14¾ x 18M, in., (37.5 x 48 cm.), serigraph on plexiglas (BP 810, DM 1955, FR 6636, Y 152,707).

BI *La Cafetiere (Otmezguine/Moreau 39), 1971,* 224/300, s., est. SF 550/630, (10-14-92, Germann, #214), 25M x 19¼ in., (657 x 489 mm.), color lithograph.

$316* *La Cafetiere (Otmezguine/Moreau 39), 1971,* #224/300, s., (06-24-93, Germann, #225), 25M, x 19¼ in., (657 x 489 mm.), color lithograph (BP 208, DM 512, FR 1727, Y 33,898, SF 460).

BI *Camera Negative (Otmezguine et Moreau 62), 1973*, s., #85/90, drystamp, est. FF1,000/1,500, (03-31-93, Briest, #E9), 29Ẑn x 22¼ in., (76 x 56.5 cm.), blue lithograph.

BI *"Chessboard In Homage To Marcel Duchamp's L.H.O.O.Q."*, s., num. 95/100 Arman in felt pen, very good cond., est. $5/700, (09-11-92, Skinner, #98, illus.), sight 15Ẑ, x 15Ẑ, in., (39.7 x 39.7 cm.), silkscreen multiple.

$160* *"The Hidden Star-1983" (CR183)*, #14/99, s., (04-04-93, Pescheteau, #154), 22Ẑ, x 30Ẑ, in., (56.2 x 76.5 cm.), drypoint in black on Arches (BP 105, DM 257, FR 873, Y 18,217).

$369* *Hommage A Beethoven (Otmezguine/Moreau 221)*, #71/99, s., tears, (11-13-92, Koller, #5233), 29Ẑn x 22Ẑn in., (76 x 56 cm.), color lithograph on Rives wove (BP 238, DM 579, FR 1953, Y 45,799, SF 522).

$424* *Hommage A Segovia (Otmezguine/Moreau 126), 1978*, s., #132/150, (06-12-93, Hauswedell/Nolt, #26), 41Ẑn x 29¾ in., (105.5 x 75.5 cm.), color serigraph on Arches (BP 278, DM 690, FR 2319, Y 44,617).

$284* *Hommage To Yves Klein (Otmezguine/Moreau 140), 1979*, 35/100, s., (06-24-93, Germann, #228), 30 x 22¼ in., (762 x 565 mm.), serigraph in 2 colors (BP 187, DM 460, FR 1552, Y 30,466, SF 414).

$240* *L'Interieur Des Choses II: Le Transistor (Otzmeguine/ Moreau 38), 1971*, #48/300, s., (09-04-92, Germann, #217), 25Ẑ'n x 19Ẑ, in., (655 x 485 mm.), color lithograph (BP 120, DM 336, FR 1145, Y 29,542, SF 299).

$29* *L'Interieur Des Choses IV: Le Fer A Repasser (Otmezguine Et Moreau 40), 1971*, s., 233/300 of 350, (06-28-93, Loudmer, #188), 25Ẑẑn x 19½ in., (655 x 495 mm.), color lithograph on Arches (BP 19, DM 49, FR 166, Y 3077).

$29* *L'Interieur Des Choses V: Le Masque A Gaz (Otmezguine Et Moreau 41),1971*, s., 77/300 of 350, (06-28-93, Loudmer, #189), 25Ẑẑn x 19M, in., (660 x 505 mm.), color lithograph on Arches (BP 19, DM 49, FR 166, Y 3077).

$221* *L'Interieur Des Choses VI: La Lampe A Souder (Otzmeguine/Moreau 42),1971*, #167/300, s., (09-04-92, Germann, #216), 25Ẑẑn x 19Ẑ, in., (655 x 486 mm.), color lithograph (BP 111, DM 310, FR 1054, Y 27,203, SF 276).

$284* *Musical Accumulations (Otmezguine/Moreau 97), 1976*, 30/100, s., (06-24-93, Germann, #230), 37Ẑẑn x 24Ẑ, in., (965 x 619 mm.), color lithograph (BP 187, DM 460, FR 1552, Y 30,466, SF 414).

BI *N.Y. International (Otmezguine/Moreau 254), 1966*, #153/225, s., stamped Chiron Press, est. SF 900/1,200, (09-04-92, Germann, #84, illus.), 16Ẑẑn x 21Ẑẑn in., (430 x 557 mm.), color serigraph.

$433* *"Les Nouveaux Realistes" (Otmezguine/Moreau 261), 1973*, s., from the portfolio Les Nouveaux Realistes, from Viva Edition, Venedig, num., (11-28-92, Grisebach, #412, illus.), 19Ẑ, x 19Ẑ'n in., (49.8 x 50 cm.), serigraph on plexiglas (BP 286, DM 690, FR 2342, Y 53,889).

$737* *Parade (Otzmeguine/Moreau 145), 1979*, #20/150, s., (09-04-92, Germann, #26, illus.), 30Ẑẑn x 22¼ in., (767 x 565 mm.), color serigraph (BP 369, DM 1033, FR 3516, Y 90,719, SF 920).

BI *Passe Temps, 1971*, album w/justification and text, s., #41, p. by De La Coppi, good cond., est. BP 1/1,500, (06-30-93, Sotheby-London, #739, illus.), 16Ẑ, x 15¾ in., (416 x 400 mm.), offset lithograph and silkscreen in color.

$432* *Rainbow Of Violins*, s., AP, (12-01-92, Karl/Faber, #326), 29½ x 20M, in., (75 x 53 cm.), color serigraph on thick wove (BP 285, DM 689, FR 2347, Y 53,785).

BI *Romantic Suite: Six*, s., est. $2/3,000, (09-24-92, Mystic, #34), each 24½ x 38 in., (62.2 x 96.5 cm.), colored lithograph.

BI *Romantic Suite: Six*, s., est. $2/3,000, (09-24-92, Mystic, #33), each 24½ x 38 in., (62.2 x 96.5 cm.), colored lithograph.

$553* *Serenata-New Romanticism (Otmezguine/Moreau 168), 1980*, H.C. 9/10, s., (04-21-93, Germann, #172, illus.), 25Ẑ, x 39Ẑn in., (645 x 998 mm.), color serigraph (BP 359, DM 884, FR 2989, Y 61,220, SF 805).

$1557* *Stranginstrument*, s., 16/100, (05-12-93, AB Stockholm, #7003), 23Ẑ, x 37 in., (60 x 94 cm.), lithograph in colors (BP 1017, DM 2512, FR 8462, Y 173,831, SK 11,550).

$890* *Suite For Violin*, s., 73/125, Multiplicata Internationale, (05-12-93, AB Stockholm, #7002), 25Ẑn x 19Ẑ'n in., (65 x 50 cm.), serigraph in colors (BP 581, DM 1436, FR 4837, Y 99,364, SK 6600).

BI *Le Telephone (Otmezguine/Moreau 37), 1971*, 294/300, s., est. SF 550/630, (10-14-92, Germann, #213, illus.), 25Ẑẑn x 19Ẑn in., (655 x 487 mm.), color lithograph.

BI *Trio A Cordes (Otmezguine und Moreau 251), 1987: Three*, Edition GKM, #82/150, s., est. DM 2,800-, (05-27-93, Lempertz, #571), 38Ẑẑn x 27Ẑn in., (99 x 69 cm.), color serigraph on thick Japan.

BI *Untitled*, s., #240/300, good cond.?, est. G 5/700, (12-09-92, Sotheby-Amstrdm, #484), sh 18½ x 25Ẑ, in., (470 x 645 mm.), color lithograph on wove.

BI *Untitled (Otmezguine/Moreau 223), 1989*, #22/99, s., est. SF 1/1,200, (04-21-93, Germann, #229, illus.), 30 x 22Ẑn in., (762 x 560 mm.), color lithograph.

BI *Untitled (Otmezguine/Moreau 232), 1990*, #50/90, est. SF 950/1,100, (11-13-92, Koller, #5238), 29Ẑẑn x 22Ẑn in., (76.1 x 56.1 cm.), lithograph on BFK Rives.

$348* *Violent Violins (Otmezguine/Moreau 119), 1978*, #97/150, s., (04-21-93, Germann, #230, illus.), 30Ẑn x 22¼ in., (766 x 565 mm.), color serigraph (BP 226, DM 556, FR 1881, Y 38,525, SF 506).

$645* *Violin Concerto (Otzmeguine/Moreau 110), 1978*, #2/150, s., d., stamped, (09-04-92, Germann, #19, illus.), 30Ẑ, x 22Ẑn in., (765 x 563 mm.), color serigraph (BP 323, DM 904, FR 3077, Y 79,394, SF 805).

$249* *Violon*, s., num., (12-01-92, Karl/Faber, #327), 23Mn x 15Ẑn in., (59.5 x 39.5 cm.), color lithograph on Arches France wove (BP 165, DM 397, FR 1353, Y 31,001).

$199* *Le Violon*, 343/600, s., (10-14-92, Germann, #216), 19Ẑẑn x 19Ẑẑn in., (500 x 500 mm.), serigraph on plexiglass (BP 117, DM 291, FR 988, Y 24,115, SF 260).

$326* *"Violons" (J.O. et MM 128), 1979*, #51/150, d., s., (10-18-92, Pescheteau, #78), 29½ x 21Ẑ, in., (75 x 55 cm.), serigraph in 3 colors on grey Canson (BP 198, DM 482, FR 1636, Y 38,925).

$272* *Yang And Bang (Otmezguine/Moreau 152), 1979*, 112/150, s., (10-14-92, Germann, #215), 30 x 22Ẑn in., (762 x 566 mm.), color serigraph (BP 160, DM 398, FR 1350, Y 32,962, SF 354).

ARMANDO   Dutch b. 1929

BI *Het Plechtige, Het Donkere, 1984: Six*, complete portfolio, s., d., #4/125, pub. Bebert, good cond., est. G 1,5/2,000, (12-09-92, Sotheby-Amstrdm, #485), overall 20Ẑn x 13Ẑ\ in., (522 x 346 mm.), lithograph on BFK Rives.

$576* *Het Plechtige, Het Donkere, 1984: Six*, complete portfolio, each s., d., #73/125, text by artist, just., #73f 137, pub. Bebert, p. Rento Brattinga, good cond., (05-27-93, Sotheby-Amstrdm, #553), overall size 20Ẑn x 13Ẑ, in., (522 x 346 mm.), lithograph on BFK Rives (BP 369, DM 924, FR 3115, Y 61,750, G 1035).

ARMINGTON, Frank M.   Canadian/American 1876-1940

BI *"Arc De Triomphe, Paris", 1924*, s., d., very good cond., est. $1/150, (05-15-93, Cleveland, #54), 8¾ x 12¼ in., (22.2 x 31.1 cm.), etching on laid.

$154* *"Woolworth Building" and "Wall Street": Two*, each s., d. (19)30, (04-02-93, Sloan, #833), each 12¼ x 8¾ in., (311 x 222 mm.), drypoint etching (BP 101, DM 248, FR 841, Y 17,534).

ARMITAGE, Kenneth   English b. 1916

BI *Komposition, 1960*, s., d., num., signs of wear, est. DM 700, (12-01-92, Karl/Faber, #328), 14Ẑn x 16¾ in., (37 x 42.5 cm.), color lithograph on wove.

ARMLEDER, John   b.Switzerland 1948

BI *Untitled, 1985*, s., #35/40, est. DM 600-, (05-27-93, Lempertz, #575), 9Ẑn x 13Ẑẑn in., (23 x 35.4 cm.), color serigraph on thick Japan.

ARMONDO

$33* *Untitled: A Pair*, s. Armondo, (04-23-93, Clearing House, #1), lithograph (BP 21, DM 52, FR 176, Y 3645).

ARMOUR, G.O. (after)

$39 *"James Piff/I Never Get Off"*, (12-11-92, G.A. Key, #20), 12 x 10 in., (30.5 x 25.4 cm.), print (BP 25, DM 61, FR 211, Y 4826).

ARMS, John Taylor American 1887-1953

$2475* *An American Cathedral (F. 107), 1921,* s., t., i., p. by Frederick Reynolds, good cond., light-staining, staining, crease, prop. Print Corner Coll. of Elizabeth and Charles Whitmore, (02-24-93, Butterfield, #2605, illus.), 17%n x 6¾ in., (433 x 171 mm.), etching p. on F.J. Head & Co. laid (BP 1726, DM 4018, FR 13,621, Y 290,425).

$374* *An American Cathedral (F. 107), 1931,* watermark, s., annot. II, p. Frederick Reynolds, full margins, good cond., mat staining, glue remains, notations, collector's stamp, (05-19-93, Butterfield, #1753), sh 18C, x 11½ in., (467 x 292 mm.), etching and aquatint on laid (BP 243, DM 608, FR 2048, Y 41,404).

$1100* *"The American Clipper Ship" (Fletcher 124), 1922,* from the Ship Series #3, s., very good cond., (05-15-93, Cleveland, #55), 12 x 18 in., (30.5 x 45.7 cm.), etching and aquatint (BP 715, DM 1769, FR 5946, Y 121,938).

$55* *American Red Cross,* margins, s., (05-22-93, Collins, #72), 3M, x 5M, in., (9.8 x 14.9 cm.), etching (BP 36, DM 89, FR 301, Y 6064).

BI *Basilica Of The Madeleine, Vezelay (F. 223), 1929,* s., d., annot. Third state, p. Peter Platt, margins, laid down, goodcond., tear, mat and light-staining, paper loss, foxing, glue remains, surfacesoiling, est. $3/500, (05-19-93, Butterfield, #1752), sh. 15 x 9B, in., (381 x 244 mm.), etching on laid.

BI *"Battle Wagon U.S.S. Alabama Outfitting At Norfolk Navy Yard, Crane Ship Kearsage Alongside" (Elvehjem, 387), 1943,* s., d. John Taylor Arms 1943, annot. III, very good cond., full margins, annot. verso, est. $1/2000, (09-11-92, Skinner, #37, illus.), 10Zzn x 17Bzn in., (25.6 x 44 cm.), etching on J. Whatman wove w/partial watermark.

$275* *"Battlewagon, USS Alabama", 1943,* s., d. John Taylor Arms 1943, annot. VI, good cond., mount staining, (03-12-93, Skinner, #33, illus.), 11M\ x 17M, in., (30.2 x 45.4 cm.), etching and aquatint on wove (BP 192, DM 458, FR 1556, Y 32,410).

$880* *"Battlewagon: U.S.S. Alabama", (Fletcher 376), 1943 and "U.S.S. Cruiser Columbia (Fletcher 390), 1945: Two,* s., full margins, (05-27-93, Swann, #18, illus.), one 11M, x 17M, in., (30.2 x 45.4 cm.), the other 12¼ x 17¾ in., (30.2 x 45.4 cm.), etchings (BP 564, DM 1412, FR 4759, Y 94,340).

$165* *"A Breton Calvary" (F. 247 ii/iii),* s., t., annot., excell. unwashed cond., (10-31-92, Cleveland, #60), 5B, x 3Z in., (14.3 x 7.9 cm.), etching (BP 106, DM 254, FR 861, Y 20,438).

BI *"Burgos" (F. 142), 1924,* s., t., good cond., est. $3/400, (05-15-93, Cleveland, #56), 8B, x 13 in., (21.9 x 33 cm.), etching.

$303* *Cavendish Church (Fletcher 381 II/II),* s., d. 1944, annot. II, (05-16-93, Hindman, #544), 9C, x 5½ in., (23.8 x 14 cm.), etching (BP 197, DM 487, FR 1638, Y 33,588).

$231* *"The Christian Science Temple, Boston" (F. 170 ii/ii), 1925,* s., annot., hinges, perfect cond., (10-31-92, Cleveland, #59), 11 x 11C, in., (27.9 x 28.9 cm.), etching (BP 148, DM 355, FR 1206, Y 28,614).

$3300* *Cobwebs (Brooklyn Bridge) (F. 95), 1921,* s., #7/75, margins, good cond., light-staining, prop. Print Corner Coll. of Elizabeth and Charles Whitmore, est. $3/5,000, (02-24-93, Butterfield, #2602, illus.), 9¾ x 7B, in., (248 x 194 mm.), etching on F.J. Head handmade laid (BP 2301, DM 5357, FR 18,162, Y 387,233).

BI *La Colegiata, Toro (F. 284), 1935,* s., d., num. Ed 100 II, margins, laid down, top mat glued, margins,good cond., mat staining, surface soiling, est. $4/600, (05-19-93, Butterfield, #1755), sh. 13Zzn x 18Czn in., (351 x 462 mm.), etching on wove.

$220* *Detail Of Choir Stall In Cathedral Of Saint Cecelia (Fletcher 316), 1938,* s., d., i. ed.150, (11-12-92, Freemn/ Fine Art, #23), plate 1¾ x2Bzrin., etching (BP 144, DM 349, FR 1176, Y 27,278).

$2475* *Early Morning North River (F. 100), 1921,* s., p. by Frederick Reynolds, margins, good cond., surface soiling, creases, pencil notations, prop. Print Corner Coll. of Elizabeth and Charles Whitmore, (02-24-93, Butterfield, #2604), 9½ x 7½ in., (241 x 191 mm.), etching & aquatint in colors on wove (BP 1726, DM 4018, FR 13,621, Y 290,425).

$1100* *Early Morning North River (F. 100), 1921,* s., p. by Frederick Reynolds, full margins, good cond., light-staining, rubbed area, surface soiling, notations, prop. Print Corner Coll. of Elizabeth and Charles Whitmore, (02-24-93, Butterfield, #2603), 9½ x 7½ in., (241 x 191 mm.), etching & aquatint on wove (BP 767, DM 1786, FR 6054, Y 129,078).

$1100* *The Enchanted Doorway, Venezia (F. 227), 1930,* s., d., i., proof, margins, good cond., glue, binding holes, surfacesoiling, (10-28-92, Butterfield, #2502, illus.), 12Mzn x 6½ in., (316 x 165 mm.), etching on antique laid papier vedatre (BP 701, DM 1699, FR 5768, Y 134,969).

$88* *Figures And Chickens On A French Street, With A Cathedral In The Background,* s., (05-20-93, Boos, #532), 6Z, x 3Azn in., (155 x 100 mm.), etching (BP 56, DM 142, FR 478, Y 9717).

$240* *"French Lace" (F. 415), 1949,* s., d., excellent cond., (05-15-93, Cleveland, #59, illus.), 8 x 4¾ in., (20.3 x 12.1 cm.), etching (BP 156, DM 386, FR 1297, Y 26,605).

$2200* *From The Ponte Vecchio, Florence (F. 159), 1925,* s., p. by Frederick Reynolds, 1st plate from the Italian Series, fullmargins, good cond., ink spot, prop. Print Corner Coll. Elizabeth and Charles Whitmore, (02-24-93, Butterfield, #2607, illus.), 11 x 15Bzn in., (279 x 389 mm.), etching & aquatint p. on F.J. Head & Co. laid (BP 1534, DM 3571, FR 12,108, Y 258,155).

$1320* *The Gothic Spirit (F. 120), 1922,* s., p. by Frederick Reynolds, 8th plate from Gargoyle Series, full margins, very good cond., surface soiling, prop. Print Corner Coll. of Elizabethand Charles Whitmore, (02-24-93, Butterfield, #2606, illus.), 11B\ x 7 in., (295 x 178 mm.), etching & stipple p. on Japan nacre (BP 921, DM 2143, FR 7265, Y 154,893).

$2300* *In Memorium, Chartres Cathedral (F. 317), 1939,* s., d., margins, good cond., mat staining, glue remains, surface soiling, notations, (05-19-93, Butterfield, #1757, illus.), sh. 9Zzn x 15¼ in., (249 x 387 mm.), etching and aquatint on J. Whatman 1928 wove (BP 1493, DM 3739, FR 12,596, Y 254,622).

$120* *"Isola Superiore" (F. 296), 1936,* s., i., proof, excellent cond., (05-15-93, Cleveland, #58), 5 x 6M, in., (12.7 x 17.5 cm.), etching (BP 78, DM 193, FR 649, Y 13,302).

$413* *Light And Shade, Taxco (Fletcher 394),* s., d. 1946, annot. II, (05-16-93, Hindman, #545), 10¼ x 13½ in., (26 x 34.3 cm.), etching (BP 269, DM 664, FR 2232, Y 45,782).

$523* *"Limoge", 1932 (Elvehjem, 246),* from French Churches Series, s., d. John Taylor Arms 1932, num. Ed 100 III, very good cond., light toning, annots. verso, (09-11-92, Skinner, #18, illus.), 10 x 13½ in., (25.4 x 34.3 cm.), etching on laid paper (BP 270, DM 753, FR 2559, Y 64,800).

BI *Medieval Pageantry (F. 270), 1933,* watermark, s., d. '34, annot. Ker Eby imp., num. Ed 100, margins, laid down, good cond., paper losses, 2 1/8" tear, mat staining, surface soiling,notations, est. $3/500, (05-19-93, Butterfield, #1754), sh. 16½ x 11B, in., (419 x 295 mm.), etching and aquatint on laid.

$303* *Notre Dame De Laon (F. 219), 1929,* s., d., annot. Third State, t. in plate, 2 French stamps, margins, good cond., foxing, surfaces soiling, paper tape, prop. Print Corner Coll. of Elizabeth and Charles Whitmore, (02-24-93, Butterfield, #2803), 14¼ x 9½ in., (362 x 241 mm.), etching on pale blue wove (BP 211, DM 492, FR 1668, Y 35,555).

$220* *Old Corner, Rouen (F. 163), 1925,* s., d., p. Frederick Reynolds, for frontispiece of The Print Connoisseur, margins, good cond., mat staining, notations, surface soiling, (10-28-92, Butterfield, #2501), 6Z, x 4Z, in., (156 x 105 mm.), etching on laid paper, watermark (BP 140, DM 340, FR 1154, Y 26,994).

$248* *"Ponte Vecchio" and "Amalfi" (Sketches), (Fletcher 262, 256), 1933: Two,* each s., d., ded., inscription; first, edit. of 15; second, edit. of13, (06-13-93, Hindman, #312), each approx. 6¾ x 4M, in., (17.1 x 12.4 cm.), etching (BP 162, DM 404, FR 1357, Y 26,097).

BI *"Puerta Principal De La Iglesia De San Pablo, Valladolid" and "Louviers Lace" (F. 278; 303), 1934; 1936: Two,* watermark, each s., d., num. Ed. 100 II, Ed. 100 III, i., each w/fullmargins, good cond., paper loss, tear, surface soiling, second w/ notations, est. $1/1,500, (05-19-93, Butterfield, #1756), one sh. 8Z, x 6C, in., (206 x 162 mm.), the other sh. 16 x 7Zzn in., (206 x 162 mm.), etching on laid.

$330* *The Rose, Beauvais (F. 161),* s., d. 1925, edit. 156, (07-03-92, Sloan, #1082), 12 x 7Z, in., (30.5 x 18.1 cm.), etching and drypoint (BP 172, DM 499, FR 1684, Y 41,137).

$330* *The Rose, Beauvais (Fletcher 161), 1925,* s., d., (03-24-93, Grogan, #48), 12¼ x 7¼ in., (31.1 x 18.4 cm.), etching (BP 223, DM 539, FR 1834, Y 38,773).

$110* *Rouen,* s., (12-17-92, Mystic, #8), 7¾ x 5¼ in., (19.7 x 13.3 cm.), etching (BP 70, DM 172, FR 587, Y 13,518).

$413* *"San Francesco" and "Gerona" (Fletcher 261, 147), 1924, 1933: Two,* each s., d., annot.; second, inscription, ded., (06-13-93, Hindman, #313), larger 5 x 6¾ in., (12.7 x 17.1 cm.), etching (BP 270, DM 672, FR 2259, Y 43,460).

$1650* *The Sarah Jane (F. 56), 1920,* s., d., num. 25/75, annot., full margins, good cond., surface scuffing, staining, hinge remains, surface soiling, prop. Print Corner Coll. of Elizabeth and Charles Whitmore, (02-24-93, Butterfield, #2601), 10¼ x 7¼ in., (260 x 184 mm.), etching & aquatint in colors on wove (BP 1151, DM 2679, FR 9081, Y 193,617).

$770* *Segovia (Fletcher 143),* s., d. 1924, (03-14-93, Hindman, #309), 13C, x 17¼ in., (34 x 43.8 cm.), etching (BP 537, DM 1282, FR 4358, Y 90,748).

$495* *"Sequoia" (Fletcher 143), 1924,* s., d., from Spanish Church Series #3, very fine cond., (10-31-92, Cleveland, #58), 13B, x 17 in., (34.6 x 45.6 cm.), etching (BP 317, DM 762, FR 2584, Y 61,315).

$385* *Somewhere In France (Fletcher 32), 1919,* s., d., (03-24-93, Grogan, #47), 12Z, x 6 in., (30.8 x 15.2 cm.), etching (BP 261, DM 629, FR 2140, Y 45,236).

$110* *"St. Catherine's Belfry, Honfleur, 1932" (Fletcher 248),* 2nd state, s., d. 1932, annot., water stains, from French series, No.34, (06-11-93, Freemn/Fine Art, #9A), 7 x 13½ in., (17.8 x 34.3 cm.), etching (BP 72, DM 179, FR 603, Y 11,671).

$247* *St. Germain L'Auxerrois, 1928,* s., p. for Chicago Society of Etchers, (05-27-93, Swann, #17), 9M, x 4M, in., (25.1 x 12.4 cm.), etching (BP 158, DM 396, FR 1336, Y 26,479).

$220* *St. Pauls, Alpes Maritimes (Lib. of Cong. 302),* s., t., d. 1927 in plate; s., d. in margin, Print Club of Cleveland Publication No. 4, 1927, (09-17-92, Sloan, #1421), 7½ x 11½ in., (19.1 x 29.2 cm.), etching (BP 124, DM 327, FR 1118, Y 27,390).

$715* *"Stockholm", 1940,* s., d., i., excell. cond., toning, (08-08-92, Litchfield, #12), 7½ x 13½ in., (19.1 x 34.3 cm.), etching and aquatint (BP 371, DM 1051, FR 3554, Y 91,257).

BI *"Street In Blois" (F. 204), 1927,* s., est. $1/200, (05-15-93, Cleveland, #57), 6M, x 4Zzn in., (17.5 x 12.5 cm.), etching.

$385* *A Swordfisherman, Nantucket (F. 52), 1920,* s., t., p. Frederick Reynolds, full margins, good cond., light-staining, pencil notations, prop. Print Corner Coll. of Elizabeth and Charles Whitmore, (02-24-93, Butterfield, #2802), 3M, x 3 in., (98 x 76 mm.), etching & aquatint in colors on F.J. Head & Co. laid (BP 268, DM 625, FR 2119, Y 45,177).

$715* *Thirty Knots Or Better (U.S.S. Destroyer 121) (F. 42), 1920,* s., p. Frederick Reynolds, margins, good cond., surface scuffs, pencil notations, prop. Print Corner Coll. of Elizabeth and Charles Whitmore, (02-24-93, Butterfield, #2801), 4B, x 9½ in., (117 x 241 mm.), aquatint & etching in colors on wove (BP 499, DM 1161, FR 3935, Y 83,900).

$220* *"Towers Of San Giminano" (F. 250 ii/ii), 1932,* from Italian Series No. 24, good cond., (10-31-92, Cleveland, #61), 10B, x 7 in., (27 x 17.8 cm.), etching (BP 141, DM 338, FR 1148, Y 27,251).

$385* *An Umbrian Street (Fletcher 168), 1925,* s., d., (03-24-93, Grogan, #46), 10¼ x 5C, in., (26 x 13.7 cm.), etching (BP 261, DM 629, FR 2140, Y 45,236).

$3575* *Venetian Mirror (Fletcher 289), 1935,* s., i. ed.100, (11-12-92, Freemn/Fine Art, #22, illus.), plate 14 x 6½ in., (35.6 x 16.5 cm.), etching (BP 2348, DM 5665, FR 19,107, Y 443,273).

$1380* *Watching The People Below, Amiens Cathedral (Flint 101), 1921,* s., d., i., p. David Strang, 1937-38, full margins, good cond., (02-11-93, Sotheby-NY, #1), 4Zzn x 8Z\ in., (125 x 207 mm.), etching (BP 974, DM 2286, FR 7735, Y 166,365).

$1870* *"Watching The People Below, Amiens Cathedral" (Fletcher 101), 1921, "Guardians Of The Spire" (F. 102), 1921 and "The Valley Of The Savery, Wyoming (F. 276), 1934: Three,* each s.; first d., time staining; third i. Trial proof XXXI/III, 3rdstate; full margins, foxmarks, good/very good cond., (09-19-92, Christie-E, #1, illus.), etching, first on blue laid paper; others on laid paper (BP 1076, DM 2800, FR 9590, Y 232,993).

ARMS, John Taylor and Kerr EBY   American
$330* *Medieval Pageantry,* s., i. Ed. 100, d. 1933, (04-02-93, Sloan, #1180), 12B, x 8¾ in., (321 x 222 mm.), etching and drypoint (BP 217, DM 530, FR 1801, Y 37,573).

$330* *Medieval Pageantry (F. 270 (V/VI)),* s. by both, i. edit. 100, d. 1933, (07-03-92, Sloan, #1085), 12B, x 8¾ in., (32.1 x 22.2 cm.), etching and drypoint (BP 172, DM 499, FR 1684, Y 41,137).

ARMSTRONG, John   American 1893-1973
$845* *Everywhere You Go, Near Lamorna, 1952,* p. Vincent Brooks, Day & Son, ref. P 42, cond. 2, (10-13-92, Phillips-London, #177, illus.), 29Zzn x 39M, in., (76 x 101.3 cm.), color lithograph (BP 492, DM 1238, FR 4206, Y 102,462).

$1111* *Everywhere You Go, Newsland Corner, 1932,* p. Vincent Brooks, Day & Son, ref. #340, cond. 1, (10-13-92, Phillips-London, #91, illus.), 29Zzn x 45Zzn in., (76 x 114.5 cm.), color lithograph (BP 647, DM 1628, FR 5530, Y 134,716).

$1442* *Farmers Use Shell, 1939,* p. Waterlow and Sons, ref. #538, cond. 1, creases, (10-13-92, Phillips-London, #154, illus.), 29Zzn x 44M, in., (75.8 x 114 cm.), color lithograph (BP 840, DM 2113, FR 7178, Y 174,851).

$2663* *Theatre-Goers Use Shell, 1938,* p. Waterlow and Sons, ref. #536, cond. 1, tear, (10-13-92, Phillips-London, #152, illus.), 30Zzn x 45Zzn in., (76.4 x 114.4 cm.), color lithograph (BP 1551, DM 3901, FR 13,255, Y 322,905).

ARMSTRONG, Neil   American b. 1930
$715* *Astronaut "Buzz" Aldrin, Jr. Descending Ladder Of Lunar Module, 1969,* NASA insignia, typewritten caption, (04-07-93, Swann, #284, illus.), 8 x 10 in., photograph, silver print (BP 473, DM 1156, FR 3914, Y 81,232).

BI *Astronaut "Buzz" Aldrin, Jr. Walking Near The Lunar Module, 1969,* est. $1/1,500, (04-07-93, Swann, #285, illus.), 10 x 8 in., photograph, silver print.

$880* *Astronaut Buzz Aldrin Jr. Assembling Scientific Apparatus, 1969,* handwritten notations, (10-14-92, Swann, #277, illus.), 14 x 11 in., (35.6 x 27.9 cm.), photograph, silver print (BP 517, DM 1288, FR 4367, Y 106,641).

$1760* *Astronaut Buzz Aldrin Jr. Walking Near The Lunar Module, 1969,* (10-14-92, Swann, #278, illus.), 8 x 10 in., (20.3 x 25.4 cm.), photograph, silver print (BP 1033, DM 2576, FR 8734, Y 213,282).

BI *Astronaut Buzz Aldrin Jr. With American Flag On The Moon, 1969,* est. $1/1,500, (10-14-92, Swann, #279, illus.), 10 x 8 in., (25.4 x 20.3 cm.), photograph, silver print.

ARNAL, Francois   b. 1924
BI *Colombins Rouges, c. 1974,* artist's proof, s., est. FF800/1,000, (05-27-93, Briest, #16), 36B, x 29½ in., (93 x 75 cm.), color serigraph.

$124* *"Composition - 1987",* d., s., (10-18-92, Pescheteau, #79), 27Zzn x 19Bzn in., (71 x 49 cm.), lithograph in colors on velin (BP 75, DM 183, FR 622, Y 14,806).

ARNESON, Robert   American b. 1930
$770* *Cherry Pie, 1975,* s., d., annot. Modesto, AP V, blindstamp pub. Landfall Press, good cond., mat staining, hinge remains, Modesto Lanzone Coll., (10-28-92, Butterfield,

#2892), 21½ x 29 in., (546 x 737 mm.), color lithograph on Arches (BP 491, DM 1189, FR 4038, Y 94,479).

BI *Five Guys, 1983: Five,* complete suite, s., d., #13/25, pub. Experimental Workshop, full margins, very good cond., crease, est. $3/5,000, (10-28-92, Butterfield, #2893, illus.), each 21¼ x 14¼ in., (540 x 362 mm.), woodcut on handmade.

ARNOLD, Eve b. 1913

BI *Marilyn Monroe Swimming In Pyramid Lake, Nevada During The Filming Of The Misfits,* 1960, p.l., sight 450 x 320mm, est. BP 5/800, (05-07-93, Sotheby-London, #315, illus.), photograph, color print.

ARNOLDI, Charles American b. 1946

$518* *Untitled #1, 1983,* s., d., #10/35, blindstamp publisher, New City Editions, full margins, very good cond.?, (05-19-93, Butterfield, #2116), 18 x 30¾ in., (457 x 781 mm.), woodcut in colors on Kasuiri (BP 336, DM 842, FR 2837, Y 57,345).

$303* *Untitled #5, 1983,* s., d. Arnoldi 1983, num. 33/70, excellent cond., (09-11-92, Skinner, #115, illus.), sight 38 x 28 in., (96.5 x 71.1 cm.), color woodblock on black paper (BP 157, DM 436, FR 1482, Y 37,542).

$5500* *Untitled, 1985,* s., d., pub. Garner Tullis Workshop, p. by Garner & Richard Tullis, apparently very good cond., (02-24-93, Butterfield, #2999, illus.), each sheet 72 x 30 in., (182.9 x 76.2 cm.), monoprint w/woodcut, embossing & debossing from eucalyptus branches in colors on 2 sheets of thick handmade (BP 3835, DM 8929, FR 30,270, Y 645,388).

$3575* *Untitled, 1985,* s., d., pub. Garner Tullis Workshop, full margins, very good cond.?, (10-28-92, Butterfield, #2894, illus.), sheet 67 x 56 in., (170.2 x 142.2 cm.), color wood relief monoprint on Tullis handmade (BP 2278, DM 5521, FR 18,747, Y 438,650).

ARNOLDI, Per

$337* *Fire Billeder Fra H.C. Andersen: Kjaerestefolkene, 1972,* portfolio, s., #12 of 125, (09-30-92, Kunsthallen, #26), color serigraph (BP 190, DM 478, FR 1616, Y 40,442, DK 1840).

ARNOUX, Guy French d. 1951

$44* *Tambours Et Trompettes,* incomplete portfolio, t., contains 2 images and 1 title page, (02-14-93, Neal, #1151), each sheet 18½ x 12 in., (47 x 30.5 cm.), (BP 31, DM 73, FR 247, Y 5306).

ARNTZ, Gerd b. 1900

$813* *"Lunapark" (Arntz: Zeit unterm Messer, S. 130/131),* i., s., d. G. Arntz 53, creases, (09-14-92, Venator/Hansten, #2432), image 19⅜n x 19⅞, in., (49 x 48.5 cm.), woodcut on 4 sheets of thin Japan (BP 430, DM 1209, FR 4096, Y 101,094).

ARONSON, David American b. 1923

$138* *Family Portrait,* s., #138/200, excell. cond?, (07-19-92, Bakker, #113), image 12½ x 17 in., (31.8 x 43.2 cm.), color lithograph (BP 71, DM 201, FR 680, Y 17,156).

AROU, G.

BI *PLM. Sports D'Hiver, 1931,* very good cond., (03-15-93, Arcole, #73), 38⅞zn x 24⅜zn in., (99 x 61.5 cm.), .

ARP, Jean (or Hans) French 1887-1966

$2599* *Blason (Arntz 234), 1961: Three,* series, one i., s., (11-28-92, Schoppmann, #359), 10⅞zn x 7 in., (27.5 x 17.8 cm.), color woodcut on eleven color handmade boards (BP 1716, DM 4141, FR 14,056, Y 323,460).

BI *Blatt-Torso (Arntz 340 b), 1960,* s., est. DM 400, (06-10-93, Hauswedell/Nolt, #11), image 25½ x 18¼ in., (64.7 x 46.3 cm.), color offset lithograph.

$830* *Blaue Form,* s., (12-01-92, Karl/Faber, #331), 12⅜n x 9⅝n in., (31 x 24 cm.), color serigraph (BP 548, DM 1323, FR 4508, Y 103,337).

$294* *Composition,* s. Arp, 89/100, (03-24-93, Kunsthallen, #20), color lithograph (BP 199, DM 480, FR 1634, Y 34,544, DK 1840).

$921* *Composition (Arntz 231 a), 1960,* s., num., (06-08-93, Karl/Faber, #504), approx. 16⅞zn x 12⅜, in., (43 x 31.5 cm.), color woodcut on BFK Rives France wove (BP 605, DM 1494, FR 5033, Y 97,823).

BI *Composition (Arntz 329), 1955,* small tear, est. SF 120/150, (10-14-92, Germann, #217), 19⅛zn x 13¾ in., (497 x 350 mm.), color lithograph.

$592* *Composition 1965,* s., #12/25, good cond., (10-27-92, Phillips-London, #182), sheet 19⅜, x 13¾ in., (498 x 349 mm.), lithograph p. in blue, black and beige on wove (BP 374, DM 907, FR 3079, Y 72,416).

$330* *(Composition In Red And Yellow),* stamp s., num. IV/XXX, margins, laid down, apparently good cond., (02-24-93, Butterfield, #2893), 25½ x 20 in., (648 x 508 mm.), silkscreen in red & yellow on Rives BFK (BP 230, DM 536, FR 1816, Y 38,723).

$996* *Composition, 1960,* s., num., (12-01-92, Karl/Faber, #330), 16⅞zn x 12⅜, in., (43 x 31.5 cm.), color woodcut on BFK Rives wove (BP 658, DM 1588, FR 5410, Y 124,004).

$972* *Composition, 1965,* s., (05-27-93, Briest, #18, illus.), 14⅛zn x 10⅜, in., (36 x 27 cm.), color lithograph and collage (BP 622, DM 1560, FR 5257, Y 104,202).

$751* *Configuration (Arntz 327 b), 1951,* #51/200, s., (04-21-93, Germann, #103, illus.), 22¼ x 14⅞zn in., (565 x 380 mm.), color lithograph (BP 487, DM 1200, FR 4059, Y 83,140, SF 1093).

$165* *Geometric Composition,* s., num. 56/75, full sheet, good cond., faint mat burn, rippling, toning, tape, (05-22-93, Weschler, #163, illus.), 10 x 7½ in., (25.4 x 19.1 cm.), etching and aquatint in colors (BP 107, DM 268, FR 903, Y 18,192).

$1277* *Komposition,* s., num., (06-05-93, Bassenge, #5874), 10⅝zn x 8¼ in., (26.5 x 21 cm.), color lithograph (BP 841, DM 2070, FR 6978, Y 136,988).

$36* *Le Musee De Grenoble Presente Les Premiers Maitres De L'Art Abstrait,1949,* crease, (10-14-92, Germann, #218), 25⅛zn x 18⅝n in., (640 x 468 mm.), poster (BP 21, DM 53, FR 179, Y 4363, SF 47).

BI *New York, Curt Valentin, 1951-1952: Twenty-Eight,* from Dreams And Projects by Hans Arp, orig. edit., hors commerce, s., includes orig. drawing and wood engraving by Arp on Japan, est. SF 7/8,000, (11-15-92, Christie-Geneva, #303, illus.), 11½ x 9¼ in., (292 x 235 mm.), wood engraving.

BI *"Ohne Titel" and "Spatziergang" (A. 87; 88): Two,* from Sturm, margins, good cond., staining, tears, paper losses, est.$4/600, (02-24-93, Butterfield, #2892), 6½ x 4½ in., (165 x 114 mm.), 6⅜, x 9¾ in., (165 x 114 mm.), woodcut on wove.

BI *Petite Figure De "Grasse", 1958,* est. FF1/1,200, (05-27-93, Briest, #17), 15⅛ x 11⅝n in., (39 x 29 cm.), serigraph in 3 colors.

$1145* *Pflanzlich - Architektonisch (Arntz 336), 1959,* s., num., (06-23-93, Kornfeld, #176), lithograph on thick wove (BP 778, DM 1937, FR 6517, Y 124,741, SF 1725).

BI *Poemes De Jean Arp: Twelve,* from Poemes De Jean Arp, est. SF 30/50,000, (11-15-92, Christie-Geneva, #302, illus.), .

$678* *Siamesisches Blatt (Arntz 130 c), 1949,* s., (06-10-93, Hauswedell/Nolt, #12), image 9¼ x 7⅞zn in., (23.5 x 20.2 cm.), woodcut on simili Japan (BP 443, DM 1104, FR 3717, Y 71,967).

$5500* *Soleil Recercle (Arntz 250-269): Eighteen,* deluxe edit., each #14/150, pub. Louis Broder, Paris, 1966, full margins, good cond., (11-05-92, Sotheby-NY, #78, illus.), each sheet approx. 19¼ x 15⅜ in., (490 x 390 mm.), woodcuts p. in colors, plus separate suite on japon nacre, separate suite on BFK Rives, woodcut p. on Auvergne (BP 3577, DM 8698, FR 29,428, Y 674,764).

$2542* *Soleil Recercle (Arntz 250a, 250b, 251, 253-254 u. 256-269), 1966: Seventeen,* s., #147/150, (06-10-93, Hauswedell/Nolt, #13), overall size 19⅞zn x 15¾ in., (50 x 40 cm.), woodcut on hand-made (BP 1663, DM 4139, FR 13,936, Y 269,823).

$805* *Le Soleil Recercle, 1966,* s., #38/60, pub. Louis Broder, full margins, good cond., foxing, (02-11-93, Sotheby-NY, #305), 10⅜n x 8⅞zn in., (255 x 220 mm.), color woodcut (BP 568, DM 1333, FR 4512, Y 97,046).

$1283* *Soleil Recercle, 1966,* s., num., watermark, (03-16-93, Schuler, #3210, illus.), 14⅛zn x 13⅛zn in., (36 x 34.5 cm.), sh 21⅜, x 17⅜n in., (36 x 34.5 cm.), color woodcut (BP 886, DM 2133, FR 7249, Y 150,023, SF 1955).

ARRIBAS, Venancio
$474* *"Dos Vistas De El Escorial": Two,* pulled by artist, unique edit., #186/225, s., (02-03-93, Duran, #52, illus.), 16Zzn x 14\zn in., (43 x 37 cm.), etching (BP 331, DM 781, FR 2647, Y 58,963, P 55,200).

ARROYO, Eduardo b. 1937
$144* *L'Homme Au Chat, 1988,* artist's proof, s., d. 1988, (03-31-93, Briest, #E11), 22Zzn x 18Z, in., (56 x 46 cm.), color lithograph (BP 95, DM 232, FR 787, Y 16,559).
$32* *Untitled,* #39/150, s., (01-28-93, Pescheteau, #64), black lithograph (BP 21, DM 51, FR 172, Y 3973).
$268* *Waldorf Astoria, 1989,* s., d., #17/75, blindstamp, (06-12-93, Hauswedell/Nolt, #27), 19B, x 25½ in., (49.8 x 64.8 cm.), color serigraph on thick wove (BP 175, DM 436, FR 1466, Y 28,202).

ARSARKEE, Charles
$22* *"Sunset Lodge",* s., (11-13-92, DuMouchelle, #2577), 10 x 7¾ in., (25.4 x 19.7 cm.), etching (BP 14, DM 35, FR 116, Y 2731).

ARTHAUD, Marcel
$80* *Quatuor Gabriel Bouillon. La Voix De Son Maitre,* cond. B, (03-16-93, Boisgirard, #44), 47¼ x 31½ in., (120 x 80 cm.), poster (BP 55, DM 133, FR 452, Y 9355).

ARTHUR
$28* *"Morning" and "Evening": A Pair,* first, s., #30/100; second, s., d. '72, (02-27-93, Dunning, #150E), 12 x 20 in., (30.5 x 50.8 cm.), lithograph (BP 20, DM 46, FR 156, Y 3305).

ARTHUR, Zinn
$550* *"Man Of A Thousand Faces": Group Of Nineteen,* James Cagney Estate, (09-30-92, Doyle, #370, illus.), photograph (BP 310, DM 780, FR 2638, Y 66,003).

ARTHUS-BERTRAND, Publisher
$603* *Voyage De La Bonite, "Vue Prise Aux Environs De Toranne", "Vue De Toranne", "Vue Prise A Toranne", "Vue Prise A Pulo Penang", "Torrent A Pula Penang", "Vue Prise A Pulo Penang" And Others: Eight,* pub. Akermann (sic) & Co., margins, excell. cond., spotting, (10-07-92, Christie-S. Ken, #91), 7½ x 12 in., (19.1 x 30.5 cm.), colored tinted lithograph (BP 352, DM 873, FR 2959, Y 72,520).
BI *Voyage De La Bonite: Plates 24-38 And Plate 41, Bayot, Bichebois, Deroy And Others: Sixteen,* margins, spotting, staining, good cond., est. BP 8/1,200, (10-07-92, Christie-S. Ken, #94), each 7¾ x 11 in., (19.7 x 27.9 cm.), colored tinted lithograph.

ARTIGUE, L.
$1150* *Amer Picon,* plate s., (03-25-93, Christie-E, #195), 60½ x 40½ in., (153.7 x 102.9 cm.), color lithograph (BP 781, DM 1889, FR 6425, Y 134,724).

ARTSCHWAGER, Richard American b. 1924
$1430* *Building Riddled With Listening Devices (Alpha), 1990,* s., d., i. '12/12 A.P.', pub. Multiples, Inc., full margins, good cond., (11-07-92, Sotheby-NY, #510, illus.), 20B, x 24 in., (524 x 610 mm.), etching and aquatint p. in tones of gray (BP 935, DM 2283, FR 7717, Y 176,500).
BI *Building Riddled With Listening Devices (Beta), 1990,* s., d., i. '12/12 A.P.', pub. Multiples, Inc., full margins, good cond., est. $2/3,000, (11-07-92, Sotheby-NY, #511), 20½ x 24 in., (521 x 610 mm.), etching and aquatint p. in tones of gray.
$1035* *Building Riddled With Listening Devices (Beta), 1990,* s., d., i. 12/12 A.P., pub. Multiples, Inc., full margins, good cond., (05-15-93, Sotheby-NY, #907, illus.), 20½ x 24 in., (52.1 x 61 cm.), etching and aquatint in tones of gray (BP 673, DM 1665, FR 5595, Y 114,732).
$1430* *Horizon, 1990,* s., d., i. '12/12 A.P.', pub. Multiples, Inc., full margins, good cond., (11-07-92, Sotheby-NY, #512, illus.), 23½ x 35B, in., (597 x 905 mm.), etching and aquatint p. in tones of gray (BP 935, DM 2283, FR 7717, Y 176,500).
BI *Interior #3, 1977,* s., d., #31/35, blindstamp, pub. Multiples, Inc., full margins, goodcond., est. $1/1,500, (05-15-93, Sotheby-NY, #906), 11M, x 9M, in., (30.2 x 25.1 cm.), etching.
$3300* *Interior, 1972,* s., d., i. 'A/P', artist's proof, pub. Brooke Alexander, Inc., full margins, good cond., creases, soiling, handling creases, (11-07-92, Sotheby-NY, #508, illus.), 28Z, x 41 in., (71.4 x 104.1 cm.), silkscreen p. in tones of gray and beige on BFK Rives (BP 2158, DM 5269, FR 17,809, Y 407,307).

ASHBROOK, Paul American b. 1867
BI *The Fisherman,* s. in plate; s., #73/100, est. $225/275, (09-17-92, Sloan, #1429), 9¼ x 7¼ in., (23.5 x 18.4 cm.), etching.

ASHE, Walter
$22* *Frank's Fruit And Vegetable,* #192/1100, (12-11-92, DuMouchelle, #1456), 21¾ x 18 in., (55.2 x 45.7 cm.), lithograph (BP 14, DM 35, FR 119, Y 2722).

ASHE-LORD, Elyse English late 19th/20th cent.
$220* *"Young Oriental Nobleman And Courtier",* s. Elyse Ashe-Lord, #45/75, (12-12-92, Wolf, #10), 9¾ x 11¼ in., (24.8 x 28.6 cm.), hand-colored drypoint (BP 141, DM 347, FR 1188, Y 27,224).

ASHTON, Henry
$357* *Immigrants Detained At Ellis Island, 1909,* pencil notations, (04-07-93, Swann, #286, illus.), 4¼ x 3¾ in., photograph, silver print (BP 236, DM 577, FR 1954, Y 40,559).
$522* *Removing Orville Wright From Accident, 1908,* penciled notations, (04-07-93, Swann, #287, illus.), 4¼ x 3¾ in., photograph, silver print (BP 345, DM 844, FR 2857, Y 59,305).

ASHTON, John William 1881-1963
$73* *Manor House,* s. Will Ashton, #21/50, (08-11-92, L. Joel, #20G), 5M, x 8¼ in., (15 x 21 cm.), etching (BP 38, DM 107, FR 363, Y 9348, A$ 99).

ASKER, Kurt
$116* *Sans Titre,* s., 17/90, drystamp, (06-28-93, Loudmer, #190), 8Zzn x 16Zzn in., (220 x 430 mm.), sh 20M, x 25Zzn in., (220 x 430 mm.), blue lithograph on beige Japan (BP 78, DM 197, FR 664, Y 12,308).

ASSADOUR b. 1943
$80* *"No Man's Land", 1972,* drystamp, #37/80, d., s., (04-04-93, Pescheteau, #155), 19Zzn x 25\zn in., (50 x 65 cm.), color etching on Arches (BP 53, DM 129, FR 437, Y 9109).
BI *"No Man's Land", 1972,* drystamp, #37/80, d., s., (01-28-93, Pescheteau, #66), 19Zzn x 25\zn in., (50 x 65 cm.), color etching on Arches.
$63* *"Polyptyque", 1972,* drystamp, #37/80, d., s., (01-28-93, Pescheteau, #65), 19Zzn x 25\zn in., (50 x 65 cm.), etching on 4 copperplates on Arches (BP 42, DM 100, FR 338, Y 7822).

ASSE, Genevieve b. 1923
BI *Sans Titre,* s., est. SF 290/380, (10-14-92, Germann, #219), 29½ x 20C, in., (750 x 518 mm.), color lithograph.

ATEGOICHON
$55 *Tenues De L'Ancienne Marine, 1943,* minor edge damage, (09-24-92, Alderfer, #257), 25 x 19¼ in., (63.5 x 48.9 cm.), (BP 32, DM 82, FR 277, Y 6616).

ATELIERS CHERET
BI *Le Figaro Est En Vente Ici, c. 1900,* Imp. Chaix, Paris, foxing, est. DM 400, (12-05-92, Bassenge, #7573), 11Bzn x 8¼ in., (28.8 x 21 cm.), color lithograph.

ATGET, Eugene French 1857-1927
$1453* *"38 Rue Descartes", c. 1900,* num. in neg., t. verso, 180 x 220mm, (05-07-93, Sotheby-London, #124, illus.), photograph, albumen print (BP 920, DM 2297, FR 7741, Y 159,987).
$1725* *"Au Chat Noir-32 Rue De La Reynie", c. 1900,* t., num. 3973 by photog., (04-06-93, Sotheby-NY, #239, illus.), 8¾ x 7 in., photograph, albumen printing-out paper print (BP 1139, DM 2779, FR 9411, Y 196,738).
$4400* *Avenue Des Gobelins, 1926-27,* num. 157 in neg., t. in Atget's hand, Berenice Abbott Coll. stamp, lit., (10-13-92, Christie-NY, #112, illus.), 8¾ x 6¾ in., (22.2 x 17.1 cm.), photograph, arrowroot process printing-out paper (BP 2563, DM 6446, FR 21,901, Y 533,527).
$7475* *Boutique 15 Rue Maitre Albert, 1911,* num. (partially cropped) in neg., num. 5811 in Atget's hand, Rue Campagne-Premiere stamp, lit., (04-08-93, Christie-NY, #52,

illus.), 9 x 6M, in., (22.9 x 17.5 cm.), photograph, arrow-root process printing-out paper, matte gelatin (BP 4902, DM 12,008, FR 40,647, Y 848,275).

BI   *"Boutique, 19 Place Dauphine"*, *1911*, t., num. 1448, est. BP 2/3,000, (05-06-93, Christie-London, #73, illus.), 8¾ x 7 in., photograph, albumen print.

BI   *"Cafe-Avenue Gde., Armee"*, *1906*, t., num. 45 (?), photog.'s credit stamp E. Atget, Rue Campagne-Premiere 17bis, est. BP 1/1,500, (05-06-93, Christie-London, #71, illus.), 7¼ x 8¾ in., photograph, albumen print.

$1840*   *Chateau De Viarmes*, *1910*, t., num. 6754 in Atget's hand, (04-08-93, Christie-NY, #51, illus.), 8½ x 7 in., (21.6 x 17.8 cm.), photograph, gold-toned silver printing-out paper (BP 1207, DM 2956, FR 10,005, Y 208,806).

$2760*   *Coiffeur, Avenue De L'Observatoire*, *1926*, Berenice Abbott Coll. stamp verso of mount, lit., (04-08-93, Christie-NY, #53, illus.), 8¾ x 6B, in., (22.2 x 16.8 cm.), photograph, gold-toned silver printing-out paper (BP 1810, DM 4434, FR 15,008, Y 313,209).

$1840*   *"Colonne Moris"* (Nesbit, p. 367, no. 7), *1910*, flush-mounted, t., num. 222 in unident. hand, (04-06-93, Sotheby-NY, #238, illus.), 8℃, x 6¾ in., photograph, albumen printing-out paper (BP 1215, DM 2964, FR 10,038, Y 209,854).

BI   *Doorway, Rue De Marly, Paris 1906*, num. 10, photog.'s credit stamp E. Atget, Rue Campagne-Premiere 17bis, est. BP 2/2,500, (05-06-93, Christie-London, #72, illus.), 7 x 8½ in., photograph, albumen print.

$350*   *French Park*, p. Bernice Abbott, label verso, (02-04-93, Sloan, #2921), sight 7 x 9 in., (17.8 x 22.9 cm.), photograph, silver gelatin print (BP 242, DM 580, FR 1962, Y 43,554).

BI   *La Grace De Dieu 121 Rue Montmatre*, *1902*, t., s., d., est. DM 1,800, (11-12-92, Lempertz, #4, illus.), 6M, x 8½ in., (17.4 x 21.6 cm.), photograph, albumen print.

BI   *Grand Trianon, Versailles, c. 1911*, num. 223 in neg., s., i., est. $2/3,000, (10-13-92, Christie-NY, #31, illus.), 6¾ x 8¼ in., (17.1 x 21 cm.), photograph, arrowroot process printing-out paper.

$3850*   *Grilles, Invalides, 1921*, #6283 by photog. in neg., t., num. by photog., prop. Museum of ModernArt, (10-15-92, Sotheby-NY, #199, illus.), 6M, x 8¾ in., (17.5 x 22.2 cm.), photograph, albumen-silver print (BP 2356, DM 5731, FR 19,435, Y 461,908).

BI   *Hotel 26 Rue De Lille, c. 1902*, t., num. 4617 in Atget's hand, est. $2/3,000, (10-13-92, Christie-NY, #29, illus.), 8¾ x 7 in., (22.2 x 17.8 cm.), photograph, gold-toned silver printing-out paper.

$1430*   *Hotel De Beauvais, c. 1900*, photog.'s t., unique notations, (04-07-93, Swann, #394, illus.), 7 x 8½ in., photograph, albumen printing-out paper print (BP 945, DM 2313, FR 7827, Y 162,463).

BI   *Hotel Du Cardinal Dubers, 10 Rue De Valois, c. 1900*, t., est. DM 1,500, (11-12-92, Lempertz, #3), 8M, x 7℥n in., (22.6 x 18 cm.), photograph, albumen print.

$2200*   *"Hotel Guebiant, 14 Rue Guillaume", "14 Rue Des Bourdounait", and "Hotel Daugny, 6 Rue Drout", c. 1900: Three*, t., notations, (10-14-92, Swann, #372, illus.), each, approx. 7 x 8½ in., (17.8 x 21.6 cm.), photograph, albumen prints (BP 1291, DM 3220, FR 10,918, Y 266,602).

BI   *Interieur, Chateau De Viarmes, c. 1910*, t., num. 695 in Atget's hand, est. $3/4,000, (10-13-92, Christie-NY, #30, illus.), 8½ x 7℥, in., (21.6 x 18.1 cm.), photograph, gold-toned printing-out paper.

BI   *Magasin, Avenue Des Gobelins, 1925*, num. 79 in Atget's hand, Berenice Abbott Coll. and West 67th Street stamps verso of mount, lit., est. $3/4,000, (04-08-93, Christie-NY, #54, illus.), 9¼ x 6¾ in., (23.5 x 17.1 cm.), photograph, gelatin silver printing-out paper.

$1725*   *Marchands Des Vins, c. 1910*, t. in Atget's hand, Berenice Abbott coll. stamp verso of mount, (04-08-93, Christie-NY, #49, illus.), 8½ x 6¾ in., (21.6 x 17.1 cm.), photograph, gold-toned silver printing-out paper (BP 1131, DM 2771, FR 9380, Y 195,756).

BI   *Market Interior, 1898*, num. 3059, est. BP 1,2/1,600, (05-06-93, Christie-London, #70, illus.), 6¾ x 8½ in., photograph, albumen print.

$6875*   *Moulin De La Galette, Montmartre, 1902*, #6311 by photog. in neg., t., #6311, i. 17 bis by photog., studio stamp, prop. Museum of Modern Art, (10-15-92,

Sotheby-NY, #203, illus.), 6M, x 9 in., (17.5 x 22.9 cm.), photograph, silver printing-out paper (BP 4207, DM 10,234, FR 34,705, Y 824,835).

$15,400*   *Notre Dame, 1923*, #6413 by photog. in neg., t., num., i. 17 bis by photog., studio stamp, prop. Museum of Modern Art, (10-15-92, Sotheby-NY, #198, illus.), 9½ x 6M, in., (24.1 x 17.5 cm.), photograph, matte albumen-silver print (BP 9424, DM 22,923, FR 77,739, Y 1,847,630).

$2645*   *"Palais De La Reine Horntese R. Lafitte", c. 1900*, (04-06-93, Sotheby-NY, #235, illus.), 7 x 8B\ in., photograph, albumen printing-out paper print (BP 1747, DM 4261, FR 14,430, Y 301,665).

$8250*   *Parc De St. Cloud (Hambourg and Szarkowski, The Ancien Regime, pl. 62), 1904*, t., #6500 by photog., studio stamp, catalog cover lot, (10-15-92, Sotheby-NY, #200, illus.), 8¾ x 7 in., (22.2 x 17.8 cm.), photograph, albumen silver print (BP 5048, DM 12,280, FR 41,646, Y 989,802).

BI   *Port Rue De Clery 42, c. 1900*, t., est. DM 1,600-, (11-12-92, Lempertz, #2, illus.), 8℥zn x 7℥n in., (22 x 17.9 cm.), photograph, albumen print.

$863*   *"Porte A La Bibliotheque Polonaise", Door Of The Polish Library, 1910*, t., num. 5279, (05-23-93, Butterfield, #3304, illus.), 8◔\ x 7 in., photograph, albumen print (BP 562, DM 1411, FR 4750, Y 95,391).

$4950*   *Portes Du Dragon De Rennes, c. 1900*, num. 3766 in Atget's hand, t., (10-13-92, Christie-NY, #28, illus.), 8½ x 6M, in., (21.6 x 17.5 cm.), photograph, gold-toned silver printing-out paper (BP 2883, DM 7252, FR 24,639, Y 600,218).

$605*   *"Prostitute Taking Her Shift, La Villette, Paris", 1921*, p. by Berenice Abbott, mounted, stamped, num. 2105-B, very good cond., (03-12-93, Skinner, #121, illus.), 9¼ x 6¾ in., photograph, silver print toned on printing-out paper (BP 422, DM 1007, FR 3424, Y 71,302).

$3575*   *"Rue Hautefeuille", c. 1925*, t., #6381; photog. stamp verso, (11-16-92, Butterfield, #5840, illus.), 7 x 8¾ in., (178.1 x 222.6 mm.), photograph, albumen print (BP 2354, DM 5700, FR 19,200, Y 444,596).

$2070*   *Selected Images: "Hotel De Roquelaure, Bd. St. Germain" and "Street Scene, Paris", early 1900's and c. 1898*, 1st t. and #5288, 2nd #3576 by photog., (04-06-93, Sotheby-NY, #236, illus.), approx. 7 x 8½ in., photograph, albumen printing-out paper (BP 1367, DM 3335, FR 11,293, Y 236,086).

$2588*   *Selected Images: "La Rue Mondetour, Nos. 13, 15, 17 Entre La Rue De La Gde. Truanderie Et Pirouette" and "Rue De La Gde. Truanderie Vue Prise De Laue Turbigo", c. 1907: Two*, each t., num. 155 and 167 by photog., (04-06-93, Sotheby-NY, #234, illus.), approx. 7 x 8½ in., photograph, albumen printing-out paper print (BP 1709, DM 4169, FR 14,119, Y 295,164).

$5500*   *St. Cloud (Cascade), 1923*, t., num. 1188 by photog., (10-15-92, Sotheby-NY, #202, illus.), 8½ x 6M, in., (21.6 x 17.5 cm.), photograph, albumen silver print (BP 3366, DM 8187, FR 27,764, Y 659,868).

$1438*   *Twenty Photographs By Eugene Atget 1856-1927: Twenty*, p. Berenice Abbott, 1956, missing num. 1, 3, 10-12, 14, and 16, eachstamped verso, photographer's/printer's credit, sig. in ink 'Berenice Abbott',edit. 92/100, in portfolio, (10-15-92, Sotheby-London, #51, illus.), each 7 x 9½ in., (17.8 x 24.1 cm.), photograph, gold toned silver prints dry mounted on card (BP 880, DM 2141, FR 7259, Y 172,525).

$4370*   *Versailles, c. 1922*, t., num. 1117 in Atget's hand, (04-08-93, Christie-NY, #50, illus.), 8½ x 7℥, in., (21.6 x 18.1 cm.), photograph, gold-toned silver printing-out paper (BP 2866, DM 7020, FR 23,763, Y 495,915).

$4950*   *Vigne Vierge, 1922/23*, num. (illegibly) by photog. in neg., t., #1162, i. 17 bis, studio stamp, prop. Museum of Modern Art, (10-15-92, Sotheby-NY, #201, illus.), 9 x 7 in., (22.9 x 17.8 cm.), photograph, matte albumen silver print (BP 3029, DM 7368, FR 24,987, Y 593,881).

ATGET, Eugene et alii

BI   *"La Femme Criminelle Et La Prostitutee"*, Felix Alcan, book by Cesare Lombroso and G. Ferrero, unique extra-illus. copy, includ. 13 plates for in text, large 8vo, Pierre MacOrlan Coll., est. $80/120,00, (04-06-93, Sotheby-NY, #237, illus.), photos various to 8½ x 5½ in., photograph.

ATKINS, Guy

$404* *Asger Jorn, The Crucial Years, 1954-1964, 1977,* (03-24-93, Kunsthallen, #22), print (BP 274, DM 660, FR 2246, Y 47,468, DK 2530).

$92* *Asger Jorn, The Final Years, 1965-1973, 1980,* (03-24-93, Kunsthallen, #23), print (BP 62, DM 150, FR 511, Y 10,810, DK 575).

$697* *Jorn In Scandinavia 1930-1953, 1968,* (03-24-93, Kunsthallen, #21), print (BP 472, DM 1138, FR 3874, Y 81,894, DK 4370).

ATKINSON, John Augustus   English 1775-1834

BI *Battle Scenes From The Napoleonic Wars, 1817: Five,* pub. Ackermann, trimmed irregularly, soiling, surface dirt, est. BP4/600, (06-30-93, Sotheby-London, #259), pen-lithograph, two hand-colored.

ATKINSON, T.L.

$50* *"Portrait Of A Soldier Wearing A Sash",* after G. Richmond, margins, (11-19-92, Bonhams-Chelsea, #26), plate 17½ x 14 in., (44.5 x 35.6 cm.), mezzotint (BP 33, DM 80, FR 269, Y 6218).

ATL, Dr.   Mexican 1875-1964

BI *Desnudo, c. 1925,* s., very good cond., creases, soiling, est. $3/4,000, (05-18-93, Sotheby-NY, #250, illus.), 18¾ x 12 in., (476 x 305 mm.), .

ATLAN, Jean   French 1913-1960

$1410* *Astarte. Ohne Titel, 1958,* s., #124/150, (05-26-93, Lempertz, #8), smallest 16⅞ᴢn x 21ᴍ, in., (43 x 55.5 cm.), largest 19¾ x 25⅞ᴢn in., (43 x 55.5 cm.), color lithograph on Rives wove (BP 912, DM 2301, FR 7743, Y 153,194).

$771* *Color Composition, c. 1950,* s., #155/220, margins, good cond., discoloration, attenuation of colors, (06-30-93, Sotheby-London, #740), 22¼ x 15⅞, in., (565 x 384 mm.), color lithograph on wove (BP 517, DM 1315, FR 4436, Y 82,610).

BI *Sagittaire, (W. 39), 1959,* watermark, s., d., num. 19/100, pub. l'Oeuvre Gravee, blindstamp, margins, mount-staining, good cond., est. BP 1,2/1,400, (12-01-92, Christie-London, #559), L. 21ᴮ, x 18⅞ᴢn in., (550 x 465 mm.), lithograph in colors on wove.

AUATI, Mario   French b. 1921

$138* *Paon Aux Roseaux,* s., t., #4/11, (06-11-93, Freemn/Fine Art, #10), 8¼ x 10¾ in., (21 x 27.3 cm.), aquatint (BP 91, DM 224, FR 756, Y 14,642).

AUBERT, Rene

$100* *Ch. De Fer De L'Etat. Versailles, Sejour Ideal A 20 Minutes De Paris,* cond. A, (03-16-93, Boisgirard, #45), 39ᴄ, x 24ᴮ, in., (100 x 62.5 cm.), poster (BP 69, DM 166, FR 565, Y 11,693).

AUBRY, Charles

$330* *Floral Study, ca. 1870,* s., num. by photog. in neg., mounted card, (04-07-93, Swann, #106, illus.), 14½ x 10 in., (36.8 x 25.4 cm.), photograph, albumen print (BP 218, DM 534, FR 1806, Y 37,491).

AUDSLEY and BOWES

$288* *Japanese Ceramics, 1880: Eight,* (04-07-93, Sotheby-Arcade, #156), sight 13½ x 9 in., (34.3 x 22.9 cm.), chromolithograph (BP 190, DM 466, FR 1576, Y 32,720).

AUDUBON

$143* *"American Ptarmigan"* and *"Ivory Gull": Two,* from Birds of America, p. J.T. Bowen, octavo edit., (02-05-93, Garth, #381, illus.), 6¾ x 10½ in., (17.1 x 26.7 cm.), hand-colored lithograph (BP 99, DM 237, FR 802, Y 17,795).

$50* *"Arctic Blue Bird",* from Birds of America, p. Endicott, octavo edit., stains, (02-05-93, Garth, #171, illus.), 16 x 12 in., (40.6 x 30.5 cm.), hand-colored lithograph (BP 35, DM 83, FR 280, Y 6222).

$28* *"Banded Three-Toed Woodpecker",* from Birds of America, (09-04-92, Garth, #561, illus.), 16 x 12 in., (40.6 x 30.5 cm.), handcolored lithograph (BP 14, DM 39, FR 134, Y 3447).

$94* *"Bank Swallow",* from Birds of America, octavo edit., p. Bowen, foxing, (10-23-92, Garth, #654, illus.), 15½ x 11 in., (39.4 x 27.9 cm.), hand colored lithograph (BP 58, DM 144, FR 487, Y 11,463).

BI *Birds: Two,* est. $120/160, (03-25-93, Boos, #650), sight 18¼ x 15¼ in., (46.4 x 38.7 cm.), print.

$253* *"Black-Throated Bunting"* and *"Lark Bunting": Two,* from Birds of America, (09-04-92, Garth, #147, illus.), 19½ x 15¼ in., (49.5 x 38.7 cm.), handcolored lithograph (BP 127, DM 355, FR 1207, Y 31,142).

$61* *"Blue Bird",* medium folio, p. Havell, London, 1881, margins trimmed, minor stains, (11-13-92, Garth, #587), 23½ x 17ᴄ, in., (59.7 x 44.1 cm.), handcolored lithograph (BP 39, DM 96, FR 323, Y 7571).

$83* *"Blue Jay",* from "Birds of America", large folio, p. J. Bien 1859, repaired tears, (11-13-92, Garth, #586), 31¾ x 25½ in., (80.6 x 64.8 cm.), colored chromolithograph (BP 54, DM 130, FR 439, Y 10,302).

$77* *"Common Pine Finch"* and *"White Bellied Swallow": Two,* from "Birds of America", octavo edit., p. J.T. Bowen, (10-23-92, Garth, #386, illus.), 10½ x 6½ in., (26.7 x 16.5 cm.), hand colored lithograph (BP 48, DM 118, FR 399, Y 9390).

$77* *"La Contis Sharp-tailed Bunting"* and *"Chestnut Sided Wood-Warbler": Two,* from "Birds of America", p. J.T. Bowen, (10-23-92, Garth, #387, illus.), 10½ x 6½ in., (26.7 x 16.5 cm.), hand colored lithograph (BP 48, DM 118, FR 399, Y 9390).

$165* *"Horn-Billed Guillemot"* and *"Tufted Puffin": Two,* from Birds of America, pub. J.T. Bowen, octavo edit., (02-05-93, Garth, #442, illus.), 5¾ x 10 in., (14.6 x 25.4 cm.), hand-colored lithograph (BP 114, DM 274, FR 925, Y 20,533).

$66* *"Horned Grebe"* and *"Red Necked Grebe": Two,* from Birds of America, p. J.T. Bowen, (02-05-93, Garth, #172, illus.), 6 x 10 in., (15.2 x 25.4 cm.), hand-colored lithograph (BP 46, DM 109, FR 370, Y 8213).

$55* *"Hudson's Bay Titmouse",* p., colored J. Bower, (02-27-93, Dunning, #106), 9½ x 6 in., (24.1 x 15.2 cm.), color book plate (BP 39, DM 90, FR 307, Y 6493).

$110* *"Indigo Bunting",* from the Birds of North America, pub. J.T. Bowen, octavo size, (12-10-92, Garth, #552), 16 x 13 in., (40.6 x 33 cm.), hand-colored lithograph (BP 71, DM 174, FR 594, Y 13,607).

$110* *"Least Bittern"* and *"Common Gallinule": Pair,* from Birds of America, 1856-60 octavo edit. pub. J.T. Bowen, (04-30-93, Garth, #391, illus.), 6½ x 10½ in., (16.5 x 26.7 cm.), handcolored lithograph (BP 70, DM 174, FR 587, Y 12,205).

$187* *"Loggerhead Shrike"* and *"Swamp Sparrow": Pair,* from Birds Of America by Audubon 1856-60 octavo edit. pub. J.T. Bowen, (04-30-93, Garth, #351, illus.), 10½ x 6½ in., (26.7 x 16.5 cm.), handcolored lithograph (BP 119, DM 296, FR 998, Y 20,748).

$83* *"Pied-Billed Dobchick", "Carolina Turtle Dove"* and *"Red Throated Diver": Three,* from Birds of America, pub. J.T. Bowen, (05-21-93, Garth, #272, illus.), 5¾ x 10 in., (14.6 x 25.4 cm.), hand-colored lithograph (BP 54, DM 135, FR 454, Y 9151).

$143* *"Pigeon Falcon"* and *"Acadian Owl": Pair,* from Birds of North America, octavo series pub. J.T. Bowen, 1856-1860, (04-30-93, Garth, #501, illus.), 10½ x 6½ in., (26.7 x 16.5 cm.), handcolored lithograph (BP 91, DM 226, FR 763, Y 15,866).

$44* *"Rednecked Grebe"* and *"Fulmor Petrel": Two,* from Birds of North America, p. J.T. Bowen, Octavo Edition, (11-13-92, Garth, #367, illus.), 6½ x 10½ in., (16.5 x 26.7 cm.), handcolored lithographs (BP 28, DM 69, FR 233, Y 5461).

$297* *"Tawny Thrush"* and *"Hermit Thrush": Two,* (09-04-92, Garth, #148, illus.), 19½ x 15¼ in., (49.5 x 38.7 cm.), handcolored lithograph (BP 149, DM 416, FR 1417, Y 36,558).

$39* *"Violet-Green Cormorant"* and *"American Scoter Duck": Two,* from Birds of North America, p. J.T. Bowen, Octavo Edition, (11-13-92, Garth, #368, illus.), 6½ x 10½ in., (16.5 x 26.7 cm.), handcolored lithographs (BP 25, DM 61, FR 206, Y 4841).

$66* *"Yellow Red - Poll Wood Warbler",* from Birds of North America, p. J.T. Bowen, (11-27-92, Garth, #476, illus.), 18 x 14 in., (45.7 x 35.6 cm.), handcolored lithograph (BP 43, DM 105, FR 358, Y 8214).

AUDUBON (after)

$39* *"Carolina Turtle Dove",* (02-12-93, DuMouchelle, #2390), 24½ x 18¾ in., (62.2 x 47.6 cm.), photolithograph (BP 27, DM 65, FR 219, Y 4703).

$715* *"Mocking Bird",* by J. Bien, plate 138, No. 32, 1860, staining, fading, full margins,prov., (06-25-93, Goldberg, #916, illus.), 38½ x 26½ in., (97.8 x 67.3 cm.), chromolithograph (BP 484, DM 1217, FR 4100, Y 75,790).

AUDUBON, J.W. American 1812-1862

$440* *"Annulated Marmot Squirrel", 1845,* J.J. Bowen, #16, plate LXXIX, (09-18-92, DuMouchelle, #7, illus.), 21 x 26¼ in., (53.3 x 66.7 cm.), lithograph (BP 253, DM 659, FR 2256, Y 54,822).

$385* *"Large Tailed Spermophile, Male", 1848,* J.T. Bowen, #28, Plate CXXXIX, (09-18-92, DuMouchelle, #8, illus.), 20¾ x 26 in., (52.7 x 66 cm.), lithograph (BP 221, DM 577, FR 1974, Y 47,969).

$385* *"Lewis' Marmot", 1847,* J.T. Bowen, #28, plate CXXXIX, (09-18-92, DuMouchelle, #10, illus.), 20½ x 26 in., (52.1 x 66 cm.), lithograph (BP 221, DM 577, FR 1974, Y 47,969).

$330* *"Mexican Marmot Squirrel, Male", 1847,* J.T. Bowen, #25, plate CXXIV, (09-18-92, DuMouchelle, #9, illus.), 21 x 26 in., (53.3 x 66 cm.), lithograph (BP 190, DM 494, FR 1692, Y 41,116).

$330* *"Spermophilus Macrourus Bennett Large Tailed Spermophile Male",* #28, plate CXXXIX, JT Bowen 1848, (02-27-93, Dunning, #1116), 18 x 24 in., (45.7 x 61 cm.), hand colored lithograph (BP 232, DM 542, FR 1844, Y 38,956).

AUDUBON, John James American 1785-1851

$385* *American Cross Fox,* (12-17-92, Mystic, #29), 21 x 27 in., (53.3 x 68.6 cm.), color lithograph (BP 244, DM 601, FR 2053, Y 47,315).

$1925* *American Goldfinch,* from "Birds of America", engraved Robert Havell, plate XXXIII, (10-30-92, Sloan, #2350, illus.), 19¼ x 12¼ in., (48.9 x 31.1 cm.), hand colored engraving (BP 1234, DM 2962, FR 10,047, Y 238,449).

$770* *American Red Fox,* (12-17-92, Mystic, #25), 21 x 27 in., (53.3 x 68.6 cm.), color lithograph (BP 489, DM 1202, FR 4107, Y 94,629).

BI *American Snipe, 1835,* plate #243, pub. Robert Havell, margins, est. $25/3500, (10-24-92, Collins, #6, illus.), 12¼ x 19½ in., (31.1 x 49.5 cm.), hand colored engraving.

$1980* *Blue Jay (Plate C11), 1825,* engraved by Robert Havell, (05-28-93, Sloan, #2674, illus.), 25¾ x 20½ in., (65.4 x 52.1 cm.), handcolored engraving (BP 1268, DM 3140, FR 10,617, Y 212,310).

$2200* *Blue Jay, 1825,* engraved Robert Havell, plate CII, margins trimmed, (10-30-92, Sloan, #2352, illus.), 25¾ x 20½ in., (65.4 x 52.1 cm.), hand colored engraving (BP 1410, DM 3385, FR 11,482, Y 272,513).

BI *Blue Jay, Corvus Cristatus,* Havell Plate CII, by Robert Havell, est. C$ 7/900, (06-08-93, Ritchie, #13, illus.), image 22 x 18 in., (55.9 x 45.7 cm.), hand-colored engraving and aquatint.

$2310* *Canada Lynx,* (12-17-92, Mystic, #22), 21 x 27 in., (53.3 x 68.6 cm.), color lithograph (BP 1466, DM 3607, FR 12,320, Y 283,888).

$385* *Canis Latrans,* plate LXXI, p. J.T. Bowen, foxing, (11-28-92, Dunning, #1015), 20 x 25 in., (50.8 x 63.5 cm.), color lithograph (BP 254, DM 613, FR 2082, Y 47,915).

$138* *Cat Bird,* No. 26 Plate CXXVIII, narrow margins, (02-13-93, Collins, #123, illus.), 19½ x 12¼ in., (49.5 x 31.1 cm.), hand-colored engraving (BP 97, DM 229, FR 774, Y 16,643).

$303* *Cervus Alces, Linn (Moose Deer. Old Male, and Young),* pub. by Havell, 1845, (09-17-92, Sloan, #2001), 17 x 24℃, in., (43.2 x 61.9 cm.), color lithograph (BP 170, DM 450, FR 1540, Y 37,724).

$35* *"Cliff Swallow" and "Black Vulture": Two,* from the Birds of North America, 1st octavo edit., good cond., (05-15-93, Cleveland, #60), one 7½ x 5 in., (19.1 x 12.7 cm.), the other 5¼ x 6¼ in., (19.1 x 12.7 cm.), hand colored lithograph (BP 23, DM 56, FR 189, Y 3880).

$3080* *Common American Wild Cat,* (12-17-92, Mystic, #35), 21 x 27 in., (53.3 x 68.6 cm.), color lithograph (BP 1955, DM 4809, FR 16,427, Y 378,518).

$4950* *Common Mouse With Canton Jar,* Audobon engraving, by J.T. Bowen, (05-29-93, Northeast, #558, illus.), sight 21 x 27 in., (53.3 x 68.6 cm.), engraving (BP 3171, DM 7851, FR 26,542, Y 530,774).

$880* *Cougar,* (09-24-92, Mystic, #10), 21 x 27 in., (53.3 x 68.6 cm.), colored lithograph (BP 515, DM 1304, FR 4429, Y 105,858).

$1430* *Crow (Plate CLVI),* watermark 1834, margins trimmed, burnt around margin edges, buckling,image in good condition, (11-12-92, Freemn/Fine Art, #24, illus.), 37⅝n x 24¾ in., (95.4 x 62.9 cm.), colored impression on paper (BP 939, DM 2266, FR 7643, Y 177,309).

$83* *DeKay's Shrew,* (12-17-92, Mystic, #27), 21 x 27 in., (53.3 x 68.6 cm.), color lithograph (BP 53, DM 130, FR 443, Y 10,200).

$110* *Florida Rat,* (12-17-92, Mystic, #24), 27 x 21 in., (68.6 x 53.3 cm.), color lithograph (BP 70, DM 172, FR 587, Y 13,518).

BI *"Fork Tailed Petrel", No. 52, plate CCLX, 1935,* by R. Havell, untinted proof, trimmed margins, crease in center, est. $5/700, (11-21-92, Goldberg, #725, illus.), image 10¼ x 17½ in., (26 x 44.5 cm.), engraving.

$138* *Fremonts Squirrel,* (09-24-92, Mystic, #11), 27 x 21 in., (68.6 x 53.3 cm.), colored lithograph (BP 81, DM 205, FR 695, Y 16,601).

$330* *"Great Auk",* plate 165, faded, toned, water stain, hole, margins reduced, (01-05-93, Bourne, #122, illus.), lithograph (BP 213, DM 537, FR 1830, Y 41,178).

$330* *"Hutchin's Barnacle Goose", Plate CCLLXXVII, c. 1933,* #56 Havell pub., fading, abrasions, full margins, (05-07-93, Goldberg, #435), 28½ x 20½ in., (72.4 x 52.1 cm.), color engraving (BP 209, DM 522, FR 1758, Y 36,336).

$495* *"Lepus Texianus",* pl. CXXXIII. "Texan Hare", (01-15-93, DuMouchelle, #2218, illus.), 22 x 28 in., (55.9 x 71.1 cm.), hand colored lithograph (BP 324, DM 809, FR 2736, Y 62,405).

$715* *Loggerhead Strike, 1829,* engraved Robert Havell, plate 57, (10-30-92, Sloan, #2354, illus.), 25¾ x 20½ in., (65.4 x 52.1 cm.), hand colored engraving (BP 458, DM 1100, FR 3732, Y 88,567).

$853* *Marsh Hare,* (12-17-92, Mystic, #31), 21 x 27 in., (53.3 x 68.6 cm.), color lithograph (BP 541, DM 1332, FR 4549, Y 104,830).

BI *Mississippi Kite Peinter,* est. $2/3,000, (09-24-92, Mystic, #9), 26 x 21 in., (66 x 53.3 cm.), colored lithograph.

$220* *Muskrat Musquash,* (12-17-92, Mystic, #28), 21 x 27 in., (53.3 x 68.6 cm.), color lithograph (BP 140, DM 343, FR 1173, Y 27,037).

$4400* *Ocelot,* (12-17-92, Mystic, #30), 21 x 27 in., (53.3 x 68.6 cm.), color lithograph (BP 2793, DM 6870, FR 23,467, Y 540,740).

$440* *Oregon Flying Squirrel,* (12-17-92, Mystic, #26), 27 x 21 in., (68.6 x 53.3 cm.), color lithograph (BP 279, DM 687, FR 2347, Y 54,074).

$248* *Pennants Marten,* (09-24-92, Mystic, #8), 27 x 21 in., (68.6 x 53.3 cm.), colored lithograph (BP 145, DM 368, FR 1248, Y 29,833).

$770* *Polar Hare,* (09-24-92, Mystic, #7), 21 x 27 in., (53.3 x 68.6 cm.), colored lithograph (BP 451, DM 1141, FR 3875, Y 92,626).

$193* *Prarie Dog,* (09-24-92, Mystic, #12), 21 x 27 in., (53.3 x 68.6 cm.), colored lithograph (BP 113, DM 286, FR 971, Y 23,217).

$468* *"Purple Martin's", Plate 22,* #5 from Havell pub., laid down, fading, staining, (05-07-93, Goldberg, #434), 19¾ x 25 in., (50.2 x 63.5 cm.), engraving (BP 296, DM 740, FR 2493, Y 51,530).

$468* *Red Tailed Squirrel,* (12-17-92, Mystic, #32), 27 x 21 in., (68.6 x 53.3 cm.), color lithograph (BP 297, DM 731, FR 2496, Y 57,515).

$1100* *Red Texan Wolf,* (09-24-92, Mystic, #6), 21 x 27 in., (53.3 x 68.6 cm.), colored lithograph (BP 644, DM 1630, FR 5536, Y 132,323).

$99* *"Rose Breasted Grosbeak" and "Black And Yellow Warbler": Two,* folios, (07-03-92, Sloan, #1068), color lithograph (BP 52, DM 150, FR 505, Y 12,341).

$1265* *Rusty Grackle, 1833,* engraved Robert Havell, plate CLVII, (10-30-92, Sloan, #2353, illus.), 25℃, x 20½ in., (64.5 x 52.1 cm.), hand colored engraving (BP 811, DM 1946, FR 6602, Y 156,695).

$660* *Scoleopaceus Courlan, 1837,* no. 76, plate CCCXXVII, p. Havel, (11-28-92, Dunning, #1016), 21 x 33¼ in., (53.3 x 84.5 cm.), color lithograph (BP 436, DM 1051, FR 3569, Y 82,141).

BI *"Spotted Sandpiper", 1836, No. 62, plate CCCX,* by R. Havell, laid down, tears, est. $6/800, (11-21-92, Goldberg, #724, illus.), 14¾ x 21¾ in., (37.5 x 55.2 cm.), engraving.

$275* *Townsend's Ground Squirrel,* (12-17-92, Mystic, #33), 21 x 27 in., (53.3 x 68.6 cm.), color lithograph (BP 175, DM 429, FR 1467, Y 33,796).

$935* *The Wolverine,* (12-17-92, Mystic, #23), 21 x 27 in., (53.3 x 68.6 cm.), color lithograph (BP 593, DM 1460, FR 4987, Y 114,907).

AUDUBON, John James (after)

$440* *"... Mexican Marmot-Squirrel..." no. 25, Plate CXXIV and "...NorthernMeadow-Mouse... " no. 26, Plate CXXIV: Two,* ident. i. on stone, (01-16-93, Skinner, #143, illus.), sheet, sight 19¼ x 25M, in., (48.9 x 65.7 cm.), hand-colored lithograph on paper (BP 288, DM 719, FR 2432, Y 55,472).

$1815* *"...Common Or Virginian Deer, Old Male And Female", 1848,* plate CXXXVI, Bowen edit., stone ident., good cond.?, foxing, toning, margins, cockling, (03-27-93, Skinner, #136, illus.), sight, sheet 19¼ x 26¼ in., (48.9 x 66.7 cm.), hand-colored lithograph on paper (BP 1219, DM 2961, FR 10,067, Y 211,243).

$440* *American Avocet, Plate CCCXVIII, 1836,* by R. Havell, mat burn, discoloration, foxing, repairs, laid down oncardboard, (12-04-92, Doyle, #27), plate 14½ x 20½ in., (368 x 521 mm.), sheet 22¼ x 28 in., (368 x 521 mm.), hand colored engraving, etching and aquatint (BP 282, DM 701, FR 2377, Y 54,931).

$1725* *American Beaver (Plate XLVI), 1844,* by J.T. Bowen, from Audubon's Viviparous Quadrupeds of North America, large margins, good cond., mat stain, foxing, creases, (01-28-93, Sotheby-NY, #527, illus.), sheet 21½ x 27 in., (546 x 686 mm.), hand-colored lithograph (BP 1139, DM 2733, FR 9249, Y 214,179).

$2530* *American Elk-Wapiti Deer (Plate LXII), 1845,* by J.T. Bowen, from Audubon's Viviparous Quadrupeds of North America, large margins, good cond., foxing, soiling, creases, tear, stitch holes, losses, (01-28-93, Sotheby-NY, #528), sheet 21¾ x 27½ in., (552 x 699 mm.), hand-colored lithograph (BP 1671, DM 4009, FR 13,566, Y 314,130).

$578* *"American Flamingo (Adult Male), No. 75, Plate 375",* from octavo edit. Birds in America pub. J.T. Bowen in 1843, (12-05-92, Neal, #721), image 8¼ x 5 in., (21 x 12.7 cm.), hand-colored lithograph (BP 362, DM 901, FR 3071, Y 71,614).

$25,300* *American Flamingo, Plate CCCCXXXI, 1838,* by R. Havell, trimmed, laid down on cardboard, foxing, discoloration, good cond., John Walton Livermore Estate, (12-04-92, Doyle, #32, illus.), 38¾ x 25¼ in., (984 x 641 mm.), hand colored engraving, etching and aquatint on J. Whatman paper (BP 16,228, DM 40,293, FR 136,683, Y 3,158,552).

$2875* *American Magpie (Pl. CCCLVII), 1837,* from Havell edit. of The Birds of America, full margins, good cond.,tears, (05-19-93, Butterfield, #1780), sh. 38¾ x 26Zzn in., (984 x 662 mm.), engraving w/aquatint and hand-coloring on J. Whatman 1837 (BP 1866, DM 4673, FR 15,745, Y 318,277).

$3450* *American Magpie (Plate CCCLVII), 1837,* by R. Havell, from Audubon's Birds of America, full margins, good cond., mat stain, fox marks, ex-coll. The New York Society Library, (01-28-93, Sotheby-NY, #522, illus.), 25В, x 21½ in., (65.1 x 54.6 cm.), sheet 39В, x 26½ in., (65.1 x 54.6 cm.), hand-colored etching, engraving and aquatint on paper, watermark (BP 2278, DM 5467, FR 18,499, Y 428,359).

$935* *"American Snipe",* plate CCXLIII, Havell edit., 1935, ident. w/in plate, laid down, fading/toning, (03-27-93, Skinner, #275), sheet 24½ x 36¾ in., (62.2 x 93.3 cm.), hand-colored engraving, etching and aquatint on wove, watermark (BP 628, DM 1525, FR 5186, Y 108,822).

$605* *"American White Pelican (Male), No. 85, Plate 423",* from octavo edit. Birds of America pub. J.T. Bowen in 1844, (12-05-92, Neal, #722), image 7¼ x 5 in., (18.4 x 12.7 cm.), hand-colored lithograph (BP 379, DM 943, FR 3215, Y 74,960).

BI *"American White Pelican" (Plate 311) and "American Brown Pelican" (Plate 421), 1971: Two,* Amsterdam, est. $800/1000, (02-18-93, Sotheby-Arcade, #84), color reproduction.

$693* *"Arctic Fox, Pl. CXXI, No. 25", 1847,* from Quadrupeds of North America, pub. J.T.Bowen, (02-13-93, Neal, #722), image 20 x 25½ in., (50.8 x 64.8 cm.), color lithograph (BP 488, DM 1149, FR 3889, Y 83,575).

$605* *Arctic Tern (Plate CCL),* by R. Havell, light struck, laid down on paper, repair entire bottommargin, mat burn, tape residue, (06-11-93, Doyle, #11), plate 19½ x 12C in., (495 x 314 mm.), sheet 37¾ x 24¾ in., (495 x 314 mm.), (BP 398, DM 983, FR 3315, Y 64,191).

$2185* *Arkansaw Flycatcher. Swallow Tailed Flycatcher. Says Flycatcher (Plate CCCLIX), 1837,* by R. Havell, from Audubon's Birds of America, full margins, good cond., soiling, foxing, repaired tear, creases, stitch holes, ex-coll. The New York Society Library, (01-28-93, Sotheby-NY, #523, illus.), 21M, x 14 in., (55.6 x 35.6 cm.), sheet 39B, x 26B, in., (55.6 x 35.6 cm.), hand-colored etching, engraving and aquatint on paper, watermark (BP 1443, DM 3462, FR 11,716, Y 271,294).

$3450* *Barnacle Goose (Plate CCXCVI), 1836,* by R. Havell, from Audubon's Birds of America, large margins, good cond., foxing, discoloration, remnants hinges, offprint, (01-28-93, Sotheby-NY, #519, illus.), sheet 25¼ x 38C in., (641 x 975 mm.), hand-colored etching, engraving and aquatint on paper, watermark (BP 2278, DM 5467, FR 18,499, Y 428,359).

$4290* *Barred Owl (Plate XLVI), 1826,* by R. Havell, narrow margins, foxing, creases, tears, skinned spots,rippling, Richard E. Benesh Estate, (01-16-93, Weschler, #148, illus.), 37½ x 25½ in., (95.3 x 64.8 cm.), hand colored engraving (BP 2804, DM 7014, FR 23,715, Y 540,847).

$330* *Bay Breasted Warbler, Plate LXIX,* by R. Havell, watermark J. Whatman 1832, mat burn, discoloration, foxing, creases, taped to mat, (12-04-92, Doyle, #17), plate 19½ x 12¼ in., (495 x 311 mm.), sheet 28 x 22C, in., (495 x 311 mm.), hand colored engraving, etching and aquatint (BP 212, DM 526, FR 1783, Y 41,199).

$1210* *Belted Kingfisher, Plate 77,* by R. Havell, (05-24-93, Grogan, #278), 24 x 18¾ in., (61 x 47.6 cm.), hand-colored etching, engraving and aquatint (BP 788, DM 1978, FR 6659, Y 133,746).

$3450* *"Black Backed Gull" (Pl. CCXLI) and "Eider Duck" (Pl. CCXLVI), 1835,* from Havell edit. of The Birds of America, margins, Black Backed Gull trimmed, good cond., losses, crease, image, surface soiling, staining, EiderDuck w/extensive losses in margins, surface abrasions in image, soiling, staining, offsetting, (05-19-93, Butterfield, #1767), one sh. 38Zzn x 26Zzn in., (983 x 662 mm.), the other sh. 25M, x 38M, in., (983 x 662 mm.), engraving w/aquatint and hand-coloring on J. Whatman Turkey Mill 1834and 1835 (BP 2240, DM 5608, FR 18,894, Y 381,933).

BI *Black Headed Gull, Plate CCCXIV, 1836,* by R. Havell, wide margins, good cond., light-staining, fox marks, creases, staining, rippling, est. $7/900, (06-12-93, Weschler, #170, illus.), 14¾ x 20 in., (37.5 x 50.8 cm.), hand-colored engraving on J. Twatman Turkey Mill paper.

$715* *Black Skimmer Or Shearwater (Plate CCCXXIII), 1836,* by R. Havell, full margins, foxing, overall staining, rippling, toning verso, Richard E. Benesh Estate, (01-16-93, Weschler, #150, illus.), 21 x 21¼ in., (53.3 x 54 cm.), hand colored engraving (BP 467, DM 1169, FR 3952, Y 90,141).

$880* *Black Skimmer Or Shearwater, 1860,* by J. Bien, plate 428 of The Birds of America, (06-13-93, Hindman, #307), sh 26½ x 25C, in., (67.3 x 64.5 cm.), chromolithograph (BP 576, DM 1432, FR 4814, Y 92,602).

$385* *"Black Throated Wax-Wing", Plate 245, "Artic Three-Toed Wookpecker",Plate 268, "American Bittern", Plate 365, "Esquimaux Curlew", Plate 537, "Gadwall Duck", Plate 388 and "Hudsonian Curlew", Plate 356, 1840-1844: Six,* by J. Bien, (06-05-93, LA Auction Ex., #12, illus.), largest 5 x 8 in., (12.7 x 20.3 cm.), hand-colored lithograph (BP 253, DM 624, FR 2104, Y 41,300).

$660* *Black Winged Hawk (plate CCCLII), 1827-1838,* by Robert Havell, from The Birds of America, (12-13-92, Hindman, #305, illus.), 32¼ x 23¼ in., hand-colored etching and aquatint (BP 422, DM 1037, FR 3535, Y 81,653).

BI *Black Winged Hawk, Plate CCLII, c. 1837,* by R. Howell, margins, good cond., fox marks, time staining, repaired tear, est. $2/3,000, (06-12-93, Weschler, #170A, illus.), 30 x 24 in., (76.2 x 61 cm.), hand-colored engraving.

$495* *Black-Billed Plover, Plate CCCXXXIV,* The Birds of America, from Original Drawings, J.J. Audubon, 1827-38,d. 1836, wide margins, staining, foxmarks, erased i., tears (backed), prov., (01-22-93, Christie-NY, #333), plate 15℀, x 21 in., (384 x 533 mm.), aquatint and engraving w/hand-coloring on J. Whatman (BP 324, DM 787, FR 2663, Y 61,952).

$2070* *Black-Tailed Hare (Plate LXIII), 1845,* by J.T. Bowen, from Audubon's Viviparous Quadrupeds of North America, large margins, good cond., mat stain, foxing, image scuffs, creases, tears, nicks, (01-28-93, Sotheby-NY, #528A), sheet 21½ x 27℃, in., (546 x 695 mm.), hand-colored lithograph (BP 1367, DM 3280, FR 11,099, Y 257,015).

$770* *Blue Grosbeak, Plate CXXII,* by R. Havell, from The Birds of America, (03-24-93, Grogan, #19), 26 x 20¾ in., (66 x 52.7 cm.), hand-colored etching, engraving and aquatint (BP 521, DM 1258, FR 4280, Y 90,471).

BI *Blue Jay, Plate CII,* by R. Havell, watermark J. Whatman 1836, repairs, foxing, discoloration, John Walton Livermore Estate, est. $2/3,000, (12-04-92, Doyle, #20), plate 25℥, x 20½ in., (651 x 521 mm.), sheet 30 x 24¼ in., (651 x 521 mm.), hand colored engraving, etching and aquatint.

$121* *"Blue Jays", "Gyrfalcon", "Shoveller Ducks": Six,* (12-10-92, Sloan, #610), largest 18¾ x 15½ in., (47.6 x 39.4 cm.), chromolithographs (BP 78, DM 191, FR 654, Y 14,968).

$110* *"Blue Mountain Warbler"* and *"Arkansas Goldfinch": Pair,* octavo edit., from Birds of America, (02-14-93, Neal, #1136), hand colored lithograph (BP 77, DM 182, FR 617, Y 13,266).

$715* *Bonapartian Gull (Plate CCCXXIV),* by R. Havell, 1836, mat burn, good cond., (06-11-93, Doyle, #13), plate 21¼ x 16½ in., (540 x 419 mm.), sheet 25 x 37½ in., (540 x 419 mm.), hand colored etching, engraving and aquatint on paper w/watermark (BP 470, DM 1162, FR 3918, Y 75,862).

$5750* *Brasilian Caracara Eagle (Pl. CLXI), 1833,* from Havell edit. of The Birds of America, margins trimmed unevenly,good cond., tears, creases, surface abrasions in image, foxing, soiling, offsetting, (05-19-93, Butterfield, #1761), sh. 38ℳ, x 26℀n in., (987 x 665 mm.), engraving w/aquatint and hand-coloring on J. Whatman 1833 (BP 3733, DM 9347, FR 31,490, Y 636,555).

$605* *"Brown Pelican (Adult Male), No 85, Plate 423",* from octavo edit. Birds of America pub. J.T. Bowen in 1844, (12-05-92, Neal, #723), image 7½ x 5 in., (19.1 x 12.7 cm.), hand-colored lithograph (BP 379, DM 943, FR 3215, Y 74,960).

$19,550* *Brown Pelican (Plate CCLI), 1835,* by R. Havell, from Audubon's Birds of America, large margins, colorsslightly faded, mat stain, foxing, soiling, tears, losses, scuffs, hinges, offprint, (01-28-93, Sotheby-NY, #515, illus.), sheet 37ℳ, x 25℀, in., (962 x 638 mm.), hand-colored etching, engraving and aquatint on paper, watermark (BP 12,910, DM 30,978, FR 104,826, Y 2,427,365).

$495* *"Brown Pelican (Young-First Winter), No. 85, Plate 424",* from octavo edit. Birds of America pub. J.T. Bowen in 1844, (12-05-92, Neal, #724), image 5¼ x 8 in., (13.3 x 20.3 cm.), hand-colored lithograph (BP 310, DM 772, FR 2630, Y 61,331).

$495* *Brown Titlark (Plate X),* by W.H. Lizars, p. and colored R. Havell, full margins, foxing, darkening, smudges, creases, rippling, Richard E. Benesh Estate, (01-16-93, Weschler, #146, illus.), (32.4 x 52.1 cm.), engraving (BP 324, DM 809, FR 2736, Y 62,405).

$978* *Burgomaster Gull (Pl. CCCXCVI), 1837,* from Havell edit. of The Birds of America, margins, good cond.,

tears, losses, staining, creases, surface soiling, (05-19-93, Butterfield, #1783), sh. 26 x 38℀n in., (660 x 973 mm.), engraving w/aquatint and hand-coloring on J. Whatman Turkey Mill 1837 (BP 635, DM 1590, FR 5356, Y 108,270).

$715* *Canada Jay, Plate CVII, 1831,* by R. Havell, watermark J. Whatman 1831, cleaned, colors faded, tapestains, good cond., (12-04-92, Doyle, #21), plate 25½ x 20½ in., (648 x 521 mm.), sheet 35¾ x 24¾ in., (648 x 521 mm.), hand colored engraving, etching and aquatint (BP 459, DM 1139, FR 3863, Y 89,263).

$4313* *Canada Lynx (Plate XVI), 1844-46,* by J.T. Bowen, from Audubon's Viviparous Quadrupeds of North America, large margins, good cond., mat stain, soiling, tears, stitch holes, (01-28-93, Sotheby-NY, #526A, illus.), sheet 21¼ x 27¼ in., (540 x 692 mm.), hand-colored lithograph (BP 2848, DM 6834, FR 23,126, Y 535,510).

$2070* *"Canada Warbler", "Connecticut Warbler"* and *"Yellow Breasted Rail" (Plates CIII, CXXXVIII and CCCXXIX), 1829, 1832 and 1837: Three,* by R. Havell, from Audubon's Birds of America, large margins, fold, backed w/ sheet wove, discoloration, 2nd and 3rd laid down, foxing or soiling, (01-28-93, Sotheby-NY, #509), hand-colored etching w/engraving and aquatint on paper, watermark (BP 1367, DM 3280, FR 11,099, Y 257,015).

$660* *Canis (Vulpes) Fulvus (American Cross Fox, Male) (Pl. VI), 1843,* from Bowen ed. of Viviparous Quadrupeds of North America, margins, good cond., mat & light-staining, surface soiling, paper loss, foxing, stains, linen tape, creases, (02-24-93, Butterfield, #2804), 15¾ x 23¼ in., (400 x 591 mm.), sheet 20ℳ, x 27℀, in., (400 x 591 mm.), lithograph w/hand-coloring on wove (BP 460, DM 1071, FR 3632, Y 77,447).

$110* *"Cape May Wood Warbler"* and *"Black-And-White Creeping Warbler": Pair,* octavo edit., from Birds of America, (02-14-93, Neal, #1138), hand colored lithograph (BP 77, DM 182, FR 617, Y 13,266).

$5290* *Carolina Pigeon, Or Turtle Dove (Plate 17), 1830,* by R. Havell, from Audubon's Birds of America, margins, soiling, foxing, discoloration, creases, tears in edges, tear, (01-28-93, Sotheby-NY, #505), 27 x 20℥, in., (686 x 524 mm.), sheet 37℥, x 25 in., (686 x 524 mm.), hand-colored etching, engraving and aquatint on paper, watermark (BP 3493, DM 8382, FR 28,365, Y 656,816).

BI *"Carolina Titmouse", Plate 127* and *"Hudson's Bay Titmouse", Plate 128, c. 1860,* J. Bien pub., fading, soiling, tuck holes, nicks, tears, est. $750/1,000, (05-07-93, Goldberg, #435B, illus.), 26 x 38½ in., (66 x 97.8 cm.), .

$1035* *Cayenne Tern (Pl CCLXXIII), 1835,* from Havell edit. of The Birds of America, margins, good cond., tears, staining, soiling, tape residue, offsetting, (05-19-93, Butterfield, #1775), 14¾ x 20½ in., (375 x 521 mm.), engraving w/aquatint and hand-coloring on J. Whatman 1835 (BP 672, DM 1682, FR 5668, Y 114,580).

$1650* *Chuck-Wills Widow, Plate LII,* by R. Havell, watermark J. Whatman 1836, large margins, discoloration, soiling, tape residue, hinged, good cond., (12-04-92, Doyle, #13, illus.), plate 26 x 20 in., (660 x 508 mm.), sheet 34¾ x 24ℳ, in., (660 x 508 mm.), hand colored engraving, etching and aquatint (BP 1058, DM 2628, FR 8914, Y 205,993).

$2860* *Cock Of The Plains, Plate CCCLXXI, 1837,* by R. Havell, tear, tape residue, foxing, discoloration, hinged to mat, (12-04-92, Doyle, #30, illus.), plate 24½ x 37 in., (622 x 940 mm.), sheet 25¼ x 38 in., (622 x 940 mm.), hand colored engraving, etching and aquatint (BP 1835, DM 4555, FR 15,451, Y 357,054).

$1320* *"Collard Peccary, Male, Plate XXXI, No. 7", 1844,* from The Viviparous Quadrupeds of North America, pub. by J.T. Bowen, (02-13-93, Neal, #723, illus.), sheet 21 x 25 in., (53.3 x 63.5 cm.), color lithograph (BP 930, DM 2189, FR 7407, Y 159,190).

BI *"Collared Peccary, (Male), No. 7, plate XXXI",* after colored lithograph pub. J.T. Bowen in 1844, est. $250/350, (12-05-92, Neal, #719), image 19 x 24 in., (48.3 x 61 cm.), photolithograph.

BI *Columbia Jay, Plate 96, 1830,* by R. Havell, watermark J. Whatman 1830, discoloration, trimmed, foxing, acid burn, fold, rippling, good cond., John Walton Livermore Estate, est. $3/4,000, (12-04-92, Doyle, #19, illus.), 37½ x 24¾ in., (953 x 629 mm.), hand colored engraving, etching and aquatint.

$1320* *"Common American Skunk, Female With Young, Plate XLII, No. 9", 1844,* from The Viviparous Quadrupeds of North America, pub. J.T. Bowen, (02-13-93, Neal, #725), sheet 27¼ x 21¼ in., (69.2 x 54 cm.), color lithograph (BP 930, DM 2189, FR 7407, Y 159,190).

$303* *"Common Buzzard",* plate CCCLXXII, Havell edit., 1837, ident. w/in plate, toning, discoloration, cockling, foxing, (03-27-93, Skinner, #296), sh 32 x 25 in., (81.3 x 63.5 cm.), hand-colored engraving, etching and aquatint on wove, watermark (BP 204, DM 494, FR 1681, Y 35,265).

$1150* *Common Cormorant (Plate CCLXVI), 1835,* by R. Havell, margins, good cond., foxing, mat stain, tears, repaired tears, (01-28-93, Sotheby-NY, #516), sheet 25¼ x 38 in., (641 x 965 mm.), hand-colored etching, engraving and aquatint on paper, watermark (BP 759, DM 1822, FR 6166, Y 142,786).

$330* *Common Crossbill, 1860,* by J. Bien, plate 200 of The Birds Of America, (06-13-93, Hindman, #306), sh 39ℭ, x 26ℭ, in., (100 x 67 cm.), chromolithograph (BP 216, DM 537, FR 1805, Y 34,726).

BI *"Common Gallinule" and "American Coot": Pair,* octavo edit., from Birds of America, est. $150/250, (02-14-93, Neal, #1132), hand colored lithograph.

$5290* *Common Or Virginian Deer (Plate CXXXVI), 1848,* by J.T. Bowen, from Audubon's Viviparous Quadrupeds of North America, large margins, good cond., mat stain, foxing, image abrasions, tears, soiling, (01-28-93, Sotheby-NY, #529, illus.), sheet 21ℬ, x 27ℤ, in., (549 x 689 mm.), hand-colored lithograph (BP 3493, DM 8382, FR 28,365, Y 656,816).

$1870* *"The Cougar, Male, Plate XCVI, No. 20", 1846,* from The Viviparous Quadrupeds of North America, pub. J.T. Bowen, (02-13-93, Neal, #728), sheet 21½ x 27ℤ, in., (54.6 x 68.9 cm.), color lithograph (BP 1317, DM 3101, FR 10,494, Y 225,519).

$99* *"Cuvier's Kinglet" and "Bay-Winged Bunting": Pair,* octavo edit., from Birds of America, (02-14-93, Neal, #1137), hand colored lithograph (BP 70, DM 164, FR 556, Y 11,939).

$1725* *"Double-Crested Cormorant" (Pl. CCLVII) and "Semipalmated Snipe Or Willet" (Pl CCLXXIV), 1835,* from Havell edit. of The Birds of America, full margins, good cond.,tears, staining, scuffing, foxing in image, (05-19-93, Butterfield, #1773), one sh. 38ℤ\n x 26ℤn in., (983 x 664 mm.), the other sh. 26ℭn x 38ℬ\ in., (983 x 664 mm.), engraving w/aquatint and hand-coloring on J. Whatman 1935 (BP 1120, DM 2804, FR 9447, Y 190,966).

BI *Fish Crow, Plate 226, 1860,* by Julius Bien, fair cond., creases, staining, fox marks, glue, tape, est. $6/800, (06-12-93, Weschler, #169), 39¼ x 26¾ in., (99.7 x 67.9 cm.), chromolithograph.

$978* *Florida Cormorant (Pl. CCLII), 1835,* from Havell edit. of The Birds of America , margins, good cond., staining, surface soiling, offsetting, (05-19-93, Butterfield, #1769), 19½ x 26½ in., (495 x 673 mm.), engraving w/aquatint and hand-coloring on J. Whatman 1834 (BP 635, DM 1590, FR 5356, Y 108,270).

$605* *Florida Jay, Plate LXXXVII,* by R. Havell, watermark J. Whatman 1832, faded, oxidized, light struck, mat burn, foxing, rippling, discoloration, John Walton Livermore Estate, (12-04-92, Doyle, #18), plate 25½ x 20 in., (648 x 508 mm.), sight 29¾ x 24¼ in., (648 x 508 mm.), hand colored engraving, etching and aquatint (BP 388, DM 964, FR 3269, Y 75,531).

$990* *Forked-Tailed Petrel, Plate CCLX, 1835,* by R. Havell, watermark J. Whatman 1836, large margins, loss, soiling, rippling, specks, John Walton Livermore Estate, (12-04-92, Doyle, #25), plate 12½ x 19½ in., (318 x 495 mm.), sheet 24¾ x 37½ in., (318 x 495 mm.), hand colored engraving, etching and aquatint on paper (BP 635, DM 1577, FR 5348, Y 123,596).

BI *"Forktailed Flycatcher" and "Tyrant Flycatcher": Two,* est. $2/250, (02-04-93, Sloan, #396), 25¼ x 17¾ in., (64.1 x 45.1 cm.), chromolithograph.

BI *Forktailed Flycacther: Two,* est. $150/200, (04-02-93, Sloan, #829), each 25¼ x 17¾ in., (641 x 451 mm.), chromolithograph.

BI *From "Octavio Edition Of Birds In America", C. 1840-70: Two,* plates 421 and 468, est. $150/200, (02-04-93, Sloan, #382), larger 7½ x 5ℤ, in., (19.1 x 13 cm.), hand-colored lithograph.

$3450* *Gannet (Pl. CCCXXVI), 1836,* from Havell edit. of The Birds of America, margins trimmed unevenly,good cond., surface soiling, staining, (05-19-93, Butterfield, #1779), sh. 25ℳ, x 39ℭ, in., (65.7 x 100 cm.), engraving w/aquatint and hand-coloring on J. Whatman 1836 (BP 2240, DM 5608, FR 18,894, Y 381,933).

$825* *Glossy Ibis, 1860,* by J. Bien, plate 358 of The Bird of America, (06-13-93, Hindman, #308), sh 26ℤ, x 39ℭ, in., (66.4 x 100 cm.), chromolithograph (BP 540, DM 1343, FR 4513, Y 86,815).

$3450* *Golden Eagle (Pl. CLXXXI), 1833,* from Havell edit. of The Birds of America, margins, trimmed, good cond., tears, one extending into image, losses, scuffing, creases, (05-19-93, Butterfield, #1764), sh. 39 x 26ℭzn in., (99.1 x 66.5 cm.), engraving w/aquatint and hand-coloring on J. Whatman 1833 (BP 2240, DM 5608, FR 18,894, Y 381,933).

$23,000* *Great American Cock Male (Pl. I),* from The Birds Of America, engraved William H. Lizars, good cond., repaired 2" fills, 2-3" repaired tears in each corner, tears, surface soiling, staining, Robert K-F Scal Estate, (05-19-93, Butterfield, #1759, illus.), sh 39ℤzn x 26¾ in., (100.5 x 67.9 cm.), engraving w/aquatint and hand coloring on J. Whatman 1826 (BP 14,930, DM 37,386, FR 125,958, Y 2,546,219).

$8050* *Great American Hen & Young (Plate VI),* from The Birds of America, engraved William H. Lizars, colored by Robert Havell Sr., margins trimmed unevenly, good cond., repaired tears, 3 inch repaired tear extending into image, tears, losses, staining, (05-19-93, Butterfield, #1760), sh 26ℤzn x 39¾ in., (68.1 x 101 cm.), engraving w/aquatint and hand-coloring on J. Whatman 1826 (BP 5226, DM 13,085, FR 44,085, Y 891,177).

$7700* *Great Horned Owl, Plate 61,* from The Birds of America, from Original Drawings, J.J. Audubon, 1827-38, d. 1828, margins, staining, creasing, tears (one backed), (01-22-93, Christie-NY, #330, illus.), sheet 38ℳ, x 26¼ in., (987 x 667 mm.), aquatint and engraving w/hand-coloring on J. Whatman Turkey Mill (BP 5038, DM 12,244, FR 41,420, Y 963,705).

$1150* *Green Black-Capt Flycatcher (Plate CXXIV), 1836,* by R. Havell, from Audubon's Birds of America, full margins, good cond., foxing, soiling, offprint, stitch holes, ex-coll. The New York Society Library, (01-28-93, Sotheby-NY, #510), 19½ x 12ℭ\ in., (49.5 x 31.4 cm.), sheet 39ℭ, x 26½ in., (49.5 x 31.4 cm.), hand-colored etching, engraving and aquatint on paper, watermark (BP 759, DM 1822, FR 6166, Y 142,786).

$825* *Green Heron, 1860,* by J. Bien, plate 367 of The Birds Of America, (06-13-93, Hindman, #305), sh 39ℭ, x 26¾ in., (100 x 67.9 cm.), chromolithograph (BP 540, DM 1343, FR 4513, Y 86,815).

$5463* *Grey Fox (Plate XXI), 1843,* by J.T. Bowen, large margins, good cond., mat stain, fox mark, stitch holes, (01-28-93, Sotheby-NY, #526B, illus.), 21ℭ, x 27½ in., (543 x 699 mm.), hand-colored lithograph w/touches gum arabic (BP 3608, DM 8656, FR 29,292, Y 678,296).

$352* *"Grey Fox, No. 5, Plate XXI",* after color lithograph pub. J.T. Bowen in 1843, (12-05-92, Neal, #715), image 19 x 24 in., (48.3 x 61 cm.), photolithograph (BP 220, DM 549, FR 1870, Y 43,613).

$1150* *"Hare Indian Dog" (Plate CXIII) and "Little Chief Hare" (Plate LXXXIII), 1848, 1846: Two,* full margins, Hare Indian Dog, surface abrasion, very minor defects,Anthony N. B. Garvan Coll., (06-05-93, Christie-NY, #66), both, sh 21ℳ, x 27¾ in., (556 x 705 mm.), lithograph w/hand-coloring on wove (BP 757, DM 1864, FR 6284, Y 123,364).

$2300* *"Harlequin Duck" (Pl. CCXCVII) and "Black Or Surf Duck" (Pl. CCCXVII), 1836,* from Havell edit. of The Birds of America, margins, good cond., Harlequin Duck w/tears, crease, staining, foxing, creases, offsetting, Black or SurfDuck w/extensive holes and tears, staining, soiling, offsetting, (05-19-93, Butterfield, #1778), one sh. 26¼ x 38½ in., (667 x 978 mm.), the other sh. 26 x 38½ in., (667 x 978 mm.), engraving w/aquatint and hand-coloring on J. Whatman 1836 (BP 1493, DM 3739, FR 12,596, Y 254,622).

$14,950* *Hooping Crane (Pl. CCLXI), 1835,* from Havell edit. of The Birds of America, full margins, good cond.,tears, loss, tape stains, staining, foxing, offsetting, (05-19-93, Butterfield, #1772, illus.), sh. 38¾ x 26☐n in., (984 x 665 mm.), engraving w/aquatint and hand-coloring on J. Whatman 1835 (BP 9705, DM 24,301, FR 81,873, Y 1,655,043).

$1320* *Horned Grebe, Plate CCLIX,* The Birds of America, from Original Drawings, J.J. Audubon 1827-38, d. 1836, cut margins, staining, colors attenuated, rubbed patch, creases, tear,foxing, (01-22-93, Christie-NY, #332), plate 14M, x 20B, in., (378 x 524 mm.), aquatint and engraving w/hand-coloring on J. Whatman (BP 864, DM 2099, FR 7101, Y 165,207).

BI *"Hudsonian Godwit" (Pl. CCLVIII) and "Fulmar Petrel" (Pl. CCLXIV), 1835,* from Havell edit. of The Birds of America, full margins, good cond.,tears, Hudsonian Godwit, surface soiling, staining, offsetting, Fulmar Petrel,-tears, losses, stains, staining, est. $2/2,500, (05-19-93, Butterfield, #1771), one sh. 26☐, x 38☐n in., (670 x 983 mm.), the other sh. 26C☐n x 38B\ in., (670 x 983 mm.), engraving w/aquatint and hand-coloring on J. Whatman 1834 and 1835.

$2588* *"Hutchin's Barnacle Goose" (Pl. CCLXXVII) and "Barnacle Goosez" (Pl.CCXCVI), 1835; 1836: Two,* from Havell edit. of The Birds of America, full margins, margin trimmed, tears, soiling, staining, foxing, offsetting, (05-19-93, Butterfield, #1776), one sh. 38☐n x 26☐, in., (983 x 664 mm.), the other sh. 26¼ x 38¾ in., (983 x 664 mm.), engraving w/aquatint and hand-coloring on J. Whatman 1836 (BP 1680, DM 4207, FR 14,173, Y 286,505).

BI *"Hutchins's Barnacle Goose", 1835,* R. Havell, plate CCLXXVII, no. 56, est. $3/400, (02-11-93, Boos, #423), sight 22☐☐n x 19Z\☐n in., (580 x 500 mm.), etching and engraving.

$440* *Iceland Or Jer Falcon, Plate 19, 1860,* by J. Bien, discoloration, badly repaired splits, hole, foxing, (12-04-92, Doyle, #34), sheet 39Z, x 26 in., (99.4 x 66 cm.), chromolithograph (BP 282, DM 701, FR 2377, Y 54,931).

$5500* *Ivory-Billed Woodpecker, Plate LXVI,* by R. Havell, watermark J. Whatman 1831, recently cleaned, old acid stain, nicks, tape stains, good cond., (12-04-92, Doyle, #16), 37M, x 25¼ in., (962 x 641 mm.), hand colored engraving, etching and aquatint (BP 3528, DM 8759, FR 29,714, Y 686,642).

$1265* *"Jager" (Pl. CCLIII) and "Buff Breasted Sandpiper" (Pl. CCLXV), 1835,* from Havell edit. of The Birds of America, margins, good cond., BuffBreasted Sandpiper w/ extensive tears, losses, tears, soiling, Jager, tears, crease, tape residue, surface soiling, staining, (05-19-93, Butterfield, #1770), one sh. 24¾ x 37¾ in., (629 x 959 mm.), the other sh. 19¼ x 38½ in., (629 x 959 mm.), engraving w/aquatint and hand-coloring on J. Whatman 1835 and J. Whatman Turkey Mill (BP 821, DM 2056, FR 6928, Y 140,042).

BI *"The Jaguar (female), No. 21, Plate CI",* after color lithograph pub. J.T. Bowen in 1846, est. $250/350, (12-05-92, Neal, #717), image 17 x 24½ in., (43.2 x 62.2 cm.), photolithograph.

$4888* *Key-West Dove (Pl. CLXVII), 1833,* from Havell edit. of The Birds of America, full margins, good cond.,tears, losses, tape remains, creases, stains, surface soiling, (05-19-93, Butterfield, #1762), sh. 24☐☐n x 37☐☐n in., (633 x 964 mm.), engraving w/aquatint and hand-coloring on J. Whatman 1833 (BP 3173, DM 7945, FR 26,769, Y 541,127).

$2300* *King Duck (Pl. CCLXXVI), 1835,* from Havell edit. of The Birds of America, good cond., tears, staining, foxing, offsetting, (05-19-93, Butterfield, #1774), sh. 26¼ x 38B, in., (667 x 981 mm.), engraving w/aquatint and hand-coloring on J. Whatman 1835 (BP 1493, DM 3739, FR 12,596, Y 254,622).

BI *"Lecontes Pine Mouse, Male And Female" (Pl.LXXX), "Jumping Mouse, Male And Female" (Pl. LXXXV),*

"Pouched Jerboa Mouse, Males" (Pl. CXXX), and "Richardson's Meadow Mouse" (Pl. CXXXV), 1845, 1846, 1847, 1848: Four, each from Bowen ed. of Viviparous Quadrupeds of North America, margins, good cond., tear, mat/light-staining, foxing, surface soiling, creases, est. $5/700, (02-24-93, Butterfield, #2806), smallest 12½ x 18½ in., (318 x 470 mm.), largest 17¼ x 22¼ in., (318 x 470 mm.), lithograph w/hand-coloring on wove.

$1430* *Little Screech Owl, Plate XCVII,* by R. Havell, from The Birds of America, (03-24-93, Grogan, #18, illus.), 26¼ x 20M, in., (66.7 x 53 cm.), hand-colored etching, engraving and aquatint (BP 968, DM 2335, FR 7949, Y 168,018).

$6050* *Long-Billed Curlew, Plate CCXXXI,* The Birds of America, from Original Drawings, J.J. Audubon, 1827-38,split, rubbed patches, scrapes, foxmarks, tears, light-staining, laid down on board, (01-22-93, Christie-NY, #331, illus.), sheet 25½ x 38½ in., (648 x 978 mm.), aquatint and engraving w/hand-coloring on wove (BP 3958, DM 9620, FR 32,544, Y 757,196).

$5500* *Long-Billed Curlew, Plate CCXXXI, 1834,* by R. Havell, trimmed, foxing, acid burn, discoloration, laid down on board, John Walton Livermore Estate, (12-04-92, Doyle, #23, illus.), 36B, x 24B\ in., (930 x 625 mm.), hand colored engraving, etching and aquatint (BP 3528, DM 8759, FR 29,714, Y 686,642).

$1430* *Long-Tailed Or Dusky Grouse, Plate CCCLXI,* The Birds of America, from Original Drawings, J.J. Audubon, 1827-38, d. 1837, trimmed margins, staining, soiling, foxmarks, scuffs, laid down on board, (01-22-93, Christie-NY, #334, illus.), sheet 25¾ x 38¼ in., (654 x 972 mm.), aquatint and engraving w/hand-coloring on J. Whatman (BP 936, DM 2274, FR 7692, Y 178,974).

$7260* *Louisiana Heron (Plate CCXVII),* by R. Havell, 1834, discoloration, mat burning, foxing, acid burn inimage, front mat laid down over print, good cond., (06-11-93, Doyle, #12, illus.), plate 20B\ x 25B, in., (524 x 651 mm.), sheet 24¾ x 31C, in., (524 x 651 mm.), (BP 4770, DM 11,799, FR 39,781, Y 770,292).

$4830* *Maria's Woodpecker. Three-Toed Woodpecker. Phillip's Woodpecker. Canadian Woodpecker. Harris's Woodpecker. Audubon's Woodpecker (Plate CCCXVII), 1838,* by Havell, from Audubon's Birds of America, large margins, good cond., mat stain, soiling, discoloration, repaired tear, filled loss, offprint, ex-coll. The New York Society Library, (01-28-93, Sotheby-NY, #521, illus.), 30¼ x 22M, in., (76.8 x 58.1 cm.), sheet 39½ x 26Z, in., (76.8 x 58.1 cm.), hand-colored engraving, etching and aquatint, watermark (BP 3190, DM 7653, FR 25,898, Y 599,702).

$5750* *"Marsh Hare" (Plate XVIII), "Bachmans' Hare" (Plate VIII), "Texan Hare" (Plate CXXXIII) and "California Hare" (Plate CXII):, 1843, 1847, 1848 and 1847: Four,* foxing, staining, tear at staining, Anthony N. B. Garvan Coll., (06-05-93, Christie-NY, #65, illus.), all sh 21¼ x 27 in., (540 x 686 mm.), lithograph w/hand-coloring (BP 3785, DM 9322, FR 31,421, Y 616,820).

$55* *"Maryland Ground Warbler",* by J.T. Bowen, octavo edit., (12-11-92, Eldred, #318), lithograph (BP 35, DM 87, FR 297, Y 6806).

$330* *"Mississippi Kite, Plate CXVII",* (05-08-93, Young, #30, illus.), 26 x 21 in., (66 x 53.3 cm.), color engraving (BP 209, DM 522, FR 1758, Y 36,336).

BI *Mocking Bird,* est. $1,5/2,000, (03-14-93, Hindman, #303), 33 x 22 in., (83.8 x 55.9 cm.), color lithograph.

$660* *Mocking-Bird, Plate XXI,* by R. Havell, watermark J. Whatman Turkey Mill 1834, recently cleaned, colors faded, acid stains verso, creases, patches, repaired split, tape stains, (12-04-92, Doyle, #11), plate 33 x 23¾ in., (838 x 603 mm.), sheet 36¾ x 25 in., (838 x 603 mm.), hand colored etching, engraving, aquatint (BP 423, DM 1051, FR 3566, Y 82,397).

$880* *Mottled Owl (Plate 97),* discoloration, badly laid down, (06-11-93, Doyle, #10), 26 x 20¼ in., (660 x 514 mm.), etching, engraving and aquatint (BP 578, DM 1430, FR 4822, Y 93,369).

BI *"Ocelot, or Leopard-Cat, No. 18, Plate LXXXVI",* after color lithograph pub. J.T. Bowen in 1846, est. $250/350, (12-05-92, Neal, #716), image 19 x 24 in., (48.3 x 61 cm.), photolithograph.

BI *"Octavia Edition Of Birds In America": Two,* c. 1840-1870, plates 421-468, est. $1/150, (04-02-93, Sloan, #804), larger 7½ x 5Z, in., (191 x 130 mm.), hand-colored lithograph.

$715* *Orchard Oriole, Plate XLII,* by R. Havell, from The Birds of America, (03-24-93, Grogan, #23), 26 x 20¾ in., (66 x 52.7 cm.), hand-colored etching, engraving and aquatint (BP 484, DM 1168, FR 3974, Y 84,009).

$3105* *Painted Finch (Plate LIII), 1836,* by Havell, from Audubon's Birds of America, full margins, good cond., image foxing, stain,; repaired tears, losses, discoloration, ex-coll. The NewYork Society Library, (01-28-93, Sotheby-NY, #506), 19½ x 12¼ in., (49.5 x 31.1 cm.), sheet 39½ x 26Z, in., (49.5 x 31.1 cm.), hand-colored etching, engraving and aquatint on paper, watermark (BP 2050, DM 4920, FR 16,649, Y 385,523).

$770* *Painted Finch, Plate LIII,* by R. Havell, watermark J. Whatman 1836, mat burn, discoloration, foxing, taped to mat, (12-04-92, Doyle, #14), plate 19½ x 12½ in., (495 x 318 mm.), sheet 28 x 22C, in., (495 x 318 mm.), hand colored engraving, etching and aquatint (BP 494, DM 1226, FR 4160, Y 96,130).

$4400* *Passenger Pigeon, Plate LXII,* by R. Havell, laid down unevenly on cardboard, foxing, soiling, large margins, good cond., John Walton Livermore Estate, (12-04-92, Doyle, #15, illus.), plate 25¾ x 20½ in., (654 x 521 mm.), sheet 38 x 25 in., (654 x 521 mm.), hand colored engraving, etching and aquatint (BP 2822, DM 7007, FR 23,771, Y 549,313).

$2588* *"Pied Oyster-catcher" (Pl. CCXXIII) and "Scaup Duck" (Pl. CCXXIX), 1834: Two,* from Havell edit. of The Birds of America, full margins, good cond.,tears, surface soiling, foxing, staining, (05-19-93, Butterfield, #1766), each sh 26Żn x 38B, in., (665 x 981 mm.), xin., (665 x 981 mm.), engraving w/aquatint and hand-coloring on J. Whatman Turkey Mill 1834 (BP 1680, DM 4207, FR 14,173, Y 286,505).

$770* *Pigeon Hawk, Plate XCII,* by R. Havell, from The Birds of America, (03-24-93, Grogan, #14), 25¾ x 20½ in., (65.4 x 52.1 cm.), hand-colored etching, engraving and aquatint (BP 521, DM 1258, FR 4280, Y 90,471).

$99* *Pileated Woodpecker,* after original Havell edition pub. by R.R. Donnelley and Sons, PLAT 111, (09-17-92, Sloan, #2002), 30 x 19¾ in., (76.2 x 50.2 cm.), color print (BP 56, DM 147, FR 503, Y 12,326).

BI *Pine Swamp Warbler, Plate CXLVIII, 1832,* by R. Havell, watermark J. Whatman 1836, discoloration, foxing, crease, taped to mat, est. $7/900, (12-04-92, Doyle, #22), plate 19¾ x 12¼ in., (502 x 311 mm.), sheet 27¾ x 22Z, in., (502 x 311 mm.), hand colored engraving, etching and aquatint.

$3910* *Polar Bear (Plate XCI), 1846,* by J.T. Bowen, from Audubon's Viviparous Quadrupeds of North America, large margins, good cond., mat stain, soiling, creases, losses, (01-28-93, Sotheby-NY, #528B, illus.), sheet 21½ x 27Z, in., (546 x 689 mm.), hand-colored lithograph w/ touches gum arabic (BP 2582, DM 6196, FR 20,965, Y 485,473).

$3080* *Polar Bear, Male, Plate XCI, 1846,* The Viviparous Quadrupeds of North America, 1845-48, full margins, soiling, binding holes, tears, very good cond., (01-22-93, Christie-NY, #336), sheet 21½ x 27¼ in., (546 x 692 mm.), hand-colored lithograph on wove (BP 2015, DM 4897, FR 16,568, Y 385,482).

$575* *Prairie Titlark (Plate 80), 1830,* by R. Havell, from Audubon's Birds of America, large margins, good cond., soiling, creases, fox marks, off-printing, stitch holes, (01-28-93, Sotheby-NY, #508), 12¼ x 19B\ in., (311 x 498 mm.), sheet 25M, x 37 in., (311 x 498 mm.), hand-colored etching, engraving and aquatint on paper, watermark (BP 380, DM 911, FR 3083, Y 71,393).

$110* *"Prairie Wood-Warbler" and "Golden Crowned Wagtail Thrush": Pair,* octavo edit., from Birds of America, (02-14-93, Neal, #1135), hand colored lithograph (BP 77, DM 182, FR 617, Y 13,266).

$880* *Puffin (Plate CCXIII), 1834,* by R. Havell, full margins, colors slightly faded, creasing, staining, toning, Richard E. Benesh Estate, (01-16-93, Weschler, #151, illus.), 12½ x 19¾ in., (31.8 x 50.2 cm.), hand colored engraving (BP 575, DM 1439, FR 4865, Y 110,943).

BI *"Puffin", "Purple Gallinule", "Fulmar Petrel", "Pied Oyster Catcher", "Foolish Guillemot", "Black Guillemot", "Razor Bill", "Booby Garnet", "Ruby-Throated Humming-bird", "Double Crested Cormorant" and one other: Eleven,* from The Amsterdam Edition, good cond., est. $1/1,500, (06-12-93, Weschler, #171, illus.), eight 14¼ x 20 in., (36.2 x 50.8 cm.), three 33 x 23¼ in., (36.2 x 50.8 cm.), offset color lithograph.

$715* *Red Cockaded Woodpecker (Plate CCCLXXXIX), 1837,* by R. Havell, full margins, foxing, mat burn, creased, toning verso,Richard E. Benesh Estate, (01-16-93, Weschler, #149, illus.), 19½ x 12¼ in., (49.5 x 31.1 cm.), hand colored engraving (BP 467, DM 1169, FR 3952, Y 90,141).

BI *"Red Texan Wolf, (Male), No. 17, Plate LXXXII",* after color lithograph pub. J.T. Bowen in 1845, est. $250/350, (12-05-92, Neal, #714), image 17 x 25 in., (43.2 x 63.5 cm.), photolithograph.

$605* *"Red Winged Starling Or Marsh Blackbird", Plate 216 and "Yellow-Breasted Chat", Plate 244: Two,* by J. Bien, from The Birds of America, (03-24-93, Grogan, #22), first, sight 37Z\ x 25B, in., (94.3 x 65.1 cm.), second, sight 34½ x 25B, in., (94.3 x 65.1 cm.), chromolithograph (BP 410, DM 988, FR 3363, Y 71,084).

$748* *Red-Breasted Sandpiper (Pl. CCCXV), 1836,* from Havell edit. of The Birds of America, margins (folded under), good cond., tears, surface soiling, staining, offsetting, (05-19-93, Butterfield, #1777), 12¼ x 19B, in., (311 x 498 mm.), engraving w/aquatint and hand-coloring on J. Whatman 1836 (BP 486, DM 1216, FR 4096, Y 82,807).

$770* *Rocky Mountain Goat, Plate CXXVIII, 1847,* by J.T. Bowen, split, crease, foxing, very good cond., John Walton Livermore Estate, (12-04-92, Doyle, #33), sheet 21 x 27 in., (533 x 686 mm.), hand colored lithograph (BP 494, DM 1226, FR 4160, Y 96,130).

$99* *"Rocky Mountain Neotoma" and "Mountain Brook Mink": Pair,* octavo edit., from Quadrupeds Of North America, (02-14-93, Neal, #1139), hand colored lithograph (BP 70, DM 164, FR 556, Y 11,939).

$385* *Roscoe's Yellow-Throat (Plate XXIV),* by R. Havell, full margins, foxing, darkening, water staining, creases, rippling, Richard E. Benesh Estate, (01-16-93, Weschler, #147, illus.), 19¼ x 12 in., (48.9 x 30.5 cm.), hand colored engraving (BP 252, DM 629, FR 2128, Y 48,538).

$345* *Ruffed Grouse (Plate 293), 1860,* by J. Bien, margins, foxing, tears, (02-18-93, Sotheby-Arcade, #83), sight 25½ x 38½ in., (64.8 x 97.8 cm.), chromolithograph (BP 238, DM 563, FR 1905, Y 41,101).

$1840* *Rusty Grackle (Plate CLVII), 1833,* by R. Havell, from Audubon's Birds of America, full margins, good cond., stray ink, foxing, soiling, stitch holes, offprint, ex-coll. The New York Society Library, (01-28-93, Sotheby-NY, #512), 25½ x 20½ in., (64.8 x 52.1 cm.), sheet 39Z, x 26 in., (64.8 x 52.1 cm.), hand-colored etching, engraving and aquatint on paper, watermark (BP 1215, DM 2916, FR 9866, Y 228,458).

$2750* *Scarlet Ibis, Plate CCCXVII, 1837,* by R. Havell, watermark J. Whatman 1838, large margins, mat burn, soiling, foxing, discoloration, tape residue, hinged to mat, (12-04-92, Doyle, #31, illus.), plate 21¾ x 19¼ in., (552 x 489 mm.), sheet 25Z, x 37¾ in., (552 x 489 mm.), hand colored engraving, etching and aquatint on paper (BP 1764, DM 4380, FR 14,857, Y 343,321).

$2070* *"Sharp-Tailed Grous" (Pl. CCCLXXXII) and "Brant Goose" (Pl. CCCXCI),1837,* from Havell edit. of The Birds of America, margins, good cond., tears, foxing, scuffing and surface soiling, tears, (05-19-93, Butterfield, #1782), one sh. 26Żn x 38¾ in., (664 x 984 mm.), the other sh. 26Żn x 38½ in., (664 x 984 mm.), engraving w/aquatint and hand-coloring on J. Whatman 1837 (BP 1344, DM 3365, FR 11,336, Y 229,160).

$132* *"Shore Lark" and "Lapland Lark Bunting": Pair,* octavo edit., from Birds of America, (02-14-93, Neal, #1134), hand colored lithograph (BP 93, DM 219, FR 741, Y 15,919).

$440* *"Snowy Heron (Male), No. 75, Plate 374",* from octavo edit. of Birds in America pub. J.T. Bowen in 1943, (12-05-92, Neal, #720), image 7½ x 5 in., (19.1 x 12.7

cm.), hand-colored lithograph (BP 276, DM 686, FR 2338, Y 54,516).

$19,800* *Snowy Heron Or White Egret, Plate CCXLII, 1835,* by R. Havell, watermark J. Whatman 1896, large margins, discoloration, soiling, very good cond., John Walton Livermore Estate, (12-04-92, Doyle, #24, illus.), plate 25M, x 20½ in., (657 x 521 mm.), sheet 38 x 25 in., (657 x 521 mm.), hand colored engraving, etching and aquatint on paper (BP 12,700, DM 31,534, FR 106,969, Y 2,471,910).

BI *Snowy Owl,* by Robet Havell, 1827-1838, pl. CXXI of The Birds of America, est. $20/25,000, (10-18-92, Hindman, #480, illus.), 37¾ x 24¾ in., (95.9 x 62.9 cm.), hand-colored etching and aquatint.

$330* *Swamp Sparrow, Plate 64,* by R. Havell, from The Birds of America, (03-24-93, Grogan, #25), 19½ x 12¼ in., (49.5 x 31.1 cm.), hand-colored etching, engraving and aquatint (BP 223, DM 539, FR 1834, Y 38,773).

$2530* *Tell-Tale Godwit Or Snipe (Plate CCCVIII), 1836,* by R. Havell, from Audubon's Birds of America, full margins, good cond., soiling, foxing, losses, traces glue, (01-28-93, Sotheby-NY, #520), 14¾ x 21 in., (375 x 533 mm.), sheet 25B, x 38Z, in., (375 x 533 mm.), hand-colored etching, engraving and aquatint w/touches gum arabic onpaper, watermark (BP 1671, DM 4009, FR 13,566, Y 314,130).

$660* *"Tell-Tale Godwit Or Snipe" Plate CCCVIII, 1836,* ident. w/in plate, watermark, J Whatman 1836, Havell Edit., (06-05-93, Skinner, #304), sheet 23¾ x 29¾ in., (60.3 x 75.6 cm.), engraving, etching and aquatint w/hand coloring on paper (BP 434, DM 1070, FR 3607, Y 70,800).

BI *Tengmalm's Owl, Plate CCCLXXX,* The Birds of America, from Orginal Drawings, J.J. Audubon, 1827-38, trimmed margins, staining, foxing, tear, taped to overmat, est. $900/1,200, (01-22-93, Christie-NY, #335, illus.), plate 20½ x 16 in., (521 x 406 mm.), aquatint and engraving w/hand-coloring on J. Whatman.

BI *Tengmalm's Owl, Plate CCCLXXX,* trimmed margins, staining, foxing, tear, taped to overmat, est. $6/900, (04-27-93, Christie-E, #1), 20½ x 16 in., (52.1 x 40.6 cm.), aquatint and engraving w/hand-coloring.

BI *"Texan Hare (Male), No. 27, Plate CXXXIII",* after color lithograph pub. J.T. Bowen in 1848, est. $250/350, (12-05-92, Neal, #718), image 17 x 24½ in., (43.2 x 62.2 cm.), photolithograph.

$385* *Towhe Bunting, Plate XXIX,* by R. Havell, discoloration, mat burn, foxing, taped to mat, (12-04-92, Doyle, #12), plate 19½ x 12¼ in., (495 x 311 mm.), sheet 27¾ x 22Z, in., (495 x 311 mm.), hand colored engraving, etching and aquatint on J. Whatman paper (BP 247, DM 613, FR 2080, Y 48,065).

$2530* *"Townsend's Rocky Mountain Hare", "Northern Hare" and "Canada Otter"(Plates III, XII and LI), 1842-44: Three,* by J.T. Bowen, from Audubon's Viviparous Quadrupeds of North America, large margins, 1st w/foxing, soiling, tears, losses, stitch holes; 2nd w/mat stain, soiling, stitch holes, offprint; foxing, image scratches, (01-28-93, Sotheby-NY, #525), each sheet approx. 20M, x 27Z, in., (530 x 689 mm.), hand-colored lithograph w/touches gum arabic (BP 1671, DM 4009, FR 13,566, Y 314,130).

$330* *Traill's Flycatcher, Plate 45,* by R. Havell, from The Birds of America, (03-24-93, Grogan, #24), 19½ x 12¼ in., (49.5 x 31.1 cm.), hand-colored etching, engraving and aquatint (BP 223, DM 539, FR 1834, Y 38,773).

$2090* *Tropic Bird, Plate CCXII, 1835,* by R. Havell, watermark J. Whatman 1836, cleaned, nicks, tape stains, very good cond., (12-04-92, Doyle, #26), plate 20¾ x 30¼ in., (527 x 768 mm.), sheet 24¾ x 37B\ in., (527 x 768 mm.), hand colored engraving, etching and aquatint on paper (BP 1341, DM 3329, FR 11,291, Y 260,924).

$3738* *Trumpeter Swan (Pl. CCCLXXVI), 1837,* from Havell edit. of The Birds of America, good cond., tears, folds across image, restoration, extensive surface scuffing in image, (05-19-93, Butterfield, #1781), 25B\ x 38½ in., (651 x 978 mm.), engraving w/aquatint and hand-coloring on J. Whatman Turkey Mill 1837 (BP 2426, DM 6076, FR 20,471, Y 413,816).

$3520* *"Tyrant Fly-Catcher (Plate LXXIX)", "Prothonotory Warbler (Plate III)", "Little Tawny Thrush (Plate CCCCXIX)", "Gray Tyrant (Plate CLXX)" and "PineGros-*

beak (Plate CCCLVII)": Five, 4 by R. Havell, (06-11-93, Doyle, #9), hand colored etching, engraving and aquatint (BP 2313, DM 5721, FR 19,288, Y 373,475).

$2300* *"Velvet Duck" (Pl. CCXLVII), "American Pied-bill Dobchick" (Pl. CCXLVIII) and "Tufted Auk" (Pl. CCXLIX), 1835: Three,* from Havell edit. of The Birds of America, large margins, good cond.,Tufted Auk, creases, repaired tear, tape remains, American Pied-bill Dobchick,staining across image, paper losses, tape, Velvet Duck, crease, staining, toning, (05-19-93, Butterfield, #1768), each sh. 24¾ x 37¾ in., (629 x 959 mm.), engraving w/aquatint and hand-coloring on J. Whatman Turkey Mill 1835 (BP 1493, DM 3739, FR 12,596, Y 254,622).

$110* *"Velvet Duck", "Fish Crow" and "Bernacle Goose": Three,* p. J.T. Bowen, (05-16-93, Hindman, #529), each 6 x 8¼ in., (15.2 x 21 cm.), hand-colored lithograph (BP 72, DM 177, FR 595, Y 12,194).

$2640* *"Velvet Duck, Male And Female, Plate CCXLVII, No. 50", 1835,* by R.Havell, from The Birds of America, pub., (02-13-93, Neal, #726, illus.), image 18 x 28 in., (45.7 x 71.1 cm.), sheet 24 x 38Z, in., (45.7 x 71.1 cm.), hand colored engraving (BP 1859, DM 4378, FR 14,815, Y 318,379).

$297* *"Violet Green Cormorant (Female In Winter) And Townsend's Cormorant (Male)",* Amsterdam edit. (elephant folio) after Havell edit., (12-05-92, Neal, #719A), image 20½ x 25 in., (52.1 x 63.5 cm.), color photolithograph (BP 186, DM 463, FR 1578, Y 36,798).

$2090* *"Virginian Opossum, Female & Young Male, Plate LXVI, No. 14", 1845,* from Quadrupeds of North America, pub. J.T. Bowen, (02-13-93, Neal, #724), sheet 21 x 27½ in., (53.3 x 69.9 cm.), (BP 1472, DM 3466, FR 11,728, Y 252,050).

$12,650* *Virginian Partridge (Plate 76), 1830,* by R. Havell, from Audubon's Birds of America, full margins, good cond., image repaired tear, water/mat stained, tears, traces glue, (01-28-93, Sotheby-NY, #507, illus.), sheet 26Z, x 39½ in., (66.4 x 100.3 cm.), hand-colored etching, engraving and aquatint on paper, watermark (BP 8354, DM 20,044, FR 67,828, Y 1,570,648).

$88* *"Virginian Rail" and "Red Phalarope": Pair,* octavo edit., from Birds of America, (02-14-93, Neal, #1133), hand colored lithograph (BP 62, DM 146, FR 494, Y 10,613).

BI *Vulpus Fulvus (American Red-Fox) (Pl. LXXXVII), 1846,* from Bowen ed. of Viviparous Quadrupeds of North America, margins, good cond., mat staining, repaired tear, paper loss, stain, linen tape, mat staining, surface soiling, stains, est. $6/800, (02-24-93, Butterfield, #2805), 16¾ x 24 in., (425 x 610 mm.), sheet 20M, x 27Z, in., (425 x 610 mm.), lithograph w/hand-coloring on wove.

$578* *White Head Pigeon, 1860,* by J. Bien, plate 280 of The Birds of America, (06-13-93, Hindman, #309), sh 39C, x 26¾ in., (100 x 67.9 cm.), chromolithograph (BP 378, DM 941, FR 3162, Y 60,823).

$660* *White Headed Eagle, 1860,* by J. Bien, heavily foxed, water staining, fading, discoloration, (12-04-92, Doyle, #35), sheet 26 x 39 in., (66 x 99.1 cm.), chromolithograph (BP 423, DM 1051, FR 3566, Y 82,397).

$3450* *White Ibis (Pl. CCXXII), 1834,* from Havell edit. of The Birds of America, full margins, tears, losses, mat light-staining, rubbing, surface soiling, (05-19-93, Butterfield, #1765, illus.), sh. 26¼ x 28½ in., (667 x 724 mm.), engraving w/aquatint and hand-coloring on J. Whatman Turkey Mill 1834 (BP 2240, DM 5608, FR 18,894, Y 381,933).

$5175* *White-Crowned Pigeon (Plate CLXXVII), 1833,* by R. Havell, from Audubon's Birds of America, large margins, good cond., light-stain, foxing, abrasions, loss, discoloration, (01-28-93, Sotheby-NY, #514, illus.), 25¼ x 20M, in., (641 x 530 mm.), sheet 38Z, x 24¾ in., (641 x 530 mm.), hand-colored etching, engraving and aquatint on paper, watermark (BP 3417, DM 8200, FR 27,748, Y 642,538).

$6440* *White-Fronted Goose (Plate CCLXXXVI), 1836,* by R. Havell, from Audubon's Birds of America, large margins, good cond., foxing, image crease, repaired tear, running into image, soiling, tears, (01-28-93, Sotheby-NY, #517, illus.), sheet 24M, x 37B, in., (632 x 956 mm.), hand-colored etching, engraving and aquatint on paper, watermark (BP 4253, DM 10,204, FR 34,531, Y 799,603).

$4370* *White-Headed Eagle (Plate CXXVI), 1831,* by R. Havell, from Audubon's Birds of America, full margins, soiling, foxing, repaired tears, laid down, (01-28-93, Sotheby-NY, #511, illus.), sheet 39 x 25¾ in., (99.1 x 65.4 cm.), hand-colored etching, engraving and aquatint on paper, watermark (BP 2886, DM 6924, FR 23,432, Y 542,588).

$385* *White-Legged Oyster-Catcher And Slender-Billed Oyster-Catcher, 1838,* plate CCCXXVII, Havell edit., ident. w/in plate, stable cond., tears,wrinkling, creasing, toning, fox marks, (10-31-92, Skinner, #445, illus.), sh 24ᴍ, x 31½ in., (63.2 x 80 cm.), engraving, etching and aquatint w/ hand-coloring on paper w/watermark (BP 252, DM 604, FR 2047, Y 47,601).

$193* *Wild Turkey,* by W.H. Lizars, Aerial Press Edition, (10-30-92, Sloan, #1303), color lithograph (BP 124, DM 297, FR 1007, Y 23,907).

$275* *Wild Turkey,* stains, losses, (09-21-92, Selkirk, #185), 36 x 24¾ in., (91.4 x 62.9 cm.), lithograph w/hand-coloring (BP 161, DM 408, FR 1396, Y 33,988).

$110* *"Wilson's Fly-Catching Warbler" and "Tennessee Swamp Warbler": Pair,* octavo edit., from Birds of America, (02-14-93, Neal, #1131), hand colored lithograph (BP 77, DM 182, FR 617, Y 13,266).

$1495* *Winter Wren. Rock Wren (Plate CCCLX), 1837,* by R. Havell, from Audubon's Birds of America, full margins, good cond., foxing, soiling, stitch holes, offprint, ex-coll. The New York Society Library, (01-28-93, Sotheby-NY, #524, illus.), 19¾ x 12ᴄ, in., (50.2 x 31.4 cm.), sheet 39½ x 26ʙ, in., (50.2 x 31.4 cm.), hand-colored etching, engraving and aquatint on paper, watermark (BP 987, DM 2369, FR 8016, Y 185,622).

$1495* *Wood Wren (Pl. CLXXIX); Black Guillemot (Pl. CCXIX), 1833; 1834: Two,* from Havell edit. of The Birds of America, margins, good cond., tears, staining, surface scuffing, soiling, creases, (05-19-93, Butterfield, #1763), one sh. 26½ x 39¼ in., (67.3 x 99.7 cm.), the other sh. 26¼ x 38½ in., (67.3 x 99.7 cm.), engraving w/aquatint and hand-coloring on J. Whatman 1833 and J. Whatman Turkey Mill 1834 (BP 970, DM 2430, FR 8187, Y 165,504).

BI *"Worm Eating Warbler", Plate 104 and ""Bachman's Warbler", Plate 108, c. 1860,* J. Gien pub., fading, soiling, nicks, tears, full margins, est. $750/1,000, (05-07-93, Goldberg, #435A, illus.), 26 x 38½ in., (66 x 97.8 cm.), chromolithograph.

$1760* *Yellow Billed Magpie, Stellers Jay, Ultra-Marine Jay, And Clark's Crow, Plate CCCLXII,* by R. Havell, watermark J. Whatman 1837, oxidized, stains, discoloration, foxing, rippling, John Walton Livermore Estate, (12-04-92, Doyle, #29), plate 26 x 21½ in., (660 x 546 mm.), sheet 38 x 25 in., (660 x 546 mm.), hand colored engraving, etching and aquatint on paper (BP 1129, DM 2803, FR 9508, Y 219,725).

$4830* *Yellow Shank (Plate CCLXXXVII), 1836,* by R. Havell, from Audubon's Birds of America, large margins, good cond., soiling, foxing, tears, ex-coll. The New York Society Library, (01-28-93, Sotheby-NY, #518, illus.), 14ʙ, x 20ʙ, in., (37.1 x 52.4 cm.), sheet 26½ x 39¾ in., (37.1 x 52.4 cm.), hand-colored etching, engraving and aquatint on paper, watermark (BP 3190, DM 7653, FR 25,898, Y 599,702).

$3080* *Yellow-Crester Heron, Plate CCCXXXVI, 1836,* by R. Havell, watermark J. Whatman 1838, cleaned, colors faded, margin trimmed, tape stains, repaired splits, acid burn, good cond., (12-04-92, Doyle, #28), 37¾ x 25 in., (959 x 635 mm.), hand colored engraving, etching and aquatint on paper (BP 1976, DM 4905, FR 16,640, Y 384,519).

$770* *Yellow-Crowned Heron, Plate 364, 1860,* by Julius Bien, good cond.?, repaired tear, crease, staining, rippling, (06-12-93, Weschler, #168, illus.), 35¼ x 23¼ in., (89.5 x 59.1 cm.), chromolithograph (BP 504, DM 1253, FR 4212, Y 81,027).

$3220* *Zenaida Dove (Plate CLXII), 1833,* by R. Havell, from Audubon's Birds of America, full margins, good cond., fox marks, soiling, creases, discoloration, offprint, ex-coll. The New York Society Library, (01-28-93, Sotheby-NY, #513, illus.), 25¾ x 20ʙ, in., (65.4 x 52.4 cm.), sheet

39ᴄ, x 26ᴄ, in., (65.4 x 52.4 cm.), hand-colored etching, engraving and aquatint on paper, watermark (BP 2126, DM 5102, FR 17,265, Y 399,801).

$715* *Zenaida Dove, Plate CLXII,* by R. Havell, from The Birds of America, (03-24-93, Grogan, #15), 26 x 20¾ in., (66 x 52.7 cm.), hand-colored etching, engraving and aquatint (BP 484, DM 1168, FR 3974, Y 84,009).

AUDUBON, John James (after) American 1812-1862
$385* *"Brown Pelican" (Plate 423), 1860,* fourth edition octavo by J.T. Bowen, (03-06-93, LA Auction Ex., #118, illus.), 9½ x 6 in., (24.1 x 15.2 cm.), hand-colored lithograph (BP 266, DM 641, FR 2163, Y 45,252).

$165* *"Song Sparrows", Plate 189, 1859,* by J. Bien, (06-05-93, LA Auction Ex., #10), image 26 x 19¼ in., (66 x 48.9 cm.), chromolithograph (BP 109, DM 268, FR 902, Y 17,700).

$165* *"Swallow-Tailed Flycatcher", Plate 54, 1860,* by. J. Bien, full margins, good cond., (06-05-93, LA Auction Ex., #11, illus.), image 26¼ x 19½ in., (66.7 x 49.5 cm.), chromolithograph (BP 109, DM 268, FR 902, Y 17,700).

AUDUBON, John James and John BACHMAN
$3960* *The Quadrupeds Of North America: Three Volumes,* 8vo, color plates, John Walton Livermore Estate, (12-04-92, Doyle, #321, illus.), (BP 2540, DM 6307, FR 21,394, Y 494,382).

AUDUBON, John James and John WOODHOUSE (after)
$3163* *Various Quadruped Subjects: Plates IX, XIII, XXXV, XLV, LV, CII, CVII, CX, CXLIV and CXLVIII, 1843-48: Ten,* by J.T. Bowen, from Audubon's Viviparous Quadrupeds of North America, good cond., sheets soiled, foxed and/or discolored, few w/tears, (01-28-93, Sotheby-NY, #526), hand-colored lithograph w/touches gum arabic (BP 2089, DM 5012, FR 16,960, Y 392,724).

AUDUBON, John John (after)
BI *"Lazuli Finch, Crimson-Necked Bull Finch, Grey Crowned Linnet, Cowpen Bird, Evening Grosbeck, Brown Longspur", Plate CCCCXXIV, 1834,* by R. Havell, full margins, good cond., est. $1/1,500, (06-05-93, LA Auction Ex., #13, illus.), image 9¾ x 13¼ in., (24.8 x 33.7 cm.), hand-colored lithograph.

AUERBACH, Frank British b. 1931
$450* *Playing Cards/Two Heads Of Jim, 1969,* s., #58/70, full margins, good cond., (11-30-92, Phillips-London, #489), sheet 40¾ x 27ʙ, in., (103.5 x 70.2 cm.), color silk-screen on thick wove (BP 297, DM 717, FR 2434, Y 56,005).

$819* *(Portrait),* s., i. A.P., p. Kelpra Studios, stamp, full margins, good cond., handling crease in image, (12-03-92, Sotheby-London, #602, illus.), 31½ x 23ᴢ, in., (802 x 589 mm.), screenprint in colors on wove (BP 528, DM 1288, FR 4396, Y 101,904).

$450* *Reclining Figure I, 1966,* s., #63/70, full margins, good cond., (11-30-92, Phillips-London, #488), sheet 27¾ x 40ᴢ, in., (70.5 x 101.9 cm.), color silkscreen on wove (BP 297, DM 717, FR 2434, Y 56,005).

AUERBACH-LEVY, William (after) American 1889-1964
$990* *"Eugene O'Neil" and "Jed Harris": Two,* margins, s.; 1 s., annotated by cutter and printer, (09-20-92, Hindman, #697, illus.), larger 11 x 8 in., (27.9 x 20.3 cm.), color woodcuts (BP 580, DM 1469, FR 5025, Y 122,358).

$440* *"Eugene O'Neill" and "Ted Harris": Two,* cut and p. by Harry de Maime, one s., (12-13-92, Hindman, #309), 10ᴍ, x 8 in., color woodcut (BP 281, DM 691, FR 2357, Y 54,435).

AUGIS (after)
$180* *SNCF. Semaine Internationale De Ski Au Mont-Blanc. "Chamonix, Les Contamines, Saint-Gervais, Les Houches, Megeve", 1949,* good cond., (03-15-93, Arcole, #74, illus.), 39ᴄᴍ x 24ᴍᴍ in., (99.5 x 62 cm.), (BP 125, DM 299, FR 1016, Y 21,322).

AUGLAY
$608* *Cornet,* (05-07-93, Christie-S. Ken, #117, illus.), 10¼ x 14¼ in., (26 x 36.2 cm.), color lithograph (BP 385, DM 961, FR 3239, Y 66,946).

AUGUSTE, Jean Eugene French 1857-1927

$880* *Untitled,* p. by Bernice Abbott, label verso, (12-10-92, Sloan, #2737), sight 7 x 9 in., (17.8 x 22.9 cm.), photograph, silver gelatin print (BP 567, DM 1392, FR 4754, Y 108,857).

BI *Untitled,* p. by Bernice Abbott, label verso, est. $3/500, (12-10-92, Sloan, #2736), sight 7 x 9 in., (17.8 x 22.9 cm.), photograph, silver gelatin print.

$660* *Untitled,* p. by Bernice Abbott, label verso, (12-10-92, Sloan, #2735), sight 7 x 9 in., (17.8 x 22.9 cm.), photograph, silver gelatin print (BP 425, DM 1044, FR 3566, Y 81,643).

AULD, Doug American contemporary

$165* *15 Minutes Of Fame (Andy Warhol), 1991,* s., #7/50, (12-13-92, Hindman, #354), 31 x 43 in., color lithograph (BP 105, DM 259, FR 884, Y 20,413).

AULT, George C. American 1891-1948

BI *Cames's House, 1934,* s., d., #25/25, full margins, good cond., light stain, smudges, est.$800/1,000, (05-13-93, Sotheby-NY, #403), 14 x 9M, in., (354 x 252 mm.), lithograph on wove.

AURIOL, Georges

BI *Selim, Enfant De Damas (U. Johnson 4), 1897,* s., full margins, (02-24-93, Picard, #10), lithograph on thin wove.

AUSBOURG, E.

$80* *Le Tribut De Zamora. Opera (...) Charles Gounod, c. 1885,* cond. A, (03-16-93, Boisgirard, #47), 31Zzn x 23Zzn in., (80.5 x 60.5 cm.), poster (BP 55, DM 133, FR 452, Y 9355).

AUSTEN, Winifred

BI *Black Backed Gulls,* s., margins, est. BP 80/120, (09-17-92, Bonhams-Chelsea, #5, illus.), plate 8Z, x 7B, in., (20.6 x 19.4 cm.), etching w/drypoint.

$82* *Black Bucked Gulls,* s., margins, (10-15-92, Bonhams-Chelsea, #121, illus.), plate 8Z, x 7B, in., (20.6 x 19.4 cm.), etching w/drypoint (BP 50, DM 122, FR 414, Y 9838).

$51* *Black Cap,* s., margins, (12-10-92, Bonhams-Chelsea, #100), plate 5C, x 7C, in., (13.7 x 18.7 cm.), etching w/ drypoint on laid paper (BP 33, DM 81, FR 276, Y 6309).

BI *Black Cap,* s., margins, est. BP 40/60, (10-15-92, Bonhams-Chelsea, #132), plate 5C, x 7C, in., (13.7 x 18.7 cm.), etching w/drypoint on laid paper.

BI *"Black Geese",* s., (12-11-92, G.A. Key, #40), 9 x 14 in., (22.9 x 35.6 cm.), colored aquatint.

BI *Blackcap,* s., margins, est. BP 70/100, (09-17-92, Bonhams-Chelsea, #48), plate 5C, x 7C, in., (13.7 x 18.7 cm.), etching w/drypoint on laid paper.

$78* *Bullfinch,* s., margins, staining, (09-17-92, Bonhams-Chelsea, #17), plate 5B, x 7½ in., (14.3 x 19.1 cm.), etching w/drypoint on laid paper (BP 44, DM 116, FR 396, Y 9711).

$128* *Chicks,* margins, creasing, surface dirt, (09-17-92, Bonhams-Chelsea, #43), plate 5 x 9 in., (12.7 x 22.9 cm.), etching on laid paper (BP 72, DM 190, FR 650, Y 15,936).

$98* *Coal Tit,* s., margins, foxing, (09-17-92, Bonhams-Chelsea, #28), plate 4C, x 5¾ in., (11.1 x 14.6 cm.), etching w/drypoint on laid paper (BP 55, DM 145, FR 498, Y 12,201).

$110* *Curlew,* margins, s. Winifred Austen, (02-13-93, Collins, #35, illus.), 7 x 9¾ in., (17.8 x 24.8 cm.), etching (BP 77, DM 182, FR 617, Y 13,266).

BI *Decoy Pool,* s., margins, est. BP 100/150, (09-17-92, Bonhams-Chelsea, #45), plate 7 x 10Z, in., (17.8 x 25.7 cm.), etching w/drypoint on laid paper.

$216* *Decoy Pool,* s., margins, (10-15-92, Bonhams-Chelsea, #131), plate 7 x 10Z, in., (17.8 x 25.7 cm.), etching w/ drypoint on laid paper (BP 132, DM 322, FR 1090, Y 25,915).

$313* *"Ducks And Ducklings At The Water's Edge",* s., margins, (09-17-92, Bonhams-Chelsea, #1, illus.), plate 6½ x 10M, in., (16.5 x 27.6 cm.), etching w/drypoint (BP 176, DM 465, FR 1590, Y 38,969).

$128* *Falcon Standing Guard,* s., margins, (09-17-92, Bonhams-Chelsea, #44), plate 7¼ x 13¼ in., (18.4 x 33.7 cm.), etching w/drypoint on laid paper (BP 72, DM 190, FR 650, Y 15,936).

$137* *Golden Eyes,* s., margins, (09-17-92, Bonhams-Chelsea, #22), plate 9M, x 7M, in., (25.1 x 20 cm.), etching w/ drypoint (BP 77, DM 203, FR 696, Y 17,057).

$353* *A Goose And Family,* s., margins, (09-17-92, Bonhams-Chelsea, #51, illus.), plate 7 x 10 in., (17.8 x 25.4 cm.), etching w/drypoint on laid paper (BP 198, DM 524, FR 1794, Y 43,949).

BI *Great Tit,* s., margins, est. BP 70/100, (09-17-92, Bonhams-Chelsea, #30), plate 5¼ x 7½ in., (13.3 x 19.1 cm.), etching w/drypoint on laid paper.

$126* *Great Tit,* s., margins, (10-15-92, Bonhams-Chelsea, #125), plate 5¼ x 7½ in., (13.3 x 19.1 cm.), etching w/ drypoint on laid paper (BP 77, DM 188, FR 636, Y 15,117).

$137* *Group Of Sparrows,* s., margins, (09-17-92, Bonhams-Chelsea, #8), plate 6¾ x 9¼ in., (17.1 x 23.5 cm.), etching w/drypoint on laid paper (BP 77, DM 203, FR 696, Y 17,057).

$137* *Grouse,* s., margins, (09-17-92, Bonhams-Chelsea, #47), plate 7Z, x 10Z\ in., (18.1 x 25.7 cm.), etching w/drypoint on laid paper (BP 77, DM 203, FR 696, Y 17,057).

BI *Guillemots,* margins, est. BP 40/60, (09-17-92, Bonhams-Chelsea, #41), plate 7 x 9¾ in., (17.8 x 24.8 cm.), aquatint.

$54* *Guillemots,* margins, (10-15-92, Bonhams-Chelsea, #129), plate 7 x 9¾ in., (17.8 x 24.8 cm.), aquatint (BP 33, DM 80, FR 273, Y 6479).

BI *Helter Skelter,* s., margins, est. BP 100/150, (09-17-92, Bonhams-Chelsea, #66, illus.), plate 6M, x 10C, in., (17.5 x 26.4 cm.), etching w/drypoint.

$234* *Helter Skelter,* s., margins, (10-15-92, Bonhams-Chelsea, #134, illus.), plate 6M, x 10C, in., (17.5 x 26.4 cm.), etching w/drypoint (BP 143, DM 348, FR 1181, Y 28,074).

BI *House Martins,* s., margins, est. BP 70/100, (09-17-92, Bonhams-Chelsea, #24), plate 6¾ x 9C, in., (17.1 x 23.8 cm.), etching w/drypoint on laid paper.

$108* *House Martins,* s., margins, (10-15-92, Bonhams-Chelsea, #124), plate 6¾ x 9C, in., (17.1 x 23.8 cm.), etching w/drypoint (BP 66, DM 161, FR 545, Y 12,957).

$333* *Intrigued By A Snail,* s., margins, back cover illus., (09-17-92, Bonhams-Chelsea, #49, illus.), plate 8M, x 8M, in., (22.5 x 22.5 cm.), etching w/drypoint (BP 187, DM 494, FR 1692, Y 41,459).

$274* *Japanese Bantam,* s., margins, (09-17-92, Bonhams-Chelsea, #9), plate 9¾ x 8 in., (24.8 x 20.3 cm.), etching w/drypoint on laid paper (BP 154, DM 407, FR 1392, Y 34,114).

$187* *Lapwings,* s., margins, (09-17-92, Bonhams-Chelsea, #4), plate 11¾ x 8¾ in., (29.8 x 22.2 cm.), etching w/drypoint on laid paper (BP 105, DM 278, FR 950, Y 23,282).

$78* *Lapwings,* s., margins, creasing, staining, (09-17-92, Bonhams-Chelsea, #55), plate 7 x 10 in., (17.8 x 25.4 cm.), etching w/drypoint on laid paper (BP 44, DM 116, FR 396, Y 9711).

$98* *The Little Songster,* s., margins, (09-17-92, Bonhams-Chelsea, #46), plate 4C\ x 6 in., (11.1 x 15.2 cm.), etching w/drypoint on thin laid paper (BP 55, DM 145, FR 498, Y 12,201).

$148* *Long-Tailed Tits,* s., margins, (09-17-92, Bonhams-Chelsea, #31), plate 8C, x 6¾ in., (21.3 x 17.1 cm.), etching w/drypoint on laid paper (BP 83, DM 220, FR 752, Y 18,426).

$78* *Magpies On A Fence,* margins, (09-17-92, Bonhams-Chelsea, #38), plate 8C, x 11C, in., (21.3 x 28.9 cm.), etching w/drypoint on laid paper (BP 44, DM 116, FR 396, Y 9711).

$83* *Making Off,* margins, s., foxed, light-stained, (11-30-92, Phillips-London, #324), plate 8M\ x 11M, in., (225 x 302 mm.), drypoint on wove (BP 55, DM 132, FR 449, Y 10,330).

$274* *A Mallard And Family,* s., margins, (09-17-92, Bonhams-Chelsea, #53), plate 6M, x 9M, in., (17.5 x 25.1 cm.), etching w/drypoint on laid paper (BP 154, DM 407, FR 1392, Y 34,114).

$240* *Mallards,* s., t., blindstamp Warwick Galleries, margins, (10-29-92, Bonhams-Chelsea, #84), plate 8Ƀ, x 12 in., (21.9 x 30.5 cm.), aquatint in colors (BP 154, DM 369, FR 1253, Y 29,729).

BI *Mallards,* s., margins, est. BP 100/150, (09-17-92, Bonhams-Chelsea, #12, illus.), plate 8¼ x 11Ƀ, in., (21 x 29.5 cm.), etching w/drypoint.

$216* *Mallards,* s., margins, (10-15-92, Bonhams-Chelsea, #122, illus.), plate 8¼ x 11Ƀ, in., (21 x 29.5 cm.), etching w/drypoint (BP 132, DM 322, FR 1090, Y 25,915).

$98* *Mallards In Flight,* s., margins, staining, (09-17-92, Bonhams-Chelsea, #35), plate 8¾ x 10M, in., (22.2 x 27.6 cm.), etching w/drypoint (BP 55, DM 145, FR 498, Y 12,201).

BI *Mallards Landing,* s., margins, est. BP 80/120, (09-17-92, Bonhams-Chelsea, #36), plate 7½ x 11Ȥ, in., (19.1 x 28.3 cm.), etching w/drypoint.

$100* *Mallards Landing,* s., margins, (10-15-92, Bonhams-Chelsea, #126), plate 7½ x 11Ȥ, in., (19.1 x 28.3 cm.), etching w/drypoint (BP 61, DM 149, FR 505, Y 11,998).

$98* *Mice Eating Corn,* margins, creasing, staining, holes, (09-17-92, Bonhams-Chelsea, #59), plate 9Ƀ, x 15 in., (24.4 x 38.1 cm.), etching w/drypoint in sepia (BP 55, DM 145, FR 498, Y 12,201).

$98* *Nightingale,* s., margins, (09-17-92, Bonhams-Chelsea, #20), plate 5Ƀ\ x 7C\ in., (14.3 x 18.7 cm.), etching w/ drypoint on laid paper (BP 55, DM 145, FR 498, Y 12,201).

$187* *Out Foraging,* s., margins, front cover illus., (09-17-92, Bonhams-Chelsea, #15), plate 7¼ x 9¾ in., (18.4 x 24.8 cm.), etching w/drypoint on laid paper (BP 105, DM 278, FR 950, Y 23,282).

$137* *Partridge,* s., margins, (09-17-92, Bonhams-Chelsea, #54), plate 9 x 11¾ in., (22.9 x 29.8 cm.), etching w/drypoint on laid paper (BP 77, DM 203, FR 696, Y 17,057).

$255* *Partridges,* s., margins, (09-17-92, Bonhams-Chelsea, #10), plate 6C, x 8¾ in., (16.2 x 22.2 cm.), etching w/ drypoint on laid paper (BP 143, DM 379, FR 1296, Y 31,748).

$118* *Pet Mice,* s., margins, (09-17-92, Bonhams-Chelsea, #58), plate 5 x 8¼ in., (12.7 x 21 cm.), etching w/drypoint on laid paper (BP 66, DM 175, FR 600, Y 14,691).

$148* *Pheasant,* s., margins, (09-17-92, Bonhams-Chelsea, #50, illus.), plate 9C, x 8C\ in., (23.8 x 21.3 cm.), etching w/ drypoint on laid paper (BP 83, DM 220, FR 752, Y 18,426).

$137* *Plover And Dunlins,* s., margins, (09-17-92, Bonhams-Chelsea, #32), plate 6¾ x 9¾ in., (17.1 x 24.8 cm.), etching w/drypoint on laid paper (BP 77, DM 203, FR 696, Y 17,057).

$78* *Rabbit And Teasels,* margins, nick to image, (09-17-92, Bonhams-Chelsea, #64), plate 3¼ x 7C, in., (8.3 x 18.7 cm.), etching w/drypoint (BP 44, DM 116, FR 396, Y 9711).

$255* *Rabbits Feeding,* s., margins, (09-17-92, Bonhams-Chelsea, #65), plate 7¾ x 5C, in., (19.7 x 13.7 cm.), etching w/drypoint (BP 143, DM 379, FR 1296, Y 31,748).

$274* *Red Setter,* s., margins, (09-17-92, Bonhams-Chelsea, #63), plate 8¾ x 11¼ in., (22.2 x 28.6 cm.), etching w/ drypoint in sepia on laid paper (BP 154, DM 407, FR 1392, Y 34,114).

$137* *Red Squirrel,* s., margins, scuff to image, (09-17-92, Bonhams-Chelsea, #61), plate 8½ x 7 in., (21.6 x 17.8 cm.), etching w/drypoint on laid paper (BP 77, DM 203, FR 696, Y 17,057).

$78* *Redwings,* margins, (09-17-92, Bonhams-Chelsea, #26), plate 7M, x 9¾ in., (20 x 24.8 cm.), etching w/drypoint on laid paper (BP 44, DM 116, FR 396, Y 9711).

BI *Rooks,* s., margins, est. BP 70/100, (09-17-92, Bonhams-Chelsea, #21), plate 9M, x 7Ȥ, in., (25.1 x 18.1 cm.), etching w/drypoint.

$72* *Rooks,* s., margins, (10-15-92, Bonhams-Chelsea, #123), plate 9M, x 7Ȥ, in., (25.1 x 18.1 cm.), etching w/drypoint (BP 44, DM 107, FR 363, Y 8638).

BI *Sedge Warbler,* s., margins, stain, est. BP 50/70, (09-17-92, Bonhams-Chelsea, #39), plate 5¾ x 7½ in., (14.6 x 19.1 cm.), etching w/drypoint on laid paper.

$54* *Sedge Warbler,* s., margins, stain, (10-15-92, Bonhams-Chelsea, #127), plate 5¾ x 7½ in., (14.6 x 19.1 cm.),

etching w/drypoint on laid paper (BP 33, DM 80, FR 273, Y 6479).

$274* *Shelduck And Family,* s., margins, (09-17-92, Bonhams-Chelsea, #29), plate 5 x 8M, in., (12.7 x 22.5 cm.), etching w/drypoint on laid paper (BP 154, DM 407, FR 1392, Y 34,114).

$235* *Shelducks,* s., margins, (09-17-92, Bonhams-Chelsea, #11), plate 8 x 10 in., (20.3 x 25.4 cm.), etching w/drypoint on laid paper (BP 132, DM 349, FR 1194, Y 29,258).

$255* *Sheltering From The Wind,* s., margins, (09-17-92, Bonhams-Chelsea, #6), plate 8 x 6¾ in., (20.3 x 17.1 cm.), etching w/drypoint on laid paper (BP 143, DM 379, FR 1296, Y 31,748).

$215* *Short-Eared Owl,* s., margins, creased, (09-17-92, Bonhams-Chelsea, #23, illus.), plate 9 x 8¾ in., (22.9 x 22.2 cm.), etching w/drypoint on laid paper (BP 121, DM 319, FR 1092, Y 26,768).

$167* *Shoveller Ducks,* s., margins, (09-17-92, Bonhams-Chelsea, #37, illus.), plate 6¾ x 9M, in., (17.1 x 25.1 cm.), etching w/drypoint on laid paper (BP 94, DM 248, FR 849, Y 20,792).

$470* *Startled Hares,* s., margins, (09-17-92, Bonhams-Chelsea, #67, illus.), plate 10½ x 7½ in., (26.7 x 19.1 cm.), etching w/drypoint on laid paper (BP 264, DM 698, FR 2388, Y 58,516).

BI *Stoat,* s., margins, est. BP 70/100, (09-17-92, Bonhams-Chelsea, #60), plate 7 x 8C, in., (17.8 x 21.3 cm.), etching w/drypoint on laid paper.

$100* *Stoat,* s., margins, (10-15-92, Bonhams-Chelsea, #135), plate 7 x 8C, in., (17.8 x 21.3 cm.), etching w/drypoint on laid paper (BP 61, DM 149, FR 505, Y 11,998).

BI *Study Of A Heron Perched On A Branch,* s., margins, est. BP 70/100, (09-17-92, Bonhams-Chelsea, #3), plate 10¾ x 8¾ in., (27.3 x 22.2 cm.), etching w/drypoint.

$372* *Surrey Fowl,* s., margins, (09-17-92, Bonhams-Chelsea, #16), plate 8¾ x 10M, in., (22.2 x 27.6 cm.), on laid paper (BP 209, DM 552, FR 1890, Y 46,315).

$98* *A Swallow Perched On A Branch,* s., margins, (09-17-92, Bonhams-Chelsea, #18), plate 7M, x 5Ƀ, in., (20 x 14.3 cm.), etching w/drypoint (BP 55, DM 145, FR 498, Y 12,201).

BI *Swallows On The Line,* s., margins, est. BP 80/120, (09-17-92, Bonhams-Chelsea, #2), plate 9Ƀ, x 13C, in., (24.4 x 34 cm.), etching w/drypoint on laid paper.

$154* *Swallows On The Line,* s., margins, (10-15-92, Bonhams-Chelsea, #120), plate 9Ƀ, x 13C, in., (24.4 x 34 cm.), etching w/drypoint on laid paper (BP 94, DM 229, FR 777, Y 18,476).

$176* *Swans In Flight,* s., margins, (09-17-92, Bonhams-Chelsea, #25, illus.), plate 8½ x 13½ in., (21.6 x 34.3 cm.), etching w/drypoint on laid paper (BP 99, DM 261, FR 894, Y 21,912).

BI *Teal By A Lake,* margins, est. BP 30/50, (12-10-92, Bonhams-Chelsea, #99), plate 9¼ x 12¾ in., (23.5 x 32.4 cm.), aquatint.

BI *Teal By A Lake,* margins, est. BP 30/50, (03-03-93, Bonhams-Chelsea, #35), plate 9¼ x 12¾ in., (23.5 x 32.4 cm.), aquatint.

BI *Teal By A Lake,* margins, est. BP 50/80, (09-17-92, Bonhams-Chelsea, #42), plate 9¼ x 12¾ in., (23.5 x 32.4 cm.), aquatint.

BI *Teal By A Lake,* margins, est. BP 30/50, (10-15-92, Bonhams-Chelsea, #130), plate 9¼ x 12¾ in., (23.5 x 32.4 cm.), aquatint.

$90* *Teal In Flight,* s., margins, (10-15-92, Bonhams-Chelsea, #133), plate 8Ȥ\ x 11¼ in., (20.6 x 28.6 cm.), etching w/drypoint on laid paper (BP 55, DM 134, FR 454, Y 10,798).

BI *Teal In Flight,* s., margins, est. BP 80/120, (09-17-92, Bonhams-Chelsea, #52), plate 8Ȥ, x 11¼ in., (20.6 x 28.6 cm.), etching w/drypoint on laid paper.

$304* *"Tomtits",* s., (06-11-93, G.A. Key, #137), 9 x 8 in., (22.9 x 20.3 cm.), mezzotint (BP 200, DM 494, FR 1666, Y 32,255).

$98* *Tree-Creeper,* s., margins, (09-17-92, Bonhams-Chelsea, #19), plate 5¼ x 7 in., (13.3 x 17.8 cm.), etching w/drypoint on laid paper (BP 55, DM 145, FR 498, Y 12,201).

$187* *Tree-Sparrows,* s., margins, (09-17-92, Bonhams-Chelsea, #14), plate 8½ x 11½ in., (21.6 x 29.2 cm.), etching w/

drypoint on laid paper (BP 105, DM 278, FR 950, Y 23,282).

BI *Wagtails On A Roof,* s., margins, est. BP 80/120, (09-17-92, Bonhams-Chelsea, #40), plate 6½ x 9 in., (16.5 x 22.9 cm.), etching w/drypoint on laid paper.

$100* *Wagtails On A Roof,* s., margins, (10-15-92, Bonhams-Chelsea, #128), plate 6½ x 9 in., (16.5 x 22.9 cm.), etching w/drypoint on laid paper (BP 61, DM 149, FR 505, Y 11,998).

$118* *White Heron,* s., margins, (09-17-92, Bonhams-Chelsea, #27), plate 8¼ x 4Z, in., (21 x 10.5 cm.), etching w/drypoint on laid paper (BP 66, DM 175, FR 600, Y 14,691).

BI *Whitethroat,* s., margins, est. BP 60/80, (09-17-92, Bonhams-Chelsea, #34), plate 5½ x 7½ in., (14 x 19.1 cm.), etching w/drypoint on laid paper.

$148* *Widgeon Landing,* s., staining, (09-17-92, Bonhams-Chelsea, #57), plate 8M, x 11¾ in., (22.5 x 29.8 cm.), etching w/drypoint on laid paper (BP 83, DM 220, FR 752, Y 18,426).

$137* *A Woodcock,* s., time staining, margins, (09-17-92, Bonhams-Chelsea, #7), plate 9M, x 8C, in., (25.1 x 21.3 cm.), etching w/drypoint (BP 77, DM 203, FR 696, Y 17,057).

$59* *Woodpecker,* margins, (09-17-92, Bonhams-Chelsea, #33), plate 4M, x 5M, in., (12.4 x 14.9 cm.), etching w/drypoint on laid paper (BP 33, DM 88, FR 300, Y 7346).

$392* *Young China,* s., margins, (09-17-92, Bonhams-Chelsea, #62, illus.), plate 6¼ x 8¼ in., (15.9 x 21 cm.), etching w/drypoint on laid paper (BP 220, DM 582, FR 1992, Y 48,805).

$78* *Young Cuckoo,* s., margins; marked w/ballpoint verso image, (09-17-92, Bonhams-Chelsea, #13), plate 7 x 8B in., (17.8 x 21.9 cm.), etching w/drypoint on laid paper (BP 44, DM 116, FR 396, Y 9711).

$69* *A Young Thrush,* margins, (09-17-92, Bonhams-Chelsea, #56), plate 4C x 5½ in., (11.1 x 14 cm.), etching w/drypoint on laid paper (BP 39, DM 102, FR 351, Y 8591).

AUSTIN, Frederick

$102* *The Woodcutter,* s., d. 1962, margins, (04-22-93, Bonhams-Chelsea, #21), (29.8 x 26 cm.), etching (BP 66, DM 164, FR 553, Y 11,215).

AUSTIN, Robert Sargent

$366* *The Bell No. 1 (C.D. 67), 1926,* s., d. 1927, full margins, pub. Twenty One Gallery, (10-27-92, Phillips-London, #232), plate 5½ x 4¼ in., (140 x 108 mm.), engraving on laid (BP 231, DM 561, FR 1903, Y 44,771).

$731* *Child In Bed (C.D. 89), 1930,* 3rd and final state, s., d., #9/40, pub. Twenty-one Gallery, full margins, good cond., (10-27-92, Phillips-London, #233), plate 5 x 5½ in., (127 x 140 mm.), etching and drypoint on smooth laid (BP 462, DM 1120, FR 3801, Y 89,419).

$383* *Plane Tree Cottage (C.D. 66), 1926,* s., very large margins, good cond., (10-27-92, Phillips-London, #231), plate 5¼ x 5½ in., (133 x 140 mm.), engraving on Van Gelder Zonnen (BP 242, DM 587, FR 1992, Y 46,850).

$480* *"The Plough", "Wherefore Plough?", "Mendicanti" and "Woman Milking AGoat" (Campbell Dodgson 31; 43; 50; and 59), 1922-1925: Four,* final states, each s., three d., full margins, good cond., (06-30-93, Sotheby-London, #279), etching on laid (BP 322, DM 819, FR 2762, Y 51,430).

$209* *The Ponte Pietra, Verona, 1928,* s., d., watermark, full margins, good cond., (10-27-92, Phillips-London, #234), plate 5¼ x 4¾ in., (133 x 121 mm.), etching on laid (BP 132, DM 320, FR 1087, Y 25,566).

AUSTRIAN SCHOOL, 19TH CENTURY

BI *"Alter Pallast Der Lombarden Konige Und Kirche St Fedele",* id. on label verso, good cond., laid down, abrasions to sky, subtle foxing, prov., est. $450/650, (06-25-93, Skinner, #277), sh 6¾ x 8¾ in., (17.1 x 22.2 cm.), etching w/aquatint and handcoloring heightened w/gum arabic on paper.

AUTHOUART, Daniel b. 1943

$63* *"C'Est Pour La Photo", 1978,* E.A., d., s., (01-28-93, Pescheteau, #67), 15C, x 11Mn in., (39 x 29 cm.), etching on Arches (BP 42, DM 100, FR 338, Y 7822).

$681* *Italia, c. 1986,* s., t., num., (06-19-93, Wachholtz, #360, illus.), 19¾ x 26Azn in., (50.2 x 68.4 cm.), color lithograph on thick copper print paper (BP 457, DM 1150, FR 3865, Y 75,491).

$749* *Route 66, c. 1986,* s., t., num., (06-19-93, Wachholtz, #361, illus.), 23zn x 30Bzn in., (59.8 x 77 cm.), color lithograph on thick copper print paper (BP 503, DM 1264, FR 4251, Y 83,028).

AUZOLLE

$70* *Savon Abeille De Marseille,* good cond., (02-13-93, Morelle/Marchan, #37), 47¼ x 62Bzn in., (120 x 160 cm.), poster (BP 49, DM 116, FR 393, Y 8442).

AUZOLLE, M.

$602* *Dentifrice Borel (...) Elixir Mousseux Et Parfume (...) Paris (...) Lille, 1899,* Lith. L. Gallice, cond. B+, (06-11-93, Boisgirard, #40), 77Bzn x 49Czn in., (198 x 125 cm.), poster (BP 396, DM 978, FR 3299, Y 63,873).

$482* *Ducellier, "Phares, Demarreurs, Dynamos", 1921,* p. Vercasson, good cond., (11-19-92, Ribeyre/Baron, #55), 62Azn x 47¼ in., (160 x 120 cm.), poster (BP 317, DM 768, FR 2589, Y 59,943).

$221* *Eau Minerale De Couzan. Source Brault,* fairly good cond., losses, tears, (02-12-93, Cheval/Robert, #50), 113C, x 41Bzn in., (288 x 105 cm.), poster (BP 156, DM 367, FR 1240, Y 26,652).

$130* *"Pecheurs, Equipez Vos Bateaux Avec Le Moteur L.L., Vous Gagnerez DuTemps Et De L'Argent",* Imp. Vercasson, good cond., (02-12-93, Cheval/Robert, #80), 51Czn x 35Mzn in., (130 x 90 cm.), poster (BP 92, DM 216, FR 730, Y 15,678).

$151* *Sels De Potasse D'Alsace. Mulhouse. "La Potasse Est La Fortune De L'Agriculteur",* Imp. Lapina, fairly good cond., (02-12-93, Cheval/Robert, #49), 47¼ x 31½ in., (120 x 80 cm.), poster (BP 106, DM 250, FR 847, Y 18,210).

AVATI, Mario French b. 1921

$308* *"Des Fruits D'Hiver" (R. Passeron 499), 1974,* s., ded., d., num., good margins, (05-06-93, Laurin, #2), black manner print in colors (BP 195, DM 485, FR 1633, Y 33,887).

$173* *Noah's Ark: Alligater, 1970,* s., d., t., #I/175, blindstamp publisher, Ferdinand Roten, full margins, very good cond., creases, (05-19-93, Butterfield, #2033), 8½ x 8½ in., (216 x 216 mm.), mezzotint on Rives BFK (BP 112, DM 281, FR 947, Y 19,152).

$105* *"Petit Duc" (P 263), 1959,* #5/100, s., drystamp, (01-28-93, Pescheteau, #68), 12Bzn x 9Zzn in., (33 x 25 cm.), aquatint on BFK Rives (BP 69, DM 166, FR 563, Y 13,037).

$403* *Still Life With Bottles, 1961,* s., d., margins, good cond., (05-19-93, Butterfield, #2032), 4M, x 3¾ in., (124 x 95 mm.), mezzotint on wove (BP 262, DM 655, FR 2207, Y 44,614).

$370* *"Le Violin Noir" (R.P. 157), 1975,* s., ded., d., #19/75, good margins, (05-06-93, Laurin, #3), black manner print in colors (BP 234, DM 583, FR 1962, Y 40,709).

AVEDON, Richard b. 1923

$7700* *B.J. Van Fleet, Nine Year Old, Ennis, Montana (7/2/82),* 1985, s., num. w/stylus in margin, s., num. 1/4 in ink (c) credi & reprod. limit. stmaps, #1/4, lit., (10-13-92, Christie-NY, #524, illus.), 54¾ x 45¼ in., (139.1 x 114.9 cm.), photograph, oversized gelatin silver print (BP 4485, DM 11,280, FR 38,328, Y 933,673).

BI *Buckminster Fuller, New York City,* 1969, p. 1975, ink s., num. 3; t., d., (c) and reprod. limitation, est. $3/5,000, (04-08-93, Christie-NY, #470, illus.), 9B, x 7B, in., (24.4 x 19.4 cm.), photograph, gelatin silver print.

$2200* *John Ford, 1975,* s. by photog. in ink, t. in unidentified hand, num. 4/50 in unidentified hand in ink, (c) reprod. limit., ed. stamps, #4/50 ed., (10-15-92, Sotheby-NY, #570, illus.), 15½ x 15½ in., (39.4 x 39.4 cm.), photograph, gelatin silver print (BP 1346, DM 3275, FR 11,106, Y 263,947).

$2760* *Marlene Dietrich In The Foreign Affair, 1948,* lit., (04-08-93, Christie-NY, #469, illus.), 10½ x 9B, in., (26.7 x 24.4 cm.), photograph, gelatin silver print (BP 1810, DM 4434, FR 15,008, Y 313,209).

$5520* *Nastassja Kinski And The Serpent, Los Angeles, California, 1981,* s., #2/200; s.; stamped t., (c), reprod. limitation, edit. num.; #2/200, (04-08-93, Christie-NY, #472, illus.), 28¾ x 43¼ in., (73 x 109.9 cm.), photograph, gelatin silver print (BP 3620, DM 8867, FR 30,016, Y 626,419).

$5750* *"Nastassja Kinsky And The Serpent", 1981,* mounted, s., #36/200 by photog., photog. (c), edit., t. stamps, p. 1982, (04-06-93, Sotheby-NY, #479, illus.), 28¾ x 42¾ in., photograph (BP 3798, DM 9264, FR 31,369, Y 655,794).

BI *Die Schriftstellerin Renate Adler,* 1969, 1975, s., #8/50, est. DM 1,200, (11-12-92, Lempertz, #5, illus.), 9Bzn x 7Bzn in., (25.2 x 20.2 cm.), photograph, gelatin silver print.

$2875* *Selected Portraits: "Ezra Pound, 1958", "Isak Dinesen, 1958" and "Marianne Moore, 1958": Group Of Three,* from Minneapolis portfolio, self-pub., 1970, s., #8/35 by photog., s.by photog. in ink, (c), edit, t. stamps, 1958, p.c. 1970, (04-06-93, Sotheby-NY, #477, illus.), each approx. 22 x 20 in., photograph (BP 1899, DM 4632, FR 15,685, Y 327,897).

$3450* *Selected Portraits: "Jimmy Durante, 1953", "Rene Clair, 1958" and "Dwight David Eisenhower, 1964": Group Of Three,* from Minneapolis portfolio, self-pub., 1970, each s., #8/35 by photog., s. by photog. in ink, his (c), edit., t. stamps, 1953-64, p.c. 1970, (04-06-93, Sotheby-NY, #478, illus.), each approx. 22 x 20 in., photograph (BP 2279, DM 5558, FR 18,822, Y 393,476).

$5060* *Truman Capote, Writer, New York City,* 1974, p. 1975, ink s., num.; t., (c), reprod. limitation and edit. stamps, lit., (04-08-93, Christie-NY, #471, illus.), 9½ x 7¾ in., (24.1 x 19.7 cm.), photograph, gelatin silver print (BP 3318, DM 8129, FR 27,515, Y 574,217).

$3300* *Verushka, Wrap By Georgio Di Sant'Angelo, New York,* (1972), 1981, s., num. 4/50 in ink, p. credit, t., d., (c) & reprod.limit. stamp, lit., (10-13-92, Christie-NY, #523, illus.), 19½ x 23¾ in., (49.5 x 60.3 cm.), photograph, gelatin silver print backed w/linen (BP 1922, DM 4834, FR 16,426, Y 400,146).

AVELINE, P.

$165* *"Enlevement D'Europe",* 18th c., after F. Boucher, pub. Paris, foxing, (12-06-92, Neal, #931), image 16¼ x 18¾ in., (41.3 x 47.6 cm.), engraving (BP 103, DM 257, FR 877, Y 20,444).

$242* *"Naissance De Bacchus",* 18th c., after F. Boucher, pub. Paris, foxing, (12-06-92, Neal, #930), image 15¾ x 18½ in., (40 x 47 cm.), engraving (BP 152, DM 377, FR 1286, Y 29,984).

AVELOT, H.

$62* *Frederique, 1927,* (01-31-93, Morelle/Marchan, #14), 31½ x 47¼ in., (80 x 120 cm.), poster (BP 42, DM 100, FR 338, Y 7735).

AVERY, Milton American 1893-1965

$1760* *Birds And Sea (L. 60), 1955,* s., num. 8/25, margins, printer's ink, very good cond., (09-19-92, Christie-E, #7), borderline 9¾ x 24 in., (248 x 610 mm.), woodcut in black and purple-brown on Japan (BP 1012, DM 2636, FR 9026, Y 219,287).

$1760* *Dance (Lunn 56), 1954,* s., d., #18/25, large margins, good cond., creases, discoloration, (11-05-92, Sotheby-NY, #2, illus.), 12 x 9¾ in., (305 x 247 mm.), sheet 16M, x 12Z, in., (305 x 247 mm.), woodcut p. in black on soft Japan (BP 1145, DM 2783, FR 9417, Y 215,924).

BI *Dawn (L. 40), 1952,* s., d., margins, foxmarks, i., taped to overmat, staining, est. $2/3,000, (11-09-92, Christie-NY, #2, illus.), border 7Czn x 9Zzn in., (182 x 230 mm.), woodcut in yellow and black on Japan.

$935* *Drawbridge (L. 10), 1936,* s., d., num. 58/60, wide margins, very good cond., (09-19-92, Christie-E, #4), plate 6C x 12M, in., (162 x 327 mm.), drypoint on wove (BP 538, DM 1400, FR 4795, Y 116,496).

BI *Flight (L. 51), 1955,* s., d., pub. Collectors of American Art, full margins, mat/light-staining, foxed, taped to overmat, est. $2,5/3,500, (11-09-92, Christie-NY, #4, illus.), border 7 x 9 in., (178 x 229 mm.), woodcut in black and brown on Japan.

$1430* *Gray Sea (L. 38), 1963,* s., d., num. 91/118, margins, very good cond., (09-19-92, Christie-E, #6, illus.), sheet 22Bzn x 28C, in., (583 x 721 mm.), lithograph in colors on Arches (BP 823, DM 2141, FR 7333, Y 178,171).

$550* *Green Fish (Lunn 41/i), 1952,* d., num., s., (05-27-93, Swann, #19), 2½ x 9 in., (6.4 x 22.9 cm.), woodcut (BP 352, DM 883, FR 2975, Y 58,962).

$1210* *Head Of A Man (L. 8), 1935,* s., pub. Laurels Portfolio, No. 4, Laurels Gallery, 1948, full margins, time staining, very good cond., (09-19-92, Christie-E, #3, illus.), plate 9Z, x 4B, in., (232 x 117 mm.), drypoint on wove (BP 696, DM 1812, FR 6205, Y 150,760).

BI *Head Of A Man (Lunn 8), 1935,* s., est. DM 4000, (06-10-93, Hauswedell/Nolt, #15, illus.), image 9Czn x 4B in., (23.3 x 11.8 cm.), drypoint on copper print paper.

$935* *Japanese Landscape (L. 15), 1939,* s., d., i. artist's proof, wide margins, very good cond., (09-19-92, Christie-E, #5), plate 3¼ x 7¾ in., (83 x 197 mm.), drypoint in brown on wove (BP 538, DM 1400, FR 4795, Y 116,496).

$15,400* *Laurels Number Four, New York, The Laurel Gallery, 1948 (Lunn 6, 8, 26, 28, 29), 1934-48: Five,* burr, #40/100, full margins, foxmarks, time staining, excell. cond.,-orig. portfolio, (11-09-92, Christie-NY, #1, illus.), 17½ x 13½ in., (445 x 343 mm.), drypoint on wove (BP 10,182, DM 24,585, FR 83,064, Y 1,911,144).

$522* *Mother And Child On A Rocking Chair, 1949,* wide margins, plate s., d., (12-08-92, Swann, #13), 23¾ x 18M in., (60.3 x 47.9 cm.), color pochoir on stiff buff paper (BP 327, DM 813, FR 2771, Y 64,700).

BI *Mother And Child On A Rocking Chair, 1949,* wide margins, plate s., est. $6/900, (05-27-93, Swann, #21), 23¾ x 17M, in., (60.3 x 45.4 cm.), color pochoir on stiff buff paper.

$1150* *Pilot Fish (Lunn 42), 1952,* s., d., i., artist's proof, full margins, staining, glued to overmat, good cond., sold after sale, (05-11-93, Christie-NY, #88, illus.), borderline 11½ x 29¾ in., (292 x 756 mm.), woodcut on Japan (BP 734, DM 1812, FR 6104, Y 126,499).

$2750* *Riders In The Park (L. 6), 1934,* s., annot., artists proof, from Laurels Portfolio, No. 4, 1948, large full margins, very good cond., staining, foxing, (10-28-92, Butterfield, #2504, illus.), 3M, x 5 in., (98 x 127 mm.), drypoint on heavy cream wove (BP 1752, DM 4247, FR 14,421, Y 337,423).

$1430* *Riders In The Park (Lunn 6), 1934,* s., pub. Laurels Portfolio, No. 4, Laurels Gallery, 1948, full margins, printer's ink, time staining, tear, very good cond., (09-19-92, Christie-E, #2), plate 3Bzn x 5 in., (100 x 127 mm.), drypoint on wove (BP 823, DM 2141, FR 7333, Y 178,171).

BI *Rooster (L. 50), 1953,* s., d., margins, light-staining, losses, taped to overmat, staining,est. $2/3,000, (11-09-92, Christie-NY, #3, illus.), border 9B, x 6Bzn in., (245 x 177 mm.), woodcut in blue and black on Japan.

$935* *Rooster (Lunn 50/ii), 1953,* wide margins, d., num., s., (05-27-93, Swann, #20, illus.), 9B, x 7¼ in., (24.4 x 18.4 cm.), woodcut in dark gray (BP 599, DM 1500, FR 5057, Y 100,236).

$990* *"Standing Nude" (Lunn, 21), 1941,* s., d. Milton Avery 1941, s. in plate, num. 20/60, good cond., lighttoning, stains verso, (09-11-92, Skinner, #87, illus.), 14¼ x 7B in., (36.2 x 19.4 cm.), drypoint on wove (BP 512, DM 1425, FR 4843, Y 122,661).

AVERY, Sid

$920* *Liz Taylor Sunning Herself On The Set Of "Giant", Marfa, Texas,* 1955, p.l., s., t., d., #13/70, (c) credit/ reprod. limitation stamps, (04-08-93, Christie-NY, #404, illus.), 14B, x 14½ in., (37.1 x 36.8 cm.), photograph, gelatin silver print (BP 603, DM 1478, FR 5003, Y 104,403).

$863* *"Marlon Brando In His Home For Article In Saturday Evening Post",* 1955, p.l., s., t., #13/70, d., photog.'s stamp, (05-23-93, Butterfield, #3305, illus.), 10 x 10 in., photograph, gelatin silver print (BP 562, DM 1411, FR 4750, Y 95,391).

AVRAMIDIS, Joannis Greek b. 1922

$181* *3 Figuren, 1967,* s., d., est. DM 400, (11-28-92, Schoppmann, #361), 14¼ x 18M, in., (36.2 x 48 cm.), lithograph in brown on weissem wove (BP 119, DM 288, FR 979, Y 22,526).

AVRIL 20th cent.
$91* *Toros, 1988,* s., d., #63/200, full margins, good cond., (12-09-92, Sotheby-Amstrdm, #486), 19½ x 25C, in., (495 x 645 mm.), color silkscreen on BFK Rives (BP 58, DM 143, FR 487, Y 11,283, G 161).

AY-O Japanese b. 1931
$303* *Abstract,* s., d. 1971, i. artist's proof, (05-16-93, Hindman, #512), 28 x 21 in., (71.1 x 53.3 cm.), color serigraph (BP 197, DM 487, FR 1638, Y 33,588).

AYLESFORD, Earl Of, David Charles READ, A. GEDDES, and other
BI *An Interesting Group Of Landscape Scenes, late 18th and early 19th cent.: Twelve,* two s., margins, good cond., est. BP 4/500, (06-30-93, Sotheby-London, #280, illus.), 12 etchings, some w/drypoint, on various papers.

AYRTON, Michael English 1921-1975
$164* *Men Fishing By A Pool,* #6/25, s., blindstamp, (05-20-93, Bonhams-Chelsea, #158), image 24¾ x 14½ in., (62.9 x 36.8 cm.), lithograph (BP 105, DM 265, FR 891, Y 18,110).

AZECHI, Umetaro Japanese b. 1902
BI *Mountaineer Standing With Striped Bird,* s., est. $4/600, (02-04-93, Sloan, #2540), 15¼ x 10½ in., (38.7 x 26.7 cm.), color woodblock.
BI *"Mountaineer With Striped Bird",* s., very good cond., est. $4/500, (05-15-93, Cleveland, #447), 15¼ x 10½ in., (38.7 x 26.7 cm.), color woodcut.

AZIPIRI, Paul
BI *Untitled, Flowers,* s., annot. Arches HC 11/12, pub. Editions Romasnet, full margins, good cond., light/water staining, hinged to overmat w/tape, soiling, hinge remains, est. $5/700, (10-28-92, Butterfield, #2895), 21 x 16¾ in., (533 x 425 mm.), color lithograph on Arches.

AZUMA, Norio Japanese/America b. 1928
$154* *Ancient City,* s., t., #8/18, (04-02-93, Sloan, #799), 30 x 24 in., (762 x 610 mm.), serigraph on canvas (BP 101, DM 248, FR 841, Y 17,534).

B., Andre
$124* *Teddy Ted And Partner, 1926,* (01-31-93, Morelle/Marchan, #222), 30Bzn x 44M, in., (77 x 114 cm.), poster (BP 83, DM 200, FR 675, Y 15,469).

BABBITT, Platt D.
$522* *Couple Posing Before Niagara Falls,* in half case, 1850's, (10-14-92, Swann, #114, illus.), photograph, half-plate ambrotype (BP 306, DM 764, FR 2591, Y 63,257).
$770* *Views Of Niagara Falls Including "The Suspension Bridge", "Horeshoe Falls", "Rapids Bear Of Cataract House", "Point View, American Side", "Luna Island", "Horeshoe Falls From Goat Island" and others: Ten,* photog.'s credit, t., (c), 1860s, (04-07-93, Swann, #257), photograph, stereograph on glass (BP 509, DM 1245, FR 4215, Y 87,480).

BABCOCK
$302* *Join The Navy,* B cond., creasing, closed tears, chartex-backing, (08-06-92, Swann, #39, illus.), 40 x 28 in., (101.6 x 71.1 cm.), (BP 158, DM 446, FR 1507, Y 38,520).

BABOULENE, Eugene
$247* *Les Rougets,* s., #168/190, good margins, (05-06-93, Laurin, #5), color lithograph (BP 157, DM 389, FR 1310, Y 27,176).

BACH, Elvira b. 1951
$516* *Femme, 1984,* s., d., #21/60, (03-31-93, Briest, #E135), 68Z, x 33Zzn in., (173 x 84 cm.), color lithograph (BP 341, DM 830, FR 2820, Y 59,338).
BI *Frau Mit Kirschen,* s., num., est. DM 2500, (12-01-92, Karl/Faber, #337), 31½ x 44Z\ in., (80 x 112 cm.), color serigraph on cardboard.
$709* *Frau Mit Palme,* s., num., (06-08-93, Karl/Faber, #509), approx. 43Bzn x 31½ in., (110 x 80 cm.), color serigraph on board (BP 466, DM 1150, FR 3874, Y 75,305).
BI *Untitled, Frau Im Baum Mit Schlange,* s., #46/89, est. DM 1,200-, (05-27-93, Lempertz, #582), 42 x 31Bzn in., (106.7 x 79.5 cm.), color serigraph on wove.

BACH, G.C. (after)
$110 *"Blumen" and "Fruchte": A Pair,* by L. Bisch, (10-09-92, G.A. Key, #47), 13 x 9½ in., (33 x 24.1 cm.), colored lithograph (BP 65, DM 164, FR 556, Y 13,415).

BACHELDER
$330* *Manchester, NH,* large folio, (03-20-93, Northeast, #101), print (BP 221, DM 540, FR 1836, Y 38,279).

BACHELDER, John B., Publisher
$550* *"The Army of the Potomac",* annot., (07-10-92, Skinner, #355), hand-colored lithograph (BP 286, DM 822, FR 2789, Y 68,879).
$523* *"Ravine Occupied By The Picket Reserves" and "Capture Of A Rebel Lunette": Two,* (07-10-92, Skinner, #392), colored lithograph (BP 272, DM 782, FR 2652, Y 65,498).

BACHER, Otto H.
$17* *Schwabelweiss,* margins, plate s., (05-22-93, Collins, #131), 3 x 8Z\ in., (7.6 x 20.6 cm.), etching (BP 11, DM 28, FR 93, Y 1874).

BACHINSKI, Walter
$147* *"Summer Flowers", 1989,* (05-12-93, Maynard, #269), 20 x 14 in., (50.8 x 35.6 cm.), color lithograph (BP 96, DM 237, FR 799, Y 16,412, C$ 187).

BACHMAN, J., Artist and Lithographer
$5175* *Bird's Eye View Of Philadelphia (R. 39), 1868,* p. P.S. Duval Son & Co. Lith., pub. John Weik, large margins, good cond., soiling, backboard stain, (01-28-93, Sotheby-NY, #455A, illus.), 25C, x 36½ in., (645 x 927 mm.), color lithograph (BP 3417, DM 8200, FR 27,748, Y 642,538).

BACHMANN, John ac. 1850-77
$4620* *Panorama Of New York And Vicinity (Reps 2696), 1866,* 1st state of 2, pub. by artist, margins, image repairs, corner made-up, tears, paper losses (backed), skinning, staining, defects, (01-22-93, Christie-NY, #319, illus.), borderline 22¼ x 35B, in., (565 x 905 mm.), chromolithograph on wove (BP 3023, DM 7346, FR 24,852, Y 578,223).

BACHMANN, Otto b. 1915
$362* *Dame Mit Blumenhut, 1977,* XXXI/LXXV, s., (10-14-92, Germann, #480), 27zn x 18M, in., (700 x 480 mm.), color lithograph (BP 212, DM 530, FR 1797, Y 43,868, SF 472).
$196* *Junges Madchen Mit Blumenhut, 1973,* #XVII/XLV, s., d., creases, (11-13-92, Koller, #5242), 24 x 18Zzn in., (61 x 47.5 cm.), lithograph on Japan (BP 127, DM 308, FR 1038, Y 24,327, SF 278).
BI *Die Menscheninsel, 1976,* s., d., est. SF 180/250, (10-14-92, Germann, #482), 18½ x 27Czn in., (470 x 690 mm.), color lithograph.

BACHRACH, Ernest G.
BI *"F.H. Day",* 1914, mono., t., s., d., mounted, est. BP 1/1,500, (12-17-92, Christie-S. Ken, #3, illus.), 6¼ x 4C, in., (15.9 x 11.1 cm.), photograph, gelatin silver print.
BI *Portrait Of A Young Boy,* 1915, s., d., mounted, est. BP 3/500, (12-17-92, Christie-S. Ken, #4, illus.), 6¼ x 4Z, in., (15.9 x 10.5 cm.), photograph, platinum print.
BI *Portrait Of A Young Man,* 1915, mono., s., d., typescript label, mounted, est. BP 4/600, (12-17-92, Christie-S. Ken, #5, illus.), 6¼ x 3M\ in., (15.9 x 9.8 cm.), photograph, warm-toned platinum print.

BACKEN, Earle b. 1927
$65* *Whitsun Etching,* s. E Backen, i., d. '66, #4/25, (08-11-92, L. Joel, #13G), 12Czn x 19C, in., (32.6 x 49.2 cm.), color etching (BP 34, DM 95, FR 323, Y 8324, A$ 88).

BACON, Francis Irish 1909-1992
$2733* *Autoportrait,* s., #XVII/XXV, creases, (05-27-93, Briest, #19), 18½ x 40zn in., (47 x 103 cm.), color lithograph (BP 1750, DM 4385, FR 14,781, Y 292,989).
$916* *The Boxer (George Dyer),* s., annot., margins, light-staining, surface dirt, tape, very good cond., (12-01-92, Christie-London, #564), L. 29Zzn x 21M, in., (758 x 556 mm.), lithograph in colors on wove (BP 605, DM 1460, FR 4976, Y 114,044).
BI *Centre Panel Of Triptych, 1987,* s., #51/180, pub. Galerie Lelong, full margins, excell. cond., est. $3/4,000, (05-11-

93, Christie-NY, #361, illus.), sheet 37¼ x 26¾ in., (946 x 679 mm.), color lithograph on Arches.

$3025* *Etude De Corps Humain, 1981,* s., #75/150, blindstamp pub. Arts-Litho, pub. Maeght editeur, very good cond., (10-28-92, Butterfield, #2898, illus.), 17¾ x 13 in., (451 x 330 mm.), color lithograph on cream wove (BP 1927, DM 4672, FR 15,863, Y 371,166).

$2300* *Etude De Corps Humain, 1981,* s., #77/150, pub. Maeght, blindstamp printer, Arts-Litho, very good cond., (05-19-93, Butterfield, #2118, illus.), 17B, x 13 in., (448 x 330 mm.), lithograph in colors on wove (BP 1493, DM 3739, FR 12,596, Y 254,622).

$2246* *"Etude De Personnage", 1985,* #35/180, s., (10-18-92, Pescheteau, #81, illus.), 37 x 26¾ in., (94 x 68 cm.), lithograph in colors on velin (BP 1361, DM 3318, FR 11,269, Y 268,179).

$2046* *Etude De Tauromachie, 1987,* s., #13/180, p., pub. Galerie Maeght-Lelong, full margins, good cond., (12-03-92, Sotheby-London, #604, illus.), 27 x 19¾ in., (685 x 505 mm.), lithograph in colors on Arches (BP 1320, DM 3217, FR 10,982, Y 254,573).

BI *Etude De Tauromachie, 1987,* s., #16/180, p. and pub. Galerie Maeght-Lelong, full margins, good cond., est. BP 1,2/1,500, (06-30-93, Sotheby-London, #744, illus.), 27 x 19M, in., (686 x 505 mm.), color lithograph on Arches.

$1518* *Etude Du Corps Humain D'Apres Ingres,* s., #20/180, (05-27-93, Briest, #23), 34B, x 23Zzn in., (88 x 60.5 cm.), color lithograph on Arches (BP 972, DM 2436, FR 8210, Y 162,736).

$4263* *Etude Pour Un Portrait, 1987,* s., #51/180, p., pub. Galerie Maeght-Lelong, full margins, good cond., (12-03-92, Sotheby-London, #606, illus.), 23M, x 19M\ in., (682 x 505 mm.), lithograph in colors on Arches (BP 2750, DM 6704, FR 22,882, Y 530,422).

BI *Etude Pour Un Portrait, 1987,* s., #16/180, p. and pub. Galerie Maeght-Lelong, full margins, good cond., est. BP 1,5/2,000, (06-30-93, Sotheby-London, #748), 26B\ x 19B in., (676 x 498 mm.), color lithograph on wove.

$2402* *Etude Pour Un Portrait, 1987,* s., #40/180, p. and pub. Galerie Maeght-Lelong, full margins, good cond., scuffs, (06-30-93, Sotheby-London, #749, illus.), 26M, x 20¼ in., (683 x 514 mm.), color lithograph on Arches (BP 1610, DM 4097, FR 13,820, Y 257,366).

$2200* *Fallen Boxer,* s., #65/200, very good cond.?, (07-19-92, Bakker, #17, illus.), image 29B, x 21¾ in., (75.2 x 55.2 cm.), color lithograph (BP 1128, DM 3207, FR 10,843, Y 273,496).

BI *Figure At A Washbasin, 1976,* #4/100, s., prov., est. C$ 3/4,000, (11-16-92, Hodgins, #119, illus.), 18½ x 14¼ in., (47 x 36.2 cm.), color etching on paper.

$7492* *Man Shaving, 1987: Triptych,* s., num. 64/99, very good cond., (12-01-92, Christie-London, #560, illus.), each L. 23Zzn x 17B, in., (605 x 448 mm.), lithographs in colors on three separate sheets of Arches (BP 4950, DM 11,941, FR 40,695, Y 932,769).

$2270* *Mannliche Figur In Einem Treppenhaus, 1976,* s., (06-05-93, Bassenge, #5876, illus.), 19¼ x 14C, in., (48.9 x 36.5 cm.), color offset print on wove (BP 1494, DM 3680, FR 12,404, Y 243,510).

BI *"Metropolitan Museum Poster", 1975,* before edit. of 170 w/letters, pub. A. Manaranche, s. Francis Bacon in green ink, num. 24/200, pub. name in matrix, Metropolitan Museum dry stamp, good cond., full margins, creasing, soiling, est. $3/5000, (09-11-92, Skinner, #111, illus.), sight 45Z, x 34 in., (114.6 x 86.4 cm.), lithograph in colors on wove.

$1610* *Metropolitan Museum Poster, 1975,* before text, s. pen, #38/200, p. A. Manaranche Lith., full margins, apparently good cond., (05-15-93, Sotheby-NY, #908), 45Z, x 33M in., (114.6 x 86 cm.), lithograph in colors (BP 1047, DM 2590, FR 8703, Y 178,472).

$5027* *Oedipe Et Le Sphinx, 1984,* s., 26/150, drystamp, 1160 x 860mm, sh 1270 x 900, (06-28-93, Loudmer, #191, illus.), color lithograph on wove (BP 3366, DM 8542, FR 28,775, Y 533,369).

$2164* *Oedipus And The Sphinx, 1984,* s., i. H.C., blindstamp, margins, creases, very good cond., L. 1170 x860mm, (12-01-92, Christie-London, #562), lithograph in colors on wove (BP 1430, DM 3449, FR 11,754, Y 269,422).

$1665* *Oedipus And The Sphinx, 1984,* s., hors commerce impression, margins, staining, good impression, L. 1,172 x 860 mm, (12-01-92, Christie-London, #563), lithograph in colors on wove (BP 1100, DM 2654, FR 9044, Y 207,296).

BI *Le Portrait De John Edwards, 1986,* s., #17/150, est. FF 15/16,000, (11-16-92, Briest, #258), 32 x 23Mzn in., (81.3 x 59.5 cm.), lithograph in colors.

BI *Portrait Of John Edwards (Right Panel), 1986,* s., i. H.C., pub. L'Ire des Vents, margins, trimmed, creases in image, est. BP 8/1,200, (11-30-92, Phillips-London, #490), sheet 26¾ x 20¾ in., (679 x 527 mm.), lithograph in colors on Arches.

BI *Portrait, 1976,* watermark, s., from Rene Crevel, La Mysticite Charnelle, est. DM 9,000-, (06-19-93, Wachholtz, #365, illus.), 10Mzn x 8M, in., (26.5 x 22.5 cm.), color etching on copper print paper.

$3163* *Repons, 1989: Triptych,* s., num. 55/60, margins, fresh cond., (12-01-92, Christie-London, #561), each L. 24 x 18Z, in., (610 x 460 mm.), lithograph in colors on 3 separate sheets of Arches (BP 2090, DM 5041, FR 17,181, Y 393,800).

BI *Studie For Tauromachie, 1987,* 126/180, s., est. SF 5,9/ 6,800, (10-14-92, Germann, #126, illus.), 35Zzn x 25C in., (890 x 645 mm.), color lithograph.

$2217* *Study For A Human Body From A Drawing By Ingres, 1982,* s., #92/180, p., pub. Galerie Maeght-Lelong, full margins, good cond., (12-03-92, Sotheby-London, #605, illus.), sheet 34B, x 23M, in., (880 x 605 mm.), lithograph in colors on Arches (BP 1430, DM 3486, FR 11,900, Y 275,849).

BI *Study For A Human Body From A Drawing By Ingres, 1982,* s., #32/180, p. and pub. Galerie Maeght-Lelong, 1984, full margins, good cond., est. BP 1,4/1,600, (06-30-93, Sotheby-London, #745, illus.), 24C, x 18¼ in., (619 x 464 mm.), color lithograph.

BI *Study For Bullfight N.1, 1978,* s., #145/150, perfect cond., est. FF60/80,000, (05-27-93, Briest, #22, illus.), 62B, x 47¼ in., (159 x 120 cm.), color lithograph.

$10,925* *Study For Bullfight No. 1, 1978,* s., #72/150, pub. Metropolitan Museum of Art, margins, sig. faded, very good cond.?, (05-11-93, Christie-NY, #357, illus.), borderline 49B, x 45¼ in., (126 x 114.9 cm.), color lithograph on wove (BP 6974, DM 17,210, FR 57,988, Y 1,201,738).

$3220* *Study For Portrait Of John Edwards, 1987,* s., #47/180, pub. Marlborough Graphics, full margins, excell. cond., (05-11-93, Christie-NY, #360, illus.), sheet 37¼ x 26¾ in., (946 x 679 mm.), color lithograph on Arches (BP 2056, DM 5072, FR 17,091, Y 354,196).

$3775* *Study For Self-Portrait, 1973,* before letters, s., #40/80, lithograpgh by G. Diamaiuto, p. by Mourlot, full margins, good cond., handling creases, scratch, discoloration, (06-30-93, Sotheby-London, #746, illus.), 33C, x 25 in., (848 x 635 mm.), color lithograph on Arches (BP 2530, DM 6439, FR 21,720, Y 404,479).

BI *Study For Self-Portrait, 1980: Set Of Three,* s., #55/150, blindstamp printer, Arts-Litho, pub. Maeght, full margins, very good cond., soiling, est. $5,5/6,500, (05-19-93, Butterfield, #2117), 18½ x 40¾ in., (47 x 103.5 cm.), lithograph in colors on one sheet of Arches.

$3025* *Study From Portrait Of Pope Innocent X, 1965,* s., annot. H.C., pub. IRCAM, full margins, good cond., (02-24-93, Butterfield, #3000, illus.), lithograph on Arches (BP 2109, DM 4911, FR 16,648, Y 354,964).

$4950* *Three Studies For A Self Portrait, 1980: Set Of Three,* s., #80/150, pub. Maeght Editeur, full margins, excellent cond., (11-09-92, Christie-NY, #239, illus.), 18½ x 40¾ in., (47 x 103.5 cm.), colored lithograph on 1 sheet of wove (BP 3273, DM 7902, FR 26,699, Y 614,296).

$5520* *Three Studies For A Self Portrait, 1980: Three,* s., #60/150, pub. Maeght Editeur, full margins, excell. cond., (05-11-93, Christie-NY, #358, illus.), sheet 18½ x 40¾ in., (47 x 103.5 cm.), color lithograph on one sheet of Arches (BP 3524, DM 8696, FR 29,299, Y 607,194).

$4950* *Three Studies For A Self Portrait, 1981,* s., #63/150, blind stamp, pub. Editions de la difference, full margins, good cond., (11-07-92, Sotheby-NY, #513, illus.), 18½ x 40¾ in., (47 x 103.5 cm.), three lithographs p. in colors, on one sheet (BP 3236, DM 7904, FR 26,713, Y 610,960).

$5500* *Three Studies For A Self-Portrait, 1980: Set Of Three,* s., #79/150, blindstamp p. Arts-Litho, pub. Maeght editeur, full margins, very good cond., surface soiling, (10-28-92, Butterfield, #2896), 18½ x 40¾ in., (47 x 103.5 cm.), color lithograph on 1 sheet of Arches (BP 3504, DM 8494, FR 28,841, Y 674,847).

$4600* *Three Studies For A Self-Portrait, 1981,* s., #57/150, blindstamp Arts-Litho, pub. Editions de la difference, full margins, good cond., creases, (05-15-93, Sotheby-NY, #909, illus.), sheet 18½ x 40¾ in., (47 x 103.5 cm.), lithograph p. in colors on one sheet (BP 2991, DM 7399, FR 24,865, Y 509,921).

$4620* *Triptych (Metropolitan Triptych), 1981: Set Of Three,* s., #93/99, pub. Ediciones Poligrafa, full margins, excellent cond., (11-09-92, Christie-NY, #241, illus.), 24B, x 43½ in., (62.5 x 110.5 cm.), colored aquatint on 1 sheet of wove (BP 3055, DM 7375, FR 24,919, Y 573,343).

BI *Triptych 1974-77: Right Panel, 1981,* s., #31/99, pub. Ediciones Poligrafa, full margins, good cond., print glued, skinned spots, est. $2/3,000, (02-11-93, Sotheby-NY, #306), 15¼ x 11B, in., (387 x 295 mm.), color aquatint on Arches.

BI *Triptych 1986-87, 1988,* s., #99/99, pub. Poligrafa, full margins, good cond., creases, soiling, est. $5/6,000, (05-15-93, Sotheby-NY, #911, illus.), 35¼ x 24B, in., (89.5 x 62.5 cm.), aquatint in colors.

$6325* *Triptych Inspired By Orestia Of Aeschlys, 1981,* s., #68/150, blind stamp, pub. Editions de la difference, full margins, good cond., creases, (11-07-92, Sotheby-NY, #514, illus.), 21¼ x 41 in., (54 x 104.1 cm.), three lithographs p. in colors, on one sheet (BP 4135, DM 10,099, FR 34,134, Y 780,671).

BI *Triptych Inspired By Orestia Of Aeschylus, 1981,* s., #80/150, blindstamp Arts-Litho, pub. Editions de la difference, full margins, good cond., est. $5,5/6,500, (05-15-93, Sotheby-NY, #910, illus.), 21 x 40¾ in., (53.3 x 103.5 cm.), lithographs printed in colors on one sheet.

$6005* *Triptych, 1983: Three,* s., #43/180, p. and pub. Galerie Maeght-Lelong, full margins, good cond., (06-30-93, Sotheby-London, #742, illus.), each sh c. 34 x 23M, in., (864 x 606 mm.), color lithograph on Arches (BP 4025, DM 10,242, FR 34,551, Y 643,416).

BI *Triptych, August 1972, 1989: Three,* s., #7/180, p. and pub. Galerie Maeght-Lelong, margins, good cond., est. BP 3/4,000, (06-30-93, Sotheby-London, #747), 35C, x 24B, in., (899 x 625 mm.), color lithograph on wove.

$7206* *Triptych, August 1972, 1989: Three,* each s., #30/180, p. and pub. Galerie Maeght-Lelong, full margins, good cond., scuff at center, (06-30-93, Sotheby-London, #743, illus.), 35C, x 24B\ in., (899 x 625 mm.), color lithograph on wove (BP 4830, DM 12,291, FR 41,461, Y 772,099).

BI *Triptych: Reponse, 1989: Three,* s., #57/60, full margins, good cond., est. BP 4/5,000, (06-30-93, Sotheby-London, #741, illus.), each sh 24C, x 18Z, in., (619 x 460 mm.), color lithograph.

$4675* *Triptyche L'Orestie D'Eschyle, 1980: Set Of Three,* s., #84/150, blindstamp p. Arts-Litho, pub. Maeght editeur, full margins, very good cond., (10-28-92, Butterfield, #2897, illus.), 21 x 40B, in., (53.3 x 103.2 cm.), color lithograph on 1 sheet of Arches (BP 2979, DM 7220, FR 24,515, Y 573,620).

BI *Triptychon, Selbstportraits,* watermark, s., A.P., i., est. DM 12,000-, (06-19-93, Wachholtz, #364), 12M, x 36B in., (32.7 x 93 cm.), color lithograph on thick copper print paper.

BI *Triptyque 1983 Droite,* s., #50/180, est. FF 8/9,000, (11-16-92, Briest, #259), 34¼ x 24 in., (87 x 61 cm.), lithograph in colors.

BI *Triptyque L'Orestie D'Eschyle, 1980: Set Of Three,* s., #85/150, pub. Maeght Editeur, full margins, excellent cond., est.$4,5/5,500, (11-09-92, Christie-NY, #240, illus.), 21 x 40B, in., (53.3 x 103.2 cm.), colored lithograph on 1 sheet of Arches.

BI *Triptyque L'Orestie D'Eschyle, 1980: Three,* s., #85/150, pub. Maeght Editeur, full margins, excell. cond., est. $4,5/5,500, (05-11-93, Christie-NY, #359, illus.), sheet 21 x 40B, in., (53.3 x 103.2 cm.), color lithograph on one sheet of Arches.

$4049* *Triptyque Sur Fond Orange: Trois,* s., #45/180, perfect cond., (05-27-93, Briest, #26), each 33Mn x 23B, in., (85 x 60 cm.), color lithograph (BP 2593, DM 6497, FR 21,898, Y 434,069).

$3085* *"Tryptique Aout 72/87",* proof #19/180, s., (04-04-93, Pescheteau, #156, illus.), 35Mn x 24Mn in., (90 x 62 cm.), color lithograph on wove (BP 2032, DM 4958, FR 16,840, Y 351,247).

$5968* *Tryptych, 1983: Three,* s., left and right panels #40/180, central panel #24/180, p., pub. Galerie Maeght-Lelong, full margins, good cond., (12-03-92, Sotheby-London, #603, illus.), each sheet approx. 34 x 24 in., (863 x 612 mm.), lithographs in colors on Arches (BP 3850, DM 9385, FR 32,034, Y 742,566).

BI *Tryptyche L'Orestie D'Eschyle, 1980: Three,* s., num. 87/150, pub. Maeght, blindstamp of printer Arts-Litho, full-margins, good cond., creases, surface soiling, est. $5/7,000, (02-24-93, Butterfield, #3001, illus.), 21 x 40B, in., (53.3 x 103.2 cm.), lithograph in colors on 1 sheet of Arches.

BACON, Peggy American 1895-1987

$2090* *Frenzied Effort (F. 57), 1925,* s., t., d., large margins, good cond., foxing, soiling, (10-28-92, Butterfield, #2505, illus.), 5M, x 9 in., (149 x 229 mm.), drypoint on cream wove (BP 1332, DM 3228, FR 10,960, Y 256,442).

BI *The Haunted House (F. 134), 1940,* s., t., pub. AAA, margins, good cond., light-staining, tape, staining, tear, soiling, est. $5/700, (05-19-93, Butterfield, #1784), 7 x 4M, in., (178 x 124 mm.), drypoint on wove.

$440* *"Haunted House",* s., t., margins, glued down, tape, foxing, toning, excell. cond., (12-12-92, Litchfield, #15), 6Zn x 4Zn in., (17.3 x 12.4 cm.), etching (BP 282, DM 693, FR 2376, Y 54,449).

BI *Outskirts Of Town (F. 184), 1952,* s., d., t., full margins, good cond., rubbed, hinge remains in sticker remains, soiling, est. $7/900, (05-19-93, Butterfield, #1785), 9An x 7Bn in., (252 x 202 mm.), etching on wove.

BI *The Priceless Find,* s., est. $4/600, (09-24-92, Mystic, #44A), 8 x 6 in., (20.3 x 15.2 cm.), lithograph.

BI *"The Priceless Find",* s. Peggy Bacon, t., good cond., crease, est. $7/900, (03-12-93, Skinner, #38, illus.), 8 x 6 in., (20.3 x 15.2 cm.), lithograph on wove.

$743* *The Promenade Deck, 1920,* s., t., full margins, good cond., pub. New Republic, 1924, (11-12-92, Freemn/Fine Art, #26), 6 x 8½ in., (15.2 x 21.6 cm.), drypoint on wove paper (BP 488, DM 1177, FR 3971, Y 92,126).

$468* *The Promenade Deck, 1920,* s., (06-11-93, Freemn/Fine Art, #11, illus.), 5M, x 8M, in., (14.9 x 22.5 cm.), drypoint (BP 307, DM 761, FR 2564, Y 49,655).

BAECHLER, Donald American b. 1956

BI *"Composition With Guitar" and "Tree", 1988: Two,* s., d., #9/22, pub. Pace Editions, excell. cond.?, est. $2,5/3,000, (05-11-93, Christie-NY, #362, illus.), each sheet 34½ x 34½ in., (876 x 876 mm.), color screenprint and woodcut on hand-made paper pulp in colors.

$4180* *"Composition With Guitar", "Composition With Suitcase" and "Tree", 1988: Set Of Three,* s., d., #6/22, pub. Pace Editions, full sheets, excellent cond., (11-09-92, Christie-NY, #242, illus.), 34½ x 34¼ in., (876 x 870 mm.), screenprint and woodcut in colors on handmade colored paper pulp (BP 2764, DM 6673, FR 22,546, Y 518,739).

$3850* *Conversation, 1990,* s., d., #5/30, pub. AC & T Corporation, full margins, soft crease, excell. cond., (11-09-92, Christie-NY, #243, illus.), 59 x 58 in., (149.9 x 147.3 cm.), colored woodcut on Japanese (BP 2545, DM 6146, FR 20,766, Y 477,786).

$2415* *Conversation, 1990,* s., d. #18/30, pub. AC&T Corp., full margins, good cond., (05-15-93, Sotheby-NY, #913, illus.), sheet 59 x 58Z, in., (149.9 x 147.6 cm.), woodcut in colors on Japanese (BP 1570, DM 3885, FR 13,054, Y 267,709).

$4300* *Donald Baechler, 1984: Six,* portfolio, pub. Delano Greenridge Editions, HC, mono., d. HC, (05-27-93, Lempertz, #585, illus.), 28n x 28Mn in., (72.5 x 72.3 cm.), 6 screenprints w/unique hand-painted variations, 6 serigraphs (BP 2754, DM 6900, FR 23,256, Y 460,978).

BI *Faces, 1986: Set Of Three,* each s., d., #3/12, p. Radierwerkstatt Kurt Zein, pub. Gallery Krinzinger, full margins, good cond., in orig. portfolio, est. BP 1,4/1,800,

(12-03-92, Sotheby-London, #608, illus.), two 8B, x 8Z in., (218 x 207 mm.), one 6½ x 6Z, in., (218 x 207 mm.), aquatints on wove.

BI *Family, 1986: Set Of Four,* s., d., #10/12, p. Radierwerkstatt Kurt Zein, pub. Gallery Krinzinger, full margins, good cond., in orig. portfolio, est. BP 1,8/2,200, (12-03-92, Sotheby-London, #607, illus.), three 13¼ x 9¾ in., (336 x 246 mm.), one 8½ x 8 in., (336 x 246 mm.), soft-ground etchings w/aquatint, on wove.

$330* *Flowers And Trees (For Klaus Wittmann), 1990,* s., d., num. 44/50, pub. Spring Street Workshop, full margins, apparently very good cond., (02-24-93, Butterfield, #3184), 15 x 9 in., (381 x 229 mm.), relief print on Chine colle attached to BFK Rives (BP 230, DM 536, FR 1816, Y 38,723).

BI *Flowers And Trees, For Klaus Wittmann, 1990,* s., d., #44/50, pub. Spring Street Workshop, full margins, very goodcond.?, est. $1/1,500, (10-28-92, Butterfield, #2899), 15 x 9 in., (381 x 229 mm.), relief print w/chine colle (pasted) on BFK Rives.

BI *Fruits, 1990: Five,* complete portfolio, s., #19/35, pub. Edition Works, good cond., est.$4/5,000, (05-15-93, Sotheby-NY, #912, illus.), each sheet 35C, x 27½ in., (89.9 x 69.9 cm.), lithograph in colors w/relief printing on Nepali handmade.

$3220* *Ricky's Rice Queen, 1990,* s., d., #9/30, pub. AC and T Corporation, full margins, good cond., (02-11-93, Sotheby-NY, #307), sheet 58¼ x 58Mzn in., (148 x 148.5 cm.), color woodcut on Japanese (BP 2272, DM 5334, FR 18,049, Y 388,186).

BI *Tangram, From, 1990,* s., d., #18/34, pub. Baron/Boisante, full margins, very good cond., in orig. portfolio, est. $8/1,200, (10-28-92, Butterfield, #2900), 11 x 8½ in., (279 x 216 mm.), color etching w/aquatint on white wove.

BI *Untitled, 1985,* s., d., #1/20, est. DM 1,800-, (05-27-93, Lempertz, #583, illus.), 19M, x 19Zzn in., (50.5 x 50.3 cm.), color linocut on Japan.

BI *Untitled, 1985,* s., d., #1/20, est. DM 1,800-, (05-27-93, Lempertz, #584), 19Zzn x 19M, in., (50 x 50.5 cm.), color linocut on Japan.

BAEDER, John American b. 1938

$303* *"Shorty's Shortstop", 1987,* s., d. Baeder 87, num. 90/200, very good cond., full margins, handling, wrinkling, (09-11-92, Skinner, #120, illus.), 15Z, x 21¼ in., (38.4 x 54 cm.), photo-silkscreen/lithograph on wove (BP 157, DM 436, FR 1482, Y 37,542).

BAER, Gil d. 1931

$241* *Elysee Montmartre (...) Bal Masque Dimanche, c. 1895,* Paris, Imp. des Services Parisiens, cond. B+, (06-11-93, Boisgirard, #41), 51Czn x 37 in., (130 x 94 cm.), poster (BP 158, DM 392, FR 1321, Y 25,570).

BAERTLING, Olle 1911-1981

$1963* *Diagonal Composition,* s., 1974-80, EA, (05-25-93, AB Stockholm, #5), 23¼ x 36Zzn in., (59 x 93.5 cm.), serigraph in colors (BP 1272, DM 3197, FR 10,762, Y 214,559, SK 2860).

$3246* *Diagonal Composition,* s., 1969-74, EA, (05-25-93, AB Stockholm, #4), 36 x 17Zzn in., (91.5 x 45.5 cm.), color serigraph (BP 2104, DM 5287, FR 17,796, Y 354,793, SK 4730).

$2415* *Diagonal Composition,* s., #38/100, (05-25-93, AB Stockholm, #3), 38Czn x 19Bzn in., (97 x 49 cm.), serigraph in colors (BP 1565, DM 3933, FR 13,240, Y 263,963, SK 3520).

$843* *Diagonal Composition,* s., 1969-1974, 49/100, (12-04-92, AB Stockholm, #7003), 36 x 17Zzn in., (91.5 x 45.5 cm.), serigraph in colors (BP 541, DM 1343, FR 4554, Y 105,243, SK 5720).

$811* *Diagonal Composition,* 1964-1974, 449/100, s., (12-04-92, AB Stockholm, #7002), 36 x 17Zzn in., (91.5 x 45.5 cm.), serigraph in colors (BP 520, DM 1292, FR 4381, Y 101,248, SK 5500).

$1638* *Diagonal Composition,* s., d. 1962-74, EA, (04-17-93, Falkkloos, #14, illus.), 35Mzn x 18Z\ in., (90 x 46 cm.), serigraph in colors (BP 1064, DM 2620, FR 8849, Y 182,142, SK 12,100).

$762* *Diagonal Composition,* s., EA, 1962-1974, (12-04-92, AB Stockholm, #7005), 36 x 18Z, in., (91.5 x 46 cm.), serigraph in colors (BP 489, DM 1214, FR 4117, Y 95,131, SK 5170).

$649* *Diagonal Composition,* s., 1969-1974, EA, (12-04-92, AB Stockholm, #7004), 36 x 17Zzn in., (91.5 x 45.5 cm.), serigraph in colors (BP 416, DM 1034, FR 3506, Y 81,024, SK 4400).

$762* *Diagonal Composition, 1962-1974,* E/A, s., (12-04-92, AB Stockholm, #7005), 36 x 18Z, in., (91.5 x 46 cm.), serigraph in colors (BP 489, DM 1214, FR 4117, Y 95,131, SK 5170).

$811* *Diagonal Composition, 1967-1974,* s., 49/100, (12-04-92, AB Stockholm, #7002), 36 x 17Zzn in., (91.5 x 45.5 cm.), serigraph in colors (BP 520, DM 1292, FR 4381, Y 101,248, SK 5500).

$649* *Diagonal Composition, 1969-1974,* E/A, s., (12-04-92, AB Stockholm, #7004), 36 x 17Zzn in., (91.5 x 45.5 cm.), serigraph in colors (BP 416, DM 1034, FR 3506, Y 81,024, SK 4400).

$843* *Flags For America'a Cup,* s., 165/250, (12-04-92, AB Stockholm, #7006), portfolio (BP 541, DM 1343, FR 4554, Y 105,243, SK 5720).

BAES, H.

BI *Bruxelles-Exposition, 1897,* minor restoration, added color, linen-backed, est. $700/1,000, (04-29-93, Swann, #131), 41 x 60 in., (104.1 x 152.4 cm.), color lithographed poster.

BAHNSEN, Axel 1907-1978

BI *Oklahoma Asphalt Plant,* c. 1945, s., t., annot. in ink, MIT exhib. label, est. $1/1,500, (10-13-92, Christie-NY, #113, illus.), 16 x 20 in., (40.6 x 50.8 cm.), photograph, gelatin silver print.

BAHUET, Louis Alfred and Gustave SURAND

$241* *Royal Muscat, Aperitif Reconstituant A Base De Lecithine, c. 1900,* Paris, Imp. and Pub. Verneau, cond. B+, (06-11-93, Boisgirard, #42), 53Azn x 38¾ in., (137 x 98.5 cm.), poster (BP 158, DM 392, FR 1321, Y 25,570).

BAIER, Jean b. 1932

$737* *Portfolio, 1971: Ten,* num., s., #XVIII/XX, s., Edition Galerie Ziegler, (09-04-92, Germann, #227), each 23½ x 23½ in., (597 x 597 mm.), color serigraph and multiple (BP 369, DM 1033, FR 3516, Y 90,719, SF 920).

BAILEY, Bill

$440* *Ringling Bros. And Barnum And Bailey, 1945,* Litho in USA, A- cond., closed tears, tape mark, written 1952, (08-06-92, Swann, #99, illus.), 27¾ x 21 in., (70.5 x 53.3 cm.), (BP 230, DM 650, FR 2196, Y 56,122).

BAILEY, David English b. 1938

$654* *Catherine Bailey And Angie Hill, 1990,* s., d., #5/12, 218 x 182mm, (05-07-93, Sotheby-London, #377, illus.), photograph, toned silver print (BP 414, DM 1034, FR 3484, Y 72,011).

$654* *Catherine Bailey In Towel Turban, 1990,* s., d., #3/25, 246 x 200mm, (05-07-93, Sotheby-London, #378, illus.), photograph, toned silver print (BP 414, DM 1034, FR 3484, Y 72,011).

BI *Catherine Bailey, Two Portraits With Towel Turban, 1990,* s., d., #3/25, 550 x 730mm, est. BP 800/1,200, (05-07-93, Sotheby-London, #375, illus.), photograph, platinum print on watercolor paper.

BI *Catherine With Skull, 1989,* s., #5/9 verso, est. BP 5/700, (10-29-92, Christie-London, #202, illus.), 5Z, x 3½ in., (13 x 8.9 cm.), photograph, toned gelatin silver print.

$1270* *Catherine, St. Paul De Vence, 1983,* s., (05-06-93, Christie-London, #118, illus.), 4½ x 6C, in., photograph, unique sun print (BP 805, DM 2000, FR 6734, Y 139,729).

BI *Figure Study,* 1960s, s., est. $4/600, (05-23-93, Butterfield, #3306), 10 x 15 in., photograph, gelatin silver print.

$254* *"Isle Of Skye 82",* s., d. D. Bailey 82, flush mounted on card, s., stamped photog.'s credit, 304 x 406mm, (05-07-93, Sotheby-London, #376, illus.), photograph, silver print (BP 161, DM 402, FR 1353, Y 27,967).

BI *"Scream",* 1983/1990, s., edit. 24/100 margin, est. $1,0/1,200, (11-16-92, Butterfield, #5841, illus.), 13 x 10 in., (330.8 x 254.5 mm.), photograph, platinum print.

BAILLIE, "Captain" William   English 1723-1792
   BI *Tacet Et Loquitor,* after Rembrandt, est. $100/150, (02-04-93, Sloan, #379), 4M, x 12 in., (12.4 x 30.5 cm.), sepia etching.

BAILLIE, James
$330* *"General Andrew Jackson-The Hero Of New Orleans",* pub. c. 1850, (12-05-92, Neal, #557), image 12½ x 9½ in., (31.8 x 24.1 cm.), hand-colored lithograph (BP 207, DM 514, FR 1753, Y 40,887).

BAILLIE, William   English 1723-1792
   BI *Tacet Et Loquitur,* after Rembrandt Van Rijn, est. $250/350, (10-30-92, Sloan, #1935), 6M, x 12 in., (17.5 x 30.5 cm.), sepia etching.
   BI *Tacet Et Loquitur,* after Rembrandt Van Rijn, est. $125/175, (12-10-92, Sloan, #946), 4M, x 12 in., (12.4 x 30.5 cm.), sepia etching.

BAINBRIDGE, John   1918-1978
$284* *Royal London, Buckingham Palace, London Underground, 1953,* excell. cond., lit., (02-04-93, Christie-S. Ken, #56, illus.), 39½ x 24½ in., (100.3 x 62.2 cm.), color lithograph backed on linen (BP 198, DM 468, FR 1586, Y 35,328).

BAIRD, S.F., T.M. BREWER and R. RIDGWAY
$1045* *A History Of North American Birds, Land Birds, 1875,* plates and woodcuts in text, 4to, John Walton Livermore Estate, (12-04-92, Doyle, #322, illus.), (BP 670, DM 1664, FR 5646, Y 130,462).

BAIREI, Kono   ac. 1884-1895
$101* *"Vogel Und Beeren",* Format Oban, (04-27-93, Dorotheum, #244), 9B, x 13Ⴀxn in., (24.5 x 35.4 cm.), color woodcut (BP 64, DM 160, FR 541, Y 11,319, SC 1120).

BAISHI, Qi   ac. lst half 20th cent.
   BI *Darstellung Eines Blutenzweiges,* s., seal, (04-27-93, Dorotheum, #421), 12Cxn x 9¼ in., (31 x 23.5 cm.), woodcut.
   BI *Elster Auf Einem Blutenzweig,* t., s., seal, (04-27-93, Dorotheum, #420), 12Cxn x 9¼ in., (31 x 23.5 cm.), .
$503* *"Flusskrebse Und Langusten",* s., signs of wear, (04-27-93, Dorotheum, #412, illus.), 14Ⴀxn x 26C, in., (38 x 67 cm.), color woodcut (BP 320, DM 796, FR 2694, Y 56,371, SC 5600).
$503* *Pflanzen- Und Tierstudien, c. 1950: Album Of Twelve,* s., seal, (04-27-93, Dorotheum, #417, illus.), 12B, x 17Ⴀxn in., (32 x 45 cm.), woodcut (BP 320, DM 796, FR 2694, Y 56,371, SC 5600).

BAJ, Enrico   Italian b. 1924
   BI *Ca,* book and portfolio w/title-page, #50/135, s., num. w/ diamond point, s. and #, pub. Soleil Noir, good cond., est. BP 1,6/2,000, (06-30-93, Sotheby-London, #750, illus.), portfolio 21B, x 15 in., (549 x 381 mm.), text on Arches, 5 color silkscreens on rhodoid.
$232* *Composition, 1976,* s., 41/100, from Pour Jorn portfolio, (09-30-92, Kunsthallen, #27), color lithograph (BP 131, DM 329, FR 1113, Y 27,841, DK 1265).
   BI *Dames Et Generaux, 1964,* book, each plate s., #59/100, w/t. page by Marcel Duchamp, s. by artist and Breton, num. 59, pub. Berggruen, and Schwarz, full margins, good cond.,est. BP 2/2,500, (12-03-92, Sotheby-London, #610, illus.), 10 etchings, nine p. in colors, one w/collage on wove, two plates onapplique supported on wove.
$233* *Le Depart A La Guerre (Petit 271), 1970,* s., num., wear, (09-25-92, Granier, #2744), 15C, x 21Ⴀxn in., (39 x 54.5 cm.), sheet 19Ⴀxn x 27Ⴀxn in., (39 x 54.5 cm.), color etching on hand-made (BP 136, DM 345, FR 1168, Y 28,123).
$361* *Figurengruppe Mit Maske,* s., dusty, (11-28-92, Schoppmann, #362), 24½ x 23¼ in., (62.2 x 59 cm.), color serigraph w/Glimmer on cardboard (BP 238, DM 575, FR 1952, Y 44,928).
$413* *"Girl" and "General": Two,* each s., General num. 29/100, Woman annot. XV/L, full margins, good cond. creases, (02-24-93, Butterfield, #3185), 27¼ x 18 in., (692 x 457 mm.), 27 x 19½ in., (692 x 457 mm.), lithograph in colors on Arches (BP 288, DM 670, FR 2273, Y 48,463).
$110* *Lace Figure,* s., num. 143/190, Carl E. Kaufman Estate, (09-20-92, Hindman, #821), 14 x 12¼ in., (35.6 x 31.1

cm.), color etching and aquatint (BP 64, DM 163, FR 558, Y 13,595).
   BI *Military Strategist, 1967,* epreuve d'essai, s., i., est. SF 6/800, (11-13-92, Koller, #5243), 25B xn x 20½ in., (66 x 52 cm.), lithograph on wove.
$388* *Tete De Femme (Petit 270), 1970,* s., num., (09-25-92, Granier, #2743), 21¼ x 14C, in., (54 x 36.5 cm.), sheet 27C, x 19M, in., (54 x 36.5 cm.), color etching on hand-made (BP 227, DM 575, FR 1945, Y 46,832).
$892* *Triptycum: Portfolio,* s., 27/60, (12-04-92, AB Stockholm, #7007), 20½ x 15¾ in., (52 x 40 cm.), aquatint in colors (BP 572, DM 1421, FR 4819, Y 111,361, SK 6050).
$233* *Viol Du General (Petit 272), 1970,* s., num., wear, (09-25-92, Granier, #2745), 14Ⴀxn x 19Ⴀxn in., (37 x 49 cm.), sheet 19M, x 27Ⴀxn in., (37 x 49 cm.), color etching on hand-made (BP 136, DM 345, FR 1168, Y 28,123).

BAKST, Leon   Russian 1866-1924
$619* *Ballett-Figuren Zu "Puppenfee" (Spencer 28): Twelve,* num. 1-12, (09-14-92, Venator/Hansten, #2433, illus.), 5Ⴀxn x 3Ⴀxn in., (14.1 x 9.1 cm.), color lithograph, partly heightened w/gold (BP 327, DM 920, FR 3118, Y 76,971).

BAKST, Leon (after)   Russian 1886-1924
$165* *Lady's Costume Design,* s., d. 1922 in stone, (10-30-92, Sloan, #891), 12B, x 9¾ in., (32.1 x 24.8 cm.), lithograph heightened w/gouache (BP 106, DM 254, FR 861, Y 20,438).

BALDACCINI (called CESAR)   b. 1921
   BI *"Compression Sur Fond Noir",* HC, s., est. FF1,000/1,500, (04-04-93, Pescheteau, #177), 12Cxn x 9Ⴀxn in., (31 x 24.6 cm.), color lithograph.
$160* *"Homme-Cheval",* E.A., s., (04-04-93, Pescheteau, #178), 22Ⴀxn x 29Ⴀ, in., (56 x 74 cm.), photolithograph on wove (BP 105, DM 257, FR 873, Y 18,217).

BALDESSARI, John   American b. 1931
   BI *Aligned Trumpeteering, 1988,* s., d., #30/50, pub. Artists Space, blindstamp printer, Cirrus, fullmargins, good cond., est. $5/700, (05-19-93, Butterfield, #2119), 21¼ x 24½ in., (540 x 622 mm.), lithograph in colors on Somerset wove.
$649* *Aligned Trumpeteering, 1988,* #25/50, pencil s., (11-20-92, Lempertz, #437), sh 24B, x 27½ in., (62.5 x 69.8 cm.), lithograph in red on offset lithograph on Velin (BP 427, DM 1035, FR 3485, Y 80,711).
$1760* *Blue Master Stroke Over Red Diagram And Two Cowboys,* s., #23/60, pub. Printed Matter, full margins, very good cond.?, (10-28-92, Butterfield, #2901), 32 x 33 in., (813 x 838 mm.), offset lithograph w/silkscreen in colors on wove (BP 1121, DM 2718, FR 9229, Y 215,951).
$13,800* *Body And Soul,* exec. 1989, prov., (02-23-93, Sotheby-NY, #338, illus.), 54 x 48 in., (137.2 x 121.9 cm.), b/w photograph w/vinyl paint, mounted on board (BP 9453, DM 22,294, FR 75,616, Y 1,611,773).
$24,200* *Cutting Ribbon, Man In Wheelchair, Painting,* exec. 1988, prov., (10-08-92, Christie-NY, #180, illus.), 75B, x 35B, in., (192.1 x 90.5 cm.), acrylic on black and white photograph (BP 14,400, DM 35,794, FR 121,486, Y 2,940,462).
$4950* *The Fallen Easel, 1988,* s., d., #5/35, pub. Multiples, Inc./Cirrus Editions, good cond., (11-07-92, Sotheby-NY, #515, illus.), nine part lithograph/silkscreen p. in colors, on four sheets of Arches/five pieces of photo-sensitized aluminum (BP 3236, DM 7904, FR 26,713, Y 610,960).
$4025* *The Fallen Easel, 1988: Nine,* s. on 1, d., AP, num., co-pub. Multiples, Inc. and Cirrus Editionsull sheets, (02-11-93, Sotheby-NY, #308, illus.), part lithograph and silkscreen p. in colors on 4 sheets Arches paper& 5 pieces photo-sensitized aluminum (BP 2840, DM 6667, FR 22,562, Y 485,232).
   BI *Falling Star, 1989-90,* s., #16/45, pub. Brooke Alexander Editions, full margins, excell. cond., est. $3/4,000, (05-11-93, Christie-NY, #365, illus.), sheet 64¾ x 23 in., (164.5 x 58.4 cm.), color photogravure and aquatint on wove.
   BI *Falling Star, 1989-90,* s., #8/45, blindstamp printer, Branstead Studio, full margins, very good cond., est. $2/3,000, (05-19-93, Butterfield, #2123), sh. 62½ x 20B, in.,

(158.8 x 52.4 cm.), photogravure and aquatint in colors on wove.

$809* *Five Pickles (With Fingerprints) In The Shape Of A Hand, 1975,* s., t., d., #10/60, pub. John Baldessari/Multiples inc., from Artistsand Photographs album, full margins, creasing, discoloration, (10-15-92, Sotheby-London, #70, illus.), 20 x 24 in., five collaged photographs in colors on one sheet on wove (BP 495, DM 1204, FR 4084, Y 97,061).

$4025* *Heaven And Hell, 1988: Two,* each sheet s., #15/45, pub. Peter Blum Editions, full margins, good cond., (02-11-93, Sotheby-NY, #309, illus.), each sheet approx. 47B, x 31½ in., (121 x 80 cm.), diptych, aquatint, roulett, etching p. in colors on 2 sheets white wove (BP 2840, DM 6667, FR 22,562, Y 485,232).

$2300* *Helmsman (With Various Fires), 1989-90,* s., #8/45, blindstamp printer, Branstead Studio, full margins, very good cond., (05-19-93, Butterfield, #2122, illus.), total sh. 98 x 55 in., (248.9 x 139.7 cm.), photogravure and aquatint in colors on 3 sheets of wove (BP 1493, DM 3739, FR 12,596, Y 254,622).

BI *Life's Balance (With Money), 1989-90,* s., #8/45, blindstamp printer, Branstead Studio, full margins, very good cond., est. $2/3,000, (05-19-93, Butterfield, #2124, illus.), sh. 51 x 42½ in., (129.5 x 108 cm.), photogravure and aquatint in colors on wove.

$614* *Love And Work, 1991,* s., (11-28-92, Schoppmann, #363), 23¾ x 9Czn in., (60.4 x 23.4 cm.), photogravure and color etching on handmade cardboard (BP 405, DM 978, FR 3321, Y 76,416).

BI *The Mondrian Story (Version III),* exec. 1973, prov., exhib., Sylvio Perlstein Coll., est. $10/15,000, (11-18-92, Sotheby-NY, #200A, illus.), 27Z, x 33Z, in., (68.9 x 84.1 cm.), photographs mounted on board w/typed text.

BI *Movie Scenario: By Sound Effect (A Murder Mystery),* exec. 1973, Sylvio Perlstein Coll., est. $20/25,000, (11-18-92, Sotheby-NY, #201, illus.), each 20 x 16 in., (50.8 x 40.6 cm.), seven photographs framed in metal.

BI *Object With Flaw, 1988,* s., #8/35, co-pub. Cirrus and Multiples, good cond., est. $4,5/5,500, (05-19-93, Butterfield, #2120, illus.), lithograph and silkscreen in colors on 3 sheets of Arches and 1 pieceof plexiglas.

$288* *Object, With Flaw, 1988: Three,* s., #3/35, co-pub. Multiples, Inc. and Cirrus Editions, excell. cond.?, plexiglas split, (05-11-93, Christie-NY, #363, illus.), overall sheet 52 x 109 in., (132.1 x 276.9 cm.), three-part color lithograph and screenprint on three sheets of Arches and one piece of plexiglas (BP 184, DM 454, FR 1529, Y 31,680).

BI *Rollercoaster, 1989,* s., #8/45, blindstamp printer, full margins, very good cond., est. $1,5/2,500, (05-19-93, Butterfield, #2121), sh. 39 x 67½ in., (99.1 x 171.5 cm.), photogravure and aquatint in colors on wove.

BI *Studio, 1988,* s., #46/150, Cirrus Editions blindstamp, pub. ART/LA 88, full margins, excell. cond., est. $2/2,500, (05-11-93, Christie-NY, #364, illus.), sheet 30¼ x 38C, in., (768 x 975 mm.), color offset lithograph w/ screenprint on Somerset.

$48,300* *Triangle, Rectangle, Circle,* exec. 1984, prov., exhib., (05-05-93, Christie-NY, #137, illus.), 74½ x 47¼ in., (189.2 x 120 cm.), three b/w photographs mounted on board (BP 30,839, DM 76,207, FR 256,778, Y 5,323,487).

BI *Two Hands, With Distant Figure, 1989-90,* s., #7/45, pub. Brooke Alexander Editions, full margins, excell. cond., est. $2/2,500, (05-11-93, Christie-NY, #366, illus.), sheet 53¼ x 34¾ in., (135.3 x 88.3 cm.), color photogravure w/aquatint on wove.

$2300* *Two Sets, One With Bench, 1989-90,* s., #7/45, pub. Brooke Alexander Editions, full margins, excell. cond., (05-11-93, Christie-NY, #367, illus.), sheet 47½ x 30 in., (120.7 x 76.2 cm.), color photogravure w/aquatint on wove (BP 1468, DM 3623, FR 12,208, Y 252,997).

BI *Two Tables: Two,* exec. 1988, prov., est. $15/20,000, (11-18-92, Sotheby-NY, #294, illus.), 60¼ x 31 in., (153 x 78.7 cm.), b/w photograph.

$717* *Untitled,* s., #19/60, (05-27-93, Lempertz, #586), 23Zzn x 9C\ in., (60.5 x 23.8 cm.), color photo-etching on wove (BP 459, DM 1151, FR 3878, Y 76,865).

$14,300* *Woman And Man With Arrow Piercing Chest,* two panels, exec. 1984, prov., exhib., (11-19-92, Christie-NY, #130, illus.), 57B\zn x 32¾ in., (147.3 x 83.2 cm.), photograph, b/w w/oil tint mounted on board (BP 9415, DM 22,800, FR 76,799, Y 1,778,386).

BALDESSIN, George Australian 1939-1978

$2027* *Banquet For No Eating,* s. George Baldessin, i. Ed.75., lit., (08-11-92, L. Joel, #52G), 23Zzn x 29Z, in., (60.5 x 74 cm.), etching and aquatint on silver foil, on paper (BP 1053, DM 2975, FR 10,075, Y 259,572, A$ 2750).

BI *Figurative Study,* s. George Baldessin, est. $3/4,000, (08-11-92, L. Joel, #157A), 29½ x 39zn in., (75 x 100.5 cm.), pencil and crayon on b/w lithograph.

$770* *(Striped Costumes And Dreams Series),* inits. G.B, d. '64, i. A.P, (08-11-92, L. Joel, #82G), 9½ x 6Mzn in., (24.2 x 16.3 cm.), color etching and aquatint (BP 400, DM 1130, FR 3827, Y 98,604, A$ 1045).

BALDUNG, Hans German 1480-1545

$433* *Die Beweinung Christi (B. 5, Curjel 42, Hollstein 53 II), 1515-17,* prov., (12-04-92, Bassenge, #6015), 8Zzn x 6 in., (22 x 15.3 cm.), woodcut (BP 278, DM 690, FR 2339, Y 54,057).

$3738* *Bewitched Groom (Holl. 237), c. 1544,* 2nd (final) state, later impression, watermark, trimmed to borderlineand into work, tear, restorations, ex-coll. H. Freiherr von und zu Aufsess, (05-13-93, Sotheby-NY, #158), 13Z, x 7M in., (333 x 200 mm.), woodcut (BP 2454, DM 6036, FR 20,359, Y 417,327).

BI *The Body Of Christ Carried By Angels Towards Heaven (Holl. 56), c. 1515-17,* later sixteenth century impression, watermark, margins, trimmed to borderline, ink, stains, foxing, est. $1,2/1,500, (05-13-93, Sotheby-NY, #157), 8B\ x 6 in., (220 x 153 mm.), woodcut.

$4910* *Der Grosse Heilige Sebastian (B.37; Curjel 35; Hollstein 128 II; Mende 38), 1514,* lit., very rare, watermark, (12-04-92, Bassenge, #6016, illus.), 12zn x 9Zzn in., (30.7 x 23 cm.), woodcut (BP 3149, DM 7820, FR 26,526, Y 612,984).

$1725* *Wild Horses Fighting (Holl. 238), 1534,* later impression, margins, wormholes touched in w/pen and ink, good cond., ex-coll. B. Hausmann, (05-13-93, Sotheby-NY, #159), 8C, x 12½ in., (212 x 316 mm.), woodcut (BP 1132, DM 2785, FR 9395, Y 192,587).

BALDUS, Edouard Denis 1813-1882

$1430* *"Chateau De Blois" and "Gare Du Boulogne Cote De L'Arrive": Two,* photog.'s credit, handwritten notations, 1860s, (04-07-93, Swann, #107, illus.), largest 13¼ x 17 in., (33.7 x 43.2 cm.), photograph, albumen print (BP 945, DM 2313, FR 7827, Y 162,463).

BI *Eglise St. Gilles, c. 1858,* s., t. in neg., est. $4/5000, (10-13-92, Christie-NY, #1, illus.), 14 x 17¼ in., (35.6 x 43.8 cm.), photograph, salt print from waxed paper neg..

BI *"Fontaine De Nimes",* 1850s, t., i., s. in neg. No. 5 E. Baldus, mounted on card w/p. facsimile sig., 432 x 334mm, est. BP 6/800, (05-07-93, Sotheby-London, #102), photograph, salt print from waxed paper neg..

BI *Palais Du Louvre Et Des Tuileries: Motifs De Decoration Interieure EtExterieure, 1875,* Ve A. Morel & Cie, set of 3 volumes, folio, est. $2,5/3,500, (10-15-92, Sotheby-NY, #82, illus.), largest 13 x 9½ in., (33 x 24.1 cm.), 300 heliogravure (photoengraving) reprods. by E. BALDUS of his own photos.

$509* *Paris And Chartres, Architectural Studies, including "L'Arc De Triomphe Du Carrousel, Paris", "Obelisk Place De La Concorde", "The Hotel De Ville, Paris" and "Cathedrale De Chartres, Facade Principale-Portail": Four,* 1860s, first mounted on card, w/p. fasimile sig.; second t., credit Heliogre de E. Baldus, smallest 190 x 272mm, largest 345 x 460mm, (05-07-93, Sotheby-London, #103), photograph, albumen prints and heliogravure (photoengraving) (BP 322, DM 805, FR 2712, Y 56,045).

$1270* *"Vues De Paries En Photographie": Ten,* c. 1860, album, one num. 12 in neg., 9 w/facsimile sig. E. Baldus, (05-06-93, Christie-London, #55, illus.), each approx. 7½ x 10½ in., photograph, albumen print (BP 805, DM 2000, FR 6734, Y 139,729).

BALDWIN and CO., M.W,
$467* *"Philadelphia" and "Lackawana & Bloomsburg Railroad Company, Kingston, Pa.": Two,* 1860s, (04-07-93, Swann, #230), one 10 x 16 in., other 12½ x 16 in., photograph (BP 309, DM 755, FR 2556, Y 53,056).

BALESTRIERI, Lionello Italian 1874-1958
$110* *The Embrace,* s. L. Balestrieri, very good cond. (?), (04-25-93, Bakker, #88), plate 17 x 24¼ in., (43.2 x 61.6 cm.), color aquatint (BP 70, DM 174, FR 588, Y 12,149).

BALLE, Mogens
$119* *Komposition,* s. Balle, 116/128, (03-24-93, Kunsthallen, #27), color lithograph (BP 81, DM 194, FR 661, Y 13,982, DK 748).
$119* *Komposition,* s. Balle, 224/300, (03-24-93, Kunsthallen, #24), color lithograph (BP 81, DM 194, FR 661, Y 13,982, DK 748).
$138* *Komposition,* s. Balle, 196/200, (03-24-93, Kunsthallen, #29), color lithograph (BP 93, DM 225, FR 767, Y 16,214, DK 863).
$73* *Komposition,* s. Balle, 224/300, (03-24-93, Kunsthallen, #25), color lithograph (BP 49, DM 119, FR 406, Y 8577, DK 460).
$92* *Komposition,* s. Balle, 70/100, (03-24-93, Kunsthallen, #26), color lithograph (BP 62, DM 150, FR 511, Y 10,810, DK 575).
$105* *Komposition,* s., 22/71, (09-30-92, Kunsthallen, #28), color lithograph (BP 59, DM 149, FR 504, Y 12,601, DK 575).
$128* *Komposition, 1976,* s. Balle 76, 161/175, (03-24-93, Kunsthallen, #28), color lithograph (BP 87, DM 209, FR 712, Y 15,039, DK 805).
$209* *"Min Datter",* (09-29-92, B. Rasmussen, #279), lithograph in colors (BP 117, DM 295, FR 1007, Y 24,949, DK 1150).
$628* *Untitled: Three,* each s. e.a., (09-29-92, B. Rasmussen, #276), lithograph in colors (BP 353, DM 887, FR 3027, Y 74,967, DK 3450).
BI *Untitled: Two,* s. 45/100 and 18/100, est. DK 2,500, (09-29-92, B. Rasmussen, #275), lithograph in colors.
$230* *Untitled: Two,* s. 28/150 and 15/150, (09-29-92, B. Rasmussen, #278), lithograph in colors (BP 129, DM 325, FR 1108, Y 27,456, DK 1265).

BALLESTER
$827* *Trinidad (Affair In Trinidad), De V. Sherman, Avec Rita Hayworth, Glenn Ford (Italian), 1952,* (01-31-93, Morelle/Marchan, #68), 12Ꜩzn x 27>zn in., (33 x 70 cm.), poster (BP 556, DM 1332, FR 4504, Y 103,169).

BALLMER, Theo Swiss 1902-1964
BI *Mouth, c. 1930,* Theo Ballmer Estate, est. $2/2,500, (04-06-93, Sotheby-NY, #327, illus.), 8¼ x 11M, in., photograph.

BALLURIAU, Paul 1860-1917
$442* *Le Petit Theatre (...) Reouverture Jeudi 10 Octobre 1901,* Asnieres, La lithographie nouvelle, cond. B, (06-11-93, Boisgirard, #43), 44M, x 31½ in., (114 x 80 cm.), poster (BP 290, DM 718, FR 2422, Y 46,897).

BALTERMANTS, Dmitri 1912-1990
$4718* *""Chto Takoe Chelovek?" ... Ikh Plach Uzhe Ne Indivdualno Eto Plach Chelovechestva/ Genrikh Boill", "What Kind Of Man Is This?" ...Their Grief Is Not Simply For Individuals It Is Grief Of Mankind/ Heinrich Boll,* 1943-44, posiibly p. 1950s, t., s., photog.'s ink credit stamp, (05-06-93, Christie-London, #173, illus.), 19 x 22½ in., photograph, gloss gelatin silver print (BP 2990, DM 7431, FR 25,016, Y 519,089).
$6900* *The Announcement Of Stalin's Death,* 1953, p. 1960s, estate stamp, earliest known print of this image, prov., (04-08-93, Christie-NY, #473, illus.), 8 x 19¾ in., (20.3 x 50.2 cm.), photograph, gelatin silver print (BP 4525, DM 11,084, FR 37,520, Y 783,023).
$4620* *Attack,* (1941). 1960s, t., inits., notations in ink, credit stamp, lit., (10-13-92, Christie-NY, #114, illus.), 7½ x 9B\ in., (19.1 x 24.4 cm.), photograph, gelatin silver print (BP 2691, DM 6768, FR 22,997, Y 560,204).
$5520* *Attack!,* 1941, p. 1960s, ink t., d., credit stamp, lit., (04-08-93, Christie-NY, #144, illus.), 10C, x 16Z\ in., (26.4 x 41 cm.), photograph, gelatin silver print (BP 3620, DM 8867, FR 30,016, Y 626,419).
$3300* *Tchaikovsky, Berlin,* (1945), late 1960s, t. in ink, notations in Russian, credit stamp, lit., (10-13-92, Christie-NY, #115, illus.), 11B, x 9 in., (29.5 x 22.9 cm.), photograph, gelatin silver print (BP 1922, DM 4834, FR 16,426, Y 400,146).

BALTHUS (after)
BI *[Figure Smoking], 1950,* i. Epreuve d'artiste XIV/XX, pub. Guilde de la Gravure, blindstamp, full margins, good cond., mat/light-stain, fox marks, creases, tape, est. $2,5/3,000, (05-13-93, Sotheby-NY, #455, illus.), 14¾ x 9 in., (376 x 230 mm.), hand-colored lithograph on wove.

BALTZ, Lewis American b. 1945
$9350* *Candlestick Point: Eighty-Four,* s., d., num. 13/21 by photog., 1984-88, p. 1988, #13/23 ed., (10-15-92, Sotheby-NY, #582, illus.), each 8 x 10 in., (20.3 x 25.4 cm.), portfolio of 84 photos incl. 12 color prints (BP 5721, DM 13,918, FR 47,198, Y 1,121,776).
$403* *"Nevada #8", 1978,* s., d., #6/40, (05-23-93, Butterfield, #3307, illus.), 6C, x 9½ in., photograph, gelatin silver print (BP 262, DM 659, FR 2218, Y 44,545).
$2875* *Selected Industrial Parks Images, 1974: Three,* from The New Industrial Parks near Irvine, California portfolio, each by photog., each s., t., d., #12/21, (04-06-93, Sotheby-NY, #491, illus.), each approx. 6 x 9 in., photograph (BP 1899, DM 4632, FR 15,685, Y 327,897).
$1725* *Selected Industrial Parks Images, 1974: Three,* from The New Industrial Parks near Irvine, California portfolio, each mounted, s., t., d., #12/21 by photog., (04-06-93, Sotheby-NY, #492, illus.), each approx. 6 x 9 in., photograph (BP 1139, DM 2779, FR 9411, Y 196,738).

BALUSCHEK, Hans 1870-1935
$295* *Arbeitervergnugen In Treptow, c. 1925,* s., (12-05-92, Bassenge, #7016), 10B, x 7M, in., (27 x 20 cm.), lithograph on wove (BP 185, DM 460, FR 1567, Y 36,551).
BI *Bei Mutter Grun, c. 1926,* s., est. DM 750, (12-05-92, Bassenge, #7017), 10½ x 7M, in., (26.7 x 20 cm.), lithograph on van-Gelder-Zonen handmade.
$1561* *"Hans Baluschek 6 Original Lithographien" (Meissner 406-411; Pommeranz-Liedtke S. 177), 1920/1921: Six,* s., t., d., i., impr. num., pub. Chryselius'scher, (06-05-93, Grisebach, #505, illus.), sh 20½ x 13¾ in., (52 x 35 cm.), lithograph on wove (BP 1028, DM 2531, FR 8530, Y 167,453).
$709* *"Die Lokomotive" (Meissner 423),* s., d., t., i., (06-05-93, Grisebach, #506, illus.), 13>zn x 10C, in., (34.4 x 26.3 cm.), lithograph on wove (BP 467, DM 1149, FR 3874, Y 76,057).

BAMBRIDGE, William
BI *Group Of Queen Victoria And Her Children Mourning The Death Of Prince Albert, 1862,* blindstamped credit, mounted on card, p. photog.'s credits, est. BP 5/800, 171 x 133mm, (05-07-93, Sotheby-London, #70, illus.), photograph, albumen print.

BAMS, Pierre
BI *Fleurs Des Alpes, c. 1935,* sig., t., est. $4/600, (10-14-92, Swann, #376, illus.), 14 x 10 in., (35.6 x 25.4 cm.), photograph, silver print.

BANDWELL, T.
BI *"Jagged Circles, With Grey Circle" and "Jagged Circles": Two,* each s., #6/50 and 60/150; label verso, prov., est. C$ 2/350, (12-01-92, Ritchie, #63), each approx. 26 x 19 in., (66 x 48.3 cm.), color serigraph.

BANGS, Frank C.
$460* *Portraits Of Beatrice Maude, 1910: Four,* three photog.'s blindstamp, s., two t., est. $800/1,000, (05-23-93, Butterfield, #3308, illus.), each approx. 6½ x 3¾ in., photograph, gelatin silver print (BP 300, DM 752, FR 2532, Y 50,846).

BANK and CO., Edinburgh, Publisher
$207* *North Berwick,* varnished, (03-03-93, Bonhams-Chelsea, #266), image 7½ x 12½ in., (19.1 x 31.8 cm.), chromolithograph (BP 143, DM 341, FR 1156, Y 24,188).

BAR-AM, Micha
$1150* *"Micha Bar-Am": Ten,* 1966-73, p. 1981, portfolio, s., #15/25, s., (05-23-93, Butterfield, #3309, illus.), each

approx. 16 x 20 in., photograph, gelatin silver print (BP 749, DM 1880, FR 6329, Y 127,114).

BARANSKI, E.
$12* *"Havas Dunaport"*, (03-12-93, DuMouchelle, #2439), 6 x 9 in., (15.2 x 22.9 cm.), etching (BP 8, DM 20, FR 68, Y 1414).

BARBARI, Jacopo de   c. 1440-c. 1511
BI *Frauen Und Manner In Einer Grossen Wanne Badend (Nagler; Die Monogrammisten III, 1842, 34)*, watermark, est. DM 1,200, (12-04-92, Bassenge, #6018), 9¼ x 13¼ in., (23.5 x 33.7 cm.), engraving.

BARBER, Charles Burton (after)
$161* *A Woman Reading Surrounded By Her Dogs*, (01-18-93, Bonhams, #71), image 17¼ x 24 in., (43.8 x 61 cm.), chromolithograph (BP 105, DM 263, FR 878, Y 20,295).

BARBEY
$299* *PLM and Cie De Navigation Paquet: Le Maroc Par Marseille. "TraverseeLa Plus Courte, La Plus Rapide, La Plus Abritee"*, good cond., (03-13-93, Laurin, #87), 39℃ x 24℃n in., (100 x 63 cm.), (BP 209, DM 498, FR 1692, Y 35,239).
$259* *PLM. Grenoble, Plaque Tournante Du Tourisme. "Grande Chartreuse, Mont-Blanc, Avignon, Nice"*, 1928, very good cond., (03-15-93, Arcole, #5), 41℁n x 29℁n in., (106.5 x 74.5 cm.), (BP 180, DM 430, FR 1462, Y 30,680).
$557* *PLM: Vers La Corne D'Or Par Le Simplon Orient-Express*, very good cond., (03-13-93, Laurin, #110), 42½ x 30½ in., (108 x 77.5 cm.), (BP 389, DM 927, FR 3152, Y 65,645).

BARBIER, Georges   French 1882-1932
$11,693* *Clotilde Et Alexandre Sakharoff, 1921*, p. H. Chachoin, excell. cond., (01-31-93, Morelle/Marchan, #15, illus.), 31℀, x 47¼ in., (79 x 120 cm.), poster (BP 7863, DM 18,838, FR 63,687, Y 1,458,708).

BARBIER, Georges (after)
BI *Figures In A Venetian Setting: Three*, est. $6/800, (09-21-92, Butterfield, #838), approx. 11℃℁n x 9℀℁n in., (30 x 25 cm.), hand-tinted pochoir.
$165* *Two Women And A Young Man In Evening Dress At A Piano*, (09-21-92, Butterfield, #840), 12℃n x 9℁n in., (31 x 24 cm.), hand-tinted pochoir (BP 97, DM 245, FR 838, Y 20,393).
$358* *A Woman Looking Into Her Compact And Applying Powder*, (09-21-92, Butterfield, #837, illus.), 11℁n x 9℃℁n in., (30.3 x 25 cm.), hand-tinted pochoir (BP 210, DM 531, FR 1817, Y 44,247).
$550* *Young Woman Standing And Stretching*, (09-21-92, Butterfield, #839, illus.), 11¾ x 9¾ in., (29.8 x 24.8 cm.), hand-tinted pochoir (BP 322, DM 816, FR 2792, Y 67,977).

BARFUSS, Ina   b. 1949
BI *Garten Eden, 1990*, s., d., est. DM 280-, (09-25-92, Granier, #2746), 23℀ x 19℁n in., (60 x 49.7 cm.), sheet 32℀, x 24℀, in., (60 x 49.7 cm.), serigraph on yellowish wove.

BARGHEER, Eduard   German 1901-1979
$148* *Dorfansicht, 1974*s., (12-05-92, Bassenge, #7023), 8¼ x 11℀, in., (21 x 29.6 cm.), lithograph (BP 93, DM 231, FR 786, Y 18,337).
BI *Badende (Rosenbach 76), 1934*, s., artist's proof, est. DM 1800, (12-05-92, Bassenge, #7020), 10℀, x 15℃, in., (27.7 x 39 cm.), etching reworked w/pencil on machine-made.
$155* *Forio (Rosenbach 146), 1956*, stone s., d., (09-25-92, Granier, #2748), 9¼ x 14 in., (23.5 x 35.6 cm.), sheet 14 x 18℀℁n in., (23.5 x 35.6 cm.), lithograph on hand-made (BP 91, DM 230, FR 777, Y 18,709).
BI *Forio, 1972*, d. 73, #51/65, s., est. DM 850, (09-18-92, Schloss Ahlden, #974), 19℀, x 25℀℁n in., (49.8 x 65.5 cm.), drypoint and aquatint on BFK Rives.
$361* *"Hauser Am Meer" (Rosenbach 123), 1952*, s., d., (11-28-92, Grisebach, #415, illus.), 8℀℁n x 11℀, in., (22.7 x 29.6 cm.), drypoint on copper print paper (BP 238, DM 575, FR 1952, Y 44,928).
$516* *Herbstliche Stadt (Rosenbach 265), 1969*, s., num., (12-05-92, Bassenge, #7022), 11℀, x 16℁℁n in., (29.5 x 41.5 cm.), color etching, drypoint and aquatint from three

plates on copper print paper (BP 323, DM 804, FR 2742, Y 63,933).
$516* *Inselfruhe (Rosenbach 254), 1967*, s., num., blindstamp, (12-05-92, Bassenge, #7021), 16℀n x 12℃, in., (41.8 x 31.5 cm.), drypoint on copper print paper (BP 323, DM 804, FR 2742, Y 63,933).
BI *Der Niger (Rosenbach 229), 1966*, s., E.A., from series Afrika, est. DM 500-, (09-25-92, Granier, #2750), 12℃, x 19℀℁n in., (31.5 x 50 cm.), sheet 16℀n x 23¼ in., (31.5 x 50 cm.), color lithograph on hand-made.
$332* *Palmenwaldchen, (19)76*, s., d., num., (12-01-92, Karl/Faber, #350), 11℀, x 16℀℁n in., (29.5 x 42 cm.), color aquatint and etching on wove (BP 219, DM 529, FR 1803, Y 41,335).
$424* *Sahara (Rosenbach 238), 1966*, s., d., t., num., artist proof, from Suite Sahara, (06-10-93, Hauswedell/Nolt, #25), image 13℀n x 19℀, in., (34.5 x 50.5 cm.), color lithograph on wove (BP 277, DM 690, FR 2325, Y 45,006).
$458* *Sudlicher Garten (Rosenbach 329), 1972*, s., d., num., blindstamp, (05-26-93, Dorling, #2536), 18℀, x 24℀ ℁n in., (48 x 63 cm.), color etching on wove (BP 296, DM 747, FR 2515, Y 49,761).
$272* *Untitled (Sudliche Stadt) (Rosenbach 218), 1965*, s., num., (09-25-92, Granier, #2749), 10℀n x 15¾ in., (25.5 x 40 cm.), sheet 13¾ x 19℀℁n in., (25.5 x 40 cm.), lithograph on hand-made (BP 159, DM 403, FR 1363, Y 32,830).

BARKER, Al
$55* *"Solitude Hunting"*, #25/50, excell. cond., (10-02-92, Guyette, #627, illus.), image 5 x 9 in., (12.7 x 22.9 cm.), etching (BP 32, DM 78, FR 262, Y 6567).

BARKER, Albert W.
$330* *"Cedar Tree Neck", "Evening-The Catskills" and "So September Ends": Three*, each s., num. 75 0/50, 24 26/51, 31 22/43, full margins, good cond.,surface soiling, pencil notations, prop. Print Corner Coll. of Elizabeth and Charles Whitmore, (02-24-93, Butterfield, #2809), one 8¾ x 6℀, in., (222 x 175 mm.), others, two 11 x 7℀n in., (222 x 175 mm.), lithograph on Basingwerk parchment (BP 230, DM 536, FR 1816, Y 38,723).
$259* *"Market Day" and "Rue St. Romaine": Two*, s., #37 8/33, 21 14/70, t., full margins, good cond., time staining,creases, tear, hinge remains, buckling, (05-19-93, Butterfield, #1975), one 13¾ x 10 in., (349 x 254 mm.), the other 8¼ x 5¾ in., (349 x 254 mm.), lithograph on Glaffonbury and Basingwerk laid (BP 168, DM 421, FR 1418, Y 28,673).
$523* *"Ridge Farm", "The Fertile Earth", and "The Outlying Farm", 1930, 1937: Three*, s., t., num. 52 8/100, very good cond., creases, mat staining, prop.Print Corner Coll. of Elizabeth and Charles Whitmore, (02-24-93, Butterfield, #2808), smallest 4¾ x 6℀, in., (121 x 175 mm.), largest 14℀, x 10¾ in., (121 x 175 mm.), lithograph on wove (BP 365, DM 849, FR 2878, Y 61,371).
$385* *"Rue St. Romaine", "The Spice Bush", and "Market Day Caudelec-En-Caux", 1928, 1931: Three*, each s., num. 21 18/70, 80 0/24 and 37 23/33, full margins, good cond., staining, creases, pencil notations, prop. Print Corner Coll. of Elizabeth and Charles Whitmore, (02-24-93, Butterfield, #2807, illus.), smallest 8¼ x 5¾ in., (210 x 146 mm.), largest 14℀, x 10℀, in., (210 x 146 mm.), lithograph on wove, BFK Rives, & F.J. Head & Co. laid (BP 268, DM 625, FR 2119, Y 45,177).
$575* *"The Sheep House", "Enchanted Meadow", "Ridge Farm" and "The OutlyingFarm": Four*, s., #83-/35, 18 29/70, 52 9/100, 51 78/100, t., full margins, good cond., time staining, handling creases, stains, (05-19-93, Butterfield, #1976), smallest 4¾ x 6℀, in., (121 x 175 mm.), largest 7½ x 10℀, in., (121 x 175 mm.), lithograph on wove (BP 373, DM 935, FR 3149, Y 63,655).
$489* *"Wild Apple", 1930, "The Spice-Bush", 1931, "The Tapestry Of Spring",1936 and "Phlox": Four*, first, second, and fourth s., #44 2/30, 80 0/24, 25 21/44, full margins, good cond., creases, foxing, notations, Print Corner Coll. Of Elizabeth andCharles Whitmore, (05-19-93, Butterfield, #1973), smallest 8℃, x 5¼ in., (213 x 133 mm.), largest 14℀℁n x 11℀n in., (213 x 133 mm.), lithograph on Rives and wove (BP 317, DM 795, FR 2678, Y 54,135).

BARKER, George   American 1844-1894
BI *View Of The Upper Falls, Niagara, c. 1876,* est. $1,2/
1,800, (10-13-92, Christie-NY, #2, illus.), sight 19½ x
15½ in., (49.5 x 39.4 cm.), photograph, mammoth albumen print.

BARKER, K.F.
$65 *"Otter Hunting",* s., (02-05-93, G.A. Key, #71), 9 x 11
in., (22.9 x 27.9 cm.), etching (BP 45, DM 108, FR
364, Y 8089).

BARKER, Robert (after)
$318* *Westminster From Albion Mills, Blackfriars, 1792,* by
Frederick Birnie, (02-17-93, Bonhams-Chelsea, #213),
image 16½ x 22 in., (41.9 x 55.9 cm.), hand-colored
aquatint (BP 220, DM 516, FR 1749, Y 37,984).

BARKER, Thomas (of Bath)
BI *Young Boy (Man 17),* glue stains, stitch marks, creases,
tears, est. BP 5/600, (06-30-93, Sotheby-London, #248),
11 x 8 in., (279 x 203 mm.), pen-lithograph on wove,
on support sheet w/dark chocolate-brown aquatint surround w/J. Whatman 1794 watermark.

BARKER, Thomas Jones (after)
BI *The Intellect And Valour Of Britain,* by Charles G.
Lewis, est. BP 1/150, (06-16-93, Bonhams-Chelsea,
#412), image 24½ x 39 in., (62.2 x 99.1 cm.), engraving.
$682* *Nelson Accepting The Surrender Of The Spanish Admiral,*
1853, by Charles G. Lewis, blindstamp, pub. Leggatt,
Hayward and Leggatt, (08-20-92, Bonhams-Chelsea, #90,
illus.), image 24¾ x 44 in., (62.9 x 111.8 cm.), engraving (BP 352, DM 988, FR 3351, Y 86,122).

BARKS, Carl   American 20th cent.
BI *No. 104, 1982-1992: Twenty-Two,* complete set, full size,
and four miniatures, pub. Walt Disney Limited Editions
by Another Rainbow, est. $25/28,000, (09-30-92,
Sotheby-NY, #433, illus.), image averaging 16 x 10 in.,
(40.6 x 25.4 cm.), and 8 x 10 in., (40.6 x 25.4 cm.),
lithograph.
BI *Twenty-One Gold Plate Prints,* 1982-1992, complete set,
18 full size and 3 miniatures, pub. Walt Disney Limited
Editions by Another Rainbow, est. $27/32,000, (09-30-92,
Sotheby-NY, #187, illus.), image average 16 x 24 in.,
(40.6 x 61 cm.), and 8 x 10 in., (40.6 x 61 cm.), lithograph.

BARLACH, Ernst   German 1870-1938
$721* *Ansteigendes Paar (Schult Band II 117), 1919,* s., sheet
5 from Der arme Vetter, (11-21-92, Lempertz, #17), 10B
x 13Zn in., (27 x 34.5 cm.), lithograph on cream wove
(BP 475, DM 1150, FR 3872, Y 89,665).
$353* *Aufbruch Und Abwehr (Schult 44), 1910-11,* s., Bl. 25
from Ernst Barlach. Der tote Tag., Cassirer, Berlin, (06-
10-93, Hauswedell/Nolt, #31), image 10>Zn x 13Zn in.,
(26.9 x 33.2 cm.), lithograph on hand-made (BP 231,
DM 575, FR 1935, Y 37,469).
$627* *Berufung (Schult 194), 1922,* s., num., (12-05-92, Bassenge, #7027), 6Zn x 5Zn in., (17 x 12.8 cm.), lithograph on Zanders handmade (BP 393, DM 978, FR
3332, Y 77,686).
$233* *Blasender Pan (Schult 280), 1928,* corner damage, (09-
25-92, Granier, #2753), 4Mzn x 3M, in., (11.2 x 9.8 cm.),
woodcut on wove (BP 136, DM 345, FR 1168, Y
28,123).
BI *Demut (S. 75), 1916,* num. 28/75, Max Slevogt litho
verso, pub. in Der Bildermann, margins,good cond., staining, est. $3/500, (02-24-93, Butterfield, #2895), 11B, x
8½ in., (295 x 216 mm.), lithograph on wove.
BI *Demut. (Schult 75), 1916,* s., Vorzugsausgabe des Bildermann, est. DM 6000, (06-10-93, Hauswedell/Nolt, #32),
image 11Zzn x 8Zzn in., (30 x 22 cm.), lithograph on
hand-made.
$2542* *Die Dome (Schult 165), 1920,* s., series Die Wandlungen Gottes, (06-10-93, Hauswedell/Nolt, #45, illus.),
image 10Zn x 14Z, in., (25.6 x 35.9 cm.), woodcut on
kaiserlichem Japan (BP 1663, DM 4139, FR 13,936, Y
269,823).
BI *Die Fliehenden (Schult 92), c. 1916-17,* s., #45/50, est.
DM 4000, (06-10-93, Hauswedell/Nolt, #33), image 10B
x 15>n in., (27 x 39.5 cm.), lithograph on hand-made.

BI *Die Fliehenden (Schult Band II 92), 1916-17,* #11/50,
s., watermark, creases, est. DM 8,500-, (11-21-92, Lempertz, #16A, illus.), stone 11Zzn x 15Zzn in., (30 x 39.8
cm.), lithograph on hand-made.
BI *Fluch (Schult 195), 1922,* s., #98/100, est. DM 2500,
(06-10-93, Hauswedell/Nolt, #38, illus.), image 19½ x
16¾ in., (49.5 x 42.5 cm.), lithograph on hand-made.
$1631* *"Fluch" (Schult 195), 1922,* watermark, s., num., pub.
Cassirer, (06-05-93, Grisebach, #512, illus.), 19Bzn x 16B,
in., (49 x 42.3 cm.), lithograph on handmade (BP 1074,
DM 2644, FR 8913, Y 174,962).
$590* *Der Getreue Eckart (Schult 245), 1924,* s., glue, (12-05-
92, Bassenge, #7028), 7Bzn x 7½ in., (18.6 x 19 cm.),
lithograph on Japan (BP 369, DM 920, FR 3135, Y
73,101).
BI *Der Gottliche Bettler from Die Wandlungen Gottes*
(Schult 166), 1920-21, s., num. 3/100, pub. Paul Cassirer,
full margins, crease across image, foxing, defects, est. BP
5/700, (11-30-92, Phillips-London, #373A), border 10Z, x
14 in., (257 x 356 mm.), woodcut on japan.
$996* *Harzreise Im Winter, 1925,* s., sheet 27 from the series
Goethe, Ausgewahlte Gedichte, pub. PaulCassirer, margin,
creases, (12-01-92, Karl/Faber, #353), 10B, x 7M, in., (27
x 20 cm.), lithograph on Japan (BP 658, DM 1588, FR
5410, Y 124,004).
$999* *Der Henker, Plate 3 (Sch. 197), 1922,* from die Ausgestossenen, s., P. Cassirer, margins, tape, very good cond,
(12-01-92, Christie-London, #302), L. 20¼ x 16>n in.,
(515 x 420 mm.), lithograph on laid (BP 660, DM 1592,
FR 5426, Y 124,377).
BI *Der Hohe Herr (Schult II 189),* illus. for Der Findling,
1922, faded, est. DM 300-, (09-25-92, Granier, #2752),
6Mzn x 5Z, in., (16.4 x 13 cm.), sheet 10>zn x 7Mzn in.,
(16.4 x 13 cm.), woodcut on hand-made.
$709* *Kniende Frau Mit Sterbendem Kind (Schult 160), 1919,*
s., num., (06-05-93, Bassenge, #5888), 8M, x 12B, in.,
(22.6 x 32 cm.), woodcut on JWZ hand-made (BP 467,
DM 1149, FR 3874, Y 76,057).
$794* *"Konigsgrab" (Schult 289), 1930,* num., (11-28-92, Grisebach, #423, illus.), 10Zzn x 14Czn in., (27.2 x 36 cm.),
lithograph on handmade (BP 524, DM 1265, FR 4294, Y
98,818).
$650* *"Kreuz-Und Sargrauber" (Schult 158), 1919,* s., #1/100,
(11-28-92, Grisebach, #420, illus.), 10Bzn x 14Bzn in.,
(26.2 x 36.3 cm.), woodcut on handmade (BP 429, DM
1036, FR 3515, Y 80,896).
BI *Liebespaar (Schult 93), C. 1916-17,* s., #31/50, est. DM
4000, (06-10-93, Hauswedell/Nolt, #34), image 10Zzn x
15C, in., (27.4 x 39 cm.), lithograph on hand-made.
BI *Magd Eines Hohen Herrn (Schult 152), 1917,* s., num.,
from Der Arme Vetter, est. DM 1000, (06-10-93,
Hauswedell/Nolt, #36), image 10½ x 13B, in., (26.7 x
34.6 cm.), lithograph on copper print paper.
$413* *Der Mude (S. 76), 1916,* num. 3/75, pub. in Der Bildermann, lithograph by Max Slevogt t. Symbole der Zeit III
verso, full margins, good cond., surface soiling, (02-24-
93, Butterfield, #2894), 11M, x 8B, in., (302 x 219 mm.),
lithograph on wove (BP 288, DM 670, FR 2273, Y
48,463).
$4229* *Der Neue Tag (Schult 294), 1932,* s., (05-26-93, Lempertz, #22, illus.), sh 18M, x 26M, in., (48 x 68.3 cm.),
lithograph on hand-made w/Van Gelder Zonen (BP
2736, DM 6900, FR 23,224, Y 459,474).
$2200* *Rasender Barbar (S. 91), 1917,* s., num. 23/50, full margins, good cond., mat staining, creases, surface soiling,
foxing, pencil notations, (02-24-93, Butterfield, #2703),
11 x 15¾ in., (279 x 400 mm.), lithograph on Van
Gelder Zonen laid (BP 1534, DM 3571, FR 12,108, Y
258,155).
$2490* *Rasender Barbar (Schult 91), 1916-17,* s., num., restored,
(12-01-92, Karl/Faber, #352, illus.), 10B, x 15C, in., (27
x 39 cm.), lithograph on hand-made (BP 1645, DM
3969, FR 13,525, Y 310,010).
BI *Russian Beggar,* prov., est. $2/250, (12-10-92, Sloan,
#581), 4 x 3Z, in., (10.2 x 7.9 cm.), woodcut.
$1475* *Schlaf Im Tod (Schult 94), 1916-17,* s., num., small tears,
(12-05-92, Bassenge, #7025), 10B, x 15B, in., (27 x 39.7
cm.), lithograph on handmade (BP 924, DM 2300, FR
7837, Y 182,753).

$361* *"Die Schuldbewusste" (Schult 37), 1912,* s., sheet 10 of series "Der tote Tag", PAN-Presse Berlin, pub. Paul Cassirer, (11-28-92, Grisebach, #417, illus.), 9Bzn x 12B in., (23.6 x 32 cm.), lithograph on copper print paper (BP 238, DM 575, FR 1952, Y 44,928).

BI *Selbstbildnis I (Schult 282), 1928,* s., est. DM 16,000, (06-10-93, Hauswedell/Nolt, #42, illus.), image 17B\ x 12C, in., (44.7 x 31.5 cm.), lithograph on Maschinen hand-made.

$2166* *"Selbstbildnis V" (Schult 297), 1928/1946,* (11-28-92, Grisebach, #424, illus.), 16Z, x 12Zzn in., (41 x 32.5 cm.), transfer lithograph on cardboard (BP 1430, DM 3451, FR 11,714, Y 269,571).

$361* *"Der Seufzerstein" (Schult 19), 1912,* s., sheet 4 of series "Der tote Tag", PAN-Presse Berlin, pub. Paul Cassirer(11-28-92, Grisebach, #416, illus.), 8Z\n x 10Zzn in., (22 x 27.5 cm.), lithograph on Japan (BP 238, DM 575, FR 1952, Y 44,928).

$2542* *Der Siebente Tag (Schult 171 B), 1920,* s., Bl. 7 from the series Die Wandlungen Gottes, Pan-Presse, (06-10-93, Hauswedell/Nolt, #37, illus.), image 10Zzn x 14Z, in., (25.5 x 35.8 cm.), woodcut on Japan (BP 1663, DM 4139, FR 13,936, Y 269,823).

$2887* *"Singende Madchen" (Schult 269), 1924,* s., num., (11-28-92, Grisebach, #422, illus.), 13¾ x 10>zn in., (35 x 26.8 cm.), lithograph on handmade (BP 1906, DM 4599, FR 15,614, Y 359,303).

$1165* *Steiniger Weg, Plate 5 (Sch. 200), 1922,* from Die Ausgestossenen, s., #41/103, pub. P. Cassirer, wide margins, tears, patch, hole, tape, folds, (12-01-92, Christie-London, #303), L. 20>zn x 16B, in., (522 x 422 mm.), lithograph on J W Zanders laid (BP 770, DM 1857, FR 6328, Y 145,045).

$2401* *Sterndeuter III (Schult 287), 1928,* s., #24/30, (06-10-93, Hauswedell/Nolt, #43, illus.), image 14½ x 10Zzn in., (36.9 x 27.5 cm.), lithograph (BP 1571, DM 3910, FR 13,163, Y 254,856).

BI *Die Sterndeuter, Die Sterngucker, III (Schult Band II 287), 1930,* s., est. DM 7,000-, (11-21-92, Lempertz, #17A, illus.), 14B, x 10Zzn in., (37.1 x 27.5 cm.), lithograph on machine-made paper.

$397* *"Sturzende Frau" (Schult 46), 1912,* s., sheet 27 of series "Der tote Tag", PAN-Presse Berlin, pub. Paul Cassirer, (11-28-92, Grisebach, #418, illus.), 10Zzn x 12>zn in., (27.2 x 30.7 cm.), lithograph on copper print paper (BP 262, DM 632, FR 2147, Y 49,409).

BI *Ungleiches Paar (Schult 120), 1919,* s., sheet 8 of series Der arme Vetter, est. DM 2400, (12-05-92, Bassenge, #7026), 10½ x 13>zn in., (26.7 x 34.5 cm.), lithograph on thin copper print cardboard.

BI *Die Verfluchung (Schult 45),* from series "Der tote Tag", s., foxing, est. SF 4/4,500, (04-21-93, Germann, #267, illus.), lithograph.

$813* *Die Wandelnde Glocke I (Sch. 252), 1924,* s., sheet 25 for Goethe's Ausgewahlte Gedichte, (10-09-92, Winterberg, #1711), 7Zzn x 7M, in., (19.5 x 20 cm.), lithograph on Japan (BP 482, DM 1208, FR 4055, Y 98,977).

$636* *Wandernder Tod (Schult 225), 1923,* s., from the portfolio Arno Holz zum 60. Geburtstag, pub. Fritz Gurlitt, (06-10-93, Hauswedell/Nolt, #40, illus.), image 10Zzn x 13>zn in., (27.2 x 34.5 cm.), lithograph on thick Japan (BP 416, DM 1036, FR 3487, Y 67,509).

$1155* *"Wem Zeit Wie Ewigeit" (Schult 79), 1916,* in "Der Bildermann", 1. Jg., Heft 13, Berlin, Hrsg. Paul Cassirer, (11-28-92, Grisebach, #419, illus.), 11B, x 8>zn in., (29.6 x 21.8 cm.), lithograph on Japan (BP 762, DM 1840, FR 6247, Y 143,746).

$268* *Der Zauberlehrling (Beschworung) (Schult 249), 1923-24,* s., Bl. 22 from Goethe. Gedichte, P. Cassirer in Berlin, (06-10-93, Hauswedell/Nolt, #41), image 6C, x 7M in., (16.2 x 20 cm.), lithograph (BP 175, DM 436, FR 1469, Y 28,447).

$879* *Zwei Gegen Einen (Schult Nr. 150), 1919,* s., sheet 36 of series Der Arme Vetter, (11-13-92, Kunsthaus, #449), 10B, x 13Zzn in., (27 x 34.7 cm.), lithograph on wove (BP 568, DM 1380, FR 4653, Y 109,098).

BARLEIGH (Barbara LEIGHTON)

$89* *Deer, Kananaskis,* #28/100, s., (10-21-92, Maynard, #202), 10½ x 10 in., (26.7 x 25.4 cm.), woodcut (BP 55, DM 135, FR 457, Y 10,840, C$ 110).

BARLOW, Francis

$1380* *Livre De Plusieurs Animaux Inventez Par Barlou (Thiebaud 56), c. 1675,* Chez De Poilly, Oblong 4to, bound as 8vo, repaired tear, repairs, fews., Barlow's mono., plates #66-78, skipping 69 and 77, s. Abeille(ge?), AnthonyN. B. Garvan Coll., (06-05-93, Christie-NY, #7, illus.), 9M, x 6Zzn in., (251 x 170 mm.), etched title and 10 etched plates (BP 908, DM 2237, FR 7541, Y 148,037).

$978* *Various Birds And Beasts Drawn From The Life (Ellis/Mengel 163, Nissen IVB 76), c. 1760: Sixty-Seven,* for T. Bowles, John Bowles & Son, Robert Sayer, repaired tear, tears,repairs, discoloration, t., after Barlow, Anthony N. B. Garvan Coll., (06-05-93, Christie-NY, #8, illus.), 9>zn x 14Zzn in., (243 x 379 mm.), on heavy paper, etched plate (BP 644, DM 1586, FR 5344, Y 104,913).

BARLOW, Myron American 1873-1938

$83* *Seated Woman,* s., (09-18-92, DuMouchelle, #2396), 16 x 11½ in., (40.6 x 29.2 cm.), etching (BP 48, DM 124, FR 426, Y 10,341).

$165* *Seated Woman Reading,* s., (09-18-92, DuMouchelle, #2395), 16½ x 11 in., (41.9 x 27.9 cm.), etching (BP 95, DM 247, FR 846, Y 20,558).

BARNARD, G.N.

BI *"Soldiers Standing With Rifles At Bunker, Atlanta" and "Courthouse, Atlanta", 1860s: Two,* notations on mount recto, est. $1,2/1,800, (04-07-93, Swann, #171, illus.), each approx. 9½ x 13 in., photograph, Albumen print.

$550* *Valley Of The Potomac,* notations, on mount recto, 1860s, (04-07-93, Swann, #172, illus.), 10½ x 15 in., photograph, Albumen print (BP 363, DM 890, FR 3010, Y 62,486).

BARNARD, G.N. (attrib.)

BI *Captured Confederate Gun, Ft. Sumpter.,* notations, on mount recto, 1860s, est. $8/1,200, (04-07-93, Swann, #173, illus.), 12¼ x 16½ in., photograph, albumen print.

BARNARD and GIBSON, BRADY, M. (attrib.)

$2420* *"Wounded Soldier At Fredericksburg", "Ft. Darling, Janes River", "Ft. Mahone", "Pontoon Landing, Janes River" and "Ruins At Richmond": Five,* notations, on mount recto, 1860s, (04-07-93, Swann, #174, illus.), largest 7½ x 10 in., photograph, albumen print (BP 1599, DM 3914, FR 13,246, Y 274,938).

BARNBAUM, Bruce American b. 1943

$935* *"Moonrise Over Cliffs And Dunes",* 1976/1992, s., d. 1992 mount, t., d., neg. num.; photog. stamp versomount, (11-16-92, Butterfield, #5842, illus.), 15½ x 18>zn in., (394.4 x 470.7 mm.), photograph, gelatin silver print (BP 616, DM 1491, FR 5021, Y 116,279).

BARNET, John American ac. 1850-1855

$1210* *"Niagara Falls, American Side" 1855,* ident. in matrix, good cond., margins 1-in. or more, staining, fox marks, hole, (10-31-92, Skinner, #139, illus.), sight 27 x 38B in., (68.6 x 98.1 cm.), lithograph w/hand coloring on paper (BP 791, DM 1900, FR 6433, Y 149,604).

BARNET, Will American b. 1911

BI *"Ariadne", 1980,* s., d., num., artist's proof, very good cond., est. $5-600, (10-31-92, Cleveland, #358), silkscreen.

$770* *Blue Bicycle (AAA 53), 1979,* s., t., d., i. AP, num. 13/50, wide margins, light-staining, good cond., (09-19-92, Christie-E, #8), borderline 26½ x 25B\ in., (673 x 651 mm.), screenprint in colors on Arches (BP 443, DM 1153, FR 3949, Y 95,938).

$358* *"The Book", 1975,* s., d., num. 48/75, very good cond., (10-31-92, Cleveland, #357, illus.), 18¼ x 26¼ in., (46.4 x 66.7 cm.), silkscreen (BP 229, DM 551, FR 1868, Y 44,345).

$247* *Dawn, 1975,* full margins, s., annot. XXIII/L, pub. Trans World Art, (12-08-92, Swann, #14), 24 x 11 in., (61 x 27.9 cm.), color serigraph (BP 155, DM 385, FR 1311, Y 30,615).

$248* *Fifth Season,* s., t., #57/100, good cond.?, (10-28-92, Butterfield, #2903), 36½ x 26 in., (927 x 660 mm.), color silkscreen on metallic silver (BP 158, DM 383, FR 1300, Y 30,429).

$522* *Introspection-5733 (Cole 147), 1972,* num., s., p. Fine Creations Inc., pub. Vera List, (05-27-93, Swann, #23), 29½ x 35 in., (74.9 x 88.9 cm.), color serigraph on Arches (BP 334, DM 838, FR 2823, Y 55,961).

$275* *"Irish Kids", 1938, "Child Reading", c. 1938 and "City Child": Three,* s., pub. AAA, 1982, (05-27-93, Swann, #24), first, woodcut; second and third, etching (BP 176, DM 441, FR 1487, Y 29,481).

$230* *"Man And Parrot" and "Child Reaching", 1937, 1940: Two,* s., second t., #42/60, pub. AAA, margins, good cond.?, foxing, surface soiling, notations, (05-19-93, Butterfield, #2125), one 5Zn x 4 in., (129 x 102 mm.), the other 7¼ x 11¼ in., (129 x 102 mm.), woodcut on Japan (BP 149, DM 374, FR 1260, Y 25,462).

$193* *Mary,* s., t., (11-12-92, Freemn/Fine Art, #26A), 15 x 12½ in., (38.1 x 31.8 cm.), litho (BP 127, DM 306, FR 1032, Y 23,931).

$193* *Reflection,* s., t., annot. A.P., margins, good cond., surface scuffing/soiling, time-staining, creases, (10-28-92, Butterfield, #2902), 22 x 14½ in., (559 x 368 mm.), color silkscreen on wove (BP 123, DM 298, FR 1012, Y 23,681).

$440* *"Reflection", 1971,* s., d. (c) Will Barnet, 1971, (03-12-93, Skinner, #53, illus.), 22Z, x 14½ in., (56.2 x 36.8 cm.), color screenprint on paper (BP 307, DM 732, FR 2490, Y 51,856).

$330* *Silent Seasons-Summer, 1975,* s., t., #144/200, pub. AA, (03-14-93, Hindman, #331), 28¾ x 22¼ in., (73 x 56.5 cm.), color lithograph (BP 230, DM 549, FR 1868, Y 38,892).

BARNI, Roberto

$360* *"Toro E Leone" and "Notte", 1982: Two,* each s., #20/30, #7/25, margins, Notte creases, defects, (10-15-92, Sotheby-London, #72, illus.), first sheet approx. 31¼ x 43¼ in., second sheet approx. 39Z, x 74 in., two drypoints w/tone, one p. in colors, on wove (BP 220, DM 536, FR 1817, Y 43,191).

BARNUM and BAILEY American 20th cent.

$798* *"The Six Glinseretty's", "Aladdin And His Wonderful Lamp" and "JamesTeddy The Human Aeroplane": Three,* (02-14-93, Hanzel, #714), each approx. 26½ x 36½ in., (67.3 x 92.7 cm.), color lithographic poster (BP 562, DM 1323, FR 4478, Y 96,237).

BARO

$210* *Fuente Vaqueros. Gran Feria Real,* good cond., (11-19-92, Ribeyre/Baron, #128), 48Zn x 25C, in., (122 x 64.5 cm.), poster (BP 138, DM 335, FR 1128, Y 26,116).

BAROCCI, Federico

$2059* *The Stigmatization Of St. Francis (B. XVII, 3),* abraded impression, narrow margins, pen and ink touches, creases, stains, discoloration, laid down, (06-30-93, Sotheby-London, #72, illus.), 9 x 5M, in., (229 x 149 mm.), etching (BP 1380, DM 3512, FR 11,847, Y 220,615).

BAROCCI, Federico (after)

BI *The Rest On The Flight Into Egypt (B. XXI, 11),* trimmed to borderline, paper loss, creasing, est. BP 1,5/2,000, (12-03-92, Sotheby-London, #6, illus.), 13½ x 11 in., (343 x 279 mm.), chiaroscuro woodcut, p. in two tones of brown.

BAROZZI, Guiseppe Gioachino (or Barocci) (after) Italian d. 1780

$300* *Five architectural engravings,* (02-04-93, Sloan, #1844), each 14 x 8½ in., (35.6 x 21.6 cm.), engraving (BP 209, DM 494, FR 1675, Y 37,318).

BARRA, Johannes 1581-1634

$2691* *Die Vier Jahreszeiten, Landschaften Mit Je Drei Sternzeichen (Wurzbach 38-41, Hollstein 40-43): Four,* after P. Stephani, watermark, (06-04-93, Bassenge, #5018, illus.), 8ZBn x 13Mn in., (22.7 x 34.1 cm.), engraving (BP 1780, DM 4370, FR 14,729, Y 290,229).

BARRABAND (after)

$1870* *"Exotic Birds: Set of Four",* (10-28-92, Doyle, #1), 15 x 11 in., (38.1 x 27.9 cm.), hand colored print (BP 1191, DM 2888, FR 9806, Y 229,448).

BARRABAND, Jacques French 1768-1809

$176* *La Grande Perruche A Collier Et Croupion Bleu,* (05-16-93, Hindman, #429), 12¾ x 10 in., (32.4 x 25.4 cm.), color engraving (BP 114, DM 283, FR 951, Y 19,510).

BARRABAND, Jacques (after) French 1768-1809

$248* *Le Rollier, Varie D'Afrique,* hand coloring by Peree, (09-20-92, Hindman, #638A), 19½ x 12½ in., (49.5 x 31.8 cm.), color etching w/hand coloring (BP 145, DM 368, FR 1259, Y 30,651).

BARRAL

$330* *Woman With Flowers And Two Gentlemen, 1929,* Exposition-Barcelona 1929, linen-backed, (04-29-93, Swann, #140), 21 x 14 in., (53.3 x 35.6 cm.), color lithograph poster (BP 210, DM 522, FR 1759, Y 36,712).

BARRAUD, Henry (after)

$627* *Rotten Row,* by William Henry Simmon, pub. Robert Turner, 1867, margins, stained,surface dirt, (06-16-93, Bonhams-Chelsea, #378), pl. 31 x 54 in., (78.7 x 137.2 cm.), engraving (BP 418, DM 1041, FR 3493, Y 66,873).

BARRAUD, Maurice Swiss 1889-1954

BI *Abandon, 1919,* proof, s., lit., est. SF 600/1,000, (09-04-92, Germann, #231), 7M, x 6M, in., (200 x 175 mm.), lithograph.

$92* *Apres Midi D'Un Faune,* E.A., s., (09-04-92, Germann, #241), 11Mn x 8Zn in., (290 x 220 mm.), etching (BP 46, DM 129, FR 439, Y 11,324, SF 115).

$971* *Attendre (Cailler 7), 1910,* s., (10-14-92, Germann, #487), 6Cn x 4Cn in., (157 x 107 mm.), etching (BP 570, DM 1421, FR 4819, Y 117,668, SF 1265).

$424* *Dame Au Gant (Cailler 100), 1918,* s., (09-04-92, Germann, #229), 8Zn x 6½ in., (205 x 165 mm.), lithograph (BP 212, DM 594, FR 2023, Y 52,191, SF 529).

BI *Les Deux Amies (Cailler 108), 1919,* from Sept pierres d'amour, s., est. SF 5/800, (09-04-92, Germann, #236), 10Mn x 6½ in., (265 x 165 mm.), lithograph.

$553* *La Drogue (Cailler 13), 1911,* s., (09-04-92, Germann, #239, illus.), 6Zn x 7Zn in., (170 x 192 mm.), etching (BP 277, DM 775, FR 2638, Y 68,070, SF 690).

$599* *Eglogues (Cailler 223), 1942,* s., (09-04-92, Germann, #230), 12Cn x 8Zn in., (310 x 220 mm.), lithograph (BP 300, DM 840, FR 2858, Y 73,732, SF 748).

$1474* *Eveil (Cailler 47), 1915,* s., (09-04-92, Germann, #242, illus.), 6Bn x 4¾ in., (160 x 120 mm.), etching (BP 739, DM 2066, FR 7032, Y 181,438, SF 1840).

BI *Femme Nue Allongee,* s., est. SF 800/1,200, (09-04-92, Germann, #237), 6Zn x 7½ in., (170 x 190 mm.), etching.

$737* *Fille De Marseille (Cailler 45), 1915,* i., (09-04-92, Germann, #233, illus.), 8Zn x 6Bn in., (205 x 160 mm.), etching (BP 369, DM 1033, FR 3516, Y 90,719, SF 920).

BI *La Gosse (Cailler 10), 1910-1912,* s., d., est. SF 5/700, (04-21-93, Germann, #278), 10B, x 8Zn in., (270 x 205 mm.), etching.

$645* *Nu A La Lanterne Chinoise,* s., (09-04-92, Germann, #238, illus.), 8Mn x 8Zn in., (215 x 220 mm.), etching (BP 323, DM 904, FR 3077, Y 79,394, SF 805).

$876* *Pantalonnade (Cailler 26), 1913,* s., d., (09-04-92, Germann, #243, illus.), 10¼ x 10Mn in., (260 x 265 mm.), etching (BP 439, DM 1228, FR 4179, Y 107,829, SF 1093).

BI *Pierrot,* s., est. SF 800/1,300, (09-04-92, Germann, #234, illus.), 9¼ x 7M, in., (235 x 200 mm.), etching.

$1059* *La Princesse (Cailler 3), 1914: Ten,* s., d., (10-14-92, Germann, #486), 11Zn x 12½ in., (300 x 318 mm.), etching (BP 622, DM 1550, FR 5256, Y 128,333, SF 1380).

$424* *La Princesse (Cailler 32), 1914,* s., d., (09-04-92, Germann, #235, illus.), 7Zn x 4½ in., (180 x 115 mm.), etching (BP 212, DM 594, FR 2023, Y 52,191, SF 529).

$184* *La Puce (Cailler 232), 1943,* E.A., s., (09-04-92, Germann, #240), 19Zn x 13¾ in., (500 x 350 mm.), lithograph (BP 92, DM 258, FR 878, Y 22,649, SF 230).

$983* *Saltimbanque, (Cailler/Darl 195), 1939,* stone mono., s.,, (11-13-92, Koller, #5246), 14B, x 11 in., (37.2 x 28 cm.), lithograph on wove (BP 635, DM 1543, FR 5204, Y 122,006, SF 1392).

BI *Selbstbildnis, 1946,* plate s., est. SF 140/180, (09-04-92, Germann, #244), 6⅞ₐₙ x 4⅜ₐₙ in., (170 x 110 mm.), lithograph.

BARRAUD, William (after)
$96* *Mr William Long On Bertha,* by Edward Hacker, pub. James Sheldon, (03-03-93, Bonhams-Chelsea, #124), image 14½ x 19 in., (36.8 x 48.3 cm.), hand-colored engraving (BP 66, DM 158, FR 536, Y 11,218).

$367* *The Pytchley Hunt, 1852,* proof before t., trimmed to plate, laid down, surface soiling, repaired tear into image, (11-30-92, Phillips-London, #264), sheet 20⅞, x 31⅞, in., (511 x 810 mm.), mixed-method engraving on chine appliqué (BP 242, DM 585, FR 1985, Y 45,675).

BARRERE, Adrien   French 1877-1931
$336* *Alcool De Menthe Ricqles,* fair cond., (11-19-92, Ribeyre/ Baron, #9, illus.), 59⅞ₐₙ x 43⅜ₐₙ in., (152 x 110 cm.), poster (BP 221, DM 536, FR 1805, Y 41,786).

$414* *Melle Napierkowska, Pathe,* creases, (01-31-93, Morelle/ Marchan, #221), 47¼ x 62⅜ ₐₙ in., (120 x 160 cm.), poster (BP 278, DM 667, FR 2255, Y 51,647).

$80* *Theatre Du Palais Royal. La Marmotte, c. 1905,* cond. B, (03-16-93, Boisgirard, #49), 78¾ x 51⅞ₐₙ in., (200 x 130 cm.), poster (BP 55, DM 133, FR 452, Y 9355).

BARRETT, Jerry (after)
BI *A Drawing Room At St. James's Palace, 1869,* by F. Stacpoole, pub. William Lucas, laid on canvas, mounted on stretcher, time-stained, foxing, est. BP 150/250, (11-30-92, Phillips-London, #33), plate 26¾ x 44⅞, in., (67.9 x 114 cm.), mixed-method engraving on india laid.

BARRIS, George   American 20th cent.
$297* *Marilyn Monroe At Mirror In Bathroom,* s., artist's proof, (10-10-92, Bonhams, #195, illus.), 8 x 10 in., (20.3 x 25.4 cm.), photograph (BP 176, DM 441, FR 1481, Y 36,158).

$408* *Marilyn Monroe Beside The Sea Holding Green Towel,* #47/99, (10-10-92, Bonhams, #220, illus.), 10 x 8 in., (25.4 x 20.3 cm.), color photograph (BP 242, DM 606, FR 2035, Y 49,671).

$408* *Marilyn Monroe By The Sea With Towel And Hand To Mouth,* stamp, blind embossed, #79/99, (10-10-92, Bonhams, #218, illus.), 10 x 8 in., (25.4 x 20.3 cm.), color photograph (BP 242, DM 606, FR 2035, Y 49,671).

$649* *Marilyn Monroe Driving Car,* s., artist's proof, (10-10-92, Bonhams, #200, illus.), 10 x 8 in., (25.4 x 20.3 cm.), photograph (BP 385, DM 964, FR 3237, Y 79,011).

$519* *Marilyn Monroe Full figure On Beach Beside Sea, Seaweed Over Shoulders,* blind embossed, artist's proof, (10-10-92, Bonhams, #212, illus.), 14 x 11 in., (35.6 x 27.9 cm.), photograph (BP 308, DM 771, FR 2589, Y 63,185).

$334* *Marilyn Monroe In Knitted Jacket At Water's Edge,* s., artist's proof, (10-10-92, Bonhams, #222, illus.), 10 x 8 in., (25.4 x 20.3 cm.), photograph (BP 198, DM 496, FR 1666, Y 40,662).

$556* *Marilyn Monroe Kneeling Beside Seashore, Holding Towel,* s., artist's proof, (10-10-92, Bonhams, #216, illus.), 14 x 11 in., (35.6 x 27.9 cm.), color photograph (BP 330, DM 826, FR 2773, Y 67,689).

$334* *Marilyn Monroe Kneeling On Beach, Wrapped In Towel,* s., #13/99, (10-10-92, Bonhams, #219, illus.), 5 x 7 in., (12.7 x 17.8 cm.), color photograph (BP 198, DM 496, FR 1666, Y 40,662).

$241* *Marilyn Monroe Lying On Beach In Knitted Jacket And Wrapped In Towel,* blind embossed, artist's proof, (10-10-92, Bonhams, #223, illus.), 8 x 10 in., (20.3 x 25.4 cm.), photograph (BP 143, DM 358, FR 1202, Y 29,340).

$315* *Marilyn Monroe Lying On Beach In Knitted Jacket And Wrapped In Towel, Hand Holding Collar,* s., #13/99, (10-10-92, Bonhams, #224, illus.), 11 x 14 in., (27.9 x 35.6 cm.), photograph (BP 187, DM 468, FR 1571, Y 38,349).

$278* *Marilyn Monroe Lying On Bed With Telephone,* s., #15/99, (10-10-92, Bonhams, #199, illus.), 11 x 14 in., (27.9 x 35.6 cm.), photograph (BP 165, DM 413, FR 1387, Y 33,845).

$445* *Marilyn Monroe Lying On Sand, Hands To Face,* artist's proof, (10-10-92, Bonhams, #225, illus.), 14 x 11 in.,

(35.6 x 27.9 cm.), photograph (BP 264, DM 661, FR 2219, Y 54,176).

$352* *Marilyn Monroe Lying On Sofa, Laughing,* s., artist's proof, (10-10-92, Bonhams, #197, illus.), 8 x 10 in., (20.3 x 25.4 cm.), photograph (BP 209, DM 523, FR 1756, Y 42,854).

$371* *Marilyn Monroe On All Fours At Seashore In Orange Bikini,* s., artist's proof, (10-10-92, Bonhams, #204, illus.), 11 x 14 in., (27.9 x 35.6 cm.), color photograph (BP 220, DM 551, FR 1850, Y 45,167).

$649* *Marilyn Monroe On Beach Wrapped In Towel,* s., #11/99, (10-10-92, Bonhams, #215, illus.), 14 x 11 in., (35.6 x 27.9 cm.), color photograph (BP 385, DM 964, FR 3237, Y 79,011).

$352* *Marilyn Monroe On Beach, Draped In Towel, Drinking Champagne,* s., #16/99, (10-10-92, Bonhams, #221, illus.), 7 x 5 in., (17.8 x 12.7 cm.), color photograph (BP 209, DM 523, FR 1756, Y 42,854).

$167* *Marilyn Monroe On Beach, Holding Towel, Stretched Out,* s., artist's proof, (10-10-92, Bonhams, #214, illus.), 10 x 8 in., (25.4 x 20.3 cm.), photograph (BP 99, DM 248, FR 833, Y 20,331).

$556* *Marilyn Monroe On Hands And Knees On Beach,* s., #8/99, (10-10-92, Bonhams, #205, illus.), 11 x 14 in., (27.9 x 35.6 cm.), photograph (BP 330, DM 826, FR 2773, Y 67,689).

$464* *Marilyn Monroe On beach, Draped In Towel, 'All Of Me',* s., #125/325, (10-10-92, Bonhams, #217, illus.), 23 x 28 in., (58.4 x 71.1 cm.), color lithographic print (BP 275, DM 689, FR 2314, Y 56,489).

$278* *Marilyn Monroe Reclining On Sofa,* s., #14/99, (10-10-92, Bonhams, #198, illus.), 11 x 14 in., (27.9 x 35.6 cm.), photograph (BP 165, DM 413, FR 1387, Y 33,845).

$204* *Marilyn Monroe Running Out Of The Surf,* s., artist's proof, (10-10-92, Bonhams, #209, illus.), 10 x 8 in., (25.4 x 20.3 cm.), photograph (BP 121, DM 303, FR 1017, Y 24,836).

$2966* *Marilyn Monroe Sitting On Beach, Hands Clasped,* s., #25/99, (10-10-92, Bonhams, #228, illus.), 7 x 5 in., (17.8 x 12.7 cm.), color photograph (BP 1760, DM 4406, FR 14,793, Y 361,091).

$352* *Marilyn Monroe Sitting On Step On Terrace, Hands Together,* blind embossed, artist's proof, (10-10-92, Bonhams, #189, illus.), 14 x 11 in., (35.6 x 27.9 cm.), photograph (BP 209, DM 523, FR 1756, Y 42,854).

$334* *Marilyn Monroe Sitting On Terrace, Chin Resting On Hand, One Eye Half Closed,* blind embossed, #3/99, (10-10-92, Bonhams, #186, illus.), 20 x 16 in., (50.8 x 40.6 cm.), photograph (BP 198, DM 496, FR 1666, Y 40,662).

$222* *Marilyn Monroe Walking From The Sea,* s., artist's proof, (10-10-92, Bonhams, #211, illus.), 10 x 8 in., (25.4 x 20.3 cm.), photograph (BP 132, DM 330, FR 1107, Y 27,027).

$220* *Marilyn Monroe, Amazing 1962,* s., #38/99, (04-26-93, Selkirk, #531), 14 x 11 in., (35.6 x 27.9 cm.), b/w photograph (BP 139, DM 345, FR 1165, Y 24,277).

$275* *Marilyn Monroe, At The Beach 1962,* s., #78/99, (04-26-93, Selkirk, #527), 10 x 8 in., (25.4 x 20.3 cm.), color photograph (BP 174, DM 431, FR 1456, Y 30,347).

$165* *Marilyn Monroe, Beach Meditation, 1962,* 25th Anniversary Edition 99, (04-26-93, Selkirk, #524), 11 x 14 in., (27.9 x 35.6 cm.), photograph, b/w proof (BP 104, DM 259, FR 873, Y 18,208).

$222* *Marilyn Monroe, Bending Down In Surf,* s., #17/99, (10-10-92, Bonhams, #203, illus.), 7 x 5 in., (17.8 x 12.7 cm.), photograph (BP 132, DM 330, FR 1107, Y 27,027).

$275* *Marilyn Monroe, Chilly Wind 1962,* s., #47/99, (04-26-93, Selkirk, #543), 14 x 11 in., (35.6 x 27.9 cm.), color photograph (BP 174, DM 431, FR 1456, Y 30,347).

$275* *Marilyn Monroe, Hands Clasped At The Beach 1962,* s., #42/99, (04-26-93, Selkirk, #542), 14 x 11 in., (35.6 x 27.9 cm.), color photograph (BP 174, DM 431, FR 1456, Y 30,347).

$241* *Marilyn Monroe, Hands To Face,* s., artist's proof, (10-10-92, Bonhams, #196, illus.), 10 x 8 in., (25.4 x 20.3 cm.), photograph (BP 143, DM 358, FR 1202, Y 29,340).

$315* *Marilyn Monroe, Holding Mirror, Checking Hair,* s., #34/99, (10-10-92, Bonhams, #183, illus.), 7 x 5 in., (17.8 x 12.7 cm.), photograph (BP 187, DM 468, FR 1571, Y 38,349).

$297* *Marilyn Monroe, In Bikini 'Feelin' The Surf',* s., #190/325, (10-10-92, Bonhams, #213, illus.), 20 x 24 in., (50.8 x 61 cm.), lithographic print (BP 176, DM 441, FR 1481, Y 36,158).

$352* *Marilyn Monroe, In Orange Outfit, Sitting,* #57/99, (10-10-92, Bonhams, #188, illus.), 10 x 8 in., (25.4 x 20.3 cm.), color photograph (BP 209, DM 523, FR 1756, Y 42,854).

$334* *Marilyn Monroe, In Profile, Leaning Against Fence With Glass Of Champagne,* s., #17/99, (10-10-92, Bonhams, #192, illus.), 14 x 11 in., (35.6 x 27.9 cm.), photograph (BP 198, DM 496, FR 1666, Y 40,662).

$187* *Marilyn Monroe, Knitted Sweater At The Beach, 1962,* 25th Anniversary Edition 99, (04-26-93, Selkirk, #521), 11 x 14 in., (27.9 x 35.6 cm.), photograph, b/w proof (BP 118, DM 293, FR 990, Y 20,636).

$464* *Marilyn Monroe, Leaning Against Fence With Champagne, Malibu, 1962,* s., #9/325, (10-10-92, Bonhams, #193, illus.), 24 x 22 in., (61 x 55.9 cm.), lithographic print (BP 275, DM 689, FR 2314, Y 56,489).

$464* *Marilyn Monroe, Leaning On Fence With Glass Of Champagne,* s., p. 14/99, (10-10-92, Bonhams, #191, illus.), 14 x 11 in., (35.6 x 27.9 cm.), photograph (BP 275, DM 689, FR 2314, Y 56,489).

$222* *Marilyn Monroe, Lying On Bench,* s., #25/99, (10-10-92, Bonhams, #190, illus.), 5 x 7 in., (12.7 x 17.8 cm.), photograph (BP 132, DM 330, FR 1107, Y 27,027).

$297* *Marilyn Monroe, Lying On Sand Beside The Sea, In A Bikini,* blind embossed Edward Weston Coll., #52/99, (10-10-92, Bonhams, #206, illus.), 8 x 10 in., (20.3 x 25.4 cm.), color photograph (BP 176, DM 441, FR 1481, Y 36,158).

$779* *Marilyn Monroe, Monrage Of Six Images In White Automobile,* s., #141/225, (10-10-92, Bonhams, #201, illus.), 18 x 28 in., (45.7 x 71.1 cm.), lithographic print (BP 462, DM 1157, FR 3885, Y 94,838).

$154* *Marilyn Monroe, On The Stoop, 1962,* 25th Anniversary Edition 99, (04-26-93, Selkirk, #522), 11 x 14 in., (27.9 x 35.6 cm.), photograph, b/w proof (BP 97, DM 241, FR 815, Y 16,994).

$315* *Marilyn Monroe, Orange Bikini, White Wrap, Enjoying The Surf,* blind embossed Edward Weston Coll., #21/99, (10-10-92, Bonhams, #207, illus.), 8 x 10 in., (20.3 x 25.4 cm.), color photograph (BP 187, DM 468, FR 1571, Y 38,349).

$2596* *Marilyn Monroe, Portrait,* unique, s., (10-10-92, Bonhams, #182, illus.), 14 x 11 in., (35.6 x 27.9 cm.), solarised color photograph (BP 1540, DM 3856, FR 12,948, Y 316,046).

$371* *Marilyn Monroe, Portrait Eyes Closed,* s., #21/99, (10-10-92, Bonhams, #184, illus.), 14 x 11 in., (35.6 x 27.9 cm.), color photograph (BP 220, DM 551, FR 1850, Y 45,167).

$315* *Marilyn Monroe, Portrait In Cyclamen Dress, Hand To Wall,* #27/99, (10-10-92, Bonhams, #187, illus.), 10 x 8 in., (25.4 x 20.3 cm.), color photograph (BP 187, DM 468, FR 1571, Y 38,349).

$297* *Marilyn Monroe, Running At Water's Edge,* s., artist's proof, (10-10-92, Bonhams, #210, illus.), 8 x 10 in., (20.3 x 25.4 cm.), photograph (BP 176, DM 441, FR 1481, Y 36,158).

$248* *Marilyn Monroe, Seaweed 1962,* s., #18/99, (04-26-93, Selkirk, #526), 10 x 8 in., (25.4 x 20.3 cm.), b/w photograph (BP 157, DM 389, FR 1313, Y 27,367).

$165* *Marilyn Monroe, Seaweed And Bikini, 1962,* 25th Anniversary Edition 99, (04-26-93, Selkirk, #523), 11 x 14 in., (27.9 x 35.6 cm.), photograph, b/w proof (BP 104, DM 259, FR 873, Y 18,208).

$464* *Marilyn Monroe, Sitting On Patio Steps Waving Goodbye,* s., #15/99, (10-10-92, Bonhams, #194, illus.), 14 x 11 in., (35.6 x 27.9 cm.), photograph (BP 275, DM 689, FR 2314, Y 56,489).

$371* *Marilyn Monroe, Sitting, Smiling In Knitted Jacket, Towel Over Knees,* blind embossed, #29/99, (10-10-92, Bonhams, #227, illus.), 8 x 10 in., (20.3 x 25.4 cm.), color photograph (BP 220, DM 551, FR 1850, Y 45,167).

$464* *Marilyn Monroe, Smiling, Hand To Shoulder 'Always Yours',* s., #99/325, (10-10-92, Bonhams, #185, illus.), 28 x 23 in., (71.1 x 58.4 cm.), color lithographic print (BP 275, DM 689, FR 2314, Y 56,489).

$371* *Marilyn Monroe, Standing Beside Sea In Knitted Jacket,* artist's proof, stamp, (10-10-92, Bonhams, #226, illus.), 14 x 11 in., (35.6 x 27.9 cm.), photograph (BP 220, DM 551, FR 1850, Y 45,167).

$464* *Marilyn Monroe, Standing In Wet Sand In White Short Robe,* #48/99, (10-10-92, Bonhams, #208, illus.), 8 x 10 in., (20.3 x 25.4 cm.), color photograph (BP 275, DM 689, FR 2314, Y 56,489).

$352* *Marilyn Monroe, Standing On Beach Against Surf In Bikini,* s., artist's proof, (10-10-92, Bonhams, #202, illus.), 14 x 11 in., (35.6 x 27.9 cm.), color photograph (BP 209, DM 523, FR 1756, Y 42,854).

$220* *Marilyn Monroe, Swinging 1962,* s., #14/99, (04-26-93, Selkirk, #525), 10 x 8 in., (25.4 x 20.3 cm.), b/w photograph (BP 139, DM 345, FR 1165, Y 24,277).

BARRIVIERA, Lino Bianchi   1906-1985
$539* *"Al Palatino, 1936" and "Inverno, 1950": Two,* first # 4/15, s., d.; second #49/50, s., d., (03-25-93, Finarte-Rome, #33), etching (BP 366, DM 885, FR 3011, Y 63,144, L 863).

$718* *"La Notte, 1956" and "Controluce, 1955": Two,* first # 18/30, s., d.; second #30/30, s., d., exhib., (03-25-93, Finarte-Rome, #9, illus.), etching (BP 488, DM 1180, FR 4011, Y 84,114, L 1150).

BARRY, Anne Meredith
$86* *Nipigon Rocks,* s., t., #26/35, (06-07-93, Ritchie, #41, illus.), 21½ x 27 in., (54.6 x 68.6 cm.), embossed color intaglio print (BP 57, DM 139, FR 470, Y 9225, C$ 110).

BARRY, D.F.
$440* *Portrait Of Indian,* photog.'s imprint, 1880's, (10-14-92, Swann, #94, illus.), image 5 x 4 in., (12.7 x 10.2 cm.), photograph, albumen cabinet card (BP 258, DM 644, FR 2184, Y 53,320).

$440* *Sitting Bull's Family, 1890,* photog.'s imprint, t., (10-14-92, Swann, #95, illus.), image 4 x 5 in., (10.2 x 12.7 cm.), photograph, albumen cabinet card (BP 258, DM 644, FR 2184, Y 53,320).

BARRY, David F. and George W. SCOTT
$2750* *Chief Joseph, Nez Perce; and Chief Sitting Bull, Sioux: Two,* cabinet cards, 1st w/paper label, studio credit; 2nd w/t., studio credt., lit., (10-13-92, Christie-NY, #54, illus.), each 6 x 3¾ in., (15.2 x 9.5 cm.), photograph (BP 1602, DM 4029, FR 13,688, Y 333,455).

BARRY, James
BI *King Lear (Pressly 38; Man 21),* trimmed into border, narrow margins, creases, est. BP 1/2,000, (06-30-93, Sotheby-London, #249), 9¼ x 12½ in., (235 x 318 mm.), pen-lithograph on laid, on support sheet w/dark chocolate-brown aquatint surround.

BARRYMORE, Lionel
$154* *Scenes Of New England: Four,* plates s., t. Lionel Barrymore, reprinted from orig. plates, (04-02-93, Garth, #268), smallest 10¾ x 13¾ in., (27.3 x 34.9 cm.), largest 12¾ x 16¾ in., (27.3 x 34.9 cm.), b/w etching (BP 101, DM 248, FR 841, Y 17,534).

BI *Untitled: Set Of Four,* est. $1/200, (12-11-92, DuMouchelle, #1286), approx. 7½ x 5¾ in., (19.1 x 14.6 cm.), etchings.

BARTHOLOMEW, Charles
$61* *Untitled: Five,* from Mother Goose ABC, (04-02-93, Garth, #38), 17¾ x 13¾ in., (45.1 x 34.9 cm.), chromolithograph (BP 40, DM 98, FR 333, Y 6945).

$165* *Untitled: Six,* from Mother Goose ABC, (04-02-93, Garth, #37), 17¾ x 13¾ in., (45.1 x 34.9 cm.), chromolithograph (BP 109, DM 265, FR 901, Y 18,786).

BARTHOLOMEW, Ralph (Jr.)   1907-1985
$1035* *Harper's Bazaar Playtex Ad, 1946,* s., t., d., lit., (04-08-93, Christie-NY, #249, illus.), 8¾ x 16⅞ in., (22.2 x 41 cm.), photograph, gelatin silver print (BP 679, DM 1663, FR 5628, Y 117,453).

BI *Steinway Piano Factory, 1936,* credit stamp twice, lit., est. $1,2/1,500, (04-08-93, Christie-NY, #248, illus.), 10⅞, x 13℃, in., (26.4 x 34 cm.), photograph, gelatin silver print.

BARTLETT
$22* *European Landscapes With Cathedral Cities: A Pair,* (04-02-93, Garth, #255), 10¾ x 12¾ in., (27.3 x 32.4 cm.), hand-colored engraving (BP 14, DM 35, FR 120, Y 2505).

BARTLETT, Charles W.   English 1860-1940
$523* *"Isogo", 1916,* s. in marker, good cond., (10-31-92, Cleveland, #243, illus.), 10½ x 15 in., (26.7 x 38.1 cm.), color woodcut (BP 335, DM 805, FR 2730, Y 64,784).

$110* *"Taj-Mahal, Agra 1916",* s., seal, toned, yoko-e, (11-20-92, Skinner, #78), oban yoko-e (BP 72, DM 175, FR 591, Y 13,680).

$248* *"Udaipur, 1916",* s. Charles W. Bartlett, very good cond. (?), (04-25-93, Bakker, #60), image 8¾ x 11M, in., (22.2 x 30.2 cm.), color woodblock print (BP 158, DM 392, FR 1325, Y 27,391).

BARTLETT, Jennifer   American b. 1941
$25,300* *At Sea, Japan, 1980,* s., #43/58, co-pub. artist and Simica Print Artists, Inc., blindstamp, good cond., discoloration, (05-15-93, Sotheby-NY, #916, illus.), each sheet 22B, x 16¾ in., (57.5 x 42.5 cm.), overall size 22B, x 100℃, in., (57.5 x 42.5 cm.), silkscreen and woodcut in colors on six sheets of handmade Kurotani Hosho (BP 16,450, DM 40,695, FR 136,757, Y 2,804,567).

$3850* *From Rhapsody: House, Tree, Beach, Birds, 1985,* complete suite, s., i. 'A-D', #20/100, pub. Harry N. Abrams, Inc., good cond., original portfolio, (11-07-92, Sotheby-NY, #517, illus.), each sheet 12 x 12 in., (305 x 305 mm.), four aquatints and etchings p. in colors on T.H. Saunders paper (BP 2517, DM 6147, FR 20,777, Y 475,191).

$10,450* *Graceland Mansion, 1978-79,* s. verso, d., i. 'PP VII', pub. Paula Cooper Gallery/Brooke Alexander, Inc., good cond., (11-07-92, Sotheby-NY, #516, illus.), overall size 24 x 120Z, in., (61 x 305.1 cm.), 5 part print, drypoint, aquatint, silkscreen, woodcut and lithographp. in colors, on five sheets of paper (BP 6832, DM 16,685, FR 56,395, Y 1,289,805).

BI *In The Garden #116, 1983,* s., d., #73/100, pub. Paula Cooper w/Simca Print Artists blindstamp,excell. cond., Late M. Anwar Kamal, M.D. Coll., est. $5/6,000, (05-11-93, Christie-NY, #368, illus.), sheet 29¼ x 38 in., (743 x 965 mm.), color screenprint on Arches.

BI *Shadow, 1985: Four,* s., d. verso of panel D, i. 'A'-'D', #17/60, co-pub. Paula Cooper and Multiples, Inc., crease, excell. cond., framed together, the Late M. Anwar Kamal, M.D. Coll., est. $12/18,000, (05-11-93, Christie-NY, #369, illus.), overall sheet 29¾ x 89 in., (75.6 x 226.1 cm.), etching, soft-ground etching, aquatint and drypoint in colors on wove.

$3163* *Untitled (Graceland Woodcut, State 1), 1979-80: Five,* complete portfolio, each t. I-V, #13/20, V s., d. 1979, pub. Cooper & Alexander, full margins good cond., crease, light-staining, (05-15-93, Sotheby-NY, #914, illus.), each sheet 27¾ x 27¾ in., (70.5 x 70.5 cm.), woodcut in different colors on white Japanese (BP 2057, DM 5088, FR 17,097, Y 350,626).

$2300* *Untitled (Graceland Woodcut, State II), 1979-80: Three,* complete portfolio, each t. I-III, #19/20, III s., d. 1979, pub. Cooper & Alexander, full margins, good cond., light-staining, (05-15-93, Sotheby-NY, #915, illus.), each sheet 33 x 32M, in., (83.8 x 83.5 cm.), woodcut in colors on white Japanese (BP 1495, DM 3700, FR 12,432, Y 254,961).

BARTLETT, William H. (after)
$358* *"Hudson Highlands, Peekskill Landing"; "View Of New York, From Weehawkean"; "View Of Hudson City And The Catskill Mountains"; "View From Ruggle's House, Newburgh" and "Village Of Sing-Sing": Six,* engraved by R. Brandard, E. Benjamin and R. Wallis, Mary Parker Porter Estate, (09-19-92, Weschler, #152), 4¼ x 7 in., (10.8 x 17.8 cm.), colored engravings (BP 210, DM 531, FR 1817, Y 44,247).

BARTLETT, William Henry   English 1809-1894
$121* *"Boston From The Dorchester Heights" and "The Ferry At Brooklyn, NewYork": A Pair,* (04-02-93, Sloan, #1169),

larger, image 4¾ x 6M, in., (121 x 175 mm.), color engraving (BP 80, DM 194, FR 660, Y 13,777).

BARTOLI (after HAMILTON)
$1320* *"The Months": Twelve,* oval, (03-20-93, Northeast, #483), frames 13 x 10 in., (33 x 25.4 cm.), hand-colored engraving (BP 885, DM 2158, FR 7346, Y 153,114).

BARTOLI, Pietro Santi
$550* *Colonna Traiana, Eretta ... All'Imperatore Traiano Augusto Nel Suo Foro In Roma ... Nuovamente Disegnata Et Intaligliata ... Con L'Esposizione LatinD'Alfonso Ciaccone: 126,* t., ded., 119 num. plates, 8 leaves letterpress explanatory text, oblong folio, t. creased, George Loch bookplate, (11-12-92, Swann, #103), engraving, old vellum (BP 361, DM 871, FR 2940, Y 68,196).

BARTOLINI, Luigi   Italian 1892-1963
$718* *Donna Del Circo,* #4/20, s., (03-25-93, Finarte-Rome, #39), aquatint and etching (BP 488, DM 1180, FR 4011, Y 84,114, L 1150).

$783* *Il Cimitero,* s., t., (05-20-93, Finarte-Milan, #16), 3Z, x 7℃zn in., (8 x 19.5 cm.), etching (BP 503, DM 1263, FR 4255, Y 86,462, L 1150).

$2620* *Il Fiume Chienti, (Bartolini, p. 72), 1929,* artist proof, s; s., d. verso, (12-15-92, Finarte-Milan, #45, illus.), 12℃, x 14℃zn in., (31.5 x 38 cm.), etching (BP 1671, DM 4107, FR 14,033, Y 324,941, L 3680).

$2349* *Il Mazzetto, 1930,* s., d., i. esemplare unico, lastra distrutta, (05-20-93, Finarte-Milan, #9, illus.), 7M, x 7℃zn in., (20 x 19.6 cm.), etching (BP 1508, DM 3790, FR 12,766, Y 259,386, L 3450).

$1410* *Il Sapone Dentro La Vasca, 1943,* proof, s., d., t., lit., (05-20-93, Finarte-Milan, #4, illus.), 12℃zn x 12℃zn in., (30.7 x 32.5 cm.), etching (BP 905, DM 2275, FR 7663, Y 155,698, L 2070).

$2193* *Merano Di Notte, 1938,* s., d., t. addio Merano, esempare primo, (05-20-93, Finarte-Milan, #14, illus.), 8℃zn x 11℃zn in., (20.8 x 30 cm.), etching (BP 1408, DM 3538, FR 11,918, Y 242,160, L 3220).

$1880* *Pesci E Stella Di Mare, 1930,* #21/50, s., d., t., (05-20-93, Finarte-Milan, #18, illus.), 7M, x 9½ in., (20 x 24.2 cm.), etching (BP 1207, DM 3033, FR 10,217, Y 207,597, L 2760).

BARTOLOZZI (after)
$47 *Four Figures Conversing,* (12-11-92, G.A. Key, #73), 7 x 11 in., (17.8 x 27.9 cm.), hand colored stipple engraving (BP 30, DM 74, FR 254, Y 5816).

BARTOLOZZI, Francesco   Italian 1725/27-1815
$374* *"Countryside Merrymaking" and "Toasting Banquet": A Pair,* fading, foxing, (05-07-93, Goldberg, #433), each 18 x 18 in., (45.7 x 45.7 cm.), hand-colored engravings (BP 237, DM 591, FR 1993, Y 41,180).

$143* *The Happy Meeting, 1795,* after Sawrey Gilpin, pub. A. Molteno, margins, (11-19-92, Bonhams-Chelsea, #87), plate 17¼ x 12½ in., (43.8 x 31.8 cm.), stipple engraving (BP 94, DM 228, FR 768, Y 17,784).

$384* *Jupiter And Io,* after Allegri da Correggio, foxing, surface dirt, trimmed, (11-19-92, Bonhams-Chelsea, #77), image 13¾ x 10 in., (34.9 x 25.4 cm.), stipple engraving in red (BP 253, DM 612, FR 2062, Y 47,755).

BI *Miss Farren (Calame-de Vesme 1075 V), 1792,* after Thomas Lawrence, est. DM 1,800, (12-04-92, Bassenge, #6512), 21M, x 13℃zn in., (55.6 x 35.1 cm.), color etching in stipple manner on hand-made.

$176* *The Musical Lesson,* after Carlo Cignani, (10-30-92, Sloan, #1944), 7½ x 9¾ in., (19.1 x 24.8 cm.), sepia engraving (BP 113, DM 271, FR 919, Y 21,801).

$281* *A Nest Of Cupids,* by Francesco Bartolozzi, pub. Anthony Malteno, 1804, margins, staining, (06-16-93, Bonhams-Chelsea, #479), pl. 10¾ x 13¾ in., (27.3 x 34.9 cm.), stipple engraving (BP 187, DM 466, FR 1565, Y 29,970).

BI *"Young Boy Playing With A Puzzle", 1795,* after Leonardo da Vinci, pub. A. Molteno, margins, est. BP 40/60, (11-19-92, Bonhams-Chelsea, #86), plate 8¾ x 7 in., (22.2 x 17.8 cm.), stipple engraving.

BARTOLOZZI, Francesco (after)
$265 *Figures In Landscapes: A Pair,* (12-11-92, G.A. Key, #104), 12 x 10 in., (30.5 x 25.4 cm.), colored stipple engraving (BP 170, DM 418, FR 1431, Y 32,793).

$160   *Figures In Landscapes: A Pair,* (04-16-93, G.A. Key, #50), 12 x 10 in., (30.5 x 25.4 cm.), colored stipple engraving (BP 105, DM 258, FR 873, Y 17,992).

$374   *"Syliva Overseen By Daphne" and "Blind Mans Buff":* A Pair, (12-11-92, G.A. Key, #87), 11 x 8 in., (27.9 x 20.3 cm.), hand-colored stipple engraving (BP 240, DM 589, FR 2019, Y 46,281).

BARTOLOZZI, Francesco, Engraver

$578*   *The Four Seasons,* (06-16-93, Bonhams-Chelsea, #478, illus.), image 5 x 4℃, in., (12.7 x 11.1 cm.), stipple engraving w/hand-coloring (BP 385, DM 959, FR 3220, Y 61,647).

BARTSCH, Adam von   1758-1821

$332*   *Selbstbildnis, 1785,* lit., (12-04-92, Bassenge, #6513), 6℞ x 5 in., (16.8 x 12.7 cm.), etching (BP 213, DM 529, FR 1794, Y 41,448).

BARYE, Antoine Louis   French 1795-1875

BI   *Le Cerf Dix Cors,* water stains, dust, good margins, collector's stamp, (06-11-93, Picard, #4), 4℞n x 6℞n in., (112 x 164 mm.), lithograph on chine fixe.

$1032*   *Ours Du Mississipi (L. Delteil, num. 6), 1836,* collector's stamp, stains, reddish stains, (04-02-93, Picard, #24), 6℞n x 9¼ in., (17.7 x 23.5 cm.), black lithograph on Chine applique on wove (BP 680, DM 1659, FR 5633, Y 117,500).

BASEBE, Charles J. and William DRUMMOND

$574*   *Edward Gower Wenman,* pub. W.H. Mason and R. Dark, 1849, foxing, back cover illus., (03-03-93, Bonhams-Chelsea, #242, illus.), image 10¼ x 8 in., (26 x 20.3 cm.), lithograph (BP 396, DM 945, FR 3207, Y 67,072).

BASELITZ, Georg   German b. 1938

$3547*   *Adler, 1980,* s., d., (06-05-93, Schoppmann, #698), woodcut on factory print (BP 2335, DM 5751, FR 19,383, Y 380,498).

$4950*   *Baume 26, VII,* s., d. G Baselitz 26. VIII. 76, num. 4/9, prov., (11-19-92, Christie-NY, #169, illus.), 24 x 16℞, in., (61 x 42.9 cm.), monotype w/brush/black ink/oil on paper (BP 3259, DM 7892, FR 26,584, Y 615,595).

$2164*   *Eine Kuh Abwarts (Jahn Band I 65), 1969,* #11/20, pencil s., (11-20-92, Lempertz, #444), sh 12℞, x 16℞n in., (32.1 x 42 cm.), etching on Velin (BP 1425, DM 3450, FR 11,622, Y 269,121).

$3080*   *Flashe (Jahn 338), 1980,* s., d., unique trial proof, pub., creases, tear, very good cond., (11-09-92, Christie-NY, #244, illus.), 34 x 24 in., (864 x 610 mm.), linocut w/ monotype in dark brown on wove (BP 2036, DM 4917, FR 16,613, Y 382,229).

BI   *Frau Im Fenster (Jahn 197 I/III), 1979,* s., d., i. No. 1, est. DM 35,000, (05-27-93, Lempertz, #597, illus.), 68℞n x 56℞n in., (173.5 x 144 cm.), linocut on drawing paper.

$682*   *Frauenkopf, 1988,* s., d., #23/30, full margins, good cond., (12-03-92, Sotheby-London, #611, illus.), sheet 12½ x 9 in., (320 x 230 mm.), drypoint w/tone on chine applique on white wove (BP 440, DM 1072, FR 3661, Y 84,858).

BI   *Hand Vor Der Stirn, 1985,* s., d., #4/20, est. DM 7,000-, (05-27-93, Lempertz, #600, illus.), 25℞n x 19℞n in., (65 x 49 cm.), woodcut on Japan.

$4658*   *Hirte (Jahn 18 II), 1965,* s., d. 65, (05-27-93, Lempertz, #594, illus.), 26℞, x 20 in., (66.3 x 50.8 cm.), etching on Richard de Bas hand-made (BP 2983, DM 7474, FR 25,192, Y 499,357).

BI   *Der Hirte (Jahn 28.2), 1965,* s., d.; plate s., est. DM 7,500, (06-12-93, Hauswedell/Nolt, #30, illus.), 12½ x 9℞n in., (31.8 x 23.7 cm.), etching w/aquatint and drypoint.

$1269*   *Der Hirte (Jahn 28; Gohr 20), 1965,* s., d., num., (05-26-93, Dorling, #2543, illus.), 12℞n x 9℞n in., (31.9 x 23.7 cm.), etching on thick wove (BP 821, DM 2070, FR 6969, Y 137,875).

$5049*   *Der Hirte (Jahn Band I 28), 1965,* #19/60, pencil s., d., (11-20-92, Lempertz, #441, illus.), sh 17℃, x 12℞, in., (44.2 x 32 cm.), etching on Velin (BP 3324, DM 8050, FR 27,116, Y 627,907).

$664*   *Komposition, (19)81,* s., d., num., (12-01-92, Karl/Faber, #355), 12℃, x 9℞n in., (31.5 x 25 cm.), etching on wove (BP 439, DM 1058, FR 3607, Y 82,669).

BI   *Komposition, 1986,* s. George Baselitz 86, 23/25, est. DK 10,000, (03-24-93, Kunsthallen, #30, illus.), etching.

BI   *Komposition, 1986,* s. G. Baselitz 86, 23/25, est. DK 12,000, (09-30-92, Kunsthallen, #29), etching.

$1010*   *Landschaft (Jahn Band I 91), 1971-1972,* pencil s., d., (11-20-92, Lempertz, #445), sh 20℞n x 26½ in., (51 x 67.3 cm.), etching on Velin (BP 665, DM 1610, FR 5424, Y 125,606).

$5410*   *Ohne Titel (Jahn Band I 126.6), 1965,* #19/20, pencil s., d., (11-20-92, Lempertz, #442, illus.), sh 17℞, x 12℞n in., (43.5 x 32.6 cm.), etching on Velin (BP 3562, DM 8626, FR 29,055, Y 672,802).

BI   *Ohne Titel (Jahn Band I 131.4), 1974,* pencil mono., d., artist's proof, sheet 10 from a series "Baume", est. DM 2,500, (11-20-92, Lempertz, #446), sh 30℞n x 20℞n in., (77.3 x 52.5 cm.), etching on Velin.

$866*   *Ohne Titel (Jahn Band I 175), 1974,* pencil mono., d., artist's proof, sheet 5 from portfolio "Adler", (11-20-92, Lempertz, #447), image 10℞n x 6℞, in., (27.5 x 16.8 cm.), wood engraving and line etching on imitated Japan (BP 570, DM 1381, FR 4651, Y 107,698).

$17,311*   *Ohne Titel (Jahn Band I 55), 1967,* artist's proof, pencil s., d., (11-20-92, Lempertz, #443, illus.), sh 19℞n x 12℃, in., (49 x 31.5 cm.), woodcut on hand-made (BP 11,398, DM 27,600, FR 92,970, Y 2,152,842).

BI   *"Ohne Titel" (Jahn 94), 1970/72,* s., d., sheet 2 of series Eine Woche, Edition Heiner Friedrich, Munchen, est. DM 2,2/2,400, (11-28-92, Grisebach, #425, illus.), 14℞n x 19℞, in., (35.7 x 48.6 cm.), drypoint with Roulette on China.

BI   *Orange Easter, Kongo, 1981,* inits., d., num. 58, good cond.?, buckling, est. $1,5/2,000, (10-28-92, Butterfield, #2904), 33½ x 25 in., (851 x 635 mm.), color linoleum cut on white wove.

BI   *Orange Eater (Kongo), 1981,* inits., d., #58, good cond.?, buckling, est. $1,4/1,800, (05-19-93, Butterfield, #2126), 33½ x 25 in., (851 x 635 mm.), linoleum cut in colors on white wove.

BI   *Portfolio (Wedewer/Jahn S. 169-183): Eight,* #25/50, s., num., d., est. DM 9/12,000, (06-24-93, Germann, #245, illus.), 29℞n x 25℃n in., (745 x 640 mm.), etching after drawing, etching, on Van Gelder paper.

BI   *Rebell (Jahn 27.2), 1965,* s., d., plate s., #36/60, series Helden, est. DM 7,500, (06-12-93, Hauswedell/Nolt, #29, illus.), 12℞, x 9℞n in., (32 x 23 cm.), etching w/ aquatint and drypoint on copper print.

$2166*   *Richard Wagner Als Frau, 1986,* s., d., (11-28-92, Schoppmann, #365), 19℞, x 12℃, in., (48.5 x 31.5 cm.), woodcut on handmade (BP 1430, DM 3451, FR 11,714, Y 269,571).

$11,063*   *Sans Titre,* s., #4/10, d. 85, lit., prov., (11-16-92, Briest, #256A), 78¾ x 59℞n in., (200 x 150 cm.), wood engraving (BP 7271, DM 17,644, FR 59,447, Y 1,380,631).

$2344*   *Schwarzes Tuch II, 1985,* #13/50, pencil s., d., (11-20-92, Lempertz, #450, illus.), sh 31℞ x 25℞, in., (79 x 63.8 cm.), wood cut on very thin Japan (BP 1543, DM 3737, FR 12,589, Y 291,506).

$1323*   *Sitzender Mann, 1976,* 24/100, s., d., (10-14-92, Germann, #220, illus.), 27℞, x 19℞n in., (702 x 500 mm.), etching in colors (BP 777, DM 1936, FR 6566, Y 160,325, SF 1725).

BI   *Sitzender Mannlicher Akt (Jahn Band II 183 III), 1974-76,* #26/100, pencil s., d., est. DM 1,800, (11-20-92, Lempertz, #449), sh 27℃, x 19¾ in., (69.6 x 50.2 cm.), etching on Velin.

BI   *Thinker (Jahn 386), 1981,* s., d., #45/50, pub. Maximillian Verlag, good cond., est. $4/5,000, (05-15-93, Sotheby-NY, #917, illus.), sheet 31℃, x 23¼ in., (79.7 x 59.1 cm.), linocut in colors.

$2640*   *Tranenkopf, 1986,* s., d., #1/25, pub. Maximilian Verlag/ Sabine Knust, full margins, excell. cond., (11-09-92, Christie-NY, #245, illus.), 30℞, x 22℃, in., (765 x 568 mm.), etching w/hand-coloring in yellow on wove (BP 1745, DM 4215, FR 14,239, Y 327,625).

$4965*   *Trinker (Jahn 386), 1981,* s., 1st state, for Erste Konzentration, portfolio II, (06-05-93, Schoppmann, #697),

31Æzn x 23B, in., (80.5 x 60 cm.), woodcut on offset (BP 3268, DM 8050, FR 27,131, Y 532,611).

BI *Untitled (Jahn 131), 1974,* mono., d., artist's proof, sheet 10 of series Baume, Galerie Heiner Friedrich, est. 1,800, (06-12-93, Hauswedell/Nolt, #31, illus.), 12Æzn x 9B\ in., (33 x 24.5 cm.), drypoint on thick wove.

BI *Untitled (Jahn 134 I/II), 1974,* mono., d., i. 1. Probedruck, plate 22 from Baume, est. DM 4,500-, (05-27-93, Lempertz, #596, illus.), 27Mzn x 19¾ in., (69.7 x 50.2 cm.), etching on wove.

BI *Untitled (Jahn 135), 1974,* mono., Dez. 74, i. 1 Probedr., tears, plate 14 from Baume, est. DM 4,500-, (05-27-93, Lempertz, #595, illus.), 29Æzn x 22Xzn in., (76 x 56 cm.), etching on wove.

$6638* *Untitled (Jahn 20), 1965,* s., num., early work, (12-05-92, Bassenge, #7031, illus.), 13Bzn x 9Mzn in., (33.8 x 24 cm.), drypoint on copper print paper (BP 4157, DM 10,349, FR 35,271, Y 822,451).

$3225* *Untitled (Jahn 239 II/II), 1980,* s., d., artist's proof, plate 1 from Adler, Baum, Frau im Fenster, (05-27-93, Lempertz, #598, illus.), 30B, x 20¾ in., (77.8 x 52.7 cm.), etching on wove (BP 2065, DM 5175, FR 17,442, Y 345,733).

BI *Untitled (Jahn 262 I/II), 1980-81,* mono., d., i. artist's proof, 1st state, plate 9 from Das Strassenbild, est. DM 4,000-, (05-27-93, Lempertz, #599, illus.), 25¾ x 19Zzn in., (65.4 x 50.3 cm.), etching on BFK Rives wove.

$424* *Untitled, 1986,* s., d., #15/30, (06-12-93, Hauswedell/Nolt, #32), 7Ozn x 9¾ in., (18.3 x 24.8 cm.), drypoint on BFK Rives (BP 278, DM 690, FR 2319, Y 44,617).

$495* *Untitled, 1990,* s., d., #9/25, (06-12-93, Hauswedell/Nolt, #33), 10½ x 5M, in., (26.6 x 15 cm.), wood cut on wove (BP 324, DM 806, FR 2708, Y 52,089).

BI *Untitled, Mit Offenen Armen Laufender Mann (Jahn 38 I), 1966,* i. artist's proof, s., est. DM 9,000, (06-05-93, Bassenge, #5896, illus.), 12>zn x 9Bzn in., (31.9 x 23.6 cm.), etching on copper print.

$2483* *Weisse Mutter, Schwarzes Kind, 1985,* s., d., num., (06-05-93, Schoppmann, #699), 25>zn x 19Bzn in., (65 x 49 cm.), woodcut on hand-made Japan (BP 1635, DM 4026, FR 13,568, Y 266,359).

BASEY, J.D.

$345* *Selected Works Of England, France And The Middle East: 222,* 1920s, most s., t., (05-23-93, Butterfield, #3311, illus.), smallest 4 x 5 in., largest 10 x 7 in., photograph, gelatin silver prints, some sepia toned, some on textured paper (BP 225, DM 564, FR 1899, Y 38,134).

$259* *Selected Works Of France: 258,* 1920s, s., t., (05-23-93, Butterfield, #3310, illus.), each approx. 4 x 5 in., photograph, gelatin silver prints, some sepia toned, some on textured paper (BP 169, DM 423, FR 1425, Y 28,628).

BASIRE, James 18th/19th cent.

$810* *The Encampment Of The English Forces Near Portsmouth, 1778,* margins, central join, staining, surface dirt, (08-20-92, Bonhams-Chelsea, #12, illus.), pl 22¼ x 73½ in., (56.5 x 186.7 cm.), engraving on wove (BP 418, DM 1173, FR 3980, Y 102,286).

$99* *The South West View Of The Steeple And Church Of South,* after J. Wilcockson, (04-02-93, Sloan, #2276), sight 20 x 13½ in., (508 x 343 mm.), engraving (BP 65, DM 159, FR 540, Y 11,272).

BASKE, Yamada

$193* *Harbor Sunset,* s. w/stamped cipher inside image, good cond., (03-28-93, Bakker, #201), sight 8½ x 13½ in., (21.6 x 34.3 cm.), color woodblock (BP 130, DM 315, FR 1070, Y 22,463).

BASKETT, C.A.

$40 *"Rochester",* s., (04-16-93, G.A. Key, #135), 8 x 11 in., (20.3 x 27.9 cm.), etching (BP 26, DM 65, FR 218, Y 4498).

BASKETT, Charles Henry

$34 *"Landermere",* s., proof plate, (10-09-92, G.A. Key, #95), 7 x 12¾ in., (17.8 x 32.4 cm.), aquatint (BP 20, DM 51, FR 172, Y 4146).

BASKIN, Leonard American b. 1922

$154* *"Birdman", c. 1969,* s., num. 32/110, (10-10-92, Goldberg, #529, illus.), 22 x 28 in., (55.9 x 71.1 cm.), etching (BP 91, DM 229, FR 768, Y 18,748).

$495* *"Callot",* s. Baskin, #24/50, exhib., (12-12-92, Wolf, #35), 17½ x 17½ in., (44.5 x 44.5 cm.), etching (BP 317, DM 780, FR 2673, Y 61,255).

$165* *Corot,* s., (06-11-93, Freemn/Fine Art, #13), 7¼ x 5¾ in., (18.4 x 14.6 cm.), wood engraving (BP 108, DM 268, FR 904, Y 17,507).

$176* *"D, H, And L Hopper", c. 1964,* s., num. 39/50, (10-10-92, Goldberg, #530), image 22 x 26 in., (55.9 x 66 cm.), etching (BP 104, DM 261, FR 878, Y 21,427).

BI *Death Bearing Angel (F. & O'S 732), 1967,* s., #53/90, margins, good cond. (?), est. $5/700, (02-24-93, Butterfield, #2810), 10 x 8M, in., (254 x 225 mm.), etching in wove.

BI *Death Of The Laureate (Fern 301), 1957,* s., t., i. artist's proof, est. $4/600, (03-24-93, Grogan, #128), woodcut.

$88* *"Distention" Male Nude,* #111/115, (06-11-93, DuMouchelle, #2103), 36 x 22 in., (91.4 x 55.9 cm.), lithograph (BP 58, DM 143, FR 482, Y 9337).

$77* *Eakins,* margins, s., (05-22-93, Collins, #130), 6 x 3¾ in., (15.2 x 9.5 cm.), wood engraving (BP 50, DM 125, FR 421, Y 8490).

$165* *"Eakins",* s., #49/50, (02-11-93, Boos, #411), image 22Mzn x 13Æzn in., (570 x 347 mm.), woodcut (BP 116, DM 273, FR 925, Y 19,892).

$39* *Grasses,* (10-03-92, Garth, #110), 18¼ x 14 in., (46.4 x 35.6 cm.), wood engraving (BP 23, DM 55, FR 188, Y 4668).

$220* *"Head Of A Man",* s., #30/144, blindstamp pub., good cond.?, (10-28-92, Butterfield, #2905), 28½ x 22 in., (724 x 559 mm.), lithograph on white wove (BP 140, DM 340, FR 1154, Y 26,994).

BI *Head Of Medicine Man (F. & O'S. 610), 1972,* s., #119/160, blindstamp, printer, good cond., foxing, est. $6/800, (05-19-93, Butterfield, #1981), sight 34 x 24 in., (864 x 610 mm.), lithograph on Rives BFK.

$165* *Jobe,* s., t., num. 14/60, (11-12-92, Freemn/Fine Art, #27, illus.), 11¾ x 11½ in., (29.8 x 29.2 cm.), etching (BP 108, DM 261, FR 882, Y 20,459).

$121* *"Joseph",* s., d. 1974 in stone, num., s., (10-08-92, Boos, #671), 13M, x 9½ in., (352 x 241 mm.), color lithograph (BP 72, DM 179, FR 607, Y 14,702).

$770* *Man Of Peace, 1952,* s., ripples throughout, creases, tear, (05-27-93, Swann, #26, illus.), sh 74½ x 39½ in., (189.2 x 100.3 cm.), woodcut on synthetic rice paper (BP 493, DM 1236, FR 4164, Y 82,547).

BI *"Maria Sybilla Merrian" (Fern & O'Sullivan 550),* s., t., num., excellent cond., est. $4-500, (10-31-92, Cleveland, #359), 17¾ x 14B, in., (45.1 x 37.1 cm.), color etching.

BI *Portrait, 1970,* init., num. H.C., taped, good cond., est. $3/500, (05-15-93, Cleveland, #447B), 15 x 9½ in., (38.1 x 24.1 cm.), color lithograph.

BI *Portrait, 1970,* init., good cond., est. $3/500, (05-15-93, Cleveland, #447A), 17 x 13½ in., (43.2 x 34.3 cm.), color lithograph.

$110* *Right Hand,* s., very good cond.?, (07-19-92, Bakker, #194), plate 12½ x 7½ in., (31.8 x 19.1 cm.), etching (BP 56, DM 160, FR 542, Y 13,675).

$144* *Thistle (F. & O'S. 313), 1957,* s., #80/150, good cond., (05-19-93, Butterfield, #1979), 13Mzn x 4Mzn in., (341 x 113 mm.), etching in colors on wove (BP 93, DM 234, FR 789, Y 15,942).

$495* *"The Tormented One" (Fern and O'Sullivan, 228), 1953,* s. Leonard Baskin, t., annot. Artist's proof, ded., good cond., foxing, creases, (09-11-92, Skinner, #82, illus.), sight 17¼ x 19 in., (43.8 x 48.3 cm.), woodcut in red and black on buff (BP 256, DM 713, FR 2422, Y 61,331).

$88* *Warthog,* s., num. 70/120, (09-20-92, Hindman, #714), 17 x 24 in., (43.2 x 61 cm.), lithograph (BP 52, DM 131, FR 447, Y 10,876).

BASKIN, Strabigmi

$88* *Human Blood Vessels,* s., (09-18-92, DuMouchelle, #2510), 40 x 20 in., (101.6 x 50.8 cm.), woodcut (BP 51, DM 132, FR 451, Y 10,964).

BASQUIAT, Jean Michel American 1960-1988

$46,000* *Tuxedo,* s., t., d. JEAN MICHEL BASQUIAT TUXEDO 1982 verso, #1/10 edit., pub.Gagosian Gallery, lit., (05-05-93, Christie-NY, #180, illus.), 102 x 60 in., (259.1 x

152.4 cm.), synthetic polymer and silkscreen inks on canvas (BP 29,370, DM 72,578, FR 244,551, Y 5,069,988).

BI *Untitled (From Leonardo), 1983,* inits., blindstamps, crease, excellent cond., est. $4/5,000, (11-09-92, Christie-NY, #246, illus.), (883 x 762 mm.), screenprint in browns on 5 sheets of Okawara.

BASSE, Willem　　　　　　　　　c. 1613-1672
$367* *Unter Einem Baum Rastendes Bauernpaar (Hollstein 31; Weigel (Suppl.)S. 64 c.; Wurzbach 56),* prov., (06-10-93, Hauswedell/Nolt, #13), etching (BP 240, DM 598, FR 2012, Y 38,956).

BASSMAN, Lillian
$2588* *Model With Dachshund, 1954,* stamp, (04-06-93, Sotheby-NY, #449, illus.), 13M, x 11 in., photograph, mounted on Artmar board (BP 1709, DM 4169, FR 14,119, Y 295,164).

BASTARD
$221* *Bieres De La Meuse,* fair cond., (02-13-93, Morelle/Marchan, #16), 37½ x 58¼ in., (96 x 148 cm.), poster (BP 156, DM 367, FR 1240, Y 26,652).

BATE, M.N. and J.C. STADLER (after G. GARRARD)
$453* *Wobourn Sheepshearing, 1871,* pub. G. Garrard, laid, tear into image, corner missing, (10-27-92, Phillips-London, #96), image 17M, x 29½ in., (454 x 749 mm.), aquatint on wove w/later hand-coloring (BP 286, DM 694, FR 2356, Y 55,413).

BATEMAN, James (after)
BI *St Peter,* (01-21-93, Bonhams-Chelsea, #94), image 13¾ x 9½ in., (34.9 x 24.1 cm.), hand-colored engraving.
BI *St. Peter,* est. BP 40/60, (11-19-92, Bonhams-Chelsea, #123), image 13¾ x 9½ in., (34.9 x 24.1 cm.), engraving w/hand coloring.
$50* *St. Peter,* laid, (06-16-93, Bonhams-Chelsea, #336), image 13¾ x 9½ in., (34.9 x 24.1 cm.), engraving w/hand-coloring (BP 33, DM 83, FR 279, Y 5333).

BATEMAN, Robert
$173* *Geese,* #611 of 950, s., (05-12-93, Maynard, #272), 20 x 28 in., (50.8 x 71.1 cm.), print (BP 113, DM 279, FR 940, Y 19,315, C$ 220).
$216* *Geese,* #265 of 950, s., num., (05-12-93, Maynard, #273), 18 x 24 in., (45.7 x 61 cm.), print (BP 141, DM 348, FR 1174, Y 24,115, C$ 275).

BATES
$192* *Pittsburgh Wall Paper,* B+ cond., fold marks, (08-06-92, Swann, #40, illus.), 42 x 28 in., (106.7 x 71.1 cm.), (BP 100, DM 284, FR 958, Y 24,490).

BATES, Maxwell　　　　　　　　1906-1980
$58* *"African Head",* #5/14, s., t., (03-10-93, Maynard, #256), image 18 x 14 in., (45.7 x 35.6 cm.), silkscreen (BP 40, DM 97, FR 328, Y 6853, C$ 72).
$173* *Beggar King, 1971,* #28/30, s., t., d. '71, prov., (05-10-93, Hodgins, #235, illus.), 16 x 12 in., (40.6 x 30.5 cm.), lithograph on paper (BP 113, DM 278, FR 938, Y 19,332, C$ 220).
BI *Bird, 1956,* First State #1/2, s., t., d. 1956, prov., est. C$3/400, (05-10-93, Hodgins, #313), 12 x 15 in., (30.5 x 38.1 cm.), lithograph on paper.
$95* *Bottles In Moonlight,* #9/11, s., t., prov., lit., (11-16-92, Hodgins, #261), 16½ x 9 in., (43.2 x 22.9 cm.), color lithograph on paper (BP 62, DM 152, FR 510, Y 11,856, C$ 121).
$164* *Bottles, 1958,* #3/14, s., t., d. 1958, prov., (11-16-92, Hodgins, #29), 16½ x 8½ in., (43.2 x 22.9 cm.), color lithograph on paper (BP 108, DM 262, FR 881, Y 20,467, C$ 209).
$260* *Cock And Hen, 1955,* #4/7, s., t., d. '55, prov., (05-10-93, Hodgins, #355), 12¼ x 15½ in., (31.1 x 39.4 cm.), lithograph on paper (BP 170, DM 418, FR 1409, Y 29,054, C$ 330).
BI *Corsican Town, 1966,* #28/34, s., t., d. '66, prov., est. C$3/400, (05-10-93, Hodgins, #334), 14 x 18 in., (35.6 x 45.7 cm.), lithograph on paper.
$173* *Garden, 1956,* #3/16, s., t., d. '56, prov., (11-16-92, Hodgins, #155), 16½ x 5½ in., (41.9 x 15.2 cm.), color lithograph on paper (BP 114, DM 276, FR 930, Y 21,590, C$ 220).

BI *Golden Bird, 1956,* #12/16, s., t., d. '56, prov., est. C$3/400, (05-10-93, Hodgins, #264), 12 x 15 in., (30.5 x 38.1 cm.), color lithograph on paper.
$121* *Nurse And Child, 1955,* #10/15, s., t., d. '55, prov., (11-16-92, Hodgins, #51), 14 x 10½ in., (35.6 x 27.9 cm.), lithograph on paper (BP 80, DM 193, FR 650, Y 15,100, C$ 154).
$282* *Punch And Two Others, 1977,* #22/48, s., t., d. 1977, prov., (05-10-93, Hodgins, #132, illus.), 18 x 22 in., (45.7 x 55.9 cm.), lithograph on paper (BP 184, DM 453, FR 1528, Y 31,512, C$ 358).
$369* *Rocking Horse, 1955,* #12/15, s., t., d. '55, prov., (05-10-93, Hodgins, #40, illus.), 10¾ x 12¾ in., (27.3 x 32.4 cm.), color lithograph on paper (BP 241, DM 593, FR 2000, Y 41,234, C$ 468).
BI *Sun,* T/P s., t., prov., est. C$4/600, (05-10-93, Hodgins, #69), 14 x 18 in., (35.6 x 45.7 cm.), color lithograph on paper.

BAUBAUT, L.
BI *PLM. Uriage Les Bains. Dauphine, Pres Grenoble,* good cond., (03-15-93, Arcole, #6), 39½ x 29½ in., (100 x 74.5 cm.), .

BAUDOUIN, P.
$189* *Air France: Paris, 1947,* p. Bedos, good cond., (11-19-92, Ribeyre/Baron, #85), 38½ x 23½ in., (99 x 60 cm.), poster (BP 124, DM 301, FR 1015, Y 23,505).

BAUDOUIN, Pierre Antoine (after)
BI *"Le Confessional" and "Le Catechisme" (L. and D. 145-6), c. 1760: Two,* by P.E. Moitte, final states, margins, staining, tear into image, defects, James R. Herbert Boone Coll., est. $5/800, (05-11-93, Christie-NY, #63), each plate 13½, x 16¾ in., (340 x 425 mm.), engraving on laid.
$748* *Le Couche De La Mariee (L. and D. 186), 1768,* by J.M. Moreau and J.B. Simonet, 3rd final state, margins, creases, staining, James R. Herbert Boone Coll., (05-11-93, Christie-NY, #65), plate 18½ x 13½ in., (470 x 333 mm.), engraving on laid (BP 477, DM 1178, FR 3970, Y 82,279).
BI *"Le Jardinier Galant", 1778,* ded., est. DM 300-, (03-24-93, Venator/Hansten, #2481), pl 16½ in x 12½ in., (43.1 x 31.3 cm.), etching.
$276* *Le Modele Honnete (L. and D. 185), c. 1760,* by J.M. Moreau and J.B. Simonet, 5th final state, margins, surface soiling, tears, creases, defects, (05-11-93, Christie-NY, #64), plate 18½ x 14½ in., (470 x 368 mm.), engraving on laid (BP 176, DM 435, FR 1465, Y 30,360).
BI *Sa Taille Et Si Ravissant (L. and D. 119), 1776,* by P.A. Le Beau, 2nd state of 3, margins, staining, James R. HerbertBoone Coll., est. $4/600, (05-11-93, Christie-NY, #62, illus.), plate 10½, x 7¼ in., (257 x 181 mm.), engraving on laid.

BAUER, Albert L.
$94* *Men Loading Log Wagon In Snowstorm,* s., d. 1930, inits. in stone, (11-13-92, DuMouchelle, #2453), 13¾ x 9¾ in., (34.9 x 24.8 cm.), lithograph (BP 61, DM 148, FR 498, Y 11,667).

BAUER, Henry　　　　　　American 20th cent.
BI *Portrait Of William Cullen Bryant,* s., stained, burned, est. $20/30, (05-15-93, Cleveland, #63), 10½ x 9 in., (26.7 x 22.9 cm.), etching.

BAUER, John　　　　　　　　　1882-1918
$2224* *Troll: Ten,* s., (05-12-93, AB Stockholm, #7004, illus.), lithograph (BP 1452, DM 3588, FR 12,087, Y 248,297, SK 16,500).

BAUER, Karl Conrad Friedrich
$515* *Goethe, c. 1895,* trimmed to image mounted, image in good cond., discolored, staining, (06-30-93, Sotheby-London, #342, illus.), 22¼ x 17¾ in., (565 x 451 mm.), colored lithograph (BP 345, DM 878, FR 2963, Y 55,181).

BAUER, M.A.J.　　　　　　　　　1864-1932
$220* *The .Queen Of Sheba At Jerusalem (Van Wisselingh 210), 1893,* s., t., (06-09-93, Bubb Kuyper, #1953), 12½ x 12½ in., (32.5 x 33 cm.), etching (BP 145, DM 360, FR 1210, Y 23,397, G 403).

$220* *A Sultan With His Attendants (Van Wisselingh 292), 1930,* plate s.; s., N82, (06-09-93, Bubb Kuyper, #1954), 9Zzn x 14¼ in., (24.6 x 36.2 cm.), etching (BP 145, DM 360, FR 1210, Y 23,397, G 403).

BAUER, Marcus

$28* *Scene In Front Of An Oriental Temple,* s., #3, (09-18-92, DuMouchelle, #84), 8½ x 7¾ in., (21.6 x 19.7 cm.), etching (BP 16, DM 42, FR 144, Y 3489).

BAUER, Maurice

BI *(Processionals: Two),* inits., paper toned, creases, good cond., est. $2/300, (06-11-93, Doyle, #14), larger 21¾ x 18½ in., (552 x 470 mm.), etching.

BAUKNECHT, Philipp 1884-1933

BI *Alp. Sonnenaufgang, 1918,* s., t., staining, foxing, est. DM 2,500-, (11-21-92, Lempertz, #27), 13Mzn x 17Mzn in., (34.1 x 44.3 cm.), woodcut on thick wove.

BI *Kirchgang II,* s., t., stains, foxing, est. DM 2,600-, (11-21-92, Lempertz, #28), 17B, x 13½ in., (44.8 x 34.3 cm.), woodcut on thin hand-made Japan.

BAUM, Paul German 1859-1932

$851* *Hollandisches Dorf,* s., prov., (06-05-93, Bassenge, #5898, illus.), 9Bzn x 7Bzn in., (23.6 x 18.6 cm.), etching (BP 560, DM 1380, FR 4650, Y 91,289).

BAUMANN, Gustave German/American 1881-1971

$1100* *"Big Timber Upper Pecos",* s. Gustave Baumann, heart chop, t., #15/100, ident. on labels, very good cond., wide margins, toning, weak chop impression, (01-02-93, Skinner, #96, illus.), 9¾ x 11¼ in., (24.8 x 28.6 cm.), color woodblock on laid paper (BP 733, DM 1802, FR 6152, Y 137,914).

$2090* *"Big Timber Upper Pecos", 1920,* s. Gustave Baumann, hand in heart chop; t., num., 15/100, d. on labels verso, very good cond., (09-11-92, Skinner, #68, illus.), sight 9Z\ x 11Z, in., (23.2 x 28.3 cm.), color woodblock on paper (BP 1081, DM 3008, FR 10,225, Y 258,952).

$1320* *Cordova Plaza, 1943,* s., t., pub. Woodcut Society in orig. mount w/text, full margins, excell. cond., (09-19-92, Christie-E, #9), borderline 7¾ x 8 in., (197 x 203 mm.), woodcut in colors on oatmeal wove (BP 759, DM 1977, FR 6769, Y 164,465).

$1870* *"Early Spring", 1916,* s., t., stamp, #29/125, 2nd printing, excell. "fresh" cond., (10-31-92, Cleveland, #63, illus.), 9½ x 11¼ in., (24.1 x 28.6 cm.), colored woodcut (BP 1198, DM 2877, FR 9760, Y 231,636).

$2200* *Harden Hollow, c. 1913,* staining, discoloration, tear, margin, s., t., i., copyright 1915 byGustave Baumann, (06-11-93, Freemn/Fine Art, #14, illus.), 19¾ x 26B, in., (50.2 x 67.6 cm.), woodcut in color (BP 1445, DM 3575, FR 12,055, Y 233,422).

$50* *"March", "June", "August", "September" and "December": Five,* illus. from James Whitcomb Riley's All the Year Round, 1912, Bobbs Merrill Co., very good cond., (05-15-93, Cleveland, #64), each 7¾ x 6¼ in., (19.7 x 15.9 cm.), color woodcut (BP 33, DM 80, FR 270, Y 5543).

$880* *"Mending the Siene"/ A Provincetown Scene, c. 1917,* s. Gustave Baumann, swan chop, t., water stainig, toning, margin trimmed to 1/4 inch, tears, creases, (05-22-93, Skinner, #90, illus.), 9¾ x 11¼ in., (24.8 x 28.6 cm.), color woodcut on paper (BP 570, DM 1431, FR 4814, Y 97,023).

BI *Pecos Valley, 1921,* s., t., stamped num. 37, inkstamp, margins, glue, good cond., staining, est. $1,5/2,500, (10-28-92, Butterfield, #2507, illus.), 9½ x 11¼ in., (241 x 286 mm.), color woodcut on oatmeal laid Galdbach paper.

$1320* *Pecos Valley, 1921,* s., t., stamp num. 37, inkstamp, margins, glued in margins to overmat, good cond., 3/8 in. tear, staining, (02-24-93, Butterfield, #2610, illus.), 9½ x 11¼ in., (241 x 286 mm.), woodcut p. in colors on oatmeal laid Gladbach paper (BP 921, DM 2143, FR 7265, Y 154,893).

$1100* *Pelican Rookery,* s., t., annot. No 25 of 120, stamp, margins, good cond., mat staining, foxing, repaired cut, (10-28-92, Butterfield, #2509, illus.), 9⅜n x 11C, in., (243 x 289 mm.), color woodcut on oatmeal paper, watermark (BP 701, DM 1699, FR 5768, Y 134,969).

$1760* *Pine And Aspen-Pecos Valley,* watermark, s., t., num. NO 54 Of 120, inkstamp, margins, good cond.,light-staining, mat staining, foxing, (02-24-93, Butterfield, #2611, illus.), 13 x 12M, in., (330 x 327 mm.), woodcut in colors on laid oatmeal paper (BP 1227, DM 2857, FR 9686, Y 206,524).

BI *Pirates! 1916: Thirteen,* complete book, i., pub. Brothers of the Book, good cond., soiling, scuffing, est. $2/4,000, (02-24-93, Butterfield, #2608, illus.), sheet 10½ x 8 in., (267 x 203 mm.), woodcuts in black on Kozuchi handmade Japanese laid, cover printed inred on black heavy laid.

BI *Redwood, 1960,* s., t., d., #54-50, inkstamp, margins, good cond., pencil notations,est. $1,5/2,500, (10-28-92, Butterfield, #2508, illus.), 12Zzn x 12M, in., (329 x 327 mm.), color woodcut on oatmeal paper.

$1540* *Road Of A Morning,* s., t. bears artist's stamp, (03-14-93, Hindman, #312), 10M, x 9M, in., (27.6 x 25.1 cm.), color woodcut (BP 1074, DM 2563, FR 8715, Y 181,497).

$1980* *Road To Town, 1937-42,* s., t., artist's ink chop, num. II 41 125, 2nd printing, wide margins, excell. cond., (11-09-92, Christie-NY, #6, illus.), border 9Z, x 11Czn in., (232 x 284 mm.), woodcut on oatmeal laid (BP 1309, DM 3161, FR 10,680, Y 245,719).

$1610* *Salt Creek, c. 1915,* s., t., artist's ink chop, num. 91 120 III, 3rd prinitng, watermark,margins, foxmark, time staining, good cond., (05-11-93, Christie-NY, #89), borderline 9½ x 11¼ in., (241 x 286 mm.), color woodcut on beige laid (BP 1028, DM 2536, FR 8546, Y 177,098).

$1540* *El Santo,* watermark, s., t., num. III 45/125, inkstamp, margins, good cond., (02-24-93, Butterfield, #2612), 9B x 11C, in., (244 x 289 mm.), woodcut p. in colors on laid oatmeal paper (BP 1074, DM 2500, FR 8476, Y 180,709).

$2420* *Summer Rain, c. 1924,* watermark, s., t., d. '56, ink chop, num. 12-50, 2nd printing, wide margins, excell. cond., (11-09-92, Christie-NY, #5, illus.), border 9Bzn x 11Z, in., (237 x 282 mm.), woodcut in colors on oatmeal laid (BP 1600, DM 3863, FR 13,053, Y 300,323).

BI *Talpa Chapel, 1920,* s., t., annot. No of 100, inkstamp, margins, good cond., light staining, tear, est. $1,4/1,600, (10-28-92, Butterfield, #2506, illus.), 5M, x 7B, in., (149 x 194 mm.), color woodcut on buff fibrous wove.

$2090* *Talpa Chapel, 1920,* s, t., annot. No. 3 of 100, glued in areas, margins, good cond., light-staining, tear, (02-24-93, Butterfield, #2609, illus.), 5M, x 7B, in., (149 x 194 mm.), woodcut in colors on buff fibrous wove (BP 1457, DM 3393, FR 11,502, Y 245,248).

BAUMBERGER, Otto Swiss 1889-1961

BI *Baumann, 1950,* excell. cond., lit., est. BP 3/500, (02-04-93, Christie-S. Ken, #45, illus.), 50 x 36 in., (127 x 91.4 cm.), color offset lithograph.

BI *Cafe St. Gothard, 1913,* fold marks, losses, repairs, est. BP 8/1,000, (02-04-93, Christie-S. Ken, #44, illus.), 50 x 36 in., (127 x 91.4 cm.), color lithograph backed on japan.

$567* *Hotel St. Gothard, Zurich, 1917,* excell. cond., lit., (02-04-93, Christie-S. Ken, #46, illus.), 50 x 35½ in., (127 x 90.2 cm.), color lithograph (BP 396, DM 934, FR 3166, Y 70,531).

$1045* *Neue Zurcher Zeitung, 1928,* Wolfsberg, A- cond., (08-06-92, Swann, #41, illus.), 50½ x 36½ in., (128.3 x 92.7 cm.), (BP 546, DM 1544, FR 5215, Y 133,291).

BI *Restaurant St. Gothard, 1913,* nicks, tears, excell. cond., est. BP 8/1,000, (02-04-93, Christie-S. Ken, #43, illus.), 50 x 35½ in., (127 x 90.2 cm.), color lithograph.

BAUMEISTER, Willi German 1889-1955

$7167* *Amenophis (Spielmann 3), 1950,* s., #62/70, margins, foxing, discoloration, stain, (05-20-93, Christie-London, #418, illus.), image 18½ x 21½ in., (47 x 54.6 cm.), sheet 24¼ x 27¼ in., (47 x 54.6 cm.), screenprint on wove (BP 4600, DM 11,563, FR 38,951, Y 791,409).

$3531* *Archaische Figur (Spielmann 70), 1921,* mono., from Reihe gestaffelte Figuren u. Apoll., (06-10-93, Hauswedell/Nolt, #55, illus.), image 16 x 7M, in., (40.7 x 20 cm.), lithograph on hand-made (BP 2310, DM 5750, FR 19,359, Y 374,801).

$2887* *"Formen" (Spielmann 23), 1953,* s., (11-28-92, Grisebach, #426, illus.), 8Mzn x 12Zzn in., (21.5 x 30.6 cm.), colored serigraph (BP 1906, DM 4599, FR 15,614, Y 359,303).

$2526* *Gravour-Fries (I) (Spielmann 16), 1952,* s., num., gebraunt, Klebestreifenreste, (11-28-92, Schoppmann, #408), 6Azn x 18M, in., (17 x 48 cm.), color serigraph on handmade (BP 1667, DM 4024, FR 13,661, Y 314,375).

$1974* *Gravour-Fries (II) (Spielmann #32),* s., #36/90, (05-26-93, Lempertz, #26, illus.), 7 x 20Bzn in., (17.8 x 53.2 cm.), color serigraph on thick wove (BP 1277, DM 3221, FR 10,840, Y 214,472).

$1162* *Gravour-Fries (III) (Spielmann 32), 1954,* s., artist's proof, (12-01-92, Karl/Faber, #356), 5Azn x 18Zzn in., (14.5 x 47.5 cm.), color serigraph on cardboard (BP 768, DM 1852, FR 6312, Y 144,671).

$5049* *Gravur-Fries, III (Spielmann 32), 1954,* #69/90, s., (11-21-92, Lempertz, #31, illus.), 5½ x 18Bzn in., (14 x 47.5 cm.), color serigraph on cream wove (BP 3324, DM 8050, FR 27,116, Y 627,907).

$9181* *Komposition In Grun (Spielmann 36), 1954,* s., #39/70, (06-10-93, Hauswedell/Nolt, #59, illus.), image 16zn x 20Z, in., (42 x 51.1 cm.), color serigraph on thick wove (BP 6005, DM 14,950, FR 50,334, Y 974,525).

$9930* *"Kreuzigung" (Spielmann 173), c. 1952-53,* s., num., (06-05-93, Grisebach, #397, illus.), 27zn x 35M, in., (70 x 91.2 cm.), lithograph on thick imitation Japan (BP 6537, DM 16,099, FR 54,262, Y 1,065,222).

$2537* *Linienfigur Auf Braun, Linie Und Flache (Spielmann 91 b.), 1935,* s., (05-26-93, Lempertz, #28, illus.), 20Czn x 16M, in., (52.8 x 42.8 cm.), color lithograph on off-white wove (BP 1641, DM 4139, FR 13,932, Y 275,641).

$1772* *Metamorphose (Spielmann 157), (19)47,* s., d., num., (06-08-93, Karl/Faber, #533, illus.), approx. 14¾ x 18M, in., (37.5 x 48 cm.), color lithograph on hand-made (BP 1165, DM 2875, FR 9683, Y 188,210).

$5320* *"Mo I" (Spielmann 41), 1955,* mono., (06-05-93, Grisebach, #396, illus.), 9Bzn x 19Czn in., (23.6 x 48.8 cm.), color serigraph on smooth offset paper (BP 3502, DM 8625, FR 29,071, Y 570,693).

$8655* *Mo, II (Spielmann 42), 1955,* #19/70, s., stains, (11-21-92, Lempertz, #32, illus.), 15¼ x 21Bzn in., (38.7 x 55.7 cm.), color serigraph on cardboard (BP 5699, DM 13,799, FR 46,482, Y 1,076,359).

BI *Mykene (Spielmann 35), 1954,* #23/100, est. DM 4,500, (05-26-93, Lempertz, #27), 14Zzn x 18¾ in., (35.7 x 47.7 cm.), color serigraph on thick wove.

$9868* *Phantom (II) (Spielmann 10), 1951,* s., #14/60, (05-26-93, Lempertz, #24, illus.), 25½ x 29Zzn in., (64.7 x 75.7 cm.), color serigraph on thick wove (BP 6384, DM 16,101, FR 54,190, Y 1,072,143).

$2632* *Schwarzes Tier (Sp. 170), c. 1952/53,* #14/35, foxed, (10-09-92, Winterberg, #1726, illus.), 14Czn x 17Azn in., (36 x 45.5 cm.), lithograph on wove (BP 1562, DM 3910, FR 13,127, Y 320,429).

$577* *"Siduri" (Spielmann 129 a/b), 1946,* s., num., (11-28-92, Grisebach, #427, illus.), 11 x 11B, in., (28 x 29.5 cm.), lithograph (BP 381, DM 919, FR 3121, Y 71,811).

BI *Souvenir D'Espagne (Spielmann 176 b), 1953,* s., num., blindstamp, est. DM 3,500, (06-05-93, Bassenge, #5899, illus.), 20zn x 13¾ in., (51 x 35 cm.), color lithograph on thick paper.

BI *Souvenir D'Espagne (Spielmann 176 b), 1953,* s., #70/220, watermark, est. DM 3000, (06-10-93, Hauswedell/Nolt, #56), image 20zn x 13¾ in., (51 x 35 cm.), color lithograph on copper print paper.

BI *Souvenir D'Espagne (Spielmann 176 b.), 1953,* s., E.A., tears, est. DM 4,200, (05-26-93, Lempertz, #29, illus.), approx. 22Mzn x 15Zzn in., (57 x 38.2 cm.), color lithograph on thick wove.

$1614* *Souvenir D'Espagne (Spielmann 176), 1953,* artist's proof, s., (04-24-93, Kunsthaus, #463), sh 22Mzn x 15zn in., (57 x 38.2 cm.), color lithograph on hand-made Marais (BP 1019, DM 2530, FR 8544, Y 178,106).

BI *Tanzerin (IV) (Spielmann 26 b.), 1954,* s., #59/80, est. DM 4,000, (05-26-93, Lempertz, #25), 24 x 17zn in., (61 x 43.4 cm.), serigraph on thick wove.

BI *Tanzerin II (Spielmann 25 b), 1953,* s., #32/32, est. DM 8000, (06-10-93, Hauswedell/Nolt, #58, illus.), image 15C, x 10Bzn in., (39 x 26.2 cm.), color serigraph on thick wove.

$1915* *"Tennisspieler II (Querformat)" (Speilmann 94), c. 1935/36,* s., num., (06-05-93, Grisebach, #517, illus.), 12Bzn x 15zn in., (31.3 x 39.6 cm.), lithograph on thin wove (BP 1261, DM 3105, FR 10,464, Y 205,428).

$1766* *Torii (Spielmann 4), 1951,* s., #28/50, (06-10-93, Hauswedell/Nolt, #57, illus.), image 17Z, x 12M, in., (43.5 x 32.7 cm.), color serigraph on wove (BP 1155, DM 2876, FR 9682, Y 187,454).

$1038* *Uns Hat Schamasch Geheissen Zu Streiten Gegen Chumbaba (Sp. 147/b), 1947,* s., one from the portfolio Sumerische Legende, num., (12-01-92, Karl/Faber, #357), 10Zzn x 14Czn in., (25.5 x 36 cm.), lithograph on simili-Japan (BP 686, DM 1654, FR 5638, Y 129,233).

BI *Untitled (Herald Und Salome), 1946,* s, indistinctly i., margins, good cond., Late Gerhard Brauer Coll., est. Dfl. 2/3,000, (05-27-93, Sotheby-Amstrdm, #807), sheet 11C, x 14½ in., (289 x 368 mm.), lithograph on wove.

BI *Untitled (Summerian Legends),* s, #57/100, margins, good cond., paper discoloration, Late Gerhard Brauer Coll., est. Dfl. 1,4/1,800, (05-27-93, Sotheby-Amstrdm, #808), 10zn x 15½ in., (255 x 394 mm.), lithograph on wove.

BAUR, Johann Wilhelm 1600-1640

$633* *Vedute De Giardini (Le B. 262-7; Holl. 31), 1636: Set Of Six,* thread margins or trimmed, stains, laid, (12-01-92, Christie-London, #196), plate 3Bzn x 5Zzn in., (100 x 128 mm.), etching (BP 418, DM 1009, FR 3438, Y 78,810).

BAWDEN, Edward b. 1903

$296* *Cabin In The Forest,* s., t., d. 1952, #2/50, very good cond., (10-27-92, Phillips-London, #237), sheet 12 x 8B, in., (305 x 219 mm.), engraving on wove (BP 187, DM 454, FR 1539, Y 36,208).

$870* *The Palm House,* s., t. in pen, waterstains, good cond., (10-27-92, Phillips-London, #235, illus.), sheet 49¼ x 30¾ in., (125.1 x 78.1 cm.), colored linocut on wove (BP 550, DM 1333, FR 4524, Y 106,422).

$207* *Saffron Waldren Church,* s., t., artist's proof, #14/50, staining, tears, (02-17-93, Bonhams-Chelsea, #250), sheet 65 x 29¾ in., (165.1 x 75.6 cm.), screenprint (BP 143, DM 336, FR 1139, Y 24,725).

$87* *Still Life Of Flowers,* s., d., 1951, mounted, creasing, (10-27-92, Phillips-London, #236), sheet 7 x 9½ in., (178 x 241 mm.), linocut in sanguine on grey prepared wove (BP 55, DM 133, FR 452, Y 10,642).

$932* *To Visit Britain's Landmarks, Walton Castle, Somerset, 1936,* p. Waterlow and Sons, ref. #474, cond. 3, (10-13-92, Phillips-London, #116, illus.), 29Azn x 44M, in., (76 x 114 cm.), color lithograph (BP 543, DM 1365, FR 4639, Y 113,011).

$343* *Westminister Abbey,* artist's proof, #58/75, s., t. ink, (05-20-93, Bonhams-Chelsea, #13), image 20¼ x 26¼ in., (51.4 x 66.7 cm.), silkscreen (BP 220, DM 553, FR 1864, Y 37,875).

BAXTER

$51 *"The Saviour Blessing The Bread",* (10-09-92, G.A. Key, #89), 8 x 6½ in., (20.3 x 16.5 cm.), colored print (BP 30, DM 76, FR 258, Y 6220).

BAXTER, George 1804-1867

BI *"The Crystal Palace",* (12-11-92, G.A. Key, #118), 5 x 11 in., (12.7 x 27.9 cm.), colored oil print.

$24* *The Great Exhibition,* (08-11-92, L. Joel, #78G), 6Z, x 12Azn in., (15.5 x 33 cm.), p. in oil color (BP 12, DM 35, FR 119, Y 3073, A$ 33).

$31 *Mother With Two Children,* (12-11-92, G.A. Key, #89), 6 x 3 in., (15.2 x 7.6 cm.), colored oil print (BP 20, DM 49, FR 167, Y 3836).

$20 *Queen Victoria,* (10-09-92, G.A. Key, #91), 5 x 3 in., (12.7 x 7.6 cm.), colored oil print (BP 12, DM 30, FR 101, Y 2439).

BAXTER, W.G. (after)

$115 *"A Quiet Game Of Nap": Two,* (08-14-92, G.A. Key, #53), 8 x 11 in., (20.3 x 27.9 cm.), colored print (BP 60, DM 169, FR 571, Y 14,502).

BAYARD, Hippolyte 1801-1887

$5812* *Portrait Of A Young Girl, c. 1845-46,* mounted on card, 165 x 128mm, (05-07-93, Sotheby-London, #100, illus.), photograph, salt print (BP 3680, DM 9189, FR 30,964, Y 639,947).

$17,254* *Study Of An Item Of Statuary, 1839,* mounted on paper, unique direct positive, prov., 118 x 72mm, (05-07-93, Sotheby-London, #99, illus.), photograph, direct positive on paper (BP 10,925, DM 27,279, FR 91,923, Y 1,899,802).

BAYEFSKY, Aba

$278* *Legends (A Folio): Twelve,* each s., #138/150, d. 1968, p. Heinrich Heine Press, (11-30-92, Ritchie, #8A), overall 21¾ x 16½ in., (55.2 x 41.9 cm.), color block print on hand made Hayle (BP 183, DM 443, FR 1504, Y 34,599, C$ 358).

BAYER, Herbert Austrian/American b. 1900

BI *Bones With Sea, Fotoplastik, 1936,* s., d.; s. twice, d., annot vintage print, credit stamp, prop. Joella Bayer, lit., est. $4/6,000, (04-08-93, Christie-NY, #93, illus.), 12½ x 16 in., (31.8 x 40.6 cm.), photograph, gelatin silver print.

$2906* *"Clinical Excerpts, The Waiting Room",* 1930s, mounted on card, p. t., credit, 188 x 317mm, (05-07-93, Sotheby-London, #234, illus.), photograph, silver print (BP 1840, DM 4594, FR 15,482, Y 319,974).

BI *Girl With Letters, Fotomontage, 1931,* s., t., d., annot., credit stamp, lit., est. $6/8,000, (10-13-92, Christie-NY, #118, illus.), 15 x 11B\ in., (38.1 x 29.5 cm.), photograph, gelatin silver print.

BI *Laszlo Moholy-Nagy, c. 1928,* t. by photog., Joella Bayer Collection, est. $2/3,000, (04-06-93, Sotheby-NY, #329, illus.), 11 x 8½ in., photograph.

$7150* *A Look Into Life, Fotomontage, 1931,* s., d. in neg., s., t., d., annotated, lit., (10-13-92, Christie-NY, #117, illus.), 14¼ x 11½ in., (36.2 x 29.2 cm.), photograph, gelatin silver print (BP 4164, DM 10,475, FR 35,590, Y 866,982).

$1380* *Marseilles, Pont Transbordeur,* 1928, p.l., s., t., d., credit stamp, (04-08-93, Christie-NY, #91, illus.), 12¾ x 8C\ in., (32.4 x 21.3 cm.), photograph, gelatin silver print (BP 905, DM 2217, FR 7504, Y 156,605).

BI *Still Life, Fotoplastik, 1936,* s. in neg., s., t., d., annotated, credit stamp, lit., est. $7/9,000, (10-13-92, Christie-NY, #116, illus.), 11 x 15C, in., (27.9 x 39.1 cm.), photograph, gelatin silver print.

$13,200* *Study Of Perspective, The Measure Of Man, 1940,* s., d., t., (10-13-92, Christie-NY, #119, illus.), 11¾ x 11¾ in., (29.8 x 29.8 cm.), other: multi-media collage on board (BP 7688, DM 19,338, FR 65,704, Y 1,600,582).

$495* *Thesaurus,* s., #35/40, (05-16-93, Hindman, #508), 22¼ x 22½ in., (56.5 x 57.2 cm.), etching (BP 322, DM 796, FR 2676, Y 54,872).

BI *Two Eggs, Fruhstuck, Berlin, 1926,* s., d., Film und Foto 1929 Werkbund-Ausstellung, Stuttgart and Deutscher Photo-Dienst (c) stamps, paper label annot. vintage, typed credit and t affixed verso, prop. Joella Bayer, exhib., lit., est. $4/6,000, (04-08-93, Christie-NY, #92, illus.), 6½ x 8¾ in., (16.5 x 22.2 cm.), photograph, gelatin silver print.

BI *Winter, Fotoplastik, 1936,* neg. s.; s. recto; s., t., d., annot. vintage print, credit stamp, prop. Joella Bayer, lit., est. $4/6,000, (04-08-93, Christie-NY, #94, illus.), 11¾ x 15½ in., (29.8 x 39.4 cm.), photograph, gelatin silver print.

BAYER, Rudolf c. 1870

BI *Blick Aus Einem Studierzimmer Gegen Die Engelsburg In Rom, 1890,* foxing, i., est. SC 6/7,000, (11-11-92, Dorotheum, #454), 12B, x 11Zzn in., (32 x 30 cm.), etching.

BAYLES, David American 20th cent.

$110* *Bristlecone Pine,* 1972, prov., (05-16-93, Hindman, #375), 19¼ x 15 in., photograph, silver print (BP 72, DM 177, FR 598, Y 12,249).

BAYNARD, Ed American b. 1940

BI *Five Flowers In A Rookwood Pot, 1979,* s., num., est. $2/300, (11-12-92, Freemn/Fine Art, #28), 17¾ x 15 in., (45.1 x 38.1 cm.), etching.

$3450* *The Lilies (T. 78:EB9), 1980,* s., d., #10/12, blindstamp, pub. Tyler Graphics Ltd., full margins, apparently good cond., (05-15-93, Sotheby-NY, #919, illus.), sheet 57¼ x 40C, in., (145.4 x 102.6 cm.), lithograph w/hand-coloring (BP 2243, DM 5549, FR 18,649, Y 382,441).

$2750* *"Pembridge Gardens" and "Blenheim Cresent", 1988: Two,* from The London Quartet, both s., d.; first num. 5/58; second i. AP,num. 9/14, Tyler Graphics blindstamps, full margins, excell. cond., (09-19-92, Christie-E, #80), both sheet 33 x 27½ in., (838 x 699 mm.), lithograph w/aquatint and woodcut in colors on wove (BP 1582, DM 4118, FR 14,103, Y 342,636).

$920* *The Print Scarf (Tyler 75:EB6), 1980,* s., d., #29/70, blindstamp, pub. Tyler Graphics, Ltd., on three sides, good cond., (05-15-93, Sotheby-NY, #918), sheet 30 x 42 in., (76.2 x 106.7 cm.), woodcut in colors on handmade natural Okawara (BP 598, DM 1480, FR 4973, Y 101,984).

$1320* *A Still Life With Orchid (Tyler 70), 1980,* s., d., num. 43/70, Tyler Graphics blindstamp, full sheet, glued down, very good cond., (09-19-92, Christie-E, #79, illus.), sheet 30 x 42 in., (76.2 x 106.7 cm.), woodcut in colors on Japan (BP 759, DM 1977, FR 6769, Y 164,465).

$3738* *The Sunflower (T. 79:EB10), 1980,* s., d., #7/12, blindstamp, pub. Tyler Graphics, Ltd., full margins, good cond., (05-15-93, Sotheby-NY, #920, illus.), sheet 57¼ x 40C, in., (145.4 x 102.6 cm.), lithograph w/hand-coloring (BP 2430, DM 6013, FR 20,205, Y 414,366).

$1760* *"Westbourne Grove" and "Notting Hill Gate", 1988: Two,* from The London Quartet, both s., d.; first num. 40/60; second num. 5/60, Tyler Graphics blindstamps, full margins, excell. cond., (09-19-92, Christie-E, #81), both sheet 33 x 27½ in., (838 x 699 mm.), lithograph w/aquatint in colors on wove (BP 1012, DM 2636, FR 9026, Y 219,287).

BAZAINE, Jean French b. 1904

$42* *Composition,* 37/300, (09-30-92, Kunsthallen, #31), color lithograph (BP 24, DM 60, FR 201, Y 5040, DK 230).

$55* *Composition, 1992,* s. Jean Bazaine 92, (03-24-93, Kunsthallen, #31), poster, offset in colors (BP 37, DM 90, FR 306, Y 6462, DK 345).

BI *Espace Marin,* s., #183/200, margins, good cond.?, est. G 4/600, (12-09-92, Sotheby-Amstrdm, #488), 16Zzn x 25Czn in., (430 x 640 mm.), color lithograph on BFK Rives.

$101* *Hollande IV, 1957,* s., #39/150, (05-27-93, Briest, #29), 14Zzn x 11¼ in., (38 x 28.5 cm.), color lithograph (BP 65, DM 162, FR 546, Y 10,828).

$433* *Komposition, 1957,* s., d., num., (11-28-92, Grisebach, #428, illus.), 14½ x 15M, in., (36.8 x 40.3 cm.), colored lithograph on wove (BP 286, DM 690, FR 2342, Y 53,889).

$67* *"Ouverture", c. 1975,* #47/75, s., (10-18-92, Pescheteau, #82), 22Zn x 14Zzn in., (56 x 38 cm.), lithograph in colors on velin (BP 41, DM 99, FR 336, Y 8000).

$164* *"Sans Titre" (Marine), 1960 and "Sans Titre", 1988: Two,* s., d., first, 42/50, second, hors commerce, (06-28-93, Loudmer, #193), first 15C, x 20M\ in., (390 x 530 mm.), second 17Bzn x 22Mzn in., (390 x 530 mm.), lithographs, first in black on wove, second, in colors on Arches (BP 110, DM 279, FR 939, Y 17,401).

BI *Untitled,* s., #122/200, margins, good cond.?, est. G 4/600, (12-09-92, Sotheby-Amstrdm, #487), 18Zzn x 27Bzn in., (475 x 710 mm.), color lithograph on BFK Rives.

$248* *(Untitled)" and "(Untitled)", 1953; 1955: Two,* 1st s., d., num. 200/300; 2nd s., d. in stone, margins; each apparently good cond., 1st w/light-staining, crease, foxing, surface soiling, (02-24-93, Butterfield, #2896), 29¾ x 21C in., (756 x 543 mm.), 9½ x 6¾ in., (756 x 543 mm.), lithograph in colors on wove (BP 173, DM 403, FR 1365, Y 29,101).

$168* *Untitled: Two,* #26/75, H.C., s., (01-28-93, Pescheteau, #69), 19Zzn x 14Czn in., (50 x 36 cm.), and 19Zzn x 15¾ in., (50 x 36 cm.), color lithograph (BP 111, DM 266, FR 901, Y 20,859).

BEAL, Gifford American 1879-1956

$80* *"Polly", 1928,* s., light struck, illus. American Prints in the Library of Congress,p. 47, (05-15-93, Cleveland, #65), 12 x 9 in., (30.5 x 22.9 cm.), drypoint (BP 52, DM 129, FR 432, Y 8868).

$165* *"The Prow",* s., taped down to mat, very good cond., (12-04-92, Doyle, #70), 9 x 11¾ in., (229 x 298 mm.), drypoint (BP 106, DM 263, FR 891, Y 20,599).

BEAL, Jack American b. 1931

$550* *"Still Life" and "Chicago", 1978; 1979: Two,* each s., t., num. 57/75 & 73/90, pub. Brooke Alexander Editions, Chicago w/Fox Graphics-Merrimac blindstamp, Still Life w/full margins, good cond., (02-24-93, Butterfield, #3186), 18 x 24¼ in., (45.7 x 61.6 cm.), 30¼ x 40 in., (45.7 x 61.6 cm.), lithograph in colors on black Arches (BP 384, DM 893, FR 3027, Y 64,539).

$165* *"Trillium", 1977,* s. Jack Beal, num. 1.150, t., excellent cond., (09-11-92, Skinner, #119, illus.), sight 8½ x 8Q in., (21.6 x 21.3 cm.), color linoleum cut on paper (BP 85, DM 238, FR 807, Y 20,444).

BEAL, Reynolds American 1867-1951

$149* *Arrived - New York Harbor, 1929,* margins, s., (05-22-93, Collins, #127), 7M, x 11M, in., (20 x 30.2 cm.), etching (BP 97, DM 242, FR 815, Y 16,428).

$138* *Becalmed, Marblehead, 1929,* margins, s., (05-22-93, Collins, #129), 7¾ x 11¾ in., (19.7 x 29.8 cm.), etching w/ ink accents (BP 89, DM 224, FR 755, Y 15,215).

$165* *Bridgeport Oyster Boats,* margins, s., (05-22-93, Collins, #94), 8¾ x 11M, in., (22.2 x 30.2 cm.), etching accented w/charcoal (BP 107, DM 268, FR 903, Y 18,192).

$220* *Curacao Boats,* margins, s., (10-24-92, Collins, #1, illus.), 7¾ x 11M, in., (19.7 x 30.2 cm.), etching (BP 136, DM 336, FR 1140, Y 26,829).

$165* *"Curacao", 1923,* s., very good cond.?, (02-07-93, Bakker, #94), plate 8 x 10 in., (20.3 x 25.4 cm.), etching (BP 114, DM 274, FR 925, Y 20,533).

$55* *Everglades Fisherman,* margins, s. Reynolds Beal, (10-24-92, Collins, #1A), 6¾ x 10¾ in., (17.1 x 27.3 cm.), etching (BP 34, DM 84, FR 285, Y 6707).

$138* *Hudson River Steamboats - Silas O. Pierce And Oswego,* margins, s., (05-22-93, Collins, #91), 7 x 10M, in., (17.8 x 27.6 cm.), etching (BP 89, DM 224, FR 755, Y 15,215).

$138* *Misty Day, Provincetown,* margins, s., (05-22-93, Collins, #92), 8 x 9¾ in., (20.3 x 24.8 cm.), etching (BP 89, DM 224, FR 755, Y 15,215).

$220* *Ship In Harbor, 1927,* s., good cond.?, (10-10-92, Litchfield, #19), plate 10 x 13¾ in., (25.4 x 34.9 cm.), etching (BP 131, DM 327, FR 1097, Y 26,784).

BI *Southern Seas, 1941,* margins, s., est. $2/300, (05-22-93, Collins, #128), 8¼ x 12M, in., (21 x 32.7 cm.), etching accented w/charcoal.

$138* *The Tanker Near The Battery, New York City,* 1929, margins, s., (05-22-93, Collins, #93), 7¾ x 11¾ in., (19.7 x 29.8 cm.), etching (BP 89, DM 224, FR 755, Y 15,215).

BEAMENT, Thomas Harold

$52* *Eskimo Berry Pickers,* s., t., (06-07-93, Ritchie, #28), 16 x 20½ in., (40.7 x 52 cm.), lithograph heightened w/ color screenprint (BP 34, DM 84, FR 284, Y 5578, C$ 66).

BEARD, Richard

$192* *Military Portrait of Capt. Richard T. Goodwin,* Beard frame, 1840's, (10-14-92, Swann, #131, illus.), photograph, sixth-plate daguerreotype (BP 113, DM 281, FR 953, Y 23,267).

BEARDEN, Romare American 1914-1988

$1210* *Bopping At Birdland (Walking Bass)(Gelburd 76), 1979,* from the Jazz series, s., i., Jorge Dumas Estate, (05-27-93, Swann, #27), 33½ x 24 in., (85.1 x 61 cm.), color lithograph (BP 775, DM 1942, FR 6544, Y 129,717).

$1210* *"Bopping In Birdland", 1979,* s., i. P.P., ded., (12-08-92, Swann, #17, illus.), 33½ x 24 in., (85.1 x 61 cm.), color lithograph (BP 758, DM 1884, FR 6423, Y 149,975).

$935* *Caribbean Landscape (Gelburd 98), 1983-85,* s., i. HC VII, (05-27-93, Swann, #28), sh 30 x 42 in., (76.2 x 106.7 cm.), color serigraph (BP 599, DM 1500, FR 5057, Y 100,236).

$605* *Circe Into Swine, c. 1979,* from the Odyssey series, full margins, s., num. XL/LXXV, image scuffs, creases, (12-08-92, Swann, #19), 17½ x 24 in., (44.5 x 61 cm.), color serigraph (BP 379, DM 942, FR 3211, Y 74,988).

$4255* *"Conjunction" and "Firebirds", 1979: Two,* each s., #100/300 and #162/300, blindstamp, pub. Transworld Art, Inc. full margins, good cond., creases, (02-11-93, Sotheby-NY, #310, illus.), each sheet approx. 28Z, x 20M in., (715 x 530 mm.), color lithograph in colors on Arches (BP 3002, DM 7048, FR 23,851, Y 512,960).

$2875* *"Conjunction" and "Firebirds", 1979: Two,* each s., #112/300 and 159/300, blindstamp, pub. Transworld Art, Inc., full margins, good cond., creases, (05-15-93, Sotheby-NY, #922), each sheet 28 x 20M, in., (71.1 x 53 cm.), lithograph in colors on Arches (BP 1869, DM 4624, FR 15,541, Y 318,701).

$935* *Dreams Of Exile, 1973,* s., t., num. 48/100, pub. Abrams Original Editions, full margins, rubbed spot, minor surface soiling, very good cond., (09-19-92, Christie-E, #82), sheet 28Z, x 22 in., (714 x 559 mm.), screenprint in colors on Arches (BP 538, DM 1400, FR 4795, Y 116,496).

$1150* *The Family, 1975,* s., ded., #11/12, pub. Transworld Art for the Bicentennial Trilogy, An American Portrait, 1776-1976, good cond., (05-15-93, Sotheby-NY, #921), sheet 19½ x 26 in., (49.5 x 66 cm.), etching and aquatint in tones of brown (BP 748, DM 1850, FR 6216, Y 127,480).

$1650* *Introduction For A Blues Queen (Uptown At Savoy)(Gelburd 77), 1979,* s., i. P.P. 4/5, (05-27-93, Swann, #29), (89.9 x 60.6 cm.), color lithograph (BP 1057, DM 2648, FR 8924, Y 176,887).

$1045* *Song Of The Sirens, c. 1979,* from the Odyssey series, full margins, s., num. XX/LXXV, (12-08-92, Swann, #18), 18 x 24 in., (45.7 x 61 cm.), color serigraph (BP 655, DM 1627, FR 5547, Y 129,524).

$2860* *The Train, 1975,* s., #29/125, blindstamp pub. Trans World Art, good cond.?, prov., (12-12-92, Weschler, #102, illus.), 17½ x 22¼ in., (44.5 x 56.5 cm.), color etching and aquatint (BP 1834, DM 4506, FR 15,443, Y 353,917).

$220* *Untitled,* s., num. 241/275, good cond., (05-22-93, Weschler, #163A), 12 x 9 in., (30.5 x 22.9 cm.), silkscreen in colors on B.F.K. Rives (BP 143, DM 358, FR 1204, Y 24,256).

BEARDSLEY, Aubrey English 1872-1898

$60* *Ad For Children's Books,* by Chaix as pub. in Les Affiches Enterprises, 1897, excell. cond., (05-15-93, Cleveland, #359), 8M n x 5M, in., (20.3 x 14.9 cm.), color lithograph (BP 39, DM 97, FR 324, Y 6651).

BI *Publisher. Children's Books (Brinckmann 127; Spielmann 241; Berckenhagen 13), 1894,* rare, London, lit., est. DM 4,500, (12-05-92, Bassenge, #7561, illus.), 29¾ x 19M, in., (75.5 x 50.5 cm.), color lithograph.

BI *The Yellow Book: Fifty-Three,* proofs, est. BP 150/200, (03-17-93, Bonhams-Chelsea, #380), subject 11¼ x 8¾ in., (28.6 x 22.2 cm.), .

BI *The Yellow Book: Fifty-Three,* proofs, est. BP 1/150, (05-20-93, Bonhams-Chelsea, #114), sheet 11¼ x 8¾ in., (28.6 x 22.2 cm.), .

BEATO, Antoine

$1210* *Egypt: Thirty-Nine,* 9 s. photog. neg., notations, 1880s, (04-07-93, Swann, #108), 8¼ x 10½ in., (21 x 26.7 cm.), photograph, albumen print (BP 800, DM 1957, FR 6623, Y 137,469).

BEATO, Felix c. 1830-1906

BI *Chinese Trader (Junk), 1871,* clipped caption, est. $500/750, (10-14-92, Swann, #97, illus.), 8 x 11 in., (20.3 x 27.9 cm.), photograph, albumen print.

BEATON, Cecil English 1904-1980

$1380* *Andrea Tagliabue, 1950's: Two,* each s. by photog., (04-06-93, Sotheby-NY, #345, illus.), one 11½ x 9½ in., other 9B, x 9C, in., photograph (BP 911, DM 2223, FR 7529, Y 157,391).

$1320* *Andrea Tagliabue: Two,* s. by photog. in ink on image, name stamp, early 1960's, (10-15-92, Sotheby-NY, #425, illus.), photograph, gelatin silver print (BP 808, DM 1965, FR 6663, Y 158,368).

BI *Anna Magnani, 50's,* stamp, est. DM 800, (11-12-92, Lempertz, #18), 7B, x 7Z \n in., (19.3 x 19.5 cm.), photograph, gelatin silver print.

BI *Audrey Hepburn In My Fair Lady, 60's,* stamp, t., est. DM 1,200, (11-12-92, Lempertz, #20, illus.), 13ZBn x 10Azn in., (35.5 x 27.8 cm.), photograph, gelatin silver print.

$634* *Audrey Hepburn In The Film Version Of "My Fair Lady", 1963,* photog.'s ink credit stamp, (05-06-93, Christie-London, #101, illus.), 13½ x 10½ in., photograph, gelatin silver print (BP 402, DM 999, FR 3362, Y 69,755).

$618* *Audrey Hepburn, 1954,* stamped photog.'s credit Cecil Beaton Photograph, studio stamp, t., num. 4/4, C.B. 4530-62, 255 x 243mm, (05-07-93, Sotheby-London, #320, illus.), photograph, silver print (BP 391, DM 977, FR 3292, Y 68,047).

$1150* *"Baba Beaton, Wanda Baillie-Hamilton, Lady Bridget Poulett" (Best ofBeaton, p. 33),* mounted, s. by photog., name stamp, 1920's, p. 1950's, (04-06-93, Sotheby-NY, #344, illus.), 17Z\ x 13Z\ in., photograph (BP 760, DM 1853, FR 6274, Y 131,159).

$1542* *"The Blitz/Western Campanile Of St. Paul's Cathedral Seen Through Victorian Shop-Front", 1940,* ink t., photog.'s ink credit stamp Cecil Beaton Photograph, annots.,prov., lit., (05-06-93, Christie-London, #98, illus.), 8½ x 8 in., photograph, gelatin silver print (BP 977, DM 2429, FR 8176, Y 169,656).

$763* *"Bowery Design", 1937,* s. Cecil Beaton, t., stamped photog.'s credit Cecil Beaton Photograph, studio stamp num. 1/2, num. stamp B 2140, annots., illus., 260 x 260mm, (05-07-93, Sotheby-London, #316, illus.), photograph, silver print (BP 483, DM 1206, FR 4065, Y 84,012).

BI *Christian Berard, 1937,* t. in ink, credit stamp, prov., est. $2/2,500, (10-13-92, Christie-NY, #121, illus.), 9½ x 9B in., (24.1 x 24.4 cm.), photograph, gelatin silver print.

$581* *Drugstore Service, 1937,* i., stamped photog.'s credit Cecil Beaton Photograph, studio stamp num. 2/2, illus., 240 x 240mm, (05-07-93, Sotheby-London, #317, illus.), photograph, silver print (BP 368, DM 919, FR 3095, Y 63,973).

BI *Evelyn Brent,* 1931, s. on mount, t., other annots., mounted, est. BP 6/900, (12-17-92, Christie-S. Ken, #16, illus.), 9¼ x 7 in., (23.5 x 17.8 cm.), photograph, gelatin silver print.

BI *Evelyn Brent,* 1931, s. on mount, t., mounted, est. BP 6/900, (12-17-92, Christie-S. Ken, #17, illus.), 9½ x 7¼ in., (24.1 x 18.4 cm.), photograph, gelatin silver print.

BI *Evelyn Brent,* c. 1931, s. on mount, t., mounted, est. BP 5/700, (12-17-92, Christie-S. Ken, #18, illus.), 9¼ x 7½ in., (23.5 x 19.1 cm.), photograph, gelatin silver print.

BI *Fashion,* 1929, 70's, d., t., est. DM 800, (11-12-92, Lempertz, #15, illus.), 17Bzn x 14¼ in., (45.7 x 36.2 cm.), photograph, gelatin silver print.

$660* *Gertrude Lawrence,* 1920s, s. in red ink, (10-13-92, Christie-NY, #120, illus.), 9½ x 7½ in., (24.1 x 19.1 cm.), photograph, gelatin silver print (BP 384, DM 967, FR 3285, Y 80,029).

BI *Graham Greene,* 1950s, t., ref. no. B656/109, photog.'s ink credit stamp, est. BP 3/500, (05-06-93, Christie-London, #100, illus.), 9M, x 7M, in., photograph, gelatin silver print.

$832* *Greta Garbo,* 1941, p. c. 1950s-60s, photog.'s credit, d., (12-17-92, Christie-S. Ken, #31, illus.), 9C, x 12C, in., (23.8 x 31.4 cm.), photograph, gelatin silver print (BP 528, DM 1299, FR 4437, Y 102,249).

BI *Greta Garbo At The Ritz, 1946,* sight 190 x 190mm, est. BP 4/500, (05-07-93, Sotheby-London, #319, illus.), photograph, silver print.

BI *"Greta Garbo" and "Audrey Hepburn", c. 1964: Two,* second w/photog.'s handstamp, both w/notations, est. $1,2/1,800, (04-07-93, Swann, #399, illus.), 10 x 8 in., photograph, silver print.

$235* *Helen, Duchess Of Northumberland, 1937,* mounted on card, s. Beaton and Heds 1837, (05-06-93, Christie-London, #97), 9¼ x 7½ in., photograph, gelatin silver print (BP 149, DM 370, FR 1246, Y 25,855).

$2990* *Jean Cocteau, c. 1935-37,* lit., (04-08-93, Christie-NY, #160, illus.), 8½ x 6C\ in., (21.6 x 16.2 cm.), photograph, gelatin silver print (BP 1961, DM 4803, FR 16,259, Y 339,310).

BI *Jeanne Moreau, 1963,* t. in ink, credit stamps, lit., est. $1,5/2,500, (10-13-92, Christie-NY, #525, illus.), 9½ x 9½ in., (24.1 x 24.1 cm.), photograph, gelatin silver print.

$371* *Joan Crawford, Portrait In White Suit, And Decorated Scarf, 1930,* s., prov., (10-10-92, Bonhams, #8, illus.), 18 x 13½ in., (45.7 x 34.3 cm.), photograph (BP 220, DM 551, FR 1850, Y 45,167).

BI *"Julie Andrews", "Vanessa Redgrave" and "Barbra Streisand": Three,* first and third w/photagrapher's handstamp, notations, 1960s, est. $1,5/2,500, (04-07-93, Swann, #400, illus.), largest 11½ x 9½ in., photograph, silver print.

BI *Lady Hudson With Greyhounds,* 1920s, double layer card mount, s., est. BP 4/600, (05-06-93, Christie-London, #95), 9¾ x 8 in., photograph, gelatin silver print.

$545* *"The Last Sitting - Dayle Haddon Modelling Givenchy Dress", 1979,* mounted on card, blindstamped P.E., pub., 402 x 297mm, (05-07-93, Sotheby-London, #321, illus.), photograph, silver print (BP 345, DM 862, FR 2904, Y 60,009).

$130* *Leslie Caron, Standing In Doorway To Garden,* prov., (10-10-92, Bonhams, #9, illus.), 10 x 8 in., (25.4 x 20.3 cm.), photograph (BP 77, DM 193, FR 648, Y 15,827).

BI *Madam Gres, 50's,* t., est. DM 1,200, (11-12-92, Lempertz, #17, illus.), 9Mzn x 9Mzn in., (24 x 24 cm.), photograph, gelatin silver print.

$659* *Marilyn Monroe,* 1956, photog.'s ink credit, (12-17-92, Christie-S. Ken, #554, illus.), 9¾ x 9 in., (24.8 x 22.9 cm.), photograph, gelatin silver print (BP 418, DM 1029, FR 3515, Y 80,988).

BI *Marilyn Monroe,* i., s., creasing, slight damage, $3,5/5,000, (12-17-92, Sotheby-NY, #178, illus.), 8¾ x 7C, in., (222 x 187 mm.), photograph.

$2750* *Marlene Dietrich, 1935 (O'Connor, p. 52),* mounted, s. by photog. in red ink, name stamp, p. l., sold after sale, (10-15-92, Sotheby-NY, #424, illus.), 15¼ x 16¾ in., (38.7 x 42.5 cm.), photograph, gelatin silver print (BP 1683, DM 4093, FR 13,882, Y 329,934).

$920* *"Miss Consuelo Villa", 1937,* photog. name stamp, (c), pub. stamp, (04-06-93, Sotheby-NY, #344A, illus.), 9B x 7B, in., photograph (BP 608, DM 1482, FR 5019, Y 104,927).

$1064* *Nancy Cunard, 1927,* p.l., s., photog.'s credit stamp, lit., (10-29-92, Christie-London, #164, illus.), 17M, x 14¼ in., (45.4 x 36.2 cm.), photograph, gelatin silver print mounted on card (BP 682, DM 1637, FR 5553, Y 131,797).

BI *Nancy Curnard,* 1930, 60's, t., est. DM 800, (11-12-92, Lempertz, #16, illus.), 9Bzn x 6Z, in., (23.6 x 15.6 cm.), photograph, gelatin silver print.

$799* *"New York, Broadway Sidewalk", 1937,* t., stamped photog.'s credit Cecil Beaton Photograph, studio stamp num. 1/1, illus., 240 x 240mm, (05-07-93, Sotheby-London, #318, illus.), photograph, silver print (BP 506, DM 1263, FR 4257, Y 87,976).

BI *Pavel Tchelitchew,* 1930s, ink s., est. $1,7/2,200, (04-08-93, Christie-NY, #159, illus.), 9½ x 7½ in., (24.1 x 19.1 cm.), photograph, gelatin silver print.

$455* *Rudolf Nureyev, 1960,* light creases, (11-12-92, Lempertz, #19), 17Zzn x 14¼ in., (43.4 x 36.2 cm.), photograph, gelatin silver print (BP 291, DM 715, FR 2437, Y 56,291).

BI *Solarized Portrait Of Greta Garbo,* (1946), late 1950s, prov., unique, est. $6/8,000, (10-13-92, Christie-NY, #410, illus.), 11B, x 9½ in., (29.5 x 24.1 cm.), photograph, gelatin silver print.

$997* *"Tallulah Bankhead",* 1930, p. 1960s, mounted on card, s., photog.'s ink credit stamp w/t., (05-06-93, Christie-London, #96, illus.), 15 x 16¾ in., photograph, gelatin silver print (BP 632, DM 1570, FR 5286, Y 109,693).

BI *Theatrical And Other Portraits: Seven,* 1940s, 50s, one photog.'s ink credit stamp; others mounted on card or traces of card remaining, lit., est. BP 800/1,000, (05-06-93, Christie-London, #99), smallest 7½ x 7 in., largest 12 x 12 in., photograph, gelatin silver print, one sepia-toned, one color print.

BEATRIZET, Nicolas c. 1515-1560

$99* *The Battle Of Trajan And Dacius,* trimmed, (06-16-93, Bonhams-Chelsea, #301), image 10¾ x 17½ in., (27.3 x 44.5 cm.), engraving on laid paper (BP 66, DM 164, FR 552, Y 10,559).

BI   *The Birth Of The Virgin (B. XV, 15),* by unknown hand, finished Beatrizet, after Bandinelli, partial margin, paper loss, laid down, est. BP 2/3,000, (06-30-93, Sotheby-London, #74), 14½ x 17 in., (368 x 432 mm.), engraving.

BI   *Christ Healing The Daughter Of Jairus (B. XV, 15), c. 1550,* after Girolamo Muciano, trimmed, stained and discolored, laid, BP 360/500, (12-01-92, Christie-London, #37), sheet 20&n x 14M, in., (519 x 378 mm.), engraving.

BI   *The Sacrifice Of Iphigenia, (B. XV, 43), 1553,* after Baccio Bandinelli ?, 1st state (of two), trimmed, stains, very-good cond., laid, est. BP 1,0/1,200, (12-01-92, Christie-London, #38, illus.), P. 13&n x 18&n in., (335 x 462 mm.), engraving.

BI   *A Standing Man With Arms Folded (Unrecorded),* after Michelangelo, polishing scratches, large margins, stained, w/tone, fingerprints, crease, defects, est. BP 4/6,000, (06-30-93, Sotheby-London, #76, illus.), 17¾ x 13&n in., (451 x 332 mm.), engraving.

BEAUDIN, Andre   French 1895-1980
$10*   *"Composition 1970",* #416/500, s., (01-28-93, Pescheteau, #70), 27&n x 19&n in., (71 x 49 cm.), color lithograph on Arches (BP 7, DM 16, FR 54, Y 1242).

$120*   *"Composition Au Vase", 1961,* s., d., #22/25, (04-04-93, Pescheteau, #157), 8¼ x 11 in., (21 x 28 cm.), color lithograph (BP 79, DM 193, FR 655, Y 13,663).

BI   *Composition, 1973,* from "Pour Paul Eluard" portfolio, s., #4/100, est. FF6/800, (05-27-93, Briest, #30), 25&n x 18½ in., (64 x 47 cm.), color lithograph.

$103*   *Feuillages, 1964,* s., #35/50, good margins, (05-06-93, Laurin, #8), color lithograph (BP 65, DM 162, FR 546, Y 11,332).

BI   *Komposition, 1961,* s., d., num., est. DM 550/650, (11-28-92, Grisebach, #429, illus.), 12¾ x 9&n in., (32.4 x 25 cm.), colored lithograph on copper print paper.

$103*   *Piege D'Araignee, 1971,* s., d., #9/50, good margins, (05-06-93, Laurin, #7), color lithograph (BP 65, DM 162, FR 546, Y 11,332).

BEAUFOY (after)
$477*   *View Of The Straits Of Messina, Sicily,* by C. Rosenberg, surface defects, (04-22-93, Bonhams-Chelsea, #151), image 15¾ x 25 in., (40 x 63.5 cm.), aquatint w/hand coloring (BP 308, DM 766, FR 2585, Y 52,446).

BEAUFRERE, Adolphe
$348*   *Femmes Au Marche De Quimperle (Morane 07-02), 1907,* second and final state, mono., d. in plate, s., annot., (06-28-93, Loudmer, #194), 6&n x 10&, in., (161 x 257 mm.), sh 8&, x 12&n in., (161 x 257 mm.), black etching on China (BP 233, DM 591, FR 1992, Y 36,923).

BEAULIEU, Pual Vancier   b. 1910
$218*   *Tete De Vieillard,* s. P.V. Beaulieu, (11-17-92, Encans, #5), 9&n x 7M, in., (25 x 20 cm.), monotype (BP 144, DM 348, FR 1171, Y 27,111, C$ 278).

BEAUMONT, Arthur E.   American 1890-1978
$193*   *"Victory Yard",* s., t., d. Arthur Beaumont 1944; label verso, #28/75, (02-16-93, Moran, #144), image 12 x 16 in., (30.5 x 40.6 cm.), lithograph on paper (BP 133, DM 315, FR 1067, Y 23,122).

BEAUSSIER, E.
$522*   *Theatre De Lyon, Les Maitres Chanteurs De Nurenberg,* Lith. Delaroche, A- cond., chipping, (08-06-92, Swann, #42, illus.), 81½ x 39½ in., (207 x 100.3 cm.), (BP 273, DM 771, FR 2605, Y 66,582).

BEAUVARLET-FIRMIN, Jacques
$660*   *"La Lecture Espagnole" and "La Conversation Espagnole" (R. Portalis et H. Beraldi, num. 20): Two,* after Van Loo, yellowed, stains, reddish stains, good margins, (04-02-93, Picard, #1), 22&n x 16&n in., (58 x 42 cm.), etching and copperplate (BP 435, DM 1061, FR 3603, Y 75,145).

BEAVER, Rick   b. c. 1950
$217*   *Feathers And Lace,* #56/100, s., t., circular, prov., (05-10-93, Hodgins, #320), 15 x 15 in., (38.1 x 38.1 cm.), serigraph on paper (BP 142, DM 349, FR 1176, Y 24,249, C$ 275).

BECHER, Bernd and Hilla   Germans b. 1930's
$2875*   *Cooling Tower,* exec. 1967, prov., exhib., Sylvio Perlstein Coll., (05-04-93, Sotheby-NY, #121, illus.), 15¾ x 11M, in., (40 x 30.2 cm.), b/w photograph mounted on cardboard (BP 1835, DM 4529, FR 15,260, Y 316,247).

$15,400*   *Cooling Towers (Wood) (B),* nine, each s., num. consecutively 1B-9B Bernhard Becher Hilla Becherverso, d. 1976 verso of first photograph, prov., (11-19-92, Christie-NY, #202, illus.), each 16 x 12&, in., (40.6 x 30.8 cm.), overall 58M, x 42M, in., (40.6 x 30.8 cm.), photograph, b/w (BP 10,140, DM 24,554, FR 82,707, Y 1,915,185).

$27,600*   *Fabrikhallen: Nine,* s., d. Bernhard and Hilla Becher 1989 verso, each num. consecutively1-9, prov., exhib., (05-05-93, Christie-NY, #215, illus.), each 17¾ x 21¾ in., (45.1 x 55.2 cm.), overall 55½ x 67½ in., (45.1 x 55.2 cm.), b/w photographs (BP 17,622, DM 43,547, FR 146,730, Y 3,041,993).

$8250*   *Industrial Buildings: Fourteen,* Schirmer/Mosel, 1961-74, mounted, s., num. 7/50 by photogs., portfolio (c) stamp, p. 1975, #7/55 ed., (10-15-92, Sotheby-NY, #579, illus.), each 15B, x 11M, in., (39.7 x 30.2 cm.), portfolio of 14 photos, gelatin silver prints (BP 5048, DM 12,280, FR 41,646, Y 989,802).

$6038*   *"Jahresgabe", 1970: Four,* s., #18/50 by photog., studio (c) stampo, (04-06-93, Sotheby-NY, #496, illus.), each approx. 10½ x 8 in., photograph (BP 3988, DM 9728, FR 32,941, Y 688,641).

BI   *Pausau, 1989,* s., num. 1/5 by photog., #1/5 ed., est. $3/5,000, (10-15-92, Sotheby-NY, #580, illus.), 23M, x 19¾ in., (60.6 x 50.2 cm.), photograph, gelatin silver print.

$7700*   *Preparation Plants (Zeche Lothringen, Bochum, Germany): Nine,* each d. 1966-76, prov., exhib., Deborah D. Dodds and Robert J. DoddsIII Coll., (11-18-92, Sotheby-NY, #243, illus.), each 9 x 12 in., (22.9 x 30.5 cm.), overall framed 35½ x 41½ in., (22.9 x 30.5 cm.), b/w photograph (BP 5070, DM 12,277, FR 41,353, Y 957,592).

$5463*   *"Spherical Gas Tank, Wesserling, NR Koln Germany, 1984" and "Water Tower, Badkreunach, 1980": Two,* exec. 1989, prov., (05-04-93, Sotheby-NY, #176, illus.), each 23½ x 19½ in., (59.7 x 49.5 cm.), b/w photograph (BP 3487, DM 8606, FR 28,997, Y 600,924).

$42,900*   *Spherical Gas Tanks,* nine, s., t., d. 1984 B. AND H. BECHER verso of first photograph; each num. consecutively 1-9 verso, prov., exhib., (11-19-92, Christie-NY, #188, illus.), each 15M, x 12&, in., (40.3 x 30.8 cm.), overall 47¾ x 36½ in., (40.3 x 30.8 cm.), photograph, b/w mounted on board (BP 28,246, DM 68,399, FR 230,397, Y 5,335,157).

$3337*   *Vier Wasserturme, 60's: Four,* ink s., #14/50, (c), (11-12-92, Lempertz, #21, illus.), 11&n x 9½ in., (30 x 24.2 cm.), photograph, gelatin silver print (BP 2134, DM 5244, FR 17,874, Y 412,842).

$341*   *Wasserturm Zeche Concordia Oberhausen, 1976,* s., d., (11-12-92, Lempertz, #22), 16¾ x 12&, in., (42.5 x 31.5 cm.), sheet 20½ x 15¾ in., (42.5 x 31.5 cm.), photograph, duotone offset print on Chromolux paper (BP 218, DM 536, FR 1826, Y 42,187).

$35,200*   *Winding Towers 1967-1978: Nine,* s., t. verso, each num. consec. 1-9 verso, exec. 1983, prov., (02-24-93, Christie-NY, #68, illus.), each 15M, x 12&, in., (40.3 x 30.8 cm.), overall 60¼ x 48 in., (40.3 x 30.8 cm.), photograph, b/w mounted on board (BP 24,547, DM 57,143, FR 193,726, Y 4,130,486).

$16,500*   *Winding Towers Germany, France, Britain Perspective Views: Six,* one s., t. verso, each num. 1-6 verso, exec. 1988, prov., (10-08-92, Christie-NY, #204, illus.), (40.6 x 31.1 cm.), b/w photographs mounted on board (BP 9819, DM 24,405, FR 82,831, Y 2,004,860).

BECHTLE, Robert   American b. 1932
$546*   *Oakland Buick, 1975,* s., annot. H/C, margins, good cond.?, crease, (05-19-93, Butterfield, #2127, illus.), 14 x 20 in., (356 x 508 mm.), lithograph in colors on wove (BP 354, DM 888, FR 2990, Y 60,445).

BI   *Through The Window,* s., d. 1966, num. 7/18, est. $3/500, (09-20-92, Hindman, #705), 12 x 18 in., (30.5 x 45.7 cm.), color lithograph.

BECK, C.A.
BI   *"Burning Of San Francisco", 1916,* s., trimmed to image, good cond., image ink loss, mat staining, creases, est. $6/800, (10-28-92, Butterfield, #2510), 21Z, x 33C, in., (537 x 848 mm.), color chromolithograph on wove.

$330* *(Burning Of San Francisco), 1916,* s. in stome, trimmed to image, good cond., ink loss in image, mat staining, creases, (02-24-93, Butterfield, #2811), 21Z, x 33C, in., (537 x 848 mm.), chromolithograph in colors on wove (BP 230, DM 536, FR 1816, Y 38,723).

BECK, Leonhard   c. 1480-1542
$144* *Die Falknerei Des Prinzen Weisskunig (Muther 34, Hollstein 18), 1513-18,* prov., illus. in Treizsaurwein, Weisskunig, (12-04-92, Bassenge, #6022), 8B, x 7B, in., (21.9 x 19.3 cm.), woodcut (BP 92, DM 229, FR 778, Y 17,978).

$3207* *Sanctus Silvinus (Hollstein 12), 1510-1518,* sheet from Sipp-, Mag- und Schwagerschaft Kaiser Maximilians I, artis proof, watermark, (06-23-93, Kornfeld, #6), woodcut (BP 2179, DM 5426, FR 18,253, Y 349,384, SF 4830).

BECK, Maurice
BI   *"Portrait Of A Chinese Man" and "A Chinese Lady":* *Two,* 1920s, mounted on card, front s., labels, 315 x 240mm and 342 x 254mm, est. BP 2/300, (05-07-93, Sotheby-London, #169), photograph, silver print.

BECK, Maurice and Peter MORGAN
$378* *Winter Shell, Now Until Next May, 1936,* p. Waterlow and Sons, ref. #452, cond. 4, (10-13-92, Phillips-London, #104), 29Zzn x 44M, in., (76 x 114 cm.), color lithograph (BP 220, DM 554, FR 1882, Y 45,835).

BECKER, Murray
$2860* *The Hindenberg Disaster,* s., i., photog.'s notations, John Faber's handstamp verso, 1937, p.l. 1958, (04-07-93, Swann, #290, illus.), 14 x 11 in., photograph, silver print (BP 1890, DM 4626, FR 15,654, Y 324,926).

$880* *The Hindenburg Disaster, 1937,* notations, (10-14-92, Swann, #284, illus.), 13½ x 10½ in., (34.3 x 26.7 cm.), photograph, silver print (BP 517, DM 1288, FR 4367, Y 106,641).

BECKLEY, Bill   American b. 1946
BI   *Song For A Hurdler, 1972,* t., s., d. in ink Song For a Hurdler, Bill Beckley, 1/72, est. BP 5/800, (10-15-92, Sotheby-London, #58, illus.), smallest 2 x 2¾ in., (5.1 x 7 cm.), largest 7 x 4¾ in., (5.1 x 7 cm.), photograph, silver prints and musical score on card.

BECKMANN, Max   American b. Germany 1884, d. 1950
BI   *Der Abend (Selbstbildnis Mit Den Battenbergs) (Hofm. 90, III, B), 1916,* sheet 10 of series Gesichter, #13/150, estate stamp, est. DM 1,450, (10-09-92, Winterberg, #1732, illus.), 9C, x 7Zzn in., (23.8 x 18 cm.), drypoint on wove.

$3248* *"Alte Frau Mit Kapothut" (Hofmaier 160 Bb.; Gallwitz 131 b.), 1920,* s., num., (11-28-92, Grisebach, #436, illus.), 11B, x 7¾ in., (29.5 x 19.7 cm.), drypoint on copper print paper (BP 2144, DM 5174, FR 17,566, Y 404,231).

$706* *Am Klavier (Hofmaier 59 B d-Gallwitz 41), 1913,* s., #32/35, (06-10-93, Hauswedell/Nolt, #62), image 4B, x 3>¹n in., (11.8 x 9.1 cm.), etching on wove (BP 462, DM 1150, FR 3871, Y 74,939).

$1604* *Am Klavier (Hofmaier 59/B/d), 1913,* s., num., (06-23-93, Kornfeld, #197), etching on wove (BP 1090, DM 2714, FR 9129, Y 174,747, SF 2415).

BI   *"Am Klavier" (Hofmaier 59 B.d.; Gallwitz 41), 1913,* s., est. DM 1,4/1,800, (11-28-92, Grisebach, #433, illus.), 4Mzn x 3C, in., (11.3 x 8.5 cm.), etching in brown on copper print paper.

$3901* *Auferstehung (Gallwitz 103; Hofmaier 132 II B a), 1918,* t., s., blindstamp, (06-05-93, Bassenge, #5905, illus.), 9Mzn x 13Zzn in., (24 x 33.2 cm.), etching on Japan (BP 2568, DM 6325, FR 21,317, Y 418,472).

$3249* *Auferstehung (Hofmaier 132 II A-Gallwitz 103), 1918,* s., d., t., (06-10-93, Hauswedell/Nolt, #69, illus.), image 9C, x 12Bzn in., (23.8 x 33 cm.), drypoint on wove (BP 2125, DM 5291, FR 17,813, Y 344,868).

$4237* *Auferstehung (Hofmaier 132 II B a-Gallwitz 103), 1918,* s., t., num., blindstamp, (06-10-93, Hauswedell/Nolt, #67),

image 9Zzn x 13Czn in., (24.6 x 33.5 cm.), drypoint on Japan (BP 2771, DM 6900, FR 23,229, Y 449,740).

BI   *Auferstehung (Hofmaier 132; Glaser 113; Gallwitz 103), 1918,* plate 12 of Gesichter, s., num. 26/60, pub. Marees Gesellschaft, 1919, blindstamp, full margins, good cond., est. Y 700/800,000, (10-14-92, Sotheby-Japan, #2, illus.), 9M, x 13 in., (251 x 330 mm.), drypoint on laid paper.

$50,168* *Berliner Reise (Glaser 187-95; Gallwitz 181i-191; Hofmaier 212-222), 1922: Ten,* J.B. Neumann, 1922, each s., #26/100, pub., H. 213, 216, and 217, printer's crease, very good cond., loose paper-covered card portfolio, (05-20-93, Christie-London, #420, illus.), sh 27½ x 21¾ in., (69.9 x 55.2 cm.), lithograph on wove (BP 32,200, DM 80,942, FR 272,652, Y 5,539,753).

$49,338* *Berliner Reise (Hofmaier 212-222), 1922: Ten,* pub. I. B. Neumann, Berlin, #76/100, s., (05-26-93, Lempertz, #33, illus.), sh, approx. 26¾ x 21Zzn in., (68 x 53.5 cm.), lithograph on wove (BP 31,917, DM 80,499, FR 270,939, Y 5,360,495).

$2119* *Bildnis Der Tanzerin Sent M'Ahesa (Hofmaier 182 II-Gallwitz 155), 1921,* s., watermark, (06-10-93, Hauswedell/Nolt, #83, illus.), image 22½ x 16¼ in., (57.2 x 41.2 cm.), lithograph on wove (BP 1386, DM 3451, FR 11,617, Y 224,923).

BI   *Bildnis Des Verwundeten Schwagers Martin Tube (Hofmaier 76), 1914,* p. in Kriegszeit Kunstlerflugblatter, Nr. 11, Nov. 1914, page folded,yellowed, tears, est. BP 3/400, (06-30-93, Sotheby-London, #343), 12 x 9M, in., (305 x 251 mm.), lithograph.

BI   *Bildnis Dr. Sakon (Hofmaier 107/Gallwitz 85), 1917,* fine impression, s., full margins, good cond., 2 small scuffs verso,Late Gerhard Brauer Coll., est. Dfl. 2,7/3,000, (05-27-93, Sotheby-Amstrdm, #712), 6¾ x 4M, in., (172 x 124 mm.), drypoint on wove.

$1986* *Bildnis Frau H. M. (Naila) (Gallwitz 252; Hofmaier 282 IV B a), 1923,* s., blindstamp, (06-05-93, Bassenge, #5902), 13Zzn x 12Bzn in., (35.5 x 32.8 cm.), woodcut on Japan (BP 1307, DM 3220, FR 10,852, Y 213,044).

$1353* *Bildnis J.B. Neumann (Hofmaier 154 II B a, Gallwitz 125 a), 1919,* s., (12-02-92, Dorling, #2527, illus.), 8¼ x 6½ in., (21 x 16.5 cm.), etching on wove (BP 873, DM 2128, FR 7262, Y 168,346).

$1554* *Bildnis Naila Mit Aufgestutzten Armen Und Glas (Hofmaier 265 A-Gallwitz 230), 1923,* s., artist's proof, (06-10-93, Hauswedell/Nolt, #79), image 8¼ x 5Zzn in., (20.9 x 15.2 cm.), drypoint on wove (BP 1016, DM 2531, FR 8520, Y 164,951).

$916* *Bildnis Reinhard Piper (Hofm. 183/B/c), 1921,* s., num., (06-23-93, Kornfeld, #200), lithograph on thin Japan (BP 622, DM 1550, FR 5213, Y 99,793, SF 1380).

$733* *Bildnis Reinhard Piper (Hofmaier Nr. 240 B), 1922,* #29/30, s., stamp, foxing, (11-13-92, Kunsthaus, #462), 8Zzn x 4Z, in., (22 x 10.4 cm.), woodcut on Japan (BP 474, DM 1151, FR 3880, Y 90,977).

$1024* *Christus Und Die Sunderin (Hofmaier 20 A c (2); Gallwitz 7), 1911,* s., sheet 3 from the series Zum neuen Testament, (12-02-92, Dorling, #2529, illus.), 10Zzn x 9¼ in., (25.5 x 23.5 cm.), lithograph on Japan (BP 661, DM 1610, FR 5497, Y 127,411).

$1412* *Dame Mit Knabe (Hofmaier 266 B a-Gallwitz 231), 1923,* s., pub. Piper & Co., (06-10-93, Hauswedell/Nolt, #80), image 8C, x 6¼ in., (21.2 x 15.8 cm.), drypoint on thin Japan paper (BP 924, DM 2299, FR 7741, Y 149,878).

$1342* *Dame Mit Knabe (Hofmaier 266 B b-Gallwitz 231), 1923,* s., Piper & Co., (06-10-93, Hauswedell/Nolt, #81), image 8C, x 6¼ in., (21.2 x 15.8 cm.), drypoint on Japan (BP 878, DM 2185, FR 7357, Y 142,448).

$10,450* *Dis Enttauschten I (G. 183; H. 214), 1922,* s., #82/100, large margins, good cond., foxing, mat stain, (11-05-92, Sotheby-NY, #80, illus.), 19¼ x 14¾ in., (490 x 375 mm.), sheet 25¼ x 19B, in., (490 x 375 mm.), lithograph (BP 6797, DM 16,527, FR 55,912, Y 1,282,051).

$1770* *Doppelbildnis J.B. Neumann Und Martha Stern (Gallwitz 178, Hofmaier 209 II), 1922,* s., (12-05-92, Bassenge, #7037), 17Zzn x 19Bzn in., (43.3 x 49 cm.), lithograph on wove (BP 1108, DM 2760, FR 9405, Y 219,304).

$1316* *Dostojewski II (Hofm. 187 B, a), 1921,* s., blindstamp, (10-09-92, Winterberg, #1733), 6Zzn x 4Z'zn in., (17 x

11.9 cm.), drypoint on hand-made (BP 781, DM 1955, FR 6564, Y 160,214).

BI *Dostojewski II (Hofmaier 186 II B a.), 1921,* s., est. DM 2,500, (05-26-93, Lempertz, #31), sh 10M, x 8Z, in., (27.7 x 20.6 cm.), etching (drypoint) on Japan.

$2402* *Ebbi: Illustration For Act II (H. 309; Gallwitz 274), 1924,* s., pub. Johannes-Presse, margins, good cond., (06-30-93, Sotheby-London, #346, illus.), sh 13 x 9½ in., (330 x 241 mm.), drypoint on wove (BP 1610, DM 4097, FR 13,820, Y 257,366).

BI *Edschmid, Kasimir; Die Furstin (Hofm. 111, IV B; 112, II B; 113, IIIB; 114, B; 115, II B; 116, IV B), 1918: Six,* Weimar, Kiepenheuer, #32/35, s., signs of wear, est. DM 7,800, (10-09-92, Winterberg, #1738, illus.), smallest 6M, x 5Bzn in., (17.5 x 13.5 cm.), largest 7C, x 5>zn in., (17.5 x 13.5 cm.), drypoint on hand-made.

$2071* *Eislauf (H. 223 B c), 1922,* s., crease, (12-01-92, Karl/Faber, #361, illus.), 15¾ x 9Mzn in., (40 x 24 cm.), lithograph on hand-made (BP 1368, DM 3301, FR 11,249, Y 257,844).

$3088* *Eislauf (H. 223), 1922,* s., pub. Verlag R.Piper & Co., full margins, good cond., (06-30-93, Sotheby-London, #347, illus.), 16 x 9½ in., (406 x 241 mm.), lithograph on laid (BP 2070, DM 5267, FR 17,768, Y 330,869).

$2401* *Eislauf (Hofmaier 223 B a-Gallwitz 192), 1922,* s., (06-10-93, Hauswedell/Nolt, #88), image 16Z, x 9Mzn in., (41 x 24 cm.), lithograph on Japan (BP 1571, DM 3910, FR 13,163, Y 254,856).

BI *Eislauf (Hofmaier 223 B c-Gallwitz 192), 1922,* s., Bl. 5 from the series Berliner Reise, est. DM 6000, (06-10-93, Hauswedell/Nolt, #89), image 16Bzn x 9Zzn in., (41.5 x 23 cm.), lithograph on hand-made.

BI *Die Enttauschten (Hofmaier 214 A), 1922,* s., d., i., artist's proof, est. DM 15,000, (05-26-93, Lempertz, #34, illus.), 23½ x 18Z\ in., (59.7 x 46 cm.), lithograph on imitated Japan.

$4290* *Fastnacht (H. 231), 1922,* s., #1/60, pub. Verlage R.Piper & Co., full margins, good cond., (06-30-93, Sotheby-London, #350, illus.), 12¾ x 9M, in., (324 x 251 mm.), drypoint on wove (BP 2875, DM 7317, FR 24,684, Y 459,659).

$5808* *"Fastnacht" (H. 231/II B d), 1922,* s., num. , pub. R. Piper, (12-01-92, Karl/Faber, #363, illus.), 12B, x 9Mzn in., (32 x 24 cm.), drypoint (BP 3837, DM 9257, FR 31,548, Y 723,108).

$1826* *Flusslandschaft (H. 268 B a), 1923,* s., hors texte, pub. Piper & Co., 1924, (12-01-92, Karl/Faber, #366, illus.), 12 x 8M, in., (30.5 x 22.5 cm.), lithograph on Japan (BP 1206, DM 2910, FR 9919, Y 227,341).

$2599* *"Flusslandschaft" (Hofmaier 268 Ba (von b); Gallwitz 233.), 1923,* s., (11-28-92, Grisebach, #438, illus.), 8¾ x 6Zzn in., (22.3 x 17 cm.), lithograph on yellow Japan (BP 1716, DM 4141, FR 14,056, Y 323,460).

BI *Frau Mit Kerze (Gl. 149; Gall. 143; Hofmeier 171 III Bc), 1920,* 2nd (final) state, s., creases, loss, foxmarks, est. BP 3/5,000, (12-01-92, Christie-London, #304, illus.), L. 11M, x 5Zzn in., (302 x 148 mm.), woodcut on laid paper.

$8600* *Frauenbad (Glaser 308; Gallwitz 204; Hofmaier 234), 1922,* s., #VIII/XX, pub. R. Piper, deckle edge on three sides, foxmarks, creasing, very good cond., (05-20-93, Christie-London, #422, illus.), plate 17¼ x 11¼ in., (43.8 x 28.6 cm.), sheet 21 x 19½ in., (43.8 x 28.6 cm.), drypoint on Japan (BP 5520, DM 13,875, FR 46,739, Y 949,647).

$5491* *Frauenbad (H. 234), 1922,* s., pub. R.Piper & Co., full margins, good cond., (06-30-93, Sotheby-London, #353, illus.), 12 x 8¾ in., (305 x 222 mm.), drypoint (BP 3680, DM 9366, FR 31,594, Y 588,342).

$7219* *"Frauenbad" (Hofmaier 234/II B c; Gallwitz 204), 1922,* s., (11-28-92, Grisebach, #211, illus.), 17 x 11¼ in., (43.2 x 28.6 cm.), drypoint on copper print paper (BP 4765, DM 11,501, FR 39,043, Y 898,444).

$944* *Frauenkopf Mit Halskette (Frau Parcus) (Gallwitz 176; Hofmaier 206 B/c (v.d.)), 1921,* s., (04-27-93, Hartung, #1938, illus.), lithograph (BP 600, DM 1495, FR 5056, Y 105,794).

$989* *Frauenkopf Mit Halskette (Frau Parcus) (Hofmaier 206 B a-Gallwitz 176), 1921,* s., (06-10-93, Hauswedell/Nolt,

#86), image 14Czn x 11 in., (36 x 28 cm.), lithograph on Japan (BP 647, DM 1610, FR 5422, Y 104,978).

$747* *Frauenkopf Mit Halskette (Frau Pracus) (H. 206 B a), 1921,* s., (12-01-92, Karl/Faber, #359), 14Czn x 10B, in., (36 x 27 cm.), lithograph on simili-Japan (BP 494, DM 1191, FR 4058, Y 93,003).

$815* *Frauenkopf Mit Halskette (H. 206), 1921,* s., (06-08-93, Karl/Faber, #542), approx. 14Czn x 11 in., (36 x 28 cm.), lithograph on hand-made (BP 536, DM 1322, FR 4454, Y 86,564).

$916* *Frauenkopf Mit Halskette (Hofm. 206/B/c), 1921,* s., (06-23-93, Kornfeld, #202), lithograph on handmade (BP 622, DM 1550, FR 5213, Y 99,793, SF 1380).

$770* *From Aus Einem Totenhaus (Ga. 28): Seven,* 3 p. on backs of others, good cond., staining, surface soiling, (02-24-93, Butterfield, #2897), lithograph on wove (BP 537, DM 1250, FR 4238, Y 90,354).

$4256* *Fruhling (Gallwitz 104; Hofmaier 133 II B a), 1918,* s., t., blindstamp, (06-05-93, Bassenge, #5906, illus.), 11Zz x 7Zzn in., (29.7 x 19.6 cm.), etching on hand-made Japan (BP 2802, DM 6900, FR 23,257, Y 456,554).

$1695* *Fruhling (Hofmaier 133 II B b-Gallwitz 104), 1918,* blindstamp, (06-10-93, Hauswedell/Nolt, #70), image 11Zz x 7¾ in., (30 x 19.7 cm.), drypoint on hand-made (BP 1109, DM 2760, FR 9293, Y 179,917).

BI *Fruhling (Kat. Karlsruhe 104, Hofmaier 133 II Ba), 1918,* t., num., s., blindstamp, plate 13 from Gesichter, est. DM 8,500-, (11-21-92, Lempertz, #35A, illus.), 11¾ x 7M, in., (29.8 x 20 cm.), etching on thick hand-made Japan.

$1412* *Die Gahnenden (Hofmaier 129 IV B b-Gallwitz 110), 1918,* blindstamp, (06-10-93, Hauswedell/Nolt, #66), image 12Zzn x 10Bzn in., (30.7 x 26.2 cm.), drypoint on hand-made (BP 924, DM 2299, FR 7741, Y 149,878).

BI *"Die Gahnenden" (Hofmaier 129/IVCb; Gallwitz 100), 1918,* sheet 7 of series Gesichter, num., 1966, s. Peter Beckmann, est. DM1,5/1,700, (11-28-92, Grisebach, #434, illus.), 11B\zn x 9Zzn in., (30.3 x 25.2 cm.), drypoint on wove.

$3260* *Geheimrat Robert (Hofmaier 66 B c), (19)14,* s., d., (06-08-93, Karl/Faber, #540, illus.), 10B, x 8¼ in., (27 x 21 cm.), drypoint on heavy wove (BP 2143, DM 5290, FR 17,814, Y 346,256).

$2750* *Gesichter: Kreuzabnahme (K. 131, Ga. 102), 1918,* s., blindstamp pub., Marees Gesellschaft, full margins, good cond., creases, surface soiling, stains, pressure marks, tears, (02-24-93, Butterfield, #2704, illus.), 12 x 10¼ in., (305 x 260 mm.), drypoint on laid (BP 1918, DM 4464, FR 15,135, Y 322,694).

$3402* *Der Grosse Mann (Hofmaier 195/II B b(von C b)), 1921,* s., fifth from the series Der Jahrmarkt, s., pub. Marees-Gesellschaft, R. Piper & Co., 1922, (12-01-92, Karl/Faber, #358, illus.), 12Czn x 8Zzn in., (31 x 20.5 cm.), drypoint on wove (BP 2248, DM 5422, FR 18,479, Y 423,556).

BI *Grosse Operation (Gallwitz 55, Hofmaier 81 VI B a), 1914,* t., s., sheet 18 of series Gesichter, blindstamp, est. DM 6,000, (12-05-92, Bassenge, #7035), 11B, x 17Czn in., drypoint.

$4229* *Grosse Operation (Hofmaier 81 VI), c. 1914,* s., sheet 18 of Gesichter series, (05-26-93, Lempertz, #30, illus.), approx. 14>zn x 20¼ in., (37 x 51.5 cm.), etching (drypoint) on handmade (BP 2736, DM 6900, FR 23,224, Y 459,474).

$6992* *Holzbrucke (Gl. 216; Gall. 212; Hofmaier 242), 1922,* i., proof, margins, excellent cond., (12-01-92, Christie-London, #305), plate 11¼ x 9¼ in., (286 x 235 mm.), drypoint on firm wove (BP 4620, DM 11,144, FR 37,979, Y 870,518).

$6858* *"In Der Trambahn" (Hofmaier 235 Ba; Gallwitz 205), 1922,* s., margins, stained, (11-28-92, Grisebach, #215, illus.), 11Bzn x 17Z, in., (28.8 x 43.5 cm.), drypoint on Japan (BP 4527, DM 10,926, FR 37,090, Y 853,516).

$57,179* *Jahrmarkt, Verlag Der Marees Gesellschaft, (Hofmaier 191-200 Ba), 1921,* R. Piper & Co., 1922, one sheet mono., copy #26, each s., blindstamp, margins, excell. cond., original mounts, impressed plate nums., loose paper-covered board portfolio, (05-20-93, Christie-London, #419, illus.), 22 x 16½ in., (55.9 x 41.9 cm.), drypoint on Japan (BP 36,700, DM 92,254, FR 310,755, Y 6,313,936).

$1527* *Junge Dame (Hofm. 269/B/a), 1923,* s., (06-23-93, Kornfeld, #205), lithograph (BP 1037, DM 2584, FR 8691, Y 166,358, SF 2300).

BI *Kinder Am Fenster (Hofmaier 237 II B d-Gallwitz 207), 1922,* s., #10/35, est. DM 7500, (06-10-93, Hauswedell/Nolt, #78, illus.), image 12M≵n x 8M, in., (31.6 x 22.6 cm.), drypoint on wove.

$4331* *"Kleine Strasse" (Hofmaier 91/II B a-b; Gallwitz 68), 1916,* s., (11-28-92, Grisebach, #213, illus.), 4Mzn x 6¾ in., (11.3 x 17.2 cm.), drypoint on Japan (BP 2859, DM 6900, FR 23,423, Y 539,017).

$1907* *Kleines Tanzendes Paar (Hofmaier 267 B a-Gallwitz 232), 1923,* s., Piper & Co., (06-10-93, Hauswedell/Nolt, #90, illus.), image 6B, x 4Zzn in., (16.9 x 10.3 cm.), woodcut on thin Japan (BP 1247, DM 3105, FR 10,455, Y 202,420).

$2837* *Kleines Tanzendes Paar (Hofmaier 267 B b), 1923,* s., (06-05-93, Bassenge, #5901), 6¾ x 3M, in., (17.2 x 9.9 cm.), woodcut on imitation Japan (BP 1868, DM 4600, FR 15,503, Y 304,334).

$2542* *Kleines Tanzendes Paar (Hofmaier 267 B b-Gallwitz 232), 1923,* s., Piper & Co., (06-10-93, Hauswedell/Nolt, #91, illus.), image 6¾ x 3Bzn in., (17.2 x 10 cm.), woodcut on Japan (BP 1663, DM 4139, FR 13,936, Y 269,823).

$2166* *"Kleines Tanzendes Paar" (Hofmaier 267 Bb; Gallwitz 232.), 1923,* s., artist's proof, (11-28-92, Grisebach, #437, illus.), 6M, x 4Zzn in., (17.5 x 10.3 cm.), woodcut on Japan (BP 1430, DM 3451, FR 11,714, Y 269,571).

$5791* *Konig Jerum Und Seine Frau,...(Hofmaier 292-Gallwitz 254), 1923,* s., Bl. 2 from Clemens Brentano: Fanferlieschen Schonefusschen, Gurlitt, (06-10-93, Hauswedell/Nolt, #82, illus.), image 7¾ x 5Zzn in., (19.7 x 14.7 cm.), drypoint on hand-made (BP 3788, DM 9430, FR 31,749, Y 614,691).

BI *Konig Und Demagoge (G. 296; H. 364), 1946,* plate VIII of Day and Dream, s., i. w/plate num., #3/90, full margins, good cond., est. $2,5/3,500, (05-13-93, Sotheby-NY, #460), 14¾ x 10 in., (375 x 253 mm.), lithograph.

$2444* *Konig Und Demagoge (Hofm. 364/B/a), 1946,* sheet 8 of series: Day and Dream, s., (06-23-93, Kornfeld, #206, illus.), lithograph on wove (BP 1660, DM 4135, FR 13,910, Y 266,260, SF 3680).

$3192* *Kreuzabnahme (Gallwitz 102; Hofmaier 131 II B a), 1918,* s., series Geischter, blindstamp, (06-05-93, Bassenge, #5904), 11Bzn x 10Czn in., (30.3 x 25.8 cm.), etching on Japan (BP 2101, DM 5175, FR 17,443, Y 342,416).

BI *Die Kriegserklarung (Hofmaier Band I, 78 II b), 1914,* s., est. DM 8,500-, (11-21-92, Lempertz, #34, illus.), 7¾ x 9Zzn in., (19.7 x 25 cm.), etching on wove.

$5628* *Liebespaar II (Hofmaier 125; Glaser 107; Gallwitz 97), 1918,* plate 5 of Gesichter, s., pub. Marees Gesellschaft, 1919, blindstamp, full margins, good cond., (10-14-92, Sotheby-Japan, #1, illus.), 8½ x 10 in., (216 x 254 mm.), drypoint on laid paper (BP 3303, DM 8236, FR 27,931, Y 682,016).

$2987* *Liegende (H. 232 B b), 1922,* s., num., pub. Piper, margin, creases, (12-01-92, Karl/Faber, #364, illus.), 11Mzn x 9Zzn in., (29 x 25 cm.), drypoint (BP 1974, DM 4761, FR 16,225, Y 371,887).

BI *Liegende (H. 232), 1922,* s., pub. R.Piper & Co., full margins, good cond., (06-30-93, Sotheby-London, #351, illus.), 11B, x 9¾ in., (295 x 248 mm.), drypoint on wove.

$2260* *Liegende (Hofmaier 232 B a-Gallwitz 202), 1922,* s., (06-10-93, Hauswedell/Nolt, #75, illus.), image 11B, x 10Zzn in., (29.6 x 25.5 cm.), drypoint on wove (BP 1478, DM 3680, FR 12,390, Y 239,890).

$916* *Lowenpaar (Hofm. 184/B/b), 1921,* s., num., (06-23-93, Kornfeld, #201), lithograph on thin Japan (BP 622, DM 1550, FR 5213, Y 99,793, SF 1380).

$1271* *Lowenpaar (Hofmaier 184 B a-Gallwitz 157), 1921,* s., (06-10-93, Hauswedell/Nolt, #85), image 15M, x 10Bzn in., (40.3 x 27.8 cm.), lithograph on thin Japan (BP 831, DM 2070, FR 6968, Y 134,911).

$5226* *Mainlandschaft (Hofmaier 128 IV B b-Gallwitz 99 b), 1918,* s., #29/60, blindstamp, (06-10-93, Hauswedell/Nolt, #65, illus.), image 9Bzn x 11Zzn in., (25.3 x 30 cm.), drypoint on hand-made (BP 3418, DM 8510, FR 28,651, Y 554,718).

$3583* *Mainlandschaft Mit Regenbogen (Gallwitz 242; Hofmaier 278A), 1923,* rich burr, t., proof, pub. R. Piper, msrgins, mount-staining, taped, (05-20-93, Christie-London, #425, illus.), plate 9½ x 8 in., (24.1 x 20.3 cm.), sheet 16½ x 13¾ in., (24.1 x 20.3 cm.), drypoint on laid paper (BP 2300, DM 5781, FR 19,473, Y 395,649).

BI *"Mainlandschaft" (Hofmaier 128/IV b; Gallwitz 99b), 1918,* sheet 6 of series "Gesichter", Munchen, pub. Marees Gesellschaft, R.Piper & Co., 1919, est. DM 14/18,000, (11-28-92, Grisebach, #212, illus.), 9¾ x 11>zn in., (24.7 x 29.3 cm.), drypoint in handmade copper print paper.

$5901* *Minette (Gallwitz 208, Hofmaier 238 VI B a), 1922,* s., ded., (12-05-92, Bassenge, #7038), 9Zzn x 7M, in., (25 x 20 cm.), drypoint on handmade (BP 3695, DM 9200, FR 31,355, Y 731,136).

$1100* *Mink Von Vorn Mit Grosser Frisur (G. 55, K. 63), 1913,* s., full margins, good cond., mat staining, surface soiling, notations, (10-28-92, Butterfield, #2606), 6C, x 4M, in., (162 x 124 mm.), drypoint on Japan paper (BP 701, DM 1699, FR 5768, Y 134,969).

$1663* *Modell (Hofmaier 124/Gallwitz 93), 1918,* s., d., full margins, good cond., traces of cellophane tape stainingin margins, Late Gerhard Brauer Coll., (05-27-93, Sotheby-Amstrdm, #713, illus.), 9¼ x 6M, in., (235 x 175 mm.), drypoint on J.W. Zanders laid paper (BP 1065, DM 2668, FR 8994, Y 178,280, G 2990).

$1444* *"Modell" (Hofmaier 35 B; Gallwitz 22), 1911,* s., d., num., (11-28-92, Grisebach, #432, illus.), 13¼ x 10B, in., (33.7 x 27 cm.), lithograph on handmade (BP 953, DM 2300, FR 7810, Y 179,714).

$3603* *Der Morgen (H. 299), 1923,* s., i. by printer, full margins, good cond., loss, glued to mount, (06-30-93, Sotheby-London, #354, illus.), 10Z, x 12 in., (257 x 305 mm.), drypoint on Japan (BP 2415, DM 6145, FR 20,731, Y 386,050).

$878* *Der Morgen (Hofmaier 299 B c; Gallwitz 237), 1923,* print stamp, (12-02-92, Dorling, #2528, illus.), 10Z, x 12 in., (25.7 x 30.5 cm.), etching on wove (BP 566, DM 1381, FR 4713, Y 109,245).

$3754* *"Der Morgen" (Hofmaier 299/Bb (von c); Gallwitz 237), 1923,* s., (11-28-92, Grisebach, #439, illus.), 9B\zn x 12 in., (25.3 x 30.5 cm.), drypoint on copper print paper (BP 2478, DM 5981, FR 20,303, Y 467,206).

$3520* *Niggertanz (Hofmaier 199), 1922,* plate 9 from Der Jahrmarkt, Verlag der Marees Gesellschaft, R. Piperand Co., s., blindstamp, full margins, light-staining, very good cond., (11-09-92, Christie-NY, #49, illus.), border 10¼ x 10Zzn in., (260 x 255 mm.), drypoint on wove (BP 2327, DM 5619, FR 18,986, Y 436,833).

$4802* *Peter Mit Der Spitzen Mutze (Hofmaier 178 A-Gallwitz 150), 1920,* plate s., d., artist's proof, prov., (06-10-93, Hauswedell/Nolt, #71, illus.), image 11Zzn x 5Zzn in., (30 x 14.5 cm.), etching on copper print paper (BP 3141, DM 7820, FR 26,327, Y 509,712).

BI *Pierrot Und Maske (Ga. 146), 1920,* pub. in Pfister, small margins, good cond., binding holes, linen tape, surface soiling, sheet slightly toned, est. $5/700, (02-24-93, Butterfield, #2898), 12¼ x 8 in., (311 x 203 mm.), lithograph on wove.

$7376* *Pierrot Und Maske (Gallwitz 146, Hofmaier 173 II B a), 1920,* s., (12-05-92, Bassenge, #7036), 12Bzn x 8Zzn in., (31.2 x 20.5 cm.), lithograph on machinemade (BP 4619, DM 11,500, FR 39,192, Y 913,889).

BI *Prosit Neujahr (Hofmaier 108 VI B b), 1917,* t., s., blindstamp, plate 17 from Gesichter, est. DM 8,500-, (11-21-92, Lempertz, #35, illus.), 9Mzn x 11Zzn in., (23.9 x 30 cm.), etching on hand-made.

$851* *Sarika (Gallwitz 203; Hofmaier 233 B e), 1922,* s., (06-05-93, Bassenge, #5909), 12Zzn x 8Zzn in., (30.6 x 22 cm.), drypoint on wove (BP 560, DM 1380, FR 4650, Y 91,289).

$1064* *Sarika (Gallwitz 203; Hofmaier 233 B f), 1922,* s., num., (06-05-93, Bassenge, #5908), 12Zzn x 8Zzn in., (30.6 x 22 cm.), drypoint on wove (BP 700, DM 1725, FR 5814, Y 114,139).

$2574* *Sarika (H. 233), 1922,* s., pub. Verlag R.Piper & Co., full margins, good cond., (06-30-93, Sotheby-London, #345, illus.), 12 x 8¾ in., (305 x 222 mm.), drypoint on Japan (BP 1725, DM 4390, FR 14,810, Y 275,796).

$1374* *Sarika (Hofm. 233/B/d), 1922,* s. in ink, num., (06-23-93, Kornfeld, #204), drypoint on bright rose Japan (BP 933, DM 2325, FR 7820, Y 149,690, SF 2070).

$847* *Sarika (Hofmaier 233 B c-Gallwitz 203), 1922,* s., num. VIV/XXX, (06-10-93, Hauswedell/Nolt, #76), image 12Zn x 8¾ in., (30.6 x 22.2 cm.), drypoint on Japan (BP 554, DM 1379, FR 4644, Y 89,906).

$721* *Sarika (Hofmaier Band II 233 B e), 1922,* s., trimmed, light-stains, (11-21-92, Lempertz, #38), 12 x 8Zn in., (30.5 x 22 cm.), etching on wove (BP 475, DM 1150, FR 3872, Y 89,665).

$916* *Sarika Mit Cigarette (Hofm. 229/B), 1922,* s., num., (06-23-93, Kornfeld, #203), lithograph on handmade (BP 622, DM 1550, FR 5213, Y 99,793, SF 1380).

$851* *Sarika Mit Zigarette (Gallwitz 198; Hofmeier 229 c), 1922,* s., (06-05-93, Schoppmann, #716), 24Cn x 14Mn in., (61.4 x 36.6 cm.), lithograph on hand-made (BP 560, DM 1380, FR 4650, Y 91,289).

$2745* *Sarika Mit Zigarette (H. 229), 1922,* s., pub. Verlag R.Piper & Co., full margins, good cond., defects, (06-30-93, Sotheby-London, #348, illus.), 24¼ x 14C, in., (616 x 365 mm.), lithograph on Japan (BP 1840, DM 4682, FR 15,794, Y 294,118).

$2013* *Sarika Mit Zigarette (Hofm. 229, B b), 1922,* VI/XX, s., (10-09-92, Winterberg, #1737, illus.), 24Bn x 14C, in., (61.8 x 36.5 cm.), lithograph on Japan (BP 1194, DM 2990, FR 10,040, Y 245,069).

$8525* *Schlafende (Gallwitz 95; Hofmaier 123), 1917,* fourth (final) state, s., full margins, good cond., hinge stain, (11-05-92, Sotheby-NY, #79), 7Z, x 5C, in., (181 x 138 mm.), drypoint on wove (BP 5545, DM 13,483, FR 45,613, Y 1,045,884).

$4600* *Schlangendame (Gallwitz 172; Hofmaier 200/II/B/a), 1921,* s., pub. Marees Gesellschaft, blindstamp, full margins, good cond., (05-13-93, Sotheby-NY, #457, illus.), 11C, x 10¼ in., (289 x 259 mm.), drypoint on Japan (BP 3020, DM 7428, FR 25,054, Y 513,565).

BI *Der Schlittschuhlaufer (Hofmaier 217 A-Gallwitz 186), 1922,* s., d., t., artist's proof, est. DM 9000, (06-10-93, Hauswedell/Nolt, #87, illus.), image 19Bn x 14\n in., (49 x 37 cm.), lithograph on thin Japan paper.

BI *"Der Schlittschuhlaufer" (H. 217 A), (19)22,* s., d., from the portfolio Berliner Reise, t., artist's proof, light-stained, tear, est. DM 10,000, (12-01-92, Karl/Faber, #360, illus.), 19Bn x 14\n in., (49 x 37 cm.), lithograph on Japan.

$7934* *Der Schornsteinfeger (Hofmaier Band II 222), 1922,* t., i. artist's proof, s., d., stains, tears, plate 10 from BerlinerReise 1922, (11-21-92, Lempertz, #37, illus.), 17Z\n x 13Cn in., (45 x 33.5 cm.), lithograph on imitiertem Japan (BP 5224, DM 12,650, FR 42,610, Y 986,693).

$7415* *Die Seiltanzer (Hofmaier 198 A-Gallwitz 170), 1921,* s., d., t., artist's proof, Bl. 8 from the series Der Jahrmarkt, (06-10-93, Hauswedell/Nolt, #73), image 10Zn x 9Zn in., (25.6 x 25 cm.), drypoint on wove (BP 4850, DM 12,075, FR 40,652, Y 787,071).

$586* *Selbstbild (Hofmaier Nr. 137 C; b), 1918,* #68/80, estate stamp, s. Peter Beckmann., posthumous edit. 1966, (11-13-92, Kunsthaus, #461), 10Zn x 10Zn in., (27.5 x 25.5 cm.), etching on wove (BP 379, DM 920, FR 3102, Y 72,732).

$4313* *Selbstbildnis (G. 289; H. 357), 1946,* plate I of Day and Dream, s., pub. Curt Valentin, full margins, goodcond., printer's creases, handling creases, skinned spots, (05-13-93, Sotheby-NY, #459, illus.), 12C, x 10C\ in., (315 x 263 mm.), lithograph on cream, Holland (BP 2832, DM 6964, FR 23,491, Y 481,523).

$12,768* *Selbstbildnis (Gallwitz 195, Hofmaier 226 III B v), 1922,* s., (06-05-93, Bassenge, #5900, illus.), 8¾ x 6Z\ in., (22.2 x 15.5 cm.), woodcut on Japan (BP 8405, DM 20,700, FR 69,770, Y 1,369,663).

$11,513* *Selbstbildnis (Hofmaier 124/Gallwitz 93), 1920,* strong impression, s., margins, good cond., slight handling marks inlower margin, Late Gerhard Brauer Coll., (05-27-93, Sotheby-Amstrdm, #714, illus.), 7Zn x 5¾ in., (195 x 146 mm.), drypoint on wove (BP 7373, DM 18,474, FR 62,266, Y 1,234,241, G 20,700).

$7965* *Selbstbildnis (Hofmaier 226/III B b (von f)), 1922,* s., pub. R. Piper & Co., tears in margins, restored, (12-01-92, Karl/Faber, #362, illus.), 8Zn x 6Z, in., (22 x 15.5 cm.), woodcut on China (BP 5263, DM 12,695, FR 43,265, Y 991,658).

$6872* *Selbstbildnis 1920 (Hofm. 172/B), 1920,* s., (06-23-93, Kornfeld, #199, illus.), drypoint on wove (BP 4668, DM 11,628, FR 39,112, Y 748,665, SF 10,350).

$11,072* *Selbstbildnis Mit Griffel (Hofm. 105/II/B/b), c. 1916,* sheet 19 of series: Gesichter, s., Ganymed-stamp, (06-23-93, Kornfeld, #198, illus.), drypoint on wove (BP 7522, DM 18,734, FR 63,017, Y 1,206,232, SF 16,675).

$14,334* *Selbstbildnis Mit Griffel (Hofmaier 105 Bb), c. 1916,* plate 19 from Gesichter, s., pub. Marees Gesellschaft, blindstamp, margins slightly trimmed, mount-staining, tape, good cond., (05-20-93, Christie-London, #421, illus.), plate 11B, x 9¼ in., (29.5 x 23.5 cm.), sheet 17C, x 14¼ in., (29.5 x 23.5 cm.), drypoint on laid (BP 9200, DM 23,127, FR 77,902, Y 1,582,818).

$63,559* *Selbstbildnis Mit Steifem Hut. (Hofmaier 180 IV B-Gallwitz 153), 1921,* s., watermark, (06-10-93, Hauswedell/Nolt, #72, illus.), image 12Cn x 9¾ in., (32.5 x 24.8 cm.), drypoint on hand-made (BP 41,574, DM 103,499, FR 348,459, Y 6,746,524).

$938* *"Spielende Kinder" (Hofmaier 136 II. C.b; Gallwitz 107.), 1918,* estate stamp, s. Peter Beckmann, num., (11-28-92, Grisebach, #435, illus.), 10Zn x 12Z, in., (25.6 x 30.8 cm.), drypoint on copper print paper (BP 619, DM 1494, FR 5073, Y 116,739).

BI *"Spielende Kinder" (Hofmaier 136/II Ba; Gallwitz 107), 1918,* s., t., d., sheet 16 of series "Gesichter", est. DM 7/8,000, (11-28-92, Grisebach, #214, illus.), 9Zn x 11Zn in., (25 x 30 cm.), drypoint on Japan.

BI *Stehender Mannlicher Akt Mit Brille (H. 151), 1919,* s., pub. I. B. Neumann, full margins, good cond., stains, est. BP 1,4/1,800, (06-30-93, Sotheby-London, #344, illus.), 9C, x 7 in., (238 x 178 mm.), drypoint on laid.

$3319* *Strand (H. 268 B d), 1922,* s., num., pub. Piper, foxed, (12-01-92, Karl/Faber, #365, illus.), 8Mn x 12Zn in., (21.5 x 32.5 cm.), drypoint on wove (BP 2193, DM 5290, FR 18,028, Y 413,222).

$25,084* *Tamerlan (Gallwitz 235; Hofmaier 284B), 1923,* burr, s., #32/60, deckle edge on three sides, mount-staining, hinge-stains, creasing, good cond., watermark, (05-20-93, Christie-London, #423, illus.), plate 15½ x 8 in., (39.4 x 20.3 cm.), sheet 23 x 18 in., (39.4 x 20.3 cm.), drypoint on laid paper (BP 16,100, DM 40,471, FR 136,326, Y 2,769,876).

$9350* *Toilette (G. 223; H. 258 IIIb), 1923,* s., pub. J.B. Neumann, large (full) margins, good cond., (11-05-92, Sotheby-NY, #81, illus.), 8M, x 6 in., (224 x 151 mm.), woodcut on cream, fibrous wove (BP 6081, DM 14,787, FR 50,027, Y 1,147,099).

$4479* *Umarmung (Glaser 210; Gallwitz 206; Hofmaier 236Bd), 1922,* s., #5/50, pub. R. Piper, mount-staining, margins, good cond., (05-20-93, Christie-London, #424, illus.), plate 16¼ x 9½ in., (41.3 x 24.1 cm.), sheet 21¼ x 15 in., (41.3 x 24.1 cm.), drypoint on wove (BP 2875, DM 7227, FR 24,342, Y 494,589).

$5147* *Umarmung (H. 236), 1922,* s., #2/50, pub. R.Piper & Co., margins, good cond., (06-30-93, Sotheby-London, #352, illus.), 16M, x 10Z, in., (429 x 257 mm.), drypoint on wove (BP 3450, DM 8779, FR 29,614, Y 551,484).

$3672* *Umarmung (Hofmaier 236 IV-Gallwitz 206), 1922,* s., X/XX, (06-10-93, Hauswedell/Nolt, #77, illus.), image 16Zn x 10½ in., (43 x 26.6 cm.), drypoint on Japan (BP 2402, DM 5979, FR 20,132, Y 389,768).

BI *Umarmung (Hofmaier Band II 236 IV B B), 1922,* #XVI/XX, s., est. DM 7,500-, (11-21-92, Lempertz, #39, illus.), 16¾ x 10Z, in., (42.5 x 25.7 cm.), etching on Japan.

BI *Vierte Klasse II (Hofmaier 58, II C), 1913,* s., tears, creases, est. DM 4,200, (10-09-92, Winterberg, #1731, illus.), 7Zn x 5B, in., (19.6 x 14.3 cm.), drypoint on wove.

$8114* *Vor Dem Auftritt (Gallwitz 250, Hofmaier 289), 1923,* s., num., (12-05-92, Bassenge, #7040, illus.), 22Mn x 14Cn in., (57 x 36 cm.), lithograph on handmade (BP 5081, DM 12,650, FR 43,114, Y 1,005,328).

BI *Weiblicher Kopf Nach Hinten Gedreht (Bildnis Fridel Battenberg) (Hofmaier 203 B a.), 1921,* s., est. DM 6,500, (05-26-93, Lempertz, #32, illus.), 18Ⓩzn x 15Ⓩn in., (47.8 x 38.3 cm.), lithograph on imitated Japan.

$3775* *Der Zeichner Gesellschaft (H. 230), 1922,* s., pub. Verlag R.Piper & Co., full margins, good cond., spots of glue, (06-30-93, Sotheby-London, #349, illus.), 13 x 9½ in., (330 x 241 mm.), drypoint on Japan (BP 2530, DM 6439, FR 21,720, Y 404,479).

$5175* *Der Zeichner In Gesellschaft (G. 200; H. 230/III), 1922,* final state, s., full margins, good cond., bleaching, crease, skinning, (05-13-93, Sotheby-NY, #458, illus.), 12M, x 9¼ in., (326 x 235 mm.), drypoint on Japan; on pale pink Japan (BP 3397, DM 8356, FR 28,186, Y 577,760).

BI *Der Zeichner In Gesellschaft (Hofmaier 230 III-Gallwitz 200), 1922,* s., est. DM 6000, (06-10-93, Hauswedell/Nolt, #74, illus.), image 12Ⓩzn x 9Mzn in., (33 x 24 cm.), drypoint on wove.

BECOM, Jeffrey

$770* *"Wall With Birdcage, Burano, Italy" and "Monastery Courtyard, Patmos, Greece": Two,* 1980/1982, each s., t., d., edit. 12/25, 9/25; photog. stamp verso, on overmat, Dixon Collection, (11-16-92, Butterfield, #5843), one 19Ⓩzn x 13½ in., (499.4 x 343.5 mm.), other 13½ x 19Mzn in., (499.4 x 343.5 mm.), photograph, cibachrome print (BP 507, DM 1228, FR 4135, Y 95,759).

BEDFORD, Francis 1816-1894

$495* *Mur Cyclopeens A Baalbeck,* photog.(?) descriptive t., 1860s, (04-07-93, Swann, #235, illus.), 10¾ x 15½ in., photograph, slbumen print (BP 327, DM 801, FR 2709, Y 56,237).

$163* *"Photographic Views Of South Devon", 1864-68: Book,* p. nums., t., photog.'s credit, (05-06-93, Christie-London, #11), approx. 5¼ x 9¾ in., photograph, 20 albumen prints (BP 103, DM 257, FR 864, Y 17,934).

BEECHEY, Sir William (after)

$132* *George The Third,* by James Ward, pub. J. P. Thompson, 1811, margins, surface dirt, other defects, (06-16-93, Bonhams-Chelsea, #460A), pl 25½ x 21¾ in., (64.8 x 55.2 cm.), mezzotint (BP 88, DM 219, FR 735, Y 14,078).

BI *John, Earl Of St. Vincent, 1816,* by Charles Turner, pub. C. Turner, creased, foxing, good cond., est.BP 120/150, (11-30-92, Phillips-London, #40), plate 24 x 16¼ in., (610 x 413 mm.), mezzotint on laid.

$133* *John, Earl Of St. Vincent, 1816,* by Charles Turner, watermark, pub. Charles Turner, bottom margin folded, image mould, good cond., (11-30-92, Phillips-London, #41), plate 24¼ x 16½ in., (616 x 419 mm.), mezzotint on laid (BP 88, DM 212, FR 719, Y 16,553).

BEECHEY, William (after)

$133* *Here Poor Boy Without A Hat, Take This Ha'Penny, 1796,* proof, by Charles Wilkin, pub. William Beechey, margins, foxing, defect, (11-30-92, Phillips-London, #208), plate 20B, x 17 in., (524 x 432 mm.), stipple engraving on laid (BP 88, DM 212, FR 719, Y 16,553).

BEERMAN, John

$1320* *The Stone's Silent Witness, 1986,* s., d., annot. W.P., blindstamp, full margins, very good cond.?, (10-28-92, Butterfield, #2906, illus.), 36 x 41 in., (91.4 x 104.1 cm.), aquatint w/etching on cream wove (BP 841, DM 2039, FR 6922, Y 161,963).

$690* *Sunset, 1990,* s., d., #8/18, blindstamp, pub. Hudson River Editions, full margins,good cond., handling creases, (05-15-93, Sotheby-NY, #923, illus.), sheet 11Ⓠ x 26¾ in., (28.9 x 67.9 cm.), aquatint in colors w/gold-leaf collage (BP 449, DM 1110, FR 3730, Y 76,488).

BEGA, Cornelis Dutch 1620-1664

$850* *Der Bauer Im Fenster (B. 19, Dutuit, Hollstein 19 II),* prov., (06-04-93, Bassenge, #5024), 3Ⓩzn x 3½ in., (9.3 x 8.9 cm.), etching (BP 562, DM 1380, FR 4652, Y 91,674).

BI *Buste Einer Jungen Frau (Bartsch 2; Weigel, Dutuit and Hollstein 2 I),* prov., est. DM 1,600, (06-10-93, Hauswedell/Nolt, #14), etching.

BI *Die Drei Trinker (Holstein Bd 1, 29),* trimmed, 1st state, est. DM 240-, (03-24-93, Venator/Hansten, #2482), pl approx. 4C, x 4Ⓩzn in., (11.1 x 11 cm.), etching.

BEGG, S. (after) British 20th cent.

$20* *The Lancashire Landing,* (05-16-93, Hanzel, #472), 11½ x 19½ in., (29.2 x 49.5 cm.), lithograph (BP 13, DM 32, FR 108, Y 2217).

BEHAM, Barthel German 1502-1540

$433* *Adam Und Eva (B. 1; Hollstein 1 II),* stained, (12-04-92, Bassenge, #6026), 3Z, x 2Ⓩzn in., (8 x 5.2 cm.), engraving (BP 278, DM 690, FR 2339, Y 54,057).

$3665* *Kampf Von Achtezehn Nackten Mannern (Hollstein und Pauli 25), c. 1530,* prov., (06-23-93, Kornfeld, #7), engraving (BP 2490, DM 6201, FR 20,859, Y 399,281, SF 5520).

$6109* *Portrait Kaiser Karl V (Hollst. und P. 90/IV), 1531,* watermark, prov., (06-23-93, Kornfeld, #8, illus.), engraving (BP 4150, DM 10,337, FR 34,769, Y 665,541, SF 9200).

BEHAM, Hans Sebald German 1500-1550

BI *12 Apostel (Pauli 45-56), 1545-46: Twelve,* mono. HSB, i., num. 1-12, d., est. DM 2,400-, (03-24-93, Venator/Hansten, #2483), each approx. 1¾ x 1Czn in., (4.5 x 3 cm.), engraving.

$722* *Christus Und Die Samariterin (B. 24; Pauli 26 I; Hollstein 26 I),* prov., (12-04-92, Bassenge, #6031), 1½ x 3Zzn in., (3.8 x 7.7 cm.), engraving (BP 463, DM 1150, FR 3901, Y 90,137).

$173* *Cimon And Pero (B. 75, Pauli, Holl. 79 iii/iii), 1544,* trimmed on or just inside platemark, foxing, good cond., (05-11-93, Christie-NY, #2), sheet 2¾ x 1M, in., (70 x 48 mm.), engraving on laid (BP 110, DM 273, FR 918, Y 19,030).

$583* *Cleopatra Seated (B. 77; P., Holl. 81), c. 1545,* Angiolini's 1st state of 2, thread margins or trimmed, residue, verygood cond., prov., (12-01-92, Christie-London, #160), plate 4Mzn x 2Ⓩzn in., (112 x 72 mm.), engraving (BP 385, DM 929, FR 3167, Y 72,585).

$2138* *Der Fahnrich (Hollstein und Pauli 203/II), 1526,* early print, (06-23-93, Kornfeld, #9, illus.), engraving (BP 1452, DM 3618, FR 12,168, Y 232,923, SF 3220).

BI *The Four Evangelists (B. 55-58; P., Holl. 57-60), c. 1541: Set Of Four,* early states, thread margins, trimmed, soiling, discoloration, generally good cond., ex-coll. A. Vivenel and Dr. Albert W. Blum, est. $1,2/1,600, (05-13-93, Sotheby-NY, #105), each approx. 1¾ x 1Z, in., (43 x 30 mm.), engraving.

$868* *The Guard Near The Powder Casks (P. 200; B. 197),* 1st state of 2, trimmed, thread margins, good cond., (06-29-93, Sotheby-London, #7, illus.), 1¾ x 1Z, in., (4.4 x 2.9 cm.), engraving (BP 575, DM 1466, FR 4940, Y 92,399).

$1372* *Hercules Und Cerberus (B. 100, Pauli 104 I), 1545,* prov., (12-04-92, Bassenge, #6037), 2¼ x 3Ⓩzn in., (5.7 x 7.7 cm.), engraving (BP 880, DM 2185, FR 7412, Y 171,286).

$770* *Hercules, 1548,* thread margins, laid down, good cond., surface soiling, surface abrasions, (02-24-93, Butterfield, #2685), 2Zzn x 3Ⓩzn in., (52 x 78 mm.), engraving on laid (BP 537, DM 1250, FR 4238, Y 90,354).

$361* *Herkules Erwurgt Den Nemaischen Lowen (B. 106; Pauli; Hollstein 99 II), 1548,* (12-04-92, Bassenge, #6039), 2 x 3Zzn in., (5.1 x 7.7 cm.), engraving (BP 232, DM 575, FR 1950, Y 45,069).

$1083* *Herkules Kampft Mit Den Trojanern (B. 101; Pauli; Hollstein 105 I), 1545,* prov., (12-04-92, Bassenge, #6038), 2 x 3Zzn in., (5.1 x 7.8 cm.), engraving (BP 695, DM 1725, FR 5851, Y 135,206).

$779* *Herkules Und Kerberus (B. 100, Pauli 104I, Hollstein 104I), 1545,* (06-04-93, Bassenge, #5025), 2Ⓩzn x 3Ⓩn in., (5.3 x 7.8 cm.), engraving (BP 515, DM 1265, FR 4264, Y 84,016).

$374* *Hiob Mit Seinen Freunden (B. 16; Pauli 17/I), 1547,* trimmed margins, stained, (12-01-92, Karl/Faber, #11), engraving (BP 247, DM 596, FR 2032, Y 46,564).

BI *The Impossibility (P. 146; B. 145), 1549,* 1st state of 5, trimmed, patch, stains, defects, est. BP 1,5/2,000, (06-29-93, Sotheby-London, #6, illus.), 3¼ x 2 in., (8.3 x 5.1 cm.), engraving.

$1516* *Joseph Und Potiphars Weib (B. 14, Pauli 15 I), 1544,* (12-04-92, Bassenge, #6030, illus.), 3Czn x 2Czn in., (8.1

x 5.5 cm.), engraving (BP 972, DM 2414, FR 8190, Y 189,263).

$939* *Judith Mit Dienerin Nach Links Schreitend (B. 11; Pauli 12),* (12-04-92, Bassenge, #6029), 4B, x 2Zzn in., (11.8 x 7.1 cm.), engraving (BP 602, DM 1495, FR 5073, Y 117,228).

$282* *Kreuztragung (B. 97 Hollstein und Pauli 823 II), 1521,* from Die Passion, mono., (05-26-93, Dorling, #2199, illus.), 5 x 3Mzn in., (12.7 x 8.8 cm.), woodcut (BP 182, DM 460, FR 1549, Y 30,639).

$9548* *The Labours Of Hercules (P. 98-109; B. 96-107), 1542-1548: Twelve,* partial thread margins, trimmed, discoloration, repaired, good cond., ex. colls., (06-29-93, Sotheby-London, #4, illus.), each approx. 2Z, x 3Z, in., (5.4 x 7.9 cm.), engraving (BP 6325, DM 16,123, FR 54,343, Y 1,016,393).

$361* *Ein Liebespaar An Einem Zaun Sitzend (B.161; Pauli; Hollstein 1229 II),* (12-04-92, Bassenge, #6042), 4Zzn x 3Mzn in., (12.6 x 8.7 cm.), woodcut (BP 232, DM 575, FR 1950, Y 45,069).

BI *Lucretia (Pauli 2; Bartsch 78), 1519,* 4th (final) state, trimmed irregularly, surface dirt, ex. coll. A.P.F. Robert-Dumesnil (L. 2200); and d'Arenberg (L. 567), est. BP 1,5/2,000, (06-29-93, Sotheby-London, #3, illus.), 2¾ x 1¾ in., (7 x 4.4 cm.), engraving.

$666* *Misfortune (B. 141; P., Holl. 144), c. 1540,* 1st state of 4, thread margins, discoloration, crease, (12-01-92, Christie-London, #163), plate 3Zzn x 2 in., (78 x 51 mm.), engraving (BP 440, DM 1062, FR 3618, Y 82,918).

$361* *Der Narr Und Die Beiden Badenden Weiber (B. 214; Hollstein 216 IV), 1541,* (12-04-92, Bassenge, #6040), 1¾ x 2¾ in., (4.5 x 7 cm.), engraving (BP 232, DM 575, FR 1950, Y 45,069).

BI *Ornament With Scroll And Dolphin's Heads (P. 240; B. 235),* 1st state of two, trimmed, repairs, defects, discolored, est. BP 5/600, (06-29-93, Sotheby-London, #9, illus.), 1½ x 3½ in., (3.8 x 8.9 cm.), engraving.

BI *Penance Of St. John Chrysostomus (B. 215; P., Holl. 70),* 4th state of 8, trimmed within platemark, repair, abrasions, est. $2/3,000, (05-13-93, Sotheby-NY, #106), 2Z\ x 3Z, in., (54 x 78 mm.), engraving.

$2777* *"Satyr Playing The Lyre" (P. 111; B. 109) and "Satyr Woman Playing Bagpipes" (P. 112; B. 110): Two,* small margins, trimmed, paper loss, good cond., (06-29-93, Sotheby-London, #5, illus.), each 1B, x 1¼ in., (4.1 x 3.2 cm.), engraving (BP 1840, DM 4689, FR 15,805, Y 295,614).

$2331* *The Seven Planets With The Signs Of The Sodiac (B. 113-20; P., Holl.115-22), 1539,* title and set of 7, thread margins or trimmed, repaired tears, good cond., prov., (12-01-92, Christie-London, #162), plate 1Zzn x 1Czn in., (43 x 30 mm.), engraving (BP 1540, DM 3715, FR 12,662, Y 290,214).

$1380* *Standard Bearer And Drummer (B. 199; P., Holl. 202), 1544,* first state of 2, trimmed, brown stains, good cond., ex-coll. Andre-Jean Hachette, (05-13-93, Sotheby-NY, #108), 2¾ x 1M, in., (70 x 49 mm.), engraving (BP 906, DM 2228, FR 7516, Y 154,069).

BI *The Standing Bearer And Drummer (P. 202; B. 199), 1525,* 2nd final state, narrow margins, scrape, good cond., Ex coll. J. O. Entres (L. 2941) and Emil Schroter (L. 2270), est. BP 1,5/1,800, (06-30-93, Sotheby-London, #78, illus.), 2¾ x 1M, in., (70 x 48 mm.), engraving.

$2166* *Die Taten Des Herkules (B. 96-101, 103-107; Pauli, Hollstein 98 I, 99I, 100 IV, 101 II, 102 IV, 103 I, 105 II, 106 V, 107 IV, 108 II, 109 II): Twelve,* (12-04-92, Bassenge, #6035), engraving (BP 1389, DM 3450, FR 11,702, Y 270,412).

$581* *"Triumpf Der Edelen Sighaften Weiber" (B. 143; P. 244/ II), 1549,* staines, (12-01-92, Karl/Faber, #13), engraving (BP 384, DM 926, FR 3156, Y 72,336).

$1736* *The Triumphal Procession Of Children (P. 242; B. 237),* thread margins, trimmed, foxmark, ex. coll. P. Mariette (L. 1788 d. 1699); G.M. La Monte (L. 1181c), (06-29-93, Sotheby-London, #8, illus.), 1 x 4Z, in., (2.5 x 10.5 cm.), engraving (BP 1150, DM 2931, FR 9880, Y 184,799).

BI *The Twelve Apostles (B. 43-54; P., Holl. 45-56), 1545: Set Of Twelve,* mainly early states, thread margins, trimmed between platemark and borderline, discolored, paper losses, generally good cond., soiling, 8 ex-coll. R. Fisher, est. $1,5/2,500, (05-13-93, Sotheby-NY, #104), each approx. 1¾ x 1Z, in., (45 x 30 mm.), engraving.

$1977* *Das Wappen Mit Dem Lowen (Bartsch 255; Pauli and Hollstein 266 II), 1544,* prov., (06-10-93, Hauswedell/ Nolt, #22, illus.), engraving in hexagon (BP 1293, DM 3219, FR 10,839, Y 209,850).

BEHMER, Marcus 1879-1958

$201* *"Johannes Auerbach, Der Selbstmorderwettbewerb, Berlin 1921",* frontispiece, artist's proof, i., s., d. P.D. 18/30, Marcus Behmer 1921, (09-14-92, Venator/Hansten, #2437), plate 3Zzn x 5⅜n in., (9.3 x 14.2 cm.), etching on hand-made (BP 106, DM 299, FR 1013, Y 24,994).

$132* *"Lebendes Fischfutter", 1910,* plate mono., d., M 10, s. Marcus Behmer, #24/30, (09-14-92, Venator/Hansten, #2435), plate 1¼ x 4B\ in., (3.2 x 11.7 cm.), etching on hand-made (BP 70, DM 196, FR 665, Y 16,414).

BEHRENS, Howard

$660* *Italian Coastal Scene,* s., num. 194/300, (05-22-93, Weschler, #164, illus.), 24¾ x 31½ in., (62.9 x 80 cm.), serigraph in colors (BP 428, DM 1073, FR 3611, Y 72,767).

$660* *Lake Como Coast,* s., num. 194/300, good cond., (05-22-93, Weschler, #165), 24¾ x 31½ in., (62.9 x 80 cm.), serigraph in colors (BP 428, DM 1073, FR 3611, Y 72,767).

BEHRENS, Peter German 1868-1940

$458* *Bildnis Richard Dehmel (MKG Hanburg V 83), c. 1905/ 06,* s., num., block mono., i., (05-26-93, Dorling, #2550, illus.), 13Mzn x 10Czn in., (34.1 x 25.8 cm.), woodcut on Kaiserlich Japan (BP 296, DM 747, FR 2515, Y 49,761).

$1773* *Der Kuss,* (06-05-93, Bassenge, #5913, illus.), 10Zzn x 8⅜n in., (27.4 x 21.8 cm.), color woodcut on Japan (BP 1167, DM 2875, FR 9689, Y 190,195).

$1100* *Der Kuss (The Kiss), 1898,* mono., lit., Barry Friedman, Ltd. Coll., (11-19-92, Sotheby-NY, #68, illus.), sight 7¾ x 6 in., (19.7 x 15.2 cm.), colored woodcut on paper (BP 724, DM 1754, FR 5908, Y 136,799).

$2434* *Der Kuss, 1898,* (12-05-92, Bassenge, #7042), 10Z\n x 8Mzn in., (27.2 x 21.5 cm.), color woodcut on Japan (BP 1524, DM 3795, FR 12,933, Y 301,574).

$1829* *Der Kuss, 1898,* from Pan IV, 2, (12-12-92, Bassenge, #8462, illus.), 10Zzn x 8Mzn in., (27.2 x 21.5 cm.), color woodcut on Japan (BP 1169, DM 2874, FR 9796, Y 226,277).

BEICH, Joachim Franz German 1665-1748

BI *"Landscape", c. 1720,* good impression, small margins, stains, tears, est. $1/150, (10-31-92, Cleveland, #8A), 9C, x 6 in., (23.8 x 15.2 cm.), etching.

BI *Landschaften In Poussins Geschmack (Andresen 7 II, 9, 10, 12, 13 I):Six,* est. DM 900, (12-04-92, Bassenge, #6514), each approx. 6B\n x 5Zzn in., (17.6 x 14.8 cm.), etching.

BEIHONG, Xu ac. mid-20th cent.

$352* *Adler,* s., seal, (04-27-93, Dorotheum, #414, illus.), 17C, x 13Zzn in., (44.1 x 33.2 cm.), (BP 224, DM 557, FR 1885, Y 39,449, SC 3920).

BEISAKU, Taguchi Japanese 19th cent.

BI *Sino-Japanese War (1894-1895),* s., t. in Japanese; bears t. verso, prov., est. C$6/800, (05-10-93, Hodgins, #285), 13½ x 28½ in., (34.3 x 72.4 cm.), 3 panel color woodcut on paper.

BEJOT, Eugene French 1867-1931

$1376* *"Du 1er Au XXe: Les Arrondissements De Paris" (J. Laran, 193 a 213),1903: Twenty-One,* ded., w/out margins, stamped, 193 fifth state of 7, others definitive state, (06-16-93, Ader Tajan, #49), etching (BP 917, DM 2284, FR 7666, Y 146,758).

$107* *Bayonne,* s., margins, (08-20-92, Bonhams-Chelsea, #117), plate 6¼ x 7¼ in., (15.9 x 18.4 cm.), drypoint etching on laid paper, watermark (BP 55, DM 155, FR 526, Y 13,512).

$50* *"La Berge Du Quai D'Anjou, Paris"*, 1925, s., good cond., (05-15-93, Cleveland, #360), 8𝔹, x 8𝔹, in., (21.9 x 21.9 cm.), etching (BP 33, DM 80, FR 270, Y 5543).

$108* *"A Country Lane"*, s., margins, (10-15-92, Bonhams-Chelsea, #147), plate 5¼ x 6 in., (13.3 x 15.2 cm.), drypoint etching (BP 66, DM 161, FR 545, Y 12,957).

$1131* *Du Ier Au XXeme, Les Arrondissements De Paris, 1905: Set Of Twenty*, text, t. and justification page, i., orig. portfolio w/etched cover, (10-27-92, Phillips-London, #184), plate 12¾ x 9𝔹, in., (324 x 244 mm.), etching on simili Japan (BP 715, DM 1733, FR 5881, Y 138,349).

$103* *Jardin Du Luxembourg*, s., margins, (05-20-93, Bonhams-Chelsea, #79), plate 8𝕄, x 5¾ in., (22.5 x 14.6 cm.), etching on laid (BP 66, DM 166, FR 560, Y 11,374).

$32* *Nantes, Le Pont De La Belle Croix*, s., margins, (02-17-93, Bonhams-Chelsea, #274), plate 6ℂ, x 9𝔹, in., (16.2 x 24.4 cm.), etching on laid paper, watermark (BP 22, DM 52, FR 176, Y 3822).

$182* *Paris, Le Pont De Sully*, s., margins, (08-20-92, Bonhams-Chelsea, #116), plate 11¾ x 10½ in., (29.8 x 26.7 cm.), drypoint etching on laid paper, watermark (BP 94, DM 264, FR 894, Y 22,983).

$76* *La Place De L'Institut*, s., margins, (01-21-93, Bonhams-Chelsea, #123), plate 6½ x 9½ in., (16.5 x 24.1 cm.), etching on laid paper (BP 50, DM 121, FR 409, Y 9512).

$76* *Le Pont Corneille, Rouen*, s., margins, (01-21-93, Bonhams-Chelsea, #124), plate 6ℂ, x 11𝕏, in., (16.2 x 28.3 cm.), etching on laid paper (BP 50, DM 121, FR 409, Y 9512).

$76* *Le Pont Neuf, 1919*, s., margins, (01-21-93, Bonhams-Chelsea, #122), plate 7𝕄, x 13ℂ, in., (20 x 34 cm.), etching on laid paper (BP 50, DM 121, FR 409, Y 9512).

$149* *Le Pont Neuf, Paris, 1905*, s., margins, (08-20-92, Bonhams-Chelsea, #115), plate 9¼ x 12 in., (23.5 x 30.5 cm.), drypoint etching on laid paper, watermark (BP 77, DM 216, FR 732, Y 18,816).

$108* *Quai De Bethune, Paris*, s., margins, (10-15-92, Bonhams-Chelsea, #148), plate 7𝕏, x 8¼ in., (18.1 x 21 cm.), drypoint etching (BP 66, DM 161, FR 545, Y 12,957).

$76* *St Germain*, s., margins, (01-21-93, Bonhams-Chelsea, #125), plate 7 x 7𝔹, in., (17.8 x 19.4 cm.), etching on laid paper (BP 50, DM 121, FR 409, Y 9512).

BELANGE, Jacques

$23,163* *Gaspar (Walch 27)*, 1st state of 2, margins, thread margins, trimmed, drying crease, repairs, defects, stains, (06-30-93, Sotheby-London, #81, illus.), 11¼ x 6𝔹, in., (286 x 168 mm.), etching (BP 15,525, DM 39,507, FR 133,274, Y 2,481,839).

BELFONDS (after)

BI *Mini Head And Shoulder Portraits: Eight*, est. BP 6/90, (04-22-93, Bonhams-Chelsea, #18), each 6𝕄, x 4 in., (17.5 x 10.2 cm.), bookplate etching.

BELL, Alistair   b. 1913

$89* *Steveston II*, #16/35, s., (10-21-92, Maynard, #204), 24 x 15 in., (61 x 38.1 cm.), color woodcut (BP 55, DM 135, FR 457, Y 10,840, C$ 110).

BI *"West Coast Tugs"*, 1 of 20, est. $3/400, (05-12-93, Maynard, #268), 8 x 13 in., (20.3 x 33 cm.), etching.

BELL, Dr. William

$316* *"Grand Canon Of The Colorado River, Mouth Of Kanab, Looking East"*, 1972, attrib., t., d., num., U.S. Army Corps of Engineers seal, (05-23-93, Butterfield, #3313, illus.), 10¾ x 7𝕄, in., photograph, albumen print (BP 206, DM 517, FR 1739, Y 34,929).

$550* *Soldier With Amputated Leg, 1865*, label, (10-14-92, Swann, #167, illus.), 9½ x 7½ in., (24.1 x 19.1 cm.), photograph, albumen print (BP 323, DM 805, FR 2730, Y 66,651).

BELL, William

BI *Selected Wheeler Survey Images, 1872: Three*, incl. Canon of Kanab Wash, Colorado River, Looking South; Utah Series. Hieroglyphic Pass, Opposite Parowan, Utah; and Colorado River Series. Headlands, Paria Canon; first two #3 and 8 in neg., photog.'s credit, t., nums. 3, 8, and 31, est. $2/3,000, (10-15-92, Sotheby-NY, #31,

illus.), largest 8 x 11 in., (20.3 x 27.9 cm.), photograph, albumen print.

BELLANGE, Jacques   1580-1638

$6138* *Die Anbetung Der Konige (Robert-Dumesnil XI, 2 I; Walch 20 II)*, (12-04-92, Bassenge, #6048, illus.), 23ℂn x 16¾ in., (58.9 x 42.5 cm.), etching (BP 3937, DM 9775, FR 33,160, Y 766,292).

$16,996* *Die Auferweckung Des Lazarus (Robert-Dumesnil V, 6, Walch 47)*, watermark, (06-04-93, Bassenge, #5033, illus.), 18𝕏, x 12𝔹n in., (46 x 31.2 cm.), etching (BP 11,244, DM 27,600, FR 93,027, Y 1,833,046).

$36,825* *Drei Heilige Frauen (Robert-Dumesnil V, 13; Walch 22)*, watermark, (06-04-93, Bassenge, #5034, illus.), 12𝔹, x 7𝕄, in., (32.1 x 20 cm.), etching (BP 24,363, DM 59,800, FR 201,560, Y 3,971,635).

$19,496* *Das Martyrium Der Hl. Lucia (Robert-Dumesnil V, 15; Walch 16)*, (12-04-92, Bassenge, #6047, illus.), 17𝕄zn x 13¾ in., (44.3 x 35 cm.), etching (BP 12,505, DM 31,050, FR 105,327, Y 2,433,958).

BI *The Raising Of Lazarus (W. 47)*, trimmed, repaired tear, damages, defects, laid down, est. BP 3/4,000, (06-30-93, Sotheby-London, #82), 17¼ x 12 in., (438 x 305 mm.), etching.

$2220* *Les Trois Saintes Femmes (R. Dumesnil, 13; N. Walch, 22)*, creases, tear, good margins, (02-03-93, Ader Tajan, #7, illus.), 12𝔹, x 7𝕄, in., (32 x 20 cm.), etching on paper w/"grappe de raisin" watermark (BP 1550, DM 3656, FR 12,395, Y 276,154).

$4093* *Virgin With The Child Standing On His Cradle (Walch 7)*, third state of four, address of Le Blond, narrow margins, trimmed within platemark, retouching, paper scrapes in image, stains, thin spots, ex-coll., (12-03-92, Sotheby-London, #10), 5½ x 8½ in., (140 x 216 mm.), etching on paper w/watermark (BP 2640, DM 6437, FR 21,970, Y 509,270).

BELLEFLEUR, Leon   b. 1910

$174* *Scene D'Hiver*, s., d., Leon Bellefleur decembre 1931, (11-17-92, Encans, #7), 3𝕏, x 3¾ in., (8 x 9.5 cm.), black lithograph (BP 115, DM 277, FR 934, Y 21,639, C$ 222).

BELLENGER, Jacques and Pierre   b. 1909

$319* *Quinquina Bourain Aux Grands Vins Blancs De Touraine, 1936*, cond. A, (03-16-93, Boisgirard, #50), 78¾ x 51ℂn in., (200 x 130 cm.), poster (BP 220, DM 530, FR 1802, Y 37,301).

BELLENGER, P.

$770* *Cycles Favor*, Chateaudun, A- cond., fraying edges, (08-06-92, Swann, #43, illus.), 46½ x 62 in., (118.1 x 157.5 cm.), (BP 402, DM 1138, FR 3842, Y 98,214).

BELLEROCHE, Albert   French 1864-1944

$880* *Femme A La Harpe*, c. 1910, (10-18-92, Hindman, #458), 20 x 13¼ in., (50.8 x 33.7 cm.), lithograph (BP 538, DM 1310, FR 4442, Y 105,579).

$990* *"Femme En Buste" (Belleroche 333)*, c. 1905, s., fine cond., (10-31-92, Cleveland, #245), 15½ x 11 in., (39.4 x 27.9 cm.), lithograph in black and sanguine (BP 634, DM 1523, FR 5167, Y 122,631).

$605* *Femme En Profile*, c. 1910, (10-18-92, Hindman, #457), 18𝔹, x 14ℂ, in., (47.3 x 36.5 cm.), lithograph (BP 370, DM 901, FR 3054, Y 72,585).

BELLING, Rudolf   1886-1972

BI *Konstruktion, (19)67*, s., d., num., est. DM 400, (12-01-92, Karl/Faber, #368), 15ℂn x 13¾ in., (38.5 x 35 cm.), lithograph on wove.

BELLMER, Hans   German/French 1902-1975

BI *Abstract With Woman*, good cond., est. $2/300, (06-11-93, Freemn/Fine Art, #16), 11½ x 15½ in., (29.2 x 39.4 cm.), etching.

$2260* *Les Anagrammes Du Corps, 1973: Ten*, s., #68/100, Editions George Visat, (06-10-93, Hauswedell/Nolt, #97), each sh 20𝕏zn x 15𝕄, in., (52.2 x 40.4 cm.), drypoint on Arches paper (BP 1478, DM 3680, FR 12,390, Y 239,890).

$275* *Auf Der Terrasse*, s., num., tears, (12-01-92, Karl/Faber, #372), 15𝕄zn x 11 in., (40.5 x 28 cm.), engraving on hand-made cardboard (BP 182, DM 438, FR 1494, Y 34,238).

BI *Les Bas Raes,* s., #12/175, est. $100/150, (06-11-93, Freemn/Fine Art, #15), 17½ x 17½ in., (44.5 x 44.5 cm.), color lithograph.

$231* *"Beatrice Ou Le Regard Mutile",* #58/100, s., (01-28-93, Pescheteau, #71), 16⅛zn x 15¾ in., (42 x 40 cm.), etching on grey wove (BP 153, DM 366, FR 1239, Y 28,681).

BI *Bellmer: 10 Photographs, 1983,* embossed stamp, facsimile sig., num. 35/50, #35/50 edit., portfolio box, lit., est. $5/7,000, (10-13-92, Christie-NY, #122, illus.), each 10¼ x 10¼ in., (26 x 26 cm.), photograph, gelatin silver prints.

$605* *La Cephalopode,* double impression, 1 image inverted, s., prov., (09-20-92, Hindman, #781), 9¾ x 8½ in., (24.8 x 21.6 cm.), etching in black and blue on rose paper (BP 354, DM 898, FR 3071, Y 74,774).

$240* *La Cephalopode,* s., #27/100, (06-10-93, Hauswedell/Nolt, #95), image 11B, x 9Bzn in., (29.5 x 23.7 cm.), etching on Arches paper (BP 157, DM 391, FR 1316, Y 25,475).

$880* *La Cephalopode Double, 1965,* s., num. 40/100, prov., (09-20-92, Hindman, #782), sheet 24 x 21¾ in., (40.6 x 43.2 cm.), etching (BP 515, DM 1306, FR 4467, Y 108,763).

$660* *Le Chapeau-Main,* pencil and ink s., d. 1947, (09-20-92, Hindman, #783), 8½ x 5Z, in., (21.6 x 13 cm.), lithograph in green and red (BP 386, DM 979, FR 3350, Y 81,572).

$677* *Deshabillage (Denoel 23), 1951,* s. artist proof, (06-28-93, Loudmer, #11), 13C, x 9¾ in., (340 x 248 mm.), sh 15Zzn x 11Bzn in., (340 x 248 mm.), color lithograph on wove (BP 453, DM 1150, FR 3875, Y 71,830).

BI *Eine Skelettfrau Vor Einer Kathedrale, 1940,* s., num., est. DM 600, (12-05-92, Bassenge, #7043), 7Zzn x 9Zzn in., (18 x 23 cm.), soft-ground etching.

$126* *Erotica,* s., 89/100, (09-30-92, Kunsthallen, #32), etching (BP 71, DM 179, FR 604, Y 15,121, DK 690).

$413* *"Fantasy Composition:, Women At The Edge Of A Desert,* s., excell. cond.?, (10-10-92, Litchfield, #20), plate 16 x 11¾ in., (40.6 x 29.8 cm.), color etching (BP 245, DM 613, FR 2060, Y 50,280).

BI *Femmes-Colonnes, 1974,* from Die Welt des Klassizismus, s., #50/80, est. DM 600, (09-18-92, Schloss Ahlden, #975), 25Zzn x 19¾ in., (65.5 x 50.2 cm.), etching in brown on Arches.

$539* *Figura Femminile,* # 53/100, s., (03-25-93, Finarte-Rome, #3), etching (BP 366, DM 885, FR 3011, Y 63,144, L 863).

$330* *From Madame Edwarda, 1965,* s., annot. 55 epreuve d'essai, (09-20-92, Hindman, #784), 7Z, x 3C, in., (18.1 x 8.6 cm.), etching (BP 193, DM 490, FR 1675, Y 40,786).

$303* *From Madame Edwarda, 1965,* s., annot. 55 epreuve d'essai, (09-20-92, Hindman, #785), 8Z, x 3M, in., (20.6 x 9.8 cm.), etching (BP 177, DM 450, FR 1538, Y 37,449).

$632* *Histoire De L'Oeil: Three,* s. Bellmer, two # 85/100, one # 65/100, (09-30-92, Kunsthallen, #33), etching (BP 357, DM 896, FR 3031, Y 75,843, DK 3450).

$1005* *Hiver,* Cephalopode Reversible, c. 1955, (06-28-93, Loudmer, #9), 12C, x 8Mzn in., (315 x 215 mm.), sh 14Zzn x 11¼ in., (315 x 215 mm.), color lithograph on Arches (BP 673, DM 1708, FR 5753, Y 106,631).

$17,250* *Les Jeux De La Poupee, 1949: Fifteen,* Les Editions Premieres, text by Paul Eluard, orig. glassine wrappers, #92/136, s. by Bellmer on colophon, (04-08-93, Christie-NY, #161, illus.), each approx. 5½ x 5½ in., (14 x 14 cm.), mounted gelatin silver print, w/one cut-out photograph on t. page, each hand-colored (BP 11,311, DM 27,711, FR 93,801, Y 1,957,558).

$4830* *Les Jeux De La Poupee: Four,* from Les Jeux de la Poupee, mounted on pages, includes t. page w/mounted, hand-colored cut-out photograph and plates I, VII and XIII, (04-08-93, Christie-NY, #162, illus.), each approx. 5½ x 5½ in., (14 x 14 cm.), photograph, hand-colored gelatin silver print (BP 3167, DM 7759, FR 26,264, Y 548,116).

$202* *Komposition,* s., artist proof, (09-25-92, Granier, #2755), 10Zzn x 7M, in., (27.5 x 20 cm.), sheet 26>zn x 20Zzn in., (27.5 x 20 cm.), etching on Japan (BP 118, DM 299, FR 1013, Y 24,381).

$185* *Komposition Mit Weiblichem Akt In Einem Innenhof,* s., num., (12-05-92, Bassenge, #7048), 7M, x 5¼ in., (20 x 13.3 cm.), etching on copper print paper (BP 116, DM 288, FR 983, Y 22,922).

$271* *Kopffusslerin, c. 1965,* #46/100, (09-14-92, Venator/Hansten, #2440), plate 11Zzn x 9Bzn in., (29.7 x 23.7 cm.), drypoint on 2 plates (BP 143, DM 403, FR 1365, Y 33,698).

$990* *Mannequin,* photog.'s facsimile sig. blindstamp on image, 1930's, p.l., (10-15-92, Sotheby-NY, #302, illus.), photograph, hand-colored silver print (BP 606, DM 1474, FR 4997, Y 118,776).

$3178* *Les Marionettes (Denoel 97-105), 1969: Eleven,* s., #15/150, (06-10-93, Hauswedell/Nolt, #96), each sh 16Bzn x 13⅛zn in., (41.5 x 34.5 cm.), color etching on hand-made (BP 2079, DM 5175, FR 17,423, Y 337,331).

$252* *"Nu Au Sofa",* #50/70, s., reddish stains, (01-28-93, Pescheteau, #72), 19Zzn x 12Zzn in., (50 x 32.5 cm.), etching en (and) bistre on Japan nacre (BP 166, DM 399, FR 1351, Y 31,289).

BI *Ohne Titel, 1953,* s., d., est. DM 800, (11-12-92, Lempertz, #24), 2Bzn x 1¾ in., (5.8 x 4.5 cm.), photograph, contact gelatin silver print.

$253* *Oracles Et Spectacles (Denoel 76), 1967,* S., (04-21-93, Germann, #279), 12B, x 9C⅛n in., (320 x 250 mm.), etching (BP 164, DM 404, FR 1368, Y 28,008, SF 368).

$398* *Oracles Et Spectacles (Mandiargues 76), 1967,* s., 1 of 120, full margins, (11-16-92, Briest, #10), 12B, x 10Zzn in., (32 x 25.5 cm.), xin., (32 x 25.5 cm.), drypoint in black (BP 262, DM 635, FR 2139, Y 49,669).

$248* *Orakel Und Spektakel (Mandiargues 76), 1967,* s., (09-14-92, Venator/Hansten, #2441), plate 6Czn x 5Zzn in., (15.7 x 15.2 cm.), drypoint and emery (BP 131, DM 369, FR 1249, Y 30,838).

$6872* *Petit Traite De Morale (Denoel 78-87), 1968: Ten,* num., s., (06-23-93, Kornfeld, #207), 15C, x 11B, in., (39 x 29.5 cm.), on Japan nacre (BP 4668, DM 11,628, FR 39,112, Y 748,665, SF 10,350).

$4675* *Petit Traite De Morale Portefeuille, 1968: Ten,* incomplete portfolio, each s., w/t. and just. pages, num. 79, pub. &p. by Georges Visat, full margins, good cond., orig. portfolio, (02-24-93, Butterfield, #2705), 11 x 8Mzn in., (279 x 214 mm.), ten drypoints in colors on Japon nacre, added suite on Japon, & on Arches (BP 3260, DM 7589, FR 25,729, Y 548,580).

$605* *Plaisir Solitaire,* s., #18/100, t. verso, good cond., skinned areas, old hinge removal,light-staining, surface soiling, creases, (10-28-92, Butterfield, #2781), 15B, x 13 in., (397 x 330 mm.), etching on Arches (BP 385, DM 934, FR 3173, Y 74,233).

BI *"Poesie", 1970,* illus., #49/100, est. FF800/1,000, (04-04-93, Pescheteau, #158), 9Zzn x 12Zzn in., (25 x 33 cm.), black lithograph on Arches.

$7700* *Poupee (Leaning Against Painted Wall), 1935-36,* lit., (10-13-92, Christie-NY, #123, illus.), 5M, x 3¾ in., (14.9 x 9.5 cm.), photograph, gelatin silver print (BP 4485, DM 11,280, FR 38,328, Y 933,673).

BI *Les Poupees,* s., num., est. DM 700, (12-01-92, Karl/Faber, #369), 9Zzn x 9¼ in., (23 x 23.5 cm.), engraving on Japon nacre.

$9860* *Die Puppe, 1934: Ten,* ded., s., d. 1953, (11-12-92, Lempertz, #23, illus.), 4Zzn x 4¼ in., (12.3 x 10.8 cm.), photograph, gelatin silver print (BP 6304, DM 15,496, FR 52,812, Y 1,219,844).

$425* *"Sans Titre": Three,* s., #20/100, #55/99, #14/100, (06-28-93, Loudmer, #13), largest 22Zzn x 17Zzn in., (560 x 455 mm.), smallest 9Zzn x 9Mzn in., (560 x 455 mm.), etchings, first in bistre on Arches wove, second in black on wove, third in black on BFK Rives (BP 285, DM 722, FR 2433, Y 45,093).

$307* *Sans Titre, c. 1970,* #23/100, s. Bellmer, (05-18-93, Encans, #170), 11Zzn x 15C, in., (30 x 39 cm.), black etching (BP 200, DM 498, FR 1682, Y 34,214, C$ 389).

$307* *Sans Titre, c. 1970,* #27/100, s. Bellmer, (05-18-93, Encans, #171), 15¾ x 11C⅛n in., (40 x 30 cm.), black etching (BP 200, DM 498, FR 1682, Y 34,214, C$ 389).

$201* *Seated Woman With Bowl, 1970,* s., annot. H.C., full margins, good cond.?, pressure marks in image, (05-19-

93, Butterfield, #2036), 12½ x 9℃, in., (318 x 238 mm.), drypoint on Arches (BP 130, DM 327, FR 1101, Y 22,252).

$773* *Set Of Five Etchings*, s., #16/70, (06-28-93, Loudmer, #12), between 8M, x 6℥n in., (225 x 170 mm.), and 12℥, x 9℥n in., (225 x 170 mm.), etchings on Arches wove (BP 518, DM 1314, FR 4425, Y 82,016).

BI *Seville*, s.n., *1940 (1944): Six*, from Lord Auch. Histoire De L'Oeil by Georges Bataille, est. SF 7/8,500, (11-15-92, Christie-Geneva, #307), 10℥n x 6M℥n in., (255 x 163 mm.), etching and copper engraving on BFK Rives.

$550* *Spider Web*, s., (09-20-92, Hindman, #780), 5M, x 3℃ in., (14.9 x 8.6 cm.), drypoint on Japan (BP 322, DM 816, FR 2792, Y 67,977).

BI *Surrealist Composition*, s. Bellmer, num. 14/50, very good cond., full margins, handling crease, est. $250/350, (09-11-92, Skinner, #102B, illus.), 11℥n x 15¾ in., (30 x 40 cm.), etching in violet on wove.

$330* *Surrealist Composition-Five Figures*, s. Bellmer, num. 30/100, very good cond., full margins, (09-11-92, Skinner, #101A, illus.), 11¾ x 15℅, in., (29.8 x 39.7 cm.), etching on Arches wove w/watermark (BP 171, DM 475, FR 1614, Y 40,887).

$2793* *Surrealistiska Och Erotiska Kompositioner*, s., (05-25-93, AB Stockholm, #6), etching in colors resp. lithograph (BP 1810, DM 4549, FR 15,313, Y 305,279, SK 4070).

BI *Tanzende Frauen, 1973*, s., #17/145, est. DM 1000, (06-10-93, Hauswedell/Nolt, #94), image 9℥℥n x 7M, in., (25 x 20 cm.), etching on Japon nacre.

$135* *Tete De Femme: Two*, s., #50/100 and 51/100, (06-28-93, Loudmer, #10), 14℃n x 7℥℥n in., (360 x 180 mm.), sh 22M℥n x 15¼ in., (360 x 180 mm.), etchings in bistre on Japan (BP 90, DM 229, FR 773, Y 14,324).

BI *Torse De La Poupee, 1935-37*, exhib., lit., est. $5/7,000, (10-13-92, Christie-NY, #124, illus.), 4℅, x 3½ in., (11.7 x 8.9 cm.), photograph, gelatin silver print.

$307* *Trois Personnages*, c. 1970, #32/100, s. Bellmer, (05-18-93, Encans, #169), 11℃ ℥n x 15¾ in., (30 x 40 cm.), black etching (BP 200, DM 498, FR 1682, Y 34,214, C$ 389).

$275* *Untitled*, s., #36/50, (05-16-93, Hindman, #499), 11¾ x 15℅, in., (29.8 x 39.7 cm.), sheet 15¼ x 22½ in., (29.8 x 39.7 cm.), etching printed on Japanese paper (BP 179, DM 442, FR 1486, Y 30,484).

$330* *(Untitled)*, s., margins, apparently good cond., (02-24-93, Butterfield, #2899), 9 x 9℃, in., (229 x 238 mm.), drypoint on wove (BP 230, DM 536, FR 1816, Y 38,723).

$385* *Untitled, 1975*, s., #44/100, pub. in Hommage aux Pris Nobel, (05-16-93, Hindman, #499A), 15½ x 11℅, in., (39.4 x 29.5 cm.), drypoint (BP 250, DM 619, FR 2081, Y 42,678).

$1175* *Untitled: Three*, #X/LXX, 63/120, 92/150 respectively, folio, all s., (05-20-93, Finarte-Milan, #21, illus.), 26℃, x 20½ in., (67 x 52 cm.), etching (BP 754, DM 1896, FR 6386, Y 129,748, L 1725).

$440* *Woman In Surreal Landscape*, s., #30/100, (05-16-93, Hindman, #500), 15½ x 11℅, in., (39.4 x 29.5 cm.), sheet 25¾ x 19¾ in., (39.4 x 29.5 cm.), etching and engraving (BP 286, DM 708, FR 2378, Y 48,775).

$783* *"Les Yeux Bleus" and "Menuiserie": Two*, #23/100, s., (05-20-93, Finarte-Milan, #19), 12℅, x 9M℥n in., (32 x 24 cm.), etching in colors on Japan (BP 503, DM 1263, FR 4255, Y 86,462, L 1150).

$268* *Zwei Frauen*, #86/100, s. Bellmer, (03-24-93, Venator/Hansten, #4469), 12½ x 9¾ in., (31.7 x 24.8 cm.), etching on hand-made (BP 181, DM 438, FR 1490, Y 31,489).

BELLOC, Auguste d. c. 1867
$80,478* *Female Nudes: Forty-Eight*, mid 1850s, p. 1860s, 23 num. in negs., mounted, lit., (05-06-93, Christie-London, #37, illus.), each approx. 8¼ x 6½ in., photograph, albumen print (BP 51,000, DM 126,757, FR 426,713, Y 8,854,439).

BELLOTTO, Bernardo Italian 1720/24-1780
$3330* *Perspective De La Facade De La Roiale Eglise Catolique (De v. 11), 1748*, 5th (final) state, narrow margins or tirmmed, nicks, made-up losses, foxing, staining, laid, (12-01-92, Christie-London, #207), plate 21℃, x

33℃n in., (543 x 843 mm.), etching (BP 2200, DM 5308, FR 18,088, Y 414,592).

$1373* *La Ville Et Le Palais Japonais A Dresde (De V. 9), 1749*, margins, trimmed to sig., remargined, pen and ink border added, otherinfilling, partially laid down, stains, surface dirt, (06-30-93, Sotheby-London, #83), 19 x 27 in., (483 x 686 mm.), etching (BP 920, DM 2342, FR 7900, Y 147,112).

BI *Vue De La Grande Place Du Vieux Marche (De Vesme 17 III), 1752*, est. DM 9,000, (12-04-92, Bassenge, #6515, illus.), etching.

$4995* *Vue Des Ruines Des Fauxbourgs De La Ville De Dresde (De V. 33)*, c. 1761-3, watermark, margins, staining, discoloration, tape, defects, (12-01-92, Christie-London, #206, illus.), plate 20M, x 25 in., (531 x 635 mm.), etching (BP 3300, DM 7961, FR 27,132, Y 621,887).

BELLOWS, A.F. and J. DUTHIE
$138* *"The Village Elms, Sunday Morning In New England"*, (06-06-93, Dunning, #1074), sight 23½ x 19½ in., (59.7 x 49.5 cm.), color engraving (BP 91, DM 224, FR 754, Y 14,804).

BELLOWS, George American 1882-1925
$4370* *Allan Donn Puts To Sea (Mason 152), 1923*, s., t., i. Bolton Brown imp., watermark, margins, light/mat staining, very good cond., (05-11-93, Christie-NY, #90, illus.), borderline 15℅, x 19℥, in., (397 x 486 mm.), lithograph on wove (BP 2790, DM 6884, FR 23,195, Y 480,695).

BI *The Appeal To The People (Mason 167), 1924*, s. by Bellows and printer Bolton Brown, est. $2,5/3,000, (05-27-93, Swann, #31, illus.), 17¾ x 18℥, in., (45.1 x 46 cm.), lithograph.

BI *"The Appeal To The People" (M. 167)*, s., by p., excell. cond., est. $3/4,000, (10-31-92, Cleveland, #71, illus.), 17¾ x 18℥, in., (45.1 x 46 cm.), lithograph.

$2875* *Artist Judging Works Of Art (Mason 18; Bellows 147), 1916*, s., num. No 24, full margins, good cond., rubbing, crease, creases, soiling, (02-11-93, Sotheby-NY, #2, illus.), 14¾ x 19℃n in., (375 x 487 mm.), lithograph on fibrous Japan (BP 2029, DM 4762, FR 16,115, Y 346,594).

$2640* *Artists Judging Works Of Art (Mason 18; Myers and Ayers 126), 1916*, s., i. Jury Duty and No 12, wide margins, offsetting, soiling, excell. cond., (11-09-92, Christie-NY, #7, illus.), border 14½ x 19 in., (368 x 483 mm.), lithograph on heavy wove (BP 1745, DM 4215, FR 14,239, Y 327,625).

BI *Auntie Mason And Her Husband (M. 180), 1923-24*, s., t., annot., good cond., glue remains, light-staining, tear in image, surface soiling, creases, est. $8/1,200, (05-19-93, Butterfield, #1786, illus.), 10 x 9℥n in., (254 x 230 mm.), lithograph on Basingwerk Parchment.

$495* *"Auntie Mason And Her Husband"*, s. Geo Bellows, and in stone, t., s. by printer Bolton Brown imp., num. 31 proofs no. 50, very good cond., imperceptible marks, annot., (03-12-93, Skinner, #18, illus.), 10 x 9 in., (25.4 x 22.9 cm.), lithograph on off-white wove (BP 345, DM 824, FR 2801, Y 58,338).

$2185* *Benediction In Georgia (M. 12), 1916*, s. Geo Bellows, JBB by artist's daughter, #75, margins, very good cond., tear, (05-19-93, Butterfield, #1790, illus.), 16℃n x 19M in., (411 x 505 mm.), lithograph on China (BP 1418, DM 3552, FR 11,966, Y 241,891).

$6613* *Between Rounds, Small, Second Stone (M. 144; B. 42), 1923*, s., t., num. No 11, large margins, good cond., tape stain, traces glue, (05-13-93, Sotheby-NY, #409, illus.), 20 x 16¾ in., (507 x 427 mm.), sh 26¾ x 21M, in., (507 x 427 mm.), lithograph on wove (BP 4342, DM 10,678, FR 36,019, Y 738,305).

BI *Dempsey And Firpo (M. 181; B. 89), 1923-24*, s., t., i. by printer, large margins, good cond., printing defect, glue stains, skinning, creases, est. $20/30,000, (05-13-93, Sotheby-NY, #410, illus.), 18¼ x 22½ in., (465 x 571 mm.), sh 22M, x 25M, in., (465 x 571 mm.), lithograph on wove.

BI *The Drunk (M. 169), 1924*, s. Geo Bellows J.B.B. by artist's daughter, very good cond., crease, est. $1/1,500, (05-19-93, Butterfield, #1789), 15℅, x 12M, in., (397 x 327 mm.), lithograph on Basingwerk Parchment.

$1100* *The Drunk No. 1 (see M. 169; M. and A. 183), 1923-4,* watermark, M. and A.'s 1st state of 2, s., init. by wife, i. Bolton Brown imp, full margins, excell. cond., (11-09-92, Christie-NY, #14, illus.), border 15B, x 13Z, in., (397 x 333 mm.), lithograph on wove paper (BP 727, DM 1756, FR 5933, Y 136,510).

BI *"The Enemy Arrive" (Mason 59), 1918,* s. by the artist's daughter, #41/70, very good cond., est. $4/600, (10-31-92, Cleveland, #64), 15¾ x 25M, in., (40 x 65.7 cm.), lithograph on chine colle (pasted).

$6050* *Evening Snow (M. 91), 1921,* s., i., margins, very good cond., sealed (?) in frame, (11-09-92, Christie-NY, #11, illus.), border 7Czn x 9¾ in., (183 x 248 mm.), lithograph on Chine (BP 4000, DM 9658, FR 32,632, Y 750,807).

$440* *Family Christmas,* s. Geo. bellows, very good/good cond., (11-21-92, Bakker, #32, illus.), image 5C, x 4C in., (13.7 x 10.2 cm.), lithograph (BP 290, DM 702, FR 2363, Y 54,720).

$715* *Garden Of Growth (Mason 161), 1923,* annot. 1st pull, s. by Bellows and printer, Bolton Brown, margins, foxing, (05-27-93, Swann, #32, illus.), 18 x 14½ in., (45.7 x 36.8 cm.), lithograph on cream wove (BP 458, DM 1147, FR 3867, Y 76,651).

BI *"Garden Of Growth" (M. 161), 1923,* s., t., s. by p., excell. cond., est. $5/700, (10-31-92, Cleveland, #69), 18 x 14B, in., (45.7 x 37.1 cm.), lithograph.

BI *"Hail To Peace, Christmas" (M. 68), 1918,* s. by artist's daughter, excell. cond., est. $150/250, (10-31-92, Cleveland, #66), 4½ x 3¼ in., (11.4 x 8.3 cm.), lithograph.

$880* *Hungry Dogs No. 2 (Mason 1; Myers and Ayres 131), 1916,* 2nd final state, s., t., num. 15, slightly trimmed margins, very good cond., (09-19-92, Christie-E, #10), borderline 13¼ x 9¾ in., (337 x 248 mm.), lithograph on wove (BP 506, DM 1318, FR 4513, Y 109,644).

$2200* *In The Park, Dark (M. 30; M. and A. p. 162), 1916,* s., t., i. 'No 17', wide margins, crease, excellent cond., (11-09-92, Christie-NY, #8, illus.), border 17 x 21Z, in., (432 x 536 mm.), lithograph on heavy cream wove (BP 1455, DM 3512, FR 11,866, Y 273,021).

$2640* *In The Park, Light (M. 31; M. and A. 132), 1916,* s., t., i. 'No 51', wide margins, rubbing, very good cond., (11-09-92, Christie-NY, #9, illus.), border 15M, x 21¼ in., (403 x 540 mm.), lithograph on heavy cream wove (BP 1745, DM 4215, FR 14,239, Y 327,625).

$770* *In The Studio (B. 159), 1916,* s., num. 18, hinged to mat, very good cond., (12-04-92, Doyle, #72), 5½ x 4¼ in., (140 x 108 mm.), lithograph (BP 494, DM 1226, FR 4160, Y 96,130).

$7475* *Introducing Georges Carpentier (M. 98; B. 116), 1921,* s., t., i. Bolton Brown imp., margins, good cond., rubbing, traces glue, (05-13-93, Sotheby-NY, #408, illus.), 14B, x 21 in., (371 x 532 mm.), sh 16Z, x 23¼ in., (371 x 532 mm.), lithograph on wove (BP 4907, DM 12,070, FR 40,714, Y 834,543).

$4620* *Introducing John L. Sullivan (Mason 27), 1916,* trimmed margins, printer's proof, soiling, creases, (05-27-93, Swann, #33), 20½ x 20½ in., (52.1 x 52.1 cm.), lithograph (BP 2959, DM 7413, FR 24,986, Y 495,283).

$2420* *Jean, 1921, First Stone; and Jean, 1921, Second Stone (M. 120; and 121): Two,* s., first t., both i. Bolton Brown, imp, margins, pale light-staining, first laid down on Japan, second laid down on board, (11-09-92, Christie-NY, #13, illus.), lithograph on Japan (BP 1600, DM 3863, FR 13,053, Y 300,323).

$51,750* *A Knockout, Second State (M. 92; B. 78), 1921,* s., t., i., margins, good cond., fox marks, glue, (05-13-93, Sotheby-NY, #406, illus.), 15C, x 21¾ in., (392 x 551 mm.), sh 17¼ x 23C, in., (392 x 551 mm.), lithograph on wove (BP 33,975, DM 83,562, FR 281,863, Y 5,777,604).

BI *"Lychnis And Her Sons" (M. 163), 1923,* s., t., s. by p., excell. cond., est. $6/800, (10-31-92, Cleveland, #70, illus.), 16½ x 13½ in., (41.9 x 34.3 cm.), lithograph.

$605* *"Morning, No. 1, Nude" (M. 76), 1921,* s. Geo. Bellows by Jean Bellows Booth, s. by p., annot., excell. cond., (10-31-92, Cleveland, #67), 11 x 7½ in., (27.9 x 19.1 cm.), lithograph (BP 388, DM 931, FR 3158, Y 74,941).

BI *"New Society Dinner Card" (M. 149), 1923,* s. by artist's daughter, excell. cond., est. $175/225, (10-31-92, Cleveland, #68), 7C\ x 5¾ in., (18.7 x 14.6 cm.), lithograph.

$770* *Nude Woman Seated With Folding Hands (Life Study-Nude Woman Seated) (M. 38), 1917,* s., t., annot. No 3, margins, good cond., light-staining, foxing, stain, hinge remains, hole, surface soiling, notations, (02-24-93, Butterfield, #2613), 12½ x 11½ in., (318 x 292 mm.), lithograph on thin Japan paper (BP 537, DM 1250, FR 4238, Y 90,354).

BI *Old Irish Woman (M. 156), 1924,* s., t., annot., full margins, good cond., loss, light-staining in image, repair, est. $5/700, (05-19-93, Butterfield, #1788), 10 x 8 in., (254 x 203 mm.), lithograph on Basingwerk Parchment.

$550* *Old Rascal (B. 167),* s., #25, very good cond., (06-11-93, Doyle, #15), 10¼ x 8¾ in., (260 x 222 mm.), lithograph (BP 361, DM 894, FR 3014, Y 58,355).

BI *Portrait Of Elsie Speicher (B. 16), 1921,* s. and by Bolton Brown, hinged, good cond., est. $2/2,500, (12-04-92, Doyle, #71), 10¾ x 7½ in., (273 x 191 mm.), lithograph.

BI *"Portrait Of Eugene Speicher, First Stone" (M. 192), 1923-4,* s., t., s. by p., excell. cond., est. $4/500, (10-31-92, Cleveland, #72), 9 x 8¼ in., (22.9 x 21 cm.), lithograph.

$1430* *Prayer Meeting, Second Stone (M. 1; M. and A. 40), 1916,* num. 18, margins, pressure mark, touched-in patches, other minor defects, (09-19-92, Christie-E, #11), borderline 18C\ x 22¼ in., (467 x 565 mm.), lithograph on thin wove laid down on wove (BP 823, DM 2141, FR 7333, Y 178,171).

$7150* *Preliminaries (Mason 24; M. and A. 36), 1916,* s., t., i. No'6, margins, touched-in spots, light-staining, paper loss, holes, taped down, (09-19-92, Christie-E, #12, illus.), borderline 15M\ x 19¾ in., (403 x 502 mm.), lithograph on Japan (BP 4113, DM 10,707, FR 36,667, Y 890,855).

BI *"The Return Of The Useless" (M. 67), 1918,* s. by artist's daughter, excell. cond., est. $4/600, (10-31-92, Cleveland, #65), 19M\ x 21½ in., (50.5 x 54.6 cm.), lithograph.

$2200* *The Sawdust Trail (M. 48; M. and A. 161), 1917,* Myers and Ayers' 1st state of 2, init. by wife, i. No 15, ripped, scrape, foxmarks, soiling, very good cond., (11-09-92, Christie-NY, #10, illus.), border 26B, x 19¾ in., (677 x 502 mm.), lithograph on Chine applique (BP 1455, DM 3512, FR 11,866, Y 273,021).

BI *Solitude (M 37),* i., num. 'no. 15', est. $3/4,000, (09-17-92, Sloan, #3107, illus.), 17¼ x 15½ in., (43.8 x 39.4 cm.), lithograph.

BI *Solitude (Mason 37; Bellows 61), 1917,* i., init. by daughter, num. 'No. 38', good cond., touched-in printing-defects, soiling, est. $1,5/1,800, (11-05-92, Sotheby-NY, #3), 17¼ x 15C, in., (437 x 392 mm.), lithograph backed w/Japan.

BI *"Solitude" (M. 37), 1917,* s., i. by The Geo. Bellows J.B.B., #15, very good cond., est. $3/4,000, (05-15-93, Cleveland, #67, illus.), 17 x 15C\ in., (43.2 x 39.1 cm.), lithograph.

$11,000* *"Splinter Beach" (Mason 28), 1916,* s., t., #, very good cond., pin hole in image, (05-15-93, Cleveland, #66, illus.), 14M, x 19B, in., (37.8 x 49.8 cm.), lithograph (BP 7152, DM 17,693, FR 59,459, Y 1,219,377).

$63,000* *A Stag At Sharkey's (Mason 46; Bellows 71), 1917,* s., t., num. No. 15, margins, good cond., crease into subject, repaired tear, glue stains, rubbing, printer's creases, soiling, Frances H. Horne Estate, (05-13-93, Sotheby-NY, #405, illus.), 18B, x 23M\ in., (473 x 606 mm.), sh 21¼ x 26¾ in., (473 x 606 mm.), lithograph on wove (BP 41,360, DM 101,728, FR 343,137, Y 7,033,605).

$690* *Study Of Mary 1923 (M. 132),* s., t., annot., good/very good cond., light staining, foxing in image, (05-19-93, Butterfield, #1787), sh. 17M, x 16Zn in., (454 x 408 mm.), lithograph on Basingwerk Parchment (BP 448, DM 1122, FR 3779, Y 76,387).

BI *The White Hope (M. 96; B. 44), 1921,* i. by printer, margins, good cond., crease through image, tears, creases, soiling, traces glue, est. $8/10,000, (05-13-93, Sotheby-NY, #407, illus.), 15 x 19 in., (381 x 482 mm.), sh 16M, x 20M, in., (381 x 482 mm.), lithograph on chine volant.

BEMMEL, Peter von German 1685-1754
BI *Bergige Und Waldige Landschaften (Andresen 1-6), 1716: Six,* lit., est. DM 1,500, (12-04-92, Bassenge, #6516, illus.), each approx. 5½ x 7Bzn in., (13.9 x 18.5 cm.), etching.
$708* *Bergige Und Waldige Landschaften (Andresen, Le Blanc Und Meyers Kunstlerlex. 1-6), 1716: Six,* (06-04-93, Bassenge, #5423, illus.), etching (BP 468, DM 1150, FR 3875, Y 76,359).

BEMMEL, Willem van Dutch 1630-1708
$217* *Wald- U. Flusslandschaft Mit Mann Und Kind (Hollstein Bd. I, 7),* s. W. Bemel fecit, (09-14-92, Venator/Hansten, #1461), plate 4Bzn x 7 in., (11 x 17.8 cm.), etching (BP 115, DM 323, FR 1093, Y 26,983).

BEN-YUSUF, Zaida
$550* *Portrait Of Esther Chamberlain,* photog.'s sig., notations, 1890's, (10-14-92, Swann, #98, illus.), 7M\ x 3½ in., (20 x 8.9 cm.), photograph, platinum print (BP 323, DM 805, FR 2730, Y 66,651).

BENAZECH, Charles ac. 1767-1794
BI *Le Prix De L'Agriculture (Le Blanc 1),* est. DM 1,500, (12-04-92, Bassenge, #6517), 9Czn x 13M, in., (23.3 x 35.3 cm.), color aquatint.

BENDA, G.K.
$1007* *Gaby Yoo Et Albert Bertson, c. 1925,* p. L. Galice, good cond., (11-19-92, Ribeyre/Baron, #160, illus.), 61¼ x 45½ in., (155.5 x 115.5 cm.), poster (BP 663, DM 1606, FR 5408, Y 125,233).
$621* *Mistinguett,* (01-31-93, Morelle/Marchan, #223), 45¼ x 62Bzn in., (115 x 160 cm.), poster (BP 418, DM 1000, FR 3382, Y 77,470).

BENDINER, Alfred American b. 1899
$176* *...And So...,* s., t., good cond., (06-11-93, Freemn/Fine Art, #17), 9½ x 13½ in., (24.1 x 34.3 cm.), lithograph (BP 116, DM 286, FR 964, Y 18,674).

BENECKE, Theodore
$935* *National Guard 7th Regt. N.Y.S.W., 1856,* after Otto Botticher, pub. Goupil and Co., staining, mat burn, foxing, trimmed margins, tears into image, discoloration, soiling, hinged w/tape, John Walton Livermore Estate, (12-04-92, Doyle, #36), 27½ x 35 in., (699 x 889 mm.), color lithograph (BP 600, DM 1489, FR 5051, Y 116,729).

BENECKE, Thomas American 19th cent.
$275* *Sleigh Riding In New York City, 1855,* (03-14-93, Hindman, #304), 21½ x 30½ in., (54.6 x 77.5 cm.), color lithograph (BP 192, DM 458, FR 1556, Y 32,410).

BENECKE, Thomas (after)
BI *Niagara Falls, Canadian Side, c. 1855,* by Adam Weingartner, pub. 1856, trimmed to image, good cond., backboard stain, smoke stains, est. $1/1,200, (01-28-93, Sotheby-NY, #453), sheet 23Z, x 33M, in., (587 x 860 mm.), color lithograph w/touches hand-coloring on heavy wove.

BENGT, Lindstrom b. 1925
$332* *Bientot Libre,* H.C. #4/5, s., lit., (04-21-93, Germann, #18, illus.), 46Zzn x 33Bzn in., (117 x 84 cm.), color aquatint w/relief embossing (BP 215, DM 531, FR 1795, Y 36,754, SF 483).

BENIGNI, L.
$2932* *PLM: Brides-Les-Bains En Savoie, "La Station De La Femme Elegante:, 1929,* Office d'edition d'art, excell. cond., (01-23-93, Ribeyre/Baron, #180, illus.), 39C, x 24Mzn in., (100 x 62 cm.), poster (BP 1918, DM 4662, FR 15,772, Y 366,959).

BENITO 20th cent.
$176* *Art Deco Lady,* s. in plate, i., (05-28-93, Sloan, #1910, illus.), 9C, x 7C, in., (23.8 x 18.7 cm.), etching w/watercolor hightlights on silver paper (BP 113, DM 279, FR 944, Y 18,872).

BENNER, Gerrit
$512* *Landscape,* s., #15/40, margins, good cond., (05-27-93, Sotheby-Amstrdm, #558), sh 19Zzn x 25¾zn in., (500 x 650 mm.), lithograph on wove (BP 328, DM 822, FR 2769, Y 54,889, G 920).
$480* *Landscape,* s., #15/40, margins, good cond., (05-27-93, Sotheby-Amstrdm, #559), sh 19Zzn x 25ZCzn in., (500 x 655 mm.), lithograph on wove (BP 307, DM 770, FR 2596, Y 51,458, G 863).
$512* *Landscape,* s., #15/40, margins, good cond., (05-27-93, Sotheby-Amstrdm, #557), sh 24M, x 38Bzn in., (632 x 966 mm.), lithograph on Japan (BP 328, DM 822, FR 2769, Y 54,889, G 920).
$480* *Landscape,* s., #78/200, margins, good cond., (05-27-93, Sotheby-Amstrdm, #556), 16Mzn x 20ZZzn in., (418 x 528 mm.), colored silkscreen on wove (BP 307, DM 770, FR 2596, Y 51,458, G 863).

BENNER, Harry M. 1875-1946
BI *Glenn Hammond Curtiss, Selected Aviation Exploits (1878-1930) and Related Early Aviation Views: Two,* album, 200 prints, most t., some d., prov., lit., (c. 1908-14), est.$14/18,000, (10-13-92, Christie-NY, #69, illus.), each 4 x 6 in., (10.2 x 15.2 cm.), oblong folio 9B, x 14 in., (10.2 x 15.2 cm.), photograph, gelatin silver prints.

BENNET, William James (after) American 1777-1844
BI *Views Of New York, Pl. 1, Broadway,* by Hutchinson, est. $400/450, (07-03-92, Sloan, #1088), 11 x 17¼ in., (27.9 x 43.8 cm.), color engraving.

BENNETT, Alfred
$139* *"Houses Of Parliament" and "Windsor Castle": Two,* s., t., margins, (08-12-92, Bonhams, #184), plate 5½ x 8¾ in., (14 x 22.2 cm.), drypoint etching (BP 72, DM 203, FR 689, Y 17,716).

BENNETT, W.J.
$110* *English Interior Scenes Of Various Royal Residences: Four,* first pub. c. 1816-1818, after C. Wild and J. Stephanoff, (06-11-93, DuMouchelle, #2261), 8 x 9¾ in., (20.3 x 24.8 cm.), hand-colored mezzotint (BP 72, DM 179, FR 603, Y 11,671).

BENNETT, William James
$3450* *Broad Way From The Bowling Green (S. & H. C. 1826-E-1114; D. 350), c. 1826,* pub. in Megarey's Views in the City of New York, by Henry J. Megareyc. 1834, margins, repaired tear into image, light-stain, soiling, foxing, gluestains, skinning, platemark slightly reinforced, (01-28-93, Sotheby-NY, #425, illus.), 11¾ x 15C\ in., (298 x 391 mm.), sheet 14Z, x 19C, in., (298 x 391 mm.), aquatint (BP 2278, DM 5467, FR 18,499, Y 428,359).
BI *Fulton St. & Market (S. & H. P. 1828-E-113; D. 362),* pub. in Megarey's Views in the City of New York, by Henry J. Megareyc. 1834, large margins, good cond., soiling, discoloration, repaired tears, est. $10/12,000, (01-28-93, Sotheby-NY, #427, illus.), 11B, x 15C, in., (295 x 391 mm.), sheet 14Z, x 19½ in., (295 x 391 mm.), aquatint.
BI *Niagara Falls, To Thomas Dixon Esq. This View Of The American Fall, Taken From Goat Island ... (K. 167; D. 367), 1829,* 1st state of 2, p. and colored John Hill, (c) Henry J. Megarey 1830,margins, good cond., losses, tears, creases, mat stain, est. $2/3,000, (01-28-93, Sotheby-NY, #423A, illus.), 15M, x 20M, in., (403 x 530 mm.), sheet 18C, x 23Z, in., (403 x 530 mm.), hand-colored aquatint on wove.
$7475* *South St. From Maiden Lane (S. & H. P. 1828-E-113; D. 306), c. 1828,* pub. in Megarey's Views in the City of New York, by Henry J. Megareyc. 1834, margins, good cond., repaired tears, light-stain, soiling, foxing, (01-28-93, Sotheby-NY, #426, illus.), 11B, x 15½ in., (295 x 394 mm.), sheet 14¼ x 19¼ in., (295 x 394 mm.), aquatint (BP 4936, DM 11,844, FR 40,080, Y 928,110).
BI *View Of The Great Fire In New York, December 16th & 17th 1835, As Seen From The Top Of The Bank Of American (D. 438), 1835,* pub. Lewis P. Clover, 1836, est. $12/1500, (02-18-93, Sotheby-Arcade, #35), sight 17¼ x 23¾ in., (43.8 x 60.3 cm.), hand colored aquatint.
BI *View Of The Great Fire In New York, Decr. 16th & 17th 1835, As Seen From The Top Of The Bank Of America (D. 438), 1835,* after Nicolino V. Calyo, pub. Lewis P. Clover 1836, margins, good cond., glue stains, discoloration, creased, nicks, backboard stain, est. $2/3,000, (01-28-93, Sotheby-NY, #447, illus.), sheet 24Z, x 31Z, in., (613 x 791 mm.), hand-colored aquatint.

$460* *View Of The Great Fire In New York, Decr. 16th & 17th 1835, As Seen From The Top Of The Bank Of America (D. 438), 1835,* after Nicolino V. Calyo, pub. Lewis P. Clover 1836, trimmed to border, tears, scrapes, discoloration, linen-backed, (01-28-93, Sotheby-NY, #448), sheet 19ʙ, x 27 in., (498 x 686 mm.), hand-colored aquatint (BP 304, DM 729, FR 2466, Y 57,114).

BI *View Of The New York Quarantine, Staten Island (Deak, William James Bennett, Master of the Aquatint View 23), 1833,* pub. Parker & Co. and Lewis P. Clover, margins, touched-in forked tear/tears/scrapes in image, soiling, est. $12/15,000, (01-28-93, Sotheby-NY, #428, illus.), image 15ᴄ\ x 22ᴄ, in., (391 x 568 mm.), sheet 18 x 24ᴢ, in., (391 x 568 mm.), hand-colored aquatint w/ touches gum arabic backed w/wove.

$575* *View Of The Ruins After The Great Fire In New York, 16th & 17th Decr. 1835, As Seen From Exchange Place)D. 439), 1835,* after Nicolino V. Caylo, pub. Lewis P. Clover 1836, trimmed to border, laid down, (01-28-93, Sotheby-NY, #449), sheet 19¾ x 26ᴄ, in., (502 x 670 mm.), hand-colored aquatint (BP 380, DM 911, FR 3083, Y 71,393).

BI *West Point, From Above Washington Valley Looking Down The River (S. & H. P. 1833-F. 21; D. 412), 1832-33,* 1st state of 3, after George Cooke, pub. Parker & Clover 1834, margins, good cond., mat stain, foxing, soiling, fox marks in sky, nicks, est. $8/12,000, (01-28-93, Sotheby-NY, #424, illus.), image 15¾ x 22ʙ, in., (400 x 575 mm.), sheet 20½ x 26¼ in., (400 x 575 mm.), hand-colored aquatint on wove.

BENOIS, Alexander   Russian 1870-1960
$426* *11 Farblithographien Mit Spielzeug,* each s., i. mono., 3 d. 1904, (09-14-92, Venator/Hansten, #2442, illus.), 3>ᴋn x 5>ᴋn in., (9.1 x 14.1 cm.), color lithograph (BP 225, DM 633, FR 2146, Y 52,972).

BENSLEY, Mick
$31 *"Blakeney, Norfolk",* (12-11-92, G.A. Key, #59), 12 x 22 in., (30.5 x 55.9 cm.), colored proof print (BP 20, DM 49, FR 167, Y 3836).

BENSON, Frank W.   American 1862-1951
$660* *"Baldpates" (Paff, 235), 1924,* s. Frank W. Benson, t., annot., good cond., stabilized tear, mount staining, (03-12-93, Skinner, #46, illus.), 7¾ x 9¾ in., (19.7 x 24.8 cm.), drypoint on wove (BP 460, DM 1099, FR 3735, Y 77,784).

$1320* *Dory Fisherman, 1935,* s., t., d., (11-08-92, Northeast, #719, illus.), 8 x 10 in., (20.3 x 25.4 cm.), etching (BP 873, DM 2107, FR 7120, Y 163,812).

$1320* *"Dry Fisherman" (Paff, 267), 1927,* s. Frank W. Benson; ident. on label verso, good cond., toning, tape, (09-11-92, Skinner, #66G), 8 x 9ᴍ, in., (20.3 x 25.1 cm.), drypoint on paper (BP 683, DM 1900, FR 6458, Y 163,549).

$286* *Ducks Alighting,* margins, s. Frank W. Benson, (02-13-93, Collins, #41, illus.), 6ᴢ\ x 4½ in., (15.6 x 11.4 cm.), etching (BP 201, DM 474, FR 1605, Y 34,491).

$413* *Ducks In Flight,* s. Frank W. Benson, d. '19, good cond., (09-27-92, Bakker, #210, illus.), plate 8¾ x 6¾ in., (22.2 x 17.1 cm.), etching and drypoint (BP 241, DM 612, FR 2070, Y 49,849).

$319* *Flock Of Canvasbacks,* margins, s. Frank W. Benson, (02-13-93, Collins, #61, illus.), 7ᴍ, x 9ʙ\ in., (20 x 24.4 cm.), etching (BP 225, DM 529, FR 1790, Y 38,471).

$330* *"Flock Of Canvasbacks",* s., excell. cond., (10-02-92, Guyette, #628, illus.), image 8½ x 10½ in., (21.6 x 26.7 cm.), etching (BP 191, DM 470, FR 1571, Y 39,403).

$358* *Four Geese Alighting,* s., (11-08-92, Northeast, #730), 7 x 6 in., (17.8 x 15.2 cm.), etching (BP 237, DM 572, FR 1931, Y 44,428).

$440* *Four Mallards In Flight,* s. Frank W. Benson, num. 33, i., very good cond., (09-27-92, Bakker, #211), plate 5¾ x 7¾ in., (14.6 x 19.7 cm.), etching and drypoint (BP 257, DM 652, FR 2206, Y 53,108).

$550* *Geese In Flight,* s., marked 23, (11-08-92, Northeast, #733), 8 x 6 in., (20.3 x 15.2 cm.), etching (BP 364, DM 878, FR 2967, Y 68,255).

$440* *Geese Taking Wing,* s. Frank W. Benson, i., very good cond., (09-27-92, Bakker, #212), plate 6¾ x 8¾ in.,

(17.1 x 22.2 cm.), etching and drypoint (BP 257, DM 652, FR 2206, Y 53,108).

$308* *Going North,* margins, s. Frank W. Benson, (02-13-93, Collins, #45, illus.), 3½ x 5½ in., (8.9 x 14 cm.), etching (BP 217, DM 511, FR 1728, Y 37,144).

$2090* *Head (Paff 29): Two, 1914,* each s., first num. 6/35, second num. 12/35, prov., (10-08-92, Grogan, #744), each 9ᴍ, x 7ᴍ, in., (25.1 x 20 cm.), drypoint (BP 1244, DM 3091, FR 10,492, Y 253,949).

$990* *"Here They Come" (Paff, 278), 1928,* s. Frank W. Benson; ident. on label verso, very good cond., (09-11-92, Skinner, #66D), 13¾ x 11ʙ, in., (34.9 x 29.5 cm.), drypoint on paper (BP 512, DM 1425, FR 4843, Y 122,661).

$66* *Heron,* s., (12-13-92, Hindman, #307), 3½ x 5½ in., drypoint (BP 42, DM 104, FR 354, Y 8165).

$1100* *Herons In Cyprus Swamp,* (03-20-93, Northeast, #740, illus.), sight 8 x 10 in., (20.3 x 25.4 cm.), etching (BP 737, DM 1799, FR 6121, Y 127,595).

$880* *Hiker Stopping For Water,* s.(11-08-92, Northeast, #731), 7 x 5 in., (17.8 x 12.7 cm.), etching (BP 582, DM 1405, FR 4746, Y 109,208).

$1210* *Hunter At Dawn,* s., (11-08-92, Northeast, #717, illus.), 8 x 10 in., (20.3 x 25.4 cm.), etching (BP 800, DM 1932, FR 6526, Y 150,161).

$413* *"In Dropping Flight" (Paff, 255), 1926,* s. Frank W. Benson; ident. on label verso, very good cond., (09-11-92, Skinner, #66B), 10ᴍ, x 13¾ in., (27.6 x 34.9 cm.), drypoint on paper (BP 214, DM 595, FR 2021, Y 51,171).

$578* *In Island Pond,* s., (11-08-92, Northeast, #732), 10 x 8 in., (25.4 x 20.3 cm.), etching (BP 382, DM 923, FR 3118, Y 71,730).

$495* *Ipswich Marshes (P. 257), 1926,* s., foxing, mat burn, hinged to mat, (12-04-92, Doyle, #74), 7¾ x 9¾ in., (197 x 248 mm.), etching w/drypoint (BP 318, DM 788, FR 2674, Y 61,798).

$495* *"Little Blue Bills" (Paff, 216), 1922,* s. Frank W. Benson, init., d. F.W.B. 22 in plate, ident. on labels verso, very good cond., (09-11-92, Skinner, #66I), 7¾ x 5¾ in., (19.7 x 14.6 cm.), drypoint on paper (BP 256, DM 713, FR 2422, Y 61,331).

$350* *"Log Driver" (P. 230),* s., mat staining, verso toned, hinges, (05-15-93, Cleveland, #70), 9ᴍ, x 11ᴍ, in., (25.1 x 30.2 cm.), drypoint (BP 228, DM 563, FR 1892, Y 38,798).

$550* *"Mallard At Evening" (Paff, 271), 1927,* s. Frank W. Benson; ident. on label verso, very good cond., (09-11-92, Skinner, #66H), 13¾ x 11¾ in., (34.9 x 29.8 cm.), drypoint on paper (BP 284, DM 792, FR 2691, Y 68,145).

$880* *A Man Poling Canoe,* s., (11-08-92, Northeast, #729), 6 x 4 in., (15.2 x 10.2 cm.), etching (BP 582, DM 1405, FR 4746, Y 109,208).

$935* *"Man With Gaff" (Paff, 247), 1925,* s. Frank W. Benson, annot., mat/time toning, staining, tape, (09-11-92, Skinner, #66C), 11ʙ, x 9ᴍ, in., (29.5 x 25.1 cm.), drypoint on paper (BP 484, DM 1346, FR 4574, Y 115,847).

$770* *"Migrating Geese" and "High-Flying Ducks" (Paff 106 and 128), 1917: Two,* each s.; first num. R-45, 2nd state of 3; second num. 68, (12-09-92, Grogan, #61), first 9ᴍ, x 7ᴍ, in., (25.1 x 20 cm.), second 7ᴍ, x 5ᴍ, in., (25.1 x 20 cm.), etching (BP 491, DM 1209, FR 4124, Y 95,474).

$303* *"On The Kedgwick",* s. below image, (08-05-92, Boos, #685), plate 7ᴢᴢn x 11ᴢᴢn in., (198 x 300 mm.), etching (BP 158, DM 448, FR 1512, Y 38,589).

$350* *"On The Redhead Grounds",* s., mat staining, (05-15-93, Cleveland, #68, illus.), 10 x 7ᴍ, in., (25.4 x 20 cm.), drypoint (BP 228, DM 563, FR 1892, Y 38,798).

$550* *Pelican,* s., (09-24-92, Mystic, #13), 5 x 4 in., (12.7 x 10.2 cm.), etching (BP 322, DM 815, FR 2768, Y 66,161).

$1870* *"Pintails",* s., num. 21, good/poor cond., (02-07-93, Bakker, #180), plate 13½ x 10½ in., (34.3 x 26.7 cm.), drypoint (BP 1294, DM 3101, FR 10,482, Y 232,703).

$715* *Plodding Home (Paff 234), 1924,* s., (12-09-92, Grogan, #58), 2ᴍ, x 2 in., (7.3 x 5.1 cm.), etching (BP 456, DM 1122, FR 3830, Y 88,655).

$440* *Pointer Dog,* s., (11-08-92, Northeast, #734), etching (BP 291, DM 702, FR 2373, Y 54,604).

$165* *Portrait Of A Gentleman, 1903,* s., prov., (10-30-92, Sloan, #1785), 4 x 4M, in., (10.2 x 12.4 cm.), etching (BP 106, DM 254, FR 861, Y 20,438).

$385* *"Redhead Alighting",* s., very good cond., (10-02-92, Guyette, #626, illus.), image 6½ x 5½ in., (16.5 x 14 cm.), etching (BP 223, DM 548, FR 1833, Y 45,970).

$550* *Redheads Landing,* s., excell. cond., (10-02-92, Guyette, #633, illus.), image 8½ x 10½ in., (21.6 x 26.7 cm.), drypoint (BP 318, DM 783, FR 2619, Y 65,672).

$475* *"Redheads" (Paff 127 ii/iii), 1917,* proof, s., #, ded. Berthe Jacques, good cond., foxing, (05-15-93, Cleveland, #69, illus.), 5¾ x 7¾ in., (14.6 x 19.7 cm.), drypoint (BP 309, DM 764, FR 2568, Y 52,655).

$286* *The Rendezvous,* margins, s. Frank W. Benson, (02-13-93, Collins, #37, illus.), 3¾ x 4M, in., (9.5 x 12.4 cm.), etching (BP 201, DM 474, FR 1605, Y 34,491).

$220* *"Rendezvous", c. 1920,* s. below image, (08-05-92, Boos, #683), plate 3¾ x 4Bzn in., (95 x 125 mm.), drypoint (BP 115, DM 325, FR 1098, Y 28,018).

$418* *Rippling Water,* margins, s. Frank W. Benson, (02-13-93, Collins, #53, illus.), 9¾ x 7M, in., (24.8 x 20 cm.), etching (BP 294, DM 693, FR 2346, Y 50,410).

$425* *Rising Geese (P. 238), 1924,* s., ded. Berthe Jacques, 1933, mat staining, tape hinges, (05-15-93, Cleveland, #71, illus.), 6¾ x 8¾ in., (17.1 x 22.2 cm.), drypoint (BP 276, DM 684, FR 2297, Y 47,112).

$385* *"Snowy Herons", 1917,* s. Frank W. Benson, num. 22, very good cond., annot., soiling, (09-11-92, Skinner, #66, illus.), 4M\ x 3M, in., (12.4 x 9.8 cm.), drypoint on Etruria paper w/watermark (BP 199, DM 554, FR 1884, Y 47,702).

$550* *"Summer Yellow Legs" (P. 186), 1920,* s., excell. cond., (10-31-92, Cleveland, #74), 4B\n x 3Zzn in., (12.5 x 9.7 cm.), drypoint (BP 352, DM 846, FR 2871, Y 68,128).

$605* *Teal (P. 243), 1925,* s., hinged to mat, tape residue, mat burn, fine cond., (12-04-92, Doyle, #73), 7¾ x 10¾ in., (197 x 273 mm.), etching w/drypoint (BP 388, DM 964, FR 3269, Y 75,531).

$400* *"Towering Widgeon" (P. 260),* s., mat burn, (05-15-93, Cleveland, #72, illus.), 9¾ x 7M, in., (24.8 x 20 cm.), drypoint (BP 260, DM 643, FR 2162, Y 44,341).

$660* *"Two Black Ducks" (Paff, 295), 1930,* s. Frank W. Benson, annot., foxing, staining, tape verso, (09-11-92, Skinner, #66E), 14¾ x 11M\ in., (37.5 x 30.2 cm.), drypoint on laid paper w/watermark (BP 341, DM 950, FR 3229, Y 81,774).

$385* *"Two Crows",* s., very good cond.?, (03-28-93, Bakker, #3), 2 x 3 in., (5.1 x 7.6 cm.), etching (BP 259, DM 628, FR 2135, Y 44,809).

$358* *Two Ducks In Flight,* s., (12-13-92, Hindman, #308), 4¾ x 6¾ in., drypoint (BP 229, DM 563, FR 1918, Y 44,290).

$154* *Two Geese Swimming,* s. below image, (08-05-92, Boos, #682), 3B\n x 5Z\n in., (100 x 145 mm.), drypoint (BP 81, DM 227, FR 768, Y 19,613).

$330* *Untitled,* s., very good cond., (10-02-92, Guyette, #629, illus.), image 10 x 12 in., (25.4 x 30.5 cm.), etching (BP 191, DM 470, FR 1571, Y 39,403).

$715* *"Wide Marshes" (Path 173), 1920,* s., excell. cond., (10-31-92, Cleveland, #73), 6M, x 10Zzn in., (17.5 x 27.5 cm.), etching (BP 458, DM 1100, FR 3732, Y 88,567).

$385* *Wild Geese,* margins, s. Frank W. Benson, (02-13-93, Collins, #36, illus.), 6¾ x 10¾ in., (17.1 x 27.3 cm.), etching (BP 271, DM 638, FR 2160, Y 46,430).

BENSON, Frank W. (after)

$101 *Seated Young Girl,* (10-09-92, G.A. Key, #139), 27 x 23½ in., (68.6 x 59.7 cm.), colored print (BP 60, DM 150, FR 510, Y 12,317).

BENT, Paul

$73* *The Wasteland,* inits. P.A.B., i., d. '77, #1/6, (08-11-92, L. Joel, #39G), 26C, x 24Czn in., (67 x 61.5 cm.), color screen print (BP 38, DM 107, FR 363, Y 9348, A$ 99).

BENTON, Fletcher

BI *Diamond In Circle, 1972,* s., d., num. 49/100, blindstamp of pub. La, full margins, apparentlygood cond., light-staining, creases, est. $3/500, (02-24-93, Butterfield, #3187), 26B, x 26B, in., (676 x 676 mm.), lithogrpah & silkscreen in colors on wove.

BI *Untitled, 1975,* s., d., annot. III, #2/70, margins, good cond.?, mat/light-staining,image foxing, Modesto Lanzone Coll., est. $8/1,200, (10-28-92, Butterfield, #2907), 20 x 20 in., (508 x 508 mm.), embossing w/graphite on paper w/encaustic.

BI *Untitled, 1975,* s., d., annot. III, num. 2/70, margins, apparently good cond., mat &light-staining, foxing in image, Modesto Lanzone Coll., est. $5/700, (02-24-93, Butterfield, #3188), 20 x 20 in., (508 x 508 mm.), embossing & graphite p. w/encaustic on paper.

BENTON, Thomas Hart American 1889-1975

$880* *Aaron (F. 42), 1941,* s., (10-30-92, Sloan, #2356, illus.), 12¾ x 9½ in., (32.4 x 24.1 cm.), lithograph (BP 564, DM 1354, FR 4593, Y 109,005).

$1210* *Aaron (F. 42), 1941,* s., margins, taped to overmat, good cond., (09-19-92, Christie-E, #14), borderline 12M x 9½ in., (327 x 241 mm.), lithograph on wove (BP 696, DM 1812, FR 6205, Y 150,760).

$1650* *Aaron (F. 42), 1941,* s., pub. AAA, good cond., light-satining, surface soiling, buckling, (10-28-92, Butterfield, #2514, illus.), 12Zzn x 9zn in., (325 x 243 mm.), lithograph on wove (BP 1051, DM 2548, FR 8652, Y 202,454).

$935* *"Aaron",* s., toning, prov., (12-12-92, Litchfield, #22), 12¾ x 9½ in., (32.4 x 24.1 cm.), lithograph (BP 600, DM 1473, FR 5049, Y 115,704).

BI *"Aaron" (F. 42), 1941,* s., excell. cond., unwashed, full margins, est. $1,5/2,000, (10-31-92, Cleveland, #78, illus.), 12M, x 9C, in., (32.7 x 23.8 cm.), lithograph.

$825* *After The Blow (F. 70), 1946,* s., pub. AAA, slightly trimmed, good cond., light staining, staining, creases, (10-28-92, Butterfield, #2517), 9Bzn x 14 in., (252 x 356 mm.), lithograph on Stratford paper (BP 526, DM 1274, FR 4326, Y 101,227).

$935* *"After The Blow" (F. 70), 1946,* s., pub. AAA, very fine cond., (10-31-92, Cleveland, #80), 13M, x 9¾ in., (35.2 x 24.8 cm.), lithograph (BP 599, DM 1438, FR 4880, Y 115,818).

$1650* *"Approaching Storm" (F. 25), 1938,* s., pub. for Print Club of Celevland, No. 18, 1940, discoloration, scuffing, excell. cond., (10-31-92, Cleveland, #76, illus.), 9¾ x 12¾ in., (24.8 x 32.4 cm.), lithograph (BP 1057, DM 2538, FR 8612, Y 204,385).

BI *At The Gate (F. 69), 1946,* s., margins, rippling, mat burn, good cond., est. $800/1,200, (12-12-92, Weschler, #103, illus.), 9¾ x 13¾ in., (24.8 x 34.9 cm.), lithograph.

$1210* *Back From The Fields (F. 66), 1945,* s., pub. AAA, full margins, good cond., light stain, backboard stain,tape hinges, paper adhering to surface, (11-05-92, Sotheby-NY, #9), 9¾ x 12M, in., (248 x 326 mm.), lithograph (BP 787, DM 1914, FR 6474, Y 148,448).

$770* *Back From The Fields (F. 66), 1945,* s., pub. AAA, full margins, good cond., light/mat staining, taped, surface soiling, (10-28-92, Butterfield, #2515), 9Bzn x 12M, in., (246 x 327 mm.), lithograph on wove (BP 491, DM 1189, FR 4038, Y 94,479).

$863* *Back From The Fields (F. 66), 1945,* s., pub. AAA, margins, good cond., light-staining, remains, thinned spots, mat staining, notations, (05-19-93, Butterfield, #1793), 9B\ x 12Bzn in., (244 x 325 mm.), lithograph on wove (BP 560, DM 1403, FR 4726, Y 95,539).

$1045* *"A Black Man Handplowing Behind A Mule",* s., Groves' Coll., (10-16-92, Neal, #135, illus.), image 8 x 13¼ in., (20.3 x 33.7 cm.), lithograph (BP 633, DM 1544, FR 5243, Y 124,776).

$1430* *The Corral (F. 21), 1948,* s., pub. AAA, margins, good cond, light stain, smudges, (11-05-92, Sotheby-NY, #7), 9¾ x 13M\ in., (246 x 352 mm.), sheet 11B\ x 15C, in., (246 x 352 mm.), lithograph (BP 930, DM 2262, FR 7651, Y 175,439).

$1045* *The Corral (F. 71), 1948,* s., pub. AAA, margins trimmed, taped to overmat, good cond., light-staining, staining, hinge remains, foxing, surface soiling, (10-28-92, Butterfield, #2518), 9B, x 13M, in., (244 x 352 mm.), lithograph on wove (BP 666, DM 1614, FR 5480, Y 128,221).

BI   *A Drink Of Water [F15], 1937,* s. in stone; s., pub. AAA, est. $1,2/1,400, (02-04-93, Sloan, #2392), 10 x 14℃, in., (25.4 x 36.5 cm.), lithograph.

$880*   *"Drink Of Water" (Fath 15),* s. plate; s., (06-24-93, Boos, #624, illus.), image 10℀n x 14℃, in., (255 x 365 mm.), sh 11℀n x 16℀, in., (255 x 365 mm.), lithograph (BP 599, DM 1503, FR 5060, Y 95,986).

$825*   *"Drink Of Water" (Fath 15), 1937,* s., pub. AAA, fine cond., (10-31-92, Cleveland, #75, illus.), 10 x 14¼ in., (25.4 x 36.2 cm.), lithograph (BP 529, DM 1269, FR 4306, Y 102,192).

$990*   *Edge Of Town (F. 22), 1938,* s., pub. AAA, full margins, good cond., light staining, (10-28-92, Butterfield, #2511, illus.), 8℀ x 10¾ in., (225 x 273 mm.), lithograph on Rives (BP 631, DM 1529, FR 5191, Y 121,472).

$1210*   *Edge Of Town (F. 22), 1938,* watermark, s., pub. AAA, full margins, very good cond., light-staining, (02-24-93, Butterfield, #2615), 9 x 10¾ in., (229 x 273 mm.), lithograph on wove (BP 844, DM 1964, FR 6659, Y 141,985).

$1980*   *"Edge Of Town",* s., AAA label, (05-20-93, Boos, #527, illus.), image 8℀n x 10℀n in., (224 x 272 mm.), paper 11℀n x 13℀n in., (224 x 272 mm.), lithograph (BP 1271, DM 3195, FR 10,761, Y 218,640).

$1100*   *Fire In The Barn Yard,* s., good cond., full margins, hinged, (06-11-93, Freemn/Fine Art, #19, illus.), 8½ x 13¼ in., (21.6 x 33.7 cm.), lithograph (BP 723, DM 1788, FR 6027, Y 116,711).

$1045*   *Five In The Barnyard (F. 64), 1944,* s., pub. AAA, full margins, laid down, good cond., tape & glue remains, mat & light-staining, (02-24-93, Butterfield, #2620, illus.), sight 8½ x 13℀, in., (216 x 333 mm.), lithograph on wove (BP 729, DM 1696, FR 5751, Y 122,624).

BI   *"Flood" (Fath 16),* s. plate; s., est. $800/1,200, (06-24-93, Boos, #625), image 9¼ x 12℀n in., (235 x 310 mm.), sh 11℀n x 14℀n in., (235 x 310 mm.), lithograph.

$6325*   *Frankie And Johnnie (Fath 11), 1936,* s., full margins, creases, soiling, tears, very good cond., (05-11-93, Christie-NY, #91, illus.), borderline 16½ x 22¼ in., (419 x 565 mm.), lithograph on Rives (BP 4038, DM 9964, FR 33,572, Y 695,743).

$770*   *Frisky Day (F. 30), 1939,* s., pub. AAA, full margins, good cond., light-staining, scuffing, (10-28-92, Butterfield, #2513), 7℀, x 12 in., (200 x 305 mm.), lithograph on GCM wove (BP 491, DM 1189, FR 4038, Y 94,479).

$1320*   *"Frisky Day" (F. 30), 1939,* s., full margins, stains, perfect cond., (10-31-92, Cleveland, #77, illus.), 7¾ x 12℀ in., (19.7 x 30.8 cm.), lithograph (BP 846, DM 2031, FR 6889, Y 163,508).

$1380*   *Goin' Home (F. 14), 1937,* s., pub. AAA, full margins, good cond., mat/light staining, (05-19-93, Butterfield, #1792, illus.), 9℃, x 11℀ in., (238 x 302 mm.), lithograph on Rives (BP 896, DM 2243, FR 7558, Y 152,773).

$935*   *Goin' Home (Fath 14), 1937,* s., (03-24-93, Grogan, #94, illus.), 9½ x 12 in., (24.1 x 30.5 cm.), lithograph (BP 633, DM 1527, FR 5197, Y 109,858).

$1100*   *Goin' Home, 1937, Fath 14,* s., pub. AAA, (09-20-92, Hindman, #683, illus.), 9½ x 12 in., (24.1 x 30.5 cm.), lithograph (BP 644, DM 1632, FR 5584, Y 135,954).

$2200*   *Haystack (Fath 21), 1938,* s., margins, scattered foxing, taped to overmat, (09-19-92, Christie-E, #13, illus.), borderline 10¼ x 12℀, in., (260 x 327 mm.), lithograph on wove (BP 1265, DM 3294, FR 11,282, Y 274,109).

$990*   *Homestead (In The Ozarks) (F. 20), 1938,* watermark, s., pub. AAA, full margins, very good cond., staining, (02-24-93, Butterfield, #2614, illus.), 10¼ x 13℀, in., (260 x 333 mm.), lithograph on wove (BP 690, DM 1607, FR 5449, Y 116,170).

$2090*   *"Homestead" and "Cradling Wheat" (F. 20 and 27), 1938, 1939: Two,* s., pub. AAA, full margins; first good cond., creases, second mat stained, glue, (11-05-92, Sotheby-NY, #6), first 10¼ x 13℀, in., (260 x 334 mm.), second 9℀, x 12 in., (260 x 334 mm.), lithograph (BP 1359, DM 3305, FR 11,182, Y 256,410).

$6050*   *Huck Finn (Fath 12), 1936,* s., full margins, skinning, good cond., repaired tears staining, (11-09-92, Christie-NY, #15, illus.), border 16℀n x 21℀, in., (420 x 550

mm.), lithograph on Rives (BP 4000, DM 9658, FR 32,632, Y 750,807).

$1320*   *"The Hymn Singer" (Fath. 74),* s. plate; s., blindstamp, (06-24-93, Boos, #626, illus.), image 15℀n x 12℀n in., (405 x 310 mm.), sh 19℀n x 15℀n in., (405 x 310 mm.), lithograph (BP 899, DM 2254, FR 7591, Y 143,979).

$2090*   *"In The Ozarks (Homestead)",* s., AAA label, (05-20-93, Boos, #528, illus.), image 10℃n x 13℀n in., (259 x 332 mm.), paper 11℃℀n x 15℀n in., (259 x 332 mm.), lithograph (BP 1341, DM 3372, FR 11,359, Y 230,786).

$660*   *Investigation,* s., abrasions, tape residue, (11-12-92, Freemn/Fine Art, #30, illus.), 13 x 10½ in., (33 x 26.7 cm.), litho on wove paper (BP 433, DM 1046, FR 3528, Y 81,835).

$550*   *"Investigation",* plate s. twice, AAA, (12-11-92, DuMouchelle, #1084), 9½ x 12½ in., (24.1 x 31.8 cm.), lithograph (BP 353, DM 867, FR 2970, Y 68,061).

$1045*   *Island Hay (F. 68), 1945,* s., pub. AAA, full margins, very good cond., mat staining, (10-28-92, Butterfield, #2516), 10 x 12℀, in., (254 x 321 mm.), lithograph on cream wove (BP 666, DM 1614, FR 5480, Y 128,221).

$935*   *"Island Hay" (Fath, 68), 1945,* s. Benton, and in stone, good cond., light/mount staining, margins trimmed to 1", annot., (09-11-92, Skinner, #44, illus.), 9℀, x 12℀, in., (25.1 x 32.1 cm.), lithograph on wove (BP 484, DM 1346, FR 4574, Y 115,847).

$1430*   *Jesse And Jake (Fath 55), 1942,* s., (05-27-93, Swann, #37, illus.), (25.1 x 34 cm.), lithograph (BP 916, DM 2295, FR 7734, Y 153,302).

$3738*   *Jesse James (Fath 13), 1936,* s., i., pub. by AAA, full margins, good cond., light-stain, repairedtears, margins running into image, creases, loss, (02-11-93, Sotheby-NY, #4, illus.), 16¼ x 25℀, in., (413 x 657 mm.), lithograph (BP 2638, DM 6192, FR 20,953, Y 450,633).

$1320*   *"Letter From Overseas" (Fath, 59), 1943,* pub. AAA, s. Benton and in stone, t. on AAA label, very good cond., orig. folder, (09-11-92, Skinner, #51, illus.), 9¾ x 13℀, in., (24.8 x 33.3 cm.), lithograph on wove (BP 683, DM 1900, FR 6458, Y 163,549).

$1210*   *Loading Corn (F. 65), 1945,* s., pub. AAA, full margins, laid down, good cond., tape & glue remains, mat & light-staining, (02-24-93, Butterfield, #2621), 9½ x 12℀, in., (241 x 327 mm.), lithograph on wove (BP 844, DM 1964, FR 6659, Y 141,985).

$1210*   *Lonesome Road (F. 18), 1938,* watermark, s., margins, foxmark, glue, skinning verso, (11-09-92, Christie-NY, #16), border 9℀n x 12½ in., (246 x 318 mm.), lithograph on wove (BP 800, DM 1932, FR 6526, Y 150,161).

BI   *The Meeting, 1941, Fath 47,* s., pub. AAA, est. $1/1,500, (09-20-92, Hindman, #686, illus.), sheet 12℀, x 16½ in., (32.1 x 41.9 cm.), lithograph on wove.

$1650*   *Morning Train (F. 58), 1943,* s., pub. AAA, full margins, very good cond., mat staining, foxing, (02-24-93, Butterfield, #2617, illus.), 9¾ x 13¾ in., (248 x 349 mm.), lithograph on wove (BP 1151, DM 2679, FR 9081, Y 193,617).

$1980*   *Morning Train Or Soldier's Farewell, 1943, Fath 58,* s., pub. AAA, (09-20-92, Hindman, #688, illus.), sheet 11℃, x 15℀, in., (28.9 x 40.3 cm.), lithograph on white wove (BP 1159, DM 2938, FR 10,051, Y 244,716).

$1760*   *"Morning Train",* s. Benton, very good cond., (11-21-92, Bakker, #1, illus.), image 9½ x 13½ in., (24.1 x 34.3 cm.), lithograph (BP 1159, DM 2806, FR 9452, Y 218,878).

$1600*   *"Morning Train" (Fath 58), 1943,* s., pub. AAA, excell. cond., (05-15-93, Cleveland, #73, illus.), 13½ x 9℃, in., (34.3 x 23.8 cm.), lithograph (BP 1040, DM 2574, FR 8649, Y 177,364).

$1980*   *The Music Lesson (Fath 60), 1943,* s., pub. AAA, catalog cover lot, (05-27-93, Swann, #38, illus.), 12½ x 10¼ in., (31.8 x 26 cm.), lithograph (BP 1268, DM 3177, FR 10,708, Y 212,264).

$1210*   *The Music Lesson (Fath 60), 1943,* s., (12-09-92, Grogan, #99A, illus.), 9¾ x 12¾ in., (24.8 x 32.4 cm.), lithograph (BP 772, DM 1899, FR 6481, Y 150,031).

$990*   *Planting (F. 28), 1939,* s., pub. AAA, full margins, good cond., tape/glue/paper remains, creases, surface soiling, (10-28-92, Butterfield, #2512), 10 x 12½ in., (254 x 318 mm.), lithograph on Rives (BP 631, DM 1529, FR 5191, Y 121,472).

$1870* *"Prodigal Son" and "Back From The Fields" (F. 29 and 66), 1939, 1945:Two,* pub. AAA; first light stain, foxing, tape stains, second repaired tears, tape stain, (11-05-92, Sotheby-NY, #8), first 10Z, x 13¼ in., (258 x 335 mm.), second 9B, x 12M\ in., (258 x 335 mm.), lithograph (BP 1216, DM 2957, FR 10,005, Y 229,420).

$1100* *Prodigal Son, 1939, Fath,* s., pub. AAA, (09-20-92, Hindman, #684, illus.), sheet 12Z, x 16½ in., (30.8 x 39.4 cm.), lithograph on white wove (BP 644, DM 1632, FR 5584, Y 135,954).

$3520* *The Race Or Homeward Bound, 1942, ref: Fath 56,* s., pub. AAA, (09-20-92, Hindman, #687, illus.), sheet 11¼ x 15¾ in., (28.6 x 40 cm.), (28.6 x 40 cm.), lithograph on white wove w/watermark (BP 2061, DM 5223, FR 17,868, Y 435,051).

$1540* *Shallow Creek (Fath 32), 1939,* s., pub. AAA, (05-27-93, Swann, #36, illus.), 9Bzn x 14¼ in., (23.7 x 36.2 cm.), lithograph (BP 986, DM 2471, FR 8329, Y 165,094).

$1870* *Slow Train Through Arkansas, 1941, Fath 46,* s., pub. AAA, (09-20-92, Hindman, #685, illus.), sheet 12½ x 16M, in., (31.8 x 42.9 cm.), lithograph on wove (BP 1095, DM 2775, FR 9492, Y 231,121).

$1540* *Spring Tryout (F. 61), 1943,* s., pub. AAA, margins trimmed, good cond., light-staining, foxing, paper tape, (02-24-93, Butterfield, #2618, illus.), 9C, x 13B\ in., (238 x 346 mm.), lithograph on wove (BP 1074, DM 2500, FR 8476, Y 180,709).

BI *Spring Tryout (F. 61), 1946,* s., margins, staining, mat/backboard burn, tape stains, est. $2/3,000, (12-12-92, Weschler, #104, illus.), 9½ x 13½ in., (24.1 x 34.3 cm.), lithograph.

BI *Sunday Morning (F. 26), 1939,* s. in stone, s., (10-30-92, Sloan, #2357), 9B, x 12C, in., (24.4 x 31.4 cm.), lithograph.

$1100* *Sunday Morning (F. 26), 1939,* watermark, s., pub. AAA, full margins, very good cond., buckling, 2 specks of ink, (02-24-93, Butterfield, #2616, illus.), 9¾ x 12¾ in., (248 x 324 mm.), lithograph on wove (BP 767, DM 1786, FR 6054, Y 129,078).

$1650* *Sunday Morning (Fath 26), 1939,* full margins, s., pub. AAA, (05-27-93, Swann, #35, illus.), 12C, x 8 in., (31.4 x 20.3 cm.), lithograph (BP 1057, DM 2648, FR 8924, Y 176,887).

$935* *"Sunday Morning", 1939,* s. Benton, good cond.?, (11-21-92, Bakker, #2, illus.), 9B\ x 12C, in., (24.4 x 31.4 cm.), lithograph (BP 616, DM 1491, FR 5021, Y 116,279).

$2530* *Threshing (F. 48), 1941,* s., full margins, light-staining, foxing, taped to overmat, tape, (05-11-93, Christie-NY, #92, illus.), borderline 9¼ x 13¾ in., (235 x 349 mm.), lithograph on wove (BP 1615, DM 3986, FR 13,429, Y 278,297).

BI *"Tom Keefer" (F. 51), 1941,* from Swamp Water Series, good cond., est. $3/400, (10-31-92, Cleveland, #79), 8¼ x 6¼ in., (21 x 15.9 cm.), lithograph.

BI *"Tom Keefer" (Fath. 51),* s. plate, i., est. $800/1,200, (06-24-93, Boos, #627), image 8zn x 6Bzn in., (205 x 160 mm.), sh 16¼ x 11Mzn in., (205 x 160 mm.), lithograph.

$1840* *Waiting For The Revolution (F. 9), 1934,* s., #11/12, full margins, good cond., mat staining, soiling, surfacescuffs, (05-19-93, Butterfield, #1791, illus.), sh. 9M, x 12C, in., (251 x 314 mm.), lithograph on wove (BP 1194, DM 2991, FR 10,077, Y 203,698).

$1840* *"The Wood Pile" and "Old Man Reading" (F. 31 and 44), 1939 and 1941:Two,* s., pub. AAA, 1st full margins; 2nd margins; generally good cond.; 1st light-stain, filled-in skinning, creases; 2nd mat,light stains, foxing, creases, (02-11-93, Sotheby-NY, #5), 8Zzn x 10Azn in., (220 x 275 mm.), 9ZBzn x 12Czn in., (220 x 275 mm.), lithograph (BP 1298, DM 3048, FR 10,314, Y 221,820).

$3300* *The Wreck Of The Ol' 97 (F. 63), 1944,* watermark, s., pub. AAA, margins, good cond., mat & light-staining, creases, paper loss, (02-24-93, Butterfield, #2619), 10¼ x 15 in., (260 x 381 mm.), lithograph on wove (BP 2301, DM 5357, FR 18,162, Y 387,233).

$4830* *Wreck Of The Ol'97 (F. 63), 1944,* s., full margins, staining, (05-11-93, Christie-NY, #93, illus.), borderline 10C x 15 in., (264 x 381 mm.), lithograph on wove (BP 3083, DM 7609, FR 25,637, Y 531,295).

BENWELL, J.H.

$64 *"A St Giles's Beauty" and "A St James's Beauty": Two,* engraved by F Bartolozzi, (04-16-93, G.A. Key, #90), 6 x 5 in., (15.2 x 12.7 cm.), rouge stipple engraving (BP 42, DM 103, FR 349, Y 7197).

BENWELL, J.H. (after)

BI *"A St. Giles's Beauty" and "A St. James's Beauty": A Pair,* engr. by F. Bartolozzi, (12-11-92, G.A. Key, #123), 6 x 5 in., (15.2 x 12.7 cm.), rouge stipple engraving.

BER, Ryback Issachar

$1320* *Shtel, Mayn Chorever Heym, 1923: Thirty-One,* complete portfolio, s., in image, d., t. and colophon, pub. Schwellen, full margins, foxing, surface soiling, water-staining, orig. cover, water-damaged, soiled, (10-28-92, Butterfield, #2718), each sheet 13 x 19¼ in., (330 x 489 mm.), offset lithograph on wove (BP 841, DM 2039, FR 6922, Y 161,963).

BERARD, Christian French 1902-1949

$72* *1e Festival International De Danse Paris, 1963,* (01-31-93, Morelle/Marchan, #16), 15¾ x 23B, in., (40 x 60 cm.), poster (BP 48, DM 116, FR 392, Y 8982).

$58* *Au Pont Des Arts, Galerie Lucie Weill, 1966,* (01-31-93, Morelle/Marchan, #124), 19Zzn x 25zn in., (50 x 65 cm.), poster (BP 39, DM 93, FR 316, Y 7236).

$79* *Theatre, 1963,* (01-31-93, Morelle/Marchan, #170), 19Zzn x 25zn in., (50 x 65 cm.), poster (BP 53, DM 127, FR 430, Y 9855).

BERBER, Mersad Yugoslavian b. 1940

$275* *Pocitely,* s., t., num. 184/200, (09-20-92, Hindman, #805), 35 x 23 in., (88.9 x 58.4 cm.), color lithograph and serigraph on Fabriano Rosaspina paper (BP 161, DM 408, FR 1396, Y 33,988).

BERCHEM, Nicolaes Dutch 1620-1683

$736* *Der Auf Dem Brunnen Sitzende Hirt, Der Die Flote Blast (B., Dutuit, Wurzbach und Hollst. 8, II),* d. in plate, prov., (10-09-92, Winterberg, #732), 10C, x 8Czn in., (26.4 x 20.8 cm.), etching (BP 437, DM 1093, FR 3671, Y 89,603).

$850* *Die Rast Vor Dem Gasthaus (B. 11, Wurzbach, Dutuit, Hollstein 11 III), c. 1652,* watermark, (06-04-93, Bassenge, #5035), 10Czn x 8¼ in., (25.9 x 20.9 cm.), etching (BP 562, DM 1380, FR 4652, Y 91,674).

$141* *Die Rastende Herde Mit Dem Hirten Unter Einem Baum (Hollstein Bd. 1,10),* trimmed, (03-24-93, Venator/Hansten, #2485), approx. 10¼ x 7Czn in., (26.1 x 19.8 cm.), etching (BP 95, DM 230, FR 784, Y 16,567).

BERCKMANS

$231* *Liqueur Severy,* very good cond., (11-19-92, Ribeyre/Baron, #10), 59Zzn x 39¾ in., (150 x 101 cm.), poster (BP 152, DM 368, FR 1241, Y 28,728).

BERDANIER, Paul F. American b. 1879

$33* *Four Ducks Landing,* s. below image, (08-05-92, Boos, #681), 3Mzn x 4Azn in., (88 x 125 mm.), etching (BP 17, DM 49, FR 165, Y 4203).

BEREND-CORINTH, Charlotte 1880-1967

$1155* *Valeska Gert Auf Dem Sofa Liegend, c. 1925,* (11-28-92, Grisebach, #440, illus.), 6M, x 17Z, in., (17.5 x 43.5 cm.), hand-colored lithograph on copper print paper (BP 762, DM 1840, FR 6247, Y 143,746).

BERENY, Rodolph

$301* *L'Homme Aux Poupees. Film D'Art Avec Charlotte Wiehe, c. 1905,* Imp. du Film d'Art, fairly good cond., (02-12-93, Cheval/Robert, #198), 61 x 44M, in., (155 x 114 cm.), poster (BP 212, DM 499, FR 1689, Y 36,300).

BERETOWSKY, Liliana Canadian 20th cent.

BI *"Averon",* #5/90, s., d. Beretowsky 84, (05-18-93, Encans, #11), 25 x 19Z, in., (63.5 x 48.5 cm.), lithograph and transfer.

BERGER, Rene French ac. 1890-1920

BI *"Sarah Bernhardt In Hamlet",* crease in image, tear, est. $150-250, (10-31-92, Cleveland, #246), 15 x 9½ in., (38.1 x 24.1 cm.), color lithograph.

BERGEVIN, A.

$649* *Avranches, Baie Du Mont Saint-Michel, c. 1910,* excell. cond., (01-23-93, Ribeyre/Baron, #50, illus.), 47¼ x 31½ in., (120 x 80 cm.), poster (BP 425, DM 1032, FR 3491, Y 81,227).

BERGHEER, Eduard   1901-1979

$62* *Wustenstadt, 1975,* s., (09-25-92, Granier, #2751), 5M, x 8¼ in., (15 x 21 cm.), lithograph on board (BP 36, DM 92, FR 311, Y 7483).

BERGMAN, Henry Eric   1893-1958

$208* *Christmas Eve,* #85/100, s., t. mono. block, (05-10-93, Hodgins, #168), 4¾ x 4¼ in., (12.1 x 10.8 cm.), wood-cut on paper (BP 136, DM 334, FR 1127, Y 23,243, C$ 264).

BERGNER, Audrey

$263* *Merry-Go-Round, Luna Park, St Kilda,* s. Audrey Bergner, i. A.P, (08-11-92, L. Joel, #37G), 19xn x 25xn in., (49 x 66 cm.), color screen print (BP 137, DM 386, FR 1307, Y 33,679, A$ 357).

BERINGUIER, Eugene   1874-1949

$1004* *Exposition D'Affiches Artistiques. Concours De Byrrh, Galerie Georges Petit, 1903,* Paris, Imp. Charles Verneau, cond. B+, (06-11-93, Boisgirard, #44), 31½ x 47¼ in., (80 x 120 cm.), poster (BP 660, DM 1632, FR 5501, Y 106,525).

BERKE, Hubert   1908-1979

BI *Der Evangelist Johannes, 1932,* s., d., i., est. DM 1,200, (12-05-92, Bassenge, #7053, illus.), 12¾ x 12Čxn in., (32.4 x 32.5 cm.), monotype, watercolored.

BI *Komposition In Grun Mit Blau Und Schwarz, 1950s,* s. Hubert Berke, foxing, est. DM 1,200-, (09-14-92, Venator/Hansten, #2447), image approx. 11xn x 16Bxn in., (30 x 43 cm.), color lithograph on Schoellers Hammer paper.

BERKMAN, Sybiel   American 20th cent.

$275* *"1", "2 Horn Plenty" And "7 The Melting Pot", 1951, 1952, 1957: Three,* Workshop Of Progress Scenes, each s., d. Sybiel Berkman in matrix, good cond., staining, (03-12-93, Skinner, #67, illus.), sight 9 x 12 in., (22.9 x 30.5 cm.), woodcuts on wove (BP 192, DM 458, FR 1556, Y 32,410).

BERKOWITZ, Leon   American contemporary

$70* *Five Exhibition Posters,* from "Middendorf Lane Gallery", Dec. 11 - Jan. 5, 2 s. Berkowitz, d.(19)79, (02-04-93, Sloan, #2925), each 24¼ x 18 in., (61.6 x 45.7 cm.), (BP 49, DM 115, FR 391, Y 8708).

BERLIT, Rudiger   1883-1939

$428* *Drei Akte, c. 1925,* mono., (12-05-92, Bassenge, #7055), 9Mxn x 11xn in., (23.9 x 29.4 cm.), woodcut on Japan (BP 268, DM 667, FR 2274, Y 53,029).

BERMAN, Eugene   Russian/American 1899-1972

$1176* *Milano, s.n. (Pietro Fornasetti), 1951: Forty-Five,* from *Viaggio In Italia* by Raffaele Carrieri, s. by artist in colophon, (11-15-92, Christie-Geneva, #321, illus.), 20xn x 15ℂ, in., (510 x 390 mm.), lithographs, 8 in color, on Rives (BP 773, DM 1876, FR 6319, Y 146,762, SF 1695).

BERMOND, A.

$199* *Hiver Comme Ete, Je Me Baigne A Agadir, c. 1950,* good cond., (03-13-93, Laurin, #88), 39ℂ, x 24Mxn in., (100 x 62 cm.), (BP 139, DM 331, FR 1126, Y 23,453).

BERMOND, Andre

$165* *Vals Casino,* Moullot, A- cond., fold through image, (08-06-92, Swann, #44, illus.), 39½ x 24½ in., (100.3 x 62.2 cm.), (BP 86, DM 244, FR 823, Y 21,046).

BERNARD, Edouard

$357* *Corset Ideale, 1922,* Vercasson, B+ cond., fold marks, repairs, (08-06-92, Swann, #46, illus.), 54 x 35½ in., (137.2 x 90.2 cm.), (BP 186, DM 527, FR 1781, Y 45,536).

$440* *Dance Panneaus: Two,* A cond., (08-06-92, Swann, #45, illus.), 11¼ x 33½ in., (28.6 x 85.1 cm.), (BP 230, DM 650, FR 2196, Y 56,122).

BERNARD, Emile   French 1868-1941

$181* *Alexandre Et Diomedes, c. 1918,* pen s., (05-15-93, Loudmer, #296), 11Mxn x 7¾ in., (290 x 197 mm.), sh 17B, x 11Ӿ, in., (290 x 197 mm.), wood engraving on wove (BP 118, DM 291, FR 978, Y 20,064).

$30,147* *Bretonneries, 1889: Set Of Eight,* small margins, s., d. in pl., (05-15-93, Loudmer, #294, illus.), smallest 9¾ x 12½ in., (247 x 317 mm.), largest 10Žxn x 13½ in., (247 x 317 mm.), zincographs on wove (BP 19,601, DM 48,491, FR 162,957, Y 3,341,869).

$116* *"La Fin De Satan", 1935: Set Of Seven,* illus., 1 of 120, d., s., (01-28-93, Pescheteau, #74), 18Žxn x 14Œxn in., (47.5 x 36 cm.), black etchings on Arches (BP 77, DM 184, FR 622, Y 14,403).

$5041* *La Lessive (Boyle Turner B3; Grivel 22), 1888,* s., losses, yellowing, (05-15-93, Loudmer, #293, illus.), 5Bxn x 15¾ in., (135 x 400 mm.), wood engraving on thin paper, contrecolle (BP 3278, DM 8108, FR 27,249, Y 558,807).

$807* *Sainte Vierge (Fragment De L'Adoration Des Bergers, 1889) (Grivel, 22),* s., d., stains, good cond., (05-15-93, Loudmer, #295, illus.), 11¼ x 7Žxn in., (285 x 180 mm.), sh 11Žxn x 9Bxn in., (285 x 180 mm.), watercolor wood cut on laid w/partial watermark (BP 525, DM 1298, FR 4362, Y 89,458).

$53* *Untitled,* s. in plate, (01-28-93, Pescheteau, #73), 18½ x 13¾ in., (47 x 35 cm.), etching on Japan ancien (BP 35, DM 84, FR 284, Y 6581).

$41* *"Venus Et Adonis" and "Cupidon": Two,* small margins, (05-06-93, Laurin, #9), etchings on wove (BP 26, DM 65, FR 217, Y 4511).

BERNARD, Francis

$1154* *Bal Des Petits Lits Blancs A L'Opera, c. 1930,* Editions Paul Martial, good cond., (11-19-92, Ribeyre/Baron, #129, illus.), 24Mxn x 15Žxn in., (62 x 39.5 cm.), poster (BP 760, DM 1840, FR 6198, Y 143,514).

$965* *Le Gaz, "Cuit, Chauffe, Eclaire", c. 1930,* ed. Paul Martial, very good cond., (11-19-92, Ribeyre/Baron, #11), 62Žxn x 47¼ in., (160 x 120 cm.), poster (BP 635, DM 1539, FR 5183, Y 120,010).

$1210* *Opera, Les Petites Lits Blanc, 1919,* Paul Martial, B-cond., tears, restoration, (08-06-92, Swann, #48, illus.), 60 x 45 in., (152.4 x 114.3 cm.), (BP 632, DM 1788, FR 6038, Y 154,337).

$715* *Salon Des Arts Menagers, 1930,* Paul-Martial, A- cond., cracking, (08-06-92, Swann, #47, illus.), 62 x 46½ in., (157.5 x 118.1 cm.), (BP 373, DM 1056, FR 3568, Y 91,199).

BERNDT(?)   German 20th cent.

BI *Landscapes: Group Of Four,* s., t., rippling, discoloration, est. $8/1,200, (12-04-92, Doyle, #75), largest 9¾ x 11½ in., (248 x 292 mm.), color woodblock print.

BERNEGGER, Alfred   Swiss 1912-1978

$111* *Selbstbildnis Mit Frau, 1934,* (09-04-92, Germann, #247), 16Žxn x 12 in., (430 x 305 mm.), linocut (BP 56, DM 156, FR 530, Y 13,663, SF 138).

BERNERS, Lord

$831* *To Visit Britains's Landmarks, Faringdon Folly, 1936,* ref. #471, cond. 3, defects, (10-13-92, Phillips-London, #101A), 29Žxn x 44M, in., (76 x 114 cm.), color lithograph (BP 484, DM 1217, FR 4136, Y 100,764).

BERNHARD, Lucian   1883-1972

BI *Internationale Automobil-Ausstellung, Berlin 1931,* pierced plastic tape, nicks, tears, sellotape stains, tape, est. BP 6/800, (02-04-93, Christie-S. Ken, #157, illus.), 27 x 37 in., (68.6 x 94 cm.), color lithograph.

$2994* *Steinway & Sons, 1910,* pierced plastic tape, creases, tears, lit., (02-04-93, Christie-S. Ken, #156, illus.), 27 x 37 in., (68.6 x 94 cm.), color lithograph (BP 2090, DM 4930, FR 16,717, Y 372,434).

BERNHARD, Ruth   German b. 1905

$935* *"Abigail With Turban", 1971,* s. on mount; s., t., d. verso mount, Dixon Collection, (11-16-92, Butterfield, #5847, illus.), 13¾ x 8 in., (349.9 x 203.6 mm.), photograph, gelatin silver print (BP 616, DM 1491, FR 5021, Y 116,279).

$2185* *"Classic Torso", 1952,* p.l., s. twice, t., photog.'s stamp, (05-23-93, Butterfield, #3315, illus.), 13½ x 10¼ in., photograph, gelatin silver print (BP 1423, DM 3573, FR 12,025, Y 241,517).

$550* *"Creation"*, 1936/1950's, ink s. on black mount, (11-16-92, Butterfield, #5846, illus.), 7½ x 9¼ in., (190.8 x 235.4 mm.), photograph, gelatin silver print (BP 362, DM 877, FR 2954, Y 68,399).

$4313* *"In The Box, Horizontal"*, 1962, p.l., s. twice, t., d., (05-23-93, Butterfield, #3314, illus.), 10½ x 19¼ in., photograph, toned gelatin silver print (BP 2809, DM 7052, FR 23,737, Y 476,733).

$3910* *In The Box-Horizontal*, 1962, p.l., s.; s., t., d., annot. No: 1 of 16 x 20 series, (04-08-93, Christie-NY, #474, illus.), 10ᴮ, x 19¼ in., (27 x 48.9 cm.), photograph, gelatin silver print (BP 2564, DM 6281, FR 21,262, Y 443,713).

$3080* *In The Box-Horizontal*, (1962), p.l., s. on mount, s., t., d., (10-13-92, Christie-NY, #526, illus.), 7½ x 13½ in., (19.1 x 34.3 cm.), photograph, gelatin silver print (BP 1794, DM 4512, FR 15,331, Y 373,469).

$3300* *In The Box-Horizontal*, s., s., d. by photog., 1962, p.l., (10-15-92, Sotheby-NY, #503A, illus.), 10½ x 19ℤ, in., (26.7 x 48.6 cm.), photograph, gelatin silver print (BP 2019, DM 4912, FR 16,658, Y 395,921).

$3575* *In The Box-Horizontal*, mounted, s. by photog., s., t., d. by photog. 1962, p.l., (10-15-92, Sotheby-NY, #503, illus.), 6ᴮ, x 12ᴮ, in., photograph, gelatin silver print (BP 2188, DM 5322, FR 18,046, Y 428,914).

$1361* *"In The Box-Vertical, 1962"*, p.l., mounted on card, s., s., t., d., 347 x 216mm, (05-07-93, Sotheby-London, #285, illus.), photograph, silver print (BP 862, DM 2152, FR 7251, Y 149,857).

$1610* *Joan Folding*, 1962, p.l., s.; s., t., d., (04-08-93, Christie-NY, #475, illus.), 10ᴮ, x 13¾ in., (27 x 34.9 cm.), photograph, gelatin silver print (BP 1056, DM 2586, FR 8755, Y 182,705).

$1100* *"Knees And Arm"*, 1976/1980's, s. mount; s., t., d. verso mount, lit., (11-16-92, Butterfield, #5844, illus.), 7ℭ, x 9¼ in., (187.7 x 235.4 mm.), photograph, gelatin silver print (BP 724, DM 1754, FR 5908, Y 136,799).

$575* *Nude Torso*, 1979, p. 1989, s., #45/50, (05-23-93, Butterfield, #3317, illus.), 7¼ x 5½ in., photograph, C-print (BP 374, DM 940, FR 3165, Y 63,557).

BI *"Star Shell, 1943"*, p.l., t., s., d., 275 x 354mm, est. BP 4/600, (05-07-93, Sotheby-London, #286, illus.), photograph, silver print.

BI *Starshell*, 1943/printed later, (05-16-93, Hindman, #331), 7½ x 9½ in., photograph, silver print.

$468* *"Starshell"*, 1943/1970's, s., t., d. verso, (11-16-92, Butterfield, #5848, illus.), 7½ x 9½ in., (190.8 x 241.7 mm.), photograph, gelatin silver print (BP 308, DM 746, FR 2513, Y 58,202).

$770* *Starshell, 1943*, photog.'s sig., notations, (04-07-93, Swann, #401, illus.), 11 x 14 in., photograph, silver print (BP 509, DM 1245, FR 4215, Y 87,480).

$330* *Starshell, 1943*, p.l., s., (06-13-93, Hindman, #426), 7½ x 9½ in., photograph, modern silver print (BP 216, DM 537, FR 1805, Y 34,726).

$1235* *"Two Forms, 1963"*, p.l., mounted on card, s., t., s., d., 340 x 257mm, (05-07-93, Sotheby-London, #287, illus.), photograph, silver print (BP 782, DM 1953, FR 6580, Y 135,983).

$990* *"Victorian House"*, 1963/1970's, s. mount; s., t. verso mount, (11-16-92, Butterfield, #5845, illus.), 13½ x 9½ in., (343.5 x 241.7 mm.), photograph, gelatin silver print (BP 652, DM 1578, FR 5317, Y 123,119).

BERNINGER, John E.

$5 *"Lehigh Canal"*, s., (09-24-92, Alderfer, #302), 5 x 5¾ in., (12.7 x 14.6 cm.), etching (BP 3, DM 7, FR 25, Y 601).

BERRIDGE, John

BI *"Brighton Pier, 1981"*, t., s., d., 300 x 235mm, est. BP 80/120, (05-07-93, Sotheby-London, #404), photograph, silver print.

BERROCAL, Miguel   Spanish b. 1933

$105* *"Jimenez De Arenos", 1988*, #38/100, d., s., (01-28-93, Pescheteau, #75), 19ℤn x 25ℤn in., (50 x 65 cm.), color serigraph (BP 69, DM 166, FR 563, Y 13,037).

$64* *Untitled, 1979*, s., d., full margins, good cond., (05-27-93, Sotheby-Amstrdm, #384), 13ℭ, x 22½ in., (340 x

572 mm.), colored etching on wove (BP 41, DM 103, FR 346, Y 6861, G 115).

$64* *Untitled, 1979*, s., d., full sheet, good cond., (05-27-93, Sotheby-Amstrdm, #385), sh 19¾ x 27ℤ, in., (502 x 689 mm.), relief print on wove (BP 41, DM 103, FR 346, Y 6861, G 115).

$102* *Untitled, 1979*, s., d., #160/190, full sheet, good cond., (05-27-93, Sotheby-Amstrdm, #386), sh 19¾ x 27ℤ, in., (502 x 689 mm.), reliefprint on wove (BP 65, DM 164, FR 552, Y 10,935, G 184).

BERRY, Carroll Thayer   American 1886-1978

$99* *"Bay Island, Maine Coast"*, s. Carroll Thayer Berry, very good cond., (09-27-92, Bakker, #251), image 10¼ x 12½ in., (26 x 31.8 cm.), color woodblock print (BP 58, DM 147, FR 496, Y 11,949).

$165* *"Church At Spurwink--Maine"*, (08-29-92, Young, #45), 7 x 10 in., (17.8 x 25.4 cm.), woodcut (BP 83, DM 232, FR 791, Y 20,345).

$165* *Limestone And Sail*, margins, s., (05-22-93, Collins, #27), 10 x 12 in., (25.4 x 30.5 cm.), wood engraving (BP 107, DM 268, FR 903, Y 18,192).

BI *Old Coaster On The Wind*, margins, s. Carroll Thayer Berry, t., est. $2/400, (10-24-92, Collins, #18), 13ᴍ, x 9 in., (35.2 x 22.9 cm.), color woodblock.

$220* *"Old Coaster-Before The Wind" and "Old Coaster-On The Wind": Two*, s., t., (05-16-93, Hindman, #543), each 13¾ x 8ᴹ, in., (34.9 x 22.5 cm.), color linocut (BP 143, DM 354, FR 1189, Y 24,388).

$220* *"Retired From The Sea" and "Pemaguid, Maine", 1947: A Pair*, s., very good cond., (07-19-92, Bakker, #9), one 9 x 12 in., (22.9 x 30.5 cm.), the other, image 7¾ x 9½ in., (22.9 x 30.5 cm.), woodblock print (BP 113, DM 321, FR 1084, Y 27,350).

BERSERIK, Herman   b. 1921

BI *Untitled, 1969*, s., d., num. proef5/5, margins, good cond.?, est. G 4/600, (12-09-92, Sotheby-Amstrdm, #492), 8ℭn x 8ℭn in., (208 x 208 mm.), color lithograph on wove.

$104* *Untitled, 1982*, s., d., #128/200, full margins, good cond., (12-09-92, Sotheby-Amstrdm, #491), 14ℭn x 19½ in., (360 x 495 mm.), etching on C.M. Fabriano wove (BP 66, DM 163, FR 557, Y 12,895, G 184).

BERSSENBRUGGE, Henri   1873-1959

$1202* *"Venetie", "Gondola" and "Ponte Paglia", 1930s-40s: Three*, one trimmed edges; each image ink i., ink t., pencil annots. w/exhib. labels, (10-29-92, Christie-London, #92), 15½ x 11½ in., (39.4 x 29.2 cm.), photograph, multiple gum prints (BP 770, DM 1849, FR 6273, Y 148,891).

BERTELLI, Luca, Publisher   ac. 1550-1580

BI *The Annunciation, c. 1575*, after Titian, 1575, (12-01-92, Christie-London, #50), P. 16½ x 10ℤn in., (419 x 275 mm.), engraving.

$1249* *The Martyrdom Of Saint Peter The Martyr, (Chiari 1), c. 1567*, trimmed, very good cond., (12-01-92, Christie-London, #49, illus.), P. 17ℭn x 23ᴮ, in., (437 x 600 mm.), engraving (BP 825, DM 1991, FR 6784, Y 155,503).

BERTHIER

$236* *Le Triomphe De Bacchus*, yellowed, good margins, (06-16-93, Ader Tajan, #22), 14ℭ, x 17ℤn in., (36.5 x 45.5 cm.), etching and stipple print (BP 157, DM 392, FR 1315, Y 25,171).

BERTHOLLE, Jean   b. 1909

BI *"Composition-1973"*, d. 73, s., est. FF4/600, (04-04-93, Pescheteau, #159), 19ℤn x 25>ℤn in., (50 x 65 cm.), color lithograph on Japan nacre.

BERTHON, Emile   French 1872-1909

BI *"Sarah Bernhardt", c. 1901*, s. in stone, from ed. 200, full margins, est. $1,500/2000, (03-12-93, Goldberg, #891, illus.), 25¾ x 19¾ in., (65.4 x 50.2 cm.), color lithograph on cream wove.

BERTHON, Paul   French 1872-1909

$605* *"Les Boules De Neige" (A. 53 2nd State B), 1900*, excellent cond., (10-31-92, Cleveland, #249, illus.), 17ᴮ, x 21 in., (44.8 x 53.3 cm.), color lithograph (BP 388, DM 931, FR 3158, Y 74,941).

BI *Les Boules De Neige, 1900,* s. in stone, s., num. 10/100, p. Chaix, margins, good cond.?, est. $1/1500, (09-21-92, Butterfield, #821), 15℃, x 21℃zn in., (391.2 x 537.5 mm.), lithograph in colors on wove.

$575* *Les Boules De Neige, 1900,* margins, apparently good condition, light-staining, (03-31-93, Butterfield, #5232), 15℃, x 21℃, in., (39.1 x 53.7 cm.), lithograph printed in colors on wove (BP 380, DM 925, FR 3142, Y 66,122).

$598* *Concert Mystique,* cond. A, (03-16-93, Boisgirard, #53), 19½ x 24℃zn in., (49.5 x 63 cm.), poster (BP 413, DM 994, FR 3379, Y 69,925).

BI *Les Elegantines, 1900,* s., #53/100, margins, apparently good condition, light-staining, est. $5/700, (03-31-93, Butterfield, #5231), 15¼ x 21¼ in., (38.7 x 54 cm.), lithograph printed in colors on wove.

$499* *La Femme A L'Oiseau,* cond. A, (03-16-93, Boisgirard, #54), 16℃zn x 21℃zn in., (42 x 53.5 cm.), poster (BP 345, DM 830, FR 2819, Y 58,349).

$546* *Lecons De Violon, 1898,* p. Chaix, margins, apparently good condition, (03-31-93, Butterfield, #5227), 7M, x 10½ in., (20 x 26.7 cm.), lithograph printed in colors on wove (BP 361, DM 878, FR 2984, Y 62,787).

$805* *Lecons De Violon, 1898,* s., larger format w/out text, p. Chaix, margins, good condition, water stain, tears, surface soiling, linen-backed, (03-31-93, Butterfield, #5230), 15M, x 21℃, in., (40.3 x 54.3 cm.), lithograph printed in colors on wove (BP 532, DM 1295, FR 4399, Y 92,571).

$1980* *Le Livre De Magda,* Imp. Chaix, A cond., (08-06-92, Swann, #49, illus.), 22½ x 15¼ in., (57.2 x 38.7 cm.), (BP 1034, DM 2926, FR 9880, Y 252,551).

$715* *"Le Livre De Magda",* Imp. Chaix Paris, (05-15-93, Dunning, #1034, illus.), 21¾ x 14½ in., (55.2 x 36.8 cm.), lithograph in color (BP 465, DM 1150, FR 3865, Y 79,260).

$748* *Le Livre De Magda, 1898,* p. Chaix, margins, apparently good condition, (03-31-93, Butterfield, #5228), 22℃ x 15 in., (56.8 x 38.1 cm.), lithograph printed in colors on wove (BP 495, DM 1203, FR 4087, Y 86,017).

BI *Le Livre De Magda/Poesies Par Armand Silvestre, 1898,* lit., rare, est. DM 2,400, (12-05-92, Bassenge, #7563), 25¼ x 19℃, in., (64.1 x 49.2 cm.), color lithograph.

$94* *"La Pointe De Brettville" (Arwas 33 2nd State B), 1899,* excellent cond., (10-31-92, Cleveland, #247), 11℃, x 23¾ in., (28.3 x 60.3 cm.), color lithograph (BP 60, DM 145, FR 491, Y 11,644).

$1495* *La Princesse Aux Crapaud,* w/out text, p. Chaix, margins, good condition, abrasion, crease, linen-backed, (03-31-93, Butterfield, #5230A, illus.), 22¾ x 17½ in., (57.8 x 44.5 cm.), lithograph printed in colors on wove (BP 988, DM 2405, FR 8169, Y 171,918).

BI *Queen Wilhelmena, 1901,* s. in stone, pub. Ullman Mfg. Co., full sheet, laid down, trimmed, good cond., light-staining, crease in image, surface scuffing, surface soiling, est. $4/600, (09-21-92, Butterfield, #822), 14½ x 12M, in., (369 x 327.6 mm.), lithograph in colors on wove.

$863* *Revue D'Art Dramatique, 1897,* p. Bourgerie&Cie., margins, apparently good condition, (03-31-93, Butterfield, #5226, illus.), 21½ x 13¾ in., (54.6 x 34.9 cm.), lithograph printed in colors on wove (BP 571, DM 1388, FR 4716, Y 99,241).

$770* *"Sa Tres Gracieuse Majeste La Reine Wilhelmine" (A. 61 2nd State B),1901,* excellent cond., (10-31-92, Cleveland, #250, illus.), 15¼ x 14 in., (38.7 x 35.6 cm.), color lithograph (BP 493, DM 1185, FR 4019, Y 95,380).

BI *"Sa Tres Gracieuse Majeste La Reine Wilhelmine" (Arwas 61), 1901,* 2nd state B, laid down, edges rough, est. $50/100, (05-15-93, Cleveland, #361), 17℃, x 21 in., (44.8 x 53.3 cm.), color lithograph.

$275* *Sa Tres Gracieuse Majeste La Reine Wilhelmine, 1901,* (05-24-93, Grogan, #377B), 15½ x 14¼ in., (39.4 x 36.2 cm.), color lithograph (BP 179, DM 450, FR 1513, Y 30,397).

$920* *Sainte Marie Des Fleurs, 1898,* p. Bourgerie & Cie., margins, good condition, handling creases, tears, stains, surface soiling, linen-backed, (03-31-93, Butterfield, #5229), 21¼ x 13℃zn in., (54 x 34.8 cm.), lithograph in colors on wove (BP 608, DM 1480, FR 5027, Y 105,796).

$1093* *Sarah Bernhardt, 1901,* margins, good condition, linen-backed, (03-31-93, Butterfield, #5233, illus.), 20 x 14¼ in., (50.8 x 36.2 cm.), lithograph printed in colors on wove (BP 723, DM 1758, FR 5973, Y 125,690).

BI *Source Des Roches,* p. Chaix, margins, good condition, staining, handling creases, repaired tear, stains, soiling, est. $4/600, (03-31-93, Butterfield, #5234), 14℃, x 17¾ in., (37.1 x 45.1 cm.), lithograph printed in colors on wove.

BI *"La Vierge Aux Lis", c. 1902,* s. in stone, full margins, tear, toning, soiling, good cond., est. $1,5/2,000, (03-12-93, Goldberg, #891A, illus.), 35¼ x 25½ in., (89.5 x 64.8 cm.), color lithograph on cream wove.

$99* *"Vision Antiques" (A. 39 2nd State B), 1899,* excellent cond., (10-31-92, Cleveland, #248), 11¼ x 23¾ in., (28.6 x 60.3 cm.), color lithograph (BP 63, DM 152, FR 517, Y 12,263).

BERTON, Armand   French 1854-1927

$307* *Etudes De Nus Feminins, c. 1900: Six,* s., two annot. fourth state, mat-staining, fingerprints, margins, (02-24-93, Picard, #11), etching or etching and aquatint on laid (BP 214, DM 498, FR 1690, Y 36,024).

BERTRAND, F.

BI *Alger, Reine Des Stations Hivernales,* fairly good cond., (03-13-93, Laurin, #30), 33Mzn x 26℃zn in., (85 x 66.5 cm.), .

BERTRAND, Huguette Arthur   b. 1922

$92* *Composition, 1962,* s. Hug. A. Bertrand, 74/260, (03-24-93, Kunsthallen, #32), color lithograph (BP 62, DM 150, FR 511, Y 10,810, DK 575).

$92* *Composition, 1962,* s. Hugh A. Bertrand, 36/38, (03-24-93, Kunsthallen, #34), color lithograph (BP 62, DM 150, FR 511, Y 10,810, DK 575).

$73* *Composition, 1962,* s. Hug. A. Bertrand, 33/50, (03-24-93, Kunsthallen, #33), color lithograph (BP 49, DM 119, FR 406, Y 8577, DK 460).

BERVE (after CALLET)

$825* *"Louis Seize" and "Marie Antoinette": A Pair,* (05-19-93, Doyle, #55), 25 x 19 in., (63.5 x 48.3 cm.), hand colored engraving (BP 536, DM 1341, FR 4518, Y 91,332).

BESLER, Basilius

$2046* *Hortus Eystettensis, 1613: Ten,* full margins, defects from binding, staining, good cond., (10-27-92, Phillips-London, #164), sheet 20M, x 16½ in., (530 x 419 mm.), wood engraving on rough handmade (BP 1293, DM 3136, FR 10,640, Y 250,275).

BESNARD, Albert   French 1849-1934

BI *La Dame En Noir (C. 83, D. 97), 1890,* 3rd final state, s., margins, good cond., discoloration, hinge remains, surface soiling, notations, est. $6/800, (05-19-93, Butterfield, #2037), 9℃ x 6¼ in., (238 x 159 mm.), etching w/drypoint and roulette on Japan.

$303* *Le Deuil (D. 51), 1886,* s., annot. Tiree a 100, plate 5 from la Femme, full margins, god cond., light-staining, discoloration, creases, surface soiling, (02-24-93, Butterfield, #2900), 12½ x 9¾ in., (318 x 248 mm.), etching on Van Gelder Zonen laid (BP 211, DM 492, FR 1668, Y 35,555).

$253* *Le Deuil (Delteil 51), c. 1886,* s., from series La Femme, (12-04-92, Bassenge, #6754), 12℃zn x 9℃, in., (31 x 24.5 cm.), etching on hand-made (BP 162, DM 403, FR 1367, Y 31,586).

$400* *La Femme A La Pelerine (L.D. 86), 1889,* fifth state of six, d., ded., s., yellowed, good margins, (06-11-93, Picard, #6), 9¼ x 6℃, in., (235 x 156 mm.), etching and drypoint on laid (BP 263, DM 650, FR 2192, Y 42,440).

$289* *L'Accouchement (Ch. Coppier, num. 43; L.Delteil, num. 49), 1886,* from "La Femme" series, definitive state annot., s., large margins, (04-02-93, Picard, #25), 12℃, x 9℃, in., (31.5 x 24.5 cm.), etching and drypoint (BP 190, DM 464, FR 1578, Y 32,904).

$784* *La Mere Malade (Ch.C., num. 75; L.D., num. 90), 1891,* 3 out of 5, ink d., s., large margins, (04-02-93, Picard, #27), etching and drypoint (BP 516, DM 1260, FR 4279, Y 89,263).

$542* *La Muse Accoudee (Delteil 17 III), 1884,* s., (12-04-92, Bassenge, #6753), 9℃zn x 7℃zn in., (23.6 x 18 cm.), etching on Ingres hand-made (BP 348, DM 863, FR 2928, Y 67,665).

$818* *PLM. Lac D'Annecy, Talloires,* fairly good cond., (03-15-93, Arcole, #3, illus.), 40≥n x 29¾ in., (103 x 75.5 cm.), (BP 570, DM 1359, FR 4619, Y 96,896).

$150 *La Paix Par La Victoire, 1917,* Maquet, significant damage, (09-24-92, Alderfer, #317), 31 x 44 in., (78.7 x 111.8 cm.), (BP 88, DM 222, FR 755, Y 18,044).

$1062* *Profil De Jeune Femme,* (06-04-93, Bassenge, #5624, illus.), 10ℂ, x 7ℤn in., (26.4 x 19.8 cm.), etching on vellum (BP 703, DM 1725, FR 5813, Y 114,538).

$1199* *La Robe De Soie (L. Delteil 66), 1887,* s., definitive state, good margins, (06-11-93, Picard, #5), 14½ x 9¼ in., (368 x 235 mm.), etching, aquatint in bistre on laid (BP 788, DM 1949, FR 6570, Y 127,215).

BESNOU, D.

$602* *3 Heures De Paris (...) Boulogne Sur Mer, c. 1895,* Paris, Imp. E. Marx, cond. A-, (06-11-93, Boisgirard, #45), 54ℬn x 36¼ in., (138 x 92 cm.), poster (BP 396, DM 978, FR 3299, Y 63,873).

BESSE, S.

$209* *Ch. De Fer Algeriens: Le Sud Algerien. "Nuit Saharienne",* very good cond., (03-13-93, Laurin, #31, illus.), 38ℤn x 24Mn in., (99 x 62 cm.), (BP 146, DM 348, FR 1183, Y 24,632).

BESY, Paul

$385* *"Indian Woman Holding Child", "Indian Women Carting Jugs Of Water OnTheir Heads", "Indian Warrior With Facial Tattoos" and "Indian In 'Dance Of The Dead' Ritual Dress", 1938: Four,* w/Paul Besy's sig., d., (04-07-93, Swann, #558, illus.), each approx. 9½ x 6½ in., photograph, silver print (BP 254, DM 623, FR 2107, Y 43,740).

BETTERMANN, Gerhard b. 1910

$109* *Die Marsch, 1939,* block t., s., d., stained, (09-25-92, Granier, #2756), 7ℂ, x 15M, in., (18.8 x 40.3 cm.), sheet 10¼ x 18¼ in., (18.8 x 40.3 cm.), woodcut on transparent paper (BP 64, DM 162, FR 546, Y 13,156).

BETZLER, Emil b. 1892

$993* *Strassenszene Mit Motorradfahrer Vor Einem Friseurladen, c. 1920,* s., (06-05-93, Bassenge, #5919, illus.), 9ℂn x 12ℂn in., (23.4 x 31 cm.), drypoint on hand-made (BP 654, DM 1610, FR 5426, Y 106,522).

BEUGNET (after)

$39* *Costumes,* (09-18-92, DuMouchelle, #2505), 4½ x 8 in., (11.4 x 20.3 cm.), engraving (BP 22, DM 58, FR 200, Y 4859).

BEUYS, Joseph German 1921-1986

$1100* *3-Tonnen Edition: Recto And Verso (S. 74), 1973,* s. in marker, stamped, pub. Edition Staeck, good cond., (11-07-92, Sotheby-NY, #521), sheet 18¼ x 18 in., (464 x 457 mm.), silkscreen p. on recto and verso on a soft (molle) sheet of PVC (BP 719, DM 1756, FR 5936, Y 135,769).

BI *3-Tonnen-Edition (Schellmann 74 c), 1973-85,* ink s., pub. Edition Staeck, good cond., est. G 1/1,500, (12-09-92, Sotheby-Amstrdm, #494), sheet 18ℤ, x 18ℤ, in., (46 x 46 cm.), silkscreen on PVC foil.

$328* *"7000 Eichen",* from Dokumenta VII, Kassel, gold pencil s., num. 143, pub. by Free International University, (11-13-92, Koller, #5247), 5ℤn x 4ℤ, in., (14.8 x 10.4 cm.), postcard on print paper (BP 212, DM 515, FR 1736, Y 40,710, SF 464).

$205* *Affiche Kunst In Europa, 1980,* s., (11-13-92, Koller, #5251), 14≥n x 31ℤ, in., (37 x 79 cm.), offset on paper (BP 132, DM 322, FR 1085, Y 25,444, SF 290).

$1809* *Bein (S 95), 1961,* s., d., num., (06-05-93, Schoppmann, #730), 12ℂ, x 12ℂ, in., (31.5 x 31.5 cm.), woodcut on hand-made (BP 1191, DM 2933, FR 9885, Y 194,057).

$1805* *Celtic Kinloch Rannoch, 1980,* s., num., Edition Demarco, (11-28-92, Schoppmann, #416), 55ℤ, x 12ℂ in., (140 x 31.5 cm.), offset w/6 color photographs on light cardboard (BP 1191, DM 2876, FR 9762, Y 224,642).

BI *Countdown (Schellmann-Kluser 291), 1981,* s., #1630/2000, est. DM 1,500, (06-12-93, Hauswedell/Nolt, #39, illus.), 31ℬn x 21¼ in., (79.5 x 54 cm.), color offset on wove.

$3575* *DM 90.000 (S. 463), 1982,* s. verso, #97/100, pub. Edition Faktotum Art, good cond., (11-07-92, Sotheby-NY, #524, illus.), overall size 27½ x 19¾ in., (699 x 502 mm.), facsimile print w/collage (BP 2337, DM 5708, FR 19,293, Y 441,249).

$650* *Einsteinzeit, 1984,* s., (11-28-92, Schoppmann, #428), 11ℤn x 16≥n in., (29.7 x 42 cm.), serigraph on paper (BP 429, DM 1036, FR 3515, Y 80,896).

BI *Erdtelephon (Schellmann-Kluser 90), 1973,* s., #87/100, Schellmann & Kluser, est. DM 12,000, (06-12-93, Hauswedell/Nolt, #37), 26ℂn x 23ℬ, in., (66.5 x 60 cm.), screen print on picture.

$2723* *Flug Des Adlers Ins Tal Und Zuruck (Schellmann 250), 1978,* s., num., #25/120, tears, (05-27-93, Lempertz, #615, illus.), 40≥n x 10¼ in., (103 x 26 cm.), color offset print (BP 1744, DM 4369, FR 14,727, Y 291,917).

BI *"Flug Des Adlers Ins Tal Und Zuruck", 1978,* #61/120, s., Edizioni Lucio Amelio, Napoli, est. SF 4, 5/5,000, (12-05-92, Mangisch, #522), 40≥n x 10¼ in., (103 x 26 cm.), lithograph on grey cardboard.

$1323* *Flug Des Adlers Ins Tal Und Zuruck, Flight Of The Eagle Into The Valley And Back (S. 195), 1978,* s., #11/120, pub. Lucio Amelio Editions, cockling, skinned patch, very good cond., sold after sale, (05-11-93, Christie-NY, #375, illus.), sheet 40½ x 10¼ in., (102.9 x 26 cm.), lithograph in violet on wove (BP 845, DM 2084, FR 7022, Y 145,529).

$248* *Food For Thought (Sch. 206), 1977,* s., stamped, (06-08-93, Karl/Faber, #558), approx. 34ℬ, x 6½ in., (88 x 16.5 cm.), offset on Maschinen hand-made (BP 163, DM 402, FR 1355, Y 26,341).

$2526* *Fragment 6, 1977,* 1 sheet of: Minneapolis-Fragmente, i. University of Minneapolis 1974, s., stamp, (11-28-92, Schoppmann, #415), 25ℂn x 35ℤn in., (64 x 89 cm.), lithograph in black on BFK Rives (BP 1667, DM 4024, FR 13,661, Y 314,375).

$5559* *Gletscher (Schellmann 88),* 1950/(1973-74), s., d., num., pub. Propylaen, streaked, (12-01-92, Karl/Faber, #379, illus.), 4½ x 14≥n in., (11.5 x 37 cm.), woodcut in brown on wove (BP 3673, DM 8860, FR 30,196, Y 692,107).

$369* *"Hase Fur Den Frieden",* silver pencil, s., num. 92, pub. by Free International University, (11-13-92, Koller, #5248), 5ℤn x 4ℤ, in., (14.8 x 10.4 cm.), postcard on art print paper (BP 238, DM 579, FR 1953, Y 45,799, SF 522).

$1702* *Hirsch-Schadel (S 524), 1985,* s., num., (06-05-93, Schoppmann, #729), 17ℤ, x 12ℬ\ in., (43.5 x 32 cm.), etching (BP 1120, DM 2759, FR 9301, Y 182,579).

$5808* *Hirschkopf (Sch. 406 B), 1985,* s., num., from the series Tears, ded., pub. Grafos, (12-01-92, Karl/Faber, #381, illus.), 3ℂ, x 4ℬn in., (8.5 x 11 cm.), etching in brown on wove (BP 3837, DM 9257, FR 31,548, Y 723,108).

$2835* *Hirschkopf (Sch. 526 B), 1985,* s., num., (06-08-93, Karl/Faber, #561, illus.), approx. 3ℂ, x 4ℬn in., (8.5 x 11 cm.), etching on white wove (BP 1864, DM 4600, FR 15,492, Y 301,115).

$5017* *Hirschkuh (Schellmann 316), 1979,* s., num., #116/180, (05-27-93, Lempertz, #619, illus.), 22ℂn x 29ℤn in., (56.3 x 76 cm.), color lithograph on wove (BP 3213, DM 8050, FR 27,134, Y 537,843).

BI *Im Kopf Und Im Topf (Schellmann 268), 1978,* s., t., #XIX/XXX, est. DM 1,800, (05-27-93, Lempertz, #616), 38ℤn x 26M, in., (99 x 68.2 cm.), serigraph on board.

$1650* *Initiation Gauloise (S. 190), 1976,* s., d., t., #74/185, pub. Verlag Schellmann & Kluser, full sheet, good cond., scuff mark, (11-07-92, Sotheby-NY, #522, illus.), sheet 21¾ x 29¾ in., (552 x 756 mm.), lithograph p. in colors on oil paper (BP 1079, DM 2635, FR 8904, Y 203,653).

BI *Initiation Gauloise, 1976,* s., i., #65/185, est. DM 2,900, (09-18-92, Schloss Ahlden, #976, illus.), 21¾ x 29ℬ in., (55.3 x 75.2 cm.), color lithograph on Oldruck paper.

$935* *Installation (S. 165), 1977,* s., num. 94/100, good cond., rubbed area, wear, pencil notations, (02-24-93, Butterfield, #3003, illus.), 12 x 17 in., (305 x 432 mm.), offset lithograph on heavy gray paper (BP 652, DM 1518, FR 5146, Y 109,716).

$542* *James Joyce*, s., num., (11-28-92, Schoppmann, #431), 11¾ x 8¼ in., (29.8 x 21 cm.), offset on cardboard (BP 358, DM 863, FR 2931, Y 67,455).

$1184* *"Junger Hase"*, s., h.c., 15/50, ded., (11-21-92, Arnold, #1, illus.), 12B, x 9Zzn in., (32 x 25 cm.), etching (BP 780, DM 1888, FR 6359, Y 147,245).

$1840* *Katalog Museum Monchengladbach (Schellmann 4)*, copy 50 of 330, pub. Stadtisches Museum, time staining, orig. box, 210 x 170 x 30mm, (05-11-93, Christie-NY, #370), piece of felt stamped in brown and the num. museum catalog of 2 leporellos and checklist of exhib. on wove (BP 1175, DM 2899, FR 9766, Y 202,398).

$6325* *Letter From London (S. 157), 1977,* s., d. 1974, #107/115, pub. Matthieu Press, scuffs, image nicks, good cond., 35 x 46 1/2 x 7/8in., (05-11-93, Christie-NY, #372, illus.), lithograph in white and black on wood (BP 4038, DM 9964, FR 33,572, Y 695,743).

$4607* *"Letter From London" (Sch. 194), 1974/77),* s., d., i., state proof 1/1, (06-08-93, Karl/Faber, #557, illus.), approx. 35Zzn x 46Zzn in., (89 x 118.2 cm.), lithograph (BP 3029, DM 7475, FR 25,175, Y 489,326).

$1417* *Meerengel Robbe 2 (Sch. 426 B), 1982,* from the series Zirkulatinszeit, num., s., pub. Grafos-Verlag, (06-08-93, Karl/Faber, #560, illus.), approx. 3Z, x 5½ in., (8 x 14 cm.), color etching and aquatint on gray hand-made (BP 932, DM 2299, FR 7743, Y 150,505).

BI *Minneapolis-Fragments: Plate 2, 5 And 6, 1977:* Three, s., i. AP, Schellmann & Kluser blindstamps, excell. cond., est. $7/8,000, (05-11-93, Christie-NY, #373, illus.), each sheet 25C, x 35 in., (645 x 889 mm.), lithograph on white Rives.

BI *Minneapolis-Fragments: Plates 2, 4 And 6, 1977:* Three, s., num. III/VI, pub. Schellmann & Kluser, cockling, excell. cond., est. $7,5/8,500, (05-11-93, Christie-NY, #374, illus.), each sheet 25C, x 35¼ in., (645 x 895 mm.), lithograph in white on black on Rives.

$2164* *Der Motor (Schellmann 336), 1980,* #65/230, pencil s., stamped, (11-20-92, Lempertz, #459), 27Mzn x 38Bzn in., (69.7 x 97.3 cm.), color offset on thin cardboard (BP 1425, DM 3450, FR 11,622, Y 269,121).

$4692* *Neues Vom Gold: Diptych,* plate sig., num., (11-28-92, Schoppmann, #414), 12Zzn x 9¾ in., (32.2 x 24.8 cm.), color serigraph (BP 3097, DM 7475, FR 25,376, Y 583,945).

BI *Neues Von Gold, 1983,* silverpen s., pub. Staeck, good cond.?, est. G 800/1,200, (12-09-92, Sotheby-Amstrdm, #498), sheet 9Zzn x 12Zzn in., (230 x 330 mm.), offset lithograph.

$863* *Pass Fur Eintritt In Die Zukunst (S. 125), 1974,* s., #33/200, pub. Lucio Amelio Editions, artist's stamp, split, stains, (05-11-93, Christie-NY, #371), sheet 16½ x 11B in., (419 x 295 mm.), graphite on smooth wove (BP 551, DM 1359, FR 4581, Y 94,929).

BI *Robbe (Schellmann 390), 1981,* s., #2/150, est. DM 4,500-, (05-27-93, Lempertz, #620, illus.), 38Zzn x 23Mzn in., (98.6 x 59.6 cm.), color lithograph on hand-made.

$2126* *"Robbe" (Sch. 390), 1981,* s., t., num., (06-08-93, Karl/Faber, #559, illus.), sh approx. 39C, x 23B, in., (100 x 60 cm.), color lithograph on wove (BP 1398, DM 3450, FR 11,617, Y 225,810).

$1844* *Schamanentrommel,* s., num., (06-05-93, Schoppmann, #728), 14Zzn x 11 in., (38 x 28 cm.), color etching on thin paper (BP 1214, DM 2990, FR 10,077, Y 197,812).

$2222* *Schiefertafel (Schellmann 52),* stamped, s., #150/200, (05-27-93, Lempertz, #612, illus.), 6Zzn x 9Zzn in., (17.3 x 25.3 cm.), print w/serigraph (BP 1423, DM 3565, FR 12,017, Y 238,208).

$390* *"Das Schweigen Von Marcel Duchamp Wird Uberbewertet" (Schellmann 74 A), 1973-85,* s., from the 3 Tonnen-Edition, num., (06-08-93, Karl/Faber, #556), approx. 18Z, x 17Zzn in., (46 x 45.5 cm.), serigraph reworked w/oil color on PVC foil (BP 256, DM 633, FR 2131, Y 41,423).

$24,750* *Show Your Wound,* exec. 1977, prov., lit., (11-18-92, Sotheby-NY, #293, illus.), 42¼ x 31¼ in., (107.3 x 79.4 cm.), photographic negative and black film between glass plates in iron frame (BP 16,296, DM 39,461, FR 132,922, Y 3,077,975).

$246* *So Kann Die Parteiendiktatur Uberwunden Werden, 1971,* s., (11-13-92, Koller, #5250), 28¾ x 20Zzn in., (73 x 51 cm.), serigraph p. on both sides of plastic paper bag (BP 159, DM 386, FR 1302, Y 30,532, SF 348).

$3300* *Spu Ib/Trace Ib (S. and K. 107b), 1974,* s., #27/98, pub. Heiner Bastian in Propylaen Verlag, excellent cond., (11-09-92, Christie-NY, #248, illus.), 20½ x 28C, in., (521 x 721 mm.), colored lithograph on pale green laid Zerkall (BP 2182, DM 5268, FR 17,799, Y 409,531).

$3300* *Spur Ia/Trace Ia (Schellmann and Kluser 107a), 1974,* s., #27/98, pub. Heiner Bastian in Propylaen Verlag, excell. cond., (11-09-92, Christie-NY, #247, illus.), 20½ x 28C, in., (521 x 721 mm.), colored lithograph on pale green laid Zerkall (BP 2182, DM 5268, FR 17,799, Y 409,531).

$3520* *Spur Ic/Trace Ic (S. and K. 107c), 1974,* s., #27/98, pub. Heiner Bastian in Propylaen Verlag, excellent cond., (11-09-92, Christie-NY, #249, illus.), 20½ x 28C, in., (521 x 721 mm.), colored lithograph on pale green laid Zerkall (BP 2327, DM 5619, FR 18,986, Y 436,833).

$3300* *Spur Id/Trace Id (S. and K. 107d), 1974,* s., #27/98, pub. Heiner Bastian in Propylaen Verlag, excell. cond., (11-09-92, Christie-NY, #250, illus.), 28C, x 20½ in., (721 x 521 mm.), colored lithograph on pale green laid Zerkall (BP 2182, DM 5268, FR 17,799, Y 409,531).

$1083* *Tafel Hamburg I-III, 1980,* s., gebraunt, (11-28-92, Schoppmann, #426), 14B, x 10Zzn in., (37.2 x 27.2 cm.), serigraph on light cardboard (BP 715, DM 1725, FR 5857, Y 134,785).

$388* *Tafel I (Schellmann/Kluser 260.I), 1980,* s., (05-26-93, Dorling, #2561), 5M, x 8¼ in., (15 x 21 cm.), serigraphy on cardboard (BP 251, DM 633, FR 2131, Y 42,156).

$540* *Tafel III (Sch. 260 c), 1980,* s., (12-01-92, Karl/Faber, #380), 14Zzn x 10B, in., (37 x 27 cm.), serigraph on cardboard (BP 357, DM 861, FR 2933, Y 67,231).

$1480* *"Taucherin",* museum edit., IX/XXV, (11-21-92, Arnold, #3, illus.), 16Zzn x 12B, in., (42 x 32 cm.), etching (BP 974, DM 2360, FR 7948, Y 184,057).

$1579* *Topfspiel (Schellmann 424), 1982,* 33/75, s., (06-24-93, Germann, #249, illus.), 17Zzn x 12Bzn in., (446 x 312 mm.), etching (BP 1039, DM 2560, FR 8628, Y 169,384, SF 2300).

$1298* *Tramstop (Schellmann 160), 1977,* s., num., (06-23-93, Kornfeld, #209), serigraph on cardboard (BP 882, DM 2196, FR 7388, Y 141,410, SF 1955).

$650* *Der Ubeseigbare, 1979,* s., d., num., (11-28-92, Schoppmann, #429), 33Zzn x 23Bzn in., (84 x 59.2 cm.), serigraph on weissem paper (BP 429, DM 1036, FR 3515, Y 80,896).

$1760* *Untitled: Three,* each s. Joseph Beuys, prov., (11-17-92, Christie-E, #106, illus.), two 12Zzn x 9 in., (33 x 22.9 cm.), one 9 x 12Zzn in., (33 x 22.9 cm.), unique offset lithograph (BP 1159, DM 2806, FR 9452, Y 218,878).

$237* *Urauffuhrung! Maifest Im Kunstverein Hannover, 1973,* red China ink, s., (04-21-93, Germany, #282), 32 x 23Mzn in., (813 x 595 mm.), offset print (BP 154, DM 379, FR 1281, Y 26,237, SF 345).

$880* *The Warhol-Beuys Event (S. 319), 1979,* s., pub. Free International University, good cond., soiling, creases, (11-07-92, Sotheby-NY, #523), 11¾ x 8¼ in., (297 x 210 mm.), (297 x 210 mm.), booklet w/brown paint (BP 575, DM 1405, FR 4749, Y 108,615).

$1265* *Zirkulationszeit (S. 316), 1982,* from Suite Zirkulationszeit, s., #22/75, pub. Grafos Verlag, full margins, surface soiling, staining, very good cond., (05-11-93, Christie-NY, #376, illus.), sheet 26 x 19¾ in., (660 x 502 mm.), etching in black and blue on Arches (BP 808, DM 1993, FR 6714, Y 139,149).

BEVERLOO, C. van (called CORNEILLE)   b. 1922

$180* *"L'Oiseau Vert", 1979,* #47/250, d., s., (10-18-92, Pescheteau, #111), 19Zzn x 25Zzn in., (50 x 65 cm.), lithograph in colors on velin (BP 109, DM 266, FR 903, Y 21,493).

BEWICK, Thomas   English 1753-1828

$193* *The Chillingham Bull,* foxing, (09-21-92, Selkirk, #181, illus.), image 7¼ x 9¼ in., (18.4 x 23.5 cm.), woodcut (BP 113, DM 286, FR 980, Y 23,854).

BEYER, Otto German 19th/20th cent.
$330* *"The Start," "The Double," "The Stone Wall," "The Finish," and "Kincsem": Five,* (10-18-92, Hindman, #513), larger 9½ x 10½ in., (24.1 x 26.7 cm.), hand colored lithographs (BP 202, DM 491, FR 1666, Y 39,592).

BEZEMER, Jan b. 1907
$128* *Circus, 1958,* s., t., d., i. Eigen Druk, margins, good cond., (05-27-93, Sotheby-Amstrdm, #560), 16Bzn x 21M in., (430 x 555 mm.), colored lithograph on wove (BP 82, DM 205, FR 692, Y 13,722, G 230).
$128* *Compositie 34, 1962,* s., t., d., margins, good cond., (05-27-93, Sotheby-Amstrdm, #561), 19Bzn x 24 in., (490 x 610 mm.), colored monotype on wove (BP 82, DM 205, FR 692, Y 13,722, G 230).
$141* *Drie Honden,* s., t., i. Eigen Druk, margins, good cond., (05-27-93, Sotheby-Amstrdm, #562), 19¾ x 27Mzn in., (502 x 697 mm.), colored lithograph on wove (BP 90, DM 226, FR 763, Y 15,116, G 253).
BI *Haan, 1954,* s., d., i. eigen druk, margins, good cond.?, prov., est. G 250/350, (12-09-92, Sotheby-Amstrdm, #499), 21B, x 17Bzn in., (550 x 440 mm.), color woodcut on wove.
BI *Vier Paarden,* s., t., i. Eigen Druk Mono, margins, good cond., est. Dfl. 3/400, (05-27-93, Sotheby-Amstrdm, #563), 19Czn x 15Mzn in., (488 x 392 mm.), colored monotype on wove.

BEZOMBES, Roger French b. 1913
$147* *"Auberge Van Gogh A Auvers",* s. in plate, E.A., s., (01-28-93, Pescheteau, #76), 20Azn x 23¼ in., (52.5 x 59 cm.), etching and aquatint (BP 97, DM 233, FR 788, Y 18,252).

BIAGIO, Civale Italian/American b. 1935
$5* *"Man, River, Landscape", 1975,* s., t., good cond., (05-15-93, Cleveland, #91), 12Z, x 16 in., (30.8 x 40.6 cm.), woodcut (BP 3, DM 8, FR 27, Y 554).

BIAIS, Maurice c. 1875-1926
$2168* *La Maison Moderne, c. 1900,* cond. B, (06-11-93, Boisgirard, #47), 42Bzn x 28¾ in., (107.5 x 73 cm.), poster (BP 1424, DM 3523, FR 11,879, Y 230,027).
$944* *La Scala, Germaine Gallois, 1901,* Paris, Imp. Artistique Minot, cond. B+, (06-11-93, Boisgirard, #46), 58Zzn x 42½ in., (149 x 108 cm.), poster (BP 620, DM 1534, FR 5173, Y 100,159).

BICKEL, Karl
$4840* *PKZ, So Kleidet, 1928,* Wolfsberg, A- cond., catalog cover lot, (08-06-92, Swann, #51, illus.), 50½ x 35 in., (128.3 x 88.9 cm.), (BP 2528, DM 7151, FR 24,152, Y 617,347).

BICKNELL, William H. American b. 1860
$770* *Rear Admiral George Dewey,* excell. cond., (02-13-93, Bourne, #210, illus.), etching (BP 542, DM 1277, FR 4321, Y 92,861).
$88* *"A Scribe" and "Group Of Early Printers": A Pair,* after Howard Pyle, s., by Bicknell and Pyle, c. 1903, bears Bibliophile Society Seal, (06-24-93, Boos, #621), each 17Zzn x 10Mzn in., (455 x 265 mm.), etching (BP 60, DM 150, FR 506, Y 9599).

BIELER, Andre Charles Canadian b. 1906
$160* *"Indians In Procession",* s., #4/10, t. verso, (03-16-93, Encans, #13), 25Z, x 19Czn in., (63.8 x 48.8 cm.), etching and embossing on paper (BP 110, DM 266, FR 904, Y 18,709, C$ 200).

BIERENBROODSPOT, Gerti b. 1940
BI *Labyrinth, 1975,* s., #90/140, good cond.?, sheet 700 x 1000 mm, est. G 3/500, (12-09-92, Sotheby-Amstrdm, #500), color lithograph on wove.
BI *Untitled, 1973,* s., d., #100/100, full margins, good cond., creases, soiling, est. G150/200, (12-09-92, Sotheby-Amstrdm, #501), 19½ x 19Mzn in., (495 x 493 mm.), color etching on wove.

BIGG, William Redmore (after)
$125* *"Black Monday Or The Departure For School" and "Duke Domum Or The Return From School": Two,* by John Jones, foxed, other defects, (06-16-93, Bonhams-Chelsea, #426), image 18 x 24½ in., (45.7 x 62.2 cm.), reprod. w/hand-coloring (BP 83, DM 208, FR 696, Y 13,332).
BI *Christening The Heir, 1799,* by William Ward, pub. William Ward, trimmed to thread margins, est. BP 200/250, (11-30-92, Phillips-London, #202), sheet 19 x 23¾ in., (483 x 603 mm.), mezzotint on wove.
$9* *A Cottage Girl Shelling Pease (sic),* by J. Ryder, trimmed, laid down, (02-17-93, Bonhams-Chelsea, #286), image 4½ x 3½ in., (11.4 x 8.9 cm.), stipple engraving (BP 6, DM 15, FR 50, Y 1075).
$108* *Saturday Evening The Husbandmans Return From Labour,* (10-15-92, Bonhams-Chelsea, #21), image 17¾ x 22½ in., (45.1 x 57.2 cm.), stipple engraving w/hand coloring (BP 66, DM 161, FR 545, Y 12,957).

BIGGS, Colonel R. A.
$1270* *"The Architecture Of Ahmedabad, The Capital Of Goozerat", 1866: Book,* p. t., green cloth, 4to., lit., (05-06-93, Christie-London, #12), photograph, 120 albumen prints (BP 805, DM 2000, FR 6734, Y 139,729).

BIGNOLOS, Rinet
BI *Fouras, La Presqu'Ile Verte Ses 3 Plages, 1933,* pub. Lucien Serre & Cie, for Chemins de fer de l'Etat; cond. 2, foxing, laid on linen, est. BP 4/600, (10-13-92, Phillips-London, #8), 39Czn x 24Mzn in., (99.5 x 62 cm.), color lithograph.

BIJL, Guillaume 20th cent.
$104* *Sculpture Trouvee, Tielt, 1987,* #43/100, pub. Promotie Actuele Kunst Tielt, margins, good cond.?, (12-09-92, Sotheby-Amstrdm, #515), sheet 23B, x 19Azn in., (600 x 500 mm.), color offset print on Job matted paper (BP 66, DM 163, FR 557, Y 12,895, G 184).

BILIOTTI, G.
$341* *Parisiana Cabriolle. Operette De MM. P.-L; Flers Et Alevy, c. 1900,* Paris, Imp. G. Bataille, cond. B, (06-11-93, Boisgirard, #48), 49B, x 37 in., (126 x 94 cm.), poster (BP 224, DM 554, FR 1868, Y 36,180).

BILL, G. and F.
$50* *"Bird's Eye View Of Mt. Vernon",* damage, restored tears in margins, (10-23-92, Garth, #633, illus.), 16 x 20 in., (40.6 x 50.8 cm.), hand colored lithograph (BP 31, DM 76, FR 259, Y 6098).

BILL, Max Swiss b. 1908
$6802* *"8x8", 1974: Eight,* #39/50, s., d., (11-13-92, Koller, #5252, illus.), image 3Zzn x 23B, in., (10 x 60 cm.), serigraph on wove (BP 4395, DM 10,678, FR 36,008, Y 844,235, SF 9628).
$410* *Combillation, 1988,* #28/50, s., d., stains, creases, (11-13-92, Koller, #5254), 47¼ x 11Azn in., (120 x 30 cm.), serigraph on wove (BP 265, DM 644, FR 2170, Y 50,887, SF 580).
$2308* *Constellations, 1974: Sixteen,* Societe Internationale d'Art XXe Siecle, Paris, #27/125, s., (11-20-92, Lempertz, #461), 20Czn x 14zn in., (51.2 x 37 cm.), color lithograph on Velin (BP 1520, DM 3680, FR 12,395, Y 287,029).
$1320* *Constellations, 1974: Sixteen,* complete portfolio, s., #20/125, w/colophon, text and t. page, p. Fernand Mourlot, pub. for Societe Internationale d'Arte XXe Siecle, very good cond., (10-28-92, Butterfield, #2908, illus.), 40 x 30 in., (101.6 x 76.2 cm.), color lithograph on Arches 88 (BP 841, DM 2039, FR 6922, Y 161,963).
BI *Constellations: Sixteen,* #20/125, s., est. SF 4/5,000, (04-21-93, Germann, #291, illus.), 19M, x 14Czn in., (505 x 360 mm.), color lithograph.
$194* *Farbkomposition In Geometrischen Feldern, 1970,* s., (09-25-92, Granier, #2761), 20½ x 20½ in., (52 x 52 cm.), sheet 31½ x 25C, in., (52 x 52 cm.), serigraph on board (BP 113, DM 288, FR 972, Y 23,416).
$593* *Komposition, 1969,* #10/100, s., d., (04-21-93, Germann, #288), 27C, x 19C, in., (695 x 492 mm.), color lithograph on Japan (BP 385, DM 948, FR 3205, Y 65,648, SF 863).
$860* *Komposition, 1971,* s., d., $44/75, blindstamp Erker Presse, (05-27-93, Lempertz, #621), 14¼ x 28Mzn in., (36.2 x 72.3 cm.), color serigraph on wove (BP 551, DM 1380, FR 4651, Y 92,196).
$1198* *Komposition, 1973,* #138/150, s., d., Erker Presse blindstamp, (09-04-92, Germann, #250, illus.), 24Zzn x 35Mzn in., (630 x 900 mm.), color lithograph (BP 600, DM 1679, FR 5716, Y 147,464, SF 1495).

$790* *Komposition, 1973,* 99/150, s., d., blindstamp, (06-24-93, Germann, #580, illus.), 24℃ x 35M℃n in., (630 x 900 mm.), color lithograph (BP 520, DM 1281, FR 4317, Y 84,746, SF 1150).

$474* *Komposition, 1979,* s., d., blindstamp, ded., (04-21-93, Germann, #153, illus.), 31½ x 25℃℃n in., (800 x 660 mm.), color lithograph (BP 308, DM 758, FR 2562, Y 52,474, SF 690).

$435* *Komposition, 1980,* s., d., blindstamp, (04-21-93, Germann, #289), 21¼ x 29℃, in., (540 x 740 mm.), color lithograph (BP 282, DM 695, FR 2351, Y 48,157, SF 633).

$284* *Komposition, 1985,* artist's proof, s., d., blindstamp, (04-21-93, Germann, #290), 14℃℃n x 11 in., (380 x 280 mm.), color lithograph (BP 184, DM 454, FR 1535, Y 31,440, SF 414).

BI *Max Bill, Transcoloration In Funf Quadraten, 1973: Five,* Meissner Edition, #19/70, s., d., num., frontispiece s., est. DM 3,000-, (05-27-93, Lempertz, #622), 32½ x 22℃℃n in., (82.5 x 58 cm.), color serigraph on white print paper.

$318* *Offenes Zentrum, 1972,* s., d., num. oeuvre Nr. 154, #12/75, blindstamp, (06-12-93, Hauswedell/Nolt, #41), 14℃n x 14℃n in., (36 x 36 cm.), color lithograph on BFK Rives (BP 208, DM 518, FR 1740, Y 33,463).

$307* *"Olympishce Spiele Munchen 1972", 1970,* s., d., num., (12-01-92, Karl/Faber, #382), 33M℃n x 24 in., (85 x 61 cm.), color serigraph on cardboard (BP 203, DM 489, FR 1668, Y 38,222).

$3633* *Portfolio. 16 Constellations. XXe Siecle, Paris, 1974,* s., (06-24-93, Germann, #579, illus.), 19M, x 14℃n in., (505 x 360 mm.), color lithograph (BP 2392, DM 5890, FR 19,852, Y 389,723, SF 5290).

$820* *Quadrat, Vier Farben, 1986,* #72/120, s., d., (11-13-92, Koller, #5255), 18℃℃n x 18℃n in., (46.5 x 46.5 cm.), serigraph on wove (BP 530, DM 1287, FR 4341, Y 101,775, SF 1160).

BI *Transcoloration In Funf Quadraten: Set Of Five,* s., d., #29/70, i. w/plate num., crayon s., num., p., pub. Meissner Edition, full margins, good cond., est. BP 1/1,200, (12-03-92, Sotheby-London, #613, illus.), sheet 31½ x 23℃, in., (800 x 600 mm.), silkscreens in colors.

$220* *Untitled,* s., d. 71, #40/90, (05-16-93, Hindman, #575), 29½ x 29½ in., (74.9 x 74.9 cm.), etching and aquatint (BP 143, DM 354, FR 1189, Y 24,388).

$901* *Vier Quadrate, 1971,* #3/200, s., d., (11-13-92, Koller, #5253), 16℃n x 16℃n in., (42 x 42 cm.), color serigraph on wove (BP 582, DM 1414, FR 4770, Y 111,828, SF 1276).

BILLE, Ejler

$126* *Composition, (N & M. 73), 1988,* s. Ejler Bille 88, 51/250, (09-30-92, Kunsthallen, #41), color lithograph (BP 71, DM 179, FR 604, Y 15,121, DK 690).

$147* *Komposition, (M. 15), 1971,* s. J. Birkmose, 1/2, (03-24-93, Kunsthallen, #43), color lithograph (BP 100, DM 240, FR 817, Y 17,272, DK 920).

$202* *Komposition, (M. 60), 1984,* s. Ejler Bille 84, prov., (03-24-93, Kunsthallen, #35), color lithograph (BP 137, DM 330, FR 1123, Y 23,734, DK 1265).

$184* *Komposition, (M. 65), 1987,* s. Ejler Bille 87, 137/200, (03-24-93, Kunsthallen, #40), color lithograph (BP 125, DM 301, FR 1023, Y 21,619, DK 1150).

$232* *Komposition, (N & M 60), 1984,* artist's proof, s. Ejler Bille 84, (09-30-92, Kunsthallen, #40), color lithograph (BP 131, DM 329, FR 1113, Y 27,841, DK 1265).

$63* *Komposition, (N & M 83), 1989,* s. Ejler Bille 89, 245/300, (09-30-92, Kunsthallen, #36), color lithograph (BP 36, DM 89, FR 302, Y 7560, DK 345).

$165* *Komposition, 1949,* s. Ejler Bille, (03-24-93, Kunsthallen, #41), offet print in colors (BP 112, DM 269, FR 917, Y 19,387, DK 1035).

$169* *Komposition, 1991,* s. Ejler Bille 91, 190/200, (09-30-92, Kunsthallen, #39), color lithograph (BP 95, DM 240, FR 811, Y 20,281, DK 920).

$169* *Komposition, 1991,* s. Ejler Bille 91, 189/200, (09-30-92, Kunsthallen, #38), color lithograph (BP 95, DM 240, FR 811, Y 20,281, DK 920).

$220* *Komposition, Bali 1990,* s. Ejler Bille, (03-24-93, Kunsthallen, #36), lithograph offset in colors (BP 149, DM 359, FR 1223, Y 25,849, DK 1380).

$128* *Kompositioner, (M. 70 and 75), 1988: Two,* s. Ejler Bille 88, (03-24-93, Kunsthallen, #38), color lithograph (BP 87, DM 209, FR 712, Y 15,039, DK 805).

$220* *Kompositioner, (M. 72-73), 1988: Two,* s. Ejler Bille, 221/250, (03-24-93, Kunsthallen, #39), color lithograph (BP 149, DM 359, FR 1223, Y 25,849, DK 1380).

$190* *Kompositioner, (N & M 74-75): Two,* s. Ejler Bille, 205/250, (09-30-92, Kunsthallen, #37), color lithograph (BP 107, DM 269, FR 911, Y 22,801, DK 1035).

$184* *Ornamentale Billeder III, (M. 11), 1971,* s. Ejler Bille, 79/120, (03-24-93, Kunsthallen, #42), color lithograph (BP 125, DM 301, FR 1023, Y 21,619, DK 1150).

$126* *Ornamentale Figurer III, (N & M 54), 1983,* s. Ejler Bille 83, (09-30-92, Kunsthallen, #34), color lithograph (BP 71, DM 179, FR 604, Y 15,121, DK 690).

$126* *Ornamentale Figurer III, (N & M 54), 1983,* s. Ejler 83, (09-30-92, Kunsthallen, #35), color lithograph (BP 71, DM 179, FR 604, Y 15,121, DK 690).

$165* *Ornamentale Figurer IV, 1983 (M. 55),* s. Ejler Bille 83, 5/125, (03-24-93, Kunsthallen, #37), color lithograph (BP 112, DM 269, FR 917, Y 19,387, DK 1035).

$293* *Untitled: Two,* s. 88, 235/250 and s. 89, 296/300, (09-29-92, B. Rasmussen, #281), lithograph in colors (BP 165, DM 414, FR 1412, Y 34,977, DK 1610).

BILLGREN, Ola   b. 1940

$179* *"Bildstoder": Four,* s., d. 79, 155/200, (04-17-93, Falkkloos, #43), 24℃℃n x 20℃℃n in., (63 x 51 cm.), color lithograph (BP 116, DM 286, FR 967, Y 19,904, SK 1320).

BINCK, Jakob   c. 1500-1569

$361* *Gotter Und Gottinnen (B. 26-45; Hollstein 75-94),* after Caraglio and Rosso, creases and stains, (12-04-92, Bassenge, #6050), engraving (BP 232, DM 575, FR 1950, Y 45,069).

BING, Ilse   American b. Germany 1899

$2860* *Arbre Et Chaise Aux Champs Elysees, 1931,* d. in ink, credit stamp on exhib. mount, (10-13-92, Christie-NY, #125, illus.), 11℃, x 8℃, in., (28.3 x 21.3 cm.), photograph, gelatin silver print (BP 1666, DM 4190, FR 14,236, Y 346,793).

BI *Blerancourt Tree Shadows, 1933,* s., d. by photog. on image, name stamp, t., d., est. $2/4,000, (10-15-92, Sotheby-NY, #445A, illus.), 8℃, x 11℃, in., (21.9 x 28.3 cm.), photograph, gelatin silver print.

$1955* *Couple, Coffee Table, Moulin Rouge, Paris, 1931,* ink s., d. recto; s., t., d., (04-08-93, Christie-NY, #163, illus.), 6℃, x 8M, in., (16.2 x 22.5 cm.), photograph, gelatin silver print (BP 1282, DM 3141, FR 10,631, Y 221,857).

$3738* *"Four Trees At Seine River, Paris", 1932,* s., d. by photog. in ink on image; s., d., t., (04-06-93, Sotheby-NY, #373, illus.), 8¼ x 11℃, in., photograph (BP 2469, DM 6022, FR 20,393, Y 426,323).

BI *Ile St. Louis, 1932,* s., d. in ink, Paris credit, d. stamp, est. $5/7,000, (10-13-92, Christie-NY, #126, illus.), 8¼ x 11℃, in., (21 x 28.3 cm.), photograph, gelatin silver print.

BI *New York Elevated, 1936,* photog.'s sig., d., est. $1,5/2,500, (04-07-93, Swann, #403, illus.), 8½ x 11 in., photograph, silver print.

$1840* *New York Skyline, 1936,* s., d. by photog. in ink on image, (04-06-93, Sotheby-NY, #372, illus.), 7℃, x 11℃, in., photograph (BP 1215, DM 2964, FR 10,038, Y 209,854).

BI *New York, El And Straw hat, 1936,* s., d. by photog. in ink on image, est. $3/4,000, (10-15-92, Sotheby-NY, #445, illus.), 11¼ x 8½ in., (28.6 x 21.6 cm.), photograph, gelatin silver print.

$2750* *New York, Wall Street With Car, 1936,* s., d. by photog. in ink on image, s., t., d. by photog., (10-15-92, Sotheby-NY, #446, illus.), 11℃, x 7℃, in., (28.3 x 18.7 cm.), photograph, gelatin silver print (BP 1683, DM 4093, FR 13,882, Y 329,934).

BI *Pont Alexandre III, Paris, 1934,* s., d. in ink, t., annot., est. $3/4,000, (10-13-92, Christie-NY, #127, illus.), 7½ x 11 in., (19.1 x 27.9 cm.), photograph, solarized gelatin silver print.

BI *Rockefeller Center, 1936,* s., d. by photog. in ink on image, est. $3/4,000, (04-06-93, Sotheby-NY, #374, illus.), 11 x 7℃, in., photograph.

BI *Self Portrait, 1945,* s., d.; s., t., d. verso, est. $4/5,000, (04-08-93, Christie-NY, #164, illus.), 5M, x 4Z\ in., (14.9 x 10.5 cm.), photograph, gelatin silver print.

BI *Staten Island, New York, 1936,* photog.'s sig., d.; sig, t., d. verso, est. $1,5/2,500, (04-07-93, Swann, #404, illus.), 11 x 8½ in., photograph, silver print.

BI *Two Anglers At The Seine, Paris, 1935,* s., d. in ink, t., (10-13-92, Christie-NY, #128, illus.), 7℃, x 11¼ in., (18.7 x 28.6 cm.), photograph, gelatin silver print.

BINGHAM, George Caleb (after)   American 1811-1879

$1100* *The Country Election (B. P9), 1854,* by John Sartain, pub. Goupil & Co., margins trimmed, good cond., light-staining, staining in image, taped, skinned areas, glue remains, foxing, staining, (02-24-93, Butterfield, #2622, illus.), 22 x 30½ in., (559 x 775 mm.), engraving, mezzotint & roulette on wove (BP 767, DM 1786, FR 6054, Y 129,078).

$880* *Stump Speaking,* engraving by Louis-Adolphe Gauthier, (05-28-93, Sloan, #2425, illus.), 22Z, x 30¼ in., (56.2 x 76.8 cm.), tinted engraving (BP 564, DM 1396, FR 4718, Y 94,360).

$3738* *Stump Speaking (Bloch P10), 1856,* by Louis-Adolphe Gautier, pub. Fishel, Adler & Schwartz, margins, good cond., tears, losses, soiling, image abrasions, long abraded area verso, (01-28-93, Sotheby-NY, #464, illus.), 22¼ x 30Z, in., (565 x 765 mm.), sh 30Z, x 34¾ in., (565 x 765 mm.), engraving, mezzotint and roulette on heavy cream wove (BP 2468, DM 5923, FR 20,043, Y 464,117).

BIRCH, William (after)

BI *The City Of New York In The State Of New York North America (S. & H.P. 1802-E-11; D. 245), c. 1802,* 2nd state of 3, engraved by Samuel Seymour, pub. William Birch, trimmed to image 3 sides, borderline below, center stains, soiling, title space tears, est. $10/14,000, (01-28-93, Sotheby-NY, #417, illus.), image 18M, x 24 in., (479 x 610 mm.), sheet 20¾ x 24 in., (479 x 610 mm.), engraving laid down.

BI *The City Of New York In The State Of New York North America (S. 7 H.P. 1802-E-11; D. 245), c. 1802,* 2nd state of 3, engraved by Seymour, pub. William Birch 1803, margins, touched-in tear/abrasion/scuff in image, tears, losses, letters partly penned-in, backed w/sheet of wove, est. $12/15,000, (01-28-93, Sotheby-NY, #418, illus.), image 18¼ x 23M, in., (464 x 606 mm.), sheet 20M, x 25℃, in., (464 x 606 mm.), hand-colored engraving.

BIRCK, A.

$518* *C.I.W.L. Et Orient-Express: Fete De Ghezireh Au Caire, 1896,* fairly good cond., (03-13-93, Laurin, #111, illus.), 61Zzn x 46Zzn in., (157 x 117 cm.), (BP 361, DM 862, FR 2932, Y 61,049).

BIRKEMOSE, Jens

$253* *Composition, 1985,* s. J. Birkemose 85, illus. in Sexus, 1/1, (09-30-92, Kunsthallen, #42), color lithograph (BP 143, DM 359, FR 1213, Y 30,361, DK 1380).

$73* *Komposition,* s. J. Birkemose, 1/2, (03-24-93, Kunsthallen, #44), color lithograph (BP 49, DM 119, FR 406, Y 8577, DK 460).

$73* *Komposition,* s. J. Birkmose, 1/2, (03-24-93, Kunsthallen, #45), color lithograph (BP 49, DM 119, FR 406, Y 8577, DK 460).

BIRKETT-FOSTER, M. (after)

$153 *"Children With Rabbits" and "Children Resting By A Cottage": A Pair,* (08-14-92, G.A. Key, #58), 8 x 7 in., (20.3 x 17.8 cm.), colored print (BP 80, DM 225, FR 760, Y 19,294).

BISCAINO, Bartolomeo   c. 1632-1657

$542* *Die Geburt Christi (B. 7, The Illustrated Bartsch 47),* reverse print, stained, (12-04-92, Bassenge, #6051), 15℃n x 10Zzn in., (38.6 x 27.8 cm.), etching (BP 348, DM 863, FR 2928, Y 67,665).

BISCAINO, Bartolomeo   Italian 1632-1657

BI *The Adoration Of The Kings (B. 8), c. 1620,* lightly bitten plate, plate tone, wiping scratches, 2nd (final) state, Daman's address, margins, repairs, stains, glued down, The Suida Manning Coll., est. $1/1,500, (05-13-93, Sotheby-NY, #213), 5 x 3M, in., (127 x 97 mm.), etching.

$4313* *The Adoration Of The Kings (B. 9), c. 1620,* 2nd state of 6, small margins, rubbed spot, foxmarks, good cond., ex-coll. L. Krones and Endris, The Suida Manning Coll., (05-13-93, Sotheby-NY, #214, illus.), 8¼ x 5M, in., (210 x 148 mm.), etching (BP 2832, DM 6964, FR 23,491, Y 481,523).

BI *The Holy Family (B. 21), c. 1650,* 2nd state of 3, trimmed, touches ink in image, repaired tear, center-crease, good cond., The Suida Manning Coll., est. $2/2,500, (05-13-93, Sotheby-NY, #217, illus.), 10 x 7¼ in., (253 x 185 mm.), etching.

$805* *The Mystic Marriage Of St. Catherine (B. 33), c. 1650,* surface dirt, good cond., The Suida Manning Coll., (05-13-93, Sotheby-NY, #219), 5¾ x 4½ in., (145 x 113 mm.), etching (BP 528, DM 1300, FR 4385, Y 89,874).

BI *The Nativity (B. 5), c. 1650,* lightly bitten plate, plate tone, wiping scratches, partial thread margins, repaired tear, stain, center crease, glued down, good cond., The Suida Manning Coll., est. $1/1,500, (05-13-93, Sotheby-NY, #210, illus.), 5 x 4 in., (128 x 100 mm.), etching.

BI *The Nativity (B. 7), c. 1650,* Daman's address, Remondini's address physically rubbed out, watermark, trimmed, foxmarks, glued, good cond., The Suida Manning Coll., est. $1,2/1,500, (05-13-93, Sotheby-NY, #212), 15½ x 10M, in., (393 x 277 mm.), etching.

BISCARETTI, C.

$148* *Anisetta Evangelisti Liquore Da Dessert (Ein Schimpanse Mit Flasche), 1925,* s. in stone, lit., (12-05-92, Bassenge, #7564), 54Zzn x 38℃n in., (138 x 97 cm.), color lithograph (BP 93, DM 231, FR 786, Y 18,337).

$660* *Anisetta Evangelisti Liquore Da Dessert, 1925,* Doyen, A- cond., (08-06-92, Swann, #52, illus.), 44 x 39 in., (111.8 x 99.1 cm.), (BP 345, DM 975, FR 3293, Y 84,184).

BISHOP, Isabel   American b. 1902

$690* *Encounter, c. 1935,* s., #28/50, full margins, good cond., (05-13-93, Sotheby-NY, #411), 8Z, x 5℃, in., (205 x 138 mm.), etching (BP 453, DM 1114, FR 3758, Y 77,035).

$880* *"Lunch Counter" (Teller 24), 1940, "Girl With Newspaper" (Teller 35), 1945, "Entrance To Union Square" (Teller 77), 1981, "Seven Students" (Teller 79), 1982-82 and "Girls At Counter" (Teller 81), 1982: Five,* s., full margins, pub. AAA 1978, 1981 and 1984, (05-27-93, Swann, #39), etching (BP 564, DM 1412, FR 4759, Y 94,340).

$605* *"Strap Hangers", "Five Women Walking", "Two With Coats" and "Girl Blowing Smoke Rings": Four,* 1st. s., soiling, tape, good cond., (06-11-93, Doyle, #16, illus.), etching, 2 w/aquatint (BP 398, DM 983, FR 3315, Y 64,191).

$302* *Two With Coats (Teller 65), 1968,* s., num. IX/XXV, p. 1981, good cond.?, (12-08-92, Swann, #20, illus.), 6M, x 4Β\ in., (17.5 x 11.7 cm.), etching w/aquatint (BP 189, DM 470, FR 1603, Y 37,432).

BI *"Two With Coats", "(Sipping Coffee)", "Five Women Walking" and "(Climbing Stairs)": Four,* 1st s., soiling, tape, good cond., est. $1/1,500, (06-11-93, Doyle, #18), etching and aquatint.

$230* *Union Square Man,* s., #VII/XXV, blindstamp, publisher, good cond., water stain, hinge remain, lightly skinned, (05-19-93, Butterfield, #1983), 3M, x 3 in., (98 x 76 mm.), etching on wove (BP 149, DM 374, FR 1260, Y 25,462).

BISHOP, Richard   American 1887-1975

$88* *Canada Geese,* s., d. 1924, (06-11-93, Freemn/Fine Art, #20), 7¾ x 10 in., (19.7 x 25.4 cm.), etching (BP 58, DM 143, FR 482, Y 9337).

$1100* *Etching For The 1936 Federal Duck Stamp: Three Canadian Geese,* s., i. Federal Duck Stamp Design accompanying stamp, (09-20-92, Hindman, #696, illus.), 5¾ x 8¾ in., (14.6 x 22.2 cm.), etching and drypoint on paper (BP 644, DM 1632, FR 5584, Y 135,954).

$605* *Flying Geese,* s. Federal Duck Stamp Design, Richard Bishop, excell. cond., (04-22-93, Guyette, #846D, illus.), etching (BP 391, DM 972, FR 3279, Y 66,520).

$138* *"Geese",* s., d. 1938, excell. cond., (10-02-92, Guyette, #630, illus.), image 8 x 5½ in., (20.3 x 14 cm.), etching (BP 80, DM 196, FR 657, Y 16,478).

$220* *"In The Bag",* s., d. 1940, excell. cond., (10-02-92, Guyette, #631, illus.), image 8 x 5½ in., (20.3 x 14 cm.), drypoint (BP 127, DM 313, FR 1048, Y 26,269).

$66* *"Rice Field Pintails" and "Through The Willows", 1936: Pair,* s., (12-11-92, DuMouchelle, #205), 10 x 8 in., (25.4 x 20.3 cm.), engravings (BP 42, DM 104, FR 356, Y 8167).

$193* *"Twilight",* s., d. 1939, excell. cond., (10-02-92, Guyette, #632, illus.), image 8 x 5½ in., (20.3 x 14 cm.), aquatint (BP 112, DM 275, FR 919, Y 23,045).

BI *Willow Ptarmigan,* s., d. (19)51, i. in plate, est. $125/175, (09-17-92, Sloan, #640), 5Zzn x 3Zzn in., (14.8 x 10 cm.), etching.

BI *"Willow Ptarmigan", 1951,* t., s., d., i. Christmas in plate, s., very good cond., est. $150/200, (05-15-93, Cleveland, #75), 15Zzn x 3Zzn in., (40.2 x 10 cm.), etching.

$77* *Wood Cock,* s., d. 1942, discoloration, tears, (04-22-93, Guyette, #852, illus.), image 7½ x 5½ in., (19.1 x 14 cm.), etching (BP 50, DM 124, FR 417, Y 8466).

BISHOP, Richard E. American 1887-1975

$176* *Wood Duck,* margins, s. Richard E. Bishop, (02-13-93, Collins, #50, illus.), 10¼ x 9Z, in., (26 x 23.2 cm.), etching (BP 124, DM 292, FR 988, Y 21,225).

BISIAUX, Pierre French b. 1924

$55* *Geometric Still Life,* s., #260/275, (07-03-92, Sloan, #294), 21½ x 16½ in., (54.6 x 41.9 cm.), color lithograph (BP 29, DM 83, FR 281, Y 6856).

BISSCHOP, C. (after) 19th cent.

$28* *Portrait Of John Motley,* (02-14-93, Hanzel, #722), 19½ x 13 in., (49.5 x 33 cm.), etching (BP 20, DM 46, FR 157, Y 3377).

BI *Portrait of John Motley,* est. $150/250, (11-01-92, Hanzel, #279), 19½ x 13 in., (49.5 x 33 cm.), etching.

BISSIER, Julius German/Swiss 1893-1965

$516* *Abstrakte Komposition, 1962,* s., (12-05-92, Bassenge, #7056), 17Bzn x 20Zzn in., (44 x 51 cm.), lithograph on Japan (BP 323, DM 804, FR 2742, Y 63,933).

$656* *Das Gelbe Haus,* artist proof, s., (11-13-92, Koller, #5256), 20M, x 9Mzn in., (53 x 24 cm.), color etching on wove (BP 424, DM 1030, FR 3473, Y 81,420, SF 928).

$2978* *Komposition 5. III. 51, 1948-1951,* s., d., i., (06-23-93, Kornfeld, #216), color monotype on wove (BP 2023, DM 5039, FR 16,949, Y 324,436, SF 4485).

$4237* *Sechs Holzschnitte, 1948-51: Eleven,* #12/16, 1971, von der Frau des Kunstlers, s., num., (06-10-93, Hauswedell/Nolt, #101, illus.), each sh 25Zzn x 18M, in., (65 x 48 cm.), woodcut on thin Japan (BP 2771, DM 6900, FR 23,229, Y 449,740).

BISSIERE, Roger French 1886/88-1964

$352* *Bois D'Automme,* s., num., blindstamp, (05-26-93, Dorling, #2565, illus.), 20Zzn x 13Mzn in., (51 x 34.1 cm.), color lithograph on BFK Rives wove (BP 228, DM 574, FR 1933, Y 38,244).

$169* *Composition,* s. Bissiere, H.C., (12-02-92, Kunsthallen, #235), lithograph (BP 109, DM 266, FR 907, Y 21,028, DK 1035).

$548* *Composition,* s. Bissiere, 9/175, (09-30-92, Kunsthallen, #43), color lithograph (BP 309, DM 777, FR 2628, Y 65,763, DK 2990).

$232* *Sans Titre,* s., #28/50, (06-28-93, Loudmer, #15), 11¾ x 7Zzn in., (298 x 198 mm.), sh 15Zzn x 11¼ in., (298 x 198 mm.), color etching and aquatint on Richard de bas laid (BP 155, DM 394, FR 1328, Y 24,615).

$193* *Sans Titre,* s., #83/125, drystamp, tears, losss, (06-28-93, Loudmer, #16), 20Zzn x 13C, in., (510 x 340 mm.), sh 25Zzn x 19Zzn in., (510 x 340 mm.), color lithograph on BFK Rives wove (BP 129, DM 328, FR 1105, Y 20,477).

BISSON, P.

$28* *"Dulton Broad II",* s., t., num. 230/350, excellent cond., (10-31-92, Cleveland, #360), 17¾ x 23¾ in., (45.1 x 60.3 cm.), etching and mezzotint (BP 18, DM 43, FR 146, Y 3468).

BISSON-FRERES

BI *"Bruges-Chapelle Du Saint Sang", "Bayeux-Abside De La Cathedrale", and "Market Square Of An Unidentified Town": Three,* 2 w/blindstamp, 2 w/photog.'s red facsimile sig. stamp, t. in unidentified hand, stamp, 1860s, prop. Museum of Modern Art, est. $2,5/3,500, (10-15-92, Sotheby-NY, #79, illus.), largest 18 x 14½ in., (45.7 x 36.8 cm.), photograph, albumen prints.

$374* *"Fragment Du Portail Meridional, 1860,* attrib., t., plate num., (05-23-93, Butterfield, #3318, illus.), 13¾ x 9½ in., photograph, salt print (BP 244, DM 612, FR 2058, Y 41,340).

$2200* *"Rome-Arc De Titus", "Venise-Porte Della Carta" and "Pise-Le Baptistere": Three Italian Studies,* 1 w/photog.'s init. blindstamp, photog.'s facsimile sig. stamp, t. inunidentified hand, studio stamp, 1860s, (10-15-92, Sotheby-NY, #80, illus.), each approx. 17½ x 14 in., (44.5 x 35.6 cm.), photograph, albumen prints (BP 1346, DM 3275, FR 11,106, Y 263,947).

BLACK, J.

$132* *Views Of London: Set Of Four,* (12-02-92, Boos, #337), plate 9 x 10¾ in., (22.9 x 27.3 cm.), hand-colored stipple engraving (BP 85, DM 208, FR 709, Y 16,424).

BLACK, James Wallace

$605* *"Devonshire Street" and "Franklin Street", 1872: Two,* photog.'s sig., t. mount recto, sig. in neg. of latter, (04-07-93, Swann, #110, illus.), each approx. 12 x 16½ in., (30.5 x 41.9 cm.), photograph, mammoth albumen print (BP 400, DM 978, FR 3311, Y 68,734).

BLACKBURN, Morris American 1902-1979

$193* *Adobe,* s., t., #4/30, (06-11-93, Freemn/Fine Art, #21), 4½ x 5¾ in., (11.4 x 14.6 cm.), etching (BP 127, DM 314, FR 1058, Y 20,477).

$300 *"Alleyway",* s., (05-20-93, Alderfer, #448), 13½ x 9 in., (34.3 x 22.9 cm.), lithograph (BP 193, DM 484, FR 1630, Y 33,127).

BLACKMAN, Charles b. 1928

$567* *Dancing Alice,* s. Charles Black, i., #56/80, (08-11-92, L. Joel, #5G, illus.), 37Zzn x 27Czn in., (96 x 69 cm.), color lithograph (BP 295, DM 832, FR 2818, Y 72,609, A$ 770).

$142* *Evening Light (1967),* s. Charles Blackman, i., #80/100, lit., (08-11-92, L. Joel, #77G), 28M, x 21Mzn in., (73.3 x 54.5 cm.), lithograph (BP 74, DM 208, FR 706, Y 18,184, A$ 192).

$263* *Sea Air,* s. Charles Blackman, i., d. 1966-67, #41/75, (08-11-92, L. Joel, #101G), 30Bzn x 21Mzn in., (77 x 54.5 cm.), color lithograph (BP 137, DM 386, FR 1307, Y 33,679, A$ 357).

$57* *Southerly Buster (1967),* s. Charles Blackman, i., #96/100, lit., (08-11-92, L. Joel, #67G), 21Zzn x 29Z, in., (53.5 x 74 cm.), lithograph (BP 30, DM 84, FR 283, Y 7299, A$ 77).

$122* *Sunset (1967),* s. Charles Blackman, i., #48/100, (08-11-92, L. Joel, #54G), 21B, x 29Z, in., (55 x 74 cm.), lithograph (BP 63, DM 179, FR 606, Y 15,623, A$ 165).

BLACKWOOD, David Lloyd American b. 1941

$1301* *Brian And Martin Winsor, March 30, 1978,* s., t., d. 1979, #16/50, (05-18-93, Joyner, #227), 20 x 31¾ in., (50.8 x 80.6 cm.), aquatint in colors (BP 847, DM 2111, FR 7129, Y 144,991, C$ 1650).

BI *The Burning Of The S.S. Diana,* s., t., d. 1968, #4/10, triptych, lit., est. C$ 4/6,000, (05-18-93, Joyner, #131), 20 x 64 in., (50.8 x 162.6 cm.), aquatint in colors.

$1198* *Captain Abraham Kean Awaiting The Return Of The Lost Party (The Icefields Series),* s., t., d. 1965, i. artist's proof, lit., (11-30-92, Ritchie, #46, illus.), 20 x 16 in., (50.8 x 40.6 cm.), color etching and aquatint w/embossing (BP 791, DM 1909, FR 6479, Y 149,098, C$ 1540).

$1474* *Captain Alb and Aunt Nance, 1982,* #24/50, s., t., d. 1982, (05-10-93, Hodgins, #225, illus.), 32 x 19¾ in., (81.3 x 50.2 cm.), etching on paper (BP 962, DM 2368, FR 7989, Y 164,711, C$ 1870).

$3071* *Fire In Indian Bay,* s., t., d. 1979, #40/50, (11-24-92, Joyner, #171), 19Zzn x 31 in., (50 x 78.8 cm.), colored aquatint (BP 2023, DM 4917, FR 16,681, Y 380,970, C$ 3960).

$2429* *The Great Peace Of Brian And Martin Winsor,* s., t., d. 1985, #47/50, (05-18-93, Joyner, #206), 31¾ x 20 in., (80.6 x 50.8 cm.), aquatint in colors (BP 1582, DM 3941, FR 13,310, Y 270,701, C$ 3080).

$1301* *January Visit Home,* s., t., d. 1975, #13/50, (05-18-93, Joyner, #228), 20 x 31½ in., (50.8 x 80 cm.), aquatint in colors (BP 847, DM 2111, FR 7129, Y 144,991, C$ 1650).

$2730* *Lone Mummer Inside,* s., t., d. 1979, #9/50, (11-24-92, Joyner, #172), 27⅛zn x 21B, in., (70 x 55 cm.), aquatint in colors (BP 1798, DM 4371, FR 14,829, Y 338,668, C$ 3520).

$1818* *Lone Mummer Inside, 1979,* A.P. #3/10, edit. of 50; s., t., d. 1979, (11-16-92, Hodgins, #117, illus.), 27B⅛n x 22 in., (71.1 x 55.9 cm.), color etching on paper (BP 1195, DM 2900, FR 9769, Y 226,881, C$ 2310).

$1454* *Man Warning Two Boys (Home In Wesleyville Series),* s., t., d. 1982, #21/50, prov., lit., (11-30-92, Ritchie, #48, illus.), 20 x 32 in., (50.9 x 81.3 cm.), color etching and aquatint (BP 960, DM 2316, FR 7864, Y 180,958, C$ 1870).

BI *March: Wesleyville From Bennet's High Island,* s., t., d. 1976, #6/35, est. C$2/3000, (05-18-93, Joyner, #110), 20 x 31¾ in., (50.8 x 80.6 cm.), aquatint in colors.

$564* *Night Island, 1981,* A/P 5/10 Ed. of 50 s., t., d. 1981, (05-10-93, Hodgins, #65, illus.), 10¾ x 13¾ in., (27.3 x 34.9 cm.), etching on paper (BP 368, DM 906, FR 3057, Y 63,024, C$ 715).

BI *Our Darling Mr. Croaker,* #11/50, s., t., d. 1984, prov., est. C$ 1,2/1,500, (05-10-93, Hodgins, #318C), 19¾ x 31¾ in., (50.2 x 80.6 cm.), color etching on paper.

$840* *"Passing Shadow", 1990,* #69/75, (03-10-93, Maynard, #311), 32 x 20 in., (81.3 x 50.8 cm.), etching (BP 586, DM 1398, FR 4746, Y 99,244, C$ 1045).

$770* *Resettlement (Bragg's Island Series),* s., t., d. 1982, #27/50, prov., label verso, (11-30-92, Ritchie, #47, illus.), 15 x 36 in., (38.1 x 81.5 cm.), color etching and aquatint (BP 508, DM 1227, FR 4164, Y 95,831, C$ 990).

$1301* *Seabird Hunters Returning Home To Braggs Island,* s., t., d. 1976, #4/35, (05-18-93, Joyner, #109), 20 x 31¾ in., (50.8 x 80.6 cm.), aquatint in color (BP 847, DM 2111, FR 7129, Y 144,991, C$ 1650).

BI *Search Party Returning,* s., t., d. 1971, #22/25, est. C$ 2,5/3,500, (05-18-93, Joyner, #205), 20 x 31¾ in., (50.8 x 80.6 cm.), aquatint in colors.

$390* *Study For Bax Ford, 1979,* #30/50, s., t., d. 1979, prov., (11-16-92, Hodgins, #316), 9¾ x 7Bzn in., (24.8 x 20.3 cm.), etching on paper (BP 256, DM 622, FR 2096, Y 48,671, C$ 495).

$520* *Study For Man Warning Two Boys II, 1982,* #30/50 s., t., d. 1982, (05-10-93, Hodgins, #124), 10¾ x 14 in., (27.3 x 35.6 cm.), etching on paper (BP 339, DM 835, FR 2818, Y 58,107, C$ 660).

$2082* *Wesleyville: Night Passage Bennett's High Island,* s., t., d. 1981, #47/50, (05-18-93, Joyner, #226), 20 x 31½ in., (50.8 x 80 cm.), aquatint in color (BP 1356, DM 3378, FR 11,408, Y 232,029, C$ 2640).

BLAEU, Jan

$275* *Monumethensis Camitatus Vernacule Monmouth Shire, c. 1650,* French text, (09-17-92, Sloan, #2684), 15 x 19½ in., (38.1 x 49.5 cm.), print (BP 154, DM 408, FR 1397, Y 34,238).

BLAIS, Jean Charles French b. 1956

$648* *Dos Nu,* s., (05-27-93, Briest, #31), 11¼ x 9B, in., (28.5 x 24.5 cm.), monotype in blue and purple (BP 415, DM 1040, FR 3505, Y 69,468).

$866* *Dos Nu,* s., (03-31-93, Briest, #E138), 12C, x 9B, in., (31.5 x 24.5 cm.), monotype in black and yellow (BP 573, DM 1393, FR 4732, Y 99,586).

BLAKE, Peter

$2899* *Alice In Wonderland, 1970: Set Of Eight,* s., #25/100, pub. Waddington Graphics, margins, good cond., light-staining, (12-03-92, Sotheby-London, #614, illus.), screen-prints on wove (BP 1870, DM 4559, FR 15,561, Y 360,707).

$1887* *"Studio Tackboard", "Costume Life Drawing", "Girl In A Poppy Field","Liberty As 'A Suffolk Child By John Constable RA'", "Costume Life Drawing: TheYellow Hat" and ": Tattooed Lady (Colored State), 1972-1985: Six,* s., two i. AP, four num., full margins, good cond., creases, (06-30-93, Sotheby-London, #751, illus.), 4 color screenprints, 1 etching w/collage on wove (BP 1265, DM 3218, FR 10,857, Y 202,186).

BLAKE, T. (after)

$83* *The Interior Of The Fives Court,* (11-12-92, Freemn/Fine Art, #31), 15½ x 22 in., (39.4 x 55.9 cm.), hand colored engraving (BP 55, DM 132, FR 444, Y 10,291).

BLAKE, William 1757-1827

BI *Chaucer's Canterbury Pilgrims (Essick XVI; Bindman 477), 1810,* Essick's late 4th state of 5, drypoint inscript., margins, staining,foxmark, tear into image, laid down on wove, taped to overmat, est. $4/6,000, (11-09-92, Christie-NY, #50, illus.), border 11M, x 37Bzn in., (302 x 941 mm.), engraving on cream wove.

BI *The Circle Of Thieves: Agnolo Brunelleschi Attacked By A Six-Footed Serpent (B. 650), 1827,* plate IV from Illustrations to Dante's Divine Comedy, margins, crease, light-staining, foxmark, defects, good cond., est. $1,4/1,800, (11-09-92, Christie-NY, #51, illus.), plate 8Bzn x 14 in., (227 x 356 mm.), engraving on laid India.

$27,600* *Illustrations Of The Book Of Job (Bentley Blake Books 421.A; Essick "Clake's Engravings to the Book of Job: An Essay On Their Graphic Form; With A Catalogue of Their States and Printings"),* Lahee, for William Blake, 8 March 1825 (i.e. March 1826), Quarto, watermark, plate 1 misdated 1828, plates tipped on stubs, first ed., drawing paper issue, prov., (06-14-93, Sotheby-NY, #85, illus.), 14½ x 10¼ in., (36.8 x 26 cm.), engraved title and 21 plates in cream-white wove (BP 18,065, DM 44,922, FR 150,985, Y 2,904,346).

$156,500* *Los And His Spectre (Cf. Bindman 485), c. 1808-12,* proof of bottom portion of plate 6, left corner tip lacking, staining, tape remains, very good cond., Dian Woodner and Andrea Woodner Coll., prov.,exhib., lit., (05-11-93, Christie-NY, #85, illus.), sheet 5Bzn x 6C, in., (144 x 162 mm.), relief etching in blue-green and black w/ extensive hand-coloring in watercolors (BP 99,904, DM 246,534, FR 830,679, Y 17,214,828).

$771* *The Messengers Tell Job Of His Misfortunes (Bindman 629), 1825,* plate 4 from Illustrations of the Book of Job, stain, good cond., (06-30-93, Sotheby-London, #261), 8½ x 6¾ in., (216 x 171 mm.), engraving on laid India (BP 517, DM 1315, FR 4436, Y 82,610).

$1430* *"Naked Came I Out Of My Mother's Womb", 1825,* plate 6 from The Book of Job, pub. by Blake, s. W. Blake inv + sc inplate, t., i., good cond., full sheet, stain, ink offset, handling marks, light staining, (09-11-92, Skinner, #15, illus.), sight 8½ x 6¾ in., (21.6 x 17.1 cm.), engraving on paper (BP 740, DM 2058, FR 6996, Y 177,178).

$771* *Satan Smiting Job With Boils (Bindman 631),* plate 6 from Illustration of the Book of Job, full margins, good cond., (06-30-93, Sotheby-London, #262), 8½ x 6¾ in., (216 x 171 mm.), engraving on laid India (BP 517, DM 1315, FR 4436, Y 82,610).

BLAKEMORE, John

$545* *Equivalents, "Ambergate, Derbyshire", "Black Rock Sands, N. Wales", "Borgie Forest" and "Linch Clough, Derbyshire", 1972-1975: Four,* t., s., d., num., from 280 x 215mm to 225 x 185mm, (05-07-93, Sotheby-London, #410), photograph, silver print (BP 345, DM 862, FR 2904, Y 60,009).

$2722* *John Blakemore, 1981: Book,* s., t., d., num. 1/20 A/P in pencil, p. t. sheet, cloth box, folio, Contrasts Gallery, (05-06-93, Christie-London, #24, illus.), largest approx. 8½ x 6¾ in., photograph, 10 gelatin silver prints (BP 1725, DM 4287, FR 14,433, Y 299,483).

$799* *"Leaves" and "Boxes", 1980: Six,* t., s., d., from 250 x 220mm to 202 x 160mm, (05-07-93, Sotheby-London, #416, illus.), photograph, silver print (BP 506, DM 1263, FR 4257, Y 87,976).

BI *Nudes, 1971: Four,* p. 1980, s., d., num., each approx. 250 x 180mm, est. BP 4/600, (05-07-93, Sotheby-London, #412, illus.), photograph, silver print.

$690* *Rocks And Water, "Linch Clough, Derbyshire", "Afan Ledr, Wales" and "River Spey, Scotland", 1974-1976:*

Three, t., s., d., num., each approx. 280 x 345mm, (05-07-93, Sotheby-London, #415, illus.), photograph, silver print (BP 437, DM 1091, FR 3676, Y 75,974).

$1090* *"Thistle", 1980: Set Of Ten,* t., s., d., #18/20, from 160 x 190mm to 250 x 196mm, (05-07-93, Sotheby-London, #414), photograph, selenium toned silver print (BP 690, DM 1723, FR 5807, Y 120,018).

$2179* *"Thistle", 1980: Ten,* portfolio, t., s., d., #6/20, each approx. 200 x 170mm, (05-07-93, Sotheby-London, #413, illus.), photograph, selenium toned silver print (BP 1380, DM 3445, FR 11,609, Y 239,925).

$1180* *Woods, 1976-1981: Six,* t., s., d., num., each approx. 350 x 290mm, (05-07-93, Sotheby-London, #411, illus.), photograph, silver print (BP 747, DM 1866, FR 6287, Y 129,927).

BLAMPIED, Edmund   English 1886-1966

$1544* *"Crossing The Stream" and "Early Morning", c. 1932: Two,* each s., former #9/100, latter #50, full margins, good cond., surfacedirt, (06-30-93, Sotheby-London, #291, illus.), one 6¾ x 8¾ in., (171 x 222 mm.), the other 8¼ x 11¾ in., (171 x 222 mm.), drypoint on cream laid (BP 1035, DM 2633, FR 8884, Y 165,434).

$385* *En Promenade,* s., #14/100, (07-03-92, Sloan, #336), 8¼ x 11¾ in., (21 x 29.8 cm.), print (BP 201, DM 583, FR 1964, Y 47,993).

$995* *"The End Of The Day" and "Come On, Boys!" (C./D. 41 and 60), 1919 and1921: Two,* s., margins, good cond., (06-30-93, Sotheby-London, #284, illus.), each 6¼ x 8½ in., (159 x 216 mm.), drypoint on wove (BP 667, DM 1697, FR 5725, Y 106,611).

$1373* *"Farm Hand" and "Cider Drinkers" (Second Plate) (C./D. 69 and 93), 1922 and 1925: Two,* s., full margins, good cond., defects, (06-30-93, Sotheby-London, #288), one 9 x 11ᴮ, in., (229 x 295 mm.), the other 10¼ x 8¼ in., (229 x 295 mm.), drypoint, both on cream laid (BP 920, DM 2342, FR 7900, Y 147,112).

$333* *The Fishermans's Return, 1922,* s., good cond., (11-30-92, Phillips-London, #325A), sheet 8ᴹ, x 14¾ in., (225 x 375 mm.), drypoint on F.J. Head laid (BP 220, DM 531, FR 1801, Y 41,444).

$1029* *"Fording The Stream", "The Fisherman's Return" and "Poor People" (C./D. 38; 70; and Unrecorded), 1914, 1922 and 1926: Three,* s., margins, good cond., (06-30-93, Sotheby-London, #283), drypoint, two on cream laid, one on Japan (BP 690, DM 1755, FR 5921, Y 110,254).

$1029* *Galloping, 1932,* s. ink, full margins, good cond., tape stains, (06-30-93, Sotheby-London, #289), 8ᴮ, x 11¼ in., (219 x 286 mm.), drypoint on cream laid (BP 690, DM 1755, FR 5921, Y 110,254).

$771* *"Grazing Horses" and "Wading" (C./D. 33; and 59), 1914 and 1920: Two,* s., margins, good cond., (06-30-93, Sotheby-London, #282), one 6¼ x 8ᴮ, in., (159 x 219 mm.), the other 6¾ x 9ᴹ, in., (159 x 219 mm.), one etching and one drypoint on cream laid (BP 517, DM 1315, FR 4436, Y 82,610).

$605* *The Harvest,* s., very good cond.?, (07-19-92, Bakker, #22), plate 9ᴮ, x 14ᴄ, in., (24.4 x 36.5 cm.), drypoint (BP 310, DM 882, FR 2982, Y 75,211).

$358* *"Hot Dogs", c. 1935: Set Of Twelve,* excellent cond., (10-31-92, Cleveland, #251), lithograph (BP 229, DM 551, FR 1868, Y 44,345).

BI *A Jersey Shore,* s., #83/100, light-staining, rust spot, surface soiling, est. BP 250/300, (11-30-92, Phillips-London, #325), plate 7½ x 10¾ in., (191 x 273 mm.), drypoint on laid.

$1201* *Morning Gossip, 1928,* s., #34/100, full margins, good cond., (06-30-93, Sotheby-London, #290, illus.), 8ᴹ, x 12 in., (225 x 305 mm.), drypoint on cream laid (BP 805, DM 2048, FR 6910, Y 128,683).

$771* *Noon Rest, c. 1930,* s., #20, margins, good cond., rubbing, (06-30-93, Sotheby-London, #292), sh 11¼ x 15 in., (286 x 381 mm.), lithograph on laid (BP 517, DM 1315, FR 4436, Y 82,610).

$550* *"Normandy Fisherman" and "To The Stable": Two,* each s., (05-24-93, Grogan, #343), first 9 x 10 in., (22.9 x 25.4 cm.), second 8ᴄ, x 11ᴢ, in., (22.9 x 25.4 cm.), etching (BP 358, DM 899, FR 3027, Y 60,794).

$165* *Ostend Shrimper, 1926,* s., #96/100, full margins, good cond., mat staining, surface soiling, (10-28-92, Butterfield, #2782), 11 x 14ᴢ₂ₙ in., (279 x 371 mm.), drypoint on cream laid paper (BP 105, DM 255, FR 865, Y 20,245).

$1458* *"Potato Planters" and "The Sick Man" (C./D. 44 and 65), 1920 and 1921: Two,* s., full margins, good cond., (06-30-93, Sotheby-London, #285, illus.), one 9ᴮ, x 12¾ in., (244 x 324 mm.), the other 7ᴮ, x 11¼ in., (244 x 324 mm.), drypoint, first on wove, second on laid (BP 977, DM 2487, FR 8389, Y 156,220).

$1286* *"Soup" and "Leisure" (C./D. 56 and 77), 1920 and 1923: Two,* s., first ded., full margins, good cond., creasing, soiling, (06-30-93, Sotheby-London, #287), one 8ᴹ, x 8 in., (225 x 203 mm.), the other 8ᴹ, x 11ᴄ, in., (225 x 203 mm.), drypoint on cream laid (BP 862, DM 2193, FR 7399, Y 137,791).

$1115* *"The Thunderstorm" and "White Horse" (C./D. 49 and 64), 1920 and 1921: Two,* s., full margins, good cond., (06-30-93, Sotheby-London, #286, illus.), one 9¾ x 12¾ in., (248 x 324 mm.), the other 7ᴹ, x 9ᴹ, in., (248 x 324 mm.), drypoint on cream laid (BP 747, DM 1902, FR 6415, Y 119,469).

$652* *Weary (Campbell Dodgson 16), 1912,* s., full margins, good cond., (06-30-93, Sotheby-London, #281, illus.), 4ᴄ, x 6½ in., (111 x 165 mm.), drypoint on cream laid (BP 437, DM 1112, FR 3751, Y 69,860).

BLANCHE, Jacques Emile   French 1861-1942

$101* *Fillettes En Buste: Two,* creases, good margins, (02-03-93, Ader Tajan, #71), brush lithograph (BP 71, DM 166, FR 564, Y 12,564).

$409* *Jeunes Filles Dans Un Jardin (U. Johnson 9), 1897,* small margins, (02-24-93, Picard, #12), color lithograph on thin wove (BP 285, DM 664, FR 2251, Y 47,993).

BI *Maurice Barres, 1897,* w/out margin, (02-24-93, Picard, #13), lithograph in brown on thin chine.

BLECHEN, Karl   1798-1840

$4237* *Kloster Im Walde (Rave 477), 1823,* (06-10-93, Hauswedell/Nolt, #223, illus.), etching china (BP 2771, DM 6900, FR 23,229, Y 449,740).

$5311* *Romanische Ruine (Rave 478), 1826,* (06-04-93, Bassenge, #5626, illus.), 7ᴹ, x 9½ in., (20 x 24.1 cm.), etching on bristol board (BP 3514, DM 8625, FR 29,070, Y 572,800).

BLECKNER, Ross   American b. 1949

BI *Ohne Titel (Globe), 1987,* #62/72, pencil num. and s., tears, est. DM 1,200, (11-20-92, Lempertz, #463), sh 39¾ x 32ᴄₐₙ in., (101 x 81.7 cm.), color serigraph on smooth white board.

$575* *Untitled, 1987,* s., #12/72, pub. Lincoln Center for List Art Posters & Prints, full margins, good cond., soiling, (05-19-93, Butterfield, #2128), 35¼ x 29ᴢ, in., (895 x 740 mm.), silkscreen in colors on wove (BP 373, DM 935, FR 3149, Y 63,655).

BLEDSOE, Judith

BI *Untitled,* s., #165/200, est. $50/70, (06-24-93, Boos, #334), sight 7ᴢₐₙ x 5ᴹ, in., (195 x 150 mm.), lithograph.

BLEW, E.W.

BI *"Desert Artistry", 1936,* mounted, s., t. by photog., est. $2/3,000, (04-06-93, Sotheby-NY, #183, illus.), 10ᴮ, x 13½ in., photograph.

BLOCH, Julius   American 1888-1966

$275* *Resting,* s., #50/50, light stained, tape residue, hinged to mat, very good cond., (12-04-92, Doyle, #77), 9¼ x 13¼ in., (235 x 337 mm.), lithograph (BP 176, DM 438, FR 1486, Y 34,332).

BI *Stokowsky,* s., t., i., est. $3/500, (06-11-93, Freemn/Fine Art, #22), 14 x 10 in., (35.6 x 25.4 cm.), lithograph.

BLOCH, M.

$42* *Huile Pour Moteur Yacco "Donne Des Chevaux Et Supprime L'Usure", c. 1925,* good cond., (11-19-92, Ribeyre/Baron, #56), 62ᴢₐₙ x 47¼ in., (160 x 120 cm.), poster (BP 28, DM 67, FR 226, Y 5223).

$105* *Un Message De la Mer,* p. Ch. Verneau, good cond., (11-19-92, Ribeyre/Baron, #159), 55ᴢ, x 39¾ in., (140 x 101 cm.), poster (BP 69, DM 167, FR 564, Y 13,058).

BLOME, Richard
$2990* *The Gentleman's Recreation, In Two Parts, The First Being An Encyclopedia Of The Arts And Sciences...The Second Part, Treats Of Horsmanship, Hawking,And Others (Harting 41; Schwerdt I, 72; Wing B-3213), 1686: Eighty-Six,* S. Roycroft for Richard Blome, 2 parts in one, folio, minor perforation to two plates, tears, browned, dampstaining, soiling, first edit., inscription, Anthony N. B. Garvan Coll., (06-05-93, Christie-NY, #14, illus.), engraved plate including 10 plates of subscriber's arms (BP 1968, DM 4848, FR 16,339, Y 320,747).

BLOND, Le
$10 *"The Figure Seller",* (10-09-92, G.A. Key, #111), 5 x 6 in., (12.7 x 15.2 cm.), colored oil print (BP 6, DM 15, FR 51, Y 1220).

BLOOM, Barbara contemporary
$1540* *"Esprit De L'Escalier (Work For The Blind)" and "Esprit De L'Escalier(One Day, Quite Some Time Ago...)",* 1985-1988: Two, s., full margins, good cond., soiling, (11-07-92, Sotheby-NY, #525), each overall size 31M, x 24Z, in., (810 x 613 mm.), two photo-lithographs w/braille and text (BP 1007, DM 2459, FR 8311, Y 190,077).

BLOSSFELDT, Karl 1865-1932
$6050* *12 Fotografien (1900-1925), 1975,* Koln: Galerie Wilde, pub. stamp w/d. & edition num. in ink on mount,#17/50 edit., lit., (10-13-92, Christie-NY, #32, illus.), each 10¼ x 8 in., (26 x 20.3 cm.), photograph, gelatin silver prints (BP 3524, DM 8863, FR 30,114, Y 733,600).
$29,700* *Cotula Turbinata, c. 1925,* t., annot. 12X by photog., (10-15-92, Sotheby-NY, #405, illus.), 11¾ x 9¼ in., (29.8 x 23.5 cm.), photograph, gelatin silver print (BP 18,174, DM 44,210, FR 149,924, Y 3,563,287).
$550* *Urformen Der Kunst (Original Forms Of Art), 1928(?),* plate #53 and 54, photog.'s handwritten numerical notations, (04-07-93, Swann, #405), largest 6 x 9 in., photograph, silver print (BP 363, DM 890, FR 3010, Y 62,486).

BLOSSFELDT, Professor Karl
$172* *"Urformen Der Kunst", 1929,* Ernst Wasmuth Verlag, pub., (05-07-93, Sotheby-London, #223), photograph (BP 109, DM 272, FR 916, Y 18,939).

BLOTELINGH, A. 19th cent.
BI *"Everhardus Bornaeus",* after P. Schick, est. $40/60, (03-12-93, DuMouchelle, #2429), 7½ x 5 in., (19.1 x 12.7 cm.), steel engraving.

BLUM, Alex American b. 1888
$55* *"Abigail Jones Property",* s., t., pub. A.A.A., Groves' Coll., (10-16-92, Neal, #141), plate 10 x 14 in., (25.4 x 35.6 cm.), etching (BP 33, DM 81, FR 276, Y 6567).
$55* *"Curiosity Shop",* s., t.; bears A.A.A. pub. label verso, Groves' Coll., (10-16-92, Neal, #140), plate 14¼ x 9¾ in., (36.2 x 24.8 cm.), etching (BP 33, DM 81, FR 276, Y 6567).

BLUM, Robert Frederick American 1857-1903
$825* *"Rialto Bridge" and "The Bead Stringers": Two, the second 1886,* each stamped in red ink, prov., (10-08-92, Grogan, #688), first 6¼ x 5 in., (15.9 x 12.7 cm.), second 12 x 8 in., (15.9 x 12.7 cm.), etching (BP 491, DM 1220, FR 4142, Y 100,243).

BLUME, Anna and Bernhard Johannes
BI *Gegenseitig, 1988,* s., d., (11-12-92, Lempertz, #28, illus.), 16⅜zn x 11B, in., (42 x 29.5 cm.), Polaroid montage.

BLUME, Bernhard Johannes German b. 1937
$9860* *Frei-Ubung Aus Odipale Komplikationen, 1978/79: Two,* s., d., t., (11-12-92, Lempertz, #25, illus.), each 81M, x 50 in., (208 x 127 cm.), photograph, gelatin silver print (BP 6304, DM 15,496, FR 52,812, Y 1,219,844).
BI *From Naturlich: Six,* s., d., est. DM 1,000-, (05-27-93, Lempertz, #623), each approx. 19Zzn x 13Zzn in., (50 x 35.5 cm.), color serigraph.
$830* *"Kubismus", (19)88,* 4-teilige Photoarbeit, s., d., t., num., (12-01-92, Karl/Faber, #384), 16Zzn x 11Zzn in.,

(42 x 30 cm.), color offset print (BP 548, DM 1323, FR 4508, Y 103,337).
BI *Memento Mori, 1984,* s., d., t., est. DM 500, (11-12-92, Lempertz, #27, illus.), 3Zzn x 3Zzn in., (10 x 10 cm.), sheet 16Zzn x 12Zzn in., (10 x 10 cm.), color photograph.
$1972* *Naturlich, 1982-1984: Five,* s., d., t., (11-12-92, Lempertz, #26, illus.), each 4Zzn x 3Zzn in., (10.3 x 10 cm.), color photographs from Polaroids (BP 1261, DM 3099, FR 10,562, Y 243,969).
BI *Naturlich, 1985,* s., d., est. DM 300-, (09-25-92, Granier, #2763), 19¾ x 13Zzn in., (50.2 x 35.5 cm.), sheet 26Zzn x 19¾ in., (50.2 x 35.5 cm.), color serigraph on cream wove.

BLUMENFELD, Erwin American,b.Germany 1897-1969
$11,000* *Blumenfeld Color: Ten, 1984,* PPS Galerie F.C. Gundlach, from orig. transparencies, each w/estate stamp, initialled, num 24/50 by pub., lit., (10-13-92, Christie-NY, #413, illus.), each 12¾ x 10 in., (32.4 x 25.4 cm.), photograph, dye transfer prints (BP 6407, DM 16,115, FR 54,754, Y 1,333,818).
$880* *Cubistic Purple Nude,* estate stamp, inits. FY, notations 19/50, 1930s(?), p. 1984, (04-07-93, Swann, #406, illus.), 12½ x 10 in., photograph, dye transfer print from the orig. transparency (BP 582, DM 1423, FR 4817, Y 99,977).
$654* *Fashion Study,* 1950s, stamped photog.'s estate credit, annot. Hand printed by ErwinBlumenfeld from the collection of..., 352 x 283mm, (05-07-93, Sotheby-London, #334, illus.), photograph, partly solarised silver print (BP 414, DM 1034, FR 3484, Y 72,011).
$2200* *Legs In Mirrors,* early 1950s, t., d., estate stamp, (10-13-92, Christie-NY, #412, illus.), 13½ x 10¾ in., (34.3 x 27.3 cm.), photograph, gelatin silver print (BP 1281, DM 3223, FR 10,951, Y 266,764).
$2300* *"Maroua Motherwell, New York" (Blumenfeld, p. 39, variant), 1942,* photog. estate stamp, (04-06-93, Sotheby-NY, #371, illus.), 13½ x 10B, in., photograph (BP 1519, DM 3705, FR 12,548, Y 262,318).
$3220* *Nude On Coca Cola Chair, 1944,* estate stamp, annot. handprinted (sic) by Erwin Blumenfeld 1944, lit., (04-08-93, Christie-NY, #250, illus.), 13¼ x 10¾ in., (33.7 x 27.3 cm.), photograph, gelatin silver print (BP 2111, DM 5173, FR 17,510, Y 365,411).
$990* *Paris: Two: "Paris, Montaparnasse", and "Paris Window With Hyacinth Vase", c. 1930,* 1st t., d. by photog. in ink, (10-15-92, Sotheby-NY, #306, illus.), one 11B, x 8M in., (29.5 x 22.5 cm.), other 11Z, x 7¾ in., (29.5 x 22.5 cm.), photograph, gelatin silver prints (BP 606, DM 1474, FR 4997, Y 118,776).
$2070* *Woman With Mirror, 1949,* estate stamp, d., annot., (04-08-93, Christie-NY, #252, illus.), 13½ x 10B, in., (34.3 x 27 cm.), photograph, gelatin silver print (BP 1357, DM 3325, FR 11,256, Y 234,907).

BLUNDELL, A.R.
BI *"Lowestoft Harbour",* s., (12-11-92, G.A. Key, #85), 4 x 6 in., (10.2 x 15.2 cm.), etching.

BLUTH, Manfred b. 1926
BI *Untitled I,* s., est. DM 450, (12-05-92, Bassenge, #7058), 16Zzn x 14C, in., (43 x 36.5 cm.), lithograph on wove.

BOAK, R. Grisswell
$22* *English Landscapes: A Pair,* s., annot., (12-02-92, Boos, #326), image 7 x 9¾ in., (17.8 x 24.8 cm.), hand-colored etching (BP 14, DM 35, FR 118, Y 2737).

BOAZ (after)
$11* *A Church,* (06-11-93, DuMouchelle, #444), approx. 18 x 24 in., (45.7 x 61 cm.), print (BP 7, DM 18, FR 60, Y 1167).

BOBAK, Molly Lamb
$108* *The Thames,* s., t., #3/10, prov., (06-07-93, Ritchie, #38), image 10 x 13½ in., (25.4 x 34.3 cm.), lithograph (BP 71, DM 175, FR 590, Y 11,585, C$ 138).

BOBERG, Jorgen
$85* *Fantastisk Fodsel,* s. Boberg, #90/100, (06-03-93, Kunsthallen, #175), etching (BP 55, DM 136, FR 458, Y 9116, DK 518).

$137* *Isolation,* s. Boberg 1964, 2/10, edit. 250, (09-30-92, Kunsthallen, #45), woodcut (BP 77, DM 194, FR 657, Y 16,441, DK 748).

$55* *Komposition,* s. Boberg, 21/125, (03-24-93, Kunsthallen, #47), etching (BP 37, DM 90, FR 306, Y 6462, DK 345).

BOCCASILE, Gino

$357* *Bantam, 1935,* S.A. Alfien and Lacroix, A cond., (08-06-92, Swann, #54, illus.), 13½ x 9¼ in., (34.3 x 23.5 cm.), (BP 186, DM 527, FR 1781, Y 45,536).

$1320* *Cappello Bantam, 1938,* Aeta, A- cond., (08-06-92, Swann, #55, illus.), 53 x 39 in., (134.6 x 99.1 cm.), (BP 689, DM 1950, FR 6587, Y 168,367).

$605* *India,* Pizzi and Pizio, A- cond., (08-06-92, Swann, #53, illus.), 38½ x 26 in., (97.8 x 66 cm.), (BP 316, DM 894, FR 3019, Y 77,168).

BOCCIONI, Umberto Italian 1882-1916

BI *I Portatori (C.-C. 446), c. 1908-1910,* s., probably p. at later date, full margins, good cond., creasing, est. BP 3/4,00, (06-30-93, Sotheby-London, #356, illus.), 5M, x 11B, in., (149 x 295 mm.), drypoint w/etching p. w/tone in dark ink.

BI *L'Ateleta (Calvesi-Coen 260), 1907,* s., probably p. at later date, full margins, good cond., scuff w/in image, creasing, (06-30-93, Sotheby-London, #355, illus.), 5M x 9 in., (149 x 229 mm.), drypoint and aquatint w/touches of etching in dark brown on thick wove.

BI *La Madre Che Cuce (C.-C. 620), 1910,* s., full margins, good cond., discoloration, est. BP 3/4,000, (06-30-93, Sotheby-London, #358, illus.), 5C, x 4C, in., (137 x 111 mm.), etching w/aquatint on thick wove.

BI *La Signora Sacchi (C.-C. 272), 1907,* s., probably p. at later date, full margins, good cond., handling marks, creases, est. BP 5/6,000, (06-30-93, Sotheby-London, #357, illus.), 11¼ x 7Z, in., (286 x 181 mm.), drypoint w/etching in brown w/tone.

BOCHE, Guy

$880* *Armistice Day, Little Italy, New York, 1918,* (10-14-92, Swann, #286, illus.), 8½ x 6½ in., (21.6 x 16.5 cm.), photograph, toned silver print (BP 517, DM 1288, FR 4367, Y 106,641).

BOCHNER, Mel American b. 1940

$1444* *Ohne Titel, 1989,* s., d., num., est. DM 3000, (11-28-92, Schoppmann, #437), 26Zzn x 41¾ in., (68.5 x 106 cm.), color etching on handmade (BP 953, DM 2300, FR 7810, Y 179,714).

$288* *Third Prelude, 1988,* t., annot. AP V/V, s., d., good cond., skinned areas, (05-19-93, Butterfield, #2129), 20B, x 23M, in., (524 x 606 mm.), sugarlift and aquatint on 2 sheets of wove (BP 187, DM 468, FR 1577, Y 31,883).

BI *Untitled, 1982/1987,* s., d., est. DM 3,000, (06-12-93, Hauswedell/Nolt, #43, illus.), 25zn x 20Zzn in., (65 x 52.5 cm.), etching on pastel on thick black wove.

BI *Untitled, 1982/1989,* s., d., est. DM 3,000, (06-12-93, Hauswedell/Nolt, #44), 27C, x 21M, in., (69.5 x 55.5 cm.), etching and mixed media on thick wove.

BOCKLIN, Arnold (after)

$619* *Sudlandische Villa Am Zypressengestade,* by Wilhelm Hecht, trimmed, (09-14-92, Venator/Hansten, #1647), approx. 18M, x 27zn in., (48 x 70 cm.), etching (BP 327, DM 920, FR 3118, Y 76,971).

BOCKMAN, Bengt b. 1936

$536* *"Bestianen": Four,* (04-17-93, Falkkloos, #68, illus.), 24 x 22zn in., (61 x 56 cm.), lithograph in colors (BP 348, DM 857, FR 2896, Y 59,602, SK 3960).

BI *Komposition Med Byggnad,* s. 49/65, est. SK 1,200, (11-07-92, Falkkloos, #68), etching.

$447* *Lusthus: Four,* 108/199, s., (04-17-93, Falkkloos, #69, illus.), 20½ x 15C, in., (52 x 39 cm.), lithograph in color (BP 290, DM 715, FR 2415, Y 49,705, SK 3300).

$164* *"Ryttarinna" and "Blue Spirit Of The Dream": Two,* both s., (04-17-93, Falkkloos, #67), one 9Zzn x 11 in., (25 x 28 cm.), the other 11Zzn x 7½ in., (25 x 28 cm.), lithograph in colors (BP 107, DM 262, FR 886, Y 18,236, SK 1210).

BOCKSTIEGEL, Peter August 1889-1951

$3258* *Abend (Becker 96), 1920,* stone mono., s., t., (09-25-92, Granier, #2769, illus.), sheet 30Zzn x 24Czn in., (78 x 61.5 cm.), color lithograph on wove (BP 1902, DM 4830, FR 16,331, Y 393,241).

$1401* *Alter Mann, Auf Dem Boden Sitzend,* (12-05-92, Bassenge, #7060), 16zn x 12Zzn in., etching on copper print paper (BP 877, DM 2184, FR 7444, Y 173,584).

$1412* *Bauer Aus Buckeburg (Becker 160), 1924,* s., d., t., artist's proof, (06-10-93, Hauswedell/Nolt, #107, illus.), image 17½ x 12Czn in., (44.4 x 31 cm.), drypoint on copper print paper (BP 924, DM 2299, FR 7741, Y 149,878).

$590* *Ein Bauernpaar Bei Der Feldarbeit,* mono. in pl., (12-05-92, Bassenge, #7061), 13Z, x 15Czn in., (33.4 x 38.5 cm.), etching on copper print paper (BP 369, DM 920, FR 3135, Y 73,101).

$194* *Bockstiegels Eltern Bei Der Kornernte Vor Dem Haus (Becker 113), 1921,* Hanna Bockstiegel Estate, Neudruck 1-30, (09-25-92, Granier, #2772), sheet 18Zzn x 20¼ in., (47.5 x 51.5 cm.), solar print (BP 113, DM 288, FR 972, Y 23,416).

$1862* *Wandere (Becker 130 II), 1922,* plate mono., s., d. 1921, t., creases, dusty, foxed, prov., (09-25-92, Granier, #2768, illus.), sheet 28Zzn x 25zn in., (73.5 x 65 cm.), etching on wove (BP 1087, DM 2760, FR 9333, Y 224,744).

BODINE, A. Aubrey 1906-1970

$2070* *Beggar At Howard And Lexington Streets, Baltimore, 1968,* estate stamp, lit., (04-08-93, Christie-NY, #254, illus.), 11B, x 9½ in., (29.5 x 24.1 cm.), photograph, toned gelatin silver print (BP 1357, DM 3325, FR 11,256, Y 234,907).

BI *Fort McHenry, c. 1940,* s., t. in ink, est. $2/2,500, (04-08-93, Christie-NY, #253, illus.), 17¼ x 14 in., (43.8 x 35.6 cm.), photograph, blue-toned gelatin silver print.

$1100* *Ocean City, Maryland, c. 1950,* s., t. in ink, (10-13-92, Christie-NY, #414, illus.), 10Z, x 13 in., (25.7 x 33 cm.), photograph, gelatin silver print (BP 641, DM 1611, FR 5475, Y 133,382).

$1650* *Pennsylvania Train Yard, Baltimore, MD., c. 1945,* s. by photog. in gold ink on image, estate stamp annot. w/t., d., process in unidentified hand, (10-15-92, Sotheby-NY, #437, illus.), 16½ x 13¾ in., (41.9 x 34.9 cm.), photograph, gelatin silver print (BP 1010, DM 2456, FR 8329, Y 197,960).

$1870* *Skipjack Reflections, 1948,* double-mounted, s., t., d., annot. by photog. in ink, t., annot., studio stamps, (10-15-92, Sotheby-NY, #436, illus.), 13¼ x 10¾ in., (33.7 x 27.3 cm.), photograph, green-toned carbro print (BP 1144, DM 2784, FR 9440, Y 224,355).

$1035* *"Symphony In Reflections", 1931,* mounted, s., t., d. by photog., annot., label, stamps, (04-06-93, Sotheby-NY, #146, illus.), 16½ x 13½ in., photograph, silver chloride print (BP 684, DM 1667, FR 5646, Y 118,043).

BI *The U.S. Capitol,* photog.'s sig., handstamp, handstamp, 1950s, est. $500/750, (04-07-93, Swann, #407), 13 x 10 in., photograph, silver print.

$920* *"Vorderburg-Rothenburg", 1932,* mounted, s., t., d. by photog., (04-06-93, Sotheby-NY, #147, illus.), 16¼ x 12¾ in., photograph, silver chloride print (BP 608, DM 1482, FR 5019, Y 104,927).

BODMER, Karl Swiss 1809-1893

$205* *"Chasse Au Faucon", "Retour Au Bercail" and "Sujets Animaliers": Ten,* faults, stains, (02-24-93, Picard, #14), lithograph, etching and procede (provenance) Comte on laid or chine applique (BP 143, DM 333, FR 1128, Y 24,055).

$3410* *"Pehriska-Ruhpa", c. 1840,* plate 28, from Travels in the Interior of North America, pub. Ackerman and Co., age toning, foxing, (11-28-92, Dunning, #1013), sh 23¼ x 16½ in., (59.1 x 41.9 cm.), etching, aquatint, roulette w/hand-coloring (BP 2251, DM 5433, FR 18,442, Y 424,393).

BODMER, Karl (after)

BI *Crow Indians,* pub. Ackerman & Co. by Hurlimann, est. $2/300, (06-11-93, Freemn/Fine Art, #23), 6¼ x 11 in., (15.9 x 27.9 cm.), engraving w/hand-coloring.

$690* *"View Of The Rocky Mountains", Plate 44 and "Mouth Of Fox River", 1839-44: Two,* from Travels in the Interior of North America, pub. Ackermann & Co.,narrow plate margins, trimmed through titles, first skinned, repaired losses/tears, filled center hole, repaired splits; second w/broken creases affecting image, image scuffs, discoloration, (01-28-93, Sotheby-NY, #469), 13¾ x 17½ in., (349 x 445 mm.), sheet 14 x 17M\ in., (349 x 445 mm.), hand-colored etching w/aquatint w/touches gum arabic (BP 456, DM 1093, FR 3700, Y 85,672).

BODMER, Walter 1903-1973

$362* *Spiel Mit Drei Figuren, 1942: Four,* 29/125, s., d., (10-14-92, Germann, #490), 15Ɐzn x 21¼ in., (405 x 540 mm.), lithograph (BP 212, DM 530, FR 1797, Y 43,868, SF 472).

BOECKLER, Georg Andrea

$3080* *Architectura Curiosa Nova..., 1664,* 4 parts in vol., foxing, tears, binding rubbed and chipped, catalog cover illus., (05-01-93, Skinner, #41), calf binding 13≯zn x 9Mzn in., (34.5 x 24 cm.), 200 engraved plates (BP 1959, DM 4876, FR 16,444, Y 341,729).

BOEHLE, Fritz 1873-1916

BI *Betender Bauer (Schrey 41),* s., d. F. Boehle 1987, est. DM 400-, (03-24-93, Venator/Hansten, #4470), pl. 11≯zn x 15¾ in., (29.3 x 40 cm.), etching on Japan.

BOEL, Coryn

$954* *The Skittleplayers (Le Blanc 37; B., Holl. 33),* after David Teniers the Younger, 1st state, w/tone and polishing scratches, countermark (?), wide margins, surface dirt, (06-29-93, Sotheby-London, #10, illus.), 4¼ x 5¾ in., (10.8 x 14.6 cm.), etching (BP 632, DM 1611, FR 5430, Y 101,554).

BOEREN, Edward

$660* *"Out Of The Gate" and "Buckeroo": Two,* mono., sig., 1 discolored, (06-11-93, Doyle, #20), larger 5 x 7 in., (127 x 178 mm.), drypoints (BP 434, DM 1073, FR 3616, Y 70,027).

BOETTI, Alighiero Italian b. 1940

$657* *Insicuro Noncurante,* t., d., s., 40 x 30 cm, (05-18-93, Auction Phila, #95, illus.), photograph (BP 431, DM 1061, FR 3578, Y 73,350, L 978).

BOEZEM, Marius

$141* *Etude Gothique, 1980,* s., t., d., #a.p.I/XV, margins, good cond., (05-27-93, Sotheby-Amstrdm, #566), sh 33Ɐzn x 21M, in., (855 x 556 mm.), silkscreen on wove (BP 90, DM 226, FR 763, Y 15,116, G 253).

$179* *L'Uomo Volante (Progetto Per Cathedrale Gotiche), 1979,* s., t., d., i. E.A., margins, good cond., (05-27-93, Sotheby-Amstrdm, #565), sh 33M, x 22Ɐzn in., (860 x 560 mm.), screenprint on wove (BP 115, DM 287, FR 968, Y 19,190, G 322).

$320* *Packed Space, 1978: Seventeen,* s., d., #36/50, pub. Editions Media, good cond., (05-27-93, Sotheby-Amstrdm, #564), overall size 10Mzn x 14Ɐzn in., (265 x 373 mm.), silkscreen (BP 205, DM 513, FR 1731, Y 34,305, G 575).

BOFA, Gus (Gustave BLANCHOT) 1883-1968

$299* *Le "Gonfle Pneus" Gonfle 15 Pneus,* cond. B, (03-16-93, Boisgirard, #123, illus.), 62Ɐzn x 46Mzn in., (158 x 118 cm.), poster (BP 206, DM 497, FR 1689, Y 34,963).

BOGART, Bram b. 1921

$1172* *Carre Jaune Sur Fond Rouge, 1989,* s., d., #97/99, good cond., (12-09-92, Sotheby-Amstrdm, #506), sheet 38C, x 38Ɐzn in., (975 x 970 mm.), color aquagravure (aquatint) (BP 748, DM 1840, FR 6277, Y 145,319, G 2070).

$1303* *Carres Jaunes Et Bleus, 1989,* s., d., #96/99, good cond., (12-09-92, Sotheby-Amstrdm, #507), sheet 37Ɐzn x 37Ɐzn in., (960 x 965 mm.), color aquagravure (aquatint) (BP 832, DM 2045, FR 6979, Y 161,562, G 2300).

$1151* *Carres Jaunes Et Bleus, 1989,* s., d., #E.A. 11/90, full sheet p. to edges, good cond., (05-27-93, Sotheby-Amstrdm, #568, illus.), sh 38Ɐzn x 38C, in., (970 x 975 mm.), colored aquatint (BP 737, DM 1847, FR 6225, Y 123,392, G 2070).

BI *Carres Noir Et Blanc, 1989,* s., d., good cond., sheet 1125 x 815 mm, est. G 2/3,000, (12-09-92, Sotheby-Amstrdm, #504), color aquagravure (aquatint).

$640* *Carres Noir Et Blanc, 1989,* s., d., #E.A. 77/90, full sheet p. to edges, good cond., (05-27-93, Sotheby-Amstrdm, #572), sh 4Ɐzn x 32Z, in., (110 x 816 mm.), colored aquagravure (aquatint) (BP 410, DM 1027, FR 3461, Y 68,611, G 1150).

$1023* *"Carres Noirs Et Blancs" and "Carres Jaunes Et Bleus", 1989: Two,* each s., d., 2nd #96/99, margins, good cond., (12-03-92, Sotheby-London, #616, illus.), one 44 x 32 in., (111.8 x 81.3 cm.), other 38 x 38C, in., (111.8 x 81.3 cm.), aquagravures in colors (BP 660, DM 1609, FR 5491, Y 127,286).

$1303* *Losange Bleu, 1989,* s., d., #99/99, good cond., sheet 1120 x 805 mm, (12-09-92, Sotheby-Amstrdm, #505), color aquagravure (aquatint) (BP 832, DM 2045, FR 6979, Y 161,562, G 2300).

$576* *Losange Bleu, 1989,* s., d., #98/99, full sheet p. to edges, good cond., (05-27-93, Sotheby-Amstrdm, #571), sh 43Ɐzn x 32C, in., (111 x 82.2 cm.), colored aquagravure (aquatint) (BP 369, DM 924, FR 3115, Y 61,750, G 1035).

$832* *Triangle Rouge Et Jaune, 1989,* s., d., #E.A. 5/20, full sheet p. to edges, good cond., (05-27-93, Sotheby-Amstrdm, #569, illus.), sh 43M, x 32C, in., (111.5 x 82.2 cm.), colored aquagravure (aquatint) (BP 533, DM 1335, FR 4500, Y 89,194, G 1495).

BI *Triangle Rouge Et Jaune, 1989,* s., d., num. E.A. 6/20, good cond., sheet 1120 x 835 mm, est. G 2/3,000, (12-09-92, Sotheby-Amstrdm, #509), color silkscreen w/ embossing.

BI *Untitled, 1970,* s., d., #43/45, margins, good cond.?, est. G 6/800, (12-09-92, Sotheby-Amstrdm, #502), 11Mzn x 18½ in., (290 x 470 mm.), blue etching on wove.

$256* *Untitled, 1970,* s., d., #12/190, full sheet, good cond., minor handling creases, (05-27-93, Sotheby-Amstrdm, #567), sh 29¾ x 21Ɐzn in., (755 x 558 mm.), colored lithograph on wove (BP 164, DM 411, FR 1385, Y 27,444, G 460).

$307* *Untitled, 1978,* s., margins, good cond., (05-27-93, Sotheby-Amstrdm, #387, illus.), 23M, x 17Ɐzn in., (607 x 450 mm.), colored lithograph on wove (BP 197, DM 493, FR 1660, Y 32,912, G 552).

$416* *Untitled, 1978,* s., margins, good cond., (05-27-93, Sotheby-Amstrdm, #388), 25C, x 18Z, in., (644 x 460 mm.), colored lithograph on wove (BP 266, DM 668, FR 2250, Y 44,597, G 748).

$384* *Untitled, 1978,* s., margins, good cond., (05-27-93, Sotheby-Amstrdm, #389), 18Ɐzn x 26Zzn in., (482 x 662 mm.), colored lithograph on wove (BP 246, DM 616, FR 2077, Y 41,166, G 690).

BOHATSCH, Erwin b. 1951

$149* *Untitled,* s., d., num. Bohatsch 88, #34/150, (04-21-93, Dorotheum, #723), linocut (BP 97, DM 238, FR 805, Y 16,495, SC 1680).

BOHEILT

$77* *"Sailing Ship",* s., (05-15-93, Dunning, #182), 24 x 36 in., (61 x 91.4 cm.), color lithograph (BP 50, DM 124, FR 416, Y 8536).

BOHEMEN, Kees van b. 1929

BI *Racer, 1970,* s. K.v.Bohemen 70, 10/100, est. DK 2,500, (09-30-92, Kunsthallen, #46), color serigraph.

BOHM, J.

$13 *"Glashauser",* holes, folds, edges torn, (03-04-93, Alderfer, #286), 37½ x 24¾ in., (95.3 x 62.9 cm.), poster (BP 9, DM 21, FR 72, Y 1514).

BOHME, Gerd 1899-1978

$361* *Im Rausch, 1920,* s., (11-28-92, Grisebach, #443, illus.), 12Ɐzn x 11B, in., (31.3 x 29.5 cm.), lithograph on factory printed paper (BP 238, DM 575, FR 1952, Y 44,928).

BOHROD, Aaron American 1907-1992

$165* *"New Orleans Street", 1938,* pub. AAA, s. Aaron Bohrod, Bohrod in stone, very good cond., tape residue, foxing, (09-11-92, Skinner, #70), 9 x 12 in., (22.9 x 30.5 cm.), lithograph on wove (BP 85, DM 238, FR 807, Y 20,444).

$44* *Untitled,* s., paper toned, (10-31-92, Cleveland, #81), 9¼ x 13Z, in., (23.5 x 33.3 cm.), lithograph (BP 28, DM 68, FR 230, Y 5450).

BOILLY, Louis (after)

$491* *"La Douce Resistance" and "On La Tire Aujourd'Hui": Two,* engraved by Tresca, restored, staining, (06-16-93, Ader Tajan, #23), 17Zzn x 14Zzn in., (45.5 x 38 cm.), stipple print (BP 327, DM 815, FR 2735, Y 52,368).

$303* *"Prends Ce Biscuit" and "Nous Etions Deux...Nous Voila Trois": Two,* reddish stains, small margins, (03-22-93, Pescheteau, #5), (BP 204, DM 497, FR 1689, Y 35,086).

BOILLY, Louis Leopold French 1761-1845

BI *Le Relais Des Diligences,* ink s., reddish stains, paper remains verso, est. FF4/6,000, (06-28-93, Loudmer, #195A), 5Zzn x 9B, in., (145 x 245 mm.), black lithograph embellished w/watercolor and ink on wove.

BOIRSART, Pierre

$22* *French Chateau,* s., (10-16-92, DuMouchelle, #2493), 13¾ x 10½ in., (34.9 x 26.7 cm.), hand-colored etching (BP 13, DM 32, FR 110, Y 2627).

BOISSEAU, Jean Jacques de French 1736-1810

$198* *Foret De Fontainbleau, 1764: Two,* (06-13-93, Hindman, #380), each 5 x 7¼ in., (12.7 x 18.4 cm.), etching (BP 130, DM 322, FR 1083, Y 20,836).

$88* *Stable Scene, 1780,* (10-18-92, Hindman, #505), 9¾ x 13B, in., (24.8 x 34.6 cm.), etching (BP 54, DM 131, FR 444, Y 10,558).

BOISSIEU, Jean Jacques de French 1736-1810

$208* *La Cascade (Le Blanc 91/III), 1809,* creased, (12-01-92, Karl/Faber, #16), etching (BP 137, DM 332, FR 1130, Y 25,896).

$361* *Les Grands Charlatans (Portalis-Beraldi I; S. 200; De Boissieu 63 IV), 1772,* watermark, (12-04-92, Bassenge, #6520), 10¼ x 13Zzn in., (26 x 33.1 cm.), etching (BP 232, DM 575, FR 1950, Y 45,069).

BI *Le Petit Hermitage (J.J. de Boissieu 90iii/V; I.F.F., 90), 1793,* definitive state, reddish stains, (05-15-93, Loudmer, #122), 8Mzn x 12Zzn in., (214 x 322 mm.), sh 10C, x 14Z, in., (214 x 322 mm.), etching on laid.

$144* *Vue Du Temple De Vesta (De Boissieu 74 III, Le Blanc 80 II), 1774,* (12-04-92, Bassenge, #6522), 11B, x 14¾ in., (29.5 x 37.5 cm.), etching (BP 92, DM 229, FR 778, Y 17,978).

$217* *Vue Du Temple Du Soleil, De L'Arc De Tite Et Fragment Du Palais Des Empereurs (De Boissieu 69 III; Le Blanc 72 III), 1773,* (12-04-92, Bassenge, #6521), 10Zzn x 13Zzn in., (25.6 x 34.8 cm.), etching (BP 139, DM 346, FR 1172, Y 27,091).

BOISSONNAS ET EGGLER STUDIO

$76* *Yulia Biriukova At Age 15,* studio blind stamp, ident. in Thoreau MacDonald's hand verso, prov., (06-07-93, Ritchie, #4, illus.), 5Z, x 4Z, in., black and white photograph on support (BP 50, DM 123, FR 415, Y 8153, C$ 97).

BOISSONNAS and EGGLER

$472* *Russian Imperial Family, 1907,* mounted on card, i., photog.'s blindstamp, s. by Head of the Imperial Suite, photog.'s credit stamp, (05-06-93, Christie-London, #147), 4 x 5½ in., photograph, oval gelatin silver print (BP 299, DM 743, FR 2503, Y 51,931).

BOISVERT, Normand Canadian b. 1950

BI *"St-Michel Des Forges",* #214/250, t., s. in plate Boisvert, (03-16-93, Encans, #15), 15¾ x 19Zzn in., (40 x 50 cm.), photolithograph.

BOL, Ferdinand Dutch 1616-1680

$939* *Bildnis Einer Jungen Frau Mit Federhut (B. 15; Dutuit 17 II; Hollstein 16 II),* prov., oval, foxed, (12-04-92, Bassenge, #6054), 2Zzn x 3Zzn in., (7.1 x 10 cm.), etching (BP 602, DM 1495, FR 5073, Y 117,228).

$3178* *Brustbildnis Eines Offiziers MIt Federgeschmucktem Barett (Bartsch 11; Dutuit 12; Hollstein 12 II), 1645,* (06-10-93, Hauswedell/Nolt, #34), etching and drypoint (BP 2079, DM 5175, FR 17,423, Y 337,331).

$21,699* *The Holy Family In The Room (B., Holl. 4), 1645,* burr, narrow to thread margins, watermark, glue, paper losses, ex. coll. Sir Edward Astley (L. 2775), (06-29-93, Sotheby-London, #11, illus.), 7¼ x 8½ in., (18.4 x 21.6 cm.), etching, drypoint and engraving (BP 14,375, DM 36,641, FR 123,500, Y 2,309,879).

BOL, Hans Dutch 1534-1593

$4461* *Das Gleichnis Vom Unkraut Saenden Feind (Van der Kellen, Wurzbach und Hollstein 10-13), 1574: Four,* watermark, (06-04-93, Bassenge, #5040, illus.), etching in Tondo (BP 2951, DM 7244, FR 24,417, Y 481,126).

BOL, Hans (after)

$722* *Flusslandschaft Mit Blick Auf Ein Dorf (Hollstein 7-18 I),* (12-04-92, Bassenge, #6055, illus.), 8Zzn x 12B, in., (22.4 x 32 cm.), engraving (BP 463, DM 1150, FR 3901, Y 90,137).

$1498* *The Months Of The Year, (Bol., 66-71, 73-7; Holl., A. Collaert, 523-8, 530-4), c. 1585: Eleven,* by A. Collaert, first state (of two), from set of twelve, each plate, made-up hall, staining, foxing, very good cond., (12-01-92, Christie-London, #84, illus.), etching w/engraving (BP 990, DM 2388, FR 8137, Y 186,504).

$1249* *A River Landscape With A Barque On A River, (Holl. 13),* by H. Cock, first state (of two), watermark, narrow margins, trimmed, thin spot, registration holes, good cond., (12-01-92, Christie-London, #87), P. 8Zzn x 12B, in., (228 x 321 mm.), etching w/engravivng (BP 825, DM 1991, FR 6784, Y 155,503).

BOLLEE, Leon 1870-1913

BI *Orville And Wilbur Wright At Le Mans, France, 1908,* notations, est. $7/1,000, (10-14-92, Swann, #280, illus.), 4C, x 6Z, in., (11.1 x 15.6 cm.), photograph, silver print.

$1045* *Orville And Wilbur Wright, Dayton, Ohio, c. 1905,* (04-07-93, Swann, #291, illus.), 8M, x 6¼ in., photograph, silver print (BP 691, DM 1690, FR 5720, Y 118,723).

$1540* *Self-Portrait In Wright Aeroplane, c. 1909,* (10-13-92, Christie-NY, #66, illus.), 11¾ x 15¾ in., (29.8 x 40 cm.), photograph, gelatin silver print (BP 897, DM 2256, FR 7666, Y 186,735).

$1150* *"Wilbur Wright Flying", "Wilbur Wright Preparing To Fly", "Spectators Waiting For Wilbur Wright To Fly" and "Le Mans", 1909: Four,* (04-08-93, Christie-NY, #41, illus.), each approx. 4¼ x 6C, in., (10.8 x 16.2 cm.), photograph, gelatin silver print (BP 754, DM 1847, FR 6253, Y 130,504).

BOLLIN, LIEBLER and HOFFMAN

$66* *Chicago And Alton RR, Great Palace Reclining Chair Route,* loss, tears, (04-02-93, Eldred, #342), 22 x 14 in., (55.9 x 35.6 cm.), colored lithograph poster (BP 43, DM 106, FR 360, Y 7515).

BOLOTOWSKY, Ilya Russian/American 1907-1981

$138* *Abstraction,* s. Ilya Bolotowsky, #5/100, very good cond., (03-12-93, Skinner, #99, illus.), 32C, x 19½ in., (82.2 x 49.5 cm.), screenprint in red, orange, blue and white in oval format on heavy wove (BP 96, DM 230, FR 781, Y 16,264).

$110* *Composition,* s., #30/125, (11-01-92, Hanzel, #275), serigraph (BP 72, DM 174, FR 585, Y 13,600).

$154* *Plate VI,* s., #79/125, prov., (05-16-93, Hindman, #619), 33¾ x 13¾ in., (85.7 x 34.9 cm.), color serigraph (BP 100, DM 248, FR 832, Y 17,071).

$440* *"Red Blue Egg" and "Red Circle": Two,* each s., num. 101/125, margins, apparently good cond., (02-24-93, Butterfield, #3189), 28 x 17¼ in., (711 x 438 mm.), 22 x 22 in., (711 x 438 mm.), silkscreen in colors on wove (BP 307, DM 714, FR 2422, Y 51,631).

$220* *Untitled,* s., #29/125, (06-13-93, Hindman, #325), approx. 21 x 23 in., (53.3 x 58.4 cm.), color serigraph (BP 144, DM 358, FR 1204, Y 23,151).

$165* *Untitled: Two,* both s., one #7/125, other #9/125, (06-13-93, Hindman, #324), larger 21Z, x 22¾ in., (53.7 x 57.8 cm.), color serigraph (BP 108, DM 269, FR 903, Y 17,363).

BOLSWERT, Boetius Adams 1580-1633

$211* *Anbetung Der Hirten (Hollstein Bd. III, 4),* trimmed, (03-24-93, Venator/Hansten, #2486), sh 19Xzn x 15C, in., (49.7 x 39 cm.), engraving (BP 143, DM 345, FR 1173, Y 24,791).

BI *The Bad Times Of The Peasants,* after David Vinckeboons, trimmed to image, est. BP 70/100, (07-16-92, Bonhams-Chelsea, #528), 8 x 11Z, in., (20.3 x 28.3 cm.), engraving.

$39* *The Bad Times Of The Peasants,* after David Vinckeboons, trimmed to image, (09-17-92, Bonhams-Chelsea,

#173), image 8 x 11Z, in., (20.3 x 28.3 cm.), engraving (BP 22, DM 58, FR 198, Y 4856).

$830* *Die Grosse Landschaft Mit Abraham Und Melchisedek (Wurzbach 7a; Hollstein 2/IV), 1634,* after G. van Coninxloo, restored tears, (12-01-92, Karl/Faber, #17), approx. 14B\n x 23Zn in., (38 x 58.5 cm.), engraving (BP 548, DM 1323, FR 4508, Y 103,337).

$464* *Large Landscapes With Farmhouse (Holl., vol. 2, 425, 427, 438), 1614: Set Of Three,* after Abraham Bloemaert, thin margins, pl. 6: crease, stain; pl. 8: restored; pl. 20: tear, (05-15-93, Loudmer, #52, illus.), approx. 5ZBn x 9>\n in., (151 x 243 mm.), etchings on laid (BP 302, DM 746, FR 2508, Y 51,436).

BOLSWERT, Schelte Adams c. 1586-1659

BI *Christi Einzug In Jerusalem (Hollstein Bd. 3, 14), 1634,* after D. Vinckboons, est. DM 800-, (09-14-92, Venator/Hansten, #1464), image 16Zn x 24Zn in., (40.8 x 63.4 cm.), engraving.

BOLTANSKI, Christian French b. 1944

$9350* *Le Repas Refuse,* exec. 1974, prov., (10-08-92, Christie-NY, #221, illus.), 39½ x 27½ in., (95.2 x 64.7 cm.), acrylic and colored crayons on black and white photograph (BP 5564, DM 13,829, FR 46,938, Y 1,136,087).

BOLTS, Hugh Pierce American 20th cent.

$165* *Drying Nets,* s., t., repaired tears, smudging, good cond., (11-12-92, Freemn/Fine Art, #32), 15½ x 17¼ in., (39.4 x 43.8 cm.), litho (BP 108, DM 261, FR 882, Y 20,459).

BOMBLED

$40* *Carte Militaire De La France,* fairly good cond., (02-12-93, Cheval/Robert, #104), 24Mn x 35Zn in., (62 x 89 cm.), poster (BP 28, DM 66, FR 224, Y 4824).

BOMMELS, Peter b. 1951

BI *Entlarvungsstation, 1985,* s., d., est. DM 300-, (09-25-92, Granier, #2773), sheet 21¼ x 15B, in., (54 x 39.7 cm.), etching on yellow copper print paper.

BOMPARD, J.-P.

$898* *PLM. Barcelonnette. "Son Monte-Pente, Son Ecole De Ski, Ses Tremplins, Sa Patinoire",* very good cond., (03-15-93, Arcole, #75, illus.), 37Zn x 23¼ in., (96 x 59 cm.), poster (BP 625, DM 1492, FR 5071, Y 106,373).

BON, E.

BI *Ch. De Fer Algeriens: Le Sud Algerien. "El Kantara". 1948,* very good cond., (03-13-93, Laurin, #32), 39C\ x 23B, in., (100 x 60 cm.), .

BONASONE, Giulio 1498-c. 1580

BI *Badende Liebende (B. XV, 177),* after 1530, after Raffael, watermark, est. DM 4,500, (06-04-93, Bassenge, #5044, illus.), 9Z, x 13Zn in., (23.2 x 35.4 cm.), engraving on haunchdunnes Japan.

BI *Badende Liebende (B. XV, 177), c. 1530,* after Raffael, est. DM 7,500, (12-04-92, Bassenge, #6062), 9Z, x 13Zn in., (23.2 x 35.4 cm.), engraving.

$1082* *The Birth Of Saint John The Baptist (B. 76; M. 71), c. 1546,* after J. del Conte, Massari's 2nd state of 4, watermark, margins, crease, made-up loss, nicks, foxing, very good cond., prov., (12-01-92, Christie-London, #200), plate 11>n x 17ZZn in., (293 x 449 mm.), engraving (BP 715, DM 1725, FR 5877, Y 134,711).

$433* *Zwei Satyre Fuhren Silen Konig Midas Vor (B. XV, 89), c. 1570,* watermark, (12-04-92, Bassenge, #6061, illus.), 5½ x 8>n in., (14 x 21.8 cm.), engraving (BP 278, DM 690, FR 2339, Y 54,057).

BONCOMPAIN, Pierre b. 1938

$140* *"Bouquet Jaune",* E.A., s., (04-04-93, Pescheteau, #161), 19Zn x 14Zn in., (49 x 38 cm.), color lithograph on Arches (BP 92, DM 225, FR 764, Y 15,940).

$160* *"Femme En Jaune",* E.A., s., (04-04-93, Pescheteau, #162), 19Zn x 14Zn in., (49 x 38 cm.), color lithograph on Arches (BP 105, DM 257, FR 873, Y 18,217).

BONE, Muirhead Scottish 1876-1953

$151* *"Naval Vessels At Dock",* laid down, (01-14-93, Bonhams, #100), image 24 x 15 in., (61 x 38.1 cm.), lithograph (BP 99, DM 247, FR 835, Y 19,037).

$880* *Picadilly Circus,* s., (12-13-92, Hindman, #263), 11¾ x 14M, in., drypoint (BP 563, DM 1383, FR 4713, Y 108,870).

$4675* *A Spanish Good Friday (Ronda) (Dodgson 412), 1925,* s., edit., large margins, good cond., light stain, soiling, creases,Edith Schumann 1988 Trust, (11-05-92, Sotheby-NY, #82, illus.), 12¾ x 8Z, in., (323 x 207 mm.), drypoint on cream simili-Japan (BP 3041, DM 7394, FR 25,013, Y 573,549).

$2070* *A Spanish Good Friday (Ronda) (Dodgson 412), 1925,* s., margins, good cond., light-stain, foxing, soiling, (05-13-93, Sotheby-NY, #460A, illus.), 12B, x 8Z, in., (320 x 205 mm.), sh 15¼ x 10Z, in., (320 x 205 mm.), drypoint on cream simili-Japan (BP 1359, DM 3342, FR 11,275, Y 231,104).

$991* *A Spanish Good-Friday Night (Ronda),* s., (04-02-93, Picard, #29), 12B, x 8Zn in., (32 x 20.5 cm.), black drypoint on laid (BP 653, DM 1593, FR 5409, Y 112,832).

$469* *Study For "Windy Night, Stockholm", 1935,* one of 21 proofs covering 4 states, margins, front cover illus., (08-20-92, Bonhams-Chelsea, #120, illus.), plate 11¾ x 7¾ in., (29.8 x 19.7 cm.), drypoint etching on laid paper (BP 242, DM 679, FR 2305, Y 59,225).

BONECHI, Lorenzo

$449* *Libretto, 1983: Five,* one s., d., #6/16; four s., d., num., margins, good cond., creasing, (10-15-92, Sotheby-London, #83, illus.), drypoint p. in blue w/tone on chine applique (BP 275, DM 668, FR 2267, Y 53,869).

BONET, Jordi 1932-1979

$409* *"Etre Conscient": Set Of Seven,* #78/90, s. Jordi Bonet, (10-20-92, Encans, #17), serigraphs (BP 229, DM 622, FR 2116, Y 51,266, C$ 500).

$45* *Untitled,* from "L'Etre conscient", num., s. Jordi Bonet, (04-20-93, Encans, #9), 15¾ x 19Z\n in., (40 x 50 cm.), lithograph (BP 29, DM 72, FR 242, Y 4965, C$ 56).

BONFILS, Felix

BI *Views Of Palestine, 1870s: Three,* two s., each t. in neg., est. $800/1,200, (04-08-93, Christie-NY, #1, illus.), each approx. 8½ x 11 in., (21.6 x 27.9 cm.), photograph, albumen prints.

BONFILS, Robert French 1886-1972

$25 *Les Allies,* damage, stain, (09-24-92, Alderfer, #243), 19 x 12C, in., (48.3 x 31.4 cm.), (BP 15, DM 37, FR 126, Y 3007).

$378* *Exposition Internationale Des Arts Decoratifs Et Industriels Modernes, Paris, 1925,* p. de Vaugirard, good cond., (11-19-92, Ribeyre/Baron, #130), 23B, x 15>n in., (60 x 39.5 cm.), poster (BP 249, DM 603, FR 2030, Y 47,009).

$479* *Paris 1925. Exposition Internationale Des Arts Decoratifs,* cond. A, (03-16-93, Boisgirard, #56), 23¼ x 14Zn in., (59 x 38 cm.), poster (BP 331, DM 796, FR 2706, Y 56,010).

$1154* *Salon D'Automne, Grand Palais Paris, 1928,* p. Marcel Picard, good cond., (11-19-92, Ribeyre/Baron, #131), 62Zn x 47¼ in., (160 x 120 cm.), poster (BP 760, DM 1840, FR 6198, Y 143,514).

BONHEUR, Rosa French 1822-1899

BI *"Lions Den",* foxing, water stain, est. $1,5/2000, (05-07-93, Goldberg, #423, illus.), 26¾ x 33¾ in., (67.9 x 85.7 cm.), engraving.

BONI, P.

$62* *"Fa"!, 1975,* s., ded., #10/50, good margins, (05-06-93, Laurin, #10), aquatint and print in color (BP 39, DM 98, FR 329, Y 6821).

BONI, Paolo Italian b. 1926

BI *Recueillement,* s., The Print Club of Cleveland publication no. 44, 1966, est. $125/175, (07-03-92, Sloan, #316), 14½ x 10 in., (36.8 x 25.4 cm.), metal relief and intaglio.

$94* *"Recueillement", 1966,* s., Print Club of Cleveland Publication No. 44, excellent cond., (10-31-92, Cleveland, #361), 14½ x 10 in., (36.8 x 25.4 cm.), relief and intaglio in colors (BP 60, DM 145, FR 491, Y 11,644).

BONILLA, Guillermo
$40　*"Semana Santa 1961",* (03-04-93, Alderfer, #263), 39 x 24¼ in., (99.1 x 61.6 cm.), poster (BP 28, DM 65, FR 223, Y 4657).

BONINGTON, Richard Parkes　　　English 1801-1828
$220*　*"Facade De L'Eglise De Brou", 1825 and "Vue D'Une Rue Des Faubourgs De Besancon", 1827 (A.C. 23 et 30): Two,* reddish stains, tear, good margins, (06-11-93, Picard, #10), one 13℃, x 9ℤzn in., (340 x 230 mm.), other 13¾ x 10ℤzn in., (340 x 230 mm.), lithographs on chine fixe (BP 145, DM 358, FR 1205, Y 23,342).
$413*　*Rue Du Gros Horloge A Rouen (A. Curtis, num. 16), 1824,* 2 out of 3, creases, large margins, (04-02-93, Picard, #30), 10¼ x 10�届, in., (26 x 27 cm.), lithograph on Chine fixe (BP 272, DM 664, FR 2254, Y 47,023).
$320*　*Rue Du Gros Horloge, Rouen (A. Curtis 16), 1824,* definitive state, creases, reddish stains, good margins, (06-11-93, Picard, #9), 9℠zn x 9ℤℤzn in., (239 x 246 mm.), lithograph on chine (BP 210, DM 520, FR 1753, Y 33,952).
$268*　*Vues Pittoresques De L'Ecosse (L.D., num. 31 (2/3), 31 (2/3), 32 (3/4), 34 (2 from 2/3), 35 (2/3), 36 (1/3 and 2/3), 37 (2/4), 38 (2/3), 39 (2/3, +1), 40 (2/3, + 1), 41 (2 impressions), 1826: Set of Fifteen,* stains, creases, reddish marks, good margins, (04-02-93, Picard, #32), lithographs, 8 on Chine fixe (BP 177, DM 431, FR 1463, Y 30,513).

BONIS, A. de (attrib.)
BI　*The Arch Of Titus,* late 1850s, stamped ADB, t. in Italian, ink stamp, mounted on paper, est. BP 3/500, (05-06-93, Christie-London, #43, illus.), 9届, x 7届, in., photograph, light albumen print.
$1633*　*"The Bridge And Castel San Angelo", "The Bridge Of The Quattro Capi" and "The Campidoglio": Three,* 1850s-60s, photog.'s ink stamp ADB, stamped, t. in Italian, mounted on paper, lit., (05-06-93, Christie-London, #45, illus.), each approx. 7℃, x 9℃, in., photograph, light albumen print (BP 1035, DM 2572, FR 8659, Y 179,668).
BI　*Cloister Of San Giovanni In Laterano, c. 1858: Two,* one t., each ink stamp ADB, mounted, photog.'s ink stamp, t. in Italian, lit., est. BP 1,2/1,600, (05-06-93, Christie-London, #40, illus.), one 9¾ x 7½ in., the other 7¼ x 9¾ in., photograph, light albumen print.
$453*　*Fountain In The Courtyard Of The Palazzo Di Venezia,* 1850-60s, stamped DB, mounted on card, stamped DB and ADB, t. in Italian, (05-06-93, Christie-London, #46, illus.), 9届, x 7届, in., photograph, albumen print (BP 287, DM 713, FR 2402, Y 49,840).
$3266*　*The Gardens Of The French Academy, c. 1858: Two,* one stamped DB, mounted on card, stamped DB abd ADB, t. in Italian; other t. in Italian, stamped ADB, mounted on paper, lit., (05-06-93, Christie-London, #41, illus.), one 9M, x 7¾ in., the other 7℃, x 9½ in., photograph, 1 albumen print, 1 light albumen print (BP 2070, DM 5144, FR 17,317, Y 359,335).
$1452*　*"The Porta Pia", "Street Scene From The Piazza Sciarra" and "Unidentified Doorway": Three,* 1850s-60s, first stamped DB; each stamped, t. in Italian, ink stamp ADB, (05-06-93, Christie-London, #47, illus.), smallest 7 x 9 in., largest 9℃, x 7½ in., photograph, albumen print (BP 920, DM 2287, FR 7699, Y 159,754).
$3448*　*Stair Of The Church Of The Cappuccini,* 1850s-60s, photog.'s DB stamp, t. in Italian, ink stamp ADB, (05-06-93, Christie-London, #44, illus.), 7 x 9届, in., photograph, albumen print (BP 2185, DM 5431, FR 18,282, Y 379,360).
$1815*　*The Tritone Fountain In The Piazza Barberini,* late 1860s, photog.'s credit stamp ADB, mounted on paper, t., ink stamp, (05-06-93, Christie-London, #39, illus.), 7½ x 9℃, in., photograph, light albumen print (BP 1150, DM 2859, FR 9624, Y 199,692).

BONIS, R.
$167*　*Ch. De Fer Du Nord: Plage Sainte-Cecile,* good cond., (01-23-93, Ribeyre/Baron, #24), 41¾ x 29¾ in., (106 x 75.5 cm.), poster (BP 109, DM 266, FR 898, Y 20,901).

BONNARD, Pierre　　　French 1867-1947
$2978*　*Au Theatre (Bouvet 67; Roger-Marx 65; Johnson 1977, 10.9), 1899,* sheet 9 of series: Quelques Aspects de la Vie de Paris, (06-23-93, Kornfeld, #229), color lithograph

on thin wove (BP 2023, DM 5039, FR 16,949, Y 324,436, SF 4485).
$1150*　*Au Theatre (R.-M. 65; B. 67; Johnson 10.9), 1899,* from Quelques aspects de la vie de Paris, pub. Vollard, full margins, repairs, losses, (02-11-93, Sotheby-NY, #62), 7M, x 15¾ in., (200 x 400 mm.), sheet 16ℤ, x 21ℤn in., (200 x 400 mm.), lithograph printed in colors on wove (BP 811, DM 1905, FR 6446, Y 138,638).
$17,499*　*Avenue Du Bois (Bouvet 59, Roger-Marx 57, Johnson 1977, 10.1), 1899,* sheet 1 of series Quelques Aspects de la Vie de Paris, p. Vollard, (06-25-93, Kornfeld, #13, illus.), 12℃n x 18ℤ, in., color lithograph (BP 11,836, DM 29,791, FR 100,338, Y 1,854,887, SF 26,450).
$819*　*Les Bas (R.-M. 88, B. 101), 1927-28,* first state, reprod., (02-24-93, Picard, #19), signature on thin chine (BP 571, DM 1330, FR 4507, Y 96,104).
$1540*　*Les Boulevards (R.-M. 74; B. 72), 1900,* pub. Das Mappenwerk der Insel, stamp verso, full margins, good cond., printer's crease, nicks, losses, (11-05-92, Sotheby-NY, #85), 10届, x 13ℤ, in., (270 x 332 mm.), sheet 10M, x 14 in., (270 x 332 mm.), lithograph p. in colors on chine volant (BP 1002, DM 2436, FR 8240, Y 188,934).
BI　*Les Boulevards (Roger-Marx 74), 1900,* stamp, est. DM 3,500, (06-05-93, Bassenge, #5923, illus.), 10届, x 13℃n in., (27 x 33.5 cm.), color lithograph on Japan.
BI　*Les Boulevards (Roger-Marx 74, Sohn 31302-5), 1900,* sheet 5 of 2, Insel-Mappe, Mai 1900, est. DM 4,000, (05-26-93, Lempertz, #38, illus.), 10ℤzn x 13M, in., (27.5 x 35.2 cm.), color lithograph on machine-made.
$12,988*　*Le Canotage (F.B. 42), 1897,* whole margins, s., 100 impressions, reddish stains, (06-11-93, Picard, #12), 10¼ x 18½ in., (260 x 470 mm.), color lithograph on thin chine (BP 8534, DM 21,108, FR 71,167, Y 1,378,037).
$275*　*Cat On A Hassock,* mono. in plate, wide margins, good cond., faint mat burn, (05-22-93, Weschler, #166), 7¼ x 4¾ in., (18.4 x 12.1 cm.), etching (BP 178, DM 447, FR 1504, Y 30,320).
$2090*　*Le Chevrier (Roger-Marx, Bouvet 12), 1893,* mono., proof impressions, pub. F. Froment, full margins, good cond., crease, soiling, mat stain, loss in tip, (11-05-92, Sotheby-NY, #83, illus.), 9℃, x 3ℤ, in., (238 x 80 mm.), lithograph on chine volant (BP 1359, DM 3305, FR 11,182, Y 256,410).
$1024*　*Conversation (Roger-Marx, Bouvet 28), 1893,* num., s., staining, full margins, 1 of 100, (02-24-93, Picard, #16), lithograph au pinceau and crayon (BP 714, DM 1662, FR 5636, Y 120,160).
$1150*　*La Coupe Et La Compotier (R.-M. 80; B. 93), 1925,* s., Frapier stamps, trial proof of 2nd state, large margins, good cond., rubbing, (05-13-93, Sotheby-NY, #463), 7¼ x 10ℤ, in., (185 x 257 mm.), sh 12¾ x 19届, in., (185 x 257 mm.), lithograph on Japan (BP 755, DM 1857, FR 6264, Y 128,391).
$660*　*La Coupe Et Le Compotier (F.B. 93), 1925,* whole margins, 3rd state, #69/100, s., drystamp, reddish marks, (04-02-93, Picard, #35), 7ℤn x 10¼ in., (18 x 26 cm.), black lithograph on creme wove (BP 435, DM 1061, FR 3603, Y 75,145).
$440*　*"Coupe Et Le Compotier" (B. 93), 1925,* s., fox stain, (10-31-92, Cleveland, #253), 7ℤ, x 10¼ in., (18.1 x 26 cm.), lithograph (BP 282, DM 677, FR 2296, Y 54,503).
$440*　*"La Derniere Croisade" (Bouvet 37 ii/ii), 1896,* tears, (10-31-92, Cleveland, #252, illus.), 12¾ x 19M, in., (32.4 x 50.5 cm.), lithograph (BP 282, DM 677, FR 2296, Y 54,503).
$2673*　*Etude De Nu (Bouv. 97/II), 1925,* s., num., (06-23-93, Kornfeld, #231), lithograph on China (BP 1816, DM 4523, FR 15,213, Y 291,208, SF 4025).
$2645*　*Femme Au Parapluie (Roger-Marx 35; Bouvet 33), 1895,* s., pub. in L'Album de la Revue blanche, full margins, good cond., foxing, repaired tear, creases, tape, John S. Spurbeck Estate, (05-13-93, Sotheby-NY, #461, illus.), 8届, x 5ℤ, in., (220 x 130 mm.), lithograph in colors (BP 1736, DM 4271, FR 14,406, Y 295,300).
$2684*　*Femme Debout Dans Sa Baignoire (Bouvet IV-Roger-Marx 81 IV), 1925,* s., mono. in stone, from Maitres et Petits-Maitres d'aujourd'hui, blindstamp, (06-10-93, Hauswedell/Nolt, #103, illus.), image 11ℤn x 7℃n in., (29.3 x 18.2 cm.), lithograph on hand-made (BP 1756, DM 4371, FR 14,715, Y 284,895).

$240* *"Femme Ecrivant" (Bouvet p. 207),* mono. in plate, (04-04-93, Pescheteau, #163), 12⅝ x 10¼ in., (32 x 26 cm.), black etching on laid (BP 158, DM 386, FR 1310, Y 27,326).

$220* *From "Dingo",* s. in plate, late impression, (12-10-92, Sloan, #3029), 10¾ x 8⅜ in., (27.3 x 21.3 cm.), soft ground etching (BP 142, DM 348, FR 1189, Y 27,214).

$3450* *Le Marchand Des Quatre-Saisons (R.-M. 63; B. 65), 1899,* from Quelques aspects de la vie de Paris, large (full?) margins, faded, mat/light-stain, margins folded back, glued to backing, John S. Spurbeck Estate, (05-13-93, Sotheby-NY, #462, illus.), 11⅜ x 13¼ in., (290 x 335 mm.), lithograph in colors on wove (BP 2265, DM 5571, FR 18,791, Y 385,174).

BI *Marchande D'Oursins,* num., est. DM 450-, (09-25-92, Granier, #2774), sheet 23⅝ x 30⅛ in., (60 x 76.5 cm.), color lithograph on Rives hand-made.

$110* *Le Parc Monceau,* s. in plate, late impression, (05-28-93, Sloan, #1923, illus.), (33.3 x 25.7 cm.), etching (BP 70, DM 174, FR 590, Y 11,795).

$345* *Le Parc Monceau (B. 114), 1937,* from Paris book edit. of 500, p. J.G. Daragnes, full margins, taped w/masking tape, good cond., mat/light-staining, creases, notations, (05-19-93, Butterfield, #2038), 13³⁄₁₆ x 10¼ in., (335 x 260 mm.), etching on Ingres laid (BP 224, DM 561, FR 1889, Y 38,193).

$145* *Le Parc Monceau (Bouvet 114), 1937,* s. in plate, from 500, (06-28-93, Loudmer, #196), 13⅜ x 10⁷⁄₁₆ in., (340 x 265 mm.), black etching on wove (BP 97, DM 246, FR 830, Y 15,385).

BI *Le Parc Monceau [B.114], 1937,* s. in plate, late impression, est. $3/350, (12-10-92, Sloan, #3018), 13⅛ x 10⅛ in., (33.3 x 25.7 cm.), etching.

$1980* *Le Pont (Bouvet 66), 1899,* from Quelques aspects de la vie de Paris, full margins, shaved, light-staining, colors attenuated, foxmarks, glue, (11-09-92, Christie-NY, #52, illus.), border 10¹⁵⁄₁₆ x 15½ in., (278 x 394 mm.), color lithograph on wove (BP 1309, DM 3161, FR 10,680, Y 245,719).

$2558* *Le Pont (Bouvet 66; Roger-Marx 64), 1899,* from Quelques aspects de la vie de Paris, pub. Vollard, full margins,good cond., mount staining, creasing, tape stain, paper loss, (12-03-92, Sotheby-London, #185, illus.), 10¾ x 16⅛ in., (273 x 410 mm.), lithograph in colors on fine wove (BP 1650, DM 4023, FR 13,731, Y 318,278).

$2661* *Portrait D'Ambroise Vollard (B. 89), c. 1924,* stains, full margins, annot., (02-24-93, Picard, #18), etching on wove (BP 1856, DM 4320, FR 14,645, Y 312,251).

$454* *Portrait De Renoir (F.B. 84), c. 1916,* pub. Vollard, (04-02-93, Picard, #34), 10⅝ x 7⅞ in., (27 x 20 cm.), etching (BP 299, DM 730, FR 2478, Y 51,691).

$110* *Portrait De Renoir Age,* sig. w/in plate, (05-20-93, Eldred, #170B), 10 x 7¾ in., (25.4 x 19.7 cm.), etching (BP 71, DM 177, FR 598, Y 12,147).

$1495* *La Redemption Par Les Betes,* book, pub. Mourlot, 1959, good cond., (02-11-93, Sotheby-NY, #64), each sheet 12¹¹⁄₁₆ x 9¹³⁄₁₆ in., (322 x 250 mm.), incl. 22 lithos in texte, separate suite of lithos p. in green (BP 1055, DM 2476, FR 8380, Y 180,229).

$230* *La Revue Blanche,* blindstamp, p. Chaix, margins, apparently good condition, restored tear, light-staining, (03-31-93, Butterfield, #5235), 11⅜ x 9⅛ in., (28.9 x 23.2 cm.), lithograph printed in colors on wove (BP 152, DM 370, FR 1257, Y 26,449).

$5395* *La Revue Blanche (F. Bouvet 30), 1894,* whole margins, (06-11-93, Picard, #11), 31½ x 24⁷⁄₁₆ in., (800 x 620 mm.), lithograph in colors on wove (BP 3545, DM 8768, FR 29,562, Y 572,414).

$920* *La Revue Blanche (Roger-Marx 32; Bouvet 30), 1894,* margins, paper tone darkened, repaired tears and creases, loss at center, water stain, paper rippled, backed w/ linen, (02-11-93, Sotheby-NY, #60), sheet 30½ x 23¹³⁄₁₆ in., (775 x 605 mm.), lithograph printed in colors (BP 649, DM 1524, FR 5157, Y 110,910).

$1540* *Rue Vue D'En Haut (R.-M. 60; B. 62; J. 10.4), 1899,* from Quelques aspects de la vie de Paris, pub. by Vollard, full margins, good cond., mat staining, stain, (11-05-92, Sotheby-NY, #84), 14⅝ x 8⅝ in., (370 x 220 mm.), sheet 20⅞ x 16 in., (370 x 220 mm.), lithograph

p. in colors on thin wove (BP 1002, DM 2436, FR 8240, Y 188,934).

$330* *"La Rue" (B. 105), 1927,* proof, foxing, (10-31-92, Cleveland, #254), 9¼ x 7 in., (23.5 x 17.8 cm.), lithograph on loose-leaf China paper (BP 211, DM 508, FR 1722, Y 40,877).

BI *"Saint Monique" (B. 111 pg. 270), 1930,* illus. No. 24, excellent cond., est. $2-300, (10-31-92, Cleveland, #255), 10½ x 8 in., (26.7 x 20.3 cm.), transfer lithograph.

$4093* *Le Salon Des Cents (B. 39), 1896,* p. Chaix, margins, good cond., creasing, foxing, (12-03-92, Sotheby-London, #186, illus.), sheet 24⅝ x 17 in., (625 x 432 mm.), lithograph in colors (BP 2640, DM 6437, FR 21,970, Y 509,270).

$1574* *Scene De Famille (F. Bouvet 2), 1892,* faded, backed, good margins, (02-03-93, Ader Tajan, #72), 8¼ x 10¼ in., (21 x 26 cm.), lithograph (BP 1099, DM 2592, FR 8788, Y 195,795).

$1985* *La Toilette Assise (Bouv. 96/I), 1925,* s., (06-23-93, Kornfeld, #230), lithograph on thick Japan (BP 1349, DM 3359, FR 11,298, Y 216,254, SF 2990).

$110* *Two Heads,* s. in plate, good cond., (11-12-92, Freemn/ Fine Art, #33), 6⅛ x 9 in., (15.6 x 22.9 cm.), etching (BP 72, DM 174, FR 588, Y 13,639).

$1495* *Woman Standing In Her Bath (R.-M. 81; B. 94), 1925,* 3rd state of 4, s., stamps, trial proof of 3rd state, full margins, good cond., crease in image, slight rubbing, foxing, (02-11-93, Sotheby-NY, #63, illus.), 11¹³⁄₁₆ x 7⅝ in., (300 x 193 mm.), lithograph on simile-Japan (BP 1055, DM 2476, FR 8380, Y 180,229).

BONNARD, Pierre (after)
$22* *Girl Reading,* Collector's Guild, (06-11-93, DuMouchelle, #216), 6 x 4 in., (15.2 x 10.2 cm.), print (BP 14, DM 36, FR 121, Y 2334).

BONNARD, Pierre and Edouard VUILLARD
$316* *"La Derniere Croisade" and "Lisez La Revue Blanche": Two (B.37; R.M.23), 1896; 1894,* margins, apparently good condition, creases, tear, toned, Albert Levinson Estate, (03-31-93, Butterfield, #5254), 12 x 19½ in., (30.5 x 49.5 cm.), 12⅜ x 18⅝ in., (30.5 x 49.5 cm.), lithograph printed on wove paper (BP 209, DM 508, FR 1727, Y 36,339).

BONNEAUD, J.
$114* *L'Invitation kA La Danse Avec Belita Et Les 4 Orchestres De Jazz: Henry Busse, Mitch Ayres, Eddie Lebaron, Lou Bring,* (01-31-93, Morelle/Marchan, #57), 47¼ x 62¹⁵⁄₁₆ in., (120 x 160 cm.), poster (BP 77, DM 184, FR 621, Y 14,222).

$70* *M.G.M. Desir D'Amour. Avec Esther Williams, Van Johnson Et Tony Martin,* Imp. Bedos & Cie, good cond., (02-12-93, Cheval/Robert, #208), 62¹⁵⁄₁₆ x 47¼ in., (160 x 120 cm.), poster (BP 49, DM 116, FR 393, Y 8442).

BONNET, Louis Marin   1736-1793
$525* *"La Belle Cachette" (J. Herold num. 869),* after J.-B. Huet, margins, reddish stains, (03-22-93, Pescheteau, #3), colored print (BP 354, DM 861, FR 2926, Y 60,792).

$908* *La Bonne Mere (J. Herold 1),* after F. Boucher, glued, second state of three, reddish stains, w/out margins, (02-03-93, Ader Tajan, #50), 13⅞ x 14⅞ in., (35.3 x 37.8 cm.), drawing manner engraving (BP 634, DM 1495, FR 5070, Y 112,949).

$7206* *"The Charmes Of The Morning" (H. 298) and "The Pleasures Of Education" (H. 299), 1777: Two,* trimmed, surface dirt, rubbed, trimmed, surface dirt, crease, rubbed, (06-30-93, Sotheby-London, #87, illus.), each c. 12½ x 9¾ in., (318 x 248 mm.), chalk-manner etching and engraving, 1st in black/blue/gold/red/white,from 5 plates, 2nd in black/blue/red/gold/ green (BP 4830, DM 12,291, FR 41,461, Y 772,099).

$393* *Deuxieme Cahier De Trophees: "Trophee De L'Agriculture" (228), "Trophee A Bacchus", "Trophee A Venus" and "Trophee A Flore": Four,* after Sallembier, stains, creases, cracks, holes, good margins, (06-16-93, Ader Tajan, #24), drawing manner engraving in sanguine (BP 262, DM 652, FR 2189, Y 41,916).

and "Trophee A Flore": Four, after Sallembier, stains, creases, cracks, holes, good margins, (06-16-93, Ader Tajan, #25), drawing manner engraving in sanguine (BP 262, DM 652, FR 2189, Y 41,916).

$6659* *Jeune Fille A La Rose (Herold pp. 60-1, no. 9; J.-R. 339), c. 1767,* after Francois Boucher, pub. Bonnet, trimmed, holes, stains, (12-01-92, Christie-London, #258, illus.), sheet 12⅛ x 8⁹⁄₁₆ in., (308 x 218 mm.), chalk-manner etching w/engraving in colors (black, blue, red and white) (BP 4400, DM 10,614, FR 36,171, Y 829,059).

BI *L'Amant Ecoute (Le Blanc 254),* lit., est. DM 2500, (06-04-93, Bassenge, #5426), 12⁵⁄₁₆ x 9³⁄₁₆ in., (31.2 x 23.3 cm.), color etching in stipple technique.

$6863* *"L'Amour Prie Venus De Lui Rendre Ses Armes" (H. 17) and "Le Reveil De Venus" (H. 20): Two,* after Boucher, 1st state of 5, trimmed, faded, (06-30-93, Sotheby-London, #88), one 13¼ x 15 in., (337 x 381 mm.), the other 12¼ x 15½ in., (337 x 381 mm.), chalk-manner engraving, in colors from 5 plates, 1st MR countermark (BP 4600, DM 11,706, FR 39,488, Y 735,348).

$2574* *"L'Eventail Casse" (H. 835) and "L'Amant Ecoute" (H. 836): Two,* margins, discoloration, surface tint, (06-30-93, Sotheby-London, #89), each c. 13¼ x 10 in., (337 x 254 mm.), stipple engraving in color (BP 1725, DM 4390, FR 14,810, Y 275,796).

$6659* *The Marriage Presents (Herold, p. 167, no. 305), 1774,* proof before title and address, pub. Bonnet, trimmed, corner made-up, thin spots, pinholes, discoloration; surface dirt verso, (12-01-92, Christie-London, #257, illus.), sheet 12½ x 9⅝ in., (318 x 244 mm.), chalk-manner etching w/engraving in colors (black, brown, blue, green, gold, two shades of red and yellow) (BP 4400, DM 10,614, FR 36,171, Y 829,059).

BI *Le Portrait Chery (Herold, p. 322, no. 851), c. 1750,* after C.-M.-A. Challe, trimmed, discoloration, staining, foxmarks, good cond., est. BP 4/500, (12-01-92, Christie-London, #232), sheet 12¹⁄₁₆ x 8¹¹⁄₁₆ in., (307 x 221 mm.), chalk-manner etching w/engraving in colors on laid paper.

BI *Le Repos De Venus (Herold, pp. 128-9, no. 203; J.-R. 384), 1774,* after Francois Boucher, 1st state of 3, pub. Bonnet, margins, partlysplit and repaired, dirt, defects, prov., est. BP 6/8,000, (12-01-92, Christie-London, #256, illus.), plate 14¹³⁄₁₆ x 19³⁄₁₆ in., (377 x 488 mm.), chalk-manner etching w/engraving in colors (black, blue, red and white) on papier bistre colle (pasted) on white paper.

BI *Le Sommeil De Venus (Herold, pp. 89-90, no. 62, P. and B., I, p. 216, J.-R. 361), 1771,* after Francois Boucher, 1st state of 3, pub. Bonnet, margins, nick, tear, staining, tape, glue, dirt, prov., est. BP 5/8,000, (12-01-92, Christie-London, #255, illus.), plate 14⅛ x 16¼ in., (358 x 412 mm.), chalk-manner etching w/engraving p. in b/w on blue papier colle on white paper.

$454* *Tete De Femme (J. Herold, num. 7), 1767,* after Ch. Eisen, before number, large margins, (04-02-93, Picard, #2), 9¹⁄₁₆ x 7¹⁄₁₆ in., (23 x 18 cm.), crayon manner engraving in black and white on paper (BP 299, DM 730, FR 2478, Y 51,691).

$343* *Tete De Femme (J.H. 133),* first state of two, reddish stains, cracks, good margins, (02-03-93, Ader Tajan, #52), 10⅝ x 8¼ in., (27 x 21 cm.), drawing manner engraving (BP 239, DM 565, FR 1915, Y 42,667).

$330* *Venus Sur Les Nuees Retenant Une Colombe (J.H., num. 33a),* after F. Boucher, num. 59, ded., wrinkles, stains, faults, (04-02-93, Picard, #3), 1³⁄₁₆ x 1⅞ in., (30.5 x 47 cm.), drawing manner engraving in sanguine (BP 217, DM 530, FR 1801, Y 37,573).

$1544* *"The Woman Ta King (Sic) Coffee" (H. 294) and "The Milk-Woman" (H. 295), 1774: Two,* from several plates, trimmed, surface dirt, (06-30-93, Sotheby-London, #86), each c. 12½ x 9¾ in., (318 x 248 mm.), chalk-manner etching and engraving in color (BP 1035, DM 2633, FR 8884, Y 165,434).

$6005* *"The Woman Ta King (Sic) Coffee" (Herold 294) and "The Milk Woman" (H. 295), 1774: Two,* trimmed, surface dirt, paper thin, stains, thin areas, defects, (06-30-93, Sotheby-London, #85, illus.), each c. 12½ x 9¾ in., (318 x 248 mm.), chalk-manner etching and engraving. 1st in

gold/black/red/blue/mauve,from 5 plates, 2nd in gold/black/blue/red (BP 4025, DM 10,242, FR 34,551, Y 643,416).

BONTECOU, Lee American b. 1931

$550* *Seventh Stone (F. 7, ULAE 21), 1965-68,* s., d., num. 12-31, blindstamp of pub. ULAE, full margins, apparently-very good cond., foxing, est. $5/700, (02-24-93, Butterfield, #3190), 14¼ x 11¼ in., (362 x 286 mm.), lithograph on Chatham British handmade (BP 384, DM 893, FR 3027, Y 64,539).

$143* *Untitled, c. 1967: Two,* one s., (05-27-93, Swann, #41), each approx. 24 x 20 in., (61 x 50.8 cm.), serigraph on muslin (BP 92, DM 229, FR 773, Y 15,330).

BOOKBINDER, Jack American 20th cent.

$99* *The Father,* s., d. 1959, (06-11-93, Freemn/Fine Art, #24), 9¼ x 13 in., (23.5 x 33 cm.), lithograph (BP 65, DM 161, FR 542, Y 10,504).

BOON, Jan 1882-1975

BI *Baum Mit Knorrigem Wurzelwerk,* s. JanBoon, est. DM 260-, (03-24-93, Venator/Hansten, #4471), 9⅝ x 14⅜ in., (24.4 x 36.5 cm.), woodcut on Japan.

BOONE, Garret American b. 1932

$5* *American Field II,* s., num., t., good cond., (05-15-93, Cleveland, #76), 10 x 8 in., (25.4 x 20.3 cm.), color serigraph (BP 3, DM 8, FR 27, Y 554).

BOOTE and Co., Arturo W.

$3740* *Vistas Y Costumbres De La Republica Argentina: Forty,* album, most w/photg.'s credit in neg., 1890s, (04-07-93, Swann, #105, illus.), approx. 6¾ x 8¾ in., (17.1 x 22.2 cm.), photograph, printing-out paper and albumen prints (BP 2472, DM 6049, FR 20,471, Y 424,903).

BORANI, Bapt. (after)

$220* *Gregorio XVI Pont. Max,* by Niccolo Guidetti and Angelo Bertini, (09-17-92, Sloan, #1999), image 14¾ x 28½ in., (37.5 x 72.4 cm.), engraving (BP 124, DM 327, FR 1118, Y 27,390).

BORCHT, Peter van der 1545-1608

$458* *Landliche Belustigungen (Hollstein 464; Wurzbach 11),* prov., (05-26-93, Dorling, #2209), 8¾ x 11¹⁵⁄₁₆ in., (22.3 x 30.4 cm.), etching (BP 296, DM 747, FR 2515, Y 49,761).

BORCHT, Pieter van der (IV) 1545-1608

$1275* *Le Jeu Des Singes: Eine Wochnerin In Ihrer Stube (Hollstein 469),* (06-04-93, Bassenge, #5045, illus.), 8¹¹⁄₁₆ x 11⁷⁄₁₆ in., (22 x 29 cm.), engraving (BP 844, DM 2070, FR 6979, Y 137,511).

BOREIN, Edward American 1872-1943

$418* *"Bronco Buster",* s., damage, (08-08-92, Litchfield, #22), 5 x 4 in., (12.7 x 10.2 cm.), etching (BP 217, DM 615, FR 2078, Y 53,350).

$1155* *The Church At Acoma,* margins, s., (05-22-93, Collins, #109), 7⅞ x 11¾ in., (20 x 29.8 cm.), etchsing (BP 748, DM 1878, FR 6318, Y 127,343).

BI *Going To The Dance No. 2 (G. 154), 1915,* s., t., #65, margins, good cond., stain, mat-staining, sheet taped toovermat, surface soiling, est. $1,2/1,400, (05-19-93, Butterfield, #1795, illus.), 5¾ x 6¹⁵⁄₁₆ in., (146 x 176 mm.), etching and drypoint on wove.

$523* *Little Bucking Horse (G. 64),* s., large margins, good cond., foxing, glue remains, (10-28-92, Butterfield, #2519), 4⅞ x 3¹⁵⁄₁₆ in., (124 x 100 mm.), etching on laid paper (BP 333, DM 808, FR 2743, Y 64,172).

$605* *Mission San Luis Rey, No. 1 (G. 244),* s., margins, good cond., light-staining, surface soiling, (10-28-92, Butterfield, #2521), 8¾ x 15⅜ in., (222 x 391 mm.), etching w/drypoint on Umbria paper (BP 385, DM 934, FR 3173, Y 74,233).

$690* *Reps (G. 52),* second (final) state, s. in plate, full margins, taped, good cond., mat staining, tape remains, notations, (05-19-93, Butterfield, #1794), 5⅛ x 8³⁄₁₆ in., (130 x 208 mm.), etching and drypoint in sepia on Umbria wove (BP 448, DM 1122, FR 3779, Y 76,387).

$1540* *Two Riders On A Canyon Rim,* s., d. Edward Borein 1917; i., (02-16-93, Moran, #142), image 6⅞ x 10⅞ in., (17.5 x 27.6 cm.), etching on paper (BP 1065, DM 2513, FR 8513, Y 184,497).

$770* *Untitled, Bucking Bronco, c. 1920,* s., remarque, mat stain, hinges, (10-31-92, Cleveland, #82), 5 x 4 in., (12.7 x 10.2 cm.), etching (BP 493, DM 1185, FR 4019, Y 95,380).

$770* *Untitled, Bucking Bronco, c. 1920,* s., remarque, sun stain, hinges, (10-31-92, Cleveland, #83, illus.), 4⅞ x 4 in., (12.4 x 10.2 cm.), etching (BP 493, DM 1185, FR 4019, Y 95,380).

BOREMAN, C. Robert
BI *"Cloud 2" and "Cloud 4": Two,* each s., t., #3/75 and 6/75, prov., est. C$ 250/400, (12-01-92, Ritchie, #42, illus.), each approx. 23¾ x 17⅝ in., (60.3 x 44.8 cm.), color etching and aquatint.

BORES, Francisco   Spanish 1898-1972
$202* *Femme,* s. Bores, 84/200, (03-24-93, Kunsthallen, #48), lithograph (BP 137, DM 330, FR 1123, Y 23,734, DK 1265).

$295* *Femme,* s. Bores, 8/25, (09-30-92, Kunsthallen, #47), color lithograph (BP 166, DM 418, FR 1415, Y 35,401, DK 1610).

BORG, Irene
BI *"Femme Couchee",* ed. #76/500, s., est. $2/300, (03-12-93, DuMouchelle, #2322), 23 x 27 in., (58.4 x 68.6 cm.), color photo lithograph.

BORGLIND, Stig   1892-1965
$1005* *Lilium Tigrinum, 1944,* (12-04-92, AB Stockholm, #7010), 10⅞ x 5⅞ in., (27.7 x 15 cm.), hand-colored engraving (BP 645, DM 1601, FR 5429, Y 125,468, SK 6820).

$572* *"Morkulla",* s., (11-07-92, Falkkloos, #62), hand-colored etching (BP 374, DM 918, FR 3087, Y 70,600, SK 3410).

BORIS, Nicholas
$440* *Three Men In A Classical Frieze-Style Pose, c. 1932,* sig., i., (10-14-92, Swann, #382, illus.), 10½ x 13½ in., (26.7 x 34.3 cm.), photograph, gold-toned silver print (BP 258, DM 644, FR 2184, Y 53,320).

BORMANN, Emma   20th cent.
BI *Firenze,* s., t., est. $2/400, (03-24-93, Grogan, #81), 7⅝ x 20½ in., (19.4 x 52.1 cm.), color woodcut.

BORN, W.
$100* *"Aus Einem Konzert": Set Of Seven,* stone mono., s., 1919, t., series pub. 1921, (11-18-92, Bubb Kuyper, #1526), all 18⅛ x 11¹³⁄₁₆ in., (46 x 30 cm.), lithograph (BP 66, DM 159, FR 537, Y 12,436, G 180).

BOROFSKY, Jonathan   American b. 1942
BI *2941345, 1985,* s., d., num. 14/125, pub. Friends of the Philadelphia Museum of Art, full sheet, thin band of skinning, excell. cond., est. $1/1,400, (09-19-92, Christie-E, #83, illus.), sheet 30⅛ x 22½ in., (765 x 572 mm.), screenprint in black and red on Arches.

$6875* *Art Is For The Spirit No. 3094248 (Gemini 1396), 1989,* marker s., #3094248, unique, blindstamp, pub. Gemini G.E.L., good cond., (11-07-92, Sotheby-NY, #526, illus.), sheet 66¾ x 54⅜ in., (169.5 x 138.1 cm.), silkscreen p. in colors w/silver leaf (BP 4495, DM 10,977, FR 37,102, Y 848,556).

$1725* *Hammering Man, 1985,* s., d., #11/35, pub. Philadelphia Museum of Art, apparently good cond., (05-15-93, Sotheby-NY, #928), sheet 53¾ x 40¼ in., (136.5 x 102.2 cm.), silkscreen in colors w/handpainted number (BP 1122, DM 2775, FR 9324, Y 191,220).

BI *Self Portrait (G. 1028), 1982,* s., d., #3/23, blindstamp pub. Gemini G.E.L., very good cond.?, est.$1,5/2,500, (10-28-92, Butterfield, #2909, illus.), 40 x 30 in., (101.6 x 76.2 cm.), color lithograph on Arches.

BORRA (after)
BI *Views Of The Ruins At Palmyra: Two,* by T. Major, margins, two sheets joined, creasing, surface dirt, est.BP 1/150, (10-07-92, Christie-S. Ken, #82), pl 12 x 28 in., (30.5 x 71.1 cm.), engraving.

BORSCH, Hieronymous (after)   c. 1450-1516
$4249* *Der Hl. Martin Mit Seinem Pferd In Einem Schiff (Wurzbach 14, Hollstein 16I, Riggs S. 314),* by Janor Lucas Duetecum, (06-04-93, Bassenge, #5046, illus.), engraving (BP 2811, DM 6900, FR 23,257, Y 458,261).

BORTNYIK, Sandor   1893-1976
BI *Album MA, 1921: Six,* Galerie Gmurzynska-Bargera, p. 1970, s., #118/140, est. DM 4,000, (05-26-93, Lempertz, #39), portfolio 18¹¹⁄₁₆ x 15⁹⁄₁₆ in., (47.5 x 39.5 cm.), color serigraph on cardboard.

BORTNYIK, Sandor   Hungarian 1893-1976
BI *Bortnyk Album Ma 1921, 1921,* album, crayon s., justification, num. 17, excell. cond., bound, est.BP 2,0/3,000, (12-03-92, Sotheby-London, #187, illus.), overall size 12¾ x 9¾ in., (324 x 248 mm.), six pochoirs.

BOS, Cornelis   c. 1508-1564
BI *The Gathering Of Manna (Holl. 24; Schele 15), c. 1550,* after Frans Floris, narrow margins, staining, very good cond., laid,est. BP 1,0/1,200, (12-01-92, Christie-London, #2, illus.), 11¹⁵⁄₁₆ x 15¹⁄₁₆ in., (304 x 383 mm.), engraving.

BOSCH, Hieronymous (after)   c. 1450-1516
$14,151* *The Temptation Of Saint Anthony, (Holl. 10), c. 1561,* indistinct watermark, trimmed, creases split and repaired, crease, rubbed spots, defects, (12-01-92, Christie-London, #76, illus.), S. 12¹⁵⁄₁₆ x 16⅞ in., (329 x 428 mm.), engraving (BP 9350, DM 22,555, FR 76,866, Y 1,761,828).

BOSCH, Hieronymus (after)
$8050* *Die Blau Schuyte (Holl. 20; Riggs 13), 1559,* by Pieter van der Heyden, watermark, trimmed, repair, damp staining,cockling, good cond., (05-13-93, Sotheby-NY, #110), 8⅞ x 11⅜ in., (226 x 289 mm.), engraving (BP 5285, DM 12,999, FR 43,845, Y 898,738).

BOSMAN, Richard   American b. 1944
$770* *Car Crash, 1981-82,* s., d., num. 24/60, pub. Brooke Alexander Editions, full margins, crease, very good cond.?, (09-19-92, Christie-E, #84, illus.), sheet 37 x 49 in., (94 x 124.5 cm.), woodcut in colors on Japan (BP 443, DM 1153, FR 3949, Y 95,938).

BI *Cat's Revenge, 1983,* s., num. 8/40, full margins, est $6/800, (09-20-92, Hindman, #717), sheet 31 x 43 in., (78.7 x 109.2 cm.), aquatint on two adjacent plates, on T.H. Saunders paper.

BI *Cat's Revenge, 1983,* s., num. 4/40, est. $4/600, (09-20-92, Hindman, #716), sheet 31 x 43 in., (78.7 x 109.2 cm.), aquatint on two adjacent plates on T.H. Saunders paper.

BI *Cat's Revenge, 1983,* s., #4/40, est. $4/600, (12-13-92, Hindman, #352), sheet 31 x 43 in., aquatint on two adjacent plates, on T.H. Saunders paper.

$660* *River, 1989,* s., #25/65, blindstamp pub. The Mezzanine Gallery, Metropolitan Museum of Art, full margins, very good cond.?, (10-28-92, Butterfield, #2910), 30 x 34 in., (762 x 864 mm.), color woodcut on Japan (BP 421, DM 1019, FR 3461, Y 80,982).

$880* *The Wave, 1987,* s., num. 12/35, Experimental Workshop blindstamps, full sheet, very good cond.?, (09-19-92, Christie-E, #85), sheet 30 x 38 in., (762 x 965 mm.), woodcut in colors on Japan (BP 506, DM 1318, FR 4513, Y 109,644).

BOSSARD, Johann Michael   1874-1950
$203* *Der Alte, 1904,* s., (09-04-92, Germann, #258), 16¹⁄₁₆ x 15¹¹⁄₁₆ in., (408 x 398 mm.), color lithograph (BP 102, DM 285, FR 969, Y 24,988, SF 253).

BOSSE, A.
$354* *Le Sculpteur (G.D. 1386),* yellowed, creases, tear, w/out margins, (06-16-93, Ader Tajan, #3), 9¹⁵⁄₁₆ x 12⅝ in., (25.2 x 32 cm.), etching and copper engraving (BP 236, DM 588, FR 1972, Y 37,756).

BOSSI, Benigno   Italian 1727-1793
$121* *Tetes D'Hommes Tournees Vers La Gauche (Leblanc II, p. 198), 1754: Two,* pl. 13, second state of 3, pl. 16, unique state, glue traces verso, (05-15-93, Loudmer, #37), first 3¼ x 2¹³⁄₁₆ in., (83 x 71 mm.), second 4¹³⁄₁₆ x 4¼ in., (83 x 71 mm.), etchings on wove (BP 79, DM 195, FR 654, Y 13,413).

$722* *Vases: Set Of Nine,* after Petitot, stains, reddish stains, mat holes, large margins, wrinkle, stain, thin margins, (04-02-93, Picard, #4), etching (BP 476, DM 1160, FR 3941, Y 82,204).

BOSSI, Silvestro (after)

$171* *Sbarco De Saraceni,* by Antonio Banzo, (10-30-92, Sloan, #871), 15½ x 19½ in., (39.4 x 49.5 cm.), engraving (BP 110, DM 263, FR 892, Y 21,182).

BI *Sbarco De Saraceni,* by Antonio Banzo, est. $225/275, (09-17-92, Sloan, #631), 15½ x 19½ in., (39.4 x 49.5 cm.), engraving.

BOTELLO, Angel   Spanish 1913-1986

$1100* *Three Girls, 1980,* s., annot. G-I, pub. by artist, margins, good cond., paper loss, tear, old masking tape, creases, (10-28-92, Butterfield, #2558), 16¾ x 14 in., (425 x 356 mm.), color linoleum cut on tissue thin fibrous paper (BP 701, DM 1699, FR 5768, Y 134,969).

BOTERO, Fernando   Colombian b. 1932

$1320* *Botero, By Pierre Restany, 1984: Sixty-One,* complete volume, one s., #115/200; s., #115/200 on just. p., pbu. Harry N. Abrams, very good cond., wear to cover, (02-24-93, Butterfield, #2662), 16¹/₁₆ x 12¼ in., (408 x 311 mm.), 61 photo-lithographs on Fabriano (BP 921, DM 2143, FR 7265, Y 154,893).

$1265* *Botero, By Pierre Restany, 1984: Sixty-One,* complete volume, s., #114/200, pub. Harry N. Abrams, very good cond., (05-19-93, Butterfield, #1838), 16¹/₁₆ x 12¼ in., (408 x 311 mm.), photo lithograph on Fabriano (BP 821, DM 2056, FR 6928, Y 140,042).

$1320* *The Dancing Couple,* s., num. 38/150, (11-12-92, Freemn/Fine Art, #33A), 15 x 10¼ in., (38.1 x 26 cm.), lithograph (BP 867, DM 2092, FR 7055, Y 163,670).

$1100* *La Maison De Raquel Vega, 1984,* s., num. 51/150, pub. Harry N. Abrams, margins, apparently very goodcond., (02-24-93, Butterfield, #2663), 13½ x 17 in., (343 x 432 mm.), photo lithograph in colors on laid (BP 767, DM 1786, FR 6054, Y 129,078).

$9775* *"Mujer Ante Al Espejo" and "Mujer Fumando", 1985: Two,* s., #89/150, full margins, excellent cond., (05-18-93, Sotheby-NY, #253, illus.), one, image 16 x 13 in., (406 x 330 mm.), the other, image 16⅛ x 13¼ in., (406 x 330 mm.), lithograph (BP 6367, DM 15,861, FR 53,562, Y 1,089,379).

$6050* *Mujer Ante El Espejo, 1985,* s., #97/150, full margins, excell. cond., (11-24-92, Christie-NY, #362, illus.), borderline 16⅛ x 13 in., (408 x 330 mm.), lithograph on wove paper (BP 3986, DM 9686, FR 32,863, Y 750,527).

$5280* *Mujer Fumando, 1985,* s., #129/150, margins, excell. cond., (11-24-92, Christie-NY, #363, illus.), borderline 16⅛ x 13⅛ in., (410 x 333 mm.), color lithograph on wove (BP 3478, DM 8453, FR 28,680, Y 655,006).

BOTH, Jan   c. 1618-1652

$3466* *Ponte Molle (B. 5; Dutuit, Hollstein 5 III),* (12-04-92, Bassenge, #6066), 7¹¹/₁₆ x 10¹³/₁₆ in., (19.6 x 27.4 cm.), etching (BP 2223, DM 5520, FR 18,725, Y 432,709).

BOTH, Jan (after Andries Both)

$522* *The Five Senses (B. 11-15): Set Of Five,* late impressions after A. Both, 2nd states, corner mounted, thread margins, tears, foxing, (10-27-92, Phillips-London, #8), plate 8⅝ x 6¾ in., (219 x 171 mm.), etching on laid (BP 330, DM 800, FR 2715, Y 63,853).

BOTHWELL, Dora (after)

$28* *"Promenade",* s., edit. #7/30, (09-18-92, DuMouchelle, #2514), 8 x 14 in., (20.3 x 35.6 cm.), silkscreen (BP 16, DM 42, FR 144, Y 3489).

BOTT, Francis   German b. 1904

BI *Abstrakte Komposition,* s., num., creases, est. DM 1,000-, (09-25-92, Granier, #2775), sheet 25⁹/₁₆ x 19⅞ in., (65 x 50.5 cm.), color lithograph on cream BFK Rives.

BI *Komposition,* s., num., signs of wear, est. DM 900, (12-01-92, Karl/Faber, #396), 13⅜ x 6½ in., (34 x 16.5 cm.), color etching on wove.

BI *Komposition,* s., num., est. DM 600, (12-05-92, Bassenge, #7062), 15¹⁵/₁₆ x 15¾ in., (40.6 x 40 cm.), color lithograph on BFK Rives.

$481* *Komposition Mit Rot,* num., s., (12-01-92, Karl/Faber, #397), 13¾ x 9⁷/₁₆ in., (35 x 24 cm.), color lithograph on wove (BP 318, DM 767, FR 2613, Y 59,885).

BOTTICHER, Otto (after)

$220* *Washington Greys 8th., Regt. N.Y.S.T., c. 1859,* (12-02-92, Christie-E, #229, illus.), hand-colored lithograph on wove (BP 142, DM 346, FR 1181, Y 27,373).

BOTTINI, Georges   French 1784-1907

$1433* *Femme Etendue Tenant Une Rose (Miami 84), 1898,* s., d., num., full margins, (02-24-93, Picard, #20), etching and aquatint in color on laid (BP 999, DM 2326, FR 7887, Y 168,153).

BOTTINI, Georges (after)

$516* *Danseuse (Cat Miami 6), 1896,* whole margins, #4/25, s., stamped, (04-02-93, Picard, #37), 7¹¹/₁₆ x 5¹³/₁₆ in., (19.5 x 14.8 cm.), color wood engraving on Japan simili (BP 340, DM 829, FR 2817, Y 58,750).

BOTTINI, Georges and Henry van der ZEE

$3264* *Au Restaurant, La Mome Casque D'Or (M. 11, L. 2821), 1897,* just., s., by both artists, d., (02-24-93, Picard, #23), wood engraving in colors on old thin Japan laid (BP 2276, DM 5299, FR 17,964, Y 383,009).

$860* *Danseuse (Miami 6, L. 374 et 1382), 1896,* d., s. by both artists, stamped, soiling, creases, large margins, (02-24-93, Picard, #21), wood engraving in color (BP 600, DM 1396, FR 4733, Y 100,915).

BOUAT, Louis

$247* *Source Verdier, Limonade "Cevenole",* SPIA, A- cond., tear, (08-06-92, Swann, #56, illus.), 62½ x 47 in., (158.8 x 119.4 cm.), (BP 129, DM 365, FR 1233, Y 31,505).

BOUBAT, Edouard   French b. 1923

$440* *Antonio; Broken Window: Two, c. 1950,* one t., each w/ credit stamp, (10-13-92, Christie-NY, #416, illus.), each 7 x 9½ in., (17.8 x 24.1 cm.), photograph, gelatin silver prints (BP 256, DM 645, FR 2190, Y 53,353).

$825* *Cynthia, 1975,* s. by photog. in ink, s., t., d., i. verso, (10-15-92, Sotheby-NY, #340, illus.), 11⅞ x 7⅞ in., (30.2 x 20 cm.), photograph, gelatin silver print (BP 505, DM 1228, FR 4165, Y 98,980).

$660* *Day Of The Dead Festival, 1980,* s., blindstamp, (10-14-92, Swann, #383, illus.), 12 x 16 in., (30.5 x 40.6 cm.), photograph, silver print (BP 387, DM 966, FR 3275, Y 79,981).

$374* *"Espagne", 1951,* p.l., s., attrib., t., d., (05-23-93, Butterfield, #3319, illus.), 14 x 9¼ in., photograph, gelatin silver print (BP 244, DM 612, FR 2058, Y 41,340).

$805* *France, Pyrenees, 1952,* p. 1976, ink s., t., d., (04-08-93, Christie-NY, #405, illus.), 13¾ x 9⅛ in., (34.9 x 23.2 cm.), photograph, gelatin silver print (BP 528, DM 1293, FR 4377, Y 91,353).

BI *Hermanos Gonzalez,* s., blindstamp, 1956, p.l., est. $4/600, (10-14-92, Swann, #384), 16 x 12 in., (40.6 x 30.5 cm.), photograph, silver print.

$1495* *Homage A Douanier Rousseau, Paris, 1980,* mono. blindstamp, s. by photog., (04-06-93, Sotheby-NY, #224, illus.), 9¼ x 14 in., photograph (BP 987, DM 2409, FR 8156, Y 170,506).

$1320* *Lella, Bretagne, (1948),* p.l., s. in ink, t., d., (10-13-92, Christie-NY, #415, illus.), 17½ x 13 in., (44.5 x 33 cm.), photograph, gelatin silver print (BP 769, DM 1934, FR 6570, Y 160,058).

$1650* *Lella, Bretagne, 1948 (Boubat par Boubat, p. 40),* s. by photog. in ink, s., t., d. verso, p. l., (10-15-92, Sotheby-NY, #339, illus.), 16⅞ x 12½ in., (42.9 x 31.8 cm.), photograph, gelatin silver print (BP 1010, DM 2456, FR 8329, Y 197,960).

$660* *"Montmartre, Paris", 1947/later,* ink s. margin; s., t., d. verso, Dixon Collection, (11-16-92, Butterfield, #5851, illus.), 13¾ x 11 in., (349.9 x 279.9 mm.), photograph, gelatin silver print (BP 435, DM 1052, FR 3545, Y 82,079).

BI *"Paris Folies Bergeres", 1962,* p.l., s. twice, t., d., est. $5/700, (05-23-93, Butterfield, #3320), 14⅜ x 9⅝ in., photograph, gelatin silver print.

BI *"Paris", 1976,* s., init., t., d., est. BP 4/600, (05-06-93, Christie-London, #146, illus.), image 14 x 9¾ in., photograph, gelatin silver print.

BI *Portugal, 1958,* ink s.; ink s., t., d. verso, est. $2/2,500, (04-08-93, Christie-NY, #406, illus.), 15⅝ x 10⅜ in., (39.7 x 26.4 cm.), photograph, gelatin silver print.

BOUCHAID, Maouail
$210* *Composition, 1988,* s., #2/4, prov., (11-16-92, Briest, #14), 52⅜ x 88⁹⁄₁₆ in., (133 x 225 cm.), engraving (BP 138, DM 335, FR 1128, Y 26,207).

BOUCHAUD, SE
$219* *PLM: Algeria Via Marseilles. "Ghardaia",* very good cond., (03-13-93, Laurin, #33), 39⅜ x 24⁷⁄₁₆ in., (100 x 62 cm.), (BP 153, DM 365, FR 1239, Y 25,810).

BOUCHER (after) French 18th century
BI *Cherubs At Play In Satyr's Garden,* est. $4/600, (02-04-93, Sloan, #1838), sight 19¾ x 9¾ in., (50.2 x 24.8 cm.), engraving.

BOUCHER, Francois (after)
$300* *La Belle Cuisiniere, c. 1780,* by P. Avelline, pub. Basan, margins, tear, good cond., (11-30-92, Phillips-London, #278), plate 18¼ x 14⅛ in., (464 x 359 mm.), etching w/engraving on laid (BP 198, DM 478, FR 1622, Y 37,337).
$55* *Les Nimphes Au Bain,* by J. Ouvrier, (09-17-92, Sloan, #618), 16½ x 11¼ in., (41.9 x 28.6 cm.), color engraving (BP 31, DM 82, FR 279, Y 6848).
$7221* *Tete De Flore (Portalis-Beraldi S. 215; Herold 192 I), 1769,* by L.-M. Bonnet, prov., (12-04-92, Bassenge, #6524, illus.), 16⅝ x 13⁷⁄₁₆ in., (42.2 x 34.1 cm.), color etching (BP 4632, DM 11,500, FR 39,011, Y 901,498).
$728* *"Venus Desarmee Par Les Amours" (L. 379),* trimmed margins, (03-22-93, Pescheteau, #9), maniere de trois crayons (BP 490, DM 1194, FR 4058, Y 84,298).

BOUCHER, Francois and Alexandre AVELINE French 18th cent.
$343* *Andromede (P.J.-Richard 203; I.F.F. 15), 1734,* fourth and final state w/address, stain, wormholes, (05-15-93, Loudmer, #124, illus.), 13¹¹⁄₁₆ x 9⅜ in., (348 x 238 mm.), etching and copper engraving on laid (BP 223, DM 552, FR 1854, Y 38,022).

BOUCHER, L.
$219* *Afrique Du Nord Et Union Francaise. Credit Lyonnais,* very good cond., (03-13-93, Laurin, #128), 40³⁄₁₆ x 29¾ in., (102 x 75.5 cm.), (BP 153, DM 365, FR 1239, Y 25,810).
$189* *Air France: Grande Bretagne, 1951,* p. Perceval, very good cond., (11-19-92, Ribeyre/Baron, #86), 39⅜ x 24 in., (100 x 61 cm.), poster (BP 124, DM 301, FR 1015, Y 23,505).

BOUCHER, Lucien 1889-1971
$378* *Reseau De La Mer Et Du Tourisme,* p. Perceval, pub. French State Railways, cond. 1, light staining, laid on linen, (10-13-92, Phillips-London, #9), 39³⁄₁₆ x 24⅝ in., (99.5 x 62.5 cm.), color lithograph (BP 220, DM 554, FR 1882, Y 45,835).

BOUCHET
$440* *"Cognac Jacquet",* pub. Vercasson, (08-05-92, Boos, #590), 62 x 46 in., (157.5 x 116.8 cm.), color lithograph (BP 230, DM 650, FR 2196, Y 56,037).

BOUDON, E.
$377* *Les Pyrenees,* good cond., (01-23-93, Ribeyre/Baron, #100), 39¾ x 79¹⁵⁄₁₆ in., (101 x 203 cm.), poster (BP 247, DM 599, FR 2028, Y 47,184).

BOUGHTON, Alice American 1865-1943
BI *Portrait Of Wynne Matthieson As Queen Katherine In "Henry VIII", 1916,* photog.'s sig., est. $1/1,500, (04-07-93, Swann, #409, illus.), 8 x 6 in., photograph, silver print.

BOUISSEAU, Jean Jacques De French 18th cent.
BI *"School Room Interior" and "Portrait Of An Elderly Woman": Two,* mono., d. 1780 and 1770 in plate, est. $300/400, (09-17-92, Sloan, #1441), larger 8½ x 12⅞ in., (21.6 x 32.7 cm.), etching.

BOUISSET, F.
$70* *5e Emprunt National. "Allies Dans La Guerre, Unis Dans La Paix", 1919,* Imp. de Vaugirard, good cond., (02-12-93, Cheval/Robert, #111), 47¼ x 30¹¹⁄₁₆ in., (120 x 78 cm.), poster (BP 49, DM 116, FR 393, Y 8442).

BOUISSET, F. (after)
$281* *Lu Biscuits (Petit Ecolier),* very good cond., (02-13-93, Morelle/Marchan, #36), 47¼ x 62¹⁵⁄₁₆ in., (120 x 160 cm.), poster (BP 198, DM 466, FR 1577, Y 33,888).

BOUISSET, Firmin 1859-1925
$642* *Chocolat Menier, Evitez Les Contrefacons, c. 1900,* Paris, Imp. Ch. Wall and Cie, cond B, restored on text, (06-11-93, Boisgirard, #49), 55⅛ x 37 in., (140 x 94 cm.), poster (BP 422, DM 1043, FR 3518, Y 68,117).

BOULANGER French 20th cent.
$220* *Figure Flying Above A Skyline,* s., #145/200, (06-11-93, Freemn/Fine Art, #25), 11½ x 11½ in., (29.2 x 29.2 cm.), etching and aquatint (BP 145, DM 358, FR 1205, Y 23,342).

BOULANGER, Louis
$516* *"Les Orientales", "Mazzeppa", "Androcles" And Others (H. Beraldi, num. 2 (2), 3, 16, 20 (2), 21 (2), 23 (3 different pls.): Set Of Eleven,* stains, good margins, (04-02-93, Picard, #38), lithographs (BP 340, DM 829, FR 2817, Y 58,750).
$330* *Le Sommeil Du Lion (H. Beraldi, num. 21, 13),* ded., reddish stains, creases, large margins, (04-02-93, Picard, #39), 8¾ x 10⅞ in., (22.2 x 27.7 cm.), lithograph on Chine fixe (BP 217, DM 530, FR 1801, Y 37,573).

BOULLIER, R.
$619* *PLM. Thonon Les Bains. "Billets De Station Thermale A Prix Reduits",1905,* very good cond., (03-15-93, Arcole, #4, illus.), 41⁵⁄₁₆ x 29½ in., (105 x 75 cm.), (BP 431, DM 1028, FR 3495, Y 73,324).

BOULT, Francis Cecil (after) English d. 1895
$330* *"An Awkward Customer" and "Bringing Up A Skirter": Two,* each s. in plate, (07-03-92, Sloan, #1073), each 14¾ x 23 in., (37.5 x 58.4 cm.), color aquatint (BP 172, DM 499, FR 1684, Y 41,137).

BOULTBEE, James (after)
$783* *The Durham Ox, 1802,* by John Whessell, pub. John Day, narrow margins, good cond., water staining, skimmed area in image, (10-27-92, Phillips-London, #95), (502 x 651 mm.), stipple engraving (BP 495, DM 1200, FR 4072, Y 95,780).

BOULTON, E* B* (after)
BI *A View Of Sydney From Mosman, c. 1860,* pub. P. E. Reynolds of Sydney, 1879, est. BP 5/700, (06-16-93, Bonhams-Chelsea, #366, illus.), image 12¾ x 31½ in., (32.4 x 80 cm.), chromolithograph.

BOURDEAU, Robert American b. 1931
$990* *"Costa Rica",* 1987/1990, s., d., edit. 4/30 mount; ink s., t., d., edit., neg. num. verso mount, (11-16-92, Butterfield, #5852, illus.), 10½ x 13½ in., (267.2 x 343.5 mm.), photograph, gelatin silver print (BP 652, DM 1578, FR 5317, Y 123,119).
$863* *"County Galway, Ireland", 1980,* s., d. twice, t., #3/30, neg. num., (05-23-93, Butterfield, #3321, illus.), 7¾ x 9¾ in., photograph, gelatin silver print (BP 562, DM 1411, FR 4750, Y 95,391).
$403* *"Cumbria, England",* 1975, p. 1985, s., d., #4/30, attrib., d., t., neg. num., (05-23-93, Butterfield, #3322, illus.), 10¼ x 13½ in., photograph, gelatin silver print (BP 262, DM 659, FR 2218, Y 44,545).
BI *"Tarn, France",* mounted, s., d., #2/30 by photog., s., t., d., #2/20 by photog. in ink, 1990, p. 1991, est. $1,5/2,000, (04-06-93, Sotheby-NY, #526, illus.), 10⅛ x 12⅞ in., photograph.

BOURDELLE, Pierre American d. 1966
$176* *War: Fifty-Two,* portfolio, s. ink on frontispiece, #112, p. Albert Carman, (05-16-93, Hindman, #556, illus.), 13 x 17 in., (33 x 43.2 cm.), color lithograph (BP 114, DM 283, FR 951, Y 19,510).

BOURDIER
$90* *Gem Beurre D'Isigny, 1933,* (02-13-93, Morelle/Marchan, #27), 47¼ x 62¹⁵⁄₁₆ in., (120 x 160 cm.), poster (BP 63, DM 149, FR 505, Y 10,854).

BOURGEOIS, Edouard French
$261* *Ch. De Fer De L'Est: Luxembourg. Grand Duche,* good cond., restored, (02-12-93, Cheval/Robert, #92), 41⁵⁄₁₆ x 29⅛ in., (105 x 74 cm.), poster (BP 184, DM 433, FR 1465, Y 31,476).
$398* *Ch. De Fer De L'Ouest: Saint-Malo, "Plage Splendide", c. 1900,* excell. cond., (01-23-93, Ribeyre/Baron, #52),

51³⁄₁₆ x 36¹³⁄₁₆ in., (130 x 93.5 cm.), poster (BP 260, DM 633, FR 2141, Y 49,812).

$272* *Dieppe, "Plage La Plus Voisine De Paris", c. 1895,* good cond., (01-23-93, Ribeyre/Baron, #51), 40³⁄₁₆ x 26⅜ in., (102 x 67 cm.), poster (BP 178, DM 433, FR 1463, Y 34,043).

$249* *PLM and Cie Transatlantique: Gorges D'El Kantara. Paquebot Charles Roux,* very good cond., (03-13-93, Laurin, #34), 42½ x 30⅞ in., (108 x 78.5 cm.), (BP 174, DM 414, FR 1409, Y 29,346).

$279* *PLM. Le Lautaret (Dauphine), c. 1900,* good cond., (03-15-93, Arcole, #7), 42½ x 31⅛ in., (108 x 79 cm.), poster (BP 194, DM 463, FR 1575, Y 33,049).

$3410* *Waterman Ideal Fountain Pen With Wright Plain,* fold/creasing/damage, Francis Aero Collection, (09-12-92, Dunning, #205, illus.), 56½ x 87 in., (143.5 x 221 cm.), poster laid on cloth (BP 1764, DM 4909, FR 16,683, Y 422,500).

BOURGEOIS, Louise   American b. 1911

BI *Sans Titre I, 1985,* s., #13/90, est. FF1,200/1,500, (05-27-93, Briest, #35), 17¹⁵⁄₁₆ x 11¼ in., (45.5 x 28.5 cm.), lithograph in 2 colors.

$686* *Two Compositions, 1985: Two,* s., #14/90 and 27/100, full margins, good cond., (06-30-93, Sotheby-London, #752, illus.), each sh c. 19⅛ x 11⅛ in., (486 x 283 mm.), lithograph in black and greyish-green on wove (BP 460, DM 1170, FR 3947, Y 73,503).

BOURKE-WHITE, Margaret   American 1904-1971

$1265* *Airplane Abstraction, 1933-34,* (04-08-93, Christie-NY, #257, illus.), 6⅝ x 4¾ in., (16.8 x 12.1 cm.), photograph, gelatin silver print (BP 830, DM 2032, FR 6879, Y 143,554).

$7700* *Airship Akron, 1931,* s. by photog. on image, (10-15-92, Sotheby-NY, #189, illus.), 17 x 23 in., (43.2 x 58.4 cm.), photograph, gelatin silver print (BP 4712, DM 11,462, FR 38,869, Y 923,815).

BI *The Caldwell's Christmas Card,* (1940), mounted as greeting card, Letterpress, t., greeting, lit., est. 7/9,000, (10-13-92, Christie-NY, #131, illus.), 6⅜ x 5 in., (16.2 x 12.7 cm.), photograph, gelatin silver print.

$288* *"Ekaterina Dzhugashvili, Mother Of Joseph Satlin",* 1931, p. 1934, from portfolio pub. Argus Press, t., (05-23-93, Butterfield, #3326, illus.), 13 x 9⅛ in., photograph, photogravure (BP 188, DM 471, FR 1585, Y 31,834).

$1320* *Factory, 1927,* photog. stamp, (11-16-92, Butterfield, #5855, illus.), 12⅛ x 9⅝ in., (308.5 x 244.9 mm.), photograph, gelatin silver print (BP 869, DM 2105, FR 7089, Y 164,159).

$5750* *The Glassblower, Corning, N.Y., 1929,* s., lit., (04-08-93, Christie-NY, #255, illus.), 12⅞ x 8¼ in., (32.7 x 21 cm.), photograph, gelatin silver print (BP 3770, DM 9237, FR 31,267, Y 652,519).

BI *Gold Miners, South Africa, 1950,* p. 1964, p. credit stamp, d. May 18 1964, lit., est. BP 8/1,000, (10-29-92, Christie-London, #157), 18¾ x 15¼ in., (47.6 x 38.7 cm.), photograph, gelatin silver print.

BI *Great Lakes Freighter Meets The Railroad At Cleveland,* late 1920s, credit stamp, label, est. $3/5,000, (04-08-93, Christie-NY, #259, illus.), 13¼ x 9⅜ in., (33.7 x 23.8 cm.), photograph, gelatin silver print.

$1045* *Harry Hackett Moulding A Steinway Piano, 1934,* ex-coll. Henry Steinway, (10-14-92, Swann, #287, illus.), 14 x 19 in., (35.6 x 48.3 cm.), photograph, silver print (BP 613, DM 1529, FR 5186, Y 126,636).

BI *"Issuance Of Equipment At A Station Near Piedmont, Italy...",* 1940s, s., label, est. $1/1,500, (05-23-93, Butterfield, #3325, illus.), 10 x 13¼ in., photograph, gelatin silver print.

$5940* *Laborers Crafting Pianos At The Steinway And Sons Factory: Seventeen,* handstamp, ex-coll. Henry Steinway (10-14-92, Swann, #289, illus.), 9 x 13 in., (22.9 x 33 cm.), photograph, silver prints (BP 3487, DM 8693, FR 29,479, Y 719,825).

BI *Landscape With River, 1955,* Life Photo stamp, est. $1,5/2,500, (10-15-92, Sotheby-NY, #196A, illus.), 10¼ x 13½ in., (26 x 34.3 cm.), photograph, gelatin silver print.

$2990* *Loom, Textile Factory, Moscow,* early 1930s, credit stamp, label, (04-08-93, Christie-NY, #258, illus.), 13⅛ x 9¼

in., (33.3 x 23.5 cm.), photograph, gelatin silver print (BP 1961, DM 4803, FR 16,259, Y 339,310).

$1495* *Ludlum Steel Company, c. 1927-30,* credit stamp, label w/t., (04-08-93, Christie-NY, #256, illus.), 13 x 9½ in., (33 x 24.1 cm.), photograph, gelatin silver print (BP 980, DM 2402, FR 8129, Y 169,655).

BI *Mail Distribution At 11th Field Hospital, Italy, c. 1944,* mounted, s. by photog. on mount, est. $1/2,000, (04-06-93, Sotheby-NY, #219, illus.), 10¼ x 13¼ in., photograph.

$1725* *"Modern City Of Johannesburg", 1950,* Erskine Caldwell, Jr. Coll., illus., (05-23-93, Butterfield, #3324, illus.), 14¾ x 19½ in., photograph, gelatin silver print (BP 1123, DM 2820, FR 9494, Y 190,671).

$1320* *Night View Of Downtown Cleveland, 1927,* photog. stamp, (11-16-92, Butterfield, #5854, illus.), 12⅞ x 9¼ in., (327.6 x 235.4 mm.), photograph, gelatin silver print (BP 869, DM 2105, FR 7089, Y 164,159).

BI *Organ Pipe Assembly, c. 1931: Two,* s. by photog., est. $4/6,000, (10-15-92, Sotheby-NY, #188, illus.), each approx. 13½ x 9½ in., (34.3 x 24.1 cm.), photograph, sepia-toned gelatin silver print w/black border.

BI *Pouring Molten Metal Into Ingot Molds, Ludlum Steel Co., 1928,* t., credit stamp, paper label, est. $5/7,000, (10-13-92, Christie-NY, #129, illus.), 13⅛ x 9 in., (33.3 x 22.9 cm.), photograph, gelatin silver print.

BI *Pro-Fascist Rally, Moravia, 1938,* handstamp, est. $8/1,200, (10-14-92, Swann, #288, illus.), 7 x 8½ in., (17.8 x 21.6 cm.), photograph, silver print.

$1100* *"Rising Cantilevers", 1927,* photog. stamp verso, typed t. label verso mount, lit., (11-16-92, Butterfield, #5853, illus.), 13½ x 10 in., (343.5 x 254.5 mm.), photograph, gelatin silver print (BP 724, DM 1754, FR 5908, Y 136,799).

BI *Selected Russian Portraits (Callahan, pp. 80-81), 1931: Two,* each mounted, s. by photog., 1st w/name stamp & label, est. $3/5,000, (10-15-92, Sotheby-NY, #190, illus.), each approx. 13 x 9 in., (33 x 22.9 cm.), photograph, sepia-toned gelatin silver prints w/black borders.

$4400* *Semionova, Premiere Ballerina, Great Theater, Moscow (Photographs, p.83), 1931,* mounted, name stamp, (10-15-92, Sotheby-NY, #190A, illus.), 9¼ x 13¼ in., (23.5 x 33.7 cm.), photograph, sepia-toned gelatin silver print w/black border (BP 2692, DM 6550, FR 22,211, Y 527,894).

$5750* *"The Spinner" (Gandhi Reading) (Callahan, pp. 174-175 variant),* mounted, photog. facsimile sig., reprod. lim. stamp, 1946, p. 1960's, (04-06-93, Sotheby-NY, #152, illus.), 9¾ x 13¼ in., photograph (BP 3798, DM 9264, FR 31,369, Y 655,794).

BI *Stalin's Mother, Tiflis (Callahan, p. 80), 1932,* mounted, s. by photog., name stamp, est. $2,5/3,500, (10-15-92, Sotheby-NY, #191, illus.), 13¼ x 9¼ in., (33.7 x 23.5 cm.), photograph, sepia-toned gelatin silver print w/black border.

$4400* *Terminal Tower With The High Level Bridge, Cleveland, 1928,* lit., (10-13-92, Christie-NY, #130, illus.), 13 x 9⅞ in., (33 x 25.1 cm.), photograph, gelatin silver print (BP 2563, DM 6446, FR 21,901, Y 533,527).

$935* *"Terminal Tower, Cleveland", c. 1927,* photog. stamp, (11-16-92, Butterfield, #5856, illus.), 13⅛ x 10⅛ in., (334 x 257.6 mm.), photograph, gelatin silver print (BP 616, DM 1491, FR 5021, Y 116,279).

$1840* *Three Hasidic Boys Reading The Torah, Czechoslovakia, 1954,* s., attrib., (05-23-93, Butterfield, #3323, illus.), 5 x 7 in., photograph, gelatin silver print (BP 1198, DM 3009, FR 10,127, Y 203,382).

$1210* *"Tool And Dye Worker On The Job", "Worker At Home (Interior Of U.L. Huse)" and "Worker On Front Porch": Three,* photog.'s notations and handstamp, Life reprod. handstamp, 1940s, (04-07-93, Swann, #292, illus.), each approx. 9½ x 7½ in., photograph, silver print (BP 800, DM 1957, FR 6623, Y 137,469).

BI *Transmission Tower Helix (cf. Callahan, p. 45), 1933,* name stamp, Archivally Reprocessed 1975 stamp, est. $10/20,000, (10-15-92, Sotheby-NY, #196, illus.), 13 x 10⅜ in., (33 x 26.4 cm.), photograph, sepia-toned gelatin silver print w/black border.

$1540* *"U.S. Supreme Court Building" and "U.S. Capitol Building", c. 1935: Two,* name stamp, N.E.A. Ref. Dept. stamp, (10-15-92, Sotheby-NY, #193, illus.), each approx. 6¾ x 4¾ in., (17.1 x 12.1 cm.), photograph, gelatin silver print (BP 942, DM 2292, FR 7774, Y 184,763).

$1650* *U.S. Supreme Court Building, c. 1935: Two,* name stamp, N.E.A. Ref. Dept. stamp, N.E.A. Service Inc. (c) stamp, (10-15-92, Sotheby-NY, #194, illus.), each approx. 13¼ x 9¼ in., (33.7 x 23.5 cm.), photograph, gelatin silver print (BP 1010, DM 2456, FR 8329, Y 197,960).

$1760* *Wall Street, 1930's,* name stamp, N.E.A. Ref. Dept. stamp, (10-15-92, Sotheby-NY, #195, illus.), 9⅜ x 6⅝ in., (23.8 x 16.8 cm.), photograph, gelatin silver print (BP 1077, DM 2620, FR 8884, Y 211,158).

$2875* *Washington Monument, c. 1935,* photog. stamp, N.E.A. Ref. Dept. stamp, (04-06-93, Sotheby-NY, #153, illus.), 6⅝ x 4½ in., photograph (BP 1899, DM 4632, FR 15,685, Y 327,897).

$1925* *Washington Monument, c. 1935,* name stamp, N.E.A. Ref. Dept. stamp, (10-15-92, Sotheby-NY, #192, illus.), 6⅝ x 4½ in., (16.8 x 11.4 cm.), photograph, gelatin silver print (BP 1178, DM 2865, FR 9717, Y 230,954).

BI *White Church In Pueblo, New Mexico, 1939,* s., t., d., annot. in crayon, label w/ink sig., p. t., d., est. $2,5/3,500, (04-08-93, Christie-NY, #260, illus.), 9⅜ x 12⅜ in., (23.8 x 31.4 cm.), photograph, gelatin silver print.

BOURNE, Samuel

$748* *Selected Works, India: 104,* 1870s, many s. in neg. or image, (05-23-93, Butterfield, #3327, illus.), from 2¾ x 3¾ in., to 8 x 10 in., photograph, albumen print (BP 487, DM 1223, FR 4117, Y 82,679).

BOURNE, Samuel and SHEPHERD & ROBERTSON

$1725* *India And Indian Life: Fifteen,* 1860s, mounted on paper, neg., s., num., various sizes from 186 x 162mm to 238 x 298mm, (05-07-93, Sotheby-London, #33, illus.), photograph, albumen print (BP 1092, DM 2727, FR 9190, Y 189,936).

BOUT, Pieter Flemish 1658-1702/19

$3610* *Die Schlittenfahrt Auf Dem Eis (B. 3; Hollstein 3 I),* prov., (12-04-92, Bassenge, #6067), 7⅝ x 10¹⁵⁄₁₆ in., (19.4 x 27.9 cm.), etching (BP 2316, DM 5749, FR 19,503, Y 450,687).

$7475* *The Skaters (Holl. 2), c. 1680-90,* 2nd (final) state, narrow margins, three sides, trimmed, stains, discoloration, good cond., ex-coll. A.F.T. Bohnenberger, (05-13-93, Sotheby-NY, #111, illus.), 7¾ x 10¾ in., (196 x 273 mm.), etching (BP 4907, DM 12,070, FR 40,714, Y 834,543).

BOUTET, Henri French 1851-1919

$186* *Madame Chrysantheme, Musique D'Andre Messager, 1893,* (01-31-93, Morelle/Marchan, #157), 23⅝ x 32⁵⁄₁₆ in., (60 x 82 cm.), poster (BP 125, DM 300, FR 1013, Y 23,204).

BI *"Parisienne", c. 1890,* s., num., stamped, excellent cond., est. $250-300, (10-31-92, Cleveland, #257), 12½ x 4¾ in., (31.8 x 12.1 cm.), drypoint.

$49* *Untitled,* (03-10-93, Maynard, #644), 8¾ x 5¼ in., (22.2 x 13.3 cm.), lithograph (BP 34, DM 82, FR 277, Y 5789, C$ 61).

BOUTET DE MONVAL, Bernard

$716* *"L'Eglise De Bagnaux" and "Le Retour Du Marche", c. 1900: Two,* t., just., s., dirt, (02-24-93, Picard, #25), color etching and aquatint on strong ivory wove (BP 499, DM 1162, FR 3941, Y 84,018).

BOUTET DE MONVAL, Maurice

$266* *Sirenes, c. 1895,* tears, stains, soiling, (02-24-93, Picard, #26), color lithograph on creme wove (BP 185, DM 432, FR 1464, Y 31,213).

BOUZONNET, Claudine (called Stella)

BI *La Vie Et La Passion Du Christ (Le Blanc 7): Thirteen,* thirteen from set of fourteen, after Nicholas Poussin, margins, surface dirt, creases, defects, est. BP 5/600, (06-30-93, Sotheby-London, #91), each c. 17¾ x 13½ in., (451 x 343 mm.), engraving.

BOVAIR, La Verne

BI *R.P.M.,* t., s. by photog., handstamp, notations, 1930s, est. $6/900, (04-07-93, Swann, #410, illus.), 19 x 15½ in., photograph, silver print.

BOVIS, Marcel

BI *Mannequins, c. 1930,* credit, reprod. limit. stamp, est $1,8/2,200, (10-13-92, Christie-NY, #132, illus.), 8⅞ x 6½ in., (22.5 x 16.5 cm.), photograph, gelatin silver print.

BOWDEN, Harry

$495* *"Badlands", 1953,* photog. stamp, (11-16-92, Butterfield, #5857, illus.), 7½ x 9½ in., (190.8 x 241.7 mm.), photograph, gelatin silver print (BP 326, DM 789, FR 2658, Y 61,560).

$690* *City Scenes In California: Six,* 1950s, t., photog.'s stamp, (05-23-93, Butterfield, #3329, illus.), 8 x 10 in., photograph, gelatin silver print (BP 449, DM 1128, FR 3797, Y 76,268).

$489* *San Francisco Scenes: Seven,* 1950s, photog.'s stamp, s., t., est. $6/800, (05-23-93, Butterfield, #3328, illus.), 8 x 9½ in., photograph, gelatin silver print (BP 318, DM 800, FR 2691, Y 54,051).

BOWEN, J.T. American 19th cent.

$495* *"Push-Ma-Ta-Ha, A Choctaw Warrior",* pub. Bowen, c. 1850, (12-05-92, Neal, #574), image 6½ x 5½ in., (16.5 x 14 cm.), hand-colored lithograph (BP 310, DM 772, FR 2630, Y 61,331).

BOWEN, Jane

$690* *"Mick Jagger", Francis Bacon" and "Jean Cocteau": Three,* 1960s, p.l., s., third t., (05-23-93, Butterfield, #3330, illus.), each approx. 10½ x 15½ in., photograph, gelatin silver print (BP 449, DM 1128, FR 3797, Y 76,268).

BOWERS, Albert (after)

$32 *Drover And Cattle In A Lane,* (02-05-93, G.A. Key, #86), 5 x 13 in., (12.7 x 33 cm.), chromolithograph (BP 22, DM 53, FR 179, Y 3982).

BOWLES, Carrington, Publisher

BI *A Journeyman Parson Going On Duty, 1785,* watermark, margins, repaired tear, est. BP 100/150, (11-30-92, Phillips-London, #141), plate 13½ x 9⅞ in., (343 x 251 mm.), mezzotint on wove.

BI *Narcissus And The Nymph Echo, c. 1770,* margins, repaired tears, thin area, est. BP 150/200, (11-30-92, Phillips-London, #139, illus.), plate 13⅞ x 10 in., (352 x 254 mm.), mezzotint on laid.

BOWLES, Thomas

$149* *The North Prospect Of London Taken From The Bowling Green At Islington,* pub. Bowles and Carver, margins, foxing, surface dirt, small tear, Late Sir Philip and Lady Hendy Coll., (06-16-93, Bonhams-Chelsea, #380), pl. 11¼ x 16½ in., (28.6 x 41.9 cm.), engraving w/hand-coloring on laid (BP 99, DM 247, FR 830, Y 15,892).

BOWLES AND CARVER, Publishers

$300* *Life And Death Contrasted Or An Essay On Woman, Or An Essay On Man: APair, c. 1820,* trimmed to thread margins on Man & to plate for Woman, image nick, (11-30-92, Phillips-London, #145), plate 13⅞ x 9¾ in., (352 x 248 mm.), engraving on thick wove (BP 198, DM 478, FR 1622, Y 37,337).

BOWLES and CARVER, Publisher

$152* *Cricket, Played By The Gentlemen's Club, White Conduit House, Islington,* pub. 1784, margins, from series Six Prints of Manly Recreations, as practised in Public Places in and about London, (03-03-93, Bonhams-Chelsea, #243), plate 7¼ x 9 in., (18.4 x 22.9 cm.), hand-colored etching (BP 105, DM 250, FR 849, Y 17,761).

BOWYER, Robert

$110* *"Moscow", "Hamburgh" and "Porto Ferrajo (Elba)": Three,* fold, from "An Illustrated Record Of Important Events...", (09-17-92, Sloan, #626), aquatint (BP 62, DM 163, FR 559, Y 13,695).

BOYD, Arthur Merric Bloomfield b. 1920

$195* *(Landscape),* s. Arthur Boyd, #100/100, (08-11-92, L. Joel, #187G), 19⅞ x 21⁷⁄₁₆ in., (50.5 x 54.5 cm.), color lithograph (BP 101, DM 286, FR 969, Y 24,971, A$ 264).

BI *Untitled,* s. Arthur Boyd, #111/X11, est. $2/300, (08-11-92, L. Joel, #178G), 13¾ x 15¾ in., (35 x 40 cm.), etching and aquatint.

BOYD, Hermia   b. 1931
$130* *(Figure In Bush),* s. Hermia Boyd, #16/50, (08-11-92, L. Joel, #186G), 19⅞ x 26¹⁵⁄₁₆ in., (50.5 x 68.5 cm.), lithograph (BP 68, DM 191, FR 646, Y 16,647, A$ 176).
$113* *(Figure In Bush),* s. Hermia Boyd, #17/50, (08-11-92, L. Joel, #177G), 19⅞ x 26¹⁵⁄₁₆ in., (50.5 x 68.5 cm.), lithograph (BP 59, DM 166, FR 562, Y 14,470, A$ 154).

BOYD, Theodore Penleigh   1890-1925
$223* *Hauling In The Nets,* s. Penleigh Boyd, i., #16/20, (08-11-92, L. Joel, #53G), 4¾ x 6⅞ in., (12.1 x 17.5 cm.), etching (BP 116, DM 327, FR 1108, Y 28,557, A$ 302).

BOYDELL, John   English 1719-1804
$633* *The Four Seasons: Four,* (09-17-92, Sloan, #1457), each, sight 14¼ x 12¼ in., (36.2 x 31.1 cm.), stipple engraving (BP 356, DM 940, FR 3216, Y 78,810).
$440* *The Four Seasons: Four,* (07-03-92, Sloan, #674), each, sight 14¼ x 12¼ in., (36.2 x 31.1 cm.), stippled engraving (BP 230, DM 666, FR 2245, Y 54,849).
$275* *William Penn's Treaty With The Indians,* after Benjamin West, (05-28-93, Sloan, #204, illus.), 17 x 23¼ in., (43.2 x 59.1 cm.), engraving (BP 176, DM 436, FR 1475, Y 29,487).

BOYLE, Keith
BI *March Light, 1987,* s., d. March/April, 1987, t., margins, very good cond., est. $2/400, (05-19-93, Butterfield, #2130), 24 x 17⅞ in., (610 x 454 mm.), lithograph in colors on wove.
$201* *Woman With Crossed Leg,* inits., #III, good cond.?, (05-19-93, Butterfield, #2131), 26¼ x 20 in., (667 x 508 mm.), lithograph on wove (BP 130, DM 327, FR 1101, Y 22,252).

BOYS, Thomas Shotter   British 1803-1874
$1480* *London As It is (Abbey Scenery 240): Eight,* plates 3, 12, 15, 18, 19, 21, 23 and 24 from the series of 26, late impression, pub. 1842, full margins, corner mounted, light stained, (10-27-92, Phillips-London, #119), sheet 21¼ x 14½ in., (540 x 368 mm.), tinted lithograph w/ hand-coloring (BP 935, DM 2268, FR 7696, Y 181,040).
$110* *"Saint Etienne Du Mont And The Pantheon, Paris",* good cond., surface dirt, (05-15-93, Cleveland, #362), 13⅞ x 11⅜ in., (35.2 x 28.9 cm.), lithograph w/hand-tinting (BP 72, DM 177, FR 595, Y 12,194).

BOYVIN, R.
$108* *Trophees D'Armes (R.D. 155, 156, 158; J.L. 105, 108, 110): Three,* from series of 6, thin or w/out margins, (06-16-93, Ader Tajan, #6), etching (BP 72, DM 179, FR 602, Y 11,519).

BRACHO, Angel   Mexican b. 1911
BI *La Cosecha, c. 1945,* s., full margins, good cond., handling creases, yellowing, tears, soiling, est. $8/1200, (05-18-93, Sotheby-NY, #251, illus.), image 27⅞ x 19¾ in., (708 x 502 mm.), linoleum cut.

BRACK, Cecil John   b. 1920
$298* *Adagio,* s. John Brack, d. '67, #147/200, lit., (08-11-92, L. Joel, #72G), 14¹⁵⁄₁₆ x 9⁵⁄₁₆ in., (37.9 x 23.7 cm.), lithograph (BP 155, DM 437, FR 1481, Y 38,161, A$ 405).
$567* *Seated Nude,* s. John Brack, d. '82, #10/50, lit., (08-11-92, L. Joel, #155G), 17⁵⁄₁₆ x 11⁷⁄₁₆ in., (44 x 29 cm.), lithograph (BP 295, DM 832, FR 2818, Y 72,609, A$ 770).
$324* *Standing Nude,* s. John Brack, d. '82, #2/50, lit., (08-11-92, L. Joel, #176G), 15½ x 10⅞ in., (39.3 x 27.7 cm.), lithograph (BP 168, DM 475, FR 1610, Y 41,491, A$ 440).

BRACKMAN, David (after)
BI *The Falcon,* #45/850, s., pub. Marine Gallery, est. BP 40/60, (02-17-93, Bonhams-Chelsea, #357), image 20 x 30 in., (50.8 x 76.2 cm.), color reproduction.

BRACQUEMOND, Felix   French 1833-1914
$778* *Au Jardin D'Acclimation (Ber. 214), 1873: Two,* first of fourth state of seven, rare, (02-24-93, Picard, #33), etching and aquatint on laid and wove (BP 543, DM 1263, FR 4282, Y 91,293).
$983* *Les Canards (Ber. 555),* stains, dirt, untrimmed margins, (02-24-93, Picard, #38), on ivory laid (BP 685, DM 1596, FR 5410, Y 115,349).
$165* *"Duverger" and "L'Enfouisseur Et Son Compere" (H. Beraldi, nums. 34 and 104),* collector's stamp, (04-02-93, Picard, #40), one 4¼ x 3¼ in., (10.8 x 8.3 cm.), other 5 x 5 in., (10.8 x 8.3 cm.), etching (BP 109, DM 265, FR 901, Y 18,786).
$3096* *Edmond De Goncourt (Inv. B.N. 386-Beraldi 54), 1881,* before i., ink s., (04-02-93, Picard, #41, illus.), 20¹⁄₁₆ x 13⅜ in., (51 x 34 cm.), etching on Japan (BP 2039, DM 4976, FR 16,900, Y 352,499).
$614* *Ex-Libris Manet, Christophe Et Aglaus Bouvenne, Sur La Meme Planche (Ber. 508-510), 1875,* rare, staining, margins, (02-24-93, Picard, #36), etching on old thin laid (BP 428, DM 997, FR 3379, Y 72,049).
BI *"L'Inconnu" (Beraldi 174 iii/III),* pub. Cadart & Chevalier, good cond., foxing, est. $2/300, (05-15-93, Cleveland, #363), 7¼ x 12½ in., (18.4 x 31.8 cm.), etching on chine colle wove.
$202* *"Leon Cladel", "Portrait Du Dr Tripier" and "L'Inconnu" (H. Beraldi 21, 96, 174): Three,* definitive state, ink s., creases, large margins, (02-03-93, Ader Tajan, #73), etching on Japan simili, third on fixed Chine (BP 141, DM 333, FR 1128, Y 25,128).
$155* *Portrait De Zacharie Astruc (Beraldi 9), 1865,* light stains, (06-28-93, Loudmer, #198), 7⁵⁄₁₆ x 5⅞ in., (185 x 150 mm.), sh 19⁵⁄₁₆ x 12⅜ in., (185 x 150 mm.), black etching on laid (BP 104, DM 263, FR 887, Y 16,446).
$220* *"Sarcelles (Teal)" (Beraldi 111 iv/iv),* pub. Cadart Luquet, good cond., full margins, (10-31-92, Cleveland, #258), 10⅝ x 12⅞ in., (27 x 32.7 cm.), etching (BP 141, DM 338, FR 1148, Y 27,251).
$372* *"Les Saules Des Mottiaux" and "Trembles Au Bord De La Seine" (H.B., num. 190 and 218): Two,* first out of 3, good margins, collector's stamp, (04-02-93, Picard, #43), one 7⅞ x 11⅝ in., (20 x 29.5 cm.), other 3⅞ x 5⅞ in., (20 x 29.5 cm.), etching (BP 245, DM 598, FR 2031, Y 42,355).
$220* *Sea Gulls,* s., bears artist's stamp, (05-16-93, Hindman, #441), 11½ x 18¾ in., (29.2 x 47.6 cm.), etching (BP 143, DM 354, FR 1189, Y 24,388).
BI *Teal,* s., stamped init., margins, good cond., creases, surface soiling, est. $2/400, (10-28-92, Butterfield, #2783), 8⅞ x 11½ in., (225 x 292 mm.), etching on tissue-thin paper.
$573* *Trembles Au Bord De La Seine (Ber. 218), 1884,* second state, creases, large margins, (02-24-93, Picard, #34), etching on old laid Japan (BP 400, DM 930, FR 3154, Y 67,238).

BRADFORD, Howard   American b. 1919
BI *Monterey Winds,* s., t., d. 1964, #26/75, est. $150/200, (02-04-93, Sloan, #362), 20 x 34 in., (50.8 x 86.4 cm.), color serigraph.
$83* *"Monterey Winds",* s., d., num. 26/75, excellent cond., (10-31-92, Cleveland, #362), 20 x 33¾ in., (50.8 x 85.7 cm.), silkscreen (BP 53, DM 128, FR 433, Y 10,281).
$99* *"Regatta Finish #2",* s., num. 13/60, excellent cond., (10-31-92, Cleveland, #364), 11 x 29¾ in., (27.9 x 75.6 cm.), silkscreen (BP 63, DM 152, FR 517, Y 12,263).
$72* *"Yellow Sky",* s., num. 37/50, excellent cond., (10-31-92, Cleveland, #363), 19¾ x 33½ in., (50.2 x 85.1 cm.), silkscreen (BP 46, DM 111, FR 376, Y 8919).

BRADFORD, William   American 1823/30-1892
BI *Section Of An Immense Berg, Which Was Nearly Half A Mile In Length, And Was Grounded Over In Five Hundred Feet Of Water, 1873,* orig. letterpress mount, est. $1/1,500, (04-07-93, Swann, #111, illus.), 10½ x 13½ in., (26.7 x 34.3 cm.), photograph, albumen print.

BRADFORD, William (after)
$575* *Crushed By Icebergs, c. 1868,* p. Storch & Kramer, pub. J.F. Bradford, trimmed to image, mounted on card, image scrapes, foxing, discoloration, (01-28-93, Sotheby-NY,

#459, illus.), 20 x 32⅞ in., (508 x 835 mm.), mount 22⅞ x 35¾ in., (508 x 835 mm.), chromolithograph (BP 380, DM 911, FR 3083, Y 71,393).

BRADFORD and CO., Lithographers   American 1854-1859

$440* *"Hunneman & Co., Builders, Boston, Mass.",* ident. w/in matrix, repaired tears, creases, margin repaired, staining, toning, laid down, (03-27-93, Skinner, #215, illus.), sight, sheet 22 x 32½ in., (55.9 x 82.6 cm.), chromolithograph on paper (BP 296, DM 718, FR 2440, Y 51,210).

$330* *"To The Firemen And Citizens Of Troy, N.Y....Presented By Union FireCompany No. Three Of Providence, R.I....1854",* ident. w/in matrix, good cond.?, staining, foxing, (03-27-93, Skinner, #214), sight, sheet 19½ x 14½ in., (49.5 x 36.8 cm.), hand-colored chromolithograph on paper (BP 222, DM 538, FR 1830, Y 38,408).

BRADLEY   American 19th cent.

$83* *Cover For "The Youths Companion, Feb. 20, 1896",* very good cond.?, (11-21-92, Bakker, #128), 14 x 9 in., (35.6 x 22.9 cm.), lithograph (BP 55, DM 132, FR 446, Y 10,322).

BRADLEY, Helen (after)

$207* *"A.H., Dear Emily" and "Oh, Just Look!":* Two num. 597, s., blindstamp, (03-17-93, Bonhams-Chelsea, #405), image 12 x 9¾ in., (30.5 x 24.8 cm.), reprod. in colors (BP 143, DM 344, FR 1171, Y 24,279).

$152* *Hollinwood Market,* num. 483, s., blindstamp, (03-17-93, Bonhams-Chelsea, #407), image 18¼ x 27¼ in., (46.4 x 69.2 cm.), reprod. in colors (BP 105, DM 253, FR 860, Y 17,828).

$152* *Our Picnic,* s., blindstamp, (03-17-93, Bonhams-Chelsea, #409), image 16 x 23¼ in., (40.6 x 59.1 cm.), reprod. in colors (BP 105, DM 253, FR 860, Y 17,828).

$152* *The Park On May Day,* #777/850, s., blindstamp, (03-17-93, Bonhams-Chelsea, #406), image 17¾ x 23 in., (45.1 x 58.4 cm.), reprod. in colors (BP 105, DM 253, FR 860, Y 17,828).

$160* *Snowman,* s., blindstamp, (03-17-93, Bonhams-Chelsea, #408), image 15 x 22 in., (38.1 x 55.9 cm.), reprod. in colors (BP 110, DM 266, FR 905, Y 18,766).

BRADLEY, John Henry   English 1832-after 1884

BI *Evening Laguna Of Venice,* good cond.?, est. $4/600, (06-11-93, Weschler, #49), 8¼ x 15¾ in., (21 x 40 cm.), etching w/tone.

BRADLEY, Martin   b. 1931

$111* *Yellow Moon,* s., #43/200, full margins, good cond., (12-09-92, Sotheby-Amstrdm, #510), 26⁹⁄₁₆ x 18⅞ in., (675 x 480 mm.), color silkscreen on Arches (BP 71, DM 174, FR 595, Y 13,763, G 196).

BRADLEY, William H.   American 1868-1962

$165* *The Ault And Wiborg, Co.: Group Of Three,* A- cond., advertisements, (08-06-92, Swann, #61, illus.), approx. 8 x 11 in., (20.3 x 27.9 cm.), (BP 86, DM 244, FR 823, Y 21,046).

$550* *Bradley, His Book (The Kiss), 1896,* A- cond., (08-06-92, Swann, #59, illus.), 9⅞ x 6¾ in., (25.1 x 17.1 cm.), (BP 287, DM 813, FR 2745, Y 70,153).

$1540* *"Bradley: His Book, Christmas", 1896,* mono. B, p. s. S.L. Busha Eng. in matrix, pub. Wayside Press, stable, backed w/tissue, losses, creases, scattered retouch, (10-09-92, Skinner, #10, illus.), sheet 42 x 29⅜ in., (106.7 x 74.6 cm.), woodcut in colors on paper (BP 914, DM 2294, FR 7778, Y 187,805).

$1430* *The Chap Book, 1894,* A- cond., (08-06-92, Swann, #57, illus.), 18½ x 12½ in., (47 x 31.8 cm.), (BP 747, DM 2113, FR 7136, Y 182,398).

BI *The Chap Book, Thanksgiving,* B+ cond., fold marks, est. $1/1,500, (08-06-92, Swann, #60, illus.), 20½ x 14 in., (52.1 x 35.6 cm.), .

$1430* *"Fringilla Or Tales-In-Verse...", 1895,* s. Bradley, ident. in matrix, pub. Burrows Brothers Co., good cond.,worm holes, glue, residue, (10-09-92, Skinner, #18, illus.), 17⅞ x 7¼ in., (45.4 x 18.4 cm.), commercial relief process in black and red on gray/brown paper (BP 849, DM 2130, FR 7222, Y 174,390).

BI *Harper's Round Table, 1895,* Thanksgiving num. (cover), A- cond., chip, est. $6/900, (08-06-92, Swann, #58, illus.), 11¾ x 8¼ in., (29.8 x 21 cm.), .

BI *May/The Chap Book, 1895,* lit., very rare, est. DM 3,500, (12-05-92, Bassenge, #7566, illus.), 22¹⁄₁₆ x 15¹⁵⁄₁₆ in., (56 x 40.5 cm.), color lithograph.

BRADY, Mathew   American 1823-1896

BI *Civil War Era, c. 1862,* est. $250/500, (03-12-93, DuMouchelle, #11, illus.), 5¾ x 8 in., photograph.

$1045* *General McClellan-Headquarters, General Motell's Brigade, Virginia, 1862,* photog. credit, t., (c) info. on mount recto, (04-07-93, Swann, #175, illus.), 10 x 14½ in., photograph, albumen print (BP 691, DM 1690, FR 5720, Y 118,723).

$2200* *General Robert E. Lee And Staff, Richmond, 1865,* on orig. mount, notations, (04-07-93, Swann, #176, illus.), 8½ x 7¼ in., photograph, albumen print (BP 1454, DM 3558, FR 12,042, Y 249,943).

$1100* *General Winfield Scott Hancock And Division Commanders, Including Generals Francis C. Barlow, John Gibbon, And David B. Birney, 1864,* (04-07-93, Swann, #177, illus.), 5 x 7½ in., photograph, Albumen print (BP 727, DM 1779, FR 6021, Y 124,972).

BI *Jacob Little, 1857,* mounted, Frederick Hill Meserve Coll., est. $3/5,000, (10-15-92, Sotheby-NY, #8, illus.), 15¾ x 12⅝ in., (40 x 32.1 cm.), photograph, imperial salt print.

BI *"Pan-American Medical Congress", 1893,* attrib., t., d., est. $4/600, (11-16-92, Butterfield, #5859, illus.), 11¾ x 14½ in., (299 x 369 mm.), photograph, albumen print.

$247* *Portrait Of General James ("Pete") Longstreet,* studio imprint, 1860s, (04-07-93, Swann, #178), photograph, Cabinet card (BP 163, DM 399, FR 1352, Y 28,062).

$605* *Portrait Of Ulysses S. Grant, 1860,* Grant's autograph and i., faded, credit, (c) info., d. in neg., (04-07-93, Swann, #113, illus.), 15 x 12 in., (38.1 x 30.5 cm.), photograph, oval albumen print (BP 400, DM 978, FR 3311, Y 68,734).

$3960* *"Recollections Of The Art Exhibition, Metropolitan Fair, New York", 14: Twenty,* album t., orig. two-toned mounts w/ photog.'s credit, (c), (04-07-93, Swann, #112, illus.), each approx. 6 x 9 in., (15.2 x 22.9 cm.), photograph, albumen print (BP 2617, DM 6405, FR 21,675, Y 449,898).

$8250* *Robert E. Lee, 1865,* s., (10-31-92, Riba, #145, illus.), photograph (BP 5394, DM 12,951, FR 43,860, Y 1,020,030).

$41,800* *Sample Book From Brady's National Photographic Art Gallery In Washington D.C.,* inc. Abraham Lincoln & his cabinet, Calhoun, Stonewall Jackson, Horace Greeley, Henry Clay, many w/Brady's sig. in neg., each num., iden., small folio, disbound, plates clean, 1860's, (10-14-92, Swann, #102, illus.), each 13½ x 8 in., (34.3 x 20.3 cm.), 480 cartes-de-visite photographs, mounted to album pages, albumen prints (BP 24,535, DM 61,174, FR 207,444, Y 5,065,439).

$1650* *Topographic And Street Views Of Charleston, South Carolina, 1865: Four,* photog. imprint, t., d., and credit mount recto, (04-07-93, Swann, #179, illus.), 7 x 9 in., photograph, albumen print (BP 1090, DM 2669, FR 9031, Y 187,457).

$935* *Young Woman In A Dark Green Dress With Velvet Trim, With A Gold Cross On A Chain Around Her Neck, ca. 1856,* photog.'s name and New York address stamped in velvet lining, (04-07-93, Swann, #126, illus.), photograph, hand-tinting (BP 618, DM 1512, FR 5118, Y 106,226).

BI *'Lilliputian Souvenir' (D.A.B., Vol 18, p. 127), c. 1863,* maquette of 14, Frederick Hill Meserve Coll., est. $2/3,000, (10-15-92, Sotheby-NY, #9, illus.), board 20¼ x 16¼ in., (51.4 x 41.3 cm.), cartes-de-visite photogs.,albumen prints, mounted on individual scallop-edged cards, all mounted on larger board.

BRADY, Mathew (Studio)

$4600* *Selected Civil War Studies, 1860's,* 49 photo., 23 half-stereo views, 19 uncut stereo pairs, 7 other, (04-06-93, Sotheby-NY, #10, illus.), various sizes to 9½ x 12 in., photograph, albumen print (BP 3038, DM 7411, FR 25,095, Y 524,635).

BRADY, Mathew (attrib.)   American 1823-1896

$1210* *"Ft. Burnham", "Harper's Ferry", "Railroad Bridge" and "Signal Station": Four,* notations, on mount recto, 1 w/ Brady imprint on mount verso, (04-07-93, Swann, #180, illus.), each approx. 7 x 10 in., photograph, Albumen print (BP 800, DM 1957, FR 6623, Y 137,469).

BRADY, Mathew and A.J. RUSSELL
BI *"Pontoon Landing, James River", "Aqueduct, Georgetown" and "Falls OfJames River": Three,* on orig. mounts, two w/Brady imprint on mount verso, 1860s, est. $1,5/2,500, (04-07-93, Swann, #181, illus.), largest 9½ x 13 in., photograph, albumen print.

BRAEKELEER, Ferdinand de (the elder) Belgian 1792-1883
BI *Les Trois Figures Pensives (Delteil 45 II),* est. DM 400, (12-04-92, Bassenge, #6755), 3¹⁄₁₆ x 3¾ in., (7.7 x 9.5 cm.), etching on hand-made.

BRAGAGLIA, Antonio Giulio 1890-1960
BI *L'Attore Lamberto Picasso, 1918-1930,* s., t., annot., credit stamp, lit., est. $20/25,000, (10-13-92, Christie-NY, #133, illus.), 8⅝ x 6 in., (21.9 x 15.2 cm.), photograph, gelatin silver print.

BRAGDON, Claude Fayette 1866-1946
BI *The Chap-Book/Price Five Cents,* before 1896, lit., est. Dm 1,800, (12-05-92, Bassenge, #7568), 18⅛ x 12⅝ in., (46 x 32 cm.), color lithograph.

BRAGG, Charles American 20th cent.
$83* *He Said That Is Was Good,* s., #275/300, (06-11-93, Freemn/Fine Art, #26), 10 x 14 in., (25.4 x 35.6 cm.), lithograph (BP 55, DM 135, FR 455, Y 8806).

BRAMI, Raoul
BI *Anais, 1990,* s., d. 90, full margins, est. FF1,800/2,000, (05-27-93, Briest, #37), 6⅞ x 5⅛ in., (17.5 x 13 cm.), pointe seche (drypoint) et encres typographiques de couleurs.

BRAMSON, Stern 1912-1989
$605* *"Baron Lavelle (Lawrence Jones) In His Home Theater, Louisville, Kentucky",* 1962/1990, collection stamp(11-16-92, Butterfield, #5860, illus.), 14⅞ x 18¹³⁄₁₆ in., (378.5 x 477.1 mm.), photograph, gelatin silver print (BP 398, DM 965, FR 3249, Y 75,239).
$715* *"Composite Photo For Newspaper Advertisement, Fourth And Broadway, Louisville, Kentucky",* 1952/1989, s., d., #7/10, (11-16-92, Butterfield, #5861, illus.), 14½ x 18⁹⁄₁₆ in., (369 x 470.7 mm.), photograph, gelatin silver print (BP 471, DM 1140, FR 3840, Y 88,919).
$288* *Premiere Of Victor Mature's "One Million B.C.",* 1940, p. 1988, d. twice, s., #2/10, (05-23-93, Butterfield, #3331, illus.), 9¾ x 12¼ in., photograph, gelatin silver print (BP 188, DM 471, FR 1585, Y 31,834).
$1150* *Untitled: Two,* 1950s, p. 1988, ink s., d.; d., #5/10 and #6/10, (04-08-93, Christie-NY, #407, illus.), 14⅝ x 18¼ in., (37.1 x 46.4 cm.), photograph, gelatin silver print (BP 754, DM 1847, FR 6253, Y 130,504).

BRANCUSI, Constantin Rumanian 1876-1957
BI *Mademoiselle Pogany II, c. 1920 (Brancusi, pl. 66),* est. $25/35,000, (10-15-92, Sotheby-NY, #288, illus.), 9 x 6⅝ in., (22.9 x 16.8 cm.), photograph, gelatin silver print.
BI *Le Nouveau-Ne II Et Tete D'Enfant Endormi (The New-born II And The Sleeping Child), 1927,* notations, prov., lit., est. 25/30,000, (10-13-92, Christie-NY, #134, illus.), 9⅜ x 11¾ in., (23.8 x 29.8 cm.), photograph, gelatin silver print.
$9200* *Vue De L'Atelier, c. 1923,* prov., exhib., lit., (04-08-93, Christie-NY, #87, illus.), 11⅜ x 15⅜ in., (28.9 x 39.1 cm.), photograph, gelatin silver print (BP 6033, DM 14,779, FR 50,027, Y 1,044,031).

BRANDES, Peter
$843* *Det Hellige Victoria Bjerg,* s. Peter Brandes 1981, (09-30-92, Kunsthallen, #50), acrylic on offset print (BP 476, DM 1195, FR 4043, Y 101,164, DK 4600).
$137* *Komposition,* s. Peter Brandes, E.A., (09-30-92, Kunsthallen, #48), etching w/collage (BP 77, DM 194, FR 657, Y 16,441, DK 748).
BI *Komposition,* s. Peter Brandes, E.A., est. DK 1,200, (09-30-92, Kunsthallen, #49), etching and collage.
$1151* *Komposition,* s. 88/90, (09-29-92, B. Rasmussen, #283), lithograph in colors (BP 647, DM 1626, FR 5547, Y 137,400, DK 6325).
$92* *Komposition,* s. Peter Brandes, 1/1, (03-24-93, Kunsthallen, #52), color lithograph (BP 62, DM 150, FR 511, Y 10,810, DK 575).
$404* *Komposition,* s. Peter Brandes, 28/100, (03-24-93, Kunsthallen, #50), color lithograph (BP 274, DM 660, FR 2246, Y 47,468, DK 2530).
$514* *Komposition,* s. Peter Brandes, 28/100, (03-24-93, Kunsthallen, #51), color lithograph (BP 348, DM 839, FR 2857, Y 60,392, DK 3220).
BI *Komposition, 1983,* s. Peter Brandes 83, est. DK 3,500, (03-24-93, Kunsthallen, #49), color lithograph.

BRANDIS, Gerald William Brender A
$43* *Dahlias,* s., t., pub. Brandstead Press, label verso, (06-07-93, Ritchie, #37, illus.), 4 x 4¼ in., (10.2 x 10.8 cm.), wood engraving (BP 28, DM 70, FR 235, Y 4613, C$ 55).

BRANDOIN, Charles (after)
$660* *The Inside Of The Pantheon In Oxford Road (C.S. Earlom 45),* by R. Earlom, pub. R. Sayer 1772, narrow margins, dirt, repairs, hinged, (10-07-92, Christie-S. Ken, #6), pl 18½ x 22 in., (47 x 55.9 cm.), mezzotint (BP 385, DM 955, FR 3238, Y 79,375).

BRANDT, Bill British 1904-1984
BI *American Soldier With French Child, 1944,* handstamps, notations, label, est. $8/1,200, (10-14-92, Swann, #290, illus.), 8 x 6 in., (20.3 x 15.2 cm.), photograph, silver print.
$2013* *"Au Marche Aux Puces" (Behind the Camera, p. 9; Shadow of Light, pl.60),* i. by photog., stamp, label, probably p. 1940's, (04-06-93, Sotheby-NY, #353, illus.), 10¾ x 8¼ in., photograph (BP 1330, DM 3243, FR 10,982, Y 229,585).
$1210* *"Aux Course D'Autueil, Paris", "Between Ullswater", "Portrait Of Jean Dubuffet In His Studio", "La Seine At Neuilly" and "Old Woman Crossing Street": Five,* photog.'s handstamp, notations, label, 1920s-40s, p.l., (04-07-93, Swann, #412, illus.), 7 x 9 in., photograph, silver print (BP 800, DM 1957, FR 6623, Y 137,469).
BI *Avebury Stone Circle, Wiltshire and Mayfair Houses, London: Two,* (1945), (1930s), p.l., each s. in ink, lit., est. $2/2,500, (10-13-92, Christie-NY, #141, illus.), each 13¼ x 11⅜ in., (33.7 x 28.9 cm.), photograph, gelatin silver prints.
$715* *"Barmaid At The Crooked Billet, Tower Hill" (Shadow Of Light, pl. 28b),* ink s., 1930's/c. 1970, (11-16-92, Butterfield, #5864, illus.), 13¼ x 11½ in., (337.2 x 292.6 mm.), photograph, gelatin silver print (BP 471, DM 1140, FR 3840, Y 88,919).
$1495* *"Bond Street Hatter's Show-Case" (Shadow of Light, pl. 4C),* s. by photog., 1930's, p.l., (04-06-93, Sotheby-NY, #347, illus.), 13 x 11 in., photograph (BP 987, DM 2409, FR 8156, Y 170,506).
$1725* *"Charlie Brown's Famous East End London Pub", 1945,* num. 10 by photog., studio stamp, Shaef Field Press Censor stamp, d.2 Mar. 1945, (04-06-93, Sotheby-NY, #350, illus.), 9⅛ x 7¼ in., photograph (BP 1139, DM 2779, FR 9411, Y 196,738).
BI *"Child And Nanny In The Nursery",* 1930s, p.l., s., illus., est. $800/1,200, (05-23-93, Butterfield, #3338, illus.), 13½ x 12 in., photograph, gelatin silver print.
$4025* *"Chiswick House Garden", 1945: Two,* t. by photog., name stamp, Shaef Field Press Censor stamp d. 14 April 1945, Harper's Bazar insertion stamp, (04-06-93, Sotheby-NY, #352, illus.), approx. 9 x 7¾ in., photograph (BP 2659, DM 6485, FR 21,959, Y 459,056).
$2310* *Coal Searcher Going Home To Jarrow (Shadow of Light, pl. 39),* mounted, s. by photog. in ink, 1930's, p.l., (10-15-92, Sotheby-NY, #432, illus.), 13½ x 11½ in., (34.3 x 29.2 cm.), photograph, gelatin silver print (BP 1414, DM 3439, FR 11,661, Y 277,145).
BI *Cocktails In A Surrey Garden,* (1930s), p.l., s. in ink, lit., est. $1,2/1,500, (10-13-92, Christie-NY, #139, illus.), 13⅛ x 11⅜ in., (33.3 x 28.9 cm.), photograph, gelatin silver print.
$770* *Cocktails In A Surrey Garden (Behind The Camera, p. 15),* ink s., (11-16-92, Butterfield, #5863, illus.), 12⅛ x 10⅜ in., (308.5 x 264 mm.), photograph, gelatin silver print (BP 507, DM 1228, FR 4135, Y 95,759).

BI *Cook And Kitchenmaids Preparing Dinner, 1937,* credit stamp, lit., est. $10/12,000, (10-13-92, Christie-NY, #137, illus.), 9 x 7¾ in., (22.9 x 19.7 cm.), photograph, gelatin silver print.

$3450* *"Couple At Charlie Brown's" (Shadow of Light, pl. 28D), 1945,* num. 11 by photog., studio stamop, Shaef Field Press Censor stamp, d. 2 Mar. 1945, (04-06-93, Sotheby-NY, #349, illus.), 9 x 7⅝ in., photograph (BP 2279, DM 5558, FR 18,822, Y 393,476).

BI *Cricket In The Park, c. 1935,* t., credit stamp, prov., lit., est. $10/12,000, (10-13-92, Christie-NY, #136, illus.), 7¼ x 9⅜ in., (18.4 x 23.8 cm.), photograph, gelatin silver print.

$863* *"Dancing The Lambeth Walk",* 1930s, p.l., s., illus., (05-23-93, Butterfield, #3334, illus.), 13⅜ x 11⅜ in., photograph, gelatin silver print (BP 562, DM 1411, FR 4750, Y 95,391).

BI *"East Durham Coal Miner Just Home From The Pit" (Shadow of Light, pl. 57),* ink s., 1930's/c. 1970, est. $800/1,200, (11-16-92, Butterfield, #5866, illus.), 13¼ x 11⅜ in., (337.2 x 289.4 mm.), photograph, gelatin silver print.

BI *East Sussex Coast,* 1958, p.l., ink s., lit., est. $1/1,500, (04-08-93, Christie-NY, #169, illus.), 13⅜ x 11½ in., (34 x 29.2 cm.), photograph, gelatin silver print.

$8625* *East Sussex Coast, 1957,* credit stamp, label w/credit/ reprod. limitation, lit., (04-08-93, Christie-NY, #172, illus.), 9 x 7¾ in., (22.9 x 19.7 cm.), photograph, gelatin silver print (BP 5656, DM 13,855, FR 46,900, Y 978,779).

$550* *East-Durham Coal Miner Just Home From The Pit,* sig., 1930's, p. 1960's, (10-14-92, Swann, #386, illus.), 13 x 11½ in., (33 x 29.2 cm.), photograph, silver print (BP 323, DM 805, FR 2730, Y 66,651).

BI *Edith And Osbert (Sitwell) Beneath The Family By Sargent, Renishaw, Yorkshire,* 1945, p.l., mounted on card, s., 335 x 287mm., est. BP 4/600, (05-07-93, Sotheby-London, #218, illus.), photograph, silver print.

BI *Ely Cathedral, 1945,* notations, handstamp, est. $2/3,000, (10-14-92, Swann, #387, illus.), 10 x 7¾ in., (25.4 x 19.7 cm.), photograph, silver print.

$1179* *"Ely Cathedral. The Octagon Tower, Nave Roof In The Foreground",* 1945, ink t., photog.'s ink credit stamp, (05-06-93, Christie-London, #109, illus.), 9⅞ x 7¾ in., photograph, gelatin silver print (BP 747, DM 1857, FR 6251, Y 129,717).

$978* *Hampstead, London,* 1945, p. 1960s, ink s., credit stamp, lit., (04-08-93, Christie-NY, #170, illus.), 13¼ x 11⅜ in., (33.7 x 28.9 cm.), photograph, gelatin silver print (BP 641, DM 1571, FR 5318, Y 110,985).

BI *Hampstead, London, 1952,* lit., est. $9/12,000, (10-13-92, Christie-NY, #420, illus.), 9⅛ x 9⅛ in., (23.2 x 23.2 cm.), photograph, gelatin silver print.

$6500* *Hampstead, London, 1956,* credit stamp, Museum of Modern Art stamp, exhib. label, exhib., lit., sold after sale, (04-08-93, Christie-NY, #173, illus.), 9½ x 7½ in., (24.1 x 19.1 cm.), photograph, gelatin silver print (BP 4262, DM 10,442, FR 35,345, Y 737,631).

$1815* *"Homes Fit For Heroes",* 1930s, t., photog.'s ink credit stamp, prov., (05-06-93, Christie-London, #107, illus.), 9 x 7⅝ in., photograph, gloss gelatin silver print (BP 1150, DM 2859, FR 9624, Y 199,692).

BI *In A Kensington Drawing Room After Dinner, 1937,* d. in ink, cred stamp, lit., est $10/12,000, (10-13-92, Christie-NY, #138, illus.), 9 x 7¾ in., (22.9 x 19.7 cm.), photograph, gelatin silver print.

$825* *London,* (1953), p.l., s. in ink, lit., (10-13-92, Christie-NY, #421, illus.), 13½ x 11½ in., (34.3 x 29.2 cm.), photograph, gelatin silver print (BP 480, DM 1209, FR 4107, Y 100,036).

BI *London, 1960,* ink num. 79; d., num., credit stamp, est. $8/10,000, (04-08-93, Christie-NY, #174, illus.), 9 x 7⅞ in., (22.9 x 20 cm.), photograph, gelatin silver print.

$660* *Night-Time, London,* photog.'s sig., 1930s, p.l., cover photo for Camera In London, (04-07-93, Swann, #411, illus.), 13¼ x 11¼ in., photograph, silver print (BP 436, DM 1067, FR 3612, Y 74,983).

BI *"No. 13. A Visitor Arrives For Luncheon. The Parlour Maid Answers The Front Door, Receives Visitors And Shows Them Into The Lounge",* 1930s, t., photog.'s ink

credit stamp, prov., est. BP 800/1,000, (05-06-93, Christie-London, #106, illus.), 7¾ x 9⅜ in., photograph, gloss gelatin silver print.

BI *"Northumbrian Miner At His Evening Meal" (Shadow of Light, pl. 47),* mounted, s. by photog., 1930's, p.l., est. $1/2,000, (04-06-93, Sotheby-NY, #349A, illus.), 13½ x 11⅜ in., photograph.

$575* *"November In The Suburb",* 1930s, p.l., s., est. $1/ 1,500, (05-23-93, Butterfield, #3337, illus.), 7½ x 10⅜ in., photograph, gelatin silver print (BP 374, DM 940, FR 3165, Y 63,557).

$1320* *Nude,* (c. 1950s), p.l., s. in ink in margin, s., (10-13-92, Christie-NY, #417, illus.), 13½ x 11¾ in., (34.3 x 29.8 cm.), photograph, gelatin silver print (BP 769, DM 1934, FR 6570, Y 160,058).

$2875* *Nude (Shadow of Light, pl. 121),* mounted, s. by photog., 1952, p.l., (04-06-93, Sotheby-NY, #363, illus.), 13½ x 11½ in., photograph (BP 1899, DM 4632, FR 15,685, Y 327,897).

$1150* *Nude (Shadow of Light, pl. 124),* mounted, s. by photog., 1948, p.l., (04-06-93, Sotheby-NY, #356A, illus.), 13⅝ x 11⅜ in., photograph (BP 760, DM 1853, FR 6274, Y 131,159).

BI *Nude (Shadow of Light, pl. 129),* mounted, s. by photog., 1956, p.l., est. $1,5/2,000, (04-06-93, Sotheby-NY, #357, illus.), 13½ x 11⅜ in., photograph.

$6325* *Nude Abstraction, 1951,* photog. name stamp, d. 1951 in unident. hand, (04-06-93, Sotheby-NY, #359, illus.), 9 x 7⅝ in., photograph (BP 4178, DM 10,190, FR 34,506, Y 721,373).

BI *Nude Abstraction, 1958,* num. 34 by photog. in ink, d. April 1958 twice, name stamp, est. $8/10,000, (04-06-93, Sotheby-NY, #358, illus.), 9 x 7¾ in., photograph.

$920* *Nude, 1950's,* s. by photog., p.l., (04-06-93, Sotheby-NY, #361, illus.), 13½ x 11¾ in., photograph (BP 608, DM 1482, FR 5019, Y 104,927).

$4600* *Nude, 1950's,* photog. studio stamp, (04-06-93, Sotheby-NY, #360, illus.), 9⅛ x 7¾ in., photograph, silver gelatin print w/pencil highlighting (BP 3038, DM 7411, FR 25,095, Y 524,635).

$2013* *Nude, 1950's,* mounted, s. by photog., p.l., (04-06-93, Sotheby-NY, #362, illus.), 13¼ x 11¼ in., photograph (BP 1330, DM 3243, FR 10,982, Y 229,585).

BI *"Nude, August" (Nude By The Window) (Shadow Of Light, pl. 126),* s., est. $2,0/2,500, (11-16-92, Butterfield, #5862, illus.), 13½ x 11⅝ in., (343.5 x 295.8 mm.), photograph, gelatin silver print.

$2300* *"Nude, Bent Elbow",* 1952, p.l., s., illus., (05-23-93, Butterfield, #3332, illus.), 13½ x 11½ in., photograph, gelatin silver print (BP 1498, DM 3761, FR 12,658, Y 254,228).

$3850* *Nude, March,* (1952), p.l., s. in white ink recto, lit., (10-13-92, Christie-NY, #418, illus.), 20 x 15⅞ in., (50.8 x 40.3 cm.), photograph, gelatin silver print (BP 2242, DM 5640, FR 19,164, Y 466,836).

$2640* *Nude, March,* (1952), p.l., s. in ink,. lit., (10-13-92, Christie-NY, #419, illus.), 13½ x 11½ in., (34.3 x 29.2 cm.), photograph, gelatin silver print (BP 1538, DM 3868, FR 13,141, Y 320,116).

$4830* *Nude, c. 1948,* credit stamp, (04-08-93, Christie-NY, #171, illus.), 9 x 7¾ in., (22.9 x 19.7 cm.), photograph, gelatin silver print (BP 3167, DM 7759, FR 26,264, Y 548,116).

$508* *"Oakwood Moor, Yorkshire",* 1944, p. early 1970s, s., lit., (05-06-93, Christie-London, #110), 13½ x 11½ in., photograph, gelatin silver print (BP 322, DM 800, FR 2694, Y 55,892).

$1380* *Parlourmaid And Under-Parlourmaid Ready To Serve Dinner,* 1933, p.l., ink s., credit stamp, lit., (04-08-93, Christie-NY, #167, illus.), 13½ x 11⅝ in., (34.3 x 29.5 cm.), photograph, gelatin silver print (BP 905, DM 2217, FR 7504, Y 156,605).

$1540* *Parlourmaid And Under-Parlourmaid Ready To Serve Dinner,* (1933), p.l., s. in ink, lit., (10-13-92, Christie-NY, #140, illus.), 13½ x 11⅝ in., (34.3 x 29.5 cm.), photograph, gelatin silver print (BP 897, DM 2256, FR 7666, Y 186,735).

$1380* *"Parlourmaid And Under-Parlourmaid Ready To Serve Dinner" (Shadow ofLight, pl. 18),* mounted, s. by photog., 1930's, p.l., (04-06-93, Sotheby-NY, #348, illus.),

13⅜ x 11½ in., photograph (BP 911, DM 2223, FR 7529, Y 157,391).

$805* *"Parlourmaid And Underparlourmaid Ready To Serve Dinner"*, 1933, p.l., s., illus., (05-23-93, Butterfield, #3335, illus.), 13½ x 11⅜ in., photograph, gelatin silver print (BP 524, DM 1316, FR 4430, Y 88,980).

$1495* *"Portrait Of A Young Girl, Eaton Place, London" (Shadow of Light, pl. 102)*, s. by photog., 1955, p.l., (04-06-93, Sotheby-NY, #356, illus.), 13⅛ x 11⅜ in., photograph (BP 987, DM 2409, FR 8156, Y 170,506).

$1870* *Portrait Of A Young Girl, Eaton Place, London, 1955 (Shadow Of Light, pl. 102)*, s. by photog. in ink, p. l., (10-15-92, Sotheby-NY, #430, illus.), 13½ x 11½ in., (34.3 x 29.2 cm.), photograph, gleatin silver print (BP 1144, DM 2784, FR 9440, Y 224,355).

$1840* *Rainswept Roofs*, c. 1930, p.l., ink s., lit., (04-08-93, Christie-NY, #166, illus.), 13½ x 11⅝ in., (34.3 x 29.5 cm.), photograph, gelatin silver print (BP 1207, DM 2956, FR 10,005, Y 208,806).

$1270* *"Religious Demonstration, Epsom Derby Day"*, 1930s, t., s., photog.'s ink credit stamp twice, prov., (05-06-93, Christie-London, #108, illus.), 6½ x 8⅜ in., photograph, gelatin silver print (BP 805, DM 2000, FR 6734, Y 139,729).

$1495* *Rene Magritte With His Picture "The Great War", Brussels*, 1966, p.l., ink s., lit., (04-08-93, Christie-NY, #165, illus.), 13½ x 11¾ in., (34.3 x 29.8 cm.), gelatin silver print (BP 980, DM 2402, FR 8129, Y 169,655).

BI *Ruins From Bombing*, 1943, p.l., s., est. $800/1,200, (05-23-93, Butterfield, #3339, illus.), 13⅝ x 11½ in., photograph, gelatin silver print.

$2300* *Rural England: "Withens (Emily Bronte's Wuthering Heights)", "Bradford-on-Avon, Looking Towards Salisbury Plain" and "Country House" (Literary Britain, pl. 11), c. 1945: Three*, from Literary Britain series, 1st w/photog. name stamp and Harper's Bazaar insertion stamp d. June 1945; 2nd t. by photog., stamp, label; 3rd w/photg. name stamp, (04-06-93, Sotheby-NY, #351, illus.), each approx. 9 x 7¾ in., photograph (BP 1519, DM 3705, FR 12,548, Y 262,318).

$1380* *Soho Bedroom*, 1936, p.l., ink s., lit., (04-08-93, Christie-NY, #168, illus.), 13½ x 11½ in., (34.3 x 29.2 cm.), photograph, gelatin silver print (BP 905, DM 2217, FR 7504, Y 156,605).

$935* *"Soho Nightclub" (Shadow Of Light, pl. 20)*, 1930's/c. 1970, ink s., (11-16-92, Butterfield, #5865, illus.), 13½ x 11½ in., (343.5 x 292.6 mm.), photograph, gelatin silver print (BP 616, DM 1491, FR 5021, Y 116,279).

BI *Sonntags Im Bois De Boulogne*, 1930s, label, est. $5/7,000, (04-08-93, Christie-NY, #175, illus.), 6⅝ x 8⅞ in., (16.8 x 22.5 cm.), photograph, gelatin silver print.

$1495* *"Stonehenge Under Snow" (Shadow of Light, pl. 117)*, mounted, s. by photog., 1947, p.l., (04-06-93, Sotheby-NY, #354, illus.), 13½ x 11½ in., photograph (BP 987, DM 2409, FR 8156, Y 170,506).

$1100* *Stonehenge Under Snow, 1947 (Shadow of Light, pl. 117)*, mounted, s. by photog. in ink, p. l., (10-15-92, Sotheby-NY, #433, illus.), 13½ x 11½ in., (34.3 x 29.2 cm.), photograph, gelatin silver print (BP 673, DM 1637, FR 5553, Y 131,974).

$1650* *Sun Bathers*, name stamp, 1950's, (10-15-92, Sotheby-NY, #435, illus.), 9¼ x 7⅝ in., (23.5 x 19.4 cm.), photograph, gelatin silver print (BP 1010, DM 2456, FR 8329, Y 197,960).

$633* *"Top Withens, West Riding, Yorkshire: After Emily Bronte"*, 1945, p.l., s., (05-23-93, Butterfield, #3340, illus.), 13½ x 11¾ in., photograph, gelatin silver print (BP 412, DM 1035, FR 3484, Y 69,968).

$920* *"Train Leaving Newcastle"*, 1930s, p.l., s., illus., (05-23-93, Butterfield, #3336, illus.), 13⅜ x 11⅜ in., photograph, gelatin silver print (BP 599, DM 1504, FR 5063, Y 101,691).

$1540* *Untitled*, s. by photog. in ink, 1950's, p. l., (10-15-92, Sotheby-NY, #427, illus.), 13½ x 11½ in., (34.3 x 29.2 cm.), photograph, gelatin silver print (BP 942, DM 2292, FR 7774, Y 184,763).

$1100* *Untitled*, s. by photog. in ink, early 1950's, p. l., (10-15-92, Sotheby-NY, #426, illus.), 13 x 11¼ in., (33 x 28.6

cm.), photograph, gelatin silver print (BP 673, DM 1637, FR 5553, Y 131,974).

BI *Untitled (Shadow of Light, pl. 125)*, s. by photog., 1952, p.l., est. $1/2,000, (10-15-92, Sotheby-NY, #429, illus.), 13⅝ x 11⅝ in., (34.6 x 29.5 cm.), photograph, gelatin silver print.

$1210* *Untitled, 1959 (Shadow of Light, pl. 144)*, mounted, s. by photog. in ink, p. l., (10-15-92, Sotheby-NY, #428, illus.), 13⅜ x 11½ in., (34 x 29.2 cm.), photograph, gelatin silver print (BP 740, DM 1801, FR 6108, Y 145,171).

$7150* *Vasterival, Normandy, 1957*, stamps, lit., (10-13-92, Christie-NY, #422, illus.), 9¼ x 7¾ in., (23.5 x 19.7 cm.), photograph, gelatin silver print (BP 4164, DM 10,475, FR 35,590, Y 866,982).

BI *A Whitechapel Blind Man*, 1930s, t. twice, in English and French, Photo Bill Brandt stamp, est. $5/7,000, (04-08-93, Christie-NY, #176, illus.), 9¾ x 7⅝ in., (24.8 x 19.4 cm.), photograph, gelatin silver print.

$1035* *Woman And Man On Riverbank With Cycle*, 1930s, photog.'s stamp, (05-23-93, Butterfield, #3333, illus.), 7¾ x 6½ in., photograph, gelatin silver print (BP 674, DM 1692, FR 5696, Y 114,403).

BRANGER, M.
BI *Portraits Of Aviators In Their Biplanes And Monoplanes, France (1908-1910), 1911: Thirteen*, 5 num. in neg.; each (c) credit identifying legend, est. $1,5/2,500, (04-08-93, Christie-NY, #43, illus.), each approx. 4⅝ x 6½ in., (11.7 x 16.5 cm.), photograph, gelatin silver print.

BRANGWYN, Sir Frank   British 1867-1956
$261* *Alcantara Bridge, Toledo (G. 236), 1916*, s., foxing, creasing, (10-27-92, Phillips-London, #239), plate 20 x 23½ in., (508 x 597 mm.), etching on wove (BP 165, DM 400, FR 1357, Y 31,927).

$468* *Beggars Under A Bridge*, glued to overmat in margins, good cond., surface staining, foxing, glue/paper remains, (10-28-92, Butterfield, #2784), etching on cream wove (BP 298, DM 723, FR 2454, Y 57,423).

$452* *Breaking Up The Duncan (G. 193)*, s., full margins, mount staining, dirt, laid, (10-07-92, Christie-S. Ken, #108), pl 21 x 32 in., (53.3 x 81.3 cm.), etching (BP 264, DM 654, FR 2218, Y 54,360).

$28* *"Brick Makers At Work"*, p. Thomas Way, plate 2, init., (06-11-93, DuMouchelle, #2266), 11½ x 10 in., (29.2 x 25.4 cm.), lithograph (BP 18, DM 46, FR 153, Y 2971).

$112* *Building The New Bourse*, s., margins, (03-17-93, Bonhams-Chelsea, #397), plate 6¾ x 6¾ in., (17.1 x 17.1 cm.), drypoint etching (BP 77, DM 186, FR 633, Y 13,136).

$235* *The Church Of St. Nicholas, Dixmunden*, s., margins, surface dirt, (01-21-93, Bonhams-Chelsea, #102), plate 22 x 26 in., (55.9 x 66 cm.), etching (BP 154, DM 374, FR 1264, Y 29,412).

$57* *Crucifixion*, s. Branwyn, (08-11-92, L. Joel, #180G), 7 x 5⅞ in., (17.8 x 15 cm.), etching (BP 30, DM 84, FR 283, Y 7299, A$ 77).

$213* *Figures In Front Of A Parisien Church*, s., margins, stained, (08-20-92, Bonhams-Chelsea, #76), plate 22 x 26 in., (55.9 x 66 cm.), etching (BP 110, DM 308, FR 1047, Y 26,897).

$44* *Forest Scene*, s., #1147, (06-11-93, DuMouchelle, #2269), 5¼ x 6½ in., (13.3 x 16.5 cm.), etching (BP 29, DM 72, FR 241, Y 4668).

$127* *Die Gerber*, s. Frank Brangwyn, creases, (03-24-93, Venator/Hansten, #4472), pl 5¹⁵⁄₁₆ x 4½ in., (15.2 x 11.4 cm.), etching on thick Japan (BP 86, DM 207, FR 706, Y 14,922).

$22* *"A Labourer Resting"*, mono., (06-11-93, DuMouchelle, #2267), 11¾ x 10 in., (29.8 x 25.4 cm.), lithograph (BP 14, DM 36, FR 121, Y 2334).

$28* *"The Mine"*, mono., (06-11-93, DuMouchelle, #2268), 12 x 8¾ in., (30.5 x 22.2 cm.), lithograph (BP 18, DM 46, FR 153, Y 2971).

$202* *A Mosque, Constantinople*, s., margins, time-stained, (01-21-93, Bonhams-Chelsea, #103), plate 18½ x 20½ in., (47 x 52.1 cm.), etching (BP 132, DM 321, FR 1087, Y 25,282).

$200* *"Outside The Temple",* margins, (11-19-92, Bonhams-Chelsea, #188), plate 23 x 29 in., (58.4 x 73.7 cm.), sepia etching (BP 132, DM 319, FR 1074, Y 24,873).

$867* *Pollard's The House Of Craftsmen, c. 1925,* fold marks, nicks, tears, (02-04-93, Christie-S. Ken, #57, illus.), 57 x 38 in., (144.8 x 96.5 cm.), color lithograph (BP 605, DM 1428, FR 4841, Y 107,849).

$348* *Pont Miare, Paris (G. 232), 1914,* s., laid on card, mount staining, (10-27-92, Phillips-London, #238), plate 20 x 23½ in., (508 x 597 mm.), etching on wove (BP 220, DM 533, FR 1810, Y 42,569).

$220* *Riverview With Figures,* s., (06-11-93, Freemn/Fine Art, #27), 27½ x 28½ in., (69.9 x 72.4 cm.), etching (BP 145, DM 358, FR 1205, Y 23,342).

$61* *"A Street In Puy" (Gaunt 222),* s., nick in image, (10-31-92, Cleveland, #259), etching (BP 39, DM 94, FR 318, Y 7556).

BI *The Studio, c. 1899,* lit., est. DM 1,500, (12-05-92, Bassenge, #7569), 33⅛ x 21 9/16 in., (84.2 x 54.7 cm.), color lithograph.

BRANGWYN, Sir Frank (after)

$191* *Old Mills, Meaux,* s., margins, (02-17-93, Bonhams-Chelsea, #227), plate 11¼ x 14½ in., (28.6 x 36.8 cm.), etching (BP 132, DM 310, FR 1051, Y 22,814).

BRAQUE, Georges French 1882-1963

$2196* *Ales, P.A.B. (Vallier 192), 1964,* from Les Petites Heures De Thouzon by Pierre Andre Benoit, num., s. P.A.B. in colophon, book, (11-15-92, Christie-Geneva, #312, illus.), 13 1/16 x 10 7/16 in., (332 x 265 mm.), etching on B.F.K. Rives (BP 1443, DM 3502, FR 11,800, Y 274,055, SF 3164).

$3921* *Ales, P.A.B., 1959,* from Dans Vos Jardins by Pierre Andre Benoit, num., s. P.A.B. in colophon, book, (11-15-92, Christie-Geneva, #310, illus.), 13⅜ x 10¼ in., (340 x 260 mm.), cartalegraphie on Arches (BP 2577, DM 6254, FR 21,069, Y 489,330, SF 5650).

$25,578* *Les Amaryllis (V. 125), 1958,* s., #53/75, p. Crommelynck et Dutrou, pub. Maeght, full margins, goodcond., (12-03-92, Sotheby-London, #190, illus.), 21½ x 17¾ in., (546 x 451 mm.), aquatint in colors on Rives wove (BP 16,500, DM 40,223, FR 137,295, Y 3,182,531).

$1579* *Andre Verdet: Le Solitaire (Vallier Nr. 142; Mourlot 67; Wunsche 65), 1959,* #14/30, s., (06-24-93, Germann, #253, illus.), 12 15/16 x 9 13/16 in., (330 x 250 mm.), color lithograph (BP 1039, DM 2560, FR 8628, Y 169,384, SF 2300).

$1998* *Aout: Frontispiece (V. 135), 1958,* s., #24/70, full margins, very good cond., (12-01-92, Christie-London, #308), overall sheet 19 11/16 x 15⅜ in., (500 x 390 mm.), aquatint in colors on Auvergne laid (BP 1320, DM 3185, FR 10,853, Y 248,755).

BI *Aout: Page 23 (V. 135, SEE P. 192), 1958,* s., #36/70, p. Crommelynck et Dutrou, pub. Louis Broder, full margins, good cond., est. BP 1,5/2,000, (06-30-93, Sotheby-London, #363, illus.), 9¾ x 12⅛ in., (248 x 308 mm.), aquatint on wove.

$706* *"Areion",* #52/200, i., s. G. Braque in plate, (02-16-93, Encans, #89), 14¾ x 22¼ in., (37.5 x 56.5 cm.), etching (BP 488, DM 1152, FR 3903, Y 84,581, C$ 888).

$6600* *Astre Et Oiseau II (V. 13), 1958,* s., #16/75, full sheet, skinning verso, good cond., (11-09-92, Christie-NY, #58, illus.), sheet 17½ x 20¾ in., (445 x 527 mm.), lithograph in colors on Arches (BP 4364, DM 10,536, FR 35,599, Y 819,062).

$8800* *Au Couchant (Oiseaux XVI) (V. 126), 1958,* s., #18/75, crease, tear/rubbing, soiling, mat staining, good cond., (11-09-92, Christie-NY, #57, illus.), sheet 19⅛ x 25 13/16 in., (485 x 655 mm.), lithograph in colors on Arches (BP 5818, DM 14,049, FR 47,465, Y 1,092,082).

BI *Au Couchant, (Oiseau XVI) (Vallier 126), 1958,* s., num. 20/75, pub. Maeght, full sheet, creases, scrape, good cond., est. Y 1,5/1,800,000, (10-14-92, Sotheby-Japan, #7, illus.), sheet 19 x 25¾ in., (483 x 654 mm.), lithograph in colors on Arches wove.

BI *Au Couchant, Oiseau XVI (Vallier 126), 1958,* #38/75, s., stains, est. DM 35,000-, (11-21-92, Lempertz, #52, illus.), 19⅛ x 25 13/16 in., (48.5 x 65.5 cm.), color lithograph on Arches wove.

$105* *"Birds In Flight",* Collector's Guild, (02-12-93, DuMouchelle, #368), approx. 13½ x 10 in., (34.3 x 25.4 cm.), etching (BP 74, DM 174, FR 589, Y 12,663).

$1024* *Blumenstilleben,* after Braque, s., 1955 in Verve, (12-12-92, Bassenge, #8471), 14 15/16 x 10⅝ in., (38 x 27 cm.), color lithograph (BP 655, DM 1609, FR 5485, Y 126,686).

$1475* *Blumenstrauss,* s., num., (12-05-92, Bassenge, #7065), 18⅞ x 11 9/16 in., (48 x 29.4 cm.), color aquatint on Arches (BP 924, DM 2300, FR 7837, Y 182,753).

$2588* *Le Canard (V. 160), 1961,* s., i. A.P., pub. Au Vent d'Arles, full margins, faded, water stains,tape stain, repaired tear, (05-13-93, Sotheby-NY, #467), 13⅝ x 17⅞ in., (345 x 455 mm.), lithograph w/embossing in colors (BP 1699, DM 4179, FR 14,096, Y 288,936).

$5870* *Le Canard (Vallier 160), 1961,* #48/75, s., (04-24-93, Kunsthaus, #478, illus.), 13 9/16 x 17 15/16 in., (34.5 x 45.5 cm.), 19⅞ x 24 13/16 in., (34.5 x 45.5 cm.), color lithograph on hand-made Auvergne (BP 3705, DM 9201, FR 31,075, Y 647,760).

BI *Cercle Dore: Couvertur Et Poeme (Mourlot 24), 1955,* s., illus., oxidation, est. FF2/4,000, (06-28-93, Loudmer, #199), 14 9/16 x 11 in., (370 x 280 mm.), sh 19 11/16 x 12 13/16 in., (370 x 280 mm.), black lithograph on Arches wove.

$2745* *Le Char III (Char Verni) (V. 98), 1955,* s., #16/75, p. Mourlot, pub. Maeght, margins, skinned spots w/in image, waterstaining, discoloration, creasing, (06-30-93, Sotheby-London, #361, illus.), sh 19⅜ x 24¼ in., (492 x 616 mm.), lithograph and embossing in color and varnished on wove (BP 1840, DM 4682, FR 15,794, Y 294,118).

$5500* *Le Char III (Char Verni) (V. 98), 1955,* s., #19/75, full margins, staining, good cond., (11-09-92, Christie-NY, #56, illus.), border 12⅝ x 16 9/16 in., (320 x 420 mm.), lithograph in colors w/varnish and blind embossing on wove (BP 3636, DM 8780, FR 29,666, Y 682,552).

$4540* *Char Noir (Char V) (Vallier 116), 1958,* ed. Maeght, (12-04-92, AB Stockholm, #7011, illus.), 9 5/16 x 11⅝ in., (23.7 x 29.6 cm.), etching and aquatint in colors (BP 2912, DM 7230, FR 24,527, Y 566,792, SK 30,800).

$4540* *Char Noir (Char V) (Vallier 116), 1958,* s., 39/75, ed. Maeght, (12-04-92, AB Stockholm, #7011), 9 5/16 x 11⅝ in., (23.7 x 29.6 cm.), etching and and color aquatint on BFK Rives (BP 2912, DM 7230, FR 24,527, Y 566,792, SK 30,800).

$4125* *Le Ciel Bleu (V. 175), 1962,* s., num. 27/75, pub. & p. by Adrien Maeght, full margins, good cond.,mat staining, foxing, glue remains, rubbed area, pencil notations, (02-24-93, Butterfield, #2707, illus.), 6½ x 9⅝ in., (165 x 244 mm.), lithograph in colors on Japon nacre (BP 2877, DM 6696, FR 22,702, Y 484,041).

$337* *"Le Ciel Bleu", 1962,* s. in plate, (10-18-92, Pescheteau, #85), 6 11/16 x 8¼ in., (17 x 21 cm.), lithograph in colors (BP 204, DM 498, FR 1691, Y 40,239).

$1106* *Ciel Gris II (Maeght 1033),* s., num., (12-05-92, Bassenge, #7064), 8 15/16 x 3⅝ in., (22.7 x 9.2 cm.), lithograph on BFK Rives (BP 693, DM 1724, FR 5877, Y 137,034).

BI *Cinq Poesies En Hommage A Georges Braque (Vallier 131), 1958,* s., #xii/xxv, pub. Edwin Englebert, margins, good cond., rubbed spot,est. BP 4,2/4,800, (12-03-92, Sotheby-London, #188, illus.), sheet 21 x 27¾ in., (533 x 705 mm.), lithograph in colors on Japon nacre.

BI *Colophon (Vallier 153),* s. H.C., est. SF 1,2/1,500, (10-14-92, Germann, #224), 8⅞ x 6 5/16 in., (225 x 160 mm.), woodcut.

$1106* *Colophon (Vallier 153),* from Tir de l'Arc, H.C., s., (09-04-92, Germann, #260), 8⅞ x 6 5/16 in., (225 x 160 mm.), woodcut (BP 554, DM 1550, FR 5277, Y 136,140, SF 1380).

BI *Composition (Nature Morte Aux Verres) (V. 11), 19112,* s., possibly retraced, # 10/50, p. Visat, pub. Maeght, 1950, full margins, good cond., est. BP 9/11,000, (06-30-93, Sotheby-London, #360, illus.), 13½ x 8¼ in., (343 x 210 mm.), etching on wove.

$5574* *Composition Sur Fond Rose (Vallier 180), 1962,* #13/40, s., (10-09-92, Winterberg, #1782, illus.), 16 9/16 x 13 3/16 in., (42 x 33.5 cm.), woodcut on Japan (BP 3307, DM 8280, FR 27,800, Y 678,598).

$5345* *Le Couple (Vall. 187; Blatt 22; Mourl 140), 1963,* s., num., (06-23-93, Kornfeld, #235), color lithograph on wove (BP 3631, DM 9044, FR 30,421, Y 582,307, SF 8050).

$4386* *Da: Si Je Mourais La-Bas (Vallier 181), 1962,* #29/70, s., (05-20-93, Finarte-Milan, #22, illus.), 11¹³/₁₆ x 11¹³/₁₆ in., (30 x 30 cm.), xilithograph in colors (BP 2815, DM 7076, FR 23,837, Y 484,320, L 6440).

$3300* *Dans Le Ciel (Oiseau XV) (V. 124), 1958,* s., #54/75, pub. Maeght, full margins, good cond., creases into image, prop. Woodward Foundation, (11-05-92, Sotheby-NY, #91), 9½ x 12¾ in., (240 x 325 mm.), lithograph p. in colors (BP 2146, DM 5219, FR 17,657, Y 404,858).

BI *De Saint-Pol-Roux.Aout (V. 135),* book w/title page and text, s., num., p. Crommelynck et Dutrou, pub.Louis Broder, 1958, good cond., est. BP 4,0/5,000, (12-03-92, Sotheby-London, #195, illus.), overall size 12½ x 9¾ in., (318 x 248 mm.), five aquatints in colors on Auvergne.

$84* *Dernier Messages,* Galerie Maeght, (09-30-92, Kunsthallen, #53), poster (BP 47, DM 119, FR 403, Y 10,080, DK 460).

$165* *"Le Derriere Le Mirroir" Series,* double page, stone 5, ex-coll., (10-16-92, DuMouchelle, #2402), image 13½ x 20 in., (34.3 x 50.8 cm.), colored lithograph (BP 100, DM 244, FR 828, Y 19,701).

$2415* *Descent Aux Enfers (Mourlot 78; see V. 171), 1961,* s., i. Epreuve d'artiste, pub. Nouveau Cercle Parisien du Livre, full margins, good cond., mat stain, nick, fox marks, (02-11-93, Sotheby-NY, #71), 9½ x 8¹¹/₁₆ in., (242 x 221 mm.), color lithograph (BP 1704, DM 4000, FR 13,537, Y 291,139).

$4909* *"Descente Aux Enfers (Komposition Mit Blattern" (Vallier 171; Mourlot 78), 1961,* s.(11-28-92, Grisebach, #249, illus.), 9⁷/₁₆ x 8⁷/₁₆ in., (24 x 21.5 cm.), color lithograph on Japan (BP 3240, DM 7821, FR 26,549, Y 610,952).

BI *Descente Aux Enfers (V. 171), 1961: Four,* suite, each s., pub. Nouveau Cercle Parisien du Livre, full margins,good cond., creases, original folder, (06-30-93, Sotheby-London, #364, illus.), each sh 12¾ x 10⅛ in., (324 x 257 mm.), color lithograph, one suite on Montval laid.

$6280* *"Descente Aux Enfers" (Vallier 171; Mourlot 79), 1961,* s., (11-28-92, Grisebach, #250, illus.), 10¼ x 7¹¹/₁₆ in., (26 x 19.5 cm.), color lithograph on Japan (BP 4145, DM 10,005, FR 33,964, Y 781,581).

$5558* *"Descente Aux Enfers" (Vallier 171; Mourlot 80), 1961,* s., Paris, Nouveau Cercle parisien du Livre, (11-28-92, Grisebach, #251, illus.), 10⅞ x 8¹/₁₆ in., (27.7 x 20.5 cm.), color lithograph on Japan (BP 3669, DM 8855, FR 30,059, Y 691,724).

BI *Deux Oiseaux,* s., #35/75, margins, good cond., light-staining, tape, hinge remains,skinned, surface soiling, mat staining, est. $4/6,000, (05-19-93, Butterfield, #1880, illus.), sh. 15 x 10¼ in., (381 x 260 mm.), lithograph in colors on wove.

$104* *"Deux Oiseaux Sur Fond Bleu",* num. F 80, s. in plate G. Braque, (06-16-93, Encans, #121), 29¹⁵/₁₆ x 21⅞ in., (76 x 55.5 cm.), lithograph on Arches (BP 69, DM 173, FR 579, Y 11,092, C$ 133).

$4995* *Equinoxe (V. 177), 1962,* s., i. H.C., pub. Maeght, margins, nick, defects, very good cond., (12-01-92, Christie-London, #311, illus.), L. 13¾ x 20⅞ in., (350 x 530 mm.), lithograph in colors on wove (BP 3300, DM 7961, FR 27,132, Y 621,887).

$1985* *Les Etoiles (Maeght, Estampes, 1029), 1959,* s., num., blindstamp, (06-23-93, Kornfeld, #236), color lithograph (BP 1349, DM 3359, FR 11,298, Y 216,254, SF 2990).

BI *Eurybia Et Eros (D. Vallier #21), c. 1932,* s., est. DM 7,000, (05-26-93, Lempertz, #41, illus.), 20¹⁵/₁₆ x 15¼ in., (53.2 x 38.8 cm.), etching on handmade.

BI *Feuillage Noir (Vallier 106), 1956,* #38/50, s., est. DM 8,500-, (11-21-92, Lempertz, #51, illus.), 17⁵/₁₆ x 14¹⁵/₁₆ in., (44 x 38 cm.), etching on Japan.

$2128* *"Feuillage Noir" (Vallier 106), 1956,* s., num., blindstamp, (06-05-93, Grisebach, #532, illus.), 17³/₁₆ x 14¹³/₁₆ in., (43.7 x 37.6 cm.), aquatint on handmade Japan (BP 1401, DM 3450, FR 11,628, Y 228,277).

$3174* *For Lettera Amorosa (Vallier 187), 1963,* s., light-stains, (11-21-92, Lempertz, #58), 6¹³/₁₆ x 7¹¹/₁₆ in., (17.3 x 19.5

cm.), color lithograph on Arches wove (BP 2090, DM 5061, FR 17,046, Y 394,727).

$2164* *For Si Je Mourais La-Bas (Vallier 181),* #29/70, s., stains, (11-21-92, Lempertz, #56), 16¼ x 11¼ in., (41.2 x 28.5 cm.), color print (BP 1425, DM 3450, FR 11,622, Y 269,121).

BI *For Si Je Mourais La-Bas (Vallier 181),* #12/40, s., est. DM 12,000-, (11-21-92, Lempertz, #57, illus.), 11⅞ x 11¾ in., (30.2 x 29.8 cm.), print on Japan nacre.

BI *For Si Je Mourais La-Bas (Vallier 181), 1962,* #13/70, num., s., light-stains, est. DM 22,000-, (11-21-92, Lempertz, #54, illus.), 16¾ x 12⅜ in., (42.6 x 31.5 cm.), color woodcut on thick wove.

BI *Frank Elgar Ressurection De L'Oiseau (Vallier 137), 1958,* complete book, w/text and justification, s. by artist and author, pub. Maeght, good cond., original slipcase, est. BP 1,6/2,000, (06-30-93, Sotheby-London, #359, illus.), overall 15⅜ x 11⅝ in., (391 x 295 mm.), four colored lithographs and three vignettes w/separate suite of fourlithographs.

$1475* *From Lettera Amorosa (Vallier 187, Mourlot 138), 1963,* #35/75, s., (11-13-92, Koller, #5262), 10⅝ x 7⅞ in., (27 x 20 cm.), lithograph on Arches wove (BP 953, DM 2316, FR 7808, Y 183,071, SF 2088).

$4400* *Gelinotte (V. 149), 1960,* s., #34/75, p. Mourlot, pub. Maeght, full margins, good cond., mat and backboard stain, (11-05-92, Sotheby-NY, #96, illus.), 8⅞ x 14⅛ in., (225 x 360 mm.), lithograph p. in colors on wove (BP 2862, DM 6959, FR 23,542, Y 539,811).

$5175* *Gelinotte (V. 149), 1960,* s., #13/75, p. Mourlot, pub. Maeght, full margins, good cond., mat/light-stain, creases, (05-13-93, Sotheby-NY, #466, illus.), 8¾ x 14⅛ in., (223 x 358 mm.), lithograph in colors (BP 3397, DM 8356, FR 28,186, Y 577,760).

BI *Helios V., (Valier 40), 1948,* s. G. Braque, 38/75, est. Dk 50,000, (09-30-92, Kunsthallen, #51), sheet 22¹³/₁₆ x 19⁵/₁₆ in., (58 x 49.1 cm.), color lithograph.

$5328* *Helios VI (V. 41), 1948,* s., #56/75, pub. Maeght, margins, crease, discoloration, very good cond., (12-01-92, Christie-London, #306, illus.), L. 18½ x 16¼ in., (470 x 413 mm.), lithograph in colors on Arches (BP 3520, DM 8492, FR 28,941, Y 663,347).

$6600* *Helios VI (V. 41), 1948,* s., #58/75, full margins, staining, glue remains, skinning verso, good cond., (11-09-92, Christie-NY, #54, illus.), border 18½ x 15¹⁵/₁₆ in., (470 x 406 mm.), lithograph in colors on Arches (BP 4364, DM 10,536, FR 35,599, Y 819,062).

$2415* *Le Jockey (V. 94), 1954,* s., #32/75, pub. Maeght, full margins, good cond., mat/masking tape/water stains, (02-11-93, Sotheby-NY, #68), 5¹¹/₁₆ x 11⁷/₁₆ in., (145 x 290 mm.), etching, aquatint, softground p. in brown, black, grey (BP 1704, DM 4000, FR 13,537, Y 291,139).

$10,350* *L'Atelier (V. 165), 1961,* s., #6/75, p. Mourlot, pub. Musees Nationaux, full margins, good cond., mat stain, soiling, stain, glue stains, creases, (05-13-93, Sotheby-NY, #468, illus.), 17 x 20½ in., (430 x 520 mm.), lithograph in colors on wove (BP 6795, DM 16,712, FR 56,373, Y 1,155,521).

BI *L'Atelier (V. 165), 1961,* s., #49/75, full margins, mat staining, good cond., est. $14/16,000, (11-09-92, Christie-NY, #59, illus.), border 17¹/₁₆ x 20⁹/₁₆ in., (434 x 522 mm.), lithograph in colors on Rives.

$1716* *"L'Echo", (Maeght 1041),* s. 297/300, (09-29-92, B. Rasmussen, #284), lithograph (BP 965, DM 2424, FR 8270, Y 204,847, DK 9430).

$4950* *L'Envol (V. 148), 1960,* s., #58/75, p., pub. Maeght, full sheet, good cond., paper tone darkened, skinned spots, (11-05-92, Sotheby-NY, #95, illus.), sheet 20 x 25¾ in., (508 x 653 mm.), lithograph p. in colors (BP 3220, DM 7829, FR 26,485, Y 607,287).

$3069* *L'Essor II (V. 162), 1961,* s., #93/100, pub. Maeght, full margins, good cond., rubbed, glue stain, (12-03-92, Sotheby-London, #194, illus.), 8¼ x 10¼ in., (210 x 260 mm.), lithograph in colors on BFK Rives (BP 1980, DM 4826, FR 16,473, Y 381,859).

$2558* *L'Oiseau Blanc (V. 159), 1961,* s., i. Epreuve d'artiste, p. Mourlot, margins, good cond., (12-03-92, Sotheby-London, #192, illus.), sheet 24 x 18⅝ in., (610 x 473 mm.), lithograph in colors on wove (BP 1650, DM 4023, FR 13,731, Y 318,278).

$7150* *L'Oiseau De Feu (Oiseau XIII) (V. 121), 1938,* s., #59/75, pub. Maeght, full margins, good cond., light stain, foxing, (11-05-92, Sotheby-NY, #90, illus.), 15¾ x 15 in., (399 x 381 mm.), etching p. in colors w/varnish (BP 4650, DM 11,308, FR 38,256, Y 877,193).

$12,011* *L'Oiseau Et Son Ombre I (V. 141), 1959,* s., #40/75, p. Mourlot, pub. Maeght, full margins, good cond., prov., (06-30-93, Sotheby-London, #362, illus.), sh 25½ x 35⅞ in., (648 x 911 mm.), colored lithograph on Rives (BP 8050, DM 20,486, FR 69,108, Y 1,286,939).

$1557* *L'Oiseau Jaune,* s., 180/300, (05-12-93, AB Stockholm, #7006, illus.), 15 15/16 x 22¼ in., (40.5 x 56.5 cm.), lithograph in colors (BP 1017, DM 2512, FR 8462, Y 173,831, SK 11,550).

BI *Lettera Amorosa: Oiseaux Fulgurants (V. 187),* s., #II/3, pub. Edwin Engleberts, margins, good cond., skinning, est.BP 2,5/3,500, (12-03-92, Sotheby-London, #193, illus.), sheet 15 x 11 in., (381 x 279 mm.), lithograph in colors on Japon nacre.

$1610* *Les Lierres Bleus,* s., #67/75, full margins, good cond., mat/light-staining, glue remains, (05-19-93, Butterfield, #1879), 8 x 13 in., (203 x 330 mm.), lithograph in colors on wove (BP 1045, DM 2617, FR 8817, Y 178,235).

$2551* *Les Marguerites (V.S. 292; Maeght 1002),* after Braque, s., H(ors) C(ommerce), (06-08-93, Karl/Faber, #576), approx. 24 7/16 x 15¾ in., (62 x 40 cm.), color etching (BP 1677, DM 4139, FR 13,940, Y 270,951).

$632* *Les Marguerites (Vallier-Maeght 1002),* s., 24/300, (12-04-92, AB Stockholm, #7015), 24 7/16 x 15 15/16 in., (62 x 40.5 cm.), aquatint in colors (BP 405, DM 1007, FR 3414, Y 78,901, SK 4290).

$44* *Marine,* #35/175, s. in plate G. Braque, edit. Maeght no 1913, illus., (06-16-93, Encans, #122), 10⅝ x 13¾ in., (27 x 35 cm.), color lithograph (BP 29, DM 73, FR 245, Y 4693, C$ 56).

$134* *"Marine",* #33/75, s. G. Braque, (03-16-93, Encans, #152), 13 9/16 x 10⅝ in., (34.5 x 27 cm.), color lithograph (BP 93, DM 223, FR 757, Y 15,669, C$ 167).

$91* *"Marine",* #30/175, s. G. Braque, (09-15-92, Encans, #130), 13 9/16 x 10⅝ in., (34.5 x 27 cm.), color lithograph (BP 49, DM 135, FR 460, Y 11,297, C$ 111).

BI *Migration (Vallier 172), 1962,* s., num. 69/90, full margins, good cond., mat stain, est. Y 9/1,100,000, (10-14-92, Sotheby-Japan, #8, illus.), 9½ x 7 in., (241 x 178 mm.), aquatint in colors on canvas textured wove.

$4237* *Milarepa. Magicien-Poete-Eremite-Tibetain (Vallier 63), 1950: Five,* s., #83/100, (06-10-93, Hauswedell/Nolt, #112, illus.), etching on hand-made Auvergne/Richard de Bas (BP 2771, DM 6900, FR 23,229, Y 449,740).

BI *Le Nid (Vallier 101), 1955,* s., #25/25, est. DM 6000, (06-10-93, Hauswedell/Nolt, #110, illus.), image 8 11/16 x 13⅛ in., (22 x 33.3 cm.), etching on Japan.

$1380* *Nous Ne Jalousons Pas Les Dieux (V. 179), 1962,* s., p., pub. Pierre Andre Benoit (PAB), p. without text, full margins, good cond., mat stain, (05-13-93, Sotheby-NY, #469), 6¼ x 7¼ in., (160 x 185 mm.), gravure (intaglio) sur carton in black on wove (BP 906, DM 2228, FR 7516, Y 154,069).

$6600* *Oiseau De Passage (V. 166), 1961,* s., #69/75, p., pub. Maeght, full margins, good cond., scratches, (11-05-92, Sotheby-NY, #97, illus.), 23¼ x 16⅛ in., (590 x 410 mm.), aquatint p. in colors on BFK Rives (BP 4293, DM 10,438, FR 35,313, Y 809,717).

$1112* *Oiseau Multicolore,* s., 117/200, (05-12-93, AB Stockholm, #7007), 10¼ x 19½ in., (26 x 49.5 cm.), aquatint in colors on BFK Rives (BP 726, DM 1794, FR 6043, Y 124,149, SK 8250).

$16,100* *Oiseau Traversant Un Nuage (Oiseau XI) (V. 110), 1957,* s., #46/75, p. Mourlot, pub. Maeght, full margins, good cond., light-stain, foxing, printer's crease, water stain, tape stain, skinning, (05-13-93, Sotheby-NY, #465, illus.), 16 x 27⅛ in., (408 x 688 mm.), lithograph in colors (BP 10,570, DM 25,997, FR 87,691, Y 1,797,477).

$5750* *Oiseau Verni, Oiseau VII (V. 93), 1954,* s., #47/75, full margins, mat staining, prop. Francesca Robinson Sanchez, (05-11-93, Christie-NY, #141, illus.), borderline 8½ x 12⅜ in., (216 x 314 mm.), lithograph w/varnish on Arches (BP 3671, DM 9058, FR 30,520, Y 632,494).

$2530* *Oiseau, Pour La Revue XXe Siecle (V. 178), 1962,* s., i. H.C., light-mat staining, skinning, (05-11-93, Christie-NY, #142), borderline 12 x 10½ in., (305 x 267 mm.), color lithograph on Arches (BP 1615, DM 3986, FR 13,429, Y 278,297).

$217* *Oiseaux Sur Fond Bleu,* (09-25-92, Granier, #2778), sheet 29 15/16 x 21⅝ in., (76 x 55 cm.), lithograph on hand-made (BP 127, DM 322, FR 1088, Y 26,192).

BI *Paris, Cahiers D'Art (Vallier 42), 1948,* from Heraclite, translated by Yves Battistini, avant-propos by Rene Char, s., num., est. SF 15/20,000, (11-15-92, Christie-Geneva, #315, illus.), 7 11/16 x 4 13/16 in., (196 x 123 mm.), etching on BFK Rives.

$350* *Les Peintres Temoins De Leurs Temps, 1961,* loss, (03-31-93, Briest, #E140), 29¾ x 20¼ in., (75.5 x 51.5 cm.), lithograph poster (BP 231, DM 563, FR 1913, Y 40,248).

$2760* *Phaeton, Char 1 (Vallier 36), 1945,* s., #17/75, full margins, light-staining, foxing, creasing, skinned patches, (05-11-93, Christie-NY, #139, illus.), borderline 12¼ x 17 in., (311 x 432 mm.), color lithograph on Arches (BP 1762, DM 4348, FR 14,650, Y 303,597).

$2659* *Pichet Et Oiseau,* Edition Galerie Maeght, s., #98/300, (10-21-92, Dobiaschofsky, #1851, illus.), 16 5/16 x 20 1/16 in., (41.5 x 51 cm.), color aquatint (BP 1651, DM 4023, FR 13,657, Y 323,873, SF 3600).

$2949* *Pichet Et Oisseau (Vallier S. 292, Maeght 1005),* #175/200, s., (09-04-92, Germann, #91, illus.), 21¼ x 29½ in., (540 x 750 mm.), color etching (BP 1478, DM 4133, FR 14,070, Y 362,999, SF 3680).

BI *Pierre Reverdy. Une Adventure Methodique (V. 49; M. 18-20),* book, 26 lithographs in text, s., num. 5, p. Mourlot, pub. Maeght, 1949, good cond., foxing, est. BP 6/800, (12-03-92, Sotheby-London, #191), each sheet 17⅞ x 13¼ in., (454 x 337 mm.), lithograph in colors on Arches.

$665* *Planche De Remarque, Ur Si Je Mourais Labas (V. 181),* s., planche de remarque, (12-04-92, AB Stockholm, #7013), 14 15/16 x 24 13/16 in., (38 x 63 cm.), woodcut in colors (BP 427, DM 1059, FR 3593, Y 83,021, SK 4510).

BI *Le Poete (V. 131), 1958,* s., #24/75, p. Mourlot, full margins, good cond., creases, mat stain,rubbed spot, discoloration, skinning, est. $7/9,000, (11-05-92, Sotheby-NY, #92, illus.), 8 x 22 in., (204 x 560 mm.), lithograph p. in colors on japon nacre.

$1417* *Les Pommes (Vallier 84), 1953,* s., num., (06-08-93, Karl/Faber, #574, illus.), 12⅜ x 19⅞ in., (31.5 x 50.5 cm.), lithograph on China (BP 932, DM 2299, FR 7743, Y 150,505).

$3950* *Pommes Et Feuilles (Vallier 114; Mourlot 47), 1958,* #15/95, s., (04-21-93, Germann, #113), 19 11/16 x 25 9/16 in., (500 x 650 mm.), lithograph in 8 colors on Arches (BP 2563, DM 6314, FR 21,351, Y 437,286, SF 5750).

$3025* *"Pommes Et Feuilles" (Vallier, 114), 1958,* p. Mourlot, pub. Maeght, s. G. Braque, num. 15/75, good cond. full margins, light/mount staining, (09-11-92, Skinner, #96, illus.), 12 x 17¾ in., (30.5 x 45.1 cm.), lithograph in eight colors on Arches wove w/watermark (BP 1565, DM 4354, FR 14,799, Y 374,799).

BI *Pommes Sur Fond Noir (V. 89), 1954,* s., #24/75, pub. Maeght, margins, trimmed, folded, lightly backed, mount-stained, defects, est. BP 2,0/2,500, (12-01-92, Christie-London, #309, illus.), L. 14 1/16 x 20 in., (357 x 508 mm.), sheet 20 15/16 x 26 15/16 in., (357 x 508 mm.), lithograph on Arches.

$4965* *Pommes Sur Fond Noir (Vallier 89), 1954,* s., num., (06-05-93, Bassenge, #5925, illus.), 13 15/16 x 19 15/16 in., (35.5 x 50.7 cm.), lithograph on Arches wove (BP 3268, DM 8050, FR 27,131, Y 532,611).

BI *Pommes Sur Fond Noire (Vallier 89), 1954,* crayon s., num. 5/75, pub. Maeght, full margins, good cond., light stain, skinning, est. Y 1/1,200,000, (10-14-92, Sotheby-Japan, #5, illus.), 13⅞ x 20 in., (352 x 508 mm.), lithograph in black.

$147* *Posters From The Galerie Maeght: Four,* (09-29-92, B. Rasmussen, #285), (BP 83, DM 208, FR 708, Y 17,548, DK 805).

$190* *Posters: Three,* Galerie Maeght, (09-30-92, Kunsthallen, #52), poster (BP 107, DM 269, FR 911, Y 22,801, DK 1035).

BI *Profil A La Palette (Vallier 82), 1953,* s., #62/75, est. DM 12,000, (06-10-93, Hauswedell/Nolt, #111, illus.), image 12¹⁵⁄₁₆ x 20³⁄₁₆ in., (33 x 51.2 cm.), color lithograph on Arches.

$6109* *Profil A La Palette (Vallier 82; Mourlot 22), 1953,* s., num., (06-23-93, Kornfeld, #234), color lithograph (BP 4150, DM 10,337, FR 34,769, Y 665,541, SF 9200).

$3163* *Profil Grec (V. 146), 1960,* s., #30/150, full margins, discoloration, surface dirt, tape, good cond., (12-01-92, Christie-London, #310), L. 13³⁄₁₆ x 9⅝ in., (335 x 245 mm.), lithograph in colors on Arches (BP 2090, DM 5041, FR 17,181, Y 393,800).

BI *Rene Char, Le Soleil Des Eaux, Paris (V. 47): Three,* Matarasso Editeur, 1949, s. on just., copy 179 of 200, ink i. by author, loose, foxing, good cond., orig. wrapper, est. $4/5,000, (05-11-93, Christie-NY, #140), 11⁹⁄₁₆ x 9³⁄₁₆ in., (293 x 234 mm.), aquatint in-texte and aquatint cover in colors, t. page, just and text on wove.

$1167* *Le Repace (V. 187, p. 44), 1963,* from Lettera Amorosa, 70/75, s., (12-04-92, AB Stockholm, #7014), 9⁷⁄₁₆ x 9¹⁄₁₆ in., (24 x 23 cm.), lithograph in colors (BP 749, DM 1859, FR 6305, Y 145,693, SK 7920).

$1167* *Le Repace, Ur Lettera Amorosa (V. 187), 1963,* s. 70/75, (12-04-92, AB Stockholm, #7014), 9⁷⁄₁₆ x 9¹⁄₁₆ in., (24 x 23 cm.), lithograph in colors (BP 749, DM 1859, FR 6305, Y 145,693, SK 7920).

$2070* *Resurrection De L'Oiseau (V. 137),* s., pub. Maeght, 1958, off-setting, discoloration, creased, good cond., rubbed, (02-11-93, Sotheby-NY, #69), each sheet approx. 14¹⁵⁄₁₆ x 11¹³⁄₁₆ in., (380 x 300 mm.), 4 orig. color lithographs and 3 vignettes, w/add. suite of 4 lithographs (BP 1461, DM 3429, FR 11,603, Y 249,548).

BI *Resurrection De L'Oiseau (V. 137), 1958,* book by Frank Elgar, s., pub. Maeght, full sheets, off-setting, discoloration, good cond., orig. slipcase, est. $3/4,000, (11-05-92, Sotheby-NY, #93), each sheet approx. 15 x 11¾ in., (380 x 300 mm.), four lithographs p. in colors and three vignettes w/additional suiteof four lithographs.

$1598* *"Si Je Mourais La-Bas" (D. Vallier 181), 1962,* illus., IX/X, s., (04-04-93, Pescheteau, #165), 18¹¹⁄₁₆ x 14³⁄₁₆ in., (47.5 x 36 cm.), color wood engraving on Auvergne (BP 1053, DM 2568, FR 8723, Y 181,942).

BI *Si Je Mourais La-Bas, Dezember 1962 (Vallier 181),* #70/70, s., est. SF 6,5/7,200, (11-13-92, Koller, #5261), 10¼ x 9⁵⁄₁₆ in., (26 x 23.7 cm.), woodcut on wove.

BI *Si Je Mourais La-Bas: Fleurs Blanches (V. 181, p. 250), 1962,* s., #36/70, pub. Louis Broder, full margins, good cond., hinge stainsverso, est. $5/6,000, (11-05-92, Sotheby-NY, #98, illus.), 19⅞ x 12½ in., (504 x 317 mm.), wood engraving p. in colors.

$3450* *Si Je Mourais La-Bas: Fleurs Blanches (see V. 181, p. 250), 1962,* s., #36/70, pub. Louis Broder, full margins, good cond., hinge stains, (02-11-93, Sotheby-NY, #72, illus.), 19¹³⁄₁₆ x 12½ in., (504 x 317 mm.), color wood engraving (BP 2434, DM 5715, FR 19,339, Y 415,913).

BI *Si Je Mourais La-Bas: Profil De Femme (V. 181, P. 47), 1962,* s., #3/70, pub. Louis Broder, full margins, good cond., est. BP 2,5/3,000, (06-30-93, Sotheby-London, #365, illus.), 17 x 12¼ in., (432 x 311 mm.), woodcut in color.

$1320* *Si Je Mourais La-Bas: Title Page (Vallier 181), 1962,* s., num. III/X, good cond., foxing, light staining, (05-22-93, Weschler, #167, illus.), 10½ x 9¼ in., (26.7 x 23.5 cm.), woodcut in blue and black on Japon Nacree (BP 855, DM 2146, FR 7221, Y 145,535).

BI *Si Je Mourais La-Bas: Untitled (V. 181, p. 247), 1962,* watermark, bears sig., #1/70, pub. Louis Broder, p. Fequet and Baudier, full margins, good cond., faint areas of white high-lighting around numbering and sig., glue remains, est. $1/1,500, (05-19-93, Butterfield, #1878), sh 18¾ x 14¼ in., (476 x 362 mm.), wood engraving w/ hand-coloring on handmade paper.

$800* *Le Signe (Vallier 92),* watermarked, #13/30, image nick, good cond., (11-30-92, Phillips-London, #377), image 11¾ x 7½ in., (298 x 191 mm.), lithograph in gold on Arches (BP 528, DM 1274, FR 4327, Y 99,564).

$2349* *Souspente (Vallier 29), 1945,* (05-20-93, Finarte-Milan, #23, illus.), 14⅜ x 9¹⁄₁₆ in., (36.5 x 23 cm.), lithograph in colors (BP 1508, DM 3790, FR 12,766, Y 259,386, L 3450).

$19,550* *St. John Perse (V. 182), 1962: Twelve,* L'Ordre des oiseaux, Paris, Au vent d'Arles, t. page, just. and text, watermark, s. by artist and author, copy 70 of 100, full margins, bound, offsetting, very good cond., w/lithographic collage (good cond.), (05-11-93, Christie-NY, #143, illus.), 17¼ x 13¾ in., (438 x 350 mm.), color aquatint in and hors-texte on Moulin Richard Le Bas (BP 12,480, DM 30,797, FR 103,769, Y 2,150,478).

$20,900* *St. John Perse (V. 182): Set of Twelve, 1962,* L'Ordre des oiseaux, Au Vent d'Arles, watermark, s. on just. by artist and author, copy 73/100, full margins, bound, very good cond., (11-09-92, Christie-NY, #60, illus.), 17¼ x 13¾ in., (438 x 350 mm.), color aquatint on Moulin Richard le Bas (BP 13,818, DM 33,365, FR 112,729, Y 2,593,696).

$3575* *Still Life With Lemon (V. 25 & p. 297), 1934,* s., pub. Chronique du jour, for Georges Braque by Carl Einstein, trimmed margins, good cond., mat staining, foxing, tape remains, (02-24-93, Butterfield, #2706, illus.), 6½ x 9¼ in., (165 x 235 mm.), color lithograph w/ pochoir on MBM wove (BP 2493, DM 5804, FR 19,675, Y 419,502).

$3631* *Thalassa I (Vallier 139), 1959,* s., num. 48/60, pub. Maeght, full margins, good cond., fox mark, hinge stains, (10-14-92, Sotheby-Japan, #6, illus.), 4⅛ x 10⅜ in., (105 x 264 mm.), aquatint in colors on Auvergne paper (BP 2131, DM 5314, FR 18,020, Y 440,015).

$4400* *Thalassa II (V. 140), 1959,* s., #34/50, pub. Maeght, full margins, good cond., loss, foxing, creases, Julie Andrews and Blake Edwards Coll., (11-05-92, Sotheby-NY, #94, illus.), 4⅛ x 12 in., (105 x 305 mm.), etching p. in colors on Auvergne (BP 2862, DM 6959, FR 23,542, Y 539,811).

$4600* *Thalassa II (V. 140), 1959,* s., #22/60, pub. Maeght, full margins, good cond., crease, mat/water stain, prop. Woodward Foundation, (02-11-93, Sotheby-NY, #70, illus.), 4⅛ x 12 in., (104 x 305 mm.), color etching (BP 3246, DM 7620, FR 25,785, Y 554,551).

$2594* *Thalassa II (V. 140), 1959,* s., (12-04-92, AB Stockholm, #7012), 4⅛ x 11⅝ in., (10.5 x 29.5 cm.), etching and aquatint in colors (BP 1664, DM 4131, FR 14,014, Y 323,845, SK 17,600).

$2594* *Thalassa II (V. 140), 1959,* s. 24/60, (12-04-92, AB Stockholm, #7012), 4⅛ x 11⅝ in., (10.5 x 29.5 cm.), color etching and aquatint on Auvergne (BP 1664, DM 4131, FR 14,014, Y 323,845, SK 17,600).

$16,200* *Theiere Et Citrons (V. 44), 1949,* crayon s., #38/75, p. and pub. Mourlot, good cond., (12-03-92, Sotheby-London, #189, illus.), 19⅝ x 23⅝ in., (498 x 600 mm.), lithograph in colors on Arches (BP 10,450, DM 25,476, FR 86,957, Y 2,015,677).

$6325* *Theiere Et Citrons (V. 44), 1949,* s., #25/75, trimmed, paint, losses, laid-down, (02-11-93, Sotheby-NY, #67, illus.), sheet 19⁹⁄₁₆ x 25⅜ in., (497 x 645 mm.), color lithograph (BP 4463, DM 10,477, FR 35,454, Y 762,508).

$22,000* *Theiere Et Pommes (Vallier 33), 1946,* black crayon s., #5/75, p. Mourlot, pub. Maeght, full margins, good cond., smudges, spots, soiling, sold after sale, (11-05-92, Sotheby-NY, #87, illus.), 11¾ x 26 in., (300 x 660 mm.), lithograph p. in colors (BP 14,309, DM 34,794, FR 117,710, Y 2,699,055).

BI *Theiere Sur Fond Gris (V. 34), 1946-47,* s., #26/74, p. Mourlot, pub. D.-H. Kahnweiler, full sheet, p. to edges, good cond., scuffs, fox marks, discoloration, nicks, surface loss, est. $6/8,000, (11-05-92, Sotheby-NY, #88, illus.), sheet 12¾ x 19¾ in., (325 x 502 mm.), lithograph p. in colors.

$3910* *Theiere Sur Fond Gris (V. 34), 1946-47,* s., #26/74, pub. D.-H. Kahnweiler, good cond., scuffs, fox marks, discoloration, nicks, surface loss, (02-11-93, Sotheby-NY, #66), sheet 12¹³⁄₁₆ x 19¾ in., (325 x 502 mm.), color lithograph (BP 2759, DM 6477, FR 21,917, Y 471,368).

$1760* *Theogonie (Vallier 20h), 1932,* from La Theogonie d'Hesiode, Ambrose Vollard, s. in brown pencil, #29/50, full margins, staining, glue remains, very good cond., (11-09-92, Christie-NY, #53, illus.), border 14⁷/₁₆ x 11¾ in., (366 x 298 mm.), etching on Van Gelder Zonen (BP 1164, DM 2810, FR 9493, Y 218,416).

$2398* *La Theogonie D'Hesiode (D. Vallier 20b a 20n), 1932: Thirteen,* illus., (06-11-93, Picard, #14), 11¹³/₁₆ x 8¹¹/₁₆ in., (300 x 220 mm.), etchings in black (BP 1576, DM 3897, FR 13,140, Y 254,430).

$2415* *La Theogonie D'Hesiode (see Vallier 20/g, p. 40),* 1932, s. crayon, #31/50, margins, good cond., mat/light stain, tape hinges, (02-11-93, Sotheby-NY, #65), 14½ x 11¾ in., (368 x 298 mm.), sheet 17⅜ x 13¹³/₁₆ in., (368 x 298 mm.), etching w/plate tone (BP 1704, DM 4000, FR 13,537, Y 291,139).

$3163* *La Theogonie D'Hesiode (see Vallier 20/h, p. 43),* 1932, plate tone, crayon s., #4/50, exec. Vollard, large margins, edge maybe trimmed, good cond., soiling, discoloration, (05-13-93, Sotheby-NY, #464), 14½ x 11¾ in., (367 x 298 mm.), sh 21 x 14¾ in., (367 x 298 mm.), etching (BP 2077, DM 5107, FR 17,228, Y 353,132).

$1760* *Theogonie III (V. 90), 1954,* #41/75, full margins, staining, good cond., (11-09-92, Christie-NY, #55, illus.), border 17 x 11⁹/₁₆ in., (432 x 293 mm.), lithograph in pale olive and gold on wove (BP 1164, DM 2810, FR 9493, Y 218,416).

$9377* *Le Tir A L'Arc (Vallier 153), 1960: Twelve,* #39/70, s., 1 sheet block mono., num. 54-57 from series Si je mourais la-bas, (11-21-92, Lempertz, #53, illus.), each 8¹⁵/₁₆ x 13¾ in., (22.8 x 34.9 cm.), 8 color lithographs, 2 color etchings, 2 woodcuts, on various papers (BP 6174, DM 14,951, FR 50,360, Y 1,166,148).

BI *Le Tir A L'Arc (Vallier 153; Wunsche 86; Hoffmann 86),* #13/70, s., num., est. SF 4/6,000, (04-21-93, Germann, #300, illus.), 9⅝ x 13⁹/₁₆ in., (245 x 345 mm.), color lithograph.

$2211* *Le Tir A L'Arc (Vallier 153; Wunsche 86; Hoffmann 86),* 13/70, s., num., (06-24-93, Germann, #254, illus.), 9⅝ x 13⁹/₁₆ in., (245 x 345 mm.), color lithograph (BP 1455, DM 3585, FR 12,082, Y 237,181, SF 3220).

$1722* *Torero,* #62/75, s., (03-25-93, Finarte-Rome, #32, illus.), lithograph in colors (BP 1169, DM 2829, FR 9620, Y 201,734, L 2760).

$1012* *Le Torero, 1955,* s., #17/75, (05-27-93, Briest, #41), 14¹⁵/₁₆ x 10⁷/₁₆ in., (38 x 26.5 cm.), color lithograph (BP 648, DM 1624, FR 5473, Y 108,491).

BI *Untitled,* s. G. Braque, #99/100, est. $2,4/3,500, (12-12-92, Wolf, #32, illus.), 12 x 28½ in., (30.5 x 72.4 cm.), color lithograph.

$413* *Untitled, 1931,* s., d., (08-08-92, Litchfield, #25), 10½ x 8¼ in., (26.7 x 21 cm.), lithograph (BP 214, DM 607, FR 2053, Y 52,712).

BI *Untitled, 1962,* from L'ordre des oiseaux, Au Vent d'Arles, watermark, s., i. HC, full margins, light-staining, skinning, tape remains, est. $4/5,000, (11-09-92, Christie-NY, #61), plate 13⁹/₁₆ x 18½ in., (344 x 470 mm.), color aquatint on Moulin Richard´le Bas.

$1161* *Varengeville (V. Zusatzkat; Maeght Nr. 1023), c. 1950,* #210/300, s., blindstamp, (10-09-92, Winterberg, #1785, illus.), 10¼ x 25½ in., (26 x 64.8 cm.), color etching on wove (BP 689, DM 1725, FR 5791, Y 141,344).

$1363* *Vaso Di Fiori,* #89/200, s., (03-25-93, Finarte-Rome, #24), lithograph in colors (BP 926, DM 2239, FR 7615, Y 159,677, L 2185).

$147* *"Verre Et Journal, 1914, (M 1050), "Compotier, (M 1012)" and "Verre Et Pichet, (M 1009): Three,* (03-24-93, Kunsthallen, #54), color lithograph (BP 100, DM 240, FR 817, Y 17,272, DK 920).

BRAQUE, Georges (after)

$1474* *Barque De Peche,* large margins, (06-16-93, Ader Tajan, #50), 11⅝ x 18¼ in., (29.5 x 46.3 cm.), color engraving (BP 983, DM 2447, FR 8212, Y 157,210).

BI *La Barque Sur La Greve (M. 1040),* s., #115/300, pub. Maeght, blindstamp, margins, creases, very good cond., est. BP 6/800, (12-01-92, Christie-London, #312), L. 12¹/₁₆ x 28¹³/₁₆ in., (306 x 732 mm.), lithograph in colors on wove.

$935* *Barque Sur La Plage, 1950,* s., num. 3/100, full margins, good cond., light-staining, buckling, (02-24-93, Butterfield, #2709, illus.), 11¾ x 18¼ in., (298 x 464 mm.),

aquatint in colors on Arches (BP 652, DM 1518, FR 5146, Y 109,716).

$978* *Barque Sur La Plage, 1950,* s., annot. E.A., full margins, good cond., light-staining, foxing, hinge remains, mat staining, notations, (05-19-93, Butterfield, #1881), 11¾ x 18⁵/₁₆ in., (298 x 465 mm.), aquatint in colors on Arches (BP 635, DM 1590, FR 5356, Y 108,270).

BI *"Bibliotheque Nationale Oeuvre Graphique",* s., #38/150, pub. Galerie Maeght, 1960, est. $5/700, (03-25-93, Boos, #609), 22 x 17½ in., (55.9 x 44.5 cm.), poster.

$609* *"Cahiers-1947",* #18/20, sig., (01-28-93, Pescheteau, #79), 22¹/₁₆ x 16⅛ in., (56 x 41 cm.), phototype on handmade Auvergne (BP 402, DM 965, FR 3265, Y 75,615).

$1298* *Les Champs (Vallier 296, Maeght 1045),* #191/200, blindstamp Maeght Editeur, s., (11-21-92, Lempertz, #60, illus.), 10¹³/₁₆ x 17¹¹/₁₆ in., (27.5 x 45 cm.), color lithograph on tone paper (BP 855, DM 2070, FR 6971, Y 161,423).

$2387* *Les Etoiles (MA. 1029), c. 1950,* s., #146/300, pub. Maeght, full margins, good cond., (12-03-92, Sotheby-London, #198), 12½ x 15 in., (318 x 381 mm.), lithograph in colors on wove (BP 1540, DM 3754, FR 12,813, Y 297,001).

$468* *Femme Devant La Poele,* s., num. 14/75, from Carnets intimes de G. Braque, pub. Verve, 1955, (09-20-92, Hindman, #759), 13¼ x 9¾ in., (33.7 x 24.8 cm.), color lithograph (BP 274, DM 694, FR 2376, Y 57,842).

$1840* *Grand Oiseau Bleu (MA. 1016),* s., #78/95, pub. Maeght, margins, good cond., water-staining, foxing,tape, glue remains, skinned areas, glue remains, soiling, creases in image, (05-19-93, Butterfield, #1882, illus.), sh. 17½ x 43¼ in., (44.5 x 109.9 cm.), lithograph in colors on wove (BP 1194, DM 2991, FR 10,077, Y 203,698).

$3410* *Grand Oiseau Bleu (Maeght 1016), c. 1950,* s., #85/95, pub. Maeght, margins, good cond., (12-03-92, Sotheby-London, #196, illus.), 21⅞ x 44¼ in., (55.6 x 112.4 cm.), lithograph in colors on wove (BP 2200, DM 5362, FR 18,304, Y 424,288).

$440* *"Hemera", "Ilya", "Neree" and "Parthenia", c. 1960: Group Of Four,* after jewelry designs by Braque, reinterpreted and engraved by Hegerde Lowenfeld, Braque's embossed sig., num., s. by Heger, (12-08-92, Swann, #26), sheet 15 x 22 in., (38.1 x 55.9 cm.), embossed gold leaf intaglio etching (BP 276, DM 685, FR 2335, Y 54,536).

$1510* *Hommage J.S. Bach,* #240/300, s., num., blindstamp, (03-16-93, Schuler, #3227, illus.), sh 22¹/₁₆ x 30⅛ in., (56 x 76.5 cm.), 17⁵/₁₆ x 23¼ in., (56 x 76.5 cm.), color etching (BP 1043, DM 2511, FR 8531, Y 176,567, SF 2300).

$358* *Journal Violon,* s. in stone, pub. H. Deschamps Grav. Lith., margins, good cond., matstaining, crease, taped, surface soiling, (02-24-93, Butterfield, #2711), 21⁵/₁₆ x 14¾ in., (541 x 375 mm.), lithograph in colors on Arches (BP 250, DM 581, FR 1970, Y 42,009).

$358* *Marine Noir (Maeght 1044 E),* s. Braque, #168/400, pub. Maeght, (03-14-93, Hindman, #270), image 19½ x 8¼ in., (49.5 x 21 cm.), color lithograph on Rives wove (BP 250, DM 596, FR 2026, Y 42,192).

$1264* *Les Martinets (Maeght 1036; Vallier S. 295),* 176/275, s., (06-24-93, Germann, #255, illus.), color lithograph (BP 832, DM 2049, FR 6907, Y 135,593, SF 1840).

$1582* *Nature Morte,* by G. Visat, s., #35/100, pub. Musee du Louvre, blindstamp, margins,creases, tape traces, mountstaining, (12-01-92, Christie-London, #313), plate 13¹⁵/₁₆ x 24⅛ in., (355 x 612 mm.), etching w/aquatint in colors on wove (BP 1045, DM 2522, FR 8593, Y 196,962).

BI *Nature Morte Oblique, by Georges Visat (Maeght 1017), c. 1960,* s., #235/300, full margins, staining, margin edges folded back, goodcond., est. $2,5/3,000, (11-09-92, Christie-NY, #62), plate 11⁹/₁₆ x 11 in., (293 x 280 mm.), etching and aquatint in colors on wove.

$80* *"Nature Morte",* #64/150, s. in plate, (04-04-93, Pescheteau, #167), 27³/₁₆ x 21¼ in., (69 x 54 cm.), color lithograph (BP 53, DM 129, FR 437, Y 9109).

$1705* *Oiseau Jaune (MA. 1031), c. 1950,* s., #288/300, pub. Maeght, full margins, good cond., (12-03-92, Sotheby-London, #197, illus.), 21¼ x 29¾ in., (540 x 756 mm.), lithograph in colors on wove (BP 1100, DM 2681, FR 9152, Y 212,144).

$1715* *Pichet Et Oiseau (M. 1005),* #37/200, s., good margins, (02-03-93, Ader Tajan, #75), 16⅛ x 20¹/₁₆ in., (41 x 51 cm.), color etching (BP 1197, DM 2824, FR 9576, Y 213,335).

$1211* *Pichet Noir Et Citrons (Maeght 1004),* #62/200, s., good margins, (02-03-93, Ader Tajan, #74), 14¾ x 17¹¹/₁₆ in., (37.5 x 45 cm.), color etching (BP 845, DM 1994, FR 6762, Y 150,641).

$1194* *Poissons (MA. 1001), c. 1950,* s., #298/300, pub. Maeght, full margins, good cond., (12-03-92, Sotheby-London, #199, illus.), 19¾ x 25¾ in., (502 x 654 mm.), engraving in colors on wove (BP 770, DM 1878, FR 6409, Y 148,563).

$160* *Profil A La Palette (Galerie Maeght) (M.A. 3),* (05-28-93, Sloan, #994, illus.), 19¾ x 28⅜ in., (50.2 x 72.1 cm.), color lithograph (BP 102, DM 254, FR 858, Y 17,156).

$715* *"Still Life",* s., #147/200, large margins, good cond., light/glue staining, skinned areas, glue remains, ink stain, creases, image surface scratch, (10-28-92, Butterfield, #2785), 18¾ x 18⅜ in., (476 x 467 mm.), color offset lithograph w/lithograph on Arches (BP 456, DM 1104, FR 3749, Y 87,730).

BI *Tabletop Still Life Of Pitcher, Mug, Pear And Lemons,* by Walter Spitzer, s. in stone, d. illegibly; s. by Braque, #25/250,prov, est. $2/3,000, (09-17-92, Sloan, #3083, illus.), 13½ x 18¼ in., (34.3 x 46.4 cm.), color lithograph.

$1430* *Tabletop Still Life With Pitcher, Mug, Pear, And Lemons, 1924,* s., #25/250, sticker, margins, folded, tears, paper losses, creases,light-staining, pencil notations, surface soiling, Muriel F. Kahn Estate, (02-24-93, Butterfield, #2708, illus.), 13⅛ x 18 in., (333 x 457 mm.), lithograph & pochoir in colors on Johannot (BP 997, DM 2321, FR 7870, Y 167,801).

$2588* *Theiere Et Raisin (Maeght 1022), c. 1955,* crayon s., #134/200, full margins, good cond., mat/light-stain, creases, tape, ink i., (05-13-93, Sotheby-NY, #472), 13⅜ x 23⅝ in., (341 x 600 mm.), etching and aquatint in colors (BP 1699, DM 4179, FR 14,096, Y 288,936).

$516* *Varengeville (Maeght, num. 1023),* yellowed, #238/300, good margins, (04-02-93, Picard, #47), 9¹³/₁₆ x 25 in., (25 x 63.5 cm.), color etching (BP 340, DM 829, FR 2817, Y 58,750).

$1029* *Vase De Fleurs Jaunes (Maeght 1039),* s., #LXXXIII/CLXXV, full margins, good cond., (06-30-93, Sotheby-London, #366), 19¼ x 13¾ in., (489 x 349 mm.), colored aquatint on wove (BP 690, DM 1755, FR 5921, Y 110,254).

$805* *[Nature Morte], 1959,* s., #18/100, pub. Editions C. Guillard, full margins, good cond., crease in image, printer's crease, mat stain, foxing, (05-13-93, Sotheby-NY, #473), 8⅛ x 18⅝ in., (205 x 472 mm.), etching and aquatint (BP 528, DM 1300, FR 4385, Y 89,874).

BRASH, Barbara b. 1959

$57* *Islet,* s. Barbara Brash, i., #16/17, (08-11-92, L. Joel, #64G), 16⅛ x 22¹¹/₁₆ in., (40.9 x 57.6 cm.), color screenprint (BP 30, DM 84, FR 283, Y 7299, A$ 77).

BRASILIER, Andre French b. 1929

$858* *Cavaliere Sur La Plage (Doschka 115), 1978,* s., #162/175, pub. Visions Nouvelles, margins, good cond., light-staining, creasing w/in image, (06-30-93, Sotheby-London, #368), sh 30 x 21⅞ in., (762 x 556 mm.), colored lithograph on wove (BP 575, DM 1463, FR 4937, Y 91,932).

$800* *Cavaliers Sur La Plage (Pichon 31), 1969,* s., #69/300, full margins, excell. cond., (11-30-92, Phillips-London, #376), sheet 22¼ x 29⅞ in., (565 x 759 mm.), color lithograph on Arches (BP 528, DM 1274, FR 4327, Y 99,564).

BI *Deux Chevaux Dans Un Box, c. 1982,* artist's proof, s., est. FF2,000/2,500, (05-27-93, Briest, #42), 29¹³/₁₆ x 21¼ in., (75.7 x 54 cm.), color lithograph.

BI *Deux Chevaux Dans Un Box, c. 1982,* epreuve d'artiste, s., est. FF 3/3,500, (11-16-92, Briest, #261), 29¹³/₁₆ x 21¼ in., (75.7 x 54 cm.), lithograph in colors.

BI *"Femme Aux Fleurs" and "Femme Sur La Plage": Two,* s., num. 98/100 and 53/80, margins, tape, discoloration, est. BP 6/800, (12-01-92, Christie-London, #565), L., and smaller 21³/₁₆ x 14¹⁵/₁₆ in., (538 x 380 mm.), lithographs p. in colors on Arches.

$1650* *Le Jardin De L'Eveche (S. 128), 1968,* s., #57/125, margins, good cond., thinned spots, creases, notations,light-staining, surface soiling, (10-28-92, Butterfield, #2613), 21 x 17 in., (533 x 432 mm.), color lithograph on Arches (BP 1051, DM 2548, FR 8652, Y 202,454).

BI *La Jupe Ecossaise, 1953,* s., d., annot. Epreuve d'Artiste X/XXV, full margins, good cond., skinned areas, glue staining, creases, est. $3/4,000, (10-28-92, Butterfield, #2609, illus.), 25½ x 18¾ in., (648 x 476 mm.), color lithograph on Japan.

BI *La Jupe Ecossaise, 1953,* s., d., annot. 'Epreuve d'Artiste X/XXV, full margins, good cond., skinned areas, glue staining, creases, est. $2/2,500, (02-24-93, Butterfield, #2713, illus.), 25½ x 18¾ in., (648 x 476 mm.), lithograph in colors on Japan.

$660* *Longchamps,* s., annot. LVII/LXXV, margins, taped, good cond., creases, rubbed area, est. $1/1,500, (02-24-93, Butterfield, #2717), 19 x 25½ in., (483 x 648 mm.), lithograph in colors on Japan (BP 460, DM 1071, FR 3632, Y 77,447).

$1796* *"Orchestre",* epreuve d'artiste, s., (10-18-92, Pescheteau, #86), 27¹⁵/₁₆ x 39⅜ in., (71 x 100 cm.), lithograph in colors on velin (BP 1088, DM 2653, FR 9012, Y 214,448).

$253* *Petit Pont Des Arts, 1965,* 24/25, s., (10-14-92, Germann, #226, illus.), 9¼ x 11¼ in., (235 x 285 mm.), color lithograph (BP 149, DM 370, FR 1256, Y 30,659, SF 330).

$990* *Promenade En Foret,* s., num. XLVII/L, margins trimmed, good cond., creases, light-brown stain, est. $1,8/2,200, (02-24-93, Butterfield, #2716, illus.), 19¾ x 25½ in., (502 x 648 mm.), lithograph in colors on Japon nacre (BP 690, DM 1607, FR 5449, Y 116,170).

$825* *Repose Au Cavalier,* s., annot. E.A., good cond., light-staining, taped, creases, (02-24-93, Butterfield, #2715), 24¼ x 17⅞ in., (616 x 454 mm.), lithograph in colors on Arches (BP 575, DM 1339, FR 4540, Y 96,808).

$750* *La Riviere (P. 73), 1973,* s., i. Epreuve d'Artiste, full margins, excellent cond., (11-30-92, Phillips-London, #376A), sheet 21¼ x 30 in., (540 x 762 mm.), lithograph in colors on japan nacre (BP 495, DM 1195, FR 4056, Y 93,342).

BI *La Robe Jaune (Doschka 57), 1972,* artist proof, s., est. SF 2,720/2,970, (10-14-92, Germann, #225), 29¾ x 22¹/₁₆ in., (755 x 560 mm.), color lithograph.

BI *Soir D'Ete,* s., #39/120, full margins, good cond., creases, est. $3,5/4,500, (10-28-92, Butterfield, #2611, illus.), 28¾ x 21⅛ in., (730 x 537 mm.), color lithograph on cream wove.

$1980* *Soir D'Ete,* s., num. 39/120, full margins, good cond., creases, (02-24-93, Butterfield, #2712, illus.), 28¾ x 21⅛ in., (730 x 537 mm.), lithograph in colors on cream wove (BP 1381, DM 3214, FR 10,897, Y 232,340).

BI *La Vase Italienne,* s., #48/150, margins, good cond.?, est. $2/3,000, (10-28-92, Butterfield, #2612), 19½ x 15 in., (495 x 381 mm.), color lithograph on cream wove.

BI *La Vase Italienne,* s., num. 48/150, margins, apparently good cond., est. $1,5/2,000, (02-24-93, Butterfield, #2714), 19½ x 15 in., (495 x 381 mm.), lithograph in colors on cream wove.

$1210* *"Vase Of Tulips",* s., #24/100, good cond.?, light-staining, creases, (10-28-92, Butterfield, #2610), 25⅝ x 18 in., (651 x 457 mm.), color lithograph on wove (BP 771, DM 1869, FR 6345, Y 148,466).

BI *Woman With Bouquet Of Sunflowers,* s. Andre Brasilier, num. 120/175, fair cond., horizontal abrasion, crease in image, handling wrinkles, est. $8/1200, (09-11-92, Skinner, #95A, illus.), 25½ x 19⅛ in., (64.8 x 48.6 cm.), color lithograph on wove.

$1029* *Woman With White Tulips,* s., #LXXXIII/CLXXV, full margins, good cond., good cond., (06-30-93, Sotheby-London, #367), 25 x 17¾ in., (635 x 451 mm.), colored lithograph on Japan nacre (BP 690, DM 1755, FR 5921, Y 110,254).

BRASKER, M. Leone

$50 *"Don't Let Them Die 1918"*, (03-04-93, Alderfer, #267), 29½ x 21¼ in., (74.9 x 54 cm.), poster (BP 34, DM 82, FR 278, Y 5821).

BRASS, Charles

$66* *"The Doctor"*, #9/150, (12-11-92, DuMouchelle, #1665), approx. 10 x 12 in., (25.4 x 30.5 cm.), lithograph (BP 42, DM 104, FR 356, Y 8167).

BRASSAI 1899-1984

BI *"Academie Julian, Rue De Dragon"*, 1931, p.l., s., annot., photog.'s stamp, est. $1/1,500, (05-23-93, Butterfield, #3342, illus.), 8⅜ x 9⅛ in., photograph, gelatin silver print.

$1650* *At Suzy, (Secret Paris, unpaginated)*, s. by photog. in ink, (c) & reprod. limit. stamps, 1930's, p. l., (10-15-92, Sotheby-NY, #326, illus.), 10⅛ x 8⅛ in., (25.7 x 20.6 cm.), photograph, gelatin silver print (BP 1010, DM 2456, FR 8329, Y 197,960).

$2090* *At Suzy, Introductions (Secret Paris, unpaginated)*, s., (c) & "Tirage de l'Auteur" stamps, c. 1932, p. l., (10-15-92, Sotheby-NY, #327, illus.), 11½ x 7⅞ in., (29.2 x 20 cm.), photograph, gelatin silver print (BP 1279, DM 3111, FR 10,550, Y 250,750).

$1725* *"At Suzy, Introductions" (Secret Paris)*, s. in ink in margins, (c) stamp, c. 1932, p.l., (04-06-93, Sotheby-NY, #240, illus.), 11½ x 8⅝ in., photograph (BP 1139, DM 2779, FR 9411, Y 196,738).

$3450* *"Bijou Of Monmartre" (MoMA, p. 76)*, s. in ink, studio and (c) stamps, 1932, p.l., (04-06-93, Sotheby-NY, #240A, illus.), 18⅛ x 13¾ in., photograph (BP 2279, DM 5558, FR 18,822, Y 393,476).

$455* *Brunnen*, wear, (11-12-92, Lempertz, #30, illus.), 11¾ x 13⅛ in., (29.9 x 33.3 cm.), photograph, gelatin silver print (BP 291, DM 715, FR 2437, Y 56,291).

BI *La Cabane Cubaine, Montmartre, c. 1932*, s., annot., t., notations, (c), stamp twice, est $4/6,000, (10-13-92, Christie-NY, #142, illus.), 9⅜ x 10⅞ in., (23.8 x 27.6 cm.), photograph, gelatin silver print.

$2300* *"Conchita With Sailors In A Cafe On The Place D'Italie"*, s. in ink, (c) stamp, c. 1933, p.l., (04-06-93, Sotheby-NY, #242, illus.), 11 x 8¼ in., photograph (BP 1519, DM 3705, FR 12,548, Y 262,318).

$1320* *A Happy Group At The Quatre Saisons, c. 1932 (Secret Paris, unpaginated)*, plate from "Portfolio of Ten Photographs by Brassai", (Witkin-Berley), mounted, s. by photog. in ink, label, p. c. 1973, #45/55 ed., (10-15-92, Sotheby-NY, #332, illus.), 8¾ x 13½ in., (22.2 x 34.3 cm.), photograph, gelatin silver print (BP 808, DM 1965, FR 6663, Y 158,368).

$1650* *Le Jardin Exotique, Monaco,* (1935), p.l., s., num. 23/30 in ink, t., d., credit & reprod. limit.stamps, (10-13-92, Christie-NY, #144, illus.), 12½ x 9¾ in., (31.8 x 24.8 cm.), photograph, gelatin silver print (BP 961, DM 2417, FR 8213, Y 200,073).

BI *Jeune Lesbienne Au Monocle,* c. 1932, p.l., ink s.; t., d., (c) credit stamp, lit., est. $2,5/3,500, (04-08-93, Christie-NY, #178, illus.), 11⅛ x 8½ in., (28.3 x 21.6 cm.), photograph, gelatin silver print.

$1150* *"Joan Miro Looking At Graffiti"*, s. in ink, (c) stamp, 1950's, p.l., (04-06-93, Sotheby-NY, #243, illus.), 8⅜ x 11⅛ in., photograph (BP 760, DM 1853, FR 6274, Y 131,159).

$770* *Leaving The Ecole Des Beaux-Arts, c. 1931 (Secret Paris, unpaginated)*, s. by photog., studio & (c) stamps, p. l., probably 1950's or 1960's, (10-15-92, Sotheby-NY, #328, illus.), 11½ x 8⅜ in., (29.2 x 21.3 cm.), photograph, gelatin silver print (BP 471, DM 1146, FR 3887, Y 92,382).

$1650* *Marlene Dietrich Poster And Bicyclist, c. 1937 (Pantheon, pl. 40)*, s., num. 12/40 by photog. in ink, (c) stamp of photog.'s widow, p. l., (10-15-92, Sotheby-NY, #333, illus.), 11⅜ x 7⅝ in., (28.9 x 19.4 cm.), photograph, gelatin silver print (BP 1010, DM 2456, FR 8329, Y 197,960).

$1265* *"Matisse At His Retrospective Exhibition, Salon L'Automne"*, 1945, p.l., s., t., photog.'s stamp, (05-23-93, Butterfield, #3341, illus.), 14 x 10¼ in., photograph, gelatin silver print (BP 824, DM 2068, FR 6962, Y 139,825).

$1980* *Nude Study,* (1934-35), 1967, s., d., num. 4/6, i., (10-13-92, Christie-NY, #147, illus.), 11½ x 15½ in., (29.2 x 39.4 cm.), photograph, cliche-verre (BP 1153, DM 2901, FR 9856, Y 240,087).

$1235* *Nude, 1939,* stamped photog.'s credit, d., 219 x 215mm, (05-07-93, Sotheby-London, #242, illus.), photograph, silver print (BP 782, DM 1953, FR 6580, Y 135,983).

$1540* *An Opium Smoker Asleep, c. 1932 (Secret Paris, unpaginated)*, s., d., i. PP.409 by photog., studio & (c) stamps, p. l., (10-15-92, Sotheby-NY, #334, illus.), 9 x 14½ in., (22.9 x 36.8 cm.), photograph, gelatin silver print (BP 942, DM 2292, FR 7774, Y 184,763).

$1760* *"Pair Of Lovers, Place D'Italie"*, s., photog. stamp, annot., 1932/later, (11-16-92, Butterfield, #5867, illus.), 11½ x 9¼ in., (292.6 x 235.4 mm.), photograph, gelatin silver print (BP 1159, DM 2806, FR 9452, Y 218,878).

$2070* *Paul Eluard, c. 1945,* crayon credit, (04-08-93, Christie-NY, #177, illus.), 11¾ x 8¼ in., (29.8 x 21 cm.), photograph, gelatin silver print (BP 1357, DM 3325, FR 11,256, Y 234,907).

$1760* *Picasso In His Atelier On Rue Des Grands Augustins, 1939 (Pantheon, pl. 55)*, s. by photog. in ink, (c) stamps, p. l., (10-15-92, Sotheby-NY, #331, illus.), 14⅝ x 10⅝ in., (37.1 x 27 cm.), photograph, gelatin silver print (BP 1077, DM 2620, FR 8884, Y 211,158).

BI *Picasso In His Atelier On Rue Des Grands Augustins, c. 1939,* studio stamp, reprod. limit. stamp, agency stamp, export date stamp,est. $2,5/3,500, (10-15-92, Sotheby-NY, #330A, illus.), 6⅜ x 9⅛ in., (16.2 x 23.2 cm.), photograph, gelatin silver print.

$3080* *Le Pont Neuf A Paris,* (1949), p.l., s. in ink, t., d. twice, (c) credit & reprod. limit. stamps, (10-13-92, Christie-NY, #423, illus.), 10¼ x 15¼ in., (26 x 38.7 cm.), photograph, gelatin silver print (BP 1794, DM 4512, FR 15,331, Y 373,469).

$990* *Portrait Of Matisse In His Studio,* 1940's, (10-14-92, Swann, #388, illus.), 11½ x 9 in., (29.2 x 22.9 cm.), photograph, silver print (BP 581, DM 1449, FR 4913, Y 119,971).

$935* *Portrait Of Matisse In His Studio,* w/presentation cover page, 1940s, (04-07-93, Swann, #413, illus.), 11½ x 9 in., photograph, silver print (BP 618, DM 1512, FR 5118, Y 106,226).

$2013* *"A Prostitute Playing Russian Billiards, Boulevard Rochechouart, Montmartre"*, s. in ink, studio (c) stamp, c. 1932, p.l., (04-06-93, Sotheby-NY, #241, illus.), 12 x 8⅜ in., photograph (BP 1330, DM 3243, FR 10,982, Y 229,585).

$1760* *A Prostitute Playing Russian Billiards, Boulevard Rochechouart, Montmartre, c. 1932 (Secret Paris, unpaginated)*, s. by photog. in ink, (c) stamp, p. l., (10-15-92, Sotheby-NY, #329, illus.), 14½ x 10¾ in., (36.8 x 27.3 cm.), photograph, gelatin silver print (BP 1077, DM 2620, FR 8884, Y 211,158).

BI *Rue De Lappe,* (c. 1932), 1989, s. in ink, (c) credit stamp, lit., est. $1,8/2,200, (10-13-92, Christie-NY, #145, illus.), 8¼ x 10½ in., (21 x 26.7 cm.), photograph, gelatin silver print.

$1840* *Rue De Lappe (c. 1932), 1989,* ink s.; (c) credit stamp, lit., (04-08-93, Christie-NY, #179, illus.), 8¼ x 10½ in., (21 x 26.7 cm.), photograph, gelatin silver print (BP 1207, DM 2956, FR 10,005, Y 208,806).

BI *Self-Portrait, Paris, 1933,* t., d., annot., est. $3000/5000, (10-13-92, Christie-NY, #143, illus.), 9⅛ x 6½ in., (23.2 x 16.5 cm.), photograph, gelatin silver print.

$1725* *"Street Fair, Place Saint-Jacques (Taken From The Window Of My ParisApartment), c. 1934,* s. #5/30 in ink in margin, studio (c), reprod. limit. stamp, (04-06-93, Sotheby-NY, #244, illus.), 11⅝ x 8¾ in., photograph (BP 1139, DM 2779, FR 9411, Y 196,738).

$2588* *"Street Walker" (MoMA, p. 37)*, s. in ink, (c) and studio, 1932, p.l., (04-06-93, Sotheby-NY, #241A, illus.), 15½ x 11¾ in., photograph (BP 1709, DM 4169, FR 14,119, Y 295,164).

$1430* *Streetwalker Near The Place D'Italie,* (c. 1932), p.l., s. in ink, d., t., (c) credit stamps, lit., (10-13-92, Christie-NY, #146, illus.), 14¾ x 10⅞ in., (37.5 x 27.6 cm.), photograph, gelatin silver print (BP 833, DM 2095, FR 7118, Y 173,396).

$2543* *Studies: Two,* 1930s, stamped photog.'s credit, 234 x 176mm and 286 x 229mm, (05-07-93, Sotheby-London, #243, illus.), photograph, silver print (BP 1610, DM 4021, FR 13,548, Y 280,004).

$4400* *Two Street Thugs, Place D'Italie, Paris, 1932 (MoMA, p. 26; Pantheon,pl. 30),* num. Pl. 172 in unidentified hand, studio stamp, archivally backed w/Japan Tissue, (10-15-92, Sotheby-NY, #330, illus.), 12 x 9⅜ in., (30.5 x 23.8 cm.), photograph, gelatin silver print (BP 2692, DM 6550, FR 22,211, Y 527,894).

BRATT, Byron H.   American b. 1952
$30* *Light Bondage,* s., t., #134/150, excell. cond., (05-15-93, Cleveland, #450), 15¾ x 11¾ in., (40 x 29.8 cm.), color mezzotint (BP 20, DM 48, FR 162, Y 3326).

$10* *The Pheonix,* s., t., #34/60, excell. cond., (05-15-93, Cleveland, #449), 15¾ x 10 in., (40 x 25.4 cm.), color mezzotint (BP 7, DM 16, FR 54, Y 1109).

BRATTER, Maurice   1905-1986
BI *Automobile Fender, c. 1932,* backed w/photographic paper, est. $2/3,000, (04-06-93, Sotheby-NY, #145, illus.), 7⅝ x 9⅝ in., photograph.

BI *Bank Check With Crystal Paperweight, c. 1930,* prov., est. $2/3,000, (10-13-92, Christie-NY, #148, illus.), 2½ x 3½ in., (6.4 x 8.9 cm.), photograph, gelatin silver print.

BRAUER, Arik   b. 1929
$332* *Sklavenleben (Koschatsky G-56), 1971,* s., num., (12-01-92, Karl/Faber, #401), 27⅜ x 19¹¹⁄₁₆ in., (69.5 x 50 cm.), color aquatint and etching on hand-made (BP 219, DM 529, FR 1803, Y 41,335).

$232* *Die Touristen Kommen,* s., #33/100, (09-18-92, Schloss Ahlden, #977), 20¾ x 23⁹⁄₁₆ in., (52.7 x 59.9 cm.), color etching on handmade (BP 136, DM 344, FR 1178, Y 28,674).

BRAUER, Erich   Austrian b. 1929
$2450* XX *Chassidische Erzahlungen" (Koschatzky G 37/I-XX), 1968-1970: Twent.* s. Brauer, #220/300, Eiteuropa Anstalt & Galerie Sydow, (05-19-93, Dorotheum, #460, illus.), 14¹⁵⁄₁₆ x 16⅛ in., (37.9 x 41 cm.), etching in color (BP 1590, DM 3982, FR 13,417, Y 271,228, SC 28,000).

BRAUN, Adolphe   French 1811-1877
$453* *Bouquet Of Tulips, 1854,* mounted on album page, 222 x 281mm, (05-07-93, Sotheby-London, #122, illus.), photograph, albumen print (BP 287, DM 716, FR 2413, Y 49,879).

$8583* *"Fleurs Photographiees De Adolphe Braun A Dornach (Ht. Rhin)", mid 1850s: Fifty,* album, two trimmed oval, embossed t. and credit, (10-29-92, Christie-London, #17, illus.), smallest approx. 7 x 9½ in., (17.8 x 24.1 cm.), largest approx. 9 x 11 in., (17.8 x 24.1 cm.), photograph, albumen prints (BP 5500, DM 13,205, FR 44,796, Y 1,063,174).

$9775* *Floral Arrangement, c. 1855,* rounded corners, mounted, (04-06-93, Sotheby-NY, #47, illus.), 12⅛ x 14½ in., photograph, albumen print (BP 6456, DM 15,748, FR 53,328, Y 1,114,849).

$635* *Floral Bouquet With Ferns, 1854,* mounted on album page, 226 x 272mm, (05-07-93, Sotheby-London, #123, illus.), photograph, albumen print (BP 402, DM 1004, FR 3383, Y 69,919).

$363* *Floral Bouquet, 1854,* mounted on album page, 224 x 276mm, (05-07-93, Sotheby-London, #121, illus.), photograph, albumen print (BP 230, DM 574, FR 1934, Y 39,969).

$1998* *Floral Composition With Tulips, 1854,* mounted on album page, 194 x 255mm, (05-07-93, Sotheby-London, #119, illus.), photograph, albumen print (BP 1265, DM 3159, FR 10,645, Y 219,996).

BI *Floral Still Life, c. 1854,* mounted, est. $7/9000, (10-13-92, Christie-NY, #5, illus.), rounded corners 12⅛ x 14¾ in., (30.8 x 37.5 cm.), photograph, albumen print.

$998* *Floral Wreath, 1854,* mounted on album page, 271 x 225mm, (05-07-93, Sotheby-London, #118, illus.), photograph, albumen print (BP 632, DM 1578, FR 5317, Y 109,888).

$726* *Irises And Marguerites, 1854,* mounted on album page, 223 x 275mm, (05-07-93, Sotheby-London, #120, illus.),

photograph, albumen print (BP 460, DM 1148, FR 3868, Y 79,938).

BRAUN, Adolphe (et cie)   1811-1877
$4400* *Views On The St. Gothard Railway, c. 1876,* album, each w/credit, t., legend offset printed in margin, i., (10-13-92, Christie-NY, #4, illus.), each 8⅝ x 11 in., (21.9 x 27.9 cm.), panorama 11 x 35½ in., (21.9 x 27.9 cm.), photograph, 44 albumen prints (BP 2563, DM 6446, FR 21,901, Y 533,527).

BRAUNER, Victor   Rumanian 1903-1966
BI *Codex D'Un Visage (Levy 8A-G), 1962: Set Of Seven,* set of seven, s., pl. 5 i. epreuve 'essai, d. 5.VIII.1961, pub. Le point Cardinal, full margins, good cond., creases, foxmarks, est. BP 3,0/4,000, (12-03-92, Sotheby-London, #200, illus.), each 18½ x 14¼ in., (470 x 362 mm.), etchings on BFK Rives wove and on Arches.

$477* *Traces Intersticles (L. 13), 1963,* s., d., #43/75, full margins, good cond., (12-03-92, Sotheby-London, #201), 12¼ x 8⅞ in., (311 x 225 mm.), lithograph in colors on Arches wove (BP 308, DM 750, FR 2560, Y 59,351).

BRAUNSDORF, Anstalt v.J.
$424* *"Vista De Pernambuco",* (02-03-93, Doyle, #12), sight 19 x 23 in., (48.3 x 58.4 cm.), hand colored lithograph (BP 296, DM 698, FR 2367, Y 52,743).

BRAVO, Claudio   Chilean b. 1936
BI *"Joven Pensativo De Frente" and "Joven Pensativo De Espaldas": A Pair,* #71/75, s., d. 1976, reserve P120,000, (12-17-92, Duran, #173, illus.), 29⅛ x 20⅞ in., (74 x 53 cm.), lithograph.

$586* *Untitled, 1974,* s., d., #33/125, good cond.?, (12-09-92, Sotheby-Amstrdm, #511, illus.), 18½ x 22³⁄₁₆ in., (470 x 563 mm.), color lithograph on wove (BP 374, DM 920, FR 3139, Y 72,660, G 1035).

BRAVO, Manuel Alvarez   Mexican b. 1902
$2530* *La Buena Fama Durmiendo,* 1930s, p. 1992, s., annot., (04-08-93, Christie-NY, #380, illus.), 7¼ x 9½ in., (18.4 x 24.1 cm.), photograph, gelatin silver print (BP 1659, DM 4064, FR 13,757, Y 287,108).

$1540* *La Buena Fama Durmiendo,* (1930s), p.l., s., annot., (10-13-92, Christie-NY, #150, illus.), 10 x 13½ in., (25.4 x 34.3 cm.), photograph, gelatin silver print (BP 897, DM 2256, FR 7666, Y 186,735).

$3025* *La Buena Fama Durmiendo, (Good Reputation Sleeping), (Livingston, pl.71), 1939,* s., i. by photog., p.l., (10-15-92, Sotheby-NY, #258, illus.), 7¼ x 9½ in., (18.4 x 24.1 cm.), photograph, gelatin silver print (BP 1851, DM 4503, FR 15,270, Y 362,927).

$1100* *Caballero De Madera, 1928 (Livingston, pl. 53),* s., i. by photog., p.l., (10-15-92, Sotheby-NY, #259, illus.), 9½ x 7¼ in., (24.1 x 18.4 cm.), photograph, gelatin silver print (BP 673, DM 1637, FR 5553, Y 131,974).

$660* *Dias De Todos Los Muertos,* photog.'s sig., 1933, p.l., (04-07-93, Swann, #414, illus.), 10 x 8 in., photograph, silver print (BP 436, DM 1067, FR 3612, Y 74,983).

BI *"Dog No. 20" and "Sparrow, Clearly, Skylight": Two,* one 1958, other 1938, both p.l., s., annot., illus., est. $1,8/2,200, (05-23-93, Butterfield, #3343, illus.), each approx. 8 x 10 in., photograph, gelatin silver print.

$1320* *"A Fish Called Sierra" and "Well-Earned Sleep": Two,* s., num., 1977 and 1966, p.l., (10-14-92, Swann, #389, illus.), 10 x 8 in., (25.4 x 20.3 cm.), photograph, silver prints (BP 775, DM 1932, FR 6551, Y 159,961).

$1320* *Fotografias, 1945 (Pasadena, p. 39),* Sociedad de Arte Moderno, 4to together w/orig. photos, Dia De Todos Muertos, s. by photog. in ink, front wrapper num. 86 in unidentified hand, 1933,p. c. 1945, (10-15-92, Sotheby-NY, #260A, illus.), 6⅝ x 4⅞ in., (16.8 x 12.4 cm.), photograph, gelatin silver prints (BP 808, DM 1965, FR 6663, Y 158,368).

$2875* *Frida Kahlo,* s., i. by photog., 1930's, p.l., (04-06-93, Sotheby-NY, #157, illus.), 9½ x 7¼ in., photograph (BP 1899, DM 4632, FR 15,685, Y 327,897).

$2300* *Frida Kahlo Con Globe,* 1930s, p.l., s., t., (04-08-93, Christie-NY, #377, illus.), 9⅝ x 7¼ in., (24.4 x 18.4 cm.), photograph, gelatin silver print (BP 1508, DM 3695, FR 12,507, Y 261,008).

$1870* *Frida Kahlo Con Globe,* (1930s), p.l., s., annot., (10-13-92, Christie-NY, #149, illus.), 9½ x 7¼ in., (24.1 x 18.4 cm.), photograph, gelatin silver print (BP 1089, DM 2740, FR 9308, Y 226,749).

$2200* *"Frida Kahlo" and "Diego Rivera": Two,* s., i. by photog., 1930's, p.l., (10-15-92, Sotheby-NY, #260, illus.), each approx. 9½ x 7 in., (24.1 x 17.8 cm.), photograph, gelatin silver print (BP 1346, DM 3275, FR 11,106, Y 263,947).

$1265* *Landscape-San Blas, Nayarit, Mexico,* c. 1940, p.l., s., annot., lit., (04-08-93, Christie-NY, #381, illus.), 4½ x 6⅜ in., (11.4 x 16.2 cm.), photograph, palladium print on hand-made paper (BP 830, DM 2032, FR 6879, Y 143,554).

$1150* *Man By The Sea With Basket, 1938,* s., annot., illus., (05-23-93, Butterfield, #3346, illus.), 5½ x 4¼ in., photograph, gelatin silver print (BP 749, DM 1880, FR 6329, Y 127,114).

BI *Mexico: Two: "Trampa Puesta" and "Gravesite With Cross", (Livingston,pl. 43),* plates from "Fifteen Photographs" portfolio, Double Elephant Press, mounted, s., num. 46/75 by photog., 1930's, p. c. 1974, est. $1,5/2,000, (10-15-92, Sotheby-NY, #261, illus.), each approx. 6¾ x 9½ in., (17.1 x 24.1 cm.), photograph, gelatin silver prints.

$920* *"Montana Negra Y Nuba Blanca", Black Mountain And White Cloud and "Retrato Postumo", Posthumous Portrait: Two,* one 1974, other 1930s, both p. 1980, s., annot., (05-23-93, Butterfield, #3347, illus.), each approx. 8 x 10 in., photograph, platinum print (BP 599, DM 1504, FR 5063, Y 101,691).

BI *"Montana Negra Y Nube Blanca" (Black Mountain And White Cloud), 1974,* s., annot., t., d., est. $800/1,200, (11-16-92, Butterfield, #5872, illus.), 10¾ x 13¾ in., (273.5 x 349.9 mm.), photograph, gelatin silver print.

$1150* *Obrero En Huelga Asesinado, 1934,* p. 1974, s., annot., t., (04-08-93, Christie-NY, #379, illus.), 7¼ x 9½ in., (18.4 x 24.1 cm.), photograph, gelatin silver print (BP 754, DM 1847, FR 6253, Y 130,504).

$575* *"Paper Game (3)", 1926-27,* p.l., s., annot., illus., (05-23-93, Butterfield, #3348, illus.), 8 x 6¾ in., photograph, gelatin silver print (BP 374, DM 940, FR 3165, Y 63,557).

$1635* *"Parabola Optica", 1931,* p.l., s. M. Alvarez Bravo Mexico, 300 x 255mm, (05-07-93, Sotheby-London, #232, illus.), photograph, platinum print (BP 1035, DM 2585, FR 8711, Y 180,026).

$2760* *Peregrino En Las Cosas De Esta Vida, 1942,* s., t., (04-08-93, Christie-NY, #376, illus.), 7½ x 9½ in., (19.1 x 24.1 cm.), photograph, gelatin silver print (BP 1810, DM 4434, FR 15,008, Y 313,209).

BI *Portrait Of The Eternal, 1932,* p. 1992, s., annot., est. $1,5/2,000, (04-08-93, Christie-NY, #378, illus.), 9½ x 7½ in., (24.1 x 19.1 cm.), photograph, gelatin silver print.

$935* *Recuerdo De Atzompan,* sig., notations, 1943, printed later, (10-14-92, Swann, #390, illus.), 7 x 9 in., (17.8 x 22.9 cm.), photograph, silver print (BP 549, DM 1368, FR 4640, Y 113,306).

BI *Retrato De Lo Eterno, 1935,* s., i. by photog., p.l., est. $2/2,500, (10-15-92, Sotheby-NY, #257A, illus.), 9½ x 7½ in., (24.1 x 19.1 cm.), photograph, gelatin silver print.

BI *"Retrato Postumo",* s., annot., num 6 of 8 label, est. $1,0/1,500, 1930's/1980, (11-16-92, Butterfield, #5871, illus.), 7½ x 9½ in., (190.8 x 241.7 mm.), photograph, platinum print.

$1380* *"Senoles Y Pronosticos" and "And By Night It Moaned": Two,* one 1938, other 1945, both p.l., s., annot., first illus., (05-23-93, Butterfield, #3344, illus.), each approx. 10 x 7 in., photograph, gelatin silver print (BP 899, DM 2256, FR 7595, Y 152,537).

BI *Tentaciones En Casa De Antonio,* plate from "Untitled" portfolio, Acorn Editions, s., i. by photog., 1930's, p. 1977, est. $2/2,500, (10-15-92, Sotheby-NY, #257, illus.), 9½ x 7⅝ in., (24.1 x 19.4 cm.), photograph, gelatin silver print.

$1150* *"Trabajadores Del Fuego", Fire Fighters, 1935,* p.l., s., annot. twice, illus., (05-23-93, Butterfield, #3345, illus.),

9⅛ x 7⅛ in., photograph, platinum print (BP 749, DM 1880, FR 6329, Y 127,114).

$1210* *Two Women,* photog.'s sig., 1930s(?), p.l., (04-07-93, Swann, #415, illus.), 11½ x 10 in., photograph, platinum print (BP 800, DM 1957, FR 6623, Y 137,469).

BRAYER, Yves   French b. 1907

$55* *"Mountain Village",* s., #54/150, discoloration, good cond., (12-04-92, Doyle, #78), 21½ x 17¼ in., (546 x 438 mm.), color lithograph (BP 35, DM 88, FR 297, Y 6866).

BI *Paysages, 1976: Four,* from "Lumiere de Moscou" portfolio, s., #31/185 (2), #31/185 (2), (05-27-93, Briest, #44), 19¹¹⁄₁₆ x 25⁹⁄₁₆ in., (50 x 65 cm.), color lithographs.

$629* *Ports: Two,* s., #68/175 and E.A. 5/35, (11-16-92, Briest, #17), one 19½ x 25⁷⁄₁₆ in., (49.6 x 64.6 cm.), other 29⅜ x 20⅞ in., (49.6 x 64.6 cm.), lithograph in colors (BP 413, DM 1003, FR 3380, Y 78,497).

$298* *Venise,* s., # Richard de Bas 74/75, good margins, (05-06-93, Laurin, #11), color lithograph on Richard de Bas wove (BP 189, DM 469, FR 1580, Y 32,787).

BREBIETTE, P.   1598-c.1650

$199* *Bacchus And Ceres (Le Blanc 75),* plate s., I. Leblond excudit, (11-18-92, Bubb Kuyper, #1824), 6¹¹⁄₁₆ x 5¹³⁄₁₆ in., (17 x 14.7 cm.), etching (BP 131, DM 317, FR 1069, Y 24,748, G 360).

BREED, Lydia N.

$55* *"Common Meeting",* s., d. 62, very good cond.?, (03-28-93, Bakker, #48), image 10½ x 16¾ in., (26.7 x 42.5 cm.), woodcut (BP 37, DM 90, FR 305, Y 6401).

BREENBERGH, Bartholomaeus   1599-1659

$1062* *Der Turm Von Leoni Bei Frascati (Hollstein 9), 1640,* estate mono., prov., (06-04-93, Bassenge, #5051), 4 x 2½ in., (10.2 x 6.4 cm.), etching (BP 703, DM 1725, FR 5813, Y 114,538).

BREENBERGH, Bartolomeus

BI *Ruins Of A Palace At Tivoli (Holl. 16),* from The Set of the Roman Ruins, thread margins, discoloration, ex-coll., est. BP 8/1,200, (12-03-92, Sotheby-London, #15), 4 x 2½ in., (102 x 64 mm.), etching.

BI *Ruins Of A Palace At Tivoli (Holl. 16),* from The Set Of The Roman Ruins, thread margins, discoloration, Ex coll. Rud. Ph. Goldschmidt (L. 2926), W. H. F. K. Graf von Lepell (L. 1672), est.BP 6/800, (06-30-93, Sotheby-London, #92), 4 x 2½ in., (102 x 64 mm.), etching.

BREFORT, A.

$251* *Saint-Germain En Laye, "A 35 Minutes De Paris, Musee National, College", c. 1890,* excell. cond., (01-23-93, Ribeyre/Baron, #25), 44⅛ x 30½ in., (112 x 77.5 cm.), poster (BP 164, DM 399, FR 1350, Y 31,414).

BREITENBACH, Josef   1896-1984

$2200* *Bertold Brecht, 1938,* estate stamp, lit., (10-13-92, Christie-NY, #152, illus.), 11¾ x 9⅜ in., (29.8 x 23.8 cm.), photograph, gelatin silver print (BP 1281, DM 3223, FR 10,951, Y 266,764).

BI *Javanese Woman And Child, 1960,* sig., notations, est. $6/900, (10-14-92, Swann, #391, illus.), 14 x 11 in., (35.6 x 27.9 cm.), photograph, silver print.

$880* *Lone Rabbit, Colorado, 1946,* estate stamp, (10-15-92, Sotheby-NY, #403, illus.), 14 x 10⅞ in., (35.6 x 27.6 cm.), photograph, gelatin silver print (BP 538, DM 1310, FR 4442, Y 105,579).

BREITNER, Georg Hendrik   Dutch 1857-1923

$177* *Untitled: Twenty-Five,* portfolio, (10-21-92, Maynard, #311), woodblock print (BP 110, DM 268, FR 909, Y 21,559, C$ 220).

BREKER, Arno   1900-1991

$232* *Deux Jeunes Filles, 1929,* s., #7/10, (06-28-93, Loudmer, #17), 6⅞ x 5⅛ in., (175 x 130 mm.), sh 13¹⁵⁄₁₆ x 10¹⁄₁₆ in., (175 x 130 mm.), sanguine etching on wove (BP 155, DM 394, FR 1328, Y 24,615).

$171* *Hande, Ein Buch Aufschlagend,* s., num., (09-25-92, Granier, #2780), sheet 17½ x 20¹¹⁄₁₆ in., (44.5 x 52.5 cm.), lithograph on wove (BP 100, DM 253, FR 857, Y 20,640).

BRENET, A.

$199* *Cie Gle Transatlantique: French Line. "Antilles, Venezuela, Colombie",* very good cond., (03-13-93, Laurin, #155), 41⁵⁄₁₆ x 26¾ in., (105 x 68 cm.), (BP 139, DM 331, FR 1126, Y 23,453).

$408* *Le Maroc Par Air Atlas. Casablanca,* very good cond., (03-13-93, Laurin, #89, illus.), 39⅜ x 24⁷⁄₁₆ in., (100 x 62 cm.), (BP 285, DM 679, FR 2309, Y 48,085).

$189* *Pilotes Dans Le Cockpit,* good cond., (11-19-92, Ribeyre/Baron, #56bis), 24⁷⁄₁₆ x 38¹⁵⁄₁₆ in., (62 x 99 cm.), poster (BP 124, DM 301, FR 1015, Y 23,505).

BRENOT, Pierre   b. 1913

$110* *Les Belles Plantes Ne S'Arrosent Pas A L'Alcool. Sante, Sobriete,* cond. B, (03-16-93, Boisgirard, #58), 38¹⁵⁄₁₆ x 51³⁄₁₆ in., (99 x 130 cm.), poster (BP 76, DM 183, FR 621, Y 12,862).

BRESCIA, Giovanni Antonio   ac. 1507-1514

$12,275* *Die Heilige Familie Mit Der Heiligen Elisabeth Und Johannes Dem Taufer (B. XIII, 320, 5. I),* trimmed, (12-04-92, Bassenge, #6070), 11⁷⁄₁₆ x 7½ in., (29.1 x 19 cm.), engraving (BP 7874, DM 19,549, FR 66,316, Y 1,532,459).

BRESDIN, Rodolphe   1825-1885

BI *Le Bon Samaritain (Van Gelder 100), 1861,* margins, good cond., paper split, repaired tear, foxing, traces of glue, est. BP 16/20,000, (06-30-93, Sotheby-London, #369, illus.), 22⅛ x 17¼ in., (562 x 438 mm.), lithograph on deux chines.

$22,599* *Le Bon Samaritain (Van Gelder 100), 1861,* stone s., d., (06-10-93, Hauswedell/Nolt, #115, illus.), image 22³⁄₁₆ x 17½ in., (56.3 x 44.5 cm.), lithograph (BP 14,782, DM 36,800, FR 123,898, Y 2,398,790).

BI *Le Chevalier Et La Mort (Van Gelder 120, Peters 33), 1886,* 3rd and final state, posthumous impression of cancelled plate, watermarked, large margins, good cond., repaired tear, est. BP 150/200, (10-27-92, Phillips-London, #44), plate 6¾ x 9¾ in., (171 x 248 mm.), etching on blue paper.

$826* *La Comedie De La Mort (D.V.G., num. 84), 1854,* large margins, (04-02-93, Picard, #49), 8⁹⁄₁₆ x 5⅞ in., (21.7 x 15 cm.), lithograph on Chine fixe (BP 544, DM 1328, FR 4509, Y 94,045).

$3736* *Comedie De La Mort (D.v.G. 84), 1854,* w/address, t., dirt, soiling, crease, (02-24-93, Picard, #45), 6⁷⁄₁₆ x 9¾ in., (164 x 248 mm.), pen lithograph on chine applique on double wove contrecolle (BP 2605, DM 6065, FR 20,561, Y 438,395).

$1527* *Frontispice Pour: Fables Et Contes (van Gelder 122/II), 1868,* s. in stone, (06-23-93, Kornfeld, #241), lithograph on thick wove (BP 1037, DM 2584, FR 8691, Y 166,358, SF 2300).

$6879* *La Fuite En Egypte (D. Van Gelder, 85),* second of second state, i., mat glued to margins, (06-16-93, Ader Tajan, #52), lithograph (BP 4586, DM 11,419, FR 38,323, Y 733,682).

$3933* *Interieur De Paysans (D.v.G. 79), 1850,* second state, untrimmed margins, (02-24-93, Picard, #44), 6¹⁄₁₆ x 4⁵⁄₁₆ in., (154 x 109 mm.), etching on thin wove applique de guingois (BP 2743, DM 6385, FR 21,646, Y 461,511).

$4916* *Je Porte Cette Pierre Depuis 50 Ans (D.v.G. 122), 1868,* before address, tears, crease, dirt, staining, (02-24-93, Picard, #47), pen lithograph (BP 3428, DM 7981, FR 27,056, Y 576,860).

$1228* *Le Marche Aux Parasols (D.v.G. 118), 1866,* first state of 2, dirt, staining, large margins, (02-24-93, Picard, #46), etching on chine applique (BP 856, DM 1994, FR 6758, Y 144,098).

$565* *Mon Reve (Van Gelder 150 II), 1883,* plate s., d., (06-10-93, Hauswedell/Nolt, #114), image 8⁹⁄₁₆ x 5⅜ in., (21.8 x 13.7 cm.), etching on Arches (BP 370, DM 920, FR 3098, Y 59,972).

$2064* *Paysage Avec Pecheurs Et Paysans (D. Van Gelder, num. 389),* (04-02-93, Picard, #48), 2¹⁵⁄₁₆ x 4⅞ in., (7.5 x 12.4 cm.), etching (BP 1360, DM 3317, FR 11,266, Y 234,999).

BI *Repos En Egypte A L'Ane Broutant (V.G. 138), 1871,* #199/243, 2nd final state, stell-faced posthumous edit., 1975, pub. Ferdinand Roten Galleries, full margins,

good cond., est. $3/500, (10-28-92, Butterfield, #2786), 9 x 7¹³⁄₁₆ in., (229 x 198 mm.), etching on Laurence Barker paper.

BRESLAUER, Marianne

$880* *Paris, Soiree A La Seine, 1927,* s., t., d. by photog., (10-15-92, Sotheby-NY, #305, illus.), 6⅞ x 9⅛ in., (17.5 x 23.2 cm.), photograph, gelatin silver print (BP 538, DM 1310, FR 4442, Y 105,579).

BI *"Weihnachtsmarkt In Berlin", 1930,* s., t., d. by photog., est. $1,5/2,500, (04-06-93, Sotheby-NY, #336, illus.), 9⅛ x 11½ in., photograph.

BRESLAUER, Marianne   b. 1909

$2300* *Sommer, 1929,* s., t., d., prov., lit., (04-08-93, Christie-NY, #95, illus.), 11½ x 9 in., (29.2 x 22.9 cm.), photograph, gelatin silver print (BP 1508, DM 3695, FR 12,507, Y 261,008).

BRESSLERN-ROTH, Norbertine von   German 1891-1978

$784* *2 Fohlen,* s., (05-19-93, Dorotheum, #416, illus.), 9¹⁄₁₆ x 8¹¹⁄₁₆ in., (23 x 22 cm.), woodcut in color (BP 509, DM 1274, FR 4294, Y 86,793, SC 8960).

$316* *Brullender Lowe,* s., (12-01-92, Karl/Faber, #404), 8¼ x 8¼ in., (21 x 21 cm.), color linocut (BP 209, DM 504, FR 1716, Y 39,343).

$138* *"Lion",* s. Bresslern-Roth, annot. Handdruck, num. 65, good cond., light toning, staining, (09-11-92, Skinner, #17A, illus.), 7¾ x 8⅜ in., (19.7 x 21.3 cm.), color woodblock on fine cream wove (BP 71, DM 199, FR 675, Y 17,098).

$514* *Lowe,* (04-21-93, Germann, #304), 9¹⁄₁₆ x 10⁷⁄₁₆ in., (230 x 265 mm.), color linocut (BP 334, DM 822, FR 2778, Y 56,902, SF 748).

$1078* *Pfefferfresser,* s., (05-19-93, Dorotheum, #417, illus.), 10⅝ x 9¹⁄₁₆ in., (27 x 23 cm.), woodcut in color (BP 700, DM 1752, FR 5904, Y 119,340, SC 12,320).

$980* *Windhunde,* s. Bresslem-Roth, i., (05-19-93, Dorotheum, #415, illus.), 8¹⁄₁₆ x 9¹⁄₁₆ in., (20.5 x 23 cm.), woodcut in color (BP 636, DM 1593, FR 5367, Y 108,491, SC 11,200).

$265* *Zwei Kroten Und Eine Schnecke,* s., (12-01-92, Karl/Faber, #406), 6⅞ x 8⁷⁄₁₆ in., (17.5 x 21.5 cm.), color linocut (BP 175, DM 422, FR 1439, Y 32,993).

BRETHERTON, Henry (after)

BI *The Hopes Of The Family-An Admission At The University The Xmas: Pair, 1773,* etched & pub. by J. Bretherton, watermark, full margins, good cond.,est. BP 100/150, (11-30-92, Phillips-London, #111), each, plate 11⅛ x 15¼ in., (283 x 387 mm.), etchings on laid.

BRETON, Louis Le   c. 1800-1866

BI *Bridge-Water (Ile Van Diemen),* p. above image-Voyage Au Pole Sud Et Dans L'Oceanie. Atlas Pittoresque. Pl. 165., below image-DEssine Par Le Breton, Lith. Par Sabatier. Gide Editeur. imp. Par Lemercier., est. $6/900, (08-11-92, L. Joel, #29G, illus.), 8³⁄₁₆ x 13¹¹⁄₁₆ in., (20.8 x 34.7 cm.), color lithograph.

$324* *Observatoire De La Baie Raffles,* p. Voyage Au Pole Sud Et Dans L'Oceanie. Atlas Pittoresque Pl. 116, p. below image-Dessine Par Le Breton. Lith Par Lassalle. Gide Editeur. Implemercier Benard & Co., (08-11-92, L. Joel, #91G), 7³⁄₁₆ x 12⁵⁄₁₆ in., (18.2 x 31.2 cm.), color lithograph (BP 168, DM 475, FR 1610, Y 41,491, A$ 440).

BI *Riviere Derwent Pres De Richemont (Ile Van Dieman),* p. above image-Voyage Au Pole Et Dans L'Oceanie. Atlas Pittoresque PL. 161., below image-Essine Par L. Le Breton.Lithe Par J Guiaud G'ide Editeur, Lith. de Thierry Freres, est. $6/900, (08-11-92, L. Joel, #35G), 7½ x 11⅝ in., (19 x 29.5 cm.), color lithograph.

BREUGHEL, Pieter (the elder) and Hans BOL (after)

$22,567* *The Seasons: "Spring" (Bast, Holl. 200), "Summer" (Bast, Holl. 202),"Autumn" (Holl. 201), "Winter" (Holl. 202), 1570: Four1570: Four,* by Peter van der Heyden, 1st state of 2, margins, crease, surface dirt, good cond., (06-29-93, Sotheby-London, #14, illus.), each approx. 8¾ x 11⅛ in., (22.2 x 28.3 cm.), engraving (BP 14,950, DM 38,107, FR 128,441, Y 2,402,278).

BREWER, H. (after)
$28 *"The Old Bridge Over The Tyne At Newcastle",* (12-11-92, G.A. Key, #56), 12 x 18 in., (30.5 x 45.7 cm.), hand colored print (BP 18, DM 44, FR 151, Y 3465).

BREWER, J. Alphege English 20th cent.
$10 *Cathedral, 1929,* s., (05-20-93, Alderfer, #428), 15½ x 8 in., (39.4 x 20.3 cm.), etching (BP 6, DM 16, FR 54, Y 1104).

BREWER, J. Alphege (after)
$47 *"Leon Cathedral",* engr. by H. C. Bewer, (12-11-92, G.A. Key, #133), 23 x 16 in., (58.4 x 40.6 cm.), colored etching (BP 30, DM 74, FR 254, Y 5816).

BREWER, James Alphege English 20th cent.
$176* *Lake Como And Sorrento, 1926, 1938: Two,* s., (06-13-93, Hindman, #372), each 19½ x 6 in., (49.5 x 15.2 cm.), color etching (BP 115, DM 286, FR 963, Y 18,520).
$7* *Liverpool Cathedral,* (05-14-93, DuMouchelle, #2536), 10 x 5 in., (25.4 x 12.7 cm.), etching (BP 5, DM 11, FR 38, Y 776).
$440* *"Rouen Cathedral", "Ratisbon From The Danube" and "Antwerp", 1913, 1915, 1925: Three,* all s., t., (06-13-93, Hindman, #373), larger 16 x 21 in., (40.6 x 53.3 cm.), color etching (BP 288, DM 716, FR 2407, Y 46,301).

BREY, Laura
$220* *"Enlist - On Which Side Of The Window Are You?",* restored, (c) 1917, (09-12-92, Dunning, #96, illus.), 39 x 26 in., (99.1 x 66 cm.), poster laid on cloth (BP 114, DM 317, FR 1076, Y 27,258).

BRIANSKY, Rita Canadian b. 1925
$45* *"Femme Assise A La Robe Orange",* s. in plate R. Briansky, (03-16-93, Encans, #27), 23⅝ x 19¹¹⁄₁₆ in., (60 x 50 cm.), serigraph (BP 31, DM 75, FR 254, Y 5262, C$ 56).

BRIDAHAM, Lester Burbank
$165* *"Alchemists Shop" and "Street In Fez": Two,* s., both #3/10, one d. 35, good cond., ded., (03-28-93, Bakker, #282), plate 8⅞ x 12 in., (22.5 x 30.5 cm.), image 7¾ x 5½ in., (22.5 x 30.5 cm.), etching (BP 111, DM 269, FR 915, Y 19,204).

BRIDGE, Joe (after)
$462* *Geo, "Jambon, Conserves. La Marque Geo Garantie La Qualite", c. 1920,* good cond., (11-19-92, Ribeyre/Baron, #12), 26³⁄₁₆ x 20⅞ in., (66.5 x 53 cm.), poster (BP 304, DM 737, FR 2481, Y 57,456).

BRIEN, G.S.
$445* *The Quick-Starting Pair, Leaping Chamois, 1929,* ref. #221, cond. 5, (10-13-92, Phillips-London, #77), 29¹⁵⁄₁₆ x 44⅞ in., (76 x 114 cm.), color lithograph (BP 259, DM 652, FR 2215, Y 53,959).

BRIGMAN, Anne 1869-1950
$4620* *The Heart Of The Storm, 1912,* s., d., lit., (10-13-92, Christie-NY, #33, illus.), 9⅝ x 7¾ in., (24.4 x 19.7 cm.), photograph, gelatin silver print (BP 2691, DM 6768, FR 22,997, Y 560,204).

BRIGNONI, Sergio Swiss b. 1903
$139* *Composizione, 1975,* artist proof, s., d., ded., (09-04-92, Germann, #264), 19⅞ x 25⁹⁄₁₆ in., (505 x 650 mm.), color lithograph (BP 70, DM 195, FR 663, Y 17,110, SF 173).
$362* *Liegende Frau,* s., (10-14-92, Germann, #492), 9¹³⁄₁₆ x 11¾ in., (250 x 298 mm.), color woodcut (BP 212, DM 530, FR 1797, Y 43,868, SF 472).

BRIL, Paul (after)
$515* *Scenes From Ovid,* margins, good cond., (06-30-93, Sotheby-London, #93), each c. 10 x 12½ in., (254 x 318 mm.), etching w/engraving on paper w/an elaborate Shield watermark (BP 345, DM 878, FR 2963, Y 55,181).

BRILLANT, Gilou
BI *Das Feuerle Feu, 1973: Eight,* #56/99, s., pub. Orangerie, est. SF 2,5/3,200, (11-13-92, Koller, #5264), sheet 25⁹⁄₁₆ x 20¼ in., (65 x 51.5 cm.), color etching, aquatint on wove.

BRINDEAU
$816* *PLM: Casablanca Maroc,* good cond., tears, (03-13-93, Laurin, #90), 38¹⁵⁄₁₆ x 24⁷⁄₁₆ in., (99 x 62 cm.), (BP 569, DM 1358, FR 4618, Y 96,170).

BRINKWORTH, Ian
$422* *Firemen Use Shell, 1938,* p. Waterlow and Sons, ref. #508, cond. 1, nick, (10-13-92, Phillips-London, #132), 29¹⁵⁄₁₆ x 44⅞ in., (76 x 114 cm.), color lithograph (BP 246, DM 618, FR 2101, Y 51,170).

BRIQUET
BI *PLM: Gabes, Centre D'Excursions. "La Plus Belle Oasis", 1921,* very good cond., (03-13-93, Laurin, #62), 42½ x 30⅞ in., (108 x 78.5 cm.), .

BRIQUET, A.
$880* *Mexican Scenes Comprising Views Of Veracruz, Tampico, Mexico City, Pueblo, Cordoba: Nine,* photog. credit, d., inventory num. in neg., descriptive labelin Spanish and English, 1890s, (04-07-93, Swann, #233), each 5 x 7 in., photograph, albumen print (BP 582, DM 1423, FR 4817, Y 99,977).

BRISCOE, Arthur
$138* *Abandoned, 1930,* s., num. 56/75, s., t. in plate, minor mat burn, some foxing, tape, (05-22-93, Weschler, #168), 8 x 15 in., (20.3 x 38.1 cm.), etching w/plate tone (BP 89, DM 224, FR 755, Y 15,215).
$133* *Brixham,* s., i. Trial, good cond., creased corner, (11-30-92, Phillips-London, #326A), sheet 8¼ x 10¾ in., (210 x 273 mm.), etching on laid (BP 88, DM 212, FR 719, Y 16,553).
$438* *Calm,* ink s., margins, (01-14-93, Bonhams, #101), plate 11½ x 15 in., (29.2 x 38.1 cm.), etching (BP 286, DM 716, FR 2421, Y 55,219).
$1115* *"The Captstan", "The Seine Net", "Hauling The Net Aboard", and "Caulking" (L. 49; 64; 77 and 126), 1925-1928: Four,* s., num., margins, good cond., discoloration, (06-30-93, Sotheby-London, #296, illus.), four etchings on cream laid (BP 747, DM 1902, FR 6415, Y 119,469).
$943* *"Clewlines And Buntlines", "Al Hands" and "We Are Bound For The Rio Grande" (L. 25; 62 and 143), 1925-1929: Three,* each s., two num., margins, good cond., defects, (06-30-93, Sotheby-London, #295), etching, one on wove, two on laid (BP 632, DM 1608, FR 5426, Y 101,039).
$686* *"Furling The Foresail", "Mooring Her" and "The Main Tack" (Laver 19;104 and 119), 1924-1928: Three,* two s., on num., margins, good cond., paper discoloration, (06-30-93, Sotheby-London, #294, illus.), three etchings, all on wove (BP 460, DM 1170, FR 3947, Y 73,503).
$165* *Heaving The Lines, 1926,* s. in ink, #54/75, mat burn, good cond., (06-11-93, Doyle, #21), 7⅛ x 11 in., (181 x 279 mm.), etching (BP 108, DM 268, FR 904, Y 17,507).
$1201* *"Making Sail", "Stowing The Main Sail" and "Abandoned" (L. 100; 152 and 157), 1928-1930: Three,* each s., ink, #75, margins, good cond., paper discoloration, skinning, (06-30-93, Sotheby-London, #298), etching on laid (BP 805, DM 2048, FR 6910, Y 128,683).
$480* *"On The Hard", "The Bucko Mate", "Gravesend Reach" and "In The Tropics" (L. 53; 69; 102 and 135), 1925-1928: Four,* s., num., margins, good cond., handling marks, paper discoloration, (06-30-93, Sotheby-London, #297), four etchings, three on laid, one on wove (BP 322, DM 819, FR 2762, Y 51,430).
$320* *Ten Knots,* #60/75, ink s., margins, (01-14-93, Bonhams, #102, illus.), plate 9¾ x 13¾ in., (24.8 x 34.9 cm.), drypoint etching (BP 209, DM 523, FR 1769, Y 40,343).

BRISSAUD, Pierre French b. 1885
$248* *La Confidance)", 1908 and "The De Ceylan", 1906: Two,* s., #6/50, (04-02-93, Picard, #51), 9¹⁄₁₆ x 8¹⁄₁₆ in., (23 x 20.5 cm.), color etching and aquatint on Japan (BP 163, DM 399, FR 1354, Y 28,236).

BRISTOL, Horace
BI *"Design With Squares And Circles", 1934,* s., d., est. $3/5,000, (05-23-93, Butterfield, #3349, illus.), 8½ x 7¼ in., photograph, gelatin silver print.
$825* *"Exercise On The Carrier Deck",* 1942/later, s., d., (11-16-92, Butterfield, #5876, illus.), 9⅞ x 9⅞ in., (251.3 x

251.3 mm.), photograph, gelatin silver print (BP 543, DM 1315, FR 4431, Y 102,599).

BI *"Fortuneteller With Glass", 1940s,* s., photog.'s chop, est. $1,5/2,000, (05-23-93, Butterfield, #3351, illus.), 2¼ x 2¼ in., photograph, gelatin silver contact print.

BI *"Invasion Of North Africa, Loading Dive Bomber On Carrier", 1942,* s., est. $1,8/2,200, (05-23-93, Butterfield, #3350, illus.), 10½ x 10½ in., photograph, gelatin silver print.

$1100* *Japanese Baths,* (1956), p.l., s.; s., d. on overmat, (10-13-92, Christie-NY, #424, illus.), 8⅝ x 12⅜ in., (21.9 x 31.4 cm.), photograph, gelatin silver print (BP 641, DM 1611, FR 5475, Y 133,382).

$523* *"Kit Scratching Nose",* 1946/1989, s., t., photog. label, (11-16-92, Butterfield, #5877, illus.), 9½ x 9½ in., (241.7 x 241.7 mm.), photograph, gelatin silver print (BP 344, DM 834, FR 2809, Y 65,042).

$605* *"Melee For The Baton",* 1956/later, s., d., (11-16-92, Butterfield, #5875, illus.), 8⅞ x 12⅞ in., (225.8 x 327.6 mm.), photograph, gelatin silver print (BP 398, DM 965, FR 3249, Y 75,239).

$770* *"Pilots In The Rain",* 1935/later, s., p. info., (11-16-92, Butterfield, #5874, illus.), 10 x 13 in., (254.5 x 330.8 mm.), photograph, gelatin silver print (BP 507, DM 1228, FR 4135, Y 95,759).

BI *San Francisco Bridge-Looking Toward City, 1936,* s. twice, t., d., est. $4/5,000, (10-13-92, Christie-NY, #153, illus.), 13½ x 10½ in., (34.3 x 26.7 cm.), photograph, gelatin silver print.

$550* *"White Chapel, New Mexico",* 1938/1991, typed t., label, s., (11-16-92, Butterfield, #5878, illus.), 7 x 9 in., (178.1 x 229 mm.), photograph, gelatin silver print (BP 362, DM 877, FR 2954, Y 68,399).

BRISTOL, Joseph W. (after)

$220* *The Great Western,* label, later addition, (11-12-92, Freemn/Fine Art, #36), 21½ x 29½ in., (54.6 x 74.9 cm.), litho, hand colored (BP 144, DM 349, FR 1176, Y 27,278).

BRISTOW, Edmund (after)

BI *Jack Hall, Fisherman Of Eton,* by Richard Graves, trimmed to plate, time-stained, area missing lowerleft corner, est. BP 70/100, (11-30-92, Phillips-London, #269), sheet 14½ x 11½ in., (368 x 292 mm.), mixed-method engraving on wove.

BRITISH SCHOOL, 19TH CENTURY

$275* *"Magpie" and "Passenger Pigeon": Two,* t., ident. on label, good cond.?, wrinkles, (12-04-92, Skinner, #359), sheet, sight 8¾ x 5¼ in., (22.2 x 13.3 cm.), color intaglio w/hand-coloring (BP 176, DM 438, FR 1486, Y 34,332).

BI *Ornithological Prints From A History Of The Birds Of Europe, 1871-1881: A Pair,* both id. w/matrix, very good cond., est. $250/350, (06-25-93, Skinner, #259), sh 10¾ x 8½ in., (27.3 x 21.6 cm.), lithograph w/handcoloring on paper.

$214* *Puppet Show For The Villagers,* (06-08-93, Ritchie, #25, illus.), sheet 29½ x 50½ in., (74.9 x 128.3 cm.), engraving (BP 141, DM 347, FR 1169, Y 22,730, C$ 275).

BROCAS, William (after)

$33* *Sunday Morning,* by Robert C. Bell, pub. by National Art Union for Ireland, 1846, (06-16-93, Bonhams-Chelsea, #416), image 16½ x 13½ in., (41.9 x 34.3 cm.), engraving (BP 22, DM 55, FR 184, Y 3520).

BROCK, Charles E. (after)

$170* *The Fall, 1892: A Set Of Four,* by Frank Paton, s. by both artists, blindstamp Print Sellers' Association, Leggatt Bros., margins, (07-16-92, Bonhams-Chelsea, #533), plate 9 x 11¾ in., (22.9 x 29.8 cm.), etching (BP 88, DM 251, FR 848, Y 21,295).

BROCKHURST, Gerald British 1890-1978

$453* *Una (D.F. 65), 1929,* s., full margins, excell. cond., prov., (10-27-92, Phillips-London, #254), pl 8$\frac{9}{16}$ x 6¼ in., (217 x 159 mm.), etching on wove (BP 286, DM 694, FR 2356, Y 55,413).

$16,100* *Adolescence, Kathleen Nancy Woodward (Fletcher 75), 1932,* 5th final state, s., full margins, mat staining, loss, very good cond., (05-11-93, Christie-NY, #94, illus.), plate 14⅜ x 10⅜ in., (365 x 264 mm.), etching on wove (BP 10,278, DM 25,362, FR 85,456, Y 1,770,982).

$261* *Almina (Anais) (D.F. 48), 1924,* full margins, excell. cond., prov., (10-27-92, Phillips-London, #247), pl te 7⅛ x 5¼ in., (181 x 133 mm.), etching on J.F. Whatman (BP 165, DM 400, FR 1357, Y 31,927).

$440* *The Amberley Boy, No. 2 (Fletcher 62), 1928,* s., Charles E. Feinberg Coll., (12-08-92, Swann, #29, illus.), 7⅝ x 5⅞ in., (19.4 x 14.9 cm.), etching (BP 276, DM 685, FR 2335, Y 54,536).

BI *Anais II (W. 67), 1930,* s., margins, good cond., est. BP 3/400, (06-30-93, Sotheby-London, #300), 8⅞ x 6⅞ in., (225 x 175 mm.), etching on wove.

BI *"The Black Cloak (Mrs. Paul Mellon)" (F. 81 III/III), 1943,* excellent cond., est. $5-700, (10-31-92, Cleveland, #262), 9¾ x 7¾ in., (24.8 x 19.7 cm.), etching.

$357* *The Black Coat, Mrs. Mary Mellon (Fletcher 81), 1943,* s., annot. 1st state, Charles E. Feinberg Coll., (12-08-92, Swann, #30, illus.), 9¾ x 7¾ in., (24.8 x 19.7 cm.), etching (BP 224, DM 556, FR 1895, Y 44,249).

$487* *The Black Silk Dress (Anais) (D.F. 58), 1927,* full margins, excell. cond., prov., (10-27-92, Phillips-London, #250, illus.), pl 8¾ x 6¼ in., (222 x 159 mm.), etching on fine wove (BP 308, DM 746, FR 2533, Y 59,572).

BI *"The Black Silk Dress (Anais)" (Fletcher 58 IX/IX), 1927,* s., hinges, est. $8-1,100, (10-31-92, Cleveland, #260, illus.), 8¾ x 6¼ in., (22.2 x 15.9 cm.), etching.

$165* *By The Window, 1922,* s., mat burn, tape residue, soiling, discoloration, hinged to mat, (12-04-92, Doyle, #79), 5⅜ x 3⅞ in., (137 x 98 mm.), etching (BP 106, DM 263, FR 891, Y 20,599).

$600* *The Dancer (D.F. 52), 1925,* s., i., 7th state, large margins, (11-30-92, Phillips-London, #329, illus.), pl 9⅜ x 5½ in., (238 x 140 mm.), etching on laid (BP 396, DM 956, FR 3245, Y 74,673).

$435* *Deux Landaises (Anais And Marguerite) (D.F. 38), 1923,* s., full margins, discolored, foxing, prov., (10-27-92, Phillips-London, #244), pl 8 x 5⅞ in., (203 x 149 mm.), etching on laid (BP 275, DM 667, FR 2262, Y 53,211).

$825* *Deux Landaises, Anais And Marguerite (Fletcher 38), 1923,* s., Charles E. Feinberg Coll., (12-08-92, Swann, #31), 8 x 6 in., (20.3 x 15.2 cm.), etching (BP 517, DM 1284, FR 4379, Y 102,256).

$1133* *Dorette (Kathleen Nancy Woodward) (D.F. 72), 1932,* 6th state, s., large margins, good cond., (11-30-92, Phillips-London, #333, illus.), pl 9¼ x 7¼ in., (235 x 184 mm.), etching on wove (BP 748, DM 1805, FR 6128, Y 141,008).

$226* *Fabian (The Ideal Head) (D.F. 23), 1921,* s., full margins, excell. cond., prov., (10-27-92, Phillips-London, #242), pl 6¾ x 4⅞ in., (171 x 124 mm.), etching on J. Whatman (BP 143, DM 346, FR 1175, Y 27,645).

BI *Genevieve (D.F. 30), 1922,* s., traces of printer's ink in margins, good cond., mounted, prov., est. BP 150/200, (10-27-92, Phillips-London, #243), pl 7⅞ x 5$\frac{15}{16}$ in., (200 x 151 mm.), etching on wove.

$917* *Henry Rushbury (D.F. 66), 1930,* s., full margins, good cond., (11-30-92, Phillips-London, #332), pl 10 x 7⅜ in., (254 x 187 mm.), etching on wove (BP 605, DM 1461, FR 4959, Y 114,126).

$770* *Henry Rushbury, No. 2 (Fletcher 66), 1930,* s., Charles E. Feinberg Coll., (12-08-92, Swann, #32), 10 x 7⅜ in., (25.4 x 18.7 cm.), etching (BP 483, DM 1199, FR 4087, Y 95,439).

$935* *James McBey (Fletcher 69), 1931,* s., Charles E. Feinberg Coll., (12-08-92, Swann, #33, illus.), 10½ x 7½ in., (26.7 x 19.1 cm.), etching (BP 586, DM 1456, FR 4963, Y 115,890).

$721* *James McBey (W. 69), 1931,* s., margins, good cond., (06-30-93, Sotheby-London, #301), 10½ x 7⅜ in., (267 x 187 mm.), etching on wove (BP 483, DM 1230, FR 4148, Y 77,253).

$296* *L'Eventail (The Fan) (D.F. 22), 1921,* s., excell. cond., full margins, prov., (10-27-92, Phillips-London, #241), pl 6⅜ x 4⅜ in., (162 x 111 mm.), etching on J. Whatman (BP 187, DM 454, FR 1539, Y 36,208).

$418* *Malvina (Alois) (D.F. 64), 1929,* s., full margins, excell. cond., prov., (10-27-92, Phillips-London, #253), pl 7¾ x

5⅞ in., (197 x 149 mm.), etching on wove (BP 264, DM 641, FR 2174, Y 51,131).

$467* *Malvina (Fletcher 64), 1929,* s., annot. special print, Charles E. Feinberg Coll., (12-08-92, Swann, #34), 7¾ x 5⅞ in., (19.7 x 14.9 cm.), etching (BP 293, DM 727, FR 2479, Y 57,883).

BI *"Mr. Albert H. Wiggin" and "Mrs. Albert H. Wiggin" (W. 73-4), 1932: Two,* margins, good cond., est. BP 2/300, (12-01-92, Christie-London, #314), plate 9¾ x 7⅜ in., (248 x 188 mm.), etching on wove.

$331* *Nadeida (D.F. 47), 1924,* s., full margins, excell. cond., mount staining, prov., (10-27-92, Phillips-London, #246, illus.), pl 5⅞ x 4⅜ in., (149 x 111 mm.), etching on J. Whatman (BP 209, DM 507, FR 1721, Y 40,489).

$309* *Noemi (White 57), 1926,* 2nd state of 6, s., margins, good cond., (06-30-93, Sotheby-London, #299), 8¼ x 5⅞ in., (210 x 149 mm.), etching on J. Whatman wove (BP 207, DM 527, FR 1778, Y 33,108).

$275* *Nude,* s. G.L. Brockhur; s., d., G.L. Brockhurst 1945 verso, (12-12-92, Wolf, #13, illus.), 7½ x 15 in., (19.1 x 38.1 cm.), lithograph (BP 176, DM 433, FR 1485, Y 34,030).

$267* *Ranunculus (Anais) (D.F. 25), 1921,* s., full margins, cockling, (11-30-92, Phillips-London, #328), pl 7⅞ x 5¾ in., (200 x 146 mm.), etching on simili japan (BP 176, DM 425, FR 1444, Y 33,230).

$495* *Ranunculus, Anais (Fletcher 25), 1921,* s., Charles E. Feinberg Coll., (12-08-92, Swann, #35, illus.), 7⅞ x 6 in., (20 x 15.2 cm.), etching (BP 310, DM 771, FR 2627, Y 61,353).

BI *Standing Nude,* s., est. $2/300, (09-17-92, Sloan, #656), 5¾ x 2⅞ in., (14.6 x 7.3 cm.), etching.

$209* *The Three Sisters (D.F. 11), 1920,* full margins, excell. cond., prov., (10-27-92, Phillips-London, #240), pl 3⅞ x 4⅞ in., (98 x 124 mm.), etching on wove (BP 132, DM 320, FR 1087, Y 25,566).

$517* *La Tresse (Anais) (D.F. 56), 1926,* s., full margins, good cond., (11-30-92, Phillips-London, #330), pl 8⁵⁄₁₆ x 6⅞ in., (211 x 175 mm.), etching on wove (BP 341, DM 824, FR 2796, Y 64,343).

$333* *The Two Melisandes (D.F. 60), 1928,* s., 3rd final state, full margins, excell. cond., (11-30-92, Phillips-London, #331), pl 6 x 3⅜ in., (152 x 86 mm.), etching on wove (BP 220, DM 531, FR 1801, Y 41,444).

BI *The Two Melisandes (F. 60), 1928,* 3rd final state, s., full margins, good cond., mat staining, foxing, est. $4/600, (05-19-93, Butterfield, #2038A), 6 x 3½ in., (152 x 89 mm.), etching on wove.

$487* *Viba (Mrs. Bobby Hazelton Ross) (D.F. 63), 1929,* s., full margins, good cond., prov., (10-27-92, Phillips-London, #252), pl 8⅜ x 6¾ in., (213 x 171 mm.), etching on wove (BP 308, DM 746, FR 2533, Y 59,572).

BI *"Viba (Mrs. Bobby Hazelton Ross) (F. 63 viii/viii), 1929,* s., excellent cond., est. $6-800, (10-31-92, Cleveland, #261, illus.), 8⅜ x 6¾ in., (21.3 x 17.1 cm.), etching.

BI *Xenia (Marguerite) (D.F. 39), 1923,* s., full margins, excell. cond., prov., (10-27-92, Phillips-London, #245), pl 7⅞ x 6 in., (200 x 152 mm.), etching on hand-made laid.

$135* *"Youth" (F. L-4),* s., repaired tears in image, (05-15-93, Cleveland, #365, illus.), 14⁹⁄₁₆ x 4¾ in., (37 x 12.1 cm.), lithograph (BP 88, DM 217, FR 730, Y 14,965).

$210* *"Zelic" (Fletcher 13), 1920,* trial proof, s., very good cond., (05-15-93, Cleveland, #364), 4⅜ x 3⅜ in., (11.1 x 8.6 cm.), etching (BP 137, DM 338, FR 1135, Y 23,279).

BROCKHUSEN, Theo von   1882-1919
$325* *Blick Auf Eine Dorfstrasse, c. 1910,* s., num., (11-28-92, Grisebach, #447, illus.), 15¹¹⁄₁₆ x 19⁷⁄₁₆ in., (39.8 x 49.3 cm.), etching on Japan (BP 215, DM 518, FR 1758, Y 40,448).

BRODECK, H.H.
$3850* *Scenes In Alaska, Including "Council Of War, Master Hanus, USN, Shatrhitch, Head Chief And Other Chiefs Of The Chilcats", "Hoonyah Indian Making Canoe", "Kan-Akl, Chief Of The Hoonyah Tribe" And Others Similar: Collection Of 63,* photographed for Northwest Trading Co., (10-31-92, Riba, #50, illus.), 57 stereo and 6 cabinet-card albumen photographs (BP 2517, DM 6044, FR 20,468, Y 476,014).

BRODER
BI *United Nations For Freedom, 1942,* U.S. Government Printing Office, B+ cond., fold marks, pin holes, est. $1/150, (08-06-92, Swann, #62, illus.), 28 x 22 in., (71.1 x 55.9 cm.), .

BRODERS, R.
$607* *Ch. De Fer De L'Etat: Villers-Sur-Mer, Normandie, 1933,* excell. cond., (01-23-93, Ribeyre/Baron, #53), 39⅜ x 24⁷⁄₁₆ in., (100 x 62 cm.), poster (BP 397, DM 965, FR 3265, Y 75,970).

$399* *Maisons-Lafitte "Son Chateau, Son Musee, Son Parc Son Champ De Course" Exposition De Alfred De Dreux, 1927,* very good cond., lit., (11-19-92, Ribeyre/Baron, #87), 40⁹⁄₁₆ x 28¾ in., (103 x 73 cm.), poster (BP 263, DM 636, FR 2143, Y 49,621).

$379* *PLM. Col Du Grand Saint-Bernard. "Au Depart De Chamonix, Le Tour Du Mont-Blanc Par Les Autocars", 1927,* very good cond., (03-15-93, Arcole, #15), 41¾ x 29¹⁵⁄₁₆ in., (106 x 76 cm.), (BP 264, DM 630, FR 2140, Y 44,895).

$838* *PLM. Funiculaire De Chamonix-Planpraz. "Le Brevent Face Au Mont-Blanc", 1928,* very good cond., (03-15-93, Arcole, #22, illus.), 41¾ x 29¾ in., (106 x 75.5 cm.), (BP 583, DM 1392, FR 4732, Y 99,266).

$399* *PLM. Grenoble. "Services Automobiles De La Route Des Alpes", c. 1922,* very good cond., (03-15-93, Arcole, #8, illus.), 42½ x 31⅛ in., (108 x 79 cm.), (BP 278, DM 663, FR 2253, Y 47,264).

$519* *PLM. La Chaine Du Mont-Blanc: L'Aiguille Du Dru "Service AutomobilesD'Excursions Pour Chamonix", 1924,* very good cond., (03-15-93, Arcole, #10, illus.), 42½ x 30⅞ in., (108 x 78.5 cm.), (BP 361, DM 862, FR 2931, Y 61,478).

$1018* *PLM. La Route Des Alpes. "De La Mer A La Haute Montagne", c. 1920-25,* very good cond., (03-15-93, Arcole, #9, illus.), 42⅛ x 29¹⁵⁄₁₆ in., (107 x 76 cm.), (BP 709, DM 1691, FR 5748, Y 120,588).

$559* *PLM. Les Gorges De La Diosaz. "Gare De Servoz, Vallee De Chamonix", c. 1930,* very good cond., (03-15-93, Arcole, #23, illus.), 39⅜ x 24⁷⁄₁₆ in., (100 x 62 cm.), (BP 389, DM 929, FR 3156, Y 66,217).

$1517* *PLM. Les Sports D'Hiver A Saint-Pierre De Chartreuse, 1930,* good cond., (03-15-93, Arcole, #77, illus.), 39⅜ x 24⁷⁄₁₆ in., (100 x 62 cm.), (BP 1056, DM 2520, FR 8566, Y 179,697).

$718* *PLM. Les Sports D'Hiver Au Mont-Revard, c. 1927,* very good cond., (03-15-93, Arcole, #76, illus.), 41¹⁵⁄₁₆ x 29¹⁵⁄₁₆ in., (106.5 x 76 cm.), (BP 500, DM 1193, FR 4054, Y 85,051).

$419* *PLM. Saint-Pierre De Chartreuse. "Autocars PLM Entre Grenoble Et Chamechaude", 1930,* very good cond., (03-15-93, Arcole, #19), 39⅜ x 24⁷⁄₁₆ in., (100 x 62 cm.), (BP 292, DM 696, FR 2366, Y 49,633).

$1152* *PLM: Agay, "Plage D'Hiver Et D'Ete Sur La Cote D'Azur", 1928,* p. L. Serre, excell. cond., (01-23-93, Ribeyre/Baron, #127, illus.), 41¹⁵⁄₁₆ x 30⁵⁄₁₆ in., (106.5 x 77 cm.), poster (BP 754, DM 1832, FR 6197, Y 144,180).

$796* *PLM: Alger, La Ville Blanche. 1920,* very good cond., (03-13-93, Laurin, #35, illus.), 41¹⁵⁄₁₆ x 29¹⁵⁄₁₆ in., (106.5 x 76 cm.), (BP 555, DM 1325, FR 4505, Y 93,813).

$1573* *PLM: Grasse. Station Climatique. "La Ville Des Fleurs Et Des Parfums", 1927,* p. L. Serre, very good cond., lit., (11-19-92, Ribeyre/Baron, #88, illus.), 42⅛ x 30⅛ in., (107 x 76.5 cm.), poster (BP 1036, DM 2508, FR 8448, Y 195,622).

$944* *PLM: La Corne D'Or. Nice, Villefranche, Monaco Par la Nouvelle Corniche, c. 1930,* p. L. Serre, very good cond., lit., (11-19-92, Ribeyre/Baron, #89, illus.), 39⅜ x 24⁷⁄₁₆ in., (100 x 62 cm.), poster (BP 622, DM 1505, FR 5070, Y 117,398).

$1891* *PLM: Marseilles Porte De L'Afrique Du Nord, 1929,* very good cond., (03-13-93, Laurin, #156, illus.), 39⁹⁄₁₆ x 24⅝ in., (100.5 x 62.5 cm.), (BP 1319, DM 3147, FR 10,702, Y 222,864).

$1466* *PLM: Saint-Honore-Les-Bains, 1928,* p. Pierre Lafitte, excell. cond., (01-23-93, Ribeyre/Baron, #153, illus.),

39⅜ x 24⁷⁄₁₆ in., (100 x 62 cm.), poster (BP 959, DM 2331, FR 7886, Y 183,479).

$657* *PLM: Simplon Orient-Express. Londres-Paris-Bucarest-Athenes-Constantinople. c. 1922,* very good cond., (03-13-93, Laurin, #112), 41¾ x 29¾ in., (106 x 75.5 cm.), (BP 458, DM 1094, FR 3718, Y 77,431).

$498* *PLM: Tunis. "L'Orient Aux Portes De Marseille", 1920,* very good cond., (03-13-93, Laurin, #63, illus.), 42⅛ x 30⅛ in., (107 x 76.5 cm.), (BP 347, DM 829, FR 2818, Y 58,692).

$1571* *PLM: Vichy, Ses Sources, "Sport, Tourisme, Theatre", 1928,* p. L. Serre, excell. cond., (01-23-93, Ribeyre/Baron, #76, illus.), 39⅜ x 24⁷⁄₁₆ in., (100 x 62 cm.), poster (BP 1028, DM 2498, FR 8451, Y 196,621).

BRODERS, Roger 1883-1953

$372* *La Flambee, Tournee Ch. Baret, 1925,* (01-31-93, Morelle/Marchan, #171, illus.), 36⅝ x 60¼ in., (93 x 153 cm.), poster (BP 250, DM 599, FR 2026, Y 46,407).

$189* *Tournee Ch. Baret Andree Divonne,* cond. B, (03-16-93, Boisgirard, #59), 77¹⁵⁄₁₆ x 54⁵⁄₁₆ in., (198 x 138 cm.), poster (BP 131, DM 314, FR 1068, Y 22,100).

BRODZKY, Horace English 1885-1969

$204* *"The Bather", 1967,* s., num., illus., excellent cond., (10-31-92, Cleveland, #263, illus.), 8⅝ x 8 in., (21.9 x 20.3 cm.), linocut (BP 131, DM 314, FR 1065, Y 25,269).

BROEK, Wim ten b. 1905

$179* *Holland Amerika Lijn, 1936,* p. Joh. Enschede, margins, paper discoloration, handling creases, foxing, minor defects at edges of sheet, lit., (05-27-93, Sotheby-Amstrdm, #373), 36⅝ x 23¼ in., (930 x 590 mm.), color lithographed poster on wove (BP 115, DM 287, FR 968, Y 19,190, G 322).

$294* *KNSM, 1948,* margins, paper discoloration, handling creases, foxing, some defects at edges of sheet, lit., (05-27-93, Sotheby-Amstrdm, #377), 36⁷⁄₁₆ x 22⁷⁄₁₆ in., (925 x 570 mm.), (BP 188, DM 472, FR 1590, Y 31,518, G 529).

$333* *KNSM-Compania Real Holandesa De Vapores, 1937,* margins, paper discoloration, handling creases, minor defects, foxing at edges of sheet, (05-27-93, Sotheby-Amstrdm, #378), 37⅜ x 22¹⁄₁₆ in., (950 x 560 mm.), color lithograph poster on wove (BP 213, DM 534, FR 1801, Y 35,699, G 598).

$141* *Lloyd Brasileiro, 1948,* p. Luii & co, margins, paper discoloration, handling creases, foxing, defects at edges of sheet, lit., (05-27-93, Sotheby-Amstrdm, #370), 38³⁄₁₆ x 23⅝ in., (970 x 600 mm.), color lithographed poster on wove (BP 90, DM 226, FR 763, Y 15,116, G 253).

$205* *New York Wereldtentoonstelling, 1938,* p. Joh. Enschede, margins, paper discoloration, creasing, foxing, minor defects at edges of sheet, lit., (05-27-93, Sotheby-Amstrdm, #368), 37 x 23⁷⁄₁₆ in., (940 x 595 mm.), color lithograph poster on wove (BP 131, DM 329, FR 1109, Y 21,977, G 368).

BROMLEY, Frederick (after Sir Francis Grant) English ac. 1856-1860

$375* *Sir Richard Sutton And The Quorn, 1855,* pub. Henry Graves, prov., (02-04-93, Sloan, #1215, illus.), image area 20⅝ x 34¾ in., (52.4 x 88.3 cm.), color engraving (BP 262, DM 617, FR 2094, Y 46,648).

BRONDY, M.

$538* *PLM: Syndicat D'Initiative De Meknes: Moulay-Idriss. "La Ville Sainte Du Djebel Zehroun", 1932,* very good cond., (03-13-93, Laurin, #91), 39¾ x 24¹³⁄₁₆ in., (101 x 63 cm.), (BP 375, DM 895, FR 3045, Y 63,406).

BROOD, Herman contemporary

$224* *Jet Up - A Rock, 1988,* s., d., #71/150, full margins, good cond., (05-27-93, Sotheby-Amstrdm, #573), 27⁹⁄₁₆ x 33¹⁄₁₆ in., (700 x 840 mm.), colored silkscreen on wove (BP 143, DM 359, FR 1211, Y 24,014, G 403).

BROODTHAERS, Marcel Belgian 1924-1976

$5775* *Chere Petite Soeur (Jamar 10), 1972,* t., mono., d., num., (11-28-92, Schoppmann, #441, illus.), 24¹³⁄₁₆ x 17⁵⁄₁₆ in., (63 x 44 cm.), black offset print on weissem paper (BP 3812, DM 9200, FR 31,233, Y 718,731).

$3967* *Citron-Citroen (Jamar 18), 1974,* black China ink mono., i. E.A., d., (11-20-92, Lempertz, #472, illus.), 40⅜ x 25⅞ in., (102.5 x 65.8 cm.), color offset print w/serigraph on smooth white paper (BP 2612, DM 6325, FR 21,305, Y 493,347).

$5775* *Citron-Citroen (Redame Pour La Mer Du Nord) (Jamar 18), 1974,* i. E.A., s., d., (11-28-92, Schoppmann, #443), 41⅛ x 25¹⁵⁄₁₆ in., (104.5 x 66 cm.), color serigraph and offset on weissem paper (BP 3812, DM 9200, FR 31,233, Y 718,731).

$2300* *Citron-Citroen (Werner 21), 1974,* init., d., #81/100, pub. Seriaal, full margins, good cond., crease, light-staining, soiling, (05-15-93, Sotheby-NY, #929, illus.), sheet 41⅛ x 26 in., (104.5 x 66 cm.), offset lithograph and silkscreen in colors (BP 1495, DM 3700, FR 12,432, Y 254,961).

$5775* *Comment Va La Memoire Et LA Fontaine (Jamar 17), 1973,* i. E.A., s., d., (11-28-92, Schoppmann, #445), 25½ x 17⁵⁄₁₆ in., (64.8 x 43.9 cm.), color offset on brown paper (BP 3812, DM 9200, FR 31,233, Y 718,731).

$5775* *Ein Eisenbahnuberfall (Jamar 11),* s., d. '72, (11-28-92, Schoppmann, #446), 33¹⁄₁₆ x 22¹⁄₁₆ in., (84 x 56 cm.), offset w/handwritten inscription on Hogelanz paper (BP 3812, DM 9200, FR 31,233, Y 718,731).

$866* *Ein Eisenbahnuberfall (Jamar 11), 1972,* w/Deckweiss mono., d., (11-20-92, Lempertz, #473), 33¹⁄₁₆ x 22¹⁄₁₆ in., (84 x 56 cm.), black offset print (BP 570, DM 1381, FR 4651, Y 107,698).

BI *Ein Eisenbahnuberfall (Jamar 11), 1972,* mono., d., #61/100, est. DM 1,800-, (05-27-93, Lempertz, #633), 32⅝ x 21⁹⁄₁₆ in., (82.8 x 54.7 cm.), offset print w/hand-printed additions.

BI *La Faute D'Orthographe, Mea Culpa (Jamar 1), 1964,* #I/XX, s., i. artist's proof, num., t., est. DM 3,000-, (05-27-93, Lempertz, #632, illus.), 17¹¹⁄₁₆ x 23¹³⁄₁₆ in., (45 x 60.5 cm.), offset print on factory-made paper.

BI *Le Manuscrit Trouve Dans Une Bouteille, 1974,* inits., #115/120, good cond., overall size 12 x 3 x 3 in., est. $3,5/4,500, (11-09-92, Christie-NY, #251, illus.), glass bottle w/stamped title.

$3609* *Musee-Museum (Jamar 12), 1972,* mono., d., num., (11-28-92, Schoppmann, #440), 19⅞ x 29½ in., (50.5 x 75 cm.), offset print on light cardboard w/3 colors on board (BP 2382, DM 5750, FR 19,519, Y 449,160).

$2300* *La Soupe De Daguerre (W. 26), 1975,* s. label verso, d., t., #59/60, pub. Multiples, Inc., good cond., colors in photographs slightly faded, soiling, (05-15-93, Sotheby-NY, #930, illus.), sheet 20¾ x 20¼ in., (52.7 x 51.4 cm.), twelve glossy color photographic prints, mounted on board, w/silkscren, in blue and black (BP 1495, DM 3700, FR 12,432, Y 254,961).

BI *La Souris Ecrit Rat, A Compte D'Auteur (Jamar 20), 1974,* red pen mono., d., i., #66/150, est. DM 3,500-, (05-27-93, Lempertz, #634, illus.), 30¹⁄₁₆ x 22⁷⁄₁₆ in., (76.4 x 57 cm.), lithograph on wove.

BROOKING, Charles (after) British 1723-1759

$121* *"A View Of The Prince Frederick...Engaging The Gloriosa...", 1753,* ident. in inscrip. w/in matrix, good cond.?, foxing, (03-19-93, Skinner, #210), sight, sheet 13½ x 18½ in., (34.3 x 47 cm.), hand-colored engraving (BP 81, DM 198, FR 673, Y 14,035).

BROOKS, Charlotte

BI *Bath Fair, Pitchman With Friend's Baby, New York, 1945,* stamp, label, credit, t., d., est. $7/900, (10-13-92, Christie-NY, #154, illus.), 7¾ x 7⅜ in., (19.7 x 18.7 cm.), photograph, gelatin silver print.

BI *Duke Ellington On Tour, 1956,* credit stamp, t., d., annot., est. $1/1,500, (04-08-93, Christie-NY, #408, illus.), 9 x 13⅛ in., (22.9 x 33.3 cm.), photograph, gelatin silver print.

BI *Lady Slipper, c. 1940,* handstamp, notations, est. $5/750, (10-14-92, Swann, #392, illus.), 12¾ x 9 in., (26.7 x 34.3 cm.), photograph, silver print.

BI *Machinery In Cold Cream Factory, 1946,* handstamp, label, notations, est. $5/700, (10-14-92, Swann, #393, illus.), 10½ x 13½ in., (26.7 x 34.3 cm.), photograph, silver print.

$550* *Mt. Vernon, Ohio-Saturday Night, 1948,* t., d., stamp, (10-13-92, Christie-NY, #155, illus.), 10¼ x 12½ in., (26 x 31.8 cm.), photograph, gelatin silver print (BP 320, DM 806, FR 2738, Y 66,691).

BI *Students Reciting Morning Prayer, 1946,* photog.'s "Standard Oil" handstamp, notations, label, est. $700/1,000, (04-07-93, Swann, #417, illus.), 10¾ x 10½ in., photograph, silver print.

BI *"Truant Girl With Family", 1968,* backed w/card, photog. studio stamp, t., d., i. in unident. hand, est. $1/2,000, (04-06-93, Sotheby-NY, #458, illus.), 12⅞ x 14¼ in., photograph.

BI *Young Black Woman And Boy, 1947,* photog.'s handstamp, notations, est. $6/900, (04-07-93, Swann, #418, illus.), 13½ x 9¾ in., photograph, silver print.

BROOKS, Frank Leonard
$103* *Father And Son (Hillside Trees),* s., t., (06-07-93, Ritchie, #27, illus.), 5⅞ x 4⁵⁄₁₆ in., (14.9 x 11 cm.), etching (BP 68, DM 167, FR 563, Y 11,049, C$ 132).

BROOKS, Mildred Bryant   American b. 1901
$165* *"Benediction",* s. Mildred Bryant Brooks, prov., (11-10-92, Moran, #155), sight 8¼ x 8½ in., (21 x 21.6 cm.), etching on paper (BP 109, DM 265, FR 894, Y 20,538).

BROOKS BANK NOTE COMPANY, Publisher American 19th cent.
BI *"Engine Of The Red Jacket Veteran Firemen's Association, Cambridge, Mass. Champion Of The New England League 1894...",* ident. w/in matrix, good cond.?, est. $800/1,200, (03-27-93, Skinner, #215A, illus.), sight, sheet 22 x 27½ in., (55.9 x 69.9 cm.), color lithograph w/additional hand-coloring on paper.

BROOKSHAW, G. (after)
$330* *Fruits: Group Of Six,* (03-24-93, Doyle, #12), 10½ x 6½ in., (26.7 x 16.5 cm.), color print (BP 223, DM 539, FR 1834, Y 38,773).

BROOKSHAW, G. and POITEAU (after)
$385* *Fruit: Group Of Six,* (03-24-93, Doyle, #11), 13 x 9½ in., (33 x 24.1 cm.), color print (BP 261, DM 629, FR 2140, Y 45,236).

BROSAMER, Hans   c. 1500-1554
$992* *Auf Einer Bank Sitzender Weiblicher Akt (Hollstein 32),* (06-08-93, Karl/Faber, #26), engraving (BP 652, DM 1610, FR 5421, Y 105,364).

$794* *Christus Am Kreuz Zwischen Maria Und Johannes (B. 5; Hollstein 8), 1545,* prov., (12-04-92, Bassenge, #6071), 3¹⁄₁₆ x 2⁵⁄₁₆ in., (7.7 x 5.9 cm.), engraving (BP 509, DM 1265, FR 4290, Y 99,126).

$165* *Laocoon, Troia,* inits., d. 1538, t. in plate, (10-30-92, Sloan, #2801), 3⅞ x 2¾ in., (9.8 x 7 cm.), engraving (BP 106, DM 254, FR 861, Y 20,438).

BROUET, Auguste   French 1872-1941
BI *Bellecourt,* s., #9/100, blindstamp, trimmed margins, good cond., tape, light-staining, skinned areas, creases, est. $2/300, (10-28-92, Butterfield, #2787), 8⅜ x 10⅞ in., (213 x 276 mm.), etching on cream wove paper, w/remarque.

$83* *Children At Play,* s., #28/50, Circle Librarie Estampes blindstamp, (05-28-93, Sloan, #223, illus.), 6⅜ x 7½ in., (16.2 x 19.1 cm.), etching (BP 53, DM 132, FR 445, Y 8900).

$193* *"Children At Play" and "Cirque Ambulant": Two,* each s., num., (10-30-92, Sloan, #431), larger 8⁹⁄₁₆ x 10⁹⁄₁₆ in., (21.7 x 26.8 cm.), etchings (BP 124, DM 297, FR 1007, Y 23,907).

$69* *Les Ciseleurs,* #17/100, s., margins, (05-20-93, Bonhams-Chelsea, #78), plate 5½ x 6¾ in., (14 x 17.1 cm.), etching on laid (BP 44, DM 111, FR 375, Y 7619).

$67* *"A Continental Market",* num. 44/75, s., margins, (01-21-93, Bonhams-Chelsea, #127), plate 7⅝ x 5⅞ in., (19.4 x 14.9 cm.), etching (BP 44, DM 107, FR 360, Y 8385).

$67* *The Cook,* num. 15/60, s., margins, (01-21-93, Bonhams-Chelsea, #129), plate 5½ x 6⅝ in., (14 x 16.8 cm.), etching on laid paper (BP 44, DM 107, FR 360, Y 8385).

$110* *"A Country Nook At Audemps" (Geffroy 30),* s., num. 13, good cond., (10-31-92, Cleveland, #264), 6½ x 7¾ in., (16.5 x 19.7 cm.), etching (BP 70, DM 169, FR 574, Y 13,626).

$98* *Deux Danseures,* #12/100, s., margins, foxed, (09-17-92, Bonhams-Chelsea, #83), plate 6¾ x 8 in., (17.1 x 20.3 cm.), etching (BP 55, DM 145, FR 498, Y 12,201).

$78* *Houses In Ruins At Audemps,* #44/50, s., margins, foxing, (05-20-93, Bonhams-Chelsea, #76), plate 10¼ x 13½ in., (26 x 34.3 cm.), etching (BP 50, DM 126, FR 424, Y 8613).

BI *Large Saint-Ouen" (G. 99),* s., num. 12/60, toned, est. $1/150, (10-31-92, Cleveland, #265), 8¼ x 12¼ in., (21 x 31.1 cm.), etching.

$144* *"Man With Basket Of Flowers On His Back", "Family Leaving", "Woman"and "Two Men Wrestling": Four,* s., #67/100, Ep d'Artiste de Presentation, Ep d'essai, 19/50, margins, good cond., hinge remains, mat/light-staining, surface soiling, foxing, (05-19-93, Butterfield, #2039), etching (the last w/aquatint) on various (BP 93, DM 234, FR 789, Y 15,942).

$60* *"Market Traders And Children Under An Archway",* s., margins, (01-21-93, Bonhams-Chelsea, #128), plate 9 x 6¼ in., (22.9 x 15.9 cm.), etching on laid paper (BP 39, DM 95, FR 323, Y 7509).

BI *"The Mattress Makers" (G. 102),* s., seal Lught 882, toned, est. $1-150, (10-31-92, Cleveland, #266), 5 x 8½ in., (12.7 x 21.6 cm.), etching.

$88* *"The Mechanical Transport Park" (G. 151),* s., num. 71/75, toning, matt remains, (10-31-92, Cleveland, #267), 5 x 9 in., (12.7 x 22.9 cm.), etching (BP 56, DM 135, FR 459, Y 10,901).

$88* *"The Odds And Ends Dealer" (G. 265),* s., num. 38/50, stamp seal Lught 882, light struck, good cond., (10-31-92, Cleveland, #268), 5 x 7¼ in., (12.7 x 18.4 cm.), etching (BP 56, DM 135, FR 459, Y 10,901).

$110* *Portrait Of Rembrandt,* s., #206, (12-02-92, Boos, #520), image 23¹³⁄₁₆ x 18½ in., (605 x 470 mm.), color etching and aquatint (BP 71, DM 173, FR 590, Y 13,687).

BI *A Tradesman Selling His Wares,* s., margins, est. BP 3/40, (03-17-93, Bonhams-Chelsea, #331), plate 4⅞ x 5⅞ in., (12.4 x 14.9 cm.), etching on laid paper.

BI *A Tradesman Selling His Wares,* s., margins, (05-20-93, Bonhams-Chelsea, #119), plate 4⅞ x 5⅞ in., (12.4 x 14.9 cm.), etching on laid.

BI *"A Tradesman Selling His Wares",* s., margins, est. BP30/50, (01-21-93, Bonhams-Chelsea, #126), plate 4⅞ x 5⅞ in., (12.4 x 14.9 cm.), etching on laid paper.

$66* *Untitled (Street Scene),* s., num., good cond., (10-31-92, Cleveland, #269), 7¼ x 4½ in., (18.4 x 11.4 cm.), etching (BP 42, DM 102, FR 344, Y 8175).

BROWN, Bolton   American 1865-1936
BI *"The Forest Yard", c. 1930,* s., good cond., est. $1/150, (10-31-92, Cleveland, #85), 8⅝ x 12 in., (21.9 x 30.5 cm.), lithograph.

BROWN, Christopher
BI *Hats, 1982,* s., d., annot. A.P. 8/20, blindstamp publisher, Magnolia Editions, full margins, good cond., soiling, traces of stray printing ink, est. $9/1,200, (05-19-93, Butterfield, #2132), sh 29½ x 29½ in., (749 x 749 mm.), lithograph in colors on wove.

BROWN, Daniel Price
$326* *Ganders,* s., d. 1982, #7/90, (05-18-93, Joyner, #237), serigraph in colors (BP 212, DM 529, FR 1786, Y 36,331, C$ 413).

$385* *Janna And Doll,* s., t., d. 1980, #48/70, (11-30-92, Ritchie, #54), 18⅜ x 15 in., (46.7 x 38.1 cm.), color serigraph (BP 254, DM 613, FR 2082, Y 47,915, C$ 495).

$326* *Young Dancers,* s., d. 1982, #7/90, (05-18-93, Joyner, #236), 23 x 22 in., (58.4 x 55.9 cm.), serigraph in colors (BP 212, DM 529, FR 1786, Y 36,331, C$ 413).

BROWN, H.K.
$288* *Caricatures: Six, 1880,* (02-18-93, Sotheby-Arcade, #62), sight 6 x 10 in., (15.2 x 25.4 cm.), chromolithograph (BP 199, DM 470, FR 1590, Y 34,310).

BROWN, James   American b. 1951
$794* *The Anchor Board III,* t., s., num., (11-28-92, Schoppmann, #453), 19⅛ x 21⁷⁄₁₆ in., (48.5 x 54.5 cm.), lithograph on thick light grey handmade (BP 524, DM 1265, FR 4294, Y 98,818).

$794* *The Anchor Board IV,* num., (11-28-92, Schoppmann, #454), 21⅝ x 18⅞ in., (55 x 48 cm.), lithograph on thick light grey handmade (BP 524, DM 1265, FR 4294, Y 98,818).

$794* *The Anchor Board V,* t., s., num., (11-28-92, Schoppmann, #455), 21⅝ x 18⅞ in., (55 x 48 cm.), lithograph on thick light grey handmade (BP 524, DM 1265, FR 4294, Y 98,818).

$377* *Self Portrait XX, 1988,* s., d. #7/35, (11-16-92, Briest, #262), 23⅝ x 17¹¹⁄₁₆ in., (60 x 45 cm.), lithograph in 2 colors (BP 248, DM 601, FR 2026, Y 47,049).

$7219* *Strassenszene (Otten 671), 1967,* s., d., prov., (11-28-92, Schoppmann, #457, illus.), 36¼ x 49⁵⁄₁₆ in., (92 x 125 cm.), offset sheet on linen laid down, painted (BP 4765, DM 11,501, FR 39,043, Y 898,444).

BROWN, James Hamilton

BI *Selected Images: Four,* 1950s, 2nd w/credit, t. on label, stamp, (10-13-92, Christie-NY, #156, illus.), 14 x 11 in., (35.6 x 27.9 cm.), 9½ x 7½ in., (35.6 x 27.9 cm.), photograph, gleatin silver prints.

BI *Untitled (Woman With Spirals) 1940-46,* est. $2/2,500, (10-13-92, Christie-NY, #157, illus.), 19 x 15¼ in., (48.3 x 38.7 cm.), photograph, gelatin silver print.

BROWN, Jane

BI *Portrait Of Magaret Drabble And Anne Stephenson At A Literary Gathering, 1985,* t., labels, 457 x 346mm, est. BP 1/200, (05-07-93, Sotheby-London, #201), photograph, silver print.

BROWN, John (after)

$3432* *Three Roman Ladies,* by Ignace Joseph de Claussin, printing w/tone, inky plate edges, margins, repaired tear, paper thin, defects, (06-30-93, Sotheby-London, #277, illus.), 11½ x 9¼ in., (292 x 235 mm.), etching on wove (BP 2300, DM 5854, FR 19,747, Y 367,727).

BROWN, Paul American 1893-1958

$523* *Sporting Scenes: Four,* each s., #7/100, d. (19)27, t. in stone, (10-30-92, Sloan, #899), each 14 x 18½ in., (35.6 x 47 cm.), color lithographs (BP 335, DM 805, FR 2730, Y 64,784).

BROWN, Robbie

$248* *Interior,* s., num. Ed. 30, margins, good cond.?, surface soiling, creases, (10-28-92, Butterfield, #2911), 23 x 34 in., (584 x 864 mm.), color silkscreen on wove (BP 158, DM 383, FR 1300, Y 30,429).

BROWN, Roger American b. 1941

$523* *The Jim And Tammy Show,* s., d. 87, #50/50, (12-13-92, Hindman, #350), 21¾ x 32¼ in., color lithograph (BP 334, DM 822, FR 2801, Y 64,704).

BROWNE, Malcolm

$935* *"Thich Quang Duc Setting Himself On Fire" and "Thich Quang Duc On Fire", 1963: Two,* (04-07-93, Swann, #293, illus.), 14 x 11 in., photograph, silver print (BP 618, DM 1512, FR 5118, Y 106,226).

BROWNE, Syd

BI *"Dooley St., Sheepshead Bay" and "The Palisades": Two,* s., t., num., very good cond., est. $6/800, (06-11-93, Doyle, #22), 9 x 6¾ in., (229 x 171 mm.), etching.

BROWNING, Irving

$1542* *"Edward Steichen, America's Foremost Photographer", c. 1935-36: Film,* 16mm, 13 mins. long, t., series t. and credit, label, (05-06-93, Christie-London, #180), b/w silent film (BP 977, DM 2429, FR 8176, Y 169,656).

BRUCKNER, M. (after)

BI *"Koln And Rhein",* marked Schoues Deutschland and Werck meisiers Kunstuerlas, est. $30/5, (03-12-93, DuMouchelle, #2465), sight 9¼ x 12½ in., (23.5 x 31.8 cm.), color print.

BRUEGHEL, Peter (after)

$412* *Antique Town (Bastelaer 3), c. 1554,* thread margins, from Large Landscapes series, pub. Hieronymous Cock and Family, minor flaws, closed tears, restoration, (05-27-93, Swann, #43), 12 x 17 in., (30.5 x 43.2 cm.), engraving on laid paper (BP 264, DM 661, FR 2228, Y 44,168).

BRUEGHEL, Pieter (the elder) Flemish c. 1525-1569

$6728* *S. Hieronymous In Deserto, Grosse Landschaft Mit Dem Hl. Hieronymous(Bastelaer 7, Hollstein 4),* (06-04-93, Bassenge, #5054, illus.), 12¹¹⁄₁₆ x 16⅝ in., (32.2 x 42.2 cm.), etching (BP 4451, DM 10,926, FR 36,825, Y 725,626).

BI *Solicitudo Rustica (Bastelaer 12, Hollstein 9 I),* watermark, est. DM 12,000, (06-04-93, Bassenge, #5055, illus.), 12¾ x 16¹³⁄₁₆ in., (32.4 x 42.7 cm.), etching w/ engraving.

BRUEGHEL, Pieter (the elder) (after)

BI *The Death Of The Virgin (Bast., Holl. 116; Lari 111; Holl., Galle, 155; Ill. B., vol. 56, p. 212, no. .060), 1574,* by Philip Galle, Bastelaer's only state, Lari's 1st state of 2, small margins, hairline, stained, laid, est. BP 3,5/4,500, (12-01-92, Christie-London, #4, illus.), 12¼ x 16⁷⁄₁₆ in., (311 x 417 mm.), engraving.

BI *Euntes In Emaus (Holl. 14), c. 1554,* by Hieronymus Cock, from The Set of Large Landscapes, trimmed on three sides, center crease partly split, creases, backed, est. $1,8/2,400, (05-13-93, Sotheby-NY, #112), 16½ x 11⅞ in., (420 x 303 mm.), engraving w/extensive hand-coloring.

$3330* *Euntes In Emmaus, (Bast. 14; Holl. 11; Lari 13), c. 1553,* from the Set of the Large Landscapes, watermark, trimmed, made-up area, discoloration, good cond., (12-01-92, Christie-London, #66, illus.), S. 11⅝ x 16⁷⁄₁₆ in., (295 x 418 mm.), engraving (BP 2200, DM 5308, FR 18,088, Y 414,592).

$11,804* *The Fair On St. George's Day (Bast., Holl. 207; L. 52),* 1st state of 2, trimmed, repairs, repaired fold, creases, defects, surface dirt, discoloration, (06-29-93, Sotheby-London, #15, illus.), 13 x 20½ in., (33 x 52.1 cm.), engraving (BP 7820, DM 19,932, FR 67,183, Y 1,256,547).

$6326* *The Fall Of The Magician Hermogenes, (Bast., Holl. 118; Lari 113), 1565,* third (final) state, watermark, small to thread margins, trimmed, fold, crease, foxmarks, (12-01-92, Christie-London, #71, illus.), P. 8⅞ x 11⅜ in., (225 x 289 mm.), engraving (BP 4180, DM 10,083, FR 34,362, Y 787,600).

$2997* *Fuga Deiparae In Aegyptum, (Bast. 15; Holl. 12; Lari 14), c. 1553,* from the Set of the Large Landscapes, watermark, margins, fold partlysplit and supported, tips repaired, nicks, tears, defects, (12-01-92, Christie-London, #67, illus.), P. 12⁵⁄₁₆ x 16⁹⁄₁₆ in., (313 x 421 mm.), engraving (BP 1980, DM 4777, FR 16,279, Y 373,132).

$10,831* *Kriegsschiff In Dreiviertel-Ansicht (Bastelaer, Hollstein 100 I), 1565,* from series Kriegsschiffe, rare, (12-04-92, Bassenge, #6072, illus.), 12⅛ x 9⅝ in., (30.8 x 24.4 cm.), etching (BP 6947, DM 17,250, FR 58,514, Y 1,352,185).

$6374* *Kriegsschiff Nach Rechts Segelnd (Bastelaer, Hollstein 101 I), 1565,* by F. Huys, from series Kriegsschiffe, trimmed, watermark, (06-04-93, Bassenge, #5056, illus.), 8¹¹⁄₁₆ x 11⁹⁄₁₆ in., (22 x 29.3 cm.), etching (BP 4217, DM 10,351, FR 34,888, Y 687,446).

$938* *Luxuria (Bast., Holl. 131; L. 24),* by Pieter van der Heyden, from set of the Seven Vices, trimmed on/within platemark, paper losses, minor defects, stains, discoloration, laid down tobacking sheet, (12-03-92, Sotheby-London, #17), 8⅞ x 11⅝ in., (225 x 295 mm.), engraving (BP 605, DM 1475, FR 5035, Y 116,710).

$2997* *Magdelena Poenitens, (Bast. 8; Holl. 5; Lari 7), c. 1553,* from the Set of the Large Landscapes, second (final) state, small tonarrow margins, trimmed, crease, nick, discoloration, prov., (12-01-92, Christie-London, #64, illus.), P. 12¾ x 16⅞ in., (324 x 428 mm.), engraving (BP 1980, DM 4777, FR 16,279, Y 373,132).

BI *A Man Of War Between Two Armed Galleys (Bast., Holl. 107; Lebeer 50),* by Frans Huys, 1st state of 2, trimmed, stain, foxing, discoloration,old tape, good cond., est. BP 2,5/3,500, (06-30-93, Sotheby-London, #94, illus.), 8¾ x 11⅜ in., (222 x 289 mm.), engraving on paper w/Shell watermark.

$2046* *Man Of War, Sailing To The Right, With The Fall Of Icarus (Bastelaer,Hollstein 101, Lebeer 44),* by Theodorus Galle, first state of two, narrow margins, pinholes, rustmark, small damages, (12-03-92, Sotheby-London, #16), 8¾ x 11½ in., (222 x 292 mm.), engraving (BP 1320, DM 3217, FR 10,982, Y 254,573).

$3996* *Nemo Non. Everyman Looks For His Own Profit, (Bast., Holl. 152; Lari140), c. 1560,* first state (of two), nick, staining, (12-01-92, Christie-London, #74, illus.), S. 8¹³⁄₁₆ x 11⅝ in., (224 x 296 mm.), engraving (BP 2640, DM 6369, FR 21,706, Y 497,510).

BI *Nundinae Rusticorum, (Bast. 13, Holl. 10; Lari 12), c. 1553,* from the Set of the Large Landscapes, first state (of two), watermark, narrow margins or trimmed, trimmed, fold, repaired tears, defects, est. BP 2,0/3,000, (12-01-92, Christie-London, #65, illus.), S. 12⅛ x 16¾ in., (308 x 425 mm.), engraving.

$1082* *The Parable Of The Good Shepherd, (Bast., Holl. 122; Lari 117), 1565,* fourth (final) state, watermark, trimmed, repaired spot, touched-in surface loss, very good cond., prov., (12-01-92, Christie-London, #69), S. 8¾ x 11⁵⁄₁₆ in., (222 x 287 mm.), engraving (BP 715, DM 1725, FR 5877, Y 134,711).

$1249* *The Parable Of The Wise And Foolish Virgins, (Bast., Holl. 123; Lari118), c. 1565,* trimmed, corners repaired, good cond., (12-01-92, Christie-London, #75), S. 8¹¹⁄₁₆ x 11⁹⁄₁₆ in., (221 x 293 mm.), engraving (BP 825, DM 1991, FR 6784, Y 155,503).

$18,227* *The Resurrection (Bast., Holl. 114; L. 84),* attrib. to Philip Galle, 2nd state of 4, w/address of Cock, watermark, trimmed, paper loss, damages, repaired tears, surface dirt, pinholes, (06-29-93, Sotheby-London, #13, illus.), 17⅛ x 12 in., (43.5 x 30.5 cm.), engraving (BP 12,075, DM 30,778, FR 103,739, Y 1,940,281).

$99,891* *The Resurrection (Bast., Holl. 114; Lari 109; Holl., Galle, 106; Ill. B., vol. 56, p. 138, no. .044), c. 1560,* by Philip Galle, Lari's 1st state of 3, thread margins, trimmed on platemark, tear, wormholes, surface glue, nick, staining, very good cond., laid, (12-01-92, Christie-London, #3, illus.), 18³⁄₁₆ x 12¹⁵⁄₁₆ in., (462 x 330 mm.), engraving (BP 66,000, DM 159,214, FR 542,591, Y 12,436,628).

$6326* *Saint Jacob Visiting The Magician Hermogenes, (Bast., Holl. 117; Lari 112), 1565,* first or second (final) state, watermark, trimmed, repaired tears, thin spots, defects, (12-01-92, Christie-London, #70, illus.), S. 8⁹⁄₁₆ x 11⁷⁄₁₆ in., (218 x 290 mm.), engraving (BP 4180, DM 10,083, FR 34,362, Y 787,600).

BI *Saint James Visiting The Magician Hermogenes (Bast., Holl. 117, L. 112), 1565,* Hollstein's 1st state of 2, d. 1565, trimmed on platemark, creases, made-up loss, defects, est. $4/6,000, (05-11-93, Christie-NY, #5), pl 8¾ x 11½ in., (222 x 292 mm.), engraving on laid.

$14,151* *The Set Of The Seven Vices, (Bast., Holl. 125-31; Lari 120-6), 1558:Set Of Seven,* watermark, small to thread margins or trimmed, repaired tear, repairs and defects, prov., (12-01-92, Christie-London, #72, illus.), P. 8⅞ x 11⁹⁄₁₆ in., (225 x 294 mm.), engraving (BP 9350, DM 22,555, FR 76,866, Y 1,761,828).

BI *Seven Virtues, (Bast., Holl. 132-8; Lari 127-33), 1559: Set Of Seven,* watermark, small margins, trimmed, repaired, defects, good cond., prov., est. BP 6/7000, (12-01-92, Christie-London, #73, illus.), P. 8¹⁵⁄₁₆ x 11⅝ in., (228 x 295 mm.), engraving.

$5208* *Solicitudo Rustico (Bastelaer 12; Hollstein 9; Lebeer 7),* from The Set of the Large Landscapes, 1st state of 2, watermark, narrow margins, nick, paper, broken through, crease, surface dirt, coll.'s mark, (06-29-93, Sotheby-London, #12, illus.), 12¾ x 16¾ in., (32.4 x 42.5 cm.), engraving (BP 3450, DM 8794, FR 29,641, Y 554,396).

$9989* *Three Men In A Tempest, Sailing To The Right, (Bast., Holl. 105; Lari 102), 1565,* by F. Huys, Lari's third (final) state, watermark, small margins, tear, thin patches, nicks, defects, prov., (12-01-92, Christie-London, #68, illus.), P. 8⅝ x 11¼ in., (219 x 285 mm.), engraving (BP 6600, DM 15,921, FR 54,259, Y 1,243,650).

BRUEGHEL, Pieter (the younger) Flemish c. 1564-1637/38

$1098* *Plaustrum Belgicum (Wibiral 11; Hollstein 11),* after Brueghel from Grossen Landschaften, (12-12-92, Bassenge, #8033), 11⅞ x 16¹⁵⁄₁₆ in., (30.2 x 43 cm.), etching (BP 702, DM 1726, FR 5881, Y 135,841).

BRUEHL, Anton American 1900-1983

BI *Textile Study, c. 1930,* stamp, est. $1,2/1,500, (10-13-92, Christie-NY, #158, illus.), 9⅝ x 7⅞ in., (24.4 x 20 cm.), photograph, toned gelatin silver print.

BRUEHL, Anton and Martin

BI *Silverware Study,* 1930s, credit stamp, est. $1/1,500, (04-08-93, Christie-NY, #261, illus.), 9¾ x 7⅝ in., (24.8 x 19.4 cm.), photograph, gelatin silver print.

BRUEHL, Martin b.c. 1900

$302* *Advertisement For Caswell, Massey Cologne Water, c. 1930,* handstamp, (10-14-92, Swann, #394, illus.), 10 x 8½ in., (25.4 x 21.6 cm.), photograph, silver print (BP 177, DM 442, FR 1499, Y 36,597).

$990* *Egg Souffle,* 1930s, credit stamp, (10-13-92, Christie-NY, #159, illus.), 7⅝ x 9¾ in., (19.4 x 24.8 cm.), photograph, gelatin silver print (BP 577, DM 1450, FR 4928, Y 120,044).

$357* *Madonna,* sig., 1930's, (10-14-92, Swann, #395, illus.), 12 x 9¾ in., (30.5 x 24.8 cm.), photograph, dye transfer print (BP 210, DM 522, FR 1772, Y 43,262).

$374* *Portrait Of Henry Bowser, 1929,* attrib., annot., photog.'s stamp, (05-23-93, Butterfield, #3352, illus.), 10 x 8 in., photograph, gelatin silver print (BP 244, DM 612, FR 2058, Y 41,340).

BRUKOFF, Barry

$633* *"Hydra Nite #3, State I" and "PDC II, State I", 1988: Two,* both t., first s., d., (05-23-93, Butterfield, #3353, illus.), one 6½ x 9½ in., other 9½ x 7¾ in., photograph, bronze-toned gelatin silver print (BP 412, DM 1035, FR 3484, Y 69,968).

BRUN, Charles le (after)

$43* *Les Noces De Tobie,* by B. Picart, margins, (08-20-92, Bonhams-Chelsea, #156), 8½ x 11 in., (21.6 x 27.9 cm.), etching (BP 22, DM 62, FR 211, Y 5430).

$83* *La Vraye Est Toujours Invincible (Battle Scene),* by I. Audran, margins, (06-16-93, Bonhams-Chelsea, #398), pl. 11¾ x 24 in., (29.8 x 61 cm.), engraving (BP 55, DM 138, FR 462, Y 8852).

BRUNEAU, Kittie Canadian b. 1929

$47* *"Adam Et Eve",* #17/50, s., d. K. Bruneau 80, (07-14-92, Encans, #94), 5⅞ x 9¹⁄₁₆ in., (15 x 23 cm.), etching (BP 24, DM 70, FR 235, Y 5877, C$ 56).

BI *"Le Quadrillage Des Mers Est Un Travail Large Et Ardu",* #3/10, t., s., d. Bruneau 75, (03-16-93, Encans, #28), 26⁹⁄₁₆ x 18¹¹⁄₁₆ in., (67.5 x 47.5 cm.), lithograph.

$159* *"Le Quadrillage Des Mers Est Un Travail Large Et Ardu",* #3/10, t., s., d. Bruneau 75, (04-20-93, Encans, #20), 26⁹⁄₁₆ x 18¹¹⁄₁₆ in., (67.5 x 47.5 cm.), lithograph (BP 103, DM 253, FR 855, Y 17,544, C$ 200).

BRUNELLESCHI, Umberto Italian b. 1879; ac. 1907-1930

$110* *An Elegant Lady,* s., (12-13-92, Hindman, #264), 21½ x 17 in., etching w/stencil coloring (BP 70, DM 173, FR 589, Y 13,609).

$660* *Lady With Harlequin,* s. in plate; s., i. 382, prov., (09-17-92, Sloan, #2601), 15⅝ x 20 in., (39.7 x 50.8 cm.), pochoir stencil (BP 371, DM 980, FR 3354, Y 82,171).

BI *Matador,* H. Chacoin, B cond., chip, creasing, folding, est. $4/600, (08-06-92, Swann, #63, illus.), 47 x 31 in., (119.4 x 78.7 cm.), .

BRUNET-DEBAINES, Alfred Louis

$22* *Landscape With Woman And Cattle,* (12-11-92, DuMouchelle, #279), 14 x 21½ in., (35.6 x 54.6 cm.), etching (BP 14, DM 35, FR 119, Y 2722).

BRUNI, Bruno b. 1935

$379* *Malinconia. Con La Mano Al Cuore, Col Cuore In Mano (Huber 309),* #75/250, s., t., (06-24-93, Germann, #256), 38⁹⁄₁₆ x 27¹⁵⁄₁₆ in., (980 x 710 mm.), color lithograph (BP 249, DM 614, FR 2071, Y 40,657, SF 552).

$332* *Per Cuneo "Una Valigia Di Ricordi" (Huber 229), 1980,* E.A., s., t., d., (06-24-93, Germann, #257), 29⁵⁄₁₆ x 21⁷⁄₁₆ in., (745 x 545 mm.), color lithograph (BP 219, DM 538, FR 1814, Y 35,615, SF 483).

$179* *Sich An Der Stange Dehnende Ballettanzerin In Rosafarbenem Rock, UndEin Schwan,* s., num., (09-25-92, Granier, #2781), 21⁵⁄₁₆ x 17¹⁄₁₆ in., (54.2 x 43.4 cm.), lithograph on brownish wove (BP 105, DM 265, FR 897, Y 21,605).

$179* *Die Venus V. Botticelli Mit Rose,* s., num., (09-25-92, Granier, #2782), 21⁵⁄₁₆ x 17⅟₁₆ in., (54.2 x 43.4 cm.), color lithograph on wove (BP 105, DM 265, FR 897, Y 21,605).

BRUNING, Max 1887-1968

$504* *Blick Auf Die Halbinsel Wasserburg Mit Verschneitem Gebirgshorizont,* s., (11-27-92, Zeller, #597), 11¹³⁄₁₆ x 13¾ in., (30 x 35 cm.), color etching (BP 332, DM 805, FR 2735, Y 62,726).

$504* *"Darling". Madchenportrait Im Profil Von Rechts, c. 1920,* s., (11-27-92, Zeller, #596), 12¹⁵⁄₁₆ x 10⅝ in., (33 x 27 cm.), color etching (BP 332, DM 805, FR 2735, Y 62,726).

$232* *Frauen: Two,* s. Max Bruning, (09-30-92, Kunsthallen, #54), etching (BP 131, DM 329, FR 1113, Y 27,841, DK 1265).

$468* *"Nach Dem Ball". Kokette Junge Frau, c. 1925,* s., (11-27-92, Zeller, #594), 18⅛ x 12⅝ in., (46 x 32 cm.), color etching (BP 308, DM 748, FR 2539, Y 58,245).

$504* *Reizvoll Entblosstes Madchen Mit Peitsche, c. 1922,* s., (11-27-92, Zeller, #595), 13⅜ x 5⅞ in., (34 x 15 cm.), color etching (BP 332, DM 805, FR 2735, Y 62,726).

$432* *Reizvoller Madchenakt, c. 1922,* s., (11-27-92, Zeller, #593), 15¾ x 8⅟₁₆ in., (40 x 20.5 cm.), color etching (BP 285, DM 690, FR 2344, Y 53,765).

$220* *Torso Of A Nude Woman,* s., c. 1945, (05-14-93, DuMouchelle, #2370), 16½ x 10 in., (41.9 x 25.4 cm.), etching (BP 143, DM 354, FR 1189, Y 24,388).

BI *Torso Of A Nude Woman,* s., est. $150/250, (12-11-92, DuMouchelle, #2283), 16½ x 11 in., (41.9 x 27.9 cm.), etching.

BRUNING, Peter 1929-1970

BI *Anonyme Kolner Schule Des 20, Jahnrhunderts (M.-L. Otten), 1969,* pencil t., s., d., est. DM 700, (11-20-92, Lempertz, #477), sh 35⅛ x 25¼ in., (89.2 x 64.2 cm.), color serigraph on offset cardboard.

BRUNO, Mark Paul American 20th cent.

$33* *Cemetery,* s., (05-16-93, Hindman, #379), 7 x 9 in., photograph, silver print (BP 22, DM 53, FR 179, Y 3675).

BRUS, Gunter b. 1938

$1299* *Die Botschaft: Six,* ed. Hundertmark 1983, portfolio, s., num., (11-28-92, Schoppmann, #463), 40 x 32 in., (101.6 x 81.3 cm.), etching (BP 857, DM 2069, FR 7025, Y 161,668).

BRUSSE, Mark b. 1937

BI *Mountain Fish, 1988: Two,* s., #19/70 and 47/80, est. FF 2,5/3,000, (11-16-92, Briest, #18), each 29¹⁵⁄₁₆ x 21¼ in., (76 x 54 cm.), lithograph.

$64* *Untitled, 1973,* s., d., i. E.A., margins, good cond., (05-27-93, Sotheby-Amstrdm, #390), 25¹¹⁄₁₆ x 17⅝ in., colored lithograph on wove (BP 41, DM 103, FR 346, Y 6861, G 115).

$179* *Untitled, 1973,* s., d., i. E.A., margins, good cond., (05-27-93, Sotheby-Amstrdm, #391), 17⅞ x 25½ in., (454 x 648 mm.), colored lithograph on wove (BP 115, DM 287, FR 968, Y 19,190, G 322).

$160* *Untitled, 1973,* s., d., #11/190, good cond., (05-27-93, Sotheby-Amstrdm, #392), 17⅞ x 25½ in., (454 x 648 mm.), colored lithograph on wove (BP 102, DM 257, FR 865, Y 17,153, G 288).

BRUSSET, P.

$638* *PLM. Mont-Genevre. Sports D'Hiver. "Six Mois De Neige", c. 1930,* very good cond., (03-15-93, Arcole, #81), 39⅜ x 24 in., (100 x 61 cm.), (BP 444, DM 1060, FR 3602, Y 75,575).

BRUTON, Margaret American 1894-1948

$275* *"Potato Face" and "Two Men In Wicker Chairs": Two,* s. Margaret Bruton, prov., (06-15-93, Moran, #190), one image 5½ x 4 in., (14 x 10.2 cm.), the other 6½ x 5 in., (14 x 10.2 cm.), (BP 181, DM 451, FR 1522, Y 29,036).

BRUYCKER, Jules de

$1215* *Mon Portrait,* s., t., #67/135, margins, good cond., Frits Coppieters Coll., (05-27-93, Sotheby-Amstrdm, #806A), 15¹¹⁄₁₆ x 11¹¹⁄₁₆ in., (399 x 297 mm.), etching on wove (BP 778, DM 1950, FR 6571, Y 130,253, G 2185).

BRY, Jan Theodor de 1561-1623

$389* *Gott Spricht Zu Adam Und Eva (Hollstein 1; Wurzbach 1),* after Marten de Vos, (06-10-93, Hauswedell/Nolt, #39), engraving in round (BP 254, DM 633, FR 2133, Y 41,291).

BRY, Johann Theodore de (attrib.) German c. 1599-1640(?)

$165* *Portraits Of Men: Three,* prov., (10-08-92, Grogan, #643A), each 5⅝ x 4⅛ in., (14.3 x 10.5 cm.), engraving (BP 98, DM 244, FR 828, Y 20,049).

BRYANT, Ashley (after)

$43 *Wooded Landscape With Trees And Flowers,* limited edit., s., 105/850, (02-05-93, G.A. Key, #33), 9¾ x 13¾ in., (24.8 x 34.9 cm.), colored print (BP 30, DM 71, FR 241, Y 5351).

BRYEN, Camille French 1907-1977

$62* *Composition, 1976,* artist's proof, before letters, s., annot., full margins, (05-06-93, Laurin, #12), color lithograph on wove (BP 39, DM 98, FR 329, Y 6821).

$209* *Komposition I Blat,* s. epreuve d'artiste, (09-29-92, B. Rasmussen, #287), etching in colors (BP 117, DM 295, FR 1007, Y 24,949, DK 1150).

$209* *Komposition I Gult,* s. 50/60, (09-29-92, B. Rasmussen, #286), etching in colors (BP 117, DM 295, FR 1007, Y 24,949, DK 1150).

$58* *Sans Titre,* s., #56/80, (06-28-93, Loudmer, #19), 13⅜ x 11 in., (340 x 280 mm.), sh 22¼ x 14¹⁵⁄₁₆ in., (340 x 280 mm.), color etching and aquatint on Arches wove (BP 39, DM 99, FR 332, Y 6154).

BI *Signe De Feu,* s., t., d. 67, #51/110, prov., est. C$ 250/400, (06-08-93, Ritchie, #49), 13¾ x 10¾ in., (34.9 x 27.3 cm.), color etching and aquatint on B.F. Rives watermarked paper.

$147* *Untitled (Loyer 54), 1962,* plate from "Vigies", epreuve d'artiste, s., full margins, (11-16-92, Briest, #20), 12⅝ x 10 in., (32 x 25.4 cm.), etching in colors (BP 97, DM 234, FR 790, Y 18,345).

BUBLEY, Esther b. 1921

BI *"Gilbert And Barker Manufacturing Company, West Springfield, Massachussetts", 1944,* photog. stamp, t., d., caption label, est. $1,0/1,500, (11-16-92, Butterfield, #5880, illus.), 7⅜ x 7½ in., (187.7 x 190.8 mm.), photograph, gelatin silver print.

BI *New York City, c. 1945,* credit stamp, label, est. $1,2/1,500, (04-08-93, Christie-NY, #262, illus.), 10⅜ x 10½ in., (26.4 x 26.7 cm.), photograph, gelatin silver print.

$715* *"Vicinity Of Jonesboro, Tennessee", 1956,* stamp, d., caption label, (11-16-92, Butterfield, #5879, illus.), 7½ x 9½ in., (190.8 x 241.7 mm.), photograph, gelatin silver print (BP 471, DM 1140, FR 3840, Y 88,919).

BUCHHEISTER, Carl 1890-1964

BI *"Komposition Do" (Buchheister/Kemp 1957/8), 1957,* s., i., ded., prov., est. DM 8/10,000, (06-05-93, Grisebach, #399, illus.), 17 x 24⁵⁄₁₆ in., (43.2 x 61.8 cm.), monotype w/mixed media w/gouache and oil in colors on thick drawing paper.

BUCHOZ, Pierre Joseph French 1731-1807

$1265* *Botanical Engravings: Two,* Latin titles, (04-16-93, Sotheby-NY, #329, illus.), first 13¾ x 9¼ in., (34.9 x 23.5 cm.), second 13¾ x 9 in., (34.9 x 23.5 cm.), hand-colored engraving (BP 830, DM 2043, FR 6905, Y 142,247).

$330* *Botanicals, 1783: Three,* from Herbier Artificiel, ident. w/in matrices and labels, good cond.?, fox marks, wrinkles, (12-04-92, Skinner, #349), approx. 12¾ x 8 in., (32.4 x 20.3 cm.), hand-colored engraving on laid paper (BP 212, DM 526, FR 1783, Y 41,199).

$330* *Botanicals, 1783: Two,* from Herbier Artificiel, ident. on labels, good cond.?, fox marks, (12-04-92, Skinner, #277, illus.), approx. 12¾ x 8 in., (32.4 x 20.3 cm.), hand-colored engraving on laid paper (BP 212, DM 526, FR 1783, Y 41,199).

$550* *Four Botanicals From Herbier Artificiel, 1783,* and various engravers, each ident. in i. in plates, very good cond.,soiling, fox marks, creasing, (10-16-92, Skinner, #449, illus.), approx. 12¾ x 8½ in., (32.4 x 21.6 cm.), engraving w/hand coloring on laid paper (BP 333, DM 812, FR 2760, Y 65,672).

$3738* *Set Of Botanical Engravings: Five,* Latin titles, (04-16-93, Sotheby-NY, #328, illus.), each 8½ x 13½ in., (21.6 x 34.3 cm.), hand-colored engraving (BP 2454, DM 6038, FR 20,404, Y 420,331).

BUCK, Samuel and Nathanial

$198* *The North East Prospect Of The City Of Salisbury,* margins, central fold, surface dirt, (06-16-93, Bonhams-Chelsea, #381), pl. 12 x 31¾ in., (30.5 x 80.6 cm.), engraving w/hand-coloring (BP 132, DM 329, FR 1103, Y 21,118).

$215* *The South East Prospect Of The City Of Bath, 1734,* trimmed, stained, other defects, (06-16-93, Bonhams-Chelsea, #382), 12¼ x 31½ in., (31.1 x 80 cm.), engraving (BP 143, DM 357, FR 1198, Y 22,931).

$59* *The South West Prospect Of Northampton, 1731,* margins, foxing, surface dirt, (09-17-92, Bonhams-Chelsea, #91), plate 11¾ x 31¼ in., (29.8 x 79.4 cm.), engraving (BP 33, DM 88, FR 300, Y 7346).

BI *The South-East Prospect Of Rippon In The County Of York,* pub. 1745, margins, dirt curling, staining, (10-07-92, Christie-S. Ken., #70), pl 12¼ x 32 in., (31.1 x 81.3 cm.), engraving.

BUCK, Samuel and Nathanial (after)

$14 *"View Of Norwich Castle",* (02-05-93, G.A. Key, #68), 5 x 9 in., (12.7 x 22.9 cm.), b/w engraving (BP 10, DM 23, FR 78, Y 1742).

BUCKLE, Samuel

BI *Portrait Of Sir David Bewster, Early 1850s,* mounted on paper, est. BP 4/600, 113 x 88mm, (05-07-93, Sotheby-London, #51, illus.), photograph, salt print from glass neg..

BUCOURT, Philibert Louis de

$182* *La Promenade Publique,* scuffed, (08-20-92, Bonhams-Chelsea, #35), image 14½ x 24 in., (36.8 x 61 cm.), engraving w/hand coloring (BP 94, DM 264, FR 894, Y 22,983).

BUCOVICH, Baron Mario

$544* *Portraits Of A Lady, 1935: Two,* s. recto, (05-06-93, Christie-London, #131), each approx. image 15 x 10¾ in., photograph, bromoil print (BP 345, DM 857, FR 2884, Y 59,853).

BUDAY, G. 20th cent.

$61* *"Wooden House In Transylvania"* and *"Transylvania Folk Ballad": Two,* #16/50 and 12/50, each s., t., num., (07-03-92, Sloan, #304), each 3¹⁵⁄₁₆ x 3½ in., (10 x 8.9 cm.), wood engraving (BP 32, DM 92, FR 311, Y 7604).

BUDZINSKI, R.

$412* *"Dance Of Death", c. 1910-20: Suite Of Eight,* each plate t., s., some spotting, (05-27-93, Swann, #44), image 6 x 5 in., (15.2 x 12.7 cm.), (15.2 x 12.7 cm.), woodcut (BP 264, DM 661, FR 2228, Y 44,168).

BUEHLER

$220* *Shell,* B cond., open tear, tearing, (08-06-92, Swann, #64, illus.), 58 x 33 in., (147.3 x 83.8 cm.), (BP 115, DM 325, FR 1098, Y 28,061).

BUELL, Alice Standish American b. 1892

$150* *Building The Barn,* s., excell. cond., (05-15-93, Cleveland, #78, illus.), 10¾ x 8¼ in., (27.3 x 21 cm.), etching (BP 98, DM 241, FR 811, Y 16,628).

$100* *"Forest Yield"* and *"Vermont Landmark": Two,* s., t., excell. cond., (05-15-93, Cleveland, #79), one 7⁵⁄₁₆ x 7¹³⁄₁₆ in., (18.6 x 19.8 cm.), other 6¾ x 9 in., (18.6 x 19.8 cm.), etching (BP 65, DM 161, FR 541, Y 11,085).

$80* *"Home Front",* s., t., excell. cond., (05-15-93, Cleveland, #77, illus.), 7½ x 10½ in., (19.1 x 26.7 cm.), etching (BP 52, DM 129, FR 432, Y 8868).

BUFAGNOTTI, Carlo and Giacomo Maria GIOVANNI

$766* *Ensemble De Sept Scenographies Theatrales,* after Antonio Chiarini and Cesare Fiore, (05-15-93, Loudmer, #5, illus.), between 7⅞ x 11⁷⁄₁₆ in., (200 x 290 mm.), and 9¹⁄₁₆ x 13⅛ in., (200 x 290 mm.), etchings on trimmed laid, Roman cross watermark (BP 498, DM 1232, FR 4141, Y 84,913).

BUFFET, Bernard French b. 1928

$5491* *Album New York (Sorlier 60), 1964,* s., #42/150, pub. A. C. Mazo, margins, good cond., (06-30-93, Sotheby-London, #372, illus.), sh 29 x 21⅜ in., (737 x 543 mm.), colored lithograph on Arches (BP 3680, DM 9366, FR 31,594, Y 588,342).

$6900* *Album New York III (S. 55), 1964,* s., #19/150, pub. A.C. Mazo, full margins, good cond., faded, light-stain, handling creases, (05-13-93, Sotheby-NY, #476, illus.), 19⅛ x 27¼ in., (485 x 693 mm.), lithograph in colors (BP 4530, DM 11,142, FR 37,582, Y 770,347).

$4775* *Album Paris: L'Arc De Triomphe (S. 40), 1962,* s., #118/150, pub. Editions Mazo et Cie, margins, good cond., paper discoloration, tape stains, skinned areas, (12-03-92, Sotheby-London, #205, illus.), sheet 21¾ x 27¾ in., (552 x 705 mm.), lithograph in colors on Rives (BP 3080, DM 7509, FR 25,631, Y 594,127).

$4604* *Album Paris: La Tour Eiffel (S. 36), 1962,* s., #118/150, pub. Editions Mazo et Cie, full margins, good cond., discoloration, creases, (12-03-92, Sotheby-London, #206, illus.), sheet 21¾ x 28⅝ in., (552 x 727 mm.), lithograph in colors on Arches (BP 2970, DM 7240, FR 24,713, Y 572,851).

$5286* *Album Paris: Le Pont Du Jour (S. 33), 1962,* s., #118/150, pub. Editions Mazo et Cie, margins, good cond., discoloration, damp staining, (12-03-92, Sotheby-London, #207, illus.), sheet 21⅝ x 28 in., (549 x 711 mm.), lithograph in colors on Rives (BP 3410, DM 8313, FR 28,374, Y 657,708).

$3410* *Album San Francisco (S. 91), 1966,* s., pub. Editions San Francisco Grafic, full margins, good cond., (12-03-92, Sotheby-London, #211, illus.), 29⅛ x 38½ in., (740 x 978 mm.), lithograph in colors on Arches (BP 2200, DM 5362, FR 18,304, Y 424,288).

$682* *Album Toreros (S. 100), 1966,* pencil additions, s., #144/150, pub. by artist, margins, good cond.,light/backboard staining, (12-03-92, Sotheby-London, #209, illus.), sheet 29½ x 20½ in., (749 x 521 mm.), lithograph in colors on Arches (BP 440, DM 1072, FR 3661, Y 84,858).

$5284* *Album Toreros (Sorlier 98), 1966,* s. 144/150, (05-25-93, AB Stockholm, #7, illus.), 27³⁄₁₆ x 19⁵⁄₁₆ in., (69 x 49 cm.), color etching on Arches (BP 3424, DM 8606, FR 28,969, Y 577,549, SK 7700).

$5435* *Album Toreros, 1966,* s. 144/150, (05-25-93, AB Stockholm, #8), 27³⁄₁₆ x 19¹¹⁄₁₆ in., (69 x 50 cm.), color lithograph on Arches (BP 3522, DM 8852, FR 29,797, Y 594,054, SK 7920).

$1740* *Arums (Rheims 88), 1979,* s., XXVIII/XXX from 150, (06-28-93, Loudmer, #200), 24¹¹⁄₁₆ x 18¹¹⁄₁₆ in., (627 x 475 mm.), sh 29¾ x 22⁷⁄₁₆ in., (627 x 475 mm.), black drypoint on BFK Rives wove (BP 1165, DM 2957, FR 9960, Y 184,615).

BI *Bateau De Peche A La Panche From St. Tropez (CS p. 283), 1979,* from the complete suite of 25, s., i. E.A., good cond., est. BP 4/600, (10-27-92, Phillips-London, #187), 18¾ x 12½ in., (476 x 318 mm.), color lithograph.

$1364* *La Cafetiere (S. 14), 1955,* s., pub. Editions Guilde de La Gravure, full margins, discoloration, (12-03-92, Sotheby-London, #203), 26¾ x 19⅝ in., (679 x 498 mm.), lithograph in colors on BFK Rives (BP 880, DM 2145, FR 7322, Y 169,715).

$2090* *La Cafetiere (S. 14), 1955,* s., #4/300, pub. Editions Guilde de la Gravure, full margins, good cond., puncture, scratches, light stain, creases, masking tape, foxing, (11-05-92, Sotheby-NY, #101), 26⅜ x 18⅞ in., (670 x 480 mm.), lithograph p. in colors (BP 1359, DM 3305, FR 11,182, Y 256,410).

BI *La Cafetiere (Sorlier 14), 1955,* s., #72/300, pub. La Guilde de la Gravure, full margins, stain in image, backboard stained, est. BP 1,4/1,600, (12-03-92, Sotheby-London, #202, illus.), 26½ x 19¼ in., (673 x 489 mm.), lithograph in colors on Rives.

$605* *La Cafetiere, 1955,* s., num. III/X, full margins, good cond., staining, creases, (02-24-93, Butterfield, #2718), 22½ x 17¼ in., (572 x 438 mm.), lithograph in colors on Japon nacre (BP 422, DM 982, FR 3330, Y 70,993).

$42* *Chemins De Fer Francais: Paris, 1967,* excell. cond., (01-23-93, Ribeyre/Baron, #26), 39⅜ x 24⁷⁄₁₆ in., (100 x 62 cm.), poster (BP 27, DM 67, FR 226, Y 5257).

BI *Le Chien Napolien (C.S. 182), 1968,* from series Mon Cirque, s., #120/120, pub. Editions Fernand Mourlot,full margins, good cond., est. BP 4/600, (11-30-92, Phillips-London, #379), sheet 28¼ x 20 in., (718 x 508 mm.), color lithograph on Arches.

$275* *City Scene,* (02-14-93, Hanzel, #688), 17 x 36 in., (43.2 x 91.4 cm.), color lithograph (BP 194, DM 456, FR 1543, Y 33,164).

$2420* *The Clown With The Green Background (Mourlot 24), 1960,* s., #114/175, (05-16-93, Hindman, #489, illus.), 26½ x 20¼ in., (67.3 x 51.4 cm.), color lithograph (BP 1573, DM 3893, FR 13,081, Y 268,263).

$690* *La Coccinelle (S. 48), 1964,* s., #27/150, pub. David et Garnier, full margins, colors slightly faded, scuffs, handling creases, soiling, skinned spots, (02-11-93, Sotheby-NY, #74), 26³⁄₁₆ x 19⁵⁄₁₆ in., (665 x 490 mm.), color lithograph (BP 487, DM 1143, FR 3868, Y 83,183).

$415* *Le Cri (Sorlier 312), 1967,* von Sorlier, s., num., (12-01-92, Karl/Faber, #411), 21⅝ x 16⁹⁄₁₆ in., (55 x 42 cm.), color lithograph on wove (BP 274, DM 661, FR 2254, Y 51,668).

$387* *Les Deux Amies,* s. in plate, 111/250, (06-28-93, Loudmer, #202), 21⁷⁄₁₆ x 15¾ in., (545 x 400 mm.), sh 28¹⁵⁄₁₆ x 19⁵⁄₁₆ in., (545 x 400 mm.), color lithograph on wove (BP 259, DM 658, FR 2215, Y 41,061).

BI *Einfahrt In Das Dorf, 1961,* s. in stone, d., sig., stone i., est. DM 1,800, (05-08-93, Schloss Ahlden, #2834, illus.), 13¾ x 10⅝ in., (35 x 27 cm.), color lithograph on Arches-handmade.

$165* *"Elephant" (Mon Cirque),* s., #36/120 Bernard Buffet, (02-27-93, Dunning, #1081, illus.), sight 27 x 19 in., (68.6 x 48.3 cm.), color lithograph (BP 116, DM 271, FR 922, Y 19,478).

BI *Les Fers A Repasser (S. 13), 1955,* s., #152/300, pub. Editions Guilde de la Gravure, blindstamp, full margins, faded, mount staining, nick, creasing, est. BP 1,5/2,000, (12-03-92, Sotheby-London, #204), sheet 22 x 30⅛ in., (559 x 765 mm.), lithograph in colors on BFK Rives.

BI *Les Fers A Repasser (S. 13), 1955,* s., #238/300, pub. Editions Guilde de la Gravure, full margins, faded, rolling, handling creases, water stain, soiling, est. $2/2,500, (11-05-92, Sotheby-NY, #100), 19¼ x 27¾ in., (490 x 706 mm.), lithograph p. in colors.

$943* *La Guepe (S. 44), 1964,* s., #90/150, pub. Editions David et Garnier, margins, crease, foxing,soiling, (06-30-93, Sotheby-London, #375, illus.), sh 21¼ x 29 in., (540 x 737 mm.), colored lithograph on Arches (BP 632, DM 1608, FR 5426, Y 101,039).

$682* *La Guepe (S. 45), 1964,* s., #126/150, pub. Editions David et Garnier, full margins, good cond., handling creases, (12-03-92, Sotheby-London, #213), 19¼ x 26 in., (489 x 660 mm.), lithograph in colors on Arches (BP 440, DM 1072, FR 3661, Y 84,858).

$1540* *La Guepe (Sorlier 44), 1964,* s., #98/150, prov., (03-14-93, Hindman, #292), 18½ x 25 in., (47 x 63.5 cm.), color lithograph (BP 1074, DM 2563, FR 8715, Y 181,497).

$7475* *Herbier (S. 67-82),* complete portfolio, s., #47, pub. A. C. Mazo, 1966, good cond., fox marks, rust spots, orig. wrappers, (02-11-93, Sotheby-NY, #76, illus.), each sheet 17⁵⁄₁₆ x 12¹³⁄₁₆ in., (440 x 325 mm.), 16 color lithographs, separate suite of 15 color lithographs, on Richard de Bas (BP 5274, DM 12,382, FR 41,900, Y 901,145).

$1544* *Herbier: La Tulipe (s. 69), 1966,* s., i. E A., artist's proof, pub. Editions A. C. Mazo, full margins,nicks, foxing, (06-30-93, Sotheby-London, #376), sh 29¼ x 21⅛ in., (743 x 537 mm.), colored lithograph on Arches (BP 1035, DM 2633, FR 8884, Y 165,434).

$2217* *"Herbier: Le Myosotis" and "La Pensee" (S. 71; and S. 76), 1966: Two,* #20/50, pub. Editions A.C. Mazo, margins, good cond., mount staining,rolling creases, (12-03-92, Sotheby-London, #210, illus.), each sheet approx. 19¼ x 14⅜ in., (489 x 365 mm.), lithograph in colors on BFK Rives (BP 1430, DM 3486, FR 11,900, Y 275,849).

$7262* *Jeux Des Dames (Sorlier 202, 204, 206, 208, 210, 212, 214, 216, 218,220), 1970: Ten,* suite, each s., num. 44/250, pub. Andre Sauret, Les Editions du Livre, full margins, good cond., handling crease, (10-14-92, Sotheby-

Japan, #9, illus.), each approx. 24 x 20½ in., (610 x 521 mm.), colored lithograph (BP 4262, DM 10,628, FR 36,040, Y 880,029).

$770* *"Jo Jo The Clown",* s., edit. #83/150, prov., (10-16-92, DuMouchelle, #2262, illus.), 24½ x 20 in., (62.2 x 50.8 cm.), color lithograph (BP 467, DM 1137, FR 3864, Y 91,940).

BI *Komposition I Gult Med Profil, Mikroskop Og Globus,* s. EA, est. DK 8,000, (09-29-92, B. Rasmussen, #288), lithograph in colors.

$853* *L'Homard (Rheims 84), 1979,* s., #xx/xxx, pub. Editions Lacouriere et Frelaut, full margins, goodcond., discoloration, (12-03-92, Sotheby-London, #214, illus.), 18¾ x 24⅝ in., (476 x 625 mm.), drypoint on Moulin de Gue (BP 550, DM 1341, FR 4579, Y 106,134).

BI *Lithographs, 1952-1966, By Simenon Georges, 1968: Twelve,* incomplete volume, Still Life With A Bottle duplicated, pub. Tudor Press, good cond., skinned areas, binding holes, losses, est. $6/800, (02-24-93, Butterfield, #2901), each sheet 12 x 9¼ in., (305 x 235 mm.), lithograph in colors.

$943* *Le Lucane (S. 51), 1964,* s., #103/150, pub. Editions David et Garnier, margins, nicks, foxing, (06-30-93, Sotheby-London, #377, illus.), sh 29¼ x 21⅛ in., (743 x 537 mm.), color lithograph on Arches (BP 632, DM 1608, FR 5426, Y 101,039).

$2049* *Marguerites (Rheims 89), 1979,* s., XIII/XXX from 150, reddish stains, (06-28-93, Loudmer, #201), 24¹¹⁄₁₆ x 18¹¹⁄₁₆ in., (627 x 475 mm.), sh 29¾ x 22⁷⁄₁₆ in., (627 x 475 mm.), black drypoint on wove (BP 1372, DM 3482, FR 11,729, Y 217,401).

$770* *Matador,* s., #40/175, (05-28-93, Sloan, #2643, illus.), 26½ x 20¼ in., (67.3 x 51.4 cm.), color lithograph (BP 493, DM 1221, FR 4129, Y 82,565).

BI *Le Microscope (M. 316), 1968,* s., est. FF 4/4,500, (11-16-92, Briest, #265), 21⅝ x 16⁹⁄₁₆ in., (55 x 42 cm.), lithograph in colors on Arches.

$283* *Le Microscope (M.316), 1968,* s., (05-27-93, Briest, #48), 21⅝ x 16⁹⁄₁₆ in., (55 x 42 cm.), color lithograph on Arches (BP 181, DM 454, FR 1531, Y 30,339).

BI *Le Microscope (Sorlier 316), 1968/1969,* s., est. SF 9/1,000, (10-14-92, Germann, #227), 28⅜ x 22¹⁄₁₆ in., (720 x 560 mm.), color lithograph.

$55* *"Mon Cirque": Two,* #157, pub. Maurlot, 4/5/68, (04-17-93, Wolf, #602), 28½ x 20 in., (72.4 x 50.8 cm.), color lithograph on Argis paper (BP 36, DM 89, FR 300, Y 6185).

$55* *"Mon Cirque": Two,* pub. Maurlot, 4/5/68, (04-17-93, Wolf, #601), 28½ x 20 in., (72.4 x 50.8 cm.), color lithograph on Argis paper (BP 36, DM 89, FR 300, Y 6185).

BI *Monsieur Loyal (S. 144), 1968,* from Mon Cirque, s., #97/120, pub. F. Mourlot, margins, creases, surface dirt, est. BP 5/700, (12-01-92, Christie-London, #317), L. 26¾ x 18¹³⁄₁₆ in., (680 x 478 mm.), lithograph in colors on Arches.

$3300* *Naples (Rheims 327-340), 1959,* complete portfolio, s., num. 112, full sheets, good cond., fox marks, (11-05-92, Sotheby-NY, #102), 14⅞ x 11⅛ in., (379 x 283 mm.), fourteen drypoints (BP 2146, DM 5219, FR 17,657, Y 404,858).

$829* *Nature Morte, 1964,* E.A., s., (09-04-92, Germann, #266), 27¾ x 20⅞ in., (705 x 530 mm.), color lithograph (BP 415, DM 1162, FR 3955, Y 102,043, SF 1035).

$4400* *New York I (Sorlier 53), 1964,* from Album New York, Editions A.C. Mazo, i. E.A., full margins, skinned patch, staining, good cond., (11-09-92, Christie-NY, #63, illus.), border 26¹⁵⁄₁₆ x 18¹⁵⁄₁₆ in., (685 x 482 mm.), color lithograph on Arches (BP 2909, DM 7024, FR 23,732, Y 546,041).

$6325* *New York III (Sorlier 55), 1964,* from Album New York, Editions A.C. Mazo, s., #73/150, full margins, colors attenuated, light-staining, taped to overmat, staining, (05-11-93, Christie-NY, #144, illus.), borderline 19¼ x 27 in., (489 x 686 mm.), color lithograph on Arches (BP 4038, DM 9964, FR 33,572, Y 695,743).

BI *"New York Skyline",* s., d. '58 in stone, margins trimmed, est. $3/600, (10-10-92, Goldberg, #528), 17 x 36 in., (43.2 x 91.4 cm.), color lithograph.

$4400* *New York VII (S. 59), 1964,* from album New York, Editions A. C. Mazo, s., i. E.A., full margins, staining, good cond., (11-09-92, Christie-NY, #64, illus.), border 25⁹/₁₆ x 19⁵/₁₆ in., (650 x 490 mm.), color lithograph on Arches (BP 2909, DM 7024, FR 23,732, Y 546,041).

$3575* *New York VIII (M. 60), 1965,* s., annot. E.A., pub. Mazo et Cie, full margins, good cond., light-staining, glue remains, thinned spots, surface soiling, pencil notations, (02-24-93, Butterfield, #2720, illus.), 25¼ x 19¼ in., (641 x 489 mm.), lithograph in colors on Arches (BP 2493, DM 5804, FR 19,675, Y 419,502).

BI *"New York",* s. Bernard Buffet, num. 120/150, very good cond., est. $4/6,000, (11-21-92, Bakker, #149, illus.), image 26½ x 19¼ in., (67.3 x 48.9 cm.), color lithograph.

$1650* *New York, 1967, Sorlier 120,* s., num. 115/150, (09-20-92, Hindman, #791, illus.), 27 x 19 in., (68.6 x 48.3 cm.), color lithograph (BP 966, DM 2448, FR 8376, Y 203,930).

$990* *Nu Accroupi (Rheims 55), 1965,* s., #104/120, full margins, (03-31-93, Briest, #E142), sh 22¹³/₁₆ x 30⅛ in., (58 x 76.5 cm.), 19¹¹/₁₆ x 25¹¹/₁₆ in., (58 x 76.5 cm.), black etching (BP 655, DM 1592, FR 5410, Y 113,845).

BI *Opstilling Med Flaske Og Brod,* s. 1964, 53/150, Sorlier, est. DK 4,000, (09-29-92, B. Rasmussen, #289), lithograph in colors.

$4078* *Paris, Parentheses, 1957; Twenty-Two,* from La Voix Humaine by Jean Cocteau, all s. by Cocteau and Buffet, (11-15-92, Christie-Geneva, #326, illus.), 18¼ x 9¼ in., (463 x 235 mm.), drypoint on Auvergne (BP 2680, DM 6504, FR 21,913, Y 508,923, SF 5876).

$578* *Parisian Scene,* s., (11-01-92, Hanzel, #210), 17½ x 22 in., (44.5 x 55.9 cm.), color lithograph (BP 378, DM 912, FR 3073, Y 71,464).

BI *Les Parisiennes (S. 19), 1958,* s., #36/250, margins, discoloration, tape, very good cond., est. BP 5/700, (12-01-92, Christie-London, #316), L. 21⁹/₁₆ x 15¾ in., (548 x 400 mm.), lithograph in colors on Rives.

$3278* *Parlament Von San Francisco, 1966,* #41/150, s., (11-13-92, Koller, #5269), 18½ x 27³/₁₆ in., (47 x 69 cm.), lithograph on wove (BP 2118, DM 5146, FR 17,353, Y 406,851, SF 4640).

BI *Paysage De Provence (M. 18), 1958,* s., #43/50, pub. Guilde de la Graveure, trimmed, good cond., mat/light-staining, tape remains, surface soiling, est. $8/1,200, (05-19-93, Butterfield, #1883), 13¼ x 10¼ in., (337 x 260 mm.), lithograph in colors Rives BFK.

$1887* *Le Petit Hibou (S. 110), 1967,* s., i. E. A., pub. Editions A. C. Mazo, margins, foxing, (06-30-93, Sotheby-London, #380), sh 2⅞ x 17½ in., (73 x 445 mm.), colored lithograph on Arches (BP 1265, DM 3218, FR 10,857, Y 202,186).

$1373* *La Petit Oiseau (S. 42), 1964,* s., #112/150, pub. Editions David et Garnier, full margins, good cond., attenuation of color, light-stained, residue, tape glue, (06-30-93, Sotheby-London, #379), 20 x 27⅛ in., (508 x 689 mm.), colored lithograph on Arches (BP 920, DM 2342, FR 7900, Y 147,112).

$1716* *Le Petit Oiseau (S. 42), 1964,* s., i. E. A., pub. Editions David et Garnier, margins, good cond., foxing, (06-30-93, Sotheby-London, #378), sh 21⅛ x 29 in., (537 x 737 mm.), color lithograph on Arches (BP 1150, DM 2927, FR 9873, Y 183,864).

$1100* *La Petite Plage (S. 103), 1967,* s., num. 88/125, pub. for l'Oeuvre Gravee by A.C. Mazo, margins, apparently good cond., (02-24-93, Butterfield, #2721), 14⅛ x 21½ in., (359 x 546 mm.), lithograph in colors on Velin d'Arches (BP 767, DM 1786, FR 6054, Y 129,078).

$3738* *Le Pont Du Jour (Sorlier 33), 1962,* s., #23/150 from Album Paris, pub. Alain Mazo et Cie, margins, good cond., discoloration, tape stain, (02-11-93, Sotheby-NY, #73, illus.), 22³/₁₆ x 26⅞ in., (546 x 683 mm.), sheet 21¹¹/₁₆ x 28¹/₁₆ in., (546 x 683 mm.), color lithograph (BP 2638, DM 6192, FR 20,953, Y 450,633).

$2588* *Le Port (S. 186), 1969,* s., #178/250, pub. Les Peintres Temoins de leur Temps, full margins, good cond., light-stain, skinning, repaired nicks, (05-13-93, Sotheby-NY, #477), 19¾ x 25⅞ in., (503 x 656 mm.), lithograph in colors (BP 1699, DM 4179, FR 14,096, Y 288,936).

$495* *Railway Station,* s., annot. E.A., full margins, good cond., surface soiling, glue staining, creases, (10-28-92, Butterfield, #2790), 13½ x 11 in., (343 x 279 mm.), color lithograph on Arches (BP 315, DM 764, FR 2596, Y 60,736).

$4976* *La Rascasse (S. 49), 1964,* s., i. E. A., pub. Editions David et Garnier, margins, good cond., foxing, Madame d'Alayer Coll., (06-30-93, Sotheby-London, #374, illus.), sh c. 21¼ x 28¼ in., (540 x 718 mm.), colored lithograph on Arches (BP 3335, DM 8487, FR 28,631, Y 533,162).

BI *La Route (Sorlier 41),* s., num. 4/220, good cond., slight mat burn, glue stains, trimmed margins, prov., est. $4/6,000, (05-22-93, Weschler, #169, illus.), 25½ x 19½ in., (64.8 x 49.5 cm.), lithograph in colors.

$2950* *La Rue (Reinz 10), 1955,* s., num., (12-05-92, Bassenge, #7067, illus.), 21⅛ x 26⅝ in., (53.6 x 67.6 cm.), drypoint on BFK Rives (BP 1847, DM 4599, FR 15,675, Y 365,506).

BI *S.l., Henri Creuzevault, 1954: Twenty-One,* from La Passio Du Christ by Buffet, est. SF 5/6,000, (11-15-92, Christie-Geneva, #319, illus.), 18⅞ x 11⅝ in., (480 x 295 mm.), drypoint on Hollande van Gelder.

$2823* *S.l., s.n., 1959: Fourteen,* from Naples by Baudelaire, Gide, Stendhal, s. Buffet, (11-15-92, Christie-Geneva, #309, illus.), 14¹⁵/₁₆ x 11⁷/₁₆ in., (380 x 290 mm.), drypoint on Arches (BP 1855, DM 4502, FR 15,169, Y 352,303, SF 4068).

$2750* *Le Sacre Coeur (S. 64), 1965,* s., #112/125, margins, good cond., light stain, creases, tape stain, stains, skinning, discoloration, (11-05-92, Sotheby-NY, #103), 23½ x 18 in., (598 x 457 mm.), lithograph p. in colors on Arches wove (BP 1789, DM 4349, FR 14,714, Y 337,382).

$1650* *Sacre Coeur (Sorlaer 64), 1965,* num. 98/125, s., time discoloration, good condition, (11-12-92, Freemn/Fine Art, #39, illus.), 23¼ x 17½ in., (59.1 x 44.5 cm.), litho printed in color (BP 1084, DM 2614, FR 8819, Y 204,588).

$2875* *Le Sacre-Coeur (S. 64), 1965,* s., #70/125, pub. Mourlot, full margins, good cond., light stain, handling creases, (02-11-93, Sotheby-NY, #75), 23½ x 18¹/₁₆ in., (597 x 459 mm.), color lithograph (BP 2029, DM 4762, FR 16,115, Y 346,594).

$2200* *San Francisco,* s. Bernard Buffet, num. 30/150, (09-25-92, Wolf, #45, illus.), 18¾ x 27 in., (47.6 x 68.6 cm.), lithograph in colors (BP 1285, DM 3261, FR 11,028, Y 265,540).

$35,750* *San Francisco (S. 83-92), 1966: Ten,* suite, s., #134/150, pub. Editions San Francisco Grafic, margins (full on two sides, trimmed on two sides), good cond., light stain, imperfections, water stain, creases, (11-05-92, Sotheby-NY, #104, illus.), sheets approx. 21 x 29¼ in., (535 x 742 mm.), ten lithographs in colors on Arches wove (BP 23,252, DM 56,540, FR 191,279, Y 4,385,965).

$419* *Le Scarabee,* s., #70/150, full margins, (11-16-92, Briest, #263), 29½ x 21¼ in., (75 x 54 cm.), lithograph in 3 colors (BP 275, DM 668, FR 2251, Y 52,290).

$916* *Squelette D'Oiseau (Rheims 48), 1964,* s., i. E.A., (06-23-93, Kornfeld, #242), drypoint on wove (BP 622, DM 1550, FR 5213, Y 99,793, SF 1380).

BI *Squelette Oiseau (R. 48), 1964,* s., num. 29/50, full margins, good cond., mat staining, surface soiling, est. $2/3,000, (02-24-93, Butterfield, #2719), 25⅜ x 29⅜ in., (645 x 746 mm.), drypoint on Arches.

BI *St. Tropez, 1978,* stone s., #13/300, est. DM 1,200, (09-18-92, Schloss Ahlden, #978), 12½ x 19¾ in., (31.8 x 50.1 cm.), color lithograph on white paper.

$600* *La Statue De La Liberte (S. 471), 1986,* s., #63/150, p. Mourlot, full margins, good cond., creases, skinned patches, (06-30-93, Sotheby-London, #381, illus.), 25¾ x 21¼ in., (654 x 540 mm.), colored lithograoh on wove (BP 402, DM 1023, FR 3452, Y 64,288).

BI *"Still Life With A Bottle", "Still Life With Fruit", and "On The Beach": Four,* s. in stone, est. $4/600, (12-10-92, Sloan, #3050), largest 12¼ x 20⅜ in., (31.1 x 51.8 cm.), color lithograph.

$1760* *Les Tentes (Sorlier 7), 1954,* s., #44/75, pub. Editions Galerie Beyeler, full margins, good cond., scratch, mat/light stain, creases, discolored verso, masking tape, (11-

05-92, Sotheby-NY, #99), 16⅞ x 23¼ in., (430 x 590 mm.), lithograph p. in colors (BP 1145, DM 2783, FR 9417, Y 215,924).

$4025* *"Le Toreador" and "Femme Au Chapeau Rose" (Sorlier 21 and 24), 1960:Two,* s., #45/175, #83/130, pub. David et Garnier, full margins, good cond., light-stain, crease; faded, creases, masking tape, (05-13-93, Sotheby-NY, #474, illus.), one 27 x 20⅞ in., (687 x 530 mm.), other 27 x 20¼ in., (687 x 530 mm.), lithograph in color (BP 2642, DM 6499, FR 21,923, Y 449,369).

BI *Torero I (Rheims 27), 1961,* s., #18/75, full margins, yellowed, tear, est. FF10/15,000, (05-27-93, Briest, #47), 29¹⁵⁄₁₆ x 22¹⁄₁₆ in., (76 x 56 cm.), black etching.

$5175* *La Tour Eiffel (S. 36), 1962,* s., #41/150, from Album Paris, pub. Alain Mazo et Cie, full margins, good cond., scuff, light-stain, creases, (05-13-93, Sotheby-NY, #475, illus.), 21 x 26⅝ in., (535 x 675 ï), lithograph in colors (BP 3397, DM 8356, FR 28,186, Y 577,760).

$3603* *Tournesol Et Melon (S. 11), 1955,* s., #41/125, pub. Galerie Beyeler, margins, light-staining, tape staining, (06-30-93, Sotheby-London, #373, illus.), sh 22 x 28½ in., (559 x 724 mm.), colored lithograph on wove (BP 2415, DM 6145, FR 20,731, Y 386,050).

$1298* *Travesti, 1951,* #V/X, plate s., d.; s., num., (11-21-92, Lempertz, #63), 22¼ x 17 in., (56.5 x 43.2 cm.), color lithograph on Japan (BP 855, DM 2070, FR 6971, Y 161,423).

BI *Visage (R. 319), 1958,* from Voyages Fantastiques, s., #22/37, pub. J. Foret, margins, creases, est. BP 3/400, (12-01-92, Christie-London, #318), plate 17³⁄₁₆ x 14⅞ in., (436 x 378 mm.), drypoint on BFK Rives.

BI *Visage (S. 17), 1958,* s., #71/105, pub. Galerie Charpentier, margins, discoloration, good cond., est. BP 6/800, (12-01-92, Christie-London, #315), L. 17⁵⁄₁₆ x 17⅛ in., (440 x 435 mm.), lithograph on Arches.

BI *Voyages Fantastiques (R. 325),* s., #15/37, p. Lacouriere and Frelaut, pub. Joseph Foret, full margins, foxing, discoloration, partially glued, good cond., est. BP 7/900, (06-30-93, Sotheby-London, #371, illus.), 17⅛ x 14¾ in., (435 x 375 mm.), drypoint on BFK Rives.

BI *Voyages Fantastiques (Rheims 309-326): Eighteen,* book w/title and text, artist's own copy, p. Lacouriere and Frelaut, pub. Joseph Foret, good cond., slightly stained, est. BP 5/7,000, (06-30-93, Sotheby-London, #370, illus.), overall 16 x 13 in., (406 x 330 mm.), drypoint, 2 copies of book, 1 on BFK Rives, 1 on Japon nacre, w/additional impressions of 9 plates, hand-colored.

BUFFET, Bernard (after)

$182* *Bouteille Et Verre,* s., untrimmed margins, (02-03-93, Ader Tajan, #77), 22¹⁄₁₆ x 16¹⁵⁄₁₆ in., (56 x 43 cm.), color lithograph (BP 127, DM 300, FR 1016, Y 22,640).

$165* *"L'Arc De Triomphe",* (01-15-93, DuMouchelle, #2431, illus.), 45 x 63 in., (114.3 x 160 cm.), poster (BP 108, DM 270, FR 912, Y 20,802).

BI *Microscope,* s., d. (19)68 in stone, s., i. E.A., pub. Charles Sorlier, est. $700/900, (09-17-92, Sloan, #2373), 21½ x 16½ in., (54.6 x 41.9 cm.), color lithograph.

$250* *"Pain Et Le Vin" (Sorlier 306), 1964,* s., very good color and cond., creases, (05-15-93, Cleveland, #451), 24¼ x 16¹¹⁄₁₆ in., (61.6 x 42.4 cm.), color lithograph (BP 163, DM 402, FR 1351, Y 27,713).

$715* *Pain Et Vin, By Charles Sorlier (S. 306), 1964,* s., large margins, good cond.?, (10-28-92, Butterfield, #2788), 22¼ x 17 in., (565 x 432 mm.), color lithograph on cream wove (BP 456, DM 1104, FR 3749, Y 87,730).

$132* *"La Plage" and "La Petite Plage": Two,* from Oeuvre Grave, (09-17-92, Sloan, #1430), each, sight 12 x 9 in., (30.5 x 22.9 cm.), color book prints (BP 74, DM 196, FR 671, Y 16,434).

BI *"Sunflowers", 1959,* s., num. VIII/X, stone s., d., margins, laid down, good cond., rubbed area, surface abrasions/soiling, est. $6/800, (10-28-92, Butterfield, #2789), 22⅞ x 17½ in., (581 x 445 mm.), hand-colored lithograph on Japan.

$75* *View Of The Arc De Triomphe,* stained, worn, (07-16-92, Bonhams-Chelsea, #456), image 43 x 62½ in., (109.2 x 158.8 cm.), lithographic reproduction on linen (BP 39, DM 111, FR 374, Y 9395).

BUFFET, Maurice

BI *Venetian Canal Scene,* s., #32/260, good cond., est. $3/500, (02-07-93, Bakker, #89), sheet 21 x 27 in., (53.3 x 68.6 cm.), color lithograph.

BUFFON

$1840* *Animals: Eight, 1778,* (02-18-93, Sotheby-Arcade, #61), sheet 17¾ x 15 in., (45.1 x 38.1 cm.), hand colored engravings (BP 1271, DM 3002, FR 10,160, Y 219,204).

$1952* *"Historia Natural, General Y Particular", 1791-1805,* 2nd spanish edit., 20 vols., bound, (10-15-92, Duran, #798, illus.), color engraving (BP 1194, DM 2906, FR 9854, Y 234,193, P 207,000).

$1265* *Monkeys, 1774: Eight,* (04-07-93, Sotheby-Arcade, #151), sight 9 x 7 in., (22.9 x 17.8 cm.), hand-colored engraving (BP 836, DM 2046, FR 6924, Y 143,717).

$690* *Monkeys, 1774: Nine,* (03-03-93, Sotheby-Arcade, #148), sight 9 x 7 in., (22.9 x 17.8 cm.), hand-colored engraving (BP 476, DM 1136, FR 3855, Y 80,626).

BUFFORD, John H., Lithographer   American ac. 1835-1871

$413* *"Hunneman & Co., Builders, Boston, Mass."/ A Fire Engine,* ident., (06-05-93, Skinner, #57), sh, sight 17 x 23¾ in., (43.2 x 60.3 cm.), chromolithograph on paper (BP 272, DM 670, FR 2257, Y 44,304).

$110* *"The New Masonic Temple, Boston",* after M.G. Wheelock, pub. William D. Stratton, 1865, poor cond., (02-07-93, Bakker, #90), image 17½ x 24½ in., (44.5 x 62.2 cm.), hand-colored lithographic poster (BP 76, DM 182, FR 617, Y 13,688).

$1430* *"View Of The Public Garden And Boston Common", 1866,* after Edwin Whitefield, ident. i., (01-16-93, Skinner, #144A), sheet, sight 25¾ x 35¼ in., (65.4 x 89.5 cm.), lithograph in black, tan and blue on paper (BP 935, DM 2338, FR 7905, Y 180,282).

$165* *"Winter Quarters Of 3d. Battery, Martin's Massachusetts Volunteers, Near Potomac Creek, Virginia" and "The Retreat": Two,* (12-02-92, Christie-E, #230), hand-colored lithograph on wove (BP 106, DM 259, FR 886, Y 20,530).

BUHLER, Robert   b. 1916

$1332* *For High Performance, Hawker Hurricanes, 1938,* p. Waterlow and Sons, ref. #529, cond. 1, creasing, (10-13-92, Phillips-London, #146), 29¹⁵⁄₁₆ x 45¹⁄₁₆ in., (76 x 114.5 cm.), color lithograph (BP 776, DM 1951, FR 6630, Y 161,513).

BUHOT, Felix   French 1847-1898

BI *La Falaise - Baie De Saint-Malo (Bourcard 165 V/II), 1889-90,* plate d., red stamped mono., collector's stamp, est. DM 10,000, (06-10-93, Hauswedell/Nolt, #119, illus.), image 8⅞ x 11¾ in., (22.5 x 29.8 cm.), sh 11¹³⁄₁₆ x 15¾ in., (22.5 x 29.8 cm.), etching w/drypoint and aquatint on wove.

$690* *La Fete Nationale Au Boulevard Clichy (Bourcard/Goodfriend 127), 1878,* Goodfriend's 6th state of 8, mono stamp, margins, light-staining, foxing, folds, surface dirt, good cond., (02-11-93, Sotheby-NY, #77), 12⁷⁄₁₆ x 9⁵⁄₁₆ in., (316 x 236 mm.), etching and aquatint on Japan (BP 487, DM 1143, FR 3868, Y 83,183).

$1201* *La Fete Nationale Au Boulevard Clichy (Goodfriend/ Bourcard 127), 1878,* 3rd state of 4, mono. stamp, margins, good cond., loss, soiling, creases, (06-30-93, Sotheby-London, #382, illus.), sh 20½ x 14⅜ in., (521 x 365 mm.), etching on wove (BP 805, DM 2048, FR 6910, Y 128,683).

$633* *French Street Scenes: A Pair,* one s. Felix Buhot, very good cond., (09-27-92, Bakker, #250), one 9⅛ x 12½ in., (23.2 x 31.8 cm.), the other 5½ x 10½ in., (23.2 x 31.8 cm.), etching and aquatint on brown paper (BP 370, DM 938, FR 3173, Y 76,403).

BI *"Hiver A Paris 1879" (B. 128),* 4th state, (01-28-93, Pescheteau, #80), etching aquatint on Japan.

BI *"Hiver A Paris Ou La Neige A Paris", 1879,* 4th state of 5, #128, est. FF 6/8,000, (10-18-92, Pescheteau, #87), etching and aquatint on Japan.

$303* *Illustration Nouvelle, Paris (Boucard and Goodfriend, 124), 1877,* frontispiece, s. Fx Buhot imp sc in plate, very good cond., (03-12-93, Skinner, #17, illus.), plate 13⅝ x 10⅞ in., (34.6 x 27.6 cm.), etching, roulette and tone on laid paper (BP 211, DM 504, FR 1715, Y 35,710).

BI *L'Hiver A Paris (Bourcard Goodfriend 128), 1879,* third state of 5, est. FF4/5,000, (06-28-93, Loudmer, #203), 9⁵⁄₁₆ x 13¹¹⁄₁₆ in., (237 x 348 mm.), sh 12³⁄₁₆ x 17⁵⁄₁₆ in., (237 x 348 mm.), etching and aquatint on Arches.

BI *L'Hiver A Paris (La Neige A Paris) (Bourcard/Goodfriend 128), 1879,* Goodfriend's fourth state of nine, crayon s., i. Paris 1879, margins, good cond., discoloration, foxing, mat staining, est. $1,5/2,000, (11-05-92, Sotheby-NY, #105), 9¼ x 17⅛ in., (234 x 435 mm.), etching, drypoint and aquatint on Arches laid.

$248* *L'Hiver A Paris Ou La Neige A Paris (Bourcard-Goodfriend 128 IV/IX),879,* pub. in L'Art, (05-16-93, Hindman, #442), 9⅜ x 13¾ in., (23.8 x 34.9 cm.), etching, aquatint and drypoint (BP 161, DM 399, FR 1341, Y 27,491).

$409* *L'Hiver A Paris or La Neige A Paris (B., G. 128), 1879,* before mention, margins, (02-24-93, Picard, #50), etching and aquatint on thin chine (BP 285, DM 664, FR 2251, Y 47,993).

BI *Ma Petite Ville (Ier Planche) (B.G. 27), 1872,* 2nd state, margins, s., surface soiling, good cond., est. BP 5/700, (11-30-92, Phillips-London, #318, illus.), plate 4½ x 6¼ in., (114 x 159 mm.), etching w/aquatint on laid.

BI *Ma Petite Ville (Ire Planche) (B.G. 27),* 2nd state of 3, s., soiling, top right corner missing, mounted, est.BP 5/700, (10-27-92, Phillips-London, #185), plate 4½ x 6¼ in., (114 x 159 mm.), etching w/aquatint on laid.

$633* *Les Oies (B., G. 166), 1887,* Bourcard's 3rd state of 4, Goodfriend's 3rd state of 6, s., t., i. 3e Etat, wide margins, light-staining, foxing, good cond., prov., prop. Montclair Art Museum, (05-11-93, Christie-NY, #149), plate 6 x 10 in., (152 x 254 mm.), etching w/aquatint and drypoint on laid (BP 404, DM 997, FR 3360, Y 69,629).

$220* *Les Petites Chaumieres (B.G. 149),* artist's stamp, sig., laid down on cardboard, mat burn, (12-04-92, Doyle, #80), 4 x 5¼ in., (102 x 133 mm.), etching, drypoint and aquatint (BP 141, DM 350, FR 1189, Y 27,466).

$368* *"Le Port Aux Mouettes", 1886 and "La Falaise", 1890 (B., G. 162 et 165): Two,* first, annot., first state; second, definitive state, margins, (02-24-93, Picard, #51), etching and aquatint on wove (BP 257, DM 597, FR 2025, Y 43,182).

$358* *Red Owl,* s., mono., (09-24-92, Mystic, #54), 9 x 11½ in., (22.9 x 29.2 cm.), etching (BP 210, DM 531, FR 1802, Y 43,065).

$770* *Le Retour Des Artistes (Bourcard-Goodfriend 125 IV/IV), 1877,* pub. L'Illustration Nouvelle, (03-14-93, Hindman, #241), 8⅛ x 12½ in., (20.6 x 31.8 cm.), etching and aquatint (BP 537, DM 1282, FR 4358, Y 90,748).

BI *"Le Retour Des Artistes" (Bourcard/Goodfriend 125 iv/iv), 1877,* tipped to window, staining, est. $3/400, (05-15-93, Cleveland, #366, illus.), 8⅛ x 12⅝ in., (20.6 x 32.1 cm.), etching.

$183* *La Ronde De Nuit (B.G. 70), 1878,* 2nd state, margins, light stained, (11-30-92, Phillips-London, #319), plate 4¾ x 3⅛ in., (121 x 79 mm.), etching on thin laid (BP 121, DM 292, FR 990, Y 22,775).

BI *Les Voisins De Campagne (Bourcard/Goodfriend 148), 1878,* s., init., t., i. Epreuve d'Artist in plate, prov., est. $800/900, (09-17-92, Sloan, #2378), 5⁵⁄₁₆ x 7⅛ in., (13.5 x 18.1 cm.), etching, drypoint and aquatint.

BI *"Les Voisins De Campagne" (B/G 148), 1878,* est. $900/1,200, (05-15-93, Cleveland, #367, illus.), 5⅝ x 7⅛ in., (14.3 x 18.1 cm.), etching, drypoint and aquatint.

$748* *Les Voisins De Campagne, Boucard, Goodfriend 148), 1877,* Bourcard's 5th final state, Goodfriend's 5th state of 6, margins, staining, i., good cond., prop. Montclair Art Museum, (05-11-93, Christie-NY, #145), plate 5⁵⁄₁₆ x 7¼ in., (135 x 184 mm.), etching w/aquatint on wove (BP 477, DM 1178, FR 3970, Y 82,279).

$2185* *Westminster Bridge, Or Westminster Clock Tower (B., G. 156), 1884,* Bourcard's 5th state of 6, Goodfriend's 6th state of 8, s., mono. stamp, i. 5e Etat-essai/ Ep. de l'avant dernier Etat, wide margins, light-staining, stain, laid down on wove, good cond., (05-11-93, Christie-NY, #148, illus.), plate 11⅛ x 15¾ in., (283 x 400 mm.),

etching on wove (BP 1395, DM 3442, FR 11,598, Y 240,348).

BI *Westminster Palace (B., G. 155), 1884,* Bourcard's 5th final state, Goodfriend's 6th state of 7, s., mono. stamp, wide margins, light-staining, platemark broken through, laid down on wove, est. $1,5/2,000, (05-11-93, Christie-NY, #147), plate 11½ x 15⅝ in., (292 x 397 mm.), etching on wove.

BI *"Westminster Palace" and "Westminster Bridge Ou Westminster Clock Tower" (G. Bourcard et J. Goodfriend, 155, 156): Two,* first, fifth or sixth state of seven, ded., frame traces, good margins; second, fifth or sixth state of eight, glue verso, good margins, (06-11-93, Picard, #15, illus.), one 11⅜ x 15¾ in., (289 x 400 mm.), other 11⅛ x 15¾ in., (289 x 400 mm.), etching, drypoint and aquatint, first, on wove; second, tinted Japan.

$715* *Westminster Palace, 1884,* artist's stamp, mat burn, light struck, laid down on cardboard, (12-04-92, Doyle, #81), 11½ x 15¾ in., (292 x 400 mm.), etching (BP 459, DM 1139, FR 3863, Y 89,263).

$605* *Westminster Palace, 1886,* pencil s., dark staining, foxing, crease, (05-22-93, Weschler, #170), 11¼ x 15¼ in., (28.6 x 38.7 cm.), etching (BP 392, DM 984, FR 3310, Y 66,703).

BULL, Charles Livingston   American 1874-1932

$160 *Eat More Fish They Feed Themselves,* Heywood Strasser and Voight Litho. Co. NY, edge loss, (09-24-92, Alderfer, #277, illus.), 30 x 20 in., (76.2 x 50.8 cm.), (BP 94, DM 237, FR 805, Y 19,247).

$95 *Keep Him Free,* Ketterlinus, edge loss, (09-24-92, Alderfer, #283), 30 x 20 in., (76.2 x 50.8 cm.), (BP 56, DM 141, FR 478, Y 11,428).

BULL, Clarence Sinclair   American 1895-1979

BI *Clark Gable,* c. 1933, photog.'s blindstamp/ink credit stamp, est. BP 2/400, (12-17-92, Christie-S. Ken, #26, illus.), 12¼ x 9¼ in., (31.1 x 23.5 cm.), photograph, warm-toned matt gelatin silver print.

$222* *Clark Gable, Photographed Beneath Stag's Head,* stamp, d. 10-10-32, blind embossed, prov., (10-10-92, Bonhams, #61, illus.), 8 x 10 in., (20.3 x 25.4 cm.), photograph (BP 132, DM 330, FR 1107, Y 27,027).

$275* *Elizabeth Taylor,* (04-26-93, Selkirk, #532), 10 x 8 in., (25.4 x 20.3 cm.), b/w photograph (BP 174, DM 431, FR 1456, Y 30,347).

$225* *Front Of Houses In Beverly Hills,* n.d. (1920s), t., photog.'s ink credit stamps, mount, (12-17-92, Christie-S. Ken, #22, illus.), 10 x 7¾ in., (25.4 x 19.7 cm.), photograph, gelatin silver print (BP 143, DM 351, FR 1200, Y 27,651).

$728* *Grace Kelly,* c. 1950, photog.'s ink credit stamp, mounted, (12-17-92, Christie-S. Ken, #28, illus.), 18 x 13 in., (45.7 x 33 cm.), photograph, gelatin silver print (BP 462, DM 1137, FR 3883, Y 89,468).

$1669* *Greta Carbo, Portrait With Fur Collar,* blind embossed, The Kobal Collection, Artist's proof, (10-10-92, Bonhams, #68, illus.), 16 x 20 in., (40.6 x 50.8 cm.), photograph (BP 990, DM 2479, FR 8324, Y 203,190).

$381* *Greta Garbo,* 1931, p.l., photog.'s blindstamp/credit stamp, (12-17-92, Christie-S. Ken, #30, illus.), 14 x 10½ in., (35.6 x 26.7 cm.), photograph, gelatin silver print (BP 242, DM 595, FR 2032, Y 46,823).

BI *Greta Garbo,* (1930s), p.l., s. in ink, num. 3/50, embossed credit stamp, est. $1,5/2,000, (10-13-92, Christie-NY, #160, illus.), 14⅛ x 10⅞ in., (35.9 x 27.6 cm.), photograph, gelatin silver print.

$260* *Greta Garbo,* blind embossed, #65/99, The Kobal Coll., (10-10-92, Bonhams, #73, illus.), 11 x 14 in., (27.9 x 35.6 cm.), photograph (BP 154, DM 386, FR 1297, Y 31,653).

$2200* *Greta Garbo As "Queen Christina": Five, c. 1933,* each w/blindstamp on image, credit stamp, (10-15-92, Sotheby-NY, #221, illus.), each approx. 12 x 9 in., (30.5 x 22.9 cm.), photograph, gelatin silver prints (BP 1346, DM 3275, FR 11,106, Y 263,947).

$649* *Greta Garbo With Floppy Hat,* blind embossed, The Kobal Collection, #65/99, (10-10-92, Bonhams, #71, illus.), 11 x 14 in., (27.9 x 35.6 cm.), photograph (BP 385, DM 964, FR 3237, Y 79,011).

$278* *Greta Garbo With Head Thrown Back,* blind embossed, #65/99, The Kobal Coll., (10-10-92, Bonhams, #72, illus.), 11 x 14 in., (27.9 x 35.6 cm.), photograph (BP 165, DM 413, FR 1387, Y 33,845).

BI *Greta Garbo, Double Image Portrait,* blind embossed, est. BP 250/350, (10-10-92, Bonhams, #74, illus.), 11 x 14 in., (27.9 x 35.6 cm.), photograph.

$1020* *Greta Garbo, Half Figure,* 1931, blind embossed, The Kobal Collection, proof, (10-10-92, Bonhams, #69, illus.), 16 x 20 in., (40.6 x 50.8 cm.), photograph (BP 605, DM 1515, FR 5087, Y 124,178).

$1205* *Greta Garbo, Hand To Forehead,* 1931, blind embossed, #65/99, The Kobal Coll., (10-10-92, Bonhams, #70, illus.), 16 x 20 in., (40.6 x 50.8 cm.), photograph (BP 715, DM 1790, FR 6010, Y 146,701).

$649* *Greta Garbo, Head And Shadow,* blind embossed, #65/99, The Kobal Coll., (10-10-92, Bonhams, #75, illus.), 11 x 14 in., (27.9 x 35.6 cm.), photograph (BP 385, DM 964, FR 3237, Y 79,011).

$303* *Greta Garbo, Her Rise And Fall, July 8, 1931,* #53/99, blind embossed sig., The Kobal Coll., (04-26-93, Selkirk, #528), 11 x 14 in., (27.9 x 35.6 cm.), b/w photograph (BP 191, DM 475, FR 1604, Y 33,436).

$303* *Greta Garbo, Inspiration, December 12, 1930,* #53/99, blind embossed sig., The Kobal Coll., (04-26-93, Selkirk, #529), 11 x 14 in., (27.9 x 35.6 cm.), b/w photograph (BP 191, DM 475, FR 1604, Y 33,436).

$1112* *Greta Garbo, Portrait Against Blackness,* blind embossed, Kobal Collection, Artist's proof, (10-10-92, Bonhams, #67, illus.), 16 x 20 in., (40.6 x 50.8 cm.), photograph (BP 660, DM 1652, FR 5546, Y 135,379).

$413* *Greta Garbo, The Kiss, August 27, 1929,* artist's proof 1/10, Limited Edition 99, blind embossed sig., (04-26-93, Selkirk, #544), 20 x 16 in., (50.8 x 40.6 cm.), b/w photograph (BP 261, DM 647, FR 2186, Y 45,575).

$385* *Greta Garbor, Mata Hari, November 19, 1931,* #53/99, blind embossed sig., The Kobal Coll., (04-26-93, Selkirk, #533, illus.), 11 x 14 in., (27.9 x 35.6 cm.), b/w photograph (BP 243, DM 603, FR 2038, Y 42,485).

$523* *"Inspiration", 1930,* s., t., d., stamp, label verso, (11-16-92, Butterfield, #5882, illus.), 7 x 6¾ in., (178.1 x 171.8 mm.), photograph, gelatin silver print (BP 344, DM 834, FR 2809, Y 65,042).

BI *Jack Conway,* c. 1930-31, s., i., t., mounted on corrugated board, est. BP 150/250, (12-17-92, Christie-S. Ken, #24), 9¾ x 8⅛ in., (24.8 x 20.6 cm.), photograph, carbon transfer print.

$185* *Joan Crawford, Portrait,* blind embossed, prov., (10-10-92, Bonhams, #62, illus.), 11 x 14 in., (27.9 x 35.6 cm.), photograph (BP 110, DM 275, FR 923, Y 22,523).

BI *Kathleen Key,* c. 1921, s., photog.'s ink credit stamp, mounted, est. BP 250/350, (12-17-92, Christie-S. Ken, #23, illus.), 9⅜ x 6⅝ in., (23.8 x 16.8 cm.), photograph, matt gelatin silver print.

BI *Luise Rainer, As 'O Lan In "The Good Earth",* 1936, est. BP 120/160, (10-10-92, Bonhams, #64, illus.), 11 x 14 in., (27.9 x 35.6 cm.), photograph.

$47* *Maria Schell, Double Portrait,* for Brothers Karamazov, prov., (10-10-92, Bonhams, #65, illus.), 10 x 8 in., (25.4 x 20.3 cm.), photograph (BP 28, DM 70, FR 234, Y 5722).

BI *Ramon Navarro,* 1931, photog.'s blindstamp/ink credit stamp, annots., est. BP 250/350, (12-17-92, Christie-S. Ken, #25, illus.), 12¼ x 9⅛ in., (31.1 x 23.2 cm.), photograph, matt gelatin silver print.

$1265* *"Refugees", 1916,* photog. name stamp, t., d., i. in unident. hand, (04-06-93, Sotheby-NY, #87, illus.), 9½ x 12½ in., photograph (BP 836, DM 2038, FR 6901, Y 144,275).

$433* *"Refuges",* 1916, t., d., i., ink credit stamp, (12-17-92, Christie-S. Ken, #21, illus.), 9⅝ x 12½ in., (24.4 x 31.8 cm.), photograph, matt gelatin silver print (BP 275, DM 676, FR 2309, Y 53,214).

$464* *W.C. Fields,* blind embossed, prov., (10-10-92, Bonhams, #66, illus.), 11 x 14 in., (27.9 x 35.6 cm.), photograph (BP 275, DM 689, FR 2314, Y 56,489).

BULL, P.C.
$302* *Farm In Kent, c. 1930,* notations, (10-14-92, Swann, #396, illus.), 4⅛ x 5⅛ in., (10.5 x 13 cm.), photograph, trichrome carbro print (BP 177, DM 442, FR 1499, Y 36,597).

BULL, Simon
$6 *"First Steps",* s., #52/250, (12-11-92, G.A. Key, #71), 2 x 3 in., (5.1 x 7.6 cm.), hand colored engraving (BP 4, DM 9, FR 32, Y 742).

BULLER, Cecil Tremayne
$727* *Adam And Eve (Notebook/Carnet: 16),* s., exec. 1920's, lit., (11-30-92, Ritchie, #33, illus.), image 3¹⁵⁄₁₆ x 2¹³⁄₁₆ in., (10 x 7.2 cm.), wood engraving (BP 480, DM 1158, FR 3932, Y 90,479, C$ 935).

BULLOCK, Wynn   American 1902-1972
$1955* *"Barbara" (Aperture, p. 86),* mounted, s. by photog., 1956, p.l., (04-06-93, Sotheby-NY, #435, illus.), 9½ x 7¼ in., photograph (BP 1291, DM 3150, FR 10,666, Y 222,970).

$3450* *Child In Forest,* 1951, p.l., s., lit., (04-08-93, Christie-NY, #410, illus.), 7½ x 9½ in., (19.1 x 24.1 cm.), photograph, gelatin silver print (BP 2262, DM 5542, FR 18,760, Y 391,512).

$3520* *Child In Forest (Monterey, 1973; Aperture, pl. 49),* mounted, plate 1 from "Photographs, 1951-1973" portfolio, s. by photog. in ink, portfolio stamp, t., d. by photog.'s widow in ink, 1951, p. c. 1973,#11/31 ed., (10-15-92, Sotheby-NY, #492, illus.), 7½ x 9½ in., (19.1 x 24.1 cm.), photograph, gelatin silver print (BP 2154, DM 5240, FR 17,769, Y 422,316).

$2750* *Child On Forest Road (Aperture, p. 13),* mounted, s. by photog., t., d., num. 1558 by photog.'s widow, 1958, p.l., (10-15-92, Sotheby-NY, #491, illus.), 8¾ x 7¼ in., (22.2 x 18.4 cm.), photograph, gelatin silver print (BP 1683, DM 4093, FR 13,882, Y 329,934).

BI *"The Forest" (Aperture, p. 45),* mounted, s. by photog., t., d. by Edna Bullock, 1956, p.l., est. $1,5/1,800, (04-06-93, Sotheby-NY, #436, illus.), 9½ x 7½ in., photograph.

$440* *Interior Of House, c. 1959,* photog.'s handstamp, (04-07-93, Swann, #419, illus.), 9¼ x 7 in., photograph, silver print (BP 291, DM 712, FR 2408, Y 49,989).

$1453* *"Old Chair, 1951",* mounted on card, s., t., d., num. 473, 238 x 184mm, (05-07-93, Sotheby-London, #304, illus.), photograph, silver print (BP 920, DM 2297, FR 7741, Y 159,987).

BI *"Pacific Grove, California", 1968,* s., t., d., neg. num., est. $1,8/2,200, (05-23-93, Butterfield, #3354, illus.), 7 x 8¼ in., photograph, gelatin silver print.

BI *"Palo, Colorado Road 1952",* mounted on card, s., t., d., num. P973.70.87, 236 x 189mm, est. BP 800/1,200, (05-07-93, Sotheby-London, #305, illus.), photograph, silver print.

BI *Posterized Dancer,* 1950s, s., est. $2/2,500, (04-08-93, Christie-NY, #411, illus.), 13⅝ x 10⅝ in., (34.6 x 27 cm.), photograph, gelatin silver print.

BI *"Reclining Nude", 1956,* s., d., t., photog. stamp, est. $2,5/3,000, (11-16-92, Butterfield, #5883, illus.), 7⅜ x 9⅜ in., (187.7 x 238.5 mm.), photograph, gelatin silver print.

$863* *"Rock", 1973,* s., t., d., neg. num. coll. stamp, (05-23-93, Butterfield, #3355, illus.), 9½ x 7½ in., photograph, gelatin silver print (BP 562, DM 1411, FR 4750, Y 95,391).

BI *"Torso In Window",* s., t., d., neg. num. verso, est. $1,8/2,200, 1954/later, (11-16-92, Butterfield, #5884, illus.), 9½ x 7½ in., (241.7 x 190.8 mm.), photograph, gelatin silver print.

BI *Untitled 1956,* mounted on card, s., d., num. B570, 240 x 173mm, est. BP 800/1,200, (05-07-93, Sotheby-London, #303, illus.), photograph, silver print.

$715* *Woman With Dog In Forest,* 1953/possibly printed later, s., (05-16-93, Hindman, #342), 9½ x 7½ in., photograph, silver print (BP 466, DM 1154, FR 3886, Y 79,621).

$2185* *Woman's Hand, 1956,* ink s., d.; ink t., d., (04-08-93, Christie-NY, #409, illus.), 7⅜ x 9⅜ in., (18.7 x 23.8 cm.), photograph, gelatin silver print (BP 1433, DM 3510, FR 11,881, Y 247,957).

BUMBECK, David
$165* *"The Olive Grove", "August Light", and "Strada Del Sole": Three,* all s., #19/60, #42/60, and #33/50, very good cond., (03-28-93, Bakker, #149), largest, plate 13½ x 15½ in., (34.3 x 39.4 cm.), etching (BP 111, DM 269, FR 915, Y 19,204).

BUNBURY, H. (after)
$145 *"A Barbers Shop",* by John Jones, d. 1785, (06-11-93, G.A. Key, #44), 18 x 26 in., (45.7 x 66 cm.), b/w engraving (BP 95, DM 236, FR 795, Y 15,385).
$25 *Six Horsemen: Two,* engr. by W. Dickinson, (12-11-92, G.A. Key, #47), 8 x 6 in., (20.3 x 15.2 cm.), monotone stipple engraving (BP 16, DM 39, FR 135, Y 3094).

BUNBURY, Henry (after)
$85* *Hints To Bad Horsemen; Plates 6-9: Four,* by Watson and Dickinson, pub. by the etchers, May 10th 1781, margins, (04-22-93, Bonhams-Chelsea, #67), plate 7⅝ x 9⅜ in., (19.4 x 23.8 cm.), bookplate etchings (BP 55, DM 137, FR 461, Y 9346).
$167* *Launce Teaching His Dog Crab To Behave As A Dog In All Things, 1794,* pub. Thomas Macklin, full margins, good cond., (11-30-92, Phillips-London, #181), plate 16¼ x 18¾ in., (413 x 476 mm.), color stipple engraving on hand-made wove (BP 110, DM 266, FR 903, Y 20,784).

BUNBURY, Henry William
$257* *Political Sketches: Five,* pub. Thomas McLean, foxing, other defects, (05-20-93, Bonhams-Chelsea, #95), lithograph (BP 165, DM 415, FR 1397, Y 28,379).

BUNBURY, Henry William (after)
$323* *"Garden Of Carlston House",* restored tears, (03-22-93, Pescheteau, #6), en (and) bistre (BP 218, DM 530, FR 1800, Y 37,402).

BUNDASCZ, R.   American 20th cent.
BI *House In A Landscape,* s., glue, est. $50/100, (05-15-93, Cleveland, #80), 8½ x 13 in., (21.6 x 33 cm.), color lithograph.

BUOTALENTI, Bernardo (after)
$99* *Apollo And The Python (B. 122),* by Agostino Carracci, unidentified state of 3, trimmed, laid down, stained, tears and other defects, (06-16-93, Bonhams-Chelsea, #302), 9½ x 13½ in., (24.1 x 34.3 cm.), etching (BP 66, DM 164, FR 552, Y 10,559).

BURCHARTZ, Max   1887-1961
$2637* *Raskolnikoff, 1919,* Galerie Flechtheim, #15/100, s., (11-13-92, Kunsthaus, #495, illus.), lithograph on handmade (BP 1704, DM 4140, FR 13,960, Y 327,293).

BURCHFIELD, Charles   American 1893-1967
BI *Sunflowers,* p. sig. Charles Burchfield, est. $1,5/2,500, (12-12-92, Wolf, #14), 16 x 20 in., (40.6 x 50.8 cm.), silkscreen.

BURCHMAN, Jerold
$248* *Untitled (Blue Vase), 1985,* s., d., pub. Garner Tullis Workshop, very good cond., surface soiling, creases, (02-24-93, Butterfield, #3191), 23½ x 31 in., (597 x 787 mm.), monotype in colors on Tumba Grafik wove (BP 173, DM 403, FR 1365, Y 29,101).

BURCKHARDT, Rudy   b. 1919
BI *Paris, 1947,* t., d. in ink, credit stamp, est. $1,2/1,500, (10-13-92, Christie-NY, #425, illus.), 7⅞ x 6¼ in., (20 x 15.9 cm.), photograph, gelatin silver print.

BURFORD, John (after)
$303* *Cambridge University Almanack,* defects, (01-21-93, Bonhams-Chelsea, #140), image 10½ x 16½ in., (26.7 x 41.9 cm.), nine engravings (BP 198, DM 482, FR 1630, Y 37,922).

BURFORD, Thomas (after)
$292* *Partridge Shooting, 1770,* margins, foxing, (10-29-92, Bonhams-Chelsea, #85), plate 9½ x 13¾ in., (24.1 x 34.9 cm.), mezzotint (BP 187, DM 449, FR 1524, Y 36,170).

BURGER, Wilhelm Friedrich
BI *Sport Jemoli, c. 1912,* large loss, tears, other defects, est. BP 450/650, (02-04-93, Christie-S. Ken, #3), 39½ x 28 in., (100.3 x 71.1 cm.), color lithograph backed on paper.

BURGESS, James   American contemporary
BI *"Flowering Plant" and "Peppers": Two,* each s., i. "A.P.", d. (one, (19)75; one (19)72), est. $150/200, (02-04-93, Sloan, #2962), larger 11¾ x 13¾ in., (29.8 x 34.9 cm.), etching.
BI *"Flowering Plants" and "Still Life Of Bud And Fruit": Two,* each s., i. "A.P.", d. (one, (19)75; one 1977), est. $125/175, (02-04-93, Sloan, #2961), each approx. 7⅞ x 13⅝ in., (20 x 34.6 cm.), etching.
BI *"Seedlings" and "Flowering Vine": Two,* each s., i. "A.P.", d. (one (19)73; one, (19)74), est. $125/175, (02-04-93, Sloan, #2960), larger 7⅞ x 14 in., (20 x 35.6 cm.), etching.
BI *Walnuts,* each s., i. "A.P.", d. 1973, est. $150/200, (02-04-93, Sloan, #2963), larger 11¾ x 15¾ in., (29.8 x 40 cm.), etching.

BURGESS, William   English 1755-1813
BI *"View Of The Church Of Tydd St. Mary" and "View Of Holbeach Church":Two,* est. $175/225, (04-02-93, Sloan, #2286), larger 8⅜ x 13 in., (213 x 330 mm.), engraving.

BURGESS, William (after)   English 1755-1813
BI *View Of Gosberton Church,* engraving by H. Burgess, pub. 182, est. $150/200, (05-28-93, Sloan, #217), sight 8½ x 13 in., (21.6 x 33 cm.), engraving.
BI *View Of Gosberton Church,* by H. Burgess, pub. 1802, est. $175/225, (04-02-93, Sloan, #2284), sight 8½ x 13 in., (216 x 330 mm.), engraving.

BURGESS, William and H.   English 18th/19th cent.
BI *Views Of Fleet Church: A Pair,* each pub. 1803, est. $175/225, (04-02-93, Sloan, #2285), each, sight 8¼ x 12⅞ in., (210 x 327 mm.), engraving.

BURGHERS, Michael   Dutch b. 1640
$138* *Britannia Saxonica,* (09-17-92, Sloan, #1413), 7⅜ x 10¾ in., (18.7 x 27.3 cm.), color engraving (BP 78, DM 205, FR 701, Y 17,181).

BURGIN, Victor
$1725* *St Laurent Demands A Whole New Lifestyle,* exec. 1976, prov., exhib., (02-23-93, Sotheby-NY, #308, illus.), (101.9 x 154.9 cm.), photograph, b/w w/printed text (BP 1182, DM 2787, FR 9452, Y 201,472).

BURGIS, William (after)
$1150* *The South Prospect Of The City Of New York, In North America (Deak 77), 1717-45,* pub. London Magazine, 1761, three 3/4 in. margins, loss, foxing, discoloration, folds, (01-28-93, Sotheby-NY, #410), 6⅝ x 21 in., (168 x 533 mm.), sheet 8¼ x 21¾ in., (168 x 533 mm.), engraving on laid paper (BP 759, DM 1822, FR 6166, Y 142,786).

BURGKMAIR, Hans   the younger b. 1500
$302* *"Triumph Of Emperor Maximillian", c. 1540: Group Of Three,* late impression of plates 5, 22 and 24, water soiling, (12-08-92, Swann, #49), woodcut (BP 189, DM 470, FR 1603, Y 37,432).

BURKE, Michael E.   American 20th cent.
$33* *Nude, 1974,* s., d., (05-16-93, Hindman, #358), 6½ x 5¼ in., photograph, silver print (BP 22, DM 53, FR 179, Y 3675).

BURKE and LEWIS
$1980* *Sacred Egyptian Beane, 1804,* after Henderson, pub. Dr. Thornton, discoloration, piece missing, very good cond., Katherine Winn Estate, (12-04-92, Doyle, #7, illus.), 21½ x 17¼ in., (546 x 438 mm.), mixed method engraving (BP 1270, DM 3153, FR 10,697, Y 247,191).

BURKETT, Christopher
$546* *"Flowering Beech Trees And Rock Wall, Blue Ridge Parkway", 1989,* p. 1990, s., t., d., (05-23-93, Butterfield, #3356, illus.), 18½ x 23¼ in., photograph, cibachrome print (BP 356, DM 893, FR 3005, Y 60,351).
$550* *"Pastel Orange Maple And Forest In Fog, Kentucky", 1990,* s., t., d., num. print #5, (11-16-92, Butterfield, #5885, illus.), 18¹³⁄₁₆ x 23⁹⁄₁₆ in., (477.1 x 598 mm.), photograph, cibachrome print (BP 362, DM 877, FR 2954, Y 68,399).

BURKHARDT, Hans   Swiss/American b. 1904
$546* *"Journey", "The Burial Of The County Museum", "Adam And Eve", "The Progression" and "Hommage To Pic-*

asso", 1956, 1975, 1977 (2), 1978: Five, each s., d., #7/10, 14/14, 4/8, and 4/121, good cond.?, (05-19-93, Butterfield, #2133), smallest 10½ x 12½ in., (267 x 318 mm.), largest 18¼ x 24 in., (267 x 318 mm.), 4 linoleum w/encaustic prints, one lithograph in colors on wove (BP 354, DM 888, FR 2990, Y 60,445).

BURLEIGH, Sidney Richmond

$110* *Harbor Scene With Figure,* mono. inside image, good cond. (?), (03-28-93, Bakker, #39), sh 6¾ x 10 in., (17.1 x 25.4 cm.), color woodblock w/hand-coloring (BP 74, DM 179, FR 610, Y 12,803).

BURLIUK, David Russian/American 1882-1967

$1665* *Marusya San, New York, 1925,* 28 pgs. of text and reproductions, dirt, s., ded., i., d. 1925, dirt,abrasions, (12-01-92, Christie-London, #533, illus.), overall S. 8⅞ x 7⁷⁄₁₆ in., (225 x 189 mm.), watercolors and reproductions on orange and ceam wove (BP 1100, DM 2654, FR 9044, Y 207,296).

BURNE-JONES, Edward Coley

$12,278* *The Legend Of The Briar Rose (Beck 48-51), 1890: Four,* set of four, s., pub. Thomas Agnew and Sons, staining, minor defects,orig. frames, (12-03-92, Sotheby-London, #151, illus.), each sheet approx. 18½ x 34¾ in., (470 x 885 mm.), photogravures (BP 7920, DM 19,308, FR 65,904, Y 1,527,684).

BURNE-JONES, Edward Coley (after)

$1887* *The Annunciation,* by Felix Jasinski, margins, s., remains, tape, glue stains, good cond., (06-30-93, Sotheby-London, #273, illus.), 23⅞ x 12⅜ in., (606 x 314 mm.), etching on vellum (BP 1265, DM 3218, FR 10,857, Y 202,186).

$1887* *Love Among The Ruins,* by Felix Jasinski, progress proof before publication by A. Tooth, s.by engraver, printing scratches w/in platemark, margins, cockled, good cond., (06-30-93, Sotheby-London, #274), 16½ x 23¼ in., (419 x 591 mm.), etching (BP 1265, DM 3218, FR 10,857, Y 202,186).

BURNETT, Calvin American b. 1921

BI *"His First Steps",* s. Calvin Burnett, num. 3/8, very good cond.?, label verso, est. $4/600, (11-21-92, Bakker, #148, illus.), sight 14¾ x 23 in., (37.5 x 58.4 cm.), lithograph.

BURNETT, Herbert American 20th cent.

$187* *Folk Dance,* s., i., (11-01-92, Hanzel, #208), 12½ x 16 in., (31.8 x 40.6 cm.), woodblock (BP 122, DM 295, FR 994, Y 23,121).

BURNS, Archibald

BI *Four Studies, 1860s,* t., mono. in neg., est. BP 6/1,000, two approx. 180 x 230mm, two approx. 170 x 105mm, (05-07-93, Sotheby-London, #54, illus.), photograph, albumen print.

BURNS, Colin W.

$61 *A Broadland Landscape,* s., #257/500, (04-16-93, G.A. Key, #47), 16 x 24 in., (40.6 x 61 cm.), colored print (BP 40, DM 99, FR 333, Y 6859).

BURNS, Marsha American b. 1945

$2475* *"Dreamers" Portfolio, 1981,* each s., edit. label, colophon s., edit. 31/60, portfolio case, Dixon Collection, (11-16-92, Butterfield, #5887, illus.), each approx. 9 x 7 in., (229 x 178.1 mm.), photograph, 12 gelatin silver prints (BP 1630, DM 3946, FR 13,292, Y 307,798).

$460* *"Enzo", "Enzo 2" and "Alessandro", 1987: Three,* from the Teenager Series, photog.'s stamp, est. $800/1,200, (05-23-93, Butterfield, #3358, illus.), 19¼ x 15¼ in., photograph, gelatin silver print (BP 300, DM 752, FR 2532, Y 50,846).

$920* *Selected Works From The Studio Series, 1978: Five,* s., photog.'s stamp, (05-23-93, Butterfield, #3357, illus.), each approx. 9 x 6½ in., photograph, gelatin silver print (BP 599, DM 1504, FR 5063, Y 101,691).

$316* *Untitled, Woman In Bathing Cap, 1978,* s., #29/50, (05-23-93, Butterfield, #3359), 8⅜ x 6⅜ in., photograph, gelatin silver print (BP 206, DM 517, FR 1739, Y 34,929).

BURNSIDE, William

$47* *Maria Montez,* Universal Pictures portrait, autograph, (10-10-92, Bonhams, #4, illus.), 8 x 10 in., (20.3 x 25.4 cm.), photograph (BP 28, DM 70, FR 234, Y 5722).

$204* *Marilyn Monroe, Arms Akimbo, Standing On Rocks,* original print, (10-10-92, Bonhams, #58, illus.), 7 x 5 in., (17.8 x 12.7 cm.), photograph (BP 121, DM 303, FR 1017, Y 24,836).

$297* *Marilyn Monroe, Standing In Surf,* orig. print, (10-10-92, Bonhams, #60, illus.), 7 x 5 in., (17.8 x 12.7 cm.), color photograph (BP 176, DM 441, FR 1481, Y 36,158).

$148* *Marilyn Monroe, Standing On Rock, Full Figure,* original print, (10-10-92, Bonhams, #59, illus.), 7 x 5 in., (17.8 x 12.7 cm.), color photograph (BP 88, DM 220, FR 738, Y 18,018).

$705* *Marilyn Monroe, Up To The Knees In Surf,* orig. print, (10-10-92, Bonhams, #57, illus.), 11½ x 8 in., (29.2 x 20.3 cm.), photograph (BP 418, DM 1047, FR 3516, Y 85,829).

BURR, George Elbert American 1859-1939

$275* *Among The Tall Saguaro Cactus,* s. George Elbert Burr, very good cond., light toning, mono. in plate, (09-11-92, Skinner, #72), 9¾ x 7¹³⁄₁₆ in., (24.8 x 19.8 cm.), drypoint on laid paper (BP 142, DM 396, FR 1345, Y 34,073).

$220* *"Capri From Sorrento - Italy",* s. George Elbert Burr, excellent cond. (?), (04-25-93, Bakker, #78), plate 10 x 6⅞ in., (25.4 x 17.5 cm.), etching (BP 140, DM 348, FR 1175, Y 24,299).

$160* *Cholla Cactus, Arizona (Seeber 220),* s., num., i., (c), good cond., tape, light struck, (05-15-93, Cleveland, #122), 7¾ x 4¹⁵⁄₁₆ in., (19.7 x 12.5 cm.), drypoint in brown ink (BP 104, DM 257, FR 865, Y 17,736).

$275* *Herdsman With Flock In Grand Canyon,* inits. in plate, s., (07-03-92, Sloan, #332), 9¾ x 11¾ in., (24.8 x 29.8 cm.), etching (BP 144, DM 416, FR 1403, Y 34,281).

BI *Leaning Pine,* mono. inits. in plate, s., t., est. C$ 2/300, (06-08-93, Ritchie, #32), 8¼ x 6¼ in., (21 x 15.9 cm.), etching and aquatint.

$33* *"Mountains In A Desert" and " Pine Tree In The Mountains": Two,* both s., (05-20-93, Boos, #530), one 5⁹⁄₁₆ x 4⁵⁄₁₆ in., (142 x 110 mm.), other 4⅝ x 3⁷⁄₁₆ in., (142 x 110 mm.), etching (BP 21, DM 53, FR 179, Y 3644).

$110* *Split Rail Fence,* margins, s., (05-22-93, Collins, #50), 9¾ x 6¾ in., (24.8 x 17.1 cm.), etching (BP 71, DM 179, FR 602, Y 12,128).

$935* *Winter Peak,* mono. GB in matrix, s. George Wlbert Burr, i., good cond., (05-22-93, Skinner, #171, illus.), 7½ x 10⅝ in., (19.1 x 27 cm.), color etching on paper (BP 606, DM 1520, FR 5115, Y 103,087).

BURRET, Jean Leonce 1866-1915

BI *Lire Le Chat Noir, c. 1897,* Imp. Bourgerie & Cie 83 Fg. St. Denis, Paris, est. DM 1,800, (12-05-92, Bassenge, #7570), 24⁵⁄₁₆ x 15¹³⁄₁₆ in., (61.8 x 40.1 cm.), color lithograph.

BURRI, Alberto Italian b. 1915

$1263* *Acquaforte F- 1975 (Brandi 50),* #26/90, s., (11-09-92, Finarte-Milan, #19), 13¾ x 9¹³⁄₁₆ in., (35 x 25 cm.), etching (BP 835, DM 2016, FR 6812, Y 156,739, L 1725).

$290* *Sans Titre, c. 1970,* s., #IV/XXV, drystamps, (06-28-93, Loudmer, #20), 15¾ x 23⁷⁄₁₆ in., (400 x 595 mm.), sh 17¹¹⁄₁₆ x 24⁷⁄₁₆ in., (400 x 595 mm.), black lithograph w/acetate collage on wove (BP 194, DM 493, FR 1660, Y 30,769).

BI *Sappho, 1973-77: Twelve,* complete portfolio, s., #30/90, num. on colophon, blindstamp pub. C Italy, very good cond., est. $5/7,000, (10-28-92, Butterfield, #2913, illus.), each sheet 10¼ x 6 in., (260 x 152 mm.), color lithograph on Umbria Italia wove.

BURTON

$798* *Shell Hill-Climb Team, 1926,* p. Waterlow & Sons, ref. #148, cond. 5, (10-13-92, Phillips-London, #58, illus.), 29¹⁵⁄₁₆ x 44⅞ in., (76 x 114 cm.), color lithograph (BP 465, DM 1169, FR 3972, Y 96,762).

BURTON, Clare Eva

$49 *"The Water Jump",* s., limited ed., #89/850, (06-11-93, G.A. Key, #20), 20 x 27 in., (50.8 x 68.6 cm.), colored print (BP 32, DM 80, FR 268, Y 5199).

BURY, Paul C.

BI *Disque, Triangle, Carre,* s., #7/50; t. label verso, pub. Maeght Edition, c. 1976-9, prov., est. C$ 2/300, (12-01-92, Ritchie, #62, illus.), 31½ x 23¾ in., (80 x 60.3 cm.), color blockprint.

BURY, Pol   Belgian b. 1922

$105* *"Cinetique Vert" and "5 Traits I": Two,* first #53/75, s.; second #55/75, s., (01-28-93, Pescheteau, #81), one 29¹⁵⁄₁₆ x 21⅝ in., (76 x 55 cm.), other 23⅝ x 31½ in., (76 x 55 cm.), color lithograph (BP 69, DM 166, FR 563, Y 13,037).

$155* *Etudes Pour Les Demoiselles D'Avignon, 1973,* from Hommage A Picasso, E.A., s., (09-18-92, Schloss Ahlden, #979), 27¹⁵⁄₁₆ x 20⅛ in., (71 x 51.1 cm.), color lithograph on handmade cardboard (BP 91, DM 230, FR 787, Y 19,157).

$155* *Spheres Et Cube: Three,* s., #117/200, 119/200, 164/200, (03-31-93, Briest, #E16), 29½ x 21⅞ in., (75 x 55.5 cm.), lithographs on Arches (BP 102, DM 249, FR 847, Y 17,824).

BUSH, Jack   Canadian 1903/09-1977

$385* *Abstraction,* s., d. 1974, #122/144, (05-16-93, Hindman, #594), 59½ x 34 in., (151.1 x 86.4 cm.), color serigraph (BP 250, DM 619, FR 2081, Y 42,678).

$220* *Untitled,* s., d. 1971, #33/100, prov., (05-16-93, Hindman, #593), 22½ x 30 in., (57.2 x 76.2 cm.), color serigraph (BP 143, DM 354, FR 1189, Y 24,388).

$220* *Untitled,* s., d. 1971, #33/100, prov., (05-16-93, Hindman, #592), 22½ x 30 in., (57.2 x 76.2 cm.), color serigraph (BP 143, DM 354, FR 1189, Y 24,388).

BUSINCK, Ludolph   c. 1590-1669

$239* *Der Apostel Andreas (Alexander/Strauss Bd. 1, Seite 100, 6; Hollstein Bd/ V, S. 180), 1625,* after G. Lallemand, (03-24-93, Venator/Hansten, #2503), 8⅛ x 6⁵⁄₁₆ in., (20.7 x 16 cm.), chiaroscuro w/three woodblocks (BP 162, DM 390, FR 1329, Y 28,081).

$265* *Die Evangelisten Matthaus Und Johannes (Hollstein 21; Strauss 93),* after G. Lalleman, (12-01-92, Karl/Faber, #28), chiaroscuro woodcut (BP 175, DM 422, FR 1439, Y 32,993).

$916* *Die Kupplerin - Die Flotenstunde (Hollstein 24; Strauss, Chiaroscuror. 96), 1635,* (06-23-93, Kornfeld, #10), chiaroscuro woodcut from 3 blocks (BP 622, DM 1550, FR 5213, Y 99,793, SF 1380).

BUSK, Hans (after)

$202* *Lady Busk,* by T.G. Dutton, pub. Vincent Brooks Day and Son, margins, (01-14-93, Bonhams, #103), image 12 x 18½ in., (30.5 x 47 cm.), hand-colored tinted lithograph (BP 132, DM 330, FR 1117, Y 25,466).

BUSSCHE, Wolf Von Dem

$1380* *"Homage To Kertesz", 1976: Twenty,* s., #33/35, (05-23-93, Butterfield, #3649, illus.), from 6 x 9 in., to 12 x 18 in., photograph, gelatin silver print (BP 899, DM 2256, FR 7595, Y 152,537).

$431* *"Homage To Stieglitz" and "Water Tower, Washington Square": Two,* 1972-76, p. 1982, s., t., d., first #65/96; second #PF/90, photog.'sstamp, (05-23-93, Butterfield, #3650, illus.), each approx. 8½ x 12¼ in., photograph, gelatin silver print (BP 281, DM 705, FR 2372, Y 47,640).

BI *"Homage to Kertesz": Twenty,* self-pub., c. 1982, portfolio, mounted, s., d., num. 21 by photog., portfolio and (c) stamp, Folio, est. $2/3,000, (04-06-93, Sotheby-NY, #489, illus.), various sizes to 17¾ x 11¾ in., photograph.

BUSSE, Gegorg Heinrich   1810-1868

$470* *Malerische Radierungen Verschiedener Gegenden Italiens (Andresen 23-34 II(, 1840-1841: Twelve,* (12-04-92, Bassenge, #6758), etching on China and wove (BP 301, DM 749, FR 2539, Y 58,677).

BUTCHER, J. (after)

$253 *A Norfolk West View Of The Quay Of Great Yarmouth, Circa 1801,* engraved R. Pollard, (10-09-92, G.A. Key, #29), 14 x 24 in., (35.6 x 61 cm.), black and white aquatint (BP 150, DM 377, FR 1278, Y 30,854).

BUTHE, Michael   German b. 1944

BI *Untitled, 1989,* s., d., #6/30, est. DM 1,200-, (05-27-93, Lempertz, #641), 21⁹⁄₁₆ x 17⁷⁄₁₆ in., (54.8 x 44.3 cm.),

etching w/hand-print and reworked w/color gouache on wove.

BUTLER, Arthur

$6 *"Across The Decks",* s., (12-11-92, G.A. Key, #57), 13 x 21 in., (33 x 53.3 cm.), lino-cut (BP 4, DM 9, FR 32, Y 742).

BUTLER, Lady (after)

$16* *The Battle Of Waterloo,* (02-17-93, Bonhams-Chelsea, #367), image 18 x 29 in., (45.7 x 73.7 cm.), chromolithograph (BP 11, DM 26, FR 88, Y 1911).

BUTLER, Reg   English b. 1913

$249* *Girl, (19)68,* s., d., num., Galerie Wolfgang Ketterer, (12-01-92, Karl/Faber, #414), 19¹¹⁄₁₆ x 19½ in., (50 x 49.5 cm.), lithograph on wove (BP 165, DM 397, FR 1353, Y 31,001).

BUTTNER, Werner   German b. 1954

BI *Figurliche Komposition Mit Zwei Maskenkopfen, 1991,* mono., d., est. DM 200-, (09-25-92, Granier, #2783), sheet 26½ x 24½ in., (67.3 x 62.2 cm.), color serigraph on copper print paper.

BYK, Suse

$8250* *Portrait Of Albert Einstein, 1926,* i., s. by Einstein, photog.'s sig. in neg., blindstamp, ex-coll. Rabindrath Tagore, (04-07-93, Swann, #451, illus.), 5⅜ x 4 in., photograph, toned platinum print (BP 5452, DM 13,343, FR 45,156, Y 937,287).

BYRNE, Harold   1899-1966

$24* *Trinity,* s. Harold Byrne, i., #8/85, (08-11-92, L. Joel, #160G), 10¹⁵⁄₁₆ x 6¹¹⁄₁₆ in., (27.8 x 17 cm.), aquatint (BP 12, DM 35, FR 119, Y 3073, A$ 33).

BYRON, F.C. (after)

$490* *Travelling In France, "Inn Yard At Calais", "A Visit To The Convent At Amiens", "Returning From A Review At The Champ De Mars In Paris" and "Changing Horses Near Clermont": Four,* pub. William Holland, trimmed, repaired tears, water damage, losses, (10-07-92, Christie-S. Ken, #39), pl 19½ x 27 in., (49.5 x 68.6 cm.), colored aquatint part p. in color (BP 286, DM 709, FR 2404, Y 58,930).

BYRON, Frederick George (after)

$238* *Inn Yard At Calais,* by Stadler and Lewes, pub. William Holland, November, 1802, (04-22-93, Bonhams-Chelsea, #143), image 15¼ x 23 in., (38.7 x 58.4 cm.), aquatint w/hand coloring (BP 154, DM 382, FR 1290, Y 26,168).

BYXBE, Lyman

$99* *Estes Park, Colorado; "Longs Peak", "Aspen Brook" and "In The Canyon": Four,* all s., t., good cond.?, (03-28-93, Bakker, #263), each approx. 5 x 3½ in., (12.7 x 8.9 cm.), 3 etchings, 1 aquatint (BP 67, DM 162, FR 549, Y 11,522).

CABALLERO, Luis   Columbian b. 1943

$95* *"Hommes",* E.A., s., (01-28-93, Pescheteau, #82), 13⅜ x 19⁵⁄₁₆ in., (34 x 49 cm.), lithograph on wove (BP 63, DM 151, FR 509, Y 11,795).

BI *Nu D'Homme,* s., #28/60, creases, est. FF1,500/1,800, (05-27-93, Briest, #49), 29½ x 20⅞ in., (75 x 53 cm.), color lithograph.

$268* *Sans Titre, 1990,* s., #95/100, (03-31-93, Briest, #E17), 47⅝ x 31⁵⁄₁₆ in., (121 x 79.5 cm.), 2-color etching and aquatint (BP 177, DM 431, FR 1464, Y 30,819).

$232* *Sans Titre, 1990,* s., d. #42/100, (06-28-93, Loudmer, #21), 38⁹⁄₁₆ x 29⁵⁄₁₆ in., (980 x 745 mm.), color aquatint on BFK Rives wove (BP 155, DM 394, FR 1328, Y 24,615).

CABAT, Louis

$103* *Une Vanne (H. Beraldi, num. 3),* reddish stains, good margins, (04-02-93, Picard, #55), 3¹⁵⁄₁₆ x 6⁵⁄₁₆ in., (10 x 16 cm.), etching on Chine applique (BP 68, DM 166, FR 562, Y 11,727).

CADMUS, Paul   American b. 1904

$1980* *"The Bath",* sig., prov., (12-02-92, Boos, #463, illus.), image 7¹⁄₁₆ x 8³⁄₁₆ in., (180 x 208 mm.), etching (BP 1277, DM 3114, FR 10,628, Y 246,361).

$2875* *Horse Play (B., J./M. 82), 1935,* watermark, s., full margins, good cond., mat staining, foxing, hingeremains, surface soiling, (05-19-93, Butterfield, #1796, illus.), 9³⁄₁₆ x

4¹³⁄₁₆ in., etching on laid (BP 1866, DM 4673, FR 15,745, Y 318,277).

$2760* *Horse Play (Johnson 82), 1935,* s., margins, good cond., discoloration, tipped to backing inupper corners, (02-11-93, Sotheby-NY, #7, illus.), 9⅛ x 4¾ in., (232 x 121 mm.), sheet 10⅜ x 5⅝ in., (232 x 121 mm.), etching on cream laid paper (BP 1948, DM 4572, FR 15,471, Y 332,731).

$690* *Italian Soldier,* s., #55.100, margins, good cond., (05-19-93, Butterfield, #1797), 7⅝ x 4½ in., (194 x 114 mm.), silkscreen in colors on wove (BP 448, DM 1122, FR 3779, Y 76,387).

$385* *Mother And Child,* full margins, s., #19/35, annot. 2, (12-08-92, Swann, #50), 4⅜ x 3½ in., (11.1 x 8.9 cm.), etching (BP 241, DM 599, FR 2044, Y 47,719).

$2310* *"Polo Spill, Aspects Of Suburban Life", 1938,* sig., t., #30/75, (12-02-92, Boos, #464, illus.), image 7¹⁄₁₆ x 9⁷⁄₁₆ in., (180 x 240 mm.), etching (BP 1490, DM 3633, FR 12,399, Y 287,421).

$5720* *"Shore Leave", 1935,* pencil sig., prov., (12-02-92, Boos, #461, illus.), image 10⁷⁄₁₆ x 11½ in., (265 x 292 mm.), etching (BP 3690, DM 8995, FR 30,703, Y 711,708).

$412* *Teddo,* full margins, num., s., (05-27-93, Swann, #45), 9⅝ x 10½ in., (24.4 x 26.7 cm.), lithograph (BP 264, DM 661, FR 2228, Y 44,168).

$550* *Teddo,* s., num. 142/200, good cond., minor handling, (05-22-93, Weschler, #172, illus.), 9¾ x 10½ in., (24.8 x 26.7 cm.), lithograph on heavy wove (BP 356, DM 894, FR 3009, Y 60,639).

$336* *"Teddo",* s., t., num. 140/200, excell. cond., (10-31-92, Cleveland, #87), 6 x 7½ in., (15.2 x 19.1 cm.), lithograph (BP 215, DM 517, FR 1754, Y 41,620).

$330* *"Teddo",* s., #6/200, t., (06-24-93, Boos, #628), image 5⅞ x 7½ in., (150 x 190 mm.), sh 9¹³⁄₁₆ x 10⅝ in., (150 x 190 mm.), lithograph (BP 225, DM 564, FR 1898, Y 35,995).

$1760* *Two Boys On A Beach No. 1, 1938, Johnson 85,* s., (09-20-92, Hindman, #702), 5⅛ x 7⅛ in., (13 x 18.1 cm.), etching (BP 1030, DM 2612, FR 8934, Y 217,526).

$2420* *"Two Boys On A Beach, No. 1",* init. in plate, s., i. artist's proof, (05-20-93, Boos, #536, illus.), sight 5⅛ x 7¹⁄₁₆ in., (130 x 180 mm.), etching (BP 1553, DM 3904, FR 13,152, Y 267,226).

$1018* *Two Models,* s. white pencil, annot. artist's proof, (09-20-92, Hindman, #703), 22¾ x 17 in., (57.8 x 43.2 cm.), lithograph in black and white on green paper (BP 596, DM 1511, FR 5168, Y 125,819).

$523* *"Waiting For Rehearsal",* s. Paul Cadmus, #115/175, t., pub.'s drystamp, very good cond., (03-12-93, Skinner, #29, illus.), 11 x 7⅞ in., (27.9 x 20 cm.), engraving on heavy handmade paper (BP 365, DM 871, FR 2960, Y 61,638).

BI *"Waiting For Rehearsal",* s., #109/175, t., blindstamp, est. $5/700, (06-24-93, Boos, #629, illus.), image 11⅛ x 7⅞ in., (282 x 200 mm.), sh 19⁵⁄₁₆ x 14⁹⁄₁₆ in., (282 x 200 mm.), etching.

$1320* *"Youth On Kite",* plate inits.; sig., prov., (12-02-92, Boos, #462, illus.), image 10⁵⁄₁₆ x 5⅜ in., (262 x 136 mm.), etching (BP 852, DM 2076, FR 7085, Y 164,240).

CADOLLE, Auguste J. (after)
$522* *"View Of Old Palace Of The Tsars", "View Of The House Of The Lost Children", "View Of The Ponds Of Presnia", "General View Of Moscow" and "Moscow And Environs", c. 1830: Five,* from the series by various hands, p. and pub. (?) by Godefray Engelmann, Paris, full margins, discoloration, (10-27-92, Phillips-London, #137), sheet 20 x 27⅜ in., (508 x 695 mm.), lithograph on wove (BP 330, DM 800, FR 2715, Y 63,853).

CAGE, John   American b. 1912
$2640* *10 Stones, 1989,* s., t., d., num. 3/20, Crown Point Press blindstamp, full margins, excell. cond., (09-19-92, Christie-E, #86), sheet 18⅛ x 22⅞ in., (460 x 581 mm.), aquatint in colors on smoked J. Whatman, watermark Mould made (BP 1519, DM 3953, FR 13,538, Y 328,931).

$2420* *11 Stones 2, 1989,* s., t., d., num. 19/20, Crown Point Press blindstamp, full margins, excell. cond., (09-19-92, Christie-E, #87, illus.), sheet 18⅛ x 22⅞ in., (460 x 581

mm.), aquatint in colors on smoked J. Whatman, watermark Mould made (BP 1392, DM 3624, FR 12,410, Y 301,520).

BI *"Ryoku 10" and "Ryoku 13", 1985: Two,* each s., d., t., annot. AP3, blindstamp of pub. Crown Point Press & printer Marcia Bartholme, full margins, good cond., est. $2,5/3,500, (02-24-93, Butterfield, #3004), 18½ x 24½ in., (470 x 622 mm.), 18¾ x 24½ in., (470 x 622 mm.), drypoint in colors on wove.

BI *"Ryoku 10" and "Ryoku 13", 1985: Two,* s., d., t., annot. AP3, blindstamp publisher, Crown Print Press, fullmargins, good cond., est. $1,5/2,500, (05-19-93, Butterfield, #2133A), one 18½ x 24½ in., (470 x 622 mm.), the other 18¾ x 24½ in., (470 x 622 mm.), drypoint in colors on wove.

CAIN, Charles William   English 1893-1962
$10* *"Aka-Kuf",* s., t., good cond., hinges, (05-15-93, Cleveland, #368), 4¼ x 8⅜ in., (10.8 x 21.3 cm.), drypoint (BP 7, DM 16, FR 54, Y 1109).

$64* *The Shamal, Mesopotamia,* s., t., margins, (08-20-92, Bonhams-Chelsea, #108), plate 4 x 8¼ in., (10.2 x 21 cm.), drypoint etching on laid paper (BP 33, DM 93, FR 314, Y 8082).

$165* *"Shortened Canvas", "Hauling The Boat Onto Shore", "From Forests Far", "Before The Breeze" and "The Canoe Builders": Five,* each s., one inits. in plate, (09-17-92, Sloan, #1423), largest 9½ x 13¾ in., (24.1 x 34.9 cm.), drypoint etching (BP 93, DM 245, FR 838, Y 20,543).

CAIRE, Nicholas   1837-1918
$25* *Dandenong State Forest At Fern Tree Gully,* Anglo-Australian Photographic Company, 13.3x18.7 cm, (08-11-92, L. Joel, #113), photograph (BP 13, DM 37, FR 125, Y 3122, A$ 33).

$25* *Interior Of The Crater At Mount Franklin,* Anglo-Australasian Photographic Company, 13x18.4 cm., (08-11-92, L. Joel, #111G), photograph (BP 13, DM 37, FR 125, Y 3122, A$ 33).

$41* *The Punt, Echuca,* Anglo-Australasian Photographic Company, 12.3x18.1 cm, (08-11-92, L. Joel, #115G), photograph (BP 21, DM 61, FR 205, Y 5121, A$ 55).

$41* *Scene On The River Campaspe,* Anglo-Australasian Photographic Company, 13.3x18.7 cm, (08-11-92, L. Joel, #114G), photograph (BP 21, DM 61, FR 205, Y 5121, A$ 55).

$164* *View Of Portion Of The City Of Sandhurst As Seen From The Hill, CampReserve,* Anglo-Australasian Photographic Company, 13.5x19 cm, (08-11-92, L. Joel, #112G), photograph (BP 85, DM 242, FR 818, Y 20,482, A$ 220).

$41* *View Of Sailor's Creek Bridge,* Anglo-Australasian Photographic Company, 12.7x18.5 cm, (08-11-92, L. Joel, #117G), photograph (BP 21, DM 61, FR 205, Y 5121, A$ 55).

$41* *View Of Sailor's Creek Falls,* Anglo-Australasian Photographic Company, 13.5x18.8 cm, (08-11-92, L. Joel, #116G), photograph (BP 21, DM 61, FR 205, Y 5121, A$ 55).

$57* *View Of Sturt Street Ballarat, Taken From The Town Hall Tower,* Anglo-Australasian Photographic Company, 11.5x18.9 cm., (08-11-92, L. Joel, #109G), photograph (BP 30, DM 84, FR 284, Y 7119, A$ 77).

$57* *View Of The "Hanging Rock", Near Mount Macedon,* Anglo-Australasian Photographic Company, 18.8x13.3 cm, (08-11-92, L. Joel, #118G), photograph (BP 30, DM 84, FR 284, Y 7119, A$ 77).

$25* *Waterfall Scene On The Coliban River Near Elphinstone,* Anglo-Australasian Photographic Company, 13.3x18.8 cm., (08-11-92, L. Joel, #110G), photograph (BP 13, DM 37, FR 125, Y 3122, A$ 33).

CAISERMAN-ROTH, Ghitta   Canadian b. 1923
$36* *Front-Back,* #5/20, s., t., (09-15-92, Encans, #25), 13¹⁵⁄₁₆ x 9¹⁄₁₆ in., (35.5 x 23 cm.), lithograph (BP 19, DM 54, FR 182, Y 4469, C$ 44).

$46* *Striped Shirts,* #18/22, t., (09-15-92, Encans, #24), 24 x 30⁵⁄₁₆ in., (61 x 77 cm.), lithograph (BP 25, DM 68, FR 232, Y 5711, C$ 56).

$104* *"The Wedding Of Samson"*, t., num. second state 4/12, s. Ghitta Caiserman, (06-16-93, Encans, #19), 16¹⁵⁄₁₆ x 24 in., (43 x 61 cm.), engraving (BP 69, DM 173, FR 579, Y 11,092, C$ 133).

CALAME, Alexandre   Swiss 1810-1864
  BI *Vallee De Hasli, Environs De La Handeck (Calabi-Schreiber 629), 1854*, No. 87, est. SF 80/120, (09-04-92, Germann, #269), 11¹³⁄₁₆ x 15⁹⁄₁₆ in., (300 x 395 mm.), lithograph.

CALAPAI, Leo
$522* *11:45 P.M.*, s., t., #19/35, very good cond., (06-11-93, Doyle, #23), 19½ x 12 in., (495 x 305 mm.), engraving and aquatint (BP 343, DM 848, FR 2860, Y 55,385).

CALAPAI, Letterio   American b. 1904
$187* *Cloud Over Pend D'Oreille*, s., t., annot. (Artist's proof), (10-18-92, Hindman, #486), 17¼ x 24 in., (43.8 x 61 cm.), etching and soft ground (BP 114, DM 278, FR 944, Y 22,436).
$275* *Counter Movements No. 7, 1946*, d., num., s., (05-27-93, Swann, #46), 9 x 12 in., (22.9 x 30.5 cm.), color intaglio etching, engraving, and aquatint (BP 176, DM 441, FR 1487, Y 29,481).

CALBET, Antoine   French 1860-1944
  BI *The Courtship*, s., very good cond.?, est. $150/200, (07-19-92, Bakker, #70), image 9½ x 12½ in., (24.1 x 31.8 cm.), color lithograph.

CALDER
$110* *"Pyramids"*, E.A., s., (02-27-93, Dunning, #63), 21¼ x 14 in., (54 x 35.6 cm.), lithograph (BP 77, DM 181, FR 615, Y 12,985).
$660* *"Quilt"*, s., (10-16-92, DuMouchelle, #1313, illus.), 22 x 30 in., (55.9 x 76.2 cm.), lithograph (BP 400, DM 975, FR 3312, Y 78,806).
$121* *"Spiral"*, E.A., s., (02-27-93, Dunning, #64), 21½ x 30 in., (54.6 x 76.2 cm.), lithograph (BP 85, DM 199, FR 676, Y 14,284).

CALDER, Alexander
$220* *Balloons*, s., i. E.A., (11-12-92, Freemn/Fine Art, #40), 12 x 9 in., (30.5 x 22.9 cm.), screen print (BP 144, DM 349, FR 1176, Y 27,278).
$413* *Butterfly*, s., num. 77/125, (11-12-92, Freemn/Fine Art, #45), 25 x 39 in., (63.5 x 99.1 cm.), litho (BP 271, DM 654, FR 2207, Y 51,209).
$337* *Composition*, s. Calder, 43/150, (09-30-92, Kunsthallen, #55), color lithograph (BP 190, DM 478, FR 1616, Y 40,442, DK 1840).
$425* *Composition, c. 1973*, plate from "Abstraction Creation Art non figuratif 1932-1936", s., 21/150,, (06-28-93, Loudmer, #205), 25¹⁵⁄₁₆ x 25¹⁵⁄₁₆ in., (660 x 660 mm.), sh 25¹⁵⁄₁₆ x 33¹⁄₁₆ in., (660 x 660 mm.), color lithograph on wove (BP 285, DM 722, FR 2433, Y 45,093).
$686* *Degoulines Sur Disque Rouge, 1969*, s., #55/75, pub. Maeght, margins, good cond., (06-30-93, Sotheby-London, #753, illus.), 42½ x 26¾ in., (108 x 67.9 cm.), color lithograph on wove (BP 460, DM 1170, FR 3947, Y 73,503).
$715* *Galactic System, 1976*, s., annot. E.A., pub. Edition de la Difference, (05-27-93, Swann, #47), sh 20½ x 28⅜ in., (52.1 x 72.1 cm.), color lithograph (BP 458, DM 1147, FR 3867, Y 76,651).
$605* *Geometric Composition*, s., num. 141/150, (09-20-92, Hindman, #711), 23½ x 17½ in., (59.7 x 44.5 cm.), color lithograph (BP 354, DM 898, FR 3071, Y 74,774).
$358* *Homage To The Pyramids*, s., i. EA, (11-12-92, Freemn/Fine Art, #44), 12 x 9¼ in., (30.5 x 23.5 cm.), litho printed in color (BP 235, DM 567, FR 1913, Y 44,389).
$1286* *Jacques Prevert. Fetes, 1971*, complete portfolio, text and justification, s. by artist and author,#XIX, hor-commerce, pub. Maeght, good cond., (06-30-93, Sotheby-London, #754, illus.), each sh c. 17⅝ x 12¾ in., (448 x 324 mm.), 8 color aquatints on Arhces (BP 862, DM 2193, FR 7399, Y 137,791).
$385* *Le Jardin Fantastique*, artist's proof, s., excell. cond.?, shrinkwrapped, (10-10-92, Litchfield, #41), sh 42¾ x 29½ in., (108.6 x 74.9 cm.), color lithograph (BP 228, DM 572, FR 1920, Y 46,871).
$468* *L'Etoile*, artist's proof, s., excell. cond.?, shrinkwrapped, (10-10-92, Litchfield, #42), sh 43¾ x 29½ in., (111.1 x

74.9 cm.), color lithograph (BP 278, DM 695, FR 2334, Y 56,976).
$110* *McGovern For McGovernment*, #97/200, s., (11-13-92, DuMouchelle, #195), 31½ x 32 in., (80 x 81.3 cm.), lithograph (BP 71, DM 173, FR 582, Y 13,653).
$505* *Ohne Titel, 1961*, s., num., yellowed, stamp, (11-28-92, Schoppmann, #466), 17¹¹⁄₁₆ x 22¼ in., (45 x 56.5 cm.), color lithograph on BFK Rives (BP 333, DM 805, FR 2731, Y 62,850).
$413* *Pyramides*, artist's proof, s., excell. cond.?, (10-10-92, Litchfield, #45), image 12½ x 9½ in., (31.8 x 24.1 cm.), color lithograph (BP 245, DM 613, FR 2060, Y 50,280).
$440* *Les Pyramides Grandes*, artist's proof, s., excell. cond.?, shrinkwrapped, (10-10-92, Litchfield, #39), 29½ x 43 in., (74.9 x 109.2 cm.), color lithograph (BP 261, DM 654, FR 2195, Y 53,567).
$330* *Safe Return, 1974*, s., num. 15/100, good cond., (05-22-93, Weschler, #173), 24 x 31 in., (61 x 78.7 cm.), lithograph in colors (BP 214, DM 537, FR 1805, Y 36,384).
$1495* *"Spiral", "Moons On The Ocean" and "Red Sun": Three*, s.; second #10/100; third #98/175 in plate, (04-07-93, Sotheby-Arcade, #44), largest 22¾ x 30 in., (57.8 x 76.2 cm.), smallest 25½ x 19½ in., (57.8 x 76.2 cm.), color lithograph (BP 988, DM 2418, FR 8183, Y 169,848).
$861* *Untitled*, H.C., s., (05-20-93, Finarte-Milan, #27), 21⅝ x 29½ in., (55 x 75 cm.), lithograph in colors (BP 553, DM 1389, FR 4679, Y 95,075, L 1265).
$550* *Untitled (Drips), c. 1970*, s., i. E.A, (05-27-93, Swann, #47A, illus.), sh 19½ x 25½ in., (49.5 x 64.8 cm.), color lithograph (BP 352, DM 883, FR 2975, Y 58,962).
  BI *Untitled (Pyramids And Sun), U.N. Cachet Design For The 30th Anniversary Of The World Federation Of The United Nations Associations, 1976*, num., canceled U.N. stamp, est. $500/750, (05-27-93, Swann, #49), sh 11 x 8½ in., (27.9 x 21.6 cm.), color lithograph.

CALDER, Alexander   1904-1987
$147* *Petit Diable*, s., #53/100, full margins, spots, (11-16-92, Briest, #25), 25¹³⁄₁₆ x 20¼ in., (65.5 x 51.5 cm.), etching in colors (BP 97, DM 234, FR 790, Y 18,345).

CALDER, Alexander   American 1898-1976
  BI *("Serpent Noir") and ("Cochaex"), c. 1970: Two*, s., i. H C, pub. Maeght, margins, good cond., est. BP 5/700, (12-03-92, Sotheby-London, #619), lithographs in colors.
  BI *"Abe Ribicoff"*, s. Calder, i. E.A., shrink wrapped, very good cond., est. $3/500, (03-12-93, Skinner, #97, illus.), sight 31⅜ x 23¼ in., (79.7 x 59.1 cm.), screenprint on paper.
  BI *Abe Ribicoff, 1974*, s., e.a., est. DM 1,500, (05-27-93, Lempertz, #642A), 30½ x 22¼ in., (77.5 x 56.5 cm.), color lithograph on wove.
$330* *Abstract*, s. Calder, num. 135/150, very good cond. (?), paper stampedTransworld Art, (04-25-93, Bakker, #66, illus.), sheet 30 x 44 in., (76.2 x 111.8 cm.), color lithograph (BP 210, DM 522, FR 1763, Y 36,448).
$495* *Abstract*, s., #38/75, (05-16-93, Hindman, #597), 14½ x 11 in., (35.6 x 27.9 cm.), color lithograph (BP 322, DM 796, FR 2676, Y 54,872).
  BI *"Abstract Compositions": Five*, est. $3/500, (05-07-93, Goldberg, #439), overall 21¾ x 15¾ in., (55.2 x 40 cm.), serigraph.
$358* *Abstraction*, s. Calder, #55/90, watermark, fair cond., staining, wrinkling, abrasions, (03-12-93, Skinner, #102, illus.), sight, sheet 22 x 31¾ in., (55.9 x 80.6 cm.), color screenprint on Rives wove (BP 250, DM 596, FR 2026, Y 42,192).
$330* *Abstraction*, s. Calder, #22/125, very good cond., mild paper toning, (03-12-93, Skinner, #98, illus.), sight, sheet 26⅜ x 38¼ in., (67 x 97.2 cm.), color screenprint on wove (BP 230, DM 549, FR 1868, Y 38,892).
$468* *(Acrobats, A Jailman, And Men With Hats)*, s., num. 69/90, margins, apparently good cond., (02-24-93, Butterfield, #3194), 14¾ x 21½ in., (375 x 546 mm.), lithograph in red & black on wove (BP 326, DM 760, FR 2576, Y 54,917).
$290* *"Anniversaire 80", 1973*, s., signs of wear, (12-01-92, Karl/Faber, #418), 19¹¹⁄₁₆ x 15¾ in., (50 x 40 cm.), color lithograph on wove (BP 192, DM 462, FR 1575, Y 36,106).

$315* *Les Astres*, hors commerce, s., #IX, (11-16-92, Briest, #266), 33⅞ x 24¹³⁄₁₆ in., (86 x 63 cm.), lithograph in colors (BP 207, DM 502, FR 1693, Y 39,311).

$682* *Autres Tetards, 1976*, s., d., i. H.C., pub. Maeght, full margins, good cond., (12-03-92, Sotheby-London, #621, illus.), sheet 30¾ x 22⅞ in., (780 x 580 mm.), lithograph in colors on Arches (BP 440, DM 1072, FR 3661, Y 84,858).

BI *Bildnis*, mono., H.C., est. DM 1000, (12-01-92, Karl/Faber, #419), 4½ x 6⁵⁄₁₆ in., (11.5 x 16 cm.), etching on wove.

$470* *Birds In Flight*, s., #48/125, (12-01-92, Ritchie, #107, illus.), 27 x 36 in., (68.6 x 91.4 cm.), color lithograph (BP 311, DM 749, FR 2553, Y 58,516, C$ 605).

BI *Black Horizontal Pyramids - Pyramides Noires, 1974*, E.A., s., pub. State Street, est. SF 1,4/1,700, (10-14-92, Germann, #130, illus.), 22¹³⁄₁₆ x 30¹¹⁄₁₆ in., (580 x 780 mm.), color lithograph.

$1474* *Black Horizontal Pyramids, 1974*, E.A., s., pub. State Street, (09-04-92, Germann, #27, illus.), 22¹³⁄₁₆ x 30¹¹⁄₁₆ in., (580 x 780 mm.), color lithograph (BP 739, DM 2066, FR 7032, Y 181,438, SF 1840).

BI *Christmas Portfolio: Two*, from the portfolio, s., #168/175, full margins, good cond., est. BP 4/500, (12-03-92, Sotheby-London, #617, illus.), each approx. 13¼ x 18½ in., (340 x 470 mm.), etchings on wove.

$882* *Circles*, E.A., s., wrinkles, (10-14-92, Germann, #232), 23¹¹⁄₁₆ x 30¼ in., (602 x 768 mm.), color lithograph (BP 518, DM 1291, FR 4377, Y 106,883, SF 1150).

$505* *Composition, 1967*, #147/200, stone mono., d., (11-20-92, Lempertz, #482), sh 25⁹⁄₁₆ x 19¹¹⁄₁₆ in., (65 x 50 cm.), color lithograph w/offset lithograph on Velin (BP 332, DM 805, FR 2712, Y 62,803).

$189* *"Construction"*, #57/75, s., (01-28-93, Pescheteau, #84), 21⅝ x 29½ in., (55 x 75 cm.), color lithograph on wove (BP 125, DM 299, FR 1013, Y 23,467).

$688* *Crags And Critters, 1975*, s., #67/150, pub. Gallerie Maeght, full margins, good cond.?, mat burn, foxing, prov., (12-12-92, Weschler, #105, illus.), 22¾ x 19½ in., (57.8 x 49.5 cm.), lithograph in red and black (BP 441, DM 1084, FR 3715, Y 85,138).

$1705* *Les Deux Lunes, 1974*, s. Hors Commerce, pub. Maeght, good cond., paper discoloration, (12-03-92, Sotheby-London, #618, illus.), 29¼ x 43⅛ in., (74.3 x 109.5 cm.), lithograph in colors (BP 1100, DM 2681, FR 9152, Y 212,144).

BI *Deux Spirales, 1974*, s., #69/75, pub. Maeght, full margins, good cond., est. BP 5/700, (12-03-92, Sotheby-London, #622, illus.), sheet 29½ x 43¼ in., (74.9 x 109.9 cm.), lithograph in colors on Arches.

BI *Dripping Ballons, 1970*, LXXV/C, s., 1015mm x 720mm, est. SF 2,2/2,400, (10-14-92, Germann, #231, illus.), color lithograph.

$921* *Dripping Ballons, 1970*, #LXXV/C, s., 1015 x 720mm, (09-04-92, Germann, #272), color lithograph (BP 462, DM 1291, FR 4394, Y 113,368, SF 1150).

BI *Eine Artistin Auf Einem Pferd*, s., epreuve d'artiste, est. DM 1200, (12-05-92, Bassenge, #7068), 21¹⁄₁₆ x 24¹³⁄₁₆ in., (53.5 x 63 cm.), color lithograph on wove.

$413* *Evolution*, s., annot. H.C., (06-13-93, Hindman, #323), 26½ x 38¼ in., (67.3 x 97.2 cm.), color lithograph (BP 270, DM 672, FR 2259, Y 43,460).

$418* *Flamme Interiore*, s., #31/75, (05-16-93, Hindman, #596), 14½ x 11 in., (35.6 x 27.9 cm.), color lithograph (BP 272, DM 672, FR 2259, Y 46,336).

$330* *Les Folles De Sachee, Une Famille De La Bas*, s., #75/75, good cond.?, creases, (12-12-92, Weschler, #106), 21 x 30 in., (53.3 x 76.2 cm.), lithograph in red and black (BP 212, DM 520, FR 1782, Y 40,837).

BI *Les Grandes Pyramides, 1975*, E.A., s., 750mm x 1090mm, est. SF 2,2/2,400, (10-14-92, Germann, #230, illus.), color lithograph.

$1567* *Les Grandes Pyramides, 1975*, E.A., s., 750 x 1090mm, (09-04-92, Germann, #271), color lithograph (BP 785, DM 2196, FR 7476, Y 192,885, SF 1955).

$193* *Head, 1943*, s., d. in stone, slightly trimmed, good cond., staining, (02-24-93, Butterfield, #3192), 8⅞ x 7⅝ in., (225 x 194 mm.), lithograph on wove (BP 135, DM 313, FR 1062, Y 22,647).

$275* *"Homage To Pyramids"*, EA, s., (06-11-93, DuMouchelle, #2096), 12 x 9 in., (30.5 x 22.9 cm.), lithograph (BP 181, DM 447, FR 1507, Y 29,178).

$496* *Komposition*, s., num., (06-08-93, Karl/Faber, #595), sh approx. 18⅛ x 18⅞ in., (46 x 48 cm.), color lithograph (BP 326, DM 805, FR 2710, Y 52,682).

$1059* *Komposition*, (10-14-92, Germann, #228), 26⅜ x 18¹⁵⁄₁₆ in., (670 x 482 mm.), (BP 622, DM 1550, FR 5256, Y 128,333, SF 1380).

$363* *Komposition*, #11/150, s., creases, signs of wear, (04-21-93, Germann, #310, illus.), 25⅞ x 32⅞ in., (657 x 835 mm.), color lithograph (BP 236, DM 580, FR 1962, Y 40,186, SF 529).

$564* *Komposition (Liegende Form), c. 1960*, s., num., (12-01-92, Karl/Faber, #416), 17¹¹⁄₁₆ x 22¹⁄₁₆ in., (45 x 56 cm.), color lithograph on BFK Rives wove (BP 373, DM 899, FR 3064, Y 70,219).

$440* *"McGovern"*, s., #126/175, styria studio, (10-10-92, Goldberg, #531, illus.), 30 x 42 in., (76.2 x 106.7 cm.), serigraph (BP 261, DM 654, FR 2195, Y 53,567).

BI *"McGovern", c. 1972*, s. Calder, #40/200, good cond., wrinkling, est. $4/600, (03-12-93, Skinner, #92, illus.), sight 28 x 22 in., (71.1 x 55.9 cm.), screenprint in red, blue and black on wove.

BI *Ohne Titel, Schwarz-roter Sichelmond, 1974*, s., creased, est. DM 600, (09-18-92, Schloss Ahlden, #980, illus.), 30½ x 22³⁄₁₆ in., (77.4 x 56.4 cm.), color lithograph on hand-made.

$1264* *Orange Ciel, 1972*, EA, s., pub. Goodstadt, (06-24-93, Germann, #261, illus.), 23¹⁄₁₆ x 30½ in., (585 x 775 mm.), color lithograph (BP 832, DM 2049, FR 6907, Y 135,593, SF 1840).

$7475* *Our Unfinished Revolution: Ten*, complete portfolio, w/ text by Leonard Boudin, each s., i. E.A., pub.Alba Editions, 1976, full margins, good cond., some offprint, creases, (02-11-93, Sotheby-NY, #313), each sheet approx. 22¹⁄₁₆ x 29¹⁵⁄₁₆ in., (561 x 760 mm.), color lithograph on Arches (BP 5274, DM 12,382, FR 41,900, Y 901,145).

$1658* *Les Pyramides Grandes, 1975*, EA, s., pub. Goodstadt, 752mm x 1103mm, (06-24-93, Germann, #259, illus.), color lithograph (BP 1091, DM 2688, FR 9060, Y 177,859, SF 2415).

$550* *"Pyramids And Spirals"*, s., i. E.A., (05-24-93, Grogan, #371, illus.), 29¾ x 43¾ in., (75.6 x 111.1 cm.), color lithograph (BP 358, DM 899, FR 3027, Y 60,794).

$863* *Pyramids And Sun, 1975*, s., annot. E.A., good cond.?, (05-19-93, Butterfield, #2135), 26 x 39⅛ in., (66 x 99.4 cm.), lithograph in colors on wove (BP 560, DM 1403, FR 4726, Y 95,539).

$605* *"Pyramids"*, s. Calder, annot. E.A.; t. verso, very good cond.?, (10-09-92, Skinner, #254, illus.), sheet 18¾ x 12¾ in., (47.6 x 32.4 cm.), lithograph in colors on cream paper (BP 359, DM 901, FR 3056, Y 73,780).

$770* *"Pyramids"*, s., #34/125, (05-24-93, Grogan, #373), 28 x 20⅜ in., (71.1 x 51.8 cm.), color lithograph (BP 501, DM 1259, FR 4238, Y 85,111).

$468* *Red Sun*, s., i. EA, (11-12-92, Freemn/Fine Art, #41), 29½ x 43½ in., (74.9 x 110.5 cm.), litho in colors (BP 307, DM 742, FR 2501, Y 58,029).

BI *Roter Und Gelber Stern*, E.A., s., signs of wear, est. SF 5/800, (04-21-93, Germann, #309), 23¼ x 35¼ in., (590 x 895 mm.), color lithograph.

$275* *Sala Gaspar, c. 1970*, s., #67/75, good cond., smudges, wear, tape, toning, (12-12-92, Weschler, #107), 25¾ x 19¾ in., (65.4 x 50.2 cm.), color lithograph on cream wove (BP 176, DM 433, FR 1485, Y 34,030).

$495* *The Santa Claus Suite, 1874*, s., #14/175, (09-21-92, Selkirk, #186), image 13½ x 18½ in., (34.3 x 47 cm.), etching (BP 290, DM 735, FR 2513, Y 61,179).

BI *Santa Claus, 1974: Nine*, s., annot. I/CLXXV, pub. Editions de l'Herne, full margins, very goodcond., est. $2/4,000, (05-19-93, Butterfield, #2134, illus.), each sh 19¾ x 25¾ in., (502 x 654 mm.), soft-ground etching on wove.

$495* *Skyscraper, 1972*, plate s., d.; s., annot. E.A., (12-08-92, Swann, #51, illus.), 22⅞ x 32⅛ in., (58.1 x 81.6 cm.), color lithograph (BP 310, DM 771, FR 2627, Y 61,353).

$221* *"Sochaux"*, H.C., s., (01-28-93, Pescheteau, #85), 26⅜ x 16⁹⁄₁₆ in., (67 x 42 cm.), color lithograph on Arches (BP 146, DM 350, FR 1185, Y 27,440).

BI *Soucoupes Dans Le Noir, 1969,* s., #54/75, pub. Maeght, full margins, good cond., crease, est. BP 5/700, (12-03-92, Sotheby-London, #620, illus.), sheet 43⅛ x 29⅜ in., (109.5 x 74.6 cm.), lithograph on Chiffon de Mandeure.

$303* *Spiral,* s., #12/120, (06-13-93, Hindman, #321), 35 x 23¾ in., (88.9 x 60.3 cm.), color lithograph (BP 198, DM 493, FR 1658, Y 31,885).

$660* *"Spiral",* s., #17/125, (05-24-93, Grogan, #374), 25½ x 19½ in., (64.8 x 49.5 cm.), color lithograph (BP 430, DM 1079, FR 3632, Y 72,952).

$198* *Spotted Pork Shop,* s., annot. H.C., (06-13-93, Hindman, #322), 29½ x 21¼ in., (74.9 x 54 cm.), color lithograph (BP 130, DM 322, FR 1083, Y 20,836).

$399* *"Sticks And Bubbles",* HC, s., (04-04-93, Pescheteau, #170), 12³⁄₁₆ x 9¼ in., (31 x 23.5 cm.), color lithograph on wove (BP 263, DM 641, FR 2178, Y 45,429).

$605* *"Structure With Blue Sun",* s., #83/150, blindstamp, good cond.?, creases, (10-28-92, Butterfield, #2916), 24 x 18 in., (610 x 457 mm.), color lithograph on Arches (BP 385, DM 934, FR 3173, Y 74,233).

$880* *(Sun And Circles),* s., annot. E.A., good cond., light-staining, creases, pencil notations, (02-24-93, Butterfield, #3195), 20⅝ x 28 in., (524 x 711 mm.), lithograph in colors on Arches (BP 614, DM 1429, FR 4843, Y 103,262).

$303* *"Tank Traps", 1975,* s., #80/95, (02-27-93, Dunning, #1064), 29¼ x 43 in., (74.3 x 109.2 cm.), color lithograph (BP 213, DM 498, FR 1693, Y 35,769).

$880* *"Third Century" and "Environment And Evolution": Two,* s., num. 10/99 & 28/125, (02-24-93, Butterfield, #3196), 26¼ x 18½ in., (667 x 470 mm.), 26⅝ x 38¾ in., (667 x 470 mm.), lithograph in colors on BFK Rives (BP 614, DM 1429, FR 4843, Y 103,262).

$220* *(Three Legged Man), 1967,* inits., s. by Carlos Fraufin, num. 396/500, pub. Maeght, margins, apparently good cond., (02-24-93, Butterfield, #3193), 23 x 33 in., (584 x 838 mm.), lithograph in colors on wove (BP 153, DM 357, FR 1211, Y 25,816).

$330* *"Triangle",* s. Calder, num. E.A., (09-25-92, Wolf, #42), 12½ x 10 in., (31.8 x 25.4 cm.), lithograph in colors (BP 193, DM 489, FR 1654, Y 39,831).

$1108* *Trois Arches, 1975,* s., #72/75, pub. Maeght, full margins, good cond., (12-03-92, Sotheby-London, #623, illus.), 29½ x 43¼ in., (74.9 x 109.9 cm.), lithograph in colors on Arches (BP 715, DM 1742, FR 5947, Y 137,862).

$608* *Untitled,* s., #87/150, full sheet p. to edges, good cond., (05-27-93, Sotheby-Amstrdm, #574, illus.), sheet 22¹³⁄₁₆ x 30¹¹⁄₁₆ in., (580 x 780 mm.), colored lithograph on wove (BP 389, DM 976, FR 3288, Y 65,180, G 1093).

$553* *Untitled,* H.C., s., margins trimmed, (09-04-92, Germann, #28, illus.), 25½ x 19½ in., (647 x 495 mm.), color lithograph (BP 277, DM 775, FR 2638, Y 68,070, SF 690).

$347* *Untitled,* XLIII/L s., prov., (05-10-93, Hodgins, #45), 12 x 8 in., (30.5 x 20.3 cm.), serigraph on paper (BP 226, DM 557, FR 1881, Y 38,775, C$ 440).

$880* *Untitled,* s., #XVI/XXV, (05-16-93, Hindman, #510), 37 x 37½ in., (94 x 95.3 cm.), color aquatint (BP 572, DM 1415, FR 4757, Y 97,550).

BI *Untitled Composition,* st. s., d. '69, est. $1/200, (02-12-93, DuMouchelle, #2328), 17½ x 25½ in., (44.5 x 64.8 cm.), color lithograph.

$81* *Untitled, 1968,* stone s.; d., (10-14-92, Germann, #229), 24 x 34¹³⁄₁₆ in., (610 x 885 mm.), color lithograph (BP 48, DM 119, FR 402, Y 9816, SF 106).

BI *Untitled, 1974,* 56/125, s., est. SF 1,2/1,500, (10-14-92, Germann, #131), 25⅜ x 19½ in., (645 x 495 mm.), color lithograph.

BI *Untitled, 1974,* #56/125, s., est. SF 7/900, (09-04-92, Germann, #273), 25⅜ x 19½ in., (645 x 495 mm.), color lithograph.

$495* *Untitled, U.N. Cachet Design For The 30th Anniversary Of The World Federation Of United Nations Associations, 1976,* #1268/1500, canceled U.N. stamp, (12-08-92, Swann, #52), 8½ x 11 in., (21.6 x 27.9 cm.), color lithograph (BP 310, DM 771, FR 2627, Y 61,353).

$1100* *Untitled, plate 2 from Anatole Jakovski, 23 Gravures de Arp, Calder,[etc.], 1935,* Editions G. Orobitz et Cie., watermark, s., p. Imprimeur Tanneur, margins, image pressure mark, foxing, losses, tears, (11-09-92, Christie-NY, #17, illus.), plate 10½ x 7¾ in., (267 x 197 mm.), engraving on laid (BP 727, DM 1756, FR 5933, Y 136,510).

$303* *"Yellow Sun",* prov., (06-11-93, DuMouchelle, #2095), 19 x 26 in., (48.3 x 66 cm.), lithograph (BP 199, DM 492, FR 1660, Y 32,149).

$280* *"Zebre", 1975,* HC, s., (04-04-93, Pescheteau, #169), 30¹¹⁄₁₆ x 22¹³⁄₁₆ in., (78 x 58 cm.), color lithograph on wove (BP 184, DM 450, FR 1528, Y 31,880).

BI *"Zebre-1975",* H.C., s., (01-28-93, Pescheteau, #83), 30¹¹⁄₁₆ x 22¹³⁄₁₆ in., (78 x 58 cm.), color lithograph on wove.

CALDER, Alexandre and Jean HELION

$231* *Untitled, 1973: Two,* plates from album Abstraction-Creation Art Non Figuratif 1932-1936, s., #11/150 and 8/150, (11-16-92, Briest, #23), each 25¹³⁄₁₆ x 33¹⁄₁₆ in., (65.5 x 84 cm.), lithograph in colors (BP 152, DM 368, FR 1241, Y 28,828).

CALDERARA, Antonio 1903-1978

$253* *Composizione, 1965,* #47/50, mono., d., (04-21-93, Germann, #311), 19¹¹⁄₁₆ x 19½ in., (500 x 495 mm.), serigraph (BP 164, DM 404, FR 1368, Y 28,008, SF 368).

BI *Epigramme, 1978: Three,* #55/75, stamps, s. by wife, est. SF 1,4/1,600, (04-21-93, Germann, #312), 8¹⁵⁄₁₆ x 8¼ in., (227 x 210 mm.), color serigraph.

BI *"Nello Spazio Quadrato", 1975: Eleven,* #30/65, mono., num., frontispiece s., est. SF 1,4/1,600, (04-21-93, Germann, #313), 8¼ x 7¹¹⁄₁₆ in., (210 x 195 mm.), color serigraph.

BI *Untitled, 1935,* mono., i. A.C. Pr.d'a, est. DM 3,500-, (05-27-93, Lempertz, #646, illus.), 5⁵⁄₁₆ x 6⁹⁄₁₆ in., (13.5 x 16.7 cm.), drypoint etching w/pencil drawing on copper print paper.

CALDWALL, James (after HENDERSON)

$957* *The Nodding Renealmia (G and B XIII), 1801,* from Dr. Thornton's Temple Of Flora, pub. London, good cond., (10-27-92, Phillips-London, #163), image 18¼ x 14 in., (464 x 356 mm.), aquatint w/stipple and line engraving in colors and finished by hand, on wove (BP 605, DM 1467, FR 4977, Y 117,064).

CALDWELL

$1100* *The Nodding Renealmia, 1801,* after Henderson, pub. Dr. Thorton, hole, acid burn verso, discoloration, good cond., Katherine Winn Estate, (12-04-92, Doyle, #4), 20¼ x 15½ in., (514 x 394 mm.), mixed method engraving (BP 706, DM 1752, FR 5943, Y 137,328).

$440* *The Oblique-Leaved Begonia, 1800,* after Reinagle, pub. Dr. Thornton, acid burn verso, water stain, discoloration, good cond., Katherine Winn Estate, (12-04-92, Doyle, #2), 20¼ x 14¾ in., (514 x 375 mm.), mixed method engraving (BP 282, DM 701, FR 2377, Y 54,931).

$440* *The Oblique-Leaved Begonia, 1800,* after Reinagle, pub. Dr. Thornton, acid burn, trimmed margins, discoloration, (12-04-92, Doyle, #3), 20¼ x 14¾ in., (514 x 375 mm.), mixed method engraving (BP 282, DM 701, FR 2377, Y 54,931).

$1045* *The Pontic Rhododendron, 1802,* after Henderson, pub. Dr. Thornton, acid burn verso, repaired margins, image ink loss, oxidation, discoloration, good cond., Katherine Winn Estate, (12-04-92, Doyle, #5), 20¾ x 15¾ in., (527 x 400 mm.), mixed method engraving (BP 670, DM 1664, FR 5646, Y 130,462).

CALETTI, Giuseppe (called Il CREMONESE) c. 1600-1660

BI *David, Den Kopf Des Goliath Betrachtend (B. 1),* est. DM 1,200, (06-04-93, Bassenge, #5058, illus.), 5⁵⁄₁₆ x 4¹¹⁄₁₆ in., (13.5 x 11.9 cm.), etching.

CALLAHAN, Harry American b. 1912

BI *"Aix-En-Provence",* 1958/later, s. verso, est. $1,5/2,000, (11-16-92, Butterfield, #5890, illus.), 9 x 7⅛ in., (229 x 181.3 mm.), photograph, gelatin silver print.

$1265* *"Aix-En-Provence",* 1958, p.l., s., (05-23-93, Butterfield, #3361, illus.), 9 x 7⅛ in., photograph, gelatin silver print (BP 824, DM 2068, FR 6962, Y 139,825).

$3300* *Aix-En-Provence, France,* (1958), c. 1964, s., t., d. in ink, label, lit., (10-13-92, Christie-NY, #427, illus.), 6¼ x 9⅝ in., (15.9 x 24.4 cm.), photograph, gelatin silver print (BP 1922, DM 4834, FR 16,426, Y 400,146).

BI *Cape Cod,* 1972, p. 1970s, s., prov., lit., est. $1,5/1,800, (04-08-93, Christie-NY, #477, illus.), 8¾ x 11½ in., (22.2 x 29.2 cm.), photograph, gelatin silver print.

$1150* *Cape Cod,* 1972, p. 1970s, s., lit., (04-08-93, Christie-NY, #476, illus.), 8¾ x 8⅞ in., (22.2 x 22.5 cm.), photograph, gelatin silver print (BP 754, DM 1847, FR 6253, Y 130,504).

$990* *"Cape Cod" (H.C.: Color),* 1978, s., info., inventory num. verso, (11-16-92, Butterfield, #5894, illus.), 7 x 9¼ in., (178.1 x 235.4 mm.), photograph, dye-transfer print (BP 652, DM 1578, FR 5317, Y 123,119).

$920* *"Cape Cod",* 1972, s., (05-23-93, Butterfield, #3364, illus.), 8⅝ x 11½ in., photograph, gelatin silver print (BP 599, DM 1504, FR 5063, Y 101,691).

$1725* *Chicago (Eleanor And Barbara On The Bed) (Eleanor, pl. 47),* s. by photog., c. 1954, p.l., (04-06-93, Sotheby-NY, #419A, illus.), 9⅛ x 9 in., photograph (BP 1139, DM 2779, FR 9411, Y 196,738).

$1210* *"Chicago" (Photographs, pl. 40),* 1949, s., t., d., (11-16-92, Butterfield, #5891, illus.), 7⅝ x 9⅝ in., (194 x 244.9 mm.), photograph, gelatin silver print (BP 797, DM 1929, FR 6498, Y 150,479).

BI *"Cuzco", Peru,* 1960s, p.l., s., t., num. #501, 300 x 278mm, est. BP 5/800, (05-07-93, Sotheby-London, #290, illus.), photograph, silver print.

BI *Cuzco, c. 1974,* s. by photog., s., t., num. 453 by photog., est. $1,5/2,500, (10-15-92, Sotheby-NY, #507, illus.), 10¼ x 10 in., (26 x 25.4 cm.), photograph, gelatin silver print.

$770* *Eleanor And Barbara At Window, 1960,* sig., (10-14-92, Swann, #399, illus.), 8 x 13½ in., (20.3 x 34.3 cm.), photograph, dye transfer print (BP 452, DM 1127, FR 3821, Y 93,311).

BI *Eleanor And Child,* 1960s, p.l., s., 303 x 279mm, est. BP 800/1,200, (05-07-93, Sotheby-London, #291, illus.), photograph, silver print.

$1035* *Eleanor, Chicago,* 1949, p.l., s., lit., (04-08-93, Christie-NY, #412, illus.), 9⅞ x 9 in., (25.1 x 22.9 cm.), photograph, gelatin silver print (BP 679, DM 1663, FR 5628, Y 117,453).

BI *Eleanor, Chicago (c. 1954),* p. later, s. w/stylus recto, s., t., d., est. $1,2/1,500, (10-13-92, Christie-NY, #429, illus.), 8⅝ x 10⅝ in., (21.9 x 27 cm.), photograph, gelatin silver print.

$1760* *"Eleanor, Chicago" (Photographs, pl. 2),* s., inventory num. verso, 1949/later, (11-16-92, Butterfield, #5895, illus.), 7 x 6⅜ in., (178.1 x 162.2 mm.), photograph, gelatin silver print (BP 1159, DM 2806, FR 9452, Y 218,878).

BI *Eleanor, Indiana,* (1948), c. 1950, s., annot., lit., est. $3/4,000, (10-13-92, Christie-NY, #428, illus.), 6 x 6 in., (15.2 x 15.2 cm.), photograph, gelatin silver print.

$3300* *Eleanor, Michigan,* (1953), c. 1964, s., t., d. in ink. label, lit., (10-13-92, Christie-NY, #426, illus.), 6⅜ x 9½ in., (16.2 x 24.1 cm.), photograph, gelatin silver print (BP 1922, DM 4834, FR 16,426, Y 400,146).

$2090* *Eleanor, Port Huron and Lake Michigan: Two,* (c. 1954), (1949), p.l., each s., prov., lit., (10-13-92, Christie-NY, #430, illus.), each 7 x 7 in., (17.8 x 17.8 cm.), photograph, gelatin silver prints (BP 1217, DM 3062, FR 10,403, Y 253,425).

$523* *Eleanor-Water's Edge,* s., #11/43, artist's chop, (05-16-93, Hindman, #330), 4½ x 5 in., photograph, silver print (BP 341, DM 844, FR 2842, Y 58,241).

$920* *"Horseneck Beach", 1978,* s., printing info., inventory num., (05-23-93, Butterfield, #3362, illus.), 7 x 7⅛ in., photograph, dye-transfer print (BP 599, DM 1504, FR 5063, Y 101,691).

$1870* *"Ireland" (H.C.: Color), 1979,* s., inventory num., (11-16-92, Butterfield, #5893, illus.), 7⅛ x 10½ in., (181.3 x 267.2 mm.), photograph, dye-transfer print (BP 1231, DM 2982, FR 10,043, Y 232,558).

BI *"Providence", 1969,* s., t., d., est. $1,5/2,000, (11-16-92, Butterfield, #5892, illus.), 6⅜ x 6⅜ in., (162.2 x 162.2 mm.), photograph, gelatin silver print.

BI *"Venice", 1978,* s., inventory num., est. $1,8/2,200, (05-23-93, Butterfield, #3360, illus.), 8¾ x 13½ in., photograph, dye-transfer print.

$1610* *"Wells Street, Chicago",* 1949, 1970s, s. twice, (05-23-93, Butterfield, #3363, illus.), 6½ x 7 in., photograph, gelatin silver print (BP 1049, DM 2632, FR 8861, Y 177,960).

BI *Wisconsin,* s. by photog., s., t., d., num. EM 41 by photog., 1949, p.l., est. $1,5/2,500, (10-15-92, Sotheby-NY, #505, illus.), 7¾ x 7⅝ in., (19.7 x 19.4 cm.), photograph, gelatin silver print.

BI *Woman On The Street, Chicago (MoMA, p. 46),* s. by photog., num. EM 68 by photog., 1961, p.l., est. $1,5/2,500, (10-15-92, Sotheby-NY, #506, illus.), 11¾ x 7⅝ in., (29.8 x 19.4 cm.), photograph, gelatin silver print.

CALLIGAN, Edwin

$223* *Everywhere You Go, General Wade's Bridge, Aberfeldy, 1933,* p. Vincent Brooks, Day & Son, ref. #373, cond. 1, light staining, (10-13-92, Phillips-London, #94), 29¾ x 44½ in., (75.5 x 113 cm.), color lithograph (BP 130, DM 327, FR 1110, Y 27,040).

$579* *To Visit Britain's Landmarks, Plas Newydd, Llangollen, 1936,* ref. #451, cond. 1, crease, (10-13-92, Phillips-London, #103), 29¹⁵⁄₁₆ x 44⅞ in., (76 x 114 cm.), color lithograph (BP 337, DM 848, FR 2882, Y 70,207).

CALLIS, Joanne   b. 1940

BI *Bird In Hat, 1980,* s., d. in ink, est. $6/800, (10-13-92, Christie-NY, #527, illus.), 22¾ x 18¼ in., (57.8 x 46.4 cm.), photograph, color coupler print.

CALLOT, Jacques   French 1592-1635

$5750* *Balli Di Sfessania (L. 379-402), c. 1620: Frontispiece and Eleven Plates,* from set of 24, 1st states of 3, before Silvestre's address and numbers, margins, foxing, discoloration, stitching holes, (05-13-93, Sotheby-NY, #305), 2⅞ x 3⅝ in., (72 x 92 mm.), etching (BP 3775, DM 9285, FR 31,318, Y 641,956).

$1610* *Balli Di Sfessania (Meaume 646-655, 657-664; Lieure 383-393 II, 395-402 II): Eighteen,* i., stained, (12-12-92, Bassenge, #8039, illus.), approx. 2¹¹⁄₁₆ x 3¹¹⁄₁₆ in., (6.8 x 9.3 cm.), etching (BP 1029, DM 2530, FR 8623, Y 199,183).

$110* *Beggars: Three,* late impressions, (12-10-92, Sloan, #611), largest 6 x 3¾ in., (15.2 x 9.5 cm.), etchings (BP 71, DM 174, FR 594, Y 13,607).

$1133* *Bildnis Des Senators Donato Dell'Antella (Meaume 430, Lieure 294),* watermark, (06-04-93, Bassenge, #5066, illus.), 7⁹⁄₁₆ x 5⅞ in., (19.2 x 14.9 cm.), etching (BP 750, DM 1840, FR 6201, Y 122,196).

BI *The Birth Of The Virgin Mary (Lieure 1358),* 2nd state of 3, 1st in series, The Life Of The Virgin, margins, est. BP 50/70, (06-16-93, Bonhams-Chelsea, #303), pl. 2¾ x 1¾ in., (7 x 4.4 cm.), etching.

BI *Les Bohemians (L. 374-377): Set Of Four,* L. 374 in 2nd state of 4, remainder 2nd state of 2, thread margins, trimmed; L. 377 narrow margins, crease, waterstain, discolored, est. $2/3,000, (05-13-93, Sotheby-NY, #302), each approx. 4⅞ x 9⅜ in., (125 x 237 mm.), etching.

$1011* *Les Bohemiens (Meaume 667 IV, 668, 669, 670 II, Lieure 374 IV, 375-378 II): Four,* stained, (12-04-92, Bassenge, #6096), each approx. 4¹⁵⁄₁₆ x 9⁵⁄₁₆ in., (12.6 x 23.7 cm.), etching (BP 648, DM 1610, FR 5462, Y 126,217).

$275* *La Carriere De Nancy (L. 589, M. 621),* 2nd state, possibly later, thread margins, i., tears, darkening, foxing, stain, creases, tape, glue, (12-12-92, Weschler, #108, illus.), 6¼ x 19¾ in., (15.9 x 50.2 cm.), etching on heavy laid paper (BP 176, DM 433, FR 1485, Y 34,030).

BI *"Carrieve Rue Neuve De Nancy..." (Lieure 5891),* s. Jac. Callot In et fecit in plate, t. in cartouche, fair cond., laid down, foxing, staining, est. $4/500, (10-16-92, Skinner, #603, illus.), image 6³⁄₁₆ x 20 in., (15.7 x 50.8 cm.), etching on wove.

$143* *Christ Washing The Feet Of A Disciple,* prov., (09-20-92, Hindman, #660), 4⅜ x 8⅜ in., (11.1 x 21.3 cm.), etching (BP 84, DM 212, FR 726, Y 17,674).

$1081* *Le Combat A La Barriere (J.L. 576 a 582, 585, 586): Nine,* creases, staining, (06-16-93, Ader Tajan, #8), etching (BP 721, DM 1794, FR 6022, Y 115,294).

BI *Le Couronnement D'Epines (Meaume 15 II, Lieure 283 II),* artist's proof, creased, watermark, est. DM 1,500, (12-04-92, Bassenge, #6087), 4³⁄₁₆ x 8¼ in., (10.6 x 21 cm.), etching.

$354* *Le Crucifiement (Lieure 287/I),* from the Passion series, watermark, 1st state, (06-08-93, Karl/Faber, #30), etching (BP 233, DM 574, FR 1934, Y 37,600).

$432* *De Droeve Ellendigheden Van Den Oorlogh, Seer Aardigh En Konstigh Afgebeeldt Door Laques Callot, Loreijns Edelman, En In Druck Uijtgegeven Door Gerret Van Schagen, (Compare Meaume 564-581; Plan 803-820), 1633: Set Of Eighteen,* complete, num., after orig. French edit. Les Miseres Et Les MalheursDe La Guerre, pub. L. Schenk, tipped in at corners, cut on or just outside borderline, (11-18-92, Bubb Kuyper, #1825), etching (BP 284, DM 689, FR 2320, Y 53,725, G 780).

BI *Les Deux Grandes Vues De Paris (L. 667-668): Two,* later impressions, margins, discoloration, est. BP 1,5/2,000, (12-03-92, Sotheby-London, #19), each approx. 6½ x 13¼ in., (165 x 337 mm.), etchings.

$149* *"Devastation D'Un Monastere" (Lieure 134 ii/iii),* from Les Petites Miseres De Las Guerre, good cond., plate mark visible, (10-31-92, Cleveland, #8B), 3¼ x 7¼ in., (8.3 x 18.4 cm.), etching (BP 95, DM 229, FR 778, Y 18,457).

$1265* *Les Fantaisies (L. 1372-1385), 1633: Set Of Title And Thirteen Plates,* t. in 2nd (final) state, others in 1st state of 2, margins, foxing, losses, good cond., (05-13-93, Sotheby-NY, #307), each approx. 2⅜ x 3¼ in., (61 x 82 mm.), etching (BP 830, DM 2043, FR 6890, Y 141,230).

$708* *Les Fantasies, 12 (Meaume 868-880, Lieure 1372-1384 II), 1633: Twelve,* prov., (06-04-93, Bassenge, #5071), each approx. 2⅜ x 3¼ in., (6 x 8.2 cm.), etching (BP 468, DM 1150, FR 3875, Y 76,359).

$297* *Figure Studies: Three,* (02-14-93, Hanzel, #666), each 3⅜ x 3½ in., (8.6 x 8.9 cm.), etching (BP 209, DM 493, FR 1667, Y 35,818).

BI *Figure Studies: Three,* est. $6/800, (11-01-92, Hanzel, #250), each 3⅜ x 3½ in., (8.6 x 8.9 cm.), etching.

$303* *Le Gentilhomme Avec Manteau (Lieure 558), 1624,* from series La Noblesse lorraine, (03-14-93, Hindman, #342), 5⅝ x 3⅝ in., (14.3 x 9.2 cm.), etching (BP 211, DM 504, FR 1715, Y 35,710).

$2164* *Les Gobbi (L. 279, 408-426), 1622,* title and 19 plates, 2nd (final) state, margins, staining, discoloration, (12-01-92, Christie-London, #210), plate 2⁹⁄₁₆ x 3³⁄₁₆ in., (65 x 81 mm.), ethcing (BP 1430, DM 3449, FR 11,754, Y 269,422).

BI *Les Grandes Miseres De La Guerre (L. 1339-1356), 1633: Eighteen,* t. in 3rd (final) state, remainder in penultimate states, watermark,wide margins, foxing, soiling, staining, est. $3/5,000, (05-13-93, Sotheby-NY, #306, illus.), each approx. 3½ x 7½ in., (90 x 190 mm.), etching.

$1725* *Les Grandes Miseres De La Guerre (L. 1339-56), 1633: Seventeen,* final states, trimmed to platemarks, staining, laid down at corners, (05-11-93, Christie-NY, #8), 7⁹⁄₁₆ x 12¼ in., (192 x 311 mm.), etching and etched title (BP 1101, DM 2717, FR 9156, Y 189,748).

BI *Les Grandes Miseres De La Guerre (L.1339-1356): Eighteen,* title, seventeen plates, later impressions, margins,discolored, stained, other defects, est. BP 8/1,200, (12-03-92, Sotheby-London, #20), each approx. 3½ x 7½ in., (89 x 191 mm.), etchings.

BI *Les Grandes Miseres De La Guerre (Meaume 564-70, 572-575, 577, 578, 580 II, Lieure 1339 III, 1340-1345, 1347-1350, 1352, 1353, 1355 II): Fourteen,* est. DM 6,000, (12-04-92, Bassenge, #6093), each approx. 3⅛ x 7⁵⁄₁₆ in., (8 x 18.6 cm.), etching.

$1249* *Les Grands Apotres (L. 1297-1312), 1631,* title and set of 15, watermark, margins, reparied tear, very good cond., (12-01-92, Christie-London, #218), plate 5⁵⁄₁₆ x 3⅜ in., (135 x 86 mm.), etching (BP 825, DM 1991, FR 6784, Y 155,503).

$497* *Judith (L. 674/II), 1631,* (06-23-93, Kornfeld, #14), etching (BP 338, DM 841, FR 2829, Y 54,145, SF 748).

$361* *Judith Mit Dem Kopf Des Holophernes (Meaume 91; Lieure 674 II),* prov., (12-04-92, Bassenge, #6090), 3⅞ x 2¹¹⁄₁₆ in., (9.9 x 6.8 cm.), etching (BP 232, DM 575, FR 1950, Y 45,069).

BI *L'Assomption De La Sainte Vierge (Meaume 96 I; Lieure 677 I),* glue traces, est. DM 1,200, (12-04-92, Bassenge, #6091), 3⁹⁄₁₆ x 2¹¹⁄₁₆ in., (9.1 x 6.9 cm.), etching.

$176* *L'Attaque De La Diligence, Lieure 1346 III/III,* plate 8 of Les Grand Miseres de la Guerra, prov., (09-20-92, Hindman, #659), 3⅛ x 7¼ in., (7.9 x 18.4 cm.), etching (BP 103, DM 261, FR 893, Y 21,753).

$1100* *L'Impruneta (L. 361, M. 624),* 5th state of 6, thread margins, creases through image, mat burn, soiling, foxing, toning, darkening, stamp, prov., (12-12-92, Weschler, #109, illus.), 15¾ x 26½ in., (40 x 67.3 cm.), etching on heavy laid paper (BP 705, DM 1733, FR 5940, Y 136,122).

$1743* *L'Impruneta (Lieure 361/VI (v.VI)),* (04-27-93, Hartung, #2415), engraving (BP 1108, DM 2760, FR 9336, Y 195,338).

$66* *Lady With A Muff, Lieure 553,* prov., (09-20-92, Hindman, #658), 5½ x 3⅝ in., (14 x 9.2 cm.), etching (BP 39, DM 98, FR 335, Y 8157).

$2444* *Lux Claustri - Oder: La Lumiere Du Cloistre (L. 599-625), Paris, Langlois 1646: Twenty-Six,* second state, (06-23-93, Kornfeld, #12), 7⅜ x 5⅝ in., (18.8 x 14.3 cm.), etching (BP 1660, DM 4135, FR 13,910, Y 266,260, SF 3680).

$1831* *Le Marche D'Esclaves (L. 369), 1629,* 2nd state of 6, margins, excellent cond., (12-01-92, Christie-London, #212, illus.), plate 4⁷⁄₁₆ x 8½ in., (113 x 216 mm.), etching (BP 1210, DM 2918, FR 9946, Y 227,963).

$1416* *Le Marche D'Esclaves (Meaume 712 II, Lieure 369 II), 1629,* (06-04-93, Bassenge, #5070, illus.), 4½ x 8⁹⁄₁₆ in., (11.5 x 21.8 cm.), etching (BP 937, DM 2299, FR 7750, Y 152,718).

$2604* *Le Martyre De Saint Sebastien (Lieure 670),* 1st state of 2, watermarks, trimmed on borderline, creases, stains, god cond., (06-29-93, Sotheby-London, #16, illus.), 6¼ x 12¾ in., (15.9 x 32.4 cm.), etching on paper (BP 1725, DM 4397, FR 14,821, Y 277,198).

$709* *"Les Miseres Et Les Malheurs De La Guerre" (L. 1339-1356/III), 1633:Eighteen,* from the series Grandes Miseres de la Guerre, (06-08-93, Karl/Faber, #34), etching (BP 466, DM 1150, FR 3874, Y 75,305).

$2022* *Les Mysteres De La Passion (Meaume 31-36 I; Lieure 679-698 I): Twenty-One,* prov., (12-04-92, Bassenge, #6088, illus.), (BP 1297, DM 3220, FR 10,924, Y 252,434).

BI *Le Nouveau Testament (Meaume 37, 38 IV, 39-47, II, Lieure 1418 V, 1419-1427): Eleven,* est. DM 2,400, (12-04-92, Bassenge, #6089), 2⅜ x 3⁷⁄₁₆ in., (6.1 x 8.7 cm.), etching.

$1082* *Le Passage De La Mer Rouge (L. 665), 1629,* 2nd state of 7, thread margins or trimmed, pen and ink touches, discoloration, tape, defects, good cond., prov., (12-01-92, Christie-London, #216), plate 5 x 9⅛ in., (127 x 232 mm.), etching (BP 715, DM 1725, FR 5877, Y 134,711).

$1271* *Le Passage De La Mer Rouge (Lieure 665 II; Meaume 1), 1629,* (06-10-93, Hauswedell/Nolt, #51, illus.), etching on strong hand-made (BP 831, DM 2070, FR 6968, Y 134,911).

$1155* *Le Passage De La Mer Rouge (Meaume 1 I; Lieure 665 II), 1629,* (12-04-92, Bassenge, #6086, illus.), 4¹⁵⁄₁₆ x 9¼ in., (12.5 x 23.5 cm.), etching (BP 741, DM 1839, FR 6240, Y 144,195).

$688* *"Le Petit Port or Le Port De Mer" and "La Chasse Aux Oiseaux" (J. Lieure 267 et 272): Two,* small losses, faults, restorations, glue traces verso, thin or w/outmargins, (06-16-93, Ader Tajan, #7), etching (BP 459, DM 1142, FR 3833, Y 73,379).

$182* *La Petite Passion (J. Lieure 537 to 548): Complete set of 12,* first state, stains, glue, faults, (02-03-93, Ader Tajan, #8), etching (BP 127, DM 300, FR 1016, Y 22,640).

BI *La Petite These (Lieure 562),* trimmed, est. DM 800, (12-01-92, Karl/Faber, #30), etching.

$1355* *Les Petits Apotres Ou Le Martyre Des Apotres (Meaume 120-135; Lieure1386-1401): Sixteen,* t., margins, prov., (10-09-92, Winterberg, #752), each approx. 2¾ x 1¾ in., (7 x 4.5 cm.), etching (BP 804, DM 2013, FR 6758, Y 164,962).

$464* *"Pillage Et Incendie D'Un Village" and "La Roue": Two,* second state of three, reddish stains, w/out margins, (02-

03-93, Ader Tajan, #9, illus.), 3¼ x 7⅜ in., (8.3 x 18.7 cm.), etching (BP 324, DM 764, FR 2591, Y 57,719).

$187* *The Place De La Carriere In Nancy (Leiure 589), 1627-28,* (12-13-92, Hindman, #253), 6⅛ x 20¼ in., etching (BP 120, DM 294, FR 1002, Y 23,135).

BI *Portrait Du Prince De Phalsbourg, (L.505), c. 1520,* narrow to thread margins or trimmed, stain, laid, good cond., est. BP700/1,000, (12-01-92, Christie-London, #214), P. 11³⁄₁₆ x 13¼ in., (284 x 337 mm.), etching.

$98* *Saint Andre (J.L. 1302),* soiling, (06-16-93, Ader Tajan, #9), 5¹¹⁄₁₆ x 3¹¹⁄₁₆ in., (14.5 x 9.4 cm.), etching (BP 65, DM 163, FR 546, Y 10,452).

$1062* *La Sainte Famille (Meaume 67, Lieure 75 II),* prov., (06-04-93, Bassenge, #5061), 6⁷⁄₁₆ x 4⁷⁄₁₆ in., (16.4 x 11.2 cm.), etching (BP 703, DM 1725, FR 5813, Y 114,538).

$468* *Six From Les Fantasies,* 1st states before number, prov., (09-20-92, Hindman, #657), each 2⅜ x 3¼ in., (6 x 8.3 cm.), etchings (BP 274, DM 694, FR 2376, Y 57,842).

$466* *Soliman (L. 364-8), 1620: Set Of Five,* watermark, small margins, good cond., trimmed, creases (partly split)and small losses, defects, (12-01-92, Christie-London, #211), plate, larger 8¹⁄₁₆ x 11⅛ in., (204 x 282 mm.), etching (BP 308, DM 743, FR 2531, Y 58,018).

$198* *The Standard Bearer,* (06-13-93, Hindman, #379), 2¼ x 3⅛ in., (5.7 x 7.9 cm.), etching (BP 130, DM 322, FR 1083, Y 20,836).

$916* *Les Supplices (L. 1402), c. 1630,* 2nd state of 8, trimmed, discoloration, very good cond., prov., (12-01-92, Christie-London, #221), sheet 4⁵⁄₁₆ x 8⁷⁄₁₆ in., (110 x 214 mm.), etching (BP 605, DM 1460, FR 4976, Y 114,044).

$12,486* *La Tentation De Saint Antoine (L. 1416), 1635,* 3rd state of 5, watermark, margins, fold, skinned patch, discoloration, defects, (12-01-92, Christie-London, #223, illus.), plate 14¹⁄₁₆ x 18⅛ in., (357 x 461 mm.), etching (BP 8250, DM 19,901, FR 67,822, Y 1,554,532).

$1725* *Varie Figure (L. 279; 407-426), c. 1622: Set of Frontispiece and Twenty Plates,* most 1st state of 2, before Silvestre's address and numbers, foxing,discoloration, surface dirt, good cond., (05-13-93, Sotheby-NY, #303), each approx. 2½ x 3⅜ in., (63 x 85 mm.), etching (BP 1132, DM 2785, FR 9395, Y 192,587).

$850* *La Vie De La Sainte Vierge (Meaume 76-89, Lieure 1357 II, 1358-1370 II): Fourteen,* (06-04-93, Bassenge, #5062, illus.), each approx. 2½ x 1⅞ in., (6.4 x 4.8 cm.), etching (BP 562, DM 1380, FR 4652, Y 91,674).

$1826* *"Vita Et Historia Beatae Mariae Virginis Matris" (L. 1357/II, 1358-1361/II(v. III), 1362/II, 1363-1370/II (v. III): Fourteen,* trimmed, (12-01-92, Karl/Faber, #32), etching (BP 1206, DM 2910, FR 9919, Y 227,341).

$1909* *Vue De La Seine Et Du Louvre (L. 667/II (v.V.)), 1628-1630,* (06-23-93, Kornfeld, #13), etching (BP 1297, DM 3230, FR 10,865, Y 207,975, SF 2875).

$220* *Vue De Pont Neuf (L. 668, M. 714),* thread margins, repaired tears top image, darkened, foxing, toning, backboard burn, (12-12-92, Weschler, #110, illus.), 6½ x 13¼ in., (16.5 x 33.7 cm.), etching on fine laid paper (BP 141, DM 347, FR 1188, Y 27,224).

BI *Vue Du Pont Neuf (L. 668),* 1st state of 5, thread margins, 3 sides, trimmed, tears, repairs, surface dirt, est. BP 1/1,500, (06-30-93, Sotheby-London, #96), 13¼ x 6¾ in., (337 x 171 mm.), etching on paper w/an interlaced C's watermark.

CALLOT, Jacques (after)

$173* *La Grande Chasse (Lieure 353, Copy 1),* after 1619, trimmed, staining, repaired tear into image, other minor-defects, Anthony N. B. Garner Coll., (06-05-93, Christie-NY, #50), pl 7⅞ x 18⅛ in., (200 x 460 mm.), etching on laid (BP 114, DM 280, FR 945, Y 18,558).

CALLOW, William (after)

$37 *Venetian Scene With Figures Before Buildings,* (04-16-93, G.A. Key, #28), 14 x 19 in., (35.6 x 48.3 cm.), chromolithograph (BP 24, DM 60, FR 202, Y 4161).

CALOGERO, Jean French ac. 1940's

$5* *"The Little Sisters",* pub. AAA, good cond., (05-15-93, Cleveland, #370), 13⅛ x 9⅛ in., (33.3 x 23.2 cm.), lithograph (BP 3, DM 8, FR 27, Y 554).

CALS, Josef

$205* *Hommage Aan G. Sutherland, 1980,* s., t., d., #102/190, full margins, good cond., (05-27-93, Sotheby-Amstrdm, #393), 14⁹⁄₁₆ x 18¹¹⁄₁₆ in., (370 x 475 mm.), lithograph and silkscreen in colors on wove (BP 131, DM 329, FR 1109, Y 21,977, G 368).

$243* *Hommage Aan G. Sutherland, 1980,* s., t., d., #166/190, full margins, good cond., (05-27-93, Sotheby-Amstrdm, #394), 14⁹⁄₁₆ x 18¾ in., (370 x 477 mm.), lithograph and silkscreen in colors on wove (BP 156, DM 390, FR 1314, Y 26,051, G 437).

$179* *Hommage Aan G. Sutherland, 1980,* s., t., d,. full margins, good cond., (05-27-93, Sotheby-Amstrdm, #395), 15¾ x 17⅝ in., (400 x 448 mm.), lithograph and silkscreen in colors on wove (BP 115, DM 287, FR 968, Y 19,190, G 322).

CALVERT, Edward (after) British 1799-1883

$330* *The Meet Of The Vine Hounds,* (06-11-93, Freemn/Fine Art, #30), 24 x 31 in., (61 x 78.7 cm.), hand-colored engraving (BP 217, DM 536, FR 1808, Y 35,013).

CALVERT, H. (after)

$147* *The Meet Of The Vine Hounds, 1844,* by W. H. Simmons, pub. Henry Graves, margins, a restrike, (10-29-92, Bonhams-Chelsea, #125A), plate 21 x 30½ in., (53.3 x 77.5 cm.), engraving w/hand coloring (BP 94, DM 226, FR 767, Y 18,209).

CALVERT, Henry (after) British b. 1798

$330* *The Wynnstay Hunt,* by W. T. Davey, prop. Donald McGurk, (10-18-92, Hindman, #512), 19¾ x 31½ in., (50.2 x 80 cm.), hand colored engraving (BP 202, DM 491, FR 1666, Y 39,592).

CALWAERT

$55* *Industrial City Scene,* s., (05-14-93, DuMouchelle, #2537), 7 x 5 in., (17.8 x 12.7 cm.), lithograph (BP 36, DM 88, FR 297, Y 6097).

CAMACHO, Jorge b. Cuba 1934

$146* *"Composition",* #17/75, s., (10-18-92, Pescheteau, #92), 18⅛ x 22⁷⁄₁₆ in., (46 x 57 cm.), lithograph in colors on velin (BP 88, DM 216, FR 733, Y 17,433).

BI *Compositions Surrealistes, 1977: Five,* s., #0/99, full margins, est. FF2,500/2,800, (05-27-93, Briest, #50), 14¹⁵⁄₁₆ x 11¼ in., (38 x 28.5 cm.), etchings.

BI *Untitled,* #62/125, s., est. FF4/600, (04-04-93, Pescheteau, #171), 25⁹⁄₁₆ x 19¹¹⁄₁₆ in., (65 x 50 cm.), color lithograph.

BI *Untitled,* #62/125, s., (01-28-93, Pescheteau, #88), 25⁹⁄₁₆ x 19¹¹⁄₁₆ in., (65 x 50 cm.), color lithograph.

CAMARO, Alexander 1901-1992

$280* *Herbstweide,* s., num., blindstamp, (12-05-92, Bassenge, #7070), 23⅛ x 17¹⁵⁄₁₆ in., (58.7 x 45.5 cm.), screen print on thick paper (BP 175, DM 437, FR 1488, Y 34,692).

BI *Komposition, (19)57,* s., d., num., est. DM 1200, (12-01-92, Karl/Faber, #420), 19⅞ x 27⁹⁄₁₆ in., (50.5 x 70 cm.), color serigraph on cardboard.

CAMERON

$28* *"On The Bradford",* t., (06-11-93, DuMouchelle, #2263), 4 x 5 in., (10.2 x 12.7 cm.), lithograph (BP 18, DM 46, FR 153, Y 2971).

CAMERON, Julia Margaret British 1815-1879

$8625* *Alfred, Lord Tennuson (Weaver, 3.10), 1869,* s., d., i. by photog., (04-06-93, Sotheby-NY, #48A, illus.), 12 x 9⅜ in., photograph, albumen print (BP 5697, DM 13,896, FR 47,054, Y 983,691).

$327* *Bishop Wilberforce, c. 1870,* mounted on card, label, annot., sight 312 x 250mm, (05-07-93, Sotheby-London, #130), photograph, autotype carbon print (BP 207, DM 517, FR 1742, Y 36,005).

$1495* *"The Body Of Elaine Before The King And Queen", c. 1875,* orig. title label, in photog. hand, (04-06-93, Sotheby-NY, #215, illus.), 4⅝ x 4 in., photograph, albumen print (BP 987, DM 2409, FR 8156, Y 170,506).

BI *Boy Holding Bow,* 1860s, est. $1,5/2,500, ex-coll. Robert Schoelkopf, (04-07-93, Swann, #115, illus.), 9½ x 7 in., (24.1 x 17.8 cm.), photograph, albumen print.

$363* *"C. H. Cameron", c. 1865,* mounted on card, t., i., s., labels, illus., 316 x 251mm, (05-07-93, Sotheby-London,

#129), photograph, albumen print (BP 230, DM 574, FR 1934, Y 39,969).

$15,438* *"Florence", 1872,* mounted on card, i., s., label, 320 x 260mm, (05-07-93, Sotheby-London, #127, illus.), photograph, albumen print (BP 9775, DM 24,408, FR 82,248, Y 1,699,846).

$1361* *Lord Overstone, 1870,* mounted on card, label verso, 360 x 251mm, (05-07-93, Sotheby-London, #128, illus.), photograph, albumen print (BP 862, DM 2152, FR 7251, Y 149,857).

$1760* *Portrait Of Sir Henry Taylor, 1864,* photog.'s sig. and notations, ex-coll. Robert Schoelkopf, (04-07-93, Swann, #116, illus.), 3¼ x 2¼ in., (8.3 x 5.7 cm.), photograph, albumen print (BP 1163, DM 2847, FR 9633, Y 199,955).

BI *The Red And White Roses (Ford, pl. 56), 1866,* s., t., i., d. 1866 by photog., est. $3/5,000, (10-15-92, Sotheby-NY, #86, illus.), 10½ x 9⅛ in., (26.7 x 23.2 cm.), photograph, albumen print.

$25,300* *Sir John Herschel (Ford, p. 24, and dust jacket), 1867,* mounted, (04-06-93, Sotheby-NY, #48, illus.), 12⅞ x 9⅞ in., photograph, albumen print (BP 16,711, DM 40,760, FR 138,025, Y 2,885,493).

$907* *"St. Agnes", 1864,* mounted on card, t., i., lit., (05-06-93, Christie-London, #59), 10 x 8 in., photograph, albumen print (BP 575, DM 1429, FR 4809, Y 99,791).

$1980* *Woman Offering A Plate Of Apples,* orig. two-toned mount, 1860, ex-coll Robert Schoelkopf, (04-07-93, Swann, #117, illus.), 8 x 6 in., (20.3 x 15.2 cm.), photograph, albumen print (BP 1308, DM 3202, FR 10,837, Y 224,949).

CAMERON, Sir David Young English 1865-1945

$30* *"Perth Bridge" (Rinder 28), 1889,* good cond., margins slightly trimmed, (05-15-93, Cleveland, #371), 6½ x 9⅞ in., (16.5 x 25.1 cm.), etching (BP 20, DM 48, FR 162, Y 3326).

$480* *Place Plumereau, Tour (Rinder 353), 1903,* 1st state of 3, s., i. w/t., full margins, foxed, prov., (06-30-93, Sotheby-London, #304, illus.), 8½ x 7 in., (216 x 178 mm.), etching w/drypoint, green paper (BP 322, DM 819, FR 2762, Y 51,430).

$69 *Scottish Loch And Mountain Scene,* s., (04-16-93, G.A. Key, #77), 7 x 11 in., (17.8 x 27.9 cm.), b/w etching (BP 45, DM 111, FR 377, Y 7759).

$86* *Village Scene,* plate s., (11-18-92, Bubb Kuyper, #1528), 5¼ x 6$^{15}/_{16}$ in., (13.4 x 17.7 cm.), etching (BP 57, DM 137, FR 462, Y 10,695, G 156).

CAMMERER, Robert German 20th cent.

$275* *Landscape,* d. 1935, (09-21-92, Selkirk, #589), 38 x 54 in., (96.5 x 137.2 cm.), engraving (BP 161, DM 408, FR 1396, Y 33,988).

CAMPAGNOLA, Domenico Italian 1484-1550/80

BI *Die Ausgiessung Des Heiligen Geistes (Bartsch XIII, 380, 3; Hind V, 210 II), 1518,* watermark, est. DM 22,500, (06-10-93, Hauswedell/Nolt, #57, illus.), engraving on hand-made.

$5750* *Venus Reclining In A Landscape (H. 13; NGA 151), 1517,* cleanly wiped, w/delicate polishing scratches, thread margins, trimmed, rubbed, foxing, good cond., ex-coll. Friedrich August of Saxony; Dr. AlbertW. Blum, (05-13-93, Sotheby-NY, #311, illus.), 3¾ x 5¼ in., (95 x 132 mm.), engraving in grey ink (BP 3775, DM 9285, FR 31,318, Y 641,956).

CAMPAGNOLA, Giulio Italian 1481/82-1516

$6728* *Der Junge Schafer (B. 6, Hind V, 199.10, The Illustrated Bartsch 25 (Commentary), 009 S 2), c. 1509,* (06-04-93, Bassenge, #5072), 4½ x 2⅞ in., (11.5 x 7.3 cm.), stipple engraving (BP 4451, DM 10,926, FR 36,825, Y 725,626).

CAMPANELLA, Angelo 1746-1811

$503* *Die 12 Apostel Des Lateran: Twelve,* complete series, prov., (09-14-92, Venator/Hansten, #1470), plate approx. 20$^{1}/_{16}$ x 12$^{15}/_{16}$ in., (51 x 33 cm.), engraving w/etching (BP 266, DM 748, FR 2534, Y 62,547).

CAMPBELL

$1495* *Architecture: Eight, c. 1760,* (02-18-93, Sotheby-Arcade, #66), sight 13 x 17 in., (33 x 43.2 cm.), copper engravings (BP 1033, DM 2439, FR 8255, Y 178,103).

CAMPBELL, Colen

BI *Vitruvius Britannicus, c. 1715-25: Nineteen,* engraved by Holsbergh, garden plans, elevations and ground plans of buildings, margins, defects from binding, discoloration, est. BP 270/300, (10-27-92, Phillips-London, #111), plate 9⅞ x 14½ in., (251 x 368 mm.), engraving on laid.

$510* *Vitruvius Britannicus, c. 1715-25: Sixteen,* from the series showing elevations and ground plans of buildings, full margins, defects from binding, good cond., mounted, (10-27-92, Phillips-London, #110), plate 14¾ x 9⅞ in., (375 x 251 mm.), engraving on thick laid (BP 322, DM 782, FR 2652, Y 62,385).

CAMPBELL, Lieut. Archibald

$495* *"An East View Of Fort Royal In The Island Of Guadaloupe",* by Peter Mazell, (06-11-93, Freemn/Fine Art, #30B), 14 x 20¾ in., (35.6 x 52.7 cm.), hand-colored engraving (BP 325, DM 804, FR 2712, Y 52,520).

$440* *"A North View Of Fort Royal In The Island Of Gaudaloupe", 1764,* by Grignion, (06-11-93, Freemn/Fine Art, #30A), 14¼ x 21 in., (36.2 x 53.3 cm.), hand-colored engraving (BP 289, DM 715, FR 2411, Y 46,684).

$495* *"A South View Of Fort Royal In The Island Of Guadaloupe", 1762,* by P. Benzech, pub. Thomas Jeffries, (06-11-93, Freemn/Fine Art, #30C), 14⅝ x 20$^{14}/_{16}$ in., hand-colored engraving (BP 325, DM 804, FR 2712, Y 52,520).

CAMPENDONK, Heinrich German 1889-1957

$550* *Am Tisch Sitzen Frau Mit Katze Und Fische (E. 42), 1919,* s., num. 7/100, margins, good cond.?, est. $7/900, (02-24-93, Butterfield, #2903), 7 x 6⅛ in., (178 x 156 mm.), woodcut on wove (BP 384, DM 893, FR 3027, Y 64,539).

$2688* *Am Tisch Sitzende Frau Mit Katze Und Fisch (Engels 42), 1919,* s., d., wide margins, good cond., (05-20-93, Christie-London, #429, illus.), image 7 x 6¼ in., (17.8 x 15.9 cm.), sh 15⅜ x 10⅝ in., (17.8 x 15.9 cm.), woodcut on thin Japan (BP 1725, DM 4337, FR 14,609, Y 296,820).

$1083* *"Am Tisch Sitzende Frau Mit Katze Und Fisch" (Engels 42), 1919,* s., (11-28-92, Grisebach, #449, illus.), 6⅞ x 6⅛ in., (17.5 x 15.5 cm.), woodcut on handmade Japan (BP 715, DM 1725, FR 5857, Y 134,785).

BI *Die Bettler (Engels 62), 1922,* s., est. DM 1800, (12-05-92, Bassenge, #7071), 5⅝ x 6¾ in., (14.3 x 17.1 cm.), woodcut.

$78* *Exlibris Paul Multhaupt (Engels 57), 1921/22,* (09-25-92, Granier, #2784), sh 7¾ x 5$^{11}/_{16}$ in., (19.7 x 14.5 cm.), woodcut on greyish copper print paper (BP 46, DM 116, FR 391, Y 9415).

$715* *Holzschnittbuch: Frau Mit Blume (E. 32), 1918,* s., num. 7/100, margins, good cond.?, (02-24-93, Butterfield, #2902), 7 x 4¾ in., (178 x 121 mm.), woodcut on wove (BP 499, DM 1161, FR 3935, Y 83,900).

BI *Interieur (Frau Am Ofen) (Engels 41), 1918,* s., d. Jan. 19, wide margins, crease, thin spots, stains, repairs atsheet edges, very good cond., est. BP 2/2,500, (05-20-93, Christie-London, #428, illus.), image 8½ x 8 in., (21.6 x 20.3 cm.), sh 17⅛ x 13¾ in., (21.6 x 20.3 cm.), woodcut on Chine volant.

$1277* *Interieur Mit Zwei Akten (Engels 36), 1918,* s., blindstamp, stamp, (06-05-93, Bassenge, #5936, illus.), 10$^{3}/_{16}$ x 8$^{11}/_{16}$ in., (25.8 x 22 cm.), woodcut on Japan (BP 841, DM 2070, FR 6978, Y 136,988).

BI *Madchenakt Mit Katze Vor Einem Fenster (Engels 30), 1917,* s., stained, foxing, est. DM 5500, (12-01-92, Karl/Faber, #421, illus.), 10⅝ x 7$^{1}/_{16}$ in., (27 x 18 cm.), woodcut on hand-made Japan.

$1551* *Das Marchen (Engels 23), 1916/1917,* s., d. 1917, (05-26-93, Lempertz, #49, illus.), 16¼ x 13⅛ in., (41.2 x 33.4 cm.), wood engraving on Japan (BP 1003, DM 2531, FR 8517, Y 168,514).

$1332* *Sitzender Harlekin (Engels 59), 1922,* s., num. No. 5, margins, repaired tear, loss, creasing, tears, defects, tape, slight discoloration, (12-01-92, Christie-London, #321), L. 14⅞ x 11$^{7}/_{16}$ in., (378 x 290 mm.), woodcut on wove (BP 880, DM 2123, FR 7235, Y 165,837).

BI *Sitzender Weiblicher Akt In Landschaft Mit Bauernhaus (Engels 51), 1920-21,* s., blindstamp, pub. in Neue Europaische Graphik: Dritte Mappe, goodcond., est. BP 6/800, (12-01-92, Christie-London, #320), L. 8¹¹⁄₁₆ x 8⅝ in., (220 x 219 mm.), woodcut on thin Japan.

$60* *"Tiere"*, pub. state, typeset caption, (05-15-93, Cleveland, #369, illus.), 3 x 9¼ in., (7.6 x 23.5 cm.), woodcut (BP 39, DM 97, FR 324, Y 6651).

$2835* *Der Tiger (Engels 15), 1916*, s., i., (06-08-93, Karl/Faber, #598, illus.), 9¹³⁄₁₆ x 12⅝ in., (25 x 32 cm.), woodcut on thin Japan (BP 1864, DM 4600, FR 15,492, Y 301,115).

$3225* *Zwei Akte Mit Pferd (Engels 34), 1918*, s., d., wide margins, creases, very good cond., (05-20-93, Christie-London, #427, illus.), image 8½ x 8 in., (21.6 x 20.3 cm.), sh 15¾ x 13⅞ in., (21.6 x 20.3 cm.), woodcut on tissue-thin Japan (BP 2070, DM 5203, FR 17,527, Y 356,117).

CAMPIGLI

$385* *Two Women, 1956*, s., d.; label verso, (10-10-92, Litchfield, #47), 16¾ x 12¾ in., (42.5 x 32.4 cm.), lithograph (BP 228, DM 572, FR 1920, Y 46,871).

CAMPIGLI, Massimo   Italian 1895-1971

$1702* *Le Balcon, 1956*, s., d., num., blindstamp, (06-05-93, Bassenge, #5937, illus.), 23¼ x 15⅜ in., (59 x 39 cm.), color lithograph on BFK Rives-copper print (BP 1120, DM 2759, FR 9301, Y 182,579).

$2349* *Case, 1965*, #III/XXXV, s., d., (05-20-93, Finarte-Milan, #29), 20¼ x 15¹⁵⁄₁₆ in., (51.5 x 40.5 cm.), lithograph in colors on Japan (BP 1508, DM 3790, FR 12,766, Y 259,386, L 3450).

$1858* *Cavallerizza (Carrieri, 13), 1952*, whole margins, #105/200, s., d. (54), (04-02-93, Picard, #56), 15⁹⁄₁₆ x 19½ in., (39.5 x 49.5 cm.), color lithograph on Rives wove (BP 1224, DM 2986, FR 10,142, Y 211,545).

$2271* *La Chambre Jeaune, 1965*, #7/90, s., d., (05-20-93, Finarte-Milan, #30, illus.), 17¹¹⁄₁₆ x 18¹¹⁄₁₆ in., (45 x 47.5 cm.), lithograph in colors (BP 1458, DM 3664, FR 12,342, Y 250,773, L 3335).

BI *Composizione Con Figure*, s., d. 53, #47/100, est. L. 5/6,000,000, (11-24-92, Sotheby-Milan, #140, illus.), 20¼ x 25¹³⁄₁₆ in., (51.5 x 65.5 cm.), lithograph in colors.

$1516* *Deux Femmes, 1952*, s., d., num., (11-28-92, Grisebach, #450, illus.), 13⅛ x 19½ in., (33.3 x 49.5 cm.), colored lithograph on wove (BP 1001, DM 2415, FR 8199, Y 188,675).

$1833* *Donna, 1959*, s., d., #94/100, (05-26-93, Lempertz, #50, illus.), 28⁹⁄₁₆ x 22⅛ in., (72.5 x 56.2 cm.), color lithograph on Rives wove (BP 1186, DM 2991, FR 10,066, Y 199,153).

$789* *Due Donne, 1944*, #P.A., s., d., (03-25-93, Finarte-Rome, #38, illus.), lithograph (BP 536, DM 1296, FR 4408, Y 92,432, L 1265).

$1801* *Due Donne, 1953*, s., d., #79/95, full margins, good cond., (06-30-93, Sotheby-London, #383, illus.), 23 x 17¼ in., (584 x 438 mm.), colored lithograph on wove (BP 1207, DM 3072, FR 10,362, Y 192,971).

$2728* *Due Figuri, 1952*, s., d., i., num. Epreuve d'artiste 5/6, pub. Guilde de la Gravure, blindstamp, margins, mount staining, surface dirt, creases, soiling, (12-03-92, Sotheby-London, #218, illus.), sheet 15 x 22¼ in., (381 x 565 mm.), lithograph in colors on Arches (BP 1760, DM 4290, FR 14,643, Y 339,430).

$1087* *Femme Au Balcon, 1956*, s., d., #36/175, pub. L'Oeuvre Gravee, full margins, handling creases, foxing, upper and lower margin papertaped to mount, (05-27-93, Sotheby-Amstrdm, #575, illus.), 23¼ x 14¹⁵⁄₁₆ in., (590 x 380 mm.), colored lithograph on BFK Rives (BP 696, DM 1744, FR 5879, Y 116,531, G 1955).

$2349* *Femme Au Metier, 1954*, #142/200, s., timbro Guilde de la Gravure, (05-20-93, Finarte-Milan, #28), 19⅛ x 13¹⁵⁄₁₆ in., (48.5 x 35.5 cm.), lithograph in colors (BP 1508, DM 3790, FR 12,766, Y 259,386, L 3450).

$498* *Frauen Mit Tauben Im Raum, (19)44*, s., num., signs of wear, (12-01-92, Karl/Faber, #422), 10⁷⁄₁₆ x 14⁹⁄₁₆ in., (26.5 x 37 cm.), lithograph on wove (BP 329, DM 794, FR 2705, Y 62,002).

$1093* *Il Teatro, 1950*, s., #60/200, Guilde de la Gravure blindstamp, margins, good cond., light-staining, mat staining, surface soiling, (05-19-93, Butterfield, #1884), 12¾ x

17½ in., (324 x 445 mm.), lithograph on Arches (BP 710, DM 1777, FR 5986, Y 121,001).

$1548* *Il Trampolino (C, 14), 1952*, whole margins, #191/200, s., d. (54), (04-02-93, Picard, #57), 9¹³⁄₁₆ x 12¹³⁄₁₆ in., (25 x 32.5 cm.), color lithograph on Rives wove (BP 1020, DM 2488, FR 8450, Y 176,250).

$425* *"Quatre Tetes" and "Personnage": Two*, first s., second s., abrasion, (06-28-93, Loudmer, #22), first 7¹⁄₁₆ x 4⁵⁄₁₆ in., (180 x 110 mm.), second 7½ x 5⅛ in., (180 x 110 mm.), lithographs, first in red on wove, second in sanguine on Japan (BP 285, DM 722, FR 2433, Y 45,093).

$1554* *Sechs Stehende Weibliche Figuren, 1958*, s., d., #173/175, (06-10-93, Hauswedell/Nolt, #122, illus.), image 23¼ x 17¹¹⁄₁₆ in., (59 x 45 cm.), color lithograph on BFK Rives (BP 1016, DM 2531, FR 8520, Y 164,951).

$1412* *Spielende Madchen, 1954*, s., d., #62/95, (06-10-93, Hauswedell/Nolt, #121, illus.), image 23⅜ x 17¹¹⁄₁₆ in., (59.4 x 45 cm.), color lithograph on BFK Rives (BP 924, DM 2299, FR 7741, Y 149,878).

$1876* *Teatro, c. 1950*, s., #110/200, pub. Guilde de la Gravure, blindstamp, margins, good cond., handling creases, discoloration, (12-03-92, Sotheby-London, #216, illus.), sheet 15⅛ x 22¼ in., (384 x 565 mm.), lithograph on wove (BP 1210, DM 2950, FR 10,070, Y 233,420).

$1610* *La Tessitrice, 1952*, s., #62/200, Guilde de la Gravure blindstamp, full margins, good cond., staining, hinge remains, soiling, notation, (05-19-93, Butterfield, #1885), 19¼ x 13⅞ in., (489 x 352 mm.), lithograph in colors on Arches (BP 1045, DM 2617, FR 8817, Y 178,235).

$4152* *Tva Damer*, s. 1952 47/115(?), (05-25-93, AB Stockholm, #9, illus.), 24¹¹⁄₁₆ x 18⁵⁄₁₆ in., (62.7 x 46.5 cm.), color lithograph on CM Fabriano (BP 2691, DM 6762, FR 22,763, Y 453,820, SK 6050).

$1248* *Tva Kvinnor Vid Ett Cafebord*, s., 1953-79/95, (12-04-92, AB Stockholm, #7016), 23¹⁄₁₆ x 17⁵⁄₁₆ in., (58.5 x 44 cm.), lithograph in colors on BFK Rives (BP 801, DM 1988, FR 6742, Y 155,805, SK 8470).

$1955* *"Two Women At A Cafe" and "The Theater", c. 1955: Two*, s., #95/95, #130/200, d., pub. Guilde de la Gravure, blindstamp, fullmargins, good cond., mat stain; water stain, discolored, Late Vitya Vronsky Babin Coll., (05-13-93, Sotheby-NY, #478), one 23⅜ x 17¼ in., (595 x 437 mm.), other 12¾ x 17⅞ in., (595 x 437 mm.), lithograph in colors, lithograph (BP 1283, DM 3157, FR 10,648, Y 218,265).

$2217* *Two Women, 1952*, s., d., #118/200, pub. Guilde de la Gravure, blindstamp, full margins, good cond., discoloration, foxing, creases, (12-03-92, Sotheby-London, #217, illus.), sheet 22¼ x 15⅛ in., (565 x 384 mm.), lithograph in colors on Arches (BP 1430, DM 3486, FR 11,900, Y 275,849).

$1610* *Untitled, Female Figure, Front And Back, 1957*, s., d., #117/175, blindstamp, margins, taped to mat, good cond., creases, glue remains, mat staining, foxing, surface soiling, (05-19-93, Butterfield, #1886), 23½ x 16 in., (597 x 406 mm.), lithograph in colors on Rives BFK (BP 1045, DM 2617, FR 8817, Y 178,235).

$330* *Verlaine Poesie*, s., plate #8/55, (05-16-93, Hindman, #466), 11 x 6¾ in., (27.9 x 17.1 cm.), lithograph (BP 215, DM 531, FR 1784, Y 36,581).

CAMPION, George Bryant

$801* *Royal House Artillery, 1846: Set Of Six*, pub. Ackermann and Co., good cond., water damage, foxing, skimming, prov., (10-27-92, Phillips-London, #83), image 17⅝ x 26¾ in., (448 x 679 mm.), tinted lithograph w/hand-colouring (BP 506, DM 1228, FR 4165, Y 97,982).

CAMPS, Gaspar

$442* *Panneau Decoratif*, cond. B+, (06-11-93, Boisgirard, #50), 30¹¹⁄₁₆ x 14¾ in., (78 x 37.5 cm.), poster (BP 290, DM 718, FR 2422, Y 46,897).

CANALETTO   Italian 1697-1768

$10,295* *Ale Porte Del Dolo (Bromberg 5)*, 3rd final state, margins, surface dirt, good cond., (06-30-93, Sotheby-London, #100), 11¾ x 16¾ in., (298 x 425 mm.), etching (BP 6900, DM 17,559, FR 59,235, Y 1,103,075).

$2974* *Das Haus Mit Dem Peristyl (Rechte Halfte) (De Vesme 13, Bromberg 14 II), 1741*, num., prov., (06-04-93, Bassenge, #5431, illus.), 11¹¹⁄₁₆ x 8⁷⁄₁₆ in., (29.7 x 21.5

cm.), etching (BP 1968, DM 4829, FR 16,278, Y 320,751).

$10,295* *Il Portico Con La Lanterna (B. 10),* 3rd final state, wide margins, good cond., (06-30-93, Sotheby-London, #101), 11¾ x 17 in., (298 x 432 mm.), etching on paper w/an R countermark (BP 6900, DM 17,559, FR 59,235, Y 1,103,075).

$3595* *Imaginary View Of Padua (De Vesme, Bomberg 11),* 2nd state of 3, small margins, corner torn, dirt, staining, front cover illus., (10-15-92, Bonhams-Chelsea, #44, illus.), plate 11¾ x 17 in., (29.8 x 43.2 cm.), etching, laid down (BP 2200, DM 5351, FR 18,147, Y 431,314).

BI *Das Kleine Monument (De Vesme 30; Palluchini-Guarnati 29b; Bromberg 33 II),* mono., est. DM 1,800, (12-04-92, Bassenge, #6529), 4⅝ x 3¼ in., (11.7 x 8.3 cm.), etching.

$2760* *Landscape With A Tower And Two Ruined Pillars (Bromberg 28),* before 1744, 2nd final state, margins, good cond., prov., (05-11-93, Christie-NY, #9, illus.), plate 5⅝ x 8¼ in., (143 x 210 mm.), etching on laid (BP 1762, DM 4348, FR 14,650, Y 303,597).

$4434* *Landscape With Ruined Monuments (Bromberg 31),* only state, trimmed within platemark, surface dirt, (12-03-92, Sotheby-London, #21), 5¾ x 8¼ in., (146 x 210 mm.), etching (BP 2860, DM 6973, FR 23,800, Y 551,698).

$2166* *Paesaggio Con Rovine Classiche (Bromberg 28),* thread margins, glue stain, minor staining, (11-30-92, Phillips-London, #281), plate 5⅝ x 8⅜ in., (143 x 213 mm.), etching on handmade laid paper (BP 1430, DM 3451, FR 11,714, Y 269,571).

$1867* *Paysage Montagneux Avec Cinq Ponts (R.B., 22),* second state, good margins, (06-16-93, Ader Tajan, #28), 8³⁄₁₆ x 5½ in., (20.8 x 14 cm.), etching (BP 1245, DM 3099, FR 10,401, Y 199,125).

$708* *Phantasieansicht Von Padua (Bromberg 11 III),* (06-04-93, Bassenge, #5430), 11⅞ x 16¾ in., (30.2 x 42.5 cm.), color etching (BP 468, DM 1150, FR 3875, Y 76,359).

$18,332* *The Portico With The Lantern (Bromberg 10),* 2nd state of 3, watermark, margins, mount-staining, foxing, good cond., (11-30-92, Phillips-London, #280, illus.), plate 11⅞ x 16⅞ in., (302 x 429 mm.), etching on laid (BP 12,100, DM 29,205, FR 99,145, Y 2,281,518).

$3450* *The Portico With The Lantern (De V., Br. 10),* c. 1741, 3rd (final) state, watermark, narrow margins, glued down, good cond., (05-13-93, Sotheby-NY, #308), 11¾ x 16⅞ in., (300 x 430 mm.), etching (BP 2265, DM 5571, FR 18,791, Y 385,174).

$14,151* *Le Portique A La Lanterne (R.B., 10),* first state of three, good margins, collector's stamp, (06-16-93, Ader Tajan, #29), 11¾ x 16¾ in., (29.8 x 42.5 cm.), etching (BP 9434, DM 23,491, FR 78,836, Y 1,509,279).

$3341* *Pra Della Valle (R. Bromberg, 8),* definitive state, small margins, (06-16-93, Ader Tajan, #26), 11⁹⁄₁₆ x 16¾ in., (29.4 x 42.5 cm.), etching (BP 2227, DM 5546, FR 18,613, Y 356,335).

$2162* *Les Prisons (R.B., 21),* third state, good margins, collector's stamp, (06-16-93, Ader Tajan, #27), 5⁹⁄₁₆ x 8¼ in., (14.1 x 21 cm.), etching (BP 1441, DM 3589, FR 12,045, Y 230,589).

BI *Title Page (De Vesme, Bromberg 1), c. 1735,* 2nd (final) state, margins, foxing, discoloration, The Suida Manning-Coll., est. $3/5,000, (05-13-93, Sotheby-NY, #298), 11⅝ x 16¾ in., (296 x 427 mm.), etching.

$5750* *View Of A Town With A Bishop's Tomb (De V. 14; Br. 16), c. 1740,* 2nd (final) state, inky plate edges, wide margins, margins, defects,good cond., collector's marks, (05-13-93, Sotheby-NY, #309, illus.), 11¾ x 11⅞ in., (300 x 302 mm.), etching (BP 3775, DM 9285, FR 31,318, Y 641,956).

$7331* *Un Villaggio Sul Fiume Brenta (Bromberg 9/II), c. 1740,* sheet 8 of series Vedute, (06-23-93, Kornfeld, #16), etching (BP 4980, DM 12,404, FR 41,725, Y 798,671, SF 11,040).

BI *The Waggon Passing Over A Bridge (B. 32),* 2nd final state, narrow margins, trimmed, paper splits, wormhole, stains, (06-30-93, Sotheby-London, #102), 5½ x 5 in., (140 x 127 mm.), etching.

CANALS, Ricardo

$186* *Danse Espagnole, 1903,* whole margins, #9/46, (04-02-93, Picard, #58), 9¹³⁄₁₆ x 12¹³⁄₁₆ in., (25 x 32.5 cm.), etching and aquatint in brown on thin Japan (BP 123, DM 299, FR 1015, Y 21,177).

CANCELLARE, Frank

$920* *Dewey Defeats Truman (1948),* c. 1950, lit., (04-08-93, Christie-NY, #263, illus.), 9⅛ x 11¼ in., (23.2 x 28.6 cm.), photograph, gelatin silver print (BP 603, DM 1478, FR 5003, Y 104,403).

$1540* *Dewey Defeats Truman, 1948,* sig., handstamp, (10-14-92, Swann, #291, illus.), 7 x 8½ in., (17.8 x 21.6 cm.), photograph, silver print (BP 904, DM 2254, FR 7643, Y 186,621).

CANE, Louis   b. 1943

$135* *"Coupe De Fruits", 1988,* epreuve d'artiste, #4/12, d., s., (10-18-92, Pescheteau, #93), 23⅝ x 18½ in., (60 x 47 cm.), lithograph in black on cream (BP 82, DM 199, FR 677, Y 16,119).

CANO Y OLMEDILLA, Don Juan De La Cruz

$99* *A Chart Of The Straits of Magellan, 1769,* (09-17-92, Sloan, #2690), 20¼ x 27 in., (51.4 x 68.6 cm.), handcolored (BP 56, DM 147, FR 503, Y 12,326).

CANOT, Pierre Charles

$376* *Ships, "View Of A Squadron Of The Imperial Russian Fleet", 1777,* after R. Paton, pub. R. Paton, foxing, waterstains, (06-09-93, Bubb Kuyper, #2073), approx. 19⁵⁄₁₆ x 25⁹⁄₁₆ in., (49 x 65 cm.), engraving (BP 248, DM 615, FR 2068, Y 39,987, G 690).

BI *A South East View Of The City Of New York, In North America, Vue Du Sud Est La Ville De New York, Dans L'Amerique Septentrionale (Stokes & Haskell C.1763-B-84; D. 115), c. 1768,* after Thomas Howdell, pub. Scenographia Americana, p. for John Bowles, Robert Sayer, Thomas Jeffrys, Carington Bowles and Henry Parker, margins, good cond., mat stain, foxing, soiling, est. $12/15,000, (01-28-93, Sotheby-NY, #411, illus.), 14⅜ x 21 in., (365 x 533 mm.), sheet 18 x 23⅜ in., (365 x 533 mm.), engraving on laid paper.

BI *A South West View Of The City Of New York, In North America, Vue De Sud Ouest De La Ville De New York Dans L'Amerique Septentroinale (S. & H. C. 1763-B-85; D. 116), c. 1768,* 3rd state of 3, after Thomas Howdell, pub. Scenographia Americana, p. for John Bowles, Carington Bowles, Robert Sayer and Henry Parker, margins, good cond., mat stain, soiling, water stain, est. $12/15,000, (01-28-93, Sotheby-NY, #412, illus.), 14⅛ x 20⅞ in., (359 x 530 mm.), sheet 18 x 23⅝ in., (359 x 530 mm.), engraving on laid paper.

BI *A View Of Louisburg In North America, Taken Near The Light House When That City Was Beseiged In 1758. Vue De Louisburg, Dans L'Amerique Septentrionale, Prise Du Fanal Durant Le Dernier Siege En 1758, 1762,* after Capt. Ince, pub. in Scenographia America, by Thos. Jeffreys, margins, good cond., discoloration, losses, creases, backboard stain, skinned spots, ex-coll. Daniel Bruce Moffet, est. $10/12,000, (01-28-93, Sotheby-NY, #439, illus.), 14⅜ x 20⅞ in., (365 x 530 mm.), sheet 15⅝ x 21⅞ in., (365 x 530 mm.), hand-colored engraving on wove.

CANOVA, Antonio (after)

$303* *Crevgante,* by Bertini, (03-17-93, Bonhams-Chelsea, #424), image 18¼ x 21½ in., (46.4 x 54.6 cm.), etching (BP 209, DM 504, FR 1714, Y 35,538).

CANTARINI, Simone   Italian 1612-1648

BI *Fortune (B. 34; Bell. 5), c. 1635-36,* i., watermark, margins, tears where glued down, center crease, good cond., The Suida Manning Coll., est. $1,5/2,000, (05-13-93, Sotheby-NY, #227, illus.), 12⅞ x 5⅝ in., (327 x 144 mm.), etching.

BI *"Holy Family And The Infant St. John" (Bartsch vol. 19),* good cond., stain, est. $3/400, (10-31-92, Cleveland, #9), 6³⁄₁₆ x 8⅜ in., (15.7 x 21.3 cm.), etching.

BI *The Rape Of Europa (B. 30; Bell. 6), c. 1639-40,* 1st state of 2, watermark, thread margins three sides, trimmed, creases, foxing, good cond., The Suida Manning Coll., est. $2/3,000, (05-13-93, Sotheby-NY, #230, illus.), 8¾ x 12¼ in., (222 x 310 mm.), etching.

BI *St. Anthony Of Padua (B. 26; Bell. 20), c. 1635-36,* plate tone, narrow margins, corner torn through, tip of margin cornerlacking, good cond., The Suida Manning Coll., est. $1,2/1,600, (05-13-93, Sotheby-NY, #229), 3⅛ x 2⅜ in., (80 x 61 mm.), etching.

BI *St. Sebastian (B. 24; Bell. 25), c. 1639,* narrow margins, stains, traces of glue, edge glued down, good cond.,The Suida Manning Coll., est. $1,2/1,500, (05-13-93, Sotheby-NY, #228, illus.), 7½ x 5 in., (191 x 127 mm.), etching.

$1610* *The Young St. John The Baptist In The Desert (B. 22; Bell. 2), c. 1635-36,* plate tone, thread margins, trimmed, nicks, rubbed spots, discoloration, stains, backed, The Suida Manning Coll., (05-13-93, Sotheby-NY, #226, illus.), 4 x 3½ in., (102 x 89 mm.), etching (BP 1057, DM 2600, FR 8769, Y 179,748).

CANTOR, A.

$932* *Builders Use Shell, 1938,* ref. #523, cond. 1, creasing, (10-13-92, Phillips-London, #142), 29¹⁵⁄₁₆ x 44⅞ in., (76 x 114 cm.), color lithograph (BP 543, DM 1365, FR 4639, Y 113,011).

CANTRE, Jozef

$269* *Het Wezen, 1919,* s., t., d., #3/32, good cond., buckling, Late Gerhard Brauer Coll., (05-27-93, Sotheby-Amstrdm, #715), 7¹⁵⁄₁₆ x 7¹¹⁄₁₆ in., (202 x 196 mm.), woodcut on wove (BP 172, DM 432, FR 1455, Y 28,838, G 483).

CANTU, Cesare and Michele SARTORIO

$4840* *Lombardia Pittoresca; O, Disegni Di Cio Che La Lombardia Chiude Di Piu Interessante Per Le Arti, La Storia, La Natura: 202,* t., by Giuseppe Elena, oblong 4to., (11-12-92, Swann, #104, illus.), lithographs, engravings (BP 3179, DM 7669, FR 25,869, Y 600,124).

CAPA, Robert   Hungarian 1913-1954

BI *Chinese Civil War, c. 1938,* photog.'s name stamp, est. $1/2,000, (10-15-92, Sotheby-NY, #556, illus.), 14 x 11 in., (35.6 x 27.9 cm.), photograph, gelatin silver print.

$1430* *Death Of A Loyalist Soldier, 1936,* p. 1960s, (04-07-93, Swann, #294, illus.), 9 x 12 in., photograph, silver print (BP 945, DM 2313, FR 7827, Y 162,463).

BI *German Prisoners, 1944,* handstamp, label, est. $7/1,000, (10-14-92, Swann, #293, illus.), 13⅞ x 10½ in., (35.2 x 26.7 cm.), photograph, silver print.

BI *Korzo, Along The Danube, Hungary, c. 1948,* credit stamp, label, est. $1,2/1,800, (10-13-92, Christie-NY, #432, illus.), 13⅝ x 10¾ in., (34.6 x 27.3 cm.), photograph, gelatin silver print.

$880* *Picasso And His Son Claude, c. 1953,* handstamp, (10-14-92, Swann, #294, illus.), 7½ x 9½ in., (19.1 x 24.1 cm.), photograph, silver print (BP 517, DM 1288, FR 4367, Y 106,641).

BI *Railroad Car Factory, Wrocaw, Poland, c. 1948,* credit stamp, label, legend, est. $1,2/1,500, (10-13-92, Christie-NY, #431, illus.), 9½ x 11 in., (24.1 x 27.9 cm.), photograph, gelatin silver print.

CAPE DORSET LUCY

BI *The Stolen Fish, 1982,* s., #36/50, est. C$350-450, (10-21-92, Maynard, #12), sheet 22 x 27 in., (55.9 x 68.6 cm.), stonecut.

CAPEDEVILLE, Jean   b. 1917

$73* "Apres La Crue III", #23/30, s., (01-28-93, Pescheteau, #89), 18½ x 22⁷⁄₁₆ in., (47 x 57 cm.), aquatint on wove (BP 48, DM 116, FR 391, Y 9064).

$50* "Sur Deux Bras", s., (04-04-93, Pescheteau, #172), 19¹¹⁄₁₆ x 25¹⁵⁄₁₆ in., (50 x 66 cm.), etching and aquatint on Arches (BP 33, DM 80, FR 273, Y 5693).

BI "Sur Deux Bras", s., (01-28-93, Pescheteau, #90), 11⅝ x 15⅜ in., (29.5 x 39 cm.), etching and aquatint on Arches.

CAPEK, Josef

$248* "Das Madchen", "Portrait Eines Mannes (3)" and "Toilette": Five, pub. in Die Aktion, good cond., sheets toned, tears, paper losses, foxing, (02-24-93, Butterfield, #2904), woodcut on wove (BP 173, DM 403, FR 1365, Y 29,101).

CAPLIN, Lee   American contemporary

BI *Self Portrait: Four,* each s., t., d. 1970, #56, 57, 58, 59/60, est. $150/250, (02-04-93, Sloan, #2973), each 18 x 16 in., (45.7 x 40.6 cm.), screenprint on heave.

CAPOGROSSI, Giuseppe   Italian 1900-1972

BI *Composition (Hase-Schmundt 34), 1962,* s., d., #61/75, p. by Mourlot, pub. XXe Siecle, full margins, good cond., mount-staining, skinned spots, est. BP 6/800, (06-30-93, Sotheby-London, #755, illus.), 12⅝ x 10 in., (321 x 254 mm.), color lithograph on wove.

$236* *Composizione (Hase-Schmundt 41), 1963,* 31/80, s., trimmed, (10-14-92, Germann, #233), 26⁹⁄₁₆ x 19⅛ in., (675 x 485 mm.), color serigraph (BP 139, DM 345, FR 1171, Y 28,599, SF 307).

$290* *Komposition Mit Archaischen Formen, (19)65,* s., d., num., (12-01-92, Karl/Faber, #423), 19⅞ x 14³⁄₁₆ in., (50.5 x 36 cm.), color lithograph on wove (BP 192, DM 462, FR 1575, Y 36,106).

$258* *Komposition Mit Zwei Figuren,* s., num., (12-05-92, Bassenge, #7072), lithograph on BFK Rives (BP 162, DM 402, FR 1371, Y 31,966).

BI *Komposition, 1965,* s., num., est. DM 500, (12-05-92, Bassenge, #7073), 19¹³⁄₁₆ x 14¼ in., (50.4 x 36.2 cm.), color lithograph on Rives.

$1535* *Untitled (Hase-Schmundt 71), 1968,* s., #86/100, p. and pub. by 2RC, full(?) margins, good cond., handling marks, (12-03-92, Sotheby-London, #624, illus.), 19⅜ x 12 in., (492 x 307 mm.), lithograph in colors on wove (BP 990, DM 2414, FR 8239, Y 190,992).

CAPONIGRO, Paul   American b. 1932

$605* *Blue Ridge Parkway,* 1965/printed later, s., prov., (05-16-93, Hindman, #343), 8¼ x 7 in., photograph, silver print (BP 395, DM 976, FR 3288, Y 67,372).

$1100* *Canyon De Chelle, 1970,* sig., (10-14-92, Swann, #402, illus.), 8½ x 12½ in., (21.6 x 31.8 cm.), photograph, silver print (BP 646, DM 1610, FR 5459, Y 133,301).

$2875* "County Wicklow, Ireland" (Wise Silence, pl. 82), 1967, mounted, s. by photog., p.l., (04-06-93, Sotheby-NY, #465, illus.), 5 x 13⅜ in., photograph (BP 1899, DM 4632, FR 15,685, Y 327,897).

BI "Petrified Forest", 1976, s., d., est. $800/1,200, (05-23-93, Butterfield, #3367, illus.), 8½ x 11¾ in., photograph, gelatin silver print.

$1100* "Redding Woods, Connecticut", 1968, s., attrib., t., d. verso, (11-16-92, Butterfield, #5896, illus.), 9¼ x 13¼ in., (235.4 x 337.2 mm.), photograph, gelatin silver print (BP 724, DM 1754, FR 5908, Y 136,799).

$605* *Redding Woods, c. 1969,* photog.'s sig., notations, (04-07-93, Swann, #423, illus.), 9 x 13 in., photograph, silver print (BP 400, DM 978, FR 3311, Y 68,734).

$805* "Redding, CT", 1969, p.l., s. twice, d., t., (05-23-93, Butterfield, #3368, illus.), 8½ x 11¼ in., photograph, gelatin silver print (BP 524, DM 1316, FR 4430, Y 88,980).

$4830* *Running White Deer, County Wicklow, Ireland, 1967,* p. 1991, s., lit., (04-08-93, Christie-NY, #478, illus.), 9 x 23⅛ in., (22.9 x 58.7 cm.), photograph, gelatin silver print (BP 3167, DM 7759, FR 26,264, Y 548,116).

$550* "Stonehenge, Half Moon", 1977, s., (11-16-92, Butterfield, #5897, illus.), 6⅞ x 8⅜ in., (174.9 x 213.1 mm.), photograph, gelatin silver print (BP 362, DM 877, FR 2954, Y 68,399).

CAPORAEL, Suzanne

BI *Wave Study #1, 1988,* s., d., #1/30, blindstamp publisher, Sette & Segura Publishing Company, full margins, est. $7/900, (05-19-93, Butterfield, #2136), 18 x 24 in., (457 x 610 mm.), lithograph on Chine colle on Arches.

BI *Wave Study #2, 1988,* s., d., #1/30, blindstamp publisher, Sette & Segura Publishing Company, full margins, very good cond., est. $7/900, (05-19-93, Butterfield, #2137), 18 x 24 in., (457 x 610 mm.), lithograph on Chine colle on Arches wove.

BI *Wave Study #3, 1988,* s., d., #1/30, blindstamp publisher, Sette & Segura Publishing, fullmargins, very good cond., est. $7/900, (05-19-93, Butterfield, #2138), 18 x 24 in., (457 x 610 mm.), lithograph on Chine colle on Arches wove.

CAPPIELLO, Leonetto 1875-1942

$1947* *Amandines De Provence. Biscuits H. Lalo, 1900,* Paris, Imp. Vercasson, cond. B, (06-11-93, Boisgirard, #51), 55⅛ x 39⁹⁄₁₆ in., (140 x 100.5 cm.), poster (BP 1279, DM 3164, FR 10,668, Y 206,578).

$566* *Anisette Marie Brizard, "L'Eternelle Favorite", 1928,* good cond., (11-19-92, Ribeyre/Baron, #17), 31½ x 23⅝ in., (80 x 60 cm.), poster (BP 373, DM 902, FR 3040, Y 70,389).

BI *"Asti Robba",* est. $8/1200, (06-24-92, Doyle, #16), 52 x 36 in., (132.1 x 91.4 cm.), color lithograph and poster.

$357* *Bally, Lyon, "Le Meilleur Marche Par La Qualilte", 1934,* p. Devambez, good cond., lit., (11-19-92, Ribeyre/Baron, #21), 23⅝ x 15¾ in., (60 x 40 cm.), poster (BP 235, DM 569, FR 1917, Y 44,397).

$683* *Bec Regina. Incandescence Par L'Alcool Ordinaire A 90 Degrees, c. 1901,* Paris, Imp. Vercasson, cond. B+, (06-11-93, Boisgirard, #52), 55⅛ x 39⅜ in., (140 x 100 cm.), poster (BP 449, DM 1110, FR 3742, Y 72,467).

$473* *Benedictine, c. 1920,* fold marks, tears, repairs, (02-04-93, Christie-S. Ken, #99, illus.), 77 x 50 in., (195.6 x 127 cm.), color lithograph backed on linen (BP 330, DM 779, FR 2641, Y 58,838).

$1301* *Buvez Du Vin Et Vivez Joyeux, 1933,* p. Devambez, good cond., (11-19-92, Ribeyre/Baron, #20), 62⅝ x 44⅞ in., (159 x 114 cm.), poster (BP 857, DM 2074, FR 6987, Y 161,796).

$1320* *Cachou Lajaunie, 1920,* Devambez, A cond., (08-06-92, Swann, #69, illus.), 59 x 39 in., (149.9 x 99.1 cm.), (BP 689, DM 1950, FR 6587, Y 168,367).

$825* *Cachou Lajaunie, Indispensable Aux Fumeurs, 1900,* Vercasson, B- cond., creasing, repairs, restored, (08-06-92, Swann, #65, illus.), 51½ x 37 in., (130.8 x 94 cm.), (BP 431, DM 1219, FR 4117, Y 105,230).

$1636* *Campari, "L'Aperitif", 1921,* good cond., lit., (11-19-92, Ribeyre/Baron, #13, illus.), 39⅜ x 27⁹⁄₁₆ in., (100 x 70 cm.), poster (BP 1077, DM 2608, FR 8786, Y 203,457).

BI *Cremant Du Roi, 1922,* plate s., est. $1/1,500, (03-25-93, Christie-E, #197), 62¾ x 47 in., (159.4 x 119.4 cm.), color lithograph.

$115* *Cremant Du Roi, 1922,* plate s., (06-08-93, Christie-E, #189), 62¾ x 47 in., (159.4 x 119.4 cm.), color lithograph (BP 76, DM 187, FR 628, Y 12,215).

$1469* *Creme Eclipse, "Eclipse Tous Les Cirages", 1937,* Editions Nouvelles Cappiello, good cond., (11-19-92, Ribeyre/Baron, #22), 62¹⁵⁄₁₆ x 47¼ in., (160 x 120 cm.), poster (BP 967, DM 2342, FR 7889, Y 182,689).

$315* *Grand Gala Au Lido. Pour Les Garibaldiens De L'Argonne,* good cond., (11-19-92, Ribeyre/Baron, #132), 21⅝ x 15⅜ in., (55 x 39 cm.), poster (BP 207, DM 502, FR 1692, Y 39,174).

$141* *Je Ne Fume Que Le Nil,* (02-13-93, Morelle/Marchan, #25), 62¹⁵⁄₁₆ x 47¼ in., (160 x 120 cm.), poster (BP 99, DM 234, FR 791, Y 17,004).

$247* *Je Ne Fume Que Le Nil, Papier A Cigarettes,* Vercasson, B+ cond., folding, creasing, chartex-backed, (08-06-92, Swann, #73, illus.), 47 x 63 in., (119.4 x 160 cm.), (BP 129, DM 365, FR 1233, Y 31,505).

BI *Je Ne Fume Que Le Nil, c. 1930,* fold marks, other minor defects, est. BP 2/400, (02-04-93, Christie-S. Ken, #103), 46 x 62½ in., (116.8 x 158.8 cm.), color lithograph backed on linen.

$273* *Job, Papier A Cigarettes, 1924,* p. Vercasson, good cond., (11-19-92, Ribeyre/Baron, #15), 35⁷⁄₁₆ x 25⁹⁄₁₆ in., (90 x 65 cm.), poster (BP 180, DM 435, FR 1466, Y 33,951).

$836* *Margarine AXA. "Garantie Fraiche", 1931,* good cond., (03-13-93, Laurin, #5, illus.), 62¹⁵⁄₁₆ x 47¼ in., (160 x 120 cm.), (BP 583, DM 1391, FR 4731, Y 98,527).

$495* *Maurin Quina, 1906,* Vercasson, B+ cond., cracking, (08-06-92, Swann, #66, illus.), 62¼ x 46 in., (158.1 x 116.8 cm.), (BP 259, DM 731, FR 2470, Y 63,138).

$2622* *La Menthe Pastille, "Desaltere", Liqueur Blanche Ou Verte E. Giffard, Angers, 1929,* p. Devambez, very good cond., (11-19-92, Ribeyre/Baron, #18), 62¹⁵⁄₁₆ x 47¼ in., (160 x 120 cm.), poster (BP 1726, DM 4180, FR 14,082, Y 326,079).

$880* *Mossant, 1938,* Edimo, A- cond., image pencil marks, (08-06-92, Swann, #72, illus.), 62 x 47 in., (157.5 x 119.4 cm.), (BP 460, DM 1300, FR 4391, Y 112,245).

$935* *Nitrolian, 1929,* Devambez, A- cond., yellowing, (08-06-92, Swann, #71, illus.), 62 x 47 in., (157.5 x 119.4 cm.), (BP 488, DM 1382, FR 4666, Y 119,260).

$1210* *Papier A Cigarettes-Job, 1912,* Vercasson, A- cond., repaired tears, (08-06-92, Swann, #68, illus.), 62½ x 46 in., (158.8 x 116.8 cm.), (BP 632, DM 1788, FR 6038, Y 154,337).

$756* *Poeles Manquette, 1925,* tears, (02-04-93, Christie-S. Ken, #101), 76 x 50 in., (193 x 127 cm.), color lithograph backed on linen (BP 528, DM 1245, FR 4221, Y 94,042).

BI *Premier Fils, 1935,* creases, est. BP 2/300, (02-04-93, Christie-S. Ken, #104), 63 x 47 in., (160 x 119.4 cm.), color lithograph backed on linen.

$420* *Le Quotidien, 1923,* p. Devambez, good cond., lit., (11-19-92, Ribeyre/Baron, #14), 62¹⁵⁄₁₆ x 47¼ in., (160 x 120 cm.), poster (BP 277, DM 670, FR 2256, Y 52,232).

$1506* *Resultat Du Concours De La Reglisse Sanguinede, Montpellier. Toux, Bronchites, Influenza Mauvaises Digestions, 1902,* Paris, Imp. Vercasson, cond. A-, (06-11-93, Boisgirard, #53, illus.), 55⅛ x 39⅜ in., (140 x 100 cm.), poster (BP 989, DM 2448, FR 8252, Y 159,788).

BI *Royal Gaillac, 1929,* fold marks, other minor defects, est. BP 3/500, (02-04-93, Christie-S. Ken, #102), 78 x 51 in., (198.1 x 129.5 cm.), color lithograph backed on linen.

$1364* *Royat. "C'Est La Sante, C'Est La Jeunesse Dans Une Atmosphere De Radium", 1923,* good cond., lit., (11-19-92, Ribeyre/Baron, #90), 78¾ x 51³⁄₁₆ in., (200 x 130 cm.), poster (BP 898, DM 2175, FR 7325, Y 169,631).

$315* *Savon La Tour, 1920,* creasing, (02-04-93, Christie-S. Ken, #100), 61 x 46 in., (154.9 x 116.8 cm.), color lithograph backed on linen (BP 220, DM 519, FR 1759, Y 39,184).

$1385* *Theatre De La Michodiere: la Fleur Des Pois De Ed. Bourdet, 1932,* p. Devambez, good cond., (11-19-92, Ribeyre/Baron, #161), 62¹⁵⁄₁₆ x 47¼ in., (160 x 120 cm.), poster (BP 912, DM 2208, FR 7438, Y 172,242).

$608* *Le Thermogene "Engendre La Chaleur Et Combat Toux, Rhumatismes...", 1924,* good cond., lit., (11-19-92, Ribeyre/Baron, #16), 62¹⁵⁄₁₆ x 47¼ in., (160 x 120 cm.), poster (BP 400, DM 969, FR 3265, Y 75,612).

$495* *Le Thermogene, Engendre La Chaleur, 1909,* Vercasson, B cond., chipping, cracking, fold marks, closed tear, (08-06-92, Swann, #67, illus.), 62½ x 47 in., (158.8 x 119.4 cm.), (BP 259, DM 731, FR 2470, Y 63,138).

$550* *Veuve Amiot, 1922,* Les Nouvelles Affiches Cappiello, B+ cond., blemishes, closed tears, (08-06-92, Swann, #70, illus.), 63 x 47½ in., (160 x 120.7 cm.), (BP 287, DM 813, FR 2745, Y 70,153).

BI *Veuve Amiot: Grands Vins Mousseux, 1922,* s. in stone, d., pub. Les Nouvelles Affiches Cappiello, margins, good cond.?, water stain, creases, est. $5/700, (09-21-92, Butterfield, #823), 60 x 44 in., (152.4 x 111.8 cm.), lithograph/poster in colors.

CAPPIELLO, Leonetto (after)

$525* *Huile Lesieur, "Huile De Table", 1933,* p. Devambez, good cond., (11-19-92, Ribeyre/Baron, #19), 23⅝ x 15¾ in., (60 x 40 cm.), poster (BP 346, DM 837, FR 2820, Y 65,290).

CAPPS, Charles Merrick American b. 1898

$154* *"Cimarron",* plate tone, s., t., tape, very fine cond., (10-31-92, Cleveland, #92), 11¾ x 9 in., (29.8 x 22.9 cm.), etching (BP 99, DM 237, FR 804, Y 19,076).

CAPTAIN, P.

BI *Lake Landscape,* s., #43/275, est. $40/60, (02-11-93, Boos, #471), 21¼ x 16 in., (540 x 406 mm.), color lithograph.

CARAGLIO, Gian Giacomo c. 1498-1570

BI *Gods And Heroes Of Antiquity (B. XV, 29, 37, 40, 41, 43), c. 1540: Five Plates,* after R. Fiorentino, very good to good impressions, margins, trimmed, creases, staining, good cond., prov., est. BP 4/500, (12-01-92, Christie-London, #199), plate 8⁷⁄₁₆ x 4⅜ in., (215 x 111 mm.), engraving.

CARAGLIO, Gian Jacopo c. 1500-1565
$722* *Apollo Hautet Marsyas,* watermark, (12-04-92, Bassenge, #6105), 14⁵⁄₁₆ x 9¹⁵⁄₁₆ in., (36.1 x 25.2 cm.), engraving (BP 463, DM 1150, FR 3901, Y 90,137).
BI *Roxanne (B. XV, 95, 62),* after Raphael, est. DM 2,400, (12-04-92, Bassenge, #6107), 8⅞ x 12⁷⁄₁₆ in., (22.6 x 31.6 cm.), engraving.

CARAGLIO, Giovanni Jacopo (after Raphael)
$550* *The Madonna With Jesus In A Cradle, Elizabeth And The Infant John (Bartsch 5, 11), c. 1520,* thread margins, plate s., repaired tear, other minor defects, (05-27-93, Swann, #50), (30.5 x 21.9 cm.), engraving on watermarked paper (BP 352, DM 883, FR 2975, Y 58,962).

CARAN D'ACHE (Emmanuel POIRE) 1859-1909
$201* *Exposition Russe. Champs De Mars, 1895,* Paris, Imp. Herold, cond. B+, (06-11-93, Boisgirard, #54), 54¾ x 35⁷⁄₁₆ in., (139 x 90 cm.), poster (BP 132, DM 327, FR 1101, Y 21,326).

CARAVA, Roy de
$1265* *Dancers, Harlem,* s., (c) by photog., 1956, p.l., (04-06-93, Sotheby-NY, #411A, illus.), 13 x 8¾ in., photograph (BP 836, DM 2038, FR 6901, Y 144,275).
$1150* *Hallway With Light Bulb,* s., (c) by photog., 1953, p.l., (04-06-93, Sotheby-NY, #411, illus.), 13 x 8¾ in., photograph (BP 760, DM 1853, FR 6274, Y 131,159).

CARAVAGGIO, Michelangelo Merisi (after) c. 1560/65-1609
$1155* *Der Hl. Thomas Steckt Den Finger In Die Seitenwunde Christi,* lit., (12-04-92, Bassenge, #6108, illus.), 8¾ x 11¼ in., (22.2 x 28.5 cm.), engraving (BP 741, DM 1839, FR 6240, Y 144,195).

CARCAN, Rene b. 1925
$147* *"Aurore-1970",* #XXI/135, s., (01-28-93, Pescheteau, #91), 18½ x 24⁷⁄₁₆ in., (47 x 62 cm.), color etching and aquatint on Auvergne (BP 97, DM 233, FR 788, Y 18,252).

CARCHIK, M.
BI *"Soaring - Sailing",* #46/260, s., est. $1/200, (01-15-93, DuMouchelle, #120), approx. 12 x 18 in., (30.5 x 45.7 cm.), lithograph.

CARCHOUNE, Serge 1888-1975
BI *Untitled,* s., #262/450, margins, good cond.?, est. G 5/700, (12-09-92, Sotheby-Amstrdm, #516), 12⁵⁄₁₆ x 15¾ in., (312 x 400 mm.), color lithograph on wove.

CARDAILBAC
$1100* *Papier Photographiques Martin, 1897,* Imp. Camis, B cond., heavy fold marks, closed tear, cracking, peeling, (08-06-92, Swann, #74, illus.), 51 x 39½ in., (129.5 x 100.3 cm.), (BP 575, DM 1625, FR 5489, Y 140,306).

CARDER, Nigel
$31 *"Elm Hill, Norwich",* s., (08-14-92, G.A. Key, #98), 12 x 9 in., (30.5 x 22.9 cm.), colored print (BP 16, DM 45, FR 154, Y 3909).

CARDINAUX, Emil 1877-1936
$1182* *Jungfrau-Bahn, 1910,* tears, nicks, lit., (02-04-93, Christie-S. Ken, #4, illus.), 40 x 28 in., (101.6 x 71.1 cm.), (BP 825, DM 1946, FR 6600, Y 147,033).
$823* *VII, Sommerskirennen Auf Dem Jungfraujoch, 1924,* mono., (05-08-93, Dobiaschofsky, #1858, illus.), 49⅝ x 35⁷⁄₁₆ in., (126 x 90 cm.), color lithograph poster (BP 537, DM 1322, FR 4461, Y 91,966, SF 1200).

CARIGIET, Alois 1902-1985
$3278* *Auf Dem Heimweg, 1968,* #290/300, s., d., (11-13-92, Koller, #5273), 17¹¹⁄₁₆ x 21⅝ in., (45 x 55 cm.), lithograph on Rives (BP 2118, DM 5146, FR 17,353, Y 406,851, SF 4640).
$239* *Die Balletteusen (H. Neuburg, Nr. 57), 1967,* #34/250, s., d., num., (06-15-93, Schuler, #3236, illus.), 16¹⁵⁄₁₆ x 25³⁄₁₆ in., (43 x 64 cm.), color lithograph (BP 157, DM 392, FR 1323, Y 25,235, SF 2760).
$711* *Bauer Mit Kind Auf Pferdeschlitten, 1952,* mono., d., (06-24-93, Germann, #587), 21⅝ x 16⅛ in., (550 x 410 mm.), lithograph (BP 468, DM 1153, FR 3885, Y 76,271, SF 1035).
$3791* *Bundner Haus, 1972,* s., d., (06-24-93, Germann, #588, illus.), 21⅝ x 25⅞ in., (550 x 657 mm.), color lithograph (BP 2496, DM 6146, FR 20,716, Y 406,672, SF 5520).
$5135* *Bundner Haus, 1974,* #245/300, s., d., (04-21-93, Germann, #317, illus.), 22¹⁄₁₆ x 29½ in., (560 x 750 mm.), color lithograph (BP 3332, DM 8208, FR 27,757, Y 568,471, SF 7475).
$3633* *Bundner Haus, 1974,* 128/250, s., d., (06-24-93, Germann, #590), 21⅝ x 29⁷⁄₁₆ in., (550 x 748 mm.), color lithograph (BP 2392, DM 5890, FR 19,852, Y 389,723, SF 5290).
$3770* *Dorfbild Mit Schafen Und Jungen Hirten, 1974,* #64/200, s., d., lit., (11-13-92, Koller, #5276), 18½ x 24³⁄₁₆ in., (47 x 61.5 cm.), lithograph on wove (BP 2436, DM 5918, FR 19,958, Y 467,916, SF 5336).
$2029* *Falke,* 115/250, s., (10-14-92, Germann, #493, illus.), 24½ x 21¼ in., (622 x 540 mm.), color lithograph (BP 1191, DM 2969, FR 10,069, Y 245,880, SF 2645).
$2459* *Figur Der Mitte, 1964,* #30/150, s., d., lit., (11-13-92, Koller, #5271), sheet 28⁹⁄₁₆ x 20¹⁄₁₆ in., (72.5 x 51 cm.), lithograph on wove (BP 1589, DM 3860, FR 13,017, Y 305,200, SF 3480).
$339* *Frau Mit Schlittengefahrt, 1964,* #91/200, s., num., d., (06-15-93, Schuler, #3242), sh 22¹⁄₁₆ x 29¹⁵⁄₁₆ in., (56 x 76 cm.), 17¹¹⁄₁₆ x 24⁷⁄₁₆ in., (56 x 76 cm.), color lithograph (BP 223, DM 556, FR 1876, Y 35,793, SF 3910).
BI *Die Funf Musiker, 1977,* s., d., ded., est. SF 2,8/3,300, (11-13-92, Koller, #5279), 16¹⁵⁄₁₆ x 24 in., (43 x 61 cm.), lithograph on Rives wove.
$2685* *Geissen Am Dorfbrunnen, 1978,* 9/250, s., d., blindstamp, (06-24-93, Germann, #589, illus.), 22³⁄₁₆ x 29¹⁵⁄₁₆ in., (563 x 760 mm.), color lithograph (BP 1767, DM 4353, FR 14,672, Y 288,028, SF 3910).
$4738* *Haus Im Camp (Neuburg 118), 1976,* s., d., (06-24-93, Germann, #591, illus.), 21¹⁵⁄₁₆ x 29⅝ in., (558 x 752 mm.), color lithograph (BP 3119, DM 7682, FR 25,891, Y 508,260, SF 6900).
$279* *Holzfaller Mit Schlittengefahrt, 1967,* s., d., i., (06-15-93, Schuler, #3241), 17¹¹⁄₁₆ x 22¹³⁄₁₆ in., (45 x 58 cm.), color lithograph (BP 184, DM 458, FR 1544, Y 29,458, SF 3220).
$1475* *Reiterin Mit Pferd Und Hund, 1966,* s., d., (11-13-92, Koller, #5278), 22¹³⁄₁₆ x 19¹¹⁄₁₆ in., (58 x 50 cm.), lithograph on wove (BP 953, DM 2316, FR 7808, Y 183,071, SF 2088).
$339* *Sattelplatz 2 (H. Neuburg, Nr. 100), 1964,* #1/80, s., d., num., (06-15-93, Schuler, #3237), 20½ x 24 in., (52 x 61 cm.), color lithograph (BP 223, DM 556, FR 1876, Y 35,793, SF 3910).
$2470* *Der Schafer, 1978,* 120/250, s., d., (10-14-92, Germann, #494), 29⅛ x 21¼ in., (740 x 540 mm.), color lithograph (BP 1450, DM 3615, FR 12,258, Y 299,321, SF 3220).
$339* *Schlittenegefahrt, 1964,* s., d., num., (06-15-93, Schuler, #3239, illus.), 14⁹⁄₁₆ x 19¹¹⁄₁₆ in., (37 x 50 cm.), color lithograph (BP 223, DM 556, FR 1876, Y 35,793, SF 3910).
$2527* *Schlittenfahrt, 1964,* 114/300, s., d., (06-24-93, Germann, #586, illus.), 19¹¹⁄₁₆ x 25⅜ in., (500 x 645 mm.), color lithograph (BP 1663, DM 4097, FR 13,809, Y 271,079, SF 3680).
$179* *Schlittengefahrt, 1964,* s., d., num., lit., (06-15-93, Schuler, #3240, illus.), 22¹⁄₁₆ x 8¼ in., (56 x 21 cm.), color lithograph (BP 118, DM 294, FR 991, Y 18,900, SF 2070).
$2290* *Skifahrer Und Vogel, 1964,* #63/200, s., d., (06-24-93, Germann, #585), 19¹¹⁄₁₆ x 25⁹⁄₁₆ in., (500 x 650 mm.), lithograph (BP 1507, DM 3713, FR 12,514, Y 245,655, SF 3335).
$3770* *Stall Von Stavons, 1974,* #140/250, s., d., pub.'s blindstamp, lit., (11-13-92, Koller, #5272), 19⁵⁄₁₆ x 23¹³⁄₁₆ in., (49 x 60.5 cm.), lithograph on wove (BP 2436, DM 5918, FR 19,958, Y 467,916, SF 5336).
BI *Tanz Mit Dem Narren,* before 1953, s., foxed, est. SF 2,6/3,400, (11-13-92, Koller, #5274, illus.), 12³⁄₁₆ x 12¹³⁄₁₆ in., (31 x 32.5 cm.), lithograph on Arches wove.
$2054* *Zwei Frauen, 1969,* #187/200, s., d., (04-21-93, Germann, #316), 24⅞ x 31⁵⁄₁₆ in., (632 x 795 mm.), color lithograph (BP 1333, DM 3283, FR 11,103, Y 227,388, SF 2990).

CARLONE, Carlo Italian 1686-1775/76
BI *Der Hl. Borromaus Erteilt Den Pestkranken Die Kommunion (De Vesme 3 II),* watermark, est. DM 2,000, (06-10-93, Hauswedell/Nolt, #182, illus.), etching.

CARLU, Jean French b. 1900
$279* *14e Salon Des Arts Menagers, 1937,* cond. A, (03-16-93, Boisgirard, #67), 38⁹⁄₁₆ x 24⁷⁄₁₆ in., (98 x 62 cm.), poster (BP 193, DM 464, FR 1576, Y 32,624).
$2203* *Fetes De Paris. "Facilites Exceptionelles De Voyage", 1935,* Alliance Graphique L. Danel, good cond., lit., (11-19-92, Ribeyre/Baron, #133), 40³⁄₁₆ x 22¹⁄₁₆ in., (102 x 56 cm.), poster (BP 1450, DM 3512, FR 11,831, Y 273,971).
$605* *International Exposition Paris, 1937,* Imp. Bedos and Cie, B+ cond., creasing, restoration, (08-06-92, Swann, #75, illus.), 59 x 40 in., (149.9 x 101.6 cm.), (BP 316, DM 894, FR 3019, Y 77,168).
$339* *A Votre Sante. Pousset Spatenbrau Munich, 1928,* cond. A, (03-16-93, Boisgirard, #66), 31½ x 23⅝ in., (80 x 60 cm.), poster (BP 234, DM 564, FR 1915, Y 39,640).
$482* *A Votre Sante...Biere Pousset Spatenbrau, Biere De Munich, 1927,* good cond., lit., (11-19-92, Ribeyre/Baron, #23), 31½ x 23⅝ in., (80 x 60 cm.), posters (BP 317, DM 768, FR 2589, Y 59,943).
$330* *Woman's Head In Profile Against A Background Made Up Of International Flags, 1937,* Exposition-Paris 1937, linen-backed, (04-29-93, Swann, #144), 23½ x 15½ in., (59.7 x 39.4 cm.), color lithograph poster (BP 210, DM 522, FR 1759, Y 36,712).

CARMAN, Albert American 20th cent.
$5* *Dancing Woman,* s., corner missing, (05-15-93, Cleveland, #87), 10 x 13 in., (25.4 x 33 cm.), lithograph in colors (BP 3, DM 8, FR 27, Y 554).

CARMEL, Gerard Titus b. 1942
$648* *7 Constructions Possibles: Seven,* s., #3/99, (05-27-93, Briest, #192), color aquatints (BP 415, DM 1040, FR 3505, Y 69,468).

CARO-DELVAILLE, Henri
BI *Maternite, c. 1900,* margins, (02-24-93, Picard, #54), color lithograph on thin chine.

CARPACCIO, Vittore (after)
$85* *"Religious Ceremony",* (12-10-92, Bonhams-Chelsea, #125), image 14½ x 29½ in., (36.8 x 74.9 cm.), chromolithograph (BP 55, DM 134, FR 459, Y 10,515).

CARPEAUX, Jean Baptiste French 1827-1875
$573* *M. Divuy (D. 3), 1860,* full margins, (02-24-93, Picard, #55), etching on thin ivory Japan (BP 400, DM 930, FR 3154, Y 67,238).

CARPENTER, Eric
$241* *Marlon Brando, Standing Portrait,* prov., (10-10-92, Bonhams, #17, illus.), 10 x 8 in., (25.4 x 20.3 cm.), photograph (BP 143, DM 358, FR 1202, Y 29,340).

CARPI, Ugo da 1480-1520
$1201* *Christ At The House Of Simon (B. XII, 17),* damaged impression of 2nd state, trimmed, fold, creases, repaired areas, backed w/Japan, (06-30-93, Sotheby-London, #98), 12 x 14½ in., (305 x 368 mm.), chiaroscuro woodcut, p. from 4 blocks in shades of brown and beige (BP 805, DM 2048, FR 6910, Y 128,683).
BI *Saturn (Bartsch XII, 125, 27 II),* after Pordenone, 2nd state, est. DM 18,000, (06-10-93, Hauswedell/Nolt, #58, illus.), chiaroscuro woodcut on thin hand-made.

CARPI, Ugo da (attrib.) 1480-1520
$1100* *Christ At The House Of Simon The Pharisee (B. XII, 40, 17), 1609,* after Raphael, Adreani's mono., good cond., thinned spots, pin holes, restored tears, creases, surface soiling, prov., (10-28-92, Butterfield, #2591, illus.), 9¾ x 14½ in., (248 x 368 mm.), chiaroscuro woodcut in black, mushroom and yellow on laid paper backed w/tissue thin Japan (BP 701, DM 1699, FR 5768, Y 134,969).

CARPIONI, Giulio Italian 1611-1674
$722* *Christus Am Olberg (B. 2 II),* (12-04-92, Bassenge, #6109, illus.), 12¹¹⁄₁₆ x 8⅝ in., (32.3 x 21.9 cm.), etching (BP 463, DM 1150, FR 3901, Y 90,137).
$5463* *Dance Of The Children (B. 19), c. 1650,* wiping scratches, 2nd (final) state, w/Cadorin's address, watermark,narrow margins, defects, glued down, good cond., The Suida Manning Coll., (05-13-93, Sotheby-NY, #235, illus.), 4¼ x 12½ in., (109 x 317 mm.), etching (BP 3587, DM 8821, FR 29,755, Y 609,914).
BI *Dance Of The Children (B. 20), c. 1650,* small margins, center crease split, backed for support, rubbed spot,soiling, fox marks, good cond., The Suida Manning Coll., est. $2,5/3,500, (05-13-93, Sotheby-NY, #236, illus.), 5 x 16⅛ in., (128 x 410 mm.), etching.
BI *Fire (B. 18), c. 1640,* from Four Elements, 2nd (final) state, scratch in sky, warm plate tone, trimmed between platemark and borderline, stains, good cond., The Suida Manning Coll., est. $1,8/2,200, (05-13-93, Sotheby-NY, #239), 4¼ x 6 in., (108 x 154 mm.), etching.
$1380* *Moderation (B. 13), c. 1640,* early but uneven impression of only state, watermark, small margins,water stain, glued down, good cond., The Suida Manning Coll., (05-13-93, Sotheby-NY, #234, illus.), 7⅛ x 5⅛ in., (180 x 130 mm.), etching (BP 906, DM 2228, FR 7516, Y 154,069).
$4025* *The Nativity (B. 8), c. 1640,* 1st state of 2, narrow to thread margins, trimmed on platemark, center crease, traces glue, good cond., The Suida Manning Coll., (05-13-93, Sotheby-NY, #238, illus.), 12⅝ x 8⅞ in., (322 x 226 mm.), etching (BP 2642, DM 6499, FR 21,923, Y 449,369).
BI *St. Jerome (B. 12), c. 1640,* plate tone, wiping scratches, 2nd state of 2, w/Cadorin's address, watermark, trimmed between platemark and borderline, stains, glued down at corners, good cond., The Suida Manning Coll., est. $1,8/2,400, (05-13-93, Sotheby-NY, #233, illus.), 8¾ x 6⅜ in., (223 x 163 mm.), etching.

CARQUEVILLE, Will
$385* *Lippincott's, October,* B+ cond., bottom restored, (08-06-92, Swann, #76, illus.), 18 x 11½ in., (45.7 x 29.2 cm.), (BP 201, DM 569, FR 1921, Y 49,107).

CARR, J. (J.H. CARSE) 1818-1900
$57* *Daylesford, Victoria,* from Australia by Edwin C. Booth pub. c. 1875, (08-11-92, L. Joel, #197G), 4¹⁵⁄₁₆ x 6¹¹⁄₁₆ in., (12.5 x 17 cm.), color engraving (BP 30, DM 84, FR 283, Y 7299, A$ 77).

CARRA, Carlo Italian 1881-1966
$861* *Fanciulle (Carra 82), 1947,* from L'Apres Midi Et Le Monologue D'Un Faune, #IV/X, s., (05-20-93, Finarte-Milan, #34), 13³⁄₁₆ x 9⁷⁄₁₆ in., (33.5 x 24 cm.), lithograph (BP 553, DM 1389, FR 4679, Y 95,075, L 1265).
$2741* *La Galleria Di Milano (M. Carra 84 s.c.), 1949,* #18/60, s., d., from Carra 1912-21, (05-20-93, Finarte-Milan, #35, illus.), 14³⁄₁₆ x 7⁹⁄₁₆ in., (36 x 19.2 cm.), lithograph (BP 1759, DM 4422, FR 14,897, Y 302,672, L 4025).
$1723* *Madre E Figlio,* edita dal Cavallino, artist proof, s., (05-20-93, Finarte-Milan, #37), 27³⁄₁₆ x 18½ in., (69 x 47 cm.), lithograph in colors (BP 1106, DM 2780, FR 9364, Y 190,261, L 2530).
$5560* *Testa Di Donna (Carra 1), 1922,* #9/25, s., d. 1924, (05-20-93, Finarte-Milan, #31, illus.), 14¼ x 9¹⁵⁄₁₆ in., (36.2 x 25.2 cm.), etching (BP 3569, DM 8971, FR 30,217, Y 613,958, L 8165).

CARRACCI, Agostino Italian 1557-1602
$466* *Adam And Eve, (B. XVIII 1; Bohlin 25), 1581,* after Annibale Carracci, small to narrow margins, loss, defects, slightly stained, laid, (12-01-92, Christie-London, #52), P. 19½ x 14³⁄₁₆ in., (496 x 360 mm.), engraving (BP 308, DM 743, FR 2531, Y 58,018).
$154* *Le Christ De Caprarole,* i., d. 1598 in plate, (10-30-92, Sloan, #2802), 4⅞ x 6¼ in., (12.4 x 15.9 cm.), engraving (BP 99, DM 237, FR 804, Y 19,076).
$2997* *Jacob And Rachel At The Well, (B. 2; Bohlin 27), 1581,* Bohlin's first state (of three), delicate tone, wiping scratches, trimmed, very good cond., laid, (12-01-92, Christie-London, #53, illus.), S. 15¹¹⁄₁₆ x 11⅝ in., (398 x 295 mm.), engraving (BP 1980, DM 4777, FR 16,279, Y 373,132).
$302* *Sainte Famille (De Grazia Bohlin 208), 1597,* after Annibale Carracci, fourth and final state, d., num., dirt spots, abrasions, good cond., (05-15-93, Loudmer, #6, illus.), 8¹¹⁄₁₆ x 6¾ in., (221 x 171 mm.), sh 9½ x 7¹¹⁄₁₆ in.,

(221 x 171 mm.), copper engraving on laid (BP 196, DM 486, FR 1632, Y 33,477).

BI   *Satyr Surprising A Sleeping Nymph (B. 128),* from Lascivicious series, trimmed to image, repaired corner, side edges reinforced, est. BP 2/300, (11-30-92, Phillips-London, #282), plate 6 x 4⅛ in., (152 x 105 mm.), etching on laid.

CARRACCI, Annibale   Italian c. 1560-1609
$199* *St. Hieronymus Mit Dem Stein In Seiner Linken Hand (B. 14),* trimmed, (12-01-92, Karl/Faber, #34), etching (BP 131, DM 317, FR 1081, Y 24,776).

CARRE, L.
$299* *PLM: Algerie. "Hivernage, Tourisme". 1921,* good cond., (03-13-93, Laurin, #36, illus.), 41¾ x 29½ in., (106 x 75 cm.), (BP 209, DM 498, FR 1692, Y 35,239).
$358* *PLM: Tlemcen. c. 1925,* very good cond., (03-13-93, Laurin, #38), 39⅜ x 24³⁄₁₆ in., (100 x 61.5 cm.), (BP 250, DM 596, FR 2026, Y 42,192).

CARRERE, P.
$70* *Le Reveil Economique: "Contre Le Monopole Des Tabacs", c. 1925,* Imp. Chachoin, fairly good cond., (02-12-93, Cheval/Robert, #116), 46⅞ x 31⅛ in., (119 x 79 cm.), poster (BP 49, DM 116, FR 393, Y 8442).

CARREY
$100* *Papier A Cigarette Job,* good cond., (02-13-93, Morelle/Marchan, #35), 13¾ x 18½ in., (35 x 47 cm.), poster (BP 70, DM 166, FR 561, Y 12,060).

CARRIERE, Eugene   French 1849-1906
$400* *Alphonse Daudet (L. Delteil 16), 1893,* whole margins, reddish stains, (06-11-93, Picard, #16), 15⁹⁄₁₆ x 11¹⁵⁄₁₆ in., (395 x 304 mm.), lithograph in bistre on chine applique on thick wove (BP 263, DM 650, FR 2192, Y 42,440).
$560* *Henri Rochefort (L.D. 27), 1896,* reddish stains, (06-11-93, Picard, #17), 21½ x 15¹³⁄₁₆ in., (546 x 402 mm.), lithograph in black on chine applique on thick wove (BP 368, DM 910, FR 3068, Y 59,416).
BI   *L'Aurore, 1897,* before text, tears, creases, lit., advertisement for daily literary journal L'Aurore, est. BP 2/400, (02-04-93, Christie-S. Ken, #105), 89 x 54 in., (226.1 x 137.2 cm.), color lithograph on two sheets, backed on linen.
$348* *Maternite (D. 38), 1899,* 1 of 100, margins, (02-24-93, Picard, #57), 3-tone lithograph on chine volant (BP 243, DM 565, FR 1915, Y 40,835).
BI   *"Les Morts D'Amour" (Delteil 8 ii/ii), c. 1885,* excell. cond., est. $100/150, (05-15-93, Cleveland, #372), 10½ x 7⅜ in., (26.7 x 18.7 cm.), lithograph.
$424* *Le Nouveau-Ne Au Bonnet (Delteil 91), 1890,* s., 1er essai, stone d., ded., (06-10-93, Hauswedell/Nolt, #123, illus.), image 9¹⁵⁄₁₆ x 7⁷⁄₁₆ in., (25.2 x 18.9 cm.), lithograph on laid down China (BP 277, DM 690, FR 2325, Y 45,006).
$778* *Paul Verlaine (D. 26), 1896,* sig., staining, creases, (02-24-93, Picard, #56), lithograph on chine on strong old laid (BP 543, DM 1263, FR 4282, Y 91,293).
$6109* *Portrait Paul Verlaine (Delteil 26), 1896,* s., (06-23-93, Kornfeld, #244), lithograph from 2 stones on China (BP 4150, DM 10,337, FR 34,769, Y 665,541, SF 9200).

CARRINGTON, Leonora   English b. 1917
$6900* *Tuesday, 1987,* s., #92/150, wide margins, excell. cond., (05-17-93, Christie-NY, #292, illus.), 25¾ x 36 in., (654 x 914 mm.), lithograph in colors on wove (BP 4501, DM 11,133, FR 37,500, Y 768,374).

CARRINGTON BOWLES, PUBLISHER
$244* *The Fond Doves,* wormholes in image, scuffing top centre, time-stained, (10-27-92, Phillips-London, #54), (349 x 251 mm.), mezzotint w/hand-colouring on wove (BP 154, DM 374, FR 1269, Y 29,847).

CARROLL, John   American 1892-1959
$55* *"Citadel-Corsica",* s., #18/40, (06-11-93, DuMouchelle, #2262), 9¼ x 11 in., (23.5 x 27.9 cm.), lithograph (BP 36, DM 89, FR 301, Y 5836).

CARROLL, Lewis   1832-1898
$2724* *Herbert Kitchin,* s., ded. by photog. 10 September 1873, mounted as cabinet card, i. verso, (05-07-93, Sotheby-

London, #74, illus.), photograph, albumen print (BP 1725, DM 4307, FR 14,513, Y 299,934).
$9444* *Julia And Ethel Arnold In Straw Boaters, c. 1872,* num. 34, and 2045 verso, 161 x 132mm, (05-07-93, Sotheby-London, #85, illus.), photograph, albumen print (BP 5980, DM 14,931, FR 50,314, Y 1,039,859).
$2179* *Julia And Ethel Arnold On Chaise Longue, c. 1872,* neg. num. 68 and 1955, and 1955 verso, 161 x 132mm, (05-07-93, Sotheby-London, #88, illus.), photograph, albumen print (BP 1380, DM 3445, FR 11,609, Y 239,925).
$13,803* *Julia And Ethel Arnold, Before The Beach, c. 1872,* 121 x 90mm, (05-07-93, Sotheby-London, #83, illus.), photograph, albumen print (BP 8740, DM 21,823, FR 73,538, Y 1,519,819).
$5812* *Julia Arnold As Allegory Of Spring, c. 1870,* mounted as cabinet card, i. 2122, (05-07-93, Sotheby-London, #78, illus.), photograph, albumen print (BP 3680, DM 9189, FR 30,964, Y 639,947).
$998* *Julia Arnold In Profile, Seated In Chair, c. 1872,* num. verso 1981, 136 x 112mm, (05-07-93, Sotheby-London, #82, illus.), photograph, albumen print (BP 632, DM 1578, FR 5317, Y 109,888).
$8354* *Julia Arnold Lying On The Floor, c. 1872,* num. verso 2094, 141 x 103mm, (05-07-93, Sotheby-London, #87, illus.), photograph, albumen print (BP 5290, DM 13,208, FR 44,507, Y 919,841).
$2179* *Julia Arnold With Parasol, c. 1872,* num. 2421 1/2, 164 x 132mm, (05-07-93, Sotheby-London, #81, illus.), photograph, albumen print (BP 1380, DM 3445, FR 11,609, Y 239,925).
$1998* *Julia Arnold, Right Hand To Cheek, c. 1872,* neg. num. 86, and 1953 verso, 85 x 75mm, (05-07-93, Sotheby-London, #86, illus.), photograph, albumen print (BP 1265, DM 3159, FR 10,645, Y 219,996).
$1725* *Julia Arnold, Seated In Chair, Facing Camera, c. 1872,* 103 x 82mm, (05-07-93, Sotheby-London, #80, illus.), photograph, albumen print (BP 1092, DM 2727, FR 9190, Y 189,936).
$14,530* *Julia Arnold, Seated On Unmade Bed, c. 1872,* neg. num. 134; num. 2046 verso, 150 x 127mm, (05-07-93, Sotheby-London, #79, illus.), photograph, albumen print (BP 9200, DM 22,972, FR 77,411, Y 1,599,868).
$2361* *Xie On Sofa, c. 1875,* mounted as cabinet card, annot. verso, (05-07-93, Sotheby-London, #76, illus.), photograph, albumen print (BP 1495, DM 3733, FR 12,579, Y 259,965).
$5812* *Xie Sleeping, 18 May 1874,* mounted as cabinet card, num. 2175, (05-07-93, Sotheby-London, #75, illus.), photograph, albumen print (BP 3680, DM 9189, FR 30,964, Y 639,947).
$9081* *Xie With Violin,* s., ded. by photog. July 1876, mounted as cabinet card, i., (05-07-93, Sotheby-London, #72, illus.), photograph, albumen print (BP 5750, DM 14,357, FR 48,380, Y 999,890).
$2543* *Xie, Standing Wearing A Tunic And Sandals, c. 1875,* mounted as cabinet card, num. verso, (05-07-93, Sotheby-London, #73, illus.), photograph, albumen print (BP 1610, DM 4021, FR 13,548, Y 280,004).
$1725* *Young Girl Standing Before A Mirror, c. 1870-75,* num. 2216 110, 150 x 125mm, (05-07-93, Sotheby-London, #84, illus.), photograph, glass neg. (BP 1092, DM 2727, FR 9190, Y 189,936).

CARRUTHERS, J.J.W.
$385* *Deep Wakes Dimple With The Dipping Oars, c. 1900,* inits., notations, (10-14-92, Swann, #404, illus.), 8½ x 9½ in., (21.6 x 24.1 cm.), photograph, platinum print (BP 226, DM 563, FR 1911, Y 46,655).

CARRUTHERS, Roy
$220* *Still Life With Safety Razor, 1981,* s., num. 52/75, blindstamp of pub. & printer Editions Press, apparently very good cond., (02-24-93, Butterfield, #3197), 30 x 22¼ in., (762 x 565 mm.), lithograph w/silkscreen in colors on cream wove (BP 153, DM 357, FR 1211, Y 25,816).

CARTER, Clarence H.   American b. 1904
$330* *"Jane Reed And Dora Hunt",* pub. AAA, s. Clarence H. Carter, t. good cond., mount staining, taperesidue, (09-11-92, Skinner, #53, illus.), 9⅛ x 13⅛ in., (23.2 x 33.3

cm.), lithograph on wove (BP 171, DM 475, FR 1614, Y 40,887).

BI *"Merry-Go-Round"*, *1979*, s., num. 43/200, very good cond., est. $2/300, (10-31-92, Cleveland, #90), 22 x 27¾ in., (55.9 x 70.5 cm.), lithograph in colors.

$385* *Olive Trees, Capri, 1932*, full margins, s., t., d., (12-08-92, Swann, #53), 5½ x 7 in., (14 x 17.8 cm.), color aquatint (BP 241, DM 599, FR 2044, Y 47,719).

BI *"The Shop Window"*, *1979*, s., d., num. 24/30, fine cond., est. $2/300, (10-31-92, Cleveland, #91, illus.), 27¾ x 19 in., (70.5 x 48.3 cm.), lithograph in colors.

BI *Untitled, 1976*, s., d., excell. cond., est. $2/300, (05-15-93, Cleveland, #456, illus.), silkscreen.

CARTER, Keith

$518* *"Dog Ghost"*, *1990*, s. twice, t., d., #5/50, (05-23-93, Butterfield, #3369, illus.), 14½ x 14½ in., photograph, toned gelatin silver print (BP 337, DM 847, FR 2851, Y 57,257).

$413* *"Humming Birds"*, *1988*, s., t., d., edit. 8/50, (11-16-92, Butterfield, #5898, illus.), 15¼ x 15¼ in., (388 x 388 mm.), photograph, toned gelatin silver print (BP 272, DM 658, FR 2218, Y 51,362).

CARTER, Samuel (after)

BI *A September Evening On Badgeworthy Water, Exmoor Forest, 1873*, by Alfred Lucas, pub. Mordaunt, Fenwick & Bissett, laid on linen, mounted on stretcher, time/light-stained, est. BP 2/300, (11-30-92, Phillips-London, #34), plate 29¾ x 45½ in., (75.6 x 115.6 cm.), mixed-method engraving on india laid.

CARTIER-BRESSON, Henri   French b. 1908

$2200* *Alberto Giacometti, 1961 (Cartier-Bresson, pl. 118)*, s. by photog. in ink, p. l., (10-15-92, Sotheby-NY, #321, illus.), 14⅛ x 9½ in., (35.9 x 24.1 cm.), photograph, gelatin silver print (BP 1346, DM 3275, FR 11,106, Y 263,947).

$1650* *Alicante, Spain*, (1932), p.l., s. in ink, embossed (c) stamp, (10-13-92, Christie-NY, #161, illus.), 9⅜ x 14 in., (23.8 x 35.6 cm.), photograph, gelatin silver stamp (BP 961, DM 2417, FR 8213, Y 200,073).

$1210* *Alicante, Spain, 1932 (Cartier-Bresson, pl. 21)*, s. by photog. in ink, (c) blindstamp, p. l., (10-15-92, Sotheby-NY, #311, illus.), 14 x 9½ in., (35.6 x 24.1 cm.), photograph, gelatin silver print (BP 740, DM 1801, FR 6108, Y 145,171).

BI *Alles De Prado, Marseilles*, (1932), p.l., s. in ink, embossed (c) stamp, lit., est. $2/2,500, (10-13-92, Christie-NY, #162, illus.), 14 x 9⅜ in., (35.6 x 23.8 cm.), photograph, gelatin silver print.

BI *"Ascot, England", 1935*, p.l., ink s., photog.'s blindstamp, lit., est. BP 8/1,200, (10-29-92, Christie-London, #160, illus.), image 13¾ x 9¼ in., (34.9 x 23.5 cm.), photograph, gelatin silver print.

$1035* *"Avenue Du Maine" (Cartier-Bresson, pl. 9)*, s. by photog., 1932, p.l., (04-06-93, Sotheby-NY, #250, illus.), 9½ x 14 in., photograph (BP 684, DM 1667, FR 5646, Y 118,043).

$546* *"Barrio Chino, Barcelona, Spain"*, 1933, p.l., s., #30/45, illus., (05-23-93, Butterfield, #3373), 14 x 9¼ in., photogravure (BP 356, DM 893, FR 3005, Y 60,351).

$3220* *Behind The Gare Saint-Lazare, Paris*, c. 1932, p.l., ink s., embossed (c) credit stamp, lit., (04-08-93, Christie-NY, #183, illus.), 14¼ x 9½ in., (36.2 x 24.1 cm.), photograph, gelatin silver print (BP 2111, DM 5173, FR 17,510, Y 365,411).

$3575* *Behind The Gare St. Lazare, Paris, 1932 (Cartier-Bresson, pl. 14)*, stamp, p. 1950's, (10-15-92, Sotheby-NY, #323, illus.), 12 x 8 in., (30.5 x 20.3 cm.), photograph, gelatin silver print (BP 2188, DM 5322, FR 18,046, Y 428,914).

$2875* *"Behind The Gare St.-Lazare, Paris" (Cartier-Bresson, pl. 14)*, s. by photog., 1932, p.l., (04-06-93, Sotheby-NY, #258, illus.), 14 x 9½ in., photograph (BP 1899, DM 4632, FR 15,685, Y 327,897).

$2750* *Behind The Gare, St. Lazare, Paris, 1932 (Cartier-Bresson, pl. 14)*, s. by photog. in ink, p. l., (10-15-92, Sotheby-NY, #324, illus.), 14⅛ x 9½ in., (35.9 x 24.1 cm.), photograph, gelatin silver print (BP 1683, DM 4093, FR 13,882, Y 329,934).

$25,300* *La Besogne A Charnee, 1934*, t., i., prov., lit., (04-08-93, Christie-NY, #182, illus.), 9¼ x 13⅝ in., (23.5 x 34.6

cm.), photograph, gelatin silver print (BP 16,590, DM 40,643, FR 137,575, Y 2,871,085).

$1361* *The Bridal Gown*, 1950s, stamped photog.'s credit, agency credit, 240 x 352mm, (05-07-93, Sotheby-London, #250, illus.), photograph, silver print (BP 862, DM 2152, FR 7251, Y 149,857).

BI *Brie, France*, (1968), p.l., s. in ink, emobssed (c) credit stamp, lit., est. $1,8/2,200, (10-13-92, Christie-NY, #528, illus.), 9¼ x 14 in., (23.5 x 35.6 cm.), photograph, gelatin silver print.

$1495* *Brussels*, 1932, p.l., ink s., lit., (04-08-93, Christie-NY, #180, illus.), 9⅜ x 14 in., (23.8 x 35.6 cm.), photograph, gelatin silver print (BP 980, DM 2402, FR 8129, Y 169,655).

$1430* *Brussels, 1932 (Cartier-Bresson, pl. 155)*, s. by photog. in ink, (c) blindstamp, p. l., (10-15-92, Sotheby-NY, #312, illus.), 9½ x 14⅛ in., (24.1 x 35.9 cm.), photograph, gelatin silver print (BP 875, DM 2129, FR 7219, Y 171,566).

$3220* *Calle Cuauhtemozctin, Mexico*, 1934, p.l., ink s., embossed (c) credit stamp, lit., (04-08-93, Christie-NY, #184, illus.), 9½ x 14⅛ in., (24.1 x 35.9 cm.), photograph, gelatin silver print (BP 2111, DM 5173, FR 17,510, Y 365,411).

$1650* *Calle Cuauhtemozctin, Mexico*, (1934), p.l., s. in ink, embossed (c) stamp, lit., (10-13-92, Christie-NY, #163, illus.), 9½ x 14 in., (24.1 x 35.6 cm.), photograph, gelatin silver print (BP 961, DM 2417, FR 8213, Y 200,073).

BI *Cardinal Pacelli, Paris*, (1938), 1950s, t., credit stmap, lit., est. $3,5/4,500, (10-13-92, Christie-NY, #166, illus.), 7 x 10 in., (17.8 x 25.4 cm.), photograph, gelatin silver print.

$2750* *Carson McCullers And George Davis, Nyack, New York, 1946 (Lonely Hunter, fig. 23)*, given to present owner by Cartier-Bresson, (10-15-92, Sotheby-NY, #320, illus.), 6½ x 9½ in., (16.5 x 24.1 cm.), photograph, gelatin silver print (BP 1683, DM 4093, FR 13,882, Y 329,934).

$522* *Celebration, Mexico, 1964*, photog.'s Magnum handstamp, (04-07-93, Swann, #295, illus.), 8 x 12 in., photograph, silver print (BP 345, DM 844, FR 2857, Y 59,305).

$1210* *Children Playing In The Ruins, Seville, Spain*, handstamps, 1933, p. 1945, (10-14-92, Swann, #296, illus.), 6¾ x 9¾ in., (17.1 x 24.8 cm.), photograph, silver print (BP 710, DM 1771, FR 6005, Y 146,631).

$4400* *Christian Berard, Paris, 1932 (cf. Galassi, p. 79)*, s., i. by photog. in ink, (10-15-92, Sotheby-NY, #313, illus.), 9⅝ x 6½ in., (24.4 x 16.5 cm.), photograph, gelatin silver print (BP 2692, DM 6550, FR 22,211, Y 527,894).

$726* *"The Decisive Moment", 1952: Book*, 1st American edit., 126 plates, dust-jacket by Henri Matisse, large 4to., (05-06-93, Christie-London, #23), photograph, (BP 460, DM 1143, FR 3849, Y 79,877).

$8250* *From One China To The Other: Twenty, 1948-49*, group of 20 photos of China and Its People, photog.'s stamp, reduction notations in unidentified hand, exhib., (10-15-92, Sotheby-NY, #325, illus.), various sizes to 7½ x 4¾ in., (19.1 x 12.1 cm.), photograph, gelatin silver prints (BP 5048, DM 12,280, FR 41,646, Y 989,802).

BI *Germany*, s. by photog. in margin, (c) stamps, 1945, p.l., est. $1/2,000, (04-06-93, Sotheby-NY, #262, illus.), 9½ x 13¾ in., photograph.

BI *Glyndebourne, 1955*, credit stamp, original label, est. $2,5/3,500, (10-13-92, Christie-NY, #434, illus.), 9⅞ x 6¾ in., (25.1 x 17.1 cm.), photograph, gelatin silver print.

$1495* *"Henri Matisse, Vence, France" (Cartier-Bresson, pl. 126)*, s. by photog., 1944, p.l., (04-06-93, Sotheby-NY, #249A, illus.), 9⅜ x 14 in., photograph (BP 987, DM 2409, FR 8156, Y 170,506).

$3025* *Henri Matisse, Vence, France, 1944 (Cartier-Bresson, pl. 126)*, s. by photog. in ink, (c) blindstamp, p. l., (10-15-92, Sotheby-NY, #317, illus.), 9½ x 14⅛ in., (24.1 x 35.9 cm.), photograph, gelatin silver print (BP 1851, DM 4503, FR 15,270, Y 362,927).

$2588* *"Hyeres, France"*, 1937, p.l., s., illus., (05-23-93, Butterfield, #3370, illus.), 9⅝ x 14¼ in., photograph, gelatin silver print (BP 1685, DM 4232, FR 14,243, Y 286,062).

$2875* *"Hyeres, France" (Cartier-Bresson, pl. 13)*, s. by photog., (c) blindstamp, 1932, p.l., (04-06-93, Sotheby-NY, #254, illus.), 9½ x 14 in., photograph (BP 1899, DM 4632, FR 15,685, Y 327,897).

$3025* *Hyeres, France, 1932 (Cartier-Bresson, pl. 13),* s. by photog. in ink, p.l., (10-15-92, Sotheby-NY, #310, illus.), 9⅝ x 14¼ in., (24.4 x 36.2 cm.), photograph, gelatin silver print (BP 1851, DM 4503, FR 15,270, Y 362,927).

$2990* *Ile De La Cite, Paris,* 1952, p.l., ink s., embossed (c) credit stamp, lit., (04-08-93, Christie-NY, #185, illus.), 9½ x 14 in., (24.1 x 35.6 cm.), photograph, gelatin silver print (BP 1961, DM 4803, FR 16,259, Y 339,310).

$2090* *Ile De La Cite, Paris,* (1952), p.l., s. in ink, embossed (c) credit stamp, lit., (10-13-92, Christie-NY, #433, illus.), 9⅜ x 14 in., (23.8 x 35.6 cm.), photograph, gelatin silver print (BP 1217, DM 3062, FR 10,403, Y 253,425).

$3300* *"Ile De La Cite, Paris" (Henri Cartier-Bresson, p. 8),* s., (11-16-92, Butterfield, #5899, illus.), 9½ x 14 in., (241.7 x 356.2 mm.), photograph, gelatin silver print (BP 2173, DM 5261, FR 17,723, Y 410,397).

$2475* *Ile De La Cite, Paris, 1952 (Cartier-Bresson, pl. 8),* s. by photog. in ink, (c) blindstamp, p. l., (10-15-92, Sotheby-NY, #319, illus.), 9½ x 14⅛ in., (24.1 x 35.9 cm.), photograph, gelatin silver print (BP 1515, DM 3684, FR 12,494, Y 296,941).

$2090* *"In Dessan, Germany, Among Liberated D.P.'s Going Home, An Informer Of The Gestapo Tried To Slip Among Them. She Is Exposed By A Forced Labor WomanShe Had Informed Upon In Berlin.",* handstamps, 1945, p. 1947, (10-14-92, Swann, #295, illus.), 6¾ x 9¾ in., (17.1 x 24.8 cm.), photograph, silver print (BP 1227, DM 3059, FR 10,372, Y 253,272).

BI *Indira Ghandi, c. 1960,* (c) stamps, est. $1,2/1,800, (10-13-92, Christie-NY, #436, illus.), 9¾ x 6½ in., (24.8 x 16.5 cm.), photograph, gelatin silver print.

$472* *John Davenport, August 1951,* i., num. 1019 and 28, 240 x 166mm, (05-07-93, Sotheby-London, #248, illus.), photograph, silver print (BP 299, DM 746, FR 2515, Y 51,971).

BI *"Last Days Of The Kuomintang, Peking", 1949,* p.l., s., photog.'s blindstamp, lit., est. BP 8/1,200, (10-29-92, Christie-London, #163, illus.), image 14⅛ x 9¼ in., (35.9 x 23.5 cm.), photograph, gelatin silver print.

$1725* *Madrid,* 1933, p.l., ink s., embossed (c) credit stamp, lit., (04-08-93, Christie-NY, #181, illus.), 9½ x 14⅛ in., (24.1 x 35.9 cm.), photograph, gelatin silver print (BP 1131, DM 2771, FR 9380, Y 195,756).

$2588* *"Madrid" (Cartier-Bresson, pl. 27),* s. by photog., (c) blindstamp, 1933, p.l., (04-06-93, Sotheby-NY, #251, illus.), 9½ x 14¼ in., photograph (BP 1709, DM 4169, FR 14,119, Y 295,164).

BI *Madrid, 1933 (Cartier-Bresson, pl. 27),* s. by photog. in ink, p. l., est. $2/2,500, (10-15-92, Sotheby-NY, #315, illus.), 9½ x 14¼ in., (24.1 x 36.2 cm.), photograph, gelatin silver print.

$2530* *Malcolm X,* 1961, p.l., ink s., (c) stamp embossed, lit., (04-08-93, Christie-NY, #479, illus.), 14 x 9½ in., (35.6 x 24.1 cm.), photograph, gelatin silver print (BP 1659, DM 4064, FR 13,757, Y 287,108).

$605* *Marc Chagall,* photog.'s handstamp, agency's label, 1970s, (04-07-93, Swann, #296, illus.), 10 x 6¾ in., photograph, silver print (BP 400, DM 978, FR 3311, Y 68,734).

BI *Martin Luther King, Jr.,* 1961, p.l., ink s., (c) stamp embossed, lit., est. $2,2/2,800, (04-08-93, Christie-NY, #480, illus.), 14 x 9⅜ in., (35.6 x 23.8 cm.), photograph, gelatin silver print.

BI *Matisse, Vence, France,* (1944), p.l., credit stmap, lit., est. $1,8/2,200, (10-13-92, Christie-NY, #165, illus.), 9⅛ x 13¾ in., (23.2 x 34.9 cm.), photograph, gelatin silver print.

$715* *Mexican Chauffeur,* stamp, 1950's, (10-14-92, Swann, #405), 9¾ x 6½ in., (24.8 x 16.5 cm.), photograph, silver print (BP 420, DM 1046, FR 3548, Y 86,646).

$1840* *"Mexico" (Cartier-Bresson, pl. 52),* s. by photog., 1964, p.l., (04-06-93, Sotheby-NY, #261, illus.), 9½ x 14¼ in., photograph (BP 1215, DM 2964, FR 10,038, Y 209,854).

$1545* *"Naples, Italy", 1963,* p.l., s., photog.'s blindstamp, lit., (10-29-92, Christie-London, #159, illus.), image 9⅜ x 14 in., (23.8 x 35.6 cm.), photograph, gelatin silver print (BP 990, DM 2377, FR 8064, Y 191,379).

$3300* *On River Steamer, Westminster To Greenwich,* credit & studio stamps, label, 1950's, (10-15-92, Sotheby-NY, #318, illus.), 8¼ x 12 in., (21 x 30.5 cm.), photograph, gelatin silver print (BP 2019, DM 4912, FR 16,658, Y 395,921).

$1610* *"On The Banks Of The Marne",* 1938, p.l., s., photog.'s blindstamp, illus., (05-23-93, Butterfield, #3371, illus.), 9½ x 14 in., photograph, gelatin silver print (BP 1049, DM 2632, FR 8861, Y 177,960).

$1100* *On The Banks Of The Marne, France,* (1938), p.l., s. in ink, embossed credit stamp, lit., (10-13-92, Christie-NY, #164, illus.), 11¾ x 17⅝ in., (29.8 x 44.8 cm.), photograph, gelatin silver print (BP 641, DM 1611, FR 5475, Y 133,382).

$2070* *"On The Banks Of The Marne, France" (Cartier-Bresson, pl. 145),* s. by photog., (c) blindstamp, 1938, p.l., (04-06-93, Sotheby-NY, #255, illus.), 9¾ x 14¼ in., photograph (BP 1367, DM 3335, FR 11,293, Y 236,086).

$1925* *On The Banks Of The Marne, France, 1938 (Cartier-Bresson, pl. 145),* s. by photog. in ink, p. l., (10-15-92, Sotheby-NY, #314, illus.), 9½ x 14⅛ in., (24.1 x 35.9 cm.), photograph, gelatin silver print (BP 1178, DM 2865, FR 9717, Y 230,954).

BI *"Palais Royal, Paris", 1960,* p.l., s., photog.'s nlindstamp, lit., est. BP 9/1,200, (10-29-92, Christie-London, #161, illus.), image 14⅛ x 9½ in., (35.9 x 24.1 cm.), photograph, gelatin silver print.

$1725* *"Palais-Royal, Paris" (Cartier-Bresson, p. 42),* s. by photog., blindstamp, 1960, p.l., (04-06-93, Sotheby-NY, #257, illus.), photograph (BP 1139, DM 2779, FR 9411, Y 196,738).

$2760* *Rue Mouffetard,* 1954, p.l., ink s., embossed (c) credit stamp, lit., (04-08-93, Christie-NY, #186, illus.), 14 x 9⅜ in., (35.6 x 23.8 cm.), photograph, gelatin silver print (BP 1810, DM 4434, FR 15,008, Y 313,209).

$2185* *"Rue Mouffetard" (Cartier-Bresson, pl. 141),* s. by photog., 1954, p.l., (04-06-93, Sotheby-NY, #256, illus.), 14⅛ x 9½ in., photograph (BP 1443, DM 3520, FR 11,920, Y 249,202).

$2750* *Rue Mouffetard, 1954 (Cartier-Bresson, pl 141),* s. by photog. in ink, p. l., (10-15-92, Sotheby-NY, #322, illus.), 14½ x 9½ in., (36.8 x 24.1 cm.), photograph, gelatin silver print (BP 1683, DM 4093, FR 13,882, Y 329,934).

$1650* *Seville, 1933 (Cartier-Bresson, pl. 90),* s. by photog. in ink, p. l., (10-15-92, Sotheby-NY, #316, illus.), 9½ x 14 in., (24.1 x 35.6 cm.), photograph, gelatin silver print (BP 1010, DM 2456, FR 8329, Y 197,960).

$1495* *"Seville, Spain" (Cartier-Bresson, pl. 90),* s. by photog., (c) blindstamp, 1932, p.l., (04-06-93, Sotheby-NY, #253, illus.), 9½ x 14⅛ in., photograph (BP 987, DM 2409, FR 8156, Y 170,506).

$2300* *"Siphnos, Greece" (Cartier-Bresson, pl. 45), 1961,* s. by photog., (c) blindstamp, (04-06-93, Sotheby-NY, #259, illus.), 9½ x 14¼ in., photograph (BP 1519, DM 3705, FR 12,548, Y 262,318).

$1955* *"Srinagar, Kashmir" (Cartier-Bresson, pl. 77),* s. by photog., (c) blindstamp, 1948, p.l., (04-06-93, Sotheby-NY, #260, illus.), 9½ x 14¼ in., photograph (BP 1291, DM 3150, FR 10,666, Y 222,970).

$1045* *Street In Madrid, 1933,* handstamps, 1933, p.l., (10-14-92, Swann, #297, illus.), 7 x 10 in., (17.8 x 25.4 cm.), photograph, silver print (BP 613, DM 1529, FR 5186, Y 126,636).

$1998* *"Tivoli, Near Rome, 1933",* stamped photog.'s credit, agency credit, illus., 353 x 238mm, (05-07-93, Sotheby-London, #249, illus.), photograph, silver print (BP 1265, DM 3159, FR 10,645, Y 219,996).

$1870* *"Trafalgar Square On The Day Of George VI's Coronation, London" (Henri Cartier-Bresson, p. 67),* 1938/later, s., photog. blindstamp, (11-16-92, Butterfield, #5900, illus.), 14⅛ x 9⅜ in., (359.4 x 238.5 mm.), photograph, gelatin silver print (BP 1231, DM 2982, FR 10,043, Y 232,558).

$1888* *"Trafalgar Square On The Day Of George VI's Coronation, London", 1938,* p.l., s., photog.'s blindstamp, lit., (10-29-92, Christie-London, #162, illus.), image 14 x 9¼ in., (35.6 x 23.5 cm.), photograph, gelatin silver print (BP 1210, DM 2905, FR 9854, Y 233,866).

$10,350* *Truman Capote (Cartier-Bresson, pl. 112), 1947,* i. by photog. w/stamp, i., (04-06-93, Sotheby-NY, #263, illus.), 6⅝ x 9⅝ in., photograph (BP 6836, DM 16,675, FR 56,465, Y 1,180,429).

$920* *Two Men At Cricket Match,* 1930s, photog.'s stamp, (05-23-93, Butterfield, #3372, illus.), 10 x 6¾ in., photograph, gelatin silver print (BP 599, DM 1504, FR 5063, Y 101,691).

$341* *U.D.S.S.R., c. 1954,* (c), t., (11-12-92, Lempertz, #31, illus.), 7¹³⁄₁₆ x 11⁹⁄₁₆ in., (19.9 x 29.3 cm.), photograph, gelatin silver print (BP 218, DM 536, FR 1826, Y 42,187).

$2013* *"Valencia" (Galassi, p. 107),* s. by photog., (c) blindstamp, 1933, p.l., (04-06-93, Sotheby-NY, #252, illus.), 9½ x 14⅛ in., photograph (BP 1330, DM 3243, FR 10,982, Y 229,585).

$1150* *The Waiter,* 1950s, Magnum Photos and ABC Press credit stamps, (04-08-93, Christie-NY, #413, illus.), 8 x 11¾ in., (20.3 x 29.8 cm.), photograph, gelatin silver print (BP 754, DM 1847, FR 6253, Y 130,504).

BI *Youngsters On Leventina, Basel, Switzerland, 1956,* credit stamp, est. $2/2,500, (10-13-92, Christie-NY, #435, illus.), 14 x 9⅜ in., (35.6 x 23.8 cm.), photograph, gelatin silver print.

CARZOU, Jean French b. 1907

$434* *Ballets De L'Opera De Paris, Palais Des Sports, 1970,* (01-31-93, Morelle/Marchan, #18), 17¹¹⁄₁₆ x 23⅝ in., (45 x 60 cm.), poster (BP 292, DM 699, FR 2364, Y 54,142).

$303* *Bateaux Echoues A Ouistreham (M. Fuange, 42), 1958,* d., #27/100, s., frame trace, good margins, (02-03-93, Ader Tajan, #78), 17¹¹⁄₁₆ x 21⅝ in., (45 x 55 cm.), color lithograph (BP 212, DM 499, FR 1692, Y 37,691).

$97* *Les Baux,* s., #31/100, crease, good cond., (06-28-93, Loudmer, #24), 12⅝ x 19³⁄₁₆ in., (320 x 488 mm.), color lithograph on wove (BP 65, DM 165, FR 555, Y 10,292).

$200* *"Couple", 1974,* d., #69/80, s., (04-04-93, Pescheteau, #173), 20½ x 27⁹⁄₁₆ in., (52 x 70 cm.), color lithograph on Japan nacre (BP 132, DM 321, FR 1092, Y 22,771).

BI *Dunkerque,* s. 66, 188/250, est. DK 1,500, (11-14-92, Bukowskis, #11), lithograph in colors.

$55* *Giselle,* (06-11-93, Freemn/Fine Art, #31), 21½ x 16¼ in., (54.6 x 41.3 cm.), lithograph in orange and black (BP 36, DM 89, FR 301, Y 5836).

$64* *Jeune Fille, 1965,* s., crease, (10-14-92, Germann, #234), 27¾ x 20¹⁄₁₆ in., (705 x 510 mm.), color lithograph (BP 38, DM 94, FR 318, Y 7756, SF 83).

$180* *"Marine-54",* d. 54, s., (04-04-93, Pescheteau, #174), 9¹³⁄₁₆ x 11 in., (25 x 28 cm.), color lithograph (BP 119, DM 289, FR 983, Y 20,494).

$101* *Nu Assis, 1973,* s., d. 76, #38/150, small margins, creases, (05-27-93, Briest, #51), 19⁵⁄₁₆ x 24¹³⁄₁₆ in., (49 x 63 cm.), color lithograph (BP 65, DM 162, FR 546, Y 10,828).

$323* *Le Palais Des Mirages, 1973,* d., annot., #18/80, s., good margins, (02-03-93, Ader Tajan, #83), 19⅛ x 25¹⁵⁄₁₆ in., (48.5 x 66 cm.), color lithograph on Japan nacre (BP 225, DM 532, FR 1803, Y 40,179).

$180* *"Paysage", 1973,* #165/175, d., s., (10-18-92, Pescheteau, #95), 21⅝ x 29½ in., (55 x 75 cm.), lithograph in colors on Arches (BP 109, DM 266, FR 903, Y 21,493).

$58* *Psychodelic Woman, 1973,* s., d., artist proof, XXIII/XXXIV, (06-28-93, Loudmer, #23), 19½ x 24¹³⁄₁₆ in., (495 x 630 mm.), sh 21⁹⁄₁₆ x 29¾ in., (495 x 630 mm.), color lithograph on BFK Rives wove (BP 39, DM 99, FR 332, Y 6154).

$197* *Venezia II (M. Fuhrange n.d.), 1985,* d., t., annot., #15/26, large margins, (06-16-93, Ader Tajan, #53), 23¼ x 19¹¹⁄₁₆ in., (59 x 50 cm.), color lithograph on Japan nacre (BP 131, DM 327, FR 1097, Y 21,011).

CASARIN, M. b. 1949

$54* *Composizione, 1986,* 36/65, s., d., (10-14-92, Germann, #235), 23¼ x 27⁹⁄₁₆ in., (590 x 700 mm.), color serigraph (BP 32, DM 79, FR 268, Y 6544, SF 71).

CASAS DE V.

$417* *Helios Material Para Fotografia, 1901,* p. Font Barcelona, (05-07-93, Christie-S. Ken, #81, illus.), 19¾ x 13 in., (50.2 x 33 cm.), color lithograph (BP 264, DM 659, FR 2222, Y 45,915).

CASPAR, Karl 1879-1956

$622* *"Passion": Ten,* pub. Delphin, s., num., signs of wear, (12-01-92, Karl/Faber, #424), 18¹¹⁄₁₆ x 16¹⁵⁄₁₆ in., (47.5 x 43 cm.), lithograph on simili-Japan (BP 411, DM 991, FR 3379, Y 77,440).

CASPEL, J.G. van 1870-1928

$2383* *De Hollandsche Revue (van Caspel Affichekunstenaar 17 and p.22; Dooijes/Brattinga 88), 1899,* Steendr., "Senefelder", restored, tears, folds, fine cond., (06-09-93, Bubb Kuyper, #2169, illus.), 31⅝ x 43⁷⁄₁₆ in., (80.3 x 110.3 cm.), color lithograph (BP 1572, DM 3898, FR 13,108, Y 253,430, G 4370).

CASPEL, V.

$955* *Foto Artikelen Capi,* p. Gederponeerd, creases, (05-07-93, Christie-S. Ken, #87, illus.), 39½ x 26½ in., (100.3 x 67.3 cm.), color lithograph (BP 605, DM 1510, FR 5088, Y 105,153).

CASSANDRE, A.M. French 1901-1968

BI *Bonnal, 1935,* ed. Alliance Graphique, est. FF 4/5,000, (11-16-92, Briest, #267), 62³⁄₁₆ x 46⅝ in., (158 x 118.5 cm.), poster.

BI *Celtique, 1934,* tears, excell. cond., lit., est. BP 2,5/3,500, (02-04-93, Christie-S. Ken, #107, illus.), 50 x 35 in., (127 x 88.9 cm.), color lithograph backed on japan.

$1382* *Ch. De Fer Du Nord: Lys Chantilly, 1930,* p. Perceval, excell. cond., (01-23-93, Ribeyre/Baron, #27, illus.), 39⅜ x 24¹³⁄₁₆ in., (100 x 63 cm.), poster (BP 904, DM 2197, FR 7434, Y 172,966).

$2727* *Chateau De La Roche Vasouy. Honfleur. "Hotel Restaurant", 1926,* p. Hachard and Cie, very good cond., lit., (11-19-92, Ribeyre/Baron, #91, illus.), 47¼ x 31½ in., (120 x 80 cm.), poster (BP 1795, DM 4348, FR 14,646, Y 339,137).

$1285* *Chemin De Fer Du Nord, (Mouron 127), 1929,* Imp. L. Danel, (03-24-93, Kunsthallen, #55), lithographic poster (BP 870, DM 2099, FR 7143, Y 150,981, DK 8050).

$1888* *Chemins De Fer Du Nord: Lys Chantilly, 1930,* p. L. Danel, very good cond., lit., (11-19-92, Ribeyre/Baron, #94, illus.), 39⅜ x 24⁷⁄₁₆ in., (100 x 62 cm.), poster (BP 1243, DM 3010, FR 10,140, Y 234,797).

$1650* *"Dubonnet", c. 1952,* (12-12-92, Christie-NY, #444, illus.), 66½ x 48 in., (168.9 x 121.9 cm.), lithograph in colors on paper laid down on linen (BP 1058, DM 2600, FR 8909, Y 204,183).

BI *Dubonnet, 1932,* by Axel Andreasen & Sons, good cond., time darkened, est. $3/5,000, (06-10-93, Sotheby-NY, #478, illus.), 67 x 48 in., (170.2 x 121.9 cm.), color lithograph laid down on canvas.

BI *Dubonnet, c. 1950,* s., est. $1,5/2,000, (06-08-93, Christie-E, #190), 66½ x 48 in., (168.9 x 121.9 cm.), color lithograph.

$2206* *Dubonnet, c. 1952,* excell. cond., (02-04-93, Christie-S. Ken, #109, illus.), 67 x 48½ in., (170.2 x 123.2 cm.), color offset lithograph on two sheets backed on linen (BP 1540, DM 3632, FR 12,317, Y 274,412).

$825* *Etoile Du Nord, 1927,* Hachard and Cie, B- cond., (08-06-92, Swann, #78, illus.), 41 x 29½ in., (104.1 x 74.9 cm.), mounted on masonite (BP 431, DM 1219, FR 4117, Y 105,230).

$5240* *Etoile Du Nord, 1927,* p. Hachard, good cond., lit., (11-19-92, Ribeyre/Baron, #92, illus.), 41⅛ x 29⁵⁄₁₆ in., (104.5 x 74.5 cm.), poster (BP 3450, DM 8355, FR 28,142, Y 651,660).

$945* *Fetes De Paris, 1935,* fold marks, tape marks, repaired tears, lit., (02-04-93, Christie-S. Ken, #108, illus.), 63 x 47½ in., (160 x 120.7 cm.), color lithograph backed on japan (BP 660, DM 1556, FR 5276, Y 117,552).

$10,476* *Grand Sport, "La Casquette Adoptee Par Tous Les Champions", 1931,* p. Hachard and Cie, good cond., lit., (11-19-92, Ribeyre/Baron, #24, illus.), 62¹⁵⁄₁₆ x 47¼ in., (160 x 120 cm.), poster (BP 6898, DM 16,703, FR 56,262, Y 1,302,823).

$1990* *Grands Reseaux Des Chemins De Fer Francais: Paris, 1930,* p. Draeger, excell. cond., (01-23-93, Ribeyre/Baron, #28, illus.), 39⅜ x 24⁷⁄₁₆ in., (100 x 62 cm.), poster (BP 1302, DM 3164, FR 10,705, Y 249,061).

BI *Italia, 1936,* by Officina Grafiche Coen & Cia, good cond., est. $2,5/3,000, (06-10-93, Sotheby-NY, #477, illus.), 39 x 24 in., (99.1 x 61 cm.), color lithograph.

$660* *L'Oiseau Bleu, Train Pullman, 1929,* L. Danel, B- cond., (08-06-92, Swann, #79, illus.), 39 x 24½ in., (99.1 x 62.2 cm.), mounted on masonite (BP 345, DM 975, FR 3293, Y 84,184).

$880* *Nord Express, 1927,* Hachard and Cie, C+ cond., (08-06-92, Swann, #77, illus.), 41 x 29½ in., (104.1 x 74.9 cm.), mounted on masonite (BP 460, DM 1300, FR 4391, Y 112,245).

$7150* *Nord Express, 1927,* by Hachard et Cie, good cond., creasing, 1.05m x 74.3cm, poster, (11-07-92, Sotheby-NY, #274, illus.), sight 41¼ x 29¼ in., lithograph in colors (BP 4675, DM 11,471, FR 38,586, Y 882,498).

$11,550* *"Normandie New York Via Le Havre Et Southampton", 1935,* pub. Alliance Graphique L. Danet, (12-12-92, Christie-NY, #443, illus.), 43 x 28 in., (109.2 x 71.1 cm.), lithograph in colors on paper laid down on linen (BP 7406, DM 18,198, FR 62,365, Y 1,429,279).

BI *Paris, 1935,* plate s., est. $1,2/1,800, (03-25-93, Christie-E, #198), 39 x 23½ in., (99.1 x 59.7 cm.), color lithograph.

$1210* *Thomson: La Main-D'Oeuvre Electro-Domestique, 1931,* by Alliance Graphique, good cond., loose sheet, (11-07-92, Sotheby-NY, #275, illus.), 10½ x 7 in., (26.7 x 17.8 ï), lithograph in colors (BP 791, DM 1941, FR 6530, Y 149,346).

BI *Unic, Chaussures D'Hommes, 1932,* tears, repairs, creases, lit., est. BP 2/4,000, (02-04-93, Christie-S. Ken, #106, illus.), 63 x 47½ in., (160 x 120.7 cm.), color lithograph backed on japan.

$1540* *Venezia,* Clacografia and Cartevaloni, A- cond., creasing, fraying, (08-06-92, Swann, #80, illus.), 39½ x 25 in., (100.3 x 63.5 cm.), (BP 804, DM 2275, FR 7685, Y 196,429).

BI *Wagons-Lits 2eme Classe, 1930,* by L. Danel Lithographers, good cond., laid down, creasing, surface abrasions, est. $6/9,000, (06-10-93, Sotheby-NY, #476, illus.), 39¼ x 24½ in., (99.7 x 62.2 cm.), color lithograph.

CASSATT, Mary American 1844-1926

$239,000* *Afternoon Tea Party (B. 151; M./S. 13), 1890-91,* mono. stamp, s., i., full margins, good cond., darkening paper, fox marks, hinge remains, (05-13-93, Sotheby-NY, #416, illus.), 13¾ x 10⅝ in., (348 x 269 mm.), sh 17 x 11⅞ in., (348 x 269 mm.), drypoint and aquatint in colors w/ touches of gold hand-coloring on heavy Arches laid (BP 156,907, DM 385,920, FR 1,301,743, Y 26,683,041).

$12,075* *The Barefoot Child (B. 160; M./S. 22), c. 1896-97,* Breeskin's 3rd state of 4, Mathew and Shapiro's final state, watermark, full margins, good cond., 3 touched-in printer's defects, (05-13-93, Sotheby-NY, #417, illus.), 9⅝ x 12½ in., (243 x 318 mm.), sh 12½ x 17¾ in., (243 x 318 mm.), drypoint and aquatint in colors on Glainges laid (BP 7927, DM 19,498, FR 65,768, Y 1,348,108).

$8800* *The Bonnet (B. 137), c. 1891,* third (final) state, s., anno. 'epreuve d'essai', full margins, goodcond., tape and hinge stains, soiling, mat stain, (11-05-92, Sotheby-NY, #12, illus.), 7⅜ x 5⅜ in., (187 x 137 mm.), drypoint p. w/ tone in dark brown ink, on fine laid w/watermark (BP 5724, DM 13,917, FR 47,084, Y 1,079,622).

$9900* *By The Pond (Breeskin 161), 1898,* 4th (final) state, s., trimmed repaired splits, glue staining in image, tears, repaired or made-up losses, laid down on board, defects, (11-09-92, Christie-NY, #17A, illus.), plate 13¹⁄₁₆ x 16¹⁵⁄₁₆ in., (331 x 430 mm.), aquatint and drypoint on laid (BP 6545, DM 15,805, FR 53,398, Y 1,228,593).

BI *In The Omnibus, Or In The Tramway (B. 145; M./S. 7), 1890-91,* 6th state (of 7), init., full margins, good cond., mat stain, fox marks, tears, stain, est. $150/200,000, (05-13-93, Sotheby-NY, #414, illus.), 14½ x 10⅝ in., (368 x 269 mm.), sh 17⅛ x 12⅛ in., (368 x 269 mm.), drypoint, soft-ground and aquatint in colors, on heavy Arches laid.

$715* *Jeanette Wearing A Bonnet, No. 1 (Breeskin 179), c. 1904,* also called Margo Wearing A Bonnet, posthumous printing, rippling, (05-27-93, Swann, #51), 9 x 6½ in., (22.9 x 16.5 cm.), hand-colored drypoint etching (BP 458, DM 1147, FR 3867, Y 76,651).

$90,500* *The Lamp Or L'Abat-Jour (B. 144; M./S. 6), 1890-91,* final state, s., i., full margins, good cond., mat stain, foxing, skinning, stains, thin spots, (05-13-93, Sotheby-NY, #413, illus.), 12⅝ x 10 in., (321 x 254 mm.), sh 17 x 11⅞ in., (321 x 254 mm.), drypoint, soft-ground and aquatint in colors, on laid (BP 59,414, DM 146,133, FR 492,919, Y 10,103,829).

BI *The Lamp Or L'Abat-Jour (Breeskin 144; Matthews/Shapiro 6), 1890-91,* proof, rich burr, s., i. No. 6 de la serie du 10 epr. en couleurs, watermark, full margins, good cond., soiling, mat stain, margin tips restored, est. $60/80,000, (05-13-93, Sotheby-NY, #412, illus.), 12⅝ x 9⅞ in., (322 x 250 mm.), sh 16⅛ x 10⅞ in., (322 x 250 mm.), drypoint, soft-ground and aquatint in colors, touches of red crayon,on laid.

$1430* *Looking Into The Hand Mirror (No. 3) (B. 202+), 1905,* watermark, margins, good cond., staining, hinge remains, (02-24-93, Butterfield, #2623), 8³⁄₁₆ x 5⅞ in., (208 x 149 mm.), drypoint on laid (BP 997, DM 2321, FR 7870, Y 167,801).

BI *Looking Into The Hand Mirror (No. 3) (B. 202+), 1905,* watermark, margins, good cond., tear, mat staining, notations, est. $7/900, (05-19-93, Butterfield, #1800), 8¼ x 5¹³⁄₁₆ in., (210 x 148 mm.), drypoint on fine laid.

$990* *"Looking Into The Hand Mirror" (Breeskin, 202+), c. 1905,* num. 3, good cond., wide margins, light staining; tape verso, (09-11-92, Skinner, #4, illus.), 8¼ x 5⅞ in., (21 x 14.9 cm.), drypoint on laid paper w/watermark (BP 512, DM 1425, FR 4843, Y 122,661).

$770* *"Looking Into The Hand Mirror", c. 1904,* full margins, excell. cond., (05-07-93, Goldberg, #425, illus.), 8¼ x 5⅞ in., (21 x 14.9 cm.), drypoint etching (BP 488, DM 1217, FR 4102, Y 84,783).

$770* *The Manicure (Breeskin 199), c. 1905,* prov., (03-24-93, Grogan, #110), 8 x 5¾ in., (20.3 x 14.6 cm.), drypoint (BP 521, DM 1258, FR 4280, Y 90,471).

$605* *The Manicure (Breeskin 199), c. 1905,* posthumous printing, (12-08-92, Swann, #55, illus.), 8¼ x 6⅞ in., (21 x 17.5 cm.), drypoint etching on antique white laid watermarked paper (BP 379, DM 942, FR 3211, Y 74,988).

$1210* *"The Manicure" (Breeskin, 199), c. 1908,* very good cond., light staining, fox mark; tape verso, (09-11-92, Skinner, #10, illus.), 8¼ x 5¹³⁄₁₅ in., (21 x 12.7 cm.), drypoint on laid paper, watermark (BP 626, DM 1742, FR 5920, Y 149,919).

$550* *"The Manicure", c. 1908,* posthumous p., (08-08-92, Litchfield, #39), 8 x 5½ in., (20.3 x 14 cm.), etching and drypoint (BP 286, DM 809, FR 2734, Y 70,198).

$24,200* *The Map (The Lesson) (Breeskin 127), 1890,* third (final) state, s., t., mono. stamp (Lugt 604), large margins, good cond., creases, soiling, ex-coll. Gordon A. Block, (11-05-92, Sotheby-NY, #11, illus.), 6⅜ x 9¼ in., (161 x 235 mm.), sheet 9⅞ x 12¾ in., (161 x 235 mm.), drypoint in dark brown ink w/a delicate veil of tone on sturdy Japanese laid (BP 15,740, DM 38,273, FR 129,481, Y 2,968,961).

$1045* *Margot Wearing A Bonnet, No. 1 (Breeskin 179), c. 1902,* posthumous printing, (12-08-92, Swann, #56), 9³⁄₁₆ x 6½ in., (23.3 x 16.5 cm.), drypoint on pale blue laid watermarked paper (BP 655, DM 1627, FR 5547, Y 129,524).

$863* *Margot Wearing A Bonnett (No. 3) (B. 181), 1902,* margins, good cond., staining, foxing, (05-19-93, Butterfield, #1798), 9⅛ x 6¼ in., (232 x 159 mm.), drypoint on Bouchet laid (BP 560, DM 1403, FR 4726, Y 95,539).

$10,350* *Margot Wearing A Large Bonnet, Seated In An Armchair (B. 192), c. 1904,* s., full margins, three skillfully repaired, losses in image, creases, specks of foxing, mat stain, skinned spots, repaired loss, (05-13-93, Sotheby-NY, #418, illus.), 11⅝ x 9⅜ in., (296 x 238 mm.), drypoint on Vanderlay laid (BP 6795, DM 16,712, FR 56,373, Y 1,155,521).

BI *Mutter Mit Kind (Breeskin 199),* est. DM 1,200, (12-04-92, Bassenge, #6759), 8¼ x 5⅞ in., (20.9 x 14.9 cm.), etching on handmade.

BI *Mutter Mit Kind Auf Ihrem Schoss,* est. DM 1800, (12-01-92, Karl/Faber, #175), 8¼ x 5⅞ in., (21 x 15 cm.), etching on Rives.

BI *Quietude (B. 139), c. 1891,* fifth (final) state, margins, good cond., foxing, est. $5/7,000, (11-05-92, Sotheby-NY, #13, illus.), 10⅛ x 6⅞ in., (258 x 175 mm.), drypoint in black ink w/light plate tone on fine laid w/watermark.

BI *Sara Smiling (B. 195), 1904,* watermark, margins, good cond., staining, creases into image, stain,foxing, est. $1/1,500, (05-19-93, Butterfield, #1799), 9⅛ x 6¼ in., (232 x 159 mm.), drypoint on laid.

$1320* *"Sara Smiling" (Breeskin 195), c. 1904 and "Looking Into The Hand Mirror-No. 3" (Breeskin 202), c. 1904: Two,* only known state, posthumous printings, (05-27-93, Swann, #53), one 7¾ x 5⁵⁄₁₆ in., (19.7 x 13.5 cm.), (19.7 x 13.5 cm.), drypoint etching (BP 845, DM 2118, FR 7139, Y 141,509).

BI *Under The Horse-Chestnut Tree (Breeskin 162), c. 1895,* 4th final state, watermark, i. No. 27, pub. by L'Estampe Nouvelle, ink stamp (L. 886), full margins, mat staining, loss, tear (backed), excell. cond., est. $60/80,000, (05-11-93, Christie-NY, #95, illus.), plate 15⅝ x 11¼ in., (397 x 286 mm.), color drypoint and aquatint on laid.

$288,500* *Woman Bathing Or La Toilette (B. 148; M./S. 10), 1890-91,* proof impression of 4th (final) state, s., i. to printer, a MonsieurLeroy, margins, good cond., crease, tip of margin corner restored, mat stain, platemark reinforced, catalog cover lot, (05-13-93, Sotheby-NY, #415, illus.), 14½ x 10½ in., (368 x 268 mm.), sh 18⅝ x 12⅜ in., (368 x 268 mm.), drypoint and aquatint in colors on heavy laid (BP 189,404, DM 465,849, FR 1,571,351, Y 32,209,445).

CASSELL

$920* *Chickens, 1877: Six,* (03-03-93, Sotheby-Arcade, #150), sight 9½ x 7½ in., (24.1 x 19.1 cm.), chromolithograph (BP 635, DM 1515, FR 5140, Y 107,502).

CASSELL, Publisher

$9* *The Thanksgiving Service At St. Paul's Cathedral On Diamond Jubilee Day, June 22nd, 1897,* photograph by the London Stereoscopic Company, Late Sir Philip Hendyand Lady Hendy Coll., (05-20-93, Bonhams-Chelsea, #133), image 17⅝ x 24 in., (44.8 x 61 cm.), reprod. (BP 6, DM 15, FR 49, Y 994).

CASSELS-BROWN, R.

$58 *"The Old Mill, Bidston, Cheshire" and "Pan": Two,* s., (04-16-93, G.A. Key, #125), 5 x 5 in., (12.7 x 12.7 cm.), b/w etching (BP 38, DM 94, FR 317, Y 6522).

CASSIERS, Henri Belgian 1858-1944

$247* *Gournay, 1927,* H. Chachoin, A- cond., creasing, closed tears, (08-06-92, Swann, #81, illus.), 58 x 39 in., (147.3 x 99.1 cm.), (BP 129, DM 365, FR 1233, Y 31,505).

$110* *Landscape With Windmill,* no. 276, s. H. Cassiers, s. by p. F. Charlet, blindstamp, (12-12-92, Wolf, #11), 18½ x 27½ in., (47 x 69.9 cm.), color etching (BP 71, DM 173, FR 594, Y 13,612).

CASSIGNEUL, Jean Pierre French b. 1935

$832* *Le Bruit De La Mer, (C. 350), 1987,* i. E.A., margins, good cond., (12-01-92, Christie-London, #566), L. 25⁹⁄₁₆ x 18¹³⁄₁₆ in., (649 x 478 mm.), lithograph in colors on Arches (BP 550, DM 1326, FR 4519, Y 103,586).

BI *Le Corsage Jaune (P.F. 25), 1970,* s., i. E.S., margins, trimmed, est. BP 4/600, (11-30-92, Phillips-London, #384), sheet 18⅝ x 15⅜ in., (473 x 391 mm.), color lithograph.

$1540* *Deauville, 1973,* s., #22/65, full margins, good cond., light/mat staining, notations, (10-28-92, Butterfield, #2614, illus.), 19⅞ x 15 in., (505 x 381 mm.), color lithograph on Arches (BP 981, DM 2378, FR 8076, Y 188,957).

$1201* *Devant La Porte (F. 47), 1972,* s., i. E. A., p. Bellini, attenuated, good cond., (06-30-93, Sotheby-London, #385), sh 32⅛ x 22⅝ in., (816 x 575 mm.), colored lithograph on Arches (BP 805, DM 2048, FR 6910, Y 128,683).

$609* *Femme A La Fontaine,* s., #140/150, good cond., (10-27-92, Phillips-London, #188), sheet 28⅞ x 21¼ in., (733 x 540 mm.), colored lithograph on Arches (BP 385, DM 933, FR 3167, Y 74,495).

BI *Filles Dans Le Foret, (Afbidet Side 11),* s. Cassigneul, 76/120, est. DK 8,000, (03-24-93, Kunsthallen, #56, illus.), color lithograph.

$298* *Flicka Vid Springbrunn,* s., 47/150, (04-17-93, Falkkloos, #77, illus.), 25³⁄₁₆ x 18⅞ in., (64 x 48 cm.), lithograph in colors (BP 194, DM 477, FR 1610, Y 33,137, SK 2200).

$550* *In The Park,* s., #26/130, toning, (05-15-93, Cleveland, #458), 20 x 16 in., (50.8 x 40.6 cm.), color lithograph (BP 358, DM 885, FR 2973, Y 60,969).

$3170* *Kvinna Vid Havet,* s. EA, (05-25-93, AB Stockholm, #10, illus.), 25³⁄₁₆ x 19⁵⁄₁₆ in., (64 x 49 cm.), color lithograph on Japan (BP 2054, DM 5163, FR 17,379, Y 346,486, SK 4620).

$425* *Lady In Profile,* s., very good cond., (05-15-93, Cleveland, #457, illus.), 22⅞ x 17 in., (58.1 x 43.2 cm.), lithograph in colors (BP 276, DM 684, FR 2297, Y 47,112).

$1100* *"Looking Out To Sea",* s., hinged to mat, very good cond., (12-04-92, Doyle, #82), 26¼ x 18⅛ in., (667 x 460 mm.), color lithograph (BP 706, DM 1752, FR 5943, Y 137,328).

$1286* *Le Marronier Bleu (Francony 135), 1977,* s., i. E. A., p. Mourlot, full margins, good cond., (06-30-93, Sotheby-London, #384), 17⅜ x 23⅜ in., (441 x 594 mm.), colored lithograph on Arches (BP 862, DM 2193, FR 7399, Y 137,791).

$748* *Portrait Of A Woman In Black,* s., #38/150, full margins, good cond., mat staining, (05-19-93, Butterfield, #1887), 21¾ x 16½ in., (552 x 419 mm.), lithograph in colors on wove (BP 486, DM 1216, FR 4096, Y 82,807).

$748* *Profile Of A Woman At The Horse Races,* s., #34/150, full margins, very good cond., (05-19-93, Butterfield, #1888), 21¾ x 16¾ in., (552 x 425 mm.), lithograph in colors on Rives BFK (BP 486, DM 1216, FR 4096, Y 82,807).

$680* *Promenade Au Parc, 1990,* before letters, s., #9/200, (03-31-93, Briest, #E143), 26³⁄₁₆ x 32¹¹⁄₁₆ in., (66.5 x 83 cm.), lithograph (BP 450, DM 1094, FR 3716, Y 78,197).

BI *The Street Lamp (S. 123), 1976,* s., num. 104/150, margins, good cond., rubbed areas, surface soiling,hinge remains, est. $9/1,200, (02-24-93, Butterfield, #2723), 21 x 15⅞ in., (533 x 403 mm.), lithograph in colors on Arches.

$600* *Tva Kvinnor I Skogen,* s., 76/120, (12-04-92, AB Stockholm, #7017), 34⅝ x 24⁷⁄₁₆ in., (88 x 62 cm.), lithograph in colors (BP 385, DM 956, FR 3241, Y 74,906, SK 4070).

$101* *"Le Village Et Profil", 1989: Two,* (10-18-92, Pescheteau, #96), each 12⅝ x 9⁷⁄₁₆ in., (32 x 24 cm.), lithograph in color on Arches (BP 61, DM 149, FR 507, Y 12,060).

$748* *Woman Watching The Racetrack,* s., #38/150, full margins, good cond., mat staining, (05-19-93, Butterfield, #1889), 21¾ x 16½ in., (552 x 419 mm.), lithograph in colors BFK Rives (BP 486, DM 1216, FR 4096, Y 82,807).

$825* *(Woman With Pink Flowers),* s., num. XXVIII/LXXV, full margins, good cond., hinge remains, skinned areas, crease, est. $1,5/2,000, (02-24-93, Butterfield, #2722, illus.), 17⅛ x 12 in., (435 x 305 mm.), lithograph in colors on Japon nacre (BP 575, DM 1339, FR 4540, Y 96,808).

CASSIGNUEL, Jean Pierre French 20th cent.

$990* *Dans Le Parc,* s., annot. E.A., (10-18-92, Hindman, #475), 19⅜ x 14⅞ in., (49.2 x 37.8 cm.), color lithograph (BP 606, DM 1474, FR 4997, Y 118,776).

CASSON, Alfred Joseph Canadian b. 1898

$326* *Above La Cloche,* t., #AP 54/60, (05-18-93, Joyner, #277), 22¾ x 28 in., (57.8 x 71.1 cm.), serigraph in colors (BP 212, DM 529, FR 1786, Y 36,331, C$ 413).

$193* *Fall Country Road With Driver And Horse,* s. in plate, pub. Sampson-Matthews, (11-30-92, Ritchie, #28, illus.), 10¾ x 9 in., (27.3 x 22.9 cm.), color serigraph (BP 127, DM 307, FR 1044, Y 24,020, C$ 248).

$239* *Grenadier Pond,* s., t., #AP 26/30, (05-18-93, Joyner, #276), 5½ x 5¾ in., (14 x 14.6 cm.), linocut in colors (BP 156, DM 388, FR 1310, Y 26,635, C$ 303).

$151* *Grizzly Bear,* s., pub. Sampson-Matthews, (06-07-93, Ritchie, #33, illus.), 8¹¹⁄₁₆ x 10¼ in., (22 x 26 cm.), color serigraph (BP 99, DM 245, FR 825, Y 16,198, C$ 193).

$151* *Hepatica,* s. in plate, pub. Sampson-Matthews, (06-07-93, Ritchie, #35), 12 x 14⅜ in., (30.5 x 36.5 cm.), color serigraph on wood veneer (BP 99, DM 245, FR 825, Y 16,198, C$ 193).

BI *Morning Reflections,* s., #53/60, lit., est. C$1,500/1,800, (06-07-93, Ritchie, #42, illus.), image 10¹¹⁄₁₆ x 13½ in., (27.2 x 34.3 cm.), color stone lithograph.

$282* *Northern Church,* t., #AP 54/60, (05-18-93, Joyner, #281), 22¾ x 28 in., (57.8 x 71.1 cm.), serigraph in colors (BP 184, DM 458, FR 1545, Y 31,428, C$ 358).

$420* *"Ontario House",* A.P. 25, (03-10-93, Maynard, #310), 12 x 16 in., (30.5 x 40.6 cm.), silkscreen (BP 293, DM 699, FR 2373, Y 49,622, C$ 523).

$260* *Snow Laden Spruce,* t., #AP 54/60, (05-18-93, Joyner, #280), 22¾ x 28 in., (57.8 x 71.1 cm.), serigraph in colors (BP 169, DM 422, FR 1425, Y 28,976, C$ 330).

$304* *Sparrow Lake,* s., t. #AP 26/30, lit., (05-18-93, Joyner, #275), 6¼ x 6¼ in., (15.9 x 15.9 cm.), linocut in colors (BP 198, DM 493, FR 1666, Y 33,879, C$ 385).

$151* *Still Life Of Daffodils And Figurine Of A Dutch Girl,* s., pub. Sampson-Matthews, (06-07-93, Ritchie, #34), 11 x 10 in., (28 x 25.4 cm.), color serigraph on wood veneer (BP 99, DM 245, FR 825, Y 16,198, C$ 193).

$282* *White Forest,* t., #AP 54/60, (05-18-93, Joyner, #279), 22¾ x 28 in., (57.8 x 71.1 cm.), serigraph in colors (BP 184, DM 458, FR 1545, Y 31,428, C$ 358).

$326* *White Pine,* t., #AP 54/60, (05-18-93, Joyner, #278), 22¾ x 28 in., (57.8 x 71.1 cm.), serigraph in colors (BP 212, DM 529, FR 1786, Y 36,331, C$ 413).

$128* *Wood Duck,* s.; t. label verso, pub. Sampson-Matthews for Canada Malting Co. Limited, (11-30-92, Ritchie, #27), 8¾ x 10½ in., (22.2 x 26.7 cm.), color serigraph (BP 84, DM 204, FR 692, Y 15,930, C$ 165).

CASSTEELS, Peter (after)
$102* *"Spring", "Summer", "Autumn" and "Winter": Four,* (04-22-93, Bonhams-Chelsea, #119), image 16¾ x 13¼ in., (42.5 x 33.7 cm.), reprod. in colors, finished by hand (BP 66, DM 164, FR 553, Y 11,215).

CASTANEDA, Emilia   Spanish b. 1943
BI *"Regard Du Passe",* s., #CXIV/CL, est. $2/300, (12-12-92, Goldberg, #519A), image 23 x 17½ in., (58.4 x 44.5 cm.), color lithograph.

CASTEELS (after)
$28* *"October 1732",* Williamsburg reprod., (06-11-93, DuMouchelle, #1546), approx. 27 x 20 in., (68.6 x 50.8 cm.), colored print (BP 18, DM 46, FR 153, Y 2971).

CASTEELS, P. (after)
$700 *"The Months In Flowers", 1730: Nine,* by H. Fletcher, (06-11-93, G.A. Key, #49), hand-colored engraving (BP 460, DM 1138, FR 3836, Y 74,271).

CASTEL
BI *"Stone Of The Temple": Four,* s., #27/30AP to #30/30AP, est. $30/50, (01-15-93, DuMouchelle, #175), image 22 x 18½ in., (55.9 x 47 cm.), color lithographs.

CASTELLON, Federico   Spanish/American 1914-1971
$50* *"Gaby" (F. 145),* s., t., edit. 76/100, fine cond., (10-31-92, Cleveland, #94), 7¼ x 4 in., (18.4 x 10.2 cm.), etching (BP 32, DM 77, FR 261, Y 6193).

BI *"The Gordian Knot" (Freundlich 1 ii/ii), 1936,* AAG edit., hinges, stains, perfect cond., (10-31-92, Cleveland, #93), 9 x 14 in., (22.9 x 35.6 cm.), lithograph.

$144* *Late Reward,* s., #40/80, full margins, good cond.?, mat/light-staining, shrink wrapped, (05-19-93, Butterfield, #2041), 21¾ x 17¹¹⁄₁₆ in., (552 x 449 mm.), lithograph in colors BFK Rives (BP 93, DM 234, FR 789, Y 15,942).

BI *Poe: The Masque Of The Red Death, 1969: Sixteen,* book, Aquarius Press, est. $75/125, (05-15-93, Cleveland, #89), lithograph.

BI *Road In Arizona (Freundlich 12), c. 1941,* s., AAA edit., est. $250/350, (05-15-93, Cleveland, #88), 9⅞ x 13¾ in., (25.1 x 34.9 cm.), lithograph.

$127* *"Self-Portrait" (F. 148),* s., t., edit. 34/100, very good cond., (10-31-92, Cleveland, #95), 7¼ x 4 in., (18.4 x 10.2 cm.), etching and aquatint (BP 81, DM 195, FR 663, Y 15,731).

$413* *"Six Etchings By Federico Castellon" (F. 182-187), 1967,* pub. AAA, s., num., excell. cond., (10-31-92, Cleveland, #96), etching and aquatint (BP 265, DM 635, FR 2156, Y 51,158).

CASTIGLIONE (after)
$160 *"Orpheus",* engraved by R Earlom, d. 1781, (04-16-93, G.A. Key, #137), 9 x 13 in., (22.9 x 33 cm.), b/w mezzotint (BP 105, DM 258, FR 873, Y 17,992).

CASTIGLIONE, G. B.
$412* *Oriental Heads: Five,* small to thread margins, plates s., foxing, soiling, creases, (05-27-93, Swann, #53A, illus.), approx. 4½ x 3¼ in., (11.4 x 8.3 cm.), etchings, all 5 mounted on a single sheet of old laid paper (BP 264, DM 661, FR 2228, Y 44,168).

CASTIGLIONE, Giovanni Benedetto   Italian 1616-1665
BI *The Allegory Of Transcience (B. 27; P. E27), 1655: Two,* trimmed along platemark, losses, rubbed spots, stains, The Suida Manning Coll., est. $1,2/1,500, (05-13-93, Sotheby-NY, #260), one 6⅞ x 10¼ in., (176 x 260 mm.), other 7 x 10⅛ in., (176 x 260 mm.), etching.

BI *Bartiger Alter Mann Mit Kappe (B. 50; Bellini 43; The Illustrated Bartsch 46, 50),* est. DM 300, (12-04-92, Bassenge, #6118), 7⁵⁄₁₆ x 5⅞ in., (18.6 x 15 cm.), etching.

$2645* *The Bodies Of SS. Peter And Paul Hidden In The Catacombs (B. 14; P. E21), c. 1647-51,* watermark, wide margins, good cond., soiling, (05-13-93, Sotheby-NY, #312), 11⅞ x 8⅛ in., (303 x 205 mm.), etching (BP 1736, DM 4271, FR 14,406, Y 295,300).

BI *Bodies Of SS. Peter And Paul Hidden In The Catacombs (B. 14; P. E.21), c. 1647-51,* watermark or countermark, thread margins, center crease, good cond.,ex-coll., The Suida Manning Coll., est. $2/3,000, (05-13-93, Sotheby-NY, #250), 11⅞ x 8¼ in., (302 x 208 mm.), etching.

$4600* *Circe Changing Ulysses' Men To Beasts (B. 22; P. E.23), c. 1650,* Bellini's 2nd (final) state, scratch, trimmed, tear, thin spot, goodcond., The Suida Manning Coll., (05-13-93, Sotheby-NY, #253), 8½ x 12⅛ in., (215 x 309 mm.), etching (BP 3020, DM 7428, FR 25,054, Y 513,565).

$1008* *La Decouverte Des Corps De Saint Pierre Et Saint Paul, c. 1650,* unique state, margins, dirt spots, restorations, (05-15-93, Loudmer, #9, illus.), 11⅞ x 8¼ in., (302 x 209 mm.), sh 15⁷⁄₁₆ x 10½ in., (302 x 209 mm.), etching and drypoint on laid (BP 655, DM 1621, FR 5449, Y 111,739).

BI *Diogenes Seeking An Honest Man (B. 21; P. E15), c. 1645-47: Two,* 2nd (final) state, p. w/plate tone, trimmed between platemark and borderline, printer's crease, stain, rubbed spot, wormholes, The Suida Manning Coll., est. $1,2/1,800, (05-13-93, Sotheby-NY, #255), one 8⅝ x 12 in., (219 x 304 mm.), other 7⅝ x 11½ in., (219 x 304 mm.), etching.

BI *The Dream Of St. Joseph (B. 10; P. E7), c. 1645-49,* 3rd state of 4, margins, staining, soiling, glued down, good cond., exhib., The Suida Manning Coll., est. $2,5/3,500, (05-13-93, Sotheby-NY, #246, illus.), 5⅜ x 7⅜ in., (137 x 187 mm.), etching.

BI *Das Fest Des Pan (B. 16; Bellini 10; The Illustrated Bartsch 46 016 S 3), 1648,* est. DM 2,500, (12-04-92, Bassenge, #6116), 9¹⁄₁₆ x 7¼ in., (23 x 18.4 cm.), etching.

$3450* *Flock Of Sheep Surrounding A Laden Donkey (B. 29; P. E5), c. 1638,* 2nd (final) state, i. completed, plate tone, wiping scratches, mono.countermark, small margin below, thread margins, restoration, crease in image,thin spots, foxing, good cond., The Suida Manning Coll., (05-13-93, Sotheby-NY, #258, illus.), 9½ x 12⅛ in., (242 x 308 mm.), etching (BP 2265, DM 5571, FR 18,791, Y 385,174).

$2588* *The Genius Of Castiglione (B. 23; P. E16), c. 1645-48,* 3rd (final) state, Rossi's address completed, watermark, trimmed between platemark and borderline, thin patches, horizontal center fold, fox marks,glue stains, exhib., The Suida Manning Coll., (05-13-93, Sotheby-NY, #256), 14⅝ x 9¾ in., (370 x 246 mm.), etching (BP 1699, DM 4179, FR 14,096, Y 288,936).

$6900* *God The Father And Angels Adoring The Christ Child (B. 7; P. E18), c.1647,* wiping scratches, watermark, crease, rust spot, fox marks, glued down, good cond., The Suida Manning Coll., (05-13-93, Sotheby-NY, #245, illus.), 8⅛ x 16 in., (206 x 405 mm.), etching (BP 4530, DM 11,142, FR 37,582, Y 770,347).

BI *The Holy Family On The Flight Into Egypt Adored By Shepherds (B. 12; P. E17), c. 1647,* light plate tone, 3rd state of 4, margins, center crease, repaired tears, glue stains, foxing, rubbed spot, glued down, exhib., The Suida Manning Coll., est. $1,5/2,000, (05-13-93, Sotheby-NY, #247), 11⅝ x 8 in., (296 x 204 mm.), etching.

$1756* *Kleine Studien Orientalischer Kopfe (B.31-52): Twenty-Two,* waterstained, (12-12-92, Bassenge, #8044, illus.), etching on China (BP 1123, DM 2760, FR 9405, Y 217,246).

$920* *Marsyas Teaching Olympos The Various Musical Modes (B. 15; P. E11), c. 1645-47: Two,* delicately bitten plate, 4th state of 5, trimmed, stains where glueddown, good cond., exhib., The Suida Manning Coll., (05-13-93, Sotheby-NY, #251), each approx. 8½ x 4½ in., (215 x 115 mm.), etching (BP 604, DM 1486, FR 5011, Y 102,713).

$1265* *Melancholia (B. 26; P. E14), c. 1645-46,* 4th (final) state, margins, printer's crease, surface dirt, stains, traces masking tape, good cond., exhib., The Suida Manning Coll., (05-13-93, Sotheby-NY, #257), 8½ x 4½ in., (217 x 115 mm.), etching (BP 830, DM 2043, FR 6890, Y 141,230).

$8338* *The Nativity With God The Father And Angels Adoring The Christ Child(B. 11; P. E6), c. 1645-47,* inky plate edges, plate tone, watermark, narrow margins, center fold,foxing, good cond., ex-coll. F. Gawet, 1837, The Suida Manning Coll., (05-13-93, Sotheby-NY, #248, illus.), 11⅝ x 8⅛ in., (294 2 5 mm.), etching (BP 5474, DM 13,464, FR 45,414, Y 930,892).

$10,350* *Noah And The Animals Entering The Ark (B. 1; Percy E24), c. 1650-55,* plate tone, wiping scratches, mono. countermark, thread margins, trimmed, center crease, stains, good cond., ex-coll. F. Gawet, The Suida Manning Coll., (05-13-93, Sotheby-NY, #240, illus.), 8 x 15¾ in., (204 x 400 mm.), etching (BP 6795, DM 16,712, FR 56,373, Y 1,155,521).

$2300* *Noah And The Animals Entering The Ark (B. 2; P. E1), c. 1630,* delicately bitten plate, plate tone, 2nd (final) state, watermark, diagonal crease, thin spots, good cond., The Suida Manning Coll., (05-13-93, Sotheby-NY, #241), 5¼ x 3¾ in., (134 x 96 mm.), etching (BP 1510, DM 3714, FR 12,527, Y 256,782).

BI *Pan Reclining Before A Large Vase (B. 18; P. E10), c. 1645,* plate tone, trimmed, small repairs, scrape, vertical fold, good cond., The Suida Manning Coll., est. $2,5/3,500, (05-13-93, Sotheby-NY, #254, illus.), 4½ x 8½ in., (113 x 215 mm.), etching.

BI *Rachel Concealing Laban's Idols (B. 4; P. E3), 1635-40,* 2nd state of 4, scratch in image, trimmed, stains, good cond., The Suida Manning Coll., est. $1,2/1,800, (05-13-93, Sotheby-NY, #242), 9⅞ x 13 in., (252 x 331 mm.), etching.

$2185* *A Satyr Resting Beneath A Herm Of Priapus (B. 17; P. E9), c. 1645,* 2nd state of 3, watermark, trimmed between platemark and borderline,rubbed spots, foxing, good cond., The Suida Manning Coll., (05-13-93, Sotheby-NY, #252, illus.), 4½ x 8⅜ in., (115 x 213 mm.), etching (BP 1434, DM 3528, FR 11,901, Y 243,943).

$6038* *Shepherds Following Their Flock (B. 30; P. E26), c. 1625-30,* plate tone, foul-biting, trimmed, stains, center fold, creases, The Suida Manning Coll., (05-13-93, Sotheby-NY, #261, illus.), 9¾ x 14⅝ in., (246 x 371 mm.), etching (BP 3964, DM 9750, FR 32,887, Y 674,110).

$4025* *Small Studies Of Heads In Oriental Headdress (B. 32-47), c. 1645-50:Set of Sixteen,* small margins, staining, glued down, good cond., exhib., The Suida Manning Coll., (05-13-93, Sotheby-NY, #264, illus.), etching (BP 2642, DM 6499, FR 21,923, Y 449,369).

$363* *Tete D'Homme Tournee Vers La Gauche,* second and final state, restored, fold, (05-15-93, Loudmer, #11), 7³⁄₁₆ x 5¹⁵⁄₁₆ in., (182 x 152 mm.), etching on trimmed laid w/Blason du Marquis de Louvois watermark (BP 236, DM 584, FR 1962, Y 40,239).

$847* *Tete De Vieillard De Profil Vers La Droite,* late 1640's, unique state, paper traces verso, (05-15-93, Loudmer, #10, illus.), 7⁵⁄₁₆ x 5⅜ in., (186 x 136 mm.), sh 7¹¹⁄₁₆ x 5¹³⁄₁₆ in., (186 x 136 mm.), etching on laid (BP 551, DM 1362, FR 4578, Y 93,892).

BI *Theseus Finding His Father's Arms (B. 24; P. E12), 1645,* 3rd (final) state, wiping scratches distinct, watermark, thread margin, trimmed between platemark and borderline, horizontal center fold, defects, good cond., The Suida Manning Coll., est. $800/1,200, (05-13-93, Sotheby-NY, #259), 11¾ x 8 in., (299 x 203 mm.), etching.

$3814* *Tobias Begrabt Die Toten (Bartsch 5; Percy E 20), c. 1647-51,* mono., watermark, (06-10-93, Hauswedell/Nolt, #59, illus.), etching (BP 2495, DM 6211, FR 20,910, Y 404,840).

$5175* *Tobit Burying The Dead (B. 5; P. E.20), c. 1647-51,* burr, stray printer's ink, mono. countermark, trimmed on and within platemark, vertical fold, foxing, masking tape, good cond., exhib., The Suida Manning Coll., (05-13-93, Sotheby-NY, #243, illus.), 8 x 11¾ in., (203 x 299 mm.), etching (BP 3397, DM 8356, FR 28,186, Y 577,760).

CASTIGLIONE, Salvatore　　　Italian ac. 1645

$222* *La Resurrection De Lazare, 1645,* after engraving by Giovanni Benedetto Castiglione, stain, very good cond., (05-15-93, Loudmer, #13), 4⅜ x 8⅜ in., (111 x 213 mm.), etching on trimmed laid (BP 144, DM 357, FR 1200, Y 24,609).

$920* *The Resurrection Of Lazarus (B. 1), c. 1645,* watermark, thread margins, trimmed on the platemark, paper loss, goodcond., The Suida Manning Coll., (05-13-93, Sotheby-NY, #266), 4⅜ x 8⅜ in., (111 x 214 mm.), etching (BP 604, DM 1486, FR 5011, Y 102,713).

CASTIGLIONI, Gianni　　　b. 1917

BI *Heuernte, 1958,* s., d., t., est. SF 140/160, (10-14-92, Germann, #495), 15¾ x 21¹⁄₁₆ in., (400 x 535 mm.), woodcut.

CASTILLO, Jorge　　　Spanish b. 1933

BI *Jorge Castillo, Die Welt Des Garcia Lorca (Kestner/Gesellschaft 24-32), 1972: Nine,* pub. Propylaen, #47/50, s., d., est. DM 2,200-, (05-27-93, Lempertz, #649), 33¹⁄₁₆ x 25 in., (84 x 63.5 cm.), etching on Arches wove.

CASTLE, John

$266* *Aladdin Pink, 1953,* ref. P 68, cond. 3, water staining, tear, (10-13-92, Phillips-London, #188), 29¹⁵⁄₁₆ x 39⅝ in., (76 x 100.7 cm.), silkscreen in black and pink (BP 155, DM 390, FR 1324, Y 32,254).

$512* *Shell X-100, Change Your Oil For Summer, 1953,* ref. P 65, cond. 1, nicks, (10-13-92, Phillips-London, #186, illus.), 29¹⁵⁄₁₆ x 39⁹⁄₁₆ in., (76 x 100.5 cm.), color lithograph (BP 298, DM 750, FR 2549, Y 62,083).

$335* *Shellspark, Gets The Best Out Of Your Tractor, 1953,* ref. P 67, cond. 2, defects, (10-13-92, Phillips-London, #187), 29¹⁵⁄₁₆ x 39¾ in., (76 x 101 cm.), color lithograph (BP 195, DM 491, FR 1667, Y 40,621).

CAT, Roland　　　b. 1943

BI *"Les Non-Violents",* #2/50, t., s., est. FF800/1,000, (04-04-93, Pescheteau, #175), 30¹¹⁄₁₆ x 19¹¹⁄₁₆ in., (78 x 50 cm.), black lithograph.

CATESBY, Mark　　　British 1679-1749

$46,000* *The Natural History Of Carolina, Florida, And The Bahama Islands: Containing The Figures Of Animals With Their Descriptions In English And French (Cpenhagen/Anker 95; Ellis/Mengel 478; Fine Bird Books 65; and others), 1771,* p. for B. White, after and by Catesby and mostly s. w/his cipher, 3rd ed., late issue, (06-14-93, Sotheby-NY, #97, illus.), 20⅞ x 14⅛ in., (53 x 35.9 cm.), 2 vol. folio, 220 hand-colored etched plates (BP 30,109, DM 74,870, FR 251,641, Y 4,840,577).

BI *"Palumbus Migratorius, The Pigeon Of Passage",* est. $500/1,000, (11-28-92, Young, #82), 10 x 14 in., (25.4 x 35.6 cm.), hand colored engraving.

$605* *"The Pigeon Of Passage/Red Oak",* (02-12-93, DuMouchelle, #2327, illus.), plate 10¼ x 14 in., (26 x 35.6 cm.), hand colored etching (BP 426, DM 1003, FR 3395, Y 72,962).

CATHELIN, Bernard   French b. 1920
  BI *Marche Mexicain, 1970,* s., #25/75, full margins, good cond., light-staining, staining, surface soiling, est. $4/600, (10-28-92, Butterfield, #2791), 25¼ x 17¾ in., (641 x 451 mm.), color lithograph on Arches.
  BI *Nature Morte Rouge,* 144/175, s., est. SF 8/1,500, (10-14-92, Germann, #236), 15¹¹⁄₁₆ x 22⁷⁄₁₆ in., (398 x 570 mm.), color lithograph.

CATLIN, George   American 1796-1872
  $1760* *Buffalo Hunt Chase, No. 6,* pub. James Ackerman, lettering slightly doubled, scratches, acid burn, laid down on board, (12-04-92, Doyle, #38), 12⅛ x 17¾ in., (308 x 451 mm.), color lithograph (BP 1129, DM 2803, FR 9508, Y 219,725).
  $77,000* *Catlin's North American Indian Portfolio, Hunting Scenes And Amusements Of The Rocky Mountains And Prairies Of America (Abbey, Travel, 653; Sabin 11532), 1844: Twenty-Four,* from Drawings and Notes of the Author..., G. Catlin, pinhole, surface nicks, paper losses, mat staining, tears, old tape, very good cond., (01-22-93, Christie-NY, #309, illus.), each sheet 18⅛ x 24¼ in., (460 x 616 mm.), hand-colored lithograph w/touches gum arabic on smooth heavy wove, mounted on card w/ink ruled frames (BP 50,376, DM 122,436, FR 414,201, Y 9,637,046).
  $1045* *Dying Buffalo Bull, In Snow Drift (Abbey, Travel, 653), 1844,* plate No. 17 from Catlin's North American Indian Portfolio, Hunting Scenes and Amusements of the Rocky Mountains and Prairies of America, from Drawings and Notes of the Author..., Day & Haghe, margins, creases, tears, paper loss, staining, soiling, (01-22-93, Christie-NY, #310), borderline 12⅛ x 17¾ in., (308 x 451 mm.), hand-colored lithograph w/touches gum arabic on wove (BP 684, DM 1662, FR 5621, Y 130,788).
  $16,100* *North American Indian Portfolio, Hunting Scenes And Amusements Of The Rocky Mountains And Prairies Of America (Abbey Travel 653 note, Howes C243, Lipperheide Mc7, Wagner-Camp-Backer 105a:2), 1844/45,* folio, after Catlin by Catlin and McGahey, lithographed by Day and Haghe, soiling, discoloration, irregular loss to top edge of ten plates, expanded edit., of Catlin's Portfolio, (05-21-93, Sotheby-NY, #20, illus.), 23½ x 16⅞ in., (597 x 429 mm.), 31 tinted lithographed plates (BP 10,431, DM 26,179, FR 88,074, Y 1,775,083).
  $31,050* *North American Indian Portfolio, Hunting Scenes And Amusements Of The Rocky Mountains And Prairies Of America (Abbey Travel 653 note, Howes C243, Lipperheide Mc7, Wagner-Camp-Becker 105a:2), 1844/85,* folio, after Catlin by Catlin and McGahey, lithographed by Day and Haghe, soiling, dampstaining, tears, repairs, expanded edit., of Catlin's Portfolio, Talfourd P. Linn Coll., (05-21-93, Sotheby-NY, #19, illus.), 23⅛ x 16¾ in., (587 x 425 mm.), 31 hand-colored lithographed plates (BP 20,117, DM 50,488, FR 169,858, Y 3,423,374).
  $28,750* *North American Indian Portfolio, Hunting Scenes And Amusements Of The Rocky Mountains And Prairies Of America (Abbey Travel 653 note, Howes C243, Sabin 11532, Wagner-Camp-Becker 105a:1), 1844,* folio, after Catlin by Catlin and McGahey, lithographed by Day and Haghe, 1st edit., prov., (05-21-93, Sotheby-NY, #18, illus.), 22⅞ x 16¾ in., (581 x 425 mm.), 25 tinted lithographed plates (BP 18,626, DM 46,748, FR 157,276, Y 3,169,791).
  $85,000* *North American Indian Portfolio, Hunting Scenes And Amusements Of The Rocky Mountains And Prairies Of America (Abbey Travel 653, Field 258, Howes C243, Sabin 11532, Schwerdt 1:100, Tooley 134, Wagner-Camp-Becker 105a:1), 1844,* folio, after Catlin by Catlin and MaGahey, lithographed by Day and Haghe, 1st edit., deluxe issue, (05-21-93, Sotheby-NY, #17, illus.), 24¼ x 18½ in., (616 x 470 mm.), 25 hand-colored lithographed plates heightened w/gum arabic and mounted on card (BP 55,070, DM 138,211, FR 464,989, Y 9,371,555).

$83* *A Winnebage,* pub. Daniel Rice and James C. Clark, Phila., 1843, (09-17-92, Sloan, #639), sheet 19 x 13¾ in., (48.3 x 34.9 cm.), handcolored lithograph (BP 47, DM 123, FR 422, Y 10,334).

CAULAERT, Jean Dominique van   French 20th cent.
  $440* *Mistinguett,* Atelier Girbal, B cond., closed tears, crack, (08-06-92, Swann, #82, illus.), 61¼ x 46 in., (155.6 x 116.8 cm.), (BP 230, DM 650, FR 2196, Y 56,122).

CAULAERT, van (after)
  $724* *Mistinguett Ca C'Est Paris,* (01-31-93, Morelle/Marchan, #239), 47¼ x 62¹⁵⁄₁₆ in., (120 x 160 cm.), poster (BP 487, DM 1166, FR 3943, Y 90,319).

CAULFIELD, Patrick   English b. 1936
  $1544* *"Jar", "Interior: Evening", "Interior: Noon", "Interior Morning", "Interior Night", "Crucifix" and "Vase On Display": Seven,* s., num., good cond., creasing, (06-30-93, Sotheby-London, #757), color silkscreen on wove (BP 1035, DM 2633, FR 8884, Y 165,434).
  $192* *Poems Of Jules Laforgue, 1973: Twenty-Six,* s., num., good cond., (12-04-92, Doyle, #83), 16 x 13¾ in., (406 x 349 mm.), book and portfolio w/20 silkscreens and 6 separate plates (BP 123, DM 306, FR 1037, Y 23,970).
  $858* *Some Poems Of Jules Laforgue With Images By Patrick Caulfield (Edition B), 1973: Two,* book w/title-page, text, justification, s. by artist, #138/200, i. Eition B, pub. Petersburg Press, good cond., (06-30-93, Sotheby-London, #756), color silkscreen accompanying separate suite of 6 color silkscreens,each on stiff wove (BP 575, DM 1463, FR 4937, Y 91,932).
  $990* *Some Poems Of Jules Laforgue: The Book And Twelve Silkscreens By TheArtist, 1973: Twenty-Two,* book, s., #12/100, very good cond.?, prov., (12-12-92, Weschler, #112, illus.), silkscreens 24 x 21¾ in., (61 x 55.2 cm.), book 16 x 14 in., (61 x 55.2 cm.), color silkscreen (BP 635, DM 1560, FR 5346, Y 122,510).
  $449* *Two Whitings,* s., #19/100, margins, soiling, creasing, (10-15-92, Sotheby-London, #91), sheet 43¼ x 60¼ in., (109.9 x 153 cm.), screenprint in colors on wove (BP 275, DM 668, FR 2267, Y 53,869).
  BI *Vessel, 1987,* s., t., #17/35, blindstamp pub. Waddington Graphics, full margins, very good cond., est. $7/900, (10-28-92, Butterfield, #2917), 37 x 25¾ in., (940 x 654 mm.), lithograph w/silkscreen in colors on cream wove.
  BI *Vessel, 1987,* s., t., #17/35, blindstamp pub., printer Waddington Graphics, full margins, very good cond., est. $5/700, (02-24-93, Butterfield, #3198), 37 x 25¾ in., (941.5 x 655.2 mm.), lithograph w/silkscreen in colors on cream wove.
  BI *Wall Plate: "Highlights", "Stucco", "Stones" and "Screen", 1987: Four,* s., #7/50, blindstamp pub. Waddington Graphics, full margins, good cond.?, est. $2,5/3,500, (10-28-92, Butterfield, #2918), each 41 x 30 in., (104.1 x 76.2 cm.), color silkscreen on cream wove.
  BI *"Wall Plate: Highlights", "Stucco", "Stones and Screen", 1987: Four,* s., num. 7/50, blindstamp of pub. & printer Waddington Graphics, fullmargins, apparently good cond., est. $1,8/2,000, (02-24-93, Butterfield, #3005), each 41 x 30 in., (104.1 x 76.2 cm.), silkscreen in colors on wove.

CAUVY, L.
  $498* *PLM: Algerie. Hivernage, Tourisme. 1925,* very good cond., (03-13-93, Laurin, #40), 41⁵⁄₁₆ x 28⅜ in., (105 x 72 cm.), (BP 347, DM 829, FR 2818, Y 58,692).

CAVAEL, Rolf   b. 1898
  $425* *Komposition "No. 76/3", 1976,* s., d., i., (06-08-93, Karl/Faber, #607), approx. 7¹¹⁄₁₆ x 6⅛ in., (19.5 x 15.5 cm.), India ink over color lithograph on board (BP 279, DM 690, FR 2322, Y 45,141).
  BI *Litho/a62/51, 1951,* t., s., num., est. DM 400, (12-05-92, Bassenge, #7075), 18⅛ x 12¹⁵⁄₁₆ in., (46 x 33 cm.), color lithograph.
  $381* *"Lithofa 61/44", 1961,* s., d., t., num., (12-01-92, Karl/Faber, #431), 17⅛ x 11¹³⁄₁₆ in., (43.5 x 30 cm.), color lithograph on wove (BP 252, DM 607, FR 2070, Y 47,435).

CAVAILLES, Jules French 1901-1977

$164* *Bouquet De Fleurs,* artist's proof, s., annot., ded., good margins, (05-06-93, Laurin, #13), color lithograph (BP 104, DM 258, FR 870, Y 18,044).

$120* *"Port Vu De La Fenetre",* artist's proof, s., (04-04-93, Pescheteau, #176), 12³⁄₁₆ x 7¹¹⁄₁₆ in., (31 x 19.5 cm.), color lithograph (BP 79, DM 193, FR 655, Y 13,663).

CAVALIERI, Giovanni Battista 1525-1597

BI *The Martyrdom Of Saint Catherine, (Le B. 28), c. 1565,* after Livio Agnesti, trimmed, tear, staining, laid, est. BP 700/800, (12-01-92, Christie-London, #45, illus.), S. 20³⁄₁₆ x 13⅛ in., (513 x 334 mm.), engraving.

$2997* *Susanna And The Elders, 1566,* tone, thread margins or trimmed, staining, very good cond., (12-01-92, Christie-London, #46, illus.), S. 12⁹⁄₁₆ x 18⅛ in., (319 x 461 mm.), etching w/engraving (BP 1980, DM 4777, FR 16,279, Y 373,132).

CAVANNA

BI *"Personnages",* #165/200, (01-28-93, Pescheteau, #92), 23⅝ x 17¹¹⁄₁₆ in., (60 x 45 cm.), color lithograph on wove.

CAWSTON, M.

$46 *Study Of Black Hunting Labradors,* s., limited edit., 103/850, (02-05-93, G.A. Key, #25), 11 x 17 in., (27.9 x 43.2 cm.), colored print (BP 32, DM 76, FR 258, Y 5724).

CAYLUS, Anne Claude Philippe 1692-1765

BI *Hieronymus Mit Dem Lowen (Nagler, mono. Bd. 1, 2162),* after Annibale Carracci, trimmed, approx., est. DM 300, (03-24-93, Venator/Hansten, #2505), approx. 15⁹⁄₁₆ x 10¹⁄₁₆ in., (39.5 x 25.5 cm.), etching.

CAZIN, Jean Charles French 1841-1901

BI *Le Pont De Pierre,* #71/300, s. in plate J.C. Cazin, (06-16-93, Encans, #123), 4¾ x 6⁵⁄₁₆ in., (12 x 16 cm.), etching.

CECCHI, Giovanni Battista 1748-1807

$81* *Le Mariage De Sainte Catherine,* after Francesco Vanni, (05-15-93, Loudmer, #38, illus.), 10¹⁄₁₆ x 7⁵⁄₁₆ in., (256 x 185 mm.), etching on laid (BP 53, DM 130, FR 438, Y 8979).

CECIL, Hugh

BI *Portrait Of Margaret Morris, c. 1920,* mounted on card, s. twice, t., label, 389 x 297mm, est. BP 3/400, (05-07-93, Sotheby-London, #166), photograph, silver print.

CECY

$85* *"Boats And Clouds I" and "Boats And Clouds II": Two,* s., t., #A.P., excell. cond., (05-15-93, Cleveland, #459), 27⅝ x 21¾ in., (70.2 x 55.2 cm.), silkscreen and embossing (BP 55, DM 137, FR 459, Y 9422).

CELMINS, Vija American b. Latvia 1939

$2300* *Concentric Bearings, B (G. 1221), 1985,* s., #35/35, blindstamp publisher, Gemini G.E.L., full margins, very good cond., (05-19-93, Butterfield, #2139, illus.), 5 x 8³⁄₁₆ in., (127 x 208 mm.), aquatint, drypoint and mezzotint on Rives BFK (BP 1493, DM 3739, FR 12,596, Y 254,622).

$3520* *Concentric Bearings, C (Gemini 1223), 1985,* s., #29/34, blindstamp, pub. Gemini G.E.L., full margins, good cond., (11-07-92, Sotheby-NY, #527, illus.), sheet 20⅛ x 20⅛ in., (511 x 511 mm.), aquatint and photogravure on BFK Rives (BP 2301, DM 5620, FR 18,996, Y 434,461).

$3220* *Concentric Bearings, D (G. 1222), 1985,* s., #33/34, Gemini G.E.L. blindstamps, full margins, excell. cond., (05-11-93, Christie-NY, #379, illus.), sheet 18 x 22⅜ in., (457 x 568 mm.), mezzotint, aquatint, drypoint and photogravure on wove (BP 2056, DM 5072, FR 17,091, Y 354,196).

$2588* *Drypoint-Ocean Surface-2nd State (G. 1225), 1985,* s., #55/55, blindstamp of pub. Gemini, G.E.L., full margins, good cond., crease, (02-11-93, Sotheby-NY, #317, illus.), 7⅜ x 9⁷⁄₁₆ in., (187 x 240 mm.), drypoint on BFK Rives paper (BP 1826, DM 4287, FR 14,507, Y 311,995).

$3163* *Drypoint-Ocean Surface-2nd State (Gemini 1225),* s., #52/55, blindstamp, pub. Gemini, G.E.L., full margins, good cond., (05-15-93, Sotheby-NY, #933), 7¾ x 9⅞ in., (19.7 x 25.1 cm.), drypoint on BFK Rives (BP 2057, DM 5088, FR 17,097, Y 350,626).

$2300* *Jupiter Moon, Constellation (Gemini 1059), 1983,* s., #45/48, Gemini G.E.L. blindstamps, full margins, excell. cond., (05-11-93, Christie-NY, #378, illus.), sheet 23⅝ x 18⅝ in., (600 x 473 mm.), mezzotint and etching on wove (BP 1468, DM 3623, FR 12,208, Y 252,997).

$2588* *Jupiter Moon-Constellation (Gemini 1059), 1983,* s., #8/48, blindstamp of pub. Gemini G.E.L., full margins, good cond., (02-11-93, Sotheby-NY, #316, illus.), 10⅞ x 7¹¹⁄₁₆ in., (277 x 195 mm.), etching and mezzotint p. in tones of gray and black on Fabriano Rosapina white paper (BP 1826, DM 4287, FR 14,507, Y 311,995).

BI *Ocean Surface, 2nd State (G. 1225), 1985,* s., #3/55, blindstamp pub. Gemini G.E.L., full margins, very good cond.?, est. $4,5/5,500, (10-28-92, Butterfield, #2920, illus.), 7¾ x 10 in., (197 x 254 mm.), drypoint on Rives BFK.

$1150* *Untitled (Desert),* s., d., #62/75, blindstamp, pub. Cirrus Editions, full margins, goodcond., discoloration, (05-15-93, Sotheby-NY, #932, illus.), 12⅜ x 16⅜ in., (31.4 x 41.6 cm.), lithograph (BP 748, DM 1850, FR 6216, Y 127,480).

$2070* *Untitled (Desert), 1971,* s., #18/65, pub. Cirrus Editions, full margins, good cond., (02-11-93, Sotheby-NY, #314, illus.), 20⅞ x 27⅜ in., (530 x 696 mm.), lithograph (BP 1461, DM 3429, FR 11,603, Y 249,548).

$2300* *"Untitled (Galaxy)" and "Untitled (Desert)": Two,* both s., d., #73/75, blindstamp, pub. Cirrus Editions, good cond., light-stain, creases, discoloration, (05-15-93, Sotheby-NY, #931, illus.), each image 12⅜ x 16⅜ in., (31.4 x 41.6 cm.), lithograph (BP 1495, DM 3700, FR 12,432, Y 254,961).

$2588* *"Untitled (Galaxy)", "Untitled (Desert)" and "Untitled (Sky)", 1975:Three,* each s., #68/75, 66/75, and 62/75, blindstamp of pub. Cirrus Editions, full margins, good cond., soiling, skinned spots, (02-11-93, Sotheby-NY, #315, illus.), each sheet 16⁷⁄₁₆ x 20³⁄₁₆ in., (417 x 512 mm.), lithograph (BP 1826, DM 4287, FR 14,507, Y 311,995).

$1980* *Untitled, Desert, 1971,* s., d., num. 45/65, pub. Cirrus, full margins, excell. cond., (09-19-92, Christie-E, #88, illus.), sheet 22⅜ x 29 in., (568 x 737 mm.), lithograph on Arches (BP 1139, DM 2965, FR 10,154, Y 246,698).

$825* *Untitled, Ocean, 1972,* s., #20/65, blindstamp pub. Cirrus, full margins, good cond., foxing, buckling, pinholes, skinned areas, mat staining, (10-28-92, Butterfield, #2919), image 6 x 42 in., (15.2 x 106.7 cm.), sheet 28¼ x 45⁹⁄₁₆ in., (15.2 x 106.7 cm.), lithograph on wove (BP 526, DM 1274, FR 4326, Y 101,227).

CELOF, Julien

$44* *Figures At A Town Gate,* s., num. below image, (08-05-92, Boos, #729), sight 19 x 22½ in., (483 x 572 mm.), aquatint (BP 23, DM 65, FR 220, Y 5604).

CELOS, E.

$2750* *Canadian Cycles, Massey Harris,* Camille Sohet and Cie, A cond., (08-06-92, Swann, #83, illus.), 51 x 36½ in., (129.5 x 92.7 cm.), (BP 1436, DM 4063, FR 13,723, Y 350,765).

CENTURY LITHOGRAPHY COMPANY, Lithographers

American 19th/20th cent.

$385* *"Palace Steamer Republic",* ident. w/in matrix, good cond.?, repaired tears, creases, (03-27-93, Skinner, #17B), sight, sheet 21¾ x 37¾ in., (55.2 x 95.9 cm.), chromolithograph on paper (BP 259, DM 628, FR 2135, Y 44,809).

CESAR (Cesar BALDACCINI) French b. 1921

BI *Automobile Compression II,* AP. #19/40, s., creases, 1022mm x 665mm, est. SF 5/600, (04-21-93, Germann, #319), color lithograph.

$500* *Compositions Abstraites: Three,* whole margins, s., num., (06-11-93, Picard, #18), between 20⅞ x 16¹⁵⁄₁₆ in., (530 x 430 mm.), and 12¹⁵⁄₁₆ x 10⅝ in., (530 x 430 mm.), color lithographs on wove (BP 329, DM 813, FR 2740, Y 53,050).

$168* *"Compression Sur Fond Noir",* HC, s., (10-18-92, Pescheteau, #97), 12³⁄₁₆ x 9⁷⁄₁₆ in., (31 x 24 cm.), lithograph in colors on velin (BP 102, DM 248, FR 843, Y 20,060).

$53* *"Mao"*, #13/50, s., (01-28-93, Pescheteau, #94), 25⁹⁄₁₆ x 19⁵⁄₁₆ in., (65 x 49 cm.), offset on papier couche (BP 35, DM 84, FR 284, Y 6581).

$208* *Papier Arache*, s. twice, num., (12-01-92, Karl/Faber, #433), 25⁹⁄₁₆ x 19¹¹⁄₁₆ in., (65 x 50 cm.), color lithograph on wove (BP 137, DM 332, FR 1130, Y 25,896).

$84* *"Le Pouce"*, #171/300, (01-28-93, Pescheteau, #93), 25⁹⁄₁₆ x 19¹¹⁄₁₆ in., (65 x 50 cm.), serigraph on papier alu (BP 55, DM 133, FR 450, Y 10,430).

BI *Quadre D'Accumulation*, #48/100, s., crease, est. SF 4,5/5,800, (11-13-92, Koller, #5280), sheet 19¹¹⁄₁₆ x 29¹⁵⁄₁₆ in., (50 x 76 cm.), lithograph on wove.

$112* *Sans Titre*, #73/500, s. Cesar; ded., s., d. Cesar 1970, (07-14-92, Encans, #184), 29⅛ x 18⁵⁄₁₆ in., (74 x 46.5 cm.), lithograph (BP 58, DM 166, FR 560, Y 14,005, C$ 133).

CESARZ

$55 *Remember The Bond*, Powers Engraving Co. NY, very good cond., (09-24-92, Alderfer, #259), 25 x 19 in., (63.5 x 48.3 cm.), (BP 32, DM 82, FR 277, Y 6616).

CEZANNE, Paul   French 1839-1906

$231* *Artist Friend*, restrike, (11-01-92, Hanzel, #218), 6⅞ x 4⅜ in., (17.5 x 11.1 cm.), etching (BP 151, DM 364, FR 1228, Y 28,561).

BI *Artist House*, restrike, est. $250/350, (11-01-92, Hanzel, #220), 5⅛ x 4¼ in., (13 x 10.8 cm.), etching.

BI *Artist's House*, est. $250/350, (02-14-93, Hanzel, #668), (13 x 10.8 cm.), restrike etching.

BI *Les Baigneurs (Large Plate) (Venturi 1157; Druick III)*, 1896-97, Druick's 3rd (final) state, watermark, full margins, good cond., slightly faded, mat/damp staining, foxing, repaired tear, crease, est. $15/25,000, (02-11-93, Sotheby-NY, #78, illus.), 16⁵⁄₁₆ x 20½ in., (415 x 520 mm.), color lithograph on fine laid.

$22,000* *Les Baigneurs (Venturi 1157, Druick 1 III/III)*, 1896-97, from 2nd ed., watermark, (03-14-93, Hindman, #302, illus.), 16⅜ x 20⅜ in., (41.6 x 51.8 cm.), color lithograph on laid (BP 15,347, DM 36,618, FR 124,505, Y 2,592,811).

$16,500* *Les Baigneurs (Venturi 1157; Druick III)*, 1896-97, Druick's third (final), full margins, good cond., faded, light/mat stain, backboard stain, fox marks, tears, creases, sold after sale, (11-05-92, Sotheby-NY, #106, illus.), 16¼ x 20⅜ in., (414 x 518 mm.), lithograph p. in colors on fine laid w/watermark (BP 10,732, DM 26,095, FR 88,283, Y 2,024,291).

$4887* *Les Baigneurs - Grande Planche (Cherpin 7/I)*, 1898, s. in stone, (06-23-93, Kornfeld, #246), lithograph on handmade (BP 3320, DM 8269, FR 27,814, Y 532,411, SF 7360).

$28,151* *Les Baigneurs. - Grande Planche (Venturi 1157; Cherpin 7/III; Johnson 1977, 23)*, 1898, s. in stone, (06-25-93, Kornfeld, #26, illus.), image 17½ x 20¼ in., (44.5 x 51.5 cm.), color lithograph on handmade paper (BP 19,040, DM 47,925, FR 161,416, Y 2,983,994, SF 42,550).

$22,064* *Les Baigneurs. - Petite Planche (Venturi 1156; Cherpin 6/II)*, 1896-1897, (06-25-93, Kornfeld, #25, illus.), image size 9⅛ x 11⅜ in., (23.2 x 28.9 cm.), sheet size 11⁵⁄₁₆ x 14¼ in., (23.2 x 28.9 cm.), color lithograph on Chine volant (BP 14,923, DM 37,562, FR 126,514, Y 2,338,775, SF 33,350).

$197* *Guillaumin Au Pendu (J. Cherpin, 2)*, 1873, yellowed, good margins, (06-16-93, Ader Tajan, #54), etching (BP 131, DM 327, FR 1097, Y 21,011).

BI *"Guillaumin Au Pendu" (Merlot 2) (Portrait Of The Artist Armand Guillaumin)*, 1873, pub. Duret 1906, excellent cond., est. $450-650, (10-31-92, Cleveland, #270, illus.), 5⅞ x 4¼ in., (14.9 x 10.8 cm.), etching.

$440* *"Guillaumin Au Pendu" and "Tete De Jeune Fille" (Melot 2, 4)*, c. 1873: Two, only state, posthumous impressions, (05-27-93, Swann, #54), 6 x 4½ in., (15.2 x 11.4 cm.), etching (BP 282, DM 706, FR 2380, Y 47,170).

$330* *"Guillaumin Au Pendu"*, c. 1873, full margins, excell. cond., (05-07-93, Goldberg, #430A), 6¼ x 4¾ in., (15.9 x 12.1 cm.), on arches (BP 209, DM 522, FR 1758, Y 36,336).

BI *Head Of A Girl*, est. $2/250, (02-14-93, Hanzel, #676), (12.1 x 9.5 cm.), restrike etching.

BI *Head Of A Girl*, restrike, est. $250/350, (11-01-92, Hanzel, #222), 4¾ x 3¾ in., (12.1 x 9.5 cm.), etching.

$374* *Paysage A Auvers, Entree De Ferme (V. 1161)*, 1873, later impression, margins, good cond., surface soiling, (05-19-93, Butterfield, #2042), 5¼ x 4⅜ in., (133 x 111 mm.), etching in sepia on wove (BP 243, DM 608, FR 2048, Y 41,404).

$13,188* *Les Petits Baigneurs (U. Johnson 22)*, 1897, whole margins, pub. Vollard, (06-11-93, Picard, #19, illus.), 8¹³⁄₁₆ x 10⅞ in., (224 x 276 mm.), color lithograph on thin chine (BP 8665, DM 21,433, FR 72,263, Y 1,399,257).

BI *Portrait De Guillaumin Pendu*, small margins, est. FF1,800/2,000, (05-27-93, Briest, #52), 9¼ x 6⅞ in., (23.5 x 17.5 cm.), etching.

$294* *"Portrait De Jeune Fille"*, s. in plate, (01-28-93, Pescheteau, #95), 9¹³⁄₁₆ x 7½ in., (25 x 19 cm.), etching in bistre on Ingres d'Arches MBM (BP 194, DM 466, FR 1576, Y 36,504).

$90* *Portrait De Peinture A. Guillamin Au Pendu*, restrike, (05-16-93, Hanzel, #463), 6 x 4¼ in., (15.2 x 10.8 cm.), etching (BP 59, DM 145, FR 486, Y 9977).

$192 *Portrait Of A Gentleman Seated*, s., (08-14-92, G.A. Key, #74), 5 x 4 in., (12.7 x 10.2 cm.), etching (BP 100, DM 282, FR 954, Y 24,212).

$660* *"Portrait Of Guillaumin" and "Tete De Femme": Two*, late impressions, (10-30-92, Sloan, #1608), larger 12½ x 9 in., (31.8 x 22.9 cm.), etching (BP 423, DM 1015, FR 3445, Y 81,754).

BI *"Portrait Of Guillaumin" and "The Artist's House": Two*, late impressions, est. $45/550, (12-10-92, Sloan, #3019), larger 5⅞ x 4¼ in., (14.9 x 10.8 cm.), etching.

BI *Selbstbilnis (Venturi 1158; Johnson 24)*, 1896/97, est. DM 3,500, (12-04-92, Bassenge, #6760), 12⅝ x 11¼ in., (32 x 28.5 cm.), gray lithograph on handmade.

$1410* *Selbstportrait (Venturi 1158; Johnson (Vollard) 24), 1898/1900*, watermark, (05-26-93, Dorling, #2588, illus.), 12¾ x 10¹³⁄₁₆ in., (32.4 x 27.5 cm.), lithograph on handmade (BP 912, DM 2301, FR 7743, Y 153,194).

$655* *Son Portrait Par Lui-Meme (Venturi 1158, Una Johnson 24, Cherpin 8),1898-1900*, full margins, (02-24-93, Picard, #58), black lithograph on MBM laid (BP 457, DM 1063, FR 3605, Y 76,860).

BI *"Tete De Femme"*, p.l., s. in plate, full margins, est. $5/700, (10-10-92, Goldberg, #425), image 4¾ x 3¾ in., (12.1 x 9.5 cm.), etching.

$330* *"Tete De Femme"*, c. 1873, s. plate, full margins, excell. cond., (05-07-93, Goldberg, #430, illus.), 5¼ x 4¼ in., (13.3 x 10.8 cm.), etching (BP 209, DM 522, FR 1758, Y 36,336).

$319* *"Tete De Jeune Fille" (M. 4 Only State)*, 1873, pub. Vollard, (10-31-92, Cleveland, #271, illus.), 4¾ x 3¾ in., (12.1 x 9.5 cm.), etching (BP 204, DM 491, FR 1665, Y 39,514).

$220* *Tete De Jeune Fille*, 1873, (12-13-92, Hindman, #261), 5⅛ x 4¼ in., etching (BP 141, DM 346, FR 1178, Y 27,218).

CEZANNE, Paul (after)

$1228* *Le Dejeuner Sur L'Herbe*, small margins, (02-24-93, Picard, #59), color lithograph on thin chine (BP 856, DM 1994, FR 6758, Y 144,098).

$220* *Portrait Of Paul Guillaumin*, later impression, w/plate tone, margins, good cond., slight toning, (05-22-93, Weschler, #174), 6¼ x 4¾ in., (15.9 x 12.1 cm.), etching on laid (BP 143, DM 358, FR 1204, Y 24,256).

CHABAS, Paul   French 1869-1934/37

$175 *"Wildflower"*, s., (05-20-93, Alderfer, #369), 10¾ x 7¼ in., (27.3 x 18.4 cm.), aquatint (BP 112, DM 282, FR 951, Y 19,324).

CHABOT, Paul de   b. 1932

$38* *"Chevaux"*, #8/99, s., (01-28-93, Pescheteau, #96), 20⅞ x 29¹⁵⁄₁₆ in., (53 x 76 cm.), color lithograph on Arches (BP 25, DM 60, FR 204, Y 4718).

CHADWICK, Lynn English b. 1914

BI *Composition, 1966,* s., d., est. DM 1,200, (06-12-93, Hauswedell/Nolt, #55), 14¾ x 11⅛ in., (37.5 x 28.2 cm.), monotype on Pergamin.

$1241* *Hommage A Lilienthal, 1968,* s., d., #24/75, (10-21-92, Dobiaschofsky, #1893), 21¼ x 29⅛ in., (54 x 74 cm.), color lithograph (BP 770, DM 1878, FR 6374, Y 151,157, SF 1680).

CHAFETZ, Sidney

$39* *Ben Franklin,* (10-03-92, Garth, #343), 9 x 8 in., (22.9 x 20.3 cm.), woodcut (BP 23, DM 55, FR 188, Y 4668).

$110* *"Debusey",* (10-03-92, Garth, #337, illus.), 22 x 18 in., (55.9 x 45.7 cm.), etching (BP 65, DM 156, FR 529, Y 13,167).

$138* *"Good Grey Poet 1971",* (10-03-92, Garth, #339, illus.), 26¼ x 22¼ in., (66.7 x 56.5 cm.), woodcut (BP 81, DM 195, FR 664, Y 16,519).

$193* *"Sholem Aleichem 1965",* (10-03-92, Garth, #338, illus.), 24¼ x 18¼ in., (61.6 x 46.4 cm.), woodcut (BP 113, DM 273, FR 929, Y 23,103).

$193* *"The Stroller II",* (10-03-92, Garth, #341, illus.), 20¼ x 13¼ in., (51.4 x 33.7 cm.), etching (BP 113, DM 273, FR 929, Y 23,103).

$248* *"Two Geniuses",* (10-03-92, Garth, #336, illus.), 29¾ x 24 in., (75.6 x 61 cm.), woodcut (BP 145, DM 351, FR 1193, Y 29,686).

$94* *"Two Hands, 1964",* (10-03-92, Garth, #342, illus.), 17 x 13½ in., (43.2 x 34.3 cm.), etching (BP 55, DM 133, FR 452, Y 11,252).

CHAGALL (after)

BI *"Mediterraneen",* est. $50/70, (08-05-92, Boos, #722), 30 x 19 in., (762 x 483 mm.), lithograph.

CHAGALL, Marc Russian/French 1887-1985

$303* *Le Geai Pare Des Plumes Du Paon I*from Fables of Fontaine, (03-14-93, Hindman, #266), 11½ x 9¼ in., (29.2 x 23.5 cm.), etching (BP 211, DM 504, FR 1715, Y 35,710).

$221* *Abendstimmung,* stone s., (09-04-92, Germann, #278), 30½ x 23⁹⁄₁₆ in., (775 x 598 mm.), color granolithograph (BP 111, DM 310, FR 1054, Y 27,203, SF 276).

$800* *Abraham And The Angels,* (05-16-93, Hanzel, #480), 11⅞ x 9⅜ in., (30.2 x 23.8 cm.), colored etching (BP 520, DM 1287, FR 4324, Y 88,682).

$2401* *Abraham Et Sarah (Mourlot 122), 1956,* s., #37/75, from Bible I, (06-10-93, Hauswedell/Nolt, #143, illus.), image 14¹⁄₁₆ x 10⁷⁄₁₆ in., (35.7 x 26.5 cm.), color lithograph on Arches paper (BP 1571, DM 3910, FR 13,163, Y 254,856).

$6160* *The Accordionist (M. 204), 1957,* s., #26/90, margins, mount-staining, tape, (12-01-92, Christie-London, #329, illus.), L. 10¹⁄₁₆ x 15¹⁵⁄₁₆ in., (255 x 405 mm.), lithograph in colors on BFK Rives (BP 4070, DM 9818, FR 33,460, Y 766,932).

BI *Adam, Eve And The Serpent (M. 914), 1977,* s., #41/50, full margins, creasing, very good cond., est. $8/12,000, (05-11-93, Christie-NY, #176, illus.), borderline 16¼ x 12¼ in., (413 x 311 mm.), color lithograph on Arches.

$23,020* *Les Adolescents (M. 741), 1975,* s., #23/50, full margins, good cond., creases, rubbing, stain, (12-03-92, Sotheby-London, #253, illus.), 25½ x 19⅞ in., (648 x 505 mm.), lithograph in colors on Arches (BP 14,850, DM 36,201, FR 123,564, Y 2,864,253).

$22,000* *The Adolescents (M. 741), 1975,* s., #20/50, full margins, light staining, very good cond., (11-09-92, Christie-NY, #79, illus.), 637 x 495 in., (x cm.), colored lithograph on Arches (BP 14,545, DM 35,121, FR 118,662, Y 2,730,206).

$3567* *Affiche Galerie Maeght (M. 354), 1962,* s., 67/90, (12-04-92, AB Stockholm, #7025), 26⅜ x 19¹¹⁄₁₆ in., (67 x 50 cm.), lithograph in colors on BFK Rives (BP 2288, DM 5681, FR 19,271, Y 445,318, SK 24,200).

$248* *Agar Dans Le Desert, c. 1960,* from Dessins Pour La Bible, (02-12-93, DuMouchelle, #352, illus.), 14 x 11 in., (35.6 x 27.9 cm.), color lithograph (BP 175, DM 411, FR 1392, Y 29,908).

BI *Der Akrobat Mit Der Geige (K. 40/III/b), 1924,* pub. Vollard, margins, good cond., mat/ıight stain, foxing, backboardstain, est. $4/4,500, (11-05-92, Sotheby-NY, #110), 16⅜ x 12½ in., (417 x 318 mm.), sheet 22 x 16⅞ in., (417 x 318 mm.), etching and drypoint p. in brownish-black on wove.

$2645* *Der Akrobat Mit Der Geige (Kornfeld 40/III/b), 1924,* pub. Vollard, margins, good cond., mat/backboard stain, fox marks, (02-11-93, Sotheby-NY, #80, illus.), 16⁷⁄₁₆ x 12½ in., (417 x 318 mm.), sheet 21¹⁵⁄₁₆ x 16¹⁵⁄₁₆ in., (417 x 318 mm.), etching and drypoint p. in brownish-black on wove (BP 1866, DM 4381, FR 14,826, Y 318,867).

BI *Der Akrobat Mit Der Geiger (Kornfeld 40), 1924,* p. Louis Fort for Vollard, full margins, restored creases, good cond., est. BP 1,5/2,000, (06-30-93, Sotheby-London, #388), 16½ x 12½ in., (419 x 318 mm.), etching on thick wove.

$358* *Les Ames Mortes: Pavel Ivanovitch Est Ramene A L'Auberge (V. 66), 1948,* pub. Teriade, p. by Louis Fort, full margins, good cond., pencil notations, (02-24-93, Butterfield, #2906), 11 x 8⅝ in., (279 x 219 mm.), etching on Arches (BP 250, DM 581, FR 1970, Y 42,009).

$1840* *"Les Ames Mortes: Tchitchikov Et Sobakevitch Discutent Affaires" and"Apparition De Tchitchikov Au Bal", 1923: Two,* plates XXXVII and LXII, pub. Teriade, 1947, full margins, good cond.,mat stain, masking tape, discolored, Late Vitya Vronsky Babin Coll., (05-13-93, Sotheby-NY, #493), one 8⅞ x 10⅞ in., (220 x 277 mm.), other 8⅜ x 10⅞ in., (220 x 277 mm.), drypoint (BP 1208, DM 2971, FR 10,022, Y 205,426).

BI *Les Amoureux (Sorlier 994), 1982,* s., #16/50, est. DM 6,500, (05-26-93, Lempertz, #74, illus.), 22¹⁄₁₆ x 17⁵⁄₁₆ in., (56 x 44 cm.), color lithograph on Arches wove.

$169* *Amoureux Avec Soleil Rouge, (Mourlot 285), 1960,* from Chagall Lithograph I, (09-30-92, Kunsthallen, #57), color lithograph (BP 95, DM 240, FR 811, Y 20,281, DK 920).

BI *Les Amoureux En Gris (M. 194), 1957,* s., #83/90, pub. Maeght, p. Draeger, full margins, very good cond.?,est. $4/6,000, (05-19-93, Butterfield, #1892), sh. 16 x 12⁹⁄₁₆ in., (406 x 319 mm.), lithograph in colors on wove.

BI *Les Amoureux Sous L'Arbre (Cramer 31), 1968,* epreuve d'artiste, s., wrinkles, est. DM 6,500, (10-09-92, Winterberg, #1831, illus.), 17⁹⁄₁₆ x 24³⁄₁₆ in., (44.6 x 61.4 cm.), etching w/aquatint on wove.

BI *Les Amoureux Sous L'Arbre (Cramer 31), 1968,* s., #4/50, pub. G. Cramer, margins, mount-staining, surface dirt, creases, est. BP 2,4/2,800, (12-01-92, Christie-London, #336), plate 17½ x 24⅛ in., (445 x 612 mm.), etching on wove.

$1897* *Arabian Nights, Plate 12: Mounting The Ebony Horse He Took Her Up Behind Him (M. 47), 1948,* s., #31/90, margins trimmed, (06-11-93, Doyle, #27), 15 x 11¼ in., (381 x 286 mm.), color lithograph (BP 1246, DM 3083, FR 10,395, Y 201,273).

BI *Arabian Nights, Plate 5: So I Came Forth Of The Sea (M. 40), 1948,* s., #31/90, margins trimmed, est. $3/5,000, (06-11-93, Doyle, #26), 14½ x 10¾ in., (368 x 273 mm.), lithograph.

$3738* *Art Flowers (M. 1006), 1983,* s., #11/50, full margins, good cond., skinned spots, (02-11-93, Sotheby-NY, #100), 19⅜ x 13⁵⁄₁₆ in., (492 x 338 mm.), color lithograph (BP 2638, DM 6192, FR 20,953, Y 450,633).

$4025* *The Artist I (M. 928), 1978,* s., #4/50, full margins, good cond., tape stain, (05-13-93, Sotheby-NY, #520), 13⅝ x 10½ in., (345 x 268 mm.), lithograph in colors (BP 2642, DM 6499, FR 21,923, Y 449,369).

$4600* *The Artist II (M. 929), 1978,* s., #4/50, full margins, good cond., soiling, tape stain, water stain, (05-13-93, Sotheby-NY, #521, illus.), 13¼ x 10 in., (337 x 255 mm.), lithograph in colors (BP 3020, DM 7428, FR 25,054, Y 513,565).

$1760* *The Artist In The Village II (Mourlot 604),* s. Marc Chagall, num. 19/50, (09-25-92, Wolf, #37, illus.), 15 x 11½ in., (38.1 x 29.2 cm.), lithograph in colors on arches paper (BP 1028, DM 2609, FR 8822, Y 212,432).

BI *The Artist's Bird (M. 655), 1972,* s., #30/30, full margins, creasing, skinned patch, good cond., est. $2,5/3,000, (05-11-93, Christie-NY, #171), borderline 13 x 9⅛ in., (330 x 232 mm.), lithograph on Arches.

$4600* *The Artist's Bouquet (M. 410), 1964,* s., #22/75, pub. Maeght, full margins, good cond., light-stain, faint mat stain, (05-13-93, Sotheby-NY, #514, illus.), 14⅝ x 11 in.,

(370 x 278 mm.), lithograph in colors (BP 3020, DM 7428, FR 25,054, Y 513,565).

$3688* *Assuerus Chasse Vashti (Mourlot 351), 1958-59,* #26/50, s., num., (11-13-92, Koller, #5284), 14 1/16 x 10 5/8 in., (35.7 x 27 cm.), lithograph on Arches wove (BP 2383, DM 5790, FR 19,524, Y 457,739, SF 5220).

BI *At Table (Mourlot 14), 1922-23,* s., #22/35, full margins, good cond., mat stain, repaired tear, reinforced thin spots, est. $2,5/3,000, (11-05-92, Sotheby-NY, #109), 4 3/4 x 5 3/4 in., (122 x 146 mm.), lithograph on cream laid.

BI *Der Auszug Aus Agypten, 1930,* #31/100, mono., sheet 33 for Bible, Paris 1956, stains, est. DM 3,000-, (11-21-92, Lempertz, #68), 9 3/4 x 12 13/16 in., (24.7 x 32.5 cm.), etching on Arches wove.

$3688* *Der Automobilist (Kornfeld 24 c), 1922,* s., num., supplementary sheet for series Mein Leben, (12-05-92, Bassenge, #7076), 8 1/8 x 7 1/16 in., (20.6 x 17.9 cm.), etching on handmade (BP 2309, DM 5750, FR 19,596, Y 456,945).

$5345* *Autoportrait Au Chapeau Orne (Kornf. 77/III), 1928,* s., i. epreuve d'artiste, (06-23-93, Kornfeld, #265), drypoint on wove (BP 3631, DM 9044, FR 30,421, Y 582,307, SF 8050).

$17,181* *Autoportrait Au Sourire (Kornfeld 42/III/b), 1924-1925,* s., num., (06-23-93, Kornfeld, #262, illus.), etching and drypoint on thick wove (BP 11,672, DM 29,071, FR 97,786, Y 1,871,773, SF 25,875).

BI *Bacchante (Mourlot 690), 1973,* s., #49/50, (05-16-93, Hindman, #490), 19 1/8 x 24 1/2 in., (48.6 x 62.2 cm.), color lithograph.

BI *"Baie De Nice (Ville De Nice)" (Sorlier S. 124/125), 1967/1970,* by Charles Sorlier after a colored lithograph by Chagall, s., est. DM 2,8/3,000, (11-28-92, Grisebach, #457, illus.), 20 3/8 x 15 7/8 in., (51.8 x 40.3 cm.), colored lithograph.

$3088* *"La Baie Des Ange" and "Carmen" (M. 350 And C. S. 108), 1961 and 1966: Two,* first pub. French Tourist Commissariat, second pub. Editions of the Metropolitan Opera, good cond., defects, (06-30-93, Sotheby-London, #398), one sh 39 1/4 x 23 7/8 in., (99.7 x 60.6 cm.), the other sh 38 3/8 x 25 3/8 in., (99.7 x 60.6 cm.), color lithographic poster (BP 2070, DM 5267, FR 17,768, Y 330,869).

$2200* *La Baie Des Anges (M. 350), 1962,* ink s., d., p. Mourlot, full margins, good cond.?, tears, surface soiling, creases, (10-28-92, Butterfield, #2796), 31 x 22 1/2 in., (787 x 572 mm.), color lithograph and poster on wove (BP 1402, DM 3398, FR 11,536, Y 269,939).

$9020* *The Baie Des Anges (M. 486a), 1967,* s., i. epreuve d'artiste, full margins, very good cond., (11-09-92, Christie-NY, #74, illus.), 14 1/2 x 16 1/2 in., (368 x 419 mm.), colored lithograph on Arches (BP 5964, DM 14,400, FR 48,652, Y 1,119,384).

$3970* *La Baie Des Anges (Sorlier S.47), 1962,* s., d.; mounting traces verso, 628mm x 1010mm, (10-14-92, Germann, #253, illus.), color lithograph (BP 2330, DM 5810, FR 19,702, Y 481,095, SF 5175).

$3105* *The Baou Of St. Jeannett II (M. 585), 1969,* s., #17/50, full margins, good cond., mat/light stains, discoloration, tape hinges, verso discolored, (02-11-93, Sotheby-NY, #96), 12 15/16 x 10 1/4 in., (330 x 260 mm.), color lithograph (BP 2191, DM 5143, FR 17,405, Y 374,322).

BI *Basket Of Fruit And Pineapples (M. 421), 1964,* s., #5/50, full margins, faded, mount staining, tape stains, est. BP7,0/8,000, (12-03-92, Sotheby-London, #238, illus.), 26 1/2 x 19 7/8 in., (673 x 505 mm.), lithograph in colors on BFK Rives.

$8579* *Basket Of Fruit And Pineapples (M. 421), 1964,* s., #5/50, full margins, pink slightly faded, mount-staining, tape stains, (06-30-93, Sotheby-London, #395, illus.), 26 1/2 x 19 7/8 in., (673 x 505 mm.), color lithograph on BFK Rives (BP 5750, DM 14,632, FR 49,361, Y 919,211).

$1410* *Die Beiden Hahne,* sheet 77 of series, 1927, 1930, 1952, s., (05-26-93, Lempertz, #60), approx. 16 9/16 x 13 3/16 in., (42 x 33.5 cm.), etching on wide Montval handmade (BP 912, DM 2301, FR 7743, Y 153,194).

$3850* *Bella (K. 41/II/b), 1924,* s., #34/100, pub. by Albert Morance, margins, thin spots, residual stains verso, good cond., (11-05-92, Sotheby-NY, #111), 8 3/4 x 4 1/2 in., (221 x 115 mm.), sheet 10 7/8 x 8 1/4 in., (221 x 115 mm.), etching and drypoint on Arches wove (BP 2504, DM 6089, FR 20,599, Y 472,335).

$4888* *Bella (K. 41/b), 1924,* s., #38/100, pub. Editions Albert Morance, full margins, good cond.,discoloration, soiling, Dora Jane Janson and late H.W. Janson Coll., (05-13-93, Sotheby-NY, #494, illus.), 8 3/4 x 4 5/8 in., (222 x 116 mm.), etching on wove (BP 3209, DM 7893, FR 26,623, Y 545,718).

$5806* *Bible (M. 117-146), 1956: Twenty-Eight,* (10-09-92, Winterberg, #1905, illus.), each approx. 13 15/16 x 10 1/4 in., (35.5 x 26 cm.), lithograph on wove (BP 3445, DM 8624, FR 28,958, Y 706,842).

$3531* *Bible (Mourlot 117-146), 1956: Sixteen,* (06-10-93, Hauswedell/Nolt, #154), book format 14 3/16 x 10 5/8 in., (36 x 27 cm.), color lithograph (BP 2310, DM 5750, FR 19,359, Y 374,801).

BI *Bible (Mourlot 117-146), 1956: Sixteen,* est. DM 10,000, (06-10-93, Hauswedell/Nolt, #155), book format 14 3/16 x 10 5/8 in., (36 x 27 cm.), color lithograph.

$5410* *Bible (Mourlot Band I 117-146): Thirty,* Editions de la Revue Verve VIII, Nos. 33/34, (11-21-92, Lempertz, #75), 14 1/4 x 10 9/16 in., (36.2 x 26.8 cm.), color lithographs, 18 in color (BP 3562, DM 8626, FR 29,055, Y 672,802).

$3410* *Bible (Verve VIII:33-34, M. 117-146), 1956,* (05-12-93, AB Stockholm, #7014), lithograph (BP 2227, DM 5502, FR 18,533, Y 380,708, SK 25,300).

$7480* *"The Bible Series": Five,* plate 30-36/100, plate 36-36/100, plate 42-36/100, plate 78-90/100, plate 93-90/100 by Chagall, artist s. MCH, (04-23-93, Clearing House, #255, illus.), hand-colored etching (BP 4752, DM 11,834, FR 39,957, Y 826,154).

$6024* *"Bible" (Mourlot 117-146): Eighteen,* (06-08-93, Karl/Faber, #615), approx. 13 15/16 x 10 5/8 in., (35.5 x 27 cm.), lithograph and heliogravure (photoengraving) (BP 3960, DM 9774, FR 32,918, Y 639,830).

$4495* *La Bible, Editions De La Revue Verve (M. 117-46), 1956,* t., text w/reproductive plates and set of 28, good cond., scuffing, discoloration, (12-01-92, Christie-London, #326), overall sheet 14 5/16 x 10 7/16 in., (363 x 265 mm.), lithograph on wove (BP 2970, DM 7164, FR 24,416, Y 559,636).

$182,770* *La Bible, L'Ancien Testament (Boston 53; Rauch 148; Johnson 175; Sorlier PP. 62-81), 1931-39: 105,* init. M. Ch., #76/100, pub. Teriade, 1956, full margins, good cond., (06-30-93, Sotheby-London, #397, illus.), sh 21 x 15 3/8 in., (533 x 391 mm.), etching, complete set of 105 plates, all hand-colored w/watercolor byartist on Arches wovw (BP 122,500, DM 311,735, FR 1,051,611, Y 19,583,199).

$4025* *Bible, Paris, Editions Verve, Vol VIII, Nos. 33-4, 1956 (M. 117-46): Book,* t., just. and text, bound, very good cond., orig. lithographic boards, (05-11-93, Christie-NY, #152), 14 3/16 x 10 7/16 in., (360 x 265 mm.), 16 color lithographs, 12 lithographs in black, 105 in reprods., on wove (BP 2569, DM 6341, FR 21,364, Y 442,746).

BI *Bible. Eaux-Fortes Originales De Marc Chagall, 1956: One Hundred,* Teriade, Editeur, #231/275, frame s., est. DM 70,000, (05-26-93, Lempertz, #67, illus.), 18 1/2 x 14 3/16 in., (47 x 36 cm.), etching on Montval wove.

BI *La Bible: Joseph Berger (V. 215), 1931-39,* inits., #47/100, pub. Teriade, full margins, good cond., mat staining, creases, surface soiling, notations, est. $1,8/2,000, (10-28-92, Butterfield, #2615), 11 3/4 x 9 3/8 in., (298 x 238 mm.), hand-colored etching on Arches.

BI *La Bible: Joseph Et Ses Freres (V. 216), 1931-39,* inits., #59/100, pub. Teriade 1956, full margins, good cond., mat/light-staining, hinge remains, surface soiling, est. $1,8/2,200, (10-28-92, Butterfield, #2616), 11 1/2 x 9 5/8 in., (292 x 244 mm.), hand-colored etching on wove.

$1540* *La Bible: Le Visage D'Israel (M. 231), 1958-59,* s., annot. Epreuve d'artiste, pub. Verve, full margins, good cond., mat/light-staining, hinge/glue remains, thinned spots, notations, surface soiling, (10-28-92, Butterfield, #2619), 14 1/8 x 10 1/2 in., (359 x 267 mm.), color lithograph on Arches (BP 981, DM 2378, FR 8076, Y 188,957).

$330* *La Bible: Passage Du Jourdain (V. 241), 1931-39,* pub. Ambroise Vollard, p. by Teriade, 1956, full margins, good cond., (02-24-93, Butterfield, #2907), 11⅝ x 9³⁄₁₆ in., (295 x 233 mm.), etching on wove (BP 230, DM 536, FR 1816, Y 38,723).

$2396* *Der Bildhauer Und Das Standbild Des Jupiter,* sheet 89 of series, 1927, 1930, 1952, s., (05-26-93, Lempertz, #63), approx. 16⁹⁄₁₆ x 13³⁄₁₆ in., (42 x 33.5 cm.), etching on wide Montval handmade (BP 1550, DM 3909, FR 13,158, Y 260,322).

BI *Blatt Aus Der Serie Paris,* #25/75, s., est. DM 8,500, (11-11-92, Ruef, #1749), 14¹⁵⁄₁₆ x 11 in., (38 x 28 cm.), color lithograph mounted on BFK Rives.

$12,413* *Die Blaue Nymphe (Mourlot 379), c. 1962,* s., artist proof XXIV/XXV, dusty, (09-25-92, Granier, #2785), sheet 29¹⁵⁄₁₆ x 21⁷⁄₁₆ in., (76 x 54.5 cm.), color lithograph on wove Arches (BP 7248, DM 18,401, FR 62,221, Y 1,498,250).

BI *Blue Nude (M. 1049), 1985,* stamp s., #36/50, Atelier Marc Chagall, Lithographie Originale blindstamp, full margins, very good cond., crease, est. $6/8,000, (05-19-93, Butterfield, #1897, illus.), sh. 32¾ x 22³⁄₁₆ in., (832 x 564 mm.), lithograph in colors on Arches.

BI *"The Blue Painter",* s., d. 1980, edit. #33/50, est. $7,5/8,500, (12-11-92, DuMouchelle, #2029, illus.), 20¾ x 14 in., (52.7 x 35.6 cm.), color lithograph.

$10,450* *The Blue Studio (M. 706), 1973,* s., #13/50, full margins, good cond., paper tone, darkened, remains of hinges, skinning, (11-05-92, Sotheby-NY, #135, illus.), 15¾ x 15 in., (400 x 380 mm.), lithograph p. in colors (BP 6797, DM 16,527, FR 55,912, Y 1,282,051).

BI *"Bodegon Con Flores Y Pez",* from "Niza" series, #55/75, s., reserve P1,500,000, (12-17-92, Duran, #164, illus.), 25⁹⁄₁₆ x 19¹¹⁄₁₆ in., (65 x 50 cm.), color lithograph.

$14,835* *Bonjour Sur Paris (M. 71), 1952,* s., #17/75, pub. Mourlot, for the One Hundredth Anniversary Album, full margins, good cond., discoloration, (12-03-92, Sotheby-London, #225, illus.), sheet 19⅞ x 26 in., (505 x 660 mm.), lithograph in colors (BP 9570, DM 23,329, FR 79,630, Y 1,845,838).

$5116* *Bouquet A L'Arc-En-Ciel (M. 743), 1975,* s., #21/50, full margins, good cond., creases, nicks, (12-03-92, Sotheby-London, #256, illus.), 14⅝ x 11¾ in., (371 x 298 mm.), lithograph in colors on Japon nacre (BP 3300, DM 8045, FR 27,461, Y 636,556).

$8018* *Le Bouquet Blanc (Sorl.-Mourl. 579), 1969,* s., i. H.C., (06-23-93, Kornfeld, #261), color lithograph on wove (BP 5447, DM 13,567, FR 45,635, Y 873,516, SF 12,075).

BI *Bouquet De Fleurs Et Panier Aux Fruits,* #23/500, est. SF 280/360, (09-04-92, Germann, #281), 35¼ x 22⅝ in., (895 x 575 mm.), color offset-lithograph.

BI *Bouquet Des Fleurs, (Mourlot 384),* s., edit. 250, est. DK 4,000, (09-30-92, Kunsthallen, #59), color lithograph.

$2387* *Branch And Flute-Player (M. 180), 1957,* s., #15/30, margins, creased, a repaired tear, good cond., (12-03-92, Sotheby-London, #228, illus.), sheet 25⅝ x 19¾ in., (651 x 502 mm.), lithograph on Canson grey (BP 1540, DM 3754, FR 12,813, Y 297,001).

$948* *Buch. Glassmalerei Fur Jerusalem (Mourlot III, s. 18): Two,* (06-24-93, Germann, #269), color lithograph (BP 624, DM 1537, FR 5180, Y 101,695, SF 1380).

$435* *Buch. Le Plafond De L'Opera De PAris (Mourlot 434): Six,* (06-24-93, Germann, #268), color lithograph (BP 286, DM 705, FR 2377, Y 46,664, SF 633).

$2200* *By The Window (M. 624), 1971,* s., #16/50, full margins, good cond., skinned spots, (11-05-92, Sotheby-NY, #132), 12½ x 16½ in., (319 x 420 mm.), lithograph p. in black and grey (BP 1431, DM 3479, FR 11,771, Y 269,906).

$192* *Cain And Abel (Mourlot 238), 1960,* from the book edit. of Drawings for the Bible, (03-24-93, Grogan, #117), 14 x 10⅜ in., (35.6 x 26.4 cm.), color lithograph (BP 130, DM 314, FR 1067, Y 22,559).

$11,058* *Carmen (Sorlier 118), 1967,* 2nd state, #55/200, s., creases, stains, 1010 x 675mm, (09-04-92, Germann, #53, illus.), color lithograph (BP 5541, DM 15,498, FR 52,758, Y 1,361,152, SF 13,800).

$9545* *Le Cercle Rouge (Sorl.-Mourl. 440), 1966,* s., i. H.C., (06-23-93, Kornfeld, #258, illus.), color lithograph (BP 6484, DM 16,151, FR 54,326, Y 1,039,874, SF 14,375).

$165* *Chagall Peintures 1947-1967,* Fondation Maeght, (03-24-93, Kunsthallen, #60), lithographic poster (BP 112, DM 269, FR 917, Y 19,387, DK 1035).

$4313* *Chagall's Studios: Frontispiece (M. 899), 1976,* s., #95/250, pub. Mourlot, full margins, good cond., light-stain, skinned spot, (05-13-93, Sotheby-NY, #519), 13 x 9½ in., (330 x 240 mm.), lithograph in colors (BP 2832, DM 6964, FR 23,491, Y 481,523).

$1150* *La Charlatan, 1927-30,* plate 71 from Les Fables de la Fontaine, s., i. w/plate, pub. Vollard, 1952, full margins, good cond., mat stain, discolored, fox marks, (02-11-93, Sotheby-NY, #84), 11⅞ x 9½ in., (302 x 242 mm.), etching on Montval (BP 811, DM 1905, FR 6446, Y 138,638).

$55* *Charlottenborg (Czwikiltzer 50), 1973,* (09-25-92, Granier, #2791), 23⅝ x 16⁹⁄₁₆ in., (60 x 42 cm.), color lithograph on wove (BP 32, DM 82, FR 276, Y 6639).

$110* *Charlottenburg,* s. Marc Chagall, (06-26-93, Wolf, #973), 23½ x 16½ in., (59.7 x 41.9 cm.), color poster (BP 74, DM 187, FR 630, Y 11,671).

$1265* *La Chene Et Le Roseau, 1927-30,* plate 12 from portfolio Les Fables de la Fontaine, s., #86/100, pub.Vollard, 1952, full margins, good cond., mat stain, glue, (02-11-93, Sotheby-NY, #83), 11⅝ x 9³⁄₁₆ in., (295 x 234 mm.), etching on cream wove (BP 893, DM 2095, FR 7091, Y 152,502).

$4611* *Le Cheval Brun (Mourlot 61), 1952,* s., num., (06-05-93, Bassenge, #5941, illus.), 14¾ x 21¼ in., (37.5 x 54 cm.), color lithograph on Arches wove (BP 3035, DM 7476, FR 25,197, Y 494,636).

$604* *Le Cheval Brun (Mourlot 61), 1952,* (10-09-92, Winterberg, #1842), 14⁷⁄₁₆ x 21¼ in., (36.7 x 54 cm.), color lithograph on wove (BP 358, DM 897, FR 3012, Y 73,533).

$6587* *Le Cheval Brun, 1952,* s., #182/200, (09-18-92, Schloss Ahlden, #981, illus.), 14¾ x 21⅞ in., (37.5 x 55.5 cm.), colored lithograph on wove (BP 3857, DM 9774, FR 33,437, Y 814,114).

$3069* *Cheval Volant Et Jongleur (M. 167), 1956,* s., i. epreuve d'artiste, foxing, good cond., (12-03-92, Sotheby-London, #233), sheet 26 x 19⅞ in., (660 x 505 mm.), lithograph on Arches (BP 1980, DM 4826, FR 16,473, Y 381,859).

$847* *Le Chien Qui Porte A Son Cou Le Dine De Son Maitre, 1927-1930,* s., (06-10-93, Hauswedell/Nolt, #134), image 11⅝ x 9⅜ in., (29.5 x 23.8 cm.), etching on hand-made Maillol (BP 554, DM 1379, FR 4644, Y 89,906).

$500* *Le Cillageous Et Le Serpent,* inits., (05-16-93, Hanzel, #449), 11½ x 9½ in., (29.2 x 24.1 cm.), etching (BP 325, DM 804, FR 2703, Y 55,426).

BI *The Circus (M. 492), 1967,* s., #10/24, full margins, good cond., est. $20/25,000, (11-05-92, Sotheby-NY, #130, illus.), 16⅝ x 12¾ in., (422 x 325 mm.), lithograph p. in colors.

$14,494* *Le Cirque (M. 501), 1967,* s., #6/24, pub. Teriade Editeur, full margins, good cond., discoloration, (12-03-92, Sotheby-London, #240, illus.), 16½ x 12½ in., (419 x 318 mm.), lithograph in colors on Arches (BP 9350, DM 22,793, FR 77,799, Y 1,803,409).

$5457* *Le Cirque (M. 515), 1967,* s., #8/24, pub. Teriade Editeur, full margins, good cond., discoloration, (12-03-92, Sotheby-London, #241, illus.), sheet 20½ x 15 in., (521 x 381 mm.), lithograph in colors on Arches (BP 3520, DM 8582, FR 29,291, Y 678,985).

$11,072* *Le Cirque A L'Etoile (Sorl.-Mourl. 436), 1965,* s., i. H.C., (06-23-93, Kornfeld, #256), color lithograph (BP 7522, DM 18,734, FR 63,017, Y 1,206,232, SF 16,675).

$5737* *"Le Cirque" (Mourlot S. 181), 1957-58,* #20/40, s., (11-13-92, Koller, #5282, illus.), 13¹⁄₁₆ x 9⅝ in., (33.2 x 24.5 cm.), lithograph on wove (BP 3707, DM 9006, FR 30,371, Y 712,052, SF 8120).

BI *Cirque, Teriade, Paris (M. 490-527), 1967,* t., text, justification and set of 38, s., copy num. XVI of 20 hors commerce copies, very good cond., est. BP 100/130,000, (12-01-92, Christie-London, #333, illus.), overall sheet 17¾ x 13½ in., (451 x 343 mm.), lithograph on Arches.

$4400* *"The Clown And The Flute, No. 2",* s. Marc Chagall, num. 49/50, (09-25-92, Wolf, #40, illus.), 16½ x 20¼ in., (41.9 x 51.4 cm.), lithograph in colors on arches paper (BP 2569, DM 6522, FR 22,055, Y 531,080).

BI *Le Clown Jaune,* est. DK 2,000, (11-14-92, Bukowskis, #12), poster.

BI *Le Clown Musicien (Mourlot 122), 1957,* s., #64/150, est. DM 8000, (06-10-93, Hauswedell/Nolt, #144, illus.), image 26⅛ x 18¹⁄₁₆ in., (66.4 x 45.8 cm.), color lithograph on Arches paper.

$9379* *Les Clowns Musiciens (M. 978), 1980,* s., #5/50, full margins, good cond., creases, skinned areas, (12-03-92, Sotheby-London, #266, illus.), 37⅜ x 23¾ in., (949 x 603 mm.), lithograph in colors on wove (BP 6050, DM 14,749, FR 50,344, Y 1,166,978).

$6900* *Come Muses Sing This Rural Song..., (M. 537), 1967,* from In the Land of the Gods, s., #6/75, full margins, light/mat staining, good cond., (05-11-93, Christie-NY, #165, illus.), borderline 18 x 14 in., (457 x 356 mm.), color lithograph on Arches (BP 4405, DM 10,870, FR 36,624, Y 758,992).

$294* *Composition,* from La Fontaines fabler, 69, (03-24-93, Kunsthallen, #58), etching (BP 199, DM 480, FR 1634, Y 34,544, DK 1840).

$1887* *Composition A L'Horloge (Cramer 33), 1967,* s., #97/125, full margins, good cond., (06-30-93, Sotheby-London, #400, illus.), 12 x 9¼ in., (305 x 235 mm.), etching w/aquatint on wove (BP 1265, DM 3218, FR 10,857, Y 202,186).

$330* *"Composition Fra Derriere Le Miroir, (Mourlot 412), 1964" and "Composition": Two,* (03-24-93, Kunsthallen, #57), color lithograph (BP 223, DM 539, FR 1834, Y 38,773, DK 2070).

$37* *Composition, (Mourlot 281), 1960,* (03-24-93, Kunsthallen, #59), lithographic poster (BP 25, DM 60, FR 206, Y 4347, DK 230).

BI *Composition, (Sorlier 602), 1970,* Galerie Maeght, est. DK 1,000, (09-30-92, Kunsthallen, #58), poster, offset print in colors.

$3335* *The Concert (M. 176), 1957,* s., #53/90, colors faded, light-stain, (02-11-93, Sotheby-NY, #89), 15½ x 22³⁄₁₆ in., (394 x 564 mm.), color lithograph (BP 2353, DM 5524, FR 18,694, Y 402,049).

$3178* *Le Concert (Mourlot 176), 1957,* s., #16/90, (06-10-93, Hauswedell/Nolt, #145, illus.), image 14¼ x 22¼ in., (36.2 x 56.5 cm.), color lithograph on strong wove (BP 2079, DM 5175, FR 17,423, Y 337,331).

BI *Le Coq Et Le Renard, c. 1927-30,* s., from the La Fontaine, Fables, 1952 Teriade Editeur, est. DM 4500, (12-01-92, Karl/Faber, #434), 11¼ x 9⅝ in., (28.5 x 24.5 cm.), etching on hand-made.

$7636* *Le Coq Jaune (Kornf. 116/b), 1960,* s., num., (06-23-93, Kornfeld, #266), color etching (BP 5188, DM 12,920, FR 43,460, Y 831,899, SF 11,500).

$193* *"Le Coq Rogue" and "Lovers With Clock", 1957: Two,* pub. Jacques Lassaigne, (05-28-93, Sloan, #1658, illus.), each, sight 9 x 15¾ in., (22.9 x 40 cm.), color lithograph (BP 124, DM 306, FR 1035, Y 20,695).

$330* *"Le Coq Rouge" and "Lovers With Clock", 1957: Two,* from Jacques Lassaigne series, (10-30-92, Sloan, #1599), each, sight 9 x 15¾ in., (22.9 x 40 cm.), color lithograph (BP 211, DM 508, FR 1722, Y 40,877).

$6643* *Les Coqs Sur Le Toit, 1968,* s., num., (06-23-93, Kornfeld, #268, illus.), 13¾ x 15¾ in., (35 x 40 cm.), color etching on wove (BP 4513, DM 11,240, FR 37,809, Y 723,717, SF 10,005).

$6356* *Le Coque Jaune (Kornfeld 116 b), 1960,* s., #65/75, (06-10-93, Hauswedell/Nolt, #139, illus.), image 17⁹⁄₁₆ x 11¼ in., (44.6 x 28.6 cm.), color etching on Arches paper (BP 4158, DM 10,350, FR 34,846, Y 674,663).

$3063* *Couple,* #139/150, s. Marc Chagall, s. in pl. Marc Chagall PINX, (05-18-93, Encans, #174), 24 x 18⅛ in., (61 x 46 cm.), lithograph (BP 1995, DM 4970, FR 16,784, Y 341,357, C$ 3885).

$2138* *Couple A La Fenetre (Mourl. 212), 1959,* s., num., (06-23-93, Kornfeld, #251), lithograph on wove (BP 1452, DM 3618, FR 12,168, Y 232,923, SF 3220).

$16,100* *Couple At Dusk (M. 972), 1980,* s., #15/50, pub. Maeght, full margins, good cond., handling creases, (05-13-93, Sotheby-NY, #522, illus.), 37¼ x 23⅞ in., (945 x 605 mm.), lithograph in colors (BP 10,570, DM 25,997, FR 87,691, Y 1,797,477).

$3069* *Couple In Ocher (M. 59), 1952,* s., bearing numbering, margins, mount/light staining, creasing in lower margin, tear, (12-03-92, Sotheby-London, #226, illus.), sheet 29¾ x 21⅜ in., (756 x 543 mm.), lithograph in colors on Arches (BP 1980, DM 4826, FR 16,473, Y 381,859).

BI *Couple In Ochre (M. 59), 1952,* s., #44/100, pub. Maeght, full margins, good cond., light stain, est.$8/10,000, (11-05-92, Sotheby-NY, #116, illus.), 24⅞ x 19¾ in., (632 x 500 mm.), lithograph p. in colors.

$5520* *Couple In Ochre (M. 59), 1952,* s., #62/100, wide margins, light/time staining, taped to overmat, (05-11-93, Christie-NY, #151, illus.), borderline 25½ x 19¾ in., (648 x 502 mm.), color lithograph on Arches (BP 3524, DM 8696, FR 29,299, Y 607,194).

$5628* *Le Couple Sous Le Rideau (Mourlot 1044), 1984,* stamp s., i. epreuve d'artiste, stamped Lithographie Originale Atelier Marc Chagall, full margins, good cond., (10-14-92, Sotheby-Japan, #11, illus.), 17¾ x 14¼ in., (451 x 362 mm.), colored lithograph on Arches wove (BP 3303, DM 8236, FR 27,931, Y 682,016).

$1760* *Couple With Two Bouquets,* s., #48/5, (02-14-93, Hanzel, #702), 23½ x 18⅜ in., (59.7 x 46.7 cm.), colored lithograph (BP 1239, DM 2919, FR 9877, Y 212,253).

$6325* *Cover For The Bible (M. 117), 1956,* s., #33/75, pub. as cover for nos. 33-34 of Verve, large margins, good cond., mat/light-stain, handling creases, (05-13-93, Sotheby-NY, #505, illus.), 15½ x 23¼ in., (395 x 592 mm.), sh 18⅝ x 25¾ in., (395 x 592 mm.), lithograph in colors (BP 4152, DM 10,213, FR 34,450, Y 706,152).

$3450* *Crucifixion (M. 425), 1964,* s., #24/30, full margins, light/mat staining, split, surface soiling, (05-11-93, Christie-NY, #161), borderline 19½ x 25½ in., (495 x 648 mm.), lithograph on Arches (BP 2202, DM 5435, FR 18,312, Y 379,496).

$4434* *Les Cyclistes (M. 171), 1956,* s., #24/30, good cond., foxing, (12-03-92, Sotheby-London, #229, illus.), sheet 26 x 19¾ in., (660 x 502 mm.), lithograph on Arches (BP 2860, DM 6973, FR 23,800, Y 551,698).

$407* *"Dame Vor Einem Spiegel", 1964,* Derriere le Miroir, Nr. 147, (11-21-92, Arnold, #5, illus.), 13⅜ x 18⅛ in., (34 x 46 cm.), color lithograph (BP 268, DM 649, FR 2186, Y 50,616).

$195,000* *Daphnis And Chloe (M. 308-349), 1960: Suite Of Forty-Two,* text by Longus, s., copy num., pub. Editions Verve, 1961, good cond.,faded, tape stain, skinned spots, orig. covers and slipcase, (05-13-93, Sotheby-NY, #508, illus.), double sh approx. 16¾ x 25¼ in., (425 x 640 mm.), single sh approx. 16¾ x 12⅝ in., (425 x 640 mm.), lithograph in colors incl. 16 double sheets (BP 128,020, DM 314,872, FR 1,062,092, Y 21,770,682).

$1535* *Daphnis And Chloe: Captain Bryaxis's Dream (M. 32*0, 1961,* pub. Editions Verve, crease, good cond., (12-03-92, Sotheby-London, #237), sheet 16½ x 25¼ in., (419 x 641 mm.), lithograph in colors on wove (BP 990, DM 2414, FR 8239, Y 190,992).

$6050* *Daphnis And Chloe: Captain Bryaxis's Dream (M. 328), 1960,* s., #40/60, full margins, good cond., scuffs, mat/light stain, crease, skinning, (11-05-92, Sotheby-NY, #124), 16¾ x 25⅝ in., (424 x 646 mm.), lithograph p. in colors (BP 3935, DM 9568, FR 32,370, Y 742,240).

$12,100* *Daphnis And Chloe: Chloe's Kiss (M. 316), 1960,* s., #47/60, full margins, good cond., fox marks, (11-05-92, Sotheby-NY, #122, illus.), 16¾ x 12⅝ in., (424 x 322 mm.), lithograph p. in colors (BP 7870, DM 19,136, FR 64,741, Y 1,484,480).

$12,650* *Daphnis And Chloe: Daphnis Discovers Dhloe (M. 310), 1960,* s., #34/60, full margins, good cond., light-stain, (05-13-93, Sotheby-NY, #509, illus.), 16¾ x 12⅝ in., (425 x 320 mm.), lithograph in colors (BP 8305, DM 20,426, FR 68,900, Y 1,412,303).

BI *Daphnis And Chloe: Dryas Discovers Chloe (M. 310), 1961,* s., #11/60, pub. Editions Verve, margins, good cond., rubbed areas, est. BP 7,0/9,000, (12-03-92, Sotheby-London, #232, illus.), sheet 21¼ x 15 in., (540 x 381 mm.), lithograph in colors on Arches.

BI *Daphnis And Chloe: Echo (M. 340), 1960,* s., #52/60, full margins, good cond., skinned spot, glue stains, est.$20/25,000, (05-13-93, Sotheby-NY, #511, illus.), 16⅞ x 25⅜ in., (430 x 645 mm.), lithograph in colors.

BI *Daphnis And Chloe: In The Cave Of The Nymphs (M. 321), 1960,* s., #44/60, full margins, good cond., mat stain, est. $35/45,000, (11-05-92, Sotheby-NY, #123, illus.), 16¾ x 25⅜ in., (427 x 646 mm.), lithograph p. in colors.

BI *Daphnis And Chloe: Lamon Discovers Daphnis (M. 309), 1961,* s., #41/60, pub. Editions Verve, margins, good cond., discoloration,est. BP 8,0/10,000, (12-03-92, Sotheby-London, #236, illus.), sheet 21¼ x 14¾ in., (540 x 375 mm.), lithograph in colors on Arches.

$7150* *Daphnis And Chloe: Little Swallow (M. 319), 1960,* s., #56/60, full margins, good cond., faded, fox mark, (11-05-92, Sotheby-NY, #122A, illus.), 16⅝ x 12½ in., (422 x 319 mm.), lithograph p. in colors (BP 4650, DM 11,308, FR 38,256, Y 877,193).

$5463* *Daphnis And Chloe: Philetas's Orchard (M. 326), 1960,* full sheet, center fold, good cond., creases, (02-11-93, Sotheby-NY, #91, illus.), 16⁹⁄₁₆ x 25 in., (420 x 635 mm.), color lithograph (BP 3855, DM 9049, FR 30,622, Y 658,590).

$6050* *Daphnis And Chloe: Summer Season (M. 337), 1960,* s., #56/60, full margins, good cond., faded, mat stain, glue stains, (11-05-92, Sotheby-NY, #125A, illus.), 16⅝ x 12⅝ in., (423 x 321 mm.), lithograph p. in colors (BP 3935, DM 9568, FR 32,370, Y 742,240).

$29,900* *Daphnis And Chloe: Temple And History Of Bacchus (M. 346), 1960,* s., #56/60, full margins, good cond., light-stain, foxing, glue stains, skinned spots, (05-13-93, Sotheby-NY, #513, illus.), 16¾ x 25½ in., (426 x 647 mm.), lithograph in colors (BP 19,630, DM 48,280, FR 162,854, Y 3,338,171).

BI *Daphnis And Chloe: Temple And History Of Bacchus (M. 346), 1961,* s., #56/60, full margins, good cond., light stain, foxing, glue stains, skinned spots, est. $30/35,000, (11-05-92, Sotheby-NY, #126, illus.), 16¾ x 25½ in., (426 x 647 mm.), lithograph p. in colors.

$9775* *Daphnis And Chloe: The Arrival Of Dionysophanes (M. 344), 1960,* s., #49/60, full margins, good cond., faded, mat/light-stain, glue stain, (05-13-93, Sotheby-NY, #512), 16¾ x 12⅞ in., (425 x 326 mm.), lithograph in colors (BP 6417, DM 15,784, FR 53,241, Y 1,091,325).

BI *Daphnis And Chloe: The Dead Dolphin And The Three Hundred Dracmas (M.338), 1960,* pub. Teriade, good cond., pinhole, skinning, est. $2/2,500, (05-13-93, Sotheby-NY, #510), 16¼ x 12¼ in., (414 x 312 mm.), lithograph in colors.

$12,100* *Daphnis And Chloe: The Meal At Dryas's House (M. 334), 1960,* s., #10/60, full margins, good cond., mat/light stain, creases, soldafter sale, (11-05-92, Sotheby-NY, #125, illus.), 17¾ x 25½ in., (450 x 647 mm.), lithograph p. in colors (BP 7870, DM 19,136, FR 64,741, Y 1,484,480).

$11,084* *Daphnis And Chloe: Winter (M. 333), 1961,* s., #34/60, pub. Editions Verve, good cond., discoloration, (12-03-92, Sotheby-London, #234, illus.), sheet 21¼ x 15 in., (540 x 381 mm.), lithograph in colors on Arches (BP 7150, DM 17,430, FR 59,495, Y 1,379,122).

$14,300* *Daphnis And Lycenion (M. 336), 1961,* from Daphnis and Chloe, s., #40/60, full margins, light/mat staining, glue, very good cond., (11-09-92, Christie-NY, #70, illus.), 16¾ x 12⅞ in., (425 x 327 mm.), colored lithograph on Arches (BP 9455, DM 22,829, FR 77,131, Y 1,774,634).

BI *Daphnis Und Gnathon,* lit., est. SF 3,5/4,500, (03-16-93, Schuler, #3238), 16⁹⁄₁₆ x 12⅝ in., (42 x 32 cm.), color lithograph.

BI *Daphnis and Chloe: The Wolf Pit (M. 312), 1960,* s., #57/60, full margins, good cond., light stain, est. $12/14,000, (11-05-92, Sotheby-NY, #121, illus.), 16⅝ x 12¾ in., (421 x 323 mm.), lithograph p. in colors.

$1626* *David A La Harpe (M. 134), 1956,* La Bible I, (10-09-92, Winterberg, #1848, illus.), 13¹⁵⁄₁₆ x 10⁵⁄₁₆ in., (35.5 x 26.2 cm.), color lithograph on wove (BP 965, DM 2415, FR 8110, Y 197,955).

$3300* *David And Bathsheba (M. 936), 1979,* s., #35/50, pub. blindstamp, Mourlot, full margins, good cond., mat stain, (11-05-92, Sotheby-NY, #138), 13¾ x 11¾ in., (350 x 300 mm.), lithograph p. in colors on japon nacre (BP 2146, DM 5219, FR 17,657, Y 404,858).

$2741* *David Devant Saul (Sorlier 261),* from La Bible (1931-39), #74/100, folio, sig., (05-20-93, Finarte-Milan, #44, illus.), 21¼ x 15⅜ in., (54 x 39 cm.), etching w/hand-coloring (BP 1759, DM 4422, FR 14,897, Y 302,672, L 4025).

$660* *"David Devant Saul"* and *"Larc En Ceil": Two, 1931-39,* from the Bible Series, very good cond., tape, annot. verso, (09-11-92, Skinner, #38M, illus.), 12 x 9⅛ in., (30.5 x 23.2 cm.), etching on wove (BP 341, DM 950, FR 3229, Y 81,774).

$25,737* *David Et Bethsabee (C. 295), 1975,* s., good cond., (06-30-93, Sotheby-London, #412, illus.), 27 x 20⅞ in., (686 x 530 mm.), color monotype on wove (BP 17,250, DM 43,897, FR 148,084, Y 2,757,634).

$825* *"David",* s., num. 49/150, (09-21-92, Selkirk, #185.1), sheet 11⅞ x 9⅝ in., (30.2 x 24.4 cm.), lithograph in colors (BP 483, DM 1224, FR 4188, Y 101,965).

BI *Day-Break (M. 1014), 1983,* s., num. 38/50, full margins, very good cond., stray pencil marks, light-staining, est. $5/7,000, (02-24-93, Butterfield, #2728, illus.), 13¾ x 10¾ in., (349 x 273 mm.), lithograph in colors on Arches wove.

$267* *Derrier Le Miroir No. 147 (M. 410-412), 1964,* pub. Galerie Maeght, good cond., (11-30-92, Phillips-London, #402B), sheet 15 x 23 in., (381 x 584 mm.), album containing 1 double page & 1 single page lithograph in blk, w/lithographic cover (BP 176, DM 425, FR 1444, Y 33,230).

$250* *Derrier Le Miroir, No. 147 (M. 410-412), 1964,* pub. Galerie Maeght, album, (11-30-92, Phillips-London, #403), sheet 15 x 23 in., (381 x 584 mm.), 1 double page & 1 single page lithograph w/lithographic cover (BP 165, DM 398, FR 1352, Y 31,114).

$110* *Derriere Le Miroir,* s. Marc Chagall, (06-26-93, Wolf, #972), 15 x 11 in., (38.1 x 27.9 cm.), color poster (BP 74, DM 187, FR 630, Y 11,671).

BI *Derriere Le Miroir (Mourlot 93-103), 1954: Nine,* Editions Pierre a Feu-A. Maeght, vols. 66-8, s., d., i. H.C., bound,offsetting, very good cond., est. $15/18,000, (11-09-92, Christie-NY, #66, illus.), 15½ x 11⁷⁄₁₆ in., (394 x 290 mm.), color lithograph, 2 in black on Arches.

$200* *Derriere Le Miroir No. 182 (M. 603A, 605),* good cond., (11-30-92, Phillips-London, #403A), sheet 15 x 21⅞ in., (381 x 556 mm.), album containing double page lithograph & lithographic cover, both p.in colors (BP 132, DM 319, FR 1082, Y 24,891).

BI *Derriere Le Miroir No. 198 (M. 649-651),* pub. Maeght, album, very good cond., est. BP 250/350, (11-30-92, Phillips-London, #404), sheet 15 x 23 in., (381 x 584 mm.), 1 double page lithograph & 1 single page color lithograph w/lithographic cover.

BI *Derriere Le Miroir Nos. 99-100 (M. 175-179, 204, 206),* good cond., est. BP 5/700, (11-30-92, Phillips-London, #402A), sheet 15 x 22 in., (381 x 559 mm.), album containing 2 double page lithographs & lithographic cover, in colors, 1 page in colors, 3 in blk & white.

$165* *"Derriere Le Miroir"* and *From Mouriot, Paris, June 1962, #356: Five,* "The Bay" Ed 75 #132 "The Trap" cover June 1964, (02-27-93, Dunning, #1179), 14¹⁵⁄₁₆ x 22¹¹⁄₁₆ in., (37.9 x 57.6 cm.), 11¹⁄₃₂ x 14¹⁵⁄₁₆ in., (37.9 x 57.6 cm.), color lithograph (BP 116, DM 271, FR 922, Y 19,478).

$167* *Derriere Le Miroir, No. 225 (M. 917),* good cond., (11-30-92, Phillips-London, #405), sheet 15 x 22 in., (381 x 559 mm.), album containing 1 double page lithograph in blue and black on wove (BP 110, DM 266, FR 903, Y 20,784).

$300* *Derriere Le Miroir, No. 235 (M. 945) (M. 946), 1979,* pub. Maeght, very good cond., (11-30-92, Phillips-London, #406), sheet 18⅛ x 22¾ in., (460 x 578 mm.), album containing 1 double page lithograph in colors & lithographic cover (BP 198, DM 478, FR 1622, Y 37,337).

$142* *Derriere Le Miroir, No. 246 (M. 992),* good cond., (11-30-92, Phillips-London, #407), sheet 15 x 22 in., (381 x 559 mm.), double page lithograph in blue, yellow & black on wove (BP 94, DM 226, FR 768, Y 17,673).

$2215* *Dessins Pour La Bible (II), (Mourlot 230-277, Verve 37-38),* (11-07-92, Falkkloos, #83), book w/24 lithographs

(BP 1448, DM 3554, FR 11,954, Y 273,389, SK 13,200).

$4329* *Dessins Pour La Bible (M. 230-277), 1960,* Editions De La Revue Verve, 1960, t., text w/reproductive plates and-set of 48, discoloration, good cond., scuffing, (12-01-92, Christie-London, #330), overall sheet 14⅛ x 10⁹⁄₁₆ in., (359 x 268 mm.), lithograph on wove (BP 2860, DM 6900, FR 23,514, Y 538,969).

BI *Dessins Pour La Bible (M. 230-80): Set of Twenty-Four, 1960,* Editions Verve, Vol. X, nos. 37-8, i., full sheets, very good cond.,original ink drawing on t. page, bound, est. $6/7,000, (11-09-92, Christie-NY, #67, illus.), 14³⁄₁₆ x 10⅝ in., (360 x 270 mm.), lithographs in colors, 24 lithographs in black, 96 reprod..

$3531* *Dessins Pour La Bible (Mourlot 230-277), 1958-59: Twenty-Four,* (06-10-93, Hauswedell/Nolt, #158), book format 14³⁄₁₆ x 10⅝ in., (36 x 27 cm.), color lithograph (BP 2310, DM 5750, FR 19,359, Y 374,801).

$4688* *Dessins Pour La Bible (Mourlot Band II 230-277): Twenty-Five,* Paris, Editions de la Revue Verve X, Nos. 37-38, 1960, (11-21-92, Lempertz, #76), 14³⁄₁₆ x 10⅝ in., (36 x 27 cm.), color lithograph (BP 3087, DM 7474, FR 25,177, Y 583,012).

$4830* *Dessins Pour La Bible, Paris Editions Verve, Vol X, Nos. 37-8, 1960 (M. 230-80),* i. Pour Myriam Freund Cordialement Marc Chagall, Reims 1961, very good cond., orig. ink drawing on t. page, bound, orig. lithographic boards, (05-11-93, Christie-NY, #157), 14³⁄₁₆ x 10⅝ in., (360 x 270 mm.), 24 color lithographs, 26 lithographs in black, 96 reprods., t., just. and text, on wove (BP 3083, DM 7609, FR 25,637, Y 531,295).

$3680* *Dessins Pour La Bible, Paris, Editions Verve, Vol. X, Nos. 37-8, 1960 (M. 230-80),* very good cond., orig. lithographic boards, (05-11-93, Christie-NY, #158), 14³⁄₁₆ x 10⅝ in., (360 x 270 mm.), 24 color lithographs, 26 lithographs in black, 96 reprods., t., just. and text, on wove (BP 2349, DM 5797, FR 19,533, Y 404,796).

$3634* *Dessins Pour La Bible. Verve Nos 37-38 (Mourlot 230 bis 280), 1960: Twenty-Four,* (04-21-93, Germann, #322, illus.), color lithograph (BP 2358, DM 5809, FR 19,643, Y 402,303, SF 5290).

BI *"Les Deux Mulets", "Le Renard Et Le Buste" and "Le Chien Qui Porte Aon Cou Le Dine De Son Maitre", 1927-30: Three,* plates 3, 46, and 81 of Les Fables de la Fontaine, pub. Vollard, 1952, full margins, good cond., foxing, skinned spots, printer's creases, one intoimage, est. $2/3,000, (02-11-93, Sotheby-NY, #82), 2 etchings on Montval, last etching on Japan.

$395* *Devant Le Village (Nach Einer Gouache), #B 138/250,* (06-24-93, Germann, #274), 33⁷⁄₁₆ x 24⁷⁄₁₆ in., (850 x 620 mm.), color lithograph (BP 260, DM 640, FR 2158, Y 42,373, SF 575).

$138* *"Les Devinereses",* from Lafontaine Fables series, plate s., (12-02-92, Boos, #505), image 11⅝ x 9⅜ in., (295 x 238 mm.), etching (BP 89, DM 217, FR 741, Y 17,171).

$5993* *Le Dimanche (M. 98), 1954,* s., #34/75, pub. Derriere le Miroir, margins, light-stained, (12-01-92, Christie-London, #327, illus.), sheet 15⁹⁄₁₆ x 11⅛ in., (396 x 283 mm.), lithograph in colors on wove (BP 3960, DM 9552, FR 32,553, Y 746,140).

$3850* *Drawings For The Bible (M. 230-277),* book, Nos. 37-38 of Verve, pub. Harcourt, Brace and Company, 1960, good cond., (11-05-92, Sotheby-NY, #120), 24 lithographs p. in colors, 23 lithographic vignettes p. in black, and lithographic cover p. in colors (BP 2504, DM 6089, FR 20,599, Y 472,335).

$3088* *Drawings For The Bible (M. 230-280), 1960,* book, Verve Nos. 37-38, English edit., pub. Verve, good cond., folio, (06-30-93, Sotheby-London, #396), 24 color lithographs, plus lithographic cover and 96 reprods. in black (BP 2070, DM 5267, FR 17,768, Y 330,869).

BI *Drawings For The Bible (Mourlot 230-277), 1958-59: Twenty-Four,* est. DM 8000, (06-10-93, Hauswedell/Nolt, #160), book format 14³⁄₁₆ x 10⅝ in., (36 x 27 cm.), color lithograph.

$3531* *Drawings For The Bible (Mourlot 230-277), 1958-59: Twenty-Four,* (06-10-93, Hauswedell/Nolt, #159), book format 14³⁄₁₆ x 10⅝ in., (36 x 27 cm.), color lithograph (BP 2310, DM 5750, FR 19,359, Y 374,801).

$3114* *Drawings For The Bible II (X:37-38, M. 230-277), 1960,* (05-12-93, AB Stockholm, #7015), lithographs in color (BP 2033, DM 5024, FR 16,924, Y 347,661, SK 23,100).

$6177* *The Easel (M. 561), 1969,* s., i. epreuve d'artiste xviii/xxv, full margins, good cond., light/backboard-staining, (06-30-93, Sotheby-London, #403, illus.), 21¼ x 19 in., (540 x 483 mm.), color lithograph on wove (BP 4140, DM 10,536, FR 35,541, Y 661,845).

$3581* *Ecuyere A L'Oiseau (M. 209), 1959,* s., #16/40, good cond., hinge remains, (12-03-92, Sotheby-London, #235), sheet 25¾ x 19⅞ in., (654 x 505 mm.), lithograph on Arches (BP 2310, DM 5631, FR 19,222, Y 445,564).

$846* *Die Eiche Und Das Schilfrohr,* sheet 12 of series, 1927, 1930, 1952, s., (05-26-93, Lempertz, #53), approx. 16⁹⁄₁₆ x 13³⁄₁₆ in., (42 x 33.5 cm.), etching on wide Montval handmade (BP 547, DM 1380, FR 4646, Y 91,917).

$7080* *Eiffel Tower With Donkey (Mourlot 97), 1954,* s., num. 16/75, full sheet, good cond., skinned spot, foxing, (10-14-92, Sotheby-Japan, #10, illus.), sheet 15½ x 11 in., (394 x 279 mm.), colored lithograph (BP 4156, DM 10,361, FR 35,136, Y 857,974).

BI *Eiffelturm (Kornfeld 85a), 1943,* s., watermark, est. DM 12,000, (12-05-92, Bassenge, #7080, illus.), 10¹³⁄₁₆ x 7⅞ in., (27.4 x 20 cm.), etching.

$7820* *The Enchanters (M. 569), 1969,* s., #31/50, wide margins, good cond., (05-11-93, Christie-NY, #167, illus.), borderline 22¼ x 15 in., (565 x 381 mm.), color lithograph on Arches (BP 4992, DM 12,319, FR 41,507, Y 860,191).

$5060* *"The Enchanters", XXIII/XXV,* s. Marc Chagall, (04-23-93, Clearing House, #254, illus.), 15 x 22 in., (38.1 x 55.9 cm.), colored lithograph (BP 3215, DM 8005, FR 27,030, Y 558,869).

$5457* *Les Enchanteurs (M. 569), 1969,* s., #30/50, full margins, good cond., discoloration, (12-03-92, Sotheby-London, #245, illus.), 22¼ x 15 in., (565 x 381 mm.), lithograph in colors on Arches (BP 3520, DM 8582, FR 29,291, Y 678,985).

$357* *The End Of Absalom (Vollard 268), 1956,* plate 72, full margins, (12-08-92, Swann, #60), 12⅜ x 9½ in., (31.4 x 24.1 cm.), etching on wove watermarked paper (BP 224, DM 556, FR 1895, Y 44,249).

$3330* *Die Erscheinung I (K. 44), 1924-5,* 3rd (final) state, s., #22/100, wide margins, i., mount-staining, good cond., (12-01-92, Christie-London, #324, illus.), plate 14¾ x 10¹¹⁄₁₆ in., (375 x 272 mm.), etching w/aquatint on Arches (BP 2200, DM 5308, FR 18,088, Y 414,592).

$916* *Die Ertrunkene Frau,* sheet 39 of series, (05-26-93, Lempertz, #56), approx. 16⁹⁄₁₆ x 13³⁄₁₆ in., (42 x 33.5 cm.), etching on wide Montval handmade (BP 593, DM 1495, FR 5030, Y 99,522).

BI *Evening Mood,* stone s., est. SF 240/280, (10-14-92, Germann, #238), 30½ x 23⁹⁄₁₆ in., (775 x 598 mm.), color lithograph.

BI *Exodus,* est. $2/250, (02-14-93, Hanzel, #669), 14¾ x 11 in., (37.5 x 27.9 cm.), lithograph.

BI *Exodus,* est. $2/300, (11-01-92, Hanzel, #238), 14¾ x 11 in., (37.5 x 27.9 cm.), lithograph.

$1947* *F. Mourlot, Chagall Lithograph I (Mourlot Band II 281-292), 1960: Twelve,* Andre Sauret, Monte Carlo(11-21-92, Lempertz, #79), 12¹³⁄₁₆ x 9¹³⁄₁₆ in., (32.5 x 25 cm.), lithograph (BP 1282, DM 3104, FR 10,456, Y 242,134).

$1298* *F. Mourlot, Chagall Lithographe II (Mourlot/Sorlier Band III 391-402), 1963: Twelve,* Andre Sauret, Monte Carlo, (11-21-92, Lempertz, #80), lithographs, 7 in color (BP 855, DM 2070, FR 6971, Y 161,423).

BI *F. Mourlot/Ch. Sorlier, Chagall Lithographe I-IV (Mourlot Band II, Mourlot/Sorlier Band III, Band IV and Sorlier Band V 281-292, 391-402, 571, 729 and 730), 1960-84: Twenty-Six,* Andre Sauret, Monte Carlo, est. DM 7,000-, (11-21-92, Lempertz, #81), lithographs, 19 in color.

$1235* *"Les Fabes De La Fontaine": Four,* s. in plate, (10-14-92, Germann, #251), 11¹³⁄₁₆ x 15⅜ in., (300 x 390 mm.), etching (BP 725, DM 1807, FR 6129, Y 149,661, SF 1610).

$11,836* *La Fable De Syringe (Mourl. 332), 1961,* s., num., (06-23-93, Kornfeld, #253, illus.), color lithograph on wove

(BP 8041, DM 20,027, FR 67,365, Y 1,289,465, SF 17,825).

$3330* *Les Fables De La Fontaine (cf. Johnson 174), 1927: Eight,* pub. A. Vollard, margins, light-staining, mount-staining, dirt, defects, (12-01-92, Christie-London, #325, illus.), plate 11¾ x 9⁷⁄₁₆ in., (298 x 240 mm.), etching on Montval laid (BP 2200, DM 5308, FR 18,088, Y 414,592).

$1059* *"Les Fables De La Fontaine": Four,* s. in plate, (10-14-92, Germann, #252), 11¹³⁄₁₆ x 15⅜ in., (300 x 390 mm.), etching (BP 622, DM 1550, FR 5256, Y 128,333, SF 1380).

$660* *Les Fables De La Fontaine: L'Aigle, La Laie Et La Chatte (V. 125), 1930,* plate s., pub. Ambroise Vollard, 1952, margins, good cond., mat staining, foxing, hinged to overmat, skinned areas, notations, surface soiling, (10-28-92, Butterfield, #2793), 11⅝ x 9⅜ in., (295 x 238 mm.), etching on heavy wove (BP 421, DM 1019, FR 3461, Y 80,982).

$1100* *Les Fables De La Fontaine: L'Alouette Et Ses Petits Avec Le Maitre D'Un Champs (V. 141), 1930,* s., num. 51, pub. Ambroise Vollard, margins, good cond., light-staining, tape remains, surface soiling, (10-28-92, Butterfield, #2794), 11⅞ x 9½ in., (302 x 241 mm.), etching on laid paper (BP 701, DM 1699, FR 5768, Y 134,969).

$330* *Les Fables De La Fontaine: Le Meunier, Son Fils Et L'Ane (V. 121), 1930,* pub. Ambroise Vollard, 1952, margins, good cond., glue & tape remains, mat & time staining, pencil notations, foxing, surface soiling, (02-24-93, Butterfield, #2905), 11¾ x 9⅔ in., (298 x 246 mm.), etching on wove (BP 230, DM 536, FR 1816, Y 38,723).

BI *Les Fables De La Fontaine: Le Meunier, Son Fils Et L'Ane (V. 121), 1930,* plate s., pub. Ambroise Bollard, 1952, margins, good cond., glue/tape remains, mat/time staining, hinged to overmat, notations, foxing, surface soiling, est. $6/800, (10-28-92, Butterfield, #2792), 11¾ x 9⅔ in., (298 x 246 mm.), etching on wove.

$688* *Fables Of Fontaine (Woman And Horse In A Landscape),* s., annot. '76, label verso, (11-12-92, Freemn/Fine Art, #47), 11⅝ x 9⅜ in., (29.5 x 23.8 cm.), etching (BP 452, DM 1090, FR 3677, Y 85,307).

$2200* *"The Face Of Israel" (Mourlot, Volume II, 231),* s., num. 8/50, prov., (08-05-92, Boos, #690, illus.), image 14⁹⁄₁₆ x 10⅝ in., (360 x 270 mm.), paper 20¹¹⁄₁₆ x 14¹⁵⁄₁₆ in., (360 x 270 mm.), color lithograph on Arches (BP 1150, DM 3250, FR 10,978, Y 280,183).

$5827* *Fairy Roses (M. 725), 1974,* s., #16/50, margins, mount-staining, creasing, laid, very good cond., (12-01-92, Christie-London, #338, illus.), L. 12⅝ x 9¹³⁄₁₆ in., (320 x 250 mm.), lithograph in colors on Japon nacre (BP 3850, DM 9288, FR 31,651, Y 725,473).

$4830* *Familiar Dream (M. 582), 1969,* s., #32/50, full margins, light-staining, good cond., (05-11-93, Christie-NY, #169, illus.), borderline 25⅝ x 19⅝ in., (651 x 498 mm.), color lithograph on Arches (BP 3083, DM 7609, FR 25,637, Y 531,295).

$6966* *Famille D'Harlequin (Mourlot Bd. III, 430), 1965,* #19/50, s., (11-13-92, Koller, #5283), 26½ x 20¹⁄₁₆ in., (67.3 x 51 cm.), lithograph on Rives wove (BP 4501, DM 10,936, FR 36,877, Y 864,590, SF 9860).

$5750* *Family With Cock (M. 567), 1969,* s., #7/50, full margins, good cond., verso, tape stain, (02-11-93, Sotheby-NY, #94, illus.), 23¹¹⁄₁₆ x 15⅞ in., (602 x 403 mm.), color lithograph (BP 4057, DM 9525, FR 32,231, Y 693,189).

$7475* *Family With Cock (M. 567), 1969,* s., i. Epreuve d'artiste IX/XXV, full margins, good cond., mat/light-stain, crease, (05-13-93, Sotheby-NY, #517, illus.), 28⅛ x 15¾ in., (713 x 400 mm.), lithograph in colors (BP 4907, DM 12,070, FR 40,714, Y 834,543).

$8740* *Fantastic Composition (M. 896), 1976,* s., #47/50, full margins, creasing, very good cond., (05-11-93, Christie-NY, #175, illus.), borderline 25 x 18⅞ in., (635 x 479 mm.), color lithograph on Arches (BP 5579, DM 13,768, FR 46,391, Y 961,390).

BI *Fantastic Composition (M. 896a), 1976,* s., #37/50, pub. Maeght, full margins, good cond., foxing, creases, light-staining, notations, est. $15/20,000, (05-19-93, Butterfield, #1895, illus.), sh. 33⅛ x 24¾ in., (841 x 629 mm.), lithograph in colors on Arches.

$2255* *"Die Farse, Die Ziege Und Das Schaf, In Genossenschaft Mit Dem Lowen",* sheet 4 of series, 1927, 1930, 1952, s., (05-26-93, Lempertz, #51), approx. 16⁹⁄₁₆ x 13³⁄₁₆ in., (42 x 33.5 cm.), etching on wide Montval handmade (BP 1459, DM 3679, FR 12,383, Y 245,002).

$619* *"La Femme Moineau", "Grigori Va Toujours" and "On Nettoie Les Pantalons" (Sorlier 56, 58, 69): Three,* s. in plate, 63/335, (06-28-93, Loudmer, #208), 11 x 8¹¹⁄₁₆ in., (280 x 220 mm.), sh 14¹⁵⁄₁₆ x 11 in., (280 x 220 mm.), black etchings on MBM wove (BP 414, DM 1052, FR 3543, Y 65,676).

$9163* *Femme Pres De La Fenetre (Sorlier-Mourl. 420), 1964,* s., i. H.C., (06-23-93, Kornfeld, #255), color lithograph (BP 6225, DM 15,504, FR 52,151, Y 998,257, SF 13,800).

$2490* *La Fenetre De L'Atelier A St. Paul, 1968,* s., num., Edition Cramer, Genf., (12-01-92, Karl/Faber, #445, illus.), 6½ x 5⅞ in., (16.5 x 15 cm.), etching (BP 1645, DM 3969, FR 13,525, Y 310,010).

$3680* *Fernand Mourlot And Charles Sorlier, The Lithographs Of Marc Chagall(I-VI), Monte Carlo, Boston And New York, Andre Sauret, Crown Publishers, Inc., Boston Book And Art Shop, Inc., 1960-86,* bound, excell. cond., (05-11-93, Christie-NY, #178), each 12¹⁵⁄₁₆ x 9¹³⁄₁₆ in., (330 x 250 mm.), 21 color lithographs, 7 lithographs in black, reprods. of artist's lithographs and text (BP 2349, DM 5797, FR 19,533, Y 404,796).

$1554* *Fernand Mourlot. Chagall Lithographe (Mourlot 281-292), 1960: Eleven,* pub. A. Sauret, (06-10-93, Hauswedell/Nolt, #161), book format 12¹³⁄₁₆ x 9¹³⁄₁₆ in., (32.5 x 25 cm.), lithograph (BP 1016, DM 2531, FR 8520, Y 164,951).

$1738* *Fernand Mourlot. Lithograph I (Mourlot 281-292): Twelve,* Sauret 1960, (04-21-93, Germann, #331), lithograph (BP 1128, DM 2778, FR 9395, Y 192,406, SF 2530).

$1185* *Fernand Mourlot. Lithograph II (Mourlot 391-402), 1957-1962: Twelve,* Sauret 1963, (04-21-93, Germann, #328), lithograph (BP 769, DM 1894, FR 6405, Y 131,186, SF 1725).

$3178* *Fernand Mourlot/Charles Sorlier. Chagall Lithographe (Mourlot 281-292, 391-402, 577, 578, 729 u. 730), 1960-74: Twenty-Four,* pub. A. Sauret, (06-10-93, Hauswedell/Nolt, #163), book format 12¹³⁄₁₆ x 9¹³⁄₁₆ in., (32.5 x 25 cm.), lithograph (BP 2079, DM 5175, FR 17,423, Y 337,331).

$1935* *La Fete Au Village (C. 66), 1979,* epreuve d'artiste, s., (10-09-92, Winterberg, #1833, illus.), 12⁷⁄₁₆ x 22¹⁄₁₆ in., (31.6 x 56 cm.), etching on wove (BP 1148, DM 2874, FR 9651, Y 235,573).

$6109* *Fleurs Devant La Fenetre (Sorl.-Mourl. 478), 1967,* s., i. H.C., (06-23-93, Kornfeld, #259), color lithograph (BP 4150, DM 10,337, FR 34,769, Y 665,541, SF 9200).

BI *Les Fleurs Rouges (S./M. 705), 1973,* s., epreuve d'artiste, prov., est. DM 40/45,000, (12-01-92, Karl/Faber, #442, illus.), 23⅝ x 16¹⁵⁄₁₆ in., (60 x 43 cm.), color lithograph on wove.

$3774* *La Flute Enchantee "Die Zauberflote, Mozart, Metropolitan Opera", 1967,* Charles Sorlier, 106/107, (05-25-93, AB Stockholm, #11), 39⅜ x 25⅜ in., (100 x 64.5 cm.), poster, lithograph in colors (BP 2446, DM 6147, FR 20,691, Y 412,504, SK 5500).

$1023* *La Fontaine Fables: Le Cure Et Le Mort, c. 1930,* s., #86/100, pub. Teriade, full margins, good cond., (12-03-92, Sotheby-London, #222), 11½ x 9½ in., (292 x 241 mm.), etching on laid (BP 660, DM 1609, FR 5491, Y 127,286).

BI *La Fontaine. Fables. Eaux-Fortes Originales De Marc Chagall, 1952:One Hundred,* s., num., est. DM 140,000, (05-26-93, Lempertz, #66, illus.), each approx. 16⁹⁄₁₆ x 13³⁄₁₆ in., (42 x 33.5 cm.), etching on wide handmade.

$671* *La Fortune Et Le Jeune Enfant, 1927-1930,* s., (06-10-93, Hauswedell/Nolt, #131), image 11⅝ x 9⁷⁄₁₆ in., (29.6 x 24 cm.), etching on hand-made Maillol (BP 439, DM 1093, FR 3679, Y 71,224).

BI *The Four Seasons (M. 727; S.p. 62), 1974,* p. Mourlot, pub. editions of The First National Bank of Chicago, margins, good cond., canvas-backed, est. BP 5/700, (12-

01-92, Christie-London, #339), L. 35⅝ x 23⅝ in., (905 x 600 mm.), lithograph in colors on wove.

$220* *Four Seasons, Chicago, 1974,* (02-14-93, Hanzel, #698), 35 x 23 in., (88.9 x 58.4 cm.), lithographic poster (BP 155, DM 365, FR 1235, Y 26,532).

$18,700* *Four Tales From The Arabian Nights: Disrobing Her With His Own Hand... (M. 39), 1948,* s., annot. Pl. 4, #42/90, pub. Pantheon Books, full margins, very good cond., discoloration, hinge remains, foxing, (10-28-92, Butterfield, #2618, illus.), image 14¾ x 11⅛ in., (375 x 283 mm.), sheet 17 x 13 in., (375 x 283 mm.), color lithograph on laid paper (BP 11,915, DM 28,880, FR 98,060, Y 2,294,479).

$15,525* *Four Tales From The Arabian Nights: Disrobing Her With His Own Hand... (Mourlot 39), 1948,* s., i. Pl. 4, #89/90, p. Albert Carman, pub. Pantheon Books, full margins, good cond., light-stain, crease, tape stain, foxing, (05-13-93, Sotheby-NY, #499, illus.), 14¾ x 11⅛ in., (373 x 283 mm.), lithograph in colors (BP 10,192, DM 25,069, FR 84,559, Y 1,733,281).

$12,650* *Four Tales From The Arabian Nights: Mounting The Ebony Horse... (M. 47), 1948,* s., i. w/plate num., #21/90, p. Albert Carman, pub. Pantheon Books, margins, good cond., traces glue, (05-13-93, Sotheby-NY, #502, illus.), 14⅞ x 11¼ in., (377 x 287 mm.), sh 19⅝ x 12⅞ in., (377 x 287 mm.), lithograph in colors (BP 8305, DM 20,426, FR 68,900, Y 1,412,303).

$6821* *Four Tales From The Arabian Nights: So I Came Forth Of The Sea And Sat Down On The Edge Of An Island In The Moonshine...(M. 40), 1948,* s., i. Pl. 5, #76/90, pub. Pantheon Books, margins, good cond., lightstaining, foxing, masking tape, (12-03-92, Sotheby-London, #224, illus.), sheet 17 x 13 in., (432 x 330 mm.), lithograph in colors (BP 4400, DM 10,727, FR 36,613, Y 848,700).

$7721* *Four Tales From The Arabian Nights: So I Came Forth Of The Sea And Sat Down On The Edge Of An Island In The Moonshine.... (M. 40), 1948,* s., i. Pl. 5, #57/90, pub. Pantheon Books, margins, good cond., discoloration, (06-30-93, Sotheby-London, #394, illus.), sh 17 x 15 in., (432 x 381 mm.), color lithograph on laid (BP 5175, DM 13,169, FR 44,425, Y 827,280).

$12,789* *Four Tales From The Arabian Nights: So She Came Down From The Tree And Drawing Near Him Strained Him To Her Bosom...(Mourlot 41), 1948,* s., pub. Pantheon Books, margins, good cond., (12-03-92, Sotheby-London, #223, illus.), sheet 16¾ x 13 in., (425 x 330 mm.), lithograph in colors on laid (BP 8250, DM 20,112, FR 68,647, Y 1,591,265).

$13,200* *Four Tales From The Arabian Nights: They Were In Forty Pairs (M. 37), 1948,* s., annot. Pl. 2, #49/90, pub. Pantheon Books, full margins, good cond., printing crease, discoloration, hinge remains, foxing, (10-28-92, Butterfield, #2617, illus.), image 14½ x 11⅛ in., (368 x 283 mm.), sheet 17 x 13 in., (368 x 283 mm.), color lithograph on laid paper (BP 8410, DM 20,386, FR 69,219, Y 1,619,632).

$2875* *Four Tales From The Arabian Nights: When Abdullah Got The Net Ashore... (M. 43), 1948,* proof of the final state, pub. Pantheon Books, full margins, good cond., loss top center, stain, (02-11-93, Sotheby-NY, #88), 14¾ x 11⁹⁄₁₆ in., (374 x 293 mm.), color lithograph (BP 2029, DM 4762, FR 16,115, Y 346,594).

$2875* *Four Tales From The Arabian Nights: When Abdullah Got The Net Ashore...(M. 43), 1948,* proof of final state, p. Albert Carman, pub. Pantheon Books, full margins, good cond., stain, (05-13-93, Sotheby-NY, #500), 14¾ x 11½ in., (376 x 293 mm.), lithograph in colors (BP 1887, DM 4642, FR 15,659, Y 320,978).

$12,075* *Four Tales From The Arabian Nights; He Went Up To The Couch...(M. 46), 1948,* s., i. w/plate num., #40/90, p. Albert Carman, pub. Pantheon Books, margins, good cond., Vitya Vronsky Babin Coll., glue traces, (05-13-93, Sotheby-NY, #501, illus.), 14⅞ x 11¼ in., (377 x 285 mm.), sh 16½ x 12⅞ in., (377 x 285 mm.), lithograph in colors (BP 7927, DM 19,498, FR 65,768, Y 1,348,108).

BI *Die Freude (S. 976), 1980,* s., num., Edition Maeght, tear, est. DM 50/60,000, (12-01-92, Karl/Faber, #444,

illus.), 37⅜ x 24⁷⁄₁₆ in., (95 x 62 cm.), color lithograph on wove.

$489* *From Les Ames Mortes: Dames Charmantes Et Charmentes A Tous Egards (V. 76), 1948,* s. in plate, platetone, margins, good cond., surface soiling, (05-19-93, Butterfield, #2044), 10¹⁵⁄₁₆ x 8⁵⁄₁₆ in., (278 x 211 mm.), etching on Arches (BP 317, DM 795, FR 2678, Y 54,135).

$460* *From Les Ames Mortes: Mort De Mets-Les-Pieds-Dans-Le-Plat (V. 54), 1948,* s. in plate, plate tone, margins, good cond., staining, surface soiling, notations, (05-19-93, Butterfield, #2043), 8¼ x 10¾ in., (210 x 273 mm.), etching on wove (BP 299, DM 748, FR 2519, Y 50,924).

$1100* *From Visions Of Paris (M. 80; 81; 82; 83; 84; 85; 86; 87), 1952: Seven, including "The Seine Bridges", "Vision Of Paris", "Mother And Child Before Notre Dame", "Place De La Concorde", "The Eiffel Tower"...,* pub. in Verve, #27-28, good cond., tear, skinned areas, creases, staining, (02-24-93, Butterfield, #2908), lithograph in colors on wove (BP 767, DM 1786, FR 6054, Y 129,078).

BI *From: De Mauvais Sujets (Kornfeld 108), 1958,* sheet 3 of series, (05-26-93, Lempertz, #70, illus.), 25¾ x 19¹⁵⁄₁₆ in., (65.4 x 50.6 cm.), color lithograph on Japan nacre.

$1057* *Der Fuchs Und Der Ziegenbock,* sheet 31 of series, 1927, 1930, 1952, s., (05-26-93, Lempertz, #55), approx. 16⁹⁄₁₆ x 13³⁄₁₆ in., (42 x 33.5 cm.), etching on wide Montval handmade (BP 684, DM 1725, FR 5805, Y 114,841).

BI *Geburt, Plate 6 Main Leben (K. 6c), 1922,* s., #102/110, pub. P. Cassirer, 1923, margins, tear, mount stain, handling creases, est. BP 900/1,200, (12-01-92, Christie-London, #322), plate 5¹⁄₁₆ x 6¹⁵⁄₁₆ in., (128 x 177 mm.), etching w/drypoint on laid paper.

$1254* *Der Geistliche Und Der Tod, 1927-1930,* s., num., from series for Fables by Lafontaine, (12-05-92, Bassenge, #7078), 11⅝ x 9⁷⁄₁₆ in., (29.5 x 24 cm.), etching on handmade (BP 785, DM 1955, FR 6663, Y 155,371).

BI *Gelber Hintergrund (Sorlier S. 65; Mourlot 602), 1969-1970,* s., d., creases, est. SF 2/2,500, (04-21-93, Germann, #323), 30¹³⁄₁₆ x 22⁷⁄₁₆ in., (782 x 570 mm.), color lithograph.

BI *Die Geschichte Von Dschullanar, Der Meermaid (Mourlot 41), 1945/46,* plate 6 from series Four Tales from the Arabian Nights, Pantheon Edition, 1948, num., s., mount staining, est. DM 50/55,000, (12-01-92, Karl/Faber, #437, illus.), 14⁹⁄₁₆ x 11 in., (37 x 28 cm.), color lithograph on hand-made.

BI *Die Geschichte Von Ebenholzpferd III (M. 46), 1945/46,* s. twice, num., brown stained, mount staining, est. DM 45/50,000, (12-01-92, Karl/Faber, #438, illus.), 14⁹⁄₁₆ x 11 in., (37 x 28 cm.), color lithograph on hand-made.

$1472* *Das Gesicht Israels (Mourlot 231, 236-239, 242-244, 248 u. 250), 1960: Ten,* from Bibel II, (09-19-92, Wachholtz, #140), 13¹⁵⁄₁₆ x 10⁵⁄₁₆ in., (35.5 x 26.2 cm.), color lithograph on wove (BP 862, DM 2184, FR 7472, Y 181,931).

BI *Gogol, Les Ames Mortes (Sorlier, Livre Des Livres P.32, The Artist And The Book 50), 1923-37,* book, in two volumes, s., #288, pub. Teriade, 1948, good cond., foxing, paper discoloration, original wrappers, est. BP 18/22,000, (06-30-93, Sotheby-London, #386, illus.), 96 etchings plus 11 etched init. letters on Arches wove.

$2189* *Grand Autoportrait Noir (M. 740), 1975,* s., 50/50, (12-04-92, AB Stockholm, #7029), 25³⁄₁₆ x 18¹¹⁄₁₆ in., (64 x 47.5 cm.), lithograph (BP 1404, DM 3486, FR 11,826, Y 273,283, SK 14,850).

$326* *Le Grand Bouquet De Fleurs,* s., (10-14-92, Germann, #240), 30¹¹⁄₁₆ x 25 in., (780 x 635 mm.), color offset lithograph (BP 191, DM 477, FR 1618, Y 39,506, SF 425).

$326* *Le Grand Bouquet De Fleurs,* s., (10-14-92, Germann, #247), 28¹¹⁄₁₆ x 25¹⁄₁₆ in., (728 x 637 mm.), color offset lithograph (BP 191, DM 477, FR 1618, Y 39,506, SF 425).

BI *Le Grand Bouquet De Fleurs,* est. SF 280/360, (09-04-92, Germann, #282), 28⁹⁄₁₆ x 25 in., (725 x 635 mm.), color lithograph.

$19,610* *La Grande Corbeille (M. 747), 1975,* s., #23/50, full margins, good cond., handling, creases, (12-03-92, Sotheby-London, #254, illus.), 26⅝ x 21 in., (676 x 533 mm.), lithograph in colors on Arches (BP 12,650, DM 30,838, FR 105,260, Y 2,439,965).

BI *La Grande Corniche (M. 485 BIS), 1967,* s., #45/50, full margins, very good cond.?, est. $18/20,000, (10-28-92, Butterfield, #2620, illus.), 19¼ x 17 in., (489 x 432 mm.), color lithograph on Arches.

$3054* *La Grande Danseuse, 1967,* s., i. E.A., num., (06-23-93, Kornfeld, #267), 13¾ x 9¾ in., (35 x 24.8 cm.), etching on Japan nacre (BP 2075, DM 5168, FR 17,382, Y 332,716, SF 4600).

$43* *The Green Bird (Sorlier p. 40),* p. Mourlot for Editions Maeght, 1962, prov., (12-01-92, Ritchie, #16), 27½ x 21 in., (69.9 x 53.3 cm.), color lithograph (BP 28, DM 69, FR 234, Y 5354, C$ 55).

$3910* *The Green Tree With Lovers (M. 959), 1980,* s., #39/50, pub. Mourlot, full margins, good cond., crease, skinning, (02-11-93, Sotheby-NY, #99), 19¾ x 15³⁄₁₆ in., (502 x 385 mm.), color lithograph (BP 2759, DM 6477, FR 21,917, Y 471,368).

$3080* *Green Tree With Lovers (Mourlot 959), 1980,* s., #37/50, (10-18-92, Hindman, #466, illus.), 19¾ x 15⅛ in., (50.2 x 38.4 cm.), color lithograph (BP 1885, DM 4585, FR 15,548, Y 369,526).

$110* *Les Grenouilles Que Demandent Un Roi (B. 30), 1927,* from La Fontaine Fables, appears good cond., (06-11-93, Doyle, #24), 9⅛ x 11½ in., (232 x 292 mm.), etching and drypoint (BP 72, DM 179, FR 603, Y 11,671).

$2899* *Grey Crucifixion (M. 617), 1970,* s., #47/50, full margins, good cond., colors faded, mount staining, (12-03-92, Sotheby-London, #257), 23⅝ x 17¾ in., (600 x 451 mm.), lithograph in colors on Arches (BP 1870, DM 4559, FR 15,561, Y 360,707).

$7150* *Grey Village (M. 423a), 1964,* s., #27/50, full margins, good cond., light stain, creases, fox marks, skinning, (11-05-92, Sotheby-NY, #128), 26⅞ x 20¼ in., (682 x 515 mm.), lithograph p. in colors (BP 4650, DM 11,308, FR 38,256, Y 877,193).

$253* *Grosser Strauss Mit Erdbeeren,* 91/500, s., (10-14-92, Germann, #248), 35⅜ x 22¹¹⁄₁₆ in., (898 x 576 mm.), color offset lithograph (BP 149, DM 370, FR 1256, Y 30,659, SF 330).

BI *Der Grune Clown, 1979,* from Derriere le Miroir, #235, stone s., (c), est. DM 650, (09-18-92, Schloss Ahlden, #982), 14¹⁵⁄₁₆ x 10⅞ in., (37.9 x 27.6 cm.), color lithograph on white paper.

$310* *Hinter Dem Spiegel (Mourlot 412), 1964,* part of pair from Derriere Le Miroir, center crease, (09-25-92, Granier, #2786, illus.), sheet 15¹⁄₁₆ x 22⅛ in., (38.2 x 56.2 cm.), color lithograph on wove (BP 181, DM 460, FR 1554, Y 37,417).

$2765* *Hommage A Elsa Triolet (Sorlier 642), 1972,* #9/20, s., (04-21-93, Germann, #325, illus.), 25³⁄₁₆ x 19⁵⁄₁₆ in., (640 x 490 mm.), color lithograph (BP 1794, DM 4420, FR 14,946, Y 306,100, SF 4025).

$1364* *Hommage A Marc Chagall, Catalogue Pour L'Exposition Au Grand Palais,1969-70 (M. 595),* book, s., #48/100, num. 48, (12-03-92, Sotheby-London, #247), 9¼ x 8 in., (235 x 203 mm.), lithograph in colors on a double sheet (BP 880, DM 2145, FR 7322, Y 169,715).

$2310* *Hommage To Marc Chagall (Mourlot 572), 1965,* s., #58/75, (03-24-93, Grogan, #116, illus.), 12½ x 9½ in., (31.8 x 24.1 cm.), color lithograph (BP 1564, DM 3773, FR 12,840, Y 271,413).

$500* *How The Women Kept A Secret from La Fables Fontaine, 1952,* full margins, good cond., (11-30-92, Phillips-London, #393), plate 11½ x 9½ in., (292 x 241 mm.), etching on japan (BP 330, DM 797, FR 2704, Y 62,228).

BI *Ile Saint-Louis (M. 225), 1959,* s., #75/75, full margins, good cond., discoloration, creasing withinimage, defects, est. BP 7,0/9,000, (12-03-92, Sotheby-London, #231, illus.), 20 x 26⅛ in., (508 x 664 mm.), lithograph in colors on Arches.

$839* *Illustration Pour Lliazd, Poesie De Mots Inconnus (E. Kornfeld 97), 1949,* whole margins, s., (06-11-93, Picard, #20), 6⅞ x 5⅛ in., (175 x 130 mm.), etching and aquatint in black on Auvergne (BP 551, DM 1364, FR 4597, Y 89,019).

$4125* *Illustrations For The Bible (M. 117-146), 1956,* book, nos. 33-34 of Verve, pub. Verve, good cond., (11-05-92, Sotheby-NY, #117), 16 lithographs p. in colors, 12 p. in black, lithographic cover in colors w/text, 105 reproductions of Bible etchings (BP 2683, DM 6524, FR 22,071, Y 506,073).

$4025* *Illustrations For The Bible (M. 117-146): Sixteen,* book, nos. 33-34 of Verve, French edit., 1956, good cond., slightly worn, spine corners reinforced, (05-13-93, Sotheby-NY, #506), lithograph in colors, 12 in black, plus lithographic cover, t. page p. in colors, w/text, 105 reprods. Bible etchings (BP 2642, DM 6499, FR 21,923, Y 449,369).

BI *Das In Sonne Getauchte Atelier (M. 712), 1974,* s., num., traces glue remains, est. DM 18/20,000, (12-01-92, Karl/Faber, #443, illus.), 17¹¹⁄₁₆ x 13¾ in., (45 x 35 cm.), color lithograph on wove.

BI *In The Land Of The Gods: By The Waters Of Aulis White With Foam...(M.535), 1967,* s., #68/75, full margins, good cond., light/backboard staining, tape,est. BP 2,5/3,000, (12-03-92, Sotheby-London, #248, illus.), 17¾ x 14⅛ in., (451 x 359 mm.), lithograph in colors on Arches.

$3260* *In The Land Of The Gods: By The Waters Of Aulis White With Foam...(M.535), 1967,* s., #68/75, pub. A. C. Mazo, full margins, good cond., light/backboard-staining, tape staining, (06-30-93, Sotheby-London, #399, illus.), 17¾ x 14⅛ in., (451 x 359 mm.), color lithograph on Arches (BP 2185, DM 5560, FR 18,757, Y 349,298).

$6900* *In The Land Of The Gods: For A Woman What Remains...(M. 536), 1967,* s., i., pub. A.C. Mazo, full margins, good cond., hinge stains, glue spots, (05-13-93, Sotheby-NY, #515, illus.), 18⅛ x 15⅜ in., (460 x 390 mm.), lithograph in colors (BP 4530, DM 11,142, FR 37,582, Y 770,347).

$5286* *In The Land Of The Gods: For A Woman, What Remains?... (M. 536), 1967,* s., #68/75, pub. A.C. Mazo, margins, good cond., light/backboard staining, water, tape, (12-03-92, Sotheby-London, #249, illus.), sheet 25½ x 19½ in., (648 x 495 mm.), lithograph in colors on Arches (BP 3410, DM 8313, FR 28,374, Y 657,708).

$17,825* *In The Sky Of The Opera (M. 973), 1980,* s., #15/50, pub. Maeght, full margins, good cond., handling creases, (05-13-93, Sotheby-NY, #523, illus.), 37¾ x 24 in., (960 x 610 mm.), lithograph in colors (BP 11,702, DM 28,782, FR 97,086, Y 1,990,064).

$3524* *Jacob Blessed By Isaac (Sorlier 211),* from La Bible (1931-39), #74/100, folio, sig., (05-20-93, Finarte-Milan, #42, illus.), 21¼ x 15⅜ in., (54 x 39 cm.), etching w/hand-coloring (BP 2262, DM 5686, FR 19,152, Y 389,134, L 5175).

$2432* *Jacob Pleurant Joseph (Sorlier 217),* from the Bible, inits., 90/100, XVIX, (12-04-92, AB Stockholm, #7022), 11⅞ x 9¾ in., (30.2 x 24.7 cm.), hand-colored etching (BP 1560, DM 3873, FR 13,139, Y 303,620, SK 16,500).

$1515* *Jacques Lassaigne, Chagall (Mourlot Band II 192-205 and 207): Fifteen,* Maeght Editeur, 1957, (11-21-92, Lempertz, #74), 9¼ x 8¼ in., (23.5 x 21 cm.), lithograph (BP 997, DM 2415, FR 8136, Y 188,409).

BI *Jacques Lassaigne: Chagall (M. 192-207), 1957,* book, p. Mourlot, pub. Maeght, good cond., bound, split in cover, est. BP 6/800, (06-30-93, Sotheby-London, #390), overall 9⅛ x 11⅞ in., (232 x 302 mm.), 15 lithographs.

$1458* *Jacques Lassaigne: Chagall (M. 192-207), 1957,* book, p. Mourlot, pub. Maeght, good cond., bound, split, (06-30-93, Sotheby-London, #391), overall 9⅛ x 11⅞ in., (232 x 302 mm.), 15 lithograph (BP 977, DM 2487, FR 8389, Y 156,220).

$332* *Jacques Lassaigne: Le Plafond De L'Opera De Paris (Mourolt 434): Seven,* book, Sauret, 1965, (04-21-93, Germann, #329), color lithograph (BP 215, DM 531, FR 1795, Y 36,754, SF 483).

$2213* *Jakob Erkennt Das Kleid Josefs, 1931/55,* mono., num., from Bible, (12-05-92, Bassenge, #7077, illus.), 11⅞ x 9¾ in., (30.1 x 24.7 cm.), handcolored etching on Arches (BP 1386, DM 3450, FR 11,759, Y 274,192).

$13,363* *Le Jardin De Pomone (Sorl.-Mourl. 541), 1968,* s., i. epreuve d'artiste, (06-23-93, Kornfeld, #260), color lithograph (BP 9078, DM 22,611, FR 76,056, Y 1,455,823, SF 20,125).

BI *Jean Leymarie. The Jerusalem Windows (M. 365-366),* book, reproductions, title page and English text, pub. 1962, by AndreSauret, lithographs trimmed and bound, good cond., folio, est. BP 5/700, (12-03-92, Sotheby-London, #239), two lithographs in colors.

$5053* *"Jeremiah" (Mourlot 139), 1956,* s., num., series "Bible", Paris, Revue Verve Nos. 33-34, (11-28-92, Grisebach, #247, illus.), 13 15/16 x 10 3/8 in., (35.5 x 26.3 cm.), color lithograph on thick wove (BP 3335, DM 8050, FR 27,328, Y 628,874).

$4256* *"Jeremias" (Mourlot 139), 1956,* s., num., from folio La Bible, (06-05-93, Grisebach, #365, illus.), 13 15/16 x 10 7/16 in., (35.5 x 26.5 cm.), color lithograph on wove (BP 2802, DM 6900, FR 23,257, Y 456,554).

$3738* *Jerusalem Windows: Tribe Of Gad 1964,* s., #1/150, for album Twelve Maquettes of Stained Glass for Jerusalem, pub. Editions Fernand Mourlot, full margins, good cond., skinned spots, creases, light-staining, soiling, offsetting, (05-19-93, Butterfield, #1898, illus.), 24 7/16 x 18 13/16 in., (621 x 478 mm.), lithograph in colors on Arches (BP 2426, DM 6076, FR 20,471, Y 413,816).

$2483* *"Jesaiah" (Mourlot 141), 1956,* s., sheet 15 of series La Bible, (06-05-93, Grisebach, #544, illus.), 13 7/8 x 10 5/16 in., (35.3 x 26.2 cm.), color lithograph on wove (BP 1635, DM 4026, FR 13,568, Y 266,359).

BI *Jesaias (Mourlot 141),* #48/75, est. DM 10,000, (05-26-93, Lempertz, #69, illus.), sh 14 1/16 x 10 5/8 in., (35.7 x 27 cm.), color lithograph.

$7636* *Le Jeu (Sorl.-Mourl. 436), 1966,* s., i. H.C., (06-23-93, Kornfeld, #257), color lithograph (BP 5188, DM 12,920, FR 43,460, Y 831,899, SF 11,500).

$8324* *Joie De Vivre (M. 472), 1967,* s., #19/50, light-staining, very good cond., (12-01-92, Christie-London, #335, illus.), L. 21 7/16 x 14 3/16 in., (545 x 360 mm.), lithograph in colors on Arches (BP 5500, DM 13,267, FR 45,215, Y 1,036,355).

$2217* *Joshua Before The Armed Angel 1931-39,* pl. 45 from Le Bible, init., #75/100, pub. Teriade 1956, full margins, good cond., crease, tape remains, (12-03-92, Sotheby-London, #221, illus.), 12 5/8 x 8 5/8 in., (321 x 219 mm.), hand colored etching on Arches (BP 1430, DM 3486, FR 11,900, Y 275,849).

$2875* *Josue Arrete Le Soleil, 1931-39,* plate 48 of the Bible, pub. Teriade, 1956, init., #III/V, full margins, good cond., light-stain, glue stain, foxing, (05-13-93, Sotheby-NY, #498), 11 x 9 1/2 in., (280 x 242 mm.), hand-colored etching (BP 1887, DM 4642, FR 15,659, Y 320,978).

$4546* *Le Joueur De Flute, (Mourlot 197), 1957,* #79/90, s., (11-09-92, Finarte-Milan, #41, illus.), 9 13/16 x 16 9/16 in., (25 x 42 cm.), lithograph in colors on Velin d'Arches (BP 3006, DM 7257, FR 24,520, Y 564,160, L 6210).

$805* *Journal D'Un Cheval, 1952,* complete vol., #24, p. Daragnes and Andre Clot, good cond., creases,soiling, surface soiling, (05-19-93, Butterfield, #1890), each sh. 11 7/8 x 9 3/8 in., (302 x 238 mm.), two etchings, four lithographs on Van Gelder (BP 523, DM 1309, FR 4409, Y 89,118).

$19,550* *Joy (M. 976), 1980,* s., #15/50, pub. Maeght, full margins, good cond., (05-13-93, Sotheby-NY, #524, illus.), 37 3/8 x 24 3/8 in., (948 x 620 mm.), lithograph in colors (BP 12,835, DM 31,568, FR 106,481, Y 2,182,650).

$3850* *Joy Of Life (Mourlot 472), 1967,* s., #49/50, (05-24-93, Grogan, #376, illus.), 14 1/2 x 21 1/2 in., (36.8 x 54.6 cm.), color lithograph (BP 2507, DM 6295, FR 21,189, Y 425,555).

$2537* *Das Kind Und Der Schulmeister,* sheet 10 of series, 1927, 1930, 1952, s., (05-26-93, Lempertz, #52), approx. 16 9/16 x 13 3/16 in., (42 x 33.5 cm.), etching on wide Montval handmade (BP 1641, DM 4139, FR 13,932, Y 275,641).

BI *Klagelied Von Jeremias (Mourlot 140),* #44/75, est. DM 14,000, (05-26-93, Lempertz, #68, illus.), sh 14 1/16 x 10 5/8 in., (35.7 x 27 cm.), color lithograph.

$846* *Der Kleine Fisch Und Der Fischer,* sheet 54 of series, 1927, 1930, 1952, s., (05-26-93, Lempertz, #58), approx. 16 9/16 x 13 3/16 in., (42 x 33.5 cm.), etching on wide Montval handmade (BP 547, DM 1380, FR 4646, Y 91,917).

$1960* *"Der Kranke Hirsch", 1927-1930,* series "La Fontaine-Fables", s. Marc Chagall, plate s., (05-19-93, Dorotheum, #435, illus.), plate 11 3/4 x 9 3/8 in., (29.8 x 23.8 cm.), sheet 16 9/16 x 12 15/16 in., (29.8 x 23.8 cm.), etching (BP 1272, DM 3186, FR 10,734, Y 216,982, SC 22,400).

$260* *"L'Acrobate Vert" (M.946),* s. in plate, (04-04-93, Pescheteau, #180), 12 15/16 x 9 1/16 in., (33 x 23 cm.), color lithograph (BP 171, DM 418, FR 1419, Y 29,603).

BI *L'Aigle, La Laie Et La Chatte, 1927-30,* s., stains, light-stains, sheet 32 from La Fontaine, Fables, est. DM2,800-, (11-21-92, Lempertz, #66, illus.), 11 11/16 x 9 7/16 in., (29.7 x 24 cm.), etching on cream hand-made by Montval.

$3734* *L'Alouette Et Ses Petits Avec Le Maitre D'Un Champ, c. 1927-30,* s., (12-01-92, Karl/Faber, #435, illus.), 11 5/8 x 9 7/16 in., (29.5 x 24 cm.), etching (BP 2467, DM 5952, FR 20,282, Y 464,890).

$4597* *L'Ange Au Chandelier (C.S. 46), 1973,* s., 4/200, (05-12-93, AB Stockholm, #7013, illus.), 20 1/2 x 16 15/16 in., (52 x 43 cm.), lithograph in colors on Arches (BP 3002, DM 7417, FR 24,984, Y 513,230, SK 34,100).

$33,458* *L'Animal Aile (C. 234), 1974,* s., good cond., (06-30-93, Sotheby-London, #410, illus.), 26 3/4 x 20 5/8 in., (679 x 524 mm.), color monotype on wove (BP 22,425, DM 57,066, FR 192,509, Y 3,584,914).

BI *L'Arc De Triomphe (M. 87), 1952,* s., #33/75, full margins, good cond., est. BP 800/1,000, (06-30-93, Sotheby-London, #393, illus.), sh 15 x 9 7/8 in., (381 x 251 mm.), lithograph on Arches.

$11,350* *L'Arc-En-Ciel (M. 596), 1969,* s., 63/75, (12-04-92, AB Stockholm, #7028), 27 3/8 x 27 3/16 in., (69.5 x 69 cm.), lithograph in colors (BP 7280, DM 18,076, FR 61,318, Y 1,416,979, SK 77,000).

BI *L'Arc-En-Ciel (Mourlot-Sorlier 596), 1969,* s., #8/75, est. DM 40,000, (06-10-93, Hauswedell/Nolt, #152), image 27 3/8 x 27 3/8 in., (69.5 x 69.5 cm.), color lithograph on Arches paper.

$1887* *L'Artiste Et Themes Bibliques (M. 722), 1974,* s., #15/50, margins, good cond., mount-staining, rubbed spots, skinning, (06-30-93, Sotheby-London, #404), sh 22 x 29 3/8 in., (559 x 746 mm.), color lithograph on Arches (BP 1265, DM 3218, FR 10,857, Y 202,186).

$1483* *L'Artiste Et Themes Bibliques (M. 722), 1974,* s., 7/50, (05-12-93, AB Stockholm, #7010), 14 3/4 x 22 7/16 in., (37.5 x 57 cm.), color lithograph on Arches (BP 968, DM 2393, FR 8060, Y 165,569, SK 11,000).

$3178* *L'Echelle (Mourlot 200), 1957,* s., #84/90, (06-10-93, Hauswedell/Nolt, #146), image 9 7/16 x 7 1/16 in., (24 x 18 cm.), color lithograph on Arches paper (BP 2079, DM 5175, FR 17,423, Y 337,331).

$3818* *L'Ecuyere (Kornf. 72/II/c), 1926-1927,* s., num., (06-23-93, Kornfeld, #263), etching and drypoint on handmade (BP 2594, DM 6460, FR 21,730, Y 415,949, SF 5750).

$258* *L'Ecuyere Au Cheval Rouge (Mourlot 191),* (09-04-92, Germann, #283), 21 1/4 x 16 9/16 in., (540 x 420 mm.), color lithograph (BP 129, DM 362, FR 1231, Y 31,758, SF 322).

$145* *L'Ecuyere Au Cheval Rouge (Mourlot 191), 1957,* (10-14-92, Germann, #237), 21 1/4 x 16 9/16 in., (540 x 420 mm.), color lithograph (BP 85, DM 212, FR 720, Y 17,571, SF 189).

$5727* *L'Homme Au Parapluie (Kornf. 73/I/d), 1926-1927,* s., num., (06-23-93, Kornfeld, #264), strich- and Flachenatzung on handmade (BP 3891, DM 9690, FR 32,595, Y 623,924, SF 8625).

$2917* *L'Homme Au Samovar (Mourlot 4), 1922-23,* proof impression?, pub. Cassirer, full margins, tip, restored, goodcond., (06-30-93, Sotheby-London, #387, illus.), 16 1/8 x 10 1/2 in., (410 x 267 mm.), lithograph on Van Gelder laid paper (BP 1955, DM 4975, FR 16,784, Y 312,547).

$318* *L'Homme Et L'Idole De Bois, 1927-30,* plate s., (06-10-93, Hauswedell/Nolt, #129), image 11 7/8 x 9 7/16 in., (30.2 x 24 cm.), etching on Montval (BP 208, DM 518, FR 1743, Y 33,754).

$2819* *L'Homme Guide Par L'Eternel (Sorlier 295),* from La Bible (1931-39), folio, #74/100, sig., (05-20-93, Finarte-

Milan, #46), 21¼ x 15⅜ in., (54 x 39 cm.), etching w/ hand-coloring (BP 1809, DM 4548, FR 15,321, Y 311,285, L 4140).

$32,399* *L'Odyssee (M. 749-830),* two volume book, pub. 1975, by Mourlot, good cond., orig. wrappers, (12-03-92, Sotheby-London, #252, illus.), each sheet approx. 16¾ x 13 in., (425 x 330 mm.), 43 lithographs in colors, 39 lithographs in grey, in texte on Archeswove (BP 20,900, DM 50,950, FR 173,908, Y 4,031,231).

$1194* *L'Odyssee, Plate 9: Ares Et Aphrodite (M. 772), 1974,* unsigned impression from the book, pub. Mourlot, good cond., skinning, (12-03-92, Sotheby-London, #255, illus.), sheet 16¾ x 12¾ in., (425 x 324 mm.), lithograph in colors (BP 770, DM 1878, FR 6409, Y 148,563).

$777* *L'Oiseau Blesse D'Une Fleche, 1927-1930,* s., zu La Fontaine. Fables, (06-10-93, Hauswedell/Nolt, #127), image 11⅝ x 9¼ in., (29.5 x 23.5 cm.), etching on hand-made (BP 508, DM 1265, FR 4260, Y 82,475).

BI *"L'Oiseau Bleu" (Sorlier S. 114/115), 1954/1968,* by Charles Sorlier after a gouache by Chagall, sig., est. DM 3,5/3,800, (11-28-92, Grisebach, #456, illus.), 22¹/₁₆ x 16¹⁵/₁₆ in., (56 x 43 cm.), colored lithograph on wove.

BI *L'Oiseau Vert (Sorlier 49), 1962,* est. SF 280/320, (10-14-92, Germann, #241), 27⁹/₁₆ x 20⅞ in., (700 x 530 mm.), color lithograph poster.

$839* *"L'Oranger",* proof HC, (04-04-93, Pescheteau, #179), 25⁹/₁₆ x 18½ in., (65 x 47 cm.), original lithograph on wove (BP 553, DM 1348, FR 4580, Y 95,525).

$11,000* *Lamon Discovers Daphinis (M. 309), 1961,* from Daphne And Chloe, s., #40/60, light stain, acid burn, (06-11-93, Doyle, #28, illus.), 16¾ x 11¾ in., (425 x 298 mm.), color lithograph (BP 7227, DM 17,877, FR 60,274, Y 1,167,109).

BI *Landscape With Rooster (M. 208), 1958,* s., #6/100, margins, light/mat staining, surface scrapes, skinning, good cond., est. $8/12,000, (05-11-93, Christie-NY, #156, illus.), borderline 15 x 22¼ in., (381 x 565 mm.), color lithograph on Arches.

BI *"Levis Stamme" and "Benjamins Stamme", (Sorlier 86 and 88): Two,* est. DK 3,500, (09-29-92, B. Rasmussen, #290), posters, lithograph (udfort som Sorlierlithografier i forbindelse medudstillingen af tolv glasmosaikker 1961).

BI *Liebespaar, 1955,* s., d., est. SF 150/250, (10-14-92, Germann, #244), 26⅞ x 23¾ in., (683 x 603 mm.), color offset lithograph.

$92* *Liebespaar, 1955,* image s., d., (09-04-92, Germann, #279), 26⅞ x 23¾ in., (683 x 603 mm.), color offset-lithograph (BP 46, DM 129, FR 439, Y 11,324, SF 115).

$72* *Liegender Akt, 1955,* s., d., (10-14-92, Germann, #246), 28¼ x 23¹¹/₁₆ in., (718 x 601 mm.), color offset lithograph (BP 42, DM 105, FR 357, Y 8725, SF 94).

$4775* *The Light Of The Circus (M. 566), 1969,* s., #21/50, full margins, good cond., (12-03-92, Sotheby-London, #244), 14⅝ x 21½ in., (371 x 546 mm.), lithograph in colors on Arches (BP 3080, DM 7509, FR 25,631, Y 594,127).

BI *The Lithographs Of Marc Chagall [I-VI], 1960-86: Set Of Twenty-One,* Fernand Mourlot and Charles Sorlier, Andre Sauret, Crown Publishers,Inc. and Boston Book and Art Shop, Inc., bound, excellent cond., est. $4,5/ 5,500, (11-09-92, Christie-NY, #81), all 330 x 250 in., (838.2 x 635 cm.), colored lithograph, 7 lithographs in black, reprod..

$4675* *The Lithographs Of Marc Chagall, Volumes I-IV, 1960-74,* catalogues raisonnes, three volumes in English, vol. III in French, pub. Andre Sauret, George Braziller, Boston Book and Art Shop, Inc. and Crown Publishers, Inc., (11-05-92, Sotheby-NY, #141), 28 orig. lithographs, 21 in colors, 7 in b/w (BP 3041, DM 7394, FR 25,013, Y 573,549).

$4400* *The Lithographs Of Marc Chagall, Volumes I-VI, 1960-86,* catalogues raisonnes, pub. Andre Sauret, George Braziller, Boston Book and Art Shop, Inc. and Crown Publishers, Inc., good cond., soiling, (11-05-92, Sotheby-NY, #140), 28 orig. lithographs, 21 in colors, 7 in b/w (BP 2862, DM 6959, FR 23,542, Y 539,811).

$1760* *The Lithographs Of Marc Chagall, Volumes II And IV, 1974,* catalogues raisonnes, pub. Andre Sauret, Boston Book and Art Shop, Inc. and Crown Publishers Inc.,

good cond., (11-05-92, Sotheby-NY, #142), 14 orig. lithographs, 9 in color, 7 in b/w (BP 1145, DM 2783, FR 9417, Y 215,924).

$777* *Le Loup Devenu Berger, 1927-1930,* s., (06-10-93, Hauswedell/Nolt, #128), image 9⁵/₁₆ x 11⅝ in., (23.7 x 29.5 cm.), etching on hand-made Maillol (BP 508, DM 1265, FR 4260, Y 82,475).

$1353* *Le Loup Et L'Agneau Et L'Aigle Et Le Hibou (Sorlier 98 and 155), c. 1927: Two,* s., #5 and 61 from 300, from "Fables de La Fontaine", mat traces verso, good cond., (06-28-93, Loudmer, #207, illus.), approx. 11⁷/₁₆ x 9⅝ in., (290 x 245 mm.), sh 16⁵/₁₆ x 13¼ in., (290 x 245 mm.), black etchings on laid (BP 906, DM 2299, FR 7745, Y 143,554).

$3850* *The Lover's Heaven (M. 393), 1963,* s., #25/40, full margins, good cond., light stain, tape hinge, (11-05-92, Sotheby-NY, #127), 12⅞ x 10⅛ in., (328 x 256 mm.), lithograph p. in colors (BP 2504, DM 6089, FR 20,599, Y 472,335).

$231* *Lovers,* (11-01-92, Hanzel, #219), 9 x 7⅞ in., (22.9 x 20 cm.), lithograph (BP 151, DM 364, FR 1228, Y 28,561).

$303* *Lovers And Ballerinas: Two,* (10-30-92, Sloan, #1598), each 13¾ x 9½ in., (34.9 x 24.1 cm.), color lithograph (BP 194, DM 466, FR 1581, Y 37,533).

$1106* *Der Lowe Und Die Jager, 1927-1930,* s., num., (12-05-92, Bassenge, #7079), 11¹¹/₁₆ x 9⁷/₁₆ in., (29.7 x 24 cm.), etching on handmade (BP 693, DM 1724, FR 5877, Y 137,034).

$2189* *La Lune Noire (M. 438), 1965,* s., 8/50, prov., (12-04-92, AB Stockholm, #7027), 10¹/₁₆ x 12¹⁵/₁₆ in., (25.5 x 33 cm.), lithograph in colors on Arches (BP 1404, DM 3486, FR 11,826, Y 273,283, SK 14,850).

BI *Lune Noire (Mourlot 293), 1959,* artist's proof, s., #34/ 40, full margins, (05-06-93, Laurin, #14, illus.), lithograph on Arches wove.

$4313* *La Lutte De Jacob Et De L'Ange (M. 657), 1972,* s., #17/50, margins, good cond., mat/light-staining, hinge remains, skinned areas, notations, (05-19-93, Butterfield, #1894, illus.), sh. 20¾ x 16 in., (527 x 406 mm.), lithograph in colors on Arches (BP 2800, DM 7011, FR 23,620, Y 477,471).

BI *The Magician Of Paris (Mourlot 597), 1969,* s., num. 49/50, full margins, good cond., est. Y 3,5/4,500,000, (10-14-92, Sotheby-Japan, #12, illus.), 35¼ x 24¾ in., (895 x 629 mm.), color lithograph on Arches wove.

BI *Le Magicien De Paris,* p. Solier, est. DK 1,800, (11-14-92, Bukowskis, #13), lithographic poster.

$194* *Der Maler Und Sein Modell (Mourlot 992), 1981,* from Derriere le Mirrior, center crease, (09-25-92, Granier, #2790), sheet 14¹⁵/₁₆ x 22¹/₁₆ in., (38 x 56 cm.), color lithograph on wove (BP 113, DM 288, FR 972, Y 23,416).

$1410* *Der Mann Und Das Holzerne Gotzenbild,* sheet 42 of series, 1927, 1930, 1952, s., (05-26-93, Lempertz, #57), approx. 16⁹/₁₆ x 13³/₁₆ in., (42 x 33.5 cm.), etching on wide Montval handmade (BP 912, DM 2301, FR 7743, Y 153,194).

BI *Marriage (M. 1017), 1983,* s., num. 38/50, full margins, good cond., skinned areas, stray ink marks, creases, est. $5/7,000, (02-24-93, Butterfield, #2729, illus.), 13⅜ x 10⅛ in., (340 x 257 mm.), lithograph in colors on Arches wove.

$3606* *Le Martyr (Mourlot/Sorlier Band IV 618), 1979,* #48/50, s., stains, (11-21-92, Lempertz, #72, illus.), 26¼ x 20⅜ in., (66.6 x 51.8 cm.), color lithograph on Arches wove (BP 2374, DM 5749, FR 19,366, Y 448,452).

$1100* *Maternite (K. 65/69), 1926: Five,* complete volume, stamp num. 521 on just. page, pub. Au San Pareil, good cond., staining,surface soiling, cover faded, split, (02-24-93, Butterfield, #2725), 8⅜ x 6¼ in., (213 x 159 mm.), five etchings on Lafuma de Voiron, watermakrs (BP 767, DM 1786, FR 6054, Y 129,078).

$5175* *Mein Leben: Der Automobilist (K. 24), 1922,* s., #80/110, pub. Paul Cassirer, full margins, good cond., light-stain, foxing, tape hinges, Late Vitya Vronsky Babin Coll., (05-13-93, Sotheby-NY, #490, illus.), 8¼ x 7 in., (208 x 179 mm.), etching and drypoint (BP 3397, DM 8356, FR 28,186, Y 577,760).

BI *Mein Leben: Der Mann Mit Dem Korb (K. 22), 1922,* s., #107/110, pub. Paul Cassirer, full margins, good cond., mat/light-stain, foxing, Late Vitya Vronsky Babin Coll., est. $2/2,500, (05-13-93, Sotheby-NY, #486), 4¾ x 3⅞ in., (120 x 98 mm.), etching and drypoint.

$6900* *Mein Leben: Der Spaziergang I (K. 26), 1922,* s., #9/110, pub. Paul Cassirer, margins, good cond., printer's crease, mat stain, rubbing, (05-13-93, Sotheby-NY, #491, illus.), 9⅞ x 7⅜ in., (250 x 188 mm.), sh 12¾ x 9 in., (250 x 188 mm.), etching and drypoint on Japan (BP 4530, DM 11,142, FR 37,582, Y 770,347).

$5750* *Mein Leben: Der Talmudlehrer (K. 9), 1922,* s., #44/110, pub. Paul Cassirer, 1923, large margins, good cond., light-stain, foxing, creases through image, creases, tape hinges, Late Vitya Vronsky Babin Coll., (05-13-93, Sotheby-NY, #484, illus.), 9¾ x 7⅜ in., (246 x 188 mm.), etching and drypoint (BP 3775, DM 9285, FR 31,318, Y 641,956).

$4600* *Mein Leben: Der Vater (Kornfeld 1), 1922,* s., #70/110, pub. Paul Cassirer, 1923, margins, good cond., light-stain, tape stains, Late Vitya Vronsky Babin Coll., (05-13-93, Sotheby-NY, #479, illus.), 11 x 8⅝ in., (278 x 218 mm.), sh 13⅝ x 11 in., (278 x 218 mm.), etching and drypoint (BP 3020, DM 7428, FR 25,054, Y 513,565).

$2300* *Mein Leben: Die Grossmutter (K. 4), 1922,* s., #101/110, pub. Paul Cassirer, 1923, full margins, good cond., light-stain, foxing, Late Vitya Vronsky Babin Coll., (05-13-93, Sotheby-NY, #482), 8¼ x 6¼ in., (209 x 160 mm.), etching and drypoint (BP 1510, DM 3714, FR 12,527, Y 256,782).

$4600* *Mein Leben: Die Grossvater (K. 3), 1922,* s., #86/110, pub. Paul Cassirer, 1923, large margins, good cond., light-stain, foxing, tape hinges, Late Vitya Vronsky Babin Coll., (05-13-93, Sotheby-NY, #481, illus.), 11 x 8½ in., (278 x 217 mm.), sh 16½ x 17½ in., (278 x 217 mm.), etching and drypoint (BP 3020, DM 7428, FR 25,054, Y 513,565).

$3738* *Mein Leben: Grab Des Vater (K. 20), 1922,* s., #106/110, pub. Paul Cassirer, 1923, full margins, good cond., mat-stain, foxing, tape hinges, Late Vitya Vronsky Babin Coll., (05-13-93, Sotheby-NY, #489), 4⅜ x 5⅞ in., (110 x 149 mm.), etching and drypoint (BP 2454, DM 6036, FR 20,359, Y 417,327).

$5750* *Mein Leben: Haus In Peskowatik (K. 8), 1922,* s., #109/110, pub. Paul Cassirer, 1923, full margins, good cond., light-stain, foxing, creases, Late Vitya Vronsky Babin Coll., (05-13-93, Sotheby-NY, #483, illus.), 7 x 8¼ in., (178 x 210 mm.), etching and drypoint (BP 3775, DM 9285, FR 31,318, Y 641,956).

$7475* *Mein Leben: Haus In Witebsk (K. 11), 1922,* s., #11/110, pub. Paul Cassirer, 1923, full margins, good cond., crease, (05-13-93, Sotheby-NY, #485, illus.), 7½ x 9⅞ in., (190 x 250 mm.), etching and drypoint (BP 4907, DM 12,070, FR 40,714, Y 834,543).

$3163* *Mein Leben: Liebende Auf Der Bank (K. 15), 1922,* s., #93/110, pub. Paul Cassirer, 1923, full margins, (margins foldedback), good cond., mat stain, Late Vitya Vronsky Babin Coll., (05-13-93, Sotheby-NY, #488), 5⅛ x 7⅛ in., (130 x 180 mm.), etching (BP 2077, DM 5107, FR 17,228, Y 353,132).

$2415* *Mein Leben: Mutter Und Sohn (K. 2), 1922,* s., #102/110, pub. Paul Cassirer, 1923, large margins, good cond., light-stain, foxing, creases, tape hinges, Late Vitya Vronsky Babin Coll., (05-13-93, Sotheby-NY, #480), 11 x 8⅝ in., (278 x 218 mm.), sh 16½ x 13½ in., (278 x 218 mm.), etching and drypoint (BP 1585, DM 3900, FR 13,154, Y 269,622).

$6050* *Mein Leben: Speisezimmer (Kornfeld 10), 1922,* s., #82/110, pub. Paul Cassirer, 1923, good cond., faint mat stain, (11-05-92, Sotheby-NY, #108, illus.), 8⅜ x 10⅞ in., (212 x 275 mm.), sheet 11⅜ x 15 in., (212 x 275 mm.), etching and drypoint (BP 3935, DM 9568, FR 32,370, Y 742,240).

$4600* *Mein Leben: Vor Dem Tore (K. 14), 1922,* s., #93/110, pub. Paul Cassirer, 1923, full margins, good cond., light-stain, foxing, tape hinges, Late Vitya Vronsky Babin Coll., (05-13-93, Sotheby-NY, #487), 8¼ x 6¼ in., (209 x 158 mm.), etching (BP 3020, DM 7428, FR 25,054, Y 513,565).

$8800* *The Mimosas (M. 544), 1968,* s., #14/50, full margins, colors attenuated, skinning, good cond., (11-09-92,

Christie-NY, #75, illus.), 610 x 445 in., (x cm.), colored lithograph on Arches (BP 5818, DM 14,049, FR 47,465, Y 1,092,082).

$2875* *La Mise En Mot (M. 584a), 1969,* s., #157/175, pub. Editions Skira, full margins, good cond., (05-13-93, Sotheby-NY, #518), 11 x 12¾ in., (280 x 323 mm.), lithograph in colors (BP 1887, DM 4642, FR 15,659, Y 320,978).

$2594* *Moise (M. 229), 1960,* s., 12/50, (12-04-92, AB Stockholm, #7024), 26⁹⁄₁₆ x 19¹¹⁄₁₆ in., (67.5 x 50 cm.), lithograph in colors on Arches (BP 1664, DM 4131, FR 14,014, Y 323,845, SK 17,600).

$3000* *Moise, Sur L'Ordre De L'Eternel, Frappe Le Rocher D'Horeb Et En FaitJaillir Une Source, from The Bible, 1956,* inits., #82/100, full margins, (11-30-92, Phillips-London, #394), plate 11⅝ x 9¼ in., (295 x 235 mm.), hand-colored etching on wove (BP 1980, DM 4779, FR 16,225, Y 373,367).

$7700* *Moon Pierrot (M. 574), 1969,* s., i. epreuve d'artiste, #XIV/XXV, full margins, light/mat staining, very good cond., (11-09-92, Christie-NY, #76, illus.), 575 x 380 in., (x 965.2 cm.), colored lithograph on Arches (BP 5091, DM 12,292, FR 41,532, Y 955,572).

$2046* *Moses (M. 114), 1956,* s., #2/50, scuffmark through image, surface losses, foxing, (12-03-92, Sotheby-London, #227), 25¾ x 16½ in., (654 x 419 mm.), lithograph in colors on wove (BP 1320, DM 3217, FR 10,982, Y 254,573).

BI   *Moses (M. 937), 1979,* s., #9/50, margins, good cond.?, est. $3/3,500, (10-28-92, Butterfield, #2622), 20½ x 15 in., (521 x 381 mm.), color lithograph on wove.

$55* *"Moses Striking Water From The Rock",* good cond., (03-28-93, Bakker, #186), plate 11¾ x 9¼ in., (29.8 x 23.5 cm.), etching (BP 37, DM 90, FR 305, Y 6401).

$457* *Moses Zerbricht Die Gesetzestafeln, 1931-39,* Bl. 39 from the series Bible, light-staining, (12-01-92, Karl/Faber, #436), 11⅝ x 9¹⁄₁₆ in., (29.5 x 23 cm.), etching on wove (BP 302, DM 728, FR 2482, Y 56,897).

$10* *"Musee National Message Biblique Marc Chagall", 1977,* by Ch. Sorlier, p. Mourlot, good cond., folds, tear, (05-15-93, Cleveland, #374), 30 x 20½ in., (76.2 x 52.1 cm.), lithographic poster (BP 7, DM 16, FR 54, Y 1109).

$7150* *The Musical Clown (M. 174), 1957,* s., #129/150, pub. Maeght, margins, good cond., creases in image, (11-05-92, Sotheby-NY, #119, illus.), 26 x 18 in., (660 x 456 mm.), sheet 28 x 18⅝ in., (660 x 456 mm.), lithograph p. in colors (BP 4650, DM 11,308, FR 38,256, Y 877,193).

$1073* *Musikalisches Bouquet,* print s., num., (10-07-92, Zeller, #794, illus.), approx. 27⁹⁄₁₆ x 20½ in., (70 x 52 cm.), color lithograph (BP 626, DM 1553, FR 5265, Y 129,044).

$1731* *Mutter Und Kind (Mourlot Band I 94), 1954,* #63/75, s., stains, trimmed, (11-21-92, Lempertz, #69), 12¹³⁄₁₆ x 10³⁄₁₆ in., (32.5 x 25.8 cm.), lithograph on Arches wove (BP 1140, DM 2760, FR 9296, Y 215,272).

$194* *Nach Dem Winter (Mourlot 651), 1972,* part of pair from Derriere le Mirroir, tears, (09-25-92, Granier, #2789), sheet 14¹⁵⁄₁₆ x 22¹⁄₁₆ in., (38 x 56 cm.), color lithograph on wove (BP 113, DM 288, FR 972, Y 23,416).

$275* *Naomi And Her Daughters-In-Law,* (09-20-92, Hindman, #773), 13½ x 10 in., (34.3 x 25.4 cm.), color lithograph (BP 161, DM 408, FR 1396, Y 33,988).

$888* *"Nice, Soleil, Fleurs",* s. Marc Chagall, (03-16-93, Encans, #153), 30½ x 22⅝ in., (77.5 x 57.5 cm.), print (BP 613, DM 1477, FR 5017, Y 103,835, C$ 1110).

$290* *Nice-Soleil-Fleurs,* (10-14-92, Germann, #242), 37¹⁵⁄₁₆ x 25⁹⁄₁₆ in., (965 x 650 mm.), color offset print (BP 170, DM 424, FR 1439, Y 35,143, SF 378).

$30,434* *Nicolas Gogol. Les Ames Mortes, 1948: Ninety-Six,* 2 volumes, frontispiece in China ink, s. Marc Chagall, (06-25-93, Kornfeld, #28, illus.), 15⅜ x 11⅝ in., (39 x 29.5 cm.), Meyer, bibliography 142, Boston 50, Rauch 46, etching (BP 20,584, DM 51,811, FR 174,507, Y 3,225,991, SF 46,000).

$24,973* *The Nymph's Cave (M. 321), 1961,* from Daphnis and Chloe, s., #34/60, pub. Verve, margins, very good cond., discoloration, (12-01-92, Christie-London, #331, illus.),

L. 16⅝ x 25¼ in., (423 x 642 mm.), lithograph in colors on Arches (BP 16,500, DM 39,804, FR 135,649, Y 3,109,188).

$12,218* *La Nymphe Bleue (Mourl. 379), 1962,* s., num., (06-23-93, Kornfeld, #254), color lithograph on wove (BP 8300, DM 20,673, FR 69,539, Y 1,331,082, SF 18,400).

$12,006* *La Nymphe Bleue (Mourlot 379), 1962,* s., #38/50, (06-10-93, Hauswedell/Nolt, #149, illus.), image 23¼ x 19⅞ in., (59 x 50.5 cm.), color lithograph on Arches paper (BP 7853, DM 19,551, FR 65,822, Y 1,274,387).

$10,925* *O Happy Bridegroom..., (M. 540), 1967,* from In the Land of the Gods, s., #47/75, light/time staining, good cond., (05-11-93, Christie-NY, #166, illus.), borderline 18 x 14⅛ in., (457 x 359 mm.), color lithograph on Arches (BP 6974, DM 17,210, FR 57,988, Y 1,201,738).

$1621* *Odysseus Macht Sich Bekannt (Sorlier 803), 1975,* #228/250, from L'Odyssee series, (05-26-93, Lempertz, #72), 16¹³⁄₁₆ x 12¹¹⁄₁₆ in., (42.7 x 32.3 cm.), color lithograph on Arches wove (BP 1049, DM 2645, FR 8902, Y 176,119).

$4400* *The Odyssey: Sisyphus (M. 785), 1974,* s., #19/30, p. and pub. by Mourlot, full margins, good cond., mat stain, (11-05-92, Sotheby-NY, #136, illus.), 16⅝ x 12¾ in., (422 x 323 mm.), lithograph p. in colors on japon nacre (BP 2862, DM 6959, FR 23,542, Y 539,811).

$4400* *The Odyssey: The Waves Swallow Up Ulysses (M. 786), 1974,* s., #19/30, p. and pub. by Mourlot, full margins, good cond., (11-05-92, Sotheby-NY, #137, illus.), 16¾ x 12⅝ in., (427 x 321 mm.), lithograph p. in colors on japon nacre (BP 2862, DM 6959, FR 23,542, Y 539,811).

BI *Offering Of Flowers, 1964, Mourlot 417,* s., num. 44/50, prov., est. $4/5,000, (09-20-92, Hindman, #771), 25 x 19 in., (63.5 x 48.3 cm.), color lithograph.

BI *Offrande De Fleurs (M. 417), 1965,* epreuve d'artiste, XVI/XXV, s., est. DM 17,500, (10-09-92, Winterberg, #1885, illus.), 24½ x 19⅛ in., (62.3 x 48.5 cm.), color lithograph on BFK Rives.

$3559* *Offrande De Fleurs (Mourlot 417), 1964,* s., (05-12-93, AB Stockholm, #7008, illus.), 24¹³⁄₁₆ x 18¹¹⁄₁₆ in., (63 x 47.5 cm.), color lithograph on BFK (BP 2324, DM 5742, FR 19,342, Y 397,343, SK 26,400).

$1840* *On The Stove (Mourlot 16), 1922-23,* s., #38/100, blindstamp pub. Karl P. Ley, full margins, good cond., foxing, (02-11-93, Sotheby-NY, #79), 4¾ x 7½ in., (120 x 190 mm.), lithograph on laid (BP 1298, DM 3048, FR 10,314, Y 221,820).

$41,800* *The Orchard (M. 341), 1960,* s., full margins, light-staining, very good cond., (11-09-92, Christie-NY, #71, illus.), 16⅝ x 25⅜ in., (422 x 645 mm.), colored lithograph on Arches (BP 27,636, DM 66,731, FR 225,458, Y 5,187,391).

$1725* *Painter And Model (M. 403), 1963,* s., #18/40, pub. Andre Suaret, full margins, good cond., foxing, scotch-taped, (02-11-93, Sotheby-NY, #92), 12¹³⁄₁₆ x 9¹³⁄₁₆ in., (325 x 249 mm.), lithograph (BP 1217, DM 2857, FR 9669, Y 207,957).

$2990* *Painter With Hat (M. 1010), 1983,* s., #11/50, full margins, good cond., (02-11-93, Sotheby-NY, #101), 18⁷⁄₁₆ x 12¼ in., (468 x 311 mm.), color lithograph (BP 2110, DM 4953, FR 16,760, Y 360,458).

$5500* *The Painter With Three Bouquets (M. 998), 1982,* s., #36/50, full margins, good cond., light stain, (11-05-92, Sotheby-NY, #139, illus.), 13 x 17¾ in., (330 x 450 mm.), lithograph p. in colors (BP 3577, DM 8698, FR 29,428, Y 674,764).

$3740* *The Painter With Three Bouquets (M. 998), 1982,* s., #15/50, full margins, crease, stain, skinned patch, taped, good cond., (11-09-92, Christie-NY, #80, illus.), 330 x 470 in., (838.2 x cm.), colored lithograph on Arches (BP 2473, DM 5971, FR 20,173, Y 464,135).

$9900* *The Painter's Bouquet (M. 483), 1967,* s., #31/75, full margins, good cond., (11-05-92, Sotheby-NY, #129, illus.), 26⅝ x 20⅛ in., (675 x 510 mm.), lithograph p. in colors (BP 6439, DM 15,657, FR 52,970, Y 1,214,575).

$9890* *Pair Of Peasants (M. 484), 1967,* s., #27/50, full margins, staining, very good cond., (05-11-93, Christie-NY, #163, illus.), borderline 25½ x 20 in., (648 x 508 mm.),

color lithograph on wove (BP 6313, DM 15,580, FR 52,495, Y 1,087,889).

$1495* *Le Paon Se Plaignant A Junon, 1927-30,* plate 24 from Les Fables de la Fontaine, s., #41/100, pub. Teriade, 1952, full margins, good cond., mat stain, tape stains, discoloration, (05-13-93, Sotheby-NY, #496), 11¾ x 9½ in., (300 x 240 mm.), etching (BP 981, DM 2414, FR 8143, Y 166,909).

$1006* *Paradis (M. 233), 1960,* from Dessins pour la Bible, (10-09-92, Winterberg, #1857), 13¹⁵⁄₁₆ x 10⁵⁄₁₆ in., (35.5 x 26.2 cm.), color lithograph on wove (BP 597, DM 1494, FR 5017, Y 122,474).

$66* *"Paradise" (Mourlot 233),* image reduced, no margins, (12-02-92, Boos, #458), 13⅞ x 10¼ in., (353 x 260 mm.), color lithograph (BP 43, DM 104, FR 354, Y 8212).

$523* *"Paris L'Opera; Le Mafond De Chagall",* (09-25-92, Wolf, #36, illus.), 24 x 38 in., (61 x 96.5 cm.), poster (BP 305, DM 775, FR 2622, Y 63,126).

$11,500* *A Paris Square (M. 573), 1969,* s., #4/75, full margins, glue, good cond., (05-11-93, Christie-NY, #168, illus.), borderline 21 x 16 in., (533 x 406 mm.), color lithograph on Arches (BP 7341, DM 18,116, FR 61,040, Y 1,264,987).

BI *Passion (M. 736), 1975,* s., #18/50, full margins, mat staining, remains of tape, foxing, est. $6/7,000, (11-09-92, Christie-NY, #78, illus.), 393 x 254 in., (998.2 x 645.2 cm.), colored lithograph on Arches.

$10,822* *Pastoral (M. 906), 1977,* s., #43/50, margins, very good cond., (12-01-92, Christie-London, #340, illus.), L. 15⅜ x 22¹³⁄₁₆ in., (390 x 580 mm.), lithograph in colors on Arches (BP 7150, DM 17,249, FR 58,783, Y 1,347,361).

$3644* *Paysage (Mourlot 154b), 1956,* second state, (05-27-93, Briest, #53), 23¼ x 18½ in., (59 x 47 cm.), lithograph on zinc (BP 2334, DM 5847, FR 19,708, Y 390,652).

$3410* *Paysage A Le Chevre (M. 562), 1969,* s., #33/50, full margins, good cond., handling creases, nick, (12-03-92, Sotheby-London, #250, illus.), sheet approx. 30 x 22¼ in., (762 x 565 mm.), lithograph in brown and black on Arches (BP 2200, DM 5362, FR 18,304, Y 424,288).

$274* *Paysage Au Coq, (Mourlot 208), 1958,* from Derriere Le Miroir, # 107-108, (09-30-92, Kunsthallen, #60), color lithograph (BP 155, DM 389, FR 1314, Y 32,881, DK 1495).

$1725* *Paysage Aux Isbas (M. 192), 1957,* s., #67/90, full margins, colors faded, light/backboard stains, (02-11-93, Sotheby-NY, #90), 9¹³⁄₁₆ x 17³⁄₁₆ in., (250 x 437 mm.), color lithograph (BP 1217, DM 2857, FR 9669, Y 207,957).

$16,799* *Le Peintre A La Palette (Mourlot 54), 1952,* 1st state, s., i. Epreuve d'Artiste, (06-23-93, Kornfeld, #248, illus.), color lithograph (BP 11,412, DM 28,425, FR 95,612, Y 1,830,156, SF 25,300).

$2728* *Peintre A La Tour Eiffel (M. 189), 1957,* s., #14/20, margins, good cond., discoloration, skinned areas, (12-03-92, Sotheby-London, #230, illus.), sheet 26 x 19⅞ in., (660 x 505 mm.), lithograph on Arches (BP 1760, DM 4290, FR 14,643, Y 339,430).

$3300* *Le Peintre Devant La Village I (Mourlot 603), 1969,* s., #54/75, (03-14-93, Hindman, #264, illus.), 16 x 11½ in., (40.6 x 29.2 cm.), color lithograph (BP 2302, DM 5493, FR 18,676, Y 388,922).

$303* *Le Peintre Et Son Double [S.992], 1981,* double page, from "Derriere le Miroir", (12-10-92, Sloan, #3026), 12½ x 18½ in., (31.8 x 47 cm.), color lithograph (BP 195, DM 479, FR 1637, Y 37,481).

BI *Le Petit Nu (Sorlier/Mourlot Band IV 634), 1971,* #13/50, s., est. DM 13,500-, (11-21-92, Lempertz, #71, illus.), 14 x 18⁹⁄₁₆ in., (35.6 x 47.2 cm.), color lithograph on Arches wove.

$1057* *Das Pferd Und Der Esel,* sheet 69 of series, 1927, 1930, 1952, s., (05-26-93, Lempertz, #59), approx. 16⁹⁄₁₆ x 13³⁄₁₆ in., (42 x 33.5 cm.), etching on wide Montval handmade (BP 684, DM 1725, FR 5805, Y 114,841).

BI *"Phantastisches Dorf" (Mourlot 429 a), c. 1964-1965,* s., num., light-staining, (11-28-92, Grisebach, #248, illus.), 25¹⁵⁄₁₆ x 19⅞ in., (66 x 50.5 cm.), color lithograph on wove.

$15,816* *Philetas's Lesson (M. 323), 1961,* from Daphnis and Chloe, s., #38/60, pub. Verve, margins, discoloration, very good cond., (12-01-92, Christie-London, #332, illus.), L. 16¾ x 12¹³⁄₁₆ in., (425 x 325 mm.), lithograph in colors on Arches (BP 10,450, DM 25,209, FR 85,910, Y 1,969,124).

$7475* *Le Pierrot, 1968*, watermark, annot. epreuve d'artiste, full margins, good cond., light-staining, foxing, creases, (05-19-93, Butterfield, #1893, illus.), sh. 29¾ x 22½ in., (756 x 572 mm.), etching and aquatint in colors on wove (BP 4852, DM 12,151, FR 40,936, Y 827,521).

$2189* *Le Pierrot, 1968*, s., 26/50, (12-04-92, AB Stockholm, #7021), 24³⁄₁₆ x 17½ in., (61.5 x 44.5 cm.), etching (BP 1404, DM 3486, FR 11,826, Y 273,283, SK 14,850).

$1650* *"La Pirouette Bleue" (M. 471)*, s. Marc Chagall, num. 9/50, (09-25-92, Wolf, #38, illus.), 14 x 10½ in., (35.6 x 26.7 cm.), lithograph in colors on arches paper (BP 964, DM 2446, FR 8271, Y 199,155).

$17,052* *Poemes, 1968*, book, s., num. pub. G.Cramer, full margins, good cond., orig. boardsand slipcase, (12-03-92, Sotheby-London, #246, illus.), overall size 15 x 11¾ in., (381 x 298 mm.), 24 woodcuts in colors on Rives wove (BP 11,000, DM 26,816, FR 91,530, Y 2,121,687).

$2588* *Poemes: "Comme Un Barbare" and "Je Me Usis Eloigne", 1968: Two*, init., i. Bon, i. bon a tirer, pub. Gerald Cramer, 1975, full margins, good cond., discoloration, glue stains, soiling, (05-13-93, Sotheby-NY, #516), sh approx. 14⅝ x 11¼ in., (372 x 285 mm.), wood engraving in colors (BP 1699, DM 4179, FR 14,096, Y 288,936).

BI *Poemes: Pour Ce Jour And Elle Vole, 1968: Two*, plates VII and XVI, pub. G. Cramer, full margins, good cond., soiling, est. BP 800/1,000, (06-30-93, Sotheby-London, #402), 14½ x 11⅛ in., (368 x 283 mm.), color woodcut on Rives.

$5457* *Le Poete (M. 442), 1966*, s., #48/50, full margins, good cond., water staining, creasing, skinned areas, (12-03-92, Sotheby-London, #242, illus.), sheet 25½ x 18¼ in., (648 x 464 mm.), lithograph in colors on Arches (BP 3520, DM 8582, FR 29,291, Y 678,985).

$3669* *Le Poisson Bleu (Mourlot 198), 1957*, #25/90, s., (04-24-93, Kunsthaus, #496, illus.), 9¹³⁄₁₆ x 16⅛ in., (25 x 41 cm.), color lithograph on hand-made Arches (BP 2316, DM 5751, FR 19,423, Y 404,878).

$523* *Poisson Blue, 1957*, pub. Jacques Lassaigne, (10-30-92, Sloan, #1602), 9 x 15 in., (22.9 x 38.1 cm.), color lithograph (BP 335, DM 805, FR 2730, Y 64,784).

$4775* *Pres De St Jeunet (M. 646), 1972*, s., i. Epreuve d'artiste, pub. Editions Andre Sauret, full margins, good cond., (12-03-92, Sotheby-London, #258, illus.), 12¼ x 9⅝ in., (311 x 244 mm.), lithograph in colors on Arches (BP 3080, DM 7509, FR 25,631, Y 594,127).

BI *Printemps De Lumiere (Sorlier 1047), 1985*, sig. stamp, #3/3/50, est. DM 5,500, (05-26-93, Lempertz, #76, illus.), 24⁷⁄₁₆ x 18½ in., (62 x 47 cm.), color lithograph on Arches wove.

$4180* *Profile With Red Flowers (Mourlot 418), 1964*, s., #19/50, pub. Mourlot, prov., (10-18-92, Hindman, #465, illus.), 15⅜ x 12⅝ in., (39.1 x 32.1 cm.), color lithograph on wove w/watermark (BP 2558, DM 6222, FR 21,100, Y 501,500).

$7673* *Psaumes De David, 1979*, book, s. hors commerce, pub. Gerald Cramer, good cond., (12-03-92, Sotheby-London, #261, illus.), each sheet approx. 11 x 8⅜ in., (279 x 213 mm.), 30 etchings in orange and black (BP 4950, DM 12,066, FR 41,186, Y 954,709).

$7700* *The Purple Bodice (M. 691), 1973*, s., #14/50, full margins, good cond., faded, light stain, (11-05-92, Sotheby-NY, #133, illus.), 24⅝ x 17¾ in., (626 x 450 mm.), lithograph p. in colors (BP 5008, DM 12,178, FR 41,199, Y 944,669).

$846* *Der Rabe, Der Den Adler Nadchahmen Wollte*, sheet 23 of series, 1927, 1930, 1952, s., (05-26-93, Lempertz, #54), approx. 16⁹⁄₁₆ x 13³⁄₁₆ in., (42 x 33.5 cm.), etching on wide Montval handmade (BP 547, DM 1380, FR 4646, Y 91,917).

BI *The Rainbow (M. 596), 1969*, s., #63/75, full margins, mat staining, creasing, excell. cond., est. $25/35,000, (05-11-93, Christie-NY, #170, illus.), borderline 27⅜ x 27⅜ in., (695 x 695 mm.), color lithograph on Arches.

$846* *Die Ratte Und Der Elefant*, sheet 85 of series, 1927, 1930, 1952, s., (05-26-93, Lempertz, #62), approx. 16⁹⁄₁₆ x 13³⁄₁₆ in., (42 x 33.5 cm.), etching on wide Montval handmade (BP 547, DM 1380, FR 4646, Y 91,917).

$881* *Das Rebhuhn Und Die Hahne*, sheet 94 of series, 1927, 1930, 1952, s., (05-26-93, Lempertz, #65), approx. 16⁹⁄₁₆ x 13³⁄₁₆ in., (42 x 33.5 cm.), etching on wide Montval handmade (BP 570, DM 1437, FR 4838, Y 95,719).

$3360* *Reception Sur Le Bateau-Mouche (Mourl. 220), 1959*, s., num., (06-23-93, Kornfeld, #252), color lithograph (BP 2283, DM 5685, FR 19,124, Y 366,053, SF 5060).

$18,400* *Red Maternity (M. 984), 1980*, s., #7/50, pub. Maeght, full margins, good cond., discoloration, handling creases, (05-13-93, Sotheby-NY, #526, illus.), 37⅛ x 23⅞ in., (943 x 605 mm.), lithograph in colors (BP 12,080, DM 29,711, FR 100,218, Y 2,054,259).

BI *The Red Rooster (M. 203), 1957*, s., #50/90, full margins, crease, paper loss, time staining, est. $2/3,000, (05-11-93, Christie-NY, #155), borderline 15 x 22 in., (381 x 559 mm.), lithograph on Arches.

$428* *The Red Rooster (M. 59), 1952*, complimentary sig., pub. in Derriere le Miroir, margins, laid-down, glued to front mat, (06-30-93, Sotheby-London, #392), 11 x 15½ in., (279 x 394 mm.), color lithograph (BP 287, DM 730, FR 2463, Y 45,859).

$1320* *The Red Rooster (M. 60), 1952*, s., #140/200, margins, sealed in mat, mat/time-staining, glue remains in image, (10-28-92, Butterfield, #2795, illus.), 14¾ x 17 in., (375 x 432 mm.), color lithograph on Arches (BP 841, DM 2039, FR 6922, Y 161,963).

$1725* *The Red Rooster (M. 60), 1952*, s., #149/200, margins, good cond., mat/light-staining, foxing, papertape remains/skinned areas, surface soiling, notations, (05-19-93, Butterfield, #1891), sh. 14¹⁵⁄₁₆ x 22 in., (379 x 559 mm.), lithograph in colors on wove (BP 1120, DM 2804, FR 9447, Y 190,966).

$2070* *La Reine De Seba, 1931-39*, plate 80 of the Bible, pub. Teriade, 1956, #72/100, margins folded back 47 mm., good cond., mat/backboard stain, scotch tape hinges, (02-11-93, Sotheby-NY, #86), 12¹¹⁄₁₆ x 8¹¹⁄₁₆ in., (322 x 221 mm.), sheet 21⅛ x 14⅝ in., (322 x 221 mm.), hand colored etching (BP 1461, DM 3429, FR 11,603, Y 249,548).

$4125* *Die Reiterin (K. 72/II/c), 1926-1927*, s., #48/50, p. Haasen, 1963, full margins, good cond., light stain, foxing, soiling, (11-05-92, Sotheby-NY, #113, illus.), 12⅞ x 9½ in., (327 x 240 mm.), etching and drypoint (BP 2683, DM 6524, FR 22,071, Y 506,073).

BI *Le Renard Et Le Bouc, 1927-30*, s., stains, light-stains, sheet 31 from La Fontaine, Fables, 1952, pub. Teriade, est. DM 3,000-, (11-21-92, Lempertz, #65, illus.), 11¾ x 9½ in., (29.8 x 24.2 cm.), etching on cream hand-made.

$777* *Le Renard Et Le Buste, 1927-1930*, s., (06-10-93, Hauswedell/Nolt, #130), image 9⅜ x 11⅝ in., (23.8 x 29.5 cm.), etching on hand-made (BP 508, DM 1265, FR 4260, Y 82,475).

BI *Rendez-Vous (M. 1022), 1983*, s., num. 38/50, full margins, good cond., creases, tape remains, light-staining, est. $6/8,000, (02-24-93, Butterfield, #2730, illus.), 16¾ x 12½ in., (425 x 318 mm.), lithograph in colors on Arches wove.

BI *Le Repos (Sorlier 1037), 1984*, sig. stamp, #33/50, est. DM 5,500, (05-26-93, Lempertz, #75, illus.), 22¹⁄₁₆ x 16⅞ in., (56 x 42.8 cm.), color lithograph on Arches wove.

$1537* *Rest (M. No. 1037)*, one of Les Quinze Dernieres Lithographies De Marc Chagall Folio M. 1035-1049), stamped sig. w/Atelier Marc Chagall blindstamp, #33/50, p. Charles Sorlier, 1985, (12-01-92, Ritchie, #96, illus.), 22⅛ x 16⅞ in., (56.2 x 42.9 cm.), color lithograph on Arches, watermark (BP 1016, DM 2450, FR 8349, Y 191,360, C$ 1980).

$395* *Reverie (Nach Einer Gouache), 1989*, #B 138/250, (06-24-93, Germann, #273), 35¹⁄₁₆ x 24⁷⁄₁₆ in., (890 x 620 mm.), color lithograph (BP 260, DM 640, FR 2158, Y 42,373, SF 575).

$1260* *La Revolution(Charles Sorlier 9), 1963*, s., 110/150, (05-12-93, AB Stockholm, #7011), 21¼ x 18½ in., (54 x 47 cm.), lithograph in colors (BP 823, DM 2033, FR 6848, Y 140,672, SK 9350).

$1323* *Der Richtende Engel (Sorlier 147), 1974,* s., d., (10-14-92, Germann, #249), 29¹⁵⁄₁₆ x 20¹¹⁄₁₆ in., (760 x 525 mm.), color lithograph (BP 777, DM 1936, FR 6566, Y 160,325, SF 1725).

BI *The River (M. 586), 1969,* s., num. epreuve d'artiste XXV/XXV, margins, good cond., est. BP 5/7,000, (12-01-92, Christie-London, #337, illus.), L. 25⁹⁄₁₆ x 19¹¹⁄₁₆ in., (650 x 500 mm.), lithograph in colors on Arches.

$525* *Romeo Et Juliette,* (05-16-93, Hanzel, #483), 25 x 39 in., (63.5 x 99.1 cm.), color lithographic poster (BP 341, DM 844, FR 2838, Y 58,198).

$13,800* *Roses And Mimosa (M. 733), 1975,* s., #14/50, full margins, light-staining, very good cond., (05-11-93, Christie-NY, #172, illus.), borderline 26 x 20½ in., (660 x 521 mm.), color lithograph on Arches (BP 8809, DM 21,739, FR 73,248, Y 1,517,985).

$413* *"Ruth Gleaning" (M246), c. 1960,* (03-25-93, Boos, #610), 14⅛ x 10⁵⁄₁₆ in., (358 x 262 mm.), color lithograph (BP 280, DM 678, FR 2307, Y 48,383).

$1355* *Sacrifice Aux Nymphes (Vgl. M. 330), 1960,* in Daphnis et Chloe, epreuve de couleurs, (10-09-92, Winterberg, #1879), 16¹¹⁄₁₆ x 12⅝ in., (42.4 x 32.1 cm.), color lithograph on wove (BP 804, DM 2013, FR 6758, Y 164,962).

$8106* *Saint-Germain-Des-Pres (Mourlot 100), 1954,* s. H.C., (05-26-93, Dorling, #2590, illus.), 14¹⁵⁄₁₆ x 11 in., (38 x 28 cm.), color lithograph on thick wove (BP 5244, DM 13,226, FR 44,514, Y 880,704).

$1980* *Samson Et Le Lion, 1931-39,* plate 54 of the Bible, pub. Teriade, 1956, init., #5/100, full margins, good cond., foxing, mat stain, stamp, (11-05-92, Sotheby-NY, #114), 10⅜ x 12¾ in., (265 x 323 mm.), etching w/touches of hand coloring (BP 1288, DM 3131, FR 10,594, Y 242,915).

$3163* *Sara And Abimelech (M. 239),* s., #48/50, full margins, good cond., soiling, scotch tape, discolored, (05-13-93, Sotheby-NY, #507), 14 x 10¾ in., (357 x 272 mm.), lithograph in colors (BP 2077, DM 5107, FR 17,228, Y 353,132).

$2467* *Der Schafer Und Seine Herde,* sheet 92 of series, 1927, 1930, 1952, s., (05-26-93, Lempertz, #64), approx. 16⁹⁄₁₆ x 1⅜ in., (42 x 3.5 cm.), etching on wide Montval handmade (BP 1596, DM 4025, FR 13,548, Y 268,036).

$1802* *"Der Scharlatan", 1927-1930,* from "La Fontaine Fables", s., light-staining, (11-25-92, Dorotheum, #485, illus.), plate size 11¹¹⁄₁₆ x 9⁷⁄₁₆ in., (29.7 x 24 cm.), sh 16⁹⁄₁₆ x 13³⁄₁₆ in., (29.7 x 24 cm.), etching (BP 1178, DM 2865, FR 9704, Y 223,075, SC 20,160).

$846* *Der Schuster Und Der Reiche,* sheet 79 of series, 1927, 1930, 1952, s., (05-26-93, Lempertz, #61), approx. 16⁹⁄₁₆ x 13³⁄₁₆ in., (42 x 33.5 cm.), etching on wide Montval handmade (BP 547, DM 1380, FR 4646, Y 91,917).

BI *Der Schwarze Mond (Mourlot/Sorlier Band III 438), 1965,* epreuve d'artiste V/XXV, s., light-stains, est. DM 12,000-, (11-21-92, Lempertz, #70, illus.), 10¹⁄₁₆ x 12¹⁵⁄₁₆ in., (25.5 x 33 cm.), color lithograph on Arches wove.

$1279* *Selbsportrait (Mourlot 282), 1960,* Wz., (09-19-92, Wachholtz, #139), 12¹³⁄₁₆ x 9¹³⁄₁₆ in., (32.5 x 25 cm.), color-lithograph on wove (BP 749, DM 1898, FR 6492, Y 158,077).

$10,640* *Selbstbildnis Mit Grimasse (Kornfeld 43 VI b), 1924/25,* s., num., (06-05-93, Bassenge, #5938, illus.), 14¾ x 10¹³⁄₁₆ in., (37.4 x 27.4 cm.), etching w/aquatint on copper print (BP 7004, DM 17,250, FR 58,142, Y 1,141,386).

$18,700* *Selbstbildnis Mit Lachendem Gesicht (K. 42), 1924-25,* s., #44/100, full margins, good cond., mat staining, paper adhering to recto, surface dirt, prop. Edith Schumann 1988 Trust, (11-05-92, Sotheby-NY, #112, illus.), 10⅞ x 8½ in., (275 x 217 mm.), etching and drypoint on MBM Perigord wove (BP 12,163, DM 29,575, FR 100,054, Y 2,294,197).

BI *Selbstbildnis Mit Lachendem Gesicht (Kornfeld 42 III b), 1924/25,* s., #16/100, est. DM 25,000, (06-10-93, Hauswedell/Nolt, #125, illus.), image 10⅞ x 8½ in., (27.7 x 21.6 cm.), drypoint on wove.

$7162* *Selbstbildnis Mit Lachendem Gesicht (Kornfeld 42), 1924-25,* s., #88/100, p. Louis Fort, full margins, good cond., creases, discoloration, (12-03-92, Sotheby-London, #219, illus.), sheet 22 x 14⅝ in., (559 x 371 mm.), etching and drypoint on MBM wove (BP 4620, DM 11,263, FR 38,443, Y 891,129).

BI *Selbstbildnis, 1979,* E.A, s., est. DM 7,000-, (11-21-92, Lempertz, #73, illus.), 15⅝ x 11¹¹⁄₁₆ in., (39.7 x 29.7 cm.), etching on wove.

BI *Selbstbildnis, Schreibend (K. 76), 1926-30,* full margins, good cond., patches of glue in upper image, foxing, light/mount-staining, est. BP 8/10,000, (06-30-93, Sotheby-London, #389, illus.), 8⅝ x 7 in., (219 x 178 mm.), etching w/tone on sturdy wove.

$2530* *Self Portrait With A Black Jacket (M. 184) 1957,* s., #23/30, full margins, mat staining, (05-11-93, Christie-NY, #154), borderline 23¾ x 18¾ in., (603 x 476 mm.), lithograph on Arches (BP 1615, DM 3986, FR 13,429, Y 278,297).

$2860* *Self-Portrait (M. 697), 1973,* s., #20/50, full margins, good cond., light/faint mat stain, (11-05-92, Sotheby-NY, #134), 22⅞ x 15¾ in., (581 x 400 mm.), lithograph p. in colors (BP 1860, DM 4523, FR 15,302, Y 350,877).

BI *Les Sept Peches Capitaux (K. 47, 49-52, 54-59, 61), 1925: Twelve,* 12 of 16, pub. Simon Kra, 1926, full margins, creases, good cond., soing, discoloration, most w/ glue/tape stains, tears, est. $2/3,000, (02-11-93, Sotheby-NY, #81), sheets approx. 8¹⁄₁₆ x 8¹⁄₁₆ in., (205 x 205 mm.), etchings w/drypoint on wove.

$3738* *Les Sept Peches Capitaux (K. 47-61),* book by Giradoux et al., incl. 15 of 16, (lacking Pl. 16, K. 62), num. 200, p. Louis Fort, pub. Simon Kra, 1926, full margins, good cond., (05-13-93, Sotheby-NY, #495), overall 9¾ x 7⅜ in., (248 x 187 mm.), etching w/drypoint and aquatint (BP 2454, DM 6036, FR 20,359, Y 417,327).

$7820* *Sequestered Garden (M. 592), 1969,* s., i. Epreuve d'artiste XXIV/XXV, full margins, good cond., light-stain, discoloration, (02-11-93, Sotheby-NY, #97, illus.), 23⅞ x 16⅛ in., (606 x 409 mm.), color lithograph (BP 5518, DM 12,953, FR 43,834, Y 942,737).

BI *"Sitzender Mann Mit Ziege" (Mourlot 10), 1922-23,* #13/35, s., est. SF 7/9,000, (11-13-92, Koller, #5285), 6¼ x 9¹⁄₁₆ in., (15.8 x 23 cm.), lithograph on wove.

$4093* *Sobakevich At Table, 1925,* from Gogol's Les Ames Mortes, s., d., i., full margins, image in goodcond., soiling, rubbing, (12-03-92, Sotheby-London, #220, illus.), 8½ x 11 in., (216 x 279 mm.), etching on wove (BP 2640, DM 6437, FR 21,970, Y 509,270).

$181* *Soleil Au Cheval Rouge,* from "Derriere le Mirior" Nr. 235, 1979, (10-14-92, Germann, #243), 14¹⁵⁄₁₆ x 19¹¹⁄₁₆ in., (380 x 500 mm.), color lithograph (BP 106, DM 265, FR 898, Y 21,934, SF 236).

$968* *Soleil Aux Amoureux (C. 143),* essai de couleur, (10-09-92, Winterberg, #1841, illus.), 12¹⁄₁₆ x 9⁵⁄₁₆ in., (30.7 x 23.7 cm.), etching w/color aquatint on Japan (BP 574, DM 1438, FR 4828, Y 117,848).

$2370* *Le Soleil De Paris (Mourlot CS 48), 1977,* s., ded., (04-21-93, Germann, #324), 30⁷⁄₁₆ x 19¹¹⁄₁₆ in., (773 x 500 mm.), color lithograph (BP 1538, DM 3788, FR 12,811, Y 262,371, SF 3450).

$2070* *Solomon Sur Son Trone, 1931-39,* plate 81 of the Bible, pub. Teriade, 1956, i., #80/100, margins, good cond., mat stain, laid down, (02-11-93, Sotheby-NY, #87), 12⁷⁄₁₆ x 9⅜ in., (316 x 238 mm.), sheet 16⅞ x 13⅜ in., (316 x 238 mm.), hand colored etching (BP 1461, DM 3429, FR 11,603, Y 249,548).

$2070* *Songe De Solomon, 1931-39,* plate 77 of the Bible, pub. Teriade, 1956, init., #53/100, margins, good cond., mat stain, ink i., masking tape hinge, (02-11-93, Sotheby-NY, #85), 12¹¹⁄₁₆ x 8⅜ in., (322 x 213 mm.), sheet 18¹⁄₁₆ x 14⅝ in., (322 x 213 mm.), hand colored etching (BP 1461, DM 3429, FR 11,603, Y 249,548).

$4804* *Le Songe Du Peintre (M. 489), 1967,* s., i. H. C., full margins, good cond., paper discoloration, (06-30-93, Sotheby-London, #401, illus.), 29⅛ x 10½ in., (740 x 267 mm.), color lithograph on Arches (BP 3220, DM 8194, FR 27,641, Y 514,733).

$3603* *Songes: La Femme-Oiseau (C. 125), 1981,* s., #41/50, pub. Cramer, full margins, good cond., (06-30-93, Sotheby-London, #408, illus.), 12 x 9¼ in., (305 x 235 mm.), color etching and aquatint on wove (BP 2415, DM 6145, FR 20,731, Y 386,050).

$3432* *Songes: La Vie (C. 126), 1981,* s., #41/50, pub. Cramer, full margins, good cond., (06-30-93, Sotheby-London, #409, illus.), 12 x 9¼ in., (305 x 235 mm.), color etching and aquatint on wove (BP 2300, DM 5854, FR 19,747, Y 367,727).

$3946* *Songes: Le Chevalet (C. 120), 1981,* s., #41/50, pub. Cramer, full margins, good cond., (06-30-93, Sotheby-London, #407, illus.), 12 x 9¼ in., (305 x 235 mm.), color etching and aquatint on wove (BP 2645, DM 6730, FR 22,704, Y 422,801).

$3260* *Songes: Le Retour De L'Enfant Prodigue (C. 113),* s., #41/50, pub. Cramer, full margins, good cond., paper discoloration, (06-30-93, Sotheby-London, #405, illus.), 12 x 9¼ in., (305 x 235 mm.), color etching and aquatint on wove (BP 2185, DM 5560, FR 18,757, Y 349,298).

$3581* *Songes: Plate II: Louanges (C. 112), 1981, 1982,* s., #41/50, pub. Cramer, full margins, good cond., (12-03-92, Sotheby-London, #267), 12¼ x 9½ in., (311 x 241 mm.), etching w/aquatint in colors on wove (BP 2310, DM 5631, FR 19,222, Y 445,564).

$3922* *Songes: Plate III: Le Retour De L'Enfant Prodigue (Cramer 113), 1981,1982,* s., #49/50, pub. Cramer, full margins, good cond., (12-03-92, Sotheby-London, #262, illus.), 12¼ x 9½ in., (311 x 241 mm.), etching w/aquatint in colors on wove (BP 2530, DM 6168, FR 21,052, Y 487,993).

$2728* *Songes: Plate V: Le Violiniste (C. 115), 1981, 1982,* s., #41/50, pub. Cramer, full margins, good cond., (12-03-92, Sotheby-London, #263), 12¼ x 9½ in., (311 x 241 mm.), etching w/aquatint in colors on wove (BP 1760, DM 4290, FR 14,643, Y 339,430).

$4093* *Songes: Plate VII: Musique (C. 117), 1981, 1982,* s., #41/50, pub. Cramer, full margins, good cond., (12-03-92, Sotheby-London, #264, illus.), 12¼ x 9½ in., (311 x 241 mm.), etching w/aquatint in colors on wove (BP 2640, DM 6437, FR 21,970, Y 509,270).

$2728* *Songes: Plate XVIII: Moise (C. 128), 1981, 1982,* s., #41/50, pub. Cramer, full margins, good cond., (12-03-92, Sotheby-London, #265), 12¼ x 9½ in., (311 x 241 mm.), etching w/aquatint in colors on wove (BP 1760, DM 4290, FR 14,643, Y 339,430).

$3946* *Songes: Tendresse (C. 119), 1981,* s., #41/50, pub. Cramer, full margins, good cond., (06-30-93, Sotheby-London, #406, illus.), 12 x 9¼ in., (305 x 235 mm.), color etching and aquatint on wove (BP 2645, DM 6730, FR 22,704, Y 422,801).

$3450* *Der Spaziergang, II (K. 27), 1922,* s., pub. Neue europaische Grazphik. Italienische und russische Kunstler. Bauhaus-Druck 4, pub. Staatlichen Bauhaus, (blindstamp), margins, good cond., (05-13-93, Sotheby-NY, #492, illus.), 6⅞ x 5⅝ in., (176 x 143 mm.), etching and drypoint on laid (BP 2265, DM 5571, FR 18,791, Y 385,174).

$8526* *Spring (M. 568), 1969,* s., #7/75, full margins, good cond., (colors faded, tape), (12-03-92, Sotheby-London, #251, illus.), 25¾ x 19¾ in., (654 x 502 mm.), lithograph in colors on Arches (BP 5500, DM 13,408, FR 45,765, Y 1,060,844).

BI *Spring Of Light (M. 1047), 1985,* stamp s., #36/50, Atelier Marc Chagall, lithographie originale blindstamp, full margins, good cond., est. $4/6,000, (05-19-93, Butterfield, #1896), 18½ x 15⁵⁄₁₆ in., (470 x 389 mm.), lithograph in colors on Arches.

$1537* *Spring Of Light (M. No. 1047),* one of Les Quinze Dernieres Lithographies De Marc Chagall Folio M. 1035-1049, stamped sig. w/Atelier Marc Chagall blindstamp, #33/50, p. Charles Sorlier, 1985, (12-01-92, Ritchie, #97, illus.), 24½ x 18½ in., (62.2 x 47 cm.), color lithograph on Arches, watermark (BP 1016, DM 2450, FR 8349, Y 191,360, C$ 1980).

$6875* *Square De Paris (Mourlot 573), 1969,* s., #57/75, (03-14-93, Hindman, #265, illus.), 20⅝ x 15¼ in., (52.4 x 38.7 cm.), color lithograph (BP 4796, DM 11,443, FR 38,908, Y 810,253).

$7260* *Square De Paris, 1969,* s., #57/75, (06-13-93, Hindman, #387), 20⅝ x 15¼ in., (52.4 x 38.7 cm.), color lithograph (BP 4752, DM 11,816, FR 39,716, Y 763,969).

$3405* *St. Germain-Des-Pres (Mourlot 100), 1954,* s. epreuve d'artiste, (12-04-92, AB Stockholm, #7023), 15¹⁄₁₆ x 11³⁄₁₆ in., (38.3 x 28.4 cm.), lithograph in colors (BP 2184, DM 5423, FR 18,395, Y 425,094, SK 23,100).

BI *Der Staffelei, Plate 18 (K. 18c), 1922,* from Mein Leben, s., #103/110, pub. P. Cassirer, 1923, margins, tear, nicks, losses, mount stain, discoloration, handling creases, est. BP 6/8,000, (12-01-92, Christie-London, #323, illus.), plate 9⅝ x 7⅜ in., (245 x 187 mm.), etching w/drypoint on laid.

$24,200* *The Story Of Exodus (M. 444-67), 1966: Set Of Twenty-Four,* Leon Amiel, s., #22/250, full margins, excell. cond., (11-09-92, Christie-NY, #73, illus.), 520 x 395 in., (x cm.), lithograph on Arches (BP 16,000, DM 38,633, FR 130,529, Y 3,003,227).

$20,700* *The Story Of Exodus, Paris And New York, Leon Amiel, 1966 (M. 444-67): Twenty-Four,* s., num. on just., copy 49 of 250, full margins, loose, foxing, excell. cond., (05-11-93, Christie-NY, #162, illus.), 20½ x 15⁹⁄₁₆ in., (520 x 395 mm.), lithographs in hors-texte, w/text and just, on Arches (BP 13,214, DM 32,609, FR 109,873, Y 2,276,977).

$20,900* *The Story Of Exodus: Twenty-Four,* folio, unbound, in wrappers, as issued, orig. cloth case and cardboard box, s., rear cover illus., (11-12-92, Swann, #44, illus.), color lithograph (BP 13,727, DM 33,117, FR 111,705, Y 2,591,445).

$21,643* *The Story Of The Exodus (M. 444-67), 1966,* L. Amiel, title, text, justification, and set of 24, s., #161/250, fiine condition, very good cond., (12-01-92, Christie-London, #334, illus.), overall sheet 20¹¹⁄₁₆ x 15½ in., (525 x 393 mm.), lithograph in colors on Arches (BP 14,300, DM 34,496, FR 117,561, Y 2,694,597).

BI *Studio Light (M. 843), 1976,* s., num. 10/50, full margins, good cond., mat staining, surface soiling, creases, est. $20/25,000, (02-24-93, Butterfield, #2727, illus.), 20¾ x 16 in., (527 x 406 mm.), lithograph in colors on Arches.

$3300* *Sujet Biblique (C. 34), 1962,* s. in ink, annot. 16.24 mars 1962, margins, good cond., mat staining,creases, prov., (02-24-93, Butterfield, #2726, illus.), 8 x 5¾ in., (203 x 146 mm.), sheet 14⅛ x 11³⁄₁₆ in., (203 x 146 mm.), monotype in black on Chine volant w/watermark (BP 2301, DM 5357, FR 18,162, Y 387,233).

$8800* *Summer Evening (M. 545), 1968,* s., #35/50, full margins, good cond., mat/light/yellow staining, creases, surface soiling, (10-28-92, Butterfield, #2621, illus.), 24 x 16½ in., (610 x 419 mm.), color lithograph on Arches (BP 5607, DM 13,591, FR 46,146, Y 1,079,755).

BI *Summer's Night (M. 696), 1973,* s., #10/50, full margins, creases, discoloration, staining, est. BP 2,0/2,500, (12-03-92, Sotheby-London, #259, illus.), 21⅞ x 15 in., (556 x 381 mm.), lithograph in colors on Arches.

$3300* *Summer's Night (M. 696), 1973,* s., #45/50, full margins, foxing, glued down verso, good cond., (11-09-92, Christie-NY, #77, illus.), 555 x 377 in., (x 957.6 cm.), colored lithograph on Arches (BP 2182, DM 5268, FR 17,799, Y 409,531).

$5500* *Der Talmudleher (Kornfeld 9), 1922,* plate 9 from Mein Leben, s., #75/110, full margins, light-staining, creasing, backed split, good cond., (11-09-92, Christie-NY, #65, illus.), plate 9½ x 7⁵⁄₁₆ in., (242 x 185 mm.), etching and drypoint on laid (BP 3636, DM 8780, FR 29,666, Y 682,552).

$5520* *Tenderness (M. 1020), 1983,* s., #43/50, full margins, good cond., (05-11-93, Christie-NY, #177, illus.), borderline 18¼ x 13 in., (464 x 330 mm.), color lithograph on Arches (BP 3524, DM 8696, FR 29,299, Y 607,194).

$21,186* *Then The Boy Displayed To The Dervish (Mourlot 36), 1948,* s., #29/90, (06-10-93, Hauswedell/Nolt, #141, illus.), image 14¾ x 19¹⁄₁₆ in., (37.5 x 48.4 cm.), color lithograph on hand-made (BP 13,858, DM 34,499, FR 116,151, Y 2,248,806).

$13,800* *They Were In Forty Pairs... (Mourlot 37), 1948,* plate 2 from Four Tales from the Arabian Nights, Pantheon Books, Inc., s., i. Pl. 2, #64/90, full margins, light-staining, taped, good cond., Mr. and Mrs. Sam B. Cantey III Estate, (05-11-93, Christie-NY, #150, illus.), borderline

14½ x 11 in., (368 x 279 mm.), color lithograph on laid (BP 8809, DM 21,739, FR 73,248, Y 1,517,985).

BI *La Tour Eiffel (C. 243), 1974,* s., good cond., est. BP 20/30,000, (06-30-93, Sotheby-London, #411, illus.), 22½ x 15 in., (572 x 381 mm.), color monotype on wove.

$3884* *La Tour Eiffel A L'Ane (Mourlot 97), 1954,* s., #38/75, (06-10-93, Hauswedell/Nolt, #142, illus.), 15⁷⁄₁₆ x 11 in., (39.2 x 28 cm.), color lithograph on wove (BP 2541, DM 6325, FR 21,294, Y 412,270).

$155* *Traumerei (Mourlot 605), 1969,* part of pair from Derriere le Mirror, center crease, (09-25-92, Granier, #2788), sheet 15¹⁄₁₆ x 19⅞ in., (38.2 x 50.5 cm.), color lithograph on wove (BP 91, DM 230, FR 777, Y 18,709).

$7188* *The Travelling Circus (M. 583), 1969,* s., #2/50, full margins, good cond., mat/light/tape stains, slight rspot, verso discolored,, (02-11-93, Sotheby-NY, #95, illus.), 14⅜ x 21³⁄₁₆ in., (365 x 538 mm.), color lithograph (BP 5072, DM 11,907, FR 40,291, Y 866,546).

$7150* *The Travelling Circus (M. 583), 1969,* s., #25/50, full margins, good cond., mat/light stain, (11-05-92, Sotheby-NY, #131, illus.), 14½ x 21 in., (367 x 535 mm.), lithograph p. in colors (BP 4650, DM 11,308, FR 38,256, Y 877,193).

$2743* *La Tribu De Ruben (Sorlier 10 epreuves d'artiste),* s., epreuve d'artiste 20/25, (05-12-93, AB Stockholm, #7012, illus.), 24³⁄₁₆ x 18⅛ in., (61.5 x 46 cm.), color lithograph on Arches (BP 1791, DM 4426, FR 14,908, Y 306,241, SK 20,350).

$413* *Two Lithographic Greeting Cards, Mourlot 904, 1977, Mourlot 957,* first num. 309/550; second num. 162/450, (09-20-92, Hindman, #774), each 5½ x 4 in., (14 x 10.2 cm.), lithograph (BP 242, DM 613, FR 2096, Y 51,044).

$1540* *Two Women And A Vase (Mourlot #217), 1959,* s., #256/3000, (05-14-93, DuMouchelle, #2049, illus.), 8 x 12½ in., (20.3 x 31.8 cm.), b/w lithograph (BP 1001, DM 2477, FR 8324, Y 170,713).

$747* *Und Moses Besichtigte Das Ganze Werk (...) Und Segnete Sie (M. 466),1966,* Bl. 23 from the series The Story of The Exodus, num., s., (12-01-92, Karl/Faber, #440), 18⅛ x 13⅜ in., (46 x 34 cm.), color lithograph on wove (BP 494, DM 1191, FR 4058, Y 93,003).

$1650* *Untitled,* s. Marc Chagall, num. 63/75, (09-25-92, Wolf, #41), 13¼ x 10¼ in., (33.7 x 26 cm.), lithograph in colors (BP 964, DM 2446, FR 8271, Y 199,155).

$66* *Untitled (Lovers With Calf And Bird),* from "Derriere le Miroir", prov., (12-10-92, Sloan, #3044), 9⁵⁄₁₆ x 8 in., (23.7 x 20.3 cm.), color lithograph (BP 43, DM 104, FR 357, Y 8164).

$12,075* *Untitled (M. 505), 1967,* from Circus, s., #10/24, full margins, time staining, skinning, goodcond., (05-11-93, Christie-NY, #164, illus.), 16½ x 12¾ in., (419 x 324 mm.), color lithograph on Arches (BP 7708, DM 19,022, FR 64,092, Y 1,328,237).

$187* *Untitled (Sorlier 572), 1969,* good cond., (10-31-92, Cleveland, #272A), 12⅜ x 9½ in., (31.4 x 24.1 cm.), color lithograph (BP 120, DM 288, FR 976, Y 23,164).

$2990* *Untitled, c. 1975,* for Louis Aragon, Celui qui dit les choses sans rien dire, s., #22/25, pub. Maeght, full margins, foxing, creasing, very good cond., (05-11-93, Christie-NY, #174, illus.), plate 15⅝ x 11¾ in., (397 x 298 mm.), color etching w/aquatint on laid Japan (BP 1909, DM 4710, FR 15,870, Y 328,897).

$929* *La Vache Bleue (M. 488), 1967,* from XXieme Siecle, Nr. 29, (10-09-92, Winterberg, #1886), 12³⁄₁₆ x 9¼ in., (31 x 23.5 cm.), color lithograph on wove (BP 551, DM 1380, FR 4633, Y 113,100).

$553* *Vence (Sorlier S. 35), 1954,* Stein s., d., (04-21-93, Germann, #332), 39³⁄₁₆ x 24⁷⁄₁₆ in., (995 x 620 mm.), color lithograph (BP 359, DM 884, FR 2989, Y 61,220, SF 805).

BI *"Le Verger (Hommage A Teriade)" (Sorlier S. 134/135), 1973,* by Charles Sorlier after a colored lithograph by Chagall, s., est. DM 3,5/3,800, (11-28-92, Grisebach, #458, illus.), 20⅜ x 16¹⁵⁄₁₆ in., (51.8 x 43 cm.), colored lithograph on wove.

$5522* *Die Verliebten In Grau, Les Amoureaux En Gris (Mourlot 194), 1957,* s., num., Maeght, (12-02-92, Dorling, #2558, illus.), 10¹³⁄₁₆ x 8¾ in., (27.5 x 22.2 cm.), color

lithograph on handmade Arches (BP 3562, DM 8684, FR 29,640, Y 687,072).

$1161* *Vers L'Autre Clarte (S. 1050), 1985,* #569/1000, blindstamp, (10-09-92, Winterberg, #1896, illus.), 16¾ x 12¹⁵⁄₁₆ in., (42.5 x 33 cm.), color lithograph on Arches wove (BP 689, DM 1725, FR 5791, Y 141,344).

$1363* *Die Vier Jahreszeiten (Sorlier 71), 1974,* poster, (06-19-93, Wachholtz, #641, illus.), plate 37 x 25³⁄₁₆ in., (94 x 64 cm.), color lithograph on thick white paper (BP 915, DM 2301, FR 7736, Y 151,092).

$20,700* *View Of Notre-Dame (M. 977), 1980,* s., #7/50, pub. Maeght, full margins, good cond., handling creases, (05-13-93, Sotheby-NY, #525, illus.), 36¼ x 23¾ in., (920 x 603 mm.), lithograph in colors (BP 13,590, DM 33,425, FR 112,745, Y 2,311,042).

$3567* *Le Village Fantastique (M. 429), 1964-65,* s., H.C., (12-04-92, AB Stockholm, #7026), 25¹⁵⁄₁₆ x 19¹¹⁄₁₆ in., (66 x 50 cm.), lithograph in colors on BFK (BP 2288, DM 5681, FR 19,271, Y 445,318, SK 24,200).

BI *Village With A Red Donkey (M. 1025), 1984,* s., num. 20/50, full margins, very good cond., hinge remains, skinnedarea, creases, light-staining, est. $6/8,000, (02-24-93, Butterfield, #2731, illus.), 10⅞ x 13½ in., (276 x 343 mm.), lithograph in colors on Arches wove.

$6872* *La Ville De Vence (Mourl. 92), 1954,* sws., s., (06-23-93, Kornfeld, #249), color lithograph on wove (BP 4668, DM 11,628, FR 39,112, Y 748,665, SF 10,350).

$2054* *Vision A Esaie, 1952/56,* plate s., #44/100, (04-24-93, Kunsthaus, #497, illus.), 12⁷⁄₁₆ x 9¹¹⁄₁₆ in., (31.6 x 24.6 cm.), etching hand-colored on hand-made Arches (BP 1296, DM 3219, FR 10,873, Y 226,661).

BI *Vision D'Apocalypse, 1967,* #29/35, s., (05-26-93, Lempertz, #71, illus.), sh 22⁷⁄₁₆ x 19⁷⁄₁₆ in., (57 x 49.3 cm.), etching and aquatint on imitated Japan.

BI *Vision De Moise, (M. 554, a),* second version, #42/75, s., est. DM 19,500, (10-09-92, Winterberg, #1887, illus.), 22¼ x 29¹⁵⁄₁₆ in., (56.5 x 76 cm.), lithograph.

$3093* *Vision De Paris (Mourlot II, 287), 1960,* s., artist's proof, mat traces verso, good cond., (06-28-93, Loudmer, #206), 13⁹⁄₁₆ x 10¹⁄₁₆ in., (345 x 255 mm.), sh 18⅞ x 12¹³⁄₁₆ in., (345 x 255 mm.), color lithograph on Arches wove (BP 2071, DM 5256, FR 17,705, Y 328,170).

$4025* *Visions Of Moses (M. 554a), 1968,* s., i. Epreuve d'artiste, pub. Maeght, good cond., crease, discolored, (02-11-93, Sotheby-NY, #93, illus.), sheet 22½ x 30 in., (572 x 762 mm.), color lithograph (BP 2840, DM 6667, FR 22,562, Y 485,232).

$2558* *Vitraux Pour Jerusalem (M. 366-372), 1962,* book, title page, reproductions, text and justification, s. by artistand author, num. 86, pub. Andre Sauret, full margins, good cond., loose, orig.paper wrappers, (12-03-92, Sotheby-London, #243, illus.), seven lithographs, 3 p. in colors, on Arches (BP 1650, DM 4023, FR 13,731, Y 318,278).

BI *Vitraux Pour Jerusalem, Monte Carlo, Andre Sauret, 1962 (M. 366-372),* s. by artist and pub., i., copy 175 of 250, full margins, loose, foxing, good cond., orig. portfolio, est. $6/8,000, (05-11-93, Christie-NY, #160), 15³⁄₁₆ x 11⁹⁄₁₆ in., (385 x 293 mm.), 3 color lithographs, 4 lithographs in black, including cover, 60 reprods., t., just. and text, on wove.

$1210* *Vocation De Jeremie, 1931-39,* plate 100 of the Bible, pub. Teriade, 1956, init., #III/V, full margins, good cond., mat/light stain, fox marks in image, discolored verso, (11-05-92, Sotheby-NY, #115), 12½ x 9½ in., (319 x 242 mm.), etching w/touches of hand coloring (BP 787, DM 1914, FR 6474, Y 148,448).

$121* *"The Window", 1957,* pub. Maeght, Mourlot Vol.I No. 175, dirt, good cond., (10-31-92, Cleveland, #272), 13¾ x 8⅝ in., (34.9 x 21.9 cm.), color lithograph (BP 78, DM 186, FR 632, Y 14,988).

$10,450* *The Wolf Pit (M. 312), 1961,* from Daphnis and Chloe, s., #37/60, full margins, light/mat staining, very good cond., (11-09-92, Christie-NY, #69, illus.), 16⅝ x 12½ in., (422 x 318 mm.), colored lithograph on Arches (BP 6909, DM 16,683, FR 56,365, Y 1,296,848).

$3450* *Woman Circus Rider (M. 153), 1956,* s., #96/100, pinholes, creasing, staining, good cond., (05-11-93, Christie-NY, #153, illus.), sheet 14¼ x 21 in., (362 x 533 mm.), color lithograph on Rives (BP 2202, DM 5435, FR 18,312, Y 379,496).

$6326* *Woman Circus Rider On Red Horse (M. 191), 1957,* s., i. epreuve d'artiste, margins, mount-staining, discoloration, tape, (12-01-92, Christie-London, #328, illus.), L. 12¹³⁄₁₆ x 9¹³⁄₁₆ in., (325 x 250 mm.), lithograph in colors on wove (BP 4180, DM 10,083, FR 34,362, Y 787,600).

BI *"XXeme Siecle" (Mourlot 470 a/b), 1966,* for XXeme Siecle, very fine cond., centerfold, est. $3/400, (05-15-93, Cleveland, #373), 12 x 18⅛ in., (30.5 x 46 cm.), color lithograph.

$4263* *XXieme Siecle, Special Issue (M. 699), 1973,* s., i. Epreuve d'artiste, full margins, good cond., (12-03-92, Sotheby-London, #260, illus.), 13¾ x 19¼ in., (349 x 489 mm.), lithograph in colors on Arches (BP 2750, DM 6704, FR 22,882, Y 530,422).

$1588* *Der Zauberer Von Paris (Sorlier 129), 1970,* s., (10-14-92, Germann, #250, illus.), 28⅛ x 20¹¹⁄₁₆ in., (715 x 510 mm.), color lithograph (BP 932, DM 2324, FR 7881, Y 192,438, SF 2070).

$1059* *Die Zauberflote (Mourlot CS 38-Sorlier (Plakate) S. 107), 1967,* (06-10-93, Hauswedell/Nolt, #153, illus.), 39⅜ x 25¹⁵⁄₁₆ in., (100 x 66 cm.), color lithograph (BP 693, DM 1724, FR 5806, Y 112,408).

CHAGALL, Marc (after)

$3334* *Les Amoureux Au Panier, 1949,* s., large margins, (02-03-93, Ader Tajan, #87), 26¹¹⁄₁₆ x 19½ in., (67.8 x 49.5 cm.), color lithograph (BP 2327, DM 5490, FR 18,615, Y 414,728).

$2990* *The Angel Of Judgement (C.S. 45), 1974,* by Charles Sorlier, s., #165/200, full margins, mat staining, taped, (05-11-93, Christie-NY, #181), borderline 20¼ x 16⅞ in., (514 x 429 mm.), color lithograph on Arches (BP 1909, DM 4710, FR 15,870, Y 328,897).

BI *"Angel Of Judgement", 1974,* Musee Nationale exhibition poster, s., d. Marc Chagall, 1977, embosse stamp, est. $1,3/1,600, (04-16-93, DuMouchelle, #2033, illus.), 20¼ x 16¾ in., (51.4 x 42.5 cm.), color lithograph.

$6900* *Angel With Candlestick (C.S. 46), 1973,* by Charles Sorlier, s., #66/200, full margins, light-staining, good cond., (05-11-93, Christie-NY, #182), borderline 20¼ x 16⅞ in., (514 x 429 mm.), color lithograph on Arches (BP 4405, DM 10,870, FR 36,624, Y 758,992).

$1498* *Carmen, Metropolitan Opera, Lincoln Center (M. CS39; S.p. 108), 1966,* by C. Sorlier, p. Mourlot, pub. Editions of the Metropolitan Opera, tear, nick, crease, defects, (12-01-92, Christie-London, #343), sheet 39½ x 25⁹⁄₁₆ in., (100.3 x 64.9 cm.), lithograph in colors on wove (BP 990, DM 2388, FR 8137, Y 186,504).

$3891* *Couple Dans Les Mimosas (C.S. 32), 1967,* by Charles Sorlier, s., 112/150, from Nice et la Cote D'Azur, (12-04-92, AB Stockholm, #7032), 24³⁄₁₆ x 18⅛ in., (61.5 x 46 cm.), lithograph in colors on Arches (BP 2496, DM 6197, FR 21,021, Y 485,768, SK 26,400).

BI *Festival De L'Ile Saint Louis,* num. from edit. of 50, s., d., est. FF15/25,000, (03-11-93, Ader Tajan, #94A), 26¹⁵⁄₁₆ x 21¼ in., (68.5 x 54 cm.), poster.

BI *Folio Containing Ten Reproductions In Colors With Accompanying Text,* est. BP70/100, (01-21-93, Bonhams-Chelsea, #119), subject 13½ x 10 in., (34.3 x 25.4 cm.), .

$7753* *Das In Mimosen Gebettete Paar (Sorlier CS 32), 1967,* s., #23/150, from Nizza und die Cote d'Azur series, (05-26-93, Lempertz, #78), 29⁵⁄₁₆ x 20⅞ in., (74.5 x 53 cm.), color lithograph on wove (BP 5016, DM 12,650, FR 42,576, Y 842,351).

$1870* *L'Horloge,* by George Visat, s. by Chagall, num. 73/300, (09-20-92, Hindman, #767, illus.), 12½ x 9½ in., (31.8 x 24.1 cm.), color etching and aquatint (BP 1095, DM 2775, FR 9492, Y 231,121).

BI *The Magic Flute (CS 38), 1967,* appears good cond., est. $2/2,500, (06-11-93, Doyle, #25), 24¾ x 38 in., (629 x 965 mm.), color lithograph and poster.

$4370* *Maternity (Charles Sorlier 7), 1954,* by Charles Sorlier, s., #114/300, wide margins, light/mat staining, glue, (05-11-93, Christie-NY, #179), borderline 20½ x 26½ in., (521 x 673 mm.), color lithograph on Arches (BP 2790, DM 6884, FR 23,195, Y 480,695).

BI *Nice And The Cote D'Azur: Couple In Mimosa (C.S. 32), 1967,* by Charles Sorlier, s., #23/150, margins, good cond., surface abrasions w/ink loss, creases, est. $1,5/2,000, (10-28-92, Butterfield, #2623), 24¼ x 18⅛ in., (616 x 460 mm.), color lithograph on Arches.

$3520* *Nice And The Cote D'Azur: Couple In Mimosa (Mourlot CS 32), 1967,* by Charles Sorlier, s. by Chagall, #1/150, (05-16-93, Hindman, #491), 24 x 18 in., (61 x 45.7 cm.), color lithograph (BP 2289, DM 5662, FR 19,027, Y 390,201).

BI *Red Poppies (M. CS2), 1949,* s., #133/400, pub. Maeght, trimmed, light and mount-staining, foxmarks, est. BP 4/6,000, (12-01-92, Christie-London, #341, illus.), L. 22⁵⁄₁₆ x 16¼ in., (567 x 412 mm.), lithograph in colors on Arches.

BI *Der Richtende Engel (Sorlier 147), 1974,* s., d., poster, est. SF 1,7/2,000, (04-21-93, Germann, #333), 29¹⁵⁄₁₆ x 20¹¹⁄₁₆ in., (760 x 525 mm.), color lithograph.

$1459* *Romeo Et Juliet, L'Opera (Charles Sorlier 10), 1964,* by Charles Sorlier, s., for the Opera, (12-04-92, AB Stockholm, #7030), 24¹³⁄₁₆ x 38¾ in., (63 x 98.5 cm.), poster, lithograph in colors (BP 936, DM 2324, FR 7882, Y 182,147, SK 9900).

$4688* *Der Strauss (Sorlier Band V CS 8, S. 197), 1955,* by Charles Sorlier, #149/300, s., stains, (11-21-92, Lempertz, #84, illus.), 25³⁄₁₆ x 19⅝ in., (64 x 49.8 cm.), color lithograph on Arches wove (BP 3087, DM 7474, FR 25,177, Y 583,012).

$4600* *The Tribe Of Benjamin (C.S. 23), 1964,* from Twelve Maquettes of Stained Glass Windows for Jerusalem, by Charles Sorlier, s., i. epreuve d' artiste, #17/25, full margins, light/time staining, good cond., (05-11-93, Christie-NY, #180), borderline 24⅛ x 18⅛ in., (613 x 460 mm.), color lithograph on Arches (BP 2936, DM 7246, FR 24,416, Y 505,995).

$1980* *The Tribe Of Joseph, 1964, Mourlot CS 22,* by Charles Sorlier, s. by Chagall, num. 99/150, pub. in album Douze Maquettes de Vitraux pour Jerusalem, (09-20-92, Hindman, #772), 24½ x 18¼ in., (62.2 x 46.4 cm.), color lithograph (BP 1159, DM 2938, FR 10,051, Y 244,716).

$4400* *The Tribe Of Levi (Charles Sorlier 14), 1964,* from Twelve Maquettes of Stained Glass Windows for Jerusalem, by Charles Sorlier, s., #186/200, full margins, staining, good cond., (11-09-92, Christie-NY, #82, illus.), 610 x 460 in., (x cm.), colored lithograph on Arches (BP 2909, DM 7024, FR 23,732, Y 546,041).

BI *"Tribu De Joseph", 1962,* est. FF800/1,000, (04-04-93, Pescheteau, #181), 12¾ x 9⁹⁄₁₆ in., (32.4 x 24.3 cm.), color lithograph.

BI *"Tribu De Joseph", 1962,* (01-28-93, Pescheteau, #97), 12¾ x 9⁹⁄₁₆ in., (32.4 x 24.3 cm.), color lithograph.

CHAGALL, Marc (attrib.) Russian/French 1887-1985

$605* *Figures With Calf,* s., #50/90, (10-30-92, Sloan, #2151), sight 14⅜ x 10½ in., (36.5 x 26.7 cm.), lithograph (BP 388, DM 931, FR 3158, Y 74,941).

CHAHINE, Edgar French 1874-1947

$97* *Au Bois De Boulogne (Tabanelli 420), 1931,* fourth and final state, s., num., s. artist's proofs, small tears, (06-28-93, Loudmer, #209), 8¹¹⁄₁₆ x 12⅜ in., (220 x 315 mm.), sh 12¹⁵⁄₁₆ x 19¹¹⁄₁₆ in., (220 x 315 mm.), black drypoint on Arches wove (BP 65, DM 165, FR 555, Y 10,292).

$155* *Carmen (T. 126), 1904,* s., t., (06-28-93, Loudmer, #210), 17¹⁵⁄₁₆ x 6½ in., (455 x 165 mm.), sh 21⅝ x 14⅜ in., (455 x 165 mm.), black drypoint on Arches laid (BP 104, DM 263, FR 887, Y 16,446).

$825* *"Demoiselle Au Tennis" (Tabenilli 32 I/III), 1899,* s., hinges, good cond., (10-31-92, Cleveland, #273, illus.), 14⅞ x 6 in., (35.6 x 15.2 cm.), etching (BP 529, DM 1269, FR 4306, Y 102,192).

$1380* *Elvira (T. 165), 1906,* only state, s., plate tone, upper margin possibly trimmed, good cond., mat staining, soiling, foxing, glue remains, notations, (05-19-93, Butterfield, #1899, illus.), 14½ x 19¾ in., (368 x 502 mm.), drypoint on Japan (BP 896, DM 2243, FR 7558, Y 152,773).

$468* *Full Length Portrait Of A Woman In A White Hat,* num. 16, s., margins, spotting, (07-16-92, Bonhams-Chelsea, #455, illus.), plate 19¾ x 13½ in., (50.2 x 34.3 cm.), drypoint etching (BP 242, DM 691, FR 2334, Y 58,625).

$550* *"Ghemmaau Turban Noir" (T 294 I/II), 1910,* s., good cond., (10-31-92, Cleveland, #275, illus.), 19¾ x 11¾ in., (50.2 x 29.8 cm.), etching (BP 352, DM 846, FR 2871, Y 68,128).

$4228* *Impressions D'Italie (T. 180-229), 1906,* complete set of 50, just., s., (02-24-93, Picard, #61), etching and drypoint (BP 2948, DM 6864, FR 23,269, Y 496,128).

$308* *Juliette (Tabanelli 107), 1903,* s., ded., #30/40, small margins, (05-06-93, Laurin, #15), drypoint (BP 195, DM 485, FR 1633, Y 33,887).

$1380* *Lara (T. 168), 1906,* 2nd final state, s., #No II/50, plate tone, upper margin possibly trimmed, good cond., mat staining, foxing, creases, tape/glue remains, surface abrasions in image, (05-19-93, Butterfield, #1900), 13¾ x 18 in., (349 x 457 mm.), drypoint on Japan (BP 896, DM 2243, FR 7558, Y 152,773).

BI *Louise France (Madame Vauquier) (T. 91), 1902,* s., margins, good cond., time/light-staining, surface soiling, stains, hinge remains, mildew residue, rubbed areas in image, est. $1,2/1,500, (10-28-92, Butterfield, #2624), 25⅜ x 17⅝ in., (645 x 448 mm.), color aquatint, drypoint and etching on Arches laid paper.

$850* *Louise France (Madame Vauquier) (Tabanelli 91), 1902,* s., (06-04-93, Bassenge, #5635), 25³⁄₁₆ x 17½ in., (64 x 44.5 cm.), color aquatint/etching on hand-made Arches (BP 562, DM 1380, FR 4652, Y 91,674).

$328* *Mademoiselle Delvair, De La Comedie Francaise (Tabanelli 73), 1901,* 1 of 15, defintive state, s., num. rubbing, full margins, (02-24-93, Picard, #60), drypoint on Japan (BP 229, DM 532, FR 1805, Y 38,489).

$323* *Midinette (M. Tabanelli 130), 1904,* definitive state, s., large margins, (02-03-93, Ader Tajan, #88), 18⅜ x 10⅛ in., (46.7 x 25.7 cm.), etching, drypoint and soft ground etching (BP 225, DM 532, FR 1803, Y 40,179).

BI *"Portrait De Femme" (Tabanelli 29 iv/IV), 1899,* good cond., weakness along plate mark, est. $6/800, (05-15-93, Cleveland, #375), 13¾ x 11¾ in., (34.9 x 29.8 cm.), drypoint.

BI *Portrait Of A Lady,* s., #14/50, est. $4/600, (10-30-92, Sloan, #2155), 9⅜ x 13⅜ in., (23.8 x 34 cm.), drypoint etching.

BI *"La Promenade" (T. 57),* pub. La Revue de L'Art 1899, good cond., est. $2-400, (10-31-92, Cleveland, #274), 4½ x 8⅝ in., (11.4 x 21.9 cm.), drypoint.

$658* *Le Promenoir (T. 110), 1903,* proof, s., annot., small margins, 1 of 50, cracks, (05-06-93, Laurin, #16), etching, aquatint and drypoint on Japan (BP 417, DM 1036, FR 3489, Y 72,395).

$147* *"La Soupe",* ink t., s., (01-28-93, Pescheteau, #100), a vue 12⅝ x 17⁵⁄₁₆ in., (32 x 44 cm.), etching and aquatint (BP 97, DM 233, FR 788, Y 18,252).

$605* *Suzette (M.T. 264), 1907,* #16/50, s., thin spots, good margins, drystamp, (02-03-93, Ader Tajan, #90), 19¹³⁄₁₆ x 13¹¹⁄₁₆ in., (50.4 x 34.7 cm.), drypoint on fixed Chine (BP 422, DM 996, FR 3378, Y 75,258).

$385* *"Two Women In A Cafe",* s., light staining, laid down on support sheet, very good cond., (12-04-92, Doyle, #85), 14 x 11¾ in., (356 x 298 mm.), etching, aquatint and drypoint (BP 247, DM 613, FR 2080, Y 48,065).

$268* *Venise. Il Bacino Di San Marco (M.T., 355), 1922,* definitive state, t., #76/100, s., large margins, (04-02-93, Picard, #62), 8⁹⁄₁₆ x 12½ in., (21.7 x 31.7 cm.), drypoint on Chine applique (BP 177, DM 431, FR 1463, Y 30,513).

$227* *Venise. Maison Du Soleil (M.T., 364), 1923,* yellowed, t., s., good margins, (04-02-93, Picard, #63), 6¼ x 8⁷⁄₁₆ in., (15.8 x 21.5 cm.), drypoint (BP 150, DM 365, FR 1239, Y 25,845).

$343* *Venise: Casin Dei Spiriti (M.T. 380), 1923,* definitive state, #36/100, s., large untrimmed margins, (02-03-93, Ader Tajan, #92), 8⁹⁄₁₆ x 12⅜ in., (21.8 x 31.5 cm.), drypoint on fixed Chine on tinted paper (BP 239, DM 565, FR 1915, Y 42,667).

$363* *Venise: La Piazza (M.T. 382), 1923,* definitive state, s., large margins, (02-03-93, Ader Tajan, #93), 12½ x 8⁹⁄₁₆ in., (31.8 x 21.8 cm.), drypoint on tinted paper (BP 253, DM 598, FR 2027, Y 45,155).

$440* *Venise: Soto Portico Molin (T. 359), 1922,* s., t., #45/100, 3rd final state, margins slightly trimmed, good cond., mat/light-staining, staining, surface soiling, (10-28-92, Butterfield, #2797), 7¹³⁄₁₆ x 10¹³⁄₁₆ in., (198 x 275 mm.), etching w/drypoint on Arches (BP 280, DM 680, FR 2307, Y 53,988).

$330* *"Woman With Yellow Hat",* s., epreuve d'etat, heavily soiled, multiple damages, stains, splits, laid down on support sheet, (12-04-92, Doyle, #84), 15½ x 11 in., (394 x 279 mm.), colored drypoint (BP 212, DM 526, FR 1783, Y 41,199).

CHAIX, Imprimerie, Publisher

$14,665* *Les Maitres De L'Affiche, 1896-1900: 256,* complete set of 240 plates w/additional 16 plates en prime, blindstamp, volumes I, II, V w/title pages, list of plates and preface, unbound, in paper folders, very good cond., (11-30-92, Phillips-London, #457), sheet 16 x 11¾ in., (406 x 298 mm.), color lithograph (BP 9680, DM 23,363, FR 79,313, Y 1,825,140).

CHALLON, A. E.

$273* *Pas De Quatre,* by T. H. Maguire, pub. J. Mitchell, September 8, 1845, stained, tearto image, (04-22-93, Bonhams-Chelsea, #141), image 18½ x 16 in., (47 x 40.6 cm.), lithograph (BP 176, DM 439, FR 1480, Y 30,016).

CHALON, Henry Bernard (after)

$345* *The Racky Pack (S. p. 92), 1814,* by William Ward, trimmed, minor defects, Anthony N. B. Garvan Coll., (06-05-93, Christie-NY, #57), sh 20¾ x 23½ in., (527 x 597 mm.), mezzotint w/hand-coloring on wove (BP 227, DM 559, FR 1885, Y 37,009).

CHALON, John James British 1778-1854

$55* *Le Porteur D'Eau, 1821,* pub. Rodwell and Martin, (10-18-92, Hindman, #511), 9 x 6¼ in., (22.9 x 15.9 cm.), hand colored lithograph (BP 34, DM 82, FR 278, Y 6599).

CHALON, L. (after)

$25 *Figure Subjects: Eight,* (12-11-92, G.A. Key, #80), 5 x 4 in., (12.7 x 10.2 cm.), black and white photogravure (BP 16, DM 39, FR 135, Y 3094).

CHAMBAS, Jean Paul b. 1947

$180* *"A L'Opera",* EA, 1/XI, s., (04-04-93, Pescheteau, #183), 25⁹⁄₁₆ x 19¹¹⁄₁₆ in., (65 x 50 cm.), pochoir on wove (BP 119, DM 289, FR 983, Y 20,494).

CHAMBERLAIN, J., Engraver

$143* *July Flowers, 1950,* s., blindstamp, pub. Frost and Reed, margins, (11-12-92, Bonhams-Chelsea, #10), plate 21½ x 17½ in., (54.6 x 44.5 cm.), color mezzotint (BP 94, DM 227, FR 764, Y 17,731).

BI *Still Life Of Roses In A Basket, 1962,* s., blindstamp, pub. Frost and Reed, margins, est. BP 50/80, (11-12-92, Bonhams-Chelsea, #11), plate 16½ x 20¼ in., (41.9 x 51.4 cm.), color mezzotint.

BI *Tetes Des Negues, 1954,* s., blindstamp, pub. Frost and Reed, margins, est. BP 40/70, (11-12-92, Bonhams-Chelsea, #25), plate 14¾ x 18½ in., (37.5 x 47 cm.), color mezzotint.

$151* *"Young Royals Playing With Spaniels In A Garden", 1954,* s., blindstamp, pub. Frost and Reed, margins, back cover lot, (11-12-92, Bonhams-Chelsea, #3, illus.), plate 25¼ x 17½ in., (64.1 x 44.5 cm.), color mezzotint (BP 99, DM 239, FR 807, Y 18,723).

$134* *"Young Royals Playing With Spaniels In A Garden", 1954,* s., blindstamp, pub. Frost and Reed, margins, back cover illus., (11-12-92, Bonhams-Chelsea, #24, illus.), plate 25¼ x 17½ in., (64.1 x 44.5 cm.), color mezzotint (BP 88, DM 212, FR 716, Y 16,615).

$160* *"Young Royals Playing With Spaniels In A Garden", 1954,* s., blindstamp, pub. Frost and Reed, margins, back cover lot, (11-12-92, Bonhams-Chelsea, #4, illus.), plate 25¼ x 17½ in., (64.1 x 44.5 cm.), color mezzotint (BP 105, DM 254, FR 855, Y 19,839).

$151* *"Young Royals Playing With Spaniels In A Garden", 1954,* s., blindstamp, pub. Frost and Reed, margins, back cover lot, (11-12-92, Bonhams-Chelsea, #5, illus.), plate 25¼ x 17½ in., (64.1 x 44.5 cm.), color mezzotint (BP 99, DM 239, FR 807, Y 18,723).

$134* *"Young Royals Playing With Spaniels In A Garden", 1954,* s., blindstamp, pub. Frost and Reed, margins, back cover illus., (11-12-92, Bonhams-Chelsea, #79, illus.), plate 25¼ x 17½ in., (64.1 x 44.5 cm.), color mezzotint (BP 88, DM 212, FR 716, Y 16,615).

$134* *"Young Royals Playing With Spaniels In A Garden", 1954,* s., blindstamp, pub. Frost and Reed, margins, back cover illus., (11-12-92, Bonhams-Chelsea, #80, illus.), plate 25¼ x 17½ in., (64.1 x 44.5 cm.), color mezzotint (BP 88, DM 212, FR 716, Y 16,615).

CHAMBERLAIN, John   American b. 1927
$707* *Composition,* s., #26/48, sig. stamp, blindstamp, (06-12-93, Hauswedell/Nolt, #60), 35⁷/₁₆ x 23¹³/₁₆ in., (90 x 60.5 cm.), color aquatint on Arches (BP 463, DM 1151, FR 3868, Y 74,398).

CHAMBERLAIN, Samuel   American 1895-1975
BI *"Church Of San Giovanni Battiste-Siracusa" and "Amalfi": Two,* each s., #30/100 and 41/100, est. $200/300, (09-17-92, Sloan, #1420), larger 6⁷/₈ x 7 in., (19.1 x 29.2 cm.), etching.
BI *"A Side Street In Beauvais" and "The Bell Tower Moulins: Two,* s.; first #5/100, full margins, light staining; second mat burn, toning, est. $3/500, (12-12-92, Weschler, #113), each 13 x 9¼ in., (33 x 23.5 cm.), etching and drypoint.
$121* *"Vitre" (Chamberlain 35), 1926,* s., edit. 37/50, paper light struck, (10-31-92, Cleveland, #97), 3⁷/₈ x 5⁵/₈ in., (9.8 x 14.3 cm.), drypoint (BP 78, DM 186, FR 632, Y 14,988).

CHAMBERLIN, Price   American 1905-1961
BI *The Knights,* s., t., d. (19)33, circulated by Print-A-Month Club, est. $200/300, (07-03-92, Sloan, #330), 6 x 8 in., (15.2 x 20.3 cm.), color linocut.
$83* *The Knights, 1933,* s., ed. 4, (11-12-92, Freemn/Fine Art, #48), 6 x 8 in., (15.2 x 20.3 cm.), hand colored lino cut (BP 55, DM 132, FR 444, Y 10,291).

CHAMPSEIX, E. Paul
BI *Chemis De Fer Du Midi, Foix Pyrenees Ariegeoises, 1930,* pub. Lucien Serre & Cie, cond. 1, laid on linen, est. BP 3/400, (10-13-92, Phillips-London, #10), 39³/₁₆ x 24⁷/₁₆ in., (99.5 x 62 cm.), color lithograph.

CHAMPSEIX, E.P.
$230* *P.O. Midi: Telepherique D'Artouste, 1130-1930 Metres,* excell. cond., (01-23-93, Ribeyre/Baron, #103), 39⅜ x 24 in., (100 x 61 cm.), poster (BP 150, DM 366, FR 1237, Y 28,786).

CHANCEL
$660* *Le Tzarewitch,* Leroy and Herve-Baille, B+ cond., discoloration, (08-06-92, Swann, #84, illus.), 47½ x 31 in., (120.7 x 78.7 cm.), (BP 345, DM 975, FR 3293, Y 84,184).

CHANT, John, Engraver
$255* *The Trial Of William Lord Ruisdell,* surface defects, (03-17-93, Bonhams-Chelsea, #306), image 22 x 34 in., (55.9 x 86.4 cm.), engraving (BP 176, DM 424, FR 1442, Y 29,909).

CHAPATTE, H.
$638* *Basses-Alpes. Neiges Inconnues Sous Le Soleil De Provence, c. 1935,* very good cond., (03-15-93, Arcole, #82, illus.), 39⅜ x 24³/₁₆ in., (100 x 61.5 cm.), (BP 444, DM 1060, FR 3602, Y 75,575).

CHAPELET, R.
$358* *Cie De Navigation Mixte: L'Algerie Par Port-vendres. "La Traversee La Plus Courte Dans Les Eaux Les Plus Arbitrees",* very good cond., (03-13-93, Laurin, #42), 39⅜ x 24⁷/₁₆ in., (100 x 62 cm.), (BP 250, DM 596, FR 2026, Y 42,192).

CHAPELET ET BEAUME
$159* *Bedouins A Pied Et Sur Ane Sur Fond De Baie Et De Village Indigene. Village Africain Et Dromadaire. Marche Au Niger Avec Touaregs Et Indigenes,* good cond., (03-13-93, Laurin, #130), 13⁹/₁₆ x 37 in., (34.5 x 94 cm.), (BP 111, DM 265, FR 900, Y 18,739).

CHAPELLIER, P.
$869* *Velocipedie Photographie,* p. P. Chapellier, defects, stamp, tears, backed on linen, (05-07-93, Christie-S. Ken, #92, illus.), 42¼ x 45¾ in., (107.3 x 116.2 cm.), color lithograph (BP 550, DM 1374, FR 4630, Y 95,684).

CHAPELLIER, Philippe
$1042* *Sauvez D'Abord Mon Spido Gaumont,* p. Philippe Chapellier, creases, defects, backed on linen, (05-07-93, Christie-S. Ken, #110, illus.), 45½ x 59 in., (115.6 x 149.9 cm.), color lithograph (BP 660, DM 1647, FR 5551, Y 114,732).

CHAPIN, James   American 1887-1975
BI *"Clown",* s., AAA edit., good cond., est. $60/100, (10-31-92, Cleveland, #98), 11½ x 9¾ in., (29.2 x 24.8 cm.), lithograph.

CHAPMAN, F.A. (after)
$275* *Revolutionary War Subjects: Pair,* engraved John McRae, (c) 1875, (11-13-92, DuMouchelle, #2368, illus.), color engravings (BP 178, DM 432, FR 1456, Y 34,132).

CHAPMAN, Henry Ford
$3850* *Etchings Of The Franciscan Missions Of California, (Cowan 217, HowesF250), 1883,* The Studio Press, s. H.C. Ford in plates, tissue-guards, minor soiling, original half morocco gilt, 1st edit., one of fifty copies, (12-16-92, Sotheby-NY, #156, illus.), 8s 17⁵/₁₆ x 12³/₁₆ in., (440 x 310 mm.), 24 etched plates (BP 2442, DM 5982, FR 20,490, Y 472,973).

CHAPMAN, J. Watkin
$22* *"Golden Pippin",* after Greuze, 1907, (03-10-93, Maynard, #646), 15½ x 12 in., (39.4 x 30.5 cm.), engraving (BP 15, DM 37, FR 124, Y 2599, C$ 28).

CHAPMAN, K.G.
$378* *Cold Coming, Winterproof Your Car With Shell Motor Oil, 1952,* p. Waterlow and Sons, ref. P 15, cond. 1, (10-13-92, Phillips-London, #167), 29¹⁵/₁₆ x 39⅝ in., (76 x 100.7 cm.), color lithograph (BP 220, DM 554, FR 1882, Y 45,835).
$711* *The New Mauritania Uses Shell, 1939,* p. Waterlow and Sons, ref. #542, cond. 1, (10-13-92, Phillips-London, #157, illus.), 29¹⁵/₁₆ x 44⅞ in., (76 x 114 cm.), color lithograph (BP 414, DM 1042, FR 3539, Y 86,213).
$579* *To Visit Britain's Landmarks, Tudor Tower, Pentlow, Essex, 1936,* p. Baynard Press, ref. #468, cond. 1, (10-13-92, Phillips-London, #111), 29¹⁵/₁₆ x 44⅞ in., (76 x 114 cm.), color lithograph (BP 337, DM 848, FR 2882, Y 70,207).

CHAR, Rene
$97* *Le Jardinier, 1959,* s., d., I/V, prov., traces of ded., t. erased, (06-28-93, Loudmer, #211), 1¹⁵/₁₆ x 1¹⁵/₁₆ in., (50 x 50 mm.), sh 5⅝ x 4⅝ in., (50 x 50 mm.), brown etching on wove (BP 65, DM 165, FR 555, Y 10,292).

CHARBONNEAU, Monique   Canadian b. 1928
$28* *"Intreme-Orient-Image 2",* #21/40, s. M. Charbonneau, (07-14-92, Encans, #99), 6⅞ x 8⅞ in., (17.5 x 22.5 cm.), etching (BP 15, DM 42, FR 140, Y 3501, C$ 33).
$36* *"Intreme-Orient-Image IV",* #21/40, s. M. Charbonneau, (09-15-92, Encans, #26), 8¹/₁₆ x 8⁷/₁₆ in., (20.5 x 21.5 cm.), drypoint and aquatint (BP 19, DM 54, FR 182, Y 4469, C$ 44).
$34* *"Intreme-Orient-Image VII",* #21/40, s. M Charbonneau, (06-16-93, Encans, #20), 11⅝ x 8⅜ in., (29.5 x 21.3 cm.), drypoint (BP 23, DM 56, FR 189, Y 3626, C$ 44).
$795* *"L'Oiseleur",* #11/12, s., d. M. Charbonneau 1969, (02-16-93, Encans, #17), 24⅛ x 23⅝ in., (61.2 x 60 cm.), wood engraving (BP 550, DM 1298, FR 4395, Y 95,244, C$ 999).

CHARCHOUNE, Serge   Russian 1888-1975
$130* *"Composition",* artist's proof, s., (04-04-93, Pescheteau, #184), 19¹¹/₁₆ x 25⁹/₁₆ in., (50 x 65 cm.), color lithograph on Arches (BP 86, DM 209, FR 710, Y 14,801).
$137* *"Composition",* E.A. s., (01-28-93, Pescheteau, #102), 25⁹/₁₆ x 18⅞ in., (65 x 48 cm.), color lithograph (BP 90, DM 217, FR 735, Y 17,010).
$147* *"Composition",* ded., d., s., (01-28-93, Pescheteau, #103), 26¾ x 20½ in., (68 x 52 cm.), color lithograph on wove (BP 97, DM 233, FR 788, Y 18,252).

CHARDEZ, Fd.
$359* *Champoing De La Romaine,* cond. B, (03-16-93, Boisgirard, #72), 24¹³/₁₆ x 18¹¹/₁₆ in., (63 x 47.5 cm.), poster (BP 248, DM 597, FR 2028, Y 41,978).

CHARDIN, Jean Baptiste Simeon (after)
$460* *Le Benedicite (Portalis and Beraldi II, 66B, no. 4), c. 1740,* by B. Lepicie, margins, surface losses, staining, James R. Herbert Boone Coll., (05-11-93, Christie-NY, #68), pl 15 x 10¾ in., (381 x 273 mm.), engraving on laid (BP 294, DM 725, FR 2442, Y 50,599).
$161* *Le Garcon Cabaretier (E. Bocher 22),* yellowed, definitive state, reddish stains, good margins, (02-03-93, Ader Tajan, #55), 11 x 8¹¹⁄₁₆ in., (28 x 22 cm.), etching and copper engraving (BP 112, DM 265, FR 899, Y 20,027).
$145* *La Maitresse D'Ecole (E. Bocher, num. 34), 1740,* 2nd state, faults, w/out margins, (04-02-93, Picard, #5), 8¹¹⁄₁₆ x 8¼ in., (22 x 21 cm.), etching and copperplate (BP 96, DM 233, FR 791, Y 16,509).

CHARGESHEIMER (Karl HARGESHEIMER)   German 1924-1972
BI *Dialog Der Madonnen, 1948,* t., est. DM 1,000, (11-12-'92, Lempertz, #34), 9⁷⁄₁₆ x 7¹⁄₁₆ in., (23.9 x 18 cm.), photograph, gelatin silver print.
BI *Das Grosse Welttheater, 40's,* i., est. DM 1,000, (11-12-92, Lempertz, #32, illus.), 8¹¹⁄₁₆ x 6⁷⁄₁₆ in., (22.1 x 16.4 cm.), photograph, gelatin silver print.
$834* *Junge Im Cowboykostum, 50's,* (11-12-92, Lempertz, #37), 11¾ x 15¹³⁄₁₆ in., (29.9 x 40.2 cm.), photograph, gelatin silver print (BP 533, DM 1311, FR 4467, Y 103,180).
BI *Medea Von Anouihl, 40's,* i., est. DM 1,000, (11-12-92, Lempertz, #33), 9⁵⁄₁₆ x 7¼ in., (23.7 x 18.4 cm.), photograph, gelatin silver print.
$4551* *Monoskripturen-Lichtgrafik, 1961: Ten,* unique, (11-12-92, Lempertz, #38, illus.), photograph, photochemical painting on gelatin silver paper (BP 2910, DM 7152, FR 24,376, Y 563,034).
$1289* *Portrat Eines Madchens, 50's,* tear, (11-12-92, Lempertz, #35, illus.), 15¾ x 11¹⁵⁄₁₆ in., (40 x 30.3 cm.), photograph, gelatin silver print (BP 824, DM 2026, FR 6904, Y 159,470).
$683* *Warten Auf Die Strassenbahn, 50's,* (11-12-92, Lempertz, #36, illus.), 11¹⁵⁄₁₆ x 15¾ in., (30.3 x 40 cm.), photograph, gelatin silver print (BP 437, DM 1073, FR 3658, Y 84,498).

CHARLET, Frantz   Belgian 1862-1928
$303* *"Les Champs Elysees",* s., good cond.?, pub. L'Estampe Moderne, 1925, embossed chop, (02-07-93, Bakker, #59), pl 10⅞ x 14⅝ in., (27.6 x 37.1 cm.), hand-colored etching (BP 210, DM 502, FR 1698, Y 37,705).
$275* *"Little Hollanders", c. 1912,* s., num. below image 199, printers blindstamp, prov., (08-05-92, Boos, #579), 24⁷⁄₁₆ x 20¹⁄₁₆ in., (620 x 510 mm.), color etching and aquatint (BP 144, DM 406, FR 1372, Y 35,023).
$33* *"Parisian Street Scene With Print Sellers",* num., s., (05-15-93, Dunning, #213), 13½ x 16 in., (34.3 x 40.6 cm.), etching and aquatint in color (BP 21, DM 53, FR 178, Y 3658).

CHARLOT, Jean   French 1898-1979
$863* *"Five Steps", "Mexican Kitchen", "Tortilleras With Rolled Petate II","The Distaff Side" and "Snake Dance" (M. 485; 486; 512; 551; 554), 1946 (2); 1947; 1951; 1952,* s., 4th d., 4th and 5th blindstamp of printer, 1st and 2nd p. Jose Sanchez at Taller de Grafica Popular, 3rd p. by Barrett, each pub. AAA, margins, good cond., hinge remains, foxing, surface soiling, (05-19-93, Butterfield, #1839), lithograph on wove (BP 560, DM 1403, FR 4726, Y 95,539).
$1045* *"Luz", "Sacrifice Of Isaac", "Bathers", and "The Yellow Robe", 1971:Four,* s. in stone, from Picture Book, nos. 9, 10, 15, 20, full margins, good cond., tape stains, foxing, yellowing, (11-23-92, Sotheby-NY, #260, illus.), 8 x 6⅛ in., (204 x 155 mm.), lithographs in colors (BP 683, DM 1673, FR 5676, Y 129,637).
$303* *Mexican Children,* plate s.; d. 1936, s., #23/240, (04-26-93, Selkirk, #155), sight 17 x 24 in., (43.2 x 61 cm.), color lithograph (BP 191, DM 475, FR 1604, Y 33,436).
$230* *Mexican Performers,* s., d. '38, (02-18-93, Sotheby-Arcade, #30), 12 x 9 in., (30.5 x 22.9 cm.), color lithograph (BP 159, DM 375, FR 1270, Y 27,401).
$825* *Picture Book (M. 117-161), 1933: Thirty-Two,* complete volume, ink s. on colophon by artist, Lynton Kistler, num. 231, i., pub. John Becker, good cond., staining, surface soiling, masking tape,skinned areas, (10-28-92, Butterfield, #2559), each sheet 11 x 8⅝ in., (279 x 219

mm.), chromolithograph on Linweave Text paper (BP 526, DM 1274, FR 4326, Y 101,227).
BI *Picture Book: The Petate No. 17 (M. 137), 1933,* s., margins, good cond., creases, mat staining, hinged, est. $5/600, (02-24-93, Butterfield, #2664), 6 x 8½ in., (152 x 216 mm.), lithograph in colors on laid.

CHARMOZ, Jacques   d. 1982
$229* *Scandale. Gaines, Soutiens-Gorges, Bas,* cond. B, (03-16-93, Boisgirard, #73), 60¹³⁄₁₆ x 44⅞ in., (154.5 x 114 cm.), poster (BP 158, DM 381, FR 1294, Y 26,777).

CHARNAY, Desire
$330* *Madagascar, c. 1863,* notations on mount recto, (04-07-93, Swann, #169), 10½ x 8 in., photograph, albumen print (BP 218, DM 534, FR 1806, Y 37,491).

CHARPENTIER, Francois Philippe   1734-1817
$1165* *La Culbute (P. and B., I, p. 362), 1766,* after Jean-Honore Fragonard, pub. Basan, wide margins, grey wash additions, staining, good cond., (12-01-92, Christie-London, #247, illus.), plate 11¹¹⁄₁₆ x 16⁵⁄₁₆ in., (297 x 415 mm.), etching w/engraving in the lavis-manner p. in bistre on Auvergne laid (BP 770, DM 1857, FR 6328, Y 145,045).

CHARPENTIER, Publisher
$283* *Lithographs: Twenty-Eight,* from Paris dans sa Splendeur after Benoist, spotting, foxing, tears, (10-07-92, Christie-S. Ken, #84), 9¾ x 14 in., (24.8 x 35.6 cm.), lithograph (BP 165, DM 409, FR 1389, Y 34,035).

CHAS-BORE
$259* *SNCF. Telepherique Du Solaize. Val. D'Isere. Savoie. "La Belle Station Sportive Francaise De Haute-Altitude",* very good cond., (03-15-93, Arcole, #83), 38¹⁵⁄₁₆ x 24 in., (99 x 61 cm.), (BP 180, DM 430, FR 1462, Y 30,680).

CHASE, Louisa   American b. Panama 1951
BI *Untitled, 1981,* s., d., num. 20/144, blindstamp of pub. Charles Cardinale Fine Creation Inc., full margins, good cond., surface soiling, creases, est. $5/700, (02-24-93, Butterfield, #3199), 26½ x 41¼ in., (67.3 x 104.8 cm.), silkscreen in colors on white wove.
$805* *Untitled, 1990,* s., d., i. 33, pub. by artist, full margins, good cond., (02-11-93, Sotheby-NY, #312), 29¹⁵⁄₁₆ x 24 in., (760 x 610 mm.), color monotype (BP 568, DM 1333, FR 4512, Y 97,046).

CHASE, William M. (after)   American 1849-1916
BI *"The Smoker, Portriat Of Frank Duveneck", c. 1875,* pub. in American Art Review, vol. 2, 1881, good cond., binding holes, est. $175/225, (10-31-92, Cleveland, #98A), 11⅜ x 6⅛ in., (28.9 x 15.6 cm.), etching.

CHASE, William Merritt   American 1849-1916
$247* *"The Court Jester" and "Man With Pipe", 1890, 1873: Two,* (05-27-93, Swann, #57), one 6¾ x 4½ in., (17.1 x 11.4 cm.), the other 9½ x 5⅛ in., (17.1 x 11.4 cm.), etching (BP 158, DM 396, FR 1336, Y 26,479).

CHASE-STATLER
$357* *Truman, Harry S., c. 1948,* s. on image, (09-17-92, Swann, #287), 7½ x 9½ in., (19.1 x 24.1 cm.), photograph (BP 201, DM 530, FR 1814, Y 44,447).

CHASSERIAU, Theodore   French 1819-1856
$383* *Arabe Montant En Selle (A.B. 22), 1849,* stains, good margins, (02-03-93, Ader Tajan, #97), 10¹³⁄₁₆ x 8¼ in., (27.5 x 21 cm.), soft ground etching on creme fixed Chine (BP 267, DM 631, FR 2138, Y 47,643).
$113* *Othello (Fisher 19), 1844,* rubbing, small margins, (02-24-93, Picard, #63), etching and roulette on simili Japan (BP 79, DM 183, FR 622, Y 13,260).
$826* *Othello. Pl. 2 (Act 1, Scene III) (A. Bouvenne, 7; J.M. Fischer, p. 44),* 2 out of 4 before i., tears, reddish stains, large margins, collector's stamp, (04-02-93, Picard, #67), 11 x 8¼ in., (28 x 21 cm.), etching and roulette on greyish Chine (BP 544, DM 1328, FR 4509, Y 94,045).
$722* *Othello. Pl. 6 (Act III, Scene III) (A.B., 11; J.M.F., p. 66),* 5 out of 7 before i., tears, reddish stains, large margins, collector's stamp, (04-02-93, Picard, #68), 10¹³⁄₁₆ x 8¹¹⁄₁₆ in., (27.4 x 22 cm.), etching and drypoint on Chine fixe (BP 476, DM 1160, FR 3941, Y 82,204).
$464* *La Romance Du Saule, Othello (A.B. 15, J.M.F. p. 90), 1844,* fifth state of six, w/i., 1844 edit., large margins,

(02-03-93, Ader Tajan, #96), 14¼ x 10¼ in., (36.2 x 26.1 cm.), etching, drypoint on fixed Chine (BP 324, DM 764, FR 2591, Y 57,719).

CHASTEL, Roger   1887-1981
  BI *Composition,* s. Chastel, epreuve d'artiste, est. DK 800, (03-24-93, Kunsthallen, #61), lithograph.

CHAVANNAZ
  $30* *Credit Lyonnais. Emprunt De La Paix, 1920,* good cond., (02-12-93, Cheval/Robert, #113), 47¼ x 31⅞ in., (120 x 81 cm.), poster (BP 21, DM 50, FR 168, Y 3618).

CHAVANNES, Pierre Puvis de   1824-1898
  BI *Le Pauvre Pecheur (Johnson 98), 1897,* stone s., from L'Album d'estampes originales de la Galerie Vollard, collector's stamp, est. DM 1,800, (06-10-93, Hauswedell/Nolt, #808), image 16⁵⁄₁₆ x 20⅞ in., (41.5 x 53 cm.), lithograph on hand-made.

CHAVEAU, F.
  $404* *Carrousel De Louis XIV,* reddish stains, creases, good margins, (02-03-93, Ader Tajan, #213), color copper engraving (BP 282, DM 665, FR 2256, Y 50,255).

CHEFFETZ, Asa   American 1896-1965
  BI *Calendula, 1931,* s., t., pub. AAA, margins, good cond.?, est. $2/400, (05-19-93, Butterfield, #1984), 8 x 6 in., (203 x 152 mm.), wood engraving on wove.

CHEMIAKIN, Michel   Russian b. 1940
  $165* *Carnaval,* s., #66/225, (12-13-92, Hindman, #334), 17 x 24¼ in., color lithograph (BP 105, DM 259, FR 884, Y 20,413).
  $132* *Carnaval,* s., #70/225, (12-13-92, Hindman, #335), 17 x 24¼ in., color lithograph (BP 84, DM 207, FR 707, Y 16,331).
  $132* *Carnaval,* s., #92/225, (12-13-92, Hindman, #336), 17 x 24¼ in., color lithograph (BP 84, DM 207, FR 707, Y 16,331).
  $135* *"Carnaval",* #78/250, s., (10-18-92, Pescheteau, #100), 29½ x 21¼ in., (75 x 54 cm.), lithograph in colors on velin (BP 82, DM 199, FR 677, Y 16,119).
  BI *"Carnival",* s., #30/225, est. $3/500, (12-12-92, Goldberg, #520), image 17 x 24¼ in., color lithograph.
  $311* *Le Quartier De Viande,* #107/225, s. M. Chemiakin, (03-16-93, Encans, #155), 24⅝ x 17¹¹⁄₁₆ in., (62.5 x 45 cm.), lithograph (BP 215, DM 517, FR 1757, Y 36,366, C$ 389).
  $85* *Still Life,* s., #176/225, (12-01-92, Ritchie, #89, illus.), 25⅛ x 18⅛ in., (63.8 x 46 cm.), color lithograph (BP 56, DM 135, FR 462, Y 10,583, C$ 110).

CHENET
  $955* *Plaques Et Papiers,* p. Chenet, folds, defects, backed on linen, (05-07-93, Christie-S. Ken, #91, illus.), 29½ x 41½ in., (74.9 x 105.4 cm.), color lithograph (BP 605, DM 1510, FR 5088, Y 105,153).

CHENEY, Philip   American b. 1927
  BI *"Cowboy Approaching Western Town"* and *"Road To Valley": Two,* s., very good cond., est. $2/300, (05-15-93, Cleveland, #90), one 12½ x 15¼ in., (31.8 x 38.7 cm.), other 8⅝ x 12¾ in., (31.8 x 38.7 cm.), lithograph.
  $94* *"Steamboat Rock, Wyoming",* s., AAA, (12-11-92, DuMouchelle, #1474), 9⅝ x 13¼ in., (24.4 x 33.7 cm.), lithograph (BP 60, DM 148, FR 508, Y 11,632).

CHERET
  $139* *Menu Surround,* (05-07-93, Christie-S. Ken, #116, illus.), 8¼ x 11½ in., (21 x 29.2 cm.), color lithograph (BP 88, DM 220, FR 741, Y 15,305).

CHERET, Jules   French 1836-1932
  $990* *"Alcazar D'Ete", Revue Fin De Siecle, c. 1890,* pub. Chaix, (08-05-92, Boos, #663, illus.), sight 47¼ x 33¼ in., (120 x 84.5 cm.), color lithograph (BP 518, DM 1462, FR 4940, Y 126,083).
  $843* *Alcazar D'Ete. Kanjarova, 1891,* Paris, Imp. Chaix, cond. B+, (06-11-93, Boisgirard, #58), 48¹³⁄₁₆ x 34⅝ in., (124 x 88 cm.), poster (BP 554, DM 1370, FR 4619, Y 89,443).
  $1205* *Alcazar D'Ete. Revue Fin De Siecle, 1890,* Paris, Imp. Chaix, cond. B+, (06-11-93, Boisgirard, #55A, illus.),

45¹¹⁄₁₆ x 31⅞ in., (116 x 81 cm.), (BP 792, DM 1958, FR 6603, Y 127,851).
  $863* *Ambassadeurs. La Jolie Fagette, 1901,* Paris, Imp. Chaix, cond. B+, (06-11-93, Boisgirard, #62), 48¹³⁄₁₆ x 34¹³⁄₁₆ in., (124 x 88.5 cm.), poster (BP 567, DM 1403, FR 4729, Y 91,565).
  $165* *The Ault And Wiborg Co., 1910: Four,* advertisements, A cond., (08-06-92, Swann, #89, illus.), 12 x 9 in., (30.5 x 22.9 cm.), (BP 86, DM 244, FR 823, Y 21,046).
  $269* *Bal Bullier, 1888,* (01-31-93, Morelle/Marchan, #20), 34⅝ x 47⅝ in., (88 x 121 cm.), poster (BP 181, DM 433, FR 1465, Y 33,558).
  $504* *La Bodiniere, 1900,* fold marks, tears, repairs, lit., (02-04-93, Christie-S. Ken, #110, illus.), 47½ x 33½ in., (120.7 x 85.1 cm.), color lithograph backed on japan (BP 352, DM 830, FR 2814, Y 62,694).
  $299* *Bullier, 1888,* cond. B, (03-16-93, Boisgirard, #74), 47¼ x 33⁷⁄₁₆ in., (120 x 85 cm.), poster (BP 206, DM 497, FR 1689, Y 34,963).
  $2200* *Casino De Paris, 1891,* image s., d., p. Chaix (Atelier Cheret), linen-backed, large margins, good cond.?, creases through image, (10-28-92, Butterfield, #2625), color lithograph on two sheets of wove (BP 1402, DM 3398, FR 11,536, Y 269,939).
  $2750* *Casino De Paris, c. 1895,* by Imprimerie Chaix, good cond., creasing, (11-07-92, Sotheby-NY, #253, illus.), sight 32½ x 22¾ in., (82.6 x 57.8 i), lithograph in colors (BP 1798, DM 4412, FR 14,841, Y 339,422).
  $542* *Champs-Elysees. Jardin De Paris, 1890,* Paris, Imp. Chaix, cond. B+, (06-11-93, Boisgirard, #55), 31½ x 23⅝ in., (80 x 60 cm.), poster (BP 356, DM 881, FR 2970, Y 57,507).
  $1104* *Champs-Elysees. Jardin De Paris, 1899,* Paris, Imp. Chaix, cond. B+, (06-11-93, Boisgirard, #59), 49³⁄₁₆ x 34⅝ in., (125 x 88 cm.), poster (BP 725, DM 1794, FR 6049, Y 117,135).
  $440* *La Closerie Des Genets, 1890,* Chaix, B+ cond., center fold mark, closed tears, (08-06-92, Swann, #86, illus.), 47 x 34 in., (119.4 x 86.4 cm.), (BP 230, DM 650, FR 2196, Y 56,122).
  $110* *Cover For "The New York Herald" December 13, 1896,* very good cond.?, (11-21-92, Bakker, #78), sight 21 x 15 in., (53.3 x 38.1 cm.), color lithograph (BP 72, DM 175, FR 591, Y 13,680).
  BI *Design,* p. Imprimerie Chaix, s. Jules Cheret, est. $7/1,000, (11-06-92, Sotheby-Arcade, #131), sight 20⅝ x 27¼ in., (52.4 x 69.2 cm.), lithograph in colors.
  $241* *La Diaphane. "Poudre De Riz. Sarah Bernhardt" (Maindron 773, Broido 931), 1890,* Imp. Chaix, fairly good cond., glued, (02-12-93, Cheval/Robert, #51A, illus.), 48⁷⁄₁₆ x 34¼ in., (123 x 87 cm.), poster (BP 170, DM 400, FR 1352, Y 29,064).
  $261* *Exposition Des Arts Incoherents, 1886,* fairly good cond., (02-12-93, Cheval/Robert, #128), 47⅝ x 33⁷⁄₁₆ in., (121 x 85 cm.), poster (BP 184, DM 433, FR 1465, Y 31,476).
  $339* *Exposition Tableaux And Dessins De A. Willette, 1888,* cond. B, (03-16-93, Boisgirard, #75), 47⁷⁄₁₆ x 33⁷⁄₁₆ in., (120.5 x 85 cm.), poster (BP 234, DM 564, FR 1915, Y 39,640).
  $61* *"Farandole",* s., ded., large margins, (03-22-93, Pescheteau, #72), sanguine lithograph on tinted (BP 41, DM 100, FR 340, Y 7063).
  $165* *Fete De Charite,* from Les Maitres de l'Affiche, PL. 89, (02-14-93, Hanzel, #687), 12¼ x 7¾ in., (31.1 x 19.7 cm.), lithograph (BP 116, DM 274, FR 926, Y 19,899).
  $410* *"La Fileuse"* and *"La Dentelliere", 1900: Two,* p. Chaix and De Malherbe, extensively torn and time stained, paper loss, laid on canvas, (10-27-92, Phillips-London, #191), sheet 47¼ x 33⅛ in., (120 x 84.1 cm.), colored lithographic poster (BP 259, DM 628, FR 2132, Y 50,153).
  $150* *"Folies-Bergere Napoli"* and *"Foles-Bergere En Voyage": Two,* (04-28-93, Doyle, #11A), larger 33 x 22 in., (83.8 x 55.9 cm.), color lithographic posters (BP 95, DM 237, FR 803, Y 16,810).
  BI *"Halle Aux Chapeaux",* s., d. 92 in stone, full margins, good cond., est. $750/1000, (03-12-93, Goldberg, #892, illus.), 14½ x 11 in., (36.8 x 27.9 cm.), color lithograph.

$2200* *Halle Aux Chapeaux, 1892,* (06-13-93, Hindman, #384), 46½ x 32½ in., (118.1 x 82.6 cm.), color lithograph poster (BP 1440, DM 3581, FR 12,035, Y 231,506).

$331* *La Jolie Fagette Aux Ambassadeurs, 1901,* (01-31-93, Morelle/Marchan, #173), 40 3/16 x 59 1/16 in., (102 x 150 cm.), poster (BP 223, DM 533, FR 1803, Y 41,292).

$770* *"La Juive Du Chateau Trompette",* designed by Cheret, pub. by Chaix, (11-13-92, DuMouchelle, #183, illus.), 97 x 34 in., (97 x 34 cm.), poster (BP 498, DM 1209, FR 4076, Y 95,569).

BI *"La Juive",* p. Chaix, est. 1,5/2,500, (08-05-92, Boos, #582), 97 x 34½ in., (246.4 x 87.6 cm.), color lithograph.

$41* *L'Amant Des Danseuses, 1892,* (01-31-93, Morelle/Marchan, #19), 10¼ x 14 3/16 in., (26 x 36 cm.), poster (BP 28, DM 66, FR 223, Y 5115).

$805* *L'Aureole Du Midi, 1903,* p. Chaix for Ateliers Cheret, keystone, good cond.?, repaired tears,stains, (05-19-93, Butterfield, #1901, illus.), sight 49⅝ x 32½ in., (125.1 x 82.6 cm.), lithograph in black and red on pulp (BP 523, DM 1309, FR 4409, Y 89,118).

$662* *Montagnes Russes,* fold marks, tears, losses, repairs, lit., (02-04-93, Christie-S. Ken, #111), 46 x 33 in., (116.8 x 83.8 cm.), color lithograph backed on linen (BP 462, DM 1090, FR 3696, Y 82,349).

BI *Musee Gravin, 1900,* before lettering, by Imprimerie Chaix, good cond., laid down on linen, losses, creases, est. $2/3,000, (03-19-93, Sotheby-NY, #299, illus.), 49¼ x 38¾ in., (125.1 x 98.4 cm.), color lithograph.

$3850* *Musee Gravin, Paris, 189?,* by Imprimerie Chaix, good cond., 1.21m x 85.7cm, (11-07-92, Sotheby-NY, #254, illus.), sight 47¾ x 33¾ in., lithograph in colors (BP 2517, DM 6177, FR 20,777, Y 475,191).

$2309* *Musee Grevin. Le Journal Lumineux, 1900,* Paris, Imp. Chaix, cond. B+, (06-11-93, Boisgirard, #61, illus.), 48 7/16 x 34⅝ in., (123 x 88 cm.), poster (BP 1517, DM 3753, FR 12,652, Y 244,987).

$703* *Musee Grevin. Magie Noire. Apparitions Instantanees Par Le Professeur Carmelli, 1887,* Paris, Imp. Chaix, cond. B, (06-11-93, Boisgirard, #56), 44 5/16 x 31⅞ in., (112.5 x 81 cm.), poster (BP 462, DM 1143, FR 3852, Y 74,589).

$1024* *Palais De Glace (M. 292, B. 362), 1893,* tears, losses, crease, (02-24-93, Picard, #65), color lithograph (BP 714, DM 1662, FR 5636, Y 120,160).

$3575* *Pantomimes Lumineuses, 1892,* by Imprimerie Chaix, good cond., loose sheet, 1.22m x 81.9cm, (11-07-92, Sotheby-NY, #256, illus.), 48 x 32¼ in., lithograph in colors (BP 2337, DM 5736, FR 19,293, Y 441,249).

BI *"Paris Courses", c. 1890,* pub. Chaix, est. $1,5/2,500, (08-05-92, Boos, #662, illus.), sight 48⅞ x 33½ in., (124.1 x 85.1 cm.), color lithograph.

BI *Pastilles Poncelet, 1896,* by Imprimerie Chaix, est. $1,5/2,000, (06-09-93, Sotheby-Arcade, #235), 47½ x 33½ in., (120.7 x 85.1 cm.), lithograph in colors.

$1045* *Pippermint, 1899,* Chaix, B+ cond., fold marks, stain, (08-06-92, Swann, #88, illus.), 48½ x 35 in., (123.2 x 88.9 cm.), (BP 546, DM 1544, FR 5215, Y 133,291).

$703* *Pippermint. Get Freres A Revel. (Hte Garonne), 1900,* Paris, Imp. Chaix, cond. B+, (06-11-93, Boisgirard, #60), 48 13/16 x 34 13/16 in., (124 x 88.5 cm.), poster (BP 462, DM 1143, FR 3852, Y 74,589).

$143* *"Polka Americaine", Ta-Ra-Ra-Boum,* p. Chaix, (08-05-92, Boos, #581), 13⅞ x 10⅝ in., (352 x 270 mm.), color lithograph (BP 75, DM 211, FR 714, Y 18,212).

BI *Premier Concours Des Balcons Fleuris, 1904,* Imp. Chaix, fairly good cond., restored, (02-12-93, Cheval/Robert, #129), 50 x 35 7/16 in., (127 x 90 cm.), poster.

$512* *Saxoleine (Maindron 785; Broido 946), 1892,* crease, paper loss, (02-24-93, Picard, #64), color lithograph (BP 357, DM 831, FR 2818, Y 60,080).

$261* *Saxoleine, 1900,* Imp. Chaix, mediocre state, (02-12-93, Cheval/Robert, #53), 48 13/16 x 34¼ in., (124 x 87 cm.), poster (BP 184, DM 433, FR 1465, Y 31,476).

$715* *Scaramouche, 1891,* Imp. Chaix, B+ cond., fold marks, closed tears, expert restoration, (08-06-92, Swann, #87, illus.), 48½ x 34 in., (123.2 x 86.4 cm.), (BP 373, DM 1056, FR 3568, Y 91,199).

BI *"Si Vous Toussez, Prenez Des" Pastilles Geraudel, 1892,* Imp. Chaix, fairly good cond., (02-12-93, Cheval/Robert, #52), 39⅜ x 29⅛ in., (100 x 74 cm.), poster.

$315* *"Skating Rink, Grandes Bailes De Mascaras", c. 1876 and "Grand Panorama", 1881: Two,* fold marks, losses, tears, lit., (02-04-93, Christie-S. Ken, #113, illus.), 30½ x 26 in., (77.5 x 66 cm.), color lithograph (BP 220, DM 519, FR 1759, Y 39,184).

$473* *La Terre, 1889,* tears, repairs, creasing, lit., (02-04-93, Christie-S. Ken, #112), 92 x 34 in., (233.7 x 86.4 cm.), color lithograph on two sheets backed on linen (BP 330, DM 779, FR 2641, Y 58,838).

BI *Theatre De La Tour Eiffel/Paris-Chicago, 1983,* p. Chaix, foxed, time stained, holes from paper loss and other defects, est. BP 2/300, (10-27-92, Phillips-London, #192), sheet 47¼ x 32⅜ in., (120 x 82.2 cm.), color lithographic poster laid on canvas.

$281* *Les Trois Mousquetaires Par Alexandre Dumas, 1887,* Paris, Imp. Chaix, cond. B+, (06-11-93, Boisgirard, #57), 68½ x 47⅝ in., (174 x 121 cm.), poster (BP 185, DM 457, FR 1540, Y 29,814).

$1100* *Untitled: Two,* for Quinquina Dubonnet, p. Imprimerie Chaix, 1895 and 1896, generally good cond., (11-06-92, Sotheby-Arcade, #132, illus.), approx. sight 22 x 15¼ in., (55.9 x 38.7 cm.), lithograph in colors (BP 719, DM 1756, FR 5936, Y 135,769).

$495* *Viviane, 1886,* Chaix, A cond., (08-06-92, Swann, #85, illus.), 29½ x 21½ in., (74.9 x 54.6 cm.), (BP 259, DM 731, FR 2470, Y 63,138).

$281* *Le Zouzou. Aperatif Francais Au Quinquina. Blanzac, Charente,* Imp. Pichot, good cond., (02-12-93, Cheval/Robert, #54), 47¼ x 62 15/16 in., (120 x 160 cm.), poster (BP 198, DM 466, FR 1577, Y 33,888).

CHERNEY, Marvin American 1925-1967

BI *The Rabbi,* s., t., #63/90, i., est. $125/175, (06-11-93, Freemn/Fine Art, #32), hand-painted lithograph.

CHERRY, Edward

$10* *"The Thames" and "Old Curiosity Shop": Two,* s., excell. cond., (05-15-93, Cleveland, #376), one 4⅜ x 5¾ in., (11.1 x 14.6 cm.), other 5¼ x 4 in., (11.1 x 14.6 cm.), etching (BP 7, DM 16, FR 54, Y 1109).

$31* *Untitled,* (05-12-93, Maynard, #558), etching (BP 20, DM 50, FR 168, Y 3461, C$ 39).

CHEUNG, Yu-Chiu

$1045* *Water Ballet, c. 1948,* credit stamp, t. in ink, labels, prov., (10-13-92, Christie-NY, #437, illus.), 14 x 17 in., (35.6 x 43.2 cm.), photograph, gelatin silver print (BP 609, DM 1531, FR 5202, Y 126,713).

CHEVALIER, Nicholas 1828-1902

$81* *The Old And New Home Stations,* from Australia by Edwin C Booth pub. c. 1875, (08-11-92, L. Joel, #196G), 4¾ x 6⅞ in., (12 x 17.5 cm.), color engraving (BP 42, DM 119, FR 403, Y 10,373, A$ 110).

CHEVALIER, Yvonne

$467* *Rouault, Georges, 15 July 1953,* s. G. Rouault, (09-17-92, Swann, #244), 4½ x 6⅞ in., (11.4 x 17.5 cm.), photograph (BP 262, DM 693, FR 2373, Y 58,142).

CHEW, Wong Moo Chinese 20th cent.

$25* *"Illustration No. 3",* s., t., #E.A., good cond., staining, (05-15-93, Cleveland, #460), 16½ x 23¼ in., (41.9 x 59.1 cm.), etching and mezzotint (BP 16, DM 40, FR 135, Y 2771).

CHIA, Sandro Italian b. 1946

$2340* *Boy And Dog,* s., proof, blindstamp SC, (05-25-93, AB Stockholm, #12), 17½ x 23 13/16 in., (44.5 x 60.5 cm.), etching (BP 1517, DM 3811, FR 12,829, Y 255,766, SK 3410).

$1216* *Boy And Dog,* blindstamp, s., (12-04-92, AB Stockholm, #7035), 17 11/16 x 23⅝ in., (45 x 60 cm.), etching (BP 780, DM 1937, FR 6569, Y 151,810, SK 8250).

BI *Bread And Wine, c. 1980,* num., s., pub. Circle Gallery, est. $1,5/2,000, (05-27-93, Swann, #59, illus.), (76.2 x 66 cm.), color lithograph.

$8114* *Children's Holiday, 1984: Six,* A.P., s., num., (12-05-92, Bassenge, #7083, illus.), 35 11/16 x 25¾ in., (90.6 x 65.4 cm.), color lithograph, assembeld together as one picture (BP 5081, DM 12,650, FR 43,114, Y 1,005,328).

$983* *Figura,* #34/40, s., (12-15-92, Finarte-Milan, #53, illus.), 21⅝ x 15⅜ in., (55 x 39 cm.), etching (BP 627, DM 1541, FR 5265, Y 121,915, L 1380).

$303* *Figure Looking Out, 1982,* s., d., #25/25, blindstamp, pub. Schellmann and Kluser w/blindstamp,very good cond.?, crease, rippling, prov., (12-12-92, Weschler, #114, illus.), 13½ x 10¾ in., (34.3 x 27.3 cm.), etching and chine colle on rag paper (BP 194, DM 477, FR 1636, Y 37,495).

BI *From Gardens And Villas Of Italy, 1985,* s., annot. IX/X, pub. Peder Bonier, full margins, good cond., surfacesoiling, handling creases, est. $1,4/1,600, (05-19-93, Butterfield, #2142), 16⅛ x 21⅝ in., (410 x 549 mm.), etching w/aquatint on Fabriano.

BI *Gardens And Villas Of Italy: In A Garden Of Florentine, 1985,* s., annot. AP, full margins, good cond., soft handling creases, surface soiling, est. $1,4/1,600, (05-19-93, Butterfield, #2141), 21½ x 15⅛ in., (546 x 384 mm.), etching w/aquatint in colors on Chine colle on Fabriano.

BI *Lunatic Boy, 1984,* s., annot. A.P., pub. Natalie Seroussi, full margins, good cond., handling creases, surface soiling, stray printing ink, est. $1,2/1,400, (05-19-93, Butterfield, #2140), 17⅞ x 11¾ in., (454 x 298 mm.), etching w/aquatint on Somerset.

$649* *Mansgestalt,* s., blindstamp, (12-04-92, AB Stockholm, #7036), 35⅝ x 23⅝ in., (90.5 x 60 cm.), etching (BP 416, DM 1034, FR 3506, Y 81,024, SK 4400).

$655* *Untitled,* artist proof, s., (12-15-92, Finarte-Milan, #34), 29½ x 21 1/16 in., (75 x 53.5 cm.), photolithograph in colors (BP 418, DM 1027, FR 3508, Y 81,235, L 920).

BI *The Waitress, 1986,* full margins, d., num. AP IX/X, est. $1/1,500, (05-27-93, Swann, #58), 17⅝ x 11 in., (44.8 x 27.9 cm.), etching.

CHIALIVA, Luigi Swiss/Italian 1842-1914

$509* *La Guardiana Di Oche: Four,* timbro, (05-20-93, Finarte-Milan, #54), 15¾ x 24 7/16 in., (40 x 62 cm.), etching on various papers (BP 327, DM 821, FR 2766, Y 56,206, L 748).

CHIC, Burnelle

$77* *"Danseuse Oriential",* c. 1940, (11-13-92, DuMouchelle, #383), 16 x 12 in., (40.6 x 30.5 cm.), silkscreen (BP 50, DM 121, FR 408, Y 9557).

CHICANOBA 1838-1912

$550* *"Inside The Temple": Triptych, c. 1880,* very good color/cond., (10-31-92, Goldberg, #723, illus.), (BP 360, DM 863, FR 2924, Y 68,002).

CHIEDEL and TAYLOR

BI *"Beaver Hunting In Canada",* s. Chiedel; s. Taylor, (06-16-93, Encans, #124), 10 13/16 x 6 7/16 in., (27.5 x 16.3 cm.), engraving.

CHIEZE, Jean Andre French 20th cent.

$88* *"Saint Fiacre, Patron Des Jardiniers, Horticulteurs, Et Fleurists",* (11-28-92, Young, #95, illus.), 12 x 10 in., (30.5 x 25.4 cm.), color woodcut (BP 58, DM 140, FR 476, Y 10,952).

CHIKAMATSU MONZAEMON Japanese 1653-1724

$700* *Yomei Tenno Shokunin Kagami "Emperor Yomei And The Mirror Of Craftsmen",* pub. Yamamoto Kyuhei and Yamamoto Kyuemon, (1750), 34 sh of text, wormed, worn, Prof. H.R.W. Kuhne Coll., (06-11-93, Sotheby-London, #520), 8⅜ x 6¼ in., (21.3 x 15.9 cm.), woodblock (BP 460, DM 1138, FR 3836, Y 74,271).

CHIKANOBU, Toyohara Japanese 1838-1912

BI *Bildnis Eines Knaben,* Format Oban, est. SC 4/5,000, (04-27-93, Dorotheum, #240), 9 13/16 x 14 9/16 in., (25 x 37 cm.), woodcut.

BI *Geishas In A Public Garden, 1875,* triptych, est. SC 6/7,000, (04-27-93, Dorotheum, #174, illus.), 29 5/16 x 14 9/16 in., (74.5 x 37 cm.), color woodcut.

$363* *Serving Food To The Dolls On Girls' Day, 1901,* from series: Setsugekka, pub. Matsumoto Heikichi, d., (04-21-93, Germann, #243), color woodcut (BP 236, DM 580, FR 1962, Y 40,186, SF 529).

CHIKUSEKI ac. c. 1900

BI *Karpfen,* s., est. SC 12/14,000, (04-27-93, Dorotheum, #200, illus.), 9 13/16 x 9 9/16 in., (25 x 24.3 cm.), color woodcut.

CHILLIDA, Eduardo Spanish b. 1924

$3432* *Adoration (Galeria Iolas-Velasco 98), 1977,* complete book, two s., w/justification and text, s. by author, #22, s., #22/35, p. by Atelier Morsang, good cond., (06-30-93, Sotheby-London, #758, illus.), 3 etchings, w/separate suite of 4 etchings on Japan on Auvergne Richard-de-Bas paper (BP 2300, DM 5854, FR 19,747, Y 367,727).

$771* *Agri I, c. 1985,* s., #33/50, full margins, good cond., (06-30-93, Sotheby-London, #760), sh 8 x 4½ in., (203 x 114 mm.), etching and collage on chine applique (BP 517, DM 1315, FR 4436, Y 82,610).

$1121* *Atz II, 1967,* s., num., (12-01-92, Karl/Faber, #450), 3¾ x 4¾ in., (9.5 x 12 cm.), etching and aquatint on China (BP 741, DM 1787, FR 6089, Y 139,567).

$1772* *Atz IV,* s., num., (06-08-93, Karl/Faber, #627), 9 1/16 x 6 11/16 in., (23 x 17 cm.), aquatint/etching on China (BP 1165, DM 2875, FR 9683, Y 188,210).

$686* *Bideak, 1982,* s., #9/50, p. and pub. by Galerie Maeght-Lelong, full margins, good cond., (06-30-93, Sotheby-London, #759, illus.), sh 29⅜ x 20⅝ in., (746 x 524 mm.), etching on chine applique (BP 460, DM 1170, FR 3947, Y 73,503).

$540* *Correlation, 1966,* s., num., (12-01-92, Karl/Faber, #449), 15⅜ x 11 in., (39 x 28 cm.), color lithograph on wove (BP 357, DM 861, FR 2933, Y 67,231).

$515* *Esku XXI, 1983,* s., #1/50, p. and pub. Galerie Maeght-Lelong, full margins, good cond., (06-30-93, Sotheby-London, #761, illus.), 5¾ x 4⅝ in., (146 x 117 mm.), etching on chine applique mounted on BFK Rives (BP 345, DM 878, FR 2963, Y 55,181).

$435* *Esku Xli (Michelin 151), 1975,* #18/50, s., (04-21-93, Germann, #336), 18⅞ x 15 1/16 in., (480 x 383 mm.), etching on Rives (BP 282, DM 695, FR 2351, Y 48,157, SF 633).

$1702* *Formen, c. 1970,* s., i. H.C., (06-05-93, Grisebach, #545, illus.), 13¼ x 14 7/16 in., (33.6 x 36.6 cm.), aquatint on handmade copper print paper (BP 1120, DM 2759, FR 9301, Y 182,579).

BI *Hommage A Rosalia De Castro, 1983,* s., #28/50, est. FF2,500/3,000, (05-27-93, Briest, #57), 25⅜ x 19½ in., (64.5 x 49.5 cm.), drypoint.

$1705* *Kate III (M. 134), 1972,* s., #49/50, pub. Maeght, full margins, good cond., (12-03-92, Sotheby-London, #626, illus.), 6⅞ x 4⅞ in., (175 x 125 mm.), aquatint on Arches (BP 1100, DM 2681, FR 9152, Y 212,144).

$442* *Komposition,* #24/100, s., (09-04-92, Germann, #284), 8 9/16 x 6 7/16 in., (218 x 164 mm.), etching (BP 221, DM 619, FR 2109, Y 54,407, SF 552).

$233* *Komposition,* stone s., (09-25-92, Granier, #2792), sheet 25 13/16 x 19⅞ in., (65.5 x 50.5 cm.), lithograph on BFK Rives (BP 136, DM 345, FR 1168, Y 28,123).

$493* *Komposition,* s., num., (05-26-93, Dorling, #2595, illus.), 6⅞ x 13⅛ in., (17.5 x 33.3 cm.), lithograph on thin cardboard (BP 319, DM 804, FR 2707, Y 53,564).

$474* *Komposition,* 63/100, s., (06-24-93, Germann, #276), 9¾ x 6⅞ in., (248 x 175 mm.), etching (BP 312, DM 768, FR 2590, Y 50,847, SF 690).

$721* *L'Emerveille Merveilleux (Michelin 91), 1973,* pencil s., (11-20-92, Lempertz, #491), sh 19⅞ x 15⅞ in., (50.5 x 40.3 cm.), woodcut on Arches-Velin (BP 475, DM 1150, FR 3872, Y 89,665).

$2885* *Leku-Aldatu (Michelin 118), 1972,* pencil s., (11-20-92, Lempertz, #490, illus.), sh 27 9/16 x 39⅜ in., (70 x 100 cm.), etching on Fabriano-Velin (BP 1900, DM 4600, FR 15,494, Y 358,786).

$938* *Nancy (Michelin 141), 1972,* s., #3/100, pub. Maeght, full margins, good cond., (12-03-92, Sotheby-London, #625, illus.), 30½ x 19⅞ in., (775 x 506 mm.), lithograph on Rives (BP 605, DM 1475, FR 5035, Y 116,710).

BI *"Olympische Spiele Munchen 1972",* s., num., est. DM 1,200, (12-01-92, Karl/Faber, #451), 40 9/16 x 26 15/16 in., (103 x 68.5 cm.), lithograph on wove.

$567* *Ozendu, 1982,* s., #24/50, (05-27-93, Briest, #55), 25⁹⁄₁₆ x 19¹¹⁄₁₆ in., (65 x 50 cm.), black drypoint (BP 363, DM 910, FR 3067, Y 60,785).

$498* *Tempo II, 1964,* s., num., (12-01-92, Karl/Faber, #448), 10⅝ x 21⅝ in., (27 x 55 cm.), lithograph on wove (BP 329, DM 794, FR 2705, Y 62,002).

CHIRICO, Giorgio de Italian 1888-1978

$649* *Gli Archaeologi, 1970,* #282/300, s., (11-21-92, Lempertz, #86), 21¹⁄₁₆ x 17¹³⁄₁₆ in., (53.5 x 45.3 cm.), lithograph on wove (BP 427, DM 1035, FR 3485, Y 80,711).

$1269* *Bagni Misteriosi (kCiranna 7), 1938,* s., num., from series "l'album 23 Gravures" Edition G. Orobitz & Cie, (05-26-93, Dorling, #2596, illus.), 9½ x 7⅞ in., (24.2 x 20 cm.), etching on wove (BP 821, DM 2070, FR 6969, Y 137,875).

$1610* *Cavalli E Ville: Cavalieri Antichi (C. 124, d'A. 29), 1954,* s., annot. P.A., blindstamp publisher Carlo Bestetti, margins, good cond., creases, shrink-wrapped, (05-19-93, Butterfield, #1902, illus.), 13½ x 17¼ in., (343 x 438 mm.), lithograph in colors on wove (BP 1045, DM 2617, FR 8817, Y 178,235).

$1488* *Cavallo E Castello (Ciranna 127), 1954,* #25/125, s., from the series Cavalli e ville, (05-20-93, Finarte-Milan, #61), 12⅝ x 16¾ in., (32 x 42.5 cm.), lithograph in colors (BP 955, DM 2401, FR 8087, Y 164,311, L 2185).

$1488* *Cavallo Fuggente (Ciranna 123), 1954,* proof, s., from the series Cavalli e ville, (05-20-93, Finarte-Milan, #60), 13⁹⁄₁₆ x 17⅛ in., (34.5 x 43.5 cm.), lithograph in colors (BP 955, DM 2401, FR 8087, Y 164,311, L 2185).

$2349* *Conversazione Misteriosa (Ciranna 91), 1934,* #26/100, s., from the series Mithologie. Bagni misteriosi, (05-20-93, Finarte-Milan, #57), 11 x 8⅞ in., (28 x 22.5 cm.), lithograph (BP 1508, DM 3790, FR 12,766, Y 259,386, L 3450).

BI *"Gladiatore" (Brandani 154), 1972,* s., t., num., margin, stained, est. DM 2000, (12-01-92, Karl/Faber, #452), 19¹¹⁄₁₆ x 14⅜ in., (50 x 36.5 cm.), color lithograph on wove.

$298* *Horses On A Beach,* s., num. 107/250, (07-16-92, Bonhams-Chelsea, #516), image 15¾ x 11¾ in., (40 x 29.8 cm.), lithograph w/hand coloring (BP 154, DM 440, FR 1486, Y 37,329).

$3133* *Il Bagnante Solitario (Ciranna 88), 1934,* s., from the series Mithologie. Bagni misteriosi, #26/120, (05-20-93, Finarte-Milan, #59, illus.), 11 x 8⅞ in., (28 x 22.5 cm.), lithograph (BP 2011, DM 5055, FR 17,027, Y 345,958, L 4600).

$1495* *Il Fiume Misterioso, 1969,* s., t., annot. P/.A., artist's blindstamp and publisher's, Alberto Carini Stampatore, margins, tape remains, skinned area, creases, stain, surface soiling, (05-19-93, Butterfield, #1903, illus.), 18⅛ x 23¹⁄₁₆ in., (460 x 586 mm.), lithograph in colors on Lana (BP 970, DM 2430, FR 8187, Y 165,504).

$3450* *Il Ritorno Del Figliuol Prodigo I (Ciranna 11), 1929,* from series Metamorphosis, s., #40/100, pub. Editions des Quatre Chemins, large margins, good cond., mat stain, masking tape stain, creases, (05-13-93, Sotheby-NY, #533, illus.), 16⅛ x 12¼ in., (411 x 312 mm.), sh 18⅞ x 15⅞ in., (411 x 312 mm.), lithograph in colors (BP 2265, DM 5571, FR 18,791, Y 385,174).

$3289* *L'Idolo Nei Bagni Misteriosi (Ciranna 86), 1934,* #26/120, s., from the series Mythologie. Bagni misteriosi, (05-20-93, Finarte-Milan, #58), 11 x 8⅞ in., (28 x 22.5 cm.), lithograph (BP 2111, DM 5307, FR 17,875, Y 363,185, L 4830).

$866* *La Lassitude De L'Infini, c. 1970,* #118/300, s., (11-21-92, Lempertz, #87), 17¹³⁄₁₆ x 24³⁄₁₆ in., (45.2 x 61.5 cm.), lithograph on wove (BP 570, DM 1381, FR 4651, Y 107,698).

$1760* *Mannequin, 1964, Ciranna 129,* s., num. 9/120, pub. Dessins par G. de Chirico, by R. Sistu, prov., (09-20-92, Hindman, #763), 15¼ x 11 in., (38.7 x 27.9 cm.), color transfer lithograph (BP 1030, DM 2612, FR 8934, Y 217,526).

BI *Self-Portrait In Costume, 1955,* s., full margins, good cond., skinned area, surface soiling, est. $2/3,000, (10-28-92, Butterfield, #2630, illus.), 25 x 19½ in., (635 x 495 mm.), lithograph on cream wove.

$880* *Sol Sul Tempio, c. 1970,* full margins, t., num., s., pub. Alberto Caprini, (05-27-93, Swann, #60, illus.), 24¼ x 18 in., (61.6 x 45.7 cm.), color lithograph (BP 564, DM 1412, FR 4759, Y 94,340).

$1263* *Sole Spento E Luna Crescente, (Brandani 45), 1969,* #77/80, s., t., (11-09-92, Finarte-Milan, #31), 23⅝ x 17¹⁵⁄₁₆ in., (60 x 45.5 cm.), lithograph in colors (BP 835, DM 2016, FR 6812, Y 156,739, L 1725).

$1760* *Trovatore Con Silos, 1974,* full margins, num., s., (05-27-93, Swann, #61, illus.), 19¼ x 14¼ in., (48.9 x 36.2 cm.), color aquatint (BP 1127, DM 2824, FR 9519, Y 188,679).

$3663* *Villa Sul Mare (C. 14), 1929,* from Metamorphosis, s., #90/100, pub. Editions de Quatre Chemins, full margins, repaired tears, creases, light-staining, surface dirt, (12-01-92, Christie-London, #344), L. 12 x 16⅛ in., (305 x 410 mm.), lithograph in colors on Arches (BP 2420, DM 5838, FR 19,897, Y 456,051).

$5116* *Zebra E Cavallo (Ciranna 161), 1969,* s., #53/76, blindstamp, full margins, good cond., handling marks, skinned patches, (12-03-92, Sotheby-London, #271, illus.), 17¼ x 23¼ in., (438 x 591 mm.), lithograph in colors on wove (BP 3300, DM 8045, FR 27,461, Y 636,556).

CHISLETT, John 1856-1938

$770* *Covered Bridge, c. 1900,* (10-14-92, Swann, #408, illus.), 7½ x 9½ in., (19.1 x 24.1 cm.), photograph, platinum print (BP 452, DM 1127, FR 3821, Y 93,311).

$1100* *Frozen Pond, c. 1905,* (10-13-92, Christie-NY, #34, illus.), 9½ x 7 in., (24.1 x 17.8 cm.), photograph, platinum print (BP 641, DM 1611, FR 5475, Y 133,382).

$770* *Harbor Scene, c. 1900,* (10-14-92, Swann, #409, illus.), 9½ x 7½ in., (24.1 x 19.1 cm.), photograph, platinum print (BP 452, DM 1127, FR 3821, Y 93,311).

$770* *Sunlight Through Trees, c. 1900,* notations, (10-14-92, Swann, #410, illus.), 7½ x 9½ in., (19.1 x 24.1 cm.), photograph, platinum print (BP 452, DM 1127, FR 3821, Y 93,311).

CHOCHOLA, Vaclav

BI *Reflektor, 1947,* s., t., d. twice, credit/exhib. stamps, exhib., est. $3/3,500, (04-08-93, Christie-NY, #115, illus.), 11¾ x 9½ in., (29.8 x 24.1 cm.), photograph, gelatin silver print.

$385* *"Vietnam, Ruins Son-La",* 1961/later, s., d.; t., d. verso, (11-16-92, Butterfield, #5901, illus.), 9⅛ x 11¼ in., (232.2 x 286.3 mm.), photograph, gelatin silver print (BP 253, DM 614, FR 2068, Y 47,880).

$1725* *Zada, 1949,* s., t., annot., d., studio stamp, (04-08-93, Christie-NY, #116, illus.), 11½ x 9¼ in., (29.2 x 23.5 cm.), photograph, gelatin silver print (BP 1131, DM 2771, FR 9380, Y 195,756).

CHODOWIECKI, Daniel Polish/German 1726-1801

$109* *12 Blatter Zu Cecilia Oder Geschichte Einer Reichen Waise (Engelmann588), 1787: Twelve,* (12-04-92, Bassenge, #6546), etching (BP 70, DM 174, FR 589, Y 13,608).

$470* *12 Blatter Zu Der Brandenburgischen Geschichte (Engelmann 712 II), 1793: Twelve,* (12-04-92, Bassenge, #6549), etching (BP 301, DM 749, FR 2539, Y 58,677).

$650* *Die Beiden Sitzenden Damen (Engelmann 11), 1758,* (12-04-92, Bassenge, #6535), 5⁹⁄₁₆ x 3¹¹⁄₁₆ in., (14.2 x 9.3 cm.), brown etching (BP 417, DM 1035, FR 3512, Y 81,149).

$1416* *Die Beiden Sitzenden Damen Am Baume (Engelmann 15), 1758,* prov., (06-04-93, Bassenge, #5441), 3¼ x 3¹⁄₁₆ in., (8.2 x 7.8 cm.), etching in reddish/brown (BP 937, DM 2299, FR 7750, Y 152,718).

$220* *Der Betteljunge Bei Dem Baume (Engelmann 7), 1758,* foxed, (12-12-92, Bassenge, #8046), 5¾ x 4½ in., (14.6 x 11.5 cm.), etching (BP 141, DM 346, FR 1178, Y 27,218).

$303* *Beweggrunde Zum Heiraten Und Ihre Folgen (Engelmann 598 II), 1788: Twelve,* (12-04-92, Bassenge, #6547), etching (BP 194, DM 483, FR 1637, Y 37,828).

$505* *Das Bibliothekzeichen Des Kunstlers (Engelmann 192), 1777,* (12-04-92, Bassenge, #6543), 3⁷⁄₁₆ x 2½ in., (8.7 x 6.3 cm.), etching (BP 324, DM 804, FR 2728, Y 63,046).

$1298* *Cabinet D'Un Peintre (Bauer 136; Engelmann 75), 1771,* (06-23-93, Kornfeld, #17, illus.), etching (BP 882, DM 2196, FR 7388, Y 141,410, SF 1955).
$1416* *Cabinet D'Un Peintre (Engelmann 75), 1771,* (06-04-93, Bassenge, #5444, illus.), 7¹⁄₁₆ x 8¹⁵⁄₁₆ in., (18 x 22.8 cm.), etching (BP 937, DM 2299, FR 7750, Y 152,718).
$1463* *Cabinet D'Un Peintre (Engelmann 75), 1771,* creased, (12-12-92, Bassenge, #8048, illus.), 7¹⁄₁₆ x 9¹⁄₁₆ in., (18 x 23 cm.), etching (BP 935, DM 2299, FR 7836, Y 180,997).
BI *Cabinet D'Un Peintre, Das Familienblatt Des Kunstlers (Engelmann 75), 1771,* prov., est. DM 3,500, (12-04-92, Bassenge, #6542), 7¹⁄₁₆ x 9 in., (18 x 22.9 cm.), etching.
$274* *Die Enthusiasten (Engelmann 734 II), 1794,* (12-04-92, Bassenge, #6551), 2⅝ x 2⁵⁄₁₆ in., (6.7 x 5.8 cm.), etching (BP 176, DM 436, FR 1480, Y 34,207).
$4957* *Friedrich Der Grosse Zu Pferde (Engelmann 9 II), 1758,* (06-04-93, Bassenge, #5440), 12¼ x 8½ in., (31.1 x 21.6 cm.), etching (BP 3280, DM 8050, FR 27,132, Y 534,620).
$347* *Das Gehirn Eines Kunstlers (Engelmann 696 II), 1792,* (12-04-92, Bassenge, #6548), 1¹³⁄₁₆ x 3⁵⁄₁₆ in., (4.6 x 8.4 cm.), etching (BP 223, DM 553, FR 1875, Y 43,321).
$217* *Gesellschaft Von Sechs Damen Mit Dem Kunstler In Einem Zimmer (Engelmann 14 II), 1758,* (12-04-92, Bassenge, #6536), 4⁹⁄₁₆ x 6⁷⁄₁₆ in., (11.6 x 16.3 cm.), etching (BP 139, DM 346, FR 1172, Y 27,091).
$542* *Der Grosse Calas, Zweite Platte (Engelmann 48 II 2 b), 1768,* (12-04-92, Bassenge, #6539), 13⁷⁄₁₆ x 17½ in., (34.2 x 44.5 cm.), etching (BP 348, DM 863, FR 2928, Y 67,665).
$383* *Der Knabe Beim Bratenwender (Engelmann 38), 1764,* prov., (12-04-92, Bassenge, #6537), 4½ x 5¾ in., (11.5 x 14.6 cm.), etching (BP 246, DM 610, FR 2069, Y 47,815).
$210* *Der Kronprinz, Nachheriger Konig Friedrich Wilhelm II (Engelmann 198), 1777,* (12-04-92, Bassenge, #6544), 4¹⁵⁄₁₆ x 3¹⁵⁄₁₆ in., (12.5 x 10.1 cm.), etching (BP 135, DM 334, FR 1135, Y 26,217).
$318* *Portrait Von Friedrich Dem Grossen (Engelmann 49 III), 1768,* (12-04-92, Bassenge, #6540), 5⅛ x 2⁹⁄₁₆ in., (13 x 6.5 cm.), etching (BP 204, DM 506, FR 1718, Y 39,700).
BI *Die Russischen Gefangenen (Engelmann 12 II b), 1758,* est. DM 1,200, (06-10-93, Hauswedell/Nolt, #183), etching.
$231* *Die Vermahlung Der Prinzessin Friderike Sophie Wilhelmine Von Preussen Mit Dem Prinzen Wilhelm V. Von Oranien (Engelmann 46), 1767,* (12-04-92, Bassenge, #6538), 13¾ x 9⁵⁄₁₆ in., (35 x 23.7 cm.), etching (BP 148, DM 368, FR 1248, Y 28,839).
BI *Die Wallfahrt Nach Franzosisch Buchholz (E.38,B.40), 1779,* margins, good cond., light-staining, tape remains, est. $1,2/1,400, (05-19-93, Butterfield, #1857A), 4⅞ x 6⅞ in., (124 x 175 mm.), etching on laid.
$1083* *Die Wallfahrt Nach Franzosisch Buchholz (Engelmann 337), 1775,* (12-04-92, Bassenge, #6545), 5 x 6¹⁵⁄₁₆ in., (12.7 x 17.6 cm.), etching (BP 695, DM 1725, FR 5851, Y 135,206).
BI *Die Wallfahrt Nach Franzosisch Buchholz (Engelmann 38; Bauer 40), 1779,* est. DM 1800, (12-01-92, Karl/Faber, #39), etching.

CHOPPY
$482* *La Houppa Et "Son Fourtoutou",* pub. Choppy, good cond., (11-19-92, Ribeyre/Baron, #164), 46¹⁄₁₆ x 30⁵⁄₁₆ in., (117 x 77 cm.), poster (BP 317, DM 768, FR 2589, Y 59,943).

CHORIS, Louis
$8050* *Voyage Pittoreque Autour Du Monde, Avec Des Portraits Des Sauvages D'Amerique, D'Asie, D'Afrique, Et Des Iles Du Grand Ocean (Lada-Mocarski 84, Sabin 12884, Streeter 4:2461), 1822,* Firmin Didot, folio, spotting, browning, soiling, 1st edit., 2nd issue, (05-21-93, Sotheby-NY, #21, illus.), 15½ x 10 in., (394 x 254 mm.), 104 plates, 12 colored (BP 5215, DM 13,089, FR 44,037, Y 887,541).
$6900* *Vues Et Paysages Des Regions Quinoxiales, Recueilles Dans Un Voyage Autour Du Monde (Lada-Mocarski 80, Sabin 12885), 1826,* Imprim chez Paul Renouaurd, folio, after Choris, offsetting, browning, soiling, 1st edit., prov., (05-21-93, Sotheby-NY, #22), 16¼ x 11 in., (413 x 279 mm.), 24 hand-colored lithographed plates (BP 4470, DM 11,220, FR 37,746, Y 760,750).

CHOUBRAC, Alfred French 1853-1902
$321* *La Bible Amusante Par Leo Taxil. Dessins De Fred'Rick, c. 1895,* Paris, Imp. Em. Levy, cond. B+, (06-11-93, Boisgirard, #65), 47¼ x 37 in., (120 x 94 cm.), poster (BP 211, DM 522, FR 1759, Y 34,058).
$145* *Casino De Paris, Ballet "Les Amoureux De Venise",* paper loss, (01-31-93, Morelle/Marchan, #21), 24⁷⁄₁₆ x 32⁵⁄₁₆ in., (62 x 82 cm.), poster (BP 98, DM 234, FR 790, Y 18,089).
$239* *Cycles Humber,* cond. B, (03-16-93, Boisgirard, #80), 57⅞ x 39⅜ in., (147 x 100 cm.), lithograph poster (BP 165, DM 397, FR 1350, Y 27,947).
BI *Esclarmonde, c. 1896,* fold marks w/corresponding defects, est. BP 150/250, (02-04-93, Christie-S. Ken, #114), 47 x 32 in., (119.4 x 81.3 cm.), color lithograph backed on linen.
$241* *Exposition Russe Hippique Et Ethnographique, 1895,* Paris, Imp. G. Massias, cond. B+, (06-11-93, Boisgirard, #63), 47¼ x 32½ in., (120 x 82.5 cm.), poster (BP 158, DM 392, FR 1321, Y 25,570).
$434* *Folies Begere "La Belle Et La Bete" Ballet,* (01-31-93, Morelle/Marchan, #22), 36⅝ x 51³⁄₁₆ in., (93 x 130 cm.), poster (BP 292, DM 699, FR 2364, Y 54,142).
$120* *Folies Bergere: Arman D'Ary,* Lith. F. Appel, good cond., (02-12-93, Cheval/Robert, #184), 46⁷⁄₁₆ x 33¹⁄₁₆ in., (118 x 84 cm.), poster (BP 85, DM 199, FR 673, Y 14,472).
$455* *Ohe! Ohe! On Va Ouvrir Le Theatre Des Folies Marigny, 7 Mai 1897,* (01-31-93, Morelle/Marchan, #175), 24⁷⁄₁₆ x 31½ in., (62 x 80 cm.), poster (BP 306, DM 733, FR 2478, Y 56,761).
$80* *Paola Del Monte,* good cond., (02-12-93, Cheval/Robert, #183), 48¹³⁄₁₆ x 35¹⁄₁₆ in., (124 x 89 cm.), poster (BP 56, DM 133, FR 449, Y 9648).
$522* *Si Vous Avez La Migraine, Achetez Le Chapeau Laurent, c. 1900,* Colombes, Ateliers Choubrac, cond. B+, (06-11-93, Boisgirard, #64), 24⁷⁄₁₆ x 31½ in., (62 x 80 cm.), poster (BP 343, DM 848, FR 2860, Y 55,385).
$114* *Theatre De L'Eldorado, Royaume Des Femmes,* (01-31-93, Morelle/Marchan, #174), 24⁷⁄₁₆ x 31½ in., (62 x 80 cm.), poster (BP 77, DM 184, FR 621, Y 14,222).

CHOUMOFF, P.
$5175* *Auguste Rodin, Selected Images, 1912-17: One-Hundred,* 26 s.; each t., some annot.; each (c) credit Faubourg St. Jacques stamp, prov., (04-08-93, Christie-NY, #86, illus.), each approx. 8¾ x 6⅝ in., (22.2 x 16.8 cm.), photograph, majority gelatin silver, few copy prints (BP 3393, DM 8313, FR 28,140, Y 587,267).

CHOUQUET, L.
$399* *Cycles Ouragan, c. 1900,* cond. A, (03-16-93, Boisgirard, #83, illus.), 83¹⁄₁₆ x 29¾ in., (211 x 75.5 cm.), poster (BP 276, DM 663, FR 2254, Y 46,656).

CHRISTENBERRY, William b. 1936
$1380* *"Corn Sign With Storm Cloud, Near Greensboro, Alabama", 1977 and "Cotton Gin, Havana Junction, Alabama (Spring)", 1976: Two,* ink s., t., d., (04-08-93, Christie-NY, #484, illus.), each 3¼ x 4⅞ in., (8.3 x 12.4 cm.), photograph, color coupler print (BP 905, DM 2217, FR 7504, Y 156,605).
BI *Gourd Tree-Pickins County, Alabama and Horses And Black Buildings-Newbern, Alabama: Two,* (1978), 1979, each s., t., d. in ink, est. $1,2/1,500, (10-13-92, Christie-NY, #529, illus.), 17⅜ x 22 in., (44.1 x 55.9 cm.), photograph, color coupler prints.

CHRISTIANSEN, Hans German 1866-1945
BI *L'Heure Du Bergere, 1898,* from L'Estampe Moderne, s. in block, est. $15/200, (12-10-92, Sloan, #578), 13⅞ x 8⅞ in., (35.2 x 22.5 cm.), color woodcut.
BI *L'Heure Du Bergere, 1898,* from "L'Estampe Moderne", est. $125/175, (02-04-93, Sloan, #348), sheet 16 x 12¼ in., (40.6 x 31.1 cm.), color woodcut.

CHRISTO   Bulgarian/American b. 1935

BI *5,600 Cubic Meter Package, Kassel (S. & B. 131), 1986,* s., annot. H.C. from For Joseph Beuys portfolio, blindstamp pub. Editions Schellmann, good cond., est. $1,2/ 1,400, (10-28-92, Butterfield, #2922), 31 x 23⅝ in., (787 x 600 mm.), silkscreen and collotype w/collage of photographs in colors on Fabraino paper.

$505* *5600 Kubikmeter-Paket, Kassel (Schelmann/Hovdenakk 11), 1968,* s., d., (11-28-92, Schoppmann, #469), 22¾ x 17¹³⁄₁₆ in., (57.8 x 45.3 cm.), offset on wove (BP 333, DM 805, FR 2731, Y 62,850).

BI *Aegina Temple (Project For The Glyptothek, Munich, Germany, And The Aegina Temple), 1988,* num., s., est. $2/3,000, (05-27-93, Swann, #62, illus.), (88.9 x 68.6 cm.), color screen print and photo collage.

BI *"Aegina Temple",* projects for Glyptothek, Munich and The Aegina Temple, s. Christo inmatrix, #184/300, shrink wrapped, very good cond., est. $2/3,000, (03-12-93, Skinner, #116, illus.), sight, sheet 35¼ x 27 in., (89.5 x 68.6 cm.), half-tone photo-collage and screenprint on paper.

BI *"Aegina Temple", c. 1988,* s., #186/300, full margins, excell. cond., est. $2/4,000, (01-23-93, Goldberg, #484, illus.), 35 x 27 in., (88.9 x 68.6 cm.), photocollage and screenprint.

$853* *America House Wrapped, Heidelberg 1969 (S. 28), 1969,* s., #162/200, pub. Editions Staeck, skinned verso, (12-03-92, Sotheby-London, #628), sheet 35¼ x 24⅝ in., (897 x 625 mm.), screenprint w/collage of polythene, on Schoeller-Hammer (BP 550, DM 1341, FR 4579, Y 106,134).

$4400* *Arc De Triomphe, Wrapped (Project For Paris), 1989,* s., d., i. AP, pub. Torsten Lilja, excell. cond., (11-09-92, Christie-NY, #256, illus.), 27¾ x 21⅞ in., (705 x 556 mm.), lithograph w/collage in colors on Arches (BP 2909, DM 7024, FR 23,732, Y 546,041).

BI *Christo, Surrounded Islands, Biscayne Bay, Greater Miami, Florida 1980/83,* s., wear, exhib., est. DM 700-, (09-25-92, Granier, #2793), 33¼ x 23⁷⁄₁₆ in., (84.5 x 59.5 cm.), color offset print.

BI *Corridor Store Front, Project (Hovdenakk 6), 1968,* s., d., i. H.C., pub. Verlag Gerd Hatje, good cond., handling marks, est. BP 800/1,200, (06-30-93, Sotheby-London, #762, illus.), 27¾ x 22¼ in., (705 x 565 mm.), color screenprint mounted on board and plexiglas w/hinges to be opened.

$3177* *Corridor Store Front, Project (Schellmann 5), 1967-68,* s., num. 14/75 on label, pub. Documenta-Foundation, good cond., (10-14-92, Sotheby-Japan, #14, illus.), overall size 27¾ x 21¾ in., (705 x 552 mm.), 2-part screenprint, front print die-cut mounted on acetate, rear print mounted on wooden support (BP 1865, DM 4649, FR 15,767, Y 384,998).

BI *Corridore Store Front (Schellmann 16), 1968,* #19/100, s., est. SF 2,2/2,800, (04-21-93, Germann, #111, illus.), 26⅞ x 21¼ in., (682 x 540 mm.), diptych screen print on laid down Klarsichfolie.

BI *Corridore Store Front - Schaufenster-Gang (Schellmann 16), 1968,* s., 19/100, est. SF 3,2/3,800, (10-14-92, Germann, #50, illus.), 26⅞ x 21¼ in., (682 x 540 mm.), serigraph.

BI *Double Show Window (S. and B. 47), 1972: A Pair,* s., d., #50/65, pub. Tanglewood Press and label, scratches, excell. cond., est. $3/4,000, both 35 3/4 x 24 x 3in., (05-11-93, Christie-NY, #381, illus.), plexiglas sheets housed in aluminum mullions w/hand-painting by artist in green.

BI *Double Show Window (Schellmann and Benecke 48), 1972: A Pair,* s., d. in ink, num. 28/65, pub. Tanglewood Press, excell. cond., est. $3,5/4,500, both 35 3/4 x 24 x 3in., (09-19-92, Christie-E, #89, illus.), pair of plexiglas sheets housed in aluminum mullions w/hand-coloringby artist in white.

$1492* *"Ericsson Display Monitor Unit 3111, Wrapped (Personal Computer)" (Schellmann/Benecke 120), 1985,* s., 47/100, (12-04-92, AB Stockholm, #7037), 27⁹⁄₁₆ x 22¹⁄₁₆ in., (70 x 56 cm.), color lithograph and collage (BP 957, DM 2376, FR 8061, Y 186,267, SK 10,120).

$1650* *Ericsson Display Monitor Unit 3111, Wrapped, Project For Personal Computer (S. and B. 120), 1985,* laid down on board, s., d., #92/100, soiling, very good cond., (11-

09-92, Christie-NY, #255, illus.), 28 x 22½ in., (711 x 572 mm.), colored lithograph w/collage of tranparent polyethylene, twine, and color photograph on Arches (BP 1091, DM 2634, FR 8900, Y 204,765).

$770* *The Gates: Project For Central Park, New York City, 1980,* s., full margins, (12-08-92, Swann, #63), 29 x 23 in., (73.7 x 58.4 cm.), offset color lithograph w/photo collage (BP 483, DM 1199, FR 4087, Y 95,439).

BI *Lower Manhattan Wrapped Buildings (Project For 2 Broadway, 20 Exchange Place), 1990,* s., i., one of 30 artist's proofs, pub. J. Rosenthal Fine Art, Ltd.,full sheet, good cond., est. $5/6,000, (11-07-92, Sotheby-NY, #530), sheet 40⅛ x 26 in., (101.9 x 66 cm.), lithograph p. in colors w/collage on Arches Cover mounted on museum board.

BI *Monuments (Schellmann 12-22), 1968,* complete portfolio, s., #79/100, w/scale-model of the Air Package, pub. 1968 Galerie Der Spiegel, good cond., original box, est. BP 2/2,500, (06-30-93, Sotheby-London, #764, illus.), overall 28¼ x 25¼ in., (718 x 641 mm.), silkscreen, 3 in color, on Bristol board.

BI *Monuments: Edifice Public Empaquete (Schellmann 21), 1968,* s., #37/100, pub. Galerie Der Spiegel, good cond., creasing, est. BP3/400, (12-03-92, Sotheby-London, #627, illus.), sheet 21½ x 27⅜ in., (545 x 695 mm.), screenprint on wove.

$851* *The Museum Of Modern Art Wrapped (Front), Project For New York (Hovdenakk 25), 1971,* s., num., (06-05-93, Schoppmann, #765), 28¾ x 22⅝ in., (73 x 57.5 cm.), color lithograph on hand-made board (BP 560, DM 1380, FR 4650, Y 91,289).

$523* *"The Museum Of Modern Art Wrapped (Project For The MOMA, New York- June 1968)",* s. Christo, t., Printers Proof II(09-25-92, Wolf, #53), 28 x 21½ in., (71.1 x 54.6 cm.), colored lithograph (BP 305, DM 775, FR 2622, Y 63,126).

$922* *The Museum Of Modern Art, Wrapped (Rear), Project For New York (Hovdenakk 25 b), 1971,* s., num., (06-05-93, Schoppmann, #764), 28¾ x 22⅝ in., (73 x 57.5 cm.), color lithograph collage w/photo and map on hand-made board (BP 607, DM 1495, FR 5038, Y 98,906).

$1705* *The Museum Of Modern Art, Wrapped, Project For New York, Some Not Realized Projects (Schellmann/Benecke 36), 1971,* s., 15/100, (05-12-93, AB Stockholm, #7016, illus.), 27¾ x 21⅞ in., (70.5 x 55.5 cm.), color lithographs w/collage (BP 1113, DM 2751, FR 9266, Y 190,354, SK 12,650).

BI *Orange Store Front, 1991,* s., #AP 27/35, inkstamp of artist and publisher, Landfall Press, verygood cond., est. $6/8,000, (05-19-93, Butterfield, #2145), 26⅛ x 30⅝ in., (664 x 778 mm.), offset lithograph w/lithograph and extensive collage in colors on heavy wove.

BI *Orange Street Front (CJ-90-68), 1991,* s., #AP 27/35, artist inkstamp, pub. Landfall Press, very good cond., est. $8/10,000, (10-28-92, Butterfield, #2923, illus.), 26⅛ x 30⅝ in., (664 x 778 mm.), offset lithograph w/lithograph and extensive collage in colors on heavy cream wove.

$948* *Packed Building, Project For The Arc De Triomphe, Paris (Schellmann 3), 1970,* E.A., s.(06-24-93, Germann, #280, illus.), 19 x 26¹⁄₁₆ in., (483 x 662 mm.), color lithograph (BP 624, DM 1537, FR 5180, Y 101,695, SF 1380).

BI *Packed Building, Project For The Ecole Militaire Paris (Schellmann 31), 1970,* E.A., s., est. DM 1,0/1,200, (06-24-93, Germann, #277, illus.), 25¹³⁄₁₆ x 19⅛ in., (655 x 485 mm.), color lithograph.

$5414* *"Packed Kunsthalle Bern, Project" (Schellmann/Benecke 43-46), 1972: Four,* s., num., Stuttgart, manus presse, (11-28-92, Grisebach, #331, illus.), 27¾ x 21⁹⁄₁₆ in., (70.5 x 54.7 cm.), serigraph on thin cardboard (BP 3574, DM 8625, FR 29,281, Y 673,802).

$374* *The Paris Review, 1990,* s., #180/250, p. to 3 sides, good cond., handling creases, (05-19-93, Butterfield, #2144), 31⅛ x 24 in., (791 x 610 mm.), offset lithograph in colors on wove (BP 243, DM 608, FR 2048, Y 41,404).

$231* *Project For The Institute Of Comtemporary Art, University Of Pennsylvania, Philadelphia,* s., #131/200, (11-16-92, Briest, #270), 22¹⁄₁₆ x 29¹⁵⁄₁₆ in., (56 x 76 cm.), lithograph in 4 colors on carton (BP 152, DM 368, FR 1241, Y 28,828).

$63* *Projekte In Der Stadt,* for Galerie Im Stadt, 1982, (09-30-92, Kunsthallen, #61), poster, offset prints in colors (BP 36, DM 89, FR 302, Y 7560, DK 345).

$2905* *Puerto De Alcala, Wrapped Project For Madrid (Schellmann 107), 1981,* s., num. 2/99, pub. Ediciones Poligrafa, full sheet, good cond., (10-14-92, Sotheby-Japan, #19, illus.), sheet 28⅛ x 21¾ in., (714 x 552 mm.), colored lithograph w/collage of fabric, twine, map and photograph (BP 1705, DM 4251, FR 14,417, Y 352,036).

$1152* *Raum-Komposition, 1978,* s., d., prov., (10-21-92, Dobiaschofsky, #1907, illus.), 27⁹⁄₁₆ x 25⁹⁄₁₆ in., (70 x 65 cm.), heliogravure, drawing, multiple (BP 715, DM 1743, FR 5917, Y 140,317, SF 1560).

$11,550* *(Some) Not Realized Projects, 1971: Five,* Landfall Press, s., num., (11-28-92, Schoppmann, #468, illus.), 28¹⁵⁄₁₆ x 23¼ in., (73.5 x 59 cm.), color lithograph on BFK Rives and special Arjomari (BP 7624, DM 18,401, FR 62,466, Y 1,437,461).

BI *(Some) Not Realized Projects: The Museum Of Modern Art, Wrapped, Project For New York (Schellman 37), 1971,* s., i. IV, pub. Landfall Press, full sheet, good cond., est. $800/1,000, (02-11-93, Sotheby-NY, #318), sheet 27¹⁵⁄₁₆ x 21⅞ in., (711 x 556 mm.), color lithograph on Arjomari.

$3300* *(Some) Not Realized Projects: Whitney Museum Of American Art, Packed, Project For New York (S. & B. 35), 1971,* s., #77/100, blindstamp pub. Landfall Press, very good cond.?, (10-28-92, Butterfield, #2921), sheet 27¾ x 21¾ in., (705 x 552 mm.), color lithograph w/collage on heavy white wove (BP 2103, DM 5097, FR 17,305, Y 404,908).

BI *(Some) Not Realized Projects: Whitney Museum Of American Art, Packed, Project For New York (S. 35), 1971,* s., i., pub. Landfall Press, full sheet, good cond., slight soiling,est. $4/5,000, (11-07-92, Sotheby-NY, #529, illus.), sheet 28 x 22 in., (711 x 559 mm.), lithograph p. in colors w/collage on Arjomari.

$2875* *(Some) Not Realized Projects: Whitney Museum Of American Art, Packed, Project For New York (Schellman 35), 1971,* s., i. IX, pub. Landfall Press, good cond., soiling, (05-15-93, Sotheby-NY, #934, illus.), sheet 28 x 22 in., (71.1 x 55.9 cm.), lithograph in colors w/collage on Arjomari (BP 1869, DM 4624, FR 15,541, Y 318,701).

BI *Surrounded Island, Project For Biscayne Bay, Greater Miami, Florida (S. and B. 132), 1987: A Pair,* s., #90/125, i., pub. Edition Schellmann, excell. cond., est. $3,5/4,000, (05-11-93, Christie-NY, #382, illus.), each sheet 15 x 15½ in., (381 x 394 mm.), color screenprint w/collage on wove.

BI *Surrounded Islands (Project For Biscayne Bay), 1983,* full margins, s., est. $700/1,000, (05-27-93, Swann, #63), (71.8 x 59.7 cm.), offset color lithograph w/photo collage.

$2990* *Surrounded Islands, 1984: Four,* ink s., #21/100, annot. Vol 2, (c) insig., (04-08-93, Christie-NY, #522, illus.), each approx. 21¾ x 16¼ in., (55.2 x 41.3 cm.), photograph, dye-transfer print (BP 1961, DM 4803, FR 16,259, Y 339,310).

$990* *Texas Mastaba, Project For 500,000 Stacked Oil Drums (S. 85), 1976,* s., annot. 12/25 AP, pub. APC Editions, Chermayeff and Geismer Associates, from portfolio America: The Third Century, apparently good cond., (02-24-93, Butterfield, #3006), 30 x 22½ in., (762 x 559 mm.), offset lithograph & silkscreen in colors w/collage on brown cardboard (BP 690, DM 1607, FR 5449, Y 116,170).

$660* *Texas Mastaba, Project For 500,000 Stacked Oil Drums (S. and B. 85),1976,* s., num. 102/200, pub. APC Editions, Chermayeff and Geismer Assoc., full sheet, excell. cond., (09-19-92, Christie-E, #90), sheet 29¹⁵⁄₁₆ x 22¼ in., (760 x 565 mm.), lithograph and screenprint in colors w/collage on brown board (BP 380, DM 988, FR 3385, Y 82,233).

$993* *Texas Mastaba, Projekt Fur 500000 Gestapelte Olfasser (Schellmann-Benecke 89), 1977,* s., num., (06-05-93, Bassenge, #5947), 27¹³⁄₁₆ x 21⅞ in., (70.7 x 55.5 cm.), color screen print on thin board (BP 654, DM 1610, FR 5426, Y 106,522).

BI *"Tonneau And Ferraille, 100 Cm", 1961,* s., t., d., annot., est. $1/2,000, (11-16-92, Butterfield, #5903, illus.), 10¾ x 7⅛ in., (273.5 x 181.3 mm.), photograph, gelatin silver print.

$880* *Two Lower Manhattan Wrapped Buildings, Project For New York City, 1979-85,* s., full margins, (12-08-92, Swann, #64, illus.), 30½ x 23½ in., (77.5 x 59.7 cm.), offset color lithograph w/photo collage (BP 552, DM 1370, FR 4671, Y 109,073).

BI *Umbrella Project For Japan And Western U.S.A., 1985,* s., est. 700/1,000, (05-27-93, Swann, #64), sh 27 x 31 in., (68.6 x 78.7 cm.), offset color lithographed poster.

$367* *The Umbrellas (Project For Japan And Western USA), 1985,* s., (05-26-93, Dorling, #2603, illus.), 29¼ x 23¹⁄₁₆ in., (74.3 x 58.5 cm.), color offset print on cardboard (BP 237, DM 599, FR 2015, Y 39,874).

$1100* *The Umbrellas, Joint Project For Japan And U.S.A., 1990,* s. in ink, full margins, apparently very good cond., (02-24-93, Butterfield, #3007), sheet 28 x 40 in., (71.1 x 101.6 cm.), offset lithgraph in colors w/collage on wove (BP 767, DM 1786, FR 6054, Y 129,078).

$1320* *Untitled, 1962,* s., d., (11-16-92, Butterfield, #5902, illus.), 7¼ x 9⅜ in., (184.5 x 238.5 mm.), photograph, gelatin silver print (BP 869, DM 2105, FR 7089, Y 164,159).

$316* *Verpackte Kunsthalle Bern (Schellmann 23), 1968,* #33/200, s., signs of wear, (04-21-93, Germann, #339), 37 x 27³⁄₁₆ in., (940 x 690 mm.), offset print (BP 205, DM 505, FR 1708, Y 34,983, SF 460).

$1348* *Verpackter Baum, Projekt (Schellmann-Benecke 33), 1970,* s., (06-05-93, Bassenge, #5945), 24⁷⁄₁₆ x 32¹¹⁄₁₆ in., (62 x 83 cm.), color screen print on thin board (BP 887, DM 2185, FR 7366, Y 144,604).

BI *Verpacktes Automobil, Projekt Fur Einen Volvo 122 S Sport Sedan (Schellmann/Benecke 113), 1984,* s., d., #78/100, est. DM 7,000, (05-27-93, Lempertz, #662, illus.), 18⁷⁄₁₆ x 27¹⁵⁄₁₆ in., (46.8 x 71 cm.), photo-lithograph, color lithograph and collage on Rives wove.

$1784* *"Wrapped Armchair (Project Height 34" x 34" x 33")",* s., 83/100, (12-04-92, AB Stockholm, #7038), 25³⁄₁₆ x 34⅝ in., (64 x 88 cm.), lithograph and collage (BP 1144, DM 2841, FR 9638, Y 222,722, SK 12,100).

$5991* *Wrapped Automobile, Project For Volvo 122 S Sport Sedan (Schellmann 113), 1984,* s., d., num. 23/100, pub. by artist and Edition Schellmann, full sheet, good cond., (10-14-92, Sotheby-Japan, #20, illus.), sheet 22⅜ x 27⅞ in., (568 x 708 mm.), colored lithograph w/collage of fabric and twine on BFK Rives mounted on museum board (BP 3516, DM 8768, FR 29,732, Y 726,006).

BI *"Wrapped Monument To Leonardo" (S. 44 et 42), 1971: Diptych,* ed. 999, #982/999, s., est. FF 8,0/10,000, (10-18-92, Pescheteau, #101), 29⅛ x 22¹⁄₁₆ in., (74 x 56 cm.), lithograph in colors and collotype on Rives.

$1634* *Wrapped Monument To Vittorio Emanuele, Project For Piazza Del Duomo, Milan (Schellmann 80), 1975,* s., num. 56/75, pub. Ediciones Poligrafa, full sheet, good cond., (10-14-92, Sotheby-Japan, #17, illus.), sheet 28 x 22 in., (711 x 559 mm.), colored lithograph on Guarro paper (BP 959, DM 2391, FR 8109, Y 198,013).

$1634* *Wrapped Monument To Vittorio Emanuele, Project For Piazza Del Duomo, Milan (Schellmann 81), 1975,* s., num. 56/75, pub. Ediciones Poligrafa, full sheet, good cond., (10-14-92, Sotheby-Japan, #18, illus.), sheet 28 x 22 in., (711 x 559 mm.), colored lithograph w/collage of text sheet, photograph and masking tape on Guarro paper (BP 959, DM 2391, FR 8109, Y 198,013).

$1634* *Wrapped Monument To Vittorio Emanuele, Project For Piazza Del Duomo,Milan (Schellmann 78), 1975,* s., num. 56/75, pub. Ediciones Poligrafa, full sheet, good cond., (10-14-92, Sotheby-Japan, #16, illus.), sheet 28 x 22 in., (711 x 559 mm.), colored lithograph w/collage of fabric, twine and staples on Guarro paper (BP 959, DM 2391, FR 8109, Y 198,013).

$246* *Wrapped Monument To Vittorio Emmanuele, Piazza Del Duomo, Mailand 1970 (Hovdenakk 44),* #595/600, s., (11-13-92, Koller, #5292), 11¹³⁄₁₆ x 16⁹⁄₁₆ in., (30 x 42 cm.), color offset on print paper (BP 159, DM 386, FR 1302, Y 30,532, SF 348).

$2743* *"Wrapped Mur Des Reformateurs, Project For Geneva" (Schellmann/Benecke 94), 1977,* s., num.(11-28-92, Grisebach, #461, illus.), 28⅛ x 22¹⁄₁₆ in., (71.4 x 56 cm.), colored lithograph w/collage, fabric, thread, photo and map on hand-made (BP 1811, DM 4370, FR 14,835, Y 341,381).

$738* *Wrapped Reichstag, 1985,* s., (11-13-92, Koller, #5291), 27³⁄₁₆ x 23⁷⁄₁₆ in., (69 x 59.5 cm.), color offset on offset paper (BP 477, DM 1159, FR 3907, Y 91,597, SF 1044).

$5410* *Wrapped Road Sign, 1963-1987,* #29/100, s., (11-20-92, Lempertz, #493, illus.), 27⅞ x 21⅞ in., (70.8 x 55.5 cm.), color lithograph w/collage on cardboard (BP 3562, DM 8626, FR 29,055, Y 672,802).

$2217* *Wrapped Road Sign, Project, 1988,* s., #HC 14/25, pub. Ediciones Poligrafa, good cond., (12-03-92, Sotheby-London, #629, illus.), sheet 27⅞ x 21⅞ in., (707 x 555 mm.), lithograph in colors w/collage of fabric and twine on white board, mounted on cardboard (BP 1430, DM 3486, FR 11,900, Y 275,849).

$895* *Wrapped Staircase (Schellmann 17), 1969,* s., #68/110, pub. Wide White Space Gallery, p. Veereman, full sheet p. to edges, good cond., (05-27-93, Sotheby-Amstrdm, #576), sh 22¹³⁄₁₆ x 15³⁄₁₆ in., (580 x 385 mm.), offset print on 300 gram Cromote (BP 573, DM 1436, FR 4840, Y 95,948, G 1610).

BI *"Wrapped Statues (Project For Die Glyptothek-Munchen W. Germany) Aegina Temple", 1988,* s., num., Landfall Press, est. DM 5000, (12-01-92, Karl/Faber, #453, illus.), 35¹⁄₁₆ x 26¹⁵⁄₁₆ in., (89 x 68.5 cm.), color serigraph and photo-collage on thick wove.

$1610* *Wrapped Statues/Project For Der Glyptothek-Munchen, W. Germany/AeginaTemple, 1988,* s., #185/300, p. Landfall Press, good cond.?, (05-19-93, Butterfield, #2143), 35¼ x 27 in., (895 x 686 mm.), photo-collage and silkscreen in colors on wove (BP 1045, DM 2617, FR 8817, Y 178,235).

$1877* *"Wrapped Sylvette" (Schellmann/Benecke 60), 1973/1974,* s., num., (11-28-92, Grisebach, #460, illus.), colored solar print with 2 collaged photos on cardboard (BP 1239, DM 2990, FR 10,151, Y 233,603).

BI *Wrapped Sylvette, 1972,* from Hommage a Picasso, i., s., E.A., creases, est. DM 1,900, (09-18-92, Schloss Ahlden, #983, illus.), 25⁹⁄₁₆ x 19⅝ in., (64.9 x 49.9 cm.), screen print, collage on white cardboard.

$1634* *Wrapped Sylvette, Project For Washington Square Village, New York (Schellmann 59), 1972,* s., i. E.A., 1/40 artist's proofs, from Hommage a Picasso, pub. Propylaen Verlag, full sheet, good cond., (10-14-92, Sotheby-Japan, #15, illus.), sheet 25⅝ x 19¾ in., (651 x 502 mm.), silkscreen and collotype in colors w/collage of city map and brown paper wrapping (BP 959, DM 2391, FR 8109, Y 198,013).

BI *Wrapped Sylvette, Project For Washington Square Village, New York, (S. & B. 60), 1973-4,* s., num. 281/300, pub. Propylaen Verlag, margins, good cond., est. BP 6/800, (12-01-92, Christie-London, #567), S. 27¹¹⁄₁₆ x 21⅞ in., (703 x 555 mm.), collotype and screenprint in colors w/collage of 2 photographs.

$886* *"Wrapped Sylvette/Project For Washington Square Village, Bleeker Str. And Houston Str." (Schellmann 59), 1972,* s., num., 3. Mappe from the series Hommage a Picasso, pub. Propylaen-Verlag, (06-08-93, Karl/Faber, #631, illus.), approx. 25⁹⁄₁₆ x 19¹¹⁄₁₆ in., (65 x 50 cm.), color light print and screen print collaged w/photo and brown packing paper (BP 582, DM 1438, FR 4842, Y 94,105).

$805* *Wrapped Tree, Project (Schellmann and Benecke 33),* from Spiegel 70, Galerie Der Spiegel, 1970, s., #100/150, full margins, creases, excell. cond., (05-11-93, Christie-NY, #380), sheet 24⅜ x 32¹¹⁄₁₆ in., (619 x 830 mm.), color screenprint on Bristol board (BP 514, DM 1268, FR 4273, Y 88,549).

BI *Wrapped Tree, Project, from Spiegel 70, Cologne, Galerie Der Spiegel,1970 (Schellmann and Benecke 33),* s., #100/150, full margins, creases, excellent cond., est. $2/3,000, (11-09-92, Christie-NY, #252, illus.), (619 x 830 mm.), colored screenprint on Bristol board.

$686* *Wrapped Venus (H. 39), 1974,* s., #25/200, pub. for portfolio Graphikmappe des Schweizerischen Kunstvereins, 1975, margins, good cond.?, (06-30-93, Sotheby-London, #763, illus.), 20 x 18½ in., (508 x 470 mm.), lithograph, offset lithograph and collage in color (BP 460, DM 1170, FR 3947, Y 73,503).

$2200* *Wrapped Venus, Project For Villa Borghese, Rome (S. and B. 75), 1975,* s., #3/50, blindstamp, full margins, excellent cond., (11-09-92, Christie-NY, #253, illus.), 28¼ x 22½ in., (718 x 572 mm.), etching and lithograph in colors w/collage on Twinrocker handmade (BP 1455, DM 3512, FR 11,866, Y 273,021).

BI *Wrapped Walk Ways (Schellmann 111), 1983,* project for St. Stephan's Green Park, Dublin, #72/100, s., d., est. SF 5/6,000, 710 x 1115mm, (09-04-92, Germann, #20, illus.), color lithograph w/collage on white cloth.

$1980* *Wrapped Walk Ways, Project For St. Stephen's Green Park, Dublin (S. and B. 111), 1983,* laid to cardboard, s., d., #64/100, pub. Editions Schellmann and Kluser, very good cond., (11-09-92, Christie-NY, #254, illus.), 28 x 44 in., (71.1 x 111.8 cm.), colored lithograph w/collage on Arches (BP 1309, DM 3161, FR 10,680, Y 245,719).

$1328* *Wrapped Woman (Schellmann-Benecke 63), 1973,* s., num., (12-05-92, Bassenge, #7084), 27¹⁵⁄₁₆ x 22¹⁄₁₆ in., (71 x 56 cm.), color screen print on thin cardboard (BP 832, DM 2070, FR 7056, Y 164,540).

CHRISTOFOROU, John

$39* *Sans Titre,* s., d., 83/100, (06-28-93, Loudmer, #211B), 30⅛ x 24¹¹⁄₁₆ in., (765 x 627 mm.), sh 34⅜ x 24¹¹⁄₁₆ in., (765 x 627 mm.), color lithograph on Arches wove (BP 26, DM 66, FR 223, Y 4138).

$39* *Sans Titre,* s., artist's proof, (06-28-93, Loudmer, #211A), 29¹⁵⁄₁₆ x 22¹³⁄₁₆ in., (760 x 580 mm.), sh 35⁷⁄₁₆ x 24¹¹⁄₁₆ in., (760 x 580 mm.), color lithograph on Arches wove (BP 26, DM 66, FR 223, Y 4138).

CHRISTY, Howard Chandler   American 1873-1952

$110* *American's All Victory Liberty Loan,* (02-14-93, Hanzel, #705), 40 x 27 in., (101.6 x 68.6 cm.), color lithographic poster (BP 77, DM 182, FR 617, Y 13,266).

$605* *"The Bookman, September" and "The Bookman, November":* Two, B+ cond., (08-06-92, Swann, #90, illus.), approx. 24 x 13 in., (61 x 33 cm.), (BP 316, DM 894, FR 3019, Y 77,168).

$330* *"Clear The Way!!", "Americans All!" and "Fight Or Buy Bonds":* Three, WWI posters, B+ cond., creasing; 2nd w/ closed tear, Christy's Lady Liberty in each, (08-06-92, Swann, #91, illus.), 30 x 20 in., (76.2 x 50.8 cm.), and 40 x 27 in., (76.2 x 50.8 cm.), (BP 172, DM 488, FR 1647, Y 42,092).

$121* *Fight Or Buy Bonds - Third Liberty Loan,* (02-14-93, Hanzel, #709), 40 x 30 in., (101.6 x 76.2 cm.), color lithographic poster (BP 85, DM 201, FR 679, Y 14,592).

$275* *"Fight Or Buy Bonds", Third Liberty Loan, 1917,* fold creasing, repair, (09-12-92, Dunning, #111), 40 x 30 in., (101.6 x 76.2 cm.), poster laid on cloth (BP 142, DM 396, FR 1345, Y 34,073).

CHRYSSA   Greek/American b. 1933

BI *Abstract Forms: Twenty,* est. $1,0/1,500, (09-24-92, Mystic, #40), each 32 x 24½ in., (81.3 x 108 cm.), colored lithographs.

BI *Calligraphies Jaunes,* s., #E.A. 2/3, est. FF1,200/1,500, (05-27-93, Briest, #58), 40³⁄₁₆ x 30⁵⁄₁₆ in., (102 x 77 cm.), color serigraph.

BI *Chinatown, 1978,* s., num., Edition Domberger, est. DM 1800, (12-01-92, Karl/Faber, #454), 38³⁄₁₆ x 31⅛ in., (97 x 79 cm.), color serigraph on wove.

BI *Komposition In Grau,* 150/300, s., est. SF 4/500, (04-21-93, Germann, #342), 37¼ x 25⅛ in., (946 x 638 mm.), color lithograph.

BI *Untitled, 1970,* s., d., i., annot. A.P., good cond., surface soiling, est. $8/10,000, (10-28-92, Butterfield, #2924), 26⅛ x 26⅞ in., (664 x 683 mm.), color lithograph on Arches.

$467* *Untitled, c. 1966: Set Of Six,* s., full margins, #30/100, pub. Prestige Art, (12-08-92, Swann, #65, illus.), each 25 x 25 in., (63.5 x 63.5 cm.), color serigraph (BP 293, DM 727, FR 2479, Y 57,883).

CHURCH, Frederick S.   American 1842-1924
$39* *The Elf,* margins, s., (05-22-93, Collins, #51), 9¼ x 5 in., (23.5 x 12.7 cm.), etching (BP 25, DM 63, FR 213, Y 4300).
$138* *Nymph With Owls,* margins, i., (10-24-92, Collins, #17), 9¾ x 14⅝ in., (24.8 x 37.1 cm.), etching (BP 85, DM 211, FR 715, Y 16,829).

CHURCHILL, Sarah
$66* *Room Interior,* s., #130/300, (02-11-93, Boos, #449), 19⅛ x 15¹⁵⁄₁₆ in., (485 x 405 mm.), color lithograph (BP 47, DM 109, FR 370, Y 7957).

CHURCHILL, Sarah   British 20th cent.
$193* *When I Was A Child,* s., (11-12-92, Freemn/Fine Art, #49), 32 x 23 in., (81.3 x 58.4 cm.), litho (BP 127, DM 306, FR 1032, Y 23,931).

CHURCHILL and DENNISON
$770* *Indian Wigwam Booth Groupe [sic] At Army Relief Fair, 1864,* t., (c), credit, (10-14-92, Swann, #169, illus.), 6 x 7½ in., (15.2 x 19.1 cm.), photograph, albumen print (BP 452, DM 1127, FR 3821, Y 93,311).

CHWAST, S.
BI *Doug Henning, "Houdini Water Torture Escape",* A-cond., est. $3/400, (08-06-92, Swann, #193, illus.), 46 x 29½ in., (116.8 x 74.9 cm.), .

CIPRIANI, G.B. (after)
$167* *The First Kiss Of Love, 1787,* by Francesco Bortolozzi, pub. R. Stanier, (09-17-92, Bonhams-Chelsea, #115), image 6¼ x 8 in., (15.9 x 20.3 cm.), stipple engraving w/hand-coloring (BP 94, DM 248, FR 849, Y 20,792).

CIPRIANI, Giovanni Battista   Italian 1727-1785 or 1790
$55* *Crucifixion,* after Grabbiani, (12-13-92, Hindman, #255), 14 x 20⅜ in., etching (BP 35, DM 86, FR 295, Y 6804).

CIRIELLO, A.
$352* *Sfolgorio De Stelle (Sensations Of 1945), De A. Stone, Avec Eleanor Powell, Cab Calloway Et Son Orchestre (Italian), 1945,* (01-31-93, Morelle/Marchan, #96), 27⁹⁄₁₆ x 39⅜ in., (70 x 100 cm.), poster (BP 237, DM 567, FR 1917, Y 43,912).

CIRY, Michel   French b. 1919
$126* *Les Deux Saules, 1941,* s. in plate, d., 6/27, small tear, good cond., (06-28-93, Loudmer, #212), 4¾ x 6¹¹⁄₁₆ in., (120 x 170 mm.), sh 10¹⁄₁₆ x 12⅝ in., (120 x 170 mm.), black drypoint on wove (BP 84, DM 214, FR 721, Y 13,369).
$193* *Emmaus 83 Num. 2, 1983,* s., d., 2/90, ink stain, (06-28-93, Loudmer, #213), 14⅜ x 12³⁄₁₆ in., (365 x 310 mm.), sh 25⁹⁄₁₆ x 19⅞ in., (365 x 310 mm.), black etching and aquatint on BFK Rives (BP 129, DM 328, FR 1105, Y 20,477).
BI *"Jesus-1963" and "Saul-1961" (P.949 and 917),* 5th state #26/30, d., s., 9th state #31/50, d., s., est. FF1,000/1,500, (04-04-93, Pescheteau, #185), one 12¹⁵⁄₁₆ x 9⅝ in., (33 x 24.5 cm.), other 14¹⁵⁄₁₆ x 11 in., (33 x 24.5 cm.), etching on Rives.
$103* *Pieta (R. Passeron, 849), 1954,* annot., s., large margin, (04-02-93, Picard, #73), 10⅛ x 7¾ in., (25.7 x 19.7 cm.), etching (BP 68, DM 166, FR 562, Y 11,727).
$182* *Stabat Mater III (R.P. 922), 1961,* definitive state, d., t., #9/50, ink s., large margins, (02-03-93, Ader Tajan, #100), 13¾ x 8⅞ in., (35 x 22.5 cm.), etching (BP 127, DM 300, FR 1016, Y 22,640).
$202* *La Vallee Aux Loups,* t., #24/150, s., reddish stains, loss, large margins, (02-03-93, Ader Tajan, #103), 7⅞ x 10⅞ in., (20 x 27.7 cm.), etching (BP 141, DM 333, FR 1128, Y 25,128).

CITROEN, Paul   German 1896-1983
$986* *Franz Osborn, 1933,* s., t., (11-12-92, Lempertz, #39, illus.), 11¾ x 9⁷⁄₁₆ in., (29.8 x 23.9 cm.), photograph, gelatin silver print (BP 630, DM 1550, FR 5281, Y 121,984).
BI *Self-Portrait With Camera (Citroen, front cover),* mounted on deckle-edged paper, 1920's, est. $2,5/3,500, (10-15-92, Sotheby-NY, #299, illus.), 2¼ x 1¾ in., (5.7 x 4.4 cm.), photograph, gelatin silver print.

BI *Still Life With Bronzes, c. 1928,* est. $8/1,000, (10-13-92, Christie-NY, #167, illus.), 9¼ x 6¾ in., (23.5 x 17.1 cm.), photograph, gelatin silver print.

CLAASEN, Hermann   German 1899-1987
BI *Hamsterer Auf Der Schiffsbrucke, 1948,* (c), t., lit., est. DM 500, (11-12-92, Lempertz, #40, illus.), 7⅞ x 11⅝ in., (20 x 29.6 cm.), photograph, gelatin silver print.

CLADEL, J.
$605* *"August Rodin: L'Oeuvre Et L'Homme", 1908,* Ltd. Ed. 1 of 25, spine missing, folio, (09-17-92, Sloan, #2652), on Japan paper, 152 plates (BP 340, DM 898, FR 3074, Y 75,324).

CLAESEN AND CO., Charles, Publisher
$48* *Mobel Und Decoration: One Hundred Thirteen,* folio w/ text, (03-17-93, Bonhams-Chelsea, #394), subject 11¾ x 8½ in., (29.8 x 21.6 cm.), chromolithograph (BP 33, DM 80, FR 271, Y 5630).

CLAGHORN, Joseph (after)   American 20th cent.
$55* *Independence Hall,* (06-11-93, Freemn/Fine Art, #35), 19½ x 29½ in., (49.5 x 74.9 cm.), offset lithograph (BP 36, DM 89, FR 301, Y 5836).

CLAIRIN, G.
$129* *"Pour La Patrie, Souscrivez A L'Emprunt Du Credit Foncier D'Algerie Et De Tunisie",* fairly good cond., (03-13-93, Laurin, #79), 46⁷⁄₁₆ x 31½ in., (118 x 80 cm.), (BP 90, DM 215, FR 730, Y 15,203).
$3025* *Theodora,* by. F. Champenois, good cond., creasing, repaired tears, Rod Stewart Collection, (11-07-92, Sotheby-NY, #251, illus.), sight 76¾ x 27 in., (194.9 x 68.6 cm.), lithograph poster p. in colors (BP 1978, DM 4853, FR 16,325, Y 373,365).

CLAISSE, Genevieve   French b. 1935
$876* *Cercles, 1967: Twelve,* #14/100, s., Edition Denise Rene blindstamp, (09-04-92, Germann, #287), 31½ x 19¹¹⁄₁₆ in., (800 x 500 mm.), color serigraph (BP 439, DM 1228, FR 4179, Y 107,829, SF 1093).

CLARK   American contemporary
$11* *Untitled,* both s., d. 73, one #58/100, other #59/100, (06-13-93, Hindman, #366), each 32 x 28 in., (81.3 x 71.1 cm.), color serigraph (BP 7, DM 18, FR 60, Y 1158).

CLARK (after H. ALKEN)
$968* *"Sporting Scenes": A Group of Twelve,* Mary Newbold Harding Estate, (02-03-93, Doyle, #1), 8 x 11¾ in., (20.3 x 29.8 cm.), color lithograph (BP 676, DM 1594, FR 5405, Y 120,413).

CLARK, C.
$1390* *LMS Bath,* p. Bemrose & Sons, creases, repairs, backed on linen, (05-07-93, Christie-S. Ken, #62, illus.), 47 x 39 in., (119.4 x 99.1 cm.), color lithograph (BP 880, DM 2198, FR 7405, Y 153,050).

CLARK, Gordon Matta
$192* *Office - Baroque, 1977,* s., #27/250, margins, good cond., handling creases, (05-27-93, Sotheby-Amstrdm, #660), 34¼ x 21⅞ in., (870 x 555 mm.), screenprint on wove (BP 123, DM 308, FR 1038, Y 20,583, G 345).

CLARK, Larry
$660* *From "Tulsa", 1971,* s., (11-16-92, Butterfield, #5904, illus.), 8 x 12 in., (203.6 x 305.3 mm.), photograph, gelatin silver print (BP 435, DM 1052, FR 3545, Y 82,079).
$1650* *Man With Gun,* photog.'s sig., 1971, p.l. 1970s, from the Tulsa series, (04-07-93, Swann, #426, illus.), 14 x 11 in., photograph, silver print (BP 1090, DM 2669, FR 9031, Y 187,457).

CLARK, Lucy   American contemporary
BI *Untitled,* s., d. March (19)76, i. "Fifth Trial Proof", est. $1/150, (02-04-93, Sloan, #2980), 5 x 6⅞ in., (12.7 x 17.5 cm.), etching on wove.

CLARK, Michael   American contemporary
$200* *Also Sally's Birthday (George Washington),* s., t., d. 1985, #2/25, (02-04-93, Sloan, #2971), 38 x 30 in., (96.5 x 76.2 cm.), color lithograph (BP 140, DM 329, FR 1117, Y 24,879).

CLARK, Roland   American 1874-1957
BI *Etchings (Siegel 139), 1938,* Derrydale Press, in 4s, num. de luxe copies, etchings, presentation copy i., prov., est. $5/7,000, (06-14-93, Sotheby-NY, #381, illus.), 16 x 12¼ in., (40.6 x 31.1 cm.), two etchings, 69 plates by Clark.
$660* *"Evening Flight",* s. Roland Clark, t., annot., ident., good cond., toning, (03-12-93, Skinner, #47, illus.), 11⅞ x 14⅞ in., (30.2 x 37.8 cm.), drypoint on wove (BP 460, DM 1099, FR 3735, Y 77,784).
$209* *Four Ducks Rising,* margins, s. Roland Clark, (02-13-93, Collins, #48, illus.), 7¾ x 5⅞ in., (19.7 x 14.9 cm.), etching (BP 147, DM 347, FR 1173, Y 25,205).
BI *Mallards Rising, 1942,* pub. by Derrydale Press, s. Roland Clark, 250/189, margins,est. $2/2,500, (02-13-93, Collins, #64B), 14 x 18 in., (35.6 x 45.7 cm.), color offset lithograph.
$264* *Scooters,* s. Roland Clark, margins, (02-13-93, Collins, #64A), 7¾ x 15 in., (19.7 x 38.1 cm.), etching (BP 186, DM 438, FR 1481, Y 31,838).
$242* *Swans Flying,* margins, s. Roland Clark, (02-13-93, Collins, #59), 11⅞ x 14¾ in., (30.2 x 37.5 cm.), etching (BP 170, DM 401, FR 1358, Y 29,185).
$121* *Widgeon,* margins, s. Roland Clark, (02-13-93, Collins, #38, illus.), 4⅞ x 3⅞ in., (12.4 x 9.8 cm.), etching (BP 85, DM 201, FR 679, Y 14,592).

CLARKE, Bob Carlos   b. 1950
$1116* *"Fork", 1991,* s., lit., (10-29-92, Christie-London, #204, illus.), approx. 35¼ x 25 in., (89.5 x 63.5 cm.), photograph, gelatin silver print (BP 715, DM 1717, FR 5825, Y 138,239).
$816* *"Jelly Baby", 17 January 1990,* mounted on card, stamped Unique Print, Bob Carlos Clarke, s., t., d., annot., stamped photog.'s credit and (c) info., 485 x 485mm, (05-07-93, Sotheby-London, #379, illus.), photograph, toned and hand-colored silver print (BP 517, DM 1290, FR 4347, Y 89,848).
BI *"Keith Richards Double Portrait, 1987",* p. before 19 April 1990, mounted on board, t., s., d., stamped Unique Print Bob Carlos Clarke, photog.'s credit, annot., 600 x 450mm, est. BP 5/800, (05-07-93, Sotheby-London, #380, illus.), photograph, toned silver print.
$635* *"Mandy Pour La Maison" 19 September 1988,* mounted on card, s., t., d., annot. in photog.'s hand, stamped photog.'s credit and (c) info., 498 x 596mm, (05-07-93, Sotheby-London, #381, illus.), photograph, gold and selenium toned silver print (BP 402, DM 1004, FR 3383, Y 69,919).
BI *"The Punishment Of Luxury" Or "Keeping Up With The Joneses", c. 1982-85,* s., lit., est. BP 6/900, (10-29-92, Christie-London, #203, illus.), image 16 x 22 in., (40.6 x 55.9 cm.), photograph, gelatin silver print.

CLARKE, Larry
$3451* *Intimate Embrace, 1972,* s., d., 276 x 352mm, (05-07-93, Sotheby-London, #288, illus.), photograph, silver print (BP 2185, DM 5456, FR 18,386, Y 379,982).

CLAUDET, Antoine   French 1798-1867
$1030* *Grou Portrait Of Children, 1850s,* hand-tinted, photog.'s credit label, morocco case, (10-29-92, Christie-London, #9), photograph, stereoscopic daguerreotype (BP 660, DM 1585, FR 5376, Y 127,586).

CLAUS, Carlfriedrich   b. 1930
$885* *Handreflexion, 1974,* s., (12-05-92, Bassenge, #7085), 17⁵⁄₁₆ x 12⅝ in., zincograph on transparent, on two pages (BP 554, DM 1380, FR 4702, Y 109,652).
$554* *Notiz: 20.12.-3.2, 1976,* t., s., num., (12-05-92, Bassenge, #7086), 4¹⁵⁄₁₆ x 4½ in., (12.5 x 11.5 cm.), etching in blue and black on thick paper (BP 347, DM 864, FR 2944, Y 68,641).
$664* *Relexion Unbewusster TV-Wirkungen, 1979,* s., t., d., num., (12-05-92, Bassenge, #7087), 5¹¹⁄₁₆ x 7⅝ in., (14.5 x 19.4 cm.), etching on thin cardboard (BP 416, DM 1035, FR 3528, Y 82,270).

CLAUS, Hugo   b. 1929
$651* *Fuga, 1979: Set Of Eight,* complete, s., #173/300, pub. De Volle Maan, good cond., in orig. portfolio, (12-09-92, Sotheby-Amstrdm, #517), each sheet approx. 22¹⁄₁₆ x 14¹⁵⁄₁₆ in., (561 x 380 mm.), color lithograph on Arches (BP 415, DM 1022, FR 3487, Y 80,719, G 1150).

$208* *James Ensor Verliefd,* s., #88/250, good cond., (12-09-92, Sotheby-Amstrdm, #518), sheet 29¹⁵⁄₁₆ x 22³⁄₁₆ in., (760 x 563 mm.), color lithograph on C.M. Fabriano wove (BP 133, DM 326, FR 1114, Y 25,790, G 368).

CLAUSEN, Franciska   Danish b. 1899
$232* *Composition Neoplasticiste, (Hommage A Mondrian), 1929,* s. F. Clausen, XXVIII/L, p. 1980 after a gouache from 1929, (09-30-92, Kunsthallen, #62), color serigraph (BP 131, DM 329, FR 1113, Y 27,841, DK 1265).
$203* *"Contre-Composition, 1983",* s. EA, (11-07-92, Falkkloos, #86), serigraph (BP 133, DM 326, FR 1096, Y 25,056, SK 1210).

CLAVE
$221* *Untitled Abstract,* #83/200, s., (03-10-93, Maynard, #636), sheet 27 x 17½ in., (68.6 x 44.5 cm.), silkscreen (BP 154, DM 368, FR 1249, Y 26,111, C$ 275).

CLAVE, Antonio   French, b. Spain b. 1913
BI *Arabesques (P. 166), 1967,* s., #26/80, blindstamp publishers L'Oeuvre Gravee, margins, good cond., est. BP 5/700, (06-30-93, Sotheby-London, #769), 15½ x 23½ in., (394 x 597 mm.), etching and aquatint on chiffon de vandan.
$466* *Bleu, Blanc, Rouge, 1991,* s., #15/75, (05-27-93, Briest, #60), 29¹⁵⁄₁₆ x 22¹⁄₁₆ in., (76 x 56 cm.), engraving on carborundum and embossing (BP 298, DM 748, FR 2520, Y 49,957).
$474* *Le Cirque,* VI/LX, s., (04-21-93, Germann, #344), 14¹⁵⁄₁₆ x 22¹⁄₁₆ in., (380 x 560 mm.), color lithograph (BP 308, DM 758, FR 2562, Y 52,474, SF 690).
BI *Composition,* #31/80, good cond., est. BP 800/1,200, (06-30-93, Sotheby-London, #766, illus.), sh 29¾ x 24¾ in., (756 x 629 mm.), etching and aquatint and embossing in color on wove.
BI *Composition,* 13/25. s., est. SF 1,6/1,800, (10-14-92, Germann, #257), 30½ x 22⁷⁄₁₆ in., (775 x 570 mm.), color etching.
$1298* *Composition,* relief sig., s., #7/80, (11-21-92, Schloss Ahlden, #2139, illus.), 25⅜ x 19½ in., (64.5 x 49.5 cm.), colored etching (BP 855, DM 2070, FR 6971, Y 161,423).
BI *Composition,* s., #95/99, good cond., est. BP 5/600, (06-30-93, Sotheby-London, #768), sh 29¾ x 22¼ in., (756 x 565 mm.), carborundum, etching and embossing, on wove.
BI *Composition,* 54/75, s., est. SF 1,6/1,800, (10-14-92, Germann, #256), 25⅜ x 19¹¹⁄₁₆ in., (645 x 500 mm.), color etching w/stamp.
$337* *Composition,* s. Clave, 11/85, (09-30-92, Kunsthallen, #63), color lithograph (BP 190, DM 478, FR 1616, Y 40,442, DK 1840).
$536* *Composition,* s., 63/100, (04-17-93, Falkkloos, #88, illus.), 19¹¹⁄₁₆ x 29¹⁵⁄₁₆ in., (50 x 76 cm.), color lithograph (BP 348, DM 857, FR 2896, Y 59,602, SK 3960).
BI *Composition,* s., est. $750/1,000, (05-15-93, Cleveland, #461, illus.), 27 x 18 in., (68.6 x 45.7 cm.), lithograph in colors.
$525* *"Composition 20-4-73",* s., (01-28-93, Pescheteau, #106), 19⁵⁄₁₆ x 15¾ in., (49 x 40 cm.), serigraph and embossing on alu (BP 347, DM 832, FR 2815, Y 65,185).
BI *Composition Au Trait Bleu, 1990,* first edition, s., est. SF 1,3/1,500, (10-14-92, Germann, #258), 29¹⁵⁄₁₆ x 21⅞ in., (760 x 555 mm.), color lithograph.
BI *Composition Au Trait Bleu, 1990,* E/A, s., est. DM 1/1,200, (06-24-93, Germann, #283), 29¹⁵⁄₁₆ x 21⅞ in., (760 x 555 mm.), color lithograph.
BI *Deux A (Passeron 297), 1972,* epreuve d'artiste, s., EA V/X, t. verso, edit. Vision Nouvelle, est.FF 4/5,000, (11-16-92, Briest, #272), 30¹¹⁄₁₆ x 25⁹⁄₁₆ in., (78 x 65 cm.), zinc engraving, collage and reliefs.
$853* *"En Noir Et Bleu", 1976,* #68/80, s., (10-18-92, Pescheteau, #102), 29¹⁵⁄₁₆ x 22¹⁄₁₆ in., (76 x 56 cm.), carborundum and lithograph on Arches (BP 517, DM 1260, FR 4280, Y 101,851).
BI *England 71 (P. 272), 1971,* s., num. 45/150, pub. Ediciones Poligrafa, defects, est. BP 3/400, (11-30-92, Phillips-London, #500), sheet 29½ x 21⅝ in., (749 x 549 mm.), lithograph in colors on paper.
$1449* *La Femme-Peintre Au Coq (Passeron 29), 1951,* s., #108/200, blindstamp La Guilde de la Gravure, margins,

good cond., discoloration, backboard staining, (12-03-92, Sotheby-London, #630, illus.), sheet 15 x 22 in., (380 x 560 mm.), lithograph in colors on wove (BP 935, DM 2279, FR 7778, Y 180,291).

$248* *(Figure)*, s. in ink, #20/150, full margins, apparently good cond., staining, crease, surface soiling, (02-24-93, Butterfield, #2909), 19¼ x 12 in., (489 x 305 mm.), lithograph on wove (BP 173, DM 403, FR 1365, Y 29,101).

$358* *"Fruits Blues", 1960-61,* s., num. 12/100, pub. L'Oeuvre Gravee, drystamp, stamp, excellent cond., (10-31-92, Cleveland, #365), 20¾ x 28¼ in., (52.7 x 71.8 cm.), color lithograph (BP 229, DM 551, FR 1868, Y 44,345).

$342* *Fruits Rouges (Passeron No. 78),* s., num. Epreuve d'Artist, t., num. Catalogue No. 295 pub. label, pub. L'oeuvre Gravee, 1960-61, (12-01-92, Ritchie, #40, illus.), 22 x 30 in., (55.9 x 76.2 cm.), color lithograph (BP 226, DM 545, FR 1858, Y 42,580, C$ 440).

$536* *Gants Et Bande Noire (Passeron 295), 1972,* s., (03-31-93, Briest, #E146), 30¹¹⁄₁₆ x 25⁹⁄₁₆ in., (78 x 65 cm.), relief on sheet of aluminum and collage (BP 354, DM 862, FR 2929, Y 61,638).

$580* *Guerrier Aux Feuilles (Catalogue Sala Gaspar, Barcelone, 1983, 122),1969,* s., 31/75, studio traces verso, good cond., (06-28-93, Loudmer, #214), 29¹⁵⁄₁₆ x 22¼ in., (760 x 565 mm.), color etching, embossing and carborundum on Arches wove (BP 388, DM 986, FR 3320, Y 61,538).

BI *Guerrier En Noir Et Jaune (Passeron 227), 1970,* s., num. VII/X, est. DM 2000, (06-10-93, Hauswedell/Nolt, #168), image 23⅝ x 15¾ in., (60 x 40 cm.), color etching w/carborundum.

$771* *Guerrier En Noir Jaune (P. 227), 1970,* s., i. E.A., a proof, pub. Vision Nouvelle, margins, good cond., marks, creases, (06-30-93, Sotheby-London, #770), 23½ x 15½ in., (597 x 394 mm.), etching and aquatint, carborundum and embossing in color on Arches onwove (BP 517, DM 1315, FR 4436, Y 82,610).

$495* *Interior With Family,* s., (09-20-92, Hindman, #799), 13¼ x 18¾ in., (33.7 x 47.6 cm.), lithograph in black and yellow (BP 290, DM 735, FR 2513, Y 61,179).

$605* *King, c. 1958,* num., s., blindstamp, pub. L'Oeuvre Graveur, creases, stains, (05-27-93, Swann, #65, illus.), sh 30 x 22 in., (76.2 x 55.9 cm.), color lithograph (BP 387, DM 971, FR 3272, Y 64,858).

$542* *L'Espagnole, c. 1965,* s., num., (11-28-92, Grisebach, #465, illus.), 16⅝ x 11¼ in., (42.2 x 28.5 cm.), colored lithograph on thick wove (BP 358, DM 863, FR 2931, Y 67,455).

$1836* *L'Homme Au Masque (Passeron 324), 1974,* s., num. 73/80, blindstamp, (06-10-93, Hauswedell/Nolt, #169, illus.), 35⅝ x 24¹³⁄₁₆ in., (90.5 x 63 cm.), color etching w/carborundum and relief print on Arches paper (BP 1201, DM 2990, FR 10,066, Y 194,884).

BI *"L'Homme Au Masque", 1974,* s., H.C. IV, est. DM 1,4/1,600, (11-28-92, Grisebach, #466, illus.), 34¹⁵⁄₁₆ x 24⅞ in., (88.8 x 63.2 cm.), color aquatint relief print on copper print paper.

$819* *La Lance Bleue (P. 351), 1975,* s., #26/75, pub. Galerie Ostermalm, good cond., (12-03-92, Sotheby-London, #634), sheet 35¼ x 29⅝ in., (895 x 572 mm.), aquatint w/carborundum in colors w/embossing on wove (BP 528, DM 1288, FR 4396, Y 101,904).

$299* *Le Lecon De Musique,* s., num. epreuve d'artist, (12-01-92, Ritchie, #39, illus.), 19¾ x 25¾ in., (50.2 x 65.4 cm.), color lithograph (BP 198, DM 477, FR 1624, Y 37,226, C$ 385).

BI *Man At Table,* s. Clave, num. 17/75, annot. in ink, good cond., light/mount staining verso, est. $6/800, (09-11-92, Skinner, #91, illus.), 8¾ x 8⅝ in., (22.2 x 21.9 cm.), lithograph in colors on wove.

$220* *Man With Black Pipe,* s., artists proof, good cond., (02-07-93, Bakker, #97), 24 x 21 in., (61 x 53.3 cm.), lithograph (BP 152, DM 365, FR 1233, Y 27,377).

$1194* *Nature Morte (P. 42), 1954,* s., #6/50, pub. by artist, full margins, good cond., handling creases, tear, (12-03-92, Sotheby-London, #632, illus.), 21¼ x 28½ in., (540 x 725 mm.), lithograph in colors on BFK Rives (BP 770, DM 1878, FR 6409, Y 148,563).

$605* *Le Patriote,* s., good cond., #17/18, (06-11-93, Freemn/Fine Art, #34), 30 x 22¼ in., (76.2 x 56.5 cm.), color lithograph (BP 398, DM 983, FR 3315, Y 64,191).

$343* *Pierre Osenat. L'Eloge De Clave (P. 175), 1958,* book, #173, p. by E. Desjobert, pub. M. Brouker, good cond., handlingmarks, (06-30-93, Sotheby-London, #767), overall 13 x 10⅜ in., (330 x 264 mm.), 7 color lithographs on Vidalon wove (BP 230, DM 585, FR 1974, Y 36,751).

$810* *Points Rouge Et Bleu, 1990,* s., #79/81, (05-27-93, Briest, #62), 29¾ x 21⅞ in., (75.5 x 55.5 cm.), engraving in carborundum and embossing (BP 519, DM 1300, FR 4381, Y 86,835).

$303* *Poisson Au Triangle Rouge, 1964,* s., #8/99, blindstamp pub. l'Oeuvre Gravee, trimmed margins, good cond., mat/light-staining, tears, (10-28-92, Butterfield, #2798), 20½ x 27½ in., (521 x 699 mm.), color lithograph on Rives BFK (BP 193, DM 468, FR 1589, Y 37,178).

BI *Poisson Sur Fond Blanc, 1961,* s., epreuve d'artiste, est. DM 1,4/1,800, (11-28-92, Grisebach, #463, illus.), 38¹⁄₁₆ x 26³⁄₁₆ in., (96.7 x 66.5 cm.), colored lithograph on thick wove.

$1290* *Retour Du Japon, 1973,* #63/75, s., (09-04-92, Germann, #288), 31¹¹⁄₁₆ x 24¹⁵⁄₁₆ in., (805 x 633 mm.), color etching w/embossing (BP 646, DM 1808, FR 6155, Y 158,789, SF 1610).

$427* *Roi-Pepe,* s., #5/90, t., num. Catalogue No. 463 pub. label, pub. L'oeuvre Gravee, 1966, (12-01-92, Ritchie, #41, illus.), 30 x 22 in., (76.2 x 55.9 cm.), color lithograph (BP 282, DM 681, FR 2319, Y 53,162, C$ 550).

BI *"Sac Et Chiffre 3", 1974,* s., H.C. III, est. DM 1,4/1,600, (11-28-92, Grisebach, #467, illus.), 35⁹⁄₁₆ x 24¹⁵⁄₁₆ in., (90.3 x 63.3 cm.), colored aquatint with relief print on copper print paper.

BI *La Sainte Famille (P. 31), 1951,* s., num. 91/200, pub. La Guilde de la Gravure, good cond., est. BP 7/1,000, (11-30-92, Phillips-London, #496), sheet 15 x 21½ in., (381 x 546 mm.), lithograph in colors on Arches.

$767* *Servando V (P. 315), 1973,* s., #1/75, good cond., creases, traces paper tape, (12-03-92, Sotheby-London, #633), sheet 29⅞ x 22¼ in., (760 x 565 mm.), etching w/carborundum over lithograph on Arches (BP 495, DM 1206, FR 4117, Y 95,434).

$516* *"Servando" (P. 315), 1973,* #20/75, s., (10-18-92, Pescheteau, #106), 29¹⁵⁄₁₆ x 22¹⁄₁₆ in., (76 x 56 cm.), carborundum and lithograph (BP 313, DM 762, FR 2589, Y 61,612).

$839* *Signe III (Passeron 296), 1972,* s., epreuve d'artiste, #V/X, edit. Vision Nouvelle, (11-16-92, Briest, #275, illus.), 30¹¹⁄₁₆ x 25⁹⁄₁₆ in., (78 x 65 cm.), lithograph in relief and collage on aluminum (BP 551, DM 1338, FR 4508, Y 104,705).

BI *Signes Et Ficelle (P. 224), 1970,* s., #45/75, pub. Vision Nouvelle, tear into image, surface soiling, est. BP 3/400, (11-30-92, Phillips-London, #499), sheet 22¼ x 30 in., (565 x 762 mm.), etching w/carborundum in blue & black on thick wove.

BI *Stilleben Mit Glas U. Blumenvase,* s., #38/50, est. DM 2000, (06-10-93, Hauswedell/Nolt, #170, illus.), image 15¾ x 23⅝ in., (40 x 60 cm.), color etching on Arches paper.

BI *Table Bleu, 1964,* s., est. DM 1,2/1,400, (11-28-92, Grisebach, #464, illus.), 20¹¹⁄₁₆ x 28⅛ in., (52.5 x 71.5 cm.), colored lithograph on wove.

$1216* *Table Et Toile De Sac (Padderon 264), 1971,* s., #33/75, edit. Vision Nouvelle, full margins, (11-16-92, Briest, #271), engraving in carborundum and colors (BP 799, DM 1939, FR 6534, Y 151,753).

BI *"Texturas",* s., reserve P50,000, (12-17-92, Duran, #178, illus.), 29¹⁵⁄₁₆ x 22¹⁄₁₆ in., (76 x 56 cm.), lithograph w/relief.

$1364* *Les Trois Maries (P. 34), 1952,* s., #82/95, pub. Kornfeld and Klipstein, full margins, good cond., creasing, (12-03-92, Sotheby-London, #631, illus.), 17 x 23¼ in., (430 x 590 mm.), lithograph in colors on BFK Rives (BP 880, DM 2145, FR 7322, Y 169,715).

$1629* *Les Trois Maries (Passeron 34), 1952,* s., #31/95, pub. Kornfeld and Klipstein, full margins, good cond., creases, (06-30-93, Sotheby-London, #765, illus.), 17 x

23¼ in., (432 x 591 mm.), color lithograph on BFK Rives (BP 1092, DM 2778, FR 9373, Y 174,542).

BI *"Two Figures"*, s., d. 1959, nicks, est. $1,5/2,000, (12-04-92, Doyle, #86), 12¼ x 9¼ in., (311 x 235 mm.), color lithograph.

$1380* *Two Kings*, s., #25/50, margins, good cond., Charles & Palmer Ducommon Estate, (05-19-93, Butterfield, #2046), 26½ x 39½ in., (67.3 x 100.3 cm.), lithograph in colors on wove (BP 896, DM 2243, FR 7558, Y 152,773).

$619* *Untitled*, s., (04-04-93, Pescheteau, #186), 29¹⁵⁄₁₆ x 22¹⁄₁₆ in., (76 x 56 cm.), carborondum engraving and embossing on wove (BP 408, DM 995, FR 3379, Y 70,477).

$546* *Untitled*, #75/75, s., (01-28-93, Pescheteau, #105), 29¹⁵⁄₁₆ x 22¹⁄₁₆ in., (76 x 56 cm.), carborundum engraving on wove (BP 361, DM 865, FR 2928, Y 67,792).

BI *Untitled: Set Of Three*, #38/170, s., est. FF 6/7,000, (10-18-92, Pescheteau, #105), each 25⁹⁄₁₆ x 19¹¹⁄₁₆ in., (65 x 50 cm.), lithograph in colors on velin.

$1840* *[Embracing Couple]*, c. 1957, s., d., i. Paris, full margins, good cond., light-stain, creases, loss, tape stain, (05-13-93, Sotheby-NY, #534, illus.), 12½ x 9¼ in., (317 x 235 mm.), hand-colored lithograph (BP 1208, DM 2971, FR 10,022, Y 205,426).

CLAXTON, William
$825* *"Chet Baker And Lili, Hollywood"*, 1955/1990, s., edit. 24/100, (11-16-92, Butterfield, #5905, illus.), 10⅛ x 10¼ in., (257.6 x 260.8 mm.), photograph, platinum print (BP 543, DM 1315, FR 4431, Y 102,599).

CLAYTON, Harrold (after)
$38 *Still Life Study Of Mixed And Summer Flowers In An Embossed China Jug On A Ledge*, (04-16-93, G.A. Key, #42), 21 x 24 in., (53.3 x 61 cm.), colored print (BP 25, DM 61, FR 207, Y 4273).

CLAYTON, K.R.   20th cent.
$66* *Three Herons*, s., (04-02-93, Sloan, #801), 9¼ x 13¾ in., (235 x 349 mm.), etching (BP 43, DM 106, FR 360, Y 7515).

BI *Three Herons*, s., est. $100/150, (02-04-93, Sloan, #354), 9¼ x 13¾ in., (23.5 x 34.9 cm.), etching.

CLEIS, Ugo   1903-1976
BI *Der Maurer*, s., num. SF 150/170, (10-14-92, Germann, #496), 19½ x 15³⁄₁₆ in., (495 x 386 mm.), woodcut.

CLEMENT
$2200* *"La Corbeille Des Fruits: Group Of Five"*, after P. Bessa, (06-23-93, Doyle, #12), 15 x 19½ in., (38.1 x 49.5 cm.), stipple engraving w/hand-coloring (BP 1495, DM 3723, FR 12,521, Y 239,678).

CLEMENT (after P. Bessa)
$1500* *"La Corbeille Des Fruits": Five*, (04-28-93, Doyle, #16), 15 x 19½ in., (38.1 x 49.5 cm.), stipple engravings w/ hand coloring (BP 954, DM 2375, FR 8034, Y 168,105).

CLEMENTE, Francesco   Italian b. 1952
BI *Conception, 1988*, s., #42/55, blindstamp, pub. 2RC Editions, full margins, good cond.,skinned spot, stain. est. $4/6,000, (05-15-93, Sotheby-NY, #936, illus.), 34¼ x 25 in., (87 x 63.5 cm.), etching and aquatint in colors.

BI *Conversion To Her, 1986*, s., #26/40, pub. Editions Schellmann, full margins, corner cut and reattached, very good cond., est. $4/5,000, (11-09-92, Christie-NY, #257, illus.), 51¾ x 61¾ in., (131.4 x 156.8 cm.), soft-ground etching and aquatint in colors on wove.

$440* *Knots, 1981*, s., num. 23/25, blindstamp of pub. Crown Point Press, full margins, apparently good cond., pressure mark in image, crease, est. $800/1,000, (02-24-93, Butterfield, #3008), 14¹⁵⁄₁₆ x 15¹⁄₁₆ in., (379 x 383 mm.), etching & aquatint in colors on wove (BP 307, DM 714, FR 2422, Y 51,631).

BI *Ohne Titel, 1984*, #14/25, pencil s., est. DM 2,500, (11-20-92, Lempertz, #495), sh 22⅜ x 18⅜ in., (56.8 x 46.7 cm.), color lithograph on Velin.

$1760* *Telemone #1, 1981*, s., num. 22/25, blindstamp of pub. Crown Point Press, margins, apparently good cond., creases, surface soiling, (02-24-93, Butterfield, #3009, illus.), 61⅛ x 19⅛ in., (155.3 x 48.6 cm.), etching &

aquatint in colors w/collage on wove (BP 1227, DM 2857, FR 9686, Y 206,524).

$935* *Tondo, 1981*, s., #23/25, inkstamp of pub. Crown Point Press, good cond., surface scuffing, (02-24-93, Butterfield, #3010, illus.), etching and aquatint in colors on Arches 88 (BP 652, DM 1518, FR 5146, Y 109,716).

$3575* *Untitled (Metropolitan Museum Of Art p. 53), 1984*, s., #148/200, blindstamp, pub. Crown Point Press, full margins, goodcond., discoloration, (11-07-92, Sotheby-NY, #531, illus.), 14⅛ x 20⅛ in., (359 x 511 mm.), woodcut p. in colors on Tosa Kozo paper (BP 2337, DM 5708, FR 19,293, Y 441,249).

$4600* *Untitled (Monotype 39), 1986*, s., i. 39, p. by artist w/ Maurice Payne, full margins, excell. cond., Keith Haring Estate, prov., lit., (05-11-93, Christie-NY, #384, illus.), plate 36½ x 20 in., (92.7 x 50.8 cm.), sheet 49 x 32½ in., (92.7 x 50.8 cm.), monotype in oil on colors on Japanese paper (BP 2936, DM 7246, FR 24,416, Y 505,995).

$2760* *Untitled, 1984*, s., #117/200, Crown Point Press blindstamp, full margins, hinges, skinned spots, creases, good cond., (05-11-93, Christie-NY, #383), sheet 16¾ x 22½ in., (425 x 572 mm.), color woodcut on Japan (BP 1762, DM 4348, FR 14,650, Y 303,597).

$2200* *Untitled, 1985*, s., i. 'AP 12', proofs, blindstamp, pub. Crown Point Press, full margins, good cond., (11-07-92, Sotheby-NY, #532), 33⅝ x 59⅛ in., (85.4 x 150.2 cm.), spit-bite, aquatint, soft ground and hard ground etching p. in colors (BP 1438, DM 3513, FR 11,873, Y 271,538).

$5500* *Untitled: Nine*, s., d. 1974, each num. consec., inscribed, prov., (02-24-93, Christie-NY, #73, illus.), overall 37½ x 31½ in., (95.3 x 80 cm.), photograph, b/w mounted on panel (BP 3835, DM 8929, FR 30,270, Y 645,388).

CLEREAU, Jean Paul   French 20th cent.
BI *Profil De Femme*, #35/175, s. Jean-Paul Clereau, (03-16-93, Encans, #156), 14⁵⁄₁₆ x 11⁵⁄₁₆ in., (36.3 x 28.8 cm.), lithograph.

CLERGUE, Lucien
BI *"Coco Au Grand Herbier"*, 1975, p. 1981, s., t., d., est. $6/800, (05-23-93, Butterfield, #3377, illus.), 17¼ x 11¾ in., photograph, fresson print.

$550* *"Picasso, President Of Bullfight, Frejus"*, s., t., d., edit. 5/20, 1962/1986, (11-16-92, Butterfield, #5906, illus.), 10 x 14⅛ in., (254.5 x 359.4 mm.), photograph, gelatin silver print (BP 362, DM 877, FR 2954, Y 68,399).

$468* *"Violinist In Arles"*, s., t., d., attrib., 1954/1983, (11-16-92, Butterfield, #5907, illus.), 10¾ x 7⅝ in., (273.5 x 194 mm.), photograph, gelatin silver print (BP 308, DM 746, FR 2513, Y 58,202).

CLERICE, Francois and Victor
$96* *La D'Moiselle Du Tabarin. Operette (...) Musique De Edmond Missa, 1910*, cond. A, (03-16-93, Boisgirard, #84), 31½ x 23⅝ in., (80 x 60 cm.), poster (BP 66, DM 160, FR 542, Y 11,225).

CLERK, John (of Eldin)
$116* *Edinburgh*, trimmed, surface dirt, (06-16-93, Bonhams-Chelsea, #385), pl. 5½ x 15¼ in., (14 x 38.7 cm.), etching on laid (BP 77, DM 193, FR 646, Y 12,372).

CLERK, Pierre Jean
$43* *Untitled, Red, Black And Yellow Swirls*, s., d., #76/125, exhib., (12-01-92, Ritchie, #51), 33¾ x 35⅞ in., (85.7 x 91.1 cm.), color serigraph (BP 28, DM 69, FR 234, Y 5354, C$ 55).

CLEVELY, J. (Jr.) (after)
$160 *"A View Of His Majestys Dock Yard At Portsmouth In The County Of Hampshire..."*, by Carington Bowles, d. 1772, (06-11-93, G.A. Key, #121), 10 x 16 in., (25.4 x 40.6 cm.), hand-colored engraving (BP 105, DM 260, FR 877, Y 16,976).

CLIFFORD, Charles   d. 1863
BI *Plaza And Cathedral, Seville, Spain, c. 1862*, from waxed paper neg., credit blindstamp, est. $1,2/1,800, (10-13-92, Christie-NY, #7, illus.), 16 x 12⅝ in., (40.6 x 32.1 cm.), photograph.

CLIFT, William   American b. 1944
- $825* *"Juan Hamilton Sculpture", 1990,* s., edit. 24/100, (11-16-92, Butterfield, #5908, illus.), 12⅞ x 10⅛ in., (327.6 x 257.6 mm.), photograph, platinum print (BP 543, DM 1315, FR 4431, Y 102,599).
- $3520* *New Mexico Portfolio: Eight,* (1972-74), privately pub. 1975, s., #43/100, (10-13-92, Christie-NY, #530, illus.), smallest 6½ x 7¾ in., (16.5 x 19.7 cm.), largest 9 x 12¾ in., (16.5 x 19.7 cm.), photograph, gelatin silver prints (BP 2050, DM 5157, FR 17,521, Y 426,822).
- BI *New Mexico: Eight,* portfolio, mounted, each s. by photog., 1972-74, p. 1975, #21/100 ed., est. $5/8,000, (10-15-92, Sotheby-NY, #576, illus.), various sizes to 9 x 12¾ in., (22.9 x 32.4 cm.), photograph, gelatin silver prints.
- $2750* *The Southwest: Two: "White House Ruin, Canyon de Chelly, Arizona" and"La Mesita from Cerro Seguro, New Mexico", 1975 & 1978,* s., t., d. by photog., s. by photog. on overmat, (10-15-92, Sotheby-NY, #576A, illus.), one 6¾ x 9⅝ in., (17.1 x 24.4 cm.), other 13⅜ x 19⅛ in., (17.1 x 24.4 cm.), photograph, gelatin silver print (BP 1683, DM 4093, FR 13,882, Y 329,934).

CLINEDIENST
- $1650* *Roosevelt, In Riding Attire, On Back Of Jumping Horse, 4 May 1904,* (c) 1902, i., d., (09-17-92, Swann, #243), image, approx. 7 x 13½ in., (17.8 x 34.3 cm.), photograph, sepia (BP 927, DM 2450, FR 8384, Y 205,428).

CLINT, G.   (after)
- $83* *Fawcett And Campbell, 1826,* by Thomas Lupton, scratch-letter proof before t., pub. Thomas Lupton, foxing, soiling, taped, (11-30-92, Phillips-London, #123), plate 20 x 14 in., (508 x 356 mm.), mezzotint on wove (BP 55, DM 132, FR 449, Y 10,330).
- BI *Madame Vestris, Miss P. Glover, Mr. Williams And Mr. Liston, 1853,* by Thomas Lupton, pub. Thomas Boys, tear into image, staining, est. BP 80/100, (11-30-92, Phillips-London, #122), sheet 21⅝ x 16½ in., (549 x 419 mm.), mezzotint on wove.

CLOSE, Chuck   American b. 1940
- BI *Georgia (P. 34), 1984,* s., t., d., #1/35, pub. Pace Editions, blue staining, excell. cond.?, est. $3,5/4,500, (05-11-93, Christie-NY, #387, illus.), sheet 59 x 46 in., (149.9 x 116.8 cm.), hand-made paper pulp in grays.
- BI *Georgie/Fingerprint, State II (Pernotto 39; Fine and Corlett 41), 1985,* s., t., d., num. 24/35, pub. Pace Editions, Graphic Studio blindstamp, full margins, excell. cond., est. $2/3,000, (09-19-92, Christie-E, #91, illus.), sheet 30 x 22⅛ in., (762 x 562 mm.), etching on grey BFK Rives.
- $1167* *"Keith/Four Times", 1975,* s., 37/50, (12-04-92, AB Stockholm, #7041), 20½ x 66⅛ in., (52 x 168 cm.), sh 29¹⁵/₁₆ x 79½ in., (52 x 168 cm.), lithograph (BP 749, DM 1859, FR 6305, Y 145,693, SK 7920).
- $2526* *Leslie (WV 48), 1986,* t., s., d., (11-28-92, Schoppmann, #472), 24¹³/₁₆ x 21⁷/₁₆ in., (63 x 54.5 cm.), color woodcut on Japan (BP 1667, DM 4024, FR 13,661, Y 314,375).
- BI *Marta/Fingerprint (P. 44), 1986,* s., t., d., #13/45, pub. Pace Editions, full margins, excell. cond., the Late M. Anwar Kamal, M.D. Coll., est. $4/4,500, (05-11-93, Christie-NY, #388, illus.), sheet 54 x 40¼ in., (137.2 x 102.2 cm.), etching on wove.
- $5175* *Phil III, 1982,* s., d., #1/15, pub. Pace Editions, full margins, very good cond.?, (05-19-93, Butterfield, #2146, illus.), 69 x 54 in., (175.3 x 137.2 cm.), black handmade paper, color pressed 1/2" grid in grays (BP 3359, DM 8412, FR 28,341, Y 572,899).
- $8050* *Phil/Manipulated (Pernotto 22), 1982,* s., t., d., #13/20, pub. Pace Editions, excell. cond.?, (05-11-93, Christie-NY, #385, illus.), sheet 68½ x 54 in., (174 x 137.2 cm.), hand-made paper pulp in grays (BP 5139, DM 12,681, FR 42,728, Y 885,491).
- $1430* *Robert, 1982,* s., d., t., #18/20, pub. Pace Editions, full margins, very good cond.?, (10-28-92, Butterfield, #2925), 22 x 17 in., (559 x 432 mm.), handmade paper, cold pressed grid (BP 911, DM 2208, FR 7499, Y 175,460).
- $3450* *Self Portrait (P. 51), 1988,* s., d., #35/50, pub. Pace Editions w/Aldo Crommelynck blindstamp, full margins,

excell. cond., (05-11-93, Christie-NY, #389, illus.), sheet 21 x 15½ in., (533 x 394 mm.), etching on Hahnemuhle (BP 2202, DM 5435, FR 18,312, Y 379,496).
- $4400* *Self Portrait, 1988,* s., d., #47/50, blindstamp, pub. Pace Editions, full margins, good cond., soiling verso, (11-07-92, Sotheby-NY, #533, illus.), 13½ x 9¾ in., (343 x 248 mm.), etching and aquatint (BP 2877, DM 7025, FR 23,745, Y 543,076).
- BI *Self Portrait/Manipulated (P. 31), 1982,* s., t., d., #17/25, pub. Pace Editions, time staining, excell. cond.?, est. $3,5/4,500, (05-11-93, Christie-NY, #386, illus.), sheet 38½ x 29 in., (978 x 737 mm.), hand-made paper pulp in grays.
- $4888* *Self-Portrait, 1988,* s., d., #41/50, blindstamp of printer Aldo Crommelynck, pub. Pace Editions, full margins, good cond., (02-11-93, Sotheby-NY, #319, illus.), 13⅜ x 9¹³/₁₆ in., (340 x 250 mm.), etching and aquatint (BP 3449, DM 8097, FR 27,399, Y 589,271).

CLOSTERMAN, Johann Baptiste   (after)
- $83* *Mr. And Mrs. Gibbons (Grinling) (C.S. 106), c. 1750,* engraved by John Smith, watermark, 2nd state of 3, trimmed to threadmargins, waterstained, repaired corners, (11-30-92, Phillips-London, #43), image 11½ x 13½ in., (292 x 343 mm.), mezzotint on laid (BP 55, DM 132, FR 449, Y 10,330).

CLOUTIER, *
- $147* *"Untitled" and "Snowshoeing", 1980: Two,* E.A. I - E.A. IX, both s., d. '80, prov., from Citadelle Hill, (11-16-92, Hodgins, #363), hand colored etching on paper (BP 97, DM 234, FR 790, Y 18,345, C$ 187).

CLOUZOT, Marianne   b. 1908
- BI *Femmes Et Cygnes, c. 1950: Series Of Six,* s., #11/30, full margins, est. FF1,800/2,000, (05-27-93, Briest, #63), 14¹⁵/₁₆ x 11 in., (38 x 28 cm.), etchings.

CLUTTERBUCK, S. Jock
- $43* *Burning Bubbles,* s., t., d. '73, #6/15, prov., (12-01-92, Ritchie, #72), 29 x 49½ in., (73.7 x 125.7 cm.), color embossed intaglio print (BP 28, DM 69, FR 234, Y 5354, C$ 55).
- $43* *San Andreas Fault,* s., t., d. 73, #7/15, prov., (12-01-92, Ritchie, #71), 29 x 50 in., (73.7 x 127 cm.), color intaglio etching (BP 28, DM 69, FR 234, Y 5354, C$ 55).
- $64* *The Temple Bar,* s., t., d. 73, #6/15, prov., (12-01-92, Ritchie, #70, illus.), 24 x 32⅜ in., (61 x 82.2 cm.), color embossed intaglio etching (BP 42, DM 102, FR 348, Y 7968, C$ 83).

COAT, Tal
- BI *Untitled,* s., #49/95, full sheet p. to edges, good cond., minor paper discoloration, creases, est. Dfl. 5/700, (05-27-93, Sotheby-Amstrdm, #687), sh 25⁷/₁₆ x 19⅛ in., (646 x 485 mm.), color lithograph on wove.

COBB, Victor   1876-1945
- $65* *Ormond College, Melbourne University,* s. Victor Cobb, i., d. 1915 in image, (08-11-92, L. Joel, #194G), 3³/₁₆ x 4¾ in., (8.1 x 12.1 cm.), etching (BP 34, DM 95, FR 323, Y 8324, A$ 88).
- BI *Scrub Tangle, Taggerty River,* s. Victor Cobb, i., est. $50/80, (08-11-92, L. Joel, #173G), 4¼ x 8¾ in., (10.8 x 22.3 cm.), etching.

COBBAERT, Jean
- $192* *Untitled,* s., i. E.A., full margins, good cond., (05-27-93, Sotheby-Amstrdm, #577), 21⁵/₁₆ x 17¹⁵/₁₆ in., (542 x 457 mm.), colored lithograph on wove (BP 123, DM 308, FR 1038, Y 20,583, G 345).
- $154* *Untitled,* s., #30/50, full sheet p. to edges, good cond., (05-27-93, Sotheby-Amstrdm, #578), sh 29⁵/₁₆ x 20⅞ in., (745 x 530 mm.), colored lithograph on wove (BP 99, DM 247, FR 833, Y 16,509, G 276).
- $1023* *"Zomer", "Herfst", Winter", and "Lente": Four,* s., #30/50, pub. Kunstcentrum Frans Masereel, w/their blindstamp, margins, good cond., (05-27-93, Sotheby-Amstrdm, #579), 25⁹/₁₆ x 19³/₁₆ in., (650 x 488 mm.), colored lithograph on wove (BP 655, DM 1642, FR 5533, Y 109,670, G 1840).

COBELLE, Charles   French b. 1902
$55* *Le Port*, s., #40/500, (06-13-93, Hindman, #389), 29¾ x
15 in., (75.6 x 38.1 cm.), color lithograph (BP 36, DM
90, FR 301, Y 5788).

COBINESS, Eddy   b. c. 1934
$87* *Cry Of The Wolves, 1979*, #19/100, s., t., d. 1979, prov.,
(11-16-92, Hodgins, #273), 18¹⁵⁄₁₆ x 15 in., (48.3 x 38.1
cm.), serigraph on paper (BP 57, DM 139, FR 467, Y
10,857, C$ 110).

COBRA-BIBLIOTEKET
$126* *Fire Forsider, 1950*, (09-30-92, Kunsthallen, #65), litho-
graph in color (BP 71, DM 179, FR 604, Y 15,121, DK
690).

COBURN, Alvin Langdon   American 1882-1966
$1650* *The Cloud, Bavaria*, early 1900's, (10-15-92, Sotheby-NY,
#99A, illus.), 14½ x 10½ in., (36.8 x 26.7 cm.), photo-
gravure (BP 1010, DM 2456, FR 8329, Y 197,960).
$1452* *"Cotton Waste", 1920: Book*, pribately p. edit., pub.
Charles W. Hobson, t. w/mono., (05-06-93, Christie-London, #22, illus.), each approx. 5¾ x 4½ in., photograph,
14 photogravures, tipped-in (BP 920, DM 2287, FR
7699, Y 159,754).
$6325* *Hampton Court, 1907: Eleven*, includ. The Lion Gates,
The East Facade, Head Of A Satyr, The Three Graces,
The Fountain Court, Looking Westward from Long
Water, tipped to double-mounts, t. by photog., front
wrapper s. and d. Alvin Langdon Coburn, 1907, rear-
wrapper s., d., i., apparently unique and unpub, (04-06-
93, Sotheby-NY, #57, illus.), various sizes to 8½ x 11½
in., photograph, waxed platinum print (BP 4178, DM
10,190, FR 34,506, Y 721,373).
BI *"London", 1909*, Duckworth and Co., Archibald Henderson Collection, est. $2/3,000, (04-06-93, Sotheby-NY,
#57a, illus.), various sizes 8½ x 6¼ in., photograph,
book w/20 tipped-in, hand-pulled photogravures.
BI *"London", 1909: Book Of Twenty*, Duckworth and Co.,
Archibald Henderson Coll., est. $2/3,000, (04-06-93,
Sotheby-NY, #57A, illus.), various sizes 8½ x 6¼ in.,
photograph, tipped-in, hand-pulled photogravure.
$3450* *"London", 1909: Twenty*, book, pub. Duckworth & Co.,
p. Ballantyne Press, excell. cond., spotting, damage, (05-
23-93, Butterfield, #3378, illus.), tipped-in, hand-pulled
photogravure (BP 2247, DM 5641, FR 18,987, Y
381,342).
$10,350* *Self-Portrait, c. 1907*, (04-06-93, Sotheby-NY, #56, illus.),
5⅜ x 4¼ in., photograph, waxed platinum print (BP
6836, DM 16,675, FR 56,465, Y 1,180,429).
BI *The Two Trees, Rothenburg, 1908*, lit., est. $1,2/1,800,
(10-13-92, Christie-NY, #35, illus.), 14⅞ x 11 in., (37.8
x 27.9 cm.), photograph, photogravure.
$106,426* *"Vortograph", 1917*, s. recto, prov., lit., (10-29-92,
Christie-London, #102, illus.), 10⅝ x 8¹⁄₁₆ in., (27 x 20.5
cm.), photograph, gelatin silver print mounted on card
(BP 68,200, DM 163,732, FR 555,459, Y 13,182,956).
$116,725* *"Vortograph", 1917*, s. recto, prov., lit., (10-29-92,
Christie-London, #100, illus.), 10⅞ x 8 in., (27.6 x 20.3
cm.), photograph, gelatin silver print mounted on card
(BP 74,800, DM 179,577, FR 609,212, Y 14,458,689).
$78,961* *"Vortograph", 1917*, prov., (10-29-92, Christie-London,
#103, illus.), 10⅝ x 8¹⁄₁₆ in., (27 x 20.5 cm.), photo-
graph, gelatin silver print mounted on card (BP 50,600,
DM 121,478, FR 412,114, Y 9,780,875).
$116,725* *"Vortograph", 1917*, s. recto, prov., (10-29-92, Christie-
London, #101, illus.), 11⅛ x 8⁵⁄₁₆ in., (28.3 x 21.1 cm.),
photograph, gelatin silver print mounted on card (BP
74,800, DM 179,577, FR 609,212, Y 14,458,689).

COCK, Hieronymous   Dutch c. 1510-1570
$2022* *Eine Ruinenlandschaft Mit Dem Hl. Hieronymus (Holl-
stein 427), 1552*, from series Romische Ruinen, (12-04-
92, Bassenge, #6123, illus.), 8⅞ x 13¹¹⁄₁₆ in., (22.5 x
34.7 cm.), etching (BP 1297, DM 3220, FR 10,924, Y
252,434).
$722* *Mercurius Argum Interficit (Wurzbach, Hollstein 14),
1558*, (12-04-92, Bassenge, #6122, illus.), 8¹³⁄₁₆ x 12¹¹⁄₁₆
in., (22.4 x 32.3 cm.), etching (BP 463, DM 1150, FR
3901, Y 90,137).
$1329* *"Prospectus Tyburtinus" (Hollstein/Brueghel 3; Hollstein/
Cock 151; Lebeer, Brueghel 1; Van Bastelaer 3)*, after P.

BRUEGHEL, H. Cock excude plate, thin spots, washed,
2nd state of 3, (11-18-92, Bubb Kuyper, #1827, illus.),
12¾ x 16¹⁵⁄₁₆ in., (32.4 x 43 cm.), engraving (BP 875,
DM 2119, FR 7137, Y 165,278, G 2400).

COCK, Hieronymous, Publisher
$3410* *The Dissolute Household (Riggs 261; Holl. 1), c. 1550-
70*, proving lines distinct, trimmed within platemark,
good cond., stains,grey wash in edges, (12-03-92,
Sotheby-London, #28), 8⅛ x 11⅛ in., (206 x 283 mm.),
engraving on paper w/watermark (BP 2200, DM 5362,
FR 18,304, Y 424,288).

COCK, Hieronymus (after Hans BOL)
$609* *Landscape With A Stag Hunt (Holl 20), 1562*, watermark,
repaired tear, thin spots, tape, (10-27-92, Phillips-London,
#10), plate 8⅞ x 12⅝ in., (225 x 321 mm.), engraving
on laid (BP 385, DM 933, FR 3167, Y 74,495).

COCK, Liliane de   American 20th cent.
$55* *Storm Near Howe, Idaho, 1969*, s., (05-16-93, Hindman,
#376), 13½ x 10½ in., photograph, silver print (BP 36,
DM 89, FR 299, Y 6125).

COCQ, Suzanne
BI *Sort En Bretoigne*, s., t., #8/25, prov., est. C$ 2/300, (12-
01-92, Ritchie, #11), 11½ x 15½ in., (29.2 x 39.4 cm.),
etching.

COCTEAU, Jean   French 1889-1963
$786* *Ballets Russes De Diaghilew, 1939*, (01-31-93, Morelle/
Marchan, #47), 34⅝ x 64¹⁵⁄₁₆ in., (88 x 165 cm.), poster
(BP 529, DM 1266, FR 4281, Y 98,054).
$459* *Junglingskopf Mit Fischen*, s., #12/80, (06-10-93,
Hauswedell/Nolt, #171), image 20⅞ x 16¾ in., (53 x
42.5 cm.), color lithograph on Arches paper (BP 300,
DM 747, FR 2516, Y 48,721).
BI *Le Livre Blanc, Paris, Edition Au Signe, 1930: Seventeen*, t. page, text and just., copy 2 of 416, t. page w/s.
drawing and i.,good cond., est. $10/15,000, (05-11-93,
Christie-NY, #183, illus.), 11¹¹⁄₁₆ x 9⅜ in., (297 x 238
mm.), color lithograph on Japon nacre, the additional
suite of 17 lithographs on Van Gelder and orig. drawing
on thin wove.
$393* *Orphee En Tournant La Tete*, annot., crease, (06-16-93,
Ader Tajan, #55), 18⅛ x 24¹³⁄₁₆ in., (46 x 63 cm.), color
lithograph (BP 262, DM 652, FR 2189, Y 41,916).
$385* *Portrait Of Rimbaud*, s., #64/97, prov., (03-14-93, Hind-
man, #271), 10¼ x 6¼ in., (26 x 15.9 cm.), color lithograph (BP 269, DM 641, FR 2179, Y 45,374).
$143* *Princepaute De Monaco, 1959*, p. Mourlot, (10-18-92,
Hindman, #476), 25⅜ x 19¼ in., (64.5 x 48.9 cm.),
color lithograph (BP 88, DM 213, FR 722, Y 17,157).
$273* *Salle Pleyel. Exposition Pouchkine, 1937*, good cond.,
(11-19-92, Ribeyre/Baron, #134), 28⅜ x 19¹¹⁄₁₆ in., (72 x
50 cm.), poster (BP 180, DM 435, FR 1466, Y 33,951).
$272* *Tete, 1947*, 32/60, stone s., 882 mm x 1040mm, (10-14-
92, Germann, #259), lithograph (BP 160, DM 398, FR
1350, Y 32,962, SF 354).
$7860* *Theatre De Monte Carlo: Ballet Russe, 1911*, p. E. Ver-
neau and H. Chachouin, very good cond., lit., (11-19-92,
Ribeyre/Baron, #162, illus.), 36¹³⁄₁₆ x 23⅝ in., (93.5 x
60 cm.), poster (BP 5175, DM 12,532, FR 42,213, Y
977,490).

COCTEAU, Jean (after)
$63* *"Toreador-1963"*, #118/200, s., d. in plate, (01-28-93,
Pescheteau, #107), 14¹⁵⁄₁₆ x 11 in., (38 x 28 cm.), color
lithograph on wove (BP 42, DM 100, FR 338, Y 7822).

COENEN, Otto   1907-1971
$296* *Mittagspause, 1931*, #12/100 (1980), estate stamp, (03-24-
93, Venator/Hansten, #4473), approx. 18⅞ x 13¾ in., (48
x 35 cm.), linocut (BP 200, DM 483, FR 1645, Y
34,779).

COGNIET (after)
$550* *Washington (Hart 666), 1839*, by Jean Nicholas Laugier,
margins folded back glued to stretcher, staining, losses,
laid down on linen, defects, (01-22-93, Christie-NY,
#308), plate 25¼ x 21 in., (641 x 533 mm.), engraving
on wove (BP 360, DM 875, FR 2959, Y 68,836).

COHEN, Arthur   American 20th cent.
$83* *"Bridge Silhouette", 1982*, s. Arthur Cohen, num. 171/
250, very good cond.?, (11-21-92, Bakker, #94), plate 7½

x 10 in., (19.1 x 25.4 cm.), etching (BP 55, DM 132, FR 446, Y 10,322).

COHEN, Bernard   American contemporary
$55* *Untitled*, s., d. 1965, #10/75 IV, (05-16-93, Hindman, #637A), 21¾ x 29½ in., (55.2 x 74.9 cm.), color lithograph (BP 36, DM 88, FR 297, Y 6097).

COHN, Max Arthur   American b. 1903
BI *Fisherman, 1947*, s., excell. cond., est. $2/250, (05-15-93, Cleveland, #96), 10 x 13½ in., (25.4 x 34.3 cm.), color silkscreen.

COIGNARD, James   French b. 1925
$1147* *"A-B"*, #56/95, s., (11-13-92, Koller, #5288), 31⁵⁄₁₆ x 23⅝ in., (79.5 x 60 cm.), carborundum and aquatint on hand-made (BP 741, DM 1801, FR 6072, Y 142,361, SF 1624).
$417* *Composition*, s., 16/30, (04-17-93, Falkkloos, #91, illus.), 21⅝ x 17⁵⁄₁₆ in., (55 x 44 cm.), engraving, hand-colored (BP 271, DM 667, FR 2253, Y 46,369, SK 3080).
$268* *Composition*, s., 58/60, (04-17-93, Falkkloos, #89), 22¹⁄₁₆ x 17⁵⁄₁₆ in., (56 x 44 cm.), etching in colors (BP 174, DM 429, FR 1448, Y 29,801, SK 1980).
$142* *Composition*, artist's proof, s., full margins, (05-27-93, Briest, #64), 12⅝ x 9¹³⁄₁₆ in., (32 x 25 cm.), color carborundum engraving (BP 91, DM 228, FR 768, Y 15,223).
$395* *Composition*, H.C., s., 658mm x 1003mm, (06-24-93, Germann, #286), color aquatint w/drypoint and collage (BP 260, DM 640, FR 2158, Y 42,373, SF 575).
$168* *"Composition A.B.C."*, #47/75, (01-28-93, Pescheteau, #108), 21⅝ x 16¹⁵⁄₁₆ in., (55 x 43 cm.), etching, collage and embossing on papier a la cuve (BP 111, DM 266, FR 901, Y 20,859).
$632* *Composition AB*, 56/95, s., (06-24-93, Germann, #285), 38³⁄₁₆ x 29½ in., (970 x 750 mm.), color aquatint w/drypoint (BP 416, DM 1025, FR 3454, Y 67,797, SF 920).
$359* *"Composition AB"*, #7/75, s., (10-18-92, Pescheteau, #107), 24¹³⁄₁₆ x 35⁷⁄₁₆ in., (63 x 90 cm.), engraving and carborundum (BP 218, DM 530, FR 1801, Y 42,866).
$314* *"Composition"*, #66/75, s., (10-18-92, Pescheteau, #108), 26⅜ x 20¹⁄₁₆ in., (67 x 51 cm.), carborundum and collage (BP 190, DM 464, FR 1576, Y 37,493).
$419* *"Computer", 1979: Portfolio*, s. 71/75, Editions F.B., (09-29-92, B. Rasmussen, #292), three etchings in color (BP 236, DM 592, FR 2019, Y 50,018, DK 2300).
$371* *Ensemble De Sept Gravures*, artist's proofs, s., whole margins, (03-31-93, Briest, #E22), largest 12¹⁵⁄₁₆ x 9¹³⁄₁₆ in., (33 x 25 cm.), smallest 5½ x 5½ in., (33 x 25 cm.), etchings, embossings, aquatints and collages (BP 245, DM 597, FR 2027, Y 42,663).
BI *"Geometrics Autour D'Un Prealable", 1982*, pub. Transworld Art, num. 68/95, pub. dry stamp, very good cond., wrinkling, est. $4/600, (09-11-92, Skinner, #110, illus.), sheet 17½ x 22 in., (44.5 x 55.9 cm.), etching/stencil hand coloring/embossing/collage on Moulin de Larroque wove.
$358* *Geometries Autour D'Un Prealable, 1982*, s., num., (11-12-92, Freemn/Fine Art, #50), 17½ x 22½ in., (44.5 x 57.2 cm.), etching, stencil, hand colored, embossing & collage on Moulin de Larroque hand made paper (BP 235, DM 567, FR 1913, Y 44,389).
$806* *Komposition, 1989*, epreuve d'artiste, s., (11-13-92, Kunsthaus, #506), 13¾ x 20½ in., (35 x 52 cm.), color etching and carborundum, collage on intaglio board (BP 521, DM 1265, FR 4267, Y 100,037).
$660* *"L'Observateur 8 Et Otoga"* and *"Denx Profilo": Two*, s., num. 53/75, blindstamp of pub. Trans World Art, full margins, good cond., (02-24-93, Butterfield, #3200), 30¹⁴ x 22¼ in., (762 x 565 mm.), 18¾ x 26³⁄₁₆ in., (762 x 565 mm.), etching & aquatint in colors w/embossing on heavy handmade (BP 460, DM 1071, FR 3632, Y 77,447).
BI *"MAC"*, #68/95, s., i., est. SF 7/900, (11-13-92, Koller, #5290), 25⁹⁄₁₆ x 19¹¹⁄₁₆ in., (65 x 50 cm.), carborundum on hand-made, worked over w/color and spachtel.
$825* *Moderato Portfolio, 1981: Three*, complete portfolio, s., num. XII/XV, t. & justification pages, num. XII/XV on justification, pub. Editions Vision Neuvelli, full margins, apparentlyvery good cond., orig. portfolio, (02-24-93,

Butterfield, #3201), 16⅛ x 12¾ in., (410 x 324 mm.), etching & aquatint w/embossing & collage in colors on handmade (BP 575, DM 1339, FR 4540, Y 96,808).
$505* *Otage Et Triangle, 1972*, s., num., (11-28-92, Schoppmann, #473), 26⁹⁄₁₆ x 20¼ in., (67.5 x 51.5 cm.), color etching w/carborundum on hangeschopftem handmade (BP 333, DM 805, FR 2731, Y 62,850).
BI *Sans Titre*, (03-16-93, Encans, #157), 20³⁄₁₆ x 14⁵⁄₁₆ in., (51.3 x 36.3 cm.), lithograph.
$2200* *Song Of The Broad Axe, 1982: Six*, portfolio, from Leaves of Grass by Walt Whitman, s., num. H.C. 3/15,p. Pasnic Atelier, pub. Trans World Art, orig. folder, (12-08-92, Swann, #68), 29½ x 22⅜ in., (74.9 x 56.8 cm.), hand-colored carborundum etching w/collage and embossment (BP 1379, DM 3425, FR 11,677, Y 272,682).
$467* *Untitled, 1979: Group Of Three*, from Computer, s., #15/75, orig. album, pub. Edition F.B., (12-08-92, Swann, #67, illus.), 16 x 12¼ in., (40.6 x 31.1 cm.), etching w/collage and hand-coloring (BP 293, DM 727, FR 2479, Y 57,883).

COIGNET, Jules   French 1798-1860
BI *Fabriques A Tivoli, 1828*, stone s., d., blindstamp, est. DM 1,200, (06-10-93, Hauswedell/Nolt, #228), lithograph on light board.

COLE, Thomas   American 1801-1848
$165* *"Voyage Of Life-Childhood", "Voyage Of Life-Youth"* and *"Voyage OfLife-Old Age": Three*, from the Voyage Of Life Series, engraved by James Smillie, p. by H.Peters, (04-25-93, Bakker, #119), each, image 15⅜ x 22¾ in., (39.1 x 57.8 cm.), engravings (BP 105, DM 261, FR 881, Y 18,224).
$341* *"The Voyage Of Life-Manhood"*, (06-02-93, Doyle, #43), 15¼ x 22¼ in., (38.7 x 56.5 cm.), engraving (BP 221, DM 544, FR 1835, Y 36,588).

COLE, Timothy
$110* *"Lowlands"*, s., good cond.?, (07-19-92, Bakker, #138), plate 6¾ x 9¼ in., (17.1 x 23.5 cm.), wood engraving (BP 56, DM 160, FR 542, Y 13,675).
$35* *Portrait Of A Woman, 1930*, after Gainesborough, s., (05-15-93, Cleveland, #97), 7¾ x 5⅞ in., (19.7 x 14.9 cm.), wood engraving on Japanese tissue (BP 23, DM 56, FR 189, Y 3880).

COLEMAN, Judy   b. 1944
$1035* *Interlude, 1989*, from the Judy Coleman Portfolio, s., t., d., #6/50, (c) insig., (04-08-93, Christie-NY, #523, illus.), 23¾ x 21¾ in., (60.3 x 55.2 cm.), photograph, gelatin silver print (BP 679, DM 1663, FR 5628, Y 117,453).

COLEMAN, William (Bill)
$243* *Thinking Woman*, s. Bill Coleman, i., d. 1962, (08-11-92, L. Joel, #70G), 10⁷⁄₁₆ x 13¾ in., (26.5 x 35 cm.), monotype (BP 126, DM 357, FR 1208, Y 31,118, A$ 330).

COLEMAN, William (Bill)   b. 1922
BI *Mother And Son*, s. Bill Coleman, i., #2/10, est. $80/150, (08-11-92, L. Joel, #146G), 7¹⁄₁₆ x 5⅛ in., (18 x 13 cm.), etching.
BI *The Trio)*, s. Bill Coleman, i. A.P., est. $80/120, (08-11-92, L. Joel, #172G), 4¹³⁄₁₆ x 3⁹⁄₁₆ in., (12.2 x 9 cm.), etching.
$122* *Xmas Shopping*, s. Bill Coleman, i. A.P., (08-11-92, L. Joel, #159G), 5¼ x 3¹⁄₁₆ in., (13.4 x 7.7 cm.), color linocut (BP 63, DM 179, FR 606, Y 15,623, A$ 165).

COLESCOTT, Warrington
BI *Secretary Seward Buys Alaska*, s., t., d. 1973, num. Artists Proof, prov., est. C$ 3/500, (12-01-92, Ritchie, #31, illus.), 17⅛ x 22¾ in., (43.5 x 57.8 cm.), color etching and aquatint.

COLIN, P.
$241* *Refrigerateur Bosch*, very good cond., (02-13-93, Morelle/Marchan, #32), 47¼ x 62¹⁵⁄₁₆ in., (120 x 160 cm.), poster (BP 170, DM 400, FR 1352, Y 29,064).

COLIN, Jean   1912-1982
$36* *Votre Vin Favori Kiravi Me Ravit!*, cond. B, (03-16-93, Boisgirard, #85), 58⅞ x 38¾ in., (149.5 x 98.5 cm.), poster (BP 25, DM 60, FR 203, Y 4210).

COLIN, Paul   French 1892-1985
  BI *16e Salon Des Arts Menagers,* plate s., trimmed, est. $4/600, (03-25-93, Christie-E, #199), 23½ x 15½ in., (59.7 x 39.4 cm.), color lithograph.

$1469* *Bal Des Petits Lits Blancs A L'Opera, 1930,* Hachard and Cie, very good cond., lit., (11-19-92, Ribeyre/Baron, #135, illus.), 21⁷⁄₁₆ x 15⅜ in., (54.5 x 39 cm.), poster (BP 967, DM 2342, FR 7889, Y 182,689).

$358* *Cei. Gle. Transatlantique,* abrasion and cracks, linen backed, (11-12-92, Freemn/Fine Art, #51), 38 x 24 in., (96.5 x 61 cm.), litho poster (BP 235, DM 567, FR 1913, Y 44,389).

$110* *La Chanson Du Bonheur, Gaite-Lyrique,* Bedos, B cond., chipping, repairs, pinhole marks, (08-06-92, Swann, #108, illus.), 23½ x 11 in., (59.7 x 27.9 cm.), (BP 57, DM 163, FR 549, Y 14,031).

$438* *Cie Gle Transatlantique French Line: Atlantique, Pacifique, Mediterranee, 1949,* very good cond., (03-13-93, Laurin, #157), 39⅜ x 24⁷⁄₁₆ in., (100 x 62 cm.), (BP 306, DM 729, FR 2479, Y 51,621).

  BI *Cie. Gle. Transatlantique/Atlantique-Pacifique-Mediterranee, c. 1937,* plate s., est. $6/800, (06-08-93, Christie-E, #192), 23½ x 15¾ in., (59.7 x 40 cm.), color lithograph.

$1093* *Cie. Gle. Transatlantique/Atlantique-Pacifique-Mediterranee, c. 1937,* plate s., (03-25-93, Christie-E, #200, illus.), 23½ x 15¾ in., (59.7 x 40 cm.), color lithograph (BP 742, DM 1796, FR 6106, Y 128,046).

$1888* *Les Comediens De Bois De Jacques Chenais, 1945,* p. Courbet, good cond., (11-19-92, Ribeyre/Baron, #171, illus.), 63³⁄₁₆ x 47⅝ in., (160.5 x 121 cm.), poster (BP 1243, DM 3010, FR 10,140, Y 234,797).

$73* *Compositions: Two,* s. Paul Colin, VI/LX, (03-24-93, Kunsthallen, #62), color lithograph (BP 49, DM 119, FR 406, Y 8577, DK 460).

$839* *Grand Guignol: La Machine Rouge. Piece De Claude Orval, 1931,* p. H. Chachouin, good cond., lit., (11-19-92, Ribeyre/Baron, #167, illus.), 23⅝ x 15¾ in., (60 x 40 cm.), poster (BP 552, DM 1338, FR 4506, Y 104,340).

$910* *La Granero, 1935,* p. Joseph Charles, (01-31-93, Morelle/Marchan, #52), 47¼ x 62¹⁵⁄₁₆ in., (120 x 160 cm.), poster (BP 612, DM 1466, FR 4956, Y 113,523).

$167* *Haut De Cagnes, "Ou La Joie De Vivre", 1971,* excell. cond., (01-23-93, Ribeyre/Baron, #133), 43⁵⁄₁₆ x 30⅛ in., (110 x 76.5 cm.), poster (BP 109, DM 266, FR 898, Y 20,901).

$827* *Jean Weidt Et Ses Ballets, 1938,* (01-31-93, Morelle/Marchan, #51, illus.), 30¹¹⁄₁₆ x 30⁵⁄₁₆ in., (78 x 77 cm.), poster (BP 556, DM 1332, FR 4504, Y 103,169).

$600* *Joe Alex Danseur Et Choregraphe, 1936,* creases, (01-31-93, Morelle/Marchan, #49), 47¼ x 62¹⁵⁄₁₆ in., (120 x 160 cm.), poster (BP 403, DM 967, FR 3268, Y 74,850).

$1448* *Katherine Dunham, 1947,* p. Bedos, (01-31-93, Morelle/Marchan, #53, illus.), 40³⁄₁₆ x 59¹⁄₁₆ in., (102 x 150 cm.), poster (BP 974, DM 2333, FR 7887, Y 180,639).

  BI *Ligue Francaise Contre Le Cancer, 1946,* Bedos and Cie, B+ cond., fold marks, cracking, est. $1/1,500, (08-06-92, Swann, #107, illus.), 61 x 45½ in., (154.9 x 115.6 cm.), .

$587* *Liqueur Izzara, 1948,* p. Bedos & Cie, very good cond., (11-19-92, Ribeyre/Baron, #26), 46⁷⁄₁₆ x 18⅞ in., (118 x 48 cm.), poster (BP 386, DM 936, FR 3153, Y 73,001).

$1489* *Mitty Tillio Et Ricaux, 1928,* p. H. Chachoin, creases, (01-31-93, Morelle/Marchan, #50, illus.), 46⁷⁄₁₆ x 61¹³⁄₁₆ in., (118 x 157 cm.), poster (BP 1001, DM 2399, FR 8110, Y 185,753).

$335* *Nancy. "Synthese De L'Histoire Lorraine", 1948,* excell. cond., (01-23-93, Ribeyre/Baron, #157), 40¹⁵⁄₁₆ x 27⁹⁄₁₆ in., (104 x 70 cm.), poster (BP 219, DM 533, FR 1802, Y 41,927).

$1678* *Odeon, c. 1935,* good cond., Atelier P. Colin, lit., (11-19-92, Ribeyre/Baron, #169, illus.), 23⅝ x 15¾ in., (60 x 40 cm.), poster (BP 1105, DM 2675, FR 9012, Y 208,681).

$379* *Paris 1937. Exposition Internationale,* cond. B, (03-16-93, Boisgirard, #87), 39⁹⁄₁₆ x 24⁷⁄₁₆ in., (100.5 x 62 cm.), poster (BP 262, DM 630, FR 2141, Y 44,317).

  BI *Paris Exposition Internationale, Mai-Novembre, 1937,* plate s., est. $6/800, (06-08-93, Christie-E, #191), 23¼ x 15½ in., (59.1 x 39.4 cm.), color lithograph.

$165* *Paris, 1945,* French National Railways, B- cond., creasing, extensive repairs, closed tears, (08-06-92, Swann, #106, illus.), 39½ x 24½ in., (100.3 x 62.2 cm.), (BP 86, DM 244, FR 823, Y 21,046).

  BI *Paris, 1945,* repaired losses, staining, other minor losses, lit., est. BP 2/300, (02-04-93, Christie-S. Ken, #116), 39 x 24 in., (99.1 x 61 cm.), color lithograph backed on linen.

$650* *Paris-Soir, "La Pegre Des Tropiques" Saisissant Documentaire Sur LesEvades Du Bagne, Par J. Lasserre, 1945/46,* p. Bedos & Cie, good cond., fragile folds, (11-19-92, Ribeyre/Baron, #25), 62¹⁵⁄₁₆ x 47¼ in., (160 x 120 cm.), poster (BP 428, DM 1036, FR 3491, Y 80,836).

$545* *Pelleas Et Melisande, Drame De M. Maeterlinck, Musique De C. Debussy, 1936,* p. Karcher, good cond., lit., (11-19-92, Ribeyre/Baron, #170), 62¹⁵⁄₁₆ x 47¼ in., (160 x 120 cm.), poster (BP 359, DM 869, FR 2927, Y 67,778).

$2056* *Salon Des Artistes Decorateurs, 1949,* orig. maquette, s., good cond., lit., (11-19-92, Ribeyre/Baron, #136), 28⅜ x 19¹¹⁄₁₆ in., (72 x 50 cm.), poster w/gouache (BP 1354, DM 3278, FR 11,042, Y 255,690).

$671* *Studio De Paris: Ces Messieurs Dames, Revue Realiste De F. Carco Avec Cora Madou, 1932,* p. Frace Affiches, good cond., lit., (11-19-92, Ribeyre/Baron, #168), 23¼ x 15¾ in., (59 x 40 cm.), poster (BP 442, DM 1070, FR 3604, Y 83,447).

$279* *Sylvie, 1928,* cond. B, (03-16-93, Boisgirard, #86), 61¹³⁄₁₆ x 44⁵⁄₁₆ in., (157 x 112.5 cm.), poster (BP 193, DM 464, FR 1576, Y 32,624).

$2098* *Theatre Saint-Georges. "Le Rire, L'Epouvante", c. 1930,* p. H. Chachouin, very good cond., (11-19-92, Ribeyre/Baron, #165, illus.), 62⅝ x 47¹⁄₁₆ in., (159 x 119.5 cm.), poster (BP 1381, DM 3345, FR 11,267, Y 260,913).

$2098* *Theatre Saint-Georges: Destination Inconnue. Drame De Mr. Bernard Zimmer, c. 1930,* p. H. Chachouin, very good cond., (11-19-92, Ribeyre/Baron, #166), 62¹⁵⁄₁₆ x 47¼ in., (160 x 120 cm.), poster (BP 1381, DM 3345, FR 11,267, Y 260,913).

$399* *Vichy Mai-Octobre, 1948,* p. Wallon, very good cond., (11-19-92, Ribeyre/Baron, #96), 38¹⁵⁄₁₆ x 24⁷⁄₁₆ in., (99 x 62 cm.), poster (BP 263, DM 636, FR 2143, Y 49,621).

$770* *Woman's Head And A Globe, 1937,* Paris 1937, linenbacked, (04-29-93, Swann, #145, illus.), 62 x 45 in., (157.5 x 114.3 cm.), color lithograph poster (BP 490, DM 1218, FR 4104, Y 85,660).

COLLAERT, Adriaen   c. 1560-1618
  BI *Johannes Der Taufer In Der Wuste (Wurzbach 4; Hollstein 147),* after H. Goltzius, trimmed. est. DM 500, (12-01-92, Karl/Faber, #41), engraving.

COLLETT (after)
$32* *The Recruiting Serjeant, 1769,* by Golder, pub. Thomas Bradford, surface defects, (03-17-93, Bonhams-Chelsea, #435), image 15¼ x 20¾ in., (38.7 x 52.7 cm.), engraving w/hand-coloring (BP 22, DM 53, FR 181, Y 3753).

COLLETT, John (after)
$435* *"The Frenchman In London" and "The Englishman In Paris", 1770: A Pair,* by C. White and J. Caldwall, pub. Robert Sayer, trimmed to plate, defects, light staining, (10-27-92, Phillips-London, #77), sheet 14⅛ x 10¼ in., (359 x 260 mm.), engraving w/later hand-coloring on laid (BP 275, DM 667, FR 2262, Y 53,211).

  BI *Slight Of Hand By A Monkey-Or The Lady's Head Unloaded, c. 1790,* pub. Carrington Bowles, watermark, thread margins, defect, tears, est. BP 150/200, (11-30-92, Phillips-London, #142), plate 13⅞ x 9⅞ in., (352 x 251 mm.), mezzotint on laid.

COLLIER, John
$805* *Peruvian Children Dancing, c. 1942,* ink s., flushmounted, (04-08-93, Christie-NY, #266, illus.), 8¼ x 13⅜ in., (21 x 34 cm.), photograph, gelatin silver print (BP 528, DM 1293, FR 4377, Y 91,353).

COLLIN, Ed.
$538* *French Line: Paquebot Colombie, c. 1955,* very good cond., (03-13-93, Laurin, #159, illus.), 33⁷⁄₁₆ x 25⁹⁄₁₆ in., (85 x 65 cm.), (BP 375, DM 895, FR 3045, Y 63,406).

COLLINS
BI *"Leith, Scotland", "Seacoast From Fissness To Montros", "Falmouth ToTruro": Three,* from Great Britain Coasting Pilot, 1793, i., est. $100/150, (09-17-92, Sloan, #2682), approx. 17½ x 22¼ in., (44.5 x 56.5 cm.), copperplate engravings.

COLLINS, James
BI *Imagining Melanie, 1974,* t., d., s., est. L. 800/1,200, (05-18-93, Auction Phila, #138), 9¹⁄₁₆ x 13⅜ in., (23 x 34 cm.), photograph.

COLLINS, John F. 1888-1990
BI *Spools And Film No. 1, 1934,* facsimile sig. stamp, lit., est. $1,5/2,000, (10-13-92, Christie-NY, #169, illus.), 9¾ x 8½ in., (24.8 x 21.6 cm.), photograph, gelatin silver print.

COLLINS, Tom
BI *Joan Bennet, Portrait In Profile,* autograph, est. BP 2/300, (10-10-92, Bonhams, #3, illus.), 13½ x 10½ in., (34.3 x 26.7 cm.), photograph.

COLLINS, W. (after)
$55 *Children Playing On A Gate By A Wood,* engraved by C. Cousen, (02-05-93, G.A. Key, #31), 8 x 9 in., (20.3 x 22.9 cm.), hand-colored engraving (BP 38, DM 91, FR 308, Y 6844).

COLTMAN, Ora American b. 1860
$190* *"Furnished Rooms, No Garage",* good cond., tears, (05-15-93, Cleveland, #98, illus.), 7¼ x 9 in., (18.4 x 22.9 cm.), woodcut (BP 124, DM 306, FR 1027, Y 21,062).

COLVILLE, Alexander Canadian b. 1920
$1561* *Kingfisher,* s., d. 1983, #49/70, (05-18-93, Joyner, #171), 35¼ x 11¾ in., (89.5 x 29.8 cm.), serigraph in colors (BP 1017, DM 2533, FR 8553, Y 173,966, C$ 1980).
$1735* *Raven,* #47/70, s., d. 1990; t. in print, (05-10-93, Hodgins, #296), 28 x 19 in., (71.1 x 48.3 cm.), serigraph on paper (BP 1132, DM 2787, FR 9404, Y 193,876, C$ 2200).

COLVIN, Calum b. 1961
$2722* *"Turkish Bath", 1986,* ink s., t., d., (05-06-93, Christie-London, #119, illus.), 38 x 30 in., photograph, cibachrome print (BP 1725, DM 4287, FR 14,433, Y 299,483).

COMBAS, Robert French b. 1957
$619* *Alchimikum Liberatum,* w/orig. drawings, s., #HC 5/5, (03-31-93, Briest, #E148), 40⁹⁄₁₆ x 33¹⁄₁₆ in., (103 x 84 cm.), color lithograph (BP 409, DM 996, FR 3383, Y 71,182).
BI *Alchimikum Liberatum, 1991,* s., d. 91, #28/75, est. FF4/5,000, (05-27-93, Briest, #65), 40⁹⁄₁₆ x 33¹⁄₁₆ in., (103 x 84 cm.), color lithograph.
BI *Les Algues, 1990,* s., d., #H.C. 3/30, full sheets p. to edges, good cond., est. Dfl. 1/1,500, (05-27-93, Sotheby-Amstrdm, #581, illus.), sh 41⁷⁄₁₆ x 34¹⁄₁₆ in., (105.3 x 86.5 cm.), colored lithograph on wove.
$416* *Meurtre, 1990,* s., d., #87/100, full sheet p. to edges, good cond., (05-27-93, Sotheby-Amstrdm, #582), sh 43⁷⁄₁₆ x 32⅝ in., (110.4 x 82.8 cm.), colored lithograph on sturdy wove (BP 266, DM 668, FR 2250, Y 44,597, G 748).
$290* *Sans Titre,* s., 85/100, 1105 x 830mm, (06-28-93, Loudmer, #217), color lithograph on wove (BP 194, DM 493, FR 1660, Y 30,769).
$674* *"Sans Titre",* #37/100, s., (10-18-92, Pescheteau, #110), 40¹⁵⁄₁₆ x 34¼ in., (104 x 87 cm.), lithograph in colors on velin (BP 408, DM 996, FR 3382, Y 80,478).
BI *Scene De Menage, 1990,* s., d., # E.A. 10/30, est. FF 5/6,000, (11-16-92, Briest, #277), 14⅞ x 10¹⁵⁄₁₆ in., (148 x 148 cm.), lithograph in color.
BI *"Trois Personnages",* H.C., #3/30, s., est. FF 3,0/3,500, (10-18-92, Pescheteau, #109), 43⁵⁄₁₆ x 32¹¹⁄₁₆ in., (110 x 83 cm.), lithograph in colors on velin.

COMETTI, A.
$134* *"Bledine" (Alimentation),* French Republique stamp, s., d. Cometti 1926 #1, (03-16-93, Encans, #140, illus.), approx. 58¹⁄₁₆ x 42⁵⁄₁₆ in., (147.5 x 107.5 cm.), poster (BP 93, DM 223, FR 757, Y 15,669, C$ 167).

COMMARMOND, P.
$314* *L'Ete...L'Etat: Saint-Brieuc, "Centre De Tourisme En Bretagne", 1930,* excell. cond., (01-23-93, Ribeyre/Baron, #54), 39⅜ x 24³⁄₁₆ in., (100 x 61.5 cm.), poster (BP 205, DM 499, FR 1689, Y 39,299).
$978* *PLM. Combloux. L'Hotel PLM Et Le Mont-Blanc, c. 1925,* very good cond., (03-15-93, Arcole, #84, illus.), 39⅜ x 24⁷⁄₁₆ in., (100 x 62 cm.), (BP 681, DM 1625, FR 5522, Y 115,849).
$219* *Salvan-Les Granges-Le Bioley. Valais, Suisse. "Chemins De Fer Martigny, Chatelard, Chamonix",* good cond., (03-15-93, Arcole, #26), 39³⁄₁₆ x 27⁹⁄₁₆ in., (99.5 x 70 cm.), (BP 152, DM 364, FR 1237, Y 25,942).

COMMARMOND, Pierre French 20th cent.
BI *Chemins De Fer Du Midi, Vernet Les Bains, 1930,* pub. Lucien Serre & Cie, cond. 1, short tear, laid on linen, est. BP3/400, (10-13-92, Phillips-London, #12, illus.), 39³⁄₁₆ x 24⁷⁄₁₆ in., (99.5 x 62 cm.), color lithograph.
BI *Tregastel, La Cote De Granite Rose, Cotes-Du Nord, c. 1930,* p. Mayeux, for French State Railways, cond. 1, laid on linen, est. BP 4/600, (10-13-92, Phillips-London, #11), 39³⁄₁₆ x 24⅝ in., (99.5 x 62.5 cm.), color lithograph.

COMTE DE NOE, Amadee Charles Henri (CHAM)
BI *Almanach Comique Illustre De 150 Vignettes Par Cham Et Maurisset Pour 1859,* s. in stone, est. DM 500, (12-05-92, Bassenge, #7571), 12¼ x 18¹³⁄₁₆ in., (31.1 x 47.8 cm.), color lithograph.

CONAL, Robbie
BI *Interior,* s., num. Ed. 30, margins, apparently good cond., surface soiling, creases, (02-24-93, Butterfield, #3202), 23 x 24 in., (584 x 610 mm.), silkscreen in colors on wove.

CONDE, Geo
$189* *Solanis, "Le Magicien Moderne", 1945,* p. Royer, very good cond., (11-19-92, Ribeyre/Baron, #172), 37 x 24¹³⁄₁₆ in., (94 x 63 cm.), poster (BP 124, DM 301, FR 1015, Y 23,505).

CONDESO, Orlando
BI *"Rays Of Brown & Gold" and "Orange & Yellow Composition": Two,* each s., d. 72, #37/50 and 38/50, prov., est. C$ 250/400, (12-01-92, Ritchie, #54, illus.), each 24⅞ x 19 in., (63.2 x 48.3 cm.), color serigraph.

CONDO, George American b. 1957
$495* *Clown, 1989,* s., num. 52/55, pub. Aldo Crommelynck, full margins, excell. cond., (09-19-92, Christie-E, #92), plate 15¾ x 14⅜ in., (400 x 365 mm.), soft-ground etching and aquatint in colors on wove, watermark (BP 285, DM 741, FR 2538, Y 61,675).

CONDY, Nicholas Matthew (after)
$303* *The "Leda" Yacht, R.W.Y.C., 1850,* by Thomas Goldsworth, pub. Messrs Fores, repaired tear, surface dirt, (01-14-93, Bonhams, #104), image 12¼ x 17¾ in., (31.1 x 45.1 cm.), hand-colored lithograph (BP 198, DM 495, FR 1675, Y 38,200).

CONNER, Bruce American b. 1933
BI *Triptych, 1970,* s., t., #2/90, good cond.?, est. $800/1000, (05-19-93, Butterfield, #2147), total 19¾ x 19¾ in., (502 x 502 mm.), lithograph on wove.

CONNOR, Linda
$374* *"Light Modulation In Twigs", 1973,* s., d., (05-23-93, Butterfield, #3380, illus.), 9½ x 7½ in., photograph, selenium-toned printing out paper (BP 244, DM 612, FR 2058, Y 41,340).

CONRAD, Julius American 20th cent.
$55* *"Old Houses-Old Tunes" and "Puppet Show": Two,* s., t., (04-02-93, Sloan, #802), larger 15⅝ x 11½ in., (397 x 292 mm.), etching (BP 36, DM 88, FR 300, Y 6262).
BI *"Old Houses-Old Tunes" and "Puppet Show": Two,* each s., t.; est. $125/175, (02-04-93, Sloan, #363), larger 15⅝ x 11½ in., (39.7 x 29.2 cm.), etching.

CONSAGRA, Pietro Italian b. 1920
BI *Composizione,* XX/XXIV, s., est. SF 200/300, (10-14-92, Germann, #261), 13¾ x 19¹³⁄₁₆ in., (350 x 503 mm.), color aquatint.

BI *Composizione,* IV/XV. P.A., s., est. SF 300/400, (10-14-92, Germann, #263), 19¹¹/₁₆ x 27⅜ in., (500 x 695 mm.), color aquatint.

BI *Composizione,* #XX/XXIV, s., est. SF 150/150, (09-04-92, Germann, #290), 13¾ x 19¹³/₁₆ in., (350 x 503 mm.), color aquatint.

BI *Composizione,* #IV/XV, P.A., s., est. SF 2/300, (09-04-92, Germann, #291), 19¹¹/₁₆ x 27⅜ in., (500 x 695 mm.), color aquatint.

BI *Elementi,* V/X p.a., s., est. SF 300/400, (10-14-92, Germann, #260), 19½ x 25⅜ in., (495 x 645 mm.), color aquatint.

BI *Elementi,* #V/X, p.a., s., est. SF 2/300, (09-04-92, Germann, #289), 19½ x 25⅜ in., (495 x 645 mm.), color aquatint.

$175* *Minnetoneka, 1972,* s., t., #66/90, full margins, (03-31-93, Briest, #E25), 19½ x 25⁹/₁₆ in., (49.5 x 65 cm.), aquatint in mauve on Arches (BP 116, DM 281, FR 956, Y 20,124).

CONSEMULLER, Erich   1902-1957
BI *Stoffprobe Aus Der Weberei,* 20's, lit., est. DM 500, (11-12-92, Lempertz, #7), 9³/₁₆ x 6¹³/₁₆ in., (23.3 x 17.3 cm.), photograph, gelatin silver print.

CONSTABLE (after)
$80* *Hampstead Heath,* by Norman Hirst, s., (02-17-93, Bonhams-Chelsea, #318), image 16 x 21¼ in., (40.6 x 54 cm.), mezzotint (BP 55, DM 130, FR 440, Y 9556).

$184* *The Jumping Horse, 1891,* pub. Dowdeswell and Dowdeswell, margins, laid down, creases, (11-12-92, Bonhams-Chelsea, #16), plate 22¼ x 29½ in., (56.5 x 74.9 cm.), hand-colored etching (BP 121, DM 292, FR 983, Y 22,815).

CONSTABLE, John   English 1776-1837
$2558* *The Ruins Of The West Window Of Netley Abbey,* margins, scuffing, other defects, (12-03-92, Sotheby-London, #152, illus.), 5¼ x 7½ in., (132 x 188 mm.), etching and drypoint (BP 1650, DM 4023, FR 13,731, Y 318,278).

CONSTABLE, John (after)
$125 *Salisbury Cathedral,* (08-14-92, G.A. Key, #29), 19 x 25 in., (48.3 x 63.5 cm.), mezzotint (BP 65, DM 183, FR 621, Y 15,763).

CONSTANDUROS, Denis
$778* *To Visit Britain's Landmarks, Llanthony Abbey, Monmouthshire, 1937,* p. Waterlow and Sons, ref. #498, cond. 1, nicks, (10-13-92, Phillips-London, #124), 29¹⁵/₁₆ x 44⅞ in., (76 x 114 cm.), color lithograph (BP 453, DM 1140, FR 3873, Y 94,337).

CONSTANT
$128* *Untitled,* s., #12/190, full margins, good cond., (05-27-93, Sotheby-Amstrdm, #583), 5⅜ x 5½ in., (137 x 140 mm.), etching on wove (BP 82, DM 205, FR 692, Y 13,722, G 230).

BI *Untitled,* s., num., est. DM 500-, (09-25-92, Granier, #2796), sheet 25⅞ x 19¹³/₁₆ in., (65.8 x 50.3 cm.), etching on hand-made.

$586* *Untitled,* s., good cond.?, creases, (12-09-92, Sotheby-Amstrdm, #519), 19½ x 27⅜ in., (496 x 695 mm.), color lithograph on wove (BP 374, DM 920, FR 3139, Y 72,660, G 1035).

$288* *Untitled, 1979,* s., #80/190, margins, good cond., (05-27-93, Sotheby-Amstrdm, #396), 5⁵/₁₆ x 5⅜ in., (135 x 137 mm.), etching w/aquatint on wove (BP 184, DM 462, FR 1558, Y 30,875, G 518).

$384* *Untitled, 1979,* s., #73/190, margins, good cond., (05-27-93, Sotheby-Amstrdm, #397), 5⁵/₁₆ x 4½ in., (135 x 115 mm.), etching w/aquatint on wove (BP 246, DM 616, FR 2077, Y 41,166, G 690).

$448* *Untitled, 1979,* s., #56/190, margins, good cond., (05-27-93, Sotheby-Amstrdm, #399), 5½ x 5¼ in., (140 x 133 mm.), etching w/aquatint on wove (BP 287, DM 719, FR 2423, Y 48,027, G 805).

CONSTANT   b. 1920
BI *New Babylon, 1963: Ten,* #e 24/60, est. DM 3,000-, (05-27-93, Lempertz, #663), 15¾ x 15¹/₁₆ in., (40 x 38.3 cm.), lithograph on wove.

BI *Ein Pianist Und Eine Sangerin,* s., num., est. DM 750, (12-05-92, Bassenge, #7089), 5½ x 5⅜ in., (14 x 13.6 cm.), etching on Arches.

$12,219* *Pousse Tout Fleurie, 1949,* s. Constant 10.VI.49, (09-30-92, Kunsthallen, #66), lithograph in 2 colors (BP 6894, DM 17,327, FR 58,604, Y 1,466,339, DK 66,700).

CONSTANT, Eugene
$654* *The Forum, Rome, 1850s,* blindstamped w/photog.'s credit, mounted on paper, 156 x 222mm, (05-07-93, Sotheby-London, #24, illus.), photograph, salt print from albumen on glass neg. (BP 414, DM 1034, FR 3484, Y 72,011).

$1053* *"The Tempel Of Vesta", "The Church Of Sta Maria Maggiore", "The ArchTitus" and "The Arch Of Constantine": Four,* 1850s, blindstamped w/photog.'s credit, mounted on paper, each approx. 164 x 220mm, (05-07-93, Sotheby-London, #26, illus.), photograph, salt print from albumen on glass neg. (BP 667, DM 1665, FR 5610, Y 115,944).

$654* *The Temple Of Vesta, 1850s,* blindstamped w/photog.'s credit, mounted on paper, 154 x 218mm, (05-07-93, Sotheby-London, #25), photograph, salt print from albumen on glass neg. (BP 414, DM 1034, FR 3484, Y 72,011).

CONSTANT, Eugene (attrib.)
$907* *"The Arch Of Constantine, Rome", "The Capitol Rome", "The Arch Of Titus Rome" and "The Tiber With The Castle Of St. Angelo And St. Peters Rome": Four,* early 1850s, mounted on card, ink t., lit., (05-06-93, Christie-London, #50), three approx. 6¼ x 9½ in., one 5⅞ x 9½ in., photograph, salt print (BP 575, DM 1429, FR 4809, Y 99,791).

CONSTANT, George   Greek/American b. 1892
$55* *"Roll The Hoop", c. 1936,* s., t., good cond., (10-31-92, Cleveland, #103), 9⅞ x 7⅞ in., (25.1 x 20 cm.), etching (BP 35, DM 85, FR 287, Y 6813).

CONSTANT-DUVAL
$94* *P.O.: Angers, "Circuits Automobiles", c. 1925,* creases, good cond., (01-23-93, Ribeyre/Baron, #30), 40¹⁵/₁₆ x 28⁹/₁₆ in., (104 x 72.5 cm.), poster (BP 61, DM 149, FR 506, Y 11,765).

$126* *P.O.: Langeais. Les Chateaux De la Loire. Circuits Automobiles, 1927,* p. L. Serre, good cond., (11-19-92, Ribeyre/Baron, #98), 41⁵/₁₆ x 29½ in., (105 x 75 cm.), poster (BP 83, DM 201, FR 677, Y 15,670).

$419* *P.O.: Uzerche. "Le Bas-Limousin",* fair cond., (01-23-93, Ribeyre/Baron, #80), 39⅜ x 27¹⁵/₁₆ in., (100 x 71 cm.), poster (BP 274, DM 666, FR 2254, Y 52,441).

$219* *PLM: La Tunisie. "Souks De Tunis, Ruines Antiques, Mosquee De Kairouan",* very good cond., (03-13-93, Laurin, #66), 41⁵/₁₆ x 29½ in., (105 x 75 cm.), (BP 153, DM 365, FR 1239, Y 25,810).

CONSTANTIN, D.
$2724* *Greece And The Holy Lands: Forty,* album, 1860s, 13 neg. s. D. Constatin a Athenes, 260 x 360mm and 160x 240mm, (05-07-93, Sotheby-London, #16, illus.), photograph, albumen print (BP 1725, DM 4307, FR 14,513, Y 299,934).

CONSTANTINE, Dimitris
$1980* *Views Of Greece's Classical Ruins, Some With Figures, Incl.:"Caryatids, Southern Portico Of Eucthum", "Temple Of Jupiter", "Theatre Of Dionysus", "The Propylea", "Temple Of Victory", "The Acroplis" and others, 1859: Twenty9,* descriptive notations, (04-07-93, Swann, #192, illus.), 11 x 15 in., photograph, albumen print (BP 1308, DM 3202, FR 10,837, Y 224,949).

CONTI, Primo   1900-1988
$251* *Natura Morta, 1972,* #III/XXXV, s., d., (03-25-93, Finarte-Rome, #16), 18⅛ x 20¹¹/₁₆ in., (46 x 52.5 cm.), lithograph in colors (BP 170, DM 412, FR 1402, Y 29,405, L 403).

CONTI, Primo   Italian contemporary
$275* *Reclining Nude,* s., d. 1982, #30/60, (03-14-93, Hindman, #300), 9⅝ x 13¾ in., (24.4 x 34.9 cm.), etching (BP 192, DM 458, FR 1556, Y 32,410).

CONTINENTAL, 16TH CENTURY
$50* *Weary Shepherd,* two sided, (11-12-92, Freemn/Fine Art, #52), 12¼ x 9¼ in., (31.1 x 23.5 cm.), woodcut (BP 33, DM 79, FR 267, Y 6200).

COOK, Beryl English b. 1926
$273* *The Baron Entertains,* #232/300, s., (04-22-93, Bonhams-Chelsea, #100), image 25¼ x 17 in., (64.1 x 43.2 cm.), silkscreen (BP 176, DM 439, FR 1480, Y 30,016).
$257* *A Bathroom,* #248/300, s., t., (05-20-93, Bonhams-Chelsea, #154), image 26¾ x 13½ in., (67.9 x 34.3 cm.), screenprint (BP 165, DM 415, FR 1397, Y 28,379).
$273* *Chartiers,* #251/300, s., t., (04-22-93, Bonhams-Chelsea, #99), image 31¾ x 22 in., (80.6 x 55.9 cm.), silkscreen (BP 176, DM 439, FR 1480, Y 30,016).
$308* *Chartiers,* #252/300, s., s., (05-20-93, Bonhams-Chelsea, #18), image 31¾ x 22 in., (80.6 x 55.9 cm.), screenprint (BP 198, DM 497, FR 1674, Y 34,011).
$273* *Gare Du Nord,* #146/300, s., t., (04-22-93, Bonhams-Chelsea, #102), image 27⅞ x 17 in., (70.8 x 43.2 cm.), silkscreen (BP 176, DM 439, FR 1480, Y 30,016).
$307* *Gare Du Nord,* #140/300, s., t., (12-10-92, Bonhams-Chelsea, #121), image 27¾ x 17 in., (70.5 x 43.2 cm.), silkscreen (BP 198, DM 486, FR 1659, Y 37,976).
$358* *Jackpot,* s., #195/300, (06-11-93, Freemn/Fine Art, #37), 11 x 29½ in., (27.9 x 74.9 cm.), color lithograph (BP 235, DM 582, FR 1962, Y 37,984).
$307* *Ladies Night,* #285/300, s., t., (04-22-93, Bonhams-Chelsea, #103), image 18 x 20⅞ in., (45.7 x 53 cm.), silkscree (BP 198, DM 493, FR 1664, Y 33,755).
$375* *Ladies' Night,* #287/300, s., t., (12-10-92, Bonhams-Chelsea, #120), image 18 x 21 in., (45.7 x 53.3 cm.), silkscreen (BP 242, DM 593, FR 2026, Y 46,388).
$257* *A Russian Tea Room,* #217/300, s., t., (05-20-93, Bonhams-Chelsea, #144), image 17½ x 23⅛ in., (44.5 x 58.7 cm.), screenprint (BP 165, DM 415, FR 1397, Y 28,379).
$273* *Tango,* #228/275, s., t., (12-10-92, Bonhams-Chelsea, #119), image 21¼ x 34 in., (54 x 86.4 cm.), silkscreen (BP 176, DM 432, FR 1475, Y 33,770).

COOK, Howard American 1901-1980
BI *"Bouganville Barracks Bags",* 1945, s., good cond., est. $6/800, (05-15-93, Cleveland, #100, illus.), 12 x 15⅝ in., (30.5 x 39.7 cm.), lithograph w/tone stone.
$412* *Country Church, Granville MA (Village Church) (F. 126), 1930,* s., #12/30, very good cond., (06-11-93, Doyle, #29), 7⅞ x 5⅞ in., (200 x 149 mm.), aquatint and roulette (BP 271, DM 670, FR 2258, Y 43,714).
$3850* *Financial District (Duffy 155), 1931,* s., d., i. '75', full margins, excellent cond., (11-09-92, Christie-NY, #18, illus.), border 13⅜ x 10⅜ in., (340 x 263 mm.), lithograph on Rives (BP 2545, DM 6146, FR 20,766, Y 477,786).
$1430* *"Grand Canyon" and "Taos Indian", 1927:* Two, s., d., annot., margins, good cond., staining, crease, soiling, prop.Print Corner Coll. of Elizabeth and Charles Whitmore, (02-24-93, Butterfield, #2625), one 12 x 15 in., (305 x 381 mm.), other 12 x 10 in., (305 x 381 mm.), woodcuts on Japan (BP 997, DM 2321, FR 7870, Y 167,801).
$550* *Herring Fisherman (Duffy 85), 1928,* s., i. imp, #50, (05-16-93, Hindman, #560), 5⅞ x 8⅞ in., (14.9 x 22.5 cm.), etching (BP 358, DM 885, FR 2973, Y 60,969).
BI *Jungle Rations, Guadal Canal (Dufy 204), 1944,* s., good cond., est. $5/700, (05-15-93, Cleveland, #99), 15⅞ x 11⅜ in., (40.3 x 28.9 cm.), lithograph.
$3666* *Manhattan Skyscraper, 1929,* s., #15/50, good cond., time-staining, ink mark, attached at sheet edge, (11-30-92, Phillips-London, #370A), sheet 19⅛ x 10 in., (486 x 254 mm.), wood engraving in black on japan (BP 2420, DM 5840, FR 19,827, Y 456,254).
$138* *Mexican Family, 1940,* s., ed. AAA, (11-12-92, Freemn/ Fine Art, #52A), mat 10¼ x 13½ in., (26 x 34.3 cm.), lithograph (BP 91, DM 219, FR 738, Y 17,111).
$220* *"Seated Woman",* s. Howard Cook, very good cond. (?), (04-25-93, Bakker, #61), image 18 x 13 in., (45.7 x 33 cm.), etching w/hand coloring (BP 140, DM 348, FR 1175, Y 24,299).

$935* *Towers,* s., t., annot., i., margins, good cond., crease, soiling, prop. PrintCorner Coll. of Elizabeth and Charles Whitmore, (02-24-93, Butterfield, #2626), 6¹⁵⁄₁₆ x 4¹⁵⁄₁₆ in., (176 x 125 mm.), etching on wove (BP 652, DM 1518, FR 5146, Y 109,716).
BI *"Wachusett" and "Grand Canyon", 1925, 1927:* Two, each s., d., t., 2nd i., margins, good cond., Wachusett w/stains in image, surface soiling, prop. Print Corner Coll. of Elizabeth and Charles Whitmore, est. $1/1,500, (02-24-93, Butterfield, #2624, illus.), one 3¹⁄₁₆ x 5¹⁄₁₆ in., (78 x 129 mm.), other 5¹⁵⁄₁₆ x 7¹⁵⁄₁₆ in., (78 x 129 mm.), etchings on wove & laid.

COOK, T. 20th cent.
$61* *The Wall Street Journal,* s., i. A.D., (12-10-92, Sloan, #582), sight 13¼ x 17¼ in., (33.7 x 43.8 cm.), lithograph (BP 39, DM 96, FR 330, Y 7546).

COOK, Thomas
$702* *The Election Series: Set Of Four,* after William Hogarth, (11-19-92, Bonhams-Chelsea, #170), image 15¾ x 21 in., (40 x 53.3 cm.), hand colored engraving (BP 462, DM 1119, FR 3770, Y 87,303).

COOKE, C., Publisher
$550* *Cooke's Edition Of Select Poet's And Novelists, 1797-1802:* Four Volumes, proof plates, (05-01-93, Skinner, #80), 8⅞ x 1¾ in., (22.5 x 4.5 cm.), 549 engraved plates (BP 350, DM 871, FR 2936, Y 61,023).

COOKE, Edward William English 1811-1880
$50* *The Thames, East Indiaman, 1424 Tons,* laid face to glass, (01-14-93, Bonhams, #105), image 11¼ x 14⅜ in., (28.6 x 36.5 cm.), hand-colored etching (BP 33, DM 82, FR 276, Y 6304).
BI *The Thames, East Indiaman, 1424 Tons,* laid face to glass, verre eglomise mount, est. BP 50/80, (08-12-92, Bonhams, #186), image 11¼ x 14⅜ in., (28.6 x 36.5 cm.), etching w/hand coloring.

COOKE, F.
BI *Englishmen, In And Out Of Uniform, With Rifles: Four,* photog. F. Cooke, Hythe label, est. $3/500, (04-07-93, Swann, #237), each 6 x 8½ in., photograph, albumen print.

COOKE, James E. (after)
BI *"Willow Grouse",* s., (12-11-92, G.A. Key, #49), 12 x 10 in., (30.5 x 25.4 cm.), colored print.

COOPER, Edward (after) British 18th/19th cent.
$77* *The Victory,* pub. Ackermann, (10-18-92, Hindman, #516), 13 x 18⅜ in., (33 x 46.7 cm.), color lithograph (BP 47, DM 115, FR 389, Y 9238).

COOPER, Thomas Sidney English 1803-1902
$16 *"The Meadow" and "The Stable": A Pair,* (12-11-92, G.A. Key, #63), 8 x 10 in., (20.3 x 25.4 cm.), hand colored stone engraving (BP 10, DM 25, FR 86, Y 1980).

COOPER, Thomas Sydney (after)
BI *Cattle By A Pond,* margins, est. BP 50/80, (03-03-93, Bonhams-Chelsea, #41), image, sheet 26½ x 19 in., (67.3 x 48.3 cm.), chromolithograph.
$60* *Cattle By A Pond,* margins, (04-22-93, Bonhams-Chelsea, #62), image 26½ x 19 in., (67.3 x 48.3 cm.), chromolithograph (BP 39, DM 96, FR 325, Y 6597).

COORNHERT, Dirck Volckertsz. Dutch 1519/22-1590
$1733* *Lob Der Tugendsamen Weiber (Hollstein 228, 229; Hollstein 179-182): Six,* after Heemsckerck, (12-04-92, Bassenge, #6125, illus.), etching (BP 1112, DM 2760, FR 9363, Y 216,355).
BI *Meeting Of Joseph And Jacob (Hollstein/Coornhert 35; Hollstein/Heemskerck 40),* after M. VAN HEEMSKERCK, mono., M. Hemskerc inventor plate, #8 of 13, History of Jacob, est. G 350/450, (11-18-92, Bubb Kuyper, #1831), 9¹¹⁄₁₆ x 7¹¹⁄₁₆ in., (24.6 x 19.5 cm.), engraving.
BI *The Queen Of Sheba Before Solomon (Holl. 77; Ill. B., vol. 55, p. 61, no. .016), 1557,* after Frans Floris, small margins, trimmed, losses, tears, made-up losses, defects, laid, est. BP 1,0/1,200, (12-01-92, Christie-London, #5), 15¹⁄₁₆ x 21⅝ in., (383 x 550 mm.), engraving.
BI *Rebekah Returning With Abraham's Servant (Hollstein/ Coornhert 23; Hollstein/Heemskerck 29), 1549,* after M.

VAN HEEMSKERCK, #6 of 8, History of Issac, est. G 350/450, (11-18-92, Bubb Kuyper, #1832), 9⅝ x 7¹¹⁄₁₆ in., (24.5 x 19.6 cm.), engraving.

COPLEY, John Singleton (after) Italian 18th/19th cent.
$99* *The Death Of The Earl Of Chatham,* by Francesco Bartolozzi, 18th/19th cent., (04-02-93, Sloan, #2281), 17¾ x 21⅝ in., (451 x 549 mm.), engraving (BP 65, DM 159, FR 540, Y 11,272).

COPPIN, John S. (after)
$77* *A Comical Hunting Scene,* s., num. #13, d. 1972, (03-25-93, Boos, #632), 15 x 17 in., (38.1 x 43.2 cm.), print (BP 52, DM 126, FR 430, Y 9021).

COPPOLA, James C.
$412* *Nude, c. 1922,* s., (10-14-92, Swann, #415, illus.), 9 x 4¾ in., (22.9 x 12.1 cm.), photograph, toned platinum print (BP 242, DM 603, FR 2045, Y 49,927).

COQUERET, Pierre Charles 1761-c. 1832
$1249* *"Interieur D'Ecurie" and "Le Marchand De Chevaux"* (Dayot 41a-b; Le B. 26-7), c. 1800: Pair, after Carle Vernet, 1st state of 2, watermark, pub. Rolland, trimmed, creases, stains, (12-01-92, Christie-London, #282), sheet 19⅛ x 21⁷⁄₁₆ in., (486 x 545 mm.), etching w/engraving (BP 825, DM 1991, FR 6784, Y 155,503).

CORA, Vladimir Mexican b. 1951
BI *"Bodegon",* s. Vladimir Cora, #4/100, exec. 1991, prov., est. $1,0/1,500, (12-12-92, A. James, #149), 30 x 42 in., (76.2 x 106.7 cm.), lithograph.

CORBASSIERE, Yves
$145* *Serenade Americaine, De J. Auer, Avec Anne Shirley, Dennis Day, 1945,* (01-31-93, Morelle/Marchan, #97), 47¼ x 62¹⁵⁄₁₆ in., (120 x 160 cm.), poster (BP 98, DM 234, FR 790, Y 18,089).

CORBIERE, de la
$210* *Ch. De Fer De L'Etat: Excursions En Normandie, "Le Nez De Jobourg, Presque'Ile Du Cotentin", 1923,* fair cond., (01-23-93, Ribeyre/Baron, #55), 41⁵⁄₁₆ x 29½ in., (105 x 75 cm.), poster (BP 137, DM 334, FR 1130, Y 26,283).

CORBINO, John Italian/American 1905-1964
$220* *Escaped Bull,* s., (09-24-92, Mystic, #14), 10¾ x 13¾ in., (27.3 x 34.9 cm.), lithograph (BP 129, DM 326, FR 1107, Y 26,465).

CORCOS, Lucille American 1908-1973
$55* *The Piano Lesson,* s. Corcos, good cond., (11-21-92, Bakker, #37), image 13½ x 9 in., (34.3 x 22.9 cm.), lithograph (BP 36, DM 88, FR 295, Y 6840).

CORDESSE, Louis
$77* *Relegations, 1976: Set Of Ten,* s., t., d., #6/7, edit. of 9, (06-28-93, Loudmer, #26), 17½ x 11⅝ in., (445 x 295 mm.), black etchings on Arches wove (BP 52, DM 131, FR 441, Y 8170).

CORDIER
$521* *100 Jahre Photographie,* p. Wilh Mehnert, creases, (05-07-93, Christie-S. Ken, #74, illus.), 46½ x 33 in., (118.1 x 83.8 cm.), color lithograph (BP 330, DM 824, FR 2776, Y 57,366).

CORINTH, Lovis German 1858-1925
$480* *Akt Mit Hochgehobenem Hemd (Muller 574), 1922,* artist's proof, s., Euphorion-Verlag, Berlin, (12-05-92, Bassenge, #7101), 10 x 7¹³⁄₁₆ in., (25.4 x 19.9 cm.), etching on wove (BP 301, DM 748, FR 2550, Y 59,472).
$5265* *Antike Legenden (Schwarz 351 II, 2), 1919: Twelve,* s., Marees-Gesellschaft, blindstamp, (12-02-92, Dorling, #2566, illus.), etching on handmade (BP 3396, DM 8280, FR 28,261, Y 655,095).
$1550* *Aus Dem Tiergarten (Schwartz 397), 1920,* s., artist's proof, (09-19-92, Wachholtz, #156), sheet 13⁵⁄₁₆ x 18¹¹⁄₁₆ in., (33.8 x 47.5 cm.), drypoint on copper print paper (BP 907, DM 2300, FR 7868, Y 191,571).
$4794* *Aus Dem Tiergarten (Schwarz 397), 1920,* s., num., (12-05-92, Bassenge, #7099, illus.), 9⅝ x 12½ in., (24.5 x 31.7 cm.), etching on wove (BP 3002, DM 7474, FR 25,473, Y 593,978).
$413* *Bacchantin (Schwarz 121), 1913,* s., margins, front cover illus., (02-17-93, Bonhams-Chelsea, #306, illus.),

plate 8½ x 4 in., (21.6 x 10.2 cm.), drypoint etching (BP 286, DM 671, FR 2272, Y 49,331).
$1701* *"Bahnhof Thier Garten" (Muller 474), 1920/21,* s., t., i. erster Zustand Nro 3, (06-08-93, Karl/Faber, #651, illus.), approx. 8⅞ x 11¹³⁄₁₆ in., (22.5 x 30 cm.), etching on hand-made (BP 1118, DM 2760, FR 9295, Y 180,669).
$2622* *Bank Im Walde II (Sch. 303), 1917,* s., i., artist's proof, (06-08-93, Karl/Faber, #641, illus.), approx. 10¼ x 15⁹⁄₁₆ in., (26 x 39.5 cm.), etching on hand-made Antique (BP 1724, DM 4254, FR 14,328, Y 278,492).
$2743* *"Bank Im Walde II" (Schwarz 303), 1917,* s., artist's proof, (11-28-92, Grisebach, #475, illus.), 10⅝ x 15¹³⁄₁₆ in., (27 x 40.2 cm.), drypoint and handmade (BP 1811, DM 4370, FR 14,835, Y 341,381).
BI *Bathers,* s., #46/75, margins, staining, est. BP 4/600, (10-07-92, Christie-S. Ken, #137), pl 7¼ x 10½ in., (18.4 x 26.7 cm.), drypoint.
$885* *Bauernhof Mit Storchennest (Schwarz 259), 1916,* s., num., (12-05-92, Bassenge, #7104), 14⅞ x 9¹³⁄₁₆ in., (37.8 x 24.9 cm.), lithograph on thick wove (BP 554, DM 1380, FR 4702, Y 109,652).
BI *Baume Mit Sonne (M. 478.), 1920/21,* s., 6 Bll. from the series Der Tiergarten, num., s., est. DM 4500, (12-01-92, Karl/Faber, #486, illus.), 9⁷⁄₁₆ x 11⁷⁄₁₆ in., (24 x 29 cm.), drypoint on wove.
$1328* *Baume Mit Sonne (Muller 478), 1920/21,* s., num., from series Die Teirgarten, (12-05-92, Bassenge, #7100), 9¹³⁄₁₆ x 11¹³⁄₁₆ in., (25 x 30 cm.), drypoint on ivory Japan (BP 832, DM 2070, FR 7056, Y 164,540).
$1245* *Bei Der Toilette (Schw. 380 IX.), 1919,* s., Bl. 9 from the series Bei den Corinthern, pub. E.A. Seemann, (12-01-92, Karl/Faber, #475), 12⅝ x 9⅝ in., (32 x 24.5 cm.), drypoint on hand-made (BP 823, DM 1984, FR 6763, Y 155,005).
$1011* *"Berg-See" (Muller 570), 1921,* sheet 3 of series "Vorfruhling im Gebirge", (11-28-92, Grisebach, #480, illus.), 12⅝ x 16¹⁵⁄₁₆ in., (32 x 43 cm.), lithograph on hand-made Japan (BP 667, DM 1611, FR 5468, Y 125,825).
$371* *Bildnis Wilhelm Trubner (Muller 453), 1913,* s., margins, soiling, foxing, minor handling creases, Late Gerhard Brauer Coll., (05-27-93, Sotheby-Amstrdm, #716, illus.), 11⁹⁄₁₆ x 9⁷⁄₁₆ in., (293 x 239 mm.), etching on wove (BP 238, DM 595, FR 2006, Y 39,773, G 667).
BI *Der Bischof Und Adelheid Beim Schach (Muller 521/B), 1920-21,* from Erich Steinthal's Goethe, s., i. #2, pub. Verlag Fritz Gurlitt, full margins, good cond., est. $1/1,500, (02-11-93, Sotheby-NY, #107), 10¹³⁄₁₆ x 8⁷⁄₁₆ in., (275 x 215 mm.), drypoint on Zanders.
$3524* *Bismarckfeier (Schwarz L 209), 1915,* s., num., (05-26-93, Lempertz, #90, illus.), 16⁹⁄₁₆ x 12⅜ in., (42 x 31.4 cm.), color lithograph heightened w/gouache on hand-made (BP 2280, DM 5750, FR 19,352, Y 382,877).
BI *Buchenwald (M. 572.), 1922,* s., est. DM 4000, (12-01-92, Karl/Faber, #491, illus.), 12⅝ x 16¹⁵⁄₁₆ in., (32 x 43 cm.), lithograph.
$1410* *Buchenwald (Muller 572), 1921,* s., artist's proof, i., from series Vorfruhling im Gebirge, (05-26-93, Dorling, #2609, illus.), 12⅝ x 16¹⁵⁄₁₆ in., (32 x 43 cm.), lithograph on handmade (BP 912, DM 2301, FR 7743, Y 153,194).
$1180* *Buchenwald (Muller 572), 1922,* s., from Vorfurhling im Gebirge, (12-05-92, Bassenge, #7107), 12¹¹⁄₁₆ x 16¹⁵⁄₁₆ in., (32.2 x 43 cm.), lithograph on wove (BP 739, DM 1840, FR 6270, Y 146,202).
$794* *"Buchenwald" (Muller 572), 1921,* sheet 5 of series "Vorfruhling im Gerbirge", artist's proof, (11-28-92, Grisebach, #482, illus.), 12⁹⁄₁₆ x 16¾ in., (31.9 x 42.5 cm.), lithograph on handmade (BP 524, DM 1265, FR 4294, Y 98,818).
BI *Calisto Und Zeus-Artemis (Schw. 401 VII.), 1920,* s., Bl. 7 from the series Leibschaften des Zeus, pub. Fritz Gurlitt, est. DM 1800, (12-01-92, Karl/Faber, #478), 9¹³⁄₁₆ x 12⅝ in., (25 x 32 cm.), color lithograph on smooth paper.
BI *Danae Und Der Goldregen (Schwarz 401 V), 1920,* s., artist's proof, Bl.5 from the series Liebschaften des Zeus, est. DM 2200, (06-10-93, Hauswedell/Nolt, #193, illus.), image 10¼ x 12¹⁵⁄₁₆ in., (26 x 33 cm.), color lithograph.
$173* *Der Dichter Mit Der Leier (Schwarz 383 I.), 1919,* s., i., artist's proof, series Der Venuswagen, (11-27-92, Zeller,

#614), 11⁷⁄₁₆ x 9¼ in., (29 x 23.5 cm.), color lithograph (BP 114, DM 276, FR 939, Y 21,531).

$384* *(Dog),* s., i. probedruck, margins, good cond., occasional foxing, very minor light staining, Late Gerhard Brauer Coll., (05-27-93, Sotheby-Amstrdm, #719), 5⅜ x 3¹⁵⁄₁₆ in., (137 x 100 mm.), etching on wove (BP 246, DM 616, FR 2077, Y 41,166, G 690).

$706* *Doppelbildnis Mit Skelett (Schwarz 278), 1916,* s., plate mono., d., (06-10-93, Hauswedell/Nolt, #187), image 5⅞ x 3¹⁵⁄₁₆ in., (14.9 x 10 cm.), etching on wove (BP 462, DM 1150, FR 3871, Y 74,939).

$1417* *Ehepaar Goeritz (M. 488), 1920/21,* print plate, M. 488 and artist's proof, (06-08-93, Karl/Faber, #652), approx. 11¹³⁄₁₆ x 8¹¹⁄₁₆ in., (30 x 22 cm.), etched plate w/one print (BP 932, DM 2299, FR 7743, Y 150,505).

$1907* *Eight Unpublished Drypoints (Muller 863, 885, 886), 1923-25: Seventeen,* #III/IIX, hors commerce, estate blindstamp, s. Thomas Corinth, (06-10-93, Hauswedell/ Nolt, #212), image 9⁵⁄₁₆ x 11¹³⁄₁₆ in., (23.6 x 30 cm.), drypoint in black/brown on simili-Japan (BP 1247, DM 3105, FR 10,455, Y 202,420).

$1826* *"Eine Vision" (M. 680/II.), 1923,* s., (12-01-92, Karl/ Faber, #493), 19⅛ x 23¹⁄₁₆ in., (48.5 x 58.5 cm.), drypoint on hand-made Van Gelder Zonen (BP 1206, DM 2910, FR 9919, Y 227,341).

$409* *Europa Und Der Stier (Schwarz 383 III), 1919,* from series Der Venuswagen, (05-26-93, Dorling, #2608, illus.), 9¹³⁄₁₆ x 8¼ in., (25 x 21 cm.), color lithograph on hand-made (BP 265, DM 667, FR 2246, Y 44,437).

$352* *Ex Libris F. Kruse (Scharz 368 B), 1919,* s., (05-26-93, Dorling, #2607, illus.), 5¹³⁄₁₆ x 4¹¹⁄₁₆ in., (14.7 x 11.9 cm.), etching on thick wove (BP 228, DM 574, FR 1933, Y 38,244).

$498* *Frau Und Krieger (Schw. 158.), 1914,* s., artist's proof, (12-01-92, Karl/Faber, #467), 18¹¹⁄₁₆ x 11 in., (47.5 x 28 cm.), lithograph on wove (BP 329, DM 794, FR 2705, Y 62,002).

$737* *Frauenraub IV (Schwarz 176.III), 1914,* #11/25, s., (09-04-92, Germann, #292, illus.), 17¹¹⁄₁₆ x 12¹³⁄₁₆ in., (450 x 325 mm.), etching (BP 369, DM 1033, FR 3516, Y 90,719, SF 920).

$2483* *Fridericus Rex, 1922: Twenty-Nine,* s., Gurlitt, (06-05-93, Bassenge, #5975), lithograph on hand-made (BP 1635, DM 4026, FR 13,568, Y 266,359).

$847* *Friedrich Von Schiller, Die Rauber (Muller 797-808), 1923: Twelve,* s., ded., (06-10-93, Hauswedell/Nolt, #209), approx. 9⁷⁄₁₆ x 6⅞ in., (24 x 17.5 cm.), lithograph (BP 554, DM 1379, FR 4644, Y 89,906).

$866* *Fruhling Am Walchensee (Muller 569), 1921,* s., from series Vorfruhling im Gebirge, 1922, pub. Euphorion, (11-21-92, Lempertz, #92), 12⁹⁄₁₆ x 17³⁄₁₆ in., (31.9 x 43.6 cm.), lithograph on wove (BP 570, DM 1381, FR 4651, Y 107,698).

$847* *Die Geburt Der Venus III (Schwarz 273 II), 1916,* s., plate t., (06-10-93, Hauswedell/Nolt, #186, illus.), image 15⅞ x 10⅞ in., (40.4 x 27.6 cm.), drypoint on wove (BP 554, DM 1379, FR 4644, Y 89,906).

$636* *Goethe, Geschichte Gottfriedens Von Berlichingen Mit Der Eisernen Hand (Muller 514-Turnier-Ritter. M. 524), 1921/22: Seven,* (06-10-93, Hauswedell/Nolt, #198), pl 3⅞ x 6⁷⁄₁₆ in., (9.9 x 16.3 cm.), etching (BP 416, DM 1036, FR 3487, Y 67,509).

$4581* *Das Hohe Lied (Schwarz L 82), 1911: Twenty-Six,* Paul Cassirer, #37/60, s., (05-26-93, Lempertz, #87, illus.), 18⅛ x 12¹⁵⁄₁₆ in., (46 x 33 cm.), color lithograph on royal Japan (BP 2964, DM 7474, FR 25,157, Y 497,718).

$1059* *Hohenfriedberg (Muller 601), 1921,* s., t., artist's proof, from the series Fridericus Rex, (06-10-93, Hauswedell/ Nolt, #201, illus.), image 12¾ x 10¹¹⁄₁₆ in., (32.4 x 27.2 cm.), color lithograph on wove (BP 693, DM 1724, FR 5806, Y 112,408).

$496* *Homerisches Gelachter (Sch. 395/IV), 1920,* s., num., E.A. Seemann, (06-08-93, Karl/Faber, #643), approx. 9⁷⁄₁₆ x 12⅝ in., (24 x 32 cm.), etching and drypoint on hand-made (BP 326, DM 805, FR 2710, Y 52,682).

BI *Im Atelier (Schw. 380 XII.), 1919,* s., sheet 12 from the series Bei den Corinthern, est. DM 7500, (12-01-92, Karl/Faber, #476, illus.), 12⅜ x 9⅝ in., (31.5 x 24.5 cm.), etching on hand-made.

$3970* *"Im Atelier" (Schwarz 380/XII), 1919,* s., sheet 12 of series "Bei den Corinthern", (11-28-92, Grisebach, #477, illus.), 12½ x 9¹¹⁄₁₆ in., (31.8 x 24.6 cm.), drypoint on handmade (BP 2620, DM 6325, FR 21,471, Y 494,088).

$465* *Im Bett I. (Schw. 37.), 1909,* s., pub. Commeterschen Kunsthandlung, (12-01-92, Karl/Faber, #463), 5½ x 7½ in., (14 x 19 cm.), etching and drypoint on hand-made (BP 307, DM 741, FR 2526, Y 57,893).

$2477* *Im Paradies (M. 539-545): Seven,* s., trimmed, (10-09-92, Winterberg, #1951), smallest 12¹³⁄₁₆ x 12³⁄₁₆ in., (32.5 x 31 cm.), largest 13¾ x 12⅝ in., (32.5 x 31 cm.), color lithograph on wove (BP 1470, DM 3679, FR 12,354, Y 301,558).

$750* *Interieur Mit Frau (Schw., 307/I, 1), 1917,* s. Zustand I, 1, mount staining, (12-01-92, Karl/Faber, #470), 9¹⁄₁₆ x 6⁵⁄₁₆ in., (23 x 16 cm.), drypoint on hand-made (BP 496, DM 1195, FR 4074, Y 93,376).

$388* *Interieur Mit Frau (Schwarz 307 II), 1917,* s., t., (05-26-93, Dorling, #2606, illus.), 9⁷⁄₁₆ x 6⁵⁄₁₆ in., (24 x 16 cm.), etching on handmade (BP 251, DM 633, FR 2131, Y 42,156).

$1394* *Joseph Deutet Dem Pharao Die Traume (Schwartz 5, V, III), 1894,* sheet 5 of series Tragikomodien, artist's proof, s.; mono., d. in plate, (10-09-92, Winterberg, #1924, illus.), 13⅜ x 16⁹⁄₁₆ in., (34 x 42 cm.), etching on hand-made (BP 827, DM 2071, FR 6953, Y 169,710).

$457* *"Kain" (Schw. 208.), 1915,* artist's proof, s. Charlotte Berend-Corinth, Nachlass Lovis Corinth,tears in margin, slight creases, (12-01-92, Karl/Faber, #468), lithograph (BP 302, DM 728, FR 2482, Y 56,897).

$597* *Kapuzinerpredigt (M. 813.), 1923,* s., 1st state, from the series of 6 Bll. Wallensteins Lager, restoredtears, traces of mounting, (12-01-92, Karl/Faber, #496), etching on wove (BP 394, DM 952, FR 3243, Y 74,328).

$1452* *Kastanienbaume (M. 700.), 1923,* s., num., light-stained, traces of old mounting, (12-01-92, Karl/Faber, #494), 9⁷⁄₁₆ x 10⅝ in., (24 x 27 cm.), drypoint on Japan (BP 959, DM 2314, FR 7887, Y 180,777).

$738* *Kastanienbaume (Muller 700), 1923,* s., (12-05-92, Bassenge, #7102), 9½ x 10⅞ in., (24.2 x 27.6 cm.), drypoint on handmade (BP 462, DM 1151, FR 3921, Y 91,438).

BI *Kind Im Bett Und Mutter (Schwarz 117), 1913,* s., artist's proof, est. DM 2400, (12-05-92, Bassenge, #7092), 9⁵⁄₁₆ x 6¼ in., (23.6 x 15.8 cm.), etching on handmade.

$1475* *Klopstockstrasse (Schwarz 304), 1917,* Erster Zustand Nro 1, s., (12-05-92, Bassenge, #7096), 11¼ x 9⁵⁄₁₆ in., (28.5 x 23.6 cm.), drypoint on thick copper print paper (BP 924, DM 2300, FR 7837, Y 182,753).

$847* *Konig Lear. (Muller 491-498), 1921: Seven,* #17/150, F. Gurlitt, estate blindstamp, (06-10-93, Hauswedell/Nolt, #207), image 5⅞ x 8¼ in., (15 x 21 cm.), etching on copper print paper (BP 554, DM 1379, FR 4644, Y 89,906).

$664* *Konig Und Konigin Von Golkonde Auf Dem Thron (Muller 507), 1920,* s., artist's proof, from Die Konigin von Golkonde series, (12-05-92, Bassenge, #7106), 10¹⁄₁₆ x 9¹⁄₁₆ in., (25.5 x 23 cm.), color lithograph on machine-made (BP 416, DM 1035, FR 3528, Y 82,270).

$7062* *Die Konigin Von Golkonde (Muller 499-505, 507-511), 1920-21: Twelve,* s., IX, num. 50, (06-10-93, Hauswedell/ Nolt, #208, illus.), overall size 20⅞ x 15¾ in., (53 x 40 cm.), color lithograph on hand-made (BP 4619, DM 11,500, FR 38,717, Y 749,602).

$605* *Krankenschwester, 1914, Schwarz 199,* s., annot. probedruck, (09-20-92, Hindman, #765), 8 x 5⅞ in., (20.3 x 14.9 cm.), drypoint on Japan tissue (BP 354, DM 898, FR 3071, Y 74,774).

$2158* *Kreuzigung (M. 554.), 1920/21,* s., Bl. 2 from the series of 10 Kompositionen, pub. Propylaen, (12-01-92, Karl/ Faber, #488), 11¼ x 9¹⁄₁₆ in., (28.5 x 23 cm.), drypoint on wove (BP 1426, DM 3440, FR 11,722, Y 268,675).

$851* *Der Kunstler Und Der Tod I (Schwarz 238 II),* s., (06-05-93, Bassenge, #5956, illus.), 10½ x 7¹¹⁄₁₆ in., (26.6 x 19.5 cm.), etching on hand-made (BP 560, DM 1380, FR 4650, Y 91,289).

$149* *Der Kuss (Muller 575),* s., (10-30-92, Sloan, #2818), 9⅜ x 7⅛ in., (23.8 x 18.1 cm.), drypoint etching (BP 95, DM 229, FR 778, Y 18,457).

$2412* *Landschaft (Schwarz 235), 1917,* s., Gurlitt, (06-05-93, Bassenge, #5955, illus.), 9¾ x 11½ in., (24.7 x 29.2 cm.), etching on hand-made (BP 1588, DM 3911, FR 13,180, Y 258,743).

$621* *Landschaft Mit Kuhen (Schwarz 306), 1917,* s., (06-10-93, Hauswedell/Nolt, #188), image 5 7/16 x 7¾ in., (13.8 x 19.7 cm.), etching on wove (BP 406, DM 1011, FR 3405, Y 65,917).

$1011* *"Leda Und Der Schwan" (Schwarz 401/BII), 1920,* s., sheet 2 of series "Die Liebschaften des Zeus", Berlin, pub. Fritz Gurlitt, (11-28-92, Grisebach, #478, illus.), 10⅝ x 13⅜ in., (27 x 34 cm.), colored lithograph on handmade (BP 667, DM 1611, FR 5468, Y 125,825).

$1038* *Liegender Akt Mit Stehenden Modellen (Sch. 157.), 1914,* s., num., (12-01-92, Karl/Faber, #466), 14 3/16 x 16¾ in., (36 x 42.5 cm.), lithograph on Japan (BP 686, DM 1654, FR 5638, Y 129,233).

$780* *Liegender Weiblicher Akt, Studie Zu Joseph Und Potiphar (Schwarz 215)1915,* s., (06-05-93, Bassenge, #5954), 7¾ x 10½ in., (19.7 x 26.7 cm.), etching on hand-made Van Gelder Zonen (BP 513, DM 1265, FR 4262, Y 83,673).

$2444* *Lovis Corinth (mull. 792-796), 1924: Five,* s., num., frontispiece, Ausgabe C, (06-23-93, Kornfeld, #277), 16⅛ x 12 in., (41 x 30.5 cm.), lithograph (BP 1660, DM 4135, FR 13,910, Y 266,260, SF 3680).

BI *Lovis Corinth, Fritz Gurlitt (Schwarz 185V), c. 1918,* p. von H. Birkholtz, remains of stains, excell. cond., est. BP 6/800, (05-20-93, Christie-London, #494, illus.), sheet 28 x 19 in., (71.1 x 48.3 cm.), lithograph in b/w, backed on Japan.

$6872* *Lovis Corinth. Probedrucke Zu Goethes Goetz, 1923: Eleven,* privatdruck Berlin, in brown leather binding, s., artist's proof, (06-23-93, Kornfeld, #276), 16 7/16 x 11 13/16 in., (41.8 x 30 cm.), on thick Japan (BP 4668, DM 11,628, FR 39,112, Y 748,665, SF 10,350).

$197* *Die Lowenbrucke Im Berliner Tiergarten (Schwarz 365), 1919,* 1st state, (03-24-93, Venator/Hansten, #4474), pl. 7⅞ x 6 9/16 in., (20 x 16.7 cm.), drypoint on China (BP 133, DM 322, FR 1095, Y 23,147).

BI *"Lowenbrucke" (Schwarz 365/II), 1919,* s., est. DM 1,9/2,100, (11-28-92, Grisebach, #476, illus.), 7⅞ x 6 5/16 in., (20 x 16 cm.), drypoint on copper print paper.

BI *"Ma Belle Mere" (Schw. 380 XIV.), 1919,* s., est. DM 4800, (12-01-92, Karl/Faber, #477, illus.), etching on hand-made.

$6638* *Obstgarten (Sch. 93.), 1912,* s., pub. Paul Cassirer, light-stained, traces of old mounting verso, (12-01-92, Karl/Faber, #465, illus.), 14 3/16 x 19⅛ in., (36 x 48.5 cm.), lithograph on Japan (BP 4386, DM 10,580, FR 36,056, Y 826,444).

$1697* *Obstgarten (Schwarz 341), 1918,* s., Gurlitt-Verlag, Berlin, (12-05-92, Bassenge, #7097), 6¾ x 10 15/16 in., (17.1 x 27.8 cm.), etching on Japan (BP 1063, DM 2646, FR 9017, Y 210,259).

$1701* *Obstgarten Im Herbst (Schwarz 108), 1912,* s., pub. Gurlitt-Verlag, (06-08-93, Karl/Faber, #636), approx. 7 11/16 x 10¼ in., (19.5 x 26 cm.), etching on hand-made (BP 1118, DM 2760, FR 9295, Y 180,669).

BI *Odysseus Und Die Freier. Akt Mit Hochgehobenem Hemd. (Schwarz 172 bzw. Muller 574), 1914/1921,* #2/25, est. DM 2,500, (05-26-93, Lempertz, #88), 15 1/16 x 11 1/16 in., (38.3 x 28.1 cm.), etching (drypoint) on Van Gelden.

BI *Orpheus (Schwarz 351 IV II), 1919,* s., Bl. 4 from the series Antike Legenden, blindstamp, est. DM 2000, (06-10-93, Hauswedell/Nolt, #190, illus.), image 9 13/16 x 12 11/16 in., (25 x 32.2 cm.), drypoint on hand-made.

$1991* *Partie Aus Dem Tiergarten (Schw. 405.), 1920,* s., artist's proof, (12-01-92, Karl/Faber, #479, illus.), 9⅝ x 7 11/16 in., (24.5 x 19.5 cm.), drypoint on hand-made (BP 1315, DM 3173, FR 10,815, Y 247,883).

BI *Prosit Neujahr 1895 (Schwarz 10), 1894,* s., est. DM 400, (12-01-92, Karl/Faber, #461), etching on Japan.

$217* *Reclining Female Nude (Schwartz 90),* s. #8/25, margins, foxing, (05-27-93, Sotheby-Amstrdm, #717), 7 7/16 x 11 7/16 in., (189 x 291 mm.), etching on wove (BP 139, DM 348, FR 1174, Y 23,263, G 391).

$433* *"Der Ritter" (Schwarz 173), 1914,* s., (11-28-92, Grisebach, #472, illus.), 5 13/16 x 4⅛ in., (14.7 x 10.5 cm.), drypoint (BP 286, DM 690, FR 2342, Y 53,889).

$542* *"Ruhender Dreiviertelakt" (Schwarz 61), 1911,* s., in "Zeitschrift fur bildende Kunst", NF, XXII, (11-28-92, Grisebach, #471, illus.), 4 15/16 x 6 15/16 in., (12.6 x 17.7 cm.), etching with soft-ground etching and plate tone on handmade (BP 358, DM 863, FR 2931, Y 67,455).

$110* *Sans Souci,* s., plate t., creases, soiling, foxing, (12-12-92, Weschler, #115), 10 x 15 in., (25.4 x 38.1 cm.), soft-ground etching (BP 71, DM 173, FR 594, Y 13,612).

$3121* *Sanssouci (Schwarz 284), 1916,* s., Gurlitt, (06-05-93, Bassenge, #5969, illus.), 9¾ x 15 9/16 in., (24.7 x 39.5 cm.), lithograph on hand-made (BP 2055, DM 5060, FR 17,055, Y 334,799).

BI *"Sanssouci" (Schwarz 284), 1916,* s., est. DM 6/7,000, (11-28-92, Grisebach, #128, illus.), 9¾ x 15 7/16 in., (24.8 x 39.2 cm.), lithograph on Japan.

$885* *Schlafender Lowe (Muller 667), 1923,* s., Verlag Fritz Gurlitt, (12-05-92, Bassenge, #7108), 7⅞ x 12⅜ in., (20 x 31.5 cm.), watercolor and chalk lithograph on hand-made (BP 554, DM 1380, FR 4702, Y 109,652).

BI *See-Ufer (M. 568.), 1920/21,* s., Bl. 1 of 5 from the series Vorfruhling im Gebirge, pub. Euphorion, light-stained, traces of old mounting, est. DM 10/12,000, (12-01-92, Karl/Faber, #489, illus.), 12⅝ x 16 15/16 in., (32 x 43 cm.), lithograph on wove.

$4252* *Selbstbildnis (M. 903),* s., i., artist's proof, watermark, (06-08-93, Karl/Faber, #660, illus.), approx. 12 13/16 x 9 1/16 in., (32.5 x 23 cm.), lithograph on Bergisch Gladbach hand-made (BP 2795, DM 6899, FR 23,235, Y 451,620).

$3485* *Selbstbildnis (M. 917.), 1916?,* s., traces of old mounting, (12-01-92, Karl/Faber, #498, illus.), 3 15/16 x 1¾ in., (10 x 4.5 cm.), etching on copper print paper (BP 2303, DM 5555, FR 18,930, Y 433,889).

BI *Selbstbildnis (Muller 464), 1920,* s., est. DM 7500, (12-01-92, Karl/Faber, #484, illus.), 11 13/16 x 9 7/16 in., (30 x 24 cm.), lithograph on hand-made.

$1412* *Selbstbildnis (Muller 470), 1920,* s., d., num. 95/100, (06-10-93, Hauswedell/Nolt, #196, illus.), image 9¼ x 5 11/16 in., (23.5 x 14.5 cm.), lithograph on wove (BP 924, DM 2299, FR 7741, Y 149,878).

BI *Selbstbildnis (S. 409), 1920,* from Pfister, good cond., staining, tape, crease, est. $5/700, (02-24-93, Butterfield, #2910), 12⅜ x 9 9/16 in., (314 x 243 mm.), lithograph on heavy wove.

$1417* *Selbstbildnis (Sch. 409), 1920,* s., num., (06-08-93, Karl/Faber, #647, illus.), approx. 12⅝ x 9 13/16 in., (32 x 25 cm.), lithograph on hand-made (BP 932, DM 2299, FR 7743, Y 150,505).

$5393* *Selbstbildnis (Schw. 414.), 1920,* Fritz Gurlitt, s. in red, trimmed, (12-01-92, Karl/Faber, #480, illus.), 9 7/16 x 7 1/16 in., (24 x 18 cm.), etching (BP 3563, DM 8596, FR 29,294, Y 671,439).

BI *Selbstbildnis (Schw. 426.), 1920,* s. in 2. Auflage von: K. Schwarz, Lovis Corinth, Fritz Gurlitt, Berlin, 1922, light-staining, traces of old mounting, est. DM 2200, (12-01-92, Karl/Faber, #482), 4½ x 3⅜ in., (11.5 x 8.5 cm.), drypoint on hand-made.

$5791* *Selbstbildnis (Schwarz 407), 1920,* s., stone s., d., (06-10-93, Hauswedell/Nolt, #194, illus.), image 11 7/16 x 9 13/16 in., (29 x 25 cm.), lithograph on wove (BP 3788, DM 9430, FR 31,749, Y 614,691).

$4149* *Selbstbildnis An Der Staffelei (Schw. 337.), 1918,* s., (12-01-92, Karl/Faber, #474, illus.), 9 7/16 x 6½ in., (24 x 16.5 cm.), etching on hand-made (BP 2741, DM 6613, FR 22,537, Y 516,559).

$1033* *Selbstbildnis Im Strohhut (Schwarz 129 B), 1913,* s., (12-05-92, Bassenge, #7093), 5⅞ x 4⅝ in., (15 x 11.7 cm.), etching on Japan (BP 647, DM 1611, FR 5489, Y 127,989).

$2323* *Selbstbildnis Mit Barett (Schw. 318), 1918,* s., (12-01-92, Karl/Faber, #472), 7⅞ x 7⅞ in., (20 x 20 cm.), drypoint on hand-made (BP 1535, DM 3703, FR 12,618, Y 289,218).

$2240* *Selbstbildnis Mit Gattin (Schw. 23.), 1904,* s., (12-01-92, Karl/Faber, #462), 7 11/16 x 6⅞ in., (19.5 x 17.5 cm.), drypoint on hand-made (BP 1480, DM 3570, FR 12,167, Y 278,884).

$3319* *Selbstbildnis Und Mannlicher Akt (Schw. 298.), 1917,* s., artist's proof, prov., (12-01-92, Karl/Faber, #469, illus.), 8¹¹⁄₁₆ x 6⅛ in., (22 x 15.5 cm.), etching on hand-made (BP 2193, DM 5290, FR 18,028, Y 413,222).

$1299* *"Selbstbildnis", 1922,* s., (11-28-92, Grisebach, #484, illus.), 7⅞ x 6¹³⁄₁₆ in., (20 x 17.3 cm.), lithograph on handmade (BP 857, DM 2069, FR 7025, Y 161,668).

$2979* *Selbstbildnis, Zeichnend (Muller 873), 1924,* s., (06-05-93, Bassenge, #5967), 12³⁄₁₆ x 9¹³⁄₁₆ in., (31 x 25 cm.), drypoint on hand-made (BP 1961, DM 4830, FR 16,279, Y 319,567).

$10,593* *Selbstbildnis, Zeichnend. (Muller 873), 1925,* s., t., Artist Proof No I, (06-10-93, Hauswedell/Nolt, #206, illus.), image 12³⁄₁₆ x 9¹³⁄₁₆ in., (31 x 25 cm.), drypoint on simili-Japan (BP 6929, DM 17,250, FR 58,076, Y 1,124,403).

$505* *"St. Georg" (Schwarz 180 II), 1916,* s., (11-28-92, Grisebach, #473, illus.), 10³⁄₁₆ x 4¹⁵⁄₁₆ in., (25.9 x 12.5 cm.), drypoint on handmade (BP 333, DM 805, FR 2731, Y 62,850).

$2655* *Strasse In Konigsberg (Schw. L 321.), 1918,* s., artist's proof, brown stained, (12-01-92, Karl/Faber, #473, illus.), 15⅜ x 9⅝ in., (39 x 24.5 cm.), lithograph on hand-made (BP 1754, DM 4232, FR 14,422, Y 330,553).

$1836* *Strasse In Konigsberg (Schwarz 306), 1918,* s., collector's stamp, (06-10-93, Hauswedell/Nolt, #189), image 15⅜ x 9¹¹⁄₁₆ in., (39 x 24.6 cm.), lithograph on hand-made (BP 1201, DM 2990, FR 10,066, Y 194,884).

$2260* *Die Sundfluth (Muller 815-822), 1923: Eight,* s., stone t., watermark, (06-10-93, Hauswedell/Nolt, #210), sh 25⁹⁄₁₆ x 31½ in., (65 x 80 cm.), lithograph on wove (BP 1478, DM 3680, FR 12,390, Y 239,890).

$2260* *Die Sundfluth (Muller 815-822), 1923: Eight,* s., stone t., watermark, (06-10-93, Hauswedell/Nolt, #211), sh 25⁹⁄₁₆ x 31½ in., (65 x 80 cm.), lithograph on wove (BP 1478, DM 3680, FR 12,390, Y 239,890).

$1063* *Tal-Grund (M. 571), 1922,* s., from series Vorfruhling im Gebirge, blindstamp, (06-08-93, Karl/Faber, #655), approx. 12⅝ x 16¹⁵⁄₁₆ in., (32 x 43 cm.), sh approx. 17¹¹⁄₁₆ x 22¹³⁄₁₆ in., (32 x 43 cm.), lithograph on cream wove (BP 699, DM 1725, FR 5809, Y 112,905).

BI *Tal-Grund (M. 571.), 1922,* s., from the series Vorfruhling im Gebirge, pub. Euphorion, est. DM 5000, (12-01-92, Karl/Faber, #490, illus.), 12⅝ x 16¹⁵⁄₁₆ in., (32 x 43 cm.), lithograph on wove.

$1135* *"Tal-Grund" (Muller 571), 1922,* s., sheet 4 of series Vorfruhling im Gebirge, pub. Euphorion, (06-05-93, Grisebach, #548, illus.), 12½ x 16⅝ in., (31.7 x 42.3 cm.), lithograph on copper print paper (BP 747, DM 1840, FR 6202, Y 121,755).

$581* *Tanzende Am Strande (Schw. 308/I), 1917,* s. Nro 1a Zustand, margin, stains, (12-01-92, Karl/Faber, #471), 11¼ x 11¼ in., (28.5 x 28.5 cm.), etching (BP 384, DM 926, FR 3156, Y 72,336).

$1235* *Tanzerinnen, (Schwarz 17), 1895,* s., pub. Gurlitt, Berlin; light stains, (10-14-92, Germann, #12, illus.), 9⅜ x 12⅛ in., (238 x 308 mm.), etching (BP 725, DM 1807, FR 6129, Y 149,661, SF 1610).

$640* *(Theft Of The Virgin),* s., #53, margins, good cond., minor paper discoloration, some foxing, Late Gerhard Brauer Coll., (05-27-93, Sotheby-Amstrdm, #718, illus.), 9⅝ x 11¹³⁄₁₆ in., (245 x 300 mm.), etching on wove (BP 410, DM 1027, FR 3461, Y 68,611, G 1150).

BI *Tierstude, Fuchse Und Schakale (Schwarz 310), 1905,* s., full margins, creasing, est. $800/1,000, (05-11-93, Christie-NY, #184, illus.), borderline 14¾ x 10⅝ in., (375 x 270 mm.), lithograph on laid.

$2655* *Tod Bei Strucks (M. 550.), 1920/21,* s., 6 Bll. from the series Totentanz, artist's proof, stained, (12-01-92, Karl/Faber, #487), 9¼ x 6⅞ in., (23.5 x 17.5 cm.), etching on hand-made (BP 1754, DM 4232, FR 14,422, Y 330,553).

$425* *Tod Und Greis (M. 548), 1920/21,* s., from series of 6 sheets, Totentanz, (06-08-93, Karl/Faber, #654), approx. 9¼ x 6⅞ in., (23.5 x 17.5 cm.), soft-ground etching on hand-made (BP 279, DM 690, FR 2322, Y 45,141).

$465* *Turnier (Schwarz L430, III), 1920,* s., (09-25-92, Granier, #2799), sheet 18⁵⁄₁₆ x 12⅝ in., (46.5 x 32 cm.), lithograph on beige machine hand-made (BP 272, DM 689, FR 2331, Y 56,126).

BI *Turnierstunde (Schw. 428 IV.), 1920,* s., Bl. 4 from the series Anna Boleyn, artist's proof, est. DM 1000, (12-01-92, Karl/Faber, #483), 12⅝ x 9¹⁄₁₆ in., (32 x 23 cm.), lithograph on hand-made.

BI *Urfeld-Walchensee (M. 675.), 1923,* s., light-stained, traces of old mounting, est. DM 5800, (12-01-92, Karl/Faber, #492, illus.), 7½ x 11⅝ in., (19 x 29.5 cm.), drypoint on wove.

BI *Der Venuswagen, 1919: Eight,* illus., s., num. 285, est. FF5/6,000, (05-27-93, Briest, #68), color lithographs.

BI *Waldlandschaft Mit Haus, 1920,* s., est. DM 5500, (12-01-92, Karl/Faber, #485, illus.), 12³⁄₁₆ x 9⅝ in., (31 x 24.5 cm.), lithograph on hand-made.

$1154* *Wallensteins Lager Von Friedrich Schiller (Muller 809), 1922,* pub. Tillger, #39/100, s., (11-21-92, Lempertz, #94), 15¼ x 12⅜ in., (38.7 x 31.5 cm.), etching on hand-made (BP 760, DM 1840, FR 6198, Y 143,514).

$411* *Weiblicher Akt Auf Einem Stuhl (Schwartz 4), 1893,* s., (04-21-93, Germann, #349, illus.), 8¼ x 6¹¹⁄₁₆ in., (210 x 170 mm.), etching (BP 267, DM 657, FR 2222, Y 45,500, SF 598).

$499* *Weiblicher Akt Im Lehnsessel (M. 154), 1914,* s., i. Probedruck, pub. F. Gurlitt, margins, rubbing, tape, (12-01-92, Christie-London, #345), L. 12⁹⁄₁₆ x 8⁷⁄₁₆ in., (319 x 214 mm.), lithograph on wove (BP 330, DM 795, FR 2710, Y 62,126).

$354* *Weiblicher Akt In Abwehr (Sch. 136), 1913,* s., num., pub. Gurlitt-Verlag, (06-08-93, Karl/Faber, #637), approx. 10⁷⁄₁₆ x 11⁷⁄₁₆ in., (26.5 x 29 cm.), lithograph on van Geldern (BP 233, DM 574, FR 1934, Y 37,600).

$258* *Weiblicher Akt In Abwehr (Schwarz 136), 1913,* s., Gurlitt-Verlag, Berlin, light staining, (12-05-92, Bassenge, #7103), 10⅝ x 11¹³⁄₁₆ in., (27 x 30 cm.), lithograph on thick wove (BP 162, DM 402, FR 1371, Y 31,966).

$443* *Weissagung (Schwarz 152), 1914,* s., (12-05-92, Bassenge, #7094), 7¹³⁄₁₆ x 9⅝ in., (19.8 x 24.5 cm.), drypoint on van Gelder-Zonen (BP 277, DM 691, FR 2354, Y 54,888).

$674* *Westminster-Abtei (Sch. 428/XIV), 1920,* s., i., artist proof from the series Anna Boleyn, (06-08-93, Karl/Faber, #648), approx. 12⅝ x 9¹³⁄₁₆ in., (32 x 25 cm.), lithograph on thick paper (BP 443, DM 1094, FR 3683, Y 71,588).

$1877* *"Wilhelm Tell" (Muller 775-787; Pommeranz-Liedtke S. 179), 1923: Thirteen,* s., (11-28-92, Grisebach, #483, illus.), 14¹⁵⁄₁₆ x 10¹³⁄₁₆ in., (38 x 27.5 cm.), colored lithograph on handmade (BP 1239, DM 2990, FR 10,151, Y 233,603).

BI *Wilhelm Tell, Zwolf Farbige Lithographien Von Lovis Corinth (Muller 775-787 and 790): Thirteen,* two t., i. Probedruck, three studio stamped, tears, est. DM 6,500-, (11-21-92, Lempertz, #95), each approx. 9¼ x 7¹⁄₁₆ in., (23.5 x 18 cm.), color lithograph.

$1239* *Windmuhle (Schw. 340), 1918,* s., (10-09-92, Winterberg, #1938), 4¾ x 6⅛ in., (12 x 15.5 cm.), drypoint on handmade (BP 735, DM 1840, FR 6180, Y 150,840).

$1264* *"Winter Am Walchensee" (Muller 858/II), 1924,* (11-28-92, Grisebach, #485, illus.), 5¹³⁄₁₆ x 7¹³⁄₁₆ in., (14.8 x 19.8 cm.), drypoint on copper print paper (BP 834, DM 2014, FR 6836, Y 157,312).

BI *Wohl Auf Kameraden, Aufs Pferd, Aufs Pferd!...(M. 814.), 1923,* s., Bl. 6 from the series Wallensteins Lager, pub. Heinrich Tilgner,est. DM 1500, (12-01-92, Karl/Faber, #497), 10¹⁄₁₆ x 8¹⁄₁₆ in., (25.5 x 20.5 cm.), etching on wove.

$770* *A Woman Smoking, 1919,* s., (12-13-92, Hindman, #265), 12½ x 9½ in., drypoint (BP 492, DM 1210, FR 4124, Y 95,262).

BI *Zwei Bauern Nach Wilhelm Leibl (Schw. L 422.), 1920,* s., s. in red, est. DM 800, (12-01-92, Karl/Faber, #481), 10⁷⁄₁₆ x 8¼ in., (26.5 x 21 cm.), lithograph on hand-made.

$295* *Zwei Stehende Weibliche Akte, Rechter Teil (Schwarz 233 B II), 1916,* s., (12-05-92, Bassenge, #7095), 7⅜ x 3¼ in., (18.8 x 8.2 cm.), drypoint on handmade Japan (BP 185, DM 460, FR 1567, Y 36,551).

CORIOLANO, Bartolomeo Italian ac. 1627-1653

BI *Alliance Von Friede Und Unabhangigkeit (Romae 1627; B./Strauss 10,3),* s., d., staining est. SC 8/10,000, (11-11-92, Dorotheum, #309, illus.), 8 11/16 x 6 3/8 in., (22 x 16.2 cm.), Claire-Obscur woodcut.

$687* *Salome (Bartsch XII, 47, 29/III), 1631,* (06-23-93, Kornfeld, #18), chiaroscuro woodcut from 3 blocks (BP 467, DM 1162, FR 3910, Y 74,845, SF 1035).

BI *Sibylle (B.XII, 5),* after Guido Reni, watermark, est. DM 1,200, (12-04-92, Bassenge, #6126), 11¼ x 8 9/16 in., (28.5 x 21.8 cm.), chiaroscuro woodcut.

CORNEC, M. Le

$252* *Le Foyer Retrouve. Exposition D'Amiens, 1919,* fair cond., (11-19-92, Ribeyre/Baron, #141), 61 13/16 x 44⅛ in., (157 x 112 cm.), poster (BP 166, DM 402, FR 1353, Y 31,339).

CORNEILLE Dutch b. 1922

$977* *Bain De Soleil, 1991,* s., d., #69/200, full margins, good cond., (12-09-92, Sotheby-Amstrdm, #547), 32 9/16 x 32 9/16 in., (827 x 827 mm.), color silkscreen on wove (BP 623, DM 1534, FR 5233, Y 121,141, G 1725).

$1172* *Un Beaute Convulsive, 1990,* s., d., #167/200, full margins, good cond., (12-09-92, Sotheby-Amstrdm, #544), 31⅞ x 39 3/16 in., (810 x 996 mm.), color silkscreen on wove (BP 748, DM 1840, FR 6277, Y 145,319, G 2070).

$320* *La Belle Allongee, 1980,* s., t., d., #50/100, full sheet, good cond., (05-27-93, Sotheby-Amstrdm, #590), sh 22 1/16 x 29 15/16 in., (560 x 760 mm.), colored lithograph on wove (BP 205, DM 513, FR 1731, Y 34,305, G 575).

BI *Bla Dame Med Hvid Maske,* est. DK 1,500, (09-29-92, B. Rasmussen, #300), offset print.

BI *Bla Dame Med Hvid Maske,* s. 13/120, est. DK 5,000, (09-29-92, B. Rasmussen, #294), lithograph in colors.

$716* *Circus, 1990,* s., d., #199/200, full margins, good cond., (12-09-92, Sotheby-Amstrdm, #545), 31 5/16 x 23 7/16 in., (796 x 596 mm.), color silkscreen on Arches (BP 457, DM 1124, FR 3835, Y 88,779, G 1265).

$283* *Le Cirque, 1990,* s., d. 90, num. XX/L, (11-16-92, Briest, #34), 41 5/16 x 29½ in., (105 x 75 cm.), lithograph in colors on Arches (BP 186, DM 451, FR 1521, Y 35,318).

$241* *Le Cirque, 1990,* s., d. 90., num. XX/L, (11-16-92, Briest, #32), 41 5/16 x 29½ in., (105 x 75 cm.), lithograph in colors on Arches (BP 158, DM 384, FR 1295, Y 30,076).

BI *Complicite, 1979,* s., d., #186/250, pub. London Arts Inc., good cond., est. G 4/600, (12-09-92, Sotheby-Amstrdm, #534), sheet 19 3/16 x 25⅞ in., (488 x 658 mm.), color lithograph on wove.

$184* *Composition, 1965,* s. Corneille 65, 53/125, (03-24-93, Kunsthallen, #65), color lithograph (BP 125, DM 301, FR 1023, Y 21,619, DK 1150).

BI *Composition, 1965,* s. Corneille 65, 35/40, est. DK 2,500, (09-30-92, Kunsthallen, #79), lithograph in colors.

BI *Composition, 1975,* s. Corneille 75, E.A., est. DK 1,800, (09-30-92, Kunsthallen, #69), color lithograph.

$316* *Composition, 1980,* s. Corneille 80, 50/300, (09-30-92, Kunsthallen, #78), color lithograph (BP 178, DM 448, FR 1516, Y 37,922, DK 1725).

$211* *Composition, 1984,* s. Corneille 84, 112/120, (09-30-92, Kunsthallen, #80), color lithograph (BP 119, DM 299, FR 1012, Y 25,321, DK 1150).

$230* *Conversion, 1980,* s., d., #176/300, pub. London Arts Inc., full sheet p. to edges, good cond., (05-27-93, Sotheby-Amstrdm, #589), sh 19 13/16 x 25⅞ in., (504 x 658 mm.), colored lithograph on wove (BP 147, DM 369, FR 1244, Y 24,657, G 414).

$251* *"Coupe Allegre", 1987 and "Couples", 1989: Two,* both s., d., 25/90, 59/85, (06-28-93, Loudmer, #219), first 12 13/16 x 10¼ in., (325 x 260 mm.), second 14 9/16 x 19 11/16 in., (325 x 260 mm.), first, color aquatint on wove; second, color lithograph on Arches wove (BP 168, DM 427, FR 1437, Y 26,631).

$316* *Deux Femmes, 1980,* s. Corneille 80, 172/300, (09-30-92, Kunsthallen, #71), color lithograph (BP 178, DM 448, FR 1516, Y 37,922, DK 1725).

$307* *Dialogue D'Oiseaux, 1973,* s., t., d., i. E.A., full sheet p. to edges, good cond., (05-27-93, Sotheby-Amstrdm, #400), sh 25 13/16 x 19⅞ in., (655 x 505 mm.), colored lithograph on wove (BP 197, DM 493, FR 1660, Y 32,912, G 552).

$1954* *Elle, C'Est-A-Dire L'Aube, 1955: Four,* complete set, s., pub. Georges Fall, full margins, good cond., discoloration, in orig. portfolio box, (12-09-92, Sotheby-Amstrdm, #520), each sheet approx. 13⅜ x 10¼ in., (340 x 260 mm.), color lithograph on BFK Rives (BP 1247, DM 3067, FR 10,466, Y 242,281, G 3450).

$367* *Enchantement DeL'Ete, (Donkersloot-Berghe 116), 1962,* s. Corneille 62, 20/120, (03-24-93, Kunsthallen, #63), color lithograph (BP 249, DM 599, FR 2040, Y 43,121, DK 2300).

$359* *Un Ete Ardent, 1968,* s., d., i. E/A, good cond., (12-09-92, Sotheby-Amstrdm, #526), sheet 30⅛ x 22¼ in., (765 x 565 mm.), color lithograph on wove (BP 229, DM 563, FR 1923, Y 44,513, G 633).

$512* *Ete Baroque, 1973,* s., t., d., full sheet p. to edges, good cond., (05-27-93, Sotheby-Amstrdm, #398, illus.), sh 25 9/16 x 19⅞ in., (650 x 505 mm.), lithograph on wove (BP 328, DM 822, FR 2769, Y 54,889, G 920).

$1107* *Ete Incendaire, 1965,* s., d., #4/125, pub. L'oeuvre Gravee, blindstamp, full margins, goodcond., discoloration, papertape, (12-09-92, Sotheby-Amstrdm, #521, illus.), 19⅛ x 15¾ in., (485 x 400 mm.), color lithograph on BFK Rives (BP 706, DM 1738, FR 5929, Y 137,260, G 1955).

BI *Un Ete Topical, 1967,* s., t., i. Epreuve d'artiste, full margins, defects, est. BP 150/200, (11-30-92, Phillips-London, #501), sheet 19½ x 25½ in., (495 x 648 mm.), lithograph in black & orange.

$316* *Femme,* (09-30-92, Kunsthallen, #77), offset lithograph in colors (BP 178, DM 448, FR 1516, Y 37,922, DK 1725).

$232* *Femme Et Chat, 1978,* s. Corneille 78, 9/25, E.A., (09-30-92, Kunsthallen, #74), lithograph (BP 131, DM 329, FR 1113, Y 27,841, DK 1265).

$220* *Femme Et Chien, 1975,* s. Corneille 75, E.A., (03-24-93, Kunsthallen, #68), color lithograph (BP 149, DM 359, FR 1223, Y 25,849, DK 1380).

$275* *Femme Et Fleur, 1979,* s. Corneille 79, 121/380, (03-24-93, Kunsthallen, #70), color lithograph (BP 186, DM 449, FR 1529, Y 32,311, DK 1725).

$230* *Femme Et Oiseau D'Ete, 1981,* s., d., #h/c 2/25, pub. The Art Part, full sheet p. to edges, good cod., (05-27-93, Sotheby-Amstrdm, #594), sh 25 9/16 x 19 11/16 in., (650 x 500 mm.), colored lithograph on wove (BP 147, DM 369, FR 1244, Y 24,657, G 414).

$232* *Femme Et Oiseau, 1978,* s. Corneille 78, 9/25 E.A., (09-30-92, Kunsthallen, #75), color lithograph (BP 131, DM 329, FR 1113, Y 27,841, DK 1265).

BI *Femme Et Oiseau, 1979,* s., d., i. E.A., full sheet p. to edges, good cond., est. Dfl. 5/700, (05-27-93, Sotheby-Amstrdm, #588), sh 27 9/16 x 18⅛ in., (700 x 460 mm.), colored lithograph on wove.

$184* *Femme Et Oiseau, 1979,* s. Corneille 79, 10/85, (03-24-93, Kunsthallen, #67), color lithograph (BP 125, DM 301, FR 1023, Y 21,619, DK 1150).

$352* *Femme Et Oiseau, 1981,* s., d,. #78/200, margins, good cond., minor foxing, (05-27-93, Sotheby-Amstrdm, #595), 18 15/16 x 13 9/16 in., (482 x 344 mm.), colored etching on wove (BP 225, DM 565, FR 1904, Y 37,736, G 633).

BI *Femme Et Oiseau, 1982,* s., d., i. E.A., full sheet p. to edges, good cond., est. Dfl. 4/600, (05-27-93, Sotheby-Amstrdm, #596), sh 21 11/16 x 15⅜ in., (551 x 390 mm.), colored lithograph on wove.

$295* *Femme Sur Un Sofa Vert, 1979,* s. Corneille 79, 172/250, (09-30-92, Kunsthallen, #70), lithograph in colors (BP 166, DM 418, FR 1415, Y 35,401, DK 1610).

$590* *Femme, 1988,* s. Corneille, 18/120, (09-30-92, Kunsthallen, #72), color serigraph (BP 333, DM 837, FR 2830, Y 70,803, DK 3220).

$126* *"Femmes Au Divan Bleu", 1980,* #100/300, s., d., (01-28-93, Pescheteau, #110), 19 11/16 x 25 9/16 in., (50 x 65 cm.), color lithograph on wove (BP 83, DM 200, FR 676, Y 15,644).

$990* *Femmes De 1973, 1979, 1980: Five,* s., #61/100, 30/100, 185/250, 85/25, 183/250, (03-31-93, Briest, #E27),

19 11/16 x 25 13/16 in., (50 x 65.5 cm.), color lithograph (BP 655, DM 1592, FR 5410, Y 113,845).

$190* *Femmes Et Chat, 1978,* s. Corneille 78, 9/25 E.A., (09-30-92, Kunsthallen, #76), lithograph (BP 107, DM 269, FR 911, Y 22,801, DK 1035).

$554* *Femmes Et Oiseau Vert, 1968,* s., t., d., #28/30, margins, good cond.?, (12-09-92, Sotheby-Amstrdm, #524), 23 1/4 x 17 5/8 in., (590 x 447 mm.), color lithograph on wove (BP 354, DM 870, FR 2967, Y 68,692, G 978).

$293* *Hommage A Satie, 1989,* s., d., #9/200, full margins, good cond., (12-09-92, Sotheby-Amstrdm, #541), 11 5/16 x 17 1/8 in., (288 x 435 mm.), color lithograph on wove (BP 187, DM 460, FR 1569, Y 36,330, G 518).

$670* *"Hymne A L'Ete": Portfolio,* s. 87, 59/200, Edition GKM, (09-29-92, B. Rasmussen, #295), 5 lithographs in colors (BP 377, DM 946, FR 3229, Y 79,981, DK 3680).

$179* *Komposition Med Kvinna Och Faglar,* s., 167/199, (04-17-93, Falkkloos, #94), 8 1/4 x 5 7/8 in., (21 x 15 cm.), serigraph (BP 116, DM 286, FR 967, Y 19,904, SK 1320).

$356* *Kvinde Og Fugl,* s. 78, 30/100, (09-29-92, B. Rasmussen, #298), lithograph in colors (BP 200, DM 503, FR 1716, Y 42,497, DK 1955).

$330* *L'Arbre Extatique, 1973,* s., t., d. 73, (03-31-93, Briest, #E26), 25 9/16 x 19 11/16 in., (65 x 50 cm.), color lithograph (BP 218, DM 531, FR 1803, Y 37,948).

$640* *L'Ile Aux Oiseaux (Donkersloot 216), 1968,* s., d., i. E.A., pub. L'Oeuvre Gravee, p. Michel Casse, full sheet, good cond., prov., (05-27-93, Sotheby-Amstrdm, #604), sh 22 1/4 x 30 1/16 in., (565 x 764 mm.), colored lithograph on Arches (BP 410, DM 1027, FR 3461, Y 68,611, G 1150).

BI *L'Oiseau Dans Un Paysage, 1992,* artist's proof, s., t., est. FF1,500/2,000, (05-27-93, Briest, #71), 34 1/4 x 29 3/4 in., (87 x 75.5 cm.), color lithograph.

$275* *L'Oiseau Ivre De Liberte, (Donkersloot-Berghe 363), 1974,* s. Corneille 74, Epreuve d'artiste, (03-24-93, Kunsthallen, #64), color lithograph (BP 186, DM 449, FR 1529, Y 32,311, DK 1725).

$330* *Natacha, 1978,* s. Corneille 78, 51/150, (03-24-93, Kunsthallen, #66), color lithograph (BP 223, DM 539, FR 1834, Y 38,773, DK 2070).

$234* *Nu Rouge A L'Oiseau, 1981,* s., d., #9/200, pub. Brentwood Interiors, good cond., (12-09-92, Sotheby-Amstrdm, #536), sheet 19 11/16 x 25 5/8 in., (500 x 651 mm.), color lithograph on wove (BP 149, DM 367, FR 1253, Y 29,014, G 414).

$213* *Odalisque, 1979,* s., d., 199/250, drystamp, (06-28-93, Loudmer, #220), 19 5/8 x 25 9/16 in., (498 x 650 mm.), color lithograph on wove (BP 143, DM 362, FR 1219, Y 22,599).

BI *Le Paradis Terrestre, 1992: Diptyque,* #E.A. 2/3, s., est. FF10/12,000, (05-27-93, Briest, #69, illus.), 37 3/8 x 59 1/16 in., (95 x 150 cm.), serigraph on canvas.

BI *Pige Og Tiger,* s. 87, 134/200, est. DK 2,000, (09-29-92, B. Rasmussen, #296), lithograph in colors.

$387* *"Sans Titre", 1977 and "Sans Titre", 1978: Two,* both s., d., hors commerce, second, drystamp, (06-28-93, Loudmer, #220A), both 25 3/8 x 19 5/16 in., (645 x 490 mm.), sh both 29 15/16 x 22 7/16 in., (645 x 490 mm.), color soft-ground etchings and aquatints on Arches wove (BP 259, DM 658, FR 2215, Y 41,061).

$479* *"Sans Titre-1959" (P.D. Van den Berghe 73),* #94/120, d., s., (04-04-93, Pescheteau, #188), a vue 21 5/8 x 14 3/16 in., (55 x 36 cm.), color lithograph on Rives (BP 316, DM 770, FR 2615, Y 54,537).

$489* *"Sans Titre-1959" (P.D. Van den Berghe 74),* #31/120, d., s., (04-04-93, Pescheteau, #187), a vue 21 5/8 x 14 3/16 in., (55 x 36 cm.), color lithograph on Johannot (BP 322, DM 786, FR 2669, Y 55,676).

$126* *"Scene D'Interieur", 1979,* #124/250, d., s., (01-28-93, Pescheteau, #109), 19 11/16 x 25 9/16 in., (50 x 65 cm.), color lithograph on wove (BP 83, DM 200, FR 676, Y 15,644).

BI *Scenes Erotiques, 1985: Triptych,* artist's proof, s., d. 85, est. FF 3/3,500, (11-16-92, Briest, #278), 14 7/8 x 10 15/16 in., (37.8 x 27.9 cm.), lithograph in colors.

$253* *She Gives Herself To Summer, 1980,* 59/300, s., d., (10-14-92, Germann, #265, illus.), 27 3/16 x 21 7/16 in., (690 x 545 mm.), color serigraph (BP 149, DM 370, FR 1256, Y 30,659, SF 330).

$1563* *Six Reves Peints, 1989: Six,* complete portfolio, s., d., #XXIII/XXX, pub. Jaski Art Productions, good cond., in orig. portfolio, (12-09-92, Sotheby-Amstrdm, #542), each approx. 17 11/16 x 14 9/16 in., (450 x 370 mm.), color silkscreen on Fabriano Artistico (BP 997, DM 2453, FR 8372, Y 193,800, G 2760).

$234* *Sous Les Palmiers, 1981,* s., d., #101/200, pub. E&S Interests, good cond., (12-09-92, Sotheby-Amstrdm, #535), sheet 19 5/8 x 25 1/2 in., (499 x 647 mm.), color lithograph on wove (BP 149, DM 367, FR 1253, Y 29,014, G 414).

BI *Suite Des Tigres Amoureux, 1986: Four,* each s., d., #72/125, pub. Galerie Moderne, full margins, good cond., contained loose in orig. portfolio, est. Dfl. 1,2/1,800, (05-27-93, Sotheby-Amstrdm, #597), each approx. 11 1/4 x 15 3/8 in., (285 x 390 mm.), colored lithograph on wove.

$1107* *Suite Des Tigres Amoureux, Troisieme Serie, 1987: Four,* portfolio, s., d., #20/125, full margins, good cond., in orig. portfolio, (12-09-92, Sotheby-Amstrdm, #540), each approx. 16 1/8 x 22 7/16 in., (410 x 570 mm.), color lithograph on wove (BP 706, DM 1738, FR 5929, Y 137,260, G 1955).

BI *Le Trio A L'Oiseau, 1992,* s., est. FF6/7,000, (05-27-93, Briest, #70), 62 15/16 x 41 5/16 in., (160 x 105 cm.), color serigraph.

BI *Untitled,* s. 83, 5/85, est. DK 2,000, (09-29-92, B. Rasmussen, #297), lithograph in colors.

$167* *Untitled,* s. e.a., (09-29-92, B. Rasmussen, #301), lithograph in colors (BP 94, DM 236, FR 805, Y 19,936, DK 920).

$660* *Untitled Abstract Composition: Four,* d. 1959, 1972, or 1973, annot., num., and/or s., (05-27-93, Swann, #74), color lithograph (BP 423, DM 1059, FR 3569, Y 70,755).

BI *Untitled, 1967,* s., d., good cond.?, est. G 800/1,200, (12-09-92, Sotheby-Amstrdm, #523), 14 3/8 x 20 13/16 in., (365 x 528 mm.), color lithograph on wove.

$651* *Untitled, 1967,* s., d., good cond.?, (12-09-92, Sotheby-Amstrdm, #522, illus.), 14 9/16 x 20 7/8 in., (370 x 530 mm.), color lithograph on wove (BP 415, DM 1022, FR 3487, Y 80,719, G 1150).

$424* *Untitled, 1973,* s., d., #68/100, margins, good cond., (12-09-92, Sotheby-Amstrdm, #527), sheet 26 3/16 x 19 5/16 in., (665 x 490 mm.), color lithograph on wove (BP 271, DM 666, FR 2271, Y 52,573, G 748).

$1824* *Untitled, 1973: Six,* part of portfolio Herbes, four s., d.; three #53/100; pub. Michel Casse, good cond., discoloration, in orig. wooden portfolio box, (12-09-92, Sotheby-Amstrdm, #525), each sheet approx. 25 15/16 x 20 1/16 in., (660 x 510 mm.), lithograph, three in colors on Arches (BP 1164, DM 2863, FR 9770, Y 226,162, G 3220).

$234* *Untitled, 1977,* s., d., #108/125, good cond., (12-09-92, Sotheby-Amstrdm, #533), sheet 25 9/16 x 19 11/16 in., (650 x 500 mm.), color lithograph on wove (BP 149, DM 367, FR 1253, Y 29,014, G 414).

$359* *Untitled, 1977,* s., d., #108/125, good cond., (12-09-92, Sotheby-Amstrdm, #530), sheet 25 9/16 x 19 11/16 in., (650 x 500 mm.), color lithograph on wove (BP 229, DM 563, FR 1923, Y 44,513, G 633).

$326* *Untitled, 1977,* s., d., #108/125, good cond., (12-09-92, Sotheby-Amstrdm, #529), sheet 25 9/16 x 19 11/16 in., (650 x 500 mm.), color lithograph on wove (BP 208, DM 512, FR 1746, Y 40,422, G 575).

$261* *Untitled, 1977,* s., d., #108/125, good cond., (12-09-92, Sotheby-Amstrdm, #531), sheet 25 9/16 x 19 11/16 in., (650 x 500 mm.), color lithograph on wove (BP 167, DM 410, FR 1398, Y 32,362, G 460).

$359* *Untitled, 1977,* s., d., #108/125, good cond., (12-09-92, Sotheby-Amstrdm, #532), sheet 25 9/16 x 19 11/16 in., (650 x 500 mm.), color lithograph on wove (BP 229, DM 563, FR 1923, Y 44,513, G 633).

$424* *Untitled, 1977,* s., d., #108/125, good cond., (12-09-92, Sotheby-Amstrdm, #528), sheet 25 9/16 x 19 11/16 in., (650 x 500 mm.), color lithograph on wove (BP 271, DM 666, FR 2271, Y 52,573, G 748).

$192* *Untitled, 1979,* s., d., #99/250, pub. London Arts, full sheet p. to edges, good cond., (05-27-93, Sotheby-Amstrdm, #584), sh 19⅝ x 25¾ in., (499 x 654 mm.), colored lithograph on wove (BP 123, DM 308, FR 1038, Y 20,583, G 345).

$294* *Untitled, 1979,* s., d., #187/250, pub. London Arts, p. Atelier Dumas Inc. w/their blindstamp, full sheet p. to edges, good cond., (05-27-93, Sotheby-Amstrdm, #585), sh 19½ x 25⅝ in., (496 x 651 mm.), colored lithograph on wove (BP 188, DM 472, FR 1590, Y 31,518, G 529).

$320* *Untitled, 1979,* s., d., #108/250, p. Atelier Dumas w/their blindstamp, full sheet p.to edges, good cond., (05-27-93, Sotheby-Amstrdm, #586), sh 19½ x 25¾ in., (496 x 654 mm.), colored lithograph on wove (BP 205, DM 513, FR 1731, Y 34,305, G 575).

$192* *Untitled, 1980,* s., d., #142/300, pub. London Arts, full sheet p. to edges, good cond., (05-27-93, Sotheby-Amstrdm, #591), sh 19¾ x 25⅞ in., (502 x 658 mm.), colored lithograph on wove (BP 123, DM 308, FR 1038, Y 20,583, G 345).

$243* *Untitled, 1981,* s., d., #119/200, pub. London Arts, full sheet p. to edges, good cond., (05-27-93, Sotheby-Amstrdm, #593), sh 25⅜ x 19⁹⁄₁₆ in., (645 x 497 mm.), colored lithograph on wove (BP 156, DM 390, FR 1314, Y 26,051, G 437).

$192* *Untitled, 1981,* s., d., #144/200, full sheet p. to edges, good cond., (05-27-93, Sotheby-Amstrdm, #592), sh 19⁹⁄₁₆ x 25⅜ in., (497 x 645 mm.), colored lithograph on wove (BP 123, DM 308, FR 1038, Y 20,583, G 345).

$293* *Untitled, 1981,* s., d., #156/200, margins, good cond., (12-09-92, Sotheby-Amstrdm, #538, illus.), sheet 19¹¹⁄₁₆ x 25⁹⁄₁₆ in., (500 x 650 mm.), color lithograph on wove (BP 187, DM 460, FR 1569, Y 36,330, G 518).

$391* *Untitled, 1982,* s., d., #39/300, margins, good cond., (12-09-92, Sotheby-Amstrdm, #537), sheet 28¾ x 20⅞ in., (730 x 530 mm.), color lithograph on wove (BP 250, DM 614, FR 2094, Y 48,481, G 690).

$208* *Untitled, 1986,* s., d., #72/200, margins, good cond.?, (12-09-92, Sotheby-Amstrdm, #539), 12⅝ x 9⅝ in., (320 x 245 mm.), color lithograph on wove (BP 133, DM 326, FR 1114, Y 25,790, G 368).

$288* *Untitled, 1989,* s., d., #15/250, full sheet p. to edges, good cond., (05-27-93, Sotheby-Amstrdm, #598), sh 26⁹⁄₁₆ x 19⅞ in., (675 x 505 mm.), colored lithograph on wove (BP 184, DM 462, FR 1558, Y 30,875, G 518).

$554* *Untitled, 1989,* s., d., #191/200, full margins, good cond., (12-09-92, Sotheby-Amstrdm, #543), 31⁷⁄₁₆ x 31½ in., (798 x 800 mm.), color silkscreen on wove (BP 354, DM 870, FR 2967, Y 68,692, G 978).

BI *Untitled, 1990,* s., d., #175/200, full sheet, good cond., est. Dfl. 5/700, (05-27-93, Sotheby-Amstrdm, #599), sh 29¼ x 29⁷⁄₁₆ in., (743 x 748 mm.), colored lithograph on wove.

BI *Untitled, 1990,* s., d., #175/200, full sheet, good cond., est. Dfl. 5/700, (05-27-93, Sotheby-Amstrdm, #601), sh 29¼ x 29⁷⁄₁₆ in., (743 x 748 mm.), colored lithograph on wove.

$512* *Untitled, 1990,* s., d., #141/200, full margins, good cond., (05-27-93, Sotheby-Amstrdm, #600), 31¹⁵⁄₁₆ x 31½ in., (811 x 800 mm.), colored silkscreen on wove (BP 328, DM 822, FR 2769, Y 54,889, G 920).

$640* *Untitled, 1991,* s., d., #122/200, full margins, good cond., (05-27-93, Sotheby-Amstrdm, #603), 32⅜ x 32⅜ in., (822 x 822 mm.), colored lithograph on wove (BP 410, DM 1027, FR 3461, Y 68,611, G 1150).

$253* *Visage De La Lune, Visage De La Terre, 1975,* s. Corneille 75, 41/100, from Pour Jorn portfolio, (09-30-92, Kunsthallen, #81), color lithograph (BP 143, DM 359, FR 1213, Y 30,361, DK 1380).

$608* *Visage, 1990,* s., d., i. E.A., full margins, good cond., (05-27-93, Sotheby-Amstrdm, #602), 31½ x 31½ in., (800 x 800 mm.), colored lithograph on wove (BP 389, DM 976, FR 3288, Y 65,180, G 1093).

$230* *Yellow Bright, 1979,* s., d., #175/250, pub. London Arts Inc., p. Atelier Dumas Inc. w/their blindstamp, full sheet p. to edges, good cond., (05-27-93, Sotheby-Amstrdm, #587), sh 19½ x 25¹¹⁄₁₆ in., (496 x 653 mm.), colored lithograph on wove (BP 147, DM 369, FR 1244, Y 24,657, G 414).

$312* *Les Yeux Noirs, 1973,* s. Corneille 73, E.A., (03-24-93, Kunsthallen, #69), color lithograph (BP 211, DM 510, FR 1734, Y 36,658, DK 1955).

BI *Les Yeux Noirs, 1973,* s. Corneille 73, E.A., est. DK 1,800, (09-30-92, Kunsthallen, #73), color lithograph.

CORNEILLE (Cornelis van BEVERLOO)   Dutch b. 1922

$860* *Composition, 1967,* s., watermark, #18/50, num., s., d., (05-27-93, Lempertz, #667), 20⅞ x 29¹⁄₁₆ in., (53.1 x 73.8 cm.), color serigraph on wove (BP 551, DM 1380, FR 4651, Y 92,196).

$593* *Femme Et Chien Vert, 1978,* 22/100, s., d., (06-24-93, Germann, #296, illus.), 27½ x 19⅝ in., (698 x 498 mm.), color lithograph (BP 390, DM 961, FR 3240, Y 63,613, SF 863).

$2150* *Femme Et Faune Familiere, 1977: Five,* Galleri Kanda Malare, #5/100, s., d., (05-27-93, Lempertz, #668, illus.), 30⅞ x 23¹¹⁄₁₆ in., (78.5 x 60.2 cm.), etching on wove (BP 1377, DM 3450, FR 11,628, Y 230,489).

BI *"Ivresse De L'Ete",* (19)74, s., d., t., est. DM 800, (12-01-92, Karl/Faber, #502), sh 29¹⁵⁄₁₆ x 22¹⁄₁₆ in., (76 x 56 cm.), color lithograph.

BI *"La Nuit Violette",* (19)75, s., d., t., num., est. DM 700, (12-01-92, Karl/Faber, #504), 25¹³⁄₁₆ x 20¹⁄₁₆ in., (65.5 x 51 cm.), color lithograph on wove.

$290* *"Regard Sur L'Oiseau",* (19)75, s., d., t., num., (12-01-92, Karl/Faber, #503), 14¾ x 17⁵⁄₁₆ in., (37.5 x 44 cm.), color lithograph on wove (BP 192, DM 462, FR 1575, Y 36,106).

BI *Self Portrait With Mask And Decorative Headdress,* (19)82, s., d., num., A.P., est. DM 800, (12-01-92, Karl/Faber, #508), sh 28¹⁵⁄₁₆ x 20⅞ in., (73.5 x 53 cm.), color lithograph on Arches wove.

$498* *She Gives Herself To Summer,* (19)80, s., d., num., (12-01-92, Karl/Faber, #507), 22¹⁄₁₆ x 21¼ in., (56 x 54 cm.), color lithograph on wove (BP 329, DM 794, FR 2705, Y 62,002).

$379* *She Gives Herself To Summer, 1980,* #60/300, s., d., (04-21-93, Germann, #16, illus.), 27³⁄₁₆ x 21⁵⁄₁₆ in., (690 x 541 mm.), color serigraph (BP 246, DM 606, FR 2049, Y 41,957, SF 552).

BI *"Sous Le Ciel Rose, La Femme",* (19)75, s., d., t., est. DM 700, (12-01-92, Karl/Faber, #505), 25¹⁵⁄₁₆ x 20¹⁄₁₆ in., (66 x 51 cm.), color lithograph.

BI *"Visage De Chat",* (19)74, s., d., t., num., est. DM 700, (12-01-92, Karl/Faber, #501), 29¹⁵⁄₁₆ x 22¹⁄₁₆ in., (76 x 56 cm.), color lithograph on wove.

$553* *Woman With Bird, 1986,* E.A., s., d., (06-24-93, Germann, #295, illus.), 19¹¹⁄₁₆ x 25¹⁵⁄₁₆ in., (500 x 660 mm.), color lithograph (BP 364, DM 897, FR 3022, Y 59,322, SF 805).

CORNEILLE, Jean

BI *Jean Clarence Lambert.Jardin Errant, 1963,* book, each s., d., w/t. page, text & just., s. by artist & author, num. 94, pub. Arturo Schwarz, est. BP 8/1,200, (12-03-92, Sotheby-London, #635, illus.), eight lithographs in colors.

CORNEILLE, and Simon VINKENOOG

$424* *Untitled, 1990,* s. by both, #33/250, full margins, good cond., (12-09-92, Sotheby-Amstrdm, #546), 22¼ x 29¾ in., (565 x 755 mm.), color silkscreen on Arches (BP 271, DM 666, FR 2271, Y 52,573, G 748).

CORNELIS, J. Belgique

BI *White-Clad Woman Holding The Symbol Of Belgium With The City Of Ghent In The Background, 1913,* Exposition-Ghent 1913, linen-backed, (04-29-93, Swann, #137), each approx. 35 x 24½ in., (88.9 x 62.2 cm.), color lithograph poster.

CORNELL

$22* *Portrait Of A Man,* #14/100, (02-12-93, DuMouchelle, #358), 19½ x 15 in., (49.5 x 38.1 cm.), etching (BP 15, DM 36, FR 123, Y 2653).

CORNELL, James and Sons   British 20th cent.

$330* *"The New York And London Packet Ship 'Victoria' 1000 Tons (Entering New York Harbor)",* s. Clifford R. James, ident. in plate, very good cond., (10-31-92, Skinner, #47, illus.), 16¼ x 22 in., (41.3 x 55.9 cm.), intaglio process printed in colors on chine appliquè (BP 216, DM 518, FR 1754, Y 40,801).

CORNER, L.R.
$121* *"Rogers & Company, Chicago Engravers And Printers", A Semi-Clad Man Working A Printing Press,* mono. sig. L.R. Corner, soiling, excell. cond., (10-31-92, Riba, #346, illus.), 22 x 15 in., (55.9 x 38.1 cm.), poster (BP 79, DM 190, FR 643, Y 14,960).

COROSONE, Paola
$65* *"Estainone Del Trombo In Fiedi",* s., t., d. 1975, embossed w/artist's stamp, num. 7, (05-12-93, Maynard, #553), (48.3 x 68.6 cm.), etching (BP 42, DM 105, FR 353, Y 7257, C$ 83).
$74* *"Vibration Di Tutte Il Corpo",* s., t., d. 1975, embossed w/artist's stamp, num. 8B, (05-12-93, Maynard, #552), sheet 27½ x 19½ in., (69.9 x 49.5 cm.), etching (BP 48, DM 119, FR 402, Y 8262, C$ 94).

COROT, Camille French 1796-1875
BI *Le Dome Florentin (Delteil 13 I), c. 1869-70,* est. DM 6000, (06-10-93, Hauswedell/Nolt, #213, illus.), image 9⁷⁄₁₆ x 6¼ in., (24 x 15.9 cm.), etching on hand-made.
$550* *Paysage D'Italie (Melot 7. Delteil 7), 1866,* wide margins, printing after third state, vertical line, (05-27-93, Swann, #75), 6⅛ x 9¼ in., (15.6 x 23.5 cm.), etching (BP 352, DM 883, FR 2975, Y 58,962).
BI *Le Repos Des Philosophes (Delteil 25 I), 1871,* est. DM 25,000, (06-10-93, Hauswedell/Nolt, #214, illus.), image 8⁹⁄₁₆ x 5⅝ in., (21.8 x 14.3 cm.), transfer lithograph on China.

COROT, Jean Baptiste Camille French 1796-1875
$385* *Environs De Rome (Melot 6), 1866,* 3rd state, foxed, (12-08-92, Swann, #71), 11⅜ x 8⅜ in., (28.9 x 21.3 cm.), etching on Japan paper (BP 241, DM 599, FR 2044, Y 47,719).
BI *Les Jardins D'Horace (L. Delteil 58), 1855,* tears, (06-11-93, Picard, #21), 14⁹⁄₁₆ x 11⅝ in., (370 x 295 mm.), cliche-verre.
$1638* *La Lecture Sous Les Arbres (D. 33), 1874,* stains, mat-staining, full margins, 100 edit., ex-coll., annot. verso, (02-24-93, Picard, #68), signature on gray chine applique (BP 1142, DM 2659, FR 9015, Y 192,208).
$1589* *Paysage D'Italie (Delteil 7 I), c. 1865,* watermark, (12-04-92, Bassenge, #6763), 6³⁄₁₆ x 9⁵⁄₁₆ in., (15.7 x 23.7 cm.), etching on hand-made (BP 1019, DM 2531, FR 8585, Y 198,377).
$9065* *Le Repos Des Philosophes (Delteil 25 I), 1871,* sheet 7 from the series Douze Autographies, artist's proof, (06-04-93, Bassenge, #5641, illus.), 8½ x 5⁹⁄₁₆ in., (21.6 x 14.2 cm.), lithograph in brown on Chine colle (BP 5997, DM 14,721, FR 49,617, Y 977,675).
$1650* *Sous Bois (D.M. 31), 1871,* large margins, good cond., surface soiling, crease, notations, hingeremains, (10-28-92, Butterfield, #2626), 10⅜ x 8½ in., (264 x 216 mm.), lithograph in sanguine on chine colle (pasted) attached to wove (BP 1051, DM 2548, FR 8652, Y 202,454).
$550* *Souvenir D'Italie (D. 5, M. 5), 1866,* large margins, good cond., light-staining, mat staining, glue staining, label verso, creases, (02-24-93, Butterfield, #2912), 12⅝ x 9⁷⁄₁₆ in., (321 x 240 mm.), etching on laid w/watermark (BP 384, DM 893, FR 3027, Y 64,539).
$1755* *Souvenir D'Italie (L. Delteil, 5), 1866,* 2 out of 4 w/i., tears, losses, large margins, dry stamp, (04-02-93, Picard, #74), 11⁹⁄₁₆ x 8¹¹⁄₁₆ in., (29.3 x 22 cm.), etching (BP 1156, DM 2821, FR 9580, Y 199,818).
$805* *Souvenir D'Ostie (D. 57), 1855,* 2nd final state, inkstamp publisher Sagot and Le Garrec, 1921, goodcond., staining, (05-19-93, Butterfield, #1905, illus.), 11⅜ x 14³⁄₁₆ in., (289 x 360 mm.), cliche verre on wove (BP 523, DM 1309, FR 4409, Y 89,118).
$330* *Souvenir De Toscane (D. I, M. I), 1865,* pub. Gazette des Beaux-Arts, margins, good cond., paper loss, tears,staining, (02-24-93, Butterfield, #2911), 4¹⁄₁₆ x 7¹⁄₁₆ in., (103 x 179 mm.), etching on laid w/watermark (BP 230, DM 536, FR 1816, Y 38,723).
$363* *Souvenir De Toscane (L. Delteil 1), 1845,* definitive state, good margins, (02-03-93, Ader Tajan, #104), 4¹³⁄₁₆ x 7 in., (12.2 x 17.8 cm.), etching (BP 253, DM 598, FR 2027, Y 45,155).

CORPRON, Carlotta 1901-1988
BI *"Egg Abstraction" and "Light Abstraction": Two,* studio stamp, 1940's, p.l., est. $2/3,000, (10-15-92, Sotheby-NY, #446A, illus.), approx. 10½ x 13½ in., (26.7 x 34.3 cm.), photograph, gelatin silver print.
$1650* *Fluid Light Design, 1940's,* s., (11-16-92, Butterfield, #5911, illus.), 4¼ x 3¼ in., (108.1 x 82.7 mm.), photograph, gelatin silver print (BP 1086, DM 2631, FR 8861, Y 205,198).
$1210* *Light Abstractions: Two, c. 1947,* 2nd s., (10-13-92, Christie-NY, #438, illus.), each 2 x 2¾ in., (5.1 x 7 cm.), photograph, gelatin silver prints (BP 705, DM 1773, FR 6023, Y 146,720).
$4025* *Negative Photogram,* 1940s, s., (04-08-93, Christie-NY, #268, illus.), 7¾ x 9¾ in., (19.7 x 24.8 cm.), photograph, gelatin silver print (BP 2639, DM 6466, FR 21,887, Y 456,764).
$1980* *Reflections In Water And Other Nature Abstractions: Six,* 1940s, each s., (10-13-92, Christie-NY, #439, illus.), various sizes to 2¼ x 2 in., (5.7 x 5.1 cm.), photograph, gelatin silver prints (BP 1153, DM 2901, FR 9856, Y 240,087).
BI *"Starfish And Coral", 1940's,* s., t., photog. stamp, est. $2/3,000, (11-16-92, Butterfield, #5910, illus.), 1⅞ x 2¼ in., (47.7 x 57.3 mm.), photograph, gelatin silver print.

CORREGGIO (after)
$509* *Jupiter And Io, 1784,* by Francesco Bartolozzi, pub. Torre and Co., trimmed, laid down, stained, (09-17-92, Bonhams-Chelsea, #104), image 13½ x 10 in., (34.3 x 25.4 cm.), stipple engraving (BP 286, DM 756, FR 2586, Y 63,372).

CORT, Cornelis 1533-1578
BI *Adam And Eve Lamenting The Death Of Abel (B. de H., Holl. 3; Ill. B., vol. 52, p. 11, no. 3), 1561,* 2nd (final) state, small to thread margins, excell. cond., laid, est.BP 1,8/2,200, (12-01-92, Christie-London, #7, illus.), 13⁹⁄₁₆ x 17⅜ in., (344 x 442 mm.), engraving.
$1205* *Die Akademie Der Schonen Kunste (Wurzbach 52; Le Blanc 150; Hollstein218), 1578,* after J. Stradanus, watermark, (06-08-93, Karl/Faber, #39), engraving (BP 792, DM 1955, FR 6585, Y 127,987).
$9157* *The Battle Of Scipio Against Hannibal, Called "The Battle Of The Elephants", (B. de H., Holl. 196; Ill. B., vol. 52, p. 227, no. 196), c. 1570,* third (final) state, crease, stain, nicks, creases, very good cond., (12-01-92, Christie-London, #90, illus.), overall P. 17¼ x 22⅞ in., (438 x 581 mm.), engraving on 2 joined sheets (BP 6050, DM 14,595, FR 49,739, Y 1,140,065).
$383* *Die Flucht Nach Agypten (Bierens de Haan, Hollstein 40 I), 1566,* (12-04-92, Bassenge, #6128), 11⁷⁄₁₆ x 7⁹⁄₁₆ in., (29.1 x 19.2 cm.), engraving (BP 246, DM 610, FR 2069, Y 47,815).
BI *Der Heilige Hieronymous (Hollstein Bd. V, 134), 1565,* after Titian, 2nd state, trimmed, est. DM 800-, (09-14-92, Venator/Hansten, #1474), sh 12¹⁄₁₆ x 10¾ in., (30.6 x 27.3 cm.), engraving.
BI *Hercules And The Pygmies (B. de H., Holl. 182; Ill. B., vol. 52, p. 206, no. 182), 1563,* after Frans Floris, thread margins, trimmed, staining very good cond., laid, est. BP 2,4/3,000, (12-01-92, Christie-London, #10, illus.), 12¹⁵⁄₁₆ x 18⁷⁄₁₆ in., (328 x 468 mm.), engraving.
$1275* *The Holy Family With St. Anne And Young St. John On A Table (BierensDe Haan, Hollstein 46 I (Von III)),* after Frans Floris, (06-04-93, Bassenge, #5085, illus.), 8⅜ x 10¹³⁄₁₆ in., (21.3 x 27.5 cm.), copper engraving (BP 844, DM 2070, FR 6979, Y 137,511).
$2164* *The Immorality Of Virtue (B. de H., Holl. 220; Ill. B. vol. 52, p. 252, no. 220), 1564,* after Frans Floris, narrow to thread margins, trimmed on or inside platemark, staining, excellent cond., laid, (12-01-92, Christie-London, #11, illus.), 12⁹⁄₁₆ x 16³⁄₁₆ in., (319 x 411 mm.), engraving (BP 1430, DM 3449, FR 11,754, Y 269,422).
BI *Prometheus An Den Felsen Des Kaukasus Gekettet (Bierens de Haan, Hollstein 192 II), 1566,* after Tizian, est. DM 1,200, (12-04-92, Bassenge, #6129), 15³⁄₁₆ x 12⅜ in., (38.5 x 31.4 cm.), engraving.
$540* *Prometheus Und Der Adler (Wurzbach 60; Le Blanc 147; Hollstein 192/II(v. III), 1566,* scratches, (12-01-92, Karl/

Faber, #42), engraving (BP 357, DM 861, FR 2933, Y 67,231).

$794* *Die Verkündigung (Bierens de Haan, Hollstein 24 I),* 1577, foxed, (12-04-92, Bassenge, #6127), 8³⁄₁₆ x 10¹¹⁄₁₆ in., (20.8 x 27.2 cm.), engraving (BP 509, DM 1265, FR 4290, Y 99,126).

CORT, Cornelis (after)
$633* *The Rest On The Flight Into Egypt (cf. B. de H., Holl. 43; Ill. B. vol. 52, no. 43, copy f), c. 1580,* after Federico Barocci, trimmed to platemark, stained, laid(12-01-92, Christie-London, #9), 15¹³⁄₁₆ x 11⁵⁄₁₆ in., (401 x 287 mm.), engraving (BP 418, DM 1009, FR 3438, Y 78,810).

CORT, Cornelis (attrib.)   1533-1578
BI *The Triumph Of The Holy Trinity (cf. B. de H., Holl. Ill; Ill. B. vol. 52, p. 132, no. 111), 1566,* after Titian, narrow to thread margins, creases, defects, staining, laid, est. BP 1,0/1,500, (12-01-92, Christie-London, #8), 20¹³⁄₁₆ x 14¹³⁄₁₆ in., (528 x 376 mm.), engraving.

CORTES, Edouard Leon   French b. 1882
BI *Parisian Street Scene,* s., #XXIII/XX, est. $6/800, (05-16-93, Hanzel, #486), 18 x 21 in., (45.7 x 53.3 cm.), color lithograph.

CORTONA, Pietro da (after)   English 18th cent.
BI *The Finding Of Romulus And Remus,* by Sir Robert Strange, est. $250/350, (04-02-93, Sloan, #2269), 20 x 15½ in., (508 x 394 mm.), engraving.

CORZAS, Francisco   Mexican b. 1936
BI *Personaje,* s., d. 74, #113/200, good cond., yellowing, handling creases, mat burn, tape marks, est. $2/3,000, (05-18-93, Sotheby-NY, #252, illus.), 25⅜ x 19⅝ in., (645 x 498 mm.), lithograph in colors.

COSGROVE, Stanley Morel   Canadian b. 1911
$178* *Bosquet D'Arbres,* #5/200, s., d. Cosgrove 83, (03-16-93, Encans, #41), 23⅝ x 18⁵⁄₁₆ in., (60 x 46.5 cm.), lithograph (BP 123, DM 296, FR 1006, Y 20,814, C$ 222).
$191* *"Debut De Printemps",* #H.C. 10/20, s., d. Cosgrove 81, (06-16-93, Encans, #29), 13¾ x 18⅛ in., (35 x 46 cm.), serigraph (BP 127, DM 317, FR 1064, Y 20,371, C$ 244).
$140* *Femme,* #5/100, s., d. Cosgrove 88, (07-14-92, Encans, #103), 15¾ x 11¹³⁄₁₆ in., (40 x 30.5 cm.), serigraph (BP 73, DM 208, FR 700, Y 17,507, C$ 167).
$133* *Nature Morte A La Coupe Et Bouteille,* #11/130, s., d. Cosgrove 81, (04-20-93, Encans, #35), 11¹³⁄₁₆ x 9¹³⁄₁₆ in., (30 x 25 cm.), serigraph (BP 86, DM 212, FR 715, Y 14,675, C$ 167).
$160* *Nature Morte Au Pichet,* s., d. Cosgrove 80, (03-16-93, Encans, #40), 9¹³⁄₁₆ x 11¹³⁄₁₆ in., (25 x 30 cm.), serigraph (BP 110, DM 266, FR 904, Y 18,709, C$ 200).
BI *"Nu Assis Au Tabouret",* #116/125, s., d. Cosgrove 79, (10-20-92, Encans, #47), 16¹⁵⁄₁₆ x 12 in., (43 x 30.5 cm.), lithograph.
$219* *"Nu Assis",* #111/125, s., d. Cosgrove 78, (05-18-93, Encans, #24), 17¼ x 13¾ in., (43.8 x 35 cm.), lithograph (BP 143, DM 355, FR 1200, Y 24,407, C$ 278).
$217* *Nu De Dos,* #85/100, s., d. Cosgrove 79, (06-16-93, Encans, #28), 16⅛ x 12³⁄₁₆ in., (41 x 31 cm.), brown etching (BP 145, DM 360, FR 1209, Y 23,144, C$ 278).
$182* *"Nu De Dos",* #118/125, s., d. Cosgrove 79, (10-20-92, Encans, #48), 20¹⁄₁₆ x 16⁹⁄₁₆ in., (51 x 42 cm.), lithograph (BP 102, DM 277, FR 942, Y 22,813, C$ 222).
$372* *Le Sentier Des Peupliers,* #66/100, s., d. Cosgrove 84, (07-14-92, Encans, #28), 29¹⁵⁄₁₆ x 24 in., (76 x 61 cm.), serigraph (BP 194, DM 552, FR 1861, Y 46,517, C$ 444).
$3532* *Sous-Bois,* # H.C., s., d. Cosgrove 88, cold stamp, (02-16-93, Encans, #24), 17¹¹⁄₁₆ x 13¾ in., (45 x 35 cm.), serigraph (BP 2443, DM 5765, FR 19,525, Y 423,146, C$ 4440).
$372* *Sous-Bois L'Hiver,* #5/100, s., d. Cosgrove 88, (07-14-92, Encans, #29), 22¹³⁄₁₆ x 28¾ in., (58 x 73 cm.), serigraph (BP 194, DM 552, FR 1861, Y 46,517, C$ 444).

COSSARD, A.
BI *"Flautist"* and *"Violinist": Two,* margins, good condition, tear extending into image, surface soiling,linen-backed,

est. $1,2/1,800, (03-31-93, Butterfield, #5236, illus.), each 10½ x 23½ in., (26.7 x 59.7 cm.), lithograph printed in colors on wove.

COSTAIN, Harold Haliday
$412* *Desert Night Scene,* 1930s, (04-07-93, Swann, #427, illus.), approx. 7 x 9 in., photograph, gold toned silver print (BP 272, DM 666, FR 2255, Y 46,808).
$357* *Fifth Avenue Street Scene During The New York World's Fair, 1939,* photog.'s handstamp, notation, (04-07-93, Swann, #428, illus.), 14 x 11 in., photograph, silver print (BP 236, DM 577, FR 1954, Y 40,559).
$302* *Gold Diggers Of 1933, 1933,* photog.'s handstamp, (04-07-93, Swann, #429, illus.), 7½ x 9½ in., photograph, silver print (BP 200, DM 488, FR 1653, Y 34,310).
$522* *Lily, c. 1940,* photographer's handstamp, (04-07-93, Swann, #430, illus.), 14 x 11 in., photograph, silver print (BP 345, DM 844, FR 2857, Y 59,305).
$3220* *Securing The Anchor Chain, Brest, France (1919), c. 1930,* credit stamp, (04-08-93, Christie-NY, #56, illus.), 13⅞ x 10⅞ in., (35.2 x 27.6 cm.), photograph, gelatin silver print (BP 2111, DM 5173, FR 17,510, Y 365,411).
$302* *Self-Portrait,* 1930s, (04-07-93, Swann, #431, illus.), 14 x 11 in., photograph, silver print (BP 200, DM 488, FR 1653, Y 34,310).
$357* *Surreal Hands (Designer Pavilion), c. 1940,* photog.'s handstamp, notations, (04-07-93, Swann, #432, illus.), 14 x 11 in., photograph, silver print (BP 236, DM 577, FR 1954, Y 40,559).
BI *Water Tower, early 1930's,* double-mounted, s., d., i. by photog., (c) stamp, exhib. labels, est.$1,2/1,800, (10-15-92, Sotheby-NY, #448, illus.), 13½ x 10½ in., (34.3 x 26.7 cm.), photograph, gelatin silver print.

COSTAIN, Harold Haliday   American ac. 20th cent.
$1045* *Floral Study, c. 1930,* handstamp, (10-14-92, Swann, #416, illus.), 10 x 8 in., (25.4 x 20.3 cm.), photograph, gold toned silver print (BP 613, DM 1529, FR 5186, Y 126,636).
BI *Housewife And Maid (Advertisement For Bisquick),* handstamps, 1930's, est. $6/900, (10-14-92, Swann, #417, illus.), 14 x 11 in., (35.6 x 27.9 cm.), photograph, silver print.
BI *Portrait Of Sculptor Leo Friedlander,* 1930's, est. $6/900, (10-14-92, Swann, #418, illus.), 14 x 11 in., (35.6 x 27.9 cm.), photograph, silver print.

COSTER, Gordon   b. 1906
$825* *Unloading Grain(?),* w/handstamp, (04-07-93, Swann, #435, illus.), 9¼ x 7½ in., photograph, silver print (BP 545, DM 1334, FR 4516, Y 93,729).
$467* *""Leadbelly" Ledbetter Playing Guitar" and ""Fats" Waller Playing Piao":Two,* handstamp, 1930's, (10-14-92, Swann, #419, illus.), 10 x 8½ in., (25.4 x 21.6 cm.), photograph, silver prints (BP 274, DM 683, FR 2318, Y 56,592).
$467* *Aviatrix In Biplane and Advertisement For United Air Lines: Two,* handstamps, 1930's, (10-14-92, Swann, #368, illus.), one 8 x 10 in., (20.3 x 25.4 cm.), other 10 x 8 in., (20.3 x 25.4 cm.), photograph, silver prints (BP 274, DM 683, FR 2318, Y 56,592).
$467* *"Housewife Washing Dishes", "Woman Drinking Coca-Cola", and "Woman Shopping: Three,* handstamps, 1930's, (10-14-92, Swann, #369, illus.), each, approx. 10 x 8 in., (25.4 x 20.3 cm.), photograph, silver prints (BP 274, DM 683, FR 2318, Y 56,592).
$770* *Industrial View,* photog.'s handstamp, 1930s, (04-07-93, Swann, #433, illus.), 9½ x 7½ in., photograph, silver print (BP 509, DM 1245, FR 4215, Y 87,480).
BI *Italian Street Fair, Chicago, 1942,* s., t., d., est. $2/2,500, (04-08-93, Christie-NY, #270, illus.), 13⅛ x 16¾ in., (33.3 x 42.5 cm.), photograph, gelatin silver print.
$550* *Luna Park Taken At Night: Two Photographs,* handstamp, 1930's, (10-14-92, Swann, #524, illus.), 8 x 10 in., (20.3 x 25.4 cm.), 10 x 8 in., (25.4 x 20.3 cm.), photograph, silver prints (BP 323, DM 805, FR 2730, Y 66,651).
BI *"Man Conferring With Tattoo Artist", "Man Getting Tattoo", and "Man Getting Tattoo (Close-Up)": Three,* handstamp, 1930's, est. $7/1,000, (10-14-92, Swann, #420, illus.), 8½ x 7½ in., (21.6 x 19.1 cm.), photograph, silver prints.

$550* *Mannequin Workshop,* 1940s, stamp, (10-13-92, Christie-NY, #171, illus.), 13⅞ x 10½ in., (35.2 x 26.7 cm.), photograph, gelatin silver print (BP 320, DM 806, FR 2738, Y 66,691).

BI *Nuclear Physics Research Station, 1946,* photog.'s handstamp, notations, est. $6/900, (04-07-93, Swann, #299, illus.), 13 x 11 in., photograph, silver print.

$660* *Photogram, 1930,* s., d., (10-14-92, Swann, #421, illus.), 8 x 10 in., (20.3 x 25.4 cm.), photograph, silver print (BP 387, DM 966, FR 3275, Y 79,981).

$1610* *"Pontiac Hood Ornament Design" and "Assembly Line": Two,* 1940s, credit stamp, (04-08-93, Christie-NY, #269, illus.), each approx. 10⅝ x 13½ in., (27 x 34.3 cm.), photograph, gelatin silver print (BP 1056, DM 2586, FR 8755, Y 182,705).

$357* *Positive/Negative Portrait Of A Woman Wearing A Fur Coat,* photog.'s handstamp, 1930s, (04-07-93, Swann, #434, illus.), 9½ x 7½ in., photograph, silver print (BP 236, DM 577, FR 1954, Y 40,559).

BI *Steel Furnaces,* 1930s, stamp, est. $1/1,500, (10-13-92, Christie-NY, #170, illus.), 13¼ x 10½ in., (33.7 x 26.7 cm.), photograph, gelatin silver print.

$522* *"Union Pacific Railroad" and "Snow Scene With Train": Two,* photog.'s handstamp, 1930s, (04-07-93, Swann, #506, illus.), one 9 x 7 in., other 6½ x 9½ in., photograph, silver print (BP 345, DM 844, FR 2857, Y 59,305).

COSTER, Howard 1885-1959

$343* *George Bernard Shaw, Autographed Portrait, 1931,* s., mount ink s., (10-29-92, Christie-London, #89), image 11¼ x 8⅞ in., (28.6 x 22.5 cm.), photograph, gelatin silver print on textured paper (BP 220, DM 528, FR 1790, Y 42,487).

BI *Portraits, c. 1930: Two,* stamped photog.'s credit, t., each approx. 262 x 215mm, est. BP 80/120, (05-07-93, Sotheby-London, #219), photograph, silver print.

COSTIGAN, John American 1888-1972

$70* *"Autumn",* s., t., AAA edit., very good cond., (05-15-93, Cleveland, #102), 8¾ x 14 in., (22.2 x 35.6 cm.), etching (BP 46, DM 113, FR 378, Y 7760).

$83* *"Autumn",* s., good/poor cond., (03-28-93, Bakker, #210), pl 8¾ x 13¾ in., (22.2 x 34.9 cm.), etching (BP 56, DM 135, FR 460, Y 9660).

$121* *"Fall Plowing", 1938,* s., t., AAA edit., good cond., (10-31-92, Cleveland, #104), 8¼ x 12⅞ in., (21 x 32.7 cm.), etching (BP 78, DM 186, FR 632, Y 14,988).

$88* *"Springtime",* AAA label verso, (08-29-92, Young, #82), 9 x 11 in., (22.9 x 27.9 cm.), etching (BP 44, DM 124, FR 422, Y 10,851).

$60* *Two Cows And Boy In A Stream,* s., light toned, (05-15-93, Cleveland, #101), 10 x 12 in., (25.4 x 30.5 cm.), etching (BP 39, DM 97, FR 324, Y 6651).

COSWAY, Maria (after)

$175* *The Hours,* by Francesco Bartolozzi, margins, stained, torn, (02-17-93, Bonhams-Chelsea, #338), plate 17¼ x 20¼ in., (43.8 x 51.4 cm.), stipple engraving (BP 121, DM 284, FR 963, Y 20,903).

COSWAY, Richard (after)

$150* *Childish Impatience, 1786,* engraved by T. Gaugain, margins, (11-30-92, Phillips-London, #162), plate 8⅛ x 8½ in., (206 x 216 mm.), stipple engraving in sepia and black on laid (BP 99, DM 239, FR 811, Y 18,668).

$102* *Melania, 1792,* by J. Conde, pub. J. Conde & Molteno, Colnaghi & Co., margins, (12-10-92, Bonhams-Chelsea, #75), plate 6 x 4¼ in., (15.2 x 10.8 cm.), engraving (BP 66, DM 161, FR 551, Y 12,618).

COTES, Francis (after)

$283* *Frances, Lady Bridges (C.S. 14), 1769,* by James Watson, 1st state of 2 (Russell 2nd state of 6), scratch-letter proof before t., pub. Sayer, trimmed to margins, good cond., (11-30-92, Phillips-London, #46), sheet 20¼ x 14¼ in., (514 x 362 mm.), mezzotint on laid (BP 187, DM 451, FR 1531, Y 35,221).

$333* *Joseph And John Gulston (C.S. 59), 1771,* by Valentine Green, scratch-letter proof before t. (Russell 1st stateof 2), unevenly trimmed to or inside platemark, repaired corner, (11-30-92, Phillips-London, #45), sheet 17½ x 20⅛ in., (445 x 511 mm.), mezzotint on laid (BP 220, DM 531, FR 1801, Y 41,444).

$83* *Maria, Lady Broughton (C.S. 2), 1772,* by J. Finlayson, 2nd final state, pub. J. Finlayson, margins folded,skinning, good cond., (11-30-92, Phillips-London, #47), plate 19⅝ x 13¾ in., (498 x 349 mm.), mezzotint on laid (BP 55, DM 132, FR 449, Y 10,330).

COTMAN, J. (after)

$36 *Continental Buildings: Four,* (02-05-93, G.A. Key, #75), each approx. 14 x 11 in., (35.6 x 27.9 cm.), sepia lithograph (BP 25, DM 60, FR 202, Y 4480).

COTMAN, John Sell English 1782-1842

$46 *"A Country House" and "A Fisherman": Two,* (04-16-93, G.A. Key, #155), etching (BP 30, DM 74, FR 251, Y 5173).

BI *Millbank On The Thames,* margins, est. BP 40/60, (02-17-93, Bonhams-Chelsea, #363), plate 6½ x 10 in., (16.5 x 25.4 cm.), soft-ground etching.

$16 *Norfolk Churches: Three,* (12-11-92, G.A. Key, #81), black and white engraving (BP 10, DM 25, FR 86, Y 1980).

$73 *"St. Botolphs Priory, Essex",* (06-11-93, G.A. Key, #13), 9 x 14 in., (22.9 x 35.6 cm.), b/w engraving (BP 48, DM 119, FR 400, Y 7745).

BI *"West End Of Braysworth Church, Suffolk",* (12-11-92, G.A. Key, #107), 12 x 10 in., (30.5 x 25.4 cm.), b/w engraving.

$43 *"West End Of Braysworth Church, Suffolk",* (02-05-93, G.A. Key, #52), 12 x 10 in., (30.5 x 25.4 cm.), b/w engraving (BP 30, DM 71, FR 241, Y 5351).

COTMAN, John Sell (after)

$46 *"Cambridge Castle" and "St Marys Chapel, Stowbridge": Two,* (02-05-93, G.A. Key, #35), one 8 x 11 in., (20.3 x 27.9 cm.), the other 6 x 11 in., (20.3 x 27.9 cm.), etched print (BP 32, DM 76, FR 258, Y 5724).

$12 *"Doorway Mintlyn Church, Norfolk",* (06-11-93, G.A. Key, #91), 9 x 6¾ in., (22.9 x 17.1 cm.), b/w engraving (BP 8, DM 20, FR 66, Y 1273).

COTTAVOZ, Ande

$226* *Collioures, 1990,* s., #168/175, good margins, (05-06-93, Laurin, #21), carborundum engraving and print in color (BP 143, DM 356, FR 1198, Y 24,865).

$144* *N.M. Aux Coquelicots, 1989,* s., #142/175, full margins, (05-06-93, Laurin, #20), carborundum engraving in color (BP 91, DM 227, FR 764, Y 15,843).

COTTET, Charles French 1863-1925

BI *Un Enterrement En Bretagne (Una Johnson 26, Cariou 8), 1897,* staining verso, (02-24-93, Picard, #69), color lithograph on thin chine.

COTTIN, Pierre (after Constant Joseph BROCHART) French 1823-1886

BI *Le Vocu Accompli (The Accomplished Vow),* est. $175/225, (02-04-93, Sloan, #390), 30¼ x 24 in., (76.8 x 61 cm.), engraving.

COTTINGHAM, Robert American b. 1935

$605* *Fox (Landwehr2), 1973,* s., #86/100, prov., (05-16-93, Hindman, #606), 20¾ x 20¾ in., (52.7 x 52.7 cm.), color lithograph (BP 393, DM 973, FR 3270, Y 67,066).

$495* *Fox, 1973,* s., num. V, arabic num. edit. of 100, blindstamp, full sheet, very good cond., (05-22-93, Weschler, #175), 23 x 23 in., (58.4 x 58.4 cm.), lithograph in colors on Arjamari (BP 321, DM 805, FR 2708, Y 54,576).

COTTON, John Wesley

$299* *Crew And Fishing Boat In Misty Sunrise,* s., d. '13, #2/50, (11-30-92, Ritchie, #11), 9½ x 13¾ in., (24.2 x 34.9 cm.), color aquatint (BP 197, DM 476, FR 1617, Y 37,212, C$ 385).

$65* *The Waits (Winter Evening With Trio Of Musicians),* t. in plate, s., i., prov., (06-07-93, Ritchie, #60, illus.), 5⅞ x 2⅞ in., (14.9 x 7.3 cm.), color aquatint (BP 43, DM 105, FR 355, Y 6973, C$ 83).

COUDRAIN, Brigette b. 1934

$101* *"Cavalier",* s., (10-18-92, Pescheteau, #113), sight 7$\frac{1}{16}$ x 5½ in., (18 x 14 cm.), etching and aquatint (BP 61, DM 149, FR 507, Y 12,060).

COUGHLIN, Jack

$85* *"Felines" and "Creature": Two*, each s., #32/100 and 33/100, prov., (12-01-92, Ritchie, #87, illus.), 12¼ x 16⅛ in., (31.1 x 41 cm.), etching (BP 56, DM 135, FR 462, Y 10,583, C$ 110).

COULET

$412* *Salle De "L'Etoile"*, A. Pomeon and Ses Fils, B cond., surface stains, closed tears, abrasions, (08-06-92, Swann, #109, illus.), 62 x 46 in., (157.5 x 116.8 cm.), (BP 215, DM 609, FR 2056, Y 52,551).

COULET, L.

$347* *Salle De L'Etoile, St. Etienne*, creases, edges chipped, backed on linen, laid on board, (05-07-93, Christie-S. Ken, #98, illus.), color lithograph (BP 220, DM 549, FR 1849, Y 38,207).

COULON, E.

$608* *Felix Potin, "Reveillon Cadeau: Foie Gras, Champagne, Marrons Glaces"*, c. 1930, p. Le Novateur, good cond., lit., (11-19-92, Ribeyre/Baron, #27), 34¼ x 60⅝ in., (87 x 154 cm.), poster (BP 400, DM 969, FR 3265, Y 75,612).

COULON, E. de

$200* *PLM. Allevard Les Bains. Dauphine. "Centre Thermal Et Touristique"*, c. 1930, very good cond., (03-15-93, Arcole, #27, illus.), 39⅜ x 24⁷⁄₁₆ in., (100 x 62 cm.), (BP 139, DM 332, FR 1129, Y 23,691).

$818* *PLM. Sports D'Hiver Alpes Et Jura. "Air Pur, Sante, Plaisir"*, 1930-32, very good cond., (03-15-93, Arcole, #85, illus.), 39⁷⁄₁₆ x 24³⁄₁₆ in., (100.1 x 61.5 cm.), (BP 570, DM 1359, FR 4619, Y 96,896).

COUNIHAN, Jack Noel   1913-1986

$65* *A Girl's Head (1968)*, s. Counihan, i., d. '68, #37/40, lit., (08-11-92, L. Joel, #79G), 17⅜ x 19 in., (44.2 x 48.3 cm.), three color lithograph (zinc plate) (BP 34, DM 95, FR 323, Y 8324, A$ 88).

$81* *A Girl's Head (1968)*, s. Counihan, i., d. '68, #2/40, lit., (08-11-92, L. Joel, #47G), 17⅜ x 19 in., (44.2 x 48.3 cm.), three color lithograph (zinc plate) (BP 42, DM 119, FR 403, Y 10,373, A$ 110).

$243* *Mexican Girl*, s. Counihan, i., d. '70, #14/120, lit., (08-11-92, L. Joel, #28G, illus.), 21³⁄₁₆ x 13¼ in., (53.8 x 33.7 cm.), linocut (BP 126, DM 357, FR 1208, Y 31,118, A$ 330).

BI *Mexican Girl*, s. Counihan, i., d. '70, #11/120, lit., est. $3/500, (08-11-92, L. Joel, #148G), 21³⁄₁₆ x 13¼ in., (53.8 x 33.7 cm.), linocut.

COURBET, Gustave   French 1819-1877

$699* *L'Apotre Jean Journet (I.F.F. 2)*, 1850, small margins, collector's stamp, (06-11-93, Picard, #23), 9⁷⁄₁₆ x 6¹¹⁄₁₆ in., (240 x 170 mm.), lithograph in black on wove (BP 459, DM 1136, FR 3830, Y 74,164).

COURCHINOUX, Edouard   1891-1968

$359* *Cycles Meteore*, 1925, cond. B, (03-16-93, Boisgirard, #88), 55⅞ x 44½ in., (142 x 113 cm.), poster (BP 248, DM 597, FR 2028, Y 41,978).

COURTIN, Pierre

BI *"La Longue Marge" (Riviere 395), c. 1971 and "La Verite Cruelle D'UnAncien Jeu" (Riviere 397): Two*, first s., #83/100; second s., #202/300, est. FF800/1,000, (06-28-93, Loudmer, #27), first 16⁵⁄₁₆ x 25³⁄₁₆ in., (415 x 640 mm.), second 17¹¹⁄₁₆ x 23⅝ in., (415 x 640 mm.), color lithographs on Arches wove.

$123* *Novembre*, 1949, s., #54/200, good margins, (05-06-93, Laurin, #22), copper engraving (BP 78, DM 194, FR 652, Y 13,533).

$72* *"Ronde"*, s., d. December 1958, (03-12-93, DuMouchelle, #2324), 9 x 9½ in., (22.9 x 24.1 cm.), etching (BP 50, DM 120, FR 407, Y 8486).

COURTOIS, Pierre-Francois   1736-1763

BI *"Tableau Des Portraits A La Mode" and "La Promenade Des Remparts De Paris" (Bocher 373, 382; P. and B., I. p. 599, nos. 1-2; L. and D. 25-6; Inventaire 18e Siecle, V, pp. 334-5, nos. 1, 3)*, 1761: A Pair, 3rd (final) state, watermark, pub. F. Chereau, wide margins, handling creases, est. BP 1,2/1,600, (12-01-92, Christie-London, #238, illus.), plate 11⁵⁄₁₆ x 15⅛ in., (287 x 384 mm.), etching w/engraving on Auvergne laid paper.

COURTOIS, Raphael

$955* *Pour Reussir En Photographie*, p. B. Chapellierjeune, repaired tear, defects, backed on linen, (05-07-93, Christie-S. Ken, #96, illus.), 63 x 47 in., (160 x 119.4 cm.), color lithograph (BP 605, DM 1510, FR 5088, Y 105,153).

COUSEN, J.

$167* *The Victory Towed Into Gibraltar After The Battle Of Trafalgar, 1867*, after Clarkson Stanfield, pub. Thomas Agnew and Sons, foxing, (11-19-92, Bonhams-Chelsea, #60), image 17⅞ x 27½ in., (45.4 x 69.9 cm.), engraving (BP 110, DM 266, FR 897, Y 20,769).

COUSSENS, Armand

$124* *Pecheurs Sur Le Quai*, s., reddish stains, large margins, (04-02-93, Picard, #78), 9¾ x 12⅝ in., (24.7 x 32 cm.), color etching (BP 82, DM 199, FR 677, Y 14,118).

$145* *"Le Pont Des Arts" and "Le Pont De La Tournelle": Two*, annot., good margins, s., (04-02-93, Picard, #76), one 8¹⁄₁₆ x 10⁵⁄₁₆ in., (20.5 x 26.2 cm.), other 10¹⁵⁄₁₆ x 15¾ in., (20.5 x 26.2 cm.), color etching (BP 96, DM 233, FR 791, Y 16,509).

$573* *"Roubaou Marechal", "Place Du Marche", "La Cuisine" and "Etameur": Four*, 2 s., 2 t., annot., untrimmed margins, (02-24-93, Picard, #70), color etching, drypoint and softground etching on wove or simili-Japan (BP 400, DM 930, FR 3154, Y 67,238).

COUTELLIER, Francois   ac. 1780-1790

$300* *M. Dutey [Mlle. Duthe] (Inventaire 18e Siecle, V, p. 341, no. 5), 1778*, pub. Coutellier and Chereau, trimmed to an oval as issued, laid, foxing, defects, (12-01-92, Christie-London, #274, illus.), sheet 14¹³⁄₁₆ x 11⁵⁄₁₆ in., (377 x 287 mm.), stipple engraving in colors (BP 198, DM 478, FR 1630, Y 37,351).

$1915* *Trois Acteurs Et Trois Actrices Celebres De La Comedie-Italienne(P. and B., I, pp. 601-2, nos. 3-8; Inventaire 18e Siecle, V, pp. 340-3, nos. 1-2, 4, 6, 8-9), 1782-3: Set Of Six*, 1st state of 2, pub. Coutellier, trimmed to oval as issued, laid, excellent cond., prov., (12-01-92, Christie-London, #273, illus.), sheet 11¼ x 8⁷⁄₁₆ in., (286 x 214 mm.), stipple engraving in colors (BP 1265, DM 3052, FR 10,402, Y 238,421).

COUTU

$16* *Snowy Owl*, #54/100, s., t., d. '73, margins, (02-17-93, Bonhams-Chelsea, #319), plate 27 x 19¾ in., (68.6 x 50.2 cm.), color etching w/aquatint (BP 11, DM 26, FR 88, Y 1911).

COUTY, Edmy

$1477* *Exposition D'Art Photographique 1896*, folds, repaired tears, defects, backed on linen, laid on board, (05-07-93, Christie-S. Ken, #130, illus.), 25¼ x 71 in., (64.1 x 180.3 cm.), lithograph (BP 935, DM 2335, FR 7869, Y 162,629).

COUZIJN, Wessel   b. 1912

BI *II, 1966: Twelve*, complete portfolio, num. 68, pub. W.A. Palm, good cond., est. G 2,8/3,500, (12-09-92, Sotheby-Amstrdm, #548, illus.), overall 17¹⁄₁₆ x 21⅝ in., (434 x 550 mm.), two color lithographs, an etching w/aquatint and nine color lithographs w/etching and aquatint.

BI *Untitled*, s., #69/100, margins, good cond., est. Dfl. 250/350, (05-27-93, Sotheby-Amstrdm, #606), sh 11 x 14¹¹⁄₁₆ in., (280 x 373 mm.), lithograph on wove.

COVARRUBIAS, Miguel   Mexican 1904-1957

BI *Rice Granary Bali*, c. 1935, s., pub. A.A.A, full margins, good cond., tape remnants, soiling, est. $8/1,200, (11-23-92, Sotheby-NY, #261, illus.), image 12¼ x 9½ in., (310 x 240 mm.), lithograph.

$275* *"Rice Granary, Bali"*, pub. AAA, s. Covarrubias, good cond., glue residue verso, (09-11-92, Skinner, #69, illus.), 12⅜ x 9⅜ in., (31.4 x 23.8 cm.), lithograph on Alexandria wove w/watermark (BP 142, DM 396, FR 1345, Y 34,073).

$468* *Rumba*, s., pub. AAA, margins, good cond., mat staining, foxing, taped, (02-24-93, Butterfield, #2812), 12 x 16 in., (305 x 406 mm.), lithograph on wove (BP 326, DM 760, FR 2576, Y 54,917).

COWARD, Richard
    BI   *John Blakemore, 1980,* s., 410 x 304mm, est. BP 1/200, (05-07-93, Sotheby-London, #409, illus.), photograph, silver print.

COWIN, Eileen
    $403* *Untitled, Two Women,* 1981, p. 1984, s., d., illus., (05-23-93, Butterfield, #3381), 14 x 18 in., photograph, c-print (BP 262, DM 659, FR 2218, Y 44,545).

COWIN, Jack L.   b. 1947
    $303* *Firehole Brown (Western Trout Series - Unique), 1981,* #63/100, s., t., d. '81, prov., (11-16-92, Hodgins, #70), 13½ x 24 in., (34.3 x 61 cm.), hand colored etching on paper (BP 199, DM 483, FR 1628, Y 37,814, C$ 385).
    $173* *Rising Brown, 1983,* #271/300, s., t., d. '83, prov., (11-16-92, Hodgins, #209, illus.), 18½ x 24½ in., (47 x 62.2 cm.), colored etching on paper (BP 114, DM 276, FR 930, Y 21,590, C$ 220).

COWLEY, Lee John (III)
    $22* *Front Of House,* s., (12-11-92, DuMouchelle, #2492), image 8 x 5½ in., (20.3 x 14 cm.), etching (BP 14, DM 35, FR 119, Y 2722).

COWLEY, Reta
    BI   *Saskatchewan Village #2,* s., t., d. 1957, est. C$2/300, (06-07-93, Ritchie, #40), 12½ x 18¾ in., (31.8 x 47.6 cm.), color serigraph.

COX, Arthur
    BI   *Barnyard Scene With Figures And Workhorse,* s., trimmed, laid down on paper, good cond.?, est. $2/300, (01-30-93, Weschler, #50), 19¼ x 23½ in., (48.9 x 59.7 cm.), mezzotint.
    $138* *Two Elegant Ladies,* (08-29-92, Young, #83), 17 x 13 in., (43.2 x 33 cm.), lithograph in colors (BP 70, DM 194, FR 662, Y 17,016).

COX, Helen   American 20th cent.
    $83* *Woman With Cat,* s., d. 1966, #26/50, (05-28-93, Sloan, #1898, illus.), 20¼ x 15½ in., (51.4 x 39.4 cm.), color lithograph (BP 53, DM 132, FR 445, Y 8900).

COX, Jacob (attrib.)
    $413* *Two Seated Indians In Ornate Costumes,* (04-30-93, Garth, #41, illus.), 18⅛ x 14¾ in., photograph (BP 263, DM 654, FR 2205, Y 45,823).

COX, Patrick Douglass   b. 1953
    $304* *The Cowhand, 1991,* s., t., d. '91, (05-10-93, Hodgins, #350), 15½ x 26½ in., (39.4 x 67.3 cm.), hand colored lithograph on paper (BP 198, DM 488, FR 1648, Y 33,970, C$ 385).
    $260* *The Right Hand Man, 1991,* #16/25, s., t., d. '91, (05-10-93, Hodgins, #150), 19¾ x 13 in., (50.2 x 33 cm.), lithograph on paper (BP 170, DM 418, FR 1409, Y 29,054, C$ 330).

COX, W.A., Engraver
    BI   *Figures In A Wooded Clearing Listening To A Mandolin Player, 1915,* pub. Virtue and Company, margins, est. BP 5/70, (03-17-93, Bonhams-Chelsea, #436), plate 19 x 22 in., (48.3 x 55.9 cm.), mezzotint in colors.

COYER, Max
    $403* *Still Life Iris, 1988,* s., d., t., annot. P.P. 5/6, blindstamp publisher, Trillium Graphics, very good cond., (05-19-93, Butterfield, #2148), 30 x 22¼ in., (762 x 565 mm.), lithograph in colors on wove (BP 262, DM 655, FR 2207, Y 44,614).

COZZENS, Frederick Schiller   American 1846-1928
    $385* *Ice Boating On The Hudson, 1984,* printed by Scribner and Son, s., (11-12-92, Freemn/Fine Art, #54, illus.), 21½ x 15½ in., (54.6 x 39.4 cm.), litho in color (BP 253, DM 610, FR 2058, Y 47,737).
    $110* *Seascape,* s. in plate, (12-17-92, Mystic, #12), 14 x 20 in., (35.6 x 50.8 cm.), chromolithograph (BP 70, DM 172, FR 587, Y 13,518).

COZZENS, Frederick Schiller (after)
    $440* *"For The America's Cup 1881-The Start, Yachts, Atlanta Mischief",* s., d. Fred S. Cozzens '83, ident. i., (01-16-93, Skinner, #9), sight 14 x 20¼ in., (35.6 x 51.4 cm.), chromolithograph on paper (BP 288, DM 719, FR 2432, Y 55,472).

    $413* *Yacht Race,* Janet-Lee Auchincloss Estate, (09-19-92, Weschler, #154), 14 x 21 in., (35.6 x 53.3 cm.), chromolithograph (BP 242, DM 613, FR 2096, Y 51,044).

CRAGG, Tony   English b. 1949
    $2200* *Laboratory Still Life 2, State 2, 1988,* s., t., d., #6/30, blindstamp, full margins, excellent cond., (11-09-92, Christie-NY, #258, illus.), 21 x 44 in., (53.3 x 111.8 cm.), aquatint in salmon red and black on wove (BP 1455, DM 3512, FR 11,866, Y 273,021).
    BI   *The Listeners, 1990: Two,* s., d., #2/15, blindstamp publisher, Crown Point Press, full margins, est. $1,5/2,000, (05-19-93, Butterfield, #2149), each 8⅜ x 8⅜ in., (213 x 213 mm.), aquatint (one p. in colors) on wove.

CRAIG, Barry
    $888* *These Men Use Shell, Explorers, 1938,* ref. #524, cond. 1, (10-13-92, Phillips-London, #143), 29¹⁵/₁₆ x 44⅞ in., (76 x 114 cm.), color lithograph (BP 517, DM 1301, FR 4420, Y 107,676).

CRAMER, Konrad   German/American 1888-1965
    BI   *Figure Studies, c. 1951: Two,* made from paper neg. of 1 of Cramer's drawings, mounted, s., i., est.$2/3,000, (10-15-92, Sotheby-NY, #481, illus.), one 5⅞ x 3½ in., (14.9 x 8.9 cm.), other 5½ x 2⅝ in., (14.9 x 8.9 cm.), photograph, gelatin silver prints.
    BI   *Figure Study, 1957,* s., d., i., annot., prov., est. $1,8/2,200, (04-08-93, Christie-NY, #484A, illus.), 12¼ x 5½ in., (31.1 x 14 cm.), photograph, gelatin silver print.
    BI   *Solarized Nude, late 1930's,* mounted, i., s. Aileen B. Cramer, est. $1,5/2,000, (04-06-93, Sotheby-NY, #135, illus.), 14⅜ x 9⅜ in., photograph.

CRANACH, Lucas
    $2728* *The Passion (B. 7-20; Holl. 10-23), 1509: Set of Fourteen,* separately p. borders, text below, margins, repairs, stains, soiling, Holl. 21 w/repairs in subject, (12-03-92, Sotheby-London, #31), each sheet approx. 14⅝ x 10⅜ in., (371 x 264 mm.), woodcuts on paper w/watermark (BP 1760, DM 4290, FR 14,643, Y 339,430).
    BI   *The Penance Of St. John Chrysostom (B., Holl. 1), 1509,* second (final) state, narrow margins, small repair, paper adhering to centre, rubbed, good cond., ex-coll., est. BP 6/8,000, (12-03-92, Sotheby-London, #33, illus.), 10 x 7⅞ in., (254 x 200 mm.), engraving.
    BI   *The Penance Of St. John Chrysostum (B., Holl. 1), 1509,* watermark, narrow margins, brown stain, fold, cockling, good cond., ex. coll. K.G. Lade(?) and Ch. J. Rosenbloom (L. 633b), est. BP 6/8,000, (06-29-93, Sotheby-London, #17, illus.), 10 x 7¾ in., (25.4 x 19.7 cm.), engraving on paper.
    $7162* *The Saxon Prince On A Boar Hunt (B. 118; Holl. 113), c. 1507,* second (final) state, thread margins, trimmed on borderline, repaired tear, borderline touched w/grey wash, thin spots, glue remains verso, good cond., ex-coll., (12-03-92, Sotheby-London, #30, illus.), 7 x 4⅞ in., (178 x 124 mm.), woodcut on paper w/watermark (BP 4620, DM 11,263, FR 38,443, Y 891,129).
    $5116* *A Saxon Prince On Horseback (B. 116; Holl. 110), 1506,* second (final) state, trimmed on borderline, paper thin, surface dirt, ex-coll., (12-03-92, Sotheby-London, #29, illus.), 7 x 4¾ in., (178 x 121 mm.), woodcut (BP 3300, DM 8045, FR 27,461, Y 636,556).
    $2728* *The Sermon Of St. John The Baptist (B. 60; Holl. 85), 1516,* trimmed to borderline, central crease, stains, thin spots, good cond., (12-03-92, Sotheby-London, #32), 13⅜ x 9¼ in., (340 x 235 mm.), woodcut on paper w/watermark (BP 1760, DM 4290, FR 14,643, Y 339,430).

CRANACH, Lucas (the elder)   German 1472-1553
    $2401* *Die Busse Des Heiligen Chrysostomus (Bartsch and Hollstein 1; Koepplin-Falck 486), 1509,* (06-10-93, Hauswedell/Nolt., #62, illus.), engraving (BP 1571, DM 3910, FR 13,163, Y 254,856).
    $3665* *Ecce Homo (Hollstein 17; Geisberg-Strauss 550), 1509,* sheet 8 of series Die Passion Christi, prov., (06-23-93, Kornfeld, #19, illus.), woodcut (BP 2490, DM 6201, FR 20,859, Y 399,281, SF 5520).
    BI   *Die Entruckung Der Hl. Maria Magdalena (B. 72; Dodgson 5; Hollstein 94 II), 1506,* est. DM 4,500, (12-04-92,

Bassenge, #6134, illus.), 9½ x 5⅝ in., (24.2 x 14.3 cm.), woodcut.

BI *The First Tournament (Tournament With Lances) (B. 124; Holl. 116), 1506,* 2nd (final) state, watermark, thread margins, trimmed, center creases, restorations, repairs, glue, stains, good cond., est. $7/10,000, (05-13-93, Sotheby-NY, #115, illus.), 10 x 14½ in., (255 x 368 mm.), woodcut.

$1228* *Friedrich III, Der Weise, Kurfurst Von Sachsen,* lit., (12-04-92, Bassenge, #6135), 12 x 10¾ in., (30.5 x 27.3 cm.), chiaroscuro woodcut by 2 plates, p. in brown and black (BP 788, DM 1956, FR 6634, Y 153,308).

$1084* *Die Heilige Verwandschaft (B. 5; Dodgson 79; Schuchardt 14; Hollst. 71),* mono., i., foxed, d. 1508, trimmed, (10-09-92, Winterberg, #757), 8¹⁵⁄₁₆ x 12¹¹⁄₁₆ in., (22.7 x 32.3 cm.), woodcut (BP 643, DM 1610, FR 5406, Y 131,970).

BI *Die Hl. Anna Mit Maria Und Dem Kinde (B. 68; Shuchardt 83; Dodgson 82; Hollstein 75),* prov., watermark, est. DM 3,500, (12-04-92, Bassenge, #6133, illus.), 9¹¹⁄₁₆ x 6⁹⁄₁₆ in., (24.6 x 16.7 cm.), woodcut.

$1840* *The Holy Kinship (B. 5, Holl. 71), c. 1510,* later impression, narrow margins, repaired tear into image, good cond., watermark, prop. Montclair Art Museum, (05-11-93, Christie-NY, #10), borderline 12¾ x 8⅞ in., (324 x 225 mm.), woodcut on laid (BP 1175, DM 2899, FR 9766, Y 202,398).

BI *Marcus Curtius Plunging Into The Chasm (B. 112; Holl. 106), c. 1507,* watermark, trimmed to borderline, thin spots, repairs, repaired tear,soiling, surface dirt, good cond., ex-coll. Dr. Albert W. Blum, est. $4/6,000, (05-13-93, Sotheby-NY, #116), 13¼ x 9⅛ in., (335 x 233 mm.), woodcut.

$2673* *Das Massenturnier Mit Lanzen - Das Erste Turnier (Hollst. 116/II; Geisb.-Str. 620), 1506,* prov., (06-23-93, Kornfeld, #21, illus.), woodcut (BP 1816, DM 4523, FR 15,213, Y 291,208, SF 4025).

$1589* *Die Ruhe Auf Der Flucht Nach Aypten, Mit Tanzenden Engeln (B. 4; Schuchardt 9; Heller 4; Dodgson 123; Hollstein 8),* (12-04-92, Bassenge, #6132), 13¼ x 9⅜ in., (33.6 x 23.8 cm.), woodcut (BP 1019, DM 2531, FR 8585, Y 198,377).

$11,500* *St. Christopher (B. 58; Holl. 79), c. 1509,* date removed, second tone block, narrow margins, horizontal center crease, repair(?), good cond., (05-13-93, Sotheby-NY, #113, illus.), 11¼ x 7⅛ in., (286 x 181 mm.), chiaroscuro woodcut p. from two blocks in black and grey (BP 7550, DM 18,569, FR 62,636, Y 1,283,912).

$2917* *St. George Slaying The Dragon (Holl. 82),* narrow margins, discoloration, stains, (06-30-93, Sotheby-London, #105), 6½ x 5 in., (165 x 127 mm.), woodcut (BP 1955, DM 4975, FR 16,784, Y 312,547).

BI *"St. James The Greater" and "St. Matthew" (B. 26 and 31; Holl. 34 and39), c. 1510-15: A Pair,* from Christ, the Apostles and St. Paul, watermark, trimmed to borderline, repairs, restorations; creases, thin spots, good cond., ex-coll. Dr. Albert W. Blum, est. $1,5/2,000, (05-13-93, Sotheby-NY, #114), each approx. 12½ x 7½ in., (316 x 190 mm.), woodcut.

$6374* *Two Tournaments With Tapestry Of Samson And The Lion (B. 126, Hollstein 117), 1509,* prov., (06-04-93, Bassenge, #5094, illus.), 11⅝ x 16¼ in., (29.5 x 41.3 cm.), woodcut (BP 4217, DM 10,351, FR 34,888, Y 687,446).

CRANE, Alan

BI *"News Of The Day" and "Supper House": Two,* s., t., hinged to mats, very good cond., est. $4/600, (12-04-92, Doyle, #89), 9¾ x 13¾ in., (248 x 349 mm.), lithograph.

$165* *"November" and "House By The Sea": Two,* both s., edit. of 40, very good cond., (03-28-93, Bakker, #64), each, image 9½ x 13¾ in., (24.1 x 34.9 cm.), lithograph (BP 111, DM 269, FR 915, Y 19,204).

CRANE, Barbara American 20th cent.

$220* *Repeat, Tress,* (05-16-93, Hindman, #355), 1⅛ x 13¾ in., photograph, silver print (BP 144, DM 355, FR 1196, Y 24,499).

CRANE, Paula

BI *Hanging Lake,* s., t., #63/300, prov., est. C$ 150/250, (12-01-92, Ritchie, #34), 28 x 21¼ in., (71.1 x 54 cm.), embossed aquatint.

CRAWFORD, Neelon American contemporary

BI *P-51. (Rolls Royce),* s., t., #11/25, est. $2/300, (02-04-93, Sloan, #2970), 15½ x 19½ in., (39.4 x 49.5 cm.), aquatint.

CRAWFORD, Ralston American 1906-1977

BI *"Composition", c. 1952,* s., num. 29/200, excellent cond., est. $1,5-2,000, (10-31-92, Cleveland, #366, illus.), 19 x 11½ in., (48.3 x 29.2 cm.), lithograph in colors.

BI *Grey Street, 1940,* s., t., pub. Cincinnati Modern Art Society, margins, light/mat/glue staining, est. $1,5/2,500, (05-11-93, Christie-NY, #96), borderline 12 x 15 in., (305 x 381 mm.), color screenprint on wove.

$17,600* *Overseas Highway, 1940,* s., t., #11/25, margins, faded, mat staining, nicks, paper losses, good cond., (11-05-92, Sotheby-NY, #14, illus.), 9⅞ x 16 in., (252 x 405 mm.), lithograph p. in colors on wove (BP 11,447, DM 27,835, FR 94,168, Y 2,159,244).

$1955* *Red And Black (U.S.S. Nevada) (F. 3), 1949,* s., t., margins, good cond., mat/light-staining, (05-19-93, Butterfield, #1801), sh. 17¼ x 23⁷⁄₁₆ in., (438 x 595 mm.), silkscreen in red and black on wove (BP 1269, DM 3178, FR 10,706, Y 216,429).

CRAWFORD, T. Hamilton Scottish b. 1860

$55* *Portrait Of A Gentleman, 1928,* s., pub. Frost and Reed, (10-18-92, Hindman, #522), 17 x 13½ in., (43.2 x 34.3 cm.), color mezzotint (BP 34, DM 82, FR 278, Y 6599).

CRAWFORD, Thomas Hamilton English early 20th century

$50* *Thomas Jefferson, 1929,* pub. Frost and Reed, (02-04-93, Sloan, #351), 14⅞ x 12¼ in., (37.8 x 31.1 cm.), color mezzotint (BP 35, DM 82, FR 279, Y 6220).

CREEKMORE, Raymond American b. 1905

BI *"Off To The Onion Patch",* s., t., AAA edit., good cond., est. $75/125, (05-15-93, Cleveland, #103), 10¹⁵⁄₁₆ x 13¹⁵⁄₁₆ in., (27.8 x 35.4 cm.), lithograph.

CREMER, Jan b. 1940

BI *The Amsterdam-New York Set Or The End Of The Far West, 1978: Six,* from set of 9, five s., d. 1963-78, #4/80, p. Printshop, margins, good cond., creases, discoloration, est. G 1/1,500, (12-09-92, Sotheby-Amstrdm, #551), each approx. 25¾ x 19⅞ in., (654 x 505 mm.), color silkscreen on wove.

$326* *Coca-Cola, 1969,* s., d., #189/190, margins, good cond., (12-09-92, Sotheby-Amstrdm, #549), 19¾ x 28⅛ in., (502 x 715 mm.), color lithograph on wove (BP 208, DM 512, FR 1746, Y 40,422, G 575).

$192* *Haystacks, 1976,* s., d., full margins, good cond., small tear in right margin, (05-27-93, Sotheby-Amstrdm, #402), 27³⁄₁₆ x 20³⁄₁₆ in., (690 x 512 mm.), colored lithograph on wove (BP 123, DM 308, FR 1038, Y 20,583, G 345).

$489* *Hotdog USA 1967, 1968,* s., d., #179/190, margins, good cond., (12-09-92, Sotheby-Amstrdm, #552, illus.), 19³⁄₁₆ x 25½ in., (488 x 648 mm.), color lithograph on wove (BP 312, DM 768, FR 2619, Y 60,632, G 863).

$307* *Landscape, 1976,* s., d., full margins, good cond., (05-27-93, Sotheby-Amstrdm, #401, illus.), 27³⁄₁₆ x 20½ in., (690 x 520 mm.), colored lithograph on wove (BP 197, DM 493, FR 1660, Y 32,912, G 552).

$228* *Provence 1, 1989,* s., d., #150/250, good cond., (12-09-92, Sotheby-Amstrdm, #550), sheet 22¼ x 29¾ in., (565 x 755 mm.), color silkscreen on wove (BP 146, DM 358, FR 1221, Y 28,270, G 403).

$182* *Provence 2, 1989,* s., d., #140/250, good cond., (12-09-92, Sotheby-Amstrdm, #553), sheet 21¼ x 29¹⁵⁄₁₆ in., (540 x 760 mm.), color silkscreen on wove (BP 116, DM 286, FR 975, Y 22,567, G 322).

CREMONINI, Leonardo Italian b. 1925

$126* *"Derriere Le Bar",* E.A. s., tear, (01-28-93, Pescheteau, #113), 24⁷⁄₁₆ x 17¹¹⁄₁₆ in., (62 x 45 cm.), color serigraph on papier couche (BP 83, DM 200, FR 676, Y 15,644).

$160* *"Les Yeux Bandes", 1976,* #22/100, d., s., (04-04-93, Pescheteau, #189), 19¹¹⁄₁₆ x 25⁹⁄₁₆ in., (50 x 65 cm.), color lithograph (BP 105, DM 257, FR 873, Y 18,217).

CRESLAND, Paul French 20th cent.

$5* *"Eglise St. Pierre", "Facade De St. Pierre" and "Lapine Agile": Three,* good cond., (05-15-93, Cleveland, #377), color etching and aquatint (BP 3, DM 8, FR 27, Y 554).

CRESPO

$458* *Ch. De Fer Algeriens: CHREA. "Sports D'Hiver"*, very good cond., (03-13-93, Laurin, #44, illus.), 38 15/16 x 24 7/16 in., (99 x 62 cm.), (BP 319, DM 762, FR 2592, Y 53,978).

CREWE, Emma (after)

$233* *The Good Mother Reading A Story, 1783,* engraved & pub. by Charles White, trimmed to plate, (11-30-92, Phillips-London, #201), image 11⅜ x 11⅝ in., (289 x 295 mm.), line and stipple engraving (BP 154, DM 371, FR 1260, Y 28,998).

CRITE, Allan Rohan American b. 1910

$523* *"Eve"*, s., good cond., (03-28-93, Bakker, #103, illus.), image 8¾ x 1¼ in., (22.2 x 3.2 cm.), wood block (BP 351, DM 853, FR 2901, Y 60,871).

$660* *Salome, 1937,* s., d. Allan R. Crite 1937, mono., good cond., rippling, (03-12-93, Skinner, #81, illus.), sight 8⅞ x 3 in., (22.5 x 7.6 cm.), woodblock w/hand coloring on paper (BP 460, DM 1099, FR 3735, Y 77,784).

CROCKER, Susan

BI *Chicago '85 State Of Illinois Center Atrium, 1985,* s., t., d., est. $500/700, (10-13-92, Christie-NY, #531, illus.), 17¾ x 13¾ in., (45.1 x 34.9 cm.), photograph, gelatin silver print.

CRODEL, Charles 1894-1973

$361* *"Madchen Mit Ziegen" (Jahn/Berger 112), 1922,* s., d., in "Die Schaffenden", II. Jg., 3. Mappe, (11-28-92, Grisebach, #488, illus.), 13 13/16 x 10 5/16 in., (35.1 x 26.2 cm.), colored lithograph on wove (BP 238, DM 575, FR 1952, Y 44,928).

BI *"Ziegenhirtin" (Steckner 161 II), 1922,* s., Die Schaffenden, III. Jg., Mappe 3, est. DM 3500, (06-10-93, Hauswedell/Nolt, #216, illus.), image 14 9/16 x 10 7/16 in., (37 x 26.5 cm.), color lithograph on wove.

CROMBIC, Charles

$326* *Laws Of Cricket: Twelve,* volume. pub. Kegan Paul, Trench, Trubner and Co. Ltd., in assoc. w/Perrier, bound w/chromolithograph promoting product, original boards, front cover illus., (10-29-92, Bonhams-Chelsea, #13, illus.), chromolithograph (BP 209, DM 502, FR 1701, Y 40,382).

CROME, John

$4633* *Norfolk Picturesque Scenery (Theobold 1-24; And 27-33), 1809-13: TheComplete Set Of 31,* pub. 1834, after artist's death, good cond., tears, repaied tears, creases, surface dirt, (06-30-93, Sotheby-London, #263, illus.), etching and soft-ground etching on laid India paper supported on pinkish wov (BP 3105, DM 7902, FR 26,657, Y 496,411).

CRON, Hans c. 1434-1480

BI *Der Schmerzensmann (The Illustrated Bartsch Bd. 13, S. 211; Nagler, Mono. Bd. 3, 803), c. 1550-80,* very rare, creased, (09-14-92, Venator/Hansten, #1475), sh 10 11/16 x 7⅜ in., (27.1 x 18.7 cm.), woodcut.

CRONQVIST, Lena b. 1938

$7322* *August Strindberg: Portfolio,* s. 98/170, Atelier Clot et Georges, 1989, (05-25-93, AB Stockholm, #13, illus.), 28¾ x 20⅞ in., (73 x 53 cm.), 30 lithographs in b/w and color (BP 4745, DM 11,925, FR 40,143, Y 800,306, SK 10,670).

$2594* *August Strindberg: Portfolio,* s., 76/170, Atelier Clot et Georges 1989, (12-04-92, AB Stockholm, #7042), 28¾ x 20⅞ in., (73 x 53 cm.), 30 color and b/w lithographs (BP 1664, DM 4131, FR 14,014, Y 323,845, SK 17,600).

$134* *Kvinna Och Pojke,* s., from Ett dromspel, (04-17-93, Falkkloos, #97), 28¾ x 20⅞ in., (73 x 53 cm.), lithograph (BP 87, DM 214, FR 724, Y 14,900, SK 990).

CROPSEY, J.F.

$90 *"American Autumn, Starucca Valley, Erie Road"*, T. Sinclair's, (09-24-92, Alderfer, #233), 15½ x 26½ in., (39.4 x 67.3 cm.), (BP 53, DM 133, FR 453, Y 10,826).

CROSBY, Charles H.

$220* *Schooner "Missionary Packet"*, small folio, (11-07-92, Northeast, #177, illus.), lithograph (BP 144, DM 353, FR 1187, Y 27,154).

CROSS, Henri Edmond French 1856-1910

$698* *In Den Champs-Elysees,* Pan, Jg. IV, H. 1, 1898, (12-01-92, Karl/Faber, #511), 7⅞ x 10¼ in., (20 x 26 cm.), color lithograph (BP 461, DM 1113, FR 3791, Y 86,902).

$1064* *"In Den Champs-Elysees", 1898,* s., pub. in PAN IV/1, blindstamp, (06-05-93, Grisebach, #555, illus.), 7⅞ x 11¼ in., (20 x 28.5 cm.), color lithograph on Japan (BP 700, DM 1725, FR 5814, Y 114,139).

CRUICKSHANK, George British 1792-1878

$220* *Collection Of Prints: Eleven,* (05-16-93, Hindman, #434), larger 10 x 13¾ in., (25.4 x 34.9 cm.), hand-colored etchings and lithographs (BP 143, DM 354, FR 1189, Y 24,388).

CRUIKSHANK

$25* *"Oliver Asking For More" (Oliver Twist),* (10-03-92, Garth, #293, illus.), 11⅜ x 10 in., (28.9 x 25.4 cm.), engraving (BP 15, DM 35, FR 120, Y 2993).

CRUIKSHANK, George English 1792-1878

$150* *Behold At Brooks's Step-Nay! (B.M. 12629), 1815,* pub. H. Humphrey, good cond., (11-30-92, Phillips-London, #109), plate 10¾ x 8⅝ in., (273 x 219 mm.), hand-colored etching on wove (BP 99, DM 239, FR 811, Y 18,668).

$3738* *The Scourge, 1811-1815,* pub. between Feb. 1, 1811 and Oct. 1, 1816, good cond., scuffing, damage from moisture, (05-19-93, Butterfield, #1905A, illus.), 8¾ x 19 in., (222 x 483 mm.), sixty-two colored broadsheet backed onto pulp w/laid (BP 2426, DM 6076, FR 20,471, Y 413,816).

$413* *Six Satirical Engravings,* fair cond., staining, rippling, tears, (06-11-93, Weschler, #45), approx. 10¼ x 14½ in., (26 x 36.8 cm.), hand-colored engraving (BP 271, DM 671, FR 2263, Y 43,820).

$99* *"A Trifling Mistake-Corrected"*, pub. 1820 by G. Humphrey, (12-06-92, Neal, #911), image 8 x 10 in., (20.3 x 25.4 cm.), hand-colored etching (BP 62, DM 154, FR 526, Y 12,266).

CRUMBO, Woody

$88* *"Sign Of Spring"*, s., (10-24-92, Dunning, #1452, illus.), 4¾ x 6¼ in., (12.1 x 15.9 cm.), etching (BP 54, DM 135, FR 456, Y 10,732).

CRUTCHFIELD, William

BI *Americana Suite: Riverboat (G. 62), 1967,* s., d., #52/56, blindstamp publisher, Gemini G.E.L., margins, good cond., foxing, hinge remains, surface soiling, est. $3/500, (05-19-93, Butterfield, #2150), 11⅕ x 19 in., (279 x 483 mm.), lithograph in colors w/hand-coloring on Rives BFK.

BI *"Captain's Table", "Titanic Rising", and "Train Of Thought", 1973, 1974, 1984: Three,* s., d., num. artist's proof, 3/35, 11/40, full margins, good cond., surface soiling, creases, Captain's Table w/hinge remains, skinned areas, est. $4/600, (02-24-93, Butterfield, #3206), from 15⅞ x 23 in., (403 x 584 mm.), to 24¼ x 17 in., (403 x 584 mm.), lithograph & silkscreen in colors on wove.

BI *"City Of Troy" and "Train Of Thought", 1972; 1984: Two,* s., d., num. 5/35 & 12/40, Train Of Thought w/ blindstamp of pub. Cirrus, City Of Troy w/blindstamp, full margins, creases, surface soiling, est. $3/500, (02-24-93, Butterfield, #3205), one 37 x 26 in., (940 x 660 mm.), other 24½ x 17 in., (940 x 660 mm.), silkscreen & lithograph in colors on wove & Arches.

$248* *"Pair", "Eucaluptus II", and "Beached City", 1971; 72: Three,* each s., d., num. 3/100, 9/125, & 3/35, Beach City w/blindstamp, eachw/full margins, good cond., creases, surface soiling, (02-24-93, Butterfield, #3203), 10 1/16 x 11 5/16 in., (256 x 287 mm.), sh 26 x 32 in., (256 x 287 mm.), silkscreen in colors on wove (BP 173, DM 403, FR 1365, Y 29,101).

BI *"Sunset", "Lemon Meringue", and "Eucalyptus II", 1984; 1975, 1971: Three,* s., d., Sunset num. 6/30, Lemon Meringue annot Color Proof I, Eucalyptus II num. 105/

125, Sunset w/blindstamp of pub. Cirrus, full margins, good cond., creases, surface soiling, est. $4/600, (02-24-93, Butterfield, #3204), from 12⅞ x 17½ in., (327 x 445 mm.), to 25⅞ x 34⅜ in., (327 x 445 mm.), silkscreen & lithograph in colors on wove & Rives BFK.

CRUTCHFIELD, William   American b. 1932
$132* *Alphabet Spire III*, s., d. 1972, #19/30, prov., (05-16-93, Hindman, #627), 24 x 36 in., (61 x 91.4 cm.), color serigraph (BP 86, DM 212, FR 714, Y 14,633).

CRUZ-DIEZ, Carlos   Venezuelan b. 1923
$1106* *Couleur Additive, 1971: Eight*, #12/200, Edition Denise Rene blindstamp, (09-04-92, Germann, #293), each 29⁷⁄₁₆ x 29½ in., (748 x 750 mm.), color serigraph (BP 554, DM 1550, FR 5277, Y 136,140, SF 1380).
   BI *Untitled, 1979*, s., d., num., est. DM 400-, (09-25-92, Granier, #2800), sheet 31¼ x 31¼ in., (79.3 x 79.3 cm.), color screenprint on cream Roches wove.

CSOKA, Stephen   American 1897-1989
   BI *"Brooklyn Landscape"*, s., t., est. $50/80, (03-25-93, Boos, #608), image 8⁷⁄₁₆ x 10¹³⁄₁₆ in., (215 x 275 mm.), etching.
   BI *Composition*, s., t., prov., est. $250/300, (09-17-92, Sloan, #2346), 3⅞ x 5⅞ in., (9.8 x 14.9 cm.), etching.
   BI *"Fatherless"*, pub. AAA, s. Csoka, t., good cond., mount staining, fox marks verso,est. $650/850, (09-11-92, Skinner, #47A, illus.), 10⅞ x 8⅞ in., (27.6 x 22.5 cm.), etching on wove.
   BI *"Fatherless"*, s., t., toning, hinges, light-staining, good cond., est. $100/150, (05-15-93, Cleveland, #104), 10¾ x 8⅞ in., (27.3 x 22.5 cm.), etching.

CUCCHI, Enzo   Italian b. 1950
$6314* *Sparire II- 1988*, #2/45, s., stamped, (11-09-92, Finarte-Milan, #27, illus.), 30¹¹⁄₁₆ x 118⅛ in., (78 x 300 cm.), etching (BP 4175, DM 10,080, FR 34,056, Y 783,569, L 8625).

CUETO, Lola
   BI *Titeres Populares Mexicanos: Two*, s., margins, good cond., The Montclair Art Museum Prop., est. $4/600, (05-17-93, Christie-NY, #293), each 6¼ x 5 in., (159 x 127 mm.), etching and aquatint on wove.

CUEVAS, Jose Luis   Mexican b. 1933/34
   BI *"Crime By Cuevas": Eleven, c. 1968*, s., #38/100, Touchstone Publishers, est. $3/5000, (03-12-93, Goldberg, #893, illus.), each roughly 30 x 22 in., (76.2 x 55.9 cm.), 11 lithographs on BFK Rives.
$330* *El Cuaderno De Paris, 1977: Eighteen*, complete portfolio, s. on colophon, #71/120, pub. Ediciones Multiarte, good cond., (10-28-92, Butterfield, #2563), 12⅜ x 13⅜ in., (314 x 340 mm.), color photo-silkscreens on Fabriano and color lithographs on Arches (BP 210, DM 510, FR 1730, Y 40,491).
$303* *Double Portrait Of Doctor Laforet(Charenton V), T. 1064), 1965*, s., d., #11/20, blindstamp, pub. Tamarind Litho Workshop, good cond., light-staining, hinge remains, surface soiling, (10-28-92, Butterfield, #2561), 22¼ x 30 in., (565 x 762 mm.), color lithograph on Arches (BP 193, DM 468, FR 1589, Y 37,178).
$457* *Interior With Figures, 1969*, s., d., num., signs of wear verso, margin tears, (12-01-92, Karl/Faber, #512), sh 21⅞ x 29¹⁵⁄₁₆ in., (55.5 x 76 cm.), color lithograph on wove (BP 302, DM 728, FR 2482, Y 56,897).
   BI *Stop The War, 1970*, s., #4/50, laid down, good cond., staining, est. $3/500, (05-19-93, Butterfield, #1840), sh. 24¹⁵⁄₁₆ x 8¹⁵⁄₁₆ in., (633 x 227 mm.), lithograph in colors on pulp.

CUITT, George
$146* *Wanderings Amongst The Ruins Of Olden Times: Sixty-Two*, frontispiece, ten missing, margins, stained, (04-22-93, Bonhams-Chelsea, #163), subject 13 x 18½ in., (33 x 47 cm.), etchings on Japanese paper (BP 94, DM 235, FR 791, Y 16,053).

CUIXART, Modest
$128* *"Coloma"*, s., #177/250, label verso, (02-03-93, Duran, #221), 25¹⁵⁄₁₆ x 19¹¹⁄₁₆ in., (66 x 50 cm.), lithograph (BP 89, DM 211, FR 715, Y 15,922, P 14,950).

CULLIN, Isaac (after)   English d. 1920
   BI *New Market*, est. $2/400, (12-17-92, Mystic, #13), 21½ x 33 in., (54.6 x 83.8 cm.), chromolithograph.

CUMMING, Gersham
   BI *Reception Of Her Most Gracious Majesty Queen Victoria, Prince AlbertAnd The Princess Royal At Dundee, 11th September, 1844*, stained, torn, est. BP80/120, (01-21-93, Bonhams-Chelsea, #145), image 14¼ x 17¾ in., (36.2 x 45.1 cm.), aquatint w/hand-coloring.
$116* *Reception Of Her Most Gracious Majesty Queen Victoria, Prince AlbertAnd The Princess Royal At Dundee, 11th September, 1844*, stained, torn, (06-16-93, Bonhams-Chelsea, #386), image 14¼ x 17¾ in., (36.2 x 45.1 cm.), aquatint w/hand-coloring (BP 77, DM 193, FR 646, Y 12,372).

CUNDALL, Joseph and Robert HOWLETT
$763* *Seven Portraits Of Crimean Braves, 1856*, mounted on album pages, i., t., each approx. 220 x 180mm, (05-07-93, Sotheby-London, #56), photograph, albumen print (BP 483, DM 1206, FR 4065, Y 84,012).

CUNEO, Terence   b. 1907
$504* *Service To Industry, British Railways, 1962*, fold marks, nicks, (02-04-93, Christie-S. Ken, #59), 39½ x 49 in., (100.3 x 124.5 cm.), color lithograph backed on linen (BP 352, DM 830, FR 2814, Y 62,694).
$666* *You Can Be Sure Of Shell, Stanlow By Night, 1952*, p. Vincent Brooks, Day & Son, ref. P 55, cond. 3, (10-13-92, Phillips-London, #182), 29¹⁵⁄₁₆ x 39¾ in., (76 x 101 cm.), color lithograph (BP 388, DM 976, FR 3315, Y 80,757).

CUNEO, Terence (after)
$1* *H.M. Queen Elizabeth II With Some Of Her Dogs*, s., blindstamp, scratched, (03-17-93, Bonhams-Chelsea, #400), image 22 x 28 in., (55.9 x 71.1 cm.), reprod. in colors (BP 1, DM 2, FR 6, Y 117).
$69* *Peterborough Royal Foxhound Show Society 1878-1978, 1980*, ball point s., pub. Felix Rosenstiel's Widow and Son Ltd., (10-29-92, Bonhams-Chelsea, #71), image 19 x 26 in., (48.3 x 66 cm.), reproduction in colors (BP 44, DM 106, FR 360, Y 8547).

CUNNINGHAM, Imogen   American 1883-1976
   BI *Ansel Adams In Yosemite, 1953 (Photographs, pl. 48)*, mounted, s., d. by photog., studio label, p. before 1974, est. $2/3,000, (10-15-92, Sotheby-NY, #285, illus.), 13¼ x 10½ in., (33.7 x 26.7 cm.), photograph, gelatin silver print.
   BI *Bill And Painting, 1963*, s., d.; t., d., partially removed typed label, est. $2/2,500, (04-08-93, Christie-NY, #383, illus.), 12¾ x 9⅞ in., (32.4 x 25.1 cm.), photograph, gelatin silver print.
   BI *"Edward Weston And Magrethe Mather, Photographers 1, 1923"*, p.l., mounted on card, photog.'s blindstamped credit, label w/t., facsimile sig., 236 x 186mm, est. BP 5/800, (05-07-93, Sotheby-London, #273, illus.), photograph, silver print.
   BI *Happy Hippy, 1967*, sig., label., est. $1/1,500, (10-14-92, Swann, #422, illus.), photograph, silver print.
$880* *Magnolia Blossom*, 1925, p. Imogen Cunningham Trust, (05-16-93, Hindman, #325, illus.), 13½ x 10¾ in., photograph, silver print (BP 574, DM 1420, FR 4783, Y 97,996).
$816* *"Magnolia Blossom, 1925"*, p.l., mounted on card, photog.'s blindstamp, label, 255 x 324mm, (05-07-93, Sotheby-London, #272, illus.), photograph, silver print (BP 517, DM 1290, FR 4347, Y 89,848).
   BI *Mary Jeanette Edwards, 1933*, s., est. $2/3,000, (10-13-92, Christie-NY, #172, illus.), 4½ x 3¾ in., (11.4 x 9.5 cm.), photograph, gelatin silver print.
   BI *"Morris Graves, 1950"*, p.l., mounted on card, photog.'s blindstamp, label w/t., d., 245 x 331mm, est. BP 4/600, (05-07-93, Sotheby-London, #274, illus.), photograph, silver print.
   BI *"Pheonix Recumbent, 1968"*, p.l., mounted on card, photog.'s blindstamp, label, 299 x 236mm, (05-07-93, Sotheby-London, #280, illus.), photograph, silver print.

$618* *Portia Hume,* 1930s, 126 x 100mm, (05-07-93, Sotheby-London, #281, illus.), photograph, toned silver print (BP 391, DM 977, FR 3292, Y 68,047).

BI *Portrait Of A Woman, 1939,* 251 x 200mm, est. BP 4/600, (05-07-93, Sotheby-London, #282, illus.), photograph, silver print.

BI *Rocks In The Gold Country,* 1930s, verso w/printing notes, 354 x 276mm, est. BP 4/600, (05-07-93, Sotheby-London, #277), photograph, silver print.

$2200* *"Snake" (Watkins To Weston, p. 140),* 1929/1960's, s., d., typed t., d., photog. label, (11-16-92, Butterfield, #5915, illus.), 13⅝ x 10¾ in., (346.7 x 273.5 mm.), photograph, gelatin silver print (BP 1449, DM 3508, FR 11,815, Y 273,598).

BI *Sunbonnet Lady, Fillmore St., San Francisco, 1950,* typewritten caption, studio stamp, est. $1,5/2,000, (10-14-92, Swann, #423, illus.), 8½ x 6½ in., (21.6 x 16.5 cm.), photograph, silver print.

BI *"Trafalgar Square, 1910",* p. 1980 by Rondal Partridge, s., photog.'s blindstamp, label, 276 x 211mm, est. BP 5/800, (05-07-93, Sotheby-London, #279, illus.), photograph, platinum palladium print on crane 100% rag paper.

$3450* *Triangles,* 1928, p.l., s., d., label, p. facsimile sig., lit., (04-08-93, Christie-NY, #382, illus.), 3⅜ x 2½ in., (8.6 x 6.4 cm.), photograph, gelatin silver print (BP 2262, DM 5542, FR 18,760, Y 391,512).

$5750* *"Triangles" (Photographs, dust jacket and pl. 12),* mounted, s., d. by photog., label, i. 1928, p. before 1976, (04-06-93, Sotheby-NY, #188, illus.), 3¾ x 2¾ in., photograph (BP 3798, DM 9264, FR 31,369, Y 655,794).

$4950* *Triangles, 1928 (Photographs, dust jacket and pl. 12),* mounted, s. by photog., studio label, p. before 1974, (10-15-92, Sotheby-NY, #284, illus.), 3¾ x 2⅜ in., (9.5 x 6 cm.), photograph, gelatin silver print (BP 3029, DM 7368, FR 24,987, Y 593,881).

$978* *"Two Callas",* 1929, p.l., photog.'s blindstamp, label, (05-23-93, Butterfield, #3382, illus.), 13½ x 10⅝ in., photograph, gelatin silver print (BP 637, DM 1599, FR 5382, Y 108,102).

$1090* *"Two Callas",* c. 1929, p.l., mounted on card, photog.'s blindstamp, label, 330 x 257mm, (05-07-93, Sotheby-London, #278, illus.), photograph, silver print (BP 690, DM 1723, FR 5807, Y 120,018).

$7150* *"The Unmade Bed" (Imogen Cunningham, pl. 54),* 1957/later, s., d. label verso, (11-16-92, Butterfield, #5914, illus.), 10⅜ x 13⅜ in., (264 x 340.3 mm.), photograph, gelatin silver print (BP 4708, DM 11,400, FR 38,400, Y 889,193).

BI *"The Unmade Bed, 1957",* p.l., mounted on card, photog.'s blindstamp, label, 267 x 331mm, est. BP 5/800, (05-07-93, Sotheby-London, #275, illus.), photograph, silver print.

$816* *"The Voice Of The Wood, 1910",* p. 1981 by Rondal Partridge, s., photog.'s blindstamp, label, 276 x 215mm, (05-07-93, Sotheby-London, #276, illus.), photograph, platinum palladium print on crane 100% rag paper (BP 517, DM 1290, FR 4347, Y 89,848).

CUNNINGHAM, William Phelps American 1904-1980

$44* *"Fruit Shop Villefranche", 1932,* s., t., Print-A-Month Club, Cleveland pub. Nov. 1932, fine cond., (10-31-92, Cleveland, #105), 9¼ x 5¾ in., (23.5 x 14.6 cm.), relief woodcut (BP 28, DM 68, FR 230, Y 5450).

$110* *Tri-County Fair,* s., t., circulated by Print-A-Month Club, (07-03-92, Sloan, #321), 6¾ x 8 in., (17.1 x 20.3 cm.), wood engraving (BP 57, DM 166, FR 561, Y 13,712).

$100* *"Tri-County Fair", 1933,* plate 19, The Print-A-Month Club of Cleveland, s., excell. cond., (05-15-93, Cleveland, #105), woodcut engraving (BP 65, DM 161, FR 541, Y 11,085).

CURREY, Francis Edmund 1814-1896

$272* *Ornithological Study, c. 1860,* mounted on card, 157 x 200mm, (05-07-93, Sotheby-London, #61, illus.), photograph, albumen print (BP 172, DM 430, FR 1449, Y 29,949).

CURRIER, C.

$39* *"The Soldier's Adieu" (C#5591),* (10-23-92, Garth, #690), 20¼ x 14½ in., (51.4 x 36.8 cm.), hand colored lithograph (BP 24, DM 60, FR 202, Y 4756).

CURRIER, N.

$3575* *Clipper Ship "Red Jacket" In The Ice Off Cape Horn,* large folio, prov., (11-07-92, Northeast, #170, illus.), 16 x 23½ in., (40.6 x 59.7 cm.), hand colored lithograph (BP 2337, DM 5736, FR 19,293, Y 441,249).

$11* *"Georgie",* (09-12-92, Dunning, #14), 17 x 12¼ in., (43.2 x 31.1 cm.), hand colored lithograph (BP 6, DM 16, FR 54, Y 1363).

$880* *Sperm Whale In A Flurry,* (08-01-92, Northeast, #257), (BP 459, DM 1305, FR 4422, Y 112,317).

CURRIER, N. American

BI *Hero And Flora Temple,* est. $8/1,200, (05-16-93, Hanzel, #475), 17 x 26 in., (43.2 x 66 cm.), color lithograph.

CURRIER, N. (after)

$110* *"Clipper Ship Sweepstakes",* label verso, creased, (03-12-93, DuMouchelle, #1026, illus.), 23 x 15¼ in., (58.4 x 38.7 cm.), (BP 77, DM 183, FR 623, Y 12,964).

CURRIER, N. (after A.F.T.) American 1813-1888

$550* *The Cares Of A Family,* time discoloration, stains in image, (11-12-92, Freemn/Fine Art, #55), 18½ x 23½ in., (47 x 59.7 cm.), litho in color (BP 361, DM 871, FR 2940, Y 68,196).

CURRIER, Nathaniel, Publisher American 1813-1888

$1760* *American Country Life, "Summers Evening" (Conningham 124; Peters 2303), 1855,* by F.F. Palmer, margins, staining, tear, foxing, (01-22-93, Christie-NY, #321, illus.), borderline 16¾ x 23⅞ in., (425 x 606 mm.), color lithograph w/hand-coloring and touches gum arabic and body color on wove (BP 1151, DM 2799, FR 9467, Y 220,275).

$660* *"American Country Life, May Morning" (Conningham 121), 1855,* Frances Flora (Fanny) Palmer, lithographer, i., (01-16-93, Skinner, #332), sheet, sight 20¼ x 26¾ in., (51.4 x 67.9 cm.), color lithograph w/additional hand-coloring on paper (BP 431, DM 1079, FR 3648, Y 83,207).

$1955* *American Country Life: Pleasures Of Winter (G. 136; P. 2304),* F.F. Palmer, del., large margins, lower publication line, good cond., discoloration, soiling, (01-28-93, Sotheby-NY, #478), 16¾ x 23⅞ in., (425 x 606 mm.), sheet 21¾ x 27½ in., (425 x 606 mm.), hand-colored lithograph (BP 1291, DM 3098, FR 10,483, Y 242,737).

$138* *"Amos",* stains, (01-08-93, Garth, #6, illus.), 17¼ x 13½ in., (43.8 x 34.3 cm.), handcolored lithograph, colors enhanced (BP 90, DM 227, FR 771, Y 17,298).

$385* *"The Battle Of New Orleans, Fought January 8, 1815",* (c) 1842, (12-05-92, Neal, #558), image 8¼ x 12½ in., (21 x 31.8 cm.), hand-colored lithograph (BP 241, DM 600, FR 2046, Y 47,702).

$920* *Broadway New York. South From The Park (G. 781; P. 4015),* margins, lower publication line, light-stained, discoloration, foxing, tear, (01-28-93, Sotheby-NY, #500), 7⅞ x 12⅝ in., (200 x 321 mm.), sheet 12½ x 16¼ in., (200 x 321 mm.), hand-colored lithograph (BP 608, DM 1458, FR 4933, Y 114,229).

$7475* *Catching A Trout. "We Hab You Now, Sar" (G. 938; P. 3232), 1854,* after A.F. Tait, lith. by N. Currier, margins, lower publication line, good cond., abraded split in center, tears extending into image, corner creased/replaced, damp-staining, soiling, colors renewed?, (01-28-93, Sotheby-NY, #481, illus.), 18⅛ x 25⅝ in., (460 x 651 mm.), sheet 21½ x 29⅛ in., (460 x 651 mm.), hand-colored lithograph w/touches gum arabic (BP 4936, DM 11,844, FR 40,080, Y 928,110).

$1100* *"The Celebrated Trotting Horse Trustee As He Appeared In His 20th Mile..." (Conningham 911), 1848,* after John Cameron, ident. i., (01-16-93, Skinner, #243), sheet 23½ x 31¾ in., (59.7 x 80.6 cm.), color lithograph w/additional hand-coloring heightened w/gum arabic on heavy paper (BP 719, DM 1799, FR 6081, Y 138,679).

$770* *Clipper Ship "Dreadnought" Off Tuskar Light,* stains, (03-12-93, DuMouchelle, #1025, illus.), 16⅛ x 24¹⁄₁₆ in., (41 x 61.1 cm.), print (BP 537, DM 1282, FR 4358, Y 90,748).

$440* *"Clipper Ship Dreadnought Off Tuskar Light" (C# 1144),* old restrike, (02-05-93, Garth, #82, illus.), 24¼ x 31¼ in., (61.6 x 79.4 cm.), hand-colored lithograph (BP 304, DM 730, FR 2466, Y 54,754).

BI *Clipper Ship Sweepstakes, 1853,* creases, discoloration, good cond., est. $1,2/1,500, (12-04-92, Doyle, #39), sight 18¾ x 24¼ in., (476 x 616 mm.), hand colored lithograph.

$2750* *"Clipper Ship 'Flying Cloud'" (Conningham 1145), 1852,* possibly p.l., ident. i., p. verso of N. Currier litho., "American Forest Scene, Maple Sugaring" 1856 (Conningham 157), (01-16-93, Skinner, #44, illus.), sheet 21⅝ x 29¾ in., (54.9 x 75.6 cm.), hand-colored lithograph heightened w/gum arabic (BP 1797, DM 4496, FR 15,202, Y 346,697).

$3025* *"Clipper Ship 'Nightengale'" (Conningham 1159), 1854,* ident.; label verso, (01-16-93, Skinner, #53, illus.), sheet, sight 18¾ x 25 in., (47.6 x 63.5 cm.), hand-colored lithograph on paper (BP 1977, DM 4946, FR 16,722, Y 381,367).

$88* *"Death Of Lieutenant Colonel Henry Clay, Jr., Of The Second Regiment Kentucky Volunteers At The Battle Of Buena Vista, February 23, 1847",* (c) 1847, (12-05-92, Neal, #556B), image 8¼ x 12½ in., (21 x 31.8 cm.), hand-colored lithograph (BP 55, DM 137, FR 468, Y 10,903).

$330* *"Gen. George Washington, The Father Of His Country",* (03-12-93, DuMouchelle, #1027, illus.), 11⅛ x 9 in., (28.3 x 22.9 cm.), print (BP 230, DM 549, FR 1868, Y 38,892).

$297* *General Andrew Jackson At New Orleans, January 8, 1815", c. 1840,* (12-05-92, Neal, #560A), image 11¼ x 8¼ in., (28.6 x 21 cm.), hand-colored lithograph (BP 186, DM 463, FR 1578, Y 36,798).

$121* *"James K. Polk - Eleventh President Of The United States",* pub. c. 1845, (12-05-92, Neal, #556A), image 11½ x 8½ in., (29.2 x 21.6 cm.), hand-colored lithograph (BP 76, DM 189, FR 643, Y 14,992).

$1035* *The Life Of A Fireman. The Fire.-"Now Then With A Will -Shake Her Up Boys!" (Gale 3783; Peters 629), 1854,* L. Maurer, del., 1st state, margins, repaired tears, tears, gesso; verso soiled, rubbed, (01-28-93, Sotheby-NY, #471), 17⅛ x 25¾ in., (435 x 654 mm.), sheet 20¼ x 27⅞ in., (435 x 654 mm.), hand-colored lithograph (BP 683, DM 1640, FR 5550, Y 128,508).

$2310* *The Life Of A Fireman. The Night Alarm. Start Her Lively, Boys. (Cunnngham 3519), 1852,* large folio, prov., (05-29-93, Northeast, #556, illus.), hand-colored lithograph (BP 1480, DM 3664, FR 12,386, Y 247,695).

$1035* *The Life Of A Fireman. The Ruins.-"Take Up"-"Man Your Rope." (G. 3788; P. 630), 1854,* L. Maurer, del., large margins, good cond., tears, abrasions, discoloration, soiling, fox marks, (01-28-93, Sotheby-NY, #472), 17 x 26 in., (432 x 660 mm.), sheet 23⅝ x 33 in., (432 x 660 mm.), hand-colored lithograph (BP 683, DM 1640, FR 5550, Y 128,508).

$176* *Presidential Portraits: Four,* Ruth K. Flower Coll., (04-18-93, Hindman, #1679), each approx. 13 x 8½ in., (33 x 21.6 cm.), hand-colored lithograph (BP 116, DM 284, FR 961, Y 19,791).

$176* *Presidential Portraits: Four,* Ruth K. Flower Coll., (04-18-93, Hindman, #1678), each approx. 13 x 8½ in., (33 x 21.6 cm.), hand-colored lithograph (BP 116, DM 284, FR 961, Y 19,791).

$83* *"The Rabbit Hunt, All But Caught",* (04-16-93, DuMouchelle, #2345), 8 x 12 in., (20.3 x 30.5 cm.), hand-colored lithograph (BP 54, DM 134, FR 453, Y 9333).

$1650* *Regatta Of The N.Y. Yacht Club, June 1st 1854, Rounding The S.W. Spit,* after Butterworth, (05-29-93, Northeast, #321), 20½ x 29½ in., (52.1 x 74.9 cm.), print (BP 1057, DM 2617, FR 8847, Y 176,925).

$1320* *Regatta Of The N.Y. Yacht Club, June 1st 1854, The Start,* (05-29-93, Northeast, #320, illus.), 20½ x 29½ in., (52.1 x 74.9 cm.), print (BP 846, DM 2094, FR 7078, Y 141,540).

$34,500* *The Road, - Winter (G. 5613; P. 2473), 1853,* on stone by Otto Knirsch, margins, lower publication line, good cond., foxing, scuff extending into image, soiling, (01-28-93, Sotheby-NY, #480, illus.), 17½ x 26¼ in., (445 x

667 mm.), sheet 21¼ x 29⅛ in., (445 x 667 mm.), hand-colored lithograph w/touches gum arabic (BP 22,783, DM 54,666, FR 184,987, Y 4,283,586).

$24,200* *The Road, Winter (C. 5171, P. 2473), 1853,* by O. Knirsch, margins, staining in image, repairs affecting image, very good cond., depicts Mr. and Mrs. Nathaniel Currier in a horse-drawn sleigh, (01-22-93, Christie-NY, #326, illus.), borderline 17½ x 26¼ in., (445 x 667 mm.), hand-colored lithograph and touches gum arabic on wove (BP 15,833, DM 38,480, FR 130,178, Y 3,028,786).

$165* *"The Steamship President" and "The Steamship Washington": Two,* small folio, (05-29-93, Northeast, #546), hand-colored lithograph (BP 106, DM 262, FR 885, Y 17,692).

$187* *Tree Of Life: Three,* Ruth K. Flower Coll., (04-18-93, Hindman, #1690), each approx. 13 x 9 in., (33 x 22.9 cm.), hand-colored lithograph (BP 123, DM 302, FR 1021, Y 21,028).

$1380* *U.S. Mail Steamship Adriatic... (G. 6826), 1856,* C. Parsons del., margins, mat stain, discoloration, repaired tears, crease, abrasions, backboard stain shows through, (01-28-93, Sotheby-NY, #477, illus.), 15⅝ x 24¼ in., (397 x 616 mm.), sheet 19¾ x 27¼ in., (397 x 616 mm.), hand-colored lithograph w/touches gum arabic (BP 911, DM 2187, FR 7399, Y 171,343).

$220* *"Washington" (C# 6503),* stains, (02-05-93, Garth, #137, illus.), 17½ x 13½ in., (44.5 x 34.3 cm.), hand-colored lithograph (BP 152, DM 365, FR 1233, Y 27,377).

$121* *"Washington", C#6537,* colors faded, stains, (03-13-93, Garth, #458, illus.), 17¼ x 13½ in., (43.8 x 34.3 cm.), hand-colored lithograph (BP 84, DM 201, FR 685, Y 14,260).

$1210* *The Whale Fishery, Laying On (Cunningham 6626), 1852,* small folio, (05-29-93, Northeast, #170, illus.), hand-colored lithograph (BP 775, DM 1919, FR 6488, Y 129,745).

$1320* *Woodcock Shooting (Cunningham 6774), 1852,* large folio, from Nature and on Stone, by F.F. Palmer, prov., (05-29-93, Northeast, #544, illus.), hand-colored lithograph (BP 846, DM 2094, FR 7078, Y 141,540).

$9488* *The Wreck Of The Steam Ship "San Francisco"... (G. 7344; P. 1391), 1854,* after F.E. Butterworth, margins, good cond., mat stain, discoloration, nicks, creases, (01-28-93, Sotheby-NY, #475, illus.), 17⅛ x 25½ in., (435 x 648 mm.), sheet 23⅞ x 29¾ in., (435 x 648 mm.), hand-colored lithograph w/touches gum arabic (BP 6266, DM 15,034, FR 50,874, Y 1,178,048).

CURRIER and IVES   ac. 1857-1907

BI *"'Trotting Cracks' At The Forge" (Conningham 6169), 1869,* ident. w/in matrix, good cond.?, tears, some into image, toning/staining, est. $4/6,000, (03-27-93, Skinner, #243A), sight, sheet 20½ x 28½ in., (52.1 x 72.4 cm.), hand-colored lithograph on paper.

$85 *Across The Continent "Westward The Course Of Empire Takes Its Way",* (09-24-92, Alderfer, #266), 17½ x 27 in., (44.5 x 68.6 cm.), lithograph (BP 50, DM 126, FR 428, Y 10,225).

$1760* *American Coast Scene, Desert Rock Light House, Maine,* discoloration, staining, mat burn, light struck, trimmed, hinged to mat, John Walton Livermore Estate, (12-04-92, Doyle, #41), image 14¾ x 20¼ in., (375 x 514 mm.), sheet 17⅛ x 22⅞ in., (375 x 514 mm.), hand colored lithograph (BP 1129, DM 2803, FR 9508, Y 219,725).

BI *"American Country Life",* d. 1855, est. $50/75, (01-15-93, DuMouchelle, #1566), approx. 15 x 11 in., (38.1 x 27.9 cm.), print remounted on cardboard.

$1430* *American Country Life-Pleasures Of Winter,* large folio, (08-01-92, Northeast, #254, illus.), (BP 746, DM 2121, FR 7186, Y 182,514).

$880* *American Farm Scenes No. 1 (Cunningham 134), 1853,* by F.F. Palmer, (05-16-93, Hindman, #531), 17¾ x 24 in., (45.1 x 61 cm.), hand-colored lithograph (BP 572, DM 1415, FR 4757, Y 97,550).

$143* *American Feathered Game,* pub. aftrer A.F. Tait, (04-02-93, Sloan, #822), sheet 23½ x 20¼ in., (597 x 514 mm.), hand colored lithograph (BP 94, DM 230, FR 781, Y 16,281).

$1150* *American Field Sports. "On A Point" (G. 163; P. 3261), 1857,* after A.F. Tait, on stone by Charles Parsons, margins, lower publication line, good cond., mat stain, discoloration, tears, nicks, repaired tears running into image, strong backboard stain, (01-28-93, Sotheby-NY, #482, illus.), 18½ x 26¾ in., (470 x 679 mm.), sh 23 x 29¾ in., (470 x 679 mm.), hand-colored lithograph w/touches gum arabic (BP 759, DM 1822, FR 6166, Y 142,786).

$8800* *American Forest Scenes. Maple Sugaring (Cunningham 157),* large folio, after a painting by A.F. Tait, prov., (05-29-93, Northeast, #550, illus.), hand-colored lithograph (BP 5637, DM 13,957, FR 47,185, Y 943,599).

$165* *"American Fruit Piece" (C#160),* (11-13-92, Garth, #66, illus.), 13⅝ x 16¾ in., (34.6 x 42.5 cm.), handcolored lithograph (BP 107, DM 259, FR 873, Y 20,479).

$138* *American Homestead Autumn,* (03-20-93, Northeast, #303), print (BP 92, DM 226, FR 768, Y 16,007).

$605* *"American Homestead Spring", c. 1869,* good color, (03-12-93, DuMouchelle, #1029, illus.), 7¹⁵⁄₁₆ x 12½ in., (20.2 x 31.8 cm.), print (BP 422, DM 1007, FR 3424, Y 71,302).

$220* *"American Homestead Summer" (C#171), 1868,* stains, repaired tear, (09-04-92, Garth, #2, illus.), 15¾ x 19½ in., (40 x 49.5 cm.), handcolored lithograph (BP 110, DM 308, FR 1050, Y 27,080).

$275* *"American Homestead Summer", c. 1868,* good color, water stain, tears, (03-12-93, DuMouchelle, #1030, illus.), 7¹⁵⁄₁₆ x 12½ in., (20.2 x 31.8 cm.), print (BP 192, DM 458, FR 1556, Y 32,410).

$770* *"American Homestead Winter", c. 1868,* good color, foxing, (03-12-93, DuMouchelle, #1028, illus.), 8 x 12½ in., (20.3 x 31.8 cm.), print (BP 537, DM 1282, FR 4358, Y 90,748).

$1495* *American Homestead: "Winter", "Spring", "Summer" and "Autumn" (G. 181, 183-185; P. 2313-2316), 1868-69: Four,* margins, good cond., discoloration, foxing, strong backboard stain, first creased; second w/dark soiling, nicks; fourth w/water stain, soiling, (01-28-93, Sotheby-NY, #479), hand-colored lithograph w/touches gum arabic (BP 987, DM 2369, FR 8016, Y 185,622).

$6325* *American Hunting Scenes. "An Early Start" (G. 187; P. 3264), 1863,* after A.F. Tait, margins, lower publication line, good cond., foxing, soiling, backboard stain, (01-28-93, Sotheby-NY, #483, illus.), 18⅝ x 27½ in., (473 x 699 mm.), sh 23¾ x 31⅞ in., (473 x 699 mm.), hand-colored lithograph w/touches gum arabic (BP 4177, DM 10,022, FR 33,914, Y 785,324).

$308* *"The Arkansaw Traveler" (C#270) and "Turn Of The Tune" (C#6248): Pair,* pub. 1870, full margins, damage, (11-13-92, Garth, #51, illus.), 15¾ x 18¾ in., (40 x 47.6 cm.), handcolored lithographs (BP 199, DM 484, FR 1630, Y 38,228).

$66* *"The Assassination Of President Lincoln" and "Death Of President Lincoln": Two,* (09-12-92, Dunning, #1, illus.), each 10¾ x 15 in., (27.3 x 38.1 cm.), xin., (27.3 x 38.1 cm.), hand colored lithograph (BP 34, DM 95, FR 323, Y 8177).

$770* *"Battle Of Baton Rouge, La. Aug 4th 1862",* spotting, (11-21-92, Goldberg, #703, illus.), 12¾ x 9½ in., (32.4 x 24.1 cm.), hand colored lithograph (BP 507, DM 1228, FR 4135, Y 95,759).

$110* *"Battle Of The Boyne" and "Death Of Pope Pius IX": Two,* foxing, (04-26-93, Selkirk, #156), lithograph (BP 69, DM 172, FR 582, Y 12,139).

$275* *Bay On Annapolis,* (08-01-92, Northeast, #258), (BP 143, DM 408, FR 1382, Y 35,099).

$248* *"Belle Hamlin And Justina" (C#2639),* stains, (10-23-92, Garth, #621, illus.), 18¼ x 22¼ in., (46.4 x 56.5 cm.), hand colored lithograph (BP 153, DM 379, FR 1286, Y 30,244).

BI *Between Two Fires,* est. $150/200, (09-17-92, Sloan, #636), 10 x 14 in., (25.4 x 35.6 cm.), color lithograph.

BI *"The Body Of His Holiness Pope Pius IX Lying In State" and "Death OfPope Pius IX": Two,* (c) 1878, est. $50/100, (02-12-93, DuMouchelle, #2470), first 8 x 12½ in., (20.3 x 31.8 cm.), second 8 x 12 in., (20.3 x 31.8 cm.), lithograph.

$248* *Bombardment Of Island Number Ten,* (08-01-92, Northeast, #260), (BP 129, DM 368, FR 1246, Y 31,653).

$413* *"Breaking In", "A New Jersey Fox Hunt-A Smoking Run" and "A New Jersey Fox Hunt-Taking Breath": Three,* discoloration, staining, fair cond., (06-11-93, Freemn/Fine Art, #39), smallest 8 x 12 in., (20.3 x 30.5 cm.), largest 9 x 12 in., (20.3 x 30.5 cm.), lithograph (BP 271, DM 671, FR 2263, Y 43,820).

BI *Broadway From The Bowling Green, 1828, c. 1855,* engraved by J.R. Hutchinson, after William Bennett, margins, light-stained, foxing, damp staining, nicks, backed w/scotch tape, est. $2/3,000, (01-28-93, Sotheby-NY, #436), 10½ x 16¼ in., (267 x 413 mm.), sh 13 x 20¼ in., (267 x 413 mm.), hand-colored engraving.

$198* *California Scenery-Seal Rocks, Point Lobos (Conningham 768),* (03-14-93, Hindman, #305), 9 x 12½ in., (22.9 x 31.8 cm.), hand-colored lithograph (BP 138, DM 330, FR 1121, Y 23,335).

$2640* *Camping In The Woods, A Good Time Coming,* large folio, (08-01-92, Northeast, #253, illus.), (BP 1377, DM 3916, FR 13,266, Y 336,950).

$4510* *Camping In The Woods, A Good Time Coming (Cunningham 773),* large folio, after a painting by A.F. Tait, prov., (05-29-93, Northeast, #547, illus.), hand-colored lithograph (BP 2889, DM 7153, FR 24,182, Y 483,594).

$3220* *Camping In The Woods. "A Good Time Coming" (G. 864; P. 3270), 1863,* after A.F. Tait, margins, lower publication line, good cond., soiling, water staining, top corner missing, tear, backboard stain, (01-28-93, Sotheby-NY, #484, illus.), 18⅝ x 27⅜ in., (473 x 695 mm.), sh 23 x 31½ in., (473 x 695 mm.), hand-colored lithograph w/touches gum arabic (BP 2126, DM 5102, FR 17,265, Y 399,801).

$200* *"Capitol Of The Nation", "Noah's Ark" and "The Riverside": Three,* (02-04-93, Sloan, #349), largest 9⅛ x 14 in., (23.2 x 35.6 cm.), lithograph (BP 140, DM 329, FR 1117, Y 24,879).

BI *The Celebrated Horse Dexter, "The King Of The Turf" (G. 976; P. 3441), 1865,* on stone by J. Cameron, margins, lower publication line, soiling, tears, image abraded area, surface scuffs, backboard stain, est. $1/1,400, (01-28-93, Sotheby-NY, #488, illus.), 16¼ x 26⅝ in., (413 x 670 mm.), sh 21½ x 30¼ in., (413 x 670 mm.), hand-colored lithograph w/touches gum arabic.

$1955* *The Celebrated Horse George M. Patchen, "The Champion Of The Turf": The Property Of Wm. Waltermire, Esq. (G. 978; P. 3510), 1860,* margins, lower publication line, good cond., soiling, foxing, tears,tear running into publication line, reinforced w/tape, (01-28-93, Sotheby-NY, #492, illus.), 16⅞ x 26¾ in., (429 x 679 mm.), sh 20⅞ x 29¾ in., (429 x 679 mm.), hand-colored lithograph (BP 1291, DM 3098, FR 10,483, Y 242,737).

$303* *"Celebrated Trotting Horse Judge Fullerton", 1874,* tears, toned, (11-20-92, Eldred, #130), 24 x 32 in., (61 x 81.3 cm.), colored lithograph (BP 199, DM 483, FR 1627, Y 37,682).

$1035* *The Celebrated Trotting Mares Maude S. And Aldine... (G. 1016; P. 3668), 1883,* margins, lower publication line, discoloration, water stains, tears,creases, abrasions, (01-28-93, Sotheby-NY, #495, illus.), 20⅝ x 33½ in., (524 x 851 mm.), sh 26½ x 37⅝ in., (524 x 851 mm.), hand-colored lithograph (BP 683, DM 1640, FR 5550, Y 128,508).

$715* *"The Celebrated Trotting Stallions 'Ethan Allen' and 'George M. Patchen'", C#938,* large folio, pub. 1858, stains, dark paper, (01-08-93, Garth, #316, illus.), 25½ x 34½ in., (64.8 x 87.6 cm.), colored lithograph (BP 465, DM 1175, FR 3994, Y 89,621).

$440* *"The Celebrated Trotting Team Edward and Swiveller...", C#940,* large folio, pub. 1882, stains, water stain, edge tears, one into image, (01-08-93, Garth, #351, illus.), 27¼ x 39½ in., (69.2 x 100.3 cm.), colored lithograph (BP 286, DM 723, FR 2458, Y 55,152).

$385* *"The Celestial Trotting Team, Edward And Swivler", 1882,* after a painting by Scott Leighton, toned, stains, (11-20-92, Eldred, #126), 26½ x 38 in., (67.3 x 96.5 cm.), colored lithograph (BP 253, DM 614, FR 2068, Y 47,880).

$1980* *"Central Park, The Drive" and "Central Park, The Lake" (C. 951-2; P.4034 and 4037), 1862: Two,* margins, abraded spots, staining, (01-22-93, Christie-NY, #322, illus.), each boderline 11⅛ x 15½ in., (283 x 394 mm.), hand-colored lithograph and touches of gum arabic on wove (BP 1295, DM 3148, FR 10,651, Y 247,810).

$1380* *The Champion Pacer Johnson... (G. 1062; P. 3602), 1884,* J. Cameron in stone, margins, lower publication line, discoloration,foxing, soiling, tears, creases, (01-28-93, Sotheby-NY, #493, illus.), 18⅛ x 27 in., (460 x 686 mm.), sh 23¼ x 32¼ in., (460 x 686 mm.), chromolithograph w/gum arabic (BP 911, DM 2187, FR 7399, Y 171,343).

BI *"The Champion Trotting Stallion NELSON..." (Conningham 982), 1891,* John Cameron, lithographer, ident. w/in matrix, stable cond., margins, trimmed, toning, staining, nicks, tears, est. $6/800, (03-27-93, Skinner, #304A), sheet 22½ x 29 in., (57.2 x 73.7 cm.), chromolithograph on paper.

$165* *Chapel Of Our Lady,* small folio, (03-20-93, Northeast, #661, illus.), print (BP 111, DM 270, FR 918, Y 19,139).

BI *"Christ Weeping Over Jerusalem",* est. $25/50, (02-12-93, DuMouchelle, #2473), 8 x 12 in., (20.3 x 30.5 cm.), lithograph.

$8625* *The City Of New York (G. 1227; P. 3992), 1876,* sketched and drawn on stone by Parsons and Atwater, margins, lower publication line, good cond., light-stain, soiling, foxing, image abrasions, loss, (01-28-93, Sotheby-NY, #499, illus.), 21⅛ x 33½ in., (537 x 851 mm.), sh 24¾ x 35⅝ in., (537 x 851 mm.), hand-colored lithograph w/touches gum arabic backed w/sheet of wove (BP 5696, DM 13,667, FR 46,247, Y 1,070,896).

$275* *Clipper Ship "Queen Of Clippers",* small folio, (11-07-92, Northeast, #293), (BP 180, DM 441, FR 1484, Y 33,942).

BI *Clipper Ship-Three Brothers, 2972 Tons (Conningham 963), 1875,* damp staining, worm holes, darkening, toning, image losses, rippling, tape, est. $7/900, (06-12-93, Weschler, #158, illus.), 19¼ x 27½ in., (48.9 x 69.9 cm.), hand-colored lithograph.

$2760* *A Collection Of Small Folio Prints Including: "The Burning Of Chicago", "The Great Fire At Boston", "The Narrows, New York", "The Old Homestead" and "Night By The Camp-Fire", c. 1850: Thirteen,* margins, all but one w/publication lines, good cond., backboard staining, foxing, (01-28-93, Sotheby-NY, #504), hand-colored lithograph (BP 1823, DM 4373, FR 14,799, Y 342,687).

$990* *"Constitution And Java", "Burning Of The Steamship Golden Gate", "Com. Farragut's Fleet Passing The Forts On The Mississippi", "Capture And Fall OfCharleston" and Others: Six,* discoloration, imperfections, John Walton Livermore Estate, (12-04-92, Doyle, #45), largest 8 x 12½ in., (203 x 318 mm.), hand colored lithograph (BP 635, DM 1577, FR 5348, Y 123,596).

$94* *"The Cottage By The Cliff" (C#1263),* stained, (10-23-92, Garth, #267, illus.), 13 x 17 in., (33 x 43.2 cm.), hand colored lithograph (BP 58, DM 144, FR 487, Y 11,463).

$17* *"Crucifixion",* c. 1880, (05-14-93, DuMouchelle, #2373), lithograph (BP 11, DM 27, FR 92, Y 1884).

$220* *"Darktown Fire Brigade, The Chief, On Duty" (C#1393), 1885,* (10-23-92, Garth, #652, illus.), 17 x 13 in., (43.2 x 33 cm.), hand colored lithograph rebacked on rice paper (BP 136, DM 336, FR 1140, Y 26,829).

$468* *"The Day Of Rest", "American Homestead Autumn" and "The Old Oaken Bucket", 1862 And 1869: Three,* Ruth K. Flower Coll., (04-18-93, Hindman, #1664), larger 10½ x 16½ in., (26.7 x 41.9 cm.), hand-colored lithograph (BP 307, DM 756, FR 2555, Y 52,626).

$1430* *"A Disputed Heat, Claiming A Foul" and "Ready For The Trot, Bring UpYour Horses": A Pair,* large folio, (11-08-92, Northeast, #716, illus.), print (BP 945, DM 2283, FR 7713, Y 177,463).

$518* *Eclipse And Sir Henry. Great Match Race For $20,000 A Side... (G. 1805; P. 3461), 1823,* margins, good cond., soiling, discoloration, water stain, foxing, soiling, glue stains, (01-28-93, Sotheby-NY, #489, illus.), sh 24⅞ x 32 in., (632 x 813 mm.), hand-colored lithograph (BP 342, DM 821, FR 2777, Y 64,316).

$660* *(Fall River Line) Steamer Pilgrim..." (Conningham 5737), 1883,* ident. w/in matrix, good cond.?, repaired, retouched abrasions, tears, (03-27-93, Skinner, #24), sight, sheet 26

x 38 in., (66 x 96.5 cm.), chromolithograph on paper (BP 443, DM 1077, FR 3661, Y 76,816).

$990* *The Falls Of Niagara, "From The Canada Side" (C. 1829; P. 4164a), 1873,* after B. Hess, by Parsons & Atwater, margins, surface scrapes, tears, staining, soiling, (01-22-93, Christie-NY, #323), borderline 18⅛ x 28⅛ in., (460 x 714 mm.), chromolithograph on wove (BP 648, DM 1574, FR 5325, Y 123,905).

$3738* *Fast Trotters On Harlem Lane N.Y. (G. 2071; P. 3482), 1870,* after John Cameron, margins, lower publication line, mat stain, soiling, surface scuffs, foxing, circular tear, repaired, lower corner re-attached, (01-28-93, Sotheby-NY, #490, illus.), 18⅜ x 28½ in., (467 x 724 mm.), sh 23⅝ x 33⅛ in., (467 x 724 mm.), hand-colored lithograph w/touches gum arabic (BP 2468, DM 5923, FR 20,043, Y 464,117).

BI *Fast Trotters On Harlem Lane N.Y. (G. 2071; P. 3482), 1870,* after John Cameron, re-margined on 3 sides, lower publication line, fox marks, abrasions, tape stains, backboard stain, est. $2/2,500, (01-28-93, Sotheby-NY, #491), 18⅜ x 28⅜ in., (467 x 721 mm.), sh 21¾ x 32⅛ in., (467 x 721 mm.), hand-colored lithograph w/touches gum arabic.

$275* *Fast Trotting In The West", 1871,* d., tears, loss, hole, staining, (11-20-92, Eldred, #128), 23½ x 31¼ in., (59.7 x 79.4 cm.), colored lithograph (BP 181, DM 438, FR 1477, Y 34,200).

$154* *Female Portraits: Four,* Ruth K. Flower Coll., (04-18-93, Hindman, #1686), 13½ x 9½ in., (34.3 x 24.1 cm.), hand-colored lithograph (BP 101, DM 249, FR 841, Y 17,317).

$143* *Fireman's Certificate, 1877,* (06-13-93, Hindman, #317), 20 x 15 in., (50.8 x 38.1 cm.), color lithograph (BP 94, DM 233, FR 782, Y 15,048).

$86* *"The First Lesson" and "Not Caught" (Conningham 1973, 4513): Two,* (06-08-93, Ritchie, #11, illus.), each approx. 13 x 20½ in., (33 x 52.1 cm.), hand-colored lithograph (BP 57, DM 140, FR 470, Y 9134, C$ 110).

$143* *"The First Smoke", C#'s 1990 and 1991: A Pair,* stains, (02-19-93, Garth, #404), one 15¼ x 11¼ in., (38.7 x 28.6 cm.), other 15½ x 11¾ in., (38.7 x 28.6 cm.), handcolored lithograph (BP 98, DM 234, FR 793, Y 16,967).

$72* *"The First Step", C#1993,* stains, (02-19-93, Garth, #329), 16¼ x 12¼ in., (41.3 x 31.1 cm.), handcolored lithograph (BP 50, DM 118, FR 399, Y 8543).

$1320* *The Four Seasons Of Life: Childhood, 1868,* mat burn, discoloration, foxing, very good cond., (06-11-93, Doyle, #31), image 15½ x 23½ in., (394 x 597 mm.), sheet 21 x 27½ in., (394 x 597 mm.), hand colored lithograph (BP 867, DM 2145, FR 7233, Y 140,053).

$3960* *A Four-Oared Shell Race, Harvard-Oxford 1869, 1884,* light struck, discoloration, laid down on cardboard, John Walton Livermore Estate, (12-04-92, Doyle, #40, illus.), image 18⅛ x 28 in., (460 x 711 mm.), sheet 22 x 30⅛ in., (460 x 711 mm.), hand colored lithograph (BP 2540, DM 6307, FR 21,394, Y 494,382).

$110* *"Frolicsome Pets" (C#2151),* (11-13-92, Garth, #210), 13¼ x 17¼ in., (33.7 x 43.8 cm.), handcolored lithograph (BP 71, DM 173, FR 582, Y 13,653).

$248* *"Fruit Piece" and "American Fruit Piece": Two,* Ruth K. Flower Coll., (04-18-93, Hindman, #1693), each 8½ x 12½ in., (21.6 x 31.8 cm.), hand-colored lithograph (BP 163, DM 401, FR 1354, Y 27,887).

$110* *"The Fruits Of Temperance", "Time Worn Abbey" and Flower Vase": Three,* (06-06-93, Dunning, #1078), hand-colored lithograph (BP 72, DM 178, FR 601, Y 11,800).

$110* *"Fruits Of The Golden Land" and "Fruits Of The Seasons": Two,* Ruth K. Flower Coll., (04-18-93, Hindman, #1705), each 8¾ x 11 in., (22.2 x 27.9 cm.), hand-colored lithograph (BP 72, DM 178, FR 600, Y 12,369).

$275* *"Fruits Of The Seasons" and "The Fall Of Richmond": Two,* (06-06-93, Dunning, #1077), hand-colored lithograph (BP 181, DM 446, FR 1503, Y 29,500).

$275* *"Fruits: Summer" and "Autumn Varieties", 1871: Two,* Ruth K. Flower Coll., (04-18-93, Hindman, #1694), each 8½ x 12¼ in., (21.6 x 31.1 cm.), hand-colored lithograph (BP 181, DM 444, FR 1501, Y 30,923).

BI *"The Garfield Family"*, (c) 1882, damage, est. $40/60, (02-12-93, DuMouchelle, #2472), 8½ x 12¾ in., (21.6 x 32.4 cm.), b/w lithograph.

$127* *"Going For A Shine"*, tears, repaired, (02-05-93, Garth, #441, illus.), 17 x 11½ in., (43.2 x 29.2 cm.), hand-colored lithograph (BP 88, DM 211, FR 712, Y 15,804).

$198* *Gray's Elegy*, (11-01-92, Hanzel, #216), 18½ x 24½ in., (47 x 62.2 cm.), lithograph (BP 129, DM 312, FR 1053, Y 24,481).

$575* *The Great Bartholdi Statue, Liberty Enlighening The World: The Gift Of France To The American People (G. 2792)*, 1885, margins, lower publication lines, creases running into image, backboard stain showing through, laid down, (01-28-93, Sotheby-NY, #502), image 24¼ x 16⅝ in., (616 x 422 mm.), lithograph (BP 380, DM 911, FR 3083, Y 71,393).

$440* *"The Great Fight Between The 'Merrimack' And 'Monitor', March 9th 1862"* (Conningham, 2612), 1862, ident. in i., (06-05-93, Skinner, #47), sh 9¼ x 13 in., (23.5 x 33 cm.), lithograph w/hand-coloring on paper (BP 290, DM 713, FR 2404, Y 47,200).

$193* *"The Great Fire At Boston..."* (Conningham 2614), 1872, ident. w/in matrix, good cond.?, tear into image, fox marks, (03-27-93, Skinner, #385), sight, sheet 9½ x 13¼ in., (24.1 x 33.7 cm.), hand-colored lithograph on paper (BP 130, DM 315, FR 1070, Y 22,463).

$605* *Great Mississippi Steamboat Race*, small folio, (11-07-92, Northeast, #297), (BP 396, DM 971, FR 3265, Y 74,673).

$2200* *"The Great Ocean Yacht Race Between The Henrietta, Fleetwing And Vesta..."* (Conningham 2634), 1867, possibly p.l., ident. i; label verso, (01-16-93, Skinner, #30, illus.), sh, sight 23⅛ x 32¾ in., (58.7 x 83.2 cm.), color lithograph w/additional hand-coloring on heavy paperboard (BP 1438, DM 3597, FR 12,161, Y 277,358).

$4400* *"The Great Race On The Mississippi"* (From New Orleans To St. Louis, 1210 miles. Between The Steamers Robert E. Lee, Captain J.W. Cannon And Natchez, Captain P.T. Leathers. Won By R.E. Lee, (Time: 3 Days, 18 Hours, 30 Minutes), pub. 1870, (12-05-92, Neal, #566, illus.), image 18½ x 29 in., (47 x 73.7 cm.), hand-colored lithograph (BP 2755, DM 6860, FR 23,379, Y 545,162).

$330* *"The Great West", "Fruit Vase" and "The Soldier's Home, The Vision":Three*, (06-06-93, Dunning, #1076), hand-colored lithograph (BP 217, DM 535, FR 1803, Y 35,400).

$22* *"Heroes Of '76" Marching To The Fight"*, C#2810, badly damaged, stained, (03-13-93, Garth, #433), 11⅝ x 15⅜ in., (29.5 x 39.1 cm.), hand-colored lithograph (BP 15, DM 37, FR 125, Y 2593).

$385* *"A Home In The Country"*, (06-06-93, Dunning, #1066), 14 x 18 in., (35.6 x 45.7 cm.), hand-colored lithograph (BP 253, DM 624, FR 2104, Y 41,300).

$495* *"A Home On The Mississippi"* (C#2876), tear, (10-23-92, Garth, #266, illus.), 19½ x 23½ in., (49.5 x 59.7 cm.), hand colored lithograph (BP 306, DM 757, FR 2566, Y 60,366).

$440* *"A Home On The Mississippi" and "The Roadside Mill", 1870-71: Two*, Ruth K. Flower Coll., (04-18-93, Hindman, #1684), each 9 x 12¼ in., (22.9 x 31.1 cm.), hand-colored lithograph (BP 289, DM 711, FR 2402, Y 49,477).

$193* *"The Hudson Near Coldspring"*, (11-13-92, DuMouchelle, #377), 8 x 12¼ in., (20.3 x 31.1 cm.), print (BP 125, DM 303, FR 1022, Y 23,954).

$220* *Hudson River - Crow Nest*, trimmed margins, appears good cond., (06-11-93, Doyle, #33), 7¾ x 12¼ in., (197 x 311 mm.), hand colored lithograph (BP 145, DM 358, FR 1205, Y 23,342).

$94* *"An Increase Of Family"* (C#3078), trimmed, stain, (10-23-92, Garth, #322, illus.), 21 x 17 in., (53.3 x 43.2 cm.), hand colored lithograph (BP 58, DM 144, FR 487, Y 11,463).

$303* *Indian Town Rivers*, (08-01-92, Northeast, #259), (BP 158, DM 449, FR 1523, Y 38,673).

$72* *"The Ivy Bridge"* (C#3141), pen and ink inscript. in boarder, stains, (09-04-92, Garth, #528, illus.), 12¾ x 17 in., (32.4 x 43.2 cm.), handcolored lithograph (BP 36, DM 101, FR 344, Y 8863).

$605* *"The King Of The Turf St. Julian..."*, C#3339, large folio, pub. 1880, stains, (01-08-93, Garth, #7, illus.), 29¾ x 37¾ in., (75.6 x 95.9 cm.), colored lithograph (BP 394, DM 995, FR 3380, Y 75,834).

$28* *"The Ladies Boquet"*, C#3374, stains, (03-13-93, Garth, #431), 18½ x 14 in., (47 x 35.6 cm.), hand-colored lithograph (BP 20, DM 47, FR 158, Y 3300).

$468* *"Lady Of The Lake", "The First Ride" and "Noah's Ark": Three*, Ruth K. Flower Coll., (04-18-93, Hindman, #1699), larger 10 x 12¼ in., (25.4 x 31.1 cm.), hand-colored lithograph (BP 307, DM 756, FR 2555, Y 52,626).

$1150* *Lady Woodruff, Miller's Damsel, General Darcy And Stella: Trotting For A Purse Of $800 Mile Heats Best 3 In. 5 In. Harness (G. 3670; P. 3625)*, 1857, after Louis Maurer, margins, lower publication line, soiling, dicoloration, filled-in loss, creases, repaired tears one running into image, corner loss, (01-28-93, Sotheby-NY, #494, illus.), 16⅞ x 27½ in., (429 x 699 mm.), sh 21⅞ x 31⅜ in., (429 x 699 mm.), hand-colored lithograph w/ touches gum arabic (BP 759, DM 1822, FR 6166, Y 142,786).

BI *Landscape, Fruit And Flowers*, time discoloration, est. $3/500, (11-12-92, Freemn/Fine Art, #56), 22½ x 29 in., (57.2 x 73.7 cm.), litho in colors.

BI *Landscape, Fruit And Flowers*, 1862, repaired tear, trimmed margins, discoloration, good cond., et. $6/9,000, (06-11-93, Doyle, #30, illus.), 19½ x 27¼ in., (495 x 692 mm.), hand colored lithograph.

$7150* *Life In The Woods: "Starting Out" and "Returning To Camp"* (Cunningham 3514 & 3513): A Pair, large folio, after paintings by A.F. Tait, (05-29-93, Northeast, #545, illus.), image 18¾ x 27½ in., (47.6 x 69.9 cm.), hand-colored lithograph (BP 4580, DM 11,340, FR 38,338, Y 766,674).

$690* *The Life Of A Fireman. The New Era. Steam And Muscle (G. 3785; P. 631)*, 1854, J. Parson, del., margins, discoloration, heavily abraded, tears, losses mainly in image, colors renewed?, (01-28-93, Sotheby-NY, #473), 17⅛ x 25⅝ in., (435 x 651 mm.), sh 19¾ x 26⅝ in., (435 x 651 mm.), hand-colored lithograph w/touches gum arabic (BP 456, DM 1093, FR 3700, Y 85,672).

$3575* *The Life Of A Hunter-Catching A Tartar*, large folio, (08-01-92, Northeast, #252, illus.), (BP 1864, DM 5303, FR 17,965, Y 456,286).

$63,000* *The Life Of A Hunter. "A Tight Fix" (G. 3790; P. 3314)*, 1861, after A.F. Tait, margins, lower publication line, good cond., tears, abrasions, 3 margin tips cut away, soiled, damp stained, backboard stained, (01-28-93, Sotheby-NY, #485, illus.), 18½ x 27 in., (470 x 686 mm.), sh 23⅝ x 29⅞ in., (470 x 686 mm.), hand-colored lithograph w/touches gum arabic (BP 41,603, DM 99,826, FR 337,802, Y 7,822,200).

$165* *"The Life" and "Age Of Man And Woman", 1850: Two*, Ruth K. Flower Coll., (04-18-93, Hindman, #1711), each 9 x 12¾ in., (22.9 x 32.4 cm.), hand-colored lithograph (BP 108, DM 267, FR 901, Y 18,554).

BI *"Little Brother" and "Daisy": Pair*, est. $150/200, (01-15-93, DuMouchelle, #2335), prints.

$94* *"Little Brothers And Sisters"* (C#3586), 1863, (09-04-92, Garth, #177, illus.), 19½ x 15½ in., (49.5 x 39.4 cm.), handcolored lithograph (BP 47, DM 132, FR 448, Y 11,571).

$165* *"Little Charlie", "The Bud And The Blossom", and "Little Violet": Three*, stains, tears, (11-13-92, Garth, #434), approx. 16¾ x 12 in., (42.5 x 30.5 cm.), handcolored lithographs (BP 107, DM 259, FR 873, Y 20,479).

$88* *"Little Lizzie" and "Little Charlie": Two*, Ruth K. Flower Coll., (04-18-93, Hindman, #1713), each 15½ x 11 in., (39.4 x 27.9 cm.), hand-colored lithograph (BP 58, DM 142, FR 480, Y 9895).

BI *"The Little Volunteer"*, 19th cent., est. $2/300, (11-21-92, Goldberg, #704), 14 x 11½ in., (35.6 x 29.2 cm.), print.

$1100* *Lula*, large folio, (08-01-92, Northeast, #255, illus.), (BP 574, DM 1632, FR 5528, Y 140,396).

$4950* *A Midnight Race On The Mississippi*, large folio, (11-08-92, Northeast, #715), print (BP 3273, DM 7902, FR 26,699, Y 614,296).

$4600* *A Midnight Race On The Mississippi (G. 4476; P. 1359), 1860,* after H.D. Manning, on stone by Frances F. Palmer, margins, good cond., soiling, discoloration, image scuffs, repaired tears, nicks, colors renewed?, (01-28-93, Sotheby-NY, #474, illus.), 18 x 27⅞ in., (457 x 708 mm.), sh 21¾ x 30 in., (457 x 708 mm.), hand-colored lithograph (BP 3038, DM 7289, FR 24,665, Y 571,145).

$1045* *"Midnight Race On The Mississippi" and "A Home On The Mississippi": Two,* mat burn, discoloration, John Walton Livermore Estate, (12-04-92, Doyle, #43), larger 9⅛ x 13 in., (232 x 330 mm.), hand colored lithograph (BP 670, DM 1664, FR 5646, Y 130,462).

$138* *"The Miniature Ship 'Red, White And Blue'",* ident., good cond., margins 1 7/8 in. or more, toning, foxing, wrinkles/creases, (10-31-92, Skinner, #286, illus.), sight 12 x 16 in., (30.5 x 40.6 cm.), lithograph w/hand coloring on paper (BP 90, DM 217, FR 734, Y 17,062).

$286* *"The Miniature Ship", "Red, White And Blue", "A Squall Off Cape Horn", "Grapeshot", "The Vase Of Flowers", "God Is Love", "A Flower Basket" and "Untitled": Seven,* foxing, (04-26-93, Selkirk, #157), color lithograph (BP 180, DM 448, FR 1514, Y 31,560).

$2645* *Mount Washington And The White Mountains (G. 4614; P. 3967), 1860,* after F. Palmer, margins, lower publication line, good cond., water staining, image abrasions, crease running through image, backboard stain, (01-28-93, Sotheby-NY, #498), 14⅞ x 20⅜ in., (378 x 518 mm.), sh 17½ x 22½ in., (378 x 518 mm.), hand-colored lithograph (BP 1747, DM 4191, FR 14,182, Y 328,408).

$770* *"Mr. August Belmont's Potomac (Hamilton Up) And Masher (Bergen Up)",* folio, t., Mr. Thad Foley Coll., (02-06-93, Julia, #227), 20 x 27¾ in., (50.8 x 70.5 cm.), print (BP 533, DM 1277, FR 4316, Y 95,819).

$110* *"My Dear Little Pet",* (05-20-93, Boos, #524), sight 12¾ x 9⅛ in., hand-colored lithograph (BP 71, DM 177, FR 598, Y 12,147).

$220* *"My Little White Kitten After The Goldfish",* stains, (06-17-93, Garth, #460), 12½ x 17¼ in., (31.8 x 43.8 cm.), hand-colored lithograph (BP 145, DM 365, FR 1228, Y 23,572).

$28* *"Natural Bridge",* (06-11-93, DuMouchelle, #1345), 8½ x 13 in., (21.6 x 33 cm.), print (BP 18, DM 46, FR 153, Y 2971).

$6050* *New England Winter Scene (C. 4420; P. 2431), 1861,* by G.H. Durrie, margins, foxmark, repaired tear, tears, losses, staining, (01-22-93, Christie-NY, #324, illus.), borderline 16½ x 23¾ in., (419 x 603 mm.), color lithograph w/hand-coloring and touches gum arabic and body color on wove (BP 3958, DM 9620, FR 32,544, Y 757,196).

$7700* *New England Winter Scene (Cunningham 4420), 1861,* large folio, after a painting by George Henry Durrie, prov., (05-29-93, Northeast, #549, illus.), hand-colored lithograph (BP 4933, DM 12,213, FR 41,287, Y 825,649).

$83* *"Noah's Ark",* small folio, tear, Mr. Thad Foley Coll., (02-06-93, Julia, #302), image 8½ x 12½ in., (21.6 x 31.8 cm.), print (BP 57, DM 138, FR 465, Y 10,329).

$413* *"Noah's Ark", "Blue Monday" and "As Kind As A Kitten": Three,* Ruth K. Flower Coll., (04-18-93, Hindman, #1685), larger 9½ x 13½ in., (24.1 x 34.3 cm.), hand-colored lithograph (BP 271, DM 667, FR 2254, Y 46,441).

BI *Ocean Express Train,* large folio, restrike by Max Williams, est. $12/1800, (08-01-92, Northeast, #256), .

$77* *"Off For The War" and "Home From The War": Two,* (09-12-92, Dunning, #2, illus.), 14 x 10 in., (35.6 x 25.4 cm.), hand colored lithograph (BP 40, DM 111, FR 377, Y 9540).

$110* *The Old Feudal Castle,* (08-01-92, Northeast, #286), (BP 57, DM 163, FR 553, Y 14,040).

$3520* *The Old Homestead In Winter (C. 4563; P. 2442), 1864,* by G.H. Durrie, wide margins, staining, soiling, foxing, good cond.,Janet Lee Auchincloss Estate, (01-22-93, Christie-NY, #325, illus.), boderline 18½ x 26⅝ in., (470 x 676 mm.), hand-colored lithograph and touches of gum arabic on wove (BP 2303, DM 5597, FR 18,935, Y 440,551).

$149* *"The Old Oaken Bucket" (C#4577),* edge stains, damage to margin, trimmed, (09-04-92, Garth, #296, illus.), 12 x 16 in., (30.5 x 40.6 cm.), handcolored lithograph (BP 75, DM 209, FR 711, Y 18,341).

$330* *"Partridge Shooting", 1870 (Conningham, 4718) and "Deer Shooting, InThe Northern Woods" (Conningham, 1539): Two,* ident., stable cond., margins 1/4-in. or more, staining, toning tearinto image, puncture, (10-31-92, Skinner, #432, illus.), sight 9½ x 13¼ in., (24.1 x 33.7 cm.), lithographs w/hand-coloring on paper (BP 216, DM 518, FR 1754, Y 40,801).

$385* *"Partridge Shooting", C#4718,* (01-08-93, Garth, #332, illus.), 11¾ x 15¾ in., (29.8 x 40 cm.), handcolored lithograph (BP 251, DM 633, FR 2151, Y 48,258).

$2875* *Pigeon Shooting. "Playing The Decoy" (G. 5181; P. 3330), 1862,* after A.F. Tait, margins, lower publication line, discoloration, soiling, repaired tear running into image center, filled-in loss/abraded area in image, circular tear in pub. line, (01-28-93, Sotheby-NY, #486, illus.), 18⅞ x 27⅝ in., (479 x 702 mm.), sh 22⅞ x 31⅝ in., (479 x 702 mm.), hand-colored lithograph w/touches gum arabic (BP 1899, DM 4556, FR 15,416, Y 356,965).

$715* *"Prairie Fires Of The Great West" (Conningham, 4859), 1871,* lithograph w/hand coloring on paper, (06-05-93, Skinner, #186), sh, sight 10 x 13¼ in., (25.4 x 33.7 cm.), lithograph w/hand-coloring on paper (BP 471, DM 1159, FR 3907, Y 76,700).

$6600* *"The Prairie Hunter" and "A Check" (Cunningham 4861 & 1021): Two,* after paintings by A.F. Tait, (05-29-93, Northeast, #542, illus.), each approx. 18¼ x 24½ in., (46.4 x 62.2 cm.), hand-colored lithograph (BP 4228, DM 10,468, FR 35,389, Y 707,699).

$193* *The Prize Fighter, The Pet Of The Fancy (Cunningham #4938),* medium folio, (05-29-93, Northeast, #191), colored lithograph (BP 124, DM 306, FR 1035, Y 20,695).

$825* *Providence And Stonington Steamship Co's Steamer, Rhode Island, Of The Providence And Stonington Lines (G. 5388), 1882,* drawn on stone by Charles Parson, large margins, mat staining, waterdamage, creases (partially torn), pin holes, paper losses, creases, tears, linen-backed, (10-28-92, Butterfield, #2523), 20½ x 33¹³⁄₁₆ in., (521 x 859 mm.), color lithograph on cream wove (BP 526, DM 1274, FR 4326, Y 101,227).

$1265* *"The Puritan And Genestra On The Homestretch..." and "The Yacht 'Dauntless' Of New York..." (G. 5395, 7351; P. 1493, 1434a), 1885 and 1869: Two,* first after Franklin Bassford, both w/margins, lower publication lines, glued down, discolored, backboard discoloration shows through; first w/tear; second w/surface scuffs, (01-28-93, Sotheby-NY, #476), one 16¾ x 24 in., (425 x 610 mm.), the other 19 x 27⅞ in., (425 x 610 mm.), hand-colored lithograph (BP 835, DM 2004, FR 6783, Y 157,065).

$495* *"Quails", "Bass Fishing" and "Mating-In The Woods": Three,* John Walton Livermore Estate, (06-02-93, Doyle, #48), larger 8½ x 12½ in., (21.6 x 31.8 cm.), hand-colored lithograph (BP 321, DM 790, FR 2664, Y 53,112).

$660* *The Queen Of The Turf "Maud S.,"Driven By W.W. Bair (Cunningham 5016), 1880,* large folio, (05-29-93, Northeast, #211, illus.), lithograph (BP 423, DM 1047, FR 3539, Y 70,770).

$605* *"The Queen Of The Turf Maud S...", C#5016,* large folio, pub. 1880, stains, (01-08-93, Garth, #321, illus.), 29¾ x 37¾ in., (75.6 x 95.9 cm.), colored lithograph (BP 394, DM 995, FR 3380, Y 75,834).

$411 *"The Race For The Queens Cup", "Royal Mail Steam Ship Scotir Of The Cunard Line", "The Celebrated Clipper Ship Dreadnought" and "The Narragansett Steamship Companies Stemaer Providence On The Fall River Line...": Four,* (06-11-93, G.A. Key, #124), 10 x 13 in., (25.4 x 33 cm.), hand-colored lithograph (BP 270, DM 668, FR 2252, Y 43,607).

$770* *"Race On The Mississippi (Steamers Eagle And Diana)", c. 1870,* tear in margin, trimmed, (11-21-92, Goldberg, #703A, illus.), 9 x 13 in., (22.9 x 33 cm.), hand colored engraving (BP 507, DM 1228, FR 4135, Y 95,759).

$193* *"The Roadside Mill",* (11-13-92, DuMouchelle, #376), 8 x 12½ in., (20.3 x 31.8 cm.), print (BP 125, DM 303, FR 1022, Y 23,954).

$165* *"Robinson Crusoe And His Pets" (Conningham 5190), 1874,* ident. i., (01-16-93, Skinner, #296), sh 11¹⁵⁄₁₆ x 15⅜ in., (30.3 x 39.1 cm.), hand-colored lithograph heightened w/gum arabic on paper (BP 108, DM 270, FR 912, Y 20,802).

$358* *The Rocky Mountains; Immigrants Crossing The Plains (Rewls 224),* trimmed margins, darkening, staining, tears, dry mounted, (01-16-93, Weschler, #145), 17½ x 25½ in., (44.5 x 64.8 cm.), colored lithograph (BP 234, DM 585, FR 1979, Y 45,134).

$9900* *Rounding The Bend On The Mississippi,* large folio, (08-01-92, Northeast, #251, illus.), (BP 5163, DM 14,686, FR 49,749, Y 1,263,561).

$330* *Salvitor And Tenny,* (08-01-92, Northeast, #261), (BP 172, DM 490, FR 1658, Y 42,119).

$314* *"Scenery Of The Upper Mississippi, An Indian Village" (C#5422),* surface damage, (09-04-92, Garth, #297, illus.), 13 x 17 in., (33 x 43.2 cm.), handcolored lithograph (BP 157, DM 440, FR 1498, Y 38,651).

$50* *"Scholars Rewards" (C#5425),* margins slightly trimmed, (11-13-92, Garth, #435), 13¼ x 17 in., (33.7 x 43.2 cm.), handcolored lithographs (BP 32, DM 78, FR 265, Y 6206).

$1980* *"Schooner Yacht Cambria", "U.S. Ship Of The Line Pennsylvania", "American Whaler", "Capturing The Whale", "The Sperm Whale In A Flurry" and "American Whalers Crushed In The Ice": Six,* discoloration, imperfection, John Walton Livermore Estate, (12-04-92, Doyle, #46), largest 8½ x 12½ in., (216 x 318 mm.), hand colored lithograph (BP 1270, DM 3153, FR 10,697, Y 247,191).

$575* *Scoring,-Coming Up For The Word. Little Fred, Needle Gun, Jessie Wales, Belle Of Brooklyn, Old Put, And Lady Whitman (G. 5832; P. 3779), 1869,* margins, trimmed through final line of text, repaired tear, good cond., discoloration, soiling, creases, (01-28-93, Sotheby-NY, #496, illus.), 17⅛ x 26⅜ in., (435 x 670 mm.), sh 22¾ x 29⅝ in., (435 x 670 mm.), hand-colored lithograph (BP 380, DM 911, FR 3083, Y 71,393).

$1150* *Shooting On The Beach (G. 5897; P. 3340),* margins, lower publication line, paper tone discolored, tears, soiling, surface scuffs, foxing, backboard stains, (01-28-93, Sotheby-NY, #487), 8⅜ x 12⅜ in., (213 x 314 mm.), sh 11 x 14 in., (213 x 314 mm.), hand-colored lithograph w/touches gum arabic (BP 759, DM 1822, FR 6166, Y 142,786).

$440* *"The Sinking Of The 'Cumberland' (Sic) By The Iron Clad 'Merrimac' Off Newport News VA. March 8th 1862" (Conningham, 5530), 1862,* ident. in i., (06-05-93, Skinner, #37), sh 12 x 15½ in., (30.5 x 39.4 cm.), lithograph w/hand-coloring on paper (BP 290, DM 713, FR 2404, Y 47,200).

$275* *Sloop Yacht "Mayflower",* small folio, (11-07-92, Northeast, #178, illus.), (BP 180, DM 441, FR 1484, Y 33,942).

$2640* *Sloop Yacht "Pocahontas" Of New York (C. 5560; P. 1459), 1881,* by C.R. Parsons, margins, split (backed), repairs, skinning, staining, tears, defects, (01-22-93, Christie-NY, #327, illus.), borderline 19¼ x 28 in., (489 x 711 mm.), color lithograph w/hand-coloring and touches gum arabic on wove (BP 1727, DM 4198, FR 14,201, Y 330,413).

$330* *Sloop Yacht "Volunteer",* small folio, (11-07-92, Northeast, #291), (BP 216, DM 529, FR 1781, Y 40,731).

$44* *"A Speaking Likeness", C#5642,* margins, trimmed, stains, (12-10-92, Garth, #530), 15½ x 11½ in., (39.4 x 29.2 cm.), hand-colored lithograph (BP 28, DM 70, FR 238, Y 5443).

$165* *"Spring" and "Summer", 1870-71: Two,* Ruth K. Flower Coll., (04-18-93, Hindman, #1683), each 14 x 10 in., (35.6 x 25.4 cm.), hand-colored lithograph (BP 108, DM 267, FR 901, Y 18,554).

BI *"St. Patrick, Apostle Of Ireland",* est. $50/75, (02-12-93, DuMouchelle, #2471), 12 x 8½ in., (30.5 x 21.6 cm.), lithograph.

$94* *"A Stagecoach Pointer", 1871,* (04-16-93, DuMouchelle, #2344), 8¾ x 12¼ in., (22.2 x 31.1 cm.), hand-colored lithograph (BP 62, DM 152, FR 513, Y 10,570).

$440* *"Surrender Of General Lee At Appomatox", "Major General Winfield Scott", "Washington" and "Battle Of Mill Spring": Four,* mid 19th cent., foxing, soiling, light staining, (01-16-93, Weschler, #144), 1st three 11¾ x 8¾ in., (29.8 x 22.2 cm.), fourth 8 x 12¼ in., (29.8 x 22.2 cm.), hand-colored lithograph (BP 288, DM 719, FR 2432, Y 55,472).

$193* *"The Three Greedy Kittens" and "My Three White Kittens": Two,* discoloration, foxing, (06-11-93, Freemn/Fine Art, #40), one 8¼ x 12⅜ in., (21 x 31.4 cm.), other 8 x 12⅜ in., (21 x 31.4 cm.), hand-colored lithograph (BP 127, DM 314, FR 1058, Y 20,477).

$688* *"Through To The Pacific" (C#6651),* trimmed, short edge tears, (10-23-92, Garth, #562, illus.), 13¼ x 17 in., (33.7 x 43.2 cm.), hand colored lithograph (BP 425, DM 1052, FR 3567, Y 83,902).

$176* *Tree Of Life, 1870: Three,* Ruth K. Flower Coll., (04-18-93, Hindman, #1689), each approx. 13 x 8 in., (33 x 20.3 cm.), hand-colored lithograph (BP 116, DM 284, FR 961, Y 19,791).

$1035* *"Trenton High Falls" and "Western River Scenery", 1866 (G. 6626, 7151; P. 4191, 1580): Two,* margins, first good cond., paper tone discolored, soiling, tear; second paper tone discolored, soiling, tears, sheet attached to mat, strong backboard staining, (01-28-93, Sotheby-NY, #501), one 8¼ x 12⅜ in., (210 x 314 mm.), the other 11⅜ x 16¾ in., (210 x 314 mm.), hand-colored lithograph w/touches gum arabic (BP 683, DM 1640, FR 5550, Y 128,508).

$935* *A Trot "For The Gate Money": 1869,* discoloration, water stains, laid down on board, (06-11-93, Doyle, #32), 16½ x 25 in., (419 x 635 mm.), hand colored lithograph (BP 614, DM 1520, FR 5123, Y 99,204).

$303* *"Trotting Cracks At The Forge", 1868,* t. removed, staining, toning, (11-20-92, Eldred, #127), 24 x 31½ in., (61 x 80 cm.), colored lithograph (BP 199, DM 483, FR 1627, Y 37,682).

$990* *"Trotting Cracks On The Snow",* toned, foxed, (01-05-93, Bourne, #171, illus.), lithograph (BP 640, DM 1610, FR 5491, Y 123,534).

$248* *"The Trotting Gelding Bill With Running Mate", 1881,* stained, (11-20-92, Eldred, #129), 24 x 32 in., (61 x 81.3 cm.), colored lithograph (BP 163, DM 395, FR 1332, Y 30,842).

$248* *"Two Souls With But A Single Thought" (C#6271), 1889,* edge repairs, (10-23-92, Garth, #653, illus.), 17 x 12¾ in., (43.2 x 32.4 cm.), hand colored lithograph (BP 153, DM 379, FR 1286, Y 30,244).

$220* *"The U.S. Sloop Of War 'Kearage' Seven Guns, Sinking The Pirate 'Alabama' Eight Guns" (Conningham 6338), 1864,* possibly p.l., ident. i., (01-16-93, Skinner, #4), sh 13½ x 17¼ in., (34.3 x 43.8 cm.), hand-colored lithograph heightened w/gum arabic on paper (BP 144, DM 360, FR 1216, Y 27,736).

$303* *United States Frigate "St. Lawrence",* small folio, (11-07-92, Northeast, #294), (BP 198, DM 486, FR 1635, Y 37,398).

$330* *United States Ship "North Carolina",* small folio, (11-07-92, Northeast, #296), (BP 216, DM 529, FR 1781, Y 40,731).

$275* *United States Ship-Of-The-Line "Pennsylvania",* small folio, (11-07-92, Northeast, #295), (BP 180, DM 441, FR 1484, Y 33,942).

$28* *"The Vase Of Flowers", C#6362,* stains, edge damage, (03-13-93, Garth, #430), 16½ x 13 in., (41.9 x 33 cm.), hand-colored lithograph (BP 20, DM 47, FR 158, Y 3300).

$330* *"Vase Of Fruit", 1864,* medium folio, good cond.?, (02-07-93, Bakker, #189), color lithograph (BP 228, DM 547, FR 1850, Y 41,065).

$149* *"View On The Rhine", C# 6450,* mint cond., (02-19-93, Garth, #405), 14¾ x 18 in., (37.5 x 45.7 cm.), handcolored lithograph (BP 102, DM 244, FR 826, Y 17,679).

$286* *"Waking Up The Old Mare", 1881,* after a painting by Scott Leighton, large folio, toned, stains, tear, (11-20-92, Eldred, #125), colored lithograph (BP 188, DM 456, FR 1536, Y 35,568).

$275* *"Washington", "The Presidents Of The United States", "George Washington", "Washington's Reception By The Ladies" and "Surrender Of Lord Cornwalis":Five,* (02-04-93, Sloan, #2025), largest 8¾ x 12⅜ in., (22.2 x 31.4 cm.), color lithograph (BP 192, DM 453, FR 1535, Y 34,208).

$193* *"Washington, Crossing The Delaware..." (Conningham 6525), 1876,* i., (01-16-93, Skinner, #115), sh 11⅝ x 14½ in., (29.5 x 36.8 cm.), hand-colored lithograph heightened w/gum arabic on paper (BP 126, DM 316, FR 1067, Y 24,332).

$61* *"The Watchers", C# 6561,* margins, water stained, (02-19-93, Garth, #403), 17½ x 13½ in., (44.5 x 34.3 cm.), handcolored lithograph (BP 42, DM 100, FR 338, Y 7238).

$2530* *The Whale Fishery. The Sperm Whale In A Flurry (Cunningham 6627),* large folio, prov., (05-29-93, Northeast, #548, illus.), hand-colored lithograph (BP 1621, DM 4013, FR 13,566, Y 271,285).

$690* *Winning "Hands Down", With A Good Second (G. 7263; P. 3869), 1887,* margins, lower publication line, good cond., mat stain, foxing, soiling, nicks, repaired loss, (01-28-93, Sotheby-NY, #497, illus.), 18½ x 28⅛ in., (470 x 714 mm.), sh 21⅞ x 30½ in., (470 x 714 mm.), hand-colored lithograph (BP 456, DM 1093, FR 3700, Y 85,672).

$18,700* *Winter In The Country, "Getting Ice" (C. 6737; P. 2546), 1864,* by G.H. Durrie, wide margins, staining, soiling, glue remains, good cond., Janet Lee Auchincloss Estate, (01-22-93, Christie-NY, #329, illus.), borderline 18½ x 27⅛ in., (470 x 689 mm.), hand-colored lithograph and touches gum arabic and body color on wove (BP 12,234, DM 29,734, FR 100,592, Y 2,340,426).

$138* *"Woodcock Shooting" (C#6775),* damage in margin, (10-23-92, Garth, #632, illus.), 14½ x 17½ in., (36.8 x 44.5 cm.), hand colored lithograph (BP 85, DM 211, FR 715, Y 16,829).

BI *"Woodcock Shooting" and "Partridge Shooting", 1852,* by F.F. Palmer, pub. New York, light/mount staining, foxing, good cond., est. BP 1,5/2,000, (10-27-92, Phillips-London, #90, illus.), (330 x 508 mm.), black lithograph w/hand-coloring on wove.

$165* *"The Wreck Of The Atlantic" and "The Burning Of The Henry Clay Near Yonkers": Two,* small folio, (05-29-93, Northeast, #623, illus.), hand-colored lithograph (BP 106, DM 262, FR 885, Y 17,692).

$110* *Yacht "Sappho" Of New York,* small folio, (11-07-92, Northeast, #292), (BP 72, DM 176, FR 594, Y 13,577).

$358* *"Yacht Puritan" (C#6811),* stains, creases, edge damage, (10-23-92, Garth, #623, illus.), 20½ x 23½ in., (52.1 x 59.7 cm.), hand colored lithograph (BP 221, DM 547, FR 1856, Y 43,659).

$105* *"A Year After Marriage", C#6826,* tears in title extend into image, (03-13-93, Garth, #434), 16½ x 13 in., (41.9 x 33 cm.), hand-colored lithograph (BP 73, DM 175, FR 594, Y 12,375).

CURRIER and IVES (after)

BI *Futurity Race At Sheepshead Bay (Conningham 1832),* est. $1,2/1,800, (06-12-93, Weschler, #159, illus.), sight 17 x 18¼ in., (43.2 x 46.4 cm.), photo offset lithograph.

CURRY, John Steuart American 1897-1946

$468* *"Coyotes Stealing A Pig" (Czestochowski, 3), 1927,* s. John Steuart Curry, J.Curry in stone, d., num. April 1928 5/35, ded., fair cond., foxing, margin trimmed, light-staining, (03-12-93, Skinner, #39, illus.), 9⅞ x 15⅛ in., (25.1 x 38.4 cm.), lithograph on wove (BP 326, DM 779, FR 2649, Y 55,156).

BI *"Elephants" (Cole 28), 1936,* s., t., d., good cond., mat burn, est. $9/1,200, (05-15-93, Cleveland, #106), 9 x 12⅝ in., (22.9 x 32.1 cm.), lithograph.

$2990* *John Brown (Cole 34), 1939,* s., wide margins, time staining, creasing, holes, tape, (05-11-93, Christie-NY, #97, illus.), borderline 14¾ x 10⅞ in., (375 x 276 mm.), lithograph on wove (BP 1909, DM 4710, FR 15,870, Y 328,897).

$2640* *John Brown (Czestochowski C-35), 1939,* s., pub. Associated American Artists, (10-18-92, Hindman, #483, illus.), 14¾ x 10¾ in., (37.5 x 27.3 cm.), lithograph (BP 1615, DM 3930, FR 13,327, Y 316,737).

$2310* *John Brown (Czestochowski C-35; Cole 34), 1939,* s., pub. AAA, 1940, full margins, good cond., light stain, foxing, (11-05-92, Sotheby-NY, #15), 14¾ x 10⅞ in., (375 x 276 mm.), lithograph (BP 1502, DM 3653, FR 12,360, Y 283,401).

$2475* *Kansas Wheat Ranch, 1929,* watermark, s., annot., full margins, good cond., mat staining, creases, proof, (02-24-93, Butterfield, #2628, illus.), 8¹⁵⁄₁₆ x 13⅞ in., (227 x 352 mm.), lithograph on wove (BP 1726, DM 4018, FR 13,621, Y 290,425).

$495* *The Missed Leap (Cole 23), 1934,* i. w/artist's name, inits. by wife, wide margins, time staining, good cond., (09-19-92, Christie-E, #15), borderline 16⅞ x 9¾ in., (429 x 248 mm.), lithograph on wove (BP 285, DM 741, FR 2538, Y 61,675).

$920* *The Missed Leap (Cole 23; Czestochowski C-19), 1932,* s., d., t., pub. AAA, margins, good cond., mat stain, fox marks, (02-11-93, Sotheby-NY, #9), 16⅞ x 9¾ in., (428 x 248 mm.), sheet 20⁹⁄₁₆ x 13⁷⁄₁₆ in., (428 x 248 mm.), lithograph (BP 649, DM 1524, FR 5157, Y 110,910).

$825* *The Missed Leap (Czestochowski C19), 1932,* s., pub. AAA, (03-14-93, Hindman, #316), 17 x 9¾ in., (43.2 x 24.8 cm.), lithograph (BP 576, DM 1373, FR 4669, Y 97,230).

$825* *"The Missed Leap",* t., #34/100, s., d. John Stewart Curry 1934, (04-17-93, Wolf, #598, illus.), image 17 x 10 in., (43.2 x 25.4 cm.), lithograph (BP 542, DM 1333, FR 4503, Y 92,770).

BI *"The Missed Leap" (Cole 23), 1934,* s., AAA edit., s. by artist's widow, fold tears, very good cond., est. $5/700, (10-31-92, Cleveland, #106), 16⅜ x 9¾ in., (41.6 x 24.8 cm.), lithograph.

$1045* *Performing Tiger (Czestochowski C-23),* s., t., d. 1934, annot. 25 prints, (03-14-93, Hindman, #317, illus.), 10⅝ x 14 in., (27 x 35.6 cm.), lithograph (BP 729, DM 1739, FR 5914, Y 123,159).

$1210* *Stallion And Jack Fighting (C. 37), 1943,* s., pub. AAA, full margins, very good cond., mat staining, (10-28-92, Butterfield, #2524, illus.), 11⅞ x 15½ in., (302 x 394 mm.), lithograph on wove, watermark (BP 771, DM 1869, FR 6345, Y 148,466).

$495* *Summer Afternoon (Czestochowski C-36), 1939,* s., pub. AAA, (05-16-93, Hindman, #557), 9¾ x 14 in., (24.8 x 35.6 cm.), lithograph (BP 322, DM 796, FR 2676, Y 54,872).

$330* *Summer Afternoon (Czestochowski C36), 1939,* s., d., (03-24-93, Grogan, #95), 10 x 14 in., (25.4 x 35.6 cm.), lithograph (BP 223, DM 539, FR 1834, Y 38,773).

$935* *"Summer Afternoon",* s., prov., (12-12-92, Litchfield, #61), lithograph (BP 600, DM 1473, FR 5049, Y 115,704).

$990* *Valley Of The Wisconsin (C. 41), 1945,* s., margins, mat staining, taped to overmat, staining, good cond., (09-19-92, Christie-E, #16), borderline 11¾ x 15⅜ in., (298 x 391 mm.), lithograph on wove, watermark (BP 569, DM 1482, FR 5077, Y 123,349).

$880* *Valley Of The Wisconsin (Czestochowski C-43), 1945,* s., annot., pub. Associated American Artists, (10-18-92, Hindman, #484), 11⅝ x 15⅝ in., (29.5 x 39.7 cm.), lithograph (BP 538, DM 1310, FR 4442, Y 105,579).

CURTIS, Asahel American 1874-1941

$1100* *Crater Lake, 1925,* d., #4827, (11-16-92, Butterfield, #5916, illus.), 11 x 14 in., (279.9 x 356.2 mm.), photograph, orotone (BP 724, DM 1754, FR 5908, Y 136,799).

$467* *Mt. Rainier, Washington, 1911,* photog.'s sig., d. in neg., Curtis studio frame, i., (04-07-93, Swann, #436), 9½ x 11¼ in., photograph, hand-colored silver print (BP 309, DM 755, FR 2556, Y 53,056).

CURTIS, E. Earle

$330* *Hooverville, c. 1932,* news agency handstamp, (04-07-93, Swann, #300, illus.), 8 x 10 in., photograph, silver print (BP 218, DM 534, FR 1806, Y 37,491).

CURTIS, Edward S. American 1868-1952

$3450* *"And He Reached His Hands To His Brothers The Stars", 1910,* s., (c) insig. on image, orig. studio frame, est. $4/5,000, (05-23-93, Butterfield, #3383, illus.), 14 x 11 in., photograph, orotone (BP 2247, DM 5641, FR 18,987, Y 381,342).

BI *Apache Cowboy, 1903,* num., d. in neg.; s. embossed (c), prov., est. $4/6,000, (04-08-93, Christie-NY, #19, illus.), 16¼ x 11⅞ in., (41.3 x 30.2 cm.), photograph, toned platinum print on textured paper.

$4400* *Apache Medicine Man With Sacred Prayer Chart (Gray-bill, p. 121), 1906,* num. 503-06 in neg. w/ photog.'s (c) blindstamp on image, (10-15-92, Sotheby-NY, #50, illus.), 9½ x 12⅝ in., (24.1 x 32.1 cm.), photograph, platinum print on wove (BP 2692, DM 6550, FR 22,211, Y 527,894).

$2990* *Apache Reaper, 1906,* num., d. in neg.; embossed (c) credit, s. recto, lit., (04-08-93, Christie-NY, #28, illus.), 13 x 17 in., (33 x 43.2 cm.), photograph, toned gelatin silver print (BP 1961, DM 4803, FR 16,259, Y 339,310).

$1495* *"Aphrodite", early 1920s,* s. by photog., (c) insig., (04-06-93, Sotheby-NY, #44, illus.), 10 x 13¼ in., photograph, blue-toned silver print (BP 987, DM 2409, FR 8156, Y 170,506).

$1380* *Aphrodite, 1920-25,* s., annot. L.A., lit., (04-08-93, Christie-NY, #39, illus.), 7⅞ x 9¾ in., (20 x 24.8 cm.), photograph, blue-toned gelatin silver print (BP 905, DM 2217, FR 7504, Y 156,605).

$248* *"Arikara Medicine Fraternity",* 1908, (10-24-92, Dunning, #1455, illus.), 14⅛ x 17 in., (35.9 x 43.2 cm.), photograph (BP 157, DM 382, FR 1297, Y 30,307).

$4600* *"At The Old Well Of Acoma" (Visions, pl. 68), 1904,* s. by photog., (c) d. blindstamp on image, (04-06-93, Sotheby-NY, #36A, illus.), 15⅞ x 19¾ in., photograph, platinum print on wove (BP 3038, DM 7411, FR 25,095, Y 524,635).

$6325* *At The Old Well Of Acoma, 1904,* s., num., (c) insignia in ink on image, lit., (04-08-93, Christie-NY, #33, illus.), 11 x 14 in., (27.9 x 35.6 cm.), photograph, orotone (BP 4148, DM 10,161, FR 34,394, Y 717,771).

BI   *At The Old Well Of Acoma, 1904,* s., num., (c) insignia, lit., est $5/7,000, (10-13-92, Christie-NY, #61, illus.), 11 x 14 in., (27.9 x 35.6 cm.), photograph, orotone.

$825* *"Basketry Of The Mission Indians",* pl. 509 from portfolio num. 15, t., d. 1924, ident., very good cond., catalog cover lot, (06-26-93, Skinner, #200G, illus.), image 11½ x 15½ in., photograph, large format sepia photogravure on vellum (BP 552, DM 1402, FR 4722, Y 87,533).

$3960* *Canon De Chelly, Navaho, 1904,* s. in gold ink on image, descriptive legend, original studio frame, lit., (10-13-92, Christie-NY, #60, illus.), 8 x 10 in., (20.3 x 25.4 cm.), photograph, orotone (BP 2306, DM 5801, FR 19,711, Y 480,175).

$4888* *"Canon Del Muerto", early 1900's,* s. photog. in neg., studio label, (04-06-93, Sotheby-NY, #30, illus.), 13½ x 10½ in., photograph, orotone (BP 3229, DM 7875, FR 26,667, Y 557,482).

BI   *"Cape Prince Of Wales", Plate 708, "A Yaudanchi Yokuts Woman", Plate507, "King Island, Village From The Sea", Plate 700, "A Digueno Home, Plate 524 and "Diegueno House, Santa Ysabel", Plate 531: Five,* 1924, p. 1928, selected works from The North American Indian, attrib.., t., plate num., pub., est. $800/1,200, (05-23-93, Butterfield, #3387, illus.), each approx. 15½ x 11½ in., photogravure on vellum.

$990* *"Carved Posts At Alert Bay",* pl. 330 from portfolio num. 10, t., d. 1914, very good cond., (06-26-93, Skinner, #213, illus.), image 11½ x 15¾ in., photograph, large format sepia photogravure on Van Gelder (BP 663, DM 1682, FR 5667, Y 105,040).

$385* *"Chemehuevi House" and "A Home In The Mesquite, Chemehuevi": Two,* both ident., good cond., (10-09-92, Skinner, #77, illus.), image 11¼ x 15½ in., (28.6 x 39.4 cm.), photogravure (BP 228, DM 573, FR 1944, Y 46,951).

$1840* *"Chief's Daughter, Nakoaktok", Plate 364, "Taos Water Girls", "Porcupine, Cheyenne", Plate 176 and "Cheyenne Profile", Plate 211, 1905-1914: Four,* selected works from The North American Indian, attrib., t., plate num., pub., est. $2,5/3,500, (05-23-93, Butterfield, #3385, illus.), each approx. 15½ x 10½ in., photogravures, 1 on Van Gelder and 3 on Japanese tissue (BP 1198, DM 3009, FR 10,127, Y 203,382).

$523* *"Datsolali, Washo Basket-Maker",* pl. 540 from portfolio num. 15, t., d., ident. 1924, very good cond., (06-26-93, Skinner, #200D, illus.), image 15½ x 11⅜ in., photograph, large format sepia photogravure on vellum (BP 350, DM 889, FR 2994, Y 55,491).

$220* *"A Diegueno Woman Of Santa Ysabel",* from (c) photograph 1924, Suffolk Eng. Co., plate #527, very good cond., (09-27-92, Bakker, #184), image 15 x 11⅜ in., (38.1 x 28.9 cm.), photogravure (BP 127, DM 319, FR 1077, Y 26,350).

$4313* *"Embarking On Flathead Lake" (Andrews, p. 131), 1910,* num. 649-10 in negs., s. by photog., blindstamp on image, (04-06-93, Sotheby-NY, #40A, illus.), 11⅞ x 16 in., photograph, platinum print on wove (BP 2849, DM 6949, FR 23,530, Y 491,902).

BI   *Evening At The Well, Hopi, 1906,* num., d. in neg.; s., embossed (c) credit, paper label, est. $2/2,500, (04-08-93, Christie-NY, #27, illus.), 5⅝ x 7½ in., (14.3 x 19.1 cm.), photograph, gelatin silver print.

$7700* *The Fisherman, Wisham, 1904,* s. in neg., lit., (10-13-92, Christie-NY, #59, illus.), 22½ x 17½ in., (57.2 x 44.5 cm.), photograph, toned gelatin silver print (BP 4485, DM 11,280, FR 38,328, Y 933,673).

$5060* *The Fisherman, Wisham, c. 1900,* s., (c) by photog. in neg., orig. studio frame, (04-07-93, Swann, #437, illus.), approx. 14 x 11 in., photograph, orotone (BP 3344, DM 8184, FR 27,696, Y 574,869).

$4620* *The Fisherman, Wishham, c. 1900,* s. in neg., letterpress labels verso, (10-14-92, Swann, #423A, illus.), 14 x 11 in., (35.6 x 27.9 cm.), photograph, orotone (BP 2712, DM 6761, FR 22,928, Y 559,864).

$1540* *"The Fishing Pool-Southern Miwok", 1924,* attri., t., d., plate num. 494, pub. credit, (11-16-92, Butterfield, #5926, illus.), 15⅜ x 11⅜ in., (391.2 x 289.4 mm.), photograph, photogravure on Van Gelder paper (BP 1014, DM 2455, FR 8271, Y 191,518).

$4600* *Fording The Stream, 1905,* s. by photog., (c) d. blindstamp on image, (04-06-93, Sotheby-NY, #38, illus.), 12½ x 16⅛ in., photograph, platinum print on wove (BP 3038, DM 7411, FR 25,095, Y 524,635).

$14,950* *Geronimo, Apache, 1905,* lit., (04-08-93, Christie-NY, #26, illus.), 13½ x 10¼ in., (34.3 x 26 cm.), photograph, toned gelatin silver print (BP 9803, DM 24,016, FR 81,294, Y 1,696,550).

$440* *"Gossiping, San Juan", Plate #598,* from The North American Indian, 1907-1930, (01-09-93, Skinner, #169), paper 18 x 22 in., (45.7 x 55.9 cm.), photograph, sepia photogravure (BP 283, DM 718, FR 2439, Y 55,007).

$798* *Hamasaka In Tlu'Wulahu Costume With Speaker's Staff-Qagyuhl,* pl. 333 from portfolio num. 10, t., d. 1914, ident., very good cond., (06-26-93, Skinner, #220, illus.), image 15½ x 10¼ in., photograph, large format sepia photogravure on Van Gelder (BP 534, DM 1356, FR 4568, Y 84,668).

$5175* *Homeward, 1898,* s., (c) insignia in ink on image, lit., (04-08-93, Christie-NY, #31, illus.), 10¾ x 13⅝ in., (27.3 x 34.6 cm.), photograph, orotone (BP 3393, DM 8313, FR 28,140, Y 587,267).

$5175* *In The Badlands, 1904,* s., embossed (c) blindstamp, lit., (04-08-93, Christie-NY, #20, illus.), 12½ x 16¼ in., (31.8 x 41.3 cm.), photograph, toned platinum print on textured paper (BP 3393, DM 8313, FR 28,140, Y 587,267).

$413* *"In The Land Of The Sioux",* 1905, (10-24-92, Dunning, #1456, illus.), 14 x 16⅞ in., (35.6 x 42.9 cm.), photograph (BP 262, DM 637, FR 2160, Y 50,470).

BI   *"In Village Santa Clara", "Soames Bar House", "Coast Mendecino Woman" and "Santa Ysabel Woman-Deigeuno",* early 1900's: *Four,* first num. X1813-05 by photog., each s. by photog. in ink, t. in unident. hand, est. $2/2,500, (04-06-93, Sotheby-NY, #41A, illus.), various sizes to 8⅛ x 6⅛ in., photograph.

$3450* *Indian Portrait, 1904,* s. by photog., blindstamp, (04-06-93, Sotheby-NY, #32, illus.), 15⅞ x 11¾ in., photograph, platinum print on wove (BP 2279, DM 5558, FR 18,822, Y 393,476).

$4313* *Indian With Headdress, 1908,* s. by photog., blindstamp on image, (04-06-93, Sotheby-NY, #36, illus.), 15⅞ x 11½ in., photograph, platinum print on wove (BP 2849, DM 6949, FR 23,530, Y 491,902).

$2070* *Indians On Horseback On Prairie, 1905,* #X1295-05 in neg., s. photog., blindstamp, (c) label, (04-06-93, Sotheby-NY, #40, illus.), 5⅞ x 7⅞ in., photograph, platinum print (BP 1367, DM 3335, FR 11,293, Y 236,086).

$920* *J. Paul Getty, 1936,* s., i. L.A. by photog. on image, studio stamp, (04-06-93, Sotheby-NY, #43, illus.), 9½ x 7⅜ in., photograph (BP 608, DM 1482, FR 5019, Y 104,927).

BI *Kwakiutl Hamatsa Initiation Rite, Selected Images, 1910-14: Nine,* each t., including Kwakiutl Grading Skull; Konimaka Dancer-Kwakiutl;Kwakiutl with Mummy; Kwakiutl (Ghost) Dancer with Skulls; 2 Kominaka (Ghost) Dancer; and 2 Kwakiutl Tree Burial; prov., lit., exhib., est. $8/10,000, (04-08-93, Christie-NY, #38, illus.), each approx. 8⅛ x 6 in., (20.6 x 15.2 cm.), photograph, gelatin silver print.

$715* *"Laguna Architecture", Plate #575, "In San Ildefonso", Plate #589 and "The Terraced Houses Of Zuni", Plate #609: Three,* from The North American Indian, 1907-1930, (01-09-93, Skinner, #124), paper 18 x 22 in., (45.7 x 55.9 cm.), photograph, sepia photogravures (BP 460, DM 1167, FR 3963, Y 89,386).

$220* *"Launching The Whaleboat, Cape Prince Of Wales",* from (c) photograph 1928, Suffolk Eng. Co., plate #707, very good cond., (09-27-92, Bakker, #183), 11¼ x 15½ in., (28.6 x 39.4 cm.), photogravure (BP 127, DM 319, FR 1077, Y 26,350).

BI *Medicine Crow (Pedhitsi-Wahpash), Apsaroke, 1908,* s. in gold ink on image, prov., lit., est. $15/18,000, (10-13-92, Christie-NY, #62, illus.), 10 x 8 in., (25.4 x 20.3 cm.), photograph, orotone.

BI *"Modern Cupeno House", Plate 511, "Otila-Maidu", Plate 492, "A Yauelmani Yokuts", Plate 498, "A Gupeno Woman", Plate 510 and "A Coast Pomo Woman", Plate 483, 1924: Five,* selected works from The North American Indian, attrib., t., plate num., pub., est. $6/800, (05-23-93, Butterfield, #3388, illus.), each approx. 15½ x 11½ in., photogravure on vellum.

BI *Navaho Type, 1903,* s., num. in neg.; embossed (c) stamp, est. $2/2,500, (04-08-93, Christie-NY, #18, illus.), 7 x 5⅛ in., (17.8 x 13 cm.), photograph, toned platinum print.

$2875* *Navajos Near Pond, 1904,* s., (c), #X170 by photog. in neg., sig. on image, (04-06-93, Sotheby-NY, #37a, illus.), 12 x 16 in., photograph, platinum print on wove (BP 1899, DM 4632, FR 15,685, Y 327,897).

$715* *"No Bear, Atsina",* plate 167 from portfolio no. 5, t., d. ...1908.., ident., good cond., (06-26-93, Skinner, #36H, illus.), image 15¾ x 11 in., photograph, large format sepia photogravure on Van Gelder (BP 479, DM 1215, FR 4093, Y 75,862).

$55,000* *The North American Indian, 1907-1930,* complete set of 20 volumes, 1st num. 56 of 272, attrib., t., d., pub. credit, (11-16-92, Butterfield, #5917, illus.), each approx. 7¼ x 5½ in., (184.5 x 139.9 mm.), approx. 1524 small format photogravures, some prints on Van Gelder and tissue paper (BP 36,213, DM 87,691, FR 295,381, Y 6,839,945).

$396,000* *The North American Indian, Being A Series Of Volumes Picturing And Describing The Indians Of The United States And Alaska, 1907-30,* complete set, 272/500 edit., 20 text vol., 20 portfolios, p. on Van Gelder Holland paper, s., d. 1907 in ink on intro. page, s. in ink by Theodore Roosevelt on Foreword page, num. 180, ltd. edit. num. 180, custon cabinet, prov., lit., (10-13-92, Christie-NY, #65, illus.), photographs (BP 230,635, DM 580,135, FR 1,971,130, Y 48,017,461).

$6050* *"An Oasis In The Badlands",* s. Curtis in neg.; photog.'s letterpress label verso, (01-09-93, Skinner, #321, illus.), image, sight 7½ x 9½ in., (19.1 x 24.1 cm.), photograph, orotone (BP 3894, DM 9871, FR 33,537, Y 756,345).

$1495* *"Oasis In The Badlands", 1905,* photog.'s (c) blindstamp on image, (05-23-93, Butterfield, #3386, illus.), 6 x 7½ in., photograph, platinum print on layered paper mount (BP 974, DM 2444, FR 8228, Y 165,248).

$18,400* *Oasis In The Badlands, Red Hawk, c. 1904,* s., embossed (c) credit stamp, lit., (04-08-93, Christie-NY, #21, illus.), 16¼ x 20¼ in., (41.3 x 51.4 cm.), photograph, toned platinum print on textured paper (BP 12,066, DM 29,558, FR 100,054, Y 2,088,062).

$10,780* *Oasis In The Badlands, c. 1904,* s., (c) insignia, i., lit., (10-13-92, Christie-NY, #58, illus.), 13½ x 16½ in., (34.3 x 41.9 cm.), photograph, toned gelatin silver print (BP 6278, DM 15,793, FR 53,659, Y 1,307,142).

$3300* *"The Oath, Crow", 1908,* s. in neg., (11-16-92, Butterfield, #5922, illus.), 9½ x 7¾ in., (241.7 x 197.2 mm.), photograph, orotone (BP 2173, DM 5261, FR 17,723, Y 410,397).

$770* *"On Quinault River", "A Primitive Quinault", "Cowichan River", "Spearing Salmon, Cowichan" and "The Mouth Of Quinault River": Five,* each ident., portfolio, very good cond., (10-09-92, Skinner, #70, illus.), image, approx. 11½ x 15¼ in., (29.2 x 38.7 cm.), photogravures (BP 457, DM 1147, FR 3889, Y 93,902).

BI *"On The Beach-Nakoaktok",* pl. 339 from portfolio num. 10, t., d. 1914, ident., very good cond., est. $6/700, (06-26-93, Skinner, #218, illus.), image 15½ x 10¾ in., photograph, sepia photogravure on Van Gelder.

$5175* *On The Little Big Horn, Apsaroke, 1906,* ink s. on image; orig. studio frame w/remnants of orig. Curtis studio label, lit., (04-08-93, Christie-NY, #34, illus.), 8 x 9¾ in., (20.3 x 24.8 cm.), photograph, orotone (BP 3393, DM 8313, FR 28,140, Y 587,267).

$5520* *Out Of The Darkness, Navaho, 1904,* s., annot. L.A., (c) insignia in ink on image, lit., (04-08-93, Christie-NY, #32, illus.), 10⅝ x 13¾ in., (27 x 34.9 cm.), photograph, orotone (BP 3620, DM 8867, FR 30,016, Y 626,419).

$935* *Photographs Of Native Americans: Seven,* 1903-1921, p. 1940's, (10-14-92, Swann, #428, illus.), photograph, large-format photogravures on deckled wove paper (BP 549, DM 1368, FR 4640, Y 113,306).

$2070* *Piki Maker, 1906,* d. in neg.; s., embossed (c) credit, lit., (04-08-93, Christie-NY, #29, illus.), 16¼ x 12½ in., (41.3 x 31.8 cm.), photograph, toned platinum print on textured paper (BP 1357, DM 3325, FR 11,256, Y 234,907).

BI *The Piki Maker, c. 1900,* sig., est. $2/3,000, (10-14-92, Swann, #424, illus.), 13 x 9½ in., (33 x 24.1 cm.), photograph, toned silver print.

$2070* *The Pima Woman, 1907,* num., d. in neg.; embossed (c) stamp, (04-08-93, Christie-NY, #30, illus.), 16 x 12 in., (40.6 x 30.5 cm.), photograph, toned platinum print on textured paper (BP 1357, DM 3325, FR 11,256, Y 234,907).

BI *"Pompompasus", The Three Brothers, At Yosemite,* p., blindstamped, Thomas Housewerth, No. 9 Montgomery St., San Francisco, soiling, yellowing, abrasions, mount trimmed, est. $3/500, (10-31-92, Riba, #55, illus.), 15¾ x 20¼ in., (40 x 51.4 cm.), albumen photograph.

$7475* *The Potter (Nampeyo) Hopi, 1910,* s., (c) insignia in ink on image, Curtis Studio label on orig. frame, lit., (04-08-93, Christie-NY, #37, illus.), 9¾ x 7¾ in., (24.8 x 19.7 cm.), photograph, orotone (BP 4902, DM 12,008, FR 40,647, Y 848,275).

$165* *"The Prarie", Chief On Horseback,* plate 88, (c) 1907, pub. John Andrew & Son, soiling, excell. cond., (10-31-92, Riba, #54, illus.), 11¾ x 15½ in., (29.8 x 39.4 cm.), photogravure, twill-weave paper (BP 108, DM 259, FR 877, Y 20,401).

BI *"Prayer To The Sun By Hopi Snake Priest", c. 1906,* #381-06 in neg., est. $2/3,000, (04-06-93, Sotheby-NY, #33, illus.), 16¼ x 12¼ in., photograph, platinum print on wove.

$2750* *"Puget Sound Indians",* s. Curtis in neg., (01-09-93, Skinner, #348, illus.), image, sight 7½ x 9½ in., (19.1 x 24.1 cm.), photograph, orotone (BP 1770, DM 4487, FR 15,244, Y 343,793).

BI *"The Rubaiyat Of Omar Khayyam": Twenty-Eight,* from Production of the Film "The Rubaiyat of Omar Khayyam", most Film Stills, each s. Curtis L.A. on image, annot. in unident. hand, est. $3/5,000, (04-06-93, Sotheby-NY, #45, illus.), various sizes to 9¼ x 7¼ in., photograph.

$5225* *Self-Portrait In Felt Hat,* printer's (John Andrew & Son, Boston) credit and photogravure p. in margin, early 1900's, (10-15-92, Sotheby-NY, #47, illus.), 10 x 7 in., (25.4 x 17.8 cm.), photograph, photogravure on Holland (BP 3197, DM 7778, FR 26,376, Y 626,875).

$495* *"Shauti-Sia",* pl. 561 from portfolio num. 16, t., d. 1925, ident., very good cond., (06-26-93, Skinner, #233, illus.), image 15½ x 11⅜ in., photograph, large format sepia photogravure on Van Gelder (BP 331, DM 841, FR 2833, Y 52,520).

$523* *"Sia Street Scene", Plate #562 and "A Paguate Entrance", Plate #578:Two,* from The North American

Indian, 1907-1930, time staining, (01-09-93, Skinner, #288), paper 18 x 22 in., (45.7 x 55.9 cm.), photograph, sepia photogravures (BP 337, DM 853, FR 2899, Y 65,383).

$1980* *"Signal Fire To The Mountain God",* s. Curtis in neg., prov., (01-09-93, Skinner, #294, illus.), image, sight 13½ x 10½ in., (34.3 x 26.7 cm.), photograph, orotone (BP 1275, DM 3231, FR 10,976, Y 247,531).

$3220* *Signal Fire To The Mountain God, 1909,* s., (c) insignia in ink on image, (04-08-93, Christie-NY, #36, illus.), 13½ x 10⅜ in., (34.3 x 26.4 cm.), photograph, orotone (BP 2111, DM 5173, FR 17,510, Y 365,411).

$1980* *Sioux Scout, c. 1900,* sig., num. in neg., (c) blindstamp, (10-14-92, Swann, #425, illus.), 15¾ x 10 in., (40 x 25.4 cm.), photograph, platinum print (BP 1162, DM 2898, FR 9826, Y 239,942).

$3450* *"Spirit Of The Past", 1908,* #540-08 in neg., s. by photog., (c) blindstamp on image, (04-06-93, Sotheby-NY, #41, illus.), 15¾ x 12 in., photograph, platinum print on wove (BP 2279, DM 5558, FR 18,822, Y 393,476).

$11,500* *The Storm, Apache, 1906,* s., (c) insignia in ink on image, orig. label, lit., (04-08-93, Christie-NY, #35, illus.), 10⅝ x 13½ in., (27 x 34.3 cm.), photograph, orotone (BP 7541, DM 18,474, FR 62,534, Y 1,305,039).

$220* *"Tablita Dancers And Singers - San Ildefonso",* 1905, (10-24-92, Dunning, #1457, illus.), 13⅝ x 16⅞ in., (34.6 x 42.9 cm.), photograph (BP 140, DM 339, FR 1151, Y 26,885).

$440* *"Tablita Dancers And Singers, San Ildefonso", Plate #588,* from The North American Indian, 1907-1930, (01-09-93, Skinner, #158), paper 18 x 22 in., (45.7 x 55.9 cm.), photograph, sepia photogravure (BP 283, DM 718, FR 2439, Y 55,007).

$11,000* *"A Taos Woman", "Yokuts Basketry Designs", "Marcos - Palm Canon-Cahuilla", "A Medicine Headdress-Blackfoot","A Comanche Mother", "Cheyenne Costume", "A Comanche Mothers" and others: Seventy,* from Curtis's The North American Indian, 1903-25, 1960s, (04-07-93, Swann, #441, illus.), large-format photogravures, nearly all on Holland Van Gel (BP 7269, DM 17,791, FR 60,208, Y 1,249,716).

$220* *"Tearing Lodge, Piegan",* John Andrew V. San., from (c) photograph 1910, plate #187, good/poorcond., (09-27-92, Bakker, #185, illus.), image 15½ x 11 in., (39.4 x 27.9 cm.), photogravure (BP 127, DM 319, FR 1077, Y 26,350).

$920* *"Three Chiefs", 1900,* s., d. in neg., (05-23-93, Butterfield, #3389, illus.), 11¾ x 15¾ in., photograph, gelatin silver print (BP 599, DM 1504, FR 5063, Y 101,691).

$2300* *"The Three Chiefs-Piegan" (Visions, p. 15; Coleman and McLuhan, p. 175),* s. and (c) by photog. in neg., s. by photog. in ink on image, (04-06-93, Sotheby-NY, #34, illus.), 12¾ x 15¾ in., photograph, platinum print on wove (BP 1519, DM 3705, FR 12,548, Y 262,318).

$6325* *Three Feathers, Nez Perce, 1905,* s., embossed (c) credit stamp recto; t. on remnant or orig. typed paper label, lit., (04-08-93, Christie-NY, #25, illus.), 16 x 12 in., (40.6 x 30.5 cm.), photograph, toned platinum print on textured paper (BP 4148, DM 10,161, FR 34,394, Y 717,771).

BI *"The Tule-Pool/Southern Yokuts",* t., d. 1924, ident., very good cond., est. $150/200, (06-26-93, Skinner, #197, illus.), image 5½ x 7½ in., sepia photogravure on vellum.

BI *"Tuvahe-Jemez",* plate 553, from (c) photo 1925 ... Suffolk Eng. Co., est. $2/250, (05-22-93, Skinner, #84), paper size 22 x 18 in., (55.9 x 45.7 cm.), photograph, large format sepia tone photogravure.

$330* *The Vanishing Race,* s. Curtis, foxing, (09-25-92, Wolf, #56A), 6 x 8 in., (15.2 x 20.3 cm.), photogravure (BP 193, DM 489, FR 1654, Y 39,831).

$825* *The Vanishing Race,* s. by photog. Curtis; num., ident. in neg., blindstamp, studio stamp, good cond., (06-26-93, Skinner, #103, illus.), image 5¾ x 7¾ in., photograph, sepia (BP 552, DM 1402, FR 4722, Y 87,533).

$1150* *"The Vanishing Race" (Andrews, frontispiece), c. 1904,* p. w/tri-colored margins, photog. studio and (c) blindstamps, (04-06-93, Sotheby-NY, #39, illus.), 6 x 7⅞ in., photograph (BP 760, DM 1853, FR 6274, Y 131,159).

$4025* *"The Vanishing Race" (Andrews, frontispiece), early 1900's,* s. by photog. in neg., label, (04-06-93, Sotheby-NY, #37, illus.), 10½ x 13½ in., photograph, orotone (BP 2659, DM 6485, FR 21,959, Y 459,056).

$660* *"The Vanishing Race", 1904,* neg. num., s., photog. blindstamp, (11-16-92, Butterfield, #5925, illus.), 12¼ x 16¼ in., (311.7 x 413.5 mm.), photograph, gelatin silver print (BP 435, DM 1052, FR 3545, Y 82,079).

$1870* *"The Vanishing Race", 1910,* s. in neg., (11-16-92, Butterfield, #5921, illus.), 8 x 10 in., (203.6 x 254.5 mm.), photograph, orotone (BP 1231, DM 2982, FR 10,043, Y 232,558).

BI *"The Vanishing Race", early 1900's,* p. w/tri-colored margins, s. E.S. Curtis in unident. hand, p. c. 1920, est. $1/1,500, (04-06-93, Sotheby-NY, #42, illus.), 6 x 8 in., photograph.

$1650* *The Vanishing Race, 1904,* photog.'s sig., (c) blindstamp, (04-07-93, Swann, #438, illus.), 6 x 7⅞ in., photograph, platinum print (BP 1090, DM 2669, FR 9031, Y 187,457).

$6600* *The Vanishing Race, Navaho, 1904,* embossed (c) credit, date stamp, lit., (10-13-92, Christie-NY, #63, illus.), 14¾ x 20⅛ in., (37.5 x 51.1 cm.), photograph, platinum print (BP 3844, DM 9669, FR 32,852, Y 800,291).

$1250* *The Vanishing Race, Navajo,* s. w/ Curtis' (c) insignia in negative., (02-04-93, Sloan, #2923), 5 9/16 x 7⅝ in., (14.1 x 19.4 cm.), photograph, sepia print (BP 865, DM 2073, FR 7007, Y 155,550).

BI *The Vanishing Race, c. 1900,* sig., label, est. $3/4,000, (10-14-92, Swann, #426, illus.), 7½ x 9½ in., (19.1 x 24.1 cm.), photograph, orotone.

$2300* *Vash Gon, Jicarilla Chief, Apache, 1904,* num. in neg., s. recto, lit., (04-08-93, Christie-NY, #24, illus.), 13½ x 7¾ in., (34.3 x 19.7 cm.), photograph, toned gelatin silver print (BP 1508, DM 3695, FR 12,507, Y 261,008).

$33* *Walapai Winter Camp,* (05-16-93, Hindman, #381), 7¼ x 5⅜ in., (18.4 x 13.7 cm.), photogravure (BP 21, DM 53, FR 178, Y 3658).

$18,400* *Walpi Man, Hopi, 1900-04,* orig. Curtis studio frame, lit., (04-08-93, Christie-NY, #23, illus.), 14⅛ x 11 in., (35.9 x 27.9 cm.), photograph, toned gelatin silver print (BP 12,066, DM 29,558, FR 100,054, Y 2,088,062).

$1870* *Water Carriers, Hopi, 1899,* sig., (c) stamp, sig. in neg., (10-14-92, Swann, #427, illus.), 5¾ x 7½ in., (14.6 x 19.1 cm.), photograph, platinum print (BP 1098, DM 2737, FR 9280, Y 226,612).

BI *"Wet Apsaroke", Plate 145, "War Chief, Apsaroke", Plate 112, "Swallow Bird, Apsaroke", Plate 139 and "Wolf Lies Down", Plate 123, 1908: Four,* selected works from The North American Indian, attrib., t., plate num., pub., (05-23-93, Butterfield, #3384, illus.), each approx. 14½ x 10½ in., photogravure on Japanese tissue.

$193* *"Woman's Primitive Dress",* 1923, (10-24-92, Dunning, #1454, illus.), 16⅜ x 12⅜ in., (41.6 x 31.4 cm.), photograph (BP 122, DM 298, FR 1009, Y 23,585).

$9350* *"Yellow Owl Mandam", "Spotted Bull, Mandan", "Four Horns Arkara", "White Shield-Arakara", "Headdress Atsina", "Old Ukiah-Pomo", "The Cheyenne Chief" and others: Fifty-Eight,* from Curtis's The North American Indian, 1903-1925, 1960s, (04-07-93, Swann, #440, illus.), photograph, large-format photogravures, nearly all on Holland Van Gelder, tissue and vellum, 7 on Curtis Tweadweave (BP 6179, DM 15,122, FR 51,177, Y 1,062,259).

BI *Yokuts Basketry Designs,* pl. 503 from portfolio num. 14, t., d. 1924, ident., very good cond., est. $750/900, (06-26-93, Skinner, #208A, illus.), image 15½ x 11½ in., photograph, large format sepia photogravure on Van Gelder.

$6325* *"Zuni Governor" (Andrews, p. 84), early 1900's,* #617-00 in neg., (04-06-93, Sotheby-NY, #31, illus.), 13½ x 9¾ in., photograph, platinum-silver print on wove (BP 4178, DM 10,190, FR 34,506, Y 721,373).

$5500* *Zuni Governor, 1903,* d. in neg., s. in ink, lit., (10-13-92, Christie-NY, #57, illus.), 8 x 4⅛ in., (20.3 x 10.5 cm.), photograph, platinum or gelatin silver print (BP 3203, DM 8057, FR 27,377, Y 666,909).

$4125* *'Canon Del Muerto',* s. Curtis, L.A., (c) by photog. in neg., label verso, early 1900s, (10-15-92, Sotheby-NY,

#51, illus.), 13½ x 10½ in., (34.3 x 26.7 cm.), photograph, orotone (BP 2524, DM 6140, FR 20,823, Y 494,901).

$8250* *'Spirit Of The Past', c. 1905,* s. by photog. in neg., label verso, (10-15-92, Sotheby-NY, #52A, illus.), 13½ x 10½ in., (34.3 x 26.7 cm.), photograph, orotone (BP 5048, DM 12,280, FR 41,646, Y 989,802).

$3850* *'The Fisherman' (Andrews, p. 134), c. 1905,* s., (c) by photog. in neg., (10-15-92, Sotheby-NY, #48A, illus.), 13½ x 10½ in., (34.3 x 26.7 cm.), photograph, orotone (BP 2356, DM 5731, FR 19,435, Y 461,908).

$6050* *'The Maid Of Dreams',* s. by photog. in neg., label, early 1900's, (10-15-92, Sotheby-NY, #54A, illus.), 13¾ x 10¾ in., (34.9 x 27.3 cm.), photograph, orotone (BP 3702, DM 9006, FR 30,540, Y 725,855).

$5775* *'The Old Well Of Acoma' (Andrews, p. 71), 1906,* s. by photog. in neg., label verso, (10-15-92, Sotheby-NY, #52, illus.), 10½ x 13½ in., (26.7 x 34.3 cm.), photograph, orotone (BP 3534, DM 8596, FR 29,152, Y 692,861).

$7150* *'The Scout, Apache',* s. by photog. in neg., 1906, (10-15-92, Sotheby-NY, #54, illus.), 10½ x 13½ in., (26.7 x 34.3 cm.), photograph, orotone (BP 4375, DM 10,643, FR 36,093, Y 857,828).

$7150* *'The Storm-Apache' (Coleman and McLuhan, p. 137), c. 1905,* s., (c) by photog. in neg., label verso, (10-15-92, Sotheby-NY, #53A, illus.), 13½ x 10½ in., (34.3 x 26.7 cm.), photograph, orotone (BP 4375, DM 10,643, FR 36,093, Y 857,828).

$1980* *'The Vanishing Race' (Andrews, frontispiece), c. 1904,* s. by photog. in ink, (10-15-92, Sotheby-NY, #49, illus.), 10 x 13⅛ in., (25.4 x 33.3 cm.), photograph, toned silver print (BP 1212, DM 2947, FR 9995, Y 237,552).

$4675* *'The Vanishing Race' (Andrews, frontispiece), c. 1904,* s., (c) by photog. in neg., labels verso, (10-15-92, Sotheby-NY, #53, illus.), 10½ x 13½ in., (26.7 x 34.3 cm.), photograph, orotone (BP 2861, DM 6959, FR 23,599, Y 560,888).

CURTIS, Edward S. (after)
$550* *"Buffalo Dance At Hano" (Plate 401), "In The Land Of The Sioux" (Plate 95), "Watching For The Signal-Apsaroke" (Plate 116), "Wolf-Apsaroke" (Plate 142): Four,* Lauriat edit., 1905-1921, p.l., (04-07-93, Swann, #439), photograph, large-format photogravures on deckled Curtis Tweadweave Cover paper (BP 363, DM 890, FR 3010, Y 62,486).

CURTIS, T.
$44* *Botanical Prints: A Pair,* spotting, (12-11-92, Eldred, #328), sight 8 x 5 in., (20.3 x 12.7 cm.), print (BP 28, DM 69, FR 238, Y 5445).

CURTIS, William   1746-1799
$242* *Blue Flowers: Four,* from The Botanical Magazine, three plate s. W. Curtis, one d. 1789, (03-13-93, Garth, #56, illus.), 13⅜ x 10¼ in., (34 x 26 cm.), hand-colored engravings (BP 169, DM 403, FR 1370, Y 28,521).

$77* *Floral: A Pair,* from The Botanical Magazine, s., d. plate W. Curtis (1797-1798), (05-21-93, Garth, #466, illus.), 13½ x 10½ in., (34.3 x 26.7 cm.), hand-colored engraving (BP 50, DM 125, FR 421, Y 8490).

$275* *From The Botanical Magazine: Two,* both plate s., d. W. Curtis 1792, (02-05-93, Garth, #229, illus.), 13¼ x 10¼ in., (33.7 x 26 cm.), hand-colored engraving (BP 190, DM 456, FR 1541, Y 34,221).

$275* *From The Botanical Magazine: Two,* both plate s., d. T. Curtis 1809, (02-05-93, Garth, #227, illus.), 13¼ x 10¼ in., (33.7 x 26 cm.), hand-colored engraving (BP 190, DM 456, FR 1541, Y 34,221).

$176* *"Iris" and "Orchid": Two,* from The Botanical Magazine, plate s., d. W. Curtis 1790 (and 1789),stains, (03-13-93, Garth, #141, illus.), 13¼ x 10¼ in., (33.7 x 26 cm.), hand-colored engraving (BP 123, DM 293, FR 996, Y 20,742).

$121* *Pink And Red Flowers: Pair,* from The Botanical Magazine, s., d. on plate W. Curtis (1793 and 1797), (04-30-93, Garth, #296, illus.), 13½ x 10¼ in., (34.3 x 26 cm.), handcolored engraving (BP 77, DM 192, FR 646, Y 13,425).

$231* *Pink Flowers: A Pair,* from The Botanical Magazine, plate s., d. W. Curtis 1797, (04-02-93, Garth, #423,

illus.), 13¼ x 10¼ in., (33.7 x 26 cm.), hand-colored engraving (BP 152, DM 371, FR 1261, Y 26,301).

$66* *Untitled: A Pair,* plate s. W. Curtis 1798, from The Botanical Magazine, (03-13-93, Garth, #31, illus.), 13½ x 10¼ in., (34.3 x 26 cm.), hand-colored engraving (BP 46, DM 110, FR 374, Y 7778).

$330* *Untitled: Four,* plate s. S. Curtis, three d. 1815, one 1822, from The Botanical Magazine, (03-13-93, Garth, #161, illus.), 13⅓ x 10¼ in., (33.9 x 26 cm.), hand-colored engraving (BP 230, DM 549, FR 1868, Y 38,892).

$209* *Untitled: Two,* from The Botanical Magazine, plate s., d. W. Curtis, 1790, (06-17-93, Garth, #331, illus.), 13⅜ x 10⅜ in., (34 x 26.4 cm.), hand-colored engraving (BP 138, DM 347, FR 1166, Y 22,394).

$187* *White Narcissus: Two,* from The Botanical Magazine, s., d. W. Curtis 1792, (03-13-93, Garth, #81, illus.), 13½ x 10⅜ in., (34.3 x 26.4 cm.), hand-colored engraving (BP 130, DM 311, FR 1058, Y 22,039).

$209* *Wild Flowers: Two,* from The Botanical Magazine, plate s., d. W. Curtis 1790 and 1791, (06-17-93, Garth, #303, illus.), 13½ x 10⅜ in., (34.3 x 26.4 cm.), hand-colored engraving (BP 138, DM 347, FR 1166, Y 22,394).

$187* *Yellow Flowers, 1790 and 1791: A Pair,* from The Botanical Magazine, plate s., d. W. Curtis, (04-02-93, Garth, #421, illus.), 13¼ x 10¼ in., (33.7 x 26 cm.), hand-colored engraving (BP 123, DM 301, FR 1021, Y 21,291).

$209* *Yellow Flowers, 1790 and 1795: A Pair,* from The Botanical Magazine by William Curtis, plate s. W. Curtis, (04-02-93, Garth, #32, illus.), 13¼ x 10¼ in., (33.7 x 26 cm.), hand-colored engraving (BP 138, DM 336, FR 1141, Y 23,796).

$143* *Yellow Flowers: A Pair,* from The Botanical Magazine, plate s., d. W. Curtis 1796 (and 1797), (03-13-93, Garth, #281, illus.), 13⅜ x 10⅜ in., (34 x 26.4 cm.), hand-colored engravings (BP 100, DM 238, FR 809, Y 16,853).

$187* *Yellow Flowers: A Pair,* from The Botanical Magazine, plate s., d. W. Curtis, 1789 and 1790, (06-17-93, Garth, #675, illus.), 13¼ x 10¼ in., (33.7 x 26 cm.), hand-colored engraving (BP 124, DM 310, FR 1044, Y 20,036).

$99* *Yellow Flowers: Three,* from the Botanical Magazine, one pl. s. S. Curtis 1814, (02-19-93, Garth, #439, illus.), 13⅜ x 10⅜ in., (34 x 26.4 cm.), handcolored engravings (BP 68, DM 162, FR 549, Y 11,747).

$215* *Yellow and Green Colored Flowers: Three,* from the Botanical Magazine, s. on pl. T. Curtis; d. 1807, 1809, 1810, (02-19-93, Garth, #437, illus.), 13⅜ x 10⅜ in., (34 x 26.4 cm.), handcolored engravings (BP 148, DM 352, FR 1192, Y 25,510).

CUSSETTI, Carlo   b. 1866
$140* *PLM. Genes, Milan, Turin, Lac Majeur, c. 1900,* cond. B, (03-16-93, Boisgirard, #89), 43⅛ x 29⅛ in., (109.5 x 74 cm.), poster (BP 97, DM 233, FR 791, Y 16,370).

$201* *Service D'Hiver. Chemin De Fer Paris Lyon Mediterranee. Florence, Rome, Naples, Venice, c. 1900,* Torino, Stabilimento Flli Pozzo, cond. B+, (06-11-93, Boisgirard, #66), 44⅛ x 30⅞ in., (112 x 78.5 cm.), poster (BP 132, DM 327, FR 1101, Y 21,326).

CUYP, A. (after)
$128* *"A Young Golfer",* by Emery Walker, margins, (03-03-93, Bonhams-Chelsea, #269), plate 24½ x 17½ in., (62.2 x 44.5 cm.), photogravure (BP 88, DM 211, FR 715, Y 14,957).

CUYP, Adrian (after)
$149* *A View On The Maese Near Maastricht,* by William Elliott, pub. J. Boydell, 1764, margins, foxing, (06-16-93, Bonhams-Chelsea, #367A), pl. 16¼ x 23⅞ in., (41.3 x 60.6 cm.), engraving (BP 99, DM 247, FR 830, Y 15,892).

D'ALBE, Bacler
$24* *"Allee Au Bord De L'Eau",* (03-22-93, Pescheteau, #2), color lithograph (BP 16, DM 39, FR 134, Y 2779).

D'ALESI, F. Hugo
$167* *P.L.M.: Billets A Prix Reduits, c. 1895,* good cond., (01-23-93, Ribeyre/Baron, #6), 42½ x 30¹¹⁄₁₆ in., (108 x 78 cm.), poster (BP 109, DM 266, FR 898, Y 20,901).

$167* *PLM: Chatel-Guyon, c. 1895,* good cond., (01-23-93, Ribeyre/Baron, #84), 42½ x 30¹¹⁄₁₆ in., (108 x 78 cm.), poster (BP 109, DM 266, FR 898, Y 20,901).

D'ALESI, Hugo (Frederic ALEXIANU)   1849-1906
$110* *Ch. De Fer De L'Est. Les Vosges,* cond. A, (03-16-93, Boisgirard, #129), 41⁵⁄₁₆ x 28¾ in., (105 x 73 cm.), poster (BP 76, DM 183, FR 621, Y 12,862).

D'ANNA, Paolo   Italian/American 20th cent.
BI *Archangel,* s. in block; s., t., est. $125/175, (10-30-92, Sloan, #840), 11 x 8 in., (27.9 x 20.3 cm.), print.

D'ARCANGELO, Allan   American b. 1930
BI *"C", 1969,* s., d., signs of wear, est. DM 600, (12-01-92, Karl/Faber, #324), 21¹⁄₁₆ x 25⅜ in., (53.5 x 64.5 cm.), color serigraph.
$109* *Cave V, 1979,* 162/175, s., d., (10-14-92, Germann, #212), 30⅞ x 26³⁄₁₆ in., (785 x 665 mm.), color serigraph (BP 64, DM 160, FR 541, Y 13,209, SF 142).
BI *"Gulf", 1969,* s., d., A/P III, est. DM 600, (12-01-92, Karl/Faber, #323), 23⁷⁄₁₆ x 25⅜ in., (59.5 x 64.5 cm.), color serigraph on cardboard.
$770* *"The Holy Family", "Highway U.S. 40", "Reflection" and "Cane V.", c.1978-80: Set Of Four,* s., full margins, (12-08-92, Swann, #77), color serigraph (BP 483, DM 1199, FR 4087, Y 95,439).
BI *Reflections, 1978,* 146/150, s., d., est. SF 2/280, (10-14-92, Germann, #211), 30 x 26⅛ in., (762 x 663 mm.), color serigraph.
BI *The Smoker, 1980,* #98/250, s., d., R.P. Shaftan, 1980 stamp, est. SF 250/350, (09-04-92, Germann, #215), 26³⁄₁₆ x 36 in., (665 x 915 mm.), color lithograph.
BI *Two Arrow Road Signs, 1970,* s., #XLIX, good cond.?, creases, inkloss, surface soiling, est. $150/250, (05-19-93, Butterfield, #2114), 40 x 29⅞ in., (101.6 x 75.9 cm.), silkscreen in colors on wove.
$193* *"Untitled", 1971,* s., d., #50/90, full margins, good cond.?, (10-28-92, Butterfield, #2926), 22⅝ x 22½ in., (575 x 572 mm.), silkscreen in black, yellow and white on wove (BP 123, DM 298, FR 1012, Y 23,681).

D'ARGENCE
$836* *PLM/ Messageries Maritimes "Paris En Orient Via Marseille", 1909,* very good cond., (03-13-93, Laurin, #161, illus.), 41⁵⁄₁₆ x 29½ in., (105 x 75 cm.), (BP 583, DM 1391, FR 4731, Y 98,527).

D'ERCOLE, Paola   Italian 20th cent.
BI *A Luca, 1978,* #15/30, s., d., i., est. SF 40/60, (09-04-92, Germann, #295), 27⁹⁄₁₆ x 19¹¹⁄₁₆ in., (700 x 500 mm.), etching.
BI *Omaggio A Merotti, 1978,* #16/32, s., d., i., est. SF 40/50, (09-04-92, Germann, #294), 27⅝ x 19⅝ in., (702 x 498 mm.), etching.
BI *Specchi Di Pietra, 1978,* #48/50, s., d., i., est. SF 40/60, (09-04-92, Germann, #297), 27⁹⁄₁₆ x 19⅝ in., (700 x 498 mm.), etching.
BI *Storia De Ogbar, 1978,* #22/50, s., d., i., est. SF 40/60, (09-04-92, Germann, #296), 27⁷⁄₁₆ x 19½ in., (697 x 495 mm.), etching.

D'EZY
BI *The De Chine,* losses, tears, est. BP 2/400, (02-04-93, Christie-S. Ken, #121), 54½ x 39½ in., (138.4 x 100.3 cm.), color lithograph.

D'OLIVIER
$577* *Female Nude And Veiled Mirror,* 1850's, sold after sale, (10-14-92, Swann, #236, illus.), 2¾ x 2¼ in., (7 x 5.7 cm.), photograph, salt print (BP 339, DM 844, FR 2864, Y 69,922).

D'OLIVIER, Count
$944* *Nude Study,* 1850s, mounted on card, 88 x 66mm, (05-07-93, Sotheby-London, #117, illus.), photograph, salt print from glass neg. (BP 598, DM 1492, FR 5029, Y 103,942).

D'ORA, Madame and Arthur BENDA (Dora Kallmus)
$2300* *Selected Portraits: Twenty-Four,* majority w/photog. credit in neg., each w/credit and/or (c) stamps, labels, (04-06-93, Sotheby-NY, #298, illus.), each approx. 6½ x 7½ in., photograph (BP 1519, DM 3705, FR 12,548, Y 262,318).

D'RYKR
$201* *Prague "Reve D'Art", 1939,* Imp. J. Goossens, good cond., (02-12-93, Cheval/Robert, #98), 59¹⁄₁₆ x 39⅜ in., (150 x 100 cm.), poster (BP 142, DM 333, FR 1128, Y 24,240).

D'YLEN, Jean
$932* *The Supreme Combination, Shell Oil & Shell Petrol, 1928,* p. EVP, ref. #168, cond. 3, (10-13-92, Phillips-London, #63, illus.). 29¹³⁄₁₆ x 44⅞ in., (75.7 x 114 cm.), color lithograph (BP 543, DM 1365, FR 4639, Y 113,011).

DA RAVENNA, Marco Dente   d. 1527
BI *Das Letzte Abendmahl (Bartsch 27),* after Marcantonio Raimondi, watermark, prov., est. DM 1,500, (06-10-93, Hauswedell/Nolt, #66, illus.), engraving.

DA VINCI, Leonardo (after)
$84* *"Young Boy Playing With A Puzzle", 1795,* by Francesco Bartolozzi, pub. A. Molteno, margins, (01-21-93, Bonhams-Chelsea, #101A), plate 17¼ x 12½ in., (43.8 x 31.8 cm.), stipple engraving (BP 55, DM 134, FR 452, Y 10,513).

DABO
$358* *PLM: La Syrie Et Le Liban. "Pays De Tourisme Et De Villegiature", c.1925,* very good cond., (03-13-93, Laurin, #114), 40¹⁵⁄₁₆ x 29⁵⁄₁₆ in., (104 x 74.5 cm.), (BP 250, DM 596, FR 2026, Y 42,192).
$398* *PLM: La Syrie Et Le Liban. Environs De Damas. Maloula, 1927,* very good cond., (03-13-93, Laurin, #116), 41⁵⁄₁₆ x 29½ in., (105 x 75 cm.), (BP 278, DM 662, FR 2252, Y 46,906).

DADO   b. 1933
BI *Morio Et Pipistrelles, 1984: Two,* s., d. 84, t., #8/10, full margins, est. FF 4/5,000, (11-16-92, Briest, #279), 29¹⁵⁄₁₆ x 22⁷⁄₁₆ in., (76 x 57 cm.), etching in black.
$50* *"Personnages-1968",* #72/500, s., (04-04-93, Pescheteau, #190), 19¹¹⁄₁₆ x 13⅜ in., (50 x 34 cm.), black lithograph on wove (BP 33, DM 80, FR 273, Y 5693).

DAHL, K.
$294* *Norvegian America Line,* p. E. Moestue, good cond., (11-19-92, Ribeyre/Baron, #99), 32½ x 20⅞ in., (82.5 x 53 cm.), offset poster (BP 194, DM 469, FR 1579, Y 36,563).

DAHL, Peter   b. 1934
$10,053* *Carl Michael Bellman: Fredmans Epistlar Med Forord Och Komentarer AvOlof Bystrom Och Sven Delblanc, 1984,* s., Gallerie Aix, (12-04-92, AB Stockholm, #7048), sh, smallest 16¹⁵⁄₁₆ x 11⅝ in., (43 x 29.5 cm.), largest 16¹⁵⁄₁₆ x 34⅝ in., (43 x 29.5 cm.), portfolio, 87 lithographs in color and b/w (BP 6448, DM 16,011, FR 54,311, Y 1,255,056, SK 68,200).
$7266* *Carl Michael Bellman: Fredmans Epistlar Med Forord Och Kommentarer Av Olof Brystrom Och Sven Delblanc, De Luxe-Utgava Med Musiken Till Epistlarna IFaksimile, 1984,* s., Gallerie Aix, (05-12-93, AB Stockholm, #7017, illus.), 16¹⁵⁄₁₆ x 11⅝ in., (43 x 29.5 cm.), lithographs, some w/color (BP 4744, DM 11,723, FR 39,489, Y 811,209, SK 53,900).
$2793* *Dansande Par,* s. 1981, 182/250, (05-25-93, AB Stockholm, #15), 20⅞ x 14⅜ in., (53 x 36.5 cm.), lithograph in colors on Tumba (BP 1810, DM 4549, FR 15,313, Y 305,279, SK 4070).
$2264* *Dansande Par I Blatt,* s., 1981, 196/250, (05-25-93, AB Stockholm, #14), 20⅞ x 14⅜ in., (53 x 36.5 cm.), lithograph in colors (BP 1467, DM 3687, FR 12,412, Y 247,459, SK 3300).
$3925* *Dansande Par I Rott,* s. 1981, proof, (05-25-93, AB Stockholm, #17), 21¹⁄₁₆ x 14⅜ in., (53.5 x 36.5 cm.), lithograph in colors (BP 2544, DM 6393, FR 21,519, Y 429,009, SK 5720).
$1510* *Dansande Par I Violett,* s. 1981, 143/250, (05-25-93, AB Stockholm, #16), 21¹⁄₁₆ x 14⅜ in., (53.5 x 36.5 cm.), lithograph in colors (BP 979, DM 2459, FR 8279, Y 165,045, SK 2200).
$486* *Dansande Par, 1981,* s., HC III/XXXV, (12-04-92, AB Stockholm, #7046), 20⅞ x 14⅜ in., (53 x 36.5 cm.).

lithograph in colors (BP 312, DM 774, FR 2626, Y 60,674, SK 3300).

$746* *Fredmans Epistel No: 82,* s., (12-04-92, AB Stockholm, #7047), 16⁵⁄₁₆ x 22⅝ in., (41.5 x 57.5 cm.), lithograph in colors (BP 479, DM 1188, FR 4030, Y 93,134, SK 5060).

$2642* *Norna,* s., proof, (05-25-93, AB Stockholm, #19), 24 x 35¹⁄₁₆ in., (61 x 89 cm.), lithograph in colors (BP 1712, DM 4303, FR 14,485, Y 288,775, SK 3850).

$2264* *Restaurant Interior,* s. 1973, 143/260, proof, (05-25-93, AB Stockholm, #20), 20¹⁄₁₆ x 30⅞ in., (51 x 78.5 cm.), lithograph in colors (BP 1467, DM 3687, FR 12,412, Y 247,459, SK 3300).

$649* *Restaurant Interior, 1973,* s., 143/260, (12-04-92, AB Stockholm, #7043), 20¹⁄₁₆ x 30⅞ in., (51 x 78.5 cm.), lithograph in colors (BP 416, DM 1034, FR 3506, Y 81,024, SK 4400).

$2108* *Six Lithographs: 1987,* s., 16/210, portfolio, ed. Galerie Aix, (12-04-92, AB Stockholm, #7049), sh 23⅝ x 31½ in., (60 x 80 cm.), lithographs in color (BP 1352, DM 3357, FR 11,388, Y 263,171, SK 14,300).

$1585* *Skuggor Mot Gron-Rod Tapet,* s., proof, (05-25-93, AB Stockholm, #18), 35¹⁄₁₆ x 24³⁄₁₆ in., (89 x 61.5 cm.), lithograph in colors (BP 1027, DM 2581, FR 8690, Y 173,243, SK 2310).

$240* *"Till Kara Mor Pa Fyrkanten",* #61, (11-07-92, Falkkloos, #101), lithograph (BP 157, DM 385, FR 1295, Y 29,622, SK 1430).

$2594* *Vin, Kvinnor Och Man, 1980: Six,* 7/250, Galerie Aix/ Edition Valen, (12-04-92, AB Stockholm, #7045), sh, approx. 26¾ x 21¼ in., (68 x 54 cm.), portfolio, lithograph in colors (BP 1664, DM 4131, FR 14,014, Y 323,845, SK 17,600).

DAHL-WOLFE, Louise American 1895-1989

$1840* *The Baroness De Rothschild, New York City,* c. 1940, p.l., ink t.; ink s., t., annot., d., George Dzugan Estate, (04-08-93, Christie-NY, #414, illus.), 13 x 10⅛ in., (33 x 25.7 cm.), photograph, gelatin silver print (BP 1207, DM 2956, FR 10,005, Y 208,806).

BI *Betty Treat, Model, Sea Island, January,* 1951, p.l., partially ink t., d.; s., partially t., est. $1,8/2,200, (04-08-93, Christie-NY, #415, illus.), 12¼ x 9½ in., (31.1 x 24.1 cm.), photograph, gelatin silver print.

$2750* *Calla Lilies, 1931 (Dahl-Wolfe, p. 8),* s. by photog., p. in 1950's, (10-15-92, Sotheby-NY, #220, illus.), 7¾ x 9 in., (19.7 x 22.9 cm.), photograph, gelatin silver print (BP 1683, DM 4093, FR 13,882, Y 329,934).

BI *Christopher Isherwood And W.H. Auden, Central Park,* (1938), p.l., s., t., d. in ink, lit., est. $1,5/2,000, (10-13-92, Christie-NY, #174, illus.), 11 x 11 in., (27.9 x 27.9 cm.), photograph, gelatin silver print.

BI *Ginger Rogers,* 1930s, est. $1,8/2,200, (04-08-93, Christie-NY, #418, illus.), 10½ x 10 in., (26.7 x 25.4 cm.), photograph, gelatin silver print.

BI *"Jean Patchett In Granada, Spain" (Dahl-Wolfe, p. 66), 1953,* s., d. by photog., annot. in unident. hand, est. $1,5/2,500, (04-06-93, Sotheby-NY, #448A, illus.), 13 x 10 in., photograph.

$1650* *Lauren Bacall Modeling Lingerie, c. 1945,* stamp, (10-13-92, Christie-NY, #178, illus.), 11⅜ x 10¾ in., (28.9 x 27.3 cm.), photograph, gelatin silver print (BP 961, DM 2417, FR 8213, Y 200,073).

BI *Margaret Bourke-White, 1942,* stamp, lit., est. $2/3,000, (10-13-92, Christie-NY, #177, illus.), 12¼ x 10¾ in., (31.1 x 27.3 cm.), photograph, gelatin silver print.

BI *Marlene Dietrich In Destry Rides Again,* 1938, p.l., s., t., d., lit., est. $1,2/1,500, (04-08-93, Christie-NY, #417, illus.), 12⅜ x 9⅜ in., (31.4 x 23.8 cm.), photograph, gelatin silver print.

$1980* *Marlene Dietrich In Destry Rides Again, 1938,* stamp, lit., (10-13-92, Christie-NY, #173, illus.), 7⅞ x 7⅝ in., (20 x 19.4 cm.), photograph, gelatin silver print (BP 1153, DM 2901, FR 9856, Y 240,087).

BI *Napier Shelley In Schiaparelli Tunic,* 1939, p.l., s., t., d., lit., est. $1,8/2,200, (04-08-93, Christie-NY, #416, illus.), 12½ x 10½ in., (31.8 x 26.7 cm.), photograph, gelatin silver print.

$1265* *"Natalie In Gres Coat, Kairouan" (Dahl-Wolfe, p. 70), 1953,* s. by photog., p. notations in unident. hand, (04-06-93, Sotheby-NY, #448, illus.), 13 x 10 in., photograph (BP 836, DM 2038, FR 6901, Y 144,275).

BI *Night Bathing,* (1939), p.l., s., lit., est. $1,8/2,200, (10-13-92, Christie-NY, #175, illus.), 10¼ x 9¾ in., (26 x 24.8 cm.), photograph, gelatin silver print.

$1380* *Twins At The Beach,* 1955, p.l., s., (c) and reprod. limitation , lit., (04-08-93, Christie-NY, #419, illus.), 10¼ x 11⅞ in., (26 x 30.2 cm.), photograph, gelatin silver print (BP 905, DM 2217, FR 7504, Y 156,605).

$2420* *Twins At The Beach,* (1955), p.l., s., lit., (10-13-92, Christie-NY, #440, illus.), 10¾ x 9 in., (27.3 x 22.9 cm.), photograph, gelatin silver print (BP 1409, DM 3545, FR 12,046, Y 293,440).

$1650* *William Edmundson, Sculptor, Nashville,* 1940s, stamp, i., (10-13-92, Christie-NY, #176, illus.), 9⅝ x 8⅜ in., (24.4 x 21.3 cm.), photograph, gelatin silver print (BP 961, DM 2417, FR 8213, Y 200,073).

DAHMEN, Karl Fred 1917-1981

$498* *Block Horizontal (A. 268.), 1980,* s., d., epr(euve) d'art(-iste), estate stamp, (12-01-92, Karl/Faber, #520), 17½ x 23⁷⁄₁₆ in., (44.5 x 59.5 cm.), color etching on thick wove (BP 329, DM 794, FR 2705, Y 62,002).

$381* *Esko (A. 257.), 1979,* s., d., t., num., (12-01-92, Karl/ Faber, #518), 7¹⁄₁₆ x 5⅞ in., (18 x 15 cm.), color etching on wove (BP 252, DM 607, FR 2070, Y 47,435).

$581* *"Kulstatte" (A. 277.), 1980,* s., d., t., num., (12-01-92, Karl/Faber, #521), 17½ x 16⅛ in., (44.5 x 41 cm.), color etching on thick wove (BP 384, DM 926, FR 3156, Y 72,336).

$922* *"Landschaft Negativ-Positiv" (Angst 175), 1975,* s., t., d., num., (06-05-93, Grisebach, #557, illus.), 30¹⁵⁄₁₆ x 19⁷⁄₁₆ in., (78.7 x 49.3 cm.), color aquatint/etching w/ embossing on copper print paper (BP 607, DM 1495, FR 5038, Y 98,906).

$332* *Malo (A. 241.), 1979,* s., d., t., num., (12-01-92, Karl/ Faber, #517), 7¹¹⁄₁₆ x 6⅛ in., (19.5 x 15.5 cm.), color etching on wove (BP 219, DM 529, FR 1803, Y 41,335).

$631* *Materie & Esprit (A. 283.), 1980,* s., d., epr(euve) d'art(-iste), (12-01-92, Karl/Faber, #522), 28⅛ x 22¼ in., (71.5 x 56.5 cm.), color etching and relief print on thick wove (BP 417, DM 1006, FR 3427, Y 78,561).

$415* *Mauritius (A. 265.), 1979,* s., d., t., num., (12-01-92, Karl/Faber, #519), 7¹¹⁄₁₆ x 5¹¹⁄₁₆ in., (19.5 x 14.5 cm.), color etching and relief print on wove (BP 274, DM 661, FR 2254, Y 51,668).

$701* *Notationen (Angst 250), 1979,* a.p., t., (12-05-92, Bassenge, #7112), 20⁹⁄₁₆ x 16⁹⁄₁₆ in., (52.2 x 42 cm.), color etching on thick copper print paper (BP 439, DM 1093, FR 3725, Y 86,854).

BI *Raum III (Angst 70.), 1966,* s., num., stamped edition rothe, stained, est. DM 600, (12-01-92, Karl/Faber, #515), 6⅞ x 6½ in., (17.5 x 16.5 cm.), etching and drypoint in ochre on wove.

BI *Second Voyage,* s., d., t., num., est. DM 900-, (09-25-92, Granier, #2803), sheet 27⁹⁄₁₆ x 20¼ in., (70 x 51.5 cm.), color lithograph on Arches hand-made.

$424* *Tagesablaufe, 1976,* s., d., t., artist's proof, (06-12-93, Hauswedell/Nolt, #64), 21⁵⁄₁₆ x 27⁷⁄₁₆ in., (54.2 x 69.7 cm.), color etching w/relief print on thick wove (BP 278, DM 690, FR 2319, Y 44,617).

$290* *Teresa (A. 233.), 1978,* s., d., num., (12-01-92, Karl/ Faber, #516), 7¹⁄₁₆ x 5⅞ in., (18 x 15 cm.), color etching and relief print on wove (BP 192, DM 462, FR 1575, Y 36,106).

DAHN, Walter German b. 1954

BI *Kosmos Aisthetos, Kosmos Noctos, 1989,* felt pen s., d., #16/16, est. DM 800, (11-12-92, Lempertz, #43), sheet 42³⁄₁₆ x 34⁷⁄₁₆ in., (627.4 x 87.5 cm.), photograph, Kodak color print.

$304* *Scared To Dance, 1975/79: Two,* s., d., t., (11-12-92, Lempertz, #42, illus.), 11⁷⁄₁₆ x 7½ in., (29 x 19 cm.), photograph, b/w xerox on DIN A 4 xerox paper (BP 194, DM 478, FR 1628, Y 37,610).

DAINTREY, Adrian b. 1902

$755* *To Visit Britain's Landmarks, The 'Jungle' Lincoln, 1936,* p. Waterlow and Sons, ref. 470, cond. 3, (10-13-92, Phillips-London, #113), 29¹⁵⁄₁₆ x 44⅞ in., (76 x 114 cm.), color lithograph (BP 440, DM 1106, FR 3758, Y 91,548).

DALBY, David (after)

$1036* *Tarrare, Winner Of The St. Leger, At Doncaster, (S.p 380), 1826,* by T. Sutherland, pub. W. Sheardown and Sons, margins, excell. cond.,laid, (10-07-92, Christie-S. Ken, #43), pl 15 x 20½ in., (38.1 x 52.1 cm.), colored aquatint (BP 605, DM 1499, FR 5083, Y 124,594).

DALI, S.

$399* *Couple On A Horse,* s., #6/95, embossed sig., foxed, (11-18-92, Bubb Kuyper, #1529), 12½ x 9 7/16 in., (31.8 x 23.9 cm.), copper engraving (BP 263, DM 636, FR 2143, Y 49,621, G 720).

DALI, Salvador Spanish 1904-1989

$230* *Abstract Figures On Horseback,* plate s.; s., #47/150, (04-07-93, Sotheby-Arcade, #15), 20 x 26 in., (50.8 x 66 cm.), color lithograph (BP 152, DM 372, FR 1259, Y 26,130).

$550* *"Ace Of Diamonds", "Jack Of Diamonds", "Queen Of Diamonds" and "KingOf Diamonds": Four,* s., #56/150, (06-11-93, Freemn/Fine Art, #42), 14¼ x 9¼ in., (36.2 x 23.5 cm.), color lithograph on Arches (BP 361, DM 894, FR 3014, Y 58,355).

$3575* *"After 50 Years Of Surrealism": Suite Of Twelve,* Transworld Art Publishers, #14/195, (02-27-93, Dunning, #1162), sh 20 x 26½ in., (50.8 x 67.3 cm.), etching (BP 2514, DM 5877, FR 19,972, Y 422,028).

$430* *Alice In Wonderland, 1976,* s., num. 16/175, pub. Transworld Art, full margins, excellent cond., (11-30-92, Phillips-London, #412), plate 15¾ x 12½ in., (400 x 318 mm.), drypoint w/extensive hand-coloring on Arches (BP 284, DM 685, FR 2326, Y 53,516).

$1650* *Alice's Adventures In Wonderland, 1969,* complete portfolio, s., stamped num. 276 on colophon, pub. Maecenas Press-Random House, full margins, very good cond., in orig. portfolio, (10-28-92, Butterfield, #2799), 16¾ x 11⅜ in., (425 x 289 mm.), etching and twlve offset lithographs in colors on Chiffon de Mandeure paper (BP 1051, DM 2548, FR 8652, Y 202,454).

$1870* *Alice's Adventures In Wonderland, 1969: Thirteen,* complete portfolio, s., stamp num. 431 on colophon, pub. Maecenas Press-Random House, full margins, good cond., in orig. portfolio, (02-24-93, Butterfield, #2732), 16¾ x 11⅜ in., (425 x 289 mm.), 1 etching & 12 offset lithographs in colors on Chiffon de Mandeure (BP 1304, DM 3036, FR 10,292, Y 219,432).

$10,350* *Aliyah,* complete portfolio, each s., i. Artist's Proof, i. on just. page, pub. Shorewood Publishers, Inc., 1968, good cond., in orig. linen covered portfolio, (05-13-93, Sotheby-NY, #536), each sh approx. 25½ x 19¾ in., (648 x 500 mm.), 25 lithographs in colors (BP 6795, DM 16,712, FR 56,373, Y 1,155,521).

$9350* *Aliyah, 1968,* complete portfolio, after orig. gouaches by Dali, s., i. 'Artist's Proof', pub. Shorewood Publishers, Inc., good cond., foxing, orig. portfolio, (11-05-92, Sotheby-NY, #149), each sheet approx. 25½ x 19¾ in., (648 x 500 mm.), 25 lithographs p. in colors (BP 6081, DM 14,787, FR 50,027, Y 1,147,099).

$9468* *Aliyah: Twenty-Five,* portfolio, s., #201/250, (05-08-93, Dobiaschofsky, #1899), 25⅜ x 19 11/16 in., (64.5 x 50 cm.), color lithograph (BP 6178, DM 15,210, FR 51,317, Y 1,057,995, SF 13,800).

$1131* *Les Amour Jaunes, 1974: Three,* 3 from the series, s., num., pub. Editions Pierre Belfont, (10-27-92, Phillips-London, #195), plate 11⅝ x 8½ in., (295 x 216 mm.), etching w/drypoint and gold leaf glitter on Arches (BP 715, DM 1733, FR 5881, Y 138,349).

BI *Les Amour Jaunes, 1974: Two,* 2 from ten series illus. text by Tristan Corbiere, s., num., pub. Editions Pierre Belfont, Paris, est. BP 6/800, (10-27-92, Phillips-London, #194), plate 11⅝ x 8½ in., (295 x 216 mm.), etching w/drypoint and gold leaf glitter on Arches.

BI *Les Amours Jaunes De Tristan Corbiere, 1974: Ten,* #48/300, s., est. DM 7,500, (05-26-93, Lempertz, #97), 15 15/16 x 12 in., (40.5 x 30.5 cm.), gravure, etching on Arches wove.

$4328* *Les Amours Jaunes De Tristan Corbiere, 1974: Ten,* #146/300, s., (11-21-92, Lempertz, #100), 15 15/16 x 12 in., (40.5 x 30.5 cm.), etching on Arches wove (BP 2850, DM 6901, FR 23,244, Y 538,242).

BI *"Les Amours Jaunes-1965-74": Two,* illus., s., est. FF2,000/2,500, (04-04-93, Pescheteau, #191), 14 15/16 x 11 in., (38 x 28 cm.), plates on Japon nacre.

BI *"Anxiety",* s., num. 194/300, Dali seal, est. $750/1000, (10-10-92, Goldberg, #435), 22¾ x 15 in., (57.8 x 38.1 cm.), color lithograph.

$6320* *Apres 50 Ans De Surrealisme, 1974: Twelve,* num., E.A., s., Transworld, (04-21-93, Germann, #42, illus.), 25 9/16 x 19 11/16 in., (650 x 500 mm.), color etching (BP 4101, DM 10,102, FR 34,162, Y 699,657, SF 9200).

$303* *Aries,* s., i., (05-28-93, Sloan, #1662, illus.), 14¾ x 10½ in., (37.5 x 26.7 cm.), color etching (BP 194, DM 481, FR 1625, Y 32,490).

BI *"Atavistic Vestiges",* s., num. 14/300, Dali seal, est. $750/1000, (10-10-92, Goldberg, #433, illus.), 22¾ x 18½ in., (57.8 x 47 cm.), color lithograph.

$3300* *Baccacio's Decameron, 1972: Ten,* s., pub. Transworld Art, (05-16-93, Hindman, #493, illus.), overall 18 x 12 in., (45.7 x 30.5 cm.), color drypoint (BP 2146, DM 5308, FR 17,838, Y 365,813).

BI *Betendes Bauernpaar, 1985,* #220/300, blindstamp, stamps verso, creases, (09-18-92, Schloss Ahlden, #986), 24 x 32 13/16 in., (61 x 83.4 cm.), multi-color solar print on hand-made.

$160* *Bird And Figure,* artist s., #190/250, (02-19-93, Garth, #444), 18¾ x 25½ in., (47.6 x 64.8 cm.), colored lithograph (BP 110, DM 262, FR 887, Y 18,984).

$770* *"The Bullfight Series",* #23/150, s. S. Dali, (04-23-93, Clearing House, #237), 21¼ x 17 in., (54 x 43.2 cm.), lithograph (BP 489, DM 1218, FR 4113, Y 85,045).

$633* *"The Bullfight Series",* #34/150, s. S. Dali, (04-23-93, Clearing House, #236), 21¼ x 17½ in., (54 x 44.5 cm.), lithograph (BP 402, DM 1001, FR 3381, Y 69,914).

$770* *Butterflies Of Anti-Matter (Albert Field Dali Archives Catalogue 1021), 1974,* from Conquest of the Cosmos series, full margins, s., annot. E.A, pub. Jean La Vigne, 1975, (05-27-93, Swann, #80), 29½ x 22 in., (74.9 x 55.9 cm.), diamond point engraving, color lithograph w/ relief embossment (BP 493, DM 1236, FR 4164, Y 82,547).

$303* *"Butterfly",* s., #249/300, (02-27-93, Dunning, #1104), 30¼ x 22¼ in., (76.8 x 56.5 cm.), lithograph (BP 213, DM 498, FR 1693, Y 35,769).

$674* *"Les Caprices De Goya" (Pl. 56-60 and 63), 1973-77: Three,* num., s., (10-18-92, Pescheteau, #115), each 17 11/16 x 12 3/16 in., (45 x 31 cm.), etching and aquatint on Rives (BP 408, DM 996, FR 3382, Y 80,478).

BI *"Les Caprices De Goya" (Pl. 64 and 78), 1973-77: Two,* num., s., est. FF 3,0/3,500, (10-18-92, Pescheteau, #118), both 17 11/16 x 12 3/16 in., (45 x 31 cm.), etching and aquatint on Rives.

BI *"Cervantes", "Cervantes", "Velasquez", and "El Cid": Four,* from the Spanish Immortals series, plate s., full margins, excell. cond., est. $4/800, (01-23-93, Goldberg, #491), 7 x 5 in., (17.8 x 12.7 cm.), etching.

BI *Le Char De David,* #123/250, full margins, est. FF 3,0/3,500, (11-16-92, Briest, #281), 20⅞ x 29½ in., (53 x 75 cm.), drypoint and aquatint in colors on Japan.

$1781* *Chateau De Stockholm (L. 771), 1976,* #98/450, s., blindstamp, (10-09-92, Winterberg, #1961, illus.), 15 9/16 x 23 5/16 in., (39.5 x 59.2 cm.), watercolored drypoint (BP 1057, DM 2646, FR 8883, Y 216,825).

$1033* *Christus Am Kreuz,* num., s., (12-05-92, Bassenge, #7113), 15 9/16 x 11 13/16 in., (39.5 x 30 cm.), etching on Japan (BP 647, DM 1611, FR 5489, Y 127,989).

$1245* *Christus Am Kreuz,* #75/100, s., (11-13-92, Kunsthaus, #518), 20 11/16 x 15 15/16 in., (52.5 x 40.5 cm.), etching on Japan (BP 805, DM 1954, FR 6591, Y 154,524).

$483* *Combat De Cavaliers, 1971,* s., fro, "Calderon" series, small tear, good cond., (06-28-93, Loudmer, #222), 12 15/16 x 20½ in., (330 x 520 mm.), sh 23 1/16 x 31⅛ in., (330 x 520 mm.), color etching on Richard de Bas wove (BP 323, DM 821, FR 2765, Y 51,247).

$1201* *Combat Des Cavaliers (Michler-Lopsinger Nr. 491 c), 1971,* s., Epreuve d'artiste, from the series Calderon (Lavie est un songe),watermark, Edition Berggruen, (06-10-93, Hauswedell/Nolt, #218, illus.), image 12 15/16 x

20⁹⁄₁₆ in., (33 x 52.3 cm.), color etching w/aquatint on copper print paper (BP 786, DM 1956, FR 6584, Y 127,481).

BI *Conquest Of The Cosmos, Part 1 "Space Time, Gelatine Watches", "Butterflies Of Anti-Matter", "Philosopher Crushed By Cosmos", "Dali Martian Equipped With A Double Microscope", and Two Others: Set Of Six,* full margins, s., annot. E.A., p. D'Art Bellini, Jacob Baal Teshuva Coll., est. $6/9,000, (12-08-92, Swann, #74, illus.), each image 29½ x 22 in., (74.9 x 55.9 cm.), diamond point engraving w/color lithography and relief embossment onArches wove.

$3867* *La Conquete Du Cosmos, 1974: Nine,* all s., 36/195, portfolio, (06-28-93, Loudmer, #224), 29¾ x 22¹⁄₁₆ in., (755 x 560 mm.), color drypoints and aquatints on Arches wove (BP 2589, DM 6571, FR 22,135, Y 410,292).

BI *La Conquette Du Cosmos II, 1977,* complete suit, each s., i., LV/CLXXXV, pub. Jean Lavigne, full margins, good cond., creases, tear, est. $5/6,000, (02-11-93, Sotheby-NY, #113, illus.), each sheet 39⅛ x 27⁷⁄₁₆ in., (993 x 697 mm.), 6 drypoints w/aquatints & embossing on BFK Rives wove.

$2175* *"La Conquista Del Cosmos",* s., #23/195, (03-17-93, Duran, #176, illus.), 38⁹⁄₁₆ x 26¾ in., (97.9 x 67.9 cm.), color engraving (BP 1500, DM 3619, FR 12,302, Y 255,102, P 258,750).

BI *"La Conquista Del Cosmos",* #23/195, s., reserve P100,000, (12-17-92, Duran, #175, illus.), 39⅜ x 26¾ in., (100 x 68 cm.), lithograph.

BI *Costa Brava,* #268/1000, s., margins, est. BP 2/300, (03-17-93, Bonhams-Chelsea, #401), image 17 x 21 in., (43.2 x 53.3 cm.), lithograph in colors.

BI *Costa Brava,* #268/1000, s., est. BP 1/200, (05-20-93, Bonhams-Chelsea, #109), image 17 x 21 in., (43.2 x 53.3 cm.), lithograph in colors.

$1100* *Le Couche Et La Mouche,* s., num. E.C. 151/250, (05-28-93, Sloan, #1661, illus.), 15½ x 22½ in., (39.4 x 57.2 cm.), color etching (BP 705, DM 1745, FR 5898, Y 117,950).

$1955* *Crazy Horse,* s., annot. E.A., pub. Yamet Arts, full margins, good cond., surface soiling, (05-19-93, Butterfield, #1907, illus.), 28½ x 21¼ in., (724 x 540 mm.), lithograph in colors w/hand-coloring, on BFK Rives (BP 1269, DM 3178, FR 10,706, Y 216,429).

$275* *"La Dance",* s. Salvadore Dali, (10-16-92, DuMouchelle, #1314, illus.), 21 x 15 in., (53.3 x 38.1 cm.), wood engraving (BP 167, DM 406, FR 1380, Y 32,836).

$825* *La Danse,* s., i. E.A., (10-30-92, Sloan, #2153), sight 22½ x 16½ in., (57.2 x 41.9 cm.), color lithograph (BP 529, DM 1269, FR 4306, Y 102,192).

$807* *Darstellungen Aus Der Gottlichen Komodie,* #103/150, s., (04-24-93, Ruef, #971), each 9¹³⁄₁₆ x 7¹⁄₁₆ in., (25 x 18 cm.), color woodcut (BP 509, DM 1265, FR 4272, Y 89,053).

$303* *Death Bed,* s., i. E.A., (10-30-92, Sloan, #2152), 6⅝ x 4⅞ in., (16.8 x 12.4 cm.), color etching (BP 194, DM 466, FR 1581, Y 37,533).

BI *Decameron Suite: Ten,* #58/150, suite, (c) Pamela Verlag, pub. Transworld Art, 1972, est. C$5/6000, (10-21-92, Maynard, #309), etching.

$1540* *"The Decameron" (Boccacio), 1972: Seven,* from set of 10, num., s., orig. linen box, pub. TransWorld Art, (05-27-93, Swann, #77), image 7 x 5 in., (44 x 12.7 cm.), sh 17½ x 12¼ in., (44 x 12.7 cm.), color drypoints (BP 986, DM 2471, FR 8329, Y 165,094).

$249* *"Devine Comedy Suite",* artist proof, s. Dali, stamp verso, (10-20-92, Encans, #168), 9⁷⁄₁₆ x 7¹⁄₁₆ in., (24 x 18 cm.), wood engraving (BP 139, DM 378, FR 1288, Y 31,211, C$ 305).

BI *"La Divina Commedia" (Harbarta 185-284), 1959-1963: One Hundred,* num., #454/4765, E. D'ART LES HEURES CLAIRES, est. SC 100/110,000, (05-19-93, Dorotheum, #462, illus.), 12¹⁵⁄₁₆ x 10¼ in., (32.9 x 26 cm.), woodcut in color.

BI *"Double Face",* s., num. 78/300, est. $750/1000, (10-10-92, Goldberg, #431, illus.), 22¾ x 15 in., (57.8 x 38.1 cm.), color lithograph.

$449* *"La Douloureuse Garde",* from La Quete du Graal, #LIX/LXXV, s., (10-18-92, Pescheteau, #114), 19¹¹⁄₁₆ x 25⁹⁄₁₆ in., (50 x 65 cm.), drypoint in colors on japon (Japan paper) nacre (BP 272, DM 663, FR 2253, Y 53,612).

$504* *Drawer, 1978,* s., #G 64/125, blindstamp, (c), (09-18-92, Schloss Ahlden, #984, illus.), 29¼ x 21⁷⁄₁₆ in., (74.3 x 54.5 cm.), color lithograph on Arches (BP 295, DM 748, FR 2558, Y 62,291).

$1865* *Europa Auf Dem Stier, c. 1980,* s., LII/CL, (09-05-92, Arnold, #8, illus.), 20⅞ x 28⅜ in., (53 x 72 cm.), color lithograph (BP 930, DM 2596, FR 8843, Y 228,919).

BI *Faust,* orig. portfolio, each s., #32/150, pub. Pierre Argillet, 1969, full margins, good cond., est. $5/6,000, (02-11-93, Sotheby-NY, #109, illus.), sheets approx. 15³⁄₁₆ x 11¼ in., (385 x 285 mm.), 10 hand colored etchings on wove.

$1430* *"Female Nudes In Chains": Three and "A Nude With Another Figure": One,* each d. 1967, s. in plate, s., #116/160 in margin, (09-23-92, Sotheby-Arcade, #136, illus.), approx. 25½ x 19¾ in., (64.8 x 50.2 cm.), lithographs in colors (BP 836, DM 2141, FR 7296, Y 171,319).

BI *La Femme Invisible (Maur 61), 1930,* i., pub., frontispiece for book Chase au Papillion, margins, good cond., est. BP 1,8/2,200, (06-30-93, Sotheby-London, #415), sh 9⅞ x 7⅝ in., (251 x 194 mm.), heliogravure (photoengraving) on wove.

$1100* *Figue Erotique, 1969,* s., d., num. 137/200, margins, good cond., mat staining, glue remains, creases, (02-24-93, Butterfield, #2733), 22¼ x 14¼ in., (565 x 362 mm.), offset lithograph & drypoint in colors w/embossing on Rives BFK (BP 767, DM 1786, FR 6054, Y 129,078).

$302* *For Teatro Figueras, 1974: Group Of Six,* Mourlot, A cond., (08-06-92, Swann, #110, illus.), 28½ x 20½ in., (72.4 x 52.1 cm.), (BP 158, DM 446, FR 1507, Y 38,520).

$80* *Franzosische Eisebahn. Alpes, 1969,* good cond., (03-15-93, Arcole, #28), 38¹⁵⁄₁₆ x 24⁷⁄₁₆ in., (99 x 62 cm.), (BP 56, DM 133, FR 452, Y 9476).

$633* *From Lautreamont, Les Chants De Maldoror (Plate 30), 1934,* watermark, aside from edit. of 210, pub. Albert Skira, full margins,good cond.?, staining, surface soiling, notations, (05-19-93, Butterfield, #1906), 8¾ x 6¾ in., (222 x 171 mm.), etching on wove (BP 411, DM 1029, FR 3467, Y 70,076).

$465* *Geburt Der Venus,* s., #G31/125, blindstamp, (09-18-92, Schloss Ahlden, #985, illus.), 29⁷⁄₁₆ x 21⁵⁄₁₆ in., (74.8 x 54.2 cm.), color lithograph on Arches (BP 272, DM 690, FR 2360, Y 57,471).

$11,275* *The Grasshopper's Child, 1934,* s., #43/100, full (large) margins, good cond., water stain, tear, crease, (11-05-92, Sotheby-NY, #148, illus.), 14½ x 11¾ in., (369 x 300 mm.), etching on Arches wove (BP 7333, DM 17,832, FR 60,326, Y 1,383,266).

$6900* *The Grasshopper's Child, 1934,* s., #40/100, large margins, good cond., mat stain, nick, discolored,skinned spots, (05-13-93, Sotheby-NY, #535, illus.), 14½ x 11¾ in., (368 x 300 mm.), sh 24½ x 19¼ in., (368 x 300 mm.), etching on Arches wove (BP 4530, DM 11,142, FR 37,582, Y 770,347).

$8250* *Grasshopper's Child, 1934,* full margins, num., s., mat burn, waterstain, paper abrasion, scratch, (05-27-93, Swann, #77A, illus.), plate 14½ x 11¾ in., (36.8 x 29.8 cm.), etching (BP 5283, DM 13,238, FR 44,619, Y 884,434).

$392* *Gravures D'Apres Francisco Goya: Pair,* s., # 30/200, 45/200, plates 29 and 30, (03-31-93, Briest, #E150), one 17½ x 12 in., (44.5 x 30.5 cm.), other 9¹⁄₁₆ x 6½ in., (44.5 x 30.5 cm.), embellished w/aquatint and etching (BP 259, DM 631, FR 2142, Y 45,078).

$4400* *Imaginations & Objects Of The Future, 1975-76,* portfolio, s., #52/250, etchings p. by J.J. Rigal, lithographs p. byDesjobert, pub. Merrill Chase Publishing Associates, full margins, good cond.,orig. folder, covers and wood box, (11-05-92, Sotheby-NY, #150), each sheet approx. 32⅞ x 25⅜ in., (835 x 645 mm.), ten mixed media graphics on Arches (BP 2862, DM 6959, FR 23,542, Y 539,811).

$6900* *Imaginations And Objects Of The Future,* portfolio, s., #216/250, etchings p. J.J. Rigal, lithographs p. Desjobert, pub. Merrill Chase Publishing Associates, 1975-76, full margins, good cond., orig. folder, w/covers, and box, (05-13-93, Sotheby-NY, #538), each sh approx. 30⅜ x 22 in., (770 x 558 mm.), ten mixed media graphics on Arches wove (BP 4530, DM 11,142, FR 37,582, Y 770,347).

$770* *Infraterrestrials Adored By A Five Year Old Dali Who Thought He Was An Insect (Albert Field Dali Archives Catalogue 1024), 1974,* from Conquest of the Cosmos series, full margins, s., annot. E.A., pub. Jean LaVigne, 1974, (05-27-93, Swann, #79), 29½ x 22 in., (74.9 x 55.9 cm.), diamond point engraving, color lithograph w/ relief embossment (BP 493, DM 1236, FR 4164, Y 82,547).

BI *Le Jugement,* s., #152/175, est. $500/750, (10-30-92, Sloan, #2154), 23 x 17 in., (58.4 x 43.2 cm.), color lithograph.

$303* *The King,* s., num. 149/400, (09-20-92, Hindman, #810), 22 x 15½ in., (55.9 x 39.4 cm.), color lithograph (BP 177, DM 450, FR 1538, Y 37,449).

$495* *"King Of Hearts" and "Queen Of Hearts": Two,* s., #87/ 150, (06-11-93, Freemn/Fine Art, #41), 14 x 9¼ in., (35.6 x 23.5 cm.), lithograph (BP 325, DM 804, FR 2712, Y 52,520).

BI *L'Apparition,* s., #25/250, full margins, est. FF 3,0/ 3,500, (11-16-92, Briest, #283), 26⅜ x 20¹⁄₁₆ in., (67 x 51 cm.), drypoint and aquatint in colors.

$398* *"L'Unicorn",* (03-10-93, Maynard, #642), etching (BP 278, DM 662, FR 2249, Y 47,023, C$ 495).

$413* *"Lady Godiva",* s., full margins, excell. cond., (05-07-93, Goldberg, #438), 15½ x 20¾ in., (39.4 x 52.7 cm.), etching w/watercolor highlights (BP 262, DM 653, FR 2200, Y 45,475).

$220* *Male Nude,* s., #210/250, (05-16-93, Hindman, #494), 26½ x 19 in., (67.3 x 48.3 cm.), color lithograph on Japan (BP 143, DM 354, FR 1189, Y 24,388).

$1967* *"Mao Tse-Toung" (Michler/Lopsinger 199-206), 1967: Eight,* Poemes illustres par Salvador Dali, s., (11-13-92, Koller, #5296), plate 9¼ x 7¹¹⁄₁₆ in., (23.5 x 19.5 cm.), heliogravure (photoengraving) w/drypoint on Arches wove (BP 1271, DM 3088, FR 10,413, Y 244,136, SF 2784).

$1235* *Maria Und Das Kind Im Stall,* s., #46/150, (05-08-93, Dobiaschofsky, #1897), 24¹³⁄₁₆ x 18½ in., (63 x 47 cm.), watercolor etching (BP 806, DM 1984, FR 6694, Y 138,004, SF 1800).

$10,350* *Marquis De Sade,* complete, original portfolio, s., # in ink 111/160, also # on just. page, pub. Shorewood Publishers, Inc., good cond., discoloration, foxing, stains, (02-11-93, Sotheby-NY, #111, illus.), each sheet 25⅜ x 19½ in., (644 x 495 mm.), 25 colored lithographs (BP 7303, DM 17,144, FR 58,016, Y 1,247,740).

BI *Mass Fur Mass (Michler/Lopsinger 268), 1968,* from Serie Shakespeare I, Epreuve d'artiste, s., est. SF 2,1/ 2,400, (11-13-92, Koller, #5295), 6⅞ x 4¹⁵⁄₁₆ in., (17.5 x 12.5 cm.), drypoint etching on parchment.

$1410* *Medusa, 1963,* s., d., #111/150, from Mythologien series, (05-26-93, Lempertz, #96), 15⅝ x 19⁹⁄₁₆ in., (39.7 x 49.7 cm.), etching on Arches wove (BP 912, DM 2301, FR 7743, Y 153,194).

$7820* *Memories Of Surrealism,* complete, orig. portfolio, s., #A XXII/XXV, from edit. of 25 artist's proofs, pub. Transworld Art Corporation, full margins, good cond., mat/ light/water stains, tape hinges, discoloration, (02-11-93, Sotheby-NY, #112, illus.), each sheet 29⅝ x 21¹⁄₁₆ in., (752 x 535 mm.), 12 etchings w/photo offset p. in colors (BP 5518, DM 12,953, FR 43,834, Y 942,737).

$2200* *"Memories Of Surrealism": Ten,* each s. Dali, (09-25-92, Wolf, #48, illus.), 20½ x 16 in., (52.1 x 40.6 cm.), lithographs in color (BP 1285, DM 3261, FR 11,028, Y 265,540).

BI *Le Monument Imperial,* #119/300, blindstamp, est. DM 750, (09-18-92, Schloss Ahlden, #990, illus.), 29¾ x 21¾ in., (75.5 x 55.3 cm.), multi-color solar print w/gold dust on Arches.

$660* *Nackter Jungling,* from Mythologie, #137/150, (04-24-93, Ruef, #970), 15⅜ x 18⅞ in., (39 x 48 cm.), etching (BP 417, DM 1034, FR 3494, Y 72,832).

$3575* *Our Historical Heritage, 1975: Eleven,* complete portfolio, s., #26/400, blindstamp pub. Leon Amiel, w/t. page and colophon, full margins, good cond., foxing, orig. portfolio and slipcase, (10-28-92, Butterfield, #2627, illus.), each sheet 25¾ x 19⅞ in., (654 x 505 mm.), hand-colored drypoint on Arches (BP 2278, DM 5521, FR 18,747, Y 438,650).

$3575* *Our Historical Heritage, 1975: Eleven,* complete portfolio, each s., #26/400, t. page, colophon, blindstamp pub., Leon Amiel, full margins, good cond., foxing, orig. portfolio, (02-24-93, Butterfield, #2734, illus.), each sheet 25¾ x 19⅞ in., (654 x 505 mm.), eleven drypoints w/ extensive hand-coloring on Arches (BP 2493, DM 5804, FR 19,675, Y 419,502).

BI *Paris, Editions Kra, 1930,* from Second Manifeste Du Surrealisme by Andre Breton, frontispiece, est. SF 5/ 6,000, book, (11-15-92, Christie-Geneva, #316, illus.), 11¼ x 9¹⁄₁₆ in., (285 x 230 mm.), color pochoir on Annam de Rives wove.

BI *Place De La Concorde (Michler/Lopsinger 101), 1963,* s., d., plate s., d., i. Epreuve d'artiste, creases, est. SF 6/ 9,000, (11-13-92, Koller, #5294, illus.), 17⁵⁄₁₆ x 23¹⁄₁₆ in., (44 x 58.5 cm.), color etching on Verge.

$529* *Le Poet Comtumace (Michler/Lopsinger 530), 1971/74,* s., from series Les amours Jaunes, (05-26-93, Dorling, #2612), 11⁵⁄₁₆ x 8¹⁄₁₆ in., (28.8 x 20.4 cm.), etching w/ Goldauflage on Arches wove (BP 342, DM 863, FR 2905, Y 57,475).

BI *Portrait De Calderon, 1971,* from Calderon-La vie est un songe, s., E.A., est. DM 1,500-, (09-25-92, Granier, #2804, illus.), sheet 26⅜ x 19⅞ in., (67 x 50.5 cm.), color etching on Richard de Bas hand-made.

$278* *Portrait De Rembrant,* #109/150, s. Dali, (08-18-92, Encans, #89), 7¹⁄₁₆ x 5⅞ in., (18 x 15 cm.), etching on paper (BP 144, DM 405, FR 1374, Y 35,048, C$ 333).

BI *Portrait De Sigismond, 1971,* s., from Calderon-La vie est un songe, est. DM 1,500-, (09-25-92, Granier, #2806), sheet 26⅜ x 19⅞ in., (67 x 50.5 cm.), color etching on Richard de Bas Hand-made.

$248* *Portrait Of A Man,* s., i., (05-28-93, Sloan, #1894, illus.), 5¾ x 4¾ in., (14.6 x 12.1 cm.), sepia etching (BP 159, DM 393, FR 1330, Y 26,592).

$461* *Prodicality (Michler 240), 1951-52,* plate XXII from Purgatoire, #143/150, s., pub. Joseph Foret and Les Heures Claires, 1963, (09-04-92, Germann, #298), 12¹⁵⁄₁₆ x 10⅜ in., (330 x 263 mm.), color woodcut (BP 231, DM 646, FR 2199, Y 56,745, SF 575).

BI *Prodicality (Michler 240), 1951/52,* 143/150., s., pub. Joseph Foret, est. SF 600/900, (10-14-92, Germann, #268), 12¹⁵⁄₁₆ x 10⅜ in., (330 x 263 mm.), color woodcut.

$2756* *Quevedos Visioner, 1975: Six,* s., 148/300, portfolio, Galerie Borjeson, (12-04-92, AB Stockholm, #7052), approx. 20½ x 14⅜ in., (52 x 36.5 cm.), hand-colored engravings (BP 1768, DM 4389, FR 14,889, Y 344,070, SK 18,700).

$715* *Reclining Nude With Water Tower,* s., #34/100, from suite Visions of Chicago, (10-18-92, Hindman, #477), 12⅜ x 19 in., (31.4 x 48.3 cm.), color dry point w/stencilling and hand coloring (BP 438, DM 1064, FR 3609, Y 85,783).

$1915* *Rhinozeros Im Profil Nach Rechts, 1968,* num., (06-05-93, Bassenge, #5983, illus.), 22¼ x 29¾ in., (56.5 x 75.5 cm.), color etching on copper print (BP 1261, DM 3105, FR 10,464, Y 205,428).

$770* *"The Search For Oil", "Morse Code" and "Jeremiah", 1975: Three,* from the Great Inventions suite, pub. Transworld Art, Our HistoricalHeritage suite, pub. Leon Amiel, (05-27-93, Swann, #78), color etching (BP 493, DM 1236, FR 4164, Y 82,547).

$1257* *Set Of Five Engravings,* all s., artist's drystamp, (06-28-93, Loudmer, #28), between 9⁷⁄₁₆ x 7½ in., (240 x 190 mm.), and 12½ x 9⅜ in., (240 x 190 mm.), black etchings and aquatints w/gouache embellishments on Japan nacre (BP 842, DM 2136, FR 7195, Y 133,369).

$251* *Set Of Six Lithographs,* 4 s. in stone, (06-28-93, Loudmer, #29), between 10¹⁄₁₆ x 7¹⁄₁₆ in., (255 x 180 mm.), and 16⁹⁄₁₆ x 11¹³⁄₁₆ in., (255 x 180 mm.), color lithographs on wove (BP 168, DM 427, FR 1437, Y 26,631).

BI *Sigismond Enchaine, 1971,* s., from Calderon-La vie est un songe, est. DM 1,500-, (09-25-92, Granier, #2805), sheet 26⅜ x 19⅞ in., (67 x 50.5 cm.), color etching on Richard de Bas hand-made.

$709* *"Sonderdruck Des Entwurfs Fur Das Plakat Der Olympia-Ausstellung Mensch Und Meere" (Michler/Lopsinger L 385), 1971,* s., i. e(preuve d') a(rtiste), poster, (06-08-93, Karl/Faber, #674), approx. 40⁹⁄₁₆ x 28¾ in., (103 x 73 cm.), offset print on poster paper (BP 466, DM 1150, FR 3874, Y 75,305).

$385* *Song Of Songs,* s., #S183/200, (05-28-93, Sloan, #1663, illus.), 15¾ x 10 in., (40 x 25.4 cm.), color etching (BP 247, DM 611, FR 2064, Y 41,282).

$7475* *The Song Of Songs Of King Solomon,* complete portfolio, each s., #VII/L, #VII, drypoints p. Jacques David, pub. Leon Amiel, 1971, full margins, good cond., orig. cover and slipcase, (05-13-93, Sotheby-NY, #537, illus.), 22⅜ x 15¼ in., (568 x 387 mm.), 12 drypoints in colors, w/ hand-coloring and glitter on Japan (BP 4907, DM 12,070, FR 40,714, Y 834,543).

BI *"Spectrums Of Sex Appeal",* s., num. 252/300, est. $750/1000, (10-10-92, Goldberg, #432, illus.), 23 x 18 in., (58.4 x 45.7 cm.), color lithograph.

BI *The Sports Suite: Two,* each s., t. #4/199, est. $2/3,000, (05-16-93, Hanzel, #80), one 16 x 19 in., (40.6 x 48.3 cm.), the other 19 x 16 in., (40.6 x 48.3 cm.), color lithograph.

$1135* *St. Georg Der Drachentoter,* s., (06-05-93, Bassenge, #5987), 18½ x 24³⁄₁₆ in., (47 x 61.5 cm.), color lithograph on Arches (BP 747, DM 1840, FR 6202, Y 121,755).

BI *Stella An Alice Grey,* #90/250, s., est. DM 1,500, (11-13-92, Kunsthaus, #519), 21⅝ x 29¹⁵⁄₁₆ in., (55 x 76 cm.), color lithograph on wove.

$413* *Surreal Love Scene,* s., #328/1000, (10-30-92, Sloan, #1771), 21 x 16¾ in., (53.3 x 42.5 cm.), color lithograph (BP 265, DM 635, FR 2156, Y 51,158).

$465* *Surrealistische Komposition,* s., num., traces lager, (09-25-92, Granier, #2807), sheet 26⅜ x 20¹⁄₁₆ in., (67 x 51 cm.), color etching on hand-made (BP 272, DM 689, FR 2331, Y 56,126).

$1495* *Symphony Bicyclette, 1970,* lithograph in color on BFK Rives, (05-19-93, Butterfield, #1908, illus.), 30¼ x 22 in., (768 x 559 mm.), lithograph in colors on BFK Rives (BP 970, DM 2430, FR 8187, Y 165,504).

$1265* *Three Abstracted Figures In Landscapes And Figures On A Stage:Four,* two d. 1968; each plate s.; s., #116/160, (03-03-93, Sotheby-Arcade, #170), approx. 25½ x 19¾ in., (64.8 x 50.2 cm.), color lithograph (BP 873, DM 2083, FR 7067, Y 147,815).

$358* *The Three Graces,* s., num. 104/300, (11-12-92, Freemn/Fine Art, #57), 24½ x 18 in., (62.2 x 45.7 cm.), litho (BP 235, DM 567, FR 1913, Y 44,389).

$358* *The Thumb, 1980,* s., num. I 40/150, pub. Levine and Levine, (09-20-92, Hindman, #811), 23 x 17 in., (58.4 x 43.2 cm.), color lithograph (BP 210, DM 531, FR 1817, Y 44,247).

$878* *Toledo (Michler/Lopsinger 98), 1964,* s., d., num., from the series Spanien, (12-02-92, Dorling, #2575, illus.), 23⁵⁄₁₆ x 17⁷⁄₁₆ in., (59.2 x 44.3 cm.), color heliograph on wove (BP 566, DM 1381, FR 4713, Y 109,245).

$387* *Le Toreador Hallucinogene,* #54/300, tears, (09-18-92, Schloss Ahlden, #987), 21¹⁵⁄₁₆ x 29¹³⁄₁₆ in., (55.8 x 75.8 cm.), multi-color solar print on handmade Lana (BP 227, DM 574, FR 1964, Y 47,831).

$1253* *Tristano E Isotta, 1970: Four,* #XII/XXV, folio, all s., (05-20-93, Finarte-Milan, #55, illus.), 17¹⁵⁄₁₆ x 12¹³⁄₁₆ in., (45.5 x 32.5 cm.), drypoint in colors (BP 804, DM 2022, FR 6810, Y 138,361, L 1840).

$4600* *Twelve Signs Of The Zodiac,* complete portfolio, each s., i. E/O, lettered E, pub. Leon Amiel, full margins, good cond., creases, hinge stains, skinned spots, (02-11-93, Sotheby-NY, #110, illus.), each sheet approx. 28¹¹⁄₁₆ x 20⅜ in., (728 x 518 mm.), 13 color lithographs (BP 3246, DM 7620, FR 25,785, Y 554,551).

BI *"Twelve Tribes Of Asher": Twelve,* single series, s. Dali, num. XXII/XXXV, est. $7/9,000, (03-06-93, Wolf, #182), 19¾ x 14½ in., (50.2 x 36.8 cm.), color etching.

$9775* *The Twelve Tribes Of Israel,* complete deluxe edit. of portfolio, French language edit., each s., #XIV/XXXV, s., num. on just. page, pub. Transworld Art Corporation, full margins, good cond., fox mark, in orig. paper folders,

(05-13-93, Sotheby-NY, #539, illus.), each sh approx. 26¼ x 20 in., (667 x 508 mm.), 13 etchings w/drypoint and stencil coloring hors-texte, and a separate suite of the 13 prints on white wove (BP 6417, DM 15,784, FR 53,241, Y 1,091,325).

BI *The Twelve Tribes Of Israel: Thirteen,* each s., #127/135, est. $6/8,000, (11-01-92, Hanzel, #269), paper 26½ x 20 in., (67.3 x 50.8 cm.), colored etching.

$382* *"Two Abstract Figures With Butterflies",* artist's proof, bears sig., margins, (02-17-93, Bonhams-Chelsea, #240), plate 30 x 21½ in., (76.2 x 54.6 cm.), color etching on wove (BP 264, DM 620, FR 2101, Y 45,628).

$275* *Universal Man,* s., (11-01-92, Hanzel, #281), 15¼ x 10 in., (38.7 x 25.4 cm.), colored etching with gold leaf (BP 180, DM 434, FR 1462, Y 34,001).

$303* *Untitled,* s., #196/200, (05-28-93, Sloan, #1665, illus.), 19¾ x 16 in., (50.2 x 40.6 cm.), color lithograph (BP 194, DM 481, FR 1625, Y 32,490).

$99* *Untitled, 1965,* (04-23-93, Clearing House, #289), 26½ x 20 in., (67.3 x 50.8 cm.), colored lithograph (BP 63, DM 157, FR 529, Y 10,934).

$3300* *"Le Vaisseau Fantome" and "Dionysus", c. 1975: Two,* s., full margins, (05-27-93, Swann, #77B), one 15¾ x 10¼ in., (40 x 26 cm.), the other 14½ x 18¾ in., (40 x 26 cm.), first, color etching; second, hand-colored etching (BP 2113, DM 5295, FR 17,847, Y 353,774).

$634* *Venice Reconstruction, 1978,* s., #166/250, (05-26-93, Lempertz, #98), 19¹³⁄₁₆ x 25⁹⁄₁₆ in., (50.3 x 65 cm.), color lithograph w/relief print on Japon nacre (BP 410, DM 1034, FR 3482, Y 68,883).

$413* *"Venus Drawers" and "Eye Of The Iris": Two,* s., num. 60/350 and 82/350, (11-12-92, Freemn/Fine Art, #58), first 21½ x 16 in., (54.6 x 40.6 cm.), second 22½ x 15½ in., (54.6 x 40.6 cm.), lithographs (BP 271, DM 654, FR 2207, Y 51,209).

BI *Venus Vor Dem Rundbogen,* #IXX/C, crease, blindstamp, est. DM 750, (09-18-92, Schloss Ahlden, #988), 29½ x 20⅞ in., (75 x 53.1 cm.), multi-color solar print on hand-made Japan.

BI *Vertige,* EA, est. DM 750, (09-18-92, Schloss Ahlden, #989, illus.), 21¾ x 29¾ in., (55.3 x 75.6 cm.), multi-color solar print w/gold dust on Arches.

$208* *Walt Disney (Michler/Lopsinger 176.), 1967,* s., from the series of 5 Bll. 5 bedeutende Amerikaner, num., (12-01-92, Karl/Faber, #523), 4¹⁵⁄₁₆ x 6¹¹⁄₁₆ in., (12.5 x 17 cm.), drypoint on Japon nacre (BP 137, DM 332, FR 1130, Y 25,896).

$220* *"Warrior's Dream",* s., t., num., (02-27-93, Dunning, #1105), 16 x 22¼ in., (40.6 x 56.5 cm.), lithograph (BP 155, DM 362, FR 1229, Y 25,971).

$550* *Watching The Birth Of A New Man,* s., #63/300, (12-13-92, Hindman, #303), 19½ x 21¾ in., (49.5 x 54.6 cm.), lithograph (BP 352, DM 864, FR 2946, Y 68,044).

BI *"Wheel Barrow",* s., num. 78/300, est. $750/1000, (10-10-92, Goldberg, #434, illus.), 17 x 23 in., (43.2 x 58.4 cm.), color lithograph.

$1650* *Zodiac Suite, 1978: Twelve,* s., #7/150, margins, very good cond.?, (10-28-92, Butterfield, #2628), each 8¾ x 8¾ in., (222 x 222 mm.), color etching on wove (BP 1051, DM 2548, FR 8652, Y 202,454).

DALI, Salvador (after)

$86* *Alice In Wonderland,* blindstamp, s., num. F IV/XXV, prov., (06-08-93, Ritchie, #56), plate 20½ x 16¼ in., (52.1 x 41.3 cm.), sheet 29¾ x 21¼ in., (52.1 x 41.3 cm.), color photolithograph (BP 57, DM 140, FR 470, Y 9134, C$ 110).

$143* *Beach Scene,* s., #256/350, (12-13-92, Hindman, #304), 14⅞ x 20¾ in., color-offset lithograph (BP 91, DM 225, FR 766, Y 17,691).

$22* *"El Cid",* Collector's Guild, (06-11-93, DuMouchelle, #2519), 9 x 7½ in., (22.9 x 19.1 cm.), etching (BP 14, DM 36, FR 121, Y 2334).

$279* *Classical Sculpture And Butterfly,* Memories of Surrealism series, blindstamp, s., num. A XXXII/XL, pub.Transworld Art Corp. w/A.E. Rich, 1971, prov., (06-08-93, Ritchie, #55), plate 20¾ x 16½ in., (52.7 x 41.9 cm.), sheet 29⅞ x 21 in., (52.7 x 41.9 cm.), color photolithograph on japon (BP 183, DM 453, FR 1525, Y 29,634, C$ 358).

$279* *Dali, Memories Of Surrealism,* Memories of Surrealism series, blindstamp, s., num. A XXXII/XL, pub.Transworld Art Corp. w/A.E. Rich, 1971, prov., (06-08-93, Ritchie, #52, illus.), plate 20¾ x 16½ in., (52.7 x 41.9 cm.), sheet 29⅞ x 21 in., (52.7 x 41.9 cm.), color photolithograph on japon (BP 183, DM 453, FR 1525, Y 29,634, C$ 358).

$275* *"La Danse",* block s., blind stamp, prov., (12-11-92, DuMouchelle, #2285, illus.), 16½ x 12 in., (41.9 x 30.5 cm.), color wood engraving (BP 176, DM 433, FR 1485, Y 34,030).

$193* *Don Quixote,* #14/125, bears sig., margins, (02-12-93, DuMouchelle, #355), 4¾ x 6¾ in., (12.1 x 17.1 cm.), etching (BP 136, DM 320, FR 1083, Y 23,275).

$257* *Dream Of Gala,* Memories of Surrealism series, blindstamp, s., num. A XXXLL/XL, pub.Transworld Art Corp. w/A.E. Rich, 1971, prov., (06-08-93, Ritchie, #53), plate 20¾ x 16½ in., (52.7 x 41.9 cm.), sheet 29⅞ x 21 in., (52.7 x 41.9 cm.), color photolithograph on japon (BP 169, DM 417, FR 1404, Y 27,297, C$ 330).

$275* *"Erinnyes",* from the "Divine Comedy", Inferno 9, block s., prov., (12-11-92, DuMouchelle, #2288, illus.), 10 x 6¾ in., (25.4 x 17.1 cm.), color wood engraving (BP 176, DM 433, FR 1485, Y 34,030).

$279* *Figure Seated On A Cube And Figure With A Butterfly,* Memories of Surrealism series, blindstamp, s., num. A XXXII/XL, pub.Transworld Art Corp. w/A.E. Rich, 1971, prov., (06-08-93, Ritchie, #54, illus.), plate 20¾ x 16½ in., (52.7 x 41.9 cm.), sheet 29⅞ x 21 in., (52.7 x 41.9 cm.), color photolithograph on japon (BP 183, DM 453, FR 1525, Y 29,634, C$ 358).

$275* *"The First Heaven",* from the "Divine Comedy", Paradise 3, block s., prov., (12-11-92, DuMouchelle, #2286, illus.), 9 x 7¼ in., (22.9 x 18.4 cm.), color wood engraving (BP 176, DM 433, FR 1485, Y 34,030).

$385* *"Forest Of Those Who Committed Suicide",* from the "Divine Comedy", Inferno 13, block s., prov., (12-11-92, DuMouchelle, #2287, illus.), 10 x 7¼ in., (25.4 x 18.4 cm.), color wood engraving (BP 247, DM 607, FR 2079, Y 47,643).

$330* *Horse And Rider,* bears sig., ed. E.A., (04-16-93, DuMouchelle, #2172, illus.), 15½ x 11¾ in., (39.4 x 29.8 cm.), etching (BP 217, DM 533, FR 1801, Y 37,108).

$83* *"Lincoln, Nude, Cross",* s., #123/475, (02-27-93, Dunning, #1126), 24 x 17 in., (61 x 43.2 cm.), lithograph (BP 58, DM 136, FR 464, Y 9798).

$440* *"Minotaur",* from the "Divine Comedy", Inferno 12, block s., prov., (12-11-92, DuMouchelle, #2289, illus.), 9¼ x 7¼ in., (23.5 x 18.4 cm.), color wood engraving (BP 282, DM 693, FR 2376, Y 54,449).

$165* *"Rhinoceros",* bears sig. Dali, (02-27-93, Dunning, #149), 4¾ x 6¾ in., (12.1 x 17.1 cm.), print (BP 116, DM 271, FR 922, Y 19,478).

$153* *The Sacrament Of The Last Supper,* bears sig., (04-22-93, Bonhams-Chelsea, #130), image 17 x 27½ in., (43.2 x 69.9 cm.), reprod. in colors (BP 99, DM 246, FR 829, Y 16,822).

$170* *The Temptation Of St. Anthony,* bears sig., #153/199, (04-22-93, Bonhams-Chelsea, #131), image 17 x 22½ in., (43.2 x 57.2 cm.), reprod. in colors (BP 110, DM 273, FR 921, Y 18,692).

BI *Untitled,* #CXXIII/LL, s., tear, est. FF4/600, (04-04-93, Pescheteau, #193), 25⁹⁄₁₆ x 19¹¹⁄₁₆ in., (65 x 50 cm.), color lithograph on Arches.

DALI, Salvador (attrib.)   Spanish 1904-1989
BI *Abstraction,* s. Dali in matrix, #108/200, good cond., foxing, paper toning, est. 5/700, (03-12-93, Skinner, #85, illus.), sight 23¼ x 15¼ in., (59.1 x 38.7 cm.), lithograph in colors w/etching on wove.

$550* *"Essence Of Time",* s., prov., (06-11-93, DuMouchelle, #2100), 28 x 20 in., (71.1 x 50.8 cm.), lithograph (BP 361, DM 894, FR 3014, Y 58,355).

$550* *"Helen Of Troy",* s., (06-11-93, DuMouchelle, #2101), 28 x 20 in., (71.1 x 50.8 cm.), lithograph (BP 361, DM 894, FR 3014, Y 58,355).

$275* *Nudes On A Beach,* s., edit. #CXI/CXX, 1970, prov., (12-11-92, DuMouchelle, #2284, illus.), 20 x 28 in.,

(50.8 x 71.1 cm.), lithograph (BP 176, DM 433, FR 1485, Y 34,030).

$523* *"Le Sacre Du Printemps",* 1966, s. Dali; s., d. Dali/1966 in matrix, num. 147/150, good cond., (09-11-92, Skinner, #90A, illus.), sight 28 x 21¼ in., (71.1 x 54 cm.), lithograph in colors on paper (BP 270, DM 753, FR 2559, Y 64,800).

DALL, Y. le
$314* *Ch. De Fer De L'Etat: Plestin Les Greves, Cotes Du Nord, c. 1930,* excell. cond., (01-23-93, Ribeyre/Baron, #64), 38¹⁵⁄₁₆ x 24 in., (99 x 61 cm.), poster (BP 205, DM 499, FR 1689, Y 39,299).

DAMARE
$414* *Casino Kursaal, 1908,* (01-31-93, Morelle/Marchan, #191), 35⁷⁄₁₆ x 48¹³⁄₁₆ in., (90 x 124 cm.), poster (BP 278, DM 667, FR 2255, Y 51,647).

DAMAVE, P.H.   b. 1921
BI *Untitled: Two,* circular, one d. 1985 in plate, #79/180, #73/200, s., (11-18-92, Bubb Kuyper, #1530), etching.

DAMERON, E.
$1129* *Le Verascope Richard,* p. B. Sirven, repaired edge tears, defects, backed on linen, (05-07-93, Christie-S. Ken, #133, illus.), 41½ x 57½ in., (105.4 x 146.1 cm.), color lithograph (BP 715, DM 1785, FR 6015, Y 124,312).

DAMIAN, Horia   Romanian b. 1922
BI *"La Colonne",* #91/100, t., s. Damian, (03-16-93, Encans, #160), 15¾ x 19³⁄₁₆ in., (40 x 48.8 cm.), lithograph.

DANBY, Francis
$2574* *View From Kingsweston Hill (Tate Gallery 130), 1823,* folds, defects, (06-30-93, Sotheby-London, #260, illus.), 9¾ x 14 in., (248 x 356 mm.), lithograph (BP 1725, DM 4390, FR 14,810, Y 275,796).

DANBY, Ken   b. 1940
BI *"December Morning",* #68/100, s., est. $750/950, (05-12-93, Maynard, #281), 14½ x 21½ in., (35.6 x 53.3 cm.), serigraph.

$237* *Heading Out,* s., d. 68, #4/50, prov., lit., (06-07-93, Ritchie, #47, illus.), 22¹⁵⁄₁₆ x 17¹⁵⁄₁₆ in., (58.4 x 45.7 cm.), lithograph (BP 156, DM 384, FR 1295, Y 25,424, C$ 303).

BI *Robert, 1971,* #80/100, s., d. '71, prov., est. C$ 7/900, (11-16-92, Hodgins, #72), 20¹⁵⁄₁₆ x 15¹⁵⁄₁₆ in., (53.3 x 40.6 cm.), lithograph on paper.

$342* *Roughriders,* s., d. 84, #6/100, lit., (11-30-92, Ritchie, #45, illus.), 18 x 24 in., (45.7 x 61 cm.), color serigraph (BP 226, DM 545, FR 1850, Y 42,564, C$ 440).

DANBY, Kenneth Edison
$434* *Cedar Break,* s., d. '79, #12/100, (05-18-93, Joyner, #155), 15 x 21½ in., (38.1 x 54.6 cm.), serigraph in colors (BP 283, DM 704, FR 2378, Y 48,367, C$ 550).

DANCE, Nathaniel (after)
$83* *Lancelot (Capability) Brown (B.M.P. p.257),* by John Keyse Sherwin, margins, good cond., (11-30-92, Phillips-London, #104), plate 14 x 10½ in., (356 x 267 mm.), engraving on laid (BP 55, DM 132, FR 449, Y 10,330).

$159* *Miss Ray (C.S. 107), 1779,* by Valentine Green, scratch-letter proof, 1st state of 2, pub. Green,good cond., coll. stamp E.M.H., (11-30-92, Phillips-London, #49), plate 19⅞ x 13¾ in., (505 x 349 mm.), mezzotint on laid (BP 105, DM 253, FR 860, Y 19,788).

DANFORTH, S. Chester   American b. 1896
$94* *"Cherry Blossom Time" and "Resting Place Of Eugene Field": Two,* both s., t.; second annot., 1/5 Artists Proof-First State, (09-20-92, Hindman, #700), larger 12 x 9 in., (30.5 x 22.9 cm.), hand colored etchings (BP 55, DM 139, FR 477, Y 11,618).

DANIELL, Samuel
$1035* *Sketches Representing The Native Tribes, Animals, And Scenery Of Southern Africa (Abbey Travel 326; Mendelssohn 413), 1820,* Richard and Arthur Taylor, for William Daniell, and William wood, after Samuel Daniell by William Daniell, smudges, crease, torn, FIRST ED., (06-14-93, Sotheby-NY, #121, illus.), OBLONG 4TO 9¾ x 13½ in., (24.8 x 34.3 cm.), 48 soft-ground etched plate (BP 677, DM 1685, FR 5662, Y 108,913).

DANIELL, Thomas
$1507* *Oriental Scenery (Abbey Travel 420): Two,* plates: 15 & 19, pub. R. Bowyer, margins, spotting, staining, repaired tear, (10-07-92, Christie-S. Ken, #93), pl 19½ x 29¾ in., (49.5 x 75.6 cm.), colored aquatint (BP 880, DM 2181, FR 7395, Y 181,239).

DANIELL, Thomas and William
BI *"Das Avatara", "Indra Sabha", "The Interior Of An Excavated Hindoo Temple, On The Island Of Salsette", "Part Of The Interior Of An Hindoo Temple, At Deo In Bahah", 1800: Four,* from the series Oriental Scenery, pub. Daniell, watermarked, full margins, good cond., foxing, discoloration, est. BP 6/700, (10-27-92, Phillips-London, #148), plate 18⅞ x 25⅝ in., (479 x 651 mm.), hand-colored aquatint.

DANIELL, William   (after Captain Robert SMITH)
$7673* *Views Of Prince Of Wale's (sic) Island; "View From Strawberry Hill", "View Of Glugor House And Spice Plantations", "View Of Suffolk House", and "View From Halliburton's Hill" (Abbey 525): Four,* all w/margins, repaired tears, one into image, creases, stains, minordefects, (12-03-92, Sotheby-London, #153, illus.), each approx. 20 x 29½ in., (510 x 750 mm.), hand colored aquatints (BP 4950, DM 12,066, FR 41,186, Y 954,709).

DANIELL, William and Thomas
$1328* *"An Antique Reservoir Near Colar, In The Mysore", "Ramseswara", "Dotall", "The Ashes Of Ravana" and "Jagannatha Sabha": Five,* from the series Oriental Scenery, pub. Thomas Daniell, full margins, colors faded, foxing, mounted, (10-27-92, Phillips-London, #147), plate 18⅞ x 25⅝ in., (479 x 651 mm.), aquatint w/hand-colouring on J. Whatman paper (BP 839, DM 2035, FR 6906, Y 162,446).

DANIELS, Rene
$198* *Elba-Sint Helena, 1987,* all init., d., one t., all #24/45, full sheets, good cond., in orig.box, (10-15-92, Sotheby-London, #92), each sheet approx. 25½ x 20 in., (64.8 x 50.8 cm.), three etchings, two w/aquatint (BP 121, DM 295, FR 999, Y 23,755).

DANVERS, V.L.
$512* *The Quick Starting Pair, Spirit & Oil, Greyhounds, 1926,* p. Waterlow & Sons, ref. #149, cond. 3, (10-13-92, Phillips-London, #59, illus.), 30 x 44⅞ in., (76.2 x 114 cm.), color lithograph (BP 298, DM 750, FR 2549, Y 62,083).

DARCIS, Louis   ac. 1787-1801
BI *"Le Jockey Au Montoir" and "Le Cheval Bouchonne" (Dayot 15c-d; Inventaire 18e Siecle, VI, p. 30, nos. 42, 48), c. 1797: Two,* from Sujets de Chevaux, after Carle Vernet, margins, pub. Noel, foxing, est. BP 250/350, (12-01-92, Christie-London, #285), plate 10¹⁄₁₆ x 12³⁄₁₆ in., (255 x 310 mm.), colored stipple engraving.

DARLEY, Felix Octavius Carr   (after)
$1045* *"Spring", "Summer" and "Autumn", 1860: Three,* from Darley's American Farm Scenes, No. 2, pub. M. Knoedler and Goupil & Co., margins, tear, soiling, good cond., (01-22-93, Christie-NY, #318), each borderline 13⅞ x 18¾ in., (352 x 476 mm.), color lithograph w/hand-coloring on wove (BP 684, DM 1662, FR 5621, Y 130,788).

DARNAUT, Hugo   Austrian 1851-1937
$28* *Book Illustration Study,* s. in plate, d. 1863, (11-01-92, Hanzel, #226), 10 x 7 in., (25.4 x 17.8 cm.), ink over print (BP 18, DM 44, FR 149, Y 3462).

DARWIN, R.   ac. 1929-1939
$445* *Everywhere You Go, Culzean Castle & Ailsa Craig, 1952,* p. Vincent Brooks, Day & Son, ref. P 54, cond. 1, (10-13-92, Phillips-London, #181), 29¹⁵⁄₁₆ x 39¾ in., (76 x 101 cm.), color lithograph (BP 259, DM 652, FR 2215, Y 53,959).

DASKALOFF
$84* *Untitled: Two,* s. 50/50 and 112/150, (09-29-92, B. Rasmussen, #303), lithograph in colors (BP 47, DM 119, FR 405, Y 10,027, DK 460).

DASSONNEVILLE, Jacques   b. 1619
$121* *"Les Deux Gueux Au Bord Du Chemin", "L'Operateur" (arracheur de dent), "La Sante Portee" and "Un Joueur De Flute" (Robert-Dumesnil 18, 20, 23 and 12 du Supplement): Four,* annot., (05-15-93, Loudmer, #139), smallest 3⅜ x 2³⁄₁₆ in., (86 x 56 mm.), largest 6⁵⁄₁₆ x 5³⁄₁₆ in., (86 x 56 mm.), etchings on laid w/Marotte de bouffon watermark (BP 79, DM 195, FR 654, Y 13,413).

DASSONVILLE, William   1879-1957
$2200* *San Francisco Skyline,* 1920s, s., (10-13-92, Christie-NY, #179, illus.), 8⅞ x 9⅞ in., (22.5 x 25.1 cm.), photograph, gelatin silver print (BP 1281, DM 3223, FR 10,951, Y 266,764).

$1320* *San Francisco: Two,* s. by photog., early 1900s, (10-15-92, Sotheby-NY, #134, illus.), one 8½ x 8⅞ in., (21.6 x 22.5 cm.), other 8 x 9⅞ in., (21.6 x 22.5 cm.), photograph, gelatin silver prints on Dassonville (BP 808, DM 1965, FR 6663, Y 158,368).

BI *Sugar Pine, c. 1910,* s. recto; studio label, est. $1,5/1,800, (04-08-93, Christie-NY, #384, illus.), 8¾ x 6⅞ in., (22.2 x 17.5 cm.), photograph, platinum print.

DATER, Judy   American b. 1941
$1725* *Imogen And Twinka At Yosemite,* 1974, p.l., s.; t., d., (04-08-93, Christie-NY, #485, illus.), 9½ x 7½ in., (24.1 x 19.1 cm.), photograph, gelatin silver print (BP 1131, DM 2771, FR 9380, Y 195,756).

$1320* *Imogen And Twinka At Yosemite,* (1074), p.l., s., t., d., (c) insig., (10-13-92, Christie-NY, #532, illus.), 13⅜ x 10⅜ in., (34 x 26.4 cm.), photograph, gelatin silver print (BP 769, DM 1934, FR 6570, Y 160,058).

$2200* *"Imogen And Twinka At Yosemite",* s., t., d., num. 34, verso, 1974/1991, (11-16-92, Butterfield, #5929, illus.), 13⅛ x 10⅛ in., (334 x 257.6 mm.), photograph, gelatin silver print (BP 1449, DM 3508, FR 11,815, Y 273,598).

$1840* *Imogen And Twinka At Yosemite",* 1974, p. 1991, s., t., d., (05-23-93, Butterfield, #3390, illus.), 13¼ x 10 in., photograph, gelatin silver print (BP 1198, DM 3009, FR 10,127, Y 203,382).

$1495* *"Imogen And Twinka",* mounted, s., t., d. by photog., 1974, p.l., (04-06-93, Sotheby-NY, #470A, illus.), 9½ x 7½ in., photograph (BP 987, DM 2409, FR 8156, Y 170,506).

BI *Nehemiah: Two, 1975,* each s., 1 t., d., est. $1,8/2,200, (10-13-92, Christie-NY, #533, illus.), 14 x 18 in., (35.6 x 45.7 cm.), photograph, gelatin silver prints.

DAUBIGNY, Charles Francois   French 1817-1878
$105* *Barbizon Riverscape,* s., d. (18)67 in plate, (07-03-92, Sloan, #305), 7¾ x 13¼ in., (19.7 x 33.7 cm.), engraving (BP 55, DM 159, FR 536, Y 13,089).

BI *"Le Berger Et La Bergere",* from L'Art, est. DM 300-, (09-14-92, Venator/Hansten, #1650), plate 11⁵⁄₁₆ x 8⁹⁄₁₆ in., (28.7 x 21.8 cm.), etching.

$275* *(Cove With Boat),* appears good cond., prov., (06-11-93, Doyle, #34), 6½ x 5¼ in., (165 x 133 mm.), etching (BP 181, DM 447, FR 1507, Y 29,178).

$157* *Le Grand Parc A Moutons (L. Delteil, 95), 1860,* definitive state, thin spots, large margins, (06-16-93, Ader Tajan, #57), 8⁷⁄₁₆ x 14¹³⁄₁₆ in., (21.5 x 37.7 cm.), etching (BP 105, DM 261, FR 875, Y 16,745).

$639* *"Le Grand Parc A Moutons", 1860 and "Les Vendanges", 1865 (L. Delteil 95, 117): Two,* first, third state of four; second, third state of five, reddish stains; both, drystamp, large margins, (06-11-93, Picard, #24), one 7³⁄₁₆ x 13⁷⁄₁₆ in., (182 x 342 mm.), other 7¹³⁄₁₆ x 13¹⁵⁄₁₆ in., (182 x 342 mm.), etchings in bistre and black on laid (BP 420, DM 1039, FR 3501, Y 67,798).

$699* *"Le Gue", 1865 and "Pommiers A Auvers", 1877 (L.D. 118, 126): Two,* first, third state of five; second, third of four; both, reddish stains, creases, large margins, (06-11-93, Picard, #26), one 9¹³⁄₁₆ x 13³⁄₁₆ in., (250 x 335 mm.), other 5½ x 9⁷⁄₁₆ in., (250 x 335 mm.), etchings on laid (BP 459, DM 1136, FR 3830, Y 74,164).

$77* *"L'Abreuvoir" and "Les Cerfs Sous Bois": Two,* Melot 72 and 82, pub. Calcographie, Louvre, (09-20-92, Hindman, #739), larger 7¼ x 5½ in., (18.4 x 14 cm.), etchings (BP 45, DM 114, FR 391, Y 9517).

BI *"Lever De Lune" (Delteil 92 II/V),* pub. Gazette Des Beaus Arts, 1859, good cond., est. $125-175, (10-31-92,

Cleveland, #276), 5¼ x 7⅝ in., (13.3 x 19.4 cm.), etching.

$409* *"Le Marais Aux Canards", "Les Cerfs" and "Le Pont" (D. 133, 134 et 135), 1862: Three,* stamped, num. verso, (02-24-93, Picard, #71), cliche-verre (BP 285, DM 664, FR 2251, Y 47,993).

$66* *"Plage De Villerville" (D. 88 IV/V), 1855,* pub. Gazette Des Beaux Arts, 1874, good cond., (10-31-92, Cleveland, #277), 5 x 8½ in., (12.7 x 21.6 cm.), etching (BP 42, DM 102, FR 344, Y 8175).

BI *La Rentree Du Troupeau (Delteil 140), 1862,* plate s., #142/150, num., mono., est. DM 2500, (06-10-93, Hauswedell/Nolt, #219), 14 3/16 x 11⅜ in., (36.1 x 28.9 cm.), cliches-verres on factory printed paper.

BI *Vaches A L'Abreuvoir (D., M. 146), 1862,* plate s., #28/150, from Le Garrec edit., 1923, inkstamp, Lugt 1766a,good cond., staining, hinge remains, skinned area, crease, est. $3/500, (10-28-92, Butterfield, #2800), 7 x 8⅜ in., (178 x 213 mm.), cliche-verre on wove.

$3597* *Le Voyage En Bateau (L.D. 99 a 107; 109 a 115), 1861: Sixteen,* complete series, definitive state, dirt stains, reddish stains, creases, large margins, (06-11-93, Picard, #25), etchings on laid on chine fixe (BP 2363, DM 5846, FR 19,710, Y 381,645).

DAULLE, Jean 1703-1763

BI *L'Ecole Champetre, 1758,* after Le Nain, est. DM 400, (12-04-92, Bassenge, #6553), 14 9/16 x 17 15/16 in., (37 x 45.7 cm.), etching w/engraving.

DAUMIER, Honore French 1808-1879

$343* *Moderne Galilee (L.D. 93)*yellowed, definitive state, good margins, collector's stamp, (02-03-93, Ader Tajan, #113), 8⅞ x 10 13/16 in., (22.5 x 27.5 cm.), lithograph on white (BP 239, DM 565, FR 1915, Y 42,667).

$177* *1830 and 1833 (L.D., 66), 1833,* pl. 303 of La Caricature, rare first state of two, yellowed, staining, (06-16-93, Ader Tajan, #63), 6⅛ x 11 13/16 in., (15.5 x 30 cm.), lithograph (BP 118, DM 294, FR 986, Y 18,878).

BI *Ah! Ciel Maman...Ah! Dieu Ma Fille...(Delteil 1413 II), 1845,* stone mono., series Pastorales, est. DM 4000, (06-10-93, Hauswedell/Nolt, #224, illus.), image 10½ x 9 3/16 in., (26.6 x 23.4 cm.), lithograph on white wove.

$3105* *Ah! Tu Veux Te Frotter A La Presse!! (Delteil 71), 1833,* (12-04-92, Bassenge, #6768), 8⅞ x 7⅞ in., (22.5 x 20 cm.), lithograph on China (BP 1992, DM 4945, FR 16,775, Y 387,640).

$2749* *Allons Donc, Chers Confreres (D. 1343/II), 1845,* sheet 7 of series: Les Gens de Justice, (06-23-93, Kornfeld, #296), lithograph (BP 1868, DM 4651, FR 15,646, Y 299,488, SF 4140).

$303* *Arrivee A Lyon (L.D. 33),* large margins, (02-03-93, Ader Tajan, #111), 9 15/16 x 7 15/16 in., (25.3 x 20.3 cm.), large margins (BP 212, DM 499, FR 1692, Y 37,691).

$646* *Aspect De La Seine De Paris A Chatou (L.D. 1716),* from "Tout ce qu'on voudra", first state of two, before i., large margins, collector's stamp, faults, (02-03-93, Ader Tajan, #121), 9 7/16 x 8⅞ in., (24 x 22.5 cm.), lithograph (BP 451, DM 1064, FR 3607, Y 80,358).

$4276* *Un Avocat Qui Evidemment Est Rempli De La Conviction La Plus Intime... Que Son Client Paiera Bien (D. 1342/II), 1845,* sheet 6 of series: Les Gens de Justice, (06-23-93, Kornfeld, #295, illus.), lithograph on wove (BP 2905, DM 7235, FR 24,337, Y 465,846, SF 6440).

$4734* *Les Baigneuses (D. 1629/II-1645/II), 1847: Seventeen,* (06-23-93, Kornfeld, #303), lithograph (BP 3216, DM 8010, FR 26,944, Y 515,742, SF 7130).

$916* *Baissez Le Rideau, La Farce Est Jouee (D. 86), 1834,* (06-23-93, Kornfeld, #291), lithograph (BP 622, DM 1550, FR 5213, Y 99,793, SF 1380).

$452* *Baissez Le Rideau, La Farce Est Jouee (L.D., 86), 1834,* pl. 421 of La Caricature, staining, restorations, good margins, (06-16-93, Ader Tajan, #64), 7⅞ x 10⅞ in., (20 x 27.7 cm.), lithograph (BP 301, DM 750, FR 2518, Y 48,208).

$230* *Bal De La Cour No.I: Mr. Royer Colas (D. 557), 1833,* margins, good cond., tears, creases, some through image, masking tapeglue/paper remains, soiling, foxing, notations, (05-19-93, Butterfield, #2048), 9 7/16 x 7⅜ in., (240 x 187 mm.), lithograph in colors w/hand-coloring on wove (BP 149, DM 374, FR 1260, Y 25,462).

$367* *Baron De Lascours (Delteil 129), 1835,* Bl. 523 in La Caricature, (06-10-93, Hauswedell/Nolt, #222), image 7½ x 8 7/16 in., (19 x 21.5 cm.), lithograph on white wove (BP 240, DM 598, FR 2012, Y 38,956).

$66* *"Les Bas Bleus",* inits. in stone, (10-08-92, Boos, #667), image 8⅞ x 7¼ in., (225 x 184 mm.), lithograph (BP 39, DM 98, FR 331, Y 8019).

$495* *"Bohemiens De Paris", c. 1841-42: Group Of Six,* (12-08-92, Swann, #78), sheet 13⅜ x 10 in., (34 x 25.4 cm.), lithograph on wove (BP 310, DM 771, FR 2627, Y 61,353).

$916* *Les Bons Bourgeois (D. 1490, 1494, 1496, 1499, 1506, 1513, 1518, 1522, 1524, 1534, 1535), 1846-1847: Eleven,* in scrapbook, (06-23-93, Kornfeld, #301), (BP 622, DM 1550, FR 5213, Y 99,793, SF 1380).

BI *Un Bouquiniste Dans L'Ivresse (Delteil 1115 II), 1844,* stone mono., series Les Beaux Jours de la Vie, est. DM 2000, (06-10-93, Hauswedell/Nolt, #223, illus.), 8 9/16 x 8 7/16 in., (21.7 x 21.4 cm.), lithograph on white wove.

$275* *"La Caricature",* plate 304, (06-11-93, Freemn/Fine Art, #42A), mat 12¼ x 10 in., (31.1 x 25.4 cm.), hand-colored lithograph (BP 181, DM 447, FR 1507, Y 29,178).

$197* *Le Cauchemar (L. Delteil, 41), 1832,* pl. 139 of La Caricature, staining, spots, good margins, (06-16-93, Ader Tajan, #58), 9 3/16 x 11⅝ in., (23.3 x 29.5 cm.), lithograph (BP 131, DM 327, FR 1097, Y 21,011).

$444* *Un Cauchemar (L.D. 25),* yellowed, good margins, (02-03-93, Ader Tajan, #109), 7 9/16 x 9⅜ in., (19.2 x 23.8 cm.), color lithograph (BP 310, DM 731, FR 2479, Y 55,231).

$1614* *La Cinquieme (sic) Acte A La Gaite (L.D. 1674),* before i., large margins, (02-03-93, Ader Tajan, #120), 9 7/16 x 8 7/16 in., (24 x 21.4 cm.), lithograph (BP 1127, DM 2658, FR 9012, Y 200,771).

$688* *Collection Of Lithographs,* as pub. La Charivari, (06-13-93, Hindman, #381), each approx. 10 x 11 in., (25.4 x 27.9 cm.), lithograph (BP 450, DM 1120, FR 3764, Y 72,398).

$1833* *Comme Je Vous Ai Bien dit Vertement Votre Fait!... (D. 1344/II), 1845,* sheet 8 of series: Les Gens de Justice, (06-23-93, Kornfeld, #297), lithograph on wove (BP 1245, DM 3102, FR 10,433, Y 199,695, SF 2760).

$268* *Comment, Adelaide, Tu As Encoe Achete Un Nouveau Chapeau (D. 2189/II), 1851,* (06-23-93, Kornfeld, #305), lithograph (BP 182, DM 453, FR 1525, Y 29,197, SF 403).

BI *"Comte Portalis, Duc DeBassano, Comte De Montlosier", "Huguet De Semonville, Robert Macaire (Thiers), Comte Roederer" and "Girod De L'Ain-J., Joseph Rousseau, Amiral Verhuel" (L.D. 121, 124-5), 1835: Three,* L.D. 124 1st state of 2, L.D. 125 2nd state of 3, crease, foxmarks, surface dirt, stamps, prov., est. BP 900/1,300, (12-01-92, Christie-London, #354), L. 10¼ x 19½ in., (260 x 495 mm.), lithograph sur blanc.

$983* *Cortege Du Commandant General Des Apothicaires (L.D., 65), 1833: Two,* pls. 299-300 of La Caricature, crease, cut, (06-16-93, Ader Tajan, #62), 11⅝ x 19 11/16 in., (29.5 x 50 cm.), color lithograph (BP 655, DM 1632, FR 5476, Y 104,842).

$236* *La Cour Du Roi Petaud (L.D., 49), 1832: Two,* pls. 192-193 of La Caricature, definitive state, creases, stains, good margins, (06-16-93, Ader Tajan, #61), 9⅝ x 20 1/16 in., (24.5 x 51 cm.), color lithograph (BP 157, DM 392, FR 1315, Y 25,171).

$2291* *La Cour, Vidant Le Delibere (D. 1340-II), 1845,* sheet 4 of series: Les Gens de Justice, (06-23-93, Kornfeld, #293, illus.), lithograph on wove (BP 1556, DM 3876, FR 13,039, Y 249,591, SF 3450).

$848* *Courage...Nous Aurons Toujours Du Pain (L.D. 9),* large margins, (02-03-93, Ader Tajan, #107), 7⅞ x 6⅛ in., (20 x 15.5 cm.), lithograph (BP 592, DM 1396, FR 4735, Y 105,486).

$1121* *Cristi!...Notre Canot A Rompu Son Amarre...(Delteil XXII, 1027), 1843,* inits. in stone, brown ink annot., collector's stamp verso RGD, creases, small stains, tear, good cond., (06-28-93, Loudmer, #225), 8 1/16 x 9¾ in., (205 x 248 mm.), sh 10⅝ x 13¾ in., (205 x 248 mm.), black lithograph on wove (BP 751, DM 1905, FR 6417, Y 118,939).

BI   *"Declaration" and "The Family": Two*, inits. in stone, late impressions, est. $25/300, (12-10-92, Sloan, #3028), each, sight 8½ x 11½ in., (21.6 x 29.2 cm.), color lithographs.

BI   *"Declaration" and "The Family": Two*, each inits. in stone, late impressions, est. $350/400, (10-30-92, Sloan, #1607), each, sight 8½ x 11½ in., (21.6 x 29.2 cm.), color lithograph.

BI   *"Declaration" and "The Family": Two*, late impressions, inits. in stone, est. $3/400, (12-10-92, Sloan, #1314), each, sight 8½ x 11½ in., (21.6 x 29.2 cm.), color lithograph.

$303*   *Des Victimes De La Revolution (L.D. 14)*, good margins, (02-03-93, Ader Tajan, #108), 5¹¹⁄₁₆ x 7⅜ in., (14.5 x 18.7 cm.), lithograph (BP 212, DM 499, FR 1692, Y 37,691).

BI   *Le Dimanche au Jardin Des Plantes (L.D. 3244), 1862*, from Souvenirs d'Artistes, 2nd (final) state, foxmarks, surface dirt, prov., est. BP 1,0/1,500, (12-01-92, Christie-London, #356), L. 10¼ x 8⁷⁄₁₆ in., (261 x 215 mm.), lithograph sur blanc.

$5147*   *Emotions Parisiennes, 1839-1842: Forty*, from set of 51, final states, margins, good cond., foxing, (06-30-93, Sotheby-London, #413, illus.), each sh c. 13½ x 9⅞ in., (343 x 251 mm.), lithograph, plates sur blanc (BP 3450, DM 8779, FR 29,614, Y 551,484).

BI   *En Chemin De Fer...Un Voisin Agreable (L.D. 3252), 1862*, 3rd (final) state, margins, foxmarks, prov., est. BP 1,8/2,500, (12-01-92, Christie-London, #365), L. 7¹¹⁄₁₆ x 9⅝ in., (195 x 245 mm.), lithograph on Chine applique.

$3330*   *En Chemin De Fer...Un Voisin Agreable (L.d. 3252), 1862*, 2nd state of 3, margins, foxmarks, tape, (12-01-92, Christie-London, #361, illus.), L. 7¹¹⁄₁₆ x 9⅝ in., (195 x 245 mm.), lithograph on chine applique (BP 2200, DM 5308, FR 18,088, Y 414,592).

BI   *En V'La Un, Il Pourrait Bien Etre Malheureux (L.D. 3249), 1862*, from Souvenirs d'Artistes, 3rd (final) state, margins, foxing, prov., est. BP 800/1,200, (12-01-92, Christie-London, #363), L. 10⁹⁄₁₆ x 8⁹⁄₁₆ in., (268 x 218 mm.), lithograph on chine applique.

BI   *"Enee Aux Enfers"*, from "Histoire Ancienne", stone s., est. $50/75, (11-13-92, DuMouchelle, #2455), 9½ x 7¾ in., (24.1 x 19.7 cm.), lithograph.

$4162*   *Enfonce Lafayette!...Attrappe Mon Vieux! (L.D. 14), 1834*, margins, foxmarks, surface dirt, tape, (12-01-92, Christie-London, #352, illus.), L. 11⁷⁄₁₆ x 16⁵⁄₁₆ in., (290 x 415 mm.), lithograph sur blanc (BP 2750, DM 6634, FR 22,607, Y 518,177).

$590*   *Le Fantome (L.D., 115), 1835*, pl. 488 of La Caricature, second state of three, creases, good margins, staining, (06-16-93, Ader Tajan, #65), 10⅝ x 8¾ in., (27 x 22.2 cm.), lithograph (BP 393, DM 979, FR 3287, Y 62,927).

$2367*   *Faut-Y Faire Une Lettre Pour L'Attendrir?... (D. 1341/III), 1845*, sheet 5 of series: Les Gens de Justice, (06-23-93, Kornfeld, #294), lithograph on wove (BP 1608, DM 4005, FR 13,472, Y 257,871, SF 3565).

$884*   *Les Femmes Socialistes (L.D. 1918, 1919, 1921 a 1925), 1849: Seven*, holes, creases, good margins, (06-16-93, Ader Tajan, #77), lithograph (BP 589, DM 1467, FR 4925, Y 94,283).

$13,363*   *Gargantua (Delteil 34/I), 1831*, (06-23-93, Kornfeld, #290, illus.), lithograph (BP 9078, DM 22,611, FR 76,056, Y 1,455,823, SF 20,125).

$12,928*   *Gargantua (L.D. 34)*, definitive state, reddish stains, good margins, (02-03-93, Ader Tajan, #112), 8⁷⁄₁₆ x 12 in., (21.4 x 30.5 cm.), lithograph (BP 9025, DM 21,288, FR 72,183, Y 1,608,160).

$10*   *"Groa Cupide Va"*, from La Caricature Journal, staining in image, (05-15-93, Cleveland, #378), 12 x 9½ in., (30.5 x 24.1 cm.), lithograph (BP 7, DM 16, FR 54, Y 1109).

$2125*   *Il Defend L'Orphelin Et La Veuve, A Moins... (Delteil 1358 II)*, sheet 22 from series Les Gens de Justice, (06-04-93, Bassenge, #5651), 9 x 7⅝ in., (22.9 x 19.4 cm.), lithograph (BP 1406, DM 3451, FR 11,631, Y 229,185).

$550*   *Il Etait Votre Amant, Madame! (D. 3280), 1864*, 2nd final state, from Croquis Dramatique, sur blanc, full margins, good cond., staining, hinge remains, surface soiling,

(10-28-92, Butterfield, #2629), 11 x 9¹⁄₁₆ in., (279 x 230 mm.), lithograph on wove (BP 350, DM 849, FR 2884, Y 67,485).

$3877*   *Jacquinot-Godart (L.D. 180)*, definitive state, large margins, collector's stamp, (02-03-93, Ader Tajan, #117), 7¹³⁄₁₆ x 8¹¹⁄₁₆ in., (19.8 x 22 cm.), lithograph on white (BP 2706, DM 6384, FR 21,647, Y 482,274).

BI   *Je N'Ai Jamais Tant Ri Qu'A L'Enterrement De La Fille A Dourdin (L.D. 3250)*, from Souvenirs d'Artistes, 2nd state of 3, margins, foxing, stamp, prov., est. BP 1,4/1,800, (12-01-92, Christie-London, #364), L. 7¹³⁄₁₆ x 10⁷⁄₁₆ in., (199 x 265 mm.), lithograph on Chine applique.

$2331*   *Je N'ai Jamais Tant Ri Qu'A L'Enterrement De La Fille A Bourdin" (L.D. 3250), 1862*, from Souvenirs d'Artistes, 2nd state of 3, margins, foxing, (12-01-92, Christie-London, #359, illus.), L. 7¹³⁄₁₆ x 10⁷⁄₁₆ in., (199 x 265 mm.), lithograph on Chine applique (BP 1540, DM 3715, FR 12,662, Y 290,214).

$382*   *Le Jour Ou Il S'Agit De Faire Une Conquete (D. 1554/III), 1847*, sheet 78 of series: Les bons bourgeois, (06-23-93, Kornfeld, #302), lithograph (BP 260, DM 646, FR 2174, Y 41,617, SF 575).

$4846*   *L'Epicier Qui N'Etait Pas Bete (L. Delteil 7)*, definitive state, large margins, collector's stamp, (02-03-93, Ader Tajan, #106), 8¹⁄₁₆ x 6¾ in., (20.5 x 17.1 cm.), on white paper (BP 3383, DM 7980, FR 27,058, Y 602,811).

BI   *"L'Hiver A La Campagne"*, good/poor cond., est. $4/500, (11-21-92, Bakker, #113), image 8½ x 11 in., (21.6 x 27.9 cm.), lithograph.

$3163*   *Madeleine Bastille (L.d. 3243), 1862*, from Souvenirs D'Artistes, 2nd (final) state, margins, foxmarks, tape, (12-01-92, Christie-London, #355), L. 9⁷⁄₁₆ x 8¹¹⁄₁₆ in., (240 x 220 mm.), lithograph on Chine applique (BP 2090, DM 5041, FR 17,181, Y 393,800).

$2974*   *Maitre Chapotard Lisant...L'Eloge De Lui-Meme (Delteil 1354 II)*, sheet 18 from series Les Gens de Justice, (06-04-93, Bassenge, #5650, illus.), 9⁹⁄₁₆ x 7⅝ in., (24.3 x 19.3 cm.), lithograph (BP 1968, DM 4829, FR 16,278, Y 320,751).

$649*   *Marionettes Politiques (D. 2003/II), 1850*, sheet 107 of Actualities, (06-23-93, Kornfeld, #304), lithograph (BP 441, DM 1098, FR 3694, Y 70,705, SF 978).

$236*   *Masques De 1831 (L.D., 42), 1832*, pl. 143 of La Caricature, staining, good margins, (06-16-93, Ader Tajan, #59), 8⁷⁄₁₆ x 11¹³⁄₁₆ in., (21.5 x 30 cm.), lithograph (BP 157, DM 392, FR 1315, Y 25,171).

$14,127*   *NADAR Elevant La Photographie A La Hauteur De L'Art (D. 3248/II), 1862*, sheet 6 of series: Le Boulevard, (06-23-93, Kornfeld, #308, illus.), lithograph on wove (BP 9597, DM 23,904, FR 80,404, Y 1,539,057, SF 21,275).

$19,978*   *Nadar Elevant La Photographie A La Hauteur De L'Art (L.D. 3248), 1862*, from Souvenirs d'Artistes, 2nd (final) state, foxmarks, stamp, prov., (12-01-92, Christie-London, #360, illus.), L. 10⁹⁄₁₆ x 8¹¹⁄₁₆ in., (268 x 221 mm.), lithograph on chine applique (BP 13,200, DM 31,843, FR 108,517, Y 2,487,301).

$3295*   *Ne Vous Y Frottez Pas (L.D. 133)*, small margins, yellowed, (02-03-93, Ader Tajan, #115), 12¹⁄₁₆ x 16¹⁵⁄₁₆ in., (30.7 x 43.1 cm.), lithograph on fixed Chine (BP 2300, DM 5426, FR 18,398, Y 409,877).

$2200*   *Ne Vous Y Frottez Pas (Liberte De La Presse) (L.D. 133), 1834*, margins, central fold, repaired tear, very good cond., (11-09-92, Christie-NY, #83, illus.), 320 x 450 in., (812.8 x cm.), lithograph on wove (BP 1455, DM 3512, FR 11,866, Y 273,021).

$2997*   *Ne Vous Y Frottez Pas!! (L.D. 133), 1834*, repaired crease, foxing, surface dirt, tears, prov., (12-01-92, Christie-London, #351, illus.), L. 12¹⁄₁₆ x 17¹⁄₁₆ in., (307 x 433 mm.), lithograph sur blanc (BP 1980, DM 4777, FR 16,279, Y 373,132).

BI   *Le Nouveau Paris (L.D. 3245), 1862*, from Souvenirs d'Artistes, 2nd (final) state, wide margins, foxmarks, surface dirt, stamp, prov., est. BP 1,0/1,500, (12-01-92, Christie-London, #362), L. 10½ x 8⅞ in., (267 x 225 mm.), lithograph sur blanc.

$1665*   *Le Nouveau Paris (L.D. 3245), 1862*, from souvenirs d'Artistes, 2nd (final) state, margins, tear, foxmarks, stamp, prov., (12-01-92, Christie-London, #357), L. 10½ x 8⅞ in., (267 x 225 mm.), lithograph on chine applique (BP 1100, DM 2654, FR 9044, Y 207,296).

$177* *Un Nouveau-Nez (L.D., 172), 1833,* rare, staining, creases, small margins, (06-16-93, Ader Tajan, #66), 8¹⁄₁₆ x 10⁹⁄₁₆ in., (20.5 x 26.8 cm.), lithograph (BP 118, DM 294, FR 986, Y 18,878).

$172* *Oh Patrie (L.D. 693 and 821): Two,* yellowed, (02-03-93, Ader Tajan, #118), 8⁹⁄₁₆ x 7¹³⁄₁₆ in., (21.8 x 19.9 cm.), lithograph, first color (BP 120, DM 283, FR 960, Y 21,396).

$850* *Oh! M'Sieu L'Avocat, Tachez de... (Delteil 1772 I), 1848,* sheet 4 from series Les Divorceuses, (06-04-93, Bassenge, #5653), 9⁹⁄₁₆ x 7½ in., (24.3 x 19.1 cm.), lithograph on hand-made (BP 562, DM 1380, FR 4652, Y 91,674).

$93* *Ou Peut Aller Cette Bande D'Hommes Armes... (L.Delteil, 1762), 1848,* from "Les Alarmistes et Les Alarmes" series, definitive state, reddish stains, good margins, creases, collector's stamp, (04-02-93, Picard, #80), 9⅝ x 8¼ in., (24.5 x 21 cm.), lithograph (BP 61, DM 149, FR 508, Y 10,589).

$2125* *Oui, On Veut Depouiller Cet Orphelin (Delteil 1347 II), 1845,* sheet 11 from the series Les Gens de Justice, (06-04-93, Bassenge, #5649), 7¼ x 10¹⁄₁₆ in., (18.4 x 25.5 cm.), lithograph (BP 1406, DM 3451, FR 11,631, Y 229,185).

$759* *Passe Ton Chemin Cochon (L. Delteil, 1), 1830,* second state w/letter, creases, reddish stains, drystamp, good margins, (06-11-93, Picard, #28), 6¹¹⁄₁₆ x 5⁷⁄₁₆ in., (170 x 138 mm.), lithograph (BP 499, DM 1234, FR 4159, Y 80,531).

$491* *Pastorales (L.D. 1391, 1393, 1399, 1402, 1406, 1416, 1426), 1846; Seven,* num. 4 rare, third state of four, others, defintive state w/letter, staining, faults, soiling, small margins, (06-16-93, Ader Tajan, #76), color lithograph (BP 327, DM 815, FR 2735, Y 52,368).

$363* *Le Patrouillotisme Chassant Le Patriotisme Du Palais Royal (L.D. 28),* second state of three, good margins, (02-03-93, Ader Tajan, #110), 8¹⁵⁄₁₆ x 11⁷⁄₁₆ in., (22.8 x 29 cm.), lithograph (BP 253, DM 598, FR 2027, Y 45,155).

$3360* *Un Peu Agee Pour Jouer Au Colosse De Rhodes (D. 3612/I), 1867,* artist's proof, (06-23-93, Kornfeld, #309), lithograph on thin wove (BP 2283, DM 5685, FR 19,124, Y 366,053, SF 5060).

$2691* *Un Plaideur Peu Satisfait (Delteil 1362 II),* sheet 26 from series Les Gens de Justice, (06-04-93, Bassenge, #5652, illus.), 9³⁄₁₆ x 7½ in., (23.4 x 19.1 cm.), lithograph (BP 1780, DM 4370, FR 14,729, Y 290,229).

$10* *"Pour Les Frais Du Culte, Sil Vous Plait" and "Avant Attrape Un CoupDe Soleil": Two,* from Actualities, good cond., (05-15-93, Cleveland, #379), one 10½ x 8½ in., (26.7 x 21.6 cm.), other 10 x 8 in., (26.7 x 21.6 cm.), lithograph (BP 7, DM 16, FR 54, Y 1109).

$2291* *Quel Dommage Que Cette Charmante Petite Femme Ne M'Ait Pas Charge DeDefendre Sa Cause... (D. 1360/II), 1846,* sheet 24 of series: Les Gens de Justice, (06-23-93, Kornfeld, #300), lithograph (BP 1556, DM 3876, FR 13,039, Y 249,591, SF 3450).

$275* *Robert Macaire (L.D. 373, 378, 394, 406): Four,* yellowed, staining, good margins, (06-16-93, Ader Tajan, #67), lithographs (BP 183, DM 457, FR 1532, Y 29,330).

$14,651* *Rue Transnonain, Le 15 Avril 1834 (L.D. 135), 1834,* margins, made-up patch, surface dirt, defects, (12-01-92, Christie-London, #353, illus.), L. 11¼ x 17⁷⁄₁₆ in., (285 x 443 mm.), lithograph sur blanc (BP 9680, DM 23,352, FR 79,582, Y 1,824,079).

$262* *"La Salle Des Ventes" and "Dans La Salle Des Ventes" (L.D. 3129, 3130): Two,* text verso, thin margins, (02-03-93, Ader Tajan, #125), 8⅜ x 10¹³⁄₁₆ in., (21.3 x 27.5 cm.), 8¼ x 10⁵⁄₁₆ in., (21.3 x 27.5 cm.), lithograph (BP 183, DM 431, FR 1463, Y 32,591).

$385* *Sire! Lisboune Est Prise-Aaaah!!, La Caricature (Journal) No 145,* soiling, good cond., (11-12-92, Freemn/Fine Art, #59), mat 12½ x 10 in., (31.8 x 25.4 cm.), hand colored lithograph (BP 253, DM 610, FR 2058, Y 47,737).

$268* *Un Train De Plaisir Aerien (D. 2265/II), 1852,* (06-23-93, Kornfeld, #306), lithograph (BP 182, DM 453, FR 1525, Y 29,197, SF 403).

$5328* *A Travers Les Ateliers (L.D. 3246), 1862,* from Souvenirs d'Artistes, 2nd (final) state, margins, foxmarks, stamp, prov., (12-01-92, Christie-London, #358, illus.), L. 9¹⁵⁄₁₆ x 8¼ in., (253 x 210 mm.), lithograph on chine applique (BP 3520, DM 8492, FR 28,941, Y 663,347).

BI *Tres Hauts Et Tres Puissans Moutards Et Moutards Legitimes (L.D. 132), 1834,* margins, trimmed, discoloration, stamp, prov., est. BP 6/800, (12-01-92, Christie-London, #349), L. 11¹³⁄₁₆ x 18¹³⁄₁₆ in., (300 x 478 mm.), lithograph sur blanc.

$2421* *Tres Hauts Et Tres Puissants Moutards Et Moutardes Legitimes (L.D. 132),* pl. 19 from Association Mensuelle, good margins, collector's stamp, (02-03-93, Ader Tajan, #114), 11¹³⁄₁₆ x 18¹³⁄₁₆ in., (30 x 47.8 cm.), on fixed Chine (BP 1690, DM 3986, FR 13,518, Y 301,157).

$444* *Untitled (Delteil XXIX, 3955), 1872,* wormholes, (05-15-93, Loudmer, #202, illus.), 3¹⁵⁄₁₆ x 8⅞ in., (100 x 225 mm.), sh 10⅛ x 14⅜ in., (100 x 225 mm.), black etching on laid w/AM watermark (BP 289, DM 714, FR 2400, Y 49,218).

BI *Le Ventre Legislatif (Delteil 131), 1834,* p. Becquet, pub. Aubert, margins, center fold, printer's crease, bleached, fox marks, tears, creases, soiling, skinned, est. $12/16,000, (05-13-93, Sotheby-NY, #540, illus.), 11⅛ x 17 in., (282 x 433 mm.), sh 14⅜ x 21⅞ in., (282 x 433 mm.), lithograph on white wove.

$26,638* *Le Ventre Legislatif (L.D. 131), 1834,* margins, crease, foxing, discoloration, nicks, (12-01-92, Christie-London, #350, illus.), L. 11¹⁄₁₆ x 17¹⁄₁₆ in., (281 x 434 mm.), lithograph sur blanc (BP 17,600, DM 42,458, FR 144,693, Y 3,316,484).

$3818* *Voici Encore Du Gibier Saisi Qu'On Adresse... (D. 1301), 1844,* sheet 9/bis of series: Les Philantropes du Jour, (06-23-93, Kornfeld, #292, illus.), lithograph on wove (BP 2594, DM 6460, FR 21,730, Y 415,949, SF 5750).

$1374* *Voila Le Ministere Public Qui Vous Dit Des Choses Tres Desagreables... (D. 1357/II), 1846,* sheet 21 of series: Les Gens de Justice, prov., (06-23-93, Kornfeld, #299), lithograph (BP 933, DM 2325, FR 7820, Y 149,690, SF 2070).

$2596* *Vous M'Avez Injurie Dans Votre Plaidoirie, Mais Je Saurai Bien Vous Forcer A M'En Rendre Raison!... (D. 1345/II), 1845,* sheet 9 of series: Les Gens de Justice, (06-23-93, Kornfeld, #298), lithograph on wove (BP 1764, DM 4393, FR 14,775, Y 282,819, SF 3910).

$2750* *Voyage En Chine (Delteil 1189-1220), 1843-45,* pub. Charivari, margins, good cond., soiling, discoloration, foxing,tipped boards, (11-05-92, Sotheby-NY, #150A), overall size approx. 13⅝ x 10⅞ in., (345 x 275 mm.), set of 32 hand colored lithographs w/touches of gum arabic on white wove (BP 1789, DM 4349, FR 14,714, Y 337,382).

DAUMONT, Emile Florentine
(after Giovanni Battista PIRANESI) French b. 1834

BI *Pont Triomphal Erige Par Un Empereur Romain,* est. $150/250, (02-04-93, Sloan, #722), image area 9 x 13⅞ in., (22.9 x 35.2 cm.), color engraving.

DAVENT, Leon ac. 1536-42

BI *Adonis Und Seine Gefahrten Erlegen Den Eber (B. 48; Zerner 77), 1547,* im Oval, after Luca Penni, est. DM 1,200, (12-04-92, Bassenge, #6137), 11⁷⁄₁₆ x 14¹³⁄₁₆ in., (29 x 37.6 cm.), engraving.

DAVENT, Leon ac. 1540-1556

BI *Mars Et Venus Servis A Table Par L'Amour Et Les Graces, (B. XVI, p. 326, no. 52, Davent, Herbert, p. 34, no. 73, Davent; Zerner LD 74), c. 1547,* wiping scratches, narrow margins on 3 sides, trimmed, shaved into subject, losses, repairs in image, defects, very good cond., BP 4/6000, (12-01-92, Christie-London, #19, illus.), P. 11½ x 17¼ in., (292 x 438 mm.), etching, w/ tone.

DAVESNE (after)
$707* *"Les Cerises" and "Les Prunes"*: Two, thin margins, (03-22-93, Pescheteau, #7), colored print (BP 476, DM 1159, FR 3941, Y 81,867).

DAVEY, John R.
$130* *Going Out*, s., margins, foxing, (10-29-92, Bonhams-Chelsea, #35), plate 8 x 9⅞ in., (20.3 x 25.1 cm.), etching (BP 83, DM 200, FR 678, Y 16,103).

DAVEY, W.T.
$412* *"The Wynnstay Hunt"*, after Henry Calvert, (03-03-93, Doyle, #20), 19 x 31½ in., (48.3 x 80 cm.), color engraving (BP 284, DM 678, FR 2302, Y 48,142).

DAVID, H.
$196* *Le Parc*, (01-31-93, Millon/Robert, #225), 5⅞ x 3⁹⁄₁₆ in., (15 x 9 cm.), etching (BP 132, DM 316, FR 1068, Y 24,451).

DAVID, Hermine   French 1886-1971
BI *"Equestrian Show" and "Park Scene"*, c. 1940: Two, s., #37/40 and 10/35, pub. Jacquart, blindstamp, full margins, good cond., mat stain, creases, nick, est. $6/800, (02-11-93, Sotheby-NY, #114), 10 x 8¼ in., (254 x 209 mm.), 8⁹⁄₁₆ x 10⅛ in., (254 x 209 mm.), drypoint.
$336* *Exposition Des Chemins De Fer De L'Etat: Bretagne "Les Grands Disparus, L'Ecole De Pont-Aven, Les Peintres Contemporains"*, 1937, good cond., (11-19-92, Ribeyre/Baron, #137), 39⅜ x 24⅝ in., (100 x 62.5 cm.), poster (BP 221, DM 536, FR 1805, Y 41,786).
$246* *"Le Luxembourg", "La Place St Augustin", "Au Zoo" and "Quelque Part Sur Les Rives Du Morbihan"*: Four, t., num., s., soiling, full margins, (02-24-93, Picard, #72), drypoint on wove (BP 172, DM 399, FR 1354, Y 28,866).
$58* *La Maison De Sylvie*, s., 88/29, drystamp, small tears, (06-28-93, Loudmer, #228), 6⅝ x 8¾ in., (168 x 223 mm.), sh 12½ x 15¼ in., (168 x 223 mm.), black drypoint on wove (BP 39, DM 99, FR 332, Y 6154).

DAVID, Joe   b. 1946
BI *'Eats-Quin,'* 1977, #24/75, (Guild Series), s., est. C$450-600, (10-21-92, Maynard, #43), sheet 22 x 14¼ in., (55.9 x 36.2 cm.), silkscreen.
BI *'Ka-Ka-Win-Chealth,'* 1977, #24/75, (Guild Series), s., est. C$450/600, (10-21-92, Maynard, #41), sheet 22 x 14 in., (55.9 x 35.6 cm.), silkscreen.
$266* *'Natural' and 'Supernatural'*: Two, 1977, #180/222, s., framed together, (10-21-92, Maynard, #42), each 19 x 6¾ in., (48.3 x 17.1 cm.), silkscreen (BP 165, DM 402, FR 1366, Y 32,400, C$ 330).

DAVIDSON, Bruce   American b. 1933
BI *Cigarette Machine, Brooklyn Gang Series*, s., prov., est. $1/1,200, (05-16-93, Hindman, #346), 16 x 10½ in., photograph, silver print.
$1210* *The Dwarf*, 1958 (Pantheon, pl. 3), photog.'s stamp, (10-15-92, Sotheby-NY, #553, illus.), 13⅝ x 9¼ in., (34.6 x 23.5 cm.), photograph, gelatin silver print (BP 740, DM 1801, FR 6108, Y 145,171).
$748* *Woman And Man From "East 100th Street"*, 1967, s., illus., (05-23-93, Butterfield, #3391, illus.), 8⅛ x 11⅛ in., photograph, gelatin silver print (BP 487, DM 1223, FR 4117, Y 82,679).

DAVIDSON, J.O. (after)
BI *A Winning Yacht*, 1885, by J. Wellstood, pub. Wellstood, large margins beyond subject, good cond., soiling, discoloration, backboard stain, est. $6/800, (01-28-93, Sotheby-NY, #461), image 24⅜ x 17⅛ in., (619 x 435 mm.), paper 31⅞ x 24 in., (619 x 435 mm.), engraving on wove.

DAVIE, Alan   English b. 1920
BI *Card Game*, (19)71, s., d., num., est. DM 900, (12-01-92, Karl/Faber, #527), 19½ x 23¼ in., (49.5 x 59 cm.), color lithograph on wove.
BI *For My Dearly Loved Master Pablo Picasso*, 1972, s., d. H.C., est. DM 400, (09-18-92, Schloss Ahlden, #991), 19¾ x 25⅞ in., (50.1 x 65.8 cm.), color lithograph on BFK Rives.
BI *"Olympische Spiele Munchen 1972"*, 1970, s., d., num., est. DM 600, (12-01-92, Karl/Faber, #528), 34¼ x 25⅜

in., (87 x 64.5 cm.), color lithograph and relief print on BFK Rives wove.

DAVIEL, J.
$438* *PLM: Marseille Alexandrie "La Route D'Egypte" Messageries Maritimes,Trains De Luxe...1927*, very good cond., (03-13-93, Laurin, #118, illus.), 42¹¹⁄₁₆ x 30¹¹⁄₁₆ in., (108.5 x 78 cm.), (BP 306, DM 729, FR 2479, Y 51,621).

DAVIES, Arthur B.   American 1862-1928
$286* *Time Of Speech*, s., t., excell. cond., (10-10-92, Litchfield, #65), plate 2 x 9¼ in., (5.1 x 23.5 cm.), etching and aquatint, grey paper pressed into gold paper (BP 170, DM 425, FR 1426, Y 34,819).

DAVIES, Lynn
$2361* *Iceberg*, c. 1990, sight 700 x 700mm, (05-07-93, Sotheby-London, #406, illus.), photograph, matt silver print (BP 1495, DM 3733, FR 12,579, Y 259,965).

DAVIES, Thomas
BI *"Wood-Scene Norton Cheshire"*, 1856, from Calotype Negative, mounted on card, est. BP 6/900, 167 x 220mm, (05-07-93, Sotheby-London, #62, illus.), photograph, lightly albumenised salt print.

DAVIS, A.J. (after)
$88* *Amherst College Mass.*, 1831, printed by Fenner Sears and Company, (11-12-92, Freemn/Fine Art, #60), 10 x 14 in., (25.4 x 35.6 cm.), engraving printed on silk with hand coloring (BP 58, DM 139, FR 470, Y 10,911).

DAVIS, Dwight A.   1852-1944
$660* *Lady In White*, c. 1905, prov., (10-13-92, Christie-NY, #36, illus.), 9½ x 7⅝ in., (24.1 x 19.4 cm.), photograph, platinum print (BP 384, DM 967, FR 3285, Y 80,029).

DAVIS, Erma   American 19th/20th cent.
BI *"Country Church" and "The Castle, Berkeley Springs, W. VA"*: Two, s., num., est. $150/250, (04-02-93, Sloan, #818), each 4¼ x 6 in., (108 x 152 mm.), etching.
$83* *"Country Church" and "The Castle, Berkeley Springs, W. VA."*: Two, s., num., (05-28-93, Sloan, #216, illus.), each 4¼ x 6 in., (10.8 x 15.2 cm.), etchings (BP 53, DM 132, FR 445, Y 8900).

DAVIS, Farust
BI *Still Life With Shoes*, 1938, s., d., num. twice, est. $1,4/1,800, (04-08-93, Christie-NY, #271, illus.), 9½ x 7½ in., (24.1 x 19.1 cm.), photograph, gelatin silver print.

DAVIS, Gene   American b. 1920
$275* *Linear Composition*, s., #110/144, (05-16-93, Hindman, #650), 79¼ x 34 in., (201.3 x 86.4 cm.), color serigraph (BP 179, DM 442, FR 1486, Y 30,484).
BI *"Two Prints From Black Watch" and "(Untitled)"*: Three, s., 1st 2 d. 1974, 3rd d. 1977, very good cond., est. $800/1,200, (06-11-93, Doyle, #90), larger 67 x 42 in., (170.2 x 106.7 cm.), color silkscreen.
$286* *Untitled (Stripes)*, s., d. 1976, #48/100, (10-30-92, Sloan, #890), 31¾ x 25½ in., (80.6 x 64.8 cm.), color screen print (BP 183, DM 440, FR 1493, Y 35,427).

DAVIS, Lynn   American b. 1940s
$4675* *Icebergs*: Two, 2nd s., d., num. 1/7, i. by photog. in ink, backed w/card, s., d., num. 1/7 by photog. in ink, reprod. limit. stamp, 1st 1980's, 2nd 1986, p. 1988,Robert Mapplethorpe Coll., (10-15-92, Sotheby-NY, #599, illus.), one 28 x 28 in., (71.1 x 71.1 cm.), other 23 x 22¾ in., (71.1 x 71.1 cm.), photograph, 1st Cibachrome, 2nd dye-transfer print (BP 2861, DM 6959, FR 23,599, Y 560,888).

DAVIS, R.B. (after)
$150* *His Majesty's Harriers*, 1815, by R. Woodman, pub. R.B. Davis, trimmed inside platemark, crease, (11-30-92, Phillips-London, #268), sheet 21⅝ x 25⅝ in., (549 x 651 mm.), stipple engraving on J. Whatman wove (BP 99, DM 239, FR 811, Y 18,668).

DAVIS, Richard Barrett (after)
$647* *"Grouse Shooting", "Snipe Shooting", "Partridge Shooting" and "Woodcock Shooting"*: Four, by R. G. Reeve, pub. Thomas McLean, November 2nd, 1836, margins, foxing, staining, (04-22-93, Bonhams-Chelsea, #153), plate 16¾ x 20¼ in., (42.5 x 51.4 cm.), aquatints w/ hand coloring (BP 418, DM 1040, FR 3507, Y 71,138).

$295* *"Road Riders, Or Funkers" and "The Few, Not Funkers":*
A Pair, by C. Hunt, margins, foxing, staining, (06-30-
93, Bonhams-Chelsea, #116), plate 14 x 31½ in., (35.6 x
80 cm.), aquatints w/hand-coloring (BP 198, DM 503,
FR 1697, Y 31,608).

DAVIS, Ronald   b. 1937
$143* *Beam*, s., d. 1975, #6/23, pub. Gemini G.E.L., bears their
chop, (05-16-93, Hindman, #513), 25 x 36 in., (63.5 x
91.4 cm.), color lithograph (BP 93, DM 230, FR 773, Y
15,852).
$440* *"Big Open Box"*, 1975, s., d. 1975, #21/39, prov., (12-
02-92, Boos, #519), sight 16⁹/₁₆ x 21¼ in., (420 x 540
mm.), color etching, aquatint and drypoint (BP 284, DM
692, FR 2362, Y 54,747).
$173* *Double Slice (G. 363), 1972*, s., d., #35/65, blindstamp
publisher, Gemini G.E.L., full margins, good cond.?,
light-staining, (05-19-93, Butterfield, #2151), 13½ x 32
in., (343 x 813 mm.), lithograph and silkscreen w/
embossing in colors on Arches Cover (BP 112, DM 281,
FR 947, Y 19,152).
$165* *Dual Windows, 1981*, s., d., num. 50/112, blindstamp,
pub. by artist for Hereditary Disease Foundation, full
margins, apparently good cond., creases, shrink-wrapped,
(02-24-93, Butterfield, #3207), 22 x 23 in., (559 x 584
mm.), silkscreen in colors on wove (BP 115, DM 268,
FR 908, Y 19,362).
BI *Dual Windows, 1981*, s., d., i. for Max, #9/112, blindstamp printer, pub. artist for Hereditary Disease Foundation, full margins, good cond.?, est. $2/300, (05-19-93,
Butterfield, #2152), 22 x 23 in., (559 x 584 mm.), silkscreen in colors on wove.
$330* *Rectangle Series: Diagonal Slice (G. 366), 1972*, s., d.,
#50/75, blindstamp pub. Gemini G.E.L., full margins,
good cond., light-staining, crease, ink residue, (10-28-92,
Butterfield, #2927), 13⅜ x 32 in., (340 x 813 mm.),
lithograph and silkscreen w/embossing in colors on
Arches cover paper (BP 210, DM 510, FR 1730, Y
40,491).
$358* *Rotation-Tilt (G. 899), 1981*, s., d., #28/34, blindstamp
pub. Gemini G.E.L., full margins, very good cond.?, (10-
28-92, Butterfield, #2929), 27¹¹/₁₆ x 17⅞ in., (703 x 454
mm.), etching w/aquatint and engraving in colors on
Arches Cover paper (BP 228, DM 553, FR 1877, Y
43,926).
$550* *Six Frame (G. 526), 1974*, s., d., t., #28/50, blindstamp
pub. Gemini G.E.L., full margins, very good cond.?, (10-
28-92, Butterfield, #2928), 25⅜ x 37 in., (645 x 940
mm.), lithograph w/silkscreen in colors on wove mounted
to white wove (BP 350, DM 849, FR 2884, Y 67,485).

DAVIS, Stuart   American 1894-1964
$13,750* *Theatre On The Beach (Cole/Myers 116), 1931*, s., i.
'artist's proof', full margins, good cond., loss, creases,
soiling, (11-05-92, Sotheby-NY, #16, illus.), 11 x 15 in.,
(280 x 382 mm.), lithograph (BP 8943, DM 21,746, FR
73,569, Y 1,686,910).

DAVIS, Warren   American 1865-1928
$138* *Nude Woman*, s., (11-13-92, DuMouchelle, #2374), 8 x
5¾ in., (20.3 x 14.6 cm.), etching (BP 89, DM 217, FR
731, Y 17,128).

DAWE, Philip, engraver
$251 *"Courtship For Money"*, 1772, (06-11-93, G.A. Key,
#68), 13 x 10 in., (33 x 25.4 cm.), colored print (BP
165, DM 408, FR 1375, Y 26,631).

DAWS, Lawrence   b. 1927
$49* *Girl And Dog*, s. Daws, i., #4/15, (08-11-92, L. Joel,
#59G), 10¼ x 7⅝ in., (26 x 19.4 cm.), color computer
print (BP 25, DM 72, FR 244, Y 6275, A$ 66).
$41* *Hills Of My Childhood*, s. Daws, i., #4/15, (08-11-92, L.
Joel, #169G), 7⅝ x 9¹⁵/₁₆ in., (19.3 x 25.2 cm.), color
computer print (BP 21, DM 60, FR 204, Y 5250, A$
55).

DAWSON, Charles E.
BI *Prunella*, A cond., est. $4/600, (08-06-92, Swann, #111,
illus.), 28 x 18½ in., (71.1 x 47 cm.), .

DAWSON, Montague   English 1895-1973
$165* *Eight Bells*, s. in plate, (12-17-92, Mystic, #40F), 20 x
30 in., (50.8 x 76.2 cm.), color photolithograph (BP 105,
DM 258, FR 880, Y 20,278).
$220* *Horn Abeam*, s. in plate, (12-17-92, Mystic, #40E), 20 x
29½ in., (50.8 x 74.9 cm.), color photolithograph (BP
140, DM 343, FR 1173, Y 27,037).
BI *"The Rising Wind", 1969*, pub. Frost and Reed, s., est.
$6/800, (05-15-93, Cleveland, #380, illus.), 36 x 24 in.,
(91.4 x 61 cm.), collotype.
$330* *Summer Breezes*, s. in plate, (12-17-92, Mystic, #40G),
17½ x 30 in., (44.5 x 76.2 cm.), color photolithograph
(BP 209, DM 515, FR 1760, Y 40,555).
$550* *"U.S.S. Constellation", 1966*, pub. Frost and Reed, full
margins, excellent cond., stains, (10-31-92, Cleveland,
#278), 20 x 29¾ in., (50.8 x 75.6 cm.), collotype (BP
352, DM 846, FR 2871, Y 68,128).

DAWSON, Montague (after)
$168* *The Action Between Java And Constitution, December
1812, 1966*, s., blindstamp, pub. Frost and Reed, (01-14-
93, Bonhams, #106), image 21 x 30 in., (53.3 x 76.2
cm.), color reproduction (BP 110, DM 275, FR 929, Y
21,180).
BI *the Days Of Adventure*, s. in plate, t., i., est. $350/500,
(07-03-92, Sloan, #1075), 20 x 30 in., (50.8 x 76.2 cm.),
photo lithograph.
$132* *The Days Of Adventure*, (04-02-93, Sloan, #857), 20 x
30 in., (508 x 762 mm.), photolithograph (BP 87, DM
212, FR 721, Y 15,029).
BI *Eight Bars*, est. $350/500, (07-03-92, Sloan, #1079), 20 x
29¾ in., (50.8 x 75.6 cm.), photolithograph.
$132* *Eight Bells*, (04-02-93, Sloan, #856), 20 x 30 in., (508 x
762 mm.), photolithograph (BP 87, DM 212, FR 721,
Y 15,029).
$168* *In Full Sail, 1972*, s., blindstamp, pub. Frost and Reed,
(01-14-93, Bonhams, #107), image 23¼ x 36⅞ in., (59.1
x 93.7 cm.), color reproduction (BP 110, DM 275, FR
929, Y 21,180).
$84* *"A Masted Vessel Under Full Sail", 1928*, s., pub. Frost
and Reed, (01-14-93, Bonhams, #108), image 25 x 17
in., (63.5 x 43.2 cm.), color reproduction (BP 55, DM
137, FR 464, Y 10,590).
$160* *Two Square Riggers, 1964*, s., blindstamp Fine Art Trade
Guild, pub. Frost and Reed, (08-12-92, Bonhams, #187),
image 24 x 29¾ in., (61 x 75.6 cm.), reproduction in
colors (BP 83, DM 234, FR 793, Y 20,393).
$385* *Under Full Sail*, s. in stone, s., embossed stamp, (07-03-
92, Sloan, #1087), 24 x 30 in., (61 x 76.2 cm.), photolithograph (BP 201, DM 583, FR 1964, Y 47,993).
$182* *The Windsor Castle, 1974*, num. 100/200. s. Mountbat-
ten of Burma, pub. Venture Prints, (08-12-92, Bonhams,
#188), image 23¾ x 30 in., (60.3 x 76.2 cm.), reproduc-
tion in colors (BP 94, DM 266, FR 902, Y 23,197).
$286* *"Yachts Racing", 1950*, s., blindstamp, pub. Frost and
Reed, (01-14-93, Bonhams, #109), image 19¾ x 29½ in.,
(50.2 x 74.9 cm.), color reproduction (BP 187, DM 468,
FR 1581, Y 36,056).

DAWSON, Robert
$220* *"Delta Farm, Sacramento River From The Great Central
Valley Project", 1984*, s., t., d., (11-16-92, Butterfield,
#5932, illus.), 10 x 13 in., (254.5 x 330.8 mm.), photo-
graph, gelatin silver print (BP 145, DM 351, FR 1182, Y
27,360).

DAY, F. Holland   American 1864-1933
$2640* *"Mother Feeding Child" and "Portrait Of A Woman",
1906, 1905: Two*, init., d. by photog., (04-07-93, Swann,
#442, illus.), largest 9½ x 7¾ in., photograph, platinum
print (BP 1745, DM 4270, FR 14,450, Y 299,932).
$1210* *Mother Holding Child, 1906*, s., (10-14-92, Swann, #431,
illus.), 9¼ x 7½ in., (23.5 x 19.1 cm.), photograph, platinum print (BP 710, DM 1771, FR 6005, Y 146,631).
$13,800* *Records Of Events At Little Good Harbor (Volume I:
1910-12; Volume II: 1912-13; Volume III: 1913-15; Volume IV: 1916-c. 1920): Four Volumes*, 1st t. w/hand lettering; many captioned and d. beneath prints or verso,
(04-08-93, Christie-NY, #69, illus.), majority 2⅜ x 3⅜
in., (6 x 8.6 cm.), photograph, silver, platinum and cyanotype (BP 9049, DM 22,169, FR 75,041, Y 1,566,046).

$1540* *Woman With Book, 1902,* s., (10-14-92, Swann, #432, illus.), 9½ x 7½ in., (24.1 x 19.1 cm.), photograph, platinum print (BP 904, DM 2254, FR 7643, Y 186,621).

BI *Young Man In Sailor Suit,* 1915, s., d., mounted, est. BP 9/1,200, (12-17-92, Christie-S. Ken, #2, illus.), 9½ x 7⅜ in., (24.1 x 18.7 cm.), photograph, warm-toned platinum print.

DAY, Richard

BI *Copelia #1, 1930,* s., t., num. 13/13, large margins, good cond., crease, est. $3/500, (02-24-93, Butterfield, #3208), lithograph on cream wove.

DAY and HAGHE PUBLISHER

$51* *The Rifles-No. 13,* trimmed and laid down, (04-22-93, Bonhams-Chelsea, #60), (42.9 x 31.8 cm.), lithograph w/ hand coloring (BP 33, DM 82, FR 276, Y 5607).

DAY and SON, Publishers English early 19th cent.

$84 *"Cottingham Of Hull, Amd Empress Of Leith",* (06-11-93, G.A. Key, #142), 12 x 20 in., (30.5 x 50.8 cm.), colored lithograph (BP 55, DM 137, FR 460, Y 8912).

$953* *The Iron Cutter Yacht Mosquito, 1852,* after T.G. Dutton, (10-20-92, B. Rasmussen, #360), lithograph in colors (BP 587, DM 1448, FR 4902, Y 116,603, DK 5520).

DAYES, Edward (after)

BI *His Majesty Reviewing The Armed Associations On The Fourth Of June 1799 In Hyde Park, 1801,* by Joseph Collyer, open-letter proof, pub. Collyer, trimmed to plate,repaired tears, est. BP 150/200, (11-30-92, Phillips-London, #237), sheet 18 x 26 in., (457 x 660 mm.), stipple engraving on laid.

$1650* *"The Promenade In St. James's Park" and "An Airing In Hyde Park": Two,* by Francois Davide Soiron And Thomas Gaugain, 1793, trimmed, laid down, foxing, (06-16-93, Bonhams-Chelsea, #417, illus.), image 16¼ x 25½ in., (41.3 x 64.8 cm.), stipple engraving w/hand-coloring (BP 1100, DM 2739, FR 9192, Y 175,981).

$470* *"A View Of Bloomsbury Square" and "A View Of Queen Square": Two,* by Robert Dodd and Robert Pollard, pub. Pollard, 1787-89, trimmed toplate, narrow margins, (10-27-92, Phillips-London, #118), image 16¼ x 20⅞ in., (413 x 530 mm.), aquatint w/engraving on wove (BP 297, DM 720, FR 2444, Y 57,492).

DAYEZ, Georges French 1907-1990

$220* *"Tolede",* #23/60, s., (04-04-93, Pescheteau, #194), 17¹¹⁄₁₆ x 23⅝ in., (45 x 60 cm.), color lithograph on Rives (BP 145, DM 354, FR 1201, Y 25,048).

$210* *"Tolede",* E.A., #18/20, s., (01-28-93, Pescheteau, #114), 25⁹⁄₁₆ x 19¹¹⁄₁₆ in., (65 x 50 cm.), color lithograph on wove (BP 139, DM 333, FR 1126, Y 26,074).

DAYOT, Armand

$149* *Grands Et Petits Maitres Hollandais,* #122/600, Georges Petit, 1907, (06-16-93, Bonhams-Chelsea, #334), photogravure (BP 99, DM 247, FR 830, Y 15,892).

DAZIARO, J. and AVANZO

BI *Russia, 1860s-1880s: Ten,* each w/ink credit stamp, est. BP 4/600, (10-29-92, Christie-London, #55, illus.), photograph, hand-colored, majority albumen prints.

DCHNEIDER, Gerard 1896-1986

$361* *Abstrakte Komposition,* blindstamp, (11-28-92, Schoppmann, #781), 15⁹⁄₁₆ x 22¹⁄₁₆ in., (39.6 x 56 cm.), color lithograph on BFK Rives (BP 238, DM 575, FR 1952, Y 44,928).

DE BENE, Maxine American 20th cent.

BI *Pale Rider,* s., t., #4/8, d. 1967, est. $125/175, (07-03-92, Sloan, #289), sight 12¾ x 16¼ in., (32.4 x 41.3 cm.), lithograph.

DE BOUTRAY French 19/20th cent.

BI *La Maison,* s., t., est. $75/125, (07-03-92, Sloan, #283), 7⅛ x 8⅛ in., (18.1 x 20.6 cm.), etching.

DE BRUYN, Nicolas 1571-1656

BI *The Passion (Holl. 78-89), 1618-9: Set Of Twelve,* watermark, narrow margins, trimmed, defects, staining, est. BP 300/400, (12-01-92, Christie-London, #105), averaging 7¹⁵⁄₁₆ x 15¾ in., (201 x 400 mm.), engraving.

DE BRY

$165* *Fretum Magellannicum, 1601,* (09-17-92, Sloan, #2686), 6½ x 12 in., (16.5 x 30.5 cm.), handcolored (BP 93, DM 245, FR 838, Y 20,543).

DE CAYLUS, Comte (attrib.)

$81* *St Andre Allant Vers Son Martyre,* wormholes, (05-15-93, Loudmer, #129), 9⅜ x 7⅜ in., (238 x 187 mm.), etching contrecolle on laid (BP 53, DM 130, FR 438, Y 8979).

DE CLERCQ, Louis 1836-1901

BI *Cadix, La Grande Rue (Calle Ancha), 1860,* from waxed paper neg., stamped mono., printed t., est. $3/5000, (10-13-92, Christie-NY, #6, illus.), 10¾ x 8¼ in., (27.3 x 21 cm.), photograph, albumen print.

DE DIENES, Andre Hungarian/American 1913-1985

$519* *Marilyn Monroe, Arms Stretched In Gateway,* blind embossed, #2/99, estate edit., (10-10-92, Bonhams, #43, illus.), 20 x 16 in., (50.8 x 40.6 cm.), photograph (BP 308, DM 771, FR 2589, Y 63,185).

$593* *Marilyn Monroe, Beside The Sea, Head Turned Over Shoulder, Smiling,* blind embossed, #10/99, (10-10-92, Bonhams, #36, illus.), 14 x 11 in., (35.6 x 27.9 cm.), photograph (BP 352, DM 881, FR 2958, Y 72,194).

$495* *Marilyn Monroe, Bookstore (AD041),* proof, Limited Edition 99, blind embossed sig., (04-26-93, Selkirk, #547), 27 x 24 in., (68.6 x 61 cm.), b/w photograph (BP 312, DM 776, FR 2620, Y 54,624).

$556* *Marilyn Monroe, Close-Up Hand To Mouth,* special effect print, blind embossed, #10/99, (10-10-92, Bonhams, #55, illus.), 14 x 11 in., (35.6 x 27.9 cm.), photograph (BP 330, DM 826, FR 2773, Y 67,689).

$334* *Marilyn Monroe, Dancing On Patio,* blind embossed, #2/99, estate edit., (10-10-92, Bonhams, #42, illus.), 24 x 20 in., (61 x 50.8 cm.), photograph (BP 198, DM 496, FR 1666, Y 40,662).

$408* *Marilyn Monroe, Dancing On The Patio,* blind embossed, #10/99, (10-10-92, Bonhams, #51, illus.), 14 x 11 in., (35.6 x 27.9 cm.), photograph (BP 242, DM 606, FR 2035, Y 49,671).

$593* *Marilyn Monroe, Hair In Turban, Holding Up Towel Decorated With NudeFigure And Butterfly,* blind embossed, #10/99, (10-10-92, Bonhams, #48, illus.), 14 x 11 in., (35.6 x 27.9 cm.), photograph (BP 352, DM 881, FR 2958, Y 72,194).

$408* *Marilyn Monroe, Half Figure In White Bathing Suit, Arms Raised Holding Up Hair,* blind embossed, #10/99, (10-10-92, Bonhams, #34, illus.), 14 x 11 in., (35.6 x 27.9 cm.), photograph (BP 242, DM 606, FR 2035, Y 49,671).

$1205* *Marilyn Monroe, In Cloak Against Telegraph Pole At Night,* blind embossed, #10/99, (10-10-92, Bonhams, #56, illus.), 14 x 11 in., (35.6 x 27.9 cm.), photograph (BP 715, DM 1790, FR 6010, Y 146,701).

$649* *Marilyn Monroe, In Sleveless Sweater,* blind embossed, #10/99, (10-10-92, Bonhams, #52, illus.), 14 x 11 in., (35.6 x 27.9 cm.), photograph (BP 385, DM 964, FR 3237, Y 79,011).

$834* *Marilyn Monroe, In Swimsuit With White Umbrella,* blind embossed, #10/99, (10-10-92, Bonhams, #33, illus.), 14 x 11 in., (35.6 x 27.9 cm.), photograph (BP 495, DM 1239, FR 4160, Y 101,534).

$334* *Marilyn Monroe, Kneeling Beside Fireplace, Wrapped In Towel,* blind embossed, #10/99, (10-10-92, Bonhams, #47, illus.), 14 x 11 in., (35.6 x 27.9 cm.), photograph (BP 198, DM 496, FR 1666, Y 40,662).

$649* *Marilyn Monroe, Kneeling On Beach With Red And White Umbrella,* blind embossed, #7/99, (10-10-92, Bonhams, #32, illus.), 14 x 11 in., (35.6 x 27.9 cm.), color photograph (BP 385, DM 964, FR 3237, Y 79,011).

$1391* *Marilyn Monroe, Kneeling On Log Beside Sea,* life time unique original print, i. 1949, (10-10-92, Bonhams, #37, illus.), 14 x 11 in., (35.6 x 27.9 cm.), photograph (BP 825, DM 2066, FR 6938, Y 169,345).

$779* *Marilyn Monroe, On Beach Leaning Over Umbrella,* blind stamp, #10/99, (10-10-92, Bonhams, #31, illus.), 14 x 11 in., (35.6 x 27.9 cm.), photograph (BP 462, DM 1157, FR 3885, Y 94,838).

$705* *Marilyn Monroe, On Bed With Milk And Eggs,* blind stamp, #10/99, (10-10-92, Bonhams, #46, illus.), 11 x 14 in., (27.9 x 35.6 cm.), photograph (BP 418, DM 1047, FR 3516, Y 85,829).

$519* *Marilyn Monroe, On Terrace Brushing Hair,* #10/99, (10-10-92, Bonhams, #49, illus.), 14 x 11 in., (35.6 x 27.9 cm.), photograph (BP 308, DM 771, FR 2589, Y 63,185).

$649* *Marilyn Monroe, Pensive,* blind embossed, #10/99, (10-10-92, Bonhams, #53, illus.), 14 x 11 in., (35.6 x 27.9 cm.), photograph (BP 385, DM 964, FR 3237, Y 79,011).

$1576* *Marilyn Monroe, Portrait, Full Face, Smiling,* life time unique original print, stamp, (10-10-92, Bonhams, #38, illus.), 14 x 11 in., (35.6 x 27.9 cm.), photograph (BP 935, DM 2341, FR 7860, Y 191,868).

$352* *Marilyn Monroe, Portrait, Smiling,* blind embossed, #10/99, (10-10-92, Bonhams, #50, illus.), 14 x 11 in., (35.6 x 27.9 cm.), photograph (BP 209, DM 523, FR 1756, Y 42,854).

$5006* *Marilyn Monroe, Reclining On Bed With Milk And Eggs,* s., orig. life time print, studio stamp, (10-10-92, Bonhams, #40, illus.), 20 x 24 in., (50.8 x 61 cm.), photograph (BP 2970, DM 7436, FR 24,968, Y 609,447).

$556* *Marilyn Monroe, Reclining On Blanket In Garden With Dumbbell,* blind embossed, #10/99, (10-10-92, Bonhams, #44, illus.), 14 x 11 in., (35.6 x 27.9 cm.), photograph (BP 330, DM 826, FR 2773, Y 67,689).

BI *Marilyn Monroe, Shoulderstand On Blanket In Garden, Legs Apart,* blind embossed, #2/99, est. BP 150/200, (10-10-92, Bonhams, #44A, illus.), 20 x 16 in., (50.8 x 40.6 cm.), photograph.

$315* *Marilyn Monroe, Silhouetted On Beach Against Sunset,* blind embossed, #10/99, (10-10-92, Bonhams, #30, illus.), 14 x 11 in., (35.6 x 27.9 cm.), photograph (BP 187, DM 468, FR 1571, Y 38,349).

$2781* *Marilyn Monroe, Sitting By Fireplace, Wrapped In Towel,* original life time print, studio stamp, (10-10-92, Bonhams, #41, illus.), 24 x 20 in., (61 x 50.8 cm.), photograph (BP 1650, DM 4131, FR 13,870, Y 338,568).

$649* *Marilyn Monroe, Smiling, Both Hands Together,* blind embossed, #10/99, (10-10-92, Bonhams, #54, illus.), 14 x 11 in., (35.6 x 27.9 cm.), photograph (BP 385, DM 964, FR 3237, Y 79,011).

$649* *Marilyn Monroe, Standing On One Leg, Arms Outstretched On Beach,* blind embossed, #10/99, (10-10-92, Bonhams, #35, illus.), 14 x 11 in., (35.6 x 27.9 cm.), photograph (BP 385, DM 964, FR 3237, Y 79,011).

$464* *Marilyn Monroe, Wrapped In Towel, Hair In Turban, On Massage Bench,* blind embossed, #10/99, (10-10-92, Bonhams, #45, illus.), 14 x 11 in., (35.6 x 27.9 cm.), photograph (BP 275, DM 689, FR 2314, Y 56,489).

$890* *Marilyn, Smiling Portrait, On The Beach,* blind embossed, #2/99, (10-10-92, Bonhams, #39, illus.), 20 x 16 in., (50.8 x 40.6 cm.), photograph (BP 528, DM 1322, FR 4439, Y 108,352).

$1650* *"Norma Jeane Standing On A Highway (AD005)", "Marilyn At The Beach Kneeling On Driftwood (AD028)", "Marilyn Wrapped In A Towel (AD009)", "Marilyn With Milk And Eggs (AD060)" and "Marilyn In A Sleeveless Sweater (AD012)": Five,* blind embossed sig., Limited Edition 99, each #4/99, one #7/99, De Dienes, Andre. MARILYN MON AMOUR. New York: St. Martin's Press, 1985, (04-26-93, Selkirk, #555, illus.), each 14 x 11 in., (35.6 x 27.9 cm.), b/w photograph (BP 1041, DM 2586, FR 8735, Y 182,079).

$649* *Norma Jeane, Barefoot Entering Farm Doorway,* blind stamp, #10/99, (10-10-92, Bonhams, #22, illus.), 14 x 11 in., (35.6 x 27.9 cm.), photograph (BP 385, DM 964, FR 3237, Y 79,011).

$556* *Norma Jeane, Barefooted On Highway,* blind embossed, #10/99, (10-10-92, Bonhams, #29, illus.), 14 x 11 in., (35.6 x 27.9 cm.), photograph (BP 330, DM 826, FR 2773, Y 67,689).

$315* *Norma Jeane, Climbing, Dressed In Jeans And Red And White Striped Shirt,* blind embossed, #7/99, (10-10-92, Bonhams, #25, illus.), 14 x 11 in., (35.6 x 27.9 cm.), photograph (BP 187, DM 468, FR 1571, Y 38,349).

$556* *Norma Jeane, In Field Holding Baby Lamb,* blind embossed, #10/99, (10-10-92, Bonhams, #28, illus.), 14 x

11 in., (35.6 x 27.9 cm.), photograph (BP 330, DM 826, FR 2773, Y 67,689).

$890* *Norma Jeane, In Jeans, Hands In Belt Loops,* blind embossed, #10/99, (10-10-92, Bonhams, #26, illus.), 14 x 11 in., (35.6 x 27.9 cm.), photograph (BP 528, DM 1322, FR 4439, Y 108,352).

$408* *Norma Jeane, In The Snow,* blind embossed, #10/99, (10-10-92, Bonhams, #27, illus.), 14 x 11 in., (35.6 x 27.9 cm.), photograph (BP 242, DM 606, FR 2035, Y 49,671).

$408* *Norma Jeane, Kneeling In Woodlands, Hair Tied With White Ribbon,* blind emboss, #10/99, (10-10-92, Bonhams, #23, illus.), 14 x 11 in., (35.6 x 27.9 cm.), photograph (BP 242, DM 606, FR 2035, Y 49,671).

$204* *Norma Jeane, Sitting On Wall, Mountain Background,* blind embossed, #10/99, (10-10-92, Bonhams, #24, illus.), 14 x 11 in., (35.6 x 27.9 cm.), photograph (BP 121, DM 303, FR 1017, Y 24,836).

$1540* *"Portrait Of Marilyn" (AD014), "Marilyn Outside Brushing Her Hair" (AD08), "Marilyn By A Fireplace Wrapped In A Towel" (AD035), "Marilyn On The Beach With Umbrella" (AD006), "Smiling Marilyn With Hollywood Sign" (AD048): Five,* blind embossed sig., Limited Edition 99, each #4/99, De Dienes, Andre. MARILYN MON AMOUR. New York: St. Martin's Press, 1985, (04-26-93, Selkirk, #554, illus.), each 14 x 11 in., (35.6 x 27.9 cm.), b/w photograph (BP 972, DM 2414, FR 8152, Y 169,940).

DE KOONING, Willem   American b. 1904

BI *21 Etchings And Poems: Revenge (G. 1), 1960,* s., annot. artist proof, pub. Morris Gallery, full margins, good cond., creases light-struck, est. $2,5/3,500, (02-24-93, Butterfield, #3069, illus.), 11¹³/₁₆ x 13⅝ in., (300 x 346 mm.), etching w/aquatint on wove.

BI *Clam Digger (Graham 10), 1971,* s., d. '70, #17/34, pub. Knoedler Gallery, full margins, good cond.,soiling, skinned spots, est. $3/4,000, (11-07-92, Sotheby-NY, #637, illus.), sheet 40½ x 28 in., (102.9 x 71.1 cm.), lithograph on J.B. Green.

$1320* *Clam Digger, 1966,* s., annot. A.P., (12-08-92, Swann, #169, illus.), 17 x 22⅜ in., (43.2 x 56.8 cm.), lithograph on Arches cream wove (BP 827, DM 2055, FR 7006, Y 163,609).

$1650* *Devil At The Keyboard,* s., num. 62/75, full margins, good cond., staining, surface soiling, (02-24-93, Butterfield, #3071, illus.), 20½ x 18¼ in., (521 x 464 mm.), lithograph in colors on wove (BP 1151, DM 2679, FR 9081, Y 193,617).

BI *From Etchings And Poems: Revenge (G. 1), 1960,* s., annot. artist proof, pub. Morris Gallery, full margins, good cond., creases, light-struck, est. $3/5,000, (10-28-92, Butterfield, #3005, illus.), 11¹³/₁₆ x 13⅝ in., (300 x 346 mm.), etching w/aquatint on cream wove.

BI *Landing Place (Graham 6), 1971,* s., d. 70, #11/54, pub. Knoedler, Hollander's Workshop blindstamp, full margins, excell. cond., est. $3/4,000, (05-11-93, Christie-NY, #479, illus.), sheet 29 x 37 in., (737 x 940 mm.), lithograph on Akawara laid.

$7188* *Landscape At Stanton Street (G. 26), 1971,* s., d., #50/60, blindstamp, co-pub. Hollanders Workshop and Fourcade, full margins, good cond., handling creases, (05-15-93, Sotheby-NY, #1052, illus.), 25⅜ x 18⅞ in., (64.5 x 47.9 cm.), lithograph on Dutch etching (BP 4674, DM 11,562, FR 38,854, Y 796,807).

BI *Lithographs For Frank O'Hara, 1988: Seventeen,* complete deluxe portfolio, each bears the bon-a-tirer facsimile sig.,annot. P P I/IV, pub. Limited Editions Club, transfer or drawings on mylar by Benjamin Shift at American Atelier, p. Trestle Editions, Ltd., excell. cond., original presentation box, est. $80/100,000, (05-19-93, Butterfield, #2231, illus.), each 14 x 11 in., (356 x 279 mm.), each sh 27½ x 23 in., (356 x 279 mm.), lithograph on handmade Japanese Yame, chine applique to handmade Twinrocker.

$8625* *The Man And The Big Blond, 1982,* s., #110/150, blindstamp of pub., Rainbow Art Foundation, good cond., scuff mark, soiling, (02-11-93, Sotheby-NY, #364, illus.), 21¼ x 26¹⁵⁄₁₆ in., (540 x 685 mm.), color lithograph (BP 6086, DM 14,287, FR 48,346, Y 1,039,783).

BI *Man And The Big Blonde, 1982,* facsimilie sig., #XIII/ CL, pub. Rainbow Art Foundation, p. American Atelier, margins, very good cond.?, est. $1/1,5000, (05-19-93, Butterfield, #2229), 21¼ x 27 in., (540 x 686 mm.), lithograph in colors on wove.

$1980* *Paris Review, 1979,* s., num. 146/200, full margins, good cond., crease, (02-24-93, Butterfield, #3072, illus.), (584 x 743 mm.), offset lithograph in colors on wove (BP 1381, DM 3214, FR 10,897, Y 232,340).

$4025* *Poems, Frank O'Hara, 1988,* entexte, facsimile sig., #356/500, pub. Limited Editions Club, mylartransfers p. at American Atelier by Benjamin Shiff, excellent cond., original binding and presentation box, (05-19-93, Butterfield, #2230), 22¾ x 17⅞ in., (578 x 454 mm.), lithograph on Japanese Kitakata (BP 2613, DM 6543, FR 22,043, Y 445,588).

$1430* *Portfolio 9: Clam Digger, 1966,* s., num. XIV/XX, blind-stamp printer Irwin Hollander, printer pub. Hollander Workshop, (09-20-92, Hindman, #712), 15¾ x 12 in., (40 x 30.5 cm.), lithograph on Arches (BP 837, DM 2122, FR 7259, Y 176,740).

$7475* *The Preacher (G. 27), 1971,* s., d., #53/60, blindstamp, co-pub. Hollanders Workshop and Fourcade, full margins, good cond., discoloration, (05-15-93, Sotheby-NY, #1053, illus.), 25¼ x 18⅞ in., (64.1 x 47.9 cm.), lithograph on Arches buff (BP 4860, DM 12,023, FR 40,405, Y 828,622).

BI *"Quatre Lithographies", 1986:* Four, XXVIII/L, s., num., d., est. SF 6/10,000, (12-05-92, Mangisch, #541), 28⅜ x 24⅝ in., (72 x 62.5 cm.), lithograph.

BI *Quatre Lithographies, 1986:* Four, portfolio, #XXVIII/L, s., d., est. SF 10/12,000, (04-21-93, Germann, #52, illus.), 28⅛ x 24⅝ in., (714 x 626 mm.), color litho-graph.

$1870* *Rainbow, Devil At The Keyboard,* s., #37/75, full mar-gins, good cond.?, surface soiling, (10-28-92, Butterfield, #3006), 20½ x 18¼ in., (521 x 464 mm.), color litho-graph on wove (BP 1191, DM 2888, FR 9806, Y 229,448).

$440* *Rainbow, Devil At The Keyboard,* linen-backed support, plate s., (05-27-93, Swann, #150), sh 36 x 25 in., (91.4 x 63.5 cm.), color lithographed poster (BP 282, DM 706, FR 2380, Y 47,170).

$124* *Rainbow, Devil At The Keyboard,* s. in stone, small creases, (03-31-93, Briest, #E59), 35⅝ x 24⁷⁄₁₆ in., (90.5 x 62 cm.), lithograph poster (BP 82, DM 199, FR 678, Y 14,259).

BI *Rainbow-Devil At The Keyboard,* stone, est. SF 450/550, (04-21-93, Germann, #580), 35⅝ x 24¹³⁄₁₆ in., (905 x 630 mm.), color lithograph.

$2875* *Revenge (Graham 1), 1960,* s., #42/50, from portfolio 21 Etchings and Poems, pub. Morris Gallery, full margins, good cond., (05-15-93, Sotheby-NY, #1051, illus.), 11¾ x 13⅝ in., (29.8 x 34.6 cm.), etching and aquatint (BP 1869, DM 4624, FR 15,541, Y 318,701).

BI *Souvenir Of Montauk (G. 9), 1971,* s., d. 70, #38/43, pub. Knoedler, Hollander's Workshop blindstamp, full margins, creases, excell. cond., est. $3,5/4,500, (05-11-93, Christie-NY, #480, illus.), sheet 43¼ x 35 in., (109.9 x 88.9 cm.), lithograph on Akawara.

$1650* *Two Figures,* s. in ink (faded), num. 89/100, blindstamp, full margins, apparentlygood cond., (02-24-93, Butterfield, #3070, illus.), 14 x 23 in., (356 x 584 mm.), offset lithograph on wove (BP 1151, DM 2679, FR 9081, Y 193,617).

$1210* *Two Women,* s., d. 1973, #24/100, (12-13-92, Hindman, #337), 14 x 11 in., lithograph (BP 774, DM 1902, FR 6481, Y 149,697).

$3025* *Two Women, 1973,* s., d., #3/100, blindstamp, pub. Styria Studio, Ltd., full margins, good cond., (11-07-92, Sotheby-NY, #638, illus.), sheet 18⅛ x 15⅛ in., (460 x 384 mm.), lithograph (BP 1978, DM 4830, FR 16,325, Y 373,365).

BI *Untitled, (19)86,* s., d., num., from the series Quatre Lithographies, est. DM 2500, (12-01-92, Karl/Faber, #875, illus.), sh 28⅛ x 24¹³⁄₁₆ in., (71.5 x 63 cm.), color lithograph.

$1245* *Untitled, (19)86,* s., d., from the series Quatre Lithogra-phies, (12-01-92, Karl/Faber, #876), sh 28⅛ x 24¹³⁄₁₆ in., (71.5 x 63 cm.), color lithograph (BP 823, DM 1984, FR 6763, Y 155,005).

$1840* *Untitled, 1987,* from Untitled, s., d. 86, #97/100, pub. Editions de la Difference, creases, tear, soiling, very good cond., (05-11-93, Christie-NY, #482, illus.), sheet 28¼ x 24¾ in., (718 x 629 mm.), color lithograph on Arches (BP 1175, DM 2899, FR 9766, Y 202,398).

BI *Untitled, From 'Quatre Lithographies', 1986,* s., num.; s., num., p. Art Estampe, good cond., est. BP 8/1,200, (12-03-92, Sotheby-London, #761), 28⅜ x 24⅝ in., (720 x 625 mm.), lithograph in colors on Arches.

$1023* *Untitled, From 'Quatre Lithographies', 1986,* s., d., #1/ 100, p. Art Estampe, good cond., (12-03-92, Sotheby-London, #760, illus.), 28⅛ x 24⅝ in., (715 x 626 mm.), lithograph in colors on Arches (BP 660, DM 1609, FR 5491, Y 127,286).

BI *Valentine (G. 16), 1971,* s., d. 70, #25/47, pub. Knoedler, Hollander's Workshop blindstamp, full margins, creases, excell. cond., est. $3/4,000, (05-11-93, Christie-NY, #481), sheet 37 x 28 in., (940 x 711 mm.), lithograph on Suzuki laid.

DE LAUNAY, N.
$187* *"La Bonne Merre",* after Fragonard, i., pub. Paris, (12-06-92, Neal, #928), plate 22⅜ x 17 in., (56.8 x 43.2 cm.), engraving (BP 117, DM 292, FR 994, Y 23,169).

DE LOSQUES (Daniel THOUROUDE)   1880-1915
$499* *Mistinguett, c. 1910,* cond. A, (03-16-93, Boisgirard, #90), 73¼ x 39⅜ in., (186 x 100 cm.), poster (BP 345, DM 830, FR 2819, Y 58,349).

DE MASSO, F.
$202* *"Saint Claude", "Saint Christophe", "Saint Jean Baptiste", "Sainte Marie Madeleine", Etc.: Twelve,* yellowed, trimmed, glued, faults, (02-03-93, Ader Tajan, #19), etch-ing and copper engraving (BP 141, DM 333, FR 1128, Y 25,128).

DE MEYER, Baron Adolf   American 1868-1946
$2300* *Camera Work Number 40: Fourteen,* pub./edit. by Alfred Steiglitz, Oct. 1912, each tipped to mount, (04-08-93, Christie-NY, #84, illus.), each approx. 8½ x 6½ in., (21.6 x 16.5 cm.), photograph, photogravures on Japanese tissue from orig. negs. and devoted exclusively to work of De Meyer (BP 1508, DM 3695, FR 12,507, Y 261,008).

BI *Cap Ferrat,* s. by photog., stamp, 1920's, p. c. 1940, (10-15-92, Sotheby-NY, #108, illus.), 14 x 11 in., (35.6 x 27.9 cm.), photograph, gelatin silver print.

$1560* *Clara Kimball Young,* 1918, s., mounted, (12-17-92, Christie-S. Ken, #9, illus.), 9½ x 7½ in., (24.1 x 19.1 cm.), photograph, warm-toned platinum print (BP 990, DM 2436, FR 8320, Y 191,717).

$805* *"The Cup", "Windows On The Bosphorus", "A Street In China", Aida, A Maid Of Tangier", "Miss J. Ranken", "Mrs. Wiggins Of Belgrove Square", "The Silver Cap" and "The Balloon Man", 1912: Eight,* from Camerawork #40, October 1912, est. $800/1,200, (05-23-93, Butter-field, #3393, illus.), each approx. 8½ x 6½ in., photogra-vure (BP 524, DM 1316, FR 4430, Y 88,980).

BI *Eleanora Duse (cf. Harper's Bazaar, Oct. 1922, p. 86), 1922,* s. by photog. in margin, archive stamp verso, p. c. 1940, est. $4/6,000, (10-15-92, Sotheby-NY, #107A, illus.), 14 x 6⅞ in., (35.6 x 17.5 cm.), photograph, gela-tin silver print.

BI *Elsa Maxwell, (c. 1940),* 1950s, s., est. $9/12,000, (10-13-92, Christie-NY, #181, illus.), 14 x 11 in., (35.6 x 27.9 cm.), photograph, gelatin silver print.

$1150* *Man With Statue, early 1900's,* (04-06-93, Sotheby-NY, #216, illus.), 3⅞ x 3⅜ in., photograph, platinum print (BP 760, DM 1853, FR 6274, Y 131,159).

$433* *Mary Pickford, Autographed Portrait, c. 1918-19,* ink s., i., pencil annots., (12-17-92, Christie-S. Ken, #74), 9¹⁄₁₆ x 6⅞ in., (23 x 17.5 cm.), photograph, gelatin silver print (BP 275, DM 676, FR 2309, Y 53,214).

BI *Olga Petrova, n.d. (1920s),* various annots., credits, est. BP 5/800, (12-17-92, Christie-S. Ken, #10), 9⅜ x 7⅜ in., (23.8 x 18.7 cm.), photograph, warm-toned platinum print.

$357* *Portrait Of A Model (For Vogue), 1918,* notations, handstamp, (10-14-92, Swann, #433, illus.), 9½ x 7½ in., (24.1 x 19.1 cm.), photograph, platinum print (BP 210, DM 522, FR 1772, Y 43,262).

BI *Portrait Of Lucian S. Kirtland, c. 1910,* photog.'s sig., est. $800/1,200, (04-07-93, Swann, #444, illus.), 8 x 6¼ in., photograph, platinum print.

BI *Portrait Of Olga, c. 1910,* s., est. $3/5,000, (10-13-92, Christie-NY, #37, illus.), 13 x 9⅝ in., (33 x 24.4 cm.), photograph, platinum print.

BI *Woman In Black Lace Gown, c. 1930,* s. on mount, est. $2,5/3,000, (10-13-92, Christie-NY, #180, illus.), 9⅝ x 7½ in., (24.4 x 19.1 cm.), photograph, gelatin silver print.

DE PASSE DE OUDE, Crispin 1565-1637

$1833* *Die Funf Sinne (Hollstein 499-504), c. 1600,* (06-23-93, Kornfeld, #75), engraving (BP 1245, DM 3102, FR 10,433, Y 199,695, SF 2760).

DE ROUGEMENT, Guy

$77* *Composition, 1977,* s., d., 9/100, losses, (06-28-93, Loudmer, #361), 23⅝ x 16 9/16 in., (600 x 420 mm.), sh 26 3/16 x 18⅞ in., (600 x 420 mm.), color lithograph on Arches wove (BP 52, DM 131, FR 441, Y 8170).

DE SCHELDE EN DE STAAD ((Antwerpe))

$66* *"European Harbor Scene",* annot., s. 14/50 Rom Maylar(?), (10-11-92, Dunning, #1533), 21½ x 31 in., (54.6 x 78.7 cm.), etching (BP 39, DM 98, FR 329, Y 8035).

DEACON, Richard b. 1949

$3450* *Muzot, 1987: Four,* inits., d., #12/25, pub. Margarete Roeder Editions, excell. cond., (05-11-93, Christie-NY, #390, illus.), each sheet 25¼ x 25¼ in., (641 x 641 mm.), etching and aquatint on wove and oil cloth (BP 2202, DM 5435, FR 18,312, Y 379,496).

DEAN, John (after George MORLAND)

$348* *A Rural Feast, 1790,* pub. John Dean, trimmed to 1/4 in. margins, defects, (10-27-92, Phillips-London, #64), 18⅛ x 23⅝ in., (460 x 600 mm.), mezzotint w/hand-coloring on laid (BP 220, DM 533, FR 1810, Y 42,569).

DEAN, John (after Joshua REYNOLDS)

$226* *Sleeping Cupid, 1797,* watermark, scratch-letter proof, pub. Dean, water stained, stains, (10-27-92, Phillips-London, #61), plate 15⅓ x 10¾ in., (389 x 273 mm.), mezzotint on laid (BP 143, DM 346, FR 1175, Y 27,645).

DEBEURE, H.

$72* *La Reine De Broadway (Cover Girl) (French),* (01-31-93, Morelle/Marchan, #119), 12 3/16 x 8 11/16 in., (31 x 22 cm.), poster (BP 48, DM 116, FR 392, Y 8982).

DEBONNET, Maurice G. American 1872-1946

BI *Coastal Fishing Village,* s. in plate, est. $100/150, (10-30-92, Sloan, #822), 6⅞ x 7⅞ in., (17.5 x 20 cm.), etching.

BI *Coastal Fishing Village,* s. in plate, est. $1/150, (12-10-92, Sloan, #316), 6⅞ x 7⅞ in., (17.5 x 20 cm.), etching.

DEBRE, Olivier French b. 1920

$189* *"Composition-1987": Two,* #32/50, mono., #36/50, s., d., (01-28-93, Pescheteau, #115), each 9¼ x 7⅞ in., (23.5 x 20 cm.), color lithograph on wove (BP 125, DM 299, FR 1013, Y 23,467).

$162* *Femme Noire, 1959,* s., #9/10, (05-27-93, Briest, #75), 29 15/16 x 19 11/16 in., (76 x 50 cm.), lithograph (BP 104, DM 260, FR 876, Y 17,367).

$404* *"Musique De Xiane", 1990,* #49/75, s., (10-18-92, Pescheteau, #119), 39 9/16 x 29 15/16 in., (100.5 x 76 cm.), lithogrpah in colors on velin (BP 245, DM 597, FR 2027, Y 48,239).

DEBUCOURT, Philibert Louis French 1755-1832

$255* *La Caleche Renversee (M. Fenaille, 307),* good margins, (06-16-93, Ader Tajan, #30), aquatint and etching in 2-tones w/embellishment (BP 170, DM 423, FR 1421, Y 27,197).

$391* *La Chasse (M. Fenaille 141),* after Claude Vernet, first state of 2, before letters, margins, (05-06-93, Laurin, #23), aquatint (BP 248, DM 616, FR 2073, Y 43,019).

$4662* *Le Chasseur (Dayot 4b), c. 1801,* after Carle Vernet, pub. Rolland, trimmed, foxing, (12-01-92, Christie-London, #284, illus.), sheet 19⅛ x 22⅜ in., (485 x 568 mm.), etching w/engraving in colors (BP 3080, DM 7431, FR 25,323, Y 580,428).

BI *Les Deux Baisers (Fenaille 7), 1786,* pub. state, margins, short tears, foxing, discoloration, est. BP 2/3,000, (12-03-92, Sotheby-London, #35, illus.), 14½ x 16½ in., (368 x 419 mm.), etching and aquatint in colors.

$3663* *Les Deux Baisers (Fenaille 7; P. and B., I, p. 693, no. 3; Inventaire 18e Siecle, Vi, p. 164, no. 4), 1786,* pub. Debucourt, margin, trimmed, soiling, (12-01-92, Christie-London, #278, illus.), sheet 13 13/16 x 16⅝ in., (351 x 422 mm.), etching w/engraving in colors (black, blue, red and yellow) (BP 2420, DM 5838, FR 19,897, Y 456,051).

$2497* *Fin De La Course (Fenaille 157; Dayot 32d; Inventaire 18e Siecle, VI, p. 69, no. 16), c. 1804,* after Carle Vernet, 1st state of 4, pub. Rolland, margins, soiling, (12-01-92, Christie-London, #283, illus.), plate 18⅛ x 23 1/16 in., (460 x 585 mm.), etching w/engraving (BP 1650, DM 3980, FR 13,563, Y 310,881).

BI *"Heur Et Malheur, Ou La Cruche Cassee" and "L'Esclade Ou Les Adieux Du Matin" (Fenaille 12-13; Inventaire 18e Siecle, VI, p. 166, nos. 8-9), 1787: Pair,* 3rd (final) state, pub. Debucourt, margins, staining, defects, prov., est. BP 5/8,000, (12-01-92, Christie-London, #276, illus.), plate 14⅝ x 11 1/16 in., (371 x 281 mm.), etching w/engraving iln colors (black, blue, red and yellow).

$275* *La Noce Au chateau,* (07-03-92, Sloan, #337), image 12 x 9 in., (30.5 x 22.9 cm.), color engraving (BP 144, DM 416, FR 1403, Y 34,281).

$5463* *La Promenade Publique (Fenaille 33), 1792,* 3rd (final) state, watermark, trimmed, registration marks on 3 sides,-mat-staining, paper losses, foxing, i., exhib., (05-13-93, Sotheby-NY, #313, illus.), 17¾ x 21¼ in., (451 x 540 mm.), etching, engraving and aquatint in colors (BP 3587, DM 8821, FR 29,755, Y 609,914).

BI *La Promenade Publique (Fenaille 33; P. and B., I, p. 695, no. 12; Inventaire 18e Siecle, VI, p. 175, no. 26), 1792,* 2nd state of 3, pub. Depeuille, trimmed to platemark, losses, reparied holes, stained, est. BP 14/18,000, (12-01-92, Christie-London, #277, illus.), sheet 17 11/16 x 25 3/16 in., (449 x 639 mm.), etching w/aquatint and engraving in colors (black, blue, red and yellow).

$295* *Route Du Marche (M.F., 409), 1819,* definitive state, trimmed, staining, (06-16-93, Ader Tajan, #31), 11 7/16 x 15¾ in., (29 x 40 cm.), aquatint in 2 tones and color (BP 197, DM 490, FR 1643, Y 31,463).

BI *Sortie D'Un Officier D'Hussard Francais (Fenaille 174/I (v.II)), 1808,* artist's proof, light-stained, est. DM 400, (12-01-92, Karl/Faber, #43), aquatint.

DECARAVA, Roy b. 1919

$1725* *"Coltrane And Elvin, New York" and "Graham, New York": Two,* 1960 and 1952, p.l., both s.; first ink s., t., d., lit., (04-08-93, Christie-NY, #481, illus.), each approx. 10 x 13 in., (25.4 x 33 cm.), photograph, gelatin silver print (BP 1131, DM 2771, FR 9380, Y 195,756).

$805* *Hallway, New York,* 1953, p. 1982, ink s., d., (c) insig., lit., (04-08-93, Christie-NY, #482, illus.), 13 x 8⅝ in., (33 x 21.9 cm.), photograph, gelatin silver print (BP 528, DM 1293, FR 4377, Y 91,353).

BI *Man In Window, New York,* 1978, p. 1982, ink s., d., (c) insig.; ink t., lit., est. $1,2/1,500, (04-08-93, Christie-NY, #483, illus.), 13 x 8⅝ in., (33 x 21.9 cm.), photograph, gelatin silverprint.

DECKER, Fred

$110* *Aerial Jungle, 1948,* s., t., d., num. 2/15, light staining, mat burn, foxing, backboard burn, toning, (05-22-93, Weschler, #176), 12 x 17½ in., (30.5 x 44.5 cm.), etching in colors (BP 71, DM 179, FR 602, Y 12,128).

DECKER, P.

$575* *Late Baroque Interior Designs: Three,* engraved by M. Engelbrecht et al., pub. Jereias Wolff, 18th cent., (04-07-93, Sotheby-Arcade, #183), sight 13½ x 17 in., (34.3 x 43.2 cm.), engraving (BP 380, DM 930, FR 3147, Y 65,326).

DECOCK, Lilianne

BI *"Two Barns, Sierra City, California", 1970's,* s., photog. stamp, est. $1,2/1,500, (11-16-92, Butterfield, #5933, illus.), 14½ x 17¹³⁄₁₆ in., (369 x 451.7 mm.), photograph, gelatin silver print.

DECURMORE, Francis

$357* *Repos Ste, Elisabeth, 1920,* Vromant et Cie Imp., A cond., creasing, (08-06-92, Swann, #112, illus.), 33½ x 24 in., (85.1 x 61 cm.), (BP 186, DM 527, FR 1781, Y 45,536).

DEFESCHE, Pieter b. 1921

BI *Hemelse En Aardse Liefde, 1991,* s., d., #23/80, full margins, good cond., est. G 2/300, (12-09-92, Sotheby-Amstrdm, #554), 16⁵⁄₁₆ x 23¹¹⁄₁₆ in., (415 x 601 mm.), color lithograph on wove.

BI *Hemelse En Aardse Liefde, 1991,* s., d., #23/80, full margins, good cond., est. G 2/300, (12-09-92, Sotheby-Amstrdm, #555), 16¹⁄₁₆ x 22⅝ in., (408 x 575 mm.), color lithograph on wove.

BI *Hemelse En Aardse Liefde, 1991,* s., d., #23/80, full margins, good cond., est. G 2/300, (12-09-92, Sotheby-Amstrdm, #556), 15½ x 23⁵⁄₁₆ in., (393 x 592 mm.), color lithograph on wove.

$130* *Hemelse En Aardse Liefde, 1991,* s., d., #23/80, full margins, good cond., (12-09-92, Sotheby-Amstrdm, #557), 16⁹⁄₁₆ x 24 in., (420 x 610 mm.), color lithograph on wove (BP 83, DM 204, FR 696, Y 16,119, G 230).

DEFOREST, Roy American b. 1930

$358* *"Untitled" and "Untitled", 1978: Two,* each s., d., 1st num. 10/30, 2nd annot. Color trial Proof, blindstamp, 2nd w/full margins, 1st apparently good cond., 2nd good cond., tear, creases, (02-24-93, Butterfield, #3209), 30 x 44½ in., (76.2 x 113 cm.), 27½ x 41½ in., (76.2 x 113 cm.), lithograph, 1 p. in white on black wove & other p. in sanguine on gray Rives BFK (BP 250, DM 581, FR 1970, Y 42,009).

$633* *Untitled, 1980,* s., d., #2/20, blindstamp publisher, Tamarind Institute, p. Paul Rangell and Catherine Kuhn, very good cond., (05-19-93, Butterfield, #2153), sh 22½ x 30 in., (572 x 762 mm.), lithograph in colors on German Etching (BP 411, DM 1029, FR 3467, Y 70,076).

$288* *Untitled, 1982,* s, #67/100, blindstamp publisher, Ernest De Soto Workshop, good cond., (05-19-93, Butterfield, #2154), 24¾ x 31¾ in., (629 x 806 mm.), lithograph in colors on wove (BP 187, DM 468, FR 1577, Y 31,883).

DEGAS, Edgar French 1834-1917

$1073* *"Au Louvre: La Peinture" and "Danseuse Mettant Son Chausson" (L. Delteil, 29 and 36): Two,* (04-02-93, Picard, #81), etching (BP 707, DM 1725, FR 5857, Y 122,168).

$358* *Autoportrait, Self-Portrait (A. 13, D. 1, R./S. 8), 1857,* 5th final state, p.l., margins, good cond., light-staining, rubbed area, surface scuff w/ink loss in image, notations, surface soiling, (10-28-92, Butterfield, #2801), 9⅛ x 5⅝ in., (232 x 143 mm.), etching on laid Japan (BP 228, DM 553, FR 1877, Y 43,926).

$2217* *Le Bidet (Adhemar Et Cachin 147; J. 111), c. 1878-80,* second of two impressions, full margins, good cond., prov., (12-03-92, Sotheby-London, #276, illus.), 6¼ x 4¾ in., (159 x 121 mm.), monotype on wove (BP 1430, DM 3486, FR 11,900, Y 275,849).

$16,985* *Les Deux Arbres (E. Janis 273), c. 1878,* stamp, (06-11-93, Picard, #33, illus.), 3¼ x 2¾ in., (83 x 70 mm.), monotype on thin wove (BP 11,160, DM 27,604, FR 93,068, Y 1,802,122).

BI *The Engraver Joseph Tourny (R.S. 5),* from cancelled plate, p. by Lacouriere, bearing blindstamp, good cond., est. BP 3/400, (11-30-92, Phillips-London, #414), plate 9 x 5¾ in., (229 x 146 mm.), etching on Vieux Japan.

BI *Jockeys (1885),* est. DM 2000, (12-01-92, Karl/Faber, #183), 18½ x 21⅝ in., (47 x 55 cm.), color lithograph.

$191* *Loges D'Actrices,* bears t. verso, posthumous restrike, prov., (05-10-93, Hodgins, #314), 6¼ x 8¼ in., (15.9 x 21 cm.), etching on paper (BP 125, DM 307, FR 1035, Y 21,343, C$ 242).

BI *Repos Sur Le Lit (Janis 98; See Adhemar Et Cachin 103), c. 1878-1879,* counterproof, margins, good cond., prov., est. BP 6/8,000, (06-30-93, Sotheby-London, #416, illus.), sh 10⅝ x 6½ in., (270 x 165 mm.), monotype on wove.

BI *Singer At A Cafe-Concert (D. 53; A. 33; R./S. 26), 1876-77,* 1st state of 2, before added work below, margins, good cond., handling creases, ex-coll. Alexis Hubert Rouart, catalogue back cover lot, est. $60/80,000, (05-13-93, Sotheby-NY, #542, illus.), 10⅛ x 7¾ in., (256 x 198 mm.), sh 13⅜ x 10¾ in., (256 x 198 mm.), crayon lithograph (on stone) on wove.

$90,750* *The Song Of The Dog (Delteil 48; Adhemar 41; Reed & Shapiro 25), 1876-77,* margins, good cond., repaired tears, spots, (11-05-92, Sotheby-NY, #151, illus.), 14 x 9 in., (355 x 230 mm.), sheet 16⅝ x 11⅝ in., (355 x 230 mm.), crayon lithograph (from transfer paper) on cream wove (BP 59,024, DM 143,524, FR 485,554, Y 11,133,603).

BI *La Sortie Du Bain (Delteil 36; Adhemar 49; Reed/Shapiro 42), 1879-80,* 1st state (of 22), watermark, margins, good cond., margin tip re-attached, discoloration, water stains, discolored, ex-coll. Eugene Mayer, est. $40/60,000, (05-13-93, Sotheby-NY, #541, illus.), 5 x 5 in., (127 x 127 mm.), sh 7 x 8⅞ in., (127 x 127 mm.), drypoint on laid.

DEGAS, Edgar (after)

$246* *Avant La Course,* w/out margins, (02-24-93, Picard, #73), lithograph on thin wove (BP 172, DM 399, FR 1354, Y 28,866).

BI *La Famille Cardinale, (cf. Boston 71), 1939: Set Of Six,* 318/325, p. Maurice Potin, good cond., bound, est. $2,5/3,000, (11-09-92, Christie-NY, #84), 330 x 258 in., (838.2 x 655.3 cm.), 6 colored aquatints, 26 black aquatints, on Rives.

$84* *"Mlle. Becat Aux Ambassadeurs",* 1 out of 650, drystamp, (01-28-93, Pescheteau, #116), 9⁷⁄₁₆ x 12⅜ in., (24 x 31.5 cm.), callichrome on tinted wove (BP 55, DM 133, FR 450, Y 10,430).

DEGAS, Edgar, and Ludovic HALEVY

$2300* *La Famille Cardinal (The Artist and the Book 71; Manet to Hockney 3),* Edgar Degas, illus., Auguste Blaizot, 1939, in 4s, (06-14-93, Sotheby-NY, #125, illus.), 12½ x 9¾ in., (31.8 x 24.8 cm.), book, 33 reprod. of monotypes, 6 hors texte, 6 in color, rest in black and bistre (BP 1505, DM 3743, FR 12,582, Y 242,029).

DEHN, Adolf American 1895-1968

$121* *"Black Mountain",* s., AAA label verso, (06-11-93, DuMouchelle, #2258), 9½ x 13½ in., (24.1 x 34.3 cm.), lithograph (BP 80, DM 197, FR 663, Y 12,838).

$88* *Boating In Central Park,* s., (02-14-93, Hanzel, #696), 8¾ x 13¼ in., (22.2 x 33.7 cm.), lithograph (BP 62, DM 146, FR 494, Y 10,613).

$121* *Celestial Excursion,* s., t., d. 1961, #5/10, (07-03-92, Sloan, #292), 14½ x 11¾ in., (36.8 x 29.8 cm.), lithograph (BP 63, DM 183, FR 617, Y 15,084).

$303* *"Central Park Lake And Skyline" (L. and O. 436), 1947,* s., AAA edit., hinges, fine cond., (10-31-92, Cleveland, #108), 8¾ x 13⅜ in., (22.2 x 34 cm.), lithograph (BP 194, DM 466, FR 1581, Y 37,533).

$176* *Circus,* s., d. 41, t., annot. 30 proofs, (03-14-93, Hindman, #315), 12¾ x 17¼ in., (32.4 x 43.8 cm.), lithograph on white wove (BP 123, DM 293, FR 996, Y 20,742).

$165* *Circus In The Mountains,* s., t., (03-14-93, Hindman, #314), 13 x 17½ in., (33 x 44.5 cm.), lithograph on white wove (BP 115, DM 275, FR 934, Y 19,446).

$150* *"Farm Yard" (L & 0 284), 1934,* plate 23 of The Print-A-Month Club, s., fine cond., soiling throughout image, (05-15-93, Cleveland, #108), 9¾ x 12¹⁵⁄₁₆ in., (24.8 x 32.9 cm.), lithograph (BP 98, DM 241, FR 811, Y 16,628).

$88* *"The Lake",* s., AAA, (12-11-92, DuMouchelle, #1475), 9½ x 13⅜ in., (24.1 x 34 cm.), lithograph (BP 56, DM 139, FR 475, Y 10,890).

BI *"Landschaft In Eldarodo" (L. & O. 172), 1930,* s., p. Meister Schulz, corners glued, good cond., est. $75/150, (05-15-93, Cleveland, #107A), 9 x 23½ in., (22.9 x 59.7 cm.), lithograph.

$187* *The Luxembourg,* s., d. 1927, t., annot. 25 prints, (03-14-93, Hindman, #313), 10¾ x 14 in., (27.3 x 35.6 cm.), lithograph on chine applique (BP 130, DM 311, FR 1058, Y 22,039).

$275* *"Moon Over South Park" and "Lake Kezar": Two,* s., d., t., num., very good cond., (06-11-93, Doyle, #35), larger 13¼ x 17¼ in., (337 x 438 mm.), lithograph (BP 181, DM 447, FR 1507, Y 29,178).

$55* *Peaceful Cove,* s., (09-20-92, Hindman, #699), 9 x 13½ in., (22.9 x 34.3 cm.), lithograph (BP 32, DM 82, FR 279, Y 6798).

$110* *R.F.D. (L. & O. 314), 1939,* s. AAA edit., very good cond., (05-15-93, Cleveland, #109), 10⅜ x 3¹³⁄₁₆ in., (26.4 x 9.7 cm.), lithograph (BP 72, DM 177, FR 595, Y 12,194).

$66* *"South Park, Colorado",* s., (11-28-92, Young, #115, illus.), 13 x 17 in., (33 x 43.2 cm.), lithograph (BP 44, DM 105, FR 357, Y 8214).

$50* *"Sunday Evening In Bois" (Lumsdaine & O'Sullivan 120), 1928,* s., d., struck, hinges, (05-15-93, Cleveland, #107), 9¾ x 14¹³⁄₁₆ in., (24.8 x 37.6 cm.), lithograph (BP 33, DM 80, FR 270, Y 5543).

$165* *Tropical Jugglers,* s., t., d. 1952, #3/30, (09-17-92, Sloan, #1431), 16 x 12 in., (40.6 x 30.5 cm.), color lithograph (BP 93, DM 245, FR 838, Y 20,543).

BI *"Venezuelan Village" (L. & O. 432), 1946,* pub. AAA edit., tape, est. $100/150, (05-15-93, Cleveland, #110), 9³⁄₁₆ x 13 in., (23.3 x 33 cm.), lithograph.

$165* *"Was It A Dream?" and "Mademoiselle Fifi": Two,* each s., #8/250, (06-13-93, Hindman, #315), 14½ x 11 in., (36.8 x 27.9 cm.), lithograph (BP 108, DM 269, FR 903, Y 17,363).

$77* *West Virginia Hills,* s., t., d. 1946, #5/40, (06-11-93, Freemn/Fine Art, #51), 12 x 16½ in., (30.5 x 41.9 cm.), lithograph (BP 51, DM 125, FR 422, Y 8170).

BI *"Willows" (Lumsdaine/O'Sullivan 125), 1928,* p. Desjeobert, excell. cond., est. $3/400, (10-31-92, Cleveland, #107), 8¹⁵⁄₁₆ x 13¹⁄₁₆ in., (22.7 x 33.2 cm.), lithograph.

DEIGHAN, Peter

$499 *"Lester Piggott's Derby Winners", "Oaks Winners", "St. Leger Winners" and "One Thousand And Two Thousand Guineas Winners": A Set Of Four,* s., #18/850, s. by Lester Piggott, (12-11-92, G.A. Key, #22), 16 x 19 in., (40.6 x 48.3 cm.), colored print (BP 320, DM 786, FR 2694, Y 61,750).

DEKAY, James E.

$250* *"Birds Of America": Twelve,* framed as four, (04-28-93, Doyle, #18), 4½ x 2¼ in., (11.4 x 5.7 cm.), color lithographs (BP 159, DM 396, FR 1339, Y 28,017).

DEL PEZZO, Lucio   b. 1933

$100* *"Composition",* #45/100, s., (04-04-93, Pescheteau, #197), 25⁹⁄₁₆ x 18⅞ in., (65 x 48 cm.), etching and aquatint on wove (BP 66, DM 161, FR 546, Y 11,386).

BI *"Composition",* #98/100, s., est. FF4/600, (04-04-93, Pescheteau, #198), 29½ x 26⅜ in., (75 x 67 cm.), color serigraph.

$84* *"Sans Titre-1975",* d., s., (01-28-93, Pescheteau, #119), 19¹¹⁄₁₆ x 25⁹⁄₁₆ in., (50 x 65 cm.), etching and aquatint on wove (BP 55, DM 133, FR 450, Y 10,430).

DELACROIX, Eugene   French 1798-1863

$2596* *Arabes D'Oran (D. 20/II), 1833,* (06-23-93, Kornfeld, #316), etching on handmade (BP 1764, DM 4393, FR 14,775, Y 282,819, SF 3910).

$2291* *Le Chant D'Ophelie (D. 114/I), 1834,* sheet 12 of series: Hamlet, 1st state, prov., (06-23-93, Kornfeld, #317), lithograph (BP 1556, DM 3876, FR 13,039, Y 249,591, SF 3450).

$5595* *Etude De Femme Vue De Dos (L.D., 21), 1833,* second state of four, whole margins, reddish stains, (06-11-93, Picard, #35), 4⁷⁄₁₆ x 6⅜ in., (113 x 162 mm.), etching on laid (BP 3676, DM 9093, FR 30,658, Y 593,634).

$173* *Faust Et Mephistopheles Galopant Dans La Nuit Du Sabbat (D. 73), 1827,* 4th state of 5, margins, good cond., losses, creases, faint staining,restorations, surface soiling, notations, (05-19-93, Butterfield, #2050), 8¼ x 11½ in., (210 x 292 mm.), lithograph on wove (BP 112, DM 281, FR 947, Y 19,152).

$28* *"French Quarter Courtyard" and "Bayou Scene": Two,* s., (11-21-92, Goldberg, #729), photograph (BP 18, DM 45, FR 150, Y 3482).

$2200* *Hamlet (Delteil 103-118), 1834-43,* set of sixteen, second (posthumous) edit., pub. Dusacq, Michel Levy Freres and Pagnerre, 1864, large margins, good cond., soiling, foxing, crease, tear, (11-05-92, Sotheby-NY, #152), lithographs on chine applique (BP 1431, DM 3479, FR 11,771, Y 269,906).

$1412* *Juive D'Alger (Delteil 18 I), 1833,* plate s., d., (06-10-93, Hauswedell/Nolt, #227, illus.), image 8⁷⁄₁₆ x 6¹³⁄₁₆ in., (21.4 x 17.3 cm.), etching on thick hand-made (BP 924, DM 2299, FR 7741, Y 149,878).

$3360* *Juive D'Alger (Delteil 18/I), 1833,* (06-23-93, Kornfeld, #315), etching on handmade (BP 2283, DM 5685, FR 19,124, Y 366,053, SF 5060).

$1486* *Juive D'Alger (L. Delteil, 18), 1833,* 1 out of 4, reddish stains, large margins, collector's stamp, (04-02-93, Picard, #83), 8⁹⁄₁₆ x 6¾ in., (21.8 x 17.1 cm.), etching (BP 979, DM 2388, FR 8111, Y 169,190).

$991* *Lion De L'Atlas (Delteil 79 III), 1829,* blindstamp, (06-04-93, Bassenge, #5655), 14¹⁵⁄₁₆ x 18³⁄₁₆ in., (38 x 46.2 cm.), lithograph on wove (BP 656, DM 1609, FR 5424, Y 106,881).

$1083* *Lionne Dechirant La Poitrine D'Un Arabe (Delteil 25 I), 1849,* (12-04-92, Bassenge, #6771), 5⅞ x 10⅝ in., (15 x 27 cm.), lithograph on China (BP 695, DM 1725, FR 5851, Y 135,206).

$424* *Lionne Dechirant La Poitrine D'Un Arabe (L.D. 25), 1849,* second state of three, creases, reddish stains, artist drystamp, small margins, (02-03-93, Ader Tajan, #132), 8⅜ x 11¹⁄₁₆ in., (21.3 x 28.1 cm.), soft ground etching in sanguine (BP 296, DM 698, FR 2367, Y 52,743).

$9506* *Macbeth Consultant Les Sorcieres (L.D. 40),* first state of five before i., good margins, (02-03-93, Ader Tajan, #136), 12¹³⁄₁₆ x 9¹³⁄₁₆ in., (32.5 x 25 cm.), lithograph (BP 6636, DM 15,653, FR 53,076, Y 1,182,485).

$372* *Mephistopheles Dans La Taverne Des Etudiants (L.D. 64), 1826,* yellowed, 2nd state out of 6 w/i. and address, reddish stains, largemargins, collector's stamp, (04-02-93, Picard, #84), 10⅝ x 8¹¹⁄₁₆ in., (27 x 22 cm.), lithograph (BP 245, DM 598, FR 2031, Y 42,355).

$560* *Mme Frederic Villot (L. Delteil, 13), 1833,* definitive state, dirt stains, thin spots, large margins, (06-11-93, Picard, #34), 3⁵⁄₁₆ x 3⅛ in., (84 x 80 mm.), etching on thick Japan (BP 368, DM 910, FR 3068, Y 59,416).

$1126* *Rencontre De Cavaliers Maures (D. 23), 1834,* rare, creases, faults, (02-24-93, Picard, #74), etching on chine applique (BP 785, DM 1828, FR 6197, Y 132,129).

$222* *Tigre Couche Dans Le Desert (L.D. 24), 1846,* definitive state w/address, large margins, (02-03-93, Ader Tajan, #133), 3¹¹⁄₁₆ x 5³⁄₁₆ in., (9.3 x 13.2 cm.), etching (BP 155, DM 366, FR 1240, Y 27,615).

$24,715* *Tigre Royal (L.D. 80),* good margins, yellowed, third state of four, (02-03-93, Ader Tajan, #137), 12⅝ x 15⅞ in., (32 x 40.3 cm.), lithograph on fixed Chine (BP 17,253, DM 40,697, FR 137,996, Y 3,074,387).

DELACROIX, Michel   b. 1933

BI *La Bonne Galette,* s., #120/225, margins, good cond.?, est. $5/700, (12-12-92, Weschler, #116), 20 x 25 in., (50.8 x 63.5 cm.), color lithograph.

$330* *Cafe - Tabac,* s. Michel Delacroix, very good cond., (09-27-92, Bakker, #261), image 18½ x 25½ in., (47 x 64.8 cm.), color lithograph (BP 193, DM 489, FR 1654, Y 39,831).

$275* *Carousel In A Park,* s. Michel Delacroix, num. cv/cc, (03-06-93, Wolf, #188), image 12½ x 17 in., (31.8 x 43.2 cm.), color lithograph (BP 190, DM 458, FR 1545, Y 32,323).

$303* *Chez Maurice,* s., excell. cond?, (07-19-92, Bakker, #48), plate 17½ x 23¼ in., (44.5 x 59.1 cm.), color lithograph (BP 155, DM 442, FR 1493, Y 37,668).

$110* *Chez Maurice,* excell. cond.?, (03-28-93, Bakker, #121), 17½ x 23¼ in., (44.5 x 59.1 cm.), color lithograph (BP 74, DM 179, FR 610, Y 12,803).

$303* *A Day In The Park,* s., excell. cond?, (07-19-92, Bakker, #31), plate 18¾ x 22¾ in., (47.6 x 57.8 cm.), color lithograph (BP 155, DM 442, FR 1493, Y 37,668).

$165* *"A Day In The Park"*, excell. cond.?, (03-28-93, Bakker, #236), plate 18¾ x 22¾ in., (47.6 x 57.8 cm.), color lithograph (BP 111, DM 269, FR 915, Y 19,204).

$275* *Grand Bal*, s. Michel Delacroix, very good cond., (09-27-92, Bakker, #260), image 19 x 23½ in., (48.3 x 59.7 cm.), color lithograph (BP 161, DM 408, FR 1378, Y 33,193).

$138* *Grand Bal*, excell. cond.?, (03-28-93, Bakker, #97), plate 19½ x 23½ in., (49.5 x 59.7 cm.), color lithograph (BP 93, DM 225, FR 765, Y 16,061).

$358* *Moulin Rouge*, s., excell. cond.?, (07-19-92, Bakker, #92), plate 19¼ x 23½ in., (48.9 x 59.7 cm.), color lithograph (BP 184, DM 522, FR 1764, Y 44,505).

$193* *Moulin Rouge*, excell. cond.?, (03-28-93, Bakker, #207), plate 19¼ x 23½ in., (48.9 x 59.7 cm.), color lithograph (BP 130, DM 315, FR 1070, Y 22,463).

$138* *Tugboat, Paris*, s., num. 23/100, good cond., (05-22-93, Weschler, #177, illus.), 19¼ x 28½ in., (48.9 x 72.4 cm.), photo-offset lithograph in colors (BP 89, DM 224, FR 755, Y 15,215).

$165* *Winter Street Scene*, excell. cond.?, (03-28-93, Bakker, #161), 18¾ x 25½ in., (47.6 x 64.8 cm.), color lithograph (BP 111, DM 269, FR 915, Y 19,204).

DELAFOSSE, Jean Baptiste   d. 1775

$60* *La Malheureuse Famille Calas (I.F.F. 55), c. 1765,* after Carmontelle, crease, stain, pinhole, restoration, (05-15-93, Loudmer, #140), 11⁹⁄₁₆ x 16¾ in., (293 x 425 mm.), copper engraving on laid (BP 39, DM 97, FR 324, Y 6651).

DELAMBERT

$189* *Flanders "Complete Avec Tous Les Accessoires", c. 1920,* p. Devambez, very good cond., (11-19-92, Ribeyre/Baron, #68), 22¹³⁄₁₆ x 14¾ in., (58 x 37.5 cm.), poster (BP 124, DM 301, FR 1015, Y 23,505).

DELANEY, Alan

BI *Cityscape, c. 1990,* #1/7, s., 970 x 1210mm, est. BP 5/800, (05-07-93, Sotheby-London, #408, illus.), photograph, silver print.

DELANO, Jack

$1430* *Locomotive Signage, 1943,* photog.'s sig., d., O.W.I. handstamp, (04-07-93, Swann, #443, illus.), 14 x 10 in., photograph, silver print (BP 945, DM 2313, FR 7827, Y 162,463).

DELAP, Tony

BI *Karnac Series: I; II; III; IV, 1972: Four,* complete suite, s., l., d., 3 num. 39/50, I num. 38/50, blindstamp ofpub. Cirrus, full margins, good cond., staining, creases, est. $1/1,500, (02-24-93, Butterfield, #3011), each 10 x 10 in., (254 x 254 mm.), lithograph w/embossing in colors on wove.

BI *Triple Trouble, 1967,* s., d., t., annot. E-75, margins, good cond., mat staining, rubbed areas, est. $3/500, (10-28-92, Butterfield, #2930), 21 x 21 in., (533 x 533 mm.), silkscreen on wove.

DELATRE

$220* *Man In Chains, Ecole Des Beaux Arts, Paris, c. 1900,* margins, (02-12-93, DuMouchelle, #348, illus.), 4 x 3¼ in., (10.2 x 8.3 cm.), engraving (BP 155, DM 365, FR 1235, Y 26,532).

DELATRE, Eugene

$555* *Elegante Au Bord Du Fleuve, c. 1900,* s., stamped, small margins, (05-06-93, Laurin, #24, illus.), color etching and aquatint (BP 352, DM 874, FR 2943, Y 61,063).

$413* *Portrait De Huysmans, 1900,* yellowed, num. 45, s., creases, cracks, (06-16-93, Ader Tajan, #79), 12⅝ x 9⁵⁄₁₆ in., (32 x 23.7 cm.), color etching and aquatint (BP 275, DM 686, FR 2301, Y 44,049).

$409* *Le Vieux Frene (L. 742), 1904,* s., stamped, creases, crack, stains, untrimmed margins, (02-24-93, Picard, #80), color aquatint on old Japan (BP 285, DM 664, FR 2251, Y 47,993).

DELAUNAY

$25,869* *Saint - Severin. II, 1926-1928,* s., (06-25-93, Kornfeld, #30, illus.), 22¼ x 16⁹⁄₁₆ in., (56.5 x 42 cm.), color lithograph on wove (BP 17,497, DM 44,040, FR 148,331, Y 2,742,103, SF 39,100).

DELAUNAY, Robert

BI *Allo! Paris!, 1926,* book, by Joseph Delteil, num. IV, init. 'W. W.', hors commerce copies,pub. Editions des Quatre Cehmins, good cond., est. $2/2,500, (11-05-92, Sotheby-NY, #153, illus.), each sheet approx. 11 x 8⅞ in., (280 x 225 mm.), ten orig. lithographs on Van Gelder.

$1840* *Allo! Paris!: Ten,* book by Joseph Delteil, #IV, i. W. W., on just. page, p. Engelmann,pub. Editions des Quatre Chemins, 1926, orig. paper covers, good cond., browning, (02-11-93, Sotheby-NY, #115), each sheet approx. 11 x 8⅞ in., (280 x 225 mm.), lithograph on Van Gelder (BP 1298, DM 3048, FR 10,314, Y 221,820).

BI *La Fenetre Sur La Ville (Loyer-Perussaux 4), 1925,* s., t., i. epreuve d'artiste, d. 1909, margins, good cond., tip, reattached, paper discoloration, est. BP 12/15,000, (06-30-93, Sotheby-London, #417, illus.), sh 25¼ x 19½ in., (641 x 495 mm.), lithograph on stiff wove.

BI *La Tour Aux Rideaux, from Allo! Paris! (L. & P. 14), c. 1926,* from series of 20 lithographs, pub. Joseph Delteil, Editions des Quatres Chemins, s., foxing, tear, crease, est. BP 2,5/3,000, (11-30-92, Phillips-London, #415, illus.), image 10¼ x 7½ in., (260 x 191 mm.), lithograph on chine volant.

DELAUNAY, Robert   French 1885-1941

BI *La Tour Eiffel (LP 3), 1926,* est. $300/400, (09-17-92, Sloan, #1450), 10⅜ x 6¼ in., (26.4 x 15.9 cm.), lithograph.

BI *La Tour Eiffel (LP 3), 1926,* est. $250/300, (10-30-92, Sloan, #1755), 10⅜ x 6¼ in., (26.4 x 15.9 cm.), lithograph.

DELAUNAY, Sonia   Russian/French 1885/86-1979

BI s. Sonia Delaunay, E.A., est. DK 12,000, (09-30-92, Kunsthallen, #83), color etching and aquatint.

$660* *Abstract,* s., d. '70, num. 51/75, (09-20-92, Hindman, #775), 27½ x 22 in., (69.9 x 55.9 cm.), color lithograph (BP 386, DM 979, FR 3350, Y 81,572).

$688* *Abstract Composition,* good cond., (06-11-93, Freemn/Fine Art, #52, illus.), 19¼ x 15¼ in., (48.9 x 38.7 cm.), aquatint (BP 452, DM 1118, FR 3770, Y 72,997).

$990* *Abstract Composition (Squares, Circles, And Rectangles), 1962,* from portfolio Huit Eaux Fortes Originales en Couleurs par Sonia Delaunay, full margins, num., s., pub. Leon Amiel, (05-27-93, Swann, #87, illus.), (48.9 x 39.4 cm.), color etching w/aquatint (BP 634, DM 1589, FR 5354, Y 106,132).

$715* *Abstract Composition, 1962,* tondo shape, full margins, num., s., (05-27-93, Swann, #85), 19½ x 15½ in., (49.5 x 39.4 cm.), color etching w/aquatint (BP 458, DM 1147, FR 3867, Y 76,651).

$990* *Abstract Composition, 1962,* s., #26/125, from Huit Eaux Fortes Originales en Couleurs par Sonia Delaunay, (12-08-92, Swann, #80, illus.), sheet 26 x 19¾ in., (66 x 50.2 cm.), color etching and aquatint (BP 620, DM 1541, FR 5255, Y 122,707).

$468* *Abstract Composition, 1964,* #80/125, s., (06-11-93, Freemn/Fine Art, #54), 19¼ x 15½ in., (48.9 x 39.4 cm.), color etching (BP 307, DM 761, FR 2564, Y 49,655).

$550* *Abstract Composition, 1964,* #44/125, s., (06-11-93, Freemn/Fine Art, #53, illus.), 19½ x 15¾ in., (49.5 x 40 cm.), color etching and aquatint (BP 361, DM 894, FR 3014, Y 58,355).

$1210* *Abstract Compositions: Two, 1962,* both s. Sonia Delaunay, num. 78/125, very good cond., full margins, pin holes, wrinkling, (09-11-92, Skinner, #98B, illus.), 19½ x 15¾ in., (49.5 x 40 cm.), color etching w/aquatint on Arches wove w/wartermarks (BP 626, DM 1742, FR 5920, Y 149,919).

$498* *Ballet Portugatis, 1974,* s., E(preuve d')A(rtiste), (12-01-92, Karl/Faber, #531), 18¹¹⁄₁₆ x 12³⁄₁₆ in., (47.5 x 31 cm.), color lithograph on Arches wove (BP 329, DM 794, FR 2705, Y 62,002).

$440* *Blanc Et Noire,* s. Sonia Delaunay, #22/25, (06-26-93, Wolf, #955), 19 x 18 in., (48.3 x 45.7 cm.), silkscreen (BP 295, DM 748, FR 2519, Y 46,684).

$711* *Boules Bleues,* E.A. XX/XXV, s., (06-24-93, Germann, #307), 29¹⁵⁄₁₆ x 22¹⁄₁₆ in., (760 x 560 mm.), color lithograph (BP 468, DM 1153, FR 3885, Y 76,271, SF 1035).

BI *Circle Composition,* s., excell. cond., est. $750/1,000, (05-15-93, Cleveland, #462, illus.), 25½ x 19⅝ in., (64.8 x 49.8 cm.), serigraph in colors.

$750* *Composition,* s. Sonia Delaunay, 5/150, (12-02-92, Kunsthallen, #237), etching in colors (BP 484, DM 1179, FR 4026, Y 93,318, DK 4600).

BI *Composition,* s. Sonia Delaunay, 5/150, est. DK 5,000, (03-24-93, Kunsthallen, #74), color etching.

$1412* *Composition,* 37/125, s., (10-14-92, Germann, #270, illus.), 26³⁄₁₆ x 19¹¹⁄₁₆ in., (665 x 500 mm.), color etching (BP 829, DM 2066, FR 7007, Y 171,110, SF 1840).

$747* *Composition,* #52/125, untrimmed large margins, (06-16-93, Ader Tajan, #81), color etching (BP 498, DM 1240, FR 4162, Y 79,672).

BI *Composition,* s. Sonia Delaunay, E.A., est. DK 7,000, (03-24-93, Kunsthallen, #72), color lithograph.

$918* *Composition,* s. Sonia Delaunay, 67/125, (03-24-93, Kunsthallen, #71), color lithograph (BP 622, DM 1499, FR 5103, Y 107,860, DK 5750).

$527* *Composition,* s. Sonia Delaunay, (09-30-92, Kunsthallen, #86), color lithograph (BP 297, DM 747, FR 2528, Y 63,243, DK 2875).

BI *Composition,* s. Sonia Delaunay, 67/125, est. DK 12,000, (09-30-92, Kunsthallen, #84), color lithograph.

$371* *Composition,* s., #53/75, (03-31-93, Briest, #E32), 22¹⁄₁₆ x 29¹⁵⁄₁₆ in., (56 x 76 cm.), color lithograph (BP 245, DM 597, FR 2027, Y 42,663).

$1248* *Composition,* s. Sonia Delaunay, 71/300, (03-24-93, Kunsthallen, #73), color serigraph (BP 845, DM 2038, FR 6937, Y 146,634, DK 7820).

$734* *Composition,* Betegnet Sonia Delaunay, 22/900, (03-24-93, Kunsthallen, #75), serigraph in colors (BP 497, DM 1199, FR 4080, Y 86,241, DK 4600).

$2001* *Composition,* s. Sonia Delaunay 1966, 8/20, (09-30-92, Kunsthallen, #85), pochoir (BP 1129, DM 2837, FR 9597, Y 240,130, DK 10,925).

$272* *Composition,* E.A., s., (10-14-92, Germann, #269), 19¹¹⁄₁₆ x 15¾ in., (500 x 400 mm.), color serigraph (BP 160, DM 398, FR 1350, Y 32,962, SF 354).

$342* *Composition,* s., #28/70, (12-01-92, Ritchie, #106, illus.), 18⅞ x 14 in., (47.9 x 35.6 cm.), color serigraph (BP 226, DM 545, FR 1858, Y 42,580, C$ 440).

$419* *Composition,* mono. in plate, epreuve d'artiste, full margins, (11-16-92, Briest, #284), 25⁹⁄₁₆ x 19¹¹⁄₁₆ in., (65 x 50 cm.), etching in colors (BP 275, DM 668, FR 2251, Y 52,290).

$180* *"Composition - 1969",* #138/150, sig. stamp, (10-18-92, Pescheteau, #122), 25⁹⁄₁₆ x 19⁵⁄₁₆ in., (65 x 49 cm.), serigraph in colors (BP 109, DM 266, FR 903, Y 21,493).

$983* *Composition Spherique,* #12/125, s., untrimmed large margins, (06-16-93, Ader Tajan, #80), 19½ x 15⁹⁄₁₆ in., (49.5 x 39.5 cm.), color etching (BP 655, DM 1632, FR 5476, Y 104,842).

BI *Composition, "Jacques Damanse 30 Ans D'Edition D'Arte",* 1979, est. DK 1,000, (03-24-93, Kunsthallen, #76), lithographic poster.

$169* *Composition, 1966,* (09-30-92, Kunsthallen, #87), poster, offset in colors (BP 95, DM 240, FR 811, Y 20,281, DK 920).

BI *Composition, 1966,* s. Sonia Delaunay, #8/20, est. DK 15,000, (06-03-93, Kunsthallen, #85, illus.), 20½ x 14¹⁵⁄₁₆ in., (52 x 38 cm.), pochoir.

$550* *Composition, 1967,* s., d. Sonia Delaunay '67, #96/100, good cond., toning, (03-12-93, Skinner, #100, illus.), sight 18⅝ x 11¾ in., (47.3 x 29.8 cm.), lithograph in colors on paper (BP 384, DM 915, FR 3113, Y 64,820).

BI *Composition, c. 1965,* s., #70/125, full margins, good cond., est. BP 6/800, (06-30-93, Sotheby-London, #418), 18½ x 27½ in., (470 x 699 mm.), color lithograph on Arches.

$441* *"Composition-1971",* #67/99, s., (01-28-93, Pescheteau, #118), 29½ x 21¼ in., (75 x 54 cm.), color lithograph on Arches (BP 291, DM 699, FR 2365, Y 54,755).

$3775* *Compositions, c. 1975: Four,* s., three num., one i. E. A., margins, good cond., creases, (06-30-93, Sotheby-London, #419, illus.), color lithograph on wove (BP 2530, DM 6439, FR 21,720, Y 404,479).

$770* *Disques, 1976,* s., num. 62/75, from Music Maestro Please portfolio, pub. Editions Sonet, apparently good cond., (02-24-93, Butterfield, #2913), 20½ x 19½ in., (521 x 495 mm.), lithograph in colors on wove (BP 537, DM 1250, FR 4238, Y 90,354).

$978* *Ellipse, 1969,* s., d., i. H.C. 17/25, full margins, good cond., (02-11-93, Sotheby-NY, #116), 21¾ x 16 in., (552 x 407 mm.), color lithograph (BP 690, DM 1620, FR 5482, Y 117,902).

$899* *"Formes Et Couleurs",* HC, s., (04-04-93, Pescheteau, #195), 12³⁄₁₆ x 9⁷⁄₁₆ in., (31 x 24 cm.), color lithograph (BP 592, DM 1445, FR 4907, Y 102,357).

$561* *"Formes Et Couleurs",* HC, s., (10-18-92, Pescheteau, #121), 12⅝ x 9⁷⁄₁₆ in., (32 x 24 cm.), lithograph in colors on velin (BP 340, DM 829, FR 2815, Y 66,985).

BI *Jacques Damase: Rhythmes-Colour, 1966,* portfolio including 11 pochoirs by Ettore Falchi after gouaches by Sonia Delaunay, title page and text, margins, good cond., orig. slip case, est. BP 2,5/3,000, (12-03-92, Sotheby-London, #277), pochoirs on hand made Moulin Richard de Bas.

$548* *Joker Vest,* proof, s., (05-20-93, Finarte-Milan, #62), 23⅝ x 17¹¹⁄₁₆ in., (60 x 45 cm.), lithograph in colors (BP 352, DM 884, FR 2978, Y 60,512, L 805).

BI *Komposition,* 67/100, s., est. SF 1,2/1,500, (10-14-92, Germann, #271), 24⅝ x 17½ in., (625 x 445 mm.), color etching.

$1412* *Komposition,* 94/125, s., (10-14-92, Germann, #132, illus.), 25⁹⁄₁₆ x 19¹¹⁄₁₆ in., (650 x 500 mm.), color aquatint (BP 829, DM 2066, FR 7007, Y 171,110, SF 1840).

$829* *Komposition,* #67/100, s., (09-04-92, Germann, #299), 24⅝ x 17½ in., (625 x 445 mm.), color etching (BP 415, DM 1162, FR 3955, Y 102,043, SF 1035).

BI *Komposition,* s., num., est. DM 2500, (12-01-92, Karl/Faber, #534), 18⅞ x 15³⁄₁₆ in., (48 x 38.5 cm.), color etching and aquatint on Arches France wove.

$790* *Komposition,* #76/125, s., (04-21-93, Germann, #363), 25¹⁵⁄₁₆ x 19¹¹⁄₁₆ in., (660 x 500 mm.), color etching (BP 513, DM 1263, FR 4270, Y 87,457, SF 1150).

$790* *Komposition,* #78/125, s., (04-21-93, Germann, #364, illus.), 23¼ x 19¹¹⁄₁₆ in., (590 x 500 mm.), color aquatint (BP 513, DM 1263, FR 4270, Y 87,457, SF 1150).

$790* *Komposition,* #78/125, s., (04-21-93, Germann, #365), 25¹⁵⁄₁₆ x 19¹¹⁄₁₆ in., (660 x 500 mm.), color aquatint (BP 513, DM 1263, FR 4270, Y 87,457, SF 1150).

$1106* *Komposition,* 56/75, s., (04-21-93, Germann, #367), 29¾ x 21⅞ in., (755 x 555 mm.), color lithograph (BP 718, DM 1768, FR 5978, Y 122,440, SF 1610).

$395* *Komposition,* #25/75, s., (04-21-93, Germann, #362), 23⁷⁄₁₆ x 16⁹⁄₁₆ in., (596 x 420 mm.), color lithograph (BP 256, DM 631, FR 2135, Y 43,729, SF 575).

$1014* *Komposition 1965,* #67/100, s., (09-04-92, Germann, #1, illus.), 24⅝ x 17½ in., (625 x 445 mm.), color etching (BP 508, DM 1421, FR 4838, Y 124,815, SF 1265).

BI *Komposition In Tondo-Form,* #76/125, s., est. SF 3,5/4,000, (04-21-93, Germann, #132, illus.), 23¼ x 18½ in., (590 x 470 mm.), color aquatint.

$869* *Komposition In Tondo-Form,* 76/125, s., (06-24-93, Germann, #311, illus.), 23¼ x 18½ in., (590 x 470 mm.), color aquatint (BP 572, DM 1409, FR 4749, Y 93,220, SF 1265).

BI *Komposition Mit Farbfeldern Und Konzentrischen Kreisen,* s., num., light-staining, est. DM 2500, (12-01-92, Karl/Faber, #532), 19⅞ x 14¹⁵⁄₁₆ in., (50.5 x 38 cm.), color lithograph on wove.

BI *Komposition, 1965,* 67/100., s., est. SF 1,2/1,500, (10-14-92, Germann, #127), 24⅝ x 17½ in., (625 x 445 mm.), color etching.

$869* *Komposition, 1974,* 48/75, s., d., (06-24-93, Germann, #308), 29¾ x 22¹⁄₁₆ in., (755 x 560 mm.), color lithograph (BP 572, DM 1409, FR 4749, Y 93,220, SF 1265).

$1045* *Large Abstract Composition, 1962,* full margins, num., s., (05-27-93, Swann, #86), 19¼ x 15⅝ in., (48.9 x 39.4 cm.), color etching w/aquatint (BP 669, DM 1677, FR 5652, Y 112,028).

$2255* *Ohne Titel, 1966,* s., #8/20, d., (05-26-93, Lempertz, #101, illus.), 20½ x 14⁹⁄₁₆ in., (52 x 37 cm.), pochoir on textured paper (BP 1459, DM 3679, FR 12,383, Y 245,002).

$740* *Olympie,* s., #H.C. XI/XXV, (05-26-93, Lempertz, #105), 23⁷⁄₁₆ x 18⅝ in., (59.5 x 47.3 cm.), color lithograph on Arches wove (BP 479, DM 1207, FR 4064, Y 80,400).

$567* *Orange,* s., i. EA, (06-08-93, Karl/Faber, #679), approx. 21¼ x 17½ in., (54 x 44.5 cm.), color lithograph (BP 373, DM 920, FR 3098, Y 60,223).

$1185* *Orange,* IX/XXV, s., (06-24-93, Germann, #309, illus.), 29¾ x 22⅛ in., (756 x 562 mm.), color lithograph (BP 780, DM 1921, FR 6475, Y 127,119, SF 1725).

$705* *Paques Russes,* s., #E.A. XI/XXXV, (05-26-93, Lempertz, #108), 21⁵⁄₁₆ x 20½ in., (54.2 x 52 cm.), color lithograph on wove (BP 456, DM 1150, FR 3871, Y 76,597).

$5639* *Rhythme Couleur, 1961,* s., d., (05-26-93, Lempertz, #100, illus.), 25⁹⁄₁₆ x 19¹¹⁄₁₆ in., (65 x 50 cm.), pochoir (BP 3648, DM 9201, FR 30,967, Y 612,668).

BI *Roi De Coeur,* s., num., light-staining, traces of mounting, est. DM 2500, (12-01-92, Karl/Faber, #533), 23¼ x 17⁵⁄₁₆ in., (59 x 44 cm.), color lithograph on Arches France wove.

BI *"Rythme Et Couleur",* s. Sonia Delaunay, (05-18-93, Encans, #178), 14¾ x 20³⁄₁₆ in., (37.5 x 51.3 cm.), pochoir w/gouache.

BI *S. Quasimodo - "La Terra Impareggiabile", 1971: Two,* M'Arte Edizioni, s., num., est. DM 1200, (12-01-92, Karl/Faber, #530), 15¹⁵⁄₁₆ x 11¹³⁄₁₆ in., (40.5 x 30 cm.), color etching on wove.

$434* *Sans Titre,* #37/125, s. Sonia Delaunay, (06-16-93, Encans, #128), 19⁵⁄₁₆ x 15¾ in., (49 x 40 cm.), drypoint and aquatint on Arches (BP 289, DM 720, FR 2418, Y 46,288, C$ 555).

$567* *Santa Barbara,* s., #2/75, (05-27-93, Briest, #78), 31½ x 24⅝ in., (80 x 62.5 cm.), color lithograph on Arches (BP 363, DM 910, FR 3067, Y 60,785).

$567* *Tourbillon,* s., (06-08-93, Karl/Faber, #680), approx. 21⅝ x 18⅛ in., (55 x 46 cm.), color lithograph (BP 373, DM 920, FR 3098, Y 60,223).

$948* *Tourbillon,* E.A. II/XXV, s., (06-24-93, Germann, #310, illus.), 29¹¹⁄₁₆ x 21¹⁵⁄₁₆ in., (754 x 557 mm.), color lithograph (BP 624, DM 1537, FR 5180, Y 101,695, SF 1380).

$440* *"Tzara",* s., d. 1961, #52/80, prov., (03-25-93, Boos, #623), sight 25⁷⁄₁₆ x 19⁷⁄₁₆ in., (646 x 493 mm.), color lithograph (BP 299, DM 723, FR 2458, Y 51,546).

BI *"Tzara",* s., d. 1961, #52/80, prov., est. $800/1,200, (12-02-92, Boos, #518), sight 25⁷⁄₁₆ x 19⁷⁄₁₆ in., (646 x 493 mm.), color lithograph.

$990* *Unitled Abstract Composition, 1962,* s., #21/125, full margins, from Huit Eaux Fortes Originales en Couleurs par Sonia Delaunay, (12-08-92, Swann, #81), 19⅜ x 15½ in., (49.2 x 39.4 cm.), color etching and aquatint (BP 620, DM 1541, FR 5255, Y 122,707).

BI *"Untitled",* s., #14/125, margins, good cond.?, est. $7/900, (10-28-92, Butterfield, #2634), 19½ x 15⅝ in., (495 x 397 mm.), color etching and aquatint on wove.

$550* *"Untitled",* s., #76/125, margins, good cond.?, Modesto Lanzone Coll., (10-28-92, Butterfield, #2633), 19½ x 15⅝ in., (495 x 397 mm.), color etching w/aquatint on cream wove (BP 350, DM 849, FR 2884, Y 67,485).

$550* *"Untitled",* s., d. 1961, #51/80, prov., (12-02-92, Boos, #517, illus.), sight 25⁹⁄₁₆ x 19¹¹⁄₁₆ in., (650 x 500 mm.), color lithograph (BP 355, DM 865, FR 2952, Y 68,433).

$1320* *"Untitled": Two,* s., #76/125, margins, good cond.?, (10-28-92, Butterfield, #2635), each 19½ x 15⅝ in., (495 x 397 mm.), color etching w/aquatint on wove (BP 841, DM 2039, FR 6922, Y 161,963).

$805* *Untitled, 1970,* s., #14/125, full margins, good cond., rubbed area in image, soiling,staining, (05-19-93, Butterfield, #2051), 19½ x 15⅝ in., (495 x 397 mm.), aquatint w/etching in colors on Arches (BP 523, DM 1309, FR 4409, Y 89,118).

$920* *Untitled, 1970,* s., annot. E.A., full margins, good cond., staining, (05-19-93, Butterfield, #2052), 29¾ x 22 in., (756 x 559 mm.), lithograph in colors on Arches (BP 597, DM 1495, FR 5038, Y 101,849).

$938* *Untitled, 1971,* #18/85, s., d., (11-21-92, Lempertz, #104), 29¹⁵⁄₁₆ x 20¹¹⁄₁₆ in., (76 x 52.5 cm.), color lithograph on wove (BP 618, DM 1496, FR 5038, Y 116,652).

$825* *Untitled, c. 1962,* s., #32/125, (05-16-93, Hindman, #497), 19½ x 15⅝ in., (49.5 x 39.7 cm.), sheet 26 x 19¾ in., (49.5 x 39.7 cm.), color etching and aquatint on Arches wove (BP 536, DM 1327, FR 4459, Y 91,453).

$715* *Untitled, c. 1962,* s., #10/125, (05-16-93, Hindman, #496), 19½ x 15½ in., (49.5 x 39.4 cm.), sheet 26 x 19¾ in., (49.5 x 39.4 cm.), color etching and aquatint on Arches wove (BP 465, DM 1150, FR 3865, Y 79,260).

$638* *Volet De Carreau,* s., i. HC, (06-08-93, Karl/Faber, #678), approx. 24 x 17¹¹⁄₁₆ in., (61 x 45 cm.), color lithograph (BP 419, DM 1035, FR 3486, Y 67,764).

DELAVAT, C.

$315* *Chemin De Fer Du Nord: Cayeux Sur Mer, c. 1930,* p. Valade, very good cond., (11-19-92, Ribeyre/Baron, #100), 38¹⁵⁄₁₆ x 28⁹⁄₁₆ in., (99 x 72.5 cm.), poster (BP 207, DM 502, FR 1692, Y 39,174).

DELAY, Alexandre

$40* *"Masculin-Feminin",* #III/X, s., (04-04-93, Pescheteau, #196), 29¹⁵⁄₁₆ x 22¹⁄₁₆ in., (76 x 56 cm.), black etching on Arches (BP 26, DM 64, FR 218, Y 4554).

DELCOURT, Maurice French d. 1914/18

$275* *"Jeune Femme En Fichu",* s. Maurice Delcourt, num. 20/98, very good cond., (09-27-92, Bakker, #262, illus.), image 3⅞ x 2¾ in., (9.8 x 7 cm.), color woodblock print (BP 161, DM 408, FR 1378, Y 33,193).

$991* *La Modiste, 1905,* full margins, s., num., (04-02-93, Picard, #85), 13¾ x 8¼ in., (35 x 21 cm.), wood engraving on Japan (BP 653, DM 1593, FR 5409, Y 112,832).

DELECHAIX, Th.

$788* *Exposition. Societe Des Amis Des Arts, 1902,* tears, (02-04-93, Christie-S. Ken, #47, illus.), 39½ x 27 in., (100.3 x 68.6 cm.), color lithograph (BP 550, DM 1298, FR 4400, Y 98,022).

DELFOS, A.

$33* *"Vischmarkt En Fontein...", 1763,* (12-11-92, DuMouchelle, #2396), 9¾ x 12¾ in., (24.8 x 32.4 cm.), etching (BP 21, DM 52, FR 178, Y 4084).

DELGADO, Alvaro

$1044* *"Variaciones Sobre El Entierro Del Conde De Orgaz", 1975: Nine,* #37/195, s., text by Rafael Alberti, Ediciones de Arte y Bibliofilia, (12-17-92, Duran, #174, illus.), 20½ x 15⅜ in., (52 x 39 cm.), lithograph (BP 663, DM 1630, FR 5568, Y 128,303, P 115,000).

DELIF, M.

$538* *Clotilde Et Alexandre Sakharoff 1923 A L'Opera De Marseille,* (01-31-93, Morelle/Marchan, #25), 23⅝ x 31½ in., (60 x 80 cm.), poster (BP 362, DM 867, FR 2930, Y 67,116).

DELKESKAMP, F.W. (after)

BI *Panorama Of The Rhine And The Adjacent Country, From Cologne To Mayence, c. 1850,* by John Clark, pub. Samuel Leigh, in orig. silk boards as pub., covers scuffed, edge damaged, est. BP 200/250, (11-30-92, Phillips-London, #249), panorama 90¼ x 8⅜ in., (229.2 x 21.3 cm.), hand-colored etching w/aquatint.

DELL, Edwin la

$24 *"Conford",* s., (10-09-92, G.A. Key, #21), 18 x 21 in., (45.7 x 53.3 cm.), colored lithograph (BP 14, DM 36, FR 121, Y 2927).

DELLA BELLA, Stefano Italian 1610-1660

$550* *Un Cavalier Portant En Croupe Une Jeune Femme (de Vesme/Massar 211),* (10-18-92, Hindman, #498), 10⅝ x 8½ in., (27 x 21.6 cm.), etching (BP 337, DM 819, FR 2776, Y 65,987).

$1133* *Dessins De Quelques Conduites De Troupes (De Vesme 246-257 II): Twelve,* (06-04-93, Bassenge, #5029), 2⁵⁄₁₆ x 5 in., (5.8 x 12.7 cm.), etching (BP 750, DM 1840, FR 6201, Y 122,196).

$2497* *Divers Desseins Tant Pour la Paix Que Pour la Guerre (De V., M. 264-9), c. 1641: Set Of Six,* 1st state of 2, watermark, trimmed, repaired tear, repaired nick, very good cond., prov., (12-01-92, Christie-London, #227, illus.), plate 3¹⁵⁄₁₆ x 9⅞ in., (100 x 251 mm.), etching (BP 1650, DM 3980, FR 13,563, Y 310,881).

$907* *La Fuite En Egypte, 1655-60,* round form, second and last state, margins, (05-15-93, Loudmer, #3, illus.), 8⁷⁄₁₆ x 8⁷⁄₁₆ in., (215 x 215 mm.), sh 13⁹⁄₁₆ x 9⅜ in., (215 x 215 mm.), etching on laid (BP 590, DM 1459, FR 4903, Y 100,543).

$880* *"Italian Landscapes": Two,* plate s., trimmed, first, good cond., glue remains, foxing; second, repaired holes, image tears, glue staining, edges reinforced, (10-28-92, Butterfield, #2592), one 9¾ x 14½ in., (248 x 368 mm.), the other 9¾ x 15¼ in., (248 x 368 mm.), engraving on laid paper (BP 561, DM 1359, FR 4615, Y 107,975).

BI *(Italian Landscapes): Two,* each s. in plate, trimmed inside platemark, 1st in good cond., glue remains, foxing; 2nd w/repaired holes, tears in image, staining, est. $8/1,000, (02-24-93, Butterfield, #2687), one 9¾ x 14½ in., (248 x 368 mm.), other 9¾ x 15¼ in., (248 x 368 mm.), engraving on laid.

$2479* *La Mort Sur Un Champ De Bataille (De Vesme 93 III),* watermark, (06-04-93, Bassenge, #5027, illus.), 8¹¹⁄₁₆ x 11⁹⁄₁₆ in., (22 x 29.4 cm.), etching (BP 1640, DM 4026, FR 13,569, Y 267,364).

$633* *Plusieurs Tetes Coiffees A la Persienne (De V., M. 181-92), 1650: Set Of Twelve,* 2nd (final) state, narrow margins or trimmed, creasing discoloration, good cond., (12-01-92, Christie-London, #226), plate, largest 3¾ x 2¾ in., (96 x 70 mm.), etching (BP 418, DM 1009, FR 3438, Y 78,810).

$202* *Portrait De Ferdinand II, 1638,* ink stain, restored corners, good cond., (05-15-93, Loudmer, #2, illus.), 8⁵⁄₁₆ x 6⅛ in., (211 x 155 mm.), etching on thin laid (BP 131, DM 325, FR 1092, Y 22,392).

BI *Raccolta Di Varii Capricii Et Nove Inventioni Di Cartelle Et Ornamenti (De V. 1027-1038): Twelve,* 3rd and final state, includ. frontispiece and t. page, narrow margins, est. BP 2/300, (10-27-92, Phillips-London, #6), plate 9¼ x 7¼ in., (235 x 184 mm.), etching on thick wove.

$916* *Raccolta Di Vasi Diversi (De V., M. 1045-50), c. 1646: Set Of Six,* 1st state of 3, narrow to thread margins, (12-01-92, Christie-London, #230), plate 3⅝ x 7⁵⁄₁₆ in., (92 x 186 mm.), etching (BP 605, DM 1460, FR 4976, Y 114,044).

$101* *Recueil De Divers Griffonements...,* thin margins, (02-03-93, Ader Tajan, #17), 8³⁄₁₆ x 6¹¹⁄₁₆ in., (20.8 x 17 cm.), etching (BP 71, DM 166, FR 564, Y 12,564).

$601* *Le Rocher Des Philosophes Ou Le Mont Parnasse,* (06-10-93, Hauswedell/Nolt, #25), etching (BP 393, DM 979, FR 3295, Y 63,794).

$867* *Die Ruhe Auf Der Flucht Nach Agypten (De Vesme 16 III),* (12-04-92, Bassenge, #6045), 3¼ x 5⁵⁄₁₆ in., (8.3 x 13.5 cm.), etching (BP 556, DM 1381, FR 4684, Y 108,240).

$275* *Scena Grotta Di Vulcano (M., DeV. 925),* small margins, good cond., tear, hinge remains, pencil notations, surface soiling, est. $5/700, (02-24-93, Butterfield, #2688), 8¹⁄₁₆ x 11¼ in., engraving on laid (BP 192, DM 446, FR 1513, Y 32,269).

$275* *Scena Qvinta D'Inferno,* margins, good cond., creases in center of image, repaired tear, holes, paper loss, hinge remains, stain, surface soiling, est. $5/700, (02-24-93, Butterfield, #2686), 8¹⁄₁₆ x 11½ in., (205 x 292 mm.), engraving on fine laid (BP 192, DM 446, FR 1513, Y 32,269).

$621* *Statue Colossale De L'Apennin (de Vesme and Massar 843 II),* sheet 6 of series Vues de la ville de Pratolino, pres de Florence, (06-10-93, Hauswedell/Nolt, #30), etching (BP 406, DM 1011, FR 3405, Y 65,917).

$464* *"Templi Antonini Pij, Et Rudorum Palatinorum Fragmenta In Foro Boario", 1656,* from Six grandes vues... de Rome, (09-14-92, Venator/Hansten, #1460), plate 12⅛ x 11⅛ in., (30.8 x 28.2 cm.), etching (BP 245, DM 690, FR 2338, Y 57,697).

DELLEPIANE, D.

$782* *Arts Graphiques, Geneve,* defects, tears, backed on linen, laid on board, (05-07-93, Christie-S. Ken, #86, illus.), 21¼ x 29¾ in., (54 x 75.6 cm.), color lithograph (BP 495, DM 1236, FR 4166, Y 86,104).

$434* *Sunflower Lady With Camera,* p. SADAG, defects, backed on linen, (05-07-93, Christie-S. Ken, #85, illus.),

19¼ x 25¾ in., (48.9 x 65.4 cm.), color lithograph (BP 275, DM 686, FR 2312, Y 47,787).

DELLEPIANNE, D.

$50* *Soldats!...Je Ne Fume Que Le Nil,* good cond., (03-13-93, Laurin, #6), 23¼ x 15¾ in., (59 x 40 cm.), (BP 35, DM 83, FR 283, Y 5893).

DELOBBE, A. (after)

$441 *Two Young Ladies Seated On A Beach,* stamp, (08-14-92, G.A. Key, #117), 19 x 34 in., (48.3 x 86.4 cm.), colored photogravure (BP 230, DM 647, FR 2191, Y 55,612).

DELORME, R.

$525* *Royan. "Les Plus Belles Plages", 1925,* p. Chaix, very good cond., (11-19-92, Ribeyre/Baron, #101), 40⁹⁄₁₆ x 27³⁄₁₆ in., (103 x 69 cm.), poster (BP 346, DM 837, FR 2820, Y 65,290).

DELPECH, Francois-Seraphin   (after Leopold BOILLY)

$226* *The Four Seasons, 1824,* fair cond., surface skimming, wormholes, (10-27-92, Phillips-London, #70), sheet 9 x 7½ in., (229 x 191 mm.), lithograph w/hand-coloring on wove (BP 143, DM 346, FR 1175, Y 27,645).

DELPECH, Jean   20th cent.

$121* *"La Liberte" and "Paris Capitale": Pair,* latter s., d. (19)47 in plate; each s., i. "Epreuve d'artiste", ded., (10-30-92, Sloan, #834), larger 20¼ x 16⅜ in., (51.4 x 41.6 cm.), engraving (BP 78, DM 186, FR 632, Y 14,988).

DELPY

$440* *36eme Salon De L'Automobile, 1949,* A cond., (08-06-92, Swann, #113, illus.), 23 x 15¼ in., (58.4 x 38.7 cm.), (BP 230, DM 650, FR 2196, Y 56,122).

DELSON, E.

BI *"Dream Of Icarus",* s., t., est. $25/50, (01-15-93, DuMouchelle, #179), 13½ x 10½ in., (34.3 x 26.7 cm.), b/w etching.

DELVAL

$80* *"Fap Anis" Celui Des Connaisseurs", c. 1925,* Pub. Wall, good cond., (02-12-93, Cheval/Robert, #55), 47¼ x 60¼ in., (120 x 153 cm.), poster (BP 56, DM 133, FR 449, Y 9648).

$276* *Fap'Anis,* plate s., lined, (03-25-93, Christie-E, #201), 62½ x 46¾ in., (158.8 x 118.7 cm.), color lithograph (BP 187, DM 453, FR 1542, Y 32,334).

$247* *Fap'Anis, Celui Des Connaisseurs,* Publicite Wall, A-cond., creased, chartex-backed, (08-06-92, Swann, #114, illus.), 47 x 63 in., (119.4 x 160 cm.), (BP 129, DM 365, FR 1233, Y 31,505).

DELVAUX, Paul   Belgian b. 1897

$1650* *The Doll(J. 65),* s., #VIII/XXV, full margins, good cond., mat stain, creases, stamp, (11-05-92, Sotheby-NY, #156), 12¼ x 9½ in., (312 x 241 mm.), lithograph p. in sanguine on japon nacre (BP 1073, DM 2610, FR 8828, Y 202,429).

$5463* *The Empress (J. 72), 1974,* s., #23/75, full margins, good cond., light-stain, handling creases, (05-13-93, Sotheby-NY, #545, illus.), 31⅞ x 23⅝ in., (810 x 600 mm.), lithograph in colors (BP 3587, DM 8821, FR 29,755, Y 609,914).

BI *Femme A La Boule (J. 54), 1971,* s., annot. E/A, full margins, good cond., creases through image, surface soiling, est. $3/5,000, (02-24-93, Butterfield, #2735, illus.), 19½ x 12⅜ in., (495 x 314 mm.), lithograph on Arches.

BI *The Flautist (J. 56), 1972,* s., #37/75, full margins, good cond., creasing, paper discoloration, est. BP 1/1,500, (06-30-93, Sotheby-London, #421), 23 x 15⅛ in., (584 x 384 mm.), lithograph on Arches.

BI *Hat 1900 (J. 62), 1972,* s., #63/75, full margins, good cond., mat/light stain, est. $10/14,000, (11-05-92, Sotheby-NY, #155, illus.), 23⅞ x 15⅝ in., (605 x 398 mm.), lithograph p. in colors.

$2960* *Hut Mit Blumen II (Jacob 36), 1969,* s., #12/75, (05-26-93, Lempertz, #109), 17¹³⁄₁₆ x 14⅛ in., (45.3 x 35.9 cm.), color lithograph on wove (BP 1915, DM 4829, FR 16,255, Y 321,599).

$2966* *Le Joueur De Flute (Jacob 56), 1972,* s., E.A., stone d., Epreuve d'artiste, (06-10-93, Hauswedell/Nolt, #228, illus.), image 22¹³⁄₁₆ x 15³⁄₁₆ in., (58 x 38.5 cm.), lithograph on Arches paper (BP 1940, DM 4830, FR 16,261, Y 314,829).

BI *L'Inscription (Jacob 85), 1973, #25/40,* s., from folio Construction d'un temple en ruine a la deesseVanade, est. DM 4,500-, (11-21-92, Lempertz, #105, illus.), 12⅝ x 17¹¹⁄₁₆ in., (32 x 45 cm.), etching on wove.

$5675* *Der Liebhaber (Jacob 50), 1971,* s., num., (06-05-93, Bassenge, #5988, illus.), 19⅞ x 26³⁄₁₆ in., (50.5 x 66.5 cm.), color lithograph on copper print (BP 3736, DM 9201, FR 31,011, Y 608,775).

BI *The Lover (Jacob 50), 1971, #37/75,* full margins, good cond., ink traces, glue, skinned spots, est. $3,5/4,000, (05-13-93, Sotheby-NY, #544, illus.), 19¾ x 26⅛ in., (500 x 663 mm.), lithograph in black w/a beige tint stone.

BI *The Mirrors (Jacob 10), 1966,* s., #25/50, full margins, good cond., light/mat stain, est. $4,5/6,500, (11-05-92, Sotheby-NY, #154, illus.), 19⅞ x 26½ in., (503 x 672 mm.), lithograph.

$938* *Nais Unclothed (J. 97), 1975,* s., #77/90, pub. Galerie Le Bateau Lavoir, full margins, good cond.,light staining, (12-03-92, Sotheby-London, #281, illus.), 12½ x 4⅜ in., (318 x 111 mm.), lithograph on Arches (BP 605, DM 1475, FR 5035, Y 116,710).

$938* *Outside, The Shadows Lengthen (J. 83), 1971-75,* from Building a Ruined Temple to the Gossess Vanade, s., #9/40, pub.Gallery Le Bateau-Lavoir, reduced margins, good cond., (12-03-92, Sotheby-London, #280), 12½ x 17½ in., (318 x 445 mm.), etching on Richard de Bas (BP 605, DM 1475, FR 5035, Y 116,710).

$496* *"Paul Delvaux. Das Graphische Werk", 1976: Two,* text by M. Jacob, Editions Andre Sauret, (06-08-93, Karl/Faber, #685), approx. 12¹⁵⁄₁₆ x 9¹³⁄₁₆ in., (33 x 25 cm.), lithograph (BP 326, DM 805, FR 2710, Y 52,682).

BI *Phryne (J. 40), 1969,* 2nd state, s., num. 10/75, full margins, mount-stained, defects, est.BP 1,5/2,000, (11-30-92, Phillips-London, #417), sheet 19⅝ x 15⅛ in., (498 x 384 mm.), lithograph w/hand-coloring on Arches.

$1692* *Phryne (Jacob 39), 1969,* s., #13/75, (05-26-93, Lempertz, #110, illus.), 17¹⁵⁄₁₆ x 14³⁄₁₆ in., (45.5 x 36 cm.), lithograph on Arches wove (BP 1095, DM 2761, FR 9292, Y 183,833).

$3631* *La Plage (Jacob 59), 1972,* s., num. 19/50, full margins, good cond., (10-14-92, Sotheby-Japan, #22, illus.), 22⅞ x 30¾ in., (581 x 781 mm.), lithograph on Arches wove (BP 2131, DM 5314, FR 18,020, Y 440,015).

BI *Reclining Nude, c. 1948,* s., #37/40, good cond., paper discoloration, est. BP 6/800, (12-03-92, Sotheby-London, #278, illus.), 9⅛ x 12⅜ in., (232 x 314 mm.), etching w/aquatint in green on wove.

$3341* *La Reine De Saba, 1982,* s., HC, (12-01-92, Karl/Faber, #535, illus.), 23⅝ x 16¹⁵⁄₁₆ in., (60 x 43 cm.), color serigraph and lithograph on wove (BP 2207, DM 5325, FR 18,148, Y 415,961).

$4678* *La Robe Du Dimanche (Jacob 18), (19)67,* s., num., stamped, (06-08-93, Karl/Faber, #684, illus.), approx. 25 x 20¹⁄₁₆ in., (63.5 x 51 cm.), color lithograph on BFK Rives wove (BP 3075, DM 7590, FR 25,563, Y 496,867).

$3536* *La Robe Du Dimanche (Jacob 18), 1967,* #43/75, s., (11-09-92, Finarte-Milan, #57, illus.), 25 x 20¹⁄₁₆ in., (63.5 x 51 cm.), lithograph in colors (BP 2338, DM 5645, FR 19,072, Y 438,819, L 4830).

$4263* *The Secret (J. 9), 1966,* s., #29/75, pub. Gallery Le Bateau Lavoir, full margins, good cond.,light staining, (12-03-92, Sotheby-London, #283, illus.), 25⅝ x 21⅝ in., (651 x 549 mm.), lithograph on Arches (BP 2750, DM 6704, FR 22,882, Y 530,422).

$1773* *"Die Sirene" (Jacob 28), 1969,* s., num., pub. in Gerhard Hauptmann, Das Meerwunder, Propylaen Verlag, (06-05-93, Grisebach, #559, illus.), 12⁵⁄₁₆ x 9¼ in., (31.2 x 23.5 cm.), color lithograph on wove (BP 1167, DM 2875, FR 9689, Y 190,195).

BI *Sleep (Jacob 44), 1970, #43/50,* s., full margins, good cond., light/mount staining, margins folded, est. BP 2,0/3,000, (12-03-92, Sotheby-London, #279, illus.), 18½ x 25½ in., (470 x 648 mm.), lithograph on Arches.

$1449* *The Speech (J. 93), 1975,* s., #46/100, pub. Galerie Le Bateau Lavoir, margins, good cond., (12-03-92, Sotheby-London, #282, illus.), 12⅝ x 9⅞ in., (321 x 251 mm.),

lithograph on Arches (BP 935, DM 2279, FR 7778, Y 180,291).

$1320* *The Visit, 1968, Jacob 19,* s., num. XII/XX, printed Lacouriere, (09-20-92, Hindman, #756, illus.), 15½ x 10¾ in., (39.4 x 27.3 cm.), etching on Japan Hodomura (BP 773, DM 1959, FR 6701, Y 163,144).

BI *Woman With Ball (Jacob 54), 1971,* s., #25/75, full margins, good cond., paper discoloration, handling creases, tape remains, skinning, est. BP 2/2,500, (06-30-93, Sotheby-London, #420, illus.), sh 27⅜ x 20⅜ in., (695 x 518 mm.), lithograph on Arches.

DELVAUX, Paul (after)

$1201* *Les Gothiques, c. 1975,* s., #37/75, blindstamp Serigraphie Atelier, full margins, good cond., (06-30-93, Sotheby-London, #422), 17⅜ x 26⅛ in., (441 x 664 mm.), color screenprint on Arches (BP 805, DM 2048, FR 6910, Y 128,683).

$1167* *Tre Kvinnor,* s., 30/75, blindstamp, (12-04-92, AB Stockholm, #7054), 23⅝ x 16¹⁵⁄₁₆ in., (60 x 43 cm.), serigraph in colors (BP 749, DM 1859, FR 6305, Y 145,693, SK 7920).

DELVILLE, F.

$147* *Montfort L'Amaury, 1926,* p. L. Serre & Cie, very good cond., (11-19-92, Ribeyre/Baron, #102), 41⁵⁄₁₆ x 29¹⁵⁄₁₆ in., (105 x 76 cm.), poster (BP 97, DM 234, FR 789, Y 18,281).

DEMARNE, Pierre   b. 1924

$90* *"Moai Aux Yeux",* unique d., s., embellished, (04-04-93, Pescheteau, #199), 14¾ x 10⅝ in., (37.4 x 27 cm.), lithograph in black (BP 59, DM 145, FR 491, Y 10,247).

DEMARTEAU, G.

$295* *Pastorale Num. 524,* restored, cracks, creases, (06-16-93, Ader Tajan, #34), 8⅛ x 10⅝ in., (20.7 x 27 cm.), drawing manner engraving in 3 crayons (BP 197, DM 490, FR 1643, Y 31,463).

$182* *La Vierge Debout De Profil A Gauche Leve Un Voile Qui Recouvre L'Enfant Jesus Endormi,* after F. Boucher, yellowed, stains, faults, creases, large margins, (02-03-93, Ader Tajan, #56), 7¹⁵⁄₁₆ x 5¹³⁄₁₆ in., (20.3 x 14.8 cm.), drawing manner engraving (BP 127, DM 300, FR 1016, Y 22,640).

DEMARTEAU, Gilles   Flemish 1729-1776

$485* *"Bergere" (Leymarie num. 481),* after F. Boucher, trimmed margins, (03-22-93, Pescheteau, #8), sanguine (BP 327, DM 795, FR 2703, Y 56,160).

$2664* *"Buste De Jeune Femme Penchee A Droite"* and *"Buste De Jeune Femme DeTrois-Quart A Gauche" (Leymarie 419-20; Inventaire 18e Siecle, VI, pp. 452-3, nos. 419-20), c. 1773: A Pair,* after Jean-Antoine Watteau, pub. Demarteau, trimmed, thin spot, pinholes, good cond., (12-01-92, Christie-London, #263, illus.), sheet 9½ x 6½ in., (241 x 165 mm.), chalk-manner etching w/engraving in black and sanguine (BP 1760, DM 4246, FR 14,470, Y 331,673).

$1445* *Denicheur De Merles,* num. 84 after F. Boucher, stains, large margins, (04-02-93, Picard, #8), 9¹³⁄₁₆ x 14⁹⁄₁₆ in., (25 x 37 cm.), crayon-manner engraving in sanguine (BP 952, DM 2322, FR 7888, Y 164,522).

BI *Deux Pastorales (Leymarie 523-4; Inventaire 18e Siecle, VI, p. 477, nos. 523-4), c. 1775: Pair,* after Jean-Baptiste Huet, pub. Demarteau, trimmed, very good cond., est. BP 1,5/2,000, (12-01-92, Christie-London, #267, illus.), sheet 8⁵⁄₁₆ x 10⅝ in., (211 x 270 mm.), etching w/engraving in the lavis-manner in black and sanguine.

BI *Grande Pastorale (Leymarie 601; Inventaire 18e Siecle, VI, p. 488, no. 23), c. 1783,* after Jean-Baptiste Huet, pub. Demarteau, narrow margin, trimmed on or inside platemark, staining, est. BP 2/3,000, (12-01-92, Christie-London, #269, illus.), sheet 11⁷⁄₁₆ x 15⅛ in., (290 x 384 mm.), etching w/engraving in the lavis-manner in colors (black, blue, red and yellow).

$3767* *Jeune Femme De Face Au Petit Chapeau Plat,* num. 419 after A. Watteau, collector's stamp, (04-02-93, Picard, #9, illus.), 9⅝ x 6½ in., (24.4 x 16.5 cm.), 3-crayon drawing manner engraving (BP 2481, DEM 6054, FR 20,562, Y 428,897).

$7991* *Jeune Fille A La Rose (Leymarie 563; Inventaire 18e Siecle, VI, p. 483, no. 563), 1777,* after Francois Boucher, pub. G.-A. Demarteau, trimmed, creases, foxing, very good cond., prov., (12-01-92, Christie-London, #265, illus.), sheet 12 3/16 x 28 7/16 in., (310 x 722 mm.), chalk-manner etching w/engraving in colors (black, greenish-blue andred) (BP 5280, DM 12,737, FR 43,406, Y 994,895).

BI *La Peinture (De Leymarie 136),* after F. Boucher, est. DM 600, (12-04-92, Bassenge, #6554), 12 15/16 x 9 5/16 in., (33 x 23.6 cm.), etching in crayon.

BI *"Portrait De Madame Huet Lisant Une Lettre" and "Portrait De Madame Huet Jouant De La Guitare" (Leymarie 408, 483; cf. P. and B., I, p. 725, no. 56; Inventaire 18e Siecle VI, p. 449, no. 408 and p. 467, no. 483), c. 1773: Two,* after Jean-Baptiste-Marie Huet, watermark, pub. Demarteau, trimmed, foxing, prov., est. BP 2/3,000, (12-01-92, Christie-London, #262, illus.), sheet 13 1/4 x 10 1/2 in., (336 x 266 mm.), chalk-manner etching w/ engraving in black and red.

BI *Les Quatre Heures De Jour (Leymarie 546-9; Inventaire 18e Siecle, VI, p. 481, nos. 546-9), c. 1775: Set Of Four,* after Jean-Baptiste Huet, pub. Demarteau, trimmed, repairs, very good cond., est. BP 6/8,000, (12-01-92, Christie-London, #268, illus.), sheet 10 7/16 x 13 11/16 in., (265 x 348 mm.), chalk-manner etching w/engraving in black and sanguine.

$110* *"Tete De Homme", c. 1785,* after Durameau, foxing, tears, folds, (05-15-93, Cleveland, #10), 16 1/4 x 13 1/2 in., (41.3 x 34.3 cm.), crayon manner engraving (BP 72, DM 177, FR 595, Y 12,194).

$3163* *Tete De Jeune Fille Tenant Une Colombe (Leymarie 474; Inventaire 18eSiecle, VI, p. 465, no. 474; J.-R. 836), c. 1774,* margins, pub. Demarteau, staining, tape, good cond., (12-01-92, Christie-London, #266, illus.), plate 9 3/8 x 7 1/16 in., (238 x 180 mm.), chalk-manner etching w/engraving in black, sanguine and chamois on firm laid paper (BP 2090, DM 5041, FR 17,181, Y 393,800).

DEMARTEAU, Gilles (called Demarteau l'Aine) 1722-1776

$749* *Etude De Femme (Lleymaire 351; Inventaire 18e Siecle, VI, p. 436, no. 351), 1772,* after Jean-Honore Fragonard, pub. Demarteau, margins, stain, nicks, creases, tape, surface dirt, (12-01-92, Christie-London, #260), plate 15 3/8 x 11 1/16 in., (391 x 281 mm.), chalk-manner etching w/ engraving in sanguine, on Auvergne laid paper (BP 495, DM 1194, FR 4068, Y 93,252).

$4329* *Jeune Dessinateur (Leymaire 188; Inventaire 18e Siecle, VI, p. 396, no. 188; J.-R. 755), c. 1768,* after Francois Boucher, pbu. Demarteau, trimmed, foxmarks, tape, very-good cond., (12-01-92, Christie-London, #259, illus.), sheet 8 7/16 x 6 5/16 in., (214 x 160 mm.), chalk-manner etching w/engraving in black and sanguine on firm laid paper (BP 2860, DM 6900, FR 23,514, Y 538,969).

DEMARTELLY, John S. American b. 1903

$330* *While The Sun Shines,* s., (03-24-93, Grogan, #93), 9 1/2 x 14 in., (24.1 x 35.6 cm.), lithograph (BP 223, DM 539, FR 1834, Y 38,773).

$523* *"White Pastures",* foxing, discoloration, taped to mat, s., (06-11-93, Freemn/Fine Art, #140A), 10 x 13 3/4 in., (25.4 x 34.9 cm.), lithograph on wove (BP 344, DM 850, FR 2866, Y 55,491).

DENANTO, Francesco a.c. 1532

BI *Large Landscape With Hermits (Passavant VI S.213 u. S. 227, Nr 26),* prov., est. DM 1200, (06-04-93, Bassenge, #5101), 15 1/4 x 20 13/16 in., (38.7 x 52.8 cm.), woodcut.

DENIS, Maurice French 1870-1943

$920* *Amour: Couverture (C. 107), 1911,* good cond., loss, staining, handling creases, hinge remains, (05-19-93, Butterfield, #1909, illus.), 20 7/8 x 16 3/4 in., (530 x 425 mm.), lithograph in colors on Chine volant (BP 597, DM 1495, FR 5038, Y 101,849).

$3071* *La Damoiselle Elue (Cailler 30), 1892,* pen s., creases, cracks, large margins, (02-24-93, Picard, #81), color lithograph on ivory wove (BP 2142, DM 4985, FR 16,901, Y 360,361).

$706* *Elle Etait La Plus Belle Que Les Reves (Cailler 114-Johnson 32/7), 1892/1898,* series Amour, pub. Ambroise Vollard, (06-10-93, Hauswedell/Nolt, #230, illus.), 16 1/16 x 11 1/4 in., (40.8 x 28.5 cm.), color lithograph on wove (BP 462, DM 1150, FR 3871, Y 74,939).

$248* *Maternite Au Cypress (C. 103),* from Pan, III 3, full margins, good cond., paper losses, repaired tears, paper tape, discoloration, surface soiling, foxing, (02-24-93, Butterfield, #2915), 9 5/8 x 6 1/16 in., (244 x 154 mm.), lithograph on wove (BP 173, DM 403, FR 1365, Y 29,101).

BI *Maternite Au Cyres, 1898,* from Pan, est. DM 220-, (03-24-93, Venator/Hansten, #4475), 9 5/8 x 6 7/8 in., (24.4 x 17.4 cm.), lithograph.

BI *Maternite Devant La Mer (Caillier 120), 1900,* stone mono., Insel-Mappe, 3. Lieferung, est. DM 1200, (06-10-93, Hauswedell/Nolt, #231), image 13 11/16 x 9 13/16 in., (34.7 x 25 cm.), color lithograph on thick, smooth wove.

$6883* *Le Reflet Dans La Fontaine (C. 100), 1900,* num., s., staining, full margins, (02-24-93, Picard, #82), color lithograph on chine (BP 4800, DM 11,174, FR 37,881, Y 807,674).

$2144* *Le Reflet Dans La Fontaine (Cailler 100), 1897,* s., #30, pub. Vollard, full margins, good cond. w/in subject, repairs, (06-30-93, Sotheby-London, #423, illus.), 16 x 9 7/8 in., (406 x 251 mm.), color lithograph on wove (BP 1437, DM 3657, FR 12,336, Y 229,722).

BI *Le Reflet Dans La Fontaine (Cailler 100; Johnson 31), 1897,* s., (sig. rubbed), pub. L'Alum d'estampes originales de la Galerie Vollard, margins, repaired tears, puckering, surface dirt, soiling, good cond., est. $6/8,000, (11-05-92, Sotheby-NY, #157, illus.), 16 1/8 x 10 in., (410 x 255 mm.), sheet 21 x 15 1/2 in., (410 x 255 mm.), lithograph p. in colors on chine volant.

$440* *La Visitation (C. 79), 1894,* from Revue Blanche, margins, apparently good cond., (02-24-93, Butterfield, #2914), 6 3/8 x 5 1/8 in., (162 x 130 mm.), lithograph in colors on wove (BP 307, DM 714, FR 2422, Y 51,631).

DENIS-VALVERANE, Louis b. 1870

$40* *La Chanson De Paris. Piece Lyrique...Musique De Francis Casadeus, c.1910,* cond. A, (03-16-93, Boisgirard, #92), 31 1/2 x 23 5/8 in., (80 x 60 cm.), poster (BP 28, DM 67, FR 226, Y 4677).

DENKMAN, Norman

$56* *Penguins,* (05-12-93, Maynard, #286), silkscreen (BP 37, DM 90, FR 304, Y 6252, C$ 72).

DENNIS, Morgan

$94* *Galway Woman With Flowers,* s., #41/75, very good cond.?, (07-19-92, Bakker, #71), plate 7 3/4 x 5 1/4 in., (19.7 x 13.3 cm.), etching (BP 48, DM 137, FR 463, Y 11,686).

$135* *Let's Go!,* s., margins, (01-18-93, Bonhams, #99), plate 4 7/8 x 3 1/2 in., (12.4 x 8.9 cm.), etching (BP 88, DM 221, FR 736, Y 17,018).

DENNY, Robyn

BI *Generations, 1978: Thirteen,* s., d., num., good cond., est. BP 1,2/1,800, (12-03-92, Sotheby-London, #638, illus.), sheet 20 5/8 x 27 3/4 in., (523 x 705 mm.), thirteen etchings w/hand-coloring on wove.

BI *"Graffiti 1" and "Graffiti 4", 1977: Two,* s., d., t., num. 15/15 & 50/50, pub. Bernard Jacobsen, blindstamp, good cond., glue remains, skinned areas, est. $7/900, (02-24-93, Butterfield, #3210), each 21 1/2 x 16 in., (546 x 406 mm.), aquatint in color on Arches wove.

BI *Mirrors, 1978: Four,* s., d., num., good con., est. BP 6/800, (12-03-92, Sotheby-London, #636, illus.), silkscreen w/collage in colors on colored wove on card.

$767* *Portraits, 1973: Six,* six plates from the set of ten, s., d., #18/30, pub. Bernard Jacobson, good cond., handling marks and creases, (12-03-92, Sotheby-London, #637, illus.), each sheet approx. 31 1/8 x 23 3/8 in., (790 x 595 mm.), lithographs in colors on wove (BP 495, DM 1206, FR 4117, Y 95,434).

DENNY, Robyn b. 1930

BI *Graffiti 24, 1977,* s. Denny, 21/30, est. DK 1,000, (09-30-92, Kunsthallen, #88), color etching.

DENON, Dominique Vivant 1747-1825

$903* *Eine Junge Zeichnerin Zeigt Bewunderern Ihr Werk (The Illustr. Bartsch B. 121; Petra ten Doesschate Chu 521),*

1819, (12-04-92, Bassenge, #6555), 8⅞ x 12¾ in., (22.5 x 32.4 cm.), lithograph (BP 579, DM 1438, FR 4878, Y 112,734).

DENTE, Marco   d. 1527
BI *Die Skelette (B. XIV, 425),* after Baccio Bandinelli, watermark, est. DM 3,500, (12-04-92, Bassenge, #6138), 11¼ x 17 in., (28.5 x 43.2 cm.), engraving.

DENTON
$2300* *Fresh Water Fish, 1901: Nine,* (03-03-93, Sotheby-Arcade, #149), sight 7½ x 10½ in., (19.1 x 26.7 cm.), chromolithograph (BP 1587, DM 3787, FR 12,849, Y 268,754).

DEPATTA, Margaret
$1380* *Untitled, 1939,* mounted, s., d. by photog., (04-06-93, Sotheby-NY, #151, illus.), 10 x 7⅞ in., photograph, photogram (BP 911, DM 2223, FR 7529, Y 157,391).

DEQUEVAUVILLER, Francois   1745-C. 1807
$921* *"Le Coucher Des Ouvrieres En Modes" (Portalis/Beraldi aus 5), 1784,* after Lavreince, (06-08-93, Karl/Faber, #40), approx. 13⁹⁄₁₆ x 16⅛ in., (34.5 x 41 cm.), engraving and etching (BP 605, DM 1494, FR 5033, Y 97,823).
$4995* *"L'Assemblee Au Concert" and "L'Assemblee Au Salon" (Bocher 5-6; P. and B., I, pp. 744-5, nos. 1-2; L. and D. 43-4; Inventaire 18e Siecle, VII, pp.44-5, nos. 62, 63), 1782: A Pair,* after Nicolas Lavreince, 1st state of 3 and 2nd state of 4, watermark, pub. Dequevauviller, small to narrow margins, foxing, staining, defects, (12-01-92, Christie-London, #239, illus.), plate 15⅞ x 19⁹⁄₁₆ in., (403 x 497 mm.), etching w/engraving on Auvergne laid paper (BP 3300, DM 7961, FR 27,132, Y 621,887).

DERAIN, Andre   French 1880-1954
$412* *"Ballade Du Pauvre Macchabe Mal Enterre...": Six,* poeme de Rene Dalize, by Derain, s. Derain on colophon, (05-27-93, Swann, #88A), sh 10¼ x 10¼ in., (26 x 26 cm.), woodcuts (BP 264, DM 661, FR 2228, Y 44,168).
$621* *Ballets Russes De Monte-Carlo,* (01-31-93, Morelle/Marchan, #45), 30¹¹⁄₁₆ x 45¼ in., (78 x 115 cm.), poster (BP 418, DM 1000, FR 3382, Y 77,470).
$4611* *Bouquet De Fleurs, c. 1940,* s., (06-05-93, Bassenge, #5988B), color woodcut on Japan (BP 3035, DM 7476, FR 25,197, Y 494,636).
$154* *Buste De Femme,* bears stamp sig., num. 8/150, prov., (09-20-92, Hindman, #753), 10½ x 10 in., (26.7 x 25.4 cm.), lithograph (BP 90, DM 229, FR 782, Y 19,033).
$491* *Cavalier, c. 1915(?),* large margins, s., (06-16-93, Ader Tajan, #82), 3⁹⁄₁₆ x 2⅝ in., (9 x 6.7 cm.), etching (BP 327, DM 815, FR 2735, Y 52,368).
$491* *Cheval, 1915(?),* s., large margins, (06-16-93, Ader Tajan, #83), 5⅛ x 7¹⁄₁₆ in., (13 x 18 cm.), drypoint on chamois paper (BP 327, DM 815, FR 2735, Y 52,368).
$764* *Couple Au bord Du Torrent (Adhemar 41), 1912,* s., num., (06-23-93, Kornfeld, #320), drypoint on thick wove (BP 519, DM 1293, FR 4348, Y 83,233, SF 1150).
BI *Eloge De Pierreries, 1947,* book, by Heron de Villefosse, num. 4, p. Mourlot, pub. Cartier, pagesuncut, good cond., foxing, est. $8/1,000, (11-05-92, Sotheby-NY, #158), each sheet approx. 11⅜ x 9½ in., (290 x 240 mm.), one orig. lithograph p. in colors on Creve-Coeur du Marais.
$393* *Femme Nue Debout, 1912(?),* s., large margins, stains, yellowed, (06-16-93, Ader Tajan, #84), 4¼ x 2⁹⁄₁₆ in., (10.8 x 6.5 cm.), etching (BP 262, DM 652, FR 2189, Y 41,916).
$715* *Nu Assis Les Jambes Croisees,* s., t., num. Tirea 25 epreuves, no. 10, full margins, good cond., light-staining, creases, mat staining, (02-24-93, Butterfield, #2916), 16 x 8½ in., (406 x 216 mm.), lithograph on Arches (BP 499, DM 1161, FR 3935, Y 83,900).
$5147* *Petronius. Satyricon, 1934,* book w/title-page and text, #22, pub. under direction of artist, 1951, good cond., handling marks, orig. paper covers and slipcase, (06-30-93, Sotheby-London, #424, illus.), overall 17¾ x 13¾ in., (451 x 349 mm.), 33 engravings w/2 orig. drawings, 2 suites of 36 pl, 1 on old laid, 1on Richard de bas, 1 in black on Malaca teinte (ti (BP 3450, DM 8779, FR 29,614, Y 551,484).

$138* *Still Life,* very good/good cond., (11-21-92, Bakker, #136), image 8 x 6¾ in., (20.3 x 17.1 cm.), woodblock print (BP 91, DM 220, FR 741, Y 17,162).

DERCHE, Ch.-E.
$538* *PLM: L'Hiver, Le Printemps Au Maroc "Marrakech: Bab Doukkala", 1929,* very good cond., (03-13-93, Laurin, #95, illus.), 38¹⁵⁄₁₆ x 24³⁄₁₆ in., (99 x 61.5 cm.), (BP 375, DM 895, FR 3045, Y 63,406).

DEROUET, Edgar and Charles LESACQ
$209* *33e Salon De L'Automobile, 1939,* cond. A, (03-16-93, Boisgirard, #94), 47⁷⁄₁₆ x 31½ in., (120.5 x 80 cm.), poster (BP 144, DM 348, FR 1181, Y 24,439).

DEROUET and CLAVEL
$357* *Le Gazogene De France "Gohin-Poulenc", 1941,* very good cond., (11-19-92, Ribeyre/Baron, #58), 47¼ x 31½ in., (120 x 80 cm.), poster (BP 235, DM 569, FR 1917, Y 44,397).

DEROUSSE, Blanche   1873-1911
$161* *La Loute,* s.; t. verso, (05-15-93, Loudmer, #298), 12⁷⁄₁₆ x 9½ in., (316 x 242 mm.), sh 23¹⁵⁄₁₆ x 17½ in., (316 x 242 mm.), etching and drypoint on Arches wove (BP 105, DM 259, FR 870, Y 17,847).

DEROY, Isidor Laurent   French 1797-1886
$45* *Montmorency River, Quebec, Canada,* s. in plate, (02-04-93, Sloan, #393), 11 x 7½ in., (27.9 x 19.1 cm.), lithograph (BP 31, DM 74, FR 251, Y 5598).

DERRITZ, Der
BI *Bord De La Mer, 1963,* s., t., d., #2/10, annot., margins, taped to overmat, very good cond., foxing, surface soiling, creases, est. $2/400, (10-28-92, Butterfield, #2802), 11½ x 18½ in., (292 x 470 mm.), woodcut and linoleum cut on Van Gelder Zonen paper.

DESBOUTIN, Marcellin
$240* *L'Homme A La Pipe (Clement Janin 63), 1879,* first state of five, s., creases, dirt stains, frame traces, large margins, (06-11-93, Picard, #37), 17¹¹⁄₁₆ x 14¾ in., (450 x 375 mm.), etching, drypoint in black on laid (BP 158, DM 390, FR 1315, Y 25,464).
$639* *L'Homme Au Grand Chapeau (C.J. 73), 1888,* ded., d., ink s., whole margins, reddish stains, (06-11-93, Picard, #38), 9⅝ x 7⁷⁄₁₆ in., (245 x 189 mm.), drypoint on thick laid (BP 420, DM 1039, FR 3501, Y 67,798).

DESCOURTIS, Charles Melchior   1753-1820
BI *Frederique-Sophie-Wilhelmine, Princesse D'Orange (P. and B., I, p. 747, no. 9), c. 1785,* proof, cond. Hentzi, margins, spots, rubbing, staining, est. BP 5/800, (12-01-92, Christie-London, #275), plate 16¹⁵⁄₁₆ x 12⅜ in., (430 x 315 mm.), etching w/engraving in colors (black, blue and red).
$5621* *Histoire De Paul Et Virginie: Six,* after F. Schall, faults, good margins, (02-03-93, Ader Tajan, #57), 12⅜ x 15¾ in., (31.5 x 40 cm.), tinted engraving (BP 3924, DM 9256, FR 31,385, Y 699,216).
$908* *L'Amant Surpris,* after F. Schall, good margins, (02-03-93, Ader Tajan, #58), 17¹³⁄₁₆ x 14⁹⁄₁₆ in., (45.2 x 37 cm.), tinted wash engraving (BP 634, DM 1495, FR 5070, Y 112,949).
$310* *Noce De Village,* after Taunay, t., stains, tear, (04-02-93, Picard, #10), 1¼ x 9¹⁄₁₆ in., (31 x 23 cm.), color tinted engraving (BP 204, DM 498, FR 1692, Y 35,295).
$1172* *"Paul Et Virginie": Five,* reddish stains, thin spots, (03-22-93, Pescheteau, #12), color (BP 789, DM 1922, FR 6533, Y 135,711).
BI *Paul Et Virginie, c. 1780,* after Jean Frederic Schall, 1 from set of 6, p. by Blin le Jeune, pub. Descourtis, trimmed to plate, defects, thin patches, est. BP 180/220, (11-30-92, Phillips-London, #284), sheet 12⅝ x 16 in., (321 x 406 mm.), mezzotint in colors.
BI *Princesse Wilhelmine De Prusse, 1791,* after Stefano Torelli, proof, margins, surface dirt, rubbing, est. BP800/1,200, (06-30-93, Sotheby-London, #108), 17¼ x 12¾ in., (438 x 324 mm.), etching and aquatint in color on wove.
$708* *La Rixe(Portalis-Beraldi 1 Nr3 II),* after Taunay, (06-04-93, Bassenge, #5471), 14⅝ x 10⅞ in., (37.2 x 27.6 cm.), color etching (BP 468, DM 1150, FR 3875, Y 76,359).

BI *Vue D'Un Pont Sur L'Aar,* est. DM 750, (12-04-92, Bassenge, #6556), 14³⁄₁₆ x 10¹⁄₁₆ in., (36 x 25.5 cm.), color etching reworked w/brush.

DESEVE

BI *"La Barge" and "Le Combattant Our Paon De Mer En Amour": Two,* from "Histoire Naturelle Des Oiseaux, Paris", est. $125/175, (02-04-93, Sloan, #1249), each image approx. 4¾ x 3 in., (12.1 x 7.6 cm.), engraving.

BI *"L'Oiseau Royal" and "Le Kamichi": Two,* from "Histoire Naturelle Des Oiseaux, Paris", est. $125/175, (02-04-93, Sloan, #1250), each image approx. 4¾ x 3 in., (12.1 x 7.6 cm.), engraving.

BI *"Le Margay" and "La Chauve Souris Fer De Lance": Two,* from "Histoire Naturelle Des Oiseaux, Paris", est. $125/175, (02-04-93, Sloan, #1248), (12.1 x 7.6 cm.), engraving.

BI *"Le Savacon" and "La Spatule": Two,* from"Histoire Naturelle Des Oiseaux, Paris", est. $125/175, (02-04-93, Sloan, #1246), (12.1 x 7.6 cm.), engraving.

BI *"Le Secretaire Ou Le Messager" and "Le Butor": Two,* from "Histoire Naturelle Des Oiseaux, Paris", est. $125/175, (02-04-93, Sloan, #1247), (12.1 x 7.6 cm.), engraving.

DESFOR, Max b. 1914

$1495* *The Korean Bridge, 1950,* lit., (04-08-93, Christie-NY, #264, illus.), 13⅜ x 10 in., (34 x 25.4 cm.), photograph, gelatin silver print (BP 980, DM 2402, FR 8129, Y 169,655).

DESGACHONS

$315* *Grand Prix De Saint-Gaudens, 1952,* good cond., (11-19-92, Ribeyre/Baron, #64), 23⅝ x 15³⁄₁₆ in., (60 x 38.5 cm.), poster (BP 207, DM 502, FR 1692, Y 39,174).

DESHAYES

$33* *"Reinparts De Carcassonne",* s., t., (06-11-93, DuMouchelle, #2272), 12 x 7¾ in., (30.5 x 19.7 cm.), etching (BP 22, DM 54, FR 181, Y 3501).

DESMARAIS, Gabriel (called GABY) Canadian 1926-1990

BI *"Marc-Aurele Fortin",* #7/50, s., d. Gaby 65, (06-16-93, Encans, #38), 9¹³⁄₁₆ x 7½ in., (25 x 19 cm.), epreuve (proof) argentique.

DESMAZIERES, Erik

$1123* *"Tour De Babel", 1976,* IV/X, s., d., (10-18-92, Pescheteau, #123), 19⁵⁄₁₆ x 24¹³⁄₁₆ in., (49 x 63 cm.), etching and brown on Arches (BP 681, DM 1659, FR 5635, Y 134,090).

DESNOYER, Francois (after)

BI *"Liseuses Au Bord De La Mer", 1950,* LXXV/C, s., est. FF1,000/1,200, (04-04-93, Pescheteau, #200), 18⅛ x 14³⁄₁₆ in., (46 x 36 cm.), color wood engraving.

DESPREZ, Jean Louis

$12,869* *Chimere (Baudicour 6; Wollin 32-33),* 3rd state of 5, printing little drily, margins, nick creasing, surface dirt, (06-30-93, Sotheby-London, #109, illus.), 12¾ x 15 in., (324 x 381 mm.), etching on paper w/an Auvergne watermark (BP 8625, DM 21,950, FR 74,045, Y 1,378,871).

BI *Promotion Medicale (Wollin 39),* 1st state of 2, trimmed into subject, repaired tears, paper split, surface dirt, damages, (06-30-93, Sotheby-London, #110, illus.), 20½ x 33 in., (521 x 838 mm.), etching, extensively hand-colored, on 2 joined sheets, on paper w/a Strasburg Lily watermark.

DESRAIS (after)

$364* *"Promenade Du Boulevard Des Italiens Ou Petit Coblentz",* (03-22-93, Pescheteau, #13), color print (BP 245, DM 597, FR 2029, Y 42,149).

DETHIER, Hendrik c. 1610-c. 1633

$991* *Bust Of A Man With Beard, In Three-Quarter Profile From The Left (Wurzbach 1, Hollstein 1), 1633,* watermark, blindstamp, (06-04-93, Bassenge, #5105, illus.), 5¹¹⁄₁₆ x 4³⁄₁₆ in., (14.5 x 10.6 cm.), etching (BP 656, DM 1609, FR 5424, Y 106,881).

DETHOMAS, Maxime

$205* *Brand (A. 74), 1894,* staining, margins, (02-24-93, Picard, #186), color lithograph (BP 143, DM 333, FR 1128, Y 24,055).

$154* *Une Mere (A. 79), 1895,* before text, (02-24-93, Picard, #187), yellow-orange lithograph (BP 107, DM 250, FR 848, Y 18,071).

DETMOLD, Edward J. and Maurice British 19th/20th cent.

$55* *"The Falcon",* ident., t. on label verso, excellent cond., toned paper, (10-27-92, Bourne, #198, illus.), image 8 x 6 in., (20.3 x 15.2 cm.), etching (BP 35, DM 84, FR 286, Y 6728).

DETMOLD, Edward Julius English 1883-1957

$343* *Two Goldfish, 1926,* #3/25, s., init., i. imp, margins, (05-20-93, Bonhams-Chelsea, #25, illus.), plate 4½ x 5⅛ in., (11.4 x 13 cm.), etching w/aquatint in colors (BP 220, DM 553, FR 1864, Y 37,875).

BI *Windmills,* s., margins, est. BP 4/60, (03-17-93, Bonhams-Chelsea, #399), plate 5¾ x 11¼ in., (14.6 x 28.6 cm.), drypoint etching.

$34* *Windmills,* s., margins, (05-20-93, Bonhams-Chelsea, #116), plate 5¾ x 11¼ in., (14.6 x 28.6 cm.), drypoint etching (BP 22, DM 55, FR 185, Y 3754).

DETOUCHE, Henry

$115* *Portrait Of A Woman,* L'Estampe Moderne blindstamp, margins, apparently good condition, tear, (03-31-93, Butterfield, #5237), 13⅞ x 9¾ in., (35.2 x 24.8 cm.), lithograph printed in colors on wove (BP 76, DM 185, FR 628, Y 13,224).

DETWILLER, Frederick

BI *Roadways And Cables N.Y.C.,* margins, s., est. $3/500, (05-22-93, Collins, #110), 18 x 11⅛ in., (45.7 x 28.3 cm.), etching.

DEVERIA, Achille French 1800-1857

$206* *Alexandre Dumas (H. Beraldi, 17),* reddish stains, creases, tears, large margins, drystamp, collector'sstamp, (04-02-93, Picard, #87), 11¹³⁄₁₆ x 9¹³⁄₁₆ in., (30 x 25 cm.), lithograph on Chine fixe (BP 136, DM 331, FR 1124, Y 23,454).

$124* *"Jeune Homme Assis" and "Buste D'Homme": Two,* yellowed, reddish stains, large margins, (04-02-93, Picard, #88), one 15⁹⁄₁₆ x 10¹⁄₁₆ in., (39.5 x 25.5 cm.), other 10¹⁄₁₆ x 11⁷⁄₁₆ in., (39.5 x 25.5 cm.), lithograph on Chine fixe (BP 82, DM 199, FR 677, Y 14,118).

DEVILLE, Henri Wilfrid

$143* *"Looking Across Fulton Market", "The Pier Eleven", "Broadway South Of 42nd St.", "Coenties Slip" "Coal Work Edison C" and "The Narrow Street": Six,* num., s., full margins, (02-24-93, Picard, #84), etching (BP 100, DM 232, FR 787, Y 16,780).

DEVINE, Jed American b. 1944

$19,550* *"The Bethesda Terrace",* self-pub., 1986, portfolio, mounted, 1982-85, p. 1986, exhib., (04-06-93, Sotheby-NY, #498, illus.), 9½ x 7½ in., photograph, 103 photog., platinum print (BP 12,913, DM 31,497, FR 106,656, Y 2,229,699).

$1265* *White Jug, 1989,* s. by photog., Chinese mono. blindstamp, (04-06-93, Sotheby-NY, #226, illus.), 9½ x 7½ in., photograph, palladium print on tissue paper (BP 836, DM 2038, FR 6901, Y 144,275).

DEWASNE, Jean b. 1921

$239* *Composition,* s. J. Dewasne, 58/62, (03-24-93, Kunsthallen, #84), lithograph in colors (BP 162, DM 390, FR 1329, Y 28,081, DK 1495).

$169* *Composition,* s. J. Dewasne, 246/275, (09-30-92, Kunsthallen, #92), color lithograph (BP 95, DM 240, FR 811, Y 20,281, DK 920).

$131* *Composition,* s. J. Dewasne, 264/275, (12-02-92, Kunsthallen, #238), serigraph in color (BP 85, DM 206, FR 703, Y 16,300, DK 805).

$147* *Composition,* s. J. Dewasne, 97/150, (03-24-93, Kunsthallen, #77), serigraph in colors (BP 100, DM 240, FR 817, Y 17,272, DK 920).

$92* *Composition,* s. J. Dewasne, 149/275, (03-24-93, Kunsthallen, #78), serigraph in colors (BP 62, DM 150, FR 511, Y 10,810, DK 575).

$184* *Composition,* s. J. Dewasne, 256/300, (03-24-93, Kunsthallen, #80), color serigraph (BP 125, DM 301, FR 1023, Y 21,619, DK 1150).

$220* *Composition,* s. J. Dewasne, 49/150, (03-24-93, Kunsthallen, #81), color serigraph (BP 149, DM 359, FR 1223, Y 25,849, DK 1380).

$184* *Composition,* s. J. Dewasne, 20/150, (03-24-93, Kunsthallen, #82), color serigraph (BP 125, DM 301, FR 1023, Y 21,619, DK 1150).

$128* *Composition,* s. J. Dewasne, 130/150, (03-24-93, Kunsthallen, #79), color serigraph (BP 87, DM 209, FR 712, Y 15,039, DK 805).

$134* *Composition, 1973,* s., (03-31-93, Briest, #E34), 29¹⁵⁄₁₆ x 22¹⁄₁₆ in., (76 x 56 cm.), color serigraph (BP 89, DM 216, FR 732, Y 15,409).

BI *Composition, 1973: Two,* s., est. FF 3/4,000, (11-16-92, Briest, #285), 26¹⁵⁄₁₆ x 18½ in., (68.5 x 47 cm.), serigraph in colors.

$128* *Composition, 1974,* s. J. Dewasne 74, (03-24-93, Kunsthallen, #83), color serigraph (BP 87, DM 209, FR 712, Y 15,039, DK 805).

BI *Composition, c. 1955,* s., yellowed, wormhole, est. FF1,200/1,500, (05-27-93, Briest, #79), 25³⁄₁₆ x 19⁵⁄₁₆ in., (64 x 49 cm.), color serigraph.

BI *Compositions: Set Of Four,* s., est. FF 8/9,000, (11-16-92, Briest, #286), 27¾ x 36¼ in., (70.5 x 92 cm.), serigraph in color.

$316* *Preface A Un Livre Futur,* s. J. Dewasne, 1949, (09-30-92, Kunsthallen, #91), book w/color lithographs (BP 178, DM 448, FR 1516, Y 37,922, DK 1725).

$210* *Untitled,* #1/100, s. verso, (01-28-93, Pescheteau, #121), 25⁹⁄₁₆ x 31½ in., (65 x 80 cm.), color serigraph (BP 139, DM 333, FR 1126, Y 26,074).

DEWEY
$70 *Our Daddy Is Fighting,* T.F. Moore Co., No. 6, torn corner, (09-24-92, Alderfer, #306), 30 x 20 in., (76.2 x 50.8 cm.), (BP 41, DM 104, FR 352, Y 8421).

DEWS, J. Steven (after)
BI *The Big Class, 1930,* #185/600, s., pub. Marine Gallery, est. BP 60/90, (02-17-93, Bonhams-Chelsea, #356), image 20 x 27¾ in., (50.8 x 70.5 cm.), color reproduction.

$106* *Eight Metres Racing Off West Solent,* s., num. 158/850, blindstamp Chelsea Green Editions, (08-12-92, Bonhams, #189), image 13¼ x 18 in., (33.7 x 45.7 cm.), reproduction in colors (BP 55, DM 155, FR 525, Y 13,510).

BI *The Racing Schooner Westward,* s., pub. Marine Gallery, est. BP 50/60, (08-12-92, Bonhams, #190), image 20 x 30 in., (50.8 x 76.2 cm.), reproduction in colors.

DEXEL, Walter   German 1890-1973
$650* *"Blick Durchs Fenster" (Vitt 6), 1918,* s., (11-28-92, Grisebach, #490, illus.), 6⅝ x 6 in., (16.8 x 15.3 cm.), woodcut on silkpaper (BP 429, DM 1036, FR 3515, Y 80,896).

$282* *Der Diplomat, Franz Von Papen, 1971,* #97/100, s. W. Dexel, glue stained, (03-24-93, Venator/Hansten, #4478), approx. 22¹³⁄₁₆ x 14⁹⁄₁₆ in., (58 x 37 cm.), serigraph w/ blue (BP 191, DM 461, FR 1568, Y 33,134).

$1977* *Moschee (Vitt 3), 1916,* s., d., t., num. 29/30, (06-10-93, Hauswedell/Nolt, #233, illus.), image 3¹⁵⁄₁₆ x 5¹⁵⁄₁₆ in., (10 x 15.1 cm.), watercolored woodcut on hand-made (BP 1293, DM 3219, FR 10,839, Y 209,850).

BI *Moschee (Vitt 3), 1916,* #29/30, s., d., t., num., est. DM 2,600-, (11-21-92, Lempertz, #111, illus.), 5¹⁵⁄₁₆ x 3⅞ in., (15.1 x 9.9 cm.), woodcut on hand-made.

$1412* *Moschee (Vitt. 3), 1916,* s., d., t., num. 4/30, (06-10-93, Hauswedell/Nolt, #234), 5¹⁵⁄₁₆ x 3¹⁵⁄₁₆ in., (15.1 x 10 cm.), woodcut on hand-made (BP 924, DM 2299, FR 7741, Y 149,878).

$433* *Ohne Titel (Vitt 39), 1969,* s., d., (11-28-92, Schoppmann, #480), 21⁹⁄₁₆ x 17¹³⁄₁₆ in., (54.7 x 45.3 cm.), color serigraph on handmade board (BP 286, DM 690, FR 2342, Y 53,889).

$2260* *Quadrate 1925 (Vitt. 16), 1925,* s., d., t., num. 34/40, (06-10-93, Hauswedell/Nolt, #237, illus.), image 9⅛ x 8⁹⁄₁₆ in., (23.2 x 21.7 cm.), watercolored woodcut on hand-made Japan (BP 1478, DM 3680, FR 12,390, Y 239,890).

$1138* *Reklame-Laterne, 1924,* ink s., d., t., (11-12-92, Lempertz, #44, illus.), 4¹¹⁄₁₆ x 3½ in., (11.9 x 8.9 cm.), sheet 6⁵⁄₁₆ x 5¹⁄₁₆ in., (11.9 x 8.9 cm.), photograph, retouched gelatin silver print (BP 728, DM 1788, FR 6095, Y 140,789).

BI *Sonne Im Fenster (Vitt 8), 1918,* #25/17, s., est. DM 2,400-, (11-21-92, Lempertz, #113), 11¹³⁄₁₆ x 7¹³⁄₁₆ in., (30 x 19.8 cm.), woodcut on Japan.

BI *Sonne Im Fenster (Vitt. 8), 1918,* s., d., num. 20/25, est. DM 2500, (06-10-93, Hauswedell/Nolt, #236), image 11⅞ x 7¹³⁄₁₆ in., (30.2 x 19.9 cm.), woodcut on hand-made Japan.

$403* *Der Staatsmann (Vitt 47), 1970,* s., num., creases, (09-25-92, Granier, #2809), sheet 25⁹⁄₁₆ x 19¹³⁄₁₆ in., (65 x 50.3 cm.), color screen print on hand-made (BP 235, DM 597, FR 2020, Y 48,642).

$1412* *Steile Strasse (Vitt. 5), 1918,* s., d., num., block mono., #24/30, (06-10-93, Hauswedell/Nolt, #235, illus.), image 7⁵⁄₁₆ x 8¹¹⁄₁₆ in., (18.6 x 22 cm.), woodcut on hand-made Japan (BP 924, DM 2299, FR 7741, Y 149,878).

BI *Steile Strasse, Der Strahl (Vitt 5), 1918,* num., i., s., d., est. DM 2,500-, (11-21-92, Lempertz, #112), 7⁵⁄₁₆ x 8¹¹⁄₁₆ in., (18.5 x 22.1 cm.), woodcut on Japan.

$686* *"Sternenbrucke (Abstrakte Komposition)" (Vitt 10), 1919,* s., t., d., (11-28-92, Grisebach, #491, illus.), 10½ x 8¹⁄₁₆ in., (26.7 x 20.5 cm.), woodcut on wove (BP 453, DM 1093, FR 3710, Y 85,376).

$2013* *Sternenbrucke (Vitt 10; Peters III/4), 1919,* s., mono., d. in block, in Bauhaus-Mappe III, Deutsche Kunstler, 1922, Bauhaus blindstamp, (10-09-92, Winterberg, #1982, illus.), 10⁷⁄₁₆ x 7⅞ in., (26.5 x 20 cm.), woodcut on Japan (BP 1194, DM 2990, FR 10,040, Y 245,069).

DEXTER, Walter
$410* *Cromer, Lms, Lner, c. 1940,* fold marks w/corresponding defects, (02-04-93, Christie-S. Ken, #60, illus.), 40 x 50 in., (101.6 x 127 cm.), color lithograph (BP 286, DM 675, FR 2289, Y 51,001).

DEYROLLE, Jean   French 1911-1967
BI *"6 Lithographie Originali A Colori Di Deyrolle", 1963: Six,* portfolio, s., #12/40, est. SF 5/5,500, (04-21-93, Germann, #369), 29½ x 19¹¹⁄₁₆ in., (750 x 500 mm.), color lithograph.

$184* *Composition,* s. J. Deyrolle 32/50, (03-24-93, Kunsthallen, #85), color lithograph (BP 125, DM 301, FR 1023, Y 21,619, DK 1150).

$209* *Untitled,* s. 3/50, (09-29-92, B. Rasmussen, #304), lithograph in colors (BP 117, DM 295, FR 1007, Y 24,949, DK 1150).

DI STETTO, A. Benois
$284* *Grindelwald, 1937,* loss, excell. cond., (02-04-93, Christie-S. Ken, #18), 39½ x 27½ in., (100.3 x 69.9 cm.), color lithograph backed on japan (BP 198, DM 468, FR 1586, Y 35,328).

DI SUVERO, Mark   American b. 1933
$920* *Tetra (Tyler 176:MdS6), 1976,* s., #7/20, blindstamp, pub. Tyler Graphics, Ltd., full margins, goodcond., (05-15-93, Sotheby-NY, #1237), sheet 50⅞ x 39½ in., (129.2 x 100.3 cm.), lithograph in yellow (BP 598, DM 1480, FR 4973, Y 101,984).

DIAMENT, R.   b. 1907
$2013* *Parachutes, 1930's,* backed w/card, s., t. in Russian, by photog., (04-06-93, Sotheby-NY, #319, illus.), photograph (BP 1330, DM 3243, FR 10,982, Y 229,585).

BI *School Children, 1937,* s. by photog., est. $1,5/2,000, (04-06-93, Sotheby-NY, #320, illus.), 16½ x 11¼ in., photograph.

BI *The Volga, Moscow, 1937,* ink s.; t., d., est. $2,5/3,500, (04-08-93, Christie-NY, #145, illus.), 11⅜ x 18¼ in., (28.9 x 46.4 cm.), photograph, gelatin silver print.

DIAMOND, Harry
BI *"Francis Bacon ANd Lucien Freud In Dean St. Soho London", 1974,* s., t., d., est. BP 5/800, (10-29-92, Christie-London, #197, illus.), image 9¾ x 14½ in., (24.8 x 36.8 cm.), photograph, gelatin silver print.

DIAZ, Gerard
$116* *"Arizona", 1981 and "Obscure", 1981: Two,* s., d., t., #25/50 and 29/50, (06-28-93, Loudmer, #31), first 18⅛ x 12¹³⁄₁₆ in., (460 x 325 mm.), second 17½ x 13⅜ in.,

(460 x 325 mm.), sepia drypoint, roulette and aquatint on Arches wove (BP 78, DM 197, FR 664, Y 12,308).

$155* *"Bruce Canyon", 1986 and "Paysage Oriental": Two,* s., d., #5/90 and 25/90, (06-28-93, Loudmer, #30), first 13¾ x 19½ in., (350 x 495 mm.), second 19½ x 13¾ in., (350 x 495 mm.), first, color etching on Moulin de Gue wove; second, aquatint and drypoint in bistre on BFK Rives (BP 104, DM 263, FR 887, Y 16,446).

DIAZ MERRY, M.

$896* *PLM and Comite De Propogande Et De Tourisme: Tanger, 1928,* very good cond., (03-13-93, Laurin, #97, illus.), 43¹¹⁄₁₆ x 31⁵⁄₁₆ in., (111 x 79.5 cm.), (BP 625, DM 1491, FR 5071, Y 105,598).

DICK, Axel   b. 1935

BI *Untitled (Grungelbe Keile), 1972,* s., #2/100, wrinkled, est. DM 150, (09-18-92, Schloss Ahlden, #992), 27⁹⁄₁₆ x 19⅝ in., (70 x 49.9 cm.), color serigraph on white cardboard.

DICK, Beau   Kwaguilth b. 1955

$151* *'Loon',* #48/100, s., (10-21-92, Maynard, #44), sheet 19½ x 12½ in., (49.5 x 31.8 cm.), silkscreen (BP 94, DM 228, FR 776, Y 18,392, C$ 187).

DICKENS, Charles   English 19th cent.

BI *Ann Hathaway's Cottage,* s., t., est. $125/175, (12-10-92, Sloan, #590), 3½ x 5½ in., (8.9 x 14 cm.), etching.

DICKENSON & SON, Publisher

$358* *"Siout", "Church Of The Holy Sepulchre, Jerusalem" and "Hall In The Palace Of The Emir Beschir": Three,* margins, staining, discoloration, (10-07-92, Christie-S. Ken, #96), each 11¾ x 16½ in., (29.8 x 41.9 cm.), colored tinted lithograph (BP 209, DM 518, FR 1757, Y 43,055).

DICKERSON, Robert Henry   b. 1924

$142* *The Play Ground,* s. R Dickerson, i., #4/26, (08-11-92, L. Joel, #168G), 11⅞ x 8¹⁵⁄₁₆ in., (30.2 x 22.8 cm.), etching (BP 74, DM 208, FR 706, Y 18,184, A$ 192).

DICKINSON, Edwin   American 1891-1978

$248* *The Marguerite,* s., very good cond.?, (03-28-93, Bakker, #28), 5 x 4½ in., (12.7 x 11.4 cm.), drypoint (BP 167, DM 405, FR 1375, Y 28,864).

DICKINSON, Messrs, Publisher

BI *Members Of The MCC Outside The Long Room, Lords,* s., blindstamp, pub. 1908, margins, surface defects, est. BP 2/300, (03-03-93, Bonhams-Chelsea, #244), plate 28 x 39 in., (71.1 x 99.1 cm.), photogravure.

$279* *Members Of The MCC Outside The Long Room, Lords,* s., pub. blindstamp, 1908, margins, surface defects, (06-30-93, Bonhams-Chelsea, #262), plate 28 x 39 in., (71.1 x 99.1 cm.), photogravure (BP 187, DM 476, FR 1605, Y 29,894).

DICKINSON BROTHERS and FOSTER, Publisher

$285* *A Lawn Meet At Badminton, 1880,* margins, laid down, staining, (11-12-92, Bonhams-Chelsea, #73, illus.), plate 26 x 45 in., (66 x 114.3 cm.), photogravure (BP 187, DM 452, FR 1523, Y 35,338).

DICKSEE, Frank (after)

$109* *The Emblem, 1903,* pub. Frost and Reed, trimmed, (11-19-92, Bonhams-Chelsea, #129), image 21½ x 16 in., (54.6 x 40.6 cm.), mezzotint w/hand coloring (BP 72, DM 174, FR 585, Y 13,556).

DICKSEE, Herbert

$268* *A Sleeping Peke, 1924,* s., blindstamp, pub. Frost and Reed, margins, (11-12-92, Bonhams-Chelsea, #83, illus.), plate 5 x 10½ in., (12.7 x 26.7 cm.), etching (BP 176, DM 425, FR 1432, Y 33,230).

$253* *Two Terriers, 1929,* s., margins, (01-18-93, Bonhams, #72), image 11¼ x 16¼ in., (28.6 x 41.3 cm.), etching (BP 165, DM 414, FR 1379, Y 31,892).

DICKSEE, Margaret Isabel (after)   English 1859-1903

$80* *Swift And Stella,* (02-04-93, Sloan, #391), 18¾ x 23 in., (47.6 x 58.4 cm.), aquatint (BP 56, DM 132, FR 447, Y 9951).

DICKSON, Jane

BI *The Ten Commandments: VIII - Thou Shalt Not Steal, 1987,* s., d., num. 2/84, blindstamp, good cond., est. $6/800, (02-24-93, Butterfield, #3211, illus.), 23⅝ x 17¾ in., (600 x 451 mm.), lithograph in colors on Dieu Donne handmade.

$85* *"Times Square", "Untitled" and "Adult Books": Three,* each s., (02-04-93, Sloan, #2972), each 8½ x 11 in., (21.6 x 27.9 cm.), color lithograph w/handcolored borders (BP 59, DM 140, FR 475, Y 10,573).

DICKSON, Jennifer

$25* *"Les Premiers Astres", 1965,* s., d., good cond., (05-15-93, Cleveland, #463), 27 x 13 in., (68.6 x 33 cm.), etching and mezzotint (BP 16, DM 40, FR 135, Y 2771).

$193* *The Prince,* s., t., #1/20, prov., (11-30-92, Ritchie, #53, illus.), image 8 x 11½ in., (20.2 x 29.2 cm.), hand colored photo-engraving (BP 127, DM 307, FR 1044, Y 24,020, C$ 248).

DIDAY, Francois   Swiss 1802-1877

BI *Eaux Fortes De F. Diday, 1875: Five,* stamped, est. SF 150/200, (09-04-92, Germann, #302), each 11¼ x 15¾ in., (285 x 400 mm.), etching on Chine Colle.

DIEBENKORN, Richard   American 1922-1993

BI *41 Etchings And Drypoint: #21, 1965,* inits., d., t., annot. a.p., pub. Crown Point Press, very good cond.,surface soiling, est. $1,4/1,800, (05-19-93, Butterfield, #2155), 8¼ x 6⅞ in., (210 x 175 mm.), etching on wove.

$9200* *Blue With Red (Yellowstone Art Center 31), 1987,* init., d., #188/200, blindstamp, pub. Crown Point Press, full margins, good cond., (05-15-93, Sotheby-NY, #941, illus.), 33½ x 23 in., (85.1 x 58.4 cm.), woodcut in colors on Echizen Kozo Mashi paper (BP 5982, DM 14,798, FR 49,730, Y 1,019,843).

$9350* *Blue With Red, 1987,* init., d., #80/200, blindstamp, pub. Crown Point Press, full margins,good cond., (11-07-92, Sotheby-NY, #539, illus.), 33⅝ x 23 in., (854 x 584 mm.), woodcut p. in colors on Echizen Kozo Mashi (BP 6113, DM 14,929, FR 50,459, Y 1,154,036).

$16,100* *Blue, 1984,* inits., d., #118/200, Crown Point Press blindstamp, full margins, excell. cond., (05-11-93, Christie-NY, #393, illus.), sheet 42½ x 26¾ in., (108 x 67.9 cm.), color woodcut on Misumata (BP 10,278, DM 25,362, FR 85,456, Y 1,770,982).

$15,400* *Blue, 1984,* inits., d., #147/200, blindstamp, full margins, excellent cond., (11-09-92, Christie-NY, #261, illus.), 42½ x 26¾ in., (108 x 67.9 cm.), colored woodcut on Misumata (BP 10,182, DM 24,585, FR 83,064, Y 1,911,144).

$14,375* *Blue, 1984,* init., d., #155/200, blindstamp, pub. Crown Point Press, full margins, good cond., crease, skinned spots, (05-15-93, Sotheby-NY, #940, illus.), 40¼ x 24¾ in., (102.2 x 62.9 cm.), woodcut in colors on Mitsumata (BP 9347, DM 23,122, FR 77,703, Y 1,593,504).

$3850* *Center Square, 1985,* s., d., num. 15/25, blindstamp of pub. Crown Point Press, full margins, apparently very good cond., (02-24-93, Butterfield, #3014, illus.), 10⅜ x 7¹⁵⁄₁₆ in., (264 x 202 mm.), etching & aquatint in dark blue & black on Rives (BP 2685, DM 6250, FR 21,189, Y 451,772).

BI *Club And Spades: Blue Club, 1981,* init., d., #12/35, blindstamp, pub. Crown Point Press, full margins,good cond., est. $5/6,000, (11-07-92, Sotheby-NY, #535, illus.), 18⅞ x 18 in., (479 x 457 mm.), etching and aquatint p. in colors.

$7150* *Clubs-Blue Ground, 1982,* inits., d., #32/35, pub. Crown Point Press, full margins, excellent cond., (11-09-92, Christie-NY, #259, illus.), 33 x 26⅜ in., (838 x 670 mm.), etching, aquatint and drypoint in black and blue (BP 4727, DM 11,414, FR 38,565, Y 887,317).

$7475* *Combination, 1981,* inits., d., i. TP, Crown Point Press blindstamp, full margins, excell. cond., (05-11-93, Christie-NY, #391, illus.), sheet 30¾ x 24⅛ in., (781 x 613 mm.), color etching and aquatint on wove (BP 4772, DM 11,775, FR 39,676, Y 822,242).

$2200* *Construct (Drypoint) (Guillemin p. 112), 1980,* init., d., #33/35, blindstamp, pub. Crown Point Press, full margins,good cond., handling creases, (11-07-92, Sotheby-NY, #534, illus.), 10⅞ x 15⅜ in., (276 x 391 mm.), etching

p. in colors (BP 1438, DM 3513, FR 11,873, Y 271,538).

$3850* *Construct, Drypoint, 1980,* s., d., #32/35, blindstamp pub. Crown Point Press, full margins, very good cond.?, (10-28-92, Butterfield, #2934, illus.), 10 x 15 in., (254 x 381 mm.), color drypoint w/etching and aquatint on Rives (BP 2453, DM 5946, FR 20,189, Y 472,393).

$1380* *Domino II, 1990,* inits., d., #24/35, blindstamp publisher, Crown Paint Press, full margins, very good cond., (05-19-93, Butterfield, #2157, illus.), 18 x 12¹⁵⁄₁₆ in., (457 x 329 mm.), etching and soft-ground w/drypoint on wove (BP 896, DM 2243, FR 7558, Y 152,773).

BI *Double X, 1987,* s., d., #20/50, Crown Point Press blindstamp, full margins, scuffs, very good cond., the Late M. Anwar Kamal, M.D. Coll., est. $1/1,400, (05-11-93, Christie-NY, #395), sheet 23⅝ x 17⅜ in., (600 x 441 mm.), woodcut on Japan.

$3025* *Eight By Eight To Benefit The Temporary Contemporary: Untitled (fromClub/Spade Group '81-'82) (G. 101), 1982,* s., d., num. 188/250, blindstamp of pub. Gemini G.E.L., full margins,very good cond., (02-24-93, Butterfield, #3012, illus.), 38¼ x 25¾ in., (972 x 654 mm.), lithograph in colors on Arches Cover (BP 2109, DM 4911, FR 16,648, Y 354,964).

$7150* *Folsom Street Variations, 1986,* inits., d., #1/60, blindstamp, full margins, excellent cond., (11-09-92, Christie-NY, #262, illus.), 25½ x 33 in., (648 x 838 mm.), aquatint in brown, green, blue and black on wove (BP 4727, DM 11,414, FR 38,565, Y 887,317).

BI *Green, 1986,* inits., d., #15/60, Crown Point Press blindstamp, full margins, excell. cond., est. $80/90,000, (05-11-93, Christie-NY, #394, illus.), sheet 53¾ x 40¾ in., (136.5 x 103.5 cm.), color etching, aquatint and drypoint on Somerset.

BI *Harvey Gantt Portfolio: Untitled, 1990,* inits., d., #133/250, blindstamp publisher, Gemini G.E.L.. full margins, very good cond., est. $1,2/1,400, (05-19-93, Butterfield, #2161), 4¹⁵⁄₁₆ x 6¹¹⁄₁₆ in., (125 x 170 mm.), lithograph in color on wove.

BI *Large Bright Blue (Guillemin p. 32 & 111), 1980,* init., d., #26/35, blindstamp, pub. Crown Point Press, full margins,good cond., skinned spot, handling creases, est. $30/40,000, (05-15-93, Sotheby-NY, #942, illus.), 23⅞ x 14¼ in., (60.6 x 36.2 cm.), etching and aquatint in color on Rives.

$24,200* *Large Light Blue (G. p. 111), 1980,* init., d., #15/35, pub. Crown Point Press, full margins, good cond., (11-07-92, Sotheby-NY, #537, illus.), 23⅞ x 14 in., (606 x 356 mm.), etching and aquatint p. in colors (BP 15,822, DM 38,640, FR 130,599, Y 2,986,917).

BI *M (Gemini 1192), 1985,* init., d. '84, #2/60, blindstamp, pub. Gemini, G.E.L., full margins,good cond., handling creases, est. $3,5/4,500, (11-07-92, Sotheby-NY, #538, illus.), 18¼ x 14 in., (464 x 356 mm.), lithograph p. in colors on Arches 88.

$805* *Ne Comprend Pas, 1990,* inits., d., #18/25, blindstamp publisher, Crown Point Press, full margins, very good cond., (05-19-93, Butterfield, #2158), 6½ x 8⅜ in., (165 x 213 mm.), aquatint, sugarlift and openbite on wove (BP 523, DM 1309, FR 4409, Y 89,118).

$917* *Nude Woman, 1962,* inits., d., num. 15/20, pub. HB blindstamp, full margins, bottom edgefolded, excellent cond., (11-30-92, Phillips-London, #504), image 13 x 22⅛ in., (330 x 562 mm.), lithograph on fine wove (BP 605, DM 1461, FR 4959, Y 114,126).

$14,950* *Ochre, 1983,* inits., d., #170/200, blindstamp of pub. Crown Point Press, full margins, good cond., (02-11-93, Sotheby-NY, #320, illus.), 25 x 35¹³⁄₁₆ in., (635 x 910 mm.), color woodcut on Mitsumata (BP 10,549, DM 24,764, FR 83,800, Y 1,802,291).

$13,200* *Ochre, 1983,* inits., d., #52/200, blindstamp, full margins, skinned patches, excellent cond., (11-09-92, Christie-NY, #260, illus.), 27⅜ x 38¼ in., (695 x 972 mm.), colored woodcut on Japan (BP 8727, DM 21,073, FR 71,197, Y 1,638,124).

BI *Oui, 1990,* inits., d., #19/25, Crown Point Press blindstamp, full margins, excell. cond., the Late M. Anwar Kamal, M.D. Coll., est. $800/1,000, (05-11-93, Christie-NY, #398), sheet 13½ x 12¾ in., (343 x 324 mm.), etching, aquatint and drypoint on wove.

$2070* *Passage I, 1990,* inits., d., #23/35, Crown Point Press blindstamp, full margins, excell. cond., the Late M. Anwar Kamal, M.D. Coll., (05-11-93, Christie-NY, #396, illus.), sheet 29½ x 20 in., (749 x 508 mm.), aquatint in black and blue on wove (BP 1321, DM 3261, FR 10,987, Y 227,698).

$1380* *Passage II, 1990,* inits., d., #22/25, Crown Point Press blindstamp, full margins, excell. cond., the Late M. Anwar Kamal, M.D. Coll., (05-11-93, Christie-NY, #397, illus.), sheet 23¼ x 20 in., (591 x 508 mm.), aquatint on wove (BP 881, DM 2174, FR 7325, Y 151,798).

$467* *Portrait Of A Man, 1962,* inits., d., num. 15/20, margins, folded at top & bottom edge, prov., (11-30-92, Phillips-London, #505), image 13¼ x 9½ in., (337 x 241 mm.), lithograph on fine japan (BP 308, DM 744, FR 2526, Y 58,121).

$1150* *Reading, 1990,* inits., d., #9/15, blindstamp publisher Crown Point Press, very goodcond.?, (05-19-93, Butterfield, #2159), 6⁷⁄₁₅ x 8⅜ in., (152 x 213 mm.), aquatint w/soft-ground and sugarlift on Rives BFK (BP 747, DM 1869, FR 6298, Y 127,311).

BI *Red-Yellow-Blue, 1986,* inits., d., #10/60, blindstamps, full margins, excellent cond., est.$18/24,000, (11-09-92, Christie-NY, #263, illus.), 26½ x 40 in., (67.3 x 101.6 cm.), etching and aquatint in colors on wove.

$12,100* *Red-Yellow-Blue, 1986,* inits., d., num. 10/60, blindstamp of pub. Crown Point Press, apparently excellent cond., minor creases, (02-24-93, Butterfield, #3015, illus.), 15⅞ x 29⅞ in., (403 x 759 mm.), etching & aquatint in colors on BFK Rives (BP 8438, DM 19,643, FR 66,593, Y 1,419,854).

$10,350* *Red-Yellow-Blue, 1986,* inits., d., #5/60, blindstamp publisher, Crown Point Press, full margins, very good cond., (05-19-93, Butterfield, #2156, illus.), 16 x 30 in., (406 x 762 mm.), etching and aquatint in colors in BFK Rives (BP 6719, DM 16,824, FR 56,681, Y 1,145,799).

$1980* *Seated Nude, 1965,* inits., d., #52/100, blindstamp pub. Original Press, good cond.?, (10-28-92, Butterfield, #2931, illus.), 24¾ x 19½ in., (629 x 495 mm.), lithograph on cream wove (BP 1262, DM 3058, FR 10,383, Y 242,945).

$1265* *Seated Nude, 1965,* init. ink, d., #44/100, blindstamp, pub. Original Press, full margins, good cond., loss hinges, handling creases, (05-15-93, Sotheby-NY, #938), 26⅜ x 20⅛ in., (67 x 51.1 cm.), lithograph on BFK Rives (BP 822, DM 2035, FR 6838, Y 140,228).

$1210* *Seated Woman In Armchair, 1965,* ink inits., d., #83/100, blindstamp pub. Original Press, full margins, very good cond.?, (10-28-92, Butterfield, #2932, illus.), 24¾ x 19¼ in., (629 x 489 mm.), lithograph on wove (BP 771, DM 1869, FR 6345, Y 148,466).

$5225* *Tri-Color II, 1981,* inits., d., #3/35, blindstamp pub. Crown Point Press, full margins, very good cond.?, surface soiling, (10-28-92, Butterfield, #2936, illus.), 19 x 18 in., (483 x 457 mm.), color soft-ground etching w/aquatint and spitbite on wove (BP 3329, DM 8069, FR 27,399, Y 641,104).

$4950* *Tri-Color, 1981,* inits., d., #3/35, blindstamp pub. Crown Point Press, full margins, very good cond.?, (10-28-92, Butterfield, #2935, illus.), 13⅜ x 9½ in., (340 x 241 mm.), color etching w/aquatint and drypoint on Arches (BP 3154, DM 7645, FR 25,957, Y 607,362).

$3300* *Tri-Colored Spade, 1982,* init., d., #46/50, blindstamp pub., Crown Point Press, full margins,very good cond.(?), (02-24-93, Butterfield, #3013, illus.), 9⅞ x 9 in., (251.3 x 229 mm.), etching and aquatint in colors on Rives (BP 2301, DM 5357, FR 18,162, Y 387,233).

$2200* *Two Way, 1982,* init., d., #2/35, blindstamp, pub. Crown Point Press, full margins, good cond., creases, one in image, (11-07-92, Sotheby-NY, #536, illus.), 24 x 14⅞ in., (610 x 378 mm.), etching (BP 1438, DM 3513, FR 11,873, Y 271,538).

$5463* *Two Way, 1982,* init., d., #8/40, blindstamp, pub. Crowne Point Press, full margins,good cond., creases, (05-15-93, Sotheby-NY, #943, illus.), 23⅞ x 14¾ in., (60.6 x 37.5 cm.), aquatint, drypoint and ink transfer method in colors (BP 3552, DM 8787, FR 29,530, Y 605,587).

$3163* *Untitled (From Club/Spade Group '81-82) (Gemini 1148), 1982,* init., d., #87/250. blindstamp, pub. Gemini, G.E.L., good cond., (05-15-93, Sotheby-NY, #939, illus.), sheet

40 x 27 in., (101.6 x 68.6 cm.), lithograph in colors on Arches Cover (BP 2057, DM 5088, FR 17,097, Y 350,626).

$4400* *Untitled (T. 2838), 1970*, s., d., #1/20, blindstamp pub. Tamarind Lithography Workshop, full margins, good cond., dents, image creases, hinge remains, (10-28-92, Butterfield, #2933, illus.), 26¼ x 18¾ in., (667 x 476 mm.), color lithograph on German Etching paper (BP 2803, DM 6795, FR 23,073, Y 539,877).

$2300* *Untitled, From Club/Spade Group '81-'82 (Gemini 1148), 1982*, from Eight by Eight To Celebrate The Temporary Contemporary, Museum of Contemp. Art, 1984, inits., d., #53/250, Gemini G.E.L. blindstamps, full margins, excell. cond., (05-11-93, Christie-NY, #392, illus.), sheet 40 x 27 in., (101.6 x 68.6 cm.), color lithograph on Arches (BP 1468, DM 3623, FR 12,208, Y 252,997).

$920* *Window, 1990*, inits., d., #12/35, blindstamp publisher Crown Point Press, very goodcond., (05-19-93, Butterfield, #2160), 8⅜ x 6⁷⁄₁₆ in., (213 x 164 mm.), aquatint w/soft-ground and sugarlift on Rives BFK (BP 597, DM 1495, FR 5038, Y 101,849).

BI *Woman Seated On Sofa, 1965*, s., d., num. 93/100, good cond., est. $4-5,000, (10-31-92, Cleveland, #367, illus.), 24 x 19 in., (61 x 48.3 cm.), lithograph.

DIEDEREN, Jef   b. 1920

$130* *Untitled, 1971*, s., d., #27/40, good cond.?, creases, (12-09-92, Sotheby-Amstrdm, #560), sheet 29¹⁵⁄₁₆ x 22⅜ in., (760 x 568 mm.), color lithograph on wove (BP 83, DM 204, FR 696, Y 16,119, G 230).

$256* *Untitled, 1975*, s., d., #177/190, full margins, good cond., (05-27-93, Sotheby-Amstrdm, #403), 21¾ x 30½ in., (552 x 775 mm.), colored woodcut on Japan (BP 164, DM 411, FR 1385, Y 27,444, G 460).

$243* *Untitled, 1975*, s., d., #174/190, full margins, handling creases, (05-27-93, Sotheby-Amstrdm, #404, illus.), 27⅜ x 23⅝ in., (695 x 600 mm.), colored woodcut on Japan (BP 156, DM 390, FR 1314, Y 26,051, G 437).

$224* *Untitled, 1975*, s, d., full margins, good cond., (05-27-93, Sotheby-Amstrdm, #405), 22⁷⁄₁₆ x 27⅜ in., (570 x 695 mm.), colored woodcut on Japan (BP 143, DM 359, FR 1211, Y 24,014, G 403).

$143* *Untitled, 1977*, s., d., #42/100, good cond., (12-09-92, Sotheby-Amstrdm, #559), sheet 19¹¹⁄₁₆ x 25¹³⁄₁₆ in., (500 x 655 mm.), lithograph on BFK Rives (BP 91, DM 224, FR 766, Y 17,731, G 253).

DIEDEREN, Jef and Bert SCHIERBEEK

$1694* *De Val, 1965: Fourteen*, complete set, num. 13, pub. W.A. Palm, good cond., (12-09-92, Sotheby-Amstrdm, #558, illus.), overall 16⁵⁄₁₆ x 20⅞ in., (414 x 530 mm.), color lithograph on Hahnemuhle Butten (BP 1081, DM 2659, FR 9073, Y 210,043, G 2990).

DIEPENBEECK, Abraham van   1596-1675

$217* *Reiterstandbild, 1657-58*, plate 2 from La Methode nouvelle... de dresser les Chevaux, Antwerpen, center crease, light-stained, (09-14-92, Venator/Hansten, #1487), sheet approx. 15⅜ x 20½ in., (39 x 52 cm.), engraving (BP 115, DM 323, FR 1093, Y 26,983).

DIETEL   20th cent.

$23* *"Paysage Marin"*, #60/150, s., (01-28-93, Pescheteau, #122), 7½ x 11⁷⁄₁₆ in., (19 x 29 cm.), color etching on wove (BP 15, DM 36, FR 123, Y 2856).

DIETMAN, Erik

$639* *"Bar A Bar Art Barbara", 1977*, s. Erik Dietman 77, #69/75, (06-03-93, Kunsthallen, #176), lithograph in colors (BP 414, DM 1023, FR 3447, Y 68,533, DK 3910).

DIETRICH, Christian Wilhelm Ernst   German 1712-1774

BI *The Birth Of Christ*, s., d. 1740 in plate, est. $6/800, (10-30-92, Sloan, #2806), 7⅜ x 10¼ in., (18.7 x 26 cm.), etching.

DIETRICH, Christian Wilhelm Ernst (called DIETRICY)   German 1712-1774

$253* *Die Badenden Nymphen In Der Felsenhohle (Linck 136 III), 1741*, prov., (12-04-92, Bassenge, #6566), 7⅞ x 10¹⁵⁄₁₆ in., (20 x 27.8 cm.), etching (BP 162, DM 403, FR 1367, Y 31,586).

$867* *Die Beiden Barenfuhrer (Linck 84 I), 1764*, prov., (12-04-92, Bassenge, #6564, illus.), 4¹⁵⁄₁₆ x 3¾ in., (12.5 x 9.5 cm.), etching (BP 556, DM 1381, FR 4684, Y 108,240).

$303* *Die Felsenschlucht (Linck 158 I), 1745*, prov., (12-04-92, Bassenge, #6567), 11⁷⁄₁₆ x 8¹¹⁄₁₆ in., (29 x 22 cm.), etching (BP 194, DM 483, FR 1637, Y 37,828).

$239* *Die Frau Mit Den Kindern Im Fenster (Linck 87 IV)*, prov., (12-04-92, Bassenge, #6565), 11⁷⁄₁₆ x 8⁹⁄₁₆ in., (29 x 21.7 cm.), mezzotint (BP 153, DM 381, FR 1291, Y 29,838).

BI *Tritonenkampfe (Linck 43-45/III), 1763: Three*, est. DM 600, (12-01-92, Karl/Faber, #50), etching.

DIETRICH, David

BI *Flora Universalis, 1833: Sixty-Four*, from the series after Linneus, De Candolle and others, pub. August Schmid, full margins, good cond., defects, est. BP 7/900, (10-27-92, Phillips-London, #171), sheet 16½ x 14⅜ in., (419 x 365 mm.), engraving and lithograph, extensively hand-colored on J. Whatman.

DIEZ, Julius   1870-1957

BI *VIII Internationale Kunstausstellung, Munchen 1901*, fold marks, tears, creases, repairs, lit., est. BP 1/1,500, (02-04-93, Christie-S. Ken, #158, illus.), 33 x 35 in., (83.8 x 88.9 cm.), color lithograph backed on linen.

DIGHTON

$550* *A Good Old Penn From The Wing Of A Good Old Cock, 1804*, (05-29-93, Northeast, #214, illus.), hand-colored engraving (BP 352, DM 872, FR 2949, Y 58,975).

DIGHTON, Richard   British 1785-1880

$243* *(Three Portraits)*, drawn, etched and pub. Richard Dighton 1818-1823, (08-11-92, L. Joel, #193G), smallest 9⅛ x 5⅞ in., (23.2 x 15 cm.), largest 11¼ x 7¹³⁄₁₆ in., (23.2 x 15 cm.), color etching (BP 126, DM 357, FR 1208, Y 31,118, A$ 330).

DIGHTON, Robert   English c. 1752-1814

$88* *Ireland In Scotland, 1807*, (10-18-92, Hindman, #509), 10½ x 8 in., (26.7 x 20.3 cm.), hand colored etching (BP 54, DM 131, FR 444, Y 10,558).

DIGHTON, Robert C.   English c. 1752-1814

BI *Untitled: Six*, from "Twelve Elegant and Humorous Prints of Rural Scenes", p. WilliamAllen, est. $250/350, (10-30-92, Sloan, #1947), each 5¾ x 9⅞ in., (14.6 x 25.1 cm.), engraving.

DIGNIMONT, Andre   1891-1965

$120* *"Le 14 juillet"*, #204/220, s., (04-04-93, Pescheteau, #201), 21⅝ x 14⁹⁄₁₆ in., (55 x 37 cm.), color lithograph on wove (BP 79, DM 193, FR 655, Y 13,663).

$59* *"Scene D'Interieur", 1952*, s. in plate, d. 1952, (01-28-93, Pescheteau, #123), 6⁵⁄₁₆ x 9⁷⁄₁₆ in., (16 x 24 cm.), etching and aquatint (BP 39, DM 93, FR 316, Y 7326).

DIGNIMONT, Jean

$1568* *Paris, Au Sans Pareil, 1927*, from Nuit De Paris by Francis Carco, includes drawing, etching, portrait of Carco, envoi-autographe, and autoportrait of Carco and marriage invitation, (11-15-92, Christie-Geneva, #320), 11⁷⁄₁₆ x 9¼ in., (290 x 235 mm.), 26 etchings on Arches Montgfolier wove, plus 5 lithographs embellished w/ watercolor and 10 wood engravings (5 color) (BP 1031, DM 2501, FR 8426, Y 195,682, SF 2260).

DIJKSTRA, Johan   1896-1978

BI *Portrait*, s., i. handdruk, full margins, good cond., creases, soiling, papertape, est. G 4/600, (12-09-92, Sotheby-Amstrdm, #565), 29¾ x 10³⁄₁₆ in., (755 x 258 mm.), linocut on wove.

DIJON, V.

BI *Paysage Avec Reuisseau, 1854*, est. $5/6000, (10-13-92, Christie-NY, #8, illus.), 10 x 11¾ in., (25.4 x 29.8 cm.), photograph, albumenized salt print.

DIKKENBOER, Daniel den

$192* *Still Life, 1952*, s., d., #5/8, margins, good cond., (05-27-93, Sotheby-Amstrdm, #607), 12¹⁵⁄₁₆ x 16⁹⁄₁₆ in., (328 x 420 mm.), colored lithograph on wove (BP 123, DM 308, FR 1038, Y 20,583, G 345).

DILL, Laddie John American b. 1943

BI *"Untitled" and "Untitled", 1985: Two,* s., d., #34/35, blindstamp pub. Cirrus, full margins, very good cond.?, est. $900/1,200, (10-28-92, Butterfield, #2937), each 20½ x 49 in., (52.1 x 124.5 cm.), color lithograph and woodcut on wove.

$495* *Untitled, 1987,* s., d., pub. Garner Tullis Workshop, very good cond., (02-24-93, Butterfield, #3016), 20½ x 27 in., (521 x 686 mm.), monotype in colors on handmade (BP 345, DM 804, FR 2724, Y 58,085).

$523* *Untitled, 1987,* s., d., pub. Garner Tullis Workshop, very good cond., (02-24-93, Butterfield, #3017), 26¾ x 20⅛ in., (679 x 511 mm.), monotype in colors on handmade (BP 365, DM 849, FR 2878, Y 61,371).

$935* *Untitled, 1987: Two,* s., d., pub. Garner Tullis Workshop, very good cond., (10-28-92, Butterfield, #2938, illus.), 19½ x 25¼ in., (495 x 641 mm.), color monotype on handmade (BP 596, DM 1444, FR 4903, Y 114,724).

DILL, Otto 1884-1957

$813* *Rabtier-Fantasien, 1920: Twelve,* Dachau, Einhorn-Verlag, #164/350, frontispiece s., (10-09-92, Winterberg, #1996), smallest 8⁷⁄₁₆ x 14³⁄₁₆ in., (21.5 x 36 cm.), largest 17¹⁵⁄₁₆ x 12³⁄₁₆ in., (21.5 x 36 cm.), lithograph on simili Japan (BP 482, DM 1208, FR 4055, Y 98,977).

DILLION, Cyril c. 1880-1970

$97* *The Chapel Tower Melbourne Grammar,* s. Cyril Dillon, i., #32/50, (08-11-92, L. Joel, #190G), etching (BP 50, DM 142, FR 482, Y 12,422, A$ 132).

DILLON

$331* *Champ De Foire Rue Fontaine,* (01-31-93, Morelle/Marchan, #26), 36¼ x 49³⁄₁₆ in., (92 x 125 cm.), poster (BP 223, DM 533, FR 1803, Y 41,292).

DILLON, Henri Patrice

$374* *L'Averse Rue L'Epic, c. 1890,* s., margins, good cond., paper loss, creases, soiling, tears, staining, rubbed area, (05-19-93, Butterfield, #2053), 22⅛ x 17½ in., (562 x 445 mm.), lithograph on Chine colle (BP 243, DM 608, FR 2048, Y 41,404).

$266* *La Place Du Trone Au Clair De Lune, c. 1895,* cracks, large margins, (02-24-93, Picard, #85), lithograph on creme wove (BP 185, DM 432, FR 1464, Y 31,213).

DILULLO

$247* *A.P.I. Voghera,* Graf. S.A.I.L.E.A., B+ cond., creasing, yellowing, (08-06-92, Swann, #115, illus.), 39¼ x 27½ in., (99.7 x 69.9 cm.), (BP 129, DM 365, FR 1233, Y 31,505).

DINE, Jim American b. 1935

$13,800* *Atheism, 1986,* s., d., i. B.A.T., pub. Pace Editions, excell. cond.?, (05-11-93, Christie-NY, #410, illus.), sheet 67¼ x 47½ in., (170.8 x 120.7 cm.), color lithograph on wove (BP 8809, DM 21,739, FR 73,248, Y 1,517,985).

$1194* *Awl (Gal. Mikro 35), 1965,* s., #71/200, pub. 11 Pop Artists III, margins, good cond., (12-03-92, Sotheby-London, #640, illus.), 24 x 19⅝ in., (610 x 500 mm.), screenprint in colors on wove (BP 770, DM 1878, FR 6409, Y 148,563).

$1540* *Awl (Mikro 35), 1965,* from 11 Pop Artists Volume 1, NY, Original Editions, s., d., num. 28/200, full sheet, very good cond., (09-19-92, Christie-E, #93), sheet 23⅞ x 19¾ in., (606 x 502 mm.), screenprint in black and red on thick wove (BP 886, DM 2306, FR 7897, Y 191,876).

$3300* *Bill Clinton, 1992,* s., d., num. 98/100, pub. for Democratic Women's Senatorial Campaign,full margins, apparently very good cond, (02-24-93, Butterfield, #3020), 12⅜ x 10⅛ in., (314 x 257 mm.), etching & woodcut in colors on wove (BP 2301, DM 5357, FR 18,162, Y 387,233).

$457* *Black And White Bathrobe, 1975,* s., d., num., (12-01-92, Karl/Faber, #539), 36 x 23¹³⁄₁₆ in., (91.5 x 60.5 cm.), lithograph on wove (BP 302, DM 728, FR 2482, Y 56,897).

$4680* *Blue Haircut,* s. 1972, 29/75, (05-25-93, AB Stockholm, #21, illus.), 21¼ x 19¹¹⁄₁₆ in., (54 x 50 cm.), etching, relief and offset lithograph (BP 3033, DM 7622, FR 25,658, Y 511,531, SK 6820).

BI *Bolt Cutters (Krens No. 143),* s., d. 1972, #73/75, pub. Petersburg Press, lit., est. C$ 4/4,500, (12-01-92, Ritchie, #95, illus.), 23¾ x 24¼ in., (60.3 x 61.6 cm.), etching.

$1210* *"Boot", "Gun", "Lips" and "Knife", c. 1968: Four,* each inits., Boot and Lips num. 101/250; Gun i. A.P., pub. Viking Press, full sheets, time staining, (09-19-92, Christie-E, #95), each sheet 10 x 8 in., (254 x 203 mm.), pochoir in colors on glazed wove (BP 696, DM 1812, FR 6205, Y 150,760).

$1364* *Braid (First State) (Williams College Catalogue 148), 1972,* s., d., #35/46, pub. Petersburg Press, margins, good cond., (12-03-92, Sotheby-London, #643, illus.), sheet 41⅜ x 30¾ in., (105.1 x 78.1 cm.), etching w/tone on German Etching (BP 880, DM 2145, FR 7322, Y 169,715).

$935* *Burning Church, c. 1956,* s., #7/10, crease, (12-08-92, Swann, #84, illus.), 30 x 11½ in., (76.2 x 29.2 cm.), woodcut on Tableau imitation Japan paper (BP 586, DM 1456, FR 4963, Y 115,890).

BI *Calico (Galerie Mikro 37), 1965,* s., #152/200, pub. 11 Pop Artists III, good cond., est. BP 5/700, (12-03-92, Sotheby-London, #639, illus.), 40⅛ x 30¼ in., (101.9 x 76.8 cm.), screenprint in colors on wove.

$4370* *Carnegie Heart, 1986,* s., d., #103/150, pub. Pace Editions, full margins, excell. cond., (05-11-93, Christie-NY, #411, illus.), sheet 30 x 22¼ in., (762 x 565 mm.), color lithograph on buff Arches (BP 2790, DM 6884, FR 23,195, Y 480,695).

$6325* *Colored Palette (Galerie Mikro 24; Sparks 12), 1963,* s., d., t., #4/23, blindstamp, pub. ULAE, full margins, good cond., scuff marks, Gertrude Kasle Coll., (11-07-92, Sotheby-NY, #544, illus.), 17⅜ x 13 in., (441 x 330 mm.), lithograph p. in colors on Chrisbrook handmade (BP 4135, DM 10,099, FR 34,134, Y 780,671).

$1430* *Dark Blue Self Portrait With White Crayon (W.C. 222), 1976,* s., d., #5/11, pub. Pace Editions, full margins, trimmed, skinned spot, excellent cond., (11-09-92, Christie-NY, #268, illus.), 29¾ x 22 in., (756 x 559 mm.), etching w/hand-coloring in gray and blue watercolor on wove (BP 945, DM 2283, FR 7713, Y 177,463).

$14,300* *Double Apple Palette With Gingham (Gal. M. 31; S. 16), 1965,* s., d., t., #13/23, blindstamp, pub. ULAE, full margins, good cond.,Gertrude Kasle Coll., (11-07-92, Sotheby-NY, #547, illus.), sheet 23½ x 28¼ in., (597 x 718 mm.), lithograph p. in colors w/collage on East Indian handmade (BP 9349, DM 22,833, FR 77,172, Y 1,764,996).

$13,800* *Double Apple Palette With Gingham (See Gal. M. 42, Sparks 16), 1965,* s., d., ded., unique proof, blindstamp, pub. ULAE, full margins, good cond., soiling, (05-15-93, Sotheby-NY, #952, illus.), sheet 23⅜ x 27½ in., (59.4 x 69.9 cm.), lithograph in colors, w/collage and hand-coloring on East Indian handmade paper (BP 8973, DM 22,197, FR 74,595, Y 1,529,764).

BI *Double Venus In The Sky At Night (D'O. & F. 166), 1984,* s., d., num. 23/50, pub. Pace Editions, excellent cond., est. $10/15,000, (02-24-93, Butterfield, #3019, illus.), 39¼ x 28¼ in., (99.7 x 71.8 cm.), silkscreen & lithograph in colors on William Morris Nonesuch buff laid.

$7475* *Double Venus In The Sky At Night (D'O.&F. 166), 1984,* s., d., #23/50, pub. Pace Editions, excellent cond., (05-19-93, Butterfield, #2161A, illus.), 39¼ x 28¼ in., (99.7 x 71.8 cm.), silkscreen and lithograph in color on Williams Morris Nonesuch buff laid (BP 4852, DM 12,151, FR 40,936, Y 827,521).

$2875* *Dutch Hearts: Untitled (Williams College 4), 1970,* s., #61/85, pub. Petersburg Press, full sheet, good cond., (02-11-93, Sotheby-NY, #323, illus.), sheet 16⁵⁄₁₆ x 20 in., (415 x 508 mm.), color lithograph w/collage on Hodgkinson handmade (BP 2029, DM 4762, FR 16,115, Y 346,594).

$3450* *Dutch Hearts: Untitled (Williams College 6), 1970,* s., #62/85, pub. Petersburg Press, good cond., soiling, (05-15-93, Sotheby-NY, #946, illus.), sheet 16⅜ x 20⅛ in., (41.6 x 51.1 cm.), lithograph in colors w/collage on Hodgkinson handmade paper (BP 2243, DM 5549, FR 18,649, Y 382,441).

BI   *Eight Sheets From An Undefined Novel State II: The Cellist Against Blue (D'O & F. 35), 1979,* s., d., #32/35, pub. Pace Editions, full margins, good cond., est. BP 8/1,200, (12-03-92, Sotheby-London, #649), 23¾ x 19⅝ in., (605 x 498 mm.), etching and soft-ground etching w/hand-coloring in red and blue on BFK Rives.

$565* *Eight Sheets From An Undefined Novel State II: The Cellist Against Blue (D'Oench & Feinberg 35), 1979,* s., d., #32/35, pub. Pace Editions, Inc., full margins, good cond., (06-30-93, Sotheby-London, #774), 23¾ x 19⅝ in., (603 x 498 mm.), etching and soft-ground etching w/hand-coloring in red and blue on BFK Rives (BP 379, DM 964, FR 3251, Y 60,538).

$938* *Eight Sheets From An Undefined Novel: The Cellist (W. 203), 1976,* s., d., #28/30, pub. Pyramid Arts Ltd., full margins, good cond., (12-03-92, Sotheby-London, #648, illus.), 23½ x 19⅞ in., (600 x 505 mm.), etching w/aquatint hand-colored in red, yellow and blue on German etching (BP 605, DM 1475, FR 5035, Y 116,710).

$943* *End Of The Crash (Galerie Mikro 6), 1960,* s., d., t., #30/32, good cond., nick, creases, (06-30-93, Sotheby-London, #776), 27 x 13⅛ in., (686 x 333 mm.), lithograph in red and black on BFK Rives (BP 632, DM 1608, FR 5426, Y 101,039).

$1725* *A Fancy Lady (W.C. 206), 1976,* from Eight Sheets from an Undefined Novel, s., d., num. e/e, PyramidArts blindstamp, full margins, time staining, excell. cond., (05-11-93, Christie-NY, #402, illus.), sheet 41⅝ x 30¾ in., (105.7 x 78.1 cm.), etching w/touched hand-coloring in watercolor on wove (BP 1101, DM 2717, FR 9156, Y 189,748).

$5775* *Five Paintbrushes (First State) (Williams College 135), 1972,* s., d., #48/75, pub. Petersburg Press, full margins, good cond., (11-07-92, Sotheby-NY, #540, illus.), 23⅝ x 35⅜ in., (600 x 899 mm.), etching on Hodgkinson handmade (BP 3776, DM 9221, FR 31,166, Y 712,787).

$10,450* *Five Paintbrushes (Sixth State) (W.C. 140), 1973,* s., d., i. A/P, pub. Petersburg Press, full margins, creases, excellent cond., (11-09-92, Christie-NY, #265, illus.), 27½ x 39½ in., (69.9 x 100.3 cm.), green-black etching on Murillo (BP 6909, DM 16,683, FR 56,365, Y 1,296,848).

$8050* *Five Paintbrushes (Sixth State) (W.C. 140), 1973,* s., d. #4/25, pub. Petersburg Press, full margins good cond., soiling, handling creases, (05-15-93, Sotheby-NY, #950, illus.), 14⅜ x 27½ in., (36.5 x 69.9 cm.), etching on Murillo paper (BP 5234, DM 12,948, FR 43,514, Y 892,362).

$3850* *Flesh Palette In A Landscape (Gal. M. 29; S. 14), 1965,* s., d., t., #9/22, blindstamp, pub. ULAE, full margins, good cond., foxing, Gertrude Kasle Coll., (11-07-92, Sotheby-NY, #545, illus.), 17⅜ x 13¾ in., (441 x 349 mm.), lithograph p. in colors on Auvergne handmade (BP 2517, DM 6147, FR 20,777, Y 475,191).

$13,200* *Flowered Robe With Sky (D. and F. 62), 1980,* s., d., #12/31, pub. Pace Editions, excellent cond., (11-09-92, Christie-NY, #271, illus.), 37½ x 29½ in., (953 x 749 mm.), lithograph in red and rust w/hand-coloring in oil, spry enamel and charcoal on wove (BP 8727, DM 21,073, FR 71,197, Y 1,638,124).

BI   *Fourteen Color Woodcut Bathrobe (D' O. & F. 112), 1982,* s., d., #15/75, pub. Pace Editions, Inc., full margins, good cond., est. BP 10/12,000, (06-30-93, Sotheby-London, #772, illus.), sh 75¾ x 42¼ in., (192.4 x 107.3 cm.), color woodcut on BFK Rives.

$711* *Gangway Birdseed, Aus "Oo La La", 1972,* 5/75, s., watermark, (06-24-93, Germann, #313, illus.), 17½ x 27⁷⁄₁₆ in., (445 x 697 mm.), offset lithograph on Hodgkinson paper (BP 468, DM 1153, FR 3885, Y 76,271, SF 1035).

BI   *The Garrity Necklace, 1986,* init., d., #24/30, pub. Pace Editions, Inc., full margins, good cond., crease, est. BP 3/4,000, (06-30-93, Sotheby-London, #779, illus.), 47¾ x 35¾ in., (121.3 x 90.8 cm.), drypoint and aquatint in color on BFK Rives.

$3850* *Glypotek, 1987-88: Set Of Forty,* Jim Dine, Pace Editions and Waddington Graphics, s., #11/90, (11-09-92, Christie-NY, #275, illus.), 27¾ x 21⅞ in., (705 x 555 mm.), glacies intaglios, on Zerkall Litho (lithograph) (BP 2545, DM 6146, FR 20,766, Y 477,786).

$4263* *Glyptotek, 1989: Seven,* seven from the set of 14, including frontispiece, each s., d., #10/60, pub. Pace Editions, Inc., full margins, good cond., (12-03-92, Sotheby-London, #651, illus.), each sheet approx. 31¼ x 23⅞ in., (795 x 606 mm.), etchings w/aquatint on colored chine colle supported on white wove (BP 2750, DM 6704, FR 22,882, Y 530,422).

BI   *Hand Painting On The Mandala (F. and C. 65), 1986,* s., d., #29/60, pub. Pace Editions, Graphicstudio, USF blindstamp, full margins, excell. cond.?, est. $18/22,000, (05-11-93, Christie-NY, #407, illus.), sheet 49¾ x 40¼ in., (126.4 x 102.2 cm.), color etching and aquatint w/hand-coloring on wove.

BI   *The Hand-Colored Viennese Hearts, 1987-90: Seven,* s., d., 1990, #22/40, pub. Pace Editions, full margins, excell. cond.?, est. $60/80,000, (05-11-93, Christie-NY, #412, illus.), each sheet 47 x 36 in., (119.4 x 91.4 cm.), color screen and etching w/hand-coloring on Arches.

BI   *The Hand-Coloured Viennese Hearts IV, 1987-1990,* s., d., num. 35/40, pub. Pace Prints, Waddington Graphics, full margins, good cond., est. Y 1/1,200,000, (10-14-92, Sotheby-Japan, #23, illus.), 33½ x 31¾ in., (851 x 806 mm.), screenprint, etching and aquatint in colors hand painted w/acrylic on Arches.

BI   *The Hand-Coloured Viennese Hearts V, 1987-1990,* s., d., num. 35/40, pub. Pace Prints, Waddington Graphics, full margins, good cond., est. Y 1/1,200,000, (10-14-92, Sotheby-Japan, #24, illus.), 33½ x 28 in., (851 x 711 mm.), screenprint, etching and aquatint in colors hand painted w/acrylic on Arches.

$1100* *Hands (W.C. 34), 1970-76,* ink s., d., #140/150, from Bathrobe, Hands, Ties, Saw, Rainbow, Boots portfolio, pub. Petersburg Press, good cond.?, creases, (10-28-92, Butterfield, #2939), 31¼ x 22½ in., (794 x 572 mm.), color lithograph on Crisbrook Waterleaf paper (BP 701, DM 1699, FR 5768, Y 134,969).

BI   *A Heart At The Opera, Metropolitan Opera Centennial Poster, 1983,* inits., #55/500, good cond., est. $800/1,200, (12-08-92, Swann, #83, illus.), 49 x 29 in., (124.5 x 73.7 cm.), offset color lithograph from 9 plates.

$4381* *Hearts Forever, 1985,* s., d., A.P. i., (06-12-93, Hauswedell/Nolt, #69, illus.), 17½ x 27⅜ in., (44.5 x 69.5 cm.), color lithograph on thick wove (BP 2868, DM 7131, FR 23,966, Y 461,012).

BI   *Historia (Devereux 150), 1971,* s., d., a/p i., est. DM 5,000, (06-12-93, Hauswedell/Nolt, #68, illus.), 20¹¹⁄₁₆ x 21⅞ in., (52.5 x 55.5 cm.), color serigraph, lithograph and etching on wove.

$2310* *Historia (Will. Coll. 150), 1971,* s., d., #6/80, pub. Petersburg Press, full sheet, good cond., (11-07-92, Sotheby-NY, #541, illus.), sheet 30¾ x 21⅞ in., (781 x 556 mm.), silkscreen, lithograph and etching in colors, hand colored w/watercolors by artist on Crisbrook Waterleaf (BP 1510, DM 3688, FR 12,466, Y 285,115).

$4888* *An Informal Tie (Galerie Mikro 10), 1961,* s., d., #1/10, p. Pratt Graphic Art Center, pub. by artist, full margins, good cond., discoloration, soiling, crease, (02-11-93, Sotheby-NY, #321), 35¹³⁄₁₆ x 17¹¹⁄₁₆ in., (910 x 450 mm.), etching w/hand coloring on BFK Rives (BP 3449, DM 8097, FR 27,399, Y 589,271).

BI   *"Jime Dine: The Red Bandana" Staatl. Kunsthalle Baden-Baden and "JimDine: Saw" Kunsthalle Bern: Two Exhibition Posters,* each s., pub. Professional Prints, 1971, lit., est. C$ 350/500, (12-01-92, Ritchie, #19, illus.), 30¾ x 22 in., (78.1 x 55.9 cm.), color lithograph.

BI   *The Kindergarten Robes (D'O & F. 146), 1983,* s., d., #27/75, pub. Pace Editions, full margins, good cond. ?, est.$15/18,000, (05-15-93, Sotheby-NY, #956, illus.), 54¾ x 71¼ in., (139.1 x 181 cm.), woodcut in colors on Lenox.

$9775* *L.A. Eye Works (D'O & F. 116), 1982,* s., d., #35/70, pub. Pace Editions, full margins, good cond. ?, handling creases, discoloration, (05-15-93, Sotheby-NY, #955, illus.), 43¼ x 37¼ in., (109.9 x 94.6 cm.), etching and aquatint in colors on Velin Arches (BP 6356, DM 15,723, FR 52,838, Y 1,083,583).

$3335* *The Little Heart In The Landscape, 1991,* s., d., #74/100, pub. Pace Editions, full margins, good cond., (05-15-93, Sotheby-NY, #954, illus.), 10 x 12⅜ in., (25.4 x 31.4

cm.), etching w/Red Moriki chine colle on Hannemuhle paper (BP 2168, DM 5364, FR 18,027, Y 369,693).

$1320* *"Mabel #7" and "Mabel #10" (W.C. 231; 234), 1977: Two,* s., #16/60, pub. Aldo Crommelynck, full margins, good cond., surfacesoiling, creases, first w/crease through center image, (10-28-92, Butterfield, #2941), 9⅛ x 7¼ in., (232 x 184 mm.), etching on d'Auvergne paper (BP 841, DM 2039, FR 6922, Y 161,963).

BI *Mabel, 1977: Eight,* s., #3/60, pub. Aldo Crommelynck, full margins, excell. cond., est. $3/4,000, (11-09-92, Christie-NY, #269, illus.), 20 x 15¼ in., (508 x 387 mm.), etching on Auvergne.

$1380* *Mabel: Eight Plates, 1977,* s., #3/60, pub. Aldo Crommelynck, full margins, excell. cond., (05-11-93, Christie-NY, #404), each approx. sheet 20 x 15¼ in., (508 x 387 mm.), etching on Auvergne (BP 881, DM 2174, FR 7325, Y 151,798).

BI *"Moon", "Knife", "Lips", "Boot", "Hat" and "Gun", c. 1968: Six,* inits., 5 i. AP, pub. Viking Press, time staining, est. $1,5/1,800, (05-11-93, Christie-NY, #399), each sheet 10 x 8 in., (254 x 203 mm.), color pochoir on glazed wove.

BI *"Multi-Colored Bathrobe", 1988,* s., d., num. 169/300 88 Dine, pub.'s dry stamp, shrink wrapped, verygood cond., est. $4/6,000, (03-12-93, Skinner, #114, illus.), sight, sheet 35¼ x 27⅛ in., (89.5 x 68.9 cm.), lithograph in colors on paper.

BI *Multi-Colored Bathrobe, 1988,* d., num., s., est. $3,5/5,000, (05-27-93, Swann, #89, illus.), sh 35 x 27 in., (88.9 x 68.6 cm.), color lithograph.

$2530* *My Nights In Santa Monica (F. and C. 66), 1985-87,* s., d. 1986, #1/20, pub. Pace Editions, Graphicstudio, USF blindstamp, full margins, excell. cond.?, (05-11-93, Christie-NY, #408, illus.), sheet 35½ x 72½ in., (90.2 x 184.2 cm.), color etching and aquatint on cream wove (BP 1615, DM 3986, FR 13,429, Y 278,297).

BI *Nancy Outside In July I (D. and F. 18), 1978,* s., d., num. 21/60, pub. Aldo Crommelynck, full margins, light/time staining, very good cond., est. $1,2/1,800, (09-19-92, Christie-E, #97), sheet 33¾ x 24¾ in., (857 x 629 mm.), etching and aquatint in colors on Arches.

$880* *Nancy Outside In July XIV: Wrestling With Spirits (D. and F. 95), 1981,* s., d., num. 8/30, pub. Aldo Crommelynck, full margins, excell. cond., (09-19-92, Christie-E, #99), sheet 36 x 25 in., (914 x 635 mm.), etching, aquatint and electric tooling in blue, grays and black on wove (BP 506, DM 1318, FR 4513, Y 109,644).

$990* *Nancy Outside In July XVII: The Reddish One (D. and F. 98), 1981,* s., d., num. 8/26, pub. Aldo Crommelynck, full margins, excell. cond., (09-19-92, Christie-E, #100), sheet 29⅞ x 22¼ in., (759 x 565 mm.), etching, photogravure and electric tooling in red/pink on pale gray BFK Rives (BP 569, DM 1482, FR 5077, Y 123,349).

BI *Nancy Outside In July XVIII: Full Of Expression (D'O & F. 99), 1981,* s., d., #9/15, pub. Aldo Crommelynck, full margins, good cond., handling creases, est. $3,5/4,500, (05-15-93, Sotheby-NY, #953, illus.), 23¼ x 19½ in., (59.1 x 49.5 cm.), photogravure, etching and aquatint in colors w/hand-coloring in pastel.

BI *The New French Tools I - Wise (O'Dench & Feinberg 171), 1984,* s., d., #30/50, pub. pace Editions, Inc., full margins, good cond., est. BP 7/900, (12-03-92, Sotheby-London, #645), 18⅛ x 16 in., (460 x 405 mm.), etching w/aquatint on Japon nacre.

$2750* *Night Palette (Gal. M. 30; S. 15), 1965,* s., d., t., #8/11, blindstamp, pub. ULAE, full margins, good cond., scuff marks, Gertrude Kasle Coll., (11-07-92, Sotheby-NY, #546, illus.), 26⅝ x 20½ in., (676 x 521 mm.), lithograph on Fabriano black (BP 1798, DM 4391, FR 14,841, Y 339,422).

$3575* *Nine Views Of Winter (2) (D'O. & F. 198), 1985,* s., d. '1986', #4/24, pub. Pace Editions, full sheet, good cond.?, (11-07-92, Sotheby-NY, #543, illus.), sheet 52⅜ x 37 in., (133 x 94 cm.), woodcut p. in colors on Arches buff (BP 2337, DM 5708, FR 19,293, Y 441,249).

$3432* *Nine Views Of Winter (9) (D'O. & F. 205), 1985,* s., d., #5/24, p. by Toby Michel, Angeles Press, pub. Pace Editions,Inc., good cond., ink traces, (06-30-93, Sotheby-London, #778, illus.), sh 52½ x 37⅛ in., (133.4 x 94.3 cm.), woodcut in ochre/red/green on wove (BP 2300, DM 5854, FR 19,747, Y 367,727).

$682* *Nude I (O'D & F. 123), 1982,* s., d., #25/30, from the suite of Eight Little Nudes, pub. Pace Editions, Inc., full margins, good cond., (12-03-92, Sotheby-London, #652), 11½ x 8⅝ in., (293 x 220 mm.), etching w/aquatint in pink and black on BFK Rives (BP 440, DM 1072, FR 3661, Y 84,858).

BI *Olympic Robe, 1988,* s., num., est. DM 9000, (12-01-92, Karl/Faber, #540, illus.), 35¹⁄₁₆ x 26¹⁵⁄₁₆ in., (89 x 68.5 cm.), color lithograph on wove.

$30,800* *A Painted Self Portrait (Williams College 15), 1970,* s., d. 1970-73, i., #7/7, pub. Petersburg Press, creases, nick, excellent cond., (11-09-92, Christie-NY, #264, illus.), (152.4 x 101.6 cm.), colored stencil w/extensive hand-coloring on Hodgkinson Mould Made (BP 20,364, DM 49,170, FR 166,127, Y 3,822,288).

$690* *Palette II (Gal. M. 57), 1969,* s., #64/75, pub. Petersburg Press, full sheet, good cond., creases, hinged w/two-sided tape, (02-11-93, Sotheby-NY, #322), sheet 27¹⁵⁄₁₆ x 19⅞ in., (710 x 505 mm.), silkscreen p. in colors on Kromecote card (BP 487, DM 1143, FR 3868, Y 83,183).

$1100* *Paris Smiles In Darkness (W.C. 219), 1976,* s., d., #23/45, pub. Aldo Crommelynck, full margins, creases, soiling, staining, (11-09-92, Christie-NY, #267), 36 x 25 in., (914 x 635 mm.), hard- and soft-ground etching and drypoint in colors on buff Arches (BP 727, DM 1756, FR 5933, Y 136,510).

$1430* *Picabia I (Cheer) (W.C. 43), 1971,* s. in crayon, d., annot. A/P, pub. Petersburg Press, apparently goodcond., (02-24-93, Butterfield, #3018), 54⅛ x 36⅞ in., (137.5 x 93.7 cm.), offset lithograph w/collage in red & black on Hodgkinson Mould Made (BP 997, DM 2321, FR 7870, Y 167,801).

$1165* *The Picture Of Dorian Gray, Edition B, Petersburg Press, (Miko cat. 47), 1968,* title, justification, text and set of 12 en-texte and en suite, s., i. Edition B, num. 168/200, good cond., (12-01-92, Christie-London, #568), overall S. 17¹⁵⁄₁₆ x 12¹¹⁄₁₆ in., (455 x 322 mm.), lithographs and etchings in colors (BP 770, DM 1857, FR 6328, Y 145,045).

$2860* *The Pine In A Storm Of Aquatint (D. and F. 31), 1978,* s., d., num. 13/45, pub. Pace, full margins, excell. cond.?, (09-19-92, Christie-E, #98, illus.), sheet 65½ x 39¾ in., (166.4 x 101 cm.), etching, aquatint and drypoint on Rives (BP 1645, DM 4283, FR 14,667, Y 356,342).

BI *Pliers II, 1969,* s., d., num. 6/21, blindstamp, full sheet, good cond., creases, one pencil mark, soiling, est. $1,5/2,000, (05-22-93, Weschler, #178, illus.), 20¼ x 25 in., (51.4 x 63.5 cm.), lithograph on hand-made paper.

$1185* *The Poet Assassinated, 1971,* #6/75, d., lit., (04-21-93, Germann, #56, illus.), 35¹⁄₁₆ x 27¾ in., (890 x 705 mm.), colored etching (BP 769, DM 1894, FR 6405, Y 131,186, SF 1725).

BI *The Poet's Twelve Hearts (cf. M. 60), 1969,* s., t., d. Jan. 1969, i., #3/10, pub. by artist, full margins, imagestain, crease, surface soiling, very good cond., est. $6,5/8,500, (05-11-93, Christie-NY, #400, illus.), sheet 21⅝ x 25⅝ in., (549 x 651 mm.), hand-colored etching in red and green watercolor on wove.

$4950* *Printing Outdoors (D. and F. 65), 1980,* s., d., #15/40, pub. Pace Editions, full margins, excellent cond., (11-09-92, Christie-NY, #272, illus.), 42¼ x 29¾ in., (107.3 x 75.6 cm.), etching and electric tooling in red and black w/hand-coloring in acrylic on wove (BP 3273, DM 7902, FR 26,699, Y 614,296).

$14,300* *Rancho Woodcut Heart (D'Oench & Feinberg 142), 1982,* s., d., #39/75, pub. Pace Editions, full sheet, good cond., tiny tear, tape remains, (11-07-92, Sotheby-NY, #542, illus.), sheet 47⅞ x 40½ in., (121.6 x 102.9 cm.), woodcut p. in colors on BFK Rives (BP 9349, DM 22,833, FR 77,172, Y 1,764,996).

$887* *The Realistic Poet Assassinated (W. 32), 1970,* s., d. 1971, i. A. P., pub. 1971 by Petersburg Press, full margins, light-staining, foxing, good cond., (12-03-92, Sotheby-London, #644, illus.), 27 x 21¼ in., (685 x 540 mm.), etching w/hand-coloring in watercolor on J. Green mould-made (BP 572, DM 1395, FR 4761, Y 110,365).

$4025* *Red And Black Diptych Robe (D'Oench & Feinberg 63), 1980,* s., d., #18/20, pub. Pace Editions, full sheets, good cond., (02-11-93, Sotheby-NY, #324), each sheet 37⅝ x 29½ in., (956 x 750 mm.), diptych, lithograph p. in colors on 2 sheets of BFK Rives newsprint gray (BP 2840, DM 6667, FR 22,562, Y 485,232).

$6325* *Red And Black Diptych Robe (D'Oench & Feinberg 63), 1980,* s., d., #8/20, pub. Pace Editions, apparently good cond., (05-15-93, Sotheby-NY, #951, illus.), each sheet 37⅝ x 29½ in., (95.6 x 74.9 cm.), diptych, lithograph in colors on two sheets of BFK Rives newsprint gray (BP 4112, DM 10,174, FR 34,189, Y 701,142).

$5520* *Red Etching Robe (W.C. 212), 1976,* s., d., #16/36, pub. Pace Editions, full margins, excell. cond., (05-11-93, Christie-NY, #403, illus.), sheet 42 x 29⅝ in., (106.7 x 75.2 cm.), color etching on wove (BP 3524, DM 8696, FR 29,299, Y 607,194).

$3019* *Rimbaud Wounded In Brussels,* s. 1973, 29/30, Petersburg Press, (05-25-93, AB Stockholm, #22), 5¹¹⁄₁₆ x 4⅛ in., (14.4 x 10.4 cm.), etching (BP 1957, DM 4917, FR 16,552, Y 329,981, SK 4400).

BI *The Robe Goes To Town (D'Oench and Feinberg 144, Fine and Corlett 62), 1983,* s., d., #40/59, Graphicstudio, USF blindstamp, scuffing along screenprint edges, excell. cond., est. $3/4,000, (05-11-93, Christie-NY, #405), sheet 57 x 36 in., (144.8 x 91.4 cm.), aquatint in white on black Arches hinged to color screenprint.

BI *The Robe Goes To Town (D. and F. 144), 1983,* s., d., #40/59, blindstamps, scuffing, excellent cond., est. $4/5,000, (11-09-92, Christie-NY, #274, illus.), 57 x 36 in., (144.8 x 91.4 cm.), white aquatint on black Arches hinged to a screenprint in colors.

$27,600* *Robe, 1983,* s., d., i. monotype, excell. cond.?, (05-11-93, Christie-NY, #406, illus.), sheet 63 x 36 in., (160 x 91.4 cm.), monotype in oil in colors w/hand-painted additions on wove (BP 17,619, DM 43,478, FR 146,497, Y 3,035,970).

$1131* *Self Portrait In A Flat Cap, 1974,* 4th state, s., d., #2/35, very good cond., (10-27-92, Phillips-London, #196), (254 x 311 mm.), etching and electric toolwork on wove (BP 715, DM 1733, FR 5881, Y 138,349).

$1035* *Self-Portrait As A Negative (Williams College 196, Sparks 33), 1975,* s., d., #37/39, ULAE blindstamp, full margins, excell. cond., (05-11-93, Christie-NY, #401), sheet 26⅛ x 20¼ in., (664 x 514 mm.), etching, drypoint and electric tooling in white on black wove (BP 661, DM 1630, FR 5494, Y 113,849).

$999* *Shoe (First State), (Williams College cat. 103), 1973,* s., d., num. 18/19, pub. Petersburg Press, margins, creasing, nick, good cond., (12-01-92, Christie-London, #569), P. 19¹¹⁄₁₆ x 25¹¹⁄₁₆ in., (500 x 653 mm.), etching on blue Hodgkinson hand-made paper (BP 660, DM 1592, FR 5426, Y 124,377).

$1540* *Silhouette Black Boots (Williams College 93),* s., d. 1972, #2/100, pub. Petersburg Press and Galerie Gerald Cramer, (05-16-93, Hindman, #523), 30 x 21¾ in., (76.2 x 55.2 cm.), lithograph (BP 1001, DM 2477, FR 8324, Y 170,713).

$4180* *Six Hearts (Williams College, 12),* s., d. 1970, t., #31/79, pub. Petersburg Press, (05-16-93, Hindman, #609, illus.), 30½ x 22 in., (77.5 x 55.9 cm.), color lithograph and collage (BP 2718, DM 6724, FR 22,595, Y 463,363).

$4888* *The Sky (D'O. & F. 164), 1984,* s., d., #5/25., Pace Editions, full sheet, good cond., (02-11-93, Sotheby-NY, #325, illus.), sheet 53¾ x 34¹³⁄₁₆ in., (136.5 x 88.5 cm.), lithograph and woodcut p. in colors on Arches buff (BP 3449, DM 8097, FR 27,399, Y 589,271).

$13,200* *Spray Painted Robe (D'Oench and Feinberg 6), 1977,* s., d., #11/27, pub. Pace Editions, excellent cond., (11-09-92, Christie-NY, #270, illus.), 41½ x 29½ in., (105.4 x 74.9 cm.), offset lithograph, etching, drypoint and electric tooling w/hand-coloring in spray enamel on wove (BP 8727, DM 21,073, FR 71,197, Y 1,638,124).

$1411* *A Sufi Baker (Williams College 199), 1976,* s., 7/30, from Eight Sheets From An Undefined Novel, (12-04-92, AB Stockholm, #7055), 23⅝ x 19¹¹⁄₁₆ in., (60 x 50 cm.), hand-colored etching (BP 905, DM 2247, FR 7623, Y 176,155, SK 9570).

$1650* *"A Sufi Baker" from Eight Sheets From An Undefined Novel, 1976,* pub. Pyramid Arts Ltd., p. T. Kettner, s., num., d. 18/30 Jim Dine 1976, t. in plate, pub./p. dry stamp, excellent cond., (09-11-92, Skinner, #112, illus.), sight 23⅝ x 19⅝ in., (60 x 49.8 cm.), etching/aquatint/hand coloring on wove German etching paper (BP 853, DM 2375, FR 8072, Y 204,436).

BI *A Temple Of Flora: Tropical Succulents (D'O. & F. 17), 1978,* s., d., i. A/P, pub. Pace Editions, Inc., full margins, good cond., est. BP 1,5/2,000, (06-30-93, Sotheby-London, #775, illus.), 23⅞ x 17¾ in., (606 x 451 mm.), etching w/hand-coloring on Fabriano Rosaspina.

$825* *Ten Winter Tools, AWL, 1973,* s., d., annot. PP 10/10, pub. Petersburg Press, full margins, good cond., creases, surface soiling, (10-28-92, Butterfield, #2940), 10¼ x 8½ in., (260 x 216 mm.), lithograph on cream wove (BP 526, DM 1274, FR 4326, Y 101,227).

BI *Thirty Bones Of My Body: Untitled (Wrench) (W.C. 69), 1972,* s., d., #8/10, pub. Petersburg Press, full margins, good cond., creases, discoloration, $1,5/2,000, (05-15-93, Sotheby-NY, #947), 8⅞ x 6 in., (22.5 x 15.2 cm.), etching on Crisbrook Waterleaf paper.

BI *Throat (Galerie Mikro 36), 1965,* s., #30/200, pub. Original Editions, good cond., est. BP 800/1,000, (06-30-93, Sotheby-London, #773, illus.), 29⅞ x 24 in., (759 x 610 mm.), color screenprint on Cartridge paper.

BI *A Tool Box (Galerie Mikro 42), 1966: Ten,* complete portfolio, s., i. Artist's Proof verso, good cond., creases, hinges, original box, est. $4/5,000, (05-15-93, Sotheby-NY, #945, illus.), each sheet 24 x 19 in., (61 x 48.3 cm.), silkscreen in colors w/collage.

$721* *Tool Box II (Galerie Mikro 42 b), 1966,* artist's proofs, pencil s., (11-20-92, Lempertz, #516), sh 23¹³⁄₁₆ x 18¹³⁄₁₆ in., (60.5 x 47.8 cm.), serigraph in 2 colors w/collage on Velin (BP 475, DM 1150, FR 3872, Y 89,665).

$303* *Tool Box Number Nine, 1966,* s. on collage, num. 20/150 verso, (11-12-92, Freemn/Fine Art, #61), 23½ x 18¾ in., (59.7 x 47.6 cm.), screen print and collage (BP 199, DM 480, FR 1619, Y 37,570).

$593* *Toolbox (From) (Dine 42), 1966,* s., #59/150, ea 337, (04-21-93, Germann, #49, illus.), 18⅞ x 23⅝ in., (480 x 600 mm.), serigraph and collage (BP 385, DM 948, FR 3205, Y 65,648, SF 863).

$385* *Torah, c. 1955,* proofs only, t., s., (05-27-93, Swann, #90), 26 x 11½ in., (66 x 29.2 cm.), woodcut on soft Tableau paper (BP 247, DM 618, FR 2082, Y 41,274).

BI *The Tree From The 'Three Sydney Close Woodcuts', 1983,* i., good cond., est. BP 5/6,000, (12-03-92, Sotheby-London, #650, illus.), sheet 46½ x 31¾ in., (118.1 x 80.6 cm.), extensive hand-coloring in watercolor over woodcut on thick hand-made.

BI *Two Florida Bathrobes (F. and C. 70), 1986,* s., d., i. Presentation proof, pub. Pace Editions, Graphicstudio, USF blindstamp, full margins, exce.. cond., est. $12/15,000, (05-11-93, Christie-NY, #409, illus.), sheet 31¾ x 46½ in., (80.6 x 118.1 cm.), color etching and lithograph on one sheet on BFK Rives.

BI *Two Hand Coloured Colorado Robes, (D'O. & F. 151), 1980-83: Diptych,* s., d. 1983, i., num. 9/10, pub. Pace Editions, very good cond., est. BP 6/8,000, (12-01-92, Christie-London, #570, illus.), S. 37¹⁵⁄₁₆ x 29½ in., (965 x 750 mm.), lithographs in colors w/extensive hand-coloring in black and turquoise on Arches.

$15,400* *Two Hearts In The Forest (D. and F. 86), 1981,* s., d., #18/24, pub. Pace Editions, printer's ink, surface soiling verso, excellent cond., (11-09-92, Christie-NY, #273, illus.), 36 x 60½ in., (91.4 x 153.7 cm.), lithograph and woodcut in colors on wove (BP 10,182, DM 24,585, FR 83,064, Y 1,911,144).

$3450* *Untitled (Robe For The 1988 Korean Olympics), 1988,* s., d., #166/300, blindstamp, Angeles Press, good cond.?, (05-19-93, Butterfield, #2162, illus.), 35 x 27⅛ in., (889 x 689 mm.), lithograph on wove (BP 2240, DM 5608, FR 18,894, Y 381,933).

$1623* *Vegetables, 1969,* s., num., (12-05-92, Bassenge, #7120), approx. 14⁹⁄₁₆ x 14⁹⁄₁₆ in., (37 x 37 cm.), collage of offset lithograph w/six mounted color photos (BP 1016, DM 2530, FR 8624, Y 201,090).

$461* *Vinyl Strip Cape, 1968,* s., (06-08-93, Karl/Faber, #691), approx. 15¾ x 7⅞ in., (40 x 20 cm.), color lithograph on wove (BP 303, DM 748, FR 2519, Y 48,964).

$286* *Wall (M. 45), 1967,* s., d., num. 14/120, Editions Alecto ink stamp, full sheet, crease, minor soiling, good cond., (09-19-92, Christie-E, #94), sheet 31 x 22⅜ in., (787 x 568 mm.), photo-etching and screenprint in colors w/letterpress on handmade (BP 165, DM 428, FR 1467, Y 35,634).

$1650* *Wall Chart (W.C. 167), 1974,* s., d., #55/75, pub. Petersburg Press, full margins, staining, foxmarks, surface soiling, creasing, shaved, skinning, (11-09-92, Christie-NY, #266, illus.), 48 x 35 in., (121.9 x 88.9 cm.), colored lithograph on wove (BP 1091, DM 2634, FR 8900, Y 204,765).

$1840* *Wall Chart I (W.C. 166), 1974,* s., d., #42/75, pub. Petersburg Press, full margins, good cond., staining, (05-15-93, Sotheby-NY, #948), 41¾ x 29¾ in., (106 x 75.6 cm.), lithograph in colors on Rives (BP 1196, DM 2960, FR 9946, Y 203,969).

$920* *Wall Chart II (W.C. 167), 1974,* s., d., #42/75, pub. Petersburg Press, full margins, good cond., soiling, (05-15-93, Sotheby-NY, #949), 41⅞ x 29⅞ in., (106.4 x 75.9 cm.), lithograph in colors on Rives (BP 598, DM 1480, FR 4973, Y 101,984).

$2387* *A Well Painted Strelitzia (D'O & F. 73), 1980,* crayon s., d., #29/33, pub. Pace Editions, Inc., good cond., (12-03-92, Sotheby-London, #647, illus.), sheet 35½ x 26¾ in., (902 x 606 mm.), etching in black w/hand painting in blue, green and red oil on Copperplate Deluxe (BP 1540, DM 3754, FR 12,813, Y 297,001).

$2200* *White Robe On Black Paper (D'Oench and Feinberg 4), 1977,* s., d., num. 89/100, pub. American Friends of the Israel Museum, full sheet, tear, excell. cond., (09-19-92, Christie-E, #96, illus.), sheet 41½ x 29½ in., (105.4 x 74.9 cm.), offset lithograph in white on black Fabriano (BP 1265, DM 3294, FR 11,282, Y 274,109).

BI *Winter Windows On Chapel Street (W. 117), 1982,* s., d., #29/40, pub. pace Editions, Inc., scratching, scuffing, one scratch extending to image, good cond., est. BP 2,5/3,000, (12-03-92, Sotheby-London, #646, illus.), each sheet approx. 25⅜ x 21⅝ in., (645 x 550 mm.), screenprint and carborundum in b/w on four sheets on Arches.

BI *Winter Windows On Chapel Street (Williams College Catalogue 117), 1982,* s., d., #29/40, scratching, scuffing, scratch extending to image, good cond., est. BP 1,5/2,000, (06-30-93, Sotheby-London, #777, illus.), each sh c. 25⅜ x 21⅝ in., (645 x 549 mm.), screenprint and carborundum in black and white on 4 sh on Arches.

DINE, Jim and Lee FRIEDLANDER

$2558* *Photographs And Etchings (Gal. Mikro 55), 1969,* complete portfolio, each s. by Dine and Friedlander, #65/75, etched t. page, just., and introduction, pub. Petersburg Press, good cond., tear, in orig black box, (12-03-92, Sotheby-London, #642), each sheet approx. 17⅞ x 29¾ in., (455 x 756 mm.), 16 etchings w/collaged photographs on Hodgkinson hand-made (BP 1650, DM 4023, FR 13,731, Y 318,278).

$2217* *Photographs and Etchings (Gal. Mikro 55), 1969,* complete portfolio, each s. by Dine and Friedlander, #54/75, etched t. page, just., and introduction, pub. Petersburg Press, good cond., tear, orig.black box, (12-03-92, Sotheby-London, #641, illus.), each sheet approx. 17⅞ x 29¾ in., (455 x 756 mm.), 16 etchings w/collaged photographs on Hodgkinson hand-made (BP 1430, DM 3486, FR 11,900, Y 275,849).

DINET, E. French 1861-1929

$1812* *L'Andalousie Au Temps Des Maures. Exposition 1900, Paris,* good cond., (03-13-93, Laurin, #20), 98⁷⁄₁₆ x 35⁷⁄₁₆ in., (250 x 90 cm.), (BP 1264, DM 3016, FR 10,255, Y 213,553).

DIRKSEN, Reyn b. 1924

$359* *Holland Amerika Line. SS Nieuw Amsterdam, 1953,* cond. A, (03-16-93, Boisgirard, #97), 37¹³⁄₁₆ x 24⁷⁄₁₆ in., (96 x 62 cm.), poster (BP 248, DM 597, FR 2028, Y 41,978).

DISERTORI, Benvenuto Italian 1887-1969

$942* *Il Pero, 1948,* s., (12-15-92, Finarte-Milan, #6, illus.), 11⅝ x 9¹⁄₁₆ in., (29.5 x 23 cm.), etching (BP 601, DM 1476, FR 5046, Y 116,830, L 1323).

$666* *Perugia, Via Dei Priori (Bellini 35), 1920,* s., (05-20-93, Finarte-Milan, #65, illus.), 14⅜ x 11 in., (36.5 x 28 cm.), etching (BP 427, DM 1075, FR 3620, Y 73,542, L 978).

DISLER, Martin b. 1949

BI *Gravure D., (19)82,* s., d., num., est. DM 2000, (12-01-92, Karl/Faber, #541A), 27³⁄₁₆ x 17¹¹⁄₁₆ in., (69 x 45 cm.), color aquatint/etching and drypoint on wove.

BI *Untitled,* s., d., num. Disler 86, #14/50, est. SC 8/12,000, (04-21-93, Dorotheum, #724), lithograph.

BI *Untitled (Willi-Cosandier/Mason Nr. 16), 1982,* 31/125, s., d., 1008mm x 760mm, est. DM 700/1,200, (06-24-93, Germann, #593), engraving and aquatint on Rives.

DITTRICH, Simon b. 1940

BI *Heinrich VIII, 1972,* s., d., #20/100, blindstamp, est. DM 300, (09-18-92, Schloss Ahlden, #993), 29⅝ x 23⅛ in., (75.2 x 58.7 cm.), color seriograph on hand-made.

DIVOLA, John

$518* *"Zuma Number 29", 1978,* s., d., illus., (05-23-93, Butterfield, #3394, illus.), 9¾ x 12 in., photograph, c-print (BP 337, DM 847, FR 2851, Y 57,257).

DIX, Otto German 1891-1969

$3300* *Alemannische Masken (K. 293/II/A/a), 1963,* s., d., t., #16/60, pub. by artist, full margins, good cond., creases, tear, soiling, foxing, (11-05-92, Sotheby-NY, #163, illus.), 22⅛ x 21⅝ in., (563 x 550 mm.), lithograph p. in colors on Van Gelder Zonen wove (BP 2146, DM 5219, FR 17,657, Y 404,858).

$3738* *"Alter Mann Mit Kind", "Grobes Selbstbildnis", Selbstportrat (Nach Links, Mit Schwarzem Kragen)" and "Selbstbildnis Mit Marcella (Augen Dunkel)" (K. 234, 303, 318 and 329), 1960-68: Four,* s.; 1st d., i. Prob., p. Ehrhardt, pub. artist; 2nd i. Probedruk, p.Emil Matthieu, pub. Wolfgang Ketterer; 3rd d., #IV/X, p. Erker Presse, pub. Rosenbach; last d., t., i. Probedruk, p. Erker Presse, blindstamp, pub. artist, full margins, good cond., creases, skinned spot, (02-11-93, Sotheby-NY, #124), lithograph (BP 2638, DM 6192, FR 20,953, Y 450,633).

$5639* *Die Barrikade (Karsch 45 II/II), 1922,* s., artist's proof, (05-26-93, Lempertz, #118, illus.), 17⅛ x 19¹¹⁄₁₆ in., (43.5 x 50 cm.), etching (etching) on wove (BP 3648, DM 9201, FR 30,967, Y 612,668).

$3531* *Bettlerin (Karsch 124), 1924,* s., Vorzugsausgabe from portfolio Hunger, (06-10-93, Hauswedell/Nolt, #246, illus.), image 14¾ x 9⅝ in., (37.5 x 24.5 cm.), lithograph on hand-made (BP 2310, DM 5750, FR 19,359, Y 374,801).

$3565* *"Bettlerin", "Meine Mutter 86 Jahre Alt II", "Frau Pfatter Friedrich", "Meine Mutter Auf Dem Totenbett I" and "Meine Mutter Auf Dem Totenbett II" (Karsch 124, 167, 199, 206, and 207), 1924-54: Five,* s., 1st pub. portfolio Hunger, pub. Neuer Deutscher Verlag; 2nd #10/25, blindstamp; 3rd d.; last 2 #6/25 & 4/22; last 4 p. Ehrhardt; all pub. artist, full margins, good cond., mat/light/hinge stains, creases, foxing, discoloration spots, masking tape, nick, skinning, (02-11-93, Sotheby-NY, #117), lithograph (BP 2516, DM 5905, FR 19,983, Y 429,777).

$493* *Bildnis Carl Jacob Burckhardt II (Karsch 282), 1961,* #50/100, i., s., (03-24-93, Venator/Hansten, #4479), image 18½ x 13¹¹⁄₁₆ in., (47 x 34.7 cm.), chalk lithograph on Rives (BP 334, DM 805, FR 2740, Y 57,925).

BI *Bildnis Max Frisch I (Karsch 316), 1967,* #11/75, s., blindstamp Erker Presse, est. DM 2,500-, (11-21-92, Lempertz, #127), 15¹⁄₁₆ x 10⁹⁄₁₆ in., (38.2 x 26.8 cm.), lithograph on BFK Rives wove.

$2245* *Bildnis Otto Klemperer (Karsch 67), 1923,* s., d., (10-09-92, Winterberg, #2002), 17¹¹⁄₁₆ x 16¹⁵⁄₁₆ in., (45 x 43 cm.), lithograph on wove (BP 1332, DM 3335, FR 11,197, Y 273,314).

$3575* *Blinder (Karsch 52), 1923,* s., d., #26/66, pub. Karl Nierendorf, full margins, good cond., lightstain, creases, repaired tear, (11-05-92, Sotheby-NY, #159, illus.), 19⅜ x 15 in., (492 x 380 mm.), lithograph (BP 2325, DM 5654, FR 19,128, Y 438,596).

$4111* *Bodenseelandschaft (Mit Schwanen) (K. 305 a), (19)65,* s., d., Mappe V. of series Europaische Graphik, (06-08-93, Karl/Faber, #703, illus.), approx. 19⁵⁄₁₆ x 25¹⁵⁄₁₆ in., (49 x 66 cm.), lithograph on Japon nacre (BP 2702, DM 6670, FR 22,464, Y 436,644).

$1610* *Christus (Kipf Nach Recht Blickend, Haare Schulterlang, Dunkel Auf Hellem Grund) (K. 220/II),* 1957, s., d., t., #9/50, pub. artist, full margins, creases into images, (02-11-93, Sotheby-NY, #121), 19¹⁄₈ x 15¹⁵⁄₁₆ in., (485 x 405 mm.), color lithograph (BP 1136, DM 2667, FR 9025, Y 194,093).

$6600* *Contessa (K. 291),* 1962, s., d., #22/80, pub. by artist, full margins, good cond., creases, skinning, nick, foxing, (11-05-92, Sotheby-NY, #161, illus.), 25¹⁄₈ x 15¹⁄₄ in., (639 x 388 mm.), lithograph p. in colors (BP 4293, DM 10,438, FR 35,313, Y 809,717).

BI *Dame Mit Reiher (Karsch 62/II),* 1923, s., d., blindstamp, est. DM 14,200-, (11-21-92, Lempertz, #120A, illus.), 15³⁄₁₆ x 10⁷⁄₈ in., (38.5 x 27.7 cm.), lithograph on thin machine-made paper.

$425* *Dr. Eckner II (K. 144), (19)48,* s., d. 53, collector's stamp, (06-08-93, Karl/Faber, #695), approx. 17¹⁄₈ x 10¹³⁄₁₆ in., (43.5 x 27.5 cm.), lithograph on copper print paper (BP 279, DM 690, FR 2322, Y 45,141).

$2559* *Ecce Home (Karsch 187),* 1949, s., t., blindstamp, light-staining, wear, (12-02-92, Dorling, #2593, illus.), 16⁵⁄₁₆ x 13³⁄₄ in., (41.5 x 35 cm.), color lithograph on copper print paper (BP 1651, DM 4024, FR 13,736, Y 318,402).

BI *"Fohse" (Vohse) (K. 22/II.), (19)22,* s., d., t., num., restored, traces of mounting, est. DM 18/20,000, (12-01-92, Karl/Faber, #544, illus.), 13⁹⁄₁₆ x 11 in., (34.5 x 28 cm.), drypoint on copper print paper.

BI *Franzosin (Karsch 226 I),* 1958, s., est. DM 2,800, (05-26-93, Lempertz, #122), 26³⁄₁₆ x 19⁵⁄₁₆ in., (66.5 x 49 cm.), lithograph on thin copper print paper.

$2588* *"Franzosin", "Madchendkopf Mit Ponyhaar", "Bildnis Max Frisch I" and"Junges Madchen" (K. 226/II, 273, 316, and 323),* 1958-68: Four, s.; 1st #21/23; 2nd d.; first 2 pub. Klihm; 3rd d., #XVII/XXX; last d., t., #31/60; last 2 p., pub. Erker Presse, blindstamp, full margins, good cond.; 1st creases, tear; 2nd skinned spot, soiled spot, masking tape stains, (02-11-93, Sotheby-NY, #122), lithograph (BP 1826, DM 4287, FR 14,507, Y 311,995).

$2260* *Frau Otto Mueller (Karsch 57 b),* 1923, s., d., #4/15, (06-10-93, Hauswedell/Nolt, #244), image 19 x 14¹⁵⁄₁₆ in., (48.3 x 38 cm.), lithograph on wove (BP 1478, DM 3680, FR 12,390, Y 239,890).

$1024* *Gefunden Beim Grabendurchstich (Auberive) (Karsch 98 a),* 1924, (12-02-92, Dorling, #2590), 7¹⁄₂ x 11¹⁄₈ in., (19 x 28.3 cm.), etching on BSB handmade machine paper (BP 661, DM 1610, FR 5497, Y 127,411).

$1559* *Grosses Selbstbildnis (K. 303 b), (19)65,* s., d., num., Mappe Europaische Graphik IV, blindstamp, (06-08-93, Karl/Faber, #701, illus.), approx. 20¹⁄₂ x 14³⁄₁₆ in., (52 x 36 cm.), lithograph on BFK Rives wove (BP 1025, DM 2530, FR 8519, Y 165,587).

$918* *Grosses Selbstbildnis (Karsch 303 a),* 1965, s., d., series Europaische Graphik, Edition Ketterer, (06-10-93, Hauswedell/Nolt, #251), image 20¹¹⁄₁₆ x 14⁵⁄₁₆ in., (52.6 x 36.4 cm.), lithograph on simili-Japan (BP 600, DM 1495, FR 5033, Y 97,442).

$12,446* *Hafenarbeiter Mit Kind (K. 327/II.), (19)68,* s., d., t., num., light-stained, traces of mounting, (12-01-92, Karl/Faber, #548), 27³⁄₄ x 20¹⁄₂ in., (70.5 x 52 cm.), color lithograph on BFK Rives wove (BP 8223, DM 19,837, FR 67,605, Y 1,549,552).

$7150* *Hahn (Vor Der Scheune) (K. 326),* 1968, s., d., t., #66/80, blindstamp pub. by artist, full margins, good cond., creases, crease extending into image, (11-05-92, Sotheby-NY, #166, illus.), 28¹⁄₄ x 20⁷⁄₈ in., (717 x 530 mm.), lithograph p. in colors (BP 4650, DM 11,308, FR 38,256, Y 877,193).

$1843* *"Hahn Und Katze" (K. 306/I), (19)65,* s., d., t., num., (06-08-93, Karl/Faber, #704, illus.), approx. 16¹⁄₈ x 23⁵⁄₈ in., (41 x 60 cm.), lithograph on Van Gelder Zonen hand-made (BP 1212, DM 2990, FR 10,071, Y 195,751).

$1844* *Halbakt (Karsch 125),* 1923, s., num., (12-05-92, Bassenge, #7123), 23⁵⁄₈ x 19⁵⁄₁₆ in., (60 x 49 cm.), litho-

graph on handmade (BP 1155, DM 2875, FR 9798, Y 228,472).

$921* *Halbakt Von Vorn (K. 314 a), (19)66,* s., d., num. III/XL, blindstamp Erker Presse St. Gallen, (06-08-93, Karl/Faber, #705), approx. 17⁵⁄₁₆ x 13³⁄₄ in., (44 x 35 cm.), lithograph on BFK Rives wove (BP 605, DM 1494, FR 5033, Y 97,823).

$706* *Halbakt Von Vorn (Karsch 314 b),* 1966, s., d., #208/300, blindstamp, (06-10-93, Hauswedell/Nolt, #252), image 17¹¹⁄₁₆ x 14 in., (45 x 35.6 cm.), lithograph on BFK Rives (BP 462, DM 1150, FR 3871, Y 74,939).

$4331* *"Halbakt" (Karsch 125),* 1923/1924, s., d., num., (11-28-92, Grisebach, #495, illus.), 23⁵⁄₈ x 19⁵⁄₁₆ in., (60 x 49 cm.), lithograph on factory made paper (BP 2859, DM 6900, FR 23,423, Y 539,017).

$8851* *Hemmenhofen II (Karsch 211 II),* 1954, s., t., num., (12-05-92, Bassenge, #7124, illus.), 19¹⁄₂ x 25 in., (49.5 x 63.5 cm.), color lithograph on handmade (BP 5542, DM 13,800, FR 47,030, Y 1,096,642).

$9589* *Herbst Am See II (Karsch 287/II),* 1961, s., artist's proof, rare, (12-05-92, Bassenge, #7128, illus.), 18⁵⁄₁₆ x 24 in., (46.5 x 61 cm.), color lithograph on van Gelder-Zonen handmade (BP 6004, DM 14,950, FR 50,951, Y 1,188,081).

$14,884* *"Herbstlandschaft" (K. 302/I/II), (19)65,* s., d., i., t., artist's proof, (06-08-93, Karl/Faber, #700, illus.), approx. 19⁷⁄₈ x 25³⁄₁₆ in., (50.5 x 64 cm.), color lithograph on Maschinen/Van Gelder Zonen hand-made (BP 9784, DM 24,151, FR 81,333, Y 1,580,882).

$3249* *Hofkirche In Dresden (Karsch 212 a B),* 1955, s., t., #50/50, (06-10-93, Hauswedell/Nolt, #249), image 18¹⁵⁄₁₆ x 25¹⁵⁄₁₆ in., (48.2 x 66 cm.), color lithograph on hand-made Van Gelder Zonen (BP 2125, DM 5291, FR 17,813, Y 344,868).

$2243* *"I.N.R.I." (Karsch 289, I.B),* i., s., d. Dix 62, foxing, (09-14-92, Venator/Hansten, #2453), image approx. 15³⁄₁₆ x 11³⁄₄ in., (38.5 x 29.8 cm.), color lithograph on hand-made (BP 1186, DM 3334, FR 11,300, Y 278,911).

BI *Internationaler Reitakt (Karsch 37II),* 1922, from the series Zirkus, s., t., d., #14/50, full margins, good cond.,- marks, creases, hinges, est. BP 4,0/5,000, (12-03-92, Sotheby-London, #284, illus.), 15³⁄₄ x 11⁵⁄₈ in., (400 x 295 mm.), drypoint on wove.

$7213* *Katze Und Hahn (Karsch 306/II),* 1966, #4/80, num., t., s., d., (11-21-92, Lempertz, #124, illus.), 17¹⁄₁₆ x 24⁵⁄₁₆ in., (43.4 x 61.8 cm.), color lithograph on machine-made Van Gelder Zonen (BP 4749, DM 11,500, FR 38,738, Y 897,028).

$6808* *Katze Und Hahn (karsch 306),* 1966, proof, pub. by artist, margins, creases, very good cond., (05-20-93, Christie-London, #431, illus.), image 17 x 24 in., (43.2 x 61 cm.), sheet 22⁷⁄₈ x 29¹⁄₂ in., (43.2 x 61 cm.), lithograph in colors on van Gelder laid paper (BP 4370, DM 10,984, FR 37,000, Y 751,767).

$7579* *"Katze" (Karsch 231/II),* 1959, s., d., (11-28-92, Grisebach, #220, illus.), 15¹⁄₁₆ x 19³⁄₄ in., (38.3 x 50.2 cm.), color lithograph on hand-made (BP 5003, DM 12,074, FR 40,990, Y 943,248).

$3172* *Kleines Kind Und Katze (Karsch 276),* 1961, s., d., proof, (05-26-93, Lempertz, #123), 25¹³⁄₁₆ x 24¹⁄₁₆ in., (65.5 x 61.1 cm.), lithograph on smooth wove (BP 2052, DM 5175, FR 17,419, Y 344,633).

$938* *Kleines Madchen Mit Blutenzweig,* 1967, s., (11-28-92, Grisebach, #498, illus.), 5⁵⁄₁₆ x 4⁵⁄₁₆ in., (13.5 x 11 cm.), lithograph in green on handmade (BP 619, DM 1494, FR 5073, Y 116,739).

$935* *Kreuzigung I (Karsch 185 a),* s., (11-11-92, Ruef, #1751, illus.), 22¹³⁄₁₆ x 13³⁄₄ in., (58 x 35 cm.), lithograph (BP 619, DM 1494, FR 5008, Y 116,265).

BI *Kupplerin (Karsch 69 II),* 1923, second (final) state, s., d., #2/65, pub. K. Nierendorf, margins, repaired tear just extending into subject, made-up areas, very good cond., est/ BP 23/26,000, (05-20-93, Christie-London, #430, illus.), image 19 x 14¹⁄₄ in., (48.3 x 36.2 cm.), sheet 23¹⁄₄ x 18¹⁄₄ in., (48.3 x 36.2 cm.), lithograph in colors on laid paper.

$53,933* *Leonie (K. 58/III b.), (19)23,* s., d., num., (12-01-92, Karl/Faber, #546, illus.), 18¹¹⁄₁₆ x 14³⁄₄ in., (47.5 x 37.5

cm.), color lithograph on Maschinen hand-made (BP 35,635, DM 85,963, FR 292,955, Y 6,714,766).

BI *Leonie (Karsch 58 III b), 1923,* s., d., #7/65, est. DM 35,000, (06-10-93, Hauswedell/Nolt, #245, illus.), image 18¾ x 14¾ in., (47.6 x 37.5 cm.), color lithograph on hand-made.

$3541* *Leuchtkugel Erhellt Die Monacuferme (Karsch 86a), 1924,* s., t., ded., (12-05-92, Bassenge, #7121), 5⅝ x 7¹¹⁄₁₆ in., (14.3 x 19.6 cm.), etching on machinemade (BP 2217, DM 5521, FR 18,815, Y 438,731).

$9737* *Liegender Akt, Sitzende Mit Zigarette (Karsch 54), 1923,* #26/36, num., s., d., (11-21-92, Lempertz, #121, illus.), 22³⁄₁₆ x 17¹⁄₁₆ in., (56.3 x 43.3 cm.), lithograph on hand-made (BP 6411, DM 15,525, FR 52,293, Y 1,210,919).

$4775* *Lili, Die Konigin Der Luft (K. 40II), 1922,* from the series Zirkus, s., t., d., #28/50, pub. by artist, reduced margins, good cond., marks, creases, (12-03-92, Sotheby-London, #286, illus.), 11¾ x 7¾ in., (298 x 197 mm.), drypoint on wove (BP 3080, DM 7509, FR 25,631, Y 594,127).

$24,892* *"Der Lustmorder" (Karsch 14a), 1920,* s., t., artist proof, tears, creases, (12-01-92, Karl/Faber, #543, illus.), 11⅝ x 9¹³⁄₁₆ in., (29.5 x 25 cm.), etching on factory printed paper (BP 16,447, DM 39,675, FR 135,209, Y 3,099,104).

$2415* *"Madchen Mit Hut" and "Witwe" (K. 139 and 218/I), 1948 and 1957: Two,* s., d., t.; 1st #5/30, p. Himmelsbach; 2nd i. Probedruk, p. Ehrhardt; both pub. artist, full margins, good cond.; 1st creases, foxing, light-stain;2nd handling creases, (02-11-93, Sotheby-NY, #119, illus.), one 19⁵⁄₁₆ x 15³⁄₁₆ in., (490 x 385 mm.), the other 18⅜ x 13⁹⁄₁₆ in., (490 x 385 mm.), color lithograph (BP 1704, DM 4000, FR 13,537, Y 291,139).

$6638* *Madchen Mit Katze I (Karsch 215 III), 1956,* artist's proof, s., (12-05-92, Bassenge, #7125, illus.), 21¾ x 14¹⁵⁄₁₆ in., (55.2 x 38 cm.), lithograph on Van-Gelder handmade (BP 4157, DM 10,349, FR 35,271, Y 822,451).

$4888* *Madchen Mit Katze I (Kopf Geradeaus) (K. 215/III), 1956,* s., d., t., #5/45, pub. artist, full margins, good cond., creases, soiling, foxing, (02-11-93, Sotheby-NY, #120, illus.), 21¾ x 15³⁄₁₆ in., (552 x 385 mm.), color lithograph (BP 3449, DM 8097, FR 27,399, Y 589,271).

$9930* *Madchen Mit Katze II (Karsch 216 III), 1956,* i. artist's proof, s., d., (06-05-93, Bassenge, #5992, illus.), 20⅞ x 15¹⁵⁄₁₆ in., (53 x 40.6 cm.), lithograph on hand-made Van-Gelder-Zonen (BP 6537, DM 16,099, FR 54,262, Y 1,065,222).

BI *"Madchen Mit Katze II" (Karsch 216 II), 1959,* s., d., t., i. artist's proof, est. DM 14/18,000, (11-28-92, Grisebach, #219, illus.), 20⅞ x 15¹⁵⁄₁₆ in., (53 x 40.5 cm.), color lithograph on Van Gelder Zonen hand-made.

$388* *Madchen Mit Sonnenblume, 1958,* stone s., d., B XII/XV, (09-25-92, Granier, #2813), sheet 25¹⁵⁄₁₆ x 22¼ in., (66 x 56.5 cm.), lithograph in green on thin white machine hand-made (BP 227, DM 575, FR 1945, Y 46,832).

$3198* *Manitschka (Karsch 61), 1923,* s., d., #28/50, margins, tear in lower right corner of sheet, creasing, short tears, small defects at edges, paper discoloration, occasional foxing, Late Gerhard Brauer Coll., (05-27-93, Sotheby-Amstrdm, #721, illus.), sheet 20⅞ x 16⁵⁄₁₆ in., (530 x 414 mm.), lithograph on wove (BP 2048, DM 5132, FR 17,296, Y 342,839, G 5750).

$2166* *"Manitschka" (Karsch 61a), 1923,* s., d., num., (11-28-92, Grisebach, #493, illus.), 13⅞ x 11⁹⁄₁₆ in., (35.2 x 29.3 cm.), lithograph on factory made paper (BP 1430, DM 3451, FR 11,714, Y 269,571).

$2645* *"Masken I", "Kind Aud Dem Kissen" and "Ruine Der Frauenkirche" (K. 135; 277 and 308/II), 1948-66: Three,* 1st t., #18/30, p. Himmelsbach; 2nd #1/30; last d., t., #4/30; last 2 p. Ehrhardt; all pub. artist, full margins, good cond., foxing, tear, skinnedspot, creases, soiling, scratches, (02-11-93, Sotheby-NY, #118), lithograph (BP 1866, DM 4381, FR 14,826, Y 318,867).

$1328* *Mission (Karsch 270), 1960,* s., (12-05-92, Bassenge, #7127), 7⅜ x 8¹¹⁄₁₆ in., (18.7 x 22 cm.), lithograph on Japan (BP 832, DM 2070, FR 7056, Y 164,540).

$4400* *Mondane Dame (K. 304/III), 1965,* s., d., t., #5/60, pub. by artist, full margins, good cond., foxing, (11-05-92, Sotheby-NY, #165, illus.), 22 x 17⅜ in., (558 x 441 mm.), lithograph p. in colors on Van Gelder Zonen laid (BP 2862, DM 6959, FR 23,542, Y 539,811).

BI *"Mondane Dame" (K. 304/III.), (19)65,* s., d., t., num., est. DM 18/20,000, (12-01-92, Karl/Faber, #547, illus.), 21⅝ x 17⅛ in., (55 x 43.5 cm.), color lithograph on hand-made.

$2887* *"Mutzli (Bildnis Frau Dix)" (Karsch 123 c.), 1924,* s., d., (11-28-92, Grisebach, #494, illus.), 9⁹⁄₁₆ x 7⁹⁄₁₆ in., (24.3 x 19.2 cm.), drypoint on copper print paper (BP 1906, DM 4599, FR 15,614, Y 359,303).

$8579* *Nachtliche Erscheinung (K. 64 II), 1923,* s., d., #28/65, pub. Karl Nierendorf, margins, good cond., handling creases, skinned spot, (06-30-93, Sotheby-London, #426, illus.), sh 25½ x 18¾ in., (648 x 476 mm.), lithograph on laid Johann-Wilhelm-Maschinen (BP 5750, DM 14,632, FR 49,361, Y 919,211).

$1316* *Nelly II (K. 122, 2 a), 1923/24,* #32/80, s., impression 1968 ed., (10-09-92, Winterberg, #2005, illus.), 7¹¹⁄₁₆ x 5⁹⁄₁₆ in., (19.5 x 14.2 cm.), etching on hand-made (BP 781, DM 1955, FR 6564, Y 160,214).

$109,249* *Otto Dix. Der Krieg (Karsch 70-119), 1924: Fifty,* (05-26-93, Lempertz, #121, illus.), etching (w/drypoint, aquatint) on wide machine-made, 5 on thin wove (BP 70,675, DM 178,249, FR 599,940, Y 11,869,731).

$3300* *Pilze (K. 232), 1960,* s., d., #29/60, pub. by artist, full margins, good cond., creases, (11-05-92, Sotheby-NY, #160, illus.), 16½ x 26¾ in., (420 x 680 mm.), lithograph p. in colors on Van Gelder Zonen laid (BP 2146, DM 5219, FR 17,657, Y 404,858).

$3544* *Pilze (K. 232/I b), (19)60,* s., d., num., (06-08-93, Karl/Faber, #697, illus.), approx. 16⁵⁄₁₆ x 26⁹⁄₁₆ in., (41.5 x 67.5 cm.), color lithograph on Van Gelder Zonen hand-made (BP 2330, DM 5750, FR 19,366, Y 376,421).

BI *Pilze (Karsch 232 I), 1960,* s., est. DM 6,000, (12-05-92, Bassenge, #7126, illus.), 16⅛ x 26¾ in., (41 x 68 cm.), color lithograph on smooth copper print paper.

$4400* *Rothaariges Madchen (K. 292/II/A), 1963,* s., d., t., #13/60, pub. by artist, full margins, good cond., creasesthrough image, foxing (one in image), (11-05-92, Sotheby-NY, #162, illus.), 21½ x 18⅛ in., (545 x 461 mm.), lithograph p. in colors on Van Galder Zonen laid (BP 2862, DM 6959, FR 23,542, Y 539,811).

$3544* *"Rothaariges Madchen" (K. 292/II), (19)63,* s., d., t., num., (06-08-93, Karl/Faber, #699, illus.), approx. 20⅞ x 17⁵⁄₁₆ in., (53 x 44 cm.), color lithograph on van Gelder Zonen hand-made (BP 2330, DM 5750, FR 19,366, Y 376,421).

$6136* *"Rothaariges Madchen" (Karsch 292/II), 1963,* s., (11-28-92, Grisebach, #221, illus.), 21³⁄₁₆ x 17¹⁵⁄₁₆ in., (53.8 x 45.5 cm.), color lithograph on handmade (BP 4050, DM 9775, FR 33,186, Y 763,659).

$7796* *"Saul & David" (K. 228 A), (19)58,* d., t., num., s., (06-08-93, Karl/Faber, #696, illus.), approx. 21⅝ x 17⁵⁄₁₆ in., (55 x 44 cm.), color lithograph on Maschinen hand-made/Van Gelder Zonen (BP 5125, DM 12,650, FR 42,601, Y 828,040).

BI *Schadel (K. 100), 1924,* s., est. DM 5,900, (10-09-92, Winterberg, #2004, illus.), 10⅛ x 7¹¹⁄₁₆ in., (25.7 x 19.6 cm.), etching on wove.

$425* *Seemann Mit Kind (K. Werkverzeichnis-Erganzung 275/I), 1961,* (06-08-93, Karl/Faber, #698), approx. 22⁵⁄₁₆ x 22⁵⁄₁₆ in., (56.6 x 56.6 cm.), sh approx. 24¹³⁄₁₆ x 29¾ in., (56.6 x 56.6 cm.), lithograph on wove (BP 279, DM 690, FR 2322, Y 45,141).

$2164* *Selbstbildnis III (Karsch 155), 1948,* #II/XV, s., d., blind-stamp, (11-21-92, Lempertz, #123, illus.), 16⁷⁄₁₆ x 13¼ in., (41.7 x 33.7 cm.), lithograph on Fabriano wove (BP 1425, DM 3450, FR 11,622, Y 269,121).

$1339* *Selbstbildnis Im Profil Beim Malen (Karsch 307 c), 1966,* s., d., poster, (05-26-93, Lempertz, #125), 31¹¹⁄₁₆ x 22½ in., (80.5 x 57.2 cm.), lithograph on offset (BP 866, DM 2185, FR 7353, Y 145,480).

$1226* *Selbstbildnis Im Profil Beim Malen (Karsch 307), 1966,* s., d., (11-21-92, Lempertz, #125), 21¹⁄₁₆ x 20⁹⁄₁₆ in., (53.5 x 52.3 cm.), lithograph on offset paper (BP 807, DM 1955, FR 6584, Y 152,469).

$1227* *"Selbstbildnis Im Profil Beim Malen" (Karsch 307 c a), 1966,* s., d., (11-28-92, Grisebach, #497, illus.), 20¹⁵⁄₁₆ x 20⅜ in., (53.3 x 51.8 cm.), lithograph on white offset paper (BP 810, DM 1955, FR 6636, Y 152,707).

$1047* *"Selbstbildnis. Danksagung Zum 70. Geburtstag" (Karsch 288), 1961/196,* s., (11-28-92, Grisebach, #496, illus.), 9¹³/₁₆ x 13⁷/₁₆ in., (25 x 34.2 cm.), lithograph on thick Japan (BP 691, DM 1668, FR 5663, Y 130,305).

$4158* *Selbstportrait (Karsch 66), 1923,* s., d., #53/60, pub. Karl Nierdorf, margins, tapestaining at intervals at edges of sheet, paperloss at right edge of sheet, short tear at left edgeof sheet, creasing, small defects at edges, Late Gerhard Brauer Coll., (05-27-93, Sotheby-Amstrdm, #720, illus.), sh 24⅝ x 18¹³/₁₆ in., (626 x 478 mm.), lithograph on wove (BP 2663, DM 6672, FR 22,488, Y 445,755, G 7475).

$1695* *Selbstportrat Im Profil (Karsch 50), 1922,* s., stone s., d., (06-10-93, Hauswedell/Nolt, #243), image 8⁵/₁₆ x 5⅞ in., (21.1 x 15 cm.), lithograph on thick, smooth wove (BP 1109, DM 2760, FR 9293, Y 179,917).

BI *Sitzendes Kind (Karsch 278), 1961,* s., d., #30/30, est. DM 2,500, (05-26-93, Lempertz, #124), 25¼ x 22⅛ in., (64.2 x 56.2 cm.), lithograph.

$6177* *Sketch (Karsch 34 II), 1922,* from series Zirkus, s., d., i., #14/50, pub. under direction of artist, margins, good cond., surface abrasion at top of image, mount-staining, skinned areas and glue remains, (06-30-93, Sotheby-London, #425, illus.), sh 19⅝ x 17 in., (498 x 432 mm.), etching and drypoint w/tone on wove (BP 4140, DM 10,536, FR 35,541, Y 661,845).

$2582* *Soldat Und Nonne (Karsch 120), 1924,* s., num., (12-05-92, Bassenge, #7122), 8¾ x 6⁷/₁₆ in., (22.2 x 16.3 cm.), etching with aquatint on handmade (BP 1617, DM 4026, FR 13,719, Y 319,911).

BI *Soldat Und Nonne, Vergewaltung (Karsch 120), 1924,* #49/70, s., est. DM 4,000-, (11-21-92, Lempertz, #122), 7¹¹/₁₆ x 5⁹/₁₆ in., (19.6 x 14.2 cm.), etching on BSB hand-made.

$7768* *Spielendes Kind (Karsch 214 b), 1955,* s., d., t., #48/50, (06-10-93, Hauswedell/Nolt, #250, illus.), image 19¾ x 26³/₁₆ in., (50.1 x 66.5 cm.), color lithograph on handmade Van Gelder Zonen (BP 5081, DM 12,649, FR 42,588, Y 824,541).

BI *Sterbender Soldat (K. 95), 1924,* #48/70, s., num. VI, est. DM 7,500, (10-09-92, Winterberg, #2003, illus.), 7⁹/₁₆ x 5¹¹/₁₆ in., (19.2 x 14.5 cm.), etching w/aquatint and drypoint.

$32,396* *"Streichholzhandler" (Karsch 11/II b), 1920,* s., t., d., num., in: Radierwerk II, 3. portfolio for "Graphischen Reihe", Dresden, Dresdner pub., (11-27-92, Grisebach, #40, illus.), 10¹/₁₆ x 11¹¹/₁₆ in., (25.5 x 29.7 cm.), drypoint on thin copper print paper (BP 21,348, DM 51,751, FR 175,779, Y 4,031,861).

BI *"Susu (Negerkind)" (Karsch 301/III), 1964,* s., t., d., i. artist's proof, est. DM 12/14,000, (11-28-92, Grisebach, #222, illus.), 25¹/₁₆ x 20¼ in., (63.7 x 51.5 cm.), color lithograph on handmade.

$1412* *Tote Vor Der Stellung Bei Tahure (Karsch 119 b), 1924,* s., I Prob, Zyklus Der Krieg, watermark, (06-10-93, Hauswedell/Nolt, #242, illus.), image 7¾ x 10³/₁₆ in., (19.7 x 25.8 cm.), etching w/aquatint on hand-made (BP 924, DM 2299, FR 7741, Y 149,878).

BI *Verschuttete (Karsch 71), 1924,* s., d., #5/70, est. DM 1,800, (05-26-93, Lempertz, #119), .

BI *Witwe (Karsch 218/II, C.),* s., artist's proof, wear, (09-25-92, Granier, #2812, illus.), sheet 24¹³/₁₆ x 19¾ in., (63 x 50.2 cm.), color lithograph on machine hand-made.

$792* *Witwe II (Karsch 218),* s., (11-11-92, Ruef, #1750), 18½ x 13¾ in., (47 x 35 cm.), lithograph on 2 stones, black and light grey-green (BP 524, DM 1266, FR 4242, Y 98,483).

$1128* *Zerschossene (Karsch 107),* #1/70, s., (05-26-93, Lempertz, #120), (BP 730, DM 1840, FR 6194, Y 122,555).

$4888* *Zwei Kinder (Mit Sonnenblume) (K. 309/III), 1966,* s., d., t., #20/80, pub. artist, full margins, good cond., crease, (02-11-93, Sotheby-NY, #125, illus.), 17¼ x 23⁷/₁₆ in., (438 x 595 mm.), color lithograph (BP 3449, DM 8097, FR 27,399, Y 589,271).

BI *Zwei Kinder (Mit Sonnenblume) (Karsch 309 III), 1966,* third (final) state, s., d., #78/80, pub. by artist, margins, foxing, light-staining, taped to glass, est. DM 2,5/3,500, (05-20-93, Christie-London, #432, illus.), image 17½ x 23½ in., (44.5 x 59.7 cm.), sheet 22⅛ x 28¾ in., (44.5 x 59.7 cm.), lithograph in colors on van Gelder laid paper.

$12,993* *"Zwei Kinder (Mit Sonnenblume)" (Karsch 309 III), 1966,* s., d., i., num., (11-28-92, Grisebach, #223, illus.), 17⁵/₁₆ x 23¼ in., (44 x 59 cm.), color lithograph on handmade (BP 8576, DM 20,699, FR 70,270, Y 1,617,050).

$6492* *Zwei Kinder, Mit Sonnenblume (Karsch 309/III), 1966,* #50/80, i., s., d., (11-21-92, Lempertz, #126, illus.), 17½ x 24³/₁₆ in., (44.5 x 61.5 cm.), color lithograph on hand-made Van Gelder Zonen (BP 4274, DM 10,351, FR 34,866, Y 807,362).

$9930* *"Zwei Kinder, Mit Sonnenblume" (Karsch 309/III), 1966,* watermark, s., d., t., num., (06-05-93, Grisebach, #388, illus.), 17⅛ x 23¼ in., (43.5 x 59 cm.), color lithograph on hand-made (BP 6537, DM 16,099, FR 54,262, Y 1,065,222).

DIXON, Ch.
$478* *By P. and O. To Australia: From London Et Marseilles Via Egypt And Ceylon, c. 1920,* very good cond., (03-13-93, Laurin, #138), 39¾ x 24¹³/₁₆ in., (101 x 63 cm.), (BP 333, DM 796, FR 2705, Y 56,335).

DIXON, Charles (after)
$168* *"Above Greenwich" and "The Lower Pool": Two,* (01-14-93, Bonhams, #110), image 9¾ x 24 in., (24.8 x 61 cm.), chromolithograph (BP 110, DM 275, FR 929, Y 21,180).

DMITRIENKO, Pierre   1925-1974
$18* *Sans Titre* #5/30, s., d. P. Dmitrienko 1970, (07-14-92, Encans, #189), 5¹¹/₁₆ x 3¹⁵/₁₆ in., (14.5 x 10 cm.), etching (BP 9, DM 27, FR 90, Y 2251, C$ 22).

$80* *"Sans Titre 1969",* d., s., (04-04-93, Pescheteau, #202), 25¹⁵/₁₆ x 21⅝ in., (66 x 55 cm.), etching and carborandum on wove (BP 53, DM 129, FR 437, Y 9109).

$168* *"Sans Titre",* #62/75, s., (01-28-93, Pescheteau, #124), 31⅛ x 23¼ in., (79 x 59 cm.), etching and aquatint on wove (BP 111, DM 266, FR 901, Y 20,859).

DOARE, Yves
$41* *L'Ange, 1981,* s., #81/100, good margins, (05-06-93, Laurin, #25), etching and aquatint (BP 26, DM 65, FR 217, Y 4511).

DOBIE, James (after Walter Dendy Sadler)   British 1854-1923
$110* *"The High Moon In The Old Coaching Days" and "The Way Of The Sun, London 1900 And 1907": Two,* (09-21-92, Selkirk, #182), one 18¼ x 13¾ in., (46.4 x 34.9 cm.), the other 14 x 18½ in., (46.4 x 34.9 cm.), hand colored etchings on brown paper (BP 64, DM 163, FR 558, Y 13,595).

DODD, Francis   Scottish 1874-1949
$487* *Charles Cundall (S. 171),* s., full margins, good cond., (10-27-92, Phillips-London, #257), plate 17⅞ x 11⅞ in., (454 x 302 mm.), drypoint (BP 308, DM 746, FR 2533, Y 59,572).

$128* *Pall Mall From The West,* s., margins, (08-20-92, Bonhams-Chelsea, #109), plate 8⅝ x 12¾ in., (21.9 x 32.4 cm.), drypoint etching (BP 66, DM 185, FR 629, Y 16,164).

$64* *Pamplona, 1928,* s., margins, (03-17-93, Bonhams-Chelsea, #330), plate 8⅜ x 13¾ in., (21.3 x 34.9 cm.), etching (BP 44, DM 106, FR 362, Y 7506).

BI *Pamplona, 1928,* s., margins, est. BP50/70, (01-21-93, Bonhams-Chelsea, #131), plate 8⅜ x 13¾ in., (21.3 x 34.9 cm.), etching.

BI *Portrait Of A Gentleman In A Three-Piece Suit,* s., margins, est. BP 30/50, (02-17-93, Bonhams-Chelsea, #354), plate 9¾ x 7¼ in., (24.8 x 18.4 cm.), etching.

$640* *Strand With Sky,* s., margins, (08-20-92, Bonhams-Chelsea, #110), plate 13¾ x 10 in., (34.9 x 25.4 cm.), drypoint etching on laid paper (BP 330, DM 927, FR 3145, Y 80,818).

$652* *Strand With Sky (Schwabe 136), 1916,* full margins, good cond., paper loss, creases, (06-30-93, Sotheby-London, #302), 13¾ x 10¼ in., (349 x 260 mm.), drypoint and etching on cream laid (BP 437, DM 1112, FR 3751, Y 69,860).

DODD, Robert English 1748-1816
$149* *Portrait Of An East Indiaman Coming Into Anchor At Spithead,* (08-20-92, Bonhams-Chelsea, #52), image 12 x 18½ in., (30.5 x 47 cm.), engraving, with hand coloring, laid face to glass (BP 77, DM 216, FR 732, Y 18,816).

DODEIGNE
$220* *Etde Pour St. Bernard I,* s., num. 11/25, full margins, apparently good cond., (02-24-93, Butterfield, #2917), (641 x 229 mm.), lithograph on Arches (BP 153, DM 357, FR 1211, Y 25,816).

DODEIGNE, Eugene b. 1923
$130* *Untitled,* s., num. E.A. 8/10, good cond.?, (12-09-92, Sotheby-Amstrdm, #561), sheet 27 15/16 x 20 11/16 in., (710 x 525 mm.), lithograph on wove (BP 83, DM 204, FR 696, Y 16,119, G 230).

DOERR, Carl (after)
BI *Emplacement De La Source St. Laurent Aux Bains De Loeche,* #1 from series, trimmed to platemark, grubby, water staining, est. BP150/250, (10-27-92, Phillips-London, #128), sheet 8½ x 11⅓ in., (216 x 288 mm.), aquatint w/hand-coloring on wove.

DOHANOS, Stevan American b. 1907
$248* *"Connecticut Yankee",* pub. AAA, s. Stevan Dohanos, t., very good cond., thinning, (09-11-92, Skinner, #45, illus.), 12⅜ x 9⅝ in., (31.4 x 24.4 cm.), lithograph on wove (BP 128, DM 357, FR 1213, Y 30,727).
$231* *"Connecticut Yankee", Man Of The Soil (Campbell No. 33), 1935,* s. Print-A-Month Club, pub. Feb. 1935, illus., tear, good cond., (10-31-92, Cleveland, #109), 12¾ x 9½ in., (32.4 x 24.1 cm.), lithograph (BP 148, DM 355, FR 1206, Y 28,614).
$303* *"Hose Co. #4",* pub. AAA, s. Stevan Dohanos, good cond., light toning, mount staining verso, tape residue, (09-11-92, Skinner, #39, illus.), 13 x 9 11/16 in., (33 x 24.6 cm.), lithograph on wove (BP 157, DM 436, FR 1482, Y 37,542).
$220* *"Man Of The Soil" (Connecticut Yankee), 1935,* s., plate 33 The Print-A-Month Club, excell. cond., (05-15-93, Cleveland, #112), 12¼ x 9½ in., (31.1 x 24.1 cm.), lithograph (BP 143, DM 354, FR 1189, Y 24,388).
$40* *"Pigeon's Roost",* s., good cond., taped, (05-15-93, Cleveland, #114), 7¾ x 5¾ in., (19.7 x 14.6 cm.), woodcut (BP 26, DM 64, FR 216, Y 4434).
$40* *"The Pooch",* s., t., good cond., taped, (05-15-93, Cleveland, #113), 5½ x 7¾ in., (14 x 19.7 cm.), woodblock (BP 26, DM 64, FR 216, Y 4434).
$220* *West Quoddy Light, 1932-3,* s., t., edit. 250, (07-03-92, Sloan, #1081), 10 x 8 in., (25.4 x 20.3 cm.), wood engraving (BP 115, DM 333, FR 1122, Y 27,425).

DOISNEAU, Robert French b. 1912
$2420* *Le Baiser De L'Hotel De Ville,* (1950), p.l., s. in ink, t., d., lit., (10-13-92, Christie-NY, #441, illus.), 9⅜ x 12⅛ in., (23.8 x 30.8 cm.), photograph, gelatin silver print (BP 1409, DM 3545, FR 12,046, Y 293,440).
BI *"Le Baiser De L'Hotel De Ville" (Three Seconds From Eternity, pl. 33),* s., init., t., d. by photog., 1950, p.l., est. $2,5/3,000, (04-06-93, Sotheby-NY, #265, illus.), 9½ x 11¾ in., photograph.
$4675* *"Le Baiser De L'Hotel De Ville" (Three Seconds, pl. 33),* 1950/later, s., inits., t., d., Dixon Collection, (11-16-92, Butterfield, #5936, illus.), 9⅝ x 12⅛ in., (244.9 x 308.5 mm.), photograph, gelatin silver print (BP 3078, DM 7454, FR 25,107, Y 581,395).
$3025* *Le Baiser De L'Hotel De Ville, 1950 (Three Seconds From Eternity, pl.33),* s. by photog. in ink, initialled, t., d., info stamp, p. l., (10-15-92, Sotheby-NY, #336, illus.), 9½ x 11¾ in., (24.1 x 29.8 cm.), photograph, gelatin silver print (BP 1851, DM 4503, FR 15,270, Y 362,927).
BI *"Un Banc Au Palais Royal",* 1950, p.l., s., t., d., est. BP 3/500, (05-06-93, Christie-London, #140), image 9½ x 13⅜ in., photograph, gelatin silver print.
$2640* *"Fernand Leger Dans Ses Oeuvres", "George Braque A Verengeville", "Les Mains De Picasso" and "Picasso Dans La Caves Aux Pots": Four,* s. by photog., photog.'s notations, 1950s, p.l., (04-07-93, Swann, #445, illus.), 11¾ x 15¾ in., photograph, silver print (BP 1745, DM 4270, FR 14,450, Y 299,932).
$1150* *"L'Enfer", Hell, "La Meute", The Pack and "Les Chaises Forees", The Gilded Chairs: Three,* selected works, 1948-69, p. 1980, s. twice, t., d., 1st and 3rd edit. 1/4, 2nd edit. 2/4, (05-23-93, Butterfield, #3395, illus.), each approx. 11½ x 9½ in., photograph, gelatin silver print (BP 749, DM 1880, FR 6329, Y 127,114).
$1210* *Man On Bed Looking At Pin-Ups,* sig., 1940's, (10-14-92, Swann, #434, illus.), 14 x 11 in., (35.6 x 27.9 cm.), photograph, silver print (BP 710, DM 1771, FR 6005, Y 146,631).
BI *Mortuary Sculpture, 1971,* s., lit., est. $1,2/1,800, (10-13-92, Christie-NY, #182, illus.), 11¾ x 15½ in., (29.8 x 39.4 cm.), photograph, gelatin silver print.
BI *"Nicole Vedros, 1955", "Louis De Broglie" and "Personalities": Three,* 1950s, photog.'s ink credit stamp, annots., est. BP 3/500, (05-06-93, Christie-London, #141), each approx. 7⅛ x 9½ in., photograph, gelatin silver print.
$990* *La Pendule,* s. by photog.'s, photog.'s notations, 1956, p. 1980, (04-07-93, Swann, #446, illus.), 16 x 12 in., photograph, silver print (BP 654, DM 1601, FR 5419, Y 112,474).
$467* *Square Du Vert-Galant,* sig., photog.'s notations, 1950's p.l., (04-07-93, Swann, #447, illus.), 11¾ x 15½ in., photograph, silver print (BP 309, DM 755, FR 2556, Y 53,056).
$3300* *Square Du Vert-Galant, 1950 (Three Seconds From Eternity, pl. 95),* s., t., d. by photog. in ink, p. 1972, (10-15-92, Sotheby-NY, #337, illus.), 11 x 14⅞ in., (27.9 x 37.8 cm.), photograph, gelatin silver print (BP 2019, DM 4912, FR 16,658, Y 395,921).
$1840* *Utrillo,* 1930s, t., credit stamp, (04-08-93, Christie-NY, #187, illus.), 9⅜ x 7⅛ in., (23.8 x 18.1 cm.), photograph, gelatin silver print (BP 1207, DM 2956, FR 10,005, Y 208,806).

DOKOUPIL, Jiri Georg b. Czec. 1954
$2867* *Portfolio Jiri Georg Dokoupil, 1986: Nine,* Delano Greenidge Editions, watermark, blindstamp, #25/33, num., s., d., (05-27-93, Lempertz, #691, illus.), 22 7/16 x 22 7/16 in., (57 x 57 cm.), serigraph on watercolor hand-made (BP 1836, DM 4600, FR 15,506, Y 307,354).

DOLA, G.
$90* *Theatre Des Varietes: La Chauve-Souris. D'Apres H. Meilhac, L. Halevy. Musique De J. Strauss, 1904,* Imp. Ch. Wall, very good cond., (02-12-93, Cheval/Robert, #154), 31½ x 22 7/16 in., (80 x 57 cm.), poster (BP 63, DM 149, FR 505, Y 10,854).

DOLA, J.
BI *Le Pays Du Sourire, 1940,* Editions Max Eschig, A cond., est. $8/1,200, (08-06-92, Swann, #116, illus.), 46 x 30½ in., (116.8 x 77.5 cm.), .
$88* *La Teresina (Spectacle),* s. J. Dola, (04-20-93, Encans, #106), 47¼ x 31½ in., (120 x 80 cm.), affiche (poster) marouflе sur toile (BP 57, DM 140, FR 473, Y 9710, C$ 111).

DOLGOROUKOV, Nicolai 1902-1980
$219* *Plus De Tracteurs Et Des Machines Agricoles, Plus De Pain, 1947,* cond. A, (03-16-93, Boisgirard, #4), 31⅞ x 22 13/16 in., (81 x 58 cm.), poster (BP 151, DM 364, FR 1237, Y 25,608).

DOLICE, Leon American 1892-1960
$55* *"In Central Park, NYC", 1922,* s., t., d., good cond., (05-15-93, Cleveland, #115), 15 x 8⅞ in., (38.1 x 22.5 cm.), etching (BP 36, DM 88, FR 297, Y 6097).

DOLS, Jean b. 1909
$47* *"Toilette",* ded., s., d. Jean Dols, 1936, (08-18-92, Encans, #93), 4 5/16 x 3 15/16 in., (11 x 10 cm.), etching (BP 24, DM 68, FR 232, Y 5925, C$ 56).

DOMBROWSKI, Ernst von b. 1896
$58* *Stillende Frau Mit Funf Schlafenden Kindern Auf Einer Holzbank,* s., stained, (09-25-92, Granier, #2814), sheet 6 9/16 x 7½ in., (16.7 x 19 cm.), woodcut on copper print paper (BP 34, DM 86, FR 291, Y 7001).

DOMELA, Cesar Dutch b. 1900
BI *"Composition-45-72",* #49/100, d., s., est. $2,000/2,500, (04-04-93, Pescheteau, #203), 30 5/16 x 24 7/16 in., (77 x 62 cm.), collage and serigraph on cardboard.

$97* *De Stijl,* s., d. artist proof, small tear, (06-28-93, Loudmer, #34), 19¹¹⁄₁₆ x 19¹¹⁄₁₆ in., (500 x 500 mm.), sh 29¹³⁄₁₆ x 20½ in., (500 x 500 mm.), color lithograph on Arches wove (BP 65, DM 165, FR 555, Y 10,292).

BI *Konstruktive Studien Von Cesar Domela, 1973: Ten,* Galerie Bargera, s., num., est. DM 1,200, (05-26-93, Lempertz, #126), 14³⁄₁₆ x 10¾ in., (36 x 27.3 cm.), serigraph.

$68* *Sans Titre,* s. artist proof, (06-28-93, Loudmer, #32), 22¹⁄₁₆ x 11¼ in., (560 x 285 mm.), sh 24⅝ x 18⅜ in., (560 x 285 mm.), color lithograph on Arches wove tinted beige (BP 46, DM 116, FR 389, Y 7215).

$87* *Sans Titre,* s. artist proof, (06-28-93, Loudmer, #33), 25¹⁵⁄₁₆ x 15¹⁵⁄₁₆ in., (660 x 405 mm.), sh 28¹⁵⁄₁₆ x 21⅝ in., (660 x 405 mm.), color lithograph on Arches wove tinted beige (BP 58, DM 148, FR 498, Y 9231).

$143* *Untitled,* s., #28/200, good cond.?, (12-09-92, Sotheby-Amstrdm, #562), sheet 27⁹⁄₁₆ x 19¹¹⁄₁₆ in., (700 x 500 mm.), color silkscreen w/collage and embossing on wove (BP 91, DM 224, FR 766, Y 17,731, G 253).

DOMERGUE, J.G. (after)

BI *Jeune Femme Nue,* #XI/XI, s., good margins, est. FF2,000, (06-16-93, Ader Tajan, #87), 14¾ x 11¹³⁄₁₆ in., (37.5 x 30 cm.), color lithograph.

DOMERGUE, Jean Gabriel French 1889-1962

$660* *Alice Soulie, 1926,* H. Chachoin, B cond., discoloration, (08-06-92, Swann, #117, illus.), 62½ x 46½ in., (158.8 x 118.1 cm.), (BP 345, DM 975, FR 3293, Y 84,184).

$414* *Ballerina, 1949,* (01-31-93, Morelle/Marchan, #58), 47¼ x 62¹⁵⁄₁₆ in., (120 x 160 cm.), poster (BP 278, DM 667, FR 2255, Y 51,647).

$552* *Colette Mars. Disques Columbia, c. 1950,* s., d. Aout 1991 by C. Mars, excell. cond., (02-04-93, Christie-S. Ken, #119), 46½ x 31 in., (118.1 x 78.7 cm.), color lithograph backed on linen (BP 385, DM 909, FR 3082, Y 68,665).

$1733* *Diane Belli, 1923,* fold marks, repairs, creasing, (02-04-93, Christie-S. Ken, #117, illus.), 62 x 46 in., (157.5 x 116.8 cm.), color lithograph backed on japan (BP 1210, DM 2854, FR 9676, Y 215,574).

$300* *"Elegante Au Chapeau Bleu",* s., (04-04-93, Pescheteau, #204), 15¾ x 12³⁄₁₆ in., (40 x 31 cm.), color lithograph on Japan nacre (BP 198, DM 482, FR 1638, Y 34,157).

$303* *"Nude With Hat", 1930,* s., num. XXXXVII/LXXV, stone s., margins, good cond., surface soiling, notations, (10-28-92, Butterfield, #2803), 12¾ x 9 in., (324 x 229 mm.), color lithograph on Japan (BP 193, DM 468, FR 1589, Y 37,178).

$100* *Opera. Samedi 24 Juin. Bal Du Grand Prix,* cond. A, (03-16-93, Boisgirard, #99), 23⅝ x 15⅜ in., (60 x 39 cm.), poster (BP 69, DM 166, FR 565, Y 11,693).

BI *"La Parisienne", 1956,* illus., s. in plate, est. FF1,000/1,500, (04-04-93, Pescheteau, #204A), 16⅛ x 12¹³⁄₁₆ in., (41 x 32.5 cm.), color lithograph.

$630* *Renee Ludger, 1925,* fold marks, creases, losses, repairs, (02-04-93, Christie-S. Ken, #118, illus.), 47½ x 37½ in., (120.7 x 95.3 cm.), color lithograph backed on japan (BP 440, DM 1037, FR 3518, Y 78,368).

$2276* *Vronska Et Alperoff, 1923,* Ateliers J.G.D., repairs, (01-31-93, Morelle/Marchan, #27, illus.), 47¼ x 62⅝ in., (120 x 159 cm.), poster (BP 1531, DM 3667, FR 12,397, Y 283,932).

DOMINGUEZ BECQUER, Jose

$290* *"La Feria De Mairena",* (03-17-93, Duran, #23, illus.), 21¼ x 15³⁄₁₆ in., (54 x 38.6 cm.), two color lithograph (BP 200, DM 483, FR 1640, Y 34,014, P 34,500).

$290* *"Los Ladrones En Una Venta",* (03-17-93, Duran, #24, illus.), 21¼ x 15³⁄₁₆ in., (54 x 38.6 cm.), two color lithograph (BP 200, DM 483, FR 1640, Y 34,014, P 34,500).

DONAGH, Rita

BI *Study For Slade Point, 1979,* est. BP 2/300, (10-15-92, Sotheby-London, #54, illus.), 8 x 16 in., (20.3 x 40.6 cm.), photograph, silver print w/pigment, mounted on card.

DONGA

$147* *Germaine Kerjean, 1934,* very good cond., (11-19-92, Ribeyre/Baron, #173), 62¹⁵⁄₁₆ x 47¼ in., (160 x 120 cm.), poster (BP 97, DM 234, FR 789, Y 18,281).

DONGEN, Kees van Dutch/French 1877-1968

$455* *Alanova, 1930,* (01-31-93, Morelle/Marchan, #46), 20½ x 29½ in., (52 x 75 cm.), poster (BP 306, DM 733, FR 2478, Y 56,761).

BI *Les Cheveux Courts,* blindstamp, Galerie des Peintres-Graveurs, p. sig., num. 1/30, full margins, light-stained, scratches, est. BP 250/350, (11-30-92, Phillips-London, #418), image 14½ x 9½ in., (368 x 241 mm.), lithograph in black on chine volant.

BI *Eine Liegende Nixe Vor Der Silhouette Von Paris,* s., num., est. DM 1,500, (12-05-92, Bassenge, #7129), 9¹³⁄₁₆ x 16⁹⁄₁₆ in., (25 x 42 cm.), color lithograph on BFK Rives.

$1063* *Les Fetards,* s., 4/100, (06-28-93, Loudmer, #390), 21⅞ x 18½ in., (555 x 470 mm.), sh 30⅛ x 22¼ in., (555 x 470 mm.), color lithograph on BFK Rives wove (BP 712, DM 1806, FR 6085, Y 112,785).

$275* *Hooded Figure On A Donkey,* illus. for Les Lepreuses, by Henry de Montherlant, (09-20-92, Hindman, #746), 9½ x 8¾ in., (24.1 x 22.2 cm.), color lithograph (BP 161, DM 408, FR 1396, Y 33,988).

$453* *Island Girl,* E.A., (10-14-92, Germann, #272), 14¾ x 11¼ in., (375 x 285 mm.), color lithograph (BP 266, DM 663, FR 2248, Y 54,896, SF 590).

$1063* *Jean-Marie Van Dongen (Au Voilier),* s., 37/100, artist's drystamp, (06-28-93, Loudmer, #386), 16⅛ x 12¹⁵⁄₁₆ in., (410 x 330 mm.), sh 22¹⁄₁₆ x 18⅛ in., (410 x 330 mm.), color lithograph on wove (BP 712, DM 1806, FR 6085, Y 112,785).

$1475* *Le Livre Des Mille Nuits Et Une Nuit, c. 1925,* Levallois, (12-05-92, Bassenge, #7579), 30⅝ x 21⅝ in., (77.8 x 55 cm.), color lithograph (BP 924, DM 2300, FR 7837, Y 182,753).

$369* *Pariser Boulevard Bei Nacht Und Regen,* num., (12-05-92, Bassenge, #7130), 10⅞ x 16⅝ in., (27.7 x 42.2 cm.), color lithograph (BP 231, DM 575, FR 1961, Y 45,719).

$967* *Polo A Alexandrie,* s., 32/100, artist's drystamp, (06-28-93, Loudmer, #396), 14¾ x 21⁷⁄₁₆ in., (375 x 545 mm.), sh 25¹⁵⁄₁₆ x 19⅞ in., (375 x 545 mm.), color lithograph on Arches (BP 647, DM 1643, FR 5535, Y 102,599).

$420* *Salon D'Automne, Peinture, Sculpture, Ensembles Decoratifs, Grand Palais, 1929,* p. Picard, good cond., creases, (11-19-92, Ribeyre/Baron, #157), 62¹⁵⁄₁₆ x 47¼ in., (160 x 120 cm.), poster (BP 277, DM 670, FR 2256, Y 52,232).

DOOLITTLE, Amos American 1754-1832

$4180* *"The Prodigal Son Receiving His Patrimony", "The Prodigal Son Revelling With Harlots", "The Prodigal Son In Misery" and "The Prodigal Son Returned To His Father" (Fowble 353-6), 1814: Set Of Four,* pub. Shelton & Kensett, trimmed margins, repaired tears, staining, creasing, (01-22-93, Christie-NY, #304, illus.), each approx. plate 13½ x 10 in., (343 x 254 mm.), hand colored etchings and stipple engravings on laid paper (BP 2735, DM 6647, FR 22,485, Y 523,154).

$13,750* *The Prodigal Son: Set of Four,* prov., (08-01-92, Northeast, #773, illus.), colored engraving (BP 7171, DM 20,398, FR 69,095, Y 1,754,946).

DOOLITTLE, James N. 1886-1954

BI *Katherine Hepburn, c. 1933,* James N. Doolittle Estate, est. $7/10,000, (04-06-93, Sotheby-NY, #143, illus.), 12½ x 10 in., photograph, color carbro print.

$990* *Portrait Of Loretta Young, c. 1935,* photog.'s sig., (04-07-93, Swann, #448, illus.), 13 x 10 in., photograph, tricolor carbo print (BP 654, DM 1601, FR 5419, Y 112,474).

BI *S.S. Saratoga, 1932,* s., lit., est. $1,8/2,200, (10-13-92, Christie-NY, #183, illus.), 16⅛ x 12¾ in., (41 x 32.4 cm.), photograph, gelatin silver print.

$1955* *"The Thinker", 1920,* i. w/Chinese characters, photog. blindstamp, mounted, s., t., d., i.by photog., notations, (04-06-93, Sotheby-NY, #144, illus.), 10⅜ x 13¼ in., photograph (BP 1291, DM 3150, FR 10,666, Y 222,970).

DORAZIO, Piero Italian b. 1927

$390* *Balken-Komposition, 1979,* s., d., num., blindstamp, ded., (06-08-93, Karl/Faber, #715), approx. 16 15/16 x 19 5/16 in., (43 x 49 cm.), color aquatint on wove (BP 256, DM 633, FR 2131, Y 41,423).

$932* *Campione, 1984: Three,* s., d., #19/25, (05-27-93, Lempertz, #694), 19 5/16 x 20 1/16 in., (49 x 51 cm.), color etching on wove (BP 597, DM 1496, FR 5041, Y 99,914).

$2212* *Color Fax, 1990: Four,* s., d., num., (04-21-93, Germann, #381), 30 5/16 x 37 3/8 in., (770 x 950 mm.), color aquatint (BP 1435, DM 3536, FR 11,957, Y 244,880, SF 3220).

$308* *Composizione,* 61/90, s., (10-14-92, Germann, #276), 27 15/16 x 19½ in., (710 x 495 mm.), color aquatint (BP 181, DM 451, FR 1529, Y 37,324, SF 401).

$361* *Composizione 61, 1961,* s., d., (11-28-92, Schoppmann, #486), 21 7/8 x 15 9/16 in., (55.5 x 39.5 cm.), color lithograph on handmade Fabriano (BP 238, DM 575, FR 1952, Y 44,928).

$645* *Composizione Rosso E Giallo, 1983,* E.A., s., d., stamped Erker-Presse, (09-04-92, Germann, #5), 33¼ x 23 7/16 in., (845 x 595 mm.), color lithograph (BP 323, DM 904, FR 3077, Y 79,394, SF 805).

$217* *Composizione, 1962,* 32/40, s., d., (10-14-92, Germann, #171), 13 9/16 x 19 11/16 in., (345 x 500 mm.), etching (BP 127, DM 318, FR 1077, Y 26,297, SF 283).

BI *Composizione, 1968,* P.a., s., d., est. SF 4/600, (10-14-92, Germann, #169), 19½ x 25 9/16 in., (495 x 650 mm.), aquatint.

$369* *Composizione, 1968,* P.a., s., d., (09-04-92, Germann, #304), 19½ x 25 9/16 in., (495 x 650 mm.), aquatint (BP 185, DM 517, FR 1760, Y 45,421, SF 460).

BI *Composizione, 1971,* 36/40, s., d., est. SF 400/600, (10-14-92, Germann, #286), 19½ x 25 9/16 in., (495 x 650 mm.), aquatint.

$645* *Composizione, 1971,* #36/40, s., d., (09-04-92, Germann, #4), 19½ x 25 9/16 in., (495 x 650 mm.), aquatint (BP 323, DM 904, FR 3077, Y 79,394, SF 805).

$417* *Composizione, 1976,* 58/84, s., d., (10-14-92, Germann, #282), 15¾ x 27 3/8 in., (400 x 695 mm.), color aquatint (BP 245, DM 610, FR 2069, Y 50,533, SF 543).

$543* *Composizione, 1976,* 15/15. p.a., s., d., (10-14-92, Germann, #99), 27 3/8 x 19 11/16 in., (695 x 500 mm.), color aquatint (BP 319, DM 795, FR 2695, Y 65,802, SF 708).

BI *Composizione, 1977,* X/XVI, p.a., s., d., est. SF 400/600, (10-14-92, Germann, #281), 19 11/16 x 27 3/8 in., (500 x 695 mm.), aquatint.

$424* *Composizione, 1977,* #X/XVI, p.a., s., d., (09-04-92, Germann, #307), 19 11/16 x 27 3/8 in., (500 x 695 mm.), aquatint (BP 212, DM 594, FR 2023, Y 52,191, SF 529).

BI *Composizione, 1978,* 54/80, s., d., stain, est. SF 700/900, (10-14-92, Germann, #277), 27 13/16 x 19 5/16 in., (707 x 490 mm.), color aquatint.

BI *Composizione, 1978,* #54/80, s., d., est. SF 5/700, (04-21-93, Germann, #372), 27 13/16 x 19 5/16 in., (707 x 490 mm.), color aquatint.

BI *Composizione, 1980,* XXVI/XXVI, s., d., est. SF 600/800, (10-14-92, Germann, #283), 19 7/8 x 27 7/16 in., (505 x 697 mm.), color aquatint.

$829* *Composizione, 1980,* #XXVI/XXVI, s., d., (09-04-92, Germann, #6, illus.), 19 7/8 x 27 7/16 in., (505 x 697 mm.), color aquatint (BP 415, DM 1162, FR 3955, Y 102,043, SF 1035).

$199* *Composizione, 1982,* 22/28, p.a., s., d., (10-14-92, Germann, #170), 11 13/16 x 9 15/16 in., (300 x 252 mm.), color aquatint (BP 117, DM 291, FR 988, Y 24,115, SF 260).

BI *Composizione, 1983,* H.C., s., d., est. SF 300/400, (10-14-92, Germann, #273), 26 3/8 x 21 7/8 in., (670 x 555 mm.), color lithograph.

$253* *Composizione, 1983,* P.A., s., d., (10-14-92, Germann, #274), 33 1/16 x 24 7/16 in., (840 x 620 mm.), color lithograph (BP 149, DM 370, FR 1256, Y 30,659, SF 330).

$236* *Composizione, 1983,* s., d., (10-14-92, Germann, #97), 32 7/8 x 23 7/16 in., (835 x 595 mm.), color lithograph (BP 139, DM 345, FR 1171, Y 28,599, SF 307).

$295* *Composizione, 1983,* H.C., s., d., Erker Presse blindstamp, (09-04-92, Germann, #303), 26 3/8 x 21 7/8 in., (670 x 555 mm.), color lithograph (BP 148, DM 413, FR 1407, Y 36,312, SF 368).

$316* *Composizione-Sarajevo, 1983,* #91/150, s., d., (04-21-93, Germann, #380), 33 1/8 x 24 7/16 in., (842 x 620 mm.), color lithograph (BP 205, DM 505, FR 1708, Y 34,983, SF 460).

BI *Delos, 1976,* s., d., t., #55/84, est. DM 1,200-, (05-27-93, Lempertz, #693), 6 3/8 x 19 9/16 in., (16.2 x 49.7 cm.), color etching on wove.

$638* *Komposition, 1961,* s., d., num., (06-08-93, Karl/Faber, #713), approx. 22 1/16 x 15 9/16 in., (56 x 39.5 cm.), color lithograph on Fabriano wove (BP 419, DM 1035, FR 3486, Y 67,764).

$316* *Komposition, 1975,* 7/25, s., d., blindstamp, Erker Presse, (06-24-93, Germann, #328), 13¾ x 19 11/16 in., (350 x 500 mm.), color lithograph (BP 208, DM 512, FR 1727, Y 33,898, SF 460).

$492* *Komposition, 1991,* s., d., (11-13-92, Koller, #5298), 27 9/16 x 19 11/16 in., (70 x 50 cm.), lithograph on wove (BP 318, DM 772, FR 2605, Y 61,065, SF 696).

$498* *Kywo, 1978,* 46/46, s., d., (10-14-92, Germann, #98), 19 11/16 x 27 3/8 in., (500 x 695 mm.), color aquatint (BP 292, DM 729, FR 2471, Y 60,349, SF 649).

$410* *Leore, 1982,* #12/95, s., d., Atelier stamp, (11-13-92, Koller, #5297), 19 11/16 x 28 15/16 in., (50 x 73.5 cm.), lithograph on Rives wove (BP 265, DM 644, FR 2170, Y 50,887, SF 580).

$672* *Moma, 1971,* #10/10. P.A., s., d., (04-21-93, Germann, #102), 19½ x 25 5/16 in., (496 x 643 mm.), color aquatint (BP 436, DM 1074, FR 3632, Y 74,394, SF 978).

$289* *Ohne Titel, 1962,* s., d., (11-28-92, Schoppmann, #487), 16 9/16 x 16 9/16 in., (42 x 42 cm.), lithograph in blue, green and yellow on handmade (BP 191, DM 460, FR 1563, Y 35,968).

$325* *Ohne Titel, 1964,* s., d., i. prova d'artista, browning, (11-28-92, Schoppmann, #488), 22 7/16 x 16 5/16 in., (57 x 41.5 cm.), lithograph in red, yellow and blue on handmade cardboard (BP 215, DM 518, FR 1758, Y 40,448).

$249* *"Olympische Spiele Munchen 1972", 1970,* s., d., num., light-stained, (12-01-92, Karl/Faber, #552), sh 41 5/16 x 27 9/16 in., (105 x 70 cm.), color lithograph on BFK Rives wove (BP 165, DM 397, FR 1353, Y 31,001).

$2211* *Portfolio. Wig-Wam, 1991: Five,* XXII/XXV, s., num., 1055mm x 720 mm, (06-24-93, Germann, #324, illus.), color serigraph, collage on gouache ground (BP 1455, DM 3585, FR 12,082, Y 237,181, SF 3220).

BI *Sans Titre, 1991,* s., 28/80, 695 x 1200mm, est. FF1,400/1,600, (06-28-93, Loudmer, #229), color aquatint on Arches wove.

$307* *Sarajevo, 1983,* s. twice, num., stamped Erker Presse St. Gallen, (12-01-92, Karl/Faber, #553), sh 33 1/16 x 24 7/16 in., (84 x 62 cm.), color lithograph on wove (BP 203, DM 489, FR 1668, Y 38,222).

BI *Senza Titolo, 1968/78,* 26/40, s., d., est. SF 3/400, (10-14-92, Germann, #143), 19 11/16 x 13 15/16 in., (500 x 355 mm.), aquatint.

$398* *Senza Titolo, 1974,* XIV/XX, s., d., (10-14-92, Germann, #284), 19 11/16 x 27 7/16 in., (500 x 697 mm.), color aquatint (BP 234, DM 582, FR 1975, Y 48,231, SF 519).

BI *Senza Titolo, 1976,* 70/83, s., d., est. SF 450/750, (10-14-92, Germann, #280), 19 11/16 x 27 3/8 in., (500 x 695 mm.), color aquatint.

$136* *Senza Titolo, 1984,* 6/6, s., d., (10-14-92, Germann, #142), 13 9/16 x 19½ in., (345 x 495 mm.), color aquatint (BP 80, DM 199, FR 675, Y 16,481, SF 177).

$240* *Senzo Titolo, 1968-78,* #26/40, s., d., (09-04-92, Germann, #305), 19 11/16 x 13 15/16 in., (500 x 355 mm.), aquatint (BP 120, DM 336, FR 1145, Y 29,542, SF 299).

$405* *Senzo Titolo, 1976,* #70/83, s., d., (09-04-92, Germann, #306), 19 11/16 x 27 3/8 in., (500 x 695 mm.), color aquatint (BP 203, DM 568, FR 1932, Y 49,852, SF 506).

$348* *Untitled, 1969,* #XIX/XX, P. artista, s., d., (04-21-93, Germann, #382), 19 9/16 x 13¾ in., (497 x 350 mm.), aquatint (BP 226, DM 556, FR 1881, Y 38,525, SF 506).

$363* *Untitled, 1974,* #38/50, s., d., (04-21-93, Germann, #374), 25 9/16 x 19 7/8 in., (650 x 505 mm.), color aquatint (BP 236, DM 580, FR 1962, Y 40,186, SF 529).

$2117* *Wig-Wam, 1991: Five,* num., s., 1055mm x 720mm, (10-14-92, Germann, #141, illus.), color serigraph (BP 1243, DM 3098, FR 10,506, Y 256,544, SF 2760).

$3317* *Wig-Wam, 1991: Five,* portfolio, #41/120, num., s., each 1055 x 720mm, (09-04-92, Germann, #106, illus.), color serigraph w/collage and green gouache (BP 1662, DM 4649, FR 15,825, Y 408,296, SF 4140).

$2054* *Wig-Wam, 1991: Five,* #41/120, s., num., d., 1055mm x 720mm, (04-21-93, Germann, #383, illus.), color serigraph, collage on gouache ground (BP 1333, DM 3283, FR 11,103, Y 227,388, SF 2990).

$316* *Zaffiro,* #26/50, s., d., (04-21-93, Germann, #375), 25⁹⁄₁₆ x 19¹¹⁄₁₆ in., (650 x 500 mm.), color aquatint (BP 205, DM 505, FR 1708, Y 34,983, SF 460).

$634* *Zaffiro, 1977,* 46/50, s., d., (10-14-92, Germann, #275, illus.), 25⅜ x 19¹¹⁄₁₆ in., (645 x 500 mm.), color aquatint (BP 372, DM 928, FR 3146, Y 76,830, SF 826).

DORE, Gustave   French 1832-1883
$660* *"La Menagerie Parisienne", 1854: Set Of Twenty-Four,* complete, foxing, p. Vayron, pub. Journal Pour Rire, (05-27-93, Swann, #91), (26.4 x 34.3 cm.), lithographs (BP 423, DM 1059, FR 3569, Y 70,755).

$110* *"Soldats Sikhs, Auxiliares Des Troupes Anglaises" and "Fakirs" (Beraldi 73), 1855-60: Two,* proof impression, both pub. Musee Francais-Anglais, (05-27-93, Swann, #92), 11⅞ x 10⅜ in., (30.2 x 26.4 cm.), lithograph on laid China paper (BP 70, DM 177, FR 595, Y 11,792).

DORIVAL
BI *La Roussalka, 1909,* Imp. F. Champenois, A cond., est. $6/900, (08-06-92, Swann, #118, illus.), 33½ x 23 in., (85.1 x 58.4 cm.), .

DORIVAL, Geo   French b. 1879
$189* *Ch. De Fer D'Alsace Et De Lorraine: Saison D'Ete, "Circuit Automobile De La Route D'Alsace", c. 1922,* good cond., (01-23-93, Ribeyre/Baron, #160), 41⅛ x 29⁵⁄₁₆ in., (104.5 x 74.5 cm.), poster (BP 124, DM 301, FR 1017, Y 23,655).

$210* *Ch. De Fer De L'Etat: Reseaux Des 600 Plages, Saint-Malo Vu De Dinard, 1912,* excell. cond., (01-23-93, Ribeyre/Baron, #57), 39⅜ x 24⁷⁄₁₆ in., (100 x 62 cm.), poster (BP 137, DM 334, FR 1130, Y 26,283).

$230* *PLM. Allevard Les Bains. "Station Blaneaire Et Centre De Tourisme", 1913,* good cond., (03-15-93, Arcole, #29), 41⁵⁄₁₆ x 29¾ in., (105 x 75.5 cm.), (BP 160, DM 382, FR 1299, Y 27,245).

$399* *PLM. La Descente De La Faucille Sur Geneve Et La Chaine Du Mont-Blanc. "Services Automobiles De La Route Du Jura", 1920,* very good cond., (03-15-93, Arcole, #30, illus.), 42½ x 30¹¹⁄₁₆ in., (108 x 78 cm.), (BP 278, DM 663, FR 2253, Y 47,264).

$378* *PLM: Visitez La Cote D'Azur. "Eze Et Le Cap Ferrat", 1919,* p. Cornille & Serre, very good cond., (11-19-92, Ribeyre/Baron, #104), 41¾ x 30¹¹⁄₁₆ in., (106 x 78 cm.), poster (BP 249, DM 603, FR 2030, Y 47,009).

DORMOY
$559* *PLM. Chamonix: Aiguille Du Midi, Mont-Blanc. "Le Plus Haut Telepherique Du Monde",* very good cond., (03-15-93, Arcole, #32), 40¹⁵⁄₁₆ x 28¾ in., (104 x 73 cm.), (BP 389, DM 929, FR 3156, Y 66,217).

DORN, Leo   American b. 1879
$110* *Fishing Village,* s. Leo Dorn, num. 24/50, good cond., (09-27-92, Bakker, #199), sight 5¾ x 6 in., (14.6 x 15.2 cm.), color woodblock print (BP 64, DM 163, FR 551, Y 13,277).

DORNY, Bertrand   French b. 1931
$73* *"Composition",* #27/50, s., (01-28-93, Peschteau, #126), 22¹⁄₁₆ x 29¹⁵⁄₁₆ in., (56 x 76 cm.), etching and aquatint on Arches (BP 48, DM 116, FR 391, Y 9064).

DORO, Theo
$587* *Ecole Du Genie Civil, c. 1930,* p. Kaplan, good cond., (11-19-92, Ribeyre/Baron, #29), 47¼ x 31½ in., (120 x 80 cm.), poster (BP 386, DM 936, FR 3153, Y 73,001).

$545* *Gold Starry, "Le Stylo Qui Marche", 1930,* p. Kaplan, good cond., (11-19-92, Ribeyre/Baron, #28), 62⅝ x 46⅞ in., (159 x 119 cm.), poster (BP 359, DM 869, FR 2927, Y 67,778).

DORVILLE, Noel
$502* *Societe La Francaise. Marque Diamant, c. 1903,* Paris, Imp. Weye and Sevestre, cond. B+, (06-11-93, Boisgi-

rard, #67, illus.), 62¹⁵⁄₁₆ x 45½ in., (160 x 115.5 cm.), poster (BP 330, DM 816, FR 2751, Y 53,263).

DOSAMANTES, Francisco   b. Mexico 1911
BI *"Lupe", c. 1940,* s., good cond., est. $3/400, (05-15-93, Cleveland, #381), 21 x 19 in., (53.3 x 48.3 cm.), lithograph.

BI *Mujer Perdido, 1957-58,* s., #1/100, margins, good cond., staining, creases, surface soiling,foxing, est. $4/600, (10-28-92, Butterfield, #2564), 22½ x 15⅛ in., (572 x 384 mm.), lithograph on wove.

$518* *"South American Country Scene", "Two Women Weaving" and "Three GirlsWith Braids", 1950: Three,* s., #9/46, full margins, good cond., hinge remains, surface soiling, (05-19-93, Butterfield, #1985), smallest 12½ x 8¼ in., (318 x 210 mm.), largest 10¼ x 13⅝ in., (318 x 210 mm.), lithograph on wove (BP 336, DM 842, FR 2837, Y 57,345).

DOTREMONT, Christian and Mogens BALLE
$312* *Composition,* s. Dotremont/Mogens Balle, 100/100, (03-24-93, Kunsthallen, #86), color lithograph (BP 211, DM 510, FR 1734, Y 36,658, DK 1955).

DOU, Gerrit (after)
$32* *The Doctor,* (02-17-93, Bonhams-Chelsea, #317), image 20¼ x 15¼ in., (51.4 x 38.7 cm.), color reproduction (BP 22, DM 52, FR 176, Y 3822).

BI *The Herring Seller,* est. BP 50/80, (04-22-93, Bonhams-Chelsea, #14), image 12 x 9 in., (30.5 x 22.9 cm.), reprod. in colors.

DOUCET, Jacques
$256* *Untitled, 1991,* s., d., #HC XXXVII/L, full margins, good cond., (05-27-93, Sotheby-Amstrdm, #608), 31⁵⁄₁₆ x 23⁹⁄₁₆ in., (796 x 598 mm.), colored lithograph on wove (BP 164, DM 411, FR 1385, Y 27,444, G 460).

$320* *Untitled, 1991,* s., d., #HC XXXVII/L, margins, good cond., (05-27-93, Sotheby-Amstrdm, #609), 31⁵⁄₁₆ x 23⁹⁄₁₆ in., (796 x 598 mm.), colored lithograph on wove (BP 205, DM 513, FR 1731, Y 34,305, G 575).

DOUGHTY, Thomas (after)
$523* *City Of Philadelphia,* by C.G. Childs, foxing, (06-11-93, Freemn/Fine Art, #57), 12¾ x 19¼ in., (32.4 x 48.9 cm.), hand-colored engraving (BP 344, DM 850, FR 2866, Y 55,491).

$1150* *To Joseph S. Lewis Esquire, This View Of Fair Mount Works ... City Of Philadelphia ... (D. 333), 1822,* engraved Cephas G. Childs, issued c. 1824, margins beyond subject, trimmed into 4th line of title, discoloration, backboard stain, fox mark, loss/tear in title, tape stains, tears, creases, (01-28-93, Sotheby-NY, #446), image 13 x 19⅜ in., (330 x 492 mm.), sheet 16½ x 21 in., (330 x 492 mm.), engraving (BP 759, DM 1822, FR 6166, Y 142,786).

DOUGLAS, E.A. (after)
$295* *Hunting Scenes: Four,* by C.R. Stock, margins, (06-30-93, Bonhams-Chelsea, #117), plate 13¼ x 29 in., (33.7 x 73.7 cm.), aquatint w/hand-coloring (BP 198, DM 503, FR 1697, Y 31,608).

DOUGLAS, E.A.S.
$20 *The Stage Coach,* s., (02-05-93, G.A. Key, #6), 8 x 13 in., (20.3 x 33 cm.), b/w engraving (BP 14, DM 33, FR 112, Y 2489).

DOUGLAS, E.A.S. (after)
$100* *"Morning. Going To Cover" and "Evening. Retiring To The Kennels": Two,* by E.G. Hester, (11-19-92, Bonhams-Chelsea, #130), image 19½ x 15½ in., (49.5 x 39.4 cm.), hand colored reproduction (BP 66, DM 159, FR 537, Y 12,436).

$230* *Starting From The Kennels, 1880,* by E.G. Hester, margins, scattered foxing, good cond., Anthony N. B.Garvan Coll., (06-05-93, Christie-NY, #70), pl 16¼ x 28¼ in., (413 x 718 mm.), aquatint in blue and black w/hand-coloring on wove (BP 151, DM 373, FR 1257, Y 24,673).

DOVICI (after)
BI *A London Street Scene,* est. $75/150, (07-17-92, DuMouchelle, #1169), 19¾ x 12 in., (50.2 x 30.5 cm.), print, hand-colored detail.

DOW, Arthur Wesley   American 1857-1922

BI   *"Blossom Tree"*, s., excell. cond., est. $2/2,400, (10-31-92, Cleveland, #111, illus.), 2½ x 4 in., (6.4 x 10.2 cm.), colored woodcut.

BI   *"Ipswich Prints", 1902: Set Of Six,* 2nd set, repaired tears to folder, good cond., est. $650/750, (10-31-92, Cleveland, #112), color relief print.

$2420* *"The Road Argilla",* s., excell. cond., (10-31-92, Cleveland, #110, illus.), 4¼ x 7 in., (10.8 x 17.8 cm.), colored woodcut (BP 1551, DM 3723, FR 12,630, Y 299,765).

$2860* *Stone Bridge,* s. Arthur Wesley Dow; annot. 15 verso, very good cond., margins approx. 1/2", (09-11-92, Skinner, #67, illus.), 2⅜ x 4 in., (6 x 10.2 cm.), color woodblock on wove (BP 1479, DM 4117, FR 13,992, Y 354,355).

BI   *[Cows And Dunes],* c. 1910, margins, good cond., est. $2,5/3,500, (05-13-93, Sotheby-NY, #419, illus.), 6½ x 4⅜ in., (164 x 112 mm.), woodcut in colors on thin Japan.

DOWLING, P.L.

BI   *P.L. Japanese Detention Center,* news agency handstamps, notations, 1940s, est. $6/900, (04-07-93, Swann, #302, illus.), 8 x 10 in., photograph, silver print.

DRAGE, E. Alice (after)

$112* *Two Terriers,* by R. Wallace Hester, s. by both artists, margins, (10-29-92, Bonhams-Chelsea, #72), plate 17½ x 13¾ in., (44.5 x 34.9 cm.), photogravure (BP 72, DM 172, FR 585, Y 13,873).

DRANSY

BI   *"Charnay Aperitif",* April 1934, p. Vercasson, est. $1/1,500, (08-05-92, Boos, #593, illus.), 76½ x 49 in., (194.3 x 124.5 cm.), color lithograph.

$398* *Visita Exposicio Colonial Paris, 1931,* very good cond., (03-13-93, Laurin, #21), 39⅜ x 24⁷⁄₁₆ in., (100 x 62 cm.), (BP 278, DM 662, FR 2252, Y 46,906).

DRANSY (after)

$201* *Nicolas Nectar* (02-13-93, Morelle/Marchan, #17), 46¹⁄₁₆ x 61⁷⁄₁₆ in., (117 x 156 cm.), poster (BP 142, DM 333, FR 1128, Y 24,240).

DRESSLER, August Wilhelm   German 1886-1970

$466* *Frau Mit Kind, 1912,* s., (12-01-92, Karl/Faber, #555), 10⅝ x 8¼ in., (27 x 21 cm.), etching on wove (BP 308, DM 743, FR 2531, Y 58,018).

$185* *Geburt,* s., t., num., blindstamp, (12-05-92, Bassenge, #7132), 9⅛ x 9¹³⁄₁₆ in., (23.2 x 25 cm.), etching w/aquatint on wood (BP 116, DM 288, FR 983, Y 22,922).

$118* *Liebespaar,* s., (12-05-92, Bassenge, #7133), 9⅛ x 7½ in., (23.2 x 19 cm.), etching on copper print paper (BP 74, DM 184, FR 627, Y 14,620).

$289* *Zwei Frauen Mit Facher Und Katze,* c. 1920, s., (11-28-92, Schoppmann, #490), 12⅝ x 8⁹⁄₁₆ in., (32 x 21.8 cm.), etching on wove (BP 191, DM 460, FR 1563, Y 35,968).

DREVET, Pierre   1663-1778

BI   *Louis Le Grand (Firmin-Didot 52I (Von III)),* after Person, est. DM 2400, (06-04-93, Bassenge, #5118), 26⅜ x 20⅞ in., (67 x 53 cm.), copper engraving.

$242* *Portrait De Pierre Gillet (I.F.F. 53),* after H. Rigaud, dust, stains, (05-15-93, Loudmer, #146), 14¹³⁄₁₆ x 11¹⁄₁₆ in., (377 x 281 mm.), copper engraving on laid w/2-headed bird on fleur-de-lis crown watermark (BP 157, DM 389, FR 1308, Y 26,826).

DREW, Pamela   b. 1910

$579* *To Visit Britain's Landmarks, John Knox Monument, Glasgow, 1936,* p. Waterlow and Sons, ref. #466, cond. 1, (10-13-92, Phillips-London, #109, illus.), 30 x 45¹⁄₁₆ in., (76.2 x 114.4 cm.), color lithograph (BP 337, DM 848, FR 2882, Y 70,207).

DREWES, Werner   German/American b. 1899

$550* *Blue Fish,* s. Drewes - 55, num. 3/XXX, ST II, very good cond., (09-27-92, Bakker, #206), image 9⅜ x 20⅞ in., (23.8 x 53 cm.), color woodblock print (BP 321, DM 815, FR 2757, Y 66,385).

$418* *Construction (Rose E230), 1944,* s., d., num. 6/30, margins, soiling, staining, creasing, old tape, (09-19-92,

Christie-E, #17), plate 14¹⁵⁄₁₆ x 6⅞ in., (379 x 175 mm.), engraving on wove (BP 240, DM 626, FR 2144, Y 52,081).

BI   *Encompassed (Rose 322), 1974,* s., num., est. DM 750, (12-05-92, Bassenge, #7134), 15¹⁵⁄₁₆ x 11⅛ in., (40.5 x 28.3 cm.), woodcut on Japan.

$248* *Flower Vase,* s. Drewes, num. 11/XL, very good cond., (09-27-92, Bakker, #208), image 21¼ x 10¼ in., (54 x 26 cm.), color woodblock print (BP 145, DM 368, FR 1243, Y 29,934).

$55*   *"Forest",* Print Club of Cleveland Publication No. 39, 1961, s. Drewes, (12-12-92, Wolf, #33), 11¼ x 24¼ in., (28.6 x 61.6 cm.), color woodblock from 4 blocks on Goyu laid paper (BP 35, DM 87, FR 297, Y 6806).

BI   *"Forest", 1959,* s., Print Club of Cleveland Publication No. 39. 1961, good cond., est. $3-400, (10-31-92, Cleveland, #113A), 11¼ x 24½ in., (28.6 x 62.2 cm.), woodcut in colors.

BI   *Grand Central Station (R. 137), 1933,* s., d., #I/XXX, full margins, good cond., restored paper losses, matstaining, est. $6/800, (05-19-93, Butterfield, #1802), 11 x 13 in., (279 x 330 mm.), soft-ground etching on wove.

$302* *New Shores, 1949,* s., (05-27-93, Swann, #93), (11.4 x 13.5 cm.), engraving w/aquatint (BP 193, DM 485, FR 1633, Y 32,376).

$403* *On Different Planes (R. 228), 1944,* s., d., #5/XXX, full margins, good cond., stain, rubbed area, glue stains, surface soiling, stray printing ink, notations, (05-19-93, Butterfield, #1803), 11¾ x 5¹⁵⁄₁₆ in., (298 x 151 mm.), engraving on wove (BP 262, DM 655, FR 2207, Y 44,614).

BI   *On Different Planes (Rose 228), 1944,* s., d., num., est. DM 1600, (12-01-92, Karl/Faber, #557), 11⅝ x 5⅞ in., (29.5 x 15 cm.), engraving on hand-made.

BI   *"Tall Trees", 1957,* excellent cond., hinges, est. $450-550, (10-31-92, Cleveland, #113, illus.), 22 x 17⅝ in., (55.9 x 44.8 cm.), woodcut.

$303* *View From The St. Louis Studios,* s. Drewes, num. pr. No. 1, very good cond., (09-27-92, Bakker, #207), image 16 x 11¼ in., (40.6 x 28.6 cm.), color woodblock print (BP 177, DM 449, FR 1519, Y 36,572).

DRIAN

$168* *Elegancias Parisienses, Moda De Paris,* good cond., (11-19-92, Ribeyre/Baron, #30), 46¹⁄₁₆ x 30¹¹⁄₁₆ in., (117 x 78 cm.), poster (BP 111, DM 268, FR 902, Y 20,893).

DROESE, Felix   b. 1950

BI   *Der Doppelte Mittelpunkt, 1989,* s., t., d., est. DM 3,000-, (09-25-92, Granier, #2817), 22¹⁵⁄₁₆ x 16⁷⁄₁₆ in., (58.3 x 41.8 cm.), woodprint w/Baumscheiben over paint on niederland newspaper.

BI   *Haus Der Waffenlosigkeit, 1988,* red ink s., est. DM 500-, (09-25-92, Granier, #2818), 26¾ x 36¼ in., (68 x 92 cm.), serigraph on hand-made.

BI   *Kompositionen (Moller 30. 1-6), 1983: Six,* s., d., Griffelkunst-Vereinigung, est. DM 1,800, (06-12-93, Hauswedell/Nolt, #71), sh 21⁷⁄₁₆ x 14¹⁵⁄₁₆ in., (54.5 x 38 cm.), etching on thick copper print.

$181* *Ohne Begleitung (Klein 30.6), 1983,* s., d., (11-28-92, Schoppmann, #493), 30 x 21 in., (76.2 x 53.3 cm.), etching on handmade copper print paper (BP 119, DM 288, FR 979, Y 22,526).

BI   *Transformation (Moller 44), 1986: Six,* s., est. DM 2,300, (11-20-92, Lempertz, #521), each approx. 11⅛ x 15⅛ in., (28.2 x 38.4 cm.), woodcut on X-ray print.

DRTIKOL, Frantisek   1888-1961

BI   *Akt,* c. 1928, blindstamp credit, est. $12/15,000, (10-13-92, Christie-NY, #187, illus.), 11 x 9½ in., (27.9 x 24.1 cm.), photograph, pigment print.

$2200* *Bromografia: Ten,* 1920s, some toned, each w/credit in neg., t., d., (10-13-92, Christie-NY, #185, illus.), various sizes to 11¼ x 8⅞ in., (28.6 x 22.5 cm.), photograph, gelatin silver print (BP 1281, DM 3223, FR 10,951, Y 266,764).

$3300* *Desire, 1928,* blindstamp credit, lit., (10-13-92, Christie-NY, #186, illus.), 3⅛ x 4 in., (7.9 x 10.2 cm.), photograph, gelatin silver print on carte postale (BP 1922, DM 4834, FR 16,426, Y 400,146).

$1980* *Fan Dancer, c. 1935,* blindstamp credit, lit., (10-13-92, Christie-NY, #188, illus.), 4⅜ x 6¼ in., (11.1 x 15.9 cm.), photograph, pigment print (BP 1153, DM 2901, FR 9856, Y 240,087).

BI *Figural Sculpture, c. 1932,* blindstamp on image, est. $2/3,000, (10-15-92, Sotheby-NY, #382, illus.), 4¼ x 5⅞ in., (10.8 x 14.9 cm.), photograph, gelatin silver print.

$10,350* *La Horreur, 1927,* blindstamped (c) credit recto; s., d., credit, t., annots., (04-08-93, Christie-NY, #119, illus.), 11¼ x 9 in., (28.6 x 22.9 cm.), photograph, pigment print (BP 6787, DM 16,627, FR 56,281, Y 1,174,535).

BI *Male Nude, c. 1926,* flush-mounted, est. $8/10,000, (04-08-93, Christie-NY, #118, illus.), 11⅝ x 9 in., (29.5 x 22.9 cm.), photograph, pigment print.

$575* *Minors At Work In Pribram Mine, 1908,* image s., est. $6/800, (05-23-93, Butterfield, #3396, illus.), 3 x 4¼ in., photograph, gelatin silver print on carte postale (BP 374, DM 940, FR 3165, Y 63,557).

BI *Mother And Child, c. 1910,* photog. blindstamp on image, est. $2,5/3,500, (04-06-93, Sotheby-NY, #298A, illus.), 10¼ x 7½ in., photograph.

$1495* *Nude Study, 1920's,* photog. credit in neg., (04-06-93, Sotheby-NY, #299, illus.), 4⅜ x 3⅛ in., photograph (BP 987, DM 2409, FR 8156, Y 170,506).

BI *Nude Torso With Cut-Out Figures (Photomontage),* 1920's, est. $4/6,000, (10-14-92, Swann, #436, illus.), 11⅜ x 9⅛ in., (28.9 x 23.2 cm.), photograph, toned silver print.

$2300* *Nude With Projected Shadow, c. 1927,* (04-08-93, Christie-NY, #117, illus.), 5 x 3⅛ in., (12.7 x 7.9 cm.), photograph, gelatin silver print on carte-postale (BP 1508, DM 3695, FR 12,507, Y 261,008).

$6900* *"Nude", c. 1927,* photog. (c) blindstamp on image, mounted, s. by photog., t., i., (04-06-93, Sotheby-NY, #300, illus.), 11⅛ x 8⅞ in., photograph, pigment print (BP 4557, DM 11,116, FR 37,643, Y 786,953).

BI *Portrait Of A Young Woman, early 1920's,* est. $2/3,000, (10-15-92, Sotheby-NY, #381, illus.), 9 x 11⅛ in., (22.9 x 28.3 cm.), photograph, gelatin silver print.

$715* *Two Women, 1925,* neg. num. 117, photog. stamp, (11-16-92, Butterfield, #5941, illus.), 4⅜ x 3⅛ in., (111.3 x 79.5 mm.), photograph, gelatin silver print on carte postale (BP 471, DM 1140, FR 3840, Y 88,919).

DRUET, Eugene
$1100* *Study Of Rodin Sculpture (Camille Claudel, Model), c. 1900,* s. by Rodin in neg., (04-07-93, Swann, #449, illus.), 15¾ x 11¾ in., photograph, silver print (BP 727, DM 1779, FR 6021, Y 124,972).

DRUITTDESH?, H.
$25 *"They Gave Their Lives",* hole, (03-04-93, Alderfer, #261), 30 x 20 in., (76.2 x 50.8 cm.), poster (BP 17, DM 41, FR 139, Y 2911).

DRUMMOND, D.
$495* *The Hinkley Locomotive Works, Boston,* C.H. Crosby & Co., Lith., margins, water stains, (10-31-92, Riba, #347, illus.), 15¾ x 26 in., (40 x 66 cm.), lithograph (BP 324, DM 777, FR 2632, Y 61,202).

DRUMMOND, William and Charles BASEBEE (after)
$417* *The Cricket Match Between Sussex And Kent At Brighton, 1849,* by G.H. Phillips, pub. E. Gambart & Co., laid on canvas, mounted on stretcher, foxed, light-stained, broken paper, (11-30-92, Phillips-London, #271), plate 27⅓ x 39⅛ in., (69.4 x 99.4 cm.), mixed-method engraving on wove (BP 275, DM 664, FR 2255, Y 51,898).

DRURY, Paul
$48* *Boxhill, 1933,* s., margins, (03-17-93, Bonhams-Chelsea, #332), plate 4 x 4½ in., (10.2 x 11.4 cm.), etching (BP 33, DM 80, FR 271, Y 5630).

DRYDEN
$210* *Champagne Veuve A. Devaux, c. 1930,* very good cond., lit., (11-19-92, Ribeyre/Baron, #31), 24¹³⁄₁₆ x 17¹⁵⁄₁₆ in., (63 x 45.5 cm.), poster (BP 138, DM 335, FR 1128, Y 26,116).

DRYSDALE, George Russell   1912-1981
$263* *Mother And Child,* s. Studio Stamp, #2/50, (08-11-92, L. Joel, #66G), 5⅜ x 5¹⁄₁₆ in., (13.6 x 12.9 cm.), etching (BP 137, DM 386, FR 1307, Y 33,679, A$ 357).

DU CAMP, Maxime   1822-1894
BI *"Mosquee Et Tombeau De Mourad Bey",* 1849-51, pub. 1852, p. t., #13, photog.'s, pub.'s, printer's credits, est. BP 4/600, (10-29-92, Christie-London, #15), 6¼ x 8¾ in., (15.9 x 22.2 cm.), photograph, Blanquart-Evrard process print, mounted on card.

DUBOSCQ, Jules (attrib.)
$605* *Floral Arrangement, ca. 1850,* inits. DS, #28 on mount, (04-07-93, Swann, #130, illus.), photograph, stereo daguerreotype (BP 400, DM 978, FR 3311, Y 68,734).

DUBOURG, M. (after)   British 18th/19th cent.
$358* *A Spanish Bullfight: Thirteen,* complete, including frontispiece engraved by John Clark, pub. 1813 by Orme, (10-18-92, Hindman, #510), 7⅛ x 9⅛ in., (18.1 x 23.2 cm.), hand colored aquatints (BP 219, DM 533, FR 1807, Y 42,951).

DUBOUT, A.
$315* *Le Schpountz, Film De Marcel Pagnol, 1952,* p. Monegasque, good cond., 160 x 1203 cm, (11-19-92, Ribeyre/Baron, #174), poster (BP 207, DM 502, FR 1692, Y 39,174).

DUBOUT, Albert   1906-1978
$461* *Cesar,* poster for film by Marcel Pagnol, good cond., (11-16-92, Briest, #287), 61⁷⁄₁₆ x 46⅞ in., (156 x 119 cm.), poster (BP 303, DM 735, FR 2477, Y 57,532).

DUBREUIL, Pierre   1872-1944
$19,550* *Green Cup, 1932,* ink mono. insig. recto; mount t.; s., t., London Salon of Photography paper label verso, only known print of this image, exhib., (04-08-93, Christie-NY, #90, illus.), 9¾ x 7¾ in., (24.8 x 19.7 cm.), photograph, oil print (BP 12,820, DM 31,406, FR 106,308, Y 2,218,566).

$5500* *Woman In Striped Corset, c. 1910,* s. twice, stamp, (10-13-92, Christie-NY, #189, illus.), 9¼ x 7⅜ in., (23.5 x 18.7 cm.), photograph, oil print (BP 3203, DM 8057, FR 27,377, Y 666,909).

DUBUFFET, Jean   French 1901-1985
$1887* *"Amas" and "Jeux Et Congres" (Webel 579 and 678), 1959: Two,* each s., t., d., i. epreuve d'artiste, margins, good cond., (06-30-93, Sotheby-London, #427, illus.), lithograph on wove (BP 1265, DM 3218, FR 10,857, Y 202,186).

$1279* *Banque D'Hourlope, 1967,* pub. Editions Alecto, p. Kelpra Studios, w/t. card and just., #186/380, full sheets p. to edges, good cond., in orig. portfolio box, (05-27-93, Sotheby-Amstrdm, #610, illus.), each sh 9¹³⁄₁₆ x 6⁷⁄₁₆ in., (250 x 164 mm.), colored screenprint (BP 819, DM 2052, FR 6917, Y 137,114, G 2300).

BI *Banque De L'Hourloupe (Webel 993-1047), 1967: Set Of Fifty-Two,* pub. Editions Alecto, #74/350, excell. cond., est. $2/2,400, (11-09-92, Christie-NY, #276, illus.), (248 x 165 mm.), screenprinted playing cards in colors.

$1725* *Banque De L'Hourloupe-Cartes A Jouer Et A Tirer, 1967,* set of 52 playing cards, w/t. card, pub. Editions Alecto, num. 283, good cond., orig. box, (10-14-92, Sotheby-Japan, #25, illus.), each card 9¾ x 6½ in., (248 x 165 mm.), colored silkscreen (BP 1013, DM 2525, FR 8561, Y 209,040).

$413* *Buste (S. 171),* s. in stone, margins, good cond., staining, surface soiling, (02-24-93, Butterfield, #2918), 12 x 6¾ in., (305 x 171 mm.), lithograph in colors on wove (BP 288, DM 670, FR 2273, Y 48,463).

$998* *"Champ De Pensee-1959",* plate II from L'Arpenteur, artist's proof, t., d., s., (04-04-93, Pescheteau, #205), a vue 20⅞ x 15¾ in., (53 x 40 cm.), color lithograph on Arches (BP 657, DM 1604, FR 5448, Y 113,629).

$379* *Compositions: Three,* 141/350, (09-30-92, Kunsthallen, #95), color serigraph on ramme (frame) (BP 214, DM 537, FR 1818, Y 45,482, DK 2070).

BI *Coucou Bazar (Webel 1158), 1973,* mono., d., est. SF 1,4/1,600, (04-21-93, Germann, #384, illus.), 25 13/16 x 17 5/16 in., (655 x 440 mm.), color lithograph.

$4025* *Danse Au Mur (Webel 59; Loreau I, 409), 1945,* ink s., i. a A.G. Cabrol, ink i. epreuve d'artiste, good cond., nick,fox marks, stains, tape hinges, glue stain, skinned spots, (05-13-93, Sotheby-NY, #546, illus.), sh 15 x 11¼ in., (380 x 285 mm.), lithograph on wove (BP 2642, DM 6499, FR 21,923, Y 449,369).

BI *Dubuffet. Grand Palais. Festival D'Automne A Paris, 1972,* mono., d., #29/200, (09-18-92, Schloss Ahlden, #994, illus.), 25 13/16 x 19⅞ in., (65.5 x 50.5 cm.), color lithograph on hand-made paper.

$4263* *Faits Memorables II (W. 1260), 1978,* s., i. epreuve de collaborateur, proof, pub. Pace Editions, Inc., margins, good cond., (12-03-92, Sotheby-London, #654, illus.), 29½ x 39½ in., (750 x 980 mm.), silkscreen in colors on Arches (BP 2750, DM 6704, FR 22,882, Y 530,422).

$1147* *Festival D'Automne A Paris, 1973,* 3/100, mono, d., traces of glue, hole, (10-14-92, Germann, #287), 27 7/16 x 20⅝ in., (697 x 524 mm.), color lithograph (BP 673, DM 1679, FR 5692, Y 138,997, SF 1495).

BI *"Festival D'Automne" (BL 1157), 1972,* #94/100, d., mono., est. FF 8/10,000, (10-18-92, Pescheteau, #127, illus.), 27⅜ x 20 11/16 in., (69.5 x 52.5 cm.), lithograph in colors on Arches.

$545* *Le Feu (Lebon I, 615), 1959,* plate XVII from 12th album "Sites et Chaussees", s., d. 59, t., (11-16-92, Briest, #291), 25 3/16 x 17 11/16 in., (64 x 45 cm.), lithograph in black on Arches (BP 358, DM 869, FR 2929, Y 68,014).

$4239* *Fougere Au Chapeau (Loreau, Fasc.IX,53),* s., t., Epreuve d'essai i., (06-12-93, Hauswedell/Nolt, #74, illus.), 25 3/16 x 19⅛ in., (64 x 48.5 cm.), color lithograph on Arches (BP 2775, DM 6899, FR 23,189, Y 446,070).

$142* *Galerie La Pochade, 1968,* stain, good cond., (11-30-92, Phillips-London, #506), sheet 29⅞ x 22¼ in., (759 x 565 mm.), color lithograph on Arches (BP 94, DM 226, FR 768, Y 17,673).

$715* *"Geometrie" and "L'Arbe D'Ombre", 1959: Two,* each s., d., t., #43/75, full margins, good cond., mat/light-staining, foxing, pin holes, surface scuffs, surface soiling, creases, (02-24-93, Butterfield, #2736), (533 x 387 mm.), lithograph on Arches (BP 499, DM 1161, FR 3935, Y 83,900).

$1290* *Insouciance (Silkeborg 475, Webel 698), 1961,* s., plate 4 from Spectacles, #25/30, t., watermark, (05-27-93, Lempertz, #697), 25¼ x 19 11/16 in., (64.1 x 50 cm.), color lithograph on Arches wove (BP 826, DM 2070, FR 6977, Y 138,293).

BI *"Jeux Et Congres" (Webel 678), 1959,* s., t., d., num., sheet 4 of series "Cadastre", est. DM 2,7/3,000, (11-28-92, Grisebach, #501, illus.), 19½ x 14⅞ in., (49.5 x 37.8 cm.), colored lithograph on handmade.

$5280* *Jeux Et Travaux (Wevel 385), 1953,* s., t. in ink, #9/60, staining, very good cond., (11-09-92, Christie-NY, #85, illus.), 660 x 503 in., (x cm.), colored lithograph on Arches (BP 3491, DM 8429, FR 28,479, Y 655,249).

$165* *Kompositioner: Three,* 41/350, (03-24-93, Kunsthallen, #87), colored serigraph on ramme (frame) (BP 112, DM 269, FR 917, Y 19,387, DK 1035).

BI *L'Arbre D'Ombre, 1969,* s., t., d., num. 42/75, full margins, good cond., mounted, est. BP 5/600, (11-30-92, Phillips-London, #507), image 21¼ x 15⅜ in., (540 x 391 mm.), lithograph on Arches.

BI *L'Homme Au Chapeau (L. XVI, p. 222; W. 811), 1961,* s., d., i., full margins, good cond., light stain, discoloration, creases, est. $10/12,000, (11-05-92, Sotheby-NY, #172, illus.), 20⅝ x 15⅛ in., (525 x 385 mm.), lithograph p. in colors on Arches.

$7093* *L'Homme Au Chapeau (Loreau XVI. 222), 1961,* ded., i. artist's proof, s., (06-05-93, Bassenge, #5997, illus.), 20½ x 14 15/16 in., (52 x 38 cm.), color lithograph on Arches (BP 4669, DM 11,500, FR 38,760, Y 760,888).

BI *Lepre (Lebon I, 607), 1959,* plate IX from 12th album in black from "Sites et Chaussees", epreuved'artiste, s., t., d. 59, est. FF 4/5,000, (11-16-92, Briest, #290), 25 x 17 15/16 in., (63.5 x 45.5 cm.), lithograph in black on Arches.

$3850* *Lion Heraldique (W. 1179), 1976,* s., d., #38/50, full margins, excellent cond., (11-09-92, Christie-NY, #277, illus.), 23 x 28 in., (584 x 711 mm.), colored screenprint on wove (BP 2545, DM 6146, FR 20,766, Y 477,786).

$3069* *Maison Forestiere (Webel 14), 1944,* s., #1/10, margins, good cond., (12-03-92, Sotheby-London, #287, illus.), sheet 12½ x 9⅞ in., (318 x 251 mm.), lithograph on Auvergne (BP 1980, DM 4826, FR 16,473, Y 381,859).

$2387* *Masse Aux Pedales (Webel 1173), 1976,* init., d., #45/50, pub. Sonja Henie-Niels Onstad Foundation, good cond., creases, (12-03-92, Sotheby-London, #653, illus.), 19⅛ x 33½ in., (485 x 850 mm.), silkscreen in colors on Arches (BP 1540, DM 3754, FR 12,813, Y 297,001).

$1153* *Le Mirivis Des Naturgies (Lebon II, 825), 1962,* epreuve d'artiste, s., d. 62, small holes, (11-16-92, Briest, #288), 13¾ x 11 13/16 in., (35 x 30 cm.), lithograph in 5 colors (BP 758, DM 1839, FR 6196, Y 143,891).

BI *Mirobolus Macadam & Cie, Hautes Pates De J Dubuffet (L. II., 120; W.98), 1946,* book by Michel Tapie, s. by artist, author and pub., num. IV, pub. Rene Drouin, staining, foxing, lithograph detached from book, est. $2/2,500, (11-05-92, Sotheby-NY, #169), overall size 12¾ x 10 in., (325 x 255 mm.), one lithograph p. in colors, Suite de Visages Bronzes on Rives.

$1540* *Mouleuse De Cafe (Loreau I, 374; Webel 44), 1944,* plate XXXIII from portfolio Matiere et Memoire, p. and pub. by Mourlot, 1945, full margins, good cond., (11-05-92, Sotheby-NY, #167), 11⅜ x 7⅝ in., (288 x 195 mm.), lithograph (BP 1002, DM 2436, FR 8240, Y 188,934).

BI *Mur Aux Souvenirs, 1958,* s., d., t., hors commerce, dusty, tears, est. FF1,200/1,500, (06-28-93, Loudmer, #229A), 18⅞ x 15 15/16 in., (480 x 405 mm.), sh 25 9/16 x 19 11/16 in., (480 x 405 mm.), black lithograph on wove.

BI *Mur Ecaille (Loreau XVI, S. 22), 1959,* t., s., num., est. DM 2400, (12-05-92, Bassenge, #7136), 20¼ x 15⅛ in., (51.5 x 38.4 cm.), lithograph on Arches.

$9350* *Les Murs (L. I, 403-417; W. 53-67), 1945,* book, p. Mourlot, num. 81, pub. Les Editions du Livre, 1950, good cond., orig. cover, soiling, (11-05-92, Sotheby-NY, #168, illus.), each folded sheet 15 x 11¼ in., (380 x 285 mm.), fifteen lithographs on Montval (BP 6081, DM 14,787, FR 50,027, Y 1,147,099).

$20,700* *Le Noctambule (L. XVI, p. 221; W. 807), 1961,* each init., #1/3, i., full margins, good cond., mat stain, old hinges stains, skinned spots, printer's ink, (02-11-93, Sotheby-NY, #127, illus.), color lithograph and set of 12 progressive color proofs (BP 14,606, DM 34,289, FR 116,031, Y 2,495,479).

BI *Le Noctambule (L. XVI, p. 221; W. 807), 1961,* each init., #1/3, i., full margins, good cond., mat stain, skinned spots, lithograph i., est. $40/60,000, (11-05-92, Sotheby-NY, #171, illus.), sheet approx. 25 x 17⅞ in., (635 x 455 mm.), lithograph p. in colors, plus set of 12 progressive color proofs, onArches wove.

$805* *Oriflammes (Loreau XXXVIII, nos. 19, 23, 28-30, 32, 33, 35, 41, 51, 53-55; W. 1455-1474): Sixteen,* complete portfolio, facsimile text by artist, inits. in ball point on just. page, #19/245 signes, p. l'Atelier Marquet, pub. Ryoan-Ji, Marseilles, 1984, full sheets, good cond., (02-11-93, Sotheby-NY, #327), each sheet 8¼ x 6¼ in., (210 x 158 mm.), color silkscreen (BP 568, DM 1333, FR 4512, Y 97,046).

$660* *Oriflammes: Fifteen, 1984,* init., justification sheet, #178/245, (12-13-92, Hindman, #324), 8⅛ x 6 in., color serigraph (BP 422, DM 1037, FR 3535, Y 81,653).

$1468* *Parade Nuptiale (Lebon 1099), 14 Avril 1972,* mono., d. 73, #51/85, excellent cond., (11-16-92, Briest, #289), 15 9/16 x 13⅛ in., (39.6 x 33.4 cm.), serigraph in 4 colors (BP 965, DM 2341, FR 7888, Y 183,202).

$2752* *Personnage,* ded., s., creases, staining, good margins, stamp, (06-16-93, Ader Tajan, #91), 11 7/16 x 7½ in., (29 x 19 cm.), aquatint (BP 1835, DM 4568, FR 15,331, Y 293,515).

BI *Pierre Seghers. L'Homme Du Commun (W. 48 and 49), 1944,* complete book, text by Seghers, #131, p. Mourlot, pub. Editions Poesie, good cond., discoloration, est. BP 1/1,200, (06-30-93, Sotheby-London, #428), 14⅝ x 7¾ in., (371 x 197 mm.), two color lithographs on Arches.

$1299* *Pierre Vagabonde, 1960,* t., s., (11-28-92, Schoppmann, #494), 12³⁄₁₆ x 12¹⁵⁄₁₆ in., (31 x 33 cm.), etching and embossing on handmade (BP 857, DM 2069, FR 7025, Y 161,668).

$2070* *Presences Fugaces: Celebrator (W. 1159), 1973,* init., d., #76/100, blindstamp, pub. Pace Editions, full margins, good cond., discoloration, (05-15-93, Sotheby-NY, #961), 19¾ x 13⅜ in., (50.2 x 34 cm.), silkscreen in colors on Dutch paper (BP 1346, DM 3330, FR 11,189, Y 229,465).

$2090* *Presences Fugances Portfolio: Epiphanor (Pace 12), 1973,* init., d., i. 'PP', pub. Pace Editions, full margins, good cond., crease, (11-07-92, Sotheby-NY, #548), 19¾ x 13⅜ in., (502 x 340 mm.), silkscreen in colors on Dutch Etching (BP 1366, DM 3337, FR 11,279, Y 257,961).

$919* *Profil Hilare (Cul-De-Lampe final) (Loreau fascicule V 115), 1949,* mono., (06-12-93, Hauswedell/Nolt, #73), 3¹⁵⁄₁₆ x 3⁹⁄₁₆ in., (10 x 9 cm.), lithograph on copper print (BP 602, DM 1496, FR 5027, Y 96,706).

$4600* *Samedi Tantot (L. XX, no. 325; W. 991), 1964,* s., #68/125, full margins, good cond., mat stain, spots, registration marks, margins touched-in w/white ink, (02-11-93, Sotheby-NY, #128, illus.), 21¾ x 15⅞ in., (552 x 403 mm.), color lithograph (BP 3246, DM 7620, FR 25,785, Y 554,551).

BI *Serenite (Arnaud 502), 1959,* #6/30, pencil t., s., d., est. DM 3,000, (11-20-92, Lempertz, #522), sh 25½ x 19⁷⁄₁₆ in., (64.7 x 49.4 cm.), lithograph in color on Arches-Velin.

$1265* *Le Sol Allegre (W. 716; L. XVI, 358), 1958,* plate VI of L'Anarchitecte, s., t., d. 58, i. epreuve d'artiste, p. Fequet et Baudier, full margins, good cond., (05-13-93, Sotheby-NY, #547), 20⅛ x 15½ in., (512 x 395 mm.), lithograph in colors on wove (BP 830, DM 2043, FR 6890, Y 141,230).

$1023* *Le Sol Allegre (Webel 716), 1958,* s., d., #17/30, p. Fequet et Baudier, full margins, good cond., (12-03-92, Sotheby-London, #288, illus.), 25 x 21⅝ in., (635 x 549 mm.), lithograph in colors on Arches (BP 660, DM 1609, FR 5491, Y 127,286).

$1248* *"Solitudes",* s., 1953, 2/10, (12-04-92, AB Stockholm, #7056), 15⅜ x 19⅛ in., (39 x 48.5 cm.), lithograph in colors on Arches (BP 801, DM 1988, FR 6742, Y 155,805, SK 8470).

BI *"Symbioses" (Webel 704), 1959,* s., t., d., num., sheet 10 of series "Banalites", est. DM 2,2/2,400, (11-28-92, Grisebach, #502, illus.), 17¹³⁄₁₆ x 15¹⁄₁₆ in., (45.2 x 38.3 cm.), colored lithograph on handmade.

BI *Vacations (L. IX, 38; Webel 380), 1953,* watermark, s., t., i. epreuve d'essai, proof, margins, repaired tears, nick, stains, very good cond., est. BP 2,2/2,600, (12-01-92, Christie-London, #366, illus.), L. 6¹¹⁄₁₆ x 9¹³⁄₁₆ in., (170 x 250 mm.), lithograph in colors on wove.

$2917* *Vacations (W. 380), 1953,* s., t., i. epreuve d'essai, full margins, good cond., defects, (06-30-93, Sotheby-London, #429), 6⅞ x 9⅞ in., (175 x 251 mm.), color lithograph on wove (BP 1955, DM 4975, FR 16,784, Y 312,547).

$848* *Vie Discrete (Loreau fascicule XVI 350), 1959,* s., d., t., #11/30, 8.Album Tables rases from suite Phenomenes, (06-12-93, Hauswedell/Nolt, #75), 18¹¹⁄₁₆ x 14⅜ in., (47.5 x 36.5 cm.), lithograph on wide margin Arches (BP 555, DM 1380, FR 4639, Y 89,235).

$8800* *Vignettes Lorgnettes (L. IV, 251-274; W. 149-172), 1948,* book, linoleum block for plate XI (W. 159), s., d. avril 63, num. 11,pub. Ernst Beyeler, 1962, good cond., orig. box, (11-05-92, Sotheby-NY, #170, illus.), each folded sheet 13 x 10 in., (330 x 255 mm.), 25 linoleum cuts and woodcuts, on Auvergne Richard de Bas (BP 5724, DM 13,917, FR 47,084, Y 1,079,622).

DUCEIN, Delvart

$138* *"Brooklyn Bridge" and "42nd Street": Two,* both s., d. below image, (08-05-92, Boos, #733), serigraph (BP 72, DM 204, FR 689, Y 17,575).

DUCHAMP, Marcel French 1887-1968

$3603* *Arturo Schwartz. The Large Glass And Related Works (Schwartz 395), 1967: Nine,* folio w/title-page, list of contents, facsimile reprods., text and just., s. by artist and author, #6, lacking 2 s. suites and barred copper plate,pub. Schwartz Gallery, good cond., orig. slipcase, (06-30-93, Sotheby-London, #430, illus.), etching w/aquatint on hand-made, watermark (BP 2415, DM 6145, FR 20,731, Y 386,050).

$4950* *Arturo Schwarz, Layout For Marcel Duchamp/Ready-Mades, Etc (1913-64)(Schwarz 366 and 379), 1964,* s., num. Draft Piston, #85/100, good cond., ink s., good cond., (11-09-92, Christie-NY, #86), 355 x 255 in., (901.7 x 647.7 cm.), photographic readymade on acetate (S. 379), together w/black leather-bound catalogue (S. 366) (BP 3273, DM 7902, FR 26,699, Y 614,296).

$3910* *Arturo Schwarz, Layout For Marcel Duchamp/Ready-Mades, Etc., 1913-64, Milan, Arturo Schwarz, 1964 (S. 366 and 379),* s., num. Draft Piston, copy 99 of 100, good cond., (05-11-93, Christie-NY, #187), photographic readymade on acetate (BP 2496, DM 6159, FR 20,754, Y 430,096).

BI *Bride (S. 413), 1937,* s. ink, d. Oct. 37, revenue stamp, good cond., creases, surface loss, spots in image, pressure mark, est. $15/20,000, (05-15-93, Sotheby-NY, #959, illus.), 13⅜ x 7¾ in., (34 x 19.7 cm.), color reproduction of the 1912 painting The Bride by Marcel Duchamp.

$7206* *The Chess Players (S. 380), 1965,* s., d., #47/50, pub. Galleria Schwarz Coll., full margins, good cond., creasing, foxing, (06-30-93, Sotheby-London, #433, illus.), 17¼ x 22½ in., (438 x 572 mm.), etching w/ground on laid (BP 4830, DM 12,291, FR 41,461, Y 772,099).

$5290* *Fluttering Hearts (S. 298b), 1961,* s., d., i., #11/125, folded, staining, good cond., Mary Sisler Estate, (05-11-93, Christie-NY, #186), sheet 12¾ x 19½ in., (324 x 495 mm.), screenprint in red and blue on wove (BP 3377, DM 8333, FR 28,079, Y 581,894).

$4804* *King And Queen (S. 405C), 1968,* 2nd final state, s., #25/30, pub. Galleria Schwarz Coll., margins, good cond., (06-30-93, Sotheby-London, #431, illus.), sh 19⅞ x 12¾ in., (505 x 324 mm.), etching and aquatint on Japon nacre (BP 3220, DM 8194, FR 27,641, Y 514,733).

$10,925* *L.H.O.O.Q. (S. 375), 1965,* s., t., full margins, good cond., (05-15-93, Sotheby-NY, #958, illus.), sheet 8¼ x 5½ in., (21 x 14 cm.), color reproduction of the Mona Lisa, pasted onto an invitation card (BP 7103, DM 17,573, FR 59,054, Y 1,211,063).

$1210* *The Large Glass And Related Works: "The Large Glass" (Pl. 58), "The Bride" (Pl. 62), "The Nine Malic Moulds & The Capillary Tubes" (Pl. 70), "The Chocolate Grinder & The Scissors" (Pl. 86)...: Five,* init. in plate, pub. Arturo Schwartz Gallery, full margins, good cond., buckling, (02-24-93, Butterfield, #2919), each sheet 16½ x 9⅞ in., (419 x 251 mm.), etching (1 w/red) on handmade paper w/watermark (BP 844, DM 1964, FR 6659, Y 141,985).

$4370* *Mirrorical Return (S. 370), 1964,* s., d., #39/100, full margins, excell. cond., (05-11-93, Christie-NY, #188, illus.), plate 7 x 5½ in., (178 x 140 mm.), etching in black and red on wove (BP 2790, DM 6884, FR 23,195, Y 480,695).

$4180* *Mirrorical Return (S. 370), 1964,* watermark G1, s., d., #86/100, full margins, crease, very good cond., (11-09-92, Christie-NY, #87, illus.), 268 x 195 in., (680.7 x 495.3 cm.), black and red etching on wove (BP 2764, DM 6673, FR 22,546, Y 518,739).

BI *Pulled At Four Pins (S. 372), 1964,* s., #88/100, pub. Galleria Schwarz Coll., full margins, good cond., creasing, repaired tear, tape staining, est. BP 3/3,500, (06-30-93, Sotheby-London, #432, illus.), 12⅜ x 8⅝ in., (314 x 219 mm.), etching on wove.

$3680* *Pulled At Four Pins (S. 372), 1964,* s., #14/100, full margins, staining, creasing, skinned patches, goodcond., (05-11-93, Christie-NY, #189), plate 12½ x 8¾ in., (318 x 222 mm.), etching on Pescia hand-made (BP 2349, DM 5797, FR 19,533, Y 404,796).

$3300* *Pulled At Four Pins (S. 372), 1964,* s., #12/100, full margins, foxing, very good cond., (11-09-92, Christie-NY, #88, illus.), 318 x 223 in., (807.7 x 566.4 cm.), etching on Pescia handmade (BP 2182, DM 5268, FR 17,799, Y 409,531).

$4057* *Un Robinet Original Revolutionnaire "Renvoi Miriorique" (Schwarz 370), 1964,* s., num., from title "...Miroirique", (12-05-92, Bassenge, #7138), 6⅞ x 5³⁄₁₆ in., (17.5 x 13.2 cm.), etching in black and some red on thick paper (BP 2540, DM 6325, FR 21,557, Y 502,664).

BI *Le Roi Et La Reine,* s., #25/30, mono. in plate, full margins, excellent cond., est. FF 35/40,000, (11-16-92, Briest, #293, illus.), 19⅞ x 12¹³⁄₁₆ in., (50.5 x 32.5 cm.), drypoint and aquatint in black on Japan.

BI *Tire A Quatre Epingles (Schwarz 372), 1964,* #88/100, full margins, tears, est. FF 32/35,000, (11-16-92, Briest, #294, illus.), 25³⁄₁₆ x 18⅛ in., (64 x 46 cm.), etching in black on handmade Pescia.

DUCHAMP, Marcel and V. HALBERSTADT
$977* *L'Opposition Et Les Cases Conjuguees Sont Reconciliees Par M. Duchamp & V. Halberstadt, 1932,* book w/cover design by Duchamp, pub. L'Echiquier, good cond., (12-09-92, Sotheby-Amstrdm, #563, illus.), approx. 11⅝ x 9¹³⁄₁₆ in., (295 x 250 mm.), (BP 623, DM 1534, FR 5233, Y 121,141, G 1725).

DUCHAMPS, Marcel
BI *Arturo Schwarz. The Large Glass And Related Works, 1967: Folio,* w/title page, list of contents, facsimile reprods., text & just., s.by artist & author, num. 6, (lacking 2 s. suites & the s. barred copper plate),pub. Schwarz Gallery, watermark, good cond., loose, est. BP 2,5/3,500, (12-03-92, Sotheby-London, #289, illus.), 9 etchings w/aquatint on hand made.

DUCHER and MATHIEU
$303* *A Reclining Female Nude,* indistinguishable sig., edit. E.A., (c) by Ducher and Mathieu, 1937, (05-14-93, DuMouchelle, #2369), image sight 15½ x 33¼ in., (39.4 x 84.5 cm.), lithograph (BP 197, DM 487, FR 1638, Y 33,588).

DUDOVICH, Marcello   1878-1962
$1039* *Grado, 1933,* p. Studio Editoriale Touristico, cond. 1, image crease; tear, (10-13-92, Phillips-London, #15, illus.), 39⅜ x 24⁵⁄₁₆ in., (100 x 61.8 cm.), color lithograph (BP 605, DM 1522, FR 5172, Y 125,985).

DUEZ, Ernest   French 1843-1896
$206* *Elegante Devant La Mer, c. 1900,* full margins, (05-06-93, Laurin, #26), color lithograph on wove (BP 131, DM 324, FR 1092, Y 22,665).

BI *Jeune Femme Accoudee Regardant La Mer, c. 1895,* dirt, staining, creases, cracks, (02-24-93, Picard, #91), lithograph and pochoir on creme wove.

BI *"Splendeur",* trial proof, very good/good cond., est. $5/600, (11-21-92, Bakker, #117), plate 10½ x 4½ in., (26.7 x 11.4 cm.), etching w/pencil drawings.

DUFRESNE, Charles   French 1876-1938
$1197* *Une Escale Au Bresil, 1920,* #10/25, s., drystamp, (04-02-93, Picard, #95), 9¹⁄₁₆ x 11¹³⁄₁₆ in., (23 x 30 cm.), black etching and drypoint on wove w/Porcabeuf watermark (BP 788, DM 1924, FR 6534, Y 136,286).

$3151* *Une Escale Au Bresil, 1920,* s. in plate, 3/25, drystamp, (06-28-93, Loudmer, #232, illus.), 9⅛ x 11¹³⁄₁₆ in., (231 x 300 mm.), sh 12⁷⁄₁₆ x 18⅛ in., (231 x 300 mm.), black etching and drypoint on Van Gelder wove w/Alfred Porcabeuf watermark (BP 2110, DM 5354, FR 18,037, Y 334,324).

$512* *La Girafe, c. 1920,* num., s., dust, full margins, (02-24-93, Picard, #92), etching and aquatint (BP 357, DM 831, FR 2818, Y 60,080).

$3597* *La Guadeloupe, 1919,* #14/25, s., drystamp, (06-11-93, Picard, #40, illus.), 8⅜ x 11⅛ in., (213 x 282 mm.), etching and wood engraving in 2 colors on simili Japan (BP 2363, DM 5846, FR 19,710, Y 381,645).

$3245* *La Partie De Cartes, 1923,* num., s., full margins, (02-24-93, Picard, #94), drypoint and pochoir on thin creme wove (BP 2263, DM 5268, FR 17,859, Y 380,779).

$516* *Planteur, 1920,* #26/35, drystamp, (04-02-93, Picard, #96), 9¼ x 7⁵⁄₁₆ in., (23.5 x 18.5 cm.), black etching on wove w/Porcabeuf watermark (BP 340, DM 829, FR 2817, Y 58,750).

$759* *Le Repos Dans L'Oasis II, 1919,* #8/35, s., (06-11-93, Picard, #41), 4¹³⁄₁₆ x 7¹³⁄₁₆ in., (122 x 198 mm.), etching

in black on Hollande wove (BP 499, DM 1234, FR 4159, Y 80,531).

$1280* *Le Triomphe De Galathee, 1923,* annot., s., creases, 5 impressions only, (04-02-93, Picard, #97), 12⅝ x 16⁹⁄₁₆ in., (32 x 42 cm.), black etching on Rives wove (BP 843, DM 2057, FR 6987, Y 145,736).

DUFY, Jean   French 1888-1964
$381* *Boulevard-Szene,* s., num., (05-26-93, Dorling, #2633, illus.), 19¹¹⁄₁₆ x 24¹⁵⁄₁₆ in., (48.4 x 63.3 cm.), color lithograph on BFK Rives wove (BP 246, DM 622, FR 2092, Y 41,395).

$550* *Montmartre,* s., #209/250, (05-16-93, Hindman, #488), 19 x 25 in., (48.3 x 63.5 cm.), color lithograph (BP 358, DM 885, FR 2973, Y 60,969).

$358* *Montmartre, Sacre-Couer,* stone s.; s., #101/250, (03-25-93, Boos, #621), 18⁹⁄₁₆ x 25³⁄₁₆ in., (472 x 640 mm.), color lithograph on Arches (BP 243, DM 588, FR 2000, Y 41,940).

DUFY, Jean (after)
$110* *Paris Street Scene,* #101/250, (01-15-93, DuMouchelle, #2440), 19 x 24 in., (48.3 x 61 cm.), lithograph (BP 72, DM 180, FR 608, Y 13,868).

DUFY, Raoul   French 1877-1953
$13,898* *Alphonse Daudet (Boston 94; Rauch 48): One Hundred,* 1937, d. 1949, (06-23-93, Kornfeld, #325), lithograph (BP 9442, DM 23,516, FR 79,101, Y 1,514,108, SF 20,930).

$352* *Anemonenstrauss,* stone s., (03-24-93, Venator/Hansten, #4480), approx. 21¹⁄₁₆ x 16¾ in., (53.5 x 42.5 cm.), color lithograph on Arches (BP 238, DM 575, FR 1957, Y 41,358).

$164* *"Baigneuse Au Coquillages " and "Portrait De Fleuret": Two,* originals, (05-06-93, Laurin, #27B), etchings (BP 104, DM 258, FR 870, Y 18,044).

BI *Baigneuse Au Poney,* full margins, (05-06-93, Laurin, #27), lithograph on Japan.

$605* *Baigneuses,* first state, #23/35, s., drystamp, large margins, (02-03-93, Ader Tajan, #144), 8¹⁵⁄₁₆ x 12¹³⁄₁₆ in., (22.8 x 32.5 cm.), lithograph (BP 422, DM 996, FR 3378, Y 75,258).

$745* *"Balcon Sur La Mer",* s., 60/190, (04-17-93, Falkkloos, #105, illus.), 13⅜ x 20¹⁄₁₆ in., (34 x 51 cm.), etching (BP 484, DM 1191, FR 4025, Y 82,842, SK 5500).

$605* *Bateaux A Dauville,* s. in stone, #15/200, (10-30-92, Sloan, #1609), 19 x 26¾ in., (48.3 x 67.9 cm.), color lithograph (BP 388, DM 931, FR 3158, Y 74,941).

$158* *"Le Champ De Ble",* t., s. Raoul Dufy, printer's stamp, (05-18-93, Encans, #183), 14¾ x 18¹¹⁄₁₆ in., (37.5 x 47.5 cm.), print (BP 103, DM 256, FR 866, Y 17,608, C$ 200).

$867* *"La Chasse", "La Peche", "L'Amour" and "La Danse", c. 1910: Four,* (04-02-93, Picard, #98), from 8¼ x 25³⁄₁₆ in., (21 x 64 cm.), to 12⅝ x 15¾ in., (21 x 64 cm.), black wood engravings, first on Arches, three others on Richard de Bas (BP 571, DM 1393, FR 4733, Y 98,713).

$467* *Deux Figures,* watermark, full margins, light-stained, (11-30-92, Phillips-London, #420), plate 13⅜ x 19⅜ in., (340 x 492 mm.), etching on Arches (BP 308, DM 744, FR 2526, Y 58,121).

$2198* *Fete Nautique (I.F.F. 23), 1921,* large margins, tears, (06-11-93, Picard, #42, illus.), 14³⁄₁₆ x 18½ in., (360 x 470 mm.), lithograph in color on thin chine (BP 1444, DM 3572, FR 12,044, Y 233,210).

$2198* *Golfe Juan-Vue De La Terrasse De La Villa Beau-Site (I.F.F. 36), 1926,* whole margins, s., annot., reddish stains, (06-11-93, Picard, #43, illus.), 14¹⁵⁄₁₆ x 18¹¹⁄₁₆ in., (380 x 475 mm.), lithograph in black on Rives wove (BP 1444, DM 3572, FR 12,044, Y 233,210).

$3996* *La Grande Baigneuse (I.F.F. 41?), c. 1928,* #27/40, s., large margins, (06-11-93, Picard, #44), 26¾ x 20½ in., (680 x 520 mm.), lithograph in color on wove (BP 2625, DM 6494, FR 21,896, Y 423,979).

$619* *Jeune Fille Sur La Plage,* s. Raoul Dufy, (04-20-93, Encans, #108), 8⅞ x 11¹³⁄₁₆ in., (22.5 x 30 cm.), print (BP 399, DM 986, FR 3328, Y 68,300, C$ 777).

$690* *"L'Amour" and "La Peche", c. 1910: Two,* bears artist's name & spurious numbering, margins, touched-in, repaird tears, scrapes, scratches, laid-down between mat and backboard, (02-11-93, Sotheby-NY, #129), one 12³⁄₁₆ x 12⅜ in., (310 x 315 mm.), the other 12¾ x 15¹⁵⁄₁₆ in., (310 x 315 mm.), woodcut on chine volant (BP 487, DM 1143, FR 3868, Y 83,183).

$3137* *Paris, Chez Camille Bloch, 1917: Thirty,* from Les Elegies Martiales by Roger Allard, d. mai 1918, prov., (11-15-92, Christie-Geneva, #301, illus.), 8⁷⁄₁₆ x 6⅛ in., (215 x 155 mm.), wood engraving on Chine (BP 2062, DM 5003, FR 16,857, Y 391,489, SF 4520).

$1725* *Le Poete Assassine, 1926,* #69, pub. Je Trouve au Sans Pareil, good cond., discoloration, creases, (02-11-93, Sotheby-NY, #130), 14⅞ x 8¾ in., (378 x 223 mm.), 36 lithographs in-texte, separate suite of lithographs on japon-ancien (BP 1217, DM 2857, FR 9669, Y 207,957).

$262* *Le Port,* (12-02-92, Kunsthallen, #240), lithograph (BP 169, DM 412, FR 1406, Y 32,599, DK 1610).

$5574* *Le Port, 1925,* sheet of series: La Mer, s., num., (06-23-93, Kornfeld, #324), 12¹¹⁄₁₆ x 17⁵⁄₁₆ in., (32.3 x 44 cm.), color lithograph on thick wove (BP 3787, DM 9431, FR 31,725, Y 607,256, SF 8395).

BI *Portraits De Femmes,* artist's proof, s., est. FF800/1,000, (05-27-93, Briest, #82), 13³⁄₁₆ x 19⁵⁄₁₆ in., (33.5 x 49 cm.), etching.

BI *Portraits De Femmes,* epreuve d'artiste, s., est. FF 2/3,000, (11-16-92, Briest, #46), 13³⁄₁₆ x 19⁵⁄₁₆ in., (33.5 x 49 cm.), etching.

$83* *Portraits De Femmes: Two,* large margins, (04-02-93, Picard, #99), 12¹⁵⁄₁₆ x 18⅞ in., (33 x 48 cm.), etching (BP 55, DM 133, FR 453, Y 9450).

$179* *"Scenes De Peche": Two,* (01-28-93, Pescheteau, #130), 12⅝ x 9¹³⁄₁₆ in., (32 x 25 cm.), etchings on wove w/ watermark (BP 118, DM 284, FR 960, Y 22,225).

BI *"Still Life",* s. Raoul Dufy within pl., i. E.A., (12-12-92, A. James, #37), sheet 26¾ x 19⅝ in., (67.9 x 49.8 cm.), lithograph.

$109* *Sur La Plage,* plate s., (09-25-92, Granier, #2821), sheet 12¹⁵⁄₁₆ x 17½ in., (33 x 44.5 cm.), color etching on hand-made (BP 64, DM 162, FR 546, Y 13,156).

$403* *Woman Sleeping With Two Butterflies And Two Boats At Sea,* s., full margins, good cond., (05-19-93, Butterfield, #2054), 8¾ x 12⁷⁄₁₆ in., (222 x 316 mm.), etching and aquatint in colors on wove (BP 262, DM 655, FR 2207, Y 44,614).

DUFY, Raoul (after)

BI *Landscape With Equestrian Scene,* est. $60/80, (02-11-93, Boos, #467), ⅝x⅞in., (16 x 22 mm.), print.

$77* *"Musee Toulouse-Lautrec-Albi", 1955,* (12-02-92, Boos, #526), sight 28 x 19½ in., (711 x 495 mm.), color lithograph, exhibition poster (BP 50, DM 121, FR 413, Y 9581).

$706* *Paysage Marocain,* #17/150, s., good margins, (02-03-93, Ader Tajan, #145), 15¹⁄₁₆ x 21⅞ in., (38.3 x 55.5 cm.), color lithograph (BP 493, DM 1163, FR 3942, Y 87,822).

$44* *"Quintette",* (02-11-93, Boos, #468), sight 11½ x 30 in., (292 x 762 mm.), lithograph (BP 31, DM 73, FR 247, Y 5304).

BI *Untitled,* #12/375, est. $70/90, (02-11-93, Boos, #470), 17 x 23½ in., (432 x 597 mm.), color lithograph.

DUFY, Raoul (after) 1877-1953

$90* *"Le Havre, Rue Pavoisee-1907",* d., s. in plate, (04-04-93, Pescheteau, #206), 29½ x 20½ in., (75 x 52 cm.), color lithograph on wove (BP 59, DM 145, FR 491, Y 10,247).

DUGMORE, A.R.

$247* *Exotic Fish, 1907,* sig., (10-14-92, Swann, #437, illus.), 5 x 7 in., (12.7 x 17.8 cm.), photograph, silver print (BP 145, DM 361, FR 1226, Y 29,932).

DUHRKOOP, Rudolf 1848-1918

$1650* *Self-Portrait, Berlin, 1912,* s. in neg., s., d. 1915, annot., (10-13-92, Christie-NY, #190, illus.), 6½ x 8½ in., (16.5 x 21.6 cm.), photograph, platinum print (BP 961, DM 2417, FR 8213, Y 200,073).

DUKE OF EDINBURGH

BI *Oyster Catchers,* s. on mount, est. BP 5/70, (04-22-93, Bonhams-Chelsea, #112), image 14½ x 18 in., photograph, b/w.

DULAU and CO., LTD., Publisher

$48* *Miniature Portrait Of Tom Cribb,* margins, (03-03-93, Bonhams-Chelsea, #29), plate 2⅝ x 2⅝ in., (6.7 x 6.7 cm.), hand-colored engraving (BP 33, DM 79, FR 268, Y 5609).

DULL, Christian American 20th cent.

BI *West Wind,* s., est. $100/150, (06-11-93, Freemn/Fine Art, #58), 9¾ x 8 in., (24.8 x 20.3 cm.), etching.

DUMARIRO, D.

$110* *Crow,* #32/250, s., (02-12-93, DuMouchelle, #350, illus.), 7¾ x 3⅞ in., (19.7 x 9.8 cm.), engraving (BP 77, DM 182, FR 617, Y 13,266).

DUMAS, Antoine Canadian b. 1932

$232* *"Croisiere A Montreal",* #42/160, s. A. Dumas 79, (08-18-92, Encans, #28), 27³⁄₁₆ x 36¼ in., (69 x 92 cm.), lithograph (BP 120, DM 338, FR 1146, Y 29,249, C$ 278).

$186* *"L'Epouse De Carriere",* #99/100, s., d. Dumas 75, stamp of la Guilde Graphique, (07-14-92, Encans, #32), 18⅞ x 22¹⁄₁₆ in., (48 x 56 cm.), serigraph (BP 97, DM 276, FR 930, Y 23,259, C$ 222).

$71* *"Lacroix Freres Et Compagnie",* #145/150, t., s., d. Dumas 77, stamp, (03-16-93, Encans, #51), 16¾ x 22³⁄₁₆ in., (42.5 x 56.3 cm.), lithograph (BP 49, DM 118, FR 401, Y 8302, C$ 89).

$93* *"Le Reve Passe",* #30/100, s. A. Dumas, (08-18-92, Encans, #27), 22¹⁄₁₆ x 18⅛ in., (56 x 46 cm.), lithograph (BP 48, DM 135, FR 459, Y 11,725, C$ 111).

DUMONT, Maurice French 1870-1899

$328* *Carmosine (A.A.B.-M. 64; A. 73), 1895,* w/letter, full margins, (02-24-93, Picard, #188), gypsotype in yellow chrome on simili-Japan (BP 229, DM 532, FR 1805, Y 38,489).

$164* *"Carmosine", 1895 and "La Fin Du Reve", 1894: Two,* first, w/out letter; second, s., d., just., full margins, (02-24-93, Picard, #95), gypsotype and lithograph on Japan simili (BP 114, DM 266, FR 903, Y 19,244).

$220* *"Relief For A Binding", c. 1895,* issued by L'Epreuve, good/poor cond., (11-21-92, Bakker, #31), plate 9⅛ x 5⅛ in., (23.2 x 13 cm.), relief etching (BP 145, DM 351, FR 1182, Y 27,360).

DUMOUCHEL, Albert 1916-1971

$325* *"La Chevre",* s., d. Dumouchel 58, (08-18-92, Encans, #29), 11 x 13⅜ in., (28 x 34 cm.), etching (BP 168, DM 473, FR 1606, Y 40,973, C$ 389).

$93* *Paysage,* #493/500, s., d. in plate Dumouchel 70, (07-14-92, Encans, #33), 18⅞ x 25⁹⁄₁₆ in., (48 x 65 cm.), lithograph (BP 48, DM 138, FR 465, Y 11,629, C$ 111).

DUNCAN, E.

BI *The H.M.S. Winchester,* after W.J. Huggins, 1830, est. $6/800, (04-07-93, Sotheby-Arcade, #21), 15⅞ x 21½ in., (40.3 x 54.6 cm.), hand-colored aquatint.

$83* *"Ships Of The General Steam Navigation Company",* after W.J. Huggins 1841; label verso, (05-15-93, Dunning, #104, illus.), engraving (BP 54, DM 134, FR 449, Y 9201).

DUNCAN, Edward (after W.J. HUGGINS)

$957* *The Honourable East India Company Ship William Fairlie, 1828,* pub. W.J. Huggins, good cond., (10-27-92, Phillips-London, #88, illus.), image 14⅛ x 21⅝ in., (359 x 549 mm.), aquatint in blue and black w/hand-coloring on wove (BP 605, DM 1467, FR 4977, Y 117,064).

$261* *The Opium Ships At Lintin In China, 1824,* pub. Huggins, 1838, good cond., (10-27-92, Phillips-London, #158), image 15 x 23 in., (381 x 584 mm.), aquatint w/ hand-coloring on wove (BP 165, DM 400, FR 1357, Y 31,927).

DUNCAN, Rodgers

$440* *Joyce, Paris, 1988,* Affiches du Marval, A cond., (08-06-92, Swann, #119, illus.), 62 x 48 in., (157.5 x 121.9 cm.), (BP 230, DM 650, FR 2196, Y 56,122).

DUNHAM, Carroll American b. 1949

BI *Accelerator, 1985,* s., d., num. 23/51, ULAE blindstamp, full sheet, excell. cond., est.$1,5/2,000, (09-19-92, Christie-E, #101), sheet 41¾ x 29¾ in., (106 x 75.6 cm.), lithograph in blacks on wove.

$770* *"Color Message A", "Color Message B" and "Color Message C", 1985-6: Set Of Three,* s., d., num. 39/52, ULAE blindstamps, full sheets, excell. cond.(09-19-92, Christie-E, #102), each, sheet 13 x 8⅝ in., (33 x 21.9 cm.), lithograph in colors on G. Amatruda Almafi (BP 443, DM 1153, FR 3949, Y 95,938).

$825* *"Color Message A", "Color Message B" and "Color Message C", 1985-6: Set Of Three,* s., d., #32/52, blindstamps, excellent cond., (11-09-92, Christie-NY, #278, illus.), 13 x 8⅝ in., (330 x 219 mm.), colored lithograph on G. Amatruda Almafi (BP 545, DM 1317, FR 4450, Y 102,383).

$1150* *Color Message A,B,C, 1985-1986: Three,* s., d., #35/52, blindstamp, pub. ULAE, good cond., (05-15-93, Sotheby-NY, #962, illus.), each sheet 13 x 8⅝ in., (33 x 21.9 cm.), lithograph in colors on G. Amatruda Almalfi handmade paper (BP 748, DM 1850, FR 6216, Y 127,480).

$2640* *Full Spectrum,* s., d., #63/68, blindstamp, excellent cond., (11-09-92, Christie-NY, #279, illus.), 41½ x 28 in., (105.4 x 71.1 cm.), lithograph and screenprint in colors on wove (BP 1745, DM 4215, FR 14,239, Y 327,625).

$2860* *Full Spectrum, 1985-87,* s., d., num. 56/68, ULAE blindstamp, full sheet, excell. cond., (09-19-92, Christie-E, #103, illus.), sheet 41½ x 28 in., (105.4 x 71.1 cm.), lithograph and screenprint in colors on wove (BP 1645, DM 4283, FR 14,667, Y 356,342).

$1955* *Full Spectrum, 1985-87,* s., d., #63/68, blindstamp, pub. ULAE, good cond., (05-15-93, Sotheby-NY, #963, illus.), sheet 41½ x 28 in., (105.4 x 71.1 cm.), lithograph and silkscreen in colors on J.B. Green (BP 1271, DM 3145, FR 10,568, Y 216,717).

$550* *Number One, 1987,* s., d., #21/50, t., blindstamp p. Vigna Antoniniana Stamperia d'Arte, full margins, very good cond., creases, (10-28-92, Butterfield, #2942), 37³⁄₁₆ x 25¹³⁄₁₆ in., (945 x 656 mm.), color aquatint w/ etching and drypoint on white wove (BP 350, DM 849, FR 2884, Y 67,485).

$770* *Number Three, 1987,* s., d., #21/50, blindstamp, full margins, very good cond., creases, (10-28-92, Butterfield, #2944), 37³⁄₁₆ x 25¹³⁄₁₆ in., (945 x 656 mm.), color aquatint w/etching and drypoint on white wove (BP 491, DM 1189, FR 4038, Y 94,479).

$660* *Number Two, 1987,* s., d., #21/50, t., blindstamp, full margins, very good cond., creases, (10-28-92, Butterfield, #2943), 37³⁄₁₆ x 25¹³⁄₁₆ in., (945 x 656 mm.), color aquatint w/etching and drypoint on white wove (BP 421, DM 1019, FR 3461, Y 80,982).

BI *Touching Two Sides, 1989-90,* s., #15/52, appears good cond., est. $6/800, (06-11-93, Doyle, #93), 24 x 27½ in., (610 x 699 mm.), drypoint.

BI *Touching Two Sides, 1989-90,* s., d., #48/52, blindstamp, pub. ULAE, good cond., est. $1,5/1,800, (05-15-93, Sotheby-NY, #964, illus.), sheet 20⅛ x 26⅜ in., (51.1 x 67 cm.), etching on Richard de Bas pink paper.

BI *Untitled, 1988-89,* s., d., appears very good cond., est. $6/800, (06-11-93, Doyle, #91), 40 x 60¼ in., (101.6 x 153 cm.), color etching.

BI *Untitled, 1988-89,* s., d., #21/53, very good cond., est. $6/800, (06-11-93, Doyle, #92), 40 x 60¼ in., (101.6 x 153 cm.), color etching.

DUNKARTON, W. (after P. REINAGLE) (and W. PETHER)

$1654* *The Night-Blowing Cereus, 1800,* from The Temple Of Flora, pub. Dr. Robert John Thornton, good cond., (10-27-92, Phillips-London, #162, illus.), plate 19¼ x 14 in., (489 x 356 mm.), mezzotint w/line engraving in colors and finished by hand on J. Whatman (BP 1045, DM 2535, FR 8601, Y 202,324).

DUNLOP, Brian James b. 1938

$243* *Pink Stockings,* s. Dunlop, i. T.P, d. '88, (08-11-92, L. Joel, #15G), 25⁹⁄₁₆ x 18⅞ in., (65 x 48 cm.), color lithograph (BP 126, DM 357, FR 1208, Y 31,118, A$ 330).

$203* *Sunlight And Shadow,* s. Dunlop, i., #18/20, (08-11-92, L. Joel, #22G), 15¹⁵⁄₁₆ x 20⅞ in., (40.5 x 53 cm.), lithograph (BP 105, DM 298, FR 1009, Y 25,996, A$ 275).

DUNN, W. Herbert American

$325* *"The Mountain Mother" (Black Boar And Cubs No. 42),* from Heart Of The West series, 1931, s., d., t., mat stain, image stains, good cond., (05-15-93, Cleveland, #116), 12 x 10 in., (30.5 x 25.4 cm.), lithograph (BP 211, DM 523, FR 1757, Y 36,027).

DUNOYER DE SEGONZAC, Andre French 1884-1974

$425* *Chevet De Notre-Dame Vu Du Quai D'Orleans (Liore Et Cailler, 1935), 1935,* second state, s., 3/35, stains, (06-28-93, Loudmer, #236), 5⁹⁄₁₆ x 7¹⁵⁄₁₆ in., (142 x 202 mm.), sh 9⁵⁄₁₆ x 14¹⁵⁄₁₆ in., (142 x 202 mm.), black etching and drypoint on laid (BP 285, DM 722, FR 2433, Y 45,093).

$1280* *Colette Ecrivant (L. et C., 671), 1932,* last state, s., (04-02-93, Picard, #101), 9³⁄₁₆ x 8¼ in., (23.4 x 21 cm.), black etching (BP 843, DM 2057, FR 6987, Y 145,736).

$206* *Daragnes II (Liore et Cailler, 140), 1924,* s., ded., (04-02-93, Picard, #100), 5¼ x 3¹⁵⁄₁₆ in., (13.4 x 10 cm.), black etching on laid (BP 136, DM 331, FR 1124, Y 23,454).

BI *Les Demoiselles De La Marne (L.S. 37), 1937,* 3rd final state, s., num., p. Leblanc, full margins, good cond.?, est. BP 7/900, (11-30-92, Phillips-London, #481), plate 16½ x 11⅛ in., (419 x 283 mm.), etching w/drypoint on laid.

BI *Les Demoiselles De La Marne (Loire-Cailler 37 III), 1921,* s., est. DM 2500, (06-10-93, Hauswedell/Nolt, #257), image 11 x 16⁷⁄₁₆ in., (28 x 41.8 cm.), drypoint on wove.

$227* *Fargue Sommeillant (L. et C., 1388), 1954,* ink s., annot., (04-02-93, Picard, #103), 5¹⁄₁₆ x 6¹⁵⁄₁₆ in., (12.9 x 17.7 cm.), black etching on Japan (BP 150, DM 365, FR 1239, Y 25,845).

$605* *Femme Au Bord De La Mer,* s. in ink, num. 8/33, full margins, good cond., creases, surface soiling, (02-24-93, Butterfield, #2793), 5¾ x 7 in., (146 x 178 mm.), etching on thin wove (BP 422, DM 982, FR 3330, Y 70,993).

$1527* *La Ferme A L'Aire, L'Apres - Midi (L.-C. 158/II), 1926,* s., num., (06-23-93, Kornfeld, #329), etching on simili-Japan (BP 1037, DM 2584, FR 8691, Y 166,358, SF 2300).

$1998* *Fernande Les Mains Croisees (Grande Planche) (A. Liore et P. Cailler96), 1923,* #4/75, good margins, (06-11-93, Picard, #46, illus.), 6¹⁵⁄₁₆ x 5⅛ in., (177 x 130 mm.), etching on old wove (BP 1313, DM 3247, FR 10,948, Y 211,989).

BI *"Le Grand Trianon",* s. A. Dunoyer de Segonzac, num. 49/75, t., pub. dry stamp, fair cond., foxing, mount/water staining, est. $4/600, (09-11-92, Skinner, #13, illus.), 7¹⁄₁₆ x 5³⁄₁₆ in., (17.9 x 13.2 cm.), etching on wove.

$424* *Labours D'Automne Pres De La Route De La Mole Dans La Foret Du Dom. (A.L. and P.C. 915),* illus., annot., ink s., large margins, (02-03-93, Ader Tajan, #147), 11⁷⁄₁₆ x 9½ in., (29 x 24.2 cm.), etching (BP 296, DM 698, FR 2367, Y 52,743).

$505* *Le Modele A Genoux or Nu A Genoux (A Liore and P. Cailler 137), 1924,* artist proof, #10/15,s., large margins, (02-03-93, Ader Tajan, #146), 8³⁄₁₆ x 7¹⁄₁₆ in., (20.8 x 18 cm.), etching (BP 353, DM 832, FR 2820, Y 62,819).

BI *La Moisson (A.L. et P.C. 848), 1930,* #7/60, ink s., whole margins, (06-11-93, Picard, #47), 18⅛ x 13⁷⁄₁₆ in., (460 x 342 mm.), etching on Japan.

$687* *La Moissonneuse Endormie (L.-C. 845), 1929,* s., num., (06-23-93, Kornfeld, #330), etching (BP 467, DM 1162, FR 3910, Y 74,845, SF 1035).

BI *"Moulin Pres De Couilly" (A. Liore et P. Cailler #1150), 1949,* illus., (03-22-93, Pescheteau, #73), etching on wove.

$329* *Petit Nu Au Panier, De Dos (Liore et Cailler, 555),* from "Petits Nus" series, s., 47/50, annot., (06-28-93, Loudmer, #237), 31¾ x 6⅛ in., (807 x 155 mm.), sh 7¹⁵⁄₁₆ x 10⁵⁄₁₆ in., (807 x 155 mm.), black etching on laid (BP 220, DM 559, FR 1883, Y 34,907).

BI   *Place De Tertre (Loire/Cailler 1143), 1949,* s.; mounting traces verso, est. SF 550/600, (10-14-92, Germann, #289), 12¹³⁄₁₆ x 9¹³⁄₁₆ in., (325 x 250 mm.), etching.

$715*   *La Vallee Et La Mer (Liore et Cailler, 1103), 1939,* s., 11/60, p. 1952, scored plate, holes, stains, (06-28-93, Loudmer, #238), 11⁷⁄₁₆ x 9⁷⁄₁₆ in., (290 x 239 mm.), sh 20³⁄₁₆ x 14⁷⁄₁₆ in., (290 x 239 mm.), black etching on laid tinted green w/beige stripes (BP 479, DM 1215, FR 4093, Y 75,862).

DUNSTAN, Bernard

$206*   *A Woman Dressing,* #19/100, s., (05-20-93, Bonhams-Chelsea, #94), image 13 x 13 in., (33 x 33 cm.), lithograph in colors (BP 132, DM 332, FR 1120, Y 22,747).

DUPAIN, Max   Australian 1911-1992

BI   *Advertising Image, c. 1935,* s. in ink, est. $2/2,500, (10-13-92, Christie-NY, #192, illus.), 11⅛ x 9⅜ in., (28.3 x 23.8 cm.), photograph, photo-collage of 3 gelatin silver prints w/airbrushing.

$825*   *The Little Nude,* sig., t., d.; sig., t. verso, 1938, p.l., (10-14-92, Swann, #438, illus.), 19¾ x 15½ in., (50.2 x 39.4 cm.), photograph, silver print (BP 484, DM 1207, FR 4094, Y 99,976).

$3520*   *Sunbaker,* (1937), p.l., s., d., (10-13-92, Christie-NY, #191, illus.), 15 x 15½ in., (38.1 x 39.4 cm.), photograph, gelatin silver print (BP 2050, DM 5157, FR 17,521, Y 426,822).

$2543*   *"Sunbaker",* 1937, p.l., s., d. Max Dupain '37, sight 490 x 582mm, (05-07-93, Sotheby-London, #241, illus.), photograph, silver print (BP 1610, DM 4021, FR 13,548, Y 280,004).

DUPARC, Marie Alexandre   French School 18th/19th cent.

$56*   *"Vue D'Une Partie Du Champ De Bramberg",* after Le Barbier, (07-14-92, Encans, #192), 10¹⁄₁₆ x 14³⁄₁₆ in., (25.5 x 36 cm.), drypoint (BP 29, DM 83, FR 280, Y 7003, C$ 67).

DUPAS, Jean   French 1882-1964

BI   *Amoureux En Promenade,* s., d. 1931, artist's proof, est. $3,5/5,000, (06-10-93, Sotheby-NY, #472, illus.), 24⅜ x 31¼ in., (61.9 x 79.4 cm.), color etching and drypoint.

BI   *"Arnold Constable",* 1928, p. Jean Dupas, est. $2,5/3,500, (12-12-92, Christie-NY, #442, illus.), framed 54 x 36½ in., (137.2 x 92.7 cm.), lithograph in colors.

$4620*   *"Bordeaux",* 1937, advertising poster, p. Jean Dupas 1937, (12-12-92, Christie-NY, #441, illus.), framed 43 x 27⅝ in., (109.2 x 70.2 cm.), lithograph in colors (BP 2962, DM 7279, FR 24,946, Y 571,711).

$3300*   *"Camden Town, Chalk Farm Or Regents Park", 1933,* advertising poster, p. Jean Dupas, (12-12-92, Christie-NY, #440, illus.), framed 43½ x 28 in., (110.5 x 71.1 cm.), lithograph in colors (BP 2116, DM 5199, FR 17,819, Y 408,365).

$3450*   *Couple Astride A Bull, 1931,* s., #4/200, prov., (03-27-93, Christie-NY, #107, illus.), 24 x 30¾ in., (61 x 78.1 cm.), hand-tinted lithograph on paper (BP 2318, DM 5628, FR 19,135, Y 401,536).

$2521*   *Regatta-Time's Pleasant Thrice Pleasant In Laughing July, London Transport, 1933,* repaired tears, other minor defects, lit., (02-04-93, Christie-S. Ken, #61), 39 x 22½ in., (99.1 x 57.2 cm.), color lithograph backed on linen (BP 1760, DM 4151, FR 14,076, Y 313,596).

$6303*   *Thence To Hyde Park, Where Much Good Company And Many Fine Ladies, London Transport, 1930,* repaired tears, creases, nicks, (02-04-93, Christie-S. Ken, #62, illus.), 39½ x 49 in., (100.3 x 124.5 cm.), color lithograph backed on linen (BP 4400, DM 10,379, FR 35,193, Y 784,053).

$6618*   *Where Is This Bower Beside The River Thames, London Transport, 1930,* repaired tears, staining, small defects, (02-04-93, Christie-S. Ken, #63, illus.), 39½ x 49 in., (100.3 x 124.5 cm.), color lithograph backed on linen (BP 4620, DM 10,897, FR 36,951, Y 823,237).

DUPIN, Leon

$467*   *Rita, 1933,* Joseph Charles, A cond., (08-06-92, Swann, #120, illus.), 35 x 39 in., (88.9 x 99.1 cm.), (BP 244, DM 690, FR 2330, Y 59,566).

DUPLESSI-BERTAUX, Jean (after)   1747-1819

$978*   *"Le Charlatan Allamond" and "Le Charlatan Francois" (Inventaire 18 Siecle p. 274-5 nos. 32-33, P. and B. II p. 394, no. 2), 1777: Two,* by I.S. Helman, margins, staining, (05-11-93, Christie-NY, #70, illus.), each plate 9⅞ x 7½ in., (251 x 191 mm.), engraving on laid (BP 624, DM 1541, FR 5191, Y 107,579).

DUPONT, Bensa

$361*   *Zan. C'est Toujours Le Meilleur!, 1898,* Paris, H. Laas, E. Pecaud and Cie, cond. B, restored in text, (06-11-93, Boisgirard, #68), 62¹⁵⁄₁₆ x 47¼ in., (160 x 120 cm.), poster (BP 237, DM 587, FR 1978, Y 38,302).

DUPONT, P.   1870-1911

$107*   *Grachtje Te Amsterdam (Dupont 41; v.W. 316),* stamp, #47, (06-09-93, Bubb Kuyper, #1974), 10¹³⁄₁₆ x 7⅞ in., (27.5 x 20 cm.), etching (BP 71, DM 175, FR 589, Y 11,379, G 196).

$63*   *Hooiopper (Dupont 22; v.W. 324),* plate s., #26, (06-09-93, Bubb Kuyper, #1975), 6⅛ x 6⅛ in., (15.5 x 15.5 cm.), etching (BP 42, DM 103, FR 347, Y 6700, G 115).

$69*   *Pont De La Tournelle (Dupont 66; v.W. 317),* stamp, #14, (06-09-93, Bubb Kuyper, #1976), 12¹⁵⁄₁₆ x 15³⁄₁₆ in., (33 x 38.5 cm.), etching (BP 46, DM 113, FR 380, Y 7338, G 127).

DUPRESSOIR, Francois Joseph   French 1800-1859

BI   *Tentation De St. Antoine, 1845-47,* from series La Galerie Imp. de l'Ermitage, creasing, stained, est. DM 200-, (09-25-92, Granier, #2622), 8⁷⁄₁₆ x 10⅞ in., (21.5 x 27.6 cm.), sheet 14³⁄₁₆ x 19¹⁄₁₆ in., (21.5 x 27.6 cm.), color lithograph.

DUPUIS, E.

$201*   *Cigarettes Khalifas: Two,* Imp. Benard, good cond., (02-12-93, Cheval/Robert, #56), 43⁵⁄₁₆ x 31½ in., (110 x 80 cm.), poster (BP 142, DM 333, FR 1128, Y 24,240).

DUPUIS, Fin

$99*   *L'Huile Sternel,* Imp. Benard, B- cond., fold marks, cracking, creasing, (08-06-92, Swann, #121, illus.), 51 x 38 in., (129.5 x 96.5 cm.), (BP 52, DM 146, FR 494, Y 12,628).

DURANDELLE, Louise Emile   1839-1917

$16,100*   *Le Nouvel Opera De Paris (1865-72): 115,* Ducher et cie, 1875-81, commissioned by Jean-Louis-Charles Garnier, Architect, 4 volumes, complete photographic atlas, oblong folio, majority num. sequentially, lit., (04-08-93, Christie-NY, #5, illus.), largest 14¾ x 11 in., (37.5 x 27.9 cm.), photograph, albumen prints from glass plate negatives (BP 10,557, DM 25,863, FR 87,548, Y 1,827,054).

DUREAU, George   American b. 1930

$193*   *"Big Beach With Seven",* s., #119/500, (06-25-93, Goldberg, #919A, illus.), 18 x 23 in., (45.7 x 58.4 cm.), serigraph (BP 131, DM 329, FR 1107, Y 20,458).

DURENDELLE, Edouard

$1100*   *Le Nouvelle Opera De Paris, Sculpture Ornementale, c. 1875,* num. in neg., orig. mount, photographer's credit, caption recto, (04-07-93, Swann, #197, illus.), 5½ x 11 in., photograph, albumen print (BP 727, DM 1779, FR 6021, Y 124,972).

DURER, Albrecht   German 1471-1528

$18,400*   *The Abduction Of Proserpine (B. 72; M., Holl. 67), 1516,* Meder a impression, rust marks, watermark, margins, repaired tear, discoloration, good cond., (05-13-93, Sotheby-NY, #125, illus.), 12¼ x 8⅜ in., (310 x 214 mm.), etching on iron (BP 12,080, DM 29,711, FR 100,218, Y 2,054,259).

$4276*   *Das Abendmahl (B. 53, M. 184/b (v.e.)), 1523,* (06-23-93, Kornfeld, #38, illus.), woodcut (BP 2905, DM 7235, FR 24,337, Y 465,846, SF 6440).

$585*   *Das Abendmahl (B.53, Meder 184 c), 1523,* stained, (12-12-92, Bassenge, #8080), 8⅜ x 11¹³⁄₁₆ in., (21.2 x 30 cm.), woodcut (BP 374, DM 919, FR 3133, Y 72,374).

$3753*   *Adoration Of The Kings (B. 87, Meder 199), c. 1503, 1511,* (06-04-93, Bassenge, #5138, illus.), 11¹³⁄₁₆ x 8³⁄₁₆ in., (30 x 20.8 cm.), woodcut (BP 2483, DM 6095, FR 20,542, Y 404,767).

$1544* *The Adoration Of The Magi (B. 3; M., Holl. 208), 1511,* Meder G impression, borderline, stain, repaired loss, foxing, Ex coll. K. E. Liphart (L. 1687) and R. Scholtz (L. 2241), (06-30-93, Sotheby-London, #115), 11⅝ x 8¾ in., (295 x 222 mm.), woodcut on paper w/a Fish-Bladder watermark (BP 1035, DM 2633, FR 8884, Y 165,434).

$2185* *The Adoration Of The Shepherds (B. 85, M., Holl. 197), c. 1503,* from The Life of the Virgin, good Meder IIc impression, trimmed, fold, tear, borderline w/touches of ink, watermark, (05-11-93, Christie-NY, #19), borderline 11¾ x 8¼ in., (298 x 210 mm.), woodcut on laid (BP 1395, DM 3442, FR 11,598, Y 240,348).

$1347* *Die Anbetung Der Konige (B. 87; M. 199/1511), c. 1503,* from Marienleben, watermark, (06-08-93, Karl/ Faber, #56), woodcut on paper (BP 885, DM 2186, FR 7361, Y 143,070).

$764* *Anbetung Der Konige (Bartsch 3; Meder 208/h (v. i.), 1511,* watermark, (06-23-93, Kornfeld, #32), woodcut (BP 519, DM 1293, FR 4348, Y 83,233, SF 1150).

$3450* *"The Angel With The Key To the Bottomless Pit" and "The Adoration OfThe Lamb" (B. 75 and 67; M., Holl. 178 and 176), 1511: A Pair,* from Apocalypse, watermark, thread margins, thin spot, stains, soiling; trimmed, fold, foxing, good cond., (05-13-93, Sotheby-NY, #142), one 15½ x 11⅛ in., (393 x 282 mm.), other 15⅜ x 11 in., (393 x 282 mm.), woodcut (BP 2265, DM 5571, FR 18,791, Y 385,174).

$6520* *The Annunciation (B. 83; M., Holl. 195), c. 1503,* from Life of the Virgin, proof, narrow margins, stains, (06-30-93, Sotheby-London, #113, illus.), 11⅝ x 8¼ in., (295 x 210 mm.), woodcut on paper w/a High Crowb watermark (BP 4370, DM 11,121, FR 37,514, Y 698,596).

$18,308* *"Apocalipsis Cu Figuris" (Meder 163-177), 1511: Fourteen,* mono. AD, (03-24-93, Venator/Hansten, #2512, illus.), approx. 15⅜ x 11 in., (39 x 28 cm.), woodcut (BP 12,398, DM 29,900, FR 101,768, Y 2,151,099).

BI *The Apocalyptic Woman (B. 71; M., Holl. 173),* from Apocalypse, German edit. 1498, repaired tears, vertical stain, thin spots, other defects, ex-coll., est. BP 2/2,500, (12-03-92, Sotheby-London, #46), 15¼ x 11 in., (390 x 280 mm.), woodcut.

$6038* *The Apocalyptic Woman (B. 72; M., Holl. 173), 1511,* from Apocalypse, watermark, narrow margins, thin spots, partially broken, good cond., (05-13-93, Sotheby-NY, #137, illus.), 15½ x 11 in., (393 x 280 mm.), woodcut (BP 3964, DM 9750, FR 32,887, Y 674,110).

$10,416* *Apollo And Diana (B. 68; M., Holl. 64),* Meder A impression, thread margins or trimmed, paper thin, pinhole(?), (06-29-93, Sotheby-London, #29, illus.), 4¼ x 2¾ in., (10.8 x 7 cm.), engraving (BP 6900, DM 17,589, FR 59,283, Y 1,108,793).

$845* *Der Apostel Bartholomaeus (Meder 45 a),* mono., d. AD 1523, prov., (03-24-93, Venator/Hansten, #2515), 4¾ x 2¹⁵⁄₁₆ in., (12 x 7.4 cm.), engraving (BP 572, DM 1380, FR 4697, Y 99,283).

BI *Apostel Thomas (B. 48; Meder 50 b), 1514,* est. DM 2,500, (12-04-92, Bassenge, #6145), 4½ x 2⅞ in., (11.5 x 7.3 cm.), engraving.

$996* *Die Armillarsphare (B. 262; M. 262), 1525,* (12-01-92, Karl/Faber, #63), woodcut (BP 658, DM 1588, FR 5410, Y 124,004).

$921* *The Ascension (B. 50, Meder 159), 1511,* prov., (06-04-93, Bassenge, #5133), 5 x 3¹¹⁄₁₆ in., (12.7 x 9.3 cm.), woodcut (BP 609, DM 1496, FR 5041, Y 99,331).

$1133* *Ascension And Coronation Of Mary (B. 94, Meder 206 b), 1510,* watermark, prov., (06-04-93, Bassenge, #5140), 11⁷⁄₁₆ x 8³⁄₁₆ in., (29 x 20.8 cm.), woodcut (BP 750, DM 1840, FR 6201, Y 122,196).

$8625* *The Assumption And Coronation Of The Virgin (B. 94, M., Holl. 206), 1510,* from The Life of the Virgin, proof, w/Latin text, thread margins, crease, staining, very good cond., watermark, (05-11-93, Christie-NY, #21A, illus.), borderline 11⅜ x 8⅛ in., (289 x 206 mm.), woodcut on laid (BP 5506, DM 13,587, FR 45,780, Y 948,741).

$2583* *Aufenthalt In Aegypten (Bartsch 90; Meder 202/Ib), c. 1504,* from Marienleben, (11-03-92, Fischer, #5014, illus.), 11⁹⁄₁₆ x 8¼ in., (29.4 x 21 cm.), woodcut (BP 1667, DM 4041, FR 13,696, Y 315,500, SF 3600).

$5477* *Die Auferstehung (B. 17; M. 17 a/b (v.d)), 1512,* num. 16 from series Die Kupferstichpassion, (12-01-92, Karl/ Faber, #53, illus.), engraving (BP 3619, DM 8730, FR 29,750, Y 681,897).

$1756* *Die Auferstehung Christi (B. 17, M. 17/b (v.d.), D. 64), 1512,* sheet 15 of series: Die Kupferstichpassion, prov., (06-23-93, Kornfeld, #26), engraving (BP 1193, DM 2971, FR 9994, Y 191,306, SF 2645).

$3163* *The Beast With Two Horns Like A Lamb (B. 74; M. Holl. 175), 1511,* from Apocalypse, narrow margins, surface dirt, thin spots, good cond., (05-13-93, Sotheby-NY, #140), 15⅜ x 11 in., (391 x 280 mm.), woodcut (BP 2077, DM 5107, FR 17,228, Y 353,132).

$3116* *The Betrothal Of The Virgin (B. 82, Meder 194), c. 1504/05, 1511,* watermark, (06-04-93, Bassenge, #5137, illus.), 11⅝ x 8¹⁄₁₆ in., (29.5 x 20.5 cm.), woodcut (BP 2062, DM 5060, FR 17,055, Y 336,066).

BI *Beweinung Christi (B. 13; Meder 122), c. 1497-1500,* Textausgabe 1511, stained, est. DM 2,800, (12-04-92, Bassenge, #6155), 15¼ x 10¹³⁄₁₆ in., (38.8 x 27.4 cm.), woodcut.

$4978* *Beweinung Christi (B. 14; M. 14 b(v.c)), 1507,* num. 12 from series Die Kupferstichpassion, (12-01-92, Karl/Faber, #52, illus.), engraving (BP 3289, DM 7934, FR 27,040, Y 619,771).

$830* *Bildnis Philipp Melanchthon (B. 105; M. 104 c/d (v.f)), 1526,* restored, (12-01-92, Karl/Faber, #58), engraving (BP 548, DM 1323, FR 4508, Y 103,337).

BI *The Birth Of The Virgin (B. 80; M., Holl. 192), 1511,* from Life of the Virgin, proof, watermark, trimmed, mended split, good cond., ex-coll. K. Krauskopf, est. $12/18,000, (05-13-93, Sotheby-NY, #145, illus.), 11¾ x 8¼ in., (297 x 210 mm.), woodcut.

$9957* *Die Busse Des Heiligen Chrysostomus (B. 63; M. 54 a/b (v.f)), c. 1497,* holes, (12-01-92, Karl/Faber, #56, illus.), engraving (BP 6579, DM 15,870, FR 54,085, Y 1,239,666).

BI *Cain Killing Abel (B. 1; M., Holl. 106), 1511,* Meder d impression, trimmed, tip of corner restored, breaks touched in, printer's crease, folds, good cond., ex-coll. Hans Brisebach, est. $2/2,500, (05-13-93, Sotheby-NY, #131), 4½ x 3¼ in., (114 x 83 mm.), woodcut.

BI *The Calvary With The Crosses (B. 59; M., Holl. 180),* Meder D impression, gap in border, touched in, surface dirt, thin patches, collector's mark, est. BP 1/1,500, (12-03-92, Sotheby-London, #48), 8¼ x 5¼ in., (212 x 143 mm.), woodcut.

$3946* *Christ Among The Doctors (B. 91; M. Holl. 203),* from the Life of the Virgin, thread margins, trimmed, break, filled in w/pen and ink, creases, Ex coll. C. Schlosser (L. 636), (06-30-93, Sotheby-London, #114, illus.), 11¾ x 8¼ in., (298 x 210 mm.), woodcut on paper w/a High Crown watermark (BP 2645, DM 6730, FR 22,704, Y 422,801).

$3450* *Christ Among The Doctors (B. 91; M., Holl. 203), 1511,* from Life of the Virgin, proof, watermark, trimmed, repaired splits along crease, repaired tear, thin spots, foxing, good cond., (05-13-93, Sotheby-NY, #146), 11¾ x 8¼ in., (297 x 209 mm.), woodcut (BP 2265, DM 5571, FR 18,791, Y 385,174).

$385* *Christ Among The Doctors (Bartsch 91, Meder 203e), c. 1503,* from the Life of the Virgin, (03-24-93, Grogan, #6), 11⅝ x 8⅛ in., (29.5 x 20.6 cm.), woodcut (BP 261, DM 629, FR 2140, Y 45,236).

$4025* *Christ Before Caiaphas (B., M., Holl. 6), 1512,* from the Passion, thread margins, trimmed, spots, surface dirt, soiling, good cond., (05-13-93, Sotheby-NY, #118), 4⅝ x 2⅞ in., (118 x 74 mm.), engraving (BP 2642, DM 6499, FR 21,923, Y 449,369).

$1042* *Christ Crowned With Thorns (B., M., Holl. 9), 1512,* from The Passion, narrow to thread margins, trimmed, replaced area, abrasions, defects, (06-29-93, Sotheby-London, #20, illus.), 4½ x 2¾ in., (11.4 x 7 cm.), engraving (BP 690, DM 1760, FR 5931, Y 110,922).

BI *Christ On The Cross (B. 24; M., Holl. 23), 1508,* watermark, thread margins, repair, discoloration, defects, prov., est. BP 4/5,000, (12-01-92, Christie-London, #179, illus.), plate 5⁵⁄₁₆ x 3⅞ in., (135 x 98 mm.), engraving.

$13,887* *Christ On The Mount Of Olives (B., M., Holl. 19), 1515,* Meder I B impression, surface tone, thread margins, trimmed, repairs, very good cond., ex. coll. S. Jancsy (L. 1529d; and F.L.), (06-29-93, Sotheby-London, #19, illus.), 8¾ x 6 in., (22.2 x 15.2 cm.), etching (BP 9200, DM 23,450, FR 79,038, Y 1,478,284).

BI *Christ On The Mount Of Olives (B., Meder, Holl. 19), 1515,* Meder b impression, rust marks, plate tone, trimmed, corner restored,thin spots, good cond., ex-coll. R.L. von Retberg (?), est. $15/25,000, (05-13-93, Sotheby-NY, #117, illus.), 8¾ x 6⅛ in., (221 x 155 mm.), etching on iron.

$2481* *Christus Am Kreuz (B. 13; M. 13 b), 1511,* from the Passion, (06-08-93, Karl/Faber, #48, illus.), engraving (BP 1631, DM 4026, FR 13,557, Y 263,516).

$11,454* *Christus Am Kreuz (B. 24; M. 23/a/b (v/e.); D. 47), 1508,* (06-23-93, Kornfeld, #27, illus.), engraving (BP 7781, DM 19,381, FR 65,191, Y 1,247,848, SF 17,250).

BI *Christus Am Kreuz Mit Der Engelbordure (B./Strauss 56, Meder 183, III b(d)), 1516,* d., staining, tears, damage, est. SC 12/14,000, (11-11-92, Dorotheum, #308, illus.), 11⅝ x 9⅝ in., (29.5 x 24.4 cm.), woodcut.

$1316* *Christus Am Oelberg (B. 19; H. 425; R. 212; W. 158; M. 19, II b), 1515,* mono., d. in plate, i., foxed, watermark, trimmed, (10-09-92, Winterberg, #759, illus.), image 8¾ x 6⅛ in., (22.2 x 15.5 cm.), etching (BP 781, DM 1955, FR 6564, Y 160,214).

$4978* *Christus Am Olberg (B. 4; Meder 4 a/b (v.e)), 1508,* num. 2 from series Die Kupferstichpassion, (12-01-92, Karl/Faber, #51, illus.), engraving (BP 3289, DM 7934, FR 27,040, Y 619,771).

$4237* *Christus Am Olberg (Bartsch 4; Meder 4 b; Strauss 48), 1508,* sheet 2 of Kupferstichpassion, S. Rosenstamm, prov., (06-10-93, Hauswedell/Nolt, #69), engraving (BP 2771, DM 6900, FR 23,229, Y 449,740).

$1680* *Christus In Der Vorholle (B. 14; M. 121/III/b. (v. d.)), c. 1510,* sheet 8 of series Die grosse Passion, (06-23-93, Kornfeld, #35), woodcut (BP 1141, DM 2843, FR 9562, Y 183,026, SF 2530).

$2138* *Christus In Emmaus (B. 48; M. 157/II (v. IV)), 1509-1511,* sheet 32 of series Die kleine Holzschnittpassion, (06-23-93, Kornfeld, #37), woodcut (BP 1452, DM 3618, FR 12,168, Y 232,923, SF 3220).

$1444* *Christus Vor Pilatus (B. 7; Meder 7 c), 1512,* from Kupferstichpassion, prov., (12-04-92, Bassenge, #6144), 4⁹⁄₁₆ x 2¹⁵⁄₁₆ in., (11.6 x 7.4 cm.), engraving (BP 926, DM 2300, FR 7801, Y 180,275).

$2596* *Christus Vor Pilatus (B.7 M. 7/(v.d.); D. 64) 1512,* sheet 5 of series Die Kupferstichpassion, prov., (06-23-93, Kornfeld, #25), engraving (BP 1764, DM 4393, FR 14,775, Y 282,819, SF 3910).

BI *Christus Vor Pilatus (Bartsch 7; Heller 208; Rethberg 96; Winkler 138; Meder 7 c), 1512,* mono. in plate, trimmed, est. DM 2,500, (10-09-92, Winterberg, #758, illus.), 4⅝ x 2¹⁵⁄₁₆ in., (11.7 x 7.5 cm.), engraving.

$1332* *A Coat Of Arms With A Skull (B. 100; M., Holl. 97), 1503,* 2nd (final) state, trimmed, corner made-up, hole, foxed, defects, prov., (12-01-92, Christie-London, #184), engraving (BP 880, DM 2123, FR 7235, Y 165,837).

$6325* *Coat Of Arms With A Skull (B. 101; M., Holl. 98), 1503,* (Meder I a/b of d), patch dry printing, good cond., surface disturbance, brown stains, foxing, (05-13-93, Sotheby-NY, #129, illus.), 8¾ x 6¼ in., (222 x 160 mm.), engraving (BP 4152, DM 10,213, FR 34,450, Y 706,152).

$12,151* *Coat-Of-Arms With A Lion And A Cock (B. 100; M., Holl. 97),* Meder A impression, watermark, trimmed on and outside borderline, abraded repaired areas, thin spots, cockling, (06-29-93, Sotheby-London, #38, illus.), 7¼ x 4½ in., (18.4 x 11.4 cm.), engraving on paper (BP 8050, DM 20,518, FR 69,158, Y 1,293,485).

BI *Coat-Of-Arms With A Skull (B. 101; M., Holl. 98), 1503,* Meder A impression, ink smudged in printing, trimmed outside borderline, crease, surface dirt, ex. coll. E. Th. Rodenacker (L. 2438); Friedrich Kalle (L. 1021); F. Debois (L. 985), est. BP 20/30,00, (06-29-93, Sotheby-London, #39, illus.), 8½ x 6 in., (21.6 x 15.2 cm.), engraving.

$2070* *The Cook And His Wife (B. 84; M., Holl. 85), c. 1496-97,* Meder a impression, watermark, trimmed to borderline, remargined, restored strip, discoloration, defects, ex-coll. J.S. Morgan, (05-13-93, Sotheby-NY, #128, illus.), 4⅜ x 3⅛ in., (110 x 78 mm.), engraving (BP 1359, DM 3342, FR 11,275, Y 231,104).

$708* *The Doubting Of Thomas (B. 49, Meder 158), 1509-11,* prov., watermark, (06-04-93, Bassenge, #5132), 4¹⁵⁄₁₆ x 3¹³⁄₁₆ in., (12.6 x 9.7 cm.), woodcut (BP 468, DM 1150, FR 3875, Y 76,359).

BI *The Dream Of The Doctor (B. 76, M., Holl. 70), c. 1498,* early Meder a-b? impression, margins, staining, glue remains, very good cond., watermark, prov., prop. Montclair Art Museum, est. $10/15,000, (05-11-93, Christie-NY, #16, illus.), plate 7⁷⁄₁₆ x 4¾ in., (189 x 121 mm.), engraving on laid.

$31,625* *The Dream Of The Doctor (B. 76; M., Holl. 70), 1497,* watermark, trimmed on borderline on three sides into work above, repaired tear, rubbed spots, repairs, stain, rubbed spot in image, good cond., ex-coll. M.J. Morgan, (05-13-93, Sotheby-NY, #126, illus.), 7⅜ x 4¾ in., (188 x 121 mm.), engraving (BP 20,762, DM 51,066, FR 172,249, Y 3,530,758).

$1451* *Einzug Christi In Jerusalem (B. 22; M. 130/II (v. V)), 1509-1511,* sheet 5 of series die kleine Holzschnittpassion, (06-23-93, Kornfeld, #36), woodcut (BP 986, DM 2455, FR 8258, Y 158,078, SF 2185).

BI *Der Engel Mit Dem Schlussel Zum Abgrund (B. 75; Meder 178), 1486,* est. DM 7,500, (12-04-92, Bassenge, #6163, illus.), 15½ x 11⅛ in., (39.3 x 28.3 cm.), woodcut.

$3955* *Der Engel Mit Dem Schlussel Zum Abgrund (Bartsch 75; Meder and Boon-Scheller 178), 1496-98,* sheet 15 of Apokalypse, (06-10-93, Hauswedell/Nolt, #76), woodcut (BP 2587, DM 6440, FR 21,683, Y 419,807).

$1690* *Der Engel Mit Dem Schlussel Zum Abgrund (Meder 178),* from Apokalypse, mono. AD, foxing, (03-24-93, Venator/Hansten, #2513), image 15⁷⁄₁₆ x 11⅛ in., (39.2 x 28.2 cm.), woodcut (BP 1144, DM 2760, FR 9394, Y 198,567).

$1760* *The Engraved Passion: Harrowing Of Hell (Christ In Limbo) (B. 16, M.Holl. 16), 1512,* Meder d impression, thread margins, good cond., repaired holes, hinge remains, skinned area, staining, soiling, notations, (10-28-92, Butterfield, #2593), 4⁹⁄₁₆ x 2¹⁵⁄₁₆ in., (116 x 75 mm.), engraving on laid paper (BP 1121, DM 2718, FR 9229, Y 215,951).

$1169* *Die Enthauptung Der Hl. Katharina (Bartsch 120; Meder 236 g),* mono. AD, (11-11-92, Dorotheum, #322A), 15⅜ x 11¼ in., (39 x 28.5 cm.), woodcut (BP 774, DM 1868, FR 6261, Y 145,362, SC 6160).

$715* *The Entombment Of Christ (B. 13),* from "The Great Passion", (10-30-92, Sloan, #2810), 15¼ x 10⅞ in., (38.7 x 27.6 cm.), woodcut (BP 458, DM 1100, FR 3732, Y 88,567).

$498* *Eroffnung Des Sechsten Siegels (B. 65; M. 168/1511), 1496-1498,* from the Apocalypse, (12-01-92, Karl/Faber, #59), woodcut (BP 329, DM 794, FR 2705, Y 62,002).

$3051* *Eustachius (St. Hubertus) (B. 57; M. 60d/f (v.k.)), c. 1501,* (04-27-93, Hartung, #2431), engraving (BP 1940, DM 4831, FR 16,342, Y 341,925).

$17,359* *Five Soldiers And A Turk On Horseback (B. 88; M., Holl. 81),* Meder A-B impression, trimmed w/in platemark, outside or on boderline, defects, repairs, surface dirt, abrasions, ex. coll. Alfred Morrison (L. 151); Felix Somary and R. Ritter von Gutmann (L. 2770), (06-29-93, Sotheby-London, #34, illus.), 5⅛ x 5¾ in., (13 x 14.6 cm.), engraving (BP 11,500, DM 29,313, FR 98,799, Y 1,847,882).

$1093* *The Flight Into Egypt (B. 89, M., Holl. 201), c. 1504-5,* from The Life of the Virgin, Meder IIIf impression, margins, tears, wormhole, staining, defects, watermark, (05-11-93, Christie-NY, #20), borderline 11¹³⁄₁₆ x 8¼ in., (300 x 210 mm.), woodcut on laid (BP 698, DM 1722, FR 5801, Y 120,229).

$330* *The Flogging,* mono. AD, d. 1512, poor cond.?, (02-07-93, Bakker, #127), sheet 4½ x 3 in., (11.4 x 7.6 cm.), engraving (BP 228, DM 547, FR 1850, Y 41,065).

$1298* *Die Flucht Nach Agypten (B. 89; M. 201/III), c. 1503,* sheet 13 of series Das Marienleben, (06-23-93, Kornfeld, #45), woodcut (BP 882, DM 2196, FR 7388, Y 141,410, SF 1955).

$3738* *"The Four Avenging Angels" and "The Seven Angels With The Trumpet" (B. 69 and 68; M., Holl. 171 and 170), 1511: A Pair,* from the Apocalypse, Latin edit., narow margins, thin spots, trimmed,repaired tear, stains; strip cut off and rejoined, ex-coll. Leopold I, (05-13-93, Sotheby-NY, #135), one 15½ x 11⅛ in., (394 x 283 mm.), other 15⅝ x 11 in., (394 x 283 mm.), woodcut (BP 2454, DM 6036, FR 20,359, Y 417,327).

$3520* *Four Naked Women, 1497,* also called The Four Witches, Lugt 1215, thread margins 3 sides, good cond., Dr. Gustave Seeligmann Coll., (12-08-92, Swann, #93, illus.), 7⅜ x 5⅛ in., (18.7 x 13 cm.), engraving on watermarked laid paper (BP 2206, DM 5480, FR 18,684, Y 436,292).

$1733* *Das Fraulein Zu Pferd Und Der Landsknecht (B. 82; Meder 84), c. 1497,* stained, (12-04-92, Bassenge, #6148), 4³⁄₁₆ x 2¹⁵⁄₁₆ in., (10.7 x 7.6 cm.), engraving (BP 1112, DM 2760, FR 9363, Y 216,355).

$435* *Frederick The Wise - Elector Of Saxony (B. 54),* Meder d/e impression, watermark, large margins, mounting, foxed, (10-27-92, Phillips-London, #13), plate 7⅝ x 5 in., (194 x 127 mm.), engraving on laid (BP 275, DM 667, FR 2262, Y 53,211).

$23,672* *Die Geburt Christi (Bartsch 2; Meder 2/b; Dodgeson 38), 1504,* prov., (06-23-93, Kornfeld, #24, illus.), engraving (BP 16,082, DM 40,054, FR 134,730, Y 2,578,930, SF 35,650).

$1547* *Die Geburt Christi (Meder 129), 1511,* from the small Passion, mono. AD, (09-14-92, Venator/Hansten, #1489), 5¹⁄₁₆ x 3⅞ in., (12.9 x 9.9 cm.), woodcut (BP 818, DM 2300, FR 7793, Y 192,365).

$6491* *Gefangennahme Christi (B. 8; M. 116/I (v. III/e)), 1510,* sheet 3 of series Die grosse Passion, watermark, (06-23-93, Kornfeld, #34, illus.), woodcut (BP 4410, DM 10,983, FR 36,944, Y 707,158, SF 9775).

BI *Die Geisselung Christi (B. 8, Meder 117), c. 1497-1500,* from Grossen Holzschnittpassion, Textausgabe before 1511, est. DM 3,500, (12-04-92, Bassenge, #6154), 15³⁄₁₆ x 10¹³⁄₁₆ in., (38.6 x 27.5 cm.), woodcut.

$30,544* *Das Grosse Pferd (B. 97; M. 94/a (v. f.)), 1505,* watermark, early print, (06-23-93, Kornfeld, #29, illus.), engraving (BP 20,750, DM 51,682, FR 173,842, Y 3,327,596, SF 46,000).

BI *Der Heilige Antonius Vor Der Stadt (B. 58, M. 51), 1519,* watermark, prov., est. DM 1,800, (12-04-92, Bassenge, #6146), 3⅞ x 5⁹⁄₁₆ in., (9.9 x 14.1 cm.), drypoint.

$878* *Die Heilige Familie (B. 43, Meder 44 III c.), c. 1512,* (12-12-92, Bassenge, #8079), 8⁵⁄₁₆ x 7⅜ in., (21.1 x 18.7 cm.), engraving (BP 561, DM 1380, FR 4703, Y 108,623).

$32,071* *Die Heilige Familie Mit Den Hasen (B. 102; M. 212/a (v. i.)), 1496-148,* early print, watermark, prov., (06-23-93, Kornfeld, #48, illus.), woodcut (BP 21,787, DM 54,266, FR 182,533, Y 3,493,954, SF 48,300).

$5345* *Die Heilige Familie Mit Funf Engeln (B. 99; M. 214/a (v. g.)),* before 1505, watermark, (06-23-93, Kornfeld, #47, illus.), woodcut (BP 3631, DM 9044, FR 30,421, Y 582,307, SF 8050).

$1300* *Die Heilige Familie Mit Zwei Engeln In Der Gewolbten Halle (B. 100, Meder 213 d), c. 1504,* prov., foxed, watermark, (12-04-92, Bassenge, #6167), 8⁹⁄₁₆ x 6 in., (21.7 x 15.3 cm.), woodcut (BP 834, DM 2070, FR 7023, Y 162,297).

BI *Der Heilige Franziskus, Die Wundmale Empfangend (B. 110; Meder 224 c), 1503-1505,* watermark, est. DM 2,000, (12-04-92, Bassenge, #6168), 8⁹⁄₁₆ x 5¹¹⁄₁₆ in., (21.7 x 14.5 cm.), woodcut.

$14,508* *Der Heilige Hubertus - Der Heilige Eustachius (B. 57; M. 60/d (v .k.) D. 32), c. 1501,* watermark, (06-23-93, Kornfeld, #28, illus.), engraving (BP 9856, DM 24,548, FR 82,573, Y 1,580,564, SF 21,850).

$774* *Die Heilige Sippe (Meder 216),* d. 1511, (09-14-92, Venator/Hansten, #1490), 8¼ x 8¹⁄₁₆ in., (21 x 20.4 cm.), woodcut (BP 409, DM 1151, FR 3899, Y 96,245).

$1909* *Die Heimsuchung (B. 84; M. 196/II (v. III/g), c. 1509,* watermark, (06-23-93, Kornfeld, #44), woodcut (BP 1297, DM 3230, FR 10,865, Y 207,975, SF 2875).

$1271* *Hercules (Bartsch 127; Meder 238, 2 a; Boon-Scheller 238 b), 1496-98,* watermark, (06-10-93, Hauswedell/Nolt, #80), woodcut on hand-made (BP 831, DM 2070, FR 6968, Y 134,911).

$3960* *Hercules At The Crossroads, Or The Effects Of Jealousy (Bartsch 73, Meder/Hollstein 63), c. 1498-1504,* Meder Plate IV, no. 20, Lugt 1494, mono., trimmed, repaired tears, other restorations, annot., prov., Dr. Gustave Seeligmann Coll. stamp verso, (12-08-92, Swann, #94, illus.), 12½ x 8⁹⁄₁₆ in., (31.8 x 21.7 cm.), engraving (BP 2482, DM 6165, FR 21,019, Y 490,828).

BI *Hercules, Or The Effects Of Jealousy (B. 73; M., Holl. 63),* Meder IIIA impression, trimmed irregularly, short nicks, losses, defects, short tear, discolored, other minor defects, est. BP 2,5/3,000, (12-03-92, Sotheby-London, #42, illus.), 12¾ x 8¾ in., (324 x 222 mm.), engraving on paper w/watermark.

BI *Hercules, Or The Effects Of Jealousy (B. 73; M., Holl. 63), 1498,* Meder IIIa impression, watermark, reparied tear, nicks, made-up, creases, est. BP 3/4,000, (12-01-92, Christie-London, #185, illus.), sheet 12⁹⁄₁₆ x 8¾ in., (319 x 222 mm.), engraving.

BI *Die Herodias Empfangt Das Haupt Des Johannes (B. 126; Meder 232 g), 1511,* prov., margin soiled, est. DM 2,500, (12-04-92, Bassenge, #6170), 7½ x 5³⁄₁₆ in., (19.1 x 13.1 cm.), woodcut.

$1955* *The Holy Family In Egypt (B. 90, M., Holl. 202), 1502,* from The Life of the Virgin, narrow margins, staining, (05-11-93, Christie-NY, #21), borderline 11⅞ x 8¼ in., (302 x 210 mm.), woodcut on laid (BP 1248, DM 3080, FR 10,377, Y 215,048).

$743* *"The Holy Family In Egypt" From "The Life Of The Virgin" (Bartsch 90,Meder, Hollstein 202),* watermark (Meder 127), thread margins, pinholes, staining, back coverlot, (06-16-93, Bonhams-Chelsea, #304, illus.), 11⅞ x 8¼ in., (30.2 x 21 cm.), woodcut (BP 495, DM 1233, FR 4139, Y 79,245).

$1044* *The Holy Family With Five Angels (Modest Woodcut) (B. 99),* Meder A, watermarks, trimmed to borderline, repaired tear, tear, (10-27-92, Phillips-London, #15), plate 8½ x 5¾ in., (216 x 146 mm.), woodcut on white laid (BP 660, DM 1600, FR 5429, Y 127,706).

$21,699* *The Holy Family With The Butterfly (B. 44; M., Holl. 42),* Meder A impression, burr, polishing scratches in sky, watermark, backed tear, paper loss, foxing, stains, (06-29-93, Sotheby-London, #24, illus.), 9 x 7⅛ in., (22.9 x 18.1 cm.), engraving (BP 14,375, DM 36,641, FR 123,500, Y 2,309,879).

$2574* *The Holy Framily With The Butterfly (B. 44; M., Holl. 42), c. 1495,* good but later impression, trimmed to image, corner restored, good cond., (06-30-93, Sotheby-London, #112), 7⅛ x 9⅛ in., (181 x 232 mm.), engraving on paper w/o a watermark (BP 1725, DM 4390, FR 14,810, Y 275,796).

$2588* *The Holy Kinship With The Lute-Playing Angels (B. 97; M., Holl. 216),1511,* watermark, margins, repair, discoloration, foxing, (05-13-93, Sotheby-NY, #147), 8⅜ x 8½ in., (213 x 217 mm.), woodcut (BP 1699, DM 4179, FR 14,096, Y 288,936).

$1840* *The Holy Trinity (B., M., Holl. 187), 1511,* strong Meder i impression, break in block, watermark, spot, creasing,-center fold, foxing, good cond., ex-coll. Naudet and F. Gawet, (05-13-93, Sotheby-NY, #143), 15½ x 11⅜ in., (395 x 290 mm.), woodcut (BP 1208, DM 2971, FR 10,022, Y 205,426).

$1725* *Joachim And The Angel (B. 78; M., Holl. 190), c. 1504,* from Life of the Virgin, proof, watermark, trimmed, repaired tear, discoloration, ex-coll. Dr. Julius Hofmann, (05-13-93, Sotheby-NY, #144), 11⅝ x 8¼ in., (296 x 210 mm.), woodcut (BP 1132, DM 2785, FR 9395, Y 192,587).

$826* *Joachim Et L'Ange (F.W.H. Hollstein, 190),* folded, faults, (06-16-93, Ader Tajan, #10), 11⁷⁄₁₆ x 8¹⁄₁₆ in., (29 x 20.5 cm.), wood engraving (BP 551, DM 1371, FR 4602, Y 88,097).

$2266* *Joachim In The Field (B. 78, Meder 190 Ohne Texte a),* c. 1504, from the Life of Mary, watermark, (06-04-93, Bassenge, #5136), 11¹¹⁄₁₆ x 8¼ in., (29.7 x 20.9 cm.), woodcut (BP 1499, DM 3680, FR 12,403, Y 244,392).

$265* *Die Jungfrau Auf Der Mondsichel (B. 76: M. 188/III a/b (v.f)),* c. 1510, trimmed, creases, (12-01-92, Karl/Faber, #61), woodcut (BP 175, DM 422, FR 1439, Y 32,993).

$1011* *Die Jungfrau Erscheint Johannes (B. 60, Meder 163 b),* 1496-1498, title sheet from Apokalypse, prov.   ., (12-04-92, Bassenge, #6158), 7⅞ x 8¼ in., (20 x 21 cm.), woodcut (BP 648, DM 1610, FR 5462, Y 126,217).

$21,186* *Die Jungfrau Mit Dem Kind Im Strahlenkranz Auf Der Mondsichel (Bartsch 33; Meder 35 a; Boon-Scheller 35),* 1514, (06-10-93, Hauswedell/Nolt, #70, illus.), engraving (BP 13,858, DM 34,499, FR 116,151, Y 2,248,806).

$882* *Die Jungfrau Mit Dem Wickelkind (B. 38; M. 0e),* 1520, stained, prov., (11-03-92, Hartung, #4036), engraving (BP 569, DM 1380, FR 4677, Y 107,732).

$6520* *Die Kanone (B. 99; M. 96 c/d),* 1518, watermark, (06-08-93, Karl/Faber, #52, illus.), steel etching (BP 4286, DM 10,579, FR 35,628, Y 692,512).

$2744* *Die Kanone (B. 99; Meder 96 II f),* 1518, (12-04-92, Bassenge, #6152), 8½ x 12¹¹⁄₁₆ in., (21.6 x 32.2 cm.), Eisenradierung (BP 1760, DM 4370, FR 14,824, Y 342,572).

$1695* *Kardinal Albrecht Von Brandenburg (Bartsch 103; Meder 101/d/e; Boon-Scheller 101),* 1523, (06-10-93, Hauswedell/Nolt, #72), engraving on thin hand-made (BP 1109, DM 2760, FR 9293, Y 179,917).

$5328* *The Kiss Of Judas (B. 7; M., Holl. 116),* 1510, from The large Passion, proof, watermark, trimmed, staining, good cond., prov., (12-01-92, Christie-London, #176, illus.), 15⁹⁄₁₆ x 11 in., (395 x 280 mm.), woodcut (BP 3520, DM 8492, FR 28,941, Y 663,347).

$103* *Der Kleine Kurier, Galloping Rider (B. 80),* init. mono. in plate, (06-08-93, Ritchie, #19, illus.), 4⅝ x 3¼ in., (11.7 x 8.3 cm.), etching (BP 68, DM 167, FR 563, Y 10,940, C$ 132).

$944* *Knoten Mit Sieben Ringformigen Geflechten, Shwarzer Mittelscheibe U.Vier Herzformigen Eckstukken (B. 143; M. 277/IIb (v.c)),* from Die sechs Knoten. 1505-07, watermark, (04-27-93, Hartung, #2432), woodcut (BP 600, DM 1495, FR 5056, Y 105,794).

BI *Kreuztragung (Bartsch 10, Meder 119),* mono., AD, foxing, before letter from 1511, est. SC 120/130,000, (11-11-92, Dorotheum, #307, illus.), 15⁷⁄₁₆ x 11⁵⁄₁₆ in., (39.2 x 28.7 cm.), woodcut.

$807* *L'Adoration Des Mages (F.W.H. Hollstein 199),* fault, loss, reddish stains, w/out margins, (02-03-93, Ader Tajan, #21), 11⅝ x 8¼ in., (29.6 x 20.9 cm.), wood engraving (BP 563, DM 1329, FR 4506, Y 100,386).

$2760* *A Landscape With A Canon (B. 99, M., Holl. 90),* 1518, Meder IId impression, trimmed on platemark, foxing, laid down, prov., (05-11-93, Christie-NY, #18), sheet 8½ x 12¾ in., (216 x 324 mm.), etching on laid (BP 1762, DM 4348, FR 14,650, Y 303,597).

$45,134* *The Landscape With The Cannon (B. 99; M., Holl. 96),* 1518, Meder A impression, 1st state before rustmarks, watermark, trimmed outside borderline or into work, repair, good cond., (06-29-93, Sotheby-London, #37, illus.), 8½ x 12½ in., (21.6 x 31.8 cm.), etching on iron on paper (BP 29,900, DM 76,214, FR 256,881, Y 4,804,556).

$15,347* *The Large Horse (B. 97; M., Holl. 94),* 1505, Meder A impression, margins, loss, thin patches, discoloration, est.BP 8/12,000, (12-03-92, Sotheby-London, #40, illus.), 6½ x 4¾ in., (165 x 121 mm.), engraving (BP 9900, DM 24,134, FR 82,378, Y 1,909,543).

$660* *The Large Passion: Resurrection (M. 124),* 1510, margins trimmed to image, good cond., paper loss, restored tears, holes, creases, wear to image, staining, surface soiling, (10-28-92, Butterfield, #2594), 15⅜ x 10⅜ in., (391 x 264 mm.), woodcut on thin wove (BP 421, DM 1019, FR 3461, Y 80,982).

$275* *The Last Supper [B. 24],* from the Small Passion, (12-10-92, Sloan, #2095), 5 x 3⅞ in., (12.7 x 9.8 cm.), wood engraving (BP 177, DM 435, FR 1486, Y 34,018).

$4276* *Das Letzte Abendmahl (B. 5, M. 114/II (v. III/g)),* 1510, sheet 1 of series Die grosse Passion, (06-23-93, Kornfeld, #33), woodcut (BP 2905, DM 7235, FR 24,337, Y 465,846, SF 6440).

$1589* *Der Liebesantrag (B. 93, Meder 77 I b),* before 1496, (12-04-92, Bassenge, #6151), 5⅝ x 5⅜ in., (14.3 x 13.7 cm.), engraving (BP 1019, DM 2531, FR 8585, Y 198,377).

$715* *The Life Of The Virgin: The Circumcision Of Christ (M. 198),* 1504, Meder e impression, from later edit. after text, c. 1580, thread margins, good cond., creases, hinge remains, surface soiling, prov., watermark, (10-28-92, Butterfield, #2595), 11⅝ x 8⁵⁄₁₆ in., (295 x 211 mm.), woodcut on laid paper (BP 456, DM 1104, FR 3749, Y 87,730).

$1841* *Lobgesang Der Auserwahlten Im Himmel (B. 67, Meder 176),* 1511, from the Apocalypse, watermark, (06-04-93, Bassenge, #5135), 15⁷⁄₁₆ x 11 in., (39.2 x 28 cm.), woodcut (BP 1218, DM 2990, FR 10,077, Y 198,555).

$8680* *The Madonna And Child On A Grassy Bench (B. 34, M., Holl. 31),* 1503, Meder A impression, narrow margins or trimmed, made up areas, laid down, defects, (06-29-93, Sotheby-London, #22, illus.), 2¾ x 4¼ in., (7 x 10.8 cm.), engraving (BP 5750, DM 14,657, FR 49,402, Y 923,994).

$2588* *The Man Of Sorrows With Arms Outstretched (B., M., Holl. 20),* c. 1500, Meder b impression, plate tone, watermark, thread margins, thin spots, foxing, soiling, good cond., (05-13-93, Sotheby-NY, #119, illus.), 4⅝ x 2¾ in., (116 x 70 mm.), engraving (BP 1699, DM 4179, FR 14,096, Y 288,936).

$4813* *Maria Mit Der Meerkatze (B. 42; M. 30 g (v.l)),* c. 1498, trimmed, (12-01-92, Karl/Faber, #55, illus.), engraving (BP 3180, DM 7671, FR 26,143, Y 599,228).

BI *Maria Verkundigung (B. 83; Meder 195 f),* c. 1503, est. DM 2,500, (12-04-92, Bassenge, #6165), 11⅝ x 8⅜ in., (29.6 x 21.3 cm.), woodcut.

$2240* *Maria Von Einem Engel Gekront (B. 37; M. 41 II b),* 1520, trimmed, prov., (12-01-92, Karl/Faber, #54), engraving (BP 1480, DM 3570, FR 12,167, Y 278,884).

BI *Marias Besuch Bei Elisabeth Und Zacharias (Meder 196),* c. 1503, from Marienleben, mono. AD, est. DM 4,200-, (03-24-93, Venator/Hansten, #2514), 11¹¹⁄₁₆ x 8¼ in., (29.7 x 20.9 cm.), woodcut.

$76,360* *Das Marienleben (B. 76-95; M. 188-207, jeweils II, von III),* c. 1503-1510: Nineteen, (06-23-93, Kornfeld, #41, illus.), woodcut (BP 51,875, DM 129,205, FR 434,604, Y 8,318,989, SF 115,000).

$2066* *Marienleben: Ten,* later printing, (11-03-92, Fischer, #5015), 11⅝ x 7¹¹⁄₁₆ in., (29.5 x 19.5 cm.), woodcut (BP 1333, DM 3232, FR 10,954, Y 252,351, SF 2880).

$1826* *Mariens Tempelgang (B. 81; M. 193/III e (v.h)),* c. 1504/05, from the Marienleben, stained, (12-01-92, Karl/Faber, #62), woodcut (BP 1206, DM 2910, FR 9919, Y 227,341).

BI *Mariens Tempelgang (B. 81; Meder 193),* c. 1504-1505, from Marienleben, 1511, stained, est. DM 1,800, (12-04-92, Bassenge, #6164), 11¹¹⁄₁₆ x 8⅛ in., (29.7 x 20.7 cm.), woodcut.

$1680* *Mariens Verehrung (B. 95; M. 207/II (v.III/f)),* c. 1504, sheet 19 of series Das Marienleben, watermark, (06-23-93, Kornfeld, #46), woodcut (BP 1141, DM 2843, FR 9562, Y 183,026, SF 2530).

$7436* *The Market Peasant And His Wife (B. 89, Meder 89 a-b),* 1519, (06-04-93, Bassenge, #5125, illus.), 4⁹⁄₁₆ x 2⅞ in., (11.6 x 7.3 cm.), copper engraving (BP 4920, DM 12,075, FR 40,701, Y 801,984).

$9459* *Der Marktbauer Und Sein Weib (B. 89; M. 89 b (v.c)),* 1519, (12-01-92, Karl/Faber, #57A, illus.), engraving (BP 6250, DM 15,077, FR 51,380, Y 1,177,664).

$939* *Der Marktbauer Und Sein Weib (B. 89; Meder 89 b),* 1519, thin spots, foxed, (12-04-92, Bassenge, #6150), 4⁷⁄₁₆ x 2¹³⁄₁₆ in., (11.3 x 7.1 cm.), engraving (BP 602, DM 1495, FR 5073, Y 117,228).

$722* *Marter Der Zehntausend Von Nikomedien (B. 117, M. 218 b),* 1497, watermark, center crease, stained, wrinkled, prov., (12-04-92, Bassenge, #6169), 15⅛ x 11 in., (38.4 x 28 cm.), woodcut (BP 463, DM 1150, FR 3901, Y 90,137).

$1298* *Marter Der Zehntausend Von Nikomedien (B. 117, M. 218/c (v.g)), 1497,* p.l., (06-23-93, Kornfeld, #49), woodcut (BP 882, DM 2196, FR 7388, Y 141,410, SF 1955).

$25,962* *Marter Des Evangelisten Johannes (B. 61, M. 164/I (v.V.)), 1496-1498,* sheet 1 of series: Die Apokalypse, watermark, (06-23-93, Kornfeld, #39, illus.), woodcut (BP 17,637, DM 43,929, FR 147,763, Y 2,828,413, SF 39,100).

$3033* *Marter Des Evangelisten Johannes (B. 61; Meder 164), 1496-1498,* from Apokalypse, prov., (12-04-92, Bassenge, #6159), 15^7/$_{16}$ x 11^1/$_8$ in., (39.2 x 28.2 cm.), woodcut (BP 1945, DM 4830, FR 16,386, Y 378,652).

$4600* *"The Martyrdom Of St. John" and "The Babylonian Whore" (B. 61 and 73;M., Holl. 164 and 177), 1511: A Pair,* from the Apocalypse, Latin edit., thread margins, trimmed, repaired tear, thin spot, discoloration, good cond.; watermark, thread margins, trimmed into subject, printer's crease, partly opened and retouched, (05-13-93, Sotheby-NY, #141), one 15^3/$_8$ x 11 in., (391 x 279 mm.), other 15^1/$_4$ x 11^1/$_8$ in., (391 x 279 mm.), woodcut (BP 3020, DM 7428, FR 25,054, Y 513,565).

$2875* *The Martyrdom Of The Ten Thousand (B. 117; M., Holl. 218), c. 1497,* Meder b, trimmed to borderline three sides, narrow margins, corners restored, restorations, repaired tears, (05-13-93, Sotheby-NY, #148), 15^1/$_2$ x 11^1/$_8$ in., (394 x 284 mm.), woodcut (BP 1887, DM 4642, FR 15,659, Y 320,978).

$14,163* *Mary And Suckling Child (B. 36, Meder a-c), 1519,* prov., (06-04-93, Bassenge, #5121, illus.), 4^1/$_2$ x 2^{13}/$_{16}$ in., (11.4 x 7.2 cm.), copper engraving (BP 9370, DM 22,999, FR 77,521, Y 1,527,502).

$3541* *Mary With Scepter And Crown Of Stars (B.32, Meder 37 c), 1516,* stamp verso, (06-04-93, Bassenge, #5120, illus.), 4^5/$_8$ x 2^7/$_8$ in., (11.7 x 7.3 cm.), copper engraving (BP 2343, DM 5750, FR 19,381, Y 381,903).

BI *"The Meeting Of Joachim And Anne At The Golden Gate" (Bartsch 79, Meder 191 g/i), 1504,* p. c. 1600, stains, tears, good cond., est. $8/1,200, (10-31-92, Cleveland, #10), 11^3/$_4$ x 8^1/$_4$ in., (29.8 x 21 cm.), woodcut.

$6000 *"Melancholia", 1514,* #1, 2nd state, s., (09-24-92, Alderfer, #236, illus.), 9^1/$_2$ x 7^1/$_2$ in., (24.1 x 19.1 cm.), etching (BP 3512, DM 8892, FR 30,196, Y 721,761).

$1805* *Michaels Kampf Mit Dem Drachen (B. 72; Meder 174), 1498,* (12-04-92, Bassenge, #6161), 15^3/$_8$ x 11 in., (39 x 28 cm.), woodcut (BP 1158, DM 2875, FR 9751, Y 225,343).

$29,511* *The Nativity (B., M., Holl. 2), 1504,* Meder B impression, watermark, trimmed, repairs, printer's crease, (06-29-93, Sotheby-London, #18, illus.), 7^1/$_4$ x 4^1/$_2$ in., (18.4 x 11.4 cm.), engraving on paper (BP 19,550, DM 49,833, FR 167,962, Y 3,141,473).

BI *Nemesis (The Great Fortune) (B. 77; M., Holl. 72),* Meder II A impression, watermark, trimmed irregularly w/in platemark, fractionally into subject, crease, surface dirt, foxing, thin patch, paper loss, repaired tear, est. BP 14/16,000, (06-29-93, Sotheby-London, #30, illus.), 12^3/$_4$ x 8^3/$_4$ in., (32.4 x 22.2 cm.), engraving on paper.

$2321* *Die Nemesis Oder Das Grosse Gluck, c. 1501-02,* mono. AD, restored, foxing, (09-14-92, Venator/Hansten, #1488), approx. 12^{15}/$_{16}$ x 8^7/$_8$ in., (33 x 22.5 cm.), engraving (BP 1227, DM 3450, FR 11,693, Y 288,610).

BI *Nemesis, The Great Fortune (B. 77, M., Holl. 72), c. 1502,* very good Meder II a-b impression, narrow to thread margins, fold, repaired tear in image, repairs, rust spot affecting image, staining, defects, watermark, prop. Montclair Art Museum, est. $4,5/5,500, (05-11-93, Christie-NY, #17, illus.), plate 12^7/$_8$ x 9 in., (327 x 229 mm.), engraving on laid.

$4025* *The Opening Of The Fifth And Sixth Seal (B. 65; M., Holl. 168), 1498,* from Apocalypse, German edit., thread margins, trimmed, thin patches,thin spots, loss into subject, glue stains, good cond., (05-13-93, Sotheby-NY, #134, illus.), 15^3/$_8$ x 11^1/$_8$ in., (392 x 283 mm.), woodcut (BP 2642, DM 6499, FR 21,923, Y 449,369).

BI *The Opening Of The Fifth And Sixth Seals (B. 65; M., Holl. 168),* from Apocalypse, Latin edit. 1511, repairs, worm hole, thin patches,other defects, est. BP 2/2,500, (12-03-92, Sotheby-London, #45), 15^1/$_4$ x 11 in., (390 x 280 mm.), woodcut.

$1062* *Philipp Melanchthon (B. 105, Meder 104 f), 1526,* (06-04-93, Bassenge, #5126), 6^3/$_4$ x 5 in., (17.2 x 12.7 cm.), copper engraving (BP 703, DM 1725, FR 5813, Y 114,538).

$8680* *Philipp Melanchthon (B. 105; M., Holl. 104), 1526,* Meder A impression, narrow margin, trimmed, repair, staining, (06-29-93, Sotheby-London, #40, illus.), 6^3/$_4$ x 5 in., (17.1 x 12.7 cm.), engraving (BP 5750, DM 14,657, FR 49,402, Y 923,994).

$2830* *Philipp Melanchthon (B. 105; M., Holl. 104), 1526,* very good Meder c impression, narrow to thread margins, trimmed, nick, surface dirt, good cond., (12-01-92, Christie-London, #186), plate 6^3/$_4$ x 4^{15}/$_{16}$ in., (172 x 125 mm.), engraving (BP 1870, DM 4511, FR 15,372, Y 352,341).

$722* *Pilatus Wascht Sich Die Hande (B. 36, Meder 145), c. 1509-11,* from Kleinen Holzschnittpassion, Textausgabe of 1511, (12-04-92, Bassenge, #6156), 5^1/$_{16}$ x 3^{13}/$_{16}$ in., (12.8 x 9.7 cm.), woodcut (BP 463, DM 1150, FR 3901, Y 90,137).

$708* *Presentation In The Temple (B. 88, Meder 200), c. 1505,* watermark, (06-04-93, Bassenge, #5139), 11^9/$_{16}$ x 8^3/$_{16}$ in., (29.4 x 20.8 cm.), woodcut (BP 468, DM 1150, FR 3875, Y 76,359).

BI *The Presentation Of The Virgin In The Temple From The Life Of The Virgin (B. 81), 1511,* meder f, narrow margins, image tear, missing area top margin, est. BP 1,5/2,000, (11-30-92, Phillips-London, #286), border 11^3/$_4$ x 8^1/$_4$ in., (298 x 210 mm.), woodcut on fine laid.

$1665* *The Prodigal Son (B., M., Holl. 28), c. 1496,* later impression, trimmed to subject, horizontal tear, losses, repairs, creases, Japan-backed, (12-01-92, Christie-London, #180), sheet 10^1/$_{16}$ x 7^1/$_2$ in., (255 x 190 mm.), engraving (BP 1100, DM 2654, FR 9044, Y 207,296).

$867* *The Prodigal Son Amid The Swine (B. 28), c. 1496,* grey impression, trimmed to plate, laid down, center image repaired tear, hole, tear, (11-30-92, Phillips-London, #285), sheet 9^1/$_4$ x 7^1/$_8$ in., (235 x 181 mm.), engraving (BP 572, DM 1381, FR 4689, Y 107,903).

$6597* *The Promenade (B. 94; M., Holl. 83),* Meder B impression, narrow to thread margins or trimmed irregularly,repairs, abrasions, surface dirt, (06-29-93, Sotheby-London, #35, illus.), 7^1/$_2$ x 4^3/$_4$ in., (19.1 x 12.1 cm.), engraving (BP 4370, DM 11,140, FR 37,547, Y 702,257).

$220* *Religious Engravings: Three,* (03-20-93, Northeast, #826), plate 3^1/$_2$ x 5 in., (8.9 x 12.7 cm.), engraving (BP 147, DM 360, FR 1224, Y 25,519).

$1841* *The Resurrection Of Christ (B. 15, Meder 124), 1511,* from the Large Passion, watermark, (06-04-93, Bassenge, #5128), 15^3/$_8$ x 10^{11}/$_{16}$ in., (39 x 27.1 cm.), woodcut (BP 1218, DM 2990, FR 10,077, Y 198,555).

$22,599* *Das Rhinozerus (Bartsch 136; Meder 273, 6; Boon-Scheller 273 f; Strauss 176), 1515,* watermark, prov., (06-10-93, Hauswedell/Nolt., #81, illus.), woodcut on soft hand-made (BP 14,782, DM 36,800, FR 123,898, Y 2,398,790).

$36,653* *Ritter, Tod Und Teufel (B. 98; M. 74/b/c (v. g.); D. 70), 1513,* prov., (06-23-93, Kornfeld, #30, illus.), engraving (BP 24,900, DM 62,019, FR 208,611, Y 3,993,137, SF 55,200).

$1955* *Saint Christopher Facing To The Right (B., M., Holl. 52), 1521,* Meder b impression, trimmed narrow margins, staining, prov., (05-11-93, Christie-NY, #14, illus.), plate 4^5/$_8$ x 2^{15}/$_{16}$ in., (117 x 75 mm.), engraving on laid (BP 1248, DM 3080, FR 10,377, Y 215,048).

BI *La Sainte Famille Aux Lievres, c. 1497,* mono. in plate, reddish stains, est. FF12,000/15,000, (06-28-93, Loudmer, #241), 15^1/$_2$ x 11^1/$_8$ in., (393 x 282 mm.), sh 19^5/$_{16}$ x 12^{11}/$_{16}$ in., (393 x 282 mm.), wood engraving on laid.

$880* *Samson Fighting With The Lion (Meder 107), 1498,* later impression, (10-18-92, Hindman, #494), 15^1/$_8$ x 11 in., (38.4 x 27.9 cm.), woodcut (BP 538, DM 1310, FR 4442, Y 105,579).

$1083* *Samson Totet Den Lowen (B. 2; Meder 107 g), c. 1496-97,* (12-04-92, Bassenge, #6153), 15^1/$_{16}$ x 10^3/$_4$ in., (38.2 x 27.3 cm.), woodcut (BP 695, DM 1725, FR 5851, Y 135,206).

$435* *Samson Wrestling With A Lion (B. 2), 1496,* a later impression, workholes, gaps, narrow margins, repaired hole, tears, reinforced margins, poor cond., (10-27-92, Phillips-London, #14), sheet 15¼ x 11⅛ in., (387 x 283 mm.), woodcut on laid (BP 275, DM 667, FR 2262, Y 53,211).

BI *Samtliche Holzschnitte, 1938,* volume, pub. Deutsche Buch, good cond., tears, creases, surface soiling, est. $6/800, (02-24-93, Butterfield, #2690), 19 x 13 in., (483 x 330 mm.), reprod. on wove.

$9534* *Sankt Georg Zu Fuss (Bartsch 53; Meder 55 a-b), c. 1707/08,* (06-10-93, Hauswedell/Nolt, #71, illus.), engraving on hand-made (BP 6236, DM 15,525, FR 52,270, Y 1,011,994).

$1983* *The Satyr Family (B. 69, Meder 65 c), 1505,* prov., (06-04-93, Bassenge, #5124), 4½ x 2¹¹⁄₁₆ in., (11.5 x 6.9 cm.), copper engraving (BP 1312, DM 3220, FR 10,854, Y 213,870).

$422* *Die Satyrfamilie,* mono., d. AD 1505, (03-24-93, Venator/Hansten, #2516), pl 4½ x 2¾ in., (11.5 x 7 cm.), engraving (BP 286, DM 689, FR 2346, Y 49,583).

$19,963* *The Sea Monster (B. 71; M., Holl. 66),* Meder A impression, watermark, trimmed outside borderline, repairs, tin spots, crease, repaired tear in image, ex. coll. A. Alferoff (L. 1727), (06-29-93, Sotheby-London, #31, illus.), 9¾ x 7⅞ in., (24.8 x 18.7 cm.), engraving on paper (BP 13,225, DM 33,710, FR 113,620, Y 2,125,080).

$1228* *Die Sechs Kriegsleute (B. 88; Meder 81 d), c. 1495/96,* (12-04-92, Bassenge, #6149), 5³⁄₁₆ x 5¹³⁄₁₆ in., (13.2 x 14.7 cm.), engraving (BP 788, DM 1956, FR 6634, Y 153,308).

$1983* *The Small Calvary (B. 59, Meder 180 c),* after 1500, prov., (06-04-93, Bassenge, #5134), 8⁷⁄₁₆ x 5¹¹⁄₁₆ in., (21.4 x 14.4 cm.), woodcut (BP 1312, DM 3220, FR 10,854, Y 213,870).

$25,171* *The Small Horse (B. 96; M., Holl. 93), 1505,* Meder A impression, watermark, narrow to thread margins, trimmed, nick, defects, (06-29-93, Sotheby-London, #36, illus.), 6½ x 4¼ in., (16.5 x 10.8 cm.), engraving on paper (BP 16,675, DM 42,504, FR 143,261, Y 2,679,476).

$25,494* *The Small Passion (B. 16, 17, 19-24, 26-33, 35-52. Meder 125, 126-133, 135, 142, 144-161), 1511: Thirty-Four,* prov., (06-04-93, Bassenge, #5129, illus.), woodcut (BP 16,867, DM 41,400, FR 139,540, Y 2,749,569).

$935* *"The Small Passion, Christ Before Pilate" (B.32, M 141),* block s., d. 1507, (12-11-92, DuMouchelle, #2052, illus.), sight 4¾ x 3½ in., (12.1 x 8.9 cm.), woodcut (BP 600, DM 1473, FR 5049, Y 115,704).

$4333* *Der Sogenannte Verzweifelnde (B. 70; Meder 95 I c), c. 1515,* thin spots, (12-04-92, Bassenge, #6147, illus.), 7⁵⁄₁₆ x 5⁵⁄₁₆ in., (18.5 x 13.5 cm.), iron etching (BP 2779, DM 6901, FR 23,409, Y 540,949).

BI *Das Sonnenweib Und Der Siebenkopfige Drachen (B. 71, Meder 173), 1496-98,* stained, est. DM 9,000, (12-04-92, Bassenge, #6160, illus.), 15½ x 11 in., (39.3 x 28 cm.), woodcut.

$4800* *Der Spaziergang (B. 94; H. 884; R. 12; M. 83, I, K), c. 1496/97,* mono. in plate, restored, (10-09-92, Winterberg, #761, illus.), 7½ x 4¹¹⁄₁₆ in., (19 x 11.9 cm.), engraving (BP 2848, DM 7130, FR 23,940, Y 584,368).

$50,342* *St. Anthony Reading (B. 58; M., Holl. 51), 1519,* Meder A impression, narrow margins, repair, hairline, very good cond., ex. coll. Felix Somary, (06-29-93, Sotheby-London, #27, illus.), 3¾ x 5¾ in., (9.5 x 14.6 cm.), engraving (BP 33,350, DM 85,008, FR 286,522, Y 5,358,953).

$6900* *St. Eustace (B. 57, M., Holl. 60), c. 1501,* good Meder i impression, trimmed to or into subject, remargined w/ ink borderline, staining, defects, paper loss, watermark, (05-11-93, Christie-NY, #15, illus.), sheet 14⅛ x 10¼ in., (359 x 260 mm.), engraving on laid (BP 4405, DM 10,870, FR 36,624, Y 758,992).

$23,435* *St. Eustace (B. 57; M., Holl. 60),* Meder A-B impression, watermark, narrow margins, rubbed, skinned, abrasions, paper discolored, folds, defects, ex. coll. E.F. Oppermann (L. 887); and another, (06-29-93, Sotheby-London, #28, illus.), 14⅛ x 10¼ in., (35.9 x 26 cm.), engraving on paper (BP 15,525, DM 39,573, FR 133,381, Y 2,494,677).

$3450* *St. Eustace (B. 57; M., Holl. 60), c. 1501,* later impression, trimmed, repair, thin patches (some reinforced),

creases, surface dirt, mat remains, (05-13-93, Sotheby-NY, #124), 14⅛ x 10¼ in., (360 x 261 mm.), engraving (BP 2265, DM 5571, FR 18,791, Y 385,174).

$4600* *St. George On Foot (B. 53; M., Holl. 55), c. 1507-08,* Meder impression, trimmed on platemark, restoration, rubbed spot, thin spots, foxing, ex-coll. P. Mariette, (05-13-93, Sotheby-NY, #127, illus.), 4½ x 2⅞ in., (113 x 72 mm.), engraving (BP 3020, DM 7428, FR 25,054, Y 513,565).

$1204* *St. George On Horseback (B. 54, Meder 56 c), 1508,* watermark, (06-04-93, Bassenge, #5122), 4¼ x 3⅜ in., (10.8 x 8.5 cm.), copper engraving (BP 797, DM 1955, FR 6590, Y 129,853).

$8680* *St. George On Horseback (B. 54; M., Holl. 56), 1508,* Meder B impression, trimmed on and into platemark, repair, scrape, ex. coll. Duke of Buccleuch (L. 402), (06-29-93, Sotheby-London, #26, illus.), 4⅛ x 3¼ in., (10.5 x 8.3 cm.), engraving (BP 5750, DM 14,657, FR 49,402, Y 923,994).

$9922* *St. Hieronyumus Im Gehause (B. 60; M. 59 b), 1514,* prov., (06-08-93, Karl/Faber, #49), engraving (BP 6522, DM 16,099, FR 54,219, Y 1,053,850).

$6799* *St. Hubertus (Meder 60), c. 1501,* mono., AD, wormholes, (11-11-92, Dorotheum, #302), 14¹⁄₁₆ x 10¼ in., (35.7 x 26 cm.), engraving (BP 4499, DM 10,866, FR 36,417, Y 845,436, SC 35,840).

$22,661* *St. Hubertus, Auch Eustachius Genannt (B. 57, Meder 60 b), c. 1501,* watermark, (06-04-93, Bassenge, #5123, illus.), 13¹⁵⁄₁₆ x 10¼ in., (35.5 x 26 cm.), copper engraving (BP 14,992, DM 36,799, FR 124,034, Y 2,444,025).

$2200* *St. Jerome In His Study, 1514, Meder 77E,* a Meder E impression, d. c. 1560, trimmed to platemark, ex-coll., (09-20-92, Hindman, #646), 9⅝ x 7½ in., (24.4 x 19.1 cm.), engraving, watermark (BP 1288, DM 3265, FR 11,168, Y 271,907).

$2875* *St. John Devouring The Book (B. 70; M., Holl. 172), 1511,* from the Apocalypse, trimmed on borderline, repaired tear, nick, stains, good cond., ex-coll. Leopold I, (05-13-93, Sotheby-NY, #136), 15½ x 11¼ in., (395 x 285 mm.), woodcut (BP 1887, DM 4642, FR 15,659, Y 320,978).

$3410* *St. Michael Fighting The Dragon (B. 72; M., Holl. 174),* from Apocalypse, Latin edit. of 1511, trimmed to borderline, stains, wormholes, repaired tear, discoloration, other defects, (12-03-92, Sotheby-London, #47, illus.), 15¼ x 11 in., (390 x 278 mm.), woodcut (BP 2200, DM 5362, FR 18,304, Y 424,288).

$18,400* *St. Michael Fighting The Dragon (B. 72; M., Holl. 174), 1498,* from Apocalypse, German edit., narrow margins, nicks, repaired tears, thin spots, good cond., ex-coll. Dr. G. Eissler, (05-13-93, Sotheby-NY, #138, illus.), 15½ x 11¼ in., (393 x 285 mm.), woodcut (BP 12,080, DM 29,711, FR 100,218, Y 2,054,259).

$4025* *St. Michael Fighting The Dragon (B. 72; M., Holl. 174), 1511,* from Apocalypse, watermark, narrow margins, printer's crease, stains, thin spots, good cond., (05-13-93, Sotheby-NY, #139), 15½ x 11⅛ in., (393 x 284 mm.), woodcut (BP 2642, DM 6499, FR 21,923, Y 449,369).

$2777* *St. Philip (B. 46; M., Holl. 48), 1526,* from the Five Apostles, narrow to thread margins, trimmed, paper thin, ex. coll. d'Arenberg (L. 567), (06-29-93, Sotheby-London, #25, illus.), 4½ x 2¾ in., (11.4 x 7 cm.), engraving (BP 1840, DM 4689, FR 15,805, Y 295,614).

$660* *St. Sebastian Bound To The Tree (Bartsch 55. Meder, Hollstein 62), c. 1501,* only state, margins trimmed, foxing, crease, pen drawn borderline, (05-27-93, Swann, #94), 4½ x 2¾ in., (11.4 x 7 cm.), engraving (BP 423, DM 1059, FR 3569, Y 70,755).

BI *St. Thomas (B. 48), c. 1514,* possibly later impression, trimmed, thread margins, corner repaired, image nicks, creased, foxing, staining, est. $2/4,000, (12-12-92, Weschler, #117), 4¾ x 2¾ in., (12.1 x 7 cm.), engraving.

$165* *St. Thomas (B. 48), c. 1514,* trimmed, corner repaired, nicks in image, creased, foxing, staining, (06-11-93, Weschler, #41), 4¾ x 2¾ in., (12.1 x 7 cm.), engraving (BP 108, DM 268, FR 904, Y 17,507).

$1870* *The Sudarium Held By 2 Angels (Bartsch, Strauss 25), 1513,* margins, glue stain, (05-27-93, Swann, #95), 4 x

5½ in., (10.2 x 14 cm.), engraving (BP 1198, DM 3001, FR 10,114, Y 200,472).

$10,416* *Three Peasants In Conversation (B. 86; M., Holl. 87)*, Meder A impression, watermark, narrow margins, inky plate edges, pinholes, repairs, crease, thin areas, (06-29-93, Sotheby-London, #33, illus.), 4⅛ x 3 in., (10.5 x 7.6 cm.), engraving on paper (BP 6900, DM 17,589, FR 59,283, Y 1,108,793).

$10,690* *Das Tier Mit Den Lammshornern (B. 74, M. 175/I (v.V))*, *1496-1498*, sheet 12 of series: Die Apokalypse, artist's proof, watermark, (06-23-93, Kornfeld, #40, illus.), woodcut (BP 7262, DM 18,088, FR 60,842, Y 1,164,615, SF 16,100).

$3734* *Das Tier Mit Den Lammshornern (B. 74; M. 175/1511)*, *1496-1498*, from the Apocalypse, prov., (12-01-92, Karl/Faber, #60, illus.), woodcut (BP 2467, DM 5952, FR 20,282, Y 464,890).

BI *Das Tier Mit Den Lammshornern (B. 74; Meder 175)*, *1498*, est. DM 7,500, (12-04-92, Bassenge, #6162), 11⁷⁄₁₆ x 11⅛ in., (29.1 x 28.3 cm.), woodcut.

$2331* *A Turkish Family (B. 85, M., Holl. 80)*, *c. 1496*, trimmed, re-margined, corner made-up, surface dirt, prov., (12-01-92, Christie-London, #182), sheet 4¼ x 3¹⁄₁₆ in., (108 x 77 mm.), engraving (BP 1540, DM 3715, FR 12,662, Y 290,214).

$6597* *The Turkish Family (B. 85; M., Holl. 80)*, watermark, trimmed on or w/in borderline, repair, (06-29-93, Sotheby-London, #32, illus.), 4⅛ x 3 in., (10.5 x 7.6 cm.), engraving on paper (BP 4370, DM 11,140, FR 37,547, Y 702,257).

$759* *Der Unglaubige Thomas (B. 49; Meder 158)*, *c. 1509-11*, stained, (12-04-92, Bassenge, #6157), 4¹⁵⁄₁₆ x 3¾ in., (12.6 x 9.6 cm.), woodcut (BP 487, DM 1209, FR 4100, Y 94,757).

$2138* *Verlobung Mariens (B. 82, M. 194/I (v. III/h.))*, *c. 1504-1505*, sheet 6 of series Das Marienleben, artist's proof, watermark, (06-23-93, Kornfeld, #43), woodcut (BP 1452, DM 3618, FR 12,168, Y 232,923, SF 3220).

$3054* *Verlobung Mariens (B. 82, M. 194/I (v.III/h))*, *c. 1504-1505*, sheet 6 of series Das Marienleben, watermark, (06-23-93, Kornfeld, #42), woodcut (BP 2075, DM 5168, FR 17,382, Y 332,716, SF 4600).

$3399* *Vier Engel, Die Winde Aufhaltend (Meder 169)*, *c. 1497-98*, mono., AD, foxing, (11-11-92, Dorotheum, #303, illus.), 15⅜ x 11 in., (39 x 28 cm.), woodcut (BP 2249, DM 5432, FR 18,206, Y 422,656, SC 17,920).

$6638* *Die Vier Hexen (B. 75; M. 69 f (v.h))*, *1497*, trimmed, (12-01-92, Karl/Faber, #57, illus.), engraving (BP 4386, DM 10,580, FR 36,056, Y 826,444).

BI *The Virgin And Child Crowned By One ANGEL (B. 37; M., Holl. 41)*, Meder IA impression, partial thread margins, stain in image, made-upareas, ext. BP 4/6,000, (12-03-92, Sotheby-London, #39, illus.), 5¼ x 3¾ in., (133 x 95 mm.), engraving.

BI *The Man Of Sorrows With Hands Bound (B., M., Holl. 21)*, *1512*, trimmed into subject, replaced areas, est. BP 3/4,000, (06-29-93, Sotheby-London, #21, illus.), 4½ x 2¾ in., (11.4 x 7 cm.), drypoint.

$5457* *The Virgin And Child Crowned By One Angel (B. 37; M., Holl. 41)*, first state of two, trimmed to work, edges touched w/India ink, nick,surface dirt, (12-03-92, Sotheby-London, #41, illus.), 5¼ x 3¾ in., (133 x 95 mm.), engraving on paper w/watermark (BP 3520, DM 8582, FR 29,291, Y 678,985).

$4340* *The Virgin And Child Crowned By Two Angels (B. 39; M., Holl. 38)*, *1518*, thread margins, trimmed, platemark touched w/brown ink, crease, thin patch, (06-29-93, Sotheby-London, #23, illus.), 5¾ x 4 in., (14.6 x 10.2 cm.), engraving (BP 2875, DM 7329, FR 24,701, Y 461,997).

$5175* *The Virgin And Child On A Grassy Bench (B. 34; M., Holl. 31)*, *1503*, watermark, trimmed to platemark, remargined, repair, thin spots, cockling, stains, ex-coll. Graf F.J. von Enzenberg, (05-13-93, Sotheby-NY, #120, illus.), 4⅜ x 2¾ in., (112 x 70 mm.), engraving (BP 3397, DM 8356, FR 28,186, Y 577,760).

$4461* *The Virgin And Child Seated By The Wall (B. 40; M., Holl. 36)*, Meder Ib impression, thread margins, repairs, (06-30-93, Sotheby-London, #111, illus.), 5¾ x 4 in.,

(146 x 102 mm.), engraving on paper w/o a watermark (BP 2990, DM 7609, FR 25,667, Y 477,981).

BI *The Virgin And Child With A Pear (B. 41, M. Holl. 33)*, *1511*, good Meder b impression, trimmed on or inside platemark, repaired split in image, corners made-up, staining, prov., est. $3/5,000, (05-11-93, Christie-NY, #12), sheet 6³⁄₁₆ x 4¼ in., (157 x 108 mm.), engraving on laid.

BI *The Virgin And Child With A Pear (B. 41, M., Holl. 33)*, *1511*, good Meder b impression, thread margins or trimmed, repaired tears or nicks, staining, good cond., prov., prop. Montclair Art Museum, est. $5/7,000, (05-11-93, Christie-NY, #11, illus.), sheet 6⁵⁄₁₆ x 4¼ in., (160 x 108 mm.), engraving on laid.

$20,463* *The Virgin And Child With The Monkey (B. 42; M., Holl. 30)*, Meder A-B impression, margins, pinhole in image, soft crease, discoloration, (12-03-92, Sotheby-London, #37, illus.), 7½ x 4¾ in., (191 x 121 mm.), engraving (BP 13,200, DM 32,180, FR 109,839, Y 2,546,099).

BI *The Virgin And Child With The Pear (B. 41, M., Holl. 33)*, Meder B impression, margins, soft crease, ex-coll., est. BP 8/12,000, (12-03-92, Sotheby-London, #38, illus.), 6¼ x 4¼ in., (159 x 108 mm.), engraving on paper w/ watermark.

$3450* *The Virgin Appearing To St. John (B. 60; M., Holl. 163)*, *1511*, from Apocalypse, from Latin edit., good margins, repaired tear, thinspots, mat staining, good cond., (05-13-93, Sotheby-NY, #132, illus.), sh 15⅞ x 10⅜ in., (403 x 263 mm.), woodcut (BP 2265, DM 5571, FR 18,791, Y 385,174).

$4370* *The Virgin With The Dragonfly (B. 44, M., Holl. 42)*, *c. 1495*, very good Meder c-d impression, trimmed on platemark, creases, surface losses, cockling, staining, watermark, Theodore W. and Josephine C. Bennett Estate, (05-11-93, Christie-NY, #13, illus.), plate 9½ x 7¼ in., (241 x 184 mm.), engraving on laid (BP 2790, DM 6884, FR 23,195, Y 480,695).

$6325* *The Virgin With The Swaddled Child (B. 38; M., Holl. 40)*, *1520*, plate tone, thread margins, nicks, foxing, good cond., ex-coll. J.S.Morgan, (05-13-93, Sotheby-NY, #121, illus.), 5⅝ x 3¾ in., (142 x 95 mm.), engraving (BP 4152, DM 10,213, FR 34,450, Y 706,152).

BI *The Vision Of The Seven Candlesticks (B. 62; M., Holl. 165)*, from Apocalypse, from Latin edit. 1511, trimmed to borderline, cornerdetached, damages, small stains at centre, thin patches, discolored, est. BP 1/1,500, (12-03-92, Sotheby-London, #44), 15½ x 11 in., (392 x 279 mm.), woodcut.

$2185* *The Vision Of The Seven Candlesticks (B. 62; M., Holl. 165)*, *1511*, from Apocalypse, from Latin edit., trimmed, plugged hole, wormholes,foxing, good cond., (05-13-93, Sotheby-NY, #133), 15½ x 11 in., (393 x 280 mm.), woodcut (BP 1434, DM 3528, FR 11,901, Y 243,943).

$1145* *Wappen Mit Dem Totenkopf (B. 101; M. 98; D. 36)*, *1503*, (06-23-93, Kornfeld, #31), engraving (BP 778, DM 1937, FR 6517, Y 124,741, SF 1725).

$3738* *Willibald Pirckheimer (B. 106; M., HOll. 103)*, *1524*, trimmed between platemark and borderline, blank paper made up, discoloration, foxing, (05-13-93, Sotheby-NY, #130), sh 7¼ x 4½ in., (183 x 113 mm.), engraving (BP 2454, DM 6036, FR 20,359, Y 417,327).

$1271* *Willibald Pirckheimer (Bartsch 106; Meder 103 I d/e; Boon-Scheller 103)*, collector stamp, (06-10-93, Hauswedell/Nolt, #73), engraving (BP 831, DM 2070, FR 6968, Y 134,911).

$1300* *Der Zwolfjahrige Jesus Im Tempel (B. 91; Meder 203)*, *c. 1504*, watermark, (12-04-92, Bassenge, #6166), 11⁵⁄₁₆ x 8⅛ in., (28.7 x 20.6 cm.), woodcut (BP 834, DM 2070, FR 7023, Y 162,297).

DURER, Albrecht (after)   German 1471-1528

$770* *Christ Carrying The Cross*, (06-13-93, Hindman, #396), approx. 15 x 11 in., (38.1 x 27.9 cm.), woodcut (BP 504, DM 1253, FR 4212, Y 81,027).

$143* *Harrowing Of Hell (Ben 16; M 16; H 16)*, *1512*, from Engraved Passion, (09-17-92, Sloan, #1437), 4½ x 2⅞ in., (11.4 x 7.3 cm.), engraving (BP 80, DM 212, FR 727, Y 17,804).

$275* *"The Martyrdom Of The Ten Thousand" and "Hercules":
Two,* later impressions, (06-13-93, Hindman, #397), each
15 x 11 in., (38.1 x 27.9 cm.), woodcut (BP 180, DM
448, FR 1504, Y 28,938).

$220* *"The Men's Bath" and "The Martyrdom Of St. Cathe-
rine": Two,* later impressions, (06-13-93, Hindman, #395),
each 15 x 11 in., (38.1 x 27.9 cm.), woodcut (BP 144,
DM 358, FR 1204, Y 23,151).

DURIEUX, Caroline   American 1896-1989
BI   *"Petite And Alouse",* s., t., est. $1/1,500, (03-12-93,
Goldberg, #1097, illus.), image 21½ x 16 in., (54.6 x
40.6 cm.), color lithograph.

DURRIE, G.H. (after)
$1540* *"West Rock, New Haven" and "East Rock, New Haven",
1853: Two,* p. Sarony & Co., margins, tears, creases,
soiling, good cond., (01-22-93, Christie-NY, #314, illus.),
both borderline 11¼ x 15½ in., (286 x 394 mm.), color
lithograph w/hand-coloring on wove (BP 1008, DM 2449,
FR 8284, Y 192,741).

DUS, Laszlo
BI   *Januar 31, 1985,* crayon s., d., margins, good cond., est.
$800/$1,200, (05-22-93, Weschler, #179, illus.), 14 x 10
in., (35.6 x 25.4 cm.), lithograph w/hand-coloring, collage, pastel, gouache and airbrush.

BI   *Piros Pont II, 1985,* crayon s., d., full sheet, good cond.,
est. $6/800, (05-22-93, Weschler, #180, illus.), 17½ x 25
in., (44.5 x 63.5 cm.), lithograph w/hand coloring, collage, pastel, gouache and airbrush.

DUSART, Cornelis   1660-1704
$1770* *The Drunken Couple (B., Dutuit, Hollstein 7), 1685,*
watermark, (06-04-93, Bassenge, #5145, illus.), 5⅛ x
4¼ in., (13 x 10.8 cm.), etching (BP 1171, DM 2874,
FR 9688, Y 190,897).

$916* *The Large Village Fair (B., Dut., Holl. 16), 1685,* 3rd
(final) state, trimmed, foxing, prov., (12-01-92, Christie-
London, #153), sheet 9¹⁵⁄₁₆ x 13¼ in., (253 x 336 mm.),
etching (BP 605, DM 1460, FR 4976, Y 114,044).

BI   *The Large Village Fair (B., Dut., Holl. 16), 1685,*
slightly later impression, watermark, narrow margins, foxing, est. BP 4/600, (12-01-92, Christie-London, #154),
plate 10⅜ x 13⁷⁄₁₆ in., (264 x 342 mm.), etching.

$850* *The Month Of July (B., Dutuit, Hollstein 26 III),* prov.,
(06-04-93, Bassenge, #5146), 8⁹⁄₁₆ x 6¹⁄₁₆ in., (21.7 x
15.4 cm.), mezzotint (BP 562, DM 1380, FR 4652, Y
91,674).

BI   *The Violin Player Seated In The Inn (Holl. 15), 1685,*
3rd (final) state, watermark, trimmed, good cond., stains,
est. $2/3,000, (05-13-93, Sotheby-NY, #149), 11 x 9¾
in., (278 x 247 mm.), etching.

BI   *The Violin-Player Seated In The Inn (B., Dut., Holl. 15),
1685,* 3rd (final) state, margins, stains, discoloration, very
good cond., est. BP 800/1,200, (12-01-92, Christie-London, #152, illus.), plate 11¼ x 9¹³⁄₁₆ in., (285 x 250
mm.), etching w/roulette work.

DUTHIE, James   American 19th cent.
$55* *The Village Alms,* (05-28-93, Sloan, #203, illus.), 18 x
25¾ in., (45.7 x 65.4 cm.), engraving (BP 35, DM 87,
FR 295, Y 5897).

DUTRIAC, G.
$259* *Engagez-Vous, Rengagez-Vous Dans Les Troupes Colo-
niales,* very good cond., (03-13-93, Laurin, #10), 46⁷⁄₁₆ x
31⅛ in., (118 x 79 cm.), (BP 181, DM 431, FR 1466,
Y 30,524).

DUTTON, T.G.
$110* *Clipper Ship "Shannon",* (11-28-92, Young, #125, illus.),
15 x 20 in., (38.1 x 50.8 cm.), colored lithograph (BP
73, DM 175, FR 595, Y 13,690).

$385* *"The Naval Review At Spithead": A Pair,* t., pub. Acker-
mann and Co., foxing, tear, water stains, margins, (02-
13-93, Bourne, #18, illus.), image 11 x 32 in., (27.9 x
81.3 cm.), lithograph (BP 271, DM 638, FR 2160, Y
46,430).

DUTTON, Thomas Goldsworth, Lithographer   British d. 1891
$880* *"The 'America', Schooner Yacht", 1851,* ident. i.; label
verso, (01-16-93, Skinner, #63), sheet, sight 14¼ x 18½
in., (36.2 x 47 cm.), color lithograph w/additional hand-

coloring on paper (BP 575, DM 1439, FR 4865, Y
110,943).

DUTTON, Thomas Goldworth   English d. 1891
$167* *The Sutlej, East Indiaman, 1200, 1848,* p. by Day &
Son, pub. W. Foster, foxed, light-stained, (11-30-92, Phillips-London, #235), sheet 14½ x 18½ in., (368 x 470
mm.), tinted hand-colored lithograph on wove (BP 110,
DM 266, FR 903, Y 20,784).

$191* *Warrior, 1861,* pub. Day and Son, tears into image, sur-
face dirt, other defects, margins, (08-12-92, Bonhams,
#191), image 15½ x 24⅜ in., (39.4 x 61.9 cm.), litho-
graph w/hand-coloring (BP 99, DM 279, FR 946, Y
24,344).

DUTTON, Thomas Goldworth (after)   English d. 1891
BI   *Clipper Ship 'SHANNON' 1450 Tons,* by Day and Son,
pub. William Foster, London, est. $400/450, (07-03-92,
Sloan, #1084), 12 x 17⅔ in., (30.5 x 44.9 cm.), color
lithograph.

DUVAL, P.
$50* *Telepherique Du Brevent,* good cond., (03-15-93, Arcole,
#86), sight 5¹¹⁄₁₆ x 4½ in., (14.5 x 11.5 cm.), on card-
board (BP 35, DM 83, FR 282, Y 5923).

DUVERNAY
$12* *Composition,* (03-15-93, Millon/Robert, #141), 25⁹⁄₁₆ x
19¹¹⁄₁₆ in., (65 x 50 cm.), serigraph (BP 8, DM 20, FR
68, Y 1421).

DUVET, Jean   French 1485-c. 1570
BI   *A King Pursued By A Unicorn (B. 40; Eisler 66),* from
series of six, trimmed irregularly into subject, pinhole,
good cond., est. BP 25/35,000, (12-03-92, Sotheby-London, #50, illus.), 9 x 15¼ in., (235 x 391 mm.), engraving on paper w/watermark.

$8498* *The Monster With Seven Heads And Ten Horns (B. 23,
Robert-Dumesnil 37, Eisler 49 II), 1561,* prov., (06-04-93,
Bassenge, #5148), 11⅝ x 8⁷⁄₁₆ in., (29.5 x 21.5 cm.),
copper engraving (BP 5622, DM 13,800, FR 46,513, Y
916,523).

BI   *The Triumph Of The Unicorn (E. 67; B. 72),* 1st state 2,
trimmed, printer's creases center, laid down, est. BP 30/
40,000, (06-30-93, Sotheby-London, #118, illus.), 9 x
15¼ in., (229 x 387 mm.), engraving, Shield watermark.

DUWE, Harald   1926-1984
$166* *Portrait Of Angela Davis, (19)71,* s., d., num., (12-01-92,
Karl/Faber, #558), 22⅝ x 16⅛ in., (57.5 x 41 cm.), seri-
graph on smooth cardboard (BP 110, DM 265, FR 902,
Y 20,667).

$99* *Selbstbildnis Mit Parteizettel, 1976,* s., d., #19/50, (06-12-
93, Hauswedell/Nolt, #77), 20⅞ x 15¾ in., (53 x 40
cm.), offset on smooth wove (BP 65, DM 161, FR 542,
Y 10,418).

DUYCK, Ed. and A. CRESPIN
$467* *Alcazar Royal, 1896,* Lith. Couweloos, A- cond., (08-06-
92, Swann, #122, illus.), 35 x 23 in., (88.9 x 58.4 cm.),
(BP 244, DM 690, FR 2330, Y 59,566).

$330* *Nieuport Bains, 1895,* Lith. AD Merlens, B+ cond., fold
marks, restoration, (08-06-92, Swann, #123, illus.), 39¼ x
23½ in., (99.7 x 59.7 cm.), (BP 172, DM 488, FR
1647, Y 42,092).

DWIGHT, Mabel   American b. 1876
$715* *"Derelicts",* s. Mabel Dwight, 1931, very good cond.,
(11-21-92, Bakker, #26, illus.), 9¾ x 12½ in., (24.8 x
31.8 cm.), lithograph (BP 471, DM 1140, FR 3840, Y
88,919).

BI   *"Farmyard",* s., AAA edit., good cond., est. $2-300, (10-
31-92, Cleveland, #114), 10 x 11 in., (25.4 x 27.9 cm.),
lithograph.

$44* *"Skating On Hope Pond",* proof, good cond., (10-31-92,
Cleveland, #115), 10¼ x 13 in., (26 x 33 cm.), lithograph (BP 28, DM 68, FR 230, Y 5450).

DYAR, Otto
BI   *Anna May Wong, Autographed Portrait,* c. 1932, photog.'s blindstamp, ink s., i., est. BP 4/600, (12-17-92,
Christie-S. Ken, #78, illus.), 13¼ x 10⅛ in., (33.7 x
25.7 cm.), photograph, warm-toned gelatin silver print.

DYCK, Anthony van 1599-1642
$1062* *Titian And His Beloved (Wibiral 21 IV, Hollstein 21 IV),* watermark, (06-04-93, Bassenge, #5153, illus.), 11¼ x 8¹¹⁄₁₆ in., (28.6 x 22.1 cm.), etching and copper engraving (BP 703, DM 1725, FR 5813, Y 114,538).

DYCK, Sir Anthony van Flemish 1599-1641
$5060* *Adam Van Noort, Before 1632(?),* small margins, glue/water stain, foxing, annot. label, (12-08-92, Swann, #95, illus.), 9½ x 6⅛ in., (24.1 x 15.6 cm.), etching w/engraving, watermark (BP 3171, DM 7878, FR 26,858, Y 627,169).
BI *Frans Francken (Holl. 6),* second state of six, narrow margin, trimmed into subject, i. in pen,repaired area, thin patch, repairs, creasing, surface dirt, other minor defects, ex-coll., est. BP 1/1,500, (12-03-92, Sotheby-London, #51), 9½ x 6 in., (243 x 157 mm.), etching on paper w/watermark.
$21,699* *Jan Snellinx (Holl. 10; Mauquoy-Hendrickx 10),* 1st state before letters, polishing scratches, watermark, wide margins, creasing, very good cond., ex. coll. H. Weber(?) (L. 1383) and M.D. (L. 1862d), (06-29-93, Sotheby-London, #42, illus.), 9½ x 6 in., (24.1 x 15.2 cm.), engraving on paper (BP 14,375, DM 36,641, FR 123,500, Y 2,309,879).

DYCK, Sir Anthony van (after)
$220* *Palamedes Palamadessen And D. Deodatus Del Mont: Two, The First Mauquoy-Hendrickx 58 III/XII, The Second M-H 78 VI/VIII,* (09-20-92, Hindman, #649), larger 9¼ x 6⅝ in., (23.5 x 16.8 cm.), etchings and engravings (BP 129, DM 326, FR 1117, Y 27,191).

DYKE, Willard van American 20th cent.
BI *Nehi, Oakland, California,* s., d. 1934, est. $1/1,500, (05-16-93, Hindman, #356), 7½ x 9½ in., photograph, silver print.

EAKINS, Thomas (attrib.) American 1844-1916
$170 *A Seated Woman With A Book,* (09-24-92, Alderfer, #226, illus.), 8 x 6 in., (20.3 x 15.2 cm.), photograph (BP 100, DM 252, FR 856, Y 20,450).

EARL, George (after)
$84* *In The Highlands,* laid down, varnished, scratched, (01-18-93, Bonhams, #75), 14½ x 22 in., (36.8 x 55.9 cm.), chromolithograph (BP 55, DM 137, FR 458, Y 10,589).
$330* *"Polo Match At Hurlingham",* (03-24-93, Doyle, #23), 11½ x 23½ in., (29.2 x 59.7 cm.), hand-colored print (BP 223, DM 539, FR 1834, Y 38,773).

EARL, Maud (after)
$84* *Champion Bock Bier,* pub. Fawcett and Co., margins, (01-18-93, Bonhams, #73), plate 9 x 11½ in., (22.9 x 29.2 cm.), photogravure (BP 55, DM 137, FR 458, Y 10,589).
$556* *English And French Bulldogs, 1914,* s., blindstamp Fine Art Trade Guild, pub. Thomas Agnew and Sons, margins, tears edges, scuffed, (01-18-93, Bonhams, #74), plate 23½ x 27 in., (59.7 x 68.6 cm.), photogravure (BP 363, DM 909, FR 3032, Y 70,087).

EARLOM, Richard British 1743-1822
$138* *Birds,* darkening, repaired tears, Maya de Montaudouin Estate, (06-11-93, Weschler, #50), 16½ x 22½ in., (41.9 x 57.2 cm.), mezzotint (BP 91, DM 224, FR 756, Y 14,642).
$345* *Head Of A Greyhound, Old Wick, c. 1760,* proof, margins, good cond., Anthony N. B. Garvan Coll., (06-05-93, Christie-NY, #54), pl 11½ x 7¼ in., (292 x 191 mm.), mezzotint on laid (BP 227, DM 559, FR 1885, Y 37,009).
$70* *"Liber Veritatis": Seven,* after Claude Gellee, pub. John Boydell, 1802-17, various sizes, foxed, staining, tears, (05-15-93, Cleveland, #12), smallest 7¼ x 9¼ in., (18.4 x 23.5 cm.), largest 9¼ x 12⅜ in., (18.4 x 23.5 cm.), etching w/mezzotint tone, 5 hand-colored, 2 uncolored (BP 46, DM 113, FR 378, Y 7760).
$230* *"Liber Veritatis": Thirty,* after Claude Gellee, pub. John Boydell, 1777, various sizes, time stained, stained, foxed, 20 good cond., (05-15-93, Cleveland, #11), each approx. 8 x 10 in., (20.3 x 25.4 cm.), etching w/mezzotint tone; one hand colored (BP 150, DM 370, FR 1243, Y 25,496).
$8250* *"Lieber Veritatis",* four volumes, after orig. designs by Claude Le Lorrain, Vol. I and II, c. 1777, vols. III and IV, c. 1817, pub. John Boydell or Messrs. Boydell, (03-25-93, Boos, #622, illus.), 300 mezzotints in vols. I-III, 168 etchings in vol. IV (BP 5603, DM 13,553, FR 46,089, Y 966,495).
BI *"Lieber Veritatis, Collection Of 300 Prints After Original Designs OfClaude Le Lorrain": Four Volumes,* volumes 1 and 2, c. 1777, volumes, 3 and 4, c. 1817, pub. John Boydell or Messrs. Boydell, est. $12/16,000, (08-05-92, Boos, #576, illus.), 300 mezzotints, vol. 1-3, 4th vol. 168 etchings.
$193* *Pastoral Scenes Of Cattle: A Pair,* plate s., first pub. Sept. 1 1775 by John Boydell, plates #101 and 103, after Claude Lorrain, (03-12-93, DuMouchelle, #2460), 7½ x 10 in., (19.1 x 25.4 cm.), etching and aquatint (BP 135, DM 321, FR 1092, Y 22,746).
$165* *Simeon And The Child, 1778,* p. and pub. John Boydell, margins glued to overmat, good cond., light-staining, foxing, surface scuffing, water/mat staining, surface soiling, (10-28-92, Butterfield, #2804), 16¾ x 12 in., (425 x 305 mm.), mezzotint on wove (BP 105, DM 255, FR 865, Y 20,245).

EASTCOTT, R.W.
$22* *"Core Plane",* #2/10, s., t., d. 24-10-73, (03-10-93, Maynard, #255), image 16¾ x 16½ in., (42.5 x 41.9 cm.), silkscreen (BP 15, DM 37, FR 124, Y 2599, C$ 28).

EASTMAN, Michael b. 1947
$1430* *Black And White In Color, 1986,* s., t., d., num. 19/50, mounted, (10-13-92, Christie-NY, #534, illus.), 29 x 36 in., (73.7 x 91.4 cm.), photograph, color coupler print (BP 833, DM 2095, FR 7118, Y 173,396).
$2760* *Montreal Balcony, 1987,* s., t., d., #20/25, (04-08-93, Christie-NY, #524, illus.), 13½ x 36½ in., (34.3 x 92.7 cm.), photograph, color coupler print (BP 1810, DM 4434, FR 15,008, Y 313,209).

EATON, Danil
$518* *Ferns, 1880: Eight,* (03-03-93, Sotheby-Arcade, #128), sight 11 x 9 in., (27.9 x 22.9 cm.), chromolithograph (BP 357, DM 853, FR 2894, Y 60,528).

EBERHARD
BI *Study Of Two Leopards,* #58/60, s., margins, est. BP 40/60, (02-17-93, Bonhams-Chelsea, #355), plate 8 x 10 in., (20.3 x 25.4 cm.), etching.

EBERSBACH, Herbert 1902-1984
BI *Bildnis Einer Alten Frau, 1921,* foxing, est. DM 300-, (09-25-92, Granier, #2822), sheet 10⅝ x 8¹¹⁄₁₆ in., (27 x 22 cm.), drypoint on copper print paper.
BI *Portrait Einer Frau, 1922,* s., d., #3, wear, est. DM 300-, (09-25-92, Granier, #2823), sheet 11 x 9¹⁄₁₆ in., (28 x 23 cm.), drypoint on copper print paper.

EBERZ, Josef 1880-1942
$332* *"Klosteranwesen", (19)18,* s., (12-01-92, Karl/Faber, #561), 14¾ x 18⁵⁄₁₆ in., (37.5 x 46.5 cm.), lithograph on hand-made (BP 219, DM 529, FR 1803, Y 41,335).
$1355* *Nachtlicher Circus (Vollmer, Bd. II, S. 5), 1920: Six,* Opus I der Reihe Graphische Capriccios, Munchen, Goltz Verlag, #190/20, frontispiece s., num., all mono., 1 sheet d. 1919 in block, (10-09-92, Winterberg, #2030), smallest 9⁷⁄₁₆ x 7¹⁄₁₆ in., (24 x 18 cm.), largest 10¾ x 7⅞ in., (24 x 18 cm.), woodcut on hand-made (BP 804, DM 2013, FR 6758, Y 164,962).

EBY, Kerr American 1889-1946
$10* *"The Aeroplane",* s., very good cond., (05-15-93, Cleveland, #118), 5⅜ x 3⅞ in., (13.7 x 9.8 cm.), etching (BP 7, DM 16, FR 54, Y 1109).
$357* *"Island Winter", "Whale's Back" and "High Island", c. 1920s: Three,* s., good cond., (05-27-93, Swann, #97), etching (BP 229, DM 573, FR 1931, Y 38,272).
$325* *"No. 1 Wall St.", 1929,* s., good cond., (05-15-93, Cleveland, #117, illus.), 16⅛ x 10⅜ in., (41 x 26.4 cm.), etching (BP 211, DM 523, FR 1757, Y 36,027).
$825* *"Pastoral Landscapes": Group Of Three,* s., good cond., (12-04-92, Doyle, #93), largest 10¼ x 15½ in., (260 x

394 mm.), etching (BP 529, DM 1314, FR 4457, Y 102,996).

$165* *Salt Marshes (K.109), 1930,* s., ed. 90, good cond., (11-12-92, Freemn/Fine Art, #62), 9⅝ x 13⅜ in., (24.4 x 34 cm.), etching (BP 108, DM 261, FR 882, Y 20,459).

$2300* *September 13, 1918, Black Cloud (L. of C. 28),* c. 1918, s., i. imp., Ed 100, full margins, mat staining, glue patches, very good cond., (05-11-93, Christie-NY, #98), plate 10¼ x 15⅞ in., (260 x 403 mm.), etching on laid (BP 1468, DM 3623, FR 12,208, Y 252,997).

ECKALUK

$87* *Pulling A Seal Through The Ice, 1976,* #2/40, s., t., d. 1976, prov., (11-16-92, Hodgins, #104), 14 x 14 in., (35.6 x 35.6 cm.), stonecut on paper (BP 57, DM 139, FR 467, Y 10,857, C$ 110).

EDEL, E.

$261* *Weberall, Illustrierte Wochenschrift, Heft-309,* p. H.S. Hermann, creases, backed on linen, (05-07-93, Christie-S. Ken, #79), 17 x 24 in., (43.2 x 61 cm.), color lithograph (BP 165, DM 413, FR 1391, Y 28,738).

EDELMAN, Yrjo   b. 1941

$166* *"Reflexion Sur L"Evolution Des Temps",* s. EA, (11-07-92, Falkkloos, #113), color lithograph (BP 109, DM 266, FR 896, Y 20,489, SK 990).

EDGERTON, Harold   1903-1990

$715* *Acrobats,* (1940), 1965, s., label w/t., (10-13-92, Christie-NY, #193, illus.), 19½ x 15⅜ in., (49.5 x 39.1 cm.), photograph, gelatin silver print (BP 416, DM 1047, FR 3559, Y 86,698).

$2200* *Bobby Jones Swinging Driver, c. 1931 (Flash, p. 61),* s., i. by photog., stamps, (10-15-92, Sotheby-NY, #472, illus.), 7⅜ x 9½ in., (18.7 x 24.1 cm.), photograph, gelatin silver print (BP 1346, DM 3275, FR 11,106, Y 263,947).

BI *"Bullet Cutting Card", "Pigeon In Flight" and "Football Kick", Selected Images (Stopping Time, p. 53 & 109-110):* Three, plates from "Ten Dye Transfer Photographs" portfolio, Palm Press, 1985, c. 1964, 1965, 1938, s. by photog., p. c. 1985, est. $2,5/4,000, (10-15-92, Sotheby-NY, #475, illus.), each, approx. 14 x 18 in., (35.6 x 45.7 cm.), photograph, dye transfer prints.

$3740* *Edgerton's M.I.T. Experiments With High Speed And Strobe Photography:Thirty,* 1930's-40's, (10-14-92, Swann, #440, illus.), 8 x 10 in., (20.3 x 25.4 cm.), photograph, silver prints (BP 2195, DM 5473, FR 18,561, Y 453,223).

$2860* *Edgerton's M.I.T. Experiments With High Speed And Strobe Photography:Thirty-Eight,* notations, 1930's-40's, est. $4/5,000, (10-14-92, Swann, #439), 8 x 10 in., (20.3 x 25.4 cm.), photograph, silver prints (BP 1679, DM 4186, FR 14,194, Y 346,583).

$825* *Jack And Bullet, 1960/1977,* s., #20/60, (11-16-92, Butterfield, #5945, illus.), 11 x 13¾ in., (279.9 x 349.9 mm.), photograph, dye-transfer print (BP 543, DM 1315, FR 4431, Y 102,599).

$6600* *Lot Of Vintage Photographs,* w/ultra high-speed multiflash and night photography, 2 pamphlets, one d.1940, several annot. by Edgerton w/locale Nola Park/Cleveland Ohio, d. Taken Aug. 31 1942/5000 ft f3.5 triX film, good cond., all mildly curled, one w/broken corner, (03-12-93, Skinner, #122, illus.), 10 x 10 in., photograph, silver prints (BP 4604, DM 10,985, FR 37,351, Y 777,843).

$1430* *"Milk Drop", "Dancer Gus Solomons" and "Two Fencers":* Three, photog.'s sig., 1930s-60s, p.l., (04-07-93, Swann, #450), largest 18 x 14 in., photograph, silver print (BP 945, DM 2313, FR 7827, Y 162,463).

$1980* *Selected Images: Three: "Milk Drop Coronet"; "Diver"; amd "CranberryJuice In Milk", (Stopping Time, pp. 103 & 127),* plates from the "Ten Dye Transfer Photographs" portfolio, 1957, 1955,1978, s. by photog., p. c. 1985, (10-15-92, Sotheby-NY, #476, illus.), each approx. 18 x 14 in., (45.7 x 35.6 cm.), photograph, dye transfer prints (BP 1212, DM 2947, FR 9995, Y 237,552).

$1980* *Selected Images: Three: "Shooting The Apple"; "Bullet Through Banana"; and "Moscow Circus Acrobats", (Stopping Time, pp. 107-108 & 126),* from the "Ten Dye

Transfer Photographs" portfolio, Palm Press, 1985,1964, c. 1964, 1963, each s. by photog., p. c. 1985, (10-15-92, Sotheby-NY, #477, illus.), each approx. 14 x 18 in., (35.6 x 45.7 cm.), photograph, dye transfer prints (BP 1212, DM 2947, FR 9995, Y 237,552).

$1100* *Selected Images: Two: "Bullet Through Playing Card" and "Fighting Finches", (Stopping Time, p. 61),* 1964, 1936, each s. by photog., p. l., (10-15-92, Sotheby-NY, #479, illus.), one 14⅛ x 18⅛ in., (35.9 x 46 cm.), other 18⅛ x 14½ in., (35.9 x 46 cm.), photograph, gelatin silver print (BP 673, DM 1637, FR 5553, Y 131,974).

$1100* *Shooting The Apple (Stopping Time, dust jacket and p. 126),* s., i. by photog., 1964, p. l., (10-15-92, Sotheby-NY, #473, illus.), 9¾ x 11⅞ in., (24.8 x 30.2 cm.), photograph, dye transfer print (BP 673, DM 1637, FR 5553, Y 131,974).

BI *Stopping Time (Stopping Time, pp. 1-2, 43, 45, 46, 51, 52, 59, 60, 61, 80, 83, 85, 92-93, 96, 97, 105, 120-121, 125, cf. 127, 133-134, 144, and 147): Twenty-Five,* including "Bob Edgerton Running", "Densmore Shute Bends The Shaft", "Water From A Faucet", "Hammer Breaks Glass Plate", "Ouch!", "Football Kick", "Fan And Smoke", "Rising Dove"...1930's-50's, p.l., est. $9/12,000, (10-15-92, Sotheby-NY, #474, illus.), var. sizes on sheets 16 x 20 in., (40.6 x 50.8 cm.), photograph, gelatin silver prints.

BI *Tennis Player, 1939/1977,* est. $6/800, s., #20/60 verso, (11-16-92, Butterfield, #5946, illus.), 8½ x 12⅛ in., (216.3 x 308.5 mm.), photograph, gelatin silver print.

EDMONDSUN, H.M.

$11* *Country Road With Oxen And Cart,* d. '37, (09-18-92, DuMouchelle, #396), engraving (BP 6, DM 16, FR 56, Y 1371).

EDRIDGE, H. (after)

$58 *"Viscount Curzon",* engraved by Charles Picart, d. 1813, (04-16-93, G.A. Key, #24), 16 x 11 in., (40.6 x 27.9 cm.), b/w stipple engraving (BP 38, DM 94, FR 317, Y 6522).

EDWARD OF NORWICH (2nd Duke of York) (Baillie-Grohman)

$460* *The Master Of Game...The Oldest English Book On Hunting, London 1904,* folio, label, worn, foxing, limited edit., #224/600 copies, s. W. A.Grohman, Anthony N. B. Garvan Coll., (06-05-93, Christie-NY, #20), facsimile plate in color and b/w (BP 303, DM 746, FR 2514, Y 49,346).

EDWARDS (after)

$220* *Botanicals: Group Of Eight,* (03-24-93, Doyle, #24), 4¾ x 8 in., (12.1 x 20.3 cm.), color print (BP 149, DM 359, FR 1223, Y 25,849).

EDWARDS, E. (after)

BI *A Group Of Charity-A Plate Dedicated To Mr. William Hickes' Support Of The Marine Society, 1774,* by John Hall, pub. J. Boydell, repaired tear, est. BP 120/180, (11-30-92, Phillips-London, #226), plate 21 x 17 in., (533 x 432 mm.), engraving on laid.

EDWARDS, George   British 1694-1773

$358* *"The Blue Jay And The Summer Red Bird From Carolina" and "The Curukui Of Marcgrave": Two,* drawn, etched from life by George Edwards, pub. 1755 and 1759, margins, (01-02-93, Litchfield, #68), 9¼ x 7¼ in., (23.5 x 18.4 cm.), hand colored etching (BP 239, DM 587, FR 2002, Y 44,885).

$86 *"Butcher-Bird And Butterfly" and "The Small Kingfisher And Blue Lizard": Two,* d. 1757, (12-11-92, G.A. Key, #97), 10 x 8 in., (25.4 x 20.3 cm.), hand colored engraving (BP 55, DM 135, FR 464, Y 10,642).

EDWARDS, George (after)   English 1694-1773

$303* *Birds: A Pair,* by Johann Michael Seligmann (Ger., 1720-1762), (12-10-92, Sloan, #1642, illus.), each, approx. 10⅜ x 8 in., (26.4 x 20.3 cm.), colored engraving (BP 195, DM 479, FR 1637, Y 37,481).

EDWARDS, Lionel   English 1877/78-1966

$108* *"The Duke Of Beaufort's Hounds...", "Forrard Away", "The Portman, Okeford Hill" and "In Beaufortshire Whitewell Woods" and others: Six Sporting Views,* plate s., t. labels, prov., (06-08-93, Ritchie, #10, illus.), largest

6½ x 9⅞ in., (16.5 x 25.1 cm.), color photomechanical print (BP 71, DM 175, FR 590, Y 11,471, C$ 138).

$122 *Military Parade*, s., d. 1959, (06-11-93, G.A. Key, #14), 13 x 22 in., (33 x 55.9 cm.), colored print (BP 80, DM 198, FR 668, Y 12,944).

EDWARDS, Lionel (after)
$75* *Forrard On, Forrard*, staining, (06-30-93, Bonhams-Chelsea, #118), image 11 x 17⅛ in., (27.9 x 43.5 cm.), chromolithograph (BP 50, DM 128, FR 432, Y 8036).
$130* *Hunting Countries, The Atherstone*, s., blindstamp Fine Art Trade Guild, pub. Eyre and Spottiswoode, (10-29-92, Bonhams-Chelsea, #126), image 13¼ x 19½ in., (33.7 x 49.5 cm.), reproduction in colors (BP 83, DM 200, FR 678, Y 16,103).
$343* *Hunting Countries, The Buccleuch, Grundistone*, s., blindstamp Fine Art Trade Guild, pub. Eyre and Spottiswoode, (10-29-92, Bonhams-Chelsea, #127), image 13¼ x 19½ in., (33.7 x 49.5 cm.), reproduction in colors (BP 220, DM 528, FR 1790, Y 42,487).
$50 *"Hunting Types, The Thruster"*, (12-11-92, G.A. Key, #9), 12 x 17 in., (30.5 x 43.2 cm.), colored print (BP 32, DM 79, FR 270, Y 6187).
$47 *"Hunting Types/The M.F.N."*, (12-11-92, G.A. Key, #16), 13 x 17 in., (33 x 43.2 cm.), colored print (BP 30, DM 74, FR 254, Y 5816).
$518* *"Lord Hugh Percy's Beagles", c. 1940 and "Trinity Foot Beagles", 1950: Two*, both s., margins, Anthony N. B. Garvan Coll., (06-05-93, Christie-NY, #80), reprod. in color on wove (BP 341, DM 840, FR 2831, Y 55,567).

EDWARDS, Sydenham Teast (after)
$275* *Botanical Prints, c. 1805: Two*, F. Sansom, engraver, ident. on labels, very good cond.?, (12-04-92, Skinner, #390), sheet approx., sight 10 x 7½ in., (25.4 x 19.1 cm.), engraving w/etching and hand-coloring on paper (BP 176, DM 438, FR 1486, Y 34,332).
$385* *Curtis Flowers, 1805, 1806: Two*, (09-17-92, Sloan, #661), handcolored engravings (BP 216, DM 572, FR 1956, Y 47,933).

EDY, John William
BI *View Of St. Anthony's Nose, On The North Shore Province Of New York,1795*, after George Bulteel Fisher, pub. J.W. Edy, St. John's, margins, broken through crease, tear, backed w/wove, est. $10/14,000, (01-28-93, Sotheby-NY, #413, illus.), image 16½ x 24½ in., (419 x 622 mm.), sheet 17⅞ x 25¼ in., (419 x 622 mm.), hand-colored aquatint.

EDZARD, Dietz   German 1893-1963
$154* *(In Love), 1922*, s., d, i. erster probedruck, margins, good cond., small tear in leftcorner, minor foxing, minor soiling, late Gerhard Brauer Coll., (05-27-93, Sotheby-Amstrdm, #723), 6¾ x 5⁵⁄₁₆ in., (172 x 135 mm.), etching on sturdy wove (BP 99, DM 247, FR 833, Y 16,509, G 276).

EEKMAN, N. M   b. 1889
$47* *Two Men*, s., #9, browned, (06-09-93, Bubb Kuyper, #1977), 8⅞ x 5¹⁄₁₆ in., (22.6 x 12.9 cm.), woodcut (BP 31, DM 77, FR 259, Y 4998, G 86).

EEKMAN, Nico   1889-1973
$231* *"Scene D'Interieur", 1973*, d., mono., (01-28-93, Pescheteau, #131), 15¾ x 19¹¹⁄₁₆ in., (40 x 50 cm.), drypoint on Arches (BP 153, DM 366, FR 1239, Y 28,681).
$70* *Untitled*, #18/110, s., (04-04-93, Pescheteau, #207), 19¹¹⁄₁₆ x 12¹³⁄₁₆ in., (50 x 32.5 cm.), wood engraving (BP 46, DM 113, FR 382, Y 7970).

EERENBEEMT, Gerard van den
BI *Untitled, 1981*, s. Gerard Leonard, #167/190, p. Bernhard Ruigrock, full margins, good cond., minor handling creases est. Dfl. 150/250, (05-27-93, Sotheby-Amstrdm, #406), 21⁵⁄₁₆ x 16¹⁵⁄₁₆ in., (542 x 430 mm.), colored screenprint on wove.
$64* *Untitled, 1981*, s. Gerard Leonard, #128/190, p. Bernhard Ruigrock, blindstamp, full margins, good cond., minor handling creases, (05-27-93, Sotheby-Amstrdm, #407), 18⅞ x 15¹¹⁄₁₆ in., (479 x 398 mm.), colored screenprint on wove (BP 41, DM 103, FR 346, Y 6861, G 115).

$115* *Untitled, 1981*, s. Gerard Leonard, p. Bernhard Ruigrock, blindstamp, full margins, good cond., minor handling creases, (05-27-93, Sotheby-Amstrdm, #408), 1⅝ x 15 in., (412 x 381 mm.), colored screenprint on wove (BP 74, DM 185, FR 622, Y 12,328, G 207).

EGGENSCHWILER, Franz   b. 1930
BI *Dreh Um Die M'Linie, 1991*, Epr.d'a., mono., d., t., est. SF 180/230, (10-14-92, Germann, #504), 22¼ x 16¹⁵⁄₁₆ in., (565 x 430 mm.), color woodcut/offset.
BI *Fellaken, 1988*, Epr.d'a, mono., d., t., est. SF 250/350, (10-14-92, Germann, #502), 19¹¹⁄₁₆ x 17¹¹⁄₁₆ in., (500 x 450 mm.), color woodcut.

EGGLESTON, William   b. 1939
$450* *Elvis' Tomb (Untitled)*, s., i. "Plate 10 of 11" and "Example 11/31", stamped 1983 verso, (02-04-93, Sloan, #2901), 20 x 23¾ in., (50.8 x 60.3 cm.), photograph, dye transfer (BP 311, DM 746, FR 2522, Y 55,998).
$525* *Gold Piano, Graceland*, s., i. "Plate 4 of 11" and "Example 21/31" verso, (02-04-93, Sloan, #2904, illus.), 14½ x 22 in., (36.8 x 55.9 cm.), photograph, dye transfer (BP 363, DM 871, FR 2943, Y 65,331).
$500* *Gold Piano, Graceland*, (02-04-93, Sloan, #2905), 14½ x 22 in., (36.8 x 55.9 cm.), photograph, dye transfer (BP 346, DM 829, FR 2803, Y 62,220).
$7500* *Graceland, Untitled Images: Eleven*, 1983, Middendorf Gallery, Inc., 1984, s., #13/31, includes folding t. sheet, colophon, sold after sale, (04-08-93, Christie-NY, #525, illus.), each approx. 22 x 14½ in., (55.9 x 36.8 cm.), photograph, dye-transfer print (BP 4918, DM 12,048, FR 40,783, Y 851,112).
BI *Interior View Of Graceland*, s., #2/3, stamped 1983 verso, est. $0, (02-04-93, Sloan, #2902), 24 x 20 in., (61 x 50.8 cm.), color photograph.
$3450* *"Troubled Waters", 1980: Four*, plates 1,5,8 and 12 from Troubled Waters portfolio, each s. by photog., photog. edit. and rights reserved stamps, (04-06-93, Sotheby-NY, #494, illus.), each approx. 17¼ x 11¼ in., photograph, dye-transfer print (BP 2279, DM 5558, FR 18,822, Y 393,476).
$1980* *Untitled (Father's Grave), 1974*, from 14 Pictures portfolio, s., label, num. 11/15, (10-13-92, Christie-NY, #535, illus.), 13 x 19 in., (33 x 48.3 cm.), photograph, dye transfer print (BP 1153, DM 2901, FR 9856, Y 240,087).

EGLAU, Otto   German 1917-1988
BI *Flughafen, 1967*, s., t., d., #16/30, full margins, good cond., minor soiling in margins, est. Dfl. 4/600, (05-27-93, Sotheby-Amstrdm, #612), 15⁹⁄₁₆ x 19⅜ in., (396 x 492 mm.), color etching on wove.
$258* *Flusslandschaft, 1957*, t., s., (12-05-92, Bassenge, #7143), 19⅝ x 22¹¹⁄₁₆ in., (49.8 x 57.6 cm.), etching (BP 162, DM 402, FR 1371, Y 31,966).
BI *"Formen Der Wuste"*, i., s., d. Eglau 60, #61/100, est. DM 300-, (03-24-93, Venator/Hansten, #4481), pl. approx. 11⁵⁄₁₆ x 20¹⁄₁₆ in., (28.7 x 50.9 cm.), color aquatint.
$169* *"Netzformen"*, i., s., d. Eglau 62, #38/100, foxing, (03-24-93, Venator/Hansten, #4482), pl. approx. 19⁹⁄₁₆ x 9⅛ in., (49.7 x 23.2 cm.), etching and color aquatint (BP 114, DM 276, FR 939, Y 19,857).
BI *New York, 1965*, s., t., d., i. Epreuve d'Artiste, full margins, good cond., minor soiling in margins, est. Dfl. 3/500, (05-27-93, Sotheby-Amstrdm, #611), 10³⁄₁₆ x 12¹⁵⁄₁₆ in., (258 x 328 mm.), color etching on wove.
$251* *Zeichen Im Watt, 1981*, 1st state, t., s., (12-05-92, Bassenge, #7144), 15½ x 19½ in., (39.3 x 49.5 cm.), color etching (BP 157, DM 391, FR 1334, Y 31,099).

EHINGER, Gabriel   1652-1736
$722* *Saul Spricht Mit Samuels Geist Bei Der Hexe Von Endor (Le Blanc 1; Hollstein 1; Pee NS 45)*, (12-04-92, Bassenge, #6173, illus.), 16⁷⁄₁₆ x 12 in., (41.8 x 30.5 cm.), etching (BP 463, DM 1150, FR 3901, Y 90,137).

EHM, Josef   1909-1989
BI *Friends In The Park, 1935*, s., t., d., est. $2,5/3,500, (10-13-92, Christie-NY, #194, illus.), 6⅝ x 5⅞ in., (16.8 x 14.9 cm.), photograph, gelatin silver print.
$1610* *Imaginary Space II*, 1936, p. 1950s, t., d., credit stamp, sold after sale, (04-08-93, Christie-NY, #120, illus.), 6¼

x 7 in., (15.9 x 17.8 cm.), photograph, gelatin silver print (BP 1056, DM 2586, FR 8755, Y 182,705).
$2750* *Nude With Black Lace, 1946,* credit stamp, sold after sale, (10-13-92, Christie-NY, #442, illus.), 12⅝ x 10½ in., (32.1 x 26.7 cm.), photograph, gelatin silver print (BP 1602, DM 4029, FR 13,688, Y 333,455).
BI *Thun Street In Mala Strana, 1947,* t., d., credit stamp, est. $3/4,000, (10-13-92, Christie-NY, #443, illus.), 15½ x 11¼ in., (39.4 x 28.6 cm.), photograph, gelatin silver print.

EHMSEN, Heinrich 1896-1964
$251* *Illustration Zu "Der Narr In Christo Emanuel Quint" Von Gerhart Hauptmann, 1927,* s., corner lightly creased, (12-05-92, Bassenge, #7146), 7⅝ x 9¾ in., (19.3 x 24.7 cm.), drypoint on strong Japan (BP 157, DM 391, FR 1334, Y 31,099).

EHRET (after)
$216* *Botanical Prints: Pair,* (05-12-93, Maynard, #557), color print (BP 141, DM 348, FR 1174, Y 24,115, C$ 275).

EHRET, Georg Dionysius
BI *Plantae Selectae C.J. Trew (Nissen 1997), 1792: Thirty-Seven,* from the series, watermarked, full margins, excellent cond., est. BP800/1,200, (10-27-92, Phillips-London, #165), plate 17 x 11 in., (432 x 279 mm.), hand-colored engraving on fine laid.

EHRHARDT, Alfred 1901-1984
BI *Dunelandschaft, c. 1935,* credit stamp, est. $1,5/1,800, (04-08-93, Christie-NY, #96, illus.), 9⅜ x 6⅜ in., (23.8 x 16.2 cm.), photograph, gelatin silver print.

EHRLICH, Franz 1907-1984
$455* *Arbeiten Von Franz Ehrlich, c. 1928,* (11-12-92, Lempertz, #8, illus.), 9$\frac{1}{16}$ x 6$\frac{7}{16}$ in., (23 x 16.3 cm.), photograph, gelatin silver print (BP 291, DM 715, FR 2437, Y 56,291).

EHRLICH, Georg
$95* *Portrait Of A Young Girl,* #18/50, s., d. 23, margins, (05-20-93, Bonhams-Chelsea, #163), plate 8⅞ x 7⅞ in., (22.5 x 20 cm.), drypoint etching (BP 61, DM 153, FR 516, Y 10,490).

EHRMANN, A.
$120* *Ca Sent Bon! Les Veinards! C'Est Surement Du Potage Maggi,* Imp. de la Cie Maggi, fairly good cond., (02-12-93, Cheval/Robert, #57), 61$\frac{13}{16}$ x 46⅞ in., (157 x 119 cm.), poster (BP 85, DM 199, FR 673, Y 14,472).

EICHENBERG, Fritz German/American 1901-1970
$220* *And Their Eyes Were Opened,* s., t., num. 106-200, full margins, good cond., light-staining, foxing, skinned areas, (02-24-93, Butterfield, #2815), 12¼ x 6 in., (311 x 152 mm.), wood engraving on Japan (BP 153, DM 357, FR 1211, Y 25,816).
$468* *The Aquarium,* s., t., num. Ed. 200, margins, good cond., (02-24-93, Butterfield, #2630), 6¼ x 4⅝ in., (159 x 117 mm.), wood engraving on wove (BP 326, DM 760, FR 2576, Y 54,917).
$1045* *City Lights, 1934,* s., d., annot. PR Proof-O.K., full margins, very good cond., surfacesoiling, (10-28-92, Butterfield, #2729), 6¼ x 4⅞ in., (159 x 124 mm.), wood engraving on cream wove (BP 666, DM 1614, FR 5480, Y 128,221).
$150* *"The Dream Of Reason",* s., t., excell. cond., (05-15-93, Cleveland, #121), 9 x 7 in., (22.9 x 17.8 cm.), woodcut (BP 98, DM 241, FR 811, Y 16,628).
$358* *"Gulliver's Travels" and "Crime And Punishment": Two,* each s., t., Crime And Punishment annot. II-Proof, margins, good cond., mat staining, buckling, (02-24-93, Butterfield, #2817), one 5¾ x 4½ in., (146 x 114 mm.), other 7⅜ x 5 in., (146 x 114 mm.), wood engraving on tissue-thin Japan (BP 250, DM 581, FR 1970, Y 42,009).
BI *Heathcliff & Linton, 1943,* s., very good cond., est. $1/200, (05-15-93, Cleveland, #120), 7½ x 5 in., (19.1 x 12.7 cm.), wood engraving.
$880* *In Praise Of Folly, 1972: Eight,* incomplete portfolio (lacking plates I & VII), s., num. 28, pub. Aquarius Press, full margins, good cond., (02-24-93, Butterfield, #2629), 20 x 14¼ in., (508 x 362 mm.), woodcuts on Japanese mulberry paper (BP 614, DM 1429, FR 4843, Y 103,262).
$303* *The Peaceable Kingdom,* s., t., num. 187/200, margins, good cond., foxing, (02-24-93, Butterfield, #2816), 12¼ x 6 in., (311 x 152 mm.), wood engraving on wove (BP 211, DM 492, FR 1668, Y 35,555).
$192* *Portrait Of Lincoln, c. 1978,* ink s., pub. Frank and Virginia Williams Coll. of Lincolniana, (05-27-93, Swann, #98), 19 x 11½ in., (48.3 x 29.2 cm.), woodcut w/lettering (BP 123, DM 308, FR 1038, Y 20,583).
$1100* *"Praise Of Folly, Erasmus", 1972: Suite Of Ten,* s., unbound sheets in paper folio, (12-08-92, Swann, #96), images 18 x 12 in., (45.7 x 30.5 cm.), wood engraving (BP 689, DM 1713, FR 5839, Y 136,341).
$165* *"Preaching To The Animals", 1936,* illus. in Fine Prints of the Year, 1936, s. Eichenberg and in block,very good cond., (09-11-92, Skinner, #74, illus.), 7⅜ x 6 in., (17.8 x 15.2 cm.), wood engraving on tissue-weight wove (BP 85, DM 238, FR 807, Y 20,444).

EICHHORN, Alfred
BI *"Oriental Princess" and "Comical Society", 1947: Two,* s., num., good cond., est. $2/300, (06-11-93, Doyle, #37), larger 8¼ x 11 in., (210 x 279 mm.), lithograph.

EICHLER, N.G.
$1230* *Et Par Prospekter Fra Sankt Petersborg,* after Mayr 1799, (11-14-92, Bukowskis, #20), copper engraving (BP 808, DM 1962, FR 6609, Y 153,501, DK 7475).

EICKEMEMYER, Rudolf (Jr.)
$460* *"Bonnie Maude", 1907,* photog.'s blindstamp w/d. on image, inits., d., est. $800/1,000, (05-23-93, Butterfield, #3398, illus.), 9¼ x 7¼ in., photograph, gelatin silver print (BP 300, DM 752, FR 2532, Y 50,846).

EICKEMEYER, Rudolf American 1862-1932
$715* *Portrait Of Black Man, 1898,* (c) label, (10-14-92, Swann, #182, illus.), 9½ x 7½ in., (24.1 x 19.1 cm.), photograph, silver print (BP 420, DM 1046, FR 3548, Y 86,646).

EIFFEL, Albert
BI *Chemin De Fer D'Orleans Et Du Midi, L'Aven Armand, c. 1930,* p. Lucien Serre & Cie, cond. 3, laid on linen, est. BP 3/400, (10-13-92, Phillips-London, #16), 38$\frac{15}{16}$ x 24⅝ in., (99 x 62.5 cm.), color lithograph.

EINBECK
$1564* *Kunst-Photographien 1899,* p. Meisenbach Riffarth & Co., creases, (05-07-93, Christie-S. Ken, #76, illus.), 16 x 34 in., (40.6 x 86.4 cm.), lithograph in sepia (BP 990, DM 2473, FR 8332, Y 172,209).

EISAI and SURIMONO
$28* *"Grasses And Poem",* laid down, crease, soiling, fading, staining, (05-07-93, Goldberg, #1352), woodblock (BP 18, DM 44, FR 149, Y 3083).

EISEN
$633* *A Beauty Holding A Katsuo (Bonito), Pausing Beside The Entrance Of ACha-Ya,* sano-ya, from series Ukiyo Bijin Juni-ka-getsu, s. Keisai Eisen ga, pub. mark, Sanoki, soiled, rubbed, wormed, (06-10-93, Sotheby-London, #219), (BP 414, DM 1031, FR 3470, Y 67,190).
$1318* *A Surimono For The Year Of The Cock,* kakuban surimono, s. Keisai w/seal, (06-10-93, Sotheby-London, #202), silver and gold pigments in details (BP 862, DM 2146, FR 7226, Y 139,900).
$2110* *Two Courtesans Feeding Birds,* surimono, kakuban, from series Sancho den momo chidori, s. Keisai, rubbed, soiled, (06-10-93, Sotheby-London, #216, illus.), (BP 1380, DM 3436, FR 11,568, Y 223,968).

EISEN 1790-1848
$99* *"Courtesan", c. 1835,* pub. Kawaguchi-ya, trimmed, creasing, soiling, fair cond., (01-23-93, Goldberg, #300), wood block (BP 65, DM 157, FR 533, Y 12,390).

EISEN, Ikeda 1790-1848
$151* *Dame, die An Ihren Geliebten Denkt, c. 1840,* Format Oban, (04-27-93, Dorotheum, #232, illus.), 9$\frac{7}{16}$ x 14$\frac{9}{16}$ in., (24 x 37 cm.), woodcut (BP 96, DM 239, FR 809, Y 16,923, SC 1680).

EISENMANN, Charles
$2200* *Portrait Of A Female Midget,* orig. mount, sig. on image, 1880s, (04-07-93, Swann, #198, illus.), 16½ x 13½ in., photograph, albumen print (BP 1454, DM 3558, FR 12,042, Y 249,943).

EISENSTAEDT, Alfred b. 1898
$2200* *Adolf Hitler Meeting Benito Mussolini At The Airport In Venice, Italy, 1934 (Eisenstaedt, p. 57),* credit stamps, labels, (10-15-92, Sotheby-NY, #414, illus.), 11¾ x 9¼ in., (29.8 x 23.5 cm.), photograph, gelatin silver print (BP 1346, DM 3275, FR 11,106, Y 263,947).
$4400* *Gala Evening In The "Scala" Of Milan, 1934 (Eisenstaedt, p. 39),* t. by photog. in ink, name stamp, studio & reprod. limit. stamps, (10-15-92, Sotheby-NY, #415, illus.), 11¾ x 8¾ in., (29.8 x 22.2 cm.), photograph, gelatin silver print (BP 2692, DM 6550, FR 22,211, Y 527,894).
BI *"Jackie Kennedy Reads Stories To Caroline In Bed, Hyannisport, Mass.", 1960,* t. by photog., stamp, notations, est. $1/2,000, (04-06-93, Sotheby-NY, #132, illus.), 10½ x 13⅜ in., photograph.
BI *Marlene Dietrich, Berlin,* t., d. by photog., 1938, p. c. 1952, est. $2/3,000, (04-06-93, Sotheby-NY, #130, illus.), 10⅜ x 13⅜ in., photograph.
$687* *"Steps", n.d. (1930s),* (10-29-92, Christie-London, #149, illus.), 9¼ x 7 in., (23.5 x 17.8 cm.), photograph, gelatin silver print mounted on card (BP 440, DM 1057, FR 3586, Y 85,098).
$1495* *Woman In A Bar, 1940's,* photog. credit stamp, annot. in unident. hand, (04-06-93, Sotheby-NY, #131, illus.), 9 x 7⅜ in., photograph (BP 987, DM 2409, FR 8156, Y 170,506).

EISHI, Hosoda Japanese 1756-1829
BI *Portrait Of A Courtesan In A Snowstorm,* signs of wear, format Chuban, est. SC 5/6,000, (04-27-93, Dorotheum, #161, illus.), 6¹³⁄₁₆ x 8¾ in., (17.3 x 22.2 cm.), .

EISHO
$1934* *Beauties On Pleasure Boats Fishing With A Four-Armed Scoop Net: Triptych,* oban, pub. Eijudo, censor's seal kiwame, s. Eisho zu, faded, trimmed,rubbed, soiled, fold marks, creases, repaired, laid-down, (06-10-93, Sotheby-London, #242), (BP 1265, DM 3149, FR 10,603, Y 205,286).

EISHOSAI CHOKI Japanese ac. c. 1772-1816
$3062* *Iwai Hanshiro IV As Yoshitsune?,* Hosoban, s. Choki ga, d. c. Kyowa 3 (1803), soiled, rubbed, worm holes restored, Prof. H.R.W. Kuhne Coll., (06-11-93, Sotheby-London, #49, illus.), 12¾ x 5¾ in., (32.4 x 14.6 cm.), woodblock (BP 2012, DM 4976, FR 16,778, Y 324,881).
$962* *Matsumoto Goroichi(?), An Onnagata Actor,* Hosoban, s. Choki ga, pub.'s mark, d. c. 1817?, soiled, wormage restored, Prof. H.R.W. Kuhne Coll., (06-11-93, Sotheby-London, #43), 12¾ x 5⅝ in., (32.4 x 14.3 cm.), woodblock (BP 632, DM 1563, FR 5271, Y 102,069).

EITEL, Walter
$357* *G.I. With Cigarette,* photog.'s sig., handstamp, 1940s, (04-07-93, Swann, #303, illus.), 19¾ x 16 in., photograph, silver print (BP 236, DM 577, FR 1954, Y 40,559).

EIZAN
$220* *Portrait Of A Courtesan,* from Bijin of the Gay Quarters, s. Chokyusai Eizan, seal, pub. seal,faded, rubbed, tate-e, (11-20-92, Skinner, #63A, illus.), oban tate-e (BP 145, DM 351, FR 1182, Y 27,360).

EIZAN Japanese 1787-1867
$440* *"Lady Hanamurasaki", c. 1800,* s. Eizan fude, worm hole, very good cond., (10-31-92, Cleveland, #24, illus.), color woodblock (BP 282, DM 677, FR 2296, Y 54,503).

EIZAN, Kikugawa (school of)
BI *Exotic Shunga Chuban,* i., est. $200/350, (01-15-93, DuMouchelle, #2295), 6¾ x 9⅝ in., (17.1 x 24.4 cm.), color woodblock print.

EIZAN, Kikugawa Kabuki Japanese 1787-1867
$330* *Actors And Actresses: Two,* block s., (12-11-92, DuMouchelle, #2266), one approx. 14 x 9 in., (35.6 x 22.9 cm.), other approx. 15 x 10 in., (35.6 x 22.9 cm.), color woodblock prints (BP 212, DM 520, FR 1782, Y 40,837).

EKS-SKOLENS TRYKKERIS KUNSTMAPPE
$220* *8 Ar 1972-1980,* portfolio, num. 458 of 500, (03-24-93, Kunsthallen, #88), (BP 149, DM 359, FR 1223, Y 25,849, DK 1380).

ELDRED, L.D.
$825* *Bark "Canton",* s. Eldred, remark 1910, mounted on acid free paper and backing, exceptional cond., (02-13-93, Bourne, #189, illus.), etching (BP 581, DM 1368, FR 4630, Y 99,493).
$1870* *"Charles W. Morgan",* s. twice, pub. 1903, remark, excell. cond., (02-13-93, Bourne, #190, illus.), etching (BP 1317, DM 3101, FR 10,494, Y 225,519).
$550* *"Rousseau",* s., remark, excell. cond., (02-13-93, Bourne, #191, illus.), etching (BP 387, DM 912, FR 3086, Y 66,329).
$55* *"Venice",* s. plate, (02-27-93, Dunning, #115), 19½ x 24 in., (49.5 x 61 cm.), color etching (BP 39, DM 90, FR 307, Y 6493).

ELFER
$223* *Shell With I.C.A., The Most Powerful Petrol You Can Buy, 1954,* ref. P 76, cond. 3, (10-13-92, Phillips-London, #190), 29¹⁵⁄₁₆ x 39⅜ in., (76 x 100 cm.), color lithograph (BP 130, DM 327, FR 1110, Y 27,040).
$168* *Shell, The Most Powerful Petrol, 1953,* ref. P 74, cond. 3, (10-13-92, Phillips-London, #189), 29¹⁵⁄₁₆ x 39¾ in., (76 x 101 cm.), color lithograph (BP 98, DM 246, FR 836, Y 20,371).

ELGORT, Arthur contemporary
$304* *Karen Spansen,* s., d., i., (11-12-92, Lempertz, #47, illus.), 16¹⁵⁄₁₆ x 13⁹⁄₁₆ in., (43 x 34.5 cm.), photograph, gelatin silver print (BP 194, DM 478, FR 1628, Y 37,610).
$304* *Patti Hansen,* s., d., i., (11-12-92, Lempertz, #48), 18⁵⁄₁₆ x 12⁵⁄₁₆ in., (46.5 x 31.3 cm.), sheet 19¹⁵⁄₁₆ x 15¹⁵⁄₁₆ in., (46.5 x 31.3 cm.), photograph, gelatin silver print (BP 194, DM 478, FR 1628, Y 37,610).
$304* *Playa Palm Beach,* s., d., t., (11-12-92, Lempertz, #49), 19¹¹⁄₁₆ x 15⅞ in., (50 x 40.3 cm.), photograph, gelatin silver print (BP 194, DM 478, FR 1628, Y 37,610).

ELIASBERG, Paul 1907-1983
BI *Erinnerung An Bassae (Jensen 21), 1962,* s., num., stains, est. DM 180-, (09-25-92, Granier, #2826), sheet 16¹⁵⁄₁₆ x 20⅞ in., (43 x 53 cm.), etching on hand-made.
BI *Ourscamp (Jensen 51), 1967,* s., est. DM 250-, (09-25-92, Granier, #2827), sheet 19¹¹⁄₁₆ x 25¹⁵⁄₁₆ in., (50 x 66 cm.), etching on hand-made Arches.

ELIOT, Maurice
BI *Lady At Dining Table, c. 1897,* s., #13/100, blindstamp, Sagot, margins, good cond., soiling, creasing, surface dirt, est. BP 5/600, (12-03-92, Sotheby-London, #291, illus.), sheet 25 x 19¼ in., (635 x 489 mm.), lithograph on sturdy wove.
$184* *"Tete De Fillette", 1897 and "Femme Nue En Pied", c. 1895-1900 (Una Johnson 38): Two,* full margins, (02-24-93, Picard, #96), color lithograph on thin chine on Japan simili (BP 128, DM 299, FR 1013, Y 21,591).

ELISOFON, Eliot
BI *"Children Playing In A Vacant Lot" and "Young Boy At Play", 1930's: Two,* each mounted, 2nd s. by photog., est. $2/3,000, (10-15-92, Sotheby-NY, #182, illus.), each approx. 10¼ x 13¼ in., (26 x 33.7 cm.), photograph, gelatin silver prints.

ELK, Ger van Dutch b. 1944
$360* *"Roquebrunne I" and "Roquebrunne II", 1979-80: Two,* each s., d., t. in ink, #A.P. VI, V/XX, margins; first soiling, (10-15-92, Sotheby-London, #95, illus.), first 19⅛ x 38⅛ in., (48.6 x 96.8 cm.), second 73¼ x 37⅜ in., (48.6 x 96.8 cm.), photographs w/silkscreen (BP 220, DM 536, FR 1817, Y 43,191).
$3300* *Study For Honda Gothic,* s., t., d. 1986 Ger van Elk verso, prov., (10-08-92, Christie-NY, #224, illus.), 40¼ x 25¾ in., (102.2 x 65.4 cm.), cibachrome in artist's frame (BP 1964, DM 4881, FR 16,566, Y 400,972).

$90* *Three Pets, 1981: Triptych,* triptych, s., t., d., #18/40, margins, apparently good cond., (10-15-92, Sotheby-London, #93, illus.), each approx. 19¼ x 12¼ in., (48.9 x 31.1 cm.), three silkscreens p. in colors on wove (BP 55, DM 134, FR 454, Y 10,798).

ELLINGSON, Bill   20th cent.

$55* *Winter Landscape,* s., edit. 35, (11-28-92, Young, #130), 20 x 29 in., (50.8 x 73.7 cm.), etching (BP 36, DM 88, FR 297, Y 6845).

ELLIOT (after)

$17* *"Pitta Venusta",* (01-15-93, DuMouchelle, #2448), 14 x 10 in., (35.6 x 25.4 cm.), hand colored print (BP 11, DM 28, FR 94, Y 2143).

ELLIOT, Daniel Giraud (after)

BI *The New And Heretofore Unfigured Species Of The Birds Of North America, 1866: Ten,* from the set of 72, p. Bowen, full margins, excellent cond., bind defects, est. BP 7/900, (10-27-92, Phillips-London, #179), sheet 18½ x 23½ in., (470 x 597 mm.), hand-colored lithograph on wove.

$220* *"The Willow Grouse", "Common Ptarmigan", "Brachyurus Vigorsii" and "Brachyurus Erythrogaster": Four,* mat burn, discoloration, imperfections, creases, repairs, laid down on board, John Walton Livermore Estate, (12-04-92, Doyle, #48), hand colored lithograph (BP 141, DM 350, FR 1189, Y 27,466).

ELLIS, Clifford and Rosemary

$711* *To Visit Britain's Landmarks, Chanter's Folly & Dry Dock, Appledall,1937,* p. Waterlow and Sons, ref. #499, cond. 1, creasing, (10-13-92, Phillips-London, #125), 29¹⁵/₁₆ x 44⅞ in., (76 x 114 cm.), color lithograph (BP 414, DM 1042, FR 3539, Y 86,213).

ELLIS, Harry C.

BI *"Andresey, France", "Chateau Of Fountainbleau, France", "Kleine Scheieg, Switzerland", "The Fountains, St. Cloud, France", c. 1910: Four,* handstamp, num., captioned, est. $8/1,200, (10-14-92, Swann, #441), 4¾ x 6¾ in., (12.1 x 17.1 cm.), photograph, bromide prints.

ELMAU

$134* *Paris Fin De Sexe,* (01-31-93, Morelle/Marchan, #192), 35⁷/₁₆ x 50⅜ in., (90 x 128 cm.), poster (BP 90, DM 216, FR 730, Y 16,717).

ELMEKKI

$24* *Visitez La Tunisie. "Terre De Traditions",* very good cond., (03-13-93, Laurin, #67), 37¹³/₁₆ x 24⁷/₁₆ in., (96 x 62 cm.), (BP 17, DM 40, FR 136, Y 2829).

ELMES, Willard Frederic

$359* *Rough Going! (...) Let's Clear Our Path, 1929,* cond. A, (03-16-93, Boisgirard, #101), 44⅛ x 36¼ in., (112 x 92 cm.), poster (BP 248, DM 597, FR 2028, Y 41,978).

ELRUY, Kerr

$193* *Fisherman At Night,* (11-13-92, DuMouchelle, #2366), 12 x 15 in., (30.5 x 38.1 cm.), etching and aquatint (BP 125, DM 303, FR 1022, Y 23,954).

ELSLEY, Arthur J. (after)

$47 *"A Chip Off The Old Block",* (12-11-92, G.A. Key, #55), 20 x 15 in., (50.8 x 38.1 cm.), black and white print (BP 30, DM 74, FR 254, Y 5816).

$47 *Young Girl With Dog And Puppies,* (12-11-92, G.A. Key, #33), 26 x 17 in., (66 x 43.2 cm.), colored print (BP 30, DM 74, FR 254, Y 5816).

ELUY, Kerr

$66* *Fisherman In Row Boat,* s., (11-13-92, DuMouchelle, #2460), 9¼ x 11½ in., (23.5 x 29.2 cm.), etching (BP 43, DM 104, FR 349, Y 8192).

ELZINGRE, Edouard

$378* *Montreux-Berner Oberland, c. 1930,* excell. cond., (02-04-93, Christie-S. Ken, #5), 40 x 25 in., (101.6 x 63.5 cm.), color lithograph (BP 264, DM 622, FR 2111, Y 47,021).

BI *XXieme Anniversaire Du Retablissement Des Jeux Olympiques 1894-1914,1914,* tears, losses, est. BP 5/700, (02-04-93, Christie-S. Ken, #48, illus.), 40½ x 29 in., (102.9 x 73.7 cm.), color lithograph.

EMERSON, Casper (Jr.)

$95 *Help Them,* American Lithographic Co., corner missing, (09-24-92, Alderfer, #295), 30 x 20 in., (76.2 x 50.8 cm.), (BP 56, DM 141, FR 478, Y 11,428).

EMERSON, Charles Chase   American 1874-1922

$70* *Three Landscapes & A Harbor Scene, c. 1890's: Four,* good cond., (05-15-93, Cleveland, #123), etching (BP 46, DM 113, FR 378, Y 7760).

EMERSON, Peter Henry   1856-1936

$660* *An Autumn Morning, 1885,* orig. mount, (04-07-93, Swann, #199), 7 x 10½ in., photograph, platinum print (BP 436, DM 1067, FR 3612, Y 74,983).

$1100* *The First Frost (East Anglia, p. 107), c. 1886,* plate XIV from Life and Landscape on the Norfolk Broads, (10-15-92, Sotheby-NY, #89, illus.), 8 x 11¼ in., (20.3 x 28.6 cm.), photograph, platinum print (BP 673, DM 1637, FR 5553, Y 131,974).

$1035* *"The First Frost" (East Anglia, p. 107), c. 1886,* plate XIV from Life and Landscape on the Norfolk Broads, mounted, (04-06-93, Sotheby-NY, #55, illus.), 8 x 11¼ in., photograph, platinum print (BP 684, DM 1667, FR 5646, Y 118,043).

$2178* *"Marsh Leaves", 1895: Book,* ordinary edit., p. plate num., t., orig. morocco-backed cloth, lit., (05-06-93, Christie-London, #20, illus.), smallest 3¼ x 5 in., largest 4½ x 9 in., photograph, 16 photogravure plates (BP 1380, DM 3430, FR 11,548, Y 239,630).

$1542* *Pictures Of East Anglian Life: Nos. V "Colts On A Norfolk Marsh", XVIII "Where Winds The Dyke", XX "Brickfield On The River Bure", XXII "Brickmaking", XXIV "Fencing In Suffolk", XXX "At The Grindstone, A Suffolk Farmyard": Six,* 1888, each plate s. P.H. Emerson, lit., (05-06-93, Christie-London, #64), largest 10½ x 8⅞ in., photograph, photogravures (BP 977, DM 2429, FR 8176, Y 169,656).

$2200* *"Quanting The Marsh Hay" and "Marshman Going To Cut School-Stuff" (East Anglin, p. 108): Two Norfolk Studies,* plates XVI & XXII, from Life and Landscape on the Norfolk Broads, (10-15-92, Sotheby-NY, #88, illus.), one 6⅛ x 9 in., (15.6 x 22.9 cm.), other 8 x 11¼ in., (15.6 x 22.9 cm.), photograph, platinum prints (BP 1346, DM 3275, FR 11,106, Y 263,947).

$880* *Reed Cutter At Work, 1886,* (10-14-92, Swann, #183, illus.), 7½ x 9½ in., (19.1 x 24.1 cm.), photograph, platinum print (BP 517, DM 1288, FR 4367, Y 106,641).

$1210* *A Reed Cutter, 1885,* (04-07-93, Swann, #200, illus.), 11 x 8 in., photograph, platinum print (BP 800, DM 1957, FR 6623, Y 137,469).

$880* *Setting Up the Bownet, 1886,* from Life and Landscape on the Norfolk Broads, Plate XVIII, lit., (10-13-92, Christie-NY, #9, illus.), 10½ x 8¾ in., (26.7 x 22.2 cm.), photograph, platinum print (BP 513, DM 1289, FR 4380, Y 106,705).

$871* *Wild Life On A Tidal Water: Nos. V "Bound For The North River", XIII "In Dock", XVI "On The Baulks", XXV "A Yarmouth Row", XXVI "The Ferry", XXX "The Last Of The Ebb, Great Yarmouth From Breydon": Six,* 1890, plate XXVI laid down, lit., (05-06-93, Christie-London, #65), largest 4½ x 7¼ in., photograph, photogravure (BP 552, DM 1372, FR 4618, Y 95,830).

EMERSON, Peter Henry and George BANKART

$990* *The Complete Angler, 1888,* Sampson Low, Marston, Searle, & Rivington, book by IZAAK WALTON & CHARLES COTTON, large 4to, #308/500, s. by editor, (10-15-92, Sotheby-NY, #91, illus.), numerous woodcuts & 54 photogravures (BP 606, DM 1474, FR 4997, Y 118,776).

EMERSON, Peter Henry and T.F. GOODALL

$880* *Wild Life On A Tidal Water: The Adventures Of A House-Boat And Her Crew, (Truthful Lens 53),* Sampson Low, Marston, Searle, & Rivington, 1890, book by PETER HENRYEMERSON, illus. w/30 photogravures after photogs. by PETER HENRY EMERSON, somein collaboration w/T.F. GOODALL; projected edit. of 500 ordinary, 100 deluxe copies, (10-15-92, Sotheby-NY, #90, illus.), photogravures (BP 538, DM 1310, FR 4442, Y 105,579).

EMKA

$192* *Baicoli, A. Colussi, 1949,* Bonetti, A- cond., (08-06-92, Swann, #124, illus.), 39 x 27½ in., (99.1 x 69.9 cm.), (BP 100, DM 284, FR 958, Y 24,490).

$247* *Focaccia Veneziana A. Colussi, 1932,* Navarra, B+ cond., spotting, fraying, (08-06-92, Swann, #125, illus.), 39 x 27½ in., (99.1 x 69.9 cm.), (BP 129, DM 365, FR 1233, Y 31,505).

EMMONS, Chansonetta Stanley　　　American 1858-1937

$1100* *"An Old Trysting Place", "Bridge Over Stanley Brook", "Cows In Pasture", "Harbor View", "House At Blueberry Mountain", "Kingfield", "Milton, Mass.","Mt. Abram" (2), "Rockfrost, Mass" and others, 1913-27: Twelve,* photog.'s sig., notations, s., (04-07-93, Swann, #452), 4¾ x 6½ in., photograph, platinum, silver, and printing-out paper prints (BP 727, DM 1779, FR 6021, Y 124,972).

EMOND, Martin　　　1895-1965

$129* *Utsikt Over Ven,* s. 18/29, (11-07-92, Falkkloos, #120), serigraph (BP 84, DM 207, FR 696, Y 15,922, SK 770).

ENDE, Edgar　　　1901-1965

$221* *Iphigenie, 1960,* s., (12-05-92, Bassenge, #7151), 13⁵⁄₁₆ x 19¹¹⁄₁₆ in., (33.8 x 50 cm.), lithograph (BP 138, DM 345, FR 1174, Y 27,382).

ENDICOTT & CO., Lithographers　　　American 1852-1886

$220* *"...Bradford and Haverhill, Mass.", "...Lawrence, Mass.", "...Haverhill, Mass.", "Great Falls, Somersworth, N.H." and "...Holyoke and South Hadley Falls": Five, c. 1858,* from Album of New England Scenery, ident. in matrices, good/fair cond., light toned, water stained, foxing, nicks, tears, handling marks, creases, prov., after John Badger Bachelder, (08-21-92, Skinner, #310), approx. sheet 15 x 20 in., (38.1 x 50.8 cm.), lithograph in black, tan (red color) on paper (BP 113, DM 315, FR 1070, Y 27,676).

$220* *"...Lawrence, Mass.", "...Lewiston, Maine", "...Bradford and Haverhill, Mass.", "Great Falls, Somersworth, N.H." and "...Haverhill, Mass.": Five, c. 1858,* from the Album of New England Scenery, each ident. w/in matrices, good/fair cond., light toned, water stained, foxing, nicks, tears, marks, creases, prov., after John Badger Bachelder, (08-21-92, Skinner, #77), approx. sheet 15 x 20 in., (38.1 x 50.8 cm.), lithographs in black and tan (red color) on paper (BP 113, DM 315, FR 1070, Y 27,676).

$385* *"...Lawrence, Mass.", "Swampscott, Mass.", "South Danvers, Mass." and "South View Salem, Mass.": Four, c. 1858,* from Album of New England Scenery, ident. in matrices, good/fair cond., light toned, water stained, foxing, nicks, tears, handling marks, creases, prov., (08-21-92, Skinner, #259), approx. sheet 15 x 20 in., (38.1 x 50.8 cm.), lithograph in black, tan (red color) on paper (BP 197, DM 552, FR 1872, Y 48,434).

$330* *"Camp 'Banks' Aug. 25th, 26th and 27th, 1858 Encampment of the 2nd Division of M.V.M. on Winter Island...",* after John Badger Bachelder, losses, margins, staining, foxing, ident. in matrices, (08-21-92, Skinner, #18), sheet 22¼ x 33 in., (56.5 x 83.8 cm.), lithograph in colors w/ additional hand coloring on paper (BP 169, DM 473, FR 1604, Y 41,515).

$330* *Encampment Of The 2nd Div Of M.V.M. On Winter Island,* (07-10-92, Skinner, #447, illus.), lithograph w/ hand coloring (BP 172, DM 493, FR 1673, Y 41,327).

$550* *"The Encampment Of The 2nd. Div. Of M. V. M. On Winter Island", c. 1860 and "On The March To The Sea": Two,* (12-02-92, Christie-E, #232, illus.), hand-colored lithograph, one on wove (BP 355, DM 865, FR 2952, Y 68,433).

$165* *Encampment Of The 2nd. Division Of M.V. On Winter Island, c. 1860: Four,* (12-02-92, Christie-E, #233, illus.), hand-colored lithograph on wove (BP 106, DM 259, FR 886, Y 20,530).

$518* *Franklin Engine No. # Brooklyn, L.I., c. 1855,* p. w/ beige tint stone, margins beyond borderline, good cond., tears, foxing, light-stain, (01-28-93, Sotheby-NY, #462), 13⅝ x 22⅛ in., (346 x 562 mm.), sheet 19⅛ x 26⅞ in., (346 x 562 mm.), hand-colored lithograph (BP 342, DM 821, FR 2777, Y 64,316).

$1100* *"Gettysburg Battle-Field", 1863,* ident. in matrix, margins, laid down, staining, nicks, after John Badger, (08-21-92,

Skinner, #99, illus.), sheet 28 x 39 in., (71.1 x 99.1 cm.), lithograph w/hand coloring on paper (BP 564, DM 1576, FR 5348, Y 138,382).

$358* *Grand Republic,* by C.R. Parson, burn marks, discoloration, (06-11-93, Freemn/Fine Art, #59, illus.), 23¼ x 33¼ in., (59.1 x 84.5 cm.), lithograph painted in colors (BP 235, DM 582, FR 1962, Y 37,984).

$138* *"Lawrence, Mass...", 1856: Three,* after John Badger Bachelder, indent. i., prov., (01-16-93, Skinner, #359), sheet 14¾ x 20 in., (37.5 x 50.8 cm.), lithograph in black and tan on paper (BP 90, DM 226, FR 763, Y 17,398).

$3300* *"New-York Clipper Ship Challenge...", 1852,* ident. i.; label verso, (01-16-93, Skinner, #56, illus.), sheet, sight 23½ x 32½ in., (59.7 x 82.6 cm.), color lithograph w/ additional hand-coloring on paper (BP 2157, DM 5396, FR 18,242, Y 416,036).

$3850* *"Ottawa City, Canada West", "Hamilton, Canada West" and "Kingston, Canada West": Three, c. 1855,* from Whitfield's Original Views of North American Cities, each ident. in matrices, good/fair cond., staining, discoloration, losses, foxing, handling marks, creases, prov., (08-21-92, Skinner, #119), approx. sheet 27 x 44 in., (68.6 x 111.8 cm.), lithograph in black, tan (red color) (BP 1973, DM 5517, FR 18,717, Y 484,338).

$495* *"Ravine Occupied by the Picket Reserves..." and "Capture of a Rebel Lunette...": Two, 1862,* after John Badger Bachelder, ident. w/in matrices, good/fair cond., light toned, water stained, foxing, nicks, tears, marks, creases, prov., (08-21-92, Skinner, #39), approx. sheet 15 x 20 in., (38.1 x 50.8 cm.), lithograph, latter w/hand coloring on paper (BP 254, DM 709, FR 2406, Y 62,272).

$1955* *Stonington Steamboat Co Steamer's: Stonington And Narragansett...,* large margins, tears, losses, soiling, creasing, image abrasions, backed w/wove, (01-28-93, Sotheby-NY, #457, illus.), image 18⅛ x 33⅛ in., (46 x 84.1 cm.), sheet 26¼ x 39¾ in., (46 x 84.1 cm.), hand-colored lithograph (BP 1291, DM 3098, FR 10,483, Y 242,737).

$259* *View Of Downtown New York City With A Crowd Watching A Parade Of Soldiers,* s. Endicott and Company Lith., Baker and Goodman pub., (06-24-93, Boos, #622), image 17½ x 26 in., (445 x 660 mm.), color lithograph (BP 176, DM 442, FR 1489, Y 28,250).

$1320* *"A View Of Manchester N.H...", 1855: Five,* after John Badger Bachelder, ident., i., prov., (01-16-93, Skinner, #385), sheet 30 x 39½ in., (76.2 x 100.3 cm.), lithograph in black, tan and blue on heavy paper (BP 863, DM 2158, FR 7297, Y 166,415).

$825* *"A View Of Manchester N.H....", 1855: Five,* ident. i., prov., after John Badger Bachelder, (01-16-93, Skinner, #318), sheet 30 x 39½ in., (76.2 x 100.3 cm.), lithograph in black, tan and blue on heavy paper (BP 539, DM 1349, FR 4561, Y 104,009).

$3520* *"View of Galena, Ill." and "View of St. Anthony, Minneapolis...": Two, c. 1855,* from Whitfield's Original Views of North American Cities, ident. in matrices, good/fair cond., losses, tears, water staining, discoloration, foxing, handling marks, creases, prov., (08-21-92, Skinner, #159), approx. sheet 26½ x 44¼ in., (67.3 x 112.4 cm.), lithograph in black, tan, latter also in blue, green (BP 1804, DM 5044, FR 17,112, Y 442,823).

ENDICOTT & CO., Lithographers (attrib.)　　　American 1852-1886

$413* *View Of Newburyport, Massachusetts,* ident. verso, (01-16-93, Skinner, #47), sheet 22¾ x 29½ in., (57.8 x 74.9 cm.), hand-colored lithograph and gum arabic on heavy paper (BP 270, DM 675, FR 2283, Y 52,068).

ENDLINGER, Johann　　　1733-1789

BI *Maria Mit Dem Kinde, Vor Einer Mauer (Heller-Andresen 1),* prov., est. DM 600, (12-04-92, Bassenge, #6571, illus.), 3¹⁵⁄₁₆ x 2¹⁵⁄₁₆ in., (10 x 7.5 cm.), etching.

ENELL, George

$660* *World's Fair, New York, 1939,* credit stamp, (10-13-92, Christie-NY, #195, illus.), 9 x 7 in., (22.9 x 17.8 cm.), photograph, gelatin silver print (BP 384, DM 967, FR 3285, Y 80,029).

ENGEL, Nissan b. 1931

$300* *"Les Quatre Saisons", 1981: Album of Four,* #51/99, s., HC, (04-04-93, Pescheteau, #208), 25⁹⁄₁₆ x 19¹¹⁄₁₆ in., (65 x 50 cm.), etchings and aquatints on Arches (BP 198, DM 482, FR 1638, Y 34,157).

ENGELMAN, Martin

$224* *Untitled, 1973,* s., d., full margins, good cond., (05-27-93, Sotheby-Amstrdm, #409), 18½ x 26⁹⁄₁₆ in., (470 x 675 mm.), colored lithograph on wove (BP 143, DM 359, FR 1211, Y 24,014, G 403).

$141* *Untitled, 1973,* s., d., full margins, good cond., (05-27-93, Sotheby-Amstrdm, #410), 18½ x 26⁹⁄₁₆ in., (470 x 675 mm.), colored lithograph on wove (BP 90, DM 226, FR 763, Y 15,116, G 253).

$205* *Untitled, 1973,* s., d., full margins, good cond., (05-27-93, Sotheby-Amstrdm, #411), 18½ x 26⁹⁄₁₆ in., (470 x 675 mm.), colored lithograph on wove (BP 131, DM 329, FR 1109, Y 21,977, G 368).

ENGELS, Pieter b. 1938

$195* *Predicted Future Inventions, 1984: Six,* complete set, s., d., #29/30, pub. Galerie Brinkman, good cond., (12-09-92, Sotheby-Amstrdm, #566), each sheet approx. 30⁵⁄₁₆ x 22¹³⁄₁₆ in., (770 x 580 mm.), lithograph on BFK Rives (BP 124, DM 306, FR 1044, Y 24,179, G 345).

ENGELS, Robert German b. 1866

BI *La Passant,* L'Estampe Moderne blindstamp, margins, good condition, staining, hinge remains, creases, surface soiling, est. $2/400, (03-31-93, Butterfield, #5239), 13⅞ x 9½ in., (35.2 x 24.1 cm.), lithograph printed in colors w/hand-coloring on wove.

ENGLISH SCHOOL, LATE 18TH CENTURY

$1403* *The King's Shilling: Set Of Four,* trimmed, (06-16-93, Bonhams-Chelsea, #444, illus.), image 21 x 17¾ in., (53.3 x 45.1 cm.), mezzotint w/fine hand-coloring (BP 935, DM 2329, FR 7816, Y 149,637).

ENGLISH SCHOOL, 19TH CENTURY

$247* *"Paying The Check",* (01-06-93, Doyle, #23), sight 14 x 21 in., (35.6 x 53.3 cm.), hand-colored engraving (BP 161, DM 405, FR 1378, Y 30,906).

$288* *Sainfoin, 1890,* trimmed, staining, other defects, Anthony N. B. Garvan Coll., (06-05-93, Christie-NY, #71, illus.), sh 23 x 28½ in., (584 x 724 mm.), aquatint in black and blue w/hand-coloring and touches of gum arabicon wove (BP 190, DM 467, FR 1574, Y 30,895).

ENGLISH SCHOOL, CIRCA 1800

$504* *"St Cecilia" and "Sappho": A Pair,* defects, (01-21-93, Bonhams-Chelsea, #73), image 16½ x 13 in., (41.9 x 33 cm.), hand-colored stipple engravings (BP 330, DM 801, FR 2711, Y 63,079).

ENGLISH SCHOOL, CIRCA 1900

$102* *A Clipper Under Full Sail,* trimmed, (12-10-92, Bonhams-Chelsea, #83), image 16¾ x 27¼ in., (42.5 x 69.2 cm.), photogravure w/hand-coloring (BP 66, DM 161, FR 551, Y 12,618).

ENSOR, James Belgian 1860-1949

$863* *Autp-Da-Fe (D. 85; T., E., 87), 1893,* s., d.; counter-signed, t., margins, good cond., crease, skinned spot, fox mark, tape, (02-11-93, Sotheby-NY, #133), 3⁷⁄₁₆ x 4¹³⁄₁₆ in., (87 x 122 mm.), sheet 9⅜ x 11⁵⁄₁₆ in., (87 x 122 mm.), etching on simili-Japan (BP 609, DM 1430, FR 4837, Y 104,039).

BI *Barques Echouees (Taevernier 49; Elesh 49 III), 1888,* s., est. DM 9,500, (12-04-92, Bassenge, #6790, illus.), 7 x 9⁵⁄₁₆ in., (17.8 x 23.6 cm.), zinc etching.

$3360* *Les Bons Juges (Croquez 88), 1894,* s., plate s., 1st state, (11-13-92, Koller, #5305), 7 x 9⅜ in., (17.8 x 23.8 cm.), etching on Verge (BP 2171, DM 5275, FR 17,787, Y 417,029, SF 4756).

$1275* *Boulevard D'Iseghem, Ostende (Taevernier 66, Elesh 66 III), 1889,* s., (06-04-93, Bassenge, #5672), 5⁷⁄₁₆ x 3¹⁵⁄₁₆ in., (13.8 x 10 cm.), etching on Japan (BP 844, DM 2070, FR 6979, Y 137,511).

$2527* *Boulevard Van Iseghem, Ostend (Taevernier 66; Elesh 66 III), 1889,* s., (12-04-92, Bassenge, #6796), 5⁷⁄₁₆ x 3⅞ in., (13.8 x 9.9 cm.), etching (BP 1621, DM 4025, FR 13,652, Y 315,481).

$1347* *Bouquet D'Arbre (Croquez 41) 1888,* s., (11-09-92, Finarte-Milan, #79, illus.), 3¾ x 5⁵⁄₁₆ in., (9.5 x 13.5 cm.), etching (BP 891, DM 2150, FR 7265, Y 167,163, L 1840).

BI *"Bouquet D'Arbres" (Delteil 41 ii/ii),* s., d., counter s. across entire plate, good cond., hinges, est. $750/1,000, (05-15-93, Cleveland, #382), 3⅞ x 5½ in., (9.8 x 14 cm.), etching on Japan.

$2459* *Les Cataclysmes (Croquez 37), 1888,* s., d., plate s., (11-13-92, Koller, #5306), 7¹⁄₁₆ x 9⅜ in., (17.9 x 23.8 cm.), etching on Verge (BP 1589, DM 3860, FR 13,017, Y 305,200, SF 3480).

BI *Les Cataclysmes Vision Devancant Le Futurisme (Taevernier 37; Elesh 37), 1888,* s., t., est. DM 9,000, (12-04-92, Bassenge, #6787), 6¹⁵⁄₁₆ x 9⁵⁄₁₆ in., (17.7 x 23.6 cm.), zinc etching.

$10,109* *La Cathedrale II (Taevernier 105; Elesh 107), 1886/1896,* s., t., (12-04-92, Bassenge, #6799, illus.), 9¹¹⁄₁₆ x 7⁷⁄₁₆ in., (24.6 x 18.9 cm.), etching (BP 6484, DM 16,100, FR 54,614, Y 1,262,047).

BI *La Cathedrale: Second Plate (T. 105), 1896,* s., t., counter-signed, margins, good cond., mount-staining, est. BP5/7,000, (06-30-93, Sotheby-London, #435, illus.), sh 12¼ x 9¼ in., (311 x 235 mm.), etching on simile-Japan.

$4331* *"Le Combat Des Demons" (Croquez 24), 1888,* s., d., (11-28-92, Grisebach, #505, illus.), 10⁵⁄₁₆ x 12 in., (26.2 x 30.5 cm.), etching on Japan (BP 2859, DM 6900, FR 23,423, Y 539,017).

$495* *The Deadly Sins Dominated By Death, 1904, Taevernier 126,* pub. in Art Contemporian, 1923, (09-20-92, Hindman, #743, illus.), 3¼ x 5¼ in., (8.3 x 13.3 cm.), etching (BP 290, DM 735, FR 2513, Y 61,179).

$4400* *The Deadly Sins: Dominated By Death (Delteil, Taevernier, Elesh 126),1904,* s., t., countersigned, t. verso, margins, good cond., mat stain, spots, rubbing, (11-05-92, Sotheby-NY, #173, illus.), 3½ x 5½ in., (90 x 140 mm.), sheet 6¼ x 9⅞ in., (90 x 140 mm.), hand colored etching on simili Japan (BP 2862, DM 6959, FR 23,542, Y 539,811).

$15,442* *The Entry Of Christ Into Brussels (Taevenier 114), 1898,* 3rd final state, s., margins, paper discolored, (06-30-93, Sotheby-London, #434, illus.), 9⅞ x 14⅛ in., (251 x 359 mm.), etching w/extensive hand-coloring by artist, on laid (BP 10,350, DM 26,338, FR 88,849, Y 1,654,559).

$6613* *Les Gendarmes (Delteil, Taevernier, Elesh 55), 1888,* s., d., t.; countersigned, t. verso, margins, light-staining, tack holes, tape, folds, good cond., collector's mark, (02-11-93, Sotheby-NY, #131, illus.), 6⅞ x 9¼ in., (175 x 235 mm.), hand colored etching on simili-Japan (BP 4666, DM 10,954, FR 37,068, Y 797,227).

$1798* *Le Grand Bassin, Ostende (A.T. 45), 1888,* whole margins, s., d., (06-11-93, Picard, #50), 7¹⁄₁₆ x 9⅜ in., (179 x 238 mm.), etching in black on simili Japan (BP 1181, DM 2922, FR 9852, Y 190,769).

$4694* *Les Insectes Singuliers (Taevernier 46; Elesh 46 V), 1888,* s., t., mono. stamp, (12-04-92, Bassenge, #6789, illus.), 4⅝ x 6³⁄₁₆ in., (11.8 x 15.7 cm.), drypoint (BP 3011, DM 7476, FR 25,359, Y 586,017).

BI *Le Jardin D'Amour (Taevernier 61; Elesh 61 II), 1888,* s., t., est. DM 15,000, (12-04-92, Bassenge, #6793), 4⁹⁄₁₆ x 3⅛ in., (11.6 x 7.9 cm.), handcolored etching on handmade paper.

BI *L'Ange Exterminateur (E. 77; T. 77), 1889,* s., t., d., counter-s., full margins, mount/light staining, skinning,-backboard staining, prov., est. BP 2,0/3,000, (12-03-92, Sotheby-London, #294, illus.), 4½ x 6 in., (114 x 152 mm.), etching w/handcoloring on laid.

$2888* *L'Ange Exterminateur (Taevernier 77; Elesh 77), 1889,* s., t., (12-04-92, Bassenge, #6798), 4⅝ x 6⅛ in., (11.7 x 15.5 cm.), etching (BP 1852, DM 4599, FR 15,602, Y 360,549).

$3249* *L'Artiste Par Lui-Meme (Elesh, Delteil u. Tavernier 4 III), 1886,* s., t., (06-10-93, Hauswedell/Nolt, #259, illus.), image 3¹⁵⁄₁₆ x 2¾ in., (10 x 7 cm.), etching on Japan (BP 2125, DM 5291, FR 17,813, Y 344,868).

$3410* *L'Assassinat (E. 38; T. 38), 1888,* s., t., d., counter-s., t., margins, light/mount stained, skinning, staining, prov., (12-03-92, Sotheby-London, #293, illus.), sheet 14 x 16½ in., (356 x 419 mm.), etching w/handcoloring on laid Arches (BP 2200, DM 5362, FR 18,304, Y 424,288).

BI *L'Ecorche (T. 57), 1888*, s., countersigned, margins, good cond., est. BP 800/1,200, (06-30-93, Sotheby-London, #436), sh 11¾ x 9⅜ in., (298 x 238 mm.), drypoint, on simili-Japan.

BI *La Mare Aux Peupliers (Taevernier 74, Elesh 74 II), 1889*, s., est. DM 4000, (06-04-93, Bassenge, #5673, illus.), 6⁵⁄₁₆ x 9⁷⁄₁₆ in., (16 x 23.9 cm.), zinc etching w/aquatint on Japan.

$5085* *Les Mauvais Medecins (Elesh u. Delteil 99. - Tavernier 97), 1895*, s., d., t., collector's stamp, (06-10-93, Hauswedell/Nolt, #263, illus.), image 7¹⁄₁₆ x 9⅞ in., (17.9 x 25.1 cm.), etching on Japan (BP 3326, DM 8280, FR 27,878, Y 539,752).

BI *Le Meuble Hante (Elesh 22; Tavernier 22), 1888*, third (final) state, s., d., t.; counters., t., margins, light/mount-stained, skinning, staining, backboard stained, prov., est. BP 2,0/3,000, (12-03-92, Sotheby-London, #292, illus.), sheet 11⅜ x 9½ in., (289 x 241 mm.), etching w/handcoloring on laid.

$1554* *Le Meuble Hante (Elesh, Delteil u. Tavernier 22 III), 1888*, s., d., t., final state, collector's stamp, (06-10-93, Hauswedell/Nolt, #261, illus.), image 5⁵⁄₁₆ x 3⁷⁄₁₆ in., (13.5 x 8.8 cm.), etching on wove (BP 1016, DM 2531, FR 8520, Y 164,951).

$8050* *La Morte Poursuivant Le Troupeau Des Humains (E. 106; D., T. 104), 1896*, Elesh's 3rd state of 4, Taeverni-er's 2nd state of 3, etched sign., s., countersigned, t., full margins, good cond., foxing, creases, skinning, (02-11-93, Sotheby-NY, #134, illus.), 9⁷⁄₁₆ x 7⁹⁄₁₆ in., (240 x 182 mm.), sheet 16¹⁄₁₆ x 11⅝ in., (240 x 182 mm.), etching on japon (Japan paper) nacre (BP 5680, DM 13,334, FR 45,123, Y 970,464).

$1684* *Musique A Ostende, (Croquez 83), 1890*, s., d., t., (11-09-92, Finarte-Milan, #45, illus.), 4⅝ x 3¹⁄₁₆ in., (11.8 x 7.8 cm.), etching (BP 1113, DM 2688, FR 9083, Y 208,985, L 2300).

$2825* *Les Patineurs (Elesh, Delteil u. Tavernier 65 II), 1889*, s., d., t., stamp, prov., (06-10-93, Hauswedell/Nolt, #262, illus.), image 6¹³⁄₁₆ x 9⁷⁄₁₆ in., (17.3 x 23.9 cm.), etching on wove (BP 1848, DM 4600, FR 15,488, Y 299,862).

BI *Les Patineurs (Taevernier 65; Elesh 65 II), 1889*, s., t., glue remains, est. DM 8,000, (12-04-92, Bassenge, #6795, illus.), 7 x 9⅜ in., (17.8 x 23.8 cm.), etching.

$1275* *Petite Vue De Mariakerke (Taevernier 122, Elesh 122), 1900*, s., d., (06-04-93, Bassenge, #5675), 2¹⁵⁄₁₆ x 3¹⁵⁄₁₆ in., (7.6 x 10.1 cm.), etching on Japan (BP 844, DM 2070, FR 6979, Y 137,511).

$3394* *Petites Figures Bizarres (Taevernier 53; Elesh 53 II), 1888*, s., t., (12-04-92, Bassenge, #6791, illus.), 5⅜ x 3⅞ in., (13.7 x 9.8 cm.), zinc etching w/aquatint (BP 2177, DM 5405, FR 18,336, Y 423,720).

$1364* *Le Pont Rustique (E; T. 76), 1889*, second state of three, s., d., counter-s., narrow margins, good cond., remains of tape, light stained, (12-03-92, Sotheby-London, #295, illus.), 3 x 4 in., (76 x 102 mm.), etching w/handcoloring on simili-Japan (BP 880, DM 2145, FR 7322, Y 169,715).

$2125* *Le Pont Rustique (Taevernier 76, Elesh 76 II), 1889*, s., (06-04-93, Bassenge, #5674), 2¹⁵⁄₁₆ x 4¹¹⁄₁₆ in., (7.6 x 11.9 cm.), etching on simili-Japan (BP 1406, DM 3451, FR 11,631, Y 229,185).

$2623* *La Reine Parysatis (Croquez 117), 1900*, t., s., d., 2nd state, (11-13-92, Koller, #5304), 6¾ x 4¾ in., (17.1 x 12 cm.), etching on Japan (BP 1695, DM 4118, FR 13,886, Y 325,555, SF 3712).

$1059* *Le Reverbere (Elesh, Delteil u. Tavernier 21 II), 1888*, s., d., t., final state, collector's stamp, (06-10-93, Hauswedell/Nolt, #260, illus.), image 3⁹⁄₁₆ x 2⁷⁄₁₆ in., (9 x 6.2 cm.), etching on Japan (BP 693, DM 1724, FR 5806, Y 112,408).

BI *Les Sacriphants (D., T. 108; E. 110), 1896*, s., d.; coun-tersigned, t. verso, margins., light/mat stains, pin hole-ded spot, good cond., Daniel A. Don Estate, est. $4/4,500, (02-11-93, Sotheby-NY, #135, illus.), 4¾ x 3⅜ in., (121 x 85 mm.), hand colored etching on simili-Japan.

$5328* *Scenes De La Vie Du Christ (D., C., T. 139; E. 141), 1921*, Galerie Georges Giroux, t., list of plates, set of 32, s., #256, margins, each mounted on simili-Japan, hinged, discoloration, good cond., (12-01-92, Christie-London, #367, illus.), overall sheet 9¹³⁄₁₆ x 12³⁄₁₆ in., (250 x 310 mm.), lithographs in colors on thin laid (BP 3520, DM 8492, FR 28,941, Y 663,347).

$5777* *Sous-Bois A Groenendael (Taevernier 63; Elesh 63 IV), 1889*, s., t., (12-04-92, Bassenge, #6794, illus.), 4¹¹⁄₁₆ x 3⅛ in., (11.9 x 8 cm.), hand-colored etching (BP 3706, DM 9201, FR 31,210, Y 721,223).

$1099* *Le Verge (A. Taevernier 2), 1886*, whole margins, s., d., (06-11-93, Picard, #49), 6⁵⁄₁₆ x 9⁷⁄₁₆ in., (160 x 240 mm.), black etching on simili Japan (BP 722, DM 1786, FR 6022, Y 116,605).

$1320* *Le Verger (Elesh 2), 1886*, 2nd state of 3, s., d., proof, wide margins, light/mat staining, tape, good cond., (11-09-92, Christie-NY, #89), 156 x 234 in., (396.2 x 594.4 cm.), etching on simili Japan (BP 873, DM 2107, FR 7120, Y 163,812).

$348* *Vue D'Ostende A L'Est (D. Tavernier 40), 1888*, rubbing, staining, (02-24-93, Picard, #97), etching on Japan (BP 243, DM 565, FR 1915, Y 40,835).

BI *Vue D'Ostende A L'Est (Taevernier 40; Elesh 40 III)*, s., t., est. DM 10,000, (12-04-92, Bassenge, #6788, illus.), 3⁷⁄₁₆ x 5⁷⁄₁₆ in., (8.8 x 13.8 cm.), etching in red, blue, yellow and green watercolor.

EPPER, Ignaz

$179* *(Mother And Child), 1925*, s., d., i. handdruck and Dr. Minnich, margins, good cond., minor foxing, creasing of margins, minor paper discoloration, (05-27-93, Sotheby-Amstrdm, #727), 24⁵⁄₁₆ x 19⁷⁄₁₆ in., woodcut on Japan (BP 115, DM 287, FR 968, Y 19,190, G 322).

BI *(Portrait Of A Man)*, s., i. fur Dr. Minnich, margins, good cond., minor foxing, creasing of margins, minor paper discoloration, est. Dfl. 3/500, (05-27-93, Sotheby-Amstrdm, #728), 24¾ x 17¹⁵⁄₁₆ in., (628 x 456 mm.), woodcut on Japan.

$166* *(Two Women)*, s., i. indistinctly, margins, good cond., minor foxing, creasing of margins, minor paper discolora-tion, Late Gerhard Brauer Coll., (05-27-93, Sotheby-Amstrdm, #729), 23⁹⁄₁₆ x 17¹⁵⁄₁₆ in., (598 x 457 mm.), woodcut on Japan (BP 106, DM 266, FR 898, Y 17,796, G 299).

ERBEN, Ulrich   b. 1940

$573* *Untitled, 1980*, s., d., #31/100, blindstamp Erker Presse, (05-27-93, Lempertz, #705), 25⁹⁄₁₆ x 22¹⁄₁₆ in., (65 x 56 cm.), color lithograph on wove (BP 367, DM 919, FR 3099, Y 61,428).

ERDE, Arthur   b. 1889

BI *Strasse Am Dorfrand*, s., est. DM 100-, (09-25-92, Granier, #2828), sheet 14¾ x 21¹⁄₁₆ in., (37.5 x 53.5 cm.), offset lithograph on machine hand-made.

ERDT, Hans Rudi   1883-1918

BI *Muller Extra, 1908*, fold marks, staining, repairs, lit., est. BP 1,5/2,000, (02-04-93, Christie-S. Ken, #159, illus.), 27½ x 38 in., (69.9 x 96.5 cm.), color lithograph backed on japan.

EREMIN, Iurii   1881-1940

$3433* *"Dinamika, 1940", Dynamic*, t., i., s., d., press agency stamp, trimmed to image, (10-29-92, Christie-London, #140, illus.), 11 x 14⅛ in., (27.9 x 35.9 cm.), photo-graph, warm-toned gelatin silver print (BP 2200, DM 5282, FR 17,918, Y 425,245).

BI *"Serebrianye Chekannye Ukrashenia Na Detiakh V AUle Richa, 1939", Silver-chased Ornaments On Children In The Aul Of Rich*, s., t., d., stamp verso, orig. mount, est. BP 7/900, (10-29-92, Christie-London, #139, illus.), 15⅛ x 10⁹⁄₁₆ in., (38.4 x 26.8 cm.), photograph, warm-toned gelatin silver print.

BI *"Tuman Okutyvlet Goru, 1930", Fog Shrouds The Hill*, t., s., d., stamp verso, est. BP 5/700, (10-29-92, Christie-London, #138, illus.), 15 x 10¾ in., (38.1 x 27.3 cm.), photograph, warm-toned gelatin silver print.

ERFURTH, Hugo   German 1874-1948
$531* *Madchenportrat, 1914,* (11-12-92, Lempertz, #51), 8¹¹⁄₁₆ x 6⁵⁄₁₆ in., (22 x 16 cm.), photograph, celloid paper print (BP 340, DM 835, FR 2844, Y 65,693).
   BI *Mannerportrat In Uniform, 1927,* est. DM 500, (11-12-92, Lempertz, #55), 8⅞ x 6⁷⁄₁₆ in., (22.6 x 16.3 cm.), photograph, collodion positive.
$1668* *Portrat Richard Muller, 1921,* s., d. in negative, (11-12-92, Lempertz, #53, illus.), 8¾ x 6⁷⁄₁₆ in., (22.2 x 16.3 cm.), sheet 13⅝ x 10 in., (22.2 x 16.3 cm.), photograph, bromoid print (BP 1066, DM 2621, FR 8934, Y 206,359).
   BI *Portrat Richard Muller, 1921,* s., d. in negative, est. DM 1,500, (11-12-92, Lempertz, #54), 8⅝ x 6¼ in., (21.9 x 15.8 cm.), sheet 13¾ x 9¹⁵⁄₁₆ in., (21.9 x 15.8 cm.), photograph, bromoid print.

ERHARD, Johann Christoph   1795-1822
$1836* *Die Bauerin Mit Dem Rechen (Apell 94 III), 1819,* early print of final state, (06-10-93, Hauswedell/Nolt, #248, illus.), etching (BP 1201, DM 2990, FR 10,066, Y 194,884).

ERHARDT, Alfred   German 1901-1984
$379* *Dunenrucken Der Kurischen Nehrung, c. 1935,* (11-12-92, Lempertz, #57, illus.), 9⅜ x 6⅞ in., (23.8 x 17.4 cm.), photograph, gelatin silver print (BP 242, DM 596, FR 2030, Y 46,889).
   BI *Kurische Nehrung, 1936,* est. DM 500, (11-12-92, Lempertz, #58, illus.), 9⁷⁄₁₆ x 6¼ in., (23.9 x 15.9 cm.), photograph, gelatin silver print.
$277* *Sando-Brucke, Schweden, 30's,* t., atelier stamp, (11-12-92, Lempertz, #59, illus.), 9⁷⁄₁₆ x 6⅞ in., (24 x 17.4 cm.), photograph, gelatin silver print (BP 177, DM 435, FR 1484, Y 34,269).

ERIC
$230* *Cote Basque: Biarritz, France, c. 1950,* good cond., (01-23-93, Ribeyre/Baron, #109), 39⅜ x 24⁷⁄₁₆ in., (100 x 62 cm.), poster (BP 150, DM 366, FR 1237, Y 28,786).

ERICH
$55* *Florals: Group Of Four,* good cond., (02-07-93, Bakker, #243), largest 20 x 16 in., (50.8 x 40.6 cm.), screenprint (BP 38, DM 91, FR 308, Y 6844).

ERIE LITHO. AND PTG. CO.
$2090* *"Buffalo Bill's Wild West Sells Floto Circus",* creasing, tears, corner missing, (09-12-92, Dunning, #34, illus.), 41 x 27 in., (104.1 x 68.6 cm.), poster (BP 1081, DM 3008, FR 10,225, Y 258,952).

ERNI, Berthe   b. 1914
   BI *Abstrakte Komposition, 1966,* s., est. SF 220/300, (10-14-92, Germann, #506), 10¼ x 16¾ in., (260 x 425 mm.), mixed media on paper.

ERNI, Hans   Swiss b. 1909
$755* *5 Ganzfigurenakte In Bewegung,* E.A., s., i. epr. d'art, (03-16-93, Schuler, #3254), 31⅛ x 22¹⁄₁₆ in., (79 x 56 cm.), sh 27⁹⁄₁₆ x 19⅞ in., (79 x 56 cm.), color lithograph (BP 521, DM 1255, FR 4266, Y 88,283, SF 1150).
$543* *Adler,* 143/200, s.; traces of mounting verso, (10-14-92, Germann, #508), 26⅛ x 19 in., (663 x 483 mm.), lithograph (BP 319, DM 795, FR 2695, Y 65,802, SF 708).
$458* *Le Chimiste (Caill. 393), 1967,* s., (06-23-93, Kornfeld, #332), color lithograph on wove (BP 311, DM 775, FR 2607, Y 49,897, SF 690).
$115* *"Cinq Jeune Fille",* s., #56/100, scuffing, (05-15-93, Cleveland, #383), 19 x 24⅝ in., (48.3 x 62.5 cm.), color lithograph (BP 75, DM 185, FR 622, Y 12,748).
$474* *Couple,* 4/75, s., (04-21-93, Germann, #388), 25¹¹⁄₁₆ x 19¹¹⁄₁₆ in., (652 x 500 mm.), color lithograph (BP 308, DM 758, FR 2562, Y 52,474, SF 690).
$498* *Couple (Cailler 291), 1960,* s., (10-14-92, Germann, #511), 25 x 18⅞ in., (635 x 480 mm.), color lithograph (BP 292, DM 729, FR 2471, Y 60,349, SF 649).
$381* *Deux Chevaux (Cailler 7), 1950,* 57/200, s., (10-14-92, Germann, #507), 15³⁄₁₆ x 19½ in., (385 x 495 mm.), color lithograph (BP 224, DM 558, FR 1891, Y 46,171, SF 496).

$2141* *Hans Erni In Bild Und Wort, 1974: Three,* portfolio, #XLIX/XC, s., Editions Le Moulin, ded., (05-08-93, Dobiaschofsky, #1930), 25¹⁵⁄₁₆ x 19⁵⁄₁₆ in., (66 x 49 cm.), color lithograph on Japan (BP 1397, DM 3439, FR 11,604, Y 239,245, SF 3120).
$588* *Homme Et Coq (Cailler 257), 1959,* s., (10-14-92, Germann, #510), 26⅜ x 20¹¹⁄₁₆ in., (670 x 525 mm.), color lithograph (BP 345, DM 861, FR 2918, Y 71,255, SF 767).
$458* *Huit Pigeons (Cailler 123), 1954,* s., i. epr. d'essai, (06-23-93, Kornfeld, #331), color lithograph on wove (BP 311, DM 775, FR 2607, Y 49,897, SF 690).
$165* *"Lady In A Chariot",* s., #12/175, (06-11-93, Freemn/Fine Art, #59A), 20 x 24 in., (50.8 x 61 cm.), lithograph in colors (BP 108, DM 268, FR 904, Y 17,507).
$138* *Nude,* s. Erni, (12-12-92, Wolf, #25, illus.), 15 x 21 in., (38.1 x 53.3 cm.), lithograph (BP 88, DM 217, FR 745, Y 17,077).
$448* *Paul Eluard. Sommes Nous Deux Ou Suis-Je Solitaire?, 1959: Thirty-One,* ex. 1, Au Vent d'Arles, Vorlage mit den Original-Federzeichnungen fur die Radierungen, (06-15-93, Schuler, #3268, illus.), etching (BP 295, DM 735, FR 2479, Y 47,302, SF 5175).
   BI *Standing Nude, c. 1965,* s., num., hinges, est. $250-350, (10-31-92, Cleveland, #369, illus.), 22¾ x 11¾ in., (57.8 x 29.8 cm.), lithograph in two colors.
$272* *Stier Und Lowe,* 3/20, s., (10-14-92, Germann, #509), 18⅛ x 11¹⁵⁄₁₆ in., (460 x 303 mm.), etching (BP 160, DM 398, FR 1350, Y 32,962, SF 354).

ERNST, Helge
$110* *Studies: Four,* s. Helge Ernst, 62/200, (03-24-93, Kunsthallen, #89), color lithograph (BP 74, DM 180, FR 611, Y 12,924, DK 690).

ERNST, Max   French 1891-1976
$747* *Affiche Pour Le Surrealisme (Sp./L.A. 11.), 1964,* s., epreuve d'artiste, (12-01-92, Karl/Faber, #580), 22⁷⁄₁₆ x 17⁵⁄₁₆ in., (57 x 44 cm.), color lithograph on Arches wove (BP 494, DM 1191, FR 4058, Y 93,003).
$155* *Affiche Pour Petit (S/L A21), 1969,* s., #17/100, before letters, (03-31-93, Briest, #E37), 31¹¹⁄₁₆ x 23¼ in., (80.5 x 59 cm.), 15-color lithograph on wove (BP 102, DM 249, FR 847, Y 17,824).
$332* *Alfred Jarry, Decervelages, Blatt IX, 1971,* XXIII/XXXIII, s., creases, (04-21-93, Germann, #400), 26⅜ x 20 in., (670 x 508 mm.), lithograph in brown on Japan (BP 215, DM 531, FR 1795, Y 36,754, SF 483).
$1935* *Animaux De Mers (L. 252, A), 1974,* s., (10-09-92, Winterberg, #2057, illus.), 12⁹⁄₁₆ x 9⁹⁄₁₆ in., (31.9 x 24.3 cm.), color lithograph on wove (BP 1148, DM 2874, FR 9651, Y 235,573).
   BI *Au Printemps Il Se Pare D'Une Notion Nuptial Importee D'Egypte, 1974,* s., from Les Oiseaux en peril, num., est. DM 5000, (12-01-92, Karl/Faber, #588, illus.), 12 x 9¹³⁄₁₆ in., (30.5 x 25 cm.), color aquatint and collage on Arches France wove.
$126* *La Ballade Du Soldat (S/L 218), 1972,* plates III and XXXIII from "Je suis le sergent..." and "Et que partent et reviennent", (11-16-92, Briest, #295), 15³⁄₁₆ x 10¼ in., (38.5 x 26 cm.), lithograph in colors on Arches wove (BP 83, DM 201, FR 677, Y 15,724).
$493* *Ballade Du Soldat XII (Spies/Leppien 218 XII B),* (05-26-93, Lempertz, #135), sh 15³⁄₁₆ x 11¼ in., (38.5 x 28.5 cm.), color lithograph on Japon nacre (BP 319, DM 804, FR 2707, Y 53,564).
$493* *Ballade Du Soldat XXXVII (Spies/Leppien 218 XXXVII B),* (05-26-93, Lempertz, #136), sh 15³⁄₁₆ x 11¼ in., (38.5 x 28.5 cm.), color lithograph on Japon nacre (BP 319, DM 804, FR 2707, Y 53,564).
$180* *"La Ballade Du Soldat", 1972: Two,* (10-18-92, Pescheteau, #133), each 14¹⁵⁄₁₆ x 11 in., (38 x 28 cm.), lithograph, one in black, other in colors (BP 109, DM 266, FR 903, Y 21,493).
$474* *Blatt II Zu Alfred Jarry "Dercervelages" (Spies/Leppien 197 II E), 1971,* #23/99, s., (04-21-93, Germann, #398), 25¹⁵⁄₁₆ x 19⅞ in., (660 x 505 mm.), lithograph in grey (BP 308, DM 758, FR 2562, Y 52,474, SF 690).
   BI *Blatt III Zu Jean Tardieu "Le Parquet Se Souleve" (Spies/Leppien 20 IV A), 1939,* 2/25, s., est. SF 800/

1,200, (10-14-92, Germann, #291), 12 15/16 x 11 1/16 in., (330 x 281 mm.), lithograph.

$332* *Blatt III Zu Jean Tardieu "Le Parquet Se Souleve" (Spies/Leppien 20 IV A), 1939,* #2/25, s., (04-21-93, Germann, #397), 12 15/16 x 11 1/16 in., (330 x 281 mm.), lithograph in red ochre (BP 215, DM 531, FR 1795, Y 36,754, SF 483).

$453* *Blatt XXIV Zu "Lewis Carrolls Wunderhorn" (Spies/Leppien 135. XXIV),1970,* 24/69, s., (10-14-92, Germann, #294), 12 15/16 x 9 3/4 in., (328 x 247 mm.), lithograph (BP 266, DM 663, FR 2248, Y 54,896, SF 590).

$2119* *La Brebis Galante (Spies-Leppien 28 G-Brusberg 49 BP), 1949: Two,* s., from Benjamin Peret. La brebis galante, Editions Premieres, (06-10-93, Hauswedell/Nolt, #267), sh 9 3/8 x 7 1/2 in., (23.8 x 19 cm.), color etching on Arches (BP 1386, DM 3451, FR 11,617, Y 224,923).

$918* *La Brebis Galante (Spies-Leppien 28), 1949,* s., e.a., (06-10-93, Hauswedell/Nolt, #268), image 4 15/16 x 4 15/16 in., (12.6 x 12.6 cm.), etching in blue on wove (BP 600, DM 1495, FR 5033, Y 97,442).

$4256* *Buttelstedt (Prasse W 208), 1920,* s., artist's proof, (06-05-93, Bassenge, #6013, illus.), 7 15/16 x 6 1/16 in., (20.2 x 15.4 cm.), woodcut on fine hand-made China (BP 2802, DM 6900, FR 23,257, Y 456,554).

$3097* *La Carte Du Monde Tourne En Derision, 1975,* from series Oiseaux en Peril, #48/100, s., (10-09-92, Winterberg, #2063, illus.), 12 x 9 15/16 in., (30.5 x 25.2 cm.), color aquatint on Arches (BP 1837, DM 4600, FR 15,446, Y 377,039).

$420* *"Chaussettes D.D.",* #50/51, s., (01-28-93, Pescheteau, #133), a vue 20 1/16 x 19 11/16 in., (51 x 50 cm.), color serigraph (BP 277, DM 666, FR 2252, Y 52,148).

$393* *"Les Chiens On Soif" (Helmut, R. Leppien, A 9), 1964: Two,* illus., num. 44.50, s., (06-16-93, Ader Tajan, #92), 17 1/8 x 12 3/16 in., (43.5 x 31 cm.), color photolithograph on bluish paper (BP 262, DM 652, FR 2189, Y 41,916).

$1093* *Les Chiens Ont Soif (Spies/ Leppien 98), 1964,* original portfolio, #173, pub. Au Pont des Arts, good cond., loss, (02-11-93, Sotheby-NY, #136), each sheet approx. 17 1/16 x 12 3/16 in., (433 x 310 mm.), 2 color etchings, hors-texte (S./L. 98/II and III); 25 lithographicreproductions of drawings (BP 771, DM 1811, FR 6127, Y 131,766).

$314* *Coeur Simple (H.R.L. A 31), 1971,* #II/X, s., creases, cracks, good margins, (06-16-93, Ader Tajan, #93), 18 1/2 x 15 3/8 in., (47 x 39 cm.), color photolithograph on Japan nacre (BP 209, DM 521, FR 1749, Y 33,490).

$696* *"Coeur Simple" (SLA 31), 1971,* s., #24/70, (10-18-92, Pescheteau, #130), 20 7/8 x 17 5/16 in., (53 x 44 cm.), lithograph in colors on Japan (BP 422, DM 1028, FR 3492, Y 83,104).

$629* *"Comme Midi Fume Un Verre" (SLA 19V), 1969,* s., (10-18-92, Pescheteau, #131), 20 7/8 x 17 5/16 in., (53 x 44 cm.), lithograph in colors on Japan (BP 381, DM 929, FR 3156, Y 75,104).

BI *Composition,* s., num. 70/100, bottom margin folded back, skimming, creases, annotation, image in good cond., label verso, est. BP 4/600, (11-30-92, Phillips-London, #421), image 10 5/8 x 13 3/4 in., (270 x 349 mm.), lithograph in colors on wove.

$469* *Composition,* s. Max Ernst, 18/79, (12-02-92, Kunsthallen, #241), color lithograph on japon (BP 303, DM 738, FR 2517, Y 58,355, DK 2875).

$411* *Composition In Dark Brown And Ochre (Spies/Leppien 135),* #21/69, s., Manus Presse blindstamp, (05-20-93, Bonhams-Chelsea, #131), image 12 1/8 x 9 in., (30.8 x 22.9 cm.), lithograph in two colors (BP 264, DM 663, FR 2234, Y 45,384).

$990* *"Composition With Birds",* s., #57/99, (11-13-92, DuMouchelle, #2035, illus.), 13 1/4 x 24 1/4 in., (33.7 x 61.6 cm.), color lithograph (BP 640, DM 1554, FR 5241, Y 122,875).

$379* *"Composition",* #15/75, s., (04-04-93, Pescheteau, #209), 20 7/8 x 17 1/2 in., (53 x 44.5 cm.), color lithograph on Japan nacre (BP 250, DM 609, FR 2069, Y 43,152).

$504* *"Composition",* H.C. VII/X, s., (01-28-93, Pescheteau, #132), 30 5/16 x 22 1/16 in., (77 x 56 cm.), color lithograph on wove (BP 333, DM 799, FR 2702, Y 62,578).

$7768* *Correspondances Dangereuses (Spies-Leppien 25 A), 1947,* s., num. 40/70, from the portfolio Brunidor Portfolio Nr. 1, (06-10-93, Hauswedell/Nolt, #266, illus.), image 11 7/8 x 8 7/8 in., (30.1 x 22.5 cm.), etching on tinted Johannot wove (BP 5081, DM 12,649, FR 42,588, Y 824,541).

$967* *Cosmos (Spies 1977, 52), 1963,* s., 15/59, (06-28-93, Loudmer, #244), 8 3/16 x 6 1/4 in., (208 x 158 mm.), sh 17 11/16 x 12 15/16 in., (208 x 158 mm.), color aquatint on BFK Rives (BP 647, DM 1643, FR 5535, Y 102,599).

$789* *Danseuse Espagnole Au Bord De La Mer (Sp./L. A 42 A.), 1973,* s., num., (12-01-92, Karl/Faber, #586), 14 3/8 x 10 13/16 in., (36.5 x 27.5 cm.), color serigraph on cardboard (BP 521, DM 1258, FR 4286, Y 98,232).

$650* *"La Dent De Scie D'Un Eclair..." (Spies/Leppien 196 C/IX), 1971,* s., sheet 9 of series "Patrick Waldberg, Aux petits agneux", Paris, Au Pont des Arts, num., (11-28-92, Grisebach, #507, illus.), 7 15/16 x 5 9/16 in., (20.2 x 14.2 cm.), colored lithograph on Japan (BP 429, DM 1036, FR 3515, Y 80,896).

BI *Dorothea Tanning. Oiseaux En Peril, 1975: Eight,* s., num. 95/100, Editions Georges Visat, est. DM 12,000, (06-10-93, Hauswedell/Nolt, #275, illus.), portfolio size 22 7/16 x 17 1/8 in., (57 x 43.5 cm.), color etching w/collage.

$1552* *Ecritures (Spies/Leppien 134 II, B), 1970,* s., num., stained, (09-25-92, Granier, #2830, illus.), sheet 17 5/16 x 23 1/16 in., (44 x 58.5 cm.), color lithograph on Japan (BP 906, DM 2301, FR 7779, Y 187,326).

$1467* *Enseigne Pour Une Ecole De Harings (Spies/Leppien A22 B/C), 1970,* artist's proof, s., (04-24-93, Kunsthaus, #548), 16 9/16 x 13 3/16 in., (42 x 33.5 cm.), photolithograph on BFK Rives hand-made (BP 926, DM 2299, FR 7766, Y 161,885).

$1742* *Ethernite (Sp./L. 205.), 1971,* s., num., Edition der Galerie Schindler, (12-01-92, Karl/Faber, #579), 11 13/16 x 7 5/16 in., (30 x 18.5 cm.), etching, aquatint and relief print in brown and black (BP 1151, DM 2777, FR 9462, Y 216,882).

$2837* *Etoile De Mer (Seestern) (Spiess-Leppien 47), 1950,* s., num., series Serie Anglaise, (06-05-93, Bassenge, #6010), color lithograph on Arches (BP 1868, DM 4600, FR 15,503, Y 304,334).

BI *Fahnenschwenker (Spies-Leppien),* from Die Ballade vom Soldaten - Lewis Carrolls Wunderhorn, Manus Prese, num., est. DM 300, (12-05-92, Bassenge, #7582), 9 15/16 x 5 1/2 in., (25.2 x 14 cm.), lithograph.

$1009* *Fahnentrager (Spies/Leppin 149 B),* s., num., (09-25-92, Granier, #2832), sheet 24 7/16 x 16 15/16 in., (62 x 43 cm.), lithograph on hand-made (BP 589, DM 1496, FR 5058, Y 121,786).

$634* *Festin II (Spies/Leppien 249 II A),* (05-26-93, Lempertz, #139, illus.), sh, approx. 18 5/16 x 13 11/16 in., (46.5 x 34.8 cm.), color lithograph on wove (BP 410, DM 1034, FR 3482, Y 68,883).

$564* *Festin XI (Spies/Leppien 249 XI A),* (05-26-93, Lempertz, #140), sh, approx. 18 5/16 x 13 11/16 in., (46.5 x 34.8 cm.), color lithograph on wove (BP 365, DM 920, FR 3097, Y 61,278).

$990* *La Foret Bleue (S. & L. 89), 1962,* s., #68/75, full margins, good cond., mat/light-staining, ink notation, sticker verso, (10-28-92, Butterfield, #2806), 12 3/8 x 9 5/8 in., (314 x 244 mm.), color lithograph on Rives BFK (BP 631, DM 1529, FR 5191, Y 121,472).

$512* *La Foret Bleue (S./L. 89), 1962,* s., #38/75, pub. XXeme Siecle, margins, good cond., (12-03-92, Sotheby-London, #300, illus.), 12 3/8 x 9 5/8 in., (314 x 244 mm.), lithograph in colors on BFK Rives (BP 330, DM 805, FR 2748, Y 63,705).

$116* *Fruits Defendus (Museum Ludwig, Cologne 1990, p. 23), 1968,* s., 10/75 and 13/75, (06-28-93, Loudmer, #242), 5 13/16 x 6 1/2 in., (148 x 165 mm.), sh 13 3/16 x 10 3/16 in., (148 x 165 mm.), black lithographs on wove (BP 78, DM 197, FR 664, Y 12,308).

$1249* *Fur Documenta III (S. and L. 100), 1964,* s., #44/100, pub. Documenta-Foundation, margins, deckle edge, minor skinning, good cond., (12-01-92, Christie-London, #369), plate 8 5/16 x 6 1/4 in., (211 x 158 mm.), etching w/ aquatint in black and ochre on Arches (BP 825, DM 1991, FR 6784, Y 155,503).

$2483* *Gelbe Dorfkirche (Prasse W 240), c. 1921,* ded., s., (06-05-93, Bassenge, #6014, illus.), 6⁷⁄₁₆ x 7¹⁵⁄₁₆ in., (16.4 x 20.1 cm.), woodcut on Japan (BP 1635, DM 4026, FR 13,568, Y 266,359).

$686* *Georges Ribemont-Dessaignes. La Ballade Du Soldat: Alors Pour Commencer/ Le Soldat Tue L'Araignee (S./L. 218 XXV), 1972,* s., #47/79, p. Pierre Chave, pub. Manus Presse, margins, good cond., (06-30-93, Sotheby-London, #438), sh 15 x 11⅛ in., (381 x 283 mm.), color lithograph on Japon nacre (BP 460, DM 1170, FR 3947, Y 73,503).

$2185* *Hibou (Leppien 64 D), 1955,* s., num., (05-26-93, Dorling, #2644), 19⁵⁄₁₆ x 14³⁄₁₆ in., (49 x 36 cm.), color lithograph on wove (BP 1414, DM 3565, FR 11,999, Y 237,397).

$2200* *Hibou (Spies and Leppien 64), 1955,* s., #206/220, full margins, light/mat staining, skinning, paper losses, remains of glue, (11-09-92, Christie-NY, #90), 484 x 356 in., (x 904.2 cm.), colored lithograph on wove (BP 1455, DM 3512, FR 11,866, Y 273,021).

$2367* *Hibou (Spies-Leppien 64/D), 1955,* s., num., (06-23-93, Kornfeld, #336), color lithograph (BP 1608, DM 4005, FR 13,472, Y 257,871, SF 3565).

$2977* *Hibou (Spies/Leppien 64 D), 1955,* s., num., (06-08-93, Karl/Faber, #732, illus.), approx. 19⅛ x 14³⁄₁₆ in., (48.5 x 36 cm.), color lithograph on Marais wove (BP 1957, DM 4830, FR 16,268, Y 316,198).

$990* *Hommage A George Rivemont Dessaignes 1972,* s., #28/99, appears very good cond., (06-11-93, Doyle, #38), 24½ x 16½ in., (622 x 419 mm.), lithograph (BP 650, DM 1609, FR 5425, Y 105,040).

BI *The Hunting Of The Snark (Sp./L. 124/IX A), 1968,* s., est. DM 1800, (12-01-92, Karl/Faber, #577), 11 x 8⁷⁄₁₆ in., (28 x 21.5 cm.), color lithograph.

$1552* *Illustration Zu Antonin Artaud, Texte U. Briefe (Spies/Leppin 113 C), 1967,* s., num., est. DM 2,200-, (09-25-92, Granier, #2829), 8⅜ x 6⅛ in., (21.3 x 15.6 cm.), color etching of 2 plates on hand-made board (BP 906, DM 2301, FR 7779, Y 187,326).

$1023* *Jacques Prevert. Les Chiens Ont Soif (S./L. 98), 1964,* book, s., title-page, text & just., num. 126, pub. Au Pont Des Arts, good cond., (12-03-92, Sotheby-London, #303), two etchings in colors, w/twenty five lithographic reprods. (BP 660, DM 1609, FR 5491, Y 127,286).

BI *Jean Tardieu. Le Parquet Se Souleve (Spies/Leppien 20), 1939,* book, s., #19/25, w/title page & poem, s., by author, w/three additional suites of the plates in different colors, all s., num., p. J.E. Wolfensberg, 1973, pub. Editions Brunidor & Editions Apeiros, full margins, good cond., orig. boards & slipcase, est. BP 8,0/10,000, (12-03-92, Sotheby-London, #297, illus.), overall size 14 x 12 in., (356 x 305 mm.), six lithographs p. i blue on chine applique.

$460* *Komposition,* s. h.c. X/X, (09-29-92, B. Rasmussen, #305), etching in colors (BP 259, DM 650, FR 2217, Y 54,912, DK 2530).

BI *Komposition (Spies/Leppien 134 II B), 1970,* 52/60, s., est. SF 1,5/1,700, (10-14-92, Germann, #293), 17⁵⁄₁₆ x 23¹⁄₁₆ in., (440 x 585 mm.), color etching on Japan.

$474* *Komposition Zu "Ecritures" (Spies/Leppien 134 II B), 1970,* #39/60, s., (04-21-93, Germann, #179, illus.), 17½ x 23¹⁄₁₆ in., (445 x 585 mm.), color lithograph on Japan (BP 308, DM 758, FR 2562, Y 52,474, SF 690).

$303* *L'Antitete, Paris, 1949,* #172/200, (06-11-93, Freemn/Fine Art, #60, illus.), 3⅜ x 2½ in., (8.6 x 6.4 cm.), etching in color (BP 199, DM 492, FR 1660, Y 32,149).

$825* *L'Oeil Bleu, 1967,* s., num. 32/99, full margins, good cond., staining, creases, pencil notations, (02-24-93, Butterfield, #2922), 8¼ x 6¼ in., (210 x 159 mm.), etching in colors on Lana (BP 575, DM 1339, FR 4540, Y 96,808).

$581* *Landschaft (Sp./L. A32A.), 1971,* s., num., (12-01-92, Karl/Faber, #582), 13⅜ x 8⁷⁄₁₆ in., (34 x 21.5 cm.), color photo-lithograph on BFK Rives wove (BP 384, DM 926, FR 3156, Y 72,336).

BI *Lena Leclerq, La Rose Et Nue (S. and L. 78), 1961:* Set Of Six, Jean Hughes, s., #50/90, good cond., loose, est. $3,5/4,000, (11-09-92, Christie-NY, #92, illus.), 338 x

260 in., (858.5 x 660.4 cm.), etchings and aquatints in colors on Arches.

$1009* *Lewis Carolls Wunderhorn (Spies/Leppin 135 B), 1970,* from series, s., num., light-stain, (09-25-92, Granier, #2831, illus.), 12¹³⁄₁₆ x 9¹¹⁄₁₆ in., (32.5 x 24.6 cm.), color lithograph on Japan (BP 589, DM 1496, FR 5058, Y 121,786).

BI *Liebespaar (Spies/Leppien 110 B), 1966,* HC II/IX, s., light-stains, est. DM 2,400-, (11-21-92, Lempertz, #135), 16⅝ x 12¹³⁄₁₆ in., (42.3 x 32.5 cm.), color etching w/ embossing on Arches wove.

$5110* *Masques (L. 49, G.), 1950,* XIII/LX of Serie Anglaise, s., (10-09-92, Winterberg, #2050, illus.), 13¹⁄₁₆ x 19¹¹⁄₁₆ in., (33.1 x 50 cm.), lithograph on Arches (BP 3032, DM 7591, FR 25,486, Y 622,109).

$4088* *Masques (Spies/Leppien 49 E), 1950,* s., #17/200, (05-26-93, Lempertz, #134), 14³⁄₁₆ x 20⅞ in., (36 x 53.1 cm.), color lithograph on Arches wove (BP 2645, DM 6670, FR 22,449, Y 444,155).

$44,951* *Maximiliana Ou L'Exercise Illegal De L'Astronomie, Iliazd, Le Degre Quarante Et Un (S. and L. 95B), 1964,* t., text, justification and set of 34 en-texte, s., #26/65, very good cond., (12-01-92, Christie-London, #368, illus.), overall sheet 17½ x 13¾ in., (445 x 350 mm.), etching in colors on Japon ancien (BP 29,700, DM 71,646, FR 244,166, Y 5,596,489).

$1079* *Maximiliana Ou L'Exercise Illegal De L'Astronomie (Sp./L. 95/XXX A.), 1964,* s., i., proof, Le Degre Quarante et Un edit., (12-01-92, Karl/Faber, #575), etching in brown on cardboard (BP 713, DM 1720, FR 5861, Y 134,338).

$847* *Das Meer (Spies-Leppien A 3 A), 1957,* s., num. 49/50, Edition Galerie Der Spiegel, (06-10-93, Hauswedell/Nolt, #276), image 9¹³⁄₁₆ x 14⅜ in., (24.9 x 36.5 cm.), color serigraph w/pencil on wove (BP 554, DM 1379, FR 4644, Y 89,906).

$1773* *Mon Fiance Est Une Idee Saugrenue, 1974,* s., num., (06-05-93, Bassenge, #6009), 12⅛ x 10⅛ in., (30.8 x 25.7 cm.), color aquatint w/collage on wove (BP 1167, DM 2875, FR 9689, Y 190,195).

$1110* *Morts Aux Vaches Et Au Champ D'Honneur (H.R. Leppien 34), 1950,* #16/90, s., large margins, (02-03-93, Ader Tajan, #148), 6⅞ x 4¹⁵⁄₁₆ in., (17.5 x 12.5 cm.), etching and aquatint (BP 775, DM 1828, FR 6198, Y 138,077).

BI *Le Musee De L'Homme (Spies/Leppien 103), 1966,* book, init., #123, pub. Galerie Alexandre Iolas, good cond., originalboards, est. BP 3/500, (06-30-93, Sotheby-London, #437), aquatint in green.

$1515* *Les Noces Interrompues (Spies/Leppien 207 A), 1971,* #31/100, s., light stains, (11-21-92, Lempertz, #136A), 13⅞ x 9½ in., (35.3 x 24.2 cm.), etching w/embossing on wove (BP 997, DM 2415, FR 8136, Y 188,409).

$1023* *Ohne Titel (S./L. 213), 1971,* s., i. essai, trial proof, pub. Georges Visat, margins, good cond., foxing, light staining, rubbed area, creasing, (12-03-92, Sotheby-London, #298, illus.), sheet 22 x 14¾ in., (559 x 375 mm.), etching w/aquatint in colors & hand coloring on wove (BP 660, DM 1609, FR 5491, Y 127,286).

$1410* *Ohne Titel (Spies/Leppien 225 B), 1972,* s., (05-26-93, Lempertz, #137), 21³⁄₁₆ x 14⅛ in., (53.8 x 35.9 cm.), color etching (and aquatint) laid down on Japon ancien (BP 912, DM 2301, FR 7743, Y 153,194).

$858* *Oiseau En Peril, c. 1975,* s., #55/100, good cond., discoloration, (06-30-93, Sotheby-London, #439), 12 x 9⅞ in., (305 x 251 mm.), soft ground etching w/aquatint and collage in color (BP 575, DM 1463, FR 4937, Y 91,932).

$206* *Oiseaux,* s. in stone, (03-31-93, Briest, #E38), 23¹³⁄₁₆ x 12¹³⁄₁₆ in., (60.5 x 32.5 cm.), color lithograph (BP 136, DM 331, FR 1126, Y 23,689).

$5486* *Oiseaux En Peril,* s., 7/100, (05-12-93, AB Stockholm, #7022, illus.), color etchings and collage on Japan (BP 3582, DM 8851, FR 29,815, Y 612,482, SK 40,700).

BI *Papier Peint (Spiess-Leppien 118), 1967,* s., num., est. DM 3500, (12-05-92, Bassenge, #7155), 17⁵⁄₁₆ x 13³⁄₁₆ in., (44 x 33.5 cm.), color etching and Durchdruckverfahren on wove.

$1160* *Paroles Peintes (Museum Ludwig, Cologne 1990, 62), 1962,* s., 22/50, (06-28-93, Loudmer, #243), 8¼ x 6⁵⁄₁₆ in., (210 x 160 mm.), sh 15⅜ x 11⁵⁄₁₆ in., (210 x 160 mm.), color aquatints on Richard de Bas laid (BP 777, DM 1971, FR 6640, Y 123,077).

BI *Patrick Waldberg, Aux Petits Agneaux (Spies/Leppien 196 I-XX), 1971:Twenty,* Au Pont des Arts, Galerie Lucie Weill, Paris, #92/101, frontispiece s., staining, est. DM 26,500-, (11-21-92, Lempertz, #136), 13¹⁵⁄₁₆ x 10¹³⁄₁₆ in., (35.5 x 27.5 cm.), color lithograph.

$565* *Patrick Waldberg. Aux Petits Agneaux (Spies-Leppien 196, III), 1971,* s., num., Galerie Lucie Weill, (06-10-93, Hauswedell/Nolt, #271), image 9⁵⁄₁₆ x 7⁵⁄₁₆ in., (23.6 x 18.5 cm.), color lithograph on Japon nacre (BP 370, DM 920, FR 3098, Y 59,972).

$9887* *Pierre Herbey. Festin (Spies-Leppien 249 A), 1974: Twenty-Four,* s., num. 47/79, Pierre Chave in Vence, (06-10-93, Hauswedell/Nolt, #274, illus.), portfolio size 19⅛ x 14¹¹⁄₁₆ in., (48.5 x 37.3 cm.), color lithograph (BP 6467, DM 16,100, FR 54,205, Y 1,049,464).

BI *Plakat Fur Worpswede (Sp./L.A 15 A.), 1967,* s., num., creases, est. DM 1400, (12-01-92, Karl/Faber, #581), 15¾ x 14⁹⁄₁₆ in., (40 x 37 cm.), color photo-lithograph on hand-made.

BI *Plate II Of Alfred Jarry "Decervelages" (Spies/Leppien 197 II E), 1971,* #23/99, s., plate i., est. SF 7/900, (09-04-92, Germann, #319), 25¹⁵⁄₁₆ x 19⅞ in., (660 x 505 mm.), lithograph in gray.

BI *Plate III of Jean Tardieu "Le Parquet Se Souleve" (Speis/Leppien 20 IV A), 1939,* #2/25, s., est. SF 7/900, (09-04-92, Germann, #318), 12¹⁵⁄₁₆ x 11¹⁄₁₆ in., (330 x 281 mm.), lithograph in red chalk.

$2200* *Poissons (Spies/Leppien 119), 1967,* s., #77/99, good cond., foxing, handling creases, hinge remains, (11-05-92, Sotheby-NY, #174), 13¼ x 17⅛ in., (335 x 435 mm.), etching p. in colors (BP 1431, DM 3479, FR 11,771, Y 269,906).

$3114* *Pyramide, Graphisme II (Spies/Leppien 213A), 1971,* #91/100, s., (11-13-92, Koller, #5309, illus.), 13³⁄₁₆ x 7¾ in., (33.5 x 19.7 cm.), etching w/relief print and watercolor on wove de Lana (BP 2012, DM 4889, FR 16,485, Y 386,496, SF 4408).

$1194* *Rene Char. Dente Prompte (S./L. A19), 1969,* book, each plate s., w/title-page, text & just., s. by artist and author, num. 55, pub. Au Pont des Arts, good cond., loose, orig. slipcase, (12-03-92, Sotheby-London, #302), set of ten photo-lithographs in colors on wove (BP 770, DM 1878, FR 6409, Y 148,563).

$4103* *Rhythmes (L. 48, F.), 1950,* XVIII/LX of Serie Anglaise, s., blindstamp, (10-09-92, Winterberg, #2049, illus.), 16¾ x 10⅝ in., (42.5 x 27 cm.), color lithograph on Arches (BP 2434, DM 6095, FR 20,464, Y 499,513).

$1766* *Rhythmes (Spies/Leppien 48), 1950,* Epreuve d'artiste II/XII, s., blindstamp, i., stained, (11-13-92, Koller, #5310), 17⅛ x 10¹¹⁄₁₆ in., (43.5 x 27.2 cm.), lithograph on Arches wove (BP 1141, DM 2772, FR 9349, Y 219,188, SF 2500).

BI *Robert Lebel. L'Oiseau Caramel (A. 20), 1969,* book, s., #38/150, w/title page, text & just., #38/150, pub. Le Soleil Noir, good cond., orig. portfolio, est. BP 1,2/1,800, (12-03-92, Sotheby-London, #301), two lithographs in colors.

$935* *Rote Blume II (Spies/Leppien 13A), 1968,* s., num., wide margins, (12-08-92, Swann, #99), 6 x 7⅞ in., (15.2 x 20 cm.), color silkscreen (BP 586, DM 1456, FR 4963, Y 115,890).

$1844* *Schiffe Im Hafen (Prasse W74),* s., (06-05-93, Bassenge, #6012), 3¼ x 4⅝ in., (8.3 x 11.8 cm.), woodcut on a letter (BP 1214, DM 2990, FR 10,077, Y 197,812).

$3547* *Das Schnabelpaar (Spiess-Leppien 56), 1953,* i. bon a tirer, s., artist's proof, (06-05-93, Bassenge, #6007), etching on Arches (BP 2335, DM 5751, FR 19,383, Y 380,498).

$3547* *Das Schnabelpaar (Spiess-Leppien 56), 1953,* i. bon a tirer, s., artist's proof, (06-05-93, Bassenge, #6006), etching w/aquatint on Arches (BP 2335, DM 5751, FR 19,383, Y 380,498).

$5311* *Das Schnabelpaar (Spiess-Leppien aus 56),* essai, artist's proof, (12-05-92, Bassenge, #7154), 9⁵⁄₁₆ x 7 in., (23.6 x 17.8 cm.), etching on Arches (BP 3326, DM 8280, FR 28,220, Y 658,035).

$2054* *Schnabelwesen, c. 1960,* #21/100, s., (04-24-93, Kunsthaus, #549, illus.), 13⁷⁄₁₆ x 9¹¹⁄₁₆ in., (34.2 x 24.6 cm.), color lithograph on hand-made Arches (BP 1296, DM 3219, FR 10,873, Y 226,661).

$1161* *Sentinelles Muettes (L. 196, III), 1971,* epreuve d'artiste, s., frontispiece for Aux petits Agneaux, (10-09-92, Winterberg, #2054, illus.), 9³⁄₁₆ x 7¹⁵⁄₁₆ in., (23.3 x 20.2 cm.), color lithograph on wove (BP 689, DM 1725, FR 5791, Y 141,344).

BI *Sign For A School For Pirates, 1970,* s., t., prov., est. C$ 2,5/3,000, (11-16-92, Hodgins, #318, illus.), 23½ x 19¼ in., (59.7 x 48.9 cm.), color lithograph on paper.

$4256* *Sonnenaufgang (Kleinstadt) (Prasse E 37), 1911,* s., i. in plate, (06-05-93, Bassenge, #6015), 6¼ x 9⅜ in., (15.8 x 23.8 cm.), etching on hand-made (BP 2802, DM 6900, FR 23,257, Y 456,554).

$1320* *Sphynx (Spies/Leppien 22), 1936,* s., annot. epreuve d'artiste: I/II, image crease, (12-08-92, Swann, #100, illus.), 10 x 8 in., (25.4 x 20.3 cm.), sanguine lithograph on Japon paper (BP 827, DM 2055, FR 7006, Y 163,609).

$652* *T/E D'Oiseau (Vogelkopf), 1972,* s. in ballpoint pen, #78/96, (05-08-93, Schloss Ahlden, #2839), 8⅞ x 6⁷⁄₁₆ in., (22.5 x 16.4 cm.), screenprint on cardboard mounted on wood (BP 425, DM 1047, FR 3534, Y 72,857).

BI *Tous Les Couloirs Du Soir Lila, 1974,* s., num., est. DM 5000, (12-01-92, Karl/Faber, #587, illus.), 12 x 9¹³⁄₁₆ in., (30.5 x 25 cm.), color aquatint and collage on wove.

$4147* *Untitled (Leppien 41.E), 1950,* #15/100, s., (09-04-92, Germann, #85, illus.), 12⅝ x 18⅞ in., (320 x 480 mm.), hand-colored etching and aquatint (BP 2078, DM 5812, FR 19,785, Y 510,463, SF 5175).

$3884* *Untitled (Spies-Leppien 31), 1949,* s., #39/99, (06-10-93, Hauswedell/Nolt, #269, illus.), image 4¾ x 3⁷⁄₁₆ in., (12 x 8.8 cm.), color etching w/aquatint on wove (BP 2541, DM 6325, FR 21,294, Y 412,270).

$715* *Untitled Composition (Three Dancing Figures In A Double Circle), c. 1970,* num., s., mat burn, (05-27-93, Swann, #100A, illus.), 20⅜ x 17 in., (51.8 x 43.2 cm.), color lithograph (BP 458, DM 1147, FR 3867, Y 76,651).

BI *Untitled, c. 1948,* s., est. DM 16/18,000, (12-01-92, Karl/Faber, #573, illus.), 8⅞ x 7¹⁄₁₆ in., (22.5 x 18 cm.), color chalk nature print on smooth paper.

$1155* *"Vital Cependant, Aimant Les Etoiles Et Les Arbres" (Spies/Leppien 196 F/XI), 1971,* s., sheet 11 of series "Patrick Waldberg, Aux petits agneaux", Paris, Au Pont des Arts(11-28-92, Grisebach, #506, illus.), 9¹⁄₁₆ x 7³⁄₁₆ in., (23 x 18.2 cm.), colored lithograph on wove (BP 762, DM 1840, FR 6247, Y 143,746).

$619* *"Vive La Mer Ubu" (S./L. 197, IV), 1971 and "Que Vous Etes Laide Ce Soir La Mere Ubu/ Est-ce Que Nous Avons Du Monde" (S./L. 197 VI), 1971: Two,* plates from "Decervelages", s., #XXIV/XXXIII, XXV/XXXIII, second, creases, (03-31-93, Briest, #E163), both 26⅜ x 20¹⁄₁₆ in., (67 x 51 cm.), first, black lithograph on Japan; second, color lithograph on Japan (BP 409, DM 996, FR 3383, Y 71,182).

$913* *Vogelkopf (Sp./L.A. 34.), 1971,* s., num., (12-01-92, Karl/Faber, #583), 9¹⁄₁₆ x 6½ in., (23 x 16.5 cm.), color serigraph and solar print (BP 603, DM 1455, FR 4959, Y 113,670).

$1319* *Wald (Spies/Leppien A. 27, A), 1970,* s., (11-13-92, Kunsthaus, #550), 29¹⁵⁄₁₆ x 37¹³⁄₁₆ in., (76 x 96 cm.), color screen print on wove (BP 852, DM 2071, FR 6983, Y 163,709).

$1328* *What Kind Of A Bird Are You? (Sp./L.A 35 A.), 1971,* num., s., (12-01-92, Karl/Faber, #584), 12⅜ x 9⁷⁄₁₆ in., (31.5 x 24 cm.), color serigraph on wove (BP 877, DM 2117, FR 7213, Y 165,339).

$1135* *What Kind Of Bird Are You? (Spies/Leppien A 35), 1971,* s., num., (06-05-93, Schoppmann, #796), 12⅜ x 9⁷⁄₁₆ in., (31.5 x 24 cm.), color serigraph on wove (BP 747, DM 1840, FR 6202, Y 121,755).

$553* *plate X for "Lewis Carrolls Wunderhorn" (Spies/Leppien 135 X B), 1970,* #39/69, s., (09-04-92, Germann, #44, illus.), 12¹³⁄₁₆ x 9¹³⁄₁₆ in., (325 x 250 mm.), color lithograph on Japan (BP 277, DM 775, FR 2638, Y 68,070, SF 690).

ERNST, Max (after)
$1045* *"Dent Prompte", by Rene Char, 1969: Ten,* porfolio, num., s. justification page by artist and author, original-paper wrapper and linen portfolio, pub. Galerie Lucie Weill, (05-27-93, Swann, #101), sh 18⅜ x 15⅝ in., (46.7 x 39.1 cm.), color lithographs (BP 669, DM 1677, FR 5652, Y 112,028).
$505* *L'Air Lave A L'Eau (Spies/Leppien A 43), 1973,* H.C., s., (11-21-92, Lempertz, #139), 19 x 14$\frac{7}{16}$ in., (48.3 x 36.7 cm.), color photolithograph on wove (BP 332, DM 805, FR 2712, Y 62,803).
$2020* *Vue De Ma Fenetre (Spies/Leppien A 5), 1960,* #11/75, s., Galerie Der Spiegel, (11-21-92, Lempertz, #138), 9$\frac{1}{16}$ x 6⅝ in., (23 x 16.8 cm.), color etching on copper print paper (BP 1330, DM 3221, FR 10,849, Y 251,213).
BI *Wald (Spies/Leppien 27A), 1970,* num., s., est. $700/1,000, (05-27-93, Swann, #102), 21 x 17½ in., (53.3 x 44.5 cm.), color serigraph.

ERNST, Max and Dorothea TANNING (after)
BI *Jean Giraudoux: Judith (S./L. A28), 1971,* book, s. by Ernst and Tanning, w/title-page, text & just., s., #50/99, pub. Matthieu AG, good cond., orig. portfolio box, est. BP 1,5/2,000, (12-03-92, Sotheby-London, #304, illus.), 6 photo-lithographs in colors w/a separate suite of 2 copies of eachlithograph in different color combinations on wove.

ERNST, Otto 1884-1967
$756* *Engelberg, c. 1920,* nicks, pin holes, (02-04-93, Christie-S. Ken, #6, illus.), 40 x 24½ in., (101.6 x 62.2 cm.), color lithograph backed on japan (BP 528, DM 1245, FR 4221, Y 94,042).

ERRO b. 1932
$421* *Composition, 1969,* s. Erro 69, (09-30-92, Kunsthallen, #96), color lithograph (BP 238, DM 597, FR 2019, Y 50,522, DK 2300).

ERRO, Gudmundur b. 1932
$103* *Charite, 1986,* s., d. 1986, (03-31-93, Briest, #E39), 23¾ x 12$\frac{13}{16}$ in., (60.3 x 32.5 cm.), color lithograph (BP 68, DM 166, FR 563, Y 11,845).
BI *Histoire De Lille, 1991: Set Of Ten,* s., d. 1991, #49/130, est. FF 8/10,000, (11-16-92, Briest, #298), 31$\frac{5}{16}$ x 23⅝ in., (79.5 x 60 cm.), lithograph in colors.
BI *Nul Ne Sera Soumis A La Torture Ni A Des Peines Ou Traitements Cruels, 1991,* s., #E.A. 23/75, est. FF10/12,000, (05-27-93, Briest, #83, illus.), 37⅜ x 56$\frac{5}{16}$ in., (95 x 143 cm.), color serigraph on canvas.

ERTE (Romain de TIRTOFF) Russian/French 1892-1990
$440* *"Anger" (The Seven Deadly Sins Series),* s., num., (10-08-92, Boos, #665), image 19¾ x 14¾ in., (502 x 375 mm.), serigraph (BP 262, DM 651, FR 2209, Y 53,463).
$171* *Avarice (Lee No. 4-172),* The Seven Deadly Sins series, s., #9/350, p. Chromacomp, for Wellsart Limited, 1983, lit., (12-01-92, Ritchie, #94), 26¼ x 20¾ in., (66.7 x 52.7 cm.), color serigraph (BP 113, DM 273, FR 929, Y 21,290, C$ 220).
BI *"Bird Cage",* s. Erte, #185/300, est. $1,5/2,000, (12-12-92, A. James, #59), 28¾ x 21⅜ in., (73 x 54.3 cm.), serigraph.
$275* *Birds And Butterflies, 1980,* from "The Numerals Suite", s., #227/350, pub. Circle Fine Art Corporation, (10-30-92, Sloan, #2365), each, sheet 22¾ x 17¼ in., (57.8 x 43.8 cm.), color screenprint (BP 176, DM 423, FR 1435, Y 34,064).
$385* *"The Blue Dress",* #25/300, s., num., (04-16-93, DuMouchelle, #1083, illus.), approx. 17 x 11 in., (43.2 x 27.9 cm.), (BP 253, DM 622, FR 2102, Y 43,292).
$385* *"Chaste Suzanna",* #202/300, s., (06-11-93, DuMouchelle, #902), 14½ x 19½ in., (36.8 x 49.5 cm.), color silkscreen (BP 253, DM 626, FR 2110, Y 40,849).
BI *"The Clasp",* s. Erte, #48/300, est. $2,0/2,500, (12-12-92, A. James, #58), 43½ x 25 in., (110.5 x 63.5 cm.), serigraph.
BI *"The Contessa",* s., num. below image, est. $4/6,000, (08-05-92, Boos, #676, illus.), image 36 x 16 in., (914 x 406 mm.), serigraphy w/hot stamping and embossing.
$4313* *Costumes Pour Les William Sisters,* s., d., stamped ERTE/ROMAIN DE TIRTOFF, 124 RUE DE BRANCAS/SEVRES (8-&-0), annot., (06-10-93, Sotheby-NY, #480, illus.), 15$\frac{1}{16}$ x 11$\frac{3}{16}$ in., (38.3 x 28.4 cm.), print (BP 2821, DM 7023, FR 23,646, Y 457,807).
BI *"Debutante",* s., num. below image, est. $1,4/1,800, (08-05-92, Boos, #675), image 26 x 18½ in., (660 x 470 mm.), color serigraph.
BI *"Deception",* s., num. below image, est. $1,4/1,800, (08-05-92, Boos, #672), image 26 x 18¾ in., (660 x 476 mm.), color serigraph.
$275* *Earth And Moon, 1980,* from "The Numerals Suite", s., #227/350, pub. Circle Fine Art Corporation, (10-30-92, Sloan, #2366), each, sheet 22¾ x 17¼ in., (57.8 x 43.8 cm.), color screenprint (BP 176, DM 423, FR 1435, Y 34,064).
$235* *Envy (Lee No. 1-172),* The Seven Deadly Sins series, s., #9/350, p. Chromacomp, for Wellsart Limited, 1983, lit., (12-01-92, Ritchie, #92, illus.), 26¼ x 20¾ in., (66.7 x 52.7 cm.), color serigraph (BP 155, DM 375, FR 1276, Y 29,258, C$ 303).
$440* *Folies Bergere,* St. Martin, A- cond., surface abrasions, (08-06-92, Swann, #127, illus.), 61½ x 46 in., (156.2 x 116.8 cm.), (BP 230, DM 650, FR 2196, Y 56,122).
BI *"Folies Bergere",* est. $8/1,200, (08-05-92, Boos, #592, illus.), 64½ x 48¾ in., (163.8 x 123.8 cm.), color poster.
BI *The Four Seasons Folio: Autumn, 1975,* s., num. 75/260, p. Superior Silkscreen, pub. blindstamp, Circle Fine Arts, full margins, good cond., handling crease, surface soiling, est. $4/600, (09-21-92, Butterfield, #824), 13 x 10$\frac{1}{16}$ in., (330.8 x 256 mm.), silkscreen in colors on paper.
$1540* *"Freedom And Captivity",* s., num. below image, (08-05-92, Boos, #674), image 26 x 18¼ in., (660 x 464 mm.), serigraph (BP 805, DM 2275, FR 7685, Y 196,128).
BI *Freedom And Captivity, 1985,* s., #276/300, pub. Chalk and Vermilion, very good cond.?, est. $1,5/2,000, (03-20-93, Weschler, #105, illus.), 18½ x 26 in., (47 x 66 cm.), color serigraph.
$605* *"French Adam And Eve",* s., #155/300 Erte, pub. 1982 by Chalk and Vermillion Fine Arts, (05-15-93, Dunning, #1057, illus.), sh 37 x 20 in., (94 x 50.8 cm.), screen print (BP 393, DM 973, FR 3270, Y 67,066).
BI *"The Harvest",* s., num. below image, est. $3/4,000, (08-05-92, Boos, #673, illus.), image 15½ x 28¼ in., (394 x 718 mm.), serigraphy w/hot stamping and embossing.
$1100* *"Indo China" and "Red Sea": Two,* s., #52/350 Erte, (02-27-93, Dunning, #1065, illus.), 18½ x 16½ in., (36.6 x 41.9 cm.), screenprint (BP 773, DM 1808, FR 6145, Y 129,855).
$275* *Lady In Catsuit: 1980,* from "The Numerals Suite", s., #227/350, pub. Circle Fine Art Corporation, (10-30-92, Sloan, #2367), each, sheet 22¾ x 17¼ in., (57.8 x 43.8 cm.), color screenprint (BP 176, DM 423, FR 1435, Y 34,064).
BI *Leo,* s., #4/35, est. $7/900, (02-14-93, Hanzel, #664), 22 x 17 in., (55.9 x 43.2 cm.), lithograph.
$495* *"Love's Captive",* s., edit. A.P. #51/60, Chromacomp Inc. blind stamp, (09-18-92, DuMouchelle, #2058), 26¼ x 22 in., (66.7 x 55.9 cm.), serigraph (BP 285, DM 741, FR 2538, Y 61,675).
BI *"Love's Captive",* s., num. below image, est. $1,3/1,600, (08-05-92, Boos, #678, illus.), image 26 x 21¾ in., (660 x 552 mm.), color serigraph.
BI *"Lovers And Idol",* s. Erte, #30/300, est. $1,5/2,000, (12-12-92, A. James, #60), 20¾ x 14¾ in., (52.7 x 37.5 cm.), serigraph.
BI *"Muff" and "Evening Dress", 1976,* each s., num. 184/300 and 156/300, pub. Circle Fine Arts, full margins, good cond., est. $4/600, (09-21-92, Butterfield, #826), each 10½ x 7½ in., (267.2 x 190.8 mm.), lithograph in colors on Arches.
$412* *O, 1980,* from The Numbers, full margins, num., s., (05-27-93, Swann, #103, illus.), 16 x 13 in., (40.6 x 33 cm.), color serigraph (BP 264, DM 661, FR 2228, Y 44,168).
BI *Pisces,* s., #8/35, est. $800/1000, (02-14-93, Hanzel, #800), 22½ x 17 in., (57.2 x 43.2 cm.), lithograph.
$880* *"La Princess Lointaine",* s., #AP 10/50, (10-16-92, DuMouchelle, #2227), 22 x 30 in., (55.9 x 76.2 cm.), silkscreen (BP 533, DM 1300, FR 4415, Y 105,075).

BI *Selection Of A Heart, 1978,* s., #219/300, from series The Twenties Remembered Again, est. $3/400, (12-13-92, Hindman, #300), 16½ x 12¼ in., color serigraph.

$171* *Sloth (Lee No. 5-173),* The Seven Deadly Sins series, s., #9/350, p. Chromacomp, for Wellsart Limited, 1983, lit., (12-01-92, Ritchie, #93), 26¼ x 20¾ in., (66.7 x 52.7 cm.), color serigraph (BP 113, DM 273, FR 929, Y 21,290, C$ 220).

$385* *"Sloth",* from Seven Deadly Sins Series, #9/350, s. Erte, (04-17-93, Wolf, #599, illus.), 24 x 16 in., (61 x 40.6 cm.), color seriograph (BP 253, DM 622, FR 2102, Y 43,292).

$412* *U, 1977,* from The Alphabet, full margins, num., s., (05-27-93, Swann, #104), (40.6 x 27.9 cm.), color serigraph (BP 264, DM 661, FR 2228, Y 44,168).

$1210* *Untitled,* s., #189/300 Erte, (05-15-93, Dunning, #1058, illus.), 27 x 20 in., (68.6 x 50.8 cm.), screen print (BP 787, DM 1946, FR 6541, Y 134,131).

BI *"Winter Flowers",* s., num. below image, est. $1,4/1,800, (08-05-92, Boos, #677), image 26 x 23 in., (660 x 584 mm.), color serigraph.

BI *Winter Resort, 1974,* s., num. 158/260, p. Frank Rowland Workshop, pub. Circle Fine Arts, margins, good cond.?, est. $7/900, (09-21-92, Butterfield, #825), 21⁹⁄₁₆ x 17¹⁄₁₆ in., (547.1 x 432.6 mm.), silkscreen in colors on Somerset paper.

BI *Winter, 1975,* s., annot. A/P, artist's proof, from The Seasons, est. $3/400, (12-13-92, Hindman, #298), 13 x 10 in., color serigraph.

$550* *Woman In White Formal Gown Standing With Pillared Candle Forms,* artists proof, #6/64, (03-07-93, Myers, #207), impression 18 x 29 in., (45.7 x 73.7 cm.), serigraph (BP 379, DM 916, FR 3090, Y 64,645).

ERTE (designed by)
$550* *"Folies Bergere",* St. Martin Publisher, (11-13-92, DuMouchelle, #182, illus.), 64 x 49 in., (64 x 49 cm.), poster (BP 355, DM 863, FR 2912, Y 68,264).

ERWITT, Elliott   b. 1928
BI *Albany: Three,* a sequence, p.l., each s., t., d.; last ink s., lit., est. $1,2/1,500, (04-08-93, Christie-NY, #421, illus.), each 10½ x 15¾ in., (26.7 x 40 cm.), photograph, gelatin silver print.

$1725* *California, 1955,* p.l., ink s.; s., annot archival print, lit., (04-08-93, Christie-NY, #420, illus.), 12⅛ x 18⅛ in., (30.8 x 46 cm.), photograph, gelatin silver print (BP 1131, DM 2771, FR 9380, Y 195,756).

$1100* *California,* (1955), p.l., t., (c) insig., lit., (10-13-92, Christie-NY, #444, illus.), 12⅛ x 18⅛ in., (30.8 x 46 cm.), photograph, gelatin silver print (BP 641, DM 1611, FR 5475, Y 133,382).

$1320* *"California Kiss",* 1955/later, s., d., annot., Dixon Collection, (11-16-92, Butterfield, #5949, illus.), 8 x 11⅞ in., (203.6 x 302.2 mm.), photograph, gelatin silver print (BP 869, DM 2105, FR 7089, Y 164,159).

BI *Conversation In Tomb,* 1950s, p.l., s., photog.'s stamp, est. $7/900, (05-23-93, Butterfield, #3399), 10½ x 15¾ in., photograph, gelatin silver print.

BI *"Des Moines, Iowa",* 1955, p.l., s., t., d., photog.'s stamp, est. $5/700, (05-23-93, Butterfield, #3401), 11⅞ x 8 in., photograph, gelatin silver print.

$522* *Dog, Mexico, c. 1968,* photog.'s sig., notations, (04-07-93, Swann, #454), 12 x 8 in., photograph, silver print (BP 345, DM 844, FR 2857, Y 59,305).

$467* *Dog, Paris, c. 1968,* photog.'s sig., notations, (04-07-93, Swann, #455), 12 x 8 in., photograph, silver print (BP 309, DM 755, FR 2556, Y 53,056).

$330* *"Florence, Italy",* 1949/later, s., t., d., Dixon Collection, (11-16-92, Butterfield, #5950, illus.), 10½ x 15¾ in., (267.2 x 400.8 mm.), photograph, gelatin silver print (BP 217, DM 526, FR 1772, Y 41,040).

$1100* *"France",* 1965/later, s., t., d., Dixon Collection, (11-16-92, Butterfield, #5951, illus.), 12 x 18¹⁄₁₆ in., (305.3 x 458 mm.), photograph, gelatin silver print (BP 724, DM 1754, FR 5908, Y 136,799).

$690* *Marching Soldiers,* 1950s, p.l., s., photog.'s stamp, (05-23-93, Butterfield, #3400), 11 x 16 in., photograph, gelatin silver print (BP 449, DM 1128, FR 3797, Y 76,268).

$460* *"Moscow, USSR",* 1966, p.l., s. twice, t., d., (05-23-93, Butterfield, #3403, illus.), 12⅛ x 18¼ in., photograph, gelatin silver print (BP 300, DM 752, FR 2532, Y 50,846).

BI *Pointer In Car,* c. 1960, p.l., s. twice, est. BP 3/500, (05-06-93, Christie-London, #192), image 8 x 12 in., photograph, gelatin silver print.

$275* *Terrier, Rio De Janeiro, Brazil, c. 1968,* sig., t., (10-14-92, Swann, #442), 11¾ x 8 in., (29.8 x 20.3 cm.), photograph, silver print (BP 161, DM 402, FR 1365, Y 33,325).

$288* *"Western USA",* 1954, p.l., s. twice, t., d., (05-23-93, Butterfield, #3403, illus.), 12 x 18 in., photograph, gelatin silver print (BP 188, DM 471, FR 1585, Y 31,834).

ESCHER, Maurits Cornelis   Dutch 1898-1972
$13,234* *Ascending And Descending (Bool/Kist/Locher 435), 1960,* s., 12/108 III, (10-14-92, Germann, #8, illus.), 17⁵⁄₁₆ x 14¹⁵⁄₁₆ in., (440 x 380 mm.), lithograph (BP 7768, DM 19,368, FR 65,677, Y 1,603,732, SF 17,250).

BI *Begegnung (Bool/Kist/Lochner/Wierda 331), (19)44,* s., num., light-stained, est. DM 10/12,000, (12-01-92, Karl/Faber, #597, illus.), lithograph on thick Japan.

$9200* *Belvedere (B./K./L./W. 426), 1958,* s., num. No. 33/107 IV, large margins, good cond., light-stain, (05-13-93, Sotheby-NY, #550, illus.), 18⅛ x 11⅝ in., (461 x 296 mm.), sh 23⅛ x 16⅛ in., (461 x 296 mm.), lithograph on cream Holland (BP 6040, DM 14,855, FR 50,109, Y 1,027,130).

$119* *Bomen En Dieren (Bool 391), 1953,* block mono., pub. Henriette Roland Holst-Stichting, (06-09-93, Bubb Kuyper, #1980), 1¾ x 3⅞ in., (4.4 x 9.9 cm.), wood engraving (BP 78, DM 195, FR 655, Y 12,656, G 219).

$2686* *Cattolica Van Stila, Calabria (Locher 139), 1930,* s., #35/40, margins, good cond., paper discoloration, minor creasing, pinhole in each corner, Late Gerhard Brauer Coll., (05-27-93, Sotheby-Amstrdm, #810), 8⅞ x 11¹¹⁄₁₆ in., (226 x 297 mm.), lithograph on Van Gelder wove (BP 1720, DM 4310, FR 14,527, Y 287,950, G 4830).

$4675* *Convex And Concave (B./K./L./W. 399), 1955,* s., num. No 7/44 II, margins, taped, good cond., mat staining, rubbedarea, hole, surface soiling, (02-24-93, Butterfield, #2737, illus.), 10¹⁵⁄₁₆ x 13¼ in., (278 x 337 mm.), sheet 14½ x 17⅛ in., (278 x 337 mm.), lithograph on cream Holland paper (BP 3260, DM 7589, FR 25,729, Y 548,580).

$1954* *De Vreeselijke Avonturen Van Scholastica (M 188-205), 1932: Eighteen,* book, num. 69, pub. Joh. Enschede en Zonen, good cond., foxing, creases, (12-09-92, Sotheby-Amstrdm, #567), 12¾ x 9¾ in., (324 x 247 mm.), woodcut (BP 1247, DM 3067, FR 10,466, Y 242,281, G 3450).

$8250* *Fish (B./K./L./W. 323), 1941,* i. Aan J. Van M. XII 1941 stencilled, margins, good cond., glued, glue in image, folds, ink i., illustration in catalogue raisonne, does not show stencil, (11-05-92, Sotheby-NY, #176), 19⅞ x 15⅛ in., (506 x 384 mm.), sheet 21⅝ x 16⅛ in., (506 x 384 mm.), woodcut p. in black, light grey and grey-green on satin (BP 5366, DM 13,048, FR 44,141, Y 1,012,146).

$3827* *Flachenfullung II (Bool/Kist/Licher/Wierda 422), (19)57,* s., num., (06-08-93, Karl/Faber, #734, illus.), approx. 12⅝ x 14⁹⁄₁₆ in., (32 x 37 cm.), lithograph on Maschinen hand-made (BP 2516, DM 6210, FR 20,913, Y 406,479).

$2431* *Landbouwers Woning, Ravello (Locher 207), 1932,* s., no. 22/25, full margins, good cond., slight soiling in margins, pinhole, minor paper discoloration at edges of sheet, occasional handling creases, Late Gerhard Brauer Coll., (05-27-93, Sotheby-Amstrdm, #813), 9³⁄₁₆ x 12¼ in., (233 x 311 mm.), lithograph on Van Gelder wove (BP 1557, DM 3901, FR 13,148, Y 260,613, G 4370).

$3070* *Libelle (Glazemaker) (Locher 281), 1936,* s., t., i. Houtsnede eigen druk, margins, good cond., soiling, occasional creasing, pinhole in top corners, staining verso, paper tape along top edge of sheet, Late Gerhard Brauer Coll., (05-27-93, Sotheby-Amstrdm, #816), 8⅛ x 10¹¹⁄₁₆ in., (207 x 272 mm.), woodgraving on thin laid (BP 1966, DM 4926, FR 16,604, Y 329,117, G 5520).

BI *Matthaus-Passion (M 302), 1938,* booklet, good cond., soiling, creases, est. G 3/500, (12-09-92, Sotheby-Amstrdm, #568), 6 x 4⅛ in., (153 x 104 mm.), woodcut on wove.

BI *Metamorphosis,* est. $5/700, (11-12-92, Freemn/Fine Art, #65), mat 9½ x 7¼ in., (24.1 x 18.4 cm.), woodcut.

$183* *New Years's Wish (Bool 371), 1950,* (11-18-92, Bubb Kuyper, #1533), 4½ x 31/16 in., (11.5 x 7.8 cm.), wood engraving (BP 120, DM 292, FR 983, Y 22,758, G 330).

$7475* *Other World (Bool/Kist/Locher/Wierda 348), 1947,* s., i. eigendruk, margins, good cond., hinge stains, (05-13-93, Sotheby-NY, #549, illus.), 12½ x 10¼ in., (318 x 260 mm.), sh 15⅝ x 12⅛ in., (318 x 260 mm.), wood engraving in colors on Japan (BP 4907, DM 12,070, FR 40,714, Y 834,543).

$6050* *Other World (Bool/Kist/Locher/Wierda 348), 1947,* s., d., w/margins, good cond., creases, mat burn, (05-22-93, Weschler, #181, illus.), 12½ x 10¼ in., (31.8 x 26 cm.), wood engraving in colors (BP 3920, DM 9837, FR 33,096, Y 667,034).

BI *Rippled Surface (B.K.L.W. 367), 1950,* s., annot. eigen druck, large margins, good cond., skinning from hinge removal, foxing, est. $2/3,000, (10-28-92, Butterfield, #2637, illus.), 10³⁄₁₆ x 12⁹⁄₁₆ in., (259 x 319 mm.), lino-leum cut in black and grey on Japan paper.

$2686* *San Cosimo, Ravello (Locher 208), 1932,* s., no. 9/24, margins, good cond., paper discoloration, some creasing, Late Gerhard Brauer Coll., (05-27-93, Sotheby-Amstrdm, #815), 12⁵⁄₁₆ x 8¾ in., (313 x 222 mm.), lithograph on wove (BP 1720, DM 4310, FR 14,527, Y 287,950, G 4830).

$2686* *Santa Serverina Calabria (Locher 11), 1931,* s., no. 21/40, margins, good cond., paper discoloration, margin, papertaped to mount, Late Gerhard Brauer Coll., (05-27-93, Sotheby-Amstrdm, #811), 9⅛ x 12³⁄₁₆ in., (232 x 310 mm.), lithograph on wove (BP 1720, DM 4310, FR 14,527, Y 287,950, G 4830).

$4830* *Sky And Water II (Bool 308), 1938,* s., i. eigendruk, full margins, excell. cond., (05-11-93, Christie-NY, #191, illus.), borderline 24¼ x 16 in., (616 x 406 mm.), wood-cut on Japan (BP 3083, DM 7609, FR 25,637, Y 531,295).

$110* *"St. Matthew Passion" (Bool, et al., 302), 1938,* program cover for BACH'S CANTATA, inits. MCE in matrix, very good cond., (03-12-93, Skinner, #68, illus.), sight 6 x 4 in., (15.2 x 10.2 cm.), woodcut printed in purple ink on paper (BP 77, DM 183, FR 623, Y 12,964).

BI *Three Worlds (B.K.L.W. 426), 1955,* s., annot. Vaevo, margins, good cond., foxing, surface soiling, creases, est. $3,5/5,500, (10-28-92, Butterfield, #2638, illus.), 14¼ x 9¾ in., (362 x 248 mm.), lithograph in two shades of grey on cream wove.

$2175* *Turello (Locher 209), 1932,* s, no. 6/24, margins, foxing, minor tear at edges of sheet, paper discoloration, Late Gerhard Brauer Coll., (05-27-93, Sotheby-Amstrdm, #812, illus.), 12¼ x 8⅞ in., (311 x 225 mm.), lithograph on wove (BP 1393, DM 3490, FR 11,763, Y 233,169, G 3910).

$2047* *Turello (Locher 209), 1932,* s., no. 5/24, margins, paper discoloration verso, occasional foxing,handling creases, papertape at left edge of sheet, good cond., Late Gerhard Brauer Coll., (05-27-93, Sotheby-Amstrdm, #814), 12¼ x 8⅞ in., (311 x 225 mm.), lithograph on wove (BP 1311, DM 3285, FR 11,071, Y 219,447, G 3680).

BI *Untitled,* Graph. Kunstanstalt, A- cond., creasing, darken-ing, est. $2/300, (08-06-92, Swann, #183, illus.), 35 x 27½ in., (88.9 x 69.9 cm.), .

$132* *Vissen, Vignet (Bool 398), 1954,* block mono., pub. Hen-riette Roland Holst-Stichting, (06-09-93, Bubb Kuyper, #1983), 2¹⁵⁄₁₆ x 3⅛ in., (7.5 x 7.9 cm.), wood engraving (BP 87, DM 216, FR 726, Y 14,038, G 242).

$94* *Vissen, Vignet (Bool 414), 1956,* block mono., pub. Hen-riette Roland Holst-Stichting, (06-09-93, Bubb Kuyper, #1984), 3³⁄₁₆ x 3³⁄₁₆ in., (8.1 x 8.1 cm.), wood engraving (BP 62, DM 154, FR 517, Y 9997, G 173).

$132* *Vlakvulingsmotief Met Vogels (Bool 361), 1949,* pub. Henriette Roland Holst-Stichting, (06-09-93, Bubb Kuyper, #1985), 2⁵⁄₁₆ x 2¹¹⁄₁₆ in., (5.9 x 6.8 cm.), wood engraving (BP 87, DM 216, FR 726, Y 14,038, G 242).

$7988* *Waterfall (Bol/Locher/Wierda 439), 1961,* full margins, good cond., mat/hinge stains, (10-14-92, Sotheby-Japan, #26, illus.), 14⅞ x 11⅞ in., (378 x 302 mm.), lithograph on cream Holland paper (BP 4689, DM 11,690, FR 39,643, Y 968,008).

$266* *Wij Komen Er Uit! Nederlandsche Exlibris-Kring 1 Jan, 1947 (Bool 371),* fine cond., (11-18-92, Bubb Kuyper, #1534), 4⅝ x 3¹⁵⁄₁₆ in., (11.8 x 10.1 cm.), woodcut (BP 175, DM 424, FR 1429, Y 33,080, G 480).

$6396* *Zuigeling (Arthur E. Escher) (Locher 125), 1929,* s., i. eigen druk., margins, small pinhole, margin, w/minor creasing, minor foxing, good cond., Late Gerhard Brauer Coll., (05-27-93, Sotheby-Amstrdm, #809, illus.), 16⅛ x 14⅜ in., (410 x 365 mm.), color woodcut on laid (BP 4096, DM 10,263, FR 34,592, Y 685,678, G 11,500).

ESCHER, Maurits Cornelis (after)

BI *Other World,* pub. by Gemeente Museum, Den Hag, good cond., est. $800/$1,200, (05-22-93, Weschler, #182, illus.), 39 x 25¼ in., (99.1 x 64.1 cm.), poster in colors.

ESLER, John K. Canadian b. 1933

BI *Boreas, 1976,* s., t., d. '76, est. C$ 1/200, (11-16-92, Hodgins, #167), 17½ x 23½ in., (44.5 x 59.7 cm.), etch-ing on paper.

$130* *Buffalo Jump, 1981,* #3/100, s., t., d. '81, prov., (11-16-92, Hodgins, #71), 23½ x 26½ in., (59.7 x 67.3 cm.), color etching on paper (BP 85, DM 207, FR 699, Y 16,224, C$ 165).

BI *Exodus, America America, 1969,* #8/25 s., t., d. '69, est. C$250/350, (05-10-93, Hodgins, #46), 27 x 25¼ in., (68.6 x 64.1 cm.), collograph on paper.

BI *Exodus, America America, 1969,* #8/25, s., t., d. '69, est. C$ 250/350, (11-16-92, Hodgins, #37), 27 x 20¼ in., (68.6 x 51.4 cm.), collograph on paper.

$43* *Fox Tail, 1979,* #75/75, s., t., d. '79; bears t. verso, prov., (05-10-93, Hodgins, #259), 7 x 6¾ in., (17.8 x 17.1 cm.), color etching on paper (BP 28, DM 69, FR 233, Y 4805, C$ 55).

BI *Pegasus #1, 1969,* #19/34, s., t., d. '69, est. C$150/250, (05-10-93, Hodgins, #171), 29 x 39 in., (73.7 x 99.1 cm.), .

BI *Worry Box #4, 1969,* #7/25, s., t., d. '69, est. C$150/250, (05-10-93, Hodgins, #186), 22 x 22 in., (55.9 x 55.9 cm.), color etching on paper.

ESPAGNAT, Georges d' French 1870-1950

$259* *La Critique. Georges Bans Directeur,* cond. A, (03-16-93, Boisgirard, #103), 27⁹⁄₁₆ x 21⅝ in., (70 x 55 cm.), poster (BP 179, DM 431, FR 1463, Y 30,285).

$512* *"Femme En Buste" and "Conversation Dans Un Jardin", c. 1895: Two,* mono., num. 3, (02-24-93, Picard, #98), wood engraving on laid (BP 357, DM 831, FR 2818, Y 60,080).

ESTES, Richard American b. 1936

$332* *Cafeteria,* mono., #144, (04-21-93, Germann, #401), 21⅞ x 25¹⁵⁄₁₆ in., (555 x 660 mm.), color offset litho-graph (BP 215, DM 531, FR 1795, Y 36,754, SF 483).

$8250* *D Train, 1988,* s., #51/125, pub. Parasol Press, Ltd., full margins, good cond., (11-07-92, Sotheby-NY, #550, illus.), 35⅞ x 71⅞ in., (91.1 x 182.6 cm.), silkscreen in colors (BP 5394, DM 13,173, FR 44,522, Y 1,018,267).

$7700* *D Train, 1988,* s., #50/125, pub. Parasol Press, margins, excellent cond., (11-09-92, Christie-NY, #281, illus.), 35½ x 71 in., (90.2 x 180.3 cm.), colored screenprint on museum board (BP 5091, DM 12,292, FR 41,532, Y 955,572).

$8800* *Holland Hotel, 1984,* gold ink s., #90/100, pub. Parasol Press, full margins, very good cond.?, (10-28-92, Butter-field, #2946, illus.), 44¾ x 71½ in., (113.7 x 181.6 cm.), color silkscreen on wove (BP 5607, DM 13,591, FR 46,146, Y 1,079,755).

$4025* *"Urban Landscapes I: St. Louis Arch", "Urban Land-scapes I: Hardware Store", "Urban Landscapes II: Meat Department" and "Urban Landscapes III: Shopping Cen-ter", 1972, 1972, 1979, 1981: Four,* each s., #14/75, J/A-Y, 26/100, an AP, pub. Parasol Press, Ltd., full margins, good cond., creases, (02-11-93, Sotheby-NY, #328, illus.), color silkscreen (BP 2840, DM 6667, FR 22,562, Y 485,232).

$8250* *Urban Landscapes III, 1981,* portfolio, each s., #66/250, pub. Parasol Press, full margins, good cond., creases, (11-07-92, Sotheby-NY, #549, illus.), approx. each sheet 19¾ x 27½ in., (502 x 699 mm.), eight silkscreens in colors on Fabriano (BP 5394, DM 13,173, FR 44,522, Y 1,018,267).

$5463* *Urban Landscapes III: "Eiffel Tower Restaurant", "Flughafen", "Manhattan", "Subway", "Bus Interior" and "Lakewood Mall", 1981: Six,* s., #134/250, pub. Parasol Press, full margins, good cond., (05-15-93, Sotheby-NY, #965, illus.), each image 14 x 20 in., (35.6 x 50.8 cm.), silkscreen in colors on Fabriano paper (BP 3552, DM 8787, FR 29,530, Y 605,587).

$2415* *"Urban Landscapes III: Subway" and "Salzburg Cathedral", 1981 and 1982: Two,* each s., #235/250 and 90/250, pub. Parasol Press, full margins, goodcond., soiling, (02-11-93, Sotheby-NY, #329, illus.), one 13¹⁵⁄₁₆ x 20 in., (355 x 508 mm.), the other 19¹⁵⁄₁₆ x 14⁹⁄₁₆ in., (355 x 508 mm.), colored silkscreen on Fabriano (BP 1704, DM 4000, FR 13,537, Y 291,139).

$2750* *Urban Landscapes No. 3, 1981: Five,* incomplete set, s., #42/50, w/colophon, blindstamp pub. Parasol Press, full margins, very good cond., scuff on two images, in orig. box, (10-28-92, Butterfield, #2945), 19¾ x 27¾ in., (502 x 705 mm.), color silkscreen on Fabriano paper (BP 1752, DM 4247, FR 14,421, Y 337,423).

BI *Urban Landscapes No. 3, New York, Parasol Press, 1981: Eight,* s., num., just., #46/250, Domberger blindstamp, full margins, excell. cond., orig. portfolio, est. $7,4/7,800, (05-11-93, Christie-NY, #413, illus.), each sheet 19¾ x 27¾ in., (502 x 705 mm.), color screenprint in Fabriano Cottone.

ESTEVE, Maurice French b. 1904

$385* *(Abstract Composition),* s., #34/75, mat burn, appears good cond., (06-11-93, Doyle, #39), 15½ x 19 in., (394 x 483 mm.), color lithograph (BP 253, DM 626, FR 2110, Y 40,849).

$211* *Agria (P-E & M 92), 1986,* (09-30-92, Kunsthallen, #105), lithograph in colors (BP 119, DM 299, FR 1012, Y 25,321, DK 1150).

$312* *Agria, 1986,* (03-24-93, Kunsthallen, #103), color lithograph (BP 211, DM 510, FR 1734, Y 36,658, DK 1955).

$2526* *Aladin, c. 1960/1965,* s., num., (11-28-92, Grisebach, #508, illus.), 18⅞ x 24⅞ in., (48 x 63.2 cm.), colored lithograph on thick wove (BP 1667, DM 4024, FR 13,661, Y 314,375).

$1475* *Ambivaloir (P-E & M side 135), 1981,* s. Esteve, 9/100, (09-30-92, Kunsthallen, #100), color lithograph (BP 832, DM 2092, FR 7074, Y 177,007, DK 8050).

$340* *Ambivaloir, (P-E & M 135), 1981,* (03-24-93, Kunsthallen, #104), poster (BP 230, DM 555, FR 1890, Y 39,948, DK 2128).

$494* *"Arizovert", 1972,* H.C., s., (10-18-92, Pescheteau, #135), 12³⁄₁₆ x 9⁷⁄₁₆ in., (31 x 24 cm.), lithograph in colors on velin (BP 299, DM 730, FR 2479, Y 58,985).

$2570* *Arizovert, (P-E & M 62), 1972,* s. Esteve, Epr.d'A, (03-24-93, Kunsthallen, #96), color lithograph (BP 1740, DM 4197, FR 14,286, Y 301,962, DK 16,100).

$771* *Badgio (Prudhomme-Esteve & Moestrup 61), 1972,* s., i. Epr. d'A., p. by Mourlot, pub. A. Mazo, full margins, good cond., handling marks, creases, (06-30-93, Sotheby-London, #781, illus.), 24⅞ x 18¾ in., (632 x 476 mm.), color lithograph on Arches (BP 517, DM 1315, FR 4436, Y 82,610).

BI *Bank Street (P-E & M44), 1967,* s. Esteve, 111/125, est. DK 10,000, (09-30-92, Kunsthallen, #103), color lithograph.

$1652* *Bebaros, (P-E & M 83), 1975,* s. Esteve, 60/100, (03-24-93, Kunsthallen, #99), color lithograph (BP 1119, DM 2698, FR 9183, Y 194,102, DK 10,350).

BI *Bouinotte (P.-E. & M. 88), 1980,* s., #4/120, pub. Sonja Henie-Niels Onstad Foundation, full margins, good cond., water stain, est. BP 8/1,200, (12-03-92, Sotheby-London, #658, illus.), 19¾ x 15½ in., (500 x 396 mm.), lithograph in colors on Arches.

$1115* *Bouinotte (P.-E. & M. 88), 1980,* s., #4/120, pub. Sonja Henie-Niels Onstad Foundation, full margins, good cond., water-stain, (06-30-93, Sotheby-London, #782, illus.), 19¾ x 15½ in., (502 x 394 mm.), color lithograph on Arches (BP 747, DM 1902, FR 6415, Y 119,469).

BI *Bredin, (P-E & M 56), 1971,* s. Esteve, Epreuve d/A., est. DK 8,000, (03-24-93, Kunsthallen, #101), color lithograph.

$2950* *La Cigale (P-E & M 24), 1956,* s. Esteve, 63/75, (09-30-92, Kunsthallen, #99), color lithograph (BP 1664, DM 4183, FR 14,149, Y 354,014, DK 16,100).

$2202* *La Cigale, (P-E & M 24), 1956,* s. Esteve, 63/75, (03-24-93, Kunsthallen, #100), 23¹¹⁄₁₆ x 18½ in., (60.2 x 47 cm.), color lithograph (BP 1491, DM 3596, FR 12,240, Y 258,724, DK 13,800).

BI *Corne A Licou (Moestrup 35), 1965,* #12/70, s., est. SF 2/3,000, (04-21-93, Germann, #403), 15⅜ x 11⅝ in., (390 x 295 mm.), lithograph in 7 colors.

$2819* *Duetto (P-E & M 53), 1969,* s. Esteve, H.C., from XXe siecle No. 33 "Panorama", (06-03-93, Kunsthallen, #185, illus.), lithograph in colors (BP 1828, DM 4512, FR 15,205, Y 302,338, DK 17,250).

$3304* *Duetto, (P-E & M 53), 1969,* s. Esteve, 39/75, (03-24-93, Kunsthallen, #95), color lithograph (BP 2237, DM 5396, FR 18,366, Y 388,204, DK 20,700).

$651* *"Duetto-1969" (CR 53),* H.C., s., (01-28-93, Pescheteau, #136), 12³⁄₁₆ x 9¼ in., (31 x 23.5 cm.), color lithograph on wove (BP 430, DM 1032, FR 3491, Y 80,829).

$2753* *Folerie, (P-E & M 82), 1975,* s. Esteve E.A., (03-24-93, Kunsthallen, #98), color lithograph (BP 1864, DM 4496, FR 15,303, Y 323,464, DK 17,250).

BI *Le Gargandin De Bourges,* Musee Bourges 1987, s. Esteve, 189/200, est. DK 5,000, (12-02-92, Kunsthallen, #243), color serigraph.

BI *Le Gargandin De Bourges, 1987,* s. Esteve, 191/200, est. DK 6,000, (09-30-92, Kunsthallen, #104), color serigraph.

$3487* *Grand Pavois, (P-E & M 25), 1956,* s. Esteve, 8/175, (03-24-93, Kunsthallen, #91), color lithograph (BP 2361, DM 5695, FR 19,383, Y 409,705, DK 21,850).

BI *Java Vrillee (P-E & M 84), 1977,* s. Esteve, 77/95, est. DK 15,000, (12-02-92, Kunsthallen, #247), color lithograph.

$1468* *Java Vrillee, (P-E & M 84), 1977,* s. Esteve 77/95, (03-24-93, Kunsthallen, #97), color lithograph (BP 994, DM 2398, FR 8160, Y 172,483, DK 9200).

BI *Jazz (Prudhomme-Esteve/Moestrup 20), 1954,* s., stains, blindstamp, est. SF 5/6,000, (09-04-92, Germann, #92, illus.), 25¹³⁄₁₆ x 19¾ in., (655 x 502 mm.), color lithograph.

$2249* *Jour De Fete (P-E & M 18), 1952,* s. Esteve 25/200, est. DK 5,000, (12-02-92, Kunsthallen, #244), lithograph in colors (BP 1451, DM 3537, FR 12,072, Y 279,831, DK 13,800).

$1279* *Jour De Fete (P.-E. & M. 18), 1952,* s., #157/200, pub. La Guilde de la Gravure, full margins, colors faded, soiling, (12-03-92, Sotheby-London, #661), 17¼ x 12⅜ in., (440 x 315 mm.), lithograph in colors on Arches (BP 825, DM 2011, FR 6865, Y 159,139).

BI *Jour De Fete, (P-E & M 18), 1952,* s. Esteve, epreuve d'artiste, est. DK 18,000, (03-24-93, Kunsthallen, #93), color lithograph.

$850* *Komposition,* s., num., (06-08-93, Karl/Faber, #735), approx. 24³⁄₁₆ x 19⁵⁄₁₆ in., (61.5 x 49 cm.), color lithograph on Arches wove (BP 559, DM 1379, FR 4645, Y 90,281).

$1725* *L' Accueil (P-E & M 21), 1954,* s. Esteve, 94/260, (12-02-92, Kunsthallen, #246), lithograph in colors (BP 1113, DM 2713, FR 9259, Y 214,632, DK 10,580).

$1023* *L'Accueil (Prudhomme-Esteve & Moestrup 21), 1954,* s., #80/260, p. Desjobert, full margins, good cond., (12-03-92, Sotheby-London, #655), 17¾ x 23¾ in., (450 x 605 mm.), lithograph in colors on Rives (BP 660, DM 1609, FR 5491, Y 127,286).

$2217* *L'Envol (P.-E. & M. 28), 1958,* s., i. Epreuve d'Artiste, artist's proof, pub. Villand-Galanis, margins slightly reduced, good cond., tape stains, (12-03-92, Sotheby-London, #656, illus.), 19¾ x 19¼ in., (653 x 490 mm.), lithograph in colors on Arches (BP 1430, DM 3486, FR 11,900, Y 275,849).

BI *Lajoupee (P-E & M 67), 1973*, s. Esteve, 42/125, est. DK 25,000, (12-02-92, Kunsthallen, #256, illus.), color lithograph.

$4864* *Lajoupee, (P-E & M 67), 1973*, s. Esteve, 42/125, (03-24-93, Kunsthallen, #90), color lithograph (BP 3294, DM 7944, FR 27,037, Y 571,496, DK 30,475).

$6531* *Lajoupee, (P-E & M 67), 1973*, s. Esteve, Epr. d' Artiste, (09-30-92, Kunsthallen, #97), color lithograph (BP 3685, DM 9261, FR 31,324, Y 783,751, DK 35,650).

BI *Loriquet, (P-E & M 86), 1977*, s. Esteve., 18/30, est. DK 20,000, (03-24-93, Kunsthallen, #92), color lithograph.

$1119* *Loupi (Cat. 55), 1971*, whole margins, #15/80, s., (06-11-93, Picard, #52), 12⅞ x 9¹⁵⁄₁₆ in., (327 x 252 mm.), color lithograph on Arches wove (BP 735, DM 1819, FR 6132, Y 118,727).

$147* *Masque Venitien (P-E & M93), 1986*, (09-30-92, Kunsthallen, #107), color lithograph (BP 83, DM 208, FR 705, Y 17,641, DK 805).

$1876* *Matinailles (P.-E. & M. 23), 1956*, s., #72/200, p., blindstamp, pub. L'Oeuvre Gravee, good cond., light-staining, tape stains, (12-03-92, Sotheby-London, #660, illus.), sheet 17¾ x 22 in., (450 x 558 mm.), lithograph in colors on Rives (BP 1210, DM 2950, FR 10,070, Y 233,420).

$1580* *Matinailles (Prudhomme 23), 1956*, #119/200, s., blindstamp, (04-21-93, Germann, #110), 17¹¹⁄₁₆ x 22¹⁄₁₆ in., (450 x 560 mm.), color lithograph (BP 1025, DM 2526, FR 8541, Y 174,914, SF 2300).

$1112* *Messidor, 1981*, 6/75, Charles Sorlier, ed., (05-12-93, AB Stockholm, #7023), color lithograph (BP 726, DM 1794, FR 6043, Y 124,149, SK 8250).

$202* *Monique Prudhomme- Esteve/Hans Moestrup, L'Oeuvre Grave, (P-E & M 92), 1986*, w/original print, (03-24-93, Kunsthallen, #106), (BP 137, DM 330, FR 1123, Y 23,734, DK 1265).

BI *Musee Bourges, c. 1986*, s., #193/200, full margins, good cond., est. BP 4/600, (06-30-93, Sotheby-London, #783, illus.), 22⅞ x 15⅜ in., (581 x 391 mm.), color pochoir on Arches.

$164* *Otochine, 1972*, s., 32/40, (06-28-93, Loudmer, #245), 14³⁄₁₆ x 19½ in., (360 x 495 mm.), sh 25⁹⁄₁₆ x 19¹¹⁄₁₆ in., (360 x 495 mm.), black lithograph w/beige background on wove (BP 110, DM 279, FR 939, Y 17,401).

BI *Le Prince (P-E & M 19), 1954*, s. Esteve, 158/220, est. DK 7,000, (12-02-92, Kunsthallen, #245), color lithograph.

$1053* *Rivanoir (P-E & M side 134), 1969*, s. Esteve, 71/150, (09-30-92, Kunsthallen, #106), color lithograph (BP 594, DM 1493, FR 5050, Y 126,365, DK 5750).

BI *Roussadou (P-E & M 75), 1974*, s. Esteve, 34/50, est. DK 12,000, (09-30-92, Kunsthallen, #102), sheet 19½ x 16⅜ in., (49.5 x 41.6 cm.), color lithograph.

$2255* *Roussadou (P-E & M 75), 1974*, s. Esteve, VII/XX, (06-03-93, Kunsthallen, #177), lithograph in colors (BP 1462, DM 3609, FR 12,163, Y 241,849, DK 13,800).

$2812* *Rouzique (P-E & M 85), 1977*, s. Esteve, 29/30, (12-02-92, Kunsthallen, #257, illus.), lithograph in colors (BP 1814, DM 4422, FR 15,094, Y 349,882, DK 17,250).

$3792* *Rouzique (P-E & M 85), 1977*, s. Esteve, 2/30, (09-30-92, Kunsthallen, #101, illus.), color lithograph (BP 2139, DM 5377, FR 18,187, Y 455,058, DK 20,700).

$1896* *Sancho Rubicon, 1989*, s. Esteve, 66/100, (09-30-92, Kunsthallen, #98), color lithograph (BP 1070, DM 2689, FR 9094, Y 227,529, DK 10,350).

$367* *Sans Titre*, artist proof, #XIX/XX, s. Esteve, (05-18-93, Encans, #188), 12⅜ x 9⁷⁄₁₆ in., (31.5 x 24 cm.), color lithograph (BP 239, DM 595, FR 2011, Y 40,900, C$ 466).

$1599* *Sirius (Cat. 40), 1966*, whole margins, #33/60, s., (06-11-93, Picard, #51), 18⁹⁄₁₆ x 14³⁄₁₆ in., (471 x 361 mm.), lithograph in colors on Rives wove (BP 1051, DM 2599, FR 8762, Y 169,655).

$551* *Toucornu, (P-E & M 36), 1965*, s. Esteve 5/35, (03-24-93, Kunsthallen, #102), color lithograph (BP 373, DM 900, FR 3063, Y 64,740, DK 3450).

BI *Untitled*, HC, s., est. FF2,000/2,500, (04-04-93, Pescheteau, #211), 12³⁄₁₆ x 9¼ in., (31 x 23.5 cm.), color lithograph.

ESTEVE, Maurice   (after)
$305* *"Le Tombeau De Mon Pere", 1961*: Two, (01-28-93, Pescheteau, #135), 11⁷⁄₁₆ x 8⅞ in., (29 x 22.5 cm.), etchings and aquatints on wove (BP 201, DM 483, FR 1635, Y 37,869).

$220* *Untitled*, (04-04-93, Pescheteau, #210), a vue 12³⁄₁₆ x 9¹⁄₁₆ in., (31 x 23 cm.), etching and aquatint (BP 145, DM 354, FR 1201, Y 25,048).

ETCHING CLUB, Publisher
$9* *Gray's Elegy*, 21 pages, pub. 1847, (01-21-93, Bonhams-Chelsea, #91), etching (BP 6, DM 14, FR 48, Y 1126).

BI *Gray's Elegy: Four*, 21 pages, pub. 1847, est. BP 40/60, (11-19-92, Bonhams-Chelsea, #45), etching.

ETIENNE
$83* *Young Girl With Dog*, s., very good cond.?, (07-19-92, Bakker, #146), plate 11¼ x 8¼ in., (28.6 x 21 cm.), color etching and aquatint (BP 43, DM 121, FR 409, Y 10,318).

ETIENNE, Martin   b. 1913
$101* *"Demeures"*, s., (10-18-92, Pescheteau, #136), 26¾ x 20¹⁄₁₆ in., (68 x 51 cm.), lithograph in colors on Arches (BP 61, DM 149, FR 507, Y 12,060).

ETNI, Hans
BI *Woman Seated In A Tree*, s., i. in crayon, est. BP 1/150, (10-27-92, Phillips-London, #197), (594 x 330 mm.), color lithograph on black paper.

ETTEN, Kruseman Van   European 19th cent.
$110* *"Gristmill"*, d. 1883, good cond., (11-21-92, Bakker, #77), plate 9 x 12½ in., (22.9 x 31.8 cm.), etching (BP 72, DM 175, FR 591, Y 13,680).

ETTINGER
$495* *"Last Shot" and "The Old Story"*: Two, s., very good cond., (04-22-93, Guyette, #853, illus.), image 7½ x 11½ in., (19.1 x 29.2 cm.), etching (BP 320, DM 795, FR 2683, Y 54,426).

ETTINGER, Churchill   American b. 1903
$220* *"Wood Cock"*, s., ident., very good cond., (04-22-93, Guyette, #847, illus.), image 8½ x 11 in., (21.6 x 27.9 cm.), etching (BP 142, DM 353, FR 1192, Y 24,189).

ETTY (after)
$22* *Portrait Of A Soldier*, (02-11-93, Boos, #473), sight 5 x 3¾ in., (127 x 95 mm.), engraving (BP 16, DM 36, FR 123, Y 2652).

EUGENE, Frank
$7700* *The Song Of The Lily (Naef, p. 346, no. 227), 1897*, s. by photog. in neg., backed w/board, probably p. c. 1908, sold after sale, (10-15-92, Sotheby-NY, #93, illus.), 27¾ x 20 in., (70.5 x 50.8 cm.), photograph, large format carbon print (BP 4712, DM 11,462, FR 38,869, Y 923,815).

EVANS, Floyd B.   1890-1966
BI *Magnolia Blossom, c. 1927*, s., mounted, est. $7/900, (10-13-92, Christie-NY, #197, illus.), 9¼ x 7⅜ in., (23.5 x 18.7 cm.), photograph, toned gelatin silver print.

$467* *Nature's Labyrinth, c. 1944*, s. by photog., address label, exhib., (04-07-93, Swann, #456, illus.), 13½ x 16 in., photograph, chlorobromide print (BP 309, DM 755, FR 2556, Y 53,056).

BI *Navajo Weavers*, sig., notations, label, 1930's, est. $1/1,500, (10-14-92, Swann, #443, illus.), 13 x 16½ in., (33 x 41.9 cm.), photograph, dye-transfer.

$330* *Night Blooming Cereus*, label, 1930's, (10-14-92, Swann, #444, illus.), 8½ x 7¼ in., (21.6 x 18.4 cm.), photograph, carbro print (BP 194, DM 483, FR 1638, Y 39,990).

$220* *Night Blooming Cereus, c. 1927*, (04-07-93, Swann, #457, illus.), 18 x 8 in., photograph, cabro print (BP 145, DM 356, FR 1204, Y 24,994).

BI *Rippling Sands, c. 1938*, s., credit label, est. $1,5/2,000, (10-13-92, Christie-NY, #196, illus.), 17¼ x 13¼ in., (43.8 x 33.7 cm.), photograph, gelatin silver print.

EVANS, Frederick   1837-1933
$13,200* *Bourges Cathedral Sth. Nave Aisle*, mounted, s., t. by photog., early 1900s, (10-15-92, Sotheby-NY, #107, illus.), 11¼ x 8⅝ in., (28.6 x 21.9 cm.), photograph,

platinum print (BP 8077, DM 19,649, FR 66,633, Y 1,583,683).

$1265* *Bourges Cathedral-West Front, early 1900's,* mounted, photog. mono. blindstamp, (04-06-93, Sotheby-NY, #59, illus.), 9¾ x 7¾ in., photograph, platinum print (BP 836, DM 2038, FR 6901, Y 144,275).

BI *Doorway,* mounted, photog.'s mono. blindstamp, early 1900's, (10-15-92, Sotheby-NY, #105A, illus.), 8⅛ x 5⅛ in., (20.6 x 13 cm.), photograph, platinum print on gray paper.

$6050* *A French Chateau (Castles In The Air),* mounted, s., t. by photog., inits., early 1900's, (10-15-92, Sotheby-NY, #104, illus.), 7½ x 7⅜ in., (19.1 x 18.7 cm.), photograph, platinum print (BP 3702, DM 9006, FR 30,540, Y 725,855).

BI *"In Nantes Cathdral", 1900,* s., t., est. $1/1,500, (05-23-93, Butterfield, #3404, illus.), 10 x 4 in., photograph, platinum print.

BI *Lincoln Cathedral,* mounted, photog.'s mono. blindstamp, early 1900s, est. $1,5/2,500, (10-15-92, Sotheby-NY, #106, illus.), 5¾ x 7⅛ in., (14.6 x 18.1 cm.), photograph, platinum print.

$2588* *Lincoln Cathedral, early 1900's,* double-mounted, i. by photog., blindstamp, label, (04-06-93, Sotheby-NY, #60, illus.), 6¾ x 5¼ in., photograph, platinum print (BP 1709, DM 4169, FR 14,119, Y 295,164).

$1320* *A Mountain Shoulder-Great Gable,* mounted, s., t. by photog., mono. blindstamp, early 1900s, (10-15-92, Sotheby-NY, #105, illus.), 9⅞ x 6⅜ in., (25.1 x 16.2 cm.), photograph, platinum print (BP 808, DM 1965, FR 6663, Y 158,368).

EVANS, Frederick H. 1852-1943

$654* *Four Studies Of Ecclesiastical Sculpture, c. 1900,* mounted together on single sheet, t., mono. FHE, various small sizes, (05-07-93, Sotheby-London, #98), photograph, platinum print (BP 414, DM 1034, FR 3484, Y 72,011).

$1540* *"Portrait Of Arthur Symons" and "Portrait Of Unidentified Man", c. 1900: Two,* photog.'s blindstamp, sig., (04-07-93, Swann, #458, illus.), each approx. 9 x 6½ in., photograph, platinum print (BP 1018, DM 2491, FR 8429, Y 174,960).

EVANS, Merlyn O. b. 1910

$755* *To Visit Britain's Landmarks, Fish Hill Tower, Broadway, 1936,* ref. #459, cond. 1, (10-13-92, Phillips-London, #106), 29¹⁵⁄₁₆ x 45¹⁄₁₆ in., (76 x 114.5 cm.), color lithograph (BP 440, DM 1106, FR 3758, Y 91,548).

EVANS, Walker American 1903-1975

$3738* *"Allie Mae Burroughs, Hale County, Alabama" (First and Last, pl. 73),* plate from "Untitled" portfolio, Ives-Sillmann, mounted, s. by photog., d., #15/100 in unident. hand, 1936, p. c. 1971, (04-06-93, Sotheby-NY, #124, illus.), 9⅜ x 7⅛ in., photograph (BP 2469, DM 6022, FR 20,393, Y 426,323).

$1650* *"Baton Rouge, LA", "Child's Grave, Hale County, AL", "Truro, MA", andSteel Mill And Company Houses, Birmingham, AL": Four,* (1935), (1936), (1931), (1936), from portfolio Walker Evans, 1971, each s., d., annot. AC, prov., lit., (10-13-92, Christie-NY, #206, illus.), various sizes to 7½ x 9¼ in., (19.1 x 23.5 cm.), photograph, gelatin silver prints (BP 961, DM 2417, FR 8213, Y 200,073).

BI *Battlefield Monument, Vicksburg, Mississippi, 1936,* lit., est. $1,5/1,800, (04-08-93, Christie-NY, #276, illus.), 9⅝ x 7½ in., (24.4 x 19.1 cm.), photograph, gelatin silver print.

$1090* *Bed Post And Stone, Truro, Massachusetts, 1936,* p. 1971, mounted on card, s., d., num. III 95/100, 151 x 194mm, (05-07-93, Sotheby-London, #284, illus.), photograph, silver print (BP 690, DM 1723, FR 5807, Y 120,018).

$489* *"Bed+Stove, Truro Mississippi",* 1936, p. 1971, s., t., d., #19/100, (05-23-93, Butterfield, #3408, illus.), 6 x 7¾ in., photograph, gelatin silver print (BP 318, DM 800, FR 2691, Y 54,051).

BI *Belle Grove Plantation, White Chapel, LA,* (c. 1935), 1960s, prov., lit., est. $2/2,500, (10-13-92, Christie-NY, #204, illus.), 9½ x 7⅝ in., (24.1 x 19.4 cm.), photograph, gelatin silver print.

BI *Blacksmith's Shop, New York City,* (1933), 1960s, s., t., d., reprod. limit. stamp, prov., est. $2,5/3,500, (10-13-92, Christie-NY, #201, illus.), 6½ x 4½ in., (16.5 x 11.4 cm.), photograph, gelatin silver print.

BI *Bloomingdale's Corner, 59th Street, New York, c. 1929,* backed w/card, dealer's stamp, est. $4/6,000, (10-15-92, Sotheby-NY, #165, illus.), 7⅞ x 8½ in., (20 x 21.6 cm.), photograph, gelatin silver print.

$2300* *"Chicago", 1946,* mounted, s. by photog., t., d., name stamp, (04-06-93, Sotheby-NY, #126, illus.), photograph (BP 1519, DM 3705, FR 12,548, Y 262,318).

BI *"Child's Grave, Alabama",* 1936, p. 1971, s., t., d., #19/100, illus., est. $6/800, (05-23-93, Butterfield, #3409, illus.), 7¼ x 9½ in., photograph, gelatin silver print.

$863* *A Child's Grave, Hale County, Alabama, Summer (1936),* from Selected Images Portfolio, 1971, s., d., #55/100, lit., (04-08-93, Christie-NY, #278, illus.), 7⅛ x 9¼ in., (18.1 x 23.5 cm.), photograph, gelatin silver print (BP 566, DM 1386, FR 4693, Y 97,935).

BI *"Coal Dock Worker" and "Steel Mill and Company Houses, Birmingham, Alabama" (Havana, pl. 77; First and Last, pl. 104): Two,* plates from "Untitled" portfolio, Ives-Sillman, s. by photog., d., #30/100 in unidentified hand, 1933 and 1936, p. c. 1971, each #30 edit. 100, est.$1,5/2,500, (10-15-92, Sotheby-NY, #180, illus.), one 7⅝ x 6 in., (19.4 x 15.2 cm.), other 7½ x 9¼ in., (19.4 x 15.2 cm.), photograph, gelatin silver prints.

$1320* *Convicts, 1930's,* dealer's stamp, (10-15-92, Sotheby-NY, #172, illus.), 6 x 4⅛ in., (15.2 x 10.5 cm.), photograph, gelatin silver print (BP 808, DM 1965, FR 6663, Y 158,368).

BI *A Cotton Field, Hale County, Alabama,* (1936), 1970s, estate stamp, lit., est. $7/900, (10-13-92, Christie-NY, #205, illus.), 7⅝ x 9⅝ in., (19.4 x 24.4 cm.), photograph, gelatin silver prints.

$1320* *Couple At Luna Park,* (1928), p.l., prov., lit., (10-13-92, Christie-NY, #198, illus.), 12⅞ x 7⅜ in., (32.7 x 18.7 cm.), photograph, gelatin silver print (BP 769, DM 1934, FR 6570, Y 160,058).

BI *Cuban Boys,* 1932, p.l., s., d., est. $1,2/1,800, (04-08-93, Christie-NY, #274, illus.), 9½ x 6 in., (24.1 x 15.2 cm.), photograph, gelatin silver print.

$2300* *Cuban Worker, 1933,* t. in unknown hand, photog.'s name, dealer's stamp verso, (04-08-93, Christie-NY, #275, illus.), 10 x 6¼ in., (25.4 x 15.9 cm.), photograph, gelatin silver print (BP 1508, DM 3695, FR 12,507, Y 261,008).

BI *Dancers, Tahiti, 1932,* notations, est. $2/3,000, (10-14-92, Swann, #445, illus.), 8 x 8½ in., (20.3 x 21.6 cm.), photograph, silver print.

$5720* *Dock Worker, Havanna, 1932,* handstamp, (10-14-92, Swann, #446, illus.), 6½ x 4½ in., (16.5 x 11.4 cm.), photograph, silver print (BP 3357, DM 8371, FR 28,387, Y 693,165).

$1150* *"Dock Workers, Havana" (Havana, pl. 76),* plate from "Selected Photographs' portfolio, Double Elephant Press, mounted, s. by photog., #18/75 in unident. hand, t., d., num. 15, 1932, p. c. 1974, (04-06-93, Sotheby-NY, #122, illus.), 11¾ x 9 in., photograph (BP 760, DM 1853, FR 6274, Y 131,159).

$1150* *"Doorway, 204 W. 13th Street, New York",* 1931, p. 1971, s., #47/75, illus., (05-23-93, Butterfield, #3406, illus.), 11 x 8¾ in., photograph, gelatin silver print (BP 749, DM 1880, FR 6329, Y 127,114).

$3300* *Frame Houses In Virginia (American Photographs, Part Two, pl. 22), 1936,* mounted on card, s., d. by photog., t., d., i. Part Two, #22, (10-15-92, Sotheby-NY, #171, illus.), 7¼ x 6⅞ in., (18.4 x 17.5 cm.), photograph, gelatin silver print (BP 2019, DM 4912, FR 16,658, Y 395,921).

BI *Havana Fortress, 1933,* t., d., stamp, s., annot., d. 12/72, prov., est. $3/5,000, (10-13-92, Christie-NY, #200, illus.), 7¼ x 9⅝ in., (18.4 x 24.4 cm.), photograph, gelatin silver print.

BI *"In Bridgeport's War Factories", 1941,* t., d., annot., photog. stamp, Dixon Collection, est. $1,8/2,200, (11-16-92, Butterfield, #5952, illus.), 6¾ x 8⅞ in., (171.8 x 225.8 mm.), photograph, gelatin silver print.

$863* *"In Bridgeport's War Factories", 1941,* t., d., annot. in unidentified hand, photog.'s stamp, (05-23-93, Butterfield, #3405, illus.), 6¾ x 8⅞ in., photograph, gelatin silver print (BP 562, DM 1411, FR 4750, Y 95,391).

$4025* *"Independence Day, Terra Alta, West Virginia", 1935,* photog. name stamp, (04-06-93, Sotheby-NY, #123, illus.), 6⅝ x 9⅛ in., photograph (BP 2659, DM 6485, FR 21,959, Y 459,056).

$5225* *Interior At Biloxi, Miss., 1945,* backed w/card, s. by photog., dealer's stamp, (10-15-92, Sotheby-NY, #171A, illus.), 5⅞ x 8½ in., (14.9 x 21.6 cm.), photograph, gelatin silver print (BP 3197, DM 7778, FR 26,376, Y 626,875).

$575* *"James Agee", 1940,* p.l., estate print, annot. From original negative, gift to friend, (05-23-93, Butterfield, #3407, illus.), 8½ x 6¾ in., photograph, gelatin silver print (BP 374, DM 940, FR 3165, Y 63,557).

$3300* *Jigsaw House At Ocean City, N.J. (American Photographs, Part Two, pl.33), 1931,* backed w/card, mounted on thick paper, s., d. by photog., t., d., i.Part Two, Cat. No. 33, (10-15-92, Sotheby-NY, #166, illus.), 5⅜ x 7 in., (13.7 x 17.8 cm.), photograph, gelatin silver print (BP 2019, DM 4912, FR 16,658, Y 395,921).

$1650* *Joe's Auto Graveyard, Pennsylvania (American Photographs, Part One, pl. 7, cropped version),* dealer's stamp, 1936, p.l., (10-15-92, Sotheby-NY, #177, illus.), 7½ x 9½ in., (19.1 x 24.1 cm.), photograph, gelatin silver print (BP 1010, DM 2456, FR 8329, Y 197,960).

$2760* *Kitchen, Burroughs Home,* 1938, p.l., s., d., lit., (04-08-93, Christie-NY, #277, illus.), 13¼ x 9⅜ in., (33.7 x 23.8 cm.), photograph, gelatin silver print (BP 1810, DM 4434, FR 15,008, Y 313,209).

$8580* *Kitchen, Havana, 1932,* s., credit stamp, label, prov., (10-13-92, Christie-NY, #199, illus.), 5⅝ x 7½ in., (14.3 x 19.1 cm.), photograph, gelatin silver print (BP 4997, DM 12,570, FR 42,708, Y 1,040,378).

$1980* *Las Brisas, Cuba, 1932,* ex-coll. James Agee, (04-07-93, Swann, #459, illus.), 10 x 7¼ in., photograph, silver print (BP 1308, DM 3202, FR 10,837, Y 224,949).

BI *Maine Pump (First and Last, pl. 57; American Photographs, Part Two, pl. 32),* plate from "Selected Photographs" portfolio, Double Elephant Press, mounted, s. by photog., #21/75 in unidentified hand, 1933, p.c. 1974, #21 edit.90, est. $1,2/1,800, (10-15-92, Sotheby-NY, #179, illus.), 11⅛ x 8⅜ in., (28.3 x 21.3 cm.), photograph, gelatin silver print.

$3025* *Manhattan Through A Window, 1930's,* dealer's stamp, (10-15-92, Sotheby-NY, #167, illus.), 7⅝ x 7½ in., (19.4 x 19.1 cm.), photograph, gelatin silver print (BP 1851, DM 4503, FR 15,270, Y 362,927).

BI *N.Y. State Farm Interior (American Photographs, Part One, pl. 15), 1931,* backed w/card, mounted on thick paper, s., d., i.by photog., t., d., i.by photog., est. $3/5,000, (10-15-92, Sotheby-NY, #168, illus.), 5¾ x 7⅞ in., (14.6 x 20 cm.), photograph, gelatin silver print.

$3025* *Negro Barber Shop Interior, Atlanta (American Photographs, Part One,pl. 6),* s. by photog., 1936, p.l., (10-15-92, Sotheby-NY, #178, illus.), 7½ x 9⅜ in., (19.1 x 23.8 cm.), photograph, gelatin silver print (BP 1851, DM 4503, FR 15,270, Y 362,927).

BI *New York Abstractions: "A Fire Escape Grating", "A Construction Crane And Skyscrapers", "Watertowers", " A Building Facade" and "Workers And Ropes And Pulleys", c. 1929: Five,* four w/pencil notations, est. $6/8,000, (04-08-93, Christie-NY, #272, illus.), each approx. 1¾ x 2⅜ in., (4.4 x 6 cm.), photograph, gelatin silver print.

$2200* *New York Cityscape, c. 1930,* dealer's stamp, (10-15-92, Sotheby-NY, #165A, illus.), 7½ x 6⅞ in., (19.1 x 17.5 cm.), photograph, gelatin silver print (BP 1346, DM 3275, FR 11,106, Y 263,947).

$4675* *New York Skyscraper, 1928-29,* (10-15-92, Sotheby-NY, #164A, illus.), 2½ x 1½ in., (6.4 x 3.8 cm.), photograph, gelatin silver print (BP 2861, DM 6959, FR 23,599, Y 560,888).

$220* *Pabst Blue Ribbon Sign,* 1940's/printed later, prov., (05-16-93, Hindman, #370), 9 x 7¼ in., photograph, silver print (BP 144, DM 355, FR 1196, Y 24,499).

BI *Phoenix Building,* dealer's stamp, 1930s, p. in 1960s or 1970s, est. $2/3,000, (10-15-92, Sotheby-NY, #175, illus.),

7½ x 9½ in., (19.1 x 24.1 cm.), photograph, gelatin silver print.

BI *Portrait Of Paul Grotz, c. 1932,* sig., notations, est. $2/3,000, ex-coll. Paul Grotz, (10-14-92, Swann, #447, illus.), photograph, silver print.

$2300* *Portrait Study, Bethehem, Pennsylvania, 1936,* estate stamp, (04-08-93, Christie-NY, #279, illus.), 7¼ x 5⅝ in., (18.4 x 14.3 cm.), photograph, gelatin silver print (BP 1508, DM 3695, FR 12,507, Y 261,008).

$2070* *"Seed Store Interior, Vicksburg, Mississippi", "Butcher's Sign Mississippi", "View Of Morgantown, West Virginia" (F.S.A. 2, 116, and 135), 1935-36:Three,* each w/photog. credit stamp, (04-06-93, Sotheby-NY, #127, illus.), photograph (BP 1367, DM 3335, FR 11,293, Y 236,086).

$1380* *Selected African Art Studies, circ. 1935: Four,* each w/ dealer's stamp, num. in unident. hand, (04-06-93, Sotheby-NY, #121, illus.), various sizes to 9½ x 7½ in., photograph (BP 911, DM 2223, FR 7529, Y 157,391).

$880* *"Shantytown, Vicksburg, Mississippi", 1936,* photog. stamp, (11-16-92, Butterfield, #5954, illus.), 7¾ x 9¾ in., (197.2 x 248.1 mm.), photograph, gelatin silver print (BP 579, DM 1403, FR 4726, Y 109,439).

$1495* *"Show Bill, Demopolis, Alabama" (MoMA, p. 123),* mounted, crop marks, notations in unident. hand; s., d. by photog.; p. c. 1971, (04-06-93, Sotheby-NY, #125, illus.), 7½ x 9½ in., photograph (BP 987, DM 2409, FR 8156, Y 170,506).

$3300* *Sidewalk And Shopfront, New Orleans (American Photographs, Part One,pl. 5), 1935,* backed w/card, mounted on thick paper, s., d. by photog., t., d., i.Part One, #5 by photog., est. $3/5,000, (10-15-92, Sotheby-NY, #169, illus.), 8¼ x 7 in., (21 x 17.8 cm.), photograph, gelatin silver print (BP 2019, DM 4912, FR 16,658, Y 395,921).

BI *Southern Interior,* dealer's stamp, i., 1930s, p. before 1974, est. $2/3,000, (10-15-92, Sotheby-NY, #174, illus.), 9⅝ x 7⅝ in., (24.4 x 19.4 cm.), photograph, gelatin silver print.

$3520* *Storefront, 1935,* s., d., t., label, prov., (10-13-92, Christie-NY, #202, illus.), 6¼ x 6½ in., (15.9 x 16.5 cm.), photograph, gelatin silver print (BP 2050, DM 5157, FR 17,521, Y 426,822).

$1100* *Street Scene, Saratoga, New York,* photog.'s handstamp, 1930s, p.l., (04-07-93, Swann, #460, illus.), 6 x 7 in., photograph, silver print (BP 727, DM 1779, FR 6021, Y 124,972).

$2070* *Subway, New York, 1938-41,* flush-mounted, dealer's archive stamp, lit., (04-08-93, Christie-NY, #280, illus.), 4¼ x 6¾ in., (10.8 x 17.1 cm.), photograph, gelatin silver print (BP 1357, DM 3325, FR 11,256, Y 234,907).

$1430* *Two Women At Counter, c. 1929,* handstamp, notations, (10-14-92, Swann, #448, illus.), 4¾ x 7 in., (12.1 x 17.8 cm.), photograph, silver print (BP 839, DM 2093, FR 7097, Y 173,291).

$2185* *Untitled, Woman Seated, c. 1935,* (04-08-93, Christie-NY, #281, illus.), 6¼ x 9¼ in., (15.9 x 23.5 cm.), photograph, gelatin silver print (BP 1433, DM 3510, FR 11,881, Y 247,957).

BI *Westchester, N.Y., Farmhouse (American Photographs, Part Two, pl. 8),1931,* mounted on thick paper, s., d. by photog., t., d., i. Part Two, #8, est. $3/5,000, (10-15-92, Sotheby-NY, #170, illus.), 6⅜ x 8¼ in., (16.2 x 21 cm.), photograph, gelatin silver print.

$2760* *Wooden Gothic House, Massachusetts, 1930,* lit., (04-08-93, Christie-NY, #273, illus.), 5⅛ x 4¼ in., (13 x 10.8 cm.), photograph, gelatin silver print (BP 1810, DM 4434, FR 15,008, Y 313,209).

EVEN

$189* *Maroc. Office Marocain Du Tourisme,* very good cond., (03-13-93, Laurin, #98), 38⁹⁄₁₆ x 24 in., (98 x 61 cm.), (BP 132, DM 315, FR 1070, Y 22,275).

EVENPOEL, Henri Jacques Edouard   Belgian 1872-1899

$1135* *Femme A L'Ombrelle Et Sa Petite Fille,* creases, drystamp, good margins, (04-02-93, Picard, #105), 12¹⁵⁄₁₆ x 9¹⁄₁₆ in., (33 x 23 cm.), color lithograph (BP 748, DM 1824, FR 6195, Y 129,227).

EVERDINGEN, Allaert van   Dutch baptized 1621,buried 1675

BI *Figurer Og Arkitektur I Landskaber,* est. DK 6/8,000, (10-20-92, B. Rasmussen, #361), etching.

$1275* *Landscape With Wooden Bridge (Dutuit 4 III, Hollstein 4 III),* mono., prov., (06-04-93, Bassenge, #5155), 6 7/16 x 7 11/16 in., (16.3 x 19.5 cm.), etching (BP 844, DM 2070, FR 6979, Y 137,511).

$891* *Landschaften In Verschiedenen Gegenden (B. und Dut. 73-74, 79-80, 82-85): Eight,* mono. in plate, foxed, prov., (10-09-92, Winterberg, #782), largest 4 15/16 x 6¼ in., (12.5 x 15.8 cm.), smallest 4 x 6 5/16 in., (12.5 x 15.8 cm.), etching (BP 529, DM 1324, FR 4444, Y 108,473).

$2899* *The Shepherd And The Lamb (Holl. 87),* first state of two, creases, margin damaged, (12-03-92, Sotheby-London, #52), 4⅞ x 6¼ in., (122 x 157 mm.), etching on paper w/watermark (BP 1870, DM 4559, FR 15,561, Y 360,707).

$660* *Two Men On The Hill (B. 46),* 1st state of 2, thread margins, thin patch, nick, surface dirt, creasing, ex. coll. A.J. Begheyn and d'Arenberg (L. 567), (06-29-93, Sotheby-London, #43, illus.), 3¾ x 5¾ in., (9.5 x 14.6 cm.), etching (BP 437, DM 1114, FR 3756, Y 70,258).

EVERGOOD, Philip American 1901-1973

$165* *Family,* s., i. A/P, (11-12-92, Freemn/Fine Art, #67), 20½ x 15 in., (52.1 x 38.1 cm.), color litho (BP 108, DM 261, FR 882, Y 20,459).

BI *Four Children,* stone s., d. '61; s., est. $1/150, (08-05-92, Boos, #671), sight 23½ x 19½ in., (597 x 495 mm.), lithograph.

$248* *"Girl And Old Dog", 1965,* s., num., t. 4/20...Philip Evergood, init., d. PE/65 in matrix, verygood cond., marks, tears, (03-12-93, Skinner, #91, illus.), 20⅝ x 15¼ in., (52.4 x 38.7 cm.), lithograph on wove (BP 173, DM 413, FR 1404, Y 29,228).

$165* *"Girl With Sunflowers", 1965,* s. Philip Evergood, s., d. in plate, t., anno. 73/150, good cond., (09-11-92, Skinner, #89, illus.), sight 8⅛ x 5⅞ in., (20.6 x 14.9 cm.), etching on paper (BP 85, DM 238, FR 807, Y 20,444).

$358* *"The Girls And The Wolves" And "Self Portrait": Two,* s. Philip Evergood, good cond., toning, handling soil, creasing, (03-12-93, Skinner, #90, illus.), sheet 26 x 19 in., (66 x 48.3 cm.), lithograph on wove (BP 250, DM 596, FR 2026, Y 42,192).

$39* *Mother And Child,* s., num. 26/100, tape residue, toning, (10-31-92, Cleveland, #370), 22 x 15 in., (55.9 x 38.1 cm.), lithograph (BP 25, DM 60, FR 204, Y 4831).

$165* *Seated Woman, 1965,* s., #27/50, (06-11-93, Freemn/Fine Art, #61), 20 x 16½ in., (50.8 x 41.9 cm.), lithograph in colors (BP 108, DM 268, FR 904, Y 17,507).

$358* *"Taming The Tiger" And "Self Portrait": Two,* s. Philip Evergood, first #5/20, t., second s. in matrix LXI, annot.artist's proof, good cond., soiling, creasing, foxing, (03-12-93, Skinner, #87, illus.), approx. 27 x 22 in., (68.6 x 55.9 cm.), lithograph on wove (BP 250, DM 596, FR 2026, Y 42,192).

$110* *"Woman In A Chekhov Mood", 1965,* s. Philip Evergood, init., d. PE/1965 in matrix, t., annot. artist'sproof, good cond., creases, soiling, (03-12-93, Skinner, #89, illus.), 20¼ x 17⅛ in., (51.4 x 43.5 cm.), lithograph in black, yellow and blue on wove (BP 77, DM 183, FR 623, Y 12,964).

EVERGOOD, Philip (after)

$14* *Girl Watching Bird,* s., edit. #13/75, (09-18-92, DuMouchelle, #2511), 17¼ x 13 in., (43.8 x 33 cm.), photolithograph (BP 8, DM 21, FR 72, Y 1744).

EVERMON, Robert

$67* *Ramboue,* #6/8, s., (10-21-92, Maynard, #205), sheet 40 x 29 in., (101.6 x 73.7 cm.), color lithograph (BP 42, DM 101, FR 344, Y 8161, C$ 83).

EVERS, Carl G. (after)

$33* *Wind And Wave,* (12-11-92, DuMouchelle, #1449), 10¾ x 11¾ in., (27.3 x 29.8 cm.), print (BP 21, DM 52, FR 178, Y 4084).

EVERS, Charles G. (after)

$55* *"USS Threshev", "USS Enterprise", "USS Long Beach", and "USS Bainbridge": Four,* (05-14-93, DuMouchelle, #2530), 14 x 19 in., (35.6 x 48.3 cm.), prints (BP 36, DM 88, FR 297, Y 6097).

EVITT, E. American 1912-1973

BI *"The Old Stone House" and "Carver House, Annapolis Md.": Two,* each s., t., est. $150/250, (07-03-92, Sloan, #309), larger 5⅞ x 4¾ in., (14.9 x 12.1 cm.), etching.

EWART, Peter b. 1918

$65* *Bow River,* s. in screen, prov., (11-16-92, Hodgins, #171), 23 15/16 x 30 in., (61.9 x 76.2 cm.), serigraph on canvas mounted on board (BP 43, DM 104, FR 349, Y 8112, C$ 83).

EWING, Louie H. American 20th cent.

$303* *Masterpieces Of Primitive American Art: Fourteen,* 1940's, pub. for Laboratory of Anthropology, s. Louie Ewing, good cond., toning, (06-26-93, Skinner, #142), sh., each 13½ x 10½ in., (34.3 x 26.7 cm.), color serigraph on paper (BP 203, DM 515, FR 1734, Y 32,149).

$165* *Modern Masterpieces Of American Indian Art: Six Images,* pub. for Laboratory of Anthropology, Santa Fe, s. Louie Ewing, good cond., toning, (06-26-93, Skinner, #113), sh., each 13½ x 10½ in., (34.3 x 26.7 cm.), color serigraph on paper (BP 110, DM 280, FR 944, Y 17,507).

EYERMAN, J.R.

BI *Elizabeth Taylor, c. 1955,* Life Photo credit stamp, est. $1/1,500, (04-08-93, Christie-NY, #422, illus.), 13 x 10⅝ in., (33 x 27 cm.), photograph, gelatin silver print.

BI *Farley Granger, c. 1955,* Life Photo credit stamp, est. $800/1,200, (04-08-93, Christie-NY, #423, illus.), 13⅜ x 10½ in., (34 x 26.7 cm.), photograph, gelatin silver print.

$1150* *Montgomery Clift Watching "The Heiress", early 1950's,* photog. Life Photo stamp, (04-06-93, Sotheby-NY, #423, illus.), 13½ x 10⅝ in., photograph (BP 760, DM 1853, FR 6274, Y 131,159).

EYRE, Ivan b. 1935

$434* *DISQ II, 1969,* #2/25 s., t., d. '69, prov., (05-10-93, Hodgins, #33, illus.), 31 x 20 in., (78.7 x 50.8 cm.), linocut on paper (BP 283, DM 697, FR 2352, Y 48,497, C$ 550).

EYRE, John b. 1771

$1459* *New South Wales 1810: "View Of Sydney From The East Side Of The CoveNos. 1 and 3", "View Of Sydney From The West Side Of The Cove No. 2 and 4": Fou,* reprints reprod. and pub. William Dymock, Sydney 1884, (08-11-92, L. Joel, #85G), 13 3/16 x 19 5/16 in., (33.5 x 49 cm.), chromolithograph (BP 758, DM 2141, FR 7251, Y 186,836, A$ 1980).

FABIANO, Fabien 1883-1962

$419* *Enveloppe Velo Michelin, 1910,* cond. A, (03-16-93, Boisgirard, #104), 46 1/16 x 29 5/16 in., (117 x 74.5 cm.), poster (BP 289, DM 697, FR 2367, Y 48,994).

FACCINI, Pietro Italian 1560-1602

BI *Interior Scene With Child And Ape And Cat By Hearth,* mono. in plate, est. $3/400, (10-30-92, Sloan, #2805), 8¼ x 6⅛ in., (21 x 15.6 cm.), etching.

FAED, John (after)

$298* *The Cottar's Saturday Night: A Set Of Five,* (08-20-92, Bonhams-Chelsea, #96), image 7 x 10 in., (17.8 x 25.4 cm.), engraving w/hand coloring (BP 154, DM 432, FR 1464, Y 37,631).

$189* *Shakespeare And His Friends,* by James Fraed, (05-20-93, Bonhams-Chelsea, #65), image 22¼ x 27½ in., (56.5 x 69.9 cm.), engraving w/hand-coloring (BP 121, DM 305, FR 1027, Y 20,870).

FAED, Thomas (after)

$201* *"The Letter" and "The Reply", 1867: Two,* pub. Henry Graves and Co., margins, (11-12-92, Bonhams-Chelsea, #21), plate 28¾ x 20¼ in., (73 x 51.4 cm.), hand-colored mezzotint (BP 132, DM 318, FR 1074, Y 24,923).

FAGGIANO, Antonio

$773* *Addenda Alle Citta Impossibili...1979,* s., (05-18-93, Auction Phila, #133), 29¾ x 32 5/16 in., (75.5 x 82 cm.), photograph, w/pastel (BP 507, DM 1248, FR 4210, Y 86,301, L 1150).

FAHLSTROM, Oyvind 1928-1976

$468* *"Column No 2 (Picasso 90)", 1973,* s., num., 5th portfolio from series Hommage a Picasso, pub. Propylaen-Verlag, (06-08-93, Karl/Faber, #736), approx. 23 1/16 x 18 7/8 in., (58.5 x 48 cm.), color serigraph on thick wove (BP 308, DM 759, FR 2557, Y 49,708).

FAIRLAND, Thomas
$80* *The Madonna And Child,* s., i. selected proof, (02-17-93, Bonhams-Chelsea, #348), image 29 3/4 x 21 in., (75.6 x 53.3 cm.), lithograph (BP 55, DM 130, FR 440, Y 9556).
$150* *The Madonna And Child,* s., i. selected proof, (11-19-92, Bonhams-Chelsea, #21), image 29 3/4 x 21 in., (75.6 x 53.3 cm.), lithograph (BP 99, DM 239, FR 806, Y 18,654).

FAISTAUER, Anton 1887-1930
$1001* *Familie,* s., crease, (11-25-92, Dorotheum, #487, illus.), 20 1/2 x 12 15/16 in., (52 x 33 cm.), hand-colored lithograph (BP 654, DM 1592, FR 5390, Y 123,917, SC 11,200).

FAIVRE, A.
$2015* *PLM. Chamonix Mont-Blanc. Sports D'Hiver, 1905,* very good cond., (03-15-93, Arcole, #87, illus.), 42 15/16 x 30 1/2 in., (109 x 77.5 cm.), (BP 1403, DM 3347, FR 11,378, Y 238,688).

FALCK
$141* *Guillot Gorju,* yellowed, good margins, (02-03-93, Ader Tajan, #22), 11 1/8 x 8 1/8 in., (28.2 x 20.6 cm.), copper engraving (BP 98, DM 232, FR 787, Y 17,539).

FALCONE, Angelo 1600-1656
$125* *Das Grabmal Des Schriftstellers (B. 13),* after Parmigianino, (12-01-92, Karl/Faber, #67), engraving (BP 83, DM 199, FR 679, Y 15,563).

FALCONET, Pierre (after)
$300* *Miss Moore (C.S. 104), 1777,* by James Watson, scratch-letter proof (Russell's 2nd state of 3), defects repaired, good cond., (11-30-92, Phillips-London, #55, illus.), sheet 13 1/3 x 9 1/4 in., (339 x 235 mm.), mezzotint on laid (BP 198, DM 478, FR 1622, Y 37,337).
$300* *Nanette Thelusson (C.S. 129), 1773,* engraved by Valentine Green, 1st state of 2, scratch-letter proof before t., printer's crease, (11-30-92, Phillips-London, #54), plate 12 7/8 x 8 7/8 in., (327 x 225 mm.), mezzotint on laid (BP 198, DM 478, FR 1622, Y 37,337).

FALCUCCI
$71* *"Monaco 23 Avril 1933",* (04-20-93, Encans, #115), 39 3/8 x 26 3/4 in., (100 x 68 cm.), lithograph on Arches (BP 46, DM 113, FR 382, Y 7834, C$ 89).
$177* *"Monaco, 17 Avril 1932",* (04-20-93, Encans, #114), 39 3/8 x 26 15/16 in., (100 x 68.5 cm.), lithograph on Arches (BP 114, DM 282, FR 952, Y 19,530, C$ 222).
$159* *"Monaco, 19 Avril 1931",* (04-20-93, Encans, #113), 39 3/8 x 26 3/4 in., (100 x 68 cm.), lithograph on Arches (BP 103, DM 253, FR 855, Y 17,544, C$ 200).
$133* *"Monaco, 6 Avril 1930",* (04-20-93, Encans, #112), 36 7/16 x 23 7/16 in., (92.5 x 59.5 cm.), lithograph on Arches (BP 86, DM 212, FR 715, Y 14,675, C$ 167).
$557* *PLM and Cie Gle Transatlantique: Paris-Alger. "Liasons Rapides Par Marseilles",* very good cond., (03-13-93, Laurin, #45), 38 15/16 x 24 5/8 in., (99 x 62.5 cm.), (BP 389, DM 927, FR 3152, Y 65,645).
$818* *PLM. Annecy. "Sa Plage",* very good cond., (03-15-93, Arcole, #88, illus.), 39 3/8 x 25 9/16 in., (100 x 65 cm.), (BP 570, DM 1359, FR 4619, Y 96,896).
$462* *PLM: Juan-Les-Pins Antibes, 1937,* p. L. Serre, very good cond., lit., (11-19-92, Ribeyre/Baron, #105), 39 3/8 x 24 5/8 in., (100 x 62.5 cm.), poster (BP 304, DM 737, FR 2481, Y 57,456).
BI *PLM: Vichy Marseille Afrique Du Nord. "Relations Frequentes Et Rapides Marseille-Vichy", 1932,* very good cond., (03-13-93, Laurin, #81), 39 3/8 x 24 7/16 in., (100 x 62 cm.), .
$587* *SNCF: Vallee De Chevreuse, "Circuits Touristiques Au Depart De Saint-Remy De Chevreuse, Abbaye De Port-Royal, Chateau De Dampierre",* excell. cond., (01-23-93, Ribeyre/Baron, #34), 39 9/16 x 25 3/8 in., (100.5 x 64.5 cm.), poster (BP 384, DM 933, FR 3158, Y 73,467).

FALCUCCI, Robert
BI *Gaz, 1939,* plate s., lined, trimmed, est. $6/800, (03-25-93, Christie-E, #202), 61 x 45 1/4 in., (154.9 x 114.9 cm.), color lithograph.

FALCUCCI, Robert 1900-1989
$299* *Champagne De Venoge, c. 1965,* cond. A, (03-16-93, Boisgirard, #105), 88 3/16 x 59 1/16 in., (224 x 150 cm.), poster (BP 206, DM 497, FR 1689, Y 34,963).

FALDA, Giovanni Battista Italian ac. 1655, d. 1678
$935* *Li Giardini Di Roma Con Le Loro Piante Alzate E Vedute In Prospettiva ... Nuovamente Dati Alle Stampe: Twenty,* including t., oblong folio, t. and few plates foxed, embossed stamp Regia Calcografia di Roma, (11-12-92, Swann, #107), 17 11/16 x 24 1/2 in., (450 x 622 mm.), engraving on wove (BP 614, DM 1482, FR 4997, Y 115,933).
$161* *Rue De La Place St Marc A L'Eglise Du Jesus (Leblanc II, p. 217), 1665,* third plate from "Il nuovo teatro delle fabriche et edificii in prospectiva di Roma moderna...", margins, (05-15-93, Loudmer, #16), 6 5/8 x 11 5/16 in., (169 x 287 mm.), sh 8 1/4 x 12 3/4 in., (169 x 287 mm.), etching on laid (BP 105, DM 259, FR 870, Y 17,847).
$1155* *Veduta Del Castello E Ponte Sant' Angelo, 1671,* (12-04-92, Bassenge, #6175, illus.), 18 3/8 x 27 3/16 in., (46.6 x 69 cm.), etching (BP 741, DM 1839, FR 6240, Y 144,195).

FALENS, Carel van (after)
BI *"Retour De Campagne",* by Pierre Filloeul, est. DM 500, (03-24-93, Venator/Hansten, #2520), 18 1/2 x 23 5/16 in., (47 x 59.2 cm.), etching.

FALIZE
$839* *Prunier Livre Vite Et Bien, "Fin Aout A Mi Juin", c. 1925,* p. Daude freres, good cond., (11-19-92, Ribeyre/Baron, #32), 84 5/8 x 55 1/8 in., (215 x 140 cm.), poster (BP 552, DM 1338, FR 4506, Y 104,340).

FALIZE, Pierre 1876-1953
$678* *Prunier Livre Vite Et Bien, c. 1925,* cond. A, (03-16-93, Boisgirard, #106), 85 13/16 x 54 5/16 in., (218 x 138 cm.), poster (BP 468, DM 1127, FR 3831, Y 79,280).

FALK, Hans b. 1918
$869* *Borse,* epr.-d'Art, s., (04-21-93, Germann, #406, illus.), 21 1/4 x 17 5/16 in., (540 x 440 mm.), color lithograph (BP 564, DM 1389, FR 4697, Y 96,203, SF 1265).
$92* *Frauenakt,* #83/125, s., (09-04-92, Germann, #328), 17 5/16 x 13 3/16 in., (440 x 335 mm.), lithograph (BP 46, DM 129, FR 439, Y 11,324, SF 115).
$229* *Strasseenszene,* #105/200, s., (11-13-92, Koller, #5313), 14 15/16 x 19 5/16 in., (38 x 49 cm.), lithograph on wove (BP 148, DM 359, FR 1212, Y 28,422, SF 324).

FALKEISEN, Johann Jokob (after WINTERLIN)
BI *Basle Du Cote Du Mide,* pub. Hasler et Cie, Bale, light staining, est. BP 150/250, (10-27-92, Phillips-London, #126), sheet 7 5/8 x 9 1/2 in., (194 x 241 mm.), aquatint w/ hand-coloring, touches of gum-arabic on wove.

FALTER, John American 1910-1982
$165* *Amish Farm,* s., t., num. 29/50, James Cagney Estate, (09-30-92, Doyle, #83), 21 1/2 x 28 1/2 in., (54.6 x 72.4 cm.), lithograph (BP 93, DM 234, FR 791, Y 19,801).

FANTIN (after)
$132* *Landscape With Dancing Figures In Classical Dress,* s. illegibly, (12-02-92, Boos, #331), image 15 1/4 x 19 1/2 in., (38.7 x 49.5 cm.), color mezzotint (BP 85, DM 208, FR 709, Y 16,424).

FANTIN-LATOUR, Henri French 1836-1904
$330* *Baigneuses (G. Hediard, 138),* definitve state, stains, large margins, (04-02-93, Picard, #107), 11 13/16 x 15 3/8 in., (30 x 39 cm.), lithograph on Chine fixe (BP 217, DM 530, FR 1801, Y 37,573).
$133* *Baigneuses (H.M. 125), 1896,* full margins, drystamp, (02-24-93, Picard, #102), signature on thin chine (BP 93, DM 216, FR 732, Y 15,607).
$605* *"Baigneuses" (Hediard 138), "La Source Dans Les Bois" (Hediard 139),"Danses" (Hediard 140), "Prelude De Lohengrin" (Hediard 146): Four,* Una Johnson, "Vollard, Editeur", no. 41, from "Suite de six planches", 1898, p. Blanchard, pub. Ambroise Vollard, 1898, (05-27-93,

Swann, #106), lithographs on loose China paper (BP 387, DM 971, FR 3272, Y 64,858).

$310* *Danses (G.H., 140), 1898,* definitive state, large margins, (04-02-93, Picard, #109), 17 x 12⅝ in., (43.2 x 32 cm.), lithograph (BP 204, DM 498, FR 1692, Y 35,295).

$206* *Evocation De Kundry (G.H., 142),* tear, large margins, (04-02-93, Picard, #110), 16¼ x 19 in., (41.2 x 48.3 cm.), lithograph on Chine fixe (BP 136, DM 331, FR 1124, Y 23,454).

$468* *Evocation d'Erda (H. 54), 1884,* 1st state of 2, s. in stone, margins, good cond., printing crease, masking & paper tape remains, paper & glue remains, tear, foxing, crease, surfacesoiling, light-staining, (02-24-93, Butterfield, #2923), 17 x 12⅛ in., (432 x 308 mm.), lithograph on fine laid w/watermark (BP 326, DM 760, FR 2576, Y 54,917).

$778* *Feuilles D'Etudes (H.,M. 178-189, L. 421): Series of Twelve,* portfolio, staining, 12 impressions, ex.coll., (02-24-93, Picard, #105), signature on Japan pelure (BP 543, DM 1263, FR 4282, Y 91,293).

$767* *"Finale De La Valkure", "A Victor Hugo" and "A Eugene Delacroix" (G.Hediard 24, 92 and 93): Three,* definitive state, stains, large margins, (02-03-93, Ader Tajan, #149), lithograph (BP 535, DM 1263, FR 4283, Y 95,410).

BI *Hector Berlioz, Sa Vie Et Ses Oeuvres: "Verite","Tuba Mirum SpargensSonum", "Symphonie Fantastique: Un Bal", "Lelio: La Harpe Eolienne", "Harold EnItalie: Dans Le Montagnes", and Others (H. 76-89), 1888: Fourteen,* p. by Lemercier, margins, good cond., staining, creases, surface soiling, est. $1/1,500, (02-24-93, Butterfield, #2738), each sheet 12¼ x 8⅛ in., (311 x 206 mm.), lithograph on Chine colle.

$246* *Portrait De M. Fantin A Dix-Sept Ans (H.M. 104), 1853,* third state of four, before mention, (02-24-93, Picard, #100), lithograph on chine remounted on ivory wove (BP 172, DM 399, FR 1354, Y 28,866).

$88* *"Tuba Mirum Spargens Sonum" and "L'Efance Du Christ: Le Repos Se La Sainte Famille": Two (Hediard 77 and 85), 1888,* pub. Hector Berlioz, sa vie et ses oeuvres, by Adolphe Jullien, (03-14-93, Hindman, #243), each 9 x 6 in., (22.9 x 15.2 cm.), lithograph on chine applique (BP 61, DM 146, FR 498, Y 10,371).

$328* *A Vistor Hugo (Hediard, Mason 92), 1889,* dust, damp stain, 25 impressions, (02-24-93, Picard, #99), lithograph on strong on Japan simili (BP 229, DM 532, FR 1805, Y 38,489).

FANTIN-LATOUR, Ignace Henri J. T.

BI *Helene (Hediard 95), 1890,* s., i. full margins, foxing, staining, est. BP 5/700, (06-16-93, Bonhams-Chelsea, #507, illus.), 22 x 31 in., (55.9 x 78.7 cm.), lithograph.

FANTUZZI, Antonio ac. 1537-1550

$433* *Jupiter Unterwirft Die Drei Gottinnen Dem Urteil Des Paris (B. 21; Zerner A.F. 55), 1543,* after Primaticcio, stained, (12-04-92, Bassenge, #6177), 7¹¹⁄₁₆ x 11 in., (19.5 x 28 cm.), engraving (BP 278, DM 690, FR 2339, Y 54,057).

BI *Venus Descendant Du Ciel Pour Secouir Adonis Blesse, (B. XVI, p. 402,no. 69, anonyme; Herbert, p. 76, no. 35, Fantuzzi; Zerner AF 27), c. 1542,* after Rosso Fiorentino, partial margins or trimmed, abrasion, discol-oration, laid, est. BP 10/12,000, (12-01-92, Christie-London, #20, illus.), S. 11¹¹⁄₁₆ x 16¹¹⁄₁₆ in., (297 x 424 mm.), etching.

$650* *Zaleukos Lasst Sich Ein Auge Ausstechen (Herbert 66; Zerner A.F. 11),c. 1542,* after Giulio Romano, (12-04-92, Bassenge, #6176), 11 x 12⁵⁄₁₆ in., (28 x 31.3 cm.), etching (BP 417, DM 1035, FR 3512, Y 81,149).

FARIA

$103* *Alcazar D'Ete Maurel,* (01-31-93, Morelle/Marchan, #225), 23⅝ x 62¹⁵⁄₁₆ in., (60 x 160 cm.), poster (BP 69, DM 166, FR 561, Y 12,849).

$221* *Aubin Et Leonel,* Imp. Formstecher, good cond., (02-12-93, Cheval/Robert, #187), 50 x 36⅝ in., (127 x 93 cm.), poster (BP 156, DM 367, FR 1240, Y 26,652).

$241* *Deverder Marionnettiste,* Affiches Faria, good cond., (02-12-93, Cheval/Robert, #188), 51³⁄₁₆ x 36¼ in., (130 x 92 cm.), poster (BP 170, DM 400, FR 1352, Y 29,064).

$161* *Jime Melomane Maestro, c. 1900,* good cond., (02-12-93, Cheval/Robert, #157), 36¼ x 24¹³⁄₁₆ in., (92 x 63 cm.), poster (BP 113, DM 267, FR 903, Y 19,416).

$151* *M. & Mme Amelys's,* Affiches L. Galice, good cond., (02-12-93, Cheval/Robert, #189), 41⅛ x 29⅛ in., (104.5 x 74 cm.), poster (BP 106, DM 250, FR 847, Y 18,210).

$165* *Mas - Andre,* (01-31-93, Morelle/Marchan, #226), 37 x 25⁹⁄₁₆ in., (94 x 65 cm.), poster (BP 111, DM 266, FR 899, Y 20,584).

$181* *Pavie. "Episode De La Compagne D'Italie" Opera Comique, c. 1900,* Imp. Formstecher, good cond., (02-12-93, Cheval/Robert, #156), 32¹¹⁄₁₆ x 25⁹⁄₁₆ in., (83 x 65 cm.), poster (BP 127, DM 300, FR 1016, Y 21,828).

FARIA (studio of)

$998* *Chamonix Mont-Blanc. Cashat's Majestic. (L'Ete), 1914,* good cond., (03-15-93, Arcole, #89, illus.), 46¹⁄₁₆ x 61¹³⁄₁₆ in., (117 x 157 cm.), (BP 695, DM 1658, FR 5635, Y 118,218).

$442* *Gare Du Nord. Plage D'Ault. Ault-Orival, 1902,* Paris, Imp. E. Delanchy and Cie, cond. B+, (06-11-93, Boisgirard, #69), 49³⁄₁₆ x 35⁷⁄₁₆ in., (125 x 90 cm.), poster (BP 290, DM 718, FR 2422, Y 46,897).

FARINATO, Orazio Italian 1559-after 1616

BI *The Madonna With Child And St. John As A Boy (B. 4),* after Paolo Farinati, watermark, est. DM 1,800, (06-04-93, Bassenge, #5159, illus.), 6⁵⁄₁₆ x 10⅝ in., (16 x 27 cm.), etching.

$282* *Pharaos Reiter Und Wagen Werden Von Den Fluten Des Roten Meeres Verschlungen (Bartsch Bd. 16, 1; Nagler mono. Bd. 3, 1),* mono., Resten by Wischton, (03-24-93, Venator/Hansten, #2521), image 13¾ x 21⅞ in., (35 x 55.5 cm.), etching (BP 191, DM 461, FR 1568, Y 33,134).

FARINATO, Paolo Italian 1524-1606

BI *Caritas (B. XVI, 4),* est. DM 1,800, (12-04-92, Bassenge, #6179, illus.), 8¾ x 9³⁄₁₆ in., (22.3 x 23.3 cm.), etching.

FARNIK

$1045* *Mein Standpunkt, Mem Rotpunkt,* maquette for poster, B+ cond., cracking, scratches throughout, (08-06-92, Swann, #128, illus.), 74½ x 49½ in., (189.2 x 125.7 cm.), (BP 546, DM 1544, FR 5215, Y 133,291).

FARNSWORTH, Jerry American b. 1895

$110* *Coastal Scene,* very good cond.?, (02-07-93, Bakker, #186), sheet 7¾ x 7¾ in., (19.7 x 19.7 cm.), monotype (BP 76, DM 182, FR 617, Y 13,688).

$110* *Landscape,* very good cond.?, (02-07-93, Bakker, #197), 8 x 8 in., (20.3 x 20.3 cm.), monotype (BP 76, DM 182, FR 617, Y 13,688).

$110* *Standing Woman,* very good cond.?, (02-07-93, Bakker, #173), image 8 x 6½ in., (20.3 x 16.5 cm.), monotype (BP 76, DM 182, FR 617, Y 13,688).

FARQUHARSON, Joseph (after)

$53 *Winter Moonlit Landscape With Sheep In Snow,* (04-16-93, G.A. Key, #53), 19 x 26 in., (48.3 x 66 cm.), b/w etching (BP 35, DM 86, FR 289, Y 5960).

FARRE, Henri French/American 1871-1934

$138* *Aviators: Two,* s., (12-17-92, Mystic, #19), each 14 x 9½ in., (35.6 x 24.1 cm.), etching (BP 88, DM 215, FR 736, Y 16,960).

FARRELL, Fred

$120* *Fishmonger's Hall,* s., blindstamp, margins, (02-17-93, Bonhams-Chelsea, #288), plate 10¼ x 14¾ in., (26 x 37.5 cm.), etching (BP 83, DM 195, FR 660, Y 14,333).

$187* *Trafalgar Square,* s., blindstamp, margins, (04-22-93, Bonhams-Chelsea, #31), plate 10¼ x 13½ in., (26 x 34.3 cm.), drypoint etching (BP 121, DM 300, FR 1014, Y 20,561).

FARRELL, Frederick A. Scottish b. 1882, ac. 1920's

$50* *The Thames At St. Pauls,* s., blindstamp, margins, (01-14-93, Bonhams, #111), plate 11 x 14 in., (27.9 x 35.6 cm.), etching (BP 33, DM 82, FR 276, Y 6304).

FARRELL, Judith   20th cent.
$55* *Cathedral Interior: Two,* each s., (09-17-92, Sloan, #638), larger 11¾ x 4¼ in., (29.8 x 10.8 cm.), etching and drypoint (BP 31, DM 82, FR 279, Y 6848).

FARRER, Henry   American 1843-1903
BI   *Harbor Scene, 1886,* s., good cond., foxing throughout image, est. $4/500, (05-15-93, Cleveland, #124), etching.
$129* *Horse And Wagon On Snow Covered Village Road,* plate s., d. 1886, s., pub. Fishel, Adler & Schwartz, (06-08-93, Ritchie, #28), image 15⅞ x 30 in., (40.3 x 76.2 cm.), etching w/remarque (BP 85, DM 209, FR 705, Y 13,702, C$ 165).
$33* *New York Bay,* margins, plate s., (05-22-93, Collins, #73), 4⅜ x 7 in., (11.1 x 17.8 cm.), etching (BP 21, DM 54, FR 181, Y 3638).
$17* *Sunset,* margins, plate s., (05-22-93, Collins, #74), 6⅜ x 9⅜ in., (16.2 x 23.8 cm.), etching (BP 11, DM 28, FR 93, Y 1874).

FASSIANOS
$377* *Bla Dame,* s. e.a., (09-29-92, B. Rasmussen, #306), lithograph in colors (BP 212, DM 532, FR 1817, Y 45,004, DK 2070).

FASSIANOS, Aleco   b. 1935
BI   *"Cycliste Brun",* s., est. FF800/1,000, (04-04-93, Pescheteau, #212), 25⁹⁄₁₆ x 19¹¹⁄₁₆ in., (65 x 50 cm.), color lithograph on wove.
$189* *"Femme Au Miroir",* remarque, s., (01-28-93, Pescheteau, #137), 25⁹⁄₁₆ x 19¹¹⁄₁₆ in., (65 x 50 cm.), color lithograph on Arches (BP 125, DM 299, FR 1013, Y 23,467).
$202* *"Nu Bleu Allonge",* artist's proof, s., (10-18-92, Pescheteau, #137), 24⁷⁄₁₆ x 34¼ in., (62 x 87 cm.), lithograph in colors on wove (BP 122, DM 298, FR 1014, Y 24,119).
$180* *"Petite Histoire": Set of Six,* s., (10-18-92, Pescheteau, #138), 20¹⁄₁₆ x 22¹³⁄₁₆ in., (14 x 11 cm.), lithograph (BP 109, DM 266, FR 903, Y 21,493).

FASSIANOS, Alexandre   Greek b. 1935
$48* *Cycliste Au Miroir,* s., #XIV/XX, (06-28-93, Loudmer, #38), 14³⁄₁₆ x 11 in., (360 x 280 mm.), 23⁷⁄₁₆ x 16 in., (360 x 280 mm.), lithograph printed in taupe on Arches wove (BP 32, DM 82, FR 275, Y 5093).
$48* *Deux Personnages Devant Un Paysage,* s. artist proof, (06-28-93, Loudmer, #37), 15³⁄₁₆ x 25⅜ in., (385 x 645 mm.), color linocut on China (BP 32, DM 82, FR 275, Y 5093).
$209* *Komposition Med Rod Figur,* s., 11/75, (04-17-93, Falkkloos, #116), 19⁵⁄₁₆ x 13⅜ in., (49 x 34 cm.), color etching (BP 136, DM 334, FR 1129, Y 23,240, SK 1540).
$93* *Triptyque,* s., full margins, (03-31-93, Briest, #E40), 9¹³⁄₁₆ x 7½ in., (25 x 19 cm.), color etchings on Arches (BP 61, DM 150, FR 508, Y 10,695).

FASZBENDER, Joseph   1903-1974
$130* *Komposition 1964,* s., d., #39/100, full margins, good cond., soiling, (12-09-92, Sotheby-Amstrdm, #572), 12½ x 6¹¹⁄₁₆ in., (317 x 170 mm.), etching w/aquatint on wove (BP 83, DM 204, FR 696, Y 16,119, G 230).

FATIN
$88* *Girl Reading,* s., (12-11-92, DuMouchelle, #69), 6 x 4 in., (15.2 x 10.2 cm.), engraving (BP 56, DM 139, FR 475, Y 10,890).

FATIN-LATOUR, Henri   French 1836-1904
BI   *Untitled, c. 1897: Two,* stains, folds, est. $2/300, (05-15-93, Cleveland, #402), 9⅛ x 6 in., (23.2 x 15.2 cm.), lithograph.

FAU, Fernand   1858-1917
BI   *14 Exposition/31 Rue Bonaparte (Brinckmann 230; Henriot 604; Wember 302), 1895,* stained, damaged,, very rare, lit., est. DM 2,400, (12-05-92, Bassenge, #7583, illus.), 23⅜ x 15¾ in., (59.4 x 40 cm.), color lithograph.

FAUCON, Bernard
$330* *"La Huitieme Chambre D'Amour", 1985,* s., t., d., edit. 15/40, annot., Dixon Collection, (11-16-92, Butterfield, #5957, illus.), 13⅝ x 12⅝ in., (346.7 x 321.2 mm.), photograph, fresson print (BP 217, DM 526, FR 1772, Y 41,040).

FAUCON, Bernard   b. 1950
$121* *Signes, 1984: Portfolio Series of Eleven,* artist proofs, s., d. 84, #13/15, (05-27-93, Briest, #85), 9⅝ x 7½ in., (24.5 x 19 cm.), black lithograph (BP 77, DM 194, FR 654, Y 12,972).

FAUGERON   French b. 1866
$697* *Cie De Navigation Mixte: Algerie Tunisie. "Passagers, Marchandises. Marseille Port-Vendres",* entoilee, (03-13-93, Laurin, #80), 38⁹⁄₁₆ x 24³⁄₁₆ in., (98 x 61.5 cm.), (BP 486, DM 1160, FR 3945, Y 82,145).

FAURER, Louis   b. 1916
$413* *"Boardwalk, Atlantic City",* 1938/1980, s., t., d., Dixon Collection, (11-16-92, Butterfield, #5958, illus.), 7⅞ x 11¾ in., (200.4 x 299 mm.), photograph, gelatin silver print (BP 272, DM 658, FR 2218, Y 51,362).
BI   *City Hall Square, Broad Street, Philadelphia, c. 1940,* s., t., d., est. $2,5/3,500, (04-08-93, Christie-NY, #424, illus.), 12¾ x 10½ in., (32.4 x 26.7 cm.), photograph, gelatin silver print.
$1610* *"Freudian Hand Clasp, New York City", 1948, "Philadelphia, Pa.", 1949, "Win, Place And Show, 3rd Ave. El, New York, NY", 1947 and "NY, NY", 1951: Four,* p. 1980-81, s., t., d., (c) insig., lit., (04-08-93, Christie-NY, #425, illus.), smallest 7 x 9⅛ in., (17.8 x 23.2 cm.), largest 11⅞ x 7¾ in., (17.8 x 23.2 cm.), photograph, gelatin silver print (BP 1056, DM 2586, FR 8755, Y 182,705).
$920* *New York City: "Repaving Times Square, N.Y., N.Y.", "Untitled (WomanWith Umbrella, Times Square)" and "Untitled (Four Men On The Street, New York)": Three,* s., d., t. or i. by photog., c. 1948-49, p.l., (04-06-93, Sotheby-NY, #391A, illus.), from 8¼ x 12½ in., to 7⅜ x 11 in., photograph (BP 608, DM 1482, FR 5019, Y 104,927).
$1760* *New York City: Two: "Man on the Street" and "Four Women at Subway Stop",* s. by photog., t., d. in unidentified hand, c. 1950 & c. 1949, p.l., (10-15-92, Sotheby-NY, #526, illus.), each approx. 7½ x 11½ in., (19.1 x 29.2 cm.), photograph, gelatin silver prints (BP 1077, DM 2620, FR 8884, Y 211,158).

FAUTRIER, Jean   French 1898-1964
BI   *Annabelle Nue, 1957,* red stamped sig., d., i., est. DM 1,700-, (05-27-93, Lempertz, #707), 12³⁄₁₆ x 9⁹⁄₁₆ in., (31 x 24.3 cm.), lithograph w/embossed print on thick paper.
$943* *Baby-Mine (Mason 232), 1947,* s., #39/50, pub. Editions Couturier, full margins, good cond., (06-30-93, Sotheby-London, #784, illus.), 11 x 13⅛ in., (279 x 333 mm.), etching w/aquatint in color on Auvergne (BP 632, DM 1608, FR 5426, Y 101,039).
BI   *Baby-Shell (M.257), 1946,* s., #17/50, pub. Jacques David, full margins, good cond., est. BP 6/800, (06-30-93, Sotheby-London, #786, illus.), 6 x 7 in., (152 x 178 mm.), etching on Auvergne.
$1215* *Ecriture Sur Fond Bleu (Engelberts 1963/1, Mason 282), 1963,* s., #86/100, full margins, (05-27-93, Briest, #86, illus.), 29¹⁵⁄₁₆ x 22¼ in., (76 x 56.5 cm.), etching, aquatint and embossing on Arches wove (BP 778, DM 1950, FR 6571, Y 130,253).
BI   *"Formes Vegetales" (MRM 242), 1947,* ed. Couturier, 2nd state H.C., s., est. FF 8/10,000, (10-18-92, Pescheteau, #140), 25¹⁵⁄₁₆ x 20¹⁄₁₆ in., (66 x 51 cm.), etching and aquatint in colors on Richard de Bas wove.
$1986* *Griffure Sur Fond Violet (Mason 281.II), 1963,* s., num., from Paroles Peintes II, (06-05-93, Schoppmann, #797), 17½ x 13¾ in., (44.5 x 35 cm.), color etching on Arches wove (BP 1307, DM 3220, FR 10,852, Y 213,044).
$524* *L'Arbre (E. 1944/12, M. 255), 1944,* hors commerce, s., 2nd state, full margins, p. Jacques David, (11-16-92, Briest, #304), 10¹³⁄₁₆ x 12¹⁵⁄₁₆ in., (27.5 x 33 cm.), etching and aquatint in colors on Japan (BP 344, DM 836, FR 2816, Y 65,394).
$1544* *Le Maquis (M. 285), 1964,* s., #59/100, pub. Editions Couturier, full margins, good cond., (06-30-93, Sotheby-London, #787, illus.), 18½ x 25³⁄₁₆ in., (470 x 640 mm.), color aquatint on Arches (BP 1035, DM 2633, FR 8884, Y 165,434).

$598* *Nu (Mason 246, I.,B.; Engleberts 1942/6), 1942,* artist's proof, full margins, (03-31-93, Briest, #E166), sh 12 15/16 x 21 5/8 in., (33 x 55 cm.), 8 7/16 x 13 3/8 in., (33 x 55 cm.), black heliogravure (photoengraving) and etching on pink Auvergne (BP 395, DM 962, FR 3268, Y 68,767).

BI *Nu Couche II 1944 (Engelberts 1944/3, Mason 140),* hors commerce, s., full margins, est. FF 5/6,000, (11-16-92, Briest, #299), 9 3/8 x 13 15/16 in., (23.8 x 35.5 cm.), etching in black on Arches wove.

$2360* *Nu Couche V (Engelberts 1944/6), 1944,* s., num., (12-05-92, Bassenge, #7156), 9 5/16 x 13 15/16 in., (23.6 x 35.4 cm.), etching on wove (BP 1478, DM 3679, FR 12,540, Y 292,405).

$797* *Nu Noir (E. 1942/8, M. 223), 1942,* #10/50, full margins, p. Jacques David, (11-16-92, Briest, #302, illus.), 13 15/16 x 19 11/16 in., (35.5 x 50 cm.), etching and aquatint in black on Rives wove (BP 524, DM 1271, FR 4283, Y 99,463).

$1201* *Le Prophete (Mason 245 II), 1944,* s., #20/50, (06-12-93, Hauswedell/Nolt, #78, illus.), 8 11/16 x 12 1/8 in., (22 x 30.8 cm.), color etching on greenish Richard de Bas wove (BP 786, DM 1955, FR 6570, Y 126,381).

BI *Rochers (Engelberts 1962/4, Mason 268), 1962,* s., #50/100, full margins, est. FF6/8,000, (05-27-93, Briest, #87), 22 1/4 x 30 1/8 in., (56.5 x 76.5 cm.), red aquatint and wash, two old roses, grey and blue on Arches wove.

$825* *Torse En Deux Couleurs (Mason 262, Engelberts 1955/2), 1955,* hors commerce, s., full margins, (03-31-93, Briest, #E165), sh 22 1/16 x 14 15/16 in., (56 x 38 cm.), 15 3/16 x 10 1/16 in., (56 x 38 cm.), violet and green celadon etching and aquatint on Arches wove (BP 545, DM 1327, FR 4508, Y 94,871).

$944* *Le maquis (E. 1963/3, M. 283), 1963,* hors commerce, s., full margins, (11-16-92, Briest, #300), 18 11/16 x 25 3/8 in., (47.5 x 64.5 cm.), aquatint and wash on Arches wove (BP 620, DM 1506, FR 5073, Y 117,809).

FAVRE, G.

$210* *Peugeot,* p. Gaillard, good cond., small paper loss, (11-19-92, Ribeyre/Baron, #59), 23 5/8 x 15 3/4 in., (60 x 40 cm.), poster (BP 138, DM 335, FR 1128, Y 26,116).

$336* *Rochet-Schneider, "La Voiture De Qualite",* very good cond., (11-19-92, Ribeyre/Baron, #60), 33 7/16 x 24 13/16 in., (85 x 63 cm.), poster (BP 221, DM 536, FR 1805, Y 41,786).

FAY, Joe

$220* *"Downtown" and "Coyote Shaman", 1986; 1987: Two,* s., d., t., good cond., creases, pin & punch holes, (02-24-93, Butterfield, #3212), 63 1/2 x 42 1/4 in., (161.3 x 107.3 cm.), 60 x 42 1/4 in., (161.3 x 107.3 cm.), monotype on heavy wove (BP 153, DM 357, FR 1211, Y 25,816).

BI *Interior Landscape, 1963,* s., d., t., #edit. 27, margins, good cond.?, light-staining, est. $3/500, (05-19-93, Butterfield, #2164), 20 x 26 1/8 in., (508 x 664 mm.), silkscreen in colors on wove.

BI *"Pink Texas" and "Red Texas", 1987,* each s., d., t., full sheets, good cond., est. $4/600, (02-24-93, Butterfield, #3213), each 42 1/4 x 60 in., (107.3 x 152.4 cm.), monotype in colors on heavy wove.

FEARNLEY, Alan (after)

$48* *The Country Ground, Hove,* #187/850, s., pub. Walton Fine Art Ltd, (03-03-93, Bonhams-Chelsea, #245), image 12 1/4 x 18 1/2 in., (31.1 x 47 cm.), color reproduction (BP 33, DM 79, FR 268, Y 5609).

FEIDLER, Heinz

$115* *(Sunset), 1935,* s., t. indistinctly, d., i. orig. lin. druck, margins, good cond., uppper and lower margin taped to mount, Late Gerhard Brauer Coll., (05-27-93, Sotheby-Amstrdm, #730), 8 11/16 x 8 1/16 in., (220 x 204 mm.), linocut on Japan (BP 74, DM 185, FR 622, Y 12,328, G 207).

FEIN, Nat

$935* *Babe Ruth Bows Out,* i., sig., 1948, p.l., (04-07-93, Swann, #311, illus.), 8 x 10 in., photograph, silver print (BP 618, DM 1512, FR 5118, Y 106,226).

FEININGER, Andreas b. 1906

$990* *"Chicago River, Chicago", 1941,* s., t., d., photog. stamp, Dixon Collection, (11-16-92, Butterfield, #5963, illus.), 10 x 8 1/8 in., (254.5 x 206.7 mm.), photograph, gelatin silver print (BP 652, DM 1578, FR 5317, Y 123,119).

BI *"Chicago, Window Shopping On State Street", 1941,* t., photog.'s stamp, est. $800/1,200, (05-23-93, Butterfield, #3410, illus.), 14 x 11 1/4 in., photograph, gelatin silver print.

$2300* *"Coney Island Beach, July 4th",* s., d. by photog., t., i., 1949, p.l., (04-06-93, Sotheby-NY, #392, illus.), 10 1/2 x 13 3/8 in., photograph (BP 1519, DM 3705, FR 12,548, Y 262,318).

$660* *Corner Of Nassau And Fulton Streets, Downtown Manhattan,* photog.'s sig., t., handstamp, 1950s, (04-07-93, Swann, #461, illus.), 9 1/2 x 7 1/2 in., photograph, silver print (BP 436, DM 1067, FR 3612, Y 74,983).

$1430* *"Dearborn Station", 1941,* photog. stamp, Dixon Collection, (11-16-92, Butterfield, #5962, illus.), 10 x 8 1/8 in., (254.5 x 206.7 mm.), photograph, gelatin silver print (BP 942, DM 2280, FR 7680, Y 177,839).

$2475* *Downtown From Brooklyn Bridge, 1940,* s. by photog. twice, p. l., (10-15-92, Sotheby-NY, #449A, illus.), 21 7/8 x 17 3/4 in., (55.6 x 45.1 cm.), photograph, gelatin silver print (BP 1515, DM 3684, FR 12,494, Y 296,941).

$2200* *Empire State Building,* s. by photog., 1940's, p. l., (10-15-92, Sotheby-NY, #449, illus.), 22 x 18 in., (55.9 x 45.7 cm.), photograph, gelatin silver print (BP 1346, DM 3275, FR 11,106, Y 263,947).

$2875* *"N.Y.-Times Square", 1940,* s., t., d. by photog., credit stamp, (04-06-93, Sotheby-NY, #393, illus.), 8 1/8 x 9 3/8 in., photograph (BP 1899, DM 4632, FR 15,685, Y 327,897).

$2750* *NY-9th Ave. Elevated,* s., t., d. by photog., stamp, 1940's, (10-15-92, Sotheby-NY, #450, illus.), 7 3/4 x 9 1/2 in., (19.7 x 24.1 cm.), photograph, gelatin silver print (BP 1683, DM 4093, FR 13,882, Y 329,934).

$1180* *"New York 1940, Bowery",* t., stamped photog.'s credit, 355 x 280mm, (05-07-93, Sotheby-London, #293, illus.), photograph, silver print (BP 747, DM 1866, FR 6287, Y 129,927).

$1100* *New York City, 1940,* s., d., various notations, photog. stamp, Dixon Collection, (11-16-92, Butterfield, #5960, illus.), 13 1/4 x 10 1/4 in., (337.2 x 260.8 mm.), photograph, gelatin silver print (BP 724, DM 1754, FR 5908, Y 136,799).

$1650* *New York Street Scene, 1940,* s., d., photog. stamp, (11-16-92, Butterfield, #5959, illus.), 9 3/4 x 8 in., (248.1 x 203.6 mm.), photograph, gelatin silver print (BP 1086, DM 2631, FR 8861, Y 205,198).

$2200* *"The Photojournalist",* 1955/1990, s., portfolio stamp, attrib., t., d., edit. 7/50, (11-16-92, Butterfield, #5961, illus.), 13 1/4 x 11 11/16 in., (337.2 x 297.2 mm.), photograph, gelatin silver print (BP 1449, DM 3508, FR 11,815, Y 273,598).

$2530* *The Photojournalist, Dennis Stock,* 1951, p.l., s., limitation stamp, #17/50, (04-08-93, Christie-NY, #426, illus.), 13 3/8 x 10 5/8 in., (34 x 27 cm.), photograph, gelatin silver print (BP 1659, DM 4064, FR 13,757, Y 287,108).

$2300* *Westside Highway, New York City,* s., d. by photog., 1940's, p.l., (04-06-93, Sotheby-NY, #394, illus.), 10 1/2 x 13 3/8 in., photograph (BP 1519, DM 3705, FR 12,548, Y 262,318).

FEININGER, Lyonel German/American 1871-1956

$2164* *Abend Am Meere (Prasse W 246), 1921,* s., plate 8 from 10 Woodcuts, (11-21-92, Lempertz, #144, illus.), 5 3/8 x 5 13/16 in., (13.6 x 14.8 cm.), woodcut on very thin Japan (BP 1425, DM 3450, FR 11,622, Y 269,121).

$847* *Abend Am Meere (Prasse W 246), 1923,* (06-10-93, Hauswedell/Nolt, #301, illus.), image 5 1/8 x 5 11/16 in., (13 x 14.5 cm.), woodcut on thin hand-made Japan (BP 554, DM 1379, FR 4644, Y 89,906).

$6356* *Die Architektur (Prasse W 232), 1920,* s., Werknummer 2040, artist's proof, series Zwolf Holzschnitte von Lyonel Feininger, Staatlichen Bauhauses, (06-10-93, Hauswedell/Nolt, #298, illus.), image 6 1/8 x 8 7/8 in., (15.5 x 22.5 cm.), woodcut on fine hand-made Japan (BP 4158, DM 10,350, FR 34,846, Y 674,663).

$3319* *Auf Der Quaimauer (Pr. W 243; WN 2106), 1921,* s., Die Schaffenden, Hrsg. Paul Westheim, pub. Euphorion, (12-01-92, Karl/Faber, #602, illus.), 6½ x 8⁷⁄₁₆ in., (16.5 x 21.5 cm.), woodcut on hand-made China (BP 2193, DM 5290, FR 18,028, Y 413,222).

$310* *Auf Der Quaimauer, 1978,* posthumous printing, (09-25-92, Granier, #2833), sheet 11 x 14³⁄₁₆ in., (28 x 36.1 cm.), woodcut on machine hand-made (BP 181, DM 460, FR 1554, Y 37,417).

$1613* *Ausfahrender Dampfer Odin (Prasse W75), 1918,* s., i. w/work num., wide margins, laid, foxmarks, very good cond., (05-20-93, Christie-London, #433, illus.), image 3¼ x 4½ in., (8.3 x 11.4 cm.), sheet 6¼ x 8¼ in., (8.3 x 11.4 cm.), woodcut on tissue-thin paper (BP 1035, DM 2602, FR 8766, Y 178,114).

$5650* *Die Ausfahrt (Prasse W 161), 1919,* s., t., Werknummer 1939, (06-10-93, Hauswedell/Nolt, #293, illus.), image 6¹¹⁄₁₆ x 7¹³⁄₁₆ in., (17 x 19.9 cm.), woodcut on thin silk Japan (BP 3696, DM 9200, FR 30,976, Y 599,724).

$5163* *Benz, 1 (Prasse W 148), 1919,* s., (12-05-92, Bassenge, #7160), 7½ x 10¼ in., (19.1 x 26 cm.), woodcut on handmade Japan (BP 3233, DM 8050, FR 27,434, Y 639,698).

BI *City With Church In The Sun (Stadt Mit Kirche In Der Sonne) (P. W-87), 1918,* s., pub. Staatliches Bauhaus, 1921, margins, good cond., light-stain,loss, est. $4/6,000, (05-13-93, Sotheby-NY, #555, illus.), 6⅜ x 9¾ in., (162 x 248 mm.), sh 8½ x 12⅛ in., (162 x 248 mm.), woodcut on thin Japan.

$4400* *Cruising Sailing Ships, 2 (Kreuzende Segelschiffe, 2) (P. W175), 1919,* s., probably a proof, pub. Hans Weigert, 1925, full margins, good cond., light stain, (11-05-92, Sotheby-NY, #179, illus.), 6¾ x 8⅞ in., (172 x 225 mm.), sheet 9½ x 13½ in., (172 x 225 mm.), woodcut on thin, yellow Japanese paper (BP 2862, DM 6959, FR 23,542, Y 539,811).

$1695* *Dampfer Odin (Prasse W 19), 1918,* s., (06-10-93, Hauswedell/Nolt, #288), image 3¹⁵⁄₁₆ x 5⁵⁄₁₆ in., (10 x 13.5 cm.), woodcut on fine Japan (BP 1109, DM 2760, FR 9293, Y 179,917).

$13,800* *Decrepit Locomotive (Altersschwache Lokomotive) (Prasse L-1), 1906,* margins, good cond., soiling, (05-13-93, Sotheby-NY, #551, illus.), 8¼ x 5⅝ in., (210 x 143 mm.), sh 9⅛ x 6⅞ in., (210 x 143 mm.), lithograph on heavy wove (BP 9060, DM 22,283, FR 75,163, Y 1,540,694).

$7415* *The Disparagers (Prasse E 38), 1911,* plate s., d., t., (06-10-93, Hauswedell/Nolt, #283, illus.), image 8¹¹⁄₁₆ x 10⁹⁄₁₆ in., (22 x 26.9 cm.), etching on hand-made (BP 4850, DM 12,075, FR 40,652, Y 787,071).

$3967* *Dorf (Prasse W 125), 1908,* s., d., i., estate stamp, light-stains, (11-21-92, Lempertz, #143, illus.), 6¾ x 8¹⁄₁₆ in., (17.1 x 20.5 cm.), woodcut on thin Japan (BP 2612, DM 6325, FR 21,305, Y 493,347).

$2990* *Dorfkirche (Prasse W210), 1920,* s., margins, mat staining, glue, good cond., (05-11-93, Christie-NY, #192, illus.), borderline 5⅝ x 6⅞ in., (143 x 175 mm.), woodcut on tan laid (BP 1909, DM 4710, FR 15,870, Y 328,897).

$1401* *Dreimaster Vor Anker (Prasse W 136 II), 1919,* s., d., (12-05-92, Bassenge, #7159), 2¾ x 2¹¹⁄₁₆ in., (7 x 6.8 cm.), woodcut on thin paper (BP 877, DM 2184, FR 7444, Y 173,584).

BI *Felsenkuste (P. W242), 1921,* s., i., margins, mount-staining, excellent cond., est. BP 1,2/1,400, (12-01-92, Christie-London, #378), L. 4¹⁵⁄₁₆ x 5 in., (125 x 127 mm.), woodcut on tissue oriental paper.

BI *Fishing Boats (Pr. W 245; WN 2108), 1921,* light-stained, traces of mounting, est. DM 2800, (12-01-92, Karl/Faber, #603), 12³⁄₁₆ x 14⁹⁄₁₆ in., (31 x 37 cm.), woodcut on hand-made Japan.

$242* *"Fishing Boats" (Prasse 245),* special edit., printed Jacques Hnizdovsky, Print Club of Cleveland Publication No. 49, 1971, excellent cond., (10-31-92, Cleveland, #118), 12⅛ x 14¾ in., (30.8 x 37.5 cm.), woodcut (BP 155, DM 372, FR 1263, Y 29,976).

BI *"Fishing Boats", 1971,* hand-printed by Jacques Hnizdovsky, Print Club of Cleveland Publication No. 49, est.

$5/700, (12-12-92, Wolf, #34), 12½ x 15 in., (31.8 x 38.1 cm.), woodcut on white laid paper.

BI *Fishing Boats, 1971,* posthumous printing, by Jacques Hrizdursky for Print Club of Cleveland, excell. cond., est. $3/500, (05-15-93, Cleveland, #127), 12⅜ x 14¾ in., (31.4 x 37.5 cm.), woodcut.

$210* *Fishing Boats, 1971,* posthumous printing, p. by Jacques Hrizdursky for Print Club of Cleveland, excell. cond., (05-15-93, Cleveland, #127A), 12⅜ x 14¾ in., (31.4 x 37.5 cm.), woodcut (BP 137, DM 338, FR 1135, Y 23,279).

$722* *Gebaude Mit Funf Sternen (Prasse W 262 B), 1928,* (11-28-92, Schoppmann, #499), 2⁹⁄₁₆ x 2⅝ in., (6.5 x 6.7 cm.), color woodcut (BP 477, DM 1150, FR 3905, Y 89,857).

$738* *Gebaude Mit Stern (Prasse W 258), 1928,* s., d., (12-05-92, Bassenge, #7162), 2¾ x 2¼ in., (7 x 5.7 cm.), woodcut on thin pape (BP 462, DM 1151, FR 3921, Y 91,438).

$3877* *Gelbe Dorfkirche (L. E. Prasse W 270), 1931,* s., (05-26-93, Lempertz, #154, illus.), 12⁵⁄₁₆ x 16¹⁄₁₆ in., (31.2 x 40.8 cm.), wood engraving on thin Japan (BP 2508, DM 6326, FR 21,290, Y 421,230).

$1650* *Gelbe Dorfkirche (P. W270), 1931,* s., pub. Die Schaffenden, large margins, light-struck, faded, good cond., glue/mat staining, creases, (10-28-92, Butterfield, #2641, illus.), 6½ x 8 in., (165 x 203 mm.), woodcut on yellow Japan paper (BP 1051, DM 2548, FR 8652, Y 202,454).

$295* *Gelbe Dorfkirche 3, 1978,* p.l., crease, (09-25-92, Granier, #2834), sheet 10¹⁵⁄₁₆ x 14¼ in., (27.8 x 36.2 cm.), woodcut on machine hand-made (BP 172, DM 437, FR 1479, Y 35,607).

$8324* *Gelmeroda (P. W237), 1920,* s., i., ded., full margins, creases, light-staining, (12-01-92, Christie-London, #377, illus.), L. 12¹⁵⁄₁₆ x 9⁷⁄₁₆ in., (330 x 240 mm.), woodcut on Japan (BP 5500, DM 13,267, FR 45,215, Y 1,036,355).

$1977* *Gelmeroda (Prasse L 20 II), 1955,* s., (06-10-93, Hauswedell/Nolt, #287), image 11⅝ x 8¹⁄₁₆ in., (29.5 x 20.5 cm.), lithograph on wove (BP 1293, DM 3219, FR 10,839, Y 209,850).

$2401* *Gelmeroda (Prasse L 20 II), 1955,* s., (06-10-93, Hauswedell/Nolt, #286), image 8⁷⁄₁₆ x 11¹³⁄₁₆ in., (21.5 x 30 cm.), lithograph on Rives paper (BP 1571, DM 3910, FR 13,163, Y 254,856).

$3107* *Gelmeroda (Prasse W 237), 1920,* estate stamp, (06-10-93, Hauswedell/Nolt, #299, illus.), image 12¹⁵⁄₁₆ x 9¹⁄₁₆ in., (33 x 23 cm.), woodcut on hand-made Japan (BP 2032, DM 5059, FR 17,034, Y 329,795).

$3734* *Gelmeroda Church (Gelmeroda) (Prasse W 11/II; WN 1808), 1918,* s., 2nd state, (12-01-92, Karl/Faber, #598, illus.), 7⅞ x 5⅞ in., (20 x 15 cm.), woodcut on thin brownish paper (BP 2467, DM 5952, FR 20,282, Y 464,890).

$1011* *Gelmeroda Mit Sonnenaufgang (Prasse W 159), 1919,* (11-28-92, Schoppmann, #498, illus.), 3⅜ x 2¼ in., (8.6 x 5.7 cm.), woodcut (BP 667, DM 1611, FR 5468, Y 125,825).

BI *"Gelmeroda", 1920,* posthumous printing, 1958, special edit. for Cleveland Print Club, Pubblication No. 36, excell. cond., est. $2/400, (05-15-93, Cleveland, #125), 13 x 9¼ in., (33 x 23.5 cm.), woodcut.

$6325* *Die Grune Brucke (P. E22), 1910-11,* s., pub. in portfolio Die zweite Jahresgabe des Kreises graphischer Kunstler und Sammler, pub. Arndt Beyer, 1922, full margins, good cond., mat stain, (11-05-92, Sotheby-NY, #178, illus.), 10⅝ x 7⅞ in., (270 x 201 mm.), etching on Zanders laid, cream, fibrous paper (BP 4114, DM 10,003, FR 33,842, Y 775,978).

$4752* *"Die Grune Brucke" (Prasse E 22), 1910/11,* s., pub. in Die zweite Jahresgabe des Kreises graphischer Kunstler und Sammler, Verlag Arndt & Beyer, 1922, (06-05-93, Grisebach, #566, illus.), 10⁷⁄₁₆ x 7¹³⁄₁₆ in., (26.5 x 19.9 cm.), etching on hand-made (BP 3128, DM 7704, FR 25,967, Y 509,762).

BI *"Die Grune Brucke" (Prasse E22), 1910-11,* s., d., i., est. DM 18/24,000, (06-05-93, Grisebach, #312, illus.), 10⅝ x 7¹³⁄₁₆ in., (27 x 19.8 cm.), etching in dark-brown on hand-made.

$4740* *Hauser Und Kirche, 1921,* s., estate stamp, prov., (04-21-93, Germann, #176, illus.), 7¹¹⁄₁₆ x 11¹³⁄₁₆ in., (196 x 300 mm.), woodcut on Japan (BP 3076, DM 7577, FR 25,622, Y 524,743, SF 6900).

BI *Holzschnitte (Pr. W 8, 110, 119, 127/II, 161, 178, 181, 207, 229, 235and 271), 1918-31: Twelve,* posthumous edit. of woodcuts for AAA, num., traces of old mounting, est. DM 7000, (12-01-92, Karl/Faber, #604), smallest 4¹⁵⁄₁₆ x 5⅞ in., (12.5 x 15 cm.), largest 12³⁄₁₆ x 7½ in., (12.5 x 15 cm.), woodcut.

BI *"Houses In Old Paris": Fifty,* hand-p. by Jacques Hrizdursky for Print Club of Cleveland, excell. cond., est. $6/800, (05-15-93, Cleveland, #126), 12 x 60 in., (30.5 x 152.4 cm.), woodcut.

BI *Kirche (Prasse W 28), 1918,* s., t., Werknummer 1819, estate stamp, est. DM 5000, (06-10-93, Hauswedell/Nolt, #289, illus.), image 5½ x 4½ in., (14 x 11.5 cm.), woodcut on thin, red silk paper.

BI *Kirche (Prasse W 28), 1918,* s., Werknummer 1819, estate stamp, est. DM 4000, (06-10-93, Hauswedell/Nolt, #290, illus.), image 5½ x 4½ in., (14 x 11.5 cm.), woodcut on thin hand-made Japan.

$1702* *"Kirche Mit Hausern, Baum Und Stern (Deep)" (Prasse W 275), 1933,* s., (06-05-93, Grisebach, #573, illus.), 2⅜ x 2⅝ in., (6.1 x 6.7 cm.), handcolored woodcut on thin stationery (BP 1120, DM 2759, FR 9301, Y 182,579).

$1554* *Kirche Von Drobsdorf (Prasse E 58), 1916/17,* estate stamp, (06-10-93, Hauswedell/Nolt, #284), image 7¹⁄₁₆ x 9³⁄₁₆ in., (17.9 x 23.3 cm.), etching on thin hand-made paper (BP 1016, DM 2531, FR 8520, Y 164,951).

$6270* *Kirchplatz (Prasse W 1 II), 1918,* s., t., (12-05-92, Bassenge, #7157, illus.), 7¹⁄₁₆ x 8¹¹⁄₁₆ in., (18 x 22 cm.), woodcut on China (BP 3926, DM 9775, FR 33,316, Y 776,855).

$3901* *"Kreuzende Segelschiffe 2" (Prasse W 175), 1919,* s., pub. in Funfte Jahresmapper des Kreises graphischer Kunstler undSammler, Verlag Arndt & Beyer, 1925, (06-05-93, Grisebach, #569, illus.), 6¾ x 8¾ in., (17.1 x 22.3 cm.), woodcut on handmade Japan (BP 2568, DM 6325, FR 21,317, Y 418,472).

$3390* *Kreuzende Segelschiffe II (Prasse W 175), 1919,* s., artist's proof, (06-10-93, Hauswedell/Nolt, #295, illus.), image 6¾ x 8⅞ in., (17.2 x 22.5 cm.), woodcut on thin Japan paper (BP 2217, DM 5520, FR 18,586, Y 359,834).

$5775* *"Kreuzende Segelschiffe II" (Prasse W175), 1919,* s., special ed. "Funfte Jahresgabe des Kreises graphischer Kunstler und Sammler", Leipzig, pub. Arndt Beyer, 1925, (11-28-92, Grisebach, #228, illus.), 6¾ x 8¾ in., (17.1 x 22.2 cm.), woodcut on handmade Japan (BP 3812, DM 9200, FR 31,233, Y 718,731).

BI *Kreuzende Segelschiffe, 2 (Cruising Ships) (Prasse W175), 1955,* s., p. by artist, s., full margins, good cond., est. Y 775/825,000, (10-14-92, Sotheby-Japan, #27, illus.), 6¾ x 8¾ in., (171 x 222 mm.), woodcut on thin Japanese laid paper.

$2750* *Locomotive On The Bridge (Prasse W81), 1918,* 2nd final state, s., pub. Zwolf Holzschnitte von Feininger, Staatliches Bauhaus, 1921, margins, very good cond., (11-09-92, Christie-NY, #93, illus.), 92 x 114 in., (233.7 x 289.6 cm.), woodcut on laid Japan (BP 1818, DM 4390, FR 14,833, Y 341,276).

$999* *Manhattan 3 (Stone 2) (P. L19), 1955,* s., edit. 240, pub. Kestner-Gesellschaft, margins, deckle edge, goodcond., (12-01-92, Christie-London, #379), L. 10¹⁄₁₆ x 8⁹⁄₁₆ in., (255 x 218 mm.), lithograph on Rives (BP 660, DM 1592, FR 5426, Y 124,377).

$3738* *Marine (P. W-77), 1918,* s., pub. Verlag der Dichtung, full margins, soiling, defects, good cond., (05-13-93, Sotheby-NY, #554, illus.), 11⅛ x 15 in., (282 x 380 mm.), woodcut on thin, soft, laid Japan (BP 2454, DM 6036, FR 20,359, Y 417,327).

BI *Marine (P. W77), 1918,* s., p. Voigt's sig., edit. 125, pub. dry stamp, margins, nicks, staining, some foxing, est. BP 2/3,000, (12-01-92, Christie-London, #372, illus.), L. 11⅛ x 14¾ in., (282 x 374 mm.), woodcut on handmade wove.

BI *Marine (Prasse W 164), 1919,* s., Werknummer 1942, estate stamp, est. DM 3500, (06-10-93, Hauswedell, #294), image 4¹¹⁄₁₆ x 5⅛ in., (11.9 x 13 cm.), woodcut on fine yellow silk paper.

$3656* *Off The Coast (Prasse L 14 II), 1951,* s., stamp, (12-02-92, Dorling, #2629, illus.), 8¹¹⁄₁₆ x 13¾ in., (22 x 35 cm.), lithograph on wove (BP 2358, DM 5749, FR 19,624, Y 454,896).

$2475* *Off The Coast, Stone 3 (P. L14), 1951,* second and final state, s., p. by Print Club of Cleveland, full margins, good cond., (11-05-92, Sotheby-NY, #180), 9⅜ x 14¾ in., (238 x 375 mm.), lithograph (BP 1610, DM 3914, FR 13,242, Y 303,644).

BI *Off The Coast, Stone 3 (Prasse L14), 1951,* 2nd (final) state, s., p. George Miller for The Print Club of Cleveland, stamp, margins, good cond., tear, scotch tape hinges, stains, skinning, est. $2,5/3,000, (02-11-93, Sotheby-NY, #138, illus.), 9⅜ x 14¾ in., (238 x 375 mm.), sheet 10⁷⁄₁₆ x 15¹⁵⁄₁₆ in., (238 x 375 mm.), lithograph.

$21,850* *The Old Locomotive (Windspiel) (P. L-2), 1906,* margins, good cond., mat stain, creases, repaired loss, (05-13-93, Sotheby-NY, #552, illus.), 6¼ x 12⅝ in., (158 x 322 mm.), sh 9¼ x 16 in., (158 x 322 mm.), lithograph in black w/bluish-black tint stone, on very thin, fibrousJapan (BP 14,345, DM 35,282, FR 119,009, Y 2,439,433).

$2070* *The Privateer (Der Reeder) (P. E-41/B), 1911-12,* s., p. Philippe Molinie at L'Imprimerie Lacouriere, c. 1950, full margins, good cond., (05-13-93, Sotheby-NY, #553), 5½ x 8½ in., (140 x 216 mm.), etching (BP 1359, DM 3342, FR 11,275, Y 231,104).

$2387* *Rathaus Von Zottelstedt 1 (Prasse W37), 1919,* s., t., full margins, good cond., crease, stain, (12-03-92, Sotheby-London, #305, illus.), 4½ x 5½ in., (114 x 140 mm.), woodcut on Japan (BP 1540, DM 3754, FR 12,813, Y 297,001).

BI *Der Reeder (An Der Waterkant) (P. E41B), 1911-12,* s., p. c. 1950 for C. Valentin, margins, deckle edge, discoloration,good cond., est. BP 1,5/2,000, (12-01-92, Christie-London, #371), plate 5½ x 8¾ in., (139 x 222 mm.), etching on Arches.

BI *Schiffe (Prasse W 151 I), 1930,* s., d., t., only state, est. DM 8000, (06-10-93, Hauswedell/Nolt, #292, illus.), image 9¹⁵⁄₁₆ x 11⅜ in., (25.2 x 28.9 cm.), woodcut on hand-made.

$220* *Schiffe Im Fjord (Tahiti) (PW 235),* posthumous printing, very good cond., (06-11-93, Doyle, #41), 6¼ x 7¼ in., (159 x 184 mm.), woodcut (BP 145, DM 358, FR 1205, Y 23,342).

BI *Schiffe Und Sonne (P. W201), 1920,* 2nd (final) state, s., i., margins, foxmarks, excellent cond., est. BP 1,0/1,200, (12-01-92, Christie-London, #375), L. 3⁷⁄₁₆ x 4¾ in., (87 x 120 mm.), woodcut on tissue Japan.

$1342* *Schiffe Und Sterne (Prasse W 178), 1919,* estate stamp, (06-10-93, Hauswedell/Nolt, #297, illus.), 5⅜ x 9¹⁄₁₆ in., (13.7 x 23 cm.), woodcut on thin hand-made Japan (BP 878, DM 2185, FR 7357, Y 142,448).

BI *Segelboote (Mit Mond) (P. W183), 1919,* 2nd state of 3, s., i., light-staining, excellent cond., est. BP 1,4/1,800, (12-01-92, Christie-London, #374), L. 5¹³⁄₁₆ x 6⅝ in., (148 x 168 mm.), woodcut on tan tissue oriental.

$2987* *Ships Along A Rocky Coast (Pr. W 213; WN 2021), 1920,* s., num., estate stamp, traces of mounting, (12-01-92, Karl/Faber, #601, illus.), 4¾ x 6⅛ in., (12 x 15.5 cm.), woodcut (BP 1974, DM 4761, FR 16,225, Y 371,887).

$201* *Ships And Stars (W. 178), 1919,* posthumous impression, #30/100, pub. AAA, 1964, p. Gehenna Press, blindstamp, margins, good cond., (05-19-93, Butterfield, #2055), 5¾ x 9 in., (146 x 229 mm.), woodcut on Japan (BP 130, DM 327, FR 1101, Y 22,252).

$358* *Ships In A Harbor, 1920,* plate s., very good cond., (07-19-92, Bakker, #25), image 6¾ x 10 in., (17.1 x 25.4 cm.), woodblock print (BP 184, DM 522, FR 1764, Y 44,505).

$1100* *Ships, Waves, And Sun (Schiffe, Wellen, Und Sonne) (P. W229),* s., large margins, good cond., glue/mat staining, creases, (10-28-92, Butterfield, #2639, illus.), 5 x 6 in.,

(127 x 152 mm.), woodcut on tissue thin laid paper (BP 701, DM 1699, FR 5768, Y 134,969).

$1620* *Skt. Nikolai (P. W250), 1923,* s., t., good cond., creases, prov., (12-03-92, Sotheby-London, #306), 8⅛ x 6¼ in., (206 x 159 mm.), woodcut on thin Japan (BP 1045, DM 2548, FR 8696, Y 201,568).

$1522* *Spaziergang (Menschen Und Hund) (Prasse W86), 1918,* s., i. w/work num., margins, laid, very good cond., (05-20-93, Christie-London, #434, illus.), image 4 x 3⅛ in., (10.2 x 7.9 cm.), sheet 5¼ x 4¼ in., (10.2 x 7.9 cm.), woodcut on deep yellow tissue paper (BP 977, DM 2456, FR 8272, Y 168,065).

$9887* *Strasse In Paris (Prasse W 97 II), 1918,* s., d., t., Werknummer 1833, (06-10-93, Hauswedell/Nolt, #291, illus.), image 21⁹⁄₁₆ x 16¼ in., (54.8 x 41.2 cm.), woodcut on thin hand-made Japan (BP 6467, DM 16,100, FR 54,205, Y 1,049,464).

$3850* *Suburb, Vorstadt (P. W254),* s., large margins, sheet faded, foxing, mat staining in image, glue staining, tape remains, (10-28-92, Butterfield, #2640, illus.), 9¼ x 14⅞ in., (235 x 378 mm.), woodcut on yellow Japanese laid paper (BP 2453, DM 5946, FR 20,189, Y 472,393).

$523* *"Sussenborn Or Dorkfkirche (Little Church)" (Prasse-W253), c. 1924,* s., d. 1920, creasing, full margins, (05-07-93, Goldberg, #421, illus.), image 5¼ x 5¾ in., (13.3 x 14.6 cm.), woodcut on Japanese cream wove (BP 331, DM 827, FR 2786, Y 57,586).

$173* *Sussenborn, 1924,* posthumous impression, estate inkstamp, margins, good cond., surfacesoiling, (05-19-93, Butterfield, #2056), 5⅝ x 5¾ in., (137 x 146 mm.), woodcut in tissue-thin Japan (BP 112, DM 281, FR 947, Y 19,152).

$14,850* *The Town At The End Of The World (Die Stadt Am Ende Der Welt) (PrasseE19), 1910,* carefully wiped, atmospheric tone, margins, good cond., mat stain, tape hinges, (11-05-92, Sotheby-NY, #177, illus.), 7¾ x 9⅞ in., (198 x 250 mm.), sheet 8⅝ x 10½ in., (198 x 250 mm.), etching and drypoint on cream wove (BP 9659, DM 23,486, FR 79,454, Y 1,821,862).

BI *Traumstadt (Prasse E 36), 1911,* s. twice, I Print, estate stamp, est. DM 8000, (06-10-93, Hauswedell/Nolt, #282, illus.), image 5⁷⁄₁₆ x 8⅜ in., (13.8 x 21.3 cm.), etching on copper print paper.

$1300* *Village,* s., i. Brucke 20-17, large margins, staining, (11-30-92, Phillips-London, #425, illus.), border 6¼ x 5¾ in., (159 x 146 mm.), woodcut on japan (BP 858, DM 2071, FR 7031, Y 161,792).

$358* *"Village", 1920,* plate s., very good cond., (07-19-92, Bakker, #40), image 6¾ x 7¾ in., (17.1 x 19.7 cm.), woodblock print (BP 184, DM 522, FR 1764, Y 44,505).

$2966* *Vor Der Kuste III (Prasse L 14 II), 1951,* s., stamped, (06-10-93, Hauswedell/Nolt, #285, illus.), image 9¹⁄₁₆ x 14¹¹⁄₁₆ in., (23 x 37.3 cm.), lithograph on wove (BP 1940, DM 4830, FR 16,261, Y 314,829).

$2164* *Vulkan (P. W132), 1919,* 2nd (final) state, s., i., margins, excellent cond., (12-01-92, Christie-London, #373), L. 3⅛ x 4¾ in., (79 x 120 mm.), woodcut on tan tissue Japan (BP 1430, DM 3449, FR 11,754, Y 269,422).

$605* *Wettsegeln (Yacht Race), 1918,* s., light struck, good cond., prov., (06-11-93, Doyle, #40), 4⅝ x 4⅞ in., (117 x 124 mm.), woodcut (BP 398, DM 983, FR 3315, Y 64,191).

$1033* *The Yacht Race (Prasse W8),* s., tear extending across top margin, foxing, mottling, taped, ex-coll. Tekla Hess, (11-30-92, Phillips-London, #423), sheet 7¼ x 9 in., (184 x 229 mm.), woodcut in black on tissue thin laid japan (BP 682, DM 1646, FR 5587, Y 128,563).

$5974* *"Zottelstedt" (Pr. W 51; WN 1837), 1920,* s., Die Schaffenden, Jg. II, Mappe 1, (12-01-92, Karl/Faber, #599, illus.), 8⅞ x 10¹³⁄₁₆ in., (22.5 x 27.5 cm.), woodcut on thin Japan (BP 3947, DM 9522, FR 32,450, Y 743,775).

$774* *Zur Ausfahrt Bereit, 1919,* #28/100, (10-09-92, Winterberg, #2075), woodcut (BP 459, DM 1150, FR 3860, Y 94,229).

FEININGER, T. Lux b. 1910

BI *A. Sharon Und M. Kallin, c. 1928/29,* lit., est. DM 500, (11-12-92, Lempertz, #11), 4⁷⁄₁₆ x 3³⁄₁₆ in., (11.3 x 8.1 cm.), photograph, gelatin silver print.

BI *Bauhaus Musicians Ernst Egeler (With Sax) And Clemens Roseler (With Trombone),* sig., notations in unidentified hand, 1920's, ex-coll. T. Lux Feininger, est. $2/3,000, (10-14-92, Swann, #377, illus.), 9 x 7 in., (22.9 x 17.8 cm.), photograph, silver print.

BI *Saxophonist, c. 1927,* stamp, est. $1,8/2,200, (10-13-92, Christie-NY, #207, illus.), 9¼ x 7 in., (23.5 x 17.8 cm.), photograph, gelatin silver print.

BI *Die Studierenden Der Wandmalerei-Werkstatt, c. 1928,* s., t., d. by photog. in ink, est. $1/1,500, (10-15-92, Sotheby-NY, #409, illus.), 3¾ x 3¼ in., (9.5 x 8.3 cm.), photograph, gelatin silver print.

BI *Theatermasken Am Bauhaus Von Schlemmer Und T.L. Feininger, 20's,* pencil and ink s., est. DM 1,000, (11-12-92, Lempertz, #10, illus.), 4¹¹⁄₁₆ x 3½ in., (11.9 x 8.9 cm.), photograph, gelatin silver print.

FEITO, Luis Spanish b. 1929

$32* *"Composition",* #36/99, s., (01-28-93, Pescheteau, #140), 29¹⁵⁄₁₆ x 22¹⁄₁₆ in., (76 x 56 cm.), color serigraph on Arches (BP 21, DM 51, FR 172, Y 3973).

$133* *Sans Titre,* num. H.C., s. Feito, (04-20-93, Encans, #116), 18¹¹⁄₁₆ x 17¼ in., (47.5 x 43.8 cm.), serigraph (BP 86, DM 212, FR 715, Y 14,675, C$ 167).

$38* *"Turmalina", 1974,* #65/110, s., (01-28-93, Pescheteau, #141), 29½ x 22¹⁄₁₆ in., (75 x 56 cm.), color serigraph on Rives (BP 25, DM 60, FR 204, Y 4718).

FEKETE, Esteban b. 1924

BI *Selbstbildnis,* artist's proof, i., s. Fekete, est. DM 300-, (03-24-93, Venator/Hansten, #4485), pl. 9⅝ x 15¹¹⁄₁₆ in., (24.5 x 39.8 cm.), etching.

FELGUEREZ, Manuel Mexico b. 1929

$43* *Dos Soluciones,* s., #23/46; t. label verso, prov., (12-01-92, Ritchie, #74), 24½ x 30½ in., (62.2 x 77.5 cm.), color serigraph (BP 28, DM 69, FR 234, Y 5354, C$ 55).

$43* *Signo Convexo,* s., #23/96; t. label verso, prov., (12-01-92, Ritchie, #61, illus.), 23½ x 29½ in., (59.7 x 74.9 cm.), color serigraph (BP 28, DM 69, FR 234, Y 5354, C$ 55).

FELIXMULLER, Conrad American 1897-1977

BI *Der Bergingenieur (Sohn 285), 1922,* s., d., i., full margins, mat/light-stain, foxing, repaired tears, repaired puncture, surface losses, creases, scuffs, ink spot, hinge stains, est.$2/4,000, (05-13-93, Sotheby-NY, #556, illus.), 21½ x 17¼ in., (545 x 438 mm.), sh 25½ x 19¾ in., (545 x 438 mm.), woodcut.

BI *Berlin, Brandenburger Tor Im Winter (S. 667), 1972,* s., num., E(preuve) d'A(rtiste), light-stained, est. DM 1800, (12-01-92, Karl/Faber, #609), 10⁷⁄₁₆ x 12³⁄₁₆ in., (26.5 x 31 cm.), etching on wove.

$1342* *Bildnis Carl Sternheim (Sohn 334), 1925,* s., watermark, (06-10-93, Hauswedell/Nolt, #306), image 19½ x 15⁹⁄₁₆ in., (49.5 x 39.5 cm.), woodcut on wove (BP 878, DM 2185, FR 7357, Y 142,448).

$1099* *Bildnis Carl Sternheim (Sohn Nr. 334 C), 1925,* s., (11-13-92, Kunsthaus, #558, illus.), 19½ x 15⁹⁄₁₆ in., (49.5 x 39.5 cm.), woodcut on Hahnemuhle handmade (BP 710, DM 1725, FR 5818, Y 136,403).

$1977* *Bildnis Christian Rohlfs (Sohn 370 c), 1927,* s., block mono., (06-10-93, Hauswedell/Nolt, #308), image 19½ x 15⁹⁄₁₆ in., (49.5 x 39.5 cm.), woodcut on hand-made Ingres (BP 1293, DM 3219, FR 10,839, Y 209,850).

$1762* *Bildnis Max Liebermann (Sohn 366 a), 1926,* s., block mono., (05-26-93, Dorling, #2645, illus.), 19½ x 15⁹⁄₁₆ in., (49.5 x 39.5 cm.), woodcut on thick wove (BP 1140, DM 2875, FR 9676, Y 191,439).

$1412* *Bildnis Max Liebermann (Sohn 366 b), 1926,* s., block mono., (06-10-93, Hauswedell/Nolt, #307), image 19½ x 15⁹⁄₁₆ in., (49.5 x 39.5 cm.), woodcut on wove (BP 924, DM 2299, FR 7741, Y 149,878).

$1463* *Bildnis Max Liebermann, 1926-1957,* Wz., s., (12-12-92, Wachholtz, #119, illus.), 19½ x 15⁹⁄₁₆ in., (49.6 x 39.5

cm.), woodcut on Hahnemuhle handmade (BP 935, DM 2299, FR 7836, Y 180,997).

$341* *Einholen Des Christbaumes Mit Dem Fahrrad (Sohn 625), 1965,* s., (09-25-92, Granier, #2837), 3 15/16 x 4 7/8 in., (10 x 12.4 cm.), woodcut on Japan (BP 199, DM 505, FR 1709, Y 41,159).

$280* *Einholen Des Christbaums Mit Dem Fahrrad (Sohn 625), 1965,* s., (12-05-92, Bassenge, #7171), 3 7/8 x 4 15/16 in., (9.8 x 12.5 cm.), woodcut on Japan (BP 175, DM 437, FR 1488, Y 34,692).

$1705* *Fabrikarbeitter (Arbeitsinvalide) (S. 259), 1921,* s., i. Holzchnitt, working proof between 1st & 2nd states, margins, good cond. within subject, damp stain, (12-03-92, Sotheby-London, #308, illus.), 19 1/8 x 11 1/2 in., (486 x 292 mm.), woodcut on wove (BP 1100, DM 2681, FR 9152, Y 212,144).

$2638* *Frau (Sohn 335), 1925,* s., num., (09-25-92, Granier, #2843, illus.), sheet 19 11/16 x 12 11/16 in., (50 x 32.2 cm.), etching on wove (BP 1540, DM 3910, FR 13,223, Y 318,407).

$1024* *Freizeit Der Berliner Elefanten (Sohn 670 c (von e), 1972,* s., d., num., i., stock mono., (12-12-92, Wachholtz, #123, illus.), 11 13/16 x 9 13/16 in., (30 x 25 cm.), color woodcut on wove (BP 655, DM 1609, FR 5485, Y 126,686).

$5367* *Genossen (Sohn 209), 1920,* s., d., t., num., (06-10-93, Hauswedell/Nolt, #304, illus.), image 21 1/8 x 27 3/16 in., (53.6 x 69 cm.), lithograph on wove (BP 3511, DM 8740, FR 29,424, Y 569,685).

$1770* *Ich Sah Und Schnitt In Holz (Sohn 474-514), 1952: Forty,* Nr. 14, 23, 27, 40, s.; num., (12-05-92, Bassenge, #7170), 3 13/16 x 4 3/4 in., (9.7 x 12 cm.), woodcut (BP 1108, DM 2760, FR 9405, Y 219,304).

$171* *Ich Zeichne Meine Eingeschlafene Mutter (Sohn 647 c.), 1968,* s., (09-25-92, Granier, #2838), sheet 7 1/2 x 10 1/4 in., (19 x 26 cm.), woodcut on white machine hand-made (BP 100, DM 253, FR 857, Y 20,640).

$289* *"Im Violinunterricht" (Sohn 645), 1968,* s., d., (11-28-92, Grisebach, #513, illus.), 3 3/4 x 4 3/4 in., (9.6 x 12.1 cm.), woodcut on handmade (BP 191, DM 460, FR 1563, Y 35,968).

$5163* *Junge Eltern (Sohn 156), 1918,* s., t., rare, prov., (12-05-92, Bassenge, #7165, illus.), 19 11/16 x 12 3/16 in., (50 x 31 cm.), woodcut (BP 3233, DM 8050, FR 27,434, Y 639,698).

$1079* *"Kohlenbergarbeiter" (Sohn 255 b),* 1921 (72), s., d., t. Neudruck 8/20, (12-01-92, Karl/Faber, #608), 9 13/16 x 12 3/16 in., (25 x 31 cm.), etching on wove (BP 713, DM 1720, FR 5861, Y 134,338).

$220* *(Kopf), 1918,* pub. in Die Aktion, margins, good cond., sheet toned, paper loss, tears, pencil notations, (02-24-93, Butterfield, #2924), 10 3/16 x 6 5/8 in., (259 x 168 mm.), woodcut on wove (BP 153, DM 357, FR 1211, Y 25,816).

$1135* *Liebespaar (Vor Industrielandschaft) (Sohn 314 b), 1923,* s., (06-05-93, Bassenge, #6024), 8 13/16 x 6 3/16 in., (22.4 x 15.7 cm.), woodcut (BP 747, DM 1840, FR 6202, Y 121,755).

$1417* *Liebespaar (Vor Industrielandschaft) (Sohn 314 b), 1923,* s., (06-08-93, Karl/Faber, #744), approx. 8 7/8 x 6 1/8 in., (22.5 x 15.5 cm.), woodcut (BP 932, DM 2299, FR 7743, Y 150,505).

$2119* *Madchen (Sohn 277 b), 1921,* s., d., num., t., #10/50, (06-10-93, Hauswedell/Nolt, #305, illus.), image 16 x 10 1/4 in., (40.7 x 26 cm.), lithograph on wove (BP 1386, DM 3451, FR 11,617, Y 224,923).

$5320* *"Max John" (Sohn 241), 1920,* s., i., (06-05-93, Grisebach, #285, illus.), 19 5/8 x 15 3/4 in., (49.8 x 40 cm.), woodcut on Japan (BP 3502, DM 8625, FR 29,071, Y 570,693).

$4434* *Menschen Im Wald (SoHN 135), 1918,* s., margins, good cond., marks, creases, (12-03-92, Sotheby-London, #307, illus.), 9 3/4 x 11 3/4 in., (248 x 298 mm.), woodcut in colors on thin wove (BP 2860, DM 6973, FR 23,800, Y 551,698).

$7093* *Menschen Im Wald (Sohn 135 b), 1918,* s., (06-05-93, Bassenge, #6021, illus.), 9 13/16 x 11 13/16 in., (25 x 30 cm.), color woodcut on hand-made (BP 4669, DM 11,500, FR 38,760, Y 760,888).

$10,994* *"Menschen Uber Der Welt" (Sohn 193), 1919,* s., d., i., restored, (06-05-93, Grisebach, #323, illus.), 26 15/16 x 19 5/16 in., (68.5 x 49 cm.), lithograph on smooth factory printed paper (BP 7237, DM 17,824, FR 60,077, Y 1,179,361).

$969* *Mutter Mit Kind (Sohn 157 b), 1918-1919,* s., d., stock mono., (09-19-92, Wachholtz, #196), 8 7/8 x 3 9/16 in., (22.5 x 9 cm.), woodcut on wove (BP 567, DM 1438, FR 4919, Y 119,763).

$117* *Neujahrsgruss Fur 1975, Erwin Nicolaus (Sohn 695), 1974,* s., num., (09-25-92, Granier, #2842), sheet 4 1/8 x 5 7/8 in., (10.5 x 15 cm.), woodcut on machine hand-made (BP 68, DM 173, FR 586, Y 14,122).

$1277* *Portrat Friedrich Engels (Sohn 232), 1920,* s., (06-05-93, Bassenge, #6023), 3 15/16 x 2 3/8 in., (10 x 6 cm.), woodcut on factory print (BP 841, DM 2070, FR 6978, Y 136,988).

$852* *Rendezvous (Sohn 699b), 1974-1975,* s., stock mono., (09-19-92, Wachholtz, #205), 11 7/8 x 9 13/16 in., (30.2 x 25 cm.), color woodcut on copper print paper (BP 499, DM 1264, FR 4325, Y 105,302).

$338* *Selbst-Bildnis Mit Zeichenstift (Sohn 369), 1927,* block mono. FM, (03-24-93, Venator/Hansten, #4487), image 19 9/16 x 15 3/4 in., (49.7 x 40 cm.), woodcut on machine made paper (BP 229, DM 552, FR 1879, Y 39,713).

$217* *"Selbstbildnis Mit Pinsel Und Palette" (Sohn 635), 1967,* s., lit., (11-28-92, Grisebach, #512, illus.), 6 7/8 x 4 15/16 in., (17.5 x 12.5 cm.), woodcut on thick wove (BP 143, DM 346, FR 1174, Y 27,007).

$461* *Selbstbildnis Mit Zeichenstift (S. 369 d), 1965,* s., (06-08-93, Karl/Faber, #745), approx. 19 1/2 x 15 3/4 in., (49.5 x 40 cm.), woodcut (BP 303, DM 748, FR 2519, Y 48,964).

$505* *Selbstportrait (Sohn 133), 1918,* s., yellowed, (09-25-92, Granier, #2835), sheet 6 5/16 x 3 15/16 in., (16 x 10 cm.), woodcut on bluish board (BP 295, DM 749, FR 2531, Y 60,954).

$2837* *Der Sohn (Sohn 155), 1918,* i., t., s., (06-05-93, Bassenge, #6022, illus.), 11 5/8 x 9 7/16 in., (29.5 x 24 cm.), woodcut on paper (BP 1868, DM 4600, FR 15,503, Y 304,334).

$155* *Titelblatt Zum "Jahr Des Malers" (Sohn 653), 1970,* stone mono., s., (09-25-92, Granier, #2839), sheet 7 1/2 x 4 3/8 in., (19.1 x 11.1 cm.), woodcut on Daunen print paper (BP 91, DM 230, FR 777, Y 18,709).

$2837* *Zwei Frauenkopfe (Sohn 76), 1915,* s., t., i., (06-05-93, Bassenge, #6020, illus.), 19 1/2 x 15 5/8 in., (49.5 x 39.7 cm.), woodcut on hand-made Japan (BP 1868, DM 4600, FR 15,503, Y 304,334).

BI *Zwei Frauenkopfe (Sohn 76), 1915,* s., t., num., very rare, est. DM 6,000, (12-05-92, Bassenge, #7164, illus.), 19 1/2 x 15 5/8 in., (49.5 x 39.7 cm.), woodcut on hand-made Japan.

$1227* *Zwei Manner (Sohn 96), 1917,* i., s., foxing, (11-28-92, Schoppmann, #501), 4 3/4 x 3 5/16 in., (12 x 8.4 cm.), woodcut on light brown wove (BP 810, DM 1955, FR 6636, Y 152,707).

$1588* *"Zwei Manner" (Sohn 96 a), 1917,* s., (11-28-92, Grisebach, #511, illus.), 4 3/4 x 3 5/16 in., (12.1 x 8.4 cm.), woodcut on wove (BP 1048, DM 2530, FR 8588, Y 197,635).

FELKEL, Carl b. 1896

$845* *For High Performance, Bristol Bombays, 1938,* p. Waterlow and Sons, ref. #530, cond. 3, (10-13-92, Phillips-London, #147, illus.), 29 15/16 x 45 1/16 in., (76 x 114.5 cm.), color lithograph (BP 492, DM 1238, FR 4206, Y 102,462).

FELL

$1259* *Automobiles Delahaye "Les Qualites De La Race",* p. Riegel, good cond., (11-19-92, Ribeyre/Baron, #61, illus.), 59 7/16 x 44 1/2 in., (151 x 113 cm.), poster (BP 829, DM 2007, FR 6762, Y 156,573).

FENOSA, Appeles

$58* *Figure En Mouvement,* s. artist's proof, (06-28-93, Loudmer, #39), 14 3/16 x 11 in., (360 x 280 mm.), sh 23 7/16 x 16 in., (360 x 280 mm.), lithograph in taupe on Arches wove (BP 39, DM 99, FR 332, Y 6154).

FENTON, Roger   1819-1869
$1453* *"Ely Cathedral From The Grammar School"*, late 1850s, mounted on card, credit., t., 353 x 436mm, (05-07-93, Sotheby-London, #66, illus.), photograph, albumen print (BP 920, DM 2297, FR 7741, Y 159,987).
$327* *"Encampment Of Horse Artillery"*, pub. Feb. 29, 1856, mounted on card, pub., p. t., photog.'s/pub. credits, 245 x 350mm, (05-07-93, Sotheby-London, #63), photograph, salt print (BP 207, DM 517, FR 1742, Y 36,005).
BI *"Greek Hero"*, c. 1857, p. t., photog.'s, pub.'s credits, lit., orig. mount, est. BP 8/1,000, (10-29-92, Christie-London, #22, illus.), 13½ x 10⅜ in., (34.3 x 26.4 cm.), photograph, salt print.
BI *"Hadrian, T. 94"*, c. 1857, p. t., photog.'s, pub.'s credits, orig. mount, est. BP 9/1,200, (10-29-92, Christie-London, #23, illus.), 12⅝ x 10 in., (32.1 x 25.4 cm.), photograph, salt print.
BI *"Lichfield Porch Of Sth. Transept"*, 1858, p. by Frith 1860s, lit., est. BP 6/800, (10-29-92, Christie-London, #28), 13¼ x 16¼ in., (33.7 x 41.3 cm.), photograph, albumen print mounted on card.
$1453* *"The Llyn Glas, Junction"*, c. 1858, mounted on card, credit, t. label, 350 x 430mm, (05-07-93, Sotheby-London, #64, illus.), photograph, albumen print (BP 920, DM 2297, FR 7741, Y 159,987).
$1361* *"On The Llugwy Near Bettws Y Coed"*, 1857, mounted on card, credit, 362 x 461mm, (05-07-93, Sotheby-London, #68, illus.), photograph, albumen print (BP 862, DM 2152, FR 7251, Y 149,857).
BI *River Scene, Probably Yorkshire*, c. 1854-57, ink s. recto, possibly from waxed paper neg., mount trimmed, est. BP7/900, (10-29-92, Christie-London, #27, illus.), 8⅛ x 7⅜ in., (20.6 x 18.7 cm.), photograph, salt print mounted on card.
BI *Salisbury Cathedral With River In Foreground And Photographer's Carriage (?)*, late 1850s, mounted on card, credit, est. BP 8/1,200, 405 x 365mm, (05-07-93, Sotheby-London, #67, illus.), photograph, albumen print.
BI *"Trajan, T. 93"*, c. 1857, p. t., photog.'s, pub.'s credits, orig. mount, est. BP 9/1,200, (10-29-92, Christie-London, #24, illus.), 13 x 10 in., (33 x 25.4 cm.), photograph, salt print.
BI *York Minster*, 1856, est. $2/300, (10-14-92, Swann, #186, illus.), image 8½ x 7½ in., (21.6 x 19.1 cm.), sheet 22 x 15 in., (21.6 x 19.1 cm.), photograph, photo-galvanograph.

FENTON, Roger/Francis FRITH
BI *Lincoln: The East End*, 1858, from neg. by Rogert Fenton, p. by Francis Frith, t. in unidentified hand, p. 1860s, est. $1/2,000, (10-15-92, Sotheby-NY, #84, illus.), 15⅞ x 13⅝ in., (40.3 x 34.6 cm.), photograph, albumen print.

FERDINAND, MAYER & CO., Lithographers
BI *Albany Street, Extended To Broadway (Peters, Amer. on Stone, p. 276)*, c. 1860, margins, good cond., losses, tear, light-stain, discoloration, ex-coll. Henry Graves and Percy R. Pyne, est. $4/5,000, (01-28-93, Sotheby-NY, #435, illus.), 10¼ x 15⅞ in., (260 x 403 mm.), sheet 14¼ x 19 in., (260 x 403 mm.), hand-colored lithograph.

FERNAND, S.
$100* *"Semer Du Ble, C'Est De L'Or Pour La France"*, 1918, Imp. de Montrouge, very good cond., (02-12-93, Cheval/Robert, #115), 21⅞ x 14³⁄₁₆ in., (55.6 x 36 cm.), poster (BP 70, DM 166, FR 561, Y 12,060).

FERNANDEZ, Agustin   b. Cuba 1928
BI *Blade*, Breakfast In Bed Series, s., d., num. II, pub. Galeria Colibri, prov., exhib., est. C$ 2/300, (12-01-92, Ritchie, #90, illus.), 30½ x 22 in., (77.5 x 55.9 cm.), color serigraph w/collage.

FERNANDEZ BARRIO, Jose
BI *"Tierras Castellanas"*, s., t., reserve P18,000, (02-03-93, Duran, #55), 20⅞ x 27¹⁵⁄₁₆ in., (53 x 71 cm.), engraving in color.

FERNEL, Fernand   c. 1872- c.1934
$502* *Sodanite. Boissons Gazeuses Instantanees. Anti-Rhume Sodanite*, c. 1900, Paris, Imp. P. Vercasson, cond. B+,

(06-11-93, Boisgirard, #70), 51³⁄₁₆ x 37 in., (130 x 94 cm.), poster (BP 330, DM 816, FR 2751, Y 53,263).

FERRANT, Angel   Spanish 1891-1959
BI *"El Anglo"*, #4/60, s., reserve P25,000, (02-03-93, Duran, #232), 13⅜ x 9⁷⁄₁₆ in., (34 x 24 cm.), etching.
$247* *"Dialogo Genesico"*, s., w/poem, (02-03-93, Duran, #233), 13⅜ x 9⁷⁄₁₆ in., (34 x 24 cm.), etching (BP 172, DM 407, FR 1379, Y 30,725, P 28,750).

FERRARESE SCHOOL, 15TH CENTURY
BI *Arithmetic (Artimetricha XXV) (Hind E. 1 25A)*, c. 1465, from set of 50 So-called Tarocchi of Mantegna, trimmed, stains, goodcond., est. BP 12/15,000, (06-30-93, Sotheby-London, #120, illus.), 7 x 3⅞ in., (178 x 98 mm.), engraving in greyish ink traces of gilding.

FERRIS, E.
$39* *Head Of A Child*, (02-12-93, DuMouchelle, #356, illus.), 9½ x 7½ in., (24.1 x 19.1 cm.), print (BP 27, DM 65, FR 219, Y 4703).

FERRIS, Edyth   American b. 1897
$193* *Spring, Independence Square*, 1956, s., #2/3, (06-11-93, Freemn/Fine Art, #61A), 33 x 10 in., (83.8 x 25.4 cm.), colored woodcut (BP 127, DM 314, FR 1058, Y 20,477).

FERRONI, Gianfranco
$588* *Cavalletto*, 1984, #39/100, s., d., (05-20-93, Finarte-Milan, #68), 14⁷⁄₁₆ x 9¾ in., (36.6 x 24.8 cm.), lithograph in colors (BP 377, DM 949, FR 3196, Y 64,929, L 863).
$666* *Oggetti E Aerografo (Mascherpa 39)*, 1979, #50/99, s., (05-20-93, Finarte-Milan, #67, illus.), 12⅜ x 11⅞ in., (31.5 x 30.2 cm.), lithograph (BP 427, DM 1075, FR 3620, Y 73,542, L 978).

FETTING, Rainer   German/American b. 1949
$523* *Man And Bird*, (19)87, s., d., num., (12-01-92, Karl/Faber, #611), 31¹¹⁄₁₆ x 17⁵⁄₁₆ in., (80.5 x 44 cm.), etching on Fabriano wove (BP 346, DM 834, FR 2841, Y 65,115).
BI *"Man And Candle II"*, (19)89, s., d., t., A/P, est. DM 1000, (12-01-92, Karl/Faber, #613), 18⅛ x 24⅝ in., (46 x 62.5 cm.), etching and aquatint in red on Arches wove.
$709* *"Man And Candle II"*, 1989, watermark, s., d., i. II A/P, (06-05-93, Grisebach, #574, illus.), 18⅛ x 24¹¹⁄₁₆ in., (46 x 62.7 cm.), red aquatint on handmade copper print paper (BP 467, DM 1149, FR 3874, Y 76,057).
$353* *Mann Und Vogel*, 1988, s., d., i. A.P., (06-12-93, Hauswedell/Nolt, #79), 31⅞ x 17½ in., (81 x 44.5 cm.), color etching on brownish Fabriano wove (BP 231, DM 575, FR 1931, Y 37,146).
BI *Shower*, 1989, s., d., t., i. A.P., est. DM 1,800, (06-12-93, Hauswedell/Nolt, #80), 23¾ x 35⅝ in., (60.3 x 90.5 cm.), color etching on thick wove.

FEURE, George de
$288* *Journal Des Ventes*, 1897, Les Maitres de l'Affiche blindstamp, p. Lemercier at Chaix, margins, good condition, (03-31-93, Butterfield, #5238), 11⅞ x 7⅞ in., (30.2 x 20 cm.), lithograph printed in color on wove (BP 190, DM 463, FR 1574, Y 33,119).
BI *Two Figures On A Balcony*, mono., est. $1,5/2,000, (06-09-93, Sotheby-Arcade, #236), 14 x 19½ in., (35.6 x 49.5 cm.), lithograph in colors.

FEURE, George de   1868-1943
BI *Chimeres Et Grimaces*, 1896/97, fold marks, staining, repaired tears, lit., est. BP 6/800, (02-04-93, Christie-S. Ken, #123, illus.), 31½ x 24 in., (80 x 61 cm.), color lithograph backed on linen stuck on card.
BI *Geneve*, c. 1890, tears, repairs, est. BP 9/1,200, (02-04-93, Christie-S. Ken, #124, illus.), 70½ x 25 in., (179.1 x 63.5 cm.), color lithograph on two sheets backed on linen.
BI *Touroff*, c. 1894, fold marks, scuffing, creases, est. BP 2/400, (02-04-93, Christie-S. Ken, #125, illus.), 51 x 37 in., (129.5 x 94 cm.), color lithograph backed on linen.

FEURE, Georges de   French 1868-1943
$819* *L'Huitre Preferee, 1896,* soiling, large margins, (02-24-93,
    Picard, #106), color lithograph on strong creme wove
    (BP 571, DM 1330, FR 4507, Y 96,104).
$409* *Le Marche Aux Puces, Bruges, 1896,* large margins, dust,
    (02-24-93, Picard, #107), color lithograph on thin chine
    (BP 285, DM 664, FR 2251, Y 47,993).

FEVRIER, C.
$179* *Office Marocain Du Tourisme, Rabat. Marokko,* good
    cond., (03-13-93, Laurin, #99), 39⅜ x 25⁹⁄₁₆ in., (100 x
    65 cm.), (BP 125, DM 298, FR 1013, Y 21,096).

FIALETTI, Odoardo   1573-1638
$2444* *Das Martyrium Des Heiligen Sebastian (Illus. Bartsch
    XXXVIII 3), c. 1606,* after Jacobo Tintoretto, early print,
    (06-23-93, Kornfeld, #50), etching (BP 1660, DM 4135,
    FR 13,910, Y 266,260, SF 3680).

FICHTER, Robert   b. 1939
    BI *Hurricane Signal, 1984,* s., t., d., num. 17/33 in ink, est.
    $1,2/1,500, (10-13-92, Christie-NY, #536, illus.), 19 x
    23¼ in., (48.3 x 59.1 cm.), photograph, cibachrome print.

FIEDLER, Herbert   1891-1962
$25* *"Composition Au Trait Blanc", #33/150,* s., (01-28-93,
    Pescheteau, #139), 30⁵⁄₁₆ x 23⅝ in., (77 x 60 cm.), pho-
    tolithograph on wove (BP 17, DM 40, FR 134, Y 3104).

FIELD, Jillian
    BI *Three Ladies,* s., est. $40/70, (03-12-93, DuMouchelle,
    #2470), 27 x 7½ in., (68.6 x 19.1 cm.), silkscreen.

FIELDING, Copley (after)
$46 *"Rough Weather" and "Teignmouth": Two,* engraved by C
    P Brandirds, (04-16-93, G.A. Key, #9), 8 x 12 in., (20.3
    x 30.5 cm.), b/w engraving (BP 30, DM 74, FR 251, Y
    5173).

FIELDING, N.
$107 *Cock Fighting: Six,* (04-16-93, G.A. Key, #102), 5 x 7
    in., (12.7 x 17.8 cm.), colored aquatints (BP 70, DM
    173, FR 584, Y 12,032).

FIENE, Ernest   German/American 1894-1965
    BI *Along The Hudson, 1928,* s., num. edition of 30, t., d.,
    est. $2/300, (03-24-93, Grogan, #89), 11 x 17 in., (27.9
    x 43.2 cm.), lithograph.
$110* *"Colonial Village",* s., d. 35, very good cond., (07-19-92,
    Bakker, #99, illus.), image 8¾ x 12 in., (22.2 x 30.5
    cm.), lithograph (BP 56, DM 160, FR 542, Y 13,675).
$77* *"Colonial Village",* s., d. 35, very good cond., (03-28-93,
    Bakker, #117), image 9 x 12¼ in., (22.9 x 31.1 cm.),
    lithograph (BP 52, DM 126, FR 427, Y 8962).
$275* *Cornhuskers, 1934,* s., d., t., i., full margins, good cond.,
    mat staining, foxing, creases, (02-24-93, Butterfield,
    #2818), 11 x 15¼ in., (279 x 387 mm.), lithograph on
    wove (BP 192, DM 446, FR 1513, Y 32,269).
$66* *"Midwinter",* s., d. 39, AAA, (12-11-92, DuMouchelle,
    #1476), 10½ x 9⅝ in., (26.7 x 24.4 cm.), lithograph (BP
    42, DM 104, FR 356, Y 8167).
$303* *New York At Night,* s., (02-14-93, Hanzel, #695), 11¾ x
    9⅛ in., (29.8 x 23.2 cm.), etching (BP 213, DM 502,
    FR 1700, Y 36,541).
$375* *"Waterfront, Manhattan" (Library Of Congress), 1931,* s.,
    d., #94/100, excell. cond., (05-15-93, Cleveland, #128,
    illus.), 11 x 18 in., (27.9 x 45.7 cm.), lithograph (BP
    244, DM 603, FR 2027, Y 41,570).
$110* *"Winter Evening",* s., d. 36, very good cond., (03-28-93,
    Bakker, #222), image 8¼ x 12 in., (21 x 30.5 cm.),
    lithograph (BP 74, DM 179, FR 610, Y 12,803).

FIERET, G.P.
$2300* *Untitled (Nude Study), 1963,* s. by photog., studio (c)
    stamp on image, (04-06-93, Sotheby-NY, #456A, illus.),
    19½ x 15⅝ in., photograph (BP 1519, DM 3705, FR
    12,548, Y 262,318).

FIERET, Gerard Petrus   b. 1924
$2420* *Untitled, Nude Study,* 1960s, s. in ink, (c) credit stamps,
    mounted, (10-13-92, Christie-NY, #537, illus.), 15⅝ x
    19⅝ in., (39.7 x 49.8 cm.), photograph, gelatin silver
    print (BP 1409, DM 3545, FR 12,046, Y 293,440).

FIETZ, Gerhard   b. 1910
$290* *Komposition Auf Schwarz, 1954,* s., d., (12-01-92, Karl/
    Faber, #614), 13⅜ x 18¹¹⁄₁₆ in., (34 x 47.5 cm.), color
    lithograph on linen (BP 192, DM 462, FR 1575, Y
    36,106).

FIGURA, Hans   American b. Hungary 1898
$110* *1930's,* s., ed. 225/250, (11-12-92, Freemn/Fine Art, #69),
    mat 17½ x 14 in., (44.5 x 35.6 cm.), color aquatint on
    silk (BP 72, DM 174, FR 588, Y 13,639).
$20* *Along The Shore,* s., #149/250, (05-15-93, Cleveland,
    #385), 7½ x 8¼ in., (19.1 x 21 cm.), colored etching
    (BP 13, DM 32, FR 108, Y 2217).
$66* *Alpine Village,* label verso; s., (11-13-92, DuMouchelle,
    #2463), 13½ x 16¾ in., (34.3 x 42.5 cm.), color etching
    (BP 43, DM 104, FR 349, Y 8192).
    BI *"Canal View", "Topographical Cityscape",* and *"View Of
    Alleyway": Three,* each s., est. $400/600, (09-17-92,
    Sloan, #1456), largest 10¼ x 12¾ in., (26 x 32.4 cm.),
    etching and aquatint, two on silk.
$55* *"Michael's Gate",* s., tape stains, hinges, good cond., (10-
    31-92, Cleveland, #279), color etching on silk (BP 35,
    DM 85, FR 287, Y 6813).
    BI *"Red Sails",* s., glue residue, fine cond., est. $75-125,
    (10-31-92, Cleveland, #280), 6½ x 7¾ in., (16.5 x 19.7
    cm.), etching in colors.
$77* *"Rottenberg"* and *"Newschwanstein": A Pair,* (02-12-93,
    DuMouchelle, #1486), approx. 10 x 12 in., (25.4 x 30.5
    cm.), etching (BP 54, DM 128, FR 432, Y 9286).
$10* *The Seine,* s., good cond., light struck, (05-15-93, Cleve-
    land, #384), 5¾ x 9 in., (14.6 x 22.9 cm.), etching in
    colors (BP 7, DM 16, FR 54, Y 1109).
$33* *"Snowy Landscape",* s., #14/250, very good cond., (12-
    04-92, Doyle, #95), 17½ x 14 in., (445 x 356 mm.),
    color aquatint (BP 21, DM 53, FR 178, Y 4120).

FILLACIER, J.
$552* *Chamonix. S.N.C.F., c. 1940,* p. Gaston Gorde, repaired
    tears, excell. cond., (02-04-93, Christie-S. Ken, #7, illus.),
    38 x 23 in., (96.5 x 58.4 cm.), color lithograph backed
    on linen (BP 385, DM 909, FR 3082, Y 68,665).

FILMER, Lady
$460* *The Marshaw Sisters, c. 1870s: Four,* ink t., (04-08-93,
    Christie-NY, #4, illus.), 11¼ x 9 in., (28.6 x 22.9 cm.),
    photograph, photocollage, albumen prints mounted on
    paper w/applied watercolor, gouache and metallic pigment
    (BP 302, DM 739, FR 2501, Y 52,202).

FINDLAY, Irene E.   20th cent.
    BI *forest Forms,* s., t., d. (19)74, #4/5; i. verso, est. $250/
    350, (07-03-92, Sloan, #1070), 9 x 14 in., (22.9 x 35.6
    cm.), etching and aquatint.

FINE ART SOCIETY LTD., Publisher
    BI *Portrait Of A Seated Lady", 1898,* indistinctly s., blinds-
    tamp, margins, staining, est. BP 40/60, (11-19-92, Bon-
    hams-Chelsea, #84), plate 20¼ x 16 in., (51.4 x 40.6
    cm.), mezzotint.

FINGER, Max
    BI *Cafe Atlantic,* fold marks, surface dirt, est. BP 4/600,
    (02-04-93, Christie-S. Ken, #160), 34 x 22 in., (86.4 x
    55.9 cm.), color lithograph.

FINI, Leonor   Italian b. 1908
    BI *Carmilla: Twenty-Three,* folio, illus. edit., #33/267, s.;
    just. pg. s., est. $6/9,000, (12-12-92, Wolf, #24, illus.),
    18 x 23 in., (45.7 x 58.4 cm.), 8 color serigraphs, 15
    color lithographs on Arches.
$176* *Carnet 2,* s., #93/275, (12-13-92, Hindman, #302), 16¾ x
    14¼ in., color drypoint (BP 113, DM 277, FR 943, Y
    21,774).
$275* *"Carnet 2",* s., 95/275, (12-12-92, Goldberg, #517),
    image 17 x 14½ in., (43.2 x 36.8 cm.), color lithograph
    (BP 176, DM 433, FR 1485, Y 34,030).
$550* *"Cinderella On A Broomstick", c. 1965, "Harmonika Zug"*
    and *"StandingWoman",* s., full margins, Standing Woman
    creases, surface scratch, (05-27-93, Swann, #111), 15½
    x 11¾ in., (39.4 x 29.8 cm.), etching, color lithograph
    (BP 352, DM 883, FR 2975, Y 58,962).
$495* *"Eliza", c. 1970* and *"Maria", c. 1970: Two,* s., full mar-
    gins, #118/200 and #159/175, stain, (12-08-92, Swann,

#104), first 7¼ x 11¾ in., (18.4 x 29.8 cm.), second, sight 18 x 16 in., (18.4 x 29.8 cm.), color lithograph (BP 310, DM 771, FR 2627, Y 61,353).

$330* *Ginger Persian Cat,* s. Leonor Fini, num. 168/180, very good cond.?, (10-09-92, Skinner, #223, illus.), sight 21 x 17¼ in., (53.3 x 43.8 cm.), color lithograph on paper (BP 196, DM 492, FR 1667, Y 40,244).

BI *Man And Woman,* s. Leonor Fini, num. EA XXIV/XXX, est. $3/500, (04-25-93, Bakker, #51), 22 x 15 in., (55.9 x 38.1 cm.), color lithograph.

BI *Mask,* s., num. E.A., est. $3/500, (05-16-93, Hanzel, #473), sight 20½ x 16 in., (52.1 x 40.6 cm.), color lithograph.

$367* *Monsieur Venus: Nineteen,* s., #50/75, good cond., (06-28-93, Loudmer, #40), between 5⅞ x 7⅞ in., (150 x 200 mm.), and 16 5/16 x 12⅝ in., (150 x 200 mm.), etchings in bistre on Japan nacre (BP 246, DM 624, FR 2101, Y 38,939).

$248* *Portrait Of A Lady,* s., #161/220, (10-30-92, Sloan, #1592), sight 21½ x 13 in., (54.6 x 33 cm.), color lithograph (BP 159, DM 382, FR 1294, Y 30,720).

BI *Three Figures,* s., est. $3/500, (05-16-93, Hanzel, #468), 14 x 14 in., (35.6 x 35.6 cm.), lithograph.

$58* *Trois Figures,* s., #259/290, editeur's drystamp, pinholes, (06-28-93, Loudmer, #41), 14 15/16 x 11¼ in., (380 x 285 mm.), sh 26 9/16 x 16¼ in., (380 x 285 mm.), color etching on handmade laid paper tinted ocre w/Auvergne watermark (BP 39, DM 99, FR 332, Y 6154).

$586* *Untitled,* s., #28/75, margins, good cond.?, (12-09-92, Sotheby-Amstrdm, #573), 22⅝ x 15⅜ in., (575 x 390 mm.), color lithograph on wove (BP 374, DM 920, FR 3139, Y 72,660, G 1035).

$132* *Untitled,* s., num. 118/185, good cond., (10-31-92, Cleveland, #371, illus.), 27½ x 20½ in., (69.9 x 52.1 cm.), lithograph in colors (BP 85, DM 203, FR 689, Y 16,351).

$283* *Visage De Femme,* #216/275, s. Leonor Fini, (04-20-93, Encans, #117), 19 11/16 x 16¾ in., (50 x 42.5 cm.), lithograph (BP 183, DM 451, FR 1522, Y 31,226, C$ 355).

$159* *"Le Visage Endormi",* s. Leonor Fini, #2/225, (02-16-93, Encans, #114), 19 11/16 x 14¾ in., (50 x 37.5 cm.), lithograph (BP 110, DM 260, FR 879, Y 19,049, C$ 200).

$105* *"Visage",* #39/250, s., (01-28-93, Pescheteau, #142), 25 9/16 x 18⅞ in., (65 x 48 cm.), color lithograph on wove (BP 69, DM 166, FR 563, Y 13,037).

FINN

BI *The Quick-Starting Pair, Shell Oil & Petrol, Coachman & Horses, 1929,* ref. #229, cond. 2, printing defects, est. BP 3/400, (10-13-92, Phillips-London, #80, illus.), 29 15/16 x 44 11/16 in., (76 x 113.5 cm.), color lithograph.

FINSLER, Hans Swiss 1891-1972

$1380* *Folded Fabric (Avant-Garde Photography in Germany, p. 12), c. 1929,* (04-06-93, Sotheby-NY, #332, illus.), 9⅛ x 6 in., photograph (BP 911, DM 2223, FR 7529, Y 157,391).

FIORENTINO, Rosso (after)

BI *The Annunciation (Bruillot 1, vol. I, Gaspare Osello; Nagler, vol. Iand vol. II, Gaspare Osello, Gabriel Fesis or Jacques Androuet Du Cerceau; Robert-Dusmesnil, vol. VIII, Rene Boyvin), before 1568,* trimmed on or inside platemark, brown stain in image, excellent cond., laid, est. BP 6/8,000, (12-01-92, Christie-London, #27, illus.), sheet 10 5/16 x 18 15/16 in., (262 x 481 mm.), engraving.

$5827* *Mars And Venus (B. XI, G. G. Caraglio, 51, copy), 1575,* trimmed on or inside platemark, staining, excell. cond., laid, (12-01-92, Christie-London, #28, illus.), sheet 16½ x 13 5/16 in., (419 x 338 mm.), engraving (BP 3850, DM 9288, FR 31,651, Y 725,473).

FIORINI, Marcel

BI *Untitled,* s., annot. Epreuve d'artiste, margins, good cond.?, est. $3/500, (05-19-93, Butterfield, #2057), 13¾ x 19⅝ in., (349 x 498 mm.), etching and aquatint in colors on wove.

FIS (Hans FISCHER) 1909-1958

$79* *Drei Figuren Aus Einem Umzug, 1958,* sig. stamp, estate stamp, (09-04-92, Germann, #334), 12⅛ x 18 11/16 in., (308 x 475 mm.), pen lithograph (BP 40, DM 111, FR 377, Y 9724, SF 98).

$240* *Katze Und Kater (Scheiddegger 96), 1947,* sig. stamp, estate stamp, (09-04-92, Germann, #335), 9 15/16 x 13⅞ in., (252 x 353 mm.), etching (BP 120, DM 336, FR 1145, Y 29,542, SF 299).

$83* *Schellenklauses (Scheidegger 184), 1951-52,* stone mono., estate stamp, (09-04-92, Germann, #330), 22⅜ x 31 5/16 in., (568 x 795 mm.), lithograph (BP 42, DM 116, FR 396, Y 10,217, SF 104).

$69* *Schreitende Katze (Scheidegger 318), 1957,* sig. stamp, (09-04-92, Germann, #336), 22¼ x 27⅞ in., (565 x 708 mm.), color lithograph (BP 35, DM 97, FR 329, Y 8493, SF 86).

BI *Le Ventre (Scheidegger 296), 1956/59,* mono. in plate, est. SF 150/170, (10-14-92, Germann, #515), 12 15/16 x 9⅞ in., (328 x 251 mm.), etching.

FISCHER, Oskar 1892-1955

$155* *Telegrafie,* s., (09-25-92, Granier, #2845), sheet 8 11/16 x 6 5/16 in., (22 x 16 cm.), linocut on machine hand-made (BP 91, DM 230, FR 777, Y 18,709).

FISCHER-HANSEN, Else

$75* *Komposition, 1973,* s. Else Fischer-Hansen, saertryk, (06-03-93, Kunsthallen, #178), lithograph in colors (BP 49, DM 120, FR 405, Y 8044, DK 460).

FISCHL, Eric American b. 1948

$4888* *Beach Balls (Glenn & Barnes p. 78), 1982,* s., d., #7/40, blindstamp, p. Aeropress, pub. Corinthian Editions, full margins, good cond., (05-15-93, Sotheby-NY, #966, illus.), sheet 54 x 38⅜ in., (137.2 x 97.5 cm.), soft ground etching, aquatintm sugar lift and spit bite in colors (BP 3178, DM 7862, FR 26,422, Y 541,847).

$2185* *Brooklyn Academy Of Music II: Untitled, 1988-89,* s., #26/75, pub. Parasol Press, Ltd., full margins, good cond., handling creases, (05-15-93, Sotheby-NY, #969, illus.), 12½ x 12¼ in., (31.8 x 31.1 cm.), etching and aquatint in colors (BP 1421, DM 3515, FR 11,811, Y 242,213).

$2588* *Digging Kids (G. & B. p. 78), 1982,* s., d., #19/40, pub. Aeropress Getler/Pall, full margins, good cond.?, (05-15-93, Sotheby-NY, #967, illus.), sheet 54 x 38⅝ in., (137.2 x 98.1 cm.), soft ground etching and aquatint in tones of gray on T.H. Saunders paper (BP 1683, DM 4163, FR 13,989, Y 286,886).

$3450* *Dog, 1989,* from portfolio Untitled, d., #33/100, pub. Parasol Press, Ltd., fullmargins, good cond., handling creases, (05-15-93, Sotheby-NY, #971, illus.), 35¼ x 54 in., (89.5 x 137.2 cm.), aquatint in colors (BP 2243, DM 5549, FR 18,649, Y 382,441).

$7150* *Floating Islands (Glenn p. 24), 1985,* complete portfolio, five etchings, s., #20/45, pub. Peter Blum Edition, full sheets, good cond., portfolio, (11-07-92, Sotheby-NY, #551, illus.), four sheets 11⅝ x 31¾ in., (295 x 806 mm.), one sheet 22¾ x 16¾ in., (295 x 806 mm.), five etchings w/aquatint, drypoint and scraping p. in colors (BP 4675, DM 11,416, FR 38,586, Y 882,498).

$2760* *Scenes And Sequences, New York, Peter Blum Edition, 1989,* s., d. 86, i. 12.11.86, num. 12, full margins, excell. cond., (05-11-93, Christie-NY, #415), sheet 13⅜ x 18½ in., (340 x 470 mm.), monotype in yellow and grey on wove (BP 1762, DM 4348, FR 14,650, Y 303,597).

$1150* *Shower, 1987,* s., #83/100, blindstamp of printer, Aldo Crommelynck, pub. Parasol Press, Ltd., full margins, good cond., creases, (02-11-93, Sotheby-NY, #330), 15 9/16 x 19½ in., (395 x 495 mm.), soft (molle) ground etching, burnishing, aquatint on Hahnemuhle (BP 811, DM 1905, FR 6446, Y 138,638).

$1100* *Shower, 1987,* s., num. 43/100, pub. Parasol Press, full margins, foxmark, excell. cond., (09-19-92, Christie-E, #104, illus.), sheet 22⅛ x 25¼ in., (56.2 x 64.1 cm.), etching and aquatint in grey and black on wove (BP 633, DM 1647, FR 5641, Y 137,055).

BI *Shower, 1987,* s., #11/100, blindstamp, p. Aldo Crommelynck, pub. Parasol Press, full margins, good cond., est. $1,2/1,500, (05-15-93, Sotheby-NY, #968), 15⅜ x 19⅜ in., (39.1 x 49.2 cm.), soft ground etching, burnishing and aquatint on Hahnemuhle paper.

BI *Untitled, 1988,* s., d., #92/200, s. by printers Shunzo Matsuda and Tadashi Toda, pub.Crown Point Press, blindstamp, full margins, good cond., est. BP 6/800, (06-30-93, Sotheby-London, #788, illus.), 9⅜ x 10½ in., (238 x 267 mm.), color woodcut.

$6900* *Untitled, 1989: Four,* complete portfolio, each s., d., #17/100, 8/100, 8/100 and 8/100, pub. Parasol Press, Ltd., full margins, good cond., creases, (05-15-93, Sotheby-NY, #970, illus.), each sheet 35⅜ x 54 in., (89.9 x 137.2 cm.), aquatint in colors (BP 4486, DM 11,099, FR 37,297, Y 764,882).

BI *Untitled, 1991,* 85/125, s., pub. Miral, est. SF 12/1500, (10-14-92, Germann, #161, illus.), 15¹⁵⁄₁₆ x 20¹⁄₁₆ in., (405 x 510 mm.), color relief print on Okawara.

$921* *Untitled, 1991,* #85/125, s., pub. Miral, (09-04-92, Germann, #338, illus.), 15¹⁵⁄₁₆ x 20¹⁄₁₆ in., (405 x 510 mm.), color relief print on Okawara paper (BP 462, DM 1291, FR 4394, Y 113,368, SF 1150).

$1320* *Untitled, Beach, 1988,* s., d., #23/200, s. by p., blindstamp pub. Crown Point Press, full margins, very good cond., skinned spots, (10-28-92, Butterfield, #2947, illus.), 9⁷⁄₁₆ x 10⁷⁄₁₆ in., (240 x 265 mm.), color woodcut on Japan (BP 841, DM 2039, FR 6922, Y 161,963).

BI *Untitled, Inner Tube, 1990,* s., d., #45/100, pub. Parasol Press, full margins, good cond., creases, buckling, est. $2/3,000, (10-28-92, Butterfield, #2948, illus.), sheet 35 x 54 in., (88.9 x 137.2 cm.), color aquatint on wove.

FISH, Janet American b. 1938

$495* *Four Glasses, 1976,* s., d., #92/150, (06-12-93, Hauswedell/Nolt, #82, illus.), 27⁹⁄₁₆ x 20¹⁄₁₆ in., (70 x 51 cm.), color lithograph on Arches (BP 324, DM 806, FR 2708, Y 52,089).

FISHBOURNE, R.W.

$1650* *"Steamer Autocrat",* pub. c. 1847, (12-05-92, Neal, #568, illus.), image 17 x 26½ in., (43.2 x 67.3 cm.), duotone lithograph (BP 1033, DM 2572, FR 8767, Y 204,436).

FISHER, A. Hugh

$358* *"Etruscan Gateway, Perugia"; "Hall Stairs"; "Winchester College"; "ThGhetto, Siena"; and San Giovano, Siena: Four,* each s., last 2 t., i., margins, good cond., 1st w/ light-staining, surface soiling, prop. Print Corner Coll. of Elizabeth and Charles Whitmore, (02-24-93, Butterfield, #2819), from 7⅞ x 6⅞ in., (200 x 175 mm.), to 10¹⁵⁄₁₆ x 6¹⁵⁄₁₆ in., (200 x 175 mm.), etching & drypoint on wove & laid (BP 250, DM 581, FR 1970, Y 42,009).

FISHER, Harrison American 1875-1934

$110* *Pictures In Color, New York, 1910: Fifteen,* (05-01-93, Skinner, #99), 17½ x 12⅜ in., (44.5 x 31.5 cm.), chromolithograph plates and frontispiece (BP 70, DM 174, FR 587, Y 12,205).

$330* *Young Red Cross Nurse Reaching Out As If To A Wounded Soldier, With Soldier Marching In The Background,* scattered foxing, s. Fisher in pl., s. on image, c. 1917, (04-29-93, Swann, #235), 19½ x 23½ in., (49.5 x 59.7 cm.), color lithograph poster (BP 210, DM 522, FR 1759, Y 36,712).

FISHER, Robert M.

$71* *Wolf In Mountain Landscape,* #10/45, s., num., (03-10-93, Maynard, #323), 16½ x 25½ in., (41.9 x 64.8 cm.), silkscreen (BP 50, DM 118, FR 401, Y 8388, C$ 88).

FISHER, Vernon American b. 1943

BI *Dark Night Full Of Stars, 1984,* s., d. '85, #11/35, blindstamp publisher, Landfall Press, very good ccond.?, est. $6/800, (05-19-93, Butterfield, #2165), 30 x 33½ in., (762 x 851 mm.), lithograph in colors on wove.

FITCH, W. and L. SNELLING (after)

$1760* *Genus Lilium: Four,* (03-24-93, Doyle, #29), 20 x 13½ in., (50.8 x 34.3 cm.), hand-colored lithograph (BP 1192, DM 2874, FR 9783, Y 206,791).

$1430* *Genus Lilium: Four,* (03-24-93, Doyle, #28), 20 x 13½ in., (50.8 x 34.3 cm.), hand-colored lithograph (BP 968, DM 2335, FR 7949, Y 168,018).

FITCH, W.H.

$3105* *Orchids, 1858: Eight,* from Warner's Select Orchidacious Plants, (03-03-93, Sotheby-Arcade, #146), sight 17 x 12 in., (43.2 x 30.5 cm.), hand-colored lithograph (BP 2142, DM 5113, FR 17,346, Y 362,818).

FITREMAN, Gerard French b. 1946

$89* *"Croix De Zut",* #31/90, s. G. Fitreman, (03-16-93, Encans, #170), 28⁹⁄₁₆ x 21⅝ in., (72.5 x 55 cm.), lithograph on Arches (BP 61, DM 148, FR 503, Y 10,407, C$ 111).

$46* *"Double Face",* #19/90, s. Fitreman, t., (09-15-92, Encans, #145), 33¹⁄₁₆ x 22¹⁄₁₆ in., (84 x 56 cm.), etching (BP 25, DM 68, FR 232, Y 5711, C$ 56).

FITSCHMANN-STEINBESSER, Marianne

$121* *"Dancing Nymphs",* s., inits. plate, (02-27-93, Dunning, #101), 8¼ x 7¼ in., (21 x 18.4 cm.), etching (BP 85, DM 199, FR 676, Y 14,284).

FITTON, Hedley English 1859-1929

BI *Amboise,* s., t. in plate, est. $100/150, (10-30-92, Sloan, #831), 16¾ x 9½ in., (42.5 x 24.1 cm.), etching and drypoint.

$60* *Amboise, 1928,* s., i. "Amboise" in plate, pub. Kennedy & Co., laid down, front mat glued down, (05-15-93, Cleveland, #386), 11¾ x 9⁷⁄₁₆ in., (29.8 x 24 cm.), etching and drypoint (BP 39, DM 97, FR 324, Y 6651).

$193* *"Cathedral Interior" and "View Along The Riverbank": Two,* each s.; one s. in plate, (09-17-92, Sloan, #1434), larger 14⅞ x 18⅞ in., (37.8 x 47.9 cm.), etching (BP 108, DM 287, FR 981, Y 24,029).

$125* *Chateau Des Contes, Ghent,* s., (02-04-93, Sloan, #721), 14½ x 15 in., (36.8 x 38.1 cm.), etching and drypoint (BP 87, DM 206, FR 698, Y 15,549).

$275* *European City Square,* s.(12-10-92, Sloan, #2088), 15⅜ x 16⅞ in., (39.1 x 42.9 cm.), drypoint etching (BP 177, DM 435, FR 1486, Y 34,018).

FITZ, Grancel 1894-1963

$1100* *Advertisement For Lucky Strikes,* 1930s, (10-15-92, Sotheby-NY, #210, illus.), 3 x 5¾ in., (7.6 x 14.6 cm.), photograph, gelatin silver print (BP 673, DM 1637, FR 5553, Y 131,974).

BI *American Family At Breakfast, c. 1935,* credit stamp, est. $1/1,500, (04-08-93, Christie-NY, #282, illus.), 13⅜ x 16¾ in., (34 x 42.5 cm.), photograph, gelatin silver print.

BI *Baseball Game, 1930's,* photog. stamp, est. $3/4,000, (11-16-92, Butterfield, #5964, illus.), 10⅛ x 11¾ in., (257.6 x 299 mm.), photograph, gelatin silver print.

$920* *Camel Cigarettes Advertisement, c. 1923,* credit stamp, (04-08-93, Christie-NY, #284, illus.), 4¼ x 2¼ in., (10.8 x 5.7 cm.), photograph, gelatin silver print (BP 603, DM 1478, FR 5003, Y 104,403).

$935* *Family At Train Station,* 1930s, (04-07-93, Swann, #462, illus.), 13 x 18 in., photograph, silver print (BP 618, DM 1512, FR 5118, Y 106,226).

$385* *Fisherman Smoking (Ad For Camel Cigarettes),* photog.'s handstamp, 1930s, (04-07-93, Swann, #463, illus.), 10½ x 13¼ in., photograph, silver print (BP 254, DM 623, FR 2107, Y 43,740).

$1320* *George Gershwin At The Piano,* handstamps, 1930's, (10-14-92, Swann, #454, illus.), 6½ x 6⅜ in., (16.5 x 16.2 cm.), photograph, silver print (BP 775, DM 1932, FR 6551, Y 159,961).

BI *Glassware Study, c. 1927,* credit stamp, est. $1/1,500, (04-08-93, Christie-NY, #283, illus.), 5⅞ x 10⅛ in., (14.9 x 25.7 cm.), photograph, gelatin silver print.

BI *Illustration For U.S. Shoe Company, 1930's,* s., t., annot., typed label, est. $800/1,000, (11-16-92, Butterfield, #5966, illus.), 10⅞ x 6⅝ in., (276.7 x 168.6 mm.), photograph, gelatin silver print.

$660* *Legs,* photog.'s blindstamp, 1930s, (04-07-93, Swann, #464, illus.), 11½ x 7 in., photograph, silver print (BP 436, DM 1067, FR 3612, Y 74,983).

$385* *Men And Women On Bleachers,* handstamp, 1930's, (10-14-92, Swann, #456, illus.), 14 x 11 in., (35.6 x 27.9 cm.), photograph, silver print (BP 226, DM 563, FR 1911, Y 46,655).

$660* *Nude Abstraction, 1930's,* photog. stamp, (11-16-92, Butterfield, #5965, illus.), 9⅝ x 8¼ in., (244.9 x 209.9 mm.), photograph, gelatin silver print (BP 435, DM 1052, FR 3545, Y 82,079).

$467* *Photomontage (Huge Baby With Mother In High Chair),* handstamp, 1930's, (10-14-92, Swann, #457, illus.), 16 x 12 in., (40.6 x 30.5 cm.), photograph, silver print (BP 274, DM 683, FR 2318, Y 56,592).

BI *Pop Warner Football, c. 1932,* est. $1,5/1,800, (10-13-92, Christie-NY, #209, illus.), 8⅝ x 12¼ in., (21.9 x 31.1 cm.), photograph, gelatin silver print from sandwiches neg.'s.

$440* *Woman Holding Mask,* handstamp, 1930's, (10-14-92, Swann, #458, illus.), 11¾ x 15¾ in., (29.8 x 40 cm.), photograph, silver print (BP 258, DM 644, FR 2184, Y 53,320).

BI *Woman With Silver Fox Stole,* photog.'s handstamp, notations, 1930s, est. $6/900, (04-07-93, Swann, #465, illus.), 12½ x 9¼ in., photograph, silver print.

FITZGERALD, R.

$97* *The Red Boy,* s., margins, (08-20-92, Bonhams-Chelsea, #5), plate 18¾ x 13¾ in., (47.6 x 34.9 cm.), mezzotint in colors (BP 50, DM 140, FR 477, Y 12,249).

FIX-MASSEAU, Pierre b. 1905

$293* *Ch. De Fer De L'Etat: Le Mont Saint-Michel, "Merveille De L'Occident",* good cond., (01-23-93, Ribeyre/Baron, #58), 39³⁄₁₆ x 24⁷⁄₁₆ in., (99.5 x 62 cm.), poster (BP 192, DM 466, FR 1576, Y 36,671).

BI *Etat, 1936,* p. Edita, cond. 1, creasing, light staining, laid on linen, est. BP 3/500, (10-13-92, Phillips-London, #20), 39⅜ x 24⁷⁄₁₆ in., (100 x 62 cm.), color lithograph.

$126* *P.L.M. Et C.I.W.L.: Cote D'Azur, Pullmann Express,* reprint, very good cond., (01-23-93, Ribeyre/Baron, #3), 34¹³⁄₁₆ x 22¼ in., (88.5 x 56.5 cm.), poster on wove (BP 82, DM 200, FR 678, Y 15,770).

$189* *Les Produits Cadet Roussel En Direct De La Campagne,* cond. B, (03-16-93, Boisgirard, #109), 47¼ x 62¹⁵⁄₁₆ in., (120 x 160 cm.), poster (BP 131, DM 314, FR 1068, Y 22,100).

$998* *SNCF. Bon Voyage Et Bonne Neige. "Alpes, Pyrenees, Jura, Vosges, Massif Central",* very good cond., (03-15-93, Arcole, #90), 38¹⁵⁄₁₆ x 47¹³⁄₁₆ in., (99 x 121.5 cm.), (BP 695, DM 1658, FR 5635, Y 118,218).

$288* *Le Transport Gratuit, 1935,* p. EDITA, (06-09-93, Sotheby-Arcade, #241), sheet approx. 38¾ x 24⅝ in., (98.4 x 62.5 cm.), lithograph in colors (BP 190, DM 471, FR 1584, Y 30,629).

FIZEAU, Louis Armand Hippolyte (circle of)

$4540* *Facade Of The Seminaire, Place St Sulpice, Paris, c. 1843,* plate 70 x 80mm, (05-07-93, Sotheby-London, #101, illus.), photograph, engraving from etched daguerrotype plate (BP 2875, DM 7178, FR 24,188, Y 499,890).

FJAESTAD, Maja 1873-1961

$238* *"Angsblommor" (Handtryck 23),* s., (04-17-93, Falkkloos, #118), 8¼ x 9¹³⁄₁₆ in., (21 x 25 cm.), woodcut in colors (BP 155, DM 381, FR 1286, Y 26,465, SK 1760).

FLACK, Audrey American b. 1931

$110* *Banana Split Sundae, 1980,* from Presidential Portfolio, 1980, s., #39/150, pub. Carter/Mondale campaign, good cond.?, (12-12-92, Weschler, #118), image 18 x 24 in., (45.7 x 61 cm.), collotype w/embossing (BP 71, DM 173, FR 594, Y 13,612).

FLAGG, James Montgomery American 1877-1960

$275* *"I Am Telling You" and "Boys And Girls": Two,* posters for War Savings Stamps, A cond., creasing, (08-06-92, Swann, #131, illus.), 30 x 20 in., (76.2 x 50.8 cm.), (BP 144, DM 406, FR 1372, Y 35,077).

$275* *I Want You For U.S. Army,* (02-14-93, Hanzel, #707), 39 x 29 in., (99.1 x 73.7 cm.), color lithographic poster (BP 194, DM 456, FR 1543, Y 33,164).

$1100* *"I Want You, For U.S. Army", c. 1917,* fold creasing, repair, two stamps, lit., (09-12-92, Dunning, #110, illus.), 40 x 30 in., (101.6 x 76.2 cm.), poster laid on cloth (BP 569, DM 1583, FR 5382, Y 136,290).

$9900* *Lost Horizon, 1936,* near mint cond., (paper), (12-12-92, Hollywd Poster, #89, illus.), poster (BP 6348, DM 15,598, FR 53,456, Y 1,225,096).

$105 *Side By Side Britannia, 1918,* very good cond., (09-24-92, Alderfer, #253, illus.), 27 x 20 in., (68.6 x 50.8 cm.), (BP 61, DM 156, FR 528, Y 12,631).

$770* *U.S. Army, "I Want You", 1941,* A- cond., (08-06-92, Swann, #130, illus.), 38 x 25 in., (96.5 x 63.5 cm.), (BP 402, DM 1138, FR 3842, Y 98,214).

$165* *Wake Up, America! - Civilization Calls,* (02-14-93, Hanzel, #711), 39 x 26 in., (99.1 x 66 cm.), color lithographic poster (BP 116, DM 274, FR 926, Y 19,899).

FLAMEN, Albert

$858* *Divers Especes De Poissons De Mer, Troisieme Partie (B. 6, 25-36): Set Of Twelve,* 2nd state of 3, otherwise 2nd final state, margins, trimmed, mounted,stains, discoloration, defects, (06-30-93, Sotheby-London, #121), each c. 4¼ x 7 in., (108 x 178 mm.), etching (BP 575, DM 1463, FR 4937, Y 91,932).

FLAMING, Francois

$193* *"Theatre De L'Opera-Comique",* p. Dourgerie and Cie, (08-05-92, Boos, #586), approx. 53 x 29¼ in., (134.6 x 74.3 cm.), color lithograph (BP 101, DM 285, FR 963, Y 24,580).

FLANAGAN, Barry English b. 1941

$256* *("Landscape In Dark Red") and ("Landscape In Dark Green"), 1976: Two,* each s., d., first #10/60, second #78/100, margins, good cond., (12-03-92, Sotheby-London, #663, illus.), sheet 15 x 22¼ in., (380 x 565 mm.), sheet 7½ x 15⅛ in., (380 x 565 mm.), linocuts in red and green respectively on wove (BP 165, DM 403, FR 1374, Y 31,853).

$375* *Loch Ness, 1976: Set Of Six,* s., d., i. w/plate numbers, #24/50, full margins, good cond., (12-03-92, Sotheby-London, #662, illus.), etchings on wove (BP 242, DM 590, FR 2013, Y 46,659).

FLAVIN, Dan American b. 1933

BI *Sails, 1986,* s., d., est. DM 1,500, (11-20-92, Lempertz, #531), 9⁹⁄₁₆ x 30¹⁄₁₆ in., (24.3 x 76.3 cm.), lithograph on paper.

FLECKENSTEIN, Louis

BI *Portrait Of Betallo Rubino, 1917,* photog.'s sig., est. $6/900, (04-07-93, Swann, #466, illus.), 12 x 9 in., photograph, toned platinum(?) print.

FLEISCHMANN, Trude b. 1895

$805* *"Autumn",* 1930s, s., photog.'s stamps, t., (05-23-93, Butterfield, #3413, illus.), 7¼ x 7 in., photograph, gelatin silver print (BP 524, DM 1316, FR 4430, Y 88,980).

$3163* *Bertha Reidinger, Dancer: Two,* each w/photog. blindstamp on image, s., i. by photog., d. December 1929, (04-06-93, Sotheby-NY, #334, illus.), photograph (BP 2089, DM 5096, FR 17,256, Y 360,744).

BI *Big Laundry, 1940's,* s., t. by photog., est. $2/3,000, (10-15-92, Sotheby-NY, #423, illus.), 13 x 11 in., (33 x 27.9 cm.), photograph, gelatin silver print.

$3300* *Camping Ground In Istria (Italy), 1931,* s., d. by photog. in ink, studio stamp, reprod. limit. stamps, (10-15-92, Sotheby-NY, #421, illus.), 18⅝ x 15⅝ in., (47.3 x 39.7 cm.), photograph, gelatin silver print (BP 2019, DM 4912, FR 16,658, Y 395,921).

$1100* *"Die Dame Im Bad", 1936 (Fotografin In Wien, p. 126),* s., i., photog. label, (11-16-92, Butterfield, #5968, illus.), 10¼ x 9¼ in., (260.8 x 235.4 mm.), photograph, gelatin silver print (BP 724, DM 1754, FR 5908, Y 136,799).

$880* *"Edgeware, London", 1936,* s., t., d., photog. stamp, (11-16-92, Butterfield, #5969, illus.), 9½ x 7½ in., (241.7 x 190.8 mm.), photograph, gelatin silver print (BP 579, DM 1403, FR 4726, Y 109,439).

BI *Helene Thimig Reinhardt, Vienna, 1936,* s., t., d., credit stamp, est. $3/4,000, (10-13-92, Christie-NY, #211, illus.), 9¾ x 9¼ in., (24.8 x 23.5 cm.), photograph, gelatin silver print.

BI *Mrs. Judith Holzmeister, 1935,* s., t., d. by photog. in ink, est. $3/4,000, (10-15-92, Sotheby-NY, #422, illus.), 19¼ x 14½ in., (48.9 x 36.8 cm.), photograph, gelatin silver print.

$1725* *"Sibylle Binder", 1932,* photog.'s blindstamp on image, s. twice, t., d., (05-23-93, Butterfield, #3412, illus.), 4⅜ x 3¼ in., photograph, sepia toned carte postale (BP 1123, DM 2820, FR 9494, Y 190,671).

$1035* *"The Thimigs", 1930,* s., t., d., illus., (05-23-93, Butterfield, #3411, illus.), 6½ x 8⅜ in., photograph, toned gelatin silver print (BP 674, DM 1692, FR 5696, Y 114,403).

$2475* *"Two People", 1932,* s., d., t., photog. stamp, (11-16-92, Butterfield, #5967, illus.), 13¼ x 10¾ in., (337.2 x 273.5 mm.), photograph, toned gelatin silver print (BP 1630, DM 3946, FR 13,292, Y 307,798).

FLETCHER, Hanslip
$111* *Trafalgar Square,* by Kenneth Hobson, margins, (04-22-93, Bonhams-Chelsea, #30), plate 10⅜ x 15¾ in., (26.4 x 40 cm.), etching w/aquatint w/hand coloring (BP 72, DM 178, FR 602, Y 12,205).

FLETCHER, John E.
BI *Lift-Off, Apollo XII, 1969,* photog.'s credit, s., i., est. $1/1,500, (10-14-92, Swann, #306, illus.), 23½ x 17½ in., (59.7 x 44.5 cm.), photograph, dye-transfer print.

FLETCHER, Martin
$302* *"Knock Out Punch",* s., mat burn, taped to mat, (12-04-92, Doyle, #96), 8 x 11¾ in., (203 x 298 mm.), lithograph (BP 194, DM 481, FR 1632, Y 37,703).

FLINT, Francis Russell (after)
$162* *The Aquaduct,* #341/500, blindstamp, (10-17-92, Bonhams, #115), image 19¼ x 27 in., (48.9 x 68.6 cm.), color reproduction (BP 99, DM 241, FR 818, Y 19,436).
$119* *The Aquaduct,* #340/500, blindstamp, (05-22-93, Bonhams, #128), image 19¼ x 27 in., (48.9 x 68.6 cm.), color reprod. (BP 77, DM 193, FR 651, Y 13,120).
BI *Dos Cabreras,* #136/500, blindstamp, est. BP 70/100, (05-22-93, Bonhams, #129), image 16 x 23¾ in., (40.6 x 60.3 cm.), color reprod..
$509* *My Father Painting At Brantome,* s., blindstamp Fine Art Trade Guild, pub. Medici Society, 1972, (05-22-93, Bonhams, #130), image 20⅞ x 29⅞ in., (53 x 75.9 cm.), color reprod. (BP 330, DM 828, FR 2784, Y 56,119).
BI *My Father Painting At Brantome, 1972,* s., blindstamp, pub. Medici Society, est. BP 5/700, (10-17-92, Bonhams, #116, illus.), image 20⅞ x 29⅞ in., (53 x 75.9 cm.), color reproduction.

FLINT, Sir William Russell   British 1880-1969
$270* *The "Frances And Jane" At Birdham, 1983,* #436/1000, pub. Museum Prints, (10-17-92, Bonhams, #15), image 12¾ x 19¼ in., (32.4 x 48.9 cm.), color reproduction (BP 165, DM 402, FR 1363, Y 32,394).
BI *The (Green) Parrot, Almeria (G & C 31),* s., blindstamp Fine Art Trade Guild, pub. W. J. Stacey, 1944, faded,est. BP 4/600, (05-22-93, Bonhams, #59), image 12⅛ x 19 in., (30.8 x 48.3 cm.), color reprod..
$1007* *Act II, Scene I,* #382/850, blindstamp, (10-17-92, Bonhams, #1), image 15½ x 22½ in., (39.4 x 57.2 cm.), color reproduction (BP 616, DM 1499, FR 5083, Y 120,816).
$883* *Act II, Scene I,* #711/850, blindstamp, (05-22-93, Bonhams, #1, illus.), image 15½ x 22½ in., (39.4 x 57.2 cm.), color reprod. (BP 572, DM 1436, FR 4830, Y 97,354).
$467* *Amanda,* #279/500, blindstamp, (10-17-92, Bonhams, #2), image 9 x 9 in., (22.9 x 22.9 cm.), color reproduction (BP 286, DM 695, FR 2357, Y 56,029).
$575* *Amazons Of A Breton Beach (W. 102), 1931,* brown ink s., num. III, margins, (10-17-92, Bonhams, #104, illus.), plate 8 x 13¼ in., (20.3 x 33.7 cm.), drypoint etching (BP 352, DM 856, FR 2903, Y 68,986).
BI *Aragonese String Makers, c. 1930,* sepia ink s., estate of Roy Mason, est. $2/3000, (10-30-92, Sloan, #2388, illus.), 9½ x 14½ in., (24.1 x 36.8 cm.), drypoint etching.
$1222* *Ariadne,* #726/850, blindstamp, (10-17-92, Bonhams, #3, illus.), image 19½ x 22½ in., (49.5 x 57.2 cm.), color reproduction (BP 748, DM 1819, FR 6169, Y 146,611).
$1324* *Ariadne,* #617/850, blindstamp, (05-22-93, Bonhams, #3), image 19½ x 22½ in., (49.5 x 57.2 cm.), color reprod. (BP 858, DM 2153, FR 7243, Y 145,976).
$934* *Awkward Encounter (G & C 54),* s., blindstamp Fine Art Trade Guild, pub. W. J. Stacey, 1956, (05-22-93, Bonhams, #63, illus.), image 16⅛ x 22 in., (41 x 55.9 cm.), color reprod. (BP 605, DM 1519, FR 5109, Y 102,977).
BI *Balance (G & C 84),* s., blindstamp Fine Art Trade Guild, Medici Society, 1965, est. BP 6/800, (05-22-93,

Bonhams, #84, illus.), image 15⅞ x 22⅜ in., (40.3 x 56.8 cm.), color reprod..
$385* *Ballet Recital,* s., pub. W.J. Stacey, (12-10-92, Sloan, #3049), 14⁵⁄₁₆ x 18¹⁵⁄₁₆ in., (36.4 x 48.1 cm.), photolithograph (BP 248, DM 609, FR 2080, Y 47,625).
$100* *The Barons Presenting Magna Carta To King John At Runnymede,* pub. Medici Society, (10-17-92, Bonhams, #105), image 20½ x 28½ in., (52.1 x 72.4 cm.), chromolithograph (BP 61, DM 149, FR 505, Y 11,998).
$683* *Basket Of Apples, Brantome,* #87/650, blindstamp, (10-17-92, Bonhams, #4), image 17¼ x 23½ in., (43.8 x 59.7 cm.), color reproduction (BP 418, DM 1017, FR 3448, Y 81,944).
BI *Basket Of Peaches,* pub. Venture Prints Ltd., 1970, est. BP 2/400, (05-22-93, Bonhams, #4), image 15 x 22 in., (38.1 x 55.9 cm.), color reprod..
$431* *La Belle Poseuse, Nerac,* #744/850, blindstamp, (10-17-92, Bonhams, #24), image 19⅝ x 26¾ in., (49.8 x 67.9 cm.), color reproduction (BP 264, DM 642, FR 2176, Y 51,710).
$679* *La Belle Poseuse, Nerac,* #465/850, blindstamp, (05-22-93, Bonhams, #25), image 19⅝ x 26¾ in., (49.8 x 67.9 cm.), color reprod. (BP 440, DM 1104, FR 3714, Y 74,862).
$645* *Beyond The Walls,* #413/850, blindstamp, (05-22-93, Bonhams, #5), image 19¾ x 14½ in., (50.2 x 36.8 cm.), color reprod. (BP 418, DM 1049, FR 3528, Y 71,114).
$34* *The Bloom Of Youth,* staining, (05-22-93, Bonhams, #113), image 11¾ x 19 in., (29.8 x 48.3 cm.), color reprod. (BP 22, DM 55, FR 186, Y 3749).
BI *The Bridge, Nerac,* blindstamp, est. BP 4/600, (10-17-92, Bonhams, #6), image 14½ x 22 in., (36.8 x 55.9 cm.), color reproduction.
$934* *Campo San Trovaso (G & C 97),* s., blindstamp Fine Art Trade Guild, pub. Frost and Reed, 1968, (05-22-93, Bonhams, #96, illus.), image 17¾ x 24 in., (45.1 x 61 cm.), color reprod. (BP 605, DM 1519, FR 5109, Y 102,977).
$863* *Campo San Trovaso (G & C 97), 1968,* s., blindstamp, pub. Frost and Reed, (10-17-92, Bonhams, #90), image 17¾ x 24 in., (45.1 x 61 cm.), color reproduction (BP 528, DM 1285, FR 4356, Y 103,539).
$791* *Carlotta On The Loire,* #599/850, blindstamp, (10-17-92, Bonhams, #7, illus.), image 19½ x 26¾ in., (49.5 x 67.9 cm.), color reproduction (BP 484, DM 1177, FR 3993, Y 94,901).
$611* *Carlotta On The Loire,* #195/850, blindstamp, (05-22-93, Bonhams, #6), image 19½ x 26¾ in., (49.5 x 67.9 cm.), color reprod. (BP 396, DM 993, FR 3342, Y 67,365).
$951* *Carmelita (G & C 70),* s., blindstamp Fine Art Trade Guild, pub. Medici Society, 1961, (05-22-93, Bonhams, #74, illus.), image 10 x 12 in., (25.4 x 30.5 cm.), color reprod. (BP 616, DM 1546, FR 5202, Y 104,851).
$1043* *Carmelita (G & C 70), 1961,* s., blindstamp, pub. Medici Society, (10-17-92, Bonhams, #68, illus.), image 10⅛ x 12⅛ in., (25.7 x 30.8 cm.), color reproduction (BP 638, DM 1553, FR 5265, Y 125,135).
$1222* *Casilda's White Petticoat (G & C 52), 1955,* s., blindstamp, pub. Frost and Reed, (10-17-92, Bonhams, #59, illus.), image 17¾ x 23⅞ in., (45.1 x 60.6 cm.), color reproduction laid down (BP 748, DM 1819, FR 6169, Y 146,611).
$503* *Castanets (G & C 62), 1959,* s., blindstamp, pub. Royal Academy, (10-17-92, Bonhams, #64), image 15⅜ x 21 in., (39.1 x 53.3 cm.), color reproduction (BP 308, DM 749, FR 2539, Y 60,348).
BI *Cecilia,* #317/500, blindstamp, est. BP 3/500, (10-17-92, Bonhams, #8), image 8¾ x 8¾ in., (22.2 x 22.2 cm.), color reproduction.
$248* *Cecilia,* s., pub. Frost & Reed, 1959, (12-10-92, Sloan, #3046), 14⅝ x 27⅞ in., (37.1 x 70.8 cm.), photolithograph (BP 160, DM 392, FR 1340, Y 30,678).
$1222* *Cecilia And Her Studies,* #387/850, blindstamp, (10-17-92, Bonhams, #9, illus.), image 10⅜ x 14⅝ in., (26.4 x 37.1 cm.), color reproduction (BP 748, DM 1819, FR 6169, Y 146,611).
$679* *Cecilia And Her Studies,* #825/850, blindstamp, (05-22-93, Bonhams, #7), image 10⅜ x 14⅝ in., (26.4 x 37.1 cm.), color reprod. (BP 440, DM 1104, FR 3714, Y 74,862).

$863* *Cecilia Contemplating Europa,* #451/850, blindstamp, (10-17-92, Bonhams, #10), image 15¼ x 12⅛ in., (38.7 x 30.8 cm.), color reproduction (BP 528, DM 1285, FR 4356, Y 103,539).

$679* *Cecilia Contemplating Europa,* #22/850, blindstamp, (05-22-93, Bonhams, #8), image 15¼ x 12⅛ in., (38.7 x 30.8 cm.), color reprod. (BP 440, DM 1104, FR 3714, Y 74,862).

$713* *Cecilia In June,* #167/500, blindstamp, (05-22-93, Bonhams, #9), image 10½ x 10½ in., (26.7 x 26.7 cm.), color reprod. (BP 462, DM 1159, FR 3900, Y 78,611).

$153* *Chattels (G & C 7),* s., blindstamp Fine Art Trade Guild, pub. W. J. Stacey, 1929, faded, (05-22-93, Bonhams, #52), image 11¼ x 14¼ in., (28.6 x 36.2 cm.), color reprod. (BP 99, DM 249, FR 837, Y 16,869).

BI *Clarissa Fishing (G & C 11), 1931,* s., blindstamp, pub. W.J. Stacey, faded, est. BP 2/400, (10-17-92, Bonhams, #49), image 12¾ x 9½ in., (32.4 x 24.1 cm.), color reproduction.

$747* *Conversation Piece (G & C 29),* s., blindstamp Fine Art Trade Guild, pub. W. J. Stacey, 1943, (05-22-93, Bonhams, #58), image 14½ x 19 in., (36.8 x 48.3 cm.), color reprod. (BP 484, DM 1215, FR 4086, Y 82,359).

$647* *Conversation Piece (G & C 29), 1943,* s., blindstamp, pub. W.J. Stacey, (10-17-92, Bonhams, #54), image 14½ x 19 in., (36.8 x 48.3 cm.), color reproduction (BP 396, DM 963, FR 3266, Y 77,624).

$1155* *Conversation, St. Martin D'Ardeche (G & C 96),* s., blindstamp Fine Art Trade Guild, pub. Medici Society, 1968, (05-22-93, Bonhams, #95), image 20 x 26½ in., (50.8 x 67.3 cm.), color reprod. (BP 748, DM 1878, FR 6318, Y 127,343).

$849* *Corisande,* #803/850, blindstamp, (05-22-93, Bonhams, #10), image 11¼ x 19 in., (28.6 x 48.3 cm.), color reprod. (BP 550, DM 1380, FR 4644, Y 93,605).

BI *The Dance Of A Thousand Flounces,* s., pub. Frost & Reed, 1952, est. $9/1,200, (12-10-92, Sloan, #3047, illus.), 17⅞ x 24⅛ in., (45.4 x 61.3 cm.), photolithograph.

BI *The Dance Of A Thousand Flounces (G & C 40), 1952,* s., blindstamp, pub. Frost and Reed, est. BP 700/1,000, (10-17-92, Bonhams, #58, illus.), image 17⅞ x 24 in., (45.4 x 61 cm.), color reproduction.

$495* *"The Danza Montana", 1960,* s., pub. Frost and Reed, 1" margins top and sides, 1 1/2" margins bottom, (10-31-92, Cleveland, #282), 18⅞ x 25 in., (47.9 x 63.5 cm.), collotype (BP 317, DM 762, FR 2584, Y 61,315).

BI *Discussion (G & C 103),* s., blindstamp Fine Art Trade Guild, pub. Medici Society, 1969, est.BP 4/600, (05-22-93, Bonhams, #101), image 18 x 26 in., (45.7 x 66 cm.), color reprod..

$611* *The Dubious Bernini (G & C 72),* s., blindstamp Fine Art Trade Guild, pub. Medici Society, 1962, faded, (05-22-93, Bonhams, #76), image 16¾ x 22½ in., (42.5 x 57.2 cm.), color reprod. (BP 396, DM 993, FR 3342, Y 67,365).

$1115* *Eve With Her Net (G & C 17), 1935,* s., blindstamp, pub. W.J. Stacey, (10-17-92, Bonhams, #50), image 16 x 11⅜ in., (40.6 x 28.9 cm.), color reproduction (BP 682, DM 1660, FR 5628, Y 133,773).

$575* *Festal Preparations, Manosque (G & C 60), 1959,* s., blindstamp, pub. Medici Society, faded, (10-17-92, Bonhams, #62), image 16⅜ x 22½ in., (41.6 x 57.2 cm.), color reproduction (BP 352, DM 856, FR 2903, Y 68,986).

$221* *The Festival Of Santa Eulalia, Andalusia,* pub. Adams Brothers and Shardlow Ltd., (05-22-93, Bonhams, #11), image 18 x 23½ in., (45.7 x 59.7 cm.), color reprod. (BP 143, DM 359, FR 1209, Y 24,366).

$575* *Fiametta,* #97/500, blindstamp, (10-17-92, Bonhams, #13), image 10½ x 10½ in., (26.7 x 26.7 cm.), color reproduction (BP 352, DM 856, FR 2903, Y 68,986).

$645* *Figures For A Baroque Fountain (G & C 46),* s., i., (05-22-93, Bonhams, #62), image 11 x 15¾ in., (27.9 x 40 cm.), sepia reprod. (BP 418, DM 1049, FR 3528, Y 71,114).

BI *Five,* #114/850, blindstamp, est. BP 6/800, (10-17-92, Bonhams, #14), image 9⅞ x 22½ in., (25.1 x 57.2 cm.), color reproduction.

$719* *A Florentine Masquerade,* #190/750, blindstamp, (10-17-92, Bonhams, #16), image 26¼ x 19½ in., (66.7 x 49.5 cm.), color reproduction (BP 440, DM 1070, FR 3629, Y 86,263).

$883* *A Florentine Masquerade,* #504/750, blindstamp, (05-22-93, Bonhams, #14), image 26¼ x 19½ in., (66.7 x 49.5 cm.), color reprod. (BP 572, DM 1436, FR 4830, Y 97,354).

$1528* *The Four Sisters, Chazalet (G & C 55),* s., blindstamp Fine Art Trade Guild, pub. Frost and Reed, 1956, (05-22-93, Bonhams, #64, illus.), image 17⅝ x 24 in., (44.8 x 61 cm.), color reprod. (BP 990, DM 2485, FR 8359, Y 168,467).

$509* *Frileuse (Wright 27), 1929,* ink s., #XXXVII, margins, (05-22-93, Bonhams, #112), pl 5½ x 2⅞ in., (14 x 7.3 cm.), drypoint etching (BP 330, DM 828, FR 2784, Y 56,119).

$1019* *Girl From Orio,* #333/850, blindstamp, (05-22-93, Bonhams, #16, illus.), image 15 x 22⅜ in., (38.1 x 56.8 cm.), color reprod. (BP 660, DM 1657, FR 5574, Y 112,348).

BI *Giselle And Julietta,* #658/850, blindstamp, est. BP 4/600, (05-22-93, Bonhams, #17), image 17¼ x 24 in., (43.8 x 61 cm.), color reprod..

$1654* *Gitanas At La Galera (G & C 106), 1970,* s., blindstamp, pub. Frost and Reed, (10-17-92, Bonhams, #97, illus.), image 26¾ x 20 in., (67.9 x 50.8 cm.), color reproduction (BP 1012, DM 2462, FR 8349, Y 198,440).

$647* *Golden Sands, Bamburgh,* s., i. Proof reserved for Nina, pub. NY Graphic Society, (10-17-92, Bonhams, #17), image 16¼ x 22 in., (41.3 x 55.9 cm.), color reproduction (BP 396, DM 963, FR 3266, Y 77,624).

$1079* *Gossip After Market, Perigord (G & C 95), 1968,* s., blindstamp pub. Medici Society, (10-17-92, Bonhams, #89, illus.), image 19½ x 26½ in., (49.5 x 67.3 cm.), color reproduction (BP 660, DM 1606, FR 5447, Y 129,454).

$629* *Gossip, St. Jeannet,* #784/850, blindstamp, (10-17-92, Bonhams, #18), image 19¼ x 26¼ in., (48.9 x 66.7 cm.), color reproduction (BP 385, DM 936, FR 3175, Y 75,465).

$747* *Gossip, St. Jeannet,* #36/850, blindstamp, (05-22-93, Bonhams, #18), image 19¼ x 26¼ in., (48.9 x 66.7 cm.), color reprod. (BP 484, DM 1215, FR 4086, Y 82,359).

BI *Gossipers, Le Castellet,* #165/850, blindstamp, est. BP 4/600, (05-22-93, Bonhams, #19), image 19½ x 26¼ in., (49.5 x 66.7 cm.), color reprod..

$1358* *Green Slippers (G & C 12),* s., blindstamp Fine Art Trade Guild, pub. W. J. Stacey, 1932, foxing, (05-22-93, Bonhams, #53), image 19½ x 13 in., (49.5 x 33 cm.), color reprod. (BP 880, DM 2208, FR 7429, Y 149,724).

BI *Griselda (G & C 58),* s., blindstamp Fine Art Trade Guild, pub. Medici Society, 1958, faded, est. BP 4/600, (05-22-93, Bonhams, #67), image 18¼ x 22¼ in., (46.4 x 56.5 cm.), color reprod..

BI *Griselda (G & C 58), 1958,* s., blindstamp, pub. Medici Society, faded, est. BP 6/800, (10-17-92, Bonhams, #61), image 18¼ x 22¼ in., (46.4 x 56.5 cm.), color reproduction.

$883* *Group Of Idlers (G & C 90),* s., blindstamp Fine Art Trade Guild, pub. Medici Society, 1967, (05-22-93, Bonhams, #90), image 19¼ x 26½ in., (48.9 x 67.3 cm.), sepia reprod. (BP 572, DM 1436, FR 4830, Y 97,354).

BI *Group Of Idlers (G & C 90), 1967,* s., blindstamp, pub. Medici Society, est. BP 5/700, (10-17-92, Bonhams, #85), image 19¼ x 26½ in., (48.9 x 67.3 cm.), sepia reproduction.

$543* *Gypsy Girl,* calendar proof, #V, s. 3 times, (05-22-93, Bonhams, #114), image 9½ x 13½ in., (24.1 x 34.3 cm.), color reprod. (BP 352, DM 883, FR 2970, Y 59,868).

$1104* *Halcyon Days (G & C 21),* s., blindstamp Fine Art Trade Guild, pub. W. J. Stacey, 1937, (05-22-93, Bonhams, #56, illus.), image 10½ x 16 in., (26.7 x 40.6 cm.), color reprod. (BP 715, DM 1795, FR 6039, Y 121,720).

$1528* *Holiday After Ramadan (G & C 85),* s., blindstamp Fine Art Trade Guild, pub. Frost and Reed, 1965, (05-22-93, Bonhams, #85, illus.), image 17½ x 24 in., (44.5 x 61 cm.), color reprod. (BP 990, DM 2485, FR 8359, Y 168,467).

$100* *The Houses Of Parliament And Westminster Abbey,* pub. Medici Society, (10-17-92, Bonhams, #106), image 20½ x 28½ in., (52.1 x 72.4 cm.), chromolithograph (BP 61, DM 149, FR 505, Y 11,998).

BI *Iberian Flounces: A Pair,* blindstamps, est. BP 1/1,500, (10-17-92, Bonhams, #19, illus.), image 11¼ x 7⅝ in., (28.6 x 19.4 cm.), color reproduction.

$1358* *Iberian Flounces: A Pair,* #302/850, blindstamp, (05-22-93, Bonhams, #20, illus.), each 11¼ x 7⅝ in., (28.6 x 19.4 cm.), color reprod. (BP 880, DM 2208, FR 7429, Y 149,724).

$467* *In A Bergundian Granary,* #VIII, one of surplus, blindstamp, (10-17-92, Bonhams, #20), image 19½ x 26½ in., (49.5 x 67.3 cm.), color reproduction (BP 286, DM 695, FR 2357, Y 56,029).

BI *In A Burgundian Granary,* #V, blindstamp, est. BP 3/400, (05-22-93, Bonhams, #115), image 19¼ x 26¼ in., (48.9 x 66.7 cm.), color reprod..

$577* *In A Burgundian Granary,* #297/850, blindstamp, (05-22-93, Bonhams, #21), image 19½ x 26½ in., (49.5 x 67.3 cm.), color reprod. (BP 374, DM 938, FR 3156, Y 63,616).

$679* *In My Studio (G & C 22),* s., blindstamp Fine Art Trade Guild, pub. W. J. Stacey, 1938, (05-22-93, Bonhams, #57), image 12½ x 18¾ in., (31.8 x 47.6 cm.), color reprod. (BP 440, DM 1104, FR 3714, Y 74,862).

$683* *In My Studio (G & C 22), 1938,* s., blindstamp, pub. W.J. Stacey, (10-17-92, Bonhams, #52), image 12½ x 18¾ in., (31.8 x 47.6 cm.), color reproduction (BP 418, DM 1017, FR 3448, Y 81,944).

$395* *Incoming Tide,* #341/750, blindstamp, (10-17-92, Bonhams, #21), image 19 x 25¾ in., (48.3 x 65.4 cm.), color reproduction (BP 242, DM 588, FR 1994, Y 47,391).

$289* *Incoming Tide,* #345/750, blindstamp, (05-22-93, Bonhams, #22), image 19 x 25¾ in., (48.3 x 65.4 cm.), color reprod. (BP 187, DM 470, FR 1581, Y 31,863).

$1358* *Interlude (G & C 94),* s., blindstamp Fine Art Trade Guild, pub. Frost and Redd, 1968, (05-22-93, Bonhams, #94), image 11⅞ x 21½ in., (30.2 x 54.6 cm.), color reprod. (BP 880, DM 2208, FR 7429, Y 149,724).

$899* *Interlude (G & C 94), 1967,* s., blindstamp, pub. Frost and Reed, (10-17-92, Bonhams, #88), image 11⅞ x 21½ in., (30.2 x 54.6 cm.), color reproduction (BP 550, DM 1338, FR 4538, Y 107,858).

$914 *"Isabell Of Lucenay",* s. Medici Society, (04-16-93, G.A. Key, #147, illus.), 19 x 25 in., (48.3 x 63.5 cm.), colored artists proof (BP 600, DM 1476, FR 4989, Y 102,777).

$934* *Isabella Of Lucenay (G & C 99),* s., blindstamp Fine Art Trade Guild, pub. Medici Society, 1969, (05-22-93, Bonhams, #98, illus.), color reprod. (BP 605, DM 1519, FR 5109, Y 102,977).

BI *Isabella Of Lucenay (G & C 99), 1969,* s., blindstamp, pub. Medici Society, est. BP 5/800, (10-17-92, Bonhams, #91, illus.), image 19¼ x 26¼ in., (48.9 x 66.7 cm.), color reproduction.

$577* *Janelle And The Volume Of Treasures,* #574/850, blindstamp, (05-22-93, Bonhams, #23), image 13¾ x 20¼ in., (34.9 x 51.4 cm.), color reprod. (BP 374, DM 938, FR 3156, Y 63,616).

$989* *Jessie And Jemima,* blindstamp, (10-17-92, Bonhams, #22, illus.), image 11⅝ x 21⅝ in., (29.5 x 54.9 cm.), color reproduction (BP 605, DM 1472, FR 4992, Y 118,656).

BI *The Judgement Of Paris,* blindstamp Fine Art Trade Guild, pub. Harcourt-Wood, est. BP 3/500, (05-22-93, Bonhams, #24), image 20 x 30 in., (50.8 x 76.2 cm.), color reprod..

$358* *Ladies In Interior,* s. in stone; pencil s., (04-02-93, Sloan, #1178), image 12½ x 18⅞ in., (318 x 479 mm.), chromolithograph (BP 236, DM 575, FR 1954, Y 40,761).

BI *Ladies In Interior,* s. in Stone; s., pub. Rudolf Lesch Fine Arts, Inc., est. $350/450, (02-04-93, Sloan, #2030), image area 12½ x 18⅞ in., (31.8 x 47.9 cm.), chromolithograph.

$1222* *Lavoir Labastide (G & C 105),* s., blindstamp Fine Art Trade Guild, pub. Medici Society, 1970, (05-22-93, Bonhams, #103, illus.), image 19 x 26½ in., (48.3 x 67.3 cm.), color reprod. (BP 792, DM 1987, FR 6685, Y 134,730).

BI *Lavoir Labastide (G & C 105), 1970,* s., blindstamp, pub. Medici Society, est. BP 700/1,000, (10-17-92, Bonhams, #96, illus.), image 19 x 26½ in., (48.3 x 67.3 cm.), color reproduction.

$934* *The Little Flower Girl, Senlis (G & C 68),* s., blindstamp Fine Art Trade Guild, pub. Frost and Reed, 1961, (05-22-93, Bonhams, #72), image 17¾ x 24 in., (45.1 x 61 cm.), color reprod. (BP 605, DM 1519, FR 5109, Y 102,977).

$539* *Little Sewing Girl, Sospel,* num. II/XII, blindstamp, (10-17-92, Bonhams, #107), image 19½ x 27 in., (49.5 x 68.6 cm.), color reproduction (BP 330, DM 802, FR 2721, Y 64,667).

$683* *Little Sewing Girl, Sospel,* #11/850, blindstamp, (10-17-92, Bonhams, #25), image 19½ x 26¾ in., (49.5 x 67.9 cm.), color reproduction (BP 418, DM 1017, FR 3448, Y 81,944).

BI *Little Sewing Girl, Sospel,* #III/XII, blindstamp, est. BP 3/400, (05-22-93, Bonhams, #116), image 19½ x 27 in., (49.5 x 68.6 cm.), color reprod..

$747* *Little Sewing Girl, Sospel,* #315/850, blindstamp, (05-22-93, Bonhams, #26), image 19½ x 26¾ in., (49.5 x 67.9 cm.), color reprod. (BP 484, DM 1215, FR 4086, Y 82,359).

$647* *The Looking Glass,* #763/850, blindstamp, (10-17-92, Bonhams, #26), image 11 x 15 in., (27.9 x 38.1 cm.), color reproduction (BP 396, DM 963, FR 3266, Y 77,624).

$679* *The Looking Glass,* #148/850, blindstamp, (05-22-93, Bonhams, #27), image 11 x 15 in., (27.9 x 38.1 cm.), color reprod. (BP 440, DM 1104, FR 3714, Y 74,862).

BI *Low Tide, St. Malo (G & C 14),* s., blindstamp Fine Art Trade Guild, pub. Frost and Reed, 1934, est.BP 5/800, (05-22-93, Bonhams, #54, illus.), image 16⅛ x 21¼ in., (41 x 54 cm.), color reprod..

$809* *Lydia On The Sands,* #148/850, blindstamp, (10-17-92, Bonhams, #27), image 19¾ x 26½ in., (50.2 x 67.3 cm.), color reproduction (BP 495, DM 1204, FR 4084, Y 97,061).

$102* *Madame Du Barry As A Bacchante,* facsimile inscription, (05-22-93, Bonhams, #117), image 14¼ x 9 in., (36.2 x 22.9 cm.), reprod. (BP 66, DM 166, FR 558, Y 11,246).

$360* *"Madame Du Barry The Reigning Beauty" and "Madame Du Barry As A Bacchante": A Pair,* (10-17-92, Bonhams, #113), image 14½ x 9 in., (36.8 x 22.9 cm.), reproduction w/facsimile inscrip. (BP 220, DM 536, FR 1817, Y 43,191).

$187* *"Madame Du Barry The Reigning Beauty" and "Madame Du Barry As A Bacchante": A Pair,* facsimile inscriptions, (05-22-93, Bonhams, #120), image 14½ x 9 in., (36.8 x 22.9 cm.), reprod. (BP 121, DM 304, FR 1023, Y 20,617).

$153* *"Madame Du Barry The Reigning Beauty" and "Madame Du Barry As A Bacchante": A Pair,* facsimile inscriptions, (05-22-93, Bonhams, #121), image 14¼ x 9 in., (36.2 x 22.9 cm.), reprod. (BP 99, DM 249, FR 837, Y 16,869).

$934* *La Mairie Manosque (G & C 65),* s., blindstamp Fine Art Trade Guild, pub. Frost and Reed, 1960, (05-22-93, Bonhams, #69), image 17¼ x 24 in., (43.8 x 61 cm.), color reprod. (BP 605, DM 1519, FR 5109, Y 102,977).

BI *Market Hall, Cordes (G & C 78),* s., blindstamp Fine Art Trade Guild, pub. Medici Society, 1963, est.BP 4/600, (05-22-93, Bonhams, #81), image 16¾ x 22¾ in., (42.5 x 57.8 cm.), color reprod..

$827* *Market Hall, Cordes (G & C 78), 1963,* s., blindstamp, pub. Medici Society, faded, (10-17-92, Bonhams, #75), image 16¾ x 22¾ in., (42.5 x 57.8 cm.), color reproduction (BP 506, DM 1231, FR 4175, Y 99,220).

BI *The Mill Pool,* #247/850, blindstamp, est. BP 5/700, (10-17-92, Bonhams, #28), image 20 x 27 in., (50.8 x 68.6 cm.), color reproduction.

$679* *The Mill Pool,* #151/850, blindstamp, i. on backboard by Cecilia Green, (05-22-93, Bonhams, #28), image 20 x 27 in., (50.8 x 68.6 cm.), color reprod. (BP 440, DM 1104, FR 3714, Y 74,862).

BI *Model And Critic,* #150/850, blindstamp, est. BP 7/900, (10-17-92, Bonhams, #29), image 14½ x 22 in., (36.8 x 55.9 cm.), color reproduction.

$849* *Model And Critic,* #150/850, blindstamp, (05-22-93, Bonhams, #29), image 14½ x 22 in., (36.8 x 55.9 cm.), color reprod. (BP 550, DM 1380, FR 4644, Y 93,605).

$989* *Model For Elegance,* #267/850, blindstamp, (10-17-92, Bonhams, #30), image 13½ x 19½ in., (34.3 x 49.5 cm.), color reproduction (BP 605, DM 1472, FR 4992, Y 118,656).

$849* *Model For Elegance,* #23/850, blindstamp, (05-22-93, Bonhams, #30), image 13½ x 19½ in., (34.3 x 49.5 cm.), color reprod. (BP 550, DM 1380, FR 4644, Y 93,605).

$605* *Models For "Goddesses",* s., pub. Frost & Reed, 1951, (12-10-92, Sloan, #3048, illus.), 18 x 25 in., (45.7 x 63.5 cm.), photolithograph (BP 390, DM 957, FR 3269, Y 74,839).

$935* *Models For Vanity (G & C 28), 1942,* s., blindstamp, pub. Frost and Reed, (10-17-92, Bonhams, #53, illus.), image 16¼ x 22 in., (41.3 x 55.9 cm.), color reproduction (BP 572, DM 1392, FR 4720, Y 112,178).

$324* *The New Heir, Stokesay (Wright 38),* 4th state, brown ink s., num. XIV, margins, (10-17-92, Bonhams, #103), plate 9 x 13½ in., (22.9 x 34.3 cm.), drypoint etching in dark brown (BP 198, DM 482, FR 1636, Y 38,872).

$934* *New Model Inspecting Drawings Of Her Predecessor (G & C 75),* s., blindstamp Fine Art Trade Guild, pub. Frost and Reed, 1963, (05-22-93, Bonhams, #78), image 13 x 21½ in., (33 x 54.6 cm.), color reprod. (BP 605, DM 1519, FR 5109, Y 102,977).

BI *New Model Inspecting Drawings Of Her Predecessor (G & C 75), 1963,* s., blindstamp, pub. Frost and Reed, est. BP 700/1,000, (10-17-92, Bonhams, #72), image 13 x 21½ in., (33 x 54.6 cm.), color reproduction.

BI *The Nuns Class, La Charite,* est. BP 150/200, (10-17-92, Bonhams, #109), image 16⅛ x 21⅞ in., (41 x 55.6 cm.), color reproduction.

$611* *The Nuns Class, La Charite (G & C 56),* s., blindstamp Fine Art Trade Guild, pub. Frost and Reed, 1957, (05-22-93, Bonhams, #65), image 16 x 21⅞ in., (40.6 x 55.6 cm.), color reprod. (BP 396, DM 993, FR 3342, Y 67,365).

$450* *Nursemaids In The Piazza, Venice (W. 16), 1929,* 2nd state of 2, full margins, s., num. XLV, sig. faded, light-stained, foxing, tape, (11-30-92, Phillips-London, #335), plate 9⅓ x 14 in., (237 x 356 mm.), drypoint on laid (BP 297, DM 717, FR 2434, Y 56,005).

BI *October Morning On The Baise (G & C 101),* s., blindstamp Fine Art Trade Guild, pub. Frost and Reed, 1969, est.BP 4/600, (05-22-93, Bonhams, #90, illus.), image 19¼ x 26½ in., (48.9 x 67.3 cm.), color reprod..

$827* *October Morning On The Baise (G & C 101), 1969,* s., blindstamp, pub. Frost and Reed, (10-17-92, Bonhams, #93, illus.), image 19¼ x 26½ in., (48.9 x 67.3 cm.), color reproduction (BP 506, DM 1231, FR 4175, Y 99,220).

$441* *A Palazzo On The Grand Canal, Venice,* #41/750, blindstamp, (05-22-93, Bonhams, #31), image 19 x 26¾ in., (48.3 x 67.9 cm.), color reprod. (BP 286, DM 717, FR 2412, Y 48,622).

$3226* *The Pendant (G & C 88),* s., blindstamp Fine Art Trade Guild, pub. Medici Society, 1966, (05-22-93, Bonhams, #88, illus.), image 20 x 27½ in., (50.8 x 69.9 cm.), color reprod. (BP 2090, DM 5246, FR 17,648, Y 355,678).

$2696* *The Pendant (G & C 88), 1966,* s., blindstamp, pub. Medici Society, (10-17-92, Bonhams, #83, illus.), image 20 x 27½ in., (50.8 x 69.9 cm.), color reproduction (BP 1650, DM 4013, FR 13,609, Y 323,455).

$217* *Phryne (W. 21), 1929,* 2nd state of 2, s., num. LXXII, light-stained, image foxing, defects, (11-30-92, Phillips-London, #337), plate 7⅛ x 6 in., (181 x 152 mm.), drypoint on wove (BP 143, DM 346, FR 1174, Y 27,007).

$385* *"Phryne",* s.; label verso, (11-13-92, DuMouchelle, #2370), 7 x 6 in., (17.8 x 15.2 cm.), etching (BP 249, DM 604, FR 2038, Y 47,785).

$539* *Picnic At La Roche,* #421/850, blindstamp, (10-17-92, Bonhams, #31), image 19½ x 26½ in., (49.5 x 67.3 cm.), color reproduction (BP 330, DM 802, FR 2721, Y 64,667).

BI *Picnic At La Roche,* #386/850, blindstamp, est. BP 4/600, (05-22-93, Bonhams, #32), image 19¼ x 26½ in., (48.9 x 67.3 cm.), color reprod..

$360* *Primavera (G & C 102), 1969,* s., blindstamp, pub. Adam Collection, faded to green, (10-17-92, Bonhams, #94), image 9 x 11¼ in., (22.9 x 28.6 cm.), color reproduction (BP 220, DM 536, FR 1817, Y 43,191).

BI *Le Quatorze Juillet,* est. BP 150/200, (10-17-92, Bonhams, #108), image 17⅝ x 24 in., (44.8 x 61 cm.), color reproduction.

$989* *Le Quatorze Juillet (G & C 53), 1956,* s., blindstamp, pub. Frost and Reed, (10-17-92, Bonhams, #60, illus.), image 17½ x 24 in., (44.5 x 61 cm.), color reproduction (BP 605, DM 1472, FR 4992, Y 118,656).

BI *A Question Of Attribution (G & C 76),* s., blindstamp Fine Art Trade Guild, pub. Frost and Reed, 1963, est.BP 5/700, (05-22-93, Bonhams, #79), image 21 x 17 in., (53.3 x 43.2 cm.), color reprod..

BI *A Question Of Attribution (G & C 76), 1963,* s., blindstamp, pub. Frost and Reed, est. BP 7/900, (10-17-92, Bonhams, #73), image 21 x 17 in., (53.3 x 43.2 cm.), color reproduction.

$1104* *A Question Of Colour (G & C 67),* s., blindstamp Fine Art Trade Guild, pub. Frost and Reed, 1961, (05-22-93, Bonhams, #71, illus.), image 17⅝ x 24 in., (44.8 x 61 cm.), color reprod. (BP 715, DM 1795, FR 6039, Y 121,720).

$1168* *Ray,* #484/850, blindstamp, (10-17-92, Bonhams, #32), image 21¼ x 14½ in., (54 x 36.8 cm.), color reproduction (BP 715, DM 1739, FR 5896, Y 140,132).

BI *Ray,* $485/850, blindstamp, est. BP 6/800, (05-22-93, Bonhams, #33), image 21¼ x 14½ in., (54 x 36.8 cm.), color reprod..

$1222* *"Ray As Madame Pompadour" and "Ray As Madame Du Barry": A Pair,* blindstamp, (05-22-93, Bonhams, #34), each, image 10½ x 10½ in., (26.7 x 26.7 cm.), color reprod. (BP 792, DM 1987, FR 6685, Y 134,730).

$1528* *Reclining Nude I (G & C 82),* s., blindstamp Fine Art Trade Guild, pub. Frost and Reed, 1965, (05-22-93, Bonhams, #82, illus.), image 12⅜ x 23 in., (31.4 x 58.4 cm.), color reprod. (BP 990, DM 2485, FR 8359, Y 168,467).

$1654* *Reclining Nude I (G & C 82), 1965,* s., blindstamp, pub. Frost and Reed, (10-17-92, Bonhams, #78), image 12⅜ x 23 in., (31.4 x 58.4 cm.), color reproduction (BP 1012, DM 2462, FR 8349, Y 198,440).

$1438* *Reclining Nude III,* #349/850, blindstamp, (10-17-92, Bonhams, #33, illus.), image 15¼ x 22¾ in., (38.7 x 57.8 cm.), color reproduction (BP 880, DM 2141, FR 7259, Y 172,525).

$2037* *Reclining Nude III,* #5/850, blindstamp, (05-22-93, Bonhams, #35, illus.), image 15¼ x 22¾ in., (38.7 x 57.8 cm.), color reprod. (BP 1320, DM 3312, FR 11,143, Y 224,587).

$374* *Red Background,* blindstamp Fine Art Trade Guild, pub. Adam Coll., 1973, (05-22-93, Bonhams, #36), image 13¼ x 19 in., (33.7 x 48.3 cm.), color reprod. (BP 242, DM 608, FR 2046, Y 41,235).

BI *Red Background, 1973,* pub. Adam Collection, blindstamp, est. BP 2/400, (10-17-92, Bonhams, #34), image 13¼ x 19 in., (33.7 x 48.3 cm.), color reproduction.

$611* *Renee,* #50/500, blindstamp, (10-17-92, Bonhams, #35), image 10½ x 10½ in., (26.7 x 26.7 cm.), color reproduction (BP 374, DM 909, FR 3084, Y 73,305).

$475* *Renee,* #389/500, blindstamp, (05-22-93, Bonhams, #37), image 10½ x 10½ in., (26.7 x 26.7 cm.), color reprod. (BP 308, DM 772, FR 2598, Y 52,370).

BI *Reproof Almeria, 1972,* pub. Medici Society, blindstamp, est. BP 4/600, (10-17-92, Bonhams, #36), image 19½ x 26½ in., (49.5 x 67.3 cm.), color reproduction.

$934* *Retreat From The Sun (G & C 73)*, s., blindstamp Fine Art Trade Guild, pub. Frost and Reed, 1962, (05-22-93, Bonhams, #77), image 17½ x 24 in., (44.5 x 61 cm.), color reprod. (BP 605, DM 1519, FR 5109, Y 102,977).

$306* *Riverside Washing, Lavardac*, blindstamp Fine Art Trade Guild, pub. Adam Coll., 1969, faded, (05-22-93, Bonhams, #38), image 13 x 18 in., (33 x 45.7 cm.), color reprod. (BP 198, DM 498, FR 1674, Y 33,738).

BI *Riverside Washing, Lavardac, 1969*, pub. Adam Collection, blindstamp, faded, est. BP 3/400, (10-17-92, Bonhams, #37), image 13 x 18 in., (33 x 45.7 cm.), color reproduction.

$719* *Rococo Aphrodite*, #212/850, blindstamp, (10-17-92, Bonhams, #38), image 16 x 26 in., (40.6 x 66 cm.), color reproduction (BP 440, DM 1070, FR 3629, Y 86,263).

BI *Rococo Aphrodite*, #488/850, blindstamp, est. BP 3/500, (05-22-93, Bonhams, #39), image 16 x 26 in., (40.6 x 66 cm.), color reprod..

$468* *Rosa And Marisa*, s., i. C F & R; pencil s. blindstamp, (04-02-93, Sloan, #1179), 17⅜ x 24 in., (441 x 610 mm.), color lithograph (BP 308, DM 752, FR 2555, Y 53,285).

BI *Rosa And Marissa (G & C 57)*, s., blindstamp Fine Art Trade Guild, pub. Frost and Reed, 1957, est.BP 7/900, (05-22-93, Bonhams, #66, illus.), image 17¾ x 24 in., (45.1 x 61 cm.), color reprod..

$509* *Rosalba (G & C 66)*, s., blindstamp Fine Art Trade Guild, pub. Medici Society, 1960, (05-22-93, Bonhams, #70), image 17⅜ x 22⅜ in., (44.1 x 56.8 cm.), color reprod. (BP 330, DM 828, FR 2784, Y 56,119).

$827* *Rosalba (G & C 66), 1960*, s., blindstamp, pub. Medici Society, (10-17-92, Bonhams, #66), image 17⅜ x 22⅜ in., (44.1 x 56.8 cm.), color reproduction (BP 506, DM 1231, FR 4175, Y 99,220).

$577* *The Royal Academy Courtyard*, #492/750, blindstamp, (05-22-93, Bonhams, #40), image 20 x 26¾ in., (50.8 x 67.9 cm.), color reprod. (BP 374, DM 938, FR 3156, Y 63,616).

$1664* *Sara (G & C 83)*, s., blindstamp Fine Art Trade Guild, pub. Medici Society, 1965, (05-22-93, Bonhams, #83, illus.), image 15½ x 25 in., (39.4 x 63.5 cm.), color reprod. (BP 1078, DM 2706, FR 9103, Y 183,462).

$1618* *Sara (G & C 83), 1965*, s., blindstamp, pub. Medici Society, (10-17-92, Bonhams, #79, illus.), image 15½ x 25 in., (39.4 x 63.5 cm.), color reproduction (BP 990, DM 2408, FR 8168, Y 194,121).

BI *The Secret Retreat (G & C 79), 1964*, s., blindstamp, pub. Medici Society, est. BP 7/900, (10-17-92, Bonhams, #76), image 16¾ x 22¾ in., (42.5 x 57.8 cm.), color reproduction.

$330* *Semi-Nude Girl*, s., plate s., (11-13-92, DuMouchelle, #2373, illus.), 7¼ x 4½ in., (18.4 x 11.4 cm.), etching (BP 213, DM 518, FR 1747, Y 40,958).

$849* *The Shower (G & C 69)*, s., blindstamp Fine Art Trade Guild, pub. Medici Society, 1961, (05-22-93, Bonhams, #73), image 16¾ x 22 in., (42.5 x 55.9 cm.), color reprod. (BP 550, DM 1380, FR 4644, Y 93,605).

BI *The Shower (G & C 69), 1961*, s., blindstamp, pub. Medici Society, est. BP 7/900, (10-17-92, Bonhams, #67), image 16¾ x 22 in., (42.5 x 55.9 cm.), color reproduction.

$849* *Silver And White*, #523/850, blindstamp, (05-22-93, Bonhams, #41), image 12⅛ x 22¼ in., (30.8 x 56.5 cm.), color reprod. (BP 550, DM 1380, FR 4644, Y 93,605).

$883* *The Silver Frock (G & C 98)*, s., blindstamp Fine Art Trade Guild, pub. Adam Coll., 1969, faded, (05-22-93, Bonhams, #97), image 5½ x 11¼ in., (14 x 28.6 cm.), color reprod. (BP 572, DM 1436, FR 4830, Y 97,354).

BI *The Silver Mirror*, est. BP 150/200, (10-17-92, Bonhams, #110), image 10¾ x 18 in., (27.3 x 45.7 cm.), color reproduction.

BI *The Silver Mirror (G & C 71)*, s., blindstamp Fine Art Trade Guild, pub. Frost and Reed, 1961, est.BP 5/700, (05-22-93, Bonhams, #75), image 11 x 18 in., (27.9 x 45.7 cm.), color reprod..

BI *The Silver Mirror (G & C 71), 1961*, s., blindstamp, pub. Frost and Reed, est. BP 800/1,000, (10-17-92, Bonhams, #69, illus.), image 11 x 18 in., (27.9 x 45.7 cm.), color reproduction.

$300* *Slippery Steps (W. 20)*, 1929, 4th state of 5, s., num. LXXII, light-staining, (11-30-92, Phillips-London, #336), plate 9½ x 6¾ in., (241 x 171 mm.), drypoint on wove (BP 198, DM 478, FR 1622, Y 37,337).

$1273* *Sonnet XXIV*, #33/750, blindstamp Adam Coll., (05-22-93, Bonhams, #42, illus.), image 14½ x 20 in., (36.8 x 50.8 cm.), color reprod. (BP 825, DM 2070, FR 6964, Y 140,353).

BI *Spanish Dancers*, s., pub. 1958 by Frost and Reed, (12-11-92, G.A. Key, #141, illus.), 17 x 23 in., (43.2 x 58.4 cm.), colored proof.

$539* *St. Malo, August 1939 (G & C 32), 1947*, s., blindstamp, pub. Frost and Reed, (10-17-92, Bonhams, #55), image 14¼ x 24 in., (36.2 x 61 cm.), color reproduction (BP 330, DM 802, FR 2721, Y 64,667).

$440* *Standing Nude Woman Holding Drapery*, s., plate s., (11-13-92, DuMouchelle, #2372, illus.), 9½ x 5 in., (24.1 x 12.7 cm.), etching (BP 284, DM 691, FR 2329, Y 54,611).

$645* *Strange Interior, Languedoc (G & C 41)*, s., blindstamp Fine Art Trade Guild, pub. Medici Society, 1952, faded, (05-22-93, Bonhams, #61), image 16½ x 22⅜ in., (41.9 x 56.8 cm.), color reprod. (BP 418, DM 1049, FR 3528, Y 71,114).

BI *Studies Of Cecilia*, est. BP 150/200, (10-17-92, Bonhams, #111), image 14¾ x 27⅞ in., (37.5 x 70.8 cm.), sepia reproduction.

BI *Studies Of Cecilia (G & C 61)*, s., blindstamp Fine Art Trade Guild, pub. Frost and Reed, 1959, est.BP 6/800, (05-22-93, Bonhams, #68, illus.), image 14¾ x 27⅞ in., (37.5 x 70.8 cm.), color reprod..

$1115* *Studies Of Cecilia (G & C 61), 1959*, s., blindstamp, pub. Frost and Reed, (10-17-92, Bonhams, #63, illus.), image 14¾ x 27⅞ in., (37.5 x 70.8 cm.), color reproduction (BP 682, DM 1660, FR 5628, Y 133,773).

$1528* *Study In White*, #15/850, blindstamp, (05-22-93, Bonhams, #43, illus.), image 9⅛ x 14½ in., (23.2 x 36.8 cm.), color reprod. (BP 990, DM 2485, FR 8359, Y 168,467).

$791* *Symposium At Lucenay*, #421/850, blindstamp, (10-17-92, Bonhams, #39), image 19½ x 27 in., (49.5 x 68.6 cm.), color reproduction (BP 484, DM 1177, FR 3993, Y 94,901).

$645* *Symposium At Lucenay*, #423/850, blindstamp, (05-22-93, Bonhams, #44), image 19½ x 27 in., (49.5 x 68.6 cm.), color reprod. (BP 418, DM 1049, FR 3528, Y 71,114).

$1324* *Teresa, Yolande And Anne Marie (G & C 91)*, s., blindstamp Fine Art Trade Guild, pub. Frost and Reed, 1966, (05-22-93, Bonhams, #91, illus.), image 11¾ x 23¼ in., (29.8 x 59.1 cm.), color reprod. (BP 858, DM 2153, FR 7243, Y 145,976).

BI *Teresa, Yolande And Anne Marie (G & C 91), 1967*, s., blindstamp, pub. Medici Society, est. BP 4/600, (10-17-92, Bonhams, #86, illus.), image 19¼ x 26½ in., (48.9 x 67.3 cm.), sepia reproduction.

BI *Three Girls*, #780/850, blindstamp, est. BP 4/600, (10-17-92, Bonhams, #40, illus.), image 12¼ x 21½ in., (31.1 x 54.6 cm.), color reproduction.

$863* *Three Groups, Viviers (G & C 74), 1962*, s., blindstamp, pub. Medici Society, (10-17-92, Bonhams, #71), image 16¾ x 22⅞ in., (42.5 x 58.1 cm.), color reproduction (BP 528, DM 1285, FR 4356, Y 103,539).

$1029* *"Three Poor Travellers, Madrid" and "Gleading Sands" (Salamon Plate II and VIII), 1929 and 1930: Two*, s, #LXXIX and X X, margins, good cond., (06-30-93, Sotheby-London, #326), one sh 7¼ x 9¼ in., (184 x 235 mm.), the other sh 17¾ x 10⅞ in., (184 x 235 mm.), two drypoint on J. Whatman wove (BP 690, DM 1755, FR 5921, Y 110,254).

$330* *Three Semi-Nude Women*, s., (11-13-92, DuMouchelle, #2371), 4¾ x 6 in., (12.1 x 15.2 cm.), etching (BP 213, DM 518, FR 1747, Y 40,958).

BI *The Trio (G & C 80), 1964*, s., blindstamp, pub. Medici Society, faded, est. BP 3/400, (10-17-92, Bonhams, #77), image 17⅛ x 23⅛ in., (43.5 x 58.7 cm.), color reproduction.

$1115* *Two Models (G & C 64), 1960*, s., blindstamp, pub. Medici Society, (10-17-92, Bonhams, #65, illus.), image

14⅝ x 11⅜ in., (37.1 x 28.9 cm.), color reproduction (BP 682, DM 1660, FR 5628, Y 133,773).

$440* *"Under The Palace Terrace"*, s., (05-15-93, Dunning, #92), 17½ x 23¾ in., (44.5 x 60.3 cm.), lithograph in color (BP 286, DM 708, FR 2378, Y 48,775).

$1273* *The Unseen Target (G & C 87)*, s., blindstamp Fine Art Trade Guild, pub. Frost and Reed, 1966, (05-22-93, Bonhams, #87, illus.), image 17¾ x 24 in., (45.1 x 61 cm.), color reprod. (BP 825, DM 2070, FR 6964, Y 140,353).

BI *Unseen Target (G & C 87), 1966*, s., blindstamp, pub. Frost and Reed, est. BP 6/800, (10-17-92, Bonhams, #82, illus.), image 17¾ x 24 in., (45.1 x 61 cm.), color reproduction.

$781* *Unwelcome Observers (G & C 36)*, s., blindstamp Fine Art Trade Guild, pub. W. J. Stacey, 1950, faded, (05-22-93, Bonhams, #60), image 15¼ x 21⅛ in., (38.7 x 53.7 cm.), color reprod. (BP 506, DM 1270, FR 4272, Y 86,108).

BI *Unwelcome Observers (G & C 36), 1950*, s., blindstamp, pub. W.J. Stacey, est. BP 5/800, (10-17-92, Bonhams, #56, illus.), image 15½ x 21 in., (39.4 x 53.3 cm.), color reproduction.

$1079* *Variations III*, #230/850, blindstamp, (10-17-92, Bonhams, #42), image 18½ x 26½ in., (47 x 67.3 cm.), color reproduction (BP 660, DM 1606, FR 5447, Y 129,454).

$1348* *Variations III*, #729/850, blindstamp, (10-17-92, Bonhams, #41), image 18½ x 26½ in., (47 x 67.3 cm.), color reproduction (BP 825, DM 2007, FR 6805, Y 161,728).

BI *Variations III*, #732/850, blindstamp, est. BP 6/800, (05-22-93, Bonhams, #45), image 18½ x 26½ in., (47 x 67.3 cm.), color reprod..

$1698* *Variations IV (G & C 86)*, s., blindstamp Fine Art Trade Guild, pub. Frost and Reed, 1966, (05-22-93, Bonhams, #86, illus.), image 17¾ x 24 in., (45.1 x 61 cm.), color reprod. (BP 1100, DM 2761, FR 9289, Y 187,211).

BI *Variations IV (G & C 86), 1966*, s., blindstamp, pub. Frost and Reed, est. BP 800/1,200, (10-17-92, Bonhams, #81), 17¾ x 24 in., (45.1 x 61 cm.), color reproduction.

BI *Variations On A Theme*, est. BP 2/250, (10-17-92, Bonhams, #112), image 21⅝ x 24⅛ in., (54.9 x 61.3 cm.), color reproduction.

$1698* *Variations On A Theme (G & C 77)*, s., blindstamp Fine Art Trade Guild, pub. Frost and Reed, 1963, (05-22-93, Bonhams, #80, illus.), image 21½ x 24½ in., (54.6 x 62.2 cm.), color reprod. (BP 1100, DM 2761, FR 9289, Y 187,211).

$3595* *"Variations On A Theme (G & C 77)", "Variations IV" (G & C 86) and "Variations III", 1963: Three*, first s., blindstamp, pub. Frost and Reed, (10-17-92, Bonhams, #74, illus.), image 21½ x 24¼ in., (54.6 x 61.6 cm.), color reproduction (BP 2200, DM 5351, FR 18,147, Y 431,314).

$2207* *Venetian Festival (G & C 89)*, s., blindstamp Fine Art Trade Guild, pub. Frost and Reed, 1965, (05-22-93, Bonhams, #89, illus.), image 17¾ x 24¼ in., (45.1 x 61.6 cm.), color reprod. (BP 1430, DM 3589, FR 12,073, Y 243,330).

$1888* *Venetian Festival (G & C 89), 1967*, s., blindstamp, pub. Frost and Reed, (10-17-92, Bonhams, #84, illus.), image 18 x 24⅛ in., (45.7 x 61.3 cm.), color reproduction (BP 1155, DM 2810, FR 9531, Y 226,515).

$395* *Victorian Diversion (G & C 37), 1951*, s., blindstamp, pub. Medici Society, faded, (10-17-92, Bonhams, #57), image 21⅝ x 16⅜ in., (54.9 x 41.6 cm.), color reproduction (BP 242, DM 588, FR 1994, Y 47,391).

$849* *La Voulte-Sur-Rhone (G & C 100)*, s., blindstamp Fine Art Trade Guild, pub. Frost and Reed, 1969, (05-22-93, Bonhams, #99), image 17½ x 24 in., (44.5 x 61 cm.), color reprod. (BP 550, DM 1380, FR 4644, Y 93,605).

$683* *La Voulte-Sur-Rhone (G & C 100), 1969*, s., blindstamp, pub. Frost and Reed, (10-17-92, Bonhams, #92), image 17⅝ x 24 in., (44.8 x 61 cm.), color reproduction (BP 418, DM 1017, FR 3448, Y 81,944).

$1188* *Waves (G & C 104)*, s., blindstamp Fine Art Trade Guild, pub. Frost and Reed, 1969, (05-22-93, Bonhams, #102, illus.), image 18 x 24 in., (45.7 x 61 cm.), color reprod. (BP 770, DM 1932, FR 6499, Y 130,981).

BI *Waves (G & C 104), 1969*, s., blindstamp, pub. Frost and Reed, est. BP 700/1,000, (10-17-92, Bonhams, #95,

illus.), image 17½ x 24 in., (44.5 x 61 cm.), color reproduction.

$645* *White Interior, Chateauneuf-Sur-Loire (G & C 93)*, s., blindstamp Fine Art Trade Guild, pub. Medici Society, 1964, (05-22-93, Bonhams, #93), image 19½ x 26⅜ in., (49.5 x 67 cm.), color reprod. (BP 418, DM 1049, FR 3528, Y 71,114).

BI *White Interior, Chateauneuf-Sur-Loire (G & C 93), 1964*, s., blindstamp, pub. Medici Society, est. BP 5/700, (10-17-92, Bonhams, #87), image 19½ x 26⅜ in., (49.5 x 67 cm.), color reproduction.

BI *Winter Sport (G & C 4), 1927*, s., blindstamp, pub. W.J. Stacey, est. BP 5/700, (10-17-92, Bonhams, #48), image 13⅜ x 18 in., (34 x 45.7 cm.), color reproduction.

$187* *Women In A Continental Street*, calendar p., s., i., (05-22-93, Bonhams, #127), image 9½ x 13 in., (24.1 x 33 cm.), color reprod. (BP 121, DM 304, FR 1023, Y 20,617).

$611* *Zoronga (G & C 18)*, s., blindstamp Fine Art Trade Guild, pub. Frost and Reed, 1936, (05-22-93, Bonhams, #55), image 15¾ x 21 in., (40 x 53.3 cm.), color reprod. (BP 396, DM 993, FR 3342, Y 67,365).

$989* *Zoronga (G & C 18), 1936*, s., blindstamp, pub. Frost and Reed, (10-17-92, Bonhams, #51, illus.), image 15¾ x 21 in., (40 x 53.3 cm.), color reproduction (BP 605, DM 1472, FR 4992, Y 118,656).

BI *The 'Frances And Jane' At Birdham*, #439/100, pub. Museum Prints, 1983, est. BP 1/150, (05-22-93, Bonhams, #15), image 12¾ x 19¼ in., (32.4 x 48.9 cm.), color reprod..

FLINT, Sir William Russell (after)

BI *Act II, Scene I*, #203/850, blindstamp, est. BP 5/700, (05-20-93, Bonhams-Chelsea, #143), image 15½ x 22½ in., (39.4 x 57.2 cm.), reprod. in colors.

BI *Carlotta On The Loire*, num. 35/850, blindstamp, est. BP 4/600, (08-20-92, Bonhams-Chelsea, #126), image 19½ x 26¾ in., (49.5 x 67.9 cm.), reproduction in colors.

BI *Cecilia And Her Studies*, num. 20/850. blindstamp, est. BP 4/600, (08-20-92, Bonhams-Chelsea, #128), image 10⅜ x 14⅝ in., (26.4 x 37.1 cm.), reproduction in colors.

BI *Cecilia And Her Studies*, num. 568/850, blindstamp, est. BP 4/600, (08-20-92, Bonhams-Chelsea, #125), image 10⅜ x 14⅝ in., (26.4 x 37.1 cm.), reproduction in colors.

BI *Eve And Yasmin And An Unfinished Picture (Gardner & Clark 59), 1958*, s., blindstamp, pub. Frost and Reed, faded, est. BP3/400, (01-21-93, Bonhams-Chelsea, #157), image 17½ x 25 in., (44.5 x 63.5 cm.), reprod. in colors.

$100* *"Four Models Seated Around A Green Armchair"*, (11-19-92, Bonhams-Chelsea, #65), image 9¼ x 13⅜ in., (23.5 x 34 cm.), color reproduction (BP 66, DM 159, FR 537, Y 12,436).

$1036* *The Four Sisters, Chazelet*, s., pub. Frost & Reed, 1957, pub. blindstamp, fading, (10-07-92, Christie-S. Ken, #32), 17½ x 24 in., (44.5 x 61 cm.), reprod. p. in color (BP 605, DM 1499, FR 5083, Y 124,594).

$58 *"Garden Of Romance"*, (02-05-93, G.A. Key, #8), 13¾ x 16 in., (34.9 x 40.6 cm.), colored print (BP 40, DM 96, FR 325, Y 7218).

BI *Gossipers Le Castelet*, num. 413/850, blindstamp, est. BP 4/600, (08-20-92, Bonhams-Chelsea, #122), image 19½ x 26¼ in., (49.5 x 66.7 cm.), reproduction in colors.

$503* *Griselda (Gardner and Clark 58)*, s., blindstamp, pub. Medici Society, 1958, faded, (10-15-92, Bonhams-Chelsea, #18), image 18¼ x 22¼ in., (46.4 x 56.5 cm.), color reproduction (BP 308, DM 749, FR 2539, Y 60,348).

BI *Group Of Idlers (Gardner And Clark 90), 1967*, s., blindstamp, pub. Medici Society, est. BP 3/500, (08-20-92, Bonhams-Chelsea, #55E), image 19¼ x 26½ in., (48.9 x 67.3 cm.), reproduction in sepia.

$1492* *Iberian Flounces: A Pair*, num. 379/850, blindstamps, (08-20-92, Bonhams-Chelsea, #55B), image 11 x 7¾ in., (27.9 x 19.7 cm.), reproduction in colors (BP 770, DM 2160, FR 7332, Y 188,408).

BI *Isabella Of Lucenay (Gardner And Clark 99), 1969*, s., blindstamp, pub. Medici Society, est. BP 5/800, (08-20-

92, Bonhams-Chelsea, #55, illus.), image 19¼ x 26¼ in., (48.9 x 66.7 cm.), reproduction in colors.

$640* *The Looking Glass,* num. 125/850, blindstamp, (08-20-92, Bonhams-Chelsea, #127), image 11 x 14¾ in., (27.9 x 37.5 cm.), reproduction in colors (BP 330, DM 927, FR 3145, Y 80,818).

BI *Market Hall, Cordes (Gardner and Clark 78), 1963,* s., blindstamp, pub. Medici Society, est. BP 4/600, (08-20-92, Bonhams-Chelsea, #121), image 16¾ x 22¾ in., (42.5 x 57.8 cm.), reproduction in colors.

BI *The Mill Pool,* num. 151/850, blindstamp, est. BP 5/700, (08-20-92, Bonhams-Chelsea, #123), image 20 x 27 in., (50.8 x 68.6 cm.), reproduction in colors.

$535* *Provencal Caprice (G. & C. 51),* s., blindstamp, pub. Medici Society, faded, (11-19-92, Bonhams-Chelsea, #147), image 17¼ x 22½ in., (43.8 x 57.2 cm.), color reproduction (BP 352, DM 853, FR 2873, Y 66,534).

$683* *Reclining Nude III,* #769/850, blindstamp, (12-10-92, Bonhams-Chelsea, #14), image 15¼ x 22½ in., (38.7 x 57.2 cm.), color reproduction (BP 440, DM 1080, FR 3690, Y 84,488).

BI *Reclining Nude III,* num. 769/850, blindstamp, est. BP 7/900, (08-20-92, Bonhams-Chelsea, #55C), image 15¼ x 22½ in., (38.7 x 57.2 cm.), reproduction in colors.

$938* *The Secret Retreat (Gardner And Clark 79), 1964,* s., blindstamp, pub. Medici Society, (08-20-92, Bonhams-Chelsea, #55D), image 16¾ x 22¾ in., (42.5 x 57.8 cm.), reproduction in colors (BP 484, DM 1358, FR 4609, Y 118,449).

$511* *The Silver Mirror (G&C 71),* s., blindstamp, pub. Frost & Reed, 1961, (04-22-93, Bonhams-Chelsea, #45), 11 x 18 in., (27.9 x 45.7 cm.), reprod. in colors (BP 330, DM 821, FR 2770, Y 56,185).

BI *The Silver Mirror (G. & C. 71), 1961,* s., blindstamp, pub. Frost and Reed, est. BP 4/600, (02-17-93, Bonhams-Chelsea, #314), image 11 x 18 in., (27.9 x 45.7 cm.), color reproduction.

BI *The Silver Mirror (Gardner And Clark 71), 1961,* s., blindstamp, pub. Frost and Reed, est. BP 5/700, (08-20-92, Bonhams-Chelsea, #54, illus.), image 11 x 18 in., (27.9 x 45.7 cm.), reproduction in colors.

BI *Strange Interior, Languedoc (G. & C. 41),* s., blindstamp, pub. Medici Society, 1952, faded, est. BP 250/350, (05-20-93, Bonhams-Chelsea, #127), image 16½ x 22½ in., (41.9 x 57.2 cm.), reprod. in colors.

BI *Two Models (Gardner And Clark 64), 1960,* s., blindstamp, pub. Medici Society, est. BP 7-900, (08-20-92, Bonhams-Chelsea, #53, illus.), image 14⅝ x 11⅜ in., (37.1 x 28.9 cm.), reproduction in colors.

$717* *Unseen Target (G&C 87), 1966,* s., blindstamp, pub. Frost & Reed, (12-10-92, Bonhams-Chelsea, #118, illus.), image 17¾ x 24 in., (45.1 x 61 cm.), color reproduction (BP 462, DM 1134, FR 3874, Y 88,694).

BI *Unwelcome Observers (G. & C. 36),* from ed. of 650, s., blindstamp, pub. W.J. Stacey, 1950, faded, est.BP 350/450, (05-20-93, Bonhams-Chelsea, #126), image 15⅜ x 21 in., (39.1 x 53.3 cm.), reprod. in colors.

BI *La Voulte-Sur-Rhone (Gardner And Clark 100), 1969,* s., blindstamp, pub. Frost and Reed, est. BP 4/600, (08-20-92, Bonhams-Chelsea, #55A), image 17½ x 24 in., (44.5 x 61 cm.), reproduction in colors.

$763* *Waves (G. & C. 104), 1969,* s., blindstamp, pub. Frost and Reed, (02-17-93, Bonhams-Chelsea, #313), image 17½ x 24 in., (44.5 x 61 cm.), color reproduction (BP 528, DM 1239, FR 4197, Y 91,137).

BI *Waves (Gardner And Clark 104), 1969,* s., blindstamp, pub. Frost and Reed, est. BP 5/700, (08-20-92, Bonhams-Chelsea, #8, illus.), image 17½ x 24 in., (44.5 x 61 cm.), reproduction in colors.

FLODIN, Hilda

BI *Potters At Work,* d. 1903, s., margins, foxing, est. BP 6/90, (05-20-93, Bonhams-Chelsea, #63), plate 5½ x 6¼ in., (14 x 15.9 cm.), etching.

FLOR, Eduard

$51* *Le Printemps, 1981,* s., t., #114/190, margins, good cond., (05-27-93, Sotheby-Amstrdm, #412), 8⅛ x 8¼ in., colored etching on wove (BP 33, DM 82, FR 276, Y 5467, G 92).

$51* *Untitled, 1981,* s., #140/190, margins, good cond., (05-27-93, Sotheby-Amstrdm, #413), 9¹³⁄₁₆ x 8¹⁄₁₆ in., (250 x 205 mm.), colored etching on wove (BP 33, DM 82, FR 276, Y 5467, G 92).

$51* *Untitled, 1981,* s., #137/190, margins, good cond., (05-27-93, Sotheby-Amstrdm, #414), 10¹⁄₁₆ x 8³⁄₁₆ in., (255 x 208 mm.), colored etching on wove (BP 33, DM 82, FR 276, Y 5467, G 92).

FLORENTINE SCHOOL

BI *Cupid Pissing On A Grind Stone (Hind. A.I. 93),* narrow margins, trimmed, good cond., ex. coll. R.L. Mayer, est. BP 4/600, (06-29-93, Sotheby-London, #44, illus.), 2 x 1¾ in., (5.1 x 4.4 cm.), engraving.

FLORENTINE SCHOOL: FINE MANNER

$805* *Dante And Virgil, With The Vision Of Beatrice (Hind A.V.2 (2)), 1481,* after Botticelli, from Dante's Divaina Comedia, pub. Nicolaus Laurentii, later impression, trimmed to borderline, holes, creases, stains, good cond., ex-coll. Dr. Albert W. Blum, (05-13-93, Sotheby-NY, #314), 3⅝ x 6⅝ in., (92 x 169 mm.), engraving (BP 528, DM 1300, FR 4385, Y 89,874).

FLORES, Pedro

$164* *"Marche Rue Mouffetard",* artist's proof, (03-17-93, Duran, #179, illus.), 5¹³⁄₁₆ x 7¹¹⁄₁₆ in., (14.8 x 19.6 cm.), aquatint (BP 113, DM 273, FR 928, Y 19,235, P 19,550).

FLORIS, Frans

BI *Victory Surrounded By Prisoners And Trophies (Holl. 4), 1552,* narrow margins, paper adhering to edge, crease, surface dirt, laid down, est. BP 2/3,000, (06-30-93, Sotheby-London, #122), 12½ x 17¼ in., (318 x 438 mm.), etching.

FLORSHEIM, Richard American 1916-1976/79

$55* *"Boats In Harbor",* s., AAA edit., good cond., (10-31-92, Cleveland, #119), 9⅞ x 14 in., (25.1 x 35.6 cm.), lithograph (BP 35, DM 85, FR 287, Y 6813).

$193* *The Bridge,* s., t., annot. Artist's Proof, full margins, very good cond., surfacesoiling, (02-24-93, Butterfield, #2820), 14 x 10 in., (356 x 254 mm.), lithograph on cream wove (BP 135, DM 313, FR 1062, Y 22,647).

$198* *"Illuminations", "Night" and "Wells": Three,* s., first #179/180, others artist's proofs, Letterio Calapia Estate, (05-16-93, Hindman, #567), larger 15¾ x 22 in., (40 x 55.9 cm.), lithographs, last two in color (BP 129, DM 318, FR 1070, Y 21,949).

BI *"Rigging" and "Full Moon": Two,* each s., t., annot. artist's proof, full margins, good cond., surfacesoiling, creases, est. $4/600, (02-24-93, Butterfield, #2823), each 13⅞ x 9⅞ in., (352 x 251 mm.), lithograph on cream wove.

$330* *"Setting Sun" and "Megalopolis": Two,* each s., t., annot. Artist's Proof, margins, good cond., (02-24-93, Butterfield, #2822), each 13¹⁵⁄₁₆ x 9¹⁵⁄₁₆ in., (354 x 252 mm.), lithograph on wove (BP 230, DM 536, FR 1816, Y 38,723).

$193* *Shoreline,* s., t., annot. artist's proof, margins, good cond., surface soiling,creases, (02-24-93, Butterfield, #2821), 10 x 13¾ in., (254 x 349 mm.), lithograph on wove (BP 135, DM 313, FR 1062, Y 22,647).

FLOWER, Cedric b. 1920

$57* *Greeks And Trojans (1968),* s. Cedric Flowers, i., d. '68, #62/100, lit., (08-11-92, L. Joel, #119G), 19⁵⁄₁₆ x 25⁹⁄₁₆ in., (49 x 65 cm.), five color lithograph (BP 30, DM 84, FR 283, Y 7299, A$ 77).

FLUXUS

$614* *Galerie Legitime,* s., num., (11-28-92, Schoppmann, #513), 20¹⁄₁₆ x 29⁵⁄₁₆ in., (51 x 74.5 cm.), color serigraph on light cardboard (BP 405, DM 978, FR 3321, Y 76,416).

$87* *Human Liberation,* s., (11-28-92, Schoppmann, #523), 20¹⁄₁₆ x 26⁹⁄₁₆ in., (51 x 67.5 cm.), color serigraph on cardboard (BP 57, DM 139, FR 471, Y 10,828).

FOGELIN, Anders b. 1933

$1963* *Landscape,* s., 1977, proof, (05-25-93, AB Stockholm, #23), 22¹⁄₁₆ x 26³⁄₁₆ in., (56 x 66.5 cm.), lithograph in colors on velin Arches (BP 1272, DM 3197, FR 10,762, Y 214,559, SK 2860).

FOGELQVIST, Jorgen b. 1927
$55* *Composition,* s. 125/185, (11-07-92, Falkkloos, #130), color lithograph (BP 36, DM 88, FR 297, Y 6788, SK 330).

FOLBERG, Neil
$690* *"Dunes Near Dakhla Oasis, Western Desert", 1985,* s., t., d., #8/100, (05-23-93, Butterfield, #3414, illus.), 14 x 18⅞ in., photograph, cibachrome print (BP 449, DM 1128, FR 3797, Y 76,268).
BI *"Portal Arch, Spider Mesa, Colorado" and "Dawn, Agua Canyon, ColoradoPlateau": Colorado: Two,* each s., d. by photog., w/ed. & (c) labels, num. 23/75 & 17/75, est.$1/2,000, (10-15-92, Sotheby-NY, #598A, illus.), each, approx. 14 x 17½ in., (35.6 x 44.5 cm.), photograph, cibachrome prints.

FOLON, Jean Michel French b. 1934
$247* *Croix Rouge Francaise,* RC Pontoise, B+ cond., closed tears, discoloration, (08-06-92, Swann, #132, illus.), 62½ x 47 in., (158.8 x 119.4 cm.), (BP 129, DM 365, FR 1233, Y 31,505).
$174* *La Gravure,* s., 17/60, good cond., (06-28-93, Loudmer, #246), 9⅜ x 13 11/16 in., (238 x 347 mm.), sh 14 15/16 x 20 13/16 in., (238 x 347 mm.), color etching and aquatint on wove (BP 117, DM 296, FR 996, Y 18,462).
BI *The Guardian,* excellent cond., est. $4-600, (10-31-92, Cleveland, #372, illus.), 11⅝ x 14⅝ in., (29.5 x 37.1 cm.), etching and aquatint in colors.
$252* *Je Vous Ecris De Chine, 1986,* s., from "Je vous ecris", ed. Francis de Lille, (11-16-92, Briest, #52), 31⅛ x 34 7/16 in., (79 x 87.5 cm.), serigraph in colors (BP 166, DM 402, FR 1354, Y 31,449).
$272* *L"Homme Et Son Double,* 22/90, s., (10-14-92, Germann, #297), 19 13/16 x 25 13/16 in., (503 x 656 mm.), etching/aquatint (BP 160, DM 398, FR 1350, Y 32,962, SF 354).
$413* *"Marathon", 1973,* s. Folon, num. 184/200, pub. dry stamp; ident. on label verso, very good cond., (09-11-92, Skinner, #99A, illus.), sight 30¼ x 22⅜ in., (76.8 x 56.8 cm.), color screenprint on paper (BP 214, DM 595, FR 2021, Y 51,171).
$593* *Opera Glasses Head, 1974,* 111/150, s., (04-21-93, Germann, #431), 37⅝ x 29⅛ in., (955 x 740 mm.), color serigraph (BP 385, DM 948, FR 3205, Y 65,648, SF 863).
$476* *Qui, 1979,* #73/90, s., prov., (11-16-92, Hodgins, #115), 11¾ x 14½ in., (29.9 x 36.8 cm.), color etching on paper (BP 313, DM 759, FR 2558, Y 59,403, C$ 605).
$124* *Le Reve,* s., #79/300, creases, (03-31-93, Briest, #E44), 25 15/16 x 19⅞ in., (66 x 50.5 cm.), color serigraph (BP 82, DM 199, FR 678, Y 14,259).
$337* *"Roland Garros 1982",* artist's proof I/X, s., (10-18-92, Pescheteau, #143), 16⅛ x 12⅝ in., (60 x 50 cm.), etching and aquatint on velin (BP 204, DM 498, FR 1691, Y 40,239).
BI *"Roland-Garros",* #27/90, s., est. FF1,000/1,500, (04-04-93, Pescheteau, #214), 23⅝ x 19 11/16 in., (60 x 50 cm.), etching and aquatint on wove.
$77* *Sans Titre,* s., 25/75, (06-28-93, Loudmer, #247), 21⅝ x 29 5/16 in., (550 x 745 mm.), sh approx. 29 5/16 x 36 13/16 in., (550 x 745 mm.), color lithograph on wove (BP 52, DM 131, FR 441, Y 8170).
$332* *Untitled,* s., waterstains, (01-28-93, Pescheteau, #143), 18½ x 21⅝ in., (47 x 55 cm.), etching and aquatint on wove (BP 219, DM 526, FR 1780, Y 41,222).
$385* *"Le Voyant", 1974,* s. Folon, num. 111/150, dry stamp; ident. on label verso, very good cond., full margins, (09-11-92, Skinner, #98A, illus.), sight 30½ x 23⅝ in., (77.5 x 60 cm.), color screenprint on paper (BP 199, DM 554, FR 1884, Y 47,702).

FONCUBERTA b. 1955
$455* *Pflanzen Und Krane, 1986,* ink s., d., (11-12-92, Lempertz, #62), 10 7/16 x 10⅜ in., (26.5 x 26.3 cm.), photograph, gelatin silver print (BP 291, DM 715, FR 2437, Y 56,291).

FONDA
$94* *Henry Fonda Paintings And Drawings, September 17-October 2, 1981,* s. Henry Fonda, i., exhibition poster, Swope Gallery, (10-08-92, Boos, #691), 29 x 22¾ in., (737 x 578 mm.), (BP 56, DM 139, FR 472, Y 11,422).

FONTANA, Franco b. 1933
$5175* *Selected Landscape Views: Eleven,* 1967-87, for portfolio Untitled, p. 1990, each ink s., t., d., #11/15, embossed credit stamp, (04-08-93, Christie-NY, #486, illus.), each approx. 20 x 13¼ in., (50.8 x 33.7 cm.), photograph, dye transfer print (BP 3393, DM 8313, FR 28,140, Y 587,267).

FONTANA, Lucio Italian 1899-1968
$1887* *Composition,* s., #72/99, pub. 2RC, blindstamp, full margins, skinned spots, (06-30-93, Sotheby-London, #789, illus.), sh 23⅝ x 19⅛ in., (600 x 486 mm.), lithograph w/embossing and puncturing on green wove (faded) (BP 1265, DM 3218, FR 10,857, Y 202,186).
$367* *Composition,* s. L. Fontana, 33/50, (03-24-93, Kunsthallen, #108), lithograph (BP 249, DM 599, FR 2040, Y 43,121, DK 2300).
$385* *Composition,* s. L. Fontana, 33/55, (03-24-93, Kunsthallen, #109), lithograph (BP 261, DM 629, FR 2140, Y 45,236, DK 2415).
$1716* *Composition, 1988,* s., #16/50, pub. 2RC, blindstamp, full margins, good cond., skinned spots, (06-30-93, Sotheby-London, #790, illus.), sh 23⅝ x 19⅛ in., (600 x 486 mm.), embossing and puncturing (BP 1150, DM 2927, FR 9873, Y 183,864).
$933* *Concetta Spaziale, 1958,* #31/70, s. twice, d., Edizioni la Salita, timbro, (03-25-93, Finarte-Rome, #15, illus.), lithograph (BP 634, DM 1533, FR 5212, Y 109,302, L 1495).
$2166* *Concetto Spaziale,* s., customs stamp, yellowing, (11-28-92, Schoppmann, #545), 25 3/16 x 18⅞ in., (64 x 48 cm.), embossing w/perforation on handmade (BP 1430, DM 3451, FR 11,714, Y 269,571).
$3069* *(Concetto Spaziale), c. 1966,* s., #49/50, blindstamp, Stamperia Duerreci, full margins, good cond., (12-03-92, Sotheby-London, #664, illus.), sheet 24¾ x 18¾ in., (630 x 500 mm.), etching w/embossing and slashing in beige on wove (BP 1980, DM 4826, FR 16,473, Y 381,859).
$2231* *Concetto Spaziale, c. 1966,* s., #42/99, blindstamp 2RC, full margins, good cond., discoloration, (06-30-93, Sotheby-London, #793, illus.), sh 23⅝ x 18½ in., (600 x 470 mm.), lithograph in green w/slashing on wove (BP 1495, DM 3805, FR 12,837, Y 239,044).
BI *Fontana,* for Moderna Museet 1967, s. L. Fontana, est. DK 3,000, (09-30-92, Kunsthallen, #109), poster.
$18,874* *Incisioni Originali, c. 1970: Set Of Six,* s., #9/50, p. by Stamperia 2RC, blindstamp, pub. Edizioni Marlborough-Duerreci, full margins, good cond., rubbing, discoloration, (06-30-93, Sotheby-London, #792, illus.), 6 pl w/embossing and puncturing, 3 w/aquatint and lithograph in color, 3 a secco (w/o ink) on wove (BP 12,650, DM 32,192, FR 108,596, Y 2,022,287).
$2046* *Red Spatial Concept, 1968,* scratch s., #167/190, good cond., creases, (12-03-92, Sotheby-London, #665, illus.), sheet 27½ x 21⅝ in., (700 x 550 mm.), silkscreen on red rhodoid w/punched holes (BP 1320, DM 3217, FR 10,982, Y 254,573).
$895* *Red Spatial Concept, 1968,* scratch s., i. E.A., full sheet, good cond., 2 small creases in upper corners, minor scratches, (05-27-93, Sotheby-Amstrdm, #615, illus.), silkscreen on red rhodoid w/punched holes (BP 573, DM 1436, FR 4840, Y 95,948, G 1610).
$1563* *Red Spatial Concept, 1968,* scratch s., i. E.A., good cond.?, (12-09-92, Sotheby-Amstrdm, #574, illus.), sheet 27 9/16 x 21⅝ in., (700 x 550 mm.), silkscreen on red rhodoid w/punched holes (BP 997, DM 2453, FR 8372, Y 193,800, G 2760).
$993* *Rote Zackenlinie,* s., (06-05-93, Grisebach, #577, illus.), 19⅛ x 26 15/16 in., (48.5 x 68.5 cm.), color serigraph on transparent foil w/perforations (BP 654, DM 1610, FR 5426, Y 106,522).
$9437* *Sei Acqueforte Originale De Lucio Fontana, c. 1966: Set Of Six,* s., #3[illegible], p. by Stamperia Duerreci, blinds-

tamp, pub. Marlborough Galleria d'Arte, title-page and etched vignettes, good cond., rubbed, handling creases, tipped to backing sheets, 7 including title-page, (06-30-93, Sotheby-London, #791, illus.), each sh c. 19⅝ x 25 in., (498 x 635 mm.), etching w/embossing and slashing, 4 in white, 1 in black and 1 a secco (w/o ink), on C.M. Fabriano (BP 6325, DM 16,096, FR 54,298, Y 1,011,143).

$1165* *Untitled Multiple*, scratch-signed, num. 38/190, defects, scratches, good cond., (12-01-92, Christie-London, #571), overall S. 27¹⁵⁄₁₆ x 22¹⁄₁₆ in., (710 x 560 mm.), screenprint in blue w/punched holes on vinyl (BP 770, DM 1857, FR 6328, Y 145,045).

FONTEBOSSO, Francesco Salvator (after)
$155* *Homme En Buste De Profil*, crease, (04-02-93, Picard, #17), 16⁹⁄₁₆ x 11⅝ in., (42 x 29.5 cm.), stipple print engraving (BP 102, DM 249, FR 846, Y 17,648).

FORAIN, Jean Louis   French 1852-1931
$180* *Apres L'Apparition (2e planche) (M.G. 82)*, annot., third state of five, s., stains, reddish, whole margins, (06-11-93, Picard, #54), 9¾ x 11⁵⁄₁₆ in., (248 x 287 mm.), etching, drypoint on laid (BP 118, DM 293, FR 986, Y 19,098).
$320* *Le Christ Depouille De Ses Vetements (M. Guerin 79)*, annot., third state of five, s., creases, large margins, (06-11-93, Picard, #53), 9⅛ x 11¼ in., (232 x 286 mm.), etching and drypoint in bistre on laid (BP 210, DM 520, FR 1753, Y 33,952).
    BI *Eine Stehende Dame (Guerin 16I), 1880*, frontispiece for "Croquis Parisiens", artist's proof, est. DM 2,400, (12-05-92, Bassenge, #7175, illus.), 5¹³⁄₁₆ x 3⅞ in., (14.7 x 9.8 cm.), etching on handmade Van-Gelder.
    BI *Femme Assise, La Tete Dans La Main Droite*, DK est. 1,200, (03-24-93, Kunsthallen, #110), lithograph.
    BI *Les Grandes Enterrements*, Simonis Empis Ed, Paris, flattened crease marks, est. DM 450, (12-05-92, Bassenge, #7629), 12¹³⁄₁₆ x 18⅛ in., (32.5 x 46 cm.), color lithograph.
$764* *Rue Laffitte (Guerin 6)*, before 1902, s., num., blindstamp, (06-23-93, Kornfeld, #339), lithograph (BP 519, DM 1293, FR 4348, Y 83,233, SF 1150).
$28* *"Sante" and "Suz Le Rhin": Two*, s., (12-17-92, Mystic, #9), each 15 x 22 in., (38.1 x 55.9 cm.), lithograph (BP 18, DM 44, FR 149, Y 3441).
    BI *Scene Of A Strike, 1897*, plate s., blindstamp The Studio, margins, good cond., crease, staining, foxing, surface soiling, est. $150/200, (10-28-92, Butterfield, #2809), 8½ x 11¼ in., (216 x 286 mm.), lithograph on cream wove.

FORAIN, Jean Louis (after)   French 1852-1931
$110* *Loin Du Front*, s., #33/300, (12-13-92, Hindman, #262), 9 x 15½ in., gillotage (BP 70, DM 173, FR 589, Y 13,609).

FORBERG, F.K.
$300* *De Figuris Veneris: Twelve*, Suite of Erotica, t., d. 1824 on frontispiece, num. I-XVII, (06-08-93, Ritchie, #17), each plate 7⅜ x 9 in., (18.7 x 22.9 cm.), heliogravure (photoengraving) (BP 197, DM 487, FR 1639, Y 31,864, C$ 385).

FORBES, Alexander (after)
$185* *There Is Much Between The Cup And The Lip*, by John Smith, time-stained, tears, (01-18-93, Bonhams, #76), image 10 x 11¾ in., (25.4 x 29.8 cm.), engraving (BP 121, DM 302, FR 1009, Y 23,320).

FORBES, Edwin   American 1839-1895
$44* *"After Dress Parade" (Pl. 13), 1876*, s., d., t. on pl., (02-19-93, Garth, #90), 17 x 21¾ in., (43.2 x 55.2 cm.), b/w engraving (BP 30, DM 72, FR 244, Y 5221).

FORBES, Edwin, Publisher   American
$468* *Life Studies Of The Great Army, 1876*, portfolio, (07-10-92, Skinner, #443), copper plate etching (BP 244, DM 699, FR 2373, Y 58,610).

FORD, B.F.   American
$90* *"Street Scene", 1948*, s., mat burn, taped, exhib., (05-15-93, Cleveland, #129), 7 x 5½ in., (17.8 x 14 cm.), etching (BP 59, DM 145, FR 486, Y 9977).

FORES, S. W., Publisher
$115* *Thos. Spring. Champion Of England, 1829*, margins, staining, (06-05-93, Christie-NY, #61), pl 16¼ x 11¼ in., (413 x 286 mm.), etching and stipple engraving on wove (BP 76, DM 186, FR 628, Y 12,336).

FORES, S.W., Publisher
    BI *The Patent Stomach Reliever, 1824*, est. BP 80/120, (11-19-92, Bonhams-Chelsea, #106), image 8 x 12¾ in., (20.3 x 32.4 cm.), etching w/hand coloring.

FORG, Gunther   German b. 1952
    BI *Barcelona Pavillon, 1989: Six*, s., d., est. DM 1,200, (11-12-92, Lempertz, #61, illus.), smallest 11⁹⁄₁₆ x 8¼ in., (29.4 x 21 cm.), largest 8¼ x 11⅝ in., (29.4 x 21 cm.), 3 gelatin silver prints and 3 color linocuts.
$22,000* *Colonia 28 Ottobre, Marina Dimassa*, s., d. 86 verso, prov., (11-18-92, Sotheby-NY, #295, illus.), each 106¼ x 47¼ in., (269.9 x 120 cm.), three b/w photographs framed in wood (BP 14,485, DM 35,077, FR 118,153, Y 2,735,978).
$6900* *Gardone*, exec. 1988, prov., (02-23-93, Sotheby-NY, #358, illus.), 106¼ x 47¼ in., (269.9 x 120 cm.), photograph, b/w in wood frame (BP 4727, DM 11,147, FR 37,808, Y 805,886).
    BI *Liken 1, Galerie Gisela Capitain, 1988: Set Of Sixteen*, s., d., num. II/V, good cond., loose, est. BP 800/1200, (12-01-92, Christie-London, #571A), overall S. 21⅝ x 15⁹⁄₁₆ in., (550 x 395 mm.), etching in colors on wove.
$607* *Ohne Titel, 1984*, s., #52/60, (11-12-92, Lempertz, #60), 7¹¹⁄₁₆ x 11⁵⁄₁₆ in., (19.6 x 28.7 cm.), and 25⁹⁄₁₆ x 19¹¹⁄₁₆ in., (19.6 x 28.7 cm.), 2 sheets w/3 color photographs (BP 388, DM 954, FR 3251, Y 75,096).
$4455* *Ohne Titel: Two*, exec. 1983, prov., (05-20-93, Christie-London, #657, illus.), 47¼ x 76 in., photograph, b/w and color (BP 2875, DM 7097, FR 23,952, Y 491,559).
$11,000* *Rom*, exec. 1987, unique, prov., (11-19-92, Christie-NY, #163, illus.), 111 x 51½ in., (281.9 x 130.8 cm.), photograph, b/w in artist's frame (BP 7243, DM 17,538, FR 59,076, Y 1,367,989).
$8050* *Rom*, exec. 1987, prov., exhib., (05-04-93, Sotheby-NY, #180, illus.), 110 x 52 in., (279.4 x 132.1 cm.), b/w photograph (BP 5139, DM 12,681, FR 42,728, Y 885,491).
$398* *Sechs Rechtecke, (19)91*, s., d., (12-01-92, Karl/Faber, #617), 21⅝ x 31½ in., (55 x 80 cm.), woodcut in green on textured cardboard (BP 263, DM 634, FR 2162, Y 49,552).
$11,500* *Untitled*, prov., (02-23-93, Sotheby-NY, #343, illus.), 106 x 48½ in., (269.2 x 123.2 cm.), b/w photograph (BP 7878, DM 18,578, FR 63,014, Y 1,343,144).

FORNAZERIS, Jacques de
$600* *Marie De Medicis, Reine De France, c. 1610*, trimmed to plate, mounted, creases, repaired tear, (11-30-92, Phillips-London, #96, illus.), plate 18¾ x 13¾ in., (476 x 349 mm.), engraving in sepia on laid (BP 396, DM 956, FR 3245, Y 74,673).

FORNEY, M.N.
$715* *The Hinkley And Williams Works, 552 Harrison Avenue, Boston, c. 1870s*, J.H. Bufford's Lith., margins, age tone, board burn, excell. cond., (10-31-92, Riba, #348, illus.), image 11½ x 26½ in., (29.2 x 67.3 cm.), lithograph (BP 467, DM 1122, FR 3801, Y 88,403).

FORSBERG, James
$220* *"Cosmic"*, s., artists proof, good cond., (02-07-93, Bakker, #169), 20 x 3¾ in., (50.8 x 9.5 cm.), color woodblock print (BP 152, DM 365, FR 1233, Y 27,377).

FORSTER, Cornelia   b. 1906
    BI *Rosina: Eight*, s., est. DM 200-, (09-25-92, Granier, #2846), sheet 15⅝ x 19¹¹⁄₁₆ in., (39 x 50 cm.), serigraph on mill print paper.

FORSYTHE, Clyde   American 1885-1962
$150 *And They Thought We Couldn't Fight*, Ketterlinus, good cond., (09-24-92, Alderfer, #297), 30 x 20 in., (76.2 x 50.8 cm.), (BP 88, DM 222, FR 755, Y 18,044).

FORTUNY, Mariano
$310* *"Arabe Assis, Mains Croisees Sur Les Genoux", "Un Pouilloux", "Tanger, Arabe Assis" (H. Beraldi, 7, 13, 17):*

Three, good margins, (04-02-93, Picard, #111), etching (BP 204, DM 498, FR 1692, Y 35,295).

FORTY ONE DEGREES   Russian early 20th cent.
$3330* *41 Degrees Ezhenedal'naia Gazeta (41 Degrees The Weekly Newspaper), Tiflis, 1919,* four sides of text, folds, fold on cover split, loss, nicks, only issue of 41 newspaper ever published, (12-01-92, Christie-London, #531, illus.), overall S. 23⅛ x 16¾ in., (588 x 426 mm.), typographical designs and text on soft (molle) buff wove (BP 2200, DM 5308, FR 18,088, Y 414,592).
$2997* *Aleski Kruchenykh And Kirill Zdanevich, Ozhirenie Roz (Obesity of Roses. On the Poems of Terent'ev and others), Tiflis, 1918,* i., good cond., cover w/drawing by Kirill Zdanevich, crease, nicks, very good cond., (12-01-92, Christie-London, #530, illus.), overall S. 8¹¹⁄₁₆ x 5¾ in., (220 x 146 mm.), pen and ink drawing and text on thin buff paper, 30 pgs. text (BP 1980, DM 4777, FR 16,279, Y 373,132).
$2331* *Igor Terent'ev And Il'ia Zdanevich, Fakt (Fact), Tiflis, 1919,* p. by the Publishing House of the Union of Towns of Georgia, excell.cond., (12-01-92, Christie-London, #529, illus.), overall S. 6¹¹⁄₁₆ x 5⁵⁄₁₆ in., (170 x 135 mm.), typographical designs on thin pink wove, w/ 31 pgs. of text (BP 1540, DM 3715, FR 12,662, Y 290,214).
$3829* *Igor' Terent'ev, Il'ia Zdanevich And Dimitrii Petrovich Gordeev, 17 Erundovykh (17 Nonsensical Instruments), Tiflis, 1919,* i., p. Publishing House of the Union of Towns of Georgia, excell. cond., (12-01-92, Christie-London, #528, illus.), overall S. 6¹¹⁄₁₆ x 5⅜ in., (170 x 136 mm.), typographical designs on thin orange and green wove w/32 pgs. of text (BP 2530, DM 6103, FR 20,798, Y 476,718).
$2997* *Sofii Georgievna Mel'nikovoi (To Sophia Georgievna Mel'nikova), Tiflis, 1919,* 190 pgs. of text and illustrations, stamp num. 68, edit. 180, 2 fold-out sheets, very good cond., nicks, spots, (12-01-92, Christie-London, #532, illus.), overall S. 7¹⁄₁₆ x 5⅜ in., (180 x 137 mm.), typographical designs, offset lithograph and reproductions on cream wove (BP 1980, DM 4777, FR 16,279, Y 373,132).

FOSTER, G.R.
$330* *"Camp Of The 9th Maine Vols., Morris Island, S.C." and "View Of The Cmps, Morris Island, S.C.": Two,* photog. sig., t. on mount recto, 1860s, (04-07-93, Swann, #182), 5½ x 8½ in., photograph, albumen print (BP 218, DM 534, FR 1806, Y 37,491).

FOSTER, Myles Birkett (after)
$229 *"Haymaking Scene" and "Female Drover With Cattle Fording A Stream" :A Pair,* (04-16-93, G.A. Key, #140), 14 x 23 in., (35.6 x 58.4 cm.), chromolithograph (BP 150, DM 370, FR 1250, Y 25,751).

FOSTER, Velma   b. 1938
BI *Set Of Three Etchings,* #14/25, s., t., prov., est. C$ 150/250, (11-16-92, Hodgins, #172), 10¹⁵⁄₁₆ x 14 in., (27.9 x 35.6 cm.), etching on paper.

FOUJITA, Tsuguharu   Japanese 1886-1968
BI *Autoportrait (Johnson 58), 1923,* pub. Vollard, margins, deckle edge, surface dirt traces, good cond., (12-01-92, Christie-London, #380), plate 16⁵⁄₁₆ x 12½ in., (415 x 317 mm.), sheet 22¹³⁄₁₆ x 17¹⁵⁄₁₆ in., (415 x 317 mm.), etching on thick wove.
BI *Autoportrait Au Chat (Buisson 27.03), 1927,* s., #35/100, pub. blindstamp, Chalcographie du Louvre, large margins,good cond., light stain, foxing, crease, traces of glue, est. $5/7,000, (11-05-92, Sotheby-NY, #181, illus.), 17¾ x 13⅞ in., (451 x 352 mm.), sheet 24¾ x 18⅞ in., (451 x 352 mm.), etching.
BI *The Birthday Party, 1950,* E.A., s., est. SF 1/1,400, (10-14-92, Germann, #300, illus.), 12¹³⁄₁₆ x 8¹¹⁄₁₆ in., (325 x 220 mm.), color lithograph.
BI *The Birthday Party, 1950,* E.A., s., foxing, est. 1/1,400, (04-21-93, Germann, #432, illus.), 12¹³⁄₁₆ x 8¹¹⁄₁₆ in., (325 x 220 mm.), color lithograph.
BI *The Birthday Party, 1950,* E.A., s., (06-24-93, Germann, #335, illus.), 12¹³⁄₁₆ x 8¹¹⁄₁₆ in., (325 x 220 mm.), color lithograph.

BI *Cafe La Petite Madeleine, c. 1925,* s., possibly retraced, i. E. E., margins, flattened creases, rubbing,soiling, est. BP 2/2,500, (06-30-93, Sotheby-London, #441, illus.), sh 10¾ x 14¾ in., (273 x 375 mm.), etching w/aquatint in brown on Japan.
BI *"Chat Au Grelot", 1924,* s., d., est. SF 6/7,000, (11-13-92, Koller, #5319), 7⁵⁄₁₆ x 12⅝ in., (18.5 x 32 cm.), etching on wove.
$3812* *Chat Etendu, c. 1930,* s., num. 11/60, full margins, good cond., creasing, discoloration, (10-14-92, Sotheby-Japan, #28, illus.), 10½ x 16¼ in., (267 x 413 mm.), lithograph on japon (Japan paper) nacre (BP 2237, DM 5579, FR 18,918, Y 461,949).
$1650* *Les Chats, 1929: Two,* one s.; each plate s., margins, good cond., light staining, mat burn, rippling, May and Howard Joynt Coll., (12-12-92, Weschler, #119), each 8 x 10 in., (20.3 x 25.4 cm.), etching and aquatint (BP 1058, DM 2600, FR 8909, Y 204,183).
$9900* *Les Chats: [Sleeping Cat With Kitten], c. 1930,* s., #V/X, margins, good cond., light stain, rubbed spots inside platemark, ex-coll. Dr. H. Stinnes, (11-05-92, Sotheby-NY, #183, illus.), 12¼ x 15¼ in., (312 x 388 mm.), sheet 15¼ x 19 in., (312 x 388 mm.), aquatint w/engraving and roulette p. in colors on chine applique, laid on japon imperial (BP 6439, DM 15,657, FR 52,970, Y 1,214,575).
$10,465* *Les Chats: [Sleeping Cat With Kittens], c. 1930,* s., #26/100, margins, good cond., (02-11-93, Sotheby-NY, #143, illus.), 12⅝ x 15¼ in., (320 x 387 mm.), sheet 17¹¹⁄₁₆ x 20⅛ in., (320 x 387 mm.), aquatint w/engraving and roulette p. in colors on chine applique, laid on sheet of japon (Japan paper) imperial (BP 7384, DM 17,335, FR 58,660, Y 1,261,603).
$5116* *Les Deux Amies, c. 1927,* s. in Japanese & English, #34/100, reduced margins, creasing, (12-03-92, Sotheby-London, #310, illus.), sheet 17 x 22¾ in., (432 x 578 mm.), etching w/aquatint & roulette in colors on chine applique supported in Japan (BP 3300, DM 8045, FR 27,461, Y 636,556).
$10,231* *Les Deux Femmes, c. 1927,* s. in Japanese & English, #38/100, margins, good cond., paper discoloration, (12-03-92, Sotheby-London, #309, illus.), 17 x 23¾ in., (432 x 603 mm.), etching w/aquatint & roulette in colors on chine applique mounted onJapan (BP 6600, DM 16,089, FR 54,917, Y 1,272,987).
BI *Deux Femmes, c. 1930,* s., #49/68, margins, creasing, staining, scuffing, tape hinge, est. BP 7/900, (12-03-92, Sotheby-London, #311), sheet 19½ x 14½ in., (495 x 368 mm.), lithograph on Japan.
BI *Deux Modeles En Buste, 1930,* crease, est. $3/4,000, (05-27-93, Swann, #112, illus.), approx. 13 x 17 in., (33 x 43.2 cm.), sheet 18 x 22 in., (33 x 43.2 cm.), lithograph on a full 4 deckle sheet of Japan paper.
$9350* *Deux Nus Assis (B. 30.36), 1930,* s., #46/100, pub. Editions Artistiques Apollo, large margins, good cond., faded, light stain, printing defect, scuff at center, soiling, water stains, foxing, loss, margins previously folded back, (11-05-92, Sotheby-NY, #184, illus.), 23½ x 16 in., (597 x 405 mm.), sheet 29 x 19⅞ in., (597 x 405 mm.), etching and aquatint p. in colors on simili Japan (BP 6081, DM 14,787, FR 50,027, Y 1,147,099).
BI *Discover France By Train, 1955,* pub. Editions Paul-Martial, cond. 1, laid on linen, est. BP 150/250, (10-13-92, Phillips-London, #21), 38¹⁵⁄₁₆ x 24⁷⁄₁₆ in., (99 x 62 cm.), color lithograph.
$23,601* *Le Dragon Des Mers, 1955,* complete book, double suite hors text, s., num. 10, pub. Editions George Guillot, good cond., foxing, time staining, ink transfer, orig. wrappers and slipcase, (10-14-92, Sotheby-Japan, #31, illus.), each page approx. 13⅛ x 10 in., (333 x 254 mm.), 25 etchings, 1 on Japan paper; 1 on Auvergne du Moulin Richard de Bas paper, orig. s. drawing and inked copper plate (BP 13,853, DM 34,540, FR 117,127, Y 2,860,034).
BI *Femme A La Cravate Rose (B. 30.26), 1930,* s., i. E.a., margins, good cond., mat stain, printer's creases, est.$4/6,000, (02-11-93, Sotheby-NY, #142, illus.), 14¹³⁄₁₆ x 11⁹⁄₁₆ in., (377 x 293 mm.), sheet 18⅛ x 14¹³⁄₁₆ in.,

(377 x 293 mm.), etching and aquatint p. in colors on chine applique.

$1320* *"La Femme Au Chat",* s. Foujita, #6/20, full margins, (12-12-92, Goldberg, #516, illus.), aquatint drypoint etching (BP 846, DM 2080, FR 7127, Y 163,346).

BI *Femme Au Doigts Croises, c. 1930,* s., i. E.A. VI/X, full margins, creases, good cond., est. Y 750/1,000,000, (10-14-92, Sotheby-Japan, #30, illus.), 15¼ x 13⅝ in., (387 x 346 mm.), etching w/roulette and stipple on Japan paper.

BI *Femme Endormie (S. and D. Buisson 30.07), 1930,* two pinholes, est. FF20/25,000, (06-28-93, Loudmer, #248), 10⅜ x 13⅜ in., (263 x 340 mm.), sh 15¾ x 18¹¹⁄₁₆ in., (263 x 340 mm.), color etching and roulette on chine applique.

$18,154* *Femmes: (Reclining Nude), 1930,* s., num. 92/100, pub. Apollo Editions Artistiques, full margins, good cond., fox marks, margins, rubbed, (10-14-92, Sotheby-Japan, #29, illus.), image 14½ x 21¾ in., (368 x 552 mm.), etching and roulette in colors on chine applique (BP 10,656, DM 26,568, FR 90,094, Y 2,199,952).

$454* *Fillette,* annot., E.A., s., large margins, (04-02-93, Picard, #113), 7¹¹⁄₁₆ x 7⁹⁄₁₆ in., (19.5 x 19.2 cm.), color print (BP 299, DM 730, FR 2478, Y 51,691).

BI *Fillette A La Poupee (Buisson 30.02), c. 1930,* s., #101/120, blindstamp, est. DM 4,500, (06-10-93, Hauswedell/Nolt, #309, illus.), image 19½ x 15⁹⁄₁₆ in., (49.5 x 39.5 cm.), color lithograph.

$6440* *Fillette Au Chat (B. 29.66), 1929,* s., #21/100, pub. Editions Artisique Apollo, large margins, good cond., faded, repaired skinning, (02-11-93, Sotheby-NY, #141, illus.), 14¾ x 11⁵⁄₁₆ in., (375 x 288 mm.), sheet 20⅜ x 16⁵⁄₁₆ in., (375 x 288 mm.), etching and aquatint p. in colors on chine applique (BP 4544, DM 10,668, FR 36,099, Y 776,371).

$378* *"Les Halles", 1963,* drystamp, H.C., s., (01-28-93, Pescheteau, #144), 14⁹⁄₁₆ x 10⅝ in., (37 x 27 cm.), color lithograph on Arches (BP 250, DM 599, FR 2027, Y 46,933).

$515* *Illustrations For (A Visit To Japan), c. 1930: Twenty-Seven,* proofs, full margins, good cond., some plates w/ soiling, handling creases, rubbing, (06-30-93, Sotheby-London, #443), each sh c. 12¾ x 9⅞ in., (324 x 251 mm.), etching w/roulette and hand-coloring on Japan (BP 345, DM 878, FR 2963, Y 55,181).

$220* *"Jeune Fille A La Rose", 1930,* very good cond., (10-31-92, Cleveland, #284), 9¼ x 6⅞ in., (23.5 x 17.5 cm.), etching and drypoint (BP 141, DM 338, FR 1148, Y 27,251).

BI *"Jeune Fille A La Rose", c. 1930,* very good cond., est. $3/400, (05-15-93, Cleveland, #130), 9 x 6⅞ in., (22.9 x 17.5 cm.), etching and drypoint.

$88* *Little Girl With Doll,* s. plate, (02-14-93, Hanzel, #426), 15 x 8½ in., (38.1 x 21.6 cm.), color woodblock (BP 62, DM 146, FR 494, Y 10,613).

$1410* *Madchen Mit Stockbrot,* s., #100/220, (05-26-93, Lempertz, #165), 25¹⁵⁄₁₆ x 19¹¹⁄₁₆ in., (66 x 50 cm.), color lithograph on wove (BP 912, DM 2301, FR 7743, Y 153,194).

$243* *Maison Close,* s., margins, (05-27-93, Briest, #88), 10⅝ x 7⅞ in., (27 x 20 cm.), black lithograph on wove (BP 156, DM 390, FR 1314, Y 26,051).

BI *Maison Close,* s., margins, est. FF 4/5,000, (11-16-92, Briest, #306), 10⅝ x 7⅞ in., (27 x 20 cm.), lithograph in black on wove.

BI *"La Mesangere - Les Halles", 1963,* dry stamp, H.C., s., est. FF 2/3,000, (10-18-92, Pescheteau, #146), 14⁹⁄₁₆ x 10⅝ in., (37 x 27 cm.), lithograph in colors on Arches.

$439* *"Nina Con Una Rosa",* s. in passe-partout, (12-17-92, Duran, #179, illus.), 10⅝ x 7⅞ in., (27 x 20 cm.), etching (BP 279, DM 685, FR 2341, Y 53,951, P 48,300).

$314* *Paris, Henry Parville, 1927: Nine,* from Les Divertissements D'Eros by Jacques Brindejont-Offenabch, first edit., (11-15-92, Christie-Geneva, #317), 9⁷⁄₁₆ x 7¹¹⁄₁₆ in., (240 x 195 mm.), hors-texte in colors and culs-de-lampe in colors on Arches (BP 206, DM 501, FR 1687, Y 39,186, SF 452).

$1650* *Le Petit Chat, 1927,* s., annot. 'Epreuve d'essai I/II, s., d. in plate, full margins, glued, good cond., staining, mat staining, hinge & tape remains, surface soiling, pencil notations, (02-24-93, Butterfield, #2739, illus.), 6 x 8⅝ in., (152 x 219 mm.), soft-ground etching on laid Japan (BP 1151, DM 2679, FR 9081, Y 193,617).

$10,175* *Petite Fille A L'Oiseau (B. 29.64), 1929,* s., #78/100, pub. Editions Artistique Apollo, full margins, good cond., faded, discoloration, creases, (11-05-92, Sotheby-NY, #182, illus.), 14⅝ x 11¼ in., (372 x 287 mm.), sheet 20¼ x 16⅜ in., (372 x 287 mm.), etching and aquatint p. in colors on chien applique (BP 6618, DM 16,092, FR 54,441, Y 1,248,313).

$5175* *Petite Fille A L'Oiseau (Buisson 29.64), 1929,* s., #21/100, pub. Editons Artistiqe Apollo, large margins, good cond., faded, repaired skinning, (02-11-93, Sotheby-NY, #140, illus.), 14⅝ x 11½ in., (371 x 292 mm.), sheet 20⁷⁄₁₆ x 16⁵⁄₁₆ in., (371 x 292 mm.), etching and aquatint p. in colors on chine applique (BP 3652, DM 8572, FR 29,008, Y 623,870).

$1278* *Portrait De Femme (S. et D. Buisson, 24-47), c. 1927,* #71/100, s., yellowed, staining, creases, good margins, (06-16-93, Ader Tajan, #94), 12⅜ x 9¼ in., (31.5 x 23.5 cm.), 2-tone etching, stipple print on tinted paper (BP 852, DM 2122, FR 7120, Y 136,305).

$354* *Profil De Femme Voilee,* #129/220, s., (06-16-93, Ader Tajan, #95), 12⅜ x 9¹³⁄₁₆ in., (31.5 x 25 cm.), lithograph (BP 236, DM 588, FR 1972, Y 37,756).

$518* *Profile Of A Woman,* watermark, s., #176/220, margins, good cond., discoloration, (05-19-93, Butterfield, #1911), 12¼ x 9⅜ in., (311 x 238 mm.), lithograph on wove (BP 336, DM 842, FR 2837, Y 57,345).

$1064* *Le Reve,* s., num., (06-05-93, Bassenge, #6032), 20¹⁄₁₆ x 25¹⁵⁄₁₆ in., (51 x 66 cm.), lithograph on wove (BP 700, DM 1725, FR 5814, Y 114,139).

$1150* *Reve D'Opera, 1951,* s., #41/50, full margins, good cond., creases, hinge and glue remains, (05-19-93, Butterfield, #1910), 9⅜ x 11½ in., (238 x 292 mm.), soft-ground etching and aquatint on Japan nacre (BP 747, DM 1869, FR 6298, Y 127,311).

$3688* *Selbstportrait Mit Katze, 1926,* #97/125, s., (11-13-92, Koller, #5318), 9¼ x 8⅞ in., (23.5 x 22.5 cm.), lithograph on wove (BP 2383, DM 5790, FR 19,524, Y 457,739, SF 5220).

BI *Tete De Femme, c. 1925,* s., countersigned in Japanese, i. essai (partially erased), margins,flattened creases, rubbed areas, soiling, est. BP 2/3,000, (06-30-93, Sotheby-London, #442, illus.), sh 14¾ x 20½ in., (375 x 521 mm.), etching on very thin Japan paper.

$275* *The Three Graces,* s. in plate, (09-17-92, Sloan, #2372), sight 20¼ x 15 in., (51.4 x 38.1 cm.), lithograph (BP 154, DM 408, FR 1397, Y 34,238).

BI *White Pussycat,* stamped sig., margins, good cond., creases, est. $2/3,000, (10-28-92, Butterfield, #2643), 13 x 17⁹⁄₁₆ in., (330 x 446 mm.), color woodcut on laid Japan paper.

BI *[Nue Allongee], c. 1930,* s., #II/VIII, margins, repaired tears, soiling, crease, est. $1/1,500, (11-05-92, Sotheby-NY, #185), 12¾ x 12¼ in., (325 x 310 mm.), lithograph.

FOUJITA, Tsuguharu (after)

BI *Dr. Lucien-Graux. La Fleur Aux Mille Petales D'Or,* album w/title-page and text, #30, pub. Editions d'Art Apollo, 1930, good cond., original paper covers, est. BP 3,5/4,000, (06-30-93, Sotheby-London, #440), 13 x 9⅞ in., (330 x 251 mm.), 5 hand-colored engravings w/aquatint on Japon Imperial.

BI *La Reve,* s., #77/250, blindstamp pub. Guy Spitzer, margins, good cond., light-staining, glue remains, surface soiling, est. $1/2,000, (10-28-92, Butterfield, #2642), 19¾ x 24 in., (502 x 610 mm.), color offset lithograph on Arches paper.

$1010* *"Le Reve",* dry stamp, #187/250, s., (10-18-92, Pescheteau, #145), sight 21¼ x 24¹³⁄₁₆ in., (54 x 63 cm.), heliogravure (photoengraving) on wove (BP 612, DM 1492, FR 5068, Y 120,597).

$1896* *Le Reve, c. 1955,* #77/150, s., blindstamp, (04-21-93, Germann, #142), 21⅝ x 24¹³⁄₁₆ in., (550 x 630 mm.), color lithograph (BP 1230, DM 3031, FR 10,249, Y 209,897, SF 2760).

BI *The Three Graces,* est. $200/300, (07-03-92, Sloan, #299), sight 20¼ x 15 in., (51.4 x 38.1 cm.), print.

FOURASTIE and ALLARD
$114* *L'Amour Mene La Danse (Happy Go Lovely) De B. Humberstone, Avec VeraEllen Et D. Niven, 1951,* (01-31-93, Morelle/Marchan, #87), 47¼ x 62¹⁵/₁₆ in., (120 x 160 cm.), poster (BP 77, DM 184, FR 621, Y 14,222).

FOWLER, W.
$160 *"South View Of The Residence Of The Late Rev. James Hervey....At Weston-Favel In The County Of Northampton",* d. 1807, (04-16-93, G.A. Key, #78), 11 x 15 in., (27.9 x 38.1 cm.), colored aquatint (BP 105, DM 258, FR 873, Y 17,992).

FOWX, Egbert Guy
BI *'Falls Church In VA',* t., credited in unidentified hand, early 1860's, est. $1/1,500, (10-15-92, Sotheby-NY, #12, illus.), 6 x 8 in., (15.2 x 20.3 cm.), photograph, oval albumen print.

FOX, Terry
$2750* *The Labyrinth: Nine,* each s., t., num., d. 1973 verso, prov., exhib., lit., Sylvio Perlstein Coll., (11-18-92, Sotheby-NY, #217, illus.), each 24 x 36 in., (61 x 91.4 cm.), b/w photograph (BP 1811, DM 4385, FR 14,769, Y 341,997).

FRACK, Mary A.
$275* *Still Life With Pears,* s., very good cond., (07-19-92, Bakker, #46, illus.), image 10½ x 11½ in., (26.7 x 29.2 cm.), color monotype (BP 141, DM 401, FR 1355, Y 34,187).

FRAGONARD, Jean Honore   French 1732-1806
$1201* *Quatres Bacchanales (Baudicour 6-9): Set Of Four,* margins, discoloration, good cond., (06-30-93, Sotheby-London, #123), 5¾ x 8¼ in., (146 x 210 mm.), etching (BP 805, DM 2048, FR 6910, Y 128,683).

FRAGONARD, Jean Honore (after)
$1535* *Les Hazards Heureux De L'Escarpolette (L. & D. 85),* by Nicholas de Launay, fifth state of seven, 's' removed from title,trimmed outside image to work, split across sheet, (12-03-92, Sotheby-London, #53), 23 x 17 in., (587 x 430 mm.), etching w/engraving (BP 990, DM 2414, FR 8239, Y 190,992).
$2300* *Les Hazards Heureux De L'Escarpolette (L. & D. 85), 1782,* engraved Nicholas de Launay, pub. Academie des Beaux-Arts, Denmark, margins, good cond., mat/light-staining, foxing, tear, surface soiling, creases,buckling, (05-19-93, Butterfield, #1858, illus.), sh. 24⅜ x 18⅜ in., (619 x 467 mm.), etching w/engraving on laid (BP 1493, DM 3739, FR 12,596, Y 254,622).
BI *Les Hazards Heureux De L'Escarpolette (L. and D. 85), 1782,* by N. Delauney, 5th state of 7, trimmed, fold, right corner made up,image split, foxing, staining, est. $4,5/6,500, (05-11-93, Christie-NY, #72, illus.), sheet 24½ x 18⅝ in., (622 x 473 mm.), engraving on laid.
$157* *La Mere De Famille,* oval, stains, glue traces, small margins, (06-16-93, Ader Tajan, #35), stipple print engraving in color (BP 105, DM 261, FR 875, Y 16,745).
$505* *"Serment D'Amour"* and *"Fontaine D'Amour": Two,* restored, margins, (03-22-93, Pescheteau, #14), color print (BP 340, DM 828, FR 2815, Y 58,476).

FRAIPONT, G.
$399* *Chemin De Fer De L'Ouest: Ligne Des Invalides A Versailles,* p. Moreau, very good cond., (11-19-92, Ribeyre/Baron, #105bis), 42⅛ x 29½ in., (107 x 75 cm.), poster (BP 263, DM 636, FR 2143, Y 49,621).
$189* *Pierrefonds, c. 1895,* good cond., (01-23-93, Ribeyre/Baron, #35), 42⅛ x 29⅛ in., (107 x 74 cm.), poster (BP 124, DM 301, FR 1017, Y 23,655).

FRAIPONT, G.   French 19th cent.
BI *Northern Railroad Company,* from Les Maitres de l'Affiche, PL. 218, est. $150/200, (02-14-93, Hanzel, #679), 11 x 8 in., (27.9 x 20.3 cm.), lithograph.

FRAIPONT, Gustave   French b. 1849
$241* *Chemin De Fer De L'Etat Et Du Midi. Royan, c. 1900,* Royan, Imp. Victor Billaud, cond. B+, (06-11-93, Boisgi-

rard, #72, illus.), 47¼ x 31½ in., (120 x 80 cm.), poster (BP 158, DM 392, FR 1321, Y 25,570).
$140* *Chemin De Fer PLM. Royat,* cond. A, (03-16-93, Boisgirard, #110), 42⅛ x 30½ in., (107 x 77.5 cm.), poster (BP 97, DM 233, FR 791, Y 16,370).
$201* *Royat. Station Thermale, c. 1895,* Paris, Fraipont et Moreau, cond. B+, (06-11-93, Boisgirard, #71), 41⁵/₁₆ x 28¾ in., (105 x 73 cm.), poster (BP 132, DM 327, FR 1101, Y 21,326).

FRAIPORT, G*
$84* *"Owls At Night",* some handcoloring, num. 50/50, s., margins, (01-21-93, Bonhams-Chelsea, #139), 13¾ x 19¼ in., (34.9 x 48.9 cm.), etching w/aquatint (BP 55, DM 134, FR 452, Y 10,513).

FRANCESCHINI, Vincenzo   b. 1680, ac. 1700-1740
$867* *Veduta Della Badia Fiorentina E Del Palazzo Del Podesta,* after Zocchi, (12-04-92, Bassenge, #6573), engraving and etching (BP 556, DM 1381, FR 4684, Y 108,240).

FRANCIA, Giacomo   Italian before 1486-1557
$2479* *Cupid And Psyche (Print Collector 30, I),* after Raphael, watermark, prov., (06-04-93, Bassenge, #5166), 7⁵/₁₆ x 10¹¹/₁₆ in., (18.6 x 27.1 cm.), copper engraving (BP 1640, DM 4026, FR 13,569, Y 267,364).

FRANCIS, Dorothy
$69* *"Innocence",* #65/195, s., t., num., (05-12-93, Maynard, #274), 16 x 11½ in., (40.6 x 27.9 cm.), print (BP 45, DM 111, FR 375, Y 7703, C$ 88).

FRANCIS, Sam   American b. 1923
$3818* *Affiche "Moderna Museet" Stockholm 1960 (Lembark-Page L. 16), 1960,* s., i. ea, (06-23-93, Kornfeld, #343), color lithograph on thick wove (BP 2594, DM 6460, FR 21,730, Y 415,949, SF 5750).
BI *Affiche Moderna Museet Stockholm (SF16) (Kornfeld 14), 1960,* s., #69/75, pub. Emil Matthieu, full margins, good cond., light-staining, est. BP 3/4,000, (12-03-92, Sotheby-London, #667, illus.), 35¾ x 24¾ in., (910 x 630 mm.), lithograph in colors on BFK Rives.
$2402* *Affiche Moderna Museet Stockholm (SF16) (Kornfeld 14), 1960,* s., #69/75, pub. Emil Matthieu, full margins, good cond., light-staining, (06-30-93, Sotheby-London, #795, illus.), 35¾ x 24¾ in., (908 x 629 mm.), color lithograph on BFK Rives (BP 1610, DM 4097, FR 13,820, Y 257,366).
$7150* *Always In And Out Of Need (G. 706), 1976,* s., annot. RTP, pub. Gemini G.E.L., very good cond.?, (10-28-92, Butterfield, #2952, illus.), 38 x 81 in., (96.5 x 205.7 cm.), lithograph in grays on Arches 88 paper (BP 4556, DM 11,042, FR 37,493, Y 877,301).
$4276* *Another Disappearance (Lemb.-P.L. 26), 1963,* s., num., blindstamp, (06-23-93, Kornfeld, #345), color lithograph (BP 2905, DM 7235, FR 24,337, Y 465,846, SF 6440).
BI *Another Disappearance (Lembark L-26), 1963,* s., i. Bon a Tirer, printer's proof, blindstamp, pub. Tamarind Lithography Workshop, good cond., crease, remains hinges, showing through to recto, est. $4,5/5,500, (05-15-93, Sotheby-NY, #972, illus.), sheet 22¼ x 30 in., (56.5 x 76.2 cm.), lithograph in colors.
$1760* *Blue Blood Stone (SF 7), 1960,* s., #16/50, pub. Gallerie Kornfeld, full sheet, good cond., short tear, soiling, creases, (11-07-92, Sotheby-NY, #553, illus.), sheet 35½ x 24⅞ in., (902 x 632 mm.), lithograph p. in colors on BFK Rives (BP 1151, DM 2810, FR 9498, Y 217,230).
$6325* *Blue-Green (L. L-56), 1963,* s., #10/40, pub. E.W. Kornfeld, good cond., (05-15-93, Sotheby-NY, #973, illus.), sheet 24¾ x 35⅜ in., (62.9 x 89.9 cm.), lithograph in colors (BP 4112, DM 10,174, FR 34,189, Y 701,142).
$11,836* *Bright Jade Ghost (Lemb.-P.L. 29), 1963,* s., i. epreuve d'artiste, (06-23-93, Kornfeld, #346, illus.), color lithograph (BP 8041, DM 20,027, FR 67,365, Y 1,289,465, SF 17,825).
$6872* *Chinese Balloons (Leb.-P.L. 30), 1963,* s., i. epreuve d'artiste, (06-23-93, Kornfeld, #347), color lithograph (BP 4668, DM 11,628, FR 39,112, Y 748,665, SF 10,350).
$3025* *Chinese Planet (SF 23), 1963,* s., #15/20, blindstamp, pub. Tamarind Lithography Workshop, good cond., paper glued to corners, skinned spots, (11-07-92, Sotheby-NY,

#555, illus.), sheet 30 x 22¼ in., (762 x 565 mm.), lithograph p. in red and blue (BP 1978, DM 4830, FR 16,325, Y 373,365).

BI *Chinese Planet, 1963,* #14/20, s., est. SF 13/18,000, (09-04-92, Germann, #108, illus.), 29¹⁵⁄₁₆ x 22¼ in., (760 x 565 mm.), color lithograph.

BI *Coldest Stone (SF. 15), 1960,* s., num., est. DM 7500, (12-01-92, Karl/Faber, #619, illus.), 24¹³⁄₁₆ x 35⁷⁄₁₆ in., (63 x 90 cm.), color lithograph on BFK Rives wove.

BI *Composition,* 4/38, s., signs of wear, est. SF 2/3,000, (10-14-92, Germann, #301, illus.), 25³⁄₁₆ x 34¹³⁄₁₆ in., (640 x 885 mm.), aquatint.

BI *Composition,* 14/39, s., signs of wear, est. SF 2/3,000, (10-14-92, Germann, #303), 25³⁄₁₆ x 35¹⁄₁₆ in., (640 x 890 mm.), etching.

$1382* *Composition,* #4/38, s., staining, (09-04-92, Germann, #8), 25³⁄₁₆ x 34¹³⁄₁₆ in., (640 x 885 mm.), aquatint (BP 693, DM 1937, FR 6594, Y 170,113, SF 1725).

BI *Composition,* #14/39, s., staining, est. SF 1,6/2,400, (09-04-92, Germann, #7), 25³⁄₁₆ x 35¹⁄₁₆ in., (640 x 890 mm.), etching.

BI *Composition,* s., #62/100, est. FF8,000/10,000, (05-27-93, Briest, #89), 37¹³⁄₁₆ x 26¾ in., (96 x 68 cm.), lithograph.

$1106* *Composition,* #14/39, s., signs of wear, (04-21-93, Germann, #433), 25³⁄₁₆ x 35¹⁄₁₆ in., (640 x 890 mm.), etching (BP 718, DM 1768, FR 5978, Y 122,440, SF 1610).

BI *Concert Hall II (SF 231), 1977,* s., #8/75, pub. Louisiana Museum, full margins, good cond., nicks, glue, est. BP 1,8/2,200, (12-03-92, Sotheby-London, #677), 25½ x 16 in., (650 x 407 mm.), lithograph in colors on BFK Rives.

$1716* *Concert Hall II (San Francisco 231), 1977,* s., #8/75, pub. Louisiana Museum, full margins, good cond., nicks, glued to backboard, (06-30-93, Sotheby-London, #805), 25½ x 16 in., (648 x 406 mm.), color lithograph on BFK Rives (BP 1150, DM 2927, FR 9873, Y 183,864).

$1495* *Concert Hall Set II (SF-231) (L. L-224), 1977,* s., #72/75, blindstamp, pub. Louisiana Museum of Modern Art, Denmark, full margins, tear, creases, handling creases, scuff mark, (05-15-93, Sotheby-NY, #975), 25⅝ x 16⅛ in., (65.1 x 41 cm.), lithograph in colors (BP 972, DM 2405, FR 8081, Y 165,724).

$3971* *Damp (Lemb.-P.L. 104), 1969,* s., num., (06-23-93, Kornfeld, #350), color lithograph (BP 2698, DM 6719, FR 22,601, Y 432,618, SF 5980).

BI *For James Kirsch (K. 43), 1972,* s., #8/32, pub. Litho Shop Inc, good cond., defects, est. BP 3/4,000, (12-03-92, Sotheby-London, #668, illus.), sheet 27½ x 41⅛ in., (69.9 x 104.5 cm.), lithograph in colors on BFK Rives.

$4439* *For James Kirsch (K. 43), 1972,* s., #8/32, pub. Litho Shop Inc, good cond., defects, (06-30-93, Sotheby-London, #801), sh 27½ x 41⅛ in., (69.9 x 104.5 cm.), color lithograph on BFK Rives (BP 2975, DM 7571, FR 25,541, Y 475,624).

$2420* *For St. Gallen (SF 49), 1963,* s., i. 'epreuve d'artiste', proof, pub. Gallerie Kornfeld, good cond., (11-07-92, Sotheby-NY, #554, illus.), sheet 25⅝ x 19¾ in., (651 x 502 mm.), lithograph p. in colors (BP 1582, DM 3864, FR 13,060, Y 298,692).

$2750* *For The Blue Sons Of The Air (L. S 21), 1990,* s., num. 73/150, pub. American Heritage Foundation, blindstamp, goodcond., (02-24-93, Butterfield, #3026, illus.), 53¾ x 32 in., (136.5 x 81.3 cm.), silkscreen in colors on PTI Supra (BP 1918, DM 4464, FR 15,135, Y 322,694).

BI *For The Blue Sons Of The Air (L. S-21), 1990,* s., #119/150, pub. American Indian Heritage Foundation, full sheet, good cond., est. $4/5,000, (02-11-93, Sotheby-NY, #338), sheet 53⁹⁄₁₆ x 31⅛ in., (136 x 79 cm.), color silkscreen.

$2990* *For The Blue Sons Of The Air (SFS-336, L. S21), 1990,* s., #31/150, pub. American Indian Heritage Foundation, excell. cond., (05-11-93, Christie-NY, #423), sheet 53½ x 32 in., (135.9 x 81.3 cm.), color screenprint on wove (BP 1909, DM 4710, FR 15,870, Y 328,897).

$4411* *For The Blue Sons Of The Air (Sam Francis Archiv SPS-336), 1990,* 55/150, s., 1365mm x 813mm, (10-14-92, Germann, #150, illus.), serigraph in colors (BP 2589, DM 6455, FR 21,891, Y 534,537, SF 5750).

$3950* *For The Blue Sons Of The Air (Sam Francis Archiv SPS-336, Sp LP05), 1990,* #12/150, s., (04-21-93, Germann, #167, illus.), 53⁹⁄₁₆ x 31⅞ in., (136 x 81 cm.), color lithograph (BP 2563, DM 6314, FR 21,351, Y 437,286, SF 5750).

BI *For The Blue Sons Of The Air, 1990,* num., s., p. Ron McPherson, blindstamp, pub. Artists for American Indians, American Indian Heritage Foundation, est. $5/7,000, (05-27-93, Swann, #112A, illus.), sh 53¼ x 32 in., (135.3 x 81.3 cm.), screenprint in colors on P. T. Supra.

$3159* *For The Blue Sons Of The Air, 1990,* 77/150, s., 1355mm x 815mm, (06-24-93, Germann, #339, illus.), color serigraph (BP 2080, DM 5122, FR 17,262, Y 338,876, SF 4600).

$2875* *For Thirteen (L. S-20), 1989,* s., #92/115, pub. La Paloma, full sheet, good cond., creases, (02-11-93, Sotheby-NY, #337, illus.), sheet 27¹⁵⁄₁₆ x 37¹³⁄₁₆ in., (710 x 960 mm.), color silkscreen (BP 2029, DM 4762, FR 16,115, Y 346,594).

BI *For Thirteen (Lembark S 20), 1989,* s., #14/115, i., est. DM 7,500, (05-27-93, Lempertz, #726, illus.), 27⅝ x 37⁹⁄₁₆ in., (70.2 x 95.4 cm.), color serigraph on thick wove.

$3300* *Freshet,* s., #75/100, prov., (05-16-93, Hindman, #631), 38 x 29½ in., (96.5 x 74.9 cm.), color lithograph (BP 2146, DM 5308, FR 17,838, Y 365,813).

$6176* *Heart Stone, (SF 30), 1963,* artist's proof, s. verso; glue, lit., (10-14-92, Germann, #43, illus.), 24¾ x 35⁹⁄₁₆ in., (628 x 903 mm.), color lithograph (BP 3625, DM 9038, FR 30,650, Y 748,425, SF 8050).

$3818* *Hurrah For The Red, White And Blue (Lemb.-P.L. 18), 1961,* s., num., (06-23-93, Kornfeld, #344), color lithograph (BP 2594, DM 6460, FR 21,730, Y 415,949, SF 5750).

$2200* *Hurrah For The Red, White And Blue (SF 17), 1961,* stamped Japanese charater sig., num. 182/400, pub. Kornfeld, full sheet, surface scrapes, skinning, old tape, very good cond., (09-19-92, Christie-E, #105, illus.), sheet 20 x 25¾ in., (50.8 x 65.4 cm.), lithograph in colors on BFK (BP 1265, DM 3294, FR 11,282, Y 274,109).

$737* *Komposition,* from One cent Life, #58/100, s., trimmed, glue, (09-04-92, Germann, #340), 16¼ x 11¼ in., (412 x 285 mm.), color lithograph (BP 369, DM 1033, FR 3516, Y 90,719, SF 920).

$4734* *Komposition,* s., #26/50, (05-08-93, Dobiaschofsky, #1974, illus.), 29¹⁵⁄₁₆ x 22¹⁄₁₆ in., (76 x 56 cm.), color lithograph (BP 3089, DM 7605, FR 25,659, Y 528,998, SF 6900).

BI *Komposition,* #IV/XX, s., est. SF 8,5/9,500, (11-13-92, Koller, #5321, illus.), 29¹⁵⁄₁₆ x 22¹⁄₁₆ in., (76 x 56 cm.), color lithograph on wove.

$425* *Komposition II, 1986,* (06-08-93, Karl/Faber, #761), sh approx. 33¹⁄₁₆ x 21⅞ in., (84 x 55.5 cm.), color lithograph on wove (BP 279, DM 690, FR 2322, Y 45,141).

$2206* *Long Blue, 1964,* artist proof, s., (10-14-92, Germann, #158, illus.), 24⅝ x 35⁷⁄₁₆ in., (625 x 900 mm.), color lithograph (BP 1295, DM 3228, FR 10,948, Y 267,329, SF 2875).

BI *Memoire De La Liberte: Untitled, 1990,* s., #93/100, p. by Magnolia Editions, good cond., est. BP 2,5/3,000, (06-30-93, Sotheby-London, #797, illus.), 29⅝ x 46 in., (75.2 x 116.8 cm.), color lithograph on wove.

$2756* *Metaphysique Du Vide, 1986,* s., XXXII/L, from Poemes Dans Le Ciel, (12-04-92, AB Stockholm, #7061), 29½ x 21⅝ in., (75 x 55 cm.), lithograph in colors (BP 1768, DM 4389, FR 14,889, Y 344,070, SK 18,700).

$9775* *Meteorite (SFS0290, L. S17, Gemini 1297), 1986,* s., #12/65, Gemini G.E.L. blindstamps, excell. cond.?, (05-11-93, Christie-NY, #420, illus.), sheet 72¼ x 42 in., (183.5 x 106.7 cm.), color screenprint on Arches (BP 6240, DM 15,399, FR 51,884, Y 1,075,239).

$3679* *Poeme Dans Le Ciel,* #HC 3/20, pencil s., (11-20-92, Lempertz, #538, illus.), sh 29¹⁵⁄₁₆ x 22¹⁄₁₆ in., (76 x 56 cm.), color lithograph on Velin (BP 2422, DM 5866, FR 19,758, Y 457,530).

BI *Poemes Dand Le Ciel: Metaphysique Du Vide, 1986,* s., #IV/L, pub. Editions de la Difference, good cond., est. BP 1,8/2,200, (12-03-92, Sotheby-London, #671), 29½ x 22 in., (750 x 558 mm.), lithograph in colors.

BI *Poemes Dand Le Ciel: Metaphysique Du Vide, 1986,* s., #IV/L, pub. Editions de la Difference, good cond., est. BP 1,8/2,200, (12-03-92, Sotheby-London, #676, illus.), 26 x 22 in., (758 x 560 mm.), lithograph in colors.

$3674* *Poemes Dans Le Ciel (Lembark L272), 1986,* s., #3/20, hors commerce, for suite Michel Waldberg Poemes dans le ciel, (06-12-93, Hauswedell/Nolt, #86, illus.), 29¹⁵⁄₁₆ x 22¹⁄₁₆ in., (76 x 56 cm.), color lithograph on thick wove (BP 2405, DM 5980, FR 20,098, Y 386,615).

$2217* *Poemes Dans Le Ciel, 1986,* s., #XXXI/L, pub. Editions de la Difference, good cond., (12-03-92, Sotheby-London, #666, illus.), 29½ x 22 in., (750 x 558 mm.), lithograph in colors (BP 1430, DM 3486, FR 11,900, Y 275,849).

BI *Poemes Dans Le Ciel: Metaphysique Du Vide, 1986,* s., #XXXIII/L, pub. Editions de la Difference, good cond., est. BP 1,4/1,800, (12-03-92, Sotheby-London, #674, illus.), 29½ x 22 in., (750 x 558 mm.), lithograph in colors.

BI *Poemes Dans Le Ciel: Metaphysique Du Vide, 1986,* s., #XXXIII/L, pub. Editions de la Difference, good cond., est. BP 1,4/1,800, (12-03-92, Sotheby-London, #673, illus.), 29½ x 21⅝ in., (750 x 555 mm.), lithograph in colors.

BI *Poemes Dans Le Ciel: Metaphysique Du Vide, 1986,* s., #XXXIII/L, pub. Editions de la Difference, good cond., est. BP 1,4/1,800, (12-03-92, Sotheby-London, #672, illus.), 29½ x 22 in., (750 x 558 mm.), lithograph in colors.

BI *Poemes Dans Le Ciel: Metaphysique Du Vide, 1986,* s., #IV/L, pub. Editions de la Difference, good cond., est. BP 1,8/2,200, (12-03-92, Sotheby-London, #670, illus.), 29½ x 22 in., (750 x 558 mm.), lithograph in colors.

BI *Poemes Dans Le Ciel: Metaphysique Du Vide, 1986,* s., #IV/L, pub. Editions de la Difference, good cond., est. BP 1,2/1,500, (12-03-92, Sotheby-London, #669, illus.), 29½ x 22 in., (750 x 558 mm.), lithograph in colors.

BI *Pointing At The Future III (G. 756), 1977,* s., annot. RTP, blindstamp pub. Gemini G.E.L., good cond.?, staining, est. $3/4,000, (10-28-92, Butterfield, #2955), 44 x 72 in., (111.8 x 182.9 cm.), lithograph in two shades of gray on 2 sheets of Arches 88 paper.

$453* *Polar Red - Louisiana, 1986/87,* s., 800mm x 1210mm, (10-14-92, Germann, #305), color offset lithograph/poster (BP 266, DM 663, FR 2248, Y 54,896, SF 590).

$2412* *Polar Red, 1973,* s., num., (06-05-93, Bassenge, #6033), 23⁷⁄₁₆ x 45¹⁄₁₆ in., (59.5 x 114.5 cm.), color offset-lithograph on thick copper print (BP 1588, DM 3911, FR 13,180, Y 258,743).

$381* *Polar Red, 1973,* 133/150, s., 665mm x 1210mm, (10-14-92, Germann, #302), color offset lithograph/poster (BP 224, DM 558, FR 1891, Y 46,171, SF 496).

$1950* *Polar Red, 1973,* s., d., #134/150, (10-21-92, Dobiaschofsky, #2001), 22¹⁄₁₆ x 47¼ in., (56 x 120 cm.), color serigraph (BP 1210, DM 2951, FR 10,015, Y 237,515, SF 2640).

$424* *Polar Red, Louisiana, 1986-87,* s., 800 x 1210mm, (09-04-92, Germann, #342), color offset-lithograph (BP 212, DM 594, FR 2023, Y 52,191, SF 529).

$911* *Sans Titre, 1986,* from "Poemes dans le ciel" portfolio, s., #51/100, (05-27-93, Briest, #92), 29¹⁵⁄₁₆ x 22¹⁄₁₆ in., (76 x 56 cm.), lithograph in four colors on BFK Rives (BP 583, DM 1462, FR 4927, Y 97,663).

$7700* *Senza Titolo III (SFE-066), 1987,* s., #27/76, blindstamp, pub. 2RC, full margins, good cond., (11-07-92, Sotheby-NY, #556, illus.), 34⅝ x 39 in., (87.9 x 99.1 cm.), aquatint p. in colors on Somerset (BP 5034, DM 12,294, FR 41,554, Y 950,383).

$6600* *Straight Line Of The Sun (G. 707, L.L. 187), 1975,* s., annot. RTP, blindstamp pub., Gemini G.E.L., full margins, good cond. (?), (02-24-93, Butterfield, #3023, illus.), sheet 51 x 90 in., (129.5 x 228.6 cm.), lithograph in blacks and grays on Arches 88 (BP 4603, DM 10,714, FR 36,324, Y 774,466).

$1150* *Sulfur Sails (SF-93, L. L107), 1969,* s., #20/20, Tamarind Lithography Workshop blindstamp, image scuff, creases, glued down in spots, (05-11-93, Christie-NY, #417), sheet 38½ x 26⅛ in., (978 x 664 mm.), color lithograph on wove (BP 734, DM 1812, FR 6104, Y 126,499).

BI *Untitled,* from series realised between 1973 and 1984, p. 1992 by Gardner Lithography, pub. Daniel Papierski, s., #12/50, good cond., est. BP 1,2/1,600, (06-30-93, Sotheby-London, #799, illus.), 29⅞ x 22 in., (759 x 559 mm.), color lithograph on wove.

BI *Untitled,* from series realised between 1973 and 1984, p. 1992 by Gardner Lithography, pub. Daniel Papierski, s., #12/50, good cond., est. BP 1,2/1,600, (06-30-93, Sotheby-London, #800, illus.), 29⅞ x 22 in., (759 x 559 mm.), color lithograph.

BI *Untitled,* from series realised between 1973 and 1984, p. 1992 by Gardner Lithography, pub. Daniel Papierski, s., #12/50, good cond., est. BP 1,2/1,500, (06-30-93, Sotheby-London, #798, illus.), 28⅞ x 22 in., (733 x 559 mm.), lithograph on wove.

BI *Untitled,* from series realised between 1973 and 1984, p. 1992 by Gardner Lithography, pub. Daniel Papierski, s., #12/50, good cond., est. BP 1,2/1,600, (06-30-93, Sotheby-London, #802), 29⅞ x 22 in., (759 x 559 mm.), lithograph on wove.

BI *Untitled,* from series realised between 1973 and 1984, p. 1992 by Gardner Lithography, pub. Daniel Papierski, s., #12/50, good cond., est. BP 1,2/1,600, (06-30-93, Sotheby-London, #803), 29⅞ x 22 in., (759 x 559 mm.), color lithograph on wove.

$2574* *Untitled,* from series realised between 1973 and 1984, p. 1992 by Gardner Lithography, pub. Daniel Papierski, s., #12/50, good cond., (06-30-93, Sotheby-London, #804), 29⅞ x 22 in., (759 x 559 mm.), color lithograph on wove (BP 1725, DM 4390, FR 14,810, Y 275,796).

BI *Untitled,* from series realised between 1973 and 1984, p. 1992 by Gardner Lithography, pub. Daniel Papierski, s., #12/50, good cond., est. BP 1,2/1,600, (06-30-93, Sotheby-London, #796, illus.), 29⅞ x 22 in., (759 x 559 mm.), color lithograph on wove.

$16,500* *Untitled (EXP-SF-61-02), 1983,* s., pub. Experimental Workshop, excellent cond., (11-09-92, Christie-NY, #287, illus.), 31¾ x 25 in., (806 x 635 mm.), woodcut monotype in oil and dry pigments in colors on handmade (BP 10,909, DM 26,341, FR 88,997, Y 2,047,655).

$19,800* *Untitled (EXP-SF-61-06), 1983,* s., pub. Experimental Workshop, excellent cond., sold after sale, (11-09-92, Christie-NY, #286, illus.), 30½ x 78½ in., (77.5 x 199.4 cm.), woodcut monotype in oil and dry pigments in colors on handmade (BP 13,091, DM 31,609, FR 106,796, Y 2,457,185).

$15,400* *Untitled (EXP-SF-63-11-83), 1983,* s., pub. Experimental Workshop, excellent cond., (11-09-92, Christie-NY, #288, illus.), 29½ x 25½ in., (749 x 648 mm.), woodcut monotype in oil and dry pigment in colors on handmade (BP 10,182, DM 24,585, FR 83,064, Y 1,911,144).

BI *Untitled (G. 751), 1977,* s., #12/25, blindstamp pub. Gemini G.E.L., good cond.?, est. $3/4,000, (10-28-92, Butterfield, #2954), 51 x 51 in., (129.5 x 129.5 cm.), lithograph on Arches 88 paper.

$5316* *Untitled (Green And Red) (Tamarind Nr. 1809), 1966,* s., num., blindstamp, (06-08-93, Karl/Faber, #757, illus.), sh approx. 30⁵⁄₁₆ x 23¹⁄₁₆ in., (77 x 58.5 cm.), color lithograph on thick wove (BP 3495, DM 8626, FR 29,049, Y 564,631).

BI *Untitled (L. L 182, SF. 202), 1975,* s., num. 20/30, blindstamp of pub. The Litho Shop, apparently very good cond., est. $1/2,000, (02-24-93, Butterfield, #3022), 37 x 27 in., (940 x 686 mm.), lithograph in black on BFK Rives.

BI *Untitled (L. L 277, SF. 319), 1987,* s., num. 39/50, blindstamp of pub. The Litho Shop, apparently very good cond., creases, est. $4/6,000, (02-24-93, Butterfield, #3024, illus.), 45 x 27¾ in., (114.3 x 70.5 cm.), lithograph in colors on BFK Rives.

BI *Untitled (L. L182), 1975,* s., #20/30, blindstamp publisher, The Litho Shop, very good cond., est. $1/2,000, (05-19-93, Butterfield, #2167), 37 x 27 in., (940 x 686 mm.), lithograph in black on Rives BFK.

BI *Untitled (L. L280, SF. 331), 1988,* s., num. 43/50, blindstamp of pub. The Litho Shop, good cond., glue remains, rubbed area, surface scuffs in image, est. $9/12,000, (02-24-93, Butterfield, #3025, illus.), 45 x 29 in., (114.3 x 73.7 cm.), lithograph in colors on PTI #120 Waterleaf.

BI *Untitled (L. P8, SFS 334), 1988,* s., #213/250, pub. artist, p. Ronald McPherson, blindstamp printshop,La Paloma, Tujunga, very good cond.?, est. $2,5/3,500, (05-19-93, Butterfield, #2168, illus.), 56⅞ x 29⅛ in., (144.5 x 74 cm.), silkscreen in colors on PTI Supra.

$920* *Untitled (L. S-1), 1968,* s., #71/300, pub. Minami Gallery, good cond., (05-15-93, Sotheby-NY, #974), sheet 40¾ x 27½ in., (103.5 x 69.9 cm.), silkscreen in colors on commercial grade matte (BP 598, DM 1480, FR 4973, Y 101,984).

$1093* *Untitled (L. S1), 1968,* s., #162/300, pub. Minami Gallery for Central Art Gallery, good cond., inkloss, creases, stray ink notations, rubbed areas, (05-19-93, Butterfield, #2166), 40⅞ x 27¾ in., (103.8 x 70.5 cm.), silkscreen in colors on commercial-grade matte (BP 710, DM 1777, FR 5986, Y 121,001).

$1650* *Untitled (L. SI), 1968,* s., num. 180/300, pub. Minami Gallery for Central Art Gallery, good cond., creases, (02-24-93, Butterfield, #3021), 40⅞ x 27¾ in., (103.8 x 70.5 cm.), silkscreen in colors on commercial-grade matte (BP 1151, DM 2679, FR 9081, Y 193,617).

$3775* *Untitled (Lembark I 46), 1984,* #14/17, p. by Jacob Samuel, pub. Litho Shop, blindstamp, full margins, good cond., (06-30-93, Sotheby-London, #806, illus.), 23⅞ x 7⅞ in., (606 x 200 mm.), color aquatint on wove (BP 2530, DM 6439, FR 21,720, Y 404,479).

BI *Untitled (Lembark P 3), 1968,* s., #128/144, poster for National Collection of Fine Arts, Smithsonian Institute, est. DM 4,000-, (05-27-93, Lempertz, #725, illus.), 29¼ x 21³⁄₁₆ in., (74.3 x 53.8 cm.), color offset lithograph on wove.

BI *Untitled (S.F. 272), 1984,* s., i., est. DM 13,000, (10-21-92, Dobiaschofsky, #2003, illus.), 42⅛ x 28¾ in., (107 x 73 cm.), color lithograph.

$1100* *Untitled (SF 243), 1968,* s., #140/300, pub. Central Art Gallery, creasing, soiling, (11-09-92, Christie-NY, #284, illus.), 41 x 27¾ in., (104.1 x 70.5 cm.), colored screenprint on wove (BP 727, DM 1756, FR 5933, Y 136,510).

$4025* *Untitled (SF 329) (Lambert L-278), 1988,* s., #44/50, pub. The Litho Shop, Inc., full sheet, good cond., creases, (02-11-93, Sotheby-NY, #335, illus.), sheet 44¹⁵⁄₁₆ x 27¹⁵⁄₁₆ in., (114.2 x 71.1 cm.), color lithograph (BP 2840, DM 6667, FR 22,562, Y 485,232).

$5225* *Untitled (SF 331), 1988,* s., #18/50, blindstamp, pub. Litho Shop, full sheet, good cond., (11-07-92, Sotheby-NY, #558), sheet 44⅞ x 29¼ in., (114 x 74.3 cm.), lithograph p. in colors (BP 3416, DM 8343, FR 28,198, Y 644,902).

$4313* *Untitled (SF-259) (L. L-240), 1980,* s., #26/32, blindstamp, pub. The Litho Shop, Inc., good cond., skinned spots, (05-15-93, Sotheby-NY, #977, illus.), sheet 27½ x 40 in., (69.9 x 101.6 cm.), lithograph in colors on BFK Rives (BP 2804, DM 6937, FR 23,314, Y 478,107).

$3450* *Untitled (SF-269) (L. L-254), 1982,* s., #49/250, apparently good cond., (05-15-93, Sotheby-NY, #976, illus.), sheet 47½ x 34¼ in., (120.7 x 87 cm.), offset lithograph in colors on Arches 88 (BP 2243, DM 5549, FR 18,649, Y 382,441).

$3680* *Untitled (SF-269, L. L254), 1982,* s., #167/250, pub. Brooke Alexander, excell. cond.?, (05-11-93, Christie-NY, #419, illus.), sheet 47¼ x 34¼ in., (120 x 87 cm.), color offset lithograph on wove (BP 2349, DM 5797, FR 19,533, Y 404,796).

$10,925* *Untitled (SF-291, L. S18, G. 1298), 1986,* s., $41/56, Gemini G.E.L. blindstamps, creases, excell. cond.?, (05-11-93, Christie-NY, #421, illus.), sheet 84 x 60 in., (213.4 x 152.4 cm.), color screenprint on wove (BP 6974, DM 17,210, FR 57,988, Y 1,201,738).

$978* *Untitled (SF-326, L. L195), 1975,* s., #26/26, The Litho Shop blindstamp, creases, excell. cond., (05-11-93, Christie-NY, #418), sheet 22 x 30 in., (559 x 762 mm.), lithograph on BFK Rives (BP 624, DM 1541, FR 5191, Y 107,579).

$4313* *Untitled (SF-330) (L. L-279), 1988,* s., #33/48, pub. The Litho Shop, Inc., full sheet, good cond., (02-11-93, Sotheby-NY, #336, illus.), sheet 44¹¹⁄₁₆ x 29⅛ in., (113.5 x 74 cm.), color lithograph (BP 3043, DM 7144, FR 24,176, Y 519,952).

$1650* *Untitled (SF. 202), 1975,* s., #20/30, blindstamp pub. The Litho Shop, very good cond.?, (10-28-92, Butterfield, #2951, illus.), 37 x 27 in., (940 x 686 mm.), lithograph in black on BFK Rives (BP 1051, DM 2548, FR 8652, Y 202,454).

$770* *Untitled (SF. 221), 1977,* s., #14/20, blindstamp pub. The Litho Shop, very good cond.?, (10-28-92, Butterfield, #2953), 28 x 42⅞ in., (71.1 x 108.9 cm.), lithograph on BFK Rives (BP 491, DM 1189, FR 4038, Y 94,479).

$4400* *Untitled (SF. 263), 1981,* s., #20/24, blindstamp pub. The Litho Shop, very good cond.?, (10-28-92, Butterfield, #2956, illus.), 42 x 29¾ in., (106.7 x 75.6 cm.), color lithograph on BFK Rives (BP 2803, DM 6795, FR 23,073, Y 539,877).

$1650* *Untitled (SF. 308A), 1987,* s., annot. AP 7/10, pub. Nantenshi Gallery, very good cond.?, (10-28-92, Butterfield, #2957, illus.), 26½ x 35 in., (673 x 889 mm.), lithograph in black, gray and silver on Arches (BP 1051, DM 2548, FR 8652, Y 202,454).

$17,600* *Untitled (SFE 031), 1985,* s., i. 'AP', 1 of 4 artist's proofs, blindstamp, pub. The Litho Shop,full margins, good cond., (11-07-92, Sotheby-NY, #557, illus.), 35⅞ x 23¾ in., (911 x 603 mm.), aquatint p. in colors (BP 11,507, DM 28,102, FR 94,981, Y 2,172,303).

$4394* *Untitled (SFS 243), 1968,* s., num., (06-08-93, Karl/Faber, #758, illus.), sh approx. 40¾ x 27⁹⁄₁₆ in., (103.5 x 70 cm.), color serigraph on thin board (BP 2889, DM 7130, FR 24,011, Y 466,702).

BI *Untitled (SFS-243, Lembrak S1), 1968,* s., #188/300, pub. Minami Gallery, tear, creasing, surface soiling, very good cond., est. $1,2/1,500, (05-11-93, Christie-NY, #416), sheet 41 x 27¾ in., (104.1 x 70.5 cm.), color screenprint on wove.

$2300* *Untitled (SFS-332, L. S19), 1988,* s., #60/114, pub. by artist, excell. cond., (05-11-93, Christie-NY, #422, illus.), sheet 30 x 22 in., (762 x 559 mm.), color screenprint on wove (BP 1468, DM 3623, FR 12,208, Y 252,997).

$3850* *Untitled (T. 2584), 1969,* s. verso, #4/20, blindstamp pub. Tamarind Lithography Workshop, verygood cond., (10-28-92, Butterfield, #2949, illus.), 22 x 30 in., (559 x 762 mm.), color lithograph on cream wove (BP 2453, DM 5946, FR 20,189, Y 472,393).

$2200* *Untitled (T. 2587), 1969,* s., annot. BAT, blindstamp pub. Tamarind Lithography Workshop, very good cond., creases, (10-28-92, Butterfield, #2950), 35 x 25 in., (889 x 635 mm.), color lithograph on Rives BFK (BP 1402, DM 3398, FR 11,536, Y 269,939).

$5163* *Untitled, 1974,* #3/40, s., (11-13-92, Koller, #5320), 26⅜ x 19¹¹⁄₁₆ in., (67 x 50 cm.), lithograph on wove (BP 3336, DM 8105, FR 27,332, Y 640,809, SF 7308).

$1837* *Untitled, 1982,* s., i. A.P., blindstamp, (06-12-93, Hauswedell/Nolt, #85, illus.), 23¹³⁄₁₆ x 17⅞ in., (60.5 x 45.4 cm.), color aquatint (BP 1202, DM 2990, FR 10,049, Y 193,307).

$3850* *Untitled, 1983,* from Eight by Eight to Celebrate the Temporary Contemporary, Museum of Contemporary Art, s., #215/250, excell. cond., (11-09-92, Christie-NY, #285, illus.), 42 x 28⅝ in., (106.7 x 72.7 cm.), colored lithograph on wove (BP 2545, DM 6146, FR 20,766, Y 477,786).

BI *Untitled, 1991,* #66/66, s., est. SF 18/22,000, (12-05-92, Mangisch, #573, illus.), 40⁹⁄₁₆ x 30⁵⁄₁₆ in., (103 x 77 cm.), etching and aquatint on copper plate in colors.

BI *Untitled, For The Central Art Gallery Tokyo, 1968,* #162/300, s., ink stain, est. SF 1,8/2,500, 1305 x 705mm, (09-04-92, Germann, #341), color serigraph.

BI *Untitled, For The Central Art Gallery Tokyo, 1968-SF 243,* 162/300, s., 1305mm x 705mm, est. SF 2/2,500, (10-14-92, Germann, #304), color serigraph.

$1650* *Untitled, For The Central Art Gallery, Tokyo, 1968,* s., #137/300, p. Litho Shop, creases, (12-08-92, Swann, #107, illus.), 40⅞ x 27¾ in., (103.8 x 70.5 cm.), color serigraph (BP 1034, DM 2569, FR 8758, Y 204,512).

$5651* *The Upper Red (Lemb.-P.L. 51), 1963,* s., i. epr. d'artiste, (06-23-93, Kornfeld, #348), color lithograph (BP 3839, DM 9562, FR 32,163, Y 615,644, SF 8510).

$2860* *The Upper Red (SF 48), 1963-5,* stamped Chinese charater sig., num. 13/300, Jahresgabe der Kestner-Gesellschaft ink stamp, full sheet, excell. cond., (09-19-92,

Christie-E, #106), sheet 19¾ x 25¾ in., (50.2 x 65.4 cm.), lithograph in colors on BFK Rives (BP 1645, DM 4283, FR 14,667, Y 356,342).

$10,034* *The Upper Yellow (Lembark L 4), 1960,* s., (05-27-93, Lempertz, #724, illus.), 24¹⁵⁄₁₆ x 35¾ in., (63.3 x 90.8 cm.), color lithograph on BFK Rives wove (BP 6426, DM 16,101, FR 54,267, Y 1,075,686).

$4611* *"Upper Yellow II" (Lembark L 73), 1964,* watermark, s., num., (06-05-93, Grisebach, #407, illus.), 29¾ x 21⅞ in., (75.5 x 55.5 cm.), color lithograph on wove (BP 3035, DM 7476, FR 25,197, Y 494,636).

$2310* *Very First Stone (Sparks 1), 1959-68,* s., d., t., #18/25, blindstamp, full margins, good cond., (11-07-92, Sotheby-NY, #552, illus.), sheet 31⅝ x 22⅝ in., (803 x 575 mm.), lithograph p. in colors, on white wove Crisbrook (BP 1510, DM 3688, FR 12,466, Y 285,115).

$1527* *Water Buffalo (Lemb.-P.L. 70), 1964,* s., num., (06-23-93, Kornfeld, #349), color lithograph (BP 1037, DM 2584, FR 8691, Y 166,358, SF 2300).

FRANCO, Battista (attrib.) Italian 1498 or 1510-1580

$444* *Suite Complete De 3 Planches D'Animaux De L'Antiquite, 1547: Three,* after Giulio Romano, losses, tears, thin spot, dirt spots, (05-15-93, Loudmer, #17, illus.), approx. 11 x 16⁹⁄₁₆ in., (280 x 420 mm.), etchings contrecollees on laid (BP 289, DM 714, FR 2400, Y 49,218).

FRANCO, Giacomo 1556-1620

$2997* *Saint Jerome In The Desert, c. 1590,* after Girolamo Muciano, narrow to thread margins, losses, rubbing, staining, laid, (12-01-92, Christie-London, #57, illus.), P. 20⁵⁄₁₆ x 14½ in., (516 x 369 mm.), engraving (BP 1980, DM 4777, FR 16,279, Y 373,132).

FRANCO, Giovanni Battista (Il Semolei) 1510-1561

$3330* *The Adoration Of The Shepherds, (B. XVI, 8; Pass. Vi, p. 178, no. 8), c. 1550,* Passavant's second state (of four), delicate tone, trimmed, defects,very good cond., laid, (12-01-92, Christie-London, #39, illus.), S. 14¾ x 20⅜ in., (375 x 518 mm.), etching w/engraving (BP 2200, DM 5308, FR 18,088, Y 414,592).

FRANCOIS, A.

$20* *Capac Cocinor: Le Soupirant. De P. Etaix, 1963,* good cond., (02-12-93, Cheval/Robert, #205), 30⁵⁄₁₆ x 22¹³⁄₁₆ in., (77 x 58 cm.), poster (BP 14, DM 33, FR 112, Y 2412).

FRANCOIS, Andre

BI *Re-Joyce,* s., i., margins, est. BP 30/50, (03-17-93, Bonhams-Chelsea, #317), plate 19¼ x 14¾ in., (48.9 x 37.5 cm.), etching in colors.

FRANCOIS, Andre b. 1915

$159* *Citroen 2 CV Prefere Total (Cheval A Double Tete), 1972,* cond. A, (03-16-93, Boisgirard, #111), 36 x 50⅜ in., (91.5 x 128 cm.), poster (BP 110, DM 264, FR 898, Y 18,592).

FRANCOIS, Geo

$798* *PLM. Evian Les Bains. "The Wonderful Savoie",* very good cond., (03-15-93, Arcole, #91, illus.), 39¾ x 24⅝ in., (101 x 62.5 cm.), (BP 556, DM 1326, FR 4506, Y 94,527).

BI *PLM. Hauteville-Lompnes. (Ain). "Station D'Altitude D'Hiver Et D'Ete", c. 1930,* good cond., (03-15-93, Arcole, #35), 41⁵⁄₁₆ x 29¹⁵⁄₁₆ in., (105 x 76 cm.), .

FRANK, Douglas

$303* *"Four Trees And Dune, Oregon", 1982,* s., t., d., edit. 3/00, (11-16-92, Butterfield, #5971, illus.), 7⅞ x 9¾ in., (200.4 x 248.1 mm.), photograph, platinum print (BP 199, DM 483, FR 1627, Y 37,682).

FRANK, Leo Austrian 1884-1948

$220* *"A Spring Gale", Before The Storm,* s. Leo Frank w/in image, ident. i. on mat and verso, good cond?, foxing, abrasions, (10-09-92, Skinner, #99, illus.), 9 x 14 in., (22.9 x 35.6 cm.), color woodblock on paper (BP 131, DM 328, FR 1111, Y 26,829).

FRANK, Mary Anglo/American b. 1933

$95* *Untitled: Three,* E.A., d., s., (01-28-93, Pescheteau, #145), serigraphs (BP 63, DM 151, FR 509, Y 11,795).

FRANK, Robert b. 1924

$990* *Allen Ginsberg,* s. Frank by photog. in ink, 1950's, (10-15-92, Sotheby-NY, #529, illus.), 7¾ x 11¼ in., (19.7 x 28.6 cm.), photograph, gelatin silver print (BP 606, DM 1474, FR 4997, Y 118,776).

$2875* *"Les Americains",* Robert Delpire, 1958, book, oblong 4to, laminated boards w/designs by Saul Steinberg, first edit., (04-06-93, Sotheby-NY, #443, illus.), photograph (BP 1899, DM 4632, FR 15,685, Y 327,897).

$3300* *Les Americains, 1958,* Robert Delpire, book illus. w/83 full-page reprods. of Frank's photos, 1st ed., (10-15-92, Sotheby-NY, #531, illus.), photograph, gelatin silver prints (BP 2019, DM 4912, FR 16,658, Y 395,921).

BI *"Les Americains, Photographies De Robert Frank", 1958,* pub., est. BP 1,5/2,000, (05-07-93, Sotheby-London, #297), photograph.

$6613* *Barcelona, Spain, 1952,* s. by photog., (04-06-93, Sotheby-NY, #440, illus.), 8½ x 12⅞ in., photograph (BP 4368, DM 10,654, FR 36,077, Y 754,220).

BI *Ben James With Miners, Wales, 1951,* s. in ink, est. $4/5,000, (10-13-92, Christie-NY, #446, illus.), 9⅝ x 13⅝ in., (24.4 x 34.6 cm.), photograph, gelatin silver print.

$3220* *Ben Walks Home, Wales, 1951,* ink s., t., d. on label, (04-08-93, Christie-NY, #431, illus.), 13 x 8⅝ in., (33 x 21.9 cm.), photograph, gelatin silver print (BP 2111, DM 5173, FR 17,510, Y 365,411).

$1760* *Black Artist With His Paintings,* 1950's, p. before Sept. 1966, (10-15-92, Sotheby-NY, #537, illus.), 9⅛ x 13½ in., (23.2 x 34.3 cm.), photograph, gelatin silver print, mounted on Crescent illus. board (BP 1077, DM 2620, FR 8884, Y 211,158).

$2760* *Byrrh, Paris, 1947,* ink s., d.; s., (c) d., archive stamp, (04-08-93, Christie-NY, #428, illus.), 10 x 13½ in., (25.4 x 34.3 cm.), photograph, gelatin silver print (BP 1810, DM 4434, FR 15,008, Y 313,209).

$4400* *Candy Store-New York City, c. 1955 (The Americans, pl. 28),* label, s. by photog. in ink, (10-15-92, Sotheby-NY, #532, illus.), 8½ x 12⅞ in., (21.6 x 32.7 cm.), photograph, gelatin silver print (BP 2692, DM 6550, FR 22,211, Y 527,894).

$1150* *"Coffee Shop, Railway Station-Indianapolis" (The Americans, p. 149),c. 1955,* s., d. by photog., Robert Frank Archive stamp, (04-06-93, Sotheby-NY, #445, illus.), 8⅝ x 13 in., photograph (BP 760, DM 1853, FR 6274, Y 131,159).

$4830* *Coney Island, 1958,* ink s., t., d., (04-08-93, Christie-NY, #432, illus.), 8¼ x 13 in., (21 x 33 cm.), photograph, gelatin silver print (BP 3167, DM 7759, FR 26,264, Y 548,116).

$6900* *Daytona Beach,* 1958, p. 1962, ink s., t., d., lit., (04-08-93, Christie-NY, #433, illus.), 12⅛ x 17 in., (30.8 x 43.2 cm.), photograph, gelatin silver print (BP 4525, DM 11,084, FR 37,520, Y 783,023).

$4400* *Elko, Nevada, 1955 (The Americans, pl. 70),* s., t., d. by photog. in ink, (10-15-92, Sotheby-NY, #533, illus.), 13 x 8½ in., (33 x 21.6 cm.), photograph, gelatin silver print (BP 2692, DM 6550, FR 22,211, Y 527,894).

$1540* *Figures On Grandstand, City Hall,* notations Robert Frank from The Americans in unident. hand, 1950s, (04-07-93, Swann, #312, illus.), 8½ x 13 in., photograph, silver print (BP 1018, DM 2491, FR 8429, Y 174,960).

$2013* *"Ford River Rouge Plant" (The Amnericans, p. 109),* s., t., d. by photog., 1955, p.c. 1960, (04-06-93, Sotheby-NY, #446A, illus.), 9 x 13½ in., photograph (BP 1330, DM 3243, FR 10,982, Y 229,585).

BI *Funeral-St Helena, South Carolina, 1955-56,* s. in ink, lit., est. $3/4,000, (10-13-92, Christie-NY, #451, illus.), 13 x 8½ in., (33 x 21.6 cm.), photograph, gelatin silver print.

$3450* *"Lincoln, Nebraska" (The Americans, p. 137),* s., t., d. by photog., 1956, p. c. 1960, (04-06-93, Sotheby-NY, #446, illus.), 8 x 11⅞ in., photograph (BP 2279, DM 5558, FR 18,822, Y 393,476).

$4400* *London,* (1951), late 1960s-early 1970s, s., t., d. in ink, lit., (10-13-92, Christie-NY, #448, illus.), 8¾ x 13½ in., (22.2 x 34.3 cm.), photograph, gelatin silver print (BP 2563, DM 6446, FR 21,901, Y 533,527).

$6900* *London Bankers, 1951,* ink s., (04-08-93, Christie-NY, #430, illus.), 13½ x 9⅜ in., (34.3 x 23.8 cm.), photograph, gelatin silver print (BP 4525, DM 11,084, FR 37,520, Y 783,023).

$4950* *London, 1951,* s., t. by photog. in ink, (c) stamp, 1951, p.l., (10-15-92, Sotheby-NY, #528, illus.), 8¾ x 13¼ in., (22.2 x 33.7 cm.), photograph, gelatin silver print (BP 3029, DM 7368, FR 24,987, Y 593,881).

$2300* *"Los Angeles", 1956,* s., t., d. by photog., (04-06-93, Sotheby-NY, #444, illus.), 9 x 13 in., photograph (BP 1519, DM 3705, FR 12,548, Y 262,318).

$3300* *Lusk Drive-In Movie, Wyo.,* s., t., d. by photog. in ink, 1956, p.l., (10-15-92, Sotheby-NY, #534, illus.), 8⅞ x 13⅜ in., (22.5 x 34 cm.), photograph, gelatin silver print (BP 2019, DM 4912, FR 16,658, Y 395,921).

BI *"Macy's Parade, NYC",* s., t., d. by photog., 1948, p.l., est. $3/4,000, (04-06-93, Sotheby-NY, #442, illus.), 10⅞ x 7⅜ in., photograph.

$7700* *New Orleans (The Americans, dust jacket & pl. 44),* s., t., d. by photog. in ink, (c) stamp, 1956, p.l., (10-15-92, Sotheby-NY, #535, illus.), 9 x 13⅜ in., (22.9 x 34 cm.), photograph, gelatin silver print (BP 4712, DM 11,462, FR 38,869, Y 923,815).

$1650* *Old Man With Pablo, 1954 (Lines of My Hand, p. 56),* prov., (10-15-92, Sotheby-NY, #530, illus.), 7½ x 11½ in., (19.1 x 29.2 cm.), photograph, gelatin silver print (BP 1010, DM 2456, FR 8329, Y 197,960).

$5225* *Opera, New York, 1959,* s., t., d. by photog. in ink, (10-15-92, Sotheby-NY, #538, illus.), 13½ x 8⅞ in., (34.3 x 22.5 cm.), photograph, gelatin silver print, backed w/card (BP 3197, DM 7778, FR 26,376, Y 626,875).

$3680* *Paris,* 1952, p. 1960s, ink s., t., d. recto, (04-08-93, Christie-NY, #429, illus.), 13⅛ x 8½ in., (33.3 x 21.6 cm.), photograph, gelatin silver print (BP 2413, DM 5912, FR 20,011, Y 417,612).

$4025* *"Paris",* s., t., d. by photog. on image, photog. (c) stamp, 1951, p.l., (04-06-93, Sotheby-NY, #441, illus.), 13⅛ x 8½ in., photograph (BP 2659, DM 6485, FR 21,959, Y 459,056).

$1980* *"Paris", 1950,* ink s., t., d., (11-16-92, Butterfield, #5974, illus.), 13 x 8⅜ in., (330.8 x 213.1 mm.), photograph, gelatin silver print (BP 1304, DM 3157, FR 10,634, Y 246,238).

$1320* *Paris, 1949,* s., t. by photog. in ink, (c) stamp, archive stamp, museum stamp, annot. by Grace Mayer, 1949, p.l., (10-15-92, Sotheby-NY, #527, illus.), 8½ x 13¾ in., (21.6 x 34.9 cm.), photograph, gelatin silver print (BP 808, DM 1965, FR 6663, Y 158,368).

$4830* *Paris, 1949-51,* ink s., t., d., flush-mounted, (04-08-93, Christie-NY, #427, illus.), 6½ x 10⅝ in., (16.5 x 27 cm.), photograph, gelatin silver print (BP 3167, DM 7759, FR 26,264, Y 548,116).

BI *Polo Match,* 1950s, s. in ink, est. $3/4,000, (10-13-92, Christie-NY, #447, illus.), 9¾ x 14 in., (24.8 x 35.6 cm.), photograph, gelatin silver print.

BI *Rome, c. 1950,* s. in ink, notations, est. $3/4,000, (10-13-92, Christie-NY, #445, illus.), 13⅜ x 9 in., (34 x 22.9 cm.), photograph, gelatin silver print.

BI *Rooming House, Bunker Hill, Los Angeles,* (1955-56), c. 1969, s., t., d., i. in ink in margin; t. in unidentified hand, (c) credit stamp, lit., est. $3/5,000, (10-13-92, Christie-NY, #450, illus.), 18⅞ x 12¼ in., (47.9 x 31.1 cm.), photograph, gelatin silver print.

$1150* *"Salt Lake City" (The Americans, p. 117), 1955,* s., t., d. by photog., Robert Frank Archive and (c) stamp, (04-06-93, Sotheby-NY, #447, illus.), 12⅞ x 8⅜ in., photograph (BP 760, DM 1853, FR 6274, Y 131,159).

BI *Sandusky, Ohio, Amusement Park, c. 1955,* s.by photog., label, (c) stamp, est. $2/2,500, (10-15-92, Sotheby-NY, #534A, illus.), 8½ x 13 in., (21.6 x 33 cm.), photograph, gelatin silver print.

$3163* *"South Carolina" (The Americans, p. 119),* s., t. by photog., i., 1955, p.c. 1960, (04-06-93, Sotheby-NY, #445A, illus.), 8½ x 12¾ in., photograph (BP 2089, DM 5096, FR 17,256, Y 360,744).

$1320* *Tennesse(sic)-Chattanooga-Main Street,* (1956), p.l., s., t., d. in ink, (c) stamp, (10-13-92, Christie-NY, #449, illus.), 9¼ x 13½ in., (23.5 x 34.3 cm.), photograph, gelatin silver print (BP 769, DM 1934, FR 6570, Y 160,058).

$4950* *"Times Square", 1948,* ink s., t., d., Dixon Collection, (11-16-92, Butterfield, #5972, illus.), 13½ x 7 in., (343.5 x 178.1 mm.), photograph, gelatin silver print (BP 3259, DM 7892, FR 26,584, Y 615,595).

$2750* *Venice,* s., t. by photog. in ink, (c) stamp, 1950's, p.l., (10-15-92, Sotheby-NY, #536, illus.), 12⅞ x 8⅝ in., (32.7 x 21.9 cm.), photograph, gelatin silver print (BP 1683, DM 4093, FR 13,882, Y 329,934).

$1235* *"Welsh Miner",* 1950s, t., num. 4, i. photog.'s credit Copyright by Robert Frank, 245 x 163mm, (05-07-93, Sotheby-London, #296, illus.), photograph, silver print (BP 782, DM 1953, FR 6580, Y 135,983).

FRANK AND SONS, Publisher

$85* *The Harbury,* finished by hand, commemorative rosette, (08-12-92, Bonhams, #192), image 18¼ x 29 in., (46.4 x 73.7 cm.), tinted photograph (BP 44, DM 124, FR 421, Y 10,834).

FRANKEL, Godfrey

$345* *"Chatham Square Barber Shop", 1946,* s., t., d., est. $6/800, (05-23-93, Butterfield, #3415, illus.), 9¾ x 7¾ in., photograph, gelatin silver print (BP 225, DM 564, FR 1899, Y 38,134).

BI *"New York",* 1947, p.l., s., t., d., annot., est. $4/600, (05-23-93, Butterfield, #3417, illus.), 10⅜ x 11 in., photograph, gelatin silver print.

$546* *"Optometrist's Shop, Rivington Street, New York",* 1947, p.l., s., t., d., annot., (05-23-93, Butterfield, #3416, illus.), 13⅝ x 11 in., photograph, gelatin silver print (BP 356, DM 893, FR 3005, Y 60,351).

$468* *"Third Avenue Elevated Stairway",* ink s., t., d. verso, 1947/later, (11-16-92, Butterfield, #5975, illus.), 10¾ x 13¾ in., (273.5 x 349.9 mm.), photograph, gelatin silver print (BP 308, DM 746, FR 2513, Y 58,202).

FRANKENTHALER, Helen American b. 1928

BI *Deep Sun (T. 201), 1983,* s., d., #54/54, blindstamp, full margins, excellent cond., est. $6/7,000, (11-09-92, Christie-NY, #291, illus.), 30 x 40½ in., (76.2 x 102.9 cm.), etching, aquatint, drypoint, engraving and mezzotint in colors on handmade.

$4313* *Deep Sun (Tyler 201:HF33), 1983,* s., d., #9/54, blindstamp, pub. Tyler Graphics, Ltd., good cond., (05-15-93, Sotheby-NY, #978, illus.), sheet 29¾ x 40⅛ in., (75.6 x 101.9 cm.), etching and aquatint in colors on handmade St. (stamp) Armand (BP 2804, DM 6937, FR 23,314, Y 478,107).

$3025* *Dream Walk (T. 178, W.C. 60), 1977,* s., d., num. 23/47, blindstamp of pub. Tyler Graphics, full margins,apparently very good cond., (02-24-93, Butterfield, #3028, illus.), 22 x 29¾ in., (559 x 756 mm.), lithgraph in colors on mauve handmade (BP 2109, DM 4911, FR 16,648, Y 354,964).

$13,200* *East And Beyond (Will. Coll. 44; Sparks 25), 1972-73,* s., d. '73-'74, #11/12, blindstamp, pub. ULAE, full margins, good cond., (11-07-92, Sotheby-NY, #561, illus.), 23⅞ x 17⅞ in., (606 x 454 mm.), woodcut p. in colors on Nepalese handmade (BP 8630, DM 21,076, FR 71,236, Y 1,629,227).

$9200* *Essence Mulberry (Williams College 62, Tyler 180), 1977,* s., d., #29/46, Tyler Graphics blindstamp, top corners reattached, creases, very good cond., (05-11-93, Christie-NY, #424, illus.), sheet 39½ x 19¾ in., (100.3 x 50.2 cm.), color woodcut on buff Maniai Gampi hand-made (BP 5873, DM 14,493, FR 48,832, Y 1,011,990).

$1210* *Experimental Impression IV (Tyler 186:HF10), 1978,* s., d. '77-78', t., blindstamp, pub. Tyler Graphics, Ltd., full margins, good cond., (11-07-92, Sotheby-NY, #562), 8⅝ x 19½ in., (219 x 495 mm.), monotype p. in colors on Dutch Etching mouldmade (BP 791, DM 1932, FR 6530, Y 149,346).

$523* *From What Red Lines Can Do (Williams College 29),* s., d. 70, #28/75, pub. Multiples, Inc., prov., (05-16-93, Hindman, #626), 32 x 20 in., (81.3 x 50.8 cm.), color serigraph (BP 340, DM 841, FR 2827, Y 57,976).

$19,800* *Gateway, 1988,* s., #2/30, blindstamp, pub. Tyler Graphics, Ltd., good cond., framedas a screen, (11-07-92, Sotheby-NY, #565, illus.), each sheet 69 x 29¾ in., (175.3 x 75.6 cm.), etching and aquatint p. in colors w/hand stenciled borders, on threesheets of TGL handmade (BP 12,945, DM 31,614, FR 106,854, Y 2,443,841).

BI *Gateway, 1988*, s., i. P/P 1, printer's proof, blindstamp, pub. Tyler Graphics Ltd.,good cond. ?, est. $18/22,000, (05-15-93, Sotheby-NY, #979, illus.), each sheet 68⅞ x 29¾ in., (174.9 x 75.6 cm.), etching and aquatint in colors, w/hand-stenciled borders, on three sheets of TGL handmade paper.

BI *Paris Review Poster (Will. Coll. 10), 1966*, s., num. 58/150, full sheet, very good cond., est. $1/2,000, (05-22-93, Weschler, #185, illus.), 30 x 22½ in., (76.2 x 57.2 cm.), lithograph in colors on Arches.

$1150* *Ramblas, 1987-88*, s., d., #46/75, pub. Editions Poligrafa, scuff, very good cond., (05-11-93, Christie-NY, #425, illus.), sheet 34¼ x 26¹⁵⁄₁₆ in., (870 x 684 mm.), color lithograph and etching on BFK Rives (BP 734, DM 1812, FR 6104, Y 126,499).

$3850* *Ramblas, 1987-88*, s., d., num. 64/75, pub. Editions Poligrafa, full sheet, excell. cond., (09-19-92, Christie-E, #107, illus.), sheet 34¼ x 27 in., (87 x 68.6 cm.), lithograph and etching in colors on BFK Rives (BP 2215, DM 5765, FR 19,744, Y 479,691).

$1870* *The Red Sea (Tyler 200), 1982*, s., d. 1978-82, i. AP, #13/14, blindstamp, full margins, excellent cond., (11-09-92, Christie-NY, #290, illus.), 24 x 28 in., (610 x 711 mm.), colored lithograph on pink handmade (BP 1236, DM 2985, FR 10,086, Y 232,068).

$3300* *Sanguine Mood (W.C. 36), 1971*, s., d., num. 26/75, pub. Chiron Press, apparently very good cond., (02-24-93, Butterfield, #3027, illus.), 22½ x 18 in., (572 x 457 mm.), pochoir & silkscreen in colors on J.B. Green/Hayle Mill English (BP 2301, DM 5357, FR 18,162, Y 387,233).

BI *Spoleto Festival Poster (F. 42), 1972*, s., t., #77/100, very good cond., est. $800/1,200, (06-11-93, Doyle, #94), 39½ x 29½ in., (100.3 x 74.9 cm.), color silkscreen.

$1925* *Spring Veil, 1986*, s., d. '87, #47/51, blindstamp, full margins, pin holes, crease, excellent cond., sold after sale, (11-09-92, Christie-NY, #292), 17¼ x 25¾ in., (438 x 654 mm.), etching, aquatint and drypoint in greens on wove (BP 1273, DM 3073, FR 10,383, Y 238,893).

$4600* *Spring Veil, 1987*, s., d., #32/51, blindstamp, pub. 2RC Edizioni d'Arte, full margins, god cond., (05-15-93, Sotheby-NY, #980, illus.), 9¼ x 13¾ in., (23.5 x 34.9 cm.), etching and aquatint in colors (BP 2991, DM 7399, FR 24,865, Y 509,921).

$990* *Sun Corner (Williams College 13), 1968*, incised sig., d., #43/50, good cond., minor scratches, (11-07-92, Sotheby-NY, #559, illus.), sheet 36⅛ x 36⅛ in., (918 x 918 mm.), silkcreen p. in colors on aluminum panel (BP 647, DM 1581, FR 5343, Y 122,192).

$4950* *Sure Violet (Williams College 70), 1979*, s., d., #35/50, blindstamp, full margins, excellent cond., (11-09-92, Christie-NY, #289, illus.), 43¼ x 31⅛ in., (109.9 x 79.1 cm.), aquatint and drypoint in colors on TGL handmade (BP 3273, DM 7902, FR 26,699, Y 614,296).

$9200* *Tahiti, 1989*, s., d., #37/45, pub. Mixografia, good cond. ?, (05-15-93, Sotheby-NY, #981, illus.), sheet 31⅞ x 54 in., (81 x 137.2 cm.), Mixografia on handmade paper (BP 5982, DM 14,798, FR 49,730, Y 1,019,843).

$660* *Untitled*, s., d. 65, #165/200, (05-16-93, Hindman, #651A), 21⅞ x 16⅞ in., (55.6 x 42.9 cm.), silkscreen (BP 429, DM 1062, FR 3568, Y 73,163).

BI *Untitled (Cleveland Orchestra Print) (Williams College 68), 1978*, s., num. AP 15/25, blindstamp, Tyler Graphics, full sheet, very goodcond., ests. $800/1,200, (05-22-93, Weschler, #184, illus.), 22 x 20 in., (55.9 x 50.8 cm.), silkscreen in colors on Arches.

$2310* *Walking Rain, 1987*, s., d., i. 'AP 9/14', numbered edit. of 54, blindstamp, pub. Tyler Graphics, Ltd., full sheet, good cond., (11-07-92, Sotheby-NY, #564, illus.), sheet 29½ x 22¼ in., (749 x 565 mm.), lithograph, soft (molle) ground etching and aquatint p. in colors onSaunders mouldmade (BP 1510, DM 3688, FR 12,466, Y 285,115).

$3850* *What Red Lines Can Do (Will. Coll. 25-29), 1970*, portfolio, s., d., #70/75, pub. Multiples, Inc., full sheets, good cond., five, (11-07-92, Sotheby-NY, #560, illus.), each sheet 38⅝ x 26 in., (981 x 660 mm.), five silkscreens p. in color (BP 2517, DM 6147, FR 20,777, Y 475,191).

$4400* *Yellow Jack, 1985-87*, s., d., #50/54, blindstamp, pub. Tyler Graphics, Ltd., good cond., (11-07-92, Sotheby-NY, #563, illus.), sheet 30 x 38 in., (762 x 965 mm.), lithograph p. in colors w/hand coloring in acrylic and pastels on Arches Cover mouldmade (BP 2877, DM 7025, FR 23,745, Y 543,076).

FRANKL, Ch.   Swiss 20th cent.

$300* *Zug*, plate mono., (04-21-93, Germann, #436), 14⁵⁄₁₆ x 20¹¹⁄₁₆ in., (364 x 525 mm.), etching (BP 195, DM 480, FR 1622, Y 33,212, SF 437).

FRANKL, Gerhart

$307* *Avignon At Sunset, 1928*, s., #34/50, margins, good cond., foxing, Late Gerhard Brauer Coll., (05-27-93, Sotheby-Amstrdm, #819), 5⅞ x 8⁹⁄₁₆ in., (150 x 218 mm.), etching on wove (BP 197, DM 493, FR 1660, Y 32,912, G 552).

$288* *Haus Auf Der Anhohe, 1927*, margins, good cond., Late Gerhard Brauer Coll., (05-27-93, Sotheby-Amstrdm, #817), 4¹⁵⁄₁₆ x 7 in., (125 x 178 mm.), etching on wove (BP 184, DM 462, FR 1558, Y 30,875, G 518).

$307* *Mont Blanc, 1928*, 3rd state, margins, good cond., Late Gerhard Brauer Coll., (05-27-93, Sotheby-Amstrdm, #820), 6⁵⁄₁₆ x 11¹⁵⁄₁₆ in., (160 x 304 mm.), etching on wove (BP 197, DM 493, FR 1660, Y 32,912, G 552).

$307* *(Mountaineous Landscape), 1928*, 3rd state, s., d., #48/50, margins, good cond., handling creases, Late Gerhard Brauer Coll., (05-27-93, Sotheby-Amstrdm, #818), 4¾ x 6¹¹⁄₁₆ in., (120 x 170 mm.), etching on wove (BP 197, DM 493, FR 1660, Y 32,912, G 552).

$307* *(Village), 1928*, margins, good cond., foxing, Late Gerhard Brauer Coll., (05-27-93, Sotheby-Amstrdm, #821), 6⅝ x 8¹¹⁄₁₆ in., (168 x 220 mm.), etching on wove (BP 197, DM 493, FR 1660, Y 32,912, G 552).

FRANKSEN, Jean Eda   American b. 1914

BI *Pueblo Indians At Market*, s., t., est. $50/75, (11-12-92, Freemn/Fine Art, #70), 9½ x 7 in., (24.1 x 17.8 cm.), litho.

FRASCONI, Antonio   American b. Argentina, 1919

$77* *"Connoisseur"*, s. Frasconi, t., (09-25-92, Wolf, #49), 6 x 3¾ in., (15.2 x 9.5 cm.), woodcut (BP 45, DM 114, FR 386, Y 9294).

$385* *"Day And Night", 1952*, Print Club of Cleveland Special Publication, excell. cond., (10-31-92, Cleveland, #120), 9⅜ x 12¹¹⁄₁₆ in., (23.8 x 32.2 cm.), woodcut (BP 247, DM 592, FR 2009, Y 47,690).

$140* *"Day And Night", 1952*, The Print Club of Cleveland Special Publication for 1952, s., excell. cond., (05-15-93, Cleveland, #464), 9⅜ x 12¹¹⁄₁₆ in., (23.8 x 32.2 cm.), woodcut (BP 91, DM 225, FR 757, Y 15,519).

$138* *The Dog And The Crocodile*, s., d. (19)50, The Print Club of Cleveland publication no. 30, 1952, (07-03-92, Sloan, #315), 16 x 11½ in., (40.6 x 29.2 cm.), woodcut (BP 72, DM 209, FR 704, Y 17,203).

$325* *The Dog And The Crocodile, 1952*, s., The Print Club of Cleveland Publication No. 30, very good cond., (05-15-93, Cleveland, #465), 16⅛ x 11⁷⁄₁₆ in., (40.6 x 29.1 cm.), woodcut in two colors (BP 211, DM 523, FR 1757, Y 36,027).

BI *Field Of Scrap, 1963*, s., d., t., #25/109, good cond., creases, stray marks, est. $2/400, (12-12-92, Weschler, #120), 24¼ x 21 in., (61.6 x 53.3 cm.), color lithograph.

$1650* *Fulton Fish Market, Sunrise, 1953*, s., t., taped, very good cond., lit., (06-11-93, Doyle, #42, illus.), 16½ x 23¾ in., (419 x 603 mm.), color woodcut (BP 1084, DM 2682, FR 9041, Y 175,066).

$193* *Migration Over The Sound, 1959*, s., d., t., #8/25, margins, good cond.?, prov., prop. Woodward Foundation, (12-12-92, Weschler, #121), 15¼ x 21 in., (38.7 x 53.3 cm.), color woodcut (BP 124, DM 304, FR 1042, Y 23,883).

$330* *Sanctuary (Baltimore Museum 428), 1959*, s., t., d., i. imp, num. 14/25, margins, light-staining, scattered foxmarks, old tapes, (09-19-92, Christie-E, #18), borderline 19¹¹⁄₁₆ x 33½ in., (484 x 851 mm.), woodcut in colors on Japan (BP 190, DM 494, FR 1692, Y 41,116).

FRASER, Alec English early 20th cent.
$55* *Low Tide,* s., t., (04-02-93, Sloan, #805), 8⅞ x 6⅞ in., (225 x 175 mm.), etching (BP 36, DM 88, FR 300, Y 6262).

FRASER, J.B. (after)
$30 *"Bhyramghattee", 1820,* by R. Havell and Son, (06-11-93, G.A. Key, #32), 22 x 17 in., (55.9 x 43.2 cm.), colored aquatint (BP 20, DM 49, FR 164, Y 3183).

FRATEL, Joseph (the elder) 1730-1783
$578* *Oeuvre De Joseph Fratel (Nagler S. 152; Beaudicour 1-10, 11 I, II, 12-16; Le Blanc 1-12), 1799: Seventeen,* pub. by A.v. Klein, (12-04-92, Bassenge, #6577), etching (BP 371, DM 921, FR 3123, Y 72,160).

FRAZETTA, Frank American b. 1928
$1650* *"Thuda - King Of The Congo", 1973,* completed color-guide for Russ Cochran's 1973 softcover reprint edit., s. Frazetta, (09-30-92, Sotheby-NY, #195, illus.), 13 x 10½ in., (33 x 26.7 cm.), hand-painted print (BP 931, DM 2340, FR 7914, Y 198,008).
BI *Weird Science-Fantasy No. 29, 1972,* edit. 30/50, s., num., pen and ink drawing on border, s., d. 9/8/72,Frazetta, est. $2,7/3,000, (09-30-92, Sotheby-NY, #314, illus.), 12¼ x 16½ in., (31.1 x 41.9 cm.), hand-colored limited edit. print, watercolor on Stratmore paper.

FRECH, Howard
$72* *Apple Tree In Blossom,* d. 1933, (09-24-92, Mystic, #16A), 14 x 11 in., (35.6 x 27.9 cm.), colored woodblock (BP 42, DM 107, FR 362, Y 8661).

FRED-MONEY
$670* *SNCF: Les Sables D'Olonne, Vendee, c. 1938,* excell. cond., (01-23-93, Ribeyre/Baron, #59), 39³⁄₁₆ x 24⁷⁄₁₆ in., (99.5 x 62 cm.), poster (BP 438, DM 1065, FR 3604, Y 83,855).

FREDDIE, Wilhelm Danish b. 1909
$169* *Composition, 1977,* s. Freddie 77, 265/300, (09-30-92, Kunsthallen, #110), color lithograph (BP 95, DM 240, FR 811, Y 20,281, DK 920).
$253* *Composition, 1977,* s. Freddie 77, 158/300, (09-30-92, Kunsthallen, #111), color lithograph (BP 143, DM 359, FR 1213, Y 30,361, DK 1380).
$379* *Composition, 1984,* s. Freddie 84, 70/250, (09-30-92, Kunsthallen, #112), color lithograph (BP 214, DM 537, FR 1818, Y 45,482, DK 2070).
$165* *Komposition, 1977,* s. Freddie 77, 195/300, (03-24-93, Kunsthallen, #111), color lithograph (BP 112, DM 269, FR 917, Y 19,387, DK 1035).
$294* *Komposition, 1977,* s. Freddie 77, 291/300, (03-24-93, Kunsthallen, #113), color lithograph (BP 199, DM 480, FR 1634, Y 34,544, DK 1840).
$220* *Komposition, 1984,* s. Freddie, 169/250, (03-24-93, Kunsthallen, #114), color lithograph (BP 149, DM 359, FR 1223, Y 25,849, DK 1380).
$257* *Portfolio,* containing Wilhelm Freddie (207/300), Svend Wiig Hansen (199/300) andGunnar Aagaard Anderson (155/300), s. 1977, (03-24-93, Kunsthallen, #112), three lithographs (BP 174, DM 420, FR 1429, Y 30,196, DK 1610).

FREDRICKS, Charles D.
BI *Mrs. Charles Noble And Child, 1857,* orig. mat and frame, studio label, negative num., d., subject ident., est. $2/3,000, (04-06-93, Sotheby-NY, #2, illus.), sight 9 x 7 in., photograph, hand colored salt print.

FREEMAN, Don American 1908-1978
BI *"Dense Fog" (McCulloch 141), 1956,* s., estate stamp, annot. LF by Lydia Cooley Freeman, est. $150/250, (05-15-93, Cleveland, #131), 13¼ x 8¾ in., (33.7 x 22.2 cm.), offset lithograph w/hand-colored impression on Christmas paper.
$220* *"Dress Rehearsal",* s., d. 1934, t., (12-05-92, Neal, #187, illus.), image 11¾ x 14 in., (29.8 x 35.6 cm.), lithograph (BP 138, DM 343, FR 1169, Y 27,258).
BI *"Handsome Cabbies",* s., foxing, taped, est. $4/500, (12-04-92, Doyle, #97), 9¼ x 10⅝ in., (235 x 270 mm.), lithograph.
$95* *"Kiosk, Cable Car, Rain" (McCulloch 142), 1956,* s. stone, (05-15-93, Cleveland, #132), 14½ x 11¼ in., (36.8 x 28.6 cm.), offset color lithograph (BP 62, DM 153, FR 514, Y 10,531).
BI *"Produce Market After Hours" (McCulloch 144),* s. w/ estate stamp, annot. LF by Lydia Cooley Freeman, excell. cond.,est. $150/250, (05-15-93, Cleveland, #133, illus.), 11⅜ x 12½ in., (28.9 x 31.8 cm.), colored off-set lithograph.
BI *"Sunday Morning Haircut" (McCulloch 145), 1956,* trial proof, s. w/estate stamp, annot. Lydia Cooley Freeman, est. $150/200, (05-15-93, Cleveland, #134), 13¾ x 13½ in., (34.9 x 34.3 cm.), off-set lithograph.
$330* *"Sunday, A.M.",* s., t., prov., stain, good cond., (10-31-92, Cleveland, #122), 8¼ x 6 in., (21 x 15.2 cm.), lithograph (BP 211, DM 508, FR 1722, Y 40,877).
$220* *"Three To Make Ready",* s., d. 1933, t., (12-05-92, Neal, #188), image 11½ x 13¾ in., (29.2 x 34.9 cm.), lithograph (BP 138, DM 343, FR 1169, Y 27,258).
BI *"Two Workers",* s., scuff, good cond., est. $250-350, (10-31-92, Cleveland, #121), 11⅛ x 8¾ in., (28.3 x 22.2 cm.), lithograph.

FREEMAN, Mark American b. 1908
$660* *"2nd Ave. El" And "South Ferry El", 1934, 1947: Two,* s., d. Mark Freeman, init. in plate, t., num., good cond., margins w/streaking, light-staining, (03-12-93, Skinner, #32, illus.), 15 x 19½ in., (38.1 x 49.5 cm.), lithograph on wove (BP 460, DM 1099, FR 3735, Y 77,784).
$292* *"The Anchor, George Washington Bridge", 1932,* s., d., t., edit., very good cond., (10-31-92, Cleveland, #123), 10⅜ x 15½ in., (26.4 x 39.4 cm.), lithograph (BP 187, DM 449, FR 1524, Y 36,170).
$413* *"Second Avenue El", 1933,* s., t., d., good cond., (10-31-92, Cleveland, #124, illus.), 10⅛ x 14¼ in., (25.7 x 36.2 cm.), lithograph (BP 265, DM 635, FR 2156, Y 51,158).
$193* *South Ferry "El",* s. Mark Freeman '47, good cond., (11-21-92, Bakker, #12), image 15 x 19½ in., (38.1 x 49.5 cm.), lithograph (BP 127, DM 308, FR 1037, Y 24,002).

FREIBERGER, Paul
$2090* *Kragen, c. 1932,* mounted, s., t. by photog., studio label, t., exhib. label, (10-15-92, Sotheby-NY, #418, illus.), 9⅜ x 11¾ in., (23.8 x 29.8 cm.), photograph, silver bromide print (BP 1279, DM 3111, FR 10,550, Y 250,750).

FREIDLAENDER, Jonny
$64* *Sao Paulo,* s., num. EA; t. label verso, prov., (12-01-92, Ritchie, #50), 29¼ x 20¼ in., (74.3 x 51.4 cm.), color lithograph (BP 42, DM 102, FR 348, Y 7968, C$ 83).

FREIJMUTH, Alfons b. 1940
$143* *Untitled, 1982,* s., d., #128/200, margins, good cond., soiling, (12-09-92, Sotheby-Amstrdm, #575), 22⁷⁄₁₆ x 16⅝ in., (570 x 423 mm.), color silkscreen on wove (BP 91, DM 224, FR 766, Y 17,731, G 253).

FREISLHIEN, P.
BI *Charles Henri Comte D'Estaing (Portalis and Beraldi, app. p. 735), c.1770,* narrow margin, trimmed, center fold, soiling, scrape, good cond., est. $900/1,200, (05-13-93, Sotheby-NY, #151), 15¾ x 10⅞ in., (400 x 275 mm.), etching and aquatint in colors.

FRELAUT, J.
$262* *La Chapelle De Becherel (Inv. F.F. 419), 1951,* #9/110, s., large margins, drystamp, (02-03-93, Ader Tajan, #150), 10³⁄₁₆ x 12 in., (25.8 x 30.5 cm.), etching (BP 183, DM 431, FR 1463, Y 32,591).
$314* *La Grenouillere (B. Frelaut, 464), 1937,* definitive state, #20/40, s., staining, mat-staining, good untrimmedmargins, (06-16-93, Ader Tajan, #96), 8³⁄₁₆ x 10⅝ in., (20.8 x 27 cm.), etching and drypoint (BP 209, DM 521, FR 1749, Y 33,490).

FREMOND, A.
$378* *PLM: Le Tourisme En Syrie. Les Ruines De Baalbeck, 1922,* very good cond., (03-13-93, Laurin, #119), 41⅛ x 29¾ in., (104.5 x 75.5 cm.), (BP 264, DM 629, FR 2139, Y 44,549).

FRENCH, Russell Lawrence
BI *Red Rock No. 13,* photog.'s sig., t., notations, 1920s, est. $500/750, (04-07-93, Swann, #467, illus.), 7½ x 9½ in., photograph, silver print.

FRENCH, S.W.
  BI *Groove, 1967,* s., d., t., #ED 10, full margins, good cond., mat/light-staining, time staining, est. $6/800, (05-19-93, Butterfield, #2169), sh 25 x 28¹⁵⁄₁₆ in., (635 x 735 mm.), silkscreen w/embossing and mixed media on wove.

FRENCH SCHOOL, 17TH CENTURY
  BI *Designs For Fire Surrounds And Doorways: Eight,* by Collot (?), margins, foxing, discoloration, est. BP 6/800, (12-03-92, Sotheby-London, #54), each approx. 7¾ x 5½ in., (195 x 140 mm.), etching on paper w/watermark.

FRENCH SCHOOL, 18TH CENTURY
  $205* *Academy Studies: Five,* possibly proofs before letters, margins, surface dirt, staining, (12-03-92, Sotheby-London, #55), etching (BP 132, DM 322, FR 1100, Y 25,507).
  BI *Le Plaisir,* watermark, wide margins, folds, nicks, creases, foxing, dirt, prov.,rare, very good impression, est. BP 1,4/1,800, (12-01-92, Christie-London, #271, illus.), plate 13¹⁵⁄₁₆ x 10⅝ in., (355 x 270 mm.), stipple engraving in colors.
  BI *Prelude De Nina,* pub. Fillion and Valmont, margins, est. BP 6/800, (12-01-92, Christie-London, #254), plate 9⅝ x 6¹⁵⁄₁₆ in., (245 x 177 mm.), etching w/engraving in colors (black, blue, brown, red and yellow).

FRENCH SCHOOL, 19TH CENTURY
  BI *For "Les Maitres De L'Affiche, Imprimerie Chaix": Four,* plates num. 58, 162, 198 and 89, good cond., est $2/300, (11-21-92, Bakker, #103), each approx. image 12 x 9 in., (30.5 x 22.9 cm.), color lithograph poster.

FRENCH SCHOOL, 20TH CENTURY
  $165* *"Souscrivez!",* p. Joseph-Charles, illegibly s., (08-05-92, Boos, #587), 47 x 31½ in., (119.4 x 80 cm.), lithograph (BP 86, DM 244, FR 823, Y 21,014).

FRENCH SCHOOL, LATE 19TH CENTURY
  $220* *"Chicoree Nouvelle",* p. La Lithographie Parisienne, (08-05-92, Boos, #588), 53¼ x 39½ in., (135.3 x 100.3 cm.), color lithograph (BP 115, DM 325, FR 1098, Y 28,018).

FRENCH, 19TH CENTURY
  $220* *Napoleon A Malmaison,* by Leney, repaired center, good cond., (11-12-92, Freemn/Fine Art, #73), plate 21½ x 14⅝ in., (54.6 x 37.1 cm.), hand colored engraving (BP 144, DM 349, FR 1176, Y 27,278).

FREUD, Lucian   British b. 1922
  BI *Bella (T. and H. 74), 1982,* init., #22/25, blindstamp, pub. Palm Tree Editions, full margins, inserted in book LUCIAN FREUD by Lawrence Gowing, good cond., orig. numbered slipcase, est. BP 1,5/1,800, (12-03-92, Sotheby-London, #680, illus.), sheet 10¾ x 8½ in., (273 x 217 mm.), etching on wove.
  $4976* *Blond Girl (G. 20; T. & H. 87), 1985,* init., #35/50, pub. James Kirkman Ltd., full margins, good cond., (06-30-93, Sotheby-London, #809, illus.), 27¼ x 21⅜ in., (692 x 543 mm.), etching on wove (BP 3335, DM 8487, FR 28,631, Y 533,162).
  BI *Blond Girl (Penny and Johnson 87), 1985,* inits., #29/50, co-pub. Brooke Alexander Editions and James Kirkman, full margins, excell. cond., the Late M. Anwar Kamal, M.D. Coll., est. $7/9,000, (05-11-93, Christie-NY, #426, illus.), sheet 34 x 28¼ in., (864 x 718 mm.), etching on Somerset.
  $4662* *Blond Girl, (South Bank cat. 87), 1985,* inits., num. 18/50, margins, good cond., (12-01-92, Christie-London, #572, illus.), P. 27⅜ x 21⅜ in., (695 x 543 mm.), etching on wove (BP 3080, DM 7431, FR 25,323, Y 580,428).
  $3996* *Blond Girl, (South Bank cat. 87), 1985,* inits., num. 32/50, margins, very good cond., (12-01-92, Christie-London, #573), P. 27⅜ x 21⅜ in., (695 x 543 mm.), etching on wove (BP 2640, DM 6369, FR 21,706, Y 497,510).
  BI *A Couple (T. and H. 84), 1982,* init., #21/25, blindstamp, pub. Palm Tree Editions, full margins, inserted in book LUCIAN FREUD by Lawrence Gowing, good cond., orig. numbered slipcase, est. BP 1,6/2,000, (12-03-92, Sotheby-London, #678, illus.), sheet 10¾ x 8½ in., (273 x 217 mm.), etching on wove.

  BI *Girl Sitting, (South Bank cat. 95), 1987,* inits., num. 30/50, margins, very good cond., est. BP 2/2,500, (12-01-92, Christie-London, #575, illus.), P. 20⅞ x 27¾ in., (530 x 705 mm.), etching on wove.
  $5116* *Girl Sitting, 1987,* init., #31/50, pub. Bernard Jacobson, full margins, good cond., laiddown, (12-03-92, Sotheby-London, #681, illus.), 20¼ x 27¼ in., (517 x 693 mm.), etching w/tone (BP 3300, DM 8045, FR 27,461, Y 636,556).
  BI *Head And Shoulders Of A Girl, 1990,* inits., #6/50, co-pub. Brooke Alexander and James Kirkman, full margins, excell. cond., est. $8/9,000, (05-11-93, Christie-NY, #428, illus.), sheet 30⅞ x 24¾ in., (784 x 629 mm.), etching on Somerset.
  $858* *Head Of A Woman (Gibson 14; Thames & Hudson 79), 1982,* init., #12/25, pub. James Kirkman Ltd., full margins, good cond., (06-30-93, Sotheby-London, #808, illus.), 5 x 5 in., (127 x 127 mm.), etching on wove (BP 575, DM 1463, FR 4937, Y 91,932).
  BI *Head Of A Woman (Thames And Hudson 79), 1982,* init., #13/25, blindstamp, pub. Palm Tree Editions, full margins, inserted in the book LUCIAN FREUD by Lawrence Gowing, good cond., orig. numbered slipcase, est. BP 1,2/1,500, (12-03-92, Sotheby-London, #675, illus.), sheet 10¾ x 8½ in., (273 x 217 mm.), etching on wove.
  $4290* *Head Of Bruce Bernard (G. 23; T. & H. 89), 1985,* init., #43/50, pub. James Kirkman Ltd., full margins, good cond., (06-30-93, Sotheby-London, #810, illus.), 20 x 8½ in., (508 x 216 mm.), etching on wove (BP 2875, DM 7317, FR 24,684, Y 459,659).
  BI *Head Of IB (G. 30), 1988,* init., #19/40, pub. James Kirkman Ltd., full margins, good cond., est. BP 2/2,500, (06-30-93, Sotheby-London, #807, illus.), 8¼ x 5¾ in., (210 x 146 mm.), etching on wove.
  BI *Maked Man On Bed, 1990,* init., #16/40, full margins, good cond., est. BP 1,2/1,800, (12-03-92, Sotheby-London, #682, illus.), 11⅝ x 11½ in., (298 x 295 mm.), etching on Somerset wove.
  $3330* *Man Posing, (South Bank cat. 91), 1985,* inits., num. 16/50, pub. J. Kirkman Ltd., margins, very good cond., (12-01-92, Christie-London, #574), P. 27⁹⁄₁₆ x 21⁷⁄₁₆ in., (700 x 545 mm.), etching on wove (BP 2200, DM 5308, FR 18,088, Y 414,592).
  $3603* *Man Resting (G. 32), 1988,* init., #19/30, pub. James Kirkman Ltd., full margins, good cond., (06-30-93, Sotheby-London, #814, illus.), 14½ x 16⅛ in., (368 x 410 mm.), etching on wove (BP 2415, DM 6145, FR 20,731, Y 386,050).
  BI *Naked Man On A Bed (G. 35), 1990,* init., #25/40, pub. James Kirkman Ltd., full margins, good cond., est. BP 1/1,500, (06-30-93, Sotheby-London, #811, illus.), 11¾ x 11¾ in., (298 x 298 mm.), etching on wove.
  $1798* *Naked Man On A Bed (Thomas Gibson Fine Art Catalogue 35), 1990,* init., #21/40, full margins, good cond., (10-15-92, Sotheby-London, #96, illus.), 11¾ x 11⅝ in., (29.8 x 29.5 cm.), etching on wove (BP 1100, DM 2676, FR 9076, Y 215,717).
  $3751* *The Painter's Mother (T. and H. 73), 1982,* init., #22/25, blindstamp, pub. Palm Tree Editions, full margins, inserted in book LUCIAN FREUD by Lawrence Gowing, good cond., orig. numbered slipcase, (12-03-92, Sotheby-London, #679, illus.), 10¾ x 8½ in., (273 x 217 mm.), etching on wove (BP 2420, DM 5899, FR 20,134, Y 466,716).
  BI *Two Men In Studio (G. 34), 1989,* init., #9/25, pub. James Kirkman Ltd., full margins, good cond., est.BP 1,5/2,000, (06-30-93, Sotheby-London, #812), 9 x 8 in., (229 x 203 mm.), etching on wove.
  $2745* *Two Men In The Studio (G. 34), 1989,* init., #5/25, pub. James Kirkman Ltd., full margins, good cond., (06-30-93, Sotheby-London, #813, illus.), 9 x 8 in., (229 x 203 mm.), etching on wove (BP 1840, DM 4682, FR 15,794, Y 294,118).
  BI *Two Men In The Studio, 1989,* inits., #12/25, co-pub. Brooke Alexander and James Kirkman, full margins, excell. cond., est. $3,5/4,500, (05-11-93, Christie-NY, #427, illus.), sheet 15¾ x 14⅛ in., (400 x 359 mm.), etching on wove.

BI *Untitled, 1992,* init., #26/30, margins, pub. Mark Matthews, very good cond.?, est. $5/7,000, (05-19-93, Butterfield, #2170, illus.), 9⅜ x 8 in., (238 x 203 mm.), etching w/plate tone on wove.

FREUDEBERG, Sigmund   Swiss 1745-1801
BI *"La Toilette", "Le Bain", and "L'Evenement Au Bae":* *Four,* est. $175/225, (10-30-92, Sloan, #888), each approx. 14⅜/16 x 10½ in., (27.8 x 33 cm.), engravings, two color.

FREUND, Gisele   b. 1912
$1289* *Colette, 1939,* ink s., (c), (11-12-92, Lempertz, #66, illus.), 11¾ x 7⅞ in., (29.8 x 20 cm.), sheet 15½ x 10¹³/16 in., (29.8 x 20 cm.), color photograph (BP 824, DM 2026, FR 6904, Y 159,470).
$1517* *Jean Cocteau, 1939,* ink s., (c), t., d., lit., (11-12-92, Lempertz, #65, illus.), 11¹¹/16 x 7¹³/16 in., (29.7 x 19.9 cm.), sheet 14¹⁵/16 x 11 in., (29.7 x 19.9 cm.), color photograph (BP 970, DM 2384, FR 8125, Y 187,678).
$990* *Julien Benda, Andre Gide, And Andre Malraux At The International Writer's Congress, Paris, 1935,* s., (c) insig., t., d., (c) credit stamps, lit., (10-13-92, Christie-NY, #213, illus.), 8 x 11½ in., (20.3 x 29.2 cm.), photograph, solarized gelatin silver print (BP 577, DM 1450, FR 4928, Y 120,044).
$412* *Portrait Of Matisse,* photog.'s sig., chopmark, (c) handstamp, 1940s, p.l., (04-07-93, Swann, #468), 15¾ x 11¾ in., photograph, chromogenic print (BP 272, DM 666, FR 2255, Y 46,808).
BI *Simon De Beauvoir, 1939,* ink s., (c), lit., est. DM 2,000, (11-12-92, Lempertz, #64, illus.), 11¹³/16 x 8¹⁵/16 in., (30 x 22.8 cm.), sheet 16⁷/16 x 11⁵/16 in., (30 x 22.8 cm.), color photograph.

FREY, Jakob   1681-1752
BI *Romische Krieger Empfangen Beutestucke,* worn, est. DM 300-, (03-24-93, Venator/Hansten, #2524), pl. approx. 12⅜ x 7½ in., (31.5 x 19 cm.), etching on thick handmade.

FRIANON
BI *"Follies-Bergere",* plate s., good cond.?, est. $2/300, (07-19-92, Bakker, #103), sheet 36½ x 24½ in., (92.7 x 62.2 cm.), color lithograph.

FRIDELL, Axel
$221* *"Gustav V",* s., d. 1932, (11-07-92, Falkkloos, #137), etching (BP 144, DM 355, FR 1193, Y 27,277, SK 1320).

FRIDLAND, Simon
$1035* *Alexander Rodchenko Reading, c. 1929,* (04-06-93, Sotheby-NY, #316, illus.), 4⅜ x 3⅛ in., photograph (BP 684, DM 1667, FR 5646, Y 118,043).

FRIED, Pal (after)
$57* *Head And Shoulder Study Of A Nude Woman,* (03-17-93, Bonhams-Chelsea, #353), image 15½ x 11½ in., (39.4 x 29.2 cm.), lithographic reprod. w/hand-coloring (BP 39, DM 95, FR 322, Y 6685).

FRIEDLAENDER, Johnny   French 1912-1992
$852* *Madrigal (Schmucking 457), 1972,* #150/150, s., glue remains, (10-09-92, Winterberg, #2137, illus.), 20⅞ x 14¹⁵/16 in., (53 x 38 cm.), color etching w/aquatint on wove (BP 505, DM 1266, FR 4249, Y 103,725).
$664* *Oiseaux Sur Fond Gris, 1978,* s., E(preuve d')A(rtiste), (12-01-92, Karl/Faber, #621), 30⁵/16 x 22⁷/16 in., (77 x 57 cm.), color lithograph on wove (BP 439, DM 1058, FR 3607, Y 82,669).

FRIEDLANDER
$105* *Tete De Tigre Rugissant, 1913,* very good cond., (11-19-92, Ribeyre/Baron, #175), 37⅜ x 27¾ in., (95 x 70.5 cm.), poster (BP 69, DM 167, FR 564, Y 13,058).

FRIEDLANDER, Issac   American 20th cent.
$99* *Ecclesiastes,* s., t., #14/30, (06-11-93, Freemn/Fine Art, #73), 13¾ x 9 in., (34.9 x 22.9 cm.), drypoint (BP 65, DM 161, FR 542, Y 10,504).

FRIEDLANDER, Johnny   French 1912-1992
BI *1949,* rare, d., s., est. FF6/8,000, (04-04-93, Pescheteau, #215), 19¹¹/16 x 12⅝ in., (50 x 32 cm.), black etching and aquatint on wove.

$150* *Les 3 Mots,* s., #29/95, t., d. 1966, (06-08-93, Ritchie, #47, illus.), 18¾ x 25¼ in., (47.6 x 64.1 cm.), color etching and aquatint (BP 99, DM 243, FR 820, Y 15,932, C$ 193).
$165* *Abstract Shades,* s., (09-24-92, Mystic, #18), 26 x 17 in., (66 x 43.2 cm.), colored lithograph (BP 97, DM 245, FR 830, Y 19,848).
$165* *Abstract Shapes,* s., (09-24-92, Mystic, #17), 30 x 22 in., (76.2 x 55.9 cm.), colored lithograph (BP 97, DM 245, FR 830, Y 19,848).
$935* *Arc-En-Ciel II (S. 417), 1971,* s., i. E.A., good cond.?, (12-12-92, Weschler, #123, illus.), 22¼ x 30 in., (56.5 x 76.2 cm.), etching and aquatint (BP 600, DM 1473, FR 5049, Y 115,704).
$83* *"Bestiaire",* s., good cond., (10-31-92, Cleveland, #373), 11¾ x 7¾ in., (29.8 x 19.7 cm.), etching (BP 53, DM 128, FR 433, Y 10,281).
$633* *"Collines",* s. Friedlaender, #19/95, (12-12-92, Wolf, #29, illus.), 18 x 23¼ in., (45.7 x 59.1 cm.), color etching (BP 406, DM 997, FR 3418, Y 78,332).
$468* *Composition,* artist's proof, s., (10-10-92, Litchfield, #83), 29½ x 21¼ in., (74.9 x 54 cm.), etching and aquatint w/ intaglio (BP 278, DM 695, FR 2334, Y 56,976).
$226* *Composition,* s., good margins, (05-06-93, Laurin, #30), color aquatint (BP 143, DM 356, FR 1198, Y 24,865).
BI *Composition,* s., #1/3, est. DM 1,200, (06-12-93, Hauswedell/Nolt, #91), 35¹¹/16 x 24¹³/16 in., (90.6 x 63 cm.), etching on Arches.
$314* *Composition Abstraite,* #5/100, s., large margins, (06-16-93, Ader Tajan, #97), 8⅞ x 6⅞ in., (22.5 x 17.5 cm.), color aquatint (BP 209, DM 521, FR 1749, Y 33,490).
$863* *Composition Sur Fond Vert, 1965,* s., #46/95, pub. Touchstone Publishers, slightly trimmed, good cond.,-creases, surface soiling, (05-19-93, Butterfield, #2058), 31¼ x 23½ in., (794 x 597 mm.), etching and aquatint in colors on wove (BP 560, DM 1403, FR 4726, Y 95,539).
$424* *Les Coqs (Schmucking 176), 1958,* s., #7/95, blindstamp, (06-12-93, Hauswedell/Nolt, #88), 20⅝ x 15¹⁵/16 in., (52.4 x 40.5 cm.), color etching on BFK Rives (BP 278, DM 690, FR 2319, Y 44,617).
$542* *Dans Le Cercle,* s., #25/95, (09-18-92, Schloss Ahlden, #998), 30¹/16 x 22⁵/16 in., (76.4 x 56.7 cm.), color lithograph on Arches (BP 317, DM 804, FR 2751, Y 66,988).
$605* *Deux Cheveaux,* s., num. 7/40, full margins, good cond., creases, (02-24-93, Butterfield, #2929), 22¼ x 17⅛ in., (565 x 435 mm.), etching, aquatint, mezzotint, & roulette on BFK Rives (BP 422, DM 982, FR 3330, Y 70,993).
$385* *Deux Compositions: A Pair,* s., full margins, (05-27-93, Briest, #93), 7¹¹/16 x 6⁵/16 in., (19.5 x 16 cm.), color aquatints w/embossing (BP 247, DM 618, FR 2082, Y 41,274).
$1299* *"En Mesure" (Schmucking 303), 1966,* s., num., (11-28-92, Grisebach, #516, illus.), 30¹³/16 x 22¹⁵/16 in., (78.2 x 58.4 cm.), colored aquatint on copper print paper (BP 857, DM 2069, FR 7025, Y 161,668).
$110* *Exercises,* s., num. 16/120, (11-12-92, Freemn/Fine Art, #74), 6¼ x 5 in., (15.9 x 12.7 cm.), color aquatint (BP 72, DM 174, FR 588, Y 13,639).
$432* *Exercises (Schmucking 258), 1964,* s., num., (12-01-92, Karl/Faber, #620), 7⁵/16 x 5⁵/16 in., (18.5 x 13.5 cm.), color etching and aquatint on Arches wove (BP 285, DM 689, FR 2347, Y 53,785).
$847* *Femme Couchee II (Schmucking 155), 1956,* s., i. artist's proof, (06-10-93, Hauswedell/Nolt, #312), image 29¹⁵/16 x 22³/16 in., (76 x 56.3 cm.), color etching and relief print on Arches (BP 554, DM 1379, FR 4644, Y 89,906).
$1063* *Formes Et Lumiere (Schm. 292), 1965,* s., num., blindstamp, (06-08-93, Karl/Faber, #771), approx. 30½ x 22⅝ in., (77.5 x 57.5 cm.), color etching on Arches wove (BP 699, DM 1725, FR 5809, Y 112,905).
$1130* *Idole (Schmucking 353), 1969,* s., i. E.A., (06-10-93, Hauswedell/Nolt, #313), image 29¹⁵/16 x 22³/16 in., (76 x 56.3 cm.), color etching and relief print on Arches (BP 739, DM 1840, FR 6195, Y 119,945).

$150* *Johnny Friedlaender Oeuvre 1961-1965,* pub. Touchstone Publishers, (11-30-92, Phillips-London, #510), lithograph in colors (BP 99, DM 239, FR 811, Y 18,668).

$290* *Komposition,* 235/290, s., stains, signs of wear, (10-14-92, Germann, #306), 33¹¹⁄₁₆ x 24¹³⁄₁₆ in., (855 x 630 mm.), color lithograph (BP 170, DM 424, FR 1439, Y 35,143, SF 378).

$425* *Komposition,* s., i. E(preuve d') A(rtiste), blindstamp, (06-08-93, Karl/Faber, #773), approx. 29½ x 17⅛ in., (75 x 43.5 cm.), color lithograph on Arches France wove (BP 279, DM 690, FR 2322, Y 45,141).

$2984* *Die Kunst Die Radierens, 1975,* portfolio, s., #134/135, pub. Manus Presse, full margins, good cond.,num. 134, (12-03-92, Sotheby-London, #684, illus.), seven etchings w/aquatint in colors on wove (BP 1925, DM 4693, FR 16,017, Y 371,283).

$356* *L'Invitation Au Vogage II, 1980,* s., #58/75, (09-18-92, Schloss Ahlden, #996), 25¹⁵⁄₁₆ x 19¹³⁄₁₆ in., (66 x 50.3 cm.), etching in colors on Arches (BP 208, DM 528, FR 1807, Y 44,000).

$427* *L'Invitation Au Voyage I, 1981,* s., #58/75, (09-18-92, Schloss Ahlden, #995), 26³⁄₁₆ x 19⅞ in., (66.5 x 50.5 cm.), etching in colors on Arches (BP 250, DM 634, FR 2168, Y 52,775).

$365* *L'Invitation Au Voyage III, 1981,* s., #58/75, (09-18-92, Schloss Ahlden, #997), 25¹⁵⁄₁₆ x 19¾ in., (66 x 50.2 cm.), etching in colors on Arches (BP 214, DM 542, FR 1853, Y 45,112).

$480* *L'Oiseau Bleu, 1963,* s., #69/95, p. G. Leblanc, just., full margins, good cond., (05-27-93, Sotheby-Amstrdm, #616), 19 x 12⅜ in., (483 x 314 mm.), etching and aquatint on wove (BP 307, DM 770, FR 2596, Y 51,458, G 863).

$413* *L'Oiseaux,* s., #119/220, pub. AAA, full margins, good cond., light/water-staining, foxing, surface soiling, image crease, tape remains, (10-28-92, Butterfield, #2810), 17½ x 13⅞ in., (445 x 352 mm.), etching w/aquatint on Arches (BP 263, DM 638, FR 2166, Y 50,675).

$550* *L'Oiseaux Sur Fond Jaune,* s., annot. Epreuve d'Artiste, L'Oeuvre Gravee blindstamp, margins, apparently good cond., water stain, surface scuffs in image, stains, light-staining, surface soiling, (02-24-93, Butterfield, #2926), 19⅝ x 10⅞ in., (498 x 276 mm.), etching, aquatint w/ roulette in colors on BFK Rives (BP 384, DM 893, FR 3027, Y 64,539).

$863* *Lobster And Flies,* s., #63/75, full margins, good cond., edge folded over, tape, surfacesoiling, (05-19-93, Butterfield, #2059), 12⅞ x 9⅜ in., (327 x 238 mm.), etching and aquatint on Paul Haasey (BP 560, DM 1403, FR 4726, Y 95,539).

$588* *"Maternite",* H.C., s., (01-28-93, Pescheteau, #146), a vue 9⁷⁄₁₆ x 7¹⁄₁₆ in., (24 x 18 cm.), etching and aquatint on wove (BP 388, DM 932, FR 3153, Y 73,007).

$679* *Miroir (Schmucking 615), 1978,* 50/95, s., (10-14-92, Germann, #307), 30⅛ x 22⁷⁄₁₆ in., (765 x 570 mm.), color etching (BP 399, DM 994, FR 3370, Y 82,283, SF 885).

$193* *Nude Composition,* s. Friedlaender, #93/100, manus presse stamp, (12-12-92, Wolf, #26), 7¼ x 13¾ in., (18.4 x 34.9 cm.), etching (BP 124, DM 304, FR 1042, Y 23,883).

$193* *Nude Composition,* s. Friedlaender, #93/100, manus stampe stamp, (12-12-92, Wolf, #28), 12¾ x 19½ in., (32.4 x 49.5 cm.), etching (BP 124, DM 304, FR 1042, Y 23,883).

$193* *"Nude Composition",* s. Friedlaender, #93/100, manus presse stamp, (12-12-92, Wolf, #27), 12¾ x 20 in., (32.4 x 50.8 cm.), etching (BP 124, DM 304, FR 1042, Y 23,883).

$395* *Paris,* 242/290, s., t., (06-24-93, Germann, #340), 33¹⁵⁄₁₆ x 25 in., (863 x 635 mm.), color lithograph (BP 260, DM 640, FR 2158, Y 42,373, SF 575).

$530* *Petecote (Schmucking 677), 1981,* s., #79/95, Editions de l'Ermitage, (06-12-93, Hauswedell/Nolt, #89), 20¾ x 19⁷⁄₁₆ in., (52.7 x 49.4 cm.), color etching on Arches (BP 347, DM 863, FR 2899, Y 55,772).

$390* *Poissons V (Schmucking 186), 1959,* s., pub. Galerie Michel, (06-08-93, Karl/Faber, #770), approx. 6⅛ x 4¾ in., (15.5 x 12 cm.), color etching and aquatint on Arches wove (BP 256, DM 633, FR 2131, Y 41,423).

$636* *Poissons, c. 1952,* s., #198/200, (06-12-93, Hauswedell/ Nolt, #87), 11⁵⁄₁₆ x 13¼ in., (28.7 x 33.6 cm.), color etching (BP 416, DM 1035, FR 3479, Y 66,926).

$679* *A Quatre Temps (Schmucking 515), 1974,* 75/95, s., (10-14-92, Germann, #308, illus.), 30⅛ x 22⁷⁄₁₆ in., (765 x 570 mm.), color aquatint (BP 399, DM 994, FR 3370, Y 82,283, SF 885).

$440* *San Paolo, c. 1975,* s., #98/275, good cond.?, (12-08-92, Swann, #116), 29½ x 20½ in., (74.9 x 52.1 cm.), color etching (BP 276, DM 685, FR 2335, Y 54,536).

$729* *Sans Titre, #38/95,* s. Friedlaender, (09-15-92, Encans, #146, illus.), 29½ x 20¹¹⁄₁₆ in., (75 x 52.5 cm.), lithograph and embossing (BP 390, DM 1085, FR 3682, Y 90,503, C$ 888).

$1010* *Trait Rouge (Schmucking Band I 247), 1962,* #147/200, pencil s., (11-20-92, Lempertz, #539), sh 29⁵⁄₁₆ x 21¾ in., (74.5 x 55.3 cm.), color etching on Velin (BP 665, DM 1610, FR 5424, Y 125,606).

$480* *Triptich B,* s., full margins, good cond., minor handling creases, (05-27-93, Sotheby-Amstrdm, #617), 30⁵⁄₁₆ x 22⅝ in., (770 x 575 mm.), etching w/aquatint in colors on wove (BP 307, DM 770, FR 2596, Y 51,458, G 863).

BI *Untitled,* s., #178/220, margins, good cond.?, discoloration, est. G 800/1,200, (12-09-92, Sotheby-Amstrdm, #576), 17½ x 13⁹⁄₁₆ in., (445 x 345 mm.), etching on wove.

$242* *Untitled,* s., good cond., (10-31-92, Cleveland, #374, illus.), 6 x 5 in., (15.2 x 12.7 cm.), etching in color (BP 155, DM 372, FR 1263, Y 29,976).

$550* *Untitled,* s., soiling, (05-15-93, Cleveland, #467, illus.), 30 x 22¾ in., (76.2 x 57.8 cm.), etching (BP 358, DM 885, FR 2973, Y 60,969).

$523* *Untitled,* s., num. 21/95, full margins, apparently good cond., staining, hinges staining through, (02-24-93, Butterfield, #2927), 25½ x 19⅛ in., (648 x 486 mm.), etching & aquatint in colors on Arches (BP 365, DM 849, FR 2878, Y 61,371).

$523* *Untitled,* s. in crayon, num. 59/99, full sheet, apparently good cond., (02-24-93, Butterfield, #2928), 30 x 22½ in., (762 x 572 mm.), etching & aquatint w/embossing in colors on wove (BP 365, DM 849, FR 2878, Y 61,371).

BI *Untitled,* s., #15/95, very good cond., est. $1/1,500, (05-19-93, Butterfield, #1912A), sh 29¾ x 22½ in., (756 x 572 mm.), aquatint and etching in colors on wove.

$805* *Untitled,* s., #87/95, very good cond., (05-19-93, Butterfield, #1911A), sh 22½ x 29¾ in., (572 x 756 mm.), aquatint and etching in colors on wove (BP 523, DM 1309, FR 4409, Y 89,118).

$1035* *Untitled,* s., #5/95, very good cond., (05-19-93, Butterfield, #1912), sh. 29⅞ x 22½ in., (759 x 572 mm.), aquatint in colors on Arches (BP 672, DM 1682, FR 5668, Y 114,580).

$150* *Untitled,* s., #149/200, good cond., light struck, (05-15-93, Cleveland, #468, illus.), 15 x 11 in., (38.1 x 27.9 cm.), lithograph in colors (BP 98, DM 241, FR 811, Y 16,628).

$305* *Untitled (Reclining Couple),* s., tears, creases, (05-15-93, Cleveland, #466), 29½ x 40½ in., (74.9 x 102.9 cm.), etching and mezzotint (BP 198, DM 491, FR 1649, Y 33,810).

$605* *"Untitled",* s., #28/95, full margins, good cond., staining, foxing, creases, surface soiling, (10-28-92, Butterfield, #2812), 23 x 30⅝ in., (584 x 778 mm.), color etching w/aquatint on Arches (BP 385, DM 934, FR 3173, Y 74,233).

$605* *Vol D'Oiseaux (F. 30), 1964,* s., #3/85, pub. AAA, full margins, good cond., (10-28-92, Butterfield, #2811), 19¼ x 23⅜ in., (489 x 594 mm.), color etching w/aquatint on Lana paper (BP 385, DM 934, FR 3173, Y 74,233).

FRIEDLANDER, Lee   American b. 1934

$758* *Photographs And Etchings IX, 1969,* s., #62/75, lit., (11-12-92, Lempertz, #68, illus.), sheet 18⁵⁄₁₆ x 29¹⁵⁄₁₆ in., (46.5 x 76 cm.), gelatin silver photograph and etching (BP 485, DM 1191, FR 4060, Y 93,777).

$910* *Photographs And Etchings VI, 1969,* s., #62/75, lit., (11-12-92, Lempertz, #67, illus.), sheet 18⁵⁄₁₆ x 29¹⁵⁄₁₆ in.,

(46.5 x 76 cm.), gelatin silver photograph and etching (BP 582, DM 1430, FR 4874, Y 112,582).

$4830* *"T.V. In Hotel Room, Galax, Virginia", "Bed In Window, Cincinnati, Ohio", "Women In Window, New York City", "Man In Window, New York City", "Plane Over Bull, Kansas City, Missouri", "Flag, New York City" and Nine Others,* 1962-72, Double Elephant Press, 1973, each s., #69/75, includes p. colophon and intro. by Walker Evans, limited edit., (04-08-93, Christie-NY, #487, illus.), smallest 5¾ x 8¾ in., (14.6 x 22.2 cm.), largest 8⅜ x 12⅝ in., (14.6 x 22.2 cm.), photograph, gelatin silver print (BP 3167, DM 7759, FR 26,264, Y 548,116).

$605* *"Tampa",* 1970, s., t., d., photog. stamp verso, Dixon Collection, (11-16-92, Butterfield, #5976, illus.), 7½ x 11⅛ in., (190.8 x 283.1 mm.), photograph, gelatin silver print (BP 398, DM 965, FR 3249, Y 75,239).

FRIEDLANDER, Lee and Jim DINE
$1725* *Untitled,* 1969-70, s., d., annot., i., artist's proof from portfolio Photograph and Etchings, pub. Petersburg Press, 1969, originally Walker Evans Coll., (05-23-93, Butterfield, #3418, illus.), sheet 18½ x 30 in., gelatin silver print and etching (BP 1123, DM 2820, FR 9494, Y 190,671).

FRIEND, Donald Stuart Leslie   1915-1989
$243* *Fishermen,* s. Donald Friend, i., #10/30, (08-11-92, L. Joel, #185G), 31⁵⁄₁₆ x 22⁷⁄₁₆ in., (79.5 x 57 cm.), color lithograph (BP 126, DM 357, FR 1208, Y 31,118, A$ 330).

FRIESZ, Achille Emilie Othon   French 1879-1949
$495* *"Calanger",* s. E. Othon Friesz, annot. Epreuve de presentation, fair cond., toning, wrinkling, creases, (09-11-92, Skinner, #12, illus.), 15½ x 19½ in., (39.4 x 49.5 cm.), color etching/aquatint on paper (BP 256, DM 713, FR 2422, Y 61,331).

$80* *"Paysage",* #5/100, sig., (04-04-93, Pescheteau, #215A), a vue 14¹⁵⁄₁₆ x 12¹⁵⁄₁₆ in., (38 x 33 cm.), black and sanguine lithograph (BP 53, DM 129, FR 437, Y 9109).

FRIESZ, Archille Emile Othon   French 1879-1949
$84* *"Paysage De Provence",* studio drystamp, #7/20, sig. stamp, (01-28-93, Pescheteau, #147), a vue 7½ x 7¹⁄₁₆ in., (19 x 18 cm.), wood engraving (BP 55, DM 133, FR 450, Y 10,430).

FRIESZ, O.
$525* *Vendanges,* #45/200, s., (02-03-93, Ader Tajan, #151), 20⅞ x 19½ in., (53 x 49.5 cm.), color aquatint (BP 366, DM 864, FR 2931, Y 65,307).

FRINK, Elisabeth   British b. 1930
$509* *"Man On Horseback",* #64/70, s., (09-17-92, Bonhams-Chelsea, #110), subject 23 x 30½ in., (58.4 x 77.5 cm.), color lithograph (BP 286, DM 756, FR 2586, Y 63,372).

FRINK, Elizabeth   British b. 1930
BI *Bullfight,* s., #57/72, very good cond., est. $2/400, (12-12-92, Weschler, #122), 21¾ x 30½ in., (55.2 x 77.5 cm.), color lithograph.

$339* *Horse And Rider V,* s., #14/70, watermarked, spotting, good cond., (10-07-92, Christie-S. Ken, #103), 21 x 17 in., (53.3 x 43.2 cm.), lithograph (BP 198, DM 491, FR 1663, Y 40,770).

FRISIUS, Simon Wynouts (Simon de VRIES)   c. 1580-1629
$267* *Bildnis Des Malers Pieter Brueghel (Hollstein 141),* (12-04-92, Bassenge, #6195), 7¹⁵⁄₁₆ x 4¾ in., (20.2 x 12.1 cm.), engraving (BP 171, DM 425, FR 1442, Y 33,333).

FRITH, Francis   1822-1898
$25,406* *"Egypt, Sinai, And Jerusalem: Series Of Twenty Photographic Views By Francis Frith",* 1862: Book, nine s., d. 1858 in negs., p. t., credit and d. on mount, descriptive text, green half morocco, lit., (05-06-93, Christie-London, #10, illus.), photograph, 20 albumen prints (BP 16,100, DM 40,016, FR 134,708, Y 2,795,247).

$1090* *F. Frith's Photo-Pictures From The Lands Of The Bible, Illustrated By Scripture Words: Forty-One,* photographed 1857, pub. c. 1862, mounted on card, p. t., quotation, each approx. 153 x 203mm, (05-07-93, Sotheby-London, #22), photograph, albumen print (BP 690, DM 1723, FR 5807, Y 120,018).

$605* *Landscape And Topographic Views Of England And Eygpt Including "The Circular Temple, Baalbec", "The Colonnade, Island Of Phila" and "The Broken Obelisk, Karnac" and more,* 1857-60s: Ten, photog. credit, caption/num. in neg., (04-07-93, Swann, #209), largest 7½ x 11½ in., photograph, albumen print (BP 400, DM 978, FR 3311, Y 68,734).

$17,600* *"Sinai And Palestine", "Upper Egypt And Ethiopia", "Lower Egypt, Thebes, And The Pyramids", and "Egypt, Sinai, And Palestine, Supplementary Volume",* (NYPL 69 & 70; Truthful Lens 64; Gernsheim 195), c. 1862: Four Volumes, W. Mackenzie, each illus. w/37 photos, total 148 photos, folio, (10-15-92, Sotheby-NY, #70, illus.), plates approx. 6 x 9 in., (15.2 x 22.9 cm.), photograph, albumen prints (BP 10,770, DM 26,198, FR 88,844, Y 2,111,578).

$220* *Travellers Boat At Ibrim,* c. 1862, sig. in neg., (10-14-92, Swann, #189), 5 x 6½ in., (12.7 x 16.5 cm.), photograph, albumen print (BP 129, DM 322, FR 1092, Y 26,660).

FRITH, W.P. (after)
$51 *"The Crossing Sweeper",* engraved by C.W. Sharpe, (02-05-93, G.A. Key, #30), 9 x 8 in., (22.9 x 20.3 cm.), hand-colored engraving (BP 35, DM 85, FR 286, Y 6346).

FRITH & CO.
$429* *Piers,* 1888-1924: Fourty-Three, all but 12 num., 18 w/ photog.'s credits, occasional t., negs., pencil num., (10-29-92, Christie-London, #67, illus.), approx. 6 x 8½ in., (15.2 x 21.6 cm.), photograph, albumen print (BP 275, DM 660, FR 2239, Y 53,140).

BI *Townscapes, Harbours And Rural Scenes,* 1889-1912: Thirty-Two, all but 14 num., 13 w/photog.'s credits, some t., num., (c) stamp, est. BP 6/900, (10-29-92, Christie-London, #75), approx. 6 x 8½ in., (15.2 x 21.6 cm.), photograph, platinum print.

FROHNER, Adolf
$299* *"Sonntagnachmittag" (Gorsen 136/III),* 1969, s., proof, i., (04-21-93, Dorotheum, #710), color etching (BP 194, DM 478, FR 1616, Y 33,101, SC 3360).

FROMANGER, Gerard   b. 1939
$606* *"Le Rouge": Album of Twenty,* #83/90, s., d., (10-18-92, Pescheteau, #148), each 35¹⁄₁₆ x 23⅝ in., (89 x 60 cm.), serigraph on bristol (BP 367, DM 895, FR 3041, Y 72,358).

FROMANTIER, Paul and Jean CARLU
$103* *Nuit Du Pre-Catelan,* 1938, (01-31-93, Morelle/Marchan, #28, illus.), 11¹³⁄₁₆ x 16⅛ in., (30 x 41 cm.), poster (BP 69, DM 166, FR 561, Y 12,849).

FRONCOLIN, Robert   French 20th cent.
BI *Cottage In Woods By Stream,* s., #171/275, est. $125/175, (10-30-92, Sloan, #846), 16 x 22¼ in., (42.5 x 24.8 cm.), color lithograph.

FROST, A.B.
$605* *From The Battery,* (c) 1896, by Charles Scribner's Sons, (02-13-93, Collins, #51, illus.), 13 x 20 in., (33 x 50.8 cm.), chromolithograph (BP 426, DM 1003, FR 3395, Y 72,962).

$242* *"Rail Shooting",* excell. cond., (04-22-93, Guyette, #849, illus.), image 19 x 27 in., (48.3 x 68.6 cm.), b/w print (BP 156, DM 389, FR 1312, Y 26,608).

FROST, A.B. (after)
$122 *Golfing Prints: Nine,* (04-16-93, G.A. Key, #120), 12 x 9 in., (30.5 x 22.9 cm.), colored prints (BP 80, DM 197, FR 666, Y 13,719).

BI *"Ruffed-Grouse Shooting/A Clean Miss And His Eyes Wiped",* (12-11-92, G.A. Key, #15), 12 x 19 in., (30.5 x 48.3 cm.), colored print.

FROST, Arthur Burdett   1851-1928
$1870* *"Quail Shooting", "Quail Shooting", "Shooting Rabbit" and "Rail Shooting": Four,* s. in plate, various sizes, (09-24-92, Mystic, #55), colored chromolithograph (BP 1095, DM 2771, FR 9411, Y 224,949).

$1540* *"Rail Shooting", "Quail In Corn Fields", "Shooting Shore Birds" and "Woodcock Shooting": Four,* s. in plate, vari-

ous sizes, (09-24-92, Mystic, #56), colored chromolithograph (BP 901, DM 2282, FR 7750, Y 185,252).
$1320* *"Shooting In The Marsh", "Shooting Snow Geese" and "Roufed Grouse Shooting": Three,* s. in plate, various sizes, (09-24-92, Mystic, #57), colored chromolithograph (BP 773, DM 1956, FR 6643, Y 158,787).

FROST, Joseph b. 1953
$57* *Twilight Calm: Pair,* s. Joseph Frost, i., #22/380, (08-11-92, L. Joel, #191G), 18⅛ x 29¹⁵⁄₁₆ in., (46 x 76 cm.), color print (BP 30, DM 84, FR 283, Y 7299, A$ 77).

FROST and REED, Publisher
$220* *"The Picnic",* (12-10-92, Doyle, #16), 19 x 26 in., (48.3 x 66 cm.), color mezzotint (BP 142, DM 348, FR 1189, Y 27,214).

FROWEIN
$110* *Centraal Museum Utrecht, 1940,* A- cond., scratching, (08-06-92, Swann, #133, illus.), 27¾ x 21 in., (70.5 x 53.3 cm.), (BP 57, DM 163, FR 549, Y 14,031).

FRUHTRUNK, Gunter 1923-1982
$388* *Epitaph Pour Arp, 1974,* s., num., edit. Denise Rene, (09-25-92, Granier, #2849), 27⁹⁄₁₆ x 28⅛ in., (70 x 71.4 cm.), color serigraph on artist's paper (BP 227, DM 575, FR 1945, Y 46,832).
$97* *Streifenkomposition,* s., num., stained, wear, (09-25-92, Granier, #2850), 31¾ x 31¾ in., (80.6 x 80.6 cm.), color serigraph on thick board (BP 57, DM 144, FR 486, Y 11,708).

FRUHTRUNK, Gunther German b. 1923
$253* *Diagonale Progression, 1973,* s., num., (11-28-92, Schoppmann, #548), 25⅜ x 25⅜ in., (64.5 x 64.5 cm.), color serigraph on light cardboard (BP 167, DM 403, FR 1368, Y 31,487).
$253* *"Emotion", c. 1974,* s., num., (11-28-92, Grisebach, #517, illus.), 25⅞ x 25⁷⁄₁₆ in., (65.8 x 64.6 cm.), colored serigraph on smooth cardboard (BP 167, DM 403, FR 1368, Y 31,487).
$332* *Epitaph Pour Arp, 1974,* #119/200, s., (09-04-92, Germann, #348), 27⅜ x 27¹⁵⁄₁₆ in., (695 x 710 mm.), color serigraph on artist's paper (BP 166, DM 465, FR 1584, Y 40,867, SF 414).
$2526* *Farbbewegungen, 1969: Six,* Koln, Galerie der Spiegel, num., s., (11-28-92, Schoppmann, #546), 26¹⁵⁄₁₆ x 36¹³⁄₁₆ in., (68.5 x 93.5 cm.), color serigraph (BP 1667, DM 4024, FR 13,661, Y 314,375).
$325* *Komposition,* s., (06-12-93, Hauswedell/Nolt, #92), 9¹⁵⁄₁₆ x 38³⁄₁₆ in., (25.3 x 97 cm.), color serigraph on offset board (BP 213, DM 529, FR 1778, Y 34,200).
$470* *Rot Aus Grun Aus Schwarz Aus Rot,* s., num., (11-28-92, Schoppmann, #547), 35⁷⁄₁₆ x 35⁷⁄₁₆ in., (90 x 90 cm.), color serigraph on cardboard (BP 310, DM 749, FR 2542, Y 58,494).
$474* *Vertikale Streifen,* #80/150, s., (04-21-93, Germann, #444), 29½ x 21⅝ in., (750 x 550 mm.), color serigraph (BP 308, DM 758, FR 2562, Y 52,474, SF 690).

FRYE, Thomas
BI *Portrait Of A Woman, 1761,* watermark, tear into image, skinning, trimmed, est. BP 3/500, (11-30-92, Phillips-London, #56), sheet 19⅝ x 13⅞ in., (498 x 352 mm.), mezzotint on laid.

FRYER, Elmer
$167* *Bette Davis With Flower Arrangement,* photog. stamp, (10-10-92, Bonhams, #1, illus.), 11 x 14 in., (27.9 x 35.6 cm.), photograph (BP 99, DM 248, FR 833, Y 20,331).
$167* *Marion Davies, White Hat With Sequinned Veil,* blind embossed, (10-10-92, Bonhams, #2, illus.), 10½ x 13 in., (26.7 x 33 cm.), photograph (BP 99, DM 248, FR 833, Y 20,331).

FUCHS, Ernst Austrian b. 1930
$737* *Baum Der Aphrodite Am Abend, c. 1985,* s., stained, (09-18-92, Schloss Ahlden, #1001), 20⅞ x 24⅞ in., (53.1 x 63.2 cm.), etching w/aquatint, handcolored on thick cardboard (BP 431, DM 1094, FR 3741, Y 91,089).
BI *Composition Symboliste,* s., trimmed margins, est. FF1,200/1,500, (05-27-93, Briest, #96), 15⁹⁄₁₆ x 11⅝ in., (39.5 x 29.5 cm.), etching and drypoint on Velin contrecollee sur Arches.
$295* *Compositions: Two,* s. Ernest Fuchs, (09-30-92, Kunsthallen, #113), etching (BP 166, DM 418, FR 1415, Y 35,401, DK 1610).
$403* *"Daphne In Eva Mystica", 1969 (Weis 147/IV),* s., #107/200, (06-04-93, Dorotheum, #122), color etching (BP 267, DM 654, FR 2206, Y 43,464, SC 4600).
BI *Elsa Im Brautkleid,* s., #25/120, est. DM 600, (09-18-92, Schloss Ahlden, #999), 25⅝ x 29¹¹⁄₁₆ in., (65.1 x 75.4 cm.), color etching on hand-made.
$7883* *"Esther" (Weis 82/V b - 84/V b, 86/IV/b, 88/IV b, 99/IV b, 109 b, 110/III b, 111/III b, 112 c), 1967: Ten,* pub Die Insel, s., num., (12-01-92, Karl/Faber, #625, illus.), 26⁹⁄₁₆ x 19¹¹⁄₁₆ in., (67.5 x 50 cm.), etching and aquatint on China (BP 5208, DM 12,565, FR 42,819, Y 981,449).
$142* *Homme-Faucon,* artist proof, full margins, (05-27-93, Briest, #97), 21¹⁄₁₆ x 14¹⁵⁄₁₆ in., (53.5 x 38 cm.), color etching and aquatint (BP 91, DM 228, FR 768, Y 15,223).
$532* *Samson (Weis 60/III b, 63/II, 71/VI, 73/II b), 1963: Four,* s., d., i., sheet 6, 12, 14 and 13 from series, Epreuve d'Artiste, watermark, (06-08-93, Karl/Faber, #778), smallest approx. 12³⁄₁₆ x 9⅝ in., (31 x 24.5 cm.), largest approx. 12³⁄₁₆ x 20⅞ in., (31 x 24.5 cm.), etching and aquatint on Japan hand-made (BP 350, DM 863, FR 2907, Y 56,506).
$33* *Seated Nude Before A Mirror,* s., (05-20-93, Boos, #531), 6⅞ x 4⅝ in., (174 x 117 mm.), etching (BP 21, DM 53, FR 179, Y 3644).
$888* *"Die Toteninsel",* s., 61/200, (11-21-92, Arnold, #2, illus.), 25³⁄₁₆ x 35⁷⁄₁₆ in., (64 x 90 cm.), color lithograph (BP 585, DM 1416, FR 4769, Y 110,434).
$132* *Treppe Der Sphinx, 1989,* s., num., wear, (09-25-92, Granier, #2851), sheet 19⅛ x 25⅞ in., (48.5 x 65.7 cm.), color serigraph on hand-made Rives (BP 77, DM 196, FR 662, Y 15,932).
$1316* *Waldidylle Vor Der Himmelsmauer (F. 205, b), 1974,* #7/100, s., (10-09-92, Winterberg, #2176, illus.), 20¼ x 26⅛ in., (51.5 x 66.4 cm.), etching w/soft-ground etching and aquatint (BP 781, DM 1955, FR 6564, Y 160,214).
$1007* *Walkure,* s., #19/20, (09-18-92, Schloss Ahlden, #1000, illus.), 25⁹⁄₁₆ x 29¹³⁄₁₆ in., (65 x 75.8 cm.), color etching on hand-made (BP 590, DM 1494, FR 5112, Y 124,459).

FUCHS, F. (after)
$220* *"Battles Of The Rebellion", 1863,* pub. Charles Magnus, (06-11-93, Freemn/Fine Art, #73A), 19½ x 20 in., (49.5 x 50.8 cm.), tinted lithograph (BP 145, DM 358, FR 1205, Y 23,342).

FUCHS, Michael
$73* *Scenes De Personnages, 1976, 1977: Two,* s., d., epreuves d'artiste, num. I/X, full margins, (11-16-92, Briest, #57), one 11³⁄₁₆ x 14¾ in., (28.4 x 37.4 cm.), other 14⁷⁄₁₆ x 10½ in., (28.4 x 37.4 cm.), etching (BP 48, DM 116, FR 392, Y 9110).

FUERTES, A.
$55* *Flying Woodcock,* issued for Ithica Gun Co., (c) 1914, wrinkled, discoloration, (10-02-92, Guyette, #635A, illus.), print (BP 32, DM 78, FR 262, Y 6567).

FUGG
$630* *"Hamburg-America Line, Southampton To New York" and "Hamburg-AmerikaLinie, To The West Indies And Central America", c. 1930: Two,* creasing, excell. cond., (02-04-93, Christie-S. Ken, #26, illus.), 40 x 25 in., (101.6 x 63.5 cm.), color lithograph (BP 440, DM 1037, FR 3518, Y 78,368).
$268* *"Hamburg-American Line, Central America, Cuba & Mexico, Winter ToursTo The Tropics" and "Hamburg-American Line, Northern Cruises": Two,* nicks, creases, (02-04-93, Christie-S. Ken, #27), 39½ x 25 in., (100.3 x 63.5 cm.), color lithograph (BP 187, DM 441, FR 1496, Y 33,337).

FUHRICH, Joseph Ritter von 1800-1876
$144* *Die Hl. Familie In der Tischlerwerkstatt (Von Boetticher 4), 1837,* foxed, (12-04-92, Bassenge, #6805), 5⅞ x 7¹³⁄₁₆ in., (15 x 19.8 cm.), etching (BP 92, DM 229, FR 778, Y 17,978).

FUHRMANN, Ernst
$518* *"Haselnuss" and "Spitzhorn", 1930: Two Botanical Studies,* t., annot., studio stamp, (04-08-93, Christie-NY, #97, illus.), each approx. 9⅛ x 6¾ in., (23.2 x 17.1 cm.), photograph, gelatin silver print (BP 340, DM 832, FR 2817, Y 58,783).

FUJI, H.
$235* *Nude,* 1980s, s. H. Fuji, 351 x 438mm, (05-07-93, Sotheby-London, #361, illus.), photograph, silver print (BP 149, DM 372, FR 1252, Y 25,875).

FUJITA, A.
$86* *Green Field,* s., t., d. 1968, #52/100, (06-08-93, Ritchie, #35), 17½ x 12½ in., (44.5 x 31.8 cm.), color woodcut (BP 57, DM 140, FR 470, Y 9134, C$ 110).

FULLER, S. and J., Publisher
$1210* *"The Meet At Melton": Fourteen,* framed as six, (12-10-92, Doyle, #17), each 8 x 22 in., (20.3 x 55.9 cm.), color lithograph (BP 780, DM 1914, FR 6537, Y 149,678).

FULLWOOD, Albert Henry   1863-1930
$65* *(Untitled),* s. A Henry Fullwood, inits. A.F, d. '03, in image, (08-11-92, L. Joel, #74G), 7⅞ x 7⅞ in., (20 x 20 cm.), etching (BP 34, DM 95, FR 323, Y 8324, A$ 88).

FULLWOOD, John   English ac. 1881-1915; d. 1931
BI *Figures In A Marshy Landscape,* s., est. $125/175, (10-30-92, Sloan, #841), 14½ x 22⅝ in., (36.8 x 57.5 cm.), etching.
$70 *Figures On A Cliff Top Path,* s., (12-11-92, G.A. Key, #144), 16 x 26 in., (40.6 x 66 cm.), black and white engraving (BP 45, DM 110, FR 378, Y 8662).
$59 *"On The Bure",* s., (10-09-92, G.A. Key, #16), 8½ x 15¾ in., (21.6 x 40 cm.), etching (BP 35, DM 88, FR 298, Y 7195).

FULTON, Hamish   English b. 1946
$14,300* *The Blue Stack Mountains Of Donegal,* t., d. 1982, prov., (10-08-92, Christie-NY, #225, illus.), 29¼ x 62½ in., (74.3 x 158.8 cm.), black and white photograph w/text mounted on board (BP 8509, DM 21,151, FR 71,787, Y 1,737,546).
$2787* *Fourteen Works, 1989,* set of fourteen, each s., #13/35 verso, pub. Paragon Press, margins, good cond., framed, loose in orig. black portfolio box, (10-15-92, Sotheby-London, #97, illus.), overall 44 x 35 in., (111.8 x 88.9 cm.), offset lithograph p. in b/red on Heritage paper (BP 1705, DM 4149, FR 14,069, Y 334,373).
$9350* *River Rock,* t. 1987, prov., (11-19-92, Christie-NY, #213, illus.), 44 x 50¾ in., (111.8 x 128.9 cm.), photograph, b/w w/text mounted on board in artist's frame (BP 6156, DM 14,908, FR 50,215, Y 1,162,791).
$11,000* *Sunrise: Four,* t., d. JULY 1982, exec. 1982, prov., (02-24-93, Christie-NY, #84, illus.), 30½ x 95½ in., (77.5 x 242.6 cm.), photograph, b/w mounted on board in artist's frame (BP 7671, DM 17,857, FR 60,539, Y 1,290,777).
$18,400* *Wheeldale Moor,* t., d. 1977, prov., (05-05-93, Christie-NY, #121, illus.), 41 x 51 in., (104.1 x 129.5 cm.), b/w photograph mounted on paper on masonite in artist's frame (BP 11,748, DM 29,031, FR 97,820, Y 2,027,995).

FULWIDER, Edwin   American b. 1913
$215* *The Train Arrival,* s., good cond., (10-31-92, Cleveland, #125, illus.), 8 x 12 in., (20.3 x 30.5 cm.), lithograph (BP 138, DM 331, FR 1122, Y 26,632).

FUNK, John   1895-1964
$522* *Tri-Boro Bridge,* s., t., 1930's, (10-14-92, Swann, #459, illus.), 10⅛ x 7⅞ in., (25.7 x 20 cm.), photograph, silver print (BP 306, DM 764, FR 2591, Y 63,257).
$550* *Triboro Bridge,* 1930s, s., t., (10-13-92, Christie-NY, #215, illus.), 10 x 8 in., (25.4 x 20.3 cm.), photograph, gelatin silver print (BP 320, DM 806, FR 2738, Y 66,691).

FUNKE, Jaromir   1896-1945
BI *Abstraction, c. 1928,* est. $3/5,000, (10-15-92, Sotheby-NY, #384, illus.), 11⅝ x 9⅜ in., (29.5 x 23.8 cm.), photograph, gelatin silver print.
$3220* *Angel Statuary From The Series Time Persists, 1930-34,* lit., (04-08-93, Christie-NY, #125, illus.), 15½ x 11¾ in.,

(39.4 x 29.8 cm.), photograph, gelatin silver print (BP 2111, DM 5173, FR 17,510, Y 365,411).
$2070* *Cubism Still Life, 1920-22,* s., d. by Anna Farova, (04-08-93, Christie-NY, #123, illus.), 5⅞ x 7¼ in., (14.9 x 18.4 cm.), photograph, gelatin silver print (BP 1357, DM 3325, FR 11,256, Y 234,907).
$3520* *Cut Paper Abstraction, 1927-29,* prov., (10-13-92, Christie-NY, #216, illus.), 4¾ x 6⅜ in., (12.1 x 16.2 cm.), photograph, gelatin silver print (BP 2050, DM 5157, FR 17,521, Y 426,822).
$6900* *The Eye (1932), 1943,* from portfolio Modern Czech Photography, s., lit., (04-08-93, Christie-NY, #126, illus.), 15⅛ x 11¼ in., (38.4 x 28.6 cm.), photograph, geltin silver print (BP 4525, DM 11,084, FR 37,520, Y 783,023).
BI *Industrial Study,* 1920s, est. $3/3,500, (04-08-93, Christie-NY, #122, illus.), 4⅛ x 3⅜ in., (10.5 x 8.6 cm.), photograph, gelatin silver print.
BI *Light Abstraction,* late 1920s, est. $3,5/4,500, (04-08-93, Christie-NY, #124, illus.), 4⅝ x 6½ in., (11.7 x 16.5 cm.), photograph, gelatin silver print.
BI *Lucien Wiskovsky, c. 1929,* s., t., d. by photog., est. $2/3,000, (10-15-92, Sotheby-NY, #383, illus.), 11⅝ x 9¼ in., (29.5 x 23.5 cm.), photograph, gelatin silver print.
$3680* *Nude Studies, c. 1940: Three,* s., (04-08-93, Christie-NY, #127, illus.), each approx. 4⅞ x 6¾ in., (12.4 x 17.1 cm.), photograph, gelatin silver print (BP 2413, DM 5912, FR 20,011, Y 417,612).
$3220* *Two Trees, c. 1920,* double-mounted, s., (04-08-93, Christie-NY, #121, illus.), 4 x 3 in., (10.2 x 7.6 cm.), photograph, blue-toned pigment print (BP 2111, DM 5173, FR 17,510, Y 365,411).

FURNISS, Harry (after)
$9 *Figures Asleep On A Park Bench,* (02-05-93, G.A. Key, #58), 12 x 17 in., (30.5 x 43.2 cm.), b/w print (BP 6, DM 15, FR 50, Y 1120).

FUSELI, Henry
BI *Woman At A Window (Man 64): Two,* 1st state of 2, detached from support sheet, trimmed close to subject, printer's crease, corners repaired, (06-30-93, Sotheby-London, #251), one 9 x 12¾ in., (229 x 324 mm.), the other 8¼ x 12½ in., (229 x 324 mm.), pen-lithograph on laid.

FUSELI, Henry (after)
BI *Beatrice, Hero, and Ursula (B.P. 87), 1791,* by John Jones, proof before t., pub. John Jones, skinning, repaired tear, good cond., est. BP 250/300, (11-30-92, Phillips-London, #126), sheet 23¼ x 19¼ in., (591 x 489 mm.), mezzotint on laid.
$100* *Frier Puck L'Allegro, 1806,* engraved & pub. by Messrs. Houghton, crease, good cond., (11-30-92, Phillips-London, #132), plate 15½ x 11¾ in., (394 x 298 mm.), stipple engraving on chine applique on wove (BP 66, DM 159, FR 541, Y 12,446).
$383* *The Nightmare, 1802,* engraved by Thomas Burke, pub. S.W. Fores, trimmed to plate, hole, (11-30-92, Phillips-London, #124, illus.), sheet 8¾ x 9⅞ in., (222 x 251 mm.), stipple engraving on wove (BP 253, DM 610, FR 2071, Y 47,666).
$183* *Prince Arthur's Vision, 1787,* by P.W. Tomkins, proof before t., pub. Thomas Macklin, skinning, repaired tears, narrow margins, (11-30-92, Phillips-London, #127), sheet 21 x 16½ in., (533 x 419 mm.), stipple engraving in sepia (BP 121, DM 292, FR 990, Y 22,775).
$383* *Queen Katharine's Dream, 1787,* scratch-letter proof prior to t., by Francesco Bartolozzi, pub. Thomas Macklin, margins, folded, repaired bottom margin, (11-30-92, Phillips-London, #133), plate 17 x 19¾ in., (432 x 502 mm.), stipple engraving on laid (BP 253, DM 610, FR 2071, Y 47,666).
$383* *The Witches, 1786,* engraved by Peltro William Tomkins, pub. Thomas Macklin, margins, spots, defects, (11-30-92, Phillips-London, #125), 10 x 11⅞ in., (254 x 302 mm.), stipple engraving in colors on wove (BP 253, DM 610, FR 2071, Y 47,666).

FUSS

BI *Hamburg Amerika Linie: Croisieres En Mediterranee Au Printemps Et EnAutomne,* good cond., (03-13-93, Laurin, #163), 33 1/16 x 23 7/16 in., (84 x 59.5 cm.), .

FUSSLI, Friedrich Salomon, Publisher   Swiss 1801-1847

$6595* *Views Of Switzerland, Including Views Of Zurich, Interlaken, Mont Blanc, Geneva, Lucerne, Basle, Bern And Rhone Glacier, By Or After Frey, Bury, Weber, Bodmer, Hegi And Others: Twenty Four,* full margins, mount staining, dirt, (10-07-92, Christie-S. Ken, #77, illus.), pl 6¾ x 8 in., (17.1 x 20.3 cm.), colored aquatint part p. in color touches of gum arabic (BP 3850, DM 9543, FR 32,360, Y 793,145).

FUSSMANN, Klaus   b. 1938

$332* *Grosses Interieur (Fussmann 32), 1973,* s., num., (12-05-92, Bassenge, #7180), 18½ x 19½ in., drypoint and aquatint on copper print paper (BP 208, DM 518, FR 1764, Y 41,135).

$332* *Hella K., Tuch Haltend (Fussmann 108), 1981,* s., num., (12-05-92, Bassenge, #7181), 16 9/16 x 17 11/16 in., (42 x 45 cm.), etching in 6 Farben from 3 plates on copper print paper (BP 208, DM 518, FR 1764, Y 41,135).

FYT, Jan   Flemish 1611-1661

$805* *Hunde (B.aus 9-16; Wurzbach; Dutuit; Hollstein aus 9-16), 1642: Five,* (12-12-92, Bassenge, #8104), approx. 6¾ x 8¾ in., (17.2 x 22.2 cm.), etching (BP 515, DM 1265, FR 4312, Y 99,592).

GABINO, Amadeo   Spanish b. 1922

$251* *"Chicago" and "Rotura De La Niebla": Two,* s. 78, 77/99, s. 77/100, (09-29-92, B. Rasmussen, #308), aquatint in colors (BP 141, DM 355, FR 1210, Y 29,963, DK 1380).

GABO, Naum   American 1890-1977

BI *Composition In Red, 1965,* s., i. e.a., margins, good cond., soiling, rubbing, est. BP 5/700, (12-03-92, Sotheby-London, #685, illus.), sheet 23⅛ x 17¾ in., (586 x 452 mm.), lithograph in red and black.

$600* *Composition In Red, 1965,* s., i. e.a. (bled), margins, good cond., soiling, rubbing, (06-30-93, Sotheby-London, #815, illus.), sh 23⅛ x 17¾ in., (587 x 451 mm.), lithograph in red and black (BP 402, DM 1023, FR 3452, Y 64,288).

$3025* *Opus 3, c. 1955,* s., t., i., good cond., mat stain, (11-05-92, Sotheby-NY, #187, illus.), 7⅞ x 4⅞ in., (200 x 124 mm.), sheet approx. 10⅝ x 7⅞ in., (200 x 124 mm.), monoprint (wood engraving) p. in dark brown ink on japon pelure (BP 1967, DM 4784, FR 16,185, Y 371,120).

$3300* *Opus 4, c. 1955,* s., t., large margins, good cond., light stain, (11-05-92, Sotheby-NY, #186, illus.), 6¼ x 5¼ in., (159 x 132 mm.), sheet 10 x 9 in., (159 x 132 mm.), monoprint (wood engraving) p. in dark brown ink on japon pelure (BP 2146, DM 5219, FR 17,657, Y 404,858).

BI *"Opus 7", 1950,* s., est. DM 6/8,000, (06-05-93, Grisebach, #369, illus.), 7 15/16 x 9 13/16 in., (20.2 x 25 cm.), wood engraving in brown on Japan.

BI *"Opus 8", 1950,* s., lit., est. DM 6/8,000, (06-05-93, Grisebach, #370, illus.), 11⅞ x 9 5/16 in., (30.2 x 23.7 cm.), wood engraving in blue on Japan.

BI *Opus Five (The Constellations), 1950,* s., full margins, annot., est. FF 10/15,000, (11-16-92, Briest, #307), 15 9/16 x 10 13/16 in., (39.5 x 27.5 cm.), monotype from wood engraving.

BI *Opus Five, c. 1950,* t., s., est. DM 12,000, (06-05-93, Bassenge, #6041, illus.), 9 7/16 x 7 15/16 in., (24 x 20.2 cm.), monotype on Japan.

BI *Opus Seven (Jorn Merkert, p. 60), 1950,* exhib., est. FF 12/15,000, (11-16-92, Briest, #308, illus.), 11 x 15¾ in., (28 x 40 cm.), monotype from wood engraving.

GADOUD, L.

$880* *Vins Camp Romains, 1935,* Affiches-Camis, A- cond., discoloration, creasing, (08-06-92, Swann, #134, illus.), 63 x 47 in., (160 x 119.4 cm.), (BP 460, DM 1300, FR 4391, Y 112,245).

GAFGEN, Wolfgang   b. 1936

BI *Sujet Divers, 1972: Four,* from "7 manieres noires" portfolio, s., #11/100, full margins, est. FF1,400/1,600, (05-27-93, Briest, #99), 29 15/16 x 21⅝ in., (76 x 55 cm.), maniere noire en (and) couleurs.

GAG, Wanda   American 1893-1946

$578* *"Garden Tools",* s., (10-31-92, Litchfield, #66), 10½ x 12¾ in., (26.7 x 32.4 cm.), lithograph (BP 378, DM 907, FR 3073, Y 71,464).

$578* *"Interior With Garden Tools", 1932,* s., d., (10-31-92, Litchfield, #65), 11¼ x 13½ in., (28.6 x 34.3 cm.), lithograph (BP 378, DM 907, FR 3073, Y 71,464).

$550* *"Moonlight Village Scene", 1926,* s., d., (10-31-92, Litchfield, #64), 14 x 16½ in., (35.6 x 41.9 cm.), lithograph (BP 360, DM 863, FR 2924, Y 68,002).

GAGLIANI, Oliver   Amerian b. 1917

$935* *"Attic", 1972,* s., d., i., (11-16-92, Butterfield, #5978, illus.), 10¼ x 12¾ in., (260.8 x 324.4 mm.), photograph, gelatin silver print (BP 616, DM 1491, FR 5021, Y 116,279).

$805* *"Grizzly Creek State Park", 1956,* s., stamped Vintage, photog.'s label, est. $800/1,200, (05-23-93, Butterfield, #3419, illus.), 4¾ x 3⅝ in., photograph, gelatin silver print (BP 524, DM 1316, FR 4430, Y 88,980).

$990* *"White Door", 1973,* s., d., i., (11-16-92, Butterfield, #5977, illus.), 10⅛ x 13 in., (257.6 x 330.8 mm.), photograph, gelatin silver print (BP 652, DM 1578, FR 5317, Y 123,119).

GAILLARD, Emile

$378* *Batavier Line, London-Rotterdam, c. 1935,* tears, excell. cond., (02-04-93, Christie-S. Ken, #28, illus.), 39½ x 24 in., (100.3 x 61 cm.), color lithograph (BP 264, DM 622, FR 2111, Y 47,021).

GAILLARD, R.

$209* *"Les Amants Surpris",* 18th c., after F. Boucher, pub. Paris, foxing, (12-06-92, Neal, #933), plate 17¼ x 14 in., (43.8 x 35.6 cm.), engraving (BP 131, DM 326, FR 1111, Y 25,895).

$165* *"L'Agreable Lecon",* after F. Boucher, pub. Paris, foxing, (12-06-92, Neal, #932), plate 17¼ x 14¼ in., (43.8 x 36.2 cm.), engraving (BP 103, DM 257, FR 877, Y 20,444).

GAINSBOROUGH, Thomas   (after)

$150* *Cottage Children, 1791,* by Henry Burke, margins, pub. R.B. Evans, good cond., (11-30-92, Phillips-London, #209), plate 22⅞ x 15⅓ in., (581 x 389 mm.), mezzotint on laid (BP 99, DM 239, FR 811, Y 18,668).

$233* *The Right Hon. William Pitt, 1808,* by William Bromley, open-letter proof, pub. Robert Bowyer, laid on canvas, mounted on stretcher, hole, foxed, time-stained, (11-30-92, Phillips-London, #57), image 24 x 16 in., (610 x 406 mm.), engraving on laid (BP 154, DM 371, FR 1260, Y 28,998).

GAKUTEI

$5626* *Crescent Moon And Shinto Decorations,* sealed Gakutei, (06-10-93, Sotheby-London, #197, illus.), (BP 3680, DM 9161, FR 30,844, Y 597,177).

$28* *"Girl And Dragon",* SURIMONO, margins laid down matt, fading, soiling, (05-07-93, Goldberg, #1407), woodblock (BP 18, DM 44, FR 149, Y 3083).

$3165* *Portrait Of A Courtesan Standing,* surimono, kakuban, s. Gakutei w/seal, (06-10-93, Sotheby-London, #212), brown ground, detail in silver w/gauffrage (BP 2070, DM 5154, FR 17,352, Y 335,952).

GALE, George A.   American 1893-1951

$50* *"Baby Of The Fleet (The A.R. Tucker)",* s. George A. Gale (M.D.G.), t., good cond., (10-31-92, Cleveland, #126), 8½ x 5 in., (21.6 x 12.7 cm.), etching (BP 32, DM 77, FR 261, Y 6193).

GALERIE BIRCH

$55* *Diverse Udstillingskataloger,* (03-24-93, Kunsthallen, #115), (BP 37, DM 90, FR 306, Y 6462, DK 345).

GALICE, Louis   French b. 1864

$181* *Bian-ka, c. 1895,* Paris, Affiches Americaines Ch. Revy, cond. B+, (06-11-93, Boisgirard, #73), 48 13/16 x 35 7/16 in.,

(124 x 90 cm.), poster (BP 119, DM 294, FR 992, Y 19,204).

$462* *Cirque D'Hiver. Les Allies En Chine, c. 1900,* Paris, Affiches Louis Galice, cond. A-, (06-11-93, Boisgirard, #74), 49$\frac{3}{16}$ x 35$\frac{1}{16}$ in., (125 x 89 cm.), poster (BP 304, DM 751, FR 2532, Y 49,019).

$50* *Grand Theatre De Bordeaux: Napoleon. Epopee En 9 Tableaux,* Ateliers Gaillard, fairly good cond., (02-12-93, Cheval/Robert, #158), 48$\frac{7}{16}$ x 33$\frac{7}{16}$ in., (123 x 85 cm.), poster (BP 35, DM 83, FR 281, Y 6030).

$64* *La Princesse Bebe. Operette (...) Musique De L. Varnay, c. 1905,* cond. A, (03-16-93, Boisgirard, #113), 39$\frac{3}{8}$ x 25$\frac{13}{16}$ in., (100 x 65.5 cm.), poster (BP 44, DM 106, FR 362, Y 7484).

GALICE, Louis (attrib.) French b. 1864

$221* *Les Soeurs Du Casino De Paris Et Du Moulin Rouge, c. 1895,* Paris, Affiches Americaines Ch. Levy, cond. B+, (06-11-93, Boisgirard, #75), 50$\frac{13}{16}$ x 35$\frac{13}{16}$ in., (129 x 91 cm.), poster (BP 145, DM 359, FR 1211, Y 23,448).

GALL, Francois French 1912-1945

$198* *Sur La Terrasse,* s., #60/100, (11-01-92, Hanzel, #212), 18$\frac{3}{4}$ x 15$\frac{1}{4}$ in., (47.6 x 38.7 cm.), lithograph (BP 129, DM 312, FR 1053, Y 24,481).

GALLAGHER, Sears American 1869-1955

$110* *Low Tide,* margins., s. Sears Gallagher, (10-24-92, Collins, #2), 6 x 8$\frac{3}{4}$ in., (15.2 x 22.2 cm.), etching (BP 68, DM 168, FR 570, Y 13,415).

GALLAND, A.

$1047* *Ch. De Fer De L'Etat: Le Mans, "Enceinte Gallo-Romaine, Golf Permanent, Circuit Automobile", c. 1930,* p. Demoulin, excell. cond., (01-23-93, Ribeyre/Baron, #60, illus.), 39$\frac{3}{8}$ x 24$\frac{7}{16}$ in., (100 x 62 cm.), poster (BP 685, DM 1665, FR 5632, Y 131,039).

$671* *Vins De France, "Sante, Gaiete, Esperance", 1937,* p. Bedos, very good cond., (11-19-92, Ribeyre/Baron, #33), 46$\frac{7}{16}$ x 31$\frac{1}{2}$ in., (118 x 80 cm.), poster (BP 442, DM 1070, FR 3604, Y 83,447).

GALLE, Cornelis (I) 1576-1650

BI *Die Jungfrau Mit Dem Kind And Den Heiligen Bernhard And Gerhard (Wurzbach 69; Hollstein 120 I),* after Francesco Vanni, watermark, prov., est. DM 600, (06-10-93, Hauswedell/Nolt, #93), engraving.

$278* *Jupiter Und Merkur Bei Philemon Und Baucis (Hollstein Bd. VII, 276),* after Jan van den Hoecke, trimmed, (09-14-92, Venator/Hansten, #1509, illus.), sh 9$\frac{13}{16}$ x 13$\frac{7}{16}$ in., (25 x 34.2 cm.), engraving and etching (BP 147, DM 413, FR 1401, Y 34,569).

GALLE, Joan 1600-1676

$645* *Bouquets De Fleurs Avec Oiseaux Et Insectes: Two,* good cond., stains, loss, (05-15-93, Loudmer, #68, illus.), 6$\frac{15}{16}$ x 5$\frac{1}{16}$ in., (177 x 129 mm.), sh 7$\frac{5}{16}$ x 5$\frac{5}{16}$ in., (177 x 129 mm.), copper engraving on laid (BP 419, DM 1037, FR 3486, Y 71,500).

GALLE, Philip 1537-1612

BI *Abraham's Sacrifice (Holl. 2; Ill. B., vol. 56, p. 18, no. .006), c.1560,* after Frans Floris, thread margins, trimmed on platemark, wormhole, tear, staining, discoloration, laid, est. BP 1,2/1,600, (12-01-92, Christie-London, #6, illus.), 13$\frac{7}{8}$ x 17$\frac{13}{16}$ in., (353 x 452 mm.), engraving.

GALLE, Philipp 1537-1612

$325* *Apollo Und Artemis Toten Niobes Kinder (Hollstein 382 II; The Illustrated Bartsch Bd. 56, 96), 1557,* (12-04-92, Bassenge, #6197), 11$\frac{11}{16}$ x 16$\frac{15}{16}$ in., (29.7 x 43.1 cm.), engraving (BP 208, DM 518, FR 1756, Y 40,574).

GALLI, Orio

$357* *Caffe Moretto, 1970,* Caslano Stampa Silkprint, A- cond., (08-06-92, Swann, #135, illus.), 50$\frac{1}{2}$ x 35$\frac{1}{2}$ in., (128.3 x 90.2 cm.), (BP 186, DM 527, FR 1781, Y 45,536).

GALLO, Frank American b. 1933

$220* *Face, 1977,* s., #80/150, (06-13-93, Hindman, #342), 39$\frac{1}{2}$ x 32 in., (100.3 x 81.3 cm.), cast paper pulp (BP 144, DM 358, FR 1204, Y 23,151).

GALVAN, Jose Maria

BI *"Frescos De San Antonio De La Florida De Goya", 1888: Sixteen,* reserve P45,000, (12-17-92, Duran, #16, illus.), 18$\frac{1}{2}$ x 14$\frac{9}{16}$ in., (47 x 37 cm.), etching.

GAME, Robert b. 1944

BI *Sky Side, 1974,* #18/20, s., t., d. 1974, prov., est. C$ 2/300, (11-16-92, Hodgins, #173), 30$\frac{1}{2}$ x 20$\frac{15}{16}$ in., (77.5 x 53.3 cm.), serigraph on paper.

GAMES, Abram b. 1914

$1732* *Shell Lubricating Oil, Stays On The Job, 1939,* ref. #540, cond. 2, crease, (10-13-92, Phillips-London, #156, illus.), 29$\frac{13}{16}$ x 44$\frac{15}{16}$ in., (75.8 x 114.2 cm.), color lithograph (BP 1009, DM 2537, FR 8621, Y 210,016).

GAMUF, Suzy Austrian b. 1906

$303* *Untitled: A Pair: Four,* (03-14-93, Hindman, #406), each 45 x 60 in., photograph, (BP 211, DM 503, FR 1711, Y 35,892).

GANDINI, Alessandro ac. 2nd half 16th cent.

BI *Maria Mit Dem Kinde, Engeln Und Heiligen,* lit., est. DM 6,000, (12-04-92, Bassenge, #6198, illus.), 14 x 9$\frac{11}{16}$ in., (35.6 x 24.6 cm.), chiaroscuro woodcut by 2 plates.

GANGOLF, Paul 1879-1945

$885* *Koksende Hure (Rathenau 23), 1926,* s., from "Die Schaffenden", (12-05-92, Bassenge, #7183, illus.), 12$\frac{5}{8}$ x 10$\frac{1}{4}$ in., (32 x 26 cm.), lithograph on handmade (BP 554, DM 1380, FR 4702, Y 109,652).

$192* *Marseille, Dampfer Im Hafen (Rathenau 2),* s., (12-05-92, Bassenge, #7182), 4$\frac{13}{16}$ x 5$\frac{15}{16}$ in., woodcut on handmade (BP 120, DM 299, FR 1020, Y 23,789).

GANKI (after) Japanese 19th cent.

$110* *Hermit And Bullfrog,* (09-17-92, Sloan, #1624), 12 x 7$\frac{1}{4}$ in., (30.5 x 18.4 cm.), woodblock (BP 62, DM 163, FR 559, Y 13,695).

BI *Hermit And Bullfrog,* est. $250/350, (07-03-92, Sloan, #892), 12 x 7$\frac{1}{4}$ in., (30.5 x 18.4 cm.), woodblock.

GANNE, Yves European 20th cent.

$28* *Tabletop Still Life,* s., #196/275, (10-30-92, Sloan, #839), 15$\frac{3}{4}$ x 21$\frac{3}{4}$ in., (40 x 55.2 cm.), color lithograph (BP 18, DM 43, FR 146, Y 3468).

GANNET, Solan

$99* *Young Of The Year,* discoloration, (06-11-93, Freemn/Fine Art, #74), 18$\frac{1}{4}$ x 22 in., (46.4 x 55.9 cm.), hand-colored engraving (BP 65, DM 161, FR 542, Y 10,504).

GANS, Louis

BI *Untitled, 1978,* s., full margins, good cond., est. Dfl. 150/250, (05-27-93, Sotheby-Amstrdm, #415), 16$\frac{1}{8}$ x 24$\frac{13}{16}$ in., (410 x 630 mm.), colored silkscreen on sturdy wove.

$64* *Untitled, 1978,* s., full margins, good cond., (05-27-93, Sotheby-Amstrdm, #416), 16$\frac{1}{8}$ x 24$\frac{13}{16}$ in., (410 x 630 mm.), colored silkscreen on sturdy wove (BP 41, DM 103, FR 346, Y 6861, G 115).

$64* *Untitled, 1978,* s., full margins, good cond., (05-27-93, Sotheby-Amstrdm, #417), 16$\frac{1}{8}$ x 24$\frac{13}{16}$ in., (410 x 630 mm.), colored silkscreen on sturdy wove (BP 41, DM 103, FR 346, Y 6861, G 115).

GANSO, Emil German/American 1895-1941

$205* *"At The Seashore", 1932,* s. The Print Club of Cleveland Publication No. 10, folds, (05-15-93, Cleveland, #139), 8 x 12 in., (20.3 x 30.5 cm.), wood engraving (BP 133, DM 330, FR 1108, Y 22,725).

$350* *"Dawn",* s., t., staining, repaired tear, fold, (05-15-93, Cleveland, #136), 12$\frac{1}{2}$ x 16 in., (31.8 x 40.6 cm.), color lithograph (BP 228, DM 563, FR 1892, Y 38,798).

$302* *Delores,* s., t., hinged to mat, very good cond., (12-04-92, Doyle, #100), 12$\frac{1}{8}$ x 8$\frac{3}{4}$ in., (308 x 222 mm.), aquatint (BP 194, DM 481, FR 1632, Y 37,703).

$250* *"Early Snow", 1938,* Iowa Cat. No. 46, s. w/estate stamp, very good cond., surface dirt, (05-15-93, Cleveland, #140, illus.), 12 x 16 in., (30.5 x 40.6 cm.), color lithograph (BP 163, DM 402, FR 1351, Y 27,713).

$286* *"Figure At Bath",* s., fine cond., (10-31-92, Cleveland, #129, illus.), 8 x 5 in., (20.3 x 12.7 cm.), etching (BP 183, DM 440, FR 1493, Y 35,427).

$220* *"Figure At The Bath"*, s., num., good cond., (10-31-92, Cleveland, #133), 13¼ x 9⅛ in., (33.7 x 23.2 cm.), lithograph (BP 141, DM 338, FR 1148, Y 27,251).

$450* *"Lingerie", 1935,* s., thin spot, (05-15-93, Cleveland, #138, illus.), 13 x 18 in., (33 x 45.7 cm.), lithograph in colors (BP 293, DM 724, FR 2432, Y 49,884).

BI *Nubbi Lighthouse,* s., est. $150/250, (12-11-92, DuMouchelle, #2282), 9½ x 13¾ in., (24.1 x 34.9 cm.), lithograph.

$138* *Nude Bathers,* s. inside plate Ganso, excellent cond. (?), (04-25-93, Bakker, #64), image 8⅞ x 6⅞ in., (22.5 x 17.5 cm.), wood engraving (BP 88, DM 218, FR 737, Y 15,242).

$297* *Nude By The Lake,* s., fine cond., (10-31-92, Cleveland, #130), 15½ x 10½ in., (39.4 x 26.7 cm.), lithograph on chine colle (pasted) on wove support (BP 190, DM 457, FR 1550, Y 36,789).

$375* *Nude With Book,* s., good cond., (05-15-93, Cleveland, #137, illus.), 12 x 21½ in., (30.5 x 54.6 cm.), lithograph in color (BP 244, DM 603, FR 2027, Y 41,570).

BI *"Nude With Chemise", c. 1934,* s., num., soiling, good cond., est. $3-400, (10-31-92, Cleveland, #127, illus.), 17 x 12 in., (43.2 x 30.5 cm.), lithograph.

$358* *Nudes At Rest",* s., num., hinges, ink in margins, fine cond., (10-31-92, Cleveland, #128, illus.), 13 x 11 in., (33 x 27.9 cm.), lithograph (BP 229, DM 551, FR 1868, Y 44,345).

$935* *Spring, c. 1937,* s., ink stains, discoloration, very good cond., (12-04-92, Doyle, #99, illus.), 11½ x 16 in., (292 x 406 mm.), color lithograph (BP 600, DM 1489, FR 5051, Y 116,729).

$50* *"Studio Mirror", 1936,* AAG edit., fine cond., (10-31-92, Cleveland, #132), 14 x 9 in., (35.6 x 22.9 cm.), wood engraving (BP 32, DM 77, FR 261, Y 6193).

BI *"Sunny Room",* s., num. 14/42, matt stain, hinges, est. $4-600, (10-31-92, Cleveland, #131, illus.), 8½ x 9⅞ in., (21.6 x 25.1 cm.), lithograph in colors.

BI *"Vase With FLowers", 1928,* s, w/estate stamp. handling marks, est. $2/300, (05-15-93, Cleveland, #141), 14 x 10 in., (35.6 x 25.4 cm.), color lithograph.

$358* *"Woman Reading",* s. Ganso, num. 4/35, very good cond. (?), (04-25-93, Bakker, #67, illus.), image 8½ x 9¾ in., (21.6 x 24.8 cm.), color lithograph (BP 227, DM 566, FR 1912, Y 39,541).

GANTNER, Bernard   French b. 1928

$124* *"Bord De Riviere",* artist's proof, ded., s., (10-18-92, Pescheteau, #153), 25⁹⁄₁₆ x 19¹¹⁄₁₆ in., (65 x 50 cm.), lithograph in colors on Arches (BP 75, DM 183, FR 622, Y 14,806).

$202* *"Paysage De Neige",* s., (10-18-92, Pescheteau, #151), 18⅞ x 25⁹⁄₁₆ in., (48 x 65 cm.), lithograph in colors on Rives (BP 122, DM 298, FR 1014, Y 24,119).

$225* *"Place De Village",* artist's proof, s., (10-18-92, Pescheteau, #154), 19¹¹⁄₁₆ x 25⁹⁄₁₆ in., (50 x 65 cm.), lithograph in colors on Arches (BP 136, DM 332, FR 1129, Y 26,866).

BI *"Pont Sur La Cascade",* #160/185, s., est. FF800/1,000, (04-04-93, Pescheteau, #216), 29¹⁵⁄₁₆ x 21¼ in., (76 x 54 cm.), color lithograph on wove.

$97* *Rue De Campagne,* s. artist's proof, d., (06-28-93, Loudmer, #45), 22¹³⁄₁₆ x 16⁹⁄₁₆ in., (580 x 420 mm.), sh 25¹⁵⁄₁₆ x 18¹¹⁄₁₆ in., (580 x 420 mm.), color lithograph on Arches (BP 65, DM 165, FR 555, Y 10,292).

$77* *Tree By Lake,* s., #97/275, (10-30-92, Sloan, #852), 15⅞ x 22 in., (40.6 x 55.9 cm.), color lithograph (BP 49, DM 118, FR 402, Y 9538).

GANTNER, OG

$121* *Paysage Boise Et Maison Au Toit Rouge,* #47/85, frame trace on large margins, (02-03-93, Ader Tajan, #152), 19¹¹⁄₁₆ x 25¹⁵⁄₁₆ in., (50 x 66 cm.), color lithograph on Japan (BP 84, DM 199, FR 676, Y 15,052).

GARBER, Daniel   American 1880-1958

$880* *Tohickon,* #5, margins, s., (05-22-93, Collins, #71), 5½ x 6½ in., (14 x 16.5 cm.), etching (BP 570, DM 1431, FR 4814, Y 97,023).

GARCIA OCHOA, Luis

BI *"Las Zahurdas De Pluton", 1976: Ten,* Francisco de Quevedo, s., portfolio, #147/225, Ediciones de Arte y Bibliofilia, reserve P225,000, (12-17-92, Duran, #169, illus.), 20¹⁄₁₆ x 15⅜ in., (51 x 39 cm.), lithograph.

GARDIER, Raoul du

$220* *"Afternoon Stroll",* s., split paper through sig., discoloration, hinged to mat, good cond., (12-04-92, Doyle, #102), 7¾ x 7¾ in., (197 x 197 mm.), colored engraving (BP 141, DM 350, FR 1189, Y 27,466).

GARDINER, Eliza   American 1871-1955

$440* *"After The Bath",* s., #20/50, good cond., (02-07-93, Bakker, #24, illus.), image 9 x 11½ in., (22.9 x 29.2 cm.), color woodblock print (BP 304, DM 730, FR 2466, Y 54,754).

$55* *"The Bathers" (Falk B.8),* very good cond., (03-28-93, Bakker, #112), image 9 x 6⅞ in., (22.9 x 17.5 cm.), wood block on gray paper (BP 37, DM 90, FR 305, Y 6401).

$358* *Boy Fishing, Harbor Background (Falk 49),* i., #8 edit. 40, very good/good cond., (03-28-93, Bakker, #57), 3¼ x 4⅛ in., (8.3 x 10.5 cm.), color woodblock (BP 241, DM 584, FR 1986, Y 41,667).

$440* *"Boy With Hoop" (Falk 48),* s., #3/25, very good cond., exhib., (03-28-93, Bakker, #128), image 6½ x 4½ in., (16.5 x 11.4 cm.), color woodblock (BP 296, DM 718, FR 2440, Y 51,210).

$418* *"Candy Apples" (Falk 7),* s., #5/25, exhib., very good cond., (03-28-93, Bakker, #61), 9¾ x 10 in., (24.8 x 25.4 cm.), color woodblock (BP 281, DM 682, FR 2318, Y 48,650).

$495* *"Circus Fans" (Falk B.2),* s., #3/30, very good cond., (03-28-93, Bakker, #89), image 12 x 8½ in., (30.5 x 21.6 cm.), wood block (BP 333, DM 808, FR 2745, Y 57,612).

$44* *"Fishing" (Falk B.3),* #8/20, very good cond., (03-28-93, Bakker, #154), image 11½ x 8⅞ in., (29.2 x 22.5 cm.), wood block (BP 30, DM 72, FR 244, Y 5121).

$770* *Floral Still Life,* s., #1/12, very good cond., (02-07-93, Bakker, #166), 16½ x 12½ in., (41.9 x 31.8 cm.), color woodblock print (BP 533, DM 1277, FR 4316, Y 95,819).

$495* *"Flowering Cactus" (Falk 50),* very good/good cond., (03-28-93, Bakker, #140), image 9¾ x 7¼ in., (24.8 x 18.4 cm.), color woodblock (BP 333, DM 808, FR 2745, Y 57,612).

$220* *"Girl Picking Flowers" (Falk 52),* very good cond., (03-28-93, Bakker, #51), 7¾ x 6 in., (19.7 x 15.2 cm.), color woodblock (BP 148, DM 359, FR 1220, Y 25,605).

BI *"The Little Spectators" (Falk #55),* s. Eliza D. Gardiner, num. 26/100, very good cond.?, est. $1/1,500, (11-21-92, Bakker, #79, illus.), image 9½ x 7¼ in., (24.1 x 18.4 cm.), color woodblock print.

$495* *"The Little Yachtsman" (Falk 42), 1923,* very good/good cond., (03-28-93, Bakker, #159), image 7 x 9¾ in., (17.8 x 24.8 cm.), color linocut (BP 333, DM 808, FR 2745, Y 57,612).

$440* *"The Lookers On" (Falk 33),* s., #1/30, exhib., very good cond., (03-28-93, Bakker, #111), image 12¾ x 10½ in., (32.4 x 26.7 cm.), color linocut (BP 296, DM 718, FR 2440, Y 51,210).

$1540* *"Love Butter", c. 1920,* s., excell./very good cond., (07-19-92, Bakker, #257, illus.), 7½ x 7 in., (19.1 x 17.8 cm.), color woodblock print (BP 790, DM 2245, FR 7590, Y 191,447).

BI *"Love Butter" (Falk #17),* s. Eliza D. Gardiner, num. 23/100, very good cond.?, est. $1/1,500, (11-21-92, Bakker, #75, illus.), image 7½ x 6¾ in., (19.1 x 17.1 cm.), color woodblock print.

$1210* *"Picaback" (Falk #28),* s. Eliza D. Gardiner, num. 19/30, very good cond.?, (11-21-92, Bakker, #80, illus.), image 9¾ x 7¼ in., (24.8 x 18.4 cm.), color woodblock print (BP 797, DM 1929, FR 6498, Y 150,479).

$358* *"Picking Poppies" (Falk 29), 1916,* s., #1/25, very good cond., exhib., (03-28-93, Bakker, #25), image 7 x 5⅜ in., (17.8 x 13.7 cm.), color woodblock (BP 241, DM 584, FR 1986, Y 41,667).

$303* *"The River" (Falk 37), c. 1919,* s., very good/good cond., (03-28-93, Bakker, #169), 7½ x 10 in., (19.1 x 25.4 cm.), color woodblock (BP 204, DM 494, FR 1681, Y 35,265).

$132* *Two Reclining Figures (Falk B.14),* s., #1/25, very good cond., (03-28-93, Bakker, #104), image 7½ x 8¾ in., (19.1 x 22.2 cm.), wood block (BP 89, DM 215, FR 732, Y 15,363).

GARDNER, Alexander   American 1821-1882
$522* *"McLean House, Appomatox"* and *"Camp Of Union Troops, Manassas", c. 182; c. 1865: Two,* notations on mount recto, handstamp, (04-07-93, Swann, #185, illus.), largest 7½ x 9¼ in., photograph, albumen print (BP 345, DM 844, FR 2857, Y 59,305).

$3850* *'A Sharpshooter's Last Sleep',* (c), studio address, t., series t., pub. credit, d., 1863, p. c. 1865, (10-15-92, Sotheby-NY, #10, illus.), 6⅞ x 8⅞ in., (17.5 x 22.5 cm.), photograph, albumen print, on 2-toned 'Incidents of the War' mount (BP 2356, DM 5731, FR 19,435, Y 461,908).

GARDNER, Alexander and Timothy O'SULLIVAN
BI   *The Halt,* notations, 1860's, est. $500/750, (10-14-92, Swann, #172, illus.), 7½ x 9½ in., (19.1 x 24.1 cm.), photograph, albumen print.

GARDNER, Alexander/ Moses P. RICE
$2070* *Abraham Lincoln (Ostendorf 77; Mellon p. 137), 1863,* p. Moses P. Rice from glass negative by Alexander Gardner, p. c. 1891, (04-06-93, Sotheby-NY, #12, illus.), 12⅞ x 10⅛ in., photograph, riceprint on Japan tissue (BP 1367, DM 3335, FR 11,293, Y 236,086).

GARDNER, Christopher   American contemporary
$187* *Map Of The Stars,* s., d. 1984, t., #2/25, (12-10-92, Sloan, #2743), 11½ x 12 in., (29.2 x 30.5 cm.), color woodcut (BP 121, DM 296, FR 1010, Y 23,132).

GARDNER, Daniel (after)   British 1750-1805
$154* *Charles Marquis Cornwallis, 1796,* by I. Jones, (09-20-92, Hindman, #676), 23⅞ x 15 in., (60.6 x 38.1 cm.), mezzotint (BP 90, DM 229, FR 782, Y 19,033).

GARDNER, George   American 20th cent.
BI   *Mr. And Mrs. Kenneth Crumb, Marathon, NY,* 1975, s., prov., est. $80/120, (05-16-93, Hindman, #380), 10 x 7¼ in., photograph, silver print.

$55* *Mr. And Mrs. Kenneth Crumb, Marathon, NY, 1975,* s., prov., (06-13-93, Hindman, #430), 10 x 7¼ in., photograph, silver print (BP 36, DM 90, FR 301, Y 5788).

GARDNER, George W.   American contemporary
$358* *"Northern New Mexico", "Mr And Mrs. Kenneth Crumb, Marathon, New York", and "Fort Drum, New York": Three,* 1967, 1975, 1969, p. later, (03-14-93, Hindman, #405), 13⅝ x 20 in., photograph, silver gelatin (BP 249, DM 595, FR 2021, Y 42,407).

GARDNER, James
$1288* *For High Performance, Vickers Wellesley's, 1939,* p. Waterlow and Sons, ref. #543, cond. 1, (10-13-92, Phillips-London, #158, illus.), 30⅟₁₆ x 45⅜ in., (76.3 x 115.3 cm.), color lithograph (BP 750, DM 1887, FR 6411, Y 156,178).

GARDUNO, Flor
$660* *"Aquamanil, Mexico", 1981/1991,* s., t., d. verso, Dixon Collection, (11-16-92, Butterfield, #5982, illus.), 12⅜ x 9⅜ in., (314.9 x 238.5 mm.), photograph, gelatin silver print (BP 435, DM 1052, FR 3545, Y 82,079).

$495* *"Minotauro", 1984,* s., t., d., Dixon Collection, (11-16-92, Butterfield, #5981, illus.), 12½ x 9⅝ in., (318.1 x 244.9 mm.), photograph, gelatin silver print (BP 326, DM 789, FR 2658, Y 61,560).

$825* *"La Mujer", 1987,* s., t., d., Dixon Collection, (11-16-92, Butterfield, #5980, illus.), 8⅞ x 12⅜ in., (225.8 x 314.9 mm.), photograph, gelatin silver print (BP 543, DM 1315, FR 4431, Y 102,599).

GARDY, Artigas J.
$56* *"Scene De Vie Courante",* s., #12/80, (10-18-92, Pescheteau, #155), 23⅝ x 29¹⁵⁄₁₆ in., (60 x 76 cm.), lithograph in colors on wove (BP 34, DM 83, FR 281, Y 6687).

GARLAND, R. (after)
$14* *"Norwich Cathedral",* engraved by B. Winkles, (02-05-93, G.A. Key, #67), 6 x 4 in., (15.2 x 10.2 cm.), b/w engraving (BP 10, DM 23, FR 78, Y 1742).

GARNERAY, Ambroise Louis (after)
$3300* *Vue De New York, Prise De Weahawk (Stokes C. 1834-E-38, D. 433), c. 1834,* by Sigismond Himely, proof before letters, pub. Basset, wide margins, soiling, foxing, tears, losses, defects, (01-22-93, Christie-NY, #307, illus.), plate 16⅜ x 20⅜ in., (416 x 518 mm.), aquatint on wove (BP 2159, DM 5247, FR 17,751, Y 413,016).

GARNETT, William   b. 1916
$1725* *Day Off, Fisherman's Wharf, San Francisco", 1938,* s., t., photog.'s stamp, (05-23-93, Butterfield, #3420, illus.), 11 x 10½ in., photograph, gelatin silver print (BP 1123, DM 2820, FR 9494, Y 190,671).

BI   *Selected Images: "Hills, San Ardo, California", "Sand Bars, ColoradoRiver" and "Butte, Marble Canyon, Arizona": Three,* s., t., d. by photog., (c) stamp, 1954 and 1975, p.l., est. $2/3,000, (04-06-93, Sotheby-NY, #466, illus.), 8¾ x 7 in., photograph.

BI   *"Zuni Boy", 1938,* s., t., photog.'s stamp, est. $1/1,500, (05-23-93, Butterfield, #3421, illus.), 13 x 10 in., photograph, gelatin silver print.

GARNIER
$460* *Sevres Porcelain, 1870: Eight,* (04-07-93, Sotheby-Arcade, #154), sight 9½ x 13 in., (24.1 x 33 cm.), lithograph (BP 304, DM 744, FR 2518, Y 52,261).

GAROUSTE, Gerard
BI   *Les Droits De L'Homme,* s., 28/100, 675 x 970mm, sh 770 x 1150mm, est. FF2,400/2,800, (06-28-93, Loudmer, #249), black etching and aquatint on Arche wove.

GARRARD, George (after)
$165* *A View From The East End Of The Brewery, Chiswell Street,* by William Ward, tears, other defects, (06-16-93, Bonhams-Chelsea, #387), image 17¼ x 21¼ in., (43.8 x 54 cm.), mezzotint (BP 110, DM 274, FR 919, Y 17,598).

BI   *A View From The East-End Of The Brewery, Chiswell Street,* by William Ward, tears, defects, est. BP1/200, (01-21-93, Bonhams-Chelsea, #142), image 17¼ x 21¼ in., (43.8 x 55.2 cm.), mezzotint.

GARRETT, Edmund H.   American 1853-1929
$11* *Near Mattakeeset,* margins, (05-22-93, Collins, #126), 4⅞ x 8⅞ in., (12.4 x 22.5 cm.), etching (BP 7, DM 18, FR 60, Y 1213).

$17* *The Wayside Inn,* margins, plate s., (05-22-93, Collins, #53), 3⅞ x 6⅛ in., (9.8 x 15.6 cm.), etching (BP 11, DM 28, FR 93, Y 1874).

GARRETT, Thomas Balfour
$2594* *The Blue Door,* s. Tom Garrett, (08-11-92, L. Joel, #70, illus.), 9¼ x 12⅜ in., (23.5 x 31.5 cm.), monotype (BP 1348, DM 3807, FR 12,893, Y 332,181, A$ 3520).

BI   *The Clearing,* s. Tom Garrett, est. $2,4/2,600, (08-11-92, L. Joel, #270), 7½ x 10⁷⁄₁₆ in., (19 x 26.5 cm.), monotype.

$1621* *Depot,* s. Tom Garrett, i. twice, (08-11-92, L. Joel, #195, illus.), 9⅟₁₆ x 14⅜ in., (23 x 36.5 cm.), monotype (BP 842, DM 2379, FR 8057, Y 207,581, A$ 2200).

$1459* *Huon Valley,* s., i. twice, (08-11-92, L. Joel, #158), 7⅞ x 7⅞ in., (20 x 20 cm.), monotype (BP 758, DM 2141, FR 7251, Y 186,836, A$ 1980).

$2027* *In The Front Yard,* s. Tom Garrett, (08-11-92, L. Joel, #234), 10¼ x 13⅜ in., (26 x 34 cm.), monotype (BP 1053, DM 2975, FR 10,075, Y 259,572, A$ 2750).

$2756* *Landlocked,* s. Tom Garrett, i., (08-11-92, L. Joel, #121), 9⅟₁₆ x 11⅝ in., (23 x 29.5 cm.), monotype (BP 1432, DM 4045, FR 13,698, Y 352,926, A$ 3740).

$1784* *On The Edge Of The Lake,* s. Tom Garrett, (08-11-92, L. Joel, #257), 11⁷⁄₁₆ x 13⅜ in., (29 x 34 cm.), monotype (BP 927, DM 2618, FR 8867, Y 228,454, A$ 2420).

$2837* *The Paper Man,* s. Tom Garrett, i. w/t. twice, (08-11-92, L. Joel, #236, illus.), 11¼ x 14³⁄₁₆ in., (28.5 x 36 cm.), monotype (BP 1474, DM 4163, FR 14,100, Y 363,299, A$ 3850).

$2432* *Placid Stream,* s. Tom Garrett, (08-11-92, L. Joel, #170, illus.), 10¹³/₁₆ x 18⁵/₁₆ in., (27.5 x 46.5 cm.), monotype (BP 1264, DM 3569, FR 12,087, Y 311,436, A$ 3300).

$2027* *Road To Nowhere,* s. Tom Garrett, i. w/t. twice, (08-11-92, L. Joel, #280), 10¼ x 10¼ in., (26 x 26 cm.), monotype (BP 1053, DM 2975, FR 10,075, Y 259,572, A$ 2750).

$3243* *Spell,* s. Tom Garrett, i. w/t. twice, (08-11-92, L. Joel, #284), 8⁷/₁₆ x 13⁹/₁₆ in., (21.5 x 34.5 cm.), monotype (BP 1685, DM 4759, FR 16,118, Y 415,290, A$ 4400).

$3081* *Subway,* s. Tom Garrett, i. w/t. twice, (08-11-92, L. Joel, #206, illus.), 10⅝ x 12 in., (27 x 30.5 cm.), monotype (BP 1601, DM 4522, FR 15,313, Y 394,545, A$ 4180).

BI *Trek,* s. Tom Garrett, i. w/t. twice, est. $3/3,500, (08-11-92, L. Joel, #177, illus.), 9¼ x 10¹³/₁₆ in., (23.5 x 27.5 cm.), monotype.

GARRETT & NICKERSON

BI *"Sketches Of Camp Boone. The First Encampment Of The Kentucky StateGuard: Held Near Louisville, From August 23rd To August 30th, 1860. Also, Photographic Views Of The Camp, And Portraits Of The General's Staff",* Louisville, Photographists, pub. G.T. Shaw, for Garrett & Nickerson,1860, est. $8/10,000, (10-15-92, Sotheby-NY, #7, illus.), large, approx. 5⅞ x 7⅞ in., (14.9 x 20 cm.), photograph, 20 salt prints.

GARRETTO

$302* *Lord, 1950,* Alfieri and Lacroix S.A., A cond., (08-06-92, Swann, #137, illus.), 12¼ x 9¼ in., (31.1 x 23.5 cm.), (BP 158, DM 446, FR 1507, Y 38,520).

$385* *Olimpic, 1937,* Boggeri, A cond., (08-06-92, Swann, #136, illus.), 13 x 9¼ in., (33 x 23.5 cm.), (BP 201, DM 569, FR 1921, Y 49,107).

GARRIC, Fernand

$120* *Les Marraines Du Siecle, 1902,* Paris, Affiches F. Garric, cond. B+, (06-11-93, Boisgirard, #76), 37 x 25⁹/₁₆ in., (94 x 65 cm.), poster (BP 79, DM 195, FR 658, Y 12,732).

GARUTTI, Alberto

$618* *Relativita Come Condizione Illimitante 1976,* s., d., t., (05-18-93, Auction Phila, #101), 30 x 158 in., photograph (BP 406, DM 998, FR 3366, Y 68,996, L 920).

GASKELL, Percival   British 1868-1934

$27 *Lakeland Scene,* s., (10-09-92, G.A. Key, #92), 4¾ x 7 in., (12.1 x 17.8 cm.), etching (BP 16, DM 40, FR 136, Y 3293).

BI *Landscape Scenes: Six,* margins, good cond., (06-30-93, Sotheby-London, #303), etching and aquatints w/etching on various papers.

GASPARNETTA, G.

$4517* *Alman Felice, Milano,* p. L. Simondeiti, creases, repair, defects, backed on linen, laid onboard, (05-07-93, Christie-S. Ken, #83, illus.), 48½ x 35 in., (123.2 x 88.9 cm.), color lithograph (BP 2860, DM 7142, FR 24,065, Y 497,357).

GASSER, Bruno   b. 1947

$147* *Erinnerung An Gras, 1984,* #7/50, s., d., (11-13-92, Koller, #5326), 19¹¹/₁₆ x 23⅝ in., (50 x 60 cm.), lithograph (BP 95, DM 231, FR 778, Y 18,245, SF 208).

GASTEIGER, A. (after)

$67* *Still Life Of Flowers,* (11-19-92, Bonhams-Chelsea, #128), image 18¼ x 11 in., (46.4 x 27.9 cm.), color reproduction (BP 44, DM 107, FR 360, Y 8332).

GATIER, A.   French c. 1930

$315* *Reges Treiben Auf Einem Pariser Platz,* s., (05-08-93, Schloss Ahlden, #2841), 10⁷/₁₆ x 18⅛ in., (26.5 x 46 cm.), color etching on copper print paper (BP 206, DM 506, FR 1707, Y 35,199).

GAUERMANN, Friedrich   1807-1862

BI *Die Steinadler Bei Dem Verenden Hirsch (Andresen 23),* est. DM 250, (12-04-92, Bassenge, #6809), 10½ x 13¼ in., (26.7 x 33.6 cm.), etching.

GAUG, Margaret A.

$248* *"Anthony And Cleopatra", "Brunhilde And Wotan", "Robinhood", Samson And Delilah", and "Venus And Cupid": Five,* each s., t., i., margins, good cond., 3 w/light-stain-

ing, surface soiling, (02-24-93, Butterfield, #2824), etching on wove (BP 173, DM 403, FR 1365, Y 29,101).

GAUGENGIGL, Ignatz M.   German/American 1855/56-1932

$154* *"The Loafer" (Library Of Congress No. 7), 1888,* s., remarqued proof, good cond., (10-31-92, Cleveland, #134), 12¼ x 9⅞ in., (31.1 x 25.1 cm.), etching on Japan (BP 99, DM 237, FR 804, Y 19,076).

$22* *Mischief,* margins, plate s., (05-22-93, Collins, #123), 8¾ x 6½ in., (22.2 x 16.5 cm.), etching (BP 14, DM 36, FR 120, Y 2426).

GAUGUIN, Paul   French 1848-1903

$1840* *Baigneuses Bretonnes (Mongan, Kornfeld, Joachim 4), 1889,* pub. Vollard after 1900, wide margins, surface split in image, light-staining, foxing, staining, time staining, (05-11-93, Christie-NY, #193), borderline 9¼ x 8 in., (235 x 203 mm.), lithograph on simili-Japan (BP 1175, DM 2899, FR 9766, Y 202,398).

$8469* *Baigneuses Bretonnes, 1889,* from "Dessins lithographiques" series, s. in pl., (05-15-93, Loudmer, #307, illus.), 9⅝ x 7⅞ in., (245 x 200 mm.), zincograph on yellow wove (BP 5507, DM 13,622, FR 45,778, Y 938,809).

$3177* *Le Calvaire Breton (Agostini-Lari 49; Guerin 68 I), 1895-1903,* mono., num., (12-04-92, Bassenge, #6810, illus.), 6¹/₁₆ x 8¹⁵/₁₆ in., (15.4 x 22.7 cm.), woodcut on handmade Japan (BP 2038, DM 5060, FR 17,164, Y 396,629).

$26,629* *Le Calvaire Breton (Mongan; Kornfeld; Joachim 50/B), 1898-1899,* ink mono. P, #22, (06-25-93, Kornfeld, #38, illus.), print and sheet size 5⅞ x 8¹⁵/₁₆ in., (14.9 x 22.7 cm.), woodcut on Japan de pelure (BP 18,011, DM 45,334, FR 152,689, Y 2,822,663, SF 40,250).

$660* *La Femme Aux Figues (G. 88, K. 25), 1894-5,* full margins, good cond., (02-24-93, Butterfield, #2930), 10½ x 16½ in., (267 x 419 mm.), etching, lavis, & soft-ground etching on Arches laid (BP 460, DM 1071, FR 3632, Y 77,447).

$412* *La Femme Aux Figues (Kornfled 25/II),* full margins, (03-31-93, Briest, #E168), sh 16⁹/₁₆ x 22⁷/₁₆ in., (42 x 57 cm.), 10⅝ x 16⁹/₁₆ in., (42 x 57 cm.), black etching on laid (BP 272, DM 663, FR 2251, Y 47,378).

BI *La Femme Aux Figues (M. Guerin 88, E. Mongan, E.W. Kornfeld et H. Joachim 25), c. 1894,* second of 10, #2/10, full margins, (05-06-93, Laurin, #32, illus.), etching on Rives wove.

$5498* *La Femme Aux Figues (Mongan-Kornfeld-Joachim 25/I/C), 1894,* num., blindstamp, (06-23-93, Kornfeld, #352, illus.), etching on simili-Japan (BP 3735, DM 9303, FR 31,292, Y 598,976, SF 8280).

BI *Femmes, Animaux Et Feuillages (Mongan, Kornfeld, Joachim 43), 1898,* num. 38 (crossed out), p. by the artist, margins, good cond., prov.,est. BP 9,0/11,000, (12-03-92, Sotheby-London, #312, illus.), 6⅜ x 11¾ in., (162 x 298 mm.), woodcut on Japon pelure, laid on wove.

$24,347* *Femmes, Animaux Et Feuillages (Mongan; Kornfeld; Joachim 43/II/A), 1898,* mono. in wood PG, No. 19, (06-25-93, Kornfeld, #39, illus.), woodcut 6⁷/₁₆ x 12 in., (16.3 x 30.5 cm.), woodcut on Japan (BP 16,467, DM 41,449, FR 139,604, Y 2,580,772, SF 36,800).

$60,867* *Mahna No Varua Ino. - Le Diable Parle (Mongan; Kornfeld; Joachim 19/IV/D), 1893-1894,* (06-25-93, Kornfeld, #37, illus.), 7¹⁵/₁₆ x 13¹⁵/₁₆ in., (20.3 x 35.5 cm.), color woodcut on thick Japan (BP 41,168, DM 103,621, FR 349,008, Y 6,451,876, SF 92,000).

BI *Manao Tupapau (Elle Pense Au Revenant-L'Esprit Des Morts Veille) (M./K./J. 23), 1894,* s., num., pub. Andre Marty, margins, crease through corner of image,handling creases, defects, good cond., est. $25/30,000, (05-13-93, Sotheby-NY, #560, illus.), 7⅛ x 10⅝ in., (181 x 270 mm.), sh 12¾ x 18⅞ in., (181 x 270 mm.), lithograph on chine volant.

BI *Manao Tupapau (G. 50; M./K./J. 23), 1894,* pub. A. marty, wide margins, foxing, light-staining, laid, est. BP 6/10,000, (12-01-92, Christie-London, #381, illus.), L. 7⅛ x 10¹¹/₁₆ in., (181 x 272 mm.), lithograph on wove.

$3450* *Maruru (Guerin 92; Mongan/Kornfeld/Joachim 22/E), 1893-94,* s. artist's son, i., #92, 100 p., pub. Pola Gauguin, 1921, full margins, good cond., foxing, printer's crease, lower corners re-attached, tape stain, repaired tears, (02-11-93, Sotheby-NY, #144, illus.), 8¹/₁₆ x 13¹⁵/₁₆ in., (204 x 355 mm.), woodcut on chine volant (BP 2434, DM 5715, FR 19,339, Y 415,913).

BI *Noa Noa (M./K./J. 13), 1893-94,* p. Louis Roy, 1894, margins, good cond., light-stain, creases, soiling, printer's ink, tack holes, est. $30/40,000, (05-13-93, Sotheby-NY, #558, illus.), 14 x 8⅛ in., (357 x 206 mm.), 15¾ x 9⅞ in., (357 x 206 mm.), woodcut in black, yellow, ochre and red, on heavy cream simili-Japan.

BI *Noa Noa (M./K./J. 13/III/E), 1893-94,* s. by artist's son, i. Paul Gauguin fait Pola Gauguin imp., num. No 7, p., pub. Pola Gauguin, 1921, full margins, good cond., water stains, crease,printer's crease, est. $8/12,000, (05-13-93, Sotheby-NY, #559, illus.), 14 x 8⅛ in., (355 x 205 mm.), woodcut on chine volant.

$27,390* *Portrait De Stephane Mallarme (Mongan; Kornfeld; Joachim 12/II/B/b),1891,* num., Charles Morice, Paul Gaugin, 1919, (06-25-93, Kornfeld, #36, illus.), plate 7⁵/₁₆ x 5¹¹/₁₆ in., etching on hand-made Japan (BP 18,526, DM 46,629, FR 157,053, Y 2,903,328, SF 41,400).

$275* *"Portrait Of Mallarme",* posthumous p., plate s., (02-11-93, Boos, #415), image 7⁵/₁₆ x 5¹¹/₁₆ in., (185 x 145 mm.), paper 13¹⁵/₁₆ x 10³/₁₆ in., (185 x 145 mm.), etching (BP 194, DM 456, FR 1541, Y 33,153).

$18,400* *Set Of "10 Zincographies" (Mongan/Kornfeld/Joachin 1-4, 6-11), 1889,* lacking Les Cigales et les Fourmis-Souvenir de la Martinique (M./K./J. 5), from 2nd edit., pub. Vollard, after 1900, full margins, good cond., handling creases, defect; soiling, skinned spot; creases, (05-13-93, Sotheby-NY, #557, illus.), each sh approx. 18¾ x 12⅝ in., (475 x 320 mm.), zincograph on simili-Japan (BP 12,080, DM 29,711, FR 100,218, Y 2,054,259).

$1312* *Soyez Amoureuse, Vous Serez Heureuse (E.W. Kornfeld 55),* large margins, (02-03-93, Ader Tajan, #153), 6⅜ x 10⅞ in., (16.2 x 27.6 cm.), woodcut on thin Japan (BP 916, DM 2160, FR 7326, Y 163,204).

$382* *Te Atua (M.-K.-J. 53/II/D), 1899,* (06-23-93, Kornfeld, #353), woodcut on Japan (BP 260, DM 646, FR 2174, Y 41,617, SF 575).

$2574* *Te Po (Kornfeld 21D), 1893-94,* p., s., num. by Pola Gauguin, 1921, margins, good cond., defects, (06-30-93, Sotheby-London, #444, illus.), sh 10⅝ x 16⅛ in., (270 x 410 mm.), woodcut on Chine (BP 1725, DM 4390, FR 14,810, Y 275,796).

$4400* *Te Po (Mongan, Kornfeld, Joachim 21), 1893-4,* from Paul Gauguin, 10 Traesnit, Copenhagen, Chr, Cato, 1921, i. PaulGauguin fait and Pola Gauguin imp by artist's son, #7, crease, very good cond., (11-09-92, Christie-NY, #94, illus.), 206 x 358 in., (523.2 x 909.3 cm.), woodcut on Chine (BP 2909, DM 7024, FR 23,732, Y 546,041).

$2271* *Tepo (Tahitisk: Lang Nat), 1894,* from Noa Noa series, (11-14-92, Bukowskis, #26, illus.), woodcut (BP 1493, DM 3622, FR 12,203, Y 283,414, DK 13,800).

GAUGUIN, Paul (after)

$18 *"Contes Barbares",* (06-11-93, G.A. Key, #24), 19 x 13 in., (48.3 x 33 cm.), colored print (BP 12, DM 29, FR 99, Y 1910).

$404* *Femme Couche Sous Un Arbre (E.W.K. supplement B VI),* large margins, (02-03-93, Ader Tajan, #154), 5 x 8⁷/₁₆ in., (12.7 x 21.5 cm.), woodcut on thin Japan (BP 282, DM 665, FR 2256, Y 50,255).

GAUL, August 1869-1921

BI *"Die Lugenflote" (Sohne Bd. 1, 13410-2), 1914,* from Kreigszeit, est. DM 180-, (03-24-93, Venator/Hansten, #4491), 5⅜ x 9⅝ in., (13.7 x 24.4 cm.), chalk lithograph.

GAUL, Winfried b. 1928

$249* *Komposition, (19)58,* s., d., num., (12-01-92, Karl/Faber, #631), 22¹/₁₆ x 14³/₁₆ in., (56 x 36 cm.), color serigraph on wove (BP 165, DM 397, FR 1353, Y 31,001).

$299* *Komposition, (19)58,* s., d., num., (12-01-92, Karl/Faber, #632), 22¹/₁₆ x 14³/₁₆ in., (56 x 36 cm.), color serigraph on wove (BP 198, DM 477, FR 1624, Y 37,226).

GAULTIER, Leonard French 1561-c. 1641

BI *Das Jungste Gericht (Le Blanc 18),* after Michelangelo, est. DM 1,000, (06-10-93, Hauswedell/Nolt, #95), engraving.

$113* *Michelangelos Jungstes Gericht (Nagler Bd. 5, S. 313),* worn, (03-24-93, Venator/Hansten, #2525), pl. 12⁵/₁₆ x 9³/₁₆ in., (31.3 x 23.3 cm.), engraving (BP 77, DM 185, FR 628, Y 13,277).

GAUTIER DAGOTY

$1091* *"Madame Dubarry Et Son Negre Zamore",* trimmed margins, i., (03-22-93, Pescheteau, #15), color print (BP 735, DM 1789, FR 6081, Y 126,332).

GAUW, Gerrit Adriaensz c. 1590-1638

$253* *Die Ruinen Des Kastells Von Brederode Bei Haarlem (Hollstein Bd 11; S 234; Nr 357),* after H. Goltzius, foxed, (12-04-92, Bassenge, #6199), 9⅜ x 12¹⁵/₁₆ in., (23.8 x 33 cm.), etching (BP 162, DM 403, FR 1367, Y 31,586).

GAVARNI, G.S. Chevallier

$314* *"Les Actrices": Fourteen, "Les Artistes": Sixteen and "Politique De Femmes": Twenty,* some creased, stains, unequal margins, (06-16-93, Ader Tajan, #98), lithograph (BP 209, DM 521, FR 1749, Y 33,490).

GAVARNI, Paul French 1804-1866

$433* *Un Covage Civilize (Armelhault-Bocher 2273 I), 1839,* (12-04-92, Bassenge, #6811), 10⁷/₁₆ x 7½ in., (26.5 x 19 cm.), lithograph on wove (BP 278, DM 690, FR 2339, Y 54,057).

$458* *Masques Et Visages (Armelhaut-Bocher 1850-1899), 1857-1858: Fifty,* series Physionomies Parisiennes, (06-23-93, Kornfeld, #355), 15¹⁵/₁₆ x 11 in., (40.5 x 28 cm.), lithograph (BP 311, DM 775, FR 2607, Y 49,897, SF 690).

$5* *"Ou Vas-Tu Si Matin" (A. & B. 119 ii/ii) and "Nous Ferez-Vous L'Honneur" (A. & B. 241 iii/iii): Two,* pub. Charivari, text verso (Matin), good cond. (Matin)(05-15-93, Cleveland, #387), one 7¾ x 6⅛ in., (19.7 x 15.6 cm.), other 7⅞ x 6⅜ in., (19.7 x 15.6 cm.), lithograph (BP 3, DM 8, FR 27, Y 554).

GAVEAU, Pierre 20th cent.

BI *"Composition",* E.A., s., (01-28-93, Pescheteau, #148), 25³/₁₆ x 19¹¹/₁₆ in., (64 x 50 cm.), color lithograph on wove.

GAVER, Carroll D.

BI *Saturday Matinee, c. 1948,* s., t. recto; exhib. label, est. $1/1,500, (04-08-93, Christie-NY, #285, illus.), 19¾ x 15⅞ in., (50.2 x 40.3 cm.), photograph, gelatin silver print.

GAVIN, J.

$321* *Loie Fuller Theatre Des Arts, "La Tragedie De Salome",* (01-31-93, Morelle/Marchan, #29), 24¹³/₁₆ x 39⅜ in., (63 x 100 cm.), poster (BP 216, DM 517, FR 1748, Y 40,045).

GAYLOR, Julius F.

$110* *"Wall Street", 1900,* s., good cond., (02-07-93, Bakker, #88, illus.), plate 11½ x 7 in., (29.2 x 17.8 cm.), etching (BP 76, DM 182, FR 617, Y 13,688).

GAYLOR, Julius F. American 20th cent.

$275* *"MacDougal Alley", "Lower New York" And "New York Harbor And Skyline", 1934, c. 1934, 1930: Three,* all s. Julius F. Gaylor, first two t., each d., good cond., handlingmarks, tape residue, (03-12-93, Skinner, #23, illus.), approx. 8 x 6 in., (20.3 x 15.2 cm.), etching w/aquatint on wove (BP 192, DM 458, FR 1556, Y 32,410).

GAYMARD, M. Antoine

$71* *"The Dogana And Santa Maria Della Salute Venice",* after J.M.W. Turner, (03-10-93, Maynard, #641), 18 x 12½ in., (45.7 x 31.8 cm.), mezzotint (BP 50, DM 118, FR 401, Y 8388, C$ 88).

$80* *"Venice From The Canale Della Giudecca",* after J.M.W. Turner, (03-10-93, Maynard, #640), 18 x 12½ in., (45.7 x 31.8 cm.), mezzotint (BP 56, DM 133, FR 452, Y 9452, C$ 99).

GEARHART, Frances

$1100* *"After The First Rains" and "Above The Trail": Two,* each s., t., margins, good cond., light-staining, foxing, pin holes,stray printing ink, surface soiling, pencil notations, prop. Print Corner Coll.of Elizabeth and Charles Whitmore, (02-24-93, Butterfield, #2631), one 9 1/16 x 10 1/8 in., (230 x 257 mm.), other 12 x 10 in., (230 x 257 mm.), woodcuts in colors on Japan paper (BP 767, DM 1786, FR 6054, Y 129,078).

$1610* *"Austerity", "Splintered Crag" and "A Tatoosh Vista": Three,* s., t., margins, good cond., light-staining, surface soiling, pinholes, stray printing ink, notations, (05-19-93, Butterfield, #1814), smallest 10 1/4 x 7 9/16 in., (260 x 192 mm.), largest 14 13/16 x 11 in., (260 x 192 mm.), block print in colors on Japan (BP 1045, DM 2617, FR 8817, Y 178,235).

$1380* *"Away Beyond", "The Peach Orchard" and "This Joyous World": Three,* s.,t., 3rd one #5/50, margins, good cond., foxing, light-staining, surface soiling, pinholes, stray printing ink, notations, (05-19-93, Butterfield, #1805), one 11 1/8 x 10 7/16 in., (283 x 265 mm.), others 9 1/4 x 10 in., (283 x 265 mm.), block print in colors on Japan (BP 896, DM 2243, FR 7558, Y 152,773).

$1725* *"Chill December" and "Winter Is Near": Two,* s., t., margins, good cond., foxing, notations, light-staining, surface soiling, pinholes, stray printing ink, (05-19-93, Butterfield, #1808), one 10 x 9 in., (254 x 229 mm.), the other 12 1/16 x 11 1/4 in., (254 x 229 mm.), block print in colors on Japan (BP 1120, DM 2804, FR 9447, Y 190,966).

$633* *"Cinerarias", "Gailiardias", "Phlox", "A Sea Captain" and "The Gearharts": Four,* 1st 3 s., 1st and 4th t., 3rd num. 50, margins, good cond., light-staining, pinholes, stray printing ink, surface soiling, notations, (05-19-93, Butterfield, #1811), smallest 6 15/16 x 3 3/4 in., (176 x 95 mm.), largest 9 9/16 x 10 1/8 in., (176 x 95 mm.), block print in colors on Japan (BP 411, DM 1029, FR 3467, Y 70,076).

$660* *The Cloud,* s., t., margins, good cond., light-staining, pin holes, stray ink, surface soiling, pencil notations, prop. Print Corner Coll. of Elizabeth and Charles Whitmore, (02-24-93, Butterfield, #2827), 10 7/8 x 9 3/8 in., (276 x 238 mm.), woodcut in colors on Japan (BP 460, DM 1071, FR 3632, Y 77,447).

$920* *"Coast Line", "Point Lobos" and "The Wave": Three,* s., 1st and 3rd #50, margins, good cond., light-staining, stray printing ink, pinholes, notations, (05-19-93, Butterfield, #1807), smallest 7 11/16 x 4 1/2 in., (195 x 114 mm.), largest 8 x 4 5/8 in., (195 x 114 mm.), block print in colors on Japan (BP 597, DM 1495, FR 5038, Y 101,849).

$935* *The Day Is Young,* s., t., margins, good cond., stray printing ink, surface soiling, pinholes, pencil notations, prop. Print Corner Coll. of Elizabeth and Charles Whitmore, (02-24-93, Butterfield, #2828), 12 1/2 x 10 1/16 in., (318 x 256 mm.), woodcut in colors on Japan (BP 652, DM 1518, FR 5146, Y 109,716).

$920* *"Eucalyptus" and "Old Pine", 1936; 1937: Two,* s., t., margins, good cond., light-staining, surface soiling, pinholes, stray printing ink, notations, (05-19-93, Butterfield, #1810), one 11 5/16 x 9 1/16 in., (303 x 230 mm.), the other 11 9/16 x 10 in., (303 x 230 mm.), block print in colors on Japan (BP 597, DM 1495, FR 5038, Y 101,849).

$770* *Fish Market,* s., t., margins, good cond., light-staining, pin holes, surface soiling, pencil notations, prop. Print Corner Coll. of Elizabeth and Charles Whitmore, (02-24-93, Butterfield, #2829), 11 1/8 x 9 in., (283 x 229 mm.), woodcut in colors on Japan (BP 537, DM 1250, FR 4238, Y 90,354).

$978* *"In The Tatoosh Country", 1933, "Trail To Winter" and "Twilight Nears": Three,* s., t., large margins, good cond., light-staining, stray printing ink, pinholes, crease, notations, prop. Print Corner Coll. of Elizabeth and Charles Whitmore, (05-19-93, Butterfield, #1804), one 11 1/16 x 10 13/16 in., (281 x 275 mm.), others 9 1/8 x 5 in., (281 x 275 mm.), block print in colors on Japan (BP 635, DM 1590, FR 5356, Y 108,270).

$1495* *"Incoming Fog", "Low Tide" and "Rain Tomorrow": Three,* s., margins, good cond., light-staining, surface soiling, pinholes, stray printing ink, notations, (05-19-93, Butterfield, #1812), 10 1/16 x 11 1/16 in., (256 x 281 mm.), block print in colors on Japan (BP 970, DM 2430, FR 8187, Y 165,504).

$935* *Lake Tahoe,* s., t., margins, good cond., light-staining, pin holes, stray ink, surface soiling, pencil notations, prop. Print Corner Coll. of Elizabeth and Charles Whitmore, (02-24-93, Butterfield, #2826, illus.), 11 x 12 in., (279 x 305 mm.), woodcut in colors on Japan (BP 652, DM 1518, FR 5146, Y 109,716).

$1495* *"March Horizons", "Solitude" and "Snow Tonight": Three,* each s., t., margins, good cond., light-staining, surface soiling, pinholes, stray printing ink, (05-19-93, Butterfield, #1809, illus.), smallest 10 5/16 x 7 3/8 in., (278 x 187 mm.), largest 12 x 9 3/16 in., (278 x 187 mm.), block print in colors on Japan (BP 970, DM 2430, FR 8187, Y 165,504).

$770* *"Mt. Hood",* s. indistinctly, good cond., (02-07-93, Bakker, #199), image 6 x 4 in., (15.2 x 10.2 cm.), color woodblock print (BP 533, DM 1277, FR 4316, Y 95,819).

$978* *"Mt. Hood", "Old Baldy", "Snow, San Gabriel Range" and "Winter": Four,* s., 1st t., last 2 #50, margins, good cond., light-staining, surfacesoiling, pinholes, stray printing ink, notations, (05-19-93, Butterfield, #1806), smallest 6 1/16 x 4 in., (154 x 102 mm.), largest 6 15/16 x 4 1/16 in., (154 x 102 mm.), block print in colors on Japan (BP 635, DM 1590, FR 5356, Y 108,270).

$1100* *"New Moon" and "Winter Looks Down On Spring", 1920, 1932: Two,* each s., t., margins, good cond., light-staining, pin holes, stray printing ink, surface soiling, pencil notations, prop. Print Corner Coll. of Elizabeth and Charles Whitmore, (02-24-93, Butterfield, #2632), each 6 1/2 x 3 5/8 in., (165 x 92 mm.), woodcuts in colors on Japan paper (BP 767, DM 1786, FR 6054, Y 129,078).

$358* *Pirate Hoard, The Gearharts,* t., margins, good cond., creases, surface soiling pin holes, pencil notation, (02-24-93, Butterfield, #2825), 8 x 7 in., (203 x 178 mm.), woodcut in colors on Japan (BP 250, DM 581, FR 1970, Y 42,009).

$1725* *"Red Rock Canyon", 1936, "Joshua Tree" and "Desert Barrier": Three,* s., 1st and 3rd t., 2nd #50, margins, good cond., light-staining, pinholes, stray printing ink, notations, (05-19-93, Butterfield, #1813, illus.), smallest 6 1/2 x 4 1/2 in., (165 x 114 mm.), largest 12 1/16 x 9 5/16 in., (165 x 114 mm.), block print in colors on Japan (BP 1120, DM 2804, FR 9447, Y 190,966).

$330* *"Rincon", c. 1925,* s., very good cond., (03-28-93, Bakker, #26), image 10 1/8 x 9 in., (25.7 x 22.9 cm.), wood block (BP 222, DM 538, FR 1830, Y 38,408).

$715* *The Sand Spit,* s., t., margins, good cond., light-staining, pinholes, stray printingink, creases, surface soiling, notations, prop. Print Corner Coll. of Elizabethand Charles Whitmore, (02-24-93, Butterfield, #2633), 8 3/4 x 11 7/8 in., (222 x 302 mm.), woodcut in colors on Japan (BP 499, DM 1161, FR 3935, Y 83,900).

GEARHART, Frances American 1869-1958

$1430* *"Incoming Fog",* s. Frances H. Gearhart, t., fine cond., mat staining, tape, creasing/wrinkling, (01-02-93, Skinner, #74, illus.), 10 x 11 in., (25.4 x 27.9 cm.), color woodblock on Japan paper (BP 953, DM 2343, FR 7998, Y 179,288).

GECCELLI, Johannes b. 1925

$397* *Abstrakte Komposition, 1967,* s., d., num., (11-28-92, Schoppmann, #551), 25 5/16 x 19 1/8 in., (64.3 x 48.5 cm.), color lithograph on handmade (BP 262, DM 632, FR 2147, Y 49,409).

GEERLINGS, Gerald K. American b. 1897

$1320* *Electrical Building At Night, Century Of Progress Fair, Chicago, 1933,* s., p. Frank Nankivell, pub. num. 24 for the Chicago Society of Etchers, (12-08-92, Swann, #120, illus.), 12 x 8 7/8 in., (30.5 x 22.5 cm.), etching (BP 827, DM 2055, FR 7006, Y 163,609).

$1650* *Grand Canal, America, Electrical Building At Night, 1933,* s., pub. Chicago Society of Etchers, (05-16-93, Hindman, #555, illus.), 11 7/8 x 8 7/8 in., (30.2 x 22.5 cm.), etching (BP 1073, DM 2654, FR 8919, Y 182,907).

$770* *The Rising Generation, 1928,* s., t., hinged to mat, very good cond., (12-04-92, Doyle, #103), 9 1/4 x 7 in., (235 x 178 mm.), drypoint (BP 494, DM 1226, FR 4160, Y 96,130).

GEFFELS, Frans c. 1615-ac. 1659-1671
BI *Die Zigeuner Bie Dem Kochfeuer (Wurzbach, Hollstein 3),* prov., from series of 7 sheets w/landscapes, ruins, architecture andpeople, est. DM 1,500, (12-04-92, Bassenge, #6200), 6⅛ x 4¹⁵⁄₁₆ in., (15.5 x 12.5 cm.), etching.

GEHR, Herbert b. 1910
BI *Construction On Antonio Gaudi's Cathedral, Sagrada Familia, Barcelona, c. 1935,* stamp, label, est. $1,5/2,500, (04-06-93, Sotheby-NY, #370, illus.), 7¼ x 9⅜ in., photograph.
BI *Einstein's Last Speech In Germany, 1932,* notations, est. $1,2/1,800, (10-14-92, Swann, #307, illus.), 6½ x 9 in., (16.5 x 22.9 cm.), photograph, silver print.
BI *Harlem Jazz Band, 1943,* credit stamp twice, est. $1,2/1,500, (10-13-92, Christie-NY, #218, illus.), 11 x 10¾ in., (27.9 x 27.3 cm.), photograph, gelatin silver print.
BI *Harlem Street Performers, 1943,* photog. credit stamp, est. $1,5/2,500, (04-06-93, Sotheby-NY, #369, illus.), 10⅞ x 10⅝ in., photograph.
BI *Harlem Study: West 125th Street, 1943,* photog.'s credit stamp, est. $1,5/2,500, (10-15-92, Sotheby-NY, #464, illus.), 10½ x 13½ in., (26.7 x 34.3 cm.), photograph, gelatin silver print.
BI *Mrs. Roosevelt And Judge Hurbert T. Delaney, Harlem, 1943,* credit stamps, t., est. $1/1,500, (04-08-93, Christie-NY, #287, illus.), 7¾ x 7⅝ in., (19.7 x 19.4 cm.), photograph, gelatin silver print.
BI *Shop Near Yellow Knife, Canada, 1938,* credit stamp, est. $800/1,200, (04-08-93, Christie-NY, #288, illus.), 7⅜ x 8¾ in., (18.7 x 22.2 cm.), photograph, gelatin silver print.
$1320* *Surreal Mask, c. 1940,* prov., (10-13-92, Christie-NY, #217, illus.), 12¼ x 9¾ in., (31.1 x 24.8 cm.), photograph, gelatin silver print (BP 769, DM 1934, FR 6570, Y 160,058).
BI *Temptation Never Takes A Vacation, Harlem, c. 1943,* credit stamps, est. $1/1,500, (04-08-93, Christie-NY, #286, illus.), 9½ x 7½ in., (24.1 x 19.1 cm.), photograph, gelatin silver print.

GEIGENBERGER, Otto 1881-1946
$498* *Vorgebirgslandschaft, 1918,* s., d., glue stained, (12-01-92, Karl/Faber, #636), 7¹¹⁄₁₆ x 9⅝ in., (19.5 x 24.5 cm.), water colored linocut (BP 329, DM 794, FR 2705, Y 62,002).

GEIGER, Raimund 1889-1968
BI *Hexensabbat (Das Fruhe Plakat III, 974), c. 1910,* p. Dr. C. Wolf u. Sohn, fold marks, tears, creases, tape, est. BP 3/5,000, (05-20-93, Christie-London, #496, illus.), sheet 44 x 33½ in., (111.8 x 85.1 cm.), lithograph in red, green and black.

GEIGER, Rupprecht German b. 1908
$1444* *"Farbsequenzen", c. 1965: Six,* s., num., Berlin, Stolpe-pub., (11-28-92, Grisebach, #521, illus.), 24⁵⁄₁₆ x 24⅜ in., (61.8 x 61.9 cm.), colored serigraph on cardboard (BP 953, DM 2300, FR 7810, Y 179,714).
$221* *Gelber Kreis, c. 1970,* s., num., (12-05-92, Bassenge, #7185), screenprint neon yellow on cardboard (BP 138, DM 345, FR 1174, Y 27,382).
$289* *Ohne Titel (WV 128), 1968,* s., num., (11-28-92, Schoppmann, #553), 22¹³⁄₁₆ x 19¹¹⁄₁₆ in., (58 x 50 cm.), serigraph in orange and yellow (BP 191, DM 460, FR 1563, Y 35,968).

GEIGER, Willi German 1878-1971
BI *(Portrait),* s., #8/30, margins, defects in margins, paper discoloration, Late Gerhard Brauer Coll., est. Dfl. 5/700, (05-27-93, Sotheby-Amstrdm, #822), 15¾ x 13¾ in., (400 x 350 mm.), etching on wove.
$101* *Stierkampfer, 1912,* plate mono., s., d., wear, (09-25-92, Granier, #2853), sheet 19 x 12½ in., (48.3 x 31.7 cm.), etching on hand-made Japan (BP 59, DM 150, FR 506, Y 12,191).
$155* *Stierkampfszene,* plate s., d. Willi Geiger 1912; s. Geiger, #36/40, foxing, (03-24-93, Venator/Hansten, #4493), pl. 7¾ x 12½ in., (19.7 x 31.7 cm.), drypoint (BP 105, DM 253, FR 862, Y 18,212).

GEISER, Karl 1898-1957
BI *Daniel Mit Zuavenmutze (Naef 9), 1942,* s., (10-14-92, Germann, #517), 14⁷⁄₁₆ x 10⅛ in., (367 x 257 mm.), etching.

GEISSLER, Paul French b. 1891
$55* *Betsy Ross House,* margins, s. Paul Geissler, (10-24-92, Collins, #9), 12 x 8½ in., (30.5 x 21.6 cm.), etching (BP 34, DM 84, FR 285, Y 6707).
$220* *"Betsy Ross House, Phila.", "Carpenter Hall, Phila.", "Girard Trust Cmpany, Phil.", "Broad Street, Phila.": Four,* (11-12-92, Freemn/Fine Art, #75), various sizes from 14 x 9 in., (35.6 x 22.9 cm.), to 12 x 8 in., (35.6 x 22.9 cm.), etchings (BP 144, DM 349, FR 1176, Y 27,278).
$17* *European City View, 1920,* s., (11-13-92, DuMouchelle, #369), 8 x 8 in., (20.3 x 20.3 cm.), etching (BP 11, DM 27, FR 90, Y 2110).

GEKKO
$50* *"Ladies Viewing Flowers",* OBAN TATE, soiling, (05-07-93, Goldberg, #1350), woodblock (BP 32, DM 79, FR 266, Y 5505).
$17* *"Water Spout",* 20th cent., seal mark, (06-11-93, DuMouchelle, #2362), 9¼ x 9¾ in., (23.5 x 24.8 cm.), color woodblock print (BP 11, DM 28, FR 93, Y 1804).

GEKKO, Ogata ac. c. 1900
BI *Samurai Mit Gezucktem Schwert,* est. SC 7/8,000, (04-27-93, Dorotheum, #227, illus.), 9¼ x 13⅜ in., (23.5 x 34 cm.), color woodcut.
BI *"Urashimataro",* Format Oban, est. SC 3/4,000, (04-27-93, Dorotheum, #239), 9⅝ x 13½ in., (24.5 x 34.3 cm.), woodcut.
$403* *"Vogel Auf Bluten",* s., Format Oban, (04-27-93, Dorotheum, #187, illus.), 9⅞ x 15¹⁄₁₆ in., (25.1 x 38.3 cm.), color woodcut (BP 256, DM 638, FR 2159, Y 45,164, SC 4480).

GELEE, Claude (called Claude le LORRAIN)
$880* *Liber Veritatis: Or A Collection Of Prints After The Original Designs... In The Collection Of His Grace The Duke Of Devonshire,* engravings after Claude by Richard Earlom, p. W. Blumer and Co., pub. Boydell and Co., (1777?-1819), folio, vol. 3 (1819), (12-12-92, Weschler, #186), engraving (BP 564, DM 1386, FR 4752, Y 108,897).

GELHAY, Edouard French b. 1856
$110* *Au Champ De Mars: Le Clou D'Exposition De 1900 "Tour Du Monde Anime",* good cond., restorations, (03-13-93, Laurin, #22), 75¹⁵⁄₁₆ x 54½ in., (193 x 138.5 cm.), (BP 77, DM 183, FR 623, Y 12,964).

GELIG
$68* *"Village Au Bord De La Mer" and "Regate", 1990: Two,* first, s.; second, s., d., ded., (06-28-93, Loudmer, #46), first 18⅞ x 24¹³⁄₁₆ in., (480 x 630 mm.), second 18⅞ x 26³⁄₁₆ in., (480 x 630 mm.), (BP 46, DM 116, FR 389, Y 7215).

GEN PAUL French 1895-1975
$145* *"Chevaux", "Sans Titre" and "Sans Titre": Three,* first, s., 96/160, dusty; second and third, artist's proof, (06-28-93, Loudmer, #48), smaller 17⁵⁄₁₆ x 13⁹⁄₁₆ in., (440 x 345 mm.), larger 21⅝ x 13⅜ in., (440 x 345 mm.), all color lithographs on Arches wove (BP 97, DM 246, FR 830, Y 15,385).
$70* *"Montmartre Et Moulin Rouge": Two,* HC 21/25, HC 2/25, s., (04-04-93, Pescheteau, #218), 13¾ x 11 in., (35 x 28 cm.), violet lithographs (BP 46, DM 113, FR 382, Y 7970).
$70* *"Musiciens": Two,* EA 5/25, HC 2/25, s., (04-04-93, Pescheteau, #217), 14³⁄₁₆ x 11 in., (36 x 28 cm.), lithographs on wove (BP 46, DM 113, FR 382, Y 7970).
$157* *Portrait D'Homme,* #53/65, s., good margins, (06-16-93, Ader Tajan, #100), 5⅞ x 3⁹⁄₁₆ in., (15 x 9 cm.), black lithograph on mauve ground on tinted paper (BP 105, DM 261, FR 875, Y 16,745).

GENDALL, J. (after)
$153* *Kew Palace, As Seen From Brentford,* by T. Sutherland, pub. R. Ackermann, January, 1819, foxing, (04-22-93, Bonhams-Chelsea, #140), image 11½ x 16½ in., (29.2 x

41.9 cm.), aquatint w/hand coloring (BP 99, DM 246, FR 829, Y 16,822).

GENERALIC, Ivan b. 1914

$131* *Landschaft Mit Bauer Und Schimmel,* #82/100, s., (11-13-92, Koller, #5327), 21⅝ x 24$\frac{13}{16}$ in., (55 x 63 cm.), color serigraph on wove (BP 85, DM 206, FR 693, Y 16,259, SF 185).

$147* *Weisser Hirsch,* #200/260, s., (11-13-92, Koller, #5328), 23¼ x 25$\frac{13}{16}$ in., (59 x 65.5 cm.), color serigraph on wove (BP 95, DM 231, FR 778, Y 18,245, SF 208).

GENIN, Rabert 1884-1943

$233* *Junge Frau Mit Obstschale,* s., num., (09-25-92, Granier, #2854), sheet 15$\frac{15}{16}$ x 12 in., (40.5 x 30.5 cm.), etching on wove (BP 136, DM 345, FR 1168, Y 28,123).

GENIN, Robert 1884-1939

$700* *"Figurliche Kompositionen": Twenty,* pub. Delphin, s., num., signs of wear, (12-01-92, Karl/Faber, #643), 17$\frac{11}{16}$ x 15¾ in., (45 x 40 cm.), lithograph on thin Seidenjapan (BP 463, DM 1116, FR 3802, Y 87,151).

GENKINGER, Fritz b. 1934

$86* *Geometrische Komposition,* s., num., (09-25-92, Granier, #2856), sheet 24$\frac{13}{16}$ x 18½ in., (63.1 x 47 cm.), color serigraph on offset board (BP 50, DM 127, FR 431, Y 10,380).

GENTHE, Arnold 1856-1915

$1430* *Anna Pavlowa, (As I Remember, facing p. 177),* mounted, s., i. by photog., t. in unidentified hand, early 1900's, probably p. 1930's, (10-15-92, Sotheby-NY, #114, illus.), 12⅝ x 9⅞ in., (32.1 x 25.1 cm.), photograph, gelatin silver print (BP 875, DM 2129, FR 7219, Y 171,566).

BI *Childe Hassam, East Hampton,* notations, 1930s, est. $1/1,500, (04-07-93, Swann, #469, illus.), 12½ x 9½ in., photograph, silver print.

$1320* *Chinatown,* mounted, s., i. by photog., early 1900's, probably p. 1930's, (10-15-92, Sotheby-NY, #113, illus.), 13½ x 9⅛ in., (34.3 x 23.2 cm.), photograph, gelatin silver print (BP 808, DM 1965, FR 6663, Y 158,368).

BI *Cloisters In The Hospital Of The Knights Of St. John (Now The Archeological Museum) In Rhodes, c. 1930,* mounted, s., i. by photog., t., est. $1,5/2,500, (10-15-92, Sotheby-NY, #119, illus.), 13 x 9¾ in., (33 x 24.8 cm.), photograph, gelatin silver print.

$1210* *The Dance: Adante (As I Remember, facing p. 203), c. 1910,* double mounted, (10-15-92, Sotheby-NY, #115, illus.), 13⅛ x 10⅛ in., (33.3 x 25.7 cm.), photograph, gelatin silver print (BP 740, DM 1801, FR 6108, Y 145,171).

$660* *European Hill Town,* mounted, s., i. by photog., early 1900s, (10-15-92, Sotheby-NY, #117, illus.), 12⅜ x 8⅜ in., (31.4 x 21.3 cm.), photograph, gelatin silver print (BP 404, DM 982, FR 3332, Y 79,184).

BI *"Genthe As A Young Man", "A Profile Portrait", Genthe With A JapaneseWoman" and "Genthe on Chesty": Four Self-Portraits,* 1890s-1930s, est. $2/3,000, (10-15-92, Sotheby-NY, #111, illus.), various sizes to 7⅞ x 9⅞ in., (20 x 25.1 cm.), photograph, gelatin silver prints.

BI *Greta Garbo, 1925,* credit in unidentified hand, est. $4/6,000, (10-15-92, Sotheby-NY, #118, illus.), 11¾ x 8⅞ in., (29.8 x 22.5 cm.), photograph, gelatin silver print.

BI *Isadora Duncan,* 1917, photog.'s credit/t. in ink, other annots. verso, est. BP 2/400, (12-17-92, Christie-S. Ken, #7), 9⅝ x 7⅝ in., (24.4 x 19.4 cm.), photograph, gelatin silver print.

$4950* *Modern Torso (As I Remember, facing p. 178), 1910-20,* mounted, (10-15-92, Sotheby-NY, #116, illus.), 13⅜ x 9¼ in., (34 x 23.5 cm.), photograph, gelatin silver print (BP 3029, DM 7368, FR 24,987, Y 593,881).

BI *Mrs. Patrick Campbell, c. 1902: Three,* two s. by photog. in image, est. $1,5/2,500, (04-06-93, Sotheby-NY, #74, illus.), various sizes 7½ x 9 in., photograph.

$460* *Portraits Of Beatrice Maude, 1910: Two,* first s., both t., (05-23-93, Butterfield, #3422, illus.), one 9½ x 7¼ in., other 4⅜ x 5¾ in., photograph, gelatin silver print (BP 300, DM 752, FR 2532, Y 50,846).

$1127* *"San Francisco, April 18th 1906",* s., t., d., mounted, (12-17-92, Christie-S. Ken, #6, illus.), 7⅝ x 13⅛ in., (19.4 x 33.3 cm.), photograph, warm-toned gelatin silver print (BP 715, DM 1760, FR 6011, Y 138,503).

$3738* *"San Francisco, April 8th, 1906" (After The Earthquake) (As I Remember, p. 95), 1906,* mounted, s., t., d., i. by photog., p. 1920's, (04-06-93, Sotheby-NY, #75, illus.), 7⅝ x 13⅛ in., photograph (BP 2469, DM 6022, FR 20,393, Y 426,323).

$3575* *Street Of The Gamblers, (As I Remember, facing p. 35; cf. Old Chinatown, pl. 47),* mounted, s., i. by photog., early 1900s, probably p. 1930s,, (10-15-92, Sotheby-NY, #112, illus.), 9⅝ x 12½ in., (24.4 x 31.8 cm.), photograph, gelatin silver print (BP 2188, DM 5322, FR 18,046, Y 428,914).

$1100* *Street Scene: Old Chinatown, San Francisco, 1900,* (11-16-92, Butterfield, #5983, illus.), 8¾ x 12¼ in., (222.6 x 311.7 mm.), photograph, gelatin silver print (BP 724, DM 1754, FR 5908, Y 136,799).

GENTLEMAN, Tom ac. 1921-1929

$1065* *To Visit Britain's Landmarks, A Strange Church, Ayot St. Lawrence, 1937,* p. Baynard Press, ref. #479, cond. 1, (10-13-92, Phillips-London, #118, illus.), 29$\frac{15}{16}$ x 45 in., (76 x 114.3 cm.), color lithograph (BP 620, DM 1560, FR 5301, Y 129,138).

GENTRY, Herbert F. American b. 1919

$104* *Composition With A Figure,* s., 80/150, (04-17-93, Falkkloos, #128), 26$\frac{3}{16}$ x 33$\frac{11}{16}$ in., (66.5 x 85.5 cm.), lithograph in colors (BP 68, DM 166, FR 562, Y 11,565, SK 770).

GEORGE, D.

$336* *Great Western Railway: Brittany. "A Land Of Quaintness And Beauty",* good cond., (11-19-92, Ribeyre/Baron, #106), 39$\frac{9}{16}$ x 24$\frac{3}{16}$ in., (100.5 x 61.5 cm.), poster (BP 221, DM 536, FR 1805, Y 41,786).

GEORGET, G.

$70* *Air France: Proche-Orient, 1962,* good cond., (03-13-93, Laurin, #120), 39⅜ x 24$\frac{7}{16}$ in., (100 x 62 cm.), (BP 49, DM 117, FR 396, Y 8250).

GEORGET, Guy b. 1911

BI *Martini, L'Aperitif,* cond. B, (03-16-93, Boisgirard, #114), 62$\frac{15}{16}$ x 47¼ in., (160 x 120 cm.), poster.

GEORGIAN SCHOOL (after) early 20th cent.

$73 *Young Ladies With Landscape Backgrounds: Two,* (04-16-93, G.A. Key, #65), each approx. 20 x 13 in., (50.8 x 33 cm.), colored mezzotint (BP 48, DM 118, FR 398, Y 8209).

GERALE, N.

$199* *Air France Aeromaritime: "Paris, Toulouse, Dakar, Pointe Noire",* very good cond., (03-13-93, Laurin, #132, illus.), 38¾ x 24$\frac{3}{16}$ in., (98.5 x 61.5 cm.), (BP 139, DM 331, FR 1126, Y 23,453).

$319* *SNCF. Plaisirs De Neige. "La Joie Qui Fortifie", 1938,* very good cond., (03-15-93, Arcole, #92), 39$\frac{3}{16}$ x 24$\frac{7}{16}$ in., (99.5 x 62 cm.), (BP 222, DM 530, FR 1801, Y 37,787).

$230* *SNCF: Bourgogne, 1939,* excell. cond., (01-23-93, Ribeyre/Baron, #161), 39⅜ x 24$\frac{7}{16}$ in., (100 x 62 cm.), poster (BP 150, DM 366, FR 1237, Y 28,786).

GERARD, Francois (after)

$59* *Charles Maurice De Talleyrand-Perigold,* by Auguste Gaspard Louis Boucher Desnoyers, margins, collector's stamp, (06-16-93, Bonhams-Chelsea, #446), pl. 23¾ x 16¼ in., (60.3 x 41.3 cm.), engraving (BP 39, DM 98, FR 329, Y 6293).

GERDES, Ludger b. 1954

BI *Ohne Titel, 1989,* pen s., d., #11/15, est. DM 500, (11-12-92, Lempertz, #71, illus.), 11$\frac{15}{16}$ x 9$\frac{7}{16}$ in., (30.4 x 23.9 cm.), color photograph.

GERICAULT, Theodore French 1791-1824

BI *An Arabian Horse (Delteil 37), 1821,* est. DM 4,500, (12-04-92, Bassenge, #6814), 7½ x 12$\frac{15}{16}$ in., (19 x 33 cm.), lithograph.

$1917* *Bouchers De Rome (L. Delteil 2),* definitive state, reddish stains, large margins, (02-03-93, Ader Tajan, #156), 6¾ x 9¾ in., (17.1 x 24.8 cm.), lithograph (BP 1338, DM 3157, FR 10,704, Y 238,462).

BI *Chariot Charge De Soldats Blesses (Delteil 11 II), 1818,* stone s., est. DM 4,000, (06-10-93, Hauswedell/Nolt, #318, illus.), image 11⁵⁄₁₆ x 11⁹⁄₁₆ in., (28.7 x 29.4 cm.), lithograph on thick wove.

$4596* *Chariot Charge De Soldats Blesses (L. Delteil 11), 1818,* definitive state, reddish stains, creases, small margins, collector's stamp, (06-11-93, Picard, #56, illus.), 11¼ x 11⅝ in., (285 x 295 mm.), lithograph on wove (BP 3020, DM 7470, FR 25,184, Y 487,639).

BI *The Coal Waggon (L.D. 36), 1821,* dirt stains, good margins, (06-11-93, Picard, #57), 7¹¹⁄₁₆ x 12³⁄₁₆ in., (195 x 310 mm.), lithograph on wove.

BI *"Deux Chevaux Gris Pommele Que L'On Promene" (Delteil 83 i/II), 1822,* collaboration w/Cogiat, est. $5/700, (05-15-93, Cleveland, #388, illus.), 11¹¹⁄₁₆ x 16⁹⁄₁₆ in., (29.7 x 42.1 cm.), lithograph on wove.

$1898* *A French Farrier (L.D. 41), 1821,* definitive state w/letter, stains, creases, tear, large margins, collector's stamp, (06-11-93, Picard, #58), 9⅝ x 13¹⁵⁄₁₆ in., (245 x 355 mm.), lithograph on wove (BP 1247, DM 3085, FR 10,400, Y 201,379).

$11,027* *Mameluck Defendant Un Trompette Blesse (L.D. 9),* rare, good margins, (02-03-93, Ader Tajan, #157, illus.), 13⅜ x 10¹⁵⁄₁₆ in., (34 x 27.8 cm.), lithograph (BP 7698, DM 18,157, FR 61,569, Y 1,371,688).

BI *Passage Du Mont Saint-Bernard (L.D. 44; R. 22), 1822,* 3rd state of 4, full margins, foxmarks, defects, staining, est. BP 4/600, (12-01-92, Christie-London, #382), L. 14¹³⁄₁₆ x 16⁷⁄₁₆ in., (377 x 418 mm.), sheet 17½ x 24⅝ in., (377 x 418 mm.), lithograph on wove.

$5815* *Pity The Sorrows Of A Poor Old Man... (L.D. 31),* rare, defintive state, large margins, yellowed, (02-03-93, Ader Tajan, #158), 12½ x 14¹³⁄₁₆ in., (31.7 x 37.6 cm.), lithograph (BP 4059, DM 9575, FR 32,468, Y 723,349).

$259* *Un Postillon Ou Les Deux Chevaux Harnaches (D. 61), 1823,* p. Villain, margins, good cond., water-staining, buckling, water stain, surface soiling, crease, staining, creasing, staining, foxing, notations, (05-19-93, Butterfield, #2061), 5¹⁄₁₆ x 7 in., (129 x 178 mm.), lithograph on wove (BP 168, DM 421, FR 1418, Y 28,673).

GERICAULT, Theodore (after)

$111* *"Cheval Noir Attache Dans Une Ecurie",* first state of three w/address, good margins, (03-22-93, Pescheteau, #16), lithograph (BP 75, DM 182, FR 619, Y 12,853).

GERICAULT, Theodore (by or after)

$182* *"Cheval Anglais", "Le Giaour" and "Cheval Que L'On Ferre" (L. Delteil 70, 71, 72): Three,* definitive state, creases, reddish stains, large margins, (02-03-93, Ader Tajan, #160), lithograph on fixed Chine (BP 127, DM 300, FR 1016, Y 22,640).

GERMAN SCHOOL, AUGSBURG c. 1500

$1415* *Der Franziskaner Pelbartus Im Garten (Schrieber 2876), c. 1500,* watermark, wide margins, worm-holing in image, foxing, staining, (12-01-92, Christie-London, #156), 9⅛ x 6³⁄₁₆ in., (232 x 157 mm.), white line wood engraving (BP 935, DM 2255, FR 7686, Y 176,170).

GERMAN/CONTINENTAL SCHOOL, 18TH/19TH CENTURY

BI *Botanical,* id. w/in plate, good cond., subtle toning, foxing, wrinkling, est. $5/700, (06-25-93, Skinner, #359), 12¾ x 8¼ in., (32.4 x 21 cm.), print, etching w/handcoloring on paper.

GERMON, W.L.

$880* *Portrait Of Abraham Lincoln And Son,* photog. ident. and studio address, 1860's, (04-07-93, Swann, #229, illus.), 8½ x 6½ in., photograph, oval albumen print (BP 582, DM 1423, FR 4817, Y 99,977).

GERNEZ, Paul Elie 1888-1948

$61* *Portraits De Femmes: Deux,* s. in plate, (05-27-93, Briest, #100), 12¹³⁄₁₆ x 9¹³⁄₁₆ in., (32.5 x 25 cm.), drypoints and etchings on Arches (BP 39, DM 98, FR 330, Y 6539).

BI *Untitled: Nineteen,* full margins, est. FF7,000/7,500, (05-27-93, Briest, #102), from 12⅝ x 9⅝ in., (32 x 24.5 cm.), to 7½ x 5⁹⁄₁₆ in., (32 x 24.5 cm.), black etchings on Rives wove.

BI *"Vielle Dame Au Tricot", "A La Fenetre" and "La Veillee": Three,* est. FF1,000/1,500, (05-27-93, Briest, #101), one 8⁷⁄₁₆ x 9¹³⁄₁₆ in., (21.5 x 25 cm.), other two 12¹³⁄₁₆ x 9¹³⁄₁₆ in., (21.5 x 25 cm.), black etchings on Arches wove.

GERRITSEN, Ad b. 1940

BI *Bericht Over Cesare Lombroso, 1973,* s., d., #12/15, margins, good cond., discoloration, est. G 4/500, (12-09-92, Sotheby-Amstrdm, #577), 19¹¹⁄₁₆ x 27½ in., (500 x 698 mm.), color lithograph on wove.

BI *Tagger Identify, 1978: Five,* s., d., #3/15, full margins, good cond., discoloration, est. G 250/350, (12-09-92, Sotheby-Amstrdm, #578), each sheet 25½ x 19⅝ in., (648 x 498 mm.), color photographic print.

GERSDORFF, Ernst

BI *Mourning Rings, c. 1935,* handstamp, notations, est. $4/600, (10-14-92, Swann, #459A, illus.), 8 x 6½ in., (20.3 x 16.5 cm.), photograph, silver print.

GERSHOWITZ, Judy

$275* *Flashback, 1965,* s., t., d., #15/40, full margins, very good cond., image scuffs, creases, surface soiling, (10-28-92, Butterfield, #2958), 17¼ x 17¼ in., (438 x 438 mm.), color silkscreen on cream wove paper (BP 175, DM 425, FR 1442, Y 33,742).

GERSTNER, Carl

$165* *Abstract,* s. ink, #142/175, pub. Denise Rene & Hans Mayer, chop, (05-16-93, Hindman, #571), 31¼ x 31¼ in., (79.4 x 79.4 cm.), color serigraph (BP 107, DM 265, FR 892, Y 18,291).

$68* *Colour Sounds II,* s., #33/175, pub. Denise Rene Editeur, blindstamped, prov., (12-01-92, Ritchie, #84), 31¼ x 31 in., (79.4 x 78.7 cm.), color serigraph (BP 45, DM 108, FR 369, Y 8466, C$ 88).

GERTSCH, Franz Swiss b. 1930

$751* *Jean Frederic Schnyder, 1970,* 1/12 ap, s., from series: documenta and no documenta realists, lit., (06-24-93, Germann, #627), 23⅜ x 34 in., (593 x 864 mm.), lithograph (BP 494, DM 1218, FR 4104, Y 80,562, SF 1093).

BI *Jean-Frederic Schnyder, 1970,* s., #290/300, portfolio Documenta, blindstamp, est. DM 2,500, (06-12-93, Hauswedell/Nolt, #99, illus.), 23³⁄₁₆ x 34 in., (58.9 x 86.4 cm.), lithograph on Arches.

BI *Komposition,* s., num., est. DM 2500, (12-01-92, Karl/Faber, #644), 23¹⁄₁₆ x 34¼ in., (58.5 x 87 cm.), lithograph on hand-made.

$22,825* *Natascha II, 1986,* s. Franz Gertsch, epreuve d'artiste, (06-25-93, Kornfeld, #40, illus.), image 41⁵⁄₁₆ x 35⅝ in., (105 x 90.5 cm.), color woodcut 3 plates on vellum (BP 15,438, DM 38,858, FR 130,877, Y 2,419,440, SF 34,500).

$453* *See,* XXVII/XXX, s., (10-14-92, Germann, #523), 22¹⁄₁₆ x 29¹⁵⁄₁₆ in., (560 x 760 mm.), color screen print (BP 266, DM 663, FR 2248, Y 54,896, SF 590).

$588* *Zwei Figuren, 1968,* 18/30, s., (10-14-92, Germann, #522), 24³⁄₁₆ x 32⅞ in., (615 x 835 mm.), color serigraph (BP 345, DM 861, FR 2918, Y 71,255, SF 767).

GERZ, Jochen German b. 1940

$2730* *A Male Token 4, 1988: Three,* t., d., (11-12-92, Lempertz, #72, illus.), smallest 15¾ x 7⅞ in., (40 x 20 cm.), largest 15¾ x 19¹¹⁄₁₆ in., (40 x 20 cm.), photograph (BP 1746, DM 4290, FR 14,622, Y 337,746).

GESMAR, C.

$414* *Guy Sarlin, 1925,* (01-31-93, Morelle/Marchan, #30), 45¹¹⁄₁₆ x 61⁷⁄₁₆ in., (116 x 156 cm.), poster (BP 278, DM 667, FR 2255, Y 51,647).

$1301* *Mistinguett, 1925,* p. H. Chachouin, good cond., (11-19-92, Ribeyre/Baron, #176, illus.), 62³⁄₁₆ x 46¹⁄₁₆ in., (158 x 117 cm.), poster (BP 857, DM 2074, FR 6987, Y 161,796).

GESMAR, Charles

$1320* *Mistinguett,* p. H. Chachoin, folds, darkening, defects, linen-backed, (11-06-92, Sotheby-Arcade, #134), 125¼ x 44⅞ in., (318.1 x 114 cm.), lithograph in colors, on two joined sheets (BP 863, DM 2108, FR 7124, Y 162,923).

GETHING, B.B.

$1271* *"Rambles By Rivers": Five,* 1850s, mounted, each approx. 200 x 250mm, (05-07-93, Sotheby-London, #59, illus.), photograph, albumen print (BP 805, DM 2009, FR 6771, Y 139,947).

GEX, E.

BI *Supreme Pernot,* G. Gerin Fils, A- cond., fold marks, creasing, est. $6/900, (08-06-92, Swann, #138, illus.), 48 x 33 in., (121.9 x 83.8 cm.),

GHEYN, Jacob de (II) Dutch 1565-1629

$1877* *Allegorie Auf Die Herrschaft Eines Weisen Konigs (Wurzbach 198, Hollstein 427): Two,* prov., stained, watermark, (12-04-92, Bassenge, #6203, illus.), 8 9/16 x 12 3/16 in., (21.7 x 31 cm.), engraving (BP 1204, DM 2989, FR 10,140, Y 234,332).

$1169* *Ein Bauer (Wurzbach 210),* s. in plate ID Gheyn, foxing, trimmed, creases, (11-11-92, Dorotheum, #304, illus.), 16⅛ x 12¾ in., engraving (BP 774, DM 1868, FR 6261, Y 145,362, SC 6160).

GHISI, Giorgio 1520-1582

$1416* *Allegorische Gestalt, Eine Kugel Haltend (B. 34, Lewis-Lewis 38), c.1565,* after Giulio Romano, (06-04-93, Bassenge, #5176), 9 5/16 x 5 3/16 in., (23.7 x 13.2 cm.), copper engraving (BP 937, DM 2299, FR 7750, Y 152,718).

BI *Apollo And The Muses, (B. XV, 58; L. & L. 23), c. 1557,* after Luca Penni, first state (of three), thread margins, trimmed, crease, very good cond., laid, est. BP 1,8/2200, (12-01-92, Christie-London, #41, illus.), S. 14⅛ x 16⅞ in., (358 x 429 mm.), engraving.

$14,151* *The Calumny Of Apelles, (B. XV, 64; L. & L. 27), 1560,* aafter Luca Penni, L. & L.'s third state (of six), tone, narrow to thread margins, excellent cond., laid, (12-01-92, Christie-London, #40, illus.), P. 14 9/16 x 12 11/16 in., (370 x 322 mm.), engraving (BP 9350, DM 22,555, FR 76,866, Y 1,761,828).

$1843* *Der Fall Trojas Und Die Flucht Des Aeneas (B. 29; L. 8/II), c. 1540,* after G.B. Scultori, watermark, prov., (06-08-93, Karl/Faber, #81, illus.), engraving (BP 1212, DM 2990, FR 10,071, Y 195,751).

$2166* *Der Fall Von Troja (B. 29; Lewis & Lewis 8 I), c. 1545,* watermark, (12-04-92, Bassenge, #6204, illus.), 15 1/16 x 19⅝ in., (38.3 x 49.8 cm.), engraving (BP 1389, DM 3450, FR 11,702, Y 270,412).

BI *The Farnese Hercules (B. 41; Boorsch/Lewis/Lewis 58), c. 1570,* 1st state of 3, watermark, trimmed to inner borderline, restorations,plugged holes center, creases, ex-coll. R. A. P. Davison, est. $1,2/1,500, (05-13-93, Sotheby-NY, #315), 12¾ x 6⅞ in., (324 x 175 mm.), engraving.

$1201* *The Farnese Hercules (B. XV, 58; Lewis And Lewis 58),* 1st state of 3, (06-30-93, Sotheby-London, #126), 12⅜ x 6⅞ in., (314 x 175 mm.), engraving on paper w/an Armorial watermark (BP 805, DM 2048, FR 6910, Y 128,683).

$302* *Venus Blessee Par Les Epines D'Un Rosier, 1556,* after Luca Penni, 3rd state of 4, cracks, restored tears, (05-15-93, Loudmer, #18, illus.), 12 3/16 x 8½ in., (310 x 216 mm.), sh 13¼ x 8¾ in., (310 x 216 mm.), copper engraving on laid (BP 196, DM 486, FR 1632, Y 33,477).

BI *Venus Und Vulkan In Einem Himmelbett (B. 35; Lewis & Lewis 18 III), c. 1550,* est. DM 6,000, (12-04-92, Bassenge, #6206), 11 3/16 x 8⅛ in., (28.4 x 20.6 cm.), engraving.

BI *Venus, Vulcan Und Drei Amoretten (B. 35; Lewis 18/III), c. 1550,* after Perino del Vaga, est. DM 800, (12-01-92, Karl/Faber, #71), engraving.

GIACOMELLI, Mario b. 1925

$920* *Brothers In The Snow,* 1968, p.l., s., photog.'s stamp, (05-23-93, Butterfield, #3423, illus.), 16 x 12 in., photograph, gelatin silver print (BP 599, DM 1504, FR 5063, Y 101,691).

$230* *Color Abstract, 1976,* s., photog.'s stamp, est. $4/600, (05-23-93, Butterfield, #3424), 11¾ x 16 in., photograph, cibachrome print (BP 150, DM 376, FR 1266, Y 25,423).

$1980* *"Il Viso" (Mario Giacomelli, p. 37), 1968,* s., photog. stamp, Dixon Collection, (11-16-92, Butterfield, #5985, illus.), 12 x 16 in., (305.3 x 407.1 mm.), photograph, gelatin silver print (BP 1304, DM 3157, FR 10,634, Y 246,238).

BI *Italy, Landscapes: Three,* 1970s, stamped photog.'s credit, each approx. 290 x 400mm or 140 x 360mm, est. BP 4/600, (05-07-93, Sotheby-London, #395), photograph, silver print.

$825* *"Paesaggio" (Mario Giacomelli, p. 6),* s., photog. stamp, Dixon Collection, (11-16-92, Butterfield, #5986, illus.), 11¾ x 15¾ in., (299 x 400.8 mm.), photograph, gelatin silver print (BP 543, DM 1315, FR 4431, Y 102,599).

GIACOMETTI, Alberto Swiss 1901-1966

$4256* *Akt Mit Blumen (Lust 32), 1960,* (06-05-93, Bassenge, #6047), 14 9/16 x 11 in., (37 x 28 cm.), lithograph on BFK Rives (BP 2802, DM 6900, FR 23,257, Y 456,554).

$404* *"Annette, Cheval Et Tabouret - 1951",* s. in plate, (10-18-92, Pescheteau, #156), 23⅝ x 29 15/16 in., (38 x 28 cm.), lithograph (BP 245, DM 597, FR 2027, Y 48,239).

BI *"Annette, Cheval Et Tabouret",* s. in plate, est. FF1,500/2,000, (04-04-93, Pescheteau, #219), 15 3/16 x 10⅝ in., (38.5 x 27 cm.), black lithograph.

$9215* *Atelierszene (Lust 231), 1969,* for Paris sans fin, mono., bo(n a) Ti(rer), (09-04-92, Germann, #43, illus.), 16 5/16 x 12⅝ in., (415 x 320 mm.), lithograph (BP 4618, DM 12,915, FR 43,965, Y 1,134,293, SF 11,500).

$4025* *Au Cafe (Lust 20), 1954,* s., i. HC 2/6, pub. Maeght, full margins, good cond., darkening of paper tone, handling creases, light foxing, (05-13-93, Sotheby-NY, #561, illus.), 14⅛ x 18⅞ in., (358 x 480 mm.), lithograph on wove (BP 2642, DM 6499, FR 21,923, Y 449,369).

BI *Bust I (L. 30), 1960,* s., #20/90, pub. Maeght, full margins, good cond., mat stain, handling creases, fox mark in image, est. $3/5,000, (05-13-93, Sotheby-NY, #562, illus.), 14 x 9⅝ in., (355 x 245 mm.), lithograph.

$773* *Buste D'Homme,* s., crease, (06-28-93, Loudmer, #250, illus.), 6 7/16 x 4¾ in., (163 x 120 mm.), sh 7⅞ x 5½ in., (163 x 120 mm.), black etching on BFK Rives on wove (BP 518, DM 1314, FR 4425, Y 82,016).

$3163* *Dans Le Miroir (L. 43), 1964,* s., #75/75, pub. Maeght, full margins, good cond., creases, discoloration, (05-13-93, Sotheby-NY, #563, illus.), 22½ x 14¾ in., (570 x 375 mm.), lithograph on white wove (BP 2077, DM 5107, FR 17,228, Y 353,132).

$935* *"Douze Portrait De Celebre Orbandale",* s., (12-08-92, Swann, #121, illus.), image 13¼ x 6¾ in., (33.7 x 17.1 cm.), etching and drypoint (BP 586, DM 1456, FR 4963, Y 115,890).

$1145* *Ex Libris Edmond Bomsel, 1961,* s., d., (06-23-93, Kornfeld, #363, illus.), 4 x 2⅞ in., (10.2 x 7.3 cm.), etching on Japan nacre (BP 778, DM 1937, FR 6517, Y 124,741, SF 1725).

$2030* *Figure Marchant (Lust 176), c. 1964: Two,* crayon s., artist's proof, (06-28-93, Loudmer, #251), 5⅞ x 3⅞ in., (150 x 98 mm.), sh approx. 9 13/16 x 12 13/16 in., (150 x 98 mm.), black etchings on wove (BP 1359, DM 3449, FR 11,620, Y 215,385).

$3547* *From The Series "Paris Sans Fin", c. 1964/66: Eighty,* watermark, num., Teriade Editeur, 1969, (06-05-93, Grisebach, #584, illus.), 16 9/16 x 12⅝ in., (42 x 32 cm.), lithograph on wove (BP 2335, DM 5751, FR 19,383, Y 380,498).

$2475* *Head Of A Man (L. 102), 1957,* s., #83/100, full margins, good cond., tape hinges, (11-05-92, Sotheby-NY, #190), 4⅞ x 5⅛ in., (125 x 130 mm.), lithograph (BP 1610, DM 3914, FR 13,242, Y 303,644).

$990* *Head Of A Man In Left Profile (Lust 168), 1962,* from Douze Portraits de Celebre Orbandale, wide margins, s., (05-27-93, Swann, #116, illus.), 5½ x 4 in., (14 x 10.2 cm.), etching (BP 634, DM 1589, FR 5354, Y 106,132).

$525* *"Homme Marchant Dans L'Atelier", 1951,* s. in plate, (01-28-93, Pescheteau, #150), 15⅜ x 21⅝ in., (39 x 55 cm.), black lithograph (BP 347, DM 832, FR 2815, Y 65,185).

$3818* *Interieur (L. 52), 1965,* s., num., (06-23-93, Kornfeld, #366), lithograph on wove (BP 2594, DM 6460, FR 21,730, Y 415,949, SF 5750).

$990* *Interior Au People, 1956, Lust 70,* s., num. 109/150, prov., Emmanuel Jacobson Estate, (09-20-92, Hindman,

#766, illus.), 8⅛ x 5½ in., (20.6 x 14 cm.), etching (BP 580, DM 1469, FR 5025, Y 122,358).

$1721* *L'Atelier,* regular edit., s., creases, wormholes, (05-27-93, Briest, #104, illus.), 22¹⁄₁₆ x 29¹⁵⁄₁₆ in., (56 x 76 cm.), black lithograph (BP 1102, DM 2762, FR 9308, Y 184,498).

BI *L'Atelier Aux Bouteilles (L. 100), 1957,* s., #20/100, pub. Maeght, full margins, tape, very good cond., est. BP 1,4/1,800, (12-01-92, Christie-London, #384), L. 14⅜ x 21¼ in., (365 x 540 mm.), lithograph on BFK Rives.

BI *L'Atelier, c. 1965,* s., i. HC, i. pour tiree, full margins, good cond., discoloration, darkening of paper tone, soiling, fox marks, est. $6/9,000, (05-13-93, Sotheby-NY, #566, illus.), 14⅜ x 21¼ in., (365 x 540 mm.), lithograph on Arches wove.

$4434* *L'Homme Qui Marche (Lust 202), 1957,* s., #194/200, pub. Maeght, margins, good cond., (12-03-92, Sotheby-London, #313), 30⅛ x 22½ in., (765 x 572 mm.), lithograph on wove (BP 2860, DM 6973, FR 23,800, Y 551,698).

$2429* *Mere De L'Artiste A La Fenetre, 1964,* s., #61/75, (05-27-93, Briest, #103), 26¾ x 19¹¹⁄₁₆ in., (68 x 50 cm.), black lithograph on wove (BP 1556, DM 3898, FR 13,137, Y 260,399).

$1145* *La Mere De L'Artiste, Assise. II (L. 51), 1963,* num., (06-23-93, Kornfeld, #365), lithograph (BP 778, DM 1937, FR 6517, Y 124,741, SF 1725).

$4995* *Nu Assis (L. 37), 1961,* s., #8/75, pub. Maeght, margins, creases, very good cond., (12-01-92, Christie-London, #383, illus.), L. 15⁹⁄₁₆ x 20½ in., (395 x 520 mm.), lithograph on BFK Rives (BP 3300, DM 7961, FR 27,132, Y 621,887).

$2584* *Nu De Face (Lust 65), 1955,* proof, s., (05-20-93, Finarte-Milan, #72, illus.), 9¹³⁄₁₆ x 2⅝ in., (25 x 6.7 cm.), etching (BP 1659, DM 4169, FR 14,043, Y 285,336, L 3795).

$4600* *Objet Inquietant II (L. 45), 1964,* s., #62/75, pub. Maeght, full margins, good cond., (05-13-93, Sotheby-NY, #565, illus.), 15¾ x 13⅜ in., (400 x 340 mm.), lithograph on wove (BP 3020, DM 7428, FR 25,054, Y 513,565).

BI *Portrait Of A Gentleman,* from "Derriere le Miroir", prov., est. $2/250, (12-10-92, Sloan, #3043), 14⅞ x 11 in., (37.8 x 27.9 cm.), lithograph.

$3163* *"Portrait Of Andre Du Bouchet" and "Portrait Of Michel Leiris" (L. 394): Two,* s., annot. Epreuve D'Essai, margins, good cond., (05-19-93, Butterfield, #1913), one 6⅜ x 4¾ in., (162 x 121 mm.), the other 6⅜ x 4⅝ in., (162 x 121 mm.), etching and aquatint in colors on BFK Rives (BP 2053, DM 5141, FR 17,322, Y 350,161).

BI *Rue D'Alesia, Galerie Maeght,* stone s., est. SF 150/200, (10-14-92, Germann, #309), 28¹⁵⁄₁₆ x 20¹¹⁄₁₆ in., (735 x 525 mm.), poster.

$2664* *Sculptures Dans L'Atelier (L. 185), 1963,* s., #86/150, margins, excellent cond., (12-01-92, Christie-London, #385), overall sheet 10¹⁄₁₆ x 7¹³⁄₁₆ in., (255 x 199 mm.), etching on wove (BP 1760, DM 4246, FR 14,470, Y 331,673).

$2860* *Sculptures, 1954, Lust 14,* s., num. 15/30, pub. Maeght in Studio series, Carl E. Kaufman Estate, (09-20-92, Hindman, #770, illus.), 23½ x 15½ in., (59.7 x 39.4 cm.), lithograph on Arches (BP 1674, DM 4244, FR 14,518, Y 353,479).

$4400* *Seated Nude (L. 53), 1965,* s., #60/100, pub. Gemini, full margins, good cond., skinned spots, (11-05-92, Sotheby-NY, #189, illus.), 24¼ x 17½ in., (615 x 444 mm.), lithograph (BP 2862, DM 6959, FR 23,542, Y 539,811).

$2341* *Sitzende Weiblicher Akt, Im Profil Nach Links (Lust 245), 1969,* i. bon a tirer, mono., sheet 41 of series Paris sans fin, artist's proof, (06-05-93, Bassenge, #6048, illus.), 14⁹⁄₁₆ x 10⅝ in., (37 x 27 cm.), lithograph on Arches (BP 1541, DM 3795, FR 12,792, Y 251,126).

$413* *Still Life,* s. ink and in plate, d. '74, (02-14-93, Hanzel, #671), plate 8 x 10 in., (20.3 x 25.4 cm.), etching (BP 291, DM 685, FR 2318, Y 49,807).

BI *Still Life,* ink s., s. in plate, d. '74, est. $800/1,200, (11-01-92, Hanzel, #221), plate 8 x 10 in., (20.3 x 25.4 cm.), lithograph.

$4620* *Studio II (Lust 15), 1954,* s., #27/30, pub. Maeght, margins, good cond., foxing, mat/light stain, (11-05-92, Sotheby-NY, #188), 14⅝ x 20½ in., (370 x 520 mm.), sheet 18 x 24 in., (370 x 520 mm.), lithograph (BP 3005, DM 7307, FR 24,719, Y 566,802).

$8094* *Tete D'Homme - Portrait Diego Giacometti (Lust 47), 1963,* s., num., (06-23-93, Kornfeld, #364), sh 25¹¹⁄₁₆ x 19¹¹⁄₁₆ in., (65.3 x 50 cm.), lithograph on wove (BP 5499, DM 13,695, FR 46,067, Y 881,795, SF 12,190).

$9469* *Tristan Et Iseute, 1959,* Fassung I, Fassung II, s., i. Epreuve d'essai, #2/7, (06-23-93, Kornfeld, #362, illus.), etching (BP 6433, DM 16,022, FR 53,893, Y 1,031,594, SF 14,260).

$2588* *[The Artist's Mother Reading] (see L. 44 and 55), 1963,* s., d., i. H.C., full margins, good cond., handling creases, (05-13-93, Sotheby-NY, #564, illus.), 21¼ x 14⅞ in., (540 x 378 mm.), lithograph (BP 1699, DM 4179, FR 14,096, Y 288,936).

GIACOMETTI, Alberto (after)

$165* *"Sculptures In The Studio",* posthumous printing from cancelled plate, exec. 1964, issued by The Collector's Guild, (05-20-93, Boos, #537), 9⅞ x 7¹³⁄₁₆ in., (251 x 199 mm.), etching (BP 106, DM 266, FR 897, Y 18,220).

GIACOMETTI, Giovanni Swiss 1868-1933

BI *Albogasio, 1907,* est. SF 170/190, (10-14-92, Germann, #524), 12¹¹⁄₁₆ x 9¹⁵⁄₁₆ in., (322 x 252 mm.), color lithograph.

$3971* *Donna Lattante (du Carrois 12), c. 1908,* s., (06-23-93, Kornfeld, #378), woodcut on cream wove (BP 2698, DM 6719, FR 22,601, Y 432,618, SF 5980).

$1967* *Frauen Am Brunnen (Carrois 35), 1921,* (11-13-92, Koller, #5329), 8⁷⁄₁₆ x 9¹³⁄₁₆ in., (21.5 x 25 cm.), woodcut on wove (BP 1271, DM 3088, FR 10,413, Y 244,136, SF 2784).

$270* *Fruhling In Den Engadiner Bergen, 1931,* #110/130, s., creases, tears, lit., (11-13-92, Koller, #5330), 15¹⁵⁄₁₆ x 19¹¹⁄₁₆ in., (40.5 x 50 cm.), lithograph on thin wove (BP 174, DM 424, FR 1429, Y 33,511, SF 382).

$5498* *Kniender Knabe Am Ufer Des Silsersees (du Carr. 25), c. 1913,* mono., (06-23-93, Kornfeld, #379, illus.), woodcut on handmade (BP 3735, DM 9303, FR 31,292, Y 598,976, SF 8280).

GIBSON, Ralph American b. 1939

BI *Arm With Bracelet, 1980,* s., d., est. $1,5/2,000, (05-23-93, Butterfield, #3426, illus.), 12½ x 8½ in., photograph, gelatin silver print.

$1100* *"The Doorman" (Darkroom, p. 71), 1975,* s., d., (11-16-92, Butterfield, #5988, illus.), 12½ x 8⅜ in., (318.1 x 213.1 mm.), photograph, gelatin silver print (BP 724, DM 1754, FR 5908, Y 136,799).

BI *The Enchanted Hand,* (1968), p.l., s., d., lit., est. $2/2,500, (10-13-92, Christie-NY, #539, illus.), 12⅜ x 8⅛ in., (31.4 x 20.6 cm.), photograph, gelatin silver print.

BI *"Lady and Man" and "Statue": Two,* sig., blindstamp, 1979, 1972, p.l., est. $1,2/1,800, (10-14-92, Swann, #460, illus.), 11 x 14 in., (27.9 x 35.6 cm.), photograph, silver prints.

$2300* *Leda,* 1974, p.l., s., d., #28/50, lit., (04-08-93, Christie-NY, #488, illus.), photograph, gelatin silver print (BP 1508, DM 3695, FR 12,507, Y 261,008).

$1840* *"Leda",* 1974, p.l., s., d., #31/50, illus., (05-23-93, Butterfield, #3425, illus.), 12¼ x 18¼ in., photograph, gelatin silver print (BP 1198, DM 3009, FR 10,127, Y 203,382).

$1062* *Ohne Titel, 1972,* from "The Somnambulist", ink s.; s. verso, (11-12-92, Lempertz, #73, illus.), 12¹¹⁄₁₆ x 8¹¹⁄₁₆ in., (32.2 x 22 cm.), sheet 13¹⁵⁄₁₆ x 11 in., (32.2 x 22 cm.), photograph, gelatin silver print (BP 679, DM 1669, FR 5688, Y 131,387).

BI *Sketch, 1984,* s., d., num. 16/75, est. $1,8/2,200, (10-13-92, Christie-NY, #538, illus.), 12⅜ x 8⅞ in., (31.4 x 22.5 cm.), photograph, gelatin silver print.

$770* *Untitled (Bar Of Light), 1972,* s., d., annot., Dixon Collection, (11-16-92, Butterfield, #5989, illus.), 12⅜ x 8⅛ in., (314.9 x 206.7 mm.), photograph, gelatin silver print (BP 507, DM 1228, FR 4135, Y 95,759).

$920* *Woman's Face In Shadow,* 1974, p.l., s., d., (05-23-93, Butterfield, #3427, illus.), 12½ x 8½ in., photograph, gelatin silver print (BP 599, DM 1504, FR 5063, Y 101,691).

GIDAL, Tim German b. 1909
$607* *Fotostructure VII, 1976,* ink s., d., t., i., (11-12-92, Lempertz, #76, illus.), 11⁹⁄₁₆ x 11⅜ in., (29.3 x 28.9 cm.), photomontage (BP 388, DM 954, FR 3251, Y 75,096).
BI *Olympia II, 1932,* ink s., d., t., est. DM 600, (11-12-92, Lempertz, #75), 8½ x 12⁵⁄₁₆ in., (21.6 x 31.3 cm.), photograph, gelatin silver print.
$493* *Der Zerbrochene Spiegel, 1903,* ink s.; s. verso, #2/3, (11-12-92, Lempertz, #74), 8¾ x 11¹³⁄₁₆ in., (22.3 x 30 cm.), photograph, gelatin silver print (BP 315, DM 775, FR 2641, Y 60,992).

GIDDENS, Philip H. American b. 1898
$28* *Along The Arno, Florence, Italy,* s., t., i., (09-17-92, Sloan, #1401), 7¼ x 3⅝ in., (18.4 x 9.2 cm.), etching (BP 16, DM 42, FR 142, Y 3486).
$39* *"Ville Franche Harbor, France",* s., num., annot., (10-08-92, Boos, #666), image 6¼ x 12 in., (159 x 305 mm.), etching (BP 23, DM 58, FR 196, Y 4739).

GIESE, Wilhelm 1883-1945
BI *Berlin, Bahnhof Friedrichstrasse Bei Regen,* s. Wilhelm Giese, est. DM 300-, (09-14-92, Venator/Hansten, #2455), plate 7¹³⁄₁₆ x 9⅝ in., (19.8 x 24.5 cm.), etching on thick Japan.

GIFFORD, Robert Swain American 1840-1905
$127* *Dutch Coastline Scene,* plate s., d. 1883, (11-13-92, DuMouchelle, #2574), etching (BP 82, DM 199, FR 672, Y 15,763).
$130* *Landscape,* s., very good cond., (05-15-93, Cleveland, #143), 7 x 10¾ in., (17.8 x 27.3 cm.), engraving (BP 85, DM 209, FR 703, Y 14,411).

GIGADO ASHIYUKI Japanese ac. c. 1813-1833
BI *Arashi Danpachi And Arashi Tomisaburo: Four,* Oban, sh from diptychs or triptychs, and a diptych, s. Gigado/Ashiyuki ga, pub.'s mark Honsei, d. 1825/30, 1831 and 1852, soiled, rubbed, trimmed, Prof. H.R.W. Kuhne Coll., est. BP 850/1,200, (06-11-93, Sotheby-London, #474, illus.), woodblock.
BI *Nakamura Utaemon III As Osono And Ichikawa Ebijuro As Keyamura Rokusuke,* Oban, s. Gigado Ashiyuki ga, pub.'s mark Wataki, Maruya Zenjiro?, d.Bunsei 9 (1826), soiled, rubbed, Prof. H.R.W. Kuhne Coll., est. BP 6/800, (06-11-93, Sotheby-London, #477, illus.), 14⅞ x 10 in., (37.8 x 25.4 cm.), woodblock.
BI *"Nakamura Utaemon III, Seki Sanjuro" and "Nakamura Matsue": Two,* Oban diptych, s. Gigado Ashiyuki ga, pub.'s mark Wataki, d. Bunsei 10(1827), wormed, laid down, Prof. H.R.W. Kuhne Coll., est. BP 6/800, (06-11-93, Sotheby-London, #478, illus.), each approx. 15⅜ x 10½ in., (39.1 x 26.7 cm.), woodblock.

GIGER, Hansruedi b. 1940
$474* *Komposition,* s., (06-24-93, Germann, #635), 27⅜ x 39⁵⁄₁₆ in., (695 x 998 mm.), light print (BP 312, DM 768, FR 2590, Y 50,847, SF 690).
$634* *N.Y. City: Five,* 51/350, s., (10-14-92, Germann, #525), offset graphics (BP 372, DM 928, FR 3146, Y 76,830, SF 826).

GIGOUX, Jean Francois 1806-1894
BI *Brustbild Von Eugene Delacroix (Beraldi 111),* prov., s., artist's proof, est. DM 600, (12-04-92, Bassenge, #6815), 11⅛ x 8⅛ in., (28.3 x 20.7 cm.), etching on handmade.

GIGUERE, Roland Canadian School b. 1929
$75* *"Feux Croises",* #22/40, s., d. Roland Giguere 74, (07-14-92, Encans, #127), 20½ x 15¹⁵⁄₁₆ in., (52 x 40.5 cm.), lithograph (BP 39, DM 111, FR 375, Y 9379, C$ 89).

GIKOW, Ruth American 1914-1982
$242* *Through A Window,* s., t., folds in margins, hinges, (10-31-92, Cleveland, #135), 15⅛ x 12⅛ in., (38.4 x 30.8 cm.), woodcut in seven colors (BP 155, DM 372, FR 1263, Y 29,976).

GILBERT, Richard
BI *Fault,* s., t., d. 75, #43/175, prov., est. C$ 2/300, (12-01-92, Ritchie, #36), 32¼ x 24 in., (81.9 x 61 cm.), color serigraph.

GILBERT, W*J* (after)
$197* *Hunting Scenes: Four,* (06-30-93, Bonhams-Chelsea, #123), image 22 x 11¼ in., (55.9 x 28.6 cm.), photogravures w/hand-coloring (BP 132, DM 336, FR 1133, Y 21,108).

GILBERT, William
$88* *"Henrietta Deburbon" and "Adelaide De France": A Pair,* after Jean Nattier, s., (12-02-92, Boos, #327), plate 5¼ x 7⅛ in., (13.3 x 18.1 cm.), color mezzotint (BP 57, DM 138, FR 472, Y 10,949).

GILBERTO, Tony American contemporary
BI *Grey Beacon,* s., t., #3/25, est. $125/175, (02-04-93, Sloan, #2958), color lithograph.
BI *Untitled: Two,* each s., (c), #19/20 and 20/20, respectively, est. $150/200, (02-04-93, Sloan, #2957), each 9¾ x 12 in., (24.8 x 30.5 cm.), color lithograph.

GILDOR, Jacob b. 1948
BI *Paris-Rue St. Denis,* E.A., s., crease, est. SF 200/300, (10-14-92, Germann, #311), 24¹³⁄₁₆ x 36 in., (630 x 915 mm.), color lithograph.

GILES, G.D.
$6 *"The Cottesmore-1905",* s., (04-16-93, G.A. Key, #21), 14 x 19 in., (35.6 x 48.3 cm.), photogravure (BP 4, DM 10, FR 33, Y 675).

GILES, G.D. (after)
BI *Polo Match,* est. $2/400, (09-20-92, Hindman, #809), 19 x 29 in., (48.3 x 73.7 cm.), photo engraving.

GILES, J. West (after J.F. HERRING)
$3307* *Fox Hunting, 1854: Set Of Four,* pub. E. Gambart and Co., stains, foxing, water staining, tear, (10-27-92, Phillips-London, #101), image 22⅞ x 33½ in., (581 x 851 mm.), lithograph w/hand-coloring, touches of gum arabic on wove (BP 2090, DM 5068, FR 17,197, Y 404,526).

GILES, Werner German 1894-1961
$165* *"Lambs At Sunset",* s., p. stamp, (c) USA, pub. 1910, Bromhead Lith. Co., (02-27-93, Dunning, #104), 13¼ x 9½ in., (33.7 x 24.1 cm.), color lithograph (BP 116, DM 271, FR 922, Y 19,478).

GILES, William
$330* *"Rock Gorge", 1982,* s., t., (11-16-92, Butterfield, #5990, illus.), 23⁷⁄₁₆ x 19⁹⁄₁₆ in., (595.2 x 496.2 mm.), photograph, gelatin silver print (BP 217, DM 526, FR 1772, Y 41,040).

GILHOOLY, David American b. 1943
$288* *How To Make Jackson Pollocks Dog, 1988,* s., d., annot. APV/VIII, blindstamp publisher, Magnolia Editions, full margins, very good cond., stain, (05-19-93, Butterfield, #2171), 21⅝ x 17½ in., (549 x 445 mm.), lithograph in colors on Rives BFK (BP 187, DM 468, FR 1577, Y 31,883).

GILL, Eric
$168* *"The Crucifixion", 1917: Set Of Twelve,* margins, (01-21-93, Bonhams-Chelsea, #113), subject 9⅛ x 6⅞ in., (23.2 x 17.5 cm.), wood engravings (BP 110, DM 267, FR 904, Y 21,026).
$1023* *Decorative Borders For Chauce's 'The Canterbury Tales' (P. 563-72, 578-79, and 580-81), 1928: Seven,* two to a sheet, proof impressions, each s., num., full margins, goodcond., (12-03-92, Sotheby-London, #171, illus.), wood engravings on chine volant (BP 660, DM 1609, FR 5491, Y 127,286).
$1108* *Initial Letters For Chaucer's 'The Canterbury Tales' (Physick 535-36,586, 593-94, 600, and 603), 1928: Five,* proof impressions, s., num.; one #5/10, full margins, good cond., (12-03-92, Sotheby-London, #170, illus.), wood enrgravings on chine volant or Japan (BP 715, DM 1742, FR 5947, Y 137,862).

GILLER, William
$330* *"The Meet At Badminton",* after William and Henry Barraud, (06-23-93, Doyle, #39), 21¾ x 31½ in., (55.2 x 80

cm.), hand-colored engraving (BP 224, DM 558, FR 1878, Y 35,952).

GILLES, Werner 1894-1961
$636* *Wachter Am Grabe Des Orpheus (Schwengers L 14), 1947,* s., d., t., i., (06-12-93, Hauswedell/Nolt, #100), 14³⁄₁₆ x 17¹⁵⁄₁₆ in., (36 x 45.5 cm.), lithograph on off-white Japan (BP 416, DM 1035, FR 3479, Y 66,926).

GILLIAM, Sam American b. 1933
$495* *"Anchor" and "Untitled": Two,* each s., d. 74 and 72, first t., num. A/P, #15/18, (06-13-93, Hindman, #340), larger 29⅜ x 41½ in., (74.6 x 105.4 cm.), color serigraph (BP 324, DM 806, FR 2708, Y 52,089).
$1210* *Coffee Thyme II,* s., t., #24/65, d. 1980, Vermillion Editions, Ltd., (12-10-92, Sloan, #2688), 30 x 40 in., (76.2 x 101.6 cm.), color lithograph w/intaglio, embossing and debossing on handmade (BP 780, DM 1914, FR 6537, Y 149,678).
$220* *"Cranes" and "Cape": Two,* each s., d. '74, #16/16, A/P, (06-13-93, Hindman, #335), larger 20¾ x 29¾ in., (52.7 x 75.6 cm.), color serigraph, first w/stitching and metal hanger (BP 144, DM 358, FR 1204, Y 23,151).
$550* *Dance '72, 1972,* s., d., i. artist's proof, full margins, mat burn, light staining, rippling, (12-12-92, Weschler, #124), 32 x 18½ in., (81.3 x 47 cm.), color silkscreen (BP 353, DM 867, FR 2970, Y 68,061).
BI *For 200,* s., t., #84/100, d. 1/1/76, est. $6/800, (12-10-92, Sloan, #2692), 17½ x 18¾ in., (44.5 x 47.6 cm.), color lithograph.
BI *For 200,* s., t., #86/100, d. 1/1/76, est. $6/800, (12-10-92, Sloan, #2694), 17½ x 18¾ in., (44.5 x 47.6 cm.), color lithograph.
BI *From The Sweet Fire And Wave,* s., d. (19)72, #54/67, est. $1,0/1,500, (12-10-92, Sloan, #2693), 24 x 18 in., (61 x 45.7 cm.), color lithograph w/intaglio on handmade.
$650* *In Celebration,* s., t., d. (19)87, # "A.P." 25/40, (02-04-93, Sloan, #2940, illus.), 32 x 40 in., (81.3 x 101.6 cm.), screenprint (BP 454, DM 1070, FR 3629, Y 80,856).
$220* *"Meeker's Press" and "Chinaberry": Two,* each s., d. 74, t., num. A/P and #9/10, (06-13-93, Hindman, #339), each 20 x 26½ in., (50.8 x 67.3 cm.), color serigraph (BP 144, DM 358, FR 1204, Y 23,151).
$330* *"Middlesboro" and "Hardstone": Two,* s., d. 76, t., #12/28 and 22/25, (05-16-93, Hindman, #514), each 22 x 21 in., (55.9 x 53.3 cm.), color paper pulp prints w/woodcut, photo etching and embossment (BP 215, DM 531, FR 1784, Y 36,581).
$660* *"Phase" and "Dusk": Two,* each s., t., annot., (06-13-93, Hindman, #336), larger 29⅝ x 29¾ in., (75.2 x 75.6 cm.), color serigraph w/stitching, collage and felt (BP 432, DM 1074, FR 3611, Y 69,452).
$22* *Pulsars HL: Three States Of A Single Poem By Harvy Lewis,* artist's book, s., copy #39/150, pub. by The Perishable Press, Ltd. 1974, (06-13-93, Hindman, #341), overall 11¼ x 6⅛ in., (28.6 x 15.6 cm.), Gilliam color serigraph (BP 14, DM 36, FR 120, Y 2315).
$770* *"Tampa" and "A Fog In The Hollow": Two,* each s., d. '74, t., num. A/P and #3/20, (06-13-93, Hindman, #337), larger 29½ x 41½ in., (74.9 x 105.4 cm.), color serigraph (BP 504, DM 1253, FR 4212, Y 81,027).
$330* *Tee 2 Trane: Two,* each s., d. 74 and 72, t., #3/10 and #9/10, (06-13-93, Hindman, #338), larger 25½ x 40 in., (64.8 x 101.6 cm.), color serigraph, first w/cotton tee-shirt (BP 216, DM 537, FR 1805, Y 34,726).
$110* *"Thursday" and "Glow": Two,* each s., d. '74, t., annot., (06-13-93, Hindman, #334), larger 14 x 20⅝ in., (35.6 x 52.4 cm.), color serigraph, first w/stitching (BP 72, DM 179, FR 602, Y 11,575).

GILLING, Lucille
$171* *The Canterbury Tales: A Folio Of Ten,* s., t., #98/100, pub. 1966, (11-30-92, Ritchie, #8, illus.), each approx. 8¼ x 12½ in., (21 x 31.7 cm.), color etching (BP 113, DM 272, FR 925, Y 21,282, C$ 220).

GILLOT, Claude (after)
BI *Pan Und Syrinx (Nagler Bd. 16, 14, Th. B. Band 14, S. 45),* by Isaac Sarrbat, prov., est. DM 1,200, (03-24-93, Venator/Hansten, #2526), 10³⁄₁₆ x 15⅞ in., (25.8 x 40.4 cm.), mezzotint.

GILLRAY, James British 1757-1815
$383* *The Bridal Night, 1797,* pub. H. Humphrey, trimmed to image, laid down, image in good cond., (10-27-92, Phillips-London, #76), sheet 11¾ x 7½ in., (298 x 191 mm.), etching w/aquatint on laid w/hand-coloring (BP 242, DM 587, FR 1992, Y 46,850).
BI *French Habits (Wright/Evans, 186-189, 192, 194, 1957), 1798,* 7 from set of 12, pub. H. Humphrey, defects, each laid on card, 1 w/tear through image, annotations, est. BP 250/300, (10-27-92, Phillips-London, #74), image 9⅞ x 7½ in., (251 x 191 mm.), etching w/hand-coloring on wove.
BI *The Genuine Works Of James Gillray, Engraved By Himself, 1830,* book, pub. Thomas McLean, disbound, defects, est. BP 3/400, (10-27-92, Phillips-London, #75), sheet 23 x 16¾ in., (584 x 425 mm.), t. page and 155 etchings.
$132* *The Reception Of The Diplomatique And His Suite, 1792,* (06-13-93, Hindman, #369), 12¼ x 15⅝ in., (31.1 x 39.7 cm.), hand-colored etching (BP 86, DM 215, FR 722, Y 13,890).
BI *The Storm Rising; Or, The Republican Flotilla In Danger, 1798,* pub. H. Humphrey, stained, trimmed, est. BP 50/70, (08-12-92, Bonhams, #193), image 10 x 26¼ in., (25.4 x 66.7 cm.), etching w/hand-coloring.
$43* *The Storm Rising; or The Republican Flotilla In Danger, 1798,* pub. H. Humphrey, time-stained, trimmed, (01-14-93, Bonhams, #112), image 10 x 26¼ in., (25.4 x 66.7 cm.), hand-colored etching (BP 28, DM 70, FR 238, Y 5421).

GILOT, Francoise French b. 1921
BI *Floral Still Life,* s., #78/7, est. $6/800, prov., (10-30-92, Sloan, #2377), 25½ x 19¾ in., (64.8 x 50.2 cm.), color lithograph.
$330* *Scorpio In Flames,* s., #1/10, Mourlot Press, Paris, 1970, prov., (10-30-92, Sloan, #2380), 8⅝ x 10⅜ in., (21.9 x 26.4 cm.), lithograph on arches paper w/gouache highlights (BP 211, DM 508, FR 1722, Y 40,877).
$303* *Scorpio In Flowers, 1970,* s., #1/10, Mourlot Press, prov., (05-28-93, Sloan, #1904, illus.), 8⅝ x 10⅜ in., (21.9 x 26.4 cm.), lithograph w/gouache on Arches (BP 194, DM 481, FR 1625, Y 32,490).

GILPIN, Henry
$770* *Black Rock And Ocean, 1978,* s., photog. stamp, (11-16-92, Butterfield, #5991, illus.), 15¼ x 19⁷⁄₁₆ in., (388 x 493 mm.), photograph, gelatin silver print (BP 507, DM 1228, FR 4135, Y 95,759).

GILPIN, Laura American 1891-1980
$2090* *Ason Kinlichinee,* sig., d., 1934, p.l., (10-14-92, Swann, #461, illus.), 13 x 10 in., (33 x 25.4 cm.), photograph, silver print (BP 1227, DM 3059, FR 10,372, Y 253,272).
$2760* *The Flower Garden, 1927,* s.; s., d., label, exhib. label, lit., (04-08-93, Christie-NY, #385, illus.), 9½ x 7½ in., (24.1 x 19.1 cm.), photograph, palladium print (BP 1810, DM 4434, FR 15,008, Y 313,209).
$2530* *My Hand And Seal, 1935-37,* s., t. twice, d., i., (04-08-93, Christie-NY, #386, illus.), 9½ x 7⅝ in., (24.1 x 19.4 cm.), photograph, gelatin silver print (BP 1659, DM 4064, FR 13,757, Y 287,108).
$8800* *Navaho Medicine Man, Red Rock, Arizona, 1932 (Enduring Grace, pl. 71),* annot. by photog., s., d., studio label, t., d., (10-15-92, Sotheby-NY, #227, illus.), 9⅝ x 7⅝ in., (24.4 x 19.4 cm.), photograph, platinum print (BP 5385, DM 13,099, FR 44,422, Y 1,055,789).
BI *Portrait Of A Woman, 1926,* s., d., est. $1,2/1,600, (05-23-93, Butterfield, #3428, illus.), 9½ x 7½ in., photograph, platinum print.

GILPIN, S. (after)
$15 *"The Kill",* engraved by John Scott, (04-16-93, G.A. Key, #70), 8 x 11 in., (20.3 x 27.9 cm.), colored engraving (BP 10, DM 24, FR 82, Y 1687).

GINGRAS, Gilles Emmanuel Canadian School b. 1932
$140* *"Premiere Neige",* #34/40, s., d. Gingras 82, t., (07-14-92, Encans, #45), 9⁷⁄₁₆ x 13¾ in., (24 x 35 cm.), etching (BP 73, DM 208, FR 700, Y 17,507, C$ 167).

$112* *"Pres Du Fleuve"*, num. E.A., s., d. Gilles E. Gingras 80, t., (07-14-92, Encans, #44), 10¹⁄₁₆ x 13¹⁵⁄₁₆ in., (25.5 x 35.5 cm.), etching (BP 58, DM 166, FR 560, Y 14,005, C$ 133).

GINNER, Charles
$487* *"Horse In Front Of A Cottage"*, *"A View Of A Village"* and *"Village Street": Three*, good cond. w/traces of ink from printing, (10-27-92, Phillips-London, #263), borderline 9 x 6½ in., (229 x 165 mm.), wood block (BP 308, DM 746, FR 2533, Y 59,572).
BI *On The Embankment*, s., margins, good cond., est. BP 3/400, (12-03-92, Sotheby-London, #169, illus.), 5½ x 7½ in., (140 x 191 mm.), woodcut w/handcloring on wove.

GINSBERG, Allen   American 20th cent.
$770* *Full Conscious Portrait of Beautiful Jack Kerouac...*, s., i., (12-10-92, Sloan, #2730, illus.), (27.3 x 35.2 cm.), photograph, b/w (BP 496, DM 1218, FR 4160, Y 95,250).
$330* *Implacable-Eyed Burroughs...*, s., d. July 7, '84, i., (12-10-92, Sloan, #2733), 14 x 11 in., (35.6 x 27.9 cm.), photograph, b/w (BP 213, DM 522, FR 1783, Y 40,821).
$385* *Jack Kerouac, William Burroughs And Others On The Beach*, s., d. 1957, i., (12-10-92, Sloan, #2732), 10⅞ x 13⅞ in., (27.6 x 35.2 cm.), photograph, b/w (BP 248, DM 609, FR 2080, Y 47,625).
$468* *Myself With Familiar Monkey...*, s., d. 1963, i., (12-10-92, Sloan, #2734), 11 x 14 in., (27.9 x 35.6 cm.), photograph, b/w (BP 302, DM 740, FR 2528, Y 57,892).
$303* *Timothy Leary Visiting Neal Cassady...*, s., d., i., (12-10-92, Sloan, #2731), 13⅞ x 10⅞ in., (35.2 x 27.6 cm.), photograph, b/w (BP 195, DM 479, FR 1637, Y 37,481).

GINSBURG, Yankel   American b. 1945
$138* *Continuity*, s., num. 164/200, (11-12-92, Freemn/Fine Art, #76), 31½ x 23½ in., (80 x 59.7 cm.), serigraph (BP 91, DM 219, FR 738, Y 17,111).
$110* *D.C. On The Grow*, s., num. 37/250, good cond., (05-22-93, Weschler, #186), 14 x 17¾ in., (35.6 x 45.1 cm.), serigraph and collage in colors (BP 71, DM 179, FR 602, Y 12,128).

GIORDANO, Luca   Italian 1632-1705
$4313* *Christ, The Virgin And St. Anne (B. 6), c. 1650*, 1st state of 2, plate tone, countermark, restoration in image, defect, stains, good cond., The Suida Manning Coll., (05-13-93, Sotheby-NY, #268), 13 x 10 in., (331 x 255 mm.), etching (BP 2832, DM 6964, FR 23,491, Y 481,523).

GIOVANNINI, Francesco
$1093* *Il Viandante*, 1940s, t., credit/exhib. stamps, (04-08-93, Christie-NY, #189, illus.), 14½ x 11¼ in., (36.8 x 28.6 cm.), photograph, gelatin silver print (BP 717, DM 1756, FR 5943, Y 124,035).
$1100* *Solitudine In Due, c. 1950*, t., credit stamp, prov., (10-13-92, Christie-NY, #452, illus.), 9¼ x 7 in., (23.5 x 17.8 cm.), photograph, gelatin silver print (BP 641, DM 1611, FR 5475, Y 133,382).

GIR, Charles   French b. 1883
$310* *"Arlequin"*, before letter, (01-31-93, Morelle/Marchan, #177), 31½ x 47¼ in., (80 x 120 cm.), poster (BP 208, DM 499, FR 1688, Y 38,673).
$248* *Casino De Paris, Le Gorille Et La Femme, 1925*, (01-31-93, Morelle/Marchan, #31), 46⁷⁄₁₆ x 60⅝ in., (118 x 154 cm.), poster (BP 167, DM 400, FR 1351, Y 30,938).
BI *Leo Madelaine*, H. Chacoin Imp., B+ cond., soiling, closed tears, est. $7/1,000, (08-06-92, Swann, #139, illus.), 62 x 46 in., (157.5 x 116.8 cm.), .
$372* *Venise, Operette De Mouezy-Eon, 1927*, (01-31-93, Morelle/Marchan, #159), 31½ x 47¼ in., (80 x 120 cm.), poster (BP 250, DM 599, FR 2026, Y 46,407).
$210* *Venise, Operette, Musique De A. Willemetz, 1927*, p. H. Chachouin, very good cond., (11-19-92, Ribeyre/Baron, #177), 46⁷⁄₁₆ x 30¹¹⁄₁₆ in., (118 x 78 cm.), poster (BP 138, DM 335, FR 1128, Y 26,116).

GIRAN, F.
$201* *Kina Perrier Nimes*, very good cond., (02-13-93, Morelle/Marchan, #48), 31½ x 39⅜ in., (80 x 100 cm.), poster (BP 142, DM 333, FR 1128, Y 24,240).

GIRARDET, Jules (after)
$385* *"The Fortune Telling"*, (10-11-92, Dunning, #1269), 7½ x 9 in., (19.1 x 22.9 cm.), (BP 228, DM 572, FR 1920, Y 46,871).

GIRARDOT, L.
BI *L'Andalousie Au Tamps Des Maures*, good cond., (03-13-93, Laurin, #23), 100⅜ x 37⅜ in., (255 x 95 cm.), .

GIRBAL, G.
$186* *Casino De Paris, 1943*, (01-31-93, Morelle/Marchan, #196), 14¹⁵⁄₁₆ x 22¹³⁄₁₆ in., (38 x 58 cm.), poster (BP 125, DM 300, FR 1013, Y 23,204).

GIRERD, Jean Pierre   Canadian School b. 1932
$372* *"Au Prix Que J'Vous Paie, Vous Avez Pas Jase Beaucoup, Beaucoup!"*, num. E. Atelier 5/8, s., d. Girerd 82, t., (07-14-92, Encans, #46), 21¹⁄₁₆ x 21¹⁄₁₆ in., (53.5 x 53.5 cm.), serigraph (BP 194, DM 552, FR 1861, Y 46,517, C$ 444).

GIRKE, Raimund   b. 1930
BI *Progressionen, 1968: Six*, pub. Spiegel Gallery, #57/95, pencil s., est. DM 2,400, (11-20-92, Lempertz, #554), 27⅝ x 27⅜ in., (70.2 x 69.5 cm.), color serigraph on hand-made cardboard.
$318* *Raute, 1970*, s., d., num., (11-28-92, Schoppmann, #557), 29¹⁵⁄₁₆ x 22¼ in., (76 x 56.5 cm.), serigraph on silver cardboard (BP 210, DM 507, FR 1720, Y 39,577).

GIROUX
BI *Roman Ruins, Arles*, 1850s, neg. num. 59, mounted on card, blindstamped credit Giroux, 371 x 270mm, est. BP 2/300, (05-07-93, Sotheby-London, #115, illus.), photograph, albumen print from waxed paper neg..

GLACKENS, William   American 1870-1938
$412* *Scribner's For February*, B+ cond., skillfully restored, (08-06-92, Swann, #140, illus.), 22 x 14½ in., (55.9 x 36.8 cm.), (BP 215, DM 609, FR 2056, Y 52,551).

GLAHA, Ben   1899-1970
$25,300* *Boulder Dam, 1935*, s., d. by photog., mounted, (04-06-93, Sotheby-NY, #191, illus.), 16¼ x 11⅛ in., photograph (BP 16,711, DM 40,760, FR 138,025, Y 2,885,493).
BI *Stairwell At Boulder Dam, 1932*, i. by photog., est. $2/3,000, (10-15-92, Sotheby-NY, #197, illus.), 11⅛ x 8⅛ in., (28.3 x 20.6 cm.), photograph, gelatin silver print.

GLARNER, Fritz   American 1899-1972
BI *Color Drawing For Relational Painting (Sparks 9), 1963*, s., d., #15/35, ULAE blindstamp, full margins, time staining, very good cond., est. $1,5/2,000, (05-11-93, Christie-NY, #429), sheet 31¾ x 23¼ in., (806 x 591 mm.), color lithograph on Crisbrook.
$385* *"Tondo"*, s. Glarner, d. '49, good cond.?, (11-21-92, Bakker, #178), sight 8 x 7 in., (20.3 x 17.8 cm.), screen print (BP 253, DM 614, FR 2068, Y 47,880).

GLASGOW, Robert MacLean
$978* *Fine Architectural Photography Photomontage*, 1930s, tipped to mount of hand-made laid paper folded as brochure w/letterpress credit, t., accompanying legend, stamped credit and 2 mounted gelatin silver prints of architectural landscapes, (04-08-93, Christie-NY, #289, illus.), 5½ x 4⅛ in., (14 x 10.5 cm.), photograph, gelatin silver print (BP 641, DM 1571, FR 5318, Y 110,985).

GLASSER, Milton
BI *(Olympia), 1974*, s., d., annot. Printers' proof, full margins, good cond., staining, foxing, est. $5/700, (02-24-93, Butterfield, #3215), 17⁷⁄₁₆ x 23⅛ in., (443 x 587 mm.), silkscreen in colors on BFK Rives.
BI *Olympia, 1974*, s., annot. printers proof, full margins, good cond., faint staining,est. $3/500, (05-19-93, Butterfield, #2172), 17⁷⁄₁₆ x 23⅛ in., (443 x 587 mm.), silkscreen in colors on Rives BFK.

GLEASON, Joe Duncan   American 1881-1959
$110* *Sailing Ship*, s. J. Duncan Gleason, (11-10-92, Moran, #161), 15 x 12 in., (38.1 x 30.5 cm.), serigraph on canvas board (BP 73, DM 176, FR 596, Y 13,692).

GLEICHMANN, Otto   German 1887-1963
$110* *A Crowded Street, c. 1919*, very good cond., (11-21-92, Bakker, #140), 7 x 5½ in., (17.8 x 14 cm.), lithograph (BP 72, DM 175, FR 591, Y 13,680).

GLEIZES, Albert   French 1881-1953
BI *Blaise Pascal. Pensees Sur L'Homme Et Sur Dieu*, book in two vols., text and title-page, #II, each s., i., pub. P. Klein, Editions de la Cicogne, 1950, est. BP 12/15,000, (06-30-93, Sotheby-London, #445, illus.), overall 13¼ x 9⅝ in., (337 x 244 mm.), 57 etchings, on Montval laid, 3 original ink drawings, a preparatoryink and watercolor drawing, a suite of plates.
$987* *Centre Noir (Jahn/Berger, Die Schaffenden, 113), 1921*, mono., d. in stone, blindstamp, (05-26-93, Dorling, #2672, illus.), 14⅛ x 10½ in., (35.8 x 26.6 cm.), lithograph on wove (BP 639, DM 1610, FR 5420, Y 107,236).
$1320* *Composition Cubiste, 1921*, s., d., full margins, good cond., minor variations in color, surfacescuffing, paper remains, restoration, mat staining, (02-24-93, Butterfield, #2740, illus.), 11⅞ x 14 in., (302 x 356 mm.), pochoir on wove (BP 921, DM 2143, FR 7265, Y 154,893).

GLEMME, Lennart   b. 1927
$45* *Utsikt, Stockholm*, s., 209/310, (04-17-93, Falkkloos, #136), 7⅞ x 18⅞ in., (20 x 48 cm.), etching (BP 29, DM 72, FR 243, Y 5004, SK 330).

GLOEDEN, Wilhelm von   German 1856-1931
$275* *Figure Study Of A Young Woman And Boy, c. 1900*, (10-29-92, Christie-London, #85), 8¾ x 6¾ in., (22.2 x 17.1 cm.), photograph, albumen print mounted on card (BP 176, DM 423, FR 1435, Y 34,064).
$9074* *Male Nudes, c. 1910: Eighty-Seven*, album, one w/p. t., photog.' scredit, i.; p. page w/ photog.'s credit, t., (05-06-93, Christie-London, #121, illus.), smallest 9 x 6¾ in., largest 14½ x 11¼ in., photograph, 21 albumen, 59 gelatin silver, 1 photogravure and others (BP 5750, DM 14,292, FR 48,112, Y 998,350).
$645* *Mannlicher Akt Mit Blumenkranz, c. 1900*, (11-12-92, Lempertz, #78, illus.), 6⁷⁄₁₆ x 4¹³⁄₁₆ in., (16.3 x 12.2 cm.), sheet 10⅝ x 8¼ in., (16.3 x 12.2 cm.), photograph, gelatin silver print (BP 412, DM 1014, FR 3455, Y 79,797).
$455* *Mannlicher Akt Mit Haarband, c. 1900*, (11-12-92, Lempertz, #77, illus.), 4⁵⁄₁₆ x 6⁵⁄₁₆ in., (11 x 16 cm.), sheet 8¼ x 10⅝ in., (11 x 16 cm.), photograph, albumin print (BP 291, DM 715, FR 2437, Y 56,291).
$575* *Portrait Of A Boy*, 1890s, photog.'s stamp, (05-23-93, Butterfield, #3651, illus.), 9 x 6½ in., photograph, albumen print (BP 374, DM 940, FR 3165, Y 63,557).

GLUME, Johann Freidrich   1711-1788
$72* *Alter Bartiger Mann, Die Hande Auf Einen Stock Gestuzt (Soldan 14), 1749*, (12-04-92, Bassenge, #6583), 5⅛ x 4¼ in., (13 x 10.8 cm.), etching (BP 46, DM 115, FR 389, Y 8989).
$116* *Der Bildhauer Friedrich Christian Glume, Bruder Des Radierers (Soldan26 II)*, prov., (12-04-92, Bassenge, #6584), 5 x 4³⁄₁₆ in., (12.7 x 10.6 cm.), etching (BP 74, DM 185, FR 627, Y 14,482).
BI *Junge Frau Mit Sonnenschirm (Huber 1788, 2; Heller-Andresen 10; Soldan 8 II), 1749*, est. DM 350, (12-04-92, Bassenge, #6581), 5⅛ x 4³⁄₁₆ in., (13 x 10.7 cm.), etching.
$181* *Mann Mit Brille Und Frau, In Einem Buch Lesend (Soldan 11), 1749*, (12-04-92, Bassenge, #6582), 4¹³⁄₁₆ x 4½ in., (12.3 x 11.5 cm.), etching (BP 116, DM 288, FR 978, Y 22,597).

GMELIN, Friedrich Wilhelm
$1210* *Dissertazioni Di Tivoli E Di Albano: Twelve*, Italian and French text, oblong folio, foxing throughout, (11-12-92, Swann, #110, illus.), 15⁹⁄₁₆ x 21¹³⁄₁₆ in., (395 x 554 mm.), etching (BP 795, DM 1917, FR 6467, Y 150,031).

GOCHOTEI UTAGAWA SADAMSU
$665* *Kataoka Gado II As Oguri Hankan*, Oban, s. Sadamaru ga in a toshidama cartouche, pub.'s mark Honsei, d.Tenpo 11 (1840), worm holes, Prof. H.R.W. Kuhne Coll., (06-11-93, Sotheby-London, #476, illus.), 15⅛ x 10⅜ in., (38.4 x 26.4 cm.), woodblock (BP 437, DM 1081, FR 3644, Y 70,557).

GODARD, E (after)
$60* *Chou De Milan Des Vertus*, (04-22-93, Bonhams-Chelsea, #27), image 19 x 24¼ in., (48.3 x 61.6 cm.), reprod. in colors (BP 39, DM 96, FR 325, Y 6597).

GODBY, James
BI *An Analysis Of The Picture Of The Transfiguration: Twenty*, after Raffaelle, volume, staining, est. BP 2/300, (11-19-92, Bonhams-Chelsea, #171), stipple engraving.

GODFREY, William Frederick
$69* *Rustic Bridge, Mt. Hamilton*, s., t., #95/100, exhib., (06-07-93, Ritchie, #26), 7¹¹⁄₁₆ x 8½ in., (19.6 x 21.6 cm.), woodcut on Japan (BP 45, DM 112, FR 377, Y 7402, C$ 88).

GODREUIL, R.
$671* *Les Fratellini, 1929*, p. Bedos & Cie, very good cond., (11-19-92, Ribeyre/Baron, #178), 60⅝ x 45¼ in., (154 x 115 cm.), poster (BP 442, DM 1070, FR 3604, Y 83,447).

GODSON, John Barclay   1882-1957
BI *The Old Toll Bar*, s. J Barclay Godson, i., num 17, est. $50/100, (08-11-92, L. Joel, #75G), 5⅜ x 11⅝ in., (13.7 x 29.5 cm.), etching.

GOEDING, Heinrich (the elder)   1531-1606
$332* *Gott Verheisst Abraham Einen Sohn (Hollstein 2), 1595*, from a series of six etchings Szenen aus dem Leben Abrahams, (12-04-92, Bassenge, #6210), 7½ x 11⅞ in., (19.1 x 30.2 cm.), etching (BP 213, DM 529, FR 1794, Y 41,448).

GOENEUTTE, Norbert   French 1854-1894
$303* *"6 Pointes Seches Parisiennes", 1887: Two*, one s. Norbert Goeneutte, pub. L. Dumont, very good/good cond., (09-27-92, Bakker, #219, illus.), image, one 9¾ x 7¼ in., (24.8 x 18.4 cm.), image, the other 5¼ x 6½ in., (24.8 x 18.4 cm.), color etching (BP 177, DM 449, FR 1519, Y 36,572).
$706* *Dans La Bergerie (I.F.F. 60; De Knyff 59)*, thin margins, from edit. of 50, ded., red artist stamp, (05-15-93, Loudmer, #302, illus.), 18¼ x 12¹⁵⁄₁₆ in., (464 x 328 mm.), etching en (and) bistre on creme wove (BP 459, DM 1136, FR 3816, Y 78,262).
$372* *Femme Vue De Face (G. de K., 106), 1894*, num. 71, inits., yellowed, creases, tears, large margins, drystamp, (04-02-93, Picard, #117), 20⅞ x 10¹⁄₁₆ in., (53 x 25.5 cm.), lithograph on wove (BP 245, DM 598, FR 2031, Y 42,355).
$578* *Jeune Femme Au Plan De Paris (G. de K., 108), 1885*, reddish stains, good margins, (04-02-93, Picard, #118), 21¹⁄₁₆ x 17¹⁵⁄₁₆ in., (53.5 x 45.5 cm.), etching and drypoint (BP 381, DM 929, FR 3155, Y 65,809).
$4436* *Portrait De Paul Gachet Fils (I.F.F. 76; De Knyff 102), 1893*, (05-15-93, Loudmer, #301, illus.), 7¹⁄₁₆ x 6 in., (180 x 153 mm.), sh 12¹⁵⁄₁₆ x 9⅞ in., (180 x 153 mm.), drypoint on wove (BP 2884, DM 7135, FR 23,978, Y 491,741).

GOERG, Edouard   French,b Australia 1893-1968/69
$185* *Le Coup De Foudre, 1956*, s., #5/75, full margins, matstaining, (05-06-93, Laurin, #33), color lithograph on Rives wove (BP 117, DM 291, FR 981, Y 20,354).
$177* *Couple En Buste Au Bouquet*, yellowed, #50/150, s., matstaining, large margins, (06-16-93, Ader Tajan, #101), 13¹⁵⁄₁₆ x 12⅜ in., (35.5 x 31.5 cm.), color lithograph (BP 118, DM 294, FR 986, Y 18,878).
BI *Illustrations Pour Vathek: Two*, s., num., small margins, glue traces, (02-24-93, Picard, #109), lithographs.
BI *"Les Modeles Et Leurs Peintre"*, s. Ed. Goerg, #9/175, t., est. $2/300, (12-12-92, A. James, #493), 27⅛ x 21⅛ in., (68.9 x 53.7 cm.), lithograph.

$102* *Un Recital, c. 1925,* s., num., dust, stains, (02-24-93, Picard, #108), etching and drypoint (BP 71, DM 166, FR 561, Y 11,969).

GOETZ, Henri American 1909-1989

BI *Composition, 1959,* s., #4/40, good margins, (05-06-93, Laurin, #34), carborundum engraving in color.

$168* *"Composition-1973" (K.M. 203),* #30/44, s., (01-28-93, Pescheteau, #151), 19¹¹⁄₁₆ x 25⁹⁄₁₆ in., (50 x 65 cm.), carborundum engraving on Arches (BP 111, DM 266, FR 901, Y 20,859).

$227* *Compositions: Two,* s., #33/45, 38/45, full margins, (03-31-93, Briest, #E47), sh 19¹¹⁄₁₆ x 25⁹⁄₁₆ in., (50 x 65 cm.), aquatints (BP 150, DM 365, FR 1240, Y 26,104).

BI *Komposition I Gront Och Gult,* s. 36/50, est. 1,500, (11-07-92, Falkkloos, #155), woodcut in colors.

BI *Sans Titre,* s., d. in stone, 14/33, est. FF800/1,000, (06-28-93, Loudmer, #254), 18¹¹⁄₁₆ x 10¼ in., (475 x 260 mm.), sh 22¹⁄₁₆ x 14¹⁵⁄₁₆ in., (475 x 260 mm.), black lithograph on wove.

GOETZE, Otto German b. 1868

BI *Five O'Clock Tea,* s. in plate, t., est. $5/800, (06-09-93, Sotheby-Arcade, #240), 12 x 9⅜ in., (30.5 x 23.8 cm.), etching and drypoint in colors.

$33* *Lady At A Balcony,* s., i., bearing blindstamp, (02-11-93, Boos, #407), 6⅝ x 3⅜ in., (260 x 175 mm.), etching and aquatint (BP 23, DM 55, FR 185, Y 3978).

GOFFEY, H.

BI *"Taffy" (Sealyham), "On Guard" (Collie Dog) and "Alert" (Alsatian): Three,* all s., i., margins, est. BP 1/150, (01-18-93, Bonhams, #77), plate 10¾ x 7¾ in., (27.3 x 19.7 cm.), drypoint etching.

GOINES, David Lance

$825* *Untitled: Group Of Ten,* 1974-1987, A cond., (08-06-92, Swann, #141, illus.), (BP 431, DM 1219, FR 4117, Y 105,230).

GOLAY, Mary

BI *Maiden Representing A Flower, One Poppies, The Other Sunflowers, c. 1900: Two,* est. $3/5,000, (06-09-93, Sotheby-Arcade, #237), sight 37½ x 15⅛ in., (95.3 x 38.4 cm.), lithograph.

$460* *Maidens Draped In Flowing Costumes, One With Red Poppies, Other WithSunflowers: Two,* creases, repaired splits; s. in stone, (06-09-93, Sotheby-Arcade, #242, illus.), sight 37¾ x 15¼ in., (95.9 x 38.7 cm.), lithograph laid down (BP 303, DM 752, FR 2530, Y 48,921).

GOLD, Maurice

BI *"Builders Corps De Ballet" and "Spider Men", c. 1960: Two,* mounted on card, stamped photog.'s credit, labels, s., 397 x 596mm, est. BP 5/800, (05-07-93, Sotheby-London, #196, illus.), photograph, silver print.

GOLDBECK, Eugene Omar American 20th cent.

$121* *Democratic National Convention, Houston, Texas,* June '28, s. ink, (05-16-93, Hindman, #368), 7 x 43 in., photograph, panoramic silver print (BP 79, DM 195, FR 658, Y 13,474).

$165* *Galveston's 5th Annual Bathing Girl Revue,* (c) stamp, (05-16-93, Hindman, #366), 32½ x 71½ in., photograph, panoramic silver print (BP 108, DM 266, FR 897, Y 18,374).

$460* *"Intoduction Division, Air Training Command, Lackland Air Base, San Antonio, Texas", 1947,* photog. (c) studio legend, t., d. in neg., s. by photog., credit stamp, label, (04-06-93, Sotheby-NY, #367A, illus.), 15⅞ x 13½ in., photograph (BP 304, DM 741, FR 2510, Y 52,464).

$220* *Old Jerusalem,* (c) stamp, (05-16-93, Hindman, #367), 62 x 9 in., photograph, panoramic silver print (BP 144, DM 355, FR 1196, Y 24,499).

GOLDBERG, Glen American b. 1953

BI *Coil Print, 1986,* s., t., #19/35, full margins, very good cond.?, est. $4/600, (10-28-92, Butterfield, #2960), 17⅞ x 13¾ in., (454 x 349 mm.), color etching w/drypoint and aquatint on cream wove.

GOLDBERG, Maurice

BI *"Bonnie Maude In Hat And Fur" and "Beatrice Maude In "The Tents Of The Arabs"": Two,* selected portraits: Bonnie Maude, 1910, first s., second photog.'s blindstamp on image, t., annot., est. $800/1,000, (05-23-93, Butterfield, #3430, illus.), each approx. 9¼ x 7¼ in., photograph, gelatin silver print.

GOLDBLATT, David

$345* *"Afrikaner Boy" and "Banksman's Chair": Two,* 1970s, p.l., s., t., d., 1st photog.'s stamp; 2nd image ink s., est.$6/800, (05-23-93, Butterfield, #3432), one 9¾ x 9¾ in., other 12½ x 10 in., photograph, gelatin silver print (BP 225, DM 564, FR 1899, Y 38,134).

$403* *"Margaret Meingama, Soweto", "At A Wedding" and "Family At Lunch": Three,* 1960s, p.l., s., t., d., 1st and 2nd image s., est. $7/900, (05-23-93, Butterfield, #3431), from 6½ x 4½ in., to 18¼ x 14¼ in., photograph, gelatin silver print (BP 262, DM 659, FR 2218, Y 44,545).

GOLDWAITE, Anne American 1869-1944

BI *Flutist,* excell. cond., est. $1/200, (01-05-93, Bourne, #234), sight 12 x 9¼ in., (30.5 x 23.5 cm.), print.

$220* *"The Little Oak Ile-Aux-Moines" and "Hill Town In France": Two,* s., t., splits, good cond., (06-11-93, Doyle, #44), 5⅞ x 6¼ in., (149 x 159 mm.), etching (BP 145, DM 358, FR 1205, Y 23,342).

GOLDYNE, Joseph

BI *Eden, Bare, Chaste, Softly Coming Awake, 1982,* s., d. Dec 1982, t., pub. artist, p. Magnolia Press, margins, very good cond., est. $7/9,000, (05-19-93, Butterfield, #2173, illus.), 47⅜ x 35¼ in., (120.3 x 89.5 cm.), monoprint w/hand-coloring on wove.

$413* *The First Spit-Bite Pearl Colored A La Poupee Depicted On A Surface Dimly Evoking The Cubist Intaglio Spirit, 1975,* inits., t., annot. proof, blindstamp pub. Magnolia Editions, full margins, good cond.(10-28-92, Butterfield, #2962), 11¹⁵⁄₁₆ x 9¹²⁄₁₆ in., (303 x 248 mm.), etching and aquatint a la poupee in colors on cream wove (BP 263, DM 638, FR 2166, Y 50,675).

$230* *Red, White And Blue Floral, 1982,* s., t., #5/50, blindstamp publisher, 3EP Ltd., full margins, very good cond., (05-19-93, Butterfield, #2174), 10 x 6 in., (254 x 152 mm.), etching and aquatints in color on wove (BP 149, DM 374, FR 1260, Y 25,462).

$1980* *Vitrine, 1978: Ten,* complete portfolio, s., t., #16/30, w/ colophon, t. and table of contents, blindstamp pub. Smith Anderson Gallery and Jeanne Gantz, full margins, very good cond.?, creases, (10-28-92, Butterfield, #2963), each sheet 13 x 9½ in., (330 x 241 mm.), aquatint w/drypoint and Chine colle (pasted) in colors on Hosho paper on Fabriano Roma Michelangelo paper (BP 1262, DM 3058, FR 10,383, Y 242,945).

GOLE, J.

$177* *"L'Electeur De Baviere" and "Deshabille De Princesse": Two,* 3 sides w/out margins, (06-16-93, Ader Tajan, #11), 9¹⁵⁄₁₆ x 7¹⁄₁₆ in., (25.2 x 18 cm.), black manner engraving (BP 118, DM 294, FR 986, Y 18,878).

GOLE, Jacob c. 1660-1737

$1372* *Bildnis Des Malers Adrian V. Ostade Mit Hut (Hollstein 103),* (12-04-92, Bassenge, #6211), 9 x 6¾ in., (22.9 x 17.1 cm.), red etching (BP 880, DM 2185, FR 7412, Y 171,286).

GOLEY, Mary 20th cent.

BI *Les Cigones (The Swans): Two,* repairs, creases, margins, trimmed, Rod Stewart Coll., est. $15/2000, (11-06-92, Sotheby-Arcade, #142), sight 40 x 15½ in., (101.6 x 39.4 cm.), lithograph in colors.

$660* *The Swans,* s. Mary Goley, pub. ident. (Depose) in matrix, good cond.?, toning, crease, (01-02-93, Skinner, #175, illus.), sheet, sight 41 x 15 in., (104.1 x 38.1 cm.), color lithograph (BP 440, DM 1081, FR 3691, Y 82,748).

GOLINKIN, Joseph American b. 1896

$345* *At Chicago (Joe Louis-Braddock Fight), 1937,* s., pub. AAA, large margins, good cond., mat staining, handling creases, (05-19-93, Butterfield, #1987), 12 x 14½ in., (305 x 368 mm.), lithograph on cream wove (BP 224, DM 561, FR 1889, Y 38,193).

BI *"At Chicago", c. 1935,* s., pub. AAA, tears, paper hinges, time stain, est. $350-450, (10-31-92, Cleveland, #137), 11⅞ x 14⅜ in., (30.2 x 36.5 cm.), lithograph.

$440* *At Chicago, c. 1937,* full margins, pub. AAA, (05-27-93, Swann, #117, illus.), 12 x 14⅜ in., (30.5 x 36.5 cm.), lithograph (BP 282, DM 706, FR 2380, Y 47,170).

$550* *"Baer And Louis" and "At Chicago": Two,* c. 1930, first num. 18/50; both s., wide margins, light-staining, very good cond., (09-19-92, Christie-E, #19), lithograph on wove (BP 316, DM 824, FR 2821, Y 68,527).

$413* *First Round Knockout (Louis And Schmeling),* s., #39/50, (03-14-93, Hindman, #311), 15¾ x 19¾ in., (40 x 50.2 cm.), lithograph (BP 288, DM 687, FR 2337, Y 48,674).

BI *In The Flesh And In The Frame, 1928,* num., s., est. $700/1,000, (05-27-93, Swann, #118), 19 x 13 in., (48.3 x 33 cm.), lithograph.

$605* *The Long Court (Dempsey And Tunney),* s., (03-14-93, Hindman, #310), 19¾ x 16⅛ in., (50.2 x 41 cm.), lithograph (BP 422, DM 1007, FR 3424, Y 71,302).

$495* *Set 'Em Up, 1933,* s., t., #21/25, full margins, time stain, (12-08-92, Swann, #122), 13 x 16 in., (33 x 40.6 cm.), lithograph (BP 310, DM 771, FR 2627, Y 61,353).

$495* *"Set Em Up",* s., very fine cond., (10-31-92, Cleveland, #136, illus.), 13 x 16 in., (33 x 40.6 cm.), lithograph (BP 317, DM 762, FR 2584, Y 61,315).

BI *[Joe Lewis Fight Scene],* c. 1945, s., #4/50, margins, laid down, Frances H. Horne Estate, est. $7/900, (05-13-93, Sotheby-NY, #420), 16 x 19⅞ in., (408 x 504 mm.), lithograph.

GOLTZIUS, Hendrik   Dutch 1558-1617

BI *Apollo (Bartsch 141; Hollstein 131; Strauss 263), 1588,* watermark, prov., est. DM 20,000, (06-10-93, Hauswedell/ Nolt, #98, illus.), engraving in oval.

$16,799* *Arkadische Landschaft Mit Rastendem Paar Und Schafer (Strauss, Hendrik Goltzius, 409/I (v.II); Hoostein Und Hirschmann 379/I (v. II)),* c. 1597-1600, (06-23-93, Kornfeld, #51, illus.), woodcut, mit (with) Deckweiss gehoht (BP 11,412, DM 28,425, FR 95,612, Y 1,830,156, SF 25,300).

$1228* *Bildnis Der Grafin Francoise D'Egmont (B. 168; Hirschmann, Hollstein183 II), 1580,* (12-04-92, Bassenge, #6218), oval 7¼ x 5⁹⁄₁₆ in., (18.4 x 14.2 cm.), engraving (BP 788, DM 1956, FR 6634, Y 153,308).

BI *Bildnis Des Malers Hans Bol (B. 161; Hirschmann, Hollstein 177 I),* est. DM 1,800, (12-04-92, Bassenge, #6217), 10¼ x 6¹⁵⁄₁₆ in., (26 x 17.7 cm.), engraving.

$2875* *The Body Of Christ Supported By Angels (B. 273; Holl. 320; S. 254), 1587,* watermark, wide margins, creases, wormhole, stains, surface dirt, defects, good cond., (05-13-93, Sotheby-NY, #153, illus.), 13¾ x 10 in., (349 x 255 mm.), engraving (BP 1887, DM 4642, FR 15,659, Y 320,978).

$290* *Ceres (B. Saenredam 67; H. 136),* trimmed, crease, (12-01-92, Karl/Faber, #74), engraving (BP 192, DM 462, FR 1575, Y 36,106).

$253* *Christus Vor Kaiphas (Hollstein Bd. 8, 24), 1597,* trimmed, (03-24-93, Venator/Hansten, #2527), pl. approx. 7¹⁵⁄₁₆ x 5¼ in., (20.1 x 13.3 cm.), engraving (BP 171, DM 413, FR 1406, Y 29,726).

$392* *The Circumcision (B. H. 12),* plate 4 from The Life of the Virgin, 3rd state of 5, trimmed to platemark, surface dirt, staining, (09-17-92, Bonhams-Chelsea, #95), plate 18⅜ x 13¾ in., (46.7 x 34.9 cm.), engraving on laid paper (BP 220, DM 582, FR 1992, Y 48,805).

BI *The Circumcision (Besnijdenis), 1594,* The Life of the Virgin, 3rd state, est. G 3,5/4,500, (11-18-92, Bubb Kuyper, #1834, illus.), 18¹¹⁄₁₆ x 13¹³⁄₁₆ in., (47.5 x 35.1 cm.), engraving.

$110* *Contemplative,* (06-11-93, Freemn/Fine Art, #75), 4¾ x 3¾ in., (12.1 x 9.5 cm.), engraving (BP 72, DM 179, FR 603, Y 11,671).

BI *Eight Deities (B. 249-56, H. 296-303, S. 289-96), 1592: Eight,* after Polidoro da Caravaggio, S. 289, 294 and 296 1st states of 4, others 2nd states of 4, margins, staining, foxing, abrasions, good cond., indistinct watermarks, est. $3/4,000, (05-11-93, Christie-NY, #22, illus.), each plate 13⅞ x 8½ in., (352 x 216 mm.), engraving on laid.

$4263* *The Emperor Commodus As Hercules (Holl. 147; S. 314),* from set of Three Famous Antique Statues At Rome, margins, slight damage, central crease, minor defects, good cond., ex-coll., (12-03-92, Sotheby-London, #63, illus.), 16¼ x 11¾ in., (415 x 298 mm.), engraving (BP 2750, DM 6704, FR 22,882, Y 530,422).

$867* *Das Festmahl Von Tarquinius Collatinus (B. 104; Hirschmann und Hollstein 171),* (12-04-92, Bassenge, #6215, illus.), 8⅛ x 9⅝ in., (20.7 x 24.4 cm.), engraving (BP 556, DM 1381, FR 4684, Y 108,240).

$830* *Die Genossen Des Kadmos, Durch Den Drachen Gewurgt (B. 262; H. 310/III(v. IV)), 1588,* after C. van Haarlem, trimmed, (12-01-92, Karl/Faber, #78), engraving (BP 548, DM 1323, FR 4508, Y 103,337).

$166* *The Great Hercules (Hirschmann 143-A),* thin spots, restorations, collector's stamp, (11-18-92, Bubb Kuyper, #1835), 15⅛ x 11³⁄₁₆ in., (38.4 x 28.4 cm.), engraving (BP 109, DM 265, FR 892, Y 20,644, G 300).

$14,584* *The Great Hercules (Holl. 143; S. 283), 1589,* 1st state of 2, trimmed, crease, tear, light stains, (06-30-93, Sotheby-London, #133), 22⅛ x 15⅞ in., (562 x 403 mm.), engraving (BP 9775, DM 24,875, FR 83,913, Y 1,562,627).

BI *The Great Standard-Bearer (Holl. 255; S. 253), 1587,* only state, trimmed within platemark but outside borderline, repairedareas in image, pinhole, central creases, other defects, tape verso, ex-coll.,est. BP 1,5/2,000, (12-03-92, Sotheby-London, #64), 11¼ x 7½ in., (285 x 193 mm.), engraving on paper w/watermark.

BI *Helios (B. 234; Holl. 371; S. 419; Bailler 31), c. 1588-90,* from three blocks, Bailler c impression, watermark, margins, printer's crease, split, surface dirt, good cond., est. $9/12,000, (05-13-93, Sotheby-NY, #154), 13¾ x 10⅜ in., (350 x 265 mm.), chiaroscuro woodcut in blk/ ochre and brown.

$1527* *Helios (Bialler 31/c; Str. 419; Hollst. und Hirschm. 371/ II), c. 15881590,* (06-23-93, Kornfeld, #53), chiaroscuro woodcut from 3 blocks (BP 1037, DM 2584, FR 8691, Y 166,358, SF 2300).

BI *Hercules And Cacus (B. 231; Holl. 373; S. 403; Bia. 25), 1588,* from three blocks, Bialler's state Ic, watermark, narrow margins, repaired tear, creases, breaks, repair, folds, soiling, Daniel A. Don Estate, est.$8/12,000, (05-13-93, Sotheby-NY, #155, illus.), 15⅞ x 12¾ in., (402 x 325 mm.), chiaroscuro woodcut in blk., tan, red and green.

$9670* *Hercules Erschlagt Cacus (Hollstein Bd. VIII, 373),* s., d. HGoltzius Inue. Ao 88, restored, (09-14-92, Venator/Hansten, #1512, illus.), 16 x 12¹⁵⁄₁₆ in., (40.7 x 33 cm.), color chiaroscuro woodcut w/2 color plates over blk. (BP 5114, DM 14,375, FR 48,715, Y 1,202,437).

BI *Hercules Killing Cacus, (B. 231; H. 373; S. 403), 1588,* Strauss's third state (of four), trimmed, colors faded, fold, creased, repaired tear, hole, defects, laid, prov., est. BP 4/6000, (12-01-92, Christie-London, #96, illus.), L. 15¹⁵⁄₁₆ x 12¹³⁄₁₆ in., (405 x 325 mm.), chiaroscuro woodcut from 3 blocks, in blk., olive-green, and ochre-yellow.

BI *Hercules Slaying Cacus (B. 231, Hirschmann 373 III, Hollstein 373 Wohl IV, The Illustr. Bartsch 3 (Commentary) 231 S 3, Bialler 25 III), 1588,* trimmed, est. DM 3500, (06-04-93, Bassenge, #5180, illus.), 15¹⁵⁄₁₆ x 12 in., (40.6 x 30.5 cm.), chiaroscuro woodcut by 3 blocks.

BI *The Holy Family (Holl. 319; S. 281),* after Spranger, trimmed irregularly, printing defects, staining, surface dirt, Ex coll. F. Gawet (L. 1069) and Jan Musin, est. BP 3/ 3,500, (06-30-93, Sotheby-London, #129, illus.), 10½ x 8¼ in., (267 x 210 mm.), engraving.

$993* *Maria Magdalena (Bialler 22/II; Str. 405/III; Hollst. und Hirschm. 363/III), c. 1585-1588,* (06-23-93, Kornfeld, #52), chiaroscuro woodcut from 3 blocks (BP 675, DM 1680, FR 5652, Y 108,182, SF 1495).

$314* *Mars And Venus Surprised By Vulcan (Hollstein 137; Strauss 216), 1585,* 3rd state of 3, w/address of L. Renard, (06-09-93, Bubb Kuyper, #2050, illus.), 16⁹⁄₁₆ x 12³⁄₁₆ in., (42 x 31 cm.), engraving (BP 207, DM 514, FR 1727, Y 33,394, G 575).

$1373* *Mars Surprised With Venus (Holl. 137; S. 216), 1585,* 1st state of 3, trimmed, crease, nick, paper thin, good cond., (06-30-93, Sotheby-London, #130), 16 x 12 in., (406 x

305 mm.), engraving on paper w/a large Strasburg Lily in Shield watermark (BP 920, DM 2342, FR 7900, Y 147,112).

$2311* *Mars Und Venus (B. 276, Hollstein 321 III), 1588,* after Bartholomaeus Spranger, (12-04-92, Bassenge, #6221), 17³⁄₁₆ x 12¹⁵⁄₁₆ in., (43.7 x 33 cm.), engraving (BP 1482, DM 3681, FR 12,485, Y 288,514).

BI *The Martyrdom Of The Apostles,* margins, good cond., staining, surface soiling, notations, est. $3/500, (10-28-92, Butterfield, #2813), 8⅛ x 10⅞ in., (206 x 276 mm.), engraving on laid paper.

BI *"The Martyrdom Of The Apostles" (Hirschmann 350-361 Only States H. 354 1/11, H. 360 1/11): Set Of Twelve,* margins, good cond. except H. 350 w/ink mark in center of image, H. 359 w/staining in margin and image, est. $3/4,000, (05-15-93, Cleveland, #13), 8¼ x 11⅜ in., (21 x 28.9 cm.), engraving in 16th cent. paper w/watermark on some sheets.

$440* *The Massacre Of The Innocents (Bartsch 23, Hollstein 17, Strauss 206),* 2nd final state, (03-24-93, Grogan, #7), 17¼ x 14⅝ in., (43.8 x 37.1 cm.), engraving (BP 298, DM 719, FR 2446, Y 51,698).

BI *Nach Stradanas, "Kampfende Pferde" (B./Strauss 293, Hirschmann 348 1),* from series "Pferde aus dem Mastelles des Juan d'Austria", est. SC 6/7,000, (11-11-92, Dorotheum, #305), 7⅞ x 7¼ in., (20 x 18.4 cm.), engraving.

BI *Nach Stradanus "Auferstehung der Toten" (B./Strauss 281, Hirschmann 35, 1),* (11-11-92, Dorotheum, #306), engraving.

BI *Pieta (B. 41, H. 50, S. 331), 1596: Two,* 2nd final state, trimmed, fold, nick, staining, watermark, prop. Montclair Art Museum, est. $700/1,000, (05-11-93, Christie-NY, #23), engraving on laid.

$3665* *Pieta (Str. 331/II; Hollst. und Hirschm. 50/II),* before 1596, watermark, prov., (06-23-93, Kornfeld, #54, illus.), engraving (BP 2490, DM 6201, FR 20,859, Y 399,281, SF 5520).

BI *The Standard-Bearer Standing Facing Right (Holl. 252; S. 215), 1585,* est. BP 1,5/2,500, (06-30-93, Sotheby-London, #128), 8⅜ x 6 in., (213 x 152 mm.), engraving on paper w/a Coat of Arms of Basel watermark.

$84* *The Twelve Apostles,* 2 from set of 12, surface dirt, margins, staining, 1 torn, (01-21-93, Bonhams-Chelsea, #118), plate 6 x 4⅛ in., (15.2 x 10.5 cm.), engravings (BP 55, DM 134, FR 452, Y 10,513).

$8498* *Die Vier Himmelsturmer (B. 258-261, Hirschmann, Hollstein 306-309 I),1588: Four,* after Cornelis Cornelisz. van Haarlem, watermark, (06-04-93, Bassenge, #5181), copper engraving in a circle (BP 5622, DM 13,800, FR 46,513, Y 916,523).

BI *Zwei Sybillen (B. 248; H. 304/II),* after Caravaggio, trimmed, est. DM 700, (12-01-92, Karl/Faber, #77), engraving.

GOLTZIUS, Hendrik (after)

$165* *Acer In Adversos Tendo Dum Signifer Hostes, Martiolis Creseit Spesque, Animique Vigor,* by Jacob De Gheyn, margins, foxing, crease, (06-16-93, Bonhams-Chelsea, #305, illus.), pl. 8½ x 6⅛ in., (21.6 x 15.6 cm.), engraving on laid paper (BP 110, DM 274, FR 919, Y 17,598).

$472* *"Aestas",* by Jacob Matham, trimmed, (03-24-93, Venator/Hansten, #2528), engraving (BP 320, DM 771, FR 2624, Y 55,458).

BI *Conserte Turbare Acies Sorte Agmine Amicas Si Puret Hostis Atrox Nostra Sarissa Vetat,* by Jacob De Gheyn, margins, foxing, creasing, BP 1/150, (06-16-93, Bonhams-Chelsea, #306), pl. 8½ x 6⅛ in., (21.6 x 15.6 cm.), engraving on laid paper.

$182* *Dupla Ego Pro Meritis Mereor Stipendia; Nempe Insigni Reliquis Strennuitate Prior,* by Jacob De Gheyn, margins, foxing, creasing, (06-16-93, Bonhams-Chelsea, #307, illus.), pl. 8½ x 6⅛ in., (21.6 x 15.6 cm.), engraving on laid paper (BP 121, DM 302, FR 1014, Y 19,411).

BI *Et Genus Et Mea Me, Virtus Terraque Marique Non Imo Patitur Nomen Habere Loco,* by Jacob De Gheyn, margins, foxing, creasing, BP 1/150, (06-16-93, Bonhams-Chelsea, #308), pl. 8½ x 6⅛ in., (21.6 x 15.6 cm.), engraving on laid paper.

$165* *Militie Caput, Et Magnum Inter Prelia Fulmen, Infracta Auspicys Pectora Reddo Meis,* by Jacob De Gheyn, margins, foxing, crease, (06-16-93, Bonhams-Chelsea, #309), pl. 8½ x 6⅛ in., (21.6 x 15.6 cm.), engraving on laid paper (BP 110, DM 274, FR 919, Y 17,598).

$198* *Munus Ego Absentis Ducis Expleo, Et Alter Ab Illo Jure Locum Teneo, Iure Capesso Vicem,* by Jacob De Gheyn, margins, foxing, crease, (06-16-93, Bonhams-Chelsea, #310), pl. 8½ x 6⅛ in., (21.6 x 15.6 cm.), engraving on laid paper (BP 132, DM 329, FR 1103, Y 21,118).

$165* *Phaeton,* after C.C. Pictor, trimmed margins, (06-26-93, Wolf, #947), engraving (BP 110, DM 280, FR 944, Y 17,507).

$182* *Tempore Si Numerem Prompte Stipendia Certo, Impavidos Animos Martia Turba Capit,* by Jacob De Gheyn, margins, foxing, creasing, (06-16-93, Bonhams-Chelsea, #311), pl. 8½ x 6⅛ in., (21.6 x 15.6 cm.), engraving on laid (BP 121, DM 302, FR 1014, Y 19,411).

$101* *"Thalie", "Clio" and "Non Me Durarum Terrent": Three,* first: loss, third: crease, dirt spots, big margins, (05-15-93, Loudmer, #71), smallest 9⅝ x 6½ in., (244 x 165 mm.), largest 10½ x 6⅞ in., (244 x 165 mm.), copper engraving on laid (BP 66, DM 162, FR 546, Y 11,196).

GONCHAROVA, Nataliia Sergeevna 1881-1962

$2830* *"Aleksei Kruchenykh And Velemir Khlebnikov, Igra V Adu" and "Poema" ("A Game In Hell" and "A Poem") (Compton p. 125), 1912,* 1st edit. G.L. Kuz'min and S.D. Dolinskii, Moscow, 1912, excellent cond., handling defects, very good cond., (12-01-92, Christie-London, #522, illus.), overall sheet 7⁵⁄₁₆ x 5¹³⁄₁₆ in., (186 x 147 mm.), lithograph on buff wove (BP 1870, DM 4511, FR 15,372, Y 352,341).

GONCHAROVA, Nataliia, Nikolai KUL'BIN, and Ol'ga ROZA NOVA

$2997* *A. Kruchenykh, Vzorval' (Explodity) (Karshan 5-6; Compton p. 125), 1913,* 28 pages of lithographic and rubber-stamped text and lithographs, nicks, spot, (12-01-92, Christie-London, #523, illus.), overall sheet 7⁵⁄₁₆ x 4¹⁵⁄₁₆ in., (186 x 125 mm.), colored lithograph and lithograph on thin buff and cream wove (BP 1980, DM 4777, FR 16,279, Y 373,132).

GOODE, Joe

$303* *"Untitled" and "Untitled", 1969: Two,* s., d., num. 31/98 and 91/98, good cond., tears, hinge remains, rubbed area, creases, surface soiling, (02-24-93, Butterfield, #3216), each sheet 22 x 30 in., (559 x 762 mm.), lithograph in colors on Arches (BP 211, DM 492, FR 1668, Y 35,555).

BI *Untitled, 1978,* inits., #23/33, blindstamp publisher, Cirrus, full margins, good cond., est. $3/500, (05-19-93, Butterfield, #2175), 17⁹⁄₁₆ x 14⁹⁄₁₆ in., (446 x 370 mm.), lithograph in colors on black wove.

GOODEN, Stephen

BI *The Book Of Revelation, 1939: Set Of Three,* s., d., pub. George C. Harrap, full margins, good cond., est. $1/1,200, (02-11-93, Sotheby-NY, #145), etching.

GOODHART, John Christian 1875-1954

$122* *The Bridge At Richmond,* s. J.C Goodhart, i. Trial Proof, (08-11-92, L. Joel, #44G), 8⅛ x 11¼ in., (20.7 x 28.6 cm.), etching (BP 63, DM 179, FR 606, Y 15,623, A$ 165).

$162* *The Ross Bridge,* s. J.C. Goodhart, i., #8/60, (08-11-92, L. Joel, #7G), 8⁹⁄₁₆ x 11⅛ in., (21.7 x 28.3 cm.), etching (BP 84, DM 238, FR 805, Y 20,745, A$ 220).

GOODNOUGH

$88* *Abstract,* s., d. 73, #4/150, very good cond.?, (02-07-93, Bakker, #179), sheet 25 x 31 in., (63.5 x 78.7 cm.), screenprint (BP 61, DM 146, FR 493, Y 10,951).

GOODNOUGH, Robert American b. 1917

$88* *Composition,* s., d. 73, #34/150, (05-16-93, Hindman, #621), 22 x 30 in., (55.9 x 76.2 cm.), color serigraph (BP 57, DM 142, FR 476, Y 9755).

$110* *From One Two Three (An Homage To Pablo Casals),* s., d. 68, #22/150, (12-13-92, Hindman, #341), 15¾ x 25¾ in., color serigraph (BP 70, DM 173, FR 589, Y 13,609).

$110* *From One Two Three (An Homage To Pablo Casals),* s., d. 68, #22/150, (12-13-92, Hindman, #338), 17¾ x 18½ in., serigraph in red and gray (BP 70, DM 173, FR 589, Y 13,609).

$440* *Untitled, 1973: Four,* each s., (10-18-92, Hindman, #489), each 23 x 30 in., (58.4 x 76.2 cm.), serigraphs (BP 269, DM 655, FR 2221, Y 52,789).

GOOST, Bertha

$17 *"Llangollen Bridge",* s., (10-09-92, G.A. Key, #88), 8 x 12 in., (20.3 x 30.5 cm.), etching (BP 10, DM 25, FR 86, Y 2073).

GORDE, G.

$259* *PLM. Alpe D'Huez. Huez, Ete-Hiver, Dauphine. "Neige, Soleil, Fleurs",* very good cond., (03-15-93, Arcole, #93), 39⅜ x 24⁷⁄₁₆ in., (100 x 62 cm.), (BP 180, DM 430, FR 1462, Y 30,680).

$379* *PLM. Pralognan La Vanoise. Savoie. Altitude 1430 m., 1936,* very good cond., (03-15-93, Arcole, #38), 39⅜ x 24³⁄₁₆ in., (100 x 61.5 cm.), (BP 264, DM 630, FR 2140, Y 44,895).

$319* *SNCF. Chamonix. Gorges De La Diosaz. Gare De Servoz, 1947,* very good cond., (03-15-93, Arcole, #37, illus.), 39⅜ x 24⁷⁄₁₆ in., (100 x 62 cm.), (BP 222, DM 530, FR 1801, Y 37,787).

GORDGE, John

$755* *Shell Motor Oil, Modern Lubrication For Modern Motors, 1929,* p. Waterlow & Sons, ref. #187, cond. 3, (10-13-92, Phillips-London, #65), 29¾ x 44¹¹⁄₁₆ in., (75.5 x 113.5 cm.), color lithograph (BP 440, DM 1106, FR 3758, Y 91,548).

GORDON, P.S.

BI *Nell's Bell, 1992,* s., d., annot. pr.p. 5/6, blindstamp publisher, Trillium Graphics, full margins, good cond., est. $6/800, (05-19-93, Butterfield, #2176), 40¼ x 25¾ in., (102.2 x 65.4 cm.), silkscreen in colors on wove.

GORDY, Dudely British late 19th cent.

BI *The Chieftain,* from Les Maitres de l'Affiche, PL. 48, est. $150/200, (02-14-93, Hanzel, #675), 1 x 6½ in., (2.5 x 16.5 cm.), color lithograph.

GORIN, Jean

$77* *"Circle In A Square" and "Red Circle Composition": Two,* both, s. artist's proof; second, tear, (06-28-93, Loudmer, #49), first 17¹¹⁄₁₆ x 17¹¹⁄₁₆ in., (450 x 450 mm.), second 17⁵⁄₁₆ x 17¹¹⁄₁₆ in., (450 x 450 mm.), color lithographs on Arches wove (BP 52, DM 131, FR 441, Y 8170).

GORIN, Jean 1899-1981

BI *"Composition-1936/73",* #48/150, est. FF1,000/1,500, (04-04-93, Pescheteau, #221), 33¹⁄₁₆ x 25¹⁵⁄₁₆ in., (84 x 66 cm.), color serigraph.

GORMAN, R.C. American b. 1933

$440* *Seated Indian Woman,* s., d. 1980, #44/230, (12-13-92, Hindman, #357), 28 x 20¾ in., color lithograph (BP 281, DM 691, FR 2357, Y 54,435).

$413* *"Woman From Paris",* s., d., #8/100, (10-24-92, Dunning, #1451, illus.), 21 x 29 in., (53.3 x 73.7 cm.), lithograph (BP 255, DM 631, FR 2141, Y 50,366).

GORNIK, April American b. 1953

$1760* *Light After The Flood, 1987,* s., t., d., num. 22/23, pub. Spring Street Workshop, full margins, excell. cond., (09-19-92, Christie-E, #108, illus.), sheet 27½ x 42 in., (69.9 x 106.7 cm.), soft-ground etching on wove (BP 1012, DM 2636, FR 9026, Y 219,287).

$1320* *Rivers Meeting, 1989,* s., d., t., num. 21/50, full margins, apparently very good cond., (02-24-93, Butterfield, #3029, illus.), 19 x 26 in., (483 x 660 mm.), aquatint & soft-ground etching in colors on wove (BP 921, DM 2143, FR 7265, Y 154,893).

BI *The Ten Commandments: II - Sabbath, 1987,* s., d., annot. W.A.P., good cond., crease, est. $6/800, (02-24-93, Butterfield, #3217), 23¾ x 17⅞ in., (603 x 454 mm.), lithograph on Dieu Donne handmade.

GOSOTEI HIROSADA Japanese ac. 1826, d. c. 1865

$1050* *Bust-Portraits Of Various Actors: Nine,* Chuban, mostly parts from polyptychs, s. Hirosada and Kunishige, pub.'s mark Kawato, Matsuki and others, d. c. 1847-49, soiled, rubbed, laid down, Prof. H.R.W. Kuhne Coll., (06-11-93, Sotheby-London, #463, illus.), each approx. 10 x 6⅞ in., (25.4 x 17.5 cm.), woodblock (BP 690, DM 1706, FR 5753, Y 111,406).

GOSSARD, A.

$788* *The Violinist, c. 1895,* foxing, excell. cond., (02-04-93, Christie-S. Ken, #125A), 12½ x 26 in., (31.8 x 66 cm.), color lithograph backed on board (BP 550, DM 1298, FR 4400, Y 98,022).

GOSSE

$239* *Valloire. Savoie, France. "Neige Soleil",* fairly good cond., (03-15-93, Arcole, #94), 38¾ x 24⁷⁄₁₆ in., (98.5 x 62 cm.), (BP 166, DM 397, FR 1350, Y 28,311).

GOTHEIN, Werner 1890-1968

$62* *Drei Engel,* s., (09-25-92, Granier, #2859), sheet 17⁵⁄₁₆ x 12¹⁵⁄₁₆ in., (44 x 33 cm.), woodcut on wove (BP 36, DM 92, FR 311, Y 7483).

GOTMAN, N.

BI *"The Mosque Of Omar",* s., est. $40/60, (02-12-93, DuMouchelle, #364), approx. 8 x 10 in., (20.3 x 25.4 cm.), engraving.

GOTSCH, Friedrich Karl 1900-1984

$1277* *Charly Chaplin (Wietek 21), 1922/23,* s., (06-05-93, Bassenge, #6060), 15⅜ x 8¼ in., (39 x 21 cm.), woodcut on hand-made (BP 841, DM 2070, FR 6978, Y 136,988).

$352* *Der Franzose Und Das Madchen In Amsterdam (Goeritz H 158 B), 1962,* s., d., num., t., block mono., (05-26-93, Dorling, #2679, illus.), 15¹⁵⁄₁₆ x 22⅝ in., (40.5 x 57.5 cm.), color woodcut on thin handmade (BP 228, DM 574, FR 1933, Y 38,244).

$1277* *Im Bett (Witek 103), 1922,* s., d., i., ded., (06-05-93, Bassenge, #6065), 9⅝ x 7¾ in., (24.4 x 19.7 cm.), etching and aquatint (BP 841, DM 2070, FR 6978, Y 136,988).

$599* *Jimmy (Goeritz H 25 B),* s., d., num., t., ded., (05-26-93, Dorling, #2677, illus.), 12¹⁵⁄₁₆ x 13¼ in., (32.9 x 33.7 cm.), woodcut on handmade (BP 388, DM 977, FR 3289, Y 65,080).

$1064* *Jimmy (Wietek 29), 1922,* s., d., i., (06-05-93, Bassenge, #6061), 12⁷⁄₁₆ x 13⅛ in., (31.6 x 33.3 cm.), woodcut (BP 700, DM 1725, FR 5814, Y 114,139).

GOTTLIEB, Adolph American 1903-1974

$1100* *"Arabesque",* s., d. 1967, #10/75, prov., (11-13-92, DuMouchelle, #2016, illus.), 22 x 30 in., (55.9 x 76.2 cm.), color serigraph (BP 711, DM 1727, FR 5823, Y 136,527).

$1210* *"Arabesque", 1967,* s., d., num. 27/75, pub. Marlborough Graphics, full margins, excell.cond., (09-19-92, Christie-E, #109, illus.), sheet 22 x 30 in., (55.9 x 76.2 cm.), screenprint in colors on wove (BP 696, DM 1812, FR 6205, Y 150,760).

BI *Burst, 1970,* from the "Peace Portfolio", full margins, d., num., s., est. $1,2/1,800, (05-27-93, Swann, #119, illus.), 20 x 15 in., (50.8 x 38.1 cm.), color serigraph.

$300* *Composition,* s., #62/90, d. 1969, crease, tear, (11-30-92, Phillips-London, #514), sheet 29⅞ x 22 in., (759 x 559 mm.), color silkscreen on wove (BP 198, DM 478, FR 1622, Y 37,337).

$250* *Composition,* s., #58/200, d. 1970, scuffs, creasing, (11-30-92, Phillips-London, #515), sheet 30⅞ x 24 in., (784 x 610 mm.), color silkscreen on wove (BP 165, DM 398, FR 1352, Y 31,114).

$825* *Imaginary Landscape,* s., d. 1972, #43/150, (05-16-93, Hindman, #591), 21¾ x 24 in., (55.2 x 61 cm.), color serigraph (BP 536, DM 1327, FR 4459, Y 91,453).

$1045* *Imaginary Landscape I, 1971,* s., d., num. 29/90, pub. Marlborough Graphics, full margins, printer's crease in image, creasing, soiling, (09-19-92, Christie-E, #112), plate 17⅝ x 23⅞ in., (44.8 x 60.6 cm.), aquatint in colors on wove (BP 601, DM 1565, FR 5359, Y 130,202).

$935* *Orange Oval, 1972,* s., d., #71/150, (05-16-93, Hindman, #517), 19 x 24 in., (48.3 x 61 cm.), color lithograph (BP 608, DM 1504, FR 5054, Y 103,647).

$1210* *"Red Ground With Green Splash", 1967,* s., d., num. 27/75, pub. Marlborough Graphics, full margins, excell.cond., (09-19-92, Christie-E, #110), sheet 23 x 31 in., (58.4 x 78.7 cm.), screenprint in reds and greens on smooth wove paper (BP 696, DM 1812, FR 6205, Y 150,760).

$1100* *Untitled,* s., d. 1969, edit. #82/98, prov., (09-18-92, DuMouchelle, #2027), 19 x 29 in., (48.3 x 73.7 cm.), color lithograph (BP 633, DM 1647, FR 5641, Y 137,055).

$825* *Untitled,* s., d. 1969, #77/95, (05-16-93, Hindman, #518), 24 x 19¼ in., (61 x 48.9 cm.), color serigraph (BP 536, DM 1327, FR 4459, Y 91,453).

$990* *"Untitled, Black Splash Under Orange Sphere", 1967,* s., d., i. Artist's Proof, margins, scuffing, sharp crease just affecting image, mat staining, (09-19-92, Christie-E, #111), sheet 24 x 18 in., (61 x 45.7 cm.), screenprint in orange, black and rust on wove (BP 569, DM 1482, FR 5077, Y 123,349).

GOTTLIEB, Harry   American 1895-1992
$440* *"Fisherman's Wharf" and "Catskill Winter", c. 1936/39: Two,* s., scattered damages, repairs, good cond., (06-11-93, Doyle, #45), larger 13 x 18¼ in., (330 x 464 mm.), lithograph (BP 289, DM 715, FR 2411, Y 46,684).

BI *Long Island Memory,* s., t. #75/93, light stain, smudging, hinged to mat, very good cond., est. $3/500, (12-04-92, Doyle, #104), 12¾ x 18 in., (324 x 457 mm.), color lithograph.

GOTTLOB, Fernand Louis   1873-1935
$2360* *2e Exposition Des Peintres Lithographes, 1899,* rare, Impies Lemercier, Paris, lit., (12-05-92, Bassenge, #7595, illus.), 47⁷⁄₁₆ x 31¼ in., (120.5 x 79.3 cm.), color lithograph (BP 1478, DM 3679, FR 12,540, Y 292,405).

GOTZ, Karl Otto   b. 1914
$4692* *14 Variationen Uber Ein Thema. Auszug Aus Der "Fakturenfibel", 1947:Fifteen,* num., s., ded., (11-28-92, Schoppmann, #559), 9¹³⁄₁₆ x 8¹¹⁄₁₆ in., (25 x 22 cm.), woodcut (BP 3097, DM 7475, FR 25,376, Y 583,945).

$649* *Belmy, 1986,* #49/60, pencil t., d., s., (11-20-92, Lempertz, #558), sh 30¹¹⁄₁₆ x 22¹³⁄₁₆ in., (78 x 58 cm.), lithograph on Velin (BP 427, DM 1035, FR 3485, Y 80,711).

$289* *Komposition Mit Kreis, c. 1963,* s., num., (11-28-92, Schoppmann, #560), 21⅛ x 15¹⁵⁄₁₆ in., (53.7 x 40.5 cm.), color lithograph on copper print board (BP 191, DM 460, FR 1563, Y 35,968).

$649* *Variation Uber 3 Themen, 1945,* pencil t., s., d., foxed, (11-20-92, Lempertz, #557), sh 10⁵⁄₁₆ x 8⁹⁄₁₆ in., (26.2 x 21.7 cm.), wood cut on thin imitated Japan (BP 427, DM 1035, FR 3485, Y 80,711).

GOUBAUD (after)
$96 *"Ninom De L'Enclos",* engraved G. Maite, (08-14-92, G.A. Key, #109), 15 x 11 in., (38.1 x 27.9 cm.), hand colored engraving (BP 50, DM 141, FR 477, Y 12,106).

GOUBAUD, Innocent Louis (after)
$133* *Rebecca, 1827,* by Thomas Lupton, pub. R. Ackermann, laid on canvas mounted on stretcher, mount staining, good cond., (11-30-92, Phillips-London, #192), plate 24 x 17 in., (610 x 432 mm.), hand-colored mezzotint on wove (BP 88, DM 212, FR 719, Y 16,553).

GOUDT, Hendrik   1585-1630
$774* *Ceres Auf Der Suche Nach Ihrer Tochter (B., Wurzbach und Hollst. 5; Dutuit und Reitlinger 6): 1610,* d. in plate, (10-09-92, Winterberg, #792, illus.), 12⁵⁄₁₆ x 9⁷⁄₁₆ in., (31.3 x 23.9 cm.), engraving (BP 459, DM 1150, FR 3860, Y 94,229).

BI *Ceres Sucht Ihre Tochter (B. 5; Wurzbach 5; Dutuit 6; Hollstein 5), 1610,* after A. Elsheimer, est. DM 3,500, (12-04-92, Bassenge, #6222), 12⅜ x 9¹¹⁄₁₆ in., (31.4 x 24.6 cm.), engraving.

$1589* *Die Enthauptung Des Hl. Johannes D. Taufers (B. 4; Dutuit 4 II; Hollstein 4 III),* after A. Elsheimer, (12-04-92, Bassenge, #6223, illus.), oval 2⅝ x 2⅛ in., (6.6 x 5.4 cm.), engraving (BP 1019, DM 2531, FR 8585, Y 198,377).

$1909* *Tobias Mit Dem Fisch Und Dem Engel. Auch: Der Grosse Tobias (Hollstein 2), 1613,* after Adam Elsheimer, d. Ao 1613, (06-23-93, Kornfeld, #56), engraving (BP 1297, DM 3230, FR 10,865, Y 207,975, SF 2875).

GOULD
$550* *Hummingbirds: A Pair,* stains, (04-02-93, Garth, #422, illus.), 27½ x 21½ in., (69.9 x 54.6 cm.), hand-colored lithograph (BP 362, DM 884, FR 3002, Y 62,621).

GOULD, Fletcher O.
BI *Shine 10 Cents, 1932,* s., t., d., labels, est. $1/1,500, (04-08-93, Christie-NY, #290, illus.), 12½ x 10½ in., (31.8 x 26.7 cm.), photograph, gelatin silver print.

GOULD, J. and H.C. RICHTER
$220* *"Buphus Comatus", "Herodias Garzetta", and "Andea Cinerea": Three,* (12-10-92, Sloan, #2107), each 21½ x 14¼ in., (54.6 x 36.2 cm.), color lithographs (BP 142, DM 348, FR 1189, Y 27,214).

$220* *"Calothorax Yarrell" and "Phoethorax Eurynome": Two,* (06-11-93, Freemn/Fine Art, #78A), one 14 8½in., other 15½ x 11 in., color lithograph (BP 145, DM 358, FR 1205, Y 23,342).

$51* *Cyanomyia Cyanocollis,* (12-10-92, Bonhams-Chelsea, #57), sheet 21¼ x 14¼ in., (54 x 36.2 cm.), hand-colored lithograph (BP 33, DM 81, FR 276, Y 6309).

$66* *Garrulus Glandarius,* foxing, Walter and Cohn, Imp., (06-11-93, Freemn/Fine Art, #78B), 14¼ x¹¹in., engraving w/hand-coloring (BP 43, DM 107, FR 362, Y 7003).

$770* *Humming Birds: Group Of Six,* (12-10-92, Doyle, #22), sight 20 x 30 in., (50.8 x 76.2 cm.), hand colored lithograph (BP 496, DM 1218, FR 4160, Y 95,250).

$187* *"Hummingbirds - Calothrax Micrurus",* p. Hullmandel and Walton, blind embossed 'Ellis-Gould Print', (12-05-92, Neal, #724B), image 14 x 9 in., (35.6 x 22.9 cm.), overall 30 x 22½ in., (35.6 x 22.9 cm.), hand-colored lithograph (BP 117, DM 292, FR 994, Y 23,169).

$22* *Mareca Punctata: Cuv.,* Hullmandel and Walton, Imp., (06-11-93, Freemn/Fine Art, #78), sight 12¼ x 19 in., (31.1 x 48.3 cm.), lithograph in color (BP 14, DM 36, FR 121, Y 2334).

$215* *Sarciophorus Pectoralis (Seagulls),* folio, (07-03-92, Sloan, #335), hand colored lithograph (BP 112, DM 325, FR 1097, Y 26,801).

$165* *Somateria Molissima,* prov., (10-30-92, Sloan, #901), sight 13½ x 20½ in., (34.3 x 52.1 cm.), color lithograph (BP 106, DM 254, FR 861, Y 20,438).

BI *Somateria Molissima,* est. $350/450, (09-17-92, Sloan, #1468), sight 13½ x 20½ in., (34.3 x 52.1 cm.), color lithograph.

GOULD, J. and H.C. RICHTER (after)
BI *"Aegiothus Rufescens",* (12-11-92, G.A. Key, #32), 19 x 13 in., (48.3 x 33 cm.), colored lithograph.

$275* *Herodles Picata,* foxing, discoloration, (11-12-92, Freemn/Fine Art, #77), length 13 x 18¼ in., (33 x 46.4 cm.), hand colored litho (BP 181, DM 436, FR 1470, Y 34,098).

GOULD, J. and W. HART
$363* *Pheasants: A Pair,* (08-05-92, Boos, #687), sight 13¾ x 20¾ in., (349 x 527 mm.), hand colored lithograph (BP 190, DM 536, FR 1811, Y 46,230).

GOULD, J.J. (Jr.)
$302* *Lippincott's December,* B+ cond., repairs, (08-06-92, Swann, #142, illus.), 13½ x 9 in., (34.3 x 22.9 cm.), (BP 158, DM 446, FR 1507, Y 38,520).

$467* *Lippincott's July, 1896,* Lippincott Co., A cond., folding, damage, (08-06-92, Swann, #143, illus.), 18½ x 14½ in., (47 x 36.8 cm.), (BP 244, DM 690, FR 2330, Y 59,566).

$275* *Lippincott's, November 1896,* A- cond., (08-06-92, Swann, #144, illus.), 16¼ x 13 in., (41.3 x 33 cm.), (BP 144, DM 406, FR 1372, Y 35,077).

GOULD, John   British 1804-1881
BI *The Birds Of Australia: Four,* pub. 1840-69, light staining, good cond., est. BP 2/250, (10-27-92, Phillips-London, #176), (540 x 364 mm.), lithograph w/hand-coloring on wove.

$243* *Eurostopodus Albogularis: White Throated Goat-Sucker,* from John Gould. The Birds of Australia 1840-1848, (08-11-92, L. Joel, #181G), 19⁵⁄₁₆ x 12¹⁵⁄₁₆ in., (49 x 32.8 cm.), hand-colored lithograph (BP 126, DM 357, FR 1208, Y 31,118, A$ 330).

$132* *"Eutrygon Terrestris",* J. GOULD & W. HART, del et lith, Walter Imp., soiling, fading, tear,nicks, (05-07-93, Goldberg, #436, illus.), 14¼ x 21 in., (36.2 x 53.3 cm.), hand-colored lithograph (BP 84, DM 209, FR 703, Y 14,534).

BI *Hydromys Leucogaster, White-Bellied Beaver-Rat,* from John Gould. The Mammels of Australia 1845-1863, est. $2/300, (08-11-92, L. Joel, #73G), 12³⁄₁₆ x 19¹¹⁄₁₆ in., (31 x 50 cm.), hand-colored lithograph.

$193* *"Lesser Redpole"* and *"Redbreasted Flycatcher": Two,* p. Hallmandel, (06-11-93, Freemn/Fine Art, #76), lithograph w/hand-coloring (BP 127, DM 314, FR 1058, Y 20,477).

$137 *Male And Female Koklass Pheasants, 1831: Two,* from John Gould's A Century Of Birds From The Himalaya Mountains, (02-05-93, G.A. Key, #7), each 18 x 12 in., (45.7 x 30.5 cm.), hand tinted lithograph (BP 95, DM 227, FR 768, Y 17,048).

$99* *"Megapodius Brenchley (From The Birds Of Paradise)",* W. Hart, del et lith., Mintern Bros. Imp., fading, tear, nicks, (05-07-93, Goldberg, #436B), 14¼ x 21 in., (36.2 x 53.3 cm.), hand-colored lithograph (BP 63, DM 157, FR 527, Y 10,901).

$99* *"Rallicula Forbesi (From The Birds Of Paradise)",* W. HART, del et lith. M intern Bros. Imp., fading, tear, nicks, (05-07-93, Goldberg, #436A), 14¼ x 21 in., (36.2 x 53.3 cm.), hand-colored lithograph (BP 63, DM 157, FR 527, Y 10,901).

GOULD, John (after)

$230* *Hummingbirds: Two Pairs,* (03-03-93, Sotheby-Arcade, #234), sight 19⅝ x 13 in., (49.8 x 33 cm.), color lithograph (BP 159, DM 379, FR 1285, Y 26,875).

$357* *"Nyroca Ferina", "Nyroca Leucophthalmos"* and *"Goosander": Three,* (06-11-93, Doyle, #46), 14 x 21 in., (356 x 533 mm.), hand colored lithograph (BP 235, DM 580, FR 1956, Y 37,878).

GOULD, John (attrib.)   British 1804-1881

$193* *"Hummingbirds",* t., prov., (06-11-93, DuMouchelle, #2265), one 14 x 10½ in., (35.6 x 26.7 cm.), the other 15½ x 9½ in., (35.6 x 26.7 cm.), hand-colored lithograph (BP 127, DM 314, FR 1058, Y 20,477).

GOULD, John and F.

BI *The Birds Of Great Britain, 1862: Ten,* p. C. Hullmandel, full margins, foxing, defects, good cond., est. BP5/600, (10-27-92, Phillips-London, #175), sheet 14½ x 21⅜ in., (368 x 543 mm.), hand-colored lithograph w/touches of gum arabic.

GOULD and HART

$220* *"Aegithalus Flamminceps",* toning, crease, split, good cond., (03-12-93, Goldberg, #903, illus.), 22⅛ x 15¼ in., (56.2 x 38.7 cm.), hand colored lithograph (BP 153, DM 366, FR 1245, Y 25,928).

GOULD and RICHTER

$440* *Hummingbird: A Pair,* s. J. Gould, H.G. Richter, (02-27-93, Dunning, #1043), sight 20 x 13 in., (50.8 x 33 cm.), color lithograph (BP 309, DM 723, FR 2458, Y 51,942).

$550* *Lamprolaima Rhami (Hummingbirds)",* toning, good cond., (03-12-93, Goldberg, #902, illus.), (56.2 x 38.7 cm.), hand colored lithograph (BP 384, DM 915, FR 3113, Y 64,820).

GOUPIL

$412* *"Run To Earth",* after Heywood Harvey, (03-03-93, Doyle, #32), 25½ x 33½ in., (64.8 x 85.1 cm.), color engraving (BP 284, DM 678, FR 2302, Y 48,142).

GOUPIL and CO., Publishers

$144* *Le Lion,* from Etudes D'Animaux D'Apres Nature, foxing, (10-15-92, Bonhams-Chelsea, #103), sheet 23½ x 19½ in., (59.7 x 49.5 cm.), lithograph w/hand coloring and gum arabic (BP 88, DM 214, FR 727, Y 17,277).

GOURDAINE, Jean Pierre Norblin de la   1745-1830

$290* *Die Predigt Johannes Des Taufers (Le Blanc 7; Franke 8), 1808,* after Rembrandt, (12-01-92, Karl/Faber, #108), etching (BP 192, DM 462, FR 1575, Y 36,106).

GOURSAT, George

$270* *Le Nouveau Monde, Second Series: Thirty-Two,* tears, defects, (02-17-93, Bonhams-Chelsea, #339), sheet 20 x 13½ in., (50.8 x 34.3 cm.), lithograph, finished by hand (BP 187, DM 438, FR 1485, Y 32,250).

GOWIN, Emmet   b. 1941

$1045* *Edith, Danville, Va., 1972,* s., t., d., (10-13-92, Christie-NY, #541, illus.), 6⅝ x 6½ in., (16.8 x 16.5 cm.), photograph, gelatin silver print (BP 609, DM 1531, FR 5202, Y 126,713).

$1980* *Edith: Three: "Edith, Berry Necklace, Danville, Virginia"; "Edith, Danville, Virginia": and "Edith, Newtown, Pennsylvania",* s., t., d., printing notations, 1971 & 1974, p. 1976-80, (10-15-92, Sotheby-NY, #575, illus.), two approx. 8 x 10 in., (20.3 x 25.4 cm.), (20.3 x 25.4 cm.), photograph, gelatin silver prints (BP 1212, DM 2947, FR 9995, Y 237,552).

$4950* *Edith: Two: "Edith, Chincoteague, Virginia" and "Edith, Danville, Virginia",* s., t., d., 2nd w/printing notations by photog., 1967 & 1972, 1st p.1974, (10-15-92, Sotheby-NY, #575A, illus.), photograph, gelatin silver print (BP 3029, DM 7368, FR 24,987, Y 593,881).

$3300* *Portraits Of Edith, Dayton, Ohio; And Danville,: Three,* (1967-73), s., t., d., prov., (10-13-92, Christie-NY, #542, illus.), each 6¼ x 6¼ in., (15.9 x 15.9 cm.), photograph, gelatin silver prints (BP 1922, DM 4834, FR 16,426, Y 400,146).

GOYA

BI *"El Famoso Martincho Poniendo Banderillas Al Quiebro" (Harris II 218),* blind stamp, est. $1,5/2,000, (12-12-92, A. James, #36), 9½ x 13½ in., (24.1 x 34.3 cm.), etching and aquatint.

GOYA (after)

$44* *Untitled,* (12-11-92, DuMouchelle, #1447A), print (BP 28, DM 69, FR 238, Y 5445).

GOYA, Francisco de   Spanish 1746-1828

BI *"Aesopus After Velaquez" (Harris, 13), 1778,* second edit. 1815-1820, trimmed to plate mark, stains, scuffs, est. $1,2-1,500, (10-31-92, Cleveland, #285), 11⅞ x 8½ in., (30.2 x 21.6 cm.), etching.

$1439* *Balthasar Carlos (L. Delteil 10; J. Harris 9), 1778,* creases, reddish stains, large margins, (06-11-93, Picard, #59), 13¾ x 8¹¹⁄₁₆ in., (350 x 220 mm.), etching and drypoint on laid w/Joan watermark (BP 945, DM 2339, FR 7885, Y 152,679).

$1977* *Banderillas De Fuego (Harris 234 III, 1; Delteil 254; Hofmann 113), 1815-16,* plate s., d., (06-10-93, Hauswedell/Nolt, #339, illus.), image 9⅝ x 13¾ in., (24.5 x 35 cm.), etching worked over w/aquatint on hand-made (BP 1293, DM 3219, FR 10,839, Y 209,850).

$1100* *Buen Viage (H. 99), 1799,* plate 64 from Los Caprichos, wide margins, trimmed, soiling, losses,good cond., (11-09-92, Christie-NY, #96, illus.), 215 x 150 in., (546.1 x 381 cm.), etching, burnished aquatint and burin on laid (BP 727, DM 1756, FR 5933, Y 136,510).

$880* *Bull Fight Scenes: Two,* (02-14-93, Hanzel, #691), each 9½ x 13½ in., (24.1 x 34.3 cm.), etching (BP 620, DM 1459, FR 4938, Y 106,126).

$330* *Bullfight,* margins, (09-18-92, DuMouchelle, #2300), 7⅞ x 12⅛ in., (20 x 30.8 cm.), etching (BP 190, DM 494, FR 1692, Y 41,116).

$193* *Bullfight,* margins, (05-14-93, DuMouchelle, #2368, illus.), 7⅞ x 12⅛ in., (20 x 30.8 cm.), etching (BP 125, DM 310, FR 1043, Y 21,395).

BI *Un Caballero Espanol En Plaza Quebrando Rejoncillos (H. 216/III, 1. Ausgabe), 1816,* est. DM 3500, (12-01-92, Karl/Faber, #205, illus.), 9⅝ x 13¹⁵⁄₁₆ in., (24.5 x 35.5 cm.), etching and aquatint on hand-made.

$328* *Caprichos (D. 101; Harris 99), 1799,* third edit., (02-24-93, Picard, #110), etching and aquatint (BP 229, DM 532, FR 1805, Y 38,489).

$1805* *A Caza De Dientes (D. 49; Harris 47 III, 1),* (12-04-92, Bassenge, #6591), 8⁷⁄₁₆ x 5⅞ in., (21.4 x 15 cm.), etching w/aquatint on hand-made (BP 1158, DM 2875, FR 9751, Y 225,343).

$867* *El Cid Campeador Lancando Otro Toro (Delteil 234 III, Harris 214 III,3), 1816,* sheet 11 of 3rd edition, 1876, (12-04-92, Bassenge, #6595), $9\frac{13}{16}$ x $13\frac{3}{4}$ in., (25 x 35 cm.), etching w/aquatint on hand-made Arches (BP 556, DM 1381, FR 4684, Y 108,240).

BI *Cogida De Un Moro Estando En La Plaza (L.D. 231, T.H. 211), 1816,* plate 8 from La Tauromaquia, from First Edition, margins, crease, stitch holes, staining, very good cond., est. $2,5/3,500, (05-11-93, Christie-NY, #87, illus.), plate $9\frac{7}{16}$ x $13\frac{3}{4}$ in., (240 x 349 mm.), etching, brunished aquatint and drypoint on Serra.

$83* *"Corrida De Un Moro",* from Tauromachia, late printing, (04-16-93, DuMouchelle, #2170), 8 x $12\frac{1}{4}$ in., (20.3 x 31.1 cm.), etching (BP 54, DM 134, FR 453, Y 9333).

$940* *"El De La Rollona" and "El Amor Y La Muerte"(Harris 39 and 45): Two,* foglio, (05-20-93, Finarte-Milan, #74, illus.), $12\frac{5}{8}$ x $8\frac{15}{16}$ in., (31 x 22.7 cm.), etching and aquatint (BP 603, DM 1517, FR 5109, Y 103,799, L 1380).

$374* *Desgracias Acaecidas En El Tendido De La Plaza De Madrid (H. 224/III,2.Ausgabe), 1855,* (12-01-92, Karl/ Faber, #206), $9\frac{5}{8}$ x $13\frac{3}{4}$ in., (24.5 x 35 cm.), etching and aquatint on Velin (BP 247, DM 596, FR 2032, Y 46,564).

$2094* *Dios La Perdone: Y Era Si Madre (D. 53; Harris 51 III),* (12-04-92, Bassenge, #6592), $7\frac{3}{4}$ x $5\frac{13}{16}$ in., (19.7 x 14.8 cm.), etching w/aquatint on handmade (BP 1343, DM 3335, FR 11,313, Y 261,423).

BI *Dios Los Cria Y Ellos Se Juntan (Harris 265 III),* sheet 18, dusty, creased, foxing, est. DM 700-, (09-25-92, Granier, #2629), .

$940* *"Donde Va Mama?" and "Ya Es Hora" (Harris 100 and 115): Two,* foglio, (05-20-93, Finarte-Milan, #77), $12\frac{3}{16}$ x $8\frac{15}{16}$ in., (31 x 22.7 cm.), etching and aquatint (BP 603, DM 1517, FR 5109, Y 103,799, L 1380).

BI *Dos Grupos De Picadores Arrollados De Seguida Por Un Solo Toro, Plate 32 (L.D. 255; T.H. 235), 1816,* margins, crease, staining, good cond., (12-01-92, Christie-London, #237), plate $9\frac{7}{16}$ x $13\frac{3}{4}$ in., (240 x 350 mm.), etching w/burnished aquatint, drypoint and engraving on laid paper.

$1331* *"Duendecitos" and "Los Chinchillas" (Harris 84 and 85 s.c.): Two,* foglio, (05-20-93, Finarte-Milan, #76), $12\frac{3}{16}$ x $8\frac{15}{16}$ in., (31 x 22.7 cm.), etching and aquatint (BP 854, DM 2147, FR 7234, Y 146,974, L 1955).

$1416* *Esto Si Que Es Leer (Delteil 66 I , Harris 64 III 1), 1799,* from the first impression, (06-04-93, Bassenge, #5503, illus.), $8\frac{3}{8}$ x $5\frac{13}{16}$ in., (21.3 x 14.7 cm.), etching w/aquatint (BP 937, DM 2299, FR 7750, Y 152,718).

$165* *The Execution,* late printing, very good cond.?, (07-19-92, Bakker, #121), plate $5\frac{1}{4}$ x $6\frac{1}{4}$ in., (13.3 x 15.9 cm.), etching (BP 85, DM 240, FR 813, Y 20,512).

$1858* *Hilan Delgado (J. Harris, 79),* first edit., reddish stains, large margins, (04-02-93, Picard, #119, illus.), $8\frac{7}{16}$ x $5\frac{7}{8}$ in., (21.5 x 15 cm.), etching and aquatint (BP 1224, DM 2986, FR 10,142, Y 211,545).

$439* *Hizonos Dios Y Maravillamos Nos (H. 253/III/7),* sheet 6 from the series Los Proverbios, (06-08-93, Karl/Faber, #295), approx. $9\frac{5}{8}$ x $13\frac{9}{16}$ in., (24.5 x 34.5 cm.), etching and aquatint on hand-made (BP 289, DM 712, FR 2399, Y 46,628).

BI *Isabel De Bourbon (L.D. 9; T.H. 8), 1778-9,* pub. Calcografia 1815-20, wide margins, tear, brown spots, staining,discoloration, rubbing, est. BP 5/700, (12-01-92, Christie-London, #235), plate $14\frac{11}{16}$ x $12\frac{1}{4}$ in., (373 x 311 mm.), etching w/drypoint on firm laid paper.

$391* *Legerete Et Adresse De Juanito Apinani Dans La Place De Madrid (L. Delteil 243, Harris 223),* from Tauromachie, third printing, large margins, (05-06-93, Laurin, #35), etching and aquatint (BP 248, DM 616, FR 2073, Y 43,019).

BI *Ligereza Y Atrevimiento De Juanito Apinani En La De Madrid (Harris 223),* from "La Tauromaquia", est. SC 4/ 5,000, (11-11-92, Dorotheum, #355), $9\frac{13}{16}$ x $14\frac{1}{2}$ in., (25 x 36.8 cm.), etching w/aquatint.

$688* *Lluvia De Toros (Th.H. 269), 1877,* yellowed, staining, creases, good margins, (06-16-93, Ader Tajan, #104), $9\frac{5}{8}$ x $13\frac{3}{4}$ in., (24.5 x 35 cm.), etching and aquatint (BP 459, DM 1142, FR 3833, Y 73,379).

$744* *Lo Merecia (Delteil 148 V, Harris 149 III 1),* (06-04-93, Bassenge, #5506), $6\frac{13}{16}$ x $8\frac{9}{16}$ in., (17.3 x 21.7 cm.), etching w/aquatint (BP 492, DM 1208, FR 4072, Y 80,242).

BI *Los Caprichos (D. 38-117; H. 36-115): Set Of Eighty,* 1st edit. (1799), margins, repair, soiling, surface dirt, good cond.,est. $120/180,000, (05-13-93, Sotheby-NY, #316, illus.), sh 11 x $7\frac{3}{8}$ in., (278 x 188 mm.), etching w/aquatint on laid.

$74,000* *Los Caprichos (D. 38-117; H. 36-115): Set Of Eighty,* 1st edit. (1799), margins, pls. 25 and 31 w/several tears, 3 just into subject, foxing, stains, good cond., (05-13-93, Sotheby-NY, #318, illus.), sh $11\frac{3}{8}$ x $8\frac{1}{4}$ in., (290 x 211 mm.), etching w/aquatint on laid (BP 48,582, DM 119,490, FR 403,050, Y 8,261,695).

$59,936* *Los Caprichos (Delteil 38-117; H. 36-115), 1799,* first edit., restorations, (06-28-93, Loudmer, #255, illus.), approx. $8\frac{7}{16}$ x 6 in., (215 x 153 mm.), approx. $11\frac{1}{4}$ x $7\frac{11}{16}$ in., (215 x 153 mm.), etching and aquatint on handmade laid (BP 40,131, DM 101,845, FR 343,080, Y 6,359,257).

$166,358* *Los Caprichos (Delteil 38-117; Harris 36-115), Eighty Plates,* complete set, Harris's trial proofs before the 1st edit. of 1799, some w/burr, 5 plates before corrections of titles, margins, repaired tear, paperloss, foxing, overall cond., fine, in presentation binding, (06-30-93, Sotheby-London, #135, illus.), etching w/aquatint on laid paper w/ o a watermark (BP 111,500, DM 283,742, FR 957,181, Y 17,824,708).

$119,365* *Los Caprichos (Delteil 38-117; Harris 36-115): Set of Eighty,* first edit. of 1799, scratch, margins, crease, surface dirt, good cond., each sheet removed, (12-03-92, Sotheby-London, #65, illus.), each sheet approx. $11\frac{5}{8}$ x $7\frac{7}{8}$ in., (295 x 200 mm.), etchings w/aquatint on laid (BP 77,000, DM 187,710, FR 640,714, Y 14,851,935).

$20,338* *Los Caprichos (Delteil 38-117; Harris II, S. 66 (36-115)), c. 1855: Eighty,* Calcografia Nacional para la Real Academia, diptych edit., stamp, collector's stamp, (04-27-93, Hartung, #2443, illus.), aquatint (BP 12,934, DM 32,201, FR 108,934, Y 2,279,278).

$921* *"Los Caprichos" (Harris 36/III-115/III/10) 1918-28), c. 1799: Eighty,* (06-08-93, Karl/Faber, #290, illus.), approx. $14\frac{3}{16}$ x 11 in., (36 x 28 cm.), etching and aquatint on heavy hand-made (BP 605, DM 1494, FR 5033, Y 97,823).

$19,838* *"Los Caprichos", 1868: Eighty,* 4th edit., Calcografia National, bound, (12-17-92, Duran, #15, illus.), etching (BP 12,591, DM 30,973, FR 105,803, Y 2,437,999, P 2,185,000).

$14,502* *"Los Caprichos", 1881-86: Eighty,* 5th edit., Colographia National, lacking #62, tears, (03-17-93, Duran, #32, illus.), $11\frac{13}{16}$ x $8\frac{7}{16}$ in., (30 x 21.4 cm.), etching and aquatint on textured paper w/grey wash (BP 9999, DM 24,130, FR 82,025, Y 1,700,915, P 1,725,000).

$8800* *"Los Caprichos": 79,* of 80, fifth edit., 1881-86, beveled plate marks, lacks plate 68, each plate tipped to a stub, bound into volume, fine cond., soiling, fading, (05-27-93, Swann, #119A, illus.), $12\frac{7}{8}$ x $8\frac{3}{4}$ in., (32.7 x 22.2 cm.), etchings w/aquatint in brownish black ink on cream wove (BP 5636, DM 14,121, FR 47,593, Y 943,396).

$4290* *Los Caprichos, "Bellos Consejos" (D. 52; H. 50), "Pobrecitas" (H. 57)and "Chiton" (H. 63): Three,* plates 15, 22 and 28 from the 1st edit., margins, stitchmarks, foxing, staining, defects, (06-30-93, Sotheby-London, #142), etching w/aquatint in black ink (BP 2875, DM 7317, FR 24,684, Y 459,659).

$3603* *Los Caprichos, "El Amor Y La Muerte" (D. 47; H. 45), "A Caza De Dientes" (D. 49; H. 47) and "Bien Tirada Esta" (D. 54; H. 52), 1799: Three,* plates 10, 12 and 17, margins, stitchmarks, rubbed area, foxed, defects, (06-30-93, Sotheby-London, #139), etching w/aquatint in brownish black ink (BP 2415, DM 6145, FR 20,731, Y 386,050).

$4804* *Los Caprichos, "Ni Asi La Distingue" (D. 44; H. 42), "Muchachos Al Avio" (D. 48; H. 46), "El Sueno De La*

Razon Produce Monstruos" (D. 80; H. 78) and"Mejor Es Holgar" (D. 110; H. 108), 1799: Four, plates 7, 11, 33 and 73 from 1st edit., wide margins, stitchmarks, foxing, discoloration, defects, (06-30-93, Sotheby-London, #137), etching w/aquatint (BP 3220, DM 8194, FR 27,641, Y 514,733).

$2059* *Los Caprichos, "Que Sacrificio!" (D. 51; H. 49) and "Quien Mas Rendido?" (D. 64; H. 62), 1799: Two,* plates 14 and 27 from 1st edit., margins, stitchmarks, printer's crease, foxing, staining, defects, (06-30-93, Sotheby-London, #141), one 7¾ x 5⅞ in., (197 x 149 mm.), the other 7⅝ x 5⅞ in., (197 x 149 mm.), etching w/aquatint in black ink (BP 1380, DM 3512, FR 11,847, Y 220,615).

$2917* *Los Caprichos, "Que Viene El Coco" (D. 40; H. 38), "El De La Rollona"(D. 41; H. 39) and "Que Se La Llevaron!" (D. 41; H. 43), 1799: Three,* plates 3, 4 and 8 from 1st edit., stitchmarks, wide margins, stains,discoloration, defects, (06-30-93, Sotheby-London, #136), etching w/aquatint in brownish black ink (BP 1955, DM 4975, FR 16,784, Y 312,547).

$4461* *Los Caprichos, "Tantalo" (D. 46; H. 44), "Volaverunt" (D. 98; H. 96)and "No Hay Quien Nos Desate?" (D. 112; H. 110), 1799: Three,* plates 9, 61 and 75, margins, stitchmarks, stain, defects, (06-30-93, Sotheby-London, #138), etching w/aquatint in brownish-black ink (BP 2990, DM 7609, FR 25,667, Y 477,981).

$5175* *Los Caprichos: Francisco Goya Y Lucientes, Pintor (D. 38; H. 36), 1799,* margins, stains, soiling, holes, (05-13-93, Sotheby-NY, #322), 8½ x 5⅞ in., (215 x 150 mm.), etching w/aquatint on laid (BP 3397, DM 8356, FR 28,186, Y 577,760).

$1029* *Los Caprichos: Mucho Hay Que Chupar (D. 82; H. 80), 1799,* plate 45, from 1st edit., remains, tape, cockling, good cond., (06-30-93, Sotheby-London, #140), 8⅛ x 6 in., (206 x 152 mm.), etching w/aquatint (BP 690, DM 1755, FR 5921, Y 110,254).

$138* *Los Caprichos: Ni Asi La Distingue (H. 42), 1799,* 12th (final) ed., 1937, p. by Ruperez in Calcografia, pub. Ministeriode Instruccion Publicain, margins, good cond., light-staining, mat staining, hinge remains, ink notations, buckling, surface soiling, (02-24-93, Butterfield, #2931), 7¾ x 5¾ in., (197 x 146 mm.), etching, aquatint, & drypoint on laid (BP 96, DM 224, FR 759, Y 16,193).

$575* *Los Caprichos: Plate 54 (D. 91; H. 89), 1799,* wide margins three sides, good cond., razor cut, surface dirt, (05-13-93, Sotheby-NY, #321), 8½ x 5⅞ in., (216 x 150 mm.), etching and aquatint (BP 377, DM 928, FR 3132, Y 64,196).

$2588* *Los Caprichos: Plates 38 And 41, 1799: Two,* full margins, stains, soiling, holes, good cond., (05-13-93, Sotheby-NY, #325, illus.), one 8½ x 5⅞ in., (216 x 150 mm.), other 7¾ x 5¾ in., (216 x 150 mm.), etching w/ aquatint on laid (BP 1699, DM 4179, FR 14,096, Y 288,936).

BI *Los Desastres De La Guerra (H. 121-200), 1863: Eighty,* complete set, full margins, good cond., mat staining, est. $6/8,000, (10-28-92, Butterfield, #2596, illus.), each plate 6¼ x 8¾ in., (159 x 222 mm.), etching w/aquatint in dark unber or black on fine laid paper.

$56,302* *Los Desastres De La Guerra (Harris 122-200/III/1/a): Eighty,* 1808-1820, 1863, (06-25-93, Kornfeld, #42, illus.), sheet size 9⅜ x 12¹⁵⁄₁₆ in., (23.8 x 33 cm.), etching (BP 38,080, DM 95,850, FR 322,833, Y 5,967,988, SF 85,100).

$35,437* *"Los Desastres De La Guerra" (H. 121/III-200/III/1. b),* c. 1810-20, 1863, (06-08-93, Karl/Faber, #291, illus.), approx. 9⅝ x 13¾ in., (24.5 x 35 cm.), etching and drypoint w/aquatint (BP 23,295, DM 57,500, FR 193,645, Y 3,763,887).

$8338* *Los Desastres De La Guerre (D. 120-199; H. 121-200): Set Of Eighty,* plus typographic explanatory sheet, 3rd edit (1903), full margins, good cond., (05-13-93, Sotheby-NY, #320), sh 13⅜ x 10¼ in., (340 x 260 mm.), etchings w/lavis, drypoint and burin, on laid (BP 5474, DM 13,464, FR 45,414, Y 930,892).

BI *Los Desastres De La Guerre (D. 120-199; H. 121-200): Set Of Eighty,* lithographic t. page and text, early 1st edit. (1863), Harris's edit.1a, watermark, margins, hole, est. $40/60,000, (05-13-93, Sotheby-NY, #317, illus.), 9⅜ x 13 in., (237 x 330 mm.), etching w/lavis, drypoint and burin, some burr on drypoint, on wove.

BI *Los Proverbios (D. 202-209; H. 248-265): Eighteen,* lithographic title page and complete set, 1st edit. of 1864, wide margins, scratch, surface dirt, discoloration, good cond., est. BP 18/22,000, (06-30-93, Sotheby-London, #143), etching w/aquatint on wove paper, 3 w/JGO from a JGO and Palmette watermark.

BI *Los Proverbios (D. 202-219; H. 248-265): Set Of Eighteen,* wide margins, good cond., bound, est. $7/9,000, (05-13-93, Sotheby-NY, #319), sh 12½ x 16⅞ in., (317 x 430 mm.), etching w/aquatint, in black ink on wove.

$1328* *Los Proverbios (H. 250, 253, 254, 259, 260, 263/jeweils III, 5. (od.6., bei 2 BII.)Ausgabe: Six,* (12-01-92, Karl/Faber, #207), 9⅝ x 13¾ in., (24.5 x 35 cm.), etching and aquatint (BP 877, DM 2117, FR 7213, Y 165,339).

$1909* *Los Proverbios (H. 266, 268 und 269/jeweils III): Three,* (12-01-92, Karl/Faber, #209, illus.), 9⁷⁄₁₆ x 13¾ in., (24 x 35 cm.), etching and aquatint on hand-made (BP 1261, DM 3043, FR 10,369, Y 237,674).

$38,981* *"Los Proverbios" (H. 248/III-265/III): Eighteen,* from 1816-24, Real Academia de Nobles Artes de San Fernando, 1864, watermark, (06-08-93, Karl/Faber, #294), 13⅜ x 19¹¹⁄₁₆ in., (34 x 50 cm.), etching and aquatint w/drypoint on heavy wove (BP 25,625, DM 63,250, FR 213,011, Y 4,140,308).

$4830* *Maja, A Maja With Dark Background (L.D. 28, T.H. 30), 1824-28,* prob. p. by Calcografia, 1859, margins, light/ mat staining, good cond., (05-11-93, Christie-NY, #86A, illus.), plate 7½ x 4¾ in., (191 x 121 mm.), etching and burnished aquatint on laid (BP 3083, DM 7609, FR 25,637, Y 531,295).

$166* *"No Te Escaparas" (H. 107/III, 10.Ausgabe), 1918-28,* (12-01-92, Karl/Faber, #203), 8⁷⁄₁₆ x 5⅞ in., (21.5 x 15 cm.), etching and aquatint on hand-made (BP 110, DM 265, FR 902, Y 20,667).

$303* *Otra Locura Suya En La Mism A Plaza, 1815, Harris 222,* plate 19 of La Tauromaquia later edit., prov., (09-20-92, Hindman, #678), 9⅝ x 14 in., (24.4 x 35.6 cm.), etching, aquatint, drypoint and burin (engraving (copper)) (BP 177, DM 450, FR 1538, Y 37,449).

BI *Otras Leyes Por El Pueblo (Disparate De Bestia) (D. 222; H. 268),* 1 of 4 additional plates prepared for Los Proverbios, 3rd final state, pub. for L'Art in 1877, margins, good cond., est. BP 7/900, (06-30-93, Sotheby-London, #145), 9⅝ x 13¾ in., (244 x 349 mm.), etching w/ aquatint.

$1024* *"Otras Leyes Por El Pueblo" and "Que Guerrero" (D. 222 et 220; H. 268 et 266): Two,* first, w/letter, staining, tears; second, w/letter, losses, (02-24-93, Picard, #112), etching and aquatint (BP 714, DM 1662, FR 5636, Y 120,160).

$1977* *Pedro Romero Matando A Toro Parado (Harris 233 II, 1), 1815-16,* (06-10-93, Hauswedell/Nolt, #338, illus.), image 9¹³⁄₁₆ x 14¹⁄₁₆ in., (24.9 x 35.7 cm.), etching worked over w/aquatint on hand-made (BP 1293, DM 3219, FR 10,839, Y 209,850).

$370* *Pepe Illo Faisant La Recorte Au Taureau (L.D. 252, H. 232),* from La Tauromachie, third printing, large margin, glue and mat traces, (05-06-93, Laurin, #36), etching and aquatint (BP 234, DM 583, FR 1962, Y 40,709).

$2260* *Pepe Illo Haciendo El Recorte Al Toro (Harris 232 III, 1; Delteil 252, Hofmann 11), 1815-16,* (06-10-93, Hauswedell/Nolt, #337, illus.), image 9⁹⁄₁₆ x 13⅞ in., (24.3 x 35.3 cm.), etching worked over w/aquatint on hand-made (BP 1478, DM 3680, FR 12,390, Y 239,890).

$487* *Pepo Illo Doing Hommage As He Plays The Bull, Plate 29 From The Tauro achia (L.D. 252), 1815,* 4th state, narrow margins, pin holes, binding trimmed to near image,foxed, old tape, (10-27-92, Phillips-London, #16), plate 8 x 12¼ in., (203 x 311 mm.), sheet 9½ x 13⅛ in., (203 x 311 mm.), black etching on laid (BP 308, DM 746, FR 2533, Y 59,572).

$314* *Le Petit Prisonnier (Th. Harris, 26), 1867,* defintive state, pub., large untrimmed margins, (06-16-93, Ader Tajan, #102), 4⅛ x 3⅜ in., (10.5 x 8.5 cm.), etching and copper print (BP 209, DM 521, FR 1749, Y 33,490).

$90* *Plate From Los Caprichos,* restrike, (05-16-93, Hanzel, #464), 8 x 5½ in., (20.3 x 14 cm.), etching (BP 59, DM 145, FR 486, Y 9977).

BI *"Le Prisoner",* posthumous p., Gazette des Beaux-Arts, Imprimere Delatre, est. $4/600, (10-10-92, Goldberg, #426), image 3¾ x 2¾ in., (9.5 x 7 cm.), etching.

BI *Que Guerrero! (Disparate Conocido) (D. 220; H. 266),* 1 of 4 additional plates prepared for Los Proverbios, 3rd final state, pub. for L'Art in 1877, wide margins, fox-marks, surface dirt, est. BP 800/1,000, (06-30-93, Sotheby-London, #144), 9½ x 14 in., (241 x 356 mm.), etching w/aquatint.

$3096* *"Que Guerrero!", "Una Reina Del Circo" and "Otras Leyes Por El Pueblo" (L. Delteil, 220 to 222; Harris, 266 to 268), 1819: Three,* stains, large margins, (04-02-93, Picard, #122), 9⅝ x 13¹⁵⁄₁₆ in., (24.5 x 35.5 cm.), black etchings and aquatints on laid (BP 2039, DM 4976, FR 16,900, Y 352,499).

$921* *La Que Mal Marida Nunca Le Falta Diga (H. 254/III/2),* (06-08-93, Karl/Faber, #296), approx. 9⅝ x 14³⁄₁₆ in., (24.5 x 36 cm.), etching and aquatint on wove (BP 605, DM 1494, FR 5033, Y 97,823).

$427* *El Que No Te Ama, Burlando Te Difama (Harris 264 III), 1875-1904,* sheet 17 from Proverbios, #2/-9, dusty, (09-25-92, Granier, #2628), plate 9⅝ x 14¹⁄₁₆ in., (24.5 x 35.7 cm.), sheet 12³⁄₁₆ x 17³⁄₁₆ in., (24.5 x 35.7 cm.), etching on copper print paper (BP 249, DM 633, FR 2140, Y 51,539).

$332* *"Que Se La Llevaron!" (H. 43/III, 3. Ausgabe.), 1868,* plate 8 from series Los Caprichos, (12-01-92, Karl/Faber, #202), 8⁷⁄₁₆ x 6⅛ in., (21.5 x 15.5 cm.), etching and aquatint on thick wove (BP 219, DM 529, FR 1803, Y 41,335).

$1805* *Que Viene El Coco (D. 40; Harris 38 III, 1), 1799,* from Los Caprichios, (12-04-92, Bassenge, #6590), 8⁷⁄₁₆ x 5¹⁵⁄₁₆ in., (21.5 x 15.1 cm.), etching w/aquatint on hand-made (BP 1158, DM 2875, FR 9751, Y 225,343).

BI *Quien Lo Creyera! Plate 62 From Los Caprichos (Delteil 99),* wide margins, good cond., foxing, old tape, est. $800/1,200, (05-22-93, Weschler, #187, illus.), 8 x 6 in., (20.3 x 15.2 cm.), etching and aquatint on laid.

$819* *Una Raina Del Circo (D. 221; H. 267),* soiling, losses, (02-24-93, Picard, #113), etching and aquatint on strong old greenish laid (BP 571, DM 1330, FR 4507, Y 96,104).

BI *Ruega Por Ella,* margins, est. BP 100/150, (09-17-92, Bonhams-Chelsea, #88), plate 8¼ x 5⅞ in., (21 x 14.9 cm.), etching.

$542* *"Se Aprovechan",* plate s., t., (10-15-92, Duran, #25, illus.), 6⁵⁄₁₆ x 9⁷⁄₁₆ in., (16 x 24 cm.), engraving (BP 332, DM 807, FR 2736, Y 65,027, P 57,500).

$1096* *"Sopla" and "Si Amanece, Nos Vamos" (Haris 104 and 106): Two,* foglio, (05-20-93, Finarte-Milan, #75), 12³⁄₁₆ x 8¹⁵⁄₁₆ in., (31 x 22.7 cm.), etching and aquatint (BP 703, DM 1768, FR 5957, Y 121,025, L 1610).

$1650* *Soplones (Harris 83), 1799,* plate 48 from Los Caprichos, from First Edition, wide margins, trimmed, losses, very good cond., (11-09-92, Christie-NY, #95), 205 x 150 in., (520.7 x 381 cm.), etching and burnished aquatint on laid (BP 1091, DM 2634, FR 8900, Y 204,765).

$143* *El Sueno De La Razon Produce Monstruos, 1795-97, Delteil 80; Harris 78,* plate 43 of Los Caprichos, later edit., Emmanuel Jacobson Estate, (09-20-92, Hindman, #677), 8¼ x 5¾ in., (21 x 14.6 cm.), etching and aquatint (BP 84, DM 212, FR 726, Y 17,674).

$1415* *Tal Para Qual. (Qui De Ressemble S'Assemble) (Th.H. 40),* first edit. 1799, staining, creases, large margins, (06-16-93, Ader Tajan, #103), 7⅞ x 5⅞ in., (20 x 15 cm.), etching and aquatint (BP 943, DM 2349, FR 7883, Y 150,917).

$275* *La Tauromaquia (H. 204-236), 1816: Forty-Three,* complete volume, num. 140, pub. Hugo Kehrer, 1923, good cond., time-staining, surface soiling, tears, notations, wear/losses to cover, (10-28-92, Butterfield, #2814), 19 x 14½ in., (483 x 368 mm.), heliogravures on wove (BP 175, DM 425, FR 1442, Y 33,742).

BI *La Tauromaquia (H. 206-208, 211, 215-217, 230/jeweils III, 5. Ausgabe), 1921: Nine,* est. DM 4000, (12-01-92,

Karl/Faber, #204, illus.), 9⅝ x 13¾ in., (24.5 x 35 cm.), etching and aquatint on hand-made.

BI *La Tauromaquia (Harris 204-236; Delteil 224-256): Thirty-Three,* explanatory sheet and complete set, plates in 1st edit. of 1816, margins, plugged hole, repaired tear, foxing, discoloration, damp stains, remains,tape hinges, good cond., est. BP 60/80,000, (06-30-93, Sotheby-London, #146), each sh, c. 12 x 15⅞ in., (305 x 403 mm.), etching w/aquatint, 5 on paper w/a Morato watermark and 8 w/a No. 1 watermark.

$660* *"Tauromaquia", c. 1905: Set Of Three,* plates 1, 3 and 7, full margins, late printings, inkless stamp of Goya, (12-08-92, Swann, #123), images 8½ x 12 in., (21.6 x 30.5 cm.), aquatint etching in sepia on laid watermarked paper (BP 414, DM 1028, FR 3503, Y 81,805).

$357* *Tauromaquia, Plate 3 and 39: Two,* discoloration, foxing, laid down on cardboard, (12-04-92, Doyle, #105), 8 x 12¼ in., (203 x 311 mm.), etching and aquatint (BP 229, DM 569, FR 1929, Y 44,569).

$1725* *Tauromaquia: Plate 14 (D. 237; H. 217), 1816,* margins, creases, foxing, soiling, tape, (05-13-93, Sotheby-NY, #328), 9¾ x 14 in., (247 x 354 mm.), etching w/aquatint on laid (BP 1132, DM 2785, FR 9395, Y 192,587).

BI *Temeridad De Martincho En La Plaza De Zaragoza (Harris 221 III, 1 - Delteil 241 - Hofmann 100), 1815-16,* est. DM 5000, (06-10-93, Hauswedell/Nolt, #334, illus.), image 9¹³⁄₁₆ x 14¹⁄₁₆ in., (24.9 x 35.7 cm.), etch-ing w/aquatint on hand-made.

$1826* *Tras El Vicio Viene El Fornicio (Bobalicon) (H. 251/III, 1.Ausgabe),* (12-01-92, Karl/Faber, #208), 9⁷⁄₁₆ x 13¾ in., (24 x 35 cm.), etching and aquatint (BP 1206, DM 2910, FR 9919, Y 227,341).

$187* *Tu Que No Puedes, 1796-1798,* plate 42 of Los Caprichos, (06-13-93, Hindman, #375), 8¼ x 5¾ in., (21 x 14.6 cm.), etching and aquatint (BP 122, DM 304, FR 1023, Y 19,678).

$921* *Valor Varonil De La Celebre Pajuelera En La De Zaragoza (H. 225/III/1),* sheet 22 from the series La Tauro-maquia, (06-08-93, Karl/Faber, #293), approx. 9¹³⁄₁₆ x 13¾ in., (25 x 35 cm.), etching and aquatint on hand-made (BP 605, DM 1494, FR 5033, Y 97,823).

$330* *Valor Varonil De La Celebre Pajuelera En La Plaza De Zaragoza, 1876,* plate 22 from La Tauromaquia, third edit., wide margins, foxing, repaired tears, (05-27-93, Swann, #120), 8¼ x 12¹⁄₁₆ in., (21 x 30.6 cm.), etching w/burnished aquatint, drypoint, and burin (BP 211, DM 530, FR 1785, Y 35,377).

BI *Y Se Le Quema La Casa (Delteil 55, Harris 53), c. 1799,* 5th edit., plate 18 from Los Caprichos, est. $2/400, (03-24-93, Grogan, #16), 8½ x 6 in., (21.6 x 15.2 cm.), etching and aquatint.

BI *"Ysele Quema La Casa" (H. 53),* Plate No. 18 from Los Caprichos, 7th edit. 1903-05, hinge, fine cond., est. $1-200, (10-31-92, Cleveland, #285A), 8⅜ x 5⅞ in., (21.3 x 14.9 cm.), etching and aquatint on heavy laid paper.

GOYA, Francisco de (after)

$640* *La Corrida De Toros: Set Of Twenty-One,* blindstamps, margins, (08-20-92, Bonhams-Chelsea, #16), plate 9⅞ x 13½ in., (25.1 x 34.3 cm.), etching, watermarks, on wove (BP 330, DM 927, FR 3145, Y 80,818).

$1131* *Los Caprichos: Eighteen,* plates: 10, 16, 22, 37, 40, 45, 46, 47, 48, 52, 55, 56, 57, 58, 63, 66, 65, and 71, (10-07-92, Christie-S. Ken, #16), pl 8½ x 6 in., (21.6 x 15.2 cm.), etching w/aquatint, reprint (BP 660, DM 1637, FR 5550, Y 136,019).

BI *Que Guerrero! (Harris 266), 1877,* 1st of series, 3rd state w/ letter, full margins, est. FF 8/10,000, (11-16-92, Briest, #204, illus.), 11¹³⁄₁₆ x 16¹⁵⁄₁₆ in., (30 x 43 cm.), etching and aquatint on Holland creme.

BI *Una Reina Del Circo (Harris 267), 1877,* 2nd of series, 3rd state w/letter, yellowing, est. FF 8/10,000, (11-16-92, Briest, #205), 11¼ x 15⅜ in., (28.6 x 39 cm.), etch-ing and aquatint on Holland cream.

GOYO, Hashiguchi   Japanese c. 1880/88-1921

$4531* *Portrait Of A Young Beauty, 1920,* format Oban, lit., (04-27-93, Dorotheum, #143, illus.), 10¹⁵⁄₁₆ x 16⅜ in., (27.8

x 41.6 cm.), color woodcut (BP 2881, DM 7174, FR 24,269, Y 507,789, SC 50,400).

GRACHAND and VISHNUPERSAUD (after)
BI *Platae Asiaticae Rariores: Forty-One,* from the series, by M. Gauci, p. Engelman, Graf and Coundet, 1830-1832, full margins, good cond., oxidizaion, defects from binding, time stained, est. BP 8/900, (10-27-92, Phillips-London, #168), sheet 21¼ x 14 in., (540 x 356 mm.), lithograph w/extensive hand-coloring on wove.

GRAESER, Camille   1892-1980
$332* *Blau-Rot 3:1 (Paradowski S. 162), 1976,* #XXXVIII/L, s., d., work number D 1976.3, (04-21-93, Germann, #464), 17¹¹⁄₁₆ x 12¹³⁄₁₆ in., (450 x 325 mm.), color serigraph (BP 215, DM 531, FR 1795, Y 36,754, SF 483).
BI *Komposition (Paradowski D 1971.5), 1971,* est. DM 6/800, (06-24-93, Germann, #636), 19¾ x 19¾ in., (501 x 501 mm.), color serigraph.
$860* *Komposition (Paradowski D 1974.1), 1974,* 13/100, s., d., (10-14-92, Germann, #528), 23⅝ x 23⅝ in., (600 x 600 mm.), color serigraph (BP 505, DM 1259, FR 4268, Y 104,217, SF 1121).
$724* *Komposition, 1971,* d., (10-14-92, Germann, #530), 19¹¹⁄₁₆ x 19¹¹⁄₁₆ in., (500 x 500 mm.), color serigraph (BP 425, DM 1060, FR 3593, Y 87,736, SF 944).
$553* *Komposition, 1971,* s., d., (09-04-92, Germann, #359), 19¾ x 19¾ in., (501 x 501 mm.), color serigraph (BP 277, DM 775, FR 2638, Y 68,070, SF 690).
$453* *Komposition, 1972,* #98/200, s., rubbed, (10-14-92, Germann, #529), 23⅝ x 23⅝ in., (600 x 600 mm.), color serigraph (BP 266, DM 663, FR 2248, Y 54,896, SF 590).

GRAF, Urs   1485-1528
BI *The Crucifixion (Holl. 3),* narrow margins, repaired tear, creasing, est. BP 5/6,000, (06-29-93, Sotheby-London, #45, illus.), 6 x 4¼ in., (15.2 x 10.8 cm.), engraving.
$840* *Eine Der Torichten Jungfrauen (Hollstein 7; Illus. Bartsch, IX, 390;is 2), c. 1505,* after Martin Schongauer, prov., (06-23-93, Kornfeld, #57), engraving (BP 571, DM 1421, FR 4781, Y 91,513, SF 1265).
$1083* *Szenen Aus Der Passion Christi (B. VII, S. 459, 2): Sixteen,* prov., (12-04-92, Bassenge, #6225), each approx. 8⁹⁄₁₆ x 6⅛ in., (21.7 x 15.6 cm.), woodcut (BP 695, DM 1725, FR 5851, Y 135,206).

GRAFF, Anton   1736-1813
$505* *Anton Graff, Nach Seinem Selbstbildnis (Nagler 21; Andresen 3 II; LeBlanc 17 nach II, vor III; Heller-Andresen 2 II), 1797,* (12-04-92, Bassenge, #6599), 14⁷⁄₁₆ x 10¹³⁄₁₆ in., (36.7 x 27.4 cm.), engraving (BP 324, DM 804, FR 2728, Y 63,046).
BI *Selbstbildnis (Andresen-Wessely 1 III; Berckenhagen 504 II),* watermark, est. DM 1,800, (06-10-93, Hauswedell/Nolt, #189), etching on hand-made.

GRAHAM, Dan
BI *Sequenza Di Intenzione Intenzionalita,* each s., d. 1972, prov., exhib., Sylvio Perlstein Coll., est. $6/8,000, (11-18-92, Sotheby-NY, #218, illus.), each framed 39 x 27¼ in., (99.1 x 69.2 cm.), five framed photographs of typed text, one w/two mounted photographs.

GRAHAM, Dan   b. 1942
BI *Homes For America, 1989: Six,* s., est. DM 1,200-, (05-27-93, Lempertz, #747), 19⅝ x 21¹⁵⁄₁₆ in., (49.8 x 55.8 cm.), color photo-offset print.

GRAHAM, Robert   American b. 1938
$108* *Dye Transfer I, 1970,* s., d., num. 10/75 Robert Graham 1970 verso, (10-15-92, Sotheby-London, #48, illus.), 8½ x 11 in., (21.6 x 27.9 cm.), photograph, color print colored w/acrylic (BP 66, DM 161, FR 545, Y 12,957)..
$539* *Dye Transfer II, 1970,* s., d., num. 10/75 Robert Graham 1970 verso, (10-15-92, Sotheby-London, #47, illus.), 9⅝ x 7½ in., (24.4 x 19.1 cm.), photograph, silver print contact sheet, colored w/acrylic (BP 330, DM 802, FR 2721, Y 64,667).

GRAMATTE, Walter   1897-1929
$2483* *Akt (Eckhardt 7), 1915,* s., t., i., (06-05-93, Bassenge, #6066), 6⁷⁄₁₆ x 8⅞ in., (16.4 x 22.5 cm.), linocut on Simili-Japan (BP 1635, DM 4026, FR 13,568, Y 266,359).
$6177* *Das Gesicht, 1924,* portfolio, s., d., w/title-page, pub. Euphorion Verlag, full margins, good cond., foxing, loose, (06-30-93, Sotheby-London, #446, illus.), each sh c. 21¼ x 15⅛ in., (540 x 384 mm.), nine etchings in various colors on wove (BP 4140, DM 10,536, FR 35,541, Y 661,845).
$1419* *Die Komponistin Sonia Friedmann (Eckhardt 39), 1920,* s., d., (06-05-93, Bassenge, #6067), 12⅝ x 11 in., (32 x 28 cm.), woodcut (BP 934, DM 2301, FR 7754, Y 152,221).
BI *Das Kreisen (Eckhardt 51), (19)18,* s., d., wrinkles, traces of old mounting, est. DM 1400, (12-01-92, Karl/Faber, #653), 10¼ x 7⅞ in., (26 x 20 cm.), lithograph on hand-made.
$636* *Das Kreisen (Eckhardt 51), 1918,* s., d., t., (06-10-93, Hauswedell/Nolt, #343, illus.), image 10¼ x 7¹³⁄₁₆ in., (26 x 19.8 cm.), lithograph on hand-made (BP 416, DM 1036, FR 3487, Y 67,509).
$664* *Liegendes Madchen (Eckhardt 164), 1923,* s., (12-05-92, Bassenge, #7188), 9⅛ x 12¹⁄₁₆ in., (23.2 x 30.7 cm.), etching on copper print paper (BP 416, DM 1035, FR 3528, Y 82,270).
$1475* *Madchen Mit Halskette (Eckhardt 176), 1923,* s., (12-05-92, Bassenge, #7190), 12 x 8¹³⁄₁₆ in., (30.5 x 22.4 cm.), etching on copper print paper (BP 924, DM 2300, FR 7837, Y 182,753).
$1419* *Madchen Mit Hand (Eckhardt 168), 1923,* s., blindstamp, (06-05-93, Bassenge, #6069, illus.), 12¹⁄₁₆ x 8⅛ in., (30.7 x 20.7 cm.), etching and etching on hand-made Japan (BP 934, DM 2301, FR 7754, Y 152,221).
$738* *Madchen Mit Hand (Eckhardt 168), 1923,* s., blindstamp, (12-05-92, Bassenge, #7189), 12¹⁄₁₆ x 8⅛ in., (30.7 x 20.7 cm.), etching on copper print paper (BP 462, DM 1151, FR 3921, Y 91,438).
$636* *Der Mann Am Spiegel (Eckhardt 135), 1919,* s., d., (06-10-93, Hauswedell/Nolt, #341, illus.), image 11⅝ x 8⁹⁄₁₆ in., (29.5 x 21.8 cm.), drypoint on thick wove (BP 416, DM 1036, FR 3487, Y 67,509).
$2490* *Mann Und Lachende Frau (E. 80/I), (19)20,* s., d., hand-colored E, tears, signs of wear, (12-01-92, Karl/Faber, #656, illus.), color lithograph, hand-coloring on blotting paper (BP 1645, DM 3969, FR 13,525, Y 310,010).
$1833* *Mudes Madchen (Eckhardt 167), 1922/23,* s., d., i., (05-26-93, Lempertz, #185, illus.), 20¾ x 13⅜ in., (52.7 x 34 cm.), etching on wove (BP 1186, DM 2991, FR 10,066, Y 199,153).
$110* *Mudes Madchen (Sonia Gramatte), 1922-23,* s., d., full margins, staining, very good cond., (10-13-92, Christie-E, #69), 8⅜ x 6½ in., (21.3 x 16.5 cm.), etching w/hand-coloring in blue on wove (BP 64, DM 161, FR 548, Y 13,338).
$208* *Robert Im Theater (E. 120/III), (19)18,* s., d., Bl. 2 from the series Der Rebell, stained, (12-01-92, Karl/Faber, #657), 6¹¹⁄₁₆ x 4¹⁵⁄₁₆ in., (17 x 12.5 cm.), drypoint on smooth paper (BP 137, DM 332, FR 1130, Y 25,896).

GRAND, Louis le
$143* *"Woman Holding A Child",* s. plate, artist stamp, #20/30, (02-27-93, Dunning, #112), 4 x 6 in., (10.2 x 15.2 cm.), print (BP 101, DM 235, FR 799, Y 16,881).

GRANDVILLE, J.-J. (after)
$24* *"Le Chene Et Le Roseau",* (03-22-93, Pescheteau, #18), lithograph on Chine applique (BP 16, DM 39, FR 134, Y 2779).

GRANET (after)
BI *Interior Of A Nunnery With A Girl Taking The Veil, 1828,* by Gleadah, pub. James Bulcock, good cond., est. BP 70/100, (11-30-92, Phillips-London, #213), sheet 21½ x 16¼ in., (546 x 413 mm.), hand-colored aquatint on J. Whatman 1827 wove.

GRANT, Allan   American b. 1920
$358* *"Fifth Avenue, New York City",* 1945/later, s., t., d., photog. stamp, (11-16-92, Butterfield, #5994, illus.), 9 x 9⅝ in., (229 x 244.9 mm.), photograph, gelatin silver print (BP 236, DM 571, FR 1923, Y 44,522).

$715* *"Heat Wave, New York City"*, 1952/later, s., photog. stamp, (11-16-92, Butterfield, #5993, illus.), 11⅛ x 9¾ in., (283.1 x 248.1 mm.), photograph, gelatin silver print (BP 471, DM 1140, FR 3840, Y 88,919).

BI *"Manolete, Mexico"*, 1946, s/. t/. d., photog.'s stamp, mount trimmed to print, est. $6/800, (05-23-93, Butterfield, #3434, illus.), 13½ x 10½ in., photograph, gelatin silver print.

$1265* *"Marilyn Monroe In Her Brentwood Home"*, 1962, p. 1976, s., t., d., photog.'s stamp, (05-23-93, Butterfield, #3433, illus.), 16½ x 14 in., photograph, gelatin silver print (BP 824, DM 2068, FR 6962, Y 139,825).

$431* *"Motorcyle Family, From The Highway 36 Series"*, 1948, photog.'s stamp, estate stamp, (05-23-93, Butterfield, #3435, illus.), 13¼ x 10¾ in., photograph, gelatin silver print (BP 281, DM 705, FR 2372, Y 47,640).

GRANT, Clement R.   American 1849-1893
$66* *Mending The Net*, s., (11-28-92, Young, #178), 18 x 23 in., (45.7 x 58.4 cm.), etching (BP 44, DM 105, FR 357, Y 8214).

GRANT, Duncan   American 1885-1978
$845* *Everywhere You Go, St. Ives, Huntingdon, 1932*, p. Vincent Brooks, Day & Son, ref. #330, cond. 3, (10-13-92, Phillips-London, #90, illus.), 29¹⁵⁄₁₆ x 45¼ in., (76 x 115 cm.), color lithograph (BP 492, DM 1238, FR 4206, Y 102,462).

GRANT, Francis (after)
BI *"The Hunt"*, engr. by Frederick Bromley, (12-11-92, G.A. Key, #42), 17 x 27 in., (43.2 x 68.6 cm.), hand colored engraving.

BI *Sir Richard Sutton And The Quorn Hounds*, pub. John O'Malley and Son, est. $3/500, (06-11-93, Freemn/Fine Art, #79), 20½ x 24½ in., (52.1 x 62.2 cm.), hand-colored engraving.

$715* *Sir Richard Sutton And The Quorn Hounds*, pub. John O'Malley and Son, (06-11-93, Freemn/Fine Art, #80), 21 x 34¼ in., (53.3 x 87 cm.), engraving w/hand-coloring (BP 470, DM 1162, FR 3918, Y 75,862).

$184* *Sutton Sykes, Sledmore*, by G. Raphael Ward, laid down, (11-12-92, Bonhams-Chelsea, #22), image 27 x 18½ in., (68.6 x 47 cm.), hand-colored mezzotint (BP 121, DM 292, FR 983, Y 22,815).

GRANT, Gordon Hope   American 1875-1962
$77* *"Arching Elms"*, s., AAA label verso, (06-11-93, DuMouchelle, #2256), 10 x 12 in., (25.4 x 30.5 cm.), lithograph (BP 51, DM 125, FR 422, Y 8170).

$468* *"Arching Elms"*, *"Old Windjammer"*, *"The Hardy Breed"*, *"Eight Bells"* and *"Between Tides"*: *Five*, s., margins, four taped to mat; mat burn, time staining, backboard burn, (12-12-92, Weschler, #125, illus.), approx. 9 x 11½ in., (22.9 x 29.2 cm.), lithograph (BP 300, DM 737, FR 2527, Y 57,914).

$138* *At The Helm*, s., #4/100, very good cond.?, (03-28-93, Bakker, #268), plate 7⅞ x 9½ in., (20 x 24.1 cm.), drypoint (BP 93, DM 225, FR 765, Y 16,061).

BI *Beaching The Dory*, s., t., est. $125/175, (10-30-92, Sloan, #833), 10 x 13¼ in., (22.9 x 30.5 cm.), lithograph.

BI *Beaching The Dory*, s., t., est. $125/175, (09-17-92, Sloan, #2344), 10 x 13¼ in., (25.4 x 33.7 cm.), lithograph.

$132* *"Beaching The Dory"*, s., (08-05-92, Boos, #561), image 9¹³⁄₁₆ x 13³⁄₁₆ in., (250 x 335 mm.), lithograph (BP 69, DM 195, FR 659, Y 16,811).

$121* *"Concarneau"*, s., (03-25-93, Boos, #603), image 7¹⁵⁄₁₆ x 9¹³⁄₁₆ in., (203 x 250 mm.), etching (BP 82, DM 199, FR 676, Y 14,175).

$83* *Dockside Politics*, s., t., (09-17-92, Sloan, #2343), 9 x 12 in., (22.9 x 30.5 cm.), lithograph (BP 47, DM 123, FR 422, Y 10,334).

$94* *Dory And Schooner On Open Waters*, s., #19/100, (09-17-92, Sloan, #2342), 7 x 10 in., (17.8 x 25.4 cm.), etching (BP 53, DM 140, FR 478, Y 11,703).

$99* *Down Sandy Hook Way*, s., (06-11-93, Freemn/Fine Art, #81), 8¾ x 11¾ in., (22.2 x 29.8 cm.), lithograph (BP 65, DM 161, FR 542, Y 10,504).

$138* *Fishermen*, s., very good cond.?, (02-07-93, Bakker, #113), plate 7¾ x 9¾ in., (19.7 x 24.8 cm.), etching (BP 95, DM 229, FR 774, Y 17,173).

$83* *"Freedom Of The Seas"*, s., (12-17-92, Mystic, #4), lithograph and etching (BP 53, DM 130, FR 443, Y 10,200).

$70* *The Life Boat, 1939*, AAA edit., s., mat staining, hinges, (05-15-93, Cleveland, #148, illus.), 9 x 11½ in., (22.9 x 29.2 cm.), lithograph (BP 46, DM 113, FR 378, Y 7760).

BI *"The Little Harbor"*, s., AAA edit., excell. cond., est. $175/250, (05-15-93, Cleveland, #145), 9⅛ x 12¹⁄₁₆ in., (23.2 x 30.6 cm.), lithograph.

$518* *New York, Skyscrapers, 1907*, s., d., laid down, margins, good cond., paper losses, soiling, pencil, (05-19-93, Butterfield, #1816, illus.), 17¹³⁄₁₆ x 10¹¹⁄₁₆ in., (452 x 271 mm.), graphite on wove (BP 336, DM 842, FR 2837, Y 57,345).

$1495* *New York, Trolley Stop, 1909*, s., d., laid down, good cond., light-staining, surface soiling, (05-19-93, Butterfield, #1815, illus.), 16 x 11¼ in., (406 x 286 mm.), watercolor and graphite on wove (BP 970, DM 2430, FR 8187, Y 165,504).

$154* *"Pigeon Cove"* and *"Under The Bows"*: *Two*, each s., AAA labels, (05-14-93, DuMouchelle, #349), 9¾ x 12½ in., (24.8 x 31.8 cm.), lithograph (BP 100, DM 248, FR 832, Y 17,071).

$85 *"The Regular"*, (03-04-93, Alderfer, #295, illus.), 28 x 20¾ in., (71.1 x 52.7 cm.), poster (BP 58, DM 139, FR 473, Y 9896).

$193* *"Schooner At Anchor"* And *"Ahoy There"*: *Two*, s. Gordon Grant, good cond., staining, toning, (03-12-93, Skinner, #35, illus.), approx. 9 x 12 in., (22.9 x 30.5 cm.), lithograph on wove (BP 135, DM 321, FR 1092, Y 22,746).

BI *Sea Harvest*, s., t., i., est. $175/225, (09-17-92, Sloan, #645), 9¾ x 11⅞ in., (24.8 x 30.2 cm.), soft ground etching and aquatint.

$130* *"Sea Harvest"*, c. 1930s, s., t., light struck, staining, foxing, (05-15-93, Cleveland, #146), 9¾ x 11⅞ in., (24.8 x 30.2 cm.), softground etching and aquatint (BP 85, DM 209, FR 703, Y 14,411).

$45* *"Stowing Jibs"*, 1938, pub. AAA, s., good cond., (05-15-93, Cleveland, #147, illus.), 8⅞ x 11½ in., (22.5 x 29.2 cm.), lithograph (BP 29, DM 72, FR 243, Y 4988).

BI *Tugboat And Schooner*, s., est. $100/150, (10-30-92, Sloan, #832), 9 x 12 in., (22.9 x 30.5 cm.), lithograph.

BI *Tugboat And Schooner*, s., est. $100/150, (09-17-92, Sloan, #617), 9 x 12 in., (22.9 x 30.5 cm.), lithograph.

$330* *Untitled: Four*, s., good cond.?, (03-28-93, Bakker, #29), each approx. 9 x 12 in., (22.9 x 30.5 cm.), lithograph (BP 222, DM 538, FR 1830, Y 38,408).

GRANT, Sir Francis (after)
BI *2nd Lord Poltimore And Hounds*, by Thomas Lewis Atkinson, blindstamp Print Sellers' Assoc., pub. Henry Graves & Co., 1874, margins, tear into image, est. BP 60/80, (03-03-93, Bonhams-Chelsea, #131), plate 24 x 32 in., (61 x 81.3 cm.), mezzotint.

$213* *2nd Lord Poltimore And Hounds*, by Thomas Lewis Atkinson, blindstamp, pub. Henry Graves and Co., 1874, margins, tear into image, defects, (06-30-93, Bonhams-Chelsea, #125), plate 24 x 32 in., (61 x 81.3 cm.), mezzotint (BP 143, DM 363, FR 1226, Y 22,822).

GRAPH
$189* *PLM: Cote D'Azur. "Ete Comme Hiver, Quand Il Pleut Ailleurs Le Soleil Resplendit"*, c. 1935, p. Dehon, good cond., (11-19-92, Ribeyre/Baron, #108), 39⅜ x 24¹³⁄₁₆ in., (100 x 63 cm.), poster (BP 124, DM 301, FR 1015, Y 23,505).

GRASSET, Eugene   Swiss 1841-1917
$2362* *Die 12 Monate In Der Jahreszeitenfolge: Twelve*, stone mono., (05-08-93, Schloss Ahlden, #2842), each 7¹⁵⁄₁₆ x 6⅛ in., (20.3 x 15.5 cm.), color lithograph on wove (BP 1541, DM 3794, FR 12,802, Y 263,940).

$1980* *Cycles And Automobiles, Marque Georges Richard*, Vaugirard G. de Malherbe, A- cond., fold marks, closed marginal tears, back cover illus., (08-06-92, Swann, #145, illus.), (BP 1034, DM 2926, FR 9880, Y 252,551).

BI *"Gismonda", 1910,* A cond., est. $6/900, (08-06-92, Swann, #146, illus.), 35 x 25 in., (88.9 x 63.5 cm.), .

$301* *Grafton Gallery, 1893,* Paris, Verdoux, Ducourtioux et Thrillard sc, cond. A-, (06-11-93, Boisgirard, #77), 29⅛ x 18⅞ in., (74 x 48 cm.), lithograph and pochoir (BP 198, DM 489, FR 1649, Y 31,936).

$341* *Jeanne D'Arc, Sarah Bernhardt, 1890,* (01-31-93, Morelle/Marchan, #178), 31½ x 47¼ in., (80 x 120 cm.), poster (BP 229, DM 549, FR 1857, Y 42,540).

BI *L'Andalousie Au Temps Des Maures. Exposition 1900,* fairly good cond., (03-13-93, Laurin, #24), 53¹⁵⁄₁₆ x 70⅞ in., (137 x 180 cm.), .

$827* *Odeon, 1890,* p. Malherbe et Cellot, (01-31-93, Morelle/Marchan, #179, illus.), 32⁵⁄₁₆ x 48¹⁄₁₆ in., (82 x 122 cm.), poster (BP 556, DM 1332, FR 4504, Y 103,169).

$502* *La Place Clichy. La Premiere Maison Du Monde Pour Ses ImportationsOrientales, 1897,* Paris, Imp. Chaix, cond. B+, (06-11-93, Boisgirard, #78), 55¹¹⁄₁₆ x 33⁷⁄₁₆ in., (141.5 x 85 cm.), poster (BP 330, DM 816, FR 2751, Y 53,263).

$498* *La Place Clichy. Soldes Des Tapis Du Salon De Peinture, c. 1895,* good cond., (03-13-93, Laurin, #7), 55⅛ x 33⅞ in., (140 x 86 cm.), (BP 347, DM 829, FR 2818, Y 58,692).

BI *Salon Des Cent,* s. in stone, pub. Affiches Artistiques - G. de Malherbe, good cond.?, light/water-staining, creases, holes, scuffs in image, surface soiling, est. $9/1200, (09-21-92, Butterfield, #827), 23¹⁄₁₆ x 14⅝ in., (585.2 x 372.1 mm.), lithograph in colors on wove.

GRASSI, Joseph (after)

BI *Comte Gregoire Czernichew (Leblanc 62), c. 1800,* engraved by J. Pichler, narrow margins, nick, repaired top left, est.BP 150/200, (11-30-92, Phillips-London, #91), plate 19¼ x 11⅝ in., (489 x 295 mm.), mezzotint on wove.

GRASSI, Raniero

$522* *Veduta Del Lungarno Di Pisa In Tempo D'Illuminazione, Verso Il Ponte Mare, 1839,* full margins, scuff marks, (10-27-92, Phillips-London, #132), image 8⅞ x 14¾ in., (225 x 375 mm.), engraving w/extensive hand-coloring and grey gouache borders (BP 330, DM 800, FR 2715, Y 63,853).

GRAU-SALA, Emilio Spanish 1911-1975

$40* *"Badinage",* s., (04-04-93, Pescheteau, #220), 13⅜ x 10¼ in., (34 x 26 cm.), etching and aquatint on laid wove (BP 26, DM 64, FR 218, Y 4554).

BI *Jeune Femme Assise Pres D'Une Fenetre,* s., #17/40, large margins, (05-06-93, Laurin, #38), color lithograph.

$56* *"Le Paddock", 1971,* s., (10-18-92, Pescheteau, #159), 25⁹⁄₁₆ x 19¹¹⁄₁₆ in., (65 x 50 cm.), lithograph in colors on Arches (BP 34, DM 83, FR 281, Y 6687).

GRAUBNER, Gotthard b. 1930

$249* *Komposition, (19)74,* s., d., (12-01-92, Karl/Faber, #659), 11⅝ x 8¹¹⁄₁₆ in., (29.5 x 22 cm.), etching (BP 165, DM 397, FR 1353, Y 31,001).

$567* *Schwamm Gouache, 1970,* s., num., (06-08-93, Karl/Faber, #804), approx. 12⅜ x 11 in., (31.5 x 28 cm.), color serigraph on Vlies paper (BP 373, DM 920, FR 3098, Y 60,223).

GRAUMANN, Erwin 1902-1988

BI *Portrait Einer Jungen Frau (Syamken R 55), 1930,* s., d., num., est. DM 300-, (09-25-92, Granier, #2861), sheet 14¹⁵⁄₁₆ x 11 in., (38 x 28 cm.), etching on hand-made.

GRAVEL, Francine b. 1944

$156* *Musique De Chambre, 1978,* #15/25, s., t., d. '78, prov., (11-16-92, Hodgins, #158), 22¹⁵⁄₁₆ x 17¹⁵⁄₁₆ in., (58.4 x 45.7 cm.), color etching and embossing on paper (BP 103, DM 249, FR 838, Y 19,468, C$ 198).

GRAVES, Henry (after)

$627* *Field Marshal, Most Noble, The Late Marquis Of Anglesey,* by Joseph Skelton, pub. Mr. Skelton, 1855, full margins, staining, (06-16-93, Bonhams-Chelsea, #418, illus.), image 20½ x 34¾ in., (52.1 x 88.3 cm.), lithograph w/hand-coloring (BP 418, DM 1041, FR 3493, Y 66,873).

GRAVES, Nancy American b. 1940

$935* *Four Times Four, 1981,* s., d., num. 5/45, Metro. Museum of Art blindstamp, full margins, excell. cond., (09-19-92, Christie-E, #113, illus.), sheet 24¼ x 24¼ in., (61.6 x 61.6 cm.), etching and aquatint in colors on wove (BP 538, DM 1400, FR 4795, Y 116,496).

$413* *Lunar Landscape,* s., d. '72, #IV, 79/100, (05-16-93, Hindman, #511), 22 x 29½ in., (55.9 x 74.9 cm.), lithograph (BP 269, DM 664, FR 2232, Y 45,782).

BI *Lunar Landscape,* s., d.'72, #IV, 79/100, est. $1/2,000, (12-13-92, Hindman, #349), 22 x 29½ in., lithograph in black and green.

BI *Medusa, 1989,* s., #41/170, pub. Institute of Contemporary Art, Philadelphia, good cond., est. $800/1,000, (05-15-93, Sotheby-NY, #983), sheet 30¼ x 29¾ in., (76.8 x 75.6 cm.), silkscreen in colors w/hand applied glitter.

$1150* *Ruis (Tyler 207:NG6), 1977,* s., d., #1/33. blindstamp, pub. Tyler Graphics Ltd., full margins, good cond., pressure mark, (05-15-93, Sotheby-NY, #982), 19⅞ x 23⅝ in., (50.5 x 60 cm.), etching, aquatint and engraving in colors w/hand-coloring (BP 748, DM 1850, FR 6216, Y 127,480).

GRAY, H.

$302* *Mam'Zelle Boyscout, 1905,* Ed. Delancey and Fil, B+ cond., fraying, closed tears, tear, (08-06-92, Swann, #147, illus.), 35 x 26½ in., (88.9 x 67.3 cm.), (BP 158, DM 446, FR 1507, Y 38,520).

GRAY, Henri (Henri BOULANGER) 1858-1924

$402* *Chemins De Fer Du Nord Et De L'Ouest. Le Treport-Mers, c. 1900,* Paris, Imp. Courmont Freres, cond. B, corner restored, (06-11-93, Boisgirard, #80), 51³⁄₁₆ x 37 in., (130 x 94 cm.), poster (BP 264, DM 653, FR 2203, Y 42,653).

$502* *Radioleine. Cie Industrielle De Petroles, c. 1900,* Paris, Imp. Bougard, cond. A-, (06-11-93, Boisgirard, #81, illus.), 61¹³⁄₁₆ x 45¹¹⁄₁₆ in., (157 x 116 cm.), poster (BP 330, DM 816, FR 2751, Y 53,263).

$1847* *Theatre De L'Opera, 1899,* before letters, cond. A-, Paris, Affiches Camis, (06-11-93, Boisgirard, #79, illus.), 51⅜ x 39⁹⁄₁₆ in., (130.5 x 100.5 cm.), poster (BP 1214, DM 3002, FR 10,121, Y 195,968).

GRAY, Joseph

$61* *Packing Through The Canyon,* margins, s., (05-22-93, Collins, #133), 11½ x 11½ in., (29.2 x 29.2 cm.), etching (BP 40, DM 99, FR 334, Y 6725).

BI *Seascapes: Six,* each s., num. in Roman numerals, good cond., paper discoloration, est. BP 2/300, (06-30-93, Sotheby-London, #306), drypoint w/etching on cream laid.

GREAVES, Derrick

$50 *"Sleeping Head",* #102/150, (12-11-92, G.A. Key, #25), 15 x 20 in., (38.1 x 50.8 cm.), etching (BP 32, DM 79, FR 270, Y 6187).

GRECO, Emilio Italian b. 1913

$384* *Reclining Female Nude, 1964,* s., t. indistinctly, d., i. prova d'artista, margins, good cond., handling creases, (05-27-93, Sotheby-Amstrdm, #618), 12⅜ x 19⁷⁄₁₆ in., (315 x 493 mm.), etching on wove (BP 246, DM 616, FR 2077, Y 41,166, G 690).

GREEN, Peter (after)

$119* *Seagulls On A Rocky Coastline,* by Joseph B. Pratt, s. by both artists, pub. Messrs. Arthur Tooth andSons, 1905, blindstamp Printsellers' Asssociation, margins, (04-22-93, Bonhams-Chelsea, #63), plate 35 x 29 in., (88.9 x 73.7 cm.), engraving (BP 77, DM 191, FR 645, Y 13,084).

GREEN, Roland English 1896-1971

$130 *Mallard Alighting On A River,* s., artist's proof, (08-14-92, G.A. Key, #112), 15 x 10 in., (38.1 x 25.4 cm.), colored print (BP 68, DM 191, FR 646, Y 16,393).

$125 *Pheasants Disturbed In An Autumn Wood,* s., artist's proof, (08-14-92, G.A. Key, #113), 15 x 9 in., (38.1 x 22.9 cm.), colored print (BP 65, DM 183, FR 621, Y 15,763).

GREEN, Roland (after)

$40 *"Woodcock And Chicks" and "Moorhen And Young": Two,* (06-11-93, G.A. Key, #61), 4 x 5 in., (10.2 x 12.7 cm.), colored print (BP 26, DM 65, FR 219, Y 4244).

GREEN, Valentine   English 1734-1813

$306* *His Grace The Duke Of Bedford With His Brothers, Lord John Russell, Lord William Russell, And Miss Vernon, 1778,* after Sir Joshua Reynolds, pub. W. Shropshire, margins, (10-15-92, Bonhams-Chelsea, #153), plate 20 x 17 in., (50.8 x 43.2 cm.), mezzotint (BP 187, DM 455, FR 1545, Y 36,713).

$50* *Marie De Levis, Vicomtesse De Sarsfield, Morte Le 5 Janvier 1781 (C.S. 119), 1785,* pub. Green, foxing, nicks, trimmed, (11-30-92, Phillips-London, #58), plate 13⅞ x 11 in., (352 x 279 mm.), mezzotint on laid (BP 33, DM 80, FR 270, Y 6223).

$244 *Portrait Of A Georgian Gentleman,* after Lemuel Francis Abbott, (04-16-93, G.A. Key, #39), 18 x 13½ in., (45.7 x 34.3 cm.), mezzotint engraving on copper (BP 160, DM 394, FR 1332, Y 27,437).

GREEN, Valentine (after Joseph WRIGHT OF DERBY)

$313* *A Philospher Showing An Experiment On The Air Pump, 1769,* poor cond., trimmed to image, laid down, defects, repaired tear, (10-27-92, Phillips-London, #62), plate 17⅜ x 22⅞ in., (441 x 581 mm.), mezzotint (BP 198, DM 480, FR 1628, Y 38,287).

GREENBAUM, Marty   American b. 1934

$22* *Blue Feamer,* s., t., #9/12, stamp d. Nov. 30, 1974, (06-13-93, Hindman, #344), overall 18 x 6¾ in., (45.7 x 17.1 cm.), artist's book, composed of screen-printed, hand-painted, sewn, burnedhand-made paper (BP 14, DM 36, FR 120, Y 2315).

GREENE, Milton H.

$556* *Ava Gardner, Portrait With White Hat,* lifetime edition, photog. stamp, (10-10-92, Bonhams, #128, illus.), 20 x 16 in., (50.8 x 40.6 cm.), photograph (BP 330, DM 826, FR 2773, Y 67,689).

BI *"Brighton 5th Street Boardwalk", "Boardwalk At Night", "Brighton" and "Winter On Bright 4th Street": Four,* 1939, one p.l., stamped photog.'s credit, s., d., largest 280 x 357mm, smallest 183 x 233mm, (05-07-93, Sotheby-London, #294, illus.), photograph, silver print.

BI *Diahann Carroll Sitting On Barrel,* photog. stamp, est. BP 250/350, (10-10-92, Bonhams, #126, illus.), 20 x 16 in., (50.8 x 40.6 cm.), color photograph.

$278* *Diahann Carroll, Portrait With Crossed Hands,* blind embossed, (10-10-92, Bonhams, #127, illus.), 20 x 16 in., (50.8 x 40.6 cm.), photograph (BP 165, DM 413, FR 1387, Y 33,845).

$371* *Judy Garland, In Black Pleated Dress With Red Velvet Coat,* photog. stamp, lifetime edit., (10-10-92, Bonhams, #122, illus.), 14 x 11 in., (35.6 x 27.9 cm.), color photograph (BP 220, DM 551, FR 1850, Y 45,167).

$204* *Lady Reclining On Running Board Of Car,* photog. stamp, prov., (10-10-92, Bonhams, #123, illus.), 11 x 14 in., (27.9 x 35.6 cm.), photograph (BP 121, DM 303, FR 1017, Y 24,836).

$978* *Marilyn Monroe,* 1953, p. 1979, ink s., d., stamped, (04-08-93, Christie-NY, #434, illus.), 15⅜ x 19⅜ in., (39.1 x 49.2 cm.), photograph, gelatin silver print (BP 641, DM 1571, FR 5318, Y 110,985).

$334* *Marilyn Monroe, "Bus Stop",* photog. stamp, (10-10-92, Bonhams, #146, illus.), 14 x 11 in., (35.6 x 27.9 cm.), color photograph (BP 198, DM 496, FR 1666, Y 40,662).

$635* *Marilyn Monroe,* 1952, p.l., sight 400 x 500mm, (05-07-93, Sotheby-London, #312, illus.), photograph, silver print (BP 402, DM 1004, FR 3383, Y 69,919).

$545* *Marilyn Monroe,* 1952, p.l., s., (c) stamp Milton H. Greene, photog.'s credit stamp copyright Milton H. Greene, 405 x 505mm, (05-07-93, Sotheby-London, #308, illus.), photograph, silver print (BP 345, DM 862, FR 2904, Y 60,009).

$581* *Marilyn Monroe,* 1952, p.l., s., (c) stamp Milton H. Greene, 505 x 405mm, (05-07-93, Sotheby-London, #314, illus.), photograph, silver print (BP 368, DM 919, FR 3095, Y 63,973).

$556* *Marilyn Monroe Embracing Statue,* blind embossed, #3/99, (10-10-92, Bonhams, #149, illus.), 16 x 20 in., (40.6 x 50.8 cm.), photograph (BP 330, DM 826, FR 2773, Y 67,689).

$779* *Marilyn Monroe Holding Decorated Guitar,* blind embossed, #3/99, (10-10-92, Bonhams, #147, illus.), 20 x 16 in., (50.8 x 40.6 cm.), photograph (BP 462, DM 1157, FR 3885, Y 94,838).

$779* *Marilyn Monroe In "Bus Stop" Costume Sitting On Doorstep,* blind embossed, #3/99, (10-10-92, Bonhams, #144, illus.), 16 x 20 in., (40.6 x 50.8 cm.), color photograph (BP 462, DM 1157, FR 3885, Y 94,838).

$1017* *Marilyn Monroe In Ballet Costume,* 1950s, p.l., s., (c) stamp Milton H. Greene, 507 x 405mm, (05-07-93, Sotheby-London, #309, illus.), photograph, silver print (BP 644, DM 1608, FR 5418, Y 111,980).

$1576* *Marilyn Monroe In Bowler Hat,* stamp, s., d. 3-14-78, #25/250, (10-10-92, Bonhams, #136, illus.), 20 x 16 in., (50.8 x 40.6 cm.), photograph (BP 935, DM 2341, FR 7860, Y 191,868).

$705* *Marilyn Monroe In Evening Dress With Fur Stole,* blind embossed, #9/99, (10-10-92, Bonhams, #150, illus.), 14 x 11 in., (35.6 x 27.9 cm.), photograph (BP 418, DM 1047, FR 3516, Y 85,829).

$816* *Marilyn Monroe In Fish Net Tights,* 1952, p.l., s., (c) stamp Milton H. Greene, 490 x 400mm, (05-07-93, Sotheby-London, #306, illus.), photograph, silver print (BP 517, DM 1290, FR 4347, Y 89,848).

$545* *Marilyn Monroe In Hat With Boa,* 1952, p. 1978, mounted on card, s. A/P Milton H. Greene, s. Milton H. Greene, s., d. Authentic Photograph stamp Milton H. Greene 4-7-78, (c) stamp Milton H. Greene 4-7-78 A/P.1/ 1 Personal, printer's label, 354 x 280mm, (05-07-93, Sotheby-London, #311, illus.), photograph, silver print (BP 345, DM 862, FR 2904, Y 60,009).

$649* *Marilyn Monroe Lying On Pillow In Fishnet Tights,* photog. stamp, blind embossed, (10-10-92, Bonhams, #133, illus.), 11 x 14 in., (27.9 x 35.6 cm.), photograph (BP 385, DM 964, FR 3237, Y 79,011).

$742* *Marilyn Monroe Removing A Stocking,* blind embossed, #3/99, (10-10-92, Bonhams, #137, illus.), 20 x 16 in., (50.8 x 40.6 cm.), photograph (BP 440, DM 1102, FR 3701, Y 90,334).

$1669* *Marilyn Monroe Sitting On Floor, Glass Balanced On Knee,* stamp, s., Artist's Proof, (10-10-92, Bonhams, #135, illus.), 16 x 20 in., (40.6 x 50.8 cm.), photograph (BP 990, DM 2479, FR 8324, Y 203,190).

$464* *Marilyn Monroe Sitting On Staircase,* blind embossed, #9/99, (10-10-92, Bonhams, #148, illus.), 20 x 16 in., (50.8 x 40.6 cm.), photograph (BP 275, DM 689, FR 2314, Y 56,489).

$334* *Marilyn Monroe Sitting On Stool, Legs Crossed, Holding Glass,* blind embossed, #3/99, (10-10-92, Bonhams, #139, illus.), 20 x 16 in., (50.8 x 40.6 cm.), photograph (BP 198, DM 496, FR 1666, Y 40,662).

BI *Marilyn Monroe Sitting On Stool, Legs Crossed, Holding Glass,* stamp, s., d. 5.22.78, #183/250, est. BP 700/ 1,100, (10-10-92, Bonhams, #134, illus.), 20 x 16 in., (50.8 x 40.6 cm.), photograph.

$593* *Marilyn Monroe Wearing Necklace And Earrings, Against A Palmist's Window,* blind embossed, #9/99, (10-10-92, Bonhams, #129, illus.), 14 x 11 in., (35.6 x 27.9 cm.), color photograph (BP 352, DM 881, FR 2958, Y 72,194).

BI *Marilyn Monroe, Glass Resting On Knee,* 1952, p. 1979, s., (c) stamp Milton H. Greene 3-14-79, stamped photog.'s credit Copyright Milton H. Greene, 405 x 508mm, est. BP 3/500, (05-07-93, Sotheby-London, #313, illus.), photograph, silver print.

BI *Marilyn Monroe, Glass Resting On Knee,* 1952, p.l., mounted on cardboard, 280 x 355mm, est. BP 3/500, (05-07-93, Sotheby-London, #307, illus.), photograph, silver print.

$545* *Marilyn Monroe, Head And Shoulders, Smiling,* 1952, p. 1979, s., (c) stamp Milton H. Greene 3-15-79 31/125, 500 x 385mm, (05-07-93, Sotheby-London, #310, illus.), photograph, silver print (BP 345, DM 862, FR 2904, Y 60,009).

$649* *Marilyn Monroe, In Red Dress Sitting, Leaning On Elbow,* blind embossed, #9/99, (10-10-92, Bonhams, #131, illus.), 14 x 11 in., (35.6 x 27.9 cm.), color photograph (BP 385, DM 964, FR 3237, Y 79,011).

$742* *Marilyn Monroe, Kneeling In Open Coat,* blind embossed, #9/99, (10-10-92, Bonhams, #142, illus.), 14 x 11 in., (35.6 x 27.9 cm.), color photograph (BP 440, DM 1102, FR 3701, Y 90,334).

$315* *Marilyn Monroe, Laughing, Hands On Thighs,* blind embossed, #9/99, (10-10-92, Bonhams, #132, illus.), 14 x 11 in., (35.6 x 27.9 cm.), photograph (BP 187, DM 468, FR 1571, Y 38,349).

$742* *Marilyn Monroe, Legs, Hands And Head,* blind embossed, photog. stamp, (10-10-92, Bonhams, #143, illus.), 11 x 14 in., (27.9 x 35.6 cm.), photograph (BP 440, DM 1102, FR 3701, Y 90,334).

$556* *Marilyn Monroe, Portrait In Bowler Hat,* blind embossed, #3/99, (10-10-92, Bonhams, #141, illus.), 20 x 16 in., (50.8 x 40.6 cm.), photograph (BP 330, DM 826, FR 2773, Y 67,689).

$1761* *Marilyn Monroe, Sitting In Gossamer Skirt,* blind embossed, #9/99, (10-10-92, Bonhams, #140, illus.), 14 x 11 in., (35.6 x 27.9 cm.), photograph (BP 1045, DM 2616, FR 8783, Y 214,390).

$1020* *Marilyn Monroe, Sitting In Red Dress, Hand In Hair,* blind embossed, #9/99, (10-10-92, Bonhams, #130, illus.), 14 x 11 in., (35.6 x 27.9 cm.), color photograph (BP 605, DM 1515, FR 5087, Y 124,178).

$334* *Marilyn Monroe, Sitting On Floor, Glass Balanced On Knee,* blind embossed, #3/99, (10-10-92, Bonhams, #138, illus.), 16 x 20 in., (40.6 x 50.8 cm.), photograph (BP 198, DM 496, FR 1666, Y 40,662).

$705* *Marilyn Monroe, Standing On Table In "Bus Stop" Costume,* blind embossed, #9/99, (10-10-92, Bonhams, #145, illus.), 14 x 11 in., (35.6 x 27.9 cm.), photograph (BP 418, DM 1047, FR 3516, Y 85,829).

$2475* *Marilyn Monroe: Two: "Marilyn in Tulle Skirt" and "Marilyn in Black",* each s., d., dedicated by photog., (c), authentication, reprod. limit. stamps, 1950, p.l., (10-15-92, Sotheby-NY, #524, illus.), one 14 x 13½ in., (35.6 x 34.3 cm.), other 17 x 15 in., (35.6 x 34.3 cm.), photograph, gelatin silver prints (BP 1515, DM 3684, FR 12,494, Y 296,941).

$1650* *Marlene Dietrich,* 1950's/1980, s., photog. stamp, notations, (11-16-92, Butterfield, #5997, illus.), 15½ x 1½ in., (394.4 x 38 mm.), photograph, gelatin silver print (BP 1086, DM 2631, FR 8861, Y 205,198).

$334* *Marlene Dietrich In Circus Costume,* (10-10-92, Bonhams, #125, illus.), 14 x 11 in., (35.6 x 27.9 cm.), photograph (BP 198, DM 496, FR 1666, Y 40,662).

$2750* *Nellie Nyad,* s., d. by photog., stamps, 1952, p.l., (10-15-92, Sotheby-NY, #525, illus.), 15¼ x 19½ in., (38.7 x 49.5 cm.), photograph, gelatin silver print (BP 1683, DM 4093, FR 13,882, Y 329,934).

$167* *Sophia Loren,* Two Women, (10-10-92, Bonhams, #124, illus.), 11 x 14 in., (27.9 x 35.6 cm.), color photograph (BP 99, DM 248, FR 833, Y 20,331).

GREENE, Roland (after)
$23 *Fledglings And Birds In Flight: Two,* (06-11-93, G.A. Key, #119), 7 x 5 in., (17.8 x 12.7 cm.), colored print (BP 15, DM 37, FR 126, Y 2440).

GREENOUGH, F.W., Publisher
$193* *"Rant Che Wai Me" and "NE Sou A Quoit": Two,* printed at I.T. Bowen, (11-12-92, Freemn/Fine Art, #78), one 10 x 9 in., (25.4 x 22.9 cm.), other 14 x 11½ in., (25.4 x 22.9 cm.), lithographs w/coloring (BP 127, DM 306, FR 1032, Y 23,931).

GREENWOOD, Marion   American 1909-1970
$44* *"Carib Caryatid",* s., very good cond., (07-19-92, Bakker, #178), image 13½ x 9½ in., (34.3 x 24.1 cm.), lithograph (BP 23, DM 64, FR 217, Y 5470).

$39* *"Folk Singer",* s., (12-11-92, DuMouchelle, #1477), 14 x 11¾ in., (35.6 x 29.8 cm.), lithograph (BP 25, DM 61, FR 211, Y 4826).

GREGORY, Yvonne   1889-1970
$1543* *Abstract Nudes: Three,* 1930s, mounted on paper, s.; photog.'s label, (c) limitation, label verso, t., each approx.

432 x 330mm, (05-07-93, Sotheby-London, #180, illus.), photograph, matt warm toned silver print (BP 977, DM 2440, FR 8221, Y 169,896).

$2179* *Babes In The Wood: Five Studies,* 1940s, mounted on card or paper, s., majority t., s., photog.'s (c) limitation, each approx. 357 x 252mm, (05-07-93, Sotheby-London, #190, illus.), photograph, matt warm toned silver print (BP 1380, DM 3445, FR 11,609, Y 239,925).

$327* *"Faith", "Hope" and "Charity", c. 1935: Three,* mounted on card, s., t., s., labels, each approx. 470 x 340mm, (05-07-93, Sotheby-London, #186), photograph, matt warm toned silver print (BP 207, DM 517, FR 1742, Y 36,005).

$872* *Female Nudes: Nine,* 1920s and 1930s, majority mounted on paper, s., t., photog.'s label,(c) limitation stamp, labels, from 452 x 357mm to 370 x 285mm, (05-07-93, Sotheby-London, #182), photograph, matt warm toned silver print (BP 552, DM 1379, FR 4646, Y 96,014).

$363* *"Figure Study", c. 1930,* mounted on paper, s., t., labels, 360 x 284mm, (05-07-93, Sotheby-London, #179, illus.), photograph, matt warm toned silver print (BP 230, DM 574, FR 1934, Y 39,969).

$1053* *Male Nudes, "Captive", "Vision" and "Rhythm": Three,* 1930s, mounted on paper or card, s., t.; photog.'s label, (c) limitation verso, labels, each approx. 447 x 327mm, (05-07-93, Sotheby-London, #181, illus.), photograph, matt warm toned silver print (BP 667, DM 1665, FR 5610, Y 115,944).

BI *Maurice Lambert, c. 1930: Two,* mounted on card, s.; photog.'s label, (c) limitation, num. verso, labels, each approx. 360 x 261mm, est. BP 5/800, (05-07-93, Sotheby-London, #178, illus.), photograph, silver print.

BI *Nude Studies, c. 1930: Five,* mounted on paper, s., t., annot., photog.'s label, labels, each approx. 365 x 276mm, est. BP 600/1,000, (05-07-93, Sotheby-London, #183), photograph, matt warm toned silver print.

$835* *Nude Studies: Two,* 1930s, mounted on paper, s., t., labels, each approx. 477 x 346mm, (05-07-93, Sotheby-London, #187, illus.), photograph, matt warm toned silver print (BP 529, DM 1320, FR 4449, Y 91,940).

$1816* *Nudes In Nature: Eight Studies,* 1940s, majority mounted on card or paper, s., t., labels, photog.'s credit, (c) limitation, each approx. 369 x 289mm, (05-07-93, Sotheby-London, #188, illus.), photograph, matt warm toned silver print (BP 1150, DM 2871, FR 9675, Y 199,956).

$363* *Nudes, c. 1935: Three,* mounted on paper, s., photog.'s label, (c) limitation, from 365 x 285mm to 285 x 215mm, (05-07-93, Sotheby-London, #189), photograph, matt warm toned silver print (BP 230, DM 574, FR 1934, Y 39,969).

BI *Stille Lifes And Landscapes: Five Studies,* mounted on card or paper, s., photog.'s label, labels, from 289 x 207mm to 485 x 352mm, est. BP 2/300, (05-07-93, Sotheby-London, #185), photograph, matt warm toned silver print.

$509* *"Study For Madonna XXVIII", c. 1930,* mounted on paper, s., t., label, 318 x 251mm, (05-07-93, Sotheby-London, #184, illus.), photograph, matt warm toned silver print (BP 322, DM 805, FR 2712, Y 56,045).

$545* *"W. Heath Robinson Esq.",* 1930s, mounted on card, t., s., labels, num. YG3889-P, 367 x 271mm, (05-07-93, Sotheby-London, #177, illus.), photograph, silver print (BP 345, DM 862, FR 2904, Y 60,009).

GREINER, Otto   1869-1916
$217* *"Civetta Del Colosseo (Frauenbildnis)" (Vogel 82/I), 1902,* s., artist's proof, prov., (11-28-92, Grisebach, #525, illus.), 11¹³⁄₁₆ x 8¹¹⁄₁₆ in., (30 x 22 cm.), lithograph on China (BP 143, DM 346, FR 1174, Y 27,007).

$996* *Der Morser (Vogel 77/II), 1900,* s., d., plate 4 of Max Klinger gewidmeten series Vom Weib, num. 6, light-stained, mount stained, (12-01-92, Karl/Faber, #210), 13⁹⁄₁₆ x 11⅝ in., (34.5 x 29.5 cm.), lithograph on simili-Japan (BP 658, DM 1588, FR 5410, Y 124,004).

GRENDEDON, Henry (after)
$215* *Don Carlos Jose Gutierrez De Los Rios,* by Charles Turner, pub. by engraver, 1815, (06-16-93, Bonhams-Chelsea, #462), image 18½ x 14½ in., (47 x 36.8 cm.), mezzotint (BP 143, DM 357, FR 1198, Y 22,931).

GRENIER, F.

BI *Chasse Au Tigre,* foxing, repairs, soiling, est. $3/500, (12-04-92, Doyle, #50), 13⅞ x 21⅜ in., (352 x 543 mm.), hand colored lithograph.

GRENIER-VALLER

$145* *The Captain Sharp - Shooter And His Troop,* (01-31-93, Morelle/Marchan, #229), 36⅝ x 49⅝ in., (93 x 126 cm.), poster (BP 98, DM 234, FR 790, Y 18,089).

GREUTER, Matthaus c. 1566-1638

$1300* *Joseph Und Potiphars Frau (Nagler, Die Monogrammisten IV, 1855, 14, Brulliot Bd.2, Hollstein 1),* lit., prov., glue remains, (12-04-92, Bassenge, #6227), 15⅜ x 11¹⁄₁₆ in., (39.1 x 28.1 cm.), engraving (BP 834, DM 2070, FR 7023, Y 162,297).

GREUZE, Jean Baptiste (after)

BI *La Cruche Cassee, 1773,* by J. Massard, pub. Greuze, muddy impression, thread margins, new bottom margin, est. BP 2/300, (11-30-92, Phillips-London, #288), sheet 20⅛ x 14⅝ in., (511 x 371 mm.), engraving on laid.

GRIESHABER, H.A.P. German 1909-1981

BI *Abschied (F. 64/74), 1964,* s., from the sheet of 39 woodcuts Osterritt, Galerie Der Spiegel, est. DM 2000, (12-01-92, Karl/Faber, #663), 12⅝ x 21¼ in., (32 x 54 cm.), color woodcut on wove.

$360* *Die Abtissin, 1966,* s., from Totentanz von Basel, Furst #66/19, (11-27-92, Zeller, #620), 17⁵⁄₁₆ x 13⅜ in., (44 x 34 cm.), color woodcut (BP 237, DM 575, FR 1953, Y 44,804).

$1875* *Affen Und Alphabete (Furst Band I 62/51), Eighteen,* Manuspresse, 1962, #36/60, s., (11-21-92, Lempertz, #165), 18⅝ x 13⅞ in., (47.3 x 35.2 cm.), woodcut on hand-made board (BP 1235, DM 2989, FR 10,070, Y 233,180).

$5991* *Alpha (Furst 68/1), 1968,* #1 of Prometheus series, (05-26-93, Lempertz, #188, illus.), 80¹¹⁄₁₆ x 40¹⁵⁄₁₆ in., (205 x 104 cm.), color serigraph print on canvas (BP 3876, DM 9775, FR 32,900, Y 650,913).

BI *Carl Orff, Carmina Burana (Furst Band I 65/41), 1965: Fourteen,* Manus-Presse, #26/XL, est. DM 40,000-, (11-21-92, Lempertz, #168, illus.), 23¼ x 16⁵⁄₁₆ in., (59 x 41.5 cm.), color woodcut.

$17,655* *Carmina Burana (Furst 65/41-54), 1965: Twenty-Eight,* s., #24/40, (06-10-93, Hauswedell/Nolt, #356), color woodcut on Japan (BP 11,548, DM 28,749, FR 96,793, Y 1,874,005).

$3069* *Carmina Burana, 1965,* portfolio, w/t. page, s. by artist and author, #XV, pub. Manus Presse, good cond., (12-03-92, Sotheby-London, #683), 13 woodcuts in colors (BP 1980, DM 4826, FR 16,473, Y 381,859).

$474* *A Daily Fight To Survive (Furst 80/18), 1980,* s., num. twice, mounting traces, (09-25-92, Granier, #2866), sheet 35³⁄₁₆ x 24⅜ in., (89.3 x 61.9 cm.), offset print on hand-made copper print paper (BP 277, DM 703, FR 2376, Y 57,212).

$916* *Drucker (Furst 65/11), 1965,* (05-26-93, Dorling, #2682, illus.), 38¹⁵⁄₁₆ x 26¾ in., (99 x 68 cm.), color woodcut on factory printed paper (BP 593, DM 1495, FR 5030, Y 99,522).

$1731* *Die Dunkle Welt Der Tiere (Furst Band I 59/20, 59/25 and 59/27): Five,* Edition Rothe, 1959, s., (11-21-92, Lempertz, #163), 21⁵⁄₁₆ x 15⁹⁄₁₆ in., (54.2 x 39.5 cm.), woodcut on factory paper (BP 1140, DM 2760, FR 9296, Y 215,272).

$974* *Erinnerung An Ernst Wilhelm Nay (Furst Band II 68/26), 1968,* #55/150, s., num., (11-21-92, Lempertz, #170), 29¹⁵⁄₁₆ x 22¹³⁄₁₆ in., (76 x 58 cm.), color woodcut on Japan (BP 641, DM 1553, FR 5231, Y 121,129).

$1095* *Eros II (Furst 54/15 b a), 1954,* s., #194/300, (06-10-93, Hauswedell/Nolt, #344), image 13¾ x 18¹¹⁄₁₆ in., (35 x 47.5 cm.), color woodcut on factory printed paper (BP 716, DM 1783, FR 6003, Y 116,230).

$1271* *Eros II (Furst 54/15), 1954,* s., #254/300, (06-10-93, Hauswedell/Nolt, #345), image 13¹⁵⁄₁₆ x 18½ in., (35.5 x 47 cm.), color woodcut on factory printed paper (BP 831, DM 2070, FR 6968, Y 134,911).

$1313* *Figuren Und Russisches B., c. 1962,* s., (06-05-93, Grisebach, #601, illus.), 11¼ x 7³⁄₁₆ in., (28.5 x 18.3 cm.), woodcut in gold w/Tuschpinselzeichnung on thin handmade (BP 864, DM 2129, FR 7175, Y 140,850).

$664* *Ein Gehorntes Wesen Rennt Durch Den Wald,* a.p., s., (12-05-92, Bassenge, #7192), 17¹¹⁄₁₆ x 11¹³⁄₁₆ in., (45 x 30 cm.), woodcut on thick Japan (BP 416, DM 1035, FR 3528, Y 82,270).

$916* *Der Grosse Bauer (Fahrmann) (Furst 62/40), 1962,* s., #54/85, (05-26-93, Lempertz, #189), 33⅜ x 25⁷⁄₁₆ in., (84.7 x 64.6 cm.), wood engraving on thick wove (BP 593, DM 1495, FR 5030, Y 99,522).

$1162* *Der Grosse Bauer (Fuerst 62/40), 1962,* s., num., from the series o du mein neckar, (12-01-92, Karl/Faber, #660), 27⁹⁄₁₆ x 18⅞ in., (70 x 48 cm.), woodcut on copper print paper (BP 768, DM 1852, FR 6312, Y 144,671).

BI *HAP Grieshaber Zum 24.X.77 Fur W. Sandberg (Furst 77/37-45), 1977: Eight,* s., num., est. DM 2,100, (12-05-92, Bassenge, #7194), Korkschnitte on Chiffon.

$424* *HAP Grieshaber. Der Holzschneider (Furst 64/18b, 22-33), 1964: Thirteen,* (06-10-93, Hauswedell/Nolt, #353), portfolio 14¹⁵⁄₁₆ x 11¼ in., (38 x 28.5 cm.), woodcut (BP 277, DM 690, FR 2325, Y 45,006).

$2245* *Herbst (F. 63/24 b), 1963,* #79/500, s., (10-09-92, Winterberg, #2232, illus.), 30⅛ x 23⅝ in., (76.5 x 60 cm.), woodcut on hand-made (BP 1332, DM 3335, FR 11,197, Y 273,314).

$1084* *Honigbarchen (F. 67/96), 1967,* #82/100, s., (10-09-92, Winterberg, #2233, illus.), 24³⁄₁₆ x 18¹¹⁄₁₆ in., (61.5 x 47.5 cm.), color woodcut on hand-made Japan (BP 643, DM 1610, FR 5406, Y 131,970).

$388* *Hunger, Kriegsgefangenenlager (Furst 80/13), 1945,* p.l. 1980, s., XIX/XX, from Engel der Geschichte, plate 2, (09-25-92, Granier, #2865), sheet 6⁹⁄₁₆ x 9⁷⁄₁₆ in., (16.7 x 24 cm.), woodcut on hand-made board (BP 227, DM 575, FR 1945, Y 46,832).

$1319* *Kamel Mit Schabracke (Furst, Nr. 59/13), 1959,* #195/500, s., (11-13-92, Kunsthaus, #575, illus.), 20½ x 18½ in., (52 x 47 cm.), color woodcut on werkdruckpapier (BP 852, DM 2071, FR 6983, Y 163,709).

$360* *Der Kaufmann, 1966,* s., from series Totentanz von Basel, Furst 66/19, (11-27-92, Zeller, #621), 17⁵⁄₁₆ x 13⅜ in., (44 x 34 cm.), color woodcut (BP 237, DM 575, FR 1953, Y 44,804).

$1083* *Kentauren (Furst 62/72),* s., (11-28-92, Schoppmann, #568), 22¹⁄₁₆ x 31½ in., (56 x 80 cm.), woodcut in black and blue on Japan (BP 715, DM 1725, FR 5857, Y 134,785).

$117* *Kreatur (Furst 65/137), 1965,* ballpoint pen s., (09-25-92, Granier, #2862), sheet 16⅛ x 11⁷⁄₁₆ in., (41 x 29 cm.), woodcut on mill print board (BP 68, DM 173, FR 586, Y 14,122).

$1676* *Kreuzigung (XII), 1969,* 55/70, s., tear, (10-14-92, Germann, #315), 28¹⁵⁄₁₆ x 38¹⁵⁄₁₆ in., (735 x 990 mm.), colored woodcut (BP 984, DM 2453, FR 8318, Y 203,102, SF 2185).

$13,418* *Der Kreuzweg Der Versohnung (Furst 69/38-69/51): Fourteen,* s., #8/70, (06-10-93, Hauswedell/Nolt, #360), image 27⁹⁄₁₆ x 31½ in., (70 x 80 cm.), color woodcut on fibrous Japan (BP 8777, DM 21,850, FR 73,564, Y 1,424,265).

$1551* *Lob Der Gartner Von Herrenhausen (Furst 66/98 K), 1966,* s., num., portfolio A, (05-26-93, Dorling, #2683, illus.), 25⁹⁄₁₆ x 18½ in., (65 x 47 cm.), color woodcut on handmade (BP 1003, DM 2531, FR 8517, Y 168,514).

$5049* *The Lord's Black Nightingale Gewidmet Grieshaber (Furst Band I 64/9), 1964: Six,* #42/65, s., (11-21-92, Lempertz, #166, illus.), 32⅜ x 24³⁄₁₆ in., (82.2 x 61.5 cm.), color woodcut on hand-made (BP 3324, DM 8050, FR 27,116, Y 627,907).

$811* *Der Maler (Furst 59/30), 1959,* s., num., (12-05-92, Bassenge, #7191), 17⁵⁄₁₆ x 14³⁄₁₆ in., (44 x 36 cm.), color woodcut (BP 508, DM 1264, FR 4309, Y 100,483).

$866* *Der Maler, Maler Mit Bild (Furst Band I 59/30), 1959,* #34/200, s., tears, (11-21-92, Lempertz, #164), 17¹³⁄₁₆ x 14⁵⁄₁₆ in., (45.2 x 36.4 cm.), color woodcut on wove (BP 570, DM 1381, FR 4651, Y 107,698).

$144* *"Paar Unter Wisenbaum", 1969,* s., series Grob, fein und gottlich, furst, #66/72, (11-27-92, Zeller, #612), 14¹⁵⁄₁₆ x

9^{13}/$_{16}$ in., (38 x 25 cm.), color woodcut (BP 95, DM 230, FR 781, Y 17,922).

$1328* *Paar Unter Zweigen (Fuerst 63/30), 1963,* s., num., (12-01-92, Karl/Faber, #661), 29^{1}/$_{8}$ x 19^{11}/$_{16}$ in., (74 x 50 cm.), woodcut on hand-made (BP 877, DM 2117, FR 7213, Y 165,339).

$9016* *Pan (Furst Band I 49/11), 1949,* s., d., (11-21-92, Lempertz, #162, illus.), 26^{3}/$_{8}$ x 18^{7}/$_{8}$ in., (67 x 48 cm.), color woodcut on thread support factory p. paper (BP 5936, DM 14,375, FR 48,421, Y 1,121,254).

$260* *Pan Im Fruhling (Furst 68/12),* s., num., (11-28-92, Schoppmann, #570), 9^{13}/$_{16}$ x 9^{13}/$_{16}$ in., (25 x 25 cm.), color woodcut on machinemade paper (BP 172, DM 414, FR 1406, Y 32,358).

$1394* *Die Rauhe Alb. (Fich. 54; F. 68/63-94, b), 1968: Thirteen,* Stuttgart, Manus Presse, #131/500, frontispiece, (10-09-92, Winterberg, #2242), 15^{3}/$_{8}$ x 19^{5}/$_{16}$ in., (39 x 49 cm.), woodcut, lithograph on wove (BP 827, DM 2071, FR 6953, Y 169,710).

$155* *Schartige Sense (Furst II 74/3 c), 1974: Six,* crease, (09-25-92, Granier, #2864), sheet, each 10^{1}/$_{4}$ x 29^{1}/$_{8}$ in., (26 x 74 cm.), color woodcut (BP 91, DM 230, FR 777, Y 18,709).

$297* *Scherben (Furst 64/46-64/51), 1964: Six,* s., #133/250, Spiegel Gallery, (06-10-93, Hauswedell/Nolt, #355), color woodcut (BP 194, DM 484, FR 1628, Y 31,525).

$5145* *Siamkatzen (F. 64/37), 1964,* s., num., stained, traces of old mounting, (12-01-92, Karl/Faber, #662, illus.), 19^{5}/$_{16}$ x 16^{1}/$_{8}$ in., (49 x 41 cm.), color woodcut on Rives wove (BP 3399, DM 8201, FR 27,947, Y 640,563).

$6003* *Siamkatzen (Furst 64/37), 1964,* s., 55/100, blindstamp, (06-10-93, Hauswedell/Nolt, #346, illus.), image 27^{9}/$_{16}$ x 29^{3}/$_{4}$ in., (70 x 75.5 cm.), color woodcut on BFK Rives (BP 3927, DM 9775, FR 32,911, Y 637,194).

$5075* *Siamkatzen (Furst 64/37b), 1936,* s., #83/100, (05-26-93, Lempertz, #190, illus.), 27^{9}/$_{16}$ x 29^{3}/$_{4}$ in., (70 x 75.5 cm.), color wood engraving on Arches (BP 3283, DM 8280, FR 27,869, Y 551,391).

$260* *Ein Stein Aus Barmherzigkeit (Furst 75/24),* s., ded., (11-28-92, Schoppmann, #571), 10^{1}/$_{16}$ x 8^{1}/$_{16}$ in., (25.5 x 20.5 cm.), color woodcut on light cardboard (BP 172, DM 414, FR 1406, Y 32,358).

$614* *Tiefebene (Furst 64/130),* s., (11-28-92, Schoppmann, #569), 15^{9}/$_{16}$ x 16^{3}/$_{4}$ in., (39.5 x 42.5 cm.), color woodcut on Japan (BP 405, DM 978, FR 3321, Y 76,416).

BI *Die Tochter (F. 64/90), 1964,* s., (12-01-92, Karl/Faber, #664), 12^{5}/$_{8}$ x 21^{1}/$_{4}$ in., (32 x 54 cm.), color woodcut.

$1276* *"Totentanz Von Basel" (F. 66/1-40), 1966: Forty,* VEB Verlag der Kunst, (06-08-93, Karl/Faber, #807), approx. 17^{11}/$_{16}$ x 14^{3}/$_{16}$ in., (45 x 36 cm.), color woodcut (BP 839, DM 2070, FR 6973, Y 135,528).

$866* *Die Tulpen (Furst Band I 64/73), 1964,* s., (11-21-92, Lempertz, #167), 12^{5}/$_{8}$ x 10^{3}/$_{4}$ in., (32.1 x 27.3 cm.), color woodcut on wove (BP 570, DM 1381, FR 4651, Y 107,698).

$1277* *"Die Tulpen" (Furst 66/107), 1966,* s., num., (06-05-93, Grisebach, #602, illus.), 12^{5}/$_{8}$ x 10^{5}/$_{8}$ in., (32 x 27 cm.), color woodcut on hand-made copper print paper (BP 841, DM 2070, FR 6978, Y 136,988).

$96* *Untitled,* s., margins, good cond., (05-27-93, Sotheby-Amstrdm, #619), 14^{9}/$_{16}$ x 9^{5}/$_{8}$ in., (370 x 245 mm.), woodcut and photograph on wove (BP 61, DM 154, FR 519, Y 10,292, G 173).

$738* *Uracher Palme (Furst 76/51c), 1976/1979,* s., num., (12-05-92, Bassenge, #7193), 42^{1}/$_{8}$ x 20^{1}/$_{16}$ in., (107 x 51 cm.), woodcut (BP 462, DM 1151, FR 3921, Y 91,438).

$360* *Der Waldbruder, 1966,* s. Widmung, from Totentanz von Basel, Fursdt #66/22c, (11-27-92, Zeller, #618), 17^{1}/$_{2}$ x 13^{3}/$_{8}$ in., (44.5 x 34 cm.), color woodcut (BP 237, DM 575, FR 1953, Y 44,804).

GRIEVE, Robert   b. 1924
$65* *Wall Theme 11,* s. Robert Grieve, i. Artist Proof, d. '82, (08-11-92, L. Joel, #149G), 25^{13}/$_{16}$ x 17^{13}/$_{16}$ in., (65.5 x 45.3 cm.), color screenprint (BP 34, DM 95, FR 323, Y 8324, A$ 88).

GRIFFITH, Brian
BI *"Les Chappel And Lene Lovich, 1979",* t., s., d., 480 x 405mm., est. BP 80/120, (05-07-93, Sotheby-London, #401), photograph, silver print.

GRIFFITH, Cecilia Beatrice   American b. 1890
BI *"Summer",* s. Griffith, mono., est. $1/150, (12-12-92, A. James, #554), 5^{5}/$_{8}$ x 5^{3}/$_{4}$ in., (13.7 x 14.6 cm.), etching.

GRIFFITH, Julius
$43* *Riders Approaching Historic Village,* inits. in plate, s., d. 1961, #2/10, (06-07-93, Ritchie, #39, illus.), 14^{1}/$_{2}$ x 22^{7}/$_{8}$ in., (36.9 x 58.1 cm.), linocut on Japan (BP 28, DM 70, FR 235, Y 4613, C$ 55).

GRIFFITH, L.O.
$198* *Untitled,* (09-20-92, Jackson, #93), 9 x 11 in., (22.9 x 27.9 cm.), etching (BP 116, DM 294, FR 1005, Y 24,472).

$132* *Untitled,* (09-20-92, Jackson, #96), 3^{1}/$_{2}$ x 3 in., (8.9 x 7.6 cm.), etching (BP 77, DM 196, FR 670, Y 16,314).

$77* *Untitled,* (09-20-92, Jackson, #95), 5 x 6 in., (12.7 x 15.2 cm.), etching (BP 45, DM 114, FR 391, Y 9517).

$121* *"Well House",* (09-20-92, Jackson, #94), 6 x 5 in., (15.2 x 12.7 cm.), etching (BP 71, DM 180, FR 614, Y 14,955).

GRIFFOULIERE, Jean Paul   b. 1946
$124* *Untitled: Album of Eight,* artist's proof, s., (10-18-92, Pescheteau, #160), each 14^{15}/$_{16}$ x 10^{1}/$_{4}$ in., (38 x 26 cm.), lithograph in colors on Arches (BP 75, DM 183, FR 622, Y 14,806).

GRIGGS, Frederick Landseer Maur   English 1876-1938
$244* *The Crescent (C. 12), 1912,* s., 1st state of 2, i. 1st state w/t., full margins, mounted at corners and lower edge, (10-27-92, Phillips-London, #267), plate 8^{1}/$_{2}$ x 11^{3}/$_{4}$ in., (216 x 298 mm.), etching on laid (BP 154, DM 374, FR 1269, Y 29,847).

$383* *Maur's Farm (Comstock 2), 1913,* s., 5th state of 8, i. 5th 5 for retouching, full margins, surface bloom, minor stain, collector's stamp, (10-27-92, Phillips-London, #264), plate 4^{3}/$_{8}$ x 7^{1}/$_{8}$ in., (111 x 181 mm.), etching on laid (BP 242, DM 587, FR 1992, Y 46,850).

$239* *The Maypole Inn, 1929,* 4th state, proof, s., margins, (02-17-93, Bonhams-Chelsea, #336), plate 6^{1}/$_{2}$ x 9^{1}/$_{2}$ in., (16.5 x 24.1 cm.), etching (BP 165, DM 388, FR 1315, Y 28,548).

$480* *"Memory Of Clavering" and "The Cross Hands" (Comstock 51 and 52), 1934 and 1935,* 3rd states, of 4 and 6 respectively, s., margins, good cond., discoloration, (06-30-93, Sotheby-London, #307, illus.), one 7^{3}/$_{8}$ x 9^{1}/$_{2}$ in., (187 x 241 mm.), the other 7^{1}/$_{4}$ x 9^{1}/$_{4}$ in., (187 x 241 mm.), etching on laid (BP 322, DM 819, FR 2762, Y 51,430).

$418* *Priory Farm (C. 4), 1913,* 2nd state of 3, full margins, discoloration, bloom on p. image, crease, (10-27-92, Phillips-London, #265), plate 4^{3}/$_{4}$ x 5^{7}/$_{8}$ in., (121 x 149 mm.), etching on laid (BP 264, DM 641, FR 2174, Y 51,131).

BI *Sellenger (C. 18), 1917,* s., 2nd state of 6, full margins, good cond., crease, mounting at top corners and bottom edge, est. BP 1/180, (10-27-92, Phillips-London, #269), (124 x 165 mm.), etching on fine laid.

GRIMALDI, Giovanni Francesco   Italian 1606-1680
$1115* *Landscape With Three Men (B. XIX, 52),* before all letters, margins, creases, (06-30-93, Sotheby-London, #147), 13 x 18^{1}/$_{4}$ in., (330 x 464 mm.), etching on paper w/a Bunch of Grapes watermark (BP 747, DM 1902, FR 6415, Y 119,469).

$403* *Paysage Avec Deux Hommes Au Sommet D'Une Montagne (Bartsch, vol. 19,31),* posterior state, margins, (05-15-93, Loudmer, #20, illus.), 7^{1}/$_{16}$ x 11 in., (179 x 280 mm.), sh 9^{3}/$_{4}$ x 13^{7}/$_{8}$ in., (179 x 280 mm.), etching on laid w/Lettres H: Oser watermark (BP 262, DM 648, FR 2178, Y 44,674).

GRIMM, Ludwig Emil   1790-1863
BI *Bettina Von Arnim, Vor Ihrem Goethedenkmal Sitzend (Stoll 52 II), 1838,* est. DM 1,200, (12-04-92, Bassenge, #6819), 10^{3}/$_{4}$ x 8^{1}/$_{2}$ in., (27.3 x 21.6 cm.), etching on wove.

GRIMM, Sammuel Hieronymous (after)

$207* *The Embarkation Of King Henry VIII At Dover May XXI.MDXX,* by James Basire, pub. 1781, laid down, stained, folds, defects, (02-17-93, Bonhams-Chelsea, #241), image 22¼ x 45¾ in., (56.5 x 116.2 cm.), engraving (BP 143, DM 336, FR 1139, Y 24,725).

GRINBERG, Alexander   1885-1979

$1100* *Sergey Eisenstein, 1927,* s., t., d., lit., (10-13-92, Christie-NY, #219, illus.), 4¼ x 3⅛ in., (10.8 x 7.9 cm.), photograph, gelatin silver print (BP 641, DM 1611, FR 5475, Y 133,382).

GRINCHTEIN, I.

$299* *Vive Le 1er Mai!, 1953,* cond. A, (03-16-93, Boisgirard, #5), 22⁷⁄₁₆ x 31½ in., (57 x 80 cm.), offset poster (BP 206, DM 497, FR 1689, Y 34,963).

GRINSSON

$72* *Drole De Frimousse (Funny Face), S. Donen, Avec A. Hepburn (French),1937,* (01-31-93, Morelle/Marchan, #103), 47¼ x 62¹⁵⁄₁₆ in., (120 x 160 cm.), poster (BP 48, DM 116, FR 392, Y 8982).

$41* *Mambo, De R. Rossen, Avec Silvana Mangano Et Les Ballets De Katherine Dunham, 1954,* (01-31-93, Morelle/Marchan, #69), 47¼ x 62¹⁵⁄₁₆ in., (120 x 160 cm.), poster (BP 28, DM 66, FR 223, Y 5115).

GRINSSON (after)

$903* *M.G.M. Autant En Emporte Le Vent Avec Clark Gable, Vivien Leigh, Olivia De Haviland Et Leslie Howard,* good cond., (02-12-93, Cheval/Robert, #209), 62¹⁵⁄₁₆ x 47¼ in., (160 x 120 cm.), poster (BP 636, DM 1498, FR 5067, Y 108,900).

GRIS, Juan   Spanish 1887-1927

$533* *Nature Morte A La Guitare,* from Form, s., (11-13-92, Koller, #5333), sheet 8¹⁄₁₆ x 12⅜ in., (20.5 x 31.5 cm.), pochoir on wove (BP 344, DM 837, FR 2822, Y 66,154, SF 754).

GRIS, Juan (after)

$303* *Du Cubisme: Metzinger, 1947,* text, margins, good cond., mat staining, foxing, (02-24-93, Butterfield, #2932), 7 x 5⁷⁄₁₆ in., (178 x 138 mm.), etching on Lana (BP 211, DM 492, FR 1668, Y 35,555).

GROEDER

$110* *"Take Me To Your Leader",* s., #152/275, (04-16-93, DuMouchelle, #1359), 31 x 25½ in., (78.7 x 64.8 cm.), color lithograph (BP 72, DM 178, FR 600, Y 12,369).

GROENEWEGEN, G.   1754-1826

$4076* *Verscheide Soorten Van Hollandse Vaartuigen, Dutch Sailing Ships (Rott., J. van den Brink), 1801,* 7 series w/82 of 84, 19th cent. hcl., oblong 4to., #D12 and E9, 2nd state of 3, stains, foxing, (06-09-93, Bubb Kuyper, #2052, illus.), approx. 5½ x 6⅛ in., (14 x 15.5 cm.), etching (BP 2689, DM 6667, FR 22,420, Y 433,479, G 7475).

GROLL, A.

BI *"Industrial Architectural Study" and "Characters In Native Costume":Two,* 1860s, label, neg. s., mounted on card, est. BP 3/400, 230 x 324mm, (05-07-93, Sotheby-London, #13), photograph, albumen print.

GROLL, A.L.

$374* *The Covered Wagon, Arizona,* s., t., margins, good cond., light-staining, foxing, soiling, notations, (05-19-93, Butterfield, #1991), 7¹⁵⁄₁₆ x 10 in., (202 x 254 mm.), drypoint on wove (BP 243, DM 608, FR 2048, Y 41,404).

GROMAIRE, Marcel   French 1892-1971

$722* *Blonde (F. Gromaire, 141), 1958,* #13/75, s., large margins, (04-02-93, Picard, #124), 10³⁄₁₆ x 7¹¹⁄₁₆ in., (25.8 x 19.5 cm.), etching (BP 476, DM 1160, FR 3941, Y 82,204).

$105* *Composition,* (09-30-92, Kunsthallen, #114), etching (BP 59, DM 149, FR 504, Y 12,601, DK 575).

BI *Figures Seated At A Table,* blindstamp, large margins, good cond., est. BP 100/150, (11-30-92, Phillips-London, #427), plate 7⅞ x 10¼ in., (200 x 260 mm.), etching on Arches.

$505* *Fille Nue Au Collier (F. Gromaire 41), 1923,* #7/30, s., tear, large margins, (02-03-93, Ader Tajan, #161), 7¹⁄₁₆ x

5⅛ in., (17.9 x 13 cm.), etching (BP 353, DM 832, FR 2820, Y 62,819).

$178* *Harlem, #166/200,* s., d. in plate Gaumaire 1951, (03-16-93, Encans, #175), 10¹³⁄₁₆ x 14¾ in., (27.5 x 37.5 cm.), lithograph (BP 123, DM 296, FR 1006, Y 20,814, C$ 222).

$378* *"Melancolia" (FG107), 1935,* #2/50, s., reddish stains, (01-28-93, Pescheteau, #152), 14¹⁵⁄₁₆ x 11 in., (38 x 28 cm.), etching in bistre on wove (BP 250, DM 599, FR 2027, Y 46,933).

$6014* *Nu Au Fauteuil Ancien (F.G. 81), 1928,* whole margins, annot., s., (06-11-93, Picard, #61, illus.), 9⁵⁄₁₆ x 6¹³⁄₁₆ in., (236 x 173 mm.), etching in brownish black on laid (BP 3951, DM 9774, FR 32,953, Y 638,090).

$3097* *Nu Au Fauteuil Courbe (F. Gromaire 75), 1928,* whole margins, #13/30, s., (06-11-93, Picard, #60, illus.), 9⁵⁄₁₆ x 7 in., (237 x 178 mm.), etching in black on Rives wove (BP 2035, DM 5033, FR 16,970, Y 328,594).

BI *Le Peintre Et Son Modele (Gromaire 134bis, repr. p. 26),* fifth and final state, inits. in plate, crayon s., 60/200, est. FF1,000/1,200, (06-28-93, Loudmer, #256), 10⅛ x 7⅞ in., (257 x 200 mm.), sh 20¹⁄₁₆ x 12¾ in., (257 x 200 mm.), black etching on BFK Rives wove.

$216* *La Rentree Des Champs (F. Gromaire 186), 1958,* s., #9/20, small margins, (05-06-93, Laurin, #39), etching on wove (BP 137, DM 340, FR 1145, Y 23,765).

GROMAIRE, Marcel (after)

$412* *The Piano Lesson, 1928,* Jacques Villon, full(?) margins, num., s. by Villon, creases, tear, (05-27-93, Swann, #120A, illus.), 18½ x 15¼ in., (47 x 38.7 cm.), aquatint in colors (BP 264, DM 661, FR 2228, Y 44,168).

GROMMAIRE, Marcel   French School 1892-1917

$182* *Le Studio De L'Artiste,* num., s., d. in plate Grommaire 1956, (09-15-92, Encans, #147), 11⁷⁄₁₆ x 14¹⁵⁄₁₆ in., (29 x 38 cm.), engraving (BP 97, DM 271, FR 919, Y 22,595, C$ 222).

GROMME, O.J.   American 20th cent.

$83* *"Flushed Grouse In Trees",* s., num., (05-15-93, Dunning, #5), 17¼ x 23 in., (43.8 x 58.4 cm.), print (BP 54, DM 134, FR 449, Y 9201).

$138* *"Flying Ducks",* s., num., (05-15-93, Dunning, #4), 17¾ x 22 in., (45.1 x 55.9 cm.), print (BP 90, DM 222, FR 746, Y 15,298).

$110* *"Grouse In Snow",* 374/850, s., (05-15-93, Dunning, #3), 17 x 22 in., (43.2 x 55.9 cm.), print (BP 72, DM 177, FR 595, Y 12,194).

GROOMS, Red   American b. 1937

BI *A Body Like Mine,* s., num. 33/150, est. $6/900, (11-12-92, Freemn/Fine Art, #78B), 23 x 17 in., (58.4 x 43.2 cm.), lithograph p. in color.

$550* *A Body Like Mine, 1978,* s., num. 64/150, Marlborough Graphics, full margins, very good cond., (02-24-93, Butterfield, #3030), 23⅞ x 18 in., (606 x 457 mm.), silkscreen in colors on wove (BP 384, DM 893, FR 3027, Y 64,539).

$908* *Chuck Berry,* s., #39/150, (06-11-93, Freemn/Fine Art, #84), 24 x 18½ in., (61 x 47 cm.), lithograph (BP 597, DM 1476, FR 4975, Y 96,340).

$1760* *Chuck Berry (A. and C. 36), 1978,* s., num. 3/150, pub. G.H.J. Graphics, margins, stain, very good cond., (09-19-92, Christie-E, #115, illus.), sheet 31¾ x 25½ in., (80.6 x 64.8 cm.), screenprint in colors w/collage on wove (BP 1012, DM 2636, FR 9026, Y 219,287).

$715* *Chuck Berry (Alexander/Cowles 36), 1978,* s., #110/150, pub. G.H.J. Graphics, (03-14-93, Hindman, #337), 24½ x 18½ in., (62.2 x 47 cm.), color serigraph and collage (BP 499, DM 1190, FR 4046, Y 84,266).

$440* *Chuck Berry, 1978,* s., num. 102/150, pub. Marlborough Graphics, full margins, good cond., crease, (02-24-93, Butterfield, #3031), 24½ x 18½ in., (622 x 470 mm.), silkscreen & collage in colors on wove (BP 307, DM 714, FR 2422, Y 51,631).

$990* *Franklin's Reception At The Court Of France, 1982,* s., d., #89/125, pub. Institute of Contemporary Art, margins, good cond.?, (10-28-92, Butterfield, #2964), 42 x 29 in., (106.7 x 73.7 cm.), color silkscreen on wove (BP 631, DM 1529, FR 5191, Y 121,472).

$330* *The Guggenheim, 1971,* s. in white crayon, num. 9/150, blindstamp of pub. & printer Bank Street atelier, good cond., creases, (02-24-93, Butterfield, #3218), 38½ x 26⅛ in., (978 x 664 mm.), lithograph in colors on Arches (BP 230, DM 536, FR 1816, Y 38,723).

$660* *Heads Up D.H. (A. and C. 49), 1980,* s., t., num. 18/26, pub. Brooke Alexander, full margins, excell. cond., (09-19-92, Christie-E, #116), sheet 26¾ x 29¾ in., (67.9 x 75.6 cm.), etching and aquatint on BFK Rives (BP 380, DM 988, FR 3385, Y 82,233).

$9350* *Little Italy, 1988-89,* cut-out, folded and assembled in plexiglas box, crayon s., #12/90, pub. by artist and Shark's Inc., box 685 x 975 x 420 mm, (11-07-92, Sotheby-NY, #569, illus.), xin., (x mm.), xin., (x mm.), three-dimensional color lithograph p. on BFK Rives (BP 6113, DM 14,929, FR 50,459, Y 1,154,036).

$990* *The Local, 1971,* from portfolio No Gas!, s., #44/75, (05-16-93, Hindman, #642), 21½ x 27¾ in., (54.6 x 70.5 cm.), color lithograph (BP 644, DM 1592, FR 5351, Y 109,744).

$2750* *Los Aficionados, 1989-1990,* s., d., num. 57/90, pub. Shark's Inc., very good cond., in plexiglassbox, (02-24-93, Butterfield, #3033, illus.), 25 x 37 in., (635 x 940 mm.), 3-dimensional lithograph in colors on wove (BP 1918, DM 4464, FR 15,135, Y 322,694).

BI *Los Aficionados, 1989-90,* s., d., #57/90, pub. Shark's Inc., very good cond., est. $6/8,000, 27 x 37 x 26, (10-28-92, Butterfield, #2966, illus.), 3-dimensional lithograph in colors on wove.

$880* *Mr. Chuck Berry, 1978,* full margins, num., s., pub. G.H.J. Graphics, (05-27-93, Swann, #121, illus.), 24½ x 18½ in., (62.2 x 47 cm.), color serigraph (BP 564, DM 1412, FR 4759, Y 94,340).

BI *Pierpont Morgan Library, 1982,* s., num. 275/300, pub. Marlborough Graphics, est. $800/1,000, (09-20-92, Hindman, #725), sheet 14⅞ x 37⅝ in., (37.8 x 95.6 cm.), color lithograph and offset lithograph.

$935* *Pierpont Morgan Library, 1982,* s., num. 87/300, pub. Marlborough Graphics, margins, apparently verygood cond., (02-24-93, Butterfield, #3032), 11¼ x 34¼ in., (286 x 870 mm.), lithograph in colors on wove (BP 652, DM 1518, FR 5146, Y 109,716).

$3850* *Portrait Of Giacometti (A. & C. 70), 1984,* s., #5/15, pub. Experimental Workshop, full sheet, good cond., (11-07-92, Sotheby-NY, #567, illus.), sheet 75¾ x 42⅜ in., (192.4 x 107.6 cm.), woodcut p. in colors (BP 2517, DM 6147, FR 20,777, Y 475,191).

$3080* *Saskia Down The Metro (Alexander & Cowles 63), 1983,* s., d. #44/250, pub. New York Graphic Society, from portfolio New York, New York, full margins, good cond., creases, (11-07-92, Sotheby-NY, #566, illus.), 23¼ x 30⅜ in., (591 x 772 mm.), silkscreen w/relief (BP 2014, DM 4918, FR 16,622, Y 380,153).

$495* *The Smoker,* s., d., num. 54/75, (11-12-92, Freemn/Fine Art, #78A), 17 x 16 in., (43.2 x 40.6 cm.), blockprint in blue ink (BP 325, DM 784, FR 2646, Y 61,376).

BI *Van Gogh With Sunflowers, 1988,* s., #8/75, pub. Shark's, Inc., full margins, good cond., est. $3/4,000, (11-07-92, Sotheby-NY, #568, illus.), 16⅛ x 21⅞ in., (410 x 556 mm.), lithograph p. in colors on Twinrocker.

$1380* *Van Gogh With Sunflowers, 1988,* s., #8/75, pub. Shark's, Inc., full margins, good cond., (02-11-93, Sotheby-NY, #340, illus.), 16⅛ x 21¹⁵⁄₁₆ in., (410 x 557 mm.), color lithograph on Twinrocker (BP 974, DM 2286, FR 7735, Y 166,365).

$1650* *Van Gogh With Sunflowers, 1988,* s., #21/75, pub. Shark's, Inc., full margins, very good cond., (10-28-92, Butterfield, #2965), 16 x 22 in., (406 x 559 mm.), color lithograph on white wove, watermark (BP 1051, DM 2548, FR 8652, Y 202,454).

$440* *You Can Have A Body Like Mine,* s., #5/25, Artist's Proof, (06-13-93, Hindman, #346), sh 31¼ x 25 in., (79.4 x 63.5 cm.), color lithograph (BP 288, DM 716, FR 2407, Y 46,301).

$440* *You Can Have A Body Like Mine,* s., #6/25 AP, (06-11-93, Freemn/Fine Art, #85), 23¾ x 18 in., (60.3 x 45.7 cm.), lithograph (BP 289, DM 715, FR 2411, Y 46,684).

$330* *You Can Have A Body Like Mine,* s., #65/150, (03-14-93, Hindman, #336), 23¾ x 18 in., (60.3 x 45.7 cm.), color lithograph (BP 230, DM 549, FR 1868, Y 38,892).

$880* *You Can Have A Body Like Mine (Alexander and Cowles 35), 1978,* s., num. 27/150, pub. G.H.J. Graphics, margins, staining, sheet rippled, good cond., (09-19-92, Christie-E, #114), sheet 31½ x 25 in., (80 x 63.5 cm.), screenprint in colors on wove (BP 506, DM 1318, FR 4513, Y 109,644).

BI *You Can Have A Body Like Mine, 1978,* full margins, num., s., pub. G.H.J. Graphics, est. $700/1,000, (05-27-93, Swann, #122, illus.), 24 x 18 in., (61 x 45.7 cm.), color serigraph.

GROOT, Annemarie de 20th cent.

$248* *Naakt, 1989,* s., d., #42/200, full margins, good cond., (12-09-92, Sotheby-Amstrdm, #580), 19³⁄₁₆ x 27³⁄₁₆ in., (488 x 690 mm.), color silkscreen on Arches (BP 158, DM 389, FR 1328, Y 30,750, G 437).

GROOVER, Jan b. 1943

$1725* *Still Life, 1981,* s., d., #3/15, (04-08-93, Christie-NY, #526, illus.), 7½ x 9½ in., (19.1 x 24.1 cm.), photograph, platinum print (BP 1131, DM 2771, FR 9380, Y 195,756).

$3080* *Untitled (Still Life Of Bottles), 1988,* #3/5, (10-13-92, Christie-NY, #545, illus.), 30 x 40 in., (76.2 x 101.6 cm.), photograph, color coupler print (BP 1794, DM 4512, FR 15,331, Y 373,469).

$4950* *Untitled (Still Life With Bottles), 1988,* s., d., num. 1/5 in ink, (10-13-92, Christie-NY, #546, illus.), 28½ x 36 in., (72.4 x 91.4 cm.), photograph, color coupler w/aluminum backing (BP 2883, DM 7252, FR 24,639, Y 600,218).

$2970* *Untitled (Still Life With Bottles), 1988,* s., d., num. 5/5 by photog. in ink, #5/5 ed., (10-15-92, Sotheby-NY, #592, illus.), 35 x 29 in., (88.9 x 73.7 cm.), photograph, dye-transfer print (BP 1817, DM 4421, FR 14,992, Y 356,329).

$1100* *Untitled (Still Life With Coffee Mug And Eggs),* s., d., num. 2/15 by photog., 1979, p. 1985, #2/15 ed., (10-15-92, Sotheby-NY, #587, illus.), 7½ x 9½ in., (19.1 x 24.1 cm.), photograph, gelatin silver print (BP 673, DM 1637, FR 5553, Y 131,974).

BI *Untitled (Three Spoons), 1981,* s., d., num. 3/15 by photog., #3/15 ed., est. $2/2,500, (10-15-92, Sotheby-NY, #588, illus.), 7½ x 9½ in., (19.1 x 24.1 cm.), photograph, platinum print.

BI *Untitled Tryptich (Building With Red Door): Three, 1977,* exhib. label, exhib., lit., est. $7/9,000, (10-13-92, Christie-NY, #543, illus.), each 11½ x 17⅛ in., (29.2 x 43.5 cm.), overall 11½ x 52 in., (29.2 x 43.5 cm.), photograph, color coupler prints.

BI *Untitled, 1979,* s., d., num. 1/3 by photog., #1/3 ed., est. $2/3,000, (10-15-92, Sotheby-NY, #589, illus.), 18¾ x 14¾ in., (47.6 x 37.5 cm.), photograph, Type-C print.

$3575* *Untitled, 1979,* s., d., num. 2/3 by photog. in ink, #2/3 ed., (10-15-92, Sotheby-NY, #590, illus.), 18¾ x 14¾ in., (47.6 x 37.5 cm.), photograph, Type-C print (BP 2188, DM 5322, FR 18,046, Y 428,914).

$2200* *Untitled, 1979,* s., d., num. 1/3 by photog. in ink, #1/3 ed., (10-15-92, Sotheby-NY, #591, illus.), 14¾ x 18⅝ in., (37.5 x 47.3 cm.), photograph, Type-C print (BP 1346, DM 3275, FR 11,106, Y 263,947).

BI *Untitled, 1989,* s., d., #1/15 by photog., est. $1,5/2,500, (04-06-93, Sotheby-NY, #496A, illus.), 9⅜ x 7½ in., photograph, platinum-palladium print on tissue.

$1650* *Untitled, Still Life, 1980-83,* s., d., num. 4/7, (10-13-92, Christie-NY, #544, illus.), 4½ x 3½ in., (11.4 x 8.9 cm.), photograph, platinum print (BP 961, DM 2417, FR 8213, Y 200,073).

GROPPER, William American 1897-1977

$275* *"Backstage", c. 1969 and "Paul Bunyan", c. 1953: Two,* s., pub. AAA, from the American Folklore series, closed tears, (05-27-93, Swann, #123), 17⅞ x 14 in., (45.4 x 35.6 cm.), color lithograph (BP 176, DM 441, FR 1487, Y 29,481).

BI *The Boss,* s., artist's proof, est. $2/300, (12-17-92, Mystic, #21), 15½ x 11 in., (39.4 x 27.9 cm.), lithograph.

$165* *Club Members,* s., #53/100, prov., (12-10-92, Sloan, #586), 5¾ x 3¾ in., (14.6 x 9.5 cm.), soft (molle) ground etching (BP 106, DM 261, FR 891, Y 20,411).

$165* *"Court Room Scene",* s. Gropper, very good cond.?, (11-21-92, Bakker, #67), image 14 x 18 in., (35.6 x 45.7 cm.), lithograph (BP 109, DM 263, FR 886, Y 20,520).

BI *"Filibuster",* s.; s. in stone; label verso, est. $4/500, (09-18-92, DuMouchelle, #2056), 14 x 18 in., (35.6 x 45.7 cm.), color lithograph.

$550* *"Liberated Village", "High Noon At Agon" and "Heirloom Lace", 1945: Three,* s., 2 from The Caucassian Set, 1950, num., p. atelier of Gaston Dorfiant, (05-27-93, Swann, #124, illus.), 12 x 16½ in., (30.5 x 41.9 cm.), lithographs (BP 352, DM 883, FR 2975, Y 58,962).

$193* *New Senate,* s., buckling, discoloration, (11-12-92, Freemn/Fine Art, #79), unframed image 14 x 18 in., (35.6 x 45.7 cm.), lithograph printed in color (BP 127, DM 306, FR 1032, Y 23,931).

$99* *The Opposition,* good cond., (06-11-93, Freemn/Fine Art, #86), 9⅞ x 12¾ in., (25.1 x 32.4 cm.), lithograph in black (BP 65, DM 161, FR 542, Y 10,504).

$110* *"Rip Van Winkle",* s. plate, s., (06-24-93, Boos, #607), sight 12 x 9¼ in., (305 x 235 mm.), lithograph (BP 75, DM 188, FR 633, Y 11,998).

$55* *Summation,* margins, s., (05-22-93, Collins, #132), 14 x 9 in., (35.6 x 22.9 cm.), lithograph (BP 36, DM 89, FR 301, Y 6064).

GROS, E.

BI *Curacao Cusenier,* Pichot, B cond., yellowing, fraying, repairs, pinholes, est. $2/300, (08-06-92, Swann, #148, illus.), 32 x 22 in., (81.3 x 55.9 cm.), .

$100* *Extra Sec Curacao Cusenier, c. 1900,* cond. B, (03-16-93, Boisgirard, #119), 61¹³⁄₁₆ x 46¹⁄₁₆ in., (157 x 117 cm.), poster (BP 69, DM 166, FR 565, Y 11,693).

GROSS, Anthony   British b. 1905

BI *Grape Pickers,* s., t., #38/250, good cond., est. BP 150/250, (10-27-92, Phillips-London, #272), plate 11 x 13½ in., (279 x 343 mm.), etching on T.H. Saunders wove.

$198* *Grape Pickers,* #73/250, s., t., margins, (10-15-92, Bonhams-Chelsea, #141), plate 11 x 14 in., (27.9 x 35.6 cm.), etching (BP 121, DM 295, FR 999, Y 23,755).

BI *Jarlan (H. 3104 Reynolds 80), 1931,* s., d., i., poor cond., tears, stains, creases, foxing, est. BP 100/150, (11-30-92, Phillips-London, #339), plate 8½ x 10¾ in., (216 x 273 mm.), etching on wove.

BI *The Valley,* s., t., num. 7/50, prov., est. $4/600, (09-20-92, Hindman, #795), 16¼ x 23½ in., (41.3 x 59.7 cm.), etching.

GROSS, Chaim   Austrian/American 1904-1991

BI *Ballet Dancers, 1967,* s., d., excell. cond., est. $250/300, (05-15-93, Cleveland, #149), 12 x 16 in., (30.5 x 40.6 cm.), lithograph.

$138* *In Front Of The Ark,* s., t., d. '62, (06-11-93, Freemn/Fine Art, #87), 13 x 10 in., (33 x 25.4 cm.), lithograph (BP 91, DM 224, FR 756, Y 14,642).

BI *In The Synagogue, 1974,* s., d., t., num. 81/110, full margins, good cond., est. $2/400, (02-24-93, Butterfield, #2833), 14¼ x 17¾ in., (362 x 451 mm.), lithograph in colors on wove.

$55* *Mother And Children,* #28/150, s., (02-12-93, DuMouchelle, #360), 15 x 18½ in., (38.1 x 47 cm.), lithograph (BP 39, DM 91, FR 309, Y 6633).

BI *"Talmidism",* s., ded. 1975 Chaim, annot. H.C., good cond., toning, est. $4/600, (09-11-92, Skinner, #38G, illus.), 7½ x 17½ in., (19.1 x 44.5 cm.), lithograph in colors on wove.

BI *Woman And Child, 1965,* s., d. Chaim Gross/'65, mono. device, good cond., surface soiling, staining, wrinkles, tape verso, est. $3/500, (09-11-92, Skinner, #88), approx. 9½ x 18½ in., (24.1 x 47 cm.), lithograph on laid paper.

BI *Women, Children And Birds, 1965,* s., d. Chaim Gross/'65, mono. device, ded., good cond., est. $3/500, (09-11-92, Skinner, #86), 18½ x 10 in., (47 x 25.4 cm.), lithograph on laid paper.

GROSSMAN, Edwin Booth   American 1887-1957

$44* *Landscape,* s., very good cond.?, (07-19-92, Bakker, #47), image 7¾ x 10 in., (19.7 x 25.4 cm.), color monotype (BP 23, DM 64, FR 217, Y 5470).

GROSSMAN, Elias M.

BI *A River Scene,* s., est. $50/75, (02-12-93, DuMouchelle, #362), 6 x 9 in., (15.2 x 22.9 cm.), engraving.

GROSSMAN, Sid

BI *Ballet Rehearsal, 1951,* backed w/card, notations, reprod. limit. stamp, est. $1/1,500, (10-15-92, Sotheby-NY, #557, illus.), 12¾ x 10⅝ in., (32.4 x 27 cm.), photograph, gelatin silver print.

GROSSMANN, Rudolf   1882-1941

$891* *Boxer (Vollmer, Bd. II; S. 319), 1921: Eight,* #94/125, from an edition of 60, s., num., (10-09-92, Winterberg, #2264), smallest 8⅞ x 9⁷⁄₁₆ in., (22.5 x 24 cm.), largest 16⁹⁄₁₆ x 12⅝ in., (22.5 x 24 cm.), watercolored lithograph on Japan (BP 529, DM 1324, FR 4444, Y 108,473).

BI *Das Dorf: Ten,* lithographs, #48/100, est. DM 1,200, (05-26-93, Lempertz, #193), sh, approx. 21⅝ x 14⅜ in., (55 x 36.5 cm.), watercolor on handmade.

$382* *Ringer (B. Jahn/F. Berger 73),* s., blindstamp, (06-23-93, Kornfeld, #389), handcolored lithograph on simili-Japan (BP 260, DM 646, FR 2174, Y 41,617, SF 575).

GROSZ, George   German/American 1893-1959

$989* *Aus Dem Zyklus Parasiten (Duckers E 55), 1919,* s., (06-10-93, Hauswedell/Nolt, #371), image 14¹⁵⁄₁₆ x 11⅝ in., (38 x 29.5 cm.), lithograph on wove (BP 647, DM 1610, FR 5422, Y 104,978).

BI *"Bafustanau" Road And Railroad Signals, c. 1930,* s., t., good cond., tape, est. $3/500, (05-15-93, Cleveland, #150), 7½ x 10⅜ in., (19.1 x 26.4 cm.), lithograph.

$3960* *"Bagdad On The Subway": Six,* portfolio depicting O'Henry's New York, s. Grosz, #46/150, pub. The Print Club, NY, 1935, (06-26-93, Wolf, #953), offset lithograph (BP 2651, DM 6729, FR 22,667, Y 420,159).

$837* *"Berlinger Fruhling", (Alexander Duckers, Bl. 2), 1920/21,* s., (09-29-92, B. Rasmussen, #309, illus.), lithograph and watercolor (BP 470, DM 1182, FR 4034, Y 99,916, DK 4600).

$93* *Bessere Leute (Duckers S I,8), 1922,* edit. Ecce Homo, (09-25-92, Granier, #2868), sheet 9⁷⁄₁₆ x 13¹⁵⁄₁₆ in., (24 x 35.5 cm.), photolithograph (BP 54, DM 138, FR 466, Y 11,225).

$1194* *Da Donnern Sie Sanftmut Und Duldung Aus Ihren Wolken Und Bringen DemGott Der Liebe Menschenopfer (Duckers M, V, 7), 1922,* plate 7 from Die Rauber, s., pub. Der Malik-Verlag, full margins, good cond., handling creases, foxing, discoloration, (12-03-92, Sotheby-London, #314, illus.), 22¾ x 15¾ in., (578 x 400 mm.), photo-lithograph on laid (BP 770, DM 1878, FR 6409, Y 148,563).

$989* *Ecce Homo (Duckers S I, 28), 1922: Three,* s., Malik-pub. Berlin, (06-10-93, Hauswedell/Nolt, #374), image 8⁷⁄₁₆ x 11¹⁵⁄₁₆ in., (21.5 x 30.3 cm.), offset on wove (BP 647, DM 1610, FR 5422, Y 104,978).

BI *"Ecce Homo" (Duckers S 1; Pommeranz-Liedtke S. 185), 1922-1923: One Hundred,* ed. C, Berlin, Malik pub., wear, prov., est. DM 5/6,000, (11-28-92, Grisebach, #208, illus.), sh 13¹¹⁄₁₆ x 9⁷⁄₁₆ in., (34.7 x 24 cm.), offset lithograph on machinemade paper.

$1986* *"Ecce Homo" (Sechzehn Aquarelle) (Duckers S I, Ausg. B II; Pommeranz-Liedtke S. 185), 1922/23: Sixteen,* Malik Verlag, (06-05-93, Grisebach, #606, illus.), sh 13⅞ x 10¼ in., (35.3 x 26 cm.), color offset lithograph on wove (BP 1307, DM 3220, FR 10,852, Y 213,044).

$2166* *"Ecce Homo", 1922-1923: One Hundred,* Berlin, Malik pub., (11-28-92, Grisebach, #526, illus.), 13¹⁵⁄₁₆ x 10¼ in., (35.5 x 26 cm.), offset lithograph (BP 1430, DM 3451, FR 11,714, Y 269,571).

BI *Ehepaar (Silberne Hochzeit) (D. E 81), 1922,* s., num., estate stamp verso, est. DM 3000, (12-01-92, Karl/Faber, #676, illus.), 19⁵⁄₁₆ x 13⅜ in., (49 x 34 cm.), lithograph on hand-made.

$385* *Er Hat Hindenburg Verspotten (Duckers/Eizenblatter 64), 1920,* s., from Deutsche Graphiker der Gegenwart, (03-

24-93, Grogan, #131), 9⁵⁄₁₆ x 7¹¹⁄₁₆ in., (23.7 x 19.5 cm.), lithograph (BP 261, DM 629, FR 2140, Y 45,236).

$423* *Er Hat Hindenburg Verspottet (Duckers E 64), 1920,* s. in stone, d., (05-26-93, Dorling, #2690), 8¹³⁄₁₆ x 6¾ in., (22.4 x 17.2 cm.), lithograph on cardboard (BP 274, DM 690, FR 2323, Y 45,958).

$837* *"Fur Regentage", (Alexander Duckers, Bl.3), 1920/21,* from Munkepunke Dionysos, (09-29-92, B. Rasmussen, #310, illus.), 11⁷⁄₁₆ x 9⁹⁄₁₆ in., (29.1 x 24.3 cm.), lithograph and watercolor (BP 470, DM 1182, FR 4034, Y 99,916, DK 4600).

$1410* *Gottes Sichtbarer Segen Ist Bei Mir (Duckers M V 6), 1922,* s., from series Die Rauber, (05-26-93, Dorling, #2692, illus.), 17⅝ x 14½ in., (44.7 x 36.8 cm.), lithograph on handmade (BP 912, DM 2301, FR 7743, Y 153,194).

$1097* *Der Held (Duckers E 107), 1933,* s., d., num., (12-02-92, Dorling, #2673), 12½ x 8¹¹⁄₁₆ in., (31.8 x 22.1 cm.), lithograph on BFK Rives wove (BP 708, DM 1725, FR 5888, Y 136,494).

$738* *Der Held (Duckers E 107), 1933,* s., (12-05-92, Bassenge, #7203), 12⅝ x 8¹¹⁄₁₆ in., (32 x 22 cm.), lithograph on wove (BP 462, DM 1151, FR 3921, Y 91,438).

$110* *"The Hero" ("Held") (Duckers, Eizenblatter, 107), 1933,* s. Grosz, anno., fair cond., light/mount staining, pin holes verso, (09-11-92, Skinner, #80A, illus.), 15¾ x 14¼ in., (40 x 36.2 cm.), lithograph on wove (BP 57, DM 158, FR 538, Y 13,629).

$628* *"Ein Madchen Aus Leipzig", (Alexander Duckers, Bl.6), 1920/21,* s., (09-29-92, B. Rasmussen, #313), 11⁷⁄₁₆ x 9⅜ in., lithograph and watercolor (BP 353, DM 887, FR 3027, Y 74,967, DK 3450).

$567* *Madison Square (Duckers M VII, 3) 1933/34,* s., sheet 3 of 6 from the series Bagdad-on-the-Subway, num., (06-08-93, Karl/Faber, #812), approx. 16⁹⁄₁₆ x 11 in., (42 x 28 cm.), color solar print on wove (BP 373, DM 920, FR 3098, Y 60,223).

$837* *"Meine Kegelbahn", (Alexander Duckers, Bl. 4), 1920/21,* from Munkepunke Dionysos, (09-29-92, B. Rasmussen, #311, illus.), 11⁷⁄₁₆ x 9⁵⁄₁₆ in., lithograph and watercolor (BP 470, DM 1182, FR 4034, Y 99,916, DK 4600).

$1412* *Menschen In Der Strasse (Duckers MI, 5), 1915/16,* from "Erste Grosz-Mappe", s., light stains, tears, (10-14-92, Germann, #13, illus.), 19¹¹⁄₁₆ x 15⅜ in., (500 x 390 mm.), lithograph (BP 829, DM 2066, FR 7007, Y 171,110, SF 1840).

$3248* *"Munkepunke Dionysos" (Duckers B 1; Pommeranz-Liedtke S. 185), 1921:Six,* s., Berlin, Gurlitt-Presse, 5 vols. of coll. "Das handgeschriebene Buch", prov., (11-28-92, Grisebach, #209, illus.), 11⁹⁄₁₆ x 9¾ in., (29.3 x 24.8 cm.), lithograph on handmade (BP 2144, DM 5174, FR 17,566, Y 404,231).

$15,654* *Die Rauber (Duckers M V, 1-9), 1922: Nine,* s., Ausgabe A, frontispiece, num., (06-23-93, Kornfeld, #391), lithograph on Japan (BP 10,635, DM 26,487, FR 89,095, Y 1,705,415, SF 23,575).

BI *Die Rauber (Duckers MV, 1-9, Ausgabe C), 1922: Nine,* s., num., Malik-Verlag, Berlin, est. DM 20,000, (12-05-92, Bassenge, #7204, illus.), sh 27¹¹⁄₁₆ x 21¼ in., (70.3 x 54 cm.), lithograph on handmade.

$2260* *Schonheitsabend In Der Motzstrasse (Duckers E 48), 1918,* s., (06-10-93, Hauswedell/Nolt, #370, illus.), image 11⅛ x 16¾ in., (28.2 x 42.5 cm.), lithograph on thick Simili-Japan (BP 1478, DM 3680, FR 12,390, Y 239,890).

$1047* *"Sport Und Liebe", (Alexander Duckers, Bl.5), 1920/21,* s., (09-29-92, B. Rasmussen, #312, illus.), 11⁷⁄₁₆ x 9⅜ in., lithograph and watercolor (BP 589, DM 1479, FR 5046, Y 124,985, DK 5750).

$217* *Storm Clouds, Cape Cod, 1949,* s., pub. Print Club Of Cleveland, full margins, good cond., mounted, (11-30-92, Phillips-London, #370), sheet 13 x 16⅛ in., (330 x 410 mm.), lithograph (BP 143, DM 346, FR 1174, Y 27,007).

BI *Strassenszene (D.E 60; Peters V/4), 1919/20,* s., 5. Mappe Bauhaus Drucke, Neue Europaische Graphik, Deutsche Kunstler, 1921, prov., est. DM 3500, (12-01-92, Karl/Faber, #674, illus.), 15⅜ x 10⅝ in., (39 x 27 cm.), photolithograph on German paper.

$885* *Taverne Du Midi (Duckers E30), 1915,* s., num., rare, (12-05-92, Bassenge, #7201), 9⅝ x 7¹⁄₁₆ in., (24.5 x 18 cm.), transfer lithograph on handmade Japan (BP 554, DM 1380, FR 4702, Y 109,652).

$1826* *Vorstadt (D. M I, 6), 1915-16,* s., Bl. 6 from the series Erste George Grosz-Mappe, pub. Malik, brownstained, creases, mount staining, (12-01-92, Karl/Faber, #677, illus.), 14⁹⁄₁₆ x 12³⁄₁₆ in., (37 x 31 cm.), lithograph on simili-Japan (BP 1206, DM 2910, FR 9919, Y 227,341).

$1370* *Zigeunermusik (D.E 75), 1921,* s., (12-01-92, Karl/Faber, #675), sh 20¹⁄₁₆ x 14¾ in., (51 x 37.5 cm.), photolithograph (BP 905, DM 2184, FR 7442, Y 170,568).

GROTZ, Paul American b. 1902

$1760* *Walker Evans, 1929,* s., d. by photog., (10-15-92, Sotheby-NY, #164, illus.), 7⅞ x 5¼ in., (20 x 13.3 cm.), photograph, gelatin silver print (BP 1077, DM 2620, FR 8884, Y 211,158).

GROUX, Henri de

$123* *"Eve Endormie", "Napoleon" and "Scene De Guerre": Three,* full margins, (02-24-93, Picard, #116), lithograph on thin chine on laid (BP 86, DM 200, FR 677, Y 14,433).

GRUAU, R.

$83* *Bal Du Moulin Rouge, Femmes Femmes Femmes,* (01-31-93, Morelle/Marchan, #197), 15¾ x 23⅝ in., (40 x 60 cm.), poster (BP 56, DM 134, FR 452, Y 10,354).

$93* *Lido C'Est Magnifique,* (01-31-93, Morelle/Marchan, #198), 15¾ x 23⅝ in., (40 x 60 cm.), poster (BP 63, DM 150, FR 507, Y 11,602).

GRUAU, Rene b. 1910

$159* *Blizzand. Collection Automne 1961,* cond. A, (03-16-93, Boisgirard, #120), 63⅜ x 47¼ in., (161 x 120 cm.), poster (BP 110, DM 264, FR 898, Y 18,592).

$159* *Relax...Compagnie Maritime Des Chargeurs Reunis,* cond. A, (03-16-93, Boisgirard, #121), 38⁹⁄₁₆ x 24⅝ in., (98 x 62.5 cm.), poster, offset and typo (BP 110, DM 264, FR 898, Y 18,592).

GRUBER, L. Fritz b. 1908

$379* *Hommage An L.F. Gruber, 1980: Four,* s., d., portfolio, edit. Zufall, Koln, (11-12-92, Lempertz, #79), largest 7⅜ x 9⅛ in., (16.8 x 23.2 cm.), smallest 9¹⁄₁₆ x 6³⁄₁₆ in., (16.8 x 23.2 cm.), 3 gelatin silver prints, 1 color photograph (BP 242, DM 596, FR 2030, Y 46,889).

GRUEN, John

BI *Still Lifes, c. 1975: Three,* each approx. 280 x 430mm, est. BP 250/350, (05-07-93, Sotheby-London, #403), photograph, toned silver print.

GRUHL

BI *Nazi, Untitled, 1938,* Wilhelm Limpert. B+ cond., closed tears, surface soiling, est. $3/400, (08-06-92, Swann, #149, illus.), 34 x 24 in., (86.4 x 61 cm.), .

GRUN

$165* *Le Grand Guignol,* Imp. Bourgerie and Cie, A cond., (08-06-92, Swann, #150, illus.), 24 x 15½ in., (61 x 39.4 cm.), (BP 86, DM 244, FR 823, Y 21,046).

GRUN, Jules Alexandre French 1868-1934

$419* *Ch. De Fer De L'Ouest: Voyages A Prix Reduits, 1901,* excell. cond., (01-23-93, Ribeyre/Baron, #61), 41¾ x 29⅛ in., (106 x 74 cm.), poster (BP 274, DM 666, FR 2254, Y 52,441).

$1245* *Chemin De Fer Du Nord. Plage De Mesnil-Val. Pres Du Treport A 3 h DeParis Grand Choix De Terrains A Vendre, 1901,* Paris, Imp. Chaix, cond. B+, back cover lot, (06-11-93, Boisgirard, #85, illus.), 41⁵⁄₁₆ x 29¹⁵⁄₁₆ in., (105 x 76 cm.), poster (BP 818, DM 2023, FR 6822, Y 132,095).

$562* *Doux Reve, Avoir Une Bicyclette Kymris, c. 1900,* Paris, Imp. Chaix, cond. B+, (06-11-93, Boisgirard, #86), 49 x 35¹⁄₁₆ in., (124.5 x 89 cm.), poster (BP 369, DM 913, FR 3079, Y 59,629).

$1345* *Folies Bergere. Napoli, 1901,* Paris, Imp. Chaix, cond. B+, (06-11-93, Boisgirard, #83), 51³⁄₁₆ x 35⁷⁄₁₆ in., (130 x 90 cm.), poster (BP 884, DM 2186, FR 7370, Y 142,706).

$266* *L'Epreuve Numero Special/La Mi-Careme Au Quartier-Latin, 1900,* Imp. Chaix, Paris, (12-05-92, Bassenge, #7596), 17¹¹⁄₁₆ x 24⁷⁄₁₆ in., (45 x 62 cm.), color lithograph (BP 167, DM 415, FR 1413, Y 32,958).
$1144* *Scala. Enfin Seuls! Revue A Grand Spectacle, 1900,* Paris, Imp. Chaix, cond. B, (06-11-93, Boisgirard, #84), 48⁷⁄₁₆ x 33¹⁄₁₆ in., (123 x 84 cm.), poster (BP 752, DM 1859, FR 6268, Y 121,379).

GRUNZWEIG, Bedrich b. 1910
$1265* *Times Square, New York, 1955,* s., t., d., (c) credit stamp, (04-08-93, Christie-NY, #291, illus.), 9½ x 13⅞ in., (24.1 x 35.2 cm.), photograph, gelatin siler print (BP 830, DM 2032, FR 6879, Y 143,554).

GRUTZKE, Johannes b. 1937
$794* *"Aus Dem Leben Richard Wagners", 1983: Seven,* s., d., num., Gilkendorf, Merlin pub., (11-28-92, Grisebach, #527, illus.), 14¹⁄₁₆ x 15¹⁄₁₆ in., (35.7 x 38.2 cm.), aquatint on copper print paper (BP 524, DM 1265, FR 4294, Y 98,818).
$148* *Aus Der Luke (Holeczek 34), 1968,* sig., artist's proof, sheet 4 of "Vernissagen" series, (12-05-92, Bassenge, #7206, illus.), 14⁹⁄₁₆ x 18⁵⁄₁₆ in., (37 x 46.5 cm.), chalk lithograph on machinemade (BP 93, DM 231, FR 786, Y 18,337).
$664* *Baseler Spiele (Holeczek 39, 40, 68, 73, 74, 82), 1974: Six,* s., num., Verlag Sydow-Zirkwitz, Frankfurt, (12-05-92, Bassenge, #7207), color mezzotint on thick paper (BP 416, DM 1035, FR 3528, Y 82,270).
$133* *Ein Jager Aus Kurpfalz (Holeczek 93), 1977,* s., num., (12-05-92, Bassenge, #7212), 10½ x 11³⁄₁₆ in., (26.7 x 28.4 cm.), mezzotint on copper print paper (BP 83, DM 207, FR 707, Y 16,479).
$148* *Nahe Der Tanzflache (Holeczek 20), 1967,* s., epreuve d'artiste, sheet 3 of "Discothek" series, (12-05-92, Bassenge, #7205), 20½ x 25¹⁵⁄₁₆ in., (52 x 66 cm.), chalk lithograph on machine (BP 93, DM 231, FR 786, Y 18,337).
$162* *Und Du? (Hoeczek 62), 1972,* s., epreuve d'artiste, (12-05-92, Bassenge, #7209), 19¼ x 23⁹⁄₁₆ in., (48.9 x 59.9 cm.), offset lithograph on thin offset cardboard (BP 101, DM 253, FR 861, Y 20,072).
$186* *Untitled Titled, 1978,* s., d., num., (09-25-92, Granier, #2869), sheet 13¾ x 11 in., (35 x 28 cm.), etching on wove (BP 109, DM 276, FR 932, Y 22,450).
$443* *Zahn Der Zeit, 1983,* s., num., (12-05-92, Bassenge, #7215), 14¹⁄₁₆ x 12¹³⁄₁₆ in., (35.7 x 32.5 cm.), mezzotint on copper print paper (BP 277, DM 691, FR 2354, Y 54,888).

GUARANA, Jacopo 1720-1808
BI *Das Urteil Des Paris (De Vesme 4),* est. DM 1,500, (12-04-92, Bassenge, #6601), 14¹⁵⁄₁₆ x 18¹⁵⁄₁₆ in., (38 x 48.2 cm.), etching.

GUAYASAMIN, Oswaldo Ecuadorian b. 1919
BI *"De Orbe Novo Decades" ("Las Decadas De Pedro Martir De Angleria"), 1984: Fifty-Seven,* #29/350, s., w/box, accompanied by note confirming destruction of plates, reserve P490,000, (12-17-92, Duran, #163, illus.), 19¹¹⁄₁₆ x 13¾ in., (50 x 35 cm.), 17 lithographs, 40 etchings.
BI *"El Grito",* #21/50, s., reserve P40,000, (12-17-92, Duran, #182, illus.), 25³⁄₁₆ x 18½ in., (64 x 47 cm.), lithograph.

GUBBELS, Klaas
$352* *Koffiepot, 1977,* s., d., full margins, good cond., minor handling creases, (05-27-93, Sotheby-Amstrdm, #420), sh 29¹³⁄₁₆ x 22³⁄₁₆ in., (758 x 563 mm.), colored lithogrpah on BFK Rives (BP 225, DM 565, FR 1904, Y 37,736, G 633).
$96* *Tafel Met Koffiepot, 1977,* s., d., full margins, good cond., minor handling creases, (05-27-93, Sotheby-Amstrdm, #418, illus.), sh 29¹³⁄₁₆ x 22³⁄₁₆ in., (758 x 563 mm.), colored lithograph on BFK Rives (BP 61, DM 154, FR 519, Y 10,292, G 173).
$128* *Tafel, 1977,* s., d., full margins, good cond., minor handling creases, (05-27-93, Sotheby-Amstrdm, #419), sh 29¹³⁄₁₆ x 22³⁄₁₆ in., (758 x 563 mm.), colored lithograph on BFK Rives (BP 82, DM 205, FR 692, Y 13,722, G 230).

GUBBELS, Klaas and K. SCHIPPERS
BI *Verlegen Schaduwen, 1981: Ten,* complete deluxe edit., s., d., #IV/CLV, pub. uitgeverij Bebert, goodcond., est. G 1,8/2,500, (12-09-92, Sotheby-Amstrdm, #581, illus.), overall 15³⁄₁₆ x 22⅝ in., (385 x 575 mm.), nine color silkscreens, a hand-colored etching and a pencil drawing by Gubbels.

GUBITZ, Friedrich Wilhelm 1786-1870
BI *Christus Als Salvator,* after Cranach, tear, crease, est. DM 1,200-, (09-25-92, Granier, #2632), 10¹³⁄₁₆ x 6⅞ in., (27.4 x 17.4 cm.), sheet 17⁵⁄₁₆ x 11¾ in., (27.4 x 17.4 cm.), color woodcut of 5 Platten.

GUDIOL, Monserrat
BI *"El Baile" and "No Te Puedes Escapar": Pair,* s., #73/75, reserve P28,000, (02-03-93, Duran, #234), 13⅜ x 9⅝ in., (34 x 24.5 cm.), engraving.

GUERARD, Eugene Johan Joseph von 1811-1900
$304* *Cataracts Near Launceston, Tasmania,* s. Eug. Guerard, in image, t., from Australian Landscapes by E Von Guerard, pub. Hamel & Ferguson, 1867, (08-11-92, L. Joel, #14G), 12¹³⁄₁₆ x 18¹³⁄₁₆ in., (32.5 x 47.8 cm.), tinted lithograph (BP 158, DM 446, FR 1511, Y 38,929, A$ 412).
$223* *The Valley Of The Ovens River,* s. E Von Guerard in image, t., (08-11-92, L. Joel, #38G), 12¾ x 20¹⁄₁₆ in., (32.4 x 51 cm.), tinted lithograph (BP 116, DM 327, FR 1108, Y 28,557, A$ 302).

GUERARD, Henri
$248* *Quai De Gare A Dieppe,* annot., collector's stamp, tears, (04-02-93, Picard, #127), 11¹³⁄₁₆ x 18¹¹⁄₁₆ in., (30 x 47.5 cm.), black etching on laid (BP 163, DM 399, FR 1354, Y 28,236).

GUERCIN (after)
$112* *Bandits Quarrelling,* by Francesco Bartolozzi, margins, staining, (03-17-93, Bonhams-Chelsea, #434), plate 9 x 12 in., (22.9 x 30.5 cm.), etching (BP 77, DM 186, FR 633, Y 13,136).

GUERCINO (Giovanni Francesco BARBIERI) 1591-1666
BI *A Man And Woman Fighting Each Other,* watermark, est. DM 2400, (06-04-93, Bassenge, #5188, illus.), 6½ x 8¼ in., (16.5 x 20.9 cm.), etching.

GUERCINO (after)
$232* *Das Martyrium Des Hl. Laurentius: Five,* by Giovanni Battista Coriolano, prov., later print, rare series, (09-14-92, Venator/Hansten, #1514), plate approx. 6⅞ x 4⁵⁄₁₆ in., (17.5 x 11 cm.), engraving (BP 123, DM 345, FR 1169, Y 28,849).
$182* *Two Gentlemen Examining A Book,* by Francesco Bartolozzi, foxed, (06-16-93, Bonhams-Chelsea, #483), image 9¼ x 8¾ in., (23.5 x 22.2 cm.), stipple engraving (BP 121, DM 302, FR 1014, Y 19,411).

GUERCINO, Giovanni Francesco 1591-1666
$290* *Ein Weib Und Ein Mann Im Handgemenge, Mit Messern,* stained, (12-01-92, Karl/Faber, #81), etching (BP 192, DM 462, FR 1575, Y 36,106).

GUERICAULT, Theodore 1791-1824
$101* *Drei Pferde, Gefuhrt Von Pferdeknecht,* (09-14-92, Venator/Hansten, #1668), image approx. 4⁵⁄₁₆ x 7⅞ in., (11 x 20 cm.), chalk lithograph (BP 53, DM 150, FR 509, Y 12,559).

GUERIN, Pierre Narcisse 1774-1833
$1155* *Le Vigilant (Thieme-Becker XV; S. 231), 1821,* artist's proof, prov., (12-04-92, Bassenge, #6820A, illus.), 10¹¹⁄₁₆ x 7¹¹⁄₁₆ in., (27.1 x 19.6 cm.), gray lithograph (BP 741, DM 1839, FR 6240, Y 144,195).
$500* *"Le Vigilant" and "Le Repos Du Monde" (H. Beraldi, p. 6), 1818: Two,* reddish stains, dirt stains, good margins, (06-11-93, Picard, #64), one 10⅝ x 7¾ in., (270 x 197 mm.), other 7¹⁄₁₆ x 9⁷⁄₁₆ in., (270 x 197 mm.), lithographs on wove (BP 329, DM 813, FR 2740, Y 53,050).

GUERRERO, Jose Spanish/American b. 1914
BI *"Abstraccion En Rojo, Morado Y Naranja",* #31/200, s., d. 1977, reserve P75,000, (12-17-92, Duran, #177, illus.), 39⅜ x 27⁹⁄₁₆ in., (100 x 70 cm.), lithograph.

GUERRERO, Pedro E. b. 1917
$2185* *"Wall Street" and "Off The 3rd Avenue (sic) Around 34th Street", 1946: Two,* s., t., d., credit stamp, (04-08-93, Christie-NY, #292, illus.), each approx. 12¾ x 10⅝ in., (32.4 x 27 cm.), photograph, gelatin silver print (BP 1433, DM 3510, FR 11,881, Y 247,957).

GUERRY, L.
BI *PLM: Palestine "Bethleem", 1898,* very good cond., (03-13-93, Laurin, #121), 41¾ x 29⅛ in., (106 x 74 cm.), .

GUIDI, P.
$1045* *Botanical (Convoluulus Arvesis), 1860s,* photog. and pub. credits and t., (04-07-93, Swann, #210, illus.), 10¾ x 8 in., photograph, albumen print w/rounded corners, hand-colored in greens and pinks (BP 691, DM 1690, FR 5720, Y 118,723).

GUIGOU, Paul French 1834-1871
$450* *La Durance A St Paul (L. 424), 1865,* full margins, drystamp, (02-24-93, Picard, #117), etching on laid (BP 314, DM 731, FR 2477, Y 52,805).

GUILBEAU, Honore American
$30* *"Duo",* s., t., very good cond., (05-15-93, Cleveland, #152), 13⅝ x 9⅛ in., (34.6 x 23.2 cm.), lithograph in colors (BP 20, DM 48, FR 162, Y 3326).
$20* *"Still Life", 1934,* s., plate No. 26 for Print-A-Month Club of Cleveland, tears, staining, good cond., (05-15-93, Cleveland, #151), 13½ x 19 15/16 in., (34.3 x 50.6 cm.), lithograph (BP 13, DM 32, FR 108, Y 2217).

GUILBERT, Paul Louis 1869-19??
$73* *"Nature Morte",* #8/100, s., water stains, (01-28-93, Pescheteau, #153), a vue 11 x 14 15/16 in., (28 x 38 cm.), color lithograph on Arches (BP 48, DM 116, FR 391, Y 9064).

GUILLAUME
$605* *Tous Disent Je Ne Fume Que Le Nil,* Affiches Camis, B+ cond., cracking, creasing, fold marks, (08-06-92, Swann, #151, illus.), 79 x 49 in., (200.7 x 124.5 cm.), (BP 316, DM 894, FR 3019, Y 77,168).

GUILLAUME, A.
$412* *"P'tites Femmes",* (12-10-92, Doyle, #21), sight 49 x 37 in., (124.5 x 94 cm.), color lithograph and poster (BP 266, DM 652, FR 2226, Y 50,965).
$80* *Tous Disent Que Je Ne Fume Que Le Nil,* Imp. Camis, fairly good cond., (02-12-93, Cheval/Robert, #59), 74 x 9 7/16 in., (188 x 24 cm.), poster (BP 56, DM 133, FR 449, Y 9648).

GUILLAUME, Albert French 1873-1942
$602* *Ambassadeurs. Duclerc Tous Les Jours, c. 1895,* Paris, Affiches Camis, cond. B, restored in text, (06-11-93, Boisgirard, #87), 51 3/16 x 39⅜ in., (130 x 100 cm.), poster (BP 396, DM 978, FR 3299, Y 63,873).
$301* *L'Homme Chic Ne Porte Que La Bretelle Ch. Guyot, c. 1900,* Imp. d'Art Lepold Verger, cond. B+, (06-11-93, Boisgirard, #88, illus.), 31½ x 24 3/16 in., (80 x 61.5 cm.), poster (BP 198, DM 489, FR 1649, Y 31,936).

GUILLAUMIN, Armand French 1841-1927
$573* *Le Bebe Endormi (Kraemer 24), 1896,* full margins, (02-24-93, Picard, #118), color lithograph on gray Ingres (BP 400, DM 930, FR 3154, Y 67,238).
$807* *Bicetre Et Chemin Des Barons, 1873,* (05-15-93, Loudmer, #305), 3¾ x 6 13/16 in., (95 x 173 mm.), etching on wove contrecolle on creme laid (BP 525, DM 1298, FR 4362, Y 89,458).
$403* *Cabaret A Ivry (I.F.F. w/out num.), 1872,* w/margins, (05-15-93, Loudmer, #306, illus.), 5 13/16 x 5⅞ in., (148 x 149 mm.), etching on wove (BP 262, DM 648, FR 2178, Y 44,674).
$423* *Chemin Creux Aux Hautes Bruyeres, Vallee De La Bievre, 1872,* ded., (05-15-93, Loudmer, #304, illus.), 5 x 3 11/16 in., (127 x 93 mm.), sh 8 13/16 x 6 7/16 in., (127 x 93 mm.), etching on wove (BP 275, DM 680, FR 2286, Y 46,891).
$899* *Jeune Fille En Buste Ou Portrait De Madeleine (I.F.F. 15), 1894,* whole margins, creases, tears, (06-11-93, Picard, #65), 18⅛ x 21 1/16 in., (460 x 535 mm.), lithograph in colors on laid (BP 591, DM 1461, FR 4926, Y 95,385).
$512* *Tete D'Enfant (Una Johnson 62; K. 26), 1897,* full margins, (02-24-93, Picard, #119), color lithograph on thin chine (BP 357, DM 831, FR 2818, Y 60,080).

GUILLEMOT, Emile
$403* *En Chase, Notes Et Croquis (Thiebau 483), Pontpoint 1887 (ie. 1889),* scuffing, limited edit. #13/150 copies, after drawings by Guillemot,Anthony N. B. Garvan Coll., (06-05-93, Christie-NY, #28), numerous collotypes on papier Imperial du Japan (BP 265, DM 653, FR 2202, Y 43,231).

GUINEGAULT, G* F*
BI *The Adoration,* #1/280, s., margins, est. BP 5/70, (04-22-93, Bonhams-Chelsea, #33), plate 15½ x 11¾ in., (39.4 x 29.8 cm.), etching w/aquatint in colors.

GUIRAMOND, Paul French b. 1926
$110* *"Nu Blanc A La Fenetre",* s. Guiramond, #16/50, (04-17-93, Wolf, #603), 27 x 20 in., (68.6 x 50.8 cm.), color lithograph (BP 72, DM 178, FR 600, Y 12,369).

GULDENSTUBBE, Trude von b. 1904
$99* *Marokkanerinnen, 1971,* stone mono. TvG, s. T. v. Guldenstubbe, #25/50, (03-24-93, Venator/Hansten, #4495), approx. 13¾ x 10⅝ in., (35 x 27 cm.), chalk lithograph (BP 67, DM 162, FR 550, Y 11,632).

GUNTHER, Max
$6* *Tall Ships,* s., d. '69, 38/10, (12-11-92, DuMouchelle, #1458), 19 x 22½ in., (48.3 x 57.2 cm.), lithograph (BP 4, DM 9, FR 32, Y 742).

GURIAN, T.F.
$17* *"Bookseller On The Seine" and "Figure On European Street": Two,* (01-15-93, DuMouchelle, #199), both 12 x 15 in., (30.5 x 38.1 cm.), lithographs (BP 11, DM 28, FR 94, Y 2143).
$28* *"Bookseller On The Seine" and "Figure On European Street": Two,* (11-13-92, DuMouchelle, #382), 12 x 15 in., (30.5 x 38.1 cm.), lithograph (BP 18, DM 44, FR 148, Y 3475).

GURSCHNER, Herbert Austrian 1901-1975
$83* *"Going To Church": A Pair,* both s. H. Gurschen, good cond.?, (11-21-92, Bakker, #112), each, image 5 x 5 in., (12.7 x 12.7 cm.), color woodblock print (BP 55, DM 132, FR 446, Y 10,322).

GURSKY, Andreas b. 1955
$2875* *"The Angler", 1989,* s., t., d., (05-23-93, Butterfield, #3436, illus.), 23¼ x 30 in., photograph, c-print (BP 1872, DM 4701, FR 15,823, Y 317,785).

GUSTON, Philip Canadian/American 1913-1980
$5750* *East Side (G. 872), 1980,* s., d., t., #37/50, blindstamp, pub. Gemini, G.E.L., full margins, good cond., (05-15-93, Sotheby-NY, #986, illus.), sheet 32⅝ x 42½ in., (82.9 x 108 cm.), lithograph (BP 3739, DM 9249, FR 31,081, Y 637,402).
$2090* *Gulf (G. 1061), 1983,* estate stamped, num. 30/36, blindstamp of pub. Gemini G.E.L., full margins, apparently very good cond., (02-24-93, Butterfield, #3034, illus.), 28 x 38½ in., (711 x 978 mm.), lithograph on Arches Cover (BP 1457, DM 3393, FR 11,502, Y 245,248).
$1760* *Remains (Gemini 954), 1981,* blindstamp, #35/50, from portfolio Eight Lithographs To Benefit The Foundation For Contemporary Performance Arts, Inc., blindstamp, pub. Gemini G.E.L., good cond., (11-07-92, Sotheby-NY, #570), sheet 19¾ x 29¾ in., (502 x 756 mm.), lithograph on Koller Transfer (BP 1151, DM 2810, FR 9498, Y 217,230).
$3163* *Sea (Gemini 869), 1980,* s., d., t., #31/50, blindstamp, pub. Gemini G.E.L., good cond., (05-15-93, Sotheby-NY, #985), sheet 30⅞ x 40¾ in., (78.4 x 103.5 cm.), lithograph on John Koller Grey handmade paper (BP 2057, DM 5088, FR 17,097, Y 350,626).
$2875* *The Street, 1970,* s., d., #94/120, pub. Skowhegan School, full margins, good cond., stray graphite mark, creases, (02-11-93, Sotheby-NY, #341, illus.), 19 15/16 x 26 3/16 in., (507 x 665 mm.), lithograph on Arches (BP 2029, DM 4762, FR 16,115, Y 346,594).
$1210* *The Street, 1970,* from Ten Lithographs by Ten Artists, Shorewood-Bank Street, s., d., i., pub. Skowhegan School of Painting and Sculpture, full margins, pale light/mat

staining, very good cond., (11-09-92, Christie-NY, #293), (572 x 765 mm.), lithograph on buff Arches (BP 800, DM 1932, FR 6526, Y 150,161).

$1210* *The Street, 1970,* s., d., annot. A.P., full margins, good cond., crease, (10-28-92, Butterfield, #2967), 19⅞ x 26¼ in., (505 x 667 mm.), lithograph on Arches (BP 771, DM 1869, FR 6345, Y 148,466).

$1650* *Studio Forms (Gemini 877), 1980,* s., d., t., #16/100, pub. Gemini G.E.L., (12-08-92, Swann, #128), 32 x 42½ in., (81.3 x 108 cm.), lithograph (BP 1034, DM 2569, FR 8758, Y 204,512).

$1980* *"Untitled" and "Untitled", 1966: Two,* both s., d., num. 33/35, 25/25, Irwin Hollander blindstamps, full margins, pale light-staining, excell. cond., (09-19-92, Christie-E, #117, illus.), both sheet 22⅜ x 30 in., (56.8 x 76.2 cm.), lithograph on Arches (BP 1139, DM 2965, FR 10,154, Y 246,698).

$2070* *Untitled, 1966,* s., i. trial proof, blindstamp, co-pub. Hollanders Workshop and artist, good cond., creases, soiling, (05-15-93, Sotheby-NY, #984), sheet 22 x 29⅞ in., (55.9 x 75.9 cm.), lithograph on BFK Rives (BP 1346, DM 3330, FR 11,189, Y 229,465).

$1380* *View (G. 1062), 1983,* s. w/estate stamp, #35/50, blindstamp publisher, Gemini G.E.L., verygood cond.?, (05-19-93, Butterfield, #2177, illus.), 30 x 42½ in., (76.2 x 108 cm.), lithograph on Arches cover (BP 896, DM 2243, FR 7558, Y 152,773).

GUTCH, John Wheeley Gough   1802-1862
BI *View Of Creswick, 1857,* t., d. in ink, penciled border, est. $2,2/2,800, (10-13-92, Christie-NY, #10, illus.), each 6¾ x 7⅜ in., (17.1 x 18.7 cm.), photograph, 3-part salt print.

GUTEKUNST, F.
$990* *Portrait Of Ulysses S. Grant, 1860s,* photog. credit, (04-07-93, Swann, #211, illus.), 18 x 15 in., photograph, albumen print (BP 654, DM 1601, FR 5419, Y 112,474).

GUTIERREZ SOLANA, Jose
$290* *"Mendigos Calentandose", c. 1932-33,* s. in plate, (03-17-93, Duran, #27, illus.), 10⅞ x 8¹³⁄₁₆ in., (27.6 x 22.4 cm.), etching (BP 200, DM 483, FR 1640, Y 34,014, P 34,500).

GUTMANN, John   b. 1904
BI *Sailor Girl, 1939,* s.; s., t., d., est. $2,5/3,500, (04-08-93, Christie-NY, #293, illus.), 9¾ x 7⅝ in., (24.8 x 19.4 cm.), photograph, gelatin silver print.
$990* *Signals: Self, 1987,* s., t., d., (c) insig., (10-13-92, Christie-NY, #547, illus.), 10⅛ x 13 in., (25.7 x 33 cm.), photograph, gelatin silver print (BP 577, DM 1450, FR 4928, Y 120,044).

GUTSCHOW, Arvid   German 1900-1984
$770* *Untitled (Shell X-Ray), c. 1930,* s., (04-07-93, Swann, #470, illus.), 8 x 6½ in., photograph, silver print (BP 509, DM 1245, FR 4215, Y 87,480).

GUYATT, Richard
$2886* *These Men Use Shell, Racing Motorists, 1939,* ref. #539, cond. 3, (10-13-92, Phillips-London, #155, illus.), 29¾ x 44¹¹⁄₁₆ in., (75.5 x 113.5 cm.), color lithograph (BP 1681, DM 4228, FR 14,365, Y 349,945).
$711* *To Visit Britain's Landmarks, Ralph Allen's Sham Castle, Bath, 1936,* p. Waterlow and Sons, ref. #461, cond. 1, creasing, (10-13-92, Phillips-London, #107), 29¹⁵⁄₁₆ x 45¹⁄₁₆ in., (76 x 114.5 cm.), color lithograph (BP 414, DM 1042, FR 3539, Y 86,213).

GUYON, Maximilienne   1868-1903
$803* *La Mode Nationale. Grand Journal De Modes, c. 1900,* Paris, Ste An. Imp. and Pub. Charles Verneau, cond. B+, (06-11-93, Boisgirard, #89), 55⅛ x 77¹⁵⁄₁₆ in., (140 x 198 cm.), poster (BP 528, DM 1305, FR 4400, Y 85,199).

GWATHMEY, Robert   American b. 1903
BI *"A" Section, c. 1960,* s., good cond., est. $1-2,000, (10-31-92, Cleveland, #138, illus.), 13 x 15 in., (33 x 38.1 cm.), lithograph in colors.
BI *"A" Section, c. 1960,* s., good cond., est. $700/1,000, (05-15-93, Cleveland, #154), 13¼ x 15⅞ in., (33.7 x 40.3 cm.), color lithograph.

BI *Cotton Pickers, c. 1948,* ink s., surface abrasions, est. $7/900, (06-11-93, Freemn/Fine Art, #89), 13¼ x 8⅞ in., (33.7 x 22.5 cm.), silkscreen in colors.
$121* *Hope For East Hampton, 1975,* num., s., (05-27-93, Swann, #125), sh 22½ x 29 in., (57.2 x 73.7 cm.), offset color lithograph poster (BP 77, DM 194, FR 654, Y 12,972).
$1430* *"Ring-Around-A-Rosy",* s. Gwathmey in matrix, good cond., tape/residue, toning, (03-12-93, Skinner, #72, illus.), 12⅝ x 15⅞ in., (32.1 x 40.3 cm.), screenprint in colors on wove (BP 998, DM 2380, FR 8093, Y 168,533).
$2415* *Strumming And Darning,* ink s. in image, cut margins, light-staining, scrapes, tape remains,surface soiling verso, good cond., (05-04-93, Christie-E, #273, illus.), 12 x 14⅛ in., (30.5 x 35.9 cm.), screenprint in colors on wove (BP 1542, DM 3804, FR 12,818, Y 265,647).
BI *Topping Tobacco,* pen s., good cond., est. $1/1,500, (06-11-93, Freemn/Fine Art, #88, illus.), 12¾ x 8½ in., (32.4 x 21.6 cm.), color silkscreen.

HAAS, Aad de   b. 1920
BI *Untitled,* p. Nel de Haas, full margins, 1151 x 70 mm, est. G 180/250, (12-09-92, Sotheby-Amstrdm, #582), linocut on Japan.
BI *Veertig Passieprenten, 1961: Forty,* complete portfolio, num. 23, pub. Uitgeverij W.A. Palm, 1968, full margins, good cond., est. G 700/1,000, (12-09-92, Sotheby-Amstrdm, #583), silkscreen.

HAAS, Ernst
$2875* *"Bullfight, Spain", 1957,* mounted on wood, s., t. by photog., labels, (04-06-93, Sotheby-NY, #422, illus.), 9¼ x 13¼ in., photograph, dye-transfer print (BP 1899, DM 4632, FR 15,685, Y 327,897).
$1725* *"The Creation": Ten, 1970-81,* p. 1982, portfolio, s., portfolio stamp, colophon s., #12/300, pub. Daniel Wolf Press, Inc., (05-23-93, Butterfield, #3437, illus.), 12½ x 19½ in., photograph, dye-transfer print (BP 1123, DM 2820, FR 9494, Y 190,671).
$1998* *Egyptian Boys, Resting, 1954,* stamped photog.'s credit Ernst Haas Magnum Photos, 202 x 297mm, (05-07-93, Sotheby-London, #252), photograph, silver print (BP 1265, DM 3159, FR 10,645, Y 219,996).
$944* *"A Study In Manpower", Extras On The Set Of "The Land Of The Pharoahs", 1954: Two,* stamped photog.'s credit Ernst Hass Magnum Photos, one t., d. stamped 27 Nov 1954, annots., each approx. 230 x 350mm, (05-07-93, Sotheby-London, #251, illus.), photograph, silver print (BP 598, DM 1492, FR 5029, Y 103,942).

HAAS, Terry
$58* *Reflets Num. 1,* artist's proof, 7/10, s., t., (06-28-93, Loudmer, #257), 7⅞ x 3¹⁵⁄₁₆ in., (200 x 100 mm.), sh 22¼ x 17⅛ in., (200 x 100 mm.), color etching and aquatint on Richard de Bas laid (BP 39, DM 99, FR 332, Y 6154).

HABBAH
$19* *Couverts,* s., 154/300, (06-28-93, Loudmer, #53), 17¹¹⁄₁₆ x 24⁷⁄₁₆ in., (450 x 620 mm.), sh 19⁹⁄₁₆ x 25⁹⁄₁₆ in., (450 x 620 mm.), color serigraph on Arches wove (BP 13, DM 32, FR 109, Y 2016).

HABERMANN, Francois Xavier
BI *"L'Entre Triumphale De Troupes Royales A Nouvelle Yorck" and "La Destruction De La Statue Royale A Nouvelle Yorck": Two,* trimmed within platemark, stains, surface dirt, est. BP 8/1,200, (12-03-92, Sotheby-London, #67), each approx. 11½ x 16¼ in., (292 x 415 mm.), etching, two plates.
BI *"Vue De La Place Capitale Dans La Ville Basse A Quebec" and "Vue De La Haute Ville A Quebec": Two,* trimmed on or within platemark, creases, surface dirt, stains, est. BP 8/1,200, (12-03-92, Sotheby-London, #68), 12½ x 16¾ in., (318 x 425 mm.), etching, two plates.

HACKERT, Jakob Phillip   1737-1807
$4590* *Phillip Hackert. Theoretisch-Practische Anleitung Zum Richtigen Und Geschmackvollen Landschaftzeichnen Nach Der Natur: Eleven,* (06-10-93, Hauswedell/Nolt,

#190, illus.), etching (BP 3002, DM 7474, FR 25,164, Y 487,209).

HADEN, F.S.   1818-1910
$314* *A Lancashire River (Schneiderman 203), 1881,* i., (06-09-93, Bubb Kuyper, #1990), 11 x 15¹³⁄₁₆ in., (28 x 40.1 cm.), etching (BP 207, DM 514, FR 1727, Y 33,394, G 575).

HADEN, Francis Seymore
$220* *"Breaking Up Of The Agamemnon", 1870,* plate s., d., good cond.?, (07-19-92, Bakker, #123), plate 7½ x 16 in., (19.1 x 40.6 cm.), etching and drypoint (BP 113, DM 321, FR 1084, Y 27,350).

HAER, Adolf de
$71* *Portrait Kurt Heymckes, 1923,* s., t., d., full margins, soiling, foxing, creasing, Late Gerhard Brauer Coll., (05-27-93, Sotheby-Amstrdm, #731), 7¹⁵⁄₁₆ x 6 in., (201 x 153 mm.), etching on wove (BP 45, DM 114, FR 384, Y 7611, G 127).

HAFFNER
$110* *Engagez-Vous Dans La Marine, 1930,* good cond., (02-12-93, Cheval/Robert, #117), 46⁷⁄₁₆ x 31⅛ in., (118 x 79 cm.), poster (BP 77, DM 182, FR 617, Y 13,266).

HAGAN, Frederick
$86* *Bee On Drawing Board,* s., #5/7; s., t., d. 1958, #5/7, artist's studio label, exhib., (06-07-93, Ritchie, #45, illus.), image 13½ x 7¹³⁄₁₆ in., (34.3 x 19.8 cm.), lithograph (BP 57, DM 139, FR 470, Y 9225, C$ 110).
$108* *Child And The Moon,* s., #8/23; s., t., d. 1955, #8/23-3 printings, artist's studio labelverso, exhib., (06-07-93, Ritchie, #44, illus.), image 10 x 13⅜ in., (25.4 x 34 cm.), color lithograph (BP 71, DM 175, FR 590, Y 11,585, C$ 138).
$128* *Desert Farm,* s., d. '45, #9/12; t. label verso, exhib., (11-30-92, Ritchie, #31), 9½ x 13¾ in., (24.1 x 35 cm.), lithograph (BP 84, DM 204, FR 692, Y 15,930, C$ 165).
$941* *Desire And Desiring", "Watchers Before The Throne", "Forgotten Games", "Walking And Listening", "Carriers And Burden", "Ladders And The Ladder", "Comforting Walls", "Barren Shelves", and Others: Folio Of Thirteen,* from Ladders, s., t., d. 54, issued and num. in various edit. sizes,lit., (11-30-92, Ritchie, #5, illus.), each approx. 12¹⁵⁄₁₆ x 9¾ in., (33 x 24.8 cm.), color lithograph, one grisaille (BP 621, DM 1499, FR 5089, Y 117,113, C$ 1210).
$107* *Doc's Catch,* s., d. '48, #14/20; t. artist's label verso, exhib., (11-30-92, Ritchie, #29, illus.), image 9³⁄₁₆ x 13¾ in., (23.3 x 35 cm.), lithograph (BP 71, DM 170, FR 579, Y 13,317, C$ 138).
   BI *Driftwood,* s., d. 57, #3/14; s., t., d. 1947, #3/14, artist's studio label, exhib., est. C$3/400, (06-07-93, Ritchie, #46), image 16 x 8¾ in., (40.7 x 22.3 cm.), lithograph.
$193* *Old Fence Post,* s., #8/20; t., d. 1947 label verso, exhib., (11-30-92, Ritchie, #32, illus.), 13¾ x 9¾ in., (35 x 24.8 cm.), lithograph (BP 127, DM 307, FR 1044, Y 24,020, C$ 248).
$599* *"Sea Saw", "Ink Island Inked", "View In View Out", "Walk In Our Past", "Cod Carry", and "Sunrise On Paper": Folio Of Six,* from Hagan In Newfoundland, s., num., issued and num. in various edit. sizes, exec. March 1976, pub. Grimsby Public Art Gallery, (11-30-92, Ritchie, #6, illus.), sheets approx. 22 x 15 in., (55.9 x 38.1 cm.), lithograph (BP 395, DM 954, FR 3240, Y 74,549, C$ 770).
$278* *Walking Boots,* s., #8/15; t., d. 1947, label verso, exhib., (11-30-92, Ritchie, #30, illus.), 9⅜ x 13¾ in., (23.8 x 35 cm.), lithograph (BP 183, DM 443, FR 1504, Y 34,599, C$ 358).

HAGEL, Otto   American 1909-1973
$522* *Franklin Delano Roosevelt,* handstamp, 1930s, (04-07-93, Swann, #313, illus.), 13⅜ x 10½ in., photograph, silver print (BP 345, DM 844, FR 2857, Y 59,305).
$1320* *Franklin Delano Roosevelt,* handstamp, 1930's, (10-14-92, Swann, #310, illus.), 13½ x 10½ in., (34.3 x 26.7 cm.), photograph, silver print (BP 775, DM 1932, FR 6551, Y 159,961).

$825* *Homecoming Vet, Broken Bow, Nebraska,* sig., notations, 1940's, (10-14-92, Swann, #309, illus.), 9¾ x 7¾ in., (24.8 x 19.7 cm.), photograph, silver print (BP 484, DM 1207, FR 4094, Y 99,976).
$1650* *Manhattan Beach (Coney Island), 1938,* s. in crayon, t., d. by Hansel Mieth, photog.'s widow, in ink, (10-15-92, Sotheby-NY, #214A, illus.), 13⅜ x 10 in., (34 x 25.4 cm.), photograph, gelatin silver print (BP 1010, DM 2456, FR 8329, Y 197,960).
$1320* *Wall Street: Four, 1938,* each s. by Hansel Mieth, photog.'s widow, p.l., (10-15-92, Sotheby-NY, #215, illus.), each approx. 13⅜ x 10⅜ in., (34 x 26.4 cm.), photograph, gelatin silver prints (BP 808, DM 1965, FR 6663, Y 158,368).

HAGEL, Otto and Hansel MIETH
   BI *North Platte, Nebr., 1938,* mounted, s., t., d. in ink on mount, t., d. in ink verso, est. $1,5/2,000, (10-15-92, Sotheby-NY, #214, illus.), 10⅜ x 13¼ in., (26.4 x 33.7 cm.), photograph, gelatin silver print.

HAGEMEYER, Johan   1884-1962
$7700* *Castle Of Today, San Francisco, 1923,* credit stamp, s., d., lit., (10-13-92, Christie-NY, #220, illus.), 4 x 3 in., (10.2 x 7.6 cm.), photograph, gelatin silver print (BP 4485, DM 11,280, FR 38,328, Y 933,673).
$3450* *Untitled (Power Lines) (Hagemeyer, pl. 21),* photog. studio stamp, mounted, s., d. by photog., 1928 p. 1940's, (04-06-93, Sotheby-NY, #172, illus.), 4 x 2⅞ in., photograph (BP 2279, DM 5558, FR 18,822, Y 393,476).
$11,000* *Untitled [Ship Abstraction] (Hagemeyer, pl. 24), 1932,* i., d. S.F. 1932 by photog., stamp, (10-15-92, Sotheby-NY, #135, illus.), 9⅛ x 7½ in., (23.2 x 19.1 cm.), photograph, gelatin silver print (BP 6731, DM 16,374, FR 55,528, Y 1,319,736).
   BI *A View Of Telegraph Hill, 1925,* t., d., lit., est. $4/6,000, (04-08-93, Christie-NY, #387, illus.), 7⅛ x 9½ in., (18.1 x 24.1 cm.), photograph, gelatin silver print.

HAGIWARA, Hidao   Japanese b. 1913
$440* *"Stone Flower - Blue Grey"; "Mask No. 9": A Pair,* s., d. Hidao Hagiwara 60, t., num. 14/30; other s., d. Hidao Hagiwara'64, t., num. 5/30, (09-25-92, Wolf, #43), 34 x 22½ in., (86.4 x 57.2 cm.), colored woodblock (BP 257, DM 652, FR 2206, Y 53,108).

HAID, J.G.   1710-1776
$235* *Les Jeunes Musiciens (Le Blanc 41),* after G Schalcken, pub. Boydell, before letters, (06-09-93, Bubb Kuyper, #2053, illus.), 17⅛ x 10⅞ in., (43.5 x 27.7 cm.), mezzotint (BP 155, DM 384, FR 1293, Y 24,992, G 431).

HAIG, Axel   b.Sweden,ac.London 1835-1921
$134 *"Assisi",* s., (08-14-92, G.A. Key, #101), 18 x 23 in., (45.7 x 58.4 cm.), etching (BP 70, DM 197, FR 666, Y 16,898).
$234* *The Doges Palace, Venice, 1898,* s., pub. Robert Dunthorne, time staining, (10-15-92, Bonhams-Chelsea, #152), image 23¾ x 32 in., (60.3 x 81.3 cm.), drypoint etching (BP 143, DM 348, FR 1181, Y 28,074).
$110* *The East Ambulatory, Burgos Cathedral,* artist's mono., d. 1909, i. in plate; i. "sample copy" w/in plate; s., (02-04-93, Sloan, #2013), 16½ x 11¾ in., (41.9 x 29.8 cm.), etching (BP 77, DM 181, FR 614, Y 13,683).
$88* *Figures Outside Cathedral,* d. 1911 in plate, s., (09-17-92, Sloan, #1435), 16½ x 22½ in., (41.9 x 57.2 cm.), etching (BP 49, DM 131, FR 447, Y 10,956).
$395* *Mont St. Michel,* s., (10-15-92, Bonhams-Chelsea, #151), image 34¼ x 24¾ in., (87 x 62.9 cm.), drypoint etching (BP 242, DM 588, FR 1994, Y 47,391).
$77* *Towing In The Prize,* mono. d. 1891 in plate; s., t., i. Wisby C.A. 1500, (12-10-92, Sloan, #951), 11⅜ x 8¼ in., (28.9 x 21 cm.), etching (BP 50, DM 122, FR 416, Y 9525).
   BI *View Inside Cathedral With Figures,* s., (12-11-92, G.A. Key, #132), 21 x 15 in., (53.3 x 38.1 cm.), etching.

HAINES, Frederick Stanley
$236* *The Flaming Maple,* s., t., prov., (11-30-92, Ritchie, #21B), 8⅜ x 9¾ in., (21.3 x 24.8 cm.), color aquatint (BP 156, DM 376, FR 1276, Y 29,371, C$ 303).
$52* *The Mill At Vercheres,* init., mono., t. in plate, s., (06-07-93, Ritchie, #20), 4¾ x 3¹⁵⁄₁₆ in., (12 x 10.1 cm.),

color aquatint and drypoint (BP 34, DM 84, FR 284, Y 5578, C$ 66).

HAINES and SON, PUBLISHER

BI *"The Moralist" and "Maternal Advice": A Pair,* pub. 1795, margins, rubbed, time-stained, defects, est. BP 3/400, (10-27-92, Phillips-London, #53), plate 13⅝ x 9⅞ in., (346 x 251 mm.), mezzotint.

HAINS, Raymond b. 1926

$1372* *The Critic Laughs (Waddington 66), 1968,* s., num., Edit. Documetan Foundation, (11-28-92, Schoppmann, #573), 13⁷⁄₁₆ x 10⁵⁄₁₆ in., (34.2 x 26.2 cm.), laminate photolithograph, serigraph, emaille-color and collage on light cardboard (BP 906, DM 2186, FR 7420, Y 170,753).

$231* *Reaper (Waddington 20), 1977,* s., (11-28-92, Schoppmann, #575), 6⅞ x 9¾ in., (17.4 x 24.7 cm.), etching on handmade (BP 152, DM 368, FR 1249, Y 28,749).

$866* *Sunrise (WV 96), 1975,* t., s., num., (11-28-92, Schoppmann, #574), 6⅞ x 9³⁄₁₆ in., (17.4 x 23.4 cm.), collotype on Schoeller Effenbein cardboard (BP 572, DM 1380, FR 4684, Y 107,778).

HAJEK-HALKE, Heinz German 1898-1983

$581* *"Aktmodell", c. 1957,* t., s., stamped photog.'s credit HHH Inventar, num. B/8/4, 595 x 479mm, (05-07-93, Sotheby-London, #389, illus.), photograph, silver print (BP 368, DM 919, FR 3095, Y 63,973).

$363* *"Blumen Fur Andrea", 1969,* s., t., stamped photog.'s credits Copyright by H. Hajek-Halke 6701, stamped, num. A/41/4, 595 x 444mm, (05-07-93, Sotheby-London, #385, illus.), photograph, silver print (BP 230, DM 574, FR 1934, Y 39,969).

BI *Das Ende,* 1966, p.l., ink s., t., (c) and edit. stamps, est. $800/1,200, (04-08-93, Christie-NY, #101, illus.), 23½ x 16¾ in., (59.7 x 42.5 cm.), photograph, gelatin silver print.

$3680* *Fall Leaf And Men Photomontage, c. 1930,* credit, reprod. limitation stamps, paper label, (04-08-93, Christie-NY, #98, illus.), 9 x 6¾ in., (22.9 x 17.1 cm.), photograph, gelatin silver print (BP 2413, DM 5912, FR 20,011, Y 417,612).

$363* *"Formbrand", 1967,* s., t., annot., stamped photog.'s credits Copyright by H. Hajek-Halke 6701, num. 914, 595 x 473mm, (05-07-93, Sotheby-London, #386, illus.), photograph, silver print (BP 230, DM 574, FR 1934, Y 39,969).

$1320* *Der Friedhof Der Fische, 1939,* credit stamps, label, (10-13-92, Christie-NY, #221, illus.), 9¼ x 8 in., (23.5 x 20.3 cm.), photograph, gelatin silver print (BP 769, DM 1934, FR 6570, Y 160,058).

BI *Mausoleum,* c. 1968, p.l., ink s., t., num., (c) and edit. stamps, est. $800/1,2000, (04-08-93, Christie-NY, #102, illus.), 23½ x 18¼ in., (59.7 x 46.4 cm.), photograph, gelatin silver print.

BI *Mittagspause, 1954,* s., d., stamp, est. DM 1,200, (11-12-92, Lempertz, #83), 11¹³⁄₁₆ x 9½ in., (30 x 24.2 cm.), photograph, gelatin silver print.

$2760* *Nude Study,* late 1930s, credit stamp, (04-08-93, Christie-NY, #99, illus.), 11½ x 9¼ in., (29.2 x 23.5 cm.), photograph, gelatin silver print (BP 1810, DM 4434, FR 15,008, Y 313,209).

$1213* *Ohne Titel, 1932,* felt pen s., d., (11-12-92, Lempertz, #82, illus.), 11¹³⁄₁₆ x 9⁹⁄₁₆ in., (30 x 24.3 cm.), photograph, gelatin silver print (BP 776, DM 1906, FR 6497, Y 150,068).

BI *Ohne Titel, c. 1963,* felt pen s., (c), est. DM 2,000, (11-12-92, Lempertz, #84, illus.), 18¹⁄₁₆ x 23½ in., (45.8 x 59.7 cm.), photograph, gelatin silver print.

BI *"Petrefakt", 1964,* s., d., annot., t., stamped photog.'s credits Copyright by H. Hajek-Halke, num. 18, stamped HHH Inventar, num. A/75/2, annot., 606 x 507mm, est. BP2/300, (05-07-93, Sotheby-London, #388, illus.), photograph, silver print.

BI *Reprints Aus Den Jahren 1927-1960: Twelve,* Edition Werner Kunze, 1978, each s., num. 11/28, est. $5/7,000, (10-13-92, Christie-NY, #222, illus.), each 13½ x 9 in., (34.3 x 22.9 cm.), photograph, gelatin silver prints.

$2806* *Spiegelakt, c. 1929,* felt pen s., stamp, (11-12-92, Lempertz, #81, illus.), 9³⁄₁₆ x 6¾ in., (23.3 x 17.2 cm.), photograph, gelatin silver print (BP 1794, DM 4410, FR 15,029, Y 347,148).

BI *Spielbank Lindau, 1925/30,* felt pen s., t., est. DM 900, (11-12-92, Lempertz, #80, illus.), 9½ x 7¹⁄₁₆ in., (24.2 x 18 cm.), photograph, gelatin silver print.

BI *Die Uble Nachrede, Idle Gossip,* 1932, p.l., s., t., annot., num., artist's inventory stamp, lit., est. $1,8/2,200, (04-08-93, Christie-NY, #100, illus.), 13¾ x 11 in., (34.9 x 27.9 cm.), photograph, gelatin silver print.

BI *"Verganglichkeit", 1963,* s., d., t., stamped photog.'s credits Copyright by H. Hajek-Halke, num. 128, stamped num. A/26/3, 670 x 575mm, est. BP 2/300, (05-07-93, Sotheby-London, #387, illus.), photograph, silver print.

$3034* *Verschiedene Titel: Twelve,* 1927-1960, 1978, s., #13, from 28 + 3 H.C., edit. Werner Kunze, Berlin, (11-12-92, Lempertz, #86, illus.), each 15⅞ x 11¹⁵⁄₁₆ in., (40.4 x 30.4 cm.), photograph, gelatin silver print (BP 1940, DM 4768, FR 16,251, Y 375,356).

BI *Windrosen, c. 1964,* felt pen s., t., (c), est. DM 1,600, (11-12-92, Lempertz, #85, illus.), 23⅝ x 18¹¹⁄₁₆ in., (60 x 47.5 cm.), photograph, gelatin silver print.

HAK, Miroslav 1911-1978

BI *Town Corner, 1943,* from portfolio Modern Czech Photography, s., est. $3/5,000, (04-08-93, Christie-NY, #135, illus.), 15⅜ x 11¼ in., (39.1 x 28.6 cm.), gelatin silver print.

HAKEWILL, James

$605* *A Picturesque Tour Of Italy From Drawings Made In 1816-1817: 63,* after Hakewill and J.M.W. Turner, folio, scattered foxing, 1st edit., (11-12-92, Swann, #111), engraving (BP 397, DM 959, FR 3234, Y 75,015).

HAKUMONKI

$143* *"Poem, 68-17B",* s., num., t., (03-25-93, Boos, #629), 19 x 8¾ in., (48.3 x 22.2 cm.), embossing and Corundum print (BP 97, DM 235, FR 799, Y 16,753).

HALABY, Samia American b. 1936

$50* *"Cleveland", 1974,* s., d., t., num. Print Club of Cleveland Publication No. 53, 1975, excellent cond., (10-31-92, Cleveland, #375), lithograph in colors (BP 32, DM 77, FR 261, Y 6193).

HALEN, Arnoud van (called AQUILA) c. 1650-1732

BI *Humana Cuncta Fumus, Umbra, Vanitas,* est. DM 1,800, (12-04-92, Bassenge, #6229, illus.), 7¹³⁄₁₆ x 5¹⁵⁄₁₆ in., (19.9 x 15.2 cm.), colored mezzotint.

HALL (after J. STEWART)

$385* *"Neo-Classical Figures": A Set Of Four,* Louis Bonadio Estate, (10-14-92, Doyle, #34), 13½ x 7⅛ in., (34.3 x 18.1 cm.), engraving (BP 226, DM 563, FR 1911, Y 46,655).

HALL, Arthur William American b. 1889

BI *Trees And Pond,* s., i., prov., $125/175, (10-30-92, Sloan, #1733), 5¹⁄₁₆ x 7¼ in., (12.9 x 18.4 cm.), drypoint etching.

HALL, H.B.

$82* *"Mount Vernon In The Olden Time",* after A. Henning, d. 1856, (06-02-93, Doyle, #63), 19 x 24¼ in., (48.3 x 61.6 cm.), hand-colored engraving (BP 53, DM 131, FR 441, Y 8798).

HALL, Harry (after)

$107* *The Great Match,* by Charles Hunt, pub. Baily Brothers, 1854, margins, repaired tears,stained, defects, (06-30-93, Bonhams-Chelsea, #198), plate 27 x 45¾ in., (68.6 x 116.2 cm.), aquatint w/hand-coloring and gum arabic (BP 72, DM 183, FR 616, Y 11,465).

$82* *The Merry Beaglers,* by J. Harris, margins, (06-30-93, Bonhams-Chelsea, #126), plate 18½ x 25 in., (47 x 63.5 cm.), mixed method engraving w/hand-coloring (BP 55, DM 140, FR 472, Y 8786).

HALL, Henry Bryan, Engraver (Jr.) American ac. 1850-1900

$330* *"Gettysburg", 1876,* ident. w/in matrix, good cond.?, staining, (03-27-93, Skinner, #332A), sight, sheet 18½ x 37¼ in., (47 x 94.6 cm.), engraving on paper (BP 222, DM 538, FR 1830, Y 38,408).

HALL, Norma Bassett
$385* *"La Gaude - France"*, s., very good cond.?, (03-28-93, Bakker, #12), image 7 x 9½ in., (17.8 x 24.1 cm.), colored woodblock (BP 259, DM 628, FR 2135, Y 44,809).

HALL, Oliver English 1869-1957
$41* *Kent Quarry*, s., margins, (03-17-93, Bonhams-Chelsea, #352), plate 7¾ x 12 in., (19.7 x 30.5 cm.), etching (BP 28, DM 68, FR 232, Y 4809).
$42 *Spanish Coastal Landscape*, s., (10-09-92, G.A. Key, #96), 6¾ x 11¾ in., (17.1 x 29.8 cm.), etching (BP 25, DM 63, FR 212, Y 5122).

HALLENSLEBEN, Ruth 1898-1977
$265* *Erz-Aufbereitung, 40's*, (c), t., (11-12-92, Lempertz, #89, illus.), 7¹¹⁄₁₆ x 6¾ in., (19.5 x 17.1 cm.), photograph, gelatin silver print (BP 169, DM 416, FR 1419, Y 32,785).
BI *Industrieaufnahme, 40's*, est. DM 500, (11-12-92, Lempertz, #88), 9⅛ x 6⅞ in., (23.2 x 17.4 cm.), photograph, gelatin silver print.
$379* *Ruhrland Am Abend, 30's*, t., (11-12-92, Lempertz, #87, illus.), 9¹⁄₁₆ x 6⅞ in., (23 x 17.4 cm.), photograph, gelatin silver print (BP 242, DM 596, FR 2030, Y 46,889).

HALLER, J. American 19th/20th cent.
BI *"Morning Calm" and "Hillside Farm": Two*, each s., est. $200/250, (10-30-92, Sloan, #1782), each 5 x 7⅞ in., (12.7 x 20 cm.), etching.

HALLEY, Peter American b. 1953
$4950* *Prison, 1988*, s., d., #15/18, pub. Editions Ilene Kurtz, p. MNM, very good cond.?, (10-28-92, Butterfield, #2968), 44 x 36 in., (111.8 x 91.4 cm.), vacuum-formed plastic relief w/screenprint in colors (BP 3154, DM 7645, FR 25,957, Y 607,362).

HALLO, Charles 1882-1969
$249* *Ch. De Fer D'Orleans. Cote Sud De Bretagne*, cond. B, (03-16-93, Boisgirard, #124), 41⁵⁄₁₆ x 29⅛ in., (105 x 74 cm.), poster (BP 172, DM 414, FR 1407, Y 29,116).

HALM, Peter
$413* *Battersea Bridge (After Whistler)*, s., num. No. 26, margins, laid down, good cond., light-staining, matstaining, surface soiling, (02-24-93, Butterfield, #2933), 23½ x 17⅜ in., (597 x 441 mm.), etching & aquatint in colors on wove (BP 288, DM 670, FR 2273, Y 48,463).

HALPERN, R.
$202* *Bureau De Claude Bernard A Saint Julien*, #1/100, s., large margins, (02-03-93, Ader Tajan, #163), lithograph (BP 141, DM 333, FR 1128, Y 25,128).

HALSMAN, Philippe 1906-1979
BI *Albert Einstein*, 1954, p.l., (c) stamp, lit., est. $1/1,500, (04-08-93, Christie-NY, #436, illus.), 13 x 10 in., (33 x 25.4 cm.), photograph, gelatin silver print.
BI *Albert Einstein*, (1954), p.l., (c) credit stamp, lit., est. $15/20,000, (10-13-92, Christie-NY, #457, illus.), 18¾ x 14¾ in., (47.6 x 37.5 cm.), photograph, gelatin silver print.
$2300* *Albert Einstein (Sight and Insight, p. 8)*, photog. name, (c) stamp, 1954, p.l., (04-06-93, Sotheby-NY, #410, illus.), 18⅛ x 14¾ in., photograph (BP 1519, DM 3705, FR 12,548, Y 262,318).
$1760* *Albert Einstein, 1954 (Sight and Insight, p. 8)*, (c) stamp, p. l., (10-15-92, Sotheby-NY, #455, illus.), 18¾ x 14¾ in., (47.6 x 37.5 cm.), photograph, gelatin silver print (BP 1077, DM 2620, FR 8884, Y 211,158).
$1430* *Churchill's Back*, handstamp. c. 1951, printed 1960's, (10-14-92, Swann, #311, illus.), 14 x 11 in., (35.6 x 27.9 cm.), photograph, silver print (BP 839, DM 2093, FR 7097, Y 173,291).
$1870* *Dali Atomicus*, (1948), p.l., credit stamp, lit., (10-13-92, Christie-NY, #453, illus.), 9¼ x 12½ in., (23.5 x 31.8 cm.), photograph, gelatin silver print (BP 1089, DM 2740, FR 9308, Y 226,749).
$1210* *Dali Atomicus*, (c) handstamp, 1948, p.l., (10-14-92, Swann, #462, illus.), 11 x 14 in., (27.9 x 35.6 cm.), photograph, silver print (BP 710, DM 1771, FR 6005, Y 146,631).
$1320* *Dali Atomicus*, photog.'s handstamp, 1948, p.l., (04-07-93, Swann, #471, illus.), 11 x 14 in., photograph, silver print (BP 872, DM 2135, FR 7225, Y 149,966).
$3738* *"Dali Atomicus" (Sight and Insight, pp. 176-7)*, photog. name stamp, 1948, p.l., (04-06-93, Sotheby-NY, #409, illus.), 13⅜ x 17⅞ in., photograph (BP 2469, DM 6022, FR 20,393, Y 426,323).
$1320* *Dali Atomicus, 1948 (Sight and Insight, pp. 176-7)*, name stamp, p. l., (10-15-92, Sotheby-NY, #453, illus.), 9⅛ x 12½ in., (23.2 x 31.8 cm.), photograph, gelatin silver print (BP 808, DM 1965, FR 6663, Y 158,368).
$1093* *Dali's Mustache Crisscrossed, 1954*, (c) stamp, (04-08-93, Christie-NY, #439, illus.), 13⅝ x 10⅝ in., (34.6 x 27 cm.), photograph, gelatin silver print (BP 717, DM 1756, FR 5943, Y 124,035).
BI *Dali's Mustache, 1954*, t., annot., (c) and West 67th Street stamps, lit., est. $1,2/1,500, (04-08-93, Christie-NY, #438, illus.), 10⅜ x 13½ in., (26.4 x 34.3 cm.), photograph, gelatin silver print.
$825* *Exploding Dali, 1953*, photog.'s handstamp, (10-14-92, Swann, #463, illus.), 11 x 14 in., (27.9 x 35.6 cm.), photograph, silver print (BP 484, DM 1207, FR 4094, Y 99,976).
$660* *Imogen Coca*, photog.'s handstamp, 1950, p.l., (04-07-93, Swann, #472, illus.), 14 x 11 in., photograph, silver print (BP 436, DM 1067, FR 3612, Y 74,983).
$1045* *Ingrid Bergman*, (1944), 1978, embossed facsimile sig., t., d., edit. num. 4/500, (c)credit stamp, (10-13-92, Christie-NY, #223, illus.), 13¼ x 9½ in., (33.7 x 24.1 cm.), photograph, gelatin silver print (BP 609, DM 1531, FR 5202, Y 126,713).
$1210* *Jean Cocteau*, photog.'s sig., 1949, p. 1950s, (04-07-93, Swann, #473, illus.), 13 x 11 in., photograph, silver print (BP 800, DM 1957, FR 6623, Y 137,469).
BI *Jen-Paul Sartre, Paris, 1951*, (c) stamp, est. $1,5/2,500, (10-15-92, Sotheby-NY, #454, illus.), 13⅝ x 10⅝ in., (34.6 x 27 cm.), photograph, gelatin silver print.
$660* *Leopard Skull*, photog.'s blindstamp, (c) handstamp, notations, 1951, p. 1958, (04-07-93, Swann, #474, illus.), 14 x 10¾ in., photograph, silver print (BP 436, DM 1067, FR 3612, Y 74,983).
BI *Marc Chagall In His Studio*, blindstamp, (c), handstamp, 1943, p.l., est. $6/900, (10-14-92, Swann, #464, illus.), 11½ x 11 in., (29.2 x 27.9 cm.), photograph, silver print.
$990* *Marilyn Monroe*, photog.'s (c) handstamp, 1954, p.l., (04-07-93, Swann, #475, illus.), 20 x 16 in., photograph, silver print (BP 654, DM 1601, FR 5419, Y 112,474).
$1650* *Marilyn Monroe Eating A Hamburger*, photog.'s handstamp, 1950s, p.l., (04-07-93, Swann, #476, illus.), 11 x 14 in., photograph, silver print (BP 1090, DM 2669, FR 9031, Y 187,457).
$1320* *Marilyn Monroe Lifting Weights*, handstamp, 1950's, p.l., (10-14-92, Swann, #465, illus.), 11 x 14 in., (27.9 x 35.6 cm.), photograph, silver print (BP 775, DM 1932, FR 6551, Y 159,961).
$920* *Marilyn Monroe, 1952: Two*, ink #89/250, t., (c), reprod. limitation and edit. stamps, (04-08-93, Christie-NY, #435, illus.), each approx. 13 x 10 in., (33 x 25.4 cm.), photograph, gelatin silver print (BP 603, DM 1478, FR 5003, Y 104,403).
$1320* *Marilyn Monroe, c. 1952*, s., t., (c) credit stamps, (10-13-92, Christie-NY, #455, illus.), 9¾ x 7⅞ in., (24.8 x 20 cm.), photograph, gelatin silver print (BP 769, DM 1934, FR 6570, Y 160,058).
BI *"Martha Graham And Eric Hawkins", 1946*, t., d., annot. vintage print, photog.'s/coll. stamps, est. $1,5/2,000, (05-23-93, Butterfield, #3438, illus.), 10⅝ x 13 in., photograph, gelatin silver print.
BI *Nixon Jumping*, (1955), p.l., credit stamp, lit., est. $1,5/1,800, (10-13-92, Christie-NY, #458, illus.), 19¼ x 15⅜ in., (48.9 x 39.1 cm.), photograph, gelatin silver print.
$770* *Nixon Jumping*, handstamp, 1955, printed 1960's, (10-14-92, Swann, #312, illus.), 14 x 11 in., (35.6 x 27.9 cm.), photograph, silver print (BP 452, DM 1127, FR 3821, Y 93,311).
BI *"Picasso's Kiln" and "Picasso's Ceramics Assistant", c. 1949: Two*, handstamps, notations in unidentified hand, est. $1/1,500, (10-14-92, Swann, #466, illus.), 13¾ x 10¾ in., (34.9 x 27.3 cm.), photograph, silver prints.

BI *Portrait Of A Morrocan Woman,* 1950s, photog.'s stamp, est. $6/800, (05-23-93, Butterfield, #3439), 11¼ x 9 in., photograph, gelatin silver print.

$660* *Portrait Of Edward Steichen, 1959,* s. by photog., (c) handstamp, (04-07-93, Swann, #477, illus.), 14 x 11 in., photograph, silver print (BP 436, DM 1067, FR 3612, Y 74,983).

BI *Portrait Of Judge Learned Hand,* blindstamp, (c), handstamp, notations, 1957, p.l., est. $6/900, (10-14-92, Swann, #467, illus.), 14 x 11 in., (35.6 x 27.9 cm.), photograph, silver print.

BI *Portrait Of Tallulah Bankhead,* (c), blindstamp, handstamp, notations, 1952, p.l., est. $6/900, (10-14-92, Swann, #468, illus.), 13¾ x 11 in., (34.9 x 27.9 cm.), photograph, silver print.

$385* *Portrait Of Vladimir Horowitz,* photog.'s blindstamp, (c), limited edit. handstamp, 1966, p. 1978, (04-07-93, Swann, #478, illus.), 11¾ x 11 in., photograph, silver print (BP 254, DM 623, FR 2107, Y 43,740).

$1540* *Portrait Of Winston Churchill, 1953,* s. by photog., handstamps, (04-07-93, Swann, #479, illus.), 13½ x 10½ in., photograph, silver print (BP 1018, DM 2491, FR 8429, Y 174,960).

$1210* *Salvador Dali, 1953,* (c) credit stamp, (10-13-92, Christie-NY, #456, illus.), 13⅝ x 10⅞ in., (34.6 x 27.6 cm.), photograph, gelatin silver print (BP 705, DM 1773, FR 6023, Y 146,720).

BI *Talullah Bankhead,* (1952), 1978, embossed facsimile sig. recto, t., d., num. 4/500, est.$15/20,000, (10-13-92, Christie-NY, #454, illus.), 13¼ x 10⅜ in., (33.7 x 26.4 cm.), photograph, gelatin silver print.

BI *Walk In Space, 1965,* s., t., d., (c) and reprod. limitation stamps, est. $1,2/1,500, (04-08-93, Christie-NY, #437, illus.), 9½ x 7½ in., (24.1 x 19.1 cm.), photograph, gelatin silver print.

HAM, Geo
$1007* *Circuit De Saint-Cloud. Juin 1949,* good cond., (11-19-92, Ribeyre/Baron, #62), 62¹⁵⁄₁₆ x 47¼ in., (160 x 120 cm.), poster (BP 663, DM 1606, FR 5408, Y 125,233).

$126* *Fiftieth Anniversary Of The Automobile International Gastronomic Rallye, 1950,* good cond., (11-19-92, Ribeyre/Baron, #63), 23¼ x 15¾ in., (59 x 40 cm.), offset poster (BP 83, DM 201, FR 677, Y 15,670).

$587* *Prix De Paris. Juin 1957. Autodrome Linas-Montlhery,* p. J. Morax, good cond., (11-19-92, Ribeyre/Baron, #65), 47¼ x 31½ in., (120 x 80 cm.), poster (BP 386, DM 936, FR 3153, Y 73,001).

HAMAGUCHI, Yozo   b. 1909
$3025* *190 Plus Une,* s., #78/100, from portfolio Reconnaissance du Cuivre, (05-28-93, Sloan, #2691, illus.), color mezzotint on Rives (BP 1938, DM 4798, FR 16,220, Y 324,362).

$2200* *Artichoke (M. Gall. 56), 1957,* s., #47/50, margins, good cond., scuff through image, mat stain, creases, (11-05-92, Sotheby-NY, #192), 11¾ x 15¾ in., (300 x 400 mm.), sheet 16½ x 20⅛ in., (300 x 400 mm.), mezzotint (BP 1431, DM 3479, FR 11,771, Y 269,906).

$2200* *Asparagus (M. Gall 59), 1957,* s., #49/50, margins, good cond., scuff, stain, creases, (11-05-92, Sotheby-NY, #193), 11⅝ x 17½ in., (296 x 443 mm.), sheet 15⅞ x 22½ in., (296 x 443 mm.), mezzotint (BP 1431, DM 3479, FR 11,771, Y 269,906).

$3575* *A Bit Of Field; And Knitting Needle (M. Gall. 164 and 165), 1985,* s., #90/150, 124/150, full margins, good cond., fox marks, (11-05-92, Sotheby-NY, #196), each 9⅛ x 21½ in., (234 x 547 mm.), mezzotints (BP 2325, DM 5654, FR 19,128, Y 438,596).

$11,000* *Blue Butterfly (15 states) (see M. Gall. 161; Tien Museum 111), 1982: Set of One and Fourteen,* s., 33/110, full margins, excell. cond., framed together, (11-09-92, Christie-NY, #100, illus.), all 52 x 52 in., (132.1 x 132.1 cm.), colored mezzotint on 15 sheets of wove (BP 7273, DM 17,561, FR 59,331, Y 1,365,103).

$2530* *Blue Butterfly (M., Gall. 161), 1982,* s., #27/110, full margins, excell. cond., (05-11-93, Christie-NY, #196), plate 1¾ x 1¾ in., (44 x 44 mm.), color mezzotint on BFK Rives (BP 1615, DM 3986, FR 13,429, Y 278,297).

$7673* *Bottle With Lemons And Red Wall (T. M. T. M. 132), 1981-89,* s., #133/145, full margins, good cond., (12-03-92, Sotheby-London, #319, illus.), 24⅜ x 18⅝ in., (619 x 473 mm.), mezzotint in colors on BFK Rives (BP 4950, DM 12,066, FR 41,186, Y 954,709).

BI *Bottle With One And One-Quarter Lemons (M. Gall. 162), 1983,* s., #32/150, full margins, excellent cond., est. $6/8,000, (11-09-92, Christie-NY, #101, illus.), 622 x 475 in., (x cm.), mezzotint on Arches.

$18,154* *Butterfly And Sun (M. Gallery 112), 1969,* s., i. e.a., full margins, good cond., (10-14-92, Sotheby-Japan, #32, illus.), 7¾ x 7¾ in., (197 x 197 mm.), colored mezzotint (BP 10,656, DM 26,568, FR 90,094, Y 2,199,952).

$3080* *Butterfly Over Leaf Hill (M. Gall. 158), 1981,* s., #37/120, full margins, excellent cond., (11-09-92, Christie-NY, #98), 60 x 40 in., (152.4 x 101.6 cm.), colored mezzotint on wove (BP 2036, DM 4917, FR 16,613, Y 382,229).

BI *Butterfly Over Leaf, 1981,* s., #113/120, est. DM 6,000-, (05-27-93, Lempertz, #756), 11⁷⁄₁₆ x 7⁹⁄₁₆ in., (29 x 19.2 cm.), color etching on white wove.

$1876* *California Cherry (T.M.T.M. 122), 1987,* s., #270/350, full margins, good cond., (12-03-92, Sotheby-London, #317, illus.), 1⅝ x 1⅝ in., (41 x 41 mm.), mezzotint in colors on BFK Rives (BP 1210, DM 2950, FR 10,070, Y 233,420).

BI *California Cherry, 1987,* s., #53/150, est. DM 5,800, (05-27-93, Lempertz, #758, illus.), 1⅝ x 1⅝ in., (4.2 x 4.2 cm.), etching on white wove.

$1980* *Corns (M. Gall. 70), 1959,* s., #33/50, good cond., creases, mat/light stain, puncture, skinned spots, scratch, soiling, (11-05-92, Sotheby-NY, #194), 9⅜ x 21⅜ in., (238 x 542 mm.), mezzotint (BP 1288, DM 3131, FR 10,594, Y 242,915).

$1760* *Eight Walnuts (M. Gall. 138), 1977,* s., #58/75, good cond., creases, (11-05-92, Sotheby-NY, #195), sheet 35½ x 24⅞ in., (901 x 631 mm.), lithograph (BP 1145, DM 2783, FR 9417, Y 215,924).

$1373* *Eight Walnuts (M. Gallery 138), 1977,* s. crayon, #16/75, blindstamp publisher N. E., margins, good cond., (06-30-93, Sotheby-London, #447), 35⅜ x 24⅝ in., (899 x 625 mm.), lithograph on wove (BP 920, DM 2342, FR 7900, Y 147,112).

$2217* *Green Cherry (Tokyo Metropolitan Teien Museum Catalogue 131), 1981-89,* s., #140/145, full margins, good cond., (12-03-92, Sotheby-London, #315, illus.), 3⅛ x 2¼ in., (79 x 57 mm.), mezzotint in colors on wove (BP 1430, DM 3486, FR 11,900, Y 275,849).

$5225* *Green Grapes (M.C.R. 62), 1958,* s., #20/50, large margins, laid down, good cond., creases through image, (10-28-92, Butterfield, #2650, illus.), 9¹³⁄₁₆ x 7¾ in., (249 x 197 mm.), color mezzotint on cream wove (BP 3329, DM 8069, FR 27,399, Y 641,104).

$2420* *Hydrangea (M. Gallery 97), 1964,* s., #43/50, full margins, light/mat staining, tape, good cond., (11-09-92, Christie-NY, #97), 36 x 57 in., (91.4 x 144.8 cm.), colored mezzotint on wove (BP 1600, DM 3863, FR 13,053, Y 300,323).

$1725* *Ladybird (M. Gallery 102), 1965,* s., i. essai, proof, foxing, mat staining, pressure marks, taped to overmat, tape, (05-11-93, Christie-NY, #194), plate 2¼ x 2½ in., (57 x 64 mm.), color mezzotint on laid (BP 1101, DM 2717, FR 9156, Y 189,748).

BI *Lemon And Cherries, (M. Gallery 68), 1959,* s., num. 51/150, margins, mount-staining, foxmarks, tape, est. BP 3/4,000, (12-01-92, Christie-London, #577, illus.), P. 7¹¹⁄₁₆ x 7¹¹⁄₁₆ in., (195 x 195 mm.), mezzotint in colors on wove.

$4400* *One Cherry (M. Gall. 90), 1962,* s., #6/50, full margins, red faded, good cond., repaired scratches in image, (10-28-92, Butterfield, #2651, illus.), 13¹¹⁄₁₆ x 11¹³⁄₁₆ in., (348 x 300 mm.), color mezzotint on BFK Rives (BP 2803, DM 6795, FR 23,073, Y 539,877).

$3080* *Papillon Rouge, 1973,* s., Print Club of Cleveland stamp, pub. 51, full margins, (12-08-92, Swann, #131, illus.), 2 x 2 in., (5.1 x 5.1 cm.), color mezzotint on Rives (BP 1930, DM 4795, FR 16,348, Y 381,755).

$3397* *Pinceaux Et Melon (M.G. 40), 1955,* whole margins, #30/50, s., (06-11-93, Picard, #70), 11⅝ x 11⅝ in., (295 x

295 mm.), black manner print on wove (BP 2232, DM 5521, FR 18,614, Y 360,424).

$3996* *Poisson Et Fruits (M. Gallery 34), 1954,* whole margins, #9/50, s., (06-11-93, Picard, #69, illus.), 11 7/16 x 15 3/8 in., (290 x 390 mm.), black manner print on Rives wove (BP 2625, DM 6494, FR 21,896, Y 423,979).

BI *Red Field (Vorpal Gallery 179), 1985-91,* s., #54/75, full margins, good cond., est. BP 3,5/4,000, (12-03-92, Sotheby-London, #316, illus.), 9 1/8 x 21 3/8 in., (232 x 543 mm.), mezzotint in colors on BFK Rives.

$1150* *Red Yarn (M. Gallery 150), 1979,* s., #18/99, full margins, good cond., (05-13-93, Sotheby-NY, #567), 1 5/8 x 1 5/8 in., (40 x 40 mm.), mezzotint in colors on white wove (BP 755, DM 1857, FR 6264, Y 128,391).

$3300* *Robina's Cherry (M. Gall. 159), 1981,* s., #64/150, full margins, mat staining, very good cond., (11-09-92, Christie-NY, #99, illus.), 78 x 60 in., (198.1 x 152.4 cm.), colored mezzotint on wove (BP 2182, DM 5268, FR 17,799, Y 409,531).

$1498* *Sole, (M. Gallery 48), 1956,* s., num. 39/50, margin, surface dirt, very good cond., (12-01-92, Christie-London, #576), P. 11 5/8 x 13 9/16 in., (295 x 345 mm.), mezzotint on BKF Rives (BP 990, DM 2388, FR 8137, Y 186,504).

$10,450* *Still Life With Pimientos (M. Gall. 38), 1955,* s., #34/50, large margins, good cond., touched-in scuffs, crease, (11-05-92, Sotheby-NY, #191, illus.), 17 1/2 x 11 3/4 in., (446 x 298 mm.), mezzotint p. in colors (BP 6797, DM 16,527, FR 55,912, Y 1,282,051).

$3541* *Stilleben Mit Kirschen,* s., num., (12-05-92, Bassenge, #7217), 7 13/16 x 7 13/16 in., (19.8 x 19.8 cm.), color aquatint, etching on copper print paper (BP 2217, DM 5521, FR 18,815, Y 438,731).

$6821* *Three Butterflies (Vorpal Gall. 167-22), 1985-91,* unique color combination s., i. t.c., full margins, good cond., (12-03-92, Sotheby-London, #318, illus.), 4 3/4 x 4 1/2 in., (121 x 114 mm.), mezzotint in colors on wove (BP 4400, DM 10,727, FR 36,613, Y 848,700).

$18,154* *Twenty-Two Cherries, 1988,* s., num. 83/150, pub. Vorpal Gallery, full margins, good cond., (10-14-92, Sotheby-Japan, #33, illus.), 21 5/8 x 9 1/2 in., (549 x 241 mm.), colored mezzotint on Rives wove (BP 10,656, DM 26,568, FR 90,094, Y 2,199,952).

$2043* *Walnut, 1982,* s., #105/150, (05-27-93, Lempertz, #757), 14 3/4 x 11 1/8 in., (37.5 x 28.2 cm.), etching on white wove (BP 1308, DM 3278, FR 11,049, Y 219,018).

$19,550* *Watermelon (M. Gall 157), 1981,* s., #64/150, full margins, excell. cond., Mine S. Crane Estate, (05-11-93, Christie-NY, #195, illus.), plate 9 5/8 x 21 1/2 in., (244 x 546 mm.), color mezzotint on wove (BP 12,480, DM 30,797, FR 103,769, Y 2,150,478).

HAMBOURG, A.

BI *"A L'Amitie",* #XVIII/XX, ded., s., creases, large margins, est. FF400, (06-16-93, Ader Tajan, #106), 10 13/16 x 8 1/4 in., (27.5 x 21 cm.), color lithograph.

HAMILTON, Hugh (after)

$150* *The Revd. Walter Blake Kirwan (C.S. 52), 1806,* by William Ward, pub. William Allen, i., defects, image creases, (11-30-92, Phillips-London, #59), sheet 26 1/2 x 28 1/4 in., (673 x 718 mm.), mezzotint on laid (BP 99, DM 239, FR 811, Y 18,668).

HAMILTON, Richard b. 1922

BI *Bathers (A) (W. 64), 1967,* s., #15/75, pub. by artist, full margins, good cond., scuff mark extending into image, crease, scuff marks, est. $2,5/3,500, (05-15-93, Sotheby-NY, #989, illus.), 19 1/2 x 29 1/2 in., (49.5 x 74.9 cm.), silkscreen in colors on Schoellerhammer paper.

BI *Bathers (W. 72), 1969,* s., #56/75, good cond.?, foxing, creases, image scuffs, est. $1,5/2,000, (10-28-92, Butterfield, #2970), 15 1/4 x 21 3/8 in., (387 x 543 mm.), dye-transfer in colors on photographic paper.

BI *Berlin Interior (W. G. 105), 1979,* s., #56/100, pub. Waddington Graphics, full margins, good cond., est.BP 5/1,000, (12-03-92, Sotheby-London, #693), 19 1/4 x 27 1/8 in., (490 x 690 mm.), photogravure w/engraving, etching, roulette and aquatint on Rives.

BI *By The Waters Of Miers (Waddington 87), 1969,* s., #38/75, est. DM 3,200, (05-27-93, Lempertz, #765), 33 9/16 x 27 3/16 in., (85.3 x 69 cm.), etching on thick wove.

$234* *By The Waters Of Miers (Waddington 87), 1972,* s., t., #68/75, pub. Petersburg Press, margins, good cond., (10-15-92, Sotheby-London, #98, illus.), 25 1/8 x 22 1/2 in., (63.8 x 57.2 cm.), etching w/aquatint on German Museum paper (BP 143, DM 348, FR 1181, Y 28,074).

$1577* *The Critic Laughs (Waddington 66), 1968,* s., (05-27-93, Lempertz, #761), 23 7/16 x 18 5/16 in., (59.5 x 46.5 cm.), photo offset-lithograph w/serigraph w/colored varnish and collage onthin board (BP 1010, DM 2530, FR 8529, Y 169,061).

$717* *Esquisse (Waddington 85), 1972,* s., t., #11/40, (05-27-93, Lempertz, #764), 14 5/8 x 17 11/16 in., (37.2 x 45 cm.), vernis mou etching color pencil on wove (BP 459, DM 1151, FR 3878, Y 76,865).

$220* *Finn MacCool, 1983,* s., t., num. 93/120, pub. Waddington Graphics, full margins, pale blue mark, very good cond., (09-19-92, Christie-E, #118), sheet 29 3/4 x 22 1/4 in., (75.6 x 56.5 cm.), photogravure w/etching and aquatint on BFK Rives (BP 127, DM 329, FR 1128, Y 27,411).

$1108* *Five Tyres Remoulded (Portfolio) (W.G. 77), 1971,* portfolio, s., #67/150, w/relief cast, pub. Professional Prints, Zug,and Eye Editions, protective sponge wrapper, good cond., orig. box w/t., (12-03-92, Sotheby-London, #691), each sheet approx. 23 5/8 x 33 1/2 in., (800 x 650 mm.), seven screenprints in black on mylar sheeting, and a collotype in colors (BP 715, DM 1742, FR 5947, Y 137,862).

$2057* *Five Tyres Remoulded (Waddington 77), 1972,* s., num., (06-05-93, Schoppmann, #851), 23 5/8 x 33 7/16 in., (60 x 85 cm.), serigraph (BP 1354, DM 3335, FR 11,240, Y 220,661).

BI *Five Tyres Remoulded (Waddington 77), 1972: Seven,* pub. Professional Prints and Eye Editions, #112/150, est. DM 4,500-, (05-27-93, Lempertz, #763, illus.), 24 1/8 x 34 1/16 in., (61.3 x 86.5 cm.), serigraph on Mylar.

BI *I'M Reading Of A Black Christmas (W. 80), 1971,* s., #1/150, pub. Petersburg Press, margins, good cond., discoloration, handling marks, est. BP 1,8/2,200, (06-30-93, Sotheby-London, #817), sh 29 3/8 x 39 3/8 in., (74.6 x 100 cm.), screenprint over collotype w/collage on wove.

$2090* *In Horne's House, 1984,* s., t., num. 93/120, Waddington Graphics blindstamp, full margins, excell. cond., (09-19-92, Christie-E, #120, illus.), sheet 30 x 22 1/8 in., (76.2 x 56.2 cm.), etching and aquatint on wove (BP 1202, DM 3130, FR 10,718, Y 260,404).

BI *Interior With Monochromes (W.G. 106), 1979,* s., #89/96, pub. Waddington Graphics, full margins, good cond., creasing, est. BP 5/1,000, (12-03-92, Sotheby-London, #688), sheet 19 5/8 x 27 1/2 in., (499 x 699 mm.), collotype and screenprint in colors on Ivorex.

BI *Kent State,* s., num., est. DM 800-, (09-25-92, Granier, #2873), sheet 28 13/16 x 36 5/8 in., (73.2 x 93 cm.), color serigraph on offset board.

BI *Kent State (Waddington 75), 1970,* s., #2315/5000, pub. Dorothea Leonhart, full margins, good cond., crease, est. BP 5/600, (06-30-93, Sotheby-London, #816), 21 3/8 x 34 3/8 in., (543 x 873 mm.), color silkscreen on Schoeller Durex.

$84* *Kent State (Waddington/Cristea 75, Whitworth 31), 1970,* s. R. Hamilton, est. 1,7/5,000, (09-30-92, Kunsthallen, #115), color serigraph (BP 47, DM 119, FR 403, Y 10,080, DK 460).

$440* *Leopold Bloom, 1983,* s., num. 92/120, Waddington Graphics blindstamp, full margins, excell. cond., (09-19-92, Christie-E, #119), sheet 29 7/8 x 22 1/4 in., (75.9 x 56.5 cm.), soft-ground etching w/engraving and aquatint on BFK Rives (BP 253, DM 659, FR 2256, Y 54,822).

$1620* *Lobby (W.G. 137), 1984,* s., #41/88, pub. Waddington Graphics, full margins, good cond., (12-03-92, Sotheby-London, #692), sheet 16 7/8 x 22 7/8 in., (428 x 580 mm.), collotype and silkscreen in colors (BP 1045, DM 2548, FR 8696, Y 201,568).

BI *Motel II (W.G. 109), 1979,* s., #25/40, pub. Waddington Graphics, full margins, good cond., est.BP 5/1,000, (12-03-92, Sotheby-London, #690), 11 x 13 5/8 in., (280 x 346 mm.), soft-ground etching w/aquatint from two plates on Rives.

BI *Multi-Colored Flower-Piece (Waddington 91), 1974,* s., #44/100, blindstamp, creases, est. DM 2,000-, (05-27-93, Lempertz, #767), 19¹³⁄₁₆ x 16⁷⁄₁₆ in., (50.3 x 41.7 cm.), color etching on wove.

$6613* *My Marilyn (Waddington 59), 1965,* s., d., #13/75, pub. Editions Alecto, full margins, folds, scuff marks, mat stain, foxing, good cond., (05-15-93, Sotheby-NY, #988, illus.), 20½ x 24¾ in., (52.1 x 62.9 cm.), silkscreen in colors on TH Saunders paper (BP 4300, DM 10,637, FR 35,746, Y 733,067).

BI *Picasso's Meninas (Cristea 88), 1973,* s., t., i. PP, #10/15, full margins, excellent cond., est. $14/18,000, (11-09-92, Christie-NY, #294, illus.), 29¾ x 22⅜ in., (756 x 568 mm.), etching, aquatint, engraving and drypoint on wove.

$7796* *"Picasso's Meninas", 1973,* s., t., num., from 2nd portfolio of series Hommage a Picasso, pub. Propylaen Verlag, (06-08-93, Karl/Faber, #822, illus.), approx. 22⁷⁄₁₆ x 19⅛ in., (57 x 48.5 cm.), etching and aquatint on wove (BP 5125, DM 12,650, FR 42,601, Y 828,040).

$938* *A Portrait Of The Artist By Francis Bacon (Katalog Waddington 76), 1970-71,* #94/140, pencil t., s., (11-20-92, Lempertz, #564), sh 23⅛ x 20¹³⁄₁₆ in., (58.7 x 52.9 cm.), collotype and color serigraph on Schoeller cardboard (BP 618, DM 1496, FR 5038, Y 116,652).

BI *A Portrait Of The Artist By Francis Bacon (W. 75), 1970-71,* s., t., #134/140, p. at E. Schreiber, pub. Petersburg Press, good cond., est. BP 4/500, (06-30-93, Sotheby-London, #819), 21⅝ x 19½ in., (549 x 495 mm.), collotype and screenprint in color on stiff wove.

$1577* *A Portrait Of The Artist By Francis Bacon (Waddington 76), 1970-71,* s., #41/140, t., blindstamp, (05-27-93, Lempertz, #762), 32⁵⁄₁₆ x 27³⁄₁₆ in., (82 x 69 cm.), collotype and color serigraph on Schoeller Elfenbein board (BP 1010, DM 2530, FR 8529, Y 169,061).

$887* *A Portrait Of The Artist By Francis Bacon (Waddington Graphics 76), 1970-71,* s., t., #92/140, pub. Petersburg Press, full margins, good cond., handling marks, creases, (12-03-92, Sotheby-London, #686), 21½ x 19¾ in., (549 x 500 mm.), collotype and screenprint in colors on sturdy wove (BP 572, DM 1395, FR 4761, Y 110,365).

$1364* *Putting On De Stijl (W. G. 107), 1979,* s., #78/90, pub. Waddington Graphics, full margins, good cond., (12-03-92, Sotheby-London, #694), 11½ x 16½ in., (295 x 417 mm.), collotype and screenprint in colors on Ivorex (BP 880, DM 2145, FR 7322, Y 169,715).

$1449* *Reaper (A) (W.G. 25), 1949,* s., #3/20, p. and pub. by artist, margins, light-staining, glue stains, tear, glued to mount, (12-03-92, Sotheby-London, #687, illus.), sheet 9⅜ x 11⅛ in., (238 x 283 mm.), drypoint, roulette and punches on unbleached Arnold (BP 935, DM 2279, FR 7778, Y 180,291).

$1998* *Reaper, (Waddington Gallery cat. 34), 1949,* s., num. 1/20, pub., mount-staining, discoloration, creased, glue-staining, (12-01-92, Christie-London, #578), P. 7⅞ x 5⅞ in., (200 x 150 mm.), etching w/aquatint in colors on wove (BP 1320, DM 3185, FR 10,853, Y 248,755).

BI *Release, (Waddington cat. 81), 1972,* s., num. 2/150, pub. Petersburg Press, margins, crease, dirt, good cond., est. BP 1,5/2,000, (12-01-92, Christie-London, #580, illus.), L. 26¾ x 33¹¹⁄₁₆ in., (680 x 855 mm.), screenprint in colors, w/collage on wove.

BI *La Scala Milano (W. 69), 1968,* s., #3/65, pub. Petersburg Press, full margins, good cond., light-staining, creases, glue staining, foxing, touched-in areas, est. $2/3,000, (10-28-92, Butterfield, #2969), 10 x 14¹¹⁄₁₆ in., (254 x 373 mm.), color photo-etching and silkscreen on wove, watermark.

$550* *Self Portrait In A Cracked Mirror, 1985,* s., num. 7/30, pub. Waddington Graphics, full margins, excell. cond., (09-19-92, Christie-E, #121), plate 11⅝ x 8⅞ in., (29.5 x 22.5 cm.), etching on wove (BP 316, DM 824, FR 2821, Y 68,527).

BI *Soft Blue Landscape (W. 104), 1979,* s., t., 15/136, pub. Waddington Graphics, full margins, good cond., creases, est. BP 5/700, (06-30-93, Sotheby-London, #818, illus.), sh 28⅝ x 36⅛ in., (727 x 918 mm.), collotype and silkscreen in color.

BI *Soft Blue Landscape (Waddington Cat. 104), 1979,* s., t., num. 98/136, pub. Waddington Graphics, est. BP 8/1,000, (11-30-92, Phillips-London, #520), image 20½ x 27½ in., (521 x 699 mm.), collotype w/screenprint in colors on Ivorex paper.

$5457* *Swingeing London 67 (W. G. 68), 1968,* s., #61/70, p. Grafica Uno, pub. Petersburg Press, full margins, good-cond., (12-03-92, Sotheby-London, #689, illus.), 13⅜ x 18½ in., (338 x 468 mm.), etching, aquatint, embossing and photo-etching w/metallic foil diestamping and collage (BP 3520, DM 8582, FR 29,291, Y 678,985).

$371* *Swinging London 1967,* num. 970, pub. Edizioni di Cultura Comtemporanea, good cond., time-stained, (11-30-92, Phillips-London, #518), sheet 27¾ x 19¾ in., (705 x 502 mm.), color lithograph on hand-made wove (BP 245, DM 591, FR 2006, Y 46,173).

$2580* *Toaster (Waddington 62), 1967,* s., #11/75, (05-27-93, Lempertz, #760), 35¹⁄₁₆ x 25³⁄₁₆ in., (89 x 63.9 cm.), color offset-lithograph w/color serigraph and collage on thick Saunders wove (BP 1652, DM 4140, FR 13,953, Y 276,587).

BI *Trichromatic Flower-Piece, 1973-74,* s., num., est. DM 1800, (12-01-92, Karl/Faber, #689), 16⁹⁄₁₆ x 11⁷⁄₁₆ in., (42 x 29 cm.), color aquatint/etching on wove.

HAMILTON, W. (after)

$43 *"Calypso Conducting Telemachus And Mentor To The Grotto",* engraved by I Eginton, (04-16-93, G.A. Key, #100), 23 x 15 in., (58.4 x 38.1 cm.), colored stipple engraving (BP 28, DM 69, FR 235, Y 4835).

$39* *"December" and "May": Two,* repub. Louis Wolf & Co., (06-11-93, DuMouchelle, #2517), both 12 x 9¾ in., (30.5 x 24.8 cm.), mezzotint in color (BP 26, DM 63, FR 214, Y 4138).

HAMILTON, William (after)

BI *Mrs. Siddons In The Tragedy Of The Grecian Daughter,* by James Caldwell, repaired tears, mould on surface, est. BP 1/200, (06-16-93, Bonhams-Chelsea, #419), image 24¼ x 17¾ in., (61.6 x 45.1 cm.), engraving w/hand-coloring.

HAMMAN, Edouard (after)

$715* *Mozart A Vienne,* by Jean-Baptiste Alfred Cornilliet, (09-20-92, Hindman, #806), 29 x 38¼ in., (73.7 x 97.2 cm.), mezzotint and engraving (BP 419, DM 1061, FR 3629, Y 88,370).

HAMMERSCHMIDT, W.

$1361* *Egypt Studies: Seven,* 1860s, mounted on card, neg., s., d.; ink t., each approx. 212 x 273mm, (05-07-93, Sotheby-London, #17), photograph, albumen print (BP 862, DM 2152, FR 7251, Y 149,857).

HAMMITT, Howard

$522* *The Everglades, c. 1927,* notations, (10-14-92, Swann, #469, illus.), 15½ x 19 in., (39.4 x 48.3 cm.), photograph, tri-color bromoil print (BP 306, DM 764, FR 2591, Y 63,257).

HAMMOND, John

$299* *Low Tide - Bay Of Fundy,* s., t., (11-30-92, Ritchie, #12, illus.), 4 x 7¹⁵⁄₁₆ in., (10.2 x 20.3 cm.), etching (BP 197, DM 476, FR 1617, Y 37,212, C$ 385).

HAMPTON, Herbert G.

BI *Cathedral Of Saint Mark, Truro, Cornwall, From South-East,* s., num. 46, est. C$ 1/150, (12-01-92, Ritchie, #7), 6⅛ x 7 in., (15.6 x 17.8 cm.), etching.

HAMPTON, Michael

$21* *Alvin Ailey City Center Dance Theater, 1974,* (01-31-93, Morelle/Marchan, #32), 26¾ x 40¹⁵⁄₁₆ in., (68 x 104 cm.), poster (BP 14, DM 34, FR 114, Y 2620).

HANBERG, W.Lee

$77* *"Montreux-Sur-Mer",* s., destroyed plate print verso, very good cond., (07-19-92, Bakker, #124), 4¾ x 5¾ in., (12.1 x 14.6 cm.), drypoint (BP 39, DM 112, FR 379, Y 9572).

HANCOCK, K.B.
BI *York Minster,* #48/1000, s., pub. Lichfield Fine Art, (02-17-93, Bonhams-Chelsea, #280), sheet 19⅛ x 23 in., (48.6 x 58.4 cm.), color reproduction.

HANDFORTH, Thomas American 1897-1948
BI *"Auxerre", "Boy" (Small Burgundian Peasant), and "The Burgundian", 1920: Three,* each s., num. 15/50, 8/50, 17/50, margins, good cond., surface soiling, pencil notations, prop. Print Corner, Coll. of Elizabeth and Charles Whitmore, est. $3/500, (02-24-93, Butterfield, #2834), from 8⁷⁄₁₆ x 6¹⁄₁₆ in., (214 x 154 mm.), to 8⁷⁄₁₆ x 6¹¹⁄₁₆ in., (214 x 154 mm.), etching on thin and MBM paper.
BI *Oriental market Scene,* s. in plate; s., #125, est. $100/150, (07-03-92, Sloan, #326), 11⅛ x 8⅝ in., (28.3 x 21.9 cm.), lithograph.
$165* *Tunisian Carriage, 1926,* s., ed. 50, (11-12-92, Freemn/Fine Art, #82), mat 6¾ x 8¼ in., (17.1 x 21 cm.), etching (BP 108, DM 261, FR 882, Y 20,459).
BI *Two Ducks, Three Ducks, Siciliam Goat, and Two Goats (In Taormina), 1923 & 1924: Four,* each s., num. 6/50, 9/50, 15/50, 6/50, margins, good cond., Two Goatsw/pin holes, surface soiling, pencil notations, prop. Print Corner, Coll. of Elizabeth and Charles Whitmore, est. $4/600, (02-24-93, Butterfield, #2835), from 3⅞ x 6⅜ in., (98 x 162 mm.), to 6¾ x 5⅛ in., (98 x 162 mm.), etching on various papers.

HANDFORTH, Thomas Schofield American 1897-1948
$55* *"Barges, Shanghai Waterfront", "Young Harlequin" and "The Merry Go Round": Three,* (03-25-93, Boos, #617), etching (BP 37, DM 90, FR 307, Y 6443).

HANKEY, William Lee English 1869-1952
$333* *Demiese,* s., artist's blindstamp, margins, (09-17-92, Bonhams-Chelsea, #74), plate 7¾ x 5 in., (19.7 x 12.7 cm.), etching (BP 187, DM 494, FR 1692, Y 41,459).
$167* *In The Garden,* s., blindstamp, light-stained, remains of glue & previous mounting, (11-30-92, Phillips-London, #341), plate 8⅞ x 7⅛ in., (225 x 181 mm.), drypoint on laid (BP 110, DM 266, FR 903, Y 20,784).
$435* *The Kiss,* s., blindstamp, good cond., (10-27-92, Phillips-London, #273), plate 10 x 7⅞ in., (254 x 200 mm.), etching w/drypoint (BP 275, DM 667, FR 2262, Y 53,211).
$116* *Mother And Child,* s., (12-17-92, Mystic, #37), 11 x 9 in., (27.9 x 22.9 cm.), etching (BP 74, DM 181, FR 619, Y 14,256).

HANKEY, William Lee (after)
$220* *Woman With Wildflowers,* (10-16-92, DuMouchelle, #2391), 14 x 17½ in., (35.6 x 44.5 cm.), print (BP 133, DM 325, FR 1104, Y 26,269).

HANNAU, H.W.
$467* *New York, Downtown, c. 1940,* photog.'s sig., notations, (04-07-93, Swann, #480, illus.), 6 x 4 in., photograph, silver print (BP 309, DM 755, FR 2556, Y 53,056).

HANS, Emil b. 1909
BI *Buch. Platon-Le Banquet: Nineteen,* s., ded., est. DM 4,5/5,500, (06-24-93, Germann, #605, illus.), etching.
$474* *Mere Et Enfants Dans L'Atelier, Du Peintre (Cailler II, Nr. 367), 1965,* 63/75, s., (06-24-93, Germann, #604), 22¼ x 30⁵⁄₁₆ in., (565 x 770 mm.), color lithograph on Japan (BP 312, DM 768, FR 2590, Y 50,847, SF 690).
$514* *Le Peintre Observant Son Modele (Cailler II, Nr. 372), 1965,* 60/75, s., (06-24-93, Germann, #603), 22¹⁄₁₆ x 29¹⁵⁄₁₆ in., (560 x 760 mm.), color lithograph (BP 338, DM 833, FR 2809, Y 55,138, SF 748).

HANSEN, Armin American 1886-1957
BI *The Old Philosopher, 1938,* s., p. by artist, margins, good cond., mat staining, est. $3/500, (05-19-93, Butterfield, #1995), 4⅞ x 4 in., (124 x 102 mm.), drypoint on laid.

HANSEN, Arne L.
$84* *"Forar I Glasvaerket",* s. 26/100, (09-29-92, B. Rasmussen, #317), lithograph in colors (BP 47, DM 119, FR 405, Y 10,027, DK 460).
$83* Komposition, (03-24-93, Kunsthallen, #117), color lithograph (BP 56, DM 136, FR 461, Y 9752, DK 518).

HANSEN, Art
BI *"Rose", (19)81,* s., d., t., num., est. DM 300, (12-01-92, Karl/Faber, #690), 14¹⁵⁄₁₆ x 11¼ in., (38 x 28.5 cm.), color lithograph on wove.

HANSEN, Diane
BI *Couple,* s., t., d. 1977-76, #17/100, prov., est. C$150/250, (12-01-92, Ritchie, #38, illus.), 21½ x 19 in., (54.6 x 48.3 cm.), color aquatint.

HANSEN, Heinrich
BI *Frederiksborg Slot,* est. DK 2,000, (10-20-92, B. Rasmussen, #362), lithograph in colors.

HANSEN, Svend
$63* *Model,* s., (09-30-92, Kunsthallen, #296), etching (BP 36, DM 89, FR 302, Y 7560, DK 345).
$349* *Seks Grafiske Arbejder,* s., (03-24-93, Kunsthallen, #337), (BP 236, DM 570, FR 1940, Y 41,006, DK 2185).

HANSEN-BAHIA, Karl Heinz 1915-1978
$295* *Vier Krieger In Greichischer Tracht, Mit Einem Lowen In Einem Boot, 1965,* s., num., (12-05-92, Bassenge, #7219), 11¹³⁄₁₆ x 16⁹⁄₁₆ in., (30 x 42 cm.), color woodcut on wove (BP 185, DM 460, FR 1567, Y 36,551).
$117* *Zwei Badende,* s., (09-25-92, Granier, #2874), sheet 14¹⁵⁄₁₆ x 11⁷⁄₁₆ in., (38 x 29 cm.), woodcut on handmade (BP 68, DM 173, FR 586, Y 14,122).

HANSI
$713* *Chemins De Fer D'Alsace Et De Lorraine: Obernai. La Procession De Sainte Odille, 1921,* p. Cornille & Serre, good cond., lit., (11-19-92, Ribeyre/Baron, #110), 41⁹⁄₁₆ x 29¾ in., (105.5 x 75.5 cm.), poster (BP 469, DM 1137, FR 3829, Y 88,671).

HANSON, Victor
BI *Wagneriana, 1935,* sig., t., d., labels, est. $4/600, (10-14-92, Swann, #470, illus.), 11 x 8½ in., (27.9 x 21.6 cm.), photograph, silver print.

HANSPERS, Olle b. 1923
$1661* *To Abraham Van Der Meulen, 1975-78,* 37/99 3rd state, blindstamp Hanspers, (05-25-93, AB Stockholm, #24), 25¹⁄₁₆ x 19½ in., (63.7 x 49.5 cm.), copper engraving (BP 1076, DM 2705, FR 9106, Y 181,550, SK 2420).

HANUSE, Roy
BI *'Double-Finned Killerwhale', 1977,* NWCIA guild, est. C$150/250, (10-21-92, Maynard, #56), print.

HAP, Carl
$120* *Chaussures Renommees. "C'Est Le Diable A User", 1897,* Imp. Lemercier, good cond., (02-12-93, Cheval/Robert, #60), 55⅛ x 39⅜ in., (140 x 100 cm.), poster (BP 85, DM 199, FR 673, Y 14,472).

HARANOBU HANUROBI SCHOOL 18th/19th cent.
BI *"Two Girls Looking Out At Young Man",* CHUBAN, fading, est. $800/1000, (05-07-93, Goldberg, #1391, illus.), woodblock.

HARARI, Hananiah American b. 1912
$660* *"Divers",* s. Harari '39, num. 11/40, very good cond., (11-21-92, Bakker, #139, illus.), image 10 x 13 in., (25.4 x 33 cm.), screen print (BP 435, DM 1052, FR 3545, Y 82,079).

HARD, J. (after)
BI *Botanical,* (12-11-92, G.A. Key, #117), 8 x 5 in., (20.3 x 12.7 cm.), hand colored print.
$24 *Botanical,* (04-16-93, G.A. Key, #89), 8 x 5 in., (20.3 x 12.7 cm.), hand-colored print (BP 16, DM 39, FR 131, Y 2699).

HARDING, Frank
$212* *"Southampton" and "Poole Harbour": A Pair,* s., t., margins, (08-12-92, Bonhams, #194), plate 4½ x 12 in., (11.4 x 30.5 cm.), drypoint etching (BP 110, DM 310, FR 1051, Y 27,020).

HARDING, J.W. (after)
$67* *Peasant And His Dog In A Landscape,* trimmed to image, cockling, (11-30-92, Phillips-London, #266), sheet 7⅞ x 6¼ in., (200 x 159 mm.), aquatint w/extensive hand-coloring on wove (BP 44, DM 107, FR 362, Y 8339).

HARDY
BI *PLM and Cie De Navigation Paquet: Paris-Tanger-Casablanca Par Marseille. "Avec Transbordement Direct", 1933,* good cond., (03-13-93, Laurin, #100), 38¹⁵⁄₁₆ x 24³⁄₁₆ in., (99 x 61.5 cm.), .

HARDY, Bert   b. 1913
$460* *"Girl At Window With Boy", "Man With Cane And Friends"* and *"Man Repairing Gas Lamp": Three,* 1940s, p.l., s., photog.'s stamp, labels, est. $7/900, (05-23-93, Butterfield, #3442), each approx. 10 x 14 in., photograph, gelatin silver print (BP 300, DM 752, FR 2532, Y 50,846).
BI *"The Halle Orchestra", "Cockney Life At The Elephant & Castle, London", Basement Room* and *"Cockney Life At The Elephant & Castle, London", Barrow Monger: Three,* 1949, p.l., s., photog.'s stamp, label, first s., t., d., annot., est. $7/900, (05-23-93, Butterfield, #3440), each approx. 9 x 14 in., photograph, gelatin silver print.
BI *"South Koreans, 1951", "Inside The Temples Of Burma, 1950"* and *"Man And Woman In Pub, 1948": Three,* 1950, p.l., s., photog.'s stamp, labels, est. $7/900, (05-23-93, Butterfield, #3441), each approx. 10 x 14 in., photograph, gelatin silver print.

HARDY, Dudley   English c. 1866-1922
BI *A Gaiety Girl,* Maitres de l'Affiche blindstamp, p. Chaix, margins, apparently good condition, light-staining, est. $3/500, (03-31-93, Butterfield, #5240), 10⅛ x 6½ in., (25.7 x 16.5 cm.), lithograph printed in colors on wove.

HARDY, Heywood   English 1843-1932
$22* *Untitled,* (03-10-93, Maynard, #630), photolithograph (BP 15, DM 37, FR 124, Y 2599, C$ 28).

HARDY, Heywood (after)
$263* *The Grouse Shoot,* s., blindstamp, pub. Boussod Valadon, 1893, (06-30-93, Bonhams-Chelsea, #57), image 18¼ x 25¼ in., (46.4 x 64.1 cm.), photogravure (BP 176, DM 449, FR 1513, Y 28,180).

HARDY, Heywood (after)   British
$275* *Coaching Scenes: Two,* Ruth K. Flower Coll., (04-18-93, Hindman, #1668), each 15 x 21¾ in., (38.1 x 55.2 cm.), color aquatint (BP 181, DM 444, FR 1501, Y 30,923).

HARDY, T.B. (after)
$114 *Coal Scenes With Shipping: A Pair,* (06-11-93, G.A. Key, #4), 13 x 19 in., (33 x 48.3 cm.), chromolithograph (BP 75, DM 185, FR 625, Y 12,095).
$68 *Fishing Boat Approaching Harbour Bar,* (06-11-93, G.A. Key, #6), 17 x 21 in., (43.2 x 53.3 cm.), chromolithograph (BP 45, DM 111, FR 373, Y 7215).
$115 *"Scarboro Sands",* (08-14-92, G.A. Key, #110), 7 x 13 in., (17.8 x 33 cm.), chromolithograph (BP 60, DM 169, FR 571, Y 14,502).

HARDY, Thomas Bush (after)
$169 *"On The Medway"* and *"Landing Fish Scarbro": A Pair,* (10-09-92, G.A. Key, #4), 13 x 19 in., (33 x 48.3 cm.), chromolithograph (BP 100, DM 252, FR 854, Y 20,610).

HARE, Jimmy   American 1856-1946
$467* *American Sailors In The Spanish-American War Playing Cards On The Deck Of A Ship, 1898,* num., photog.'s partial sig., (04-07-93, Swann, #314, illus.), 7½ x 9½ in., photograph, silver print (BP 309, DM 755, FR 2556, Y 53,056).
$1045* *Children Gathered To Welcome The Wright Brothers, c. 1908,* (04-07-93, Swann, #315, illus.), 4½ x 6½ in., photograph, silver print (BP 691, DM 1690, FR 5720, Y 118,723).
$2070* *Finish Of First American Auto Race At Springfield, L.I., 1900,* t., d., annot. A.L., publication stamp, only vintage print known to exist, (04-08-93, Christie-NY, #40, illus.), 6¾ x 9 in., (17.1 x 22.9 cm.), photograph, gelatin silver print (BP 1357, DM 3325, FR 11,256, Y 234,907).
BI *Have You Shared, 1917,* handstamp, penciled marks, est. $1/1,500, (04-07-93, Swann, #316, illus.), 7¼ x 9¼ in., photograph, silver print.
$1980* *We'll See It Thru, 1917,* unique, ex-coll. Jimmy Hare and Cecil Carnes, (10-14-92, Swann, #313, illus.), 6½ x 9½ in., (16.5 x 24.1 cm.), photograph, silver print (BP 1162, DM 2898, FR 9826, Y 239,942).

$3300* *Wilbur Wright Getting Ready To Fly At Fort Myer, VA., 1908,* (10-15-92, Sotheby-NY, #65, illus.), 6⅝ x 5 in., (16.8 x 12.7 cm.), photograph, gelatin silver print (BP 2019, DM 4912, FR 16,658, Y 395,921).
$880* *Williamsburg Bridge, From Midway To Top Of Tower, c. 1900,* s., t., (10-13-92, Christie-NY, #38, illus.), 7⅝ x 9⅝ in., (19.4 x 24.4 cm.), photograph, gelatin silver print (BP 513, DM 1289, FR 4380, Y 106,705).
$2300* *The Wright Brothers Flying, Ft. Myer, Virginia, 1908,* s., i. by photog., (04-06-93, Sotheby-NY, #83, illus.), 4⅝ x 6½ in., photograph (BP 1519, DM 3705, FR 12,548, Y 262,318).

HARFORD
$93* *Helene Mai,* (01-31-93, Morelle/Marchan, #231), 26¾ x 38³⁄₁₆ in., (68 x 97 cm.), poster (BP 63, DM 150, FR 507, Y 11,602).

HARING, Keith   American 1958-1990
$10,450* *Apocalypse, 1988: Set Of Ten,* William Burroughs, George Mulder Fine Art, s. in ink, d., num., copy65 of 90, ink stamps verso, excellent cond., (11-09-92, Christie-NY, #295, illus.), 38 x 38 in., (965 x 965 mm.), colored screenprint on Museum Board on P.V.C. Folie (BP 6909, DM 16,683, FR 56,365, Y 1,296,848).
$330* *"Art Attack On AIDS",* s., d. '88, #30/100, (02-11-93, Boos, #416, illus.), sight 38⅜ x 27¹⁵⁄₁₆ in., (975 x 710 mm.), lithographic poster (BP 233, DM 547, FR 1850, Y 39,783).
$1980* *Best Buddies, 1990,* t., num. 107/200 by estate, estate stamp, sig., p. by Jean-Paul Russell, Durham Press, full margins, very good cond., (02-24-93, Butterfield, #3041, illus.), 22 x 27½ in., (559 x 699 mm.), silkscreen in colors on wove (BP 1381, DM 3214, FR 10,897, Y 232,340).
$954* *Dancing In Love, 1987,* s., (10-07-92, Zeller, #866), 5⅛ x 3⅞ in., (13 x 9.8 cm.), color offset (BP 557, DM 1380, FR 4681, Y 114,732).
$358* *"Fight AIDS Worldwide",* Limited Edition Lithograph 1990, #597/1000, very good cond., (02-07-93, Bakker, #56), image 10½ x 8 in., (26.7 x 20.3 cm.), color lithograph (BP 248, DM 594, FR 2007, Y 44,550).
$1582* *Figurative Composition, 1985,* s., d., num., thumb print blindstamp, margins, very good cond., (12-01-92, Christie-London, #581), P. 27⅜ x 19¹¹⁄₁₆ in., (695 x 500 mm.), drypoint and screenprint in colors on BFK Rives (BP 1045, DM 2522, FR 8593, Y 196,962).
BI *Flowers, 1990: Set Of Five,* s., d., #61/100, p. by Studio Heinrici, pub. Shafrazi editions, blindstamp, excell. cond., loose, est. BP 10/12,000, (06-30-93, Sotheby-London, #820, illus.), each sh c. 51⅛ x 39⅝ in., (129.9 x 100.6 cm.), color silkscreen.
$1093* *Focus On Aids I, 1987,* s., d. '88, i. Joel, pub. for Focus on Aids, margins, good cond.?, (05-19-93, Butterfield, #2178), 15¼ x 10¾ in., (387 x 273 mm.), silkscreen w/hand-coloring on silk (BP 710, DM 1777, FR 5986, Y 121,001).
BI *From Ludo, 1985,* s., d., num. 60/90, pub. Editions F.B., full margins, good cond., hinge remains, surface soiling, est. $1/1,500, (02-24-93, Butterfield, #3036, illus.), sheet 26 x 19⅛ in., (660 x 486 mm.), silkscreen in red & black on Arches.
$605* *Happy New Year,* s., d. '89, i. Patrick, (11-12-92, Freemn/Fine Art, #82A), 10 x 16 in., (25.4 x 40.6 cm.), lithograph (BP 397, DM 959, FR 3234, Y 75,015).
$1023* *Lithograph For 'International Volunteer Day', 1988,* s., d., #337/1000, good cond., (12-03-92, Sotheby-London, #696, illus.), 11¼ x 8½ in., (285 x 215 mm.), lithograph in colors on Arches rag (BP 660, DM 1609, FR 5491, Y 127,286).
$1364* *Ludo, 1985: Two,* two plates from the set of five, each s., d., #41/90 and #42/90, pub.Editions F.B., good cond., (12-03-92, Sotheby-London, #695), each sheet approx. 25¾ x 19 in., (655 x 482 mm.), lithograph in red and black on Arches (BP 880, DM 2145, FR 7322, Y 169,715).
$1501* *Montreux 1983- Jazz-Festival,* #56/80, s., d., (04-21-93, Germann, #47, illus.), 39³⁄₁₆ x 27⅜ in., (995 x 695 mm.), color lithograph (BP 974, DM 2399, FR 8114, Y 166,168, SF 2185).

$2092* *Montreux 1983. 17eme Festival De Jazz, 1983,* s., d., (c), (09-18-92, Schloss Ahlden, #1002, illus.), 39⁵⁄₁₆ x 27½ in., (99.9 x 69.9 cm.), color serigraph on heavy white paper (BP 1225, DM 3104, FR 10,619, Y 258,559).

$1198* *Montreux Jazz Festival, 1983,* #59/80, s., 1000 x 700mm, (09-04-92, Germann, #385), color serigraph (BP 600, DM 1679, FR 5716, Y 147,464, SF 1495).

$1412* *Montreux Jazz Festival, 1983,* AP XX/XX, s., d., 1000mm x 700mm, (10-14-92, Germann, #318, illus.), color serigraph (BP 829, DM 2066, FR 7007, Y 171,110, SF 1840).

BI *"New York Book Is Book Country",* s., good cond., est. $2/300, (07-19-92, Bakker, #186), 19¾ x 25 in., (50.2 x 63.5 cm.), color lithograph.

BI *Ohne Titel (Fliegender, Mensch Tragender Delphin), 1987,* s., d., est. DM 2,000, (11-20-92, Lempertz, #567), sh 29⁷⁄₁₆ x 35⅜ in., (74.8 x 89.8 cm.), serigraph on Velin.

BI *Safe Sex! 1987,* felt-tip pen s., tears, est. DM 800, (11-20-92, Lempertz, #566), 29½ x 27⅜ in., (75 x 69.5 cm.), offset print on in black and red on smooth offset paper.

$4025* *Silence Equals Death, 1989,* s., d., #150/200, blindstamp printer, pub. Outreach Fund for AIDS, full margins, very good cond.?, (05-19-93, Butterfield, #2179), 33 x 33 in., (838 x 838 mm.), silkscreen in colors on Moulin des Berger (BP 2613, DM 6543, FR 22,043, Y 445,588).

$1430* *Three Lithographs: Untitled (S. p. 134), 1985,* s., d., #5/80, pub. Edition Schellmann, full margins, very good cond.?, (10-28-92, Butterfield, #2971), sheet 32 x 40 in., (81.3 x 101.6 cm.), lithograph w/collotype in black and red (rosso) on BFK Rives (BP 911, DM 2208, FR 7499, Y 175,460).

BI *Untitled,* from Apocalypse suite, s., d. 88, est. $2,5/3,500, (06-13-93, Hindman, #354), 38 x 38 in., (96.5 x 96.5 cm.), silkscreen.

$1535* *Untitled, 1985,* s., d., #46/60, p. Matthieu, blindstamp, pub. Editions Schellmann, good cond., (12-03-92, Sotheby-London, #697, illus.), sheet 31¼ x 39 in., (795 x 990 mm.), lithograph w/collotype in black and red on BFK Rives (BP 990, DM 2414, FR 8239, Y 190,992).

$843* *Untitled, 1985,* s., 41/60, Edition Schellman, blindstamp, (12-04-92, AB Stockholm, #7062, illus.), 30⁵⁄₁₆ x 37¹³⁄₁₆ in., (77 x 96 cm.), lithograph and collotype in colors on BFK Rives (BP 541, DM 1343, FR 4554, Y 105,243, SK 5720).

$1330* *Untitled, 1985,* s., 41/60, Edition Schellman, (12-04-92, AB Stockholm, #7063), 30⁵⁄₁₆ x 37¹³⁄₁₆ in., (77 x 96 cm.), lithograph and collotype in colors on BFK Rives (BP 853, DM 2118, FR 7185, Y 166,042, SK 9020).

$2090* *Untitled, 1985,* s., d., num. 20/60, pub. Edition Schellmann, full margins, apparentlyvery good cond., (02-24-93, Butterfield, #3035, illus.), 30½ x 38 in., (775 x 965 mm.), lithograph & collotype in black & red on BFK Rives (BP 1457, DM 3393, FR 11,502, Y 245,248).

$1877* *Untitled, 1986,* i. A.P., s., d., num., (11-28-92, Schoppmann, #576), 25¹⁵⁄₁₆ x 19½ in., (66 x 49.5 cm.), color serigraph on handmade (BP 1239, DM 2990, FR 10,151, Y 233,603).

$1087* *Untitled, 1987,* s., d., #65/170, full margins, good cond., (05-27-93, Sotheby-Amstrdm, #620, illus.), 25³⁄₁₆ x 31⅜ in., (640 x 797 mm.), silkscreen on wove (BP 696, DM 1744, FR 5879, Y 116,531, G 1955).

$880* *Untitled, 1987,* s., d., annot. AI, blindstamp of pub. Sette Publishing Co., full margins, apparently very good cond., (02-24-93, Butterfield, #3038), 12¼ x 8¼ in., (311 x 210 mm.), silkscreen in colors on wove (BP 614, DM 1429, FR 4843, Y 103,262).

$1045* *Untitled, 1987,* s., d., annot. AI, blindstamp of pub. Sette Publishing Co., full margins, apparently good cond., (02-24-93, Butterfield, #3040, illus.), 8⅜ x 12½ in., (213 x 318 mm.), silkscreen in colors on wove (BP 729, DM 1696, FR 5751, Y 122,624).

$990* *Untitled, 1987,* s., d., num. 4/100, blindstamp on pub. Sette Publishing Co., full margins, apparently good cond., (02-24-93, Butterfield, #3037), 8½ x 12¼ in., (216 x 311 mm.), silkscreen in colors on wove (BP 690, DM 1607, FR 5449, Y 116,170).

$990* *Untitled, 1987,* s., d., num. 14/100, blindstamp of pub. Sette Publishing Co., full margins, apparently very good cond., (02-24-93, Butterfield, #3039), 8¼ x 12¼ in., (210 x 311 mm.), silkscreen in colors on wove (BP 690, DM 1607, FR 5449, Y 116,170).

HARING, Keith and Andy WARHOL

$632* *Plakat. 20th Montreux Jazz July 3rd-19th, 1986,* s., d., (06-24-93, Germann, #372, illus.), 38⁹⁄₁₆ x 27⅜ in., (980 x 695 mm.), color serigraph (BP 416, DM 1025, FR 3454, Y 67,797, SF 920).

HARLOW, George Henry (after)

$75* *Congratulations,* by J. Thomson, (06-16-93, Bonhams-Chelsea, #484), image 9½ x 7½ in., (24.1 x 19.1 cm.), stipple engraving w/hand-coloring (BP 50, DM 125, FR 418, Y 7999).

HARLOW, Louis K. American 1850-1930

BI *Pigrims Arriving On Shore And Advertising "Holiday Publications",* Louis Prang, mounted to stiff sh., right corner lacking, est. $100/150, (04-29-93, Swann, #320), 21 x 15½ in., (53.3 x 39.4 cm.), color lithograph poster.

HARNEST, Fritz b. 1905

BI *"Acht Holzschnitte", 1959: Eight,* pub. Galerie Otto Stangl, linen case, s., est. DM 1400, (12-01-92, Karl/Faber, #693), 18⁵⁄₁₆ x 12¹³⁄₁₆ in., (46.5 x 32.5 cm.), color woodcut on hand-made Japan.

HARPER'S WEEKLY

$154* *"The Battle Of New Orleans, Fought January 8, 1815",* pub. January 12, 1861 as page 20, (12-05-92, Neal, #560), image 7 x 14 in., (17.8 x 35.6 cm.), wood engraving (BP 96, DM 240, FR 818, Y 19,081).

HARPIGNIES, Henri French 1819-1916

$227* *"Dessous De Foret" and "Charrette Devant Une Ferme" (H. Beraldi, 23,33), 1850: Two,* reddish stains, good margins, (04-02-93, Picard, #128), one 4¹⁵⁄₁₆ x 8¹⁄₁₆ in., (12.5 x 20.5 cm.), other 3⅛ x 4⁵⁄₁₆ in., (12.5 x 20.5 cm.), etchings (BP 150, DM 365, FR 1239, Y 25,845).

HARRIS, J. (after C.C. HENDERSON)

$487* *Going To The Moors, 1847,* plate 1 from Fore's Sporting Traps, staining, paper loss, foxing, (10-27-92, Phillips-London, #93), (445 x 667 mm.), aquatint w/hand-coloring on wove (BP 308, DM 746, FR 2533, Y 59,572).

HARRIS, J. and C. QUENTERY (after Harry HALL)

$383* *Rataplan,* foxing, (10-27-92, Phillips-London, #100), plate 23 x 29⅞ in., (584 x 759 mm.), aquatint w/hand-coloring, touches of gum arabic; laid on board (BP 242, DM 587, FR 1992, Y 46,850).

HARRIS, J. and W. SUMMERS

$440* *"Fores's National Sports, Racing Plate 4, Returning To Weight",* after J.F. Herring, Sr., (02-17-93, Doyle, #40), 24½ x 44½ in., (62.2 x 113 cm.), hand colored engraving (BP 304, DM 715, FR 2420, Y 52,556).

HARRIS, Lawren Stewart Canadian 1885-1970

$369* *In The Ward,* s., (05-18-93, Joyner, #283), 5½ x 7 in., (14 x 17.8 cm.), print (BP 240, DM 599, FR 2022, Y 41,123, C$ 468).

HARRIS, Mildred F.

$28* *Mermaid Inn, Rye, 1925,* s., d., t., (02-14-93, Neal, #1144), image 10 x 7 in., (25.4 x 17.8 cm.), etching (BP 20, DM 46, FR 157, Y 3377).

HARRIS & EWING

$192* *Coolidge, Calvin,* s., i., (09-17-92, Swann, #72), image 9 x 6 in., (22.9 x 15.2 cm.), photograph (BP 108, DM 285, FR 976, Y 23,904).

HARRISON, John Cyril

$140 *"Black Game In The Birches",* s., #247/350, (12-11-92, G.A. Key, #50), 12 x 17 in., (30.5 x 43.2 cm.), colored print (BP 90, DM 221, FR 756, Y 17,325).

$76 *"First Drive",* s., #242/500, faded, (04-16-93, G.A. Key, #58), 14 x 17 in., (35.6 x 43.2 cm.), colored print (BP 50, DM 123, FR 415, Y 8546).

$182 *Partridge In Flight Over Corn Fields,* s., #78/500, (08-14-92, G.A. Key, #111, illus.), 12 x 17 in., (30.5 x 43.2 cm.), colored print (BP 95, DM 267, FR 904, Y 22,951).

HARRISON, John Cyril (after)

$185 *"Blackcock Beneath The Cairngorns"*, s., #477/500, (10-09-92, G.A. Key, #150), 11¾ x 18 in., (29.8 x 45.7 cm.), colored print (BP 110, DM 276, FR 934, Y 22,561).

$185 *"First Fall Of Snow"*, s., #355/500, (10-09-92, G.A. Key, #151), 13 x 17¾ in., (33 x 45.1 cm.), colored print (BP 110, DM 276, FR 934, Y 22,561).

HARRISON, Ted

$243* *"Ducks"*, (19)83, #72/50, s., t., num., (03-10-93, Maynard, #316), image 14 x 9½ in., (35.6 x 24.1 cm.), serigraph (BP 170, DM 404, FR 1373, Y 28,710, C$ 303).

$199* *"Ravens"*, (19)83, #12/50, s., t., num., (03-10-93, Maynard, #315), image 9½ x 14 in., (24.1 x 35.6 cm.), serigraph (BP 139, DM 331, FR 1124, Y 23,511, C$ 248).

HARRISON, Ted   b. 1926

$251* *Ball Game*, #110/200, s., t., d. '91, (11-16-92, Hodgins, #310, illus.), 16¼ x 24¼ in., (41.3 x 61.6 cm.), serigraph on paper (BP 165, DM 400, FR 1349, Y 31,324, C$ 319).

$282* *Horses, 1990*, #132/180, s., t., d. 1990, prov., (05-10-93, Hodgins, #204, illus.), (41.3 x 61.6 cm.), serigraph on paper (BP 184, DM 453, FR 1528, Y 31,512, C$ 358).

HART, Pop   American 1868-1933

$55* *Cock Fight*, s., (09-24-92, Mystic, #25), 12 x 16 in., (30.5 x 40.6 cm.), lithograph (BP 32, DM 82, FR 277, Y 6616).

HART, Pro (Kevin CHARLES)   b. 1928

$81* *Cook At Whitby*, s. Pro Hart, i., d. '70, #94/100, lit., (08-11-92, L. Joel, #153G), 16⅛ x 18⅛ in., (41 x 46 cm.), color lithograph (BP 42, DM 119, FR 403, Y 10,373, A$ 110).

BI *Cook Loading Stores*, s. Pro Hart, i., d. '70, #98/100, lit., est. $1/200, (08-11-92, L. Joel, #143G), 17½ x 17¹⁵/₁₆ in., (44.5 x 45.5 cm.), color lithograph.

$81* *Death Of Cook*, s. Pro Hart, i., d. '70, #99/100, lit., (08-11-92, L. Joel, #103G), 20½ x 27¾ in., (52 x 70.5 cm.), color lithograph (BP 42, DM 119, FR 403, Y 10,373, A$ 110).

$81* *The Endeavour At Whitby*, s. Pro Hart, i., #97/100, lit., (08-11-92, L. Joel, #166G), 18⅛ x 24 in., (46 x 61 cm.), color lithograph (BP 42, DM 119, FR 403, Y 10,373, A$ 110).

$130* *The Landing*, s. Pro Hart, i., d. '70, #88/100, lit., (08-11-92, L. Joel, #93G), 25⁹/₁₆ x 27¾ in., (65 x 70.5 cm.), color lithograph (BP 68, DM 191, FR 646, Y 16,647, A$ 176).

HARTIGAN, Grace   American b. 1922

$1320* *Pastoral*, s. ink, d. 1953, t., num. 25, prov., (09-20-92, Hindman, #730), 7 x 10 in., (17.8 x 25.4 cm.), color serigraph (BP 773, DM 1959, FR 6701, Y 163,144).

HARTING, G.W.

$1760* *The Open Air Store, c. 1925,* double mounted, s. by photog., s., t., i. w/studio address & list of 1-man shows in 1925 by photog. w/exhib. labels, (10-15-92, Sotheby-NY, #129, illus.), 9⅜ x 7¼ in., (23.8 x 18.4 cm.), photograph, toned silver print (BP 1077, DM 2620, FR 8884, Y 211,158).

HARTLEY, Marsden   American 1877-1943

$1760* *Mountain Landscape*, ink s., margins, good cond., ink residue, creases, (10-28-92, Butterfield, #2525, illus.), 11¾ x 9¾ in., (298 x 248 mm.), color monotype on Japan paper (BP 1121, DM 2718, FR 9229, Y 215,951).

HARTLY, Alfred

$33* *The Town Of Cornwall*, s., (09-18-92, DuMouchelle, #244), etching (BP 19, DM 49, FR 169, Y 4112).

HARTSOOK

$241* *Mary Pickford, Head And Shoulders*, autograph, (10-10-92, Bonhams, #81, illus.), 9½ x 7½ in., (24.1 x 19.1 cm.), photograph (BP 143, DM 358, FR 1202, Y 29,340).

$297* *Mary Pickford, Profile Portrait*, autograph, (10-10-92, Bonhams, #83, illus.), 9½ x 7½ in., (24.1 x 19.1 cm.), photograph (BP 176, DM 441, FR 1481, Y 36,158).

BI *Mary Pickford, Standing*, autograph, est. BP 2/300, (10-10-92, Bonhams, #82, illus.), 9½ x 7½ in., (24.1 x 19.1 cm.), photograph.

HARTUNG, Hans   German 1904-1989

BI *Abstrakte Komposition, 1973,* i. E.A., s., est. DM 2,400, (11-28-92, Schoppmann, #577), 22¹³/₁₆ x 30¹¹/₁₆ in., (58 x 78 cm.), color lithograph on wove.

$233* *Affiche Pour Les Jeux Olympiques De Munich 1972*, #133/200, s. Hartung, (07-14-92, Encans, #216), 39¹⁵/₁₆ x 25 in., (101.5 x 63.5 cm.), lithograph in color (BP 121, DM 346, FR 1166, Y 29,136, C$ 278).

BI *Barcelona 10, 1971,* s., num., est. DM 1500, (12-01-92, Karl/Faber, #700), 19⁵/₁₆ x 29½ in., (49 x 75 cm.), lithograph on wove.

$550* *Black Horizontals,* s., #30/75, blindstamp pub. Atelier Lacouriere, full margins, good cond., surface soiling, creases, tape remains, skinned areas, (10-28-92, Butterfield, #2652), 15 x 20⅜ in., (381 x 518 mm.), etching on Arches (BP 350, DM 849, FR 2884, Y 67,485).

$379* *Composition,* s. Hartung, 168/200, est. DK 1,800, (09-30-92, Kunsthallen, #116), color lithograph (BP 214, DM 537, FR 1818, Y 45,482, DK 2070).

$411* *Composition,* s., annot., good margins, (05-06-93, Laurin, #40), color lithograph (BP 260, DM 647, FR 2179, Y 45,219).

BI *Composition I , 1970,* s., HC, num., wrinkles, est. DM 1500, (12-01-92, Karl/Faber, #699), 18⅞ x 13⅜ in., (48 x 34 cm.), lithograph on wove.

$280* *"Composition Pour XXeme Siecle"*, outside regular edit., s. Hartung, (05-18-93, Encans, #193), 15⅜ x 10⅝ in., (39 x 27 cm.), color lithograph (BP 182, DM 454, FR 1534, Y 31,205, C$ 355).

$304* *Composition, 1970,* large margins, s., #6/75, (05-27-93, Briest, #106), 23⁷/₁₆ x 34¹/₁₆ in., (59.5 x 86.5 cm.), lithograph (BP 195, DM 488, FR 1644, Y 32,590).

BI *Compositions: Two,* s., epreuve d'artiste, #38/75, restorations, est. FF 2,5/3,000, (11-16-92, Briest, #309), 41⁵/₁₆ x 29¾ in., (105 x 75.5 cm.), lithograph in black.

$686* *"Farandole 11", c. 1975,* s., num., (11-28-92, Grisebach, #529, illus.), 19½ x 29¼ in., (49.6 x 74.3 cm.), lithograph on think copper print paper (BP 453, DM 1093, FR 3710, Y 85,376).

$938* *"Farandole 15", c. 1975,* s., num., (11-28-92, Grisebach, #530, illus.), 19⁷/₁₆ x 29⁷/₁₆ in., (49.3 x 74.7 cm.), lithograph on thick copper print paper (BP 619, DM 1494, FR 5073, Y 116,739).

BI *Farandole: Fifteen,* num. HC, s., t. HC, frontispiece s., ded., est. DM 9,000, (11-20-92, Lempertz, #573), 19⁹/₁₆ x 15¼ in., (49.7 x 38.7 cm.), lithograph on Velin.

$168* *"Hommage A Messian"*, #41/120, s., (01-28-93, Pescheteau, #155), 14¹⁵/₁₆ x 13⅜ in., (38 x 34 cm.), etching and aquatint on yellow background wove (BP 111, DM 266, FR 901, Y 20,859).

BI *IV, 1972,* #3/75, pencil s., est. DM 1,200, (11-20-92, Lempertz, #571), 18½ x 27⅜ in., (47 x 69.5 cm.), lithograph on Velin.

$332* *Komposition,* after 1965, s., num., (12-05-92, Bassenge, #7223), 14 x 9⅞ in., (35.6 x 25.1 cm.), lithograph on Arches (BP 208, DM 518, FR 1764, Y 41,135).

$664* *Komposition,* s., num., Erker Presse St. Gallen, (12-01-92, Karl/Faber, #701), 31½ x 19¹¹/₁₆ in., (80 x 50 cm.), lithograph on BFK Rives wove (BP 439, DM 1058, FR 3607, Y 82,669).

$1577* *Komposition "L 19" (Schm. L 19), 1957,* s., EA, (12-01-92, Karl/Faber, #696), 19¹¹/₁₆ x 12¹⁵/₁₆ in., (50 x 33 cm.), color lithograph on BFK Rives wove (BP 1042, DM 2514, FR 8566, Y 196,340).

$747* *Komposition "L 36" (Schm. L. 36), 1957,* s., num., traces of mounting, (12-01-92, Karl/Faber, #697), 19½ x 12⅜ in., (49.5 x 31.5 cm.), color lithograph on wove (BP 494, DM 1191, FR 4058, Y 93,003).

$664* *Komposition "L 36" (Schmucking L 36), 1957,* s., num., (12-05-92, Bassenge, #7221), 19¹¹/₁₆ x 12⅜ in., (50 x 31.5 cm.), lithograph on copper print paper (BP 416, DM 1035, FR 3528, Y 82,270).

$705* *Komposition (Schmucking L 10), 1957,* s., num., (05-26-93, Dorling, #2703, illus.), 20¹¹/₁₆ x 12⅝ in., (52.6 x 32 cm.), color lithograph on BFK Rives (BP 456, DM 1150, FR 3871, Y 76,597).

$996* *Komposition 05 (Schmucking R 05), 1947/48,* s., d., stained, (12-01-92, Karl/Faber, #695), 6⅛ x 4½ in., (15.5 x 11.5 cm.), etching on wove (BP 658, DM 1588, FR 5410, Y 124,004).

$891* *Komposition 10, 1953,* epreuve d'artiste, s., blindstamp, (10-09-92, Winterberg, #2299), 15¹⁄₁₆ x 21⅞ in., (38.3 x 55.5 cm.), drypoint on Arches (BP 529, DM 1324, FR 4444, Y 108,473).

$498* *Komposition L 96 (Schm. L 96), 1963,* s., crease, (12-01-92, Karl/Faber, #698), 27³⁄₁₆ x 18⅞ in., (69 x 48 cm.), lithograph on smooth thin paper (BP 329, DM 794, FR 2705, Y 62,002).

$363* *Komposition L-19-1976,* H.C., s., d., (04-21-93, Germann, #508), 22¹⁄₁₆ x 17¹⁵⁄₁₆ in., (560 x 455 mm.), lithograph (BP 236, DM 580, FR 1962, Y 40,186, SF 529).

BI *Komposition Mit Gelb, 1974,* H.C., s., est. SF 1,3/1,600, 750mm x 1050mm, (10-14-92, Germann, #321, illus.), color lithograph.

BI *Komposition Mit Rotbraun, 1974,* 2/75, s., est. SF 1,3/1,600, 750mm x 1050mm, (10-14-92, Germann, #322), color lithograph.

$1761* *Komposition R1 (Schmucking S.30), 1953,* #4/75, s., (04-24-93, Kunsthaus, #586), 15⁹⁄₁₆ x 20¹³⁄₁₆ in., (39.6 x 52.8 cm.), color lithograph on copper on hand-made Arches (BP 1111, DM 2760, FR 9322, Y 194,328).

$493* *Komposition, 1966,* s., num., Jubilaumsmappe "B" der Kerstner-Gesellschaft, (05-26-93, Dorling, #2704, illus.), 14⅜ x 9¹⁵⁄₁₆ in., (36.5 x 25.2 cm.), lithograph on vollrandigem handmade (BP 319, DM 804, FR 2707, Y 53,564).

$425* *Komposition, 1966,* s., artist proof, (06-08-93, Karl/Faber, #824), approx. 15⅜ x 21⅝ in., (39 x 55 cm.), lithograph (BP 279, DM 690, FR 2322, Y 45,141).

$363* *Komposition, 1973,* s., (06-24-93, Germann, #379), 30⅛ x 21⅞ in., (765 x 555 mm.), woodcut (BP 239, DM 589, FR 1984, Y 38,940, SF 529).

BI *Komposition, Nach 1965,* s., num., est. DM 1,200, (12-05-92, Bassenge, #7222), lithograph on handmade BFK Rives.

$435* *L 33 (Schmucking 96), 1957,* 8/100, s., (06-24-93, Germann, #376), 25¹¹⁄₁₆ x 19¹¹⁄₁₆ in., (653 x 500 mm.), lithograph in 2 colors (BP 286, DM 705, FR 2377, Y 46,664, SF 633).

$453* *Ohne Titel,* H.C., s., 1050mm x 750mm, (10-14-92, Germann, #320), lithograph (BP 266, DM 663, FR 2248, Y 54,896, SF 590).

$721* *Ohne Titel,* #80/209, pencil s., stamped, (11-20-92, Lempertz, #570), sh 21¾ x 29¹³⁄₁₆ in., (55.3 x 75.7 cm.), color lithograph on BFK Rives Velin (BP 475, DM 1150, FR 3872, Y 89,665).

BI *R 15 (Schmucking S. 44), 1953,* #239/250, pencil s., est. DM 1,100, (11-20-92, Lempertz, #569), sh 25³⁄₁₆ x 19³⁄₁₆ in., (64 x 48.8 cm.), etching on Arches Velin.

BI *"R 20" (Schmucking 20), 1953,* s., i. artist's proof, est. DM 1,000, (06-12-93, Hauswedell/Nolt, #112), 20¼ x 14⅞ in., (51.5 x 37.8 cm.), etching on Arches.

$1201* *"R 3" (Schmucking R 3), 1953,* s., (06-12-93, Hauswedell/Nolt, #111, illus.), 3⅞ x 11 in., (9.8 x 28 cm.), color etching on copper print (BP 786, DM 1955, FR 6570, Y 126,381).

$356* *Radibutz,* s., blindstamp, (04-21-93, Germann, #509), 22¹⁄₁₆ x 29¹⁵⁄₁₆ in., (560 x 760 mm.), lithograph (BP 231, DM 569, FR 1924, Y 39,411, SF 518).

$232* *Sans Titre,* s., 16/100, (06-28-93, Loudmer, #259), 18⅞ x 10⅝ in., (480 x 270 mm.), sh 25¹³⁄₁₆ x 19¹³⁄₁₆ in., (480 x 270 mm.), color lithograph on BFK Rives wove (BP 155, DM 394, FR 1328, Y 24,615).

$430* *Untitled,* s., #5/75, (05-27-93, Lempertz, #771), 15⁹⁄₁₆ x 20¹⁄₁₆ in., (39.5 x 51 cm.), etching on wove (BP 275, DM 690, FR 2326, Y 46,098).

BI *Untitled,* s., full margins, good cond., minor handling creases, minor defects in edges of sheet, est. Dfl. 800/1,200, (05-27-93, Sotheby-Amstrdm, #621, illus.), sh 30¹⁄₁₆ x 41⁷⁄₁₆ in., (76.3 x 105.3 cm.), lithograph on wove.

BI *Untitled,* s., #14/75, full margins, good cond., minor handling creases, est. Dfl. 800/1,200, (05-27-93, Sotheby-Amstrdm, #623), 25 x 28⁷⁄₁₆ in., (635 x 723 mm.), lithograph on BFK Rives.

BI *Untitled,* s., i. E.A., full margins, good cond., minor handling creases, est. Dfl. 800/1,200, (05-27-93, Sotheby-Amstrdm, #624), 21⁹⁄₁₆ x 31⅞ in., (547 x 810 mm.), lithograph on BFK Rives.

BI *Untitled,* s., #34/75, full margins, good cond., minor handling creases, est. Dfl. 800/1,200, (05-27-93, Sotheby-Amstrdm, #622, illus.), sh 29¹⁵⁄₁₆ x 41⁹⁄₁₆ in., (76 x 105.5 cm.), lithograph on BFK Rives.

BI *Untitled,* s., #12/75, full margins, good cond., minor handling creases, est. Dfl. 800/1,200, (05-27-93, Sotheby-Amstrdm, #626), 31¹¹⁄₁₆ x 23⅝ in., (805 x 600 mm.), lithograph on BFK Rives.

$300* *Untitled,* illus., #52/75, faults, (04-04-93, Pescheteau, #222), 23¼ x 33⅞ in., (59 x 86 cm.), color serigraph (BP 198, DM 482, FR 1638, Y 34,157).

$543* *Untitled, 1989,* mono., (09-25-92, Granier, #2875), sheet 19⅜ x 13⁹⁄₁₆ in., (49.2 x 34.5 cm.), etching on thick hand-made (BP 317, DM 805, FR 2722, Y 65,540).

BI *VI, 1972,* #3/75, pencil s., est. DM 1,200, (11-20-92, Lempertz, #572), 18½ x 28⅜ in., (47 x 72 cm.), lithograph on Velin.

HARTUNG, Karl 1908-1967

BI *Ohne Titel,* #25/25, ballpoint pen s., est. DM 1,000, (11-20-92, Lempertz, #575), sh 13⅞ x 19¹³⁄₁₆ in., (35.2 x 50.3 cm.), serigraph in color on thick Velin.

$86* *Phantastisches Gerippe, 1946,* s., d., (09-25-92, Granier, #2876), sheet 11¼ x 12¼ in., (28.6 x 31.1 cm.), lithograph on drawing board (BP 50, DM 127, FR 431, Y 10,380).

HARTUNG, Wilhelm 1879-1957

BI *XXII Fete Federale De Chant, Neuchatel, 1912,* fold marks, creasing, est. BP 6/800, (02-04-93, Christie-S. Ken, #49, illus.), 47 x 31 in., (119.4 x 78.7 cm.), color lithograph.

HARUNOBU, Suzuki Japanese 1724-1770

BI *From The Series "Ehon Haru No Nishiki",* est. SC 8/10,000, (04-27-93, Dorotheum, #223, illus.), 10¼ x 6¹¹⁄₁₆ in., (26 x 17 cm.), woodcut.

BI *Portrait Of A Young Beauty With A Book,* format Chuban, signs of wear, est. SC 10/12,000, (04-27-93, Dorotheum, #172, illus.), 6⅛ x 8⅞ in., (15.5 x 22.5 cm.), color woodcut.

BI *Portrait Of A Young Girl As Sambaso Dancer,* format Chuban, est. SC 6/8,000, (04-27-93, Dorotheum, #147, illus.), 7⅛ x 9¹⁵⁄₁₆ in., (18.1 x 25.2 cm.), .

BI *Portrait Of Two Young Girls With A Boy,* format Chuban, signs of wear, est. SC 6/7,000, (04-27-93, Dorotheum, #173, illus.), 8¼ x 11⅝ in., (21 x 29.5 cm.), color woodcut.

BI *Women In The Moonlight,* signs of wear, format Chuban, est. SC 6/7,000, (04-27-93, Dorotheum, #153, illus.), 8¹⁄₁₆ x 11 in., (20.5 x 28 cm.), color woodcut.

BI *"Zwei Madchen Beim Schreinbesuch",* format Chuban, est. SC 5/6,000, (04-27-93, Dorotheum, #154, illus.), 8⁵⁄₁₆ x 11¼ in., (21.1 x 28.5 cm.), color woodcut.

HARUNOBU and KORYUSAI (attrib.)

$11,428* *Shunga Prints,* chuban yoko-e, faded, laid-down, (06-10-93, Sotheby-London, #222, illus.), approx. 7⅜ x 9¹³⁄₁₆ in., (18.7 x 25 cm.), (BP 7475, DM 18,609, FR 62,654, Y 1,213,035).

HARVEY, Harold Leroy American 1899-1971

$247* *Portrait Of Ruth St. Denis,* notations, 1930's, (10-14-92, Swann, #430, illus.), 4¾ x 3¾ in., (12.1 x 9.5 cm.), photograph, silver print (BP 145, DM 361, FR 1226, Y 29,932).

BI *Abstraction, 1932,* credit by photog., i. in unidentified hand, w/partial reprod. limit.stamp, est. $1,2/1,800, (10-15-92, Sotheby-NY, #133, illus.), 11¾ x 8⅞ in., (29.8 x 22.5 cm.), photograph, gelatin silver print.

BI *Flame, 1932,* photog.'s sig., notations, est. $800/1,200, (04-07-93, Swann, #481, illus.), 9 x 6⅝ in., photograph, silver print.

BI *Industrial Still Life,* 1930's, est. $8/1,200, (10-14-92, Swann, #471, illus.), 7¾ x 9⅝ in., (19.7 x 24.4 cm.), photograph, toned silver prints.

BI *Photo Collage (Woman And Bridge),* partially hand-colored, 1930's, est. $1/1,500, (10-14-92, Swann, #472, illus.), 13⅛ x 10 in., (33.3 x 25.4 cm.), photograph, silver print.

$1650* *Photogram,* matted 1924, from photog.'s estate, (10-15-92, Sotheby-NY, #132, illus.), 9⅝ x 7⅞ in., (24.4 x 20 cm.), photograph, toned gelatin silver print heightened w/ gouache (BP 1010, DM 2456, FR 8329, Y 197,960).

$715* *Photomontage (Man On Stairs),* 1930's, (10-14-92, Swann, #473, illus.), 9½ x 7½ in., (24.1 x 19.1 cm.), photograph, toned silver print (BP 420, DM 1046, FR 3548, Y 86,646).

$495* *Photomontage (Man On Stairs), c. 1932,* notations, (04-07-93, Swann, #482, illus.), 14 x 11 in., photograph, toned silver print (BP 327, DM 801, FR 2709, Y 56,237).

$495* *Photomontage (Woman And Machine),* notations, 1930's, (10-14-92, Swann, #474, illus.), 14 x 10⅞ in., (35.6 x 27.6 cm.), photograph, toned silver print (BP 291, DM 724, FR 2457, Y 59,985).

BI *Portrait Of A Woman, c. 1930,* prov., est. $2/2,500, (10-13-92, Christie-NY, #224, illus.), 13 x 10¼ in., (33 x 26 cm.), photograph, toned gelatin silver photocollage.

BI *Rooftops, early 1930's,* Harold Harvey Estate, est. $2/3,000, (04-06-93, Sotheby-NY, #141, illus.), 12½ x 8¼ in., photograph.

BI *Ruth In Uranium, c. 1935,* s., t., est. $1,2/1,800, (04-08-93, Christie-NY, #294, illus.), 12¾ x 8⅞ in., (32.4 x 22.5 cm.), photograph, toned gelatin silver print.

$633* *"Silhouette", "Portrait Of A Woman" and "The Dancer", 1917: Three,* s., d., annot., first and third t., attrib., (05-23-93, Butterfield, #3443, illus.), each approx. 9 x 7 in., photograph, gelatin silver print on wove textured paper (BP 412, DM 1035, FR 3484, Y 69,968).

BI *Study Of A Rose, early 1930's,* Harold Harvey Estate, est. $1,5/2,500, (04-06-93, Sotheby-NY, #140, illus.), 9⅛ x 8⅜ in., photograph, toned silver print on multiple-mount.

BI *Today And Yesterday, N.Y., 1936,* s., t., d., est. $1,5/2,000, (10-13-92, Christie-NY, #225, illus.), 13¼ x 9⅝ in., (33.7 x 24.4 cm.), photograph, blue-toned gelatin silver print.

HASEGAWA, Kiyoshi 1891-1980

$1449* *Avions (C.R. 259), c. 1929,* stamped sig., full margins, good cond. within subject, foxing, (12-03-92, Sotheby-London, #340), 6⅞ x 10¼ in., (175 x 260 mm.), drypoint on wove (BP 935, DM 2279, FR 7778, Y 180,291).

$2046* *Baigneuse Assise (C.R. 214), 1926,* stamped sig., full margins, good cond. within subject, handling creases, (12-03-92, Sotheby-London, #328, illus.), 11½ x 8½ in., (292 x 216 mm.), drypoint on wove (BP 1320, DM 3217, FR 10,982, Y 254,573).

$3069* *Baigneuse Couchee (C.R. 374), c. 1940,* s., i. epreuve d'etat, full margins, good cond., handling creases, (12-03-92, Sotheby-London, #341, illus.), 8 x 11 in., (203 x 279 mm.), engraving on wove (BP 1980, DM 4826, FR 16,473, Y 381,859).

$6864* *Femme Au Poisson, 1969,* artist's proof, s., d., ded., artist's drystamp, (06-28-93, Loudmer, #261), 5⅞ x 3⅛ in., (150 x 80 mm.), sh 12⅝ x 9$^{13}/_{16}$ in., (150 x 80 mm.), black copper engraving on wove (BP 4596, DM 11,664, FR 39,290, Y 728,276).

$1620* *Fleurs (C.R. 212), c. 1925,* stamped sig., full margins, good cond. within subject, handling creases, (12-03-92, Sotheby-London, #331, illus.), 10¼ x 8 in., (260 x 203 mm.), drypoint on wove (BP 1045, DM 2548, FR 8696, Y 201,568).

$1449* *Fruits (C.R. 330), c. 1930,* stamped sig., full margins, good cond. within subject, foxing, (12-03-92, Sotheby-London, #327, illus.), 7½ x 9½ in., (191 x 241 mm.), drypoint on wove (BP 935, DM 2279, FR 7778, Y 180,291).

$2558* *Graminees Dans Un Vase En Opaline (C.R. 453), 1968,* stamped sig., full margins, good cond., (12-03-92, Sotheby-London, #343, illus.), 13¼ x 10½ in., (337 x 267 mm.), mezzotint on wove (BP 1650, DM 4023, FR 13,731, Y 318,278).

$1790* *Herbes Dans Un Verre (C.R. 356), 1940,* stamped sig., full margins, good cond. within subject, handling creases, (12-03-92, Sotheby-London, #329, illus.), 10½ x 8¼ in., (267 x 210 mm.), drypoint on wove (BP 1155, DM 2815, FR 9608, Y 222,720).

$1449* *Jeunesse (C.R. 375), c. 1940,* stamped sig., full margins, good cond., handling creases, (12-03-92, Sotheby-London, #335, illus.), 9⅝ x 7⅜ in., (244 x 187 mm.), engraving on wove (BP 935, DM 2279, FR 7778, Y 180,291).

$1876* *Nature Morte (C.R. 448), 1966,* stamped sig., full margins, good cond., handling marks, foxing, (12-03-92, Sotheby-London, #342, illus.), 13¼ x 10½ in., (337 x 267 mm.), mezzotint on wove (BP 1210, DM 2950, FR 10,070, Y 233,420).

$2728* *Nature Morte A La Poupee (C.R. 415), 1960,* stamped sig., full margins, good cond. within subject, handling creases, (12-03-92, Sotheby-London, #336, illus.), 10¼ x 14⅛ in., (260 x 359 mm.), mezzotint on wove (BP 1760, DM 4290, FR 14,643, Y 339,430).

$3581* *Oiseau Apprivoise, Fleurs Et Graines (C.R. 424), 1962,* stamped sig., full margins, good cond., (12-03-92, Sotheby-London, #337, illus.), 10¼ x 14⅛ in., (260 x 359 mm.), mezzotint on wove (BP 2310, DM 5631, FR 19,222, Y 445,564).

$3240* *Oiseau Et Papilons (C.R. 421), 1961,* stamped sig., full margins, good cond., (12-03-92, Sotheby-London, #338, illus.), 13⅞ x 10½ in., (352 x 267 mm.), mezzotint on wove (BP 2090, DM 5095, FR 17,391, Y 403,135).

$3240* *Oiseau Sur Une Fleur De Lumiere (C.R. 445), c. 1962,* s., #36/40, full margins, good cond., (12-03-92, Sotheby-London, #339, illus.), 4 x 5½ in., (102 x 140 mm.), mezzotint on wove (BP 2090, DM 5095, FR 17,391, Y 403,135).

BI *Paysage De Banlieue (Meudon) (C.R. 242), 1929,* stamped sig., full margins, good cond. within subject, handling creases, est. BP 8/1,000, (12-03-92, Sotheby-London, #333, illus.), 8½ x 11¼ in., (216 x 286 mm.), drypoint on wove.

BI *Pensee Et Muguet Dans Un Petit Verre (C.R. 366), c. 1940,* stamped sig., full margins, good cond. within subject, creases, est.BP 6/800, (12-03-92, Sotheby-London, #334, illus.), 9½ x 7⅜ in., (241 x 187 mm.), engraving on wove.

$2473* *Petit Aquarium (C.R. 240), 1929,* s., t., #16/50, full margins, good cond. within subject, handling creases, (12-03-92, Sotheby-London, #330, illus.), 10½ x 11 in., (267 x 279 mm.), drypoint on wove (BP 1595, DM 3889, FR 13,274, Y 307,702).

$1620* *Pigeon (C.R. 174), c. 1920,* stamped sig., full margins, good cond. within subject, creases, (12-03-92, Sotheby-London, #324, illus.), 5⅝ x 4⅞ in., (143 x 124 mm.), drypoint on wove (BP 1045, DM 2548, FR 8696, Y 201,568).

BI *Planete (C.R. 189), 1925,* stamped sig., full margins, good cond. within subject, handling creases, est. BP 5/700, (12-03-92, Sotheby-London, #322, illus.), 4¾ x 3½ in., (121 x 89 mm.), drypoint on wove.

$1535* *Pommes Et Raisins (C.R. 269), 1931,* stamped sig., full margins, good cond. within subject, foxing, handling creases, (12-03-92, Sotheby-London, #326, illus.), (165 x 279 mm.), drypoint on wove (BP 990, DM 2414, FR 8239, Y 190,992).

$938* *Profil Avec Poisson (C.R. 161), c. 1920,* stamped sig., full margins, good cond. within subject, creases, (12-03-92, Sotheby-London, #321, illus.), 5¼ x 4½ in., (133 x 114 mm.), drypoint on wove (BP 605, DM 1475, FR 5035, Y 116,710).

$3707* *Renard Et Raisins (Fables De La Fontaine), 1963,* s., 59/80, blindstamp kiyoshi Hasegawa, (05-12-93, AB Stockholm, #7024, illus.), 14⅛ x 10$^{9}/_{16}$ in., (35.8 x 26.8 cm.), mezzotint on Rives (BP 2421, DM 5981, FR 20,147, Y 413,866, SK 27,500).

$1023* *Souvenir (C.R. 176), 1925,* stamped sig., full margins, good cond. within subject, crease, defects, (12-03-92, Sotheby-London, #323, illus.), 5⅜ x 3⅛ in., (137 x 79 mm.), drypoint on wove (BP 660, DM 1609, FR 5491, Y 127,286).

BI *Tete Penchee (Catalogue Raisonne 171), c. 1920,* stamped sig., full margins, good cond. within subject, creases, tapestain, est. BP 6/800, (12-03-92, Sotheby-London, #320, illus.), 8 x 5¾ in., (203 x 146 mm.), drypoint on wove.

$2046* *Vieux Moulin, Le Cannet (C.R. 252), 1929,* stamped sig., full margins, good cond. within subject, slight foxing, (12-03-92, Sotheby-London, #332, illus.), 7¾ x 10¼ in., (197 x 260 mm.), mezzotint on wove (BP 1320, DM 3217, FR 10,982, Y 254,573).

$2132* *Village De Voix (C.R. 235), c. 1926,* stamped sig., full margins, good cond. within subject, crease, (12-03-92, Sotheby-London, #325, illus.), 7¾ x 11 in., (197 x 279 mm.), mezzotint on wove (BP 1375, DM 3353, FR 11,444, Y 265,273).

HASEGAWA, Shoichi Japanese b. 1929

BI *Soleil Couchant,* s., t., d. 1976, est. $125/175, (10-30-92, Sloan, #962), 19½ x 23½ in., (49.5 x 59.7 cm.), color intaglio.

BI *Soleil Couchant,* s., t., d. 1976, est. $250/350, (09-17-92, Sloan, #2359), 19½ x 23½ in., (49.5 x 59.7 cm.), color intaglio.

$105* *"Sosei",* s. 4/120, (09-29-92, B. Rasmussen, #318), lithograph in colors (BP 59, DM 148, FR 506, Y 12,534, DK 575).

BI *"To Sazare Ishi",* s., t., good cond., est. $3/400, (10-31-92, Cleveland, #36A), 22⅝ x 17¼ in., (57.5 x 43.8 cm.), mixed media etching.

HASHIMOTO, Okiie Japanese b. 1899

$198* *Rocks In A Pool,* s., sealed in image, num., annot. below image, (10-08-92, Boos, #169), image 19⅞ x 15¹¹⁄₁₆ in., (505 x 398 cm.), color wood block print (BP 118, DM 293, FR 994, Y 24,058).

$121* *Untitled,* s., d. 1958, #16/60, (05-16-93, Hindman, #385), color woodcut (BP 79, DM 195, FR 654, Y 13,413).

HASKELL, Ernest American 1876-1925

$77* *Sentinels Of North Creek, 1924,* s., full margins, good cond., pub. New Republic, (11-12-92, Freemn/Fine Art, #83), plate 5 x 8 in., (12.7 x 20.3 cm.), etching on wove paper (BP 51, DM 122, FR 412, Y 9547).

HASKELL and ALLEN, Publishers

BI *"Leaving Brighton Hotel For The Mill-Dam, Winter", 1871,* good cond., margins 1 1/4 in. or more, mount staining, time toning, est. $6-800, (10-31-92, Skinner, #314, illus.), sight 21¾ x 27½ in., (55.2 x 69.9 cm.), chromolithograph w/hand coloring on paper.

$39* *"Scene On The Delaware River",* stains, paper damage, (03-13-93, Garth, #187, illus.), 14¼ x 17½ in., (36.2 x 44.5 cm.), hand-colored lithograph (BP 27, DM 65, FR 221, Y 4596).

$385* *The Schooner "Edward A. Horton",* (11-07-92, Northeast, #171, illus.), 20 x 27½ in., (50.8 x 69.9 cm.), colored lithograph (BP 252, DM 618, FR 2078, Y 47,519).

HASKINS, Sam

BI *Woman And Woodscape, Double Exposure, c. 1970,* label, sight 590 x 486mm, est. BP 150/250, (05-07-93, Sotheby-London, #199), photograph, color print.

HASS, Erwin b. 1887

$304* *Die Rohre, 1925,* d., (11-12-92, Lempertz, #12), 3⅝ x 5⁹⁄₁₆ in., (9.2 x 13.1 cm.), photograph, gelatin silver print (BP 194, DM 478, FR 1628, Y 37,610).

HASSAM, Childe American 1859-1935

$6050* *The "Home Sweet Home" Cottage, Easthampton (Clayton 174), 1921,* w/cipher, i. imp, margins, light-staining, surface soiling, foxing, (09-19-92, Christie-E, #20, illus.), plate 9⅞ x 11¾ in., (251 x 298 mm.), etching on wove (BP 3480, DM 9060, FR 31,026, Y 753,800).

BI *The Big Horse Chestnut Tree (C./Cl. 304), 1928,* s.,#i., full margins, good cond., mat stain, foxing, tack holes, est. $4/5,000, (02-11-93, Sotheby-NY, #15, illus.), 8⅞ x 11¹³⁄₁₆ in., (225 x 300 mm.), etching.

$2530* *The Big Horse Chestnut Tree (C./Cl. 304), 1928,* s. w/cypher, i. imp, full margins, good cond., mat stain, foxing, tack holes, (05-13-93, Sotheby-NY, #422, illus.), 8⅞ x 11¾ in., (225 x 300 mm.), etching (BP 1661, DM 4085, FR 13,780, Y 282,461).

$990* *Birches (Clayton 214), 1922,* s. w/cipher, (05-27-93, Swann, #129, illus.), 10¼ x 5⅞ in., (26 x 14.9 cm.), drypoint etching (BP 634, DM 1589, FR 5354, Y 106,132).

$5750* *The Broad Curtain (Griffith 29), 1918,* s. w/cipher, margins, watermark, creases, light-staining, losses, good cond., (05-11-93, Christie-NY, #103, illus.), borderline 10⅞ x 14⅞ in., (276 x 378 mm.), lithotint on wove (BP 3671, DM 9058, FR 30,520, Y 632,494).

BI *Calvary Church In Snow,* mono., prov., est. $1,200/1,400, (09-17-92, Sloan, #3080, illus.), 6⅞ x 4⅝ in., (17.5 x 11.7 cm.), etching.

$715* *Church Doorway, Snow, 1916,* mono., tack holes, very good cond., prov., (06-11-93, Doyle, #48), 7 x 5⅜ in., (178 x 137 mm.), etching (BP 470, DM 1162, FR 3918, Y 75,862).

$460* *Colonial Church, Gloucester (Griffith 41), 1918,* s., full margins, good cond., light-stain, bleach stain, creases, (02-11-93, Sotheby-NY, #12), 13⅜ x 10¼ in., (340 x 260 mm.), lithograph on buff wove (BP 325, DM 762, FR 2578, Y 55,455).

$715* *Cos Cob (C./C. 32), 1915,* cypher, margins, good cond., sheet toned, hinge remains, surface soiling, (02-24-93, Butterfield, #2634), 7 x 5 in., (178 x 127 mm.), etching on Van Gelder Zonen (BP 499, DM 1161, FR 3935, Y 83,900).

$2090* *Easthampton (Cortissoz/Clayton 134), 1917,* s., i., full margins, good cond., puncture, light stain, tear, (11-05-92, Sotheby-NY, #19), 7½ x 11⅜ in., (190 x 290 mm.), etching (BP 1359, DM 3305, FR 11,182, Y 256,410).

$805* *Elms In May (Cortissoz/Clayton 43), 1909,* s., i., light-stain, discoloration, glued, (02-11-93, Sotheby-NY, #10), 6⅞ x 10⅞ in., (174 x 276 mm.), etching (BP 568, DM 1333, FR 4512, Y 97,046).

BI *Fifth Avenue, Noon (C. 77), 1916,* 2nd final state, s. w/ cipher, i. imp., full margins, staining, surface skinning, tack holes, losses, very good cond., est. $6/7,000, (05-11-93, Christie-NY, #102, illus.), plate 9⅞ x 7⅛ in., (251 x 181 mm.), etching and drypoint on wove.

BI *Home Sweet Home Cottage, No. 3, Easthampton (C./Cl. 292), 1928,* s., i., full margins, good cond., light stain, repaired puncture, thin spot, crease through image, est. $2,5/3,500, (11-05-92, Sotheby-NY, #23), 9¼ x 11 in., (236 x 280 mm.), etching.

$1380* *Home Sweet Home Cottage, No. 3, Easthampton (C./Cl. 292), 1928,* s., i., full margins, good cond., mat stain, puncture, thin spot,crease through part of image, discoloration, (02-11-93, Sotheby-NY, #14, illus.), 9⁵⁄₁₆ x 11 in., (236 x 280 mm.), etching (BP 974, DM 2286, FR 7735, Y 166,365).

$1840* *House On Main Street, Easthampton (C./Cl. 213), 1922,* s., i., full margins, good cond., light-stain, (02-11-93, Sotheby-NY, #13), 6⅛ x 12³⁄₁₆ in., (155 x 310 mm.), etching (BP 1298, DM 3048, FR 10,314, Y 221,820).

$2200* *House On Main Street, Easthampton (Clayton 213), 1922,* s. w/cypher, annot. imp., (05-16-93, Hindman, #538), 6 x 12⅛ in., (15.2 x 30.8 cm.), etching (BP 1430, DM 3539, FR 11,892, Y 243,875).

$2530* *House On The Main Street, Easthampton (C. 213), 1922,* s. w/cipher, i. imp., margins, light-staining, tack holes, good cond., (05-11-93, Christie-NY, #104, illus.), plate 6¹⁄₁₆ x 12³⁄₁₆ in., (154 x 310 mm.), etching on wove (BP 1615, DM 3986, FR 13,429, Y 278,297).

$1650* *House On The Main Street, Easthampton (C./Cl. 213), 1922,* s., i., full margins, good cond., light stain, foxing, gluded to front mat, (11-05-92, Sotheby-NY, #22), 5⅞ x 12¼ in., (150 x 310 mm.), etching (BP 1073, DM 2610, FR 8828, Y 202,429).

$1840* *House On The Main Street, Easthampton (Cortissoz/Clayton 213), 1922,* s., i. imp, margins, good cond., light-stain, tack holes, (05-13-93, Sotheby-NY, #421), 6 x 12⅛ in., (153 x 309 mm.), etching (BP 1208, DM 2971, FR 10,022, Y 205,426).

$8800* *The Lion Gardiner House, Easthampton (C./Cl. 159), 1920,* s., i., full margins, good cond., pencil notations, soiling, tape stains, discoloration, tack holes, (11-05-92, Sotheby-NY, #20, illus.), 9⅞ x 10 in., (250 x 254 mm.), etching (BP 5724, DM 13,917, FR 47,084, Y 1,079,622).

BI *Madonna Of The North End,* mono., d. 1916 in plate; mono. in margin, prov., est. $2/3,000, (09-17-92, Sloan, #3081, illus.), 6½ x 4⁹⁄₁₆ in., (16.5 x 11.6 cm.), etching.

$770* *Old Lace (C. 56; Lib. of Cong. 68)*, mono., i., d. 1915 in plate; s., mono., prov., (09-17-92, Sloan, #3082), 6⅞ x 6⅞ in., (17.5 x 17.5 cm.), etching (BP 432, DM 1143, FR 3913, Y 95,867).

$1650* *Portsmouth Custom's House*, s. artist's proof, (03-20-93, Northeast, #745, illus.), plate 6½ x 7 in., (16.5 x 17.8 cm.), etching (BP 1106, DM 2698, FR 9182, Y 191,393).

BI *The Steps (Clayton 52)*, 1915, s. w/cipher, i. imp., full margins, good cond., est. $5,5/6,500, (05-11-93, Christie-NY, #100, illus.), plate 10¾ x 7⅝ in., (273 x 194 mm.), etching on thick laid.

$2070* *Toby's, Cos Cob (C. 55)*, 1915, s. w/cipher, i. imp., wide margins, staining, tack holes, tears, skinning, defects, (05-11-93, Christie-NY, #101, illus.), plate 6¾ x 9 in., (171 x 229 mm.), etching on old bible paper (BP 1321, DM 3261, FR 10,987, Y 227,698).

BI *Virginia And A New York Winter Window (C. 378)*, 1934, s. w/cipher, i. imp., full margins, mat staining, tack holes, foxmark, tape, very good cond., est. $14/18,000, (05-11-93, Christie-NY, #108, illus.), plate 10½ x 13 in., (267 x 330 mm.), etching on wove.

$1035* *Walt Whitman's Birth-Place (C. 284)*, 1927, s. w/cipher, i. imp., full margins, staining, creases, tape where previously folded back, tack holes, very good cond., (05-11-93, Christie-NY, #107), plate 4½ x 6⁷⁄₁₆ in., (114 x 164 mm.), etching on wove (BP 661, DM 1630, FR 5494, Y 113,849).

BI *"The Wild Cherry Tree" (Kleeman 44, Griffith 37)*, s. w/ artist's cipher, very good cond., est. $2-3,000, (10-31-92, Cleveland, #139, illus.), 10¾ x 11⅜ in., (27.3 x 28.9 cm.), lithograph.

$3575* *The 'Home Sweet Home' Cottage, Easthampton (C./Cl. 174)*, 1921, s., i., margins, good cond., light stain, creases, tack holes, blue pencil lines verso, (11-05-92, Sotheby-NY, #21), 9⅞ x 11¾ in., (251 x 300 mm.), sheet 11 x 16½ in., (251 x 300 mm.), etching on laid (BP 2325, DM 5654, FR 19,128, Y 438,596).

HASSEBRAUCK, Ernst   1905-1974
$295* *Hafen*, t., s., (12-05-92, Bassenge, #7227), 9¹¹⁄₁₆ x 12⅝ in., (24.6 x 32 cm.), drypoint (BP 185, DM 460, FR 1567, Y 36,551).

$295* *Herrenbildnis*, t., s., margin foxed, (12-05-92, Bassenge, #7225), 12⅝ x 9⅜ in., (32 x 23.8 cm.), etching on handmade Van-Gelder (BP 185, DM 460, FR 1567, Y 36,551).

$332* *Zwei Frauen*, t., s., creased, (12-05-92, Bassenge, #7226), 9⅛ x 8¼ in., (23.2 x 20.9 cm.), etching on wove (BP 208, DM 518, FR 1764, Y 41,135).

HASUI
$154* *"Mt. Fuji", TANZAKA YOKOE*, excell. cond., left and lower margins trimmed, (05-07-93, Goldberg, #1356, illus.), woodblock (BP 98, DM 243, FR 820, Y 16,957).

$2110* *Snow At Miyajima*, oban tate-e, from series Tabi Miyage Dai Nishu, d. Taisho 10 (1921),pub. mark Watanabe, s. Hasui w/ seal Hasui, (06-10-93, Sotheby-London, #291), (BP 1380, DM 3436, FR 11,568, Y 223,968).

$440* *Temple In Daylight Rain*, 1929, d. Showa 4; #62/100 verso, pub. Kawaguchi, seal, tate-e, (11-20-92, Skinner, #91, illus.), oban tate-e (BP 290, DM 702, FR 2363, Y 54,720).

$1045* *"Zozoji In Shiba"*, from Twelve Views of Tokyo, s., d. Taisho 14 (1924), pub. Watanabe, very good cond., tate-e, (11-20-92, Skinner, #110, illus.), oban tate-e (BP 688, DM 1666, FR 5612, Y 129,959).

HASUI, Kawase   Japanese 1883-1957
$193* *Figures In Rain Outside Temple*, (09-17-92, Sloan, #1610), sight 14 x 9¼ in., (35.6 x 23.5 cm.), woodblock (BP 108, DM 287, FR 981, Y 24,029).

$50* *Golden Moon With Tree*, (05-16-93, Hanzel, #1102), 14 x 9½ in., (35.6 x 24.1 cm.), color woodblock (BP 33, DM 80, FR 270, Y 5543).

$187* *Matsushima Island, Near Sendai*, (09-17-92, Sloan, #1637), 9½ x 14⅛ in., (24.1 x 35.9 cm.), woodblock (BP 105, DM 278, FR 950, Y 23,282).

$220* *Moon At Magome, Near Omori, Tokyo*, (09-17-92, Sloan, #1606), 14⅛ x 9½ in., (35.9 x 24.1 cm.), woodblock (BP 124, DM 327, FR 1118, Y 27,390).

$132* *Moon In Magume*, s., (12-13-92, Hindman, #359), 14½ x 9 in., color woodcut (BP 84, DM 207, FR 707, Y 16,331).

$120* *Moonlit Seascape*, (05-16-93, Hanzel, #1104), 14 x 9 in., (35.6 x 22.9 cm.), color woodblock (BP 78, DM 193, FR 649, Y 13,302).

$330* *"Night Rain In Matsuzaki"*, s. in plate, artist's seal, i., (09-25-92, Wolf, #14), 14 x 9½ in., (35.6 x 24.1 cm.), woodblock (BP 193, DM 489, FR 1654, Y 39,831).

$30* *Nishiki Seacoast At Atami*, s. in block, artist's red stamp, paper missing in margins, (05-15-93, Cleveland, #17, illus.), 9⅜ x 9⅞ in., (23.8 x 25.1 cm.), color woodblock (BP 20, DM 48, FR 162, Y 3326).

$358* *Rain At Shinagawa, Tokyo*, (09-17-92, Sloan, #1607), 14⅛ x 9½ in., (35.9 x 24.1 cm.), woodblock (BP 201, DM 531, FR 1819, Y 44,572).

$468* *"Snow At Saishoin Temple, Hirosaki" and "Fisherman On Lake Knak": Two*, (09-17-92, Sloan, #1651), larger 10½ x 15 in., (26.7 x 38.1 cm.), woodblock (BP 263, DM 695, FR 2378, Y 58,267).

$60* *Snowy Landscape With Pagoda*, (05-16-93, Hanzel, #1103), 9½ x 14 in., (24.1 x 35.6 cm.), color woodblock (BP 39, DM 97, FR 324, Y 6651).

$358* *Twin Islands At Matashima*, s. w/brush, bearing artist's seal, (10-18-92, Hindman, #533), 9¼ x 14¼ in., (23.5 x 36.2 cm.), color woodcut (BP 219, DM 533, FR 1807, Y 42,951).

BI *Untitled*, s., est. $2/400, (06-26-93, Wolf, #957), 14½ x 9½ in., (36.8 x 24.1 cm.), color woodblock.

HATCH & SEVERYN
$138* *"Mount Savage Iron Works, Allegany Co. Md."*, large folio, wear, damage, suface appears to have been varnished, (11-13-92, Garth, #452, illus.), 26½ x 29¾ in., (67.3 x 75.6 cm.), handcolored lithograph (BP 89, DM 217, FR 731, Y 17,128).

HATER, Stanley William   American
$303* *Abstract Composition*, init. SH, d. 1950, (06-11-93, Freemn/Fine Art, #91), 6 x 4 in., (15.2 x 10.2 cm.), etching (BP 199, DM 492, FR 1660, Y 32,149).

HATHAWAY, John W.   American
$99* *Still Life, 1943*, s., t., d. 1943, (06-11-93, Freemn/Fine Art, #92), 9⅛ x 11¾ in., (23.2 x 29.8 cm.), woodcut w/ hand-coloring (BP 65, DM 161, FR 542, Y 10,504).

HATHERELL, William (after)
$143* *The King's Derby (1909)*, pub. Bovril Ltd., repaired tears, laid down, (11-12-92, Bonhams-Chelsea, #66), image 18 x 29¼ in., (45.7 x 74.3 cm.), hand-colored reproduction (BP 94, DM 227, FR 764, Y 17,731).

HAUSER, Carry   Austrian 1895-1985
$133* *Christkind Mit Engeln*, s., ded., (12-01-92, Karl/Faber, #703), 4½ x 4⁵⁄₁₆ in., (11.5 x 11 cm.), lithograph on Maschinen paper (BP 88, DM 212, FR 722, Y 16,559).

$300* *Liegendes Paar*, mono., d., #10/30, stained, (11-25-92, Dorotheum, #471, illus.), woodcut (BP 196, DM 477, FR 1616, Y 37,138, SC 3360).

HAUSER, Erich   b. 1930
$505* *"Sechs Radierungen", c. 1965: Six*, s., num., Berlin, Stolpe pub., (11-28-92, Grisebach, #531, illus.), 27¼ x 23⅝ in., (69.2 x 60 cm.), etching on wove (BP 333, DM 805, FR 2731, Y 62,850).

HAUSMANN, Raoul   Austrian 1886-1971
BI *Dadasophie*, stone mono., estate stamp sig., est. DM 250-, (09-25-92, Granier, #2878), sheet 14⁹⁄₁₆ x 12⅝ in., (37 x 32 cm.), woodcut on transparent hand-made.

$2483* *Untitled, c. 1915*, s., (06-05-93, Bassenge, #6082, illus.), 5¼ x 2⅜ in., (13.3 x 6 cm.), woodcut on hand-made China (BP 1635, DM 4026, FR 13,568, Y 266,359).

HAVELL
$66* *Oriental Figures: Four*, stains, (10-03-92, Garth, #1, illus.), 11½ x 10½ in., (29.2 x 26.7 cm.), handcolored engravings (BP 39, DM 93, FR 318, Y 7900).

HAVELL, Robert   English 1793-1878
$295* *Snipe Shooting Near Uxbridge*, margins, (06-30-93, Bonhams-Chelsea, #58), plate 10¾ x 14½ in., (27.3 x 36.8 cm.), aquatint w/hand-coloring (BP 198, DM 503, FR 1697, Y 31,608).

$84* *A View Of The Grand Fleet In The Order Of Sailing Under The Command Of Admiral Earl Howe, In 1790, 1834,* pub. Colnaghi, Son and Co., (01-14-93, Bonhams, #113), image 10¼ x 20½ in., (26 x 52.1 cm.), hand-colored aquatint (BP 55, DM 137, FR 464, Y 10,590).

HAVELL, Robert   (after Henry ALKEN)
BI   *"The Holyhead And Chester Mails" and "The Birmingam Mail Near Aylesbury": Two,* pub. R. Havell, trimmed, light staining, foxing, est. BP 2/250, (10-27-92, Phillips-London, #107), image 8 x 11 in., (203 x 279 mm.), aquatint w/hand-coloring on wove.

HAVELL, William   1782-1857
$397* *Landschaft Mit Bizarren Eichen, Vorne Ein Sitzender Hirte, 1804,* (12-04-92, Bassenge, #6825), 12³⁄₁₆ x 8¹¹⁄₁₆ in., (31 x 22.1 cm.), lithograph on gray handmade (BP 255, DM 632, FR 2145, Y 49,563).

HAVILAND, Paul   1880-1915
BI   *Edward Steichen (Lunn, Photo-Secession, p. 23), 1910,* est. $4/6,000, (04-06-93, Sotheby-NY, #65A, illus.), 8¼ x 6⅛ in., photograph, platinum print.
$4125* *Edward Steichen, c. 1914,* (10-15-92, Sotheby-NY, #97, illus.), 6¾ x 4⅝ in., (17.1 x 11.7 cm.), photograph, platinum print (BP 2524, DM 6140, FR 20,823, Y 494,901).

HAVILAND, Paul Burty   1880-1950
$1725* *Self-Portrait, Kissing, c. 1910,* (04-08-93, Christie-NY, #72, illus.), 9⅝ x 7½ in., (24.4 x 19.1 cm.), photograph, platinum print (BP 1131, DM 2771, FR 9380, Y 195,756).

HAVINDEN, John   b. 1909
BI   *Still Life With Handbags,* 1930s, s., est. BP 3/500, (05-06-93, Christie-London, #102), 11 x 10⅛ in., photograph, gelatin silver print.

HAWES, Josiah Johnson
$330* *Boston Street Scene,* 1860's, (10-14-92, Swann, #191, illus.), photograph, circular albumen print (BP 194, DM 483, FR 1638, Y 39,990).

HAWORTH, Miriam
$88* *"Cartes A Jouer": Pair,* (12-11-92, DuMouchelle, #1669), approx. 14 x 20 in., (35.6 x 50.8 cm.), colored engravings (BP 56, DM 139, FR 475, Y 10,890).

HAXTON, Elaine Alys   b. 1909
$162* *Le Gong Dancer,* s. Elaine Haxton, i., d. '73, #1/10 1st State, (08-11-92, L. Joel, #65G), 13¾ x 12 in., (35 x 30.5 cm.), color drypoint etching aquatint and gold leaf (BP 84, DM 238, FR 805, Y 20,745, A$ 220).

HAYDEN, Seymour   British 1818-1910
$17* *Ballersea Reach,* margins, plate s., (05-22-93, Collins, #10), 9 x 9 in., (22.9 x 22.9 cm.), etching (BP 11, DM 28, FR 93, Y 1874).

HAYES, William   b. 1794
$165* *"Goldfinches" and "Falcon": Two,* from "Natural History of British Birds", London, 1771-1775, folio, (07-03-92, Sloan, #333), hand colored etching (BP 86, DM 250, FR 842, Y 20,568).

HAYMAN, Francis   (after)
BI   *The Triumph Of Brittania,* by S.F. Ravenet, pub. J. Boydell, narrow margins, thin in places, defects, est. BP 80/120, (11-30-92, Phillips-London, #224), plate 19¾ x 25⅝ in., (502 x 651 mm.), mixed-method engraving on laid.

HAYNES, E. Leslie, engraver
BI   *"Portrait Of A Lady", 1903,* s., blindstamp, pub. Henry Graves and Co. Ltd., est. BP 50/70, (11-19-92, Bonhams-Chelsea, #85), image 17¾ x 13¾ in., (45.1 x 34.9 cm.), mezzotint.

HAYNES, F. Jay   American 1853-1921
BI   *"Minerva Terrace, Mammoth Hot Springs, Yellowstone National Park",* 1880s, attrib., t. in neg., p. on mount, est. $3/4,000, (05-23-93, Butterfield, #3444, illus.), 18 x 22 in., photograph, albumen print.
$3575* *Mining View,* num. 3175 in neg., 1880's, (10-15-92, Sotheby-NY, #46, illus.), 16¾ x 21½ in., (42.5 x 54.6 cm.), photograph, albumen print (BP 2188, DM 5322, FR 18,046, Y 428,914).

$3575* *'Grand Canyon Of The Yellowstone',* photog.'s credit, t., num. 3126 in neg., mounted, label w/photog.'s credit & t., 1880's, (10-15-92, Sotheby-NY, #45, illus.), 17¼ x 21¾ in., (43.8 x 55.2 cm.), photograph, albumen print (BP 2188, DM 5322, FR 18,046, Y 428,914).

HAYNES, F.J.
$385* *Old Faithful,* 1890s, (04-07-93, Swann, #216, illus.), 21 x 16 in., photograph, hand-colored printing-out paper print (BP 254, DM 623, FR 2107, Y 43,740).

HAYSLETTE   contemporary
$110* *"East Of Myako",* s. #103/175, (03-12-93, DuMouchelle, #2471), 38 x 50 in., (96.5 x 127 cm.), silkscreen (BP 77, DM 183, FR 623, Y 12,964).

HAYSLETTE, Max
BI   *Abstract In Black And Blue,* s., #121/150, prov., est. C$ 2/300, (12-01-92, Ritchie, #78), 39¼ c 59⅞ in., (99.7 x 152.1 cm.), color serigraph.
BI   *Along The Noatak,* s., stamped mono., #34/183; s., t., d. May 25, 1977 on backing, pub.Olympus Graphicus, prov., est. C$ 150/250, (12-01-92, Ritchie, #77), 39¾ x 23 in., (101 x 58.4 cm.), color serigraph.
$64* *High Meadow,* s., #44/179, prov., (12-01-92, Ritchie, #76, illus.), 38¼ x 35⅛ in., (97.2 x 89.2 cm.), color serigraph (BP 42, DM 102, FR 348, Y 7968, C$ 83).
$64* *Oiseau Exotique,* s., #23/180; s., t., d. July 7, 1977 on backing, pub. Olympus Graphicus, prov., (12-01-92, Ritchie, #67, illus.), 52¾ x 40⅝ in., (134 x 103.2 cm.), color serigraph (BP 42, DM 102, FR 348, Y 7968, C$ 83).
BI   *Rain Kite Descending,* s. in Roman and characters, t., #12/176; s., t., d. April 12, 1977 on backing, pub. Olympus Graphicus, prov., est. C$ 2/350, (12-01-92, Ritchie, #68), 27½ x 52¾ in., (69.9 x 134 cm.), color serigraph.
BI   *Series 70, Number 3,* s., #95/170; t., prov., est. C$ 2/300, (12-01-92, Ritchie, #79), 42¾ x 53½ in., (108.6 x 135.9 cm.), color serigraph.

HAYTER, Stanley William   English 1901-1988
$1210* *The Aquarius Suite (B. and M. 337-40), 1970: Set Of Four,* s., d., two num. 95/150, two num. 92/150, pub. Barney Weinger Gallery, full margins, scuff, excell. cond., (09-19-92, Christie-E, #24), sheet, each 23 x 28 in., (584 x 711 mm.), screenprint in colors on Bristol board (BP 696, DM 1812, FR 6205, Y 150,760).
$880* *"The Aquarius Suite" (Black and Moorhead 337-340), 1970: Set Of Four,* s., d., #146/150, full margins, very good cond., (12-08-92, Swann, #135), 23 x 28 in., (58.4 x 71.1 cm.), color serigraph (BP 552, DM 1370, FR 4671, Y 109,073).
$275* *Caribbean Sea, 1969,* s., t., d., full margins, creases, foxing, tape remains, (12-08-92, Swann, #134), 25½ x 19 in., (64.8 x 48.3 cm.), color intaglio etching (BP 172, DM 428, FR 1460, Y 34,085).
$770* *Chas De L' Aiguelle, 1946,* s., t., d., num. 11/30, full margins, very good cond., (09-19-92, Christie-E, #21), plate 11⅞ x 7¼ in., (302 x 184 mm.), engraving on BFK Rives (BP 443, DM 1153, FR 3949, Y 95,938).
BI   *Combat (B./ M. 210), 1953,* s., d., #114/220, p. Hayter and Atelier 17, pub. La Guilde Internationale de la Gravure, blindstamp, margins, good cond., defects, est. BP 800/1,200, (06-30-93, Sotheby-London, #451, illus.), 11⅝ x 7⅞ in., (295 x 200 mm.), engraving, soft-ground etching and scorper in color on Marais wove.
BI   *Combat (B./ M. 210), 1953,* s., d., #55/220, p. Hayter and Atelier, pub. La Guilde Internationalede la Gravure, margins, good cond., est. BP 800/1,200, (06-30-93, Sotheby-London, #450), 22 x 14¾ in., (559 x 375 mm.), engraving, w/scorper and soft-ground etching in color.
$830* *Composition, 1951,* s., d. 51, #139/200, full margins, creases, (05-27-93, Briest, #107), 12¹⁵⁄₁₆ x 16¹⁵⁄₁₆ in., (33 x 43 cm.), etching and print (BP 532, DM 1332, FR 4489, Y 88,979).
BI   *Composition, 1951,* s., d. 51, #139/200, full margins, tears, scratch, est. FF 6/7,000, (11-16-92, Briest, #311, illus.), 12¹⁵⁄₁₆ x 16¹⁵⁄₁₆ in., (33 x 43 cm.), etching and print in colors.
BI   *Le Couple (B & M 206), 1952,* s., d., t., i., proof impression, full margins, pub. Guilde de la Gravure

Geneva, good cond., est. BP 7/900, (11-30-92, Phillips-London, #428), plate 17¾ x 11⅝ in., (451 x 295 mm.), engraving, soft ground etching, & scorper in colors.

BI *Le Couple (B./M. 206), 1952,* s., #4/20, i. He (?), pub. La Guilde International de la Gravure, full margins, good cond., foxing, est. $2/2,500, (05-13-93, Sotheby-NY, #569), 17⅜ x 11⅝ in., (442 x 296 mm.), engraving, soft-ground etching and embossing in colors on wove.

$924* *Dance Du Soleil,* s., 170/200, (12-04-92, AB Stockholm, #7064), 15½ x 9⁷⁄₁₆ in., (39.3 x 24 cm.), aquatint, etching and reliefprint in colors on Arches (BP 593, DM 1472, FR 4992, Y 115,356, SK 6270).

BI *Danse Du Soleil (B./ M. 197), 1951,* s., #181/200, pub. by La Guilde Internationale de la Gravure, full margins, good cond., light-staining, foxing, skinning, est. BP 800/1,200, (06-30-93, Sotheby-London, #449, illus.), 15⅝ x 9⅜ in., (391 x 238 mm.), engraving, soft-ground etching and scorper in color on Arches.

$176* *Expansion,* s., d. 70, t., num. 59/100, prov., (09-20-92, Hindman, #794), 17⅛ x 19⅜ in., (43.5 x 49.2 cm.), color etching, aquatint and soft-ground (BP 103, DM 261, FR 893, Y 21,753).

$990* *Facile Proie, 1938,* s., d., t., annot. essai etat, (12-08-92, Swann, #133, illus.), 6 x 8 in., (15.2 x 20.3 cm.), sheet 10 x 13 in., (15.2 x 20.3 cm.), engraving w/soft-ground and burnishing on laid paper, watermark (BP 620, DM 1541, FR 5255, Y 122,707).

BI *Feu Sous L'Eau, 1955,* s., d. 55, t., #12/50, full margins, est. FF6/8,000, (05-27-93, Briest, #108), 17¹¹⁄₁₆ x 12⅜ in., (45 x 31.5 cm.), etching and print.

BI *Feu Sous L'Eau, 1955,* s., d. 55, t., #12/50, full margins, est. FF 8/10,000, (11-16-92, Briest, #310, illus.), 17¹¹⁄₁₆ x 12⅜ in., (45 x 31.5 cm.), etching and stamp in colors.

$440* *"Gemini", 1970,* s., t., d., num. 95/100, staining, good cond., (10-31-92, Cleveland, #290, illus.), 19 x 23 in., (48.3 x 58.4 cm.), color lithograph (BP 282, DM 677, FR 2296, Y 54,503).

$1279* *Jeux D'Eau (Water Play) (Hacker 56), 1953,* s., d., t., i. Trial print, full margins, good cond., (12-03-92, Sotheby-London, #344, illus.), 14½ x 12¼ in., (368 x 311 mm.), engraving, soft ground etching w/texture, & burnisher in colors, on hand-made textured wove (BP 825, DM 2011, FR 6865, Y 159,139).

$990* *L' Escoutay (Hacker 53), 1951,* s., d., num. 19/200, International Graphic Arts Society, Inc. blindstamp, full margins, crease where obviously folded, very good cond., (09-19-92, Christie-E, #22), plate 7⅝ x 12 in., (194 x 305 mm.), soft-ground etching and engraving in colors on wove, watermark (BP 569, DM 1482, FR 5077, Y 123,349).

BI *La Lecon D'Anatomie (B & M 214), 1954,* s., d., t., i. E 1/10, artist proof edition, pub. L'Oeuvre Gravee, full margins, est. BP 9/1,100, (11-30-92, Phillips-London, #429, illus.), plate 15⅞ x 11¾ in., (403 x 298 mm.), engraving, aquatint, soft (molle) ground-etching and scorper in colors on B.F.K. Rives.

$1495* *"Lutteurs", "Ormond" and "Hang Glider" (B./M. 378 and 398), 1974, 1976, 1978,* s., d., t., two #7/50 and 37/75; last i. E 2/5, p. Hector Saunier, pub. North Carolina Society, full margins, good cond.; 1st w/printer's crease, creases, nick; 2nd w/slit in image, tear, (02-11-93, Sotheby-NY, #150), etching, two w/soft ground etching in color (BP 1055, DM 2476, FR 8380, Y 180,229).

$1955* *Maternite Ailee (B./M. 187), 1948-53,* s., d., t., i. 37/50, p. artist and Hector Saunier, pub. Graphics International, 1972, full margins, good cond., masking tape stains, (02-11-93, Sotheby-NY, #148), 13½ x 7¹⁵⁄₁₆ in., (343 x 202 mm.), etching and engraving p. in colors (BP 1379, DM 3238, FR 10,959, Y 235,684).

$1380* *Meduse (B./M. 246), 1958,* s., d., t., #45/50, full margins, good cond., (02-11-93, Sotheby-NY, #149), 11⅝ x 14½ in., (296 x 368 mm.), color etching (BP 974, DM 2286, FR 7735, Y 166,365).

BI *Meduse, 1958,* s., d., t., #37/50, full margins, good cond., paper loss, skinned area, surface soiling, est. $800/1000, (05-19-93, Butterfield, #1915), 11⅝ x 14½ in., (295 x 368 mm.), etching and aquatint in colors on BFK Rives.

$1540* *Nine Engravings 1933-1946,* complete portfolio, s., #21/100, #21, pub. AAA, 1974, full margins, good cond., ink smudges, fox marks, orig. portfolio, (11-05-92, Sotheby-NY, #199), each sheet approx. 15¾ x 11⅜ in., (400 x 290 mm.), set of nine engravings (BP 1002, DM 2436, FR 8240, Y 188,934).

$1870* *Nine Engravings 1933-1946: Nine,* complete portfolio, each s., #73/100, num. 73 on just. page; p. Atelier 17, 1973, pub. AAA, 1974, full margins, orig. portfolio, (04-26-93, Selkirk, #154), 15¾ x 11½ in., (40 x 29.2 cm.), engraving (BP 1180, DM 2931, FR 9899, Y 206,356).

$6270* *"Nine Engravings",* 1933-46, AAA, 1974, s., d., t., num., (12-01-92, Karl/Faber, #705, illus.), engraving on thick wove (BP 4143, DM 9994, FR 34,058, Y 780,627).

$1650* *Paysage Lunaire, 1955,* s., t., d., i. E(?), num. 3/5, full margins, creasing, soiling, hole, old tape, (09-19-92, Christie-E, #23, illus.), plate 14¾ x 11⅜ in., (375 x 289 mm.), engraving and mixed media itaglio on Japan (BP 949, DM 2471, FR 8462, Y 205,582).

$1840* *Stanley William Hayter, Nine Engravings 1933-1946, New York, Associated American Artists, 1974: Nine,* s., d., num., t.; t., just. and text, copy 57 of 120, full margins, loose, foxmark, excell. cond., orig. portfolio, includ. Cirque; Cheiromancy; Facile Proie; Invocation; Nostradam; Espana; Unfolding; Le Chas de l'Aiguille; and New Year Greeting Card (B. and M.), (05-11-93, Christie-NY, #199, illus.), 16¼ x 12⁷⁄₁₆ in., (412 x 316 mm.), engraving on Barcham Green (BP 1175, DM 2899, FR 9766, Y 202,398).

$2164* *Stanley William Hayter. Nine Engravings 1933-1946, 1974: Nine,* AAA, #20/100, s., d., t., (11-20-92, Lempertz, #577), portfolio 16⅛ x 12¹⁵⁄₁₆ in., (41 x 32.8 cm.), etching and hand-made Barcham Green Velin (BP 1425, DM 3450, FR 11,622, Y 269,121).

BI *"Still", 1974: Three,* text by S. Beckett, M'Arte Edizioni, Mailand, num., est. DM 2000, (12-01-92, Karl/Faber, #706), 15¹⁵⁄₁₆ x 11¹³⁄₁₆ in., (40.5 x 30 cm.), etching and aquatint on wove.

$4888* *Tarantelle (Black/Moorhead 156), 1943,* d., s., t., #41/50, pub. Curt Valentin, full margins, good cond., scrape, scuffs, scattered fox marks, masking tape, discoloration, foxing, (02-11-93, Sotheby-NY, #146, illus.), 21¹¹⁄₁₆ x 12¹⁵⁄₁₆ in., (551 x 330 mm.), sheet 24¾ x 15¹⁄₁₆ in., (551 x 330 mm.), engraving, soft (molle) ground etching, embossing on cream wove paper (BP 3449, DM 8097, FR 27,399, Y 589,271).

BI *Tarantelle, 1943,* s., d., t., #41/50, full margins, good cond., scuffs, light stain, fox marks, tape, discoloration, foxing, est. $6/8,000, (11-05-92, Sotheby-NY, #197, illus.), 21¾ x 13 in., (551 x 330 mm.), sheet 24¾ x 15 in., (551 x 330 mm.), engraving, etching, and embossing on cream wove.

$1701* *Trois Personnages, (19)51,* s., d., t., num., (06-08-93, Karl/Faber, #834, illus.), approx. 19⁵⁄₁₆ x 13⁹⁄₁₆ in., (49 x 34.5 cm.), aquatint/etching w/drypoint and soft-ground etching on hand-made (BP 1118, DM 2760, FR 9295, Y 180,669).

$3680* *Tropic Of Cancer (Black and Moorehead 190), 1949,* s., t., d., #37/50, full margins, mat staining, glue, good cond., (05-11-93, Christie-NY, #197, illus.), plate 21¾ x 27½ in., (552 x 699 mm.), engraving, hard- and soft-ground etching on Barcham Green (BP 2349, DM 5797, FR 19,533, Y 404,796).

$1495* *Unfolding (B./M. 166), 1945-46,* s., t., d. 1946, i. Trial proof, margins, good cond., scrape, scratches, mat stain, (02-11-93, Sotheby-NY, #147), 5½ x 6¾ in., (140 x 172 mm.), sheet 8⅛ x 9¹¹⁄₁₆ in., (140 x 172 mm.), etching (BP 1055, DM 2476, FR 8380, Y 180,229).

BI *Unfolding (Black/Moorehead 166), 1945-46,* s., d., t., #55/100, p. Hector Saunier and Rigmor Poenaru, pub. AAA in portfolio Hayter-Nine Engravings, 1974, full margins, good cond., fox mark, est. $6/800, (05-13-93, Sotheby-NY, #568), 5⅜ x 6¾ in., (138 x 173 mm.), engraving.

BI *Untitled, 1945,* s., #92/200, margins, good cond., skinning, mat/light-staining, foxing, est. $2/3,000, (10-28-92, Butterfield, #2653), 15½ x 9⅜ in., (394 x 238 mm.), color engraving, soft-ground etching and roulette on heavy cream wove.

BI *"La Villette" (Hacker 102),* from Paysage Urban Suite, very fine cond., hinge, est. $2-3,000, (10-31-92, Cleveland, #289, illus.), 7⅜ x 9¾ in., (18.7 x 24.8 cm.), engraving.

$1980* *Warriors, 1953,* s., d., t., large margins, good cond., mat stain, (11-05-92, Sotheby-NY, #198), 18¾ x 13¼ in., (477 x 335 mm.), sheet 22½ x 16⅞ in., (477 x 335 mm.), etching and aquatint p. in colors (BP 1288, DM 3131, FR 10,594, Y 242,915).

BI *White Horses (Black and Moorhead 308), 1967,* s., d., t., ded., 9/50, erased traces of ded., est. FF4/6,000, (06-28-93, Loudmer, #262, illus.), 15⁹⁄₁₆ x 19⅛ in., (395 x 485 mm.), sh 19⁹⁄₁₆ x 25⅝ in., (395 x 485 mm.), color copper engraving on BFK Rives wove.

$1840* *Winged Figures (B. and M. 205), 1952,* s., d., i. Ep d' artiste, full margins, light/mat staining, surface soiling, good cond., Mr. and Mrs. Sam B. Cantey III Estate, (05-11-93, Christie-NY, #198), plate 15⅝ x 12⅞ in., (397 x 327 mm.), color engraving and woodcut on wove (BP 1175, DM 2899, FR 9766, Y 202,398).

$1449* *Winged Figures (H. 54), 1952,* s., d., #35/90, full margins, good cond., (12-03-92, Sotheby-London, #345, illus.), 15¾ x 12⅞ in., (400 x 327 mm.), engraving w/ scorper & soft-ground etching p. in colors on hand-made laid (BP 935, DM 2279, FR 7778, Y 180,291).

HAZARD, Garnet
$65* *Harvest (Saskatchewan),* s., t.; num. Proof pub.'s paper label verso backing, prov., (06-07-93, Ritchie, #32), 7⅝ x 9⅞ in., (19.3 x 25.1 cm.), etching (BP 43, DM 105, FR 355, Y 6973, C$ 83).

HAZENPLUG, Frank   b. 1873
BI *The Chap-Book, c. 1895,* very rare, est. DM 2,500, (12-05-92, Bassenge, #7597, illus.), 20¹¹⁄₁₆ x 13¹⁵⁄₁₆ in., (52.6 x 35.4 cm.), color lithograph.

HEAP, George (attrib.)
$575* *The East Prospect Of The City Of Philadelphia, In The Province Of Pennsylvania, c. 1752,* pub. London Magazine 1761, discoloration, mat stain, tape hinges, folds, (01-28-93, Sotheby-NY, #438), 6½ x 19⅛ in., (165 x 486 mm.), sheet 8¼ x 21½ in., (165 x 486 mm.), engraving on laid (BP 380, DM 911, FR 3083, Y 71,393).

HEARD, Graeme
$24* *Gabriel,* s. Graeme Heard, i., #2/100, (08-11-92, L. Joel, #183G), 13⅝ x 9¹¹⁄₁₆ in., (34.6 x 24.6 cm.), linocut (BP 12, DM 35, FR 119, Y 3073, A$ 33).

HEARD, Peter
BI *"Chocks Away!",* #151/300, s., t., est. BP 80/120, (05-20-93, Bonhams-Chelsea, #149), image 20 x 17⅝ in., (50.8 x 44.8 cm.), screenprint.

BI *Leander Blues?,* #151/300, s., t., est. BP 80/120, (05-20-93, Bonhams-Chelsea, #19), image 25½ x 21⅛ in., (64.8 x 53.7 cm.), screenprint.

HEARTFIELD, John   1891-1968
$660* *Boot With Helmet, 1932,* leaf extracted from A.I.Z. (Arbeiter Illustrierte Zeitung, no. 26, June 26, 1932), (04-07-93, Swann, #317), 15 x 11 in., photograph, photogravure reprod. of photomontage (BP 436, DM 1067, FR 3612, Y 74,983).

$3450* *The Executioner And Justice, c. 1960,* lit., (04-08-93, Christie-NY, #105, illus.), 37⅞ x 30⅛ in., (96.2 x 76.5 cm.), photograph, gelatin silver print (BP 2262, DM 5542, FR 18,760, Y 391,512).

BI *Der Friedfertige Raubfisch, The Peaceful Fish Of Prey, c. 1960,* lit., est. $3/5,000, (04-08-93, Christie-NY, #103, illus.), 36⅝ x 25⅞ in., (93 x 65.7 cm.), photograph, gelatin silver print.

$1955* *John Heartfield, Tretjakov, Sergei, And Telingater, Solomon, Moscow:Ogis, 1936: Seventy-Nine,* in Russian, pages of reprods. after John Heartfield photomontages, graphic design, book covers and collages, (04-08-93, Christie-NY, #108, illus.), photograph, monograph (monografia) (BP 1282, DM 3141, FR 10,631, Y 221,857).

$2990* *Niemals Wieder!, Never Again!, c. 1960,* lit., (04-08-93, Christie-NY, #106, illus.), 36⅝ x 26¾ in., (93 x 67.9 cm.), photograph, gelatin silver print (BP 1961, DM 4803, FR 16,259, Y 339,310).

BI *Selected Plates From Arbeiter Illustriete Zeitung (AIZ): Five,* lit., est. $2,2/2,800, (04-08-93, Christie-NY, #107, illus.), each 14⅞ x 10½ in., (37.8 x 26.7 cm.), photograph, photogravure pages.

$4600* *They Twist And Turn And Call Themselves German Judges, At The Arsonist Trial In Leipzig, c. 1960,* lit., (04-08-93, Christie-NY, #104, illus.), 37⅛ x 27¼ in., (94.3 x 69.2 cm.), photograph, gelatin silver print (BP 3016, DM 7390, FR 25,014, Y 522,015).

HEASLIP, William
$220* *The Intruder,* s., t., full margins, good cond., (02-24-93, Butterfield, #2836), 8⅞ x 12¹⁄₁₆ in., (225 x 306 mm.), etching & aquatint on wove (BP 153, DM 357, FR 1211, Y 25,816).

HEATH, Lieutenant L.G. (after)
$510* *Hong Kong, 1846,* 3 plates p. on 1 sheet, good cond., w/out margins, panorama, (10-27-92, Phillips-London, #155), sheet 6 x 28¾ in., (152 x 730 mm.), engraving w/hand-coloring on wove (BP 322, DM 782, FR 2652, Y 62,385).

HEATON-COOPER, S.A. (after)
$8 *Broadland Views: Four,* (12-11-92, G.A. Key, #121), 3 x 5 in., (7.6 x 12.7 cm.), colored print (BP 5, DM 13, FR 43, Y 990).

HEBALD, Milton   American b. 1917
BI *The Dragon,* ed. 27/100, est. $100/150, (11-12-92, Freemn/Fine Art, #85), mat 17⅛ x 12½ in., (43.5 x 31.8 cm.), litho in color.

BI *The Reluctant Donkey,* s., 27/100, est. $100/150, (11-12-92, Freemn/Fine Art, #84), mat 19⅛ x 13⅛ in., (48.6 x 33.3 cm.), litho in color.

HEBERT, Adrien   Canadian 1890-1967
BI *Des Maisons, Edifices Publics Et Religieux, Monuments Historiques DuQuebec: Sixteen,* s. in plate Adrien Hebert, (06-16-93, Encans, #61), 5⅞ x 4½ in., (15 x 11.5 cm.), engraving.

HEBRIG-STREHL, Paul
BI *Sports E Giuochi Invernali In Germania, c. 1930,* cond. 1, defects, image crease, est. BP 150/200, (10-13-92, Phillips-London, #25), 39⅞ x 24¹³⁄₁₆ in., (101.3 x 63 cm.), color offset lithograph.

HECHT, Joseph
$409* *Chat (T.-R. et P. 282), 1938,* s., num., damp ring, untrimmed margins, 45 proof, (02-24-93, Picard, #123), copper engraving on laid (BP 285, DM 664, FR 2251, Y 47,993).

$127* *"Heron I", 1920-23 and "Buse Blesse", 1944-45 (Tonneau-Ryckelynck etPlumart 035 et 329): Two,* s., num., full margins, 30 to 31 proof, (02-24-93, Picard, #122), copper engraving on laid (BP 89, DM 206, FR 699, Y 14,903).

HECKEL, Erich   German 1883-1970
$9887* *A. N. Holzschnitt (Dube 322 B), 1919,* s., d., Elf Holzschnitte, Neumann, prov., (06-10-93, Hauswedell/Nolt, #401, illus.), image 18³⁄₁₆ x 11¹³⁄₁₆ in., (46.2 x 30 cm.), woodcut on wove (BP 6467, DM 16,100, FR 54,205, Y 1,049,464).

$2497* *Alter Fischer (D. L68), 1908,* s., d. 7(?), t., full margins, crease, tear, dirt, discoloration, (12-01-92, Christie-London, #387), L. 17½ x 14¹¹⁄₁₆ in., (445 x 373 mm.), lithograph on wove (BP 1650, DM 3980, FR 13,563, Y 310,881).

BI *Am Strand (D. H 336/III B), 1923,* s., Mappe der Gegenwart, 42. Druck der Marees-Gesellschaft, Munchen,restored tears, est. DM 6000, (12-01-92, Karl/Faber, #711, illus.), 16⅛ x 10¼ in., (41 x 26 cm.), woodcut on Maschinen paper.

$2270* *"Am Strand" (Dube 336/IIIB), 1923,* s., pub. in Mappe der Gegenwart, Munchen, blindstamp, (06-05-93, Grisebach, #622, illus.), 16¹⁄₁₆ x 10⅛ in., (40.8 x 25.7 cm.), woodcut on wove (BP 1494, DM 3680, FR 12,404, Y 243,510).

$777* *Anemonen (Dube 360 II B), 1954,* s., d., blindstamp, (06-10-93, Hauswedell/Nolt, #392), image 15¹¹⁄₁₆ x 10¹³⁄₁₆ in., (38.2 x 27.4 cm.), lithograph on wove (BP 508, DM 1265, FR 4260, Y 82,475).

$310* *Badende (Dube 334), 1922,* (09-25-92, Granier, #2879), sheet 7⅜ x 4⅞ in., (18.7 x 12.4 cm.), woodcut on beige book print paper (BP 181, DM 460, FR 1554, Y 37,417).

$733* *Badende Kinder (Dube, Nr. 354 III), 1952,* d., s., (11-13-92, Kunsthaus, #591), 14⅝ x 10⁵⁄₁₆ in., (37.2 x 26.2 cm.), lithograph on wove (BP 474, DM 1151, FR 3880, Y 90,977).

BI *Bei Ghent (D. 238), 1916,* num. 28/75, pub. in Der Bildermann, margins, good cond., staining, creases, surface soiling, est. $4/600, (02-24-93, Butterfield, #2935), 10⅞ x 8¼ in., (276 x 210 mm.), lithograph on wove.

$3054* *Beim Vorlesen (D. 272/II/B), 1914,* s., d., blindstamp, (06-23-93, Kornfeld, #399), woodcut on thick wove (BP 2075, DM 5168, FR 17,382, Y 332,716, SF 4600).

$2825* *Beim Vorlesen (Dube 272 II B), 1914,* s., d., blindstamp, (06-10-93, Hauswedell/Nolt, #395), image 11⅞ x 7⅞ in., (30.1 x 20 cm.), engraving on thick hand-made (BP 1848, DM 4600, FR 15,488, Y 299,862).

$3583* *Beim Vorlesen (Dube H272 B), 1914,* second (final) state, s., d., s. by printer Voigt, pub. in Verlag der Dichtung, 1. Mappe, 1922, blindstamp, margins, foxing, creasing, good cond., (05-20-93, Christie-London, #440, illus.), image 11¾ x 8 in., (29.8 x 20.3 cm.), sheet 19¾ x 13¾ in., (29.8 x 20.3 cm.), woodcut on Japan w/wirelines (BP 2300, DM 5781, FR 19,473, Y 395,649).

$1382* *Berge Im Winter (Dube III 377), 1964,* s., d., t., blindstamp, (09-04-92, Germann, #388), 18¹¹⁄₁₆ x 24¹¹⁄₁₆ in., (475 x 627 mm.), color lithograph (BP 693, DM 1937, FR 6594, Y 170,113, SF 1725).

BI *Bildnis (Dube Band III 453 II C), 1965,* t., s., from Europaische Graphik IV, est. DM 2,200-, (11-21-92, Lempertz, #184), 20¹⁵⁄₁₆ x 15¹⁄₁₆ in., (53.2 x 38.2 cm.), color woodcut on BFK Rives wove.

BI *Bildnis E.G. (Dube L260), 1920,* s., d., margins, pen strokes, staining, good cond., est. BP 1/1,500, (05-20-93, Christie-London, #442, illus.), image 19½ x 15¼ in., (49.5 x 38.7 cm.), sheet 22¾ x 19⅜ in., (49.5 x 38.7 cm.), .

BI *"Bildnis E.G." (Dube 260), 1920,* s., d., est. DM 3,5/3,700, (11-28-92, Grisebach, #533, illus.), 19⁵⁄₁₆ x 15⅛ in., (49 x 38.4 cm.), lithograph on handmade.

$1588* *"Birnen" (Dube 342), 1948,* s., d., num., (11-28-92, Grisebach, #535, illus.), 12¹³⁄₁₆ x 16⅝ in., (32.6 x 42.3 cm.), colored lithograph on thick wove (BP 1048, DM 2530, FR 8588, Y 197,635).

$2213* *Die Brandung (Dube 289 II), 1915,* s., t., d., (12-05-92, Bassenge, #7230), 14⁷⁄₁₆ x 10⁷⁄₁₆ in., (36.7 x 26.5 cm.), woodcut on handmade (BP 1386, DM 3450, FR 11,759, Y 274,192).

$235,860* *Brucke Mappe 1911 - VI. Mappe, Erich Heckel, 1910-1911,* (06-25-93, Kornfeld, #23, illus.), portfolio 22¾ x 17⁵⁄₁₆ in., (57.8 x 44 cm.), 1 color woodcut, 1 lithograph, 1 drypoint (BP 159,527, DM 401,532, FR 1,352,408, Y 25,001,060, SF 356,500).

BI *"Clown Und Knabe" (Dube 150/II), 1924,* s., d., est. DM 4/4,200, (11-28-92, Grisebach, #532, illus.), 9¹¹⁄₁₆ x 6½ in., (24.6 x 16.5 cm.), drypoint on handmade.

$4944* *Drei Frauen Am Wasser (Dube 338 I A), 1923,* s., d., (06-10-93, Hauswedell/Nolt, #403, illus.), image 15¾ x 12⅝ in., (40 x 32 cm.), woodcut on thin Japan (BP 3234, DM 8051, FR 27,105, Y 524,785).

$4805* *Drei Frauen Am Wasser (Dube 338 I B), 1923,* s., d., num., (09-19-92, Wachholtz, #242, illus.), 15¾ x 12⅝ in., (40 x 32 cm.), woodcut on Simili Japan (BP 2813, DM 7130, FR 24,391, Y 593,870).

$5085* *Ehepaar (Dube 213), 1914,* s., d., (06-10-93, Hauswedell/Nolt, #390, illus.), image 14¾ x 12½ in., (37.4 x 31.8 cm.), lithograph on hand-made (BP 3326, DM 8280, FR 27,878, Y 539,752).

$846* *Eucalyptusblatter (Dube L 388), 1966,* s., d., num., Jubilaumsmappe "B" der Kestner-Gesellschaft, (05-26-93, Dorling, #2715), 20³⁄₁₆ x 13¹¹⁄₁₆ in., (51.3 x 34.7 cm.), color lithograph on vollrandigem BFK Rives wove (BP 547, DM 1380, FR 4646, Y 91,917).

BI *Die Fahrt (D. 241/II/B), 1916,* num. 28/75, pub. in Die Bilderman, margins, good cond., staining, est. $7/900, (02-24-93, Butterfield, #2936), 10⅛ x 8⅜ in., (257 x 213 mm.), lithograph on wove.

$1498* *Flusslandschaft (D. R148), 1924,* s., d., wide margins, light-staining, good cond., (12-01-92, Christie-London, #389), plate 5¹¹⁄₁₆ x 7¹³⁄₁₆ in., (145 x 198 mm.), drypoint on fibrous Japan (BP 990, DM 2388, FR 8137, Y 186,504).

$671* *Fordelandschaft (Dube 362 II), 1954,* s., d., (06-10-93, Hauswedell/Nolt, #393), image 11¾ x 15⁷⁄₁₆ in., (29.8 x 39.2 cm.), lithograph on wove (BP 439, DM 1093, FR 3679, Y 71,224).

BI *Franzosische Flusslandschaft (Dube 135), 1916,* s., d., est. DM 6,000, (05-26-93, Lempertz, #209, illus.), 11¹³⁄₁₆ x 18¾ in., (30 x 47.7 cm.), etching (drypoint) on copper print.

$2640* *Franzosische Flusslandshcaft (Dube R 136), 1916,* s., d., i. Ostende, pub. Verlag Neue Kunst Hans Goltz, margins, goodcond., creases, foxing, ink spot, nicks, (11-05-92, Sotheby-NY, #200, illus.), 6¼ x 7⅛ in., (158 x 181 mm.), sheet 11¾ x 18½ in., (158 x 181 mm.), drypoint p. in greenish-black on heavy wove (BP 1717, DM 4175, FR 14,125, Y 323,887).

$4662* *Frauen Am Strand (D. H320), 1919,* s., d., s., pub. Elf Holzschnitte, wide margins, foxing, mount-staining, laid, (12-01-92, Christie-London, #388, illus.), L. 18⅛ x 12¹³⁄₁₆ in., (460 x 325 mm.), woodcut on wove (BP 3080, DM 7431, FR 25,323, Y 580,428).

$1844* *Frauenkopf (Dube 269 A), 1922,* s., (12-05-92, Bassenge, #7236), 10⁹⁄₁₆ x 8⁷⁄₁₆ in., (26.8 x 21.4 cm.), lithograph on Japan (BP 1155, DM 2875, FR 9798, Y 228,472).

$516* *Der Freund (Dube 173 II), 1954,* s., (12-05-92, Bassenge, #7234), 9¾ x 6⅜ in., drypoint on geschopftem paper (BP 323, DM 804, FR 2742, Y 63,933).

$3390* *Gartnerei (Dube 254), 1913,* s., d. '14, full margins, good cond., some minor handling creases, Late Gerhard Brauer Coll., (05-27-93, Sotheby-Amstrdm, #732, illus.), 10¼ x 8⅞ in., (260 x 225 mm.), woodcut on buff laid paper (BP 2171, DM 5440, FR 18,334, Y 363,422, G 6095).

$6109* *Geschwister (D. 260), 1913,* s., d., ded., (06-23-93, Kornfeld, #398, illus.), woodcut on tan (red color) handmade (BP 4150, DM 10,337, FR 34,769, Y 665,541, SF 9200).

$1419* *Geshwister (Dube 284 III), 1929,* s., (06-05-93, Bassenge, #6095), 10⁹⁄₁₆ x 8⁷⁄₁₆ in., (26.8 x 21.4 cm.), lithograph on hand-made Japan (BP 934, DM 2301, FR 7754, Y 152,221).

$1588* *Handstand (Dube 2301), 1916,* s., d., #1/100, (10-14-92, Germann, #10, illus.), 16⁹⁄₁₆ x 12⅝ in., (420 x 320 mm.), lithograph (BP 932, DM 2324, FR 7881, Y 192,438, SF 2070).

$2497* *Haus (D. L52), 1907,* s., d., margins, staining, creases, defects, tears, (12-01-92, Christie-London, #386), L. 10¹¹⁄₁₆ x 12¹¹⁄₁₆ in., (271 x 322 mm.), sheet 14⅝ x 18⁹⁄₁₆ in., (271 x 322 mm.), lithograph on grey wove (BP 1650, DM 3980, FR 13,563, Y 310,881).

$17,917* *Hockende (Dube H263 IIB), 1913,* second (final) state, s., d. 14, s. by printer Voigt, pub. in Elf Holzschnitte, 1912-1919, Erich Heckel bei J.B. Neumann, 1921, wide margins, foxmars, light-staining, very good cond., (05-20-93, Christie-London, #439, illus.), image 16¼ x 11¾ in., (41.3 x 29.8 cm.), sheet 24 x 20¼ in., (41.3 x 29.8 cm.), woodcut on wove (BP 11,500, DM 28,908, FR 97,375, Y 1,978,467).

$6262* *Im Dangaster Moor (Dube 157/a), 1908,* s., d., t., (06-23-93, Kornfeld, #397, illus.), woodcut on thick Japan (BP 4254, DM 10,596, FR 35,640, Y 682,209, SF 9430).

$1919* *Der Irre (Dube 127), 1914,* s., d., margins, good cond., minor foxing, tape staining at edges ofsheet verso, Late Gerhard Brauer Coll., (05-27-93, Sotheby-Amstrdm, #733, illus.), 5¹⁵⁄₁₆ x 9⁵⁄₁₆ in., (151 x 237 mm.), etching on wove (BP 1229, DM 3079, FR 10,379, Y 205,725, G 3450).

$6271* *Der Irre (Dube L215), 1914,* s., d., margins, light-staining, very good cond., (05-20-93, Christie-London, #441, illus.), image 10¾ x 8½ in., (27.3 x 21.6 cm.), sheet 15 x 11 in., (27.3 x 21.6 cm.), lithograph w/extensive hand-coloring in black, blue and yellow on smooth wove (BP 4025, DM 10,118, FR 34,082, Y 692,469).

$1217* *Junge Frau (Dube H 392), 1949,* s., num., blindstamp, (05-08-93, Zeller, #886, illus.), 15¹⁵⁄₁₆ x 11⁹⁄₁₆ in., (40.5

x 29.4 cm.), woodcut (BP 794, DM 1955, FR 6596, Y 135,993).

$5037* *Junger Clown (Dube H 244 b), 1929,* s., d., (09-19-92, Wachholtz, #243, illus.), 11⁹⁄₁₆ x 6¹⁄₁₆ in., (29.4 x 15.4 cm.), color woodcut on handmade (BP 2949, DM 7474, FR 25,569, Y 622,544).

$4944* *Kanal Bei Ostende (Dube 135 A), 1916,* s., d., i. artist's proof, (06-10-93, Hauswedell/Nolt, #385, illus.), image 5¾ x 7⅝ in., (14.6 x 19.4 cm.), drypoint on wove (BP 3234, DM 8051, FR 27,105, Y 524,785).

BI *Katalog Der Ausstellung, "Erich Heckel" In Der Kunst-hutte, Chemnitz,1931 (D. 346-7), 1930,* discoloration, good cond., est. BP 2/300, (12-01-92, Christie-London, #391), overall sheet 8⅜ x 6⁷⁄₁₆ in., (212 x 163 mm.), woodcuts on wove.

$634* *Kinderbildnis (Dube H 386), 1948,* s., d., (05-26-93, Dorling, #2711, illus.), 7½ x 6⅛ in., (19 x 15.5 cm.), woodcut on light cardboard (BP 410, DM 1034, FR 3482, Y 68,883).

$4511* *Kniende Am Stein (Dube 258 a A), 1913,* s., d., eleven wood engravings, (05-26-93, Lempertz, #208, illus.), 27⁹⁄₁₆ x 21⅞ in., (70 x 55.5 cm.), wood engraving on thick wove (BP 2918, DM 7360, FR 24,772, Y 490,113).

$433* *"Krankes Madchen" (Dube 266 B; Sohn 108-12), 1913,* (11-28-92, Grisebach, #534, illus.), 7½ x 5½ in., (19.1 x 14 cm.), woodcut on wove (BP 286, DM 690, FR 2342, Y 53,889).

$4520* *Leichenzug (Dube 50), 1907,* s., d., t., (06-10-93, Hauswedell/Nolt, #388, illus.), image 10⁷⁄₁₆ x 12⅝ in., (26.5 x 32 cm.), lithograph on hand-made (BP 2957, DM 7360, FR 24,781, Y 479,779).

BI *"Lesende" (D. 178/II), (19)54,* s., est. DM 2500, (12-01-92, Karl/Faber, #713), 9⅝ x 12⅝ in., (24.5 x 32 cm.), drypoint on rough wove.

BI *Lesendes Madchen (Dube 174), 1954,* s., d., full margins, good cond., minor soiling, creasing in margins, Late Gerhard Brauer Coll., est. Dfl. 1/1,500, (05-27-93, Sotheby-Amstrdm, #734), 9¾ x 7¾ in., (247 x 197 mm.), etching on wove.

$498* *Liegende (D. L 340 B), (19)48,* s., d., num., (12-01-92, Karl/Faber, #717), 7½ x 12³⁄₁₆ in., (19 x 31 cm.), lithograph on wove (BP 329, DM 794, FR 2705, Y 62,002).

$1240* *Liegende (Dube 259 II b.-Sohn HDO 118-8), 1913-1914,* s., (09-19-92, Wachholtz, #240, illus.), 7¹⁄₁₆ x 4⅛ in., (18 x 10.5 cm.), woodcut on werkdruckpapier (BP 726, DM 1840, FR 6294, Y 153,257).

$20,480* *Madchen Am Meer (Dube 314 A), 1918,* s., d., portfolio Elf Holzschnitte, Neumann, (06-10-93, Hauswedell/Nolt, #399, illus.), image 17¹⁵⁄₁₆ x 12¹³⁄₁₆ in., (45.6 x 32.5 cm.), woodcut worked over w/watercolor on wove (BP 13,396, DM 33,350, FR 112,281, Y 2,173,867).

BI *"Madchen" Mit Turban (Dube H 211), 1911,* s., d., t., est. DM 13/15,000, (12-01-92, Karl/Faber, #708, illus.), 12⅜ x 8¼ in., (31.5 x 21 cm.), woodcut on hand-made.

BI *Madchenkopf (D. 16), 1907,* margins, good cond., staining, tear, creases, est. $3/500, (02-24-93, Butterfield, #2934), 7⅝ x 6¼ in., (194 x 159 mm.), lithograph on wove.

BI *Madchenkopf (D. 264), 1913,* pub. in Genius, 1920, margins, good cond., staining, creases, surfacesoiling, est. $6/800, (02-24-93, Butterfield, #2937), 10³⁄₁₆ x 6¾ in., (259 x 171 mm.), woodcut on wove.

BI *"Mannerbildnis" (Dube H 318/III B), 1919,* s., est. DM 80/100,000, (11-27-92, Grisebach, #18, illus.), 18⅛ x 12¾ in., (46.1 x 32.4 cm.), color woodcut on hand-made.

$18,046* *"Mude" (Dube 265/II), 1913,* s., d., i., (11-28-92, Grisebach, #155, illus.), 18⁵⁄₁₆ x 13³⁄₁₆ in., (46.5 x 33.5 cm.), woodcut on handmade (BP 11,912, DM 28,749, FR 97,599, Y 2,245,924).

BI *Der Narr (D. H 309/II (von IV); Peters V/5), (19)17,* s., d., 5. Mappe Bauhaus Drucke, Neue Europaische Graphik, Deutsche Kunstler, Weimar, 1921, prov., est. DM 7000, (12-01-92, Karl/Faber, #710, illus.), 13¹⁵⁄₁₆ x 10⅝ in., (35.5 x 27 cm.), woodcut on hand-made.

$1540* *Ocean Front,* s. E. Heckel 16, very good cond., (09-27-92, Bakker, #268, illus.), image 5¾ x 7¾ in., (14.6 x 19.7 cm.), drypoint (BP 899, DM 2283, FR 7719, Y 185,878).

$1551* *Otto Mueller (Dube 291 I/II), 1933,* s., d., #9/10, (05-26-93, Lempertz, #211), 20⅞ x 13¹⁵⁄₁₆ in., (53 x 35.5 cm.), lithograph on thick handmade (BP 1003, DM 2531, FR 8517, Y 168,514).

$1394* *Regenbogen (D. 378, b, B), 1964,* #6/300, s., d., blindstamp, (10-09-92, Winterberg, #2323, illus.), 17⁹⁄₁₆ x 22⁹⁄₁₆ in., (44.6 x 57.3 cm.), color lithograph on BFK Rives (BP 827, DM 2071, FR 6953, Y 169,710).

$3884* *Romische Tanzerin (Dube 63), 1909,* s., d., t., (06-10-93, Hauswedell/Nolt, #383, illus.), image 5½ x 3⅞ in., (13.9 x 9.9 cm.), drypoint on copper print (BP 2541, DM 6325, FR 21,294, Y 412,270).

$3583* *Romische Tanzerin (Dube R63), 1909,* s., d., wide margins, very good cond., (05-20-93, Christie-London, #435, illus.), plate 5⅜ x 3⅞ in., (13.7 x 9.8 cm.), sheet 18⅝ x 14¼ in., (13.7 x 9.8 cm.), drypoint on firm wove paper (BP 2300, DM 5781, FR 19,473, Y 395,649).

BI *Ruhende (Dube Band II, 216 II), 1914,* #27/100, s., from portfolio Siebzehn Steinzeichnungen, est. DM 9,900-, (11-21-92, Lempertz, #179A, illus.), 10½ x 8⁷⁄₁₆ in., (26.6 x 21.5 cm.), color lithograph on ivory hand-made.

$706* *Schlafende Frau (Dube 352 II B), 1954,* s., d., t., blindstamp, (06-10-93, Hauswedell/Nolt, #391), image 14⁷⁄₁₆ x 10¹⁄₁₆ in., (36.7 x 25.5 cm.), lithograph on wove (BP 462, DM 1150, FR 3871, Y 74,939).

$1180* *Schlafende Frau (Dube 352 II), 1952,* s., (12-05-92, Bassenge, #7237), 14⁷⁄₁₆ x 10⁵⁄₁₆ in., (36.7 x 26.2 cm.), lithograph (BP 739, DM 1840, FR 6270, Y 146,202).

$4149* *Schneetreiben (D. H 278/II), (19)14,* s., d., (12-01-92, Karl/Faber, #709, illus.), 17⅛ x 11⅝ in., (43.5 x 29.5 cm.), woodcut on blotting paper (BP 2741, DM 6613, FR 22,537, Y 516,559).

$4507* *Schneetreiben (Dube, Bd. I, 278 III), 1914,* s., d., creases, (11-13-92, Koller, #5336), 17³⁄₁₆ x 11⅝ in., (43.7 x 29.6 cm.), woodcut on wove (BP 2912, DM 7075, FR 23,859, Y 559,389, SF 6380).

$330* *Schreitende (D. 325B), 1921,* pub. in Die Gaeste, margins, apparently good cond., (02-24-93, Butterfield, #2938), 9¹¹⁄₁₆ x 7¼ in., (246 x 184 mm.), woodcut on wove (BP 230, DM 536, FR 1816, Y 38,723).

$400* *Schwarze Und Weisse Kugel (11. Jahresblatt) (D. 372), 1940,* 2nd (final) state, s., d., foxmarks, light-staining, (12-01-92, Christie-London, #392), L. 5⅞ x 5¹⁄₁₆ in., (150 x 129 mm.), sheet 8¹⁄₁₆ x 8¼ in., (150 x 129 mm.), woodcut on fibrous Japan (BP 264, DM 638, FR 2173, Y 49,801).

$2819* *Segelboot (Dube 143), 1907,* s., d., Jahresmappe der Kunstlergruppe "Brucke", (05-26-93, Lempertz, #205), 16⁵⁄₁₆ x 12⁵⁄₁₆ in., (41.5 x 31.3 cm.), wood engraving on thick copper print (BP 1824, DM 4599, FR 15,481, Y 306,280).

$1059* *Segelboote (Dube 43), 1908,* s., i. 1. artist's proof, (06-10-93, Hauswedell/Nolt, #382, illus.), image 5⅜ x 6⁹⁄₁₆ in., (13.7 x 16.7 cm.), etching on copper print board (BP 693, DM 1724, FR 5806, Y 112,408).

BI *Sleeping Girl (Dube, Nr. 352B),* est. DM 2,000, (11-13-92, Kunsthaus, #590), 14⁷⁄₁₆ x 10⁵⁄₁₆ in., (36.7 x 26.2 cm.), lithograph on wove.

$3531* *Sonnenaufgang (Dube 284 II B), 1914,* s., d., Kreis graphischer Kunstler und Sammler, portfolio 2, 1921, Beyer, (06-10-93, Hauswedell/Nolt, #396, illus.), image 14⁵⁄₁₆ x 10⅝ in., (36.4 x 27 cm.), woodcut on hand-made (BP 2310, DM 5750, FR 19,359, Y 374,801).

$1907* *Der Spaziergang (Dube 317 I/II), 1919,* s., d., (06-10-93, Hauswedell/Nolt, #400, illus.), image 18⅛ x 12¹³⁄₁₆ in., (46 x 32.6 cm.), woodcut on hand-made rag (BP 1247, DM 3105, FR 10,455, Y 202,420).

BI *Stehendes Kind (Franzi Stehend) (Dube W204 b2; Bolliger & Kornfeld 22), 1911,* s., d., issued in VI. Jahresmappe der Kunstlergruppe Brucke, margins, inconspicuous marks, backed tear, pencil strokes, staining, foxmarks, lesser defects, good cond., est. BP 100/120,000(05-20-93, Christie-London, #436, illus.), image 14½ x 11 in., (36.8 x 27.9 cm.), sheet 20¼ x 15 in., (36.8 x 27.9 cm.), woodcut p. in black, deep-green and red on firm wove.

$2051* *Stilleben Mit Vasen Und Tischkarten (Dube, Nr. 381 C), 1965,* s., d., #44/65, (11-13-92, Kunsthaus, #593, illus.), 20¹⁄₁₆ x 14¹⁵⁄₁₆ in., (51 x 38 cm.), color lithograph on

BFK Rives hand-made (BP 1325, DM 3220, FR 10,858, Y 254,561).

$7448* *Stralsund (Dube 243 II B), 1912,* s., portfolio Elf Holzschnitte, 1912-1919, Neumann, (06-05-93, Bassenge, #6088, illus.), 12⅛ x 14¼ in., (30.8 x 36.2 cm.), woodcut (BP 4903, DM 12,075, FR 40,699, Y 798,970).

$8157* *"Stralsund" (Dube 243/II), 1912,* s., d., (06-05-93, Grisebach, #286, illus.), 11 15/16 x 14¼ in., (30.3 x 36.2 cm.), woodcut on thick hand-made (BP 5370, DM 13,225, FR 44,574, Y 875,027).

$12,542* *Szene Im Wald (Dube L 153), 1910,* s., d., issued in VI Jahresmappe der Kunstlergruppe Brucke, 1911, margins, foxmarks, creases, very good cond., (05-20-93, Christie-London, #438, illus.), image 10¾ x 13¼ in., (27.3 x 33.7 cm.), sheet 15¾ x 21¼ in., (27.3 x 33.7 cm.), lithograph on firm wove (BP 8050, DM 20,236, FR 68,163, Y 1,384,938).

$2020* *Tulpen (Dube Band I 353 III b), 1952,* s., d., (11-21-92, Lempertz, #183, illus.), 14 13/16 x 12⅞ in., (37.7 x 32.7 cm.), color lithograph on wove (BP 1330, DM 3221, FR 10,849, Y 251,213).

$948* *Vernschneite Berge (Dube III 390), 1967,* #42/60, s., d., t., (04-21-93, Germann, #510, illus.), 11 13/16 x 16⅛ in., (300 x 410 mm.), lithograph (BP 615, DM 1515, FR 5124, Y 104,949, SF 1380).

BI *Verschneite Berge (Dube III 390), 1967,* #42/60, s., d., t., est. SF 1/1,300, (09-04-92, Germann, #389), 11 13/16 x 16⅛ in., (300 x 410 mm.), lithograph.

BI *Vorm Spiegel (Dube Band II, 265 II), 1920,* s., d., i., est. DM 23,000-, (11-21-92, Lempertz, #180, illus.), 19 5/16 x 15 1/16 in., (49 x 38.3 cm.), lithograph on cream factory-made paper.

BI *Weib (Dube 133), 1907,* s., est. DM 8,000, (12-05-92, Bassenge, #7229, illus.), 7½ x 5⅛ in., (19 x 13 cm.), woodcut on thick handmade.

$5477* *Weisse Dahlien (D. L 272/II), (19)22,* s., d., (12-01-92, Karl/Faber, #715, illus.), 23 1/16 x 16 9/16 in., (58.5 x 42 cm.), watercolor/lithograph on simili-Japan (BP 3619, DM 8730, FR 29,750, Y 681,897).

$24,704* *Weisse Pferde (Dube 242 IV), 1912,* s., d., crease, repaired, (10-14-92, Germann, #11, illus.), 16¾ x 15¾ in., (425 x 400 mm.), wood cut (BP 14,500, DM 36,154, FR 122,600, Y 2,993,698, SF 32,200).

BI *"Winter I(n) Angeln" (Dube Nr. 361, II), 1954,* t., d., s., est. DM 2,500, (11-13-92, Kunsthaus, #592, illus.), 10½ x 14¾ in., (26.7 x 37.4 cm.), lithograph on wove.

$1803* *Der Zeichner (Dube Band I 385), 1948,* t., s., d., lightstains, (11-21-92, Lempertz, #182), 11⅞ x 9⅝ in., (30.2 x 24.5 cm.), woodcut on Japan (BP 1187, DM 2875, FR 9683, Y 224,226).

$709* *Zirkus (Dube 349), 1930,* (06-05-93, Bassenge, #6091), 9 7/16 x 12 5/16 in., (24 x 31.2 cm.), woodcut of 2 blocks on hand-made (BP 467, DM 1149, FR 3874, Y 76,057).

$1271* *Zwei Am Meer (Dube 326 A), 1920,* s., d., (06-10-93, Hauswedell/Nolt, #402, illus.), image 7 x 5⅜ in., (17.8 x 13.6 cm.), woodcut on wove (BP 831, DM 2070, FR 6968, Y 134,911).

$35,834* *Zwei Frauen (Dube H182 I), 1910,* first state (of two), s., d., t., i., margins, paper split from printing, foxmarks, surface dirt, skinning, remarkably fresh cond., (05-20-93, Christie-London, #437, illus.), image 11 5/16 x 14 9/16 in., (28.7 x 37 cm.), sheet 13 3/16 x 17 15/16 in., (28.7 x 37 cm.), woodcut on smooth wove (BP 23,000, DM 57,815, FR 194,750, Y 3,956,935).

$7910* *Zwei Madchen (Dube 117), 1909,* s., d., t., (06-10-93, Hauswedell/Nolt, #389, illus.), image 13 5/16 x 10¾ in., (33.8 x 27.3 cm.), lithograph on copper print board (BP 5174, DM 12,881, FR 43,366, Y 839,614).

$2483* *Zwei Manner Am Meer (Dube 327 I), 1920,* s., d., (06-05-93, Bassenge, #6090), 18 3/16 x 12⅞ in., (46.2 x 32.7 cm.), woodcut (BP 1635, DM 4026, FR 13,568, Y 266,359).

BI *"Zwei Manner Am Tisch" (Dube 250/II), 1913,* s., stained, est. DM 7/9,000, (11-28-92, Grisebach, #156, illus.), 9⅜ x 10 5/16 in., (23.8 x 26.2 cm.), woodcut on handmade.

$3850* *Zwei Verwundete (Dube W494), 1915,* watermark, 2nd final state, s., d., i., full margins, mat staining, edges folded back, good cond., (11-09-92, Christie-NY, #102, illus.), 350 x 283 in., (889 x 718.8 cm.), woodcut on laid (BP 2545, DM 6146, FR 20,766, Y 477,786).

HECKER, Franz 1870-1944

$698* *Bauer (Hamm. 13), 1909,* s., wear, (09-25-92, Granier, #2634), 5⅞ x 4¾ in., (15 x 12 cm.), sheet 12 11/16 x 9 15/16 in., (15 x 12 cm.), etching on brown hand-made (BP 408, DM 1035, FR 3499, Y 84,249).

$698* *Beim Kuhhuten (Hamm 60), c. 1923,* s., t., num., (09-25-92, Granier, #2638), 4⅝ x 6⅞ in., (11.7 x 17.5 cm.), sheet 9 15/16 x 11⅝ in., (11.7 x 17.5 cm.), etching in brown on beige copper print paper (BP 408, DM 1035, FR 3499, Y 84,249).

$1319* *Musikanten (Hamm. 24), 1909,* s., wear, trimmed, (09-25-92, Granier, #2637), image 10 3/16 x 14⅜ in., (25.8 x 36.5 cm.), sheet 12 x 16 7/16 in., (25.8 x 36.5 cm.), etching in olive green on copper print paper (BP 770, DM 1955, FR 6612, Y 159,203).

$2172* *Primula Veris (Hamm. 19), 1909,* s., num., dusty, (09-25-92, Granier, #2636, illus.), 9⅝ x 13⅞ in., (24.5 x 35.2 cm.), sheet 17 15/16 x 23 9/16 in., (24.5 x 35.2 cm.), color etching on copper print board (BP 1268, DM 3220, FR 10,887, Y 262,161).

$1319* *Quartett (Hamm. 2), 1908,* s., t., num., creases, (09-25-92, Granier, #2633), 11 7/16 x 14⅝ in., (29 x 37.2 cm.), sheet 18⅝ x 25¾ in., (29 x 37.2 cm.), etching on brownish beige copper print board (BP 770, DM 1955, FR 6612, Y 159,203).

$698* *Studienkopf (Hamm. 14), 1909,* s., wear, (09-25-92, Granier, #2635), 4⅝ x 3⅞ in., (11.8 x 9.8 cm.), sheet 14 13/16 x 9 13/16 in., (11.8 x 9.8 cm.), etching on brownish beige wove paper (BP 408, DM 1035, FR 3499, Y 84,249).

HEDIGER, Kurt b. 1932

BI *Flusslandschaft, 1966,* 8/140, s., d., hole, est. SF 30/40, (10-14-92, Germann, #533), 20 1/16 x 16 9/16 in., (510 x 420 mm.), lithograph.

$22* *Flusslandschaft, 1966,* #8/140, s., d., (09-04-92, Germann, #390), 20 1/16 x 16 9/16 in., (510 x 420 mm.), lithograph (BP 11, DM 31, FR 105, Y 2708, SF 28).

HEDSTROM, Trond

$880* *The 9:45 Express, c. 1950,* s., credit stamp, label w/t. in ink, flush mounted, prov., (10-13-92, Christie-NY, #459, illus.), 15⅝ x 9¾ in., (39.7 x 24.8 cm.), photograph, gelatin silver print (BP 513, DM 1289, FR 4380, Y 106,705).

HEEMSKERCK, Jacoba van

$3070* *Sechs Holzschnitte: Six,* portfolio, each s., pub. Verlag Der Sturm, margins, good cond., minor creasing, some foxing, in orig. portfolio, Late Gerhard Brauer Coll., (05-27-93, Sotheby-Amstrdm, #735, illus.), each sheet 14 15/16 x 20¼ in., (380 x 515 mm.), woodcut on Japan (BP 1966, DM 4926, FR 16,604, Y 329,117, G 5520).

HEEMSKERCK, Maarten van Dutch 1498-1574

$217* *Die Geschichte Von Dinah Und Shechem (Hollstein 410-413 II): Four,* (12-04-92, Bassenge, #6230), 7⅞ x 9⅝ in., (20 x 24.5 cm.), engraving (BP 139, DM 346, FR 1172, Y 27,091).

$1910* *The Seven Wonders Of The World And The Ruins Of The Colisuem (Holl. 357-364): Set Of Eight,* 1st state of 3, watermark, trimmed, paper losses, stains, good cond., (06-29-93, Sotheby-London, #46, illus.), each approx. 8¼ x 10¼ in., (21 x 26 cm.), engraving on paper (BP 1265, DM 3225, FR 10,871, Y 203,321).

HEEMSKERCK VAN BEEST, Jacoba 1876-1923

$879* *Komposition (Sohn HDO Bd. 1. Nr. 103-6), 1920-1921,* s., 6 sheet of 3 portfolio Bauhaus, blindstamp, (11-13-92, Kunsthaus, #594), 11 13/16 x 15¾ in., (30 x 40 cm.), linocut on Japan (BP 568, DM 1380, FR 4653, Y 109,098).

HEEMSKERK, Maarten van (after)

$1498* *"Clades" or Disasters Of The Jewish Nations, (Holl. 202-223): Set OfTwenty-One,* by P. Galle, thread margins or trimmed, small paper adhesion, staining, very good cond., (12-01-92, Christie-London, #78), averaging S. 5¼ x 7¾ in., (133 x 197 mm.), engraving (BP 990, DM 2388, FR 8137, Y 186,504).

$1498* *The History Of Bel And The Dragon, (Holl. 534-43), c. 1565: Set Of Ten,* first state (of three), wide margins, thin spot, staining, defects, (12-01-92, Christie-London, #81), averaging P. 7¹⁵⁄₁₆ x 9¾ in., (201 x 248 mm.), engraving (BP 990, DM 2388, FR 8137, Y 186,504).

$169* *Schlusselubergabe Nach Der Belagerung Von Schmalkalden (Hollstein Bd. IV, 226), 1556,* by Dirk Volkertsz Coornhert, (03-24-93, Venator/Hansten, #2530), plate 6¼ x 9⅛ in., (15.8 x 23.1 cm.), engraving (BP 114, DM 276, FR 939, Y 19,857).

$749* *The Story Of Esther, Plates 1-3, 5-8, (Holl. 248-50, 252-5), c. 1560: Set Of Eight,* tone, good cond., (12-01-92, Christie-London, #79), averaging P. 7¹⁵⁄₁₆ x 9⅝ in., (203 x 245 mm.), engraving (BP 495, DM 1194, FR 4068, Y 93,252).

HEERUP, Henry   Danish b. 1909

$293* *"Bolgekysset", "Kjaerlighedsankeret" and "Intuition", (Moestrup 208 ad 260): Three,* s., (09-29-92, B. Rasmussen, #321), lithograph (BP 165, DM 414, FR 1412, Y 34,977, DK 1610).

$147* *Composition,* s. Heerup, (09-30-92, Kunsthallen, #118), linocut (BP 83, DM 208, FR 705, Y 17,641, DK 805).

$110* *Elskende Par I Ornamentskov, 1970,* s. Heerup, 99/150, (03-24-93, Kunsthallen, #128), color lithograph (BP 74, DM 180, FR 611, Y 12,924, DK 690).

BI *Eventyr Af H.C. Andersen, 1983: Six,* complete set, each s., d., #2/125, margins, good cond., est. Dfl. 2,5/3,000, (05-27-93, Sotheby-Amstrdm, #625), each 16¾ x 23⅝ in., (425 x 600 mm.), color lithograph on wove.

$274* *Flojte Huggas Billedbog, 1953,* p. Permild & Rosengreen, (09-30-92, Kunsthallen, #119), color lithograph (BP 155, DM 389, FR 1314, Y 32,881, DK 1495).

$110* *Foraeldre, (M. 224), 1970,* s. Heerup, 61/150, (03-24-93, Kunsthallen, #127), color lithograph (BP 74, DM 180, FR 611, Y 12,924, DK 690).

$138* *Foraret,* s. Heerup, 894/999, (03-24-93, Kunsthallen, #125), color lithograph (BP 93, DM 225, FR 767, Y 16,214, DK 863).

$92* *Fredsduva,* s. EA, (11-07-92, Falkkloos, #179), serigraph (BP 60, DM 148, FR 496, Y 11,355, SK 550).

$92* *Hymne Til Foraret, (M. 281), 1980,* s. Heerup, 27/350, (03-24-93, Kunsthallen, #124), color lithograph (BP 62, DM 150, FR 511, Y 10,810, DK 575).

$147* *Kattekillingen, 1971,* s. Heerup, 126/200, from the series Go'Da Dyr, (03-24-93, Kunsthallen, #132), color lithograph (BP 100, DM 240, FR 817, Y 17,272, DK 920).

$156* *Loven,* s. Heerup, 118/267, (03-24-93, Kunsthallen, #123), color lithograph (BP 106, DM 255, FR 867, Y 18,329, DK 978).

$110* *Medaljon, (M. 118). 1956,* s. Heerup, (03-24-93, Kunsthallen, #131), linoprint (BP 74, DM 180, FR 611, Y 12,924, DK 690).

$230* *"Mor Og Barn", (Moestrup 122),* s., (09-29-92, B. Rasmussen, #322), linocut (BP 129, DM 325, FR 1108, Y 27,456, DK 1265).

$110* *Oresundsmode, (Jvf. M. 227), 1990,* s. Heerup 212/225, (03-24-93, Kunsthallen, #126), color lithograph (BP 74, DM 180, FR 611, Y 12,924, DK 690).

$101* *Pa Livsvjen, (M. 160), 1960,* s. Heerup, (03-24-93, Kunsthallen, #130), linoprint (BP 68, DM 165, FR 561, Y 11,867, DK 633).

$358* *Portfolio, 1945,* s., #296 of 350, p. Chr. Sorensen, (09-30-92, Kunsthallen, #117), color lithograph (BP 202, DM 508, FR 1717, Y 42,962, DK 1955).

$92* *Rod Kvinna,* s. EA, (11-07-92, Falkkloos, #180), serigraph (BP 60, DM 148, FR 496, Y 11,355, SK 550).

$74* *Rod Sol,* s. EA, (11-07-92, Falkkloos, #178), serigraph (BP 48, DM 119, FR 399, Y 9134, SK 440).

BI *Sagadrom, (M. 206a), 1968,* s. Heerup, 126/300, est. DK 1,000, (03-24-93, Kunsthallen, #129), color lithograph.

HEESER, Edwin Bower

$1020* *Jean Harlow Standing On A Rock, Arms High, Griffith Park, 1929,* blind embossed, proof, (10-10-92, Bonhams, #160, illus.), 30 x 24 in., (76.2 x 61 cm.), photograph (BP 605, DM 1515, FR 5087, Y 124,178).

HEESER, Peter   b. 1938

BI *Komposition, 1971,* s., d., creases, est. DM 200, (09-18-92, Schloss Ahlden, #1003), 30¹³⁄₁₆ x 20⅝ in., (78.3 x

52.4 cm.), etching in black, light-and-medium green on hand-made.

HEFFERNAN, Edward Bonaventura   b. 1912

$24* *1888 Building,* s. Edward Heffernan, i. 1888 Building, #35/100, (08-11-92, L. Joel, #165G), 8¹⁵⁄₁₆ x 14 in., (22.7 x 35.6 cm.), linocut (BP 12, DM 35, FR 119, Y 3073, A$ 33).

HEGENBARTH, Josef   1884-1962

$1826* *"Salambo", 1922: Twenty,* s., num., (12-01-92, Karl/Faber, #720), 21¼ x 14¹⁵⁄₁₆ in., (54 x 38 cm.), drypoint and lithograph on japanartigem cardboard (BP 1206, DM 2910, FR 9919, Y 227,341).

$325* *"Toilettenszene (2. Fassung)" (Lewinger 111), 1920,* s., (11-28-92, Grisebach, #536, illus.), 11⅝ x 11¼ in., (29.6 x 28.5 cm.), drypoint on wove (BP 215, DM 518, FR 1758, Y 40,448).

$922* *Vorstadjuche,* s., t., (06-05-93, Bassenge, #6101, illus.), 9¹¹⁄₁₆ x 11⅝ in., (24.6 x 29.6 cm.), etching on yellowish Japan (BP 607, DM 1495, FR 5038, Y 98,906).

HEGER, Frantz   1766-1831

$3399* *Anischt Des Hauptplatzes Vor Der Altstadt Prag, 1793,* d., staining, (11-11-92, Dorotheum, #382, illus.), 18⅛ x 25⅜ in., (46 x 64.5 cm.), hand-colored line etching (BP 2249, DM 5432, FR 18,206, Y 422,656, SC 17,920).

$2974* *Prag-Anischt Des Huberner Platzes Gegen Die Pflastergasse, 1792,* d., foxing, (11-11-92, Dorotheum, #380, illus.), 18½ x 24¹³⁄₁₆ in., (47 x 63 cm.), hand-colored line etching (BP 1968, DM 4753, FR 15,929, Y 369,809, SC 15,680).

HEICK, William

$431* *"The Fillmore, San Francisco",* 1947, p.l., s., d. twice, t., annot., (05-23-93, Butterfield, #3445, illus.), 10 x 8 in., photograph, gelatin silver print (BP 281, DM 705, FR 2372, Y 47,640).

$288* *"Seattle, Wash. Ladies Waiting To Welcome Gen'l McArthur Upon His Return From The Far East",* 1951, p.l., s., t., d., annot., est. $5/700, (05-23-93, Butterfield, #3446, illus.), 8 x 10 in., photograph, gelatin silver print (BP 188, DM 471, FR 1585, Y 31,834).

HEIDELBACH, Karl   b. 1923

BI *Bauernstuhl,* relief stamp H., A/P, s., d. Heidelbach 75, ded., est. DM 300-, (03-24-93, Venator/Hansten, #4497), approx. 24⅝ x 18⅛ in., (62.5 x 46 cm.), mixed media w/screenprint on Fabriano Cotton.

HEIJBOER, Anton   b. 1924

$2605* *Het Bloed Is Een Steen Geworden, 1964,* waxed crayon s., d.; #6/9, i. eigen druk, full margins, good cond.?, (12-09-92, Sotheby-Amstrdm, #584, illus.), 34⅝ x 22¼ in., (880 x 565 mm.), color etching on laid paper (BP 1662, DM 4089, FR 13,953, Y 323,001, G 4600).

$195* *Le Saint..., 1985,* colored chalk s., d.,; i. handdruk by the artist E.A., full margins,good cond.?, (12-09-92, Sotheby-Amstrdm, #587), 8⅜ x 8¹⁵⁄₁₆ in., (213 x 228 mm.), hand-colored etching w/aquatint on wove (BP 124, DM 306, FR 1044, Y 24,179, G 345).

$195* *Untitled, 1974,* waxed crayon s., d.; #8/9, margins, good cond.?, (12-09-92, Sotheby-Amstrdm, #586), sheet 7³⁄₁₆ x 10 in., (182 x 254 mm.), etching on 2 plates on wove (BP 124, DM 306, FR 1044, Y 24,179, G 345).

$977* *Wit Wezen, 1970,* brown chalk s., d., margins, good cond.?, (12-09-92, Sotheby-Amstrdm, #585), 23¹¹⁄₁₆ x 38¹⁵⁄₁₆ in., (602 x 990 mm.), color etching on laid paper (BP 623, DM 1534, FR 5233, Y 121,141, G 1725).

HEIJDEN, J.C.J. van der   b. 1928

$104* *Untitled,* s., #166/250, good cond., (12-09-92, Sotheby-Amstrdm, #589), sheet 10¹³⁄₁₆ x 8⅞ in., (275 x 225 mm.), color screenprint on wove (BP 66, DM 163, FR 557, Y 12,895, G 184).

$117* *Untitled, 1968,* s., d., #4/190, pub. Prent 190, good cond., creases, (12-09-92, Sotheby-Amstrdm, #588), sheet 25¹¹⁄₁₆ x 19¹¹⁄₁₆ in., (652 x 500 mm.), color etching and embossing on wove (BP 75, DM 184, FR 627, Y 14,507, G 207).

HEINDORFF, Michael

    BI *Tasso's Trees, 1971: Nine,* s., d. num., good cond., est. BP 8/1,200, (12-03-92, Sotheby-London, #698, illus.), screenprints in colors on wove.

HEINE, Thomas Theodor   1867-1948

    $1844* *Simplicissimus, 1896,* rare, Albert Langen's Verlag, Muchen, lit., signs of wear, (12-05-92, Bassenge, #7598, illus.), 31½ x 23¼ in., (80 x 59 cm.), color lithograph (BP 1155, DM 2875, FR 9798, Y 228,472).

HEINECKEN, Robert   b. 1931

    $248* *Collage, 1977,* #5/6, (05-16-93, Hindman, #353), 16 x 20 in., photograph, collage w/polaroid (BP 162, DM 400, FR 1348, Y 27,617).

    $518* *"Recto/Verso #1", 1988,* s., d., edit. AP 2/10, (05-23-93, Butterfield, #3447, illus.), 9 x 10¾ in., photograph, cibachrome print (BP 337, DM 847, FR 2851, Y 57,257).

HEINEMANN, William, Publisher

    $50* *Great Masters: Twenty Folios,* full margins, pub. 1904, (06-16-93, Bonhams-Chelsea, #335), photogravure (BP 33, DM 83, FR 279, Y 5333).

HEINTZELMAN, Arthur W.   American 1890-1965

    $121* *The Donkey Cart,* s. in plate, d. 1923, (11-01-92, Hanzel, #233), 10 x 7½ in., (25.4 x 19.1 cm.), etching (BP 79, DM 191, FR 643, Y 14,960).

    $70* *"L'Artiste Italian", 1931,* s., good cond., tape, surface dirt, (05-15-93, Cleveland, #156), 2¼ x 1¾ in., (5.7 x 4.4 cm.), etching (BP 46, DM 113, FR 378, Y 7760).

    $143* *Man In A Beret,* plate s., annot. Ciboure 27; num., s., (12-02-92, Boos, #456), plate 10½ x 7¼ in., (26.7 x 18.4 cm.), etching and drypoint (BP 92, DM 225, FR 768, Y 17,793).

    $90* *Portrait Of A Young Girl,* s., excell. cond., (05-15-93, Cleveland, #155), 9⅜ x 8¼ in., (23.8 x 21 cm.), etching (BP 59, DM 145, FR 486, Y 9977).

    $138* *The Rehearsal,* s., (12-10-92, Sloan, #585), 9¾ x 7¾ in., (24.8 x 19.7 cm.), drypoint etching (BP 89, DM 218, FR 746, Y 17,071).

HEISIG, Bernhard   b. 1925

    BI *Bildnis Einer Sitzenden Frau, c. 1979,* s., num., blindstamp, est. DM 750, (12-05-92, Bassenge, #7244), 23¼ x 15¾ in., (59 x 40 cm.), chalk lithograph on wove.

HEISMANN, Paul   b. 1912

    BI *Flower Study, c. 1940,* est. $1,2/1,800, (04-08-93, Christie-NY, #389, illus.), 10 x 8 in., (25.4 x 20.3 cm.), photograph, gelatin silver print.

    BI *Light Abstraction, c. 1940,* orig. in artist's coll., est. $1,5/2,500, (04-06-93, Sotheby-NY, #376, illus.), 7¾ x 9½ in., photograph.

    BI *Nude And Cactus Abstraction, c. 1940,* est. $1,2/1,800, (04-08-93, Christie-NY, #388, illus.), 14 x 11 in., (35.6 x 27.9 cm.), photograph, gelatin silver print.

    BI *Surrealistic Portraiture, c. 1941,* mounted, label, est. $1/1,500, (04-06-93, Sotheby-NY, #375, illus.), 13⅞ x 10¾ in., photograph.

HEIZER, Michael   American b. 1944

    BI *Dragged Mass (T. 235:MH84), 1983,* s., d., #15/40, blindstamp, pub. Tyler Graphics, Ltd., good cond., est. $800/1,000, (05-15-93, Sotheby-NY, #991), sheet 31⅞ x 46⅜ in., (81 x 117.8 cm.), lithograph, silkscreen and etching in colors on white handmade TGL paper.

    $690* *Levitated Mass (Tyler 234:MH83), 1983,* s., d., #40/40, blindstamp, pub. Tyler Graphics, Ltd., good cond., (05-15-93, Sotheby-NY, #990), sheet 31⅞ x 46½ in., (81 x 118.1 cm.), lithograph, silkscreen and etching in colors on white handmade TGL paper (BP 449, DM 1110, FR 3730, Y 76,488).

HELD, Al   American b. 1928

    BI *Out And In, 1987,* s., d., #32/50, Crown Point Press ink stamp, full margins, surface scuffs, creasing, good cond., est. $8/9,000, (05-11-93, Christie-NY, #430, illus.), sheet 39¾ x 52½ in., (101 x 133.4 cm.), color etching and aquatint on wove.

    $1650* *Stoneridge #6, State II, 1985,* s., d. 84, i. (c), num. 16/20, pub. Pace Editions, full sheet, excell. cond., (09-19-92, Christie-E, #122, illus.), sheet 26¾ x 39¼ in., (67.9

x 99.7 cm.), etching on heavy wove paper (BP 949, DM 2471, FR 8462, Y 205,582).

    $1150* *Straits Of Malacca II, 1988,* s., d. '89, #5/20, pub. Crown Point Press, full margins, good cond., (02-11-93, Sotheby-NY, #342, illus.), 35¼ x 44½ in., (89.5 x 113 cm.), etching (BP 811, DM 1905, FR 6446, Y 138,638).

HELDT, Werner   1904-1954

    $9220* *Berlin (Seel 629-635), 1949: Six,* s., num., (12-05-92, Bassenge, #7251), lithograph (BP 5773, DM 14,375, FR 48,990, Y 1,142,362).

    $891* *Blick Aus Dem Fenster Mit Mandoline (Seel 372), 1946,* #110, mono., d., (10-09-92, Winterberg, #2336), 7¹⁵⁄₁₆ x 6⁹⁄₁₆ in., (20.2 x 16.7 cm.), linocut on wove (BP 529, DM 1324, FR 4444, Y 108,473).

    $1328* *Hauser Und Trummer (Seel 462), 1947,* s., num., (12-05-92, Bassenge, #7249, illus.), 11¹³⁄₁₆ x 8¼ in., (30 x 21 cm.), lithograph on wove (BP 832, DM 2070, FR 7056, Y 164,540).

HELFOND, Riva

    BI *"Elec. Plant" and "No. 6 Colliery": Two,* s., t.; second t., i., sig. erased/rewritten, tape stains; both hinged to mat, foxing, good cond., est. $1,4/1,600, (12-04-92, Doyle, #108), larger 14¼ x 15 in., (362 x 381 mm.), lithograph.

    BI *"Lansford, PA" and "A Miner": Two,* both s., t., hinged to mats, good cond.; first w/smudging, soiling, missing corner, est. $4/600, (12-04-92, Doyle, #106), larger 10¼ x 15 in., (260 x 381 mm.), lithograph.

    BI *"Refuges", "Harvest Of War" and "Devastation": Three,* first two s., mat burn, soiling, smudging, hinged to mats, good cond., est. $7/900, (12-04-92, Doyle, #107), larger 9½ x 13½ in., (241 x 343 mm.), lithograph.

HELHESTEN

    $239* *1, Argang, Nr. 1-6,* (03-24-93, Kunsthallen, #133), w/original print (BP 162, DM 390, FR 1329, Y 28,081, DK 1495).

HELION, Jean   French b. 1904

    BI *Abstrakte Komposition, (19)38,* s., d., num., margin creases, est. DM 1000, (12-01-92, Karl/Faber, #723), 8¼ x 5⁵⁄₁₆ in., (21 x 13.5 cm.), lithograph on Japan.

    BI *Choeur De Journalier N.1, 1951,* artist proof, s., d. 51, est. FF2,500/3,000, (05-27-93, Briest, #109), 25¹³⁄₁₆ x 19¹¹⁄₁₆ in., (65.5 x 50 cm.), black lithograph.

    $97* *Figure Dressee, 1936-1969,* s. artist's proof, d., est. FF5/600, (06-28-93, Loudmer, #55), 26⅜ x 18⅞ in., (670 x 480 mm.), black lithograph on Arches wove (BP 65, DM 165, FR 555, Y 10,292).

    $135* *"Retour Du Marche 1973",* #235/250, s., (10-18-92, Pescheteau, #165), 19¹¹⁄₁₆ x 25⁹⁄₁₆ in., (50 x 65 cm.), lithograph in colors on Arches (BP 82, DM 199, FR 677, Y 16,119).

    $909* *Sans Titre, 1934,* s., d., ded., annot. fourth state, small stains, (06-28-93, Loudmer, #263), 9⁵⁄₁₆ x 7¹⁄₁₆ in., (236 x 180 mm.), sh 12⅝ x 9¹⁵⁄₁₆ in., (236 x 180 mm.), black etching on wove (BP 609, DM 1545, FR 5203, Y 96,446).

HELLA-IRRNO

    $259* *Val D'Isere. Col De L'Iseran. 1850 m.,* good cond., (03-15-93, Arcole, #40), 39⅜ x 24⁷⁄₁₆ in., (100 x 62 cm.), (BP 180, DM 430, FR 1462, Y 30,680).

HELLER, Ben   b. 1913

    $805* *Joe Di Maggio, 1938,* p.l., credit stamp, (04-08-93, Christie-NY, #295, illus.), 13⅝ x 8⅜ in., (34.6 x 21.3 cm.), photograph, gelatin silver print (BP 528, DM 1293, FR 4377, Y 91,353).

    $1320* *Joe Di Maggio Signing Programs At The 1938 World Series, 1938,* (10-15-92, Sotheby-NY, #208, illus.), 9⅞ x 11⅞ in., (25.1 x 30.2 cm.), photograph, gelatin silver print (BP 808, DM 1965, FR 6663, Y 158,368).

    BI *Joe DiMaggio, 1938,* p.l., est. $6/900, (10-14-92, Swann, #314, illus.), 10 x 8 in., (25.4 x 20.3 cm.), photograph, silver print.

    $357* *Lou Gehrig And His Wife, 1938,* p.l., (10-14-92, Swann, #315, illus.), 10 x 8 in., (25.4 x 20.3 cm.), photograph, silver print (BP 210, DM 522, FR 1772, Y 43,262).

    $550* *Man Working On Machinery,* photog.'s sig., handstamp, (04-07-93, Swann, #483, illus.), 13¼ x 10 in., photograph, silver print (BP 363, DM 890, FR 3010, Y 62,486).

$1380* *Mr. And Mrs. Lou Gehrig,* photog. name stamp, c. 1938, p.l., (04-06-93, Sotheby-NY, #368, illus.), 13¾ x 10⅝ in., photograph (BP 911, DM 2223, FR 7529, Y 157,391).

BI *New York Yankees, 1938 World Champions,* 1938, p.l., est. $6/900, (10-14-92, Swann, #316, illus.), 11 x 14 in., (27.9 x 35.6 cm.), photograph, silver print.

BI *Tot Lot,* news agency handstamp, caption label, 1930s, est. $500/750, (04-07-93, Swann, #318, illus.), photograph, silver print.

HELLER, Frank J.

$1210* *Abstraction (Amusement Park), c. 1945,* mounted, s., t. by photog.; s., t., i. by photog. in ink, exhib. label, (10-15-92, Sotheby-NY, #441, illus.), 19⅛ x 15½ in., (48.6 x 39.4 cm.), photograph, gelatin silver print (BP 740, DM 1801, FR 6108, Y 145,171).

BI *"Abstraction", c. 1945,* mounted, s., t. by photog., studio stamp, exhib. stamp, est. $2/2,500, (04-06-93, Sotheby-NY, #154, illus.), 19⅛ x 15½ in., photograph.

$385* *Jonquils, 1949,* notations, handstamps, (04-07-93, Swann, #484, illus.), 14 x 11 in., photograph, silver print (BP 254, DM 623, FR 2107, Y 43,740).

BI *Spring Blooms, c. 1945,* s., t., credit stamp, exhib. stamps & labels, prov., est. $1,2/1,800, (10-13-92, Christie-NY, #226, illus.), 19½ x 15½ in., (49.5 x 39.4 cm.), photograph, gelatin silver print.

HELLEU, Paul Cesar French 1859-1927

$330* *Adolescense,* s. in plate; s., i. w/in plate; i. illegibly, (10-30-92, Sloan, #2362), 14½ x 11⅛ in., (36.8 x 28.3 cm.), drypoint etching (BP 211, DM 508, FR 1722, Y 40,877).

$1065* *Adolescente,* annot. first state, sig., creases, large margins, (02-24-93, Picard, #125), drypoint on laid (BP 743, DM 1729, FR 5861, Y 124,971).

BI *Buste D'Une Femme Tournee A Gauche, c. 1900,* s., margins, repaired tear, rubbing, staining, defects, est. BP 1,4/1,800, (12-01-92, Christie-London, #395), plate 15¾ x 11¹¹⁄₁₆ in., (400 x 297 mm.), drypoint in colors on wove.

$1320* *Le Chapeau A Plume,* s., (10-30-92, Sloan, #2364, illus.), 17⅜ x 22⅞ in., (44.1 x 58.1 cm.), color drypoint etching (BP 846, DM 2031, FR 6889, Y 163,508).

$495* *Ed. Sagot,* Imp. Chaix, A- cond., creasing, (08-06-92, Swann, #153, illus.), 41½ x 29 in., (105.4 x 73.7 cm.), (BP 259, DM 731, FR 2470, Y 63,138).

BI *Ed. Sagot Estampes Et Affiches Illustrees, 1901,* est. $4/600, (10-18-92, Hindman, #456), 40¼ x 27¾ in., (102.2 x 70.5 cm.), lithograph in sanguine, mounted on linen.

BI *Ed. Sagot/Estampes & Affiches Illustrees,* very rare, before 1901, Imp. Chaix, Paris, lit., est. DM 3,000, (12-05-92, Bassenge, #7599, illus.), 41¾ x 29½ in., (106 x 75 cm.), lithograph.

$495* *Edition Sagot Estampes Et Affiches Illustres, c. 1900,* s. in stone, first edit. p. by Chaix, full sheet, good cond., light staining, crease, soft handling creases, (05-22-93, Weschler, #188), 37¼ x 26½ in., (94.6 x 67.3 cm.), lithograph in beige and sanguine on soft-wove (BP 321, DM 805, FR 2708, Y 54,576).

$1887* *Ellen 13 Ans, c. 1900,* s., margins, good cond., mount-staining, Ex. coll. (Lugt 2086), (06-30-93, Sotheby-London, #454), sh 23 x 17⅜ in., (584 x 441 mm.), drypoint in bistre w/tone on wove (BP 1265, DM 3218, FR 10,857, Y 202,186).

BI *Ellen A 5 1/2 Ans,* s., margins, inside front cover illus., est. BP8/1,200, (01-21-93, Bonhams-Chelsea, #116), plate 8⅜ x 12½ in., (21.3 x 31.8 cm.), drypoint etching.

$848* *Femme Au Chapeau De Plumes,* c. 1900, s., ded., margins, w/burr, foxing on image, waterstained, (10-07-92, Christie-S. Ken, #102), pl 15¾ x 11¾ in., (40 x 29.8 cm.), drypoint on wove (BP 495, DM 1227, FR 4161, Y 101,984).

BI *Femme Au Chapeau, c. 1900,* s., margins, tear, skinning, foxed, est. BP 1,5/2,000, (12-01-92, Christie-London, #393, illus.), plate 21⅝ x 13¼ in., (550 x 337 mm.), drypoint on wove.

BI *Girl In Profile With Her Hands Clasped Under Her Chin,* s., full margins, defects, light-stained, est. BP 1,5/2,000, (11-30-92, Phillips-London, #430, illus.), image 20⅝ x 13¾ in., (524 x 349 mm.), drypoint on wove.

$4995* *Helen Helleu (M. LXV), c. 1900,* burr s., margins, repaired tear, staining, nicks, good cond., (12-01-92, Christie-London, #394, illus.), plate 13³⁄₁₆ x 12⅛ in., (335 x 308 mm.), drypoint in colors on wove (BP 3300, DM 7961, FR 27,132, Y 621,887).

BI *Jean Malade, c. 1905,* s., margins, light/time staining, foxing, repaired tear, laid down on laid, est. $2,5/3,000, (05-11-93, Christie-NY, #201), plate 10½ x 13½ in., (267 x 343 mm.), drypoint on laid.

$2200* *Jeune Brune Au Chapeau Plume, circa 1900,* s., i. 55, margins, blindstamp, staining, laid down on board, (11-09-92, Christie-NY, #103), 571 x 352 in., (x 894.1 cm.), colored drypoint on wove (BP 1455, DM 3512, FR 11,866, Y 273,021).

$1651* *Jeune Femme Brune En Buste Avec Une Toque,* annot., s., tear, large margins, (04-02-93, Picard, #130), 21¼ x 13³⁄₁₆ in., (54 x 33.5 cm.), 3-tone drypoint (BP 1087, DM 2653, FR 9012, Y 187,977).

$805* *Jeune Femme Debout, Pres D'Un Buste Sculpte,* s., creases, large margins, (04-02-93, Picard, #129), 15⁹⁄₁₆ x 11⅝ in., (39.5 x 29.5 cm.), drypoint (BP 530, DM 1294, FR 4394, Y 91,654).

$3046* *Jeune Femme Rousse,* s., good margins, (06-16-93, Ader Tajan, #107), 21⅝ x 13³⁄₁₆ in., (55 x 33.5 cm.), drypoint in 2 tones (BP 2031, DM 5056, FR 16,969, Y 324,872).

$1439* *Jeune Femme Rousse Au Grand Chapeau. Main Sous Le Menton,* red crayon s., Esquisse d'un nu verso, dirt spots, loss, good margins, (06-11-93, Picard, #71), 12¹⁵⁄₁₆ x 12¹⁵⁄₁₆ in., (330 x 330 mm.), drypoint on laid in 2 tones (BP 945, DM 2339, FR 7885, Y 152,679).

$1155* *Junge Frau Im Profil, Vom Rucken Gesehen,* s., (12-04-92, Bassenge, #6827, illus.), 10⅞ x 5¹³⁄₁₆ in., (27.7 x 14.8 cm.), etching on handmade (BP 741, DM 1839, FR 6240, Y 144,195).

$605* *Katherine,* s., i. w/in image, (10-30-92, Sloan, #2363), sight 20⅜ x 15¼ in., (51.8 x 38.7 cm.), drypoint etching (BP 388, DM 931, FR 3158, Y 74,941).

$899 *Lady With Ginger Hair Seated Writing At A Table With Figurines Standing On It,* s., water stained, (04-16-93, G.A. Key, #109, illus.), 11 x 15 in., (27.9 x 38.1 cm.), drypoint etching (BP 590, DM 1452, FR 4907, Y 101,091).

$1980* *Madame Helleu, c. 1910,* s., t. by another hand, margins, good cond., fox mark, creases, tapestain, discoloration, William L. Harris Estate, (11-05-92, Sotheby-NY, #201), 15½ x 10¾ in., (395 x 274 mm.), sheet 20 x 15¼ in., (395 x 274 mm.), drypoint p. in black and brown (BP 1288, DM 3131, FR 10,594, Y 242,915).

$1024* *Meditation (Karshan 46), 1894,* s., num., oxidation both sides, soiling verso, crease, full margins,100 proof, drystamp, (02-24-93, Picard, #124), drypoint on laid (BP 714, DM 1662, FR 5636, Y 120,160).

$2530* *Portrait De Femme De Trois-Quarts, c. 1910,* s., (05-16-93, Hindman, #447), 15½ x 11¾ in., (39.4 x 29.8 cm.), drypoint (BP 1645, DM 4069, FR 13,676, Y 280,457).

BI *Portrait Of A Lady With A Fur Hat And A Fur-Collared Coat,* s. Helleu, est. 1/1,500, (09-25-92, Wolf, #9, illus.), 15½ x 10¾ in., (39.4 x 27.3 cm.), etching and drypoint.

BI *Portrait Of A Lady With A Hat,* s. Helleu, est. $1/2,000, (09-25-92, Wolf, #8), 15¾ x 11½ in., (40 x 29.2 cm.), drypoint.

$1650* *"Portrait Of A Woman",* s., good cond., (10-31-92, Cleveland, #291, illus.), 15½ x 9⅞ in., (39.4 x 25.1 cm.), etching and drypoint (BP 1057, DM 2538, FR 8612, Y 204,385).

BI *A Quatre Mains (Ellen And Her Grandmother At The Piano), 1897,* s., margins, surface abrasions w/in image, restorations, backed w/Japan, est. BP 800/1,200, (06-30-93, Sotheby-London, #453, illus.), sh 22¼ x 17 in., (565 x 432 mm.), drypoint on wove.

$2200* *Reverie, circa 1905,* s., i. tiree a 10, full margins, staining, margins folded back, (11-09-92, Christie-NY, #104), 407 x 305 in., (x 774.7 cm.), drypoint on wove (BP 1455, DM 3512, FR 11,866, Y 273,021).

$231* *Salon De La Marine. Palais De Chaillot, 1949,* good cond., (11-19-92, Ribeyre/Baron, #139), 40⁹⁄₁₆ x 28⅜ in., (103 x 72 cm.), poster (BP 152, DM 368, FR 1241, Y 28,728).

BI *Seated Lady Fur Stole,* bearing pencil sig., margins, skinning, glue stains, est. BP 800/1,000, (06-30-93, Sotheby-London, #452), sh 26 x 17¾ in., (660 x 451 mm.), color drypoint w/plate tone on wove.

$900* *"Seated Woman With Black Muff", c. 1900,* s., burr, small margins, creases, staining, verso toned, (05-15-93, Cleveland, #391, illus.), 21⅜ x 13⅛ in., (54.3 x 33.3 cm.), drypoint (BP 585, DM 1448, FR 4865, Y 99,767).

$1160* *Sept Croquis, 1895,* orange crayon s., dusty, tear, (06-28-93, Loudmer, #265, illus.), 17¹⁵⁄₁₆ x 8⅞ in., (455 x 225 mm.), sh 24⁷⁄₁₆ x 15¹⁵⁄₁₆ in., (455 x 225 mm.), drypoint on wove (BP 777, DM 1971, FR 6640, Y 123,077).

$3450* *Three Portraits Of Women, c. 1910: Three,* two s.; last bears sig. of artist, margins; 1st foxing, water stain,laid down; two taped, soiling, (02-11-93, Sotheby-NY, #151, illus.), drypoint, first in color (BP 2434, DM 5715, FR 19,339, Y 415,913).

$1725* *Viola Et Aileen, c. 1900,* s., wide margins, light/time staining, losses, tears, skinning, (05-11-93, Christie-NY, #200, illus.), plate 13⅜ x 21½ in., (340 x 546 mm.), color drypoint on wove (BP 1101, DM 2717, FR 9156, Y 189,748).

$1870* *"Le Visage Encadre" (Madame Helleu), c. 1900,* s. Helleu, good cond., wide margins, tears, soiling, (03-12-93, Skinner, #4, illus.), 11 x 15¾ in., (27.9 x 40 cm.), drypoint in color on wove (BP 1304, DM 3113, FR 10,583, Y 220,389).

$7993* *Les Watteau Du Louvre (R. de Montesquiou LVI. I.F.F. 48), c. 1895,* red crayon s., whole margins, (06-11-93, Picard, #72, illus.), 11¹¹⁄₁₆ x 15¾ in., (297 x 400 mm.), drypoint on wove in 2 tones (BP 5252, DM 12,990, FR 43,797, Y 848,064).

$1760* *"Woman In Fur Hat" and "Woman In Feathered Hat": Two,* s., c. 1900, full margins, good cond., (06-05-93, LA Auction Ex., #135), first 16¼ x 11½ in., (41.3 x 29.2 cm.), second 16½ x 12½ in., (41.3 x 29.2 cm.), drypoint on wove (BP 1159, DM 2853, FR 9617, Y 188,801).

$2588* *Woman Wearing A Hat, 1900,* s., margins, good cond., light-staining, glue staining, paper loss, tears, foxing, surface soiling, notations, (05-19-93, Butterfield, #1916, illus.), 15¾ x 11¹¹⁄₁₆ in., (400 x 297 mm.), drypoint on wove (BP 1680, DM 4207, FR 14,173, Y 286,505).

$935* *Young Girl Sewing, c. 1896,* s. Helleu, good cond., mount/light staining, (09-11-92, Skinner, #5, illus.), 11³⁄₁₆ x 8³⁄₁₆ in., (28.4 x 20.8 cm.), etching on wove (BP 484, DM 1346, FR 4574, Y 115,847).

HELLINGRATH, Berthold   b. 1877
$117* *Danziger Hafen,* s., (09-25-92, Granier, #2640), 9¹³⁄₁₆ x 12⁵⁄₁₆ in., (24.9 x 31.2 cm.), sheet 14¾ x 19½ in., (24.9 x 31.2 cm.), etching in brown on copper print paper (BP 68, DM 173, FR 586, Y 14,122).

HELMAN   English 19th cent.
$110* *Amour-Sana Etabli Roi Des Eleuths...,* (04-02-93, Sloan, #831), 10 x 16¾ in., (254 x 425 mm.), engraving (BP 72, DM 177, FR 600, Y 12,524).

HEMY, Thomas M. (after)
$303* *Fight For The Association Championship 1894/5, Sunderland V Aston Villa, A Corner Kick,* pub. Henry Graves and Co., 1895, margins, laid down, tears, defects, (03-03-93, Bonhams-Chelsea, #4), plate 23¾ x 35 in., (60.3 x 88.9 cm.), photogravure (BP 209, DM 499, FR 1693, Y 35,405).

HENDEE, A.
$50 *Eat Less Wheat Meat Fats Sugar,* Edwards and Deutsch Litho. Co., minor breaks, (09-24-92, Alderfer, #273), 29 x 21 in., (73.7 x 53.3 cm.), (BP 29, DM 74, FR 252, Y 6015).

HENDERSON (after)
$440* *Indian Reed, 1804,* engraved by Caldwell, pub. in Dr. Thornton's Temple of Flora, unevenly trimmed margins, good cond., tear, mat & light-staining, foxing, surface scuffing, creases, surface soiling, binding holes, pencil notations, (02-24-93, Butterfield, #2939), 21 x 16 in., (533 x 406 mm.), mezzotint, aquatint, & line engraving

p. in colors w/hand-coloring onJ. Whatman w/watermark (BP 307, DM 714, FR 2422, Y 51,631).

HENDERSON (after)   British 18th/19th cent.
$77* *The Sacred Egyptian Bean, 1811,* pub. Dr. Thornton, (12-13-92, Hindman, #256), 12 x 8⅝ in., color mezzotint (BP 49, DM 121, FR 412, Y 9526).

HENDERSON, Charles Cooper   English 1803-1877
$106* *"Waking Up",* s., d., pub. 1843, (04-20-93, Encans, #119), 12¹³⁄₁₆ x 20¹¹⁄₁₆ in., (32.5 x 52.5 cm.), print (BP 68, DM 169, FR 570, Y 11,696, C$ 133).

HENDERSON, Charles Cooper (after)
$213* *Fones's Coaching Recollections "Waking Up", Plate IV,* by C. Hunt, pub. Fones, 1843, (06-30-93, Bonhams-Chelsea, #243), image 17¼ x 26½ in., (43.8 x 67.3 cm.), aquatint w/hand-coloring (BP 143, DM 363, FR 1226, Y 22,822).

BI *Fores's Coaching Recollections "Waking Up", Plate IV,* by C. Hunt, pub. Fores, 1843, est. BP 180/220, (03-03-93, Bonhams-Chelsea, #215), image 17¼ x 26½ in., (43.8 x 67.3 cm.), hand-colored aquatint.

$2746* *Fores's Coaching Recollections, 1842, Plates I-VI: A Set Of Six,* by J. Harris and H. Papprill, pub. Messrs Fores, foxing, back cover illus., (10-29-92, Bonhams-Chelsea, #195, illus.), image 17¼ x 26½ in., (43.8 x 67.3 cm.), aquatint w/hand coloring (BP 1760, DM 4225, FR 14,332, Y 340,146).

BI *Got Hold,* pub. R. Ackermann, est. $200/250, (07-03-92, Sloan, #327), 12¾ x 23¾ in., (32.4 x 60.3 cm.), color lithograph.

$18 *"Stuck Fast",* engraved by E Duncan, (from Fore's Coaching Incidents), (04-16-93, G.A. Key, #40), 12 x 23 in., (30.5 x 58.4 cm.), colored aquatint (BP 12, DM 29, FR 98, Y 2024).

BI *The Turnpike Gate,* by J. Harris, pub. R. Ackermann, March 1st, 1839, trimmed, laid down, est. BP 1/150, (06-30-93, Bonhams-Chelsea, #244), image 14½ x 20¾ in., (36.8 x 52.7 cm.), aquatint, hand-coloring.

HENDERSON, Leslie
$110* *Figural Prints: Twenty,* all s., good cond., (03-28-93, Bakker, #220), largest, plate 9 x 5½ in., (22.9 x 14 cm.), mezzotints (BP 74, DM 179, FR 610, Y 12,803).

HENDERSON, P. (after)   English 19th cent.
$110* *The Egg Plant,* by Warner, pub. Thornton, June 1, 1803, (04-02-93, Sloan, #1160), 17¾ x 12½ in., (451 x 318 mm.), hand colored lithograph (BP 72, DM 177, FR 600, Y 12,524).

HENDERSON, Will
$248* *Reclining Goddesses: Two,* s., margins, good cond.?, darkening, time staining, (06-11-93, Weschler, #48), 10¾ x 14¾ in., (27.3 x 37.5 cm.), mezzotint w/hand-coloring (BP 163, DM 403, FR 1359, Y 26,313).

HENLE, Fritz   b. 1909
BI *Photographs Of The Caribbean: Dry Goods Store; Young Women In Colonnade; Woman At Window; Elderly Man: Four,* handstamp, 1950's, est. $1,2/1,800, (10-14-92, Swann, #475, illus.), each 4¾ x 3¾ in., (12.1 x 9.5 cm.), photograph, silver prints.

HENRI, Florence   b. 1893
BI *Fenster, Paris,* (1929), 1974, s., t., d. twice, (c) credit stamp, est. $1,2/1,800, (10-13-92, Christie-NY, #227, illus.), 10 x 7⅛ in., (25.4 x 18.1 cm.), photograph, gelatin silver print.

BI *"Hans Arp", "Fernand Leger" and "Jean Pougny": Selected Portraits ofArtists: Three,* each s., 1st num. 8/9, 3rd num. 9/9 on image, sig. stamp, info. stamp, t., d., num. in unidentified hand, 1934, p. 1976, each either #8 or 9 in 9, est. $2/3,000, (10-15-92, Sotheby-NY, #402, illus.), from 8½ x 6⅞ in., (21.6 x 17.5 cm.), to 19¾ x 15¼ in., (21.6 x 17.5 cm.), photograph, gelatin silver prints.

$1365* *Portrat Escha Christiansen, 30's,* ink s., t., small tear, (11-12-92, Lempertz, #94, illus.), 11¹³⁄₁₆ x 9⁷⁄₁₆ in., (30 x 24 cm.), photograph, gelatin silver print (BP 873, DM 2145, FR 7311, Y 168,873).

BI *Portrat Tullia Kaiser, c. 1930,* t., est. DM 800, (11-12-92, Lempertz, #92, illus.), 11¾ x 9⁷⁄₁₆ in., (29.8 x 23.9 cm.), photograph, gelatin silver print.

$2806* *Portrat Tullia Kaiser, c. 1930,* t., d., lit., (11-12-92, Lempertz, #91, illus.), 9¼ x 11⁵⁄₈ in., (23.5 x 29.6 cm.), photograph, gelatin silver print (BP 1794, DM 4410, FR 15,029, Y 347,148).

$2048* *Rom, 1934,* slight tear in margin, lit., (11-12-92, Lempertz, #93, illus.), 11³⁄₈ x 9³⁄₈ in., (28.9 x 23.8 cm.), photograph, gelatin silver print (BP 1309, DM 3219, FR 10,969, Y 253,371).

$880* *Structure (Interior Of Palais De L'Air, Paris World's Fair), 1937,* s., d. by photog. in ink, (10-15-92, Sotheby-NY, #401, illus.), 2⅜ x 2⅛ in., (6 x 5.4 cm.), photograph, gelatin silver print (BP 538, DM 1310, FR 4442, Y 105,579).

$1062* *Weibliches Portrat, 1938,* s., d., (11-12-92, Lempertz, #95, illus.), 11⁵⁄₈ x 8⁵⁄₈ in., (29.6 x 21.9 cm.), photograph, gelatin silver print (BP 679, DM 1669, FR 5688, Y 131,387).

HENRI, Paolo

$642* *Cie Des Chemins De Fer De L'Ouest. Granville Mont Saint-Michel, c. 1900,* Paris, Affiches Artistiques Pierrefort, cond. B+, (06-11-93, Boisgirard, #90), 50¹³⁄₁₆ x 36¹³⁄₁₆ in., (129 x 93.5 cm.), poster (BP 422, DM 1043, FR 3518, Y 68,117).

$1100* *Cycles Gladiator,* Kossuth, B cond., fold marks, surface soiling, repair discoloring, (08-06-92, Swann, #154, illus.), 34½ x 54½ in., (87.6 x 138.4 cm.), (BP 575, DM 1625, FR 5489, Y 140,306).

HENRI, Victor

$174* *Joli Sport,* creases, edges taped, laid on board, (05-07-93, Christie-S. Ken, #107, illus.), 34½ x 47 in., (87.6 x 119.4 cm.), color lithograph (BP 110, DM 275, FR 927, Y 19,159).

HENRY, Edward Lamson   American 1841-1919

BI *"Woman In Doorway" and "Buggy Ride": Two,* inits. in plate, est. $275/325, (12-10-92, Sloan, #1317), 7⅞ x 6 in., (20 x 15.2 cm.), etchings p. on uncut plate.

HEPWORTH, Barbara   English 1903-1975

$303* *Abstract,* s., #37/60, prov., (05-16-93, Hindman, #576), 26½ x 20 in., (67.3 x 50.8 cm.), color lithograph (BP 197, DM 487, FR 1638, Y 33,588).

$275* *Argos,* (05-16-93, Hindman, #598), 32 x 23¼ in., (81.3 x 59.1 cm.), color lithograph (BP 179, DM 442, FR 1486, Y 30,484).

$512* *Composition With Circles And Lines,* s., #48/60, margins, good cond., (12-03-92, Sotheby-London, #699), 21⅞ x 28½ in., (555 x 722 mm.), lithograph in colors on wove (BP 330, DM 805, FR 2748, Y 63,705).

$319* *"Composition With Six Semi-Circles",* num. 15/60, s., (01-21-93, Bonhams-Chelsea, #101), subject 32 x 23 in., (81.3 x 58.4 cm.), lithograph in colors (BP 209, DM 507, FR 1716, Y 39,925).

BI *Komposition,* s., num., est. DM 1000, (12-01-92, Karl/Faber, #726), 22¹³⁄₁₆ x 19¹¹⁄₁₆ in., (58 x 50 cm.), color lithograph on wove.

$425* *Orchid, 1970,* s., num., Marlborough Fine Art Ltd., stamp, (06-08-93, Karl/Faber, #851), approx. 18⅛ x 15⁹⁄₁₆ in., (46 x 39.5 cm.), color serigraph on TH Saunders England wove (BP 279, DM 690, FR 2322, Y 45,141).

BI *Untitled,* s., d., #177/200, pub. Cercle Graphique w/their blindstamp, full sheet, good cond., minor soiling, minor handling creases, est. Dfl. 4/600, (05-27-93, Sotheby-Amstrdm, #627), sh 21⅞ x 29¹⁵⁄₁₆ in., (555 x 760 mm.), color lithograph on wove.

HERBERT, Harold Brocklebank   1892-1945

$324* *Fishing Boats, Martigues,* s. Harold B Herbert, i., #8/50, lit., (08-11-92, L. Joel, #81G), 9¹⁵⁄₁₆ x 6¹⁵⁄₁₆ in., (25.2 x 17.7 cm.), etching (BP 168, DM 475, FR 1610, Y 41,491, A$ 440).

HERBERT, J.R. (after)

$115 *A Court Room Scene,* engraved by S.W. Reynolds, (08-14-92, G.A. Key, #15), 20 x 31 in., (50.8 x 78.7 cm.), print (BP 60, DM 169, FR 571, Y 14,502).

HERBIG, Otto   1889-1971

$258* *Mit Bauklotzen Spielendes Kind, 1922,* s., num., blindstamp, (12-05-92, Bassenge, #7254), 16¹⁵⁄₁₆ x 8¹¹⁄₁₆ in., (43 x 22 cm.), lithograph on handmade (BP 162, DM 402, FR 1371, Y 31,966).

$185* *Mutter Und Kind, 1924,* s., t., (12-05-92, Bassenge, #7255), 14⁷⁄₁₆ x 20¹⁄₁₆ in., (36.7 x 51 cm.), lithograph on imitation Japan (BP 116, DM 288, FR 983, Y 22,922).

HERBIN, Auguste   French 1882-1960

$642* *Composition,* 33/100, (03-24-93, Kunsthallen, #134), color lithograph (BP 435, DM 1049, FR 3569, Y 75,432, DK 4025).

$3457* *Ete, 1959,* s., d., #55/150, (10-21-92, Dobiaschofsky, #2034), 19¹¹⁄₁₆ x 14¹⁵⁄₁₆ in., (50 x 38 cm.), color serigraph (BP 2146, DM 5231, FR 17,756, Y 421,072, SF 4680).

$419* *Fou, 1953,* from Maitres d'Aujourd'hui, s., d. 53, Editions Art d'Aujourd'hui, (11-16-92, Briest, #59), 25³⁄₁₆ x 19⁵⁄₁₆ in., (64 x 49 cm.), serigraph in colors (BP 275, DM 668, FR 2251, Y 52,290).

$3293* *Komposition,* s., d. 1957, #97/100, (05-08-93, Dobiaschofsky, #2021, illus.), 25³⁄₁₆ x 25 in., (64 x 63.5 cm.), color serigraph (BP 2149, DM 5290, FR 17,848, Y 367,974, SF 4800).

BI *Komposition,* stamped sig., #55/150, est. SF 2,600-, (05-08-93, Dobiaschofsky, #2019), 16⁵⁄₁₆ x 21⅝ in., (41.5 x 55 cm.), color serigraph.

$3458* *Midi, 1959,* s., d., #55/150, (05-08-93, Dobiaschofsky, #2020, illus.), 20½ x 14¹⁵⁄₁₆ in., (52 x 38 cm.), color serigraph (BP 2256, DM 5555, FR 18,743, Y 386,412, SF 5040).

$3458* *Minuit, 1959,* s., d., #55/150, (05-08-93, Dobiaschofsky, #2018), 20½ x 14¹⁵⁄₁₆ in., (52 x 38 cm.), color serigraph (BP 2256, DM 5555, FR 18,743, Y 386,412, SF 5040).

$3191* *"Vendredi", 1959,* s., d., #4/150, (10-21-92, Dobiaschofsky, #2035, illus.), 14¹⁵⁄₁₆ x 19¹¹⁄₁₆ in., (38 x 50 cm.), color serigraph (BP 1981, DM 4828, FR 16,389, Y 388,672, SF 4320).

HERDEG

BI *St. Moritz-Diver, c. 1930,* p. Wolsberg, cond. 1, defects, est. BP 150/200, (10-13-92, Phillips-London, #27), 40¹⁄₁₆ x 25⁵⁄₁₆ in., (101.7 x 64.3 cm.), color lithograph.

HERDMAN-SMITH, R.   British contemporary

$33* *"Canterbury, Christ Church Gate",* pen s., (02-12-93, DuMouchelle, #1365), approx. 10 x 7 in., (25.4 x 17.8 cm.), hand colored etching (BP 23, DM 55, FR 185, Y 3980).

HERDMAN-SMITH, Robert

$96 *"The Little Shrine" and "The Yellow Junk": A Pair,* (08-14-92, G.A. Key, #59), 7 x 8 in., (17.8 x 20.3 cm.), colored etching (BP 50, DM 141, FR 477, Y 12,106).

HERIOT, George

BI *Fall Of Montmorenci (sic) In Winter, 1807,* pl. 7 from Travels Through Canada, p. F.C. Lewis, prov., lit., est. C$3/400, (06-07-93, Ritchie, #13, illus.), plate 5⁹⁄₁₆ x 8⅛ in., (14.1 x 20.7 cm.), aquatint hand-colored w/watercolor before letters.

HERMANN, Hans   German b. 1952

$28* *"Dutch Harbor Scene",* d. 1902, s. in plate, (10-11-92, Dunning, #1530), 15¾ x 19½ in., (40 x 49.5 cm.), lithograph (BP 17, DM 42, FR 140, Y 3409).

HERMES, Eric

$709* *Montreux-Oberland-Bernois, Chemin De Fer Suisse, 1929,* staining, holes top image, (02-04-93, Christie-S. Ken, #8, illus.), 40 x 25 in., (101.6 x 63.5 cm.), color lithograph (BP 495, DM 1167, FR 3959, Y 88,195).

HERNANDEZ, Jose

BI *"Los Cuatro Estamentos: Intelectualidad, Iglesia, Aristocracia Y Burguesia": Four,* #31/50, s., d. 74, reserve P150,000, (12-17-92, Duran, #172, illus.), 29¹⁵⁄₁₆ x 22⁷⁄₁₆ in., (76 x 57 cm.), etching.

HERNI, Hans

$39* *Spirale, 1973,* pl. from "Abstraction Creation Art non Figuratif 1932-36" book, s., 11/150, (06-28-93, Loudmer, #56), 20¹⁄₁₆ x 23¼ in., (510 x 590 mm.), sh 25¹⁵⁄₁₆ x

32¹⁵⁄₁₆ in., (510 x 590 mm.), color lithograph on wove (BP 26, DM 66, FR 223, Y 4138).

HEROLD, Jacques   1910-1987
$112* *"Composition Vegetale"*, artist's proof, s., (10-18-92, Pescheteau, #166), 25⁹⁄₁₆ x 19¹¹⁄₁₆ in., (65 x 50 cm.), lithograph in colors on Arches (BP 68, DM 165, FR 562, Y 13,373).

HERON, Patrick   English b. 1920
$110* *"Blue Day Disc", 1979*, pub. Kelpra Studio, s. Patrick Heron 79, #2/50, pub.'s and printer'sdrystamps, very good cond., wrinkling, (03-12-93, Skinner, #93, illus.), sight 21⅜ x 27 in., (54.3 x 68.6 cm.), aquatint and etching in colors on wove (BP 77, DM 183, FR 623, Y 12,964).
BI *Color Compositions, 1979 and 1980: Two*, s., d., i., full margins, good cond., est. BP 800/1,000, (12-03-92, Sotheby-London, #701, illus.), each sheet approx. 26¾ x 35⅝ in., (680 x 905 mm.), aquatints in colors.

HEROUX, Bruno   1868-1944
$127* *"Sauerkraut U Wurstchen"*, i., s. BHeroux, (03-24-93, Venator/Hansten, #4500), pl. 8¼ x 5⁹⁄₁₆ in., (20.9 x 14.1 cm.), etching and drypoint (BP 86, DM 207, FR 706, Y 14,922).

HERPIN, A.
$662* *Malo-Les-Bains, Pres Dunkerque, 1898*, Chatelles, Imp. L. Geisler, cond. B+, (06-11-93, Boisgirard, #91), 45¹¹⁄₁₆ x 37¹³⁄₁₆ in., (116 x 96 cm.), poster (BP 435, DM 1076, FR 3627, Y 70,239).

HERREGOUTS, Jean Baptist   1640-1721
BI *Johannes Der Evangelist And Johannes Der Taufer Von Engeln Umgeben (Wurzbach and Hollstein 1)*, watermark, est. DM 2,000, (06-10-93, Hauswedell/Nolt, #101, illus.), etching on hand-made.

HERRING, Ben (after)
$220* *"Achievement" and "Hermit": Two*, (11-12-92, Freemn/ Fine Art, #86), each 13½ x 19 in., (34.3 x 48.3 cm.), colored engravings (BP 144, DM 349, FR 1176, Y 27,278).
BI *The Silks And Satins Of The Turf*, by J. Summers, pub. Thomas McLean, trimmed, 3 sides, losses, repairedtear, est. BP 4/600, (10-07-92, Christie-S. Ken, #54), sh 24 x 46 in., (61 x 116.8 cm.), colored aquatint part p. in color.

HERRING, Benjamin (Jr.)   English 1830-1871
$107* *The Silks And Satins Of The Field*, pub. Thomas McLean, 1868, (12-01-92, Ritchie, #1, illus.), image 20 x 43 in., (50.8 x 109.2 cm.), hand-colored aquatint (BP 71, DM 171, FR 581, Y 13,322, C$ 138).

HERRING, J.F. (Sr.) (after)
$440* *Teddington-Winner Of The Derby Stakes At Epson, 1851*, pub. 1851 by Messieurs Fores, (06-11-93, Freemn/ Fine Art, #93), 17¼ x 27¼ in., (43.8 x 69.2 cm.), hand-colored engraving (BP 289, DM 715, FR 2411, Y 46,684).

HERRING, J.F. (after)
$38 *Busy Hunting Scene*, (04-16-93, G.A. Key, #59), 25 x 34 in., (63.5 x 86.4 cm.), colored print (BP 25, DM 61, FR 207, Y 4273).
$275* *"Extraordinary Trotting Match   Against Time"*, (01-06-93, Doyle, #34), sight 24 x 32 in., (61 x 81.3 cm.), color print (BP 179, DM 450, FR 1535, Y 34,409).
$247* *Mendicant*, discoloration, image scratches, trimmed, laid down on paper, (12-04-92, Doyle, #51), 12¾ x 17 in., (324 x 432 mm.), color aquatint (BP 158, DM 393, FR 1334, Y 30,836).

HERRING, J.R. (Sr.) (after)
$129 *A Carriage Race*, (06-11-93, G.A. Key, #129), 21 x 41 in., (53.3 x 104.1 cm.), colored aquatint (BP 85, DM 210, FR 707, Y 13,687).

HERRING, John Frederick
BI *The Meet*, by John Harris, pub. R. Dobson, October 1867, est. C$ 2/300, (06-08-93, Ritchie, #3), plate 22 x 33½ in., (55.9 x 85.1 cm.), sheet 24 x 36 in., (55.9 x 85.1 cm.), color aquatint w/hand-coloring.

HERRING, John Frederick (Sr.)   British 1795-1865
$495* *Breaking Cover, 1867*, full margins, (02-13-93, Collins, #2, illus.), 17¼ x 30½ in., (43.8 x 77.5 cm.), hand-colored aquatint (BP 349, DM 821, FR 2778, Y 59,696).
$495* *The Death, 1867*, full margins, (02-13-93, Collins, #3, illus.), 17¼ x 30½ in., (43.8 x 77.5 cm.), hand-colored aquatint (BP 349, DM 821, FR 2778, Y 59,696).
$495* *The Meet, 1867*, full margins, (02-13-93, Collins, #1, illus.), 17¼ x 30½ in., (43.8 x 77.5 cm.), hand colored aquatint (BP 349, DM 821, FR 2778, Y 59,696).

HERRING, John Frederick (Sr.) (after)
$605* *Fox Hunting Plate 2: The Find, 1852*, by J. Harris, series Fores's, National Sports, (03-14-93, Hindman, #231), 24½ x 44⅜ in., (62.2 x 112.7 cm.), hand-colored etching and aquatint (BP 422, DM 1007, FR 3424, Y 71,302).
$66* *Fox Hunting, The Start*, p. by M. & N. Hanhart, (11-28-92, Young, #226), 24 x 34 in., (61 x 86.4 cm.), lithograph (BP 44, DM 105, FR 357, Y 8214).
$154* *The Seasons, "Summer" and "Winter": Two*, (04-02-93, Sloan, #825), larger, image 17⅝ x 27⅜ in., (448 x 695 mm.), hand colored engraving (BP 101, DM 248, FR 841, Y 17,534).
BI *The Seasons, Summer And Winter: Two*, est. $200/300, (09-17-92, Sloan, #649), larger, image 17⅝ x 27⅜ in., (44.8 x 69.5 cm.), handcolored engravings.

HERRING, John Frederick (Sr.) (circle of)
$43* *Sailor, Jerry, Lottery*, pub. Gebr Rocca, prov., (06-08-93, Ritchie, #2), image 16 x 21¾ in., (40.6 x 55.2 cm.), color stone lithograph heightened w/watercolor (BP 28, DM 70, FR 235, Y 4567, C$ 55).

HERRING, John Frederick (after)
$255* *Beeswing*, by Charles Hunt, surface dirt, foxing, (03-03-93, Bonhams-Chelsea, #183), image 15 x 19¾ in., (38.1 x 50.2 cm.), hand-colored aquatint (BP 176, DM 420, FR 1425, Y 29,797).
BI *Beeswing, Winner Of The Ascot Gold Cup 1842, 1842*, pub. J. Moore, margins, discoloration, thinning, scuff, est. BP 80/120, (07-16-92, Bonhams-Chelsea, #539), plate 16 x 19¼ in., (40.6 x 48.9 cm.), aquatint w/hand coloring.
$989* *Birmingham, The Winner Of The Great St. Leger Stakes At Doncaster, 1830*, by Richard Gilson Reeve, pub. S. and J. Foller, 1830, (03-03-93, Bonhams-Chelsea, #184, illus.), image 12 x 16½ in., (30.5 x 41.9 cm.), hand-colored aquatint (BP 682, DM 1629, FR 5525, Y 115,564).
$603* *Cadland, The Winner Of The Derby Stakes At Epsom, by R. G. Reeve (S.p147), 1828*, pub. J. F. Herring and S. & J. Fuller, margins, excellent cond., hinged, (10-07-92, Christie-S. Ken, #41), pl 15 x 19½ in., (38.1 x 49.5 cm.), colored aquatint (BP 352, DM 873, FR 2959, Y 72,520).
$175* *Charles XIIth And Euclid*, by Charles Hunt, pub. J. Moore, 1840, foxed, stained, (03-03-93, Bonhams-Chelsea, #186), image 12½ x 16¾ in., (31.8 x 42.5 cm.), hand-colored aquatint (BP 121, DM 288, FR 978, Y 20,449).
$957* *Chorister, The Winner Of The Great St. Leger Stakes At Doncaster, 1831*, by Charles Hunt, pub. S. and J. Fuller, 1832, (03-03-93, Bonhams-Chelsea, #187), image 11¾ x 16 in., (29.8 x 40.6 cm.), hand-colored aquatint (BP 660, DM 1576, FR 5346, Y 111,825).
$104* *Doncaster Great St. Leger, 1839*, by Charles Hunt, pub. L. Brall and Sons, 1870, margins, tears, stains, defects, (03-03-93, Bonhams-Chelsea, #188), plate 24½ x 32½ in., (62.2 x 82.6 cm.), hand-colored aqautint (BP 72, DM 171, FR 581, Y 12,152).
$1116* *Fore's National Sports, Fox Hunting: Plates 1-4: Four*, by J. Harris, pub. 1852, margins, (06-30-93, Bonhams-Chelsea, #127, illus.), plate 24½ x 44¼ in., (62.2 x 112.4 cm.), aquatint w/hand-coloring (BP 748, DM 1903, FR 6421, Y 119,576).
$165* *Full Cry*, from Herring's Fox Hunting Scenes, pub. R. Dodson, (11-12-92, Freemn/Fine Art, #87), 17½ x 30½ in., (44.5 x 77.5 cm.), hand colored engraving (BP 108, DM 261, FR 882, Y 20,459).
$617* *Herring's Fox Hunting Scene: "Full Cry" and "The Death", 1874: Two*, restored, large margins, staininig,

(05-06-93, Laurin, #41), color prints (BP 391, DM 972, FR 3271, Y 67,884).

$91* *Herring's Sketched On The Road, No. 2-Post Horses,* by Charles Hunt, pub. Baily Brothers, 1847, trimmed, torn, defects, (06-30-93, Bonhams-Chelsea, #245), image 21¾ x 29½ in., (55.2 x 74.9 cm.), aquatint w/hand-coloring and gum arabic (BP 61, DM 155, FR 524, Y 9750).

$2261* *Jerry, The Winner Of The Great St. Leger At Doncaster (S.p 145), 1824,* by T.Sutherland, pub. W. Sheardon and Son, watermarked, margins, spotting, excell. cond., hinged, (10-07-92, Christie-S. Ken, #45, illus.), pl 15¾ x 20½ in., (40 x 52.1 cm.), colored aquatint (BP 1320, DM 3272, FR 11,094, Y 271,918).

$603* *Margrave, Winner Of The Great St. Leger Stakes At Doncaster (S.p 146), 1832,* by C. Hunt, pub. J. F. Herring and S. & J. Fuller, trimmed, abrasion,side of image, laid, (10-07-92, Christie-S. Ken, #42), sh 15 x 18 in., (38.1 x 45.7 cm.), colored aquatint (BP 352, DM 873, FR 2959, Y 72,520).

BI *Priam, The Winner Of The Derby Stakes At Epsom, 1830,* by Richard Gilson Reeve, pub. S. and J. Fuller, 1830, est. BP 3/500, (03-03-93, Bonhams-Chelsea, #189), image 12¾ x 17 in., (32.4 x 43.2 cm.), hand-colored aquatint.

$495* *Priam, The Winner Of The Derby Stakes At Epsom, 1830,* by Richard Gilson Reeve, pub. S. and J. Fuller, 1830, (06-16-93, Bonhams-Chelsea, #420), image 12¾ x 17 in., (32.4 x 43.2 cm.), aquatint w/hand-coloring (BP 330, DM 822, FR 2758, Y 52,794).

$1884* *Reveller, The Winner Of The Great St. Leger At Doncaster (S.p 145), 1818,* T. Sutherland, pub. W. Sheardown & Son, watermarked, margins, spotting, excellent cond., hinged, (10-07-92, Christie-S. Ken, #44), pl 15 x 20½ in., (38.1 x 52.1 cm.), colored aquatint (BP 1100, DM 2726, FR 9244, Y 226,578).

$117* *Stable Companions, 1964,* by Lawrence Josset, s., blindstamp, pub. Frost and Reed, margins, (11-12-92, Bonhams-Chelsea, #17), plate 16 x 21 in., (40.6 x 53.3 cm.), mezzotint (BP 77, DM 185, FR 625, Y 14,507).

$93* *Stable Companions, 1964,* by Lawrence Josset, s., blindstamp, pub. Frost and Reed, margins, (11-12-92, Bonhams-Chelsea, #19), plate 16 x 21 in., (40.6 x 53.3 cm.), mezzotint (BP 61, DM 147, FR 497, Y 11,531).

$126* *Stable Companions, 1964,* by Lawrence Josset, s., blindstamp, pub. Frost and Reed, margins, (11-12-92, Bonhams-Chelsea, #18), plate 16 x 21 in., (40.6 x 53.3 cm.), mezzotint (BP 83, DM 200, FR 673, Y 15,623).

BI *Stable Companions, 1964,* by Lawrence Josset, s., blindstamp, pub. Frost and Reed, margins, est. BP 60/90, (11-12-92, Bonhams-Chelsea, #64), plate 16 x 21 in., (40.6 x 53.3 cm.), mezzotint.

$93* *Stable Companions, 1964,* by Lawrence Josset, s., blindstamp, pub. Frost and Reed, margins, (11-12-92, Bonhams-Chelsea, #63), plate 16 x 21 in., (40.6 x 53.3 cm.), mezzotint (BP 61, DM 147, FR 497, Y 11,531).

HERRMANN, Paul
$110* *"Guitar Serenade", "Couple In A Row Boat" and "Shepherdess": Three Prints,* each s., num. 110/120, 102/120, 109/120 respectively, good cond., smudging, (05-22-93, Weschler, #190, illus.), each 15¾ x 11½ in., (40 x 29.2 cm.), etching and drypoint on wove (BP 71, DM 179, FR 602, Y 12,128).

$109* *Margot Ohne Hut,* s., margins, foxing, minor paper discoloration, creasing, good cond., Late Gerhard Brauer Coll., (05-27-93, Sotheby-Amstrdm, #736), 9¹¹⁄₁₆ x 7¾ in., (246 x 197 mm.), etching on wove (BP 70, DM 175, FR 590, Y 11,685, G 196).

HERSHEY, Nona   American b. 1946
$55* *May 1981,* s., #8/25, good cond., (06-11-93, Freemn/Fine Art, #94), 25¾ x 19¼ in., (65.4 x 48.9 cm.), mezzotint (BP 36, DM 89, FR 301, Y 5836).

HERVE, Lucien
$1540* *Le Corbusier, 1955,* credit stamp, initialed, t., d. on mount; s., t., d., num. 31 in ink, (10-13-92, Christie-NY, #460, illus.), 8¼ x 6⅛ in., (21 x 15.6 cm.), photograph, gelatin silver print (BP 897, DM 2256, FR 7666, Y 186,735).

HERVIER, Adolphe   Dutch 1871-1891
$368* *Barque En Mer Chargee De Tonneaux (Ber. 86), 1852,* staining, good margins, (02-24-93, Picard, #127), lithograph on chine applique (BP 257, DM 597, FR 2025, Y 43,182).

$348* *Etchings (Ber. 46-51), 1875: Six,* complete series, staining, soiling, tears of cover, (02-24-93, Picard, #126), etching and aquatint (BP 243, DM 565, FR 1915, Y 40,835).

HERZIG, E.
$80* *Ch. De Fer Algeriens De L'Etat: Le Sud Algerien. "Le Figuig", 1925,* good cond., (03-13-93, Laurin, #46), 42⅛ x 29⅛ in., (107 x 74 cm.), (BP 56, DM 133, FR 453, Y 9428).

HESLER, Alexander   1823-1895
$715* *Portrait Of A Man, c. 1855,* modern seal, (04-07-93, Swann, #145, illus.), photograph, half-plate daguerrotype, hand-tinting, case (BP 473, DM 1156, FR 3914, Y 81,232).

$605* *Portrait Of Lincoln,* 1860's, printed 1890's, printed by George B. Ayres from Hesler's orig. neg., penciled notations, (10-14-92, Swann, #205, illus.), 8 x 6 in., (20.3 x 15.2 cm.), photograph, oval albumen print (BP 355, DM 885, FR 3002, Y 73,316).

HESSER, Edwin Bower
BI *Jean Harlow In The Water, Arms Back, Griffith Park, 1929,* blind embossed, proof, est. BP 180/250, (10-10-92, Bonhams, #167, illus.), 14 x 11 in., (35.6 x 27.9 cm.), photograph.

BI *Jean Harlow Leaning On Boulder, Griffith Park, 1929,* blind embossed, proof, est. BP 180/250, (10-10-92, Bonhams, #168, illus.), 14 x 11 in., (35.6 x 27.9 cm.), photograph.

BI *Jean Harlow Standing In Wooded Glade, Hands Raised Behind her, Griffith Park, 1929,* est. BP 350/450, (10-10-92, Bonhams, #162, illus.), 22 x 20 in., (55.9 x 50.8 cm.), photograph.

$315* *Jean Harlow Standing On Rock, Arms Held Wide, Griffith Park, 1929,* blind embossed, proof, est. BP 180/250, (10-10-92, Bonhams, #169, illus.), 14 x 11 in., (35.6 x 27.9 cm.), photograph (BP 187, DM 468, FR 1571, Y 38,349).

$315* *Jean Harlow Standing on Rock, Arms High, Griffith Park, 1929,* blind embossed, proof, (10-10-92, Bonhams, #171, illus.), 14 x 11 in., (35.6 x 27.9 cm.), photograph (BP 187, DM 468, FR 1571, Y 38,349).

BI *Jean Harlow, In Griffith Park, 1929, Arms Raised,* proof, est. BP 350/450, (10-10-92, Bonhams, #165, illus.), 30 x 24 in., (76.2 x 61 cm.), photograph.

$1112* *Jean Harlow, In The Water, Arms Back, Griffith Park, 1929,* blind embossed, (10-10-92, Bonhams, #161, illus.), 29 x 24 in., (73.7 x 61 cm.), sepia photograph (BP 660, DM 1652, FR 5546, Y 135,379).

$241* *Jean Harlow, Seated On Rock, Arms Raised, Griffith Park, 1929,* blind embossed, proof, (10-10-92, Bonhams, #170, illus.), 14 x 11 in., (35.6 x 27.9 cm.), photograph (BP 143, DM 358, FR 1202, Y 29,340).

$371* *Jean Harlow, Seated With Arms Stretched Upward, Griffith Park, 1929,* blind embossed, proof, est. BP 180/250, (10-10-92, Bonhams, #172, illus.), 14 x 11 in., (35.6 x 27.9 cm.), photograph (BP 220, DM 551, FR 1850, Y 45,167).

BI *Jean Harlow, Sitting On Rock, one Knee Raised, Griffith Park, 1929,* proof, est. BP 350/450, (10-10-92, Bonhams, #164, illus.), 22 x 20 in., (55.9 x 50.8 cm.), photograph.

BI *Jean Harlow, Standing Beside Water, Hands Held Forward, Griffith Park, 1929,* proof, est. BP 350/450, (10-10-92, Bonhams, #163, illus.), 22 x 20 in., (55.9 x 50.8 cm.), photograph.

BI *Jean Harlow, Standing In Water, Leaning Forwards, Griffith, 1929,* proof, est. BP 350/450, (10-10-92, Bonhams, #166, illus.), 22 x 20 in., (55.9 x 50.8 cm.), photograph.

HESTER, E.G.
$154* *"Winter Going North",* (06-24-93, Boos, #347), sight 15 x 20¾ in., (381 x 527 mm.), colored engraving (BP 105, DM 263, FR 886, Y 16,798).

HESTER, Wallace, engraver
BI   *"A Mother And Two Children"*, 1903, s., blindstamp, pub. Frost and Reed, est. BP 60/80, (11-19-92, Bonhams-Chelsea, #83), image 13¾ x 11 in., (34.9 x 27.9 cm.), mezzotint.

HEWARD, John   Canadian b. 1934
BI   *"Markings"*, s., d., num. Heward 73-4/49, (06-16-93, Encans, #56), 24 x 20¹⁄₁₆ in., (61 x 51 cm.), lithograph.

HEYBOER, Anton   contemporary
$993*   *System Mit Figueren, 1959*, s. in brush, d., num., (06-23-93, Kornfeld, #401), plate 11¹¹⁄₁₆ x 22¹³⁄₁₆ in., (29.7 x 58 cm.), etching of 5 plates, printed together on handmade (BP 675, DM 1680, FR 5652, Y 108,182, SF 1495).

HEYDECKER, Joe   b. 1916
BI   *World War II, Paris, Minsk And Warsaw, 1940-1943: Five*, each p.l., ink s., d., located, lit., est. BP 4/600, (10-29-92, Christie-London, #97, illus.), each approx. 8½ x 11 in., (21.6 x 27.9 cm.), photograph, gelatin silver print.

HEYDEN, Jan van der   Dutch 1637-1712
BI   *Winter (Holl. 66), 1570*, after Hans Bol, from Four Seasons, margins, watermark, foxing, discoloration, good cond., est. $1,5/2,500, (05-13-93, Sotheby-NY, #160), 8⅞ x 11¼ in., (225 x 287 mm.), engraving.

HEYENDECHER
$105   *USA Bond Weapons For Liberty*, American Litho. Co., holes, corner tears, (09-24-92, Alderfer, #301), 30 x 20 in., (76.2 x 50.8 cm.),   (BP 61, DM 156, FR 528, Y 12,631).

HEYNE, NEUSUSS, PFAFFE
$379*   *Joseph Beuys, 1972*, s., from VIPs der documenta 5, Kassel, (11-12-92, Lempertz, #96), 15⅞ x 11¹⁵⁄₁₆ in., (40.3 x 30.3 cm.), photograph, gelatin silver print (BP 242, DM 596, FR 2030, Y 46,889).

HEYSEN, Hans   1877-1968
$567*   *Farm Trees (J.O Thiele's Barn, Hahndorf)*, s. Hans Heysen, d. 1919, (08-11-92, L. Joel, #1G, illus.), 5¹³⁄₁₆ x 7¾ in., (14.8 x 19.7 cm.), etching (BP 295, DM 832, FR 2818, Y 72,609, A$ 770).

HEYWOOD, John Carl
$257*   *Japan Colle With Culture*, s., stamped w/character seal, t., d. 1987, #46/70, prov., label verso, (11-30-92, Ritchie, #43), 14⅞ x 11⅝ in., (37.8 x 29.5 cm.), etching w/china colle (BP 170, DM 409, FR 1390, Y 31,985, C$ 330).

HIBEL, Edna   American b. 1917
$165*   *"Bethsheba And David"*, #175/185, s., (02-12-93, DuMouchelle, #2331, illus.), 17½ x 15 in., (44.5 x 38.1 cm.), lithograph (BP 116, DM 274, FR 926, Y 19,899).
$99*   *Breton Girl*, s., t., prov., (09-20-92, Hindman, #732), 13¾ x 10¾ in., (34.9 x 27.3 cm.), lithograph w/green tint stone (BP 58, DM 147, FR 503, Y 12,236).
$248*   *"Jerusalem"*, I, #101/208 edit. of 298, s., (02-12-93, DuMouchelle, #2329, illus.), 28 x 37 in., (71.1 x 94 cm.), lithograph (BP 175, DM 411, FR 1392, Y 29,908).
$165*   *"Mother And Child"*, II, #152/152 edit. of 302, s., (02-12-93, DuMouchelle, #2330, illus.), 17 x 11½ in., (43.2 x 29.2 cm.), b/w lithograph (BP 116, DM 274, FR 926, Y 19,899).

HICKS, David (after)
$17*   *"The Dawn Of Day" and "The Close Of Day": Two*, margins, surface defects, (12-10-92, Bonhams-Chelsea, #123), plate 18 x 23¾ in., (45.7 x 60.3 cm.), photogravure (BP 11, DM 27, FR 92, Y 2103).

HIDER, Frank (after)
$126   *Rural Village Scenes With Figures, Buildings And Farmyard Animals: A Pair*, (10-09-92, G.A. Key, #5), 21 x 28½ in., (53.3 x 72.4 cm.), oleograph (BP 75, DM 188, FR 636, Y 15,366).

HIGGINS, Eugene   American 1874-1958
$77*   *"Late Hours"*, s., annot. imp, glue residue recto, (10-31-92, Cleveland, #140), 4⅝ x 3¾ in., (11.7 x 9.5 cm.), etching (BP 49, DM 118, FR 402, Y 9538).
BI   *[Night]*, c. 1930, ink s., good cond., tear, loss, est. $2,8/3,200, (05-13-93, Sotheby-NY, #423, illus.), 4⅞ x 6 in., (124 x 153 mm.), monotype in green on wove.

HILAIRE, Camille   French b. 1916
$210*   *"Le Cirque"*, s., (01-28-93, Pescheteau, #159), 20⅞ x 29⅛ in., (53 x 74 cm.), color lithograph on Arches (BP 139, DM 333, FR 1126, Y 26,074).
$160*   *"Clowns Musiciens"*, artist's proof, s., (04-04-93, Pescheteau, #223), 20⅞ x 14⁹⁄₁₆ in., (53 x 37 cm.), color lithographs on wove (BP 105, DM 257, FR 873, Y 18,217).
$130*   *"Deux Baigneuses"*, EA s., (04-04-93, Pescheteau, #225), 14¹⁵⁄₁₆ x 11 in., (38 x 28 cm.), color lithograph on wove (BP 86, DM 209, FR 710, Y 14,801).
$96*   *Forest*, s., #138/250, full margins, good cond., minor soiling, minor handling creases, (05-27-93, Sotheby-Amstrdm, #629), sh 15⁹⁄₁₆ x 21⅝ in., (395 x 550 mm.), color lithograph on BFK Rives (BP 61, DM 154, FR 519, Y 10,292, G 173).
$96*   *Palmtrees*, s., i. E.A., full margins, good cond., minor soiling, minor handlingcreases, minor defects in edges of sheet, (05-27-93, Sotheby-Amstrdm, #628), sh 15⁹⁄₁₆ x 21⅝ in., (395 x 550 mm.), color lithograph on wove (BP 61, DM 154, FR 519, Y 10,292, G 173).
$432*   *Scenes De Cirque: Six*, num. 12 and 64/80, s., large untrimmed margins, (06-16-93, Ader Tajan, #108), 20⅞ x 14⅜ in., (53 x 36.5 cm.), color lithographs, 2 on Japan nacre (BP 288, DM 717, FR 2407, Y 46,075).
$123*   *Le Verger Au Printemps*, s., #XI/CXX, w/out margins, (05-06-93, Laurin, #42), color print on Japan nacre (BP 78, DM 194, FR 652, Y 13,533).

HILDREN, Ken
$9   *"The Giants Causeway, Co. Antrim"*, s., limited edit., 70/75, (02-05-93, G.A. Key, #10), 13 x 17 in., (33 x 43.2 cm.), colored print (BP 6, DM 15, FR 50, Y 1120).

HILFIKER
BI   *Brienz Rothorn Bahn, 1931*, pin holes, tears, creases, brown tape, slight corresponding stainingon image, est. BP 3/500, (02-04-93, Christie-S. Ken, #9, illus.), 40 x 25 in., (101.6 x 63.5 cm.), photomontage and lithograph.

HILL, A.R.
$357*   *Gunboat On Bo De River, Vietnam, 1969*, handwritten notations, caption label, handstamp; handwritten notations verso, (04-07-93, Swann, #319, illus.), 10 x 8 in., photograph, silver print (BP 236, DM 577, FR 1954, Y 40,559).

HILL, David Octavius and Robert ADAMSON
$326*   *Greyfriars With D.O. Hill, His Nieces The Misses Watson And An Unknown Man*, 1840s p.l., lit., prov., (10-29-92, Christie-London, #11, illus.), 8¼ x 6 in., (21 x 15.2 cm.), photograph, carbon print, mounted on card (BP 209, DM 502, FR 1701, Y 40,382).
$2904*   *John Henning And Mrs. Cleghorn*, mid 1840s, i., watermark, lit., (05-06-93, Christie-London, #29, illus.), 8¼ x 6⅛ in., photograph, calotype (BP 1840, DM 4574, FR 15,398, Y 319,507).
$5081*   *Mr. Finlay The Deer Stalker*, mid 1840s, lit., (05-06-93, Christie-London, #31, illus.), 8 x 5¾ in., photograph, calotype (BP 3220, DM 8003, FR 26,941, Y 559,027).
$481*   *Newhaven Boys*, 1840s p.l., lit., prov., (10-29-92, Christie-London, #12, illus.), 5⅝ x 7¾ in., (14.3 x 19.7 cm.), photograph, carbon print, mounted on card (BP 308, DM 740, FR 2510, Y 59,581).
BI   *Portraits Of Gentlemen: Eight*, 1840s, p.l., lit., prov., est. BP 1,5/2,000, (10-29-92, Christie-London, #13), each approx. 8 x 6 in., (20.3 x 15.2 cm.), photograph, carbon prints mounted on card.
BI   *Portraits Of Gentlemen: Eight*, 1840s, p.l. by Andrew Elliot, mounted on card, prov., lit., est. BP 900/1,200, (05-06-93, Christie-London, #32), each approx. 8 x 6 in., photograph, carbon print.
$2359*   *Three Newhaven Fisherwomen*, mid 1840s, lit., (05-06-93, Christie-London, #30, illus.), 7¾ x 5½ in., photograph, calotype (BP 1495, DM 3716, FR 12,508, Y 259,545).

HILL, J.
$5500*   *Capturing A Sperm Whale*, painted by William Page from sketch by Cornelius B. Hulsart, pub. Hulsart, 1835, (05-29-93, Northeast, #52, illus.), image 16¼ x 24½ in., (41.3 x 62.2 cm.), color aquatint, engraved, printed and hand-colored (BP 3523, DM 8723, FR 29,491, Y 589,749).

$798* *West Point Military Academy,* (06-11-93, Freemn/Fine Art, #95, illus.), 11¾ x 16⅛ in., (29.8 x 41 cm.), color aquatint (BP 524, DM 1297, FR 4373, Y 84,668).

HILL, J. Hollyer, Engraver
$93* *The Flautist, 1950,* s., blindstamp, pub. Frost and Reed, margins, (11-12-92, Bonhams-Chelsea, #6), plate 14½ x 20¼ in., (36.8 x 51.4 cm.), color mezzotint (BP 61, DM 147, FR 497, Y 11,531).

HILL, J.W. and B.F. SMITH
$990* *"Philadelphia From Camden, 1850",* (06-11-93, Freemn/ Fine Art, #57A), 22¾ x 38¼ in., (57.8 x 97.2 cm.), tinted lithograph (BP 650, DM 1609, FR 5425, Y 105,040).

HILL, John
$2740* *Hudson (K. 91), 1820,* after William Guy Wall, 1st state of 2, plate 13 of Hudson River Portfolio, pub. Henry J. Megarey 1821-25, margins, good cond., discoloration, off-print of text sheet shows through, rippling, foxing, (01-28-93, Sotheby-NY, #423), image 14½ x 21½ in., (368 x 546 mm.), sheet 18 x 24¼ in., (368 x 546 mm.), hand-colored aquatint (BP 1809, DM 4342, FR 14,692, Y 340,204).

$9488* *New York, From Governor Island (K. 89), 1820,* after William Guy Wall, 1st state of 3, plate 20 of Hudson River Portfolio, pub. Henry J. Megarey 1821-25, margins, good cond., mat stains, fox marks, soiling, creases, (01-28-93, Sotheby-NY, #422, illus.), image 14 x 21 in., (356 x 533 mm.), sheet 19 x 24¾ in., (356 x 533 mm.), hand-colored aquatint (BP 6266, DM 15,034, FR 50,874, Y 1,178,048).

$1495* *View Near Hudson (Koke 81), 1820,* after William Guy Wall, 1st state of 2, plate 12 of Hudson River Portfolio, pub. Henry J. Megarey 1821-25, margins, long image tear backed w/tape, creases, discoloration, foxing, (01-28-93, Sotheby-NY, #421, illus.), image 14¼ x 21⅛ in., (362 x 537 mm.), sheet 18 x 24¼ in., (362 x 537 mm.), hand-colored aquatint (BP 987, DM 2369, FR 8016, Y 185,622).

HILL, John William (after)
BI *Boston,* by Charles Mottram, possibly later, est. BP 5/700, (06-16-93, Bonhams-Chelsea, #355, illus.), pl 28¼ x 41 in., (71.8 x 104.1 cm.), engraving w/hand-coloring.

$770* *"Boston",* C. Mottram, engraver, ident. w/in matrix, good cond.?, abrasions, wrinkling, (03-27-93, Skinner, #39), sight, sheet 27¾ x 40¼ in., (70.5 x 102.2 cm.), hand-colored engraving on paper (BP 517, DM 1256, FR 4271, Y 89,618).

HILL, Paul
BI *"Man Against Snow, Austria", 1974,* t., s., d., labels, 356 x 255mm, est. BP 3/500, (05-07-93, Sotheby-London, #202, illus.), photograph, silver print.

HILLENIUS, Jaap
$128* *Blauw (Regen), 1975,* s., t., d., full sheet, good cond., creases, (05-27-93, Sotheby-Amstrdm, #630), sh 25⁷⁄₁₆ x 19½ in., (646 x 496 mm.), lithograph w/watercolor on wove (BP 82, DM 205, FR 692, Y 13,722, G 230).

HILLER, Karel   1891-1939
BI *Heliographie, 1939,* init., d. in neg., lit., est. $7/8,000, (04-08-93, Christie-NY, #128, illus.), 15¼ x 11½ in., (38.7 x 29.2 cm.), photograph, gelatin silver print.

HILLERS, John K.
$660* *Bullion Canon, Utah,* photog. caption, credit in negative, 1870s, (04-07-93, Swann, #217, illus.), 13 x 10 in., photograph, albumen print (BP 436, DM 1067, FR 3612, Y 74,983).
BI *Selected Utah Views (Myself in the Water, figs. 10 and 14): Four,* s., t. by photog. in neg., est. $2,5/3,500, (10-15-92, Sotheby-NY, #37, illus.), each 9⅞ x 13 in., (25.1 x 33 cm.), photograph, albumen prints.
BI *Selected Zuni Pueblo Views (Myself in the Water, figs. 66, 68, 69): Nineteen,* t., s. by photog. in neg., seven i., label verso, Alonzo Bell Coll.,est. $6/9,000, (10-15-92, Sotheby-NY, #36, illus.), each, approx. 10 x 13 in., (25.4 x 33 cm.), photograph, albumen prints.
$1320* *Selected 'De Chelley Canon' Views (Myself in the Water, figs. 90 and 91): Six,* 1st 4 s., t. by photog. in neg., 1st 2 w/labels verso, Alonzo Bell Coll., 1879 or 1881, (10-15-92, Sotheby-NY, #40, illus.), each 9⅞ x 13 in., (25.1 x 33 cm.), photograph, albumen prints (BP 808, DM 1965, FR 6663, Y 158,368).

$1870* *'Eroded Sandstone, Kanab Canon, Utah', c. 1872,* s., t. by photog. in neg., (10-15-92, Sotheby-NY, #38, illus.), 9⅞ x 13 in., (25.1 x 33 cm.), photograph, albumen print (BP 1144, DM 2784, FR 9440, Y 224,355).

$1980* *'Governors Of Zuni' (Myself in the Water, fig. 74), 1879,* s., t. by photog. in neg., i. in unidentified hand, label verso, (10-15-92, Sotheby-NY, #35, illus.), 9½ x 12 in., (24.1 x 30.5 cm.), photograph, albumen print (BP 1212, DM 2947, FR 9995, Y 237,552).

$4400* *'Group Of Zuni Albinos' (Photodiscovery, pl. 109),* s., t. by photog. in neg., i. Also Bell, April 5-97, A. Bell, 665 E.142nd St., label verso, 1879 or 1881, (10-15-92, Sotheby-NY, #34, illus.), 9½ x 11⅞ in., (24.1 x 30.2 cm.), photograph, albumen print (BP 2692, DM 6550, FR 22,211, Y 527,894).

$2475* *'Mummy Cave, Canon Del Muerte, Ariz.' (Myself in the Water, fig. 93),* s., t. by photog. in neg., 1881, (10-15-92, Sotheby-NY, #41, illus.), 13 x 9⅞ in., (33 x 25.1 cm.), photograph, albumen print (BP 1515, DM 3684, FR 12,494, Y 296,941).

BI *'Pueblo De Santa Clara, N.M.', c. 1880,* s., t. by photog. in neg., est. $1,5/2,000, (10-15-92, Sotheby-NY, #42, illus.), 9¾ x 13 in., (24.8 x 33 cm.), photograph, albumen print.

$2475* *'The Caciques Of Zuni',* s., t. by photog. in neg., label verso, 1879 or 1881, (10-15-92, Sotheby-NY, #33, illus.), 9½ x 12 in., (24.1 x 30.5 cm.), photograph, albumen print (BP 1515, DM 3684, FR 12,494, Y 296,941).

$2200* *'Zuni Water Carrier',* s., t. in neg., i., label verso, 1879 or 1881, Alonzo Bell Coll., (10-15-92, Sotheby-NY, #32, illus.), 12 x 8¾ in., (30.5 x 22.2 cm.), photograph, albumen print (BP 1346, DM 3275, FR 11,106, Y 263,947).

HILLERS, John K. (et alii)
BI *Selected American Views (Myself in the Water, figs. 14, 95, 108, 111, 114, and 117): Twenty-Six,* 17 t., 3 s. by Hillers in neg., 1870's-90's, est. $2/3,000, (10-15-92, Sotheby-NY, #39, illus.), largest 10 x 13 in., (25.4 x 33 cm.), photograph, albumen prints.

HILLIER, Tristram   British b. 1905
$1111* *To Visit Britain's Landmarks, Jezreel's Temple, Kent, 1936,* p. Baynard Press, ref. #469, cond. 3, (10-13-92, Phillips-London, #112, illus.), 29¹⁵⁄₁₆ x 45¹⁄₁₆ in., (76 x 114.5 cm.), color lithograph (BP 647, DM 1628, FR 5530, Y 134,716).

$3218* *Tourists Prefer Shell, 1936,* pen/ink s., p. Baynard Press, ref. #448, cond. 3, (10-13-92, Phillips-London, #100, illus.), 29¹⁵⁄₁₆ x 44⅞ in., (76 x 114 cm.), color lithograph (BP 1874, DM 4714, FR 16,018, Y 390,202).

HILTON, Hedley
$60* *A Continental Town By A River,* s., margins, (04-22-93, Bonhams-Chelsea, #134), plate 11½ x 12⅞ in., (29.2 x 32.7 cm.), drypoint etching (BP 39, DM 96, FR 325, Y 6597).

HILTON, John W.   American b. 1904
$330* *Hilton Paints The Desert: Twelve,* s., i. John Hilton, unbound book, James Cagney Estate, (09-30-92, Doyle, #47), 16 x 20 in., (40.6 x 50.8 cm.), photo-offset reproduction (BP 186, DM 468, FR 1583, Y 39,602).

HIMELY, Sigismond   French 1801-1872
$6900* *New-York, 1851,* after Heine, J. Kummer & Dopler, pub. Goupil & Co. and W. Schaus, margins, good cond., repaired tears and losses, mat stain, soiling gesso-ed over,creases, (01-28-93, Sotheby-NY, #437, illus.), plate 28⅞ x 43 in., (73.3 x 109.2 cm.), sheet 30¾ x 44⅛ in., (73.3 x 109.2 cm.), hand-colored engraving (BP 4557, DM 10,933, FR 36,997, Y 856,717).

$6900* *Vue De New York, Prise De Weahawk, A View Of New York, Taken From Veahawk (S.- & H. C. 1834-E-38; D. 433), c. 1834,* 2nd state of 2, after Ambroise-Louis Garneray, pub. in Vues des Cotes de France dans l'Ocean et dans la Mediterranee, by Hocquart and Bailly Ward &Co. c. 1830-35, margins, good cond., water stain just through image tip, soiling, creases, nicks, colors possibly renewed, (01-28-93, Sotheby-NY, #430, illus.), 16¼ x 20¼ in., (413 x 514 mm.), sheet 17⅜ x 21¼ in., (413 x 514 mm.), hand-colored aquatint on white wove (BP 4557, DM 10,933, FR 36,997, Y 856,717).

$8050* *Vue De New York, Prise De Weahawk, A View Of New York, Taken From Veahawk (S. & H. C. 1834-E-38; D. 433), c. 1834,* 2nd state of 2, after Ambroise-Louis Garneray, pub. in Vues des Cotes de France dans l'Ocean et dans la Mediterranee, by Hocquart and Bailey Ward &Co., margins, good cond., mat stain, fox marks, repaired tear, soiling, skinned spot, tape stains, (01-28-93, Sotheby-NY, #429, illus.), image 12¾ x 17½ in., (324 x 445 mm.), sheet 15¾ x 19¾ in., (324 x 445 mm.), hand-colored aquatint w/touches gum arabic on wove (BP 5316, DM 12,756, FR 43,164, Y 999,503).

HINDS, Susan American 1929-1988
 BI *Untitled: Three,* est. $2/300, (12-11-92, DuMouchelle, #1287), prints.

HINE, Lewis American 1874-1940
$1045* *Bowery Mission Bread Line,* (1907), p. 1941, prov., lit., (10-13-92, Christie-NY, #76, illus.), 4⅝ x 5⅞ in., (11.7 x 14.9 cm.), photograph, gelatin silver print (BP 609, DM 1531, FR 5202, Y 126,713).

$385* *Boy At Wharf, c. 1910,* handstamps, (10-14-92, Swann, #476, illus.), 5 x 7 in., (12.7 x 17.8 cm.), photograph, silver print (BP 226, DM 563, FR 1911, Y 46,655).

$5060* *Boy Harvesting Tobacco,* photog.'s sig., Interpretive Photo. handstamp, c. 1910, p.l., ex-coll. Naomi and Walter Rosenblum, (04-07-93, Swann, #485, illus.), approx. 10½ x 13¼ in., photograph, silver print (BP 3344, DM 8184, FR 27,696, Y 574,869).

 BI *"Boy In A Cotton Mill" and "Three Children In A Cotton Mill": Two,* one 1909, other 1908, num., est. $1,5/2,000, (05-23-93, Butterfield, #3449, illus.), one 4¾ x 6¾ in., other 5 x 6¾ in., photograph, gelatin silver print.

$2200* *Child Labor Propaganda Sign, c. 1900,* (10-13-92, Christie-NY, #78, illus.), 3½ x 5⅞ in., (8.9 x 14.9 cm.), photograph, gelatin silver print (BP 1281, DM 3223, FR 10,951, Y 266,764).

 BI *Climbing Into America,* (1905), 1930s, stamp, prov., est. 4/6,000, (10-13-92, Christie-NY, #74, illus.), 6¾ x 5 in., (17.1 x 12.7 cm.), photograph, gelatin silver print.

$770* *Family Engaged In Homework (Sewing Trousers), Mulberry Street,* photog.'s Interpretive Photo. handstamp, typewritten caption, c later, c. 1908, p. 1920s, (04-07-93, Swann, #486, illus.), approx. 7½ x 9½ in., photograph, silver print (BP 509, DM 1245, FR 4215, Y 87,480).

$1035* *Group Of Men At A Mill, 1910,* stamp, (05-23-93, Butterfield, #3450, illus.), 5 x 7 in., photograph, gelatin silver print (BP 674, DM 1692, FR 5696, Y 114,403).

$1650* *The Heart Of The Turbine, Industrial Design In New York City Power House, 1930,* photog.'s studio stamp, label, (10-15-92, Sotheby-NY, #143, illus.), 9½ x 7½ in., (24.1 x 19.1 cm.), photograph, gelatin silver print (BP 1010, DM 2456, FR 8329, Y 197,960).

 BI *"Italian Immigrant At The Hull House Workshop" and "Red Cross SeriesPhotograph", 1910: Two,* first t., d., each photog.'s stamp, est. $7/900, (05-23-93, Butterfield, #3452, illus.), one 5 x 7 in., other 6¾ x 4¾ in., photograph, gelatin silver print.

$1320* *Little Orphan Annie, In A Pittsburg Institution,* (1909). p. c. 1942 by Photo League, prov., lit., (10-13-92, Christie-NY, #73, illus.), 6½ x 4½ in., (16.5 x 11.4 cm.), photograph, gelatin silver print (BP 769, DM 1934, FR 6570, Y 160,058).

$690* *"Little Orphan Annie, In A Pittsburgh Institution",* 1909, p. 1942, p. posthumously by Photo League of NY, (05-23-93, Butterfield, #3453, illus.), 6¾ x 4¾ in., photograph, gelatin silver print (BP 449, DM 1128, FR 3797, Y 76,268).

 BI *Machine Shop and Family Tailoring: Two, c. 1910,* est. $1,5/1,800, (10-13-92, Christie-NY, #75, illus.), each 4⅝ x 6⅝ in., (11.7 x 16.8 cm.), photograph, gelatin silver prints.

 BI *Mechanic In Car Shop, "Old Faithful",* 1920s, s., t., Interpretive Photography stamp, est. $2,5/3,500, (04-08-93, Christie-NY, #60, illus.), 16¾ x 12¾ in., (42.5 x 32.4 cm.), photograph, gelatin silver print.

 BI *Mother And Children With Dachshund, c. 1910,* picture agency stamp, est. $1/1,500, (04-08-93, Christie-NY, #59, illus.), 7⅝ x 9⅝ in., (19.4 x 24.4 cm.), photograph, gelatin silver print.

$7150* *One Of The Many Young Spinners In Carolina Cotton Mills,* (1908), 1930s, t., d. in photo., label, prov., (10-13-92, Christie-NY, #79, illus.), 10⅝ x 13½ in., (27 x 34.3 cm.), photograph, gelatin silver print (BP 4164, DM 10,475, FR 35,590, Y 866,982).

 BI *Packing Candies Under Good Conditions, N.Y. City,* handstamp, 1920's, est. $1/1,500, (10-14-92, Swann, #477, illus.), 4¾ x 6¾ in., (12.1 x 17.1 cm.), photograph, silver print.

 BI *Pittsburgh Steel Plants At Night, c. 1920,* t. w/notations, est. $4/6,000, (10-13-92, Christie-NY, #77, illus.), 12¾ x 18⅛ in., (8.9 x 14.9 cm.), photograph, toned gelatin silver print.

$51,750* *Powerhouse Mechanic (1925), 1939,* s., Interpretive Photography credit stamp, accompanied by section oforig. backboard w/credit stamp and Walter and Naomi Rosenblum p. label w/typedt. and d. affixed verso of backboard, lit., (04-08-93, Christie-NY, #61, illus.), 19⅛ x 13⅛ in., (48.6 x 33.3 cm.), photograph, gelatin silver print (BP 33,934, DM 83,133, FR 281,403, Y 5,872,674).

$15,400* *Powerhouse Mechanic Or Steamfitter (Gutman, p. 32), 1925,* s. by photog. in ink, studio stamp, p. before 1940, sold after sale, (10-15-92, Sotheby-NY, #141, illus.), 6½ x 4½ in., (16.5 x 11.4 cm.), photograph, gelatin silver print (BP 9424, DM 22,923, FR 77,739, Y 1,847,630).

$920* *"Small Boy Works As Helper...Somersworth, N.H.", 1909,* num. 767 in unident. hand, typed caption label, (04-06-93, Sotheby-NY, #217, illus.), 4¾ x 6¾ in., photograph (BP 608, DM 1482, FR 5019, Y 104,927).

$4025* *"Swinging Along With A Load Of "Homework", East Side", 1910,* mounted, label, p. 1920's or 1930's, (04-06-93, Sotheby-NY, #84, illus.), 13½ x 10½ in., photograph (BP 2659, DM 6485, FR 21,959, Y 459,056).

$8800* *Topping The Mast,* s. by photog., studio stamp, 1931, p. before 1940, sold after sale, (10-15-92, Sotheby-NY, #142, illus.), 13⅜ x 10½ in., (34 x 26.7 cm.), photograph, gelatin silver print (BP 5385, DM 13,099, FR 44,422, Y 1,055,789).

$920* *Two Boys In A Broom Factory, 1908,* num., (05-23-93, Butterfield, #3451, illus.), 4⅝ x 6⅝ in., photograph, gelatin silver print (BP 599, DM 1504, FR 5063, Y 101,691).

$935* *"Two Boys In A Mill" and "Three Girls In A Factory", c. 1910: Two,* first ink #3850, captioned, second ink #4907, (11-16-92, Butterfield, #6005, illus.), each approx. 4¼ x 6¼ in., (108.1 x 159 mm.), photograph, gelatin silver print (BP 616, DM 1491, FR 5021, Y 116,279).

$358* *Women And Girls On Porch Steps, 1910,* neg. num. 2016-A, annot. verso, (11-16-92, Butterfield, #6006, illus.), 2½ x 4 in., (63.6 x 101.8 mm.), photograph, gelatin silver print (BP 236, DM 571, FR 1923, Y 44,522).

 BI *"Workers, Barker Cotton Mill", "New York City Family" and "Five Boys": Three,* 1909-14, two annots., each num., est. 1,5/2,000, (05-23-93, Butterfield, #3448, illus.), each approx. 4½ x 6½ in., photograph, gelatin silver print.

$303* *Young Workers, c. 1910,* prov., (06-13-93, Hindman, #425), 4⅜ x 6⅜ in., photograph, silver print (BP 198, DM 493, FR 1658, Y 31,885).

 BI *Young Workers, c. 1910,* prov., est. $1/1,500, (05-16-93, Hindman, #324), 4⅜ x 6⅜ in., photograph, silver print.

$645* *Zeitungsjunge, 20's,* (11-12-92, Lempertz, #97, illus.), 5½ x 3¼ in., (13.9 x 8.2 cm.), photograph, gelatin silver print (BP 412, DM 1014, FR 3455, Y 79,797).

HINE, Sheldon
 BI *"Barrel Of A Gun", "Watch Mechanism" and "Shadow Of An Egg": Three,* photog.'s sig., 1930's, est. $800/1,200, (04-07-93, Swann, #487, illus.), 7 x 9 in., photograph, silver print.

HINES, Fred (after)
$24 *River Scenes With Swans: Three,* (04-16-93, G.A. Key, #93), 7 x 4 in., (17.8 x 10.2 cm.), b/w prints (BP 16, DM 39, FR 131, Y 2699).

HINGRE, L.

BI *Paris-Marseille,* d. 1902, generally good cond., repaired tears, prop. Rod Stewart, est. $3/400, (11-06-92, Sotheby-Arcade, #137), sight 17½ x 11½ in., (44.5 x 29.2 cm.), lithograph in colors.

HINMAN, Charles American b. 1932

$308* *Untitled, 1973,* from Peace Portfolio II, s., #11/90, good cond.?, (12-12-92, Weschler, #126A), 32¼ x 22 in., (81.9 x 55.9 cm.), color silkscreen (BP 197, DM 485, FR 1663, Y 38,114).

HINTON, Alfred Horsley 1863-1908

BI *"Tide Bereft",* before 1898, composed from 2 negs., mounted on card, t., s., annot.,481 x 293mm, est. BP 1/1,500, (05-07-93, Sotheby-London, #163, illus.), photograph, platinum print.

HIPKINS

$748* *Musical Instruments, 1888: Eight,* (04-07-93, Sotheby-Arcade, #289), sight 13 x 9 in., (33 x 22.9 cm.), chromolithograph (BP 494, DM 1210, FR 4094, Y 84,981).

HIRAKAWA, Isamu

$93* *Paris,* s., #69/75, good margins, (05-06-93, Laurin, #43), color lithograph (BP 59, DM 146, FR 493, Y 10,232).

HIRATSUKA, Un'ichi Japanese b. 1895

BI *"Pagoda At Bukkuku-Ji Temple" and "Workers In A Rice Field": Two,* each s., Un-ichi- Hiratsuka, artist's seal, 1st d. 1952, 2nd d. 1942,each good cond.; toning verso, est. $1/1,500, (04-02-93, Weschler, #268, illus.), each 13 x 18 in., (33 x 45.7 cm.), wood engraving.

$750* *Waiting Booth Of Hasso-An Tea House, Nara,* s., t., d. 1960, #10/80, (02-04-93, Sloan, #2571), 23½ x 17 in., (59.7 x 43.2 cm.), woodcut (BP 524, DM 1235, FR 4188, Y 93,295).

HIROAKI, Takahashi 1871-1944

$1208* *Blick Auf Den Fuji,* t., (04-27-93, Dorotheum, #195, illus.), 15¹⁄₁₆ x 6¹¹⁄₁₆ in., (38.2 x 17 cm.), color woodcut (BP 768, DM 1913, FR 6470, Y 135,380, SC 13,440).

$252* *"Der Mond Vor Sekiguchi",* t., s., (04-27-93, Dorotheum, #205, illus.), 6⅞ x 15⅜ in., (17.5 x 39.1 cm.), color woodcut (BP 160, DM 399, FR 1350, Y 28,242, SC 2800).

$654* *"Spaziergang Bei Vollmond",* t., (04-27-93, Dorotheum, #204, illus.), 6¹³⁄₁₆ x 15⅜ in., (17.3 x 39 cm.), color woodcut (BP 416, DM 1035, FR 3503, Y 73,294, SC 7280).

HIROAKI, Takahashi Japanese c. 1811-1945

$275* *"Full Moon At Ishigama Alongside Biwa Lake",* block s., (01-15-93, DuMouchelle, #2160, illus.), 14¾ x 6½ in., (37.5 x 16.5 cm.), color woodblock print (BP 180, DM 450, FR 1520, Y 34,670).

$121* *"Otome Pass At Foot Of Fuji",* block s., (01-15-93, DuMouchelle, #2157, illus.), 6½ x 14¾ in., (16.5 x 37.5 cm.), color woodblock print (BP 79, DM 198, FR 669, Y 15,255).

BI *"Rain At Izurnibashi Bridge",* block s., est. $4/600, (01-15-93, DuMouchelle, #2158, illus.), 6½ x 14¾ in., (16.5 x 37.5 cm.), color woodblock print.

$275* *"Village Sawatori In Joshu District",* block s., (01-15-93, DuMouchelle, #2159, illus.), 14¾ x 6½ in., (37.5 x 16.5 cm.), color woodblock print (BP 180, DM 450, FR 1520, Y 34,670).

HIROAKI, Takahashi Japanese c.1811-1945

BI *"Row Of Cypress Trees At Nakko",* block s., est. $4/600, (01-15-93, DuMouchelle, #2156, illus.), 14¾ x 6½ in., (37.5 x 16.5 cm.), color woodblock print.

HIROSADA, Utagawa ac. 1820-1860

$302* *Kopfportrait Eines Schauspielers Mit Aufwendiger Haartracht,* Format Chuban, (04-27-93, Dorotheum, #213, illus.), 6¹¹⁄₁₆ x 9¹³⁄₁₆ in., (17 x 25 cm.), (BP 192, DM 478, FR 1618, Y 33,845, SC 3360).

HIROSHIGA

BI *"The Camphor Tree With Entwined Branches In The Grove Of Azuma",* from "The Hundred Famous Views of Edo", t., block s., est. $200/350, (01-15-93, DuMouchelle, #2297, illus.), 13¼ x 8⅛ in., (33.7 x 20.6 cm.), color woodblock print.

HIROSHIGE

$2461* *"The Bikuni Bridge In Snow" and "Cherry Blossom Over Arashiyama": Two,* oban tate-e and oban yoko-e, from series The Hundred Views of Edo and The Famous Places of Kyoto respectively, both s. Hiroshige-ga, latter w/seal of pub., Kawaguchi-ban, margins, trimmed, paper thinned, (06-10-93, Sotheby-London, #256), (BP 1610, DM 4007, FR 13,492, Y 261,225).

$275* *Cherry Blossoms,* (10-11-92, Hanzel, #956E), 13¼ x 8¾ in., (33.7 x 22.2 cm.), color woodblock print (BP 163, DM 408, FR 1372, Y 33,479).

$132* *Figures At A Mountain Retreat,* mid-19th century, (12-05-92, Eldred, #536), woodblock (BP 83, DM 206, FR 701, Y 16,355).

$2110* *Fox-Fires At The Foot Of An Elm Tree On New Year's Eve At O-Ji,* oban tate-e, from series The Hundred Views of Edo, s. Hiroshige ga, scuffed areas, puncture, trimmed, laid-down, (06-10-93, Sotheby-London, #249), (BP 1380, DM 3436, FR 11,568, Y 223,968).

$14,065* *From The Series Edo Meisho, "The Famous Places Of Edo": Thirty-Four,* oban yoko-e, 20 prints mounted in an album, pub. Yamada Shojiro, censor's seals, s. Hiroshige ga, fold mark, rubbed, soiled, (06-10-93, Sotheby-London, #258, illus.), (BP 9200, DM 22,903, FR 77,111, Y 1,492,941).

$1055* *Fukagawa Mannenbashi, "The Mannen Bridge At Fukagawa",* oban, from series The Hundred Views Of Edo, censor's aratame seal, d. Year of the Snake (1857), faded, repaired tear, thinned area, (06-10-93, Sotheby-London, #254), (BP 690, DM 1718, FR 5784, Y 111,984).

$99* *"Ishibe",* HOEIDO TOKAIDO, soiling, corners torn, (05-07-93, Goldberg, #1383), woodblock (BP 63, DM 157, FR 527, Y 10,901).

$2813* *Kameyama From Hoeido's Takaido Series,* oban yoko-e, s. Hiroshige ga, pub. mark, Hoeido, foxed, centre-fold mark, (06-10-93, Sotheby-London, #250), (BP 1840, DM 4581, FR 15,422, Y 298,588).

$165* *Kyoto,* from 53 Stations of the Tokaido, no date seals, (12-05-92, Eldred, #533), woodblock (BP 103, DM 257, FR 877, Y 20,444).

$165* *Landscape With Dwellings,* block s., (04-16-93, DuMouchelle, #2308, illus.), 13 x 8¾ in., (33 x 22.2 cm.), woodblock (BP 108, DM 267, FR 901, Y 18,554).

$165* *Mariko,* from 53 Stations of the Tokaido, no date seals, (12-05-92, Eldred, #531), woodblock (BP 103, DM 257, FR 877, Y 20,444).

$55* *"Masaki Atari Yori Suijin-No-Mori Uchikawa Sekiya-No-Sato-Wo-Miro-Zu", 1857,* from Views of Edo, toned, (12-05-92, Eldred, #535), woodblock (BP 34, DM 86, FR 292, Y 6815).

BI *"Monkey Bridge",* KAKEMONO-E, poor cond., laid down, torn, fading, soiling, portion print broken away, est. $75/150, (05-07-93, Goldberg, #1354), woodblock.

$45* *Mountain Peak By The Sea,* (05-16-93, Hanzel, #1098), 9 x 6½ in., (22.9 x 16.5 cm.), color woodblock (BP 29, DM 72, FR 243, Y 4988).

$45* *Mountainous Landscape,* (05-16-93, Hanzel, #1096), 9 x 6½ in., (22.9 x 16.5 cm.), color woodblock (BP 29, DM 72, FR 243, Y 4988).

$50* *Mountains And Lake With Sailboats,* (05-16-93, Hanzel, #1097), 8¾ x 6½ in., (22.2 x 16.5 cm.), color woodblock (BP 33, DM 80, FR 270, Y 5543).

$220* *Muja,* from 53 Stations of the Tokaido, (12-05-92, Eldred, #534), woodblock (BP 138, DM 343, FR 1169, Y 27,258).

$3867* *Serie Des 53 Stations Du Tokaido,* La Station 9, Oiso, format oban yoko-e, s., creases, stains, (06-28-93, Loudmer, #165), (BP 2589, DM 6571, FR 22,135, Y 410,292).

$1450* *Serie Des 53 Stations Du Tokaido,* La Station 6, Totsuka, format oban yoko-e, s., c. 1833, crease, (06-28-93, Loudmer, #164), (BP 971, DM 2464, FR 8300, Y 153,846).

BI *Shimada,* from 53 Stations of the Tokaido, est. $750/850, (12-05-92, Eldred, #538), woodblock.

$248* *"Shinagawa",* from Fifty-Three Stations of the Tokaido, pub. Hoeido, 2nd state, Kiwame seal, trimmed, soiled, stained, (11-20-92, Skinner, #40, illus.), oban yoko-e (BP 163, DM 395, FR 1332, Y 30,842).

$492* *Shinmachi On The Kiso Road*, oban yoko-e, from series The Sixty-nine Stations on the Kiso Road, pub. seal Kinjudo, s. Hiroshige ga, fold mark, repaired, new margins, (06-10-93, Sotheby-London, #253), (BP 322, DM 801, FR 2697, Y 52,224).

$966* *Shono And Kusatsu From The So-Called "Upright Tokaido" Series: Two*, oban, pub. Tsutakichi, censor's aratame seal d. Year of the Hare, s.Hiroshige hitsu, late edit., fair state, (06-10-93, Sotheby-London, #255), (BP 632, DM 1573, FR 5296, Y 102,537).

BI *Six Men Carrying Burdens Along The Road*, from 53 Stations of the Tokaido, soiled, est. $150/250, (12-05-92, Eldred, #540), woodblock.

$4571* *Small Series Of Tokaido: Fifty-Five*, koban yoko-e, pub. Aritaya, s. Hiroshige ga, (06-10-93, Sotheby-London, #260), (BP 2990, DM 7443, FR 25,060, Y 485,193).

$165* *Tokiwa And Her Children In Snow*, no date seals, (12-05-92, Eldred, #532), woodblock (BP 103, DM 257, FR 877, Y 20,444).

$110* *Untitled*, block s., (04-16-93, DuMouchelle, #2309, illus.), 6 x 8¼ in., (15.2 x 21 cm.), woodblock (BP 72, DM 178, FR 600, Y 12,369).

BI *Untitled: A Pair*, est. $225/275, (12-05-92, Eldred, #537), woodblock.

$4923* *Waiting For The Moonrise At Takanawa: Three*, oban triptych, t., s. Ichiryusai Hiroshige hitsu, faded, soiled, rubbed, tears, (06-10-93, Sotheby-London, #259, illus.), (BP 3220, DM 8017, FR 26,990, Y 522,556).

$99* *"Yoshiware"*, TOTO MEISHO, fading, soiling, (05-07-93, Goldberg, #1385), woodblock (BP 63, DM 157, FR 527, Y 10,901).

HIROSHIGE   Japanese 1797-1858
$143* *"A Bridge In Winter" and "A Mountainous Winter Landscape With Figures": Two*, (03-25-93, Boos, #266), color woodblock print (BP 97, DM 235, FR 799, Y 16,753).

HIROSHIGE (I)   1797-1858
$770* *"100 Famous Views Of Edo"*, #105, Ommaya Riverbank, 1857, late impression, foxing, (10-31-92, Goldberg, #642, illus.), (BP 503, DM 1209, FR 4094, Y 95,203).

$550* *"100 Famous Views Of Edo"*, #41, Hachiman Shrine, 1858, late impression, oban, (10-31-92, Goldberg, #640), (BP 360, DM 863, FR 2924, Y 68,002).

$880* *"100 Famous Views Of Edo"*, #9, 1857, verticle oban, good colors/cond., (10-31-92, Goldberg, #641), (BP 575, DM 1381, FR 4678, Y 108,803).

$660* *"100 Famous Views Of Edo"*, Toto Meisho, c. 1845, horizontal oban, w/seals, pub. mark, (10-31-92, Goldberg, #644), (BP 432, DM 1036, FR 3509, Y 81,602).

HIROSHIGE (II)
$55* *The Bay*, (05-16-93, Hanzel, #1110), 6½ x 8¾ in., (16.5 x 22.2 cm.), color woodblock (BP 36, DM 88, FR 297, Y 6097).

$70* *Boats On The Bay*, (05-16-93, Hanzel, #1108), 6½ x 8¾ in., (16.5 x 22.2 cm.), color woodblock (BP 46, DM 113, FR 378, Y 7760).

$45* *Mountains*, (05-16-93, Hanzel, #1109), 6¼ x 8¾ in., (15.9 x 22.2 cm.), color woodblock (BP 29, DM 72, FR 243, Y 4988).

HIROSHIGE (II)   Japanese 1829-1869
$70* *"Kanaya, Oi-Gawa Engan"*, c. 1865, from series 53 Stations of the Tokaido, s. Rissho, (05-15-93, Cleveland, #18), 9¼ x 6⅞ in., (23.5 x 17.5 cm.), color woodblock (BP 46, DM 113, FR 378, Y 7760).

$70* *"No. 48 Seki Honjin Hayadachi Early Departure Of Daimyo"*, c. 1865, from series 53 Stations of the Tokaido, s. Rissho, (05-15-93, Cleveland, #19), 9¼ x 6⅞ in., (23.5 x 17.5 cm.), color woodblock (BP 46, DM 113, FR 378, Y 7760).

HIROSHIGE (after)
$138* *Prints: Five*, (03-12-93, DuMouchelle, #464), 10¾ x 6¾ in., (27.3 x 17.1 cm.), wood block print (BP 96, DM 230, FR 781, Y 16,264).

$22* *"Rainstorm On Ohashi"*, (03-25-93, Boos, #640), image 13 x 8¼ in., (33 x 21 cm.), color woodblock print (BP 15, DM 36, FR 123, Y 2577).

$39* *Untitled*, (06-11-93, DuMouchelle, #416), 10½ x 7 in., (26.7 x 17.8 cm.), woodblock print (BP 26, DM 63, FR 214, Y 4138).

$132* *Untitled: Two*, (06-13-93, Hindman, #406), each 8½ x 13½ in., (21.6 x 34.3 cm.), color woodcut (BP 86, DM 215, FR 722, Y 13,890).

HIROSHIGE, Ando   Japanese 1797-1858
$806* *"Akasaka"*, 1855, format Oban, (04-27-93, Dorotheum, #149, illus.), 14¹/₁₆ x 9⁵/₁₆ in., (35.7 x 23.6 cm.), color woodcut (BP 513, DM 1276, FR 4317, Y 90,328, SC 8960).

$193* *"Driving Rain" and "Travelers In Marshy Landscape": Two*, (04-02-93, Sloan, #1887), each 9½ x 14 in., (241 x 356 mm.), color woodcut (BP 127, DM 310, FR 1053, Y 21,974).

$125* *Figures And Cherry Blossoms Outside Temple*, (02-04-93, Sloan, #929), 9½ x 14½ in., (24.1 x 36.8 cm.), color woodcut (BP 87, DM 206, FR 698, Y 15,549).

$154* *Figures Passing Through Landscape*, (12-13-92, Hindman, #383), 9 x 13½ in., color woodcut (BP 98, DM 242, FR 825, Y 19,052).

BI *From The Series "Edo Meisho"*, c. 1855, format Oban, est. SC 12/15,000, (04-27-93, Dorotheum, #167, illus.), 14¼ x 9³/₁₆ in., (36.2 x 23.4 cm.), color woodcut.

$252* *From The Series "Tokaido Gojusan Tsugi No Uchi"*, (04-27-93, Dorotheum, #158, illus.), 14¾ x 10⅛ in., (37.5 x 25.7 cm.), color woodcut (BP 160, DM 399, FR 1350, Y 28,242, SC 2800).

$806* *From The Series "Toto Meisho"*, appears 1833-1843 in publication Kikakudo, format Oban, (04-27-93, Dorotheum, #157, illus.), 14¹¹/₁₆ x 10¹/₁₆ in., (37.3 x 25.6 cm.), color woodcut (BP 513, DM 1276, FR 4317, Y 90,328, SC 8960).

$4531* *"Kambara"*, 1833/34, from the series Tokaido gojusan tsugi no uchi (53 Stationen der Ostmeerstrasse), format Oban, (04-27-93, Dorotheum, #163, illus.), 14³/₁₆ x 9⅝ in., (36 x 24.5 cm.), woodcut (BP 2881, DM 7174, FR 24,269, Y 507,789, SC 50,400).

$302* *"Kusatsu"*, from the 53 Stations of Tokaido, format Oban, (04-27-93, Dorotheum, #156, illus.), 14⅜ x 9¹⁵/₁₆ in., (36.5 x 25.2 cm.), color woodcut (BP 192, DM 478, FR 1618, Y 33,845, SC 3360).

$468* *Landscape With Mount Fuji*, (06-13-93, Hindman, #407), 9 x 13¾ in., (22.9 x 34.9 cm.), color woodcut (BP 306, DM 762, FR 2560, Y 49,248).

$935* *Processions With Umbrellas In Landscape: Triptych*, (10-18-92, Hindman, #526, illus.), each 14½ x 9¾ in., (36.8 x 24.8 cm.), color woodcut (BP 572, DM 1392, FR 4720, Y 112,178).

$165* *Samurai Fight Scene*, from "Soga Bros." series, (02-04-93, Sloan, #928), (36.5 x 24.8 cm.), color woodcut (BP 115, DM 272, FR 921, Y 20,525).

$8250* *"Seba, No. 32"*, c. 1845, from the series The Sixty Nine Stations of the Kisokaido, s. Hiroshige ga, Seal: Ichiyusai, pub. Kinjudo, later impression, 2nd state, center fold,ine cond., (10-31-92, Cleveland, #25, illus.), 8⅞ x 13⅞ in., (22.5 x 35.2 cm.), woodblock (BP 5287, DM 12,692, FR 43,058, Y 1,021,925).

$143* *Tsuki-No-Misaki (Moon Cape)*, from One Hundred Famous Views Of Edo, (09-17-92, Sloan, #1650), 9 x 13¼ in., (22.9 x 33.7 cm.), woodblock (BP 80, DM 212, FR 727, Y 17,804).

$238* *Untitled*, c. 1849, s., (11-16-92, Hodgins, #338, illus.), 8½ x 13½ in., (21.6 x 34.3 cm.), color woodblock on paper (BP 156, DM 380, FR 1279, Y 29,702, C$ 303).

$248* *View Of Bridge Over river susmida*, (07-03-92, Sloan, #902), woodblock (BP 130, DM 375, FR 1265, Y 30,915).

$187* *Waves At Naruto*, (12-13-92, Hindman, #382), 14¾ x 28½ in., woodblock (BP 120, DM 294, FR 1002, Y 23,135).

$806* *"Yokkaichi"*, from the series Tokaido gojusan tsugi no uchi, signs of wear, formatOban, (04-27-93, Dorotheum, #168, illus.), 14¹/₁₆ x 9⁵/₁₆ in., (35.7 x 23.6 cm.), color woodcut (BP 513, DM 1276, FR 4317, Y 90,328, SC 8960).

HIROSHIGE, Ando (after)
BI *Ehon Tebiki-Gusa: Book Of Forty-Two,* est. $250/350, (02-04-93, Sloan, #931), each 7⅛ x 4¾ in., (18.1 x 12.1 cm.), woodcut.
$150* *Eight Views,* from One Hundred Famous Views of Edo, (02-04-93, Sloan, #922), each 5¾ x 3¾ in., (14.6 x 9.5 cm.), color woodcut (BP 105, DM 247, FR 838, Y 18,659).
BI *"Evening Snow At Asika-Yama", "Night Snow" and "Nagakubo": Three,* est. $2/250, (02-04-93, Sloan, #926), each, sight 7¼ x 11¼ in., (18.4 x 28.6 cm.), color woodcut.
$200* *Two,* from "Fifty-three Stations of the Tokaido", (02-04-93, Sloan, #924), each 7⅜ x 10¼ in., (18.7 x 26 cm.), color woodcut (BP 140, DM 329, FR 1117, Y 24,879).

HIROSHIGE, Ando (I) 1797-1858
$674* *Nihon-Bashi Nach Schneefall, Bei Sonnenaufgang,* oban, yoko-e, s., censor's stamp, (06-08-93, Karl/Faber, #434), color woodcut (BP 443, DM 1094, FR 3683, Y 71,588).

HIROSHIGE, Ando (after)
BI *Ehon Tebiki-Gusa,* book of 42, est. $2/300, (04-02-93, Sloan, #1877), each 7⅛ x 4¾ in., (181 x 121 mm.), woodcut.
$165* *"Evening Snow At Asuka-Yama", "Night Snow" and "Nagakubo": Three,* (04-02-93, Sloan, #1874), each, sight 7¼ x 11¼ in., (184 x 286 mm.), color woodcut (BP 109, DM 265, FR 901, Y 18,786).

HIROSHIGE, Ando and Utagawa KUNISADA Japanese 18th cent.
$150* *Kabuki Actor And Actress In Landscape,* (02-04-93, Sloan, #927), 14¼ x 9¾ in., (36.2 x 24.8 cm.), color woodcut (BP 105, DM 247, FR 838, Y 18,659).

HIROSHIGE, Ichiryusai Japanese 1797-1858
$217* *Scene De Rue,* (06-16-93, Encans, #145), 13¹⁵⁄₁₆ x 9¹⁄₁₆ in., (35.5 x 23 cm.), wood engraving (BP 145, DM 360, FR 1209, Y 23,144, C$ 278).

HIROSHIGE, Utagawa
BI *Akasake,* from Sketches of Famous Places on Fifty-Three Stations (Upright Tokaido), t., s. Hiroshige hitsu, censor's seal, publisher's seal Tsutayo Kichizo, d. seal Seventh U (1855), good cond., est. $3/500, (04-02-93, Weschler, #263),
BI *Kanagawa,* from Sketches of Famous Places on the Fifty-Three Stations (Upright Tokaido), t., s. Hiroshige hitsu, censor's seal, d. seal Seventh U (1855), publisher's seal Tsuta-ya Kichizo, good cond., est. $3/500, (04-02-93, Weschler, #262), .
$275* *Kawaski,* from Sketches of Famous Places on the Fifty-Three Stations (Upright Tokaido), t., s. Hiroshige hitsu, censor's seal, publisher's seal Tsutaya Kichizo, d. seal Seventh U (1855), good cond., (04-02-93, Weschler, #264, illus.), (BP 181, DM 442, FR 1501, Y 31,310).
$553* *Kinokuni-Zaka, Akasaka Tameike Enkei (R. Lane S. 248), 1857,* from series: 100 beruhmte Ansichten von Edo, Oban Tate-e, s., censurestamp, Uoyo Eikichi, (04-21-93, Germann, #249, illus.), color woodcut (BP 359, DM 884, FR 2989, Y 61,220, SF 805).
BI *Kusatus,* from Sketches of Famous Places on the Fifty-Three Stations (Upright Tokaido), t., s. Hiroshige hitsu, censor's seal, publisher's seal Tsutaya Kichizo, d. seal Seventh U (1855), good cond., est. $3/500, (04-02-93, Weschler, #265), .
$395* *Der Tomioka Hachimangu Schrein In Fukagawa, c. 1840,* from series: Edo Meisho, Oban yokoe, censure stamp, Kiwane, mounted,creases, (04-21-93, Germann, #254), color woodcut (BP 256, DM 631, FR 2135, Y 43,729, SF 575).

HIROSHIGE, Utagawa Japanese
$395* *Chu-Tanzakue. Vogel Und Blumen,* oban, s., (04-21-93, Germann, #248), blue woodcut (BP 256, DM 631, FR 2135, Y 43,729, SF 575).

HIROSHIGE, Utagawa (Ando) Japanese
$316* *Die Station Hamamatsu, 1843-1847,* from series 53 Stationsn of okaido, Oban-yokoe, s., censure stamp, Hama, (04-21-93, Germann, #251), color woodcut (BP 205, DM 505, FR 1708, Y 34,983, SF 460).

HIROSHIGE, Utagawa (II) 1829-1869
BI *"Festlicher Abend Am Fluss",* from series Hundert Beruhmte Orte Der Provinzen (Shokoku Meisho Hyakkei), 1859, 1864, format Oban, est. SC 8/9,000, (04-27-93, Dorotheum, #234, illus.), 9¹³⁄₁₆ x 14⁹⁄₁₆ in., (25 x 37 cm.), woodcut.

HIROSHIGE, Utagawa (II) Japanese
$435* *Die Reisenden Vor Dem Fujiyama, 1855,* from series: Chusingura., Oban, s., censure stamp, Aratame, pub. Fujioka, (04-21-93, Germann, #250), color woodcut (BP 282, DM 695, FR 2351, Y 48,157, SF 633).

HIROSHIGE II
$580* *Serie 100 Vues De Provinces, Le Pont De Kintai Sous La Neige,* s., 1860, stains, restorations, (06-28-93, Loudmer, #174), (BP 388, DM 986, FR 3320, Y 61,538).

HIROSHIGE II Japanese 1829-1869
$138* *"Futakawa, Saru-Ga-Baba No. 34", c. 1865,* Series: 53 Stations of the Takaido, s. Rissho, (10-31-92, Cleveland, #26), woodblock (BP 88, DM 212, FR 720, Y 17,094).
$132* *"Narumi, Meibutsu Arimatsu-Shi Beri No. 41", c. 1865,* Series: 53 Station of the Tokaido, s. Rissho, (10-31-92, Cleveland, #27), 9¼ x 6⅞ in., (23.5 x 17.5 cm.), woodblock (BP 85, DM 203, FR 689, Y 16,351).

HIROSHIGE and TOYOKUNI III
BI *Man And Woman Before A Landscape Scene,* est. $250/350, (12-05-92, Eldred, #543, illus.), woodblock.

HIRSCH, Joseph American 1910-1981
$275* *"Bass Viol" and "Coffee": Two,* s., pub. AAA, (03-14-93, Hindman, #321), 14¼ x 9 in., (36.2 x 22.9 cm.), lithographs (BP 192, DM 458, FR 1556, Y 32,410).
$385* *"The Brief",* s. Joseph Hirsch, good cond.?, (11-21-92, Bakker, #48), image 12¾ x 8½ in., (32.4 x 21.6 cm.), lithograph (BP 253, DM 614, FR 2068, Y 47,880).
$120* *Court Stenotypist Checking Record,* s., num., excell. cond., (05-15-93, Cleveland, #157), 15¼ x 11⅛ in., (38.7 x 28.3 cm.), lithograph (BP 78, DM 193, FR 649, Y 13,302).
$345* *"Harmonica Player" and "Negro Father And Son": Two,* s., margins, good cond., mat staining, (05-19-93, Butterfield, #1996), one 10 x 8⅛ in., (254 x 206 mm.), the other 9¹³⁄₁₆ x 11⁹⁄₁₆ in., (254 x 206 mm.), lithograph on wove (BP 224, DM 561, FR 1889, Y 38,193).
$248* *"The Hecklers",* s., AAA, (12-02-92, Boos, #459), sight 9¹³⁄₁₆ x 15³⁄₁₆ in., (250 x 385 mm.), lithograph (BP 160, DM 390, FR 1331, Y 30,857).
$50* *"The Lovers", c. 1960,* s., num. 93/150, good cond., (10-31-92, Cleveland, #141), lithograph (BP 32, DM 77, FR 261, Y 6193).

HIRSCH, S.L. Emil German 20th cent.
BI *Umzug Der Penaten,* s., i.; s., t., d. (19)25 in plate, est. $150/200, (10-30-92, Sloan, #2817), 2¹³⁄₁₆ x 9¼ in., (7.1 x 23.5 cm.), etching.

HIRSCH, Stefan American 20th cent.
$35* *Portriat Of John Laurette, 1929,* s., d., very good cond., (05-15-93, Cleveland, #158), 13½ x 9½ in., (34.3 x 24.1 cm.), lithograph (BP 23, DM 56, FR 189, Y 3880).

HIRSCHFELD, Al American b. 1903
$193* *"Betty Davis",* s., #136/150, (02-11-93, Boos, #418), sight 12⅝ x 9¹³⁄₁₆ in., (320 x 250 mm.), etching (BP 136, DM 320, FR 1082, Y 23,267).
$170* *Bob Hope, 1983,* s., #70/200, (02-04-93, Sloan, #1237), 12⅝ x 9⅝ in., (32.1 x 24.4 cm.), etching (BP 119, DM 280, FR 949, Y 21,147).
$633* *Harlem, 1941,* text, (02-14-93, Hanzel, #663), folio (BP 446, DM 1050, FR 3552, Y 76,339).
$220* *"Railway Station, Moscow",* s., #8/15, very good cond.?, (07-19-92, Bakker, #42), image 15⅛ x 11⅜ in., (38.4 x 28.9 cm.), lithograph (BP 113, DM 321, FR 1084, Y 27,350).
BI *Shirbaraku,* s., #129/275, est. $300/400, (09-17-92, Sloan, #2366), 30 x 21¾ in., (76.2 x 55.2 cm.), color lithograph.
$121* *Shirbaraku,* s., #129/275, (10-30-92, Sloan, #1730), 30 x 21¾ in., (76.2 x 55.2 cm.), color lithograph (BP 78, DM 186, FR 632, Y 14,988).

BI *Three Samurais*, s., #105/275, est. $300/400, (09-17-92, Sloan, #2365), sheet 21¾ x 30 in., (55.2 x 76.2 cm.), color lithograph.

$275* *Woody Allen And Diane Keaton*, artist's proof, excell. cond., full margins, (10-10-92, Litchfield, #109), plate 13 x 9¾ in., (33 x 24.8 cm.), etching and aquatint (BP 163, DM 408, FR 1372, Y 33,479).

HIRSCHFELD, Albert
$110* *"Plastered"*, good cond.?, (03-28-93, Bakker, #258), image 10 x 9 in., (25.4 x 22.9 cm.), color lithograph (BP 74, DM 179, FR 610, Y 12,803).

HIRSCHVOGEL, Augustin   1503-1553
$248* *Christ Before Caiaphus, 1549*, from Konkordanz, prov., (09-20-92, Hindman, #648), 4½ x 5⅝ in., (11.4 x 14.3 cm.), etching (BP 145, DM 368, FR 1259, Y 30,651).

BI *Ecce Homo (Holl. 134; B. IX, 171), 1549*, lacking text, narrow margin, trimmed within platemark, surface dirt,excoll., est. BP 8/1,000, (12-03-92, Sotheby-London, #69, illus.), 4½ x 5½ in., (113 x 142 mm.), etching.

BI *"Koncordanz Und Vergleichung Des Alten Und Neuen Testaments" (Schwarz III; Hollstein 134): Eleven*, prov., est. DM 2,400, (12-04-92, Bassenge, #6232), etching.

HIRSTSUKA, Un Ichi
$330* *"Selected Woodcuts", c. 1961*, EHON, good cond., soiling, fading, (05-07-93, Goldberg, #1357), woodblock (BP 209, DM 522, FR 1758, Y 36,336).

HISTED
$343* *"George Bernard Shaw, Early 1900s" and "(?)Hans Neumann, 1905": Two*, s.; one i., s., (10-29-92, Christie-London, #88), first 11¼ x 9¼ in., (28.6 x 23.5 cm.), second 11 x 8½ in., (28.6 x 23.5 cm.), photograph, platinum print mounted on grey card (BP 220, DM 528, FR 1790, Y 42,487).

HITA, Jose Maventura
$65 *Feria De Sevilla, 1954*, very good cond., (09-24-92, Alderfer, #241), 19¼ x 12⅞ in., (48.9 x 32.7 cm.), (BP 38, DM 96, FR 327, Y 7819).

HITCHENS, Ivon   English b. 1893
$686* *For John Constable, 1976*, s., i., #8/100, pub. Bernard Jacobson, full margins, good cond.?, (06-30-93, Sotheby-London, #821), 14½ x 33⅛ in., (368 x 841 mm.), color screenprint on wove (BP 460, DM 1170, FR 3947, Y 73,503).

HITZLER, Franz   b. 1946
$1276* *Komposition, (19)87*, s., d., (06-08-93, Karl/Faber, #863), approx. 14⁹⁄₁₆ x 9¹⁄₁₆ in., (37 x 23 cm.), mixed media over etching on wove (BP 839, DM 2070, FR 6973, Y 135,528).

$722* *Untitled*, s., d., (11-28-92, Schoppmann, #586), 31¹¹⁄₁₆ x 23¹³⁄₁₆ in., (80.5 x 60.5 cm.), gouache on gerissener color lithograph on Zeichen paper (BP 477, DM 1150, FR 3905, Y 89,857).

BI *Untitled (Jahn 8), 1977*, s., d., #7/8, est. DM 1,200, (06-12-93, Hauswedell/Nolt, #123, illus.), 17½ x 11¾ in., (44.5 x 29.8 cm.), drypoint on thick wove.

BI *Untitled (Jahn 82 VII), 1979*, s., d., #1/9, est. DM 1,200, (06-12-93, Hauswedell/Nolt, #127), 17½ x 13³⁄₁₆ in., (44.5 x 33.5 cm.), etching worked over w/aquatint on thick wove.

HIZAKURIGE
$44* *"The Comic Journey Along The Tiksido Road", "Fujisawa Station", and "Travellers Give Candy To The Dog": Three*, block s., (01-15-93, DuMouchelle, #2300, illus.), 8½ x 13 in., (21.6 x 33 cm.), color woodblock print (BP 29, DM 72, FR 243, Y 5547).

HNIZDOVSKY, Jacques   American 1915-1985
$39* *"Aconium" and "Aconium II", 1975: Pair*, 13/250, s., t. d.; #10/50, s., t., d., (02-14-93, Neal, #1148), each image 9½ x 7 in., (24.1 x 17.8 cm.), woodcut, second in color (BP 27, DM 65, FR 219, Y 4703).

$6* *Ear Of Corn, 1969*, Hnizdovsky, (10-03-92, Garth, #109), 16¾ x 21 in., (42.5 x 53.3 cm.), woodcut (BP 4, DM 8, FR 29, Y 718).

$55* *"Walnuts"*, s., t., annot., trial proof, good cond., (10-31-92, Cleveland, #142), 8 x 10 in., (20.3 x 25.4 cm.), woodcut (BP 35, DM 85, FR 287, Y 6813).

HOBBS, Morris Henry   American b. 1892
BI *"Alice"*, s. Morris Henry Hobbs, t., pub. AAA, est. $150/200, (12-12-92, A. James, #517), sight 8⅞ x 6⅞ in., (22.5 x 17.5 cm.), etching.

$88* *"Anne"*, s., (11-13-92, DuMouchelle, #2454), 5¾ x 4¼ in., (14.6 x 10.8 cm.), etching (BP 57, DM 138, FR 466, Y 10,922).

$85* *"Brittany Seaport", 1932*, s., plate No. E for Print-A-Month Club, excell. cond., (05-15-93, Cleveland, #160), etching (BP 55, DM 137, FR 459, Y 9422).

$358* *"Louise"*, s., t., pub. AAA, (05-22-93, Neal, #596, illus.), plate 4 x 3½ in., (10.2 x 8.9 cm.), etching (BP 232, DM 582, FR 1958, Y 39,471).

$110* *Mardi Gras*, s., (12-17-92, Mystic, #36), 12 x 9 in., (30.5 x 22.9 cm.), etching (BP 70, DM 172, FR 587, Y 13,518).

$495* *"New Orleans, Mardi Gras At Royal And Conti Streets" and "Exchange Alley": Two*, each s.(05-29-93, Northeast, #620, illus.), etching (BP 317, DM 785, FR 2654, Y 53,077).

$352* *"Penelope"*, s., t., pub. AAA, (05-22-93, Neal, #597, illus.), plate 6½ x 5½ in., (16.5 x 14 cm.), etching (BP 228, DM 572, FR 1926, Y 38,809).

$40* *"Pirates Alley, New Orleans", c. 1932*, s., t., paper toned, water damage, (05-15-93, Cleveland, #159), 9 x 6 in., (22.9 x 15.2 cm.), etching (BP 26, DM 64, FR 216, Y 4434).

HOBOKEN, G.B.R. van   1893-1971
$140* *Liebespaar, 1918*, (09-25-92, Granier, #2883), 3¾ x 2⁹⁄₁₆ in., (9.5 x 6.5 cm.), woodcut on Japan (BP 82, DM 208, FR 702, Y 16,898).

HOCH, Franz Xaver   1869-1916
$127* *Eifeldorf*, stone s., d. F. Hoch 1903, (03-24-93, Venator/Hansten, #4501), approx. 14⅜ x 18½ in., (36.5 x 47 cm.), color lithograph (BP 86, DM 207, FR 706, Y 14,922).

HOCH, Hannah   German 1889-1979
BI *Leere Strasse, 1912*, est. DM 800, (05-26-93, Lempertz, #226), 17¹¹⁄₁₆ x 13¾ in., (45 x 35 cm.), wood cut on hand-made.

HOCKNEY, David   English b. 1937
$978* *Abstract Flowers 1990*, s., i., margins, good cond., handling creases, hinge remains, skinnedarea, (05-19-93, Butterfield, #2187), 13⅝ x 8¼ in., (346 x 210 mm.), color print on linen on an office copier (BP 635, DM 1590, FR 5356, Y 108,270).

$41,400* *Afternoon Swimming (T. 266:DH53), 1980*, s., d. 79, #54/55, blindstamp of pub., Tyler Graphics, Ltd., full sheet, good cond., catalog cover illus., (02-11-93, Sotheby-NY, #349, illus.), sheet 31½ x 39½ in., (80 x 100.4 cm.), color lithograph on Arches Cover (BP 29,213, DM 68,577, FR 232,063, Y 4,990,958).

$3850* *Apples Pears And Grapes, May 1986, 1986*, produced on an office copier, specially designed frame, s., d., #29/50, blindstamp, excellent cond., (11-09-92, Christie-NY, #309, illus.), 8½ x 14 in., (216 x 356 mm.), colored handmade print on Arches (BP 2545, DM 6146, FR 20,766, Y 477,786).

$5500* *Apples, Grapes, Lemon On A Table, 1988*, s., d., #3/91, blindstamp, from Brooklyn Academy of Music portfolio,-pub. Parasol Press, Ltd., good cond., (11-07-92, Sotheby-NY, #589, illus.), overall size 16⅞ x 22 in., (429 x 559 mm.), color handmade print, exec. on an office copier, on two sheets of Arches (BP 3596, DM 8782, FR 29,682, Y 678,845).

$4180* *Apples, Grapes, Lemon On A Table, 1988*, from Brooklyn Academy of Music 1988-89 Artists Prints Portfolio, Parasol Press, 1988-89, produced on Toshiba and Canon copiers, s., d. 86, #33/91, blindstamp, colors slightly attenuated, glued down, soiled, skinned patches verso, defects, (11-09-92, Christie-NY, #312, illus.), 17 x 22¼ in., (432 x 565 mm.), colored handmade print on 2 sheet of Arches (BP 2764, DM 6673, FR 22,546, Y 518,739).

$3922* *Apples, Pears And Grapes (Knoed. Gall. 3), 1986*, s., d., #30/50, good cond., (12-03-92, Sotheby-London, #731, illus.), sheet 8½ x 13¾ in., (215 x 350 mm.), home made print in colors exec. on office copier on rag Arches text (BP 2530, DM 6168, FR 21,052, Y 487,993).

$7492* *Artist And Model, (S.A.C.E. 160), 1973-4,* s., d., num. 22/100, pub. Petersburg Press, excell. cond., (12-01-92, Christie-London, #595, illus.), P. 22⅝ x 17⅜ in., (574 x 442 mm.), etching on Arches (BP 4950, DM 11,941, FR 40,695, Y 932,769).

$115 *"The Artist's Eye, National Gallery, 1st July-31st August, 1981",* s., (08-14-92, G.A. Key, #41), 29 x 19 in., (73.7 x 48.3 cm.), photographic poster (BP 60, DM 169, FR 571, Y 14,502).

BI *Big Celiaprint #2 (G. 981), 1982,* s., d. 81, #78/100, blindstamps, excellent cond., est. $10/14,000, (11-09-92, Christie-NY, #304, illus.), 52¾ x 57¾ in., (134 x 146.7 cm.), lithograph on Arches.

$9200* *Black Tulips (T. 258:DH45), 1980,* s., d., #53/100, blindstamp, pub. Tyler Graphics, Ltd., good cond., creases, (05-15-93, Sotheby-NY, #1002, illus.), sheet 44¼ x 30 in., (112.4 x 76.2 cm.), lithograph on cream BFK Rives (BP 5982, DM 14,798, FR 49,730, Y 1,019,843).

$1100* *The Blue Guitar (S.A.C. 199), 1977,* title page, from suite of 20, s., num. 75/200, pub. Petersburg Press, full margins, apparently very good cond., (02-24-93, Butterfield, #3047), 16¾ x 13⅝ in., (425 x 346 mm.), softground etching w/aquatint in colors on wove (BP 767, DM 1786, FR 6054, Y 129,078).

$37,515* *The Blue Guitar (S.A.C. 199-218), 1976-77,* complete set, each plate s., #109/200, w/list of plates and just., pub. Petersburg Press, 1977, fine cond., orig. portfolio box, (12-03-92, Sotheby-London, #713, illus.), each sheet approx. 20½ x 17⅛ in., (517 x 454 mm.), hard and soft-ground etchings w/aquatint in colors on Inveresk mouldmade (BP 24,200, DM 58,995, FR 201,369, Y 4,667,786).

BI *The Blue Guitar (S.A.C. 199-218), Titles Include: "The Blue Guitar","The Old Guitarist", "A Tune", "It Picks Its Way", "Franco-American Mail", "Parade" and "Discord Merely Magnifies" And Others, 1977: Twenty,* complete portfolio, s., #91/200, stamp t., including t./justification, pub., p. Petersburg Press, full margins, very good cond., original leather portfolio box, est. $45/55,000, (05-19-93, Butterfield, #2182, illus.), each sh 20⅝ x 18 in., (524 x 457 mm.), etching w/aquatint and softground in color on Inveresk mould-made.

$2475* *The Blue Guitar: Tick It, Tock It, Turn It True (S.A.C. 213), 1977,* s., #87/200, pub. Petersburg Press, full margins, good cond., (11-07-92, Sotheby-NY, #575), 16½ x 13⅝ in., (419 x 346 mm.), etching and aquatint p. in colors on Inveresk mouldmade (BP 1618, DM 3952, FR 13,357, Y 305,480).

BI *Bora Bora (T. 256), 1980,* s., d. 79, #22/100, Tyler Graphics blindstamp, rubbing, foxing, verygood cond., est. $7/9,000, (05-11-93, Christie-NY, #437, illus.), sheet 34½ x 48 in., (87.6 x 121.9 cm.), color lithograph on Arches.

$2046* *Bowl Of Fruit (Knoed. Gall. 12), 1986,* s., d., #31/46, good cond., (12-03-92, Sotheby-London, #724, illus.), sheet 11 x 8½ in., (280 x 215 mm.), home made print in colors exec. on office copier on rag Arches text (BP 1320, DM 3217, FR 10,982, Y 254,573).

BI *Caribbean Tea Time, 1987,* s., #2/36, blindstamp, pub. Tyler Graphics, Ltd., full sheets, original sculptural painted frame, designed by artist, est. $125/175,000, (11-07-92, Sotheby-NY, #586, illus.), overall size approx. 47⅞ x 136½ in., (121.6 x 346.7 cm.), double sided four panel folding screen; offset lithograph in colors w/collage and silkscreen on wood panel.

$8250* *Celia 8365 Melrose Avenue, Hollywood (S.A.C. 147; F. 448), 1973,* s., t., d., i. Artist's proof IX, blindstamps, scratches, scrapes, staining, surface soiling, (11-09-92, Christie-NY, #300, illus.), 47½ x 31½ in., (120.7 x 80 cm.), lithograph on Arches (BP 5455, DM 13,170, FR 44,498, Y 1,023,827).

BI *Celia 8365 Melrose Avenue, Hollywood (S.A.C. 147; G. 448), 1973,* s., d., t., #35/46, blindstamp, pub. Gemini, G.E.L., full margins, good cond., creases, discoloration verso, est. $10/12,000, (11-07-92, Sotheby-NY, #577,

illus.), sheet 47⅝ x 31⅝ in., (121 x 80.3 cm.), lithograph.

$9350* *Celia In An Armchair (G. 918), 1981,* s., d. '80, #66/74, blindstamp, pub. Gemini G.E.L., full margins, good cond., (11-07-92, Sotheby-NY, #584, illus.), sheet 40 x 48 in., (101.6 x 121.9 cm.), lithograph on Arches Cover (BP 6113, DM 14,929, FR 50,459, Y 1,154,036).

$3751* *Celia With Chair (Knoed. Gall. 19), 1986,* s., d., #33/50, good cond., (12-03-92, Sotheby-London, #730, illus.), sheet 8½ x 10⅞ in., (215 x 275 mm.), home made print in colors exec. on office copier on rag Arches text (BP 2420, DM 5899, FR 20,134, Y 466,716).

$13,200* *Celia With Green Hat (T. 274:DH61), 1985,* s., d. '84, i. 'P.P II', blindstamp, pub. Tyler Graphics, Ltd., goodcond., (11-07-92, Sotheby-NY, #585, illus.), sheet 29⅞ x 22 in., (759 x 559 mm.), lithograph p. in colors on HMP handmade (BP 8630, DM 21,076, FR 71,236, Y 1,629,227).

$7206* *Celia With Green Plant (Gemini 919), 1981,* s., d. '80, #71/90, pub. Gemini G.E.L., blindstamp, good cond., rubbing, (06-30-93, Sotheby-London, #842, illus.), sh 29¾ x 39⅜ in., (75.6 x 100 cm.), color lithograph on Arches cover (BP 4830, DM 12,291, FR 41,461, Y 772,099).

$2300* *Celia, Adjusting Her Eyelash (G. 837), 1979,* s., d., #93/100, Gemini G.E.L. blindstamps, excell. cond., the Late M. Anwar Kamal, M.D. Coll., sold after sale, (05-11-93, Christie-NY, #435), sheet 23 x 31 in., (584 x 787 mm.), lithograph on pale grey Twinrocker (BP 1468, DM 3623, FR 12,208, Y 252,997).

BI *Celia-Recling (G. 838), 1979,* s., d., #98/100, blindstamps, excellent cond., $3/3,500, (11-09-92, Christie-NY, #302, illus.), 23 x 21¾ in., (584 x 552 mm.), lithograph on buff Twinrocker.

$4025* *Celia-Reclining (Gemini 838), 1979,* s., d., #98/100, blindstamp of pub. Gemini, G.E.L., full sheet, goodcond., (02-11-93, Sotheby-NY, #346, illus.), sheet 22¹⁵⁄₁₆ x 21⁹⁄₁₆ in., (584 x 548 mm.), lithograph on Twinrocker (BP 2840, DM 6667, FR 22,562, Y 485,232).

$830* *"Chair 38 The Colony, Malibu" (S.A.C. 143), (19)73,* s., d., t., num., (12-01-92, Karl/Faber, #733), 13⁹⁄₁₆ x 11⅝ in., (34.5 x 29.5 cm.), lithograph on hand-made handgeschopftem (BP 548, DM 1323, FR 4508, Y 103,337).

$853* *China Diary, 1982,* s., d., #156/1000, orig. wrapper, num. 156, w/book by Stephen Spender, s. by artist and author, good cond., orig. folder, num. 159, (12-03-92, Sotheby-London, #716), lithograph in colors (BP 550, DM 1341, FR 4579, Y 106,134).

BI *China Diary, 1982,* s., d., #813/1000, s. by artist and author, #813, original cardboard,good cond., est. BP 5/700, (06-30-93, Sotheby-London, #825), color lithograph.

$825* *China Diary, 1982: Two,* s., d., num. 942/1000, p. by Petersburg Press, including complete volume, s. in ink by artist & author, pub. Thames and Hudson, Ltd., each in good cond., book contained in orig. cardboard box, est. $1,5/2,000, (02-24-93, Butterfield, #3049), lithograph 19½ x 21½ in., (495 x 546 mm.), lithograph in colors on Somerset satin-finish mould-made rag paper (BP 575, DM 1339, FR 4540, Y 96,808).

$978* *China Diary, 1982: Two,* s., d., #896/1000, p. Petersburg Press, including complete vol., inks. by artist and author, Stephen Spender, pub. Thames and Hudson, Ltd., (05-19-93, Butterfield, #2186), lithograph 19½ x 21½ in., (495 x 546 mm.), lithograph in colors on Somerset satin-finish mould-made rag (BP 635, DM 1590, FR 5356, Y 108,270).

$1998* *Christopher Isherwood And Don Bacardy, (S.A.C.E. 186), 1976,* s., d., num. 79/96, pub. Gemini GEL, very good cond., (12-01-92, Christie-London, #600), S. 28¹¹⁄₁₆ x 37⅜ in., (728 x 950 mm.), lithograph in black and gray on blue-gray Barker hand-made paper (BP 1320, DM 3185, FR 10,853, Y 248,755).

$1320* *The Commissioner (T. 265), 1980,* s., d. '79, num. 37/50, blindstamp of pub. Tyler Graphics, good cond., thinned spots, hinge removal, yellow stain, printing creases, (02-24-93, Butterfield, #3048, illus.), 15¼ x 19⅞ in., (387 x 505 mm.), lithograph in red-brown on light orange W. Zanders laid w/watermark (BP 921, DM 2143, FR 7265, Y 154,893).

BI *Contrejour In The French Style (S.A.C. 167), 1974,* s., d., #57/75, pub. Petersburg Press, full margins, mat staining, excell. cond., est. $15/18,000, (05-11-93, Christie-NY, #433, illus.), sheet 39⅛ x 36⅛ in., (99.4 x 91.8 cm.), color etching and aquatint on wove.

$8338* *Conversation In The Studio (T. 271:DH58), 1984,* hand-painted frame, s., d., #32/45, blindstamp, pub. Tyler Graphics,Ltd., good cond., (05-15-93, Sotheby-NY, #1005, illus.), sheet 24¼ x 28¾ in., (61.6 x 73 cm.), lithograph in colors on TGL handmade paper (BP 5421, DM 13,412, FR 45,070, Y 924,288).

BI *Corpses On Fire (David Hockney Prints 91), 1969,* s. David Hockney, 79/100, est. DK 8,000, (09-30-92, Kunsthallen, #127), etching.

$2899* *Dancing Flowers (Knoed. Gall. 22), 1986,* s., d., #38/60, good cond., (12-03-92, Sotheby-London, #725), 1/2 overall size 21⅝ x 25¼ in., (550 x 640 mm.), home made print exec. on six sheets of rag Arches text (BP 1870, DM 4559, FR 15,561, Y 360,707).

$5175* *Dark Mist (Scottish Arts Council 134, Gemini 444), 1973,* s., t., d., #13/25, Gemini G.E.L. blindstamps, full margins, excell.cond., (05-11-93, Christie-NY, #431, illus.), sheet 35 x 28½ in., (889 x 724 mm.), color lithograph on Angoumois a la main (BP 3304, DM 8152, FR 27,468, Y 569,244).

$9350* *David And Ann On The Subway, N.Y., 1982,* mounted on gray card, s., t., d., num. 15 by photog. in white ink, #15/15 ed., (10-15-92, Sotheby-NY, #586, illus.), 39¾ x 26¾ in., (101 x 67.9 cm.), photograph, gelatin silver print (BP 5721, DM 13,918, FR 47,198, Y 1,121,776).

$300* *David's Evening On Wheels,* s. black crayon, (02-04-93, Sloan, #2391), 27⅜ x 18½ in., (69.5 x 47 cm.), offset color lithograph poster (BP 209, DM 494, FR 1675, Y 37,318).

$2558* *The Drooping Plant (Knoed. Gall. 25), 1986,* s., d., #30/46, good cond., (12-03-92, Sotheby-London, #734), sheet 11 x 8½ in., (280 x 215 mm.), home made print in colors exec. on office copier on rag Arches text (BP 1650, DM 4023, FR 13,731, Y 318,278).

$1696* *Felicite Sleeping, With Parrot (Scottish Arts Council 163), 1974,* s., d., #2/100, (06-12-93, Hauswedell/Nolt, #128, illus.), 8¹¹⁄₁₆ x 9¼ in., (22 x 23.5 cm.), color etching worked over w/Vernis-mou and aquatint on Arches (BP 1110, DM 2760, FR 9278, Y 178,470).

$7150* *Flowers Made Of Paper And Black Ink (Scottish Arts Council 120), 1971,* s., d., t., #13/50, pub. Petersburg Press, good cond., creases, soiling, (11-07-92, Sotheby-NY, #571, illus.), sheet 39⅛ x 37⅝ in., (99.4 x 95.6 cm.), lithograph on Hodgkinson mouldmade (BP 4675, DM 11,416, FR 38,586, Y 882,498).

$943* *For John Constable (S. A. C. 189), 1976,* s., d., #5/100, pub. Bernard Jacobson, good cond., skinned, (06-30-93, Sotheby-London, #832), 10¾ x 14 in., (273 x 356 mm.), hard/soft-ground etching on Crisbrook handmade (BP 632, DM 1608, FR 5426, Y 101,039).

$2185* *French Shop (S.A.C. 122), 1927,* s., d., #447/500, pub. The Observer, margins, good cond., yellow stains in margin and platemark, hinge remains, skinned areas, surface soiling, (05-19-93, Butterfield, #2180, illus.), 21⅛ x 17⅞ in., (537 x 454 mm.), etching and aquatint in black and red on wove (BP 1418, DM 3552, FR 11,966, Y 241,891).

$1320* *French Shop (S.A.C. 122), 1971,* s., d., i. 'A.P. XXXX-VIII/LX', proofs, pub. Observer, full margins, good cond., fox mark, mat stain, (11-07-92, Sotheby-NY, #573), 21¼ x 17⅞ in., (540 x 454 mm.), etching and aquatint p. in black and red on BFK Rives (BP 863, DM 2108, FR 7124, Y 162,923).

$917* *French Shop (S.A.C. 122), 1971,* s., d. '71, num. 374/500, pub. The Observer, time-staining, good cond., (11-30-92, Phillips-London, #527), plate 21 x 17⅞ in., (533 x 454 mm.), etching w/aquatint in black & red on wove (BP 605, DM 1461, FR 4959, Y 114,126).

$825* *French Shop (S.A.C. 122), 1971,* s., d., num. 2/500, pub. Observer, full margins, time staining, skinned patches, pressure marks, staining, (09-19-92, Christie-E, #125), sheet 24⅝ x 21⅛ in., (62.5 x 53.7 cm.), etching and aquatint in black and red on wove (BP 475, DM 1235, FR 4231, Y 102,791).

$999* *French Shop, (S.A.C.E. 122), 1971,* s., num. 157/500, pub. Observer, margins, scuffing, tape, discoloration, good

cond., (12-01-92, Christie-London, #588), P. 21¹⁄₁₆ x 17¹³⁄₁₆ in., (535 x 453 mm.), etching p. in black and red on wove (BP 660, DM 1592, FR 5426, Y 124,377).

$2090* *Friends: Gregory Evans (G. 712, S.A.C. 176), 1976,* s., d., annot. A.P. VIII, blindstamp of pub. Gemini G.E.L., apparentlygood cond., staining, (02-24-93, Butterfield, #3045, illus.), 37 x 29⁹⁄₁₆ in., (940 x 751 mm.), lithograph on buff Arches Cover (BP 1457, DM 3393, FR 11,502, Y 245,248).

$2090* *Friends: Joe McDonald (G. 717, S.A.C. 175), 1976,* s. in blue pencil, d., num. 58/99, blindstamp of pub. Gemini G.E.L.,apparently good cond., creases, (02-24-93, Butterfield, #3044, illus.), 41½ x 29½ in., (105.4 x 74.9 cm.), lithograph on Arches Cover (BP 1457, DM 3393, FR 11,502, Y 245,248).

BI *Friends: Peter Schlesinger (G. 734, S.A.C. 185), 1976,* s., annot. R.T.P., blindstamp of pub. Gemini G.E.L., good cond.,hinge remains, est. $1/1,500, (02-24-93, Butterfield, #3046), 15⅞ x 11⅞ in., (403 x 302 mm.), lithograph in brick red on Arches Cover.

$749* *Fundevogel, (S.A.C.E. 75-80), 1969: Set Of Six,* from Illustrations for Six Fairy Tales from the Brothers Grimm, watermark s., num. 71/100, pub. Portfolio Edition, Petersburg Press, 1970, crease, (12-01-92, Christie-London, #582), overall S. 17¹⁵⁄₁₆ x 12⁵⁄₁₆ in., (455 x 313 mm.), etchings on Hodgkinson handmade (BP 495, DM 1194, FR 4068, Y 93,252).

BI *Fundevogel, (S.A.C.E. 75-80), 1969: Set Of Six,* from Illustrations for six Fairy Tales from the Brothers Grimm, watermark, pub. in Portfolio edit., s., num. 71/100, Petersburg Press, 1970, crease, est. BP 400/500, (12-01-92, Christie-London, #583), overall S. 17¹⁵⁄₁₆ x 12⁵⁄₁₆ in., (455 x 313 mm.), etching on Hodgkinson handmade paper.

$1364* *"George Sand" and "Gustave Flaubert" (S.A.C. 151; and 152), 1973: Two,* s., d., #16/25, , #19/25, pub. Petersburg Press, margins, good cond.,creases, (12-03-92, Sotheby-London, #706), each sheet 31⅜ x 22½ in., (795 x 570 mm.), etchings w/aquatint in black and red on Crisbrook hand-made (BP 880, DM 2145, FR 7322, Y 169,715).

$1162* *Glass Table With Objects (Scottish Arts Council 68), 1969,* s., d., num., creases, (12-01-92, Karl/Faber, #728), 8¹¹⁄₁₆ x 14¾ in., (22 x 37.5 cm.), color lithograph on BFK Rives wove (BP 768, DM 1852, FR 6312, Y 144,671).

BI *"Gold" and "Straw On The Left, Gold On The Right", 1969: Two,* plates 34 and 36 from Illustrations for six Fairy Tales from the Brothers Grimm, (S.A.C.E. 103, 103), watermark inits., s., num. 71/100, pub. Petersburg Press, 1970, margins, discoloration, dirt, creases, good cond., est. BP 7/900, (12-01-92, Christie-London, #584), P. and smaller 13⁹⁄₁₆ x 10⁷⁄₁₆ in., (345 x 265 mm.), etching on Hodgkinson handmade paper.

BI *The Grand Canyon Looking North, 1982,* ink s., t., d., num. 15, lit., est. $25/30,000, (04-08-93, Christie-NY, #527, illus.), 44 x 99 in., (111.8 x 251.5 cm.), photograph, color coupler print collage.

$2475* *Gregory (S.A.C. 169), 1974,* s., #35/75, pub. Petersburg Press, full margins, good cond., creases, (11-07-92, Sotheby-NY, #574), 27 x 21⅜ in., (686 x 543 mm.), etching p. in colors on Inveresk mouldmade (BP 1618, DM 3952, FR 13,357, Y 305,480).

$3300* *Gregory And Shinro, Nara, Japan, 1983,* mounted on gray card, s., t., d., num. #3 by photog. in white ink, #3/15 ed., (10-15-92, Sotheby-NY, #585, illus.), 35 x 29 in., (88.9 x 73.7 cm.), photocollage of Type-C prints (BP 2019, DM 4912, FR 16,658, Y 395,921).

BI *Gregory, (S.A.C.E. 169), 1974,* s., d., num. 51/75, pub. Petersburg Press, 1975, dirt, discoloration, good cond., (12-01-92, Christie-London, #597), P. 27 x 21⅜ in., (686 x 543 mm.), soft-ground etching in colors, on Inveresk mould-made paper.

BI *Grey Blooms, May 1986, 1986,* produced by an office copier, specially designed frame, s., d., #43/50, blindstamp, excellent cond., est. $4/6,000, (11-09-92, Christie-NY, #310, illus.), 14 x 17 in., (356 x 432 mm.), handmade print on 2 sheet of Arches.

BI *A Hollywood Collection (S.A.C. 41-46), 1965: Set Of Six,* s., d., i., copy artist's proof VII, pub. Editions Alecto, excellentcond., sig., est. $24/28,000, (11-09-92, Christie-NY, #298, illus.), 30¼ x 22½ in., (768 x 572 mm.), colored lithograph on BFK Rives.

BI *A Hollywood Collection (S.A.C. 41-46), 1965: Six,* s., #63/85, d. '63, p. Gemini G.E.L., pub. Editions Alecto, scuffing, very good cond., est. BP 10/12,000, (11-30-92, Phillips-London, #528, illus.), sheet 30¼ x 22¼ in., (768 x 565 mm.), color lithograph on wove.

$2875* *A Hollywood Collection: Picture Of Melrose Avenue In An Ornate Gold Frame (Scottish Arts Council 44), 1965,* s., d., #55/85, pub. Editions Alecto, repaired puncture, tear, pin holes, soilig(05-15-93, Sotheby-NY, #992, illus.), sheet 30⅛ x 22 in., (76.5 x 55.9 cm.), lithograph in colors on BFK Rives (BP 1869, DM 4624, FR 15,541, Y 318,701).

BI *Hollywood Window, 1973,* ink mono., #60/80, from portfolio "Twenty Pictures, edit. from Gallerie Sonnabend, New York 1976, est. DM 1,800, (11-12-92, Lempertz, #99), 8¼ x 10⅝ in., (20.9 x 27 cm.), Kodak-Color print color photograph.

$2875* *Homage To Michelangelo (S.A.C. 173), 1975,* s., d., #125/200, blindstamp of printer, Atelier Crommelynk, pub. Studio Bruckmann, full margins, good cond., soiling, (02-11-93, Sotheby-NY, #345, illus.), 18⅛ x 26⅜ in., (460 x 670 mm.), etching and aquatint p. in red (rosso) & black on Rives mouldmade (BP 2029, DM 4762, FR 16,115, Y 346,594).

$1980* *Homage To Michelangelo (S.A.C. 173), 1975,* s., d., num. 23/200, pub. Bruckman, full margins, excell. cond., (09-19-92, Christie-E, #126, illus.), sheet 23½ x 31 in., (59.7 x 78.7 cm.), etching and aquatint in black and red on Rives (BP 1139, DM 2965, FR 10,154, Y 246,698).

$1582* *Hommage To Michelangelo, (S.A.C.E. 173), 1975,* s., d., num. 31/200, pub. Studio Bruckmann, margins, crease, very good cond., (12-01-92, Christie-London, #598), P. 18⅛ x 26⅜ in., (460 x 670 mm.), etching w/aquatint p. in black and red on Rives mould made paper (BP 1045, DM 2522, FR 8593, Y 196,962).

$25,300* *Hotel Acatlan: First Day (T. 279), 1985,* s., d. 84/5, #34/70, Tyler Graphics blindstamp, excell. cond.?, (05-11-93, Christie-NY, #440, illus.), each sheet 37 x 28½ in., (940 x 724 mm.), color lithograph on two sheets of HMP hand-made (BP 16,151, DM 39,855, FR 134,289, Y 2,782,972).

BI *Hotel Acatlan: First Day (T. 279), 1985,* s., d. 84/5, #34/70, blindstamp, excellent cond., est. $30/40,000, (11-09-92, Christie-NY, #307), 37 x 28½ in., (940 x 724 mm.), colored lithograph on 2 sheets of HMP handmade.

$17,158* *Hotel Acatlan: First Day (T. 279: DH66), 1985,* s., d. 84/5, #33/70, pub. Tyler Graphics, blindstamp, full margins, good cond., (06-30-93, Sotheby-London, #834, illus.), overall 28¾ x 73¾ in., (73 x 187.3 cm.), color lithograph on HMP handmade on 2 sh (BP 11,500, DM 29,265, FR 98,723, Y 1,838,423).

$18,874* *Hotel Acatlan: Second Day (T. 283: DH70), 1985,* s., d. 1984-5, #71/98, pub. Tyler Graphics, blindstamp, full margins,good cond., (06-30-93, Sotheby-London, #836, illus.), overall 28¾ x 75¼ in., (73 x 191.1 cm.), color lithograph on TGL handmade on 2 sh (BP 12,650, DM 32,192, FR 108,596, Y 2,022,287).

BI *Hotel Acatlan: Second Day (Tyler 283:DH70), 1985: Diptych,* s., d. 1984-5, num. 19/98, blindstamp pub. Tyler Graphics, full sheets, good cond.?, est. Y 5/5,500,000, (10-14-92, Sotheby-Japan, #37, illus.), overall 28⅝ x 75⅞ in., (72.7 x 192.7 cm.), colored lithograph on 2 sheets white TGL handmade.

$33,000* *Hotel Acatlan: Two Weeks Later (T. 286), 1985,* s., d., #29/98, blindstamp, excellent cond., (11-09-92, Christie-NY, #308, illus.), 29 x 74½ in., (73.7 x 189.2 cm.), colored lithograph on 2 sheets of HMP handmade (BP 21,818, DM 52,682, FR 177,994, Y 4,095,309).

$23,725* *Hotel Acatlan: Two Weeks Later (T. 286), 1985,* s., 92/98, blindstamp Tyler Graphics, (05-12-93, AB Stockholm, #7027, illus.), approx. 73⅝ x 28⅜ in., (187 x 72 cm.), color lithographs on HMP handmade (BP 15,491, DM 38,278, FR 128,940, Y 2,648,766, SK 176,000).

$26,595* *Hotel Acatlan: Two Weeks Later (T. 286: DH73), 1985,* s., d., #42/98, pub. Tyler Graphics, blindstamp, good cond., (06-30-93, Sotheby-London, #837, illus.), overall 28½ x 73⅝ in., (72.4 x 187 cm.), color lithograph on HMP handmade on 2 full sh (BP 17,825, DM 45,361, FR 153,021, Y 2,849,566).

$5999* *The Hypnotist (S.A.C. 16), 1963,* s., num. 37/50, d. '63, p. by Peter Mathews, margins, very good cond., (11-30-92, Phillips-London, #524, illus.), plate 19⅝ x 19⅝ in., (498 x 498 mm.), etching in black & red on hand-made wove (BP 3960, DM 9557, FR 32,445, Y 746,609).

$599* *Igor Stravinsky, Metropolitan Opera, 1981,* pen s., creasing w/corresponding defects, lit., (02-04-93, Christie-S. Ken, #66, illus.), 81 x 35 in., (205.7 x 88.9 cm.), color silkscreen (BP 418, DM 986, FR 3345, Y 74,512).

$652* *Illustration For Six Fairy Tales From The Brothers Grimm: The Cook (S. A. C. 76), 1969,* s., i. A.P. XV, pub. Petersburg Press, margins, good cond., (06-30-93, Sotheby-London, #827), 7¼ x 8 in., (184 x 203 mm.), etching and aquatint on Hodgkinson handmade (BP 437, DM 1112, FR 3751, Y 69,860).

$1364* *Illustrations For Fourteen Poems By C. P. Cavafy, 1966,* book, s., #441/500, pub. Editions Alecto, good cond., (12-03-92, Sotheby-London, #704), 12 etchings (BP 880, DM 2145, FR 7322, Y 169,715).

BI *Illustrations For Fourteen Poems From C P Cavafy Edition D (S.A.C. 47-58), 1966: Twelve,* complete portfolio, each s., d., #71/75, text by Cavafy, #51-75, pub. Editions Alecto Ltd., full margins, good cond., discoloration, soiling, straymark, original portfolio box, est. $7/9,000, (05-15-93, Sotheby-NY, #993, illus.), each sheet 22¼ x 15⅞ in., (56.5 x 40.3 cm.), 12 etchings and aquatints.

$4600* *Illustrations For Six Fairy Tales From The Brothers Grimm, Edition A (S.A.C. 70-108), 1970,* book, s., i. Ed. A, #98/100, and portfolio, each s., i. ink Grimm Ed. A 98/100, pub. Petersburg Press, good cond., (05-15-93, Sotheby-NY, #994, illus.), each sheet 17¾ x 12⅛ in., (45.1 x 30.8 cm.), 39 unsigned etchings w/six etchings (BP 2991, DM 7399, FR 24,865, Y 509,921).

BI *Illustrations For Six Fairy Tales From The Brothers Grimm: Rumpelstilzchen (S. A. C. 103-108), 1970,* chapter from portfolio edit., s., #14/100, pub. Petersburg Press, good cond., est. BP 5/600, (06-30-93, Sotheby-London, #829), each sh c. 17¾ x 12¼ in., (451 x 311 mm.), 6 etchings.

$767* *Illustrations For Thirteen Poems From C. P. Cavafy: One Night (Scottish Arts Council 56), 1966,* s., d., #14/75, pub. Editions Alecto, margins, good cond., hinged tomount, (12-03-92, Sotheby-London, #702), 19¼ x 13¾ in., (490 x 348 mm.), etching w/aquatint on Crisbrook hand-made (BP 495, DM 1206, FR 4117, Y 95,434).

$686* *Illustrations For Thirteen Poems From CP Cavafy: One Night (ScottishArts Council 56), 1966,* s., d., #74/75, pub. Editions Alecto, 1967, stamp, margins, good cond., pressure mark, (06-30-93, Sotheby-London, #826, illus.), sh 19¼ x 14⅛ in., (489 x 359 mm.), etching (BP 460, DM 1170, FR 3947, Y 73,503).

$14,383* *An Image Of Gregory (T. 285), 1984-85,* s., blindstamp Tyler Graphics, 46/75, (05-12-93, AB Stockholm, #7026, illus.), 46¹⁄₁₆ x 35¹⁄₁₆ in., (117 x 89 cm.), color lithograph with collage (BP 9391, DM 23,206, FR 78,168, Y 1,605,783, SK 106,700).

$990* *In Despair (S.A.C. 57), 1966,* illus. for 13 Poems from C.P. Cavafy, s., d., num. 17/75, pub. Editions Alecto, full margins, mat staining, (02-24-93, Butterfield, #3042, illus.), 13¾ x 8⅞ in., (349 x 225 mm.), etching on Crisbrook handmade (BP 690, DM 1607, FR 5449, Y 116,170).

$1299* *"In Despair" (Scottish Arts Council 57), 1966,* s., d., num. twice, (11-28-92, Grisebach, #546, illus.), 13¹¹⁄₁₆ x 8⅞ in., (34.8 x 22.5 cm.), etching on handmade (BP 857, DM 2069, FR 7025, Y 161,668).

$1097* *In The Dull Village, 1966,* s., d., num., in Fourteen poems by C.P. Cavafy, lit., (12-02-92, Dorling, #2717), 12¹⁵⁄₁₆ x 8⅞ in., (33 x 22.5 cm.), etching (BP 708, DM 1725, FR 5888, Y 136,494).

$171* *Jacques De Bascher De Beaumarchais, 1973 (Baggott No. 41, Hockney Possters),* s., #265/450, lit., (12-01-92, Ritchie, #18, illus.), 25¼ x 17¾ in., (64.1 x 45.1 cm.), color lithograph (BP 113, DM 273, FR 929, Y 21,290, C$ 220).

$2300* *"Joe MacDonald + Peter Schlenger On The Banks Of The Nile, Luxor", 1978,* s., t., d. by photog., (04-06-93, Sotheby-NY, #486A, illus.), photograph (BP 1519, DM 3705, FR 12,548, Y 262,318).

$2470* *Joe McDonald (Scottish Arts Council 175), 1976,* 73/99, s. Gemini, 1053mm x 750mm, (10-14-92, Germann, #164, illus.), lithograph (BP 1450, DM 3615, FR 12,258, Y 299,321, SF 3220).

$2300* *"Joe McDonald + Peter Schlenger On The Banks Of The Nile, Luxor", 1978,* s., t., d. by photog., (04-06-93, Sotheby-NY, #486a, illus.), photograph (BP 1519, DM 3705, FR 12,548, Y 262,318).

BI *Joe With David Hart (Tyler 262), (19)79,* s., d., num., est. DM 5,000, (12-01-92, Karl/Faber, #736, illus.), 46⅞ x 31½ in., (119 x 80 cm.), color lithograph on Arches wove.

$1380* *Joe With David Harte (T. 262;DH49), 1980,* s., d. 79, #6/39, blindstamp of pub., Tyler Graphics, Ltd., full sheet, good cond., soiling, rubbed spot, (02-11-93, Sotheby-NY, #348, illus.), sheet 47¹⁄₁₆ x 31⁹⁄₁₆ in., (119.5 x 80.2 cm.), color lithograph on Arches cover mould-made (BP 974, DM 2286, FR 7735, Y 166,365).

$2860* *Joe With Green Window (Tyler 261), 1980,* s., d. 79, #23/54, blindstamp, excellent cond., (11-09-92, Christie-NY, #303), 44 x 30 in., (111.8 x 76.2 cm.), colored lithograph on cream BFK Rives (BP 1891, DM 4566, FR 15,426, Y 354,927).

$377* *John Hockney (G. 921), 1981,* crayon s., d. '80, #71/100, pub. Gemini G.E.L., blindstamp, good cond., (06-30-93, Sotheby-London, #838), sh 16 x 14¾ in., (406 x 375 mm.), lithograph on Arches Cover paper (BP 253, DM 643, FR 2169, Y 40,394).

$489* *John Hockney (G. 921), 1981,* s., d., #88/100, blindstamp publisher, Gemini G.E.L., good cond.?, (05-19-93, Butterfield, #2185), 16⅛ x 14¹⁵⁄₁₆ in., (410 x 379 mm.), lithograph on Arches cover (BP 317, DM 795, FR 2678, Y 54,135).

$2558* *Jug On A Table (Knoed. Gall. 28), 1986,* s., d., #21/36, good cond., (12-03-92, Sotheby-London, #719, illus.), 8½ x 11 in., (215 x 280 mm.), home made print in colors exec. on office copier on rag Arches text (BP 1650, DM 4023, FR 13,731, Y 318,278).

$3751* *Lemons & Oranges (Knoed. Gall. 4), 1986,* s., d., #35/50, good cond., (12-03-92, Sotheby-London, #732, illus.), 8½ x 13¾ in., (215 x 350 mm.), home made print in colors exec. on office copier on rag Arches text (BP 2420, DM 5899, FR 20,134, Y 466,716).

$5457* *Lithograph Of Water Made Of Line (Tyler Graphics 246), 1980,* s., d., #23/42, blindstamp, pub. Tyler Graphics, full margins, good cond., discolored area, (12-03-92, Sotheby-London, #709, illus.), sheet 28½ x 33⅞ in., (725 x 860 mm.), lithograph in colors on TGL hasnd-made (BP 3520, DM 8582, FR 29,291, Y 678,985).

$6555* *Lithograph Of Water Made Of Lines (T. 246), 1980,* s., d. 78, #30/39, Tyler Graphic blindstamp, full margins, skinned patch, excell. cond., (05-11-93, Christie-NY, #436, illus.), sheet 26 x 34¼ in., (660 x 870 mm.), lithograph in blue on TGL hand-made (BP 4184, DM 10,326, FR 34,793, Y 721,043).

$4600* *Lithograph Of Water Made Of Lines (Tyler 246:DH33), 1980,* s., d. '78, #26/39, blindstamp, pub. Tyler Graphics, Ltd., full margins, good cond., discoloration, soiling, (05-15-93, Sotheby-NY, #998, illus.), 20⅛ x 27 in., (51.1 x 68.6 cm.), lithograph in blue on white handmade TGL paper (BP 2991, DM 7399, FR 24,865, Y 509,921).

$6038* *Lithograph Of Water Made Of Lines And A Green Wash (T.247:DH34),* s., d. 1978-80, #14/36, blindstamp, pub. Tyler Graphics, Ltd., fullmargins, good cond., (05-15-93, Sotheby-NY, #999, illus.), 19¾ x 27 in., (50.2 x 68.6 cm.), lithograph in colors on white TGL handmade paper (BP 3926, DM 9712, FR 32,638, Y 669,327).

$6900* *Lithograph Of Water Made Of Lines And A Green Wash (Tyler 247:DH34),1980,* s., d. 1979-80, #5/36, blindstamp of pub., Tyler Graphics, Ltd., good cond., (02-11-93, Sotheby-NY, #347, illus.), 20¹⁄₁₆ x 27⁹⁄₁₆ in., (510 x 700 mm.), color lithograph on white, handmade TGL (BP 4869, DM 11,430, FR 38,677, Y 831,826).

$5750* *Lithograph Of Water Made Of Lines, A Green Wash, And A Light Blue Wash (T. 248), 1980,* s., d. 1978-80, #30/37, blindstamp publisher, Tyler Graphics, full margins, very good cond.?, (05-19-93, Butterfield, #2183, illus.), 20¼ x 27¾ in., (514 x 705 mm.), lithograph in colors on TGL handmade (BP 3733, DM 9347, FR 31,490, Y 636,555).

$8250* *Lithograph Of Water Made Of Lines, A Green Wash, And A Light Blue Wash (T. 248:DH35), 1980,* s., d. '78-80, #9/37, blindstamp, pub. Tyler Graphics, Ltd., full margins, good cond., (11-07-92, Sotheby-NY, #582, illus.), 21⅞ x 27¾ in., (556 x 705 mm.), lithograph p. in colors on white TGL handmade (BP 5394, DM 13,173, FR 44,522, Y 1,018,267).

$10,450* *Lithograph Of Water Made Of Thick And Thin Lines, A Green Wash, A Light Blue Wash, And A Dark Blue Wash (Tyler 245:DH32), 1980,* s., d., #58/80, blindstamp, pub. Tyler Graphics, Ltd., full margins,good cond., hinge stains, soiling, (11-07-92, Sotheby-NY, #581, illus.), 19¾ x 27⅜ in., (502 x 695 mm.), lithograph p. in colors on white TGL handmade (BP 6832, DM 16,685, FR 56,395, Y 1,289,805).

$9775* *Lithographic Water MAde Of Lines, Crayon, And Two Blue Washes (T. 252:DH39), 1980,* s., d. 1978-80, #64/85, blindstamp, pub. Tyler Graphics, Ltd., full margins, good cond., light-stain, foxing, (05-15-93, Sotheby-NY, #1000, illus.), 21½ x 29 in., (54.6 x 73.7 cm.), lithograph in colors on white handmade TGL paper (BP 6356, DM 15,723, FR 52,838, Y 1,083,583).

BI *Lithographic Water Made Of Lines And Crayon (T. 254:DH 41), 1980,* s., d. 1978-80, #30/42, blindstamp, pub. Tyler Graphics, Ltd., full margins, good cond., foxing, est. $6/8,000, (05-15-93, Sotheby-NY, #1001, illus.), 21½ x 29⅛ in., (54.6 x 74 cm.), lithograph in tones of blue on white handmade TGL paper.

$3300* *Lithographic Water Made Of Lines, Crayon, And Two Blue Washes (T. 252:DH39), 1980,* s., d. '78, #31/42, blindstamp, pub. Tyler Graphics, Ltd., full margins, good cond., repaired tear, (11-07-92, Sotheby-NY, #580, illus.), sheet 29 x 34⅛ in., (737 x 867 mm.), lithograph p. in blue on white TGL handmade (BP 2158, DM 5269, FR 17,809, Y 407,307).

$4180* *A Lot More Of Ann Combing Her Hair (G. 828), 1979,* s., d., #18/67, blindstamps, gray stain, slightly rubbed, good cond., (11-09-92, Christie-NY, #301, illus.), 49⅜ x 36 in., (125.4 x 91.4 cm.), lithograph on Toyoshi (BP 2764, DM 6673, FR 22,546, Y 518,739).

$1364* *Man Looking For His Glasses (Knoedler Gallery 10), 1986,* s., d., #30/50, good cond., (12-03-92, Sotheby-London, #717, illus.), sheet 8½ x 11 in., (214 x 280 mm.), home made print in colors exec. on office copier on rag Arches text (BP 880, DM 2145, FR 7322, Y 169,715).

BI *The Master Printer Of Los Angeles, Portrait Of Ken Tyler, (S.A.C.E. 149), 1973,* s., d., t. in crayon, num. 25/27, pub. Gemini GEL, blindstamp, margins, creasing, discoloration, tear, est. BP 1,5/2,500, (12-01-92, Christie-London, #593), L. 38⅛ x 27⅝ in., (968 x 702 mm.), lithograph in colors on Arches.

BI *Maurice Payne (Scottish Arts Council 123), 1971,* #71/75, pencil s., est. DM 4,500, (11-20-92, Lempertz, #582, illus.), sh 35⁹⁄₁₆ x 27¾ in., (90.3 x 70.5 cm.), etching on Velin.

$2333* *Mirror, Mirror On The Wall (S.A.C. 10), 1961,* s., d. '61, light-staining, good cond., (11-30-92, Phillips-London, #523, illus.), plate 15¾ x 19¾ in., (400 x 502 mm.), etching w/aquatint in red & black on hand-made wove (BP 1540, DM 3717, FR 12,618, Y 290,355).

$916* *Mo McDermott, (S.A.C.E. 178), 1976,* s., d., num. 94/100, stain, mount-staining, (12-01-92, Christie-London, #599), S. 32¹³⁄₁₆ x 23¾ in., (833 x 603 mm.), lithograph on buff Arches (BP 605, DM 1460, FR 4976, Y 114,044).

$4888* *The Moving Focus: A Picture Of Two Chairs, 1986,* s., d. 1985-86, #4/60, blindstamp, pub. Tyler Graphics, Ltd., good cond., (05-15-93, Sotheby-NY, #1006, illus.), sheet 18⅝ x 21⅞ in., (47.3 x 55.6 cm.), lithograph and etching in colors on white handmade HMP paper (BP 3178, DM 7862, FR 26,422, Y 541,847).

BI *A Moving Still Life,* from the Blue Guitar Series, est. $1500/2000, s., num. 186/200, (11-12-92, Freemn/Fine Art, #88A), 14½ x 20 in., (36.8 x 50.8 cm.), etching in color.

BI *My Bonnie Lies Over The Ocean (S.A.C. 13), 1962,* s., d., pub. by artist, margins, staining, tear affecting image(-backed), remains of glue, est. $2/3,000, (11-09-92, Christie-NY, #297, illus.), 17¾ x 17¾ in., (451 x 451 mm.), etching, aquatint and collage in colors on J. Whatman.

BI *My Father's Bedside Table, St. Luke's Hospital, Bradford and Doorway:Two,* (1973), 1970s, s. in ink in margin, lit., est. $2/2,500, (10-13-92, Christie-NY, #548, illus.), one 2⅝ x 3⅞ in., (6.7 x 9.8 cm.), other 5⅝ x 3¾ in., (6.7 x 9.8 cm.), photograph, color coupler prints.

BI *My Mother At Age Twenty, 1973,* s., d., #7/10, full margins, very good cond., mat staining, est. $1,5/2,000, (10-28-92, Butterfield, #2972), 8⅛ x 6½ in., (206 x 165 mm.), aquatint w/sugarlift on white wove.

BI *My Mother At The Age Of Twenty (From A Photograph) As A Study For Felicite In 'A Simple Heart' Of Gustave Flaubert, 1973,* s., d., #7/10, pub. Petersburg Press, full margins, very good cond.,mat staining, est. $1/1,500, (05-19-93, Butterfield, #2181), sh 11¹⁄₁₆ x 9¼ in., (281 x 235 mm.), aquatint w/sugarlift on Augoumois a la Main.

$221* *"The New World Festival Of The Arts, Miami 1982" and "David Hockney At Andre Emmerich": Two,* pen s., creases, lit., (02-04-93, Christie-S. Ken, #69), 38½ x 36 in., (97.8 x 91.4 cm.), color offset reproduction (BP 154, DM 364, FR 1234, Y 27,491).

$1201* *Nicholas Wilder (Scottish Arts Council 179), 1976,* s., d., #53/95, blindstamp, stamp, (06-12-93, Hauswedell/Nolt, #131, illus.), 32⅞ x 24⅝ in., (83.5 x 62.5 cm.), lithograph on light Rives (BP 786, DM 1955, FR 6570, Y 126,381).

$5286* *Office Chair, 1988,* s., d., #26/40, good cond., (12-03-92, Sotheby-London, #733), 50⅝ x 21⅞ in., (128.6 x 55.6 cm.), home made print in colors exec. on office copier on rage Arches text (BP 3410, DM 8313, FR 28,374, Y 657,708).

$704* *The Older Rapunsel (S.A.C. 84), 1969,* s., pub. Petersburg Press, full margins, good cond., (05-27-93, Sotheby-Amstrdm, #631, illus.), 8¾ x 9¾ in., (223 x 247 mm.), etching w/aquatint on Hodgkinson hand-made paper (BP 451, DM 1130, FR 3807, Y 75,472, G 1265).

$2300* *Olympische Spiele Munchen 1972, 1970,* s., d., #41/200, p. Matthieu AG, pub. Edition Olympia, full margins,good cond., creases, (02-11-93, Sotheby-NY, #343, illus.), 34⁷⁄₁₆ x 25⅜ in., (875 x 645 mm.), color lithograph (BP 1623, DM 3810, FR 12,892, Y 277,275).

BI *Olympische Spiele Munchen 1972, 1970,* s., d., num. 48/200, pub. Editions Olympia 1972 GmBH, margins, dirt,-good cond., est. BP 1,2/1,400, (12-01-92, Christie-London, #586), L. 32½ x 25⅜ in., (825 x 645 mm.), lithograph in colors on Rives.

$3163* *Olympische Spiele Munchen 1972, 1970,* before letters, s., d., #75/200, p. Matthieu AG, pub. Editions Olympia, full margins, good cond., (05-15-93, Sotheby-NY, #995), 34½ x 25⅜ in., (87.6 x 64.5 cm.), lithograph in colors (BP 2057, DM 5088, FR 17,097, Y 350,626).

$2860* *On The Banks Of The Nile, 1978,* (10-14-92, Swann, #478, illus.), photograph, silver print (BP 1679, DM 4186, FR 14,194, Y 346,583).

BI *One Night,* from Fourteen Poems by C.P. Cavafy, pub. Alecto, 1967, est. $7/800, (08-11-92, L. Joel, #3G), 13¹¹⁄₁₆ x 8⅞ in., (34.8 x 22.5 cm.), etching and aquatint.

BI *"The Pacific Ocean At Malibu" and "A Neat Window, Santa Monica", April 1973,* p. c. 1976, mono., num. DH 80/80, from portfolio 20 Photographic Plates by David Hockney, each 208 x 268mm, est. BP 3/500, (05-07-93, Sotheby-London, #383), photograph, color print.

BI *The Pacific Ocean At Malibu, 1973,* ink mono., #60/80, from portfolio "Twenty Pictures", edit. from Galerie Sonnabend, New York 1976, est. DM 1,800, (11-12-92, Lempertz, #98, illus.), 8¼ x 10⅝ in., (20.9 x 27 cm.), Kodak-Color print color photograph.

BI *Panama Hat, (S.A.C.E. 127), 1972,* s., d., num. 6/125, pub. Brooke Alexander, margins, tape, very good cond., est. BP 7/9,000, (12-01-92, Christie-London, #590, illus.), S. 16⁹⁄₁₆ x 13³⁄₁₆ in., (420 x 335 mm.), etching w/aquatint on Crisbrook handmade paper.

$1887* *Paper Pools (T. 269), 1980,* s., d., #763/100, pub. Tyler Graphics, blindstamp, margins, good cond., s., pub. Thames and Hudson, (06-30-93, Sotheby-London, #840), sh 10½ x 9 in., (267 x 229 mm.), color lithograph on wove (BP 1265, DM 3218, FR 10,857, Y 202,186).

$1972* *Paper Pools (Tyler Graphics 269), 1980,* s., #212/1000, pub. Tyler Graphics, blindstamp, full margins, good cond., pub. Thames and Hudson, (06-30-93, Sotheby-London, #841, illus.), sh 10½ x 9 in., (267 x 229 mm.), color lithograph on Arches (BP 1322, DM 3363, FR 11,346, Y 211,293).

BI *Parade (Scottish Arts Council 204), 1976-77,* #168/200, pencil s., sheet 6 from series The Blue Guitar, est. DM 3,200, (11-20-92, Lempertz, #583), sh 20¹³⁄₁₆ x 18¹⁄₁₆ in., (52.8 x 45.8 cm.), etching on Velin.

$19,550* *Pembroke Studio Interior (T. 277), 1985,* frame designed by artist, s., d. 84, #31/70, Tyler Graphics blindstamp, full margins, rubbed spots, cockling, excell. cond., (05-11-93, Christie-NY, #439, illus.), sheet 41 x 49½ in., (104.1 x 125.7 cm.), color lithograph on TGL hand-made (BP 12,480, DM 30,797, FR 103,769, Y 2,150,478).

$21,448* *Pembroke Studio Interior (T. 277; DH64), 1985,* s., d., #19/70, pub. Tyler Graphics, full margins, good cond., frame,hand painted by artist, (06-30-93, Sotheby-London, #822, illus.), sh 40⅜ x 49⅝ in., (102.6 x 126 cm.), color lithograph on TGL handmade (BP 14,375, DM 36,582, FR 123,406, Y 2,298,082).

BI *Pembroke Studio Interior, (Tyler 277: DH 64), 1984,* s., d., i., pub. Tyler Graphics, margins, excell. cond., est. BP 15/20,000, overall S. 1,175 x 1,395 mm, (12-01-92, Christie-London, #596, illus.), lithograph p. in colors on TG2 handmade wove.

$4290* *Pembroke Studio With Blue Chairs And Lamp (T. 275: DH62), 1985,* s., d. '84, #33/98, pub. Tyler Graphics, blindstamp, good cond., (06-30-93, Sotheby-London, #843, illus.), 17⅜ x 19½ in., (441 x 495 mm.), color lithograph on white HMP handmade (BP 2875, DM 7317, FR 24,684, Y 459,659).

BI *Pembroke Studio With Chairs And Lamp (T. 275), 1985,* s., d. 84, #6/98, Tyler Graphics blindstamp, foxing, very good cond., est. $7,5/8,000, (05-11-93, Christie-NY, #438, illus.), sheet 18¾ x 21¾ in., (476 x 552 mm.), color lithograph on HMP hand-made.

$5750* *The Perspective Lesson (T. 284:DH71), 1985,* s., d. 1984, #2/50, blindstamp, pub. Tyler Graphics, Ltd., good cond., (05-15-93, Sotheby-NY, #1008, illus.), sheet 29⅞ x 22 in., (75.9 x 55.9 cm.), lithograph in colors on gray hand-made HMP paper (BP 3739, DM 9249, FR 31,081, Y 637,402).

BI *"Peter Showering 1975",* p. c. 1976, mono., num. 47/80, from portfolio 20 Photographic Platesby David Hockney, 240 x 175mm, est. BP 600/1,000, (05-07-93, Sotheby-London, #384, illus.), photograph, color print.

$1011* *"Peter" (Scottish Arts Council 110), 1969,* s., d., num., (11-28-92, Grisebach, #547, illus.), 26⅞ x 21¼ in., (68.2 x 54 cm.), etching on copper print paper (BP 667, DM 1611, FR 5468, Y 125,825).

$935* *Portrait Of Felix Mann (S.A.C. 113), 1969,* s., num. 44/65, Galerie Wolfgang Ketterer blindstamp, full sheet, excell. cond., (09-19-92, Christie-E, #124), sheet 25¾ x 19¾ in., (65.4 x 50.2 cm.), lithograph in grey on Arches (BP 538, DM 1400, FR 4795, Y 116,496).

$4775* *A Portrait Of Rolf Nelson (S. A. C. 63), 1965-68,* s., d., #1/12, p. Kenneth Tyler at Gemini G. E. L., blindstamp, goodcond., scratches, creasing, discoloration, (12-03-92, Sotheby-London, #703, illus.), 41⅜ x 29½ in., (105.1 x 74.9 cm.), lithograph in colors and finished by hand on BFK Rives (BP 3080, DM 7509, FR 25,631, Y 594,127).

$7188* *Potted Daffodils (T.259:DH46), 1980,* s., d., #33/98, blindstamp, pub. Tyler Graphics, Ltd., good cond., tape hinges showing through to recto, (05-15-93, Sotheby-NY, #1003, illus.), sheet 44¼ x 30 in., (112.4 x 76.2 cm.), lithograph on cream BFK Rives (BP 4674, DM 11,562, FR 38,854, Y 796,807).

BI *Pretty Tulips (S. A. C. 115), 1969,* s., d., t., #5/200, pub. Petersburg Press, 1970, good cond., ex coll.Elton John, est. BP 5/7,000, (06-30-93, Sotheby-London, #833, illus.), sh 28½ x 19⅞ in., (724 x 505 mm.), color lithograph.

$9775* *Pretty Tulips (S.A.C. 115), 1969,* s., d., t., #75/200, pub. Petersburg Press, good cond., crease, soiling, (05-15-93, Sotheby-NY, #996, illus.), sheet 28⅜ x 19⅞ in., (72.1 x 50.5 cm.), lithograph in colors (BP 6356, DM 15,723, FR 52,838, Y 1,083,583).

BI *"Pretty Tulips" (Scottish Arts Council, 115), 1970,* pub. Petersburg Press, 1969, s., d. David Hockney 1970, very good cond., deformations, catalogue cover lot, est. $18/22,000, (03-12-93, Skinner, #105, illus.), sheet 28⅛ x 20 in., (71.4 x 50.8 cm.), lithograph in colors on wove.

BI *Pretty Tulips, (S.A.C.E. 115), 1969,* s., d., num. 82/200, pub. Petersburg Press, margins, light-staining,tape, discoloration, very good cond., est. BP 5/7,000, (12-01-92, Christie-London, #585, illus.), S. 28⁹⁄₁₆ x 19⅞ in., (725 x 505 mm.), lithograph in colors on Crisbrook handmade wove.

$1364* *"The Princess Searching" and "The Church Tower And The Clock": Illustrations For Six Fairy Tales From The Brothers Grimm (S.A.C. 74; and 79), 1969:Two,* s., #21/100, pub. Petersburg Press, full margins, good cond., rubbing, creasing, (12-03-92, Sotheby-London, #705, illus.), each sheet approx. 17⅜ x 15½ in., (440 x 395 mm.), etchings w/aquatint on Hodgkinson hand-made (BP 880, DM 2145, FR 7322, Y 169,715).

$711* *Rapunzel, Rapunzel, Let Down Your Hair (Hockney 272),* #33/100, s., (04-21-93, Germann, #515, illus.), 22⁷⁄₁₆ x 15⁹⁄₁₆ in., (570 x 395 mm.), etching (BP 461, DM 1137, FR 3843, Y 78,711, SF 1035).

$1876* *Red And Blue Wicker (Knoed. Gall. 21), 1986,* s., d., #25/39, good cond., (12-03-92, Sotheby-London, #721, illus.), 10⅝ x 8½ in., (270 x 215 mm.), home made print in colors exec. on office copier on rag Arches text (BP 1210, DM 2950, FR 10,070, Y 233,420).

$16,500* *Red Celia (T. 273), 1985,* i. proof for Celia love David H 1984, blindstamp, excellent cond., (11-09-92, Christie-NY, #305, illus.), 30 x 21¾ in., (762 x 552 mm.), red lithograph on HMP handmade (BP 10,909, DM 26,341, FR 88,997, Y 2,047,655).

$4830* *Red Flowers And Green Leaves, Separate, May 1988,* specially designed frame chosen by artist, s., d., #36/70, pub. Metropolitan Museum of Art, artist's blindstamp, excell. cond.?, (05-11-93, Christie-NY, #442, illus.), overall sheet 14 x 17 in., (356 x 432 mm.), hand-made print in colors produced on office copier on two sheets ofwove (BP 3083, DM 7609, FR 25,637, Y 531,295).

$3410* *The Red Pot (Knoed. Gall. 27), 1986,* s., d., #28/60, good cond., (12-03-92, Sotheby-London, #726), sheet 13¾ x 8½ in., (350 x 215 mm.), home made print in colors exec. on office copier on rag Arches text (BP 2200, DM 5362, FR 18,304, Y 424,288).

$1595* *Red Square And The Forbidden City,* from China Diary, s., d. '82, #760/1000, folded to form four panels, (04-26-93, Selkirk, #314), each panel 9¹¹⁄₁₆ x 7⅛ in., (24.6 x 18.1 cm.), color lithograph (BP 1007, DM 2500, FR 8444, Y 176,010).

BI *Rocks Nevada (SAC62), 1968,* s., i. artist's proof, est. DM 2,400, (06-05-93, Bassenge, #6118), 25⁹⁄₁₆ x 19⅝ in., (65 x 49.8 cm.), color lithograph on wove.

BI *Rocks, Nevada (S.A.C. 62), 1968,* s., d., #17/95, pub. Petersburg Press, very good cond., est. BP 800/1,000, (10-27-92, Phillips-London, #202), sheet 25⅝ x 19⅝ in., (651 x 498 mm.), color lithograph on B.F.K. Rives.

$3240* *The Round Plate (Knoed. Gall. 23), 1986,* s., d., #20/46, good cond., (12-03-92, Sotheby-London, #720, illus.), sheet 8¼ x 10¾ in., (210 x 275 mm.), home made print in colors exec. on office copier on rag Arches text (BP 2090, DM 5095, FR 17,391, Y 403,135).

$14,494* *Rue De Seine (S.A.C. 121), 1971,* s., d. '72, i. A.P, pub. Petersburg Press, margins, good cond., discoloration, (12-03-92, Sotheby-London, #712, illus.), sheet 35½ x 27¾ in., (895 x 704 mm.), etching w/aquatint on J Green mould made (BP 9350, DM 22,793, FR 77,799, Y 1,803,409).

$7700* *Rue De Seine (S.A.C. 121), 1971,* s., d. '72, #48/150, pub. Liberties and Release, full margins, very good cond. (?), (02-24-93, Butterfield, #3043, illus.), 21⅛ x 17⅛ in., (537.5 x 435.8 mm.), etching and aquatint on wove (BP 5370, DM 12,500, FR 42,378, Y 903,544).

BI *Rue De Seine, (S.A.C.E. 121), 1971,* s., d. '72, i. Artist's Proof, pub. Petersburg Press, 1971, very good cond., est. BP 7/9,000, (12-01-92, Christie-London, #587, illus.), P. 21¹⁄₁₆ x 17³⁄₁₆ in., (535 x 437 mm.), etching on J Green mould made paper.

$599* *"San Francisco Opera, Summer Festival Season, 1982" and "Parade": Two,* pen s., excell. cond., lit., (02-04-93, Christie-S. Ken, #67), 39 x 34 in., (99.1 x 86.4 cm.), color offset reproduction (BP 418, DM 986, FR 3345, Y 74,512).

$1150* *Selected Images: "The Pines, Fire Island", "Peter Showering, Paris" and "Peter Washing, Belgrade": Three,* from Twenty Photographic Pictures by David Hockney protfolio, Sonnabend Editions, each init., #80/80 by photog., 1970-75, p. 1976, (04-06-93, Sotheby-NY, #485, illus.), each approx. 7 x 9½ in., photograph, Type-C print (BP 760, DM 1853, FR 6274, Y 131,159).

$880* *Sidney In His Office (S.A.C. 190; G. 770), 1976,* white pencil s., num. 42/60, Gemini G.E.L. blindstamps, full sheet, excell. cond., (09-19-92, Christie-E, #127), sheet 24 x 20¾ in., (61 x 52.7 cm.), lithograph on light grey wove (BP 506, DM 1318, FR 4513, Y 109,644).

BI *Sidney In His Office (SAC 190), 1977,* s., num., est. DM 6,000, (12-05-92, Bassenge, #7258), 23⅝ x 20½ in., (60 x 52 cm.), lithograph.

$1494* *"Simplified Faces" (S.A.C. 165), (19)73,* s., d., num., state I, (12-01-92, Karl/Faber, #735, illus.), 12¹³⁄₁₆ x 12¹³⁄₁₆ in., (32.5 x 32.5 cm.), colored soft-ground etching on wove (BP 987, DM 2381, FR 8115, Y 186,006).

$943* *Small Study Of Lightning (S. A. C. 132), 1973,* s., d., #34/75. pub. Gemini G.E.L., blindstamp, full margins, good cond., (06-30-93, Sotheby-London, #831), 13 x 9¼ in., (330 x 235 mm.), color lithograph on Amgoumois handmade (BP 632, DM 1608, FR 5426, Y 101,039).

BI *"The Steering Wheel", 1982,* s., t., d., #19 by photog., est. $8/12,000, (04-06-93, Sotheby-NY, #487, illus.), mount size 30 x 32½ in., photograph, photocollage Type-C print, mounted on gray card.

$9900* *The Steering Wheel, Oct. 1982,* s., t., d., #6/20 in white ink on mount, mounted on gray board, lit., (10-13-92, Christie-NY, #549, illus.), 19⅜ x 24⅝ in., (49.2 x 62.5 cm.), photograph, color coupler print photocollage (BP 5766, DM 14,503, FR 49,278, Y 1,200,437).

$2200* *Still Life (Scottish Arts Council 111), 1969,* s., d., num. 51/75, pub. Petersburg Press, trimmed margins, pale foxmarks, surface soiling, rubbing, (09-19-92, Christie-E, #123, illus.), plate 21⅛ x 26¾ in., (53.7 x 67.9 cm.), etching and aquatint on J. Green mouldmade (BP 1265, DM 3294, FR 11,282, Y 274,109).

$2387* *Still Life With Curtains (Knoed. Gall. 1), 1986,* s., d., #28/48, good cond., (12-03-92, Sotheby-London, #727), 8½ x 11 in., (215 x 280 mm.), home made print in colors exec. on office copier on rag Arches text (BP 1540, DM 3754, FR 12,813, Y 297,001).

$2200* *Still Life With Hats,* plate from Twenty Photographic Pictures by David Hockney portfolio, initialled, num. 25/80 by photog. in ink, 1973, p. c. 1976, #25/100 ed., (10-15-92, Sotheby-NY, #583, illus.), 9⅜ x 7 in., (23.8 x 17.8 cm.), photograph, Type-C print (BP 1346, DM 3275, FR 11,106, Y 263,947).

BI *Straw Into Gold,* #62/100, s., prov., est. C$ $3,5/4,000, (11-16-92, Hodgins, #315), 13¼ x 5¹⁵⁄₁₆ in., (33.7 x 15.2 cm.), etching on paper.

$333* *Straw On The Left, Gold On The Right (S.A.C.E. 105), 1969,* from Six Fairy Tales, s., #54/100, good cond.?, (11-30-92, Phillips-London, #526), plate 5⅞ x 9½ in., (149 x 241 mm.), etching on wove (BP 220, DM 531, FR 1801, Y 41,444).

$7492* *The Student, Homage To Picasso, (S.A.C.E. 153), 1973,* s., d., num. A/P 13/15, very good cond., (12-01-92, Christie-London, #594, illus.), P. 22⅝ x 17⁵⁄₁₆ in., (575 x 440 mm.), etching w/aquatint on Arches (BP 4950, DM 11,941, FR 40,695, Y 932,769).

$8800* *The Student: Homage To Picasso (S.A.C. 153), 1973,* s., d., i. 'P.P. IV/XV', printer's proof, pub. Propylaen Verlag, fullmargins, good cond., (11-07-92, Sotheby-NY, #578, illus.), 22⅝ x 17⅜ in., (575 x 441 mm.), etching (BP 5754, DM 14,051, FR 47,491, Y 1,086,152).

BI *Study Of Lightning Medium (S.A.C. 133), 1973,* s., d., #23/60, blindstamp, pub. Gemini, margins, good cond., est. BP8/1,000, (12-03-92, Sotheby-London, #715), sheet 31 x 23¼ in., (790 x 590 mm.), lithograph in colors on Arches mould-made.

BI *Study Of Lightning Medium, (S.A.C.E. 133), 1973,* s., d., num. 18/60, pub. Gemini GEL, margins, staining, foxed, discolored, est. BP 800/1,000, (12-01-92, Christie-London, #592), L. 24⅞ x 19 in., (632 x 483 mm.), lithograph in colors on Arches.

$1286* *Study Of Lightning, Medium (S. A. C. 133), 1973,* s., d., #23/60, pub. Gemini, blindstamp, full margins, good cond., stains, (06-30-93, Sotheby-London, #830, illus.), 30 x 22¾ in., (762 x 578 mm.), color lithograph on wove (BP 862, DM 2193, FR 7399, Y 137,791).

BI *Sun, (S.A.C.E. 136), 1973,* from the Weather Series, s., d. crayon, num. 76/98, pub. Gemini GEL, margins, fold, rubbing, surface dirt, est. BP 8/12,000, (12-01-92, Christie-London, #591, illus.), L. 30¹⁵⁄₁₆ x 25¼ in., (786 x 642 mm.), lithograph p. in colors on Arjomari mould made paper.

$36,800* *Sunday Morning Mayflower Hotel N.Y., 1982,* ink s., t., d., num. 8, lit., (04-08-93, Christie-NY, #528, illus.), 50 x 77 in., (127 x 195.6 cm.), photograph, color coupler print collage (BP 24,131, DM 59,116, FR 200,109, Y 4,176,123).

$3410* *The Tall Tree (Knoed. Gall. 30), 1986,* s., d., #36/60, good cond., (12-03-92, Sotheby-London, #729, illus.), overall size 27¾ x 8½ in., (705 x 215 mm.), home made print in colors exec. on office copier on two sheets of ragArches text (BP 2200, DM 5362, FR 18,304, Y 424,288).

$2217* *Three Black Flowers (Knoed. Gall. 29), 1986,* s., d., #33/50, good cond., (12-03-92, Sotheby-London, #722, illus.), sheet 10¾ x 8¼ in., (275 x 210 mm.), home made print exec. on office copier on rag Arches text (BP 1430, DM 3486, FR 11,900, Y 275,849).

$1320* *Three Kings And A Queen (Scottish Arts Council 7), 1961,* s., d., pub. by artist, full margins, tears, pinholes, surface soiling, (11-09-92, Christie-NY, #296, illus.), 22½ x 31½ in., (572 x 800 mm.), etching on handmade (BP 873, DM 2107, FR 7120, Y 163,812).

BI *The Tower Had One Window,* #53/100, s., prov., est. C$ 3,5/4,000, (11-16-92, Hodgins, #118, illus.), 13½ x 10½ in., (34.3 x 26.7 cm.), etching on paper.

BI *Tree (Scottish Arts Council 61), 1968,* #36/95, pencil s., d., est. DM 5,200, (11-20-92, Lempertz, #581), sh 25¹¹⁄₁₆ x 19⅝ in., (65.2 x 49.8 cm.), color lithograph on Velin.

BI *Tree (Scottish Arts Council 68), 1968,* 57/95, s., d., pub. Petersburg Press, est. SF 2,8/3,500, (10-14-92, Germann, #115, illus.), 25⁹⁄₁₆ x 19¹¹⁄₁₆ in., (650 x 500 mm.), color lithograph.

BI *Tree, 1968,* #57/95, s., d., pub. Petersburg Press, lit., est. SF 1,5/1,800, (09-04-92, Germann, #45, illus.), 25⁹⁄₁₆ x 19¹¹⁄₁₆ in., (650 x 500 mm.), color lithograph.

$6325* *Tulips (S.A.C. 158), 1973,* s., #34/75, pub. Petersburg Press, full margins, good cond., crease, (11-07-92, Sotheby-NY, #579, illus.), 27⅛ x 21¼ in., (689 x 540 mm.), etching and aquating on German mouldmade museum board (BP 4135, DM 10,099, FR 34,134, Y 780,671).

$6821* *Tulips (S.A.C. 158), 1973,* s., d., #58/75, p. Maurice Payne, pub. Petersburg Press, full margins, good cond., (12-03-92, Sotheby-London, #708, illus.), 27 x 21¼ in., (685 x 540 mm.), etching w/aquatint on wove (BP 4400, DM 10,727, FR 36,613, Y 848,700).

BI *Tulips (S.A.C. 158), 1973,* s., d., #38/75, pub. Petersburg Press, full margins, good cond., tape hinges, foxing, est. $6/8,000, (05-15-93, Sotheby-NY, #1004, illus.), 27 x 21½ in., (68.6 x 54.6 cm.), etching on German mould-made Museum Board.

$9437* *Twenty Photographic Pictures,* portfolio, init., #51/80, title-page, list of contents and justification (#45), pub. Sonnabend Editions, good cond., loose, (06-30-93, Sotheby-London, #828, illus.), 20 photographic prints (BP 6325, DM 16,096, FR 54,298, Y 1,011,143).

BI *Twenty Photographic Pictures: Sixteen,* Sonnabend Editions, inits., num. 80/80 by photog., 1970-75m p. 1976,folio, #80/100 ed., 4 missing plates, est. $8/10,000, (10-15-92, Sotheby-NY, #584, illus.), each, approx. 7 x 9½ in., (17.8 x 24.1 cm.), photograph, portfolio of 16 (of 20) Type-C prints.

$1299* *"Two Boys Aged 23 Or 24" (Scottish Arts Council 48), 1966,* s., d., num., (11-28-92, Grisebach, #545, illus.), 13¾ x 8¾ in., (35 x 22.3 cm.), etching and aquatint on copper print paper (BP 857, DM 2069, FR 7025, Y 161,668).

$472* *"Two Lemon And Four Limes, Santa Monica",* p. c. 1976, mono., num. DH 80/80, from portfolio 20 Photographic Plates by David Hockney, 208 x 269mm, (05-07-93, Sotheby-London, #382, illus.), photograph, color print (BP 299, DM 746, FR 2515, Y 51,971).

$5286* *Two Red Chairs (Knoed. Gall. 11), 1986,* s., d., #21/44, good cond., (12-03-92, Sotheby-London, #718, illus.), sheet 8¼ x 10⅞ in., (210 x 276 mm.), home made print in colors exec. on office copier on rag Arches text (BP 3410, DM 8313, FR 28,374, Y 657,708).

$12,011* *Two Vases In The Louvre (S. A. C. 168), 1974,* s., d., #33/75, pub. Petersburg Press, full margins, good cond., (06-30-93, Sotheby-London, #839, illus.), 29¼ x 29⅛ in., (743 x 740 mm.), color etching on Inveresk mould-made (BP 8050, DM 20,486, FR 69,108, Y 1,286,939).

BI *Two Vases In The Louvre (S.A.C. 168), 1974,* s., d., #33/75, pub. Petersburg Press, full margins, good cond., est.BP 8/10,000, (12-03-92, Sotheby-London, #711, illus.), 29¼ x 29⅛ in., (743 x 740 mm.), etching in colors on Inveresk mould made.

BI *Tyler Dining Room (T. 278), 1985,* s., d. 84, #82/98, blindstamps, full margins, excellent cond., est. $20/25,000, (11-09-92, Christie-NY, #306, illus.), 32 x 40 in., (81.3 x 101.6 cm.), colored lithograph on TGL hand-made.

$14,950* *Tyler Dining Room (T. 278:DH65), 1985,* s., d. '84, #82/98, blindstamp of pub., Tyler Graphics, Ltd., full margins, good cond., (02-11-93, Sotheby-NY, #351, illus.), sheet 32¹⁄₁₆ x 39¾ in., (81.5 x 101 cm.), color lithograph on TGL handmade (BP 10,549, DM 24,764, FR 83,800, Y 1,802,291).

BI *Tyler Dining Room (T. 278; DH65), 1985,* d. '84, #89/98, pub. Tyler Graphics, blindstamp, full margins, good cond., est. BP 10/14,000, (06-30-93, Sotheby-London, #823, illus.), sh 31⅞ x 39⅝ in., (81 x 100.6 cm.), color lithograph on TGL handmade.

$23,873* *View Of Hotel Well I (T. 280 DH:67), 1985,* s/, i. P.P.I., blindstamp, pub. Tyler Graphics, full margins, good cond., orig. frame, designed by artist, (12-03-92, Sotheby-London, #714, illus.), overall 26⅝ x 47 in., (67.6 x 119.4 cm.), lithograph in colors on TGL hand-made (BP 15,400, DM 37,542, FR 128,143, Y 2,970,387).

BI *View Of Hotel Well I (T. 280:DH67), 1985,* s., d., i. 'A.P. XI/XIV', blindstamp, pub. Tyler Graphics, Ltd., fullmargins, good cond., est. $25/35,000, (11-07-92, Sotheby-NY, #587, illus.), approx. overall size 36⅞ x 46⅞ in., (93.7 x 119.1 cm.), lithograph p. in colors on white handmade TGL.

$22,425* *View Of Hotel Well I (T. 280:DH67), 1985,* s., d., i. A.P. XI/XIV, blindstamp of pub., Tyler Graphics, Ltd., full margins, good cond., (02-11-93, Sotheby-NY, #352, illus.), overall size 36⅞ x 46⅞ in., (93.6 x 119.1 cm.), color lithograph on white handmade TGL (BP 15,823, DM 37,146, FR 125,701, Y 2,703,436).

$15,442* *Views Of Hotel Well I (T. 280: DH67), 1985,* s., d. 1984-5, #33/75, pub. Tyler Graphics, blindstamp, full margins,good cond., original frame, designed by artist, (06-30-93, Sotheby-London, #844, illus.), sh 30⅞ x 41⅛ in., (78.4 x 104.5 cm.), color lithograph on TGL hand-made (BP 10,350, DM 26,338, FR 88,849, Y 1,654,559).

BI *Views Of Hotel Well I (Tyler 280:DH67), 1985,* s., d., num. 28/75, blindstamp pub. Tyler Gaphics, Ltd., full margins, excell. cond., in frame designed by artist, est. Y 3,8/4,500,000, (10-14-92, Sotheby-Japan, #34, illus.), overall 26⅝ x 47 in., (67.6 x 119.4 cm.), colored lithograph on white TGL handmade.

$24,879* *Views Of Hotel Well II (T. 280; DH68), 1985,* s., d., #37/75, pub. Tyler Graphics, blindstamp, full margins, good cond., original frame, designed by artist, (06-30-93, Sotheby-London, #845, illus.), sh 25 x 31¾ in., (635 x 806 mm.), color lithograph on HMP handmade (BP 16,675, DM 42,434, FR 143,147, Y 2,665,702).

$23,106* *Views Of Hotel Well II (Tyler 281:DH68), 1985,* s., d., num. 68/75, blindstamp pub. Tyler Graphics, full margins, excell. cond., in frame designed by artist, (10-14-92, Sotheby-Japan, #35, illus.), overall 29⅜ x 36⅜ in., (746 x 924 mm.), colored lithograph on white HMP handmade (BP 13,562, DM 33,815, FR 114,670, Y 2,800,048).

$41,400* *Views Of Hotel Well III (T. 282), 1985,* frame designed by artist, s., d. 1984-5, #15/80, Tyler Graphics blindstamp, full margins, excell. cond.?, (05-11-93, Christie-NY, #441, illus.), sheet 48½ x 38 in., (123.2 x 96.5 cm.), color lithograph on TGL hand-made (BP 26,428, DM 65,217, FR 219,745, Y 4,553,954).

$41,800* *Views Of Hotel Well III (T. 282:DH69), 1985,* s., d. '1984-5', #49/80, blindstamp, pub. Tyler Graphics, Ltd., fullmargins, good cond., sculptural wood frame designed by artist, (11-07-92, Sotheby-NY, #588, illus.), approx. overall size 55⅛ x 44⅞ in., (140 x 114 cm.), lithograph p. in colors on white TGL handmade (BP 27,329, DM 66,741, FR 225,580, Y 5,159,220).

$30,027* *Views Of Hotel Well III (T. 282; DH69), 1985,* s., d. 1984-5, #33/80, pub. Tyler Graphics, blindstamp, full margins,good cond., original colored frame, designed by artist, (06-30-93, Sotheby-London, #824, illus.), sh 48¼ x 38⅜ in., (122.6 x 97.5 cm.), color lithograph on TGL handmade (BP 20,125, DM 51,214, FR 172,768, Y 3,217,293).

$23,725* *Views Of Hotel Well III (Tyler 282),* s., blindstamp Tyler Graphics, (05-12-93, AB Stockholm, #7025, illus.), 46¹⁄₁₆ x 35¹⁄₁₆ in., (117 x 89 cm.), color lithograph on TGL handmade (BP 15,491, DM 38,278, FR 128,940, Y 2,648,766, SK 176,000).

BI *Views Of Hotel Well III (Tyler 282:DH69), 1985,* s., d., num. 60/80, blindstamp pub. Tyler Graphics, full margins, excell. cond., in frame designed by artist, est. Y 6,2/7,500,000, (10-14-92, Sotheby-Japan, #36, illus.), overall 46⅜ x 35⅛ in., (117.8 x 89.2 cm.), colored lithograph on white TGL handmade.

$978* *Violets, 1992,* s., i., small margins, good cond., handling creases, inkloss, tears, (05-19-93, Butterfield, #2188), 16⅝ x 10⅞ in., (422 x 276 mm.), color print on Parsons on an office copier (BP 635, DM 1590, FR 5356, Y 108,270).

$767* *Walking (Knoed. Gall. 17), 1986,* s., d., #45/59, good cond., (12-03-92, Sotheby-London, #728), sheet 17 x 10⅞ in., (430 x 275 mm.), home made print in colors exec. on office copier on rag Arches text (BP 495, DM 1206, FR 4117, Y 95,434).

BI *Walking Past Two Chairs, 1984-86,* s., d., #14/38, pub. Tyler Graphics, Ltd., good cond., frame, designed and hand painted by artist, paint losses, soiling, est. $50/70,000, (05-15-93, Sotheby-NY, #1007, illus.), overall 28¼ x 45¾ in., (71.8 x 116.2 cm.), lithograph in colors on white handmade TGL paper overlaid w/a color silkscreen image printed on plexiglas.

$28,175* *Wallace Stevens, The Blue Guitar, London And New York, Petersburg Press, 1977 (S.A.C. 199-218), 1976-77: Twenty,* s., num., t., text, just. stamped t., copy 156 of 200, full margins,excell. cond., orig. portfolio, (05-11-93, Christie-NY, #434, illus.), each sheet 20⅝ x 17⅞ in., (524 x 454 mm.), hard- and soft-ground etching and aquatint in colors on Inveresk Mouldmade (BP 17,986, DM 44,384, FR 149,549, Y 3,099,219).

$2500* *Water Pouring Into Swimming Pool, Santa Monica (S.A.C.E. 38), 1964,* s., d. '64, num. 11/75, pub. Editions Alecto, 1965, blindstamp, bodycolor, good cond., (11-30-92, Phillips-London, #525), sheet 20 x 26 in., (508 x 660 mm.), color lithograph on Japan (BP 1650, DM 3983, FR 13,521, Y 311,139).

$1364* *Waving (Knoed. Gall. 14), 1986,* s., d., #29/45, good cond., (12-03-92, Sotheby-London, #723, illus.), sheet 10⅞ x 8⅜ in., (275 x 212 mm.), home made print in colors exec. on office copier on rag Arches text (BP 880, DM 2145, FR 7322, Y 169,715).

$7673* *The Weather Series: Rain (S.A. C. 137), 1973,* s., d., #54/98, in crayon, t., pub. Gemini G.E.L., blindstamp, margins, good cond., board staining, handling creases, (12-03-92, Sotheby-London, #707, illus.), sheets 39 x 31¾ in., (990 x 805 mm.), lithograph in colors on Arches mould made (BP 4950, DM 12,066, FR 41,186, Y 954,709).

$8050* *The Weather Series: Snow (S.A.C. 140, Gemini 445), 1973,* s., d., t., #68/98, blindstamp, pub. Gemini, G.E.L., full margins, good cond., tape hinges, creases, (05-15-93, Sotheby-NY, #997, illus.), 33½ x 28 in., (85.1 x 71.1 cm.), lithograph in colors on Arjomari mouldmade paper (BP 5234, DM 12,948, FR 43,514, Y 892,362).

$4950* *The Weather Series: Wind (S.A.C. 141; Gemini 440), 1973,* s., d., #36/98 in red crayon, t., blindstamp, pub. Gemini G.E.L., full margins, good cond., (11-07-92, Sotheby-NY, #576, illus.), 31⅛ x 24 in., (791 x 610 mm.), lithograph and silkscreen p. in colors on Arjomari mouldmade (BP 3236, DM 7904, FR 26,713, Y 610,960).

$6600* *White Pelican, 1985-86,* s., d., #78/80, blindstamp pub. Tyler Graphics, very good cond., creases, (10-28-92, Butterfield, #2974, illus.), 18¾ x 22⅛ in., (476 x 562 mm.), color etching and offset lithograph on white HMP handmade (BP 4205, DM 10,193, FR 34,609, Y 809,816).

BI *White Porcelain, 1986,* s., d. 85-86, #32/80, blindstamp, taped vero, excellent cond., est. $10/14,000, (11-09-92, Christie-NY, #311, illus.), 18½ x 22 in., (470 x 559 mm.), etching and offset lithograph in colors on HMP handmade.

$748* *William Burroughs (G. 920), 1981,* s., d. '80, #91/100, blindstamp publisher, Gemini G.E.L., full margins, good cond.?, (05-19-93, Butterfield, #2184), sh 20⅝ x 17⅝ in., (524 x 448 mm.), lithograph on John Koller HMP (BP 486, DM 1216, FR 4096, Y 82,807).

$546* *"William Burroughs" and "James" (Gemini 920; and 922), 1980: Two,* both s., d., #34/100, blindstamp, pub. Gemini, good cond., soiling, rubbed, (12-03-92, Sotheby-London, #710), sheet 20⅝ x 17¼ in., (524 x 440 mm.), sheet 24⅛ x 20 in., (524 x 440 mm.), lithographs (BP 352, DM 859, FR 2931, Y 67,936).

$4180* *Wind (S.A.C. 141; Gemini 440), 1973,* from The Weather Series, s., d., t., #92/98, blindstamps, full margins, scuff, surface loss, scratches, mat staining, very good cond., (11-09-92, Christie-NY, #299, illus.), 40 x 31 in., (101.6 x 78.7 cm.), lithograph and screenprint in colors on wove (BP 2764, DM 6673, FR 22,546, Y 518,739).

$932* *A Wooded Landscape (Midland Group/Petersburg Press 75), 1969,* watermark, #90/100, s., plate 6 from Six fairy tales, (05-27-93, Lempertz, #785), 15⁹⁄₁₆ x 10¾ in., (39.5 x 27.3 cm.), etching and aquatint on wove (BP 597, DM 1496, FR 5041, Y 99,914).

$1038* *Yves Marie (S.A.C. 159), (19)4,* s., d., num., (12-01-92, Karl/Faber, #734), 26¾ x 22¹⁄₁₆ in., (68 x 56 cm.), lithograph on Arches France wove (BP 686, DM 1654, FR 5638, Y 129,233).

HOCY, A.

$159* *Banque Imperiale Ottomane, Emprunte Francais 1920 "Paris, Londres, Constantinople, Marseille, Manchester",* good cond., (03-13-93, Laurin, #122), 47¼ x 31½ in., (120 x 80 cm.), (BP 111, DM 265, FR 900, Y 18,739).

HODGE, Spencer (after)

$54* *Barn Owls,* num. 165/600, s., (08-20-92, Bonhams-Chelsea, #21), image 19¾ x 24 in., (50.2 x 61 cm.), reproduction in colors (BP 28, DM 78, FR 265, Y 6819).

HODGES, C.H. (after S. Gilpin)

BI *Pot OOOO OOOO, 1790,* toning of paper, tape, est. $800/1,200, (06-11-93, Doyle, #50), 17 x 19¾ in., (432 x 502 mm.), mezzotint.

HODGES, Charles Howard

$133* *Rutger Jan Schimmelpenick (Van der Felyz 710), 1806,* 2nd state of 2, repaired tear, defects, trimmed, good cond., (11-30-92, Phillips-London, #60), sheet 26¾ x 16½ in., (679 x 419 mm.), mezzotint on laid (BP 88, DM 212, FR 719, Y 16,553).

BI *Rutger Jan Schimmelpenninck (Van der Felyz 710), 1806,* 2nd state of 2, full margins, good cond., est. BP 1/150,

(11-30-92, Phillips-London, #61), plate 26½ x 16½ in., (673 x 419 mm.), mezzotint.

HODGES, W. P. (after)

$173* *Hare Hunting, Plate 1, SoHo! (S. p. 159), 1836,* by R.G. Reeve, trimmed, good cond.?, Anthony N. B. Garvan Coll., (06-05-93, Christie-NY, #63), sh 15¾ x 22 in., (400 x 559 mm.), aquatint w/hand-coloring on wove (BP 114, DM 280, FR 945, Y 18,558).

HODGKIN, Howard   English b. 1932

$1108* *After Lunch (T. 27), 1980,* by Ken Farly, crayon init., d., #88/100, pub. Petersburg Press, goodcond., (12-03-92, Sotheby-London, #745, illus.), 22¼ x 30 in., (564 x 761 mm.), etching and aquatint, hand-colored on Arches (BP 715, DM 1742, FR 5947, Y 137,862).

$938* *All Alone In The Museum Of Modern Art (T. 24), 1979,* by Ken Farley, crayon s., d., #95/100, pub. Petersburg Press, good cond., (12-03-92, Sotheby-London, #742, illus.), 29½ x 38 in., (748 x 985 mm.), etching w/hand-coloring on BFK Rives (BP 605, DM 1475, FR 5035, Y 116,710).

$515* *Artificial Flowers, 1975,* s., #145/250, margins, good cond., (06-30-93, Sotheby-London, #847), 11¼ x 15⅝ in., (286 x 397 mm.), color screenprint (BP 345, DM 878, FR 2963, Y 55,181).

$1150* *Artist And Model (In Green And Yellow) (T. 30), 1980,* i. in red crayon, d., #9/100, pub. Petersburg Press, full sheet, good cond., (02-11-93, Sotheby-NY, #354), sheet 32¹/₁₆ x 40⁹/₁₆ in., (81.5 x 103 cm.), etching and aquatint p. in colors w/hand-coloring on Stoneridge mouldmade etching (BP 811, DM 1905, FR 6446, Y 138,638).

BI *Artist And Model (In Green And Yellow) (T. 30), 1980,* init. crayon, d., #80/100, pub. Petersburg Press, good cond., est. $11,200, (05-15-93, Sotheby-NY, #1011, illus.), sheet 32⅛ x 40½ in., (81.6 x 102.9 cm.), etching and aquatint in colors w/hand-coloring on Stoneridge mould-made etching paper.

$1540* *Artist And Model (In Green And Yellow) (Tate 30), 1980,* inits., d. in red crayon, num. 41/100, pub. Petersburg Press, full sheet, creases, excell. cond., (09-19-92, Christie-E, #128), sheet 32 x 40½ in., (81.3 x 102.9 cm.), soft-ground etching in colors w/hand-coloring on Stoneridge mould made (BP 886, DM 2306, FR 7897, Y 191,876).

BI *Artist And Model, In Green And Yellow (T. 30), 1980,* inits., d., #45/100, pub. Petersburg Press, excell. cond., est. $1,4/1,800, (05-11-93, Christie-NY, #445), sheet 32 x 40¾ in., (81.3 x 103.5 cm.), color lithograph w/hand-coloring on Stoneridge mould made.

BI *Artist And Model, In Green And Yellow (Tate 29), 1980,* s., d., num. 9/100, p. and hand colored by Ken Farley, pub. Petersburg Press, full sheet, good cond., est. Y 150/190,000, (10-14-92, Sotheby-Japan, #38, illus.), sheet 32¼ x 40⅞ in., (81.9 x 103.8 cm.), softground etching w/ hand coloring in w/c and gouache.

BI *Black Moonlight (T. 32), 1980,* by Cinda Sparling, s., #8/50, pub. Bernard Jacobson, good cond., est.BP 1,2/1,800, (12-03-92, Sotheby-London, #741, illus.), overall size approx. 44 x 55⅜ in., (111.8 x 140.7 cm.), lithograph in black and greys hand-colored on buff BFK Rives.

$2420* *Black Moonlight (T. 32), 1980,* inits., d., num. 33/50, pub. Bernard Jacobson, full sheets, excell. cond., shrink-wrapped separately, (09-19-92, Christie-E, #129), overall sheet 44 x 55¼ in., (111.8 x 140.3 cm.), lithograph in colors w/hand-coloring on 2 sheets of tan wove (BP 1392, DM 3624, FR 12,410, Y 301,520).

$2530* *Bleeding (Knowles 36), 1981,* init., d., i. 'P.P.1', printer's proof, pub. Bernard Jacobson, good cond., (11-07-92, Sotheby-NY, #590, illus.), sheet 35⅝ x 59½ in., (90.5 x 151.1 cm.), lithograph p. in colors w/hand coloring in gouache (BP 1654, DM 4040, FR 13,654, Y 312,269).

$2402* *Bleeding (T. 36), 1981,* init., d., #18/100, pub. Bernard Jacobson, good cond., rubbing, creasing, (06-30-93, Sotheby-London, #850, illus.), sh 36⅛ x 45½ in., (91.8 x 115.6 cm.), color lithograph w/hand-coloring by Cinda Sparling on buff Arches (BP 1610, DM 4097, FR 13,820, Y 257,366).

$1725* *Bleeding (T. 36), 1982,* inits., d. 81, #72/100, pub. Bernard Jacobson, crease, excell. cond.?, (05-11-93, Christie-NY, #447), sheet 36¼ x 59⅞ in., (92.1 x 152.1 cm.), color lithograph w/hand-coloring on buff Velin Arches mould made (BP 1101, DM 2717, FR 9156, Y 189,748).

BI *Bleeding (Tate 36),* inits., d. 81, #72/100, pub. Bernard Jacobson, crease, excellent cond., est. $2,5/3,500, (11-09-92, Christie-NY, #313, illus.), 36¼ x 59⅞ in., (92.1 x 152.1 cm.), colored lithograph w/hand-coloring on buff Velin Arches mould.

$2760* *Blood (T. 41), 1983,* inits., d., #20/50, pub. Petersburg Press, excell. cond., the Late M. Anwar Kamal, M.D. Coll., (05-11-93, Christie-NY, #449), sheet 31 x 40 in., (78.7 x 101.6 cm.), color lithograph w/hand-coloring on Arches (BP 1762, DM 4348, FR 14,650, Y 303,597).

BI *Blue Listening Ear, 1986,* inits., d., num. 41/100, pub. B. Jacobsen, very good cond., est. BP 1,0/1,500, (12-01-92, Christie-London, #602), S. 18½ x 25⁹/₁₆ in., (470 x 650 mm.), etching w/carborundum in colors, w/hand-coloring.

$4888* *David's Pool (T. 39), 1985,* i., d., #74/100, pub. Petersburg Press, full sheet, good cond., (02-11-93, Sotheby-NY, #355, illus.), sheet 25⅜ x 30¹³/₁₆ in., (645 x 783 mm.), etching and aquatint p. in colors w/hand-coloring in blue ink on Hahnmule mouldmade (BP 3449, DM 8097, FR 27,399, Y 589,271).

$3680* *David's Pool (Tate 16), 1979,* inits., d. 85, #35/100, pub. Petersburg Press, excell. cond., the Late M. Anwar Kamal, M.D. Coll., (05-11-93, Christie-NY, #443, illus.), sheet 25 x 31 in., (635 x 787 mm.), soft-ground etching and aquatint in colors w/hand-coloring on Hahnemuhle (BP 2349, DM 5797, FR 19,533, Y 404,796).

$1194* *David's Pool Black (T. 42), 1985,* by Cinda Sparling, crayon init., d., #55/100, pub. Petersburg Press,good cond., (12-03-92, Sotheby-London, #744, illus.), 25 x 31⅛ in., (637 x 791 mm.), etching and aquatint, hand-colored on Hahnemuhle mould-made (BP 770, DM 1878, FR 6409, Y 148,563).

BI *The Green Room, 1986,* init., d., #48/100, pub. Bernard Jacobson, good cond., est. BP 1,5/2,000, (12-03-92, Sotheby-London, #747, illus.), sheet 90⅝ x 24 in., (500 x 610 mm.), aquatint in colors w/hand-coloring on wove.

BI *The Green Room, 1986,* init., d., #82/100, pub. Bernard Jacobson, good cond., est. BP 800/1,000, (06-30-93, Sotheby-London, #849, illus.), sh 192¾ x 24 in., (489.6 x 61 cm.), color aquatint w/hand-coloring.

$1650* *The Green Room, 1986,* inits., d., num. 34/100, pub. Bernard Jacobson, full sheet, excell. cond.?, shrink-wrapped, (09-19-92, Christie-E, #130, illus.), sheet 20 x 24⅛ in., (50.8 x 61.3 cm.), carborundum etching in colors w/ hand-coloring on wove (BP 949, DM 2471, FR 8462, Y 205,582).

BI *Indian Tree,* s., d. '67, #64/75, foxing, staining, est. BP 4/600, (10-27-92, Phillips-London, #203), sheet 20 x 25¼ in., (508 x 641 mm.), color lithograph on wove.

$275* *Indian View C,* s., d. 71, #43/75, (05-16-93, Hindman, #578), 22¾ x 30½ in., (57.8 x 77.5 cm.), color serigraph (BP 179, DM 442, FR 1486, Y 30,484).

$1876* *Indian Views, 1971: Ten,* from set of twelve, s., d., num., good cond., soiling marks, (12-03-92, Sotheby-London, #737, illus.), 22¾ x 30⅜ in., (578 x 773 mm.), color screenprint (BP 1210, DM 2950, FR 10,070, Y 233,420).

BI *Indian Views: A, C, F, G, H And J, 1971: Six,* from set of 12, s., d., good cond., soiling, handling creases, est. BP 800/1,000, (06-30-93, Sotheby-London, #846, illus.), each sh c. 22¾ x 30⅞ in., (578 x 784 mm.), color screenprint.

BI *Indian Views: Six Plates,* s., margins, creases, scratches, surface dirt, est. BP 800/1200, (12-01-92, Christie-London, #601), averaging S. 22⅝ x 30⅞ in., (575 x 785 mm.), screenprint in colors on wove.

BI *Interior Day, 1974,* s., d., #38/75, good cond., est. BP 2/400, (12-03-92, Sotheby-London, #738), sheet 17¼ x 23½ in., (444 x 597 mm.), aquatint in colors on wove.

$4025* *Julian And Alexis (T. 6), 1977,* s., d., i. AP, artist's proof, pub. Bernard Jacobson Gallery, good cond. ?, (05-15-93, Sotheby-NY, #1010, illus.), sheet 27⅜ x 39¾ in., (69.5 x 101 cm.), lithograph in colors w/hand-coloring in gouache on cream Velin Arches mouldmade paper (BP 2617, DM 6474, FR 21,757, Y 446,181).

BI *Komposition, (19)67,* s., d., num., est. DM 1400, (12-01-92, Karl/Faber, #737), 19⅞ x 25⁹⁄₁₆ in., (50.5 x 64 cm.), color lithograph.

$2558* *Lotus (T. 25), 1980,* s., d., #90/100, pub. Bernard Jacobson, good cond., (12-03-92, Sotheby-London, #740, illus.), 29⅛ x 36 in., (740 x 916 mm.), screenprint in colors (BP 1650, DM 4023, FR 13,731, Y 318,278).

$3025* *Lotus (T. 25), 1980,* s., d., num. 36/100, pub. Bernard Jacobson, margins, apparently goodcond., crease, surface soiling, (02-24-93, Butterfield, #3050, illus.), 29 x 36¼ in., (737 x 921 mm.), silkscreen in colors w/embossing on wove (BP 2109, DM 4911, FR 16,648, Y 354,964).

$4950* *Monsoon, 1987,* init., d., i. 'B.A.T', pub. Waddington Graphics, good cond., (11-07-92, Sotheby-NY, #591, illus.), sheet 42½ x 52⅞ in., (108 x 134.3 cm.), lithograph p. in colors w/hand coloring (BP 3236, DM 7904, FR 26,713, Y 610,960).

$1150* *Monsoon, Black, 1988,* inits., i. AP5, pub. Waddington Graohics, Solo Press blindstamp, excell. cond., (05-11-93, Christie-NY, #451), sheet 53¼ x 42½ in., (135.3 x 108 cm.), lithograph on wove (BP 734, DM 1812, FR 6104, Y 126,499).

$1380* *Mourning (T. 37), 1982,* inits., d., #50/50, pub. Bernard Jacobson, excell. cond.?, (05-11-93, Christie-NY, #448), sheet 36 x 60 in., (91.4 x 152.4 cm.), lithograph w/hand-coloring in gouache and watercolor on Arches (BP 881, DM 2174, FR 7325, Y 151,798).

$1194* *Nick's Room (T. 4), 1977,* s., i. A.P., pub. Petersburg Press, good cond., (12-03-92, Sotheby-London, #736), sheet 20½ x 24⅛ in., (520 x 613 mm.), lithograph w/hand-coloring (BP 770, DM 1878, FR 6409, Y 148,563).

$1887* *One Down (Tate Gallery Catalogue 38),* init., d., #30/100, pub. Bernard Jacobson, good cond., tear, (06-30-93, Sotheby-London, #848, illus.), 36⅛ x 48 in., (91.8 x 121.9 cm.), lithograph in black and greys, w/hand-coloring by Cinda Sparling (BP 1265, DM 3218, FR 10,857, Y 202,186).

BI *Red Listening Ear, 1986,* inits., num. 94/100, pub. B. Jacobson, very good cond., est. BP 1,0/1,500, (12-01-92, Christie-London, #603), S. 18¹¹⁄₁₆ x 25⁹⁄₁₆ in., (475 x 650 mm.), etching w/carborundum p. in colors, w/handcoloring on wove.

$3220* *Red Palm, 1986,* inits., #3/85, Waddington Graphics blindstamp, excell. cond.?, the Late M. Anwar Kamal, M.D. Coll., (05-11-93, Christie-NY, #450, illus.), sheet 42½ x 53¼ in., (108 x 135.3 cm.), color lithograph w/hand-coloring on wove (BP 2056, DM 5072, FR 17,091, Y 354,196).

BI *Sarajevo: Arrow Composition In Red And Green, 1983,* inits., d., #82/150, good cond., handling creases, surface soiling, est. $5/700, (05-19-93, Butterfield, #2190), 33½ x 24⁵⁄₁₆ in., (851 x 618 mm.), lithograph in colors on wove.

$1380* *Souvenir (T. 34), 1981,* inits., d., #74/100, pub. Petersburg Press, excell. cond., the Late M. Anwar Kamal, M.D. Coll., (05-11-93, Christie-NY, #446), sheet 45 x 55 in., (114.3 x 139.7 cm.), screenprint in grays and black on Arches (BP 881, DM 2174, FR 7325, Y 151,798).

BI *Souvenir (T. 34), 1981,* init., d., i. AP 3, pub. Petersburg Press, good cond. ?, est. $2,5/3,500, (05-15-93, Sotheby-NY, #1013, illus.), sheet 45⅛ x 55⅛ in., (114.6 x 140 cm.), silkscreen in tones of gray and black.

$1430* *Still LIfe (T. 26), 1980,* inits., d., num. 55/100, pub. Bernard Jacobson, apparently very goodcond., (02-24-93, Butterfield, #3051, illus.), 31¼ x 28¾ in., (794 x 730 mm.), silkscreen in colors on black wove (BP 997, DM 2321, FR 7870, Y 167,801).

$1535* *Still Life (T. 26), 1980,* init., d., #95/100, pub. Bernard Jacobson, good cond., (12-03-92, Sotheby-London, #746, illus.), 36¾ x 30⅞ in., (936 x 785 mm.), screenprint in colors on wove (BP 990, DM 2414, FR 8239, Y 190,992).

BI *Still Life (T. 26), 1981,* init., d., #77/100, pub. Bernard Jacobson, good cond., est. BP 1/1,500, (06-30-93, Sotheby-London, #851), sh 31¼ x 28¾ in., (794 x 730 mm.), color screenprint on wove.

$1540* *Still Life (Tate Gallery 26), 1980,* init., 67/100, (12-04-92, AB Stockholm, #7065), 31½ x 28¾ in., (80 x 73 cm.), serigraph in colors (BP 988, DM 2453, FR 8320, Y 192,260, SK 10,450).

$3450* *A Storm (Tate 5), 1977,* s., d., i. AP, pub. Petersburg Press, good cond., (05-15-93, Sotheby-NY, #1009), sheet 20⅝ x 24⅜ in., (52.4 x 61.9 cm.), lithograph in colors w/hand-coloring in gouache on Lexington handmade paper (BP 2243, DM 5549, FR 18,649, Y 382,441).

$1150* *Thinking Aloud In The Museum Of Modern Art (T. 23), 1979,* inits., d., #97/100, pub. Petersburg Press, full margins, excell. cond., the Late M. Anwar Kamal, M.D. Coll., (05-11-93, Christie-NY, #444), sheet 30¾ x 40½ in., (78.1 x 102.9 cm.), etching on gray Hodgkinson hand-made (BP 734, DM 1812, FR 6104, Y 126,499).

BI *"Thinking Aloud In The Museum Of Modern Art" and "All Alone In The Museum Of Modern Art" (Tate 23 and 24), 1979: Two,* each s. in red crayon, d., #13/100 and 14/100, pub. Petersburg Press, full sheets, good cond., est. $2/3,000, (02-11-93, Sotheby-NY, #353, illus.), sheet 30¹¹⁄₁₆ x 40³⁄₁₆ in., (78 x 102 cm.), 295¼ x 385¹³⁄₁₆ in., (78 x 102 cm.), etching, 2nd w/hand coloring in black watercolor on gray BFK Rives mouldmade paper, 1st on Hodgkinson handmade paper.

$2108* *"Those...Plants", "Artist And Model" and "Artist And Model In Green And Yellow" (Tate Gallery 28-30), 1980: Three,* init., ed. Petersburg Press, (12-04-92, AB Stockholm, #7066), 32⁵⁄₁₆ x 40¹⁵⁄₁₆ in., (82 x 104 cm.), hand-colored etching (BP 1352, DM 3357, FR 11,388, Y 263,171, SK 14,300).

$3240* *Two To Go (T. 39), 1982,* init., d., i. 9 A.P., good cond., handling creases, (12-03-92, Sotheby-London, #743, illus.), sheet 36 x 48⅛ in., (91.4 x 122.2 cm.), lithograph w/hand-coloring on wove (BP 2090, DM 5095, FR 17,391, Y 403,135).

BI *Untitled, 1983,* s., i. A.P., num. 34/45, good cond., est. $5/700, (05-22-93, Weschler, #191), 33 x 25 in., (83.8 x 63.5 cm.), screenprint in colors.

HODGSON, David (after)

$65 *"Ruins In The Bishops Garden, Norwich" and "Gatehouse To The BishopsPalace, Norwich": Two,* (02-05-93, G.A. Key, #39), one 6 x 8 in., (15.2 x 20.3 cm.), the other 8 x 6 in., (15.2 x 20.3 cm.), b/w engraving (BP 45, DM 108, FR 364, Y 8089).

HODGSON, Tom Sherlock Canadian b. 1924

BI *Sans Titre,* s. Tom Hodgson, (03-16-93, Encans, #65), 15¾ x 20¹¹⁄₁₆ in., (40 x 52.5 cm.), lithograph.

HODICKE, Karl Horst German B. 1938

BI *Ohne Titel, 1988,* pencil s., d., est. DM 1,000, (11-20-92, Lempertz, #590), sh 29½ x 55⅛ in., (75 x 140 cm.), color serigraph on thick Velin.

HODLER, Ferdinand Swiss 1853-1918

$326* *Bildnis Des Herrn Willy Russ,* s., (10-14-92, Germann, #539), 25⁹⁄₁₆ x 19¹¹⁄₁₆ in., (649 x 500 mm.), heliograph on China (BP 191, DM 477, FR 1618, Y 39,506, SF 425).

$1323* *Eiger, Monch Und Jungfrau Uber Dem Nebel,* s., (10-14-92, Germann, #538, illus.), 19⅝ x 25⁹⁄₁₆ in., (499 x 650 mm.), heliograph on China (BP 777, DM 1936, FR 6566, Y 160,325, SF 1725).

$1500* *Die Einmutigkeit,* 3-15, s., (10-14-92, Germann, #537, illus.), 19⅝ x 25½ in., (498 x 647 mm.), heliograph on China (BP 880, DM 2195, FR 7444, Y 181,774, SF 1955).

$1941* *Die Enttauschten,* s., (10-14-92, Germann, #542, illus.), 19¹¹⁄₁₆ x 25⁹⁄₁₆ in., (500 x 650 mm.), heliograph on China (BP 1139, DM 2841, FR 9633, Y 235,216, SF 2530).

$1198* *Eurhythmie,* #3/15, Piper & Co. blindstamp, s., (09-04-92, Germann, #400), 19¹¹⁄₁₆ x 25⁹⁄₁₆ in., (500 x 650 mm.), heliogravure (photoengraving) (BP 600, DM 1679, FR 5716, Y 147,464, SF 1495).

$601* *Frauenkopf Im Profil,* s., (11-25-92, Dorotheum, #469, illus.), 14⁹⁄₁₆ x 10⅝ in., (37 x 27 cm.), lithograph (BP 393, DM 956, FR 3236, Y 74,400, SC 6720).

BI *Fruhlingserwachen, 1912,* s., est. DM 2,500, (05-26-93, Lempertz, #224), 32⅞ x 23¹⁄₁₆ in., (83.5 x 58.5 cm.), lithograph on paper.

$3278* *Fruhlingssehnsucht, c. 1900-91,* s., prov., (11-13-92, Koller, #5342), 26¾ x 1615⁄16 in., (68 x 43 cm.), lithograph on cardboard (BP 2118, DM 5146, FR 17,353, Y 406,851, SF 4640).

$1145* *Fruhlingssehnsucht, c. 1910,* II Fassung, s., (06-23-93, Kornfeld, #404), 26¾ x 17 3⁄16 in., (68 x 43.7 cm.), lithograph on wove (BP 778, DM 1937, FR 6517, Y 124,741, SF 1725).

$1412* *Heilige Stunde,* s., (10-14-92, Germann, #541, illus.), 19 11⁄16 x 25 9⁄16 in., (500 x 650 mm.), heliograph on China (BP 829, DM 2066, FR 7007, Y 171,110, SF 1840).

$1106* *Die Heilige Stunde, Sechs Figuren,* #3/15, Piper & Co. blindstamp, s., (09-04-92, Germann, #399, illus.), 19 11⁄16 x 25 9⁄16 in., (500 x 650 mm.), heliogravure (photoengraving) (BP 554, DM 1550, FR 5277, Y 136,140, SF 1380).

$1737* *Die Hellige Stunde,* s., 605mm x 1025mm, (06-24-93, Germann, #650), lithograph (BP 1143, DM 2816, FR 9492, Y 186,333, SF 2530).

$350* *Kastanienbaum,* #3/15, Piper & Co. blindstamp, s., (09-04-92, Germann, #402, illus.), 25 9⁄16 x 19 11⁄16 in., (650 x 500 mm.), heliogravure (photoengraving) (BP 175, DM 491, FR 1670, Y 43,082, SF 437).

$1145* *Kunsthaus Zurich, Sechste Ausstellung Der Gesellschaft Schweizer. Maler, Bildhauer und Architekten, 1915,* poster, mono. in stone, (06-23-93, Kornfeld, #405), 38 9⁄16 x 26⅜ in., (98 x 67 cm.), color lithograph on wove (BP 778, DM 1937, FR 6517, Y 124,741, SF 1725).

$1676* *Die Nacht,* s., (10-14-92, Germann, #540, illus.), 19 11⁄16 x 25 9⁄16 in., (500 x 650 mm.), heliograph on China (BP 984, DM 2453, FR 8318, Y 203,102, SF 2185).

$139* *Portrait Eines Mannes,* #3/15, Piper & Co. blindstamp, s., (09-04-92, Germann, #401), 25 9⁄16 x 19 11⁄16 in., (650 x 500 mm.), heliogravure (photoengraving) (BP 70, DM 195, FR 663, Y 17,110, SF 173).

$175* *Portrait Eines Mannes,* #3/15, Piper & Co. blindstamp, s., (09-04-92, Germann, #396), 25 9⁄16 x 19 11⁄16 in., (650 x 500 mm.), heliogravure (photoengraving) (BP 88, DM 245, FR 835, Y 21,541, SF 219).

$147* *Schreitende,* stone s., (11-13-92, Koller, #5341), 18½ x 10 7⁄16 in., (47 x 26.5 cm.), lithograph on wove (BP 95, DM 231, FR 778, Y 18,245, SF 208).

$461* *Schreitendes Weib,* #3/15, Piper & Co. blindstamp, s., (09-04-92, Germann, #403, illus.), 25 9⁄16 x 19 11⁄16 in., (650 x 500 mm.), heliogravure (photoengraving) (BP 231, DM 646, FR 2199, Y 56,745, SF 575).

$258* *Sterbende Frau, Augustine Dupin,* #3/15, Piper & Co. blindstamp, s., (09-04-92, Germann, #397, illus.), 19 11⁄16 x 25 9⁄16 in., (500 x 650 mm.), heliogravure (photoengraving) (BP 129, DM 362, FR 1231, Y 31,758, SF 322).

$2294* *Sterbender Fahnrich Zu "Marignano",* s., (10-14-92, Germann, #544, illus.), 25⅜ x 19 11⁄16 in., (644 x 500 mm.), heliograph on China (BP 1346, DM 3357, FR 11,385, Y 277,993, SF 2990).

$1567* *Der Tell,* #3/15, Piper & Co. blindstamp, s., (09-04-92, Germann, #395, illus.), 25 9⁄16 x 19 11⁄16 in., (650 x 500 mm.), heliogravure (photoengraving) (BP 785, DM 2196, FR 7476, Y 192,885, SF 1955).

$1147* *Was Die Blumen Sagen,* s., (10-14-92, Germann, #543, illus.), 25 9⁄16 x 19 11⁄16 in., (650 x 500 mm.), heliograph on China (BP 673, DM 1679, FR 5692, Y 138,997, SF 1495).

$599* *Weib Am Bergbach,* #3/15, Piper & Co. blindstamp, s., (09-04-92, Germann, #398, illus.), 25 9⁄16 x 19 11⁄16 in., (650 x 500 mm.), heliogravure (photoengraving) (BP 300, DM 840, FR 2858, Y 73,732, SF 748).

HOEFNAGEL, Jacob

BI *Archetypa Studiaque Patris Georgii Hoefnagelii, 1592: Fifty-Two,* complete set, wide margins, stitch marks, page numbers i. in ink, penultimate plate lacking right half, waterstained, other stains, creases, surfacedirt, loose, est. BP 6/8,000, (06-30-93, Sotheby-London, #148, illus.), each sh, c. 9¼ x 11⅜ in., (235 x 289 mm.), engraving, 4 title-pages and 48 plates, on paper w/a High Crown watermark.

HOEHME, Gerhard 1920-1989

$771* *"...Mit 4 Punkten",* #148/250, t., d., s., (04-24-93, Kunsthaus, #605), 8⅞ x 16¾ in., (22.5 x 42.5 cm.), color etching and aquatint on hand-made intaglio (BP 487, DM 1208, FR 4082, Y 85,081).

$1075* *Montepulciano (Heuer 147), 1987,* s., d., t., #96/100, (05-27-93, Lempertz, #795), 31 11⁄16 x 27¼ in., (80.5 x 69.2 cm.), color etching on wove (BP 688, DM 1725, FR 5814, Y 115,244).

$1467* *Schatten-Blume-Frucht: Seventy,* s., t., ded., (04-24-93, Kunsthaus, #604, illus.), 22 7⁄16 x 20 1⁄16 in., (57 x 51 cm.), mixed media/monotype on photo paper (BP 926, DM 2299, FR 7766, Y 161,885).

$674* *Schnittmusterbild, (19)70,* s., d., num., (06-08-93, Karl/Faber, #875), approx. 23 1⁄16 x 17 5⁄16 in., (58.5 x 44 cm.), color serigraph on board (BP 443, DM 1094, FR 3683, Y 71,588).

$866* *Die Schnur Ist Die Plastische Form Des Heraklit'Schen Denkens, 1984:Three,* #40/60, s., (11-20-92, Lempertz, #595), 19 5⁄16 x 19 5⁄16 in., (49 x 49 cm.), etching on white Velin (BP 570, DM 1381, FR 4651, Y 107,698).

$1419* *Vibrierendes Leben (Heuer 47), 1959,* i., t., s., num., (06-05-93, Schoppmann, #872), 19 7⁄16 x 12½ in., (49.3 x 31.7 cm.), color etching on copper print (BP 934, DM 2301, FR 7754, Y 152,221).

$1577* *Vibrierendes Leben (Heuer 47), 1959,* s., d., t., i., #19/50, (05-27-93, Lempertz, #793), 28 11⁄16 x 19 15⁄16 in., (72.8 x 50.6 cm.), color etching on wove (BP 1010, DM 2530, FR 8529, Y 169,061).

HOEPFFNER, Marta b. 1912

BI *Bewegung, 1940,* s., d., t., stamps, lit., est. $3/4,000, (10-13-92, Christie-NY, #228, illus.), 15½ x 11¼ in., (39.4 x 28.6 cm.), photograph, gelatin silver print.

BI *Torso, 1940,* s., d., t., credit stamps, lit., est. $3/4,000, (10-13-92, Christie-NY, #229, illus.), 15⅝ x 11⅝ in., (39.7 x 29.5 cm.), photograph, gelatin silver print.

HOERLE, Heinrich 1895-1936

$13,392* *Kruppel (Backes 35), 1920: Twelve,* #14/100, s., (05-26-93, Lempertz, #228, illus.), 23¼ x 18⅛ in., (59 x 46 cm.), lithograph on thick wove (BP 8663, DM 21,850, FR 73,542, Y 1,455,020).

HOERNES, Tanna Austrian 1887-1972

BI *"Chicago Palmolive Building",* s., num. 38/250, good cond., staining, est. $150-250, (10-31-92, Cleveland, #301), 16¾ x 11¼ in., (42.5 x 28.6 cm.), color etching.

BI *Place Du Tertres, Paris,* s., est. $400/500, (09-17-92, Sloan, #2368), 11½ x 9 in., (29.2 x 22.9 cm.), color etching and aquatint.

$187* *Roman Coliseum,* s., (04-02-93, Sloan, #1165), 15⅞ x 18 in., (403 x 457 mm.), color etching and aquatint (BP 123, DM 301, FR 1021, Y 21,291).

BI *"Salzburg, The Salzach River",* s., good cond., est. $150-250, (10-31-92, Cleveland, #302), 4½ x 6¾ in., (11.4 x 17.1 cm.), etching on silk.

HOESEN, Beth van

$220* *Erika, 1966,* s., t., d., #48/50, blindstamp pub. Made in California, full margins, very good cond., (10-28-92, Butterfield, #3156), 15¾ x 14¼ in., (400 x 362 mm.), etching on Rives BFK (BP 140, DM 340, FR 1154, Y 26,994).

HOFER, Karl German 1878-1956

$1059* *Drei Frauen (Rathenau 61), 1929,* s., #61/100, (06-10-93, Hauswedell/Nolt, #411, illus.), image 9¾ x 7 11⁄16 in., (24.8 x 19.6 cm.), drypoint on copper print board (BP 693, DM 1724, FR 5806, Y 112,408).

$1877* *"Drei Frauen Beim Baden" (Rathenau 183), 1923,* s., sheet 11 of series: "Zenana", Munchen, pub. Marees Gesellschraft, R. Piper & Co., (11-28-92, Grisebach, #555, illus.), 12 5⁄16 x 10 13⁄16 in., (31.2 x 27.5 cm.), lithograph on Japan (BP 1239, DM 2990, FR 10,151, Y 233,603).

$599* *Drei Mannerkopfe Im Profil (Rathenau L 110), 1929,* in Die Schaffenden, s., pub. Euphorion, (09-04-92, Germann, #404, illus.), 11 x 9¼ in., (280 x 235 mm.), lithograph (BP 300, DM 840, FR 2858, Y 73,732, SF 748).

$1271* *Gehoft (Rathenau 143), c. 1925,* s., t., (06-10-93, Hauswedell/Nolt, #413), image 8 7⁄16 x 14 13⁄16 in., (21.5 x

37.7 cm.), lithograph on thick wove (BP 831, DM 2070, FR 6968, Y 134,911).

$851* *Madchen Mit Christblume (Rathenau 85 II, Soldan 85), 1947,* s., stamp, (06-05-93, Bassenge, #6132, illus.), 14⅜ x 8⅛ in., (36.5 x 20.7 cm.), lithograph on machine-made (BP 560, DM 1380, FR 4650, Y 91,289).

BI *Madchen Mit Facher (Rathenau L 43). c. 1923,* s., mount staining, est. DM 2600, (12-01-92, Karl/Faber, #742), 14³⁄₁₆ x 5½ in., (36 x 14 cm.), photolithograph on wove.

$1009* *Novize II (Rathenau L 30), 1922,* stone mono., s., (09-25-92, Granier, #2884), sheet 19⁵⁄₁₆ x 12¹¹⁄₁₆ in., (49 x 32.3 cm.), lithograph on Zanders hand-made (BP 589, DM 1496, FR 5058, Y 121,786).

$709* *"Schlafende" (Rathenau 41), 1922,* watermark, s., pub. in Zweite Jahresgabe des Kreises graphischer Kunstler und Sammler, Verlag Arndt & Beyer, (06-05-93, Grisebach, #643, illus.), 10⁹⁄₁₆ x 9¹⁵⁄₁₆ in., (26.8 x 25.3 cm.), lithograph on handmade (BP 467, DM 1149, FR 3874, Y 76,057).

BI *Sitzendes Madchen (Rathenau L. 70), 1929,* s., est. DM 1,200, (12-05-92, Bassenge, #7265, illus.), 11⅝ x 10½ in., (29.5 x 26.7 cm.), lithograph.

$1191* *"Sitzendes Madchen" (Rathenau 70), 1929,* s., in: "Die Schaffenden", 6 Jahrgang, 1. Mappe, Berlin, Euphorion pub., (11-28-92, Grisebach, #554, illus.), 11⅝ x 9¹⁵⁄₁₆ in., (29.5 x 25.3 cm.), lithograph on Japan (BP 786, DM 1897, FR 6441, Y 148,227).

$581* *Vorderakt Mit Gefalteten Handen (R. L 61), c. 1923,* s., num., margin tears, (12-01-92, Karl/Faber, #743), 12³⁄₁₆ x 7⅞ in., (31 x 20 cm.), lithograph on hand-made (BP 384, DM 926, FR 3156, Y 72,336).

HOFF, Adriaan Van't 1893-1939

BI *Holland Amerika Linie, 1928,* tears, losses, repairs, lit., est. BP 1,2/1,600, (02-04-93, Christie-S. Ken, #29, illus.), 40 x 30 in., (101.6 x 76.2 cm.), color lithograph backed on japan.

HOFF, Charles

$550* *The Hindenburg Explosion,* 1937, p. 1940s, (04-07-93, Swann, #320), 10½ x 13 in., photograph, honey-toned silver print (BP 363, DM 890, FR 3010, Y 62,486).

$1540* *The Hindenburg Explosion,* handstamps, notations, 1937, p.l., (10-14-92, Swann, #317, illus.), 8 x 10 in., (20.3 x 25.4 cm.), photograph, silver print (BP 904, DM 2254, FR 7643, Y 186,621).

HOFF, Margo American b. 1912

$110* *Picasso's Bather,* s., t., #85/200, (11-01-92, Hanzel, #276), 17½ x 12½ in., (44.5 x 31.8 cm.), lithograph (BP 72, DM 174, FR 585, Y 13,600).

$110* *Vespers,* s., t., (11-01-92, Hanzel, #211), 23½ x 24 in., (59.7 x 61 cm.), linocut (BP 72, DM 174, FR 585, Y 13,600).

HOFFMAN, Irwin D. American b. 1901

$110* *"African Golfers", 1936,* good cond., s., t., (06-11-93, Freemn/Fine Art, #95B), 9 x 12 in., (22.9 x 30.5 cm.), etching (BP 72, DM 179, FR 603, Y 11,671).

BI *African Golfers, 1936,* s., t., good cond., est. $150/200, (11-12-92, Freemn/Fine Art, #89), unframed 8 x 11 in., (20.3 x 27.9 cm.), etching.

$95* *"Barber Shop",* s., t., AAA edit., excell. cond., (05-15-93, Cleveland, #161), 8 x 11 in., (20.3 x 27.9 cm.), etching (BP 62, DM 153, FR 514, Y 10,531).

$303* *"Barber Shop", "Mexican Folk Band", "Pastoral Puerto Rico", and "Puerto Rican Folk Song": Four,* each s., t., pub. AAA, full margins, good cond., surface soiling, (02-24-93, Butterfield, #2837), etching on wove (BP 211, DM 492, FR 1668, Y 35,555).

$65* *"Lace Makers", 1944,* s., t., light struck, (05-15-93, Cleveland, #162), 9¾ x 11¾ in., (24.8 x 29.8 cm.), etching and drypoint (BP 42, DM 105, FR 351, Y 7205).

$193* *"Miner At Rest", 1937,* s. Irwin D. Hoffman, annot. artist's proof, very good cond., (09-11-92, Skinner, #43, illus.), 10⅞ x 7⅞ in., (27.6 x 20 cm.), etching on wove (BP 100, DM 278, FR 944, Y 23,913).

HOFFMANN, Hans

$1760* *Composition In Blue, 1952,* s., #62/120, margins, paper loss, (12-08-92, Swann, #142, illus.), 16⅞ x 14 in., (42.9 x 35.6 cm.), color silkscreen laid down on board (BP 1103, DM 2740, FR 9342, Y 218,146).

HOFFMANN, Heinrich

BI *German Soldiers Playing For French Children, 1915,* handstamp, label, est. $6/900, (10-14-92, Swann, #352, illus.), 4½ x 6½ in., (11.4 x 16.5 cm.), photograph, silver print.

HOFFMANN, Irwin D. American b. 1901

$143* *El Jibaro,* s., t., (11-01-92, Hanzel, #209), 12 x 10 in., (30.5 x 25.4 cm.), etching (BP 93, DM 226, FR 760, Y 17,681).

HOFMAN, Pieter Adrianus Hendrik 1885-1965

BI *L'Etranger, c. 1922,* excell. cond., est. BP 4/500, (02-04-93, Christie-S. Ken, #126, illus.), 42½ x 29 in., (108 x 73.7 cm.), color lithograph backed.

HOFMAN, Vlastislav 20th cent.

BI *"Raskolnikoff", c. 1920,* very good/good cond., est. $150/250, (11-21-92, Bakker, #13), image 7 x 5 in., (17.8 x 12.7 cm.), linocut.

HOFMANN, Ludwig von

$122* *(Women),* s., #4/20, margins, good cond., minor handling creases, upper corners of sheet glued to mount, Late Gerhard Brauer Coll., (05-27-93, Sotheby-Amstrdm, #738), 7¹⁵⁄₁₆ x 10¹³⁄₁₆ in., (202 x 274 mm.), woodcut on Japan (BP 78, DM 196, FR 660, Y 13,079, G 219).

HOFMANN, Otto

BI *(Untitled)" and "(Cubist Still Life)": Two,* 1 s., both in good cond., est. $2/300, (06-11-93, Doyle, #49), (210 x 279 mm.), color lithograph.

HOGAN, John R. 1888-1946

BI *Skirting Davy Jones Locker, c. 1938,* s., t., est. $1/1,500, (10-13-92, Christie-NY, #230, illus.), 14½ x 19 in., (36.8 x 48.3 cm.), photograph, blue-toned gelatin silver print.

HOGARTH (after)

$17* *"Garrick In The Character Of Richard III",* (12-11-92, DuMouchelle, #258), 15 x 20 in., (38.1 x 50.8 cm.), engraving (BP 11, DM 27, FR 92, Y 2104).

HOGARTH, William English 1697-1764

$303* *"Beer Street" and "The Enraged Musician," 1741 and 1751: Two,* later impressions, (10-18-92, Hindman, #506), larger 14¼ x 16¼ in., (36.2 x 41.3 cm.), etchings (BP 185, DM 451, FR 1530, Y 36,353).

BI *Captain Tho Coram,* est. $300/400, (09-17-92, Sloan, #2362), 22¼ x 15⅞ in., (56.5 x 40.3 cm.), etching and engraving.

BI *A Catalogue Of Hogarth's Original Works Including The Rake's Progress, Marriage A-La-Mode, Election Entertainment Four Plates, The Four Times Of Day, Four Stages Of Cruelty, And Others: Eighty-Nine,* pub. 1784, full margins, foxed, time-stained, bound, prov., est. BP 3/5,000, (10-27-92, Phillips-London, #43, illus.), sheet 25 x 18½ in., (635 x 470 mm.), etching on laid.

BI *"Credulity, Superstition And Fanaticism" (P. 232), 1762,* Heath edit. 1822, good cond., est. $1/200, (10-31-92, Cleveland, #12), etching and engraving.

$182* *An Election Entertainment, Plate 1,* pub. 1755, margins, (06-16-93, Bonhams-Chelsea, #421), pl. 16¾ x 22 in., (42.5 x 55.9 cm.), engraving w/hand-coloring (BP 121, DM 302, FR 1014, Y 19,411).

BI *The Four Stages Of Cruelty, 1751: Four,* margins, time-staining, est. BP 1/200, (12-10-92, Bonhams-Chelsea, #105), plate 15¼ x 12¾ in., (38.7 x 32.4 cm.), etching.

$127* *The Four Stages Of Cruelty, 1751: Four,* margins, time-staining, (02-17-93, Bonhams-Chelsea, #268), plate 15¼ x 12¾ in., (38.7 x 32.4 cm.), etching (BP 88, DM 206, FR 699, Y 15,170).

BI *France Plate 1 (Soldiers Outside The Soup Of Meagre A La Sabot Royal),* est. $300/400, (09-17-92, Sloan, #2361), 12½ x 15¼ in., (31.8 x 38.7 cm.), etching and engraving.

$330* *From The Prentice Series, 18th Century: Eleven,* p. for Bowles and Craver, (01-02-93, Litchfield, #117), steel engraving (BP 220, DM 541, FR 1846, Y 41,374).

$410* *A Harlot's Progress, Plates 1-6: Six,* margins, surface dirt, (12-10-92, Bonhams-Chelsea, #103), plate 12½ x

15¼ in., (31.8 x 38.7 cm.), etching (BP 264, DM 649, FR 2215, Y 50,717).

$119* *A Harlot's Progress, Plates I-VI: Six,* margins, staining, (12-10-92, Bonhams-Chelsea, #44), plate 12¾ x 15½ in., (32.4 x 39.4 cm.), engraving on wove (BP 77, DM 188, FR 643, Y 14,720).

BI *A Harlot's Progress, Plates I-VI: Six,* margins, staining, est. BP 1/150, (12-10-92, Bonhams-Chelsea, #45), plate 12¾ x 15½ in., (32.4 x 39.4 cm.), engraving on wove.

$39* *"Henry The VIII And Anne Boleyn" (Paulson 116), 1728-9,* Heath edit. 1822, good cond., (10-31-92, Cleveland, #11), etching and engraving (BP 25, DM 60, FR 204, Y 4831).

$85* *The Idle Prentice And The Industrious Prentice: Four Plates,* scuffed, defects, (07-16-92, Bonhams-Chelsea, #472), image 10 x 13 in., (25.4 x 33 cm.), engraving (BP 44, DM 126, FR 424, Y 10,648).

$38 *"The Industrious Prentice": Two,* d. 1747, (04-16-93, G.A. Key, #134), 8 x 11 in., (20.3 x 27.9 cm.), b/w engraving (BP 25, DM 61, FR 207, Y 4273).

BI *Industry And Idleness (Paulson 169-179 II bzw.III), 1747: Twelve,* est. DM 3500, (06-04-93, Bassenge, #5512, illus.), woodcut.

BI *The Invasion, "France" and "England", 1756: Two,* margins, foxing, est. BP 60/100, (12-10-92, Bonhams-Chelsea, #106), plate 12½ x 15¼ in., (31.8 x 38.7 cm.), engraving.

$111* *The Invasion: "France" and "England", 1756: Two,* margins, foxing, (02-17-93, Bonhams-Chelsea, #267), plate 12½ x 15¼ in., (31.8 x 38.7 cm.), engraving (BP 77, DM 180, FR 611, Y 13,258).

BI *John Wilkes Esq. (Paulson 214 I), 1673,* est. DM 500, (12-04-92, Bassenge, #6609), 13¹⁵/₁₆ x 9 in., (35.5 x 22.9 cm.), etching.

$2362* *Marriage A La Mode, 1795-1800: Six,* by Richard Earlom, after Hogarth, (05-08-93, Schloss Ahlden, #2156), each approx. 18⅞ x 24⁷/₁₆ in., (48 x 62 cm.), mezzotint (BP 1541, DM 3794, FR 12,802, Y 263,940).

$410* *Marriage A La Mode, Plates 1-VI, 1745: Six,* by Baron, Scotin and Ravenet, margins, foxing, (12-10-92, Bonhams-Chelsea, #104), plate 15¼ x 18¼ in., (38.7 x 46.4 cm.), etching (BP 264, DM 649, FR 2215, Y 50,717).

$165* *Midnight Modern Conversation,* (04-02-93, Sloan, #2265), sight 12¾ x 18 in., (324 x 457 mm.), engraving (BP 109, DM 265, FR 901, Y 18,786).

$467* *"Morning", "Noon", "Evening" and "Night", 1738: Four,* margins, stained, tears, (10-15-92, Bonhams-Chelsea, #97), plate 19¼ x 16 in., (48.9 x 40.6 cm.), engraving (BP 286, DM 695, FR 2357, Y 56,029).

$550* *"Night" and "Morning" "Evening" "Noon": Two,* pub. 1738, (02-27-93, Dunning, #1130), sight 19¼ x 15½ in., (48.9 x 39.4 cm.), engraving w/hand coloring (BP 387, DM 904, FR 3073, Y 64,927).

$55* *"Pit Ticket, Royal Sport" (Cockfighting Scene),* design'd and engrav'd by Willm Hogarth, Royal Sport Publ Nov 5, 1750, (02-27-93, Dunning, #1102, illus.), 12¾ x 15 in., (32.4 x 38.1 cm.), engraving (BP 39, DM 90, FR 307, Y 6493).

$1554* *The Rake's Progress (Burke-Caldwell 149, 151, 153, 155, 157, 159, 161, 163), 1735: Eight,* (06-10-93, Hauswedell/Nolt, #194, illus.), etching (BP 1016, DM 2531, FR 8520, Y 164,951).

BI *"A Rake's Progress" (Paulson 132-139, all final states): Eight,* complete set, homogeneous set p. after 1763, but before re-engraving and posthumuus reissue, very fine cond., thin spots, surface dirt, crease, repaired tear, est. $1,5/2,500, (05-15-93, Cleveland, #392), 13⅞ x 16 in., (35.2 x 40.6 cm.), etching and engraving.

$68* *Rake's Progress, Plates 1-6: Six,* margins, spotting, (12-10-92, Bonhams-Chelsea, #47), plate 14¼ x 16 in., (36.2 x 40.6 cm.), engraving on wove (BP 44, DM 108, FR 367, Y 8412).

$129* *Rake's Progress, Plates 1-8: Eight,* margins, spotting, (12-10-92, Bonhams-Chelsea, #46), plate 14¼ x 16 in., (36.2 x 40.6 cm.), engraving on wove (BP 83, DM 204, FR 697, Y 15,957).

$110* *"Scholars At Lecture" and "The Company Of Undertakers": Two,* (11-01-92, Hanzel, #234), 20½ x 7½ in.,

(52.1 x 19.1 cm.), engravings on one sheet of paper (BP 72, DM 174, FR 585, Y 13,600).

$34 *"Strolling Actresses Dressing In A Barn",* (04-16-93, G.A. Key, #68), 6 x 9 in., (15.2 x 22.9 cm.), b/w engraving (BP 22, DM 55, FR 186, Y 3823).

$433* *Tailpiece, Or The Bathos (Burke 267; Paulson 216), 1764,* (12-04-92, Bassenge, #6610), 12¾ x 13¼ in., (32.4 x 33.6 cm.), engraving w/etching on China (BP 278, DM 690, FR 2339, Y 54,057).

BI *To The Right Hon. Earl Onslow,* est. $300/400, (09-17-92, Sloan, #2363), 21 x 16 in., (53.3 x 40.6 cm.), etching and engraving.

$440* *Untitled: Group Of Thirteen,* staining, worn margins, (01-02-93, Litchfield, #80), steel engraving (BP 293, DM 721, FR 2461, Y 55,165).

$550* *Various Titles, 1740-1806: Twenty-Two,* margins, good cond., tears, paper losses, creases, surface soiling; p. by Thomas Davison, margins, good cond., water & light-staining, foxing, tears, surface soiling, pencil notations, (02-24-93, Butterfield, #2691), engravings on wove and J. Whatman paper (BP 384, DM 893, FR 3027, Y 64,539).

HOGARTH, William (after)

$88* *Captain Thomas Coram,* by William Nutter, 18th/19th cent., pub. 1796 by R. Cribb, (04-02-93, Sloan, #2288), 22¾ x 15¾ in., (578 x 400 mm.), engraving (BP 58, DM 141, FR 480, Y 10,019).

$101* *The Four Stages Of Cruelty,* margins, staining, (01-21-93, Bonhams-Chelsea, #20), plate 15¼ x 12¾ in., (38.7 x 32.4 cm.), etchings (BP 66, DM 161, FR 543, Y 12,641).

$88* *Frontpiece For Samuel Butler,* (02-12-93, DuMouchelle, #1184), approx. 10¾ x 13½ in., (27.3 x 34.3 cm.), engraving (BP 62, DM 146, FR 494, Y 10,613).

$85* *A Harlot's Progress, Plates 2-6: Four,* (12-10-92, Bonhams-Chelsea, #107), image 11¼ x 14¾ in., (28.6 x 37.5 cm.), etching (BP 55, DM 134, FR 459, Y 10,515).

$149* *Hudibras: Five,* after William Hogarth, margins, dirt, defects, (07-16-92, Bonhams-Chelsea, #471), plate 21½ x 14¼ in., (54.6 x 36.2 cm.), engraving (BP 77, DM 220, FR 743, Y 18,665).

$275* *The Idle Prentice And The Industrious Prentice: Four,* (09-21-92, Selkirk, #180), 10½ x 13¾ in., (26.7 x 34.9 cm.), engraving (BP 161, DM 408, FR 1396, Y 33,988).

$550* *"Marriage A La Mode": Six,* (01-06-93, Doyle, #35), 15 x 18 in., (38.1 x 45.7 cm.), etching (BP 359, DM 901, FR 3069, Y 68,819).

$154* *Marriage A-La-Mode, Plates I-VI, 1745: Six,* by G. Scotin, B. Baron, F. Ravenet, pub. Hogarth, surface defects, (12-10-92, Bonhams-Chelsea, #43), plate 15¼ x 18½ in., (38.7 x 47 cm.), engraving (BP 99, DM 244, FR 832, Y 19,050).

$594* *Marriage A-La-Mode: Six,* by Thomas Cook, pub. G. and J. Robinson, 1797, (06-16-93, Bonhams-Chelsea, #422), image 13¾ x 17¼ in., (34.9 x 43.8 cm.), engraving (BP 396, DM 986, FR 3309, Y 63,353).

$67* *Set Of Six Bookplates,* (11-19-92, Bonhams-Chelsea, #52), image 6¼ x 8 in., (15.9 x 20.3 cm.), engraving (BP 44, DM 107, FR 360, Y 8332).

$47* *Shrimps!,* by Francesco Bartolozzi, pub. Jane Hogarth, 1782, margins, (06-16-93, Bonhams-Chelsea, #423), pl. 10¾ x 8 in., (27.3 x 20.3 cm.), stipple engraving (BP 31, DM 78, FR 262, Y 5013).

BI *The Strolling Players,* est. BP 6/80, (06-16-93, Bonhams-Chelsea, #424), image 15¾ x 20 in., (40 x 50.8 cm.), reprod. w/hand-coloring.

$46 *Various Subjects: Six,* various sizes, (04-16-93, G.A. Key, #113), b/w engraving (BP 30, DM 74, FR 251, Y 5173).

HOGENBERG, Nicolaus   d. 1539

$2166* *Kurtze Erzeichniss Wie Keyser Carolus Der V. In Africa Dem Konig VonThunis...Mit Kriegrustung Zu Huffe Komt, 1535: Eight,* watermark, lit., stained, (12-04-92, Bassenge, #6235), etching (BP 1389, DM 3450, FR 11,702, Y 270,412).

HOGFELDT, Robert   1894-1986

$591* *"Underbarnet",* s. 11/50, (11-07-92, Falkkloos, #193), lithograph w/watercolor (BP 386, DM 948, FR 3189, Y 72,945, SK 3520).

HOHENSTEIN, Adolfo b. 1854

$1418* *Chiozza E Turchi, 1899,* crease upper image, excell. cond., (02-04-93, Christie-S. Ken, #87, illus.), 20 x 11 in., (50.8 x 27.9 cm.), color lithograph (BP 990, DM 2335, FR 7917, Y 176,390).

HOHLWEIN, Ludwig 1874-1949

$536* *Berijdt Duitschlands Schoone Wegen, 1935,* creases, lit., (02-04-93, Christie-S. Ken, #165, illus.), 39 x 25 in., (99.1 x 63.5 cm.), color lithograph backed on linen (BP 374, DM 883, FR 2993, Y 66,675).

$770* *"Direct China Cotton Importers Wonalancet Company, Nasua, N.H.",* s., i., t., Ludwig Hohlwein Munchen" in matrix, pub. G. Schuh and Cie, ident, very good cond., nicks, tears, (05-22-93, Skinner, #59, illus.), sheet 32 x 23 in., (81.3 x 58.4 cm.), color lithograph on paper (BP 499, DM 1252, FR 4212, Y 84,895).

$1733* *Engleder Und Finkenzeller, c. 1913,* pierced plastic tape, sellotape stains, tape, lit., (02-04-93, Christie-S. Ken, #164, illus.), 35 x 49 in., (88.9 x 124.5 cm.), color lithograph (BP 1210, DM 2854, FR 9676, Y 215,574).

BI *Hellabrunn, 1937,* pierced plastic tape, defects, excell. cond., lit., est. BP 1,5/2,000, (02-04-93, Christie-S. Ken, #166), 47 x 33 in., (119.4 x 83.8 cm.), color lithograph.

BI *Marco Polo-Tee, 1914,* fold marks, tears, repairs, lit., est. BP 2/4,000, (02-04-93, Christie-S. Ken, #163, illus.), 43½ x 30 in., (110.5 x 76.2 cm.), color lithograph backed on japan.

$770* *"Peruvian Cotton/Carders Wonalancet Company, Nashua, N.H.",* s., i., t. Ludwig Hohlwein Munchen, pub. G. Schuh and Cie, ident., veood cond., nicks, tears, (05-22-93, Skinner, #60, illus.), sheet 31 x 23 in., (78.7 x 58.4 cm.), color lithograph on paper (BP 499, DM 1252, FR 4212, Y 84,895).

$1320* *Yellowstone-Park (S. 31), 1910,* p. by G. Schuh & Cie., margins, good cond., tears, creases, surface soiling, (02-24-93, Butterfield, #2742), 34¼ x 48¼ in., (87 x 122.6 cm.), lithograph in colors on wove (BP 921, DM 2143, FR 7265, Y 154,893).

BI *Zoologischer Garten Munchen, 1912,* pierced plastic tape, creases, stains, excell. cond., est. BP 1,5/2,000, (02-04-93, Christie-S. Ken, #162, illus.), 49 x 36 in., (124.5 x 91.4 cm.), color lithograph.

$4255* *Zoologischer Garten, 1912,* pierced plastic/paper tape, tears, creases, lit., (02-04-93, Christie-S. Ken, #161, illus.), 49½ x 36 in., (125.7 x 91.4 cm.), color lithograph (BP 2970, DM 7006, FR 23,758, Y 529,295).

HOKKEI

$1758* *"It Is Favourable To Dig A Well" (Ido Hori Yoshi),* surimono, kakuban, from series Hanazono bantsuzuki, s. Hokkei, (06-10-93, Sotheby-London, #199), details in silver and gold, gauffrage (embossing) (BP 1150, DM 2863, FR 9638, Y 186,604).

$5626* *Okyo Riding On A Goose With Trailing Clouds And Playing A Sho (Reed Instrument): Two,* surimono, kakuban, from series Mogyu, s. Hokkei, rubbed, (06-10-93, Sotheby-London, #198), (BP 3680, DM 9161, FR 30,844, Y 597,177).

$3516* *Turtles,* surimono, kakuban, s. Go Hokkei w/seal, rubbed, (06-10-93, Sotheby-London, #196, illus.), (BP 2300, DM 5725, FR 19,276, Y 373,209).

HOKUSAI

BI *"The 36 Views Of Mount Fuji",* t. Senju in Musaoki Province, block s., est. $200/300, (01-15-93, DuMouchelle, #2309, illus.), 9⅞ x 14½ in., (25.1 x 36.8 cm.), color woodblock print.

$3868* *Five Prints From The Tokaido Series With Poems,* koban yoko-e, each w/poems, s. Gakojin Hokusai ga, wormage, laid-down, (06-10-93, Sotheby-London, #240, illus.), each approx. 5¹⁄₁₆ x 7¹⁄₁₆ in., (12.8 x 18 cm.), (BP 2530, DM 6299, FR 21,206, Y 410,572).

$4219* *Genroku Kasen Kai Awase, "A Matching Game With The Genroku Poem Shells": Two,* 2 surimono, s. Getchirojin Iitsu hitsu and Gakyojin Hokusai ga respectively, soiled, rubbed, (06-10-93, Sotheby-London, #214, illus.), one 7¹⁵⁄₁₆ x 7¹⁄₁₆ in., (20.2 x 18 cm.), the other 5¼ x 7⅛ in., (20.2 x 18 cm.), (BP 2760, DM 6870, FR 23,130, Y 447,829).

$20,218* *Hunters Around A Log-Fire, The Snowy Mountain,* oban yoko-e, from series Hyakunin Isshu Ubagaetoki, censor's seal, pub. mark, Eijudo, s. Zen Hokusai Manji, rubbed, creased, soiled, wormed, (06-10-93, Sotheby-London, #238, illus.), 10¹⁄₁₆ x 14¾ in., (25.6 x 37.5 cm.), (BP 13,225, DM 32,923, FR 110,844, Y 2,146,057).

$7912* *Imperial Guards Around A Bonfire,* oban yoko-e, from series Hyakunin Isshu Ubaga Etoki, censor's seal, pub. marks, Eijudo, s. Zen Hokusai Manji, fold-mark, soiled, trimmed, (06-10-93, Sotheby-London, #239, illus.), 9½ x 14⁷⁄₁₆ in., (24.2 x 36.6 cm.), (BP 5175, DM 12,884, FR 43,377, Y 839,826).

$6050* *"Kirifura Fall In Kurokawa Mountain",* from Journey to Waterfalls of All the Provinces, s., pub. Eijudo, seal, fading, mat line, center crease, wrinkles, tate-e, (11-20-92, Skinner, #60, illus.), oban tate-e (BP 3983, DM 9646, FR 32,492, Y 752,394).

$5626* *The Portrait Of A Court Lady,* surimono, kakuban, s. Katsushika Rofu, Iitsu hitsu, soiled, rubbed, (06-10-93, Sotheby-London, #194, illus.), gauffrage, silver and gold pigments (BP 3680, DM 9161, FR 30,844, Y 597,177).

$1183* *"Senju In Musashi Province",* from Thirty Six Views of Mt. Fuji, posthumous edit., (10-31-92, Litchfield, #355), 14½ x 9¾ in., (36.8 x 24.8 cm.), woodblock print (BP 773, DM 1857, FR 6289, Y 146,266).

$2110* *The Seven Lucky Gods (Shichi Fukujin),* surimono, kakuban, s. Katsushika Hokusai ga, soiled, rubbed, (06-10-93, Sotheby-London, #204, illus.), (BP 1380, DM 3436, FR 11,568, Y 223,968).

$4923* *Soshu Umezawa, From The Thirty-Six Views Of Fuji,* oban yoko-e: blue outlines; s. Zen Hokusai Iitsu hitsu, fold mark, rubbed, soiled, wormed, laid-down, (06-10-93, Sotheby-London, #241), 10⅛ x 14¾ in., (25.7 x 37.5 cm.), (BP 3220, DM 8017, FR 26,990, Y 522,556).

$6153* *Still Life Of Soma-Yaki (Soma Ware),* surimono, kakuban, from series Uma Zukushi, s. Fusenkyo Iitsu hitsu, (06-10-93, Sotheby-London, #195, illus.), details in gold and silver (BP 4025, DM 10,020, FR 33,734, Y 653,115).

BI *"Surimono",* OBAN YOKOE, soiling, creasing, trimmed, fair cond., est. $3/400, (05-07-93, Goldberg, #1390, illus.), woodblock.

$35,162* *The Waterfall Of Amida,* oban yoko-e, from series Shokoku Takimeguri, s. Zen Hokusai Iitsu hitsu, full margins, (06-10-93, Sotheby-London, #237, illus.), 15⁵⁄₁₆ x 10¼ in., (38.9 x 26.1 cm.), (BP 23,000, DM 57,258, FR 192,774, Y 3,732,300).

$5274* *The Waterfall Of Roben On Oyama In Soshu Province,* oban tate-e, series Shokoku Taki Meguri, censor's seal, pub. mark, Eijudo, s. Zen Hokusai Iitsu hitsu, faded, rubbed, soiled, trimmed, wormed, (06-10-93, Sotheby-London, #244, illus.), (BP 3450, DM 8588, FR 28,914, Y 559,813).

$1934* *Women Making Paper Dolls,* surimono, kakuban, s. Kukushin Hokusai ga, creased, rubbed, (06-10-93, Sotheby-London, #215), (BP 1265, DM 3149, FR 10,603, Y 205,286).

$5626* *The Yatsuhashi (Eight Bridges) In Mikawa Province,* oban yoko-e, from series Shokoku Meikyo Kiran, censor's seal, pub. mark, Eijudo, s. Zen Hokusai Iitsu hitsu, faded, soiled, rubbed, (06-10-93, Sotheby-London, #243, illus.), 9¾ x 14¹¹⁄₁₆ in., (24.8 x 37.3 cm.), (BP 3680, DM 9161, FR 30,844, Y 597,177).

HOKUSAI (after) Japanese 1760-1849

$385* *The Great Wave,* (06-13-93, Hindman, #405), 9¾ x 14½ in., (24.8 x 36.8 cm.), color woodcut (BP 252, DM 627, FR 2106, Y 40,514).

HOKUSAI, Katsushika Japanese 1760-1849

$453* *"Eijiri",* from the series 36 Postcards of Fuji, signs of wear, format Oban, (04-27-93, Dorotheum, #175, illus.), 14⁹⁄₁₆ x 9¹⁵⁄₁₆ in., (37 x 25.3 cm.), color woodcut (BP 288, DM 717, FR 2426, Y 50,768, SC 5040).

BI *From The "100 Geschichten Von Der Amme Erzahlt",* format Oban, est. SC 5/6,000, (04-27-93, Dorotheum, #155, illus.), 14¾ x 10¼ in., (37.4 x 26 cm.), color woodcut.

BI *From The Series "53 Stationen Der Tokaido", 1806,* illus. 29, Format Chuban, est. SC 6/7,000, (04-27-93, Dorotheum, #235), 6¹¹⁄₁₆ x 8¹¹⁄₁₆ in., (17 x 22 cm.), .

$604* *From The Series "Kana Dehon Chushingura",* format Oban, (04-27-93, Dorotheum, #165, illus.), 13¹⁵⁄₁₆ x 9¼ in., (35.5 x 23.5 cm.), color woodcut (BP 384, DM 956, FR 3235, Y 67,690, SC 6720).

$654* *From The Series "Kana Dehon Chushingura",* format Oban, (04-27-93, Dorotheum, #166, illus.), 13¹⁵⁄₁₆ x 9¼ in., (35.5 x 23.5 cm.), color woodcut (BP 416, DM 1035, FR 3503, Y 73,294, SC 7280).

$806* *"Laternengeist",* t., 2. Afl., format Chuban, (04-27-93, Dorotheum, #164, illus.), 7⅛ x 9⁵⁄₁₆ in., (18.1 x 23.7 cm.), color woodcut (BP 513, DM 1276, FR 4317, Y 90,328, SC 8960).

$1510* *People On A Road,* in the Quer-Oban, (04-27-93, Dorotheum, #176, illus.), 14³⁄₁₆ x 8¾ in., (36 x 22.3 cm.), color woodcut (BP 960, DM 2391, FR 8088, Y 169,226, SC 16,800).

$503* *Portrait Of Two Actors Onoe Matsusuke As Samurai And Segawa KikujiroAs Lover,* from the series Chushingura, s., (04-27-93, Dorotheum, #160, illus.), 5⁷⁄₁₆ x 11¹⁵⁄₁₆ in., (13.8 x 30.3 cm.), woodcut (BP 320, DM 796, FR 2694, Y 56,371, SC 5600).

$1812* *Portrayal Of A Farmer,* (04-27-93, Dorotheum, #159, illus.), 8⅞ x 19¹¹⁄₁₆ in., (22.6 x 50 cm.), color woodcut (BP 1152, DM 2869, FR 9705, Y 203,071, SC 20,160).

$302* *Studie Versch, Meerestiere,* signs of wear, s., Format Chuban, (04-27-93, Dorotheum, #201, illus.), 7³⁄₁₆ x 9⅝ in., (18.2 x 24.4 cm.), woodcut (BP 192, DM 478, FR 1618, Y 33,845, SC 3360).

BI *Waterfall,* format Oban, est. SC 9/10,000, (04-27-93, Dorotheum, #150, illus.), 10¼ x 14⅝ in., (26 x 37.2 cm.), color woodcut.

HOKUSAI, Katsushika (after)   Japanese 1760-1849
$200* *"Under The Wave Off Kanagawa" and "Hodogaya On The Tokaido": Two,* from "Thirty-six Views of Mr. Fuji", (02-04-93, Sloan, #925), sight, each 7¼ x 11¼ in., (18.4 x 28.6 cm.), color woodcut (BP 140, DM 329, FR 1117, Y 24,879).

HOLBEIN, Hans (after)   English 18th cent.
BI *The Country Attorney And His Client,* by Anthony Walker, pub. Boydell, 1764, est. $3/400, (04-02-93, Sloan, #2277), 16¾ x 21¼ in., (425 x 540 mm.), engraving.

HOLBEIN, Hans (the younger)   1497/98-1543
BI *Erasmus Von Rotterdam (Passavant III, 390, 57; Hollstein 9), c. 1538,* est. DM 1,200, (12-04-92, Bassenge, #6236), 11¼ x 5¹³⁄₁₆ in., (28.5 x 14.8 cm.), woodcut.

HOLBEIN, Hans (the younger) (after)
BI *Erasmus Of Rotterdam (Holl. 9),* by Veit Specklin, w/ inscription Corporis effigium, trimmed, paper disturbance, thin spots, discoloration, creasing, est. BP 1/2,000, (06-30-93, Sotheby-London, #149), 11¼ x 6½ in., (286 x 165 mm.), woodcut on paper w/a Small Jug watermark.

HOLBEIN(?) (after)
$70 *Figure Subjects: Two,* (12-11-92, G.A. Key, #101), 10 x 11 in., (25.4 x 27.9 cm.), colored print (BP 45, DM 110, FR 378, Y 8662).

HOLE
BI *Hannibal's Defeat Of The Romans At The Battle Of Cannae, 216 B.C.: Two,* from Sir Walter Raleigh's "History...", London, 1614, est. $400/500, (09-17-92, Sloan, #2687), 13 x 15½ in., (33 x 39.4 cm.), engraving.

HOLE, William
$198* *"Shepherd And Sheep In Snowy Woodlands", 1909,* after Joseph Farquharson, s. by both artists, pub. Frost and Reed, (10-15-92, Bonhams-Chelsea, #107), image 18½ x 28 in., (47 x 71.1 cm.), mixed method engraving (BP 121, DM 295, FR 999, Y 23,755).

HOLLAND, George (after)   American 19th cent.
$110* *A View Of The Federal Hall Of The City Of New York,* by Currier, (04-02-93, Sloan, #823), 16½ x 20½ in., (419 x 521 mm.), color lithograph (BP 72, DM 177, FR 600, Y 12,524).

HOLLAND, Tom   American b. 1936
$173* *Diablo, 1971,* s., d., t., annot. A/P, blindstamp publisher, full margins, good cond., stains, (05-19-93, Butterfield, #2193), 18 x 23¾ in., (457 x 603 mm.), silkscreen w/ collage and embossing in metallic silver on wove (BP 112, DM 281, FR 947, Y 19,152).

$220* *"Nerin" and "Ryder", 1971; 1972: Two,* s., d., t., num. 52/60 and 23/55, blindstamp of pub. Cirrus, full margins, good cond., hinge remains, creases, (02-24-93, Butterfield, #3219), 11 x 20½ in., (27.9 x 52.1 cm.), 30 x 42⅛ in., (27.9 x 52.1 cm.), silkscreen w/collage & lithograph in colors on Rives & wove (BP 153, DM 357, FR 1211, Y 25,816).

BI *Untitled, 1988,* s., d., pub. Garner Tullis Workshop, good cond., pinholes, est. $1,5/2,000, (02-24-93, Butterfield, #3053), 30¼ x 44⅜ in., (76.8 x 112.7 cm.), monotype in colors w/collage on Somerset.

$825* *Untitled, 1988,* s., d., t., pub. Garner Tullis Workshop, good cond., (02-24-93, Butterfield, #3054), 30¼ x 44½ in., (76.8 x 113 cm.), monotype in colors on wove (BP 575, DM 1339, FR 4540, Y 96,808).

BI *Untitled, 1988,* s., d., pub. Garner Tullis Workshop, good cond., pinholes, surface soiling, est. $2/2,500, (02-24-93, Butterfield, #3052), (76.8 x 112.4 cm.), monotype & collage in colors on Somerset.

BI *Untitled, 1988,* s., d., pub. Garner Tullis Workshop, very good cond., est. $1/1,500, (10-28-92, Butterfield, #2975), 29¼ x 43¼ in., (74.3 x 109.9 cm.), color monotype w/ collage on cream wove.

BI *Untitled, 1988,* s., d., pub. Garner Tullis Workshop, very good cond., est. $8/1,000, (05-19-93, Butterfield, #2194), 29¼ x 43¼ in., (74.3 x 109.9 cm.), monotype w/collage in colors on cream wove.

HOLLAND, W., publisher
$46 *"Four Stages Of Matrimony",* d. May 1811, (06-11-93, G.A. Key, #45), 16 x 12 in., (40.6 x 30.5 cm.), hand-colored engraving (BP 30, DM 75, FR 252, Y 4881).

HOLLAR, Wenzel   German 1607-1677
$1417* *Ceres Sucht Ihre Tochter (Parthey 273), 1646,* after A. Elsheimer, watermark, (06-08-93, Karl/Faber, #87, illus.), etching (BP 932, DM 2299, FR 7743, Y 150,505).

BI *A Chalice (Parthey, Pennington 2109), 1640,* after A. Mantegna (?), margins, fold, staining, surface soiling, paper tape, very good cond., watermark, prov., prop. Montclair Art Museum, est. $1,4/1,600, (05-11-93, Christie-NY, #24), plate 18 x 9⅜ in., (457 x 238 mm.), etching on laid.

BI *Costume Designs: Twelve,* bookplates, trimmed, framed as 2, BP 250/350, (06-16-93, Bonhams-Chelsea, #314), image 5 x 2¾ in., (12.7 x 7 cm.), etching.

$188* *Elephant,* margins, (12-10-92, Bonhams-Chelsea, #52), plate 6¾ x 10½ in., (17.1 x 26.7 cm.), etching on laid paper (BP 121, DM 297, FR 1016, Y 23,256).

$550* *Fables: Ten,* animals and men, Letterio Calapia Estate, (05-16-93, Hindman, #409), each approx. 10⅛ x 6⅞ in., (25.7 x 17.5 cm.), etching (BP 358, DM 885, FR 2973, Y 60,969).

BI *Flache Schale M. Verziertem Fuss (Parthey 2629), 1646,* after H. Holbein, plate s., d., trimmed, dusty, est. DM 250-, (09-25-92, Granier, #2645), 6⁷⁄₁₆ x 4¹³⁄₁₆ in., (16.3 x 12.3 cm.), etching.

$1416* *The Peasant Scuffle (Parthey 599 I, Hollstein 221 a I), 1646,* after P. Brueghel, (06-04-93, Bassenge, #5197, illus.), 9⅝ x 13⅛ in., (24.4 x 33.3 cm.), etching (BP 937, DM 2299, FR 7750, Y 152,718).

$289* *Der Satyr Bei Den Bauern (Parthey 424; Hollstein 30), 1644,* after A. Elsheimer, (12-04-92, Bassenge, #6237), 2⅞ x 3¹¹⁄₁₆ in., (7.3 x 9.4 cm.), etching (BP 185, DM 460, FR 1561, Y 36,080).

BI *"Willebroek Bey Boom" (Parthey 901),* after J. Brueghel, est. DM 1,800, (12-01-92, Karl/Faber, #83), etching.

HOLLAR, Wenzel (after)
$40* *A 17th Century View Of London,* staining, (02-17-93, Bonhams-Chelsea, #249), sheet 18 x 88 in., (45.7 x 223.5 cm.), reproduction (BP 28, DM 65, FR 220, Y 4778).

HOLLIDAY, Doc
$3520* *Studio Portrait Purported To Be Of Wyatt And Morgan Earp And Doc Holliday, c. 1880,* (10-14-92, Swann, #193, illus.), photograph, albumen cabinet card (BP 2066, DM 5151, FR 17,469, Y 426,563).

HOLLYER, Frederick   1837-1933
$327* *Walford Graham Robertson,* c. 1880s, mounted on grey card, (05-06-93, Christie-London, #67, illus.), 5⅝ x 3⅞ in., photograph, platinum print (BP 207, DM 515, FR 1734, Y 35,978).

HOLM, Jens M.   Danish 1776-1859
$695* *"Sjellandsyndigste Egne",* after H.G.F. Holm, (10-20-92, B. Rasmussen, #363), etching in colors (BP 428, DM 1056, FR 3575, Y 85,036, DK 4025).

HOLMAN
$12* *"Harbor Scene",* ed. AP, s., t., (03-12-93, DuMouchelle, #2450), 5 x 7 in., (12.7 x 17.8 cm.), etching (BP 8, DM 20, FR 68, Y 1414).

HOLST, Richard Roland
$544* *Glasblazer, 1904,* s., margins, glued to backboard, foxing, light-staining, (05-27-93, Sotheby-Amstrdm, #823), 14¹³⁄₁₆ x 9½ in., (377 x 242 mm.), lithograph on wove (BP 348, DM 873, FR 2942, Y 58,319, G 978).

HOLST, Roland
$1320* *Raden Van Arbeid,* s., d. 1920, Barry Friedman, Ltd. Coll., (11-19-92, Sotheby-NY, #149, illus.), 44½ x 31⅛ in., (113 x 79.1 cm.), lithograph in colors on paper (BP 869, DM 2105, FR 7089, Y 164,159).

HOLSTEIN, Pieter
$64* *Kracht, 1979,* s., good cond., minor handling creases in margins, (05-27-93, Sotheby-Amstrdm, #421), 10¹¹⁄₁₆ x 12¹³⁄₁₆ in., (272 x 326 mm.), hand colored etching on wove (BP 41, DM 103, FR 346, Y 6861, G 115).
$96* *Ontmoeting, 1979,* s., good cond., (05-27-93, Sotheby-Amstrdm, #423), 10¹¹⁄₁₆ x 12¹³⁄₁₆ in., (272 x 326 mm.), hand colored etching on wove (BP 61, DM 154, FR 519, Y 10,292, G 173).
$115* *Romance, 1979,* s., good cond., minor handling creases, (05-27-93, Sotheby-Amstrdm, #422), 10¹¹⁄₁₆ x 12¹³⁄₁₆ in., (272 x 326 mm.), hand colored etching on wove (BP 74, DM 185, FR 622, Y 12,328, G 207).

HOLTZ, Karl   1889-1978
$830* *Pariser Strassenszene, c. 1925,* s., ded., (11-28-92, Grisebach, #559, illus.), 13⅜ x 10¾ in., (34 x 27.3 cm.), lithograph on copper print paper (BP 548, DM 1322, FR 4489, Y 103,298).
$614* *"Toulon", c. 1925,* s., t., (11-28-92, Grisebach, #560, illus.), 8¹⁵⁄₁₆ x 11⅝ in., (22.8 x 29.5 cm.), lithograph on copper print paper (BP 405, DM 978, FR 3321, Y 76,416).

HOLTZ, Karl   1899-1978
$709* *Berliner Tageblatt, 1920,* s., (06-05-93, Bassenge, #6137, illus.), 9¹⁄₁₆ x 13⁹⁄₁₆ in., (23 x 34.5 cm.), lithograph on imitation Japan (BP 447, DM 1149, FR 3874, Y 76,057).
BI *Nachtlicher Boulevard In Paris, c. 1925,* stamp verso, est. DM 1,800, (12-05-92, Bassenge, #7271), 5¹⁵⁄₁₆ x 10³⁄₁₆ in., (15.2 x 25.8 cm.), lithograph on copper print paper.

HOLWEIN, Ludwig
BI *"Turf", c. 1904: Set Of Five,* est. SF 2,5/3,000, (11-15-92, Christie-Geneva, #6, illus.), 19⅛ x 19⅛ in., (48.5 x 48.5 cm.), woodcut prints.

HOMANN
BI *Danubii Cum Adiacentibus Regnis,* est. $400/600, (09-17-92, Sloan, #2688), 18¾ x 22 in., (47.6 x 55.9 cm.), handcolored.
$165* *Danubii Cum Adiacentibus Regnis,* (12-10-92, Sloan, #1311), 18¾ x 22 in., (47.6 x 55.9 cm.), handcolored (BP 106, DM 261, FR 891, Y 20,411).

HOMER, Winslow   American 1836-1910
BI *"The Bathers",* from Harper's Weekly, Aug. 2, 1873, good cond., margins, trimmed, est$1-150, (10-31-92, Cleveland, #143), 13⅞ x 9⅛ in., (35.2 x 23.2 cm.), wood engraving.

$2310* *Mending The Tears, 1888,* plate s., i., (c) 1888 Winslow Homer, G. Ritchie Imp., remarque, (06-11-93, Freemn/Fine Art, #96, illus.), 17¼ x 22¾ in., (43.8 x 57.8 cm.), etching (BP 1518, DM 3754, FR 12,658, Y 245,093).
$30* *"The Noon Recess", 1878,* from Harper's Weekly, staining, foxing, (05-15-93, Cleveland, #163), 9 x 13½ in., (22.9 x 34.3 cm.), wood engraving (BP 20, DM 48, FR 162, Y 3326).
$60* *The Nooning,* pub., (05-16-93, Hanzel, #444), 8¾ x 13¾ in., (22.2 x 34.9 cm.), engraving (BP 39, DM 97, FR 324, Y 6651).
$4180* *Perils Of The Sea (Goodrich 99), 1988,* (05-16-93, Hindman, #535, illus.), 16½ x 21⅞ in., (41.9 x 55.6 cm.), etching (BP 2718, DM 6724, FR 22,595, Y 463,363).
$8140* *Saved (G. 102),* plate s. Winslow Homer Sc., i. G.W.H. Ritchie Imp., (c) 1889 by C. Klackner, creasing, discoloration, good cond., catalog cover lot, (06-11-93, Freemn/Fine Art, #97, illus.), 23 x 32¾ in., (58.4 x 83.2 cm.), etching (BP 5348, DM 13,229, FR 44,603, Y 863,660).
$110* *Shipbuilding, Gloucester Harbor,* from Harper's Weekly, Oct. 11, 1873, inits. in plate W.H., (10-24-92, Collins, #23), 9¼ x 13½ in., (23.5 x 34.3 cm.), woodblock print (BP 68, DM 168, FR 570, Y 13,415).

HOMER, Winslow (after)
$1540* *From Harper's Weekly, 1861-1874: Collection Of Fourteen,* w/text verso, margins, light-staining, losses, short tears, time staining, other minor defects, (09-19-92, Christie-E, #25, illus.), wood engraving on newsprint (BP 886, DM 2306, FR 7897, Y 191,876).
$7* *"Sloop Bermuda"* and *"Sponge Fishing, Bahamas": Two,* (01-15-93, DuMouchelle, #2439), each 13 x 18 in., (33 x 45.7 cm.), prints (BP 5, DM 11, FR 39, Y 883).

HOMER, Winslow (after)   American 1836-1910
$990* *The Fog Warning, 1885,* s. Hamilton Hamilton, bears sig. N. Homer, (11-12-92, Freemn/Fine Art, #90, illus.), plate 20 x 31 in., (50.8 x 78.7 cm.), etching (BP 650, DM 1569, FR 5291, Y 122,753).

HONDA, Kazuhisa   Japanese b. 1948
$77* *"A",* s., t., d., num. 25/65, excell. cond., (10-31-92, Cleveland, #37), 17½ x 11½ in., (44.5 x 29.2 cm.), mezzotint (BP 49, DM 118, FR 402, Y 9538).
$330* *"Awakening": Six,* all s., num. 3/75, p. 1981, excell. cond., portfolio, (10-31-92, Cleveland, #39), 5½ x 6¾ in., (14 x 17.1 cm.), mezzotint (BP 211, DM 508, FR 1722, Y 40,877).
$300* *Awakening: Six,* s., #HC v/vii, p. 1981 by John Szoke Graphics and Elaine Daughtery Fine Arts, excell. cond., (05-15-93, Cleveland, #20), 5½ x 6¾ in., (14 x 17.1 cm.), mezzotint (BP 195, DM 483, FR 1622, Y 33,256).
$660* *"Mezzotint": Seven,* all s., num. 21/75, p. by artist 1983, excell. cond., portfolio, (10-31-92, Cleveland, #40), 2¾ x 3¾ in., (7 x 9.5 cm.), 5 colored mezzotints, 2 b/w mezzotints (BP 423, DM 1015, FR 3445, Y 81,754).
$75* *"Milk",* s., d., t., #15/75, excellent cond., (05-15-93, Cleveland, #22), 7⅞ x 11¾ in., (20 x 29.8 cm.), color mezzotint (BP 49, DM 121, FR 405, Y 8314).
$55* *"N",* s., t., d., num. 39/75, (10-31-92, Cleveland, #38), 17½ x 11½ in., (44.5 x 29.2 cm.), mezzotint (BP 35, DM 85, FR 287, Y 6813).
$95* *"Ten Wheats", 1981,* s., t., d. #7/75, excellent cond., (05-15-93, Cleveland, #21), 11¾ x 7¾ in., (29.8 x 19.7 cm.), color mezzotint (BP 62, DM 153, FR 514, Y 10,531).

HONDIUS
BI *"A General Plot...Six Counties Of Norfolke, Suffolke, Cambridge...",1632,* margins trimmed, est. $225/300, (09-17-92, Sloan, #2689), 17¼ x 21¾ in., (43.8 x 55.2 cm.), print.

HONEGGER, Gottfried   b. 1917
BI *Madchenkopf,* artist's proof, s., est. SF 80/120, (10-14-92, Germann, #546), 17¹¹⁄₁₆ x 12¹³⁄₁₆ in., (450 x 325 mm.), lithograph.

HONTY, Tibor
$1495* *The Old Jewish Cemetery, Prague, 1942,* annot. by photog.'s wife, studio stamp, (04-08-93, Christie-NY, #129, illus.), 8¼ x 11½ in., (21 x 29.2 cm.), photograph, gelatin silver print (BP 980, DM 2402, FR 8129, Y 169,655).

HOOCH, Peter de (after)
$38 *"A Dutch Interior With Soldiers"*, Medici Society, (04-16-93, G.A. Key, #17), 17 x 14 in., (43.2 x 35.6 cm.), colored print (BP 25, DM 61, FR 207, Y 4273).

HOOK, S.
$755* *La Corse 'En Yacht', A Cinq Heures De Nice Par La Cie Fraissinet*, p. Affiche Gaillard, cond. 1, yellowing, defects, laid on linen, (10-13-92, Phillips-London, #29, illus.), 38¹⁵⁄₁₆ x 24¹³⁄₁₆ in., (99 x 63 cm.), color lithograph (BP 440, DM 1106, FR 3758, Y 91,548).

HOOKER, William and R.A. SALISBURY
$487* *Paradisus Londinensis Or Specimens Of The Most Beautiful Flowering Plants Grown In Or Near London, 1805: One Hundred And Eight Plates*, from the series, pub. London, original leather binding, disbound, fair cond., (10-27-92, Phillips-London, #170), sheet 9⅝ x 7½ in., (244 x 191 mm.), engraving w/hand-coloring on wove (BP 308, DM 746, FR 2533, Y 59,572).

HOOPER, George   b. 1910
$246* *Everywhere You Go, Kintbury, Berkshire, 1952*, p. Vincent Brooks, Day & Son, ref. P 40, cond. 3, (10-13-92, Phillips-London, #176), 29¾ x 39⅞ in., (75.5 x 101.3 cm.), color lithograph (BP 143, DM 360, FR 1224, Y 29,829).

HOOVER, Ellison
$66* *"St. Sulpice"*, s., AAA, (12-11-92, DuMouchelle, #1478, illus.), 12½ x 9¼ in., (31.8 x 23.5 cm.), lithograph (BP 42, DM 104, FR 356, Y 8167).

HOOVER, Ellison   American 1888-1955
$165* *Racing The Storm*, s. Ellison Hoover, good cond., light/mount staining, margins broken/fragile, tape, (09-11-92, Skinner, #47, illus.), 9⅜ x 12⅞ in., (23.8 x 32.7 cm.), lithograph on wove (BP 85, DM 238, FR 807, Y 20,444).

HOPF, Sonia
$19* *Zoe, 1987: Two*, both s., 29/50, (06-28-93, Loudmer, #57), 9¹³⁄₁₆ x 7¹¹⁄₁₆ in., (250 x 195 mm.), sh 18⅛ x 14¹⁵⁄₁₆ in., (250 x 195 mm.), 2 states on black etchings on wove (BP 13, DM 32, FR 109, Y 2016).

HOPFER, Daniel   German c. 1470-1536
BI *Buste Neros (Hollstein 85, II)*, mono., est. DM 300-, (03-24-93, Venator/Hansten, #2531), pl. 8⅞ x 6¼ in., (22.6 x 15.8 cm.), etching.
$2997* *The Crucified Christ In A Decorated Niche (B. 13; Holl. 18)*, 1st state of 2, w/delicate tone, watermark, narrow margins, horizontal and vertical crease, pinholes, good cond., prov., (12-01-92, Christie-London, #187, illus.), plate 8¹³⁄₁₆ x 5⅞ in., (224 x 149 mm.), etching (BP 1980, DM 4777, FR 16,279, Y 373,132).
$289* *Venus Und Amor (B. 46; Hollstein 54 II)*, (12-04-92, Bassenge, #6240), 8⅞ x 6⅛ in., (22.5 x 15.5 cm.), eisenradierung (BP 185, DM 460, FR 1561, Y 36,080).

HOPFER, Hieronymus   German c. 1500-1563
BI *The Abduction On The Unicorn (B. 42; Holl. 47)*, after A. Durer, 2nd (final) state, watermark, narrow margins, foxmarks, crease, very good cond., est. BP 4/600, (12-01-92, Christie-London, #191), plate 11¼ x 8⁷⁄₁₆ in., (285 x 214 mm.), etching.
$303* *Death Of The Virgin*, mono. in plate, (10-30-92, Sloan, #2807), 11⅜ x 8⅝ in., (28.9 x 21.9 cm.), etching (BP 194, DM 466, FR 1581, Y 37,533).
$581* *Memento Mori Als Ornamentfullung (Hollstein Bd. XV, 79)*, mono. IH, prov., (09-14-92, Venator/Hansten, #1516, illus.), plate 11⁵⁄₁₆ x 3⅞ in., (28.8 x 9.8 cm.), eisenradierung (BP 307, DM 864, FR 2927, Y 72,246).
BI *Die Personifikation Der Siegreichen Stadtgottin Roma, Auf Trophaen Sitzend (B. 37, Hollstein 41 I)*, prov., est. DM 1,800, (12-04-92, Bassenge, #6243), 8⅞ x 6³⁄₁₆ in., (22.5 x 15.7 cm.), etching.
BI *Saint Jerome In Penitence (B. 19; Holl. 22)*, after A. Durer, 1st state of 2, watermark, narrow margins, crease, paer mounting, prov., est. BP 6/800, (12-01-92, Christie-London, #189), plate 8¹⁵⁄₁₆ x 5¹³⁄₁₆ in., (227 x 148 mm.), etching.

HOPFER, Lambert   German c. 1525-1550
$2630* *Christi Leben Und Leiden (Hollstein Bd. 15 A, 2-13, 15), Thirteen*, after engraving-Passion by Albrecht Durer, mono. LH, num. 175-184, 194, 196, 197, prov., (09-14-92, Venator/Hansten, #1517), plate, largest 6 x 3⁹⁄₁₆ in., (15.3 x 9 cm.), smallest 5½ x 3½ in., (15.3 x 9 cm.), etching w/drypoint (BP 1391, DM 3910, FR 13,249, Y 327,033).
BI *Die Gefangennahme Christi (Bartsch 4; Hollstein I)*, after A. Durer, watermark, 1st state, prov., est. DM 1,200, (06-10-93, Hauswedell/Nolt, #109), etching on hand-made.

HOPKINS, Arthur   English 1848-1930
$144* *The Lawn Tennis Championship Meeting At Wimbledon, The Fifth Round Of The All Comer's Match, 1881*, (03-03-93, Bonhams-Chelsea, #13), image 8¾ x 11⅝ in., (22.2 x 29.5 cm.), hand-colored etching (BP 99, DM 237, FR 804, Y 16,826).

HOPNER (after)
$100 *"Countess Of Orford"*, (08-14-92, G.A. Key, #31), 18 x 14 in., (45.7 x 35.6 cm.), colored print (BP 52, DM 147, FR 497, Y 12,610).

HOPPE, Emil Otto   1878-1972
BI *"Martin Hardie", c. 1910*, ink s., i., photog.'s ink credit, est. BP 3/500, (10-29-92, Christie-London, #90, illus.), 9⅞ x 7⅛ in., (25.1 x 18.1 cm.), photograph, warm-toned gelatin silver print.

HOPPE, Robert
BI *Radio City Music Hall*, s., num. SP 18, est. $6/800, (05-22-93, Weschler, #192, illus.), 31 x 21 in., (78.7 x 53.3 cm.), lithograph in colors.

HOPPER, Edward   American 1882-1967
BI *East Side Interior (Zigrosser 8; Levin pl. 85), 1922*, s., annot., full margins, good cond., mat stain, est. $24/28,000, (05-13-93, Sotheby-NY, #424, illus.), 8 x 9⅞ in., (202 x 251 mm.), etching.
$5500* *Night Shadows (Z. 22), 1921*, pub. New Republic, 1924, s., (06-11-93, Freemn/Fine Art, #98, illus.), 7 x 8¼ in., (17.8 x 21 cm.), etching (BP 3614, DM 8939, FR 30,137, Y 583,554).
$8250* *Night Shadows (Zigrosser 22), 1921*, s., full margins, crease, good cond., pub. New Republic 1924, cover lot, (11-12-92, Freemn/Fine Art, #91, illus.), plate 7 x 8¼ in., (17.8 x 21 cm.), etching on wove paper (BP 5419, DM 13,072, FR 44,094, Y 1,022,939).
$8800* *Night Shadows (Zigrosser 22; Levin pl. 82), 1921*, s., full margins, good cond., thumb print verso, (11-05-92, Sotheby-NY, #24, illus.), 6⅞ x 8⅜ in., (176 x 212 mm.), etching on wove (BP 5724, DM 13,917, FR 47,084, Y 1,079,622).
$2420* *Portrait Of Jean Cheruy (Zigrosser 47), 1915-18*, s., margins, paper crackle, (12-08-92, Swann, #145), 4 x 3½ in., (10.2 x 8.9 cm.), etching on wove (BP 1517, DM 3768, FR 12,845, Y 299,950).

HOPPNER, John   British 1758-1810
$366* *Lady Charlotte Greville (C.S., R. 29), 1796*, by John Young, 3rd (final) state, watermark, pub. Young, wide margins, surface dirt, good cond., prov., (12-01-92, Christie-London, #289), plate 19¹⁵⁄₁₆ x 13⅞ in., (506 x 353 mm.), mezzotint (BP 242, DM 583, FR 1988, Y 45,568).

HOPPNER, John (after)
$283* *Admiral, Lord Nelson, 1806*, by Charles Turner, creasing, trimmed, good cond., (11-30-92, Phillips-London, #65), sheet 25⅛ x 17 in., (638 x 432 mm.), mezzotint on laid (BP 187, DM 451, FR 1531, Y 35,221).
$159* *Her Grace, The Duchess Of Bedford, 1803*, by S.W. Reynolds, pub. S.W. Reynolds, skinning, repaired damage, goodcond., (11-30-92, Phillips-London, #62), plate 26 x 17⅞ in., (660 x 454 mm.), mezotint on laid (BP 105, DM 253, FR 860, Y 19,788).
$200* *Miss Greville (C.S. 29), 1796*, by John Young, 1st state of 2, scratch-letter proof before t., pub. John Young, skinning, trimmed to plate, (11-30-92, Phillips-London, #67), sheet 20 x 14 in., (508 x 356 mm.), mezzotint on laid (BP 132, DM 319, FR 1082, Y 24,891).

$50* *The Right Honourable Lord Grenville, 1800,* by S.W. Reynolds, pub. John Jeffryes, foxed, light-stained, folded &pinned on stretcher, (11-30-92, Phillips-London, #63), image 16½ x 13¼ in., (419 x 337 mm.), mezzotint in colors, on wove (BP 33, DM 80, FR 270, Y 6223).

$264* *The Show,* by J. Young, pub. by engraver, margins, tears, other defects, (06-16-93, Bonhams-Chelsea, #465), pl. 23¼ x 17 in., (59.1 x 43.2 cm.), mezzotint (BP 176, DM 438, FR 1471, Y 28,157).

HOPPNER, John (after)   1785-1810

$383* *Eliza (C.S., R. 74), 1786,* by John Young, 3rd (final) state, pub. Young, margins, spot, staining, prov., (12-01-92, Christie-London, #290), plate 14¹³⁄₁₆ x 10¹³⁄₁₆ in., (376 x 274 mm.), mezzotint, on Auvergne laid paper (BP 253, DM 610, FR 2080, Y 47,684).

$117* *Mrs. Benwell (Frankau 24; C.S., R. 7), c. 1785,* by William Ward, 3rd (final) state, watermark, pub. J.R. Smith, margins, crease, repair, surface dirt, (12-01-92, Christie-London, #288), plate 14¹⁵⁄₁₆ x 10⅞ in., (380 x 277 mm.), mezzotint (BP 77, DM 186, FR 636, Y 14,567).

HORN

$1100* *Path Through Woods, 1900's,* s., (11-16-92, Butterfield, #6009, illus.), 23¹³⁄₁₆ x 17⁹⁄₁₆ in., (604.3 x 445.3 mm.), photograph, sepia-toned gelatin silver print (BP 724, DM 1754, FR 5908, Y 136,799).

HORNBY, Lester   American 1882-1956

$110* *Bait Casting,* margins, s. L. G. Hornby, (02-13-93, Collins, #87, illus.), 9⅞ x 12⅞ in., (25.1 x 32.7 cm.), etching (BP 77, DM 182, FR 617, Y 13,266).

$275* *"Dans Le Jardin Du Palais Royal" and "A La Gaite, Montparnesse": Two,* s., t., very good cond., (06-11-93, Doyle, #51), larger 7⅞ x 11¾ in., (200 x 298 mm.), drypoint (BP 181, DM 447, FR 1507, Y 29,178).

$44* *L Arc-En Ciel,* s. L.G. Hornby, t., (10-24-92, Collins, #21), 5¾ x 8½ in., (14.6 x 21.6 cm.), etching (BP 27, DM 67, FR 228, Y 5366).

$20* *"Trolling",* s., t., cardboard remnants, (05-15-93, Cleveland, #166), 7 x 10 in., (17.8 x 25.4 cm.), etching (BP 13, DM 32, FR 108, Y 2217).

HORNUNG, J.

$147* *P.L.M.: Stations D'altitude, "Alpes, Monts, Jura, Cevennes", 1932,* fair cond., (01-23-93, Ribeyre/Baron, #4), 38¹⁵⁄₁₆ x 24⁷⁄₁₆ in., (99 x 62 cm.), poster (BP 96, DM 234, FR 791, Y 18,398).

HORNUNG, Preben

$379* *Compositions: Two,* s. Hornung, (09-30-92, Kunsthallen, #129), color lithograph (BP 214, DM 537, FR 1818, Y 45,482, DK 2070).

$128* *Figurkomposition, 1986,* s. Hornug, E.A., (03-24-93, Kunsthallen, #135), color lithograph (BP 87, DM 209, FR 712, Y 15,039, DK 805).

$404* *Portfolio: Four,* s. 36/125, (03-24-93, Kunsthallen, #136), color etching (BP 274, DM 660, FR 2246, Y 47,468, DK 2530).

HORNY, Conrad   1764-1807

BI *A Tivoli, 1795,* after J.C. Reinhart, margin foxed, (12-04-92, Bassenge, #6830), 9¹³⁄₁₆ x 7⁹⁄₁₆ in., (25 x 19.2 cm.), etching.

HORNYANSKY, Nicholas   1896-1965

$299* *Days End Around The Campus (University Of Toronto),* s., t., (11-30-92, Ritchie, #17, illus.), 4⅛ x 6 in., (10.5 x 15.3 cm.), color aquatint (BP 197, DM 476, FR 1617, Y 37,212, C$ 385).

$214* *Grace Church On-The-Hill,* s., t., (11-30-92, Ritchie, #19, illus.), 7⅞ x 10½ in., (20 x 26.6 cm.), aquatint (BP 141, DM 341, FR 1157, Y 26,633, C$ 275).

$86* *Laurentian Village,* s., t., (06-07-93, Ritchie, #21, illus.), 3¾ x 4¼ in., (9.5 x 10.8 cm.), color aquatint (BP 57, DM 139, FR 470, Y 9225, C$ 110).

$193* *The Masks And Their Maker,* s., t., #14/50, (11-30-92, Ritchie, #20, illus.), 9⅜ x 7⅝ in., (23.8 x 19.4 cm.), aquatint (BP 127, DM 307, FR 1044, Y 24,020, C$ 248).

$299* *"Orchids" and "Rose": Two,* s., t., prov., (11-30-92, Ritchie, #21A), each 8½ x 6¾ in., (21.6 x 17.1 cm.),

color aquatint (BP 197, DM 476, FR 1617, Y 37,212, C$ 385).

$150* *Royal Archives, Ottawa,* s., t., (11-30-92, Ritchie, #21), 4 x 4¼ in., (10.2 x 10.8 cm.), color aquatint (BP 99, DM 239, FR 811, Y 18,668, C$ 193).

$214* *The Soldiers' Tower And University College From The North (Toronto),* s., t., (11-30-92, Ritchie, #18), 4⅛ x 5⅞ in., (10.5 x 15 cm.), color aquatint (BP 141, DM 341, FR 1157, Y 26,633, C$ 275).

$113* *St. Andrews, Niagra On The Lake,* s., t., prov., (11-16-92, Hodgins, #159), 5¼ x 4 in., (13.3 x 10.2 cm.), aquatint on paper (BP 74, DM 180, FR 607, Y 14,102, C$ 143).

$280* *Twilight In Old Down-Town (Toronto),* s., t., (06-07-93, Ritchie, #19, illus.), 5¹⁄₁₆ x 3⅞ in., (12.9 x 9.9 cm.), color aquatint (BP 184, DM 454, FR 1530, Y 30,036, C$ 358).

$69* *"View Of Cathedral" and "Shoreline": Two,* each cancelled w/X in plate, (06-07-93, Ritchie, #24), larger 5¼ x 4¼ in., (13.3 x 10.8 cm.), copper etching (BP 45, DM 112, FR 377, Y 7402, C$ 88).

HORST, Horst P.   American b. 1906

$910* *Agenta Fischer, c. 1930,* ink s., (11-12-92, Lempertz, #100, illus.), 8½ x 6⁷⁄₁₆ in., (21.6 x 16.4 cm.), photograph, gelatin silver print (BP 582, DM 1430, FR 4874, Y 112,582).

$1180* *Black Bodice, New York, 1948,* p.l., s., #9/25, 352 x 277mm, (05-07-93, Sotheby-London, #329, illus.), photograph, platinum print on Strathmore script cotton fibre paper (BP 747, DM 1866, FR 6287, Y 129,927).

$1543* *Calvin Klein Fashion, New York, 1983,* s. Horst, s., t., #2/10, sight 500 x 370mm, (05-07-93, Sotheby-London, #333, illus.), photograph, platinum palladium print (BP 977, DM 2440, FR 8221, Y 169,896).

$3575* *"Chanel, Paris" and "Gertrude Stein and Horst, Paris" (Lawford, p. 154 & Salute to the Thirties, pl. 3): Two,* each s. by photog., 1937 & 1930s, p.l., (10-15-92, Sotheby-NY, #225, illus.), each approx. 10 x 9½ in., (25.4 x 24.1 cm.), photograph, gelatin silver prints (BP 2188, DM 5322, FR 18,046, Y 428,914).

BI *"Coco Chanel", 1950s,* p. 1982, s., i., t., d. 1982, photog.'s credit stamp, Jocelyn Kargere Coll., est. BP 8/1,200, (10-29-92, Christie-London, #171, illus.), image 7⅜ x 9⅜ in., (18.7 x 23.8 cm.), photograph, colour print.

BI *Dogwood,* s. Horst, 495 x 600mm, est. BP 1,5/2,000, (05-07-93, Sotheby-London, #332, illus.), photograph, platinum print.

BI *Edith Sitwell,* s. by photog., #6/10 in unident. hand, 1948, p. 1980's, (04-06-93, Sotheby-NY, #385A, illus.), 17½ x 14¼ in., photograph, platinum-palladium print.

$1980* *Electric Beauty,* (1938), s., t., d., num. 1/10, (c) credit stamps, lit., (10-13-92, Christie-NY, #232, illus.), 17⅝ x 14¼ in., (44.8 x 36.2 cm.), photograph, platinum-palladium print (BP 1153, DM 2901, FR 9856, Y 240,087).

$944* *Fashion Story, Clasp, New York, 1950,* p.l., s. twice, stamped photog.'s credit, 501 x 402mm, (05-07-93, Sotheby-London, #331, illus.), photograph, silver bromide print (BP 598, DM 1492, FR 5029, Y 103,942).

$1430* *Female Torso,* photog.'s sig., 1930s, p.l., (04-07-93, Swann, #488, illus.), 9 x 7 in., photograph, platinum print (BP 945, DM 2313, FR 7827, Y 162,463).

BI *Gertrude Stein With Basket, 1946,* s., est. $2,5/3,500, (10-13-92, Christie-NY, #234, illus.), 7½ x 7½ in., (19.1 x 19.1 cm.), photograph, gelatin silver print.

$544* *Gertrude Stein With Her Poodle Basket, Paris, 1946,* p.l., s. twice, (05-06-93, Christie-London, #190), image 10⅞ x 10⅛ in., photograph, gelatin silver print (BP 345, DM 857, FR 2884, Y 59,853).

$1430* *"Gertrude Stein, Horst, And Eric", 1946/later,* s., inventory num., Dixon Collection, (11-16-92, Butterfield, #6010, illus.), 10⅛ x 9¾ in., (257.6 x 248.1 mm.), photograph, gelatin silver print (BP 942, DM 2280, FR 7680, Y 177,839).

BI *Gloria Vanderbilt,* s., t., #1/25, photog.'s (c) stamp, est. BP 1/1,500, (05-06-93, Christie-London, #189), 9½ x 7½ in., photograph, platinum-palladium print.

BI *"Hands",* 1941, p.l., s. twice, #3/15, lit., est. BP 2/2,500, (05-06-93, Christie-London, #188, illus.), image 19 x 13½ in., photograph, platinum-palladium print.

BI *Helen Bennett Modelling Schiaparelli Dress, New York,* 1940, p.l., s. Horst, sight 235 x 185mm, est. BP 5/800, (05-07-93, Sotheby-London, #330, illus.), photograph, color print.

$1543* *Mainbocher Corset,* 1939, p. 1986, s. Horst, image 240 x 190mm, (05-07-93, Sotheby-London, #328, illus.), photograph, silver print (BP 977, DM 2440, FR 8221, Y 169,896).

$2060* *"The Mainbocher Corset", Paris 1939,* p.l., s., stamped, t., num., lit., (10-29-92, Christie-London, #165, illus.), image 9½ x 7½ in., (24.1 x 19.1 cm.), photograph, gelatin silver print (BP 1320, DM 3169, FR 10,752, Y 255,172).

$2860* *Mainbocher Corset, Paris,* (1939), p.l., s., lit., (10-13-92, Christie-NY, #233, illus.), 12¾ x 9⅝ in., (32.4 x 24.4 cm.), photograph, gelatin silver print (BP 1666, DM 4190, FR 14,236, Y 346,793).

$2475* *Marlene Dietrich, 1947,* CNP (c) blindstamp on image, Vogue Studio stamp, Conde Nast Publications' (c) date stamp, (10-15-92, Sotheby-NY, #226, illus.), 9½ x 7½ in., (24.1 x 19.1 cm.), photograph, gelatin silver print (BP 1515, DM 3684, FR 12,494, Y 296,941).

$4025* *Phallic Lily, New York,* 1949, p.l., s.; s., edit. #13/25, (04-08-93, Christie-NY, #297, illus.), 15½ x 19¼ in., (39.4 x 48.9 cm.), photograph, platinum-palladium print (BP 2639, DM 6466, FR 21,887, Y 456,764).

$13,200* *Round The Clock, 1987,* s. by photog. in ink, s. twice, (c) by photog., i. Edition on paper 15 + 3 a.p., #1/15, #1 edit. 18, (10-15-92, Sotheby-NY, #226A, illus.), 23¼ x 19½ in., (59.1 x 49.5 cm.), photograph, platinum print (BP 8077, DM 19,649, FR 66,633, Y 1,583,683).

$2300* *"The Sting" (Two Callas),* photog. facsimile sig., blindstamp, s. by photog., t., d., #8/25 in unident. hand, 1945, p.l., (04-06-93, Sotheby-NY, #386, illus.), 15½ x 19⅜ in., photograph, platinum-palladium print (BP 1519, DM 3705, FR 12,548, Y 262,318).

$1815* *Suzy Parker In Balenciaga Dress, Vogue, Paris,* 1952, p.l., s. recto, s., #3/25, (05-06-93, Christie-London, #187, illus.), image 19 x 15 in., photograph, platinum-palladium print (BP 1150, DM 2859, FR 9624, Y 199,692).

BI *White Sleeve, Fashion Shot With Doris Zelensky, Paris,* (1936), p.l., s., num. 9/25, lit., est. $4/6,000, (10-13-92, Christie-NY, #231, illus.), 23 x 17¼ in., (58.4 x 43.8 cm.), photograph, platinum print.

HORST, Janssen b. 1919

$210* *"Visages",* d. 75, mono., (01-28-93, Pescheteau, #161), 16⅛ x 11¹³⁄₁₆ in., (41 x 30 cm.), black etching on wove (BP 139, DM 333, FR 1126, Y 26,074).

HORTER, Earl American 1881-1940

$22* *Continental Architectural Rendering,* s., (06-11-93, Freemn/Fine Art, #104), 10¾ x 8½ in., (27.3 x 21.6 cm.), etching (BP 14, DM 36, FR 121, Y 2334).

$33* *Continental Street Scenes: Two,* s., (06-11-93, Freemn/ Fine Art, #105), one 9¾ x 7¾ in., (24.8 x 19.7 cm.), other 10¼ x 5¾ in., (24.8 x 19.7 cm.), etching (BP 22, DM 54, FR 181, Y 3501).

$66* *Country Snow Scene,* s., (06-11-93, Freemn/Fine Art, #99), 8¼ x 11 in., (21 x 27.9 cm.), lithograph (BP 43, DM 107, FR 362, Y 7003).

$83* *"Gloucester",* s., (03-24-93, Grogan, #84), 7½ x 12 in., (19.1 x 30.5 cm.), aquatint (BP 56, DM 136, FR 461, Y 9752).

$143* *"The Kitchen, New Orleans",* s., pub. A.A.A., label verso, (10-16-92, Neal, #973), plate 12⅜ x 10⅜ in., (31.4 x 26.4 cm.), sheet 15 x 12½ in., (31.4 x 26.4 cm.), aquatint etching (BP 87, DM 211, FR 718, Y 17,075).

BI *"The Kitchen, New Orleans",* s. E. Horter, pub. AAA, est. $1/150, (12-12-92, A. James, #322), sheet 15 x 12½ in., (38.1 x 31.8 cm.), aquatint etching.

$99* *Locust Street, Philadelphia,* s., (06-11-93, Freemn/Fine Art, #106), 6 x 11¾ in., (15.2 x 29.8 cm.), etching (BP 65, DM 161, FR 542, Y 10,504).

$22* *Marketplace,* s., (06-11-93, Freemn/Fine Art, #103), 9¼ x 7½ in., (27.3 x 21.6 cm.), etching (BP 14, DM 36, FR 121, Y 2334).

BI *Ye Olde Curiosity Shop, Nantucket,* s., t., est. $100/150, (06-11-93, Freemn/Fine Art, #100), 8 x 13¼ in., (20.3 x 33.7 cm.), etching.

HORVAT, Frank

$920* *Bar In Soho, London,* s. by photog. in ink in margin, t., d., 1959, p.l., (04-06-93, Sotheby-NY, #222, illus.), 12⅜ x 10⅜ in., photograph (BP 608, DM 1482, FR 5019, Y 104,927).

BI *Deborah Dixon In Italian High Fashion (With Spaghetti), Rome,* s., t., d. by photog., 1962, p. 1989, est. $1,5/ 2,000, (10-15-92, Sotheby-NY, #561, illus.), 17¼ x 11⅝ in., (43.8 x 29.5 cm.), photograph, gelatin silver print.

$690* *"Givenchy Fashion At Longchamp Races",* 1959, p.l., s. twice, d., annot., (05-23-93, Butterfield, #3454, illus.), 10½ x 14½ in., photograph, gelatin silver print (BP 449, DM 1128, FR 3797, Y 76,268).

HORY, Elmyr de French 20th cent.

$483* *"El Abrazo",* after Picasso, s., #23/75, (03-17-93, Duran, #182, illus.), 29½ x 21¼ in., (74.9 x 54 cm.), lithograph (BP 333, DM 804, FR 2732, Y 56,650, P 57,500).

$158* *"El Concierto",* s., #16/75, (02-03-93, Duran, #225), 29½ x 20⅞ in., (75 x 53 cm.), color lithograph (BP 110, DM 260, FR 882, Y 19,654, P 18,400).

$316* *"Joven De Modigliani",* s., #16/75, (02-03-93, Duran, #226, illus.), 29½ x 20⅞ in., (75 x 53 cm.), lithograph (BP 221, DM 520, FR 1764, Y 39,308, P 36,800).

$184* *"Joven Entre Las Flores",* s., #25/75, (03-17-93, Duran, #180, illus.), 29½ x 21¼ in., (74.9 x 54 cm.), lithograph (BP 127, DM 306, FR 1041, Y 21,581, P 21,850).

$148* *"Paisaje Con Casas Y Arboles",* s., #6/75, (02-03-93, Duran, #224), 29½ x 20⅞ in., (75 x 53 cm.), color lithograph (BP 103, DM 244, FR 826, Y 18,410, P 17,250).

$271* *"Paisaje Con Lago",* s., #19/75, (03-17-93, Duran, #181, illus.), 21¼ x 29⁵⁄₁₆ in., (54 x 74.5 cm.), lithograph (BP 187, DM 451, FR 1533, Y 31,785, P 32,200).

HOSIASSON, Roziaccom

BI *Composition En Rouge,* s. artist's proof, small restored tear, ded. partially erased, est. FF4/500, (06-28-93, Loudmer, #59), 23¼ x 17⅛ in., (590 x 435 mm.), sh 31½ x 23⅝ in., (590 x 435 mm.), color lithograph on Arches wove.

HOSOE, Eikoh b. 1933

$920* *Bee And Woman,* 1964, p.l., s., #2/50; s., t., d., (04-08-93, Christie-NY, #490, illus.), 12¾ x 12½ in., (32.4 x 31.8 cm.), photograph, gelatin silver print (BP 603, DM 1478, FR 5003, Y 104,403).

BI *Breast With Rose,* 1962, p. 1990, s. twice, d., est. $6/ 800, (05-23-93, Butterfield, #3457, illus.), 8½ x 12½ in., photograph, gelatin silver print.

$1320* *Butoh Actor From Simon: A Private Landscape, 1970,* s. twice, (10-13-92, Christie-NY, #550, illus.), 14 x 9¼ in., (35.6 x 23.5 cm.), photograph, gelatin silver print (BP 769, DM 1934, FR 6570, Y 160,058).

$1100* *"Embrace #21",* 1971/later, English and Japanese sig., s., t., d., Dixon Collection, (11-16-92, Butterfield, #6012, illus.), 14½ x 21⁹⁄₁₆ in., (369 x 547.1 mm.), photograph, gelatin silver print (BP 724, DM 1754, FR 5908, Y 136,799).

$920* *"Fish And Woman",* 1964, p.l., Japanese sig., s., t., d., (05-23-93, Butterfield, #3456, illus.), 9¾ x 9 in., photograph, gelatin silver print (BP 599, DM 1504, FR 5063, Y 101,691).

$1320* *Kamaitachi #2,* (1968), p.l., s. in margin; s., t., d., (10-13-92, Christie-NY, #551, illus.), 12 x 9 in., (30.5 x 22.9 cm.), photograph, gelatin silver print (BP 769, DM 1934, FR 6570, Y 160,058).

$825* *"Kamatachi #26",* 1968/later, sig., t., d., Dixon Collection, (11-16-92, Butterfield, #6013, illus.), 14½ x 21⁷⁄₁₆ in., (369 x 543.9 mm.), photograph, gelatin silver print (BP 543, DM 1315, FR 4431, Y 102,599).

$489* *"Man And Woman #24",* 1960, p. 1989, s., d., photog.'s blindstamp, t., d., annot. For FOP, (05-23-93, Butterfield, #3458, illus.), 6 x 10 in., photograph, gelatin silver print (BP 318, DM 800, FR 2691, Y 54,051).

$440* *"Man And Woman #24" (Eikoh Hosoe, pl. 1),* 1960/1988, inits., d., s., t., i., (11-16-92, Butterfield, #6014, illus.), 6⅛ x 10 in., (155.9 x 254.5 mm.), photograph, gelatin silver print (BP 290, DM 702, FR 2363, Y 54,720).

$1150* *Man And Woman #33,* 1960, p.l., s., #5/50; s., t., d., (04-08-93, Christie-NY, #489, illus.), 14⅜ x 20⅝ in., (36.5 x 52.4 cm.), photograph, gelatin silver print (BP 754, DM 1847, FR 6253, Y 130,504).

BI *Sunflower Children, Arles, France, 1983,* s. in margin; s., t., d., est. $1,5/2,000, (10-13-92, Christie-NY, #552, illus.), 8 x 11 in., (20.3 x 27.9 cm.), photograph, gelatin silver print.

$1150* *"Woman And Bee",* 1964, p. 1990, s. twice, t., d., #5/50, (05-23-93, Butterfield, #3455, illus.), 12½ x 12½ in., photograph, gelatin silver print (BP 749, DM 1880, FR 6329, Y 127,114).

HOUBRAC, A.

$3474* *Le Petit Bleu,* p. Bourgerie & Co., defects, repaired tears, backed on linen, (05-07-93, Christie-S. Ken, #127, illus.), 36½ x 50½ in., (92.7 x 128.3 cm.), color lithograph (BP 2200, DM 5492, FR 18,508, Y 382,515).

$3474* *Le Petit Bleu,* p. Bourgerie & Cie, defects, backed on linen, (05-07-93, Christie-S. Ken, #126, illus.), 36½ x 50¾ in., (92.7 x 128.9 cm.), color lithograph (BP 2200, DM 5492, FR 18,508, Y 382,515).

HOUBRAKEN, Jakob 1698-1780

$121* *Portraits De J.A. Appelman, C. Bicker, A.R. Crombout, C. De Graeff, J.V. Hout, J. Huydecoper, G.V. Slingelandt, N. Struyck, M.V. Oostenryk: Nine,* stains, loss, wormholes, (05-15-93, Loudmer, #79), from 7 x 9⁹⁄₁₆ in., (178 x 236 mm.), to 4½ x 7⅛ in., (178 x 236 mm.), copper engraving on laid w/flower watermarks (BP 79, DM 195, FR 654, Y 13,413).

HOUSE, Gordon American contemporary

$55* *Celt Green,* s., d. 78/79, t., #12/80, prov., (05-16-93, Hindman, #617), 37 x 27 in., (94 x 68.6 cm.), color serigraph (BP 36, DM 88, FR 297, Y 6097).

$55* *Triangle F,* s., d. 71, t., #53/75, (05-16-93, Hindman, #615), 33½ x 17 in., (85.1 x 43.2 cm.), color serigraph (BP 36, DM 88, FR 297, Y 6097).

HOUSTIE, Ben

$40* *"Eagle And Sun", 1992,* s., t., #52/84, (03-10-93, Maynard, #319), print (BP 28, DM 67, FR 226, Y 4726, C$ 50).

$22* *"Frogs", 1992,* s., t., #65/200, (03-10-93, Maynard, #318), print (BP 15, DM 37, FR 124, Y 2599, C$ 28).

HOUSTON, Deryk

$111* *"Orchard",* #19/160, (03-10-93, Maynard, #327), 18 x 24 in., (45.7 x 61 cm.), silkscreen (BP 77, DM 185, FR 627, Y 13,114, C$ 138).

HOUSTON, R.

$1100* *"The Portrature Of White Hofe: "Babraham" "Newmarket" "Old Partner" "Lamrey" "Crab",* pub. 1756, (02-27-93, Dunning, #1197), 13¾ x 17 in., (34.9 x 43.2 cm.), hand colored aquatint (BP 773, DM 1808, FR 6145, Y 129,855).

HOUSTON, Robert

BI *Lake Scene At Sunset,* s., (12-11-92, G.A. Key, #17), 7 x 9 in., (17.8 x 22.9 cm.), etching.

$8 *Lake Scene At Sunset,* s., (04-16-93, G.A. Key, #118), 7 x 9 in., (17.8 x 22.9 cm.), etching (BP 5, DM 13, FR 44, Y 900).

HOWARD, F.

$55* *"First Blossom Of Spring", c. 1896,* stone s., (08-05-92, Boos, #732), sight 15½ x 19½ in., (394 x 495 mm.), color lithograph (BP 29, DM 81, FR 274, Y 7005).

HOWARD, Thomas

BI *Execution Of Ruth Snyder,* handstamp, notations, 1928, p. 1930's, est. $1/1,500, (10-14-92, Swann, #318, illus.), 2⅜ x 3⅛ in., (6 x 7.9 cm.), photograph, silver print.

HOWITT, Samuel (after)

$230* *A Collection Of Eleven Sporting Subjects, c. 1800,* margins, very good cond., Anthony N. B. Garvan Coll., (06-05-93, Christie-NY, #55), all approx. 6 x 8 in., (152 x 203 mm.), etching and aquatint w/hand-coloring, various paper (BP 151, DM 373, FR 1257, Y 24,673).

$152 *"Grouse Shooting", "Pheasant Shooting", "Snipe Shooting" and "Duck Shooting": Four,* (04-16-93, G.A. Key, #68A), 5 x 7 in., (12.7 x 17.8 cm.), hand-colored engraving (BP 100, DM 246, FR 830, Y 17,092).

$22* *Pheasant Shooting,* by J. Clark and H. Merke, (03-03-93, Bonhams-Chelsea, #77), image 12 x 17¼ in., (30.5 x 43.8 cm.), color reproduction of aquatint (BP 15, DM 36, FR 123, Y 2571).

HOWLETT, Robert 1831-1858

BI *The Stern Of "The Great Eastern", With Figures, 1857,* d. Dec. 3, 57 in neg., mounted, photog. blindstamp, est. $2,5/3,500, (04-06-93, Sotheby-NY, #49, illus.), 10⅞ x 13⅝ in., photograph, early albumen print.

HOWLETT, Robert and Georges DOWNES

$2179* *Isambard Kingdom Brunel Seated Beside The Launching Chains Of The Leviathan, November 1857,* stereoscopic card, (05-07-93, Sotheby-London, #7, illus.), photograph, albumen print (BP 1380, DM 3445, FR 11,609, Y 239,925).

HOWSON, Peter

$119* *The Boxer,* #25/40, s., (04-22-93, Bonhams-Chelsea, #89), image 11⅞ x 7⅝ in., (30.2 x 19.4 cm.), lithograph (BP 77, DM 191, FR 645, Y 13,084).

HOXIE, George b. 1907

BI *First Hour, 30 Cents,* 1940s, s., t., exhib. label, est. $8/1,000, (10-13-92, Christie-NY, #235, illus.), 13½ x 15¾ in., (34.3 x 40 cm.), photograph, gelatin silver print.

BI *George Lewis, c. 1945,* s., crayon i.; t., est. $1,2/1,800, (04-08-93, Christie-NY, #296, illus.), 16⅞ x 13⅝ in., (42.9 x 34.6 cm.), photograph, gelatin silver print.

$357* *Machinery Study,* sig., notations, handstamp, 1930's, (10-14-92, Swann, #480, illus.), 12½ x 7½ in., (31.8 x 19.1 cm.), photograph, silver print (BP 210, DM 522, FR 1772, Y 43,262).

$440* *Photogram,* photog.'s handstamp, 1940s, (04-07-93, Swann, #489, illus.), 8 x 9½ in., photograph, silver print (BP 291, DM 712, FR 2408, Y 49,989).

$412* *Portrait Of Paul Outerbridge,* photog.'s notations, 1940s, (04-07-93, Swann, #490, illus.), 9½ x 7½ in., photograph, silver print (BP 272, DM 666, FR 2255, Y 46,808).

HOYLAND, John English b. 1934

BI *Abstract,* s., d. '86, #20/40, est. BP 2/400, (10-07-92, Christie-S. Ken, #104), pl 10¾ x 9½ in., (27.3 x 24.1 cm.), etching p. in color.

BI *Hommage To Rothko: Untitled, 1973,* s., d., #61/75, pub. Mark Rothko Memorial Trust, full margins, good cond., creases, est. $5/700, (05-19-93, Butterfield, #2195), 20⅞ x 29¾ in., (530 x 756 mm.), lithograph in colors on T.H. Saunders.

HOYNINGEN-HUENE, George 1900-1968

$726* *"Dolores Del Rio", c. 1940,* s. Horst, i. Photo by Hoyningen-Huene, (05-06-93, Christie-London, #191), photograph, gelatin silver print from a 10 x 8in. neg. (BP 460, DM 1143, FR 3849, Y 79,877).

$3850* *"Horst And Model, Swimwear By Izod" (Hoyningen-Huene, cover),* 1930/later, p. by Horst, t., d., edit. 15/25, annot., Dixon Collection, (11-16-92, Butterfield, #6015, illus.), 19¹⁄₁₆ x 14¾ in., (483.5 x 375.3 mm.), photograph, platinum print (BP 2535, DM 6138, FR 20,677, Y 478,796).

$3025* *"Horst" (Horst),* 1931/later, by Horst, annot., Dixon Collection, (11-16-92, Butterfield, #6016, illus.), 7¾ x 9⅝ in., (197.2 x 244.9 mm.), photograph, platinum print (BP 1992, DM 4823, FR 16,246, Y 376,197).

$4600* *Male Studies: "Nude Torso" and "Study of A Young Man In White", 1930': Two,* (04-06-93, Sotheby-NY, #383, illus.), each approx. 9 x 7 in., photograph (BP 3038, DM 7411, FR 25,095, Y 524,635).

$4370* *Nude Study,* late 1930s, authenticated and annot. by Jorgensen, (04-08-93, Christie-NY, #298, illus.), 10 x 13⅜ in., (25.4 x 34 cm.), photograph, gelatin silver print (BP 2866, DM 7020, FR 23,763, Y 495,915).

$4180* *Tamara Toumanova, c. 1932,* (10-13-92, Christie-NY, #236, illus.), 7¾ x 13½ in., (19.7 x 34.3 cm.), photograph, toned gelatin silver print (BP 2434, DM 6124, FR 20,806, Y 506,851).

HRDLICKA, Alfred b. 1928

BI *Bildhauer-Atelier, 1973,* s., d., num., printer's crease, est. DM 300-, (09-25-92, Granier, #2886), sheet 19¾ x 25⁹⁄₁₆ in., (50.2 x 65 cm.), etching on BFK Rives.

BI *Die Dantonisten Am Morgen Ihrer Hinrichtung, 5 April 1794, 1989,* s., d., 37/70, pl. from "La Revolution Francaise" series, est. FF800/1,000, (06-28-93, Loudmer, #60), 14³⁄₁₆ x 23⅝ in., (360 x 600 mm.), sh 29¹⁵⁄₁₆ x 27¾ in., (360 x 600 mm.), black mezzotint on wove.

$540* *Figurliche Komposition, 1970,* s., d., num., mount staining, (12-01-92, Karl/Faber, #752), 9⅝ x 11¹³⁄₁₆ in., (24.5 x 30 cm.), mezzotint and drypoint on thin cardboard (BP 357, DM 861, FR 2933, Y 67,231).

$221* *Franz Josef Strauss (Lewin 754 II), 1978,* s., num., (12-05-92, Bassenge, #7275), 23³⁄₁₆ x 19½ in., (58.9 x 49.6 cm.), drypoint on copper print paper (BP 138, DM 345, FR 1174, Y 27,382).

$221* *Gute Kinderstube (Lewin 512), 1973,* s., num., (12-05-92, Bassenge, #7273), 15¾ x 19½ in., (40 x 49.5 cm.), etching on copper print paper (BP 138, DM 345, FR 1174, Y 27,382).

BI *Hommage A Basaglia (Lewin Band III.2, 711-715), 1980: Five,* #47/56, s., est. DM 1,500, (11-20-92, Lempertz, #598), 26⁹⁄₁₆ x 20½ in., (67.5 x 52 cm.), aquatint and mezzotint on Velin on BFK Rives.

$140* *Intermezzo In Munster,* s., (09-25-92, Granier, #2887), sheet 22⁹⁄₁₆ x 30¼ in., (57.3 x 76.8 cm.), lithograph on hand-made (BP 82, DM 208, FR 702, Y 16,898).

$369* *Jeunesse Dore (Lewin 751), 1978,* s., num., (12-05-92, Bassenge, #7274), 15⅝ x 19⁷⁄₁₆ in., (39.7 x 49.3 cm.), zinc etching on copper print paper (BP 231, DM 575, FR 1961, Y 45,719).

$929* *Lyon 1793 (L. 1070), 1985,* sheet 28 of series Die Franzosische Revolution, #37/70, s., (10-09-92, Winterberg, #2396, illus.), 23⁵⁄₁₆ x 39⅛ in., (59.2 x 99.4 cm.), drypoint, Roulette, and mezzotint on wove (BP 551, DM 1380, FR 4633, Y 113,100).

$929* *Nouveau Regime - Ancien Regime (L. 1044, III), 1985,* sheet 2 of series Die Franzosische Revolution, #37/70, s., (10-09-92, Winterberg, #2393, illus.), 23⁷⁄₁₆ x 39³⁄₁₆ in., (59.5 x 99.6 cm.), etching w/drypoint, Roulette and mezzotint on wove (BP 551, DM 1380, FR 4633, Y 113,100).

BI *Portraitstudie, 1983,* s., est. SF 150/200, (10-14-92, Germann, #325), 22⁷⁄₁₆ x 30 in., (570 x 762 mm.), lithograph.

$367* *Selbstportrat (Lewin 75 B), 1959,* s. 1961, d., #79/90, blindstamp, (06-12-93, Hauswedell/Nolt, #138), 9⅛ x 9¹⁵⁄₁₆ in., (23.2 x 25.3 cm.), etching on BFK Rives (BP 240, DM 597, FR 2008, Y 38,619).

$194* *Soldat Mit Gefangenen,* s., #7/99, (09-18-92, Schloss Ahlden, #1005), 25¹³⁄₁₆ x 19⁹⁄₁₆ in., (65.5 x 49.7 cm.), etching on BFK Rives (BP 114, DM 288, FR 985, Y 23,977).

$147* *Untitled,* s., (11-13-92, Koller, #5340), 20¹⁄₁₆ x 24³⁄₁₆ in., (51 x 61.5 cm.), lithograph on wove (BP 95, DM 231, FR 778, Y 18,245, SF 208).

BI *Zwei Aufgehangte, 1969,* s., d., E.A., est. DM 250, (09-18-92, Schloss Ahlden, #1004), 19⅝ x 25¹¹⁄₁₆ in., (49.8 x 65.2 cm.), etching on BFK Rives.

$117* *Zweikampf,* s., crease, (09-25-92, Granier, #2888), sheet 25⅞ x 20⁵⁄₁₆ in., (65.8 x 51.6 cm.), lithograph on hand-made (BP 68, DM 173, FR 586, Y 14,122).

BI *Zweikampf, 1958,* s., est. DM 400, (12-01-92, Karl/Faber, #753), 15³⁄₁₆ x 11 in., (38.5 x 28 cm.), lithograph on wove.

HRISCH, Holman W.

$55 *Fairies With Owl And Ravens: Two,* s., (02-05-93, G.A. Key, #43), each 5 x 4 in., (12.7 x 10.2 cm.), colored etching (BP 38, DM 91, FR 308, Y 6844).

HUARD, Charles 1874-1965

$100* *Bejot Bracquemond Bourget Gascogne Huard Luigini, c. 1900,* cond. B, (03-16-93, Boisgirard, #127), 29⅛ x 22¼ in., (74 x 56.5 cm.), poster (BP 69, DM 166, FR 565, Y 11,693).

HUBBELL, Marion Bingham American 20th cent.

BI *"Reflections, Nailed Down IV" and "Reflections, Upside Down Times I": Two,* s. Marion Bingham Hubbell, num. 4/4, 3/4, very good cond.?, est. $7/900, (11-21-92, Bakker, #49), image, one 15¼ x 7½ in., (38.7 x 19.1 cm.), the other 7¾ x 10½ in., (38.7 x 19.1 cm.), color lithograph.

HUBBUCH, Karl 1891-1979

$1155* *"Freiburg" (Riester 82), 1924,* s., num., (11-28-92, Grisebach, #564, illus.), 11⅞ x 12⅜ in., (30.1 x 31.4 cm.), drypoint on copper print paper (BP 762, DM 1840, FR 6247, Y 143,746).

BI *Die Mussestunde Des Herrn Obermtsrichters, 1923,* i. II, s., num., est. DM 800, (11-28-92, Schoppmann, #592), 10¹³⁄₁₆ x 10³⁄₁₆ in., (27.5 x 25.9 cm.), etching on copper print board.

$7219* *"Notausgange Der Ehe (George Grosz Gewidmet)" (Riester 69), 1923,* s., num., foxed, (11-28-92, Grisebach, #216, illus.), 15⁷⁄₁₆ x 14⅛ in., (39.2 x 35.8 cm.), lithograph on thin cardboard (BP 4765, DM 11,501, FR 39,043, Y 898,444).

$369* *Sitzende Junge Frau Im Profil Nach Rechts,* s., num., (12-05-92, Bassenge, #7280), 9⅜ x 7⁹⁄₁₆ in., (23.8 x 19.2 cm.), etching on copper print paper (BP 231, DM 575, FR 1961, Y 45,719).

$1106* *Die Tragodie Eine Schone Frau Zu Haben, 1921,* s., t., d., (12-05-92, Bassenge, #7279), 9¾ x 12¹¹⁄₁₆ in., (24.7 x 32.3 cm.), drypoint on thin cardboard (BP 693, DM 1724, FR 5877, Y 137,034).

$6497* *"Der Untertan" (Riester 79), 1923,* s., d., num., (11-28-92, Grisebach, #217, illus.), 13³⁄₁₆ x 18¹³⁄₁₆ in., (33.5 x 47.8 cm.), lithograph on copper print paper (BP 4288, DM 10,350, FR 35,138, Y 808,587).

$1631* *"Der Zersplitterte Baum" (Riester 61), 1922,* s., d., (06-05-93, Grisebach, #652, illus.), 7⁵⁄₁₆ x 8½ in., (18.5 x 21.6 cm.), drypoint on copper print paper (BP 1074, DM 2644, FR 8913, Y 174,962).

HUBER, Wolf German 1490-1553

$22,908* *Die Darbringung Im Tempel (Hollstein 4; Geisberg-Strauss 878, Winzinger 264), c. 1512-1513,* (06-23-93, Kornfeld, #58, illus.), woodcut (BP 15,563, DM 38,761, FR 130,381, Y 2,495,697, SF 34,500).

HUBERLAND, Morris

$374* *"Harlem",* 1940s, s., t., d., photog.'s stamp, (05-23-93, Butterfield, #3459, illus.), 9½ x 7½ in., photograph, gelatin silver print (BP 244, DM 612, FR 2058, Y 41,340).

HUCET, Urbain

$108* *Sunday In The Ile De France,* plate t.; s., #59/350, stamped pub.'s blindstamp, (06-08-93, Ritchie, #45), image 26 x 19½ in., (66 x 49.5 cm.), color lithograph (BP 71, DM 175, FR 590, Y 11,471, C$ 138).

HUDSON, Erlund

$68* *Fireside Study,* s., i., margins, (04-22-93, Bonhams-Chelsea, #86), image 7 x 4¾ in., (17.8 x 12.1 cm.), etching (BP 44, DM 109, FR 369, Y 7477).

HUDSON, L. 19th-20th century

$750* *Courting Scenes: A Pair,* each bears sig., i. on labels, (02-04-93, Sloan, #1492), each 10½ x 6¼ in., (26.7 x 15.9 cm.), chromolithograph on panel (BP 524, DM 1235, FR 4188, Y 93,295).

HUEBLER

$96* *Although It Is Customary..., 1979,* s., d., #12/25, margins, good cond., (05-27-93, Sotheby-Amstrdm, #633), sh 19⅞ x 14⅛ in., (505 x 358 mm.), color silkscreen on wove (BP 61, DM 154, FR 519, Y 10,292, G 173).

HUEBLER, Douglas American b. 1924

$4950* *Site Sculpture Project: Cape Cod Star Shape Exchange,* s. twice, d. 1968, two maps, prov., exhib., Sylvio Perlstein Coll., (11-18-92, Sotheby-NY, #219, illus.), photographs 36¼ x 28 in., (92.1 x 71.1 cm.), maps framed 36¼ x 28 in., (92.1 x 71.1 cm.), ink on paper and collage framed together w/six b/w photographs framed together (BP 3259, DM 7892, FR 26,584, Y 615,595).

$4888* *Variable Piece #64,* s., t., d. October, 1971, prov., exhib., (02-23-93, Sotheby-NY, #311, illus.), framed 27½ x 35¼ in., (69.9 x 89.5 cm.), 3 photographs, 1 typed sheet of paper mounted on paper board (BP 3348, DM 7897, FR 26,784, Y 570,895).

$4025* *Variable Piece #99, Israel: Seven,* s., t., d. July, 1973, prov., exhib., lit., Sylvio Perlstein Coll., (05-04-93, Sotheby-NY, #131, illus.), 31 x 31 in., (78.7 x 78.7 cm.), color photograph, typed text on paper and pastel on board mounted onboard (BP 2569, DM 6341, FR 21,364, Y 442,746).

HUET, Jean Baptiste   1745-1811
BI *Das Letzte Abendmahl, Unter Draperie In Grossem Palastraum, 1792,* after Francois Boucher, trimmed, est. DM 600-, (09-14-92, Venator/Hansten, #1518), sh 8¹¹⁄₁₆ x 12¹¹⁄₁₆ in., (22 x 32.2 cm.), etching.

HUET, Paul   French 1803-1869
$839* *Le Heron (L. Delteil, 7), 1833,* first state of three before letter, reddish, creases, tear, good margins, (06-11-93, Picard, #73), 9⅝ x 13¾ in., (245 x 350 mm.), etching on chine fixe (BP 551, DM 1364, FR 4597, Y 89,019).

$320* *La Maison Du Garde (L.D., 9), 1833,* second state of three w/letter, reddish stains, drystamp, good margins, (06-11-93, Picard, #74), 8⁷⁄₁₆ x 11¹³⁄₁₆ in., (215 x 300 mm.), etching on chine fixe (BP 210, DM 520, FR 1753, Y 33,952).

$716* *Palais Des Papes A Avignon (D. 20), 1834,* definitive state, staining, untrimmed margins, ex-coll., rare, (02-24-93, Picard, #129), etching on old laid (BP 499, DM 1162, FR 3941, Y 84,018).

$81* *Saulee Aux Environs De Paris (L. Delteil 19), 1830(?),* definitive state, dirt spots, large margins, (02-03-93, Ader Tajan, #164), 5 x 9⅝ in., (12.7 x 24.5 cm.), etching (BP 57, DM 133, FR 452, Y 10,076).

HUFFMAN, Laton Alton   American 1854-1931
$138* *"Buffalo Grazing",* s. in plate, (10-24-92, Dunning, #1485, illus.), 9 x 13⅞ in., (22.9 x 35.2 cm.), callotype (BP 88, DM 213, FR 722, Y 16,864).

$1760* *"Hot Noon Beside The Roundup Camp", BBW205, "The Day's Work", BB10 157-161, "Sioux Chief Spotted Eagle, Wana Logo Lisea, 1880", "A Crow Warrior" D45, "Portrait Of Two Indian Men" D135 and "Chief American Horse", D22: Ten,* vintage, (11-28-92, Dunning, #1058), photograph (BP 1162, DM 2804, FR 9519, Y 219,042).

$275* *Northern Range Montana, January, 1882,* t., stamped sig., (11-28-92, Dunning, #1057), 13½ x 10½ in., (34.3 x 26.7 cm.), photograph (BP 182, DM 438, FR 1487, Y 34,225).

HUG, Fritz   1921-1989
$114* *Edelhirsch, 1971,* s., (11-13-92, Koller, #5344), sheet 14¹⁵⁄₁₆ x 11 in., (38 x 28 cm.), lithograph on print paper (BP 74, DM 179, FR 603, Y 14,149, SF 162).

$287* *Fluchtende Wildschweine, 1986,* i., s., d., (11-13-92, Koller, #5346), 14¹⁵⁄₁₆ x 21¼ in., (38 x 54 cm.), lithograph on wove (BP 185, DM 451, FR 1519, Y 35,621, SF 406).

$180* *Hunde, 1986,* i., s., d., (11-13-92, Koller, #5347), 21¼ x 29¹⁵⁄₁₆ in., (54 x 76 cm.), lithograph on wove (BP 116, DM 283, FR 953, Y 22,341, SF 255).

$348* *Igel, 1982,* Epreuve X/XIX, s., d., (04-21-93, Germann, #539), 14¹⁵⁄₁₆ x 20⅞ in., (380 x 530 mm.), color lithograph (BP 226, DM 556, FR 1881, Y 38,525, SF 506).

$246* *Nilpferd Mit Jungen, 1986,* i., s., d., (11-13-92, Koller, #5348), sheet 21¼ x 14¹⁵⁄₁₆ in., (54 x 38 cm.), lithograph on wove (BP 159, DM 386, FR 1302, Y 30,532, SF 348).

$308* *Zwei Vogel, 1967,* 198/250, s., d., (10-14-92, Germann, #548), 12⅝ x 18½ in., (320 x 470 mm.), color lithograph (BP 181, DM 451, FR 1529, Y 37,324, SF 401).

HUGENTOBLER, Iwan Edwin   1886-1972
$553* *Dragoneroffizier Zu Pferde, 1917,* s., d., (06-24-93, Germann, #657), 25 x 31¹¹⁄₁₆ in., (635 x 805 mm.), lithograph (BP 364, DM 897, FR 3022, Y 59,322, SF 805).

BI *Zwei Reiter, 1915,* s. in plate, d., est. SF 220/240, (10-14-92, Germann, #551), 21½ x 15¹⁄₁₆ in., (546 x 382 mm.), aquatint/drypoint.

HUGGINS, William John   English 1781-1845
$43* *A Man-Of-War In Open Seas,* plate s., (12-01-92, Ritchie, #2), 8⅛ x 10⅛ in., (20.6 x 25.7 cm.), hand-colored engraving (BP 28, DM 69, FR 234, Y 5354, C$ 55).

HUGHES, Arthur (after)
$132* *The Violinist,* foxing, (06-16-93, Bonhams-Chelsea, #508), image 27 x 16 in., (68.6 x 40.6 cm.), photogravure w/ hand-coloring (BP 88, DM 219, FR 735, Y 14,078).

BI *The Violinist,* foxing, est. BP1/200, (01-21-93, Bonhams-Chelsea, #147), image 27 x 16 in., (68.6 x 40.6 cm.), photogravure w/hand-coloring.

HUGHES, Griffith   English 18th cent.
$110* *"Guaiacum", "Incrusted Sea Rods", and "Physic-Nut", 1750: Three,* from "Natural History of Barbados", 4to., (12-10-92, Sloan, #1017), handcolored etchings (BP 71, DM 174, FR 594, Y 13,607).

HUGHES, Patrick
BI *"Moonroom" and "Sunscraper", 1980: Two,* s., t., first #33/90, second. #63/90, good cond., (12-12-92, Weschler, #127), each 27 x 21 in., (68.6 x 53.3 cm.), silkscreen.

HUGHES-STANTON, Blair
BI *The Pilgrims Progress, 1928,* set of six w/two vignettes, each s., d., t., #7/12, full margins, good cond., est. BP 4/600, (12-03-92, Sotheby-London, #172, illus.), wood engravings on Japan.

HUGNET, Georges   1906-1974
BI *Huit Jours A Trebaumec (L'Amour Fou, figs. 195 and 196),* book designed by Henri Mercher, illus. w/82 mounted photos of photo-collages made by Hugnet in 1947, text handwritten ink by photog., folio, leavesloose, lettered A, s. by Hugnet and Mercher, est. $8/12,000, (04-06-93, Sotheby-NY, #264A, illus.), photos approx. 4¾ x 3½ in., photograph.

BI *Nous Inventames..., 1934,* label, prov., est. $2,5/3,000, (10-13-92, Christie-NY, #237, illus.), 9 x 7 in., (22.9 x 17.8 cm.), photograph, collage of halftone elements.

BI *Untitled,* from book "1961", inits., d. in ink, prov., est. $1,8/2,200, (10-13-92, Christie-NY, #553, illus.), 9¼ x 6 in., (23.5 x 15.2 cm.), photograph, half-tone collage.

HUGO, Charles   French 1826-1871
BI *Portrat Victor Hugo, 1852/53,* lit., est. DM 5,000, (11-12-92, Lempertz, #101, illus.), 3¹¹⁄₁₆ x 2⅞ in., (9.3 x 7.3 cm.), photograph, salt print (calotype).

BI *Portrat Victor Hugo, 1852/53,* lit., est. DM 5,000, (11-12-92, Lempertz, #102, illus.), 3⅞ x 2¹³⁄₁₆ in., (9.9 x 7.2 cm.), photograph, salt print (calotype).

BI *Portrat Victor Hugo, 1852/53,* lit., est. DM 4,500, (11-12-92, Lempertz, #103, illus.), 4⅛ x 3⅛ in., (10.4 x 8 cm.), photograph, salt print (calotype).

HUGO, Leopold
$230* *Selected Works, Cypress Trees At Monterey Bay: Two,* 1920s, edit., photog.'s stamp, second s., (05-23-93, Butterfield, #3461, illus.), one 6 x 4 in., other 9 x 7⅛ in., photograph, gelatin silver print (BP 150, DM 376, FR 1266, Y 25,423).

$230* *Selected Works, Trees At Monterey Bay: Two,* 1920s, first s., each edit., photog.'s stamp, (05-23-93, Butterfield, #3462, illus.), one 9 x 7 in., other 8 x 6 in., photograph, gelatin silver print (BP 150, DM 376, FR 1266, Y 25,423).

$374* *Selected Works, Views Of The Monterey Coast: Nine,* 1920s, several toned, s., (05-23-93, Butterfield, #3460, illus.), from 5 x 7 in., to 10 x 12 in., photograph, gelatin silver print (BP 244, DM 612, FR 2058, Y 41,340).

HUGO D'ALESI (Frederic ALEXIANU)   1849-1906
$181* *P.L.M. Le Mont Cervin, c. 1895,* Paris-Bordeaux, Imp. Bellier and Cie, cond. B, (06-11-93, Boisgirard, #93), 41¾ x 29¾ in., (106 x 75.5 cm.), poster (BP 119, DM 294, FR 992, Y 19,204).

$221* *Paris Lyon Mediterranee. Hyres, c. 1895,* Paris, Ateliers F. Hugo d'Alesi, cond. B+, (06-11-93, Boisgirard, #94), 42½ x 29¹⁵⁄₁₆ in., (108 x 76 cm.), poster (BP 145, DM 359, FR 1211, Y 23,448).

HUGO D'ALESI, F.

$180* *PLM. Le Vercours. Dauphine. Billets A Prix Reduits, c. 1900,* fairly good cond., (03-15-93, Arcole, #41), 41¾ x 29⅛ in., (106 x 74 cm.), (BP 125, DM 299, FR 1016, Y 21,322).

$239* *PLM: Algerie. Gorges D'El Kantara Et Cavaliers Arabes. 1892,* good cond., (03-13-93, Laurin, #48), 41¾ x 29½ in., (106 x 75 cm.), (BP 167, DM 398, FR 1353, Y 28,167).

$199* *Tunisie, c. 1890,* good cond., (03-13-93, Laurin, #68), 40³⁄₁₆ x 28⅜ in., (102 x 72 cm.), (BP 139, DM 331, FR 1126, Y 23,453).

HUGON, R.

$419* *"P.O. And Midi: Pyrenees Auvergne, Plaisirs De Neige", 1936 and "AirFrance Et Ch. De Fer Francais: 'Avec Les Billets Combines Air Fer, Vous Quittez L'Un, Vous Prenez L'Autre'": Two,* good cond., (01-23-93, Ribeyre/Baron, #5), one 39⁹⁄₁₆ x 24⁷⁄₁₆ in., (99.5 x 62 cm.), other 39⅜ x 24⁷⁄₁₆ in., (99.5 x 62 cm.), poster (BP 274, DM 666, FR 2254, Y 52,441).

$309* *SNCF. 8 Jours De Neige, Une Annee De Joues Roses, 1938,* good cond., (03-15-93, Arcole, #97), 38¹⁵⁄₁₆ x 24⅝ in., (99 x 62.5 cm.), (BP 215, DM 513, FR 1745, Y 36,603).

$419* *SNCF. Plaisirs De Neige, 1938,* very good cond., (03-15-93, Arcole, #95), 39⅜ x 24⁷⁄₁₆ in., (100 x 62 cm.), (BP 292, DM 696, FR 2366, Y 49,633).

$210* *SNCF: Lunchon Superbagneres, 1937,* excell. cond., (01-23-93, Ribeyre/Baron, #114), 39⅜ x 24⁷⁄₁₆ in., (100 x 62 cm.), poster (BP 137, DM 334, FR 1130, Y 26,283).

HUJAR, Peter American b. 1934

$920* *Candy Darling, 1973,* s., t., d. by photog., (04-06-93, Sotheby-NY, #468, illus.), photograph (BP 608, DM 1482, FR 5019, Y 104,927).

$550* *David Wojnarowicz, c. 1984,* estate stamp, (10-15-92, Sotheby-NY, #562, illus.), photograph, gelatin silver print (BP 337, DM 819, FR 2776, Y 65,987).

HULL, E.

$112* *A Neat Start Pleasant, But Wrong,* pub. Charles Tilt, 1833, (03-03-93, Bonhams-Chelsea, #216), image 6½ x 10 in., (16.5 x 25.4 cm.), hand-colored lithograph (BP 77, DM 184, FR 626, Y 13,087).

HULME, F.W. (after)

$14 *"Sherborne Lodge, Dorset",* (02-05-93, G.A. Key, #57), 7 x 11 in., (17.8 x 27.9 cm.), tinted lithograph (BP 10, DM 23, FR 78, Y 1742).

HULOT, S.

$105* *Ch. De Fer De L'Etat: Dreux, "Vieille Cite Dans La Verdure", 1925,* excell. cond., (01-23-93, Ribeyre/Baron, #62), 39⁹⁄₁₆ x 24⅝ in., (100.5 x 62.5 cm.), poster (BP 69, DM 167, FR 565, Y 13,141).

$398* *Ch. De Fer De L'Etat: Sables D'Or Les Pins, "Casino, Golf, Tennis", c. 1930,* excell. cond., (01-23-93, Ribeyre/Baron, #63), 39⅜ x 24⁷⁄₁₆ in., (100 x 62 cm.), poster (BP 260, DM 633, FR 2141, Y 49,812).

HUMAIR, Daniel b. 1929

$110* *Untitled,* #208/290, (04-04-93, Pescheteau, #226), 27³⁄₁₆ x 17¹¹⁄₁₆ in., (69 x 45 cm.), color photolithograph (BP 72, DM 177, FR 600, Y 12,524).

$96* *Untitled, 1979,* s., #177/190, full sheet p. to edges, good cond., (05-27-93, Sotheby-Amstrdm, #424), sh 29½ x 21⅛ in., (750 x 537 mm.), colored lithograph on wove (BP 61, DM 154, FR 519, Y 10,292, G 173).

$128* *Untitled, 1979,* s., #186/190, full sheet p. to edges, good cond., (05-27-93, Sotheby-Amstrdm, #425, illus.), sh 29⁵⁄₁₆ x 20⅞ in., (745 x 530 mm.), colored lithograph on wove (BP 82, DM 205, FR 692, Y 13,722, G 230).

$96* *Untitled, 1979,* s., #84/190, full sheet p. to edges, good cond., (05-27-93, Sotheby-Amstrdm, #426), sh 21⅛ x 29½ in., (537 x 750 mm.), colored lithograph on wove (BP 61, DM 154, FR 519, Y 10,292, G 173).

HUMBLOT, Robert

$206* *Le Guilvinec,* s., annot., good margins, (05-06-93, Laurin, #44), color lithograph (BP 131, DM 324, FR 1092, Y 22,665).

HUNDERTWASSER, Friedensreich Austrian b. 1928

$943* *10002 Nights Homo Homus Come Va How Do You Do (K. 83), 1982,* s., #3110/10002, pub. Die Galerie, good cond., (06-30-93, Sotheby-London, #459, illus.), sh 27⅜ x 19⅝ in., (695 x 498 mm.), color lithograph w/silkscreen and metallic addition on wove (BP 632, DM 1608, FR 5426, Y 101,039).

$1115* *10002 Nights Homo Homus Come Va How Do You Do (K. 83), 1982,* s., #3135/10002, pub. Die Galerie, good cond., rubbing, (06-30-93, Sotheby-London, #460), sh 27⅜ x 19⅝ in., (695 x 498 mm.), color lithograph w/ silkscreen and metallic addition on wove (BP 747, DM 1902, FR 6415, Y 119,469).

$1415* *10002 Nights Homo Humus Come A Va How Do You Do, (K. 83), 1984,* ink s., num. 8567/10002, pub. Die Galerie, Offenbach-am-Main, good cond., (12-01-92, Christie-London, #612), S. 27³⁄₁₆ x 19½ in., (690 x 495 mm.), screenprint and photolithograph in colors, w/metal imprint, on wove (BP 935, DM 2255, FR 7686, Y 176,170).

$1941* *10002 Nights Homo Humus Come Va How Do You Do (Kotschatzky 83), 1984,* 2605/10001., s., (10-14-92, Germann, #330, illus.), 27⁵⁄₁₆ x 19⅝ in., (693 x 498 mm.), color serigraph w/metal stamp (BP 1139, DM 2841, FR 9633, Y 235,216, SF 2530).

$1791* *Die Augen Des Machu Picchu (HWG 23), 1966,* s. Hundertwasser, 94/132, (09-30-92, Kunsthallen, #131), color lithograph (BP 1010, DM 2540, FR 8590, Y 214,929, DK 9775).

BI *The Boy With The Green Hair (Koschatsky 26), 1967,* s., d., #6/100, pub. Galerie Karl Flinker, full margins, good cond.,light/mount-staining, defects, discoloration, est. BP 1/1,500, (06-30-93, Sotheby-London, #455, illus.), 20½ x 14⅝ in., (521 x 371 mm.), color lithograph on wove.

$1100* *Columbus Rainy Day In India (K. 49), 1971-72,* stamp s., num. 00692/3000, pub. Ars Viva, p. by Dietz Offizin, margins, apparently good cond., (02-24-93, Butterfield, #2743), 17¾ x 23 in., (451 x 584 mm.), silkscreen in colors w/metal imprints on wove (BP 767, DM 1786, FR 6054, Y 129,078).

$935* *Crusade Of The Crossroads (K. 53), 1971-72,* stamp s., num. 1381/3000, from Look At It On A Rainy Day portfolio, pub. Ars Viva, margins, apparently good cond., (02-24-93, Butterfield, #2744), 15 x 21⅝ in., (381 x 549 mm.), silkscreen in colors w/metal imprints & ground glass on tarred brownpaper (BP 652, DM 1518, FR 5146, Y 109,716).

$2750* *Exodus Into Space (K. 47), 1972-72,* ink s., #172/300, stamp num. 1714/3000, from portfolio Look at it ona Rainy Day, blindstamp pub. Ars Viva, full margins, good cond., discoloration, glue/paper remains, (10-28-92, Butterfield, #2654, illus.), 16⅜ x 23⅜ in., (416 x 594 mm.), color silkscreen w/metal imprints on wove (BP 1752, DM 4247, FR 14,421, Y 337,423).

$3001* *Fall In Cloud-Fall In Fog-Fall Out (Gruener Janura, 1980; Werkverzeicnis Nr. 780), 1973,* 156/199, s., d., (06-24-93, Germann, #384, illus.), 11⁷⁄₁₆ x 13¾ in., (290 x 350 mm.), 3-D object nach Zolle w/color serigraph on 5 sheets of plexiglas (BP 1976, DM 4865, FR 16,399, Y 321,927, SF 4370).

$147* *Fem Kompositioner: Five,* s. Poul Janus Ipsen 1974, (03-24-93, Kunsthallen, #141), etching (BP 100, DM 240, FR 817, Y 17,272, DK 920).

$1433* *Flucht Ins All (Hundertwasser 650 A), 1971-72,* plate 4 from Regentag, embossed stamp, #2782/3000, (05-27-93, Lempertz, #800), 19⁷⁄₁₆ x 26⅜ in., (49.3 x 67 cm.), color serigraph on half board (BP 918, DM 2299, FR 7750, Y 153,623).

$2739* *Gib Acht Wenn Du Uber Die Prarie Gehst (HWG 68 A & B), 1976,* s. Hundertwasser, 51/214, (09-30-92, Kunsthallen, #130), color etching and aquatint (BP 1545, DM 3884, FR 13,137, Y 328,693, DK 14,950).

BI *Good Morning City (K. 41), 1969-70,* s., #3646/10,000, pub. Dorothea Leonhart, margins, good cond., handling creases, paper discoloration, est. BP 1,2/1,500, (06-30-93, Sotheby-London, #456, illus.), 30⅛ x 19¼ in., (765 x 489 mm.), color silkscreen on stiff card.

$1561* *Good Morning City (Koschatzky 41),* s., d., num., relief stamp, (06-05-93, Schoppmann, #878), 30⅛ x 18½ in.,

(76.5 x 47 cm.), color serigraph and metal embossing on hand-made board (BP 1028, DM 2531, FR 8530, Y 167,453).

$1378* *Good Morning City (Koschatzky 41), 1969-1970,* s., 3646/10,000, blindstamp, (12-04-92, AB Stockholm, #7067), 30⅛ x 19⁵⁄₁₆ in., (76.5 x 49 cm.), serigraph in colors (BP 884, DM 2195, FR 7445, Y 172,035, SK 9350).

$2213* *Good Morning City - Bleeding Town, 1969,* s., d., num., (12-05-92, Bassenge, #7281), 33¼ x 21¹⁵⁄₁₆ in., (84.5 x 55.8 cm.), color screenprint with Folienpragung on thin Fabriano cardboard (BP 1386, DM 3450, FR 11,759, Y 274,192).

$1468* *Good Morning City Bleeding Town (Series KK), c. 1971,* num. 7108, d., p. by Studio Quattro, good cond., creases, (11-30-92, Phillips-London, #533), sheet 33½ x 22 in., (851 x 559 mm.), color silkscreen & embossing on thick wove (BP 969, DM 2339, FR 7939, Y 182,701).

$1248* *Good Morning City, (HWG 41), 1969-79,* s. Hundertwasser 686, Serie Q, 3301/10,000, (03-24-93, Kunsthallen, #137), color serigraph (BP 845, DM 2038, FR 6937, Y 146,634, DK 7820).

$4302* *Good Morning City, 1969-70,* s., 4325/10000, blindstamp Fabriano, (05-25-93, AB Stockholm, #25, illus.), 30⅛ x 19⁵⁄₁₆ in., (76.5 x 49 cm.), serigraph in colors m. metall-pragling (BP 2788, DM 7007, FR 23,586, Y 470,215, SK 6270).

$2420* *Good Morning City, Bleeding Town, #8085/10,000,* (10-18-92, Hindman, #479, illus.), 33½ x 22 in., (85.1 x 55.9 cm.), color lithograph (BP 1481, DM 3602, FR 12,216, Y 290,342).

$1837* *Good Morning City, Bleeding Town (Oeuvre Kat. 686), 1969,* s., d., Form, t., #7616/10000, stamped, (06-12-93, Hauswedell/Nolt, #140), 30⅛ x 17½ in., (76.5 x 44.5 cm.), color screenprint w/metal embossing on Fabriano wove (BP 1202, DM 2990, FR 10,049, Y 193,307).

BI *Good Morning City: Color Series T (Koschatzky 41), 1969-70,* s., d., i. pen and black ink, #3848, pub. D. Leonhart, margins, tape, very good cond., est. BP 800/1,000, (05-20-93, Christie-London, #444, illus.), image 32 x 20¾ in., (81.3 x 52.7 cm.), sheet 33¼ x 22 in., (81.3 x 52.7 cm.), screenprint in colors, w/metal imprints on wove.

BI *Good Morning City: Color Series X (Koschatzky K. 41), 1969-70,* s., d., i. pen and black ink, #4444 (corrected), pub. D. Leonhart, margins, deckle edge, very good cond., est. BP 800/1,000, (05-20-93, Christie-London, #445, illus.), image 32 x 20¾ in., (81.3 x 52.7 cm.), sheet 33¼ x 22 in., (81.3 x 52.7 cm.), screenprint in colors w/ metal imprints on wove.

$1199* *Good Morning City: Colour Series RR (K. 41), 1969-70,* ink s., d., i., num. 8477, pub. D. Leonhart, margins, mounting, dirt,very good cond., (12-01-92, Christie-London, #604), L. 31⅞ x 20¹¹⁄₁₆ in., (810 x 525 mm.), screenprint in colors, w/metal imprints on wove (BP 792, DM 1911, FR 6513, Y 149,278).

$1249* *Good Morning City; Series W (K. 41), 1969-70,* s., d., i. in ink, num. 4281, pub. D. Leonhart, margins, very good cond., (12-01-92, Christie-London, #605), L. 31⅞ x 20¹¹⁄₁₆ in., (810 x 525 mm.), screenprint in colors, w/ metal imprints on wove (BP 825, DM 1991, FR 6784, Y 155,503).

BI *Homage To Schroder - Sonnenstern (K. 56), 1972,* ink s., #18/46, s. Schroder-Sonnenstern, pub. Ars Viva, margins, goodcond. (?), discoloration, est. BP 1,5/2,000, (12-03-92, Sotheby-London, #352, illus.), approx. 36½ x 24 in., (927 x 610 mm.), silkscreen on wove.

BI *Homage To Schroder-Sonnenstern (K. 56), 1972,* s., #18/46, s. by Schroder-Sonnenstern, pub. Ars Viva, margins, goodcond.?, discoloration, est. BP 7/900, (06-30-93, Sotheby-London, #463), c. 36½ x 24 in., (927 x 610 mm.), silkscreen on wove.

BI *Homage To Schroder-Sonnenstern (K. 56), 1972,* ink s., #294/416, s. by Sonnenstern, d., pub. Ars Viva, margins, good cond.?, creases, est. $1/1,500, (10-28-92, Butterfield, #2655), 34 x 25½ in., (864 x 648 mm.), color silkscreen w/metal imprints on wove.

$1468* *Homage To Schroder-Sonnerstern, 1972,* stamped sig., num. 218/416, s., d. by Sonnerstern, pub. Dietz Offizia,

full margins, good cond., 1 cm. tear, (11-30-92, Phillips-London, #532), sheet 39⅞ x 27¾ in., (101.3 x 70.5 cm.), color silkscreen & embossing on thick cream wove (BP 969, DM 2339, FR 7939, Y 182,701).

BI *Hommage A Schroder-Sonnenstern (Hundertwasser 715), 1972,* s., #405/416, est. DM 2,500-, (05-27-93, Lempertz, #802), 39⅜ x 27½ in., (100 x 69.8 cm.), color serigraph w/metal embossing and thread application on thick wove.

$435* *Hommage A Schroder-Sonnenstern (Koschatzky 56; Werkverzeichnis 715),1972,* #3906/4200, stamp sig., (04-21-93, Germann, #547), 39⅜ x 27⁹⁄₁₆ in., (100 x 70 cm.), color serigraph w/metal embossing (BP 282, DM 695, FR 2351, Y 48,157, SF 633).

BI *Hommage A Schroder-Sonnenstern (Koschatzky 56b), 1972,* #2213/4200, stamped sig., est. DM 1,200, (11-20-92, Lempertz, #600), sh 39⅜ x 27⁹⁄₁₆ in., (100 x 70 cm.), poster w/metal embossing on thick gray-green hand-made.

$1343* *Hommage A Schroder-Sonnenstern (Koschatzky Nr. 56; Werkverzeichnis 71), 1972,* #343/416, s., d., relief stamp, (04-21-93, Germann, #548), 39⅜ x 27⁹⁄₁₆ in., (100 x 70 cm.), serigraph in 8 colors w/metal stamp in 5 colors on gray-brown paper (BP 871, DM 2147, FR 7259, Y 148,677, SF 1955).

$1515* *Hommage A Schroder-Sonnenstern (Koschatzky, Hundertwasser 56a), 1972,* #407/416, ink s., (11-20-92, Lempertz, #599), sh 39⅜ x 27½ in., (100 x 69.8 cm.), serigraph in color w/metal embossing and felting on thick Velin (BP 997, DM 2415, FR 8136, Y 188,409).

$747* *Hommage A Schroder-Sonnenstern, 1971,* num., (12-01-92, Karl/Faber, #757), sh 39⅜ x 27⁹⁄₁₆ in., (100 x 70 cm.), color serigraph w/metal print on thick hand-made cardboard (BP 494, DM 1191, FR 4058, Y 93,003).

$543* *Hommage A Schroder-Sonnenstern, 1972,* 93143/4200, estate stamp, 1005mm x 700mm, (10-14-92, Germann, #331), color serigraph w/metal stamp (BP 319, DM 795, FR 2695, Y 65,802, SF 708).

$2120* *Hommage To Schroder-Sonnenstem (Oeuvre-Kat. 715), 1972,* s., #404/420, 1st state, ded., (06-12-93, Hauswedell/Nolt, #141), 33⅞ x 25⁹⁄₁₆ in., (86 x 65 cm.), color serigraph on metal embossing and velvet (BP 1388, DM 3451, FR 11,597, Y 223,087).

$1858* *Homo Humus Come Va - 10002 Nights (Werk-Nr. 860), 1983/84,* #9812/10002, s., num., stamps, (10-09-92, Winterberg, #2410), 25³⁄₁₆ x 17⁵⁄₁₆ in., (64 x 44 cm.), serigraph on photolithograph on Fabriano (BP 1102, DM 2760, FR 9267, Y 226,199).

$1701* *"Il Rotolante - Creeper I" (Werk-Nr. 859), 1982-83,* s., d., i., num., stamp, blindstamp, (06-08-93, Karl/Faber, #894), approx. 19¹¹⁄₁₆ x 13¾ in., (50 x 35 cm.), color photolithograph w/screen and metal print on wove (BP 1118, DM 2760, FR 9295, Y 180,669).

$1742* *"Il Rotolante" - "Creeper I" (Werk-Nr. 859), 1982-83,* s., d., num., (12-01-92, Karl/Faber, #759, illus.), 19¹¹⁄₁₆ x 13¾ in., (50 x 35 cm.), color photolithograph w/screen and metal print on wove (BP 1151, DM 2777, FR 9462, Y 216,882).

$770* *Image From Rainy Day Portfolio, 1971,* stamped w/sig., t., d., num. 1885/3000, pub./p. stamps, good cond., wrinkling, (09-11-92, Skinner, #106, illus.), sight 19½ x 26½ in., (49.5 x 67.3 cm.), color silkscreen on paper (BP 398, DM 1108, FR 3767, Y 95,403).

BI *In Gamba, 1990,* #162/905, d., est. DM 450, (09-18-92, Schloss Ahlden, #1006), 11⅝ x 8¼ in., (29.5 x 21 cm.), offset print w/metal embossing on white coated paper.

$3663* *Irinaland Uber Dem Balkan, Plate 7, (K. 70), 1971,* from Look At It On A Rainy Day, num. 357, sig., num. 36/300, pub. Ars Viva, margins, very good cond., (12-01-92, Christie-London, #606A), L. 16⁵⁄₁₆ x 23⅛ in., (415 x 588 mm.), screenprint in colors, w/metal imprints on wove (BP 2420, DM 5838, FR 19,897, Y 456,051).

$3996* *Kolumbus Regentag In Indian, Plate 6, 1971,* from Look At It On A Rainy Day, copy num. 1606, sig., num. 161/300, pub. Ars Viva, margins, surface dirt, very good cond., (12-01-92, Christie-London, #606), L. 17⅞ x 23³⁄₁₆ in., (454 x 589 mm.), screenprints in colors, w/metal imprints on wove (BP 2640, DM 6369, FR 21,706, Y 497,510).

BI *Komposition, 1971-72,* regentag, s. Hundertwasser, s. Hundertwasser, 2869/3000, est. 2,500, (03-24-93, Kunsthallen, #139), color serigraph.

$2217* *Last Tears (K. 75), 1979,* ink s., i. 20 Dezember 1979 Wien, i. 662a, pub. Greuner Janura AG, full margins, good cond., (12-03-92, Sotheby-London, #350, illus.), 20¼ x 14¼ in., (514 x 362 mm.), woodcut in colors on Japan (BP 1430, DM 3486, FR 11,900, Y 275,849).

BI *The Last Tears, (K. 75), 1979,* ink s., d., i., num. 167/200, pub. Gruener Janura AG, Glarus, full margins, very good cond., est. BP 1,8/2,500, (12-01-92, Christie-London, #610), L. 20³⁄₁₆ x 13¼ in., (513 x 337 mm.), woodcut p. in colors.

$15,483* *Look At It On A Rainy Day, Ars Viva, Zurich, (K. 44-53), 1971: Set OfTen,* each plate num. 1837, pl. 7, sig., num. 184/300, pl. 2 w/creases, very good cond., loose, num. 1837, (12-01-92, Christie-London, #608, illus.), overall S. 21⁷⁄₁₆ x 28⁷⁄₁₆ in., (545 x 723 mm.), screenprints in colors, w/metal imprints, on wove (BP 10,230, DM 24,678, FR 84,101, Y 1,927,664).

$17,158* *Midori No Namida (Works Nos. 688A, 692A, 659A and 90A), 1976,* complete portfolio, each s., d., #121/200, i., pub. Gruner Janura, each loose in folder of collaged Kurotoni paper, including a furoshiki designed by Hundertwasser, good cond., (06-30-93, Sotheby-London, #457, illus.), 5 color woodcuts on Japan (BP 11,500, DM 29,265, FR 98,723, Y 1,838,423).

$55* *"Min Gamle Get",* s. Poul Janus Ipsen 1983, 76/100, (03-24-93, Kunsthallen, #143), color lithograph (BP 37, DM 90, FR 306, Y 6462, DK 345).

$1047* *"Mit Der Liebe Warten Tut Weh, Wenn Die Liebe Woanders Ist", (HWG 46), 1971,* from the series Look at it on a rainy day, 388/3000, (09-29-92, B. Rasmussen, #323), serigraph in 29 colors (BP 589, DM 1479, FR 5046, Y 124,985, DK 5750).

$422* *My Love I-IV, 1980-1981: Four,* s. Oplag 100, (03-24-93, Kunsthallen, #140), color lithograph (BP 286, DM 689, FR 2346, Y 49,583, DK 2645).

$1876* *Night Train (K. 72), 1978,* color variant 3 of 5, ink s., i. Wien den 19 mai 1978, #185/285, pub.Gruener Janura Ag, good cond., scuffs, (12-03-92, Sotheby-London, #351, illus.), sheet 22 x 28⅞ in., (559 x 733 mm.), silkscreen in colors on white wove (BP 1210, DM 2950, FR 10,070, Y 233,420).

BI *Night Train; Colour Variant 2 , (K. 72), 1978,* ink s., d., i., num. 70/285, pub. Gruener Janura AG, Glarus, dirt, ink at sheet edges, est. BP 1,8/2,500, (12-01-92, Christie-London, #609), S. 21¹⁵⁄₁₆ x 28¹⁵⁄₁₆ in., (558 x 735 mm.), screenprint in colors, w/metal imprints on wove.

$1210* *Olympic Games Munich 1972 (K. 54), 1972,* stamp #2495/3999, pub. Edition Olympia, good cond.?, (10-28-92, Butterfield, #2823), 40¼ x 25¼ in., (102.2 x 64.1 cm.), color silkscreen w/metallic imprints on wove (BP 771, DM 1869, FR 6345, Y 148,466).

$1505* *Plakat Olympische Spiele Munchen (Hundertwasser 700), 1972,* #2522/3999, 2nd state, (05-27-93, Lempertz, #801), 40³⁄₁₆ x 25⅛ in., (102.1 x 63.8 cm.), color serigraph w/metal embossing on pack paper (BP 964, DM 2415, FR 8140, Y 161,342).

$73* *Portraet Af En Ener,* s. Poul Janus Ipsen 1973, 8/50, (03-24-93, Kunsthallen, #142), color etching (BP 49, DM 119, FR 406, Y 8577, DK 460).

$3751* *The Rain Falls Far From US (K. 61), 1972,* from Midori No Namida, ink s., d. 1976, #77/20, p. M.U.Surishi, pub.Gruener Januar AG, 1975, full margins, colors faded, good cond., (12-03-92, Sotheby-London, #348, illus.), 14½ x 20 in., (368 x 508 mm.), woodcut in colors on Japan (BP 2420, DM 5899, FR 20,134, Y 466,716).

BI *Regentag (K. 44-53), 1971: Ten,* s., #191/300, stamp s. and stamp #01902/3000, pub. Ars Viva, margins,discoloration, fading colors, backboard-staining, in original box, est. BP 8/10,000, (06-30-93, Sotheby-London, #458, illus.), color silkscreen.

$1896* *Regentag Auf Liebe Wellen (Koschatzky Nr. 51; Werkverzeichnis 715), 1971-1972,* #2210/3000, stamp sig., sheet 8 of Portfolio "Look at it on a rainy day", (04-21-93, Germann, #549, illus.), 19½ x 26⅜ in., (495 x 670 mm.), serigraph in 23 colors w/metal embossing in 3 colors and 1 reflecting glass particle layer (BP 1230, DM 3031, FR 10,249, Y 209,897, SF 2760).

$3996* *Regentag Auf Liebe Wellen, Plate 8, (K. 51), 1971,* from Look At It On A Rainy Day, num. 2518, 298/300, pub., Ars Viva, margins, excell. cond., (12-01-92, Christie-London, #607), L. 15⅞ x 23½ in., (403 x 597 mm.), screenprint in colors w/metal imprints on wove (BP 2640, DM 6369, FR 21,706, Y 497,510).

$880* *Regentag On Waves Of Love (K. 51), 1971-72,* stamp s., from portfolio Look at it on a Rainy Day, blindstamp p. Dietz Offizin, pub. Ars Viva, margins, good cond.?, (10-28-92, Butterfield, #2822), 16 x 23½ in., (406 x 597 mm.), color silkscreen w/metal imprints and ground glass on wove (BP 561, DM 1359, FR 4615, Y 107,975).

$4775* *Rotaprint-Mappe Des Wiener Art Club (Koschatsky 1-9), 1951,* portfolio, lithographed title on covers, (lacking Plate 9), p. by Rotaprint Burodruckmaschinen, pub. Alfred Schmeller, Art Club, good cond., handling marks & creases, tape hinges, covers stained & soiled, (12-03-92, Sotheby-London, #346, illus.), overall size 11¾ x 8¼ in., (298 x 210 mm.), eight lithographs in colors on wove (BP 3080, DM 7509, FR 25,631, Y 594,127).

$4038* *Sad Not So Sad Is Rainshine From Rainday On A Rainy Day,* s. Hundertwasser Venezia 1968, 680, A2, 95/250, (03-24-93, Kunsthallen, #138), color serigraph (BP 2734, DM 6595, FR 22,446, Y 474,445, DK 25,300).

$4300* *Sad Not So Sad Is Rainshine From Rainday On A Rainy Say (Koschatzky 39b), 1970,* s., d. pen, black ink, #167.250, pub., deckle edge, good cond., (05-20-93, Christie-London, #443, illus.), image 27½ x 20 in., (69.9 x 50.8 cm.), sheet 29¼ x 22 in., (69.9 x 50.8 cm.), screenprint in colors w/metal imprints on wove (BP 2760, DM 6938, FR 23,370, Y 474,823).

$2867* *Seereise II, Reise Zur See Und Mit Der Bahn (Hundertwasser 652), 1967,* s., d., i., watermark, #109/267, (05-27-93, Lempertz, #799, illus.), 25¹³⁄₁₆ x 19¾ in., (65.5 x 50.2 cm.), color lithograph on wove (BP 1836, DM 4600, FR 15,506, Y 307,354).

$3603* *Spectacles In The Small Face (K. 33), 1967,* from Nana Hyaku Mizu, s., d., i., pub. Gruener Janura AG, margins, (06-30-93, Sotheby-London, #462, illus.), sh 13¾ x 17 in., (349 x 432 mm.), color woodcut on wove (BP 2415, DM 6145, FR 20,731, Y 386,050).

$3123* *Spiral Sun And Moon House: The Neighbours (K. 32), 1967,* from Nana Hyaku Mizu, s., d., i., pub. Gruener Janura AG, margins, good cond., creasing, (06-30-93, Sotheby-London, #461, illus.), sh 13⅞ x 20½ in., (352 x 521 mm.), color woodcut on Japan (BP 2093, DM 5327, FR 17,969, Y 334,619).

$3829* *Town In Town, (K. 78), 1979,* s., d., i. in ink, num. 306/350, pub. Gruener Janura AG, Glarus, margins, dirt, very good cond., (12-01-92, Christie-London, #611, illus.), S. 17⁹⁄₁₆ x 26⅜ in., (446 x 670 mm.), screenprint in colors, w/metal imprints, on wove (BP 2530, DM 6103, FR 20,798, Y 476,718).

$3751* *Two Clouds Raining Seven Colours (K. 60), 1972,* from Midori No Namida, ink s., d. 1976, #77/200, p. M.U. Surishi, pub. Gruener Januar AG, 1975, full margins, (slightly trimmed lower left) colors faded, good cond., (12-03-92, Sotheby-London, #347, illus.), 11½ x 20½ in., (292 x 521 mm.), woodcut in colors on Japan (BP 2420, DM 5899, FR 20,134, Y 466,716).

$4775* *Two Trees On Board Of Regentag (K. 58), 1971,* from Midori No Namida, ink s., d. 17 Januar 1976 Wien, #105/200, p. M.U. Surishi, pub. Gruener Janura AG, 1975, full margins, good cond., (12-03-92, Sotheby-London, #349, illus.), 16⅝ x 20⅛ in., (422 x 511 mm.), woodcut in colors on Japan (BP 3080, DM 7509, FR 25,631, Y 594,127).

HUNT, Bryan American b. 1947

BI *Ghosts: Three Plates, 1979: Three,* s., d. 78, #15/31, pub. Parasol Press, blindstamps, full margins, excellent cond., est. $3/4,000, (11-09-92, Christie-NY, #314, illus.), 30¼ x 22⅛ in., (768 x 562 mm.), etching and aquatint on oatmeal Angoumois a la Main.

BI *Untitled, 1979,* from Ghosts, s., d. 78, num. 5/31, pub. Parasol Press, Crown Point Press blindstamp, full margins, excell. cond., est. $7/900, (09-19-92, Christie-E,

132), sheet 30¼ x 22⅛ in., (76.8 x 56.2 cm.), etching and aquatint on oatmeal Angoumois a la Main.

$605* *Window, 1986,* s., d., #10/200, s. by p. w/inkstamp, blindstamp pub. Crown Point Press, full margins, very good cond., (10-28-92, Butterfield, #2976), 13 x 9¼ in., (330 x 235 mm.), color woodcut on Japan (BP 385, DM 934, FR 3173, Y 74,233).

HUNT, C.   (after)
$138* *Cheltenham Annual Grand Steeplechase,* (11-12-92, Freemn/Fine Art, #93), 16 x 23½ in., (40.6 x 59.7 cm.), hand colored engraving (BP 91, DM 219, FR 738, Y 17,111).

HUNT, C.   (after F.C. TURNER)
$242* *The Young English Fox Hunter: "Full Cry" and "The Death": Two,* Mary Newbold Harding Estate, (02-03-93, Doyle, #60), 19½ x 26¾ in., (49.5 x 67.9 cm.), color engraving (BP 169, DM 398, FR 1351, Y 30,103).

HUNT, C.   (after J.F. HERRING)
$308* *Amato, The Winner Of The Derby Stakes At Epsom, 1838,* (11-30-92, Selkirk, #710), impression 15 x 18¾ in., (38.1 x 47.6 cm.), hand colored lithograph (BP 203, DM 491, FR 1666, Y 38,332).

HUNT, C.   (after J.F. Herring)
BI *Gray Momus,* foxing, discoloration, est. $2/300, (06-11-93, Doyle, #52), 12 x 16¾ in., (305 x 425 mm.), hand colored aquatint.

HUNT, Charles
$427* *Belle Of The Hunt,* pub. W. Soffe, repaired tear, (06-30-93, Bonhams-Chelsea, #129), image 15 x 21 in., (38.1 x 53.3 cm.), aquatint w/hand-coloring (BP 286, DM 728, FR 2457, Y 45,752).

$230* *Bendigo (Wm. Thompson, Champion Of England) (S. p. 325), 1846,* trimmed margins, light-staining, minor defects, Anthony N. B. GarvanColl., (06-05-93, Christie-NY, #67), sh 21 x 15¼ in., (533 x 387 mm.), aquatint w/hand-coloring on wove (BP 151, DM 373, FR 1257, Y 24,673).

BI *The Grand Military Steeple Chase Near Newmarket, March 24th, 1856: Plates I, II and III: Three,* pub. Ackermann and Co., 1856, margins, staining, est. BP 1/150, (06-30-93, Bonhams-Chelsea, #204), plate 17¼ x 22¾ in., (43.8 x 57.8 cm.), aquatint w/hand-coloring.

$240* *The Grand Military Steeple Chase Near Newmarket, Plates I-IV: Four,* margins, (10-29-92, Bonhams-Chelsea, #156), plate 17½ x 23 in., (44.5 x 58.4 cm.), aquatint, restrike, w/hand coloring (BP 154, DM 369, FR 1253, Y 29,729).

$192* *"Liverpool Grand Steeple Chase: Plates 2 and 4",* (09-09-92, Doyle, #49), sight 18 x 30 in., (45.7 x 76.2 cm.), color prints (BP 97, DM 272, FR 923, Y 23,602).

HUNT, Charles   (after)
BI *The Dublin, 1856, Charging The Stone Wall,* image repairs, est. BP 1/200, (03-03-93, Bonhams-Chelsea, #185), image 15 x 20¼ in., (38.1 x 51.4 cm.), hand-colored aquatint.

$131* *The Dublin, 1856-Charging The Stone,* repairs, (06-30-93, Bonhams-Chelsea, #205), image 15 x 20¼ in., (38.1 x 51.4 cm.), aquatint w/hand-coloring (BP 88, DM 223, FR 754, Y 14,036).

HUNT, Charles   (after G.H. ALKEN)
$385* *"Steeple Chase": Set of Four,* (01-06-93, Doyle, #1A), 11 x 17¾ in., (27.9 x 45.1 cm.), hand colored lithograph (BP 251, DM 631, FR 2148, Y 48,173).

HUNT, Charles   (after James POLLARD)
BI *Chances Of The Steeplechase: Set Of Eight,* late impressions, skimming, est. BP 1/1,500, (10-27-92, Phillips-London, #103), image 13½ x 18¾ in., (343 x 476 mm.), aquatint w/hand-coloring on wove.

HUNT, Donna Rae
$22* *"Fleurs D'Hiver",* d. 1967, #1/22, s., (10-16-92, DuMouchelle, #2484), approx. 15½ x 18 in., (39.4 x 45.7 cm.), lithograph (BP 13, DM 32, FR 110, Y 2627).

HUNT, G. and J.R. MACKREL   (after F.C. Turner)
$244* *Tiperary Glory - The Marquis At Home,* from set of four, repaired paper damage, water staining, (10-27-92,

Phillips-London, #102), image 17 x 24 in., (432 x 610 mm.), aquatint w/hand-coloring on wove (BP 154, DM 374, FR 1269, Y 29,847).

HUNT, George, Engraver
BI *"Smugglers Alarmed" and "Smugglers Attacked": A Pair,* foxing, defects, est. BP2/300, (01-21-93, Bonhams-Chelsea, #74), image 20½ x 16¼ in., (52.1 x 41.3 cm.), hand-colored aquatints.

BI *"Smugglers Alarmed" and "Smugglers Attacked": A Pair,* foxing, other surface defects, est. BP 2/250, (06-16-93, Bonhams-Chelsea, #425), image 20½ x 16¼ in., (52.1 x 41.3 cm.), aquatint w/hand-coloring.

HUNT, H. Alken
$165* *Fox Hunting: Four,* pub. T. McLean, 1820, (11-13-92, DuMouchelle, #363), 7 x 11 in., (17.8 x 27.9 cm.), hand colored prints (BP 107, DM 259, FR 873, Y 20,479).

HUNT, Richard   American b. 1933
BI *'Hamatsa Dance Screen', 1977,* NWCIA guild, est. $150/300, (10-21-92, Maynard, #57), print.

HUNT, William Holman
$341* *The Abundance Of Egypt (Hartnoll 9),* pub. state, margins, surface dirt, (12-03-92, Sotheby-London, #158), 6⅛ x 4¾ in., (156 x 121 mm.), etching on laid India (BP 220, DM 536, FR 1830, Y 42,429).

HUNT, William Holman   (after)
BI *Finding Of The Savious In The Temple,* by A. Blanchard, s. by Holman Hunt and Blanchard, pub. Gambert & Co.,full margins, water stains, dirt, defective, laid down, est. BP 1/2,000, (10-07-92, Christie-S. Ken, #33), pl 20¾ x 29½ in., (52.7 x 74.9 cm.), engraving.

HUNT, William Morris   American 1824-1879
$66* *Two Boys Swimming,* plate s. W.H. 1877, (12-11-92, Eldred, #346), image 19½ x 12¾ in., (49.6 x 32.4 cm.), engraving (BP 42, DM 104, FR 356, Y 8167).

BI *[Girl At Fountain], 1857,* pub. Phillips and Sampson, margins, good cond., discoloration, est. $1,5/2,000, (05-13-93, Sotheby-NY, #425), 9¾ x 7⅜ in., (246 x 188 mm.), lithograph on chine applique.

HUNT, Willima Holman   (after)
$396* *The Flight Into Egypt,* s., blindstamp, pub. The Fine Art Society, 1887, foxing, (06-16-93, Bonhams-Chelsea, #509, illus.), image 20 x 32 in., (50.8 x 81.3 cm.), photogravure (BP 264, DM 657, FR 2206, Y 42,235).

HUNT and SON, G.C.
$171* *"The Paddock", "The First Fence", "The Stone Wall", "The Brook", "The Last Fence" and "An Exciting Finish": Six Steeplechase Episodes,* pub. G.P. Queen, 1877, (06-08-93, Ritchie, #1, illus.), each plate 11½ x 16¾ in., (29.2 x 42.5 cm.), hand-colored aquatint (BP 112, DM 277, FR 934, Y 18,163, C$ 220).

HUNTER, David   American 20th cent.
$215* *Elon,* D. Hunter, (10-03-92, Garth, #294, illus.), 12½ x 10½ in., (31.8 x 26.7 cm.), etching (BP 126, DM 304, FR 1035, Y 25,736).

$132* *Nashum (Smith 375),* s., t., #69/100, (07-03-92, Sloan, #293), 2⅜ x 1⅞ in., (6 x 4.8 cm.), etching (BP 69, DM 200, FR 673, Y 16,455).

$55* *"Tola",* #84/100, s., t., num., (12-11-92, Eldred, #292), 2⅜ x 2 in., (6 x 5.1 cm.), etching (BP 35, DM 87, FR 297, Y 6806).

HUNTER, Mel   American 20th cent.
$28* *"Cranes Over Lake",* (05-15-93, Dunning, #59), 15¾ x 20¼ in., (40 x 51.4 cm.), print (BP 18, DM 45, FR 151, Y 3104).

HUNTER, William   1896-1963
$227* *The Black Swan,* s. William Hunter, i., #17/95, (08-11-92, L. Joel, #2G), 5⅜ x 6⁹⁄₁₆ in., (13.7 x 16.6 cm.), color aquatint (BP 118, DM 333, FR 1128, Y 29,069, A$ 308).

$146* *The Lower Yarra,* s. William Hunter, i., #10/50, (08-11-92, L. Joel, #71G), 6³⁄₁₆ x 9⁹⁄₁₆ in., (15.7 x 24.3 cm.), aquatint (BP 76, DM 214, FR 726, Y 18,696, A$ 198).

$122* *Mount Macedon,* s. William Hunter, i., (08-11-92, L. Joel, #102G), 3¹³⁄₁₆ x 6¹⁵⁄₁₆ in., (9.7 x 17.6 cm.), color aquatint (BP 63, DM 179, FR 606, Y 15,623, A$ 165).

$162* *The Old Moorings, Williamstown,* s. William Hunter, i. #3/50, (08-11-92, L. Joel, #27G), 9³⁄₁₆ x 12⁵⁄₁₆ in., (23.3 x 31.3 cm.), aquatint (BP 84, DM 238, FR 805, Y 20,745, A$ 220).

$243* *Three Trees,* s. William Hunter, i., #7/50, (08-11-92, L. Joel, #100G), 9⅝ x 6¾ in., (24.5 x 17.2 cm.), aquatint (BP 126, DM 357, FR 1208, Y 31,118, A$ 330).

$97* *The Wanderer,* s. William Hunter, i., #1/50, (08-11-92, L. Joel, #152G), 5⁹⁄₁₆ x 8¹⁄₁₆ in., (14.2 x 20.4 cm.), aquatint (BP 50, DM 142, FR 482, Y 12,422, A$ 132).

$122* *White Horses,* s. William Hunter, i., #3/50, (08-11-92, L. Joel, #41G), 9⁹⁄₁₆ x 8¹³⁄₁₆ in., (24.3 x 22.4 cm.), color aquatint (BP 63, DM 179, FR 606, Y 15,623, A$ 165).

HUNTINGTON, Daniel P. American 1816-1906

$193* *Washington And His Generals,* (04-02-93, Sloan, #1175), 23½ x 35 in., (597 x 889 mm.), color engraving (BP 127, DM 310, FR 1053, Y 21,974).

HUNTINGTON, F.J.

$110* *Astrological Prints, 1835,* pub. F.J. Huntington, (03-27-93, Julia, #108), 13½ x 15 in., (34.3 x 38.1 cm.), hand-colored prints (BP 74, DM 179, FR 610, Y 12,803).

HUNTLEY, Victoria

$66* *Sunburst Through Dark Clouds,* s., d. 1956, (06-11-93, Freemn/Fine Art, #107), 9¼ x 12½ in., (23.5 x 31.8 cm.), lithograph (BP 43, DM 107, FR 362, Y 7003).

HUNTLEY, Victoria H. American 1900-1971

$83* *"Wild Birds", 1949,* s., d., very good cond., (10-31-92, Cleveland, #144), 11⅞ x 15⅞ in., (30.2 x 40.3 cm.), lithograph (BP 53, DM 128, FR 433, Y 10,281).

HUPPI, Alfonso b. 1935

BI *Taschengalerie, 1972,* Galerie der Spiegel, 15 s., num., (11-28-92, Schoppmann, #594), 16¹⁵⁄₁₆ x 4⁵⁄₁₆ in., (43 x 11 cm.), color serigraph.

HURD, Peter American 1904-1984

$330* *"Approaching Storm" and "Today It Rained", c. 1975: Two,* both s., first #81/260; second #237/260, p. American Atelier, pub. Circle Fine Art, (12-08-92, Swann, #146), first 15 x 26 in., (38.1 x 66 cm.), second 18½ x 26 in., (38.1 x 66 cm.), color lithograph (BP 207, DM 514, FR 1752, Y 40,902).

$220* *"Don Jose",* t., i., s., ded., hinges, minor flaws, skinned spot, excell. cond., (05-15-93, Cleveland, #167, illus.), 14¾ x 11¾ in., (37.5 x 29.8 cm.), lithograph (BP 143, DM 354, FR 1189, Y 24,388).

$110* *Don Patricio,* s., t., annot. ed 50, (10-18-92, Hindman, #485), 14 x 10⅛ in., (35.6 x 25.7 cm.), lithograph (BP 67, DM 164, FR 555, Y 13,197).

$358* *Home For Supper,* s., t., #76/100, (05-16-93, Hindman, #562), 7½ x 10½ in., (19.1 x 26.7 cm.), lithograph (BP 233, DM 576, FR 1935, Y 39,685).

$345* *Windmill, 1940,* stone s., margins, good cond., mat/light-staining, (05-19-93, Butterfield, #1997), 8½ x 10 in., (216 x 254 mm.), lithograph on wove (BP 224, DM 561, FR 1889, Y 38,193).

HURLEY, Frank 1885-1962

$721* *The Endurance, 1915,* (10-29-92, Christie-London, #95), 19⅜ x 14½ in., (49.2 x 36.8 cm.), photograph, gelatin silver print mounted on card (BP 462, DM 1109, FR 3763, Y 89,310).

HURLEY, R.

BI *Flight Over Mariamvale Landscape,* s., t., d. '82, stamped inits. R H, prov., est. C$ 2/300, (12-01-92, Ritchie, #80, illus.), 19¾ x 26¼ in., (50.2 x 66.7 cm.), lino-cut.

BI *Hommage To The Owl,* s., t., d. 84, stamped mono., prov., est. C$ 2/300, (12-01-92, Ritchie, #81), 25 x 18½ in., (63.5 x 47 cm.), lino-cut.

HURRELL, George 1904-1992

$748* *"Anna Mae Wong",* 1930s, p. c. 1980, s., #2/110, (05-23-93, Butterfield, #3469, illus.), 13½ x 10½ in., photograph, gelatin silver print (BP 487, DM 1223, FR 4117, Y 82,679).

$413* *Bette Davis,* hand s. test print #28/190, (04-26-93, Selkirk, #550), 14 x 11 in., (35.6 x 27.9 cm.), photograph (BP 261, DM 647, FR 2186, Y 45,575).

$1870* *"Bianca Jagger", 1977,* ink s., verso, unique in this size, (11-16-92, Butterfield, #6018, illus.), 61⁹⁄₁₆ x 54⅛ in., (156.4 x 137.4 cm.), photograph, gelatin silver print (BP 1231, DM 2982, FR 10,043, Y 232,558).

$770* *"Charles Boyer",* 1930's/c. 1980, s., edit. 219/250, Dixon Collection(11-16-92, Butterfield, #6021, illus.), 19¹⁄₁₆ x 15½ in., (483.5 x 394.4 mm.), photograph, gelatin silver print (BP 507, DM 1228, FR 4135, Y 95,759).

$385* *Clark Gable,* mounted proof of Limited Edition, (04-26-93, Selkirk, #548, illus.), 20 x 16 in., (50.8 x 40.6 cm.), photograph (BP 243, DM 603, FR 2038, Y 42,485).

BI *Doris Duke, 1939,* s., t., d. by photog. in ink, stamp, est. $3/5,000, (10-15-92, Sotheby-NY, #224, illus.), 12⅞ x 9¼ in., (32.7 x 23.5 cm.), photograph, gelatin silver print.

$489* *"Dorothy Lamour",* 1930s, p. c. 1980, s., #112/190, (05-23-93, Butterfield, #3465, illus.), 23½ x 19½ in., photograph, gelatin silver print (BP 318, DM 800, FR 2691, Y 54,051).

BI *"Douglas Fairbanks",* 1930s, p. c. 1980, s., #112/190, est. $800/1,200, (05-23-93, Butterfield, #3466, illus.), 23½ x 19½ in., photograph, gelatin silver print.

$1870* *"Errol Flynn",* 1939/1977, ink s., unique in this size, (11-16-92, Butterfield, #6019, illus.), 62⅜ x 45¹⁵⁄₁₆ in., (158.4 x 116.7 cm.), photograph, gelatin silver print (BP 1231, DM 2982, FR 10,043, Y 232,558).

BI *Gary Cooper,* s., #218/250, est. BP 6/800, (10-10-92, Bonhams, #176, illus.), 20 x 16 in., (50.8 x 40.6 cm.), photograph.

$607* *Greta Garbo,* 1930, p.l., ink s., mounted, (12-17-92, Christie-S. Ken, #55, illus.), 14 x 11 in., (35.6 x 27.9 cm.), photograph, matt gelatin silver print (BP 385, DM 948, FR 3237, Y 74,598).

BI *Greta Garbo And John Barrymore,* still from "Grand Hotel", s., #6/190, est. BP 6/800, (10-10-92, Bonhams, #174, illus.), 14 x 11 in., (35.6 x 27.9 cm.), photograph.

$546* *"Hedy Lamarr",* 1930s, p. c. 1980, s., #112/190, (05-23-93, Butterfield, #3467, illus.), 23½ x 19½ in., photograph, gelatin silver print (BP 356, DM 893, FR 3005, Y 60,351).

$2530* *Hurrel, 1979: "Greta Garbo And John Barrymore", "Gary Cooper", "JoanCrawford", "Bette Davis", "Marlene Dietrich", "Clark Gable", "Jean Harlow", "Rita Hayworth", "Katherine Hepburn" and "Loretta Young And Tyrone Power": Ten,* Creative Art Investments, Inc., s., n#242/250 in ink, num. 242 from 250, lit., (04-08-93, Christie-NY, #299, illus.), each approx. 18⅞ x 13½ in., (47.9 x 34.3 cm.), photograph, gelatin silver print (BP 1659, DM 4064, FR 13,757, Y 287,108).

BI *Hurrell II, 1980: "Dorothy Lamour", "Ramon Novarro", "Greta Garbo", "Johnny Weissmuller", "Douglas Fairbanks", "Robert Taylor", "Hedy Lamarr" and "Jane Russell": Eight,* Creative Art Images, Inc., s., #21/250 in ink, num. 21 edit 250, lit., est. $2,5/3,500, (04-08-93, Christie-NY, #300, illus.), each approx. 19 x 15½ in., (48.3 x 39.4 cm.), photograph, gelatin silver print.

$3520* *Hurrell II, 1980: Eight,* Los Angeles: Creative Art Images, Inc., each s., num. 8/190, lit., (10-13-92, Christie-NY, #240, illus.), each 23¼ x 19½ in., (59.1 x 49.5 cm.), photograph, gelatin silver prints (BP 2050, DM 5157, FR 17,521, Y 426,822).

$2200* *Hurrell II, c. 1980,* Creative Art Images, c. 1980, portfolio of 8 photogs., each s., #69/190 by photog. in ink, 1920's-40's, p. c. 1980, (10-15-92, Sotheby-NY, #223, illus.), each approx. 20 x 24 in., (50.8 x 61 cm.), photograph, gelatin silver prints (BP 1346, DM 3275, FR 11,106, Y 263,947).

$2200* *Hurrell III,* Creative Art Images, c. 1980, portfolio of 10 photos, each s., num. 172/190 by photog. in ink, 1920's-40's, p. c. 1980, #172/190 ed., (10-15-92, Sotheby-NY, #223A, illus.), each approx. 20 x 24 in., (50.8 x 61 cm.), photograph, gelatin silver prints (BP 1346, DM 3275, FR 11,106, Y 263,947).

$1955* *"Hurrell III": Ten,* 1920s-40s, p. 1980, s., #114/250, colophon s., orig. portfolio case, (05-23-93, Butterfield, #3464, illus.), 16 x 20 in., photograph, gelatin silver print (BP 1273, DM 3197, FR 10,759, Y 216,094).

$3520* *Hurrell III, 1980: Ten,* Los Angeles: Creative Art Images, Inc., each s., num. 83/190, lit., (10-13-92,

Christie-NY, #241, illus.), each 23½ x 19¼ in., (59.7 x 48.9 cm.), photograph, gelatin silver prints (BP 2050, DM 5157, FR 17,521, Y 426,822).

$2875* *"Hurrell": Ten,* 1920s-40s, p. 1980, s., #99/250, colophon s., orig. portfolio case, (05-23-93, Butterfield, #3463, illus.), each approx. 16 x 20 in., photograph, gelatin silver print (BP 1872, DM 4701, FR 15,823, Y 317,785).

BI *Jane Russell,* 1940, p.l., ink s., est. BP 2/400, (12-17-92, Christie-S. Ken, #63, illus.), 10 x 11 in., (25.4 x 27.9 cm.), photograph, matt gelatin silver print.

BI *Jean Harlow,* 1935, p.l., ink s., est. BP 2/400, (12-17-92, Christie-S. Ken, #62, illus.), 14 x 11 in., (35.6 x 27.9 cm.), photograph, matt gelatin silver print.

$385* *Jean Harlow,* mounted proof of Limited Edition, (04-26-93, Selkirk, #541, illus.), 14 x 11 in., (35.6 x 27.9 cm.), photograph (BP 243, DM 603, FR 2038, Y 42,485).

BI *Jean Harlow, 1934,* s., annot., credit, d., Metro-Goldwyn-Mayer stamps, est. $2/3,000, (10-13-92, Christie-NY, #238, illus.), 9⅜ x 12¼ in., (23.8 x 31.1 cm.), photograph, gelatin silver print.

BI *Jean Harlow, Leaning On Polar Bear,* s., #178/250, est. BP 7/900, (10-10-92, Bonhams, #173, illus.), 20 x 16 in., (50.8 x 40.6 cm.), photograph.

BI *Joan And Christina Crawford,* blindstamp, i. in ink on image, early 1940s, est. $1,5/2,500, (10-15-92, Sotheby-NY, #222, illus.), 13 x 10¼ in., (33 x 26 cm.), photograph, gelatin silver print.

$607* *Joan Crawford,* 1935, p.l., ink s., lit., (12-17-92, Christie-S. Ken, #61, illus.), 14 x 11 in., (35.6 x 27.9 cm.), photograph, matt gelatin silver print (BP 385, DM 948, FR 3237, Y 74,598).

BI *Joan Crawford,* 1933, p.l., ink s., num. 2/30, est. BP 2/400, (12-17-92, Christie-S. Ken, #59, illus.), 14 x 11 in., (35.6 x 27.9 cm.), photograph, matt gelatin silver print.

BI *Joan Crawford,* 1932, p.l., ink s., num. 3/30, est. BP 2/400, (12-17-92, Christie-S. Ken, #58, illus.), 14 x 11 in., (35.6 x 27.9 cm.), photograph, matt gelatin silver print.

$607* *Joan Crawford,* 1932, p.l., ink s., num. 3/30, (12-17-92, Christie-S. Ken, #57, illus.), 14 x 11 in., (35.6 x 27.9 cm.), photograph, matt gelatin silver print (BP 385, DM 948, FR 3237, Y 74,598).

$385* *Joan Crawford,* test print, num. XIII/XV, (04-26-93, Selkirk, #549), 20 x 16 in., (50.8 x 40.6 cm.), photograph (BP 243, DM 603, FR 2038, Y 42,485).

$495* *Joan Crawford And Her Mother, 1931,* photog. blindstamp, typed caption labels, (11-16-92, Butterfield, #6022, illus.), 9½ x 7½ in., (241.7 x 190.8 mm.), photograph, gelatin silver print (BP 326, DM 789, FR 2658, Y 61,560).

BI *Joan Crawford, Arm Raised Leaning Against Wall,* s., #218/250, est. BP 6/800, (10-10-92, Bonhams, #178, illus.), 20 x 16 in., (50.8 x 40.6 cm.), photograph.

$408* *Johnny Weissmuller, Paris, 1924,* artist's proof, s., (10-10-92, Bonhams, #179, illus.), 29 x 22 in., (73.7 x 55.9 cm.), photograph (BP 242, DM 606, FR 2035, Y 49,671).

BI *Katharine Hepburn, Portrait,* s., #6/190, est. BP 5/700, (10-10-92, Bonhams, #181, illus.), 14 x 11 in., (35.6 x 27.9 cm.), photograph.

BI *Loretta Young And Tyrone Power,* s., #18/190, (10-10-92, Bonhams, #177, illus.), 14 x 11 in., (35.6 x 27.9 cm.), photograph.

BI *Marlene Dietrich,* 1934, p.l., ink s., num. 3/30, est. BP 2/400, (12-17-92, Christie-S. Ken, #60, illus.), 10 x 11 in., (25.4 x 27.9 cm.), photograph, matt gelatin silver print.

$1224* *Marlene Dietrich Seated With Arm Across Knee,* s., #18/190, (10-10-92, Bonhams, #175, illus.), 11 x 14 in., (27.9 x 35.6 cm.), photograph (BP 726, DM 1818, FR 6105, Y 149,014).

$2200* *"Marlene Dietrich",* 1939/1977, ink s., unique in this size, (11-16-92, Butterfield, #6017, illus.), 62¹³⁄₁₆ x 44⁹⁄₁₆ in., (159.6 x 113.2 cm.), photograph, gelatin silver print (BP 1449, DM 3508, FR 11,815, Y 273,598).

BI *Norma Shearer,* 1932, p.l., ink s., num. 3/30, lit., est. BP 2/400, (12-17-92, Christie-S. Ken, #56, illus.), 10 x 11 in., (25.4 x 27.9 cm.), photograph, matt gelatin silver print.

BI *"Ramon Navarro",* 1930, p. c. 1980, s., #2/110, est. $6/800, (05-23-93, Butterfield, #3468, illus.), 13½ x 10½ in., photograph, gelatin silver print.

$1320* *"Ramon Navarro",* 1930/later, s., edit. 249/250, t., (11-16-92, Butterfield, #6020, illus.), 15½ x 19¹⁄₁₆ in., (394.4 x 483.5 mm.), photograph, gelatin silver print (BP 869, DM 2105, FR 7089, Y 164,159).

BI *Rita Hayworth,* s., #18/190, est. BP 5/700, (10-10-92, Bonhams, #180, illus.), 11 x 14 in., (27.9 x 35.6 cm.), photograph.

$468* *Rita Hayworth,* test print, hand s., #15/250, (04-26-93, Selkirk, #552, illus.), 16 x 20 in., (40.6 x 50.8 cm.), photograph (BP 295, DM 734, FR 2478, Y 51,644).

$413* *Tyrone Power And Loretta Young,* test print, hand s., #21/190, (04-26-93, Selkirk, #551, illus.), 14 x 11 in., (35.6 x 27.9 cm.), photograph (BP 261, DM 647, FR 2186, Y 45,575).

HURST, Hal (after)

BI *Cycling In Hyde Park,* est. BP 80/120, (06-30-93, Bonhams-Chelsea, #38), image 13 x 19¼ in., (33 x 48.9 cm.), chromolithograph.

HURST and ROBINSON, Publishers

$639* *The North Bank Of The Thames From Westminster Bridge To London Bridge, 1825,* album, staining, tearing, (07-16-92, Bonhams-Chelsea, #508), subject 11½ x 22 in., (29.2 x 55.9 cm.), lithograph (BP 330, DM 944, FR 3187, Y 80,045).

HUSS, Michel b. 1954

$326* *Jeux De Plage II, 1991,* 11/90, s., (10-14-92, Germann, #333), 26⅞ x 21⁵⁄₁₆ in., (682 x 542 mm.), color serigraph w/collage (BP 191, DM 477, FR 1618, Y 39,506, SF 425).

$272* *Jeux De Plage V, 1991,* 49/90, s., (10-14-92, Germann, #332), 30¹⁄₁₆ x 22³⁄₁₆ in., (763 x 564 mm.), color serigraph w/collage (BP 160, DM 398, FR 1350, Y 32,962, SF 354).

HUSSEY, Harold

$288* *A Friend To The Farmer, Shell Tractor Oil, The Robin, 1952,* p. John Waddington, ref. P 24, cond. 3, (10-13-92, Phillips-London, #170), 29¾ x 39¾ in., (75.5 x 101 cm.), color lithograph (BP 168, DM 422, FR 1434, Y 34,922).

HUTCHENBURG, Jan van Dutch 1647-1733

BI *Levee Du Siege De Coni Ville De Piemont, 1691,* s. in block "Hutchenbury Fec.", excell. cond., toning, est. 1/2000, (08-29-92, Goldberg, #367A, illus.), image 18¼ x 22 in., (46.4 x 55.9 cm.), engraving.

BI *Vue Et Representation De La Bataille De Peterwaradin Donne Le 5 D Aout 1716,* s. in block "Hutchenbury Pinxit et Excudit", excell. cond., toning, est. 1/2000, (08-29-92, Goldberg, #367, illus.), image 17¾ x 11¾ in., (45.1 x 29.8 cm.), engraving.

HUTCHINSON (after William James BENNET) (after) American

$80* *Views Of New York, Pl.1., Broadway,* (02-04-93, Sloan, #752), 11 x 17¼ in., (27.9 x 43.8 cm.), color engraving (BP 56, DM 132, FR 447, Y 9951).

HUTCHINSON, Ken

$66* *1931 Model Ford Pick Up Containing Decoys,* s., d. 1988, #27/250, (10-02-92, Guyette, #625, illus.), image 19 x 30 in., (48.3 x 76.2 cm.), color photograph (BP 38, DM 94, FR 314, Y 7881).

HUTCHINSON, Leonard 1896-1980

$369* *Winter On The Lake,* #27/50 s., t., (05-10-93, Hodgins, #41, illus.), 10 x 10½ in., (25.4 x 26.7 cm.), wood engraving on paper (BP 241, DM 593, FR 2000, Y 41,234, C$ 468).

HUTH, Robert W. 1890-1977

$564* *Kunsttanzer, 1924,* Erschienen in der Kestner-Mappe, (05-26-93, Dorling, #2727, illus.), 14¾ x 19¹⁵⁄₁₆ in., (37.5 x 50.6 cm.), lithograph on cardboard (BP 365, DM 920, FR 3097, Y 61,278).

$1064* *Madchen Vor Dem Spiegel, 1922,* s., blindstamp, (06-05-93, Bassenge, #6147, illus.), 9⅜ x 6⅞ in., (23.8 x 17.5 cm.), drypoint on J. W. Zanders-machine-made (BP 700, DM 1725, FR 5814, Y 114,139).

HUTTY, Alfred   American 1877/78-1954

$165* *Charleston S.C.*, margins, s., (05-22-93, Collins, #8), 9¾ x 6⅞ in., (24.8 x 17.5 cm.), etching (BP 107, DM 268, FR 903, Y 18,192).

$154* *Hills And Trees*, s., t., i., (10-30-92, Sloan, #1734), 8 x 8¹¹⁄₁₆ in., drypoint etching (BP 99, DM 237, FR 804, Y 19,076).

$440* *"Huguenot Church" and "Bishop's Gate": Two*, s., (12-17-92, Mystic, #2), one 5½ x 6¼ in., (14 x 15.9 cm.), the other 5¾ x 7¼ in., (14 x 15.9 cm.), etching (BP 279, DM 687, FR 2347, Y 54,074).

$200* *"In Cypress Gardens"*, s., mat burn, mat/glue residue, (05-15-93, Cleveland, #167A), 14 x 9½ in., (35.6 x 24.1 cm.), etching (BP 130, DM 322, FR 1081, Y 22,170).

$55* *Magnolia Gardens*, margins, s. Alfred Hutty, (10-24-92, Collins, #22), 6 x 6 in., (15.2 x 15.2 cm.), etching (BP 34, DM 84, FR 285, Y 6707).

$132* *"New England Fishing Village"*, s., t., rem. snail, tape residue, good cond., (10-31-92, Cleveland, #145), 6½ x 7⅜ in., (16.5 x 18.7 cm.), etching (BP 85, DM 203, FR 689, Y 16,351).

$110* *"Northern Pines"*, s., mat burn, tears, taped, (05-15-93, Cleveland, #167C), 8½ x 10½ in., (21.6 x 26.7 cm.), etching (BP 72, DM 177, FR 595, Y 12,194).

$120* *"Old Sycamore"*, s., mat burn, staining, tape, (05-15-93, Cleveland, #167B), 9 x 11¾ in., (22.9 x 29.8 cm.), etching (BP 78, DM 193, FR 649, Y 13,302).

HUYBERTS, Cornelis   Dutch 1669-1712

$468* *Pugna Cum Elephantes (A Roman Battle)*, (04-02-93, Sloan, #2279, illus.), sight 16⅛ x 20⅝ in., (410 x 524 mm.), engraving (BP 308, DM 752, FR 2555, Y 53,285).

HUYSUM, Jan van   Dutch 1682-1749

$201* *Still Life Of Mixed Flowers In An Ornamental Stone Vase, 1947*, by J. Chamberlain, s., blindstamp, pub. Frost and Reed, margins, (11-12-92, Bonhams-Chelsea, #9, illus.), plate 18 x 13¾ in., (45.7 x 34.9 cm.), color mezzotint (BP 132, DM 318, FR 1074, Y 24,923).

HUYSUM, Jan van (after)

$2530* *"A Fruit Piece" and "A Flower Piece", 1781: Two*, by Richard Earlom, artists' names in scratch lettering, pub. J. Boydell, narrow margins, stained, laid down, prop. R. Thornton Wilson, (05-11-93, Christie-NY, #25), each plate 22 x 16½ in., (559 x 419 mm.), mezzotint on laid (BP 1615, DM 3986, FR 13,429, Y 278,297).

$1610* *"A Fruit Piece" and "A Flower Piece", 1781: Two*, by Richard Earlom, final pub. states, pub. J. Boydell, narrow margins, surface soiling, foxing, staining, (05-11-93, Christie-NY, #26), each plate 22 x 16½ in., (559 x 419 mm.), mezzotint on laid (BP 1028, DM 2536, FR 8546, Y 177,098).

$318* *A Fruit Piece, In The Cabinet At Houghton, 1781*, by Richard Earlom, pub. John Boydell, repaired tears, trimmed, laid down, (11-12-92, Bonhams-Chelsea, #12), sheet 21¼ x 15¼ in., (54 x 38.7 cm.), hand-colored mezzotint (BP 209, DM 504, FR 1700, Y 39,430).

HWANG, Kyu Baik   Korean b. 1932

$350* *Bundle*, artist's proof, t., s., d. 1974, (02-04-93, Sloan, #1835), 13 x 10½ in., (33 x 26.7 cm.), color engraving (BP 244, DM 576, FR 1954, Y 43,538).

$160* *Flower-B.*, s., d. 1975, (02-04-93, Sloan, #1836), 13 x 10½ in., (33 x 26.7 cm.), color engraving (BP 112, DM 263, FR 893, Y 19,903).

HYDE, Helen   American 1868-1919

$220* *"Child Coming Out Of Her Bath", "Child With Geese" and "The Daruma Brh", c. 1910-14: Three*, s., (05-27-93, Swann, #135), color woodcuts (BP 141, DM 353, FR 1190, Y 23,585).

BI *From The Rice Fields (M. & M. 38), 1901*, s., num. indistinctly, colors slightly faded, good cond., light-staining, paper remains, paper loss, glue/paper remains, creases, buckling, est. $6/800, (05-19-93, Butterfield, #1817), 19¾ x 4⅝ in., (502 x 117 mm.), woodcut in colors on Japan attached to textured wove w/fabric collage.

$413* *"From The Rice Fields", 1901 (Mason and Mason 38)*, s., i. 151. (c) 1901... Helen Hyde, block mono., good cond., margins, cockling, (10-09-92, Skinner, #39, illus.),

21½ x 4⅝ in., (54.6 x 11.7 cm.), color woodblock on tissue (BP 245, DM 615, FR 2086, Y 50,366).

$550* *"Going To Market" 1912 and "The Sacred Calf...In The Bazaar At Agra"1910: Two*, both s. Helen Hyde, very good/good cond., (04-25-93, Bakker, #173, illus.), image 11½ x 4¼ in., (29.2 x 10.8 cm.), image 9 x 9¾ in., (29.2 x 10.8 cm.), color woodblock prints (BP 349, DM 870, FR 2938, Y 60,747).

$220* *The Greeting, Mason 87*, s., num. 230, bearing artist's chop, prov., (09-20-92, Hindman, #682), 11⅛ x 10⅛ in., (28.3 x 25.7 cm.), color woodcut (BP 129, DM 326, FR 1117, Y 27,191).

$605* *"In Their Holiday Clothes" (Mason 119)*, s., perfect cond., orig. folder, print tipped corners to folder (as issued), (10-31-92, Cleveland, #147, illus.), 13¼ x 5⅛ in., (33.7 x 13 cm.), color woodblock (BP 388, DM 931, FR 3158, Y 74,941).

$358* *"Miss Apricot Cloud Of Shanghai" and "Daruma Branch": Two*, s. Helen Hyde, s. in plate, d. 1908, 1910, very good/good cond. (?), (04-25-93, Bakker, #57), image 7½ x 5 in., (19.1 x 12.7 cm.), image 4¾ x 4½ in., (19.1 x 12.7 cm.), color woodblock prints (BP 227, DM 566, FR 1912, Y 39,541).

$770* *Mt. Orizaba, 1912*, s. in image, (05-27-93, Swann, #133), 9⅝ x 9 in., (24.4 x 22.9 cm.), color woodcut (BP 493, DM 1236, FR 4164, Y 82,547).

$605* *New Brooms (M. & M. 88), 1910*, num. 9, margins, good cond., (02-24-93, Butterfield, #2635), 6⅝ x 4⅞ in., (168 x 124 mm.), woodcut in colors on tissue paper (BP 422, DM 982, FR 3330, Y 70,993).

BI *Playtime*, s. ink, paper toned, colors faded, tipped to mat, fold in image, est.$350-550, (10-31-92, Cleveland, #146), 6 x 20⅝ in., (15.2 x 52.4 cm.), woodblock in colors.

$468* *"The Sacred Calf ... In The Bazaar At Agra", "Miss Apricot, Cloud OfShanghai" and "The Hired Baby": Three*, all s. Helen Hyde, very good/good cond., (11-21-92, Bakker, #108, illus.), largest image 9 x 10 in., (22.9 x 25.4 cm.), color woodblock print on toned paper (BP 308, DM 746, FR 2513, Y 58,202).

$165* *"The White Peacock", 1914*, s. Helen Hyde, good cond.?, (11-21-92, Bakker, #109), 8⅜ x 10 in., (21.3 x 25.4 cm.), color woodblock print (BP 109, DM 263, FR 886, Y 20,520).

$550* *The White Peacock, 1914*, full margins, num., s., (05-27-93, Swann, #134, illus.), 8½ x 10⅛ in., (21.6 x 25.7 cm.), color woodcut (BP 352, DM 883, FR 2975, Y 58,962).

$70* *Young Girl With Flowers*, s., (05-16-93, Hanzel, #1116), 6¾ x 1¾ in., (17.1 x 4.4 cm.), color woodblock (BP 46, DM 113, FR 378, Y 7760).

HYLAND, Fred

BI *Harper's Magazine*, Maitres de l'Affiche blindstamp, p. Chaix, margins, apparently good condition, est. $3/500, (03-31-93, Butterfield, #5241), 12⅛ x 7⅞ in., (30.8 x 20 cm.), lithograph printed in colors on wove.

HYNES, Paul

BI *Feathers, 1940*, s., t., prov., est. $1,2/1,800, (10-13-92, Christie-NY, #242, illus.), 13¾ x 16 in., (34.9 x 40.6 cm.), photograph, gelatin silver print.

IBELS, H.S.

$66* *"The Times"*, (02-27-93, Dunning, #113), 11 x 8 in., (27.9 x 20.3 cm.), lithograph (BP 46, DM 108, FR 369, Y 7791).

IBELS, Henri Gabriel   1867-1936

$292* *"La Dispute"*, s. in plate, crayon s., (10-18-92, Pescheteau, #168), 13¾ x 10⅝ in., (35 x 27 cm.), lithograph in colors on Japan (BP 177, DM 431, FR 1465, Y 34,866).

BI *Exposition H.G. Ibels A La Bodiniere, 1894*, fold marks, losses, tears, repairs, lit., est. BP 3/500, (02-04-93, Christie-S. Ken, #128), 23 x 16½ in., (58.4 x 41.9 cm.), color lithograph backed on linen.

BI *Horloge, J. Mevisto, c. 1892*, tears, defects, est. BP 4/600, (02-04-93, Christie-S. Ken, #127, illus.), 71 x 25 in., (180.3 x 63.5 cm.), color lithograph on two sheets backed on linen.

IBELS, Louise Catherine

BI *Clochard Et Clocharde*, s., #5/20, est. C$ 1/150, (12-01-92, Ritchie, #9, illus.), 10⅝ x 10¾ in., (27 x 27.3 cm.), etching on laid paper.

BI *La Rue De Venise*, s., t., #5/30, est. C$ 1/150, (12-01-92, Ritchie, #10), 18⅝ x 12¼ in., (47.3 x 31.1 cm.), etching.

ICART, Louis   French 1888-1950

$1760* *1930*, (c) 1929 L. Icart, s., artist's blindstamp, good cond., full sheet, tears, (11-06-92, Sotheby-Arcade, #157), 15 x 18 in., (38.1 x 45.7 cm.), etching/drypoint in colors w/hand-coloring (BP 1151, DM 2810, FR 9498, Y 217,230).

$2185* *Accord Parfait, (Perfect Harmony) (H., C. & I. 417), 1932*, s., blindstamp, (c), d. in plate, margins, good condition, mat and light-staining, paper and glue remains, handling creases, (03-31-93, Butterfield, #5219), 13⅛ x 17¼ in., (33.3 x 43.8 cm.), sheet 18 x 22 in., (33.3 x 43.8 cm.), etching and drypoint printed in colors w/a touch of hand-coloring on wove (BP 1445, DM 3515, FR 11,940, Y 251,265).

BI *Der Apfelkorb*, s. Louis Icart, num. 216, est. SC 20/22,000, (05-19-93, Dorotheum, #436, illus.), sheet 17¹¹⁄₁₆ x 12¹⁵⁄₁₆ in., (45 x 33 cm.), etching in color.

$1045* *Au Revoir, 1927, Holland-Catania-Ken 305*, s., annot. epreuve d'artiste, bears artist stamp, prov., (09-20-92, Hindman, #789, illus.), 15 x 19¼ in., (38.1 x 48.9 cm.), color drypoint and aquatint (BP 612, DM 1551, FR 5305, Y 129,156).

$550* *Autumn Leaves, 1926 (H. 294)*, s., annot. 222, (11-12-92, Freemn/Fine Art, #94), plate 20 x 15¾ in., (50.8 x 40 cm.), drypoint and aquatint (BP 361, DM 871, FR 2940, Y 68,196).

$605* *"Aux Champs Elysees", 1938*, s., artist's device, (10-11-92, Dunning, #1242), 22 x 15½ in., (55.9 x 39.4 cm.), etching in colors, acetoned (BP 359, DM 899, FR 3017, Y 73,655).

BI *Backstage (H., C. & I. 298), 1926*, s., blindstamp, trimmed, good condition, mat staining, brown staining, rubbed areas, surface soiling, est. $1/1,500, (03-31-93, Butterfield, #5207), 11⁹⁄₁₆ x 8⅜ in., (29.4 x 21.3 cm.), sheet 20⅝ x 15 in., (29.4 x 21.3 cm.), drypoint printed in colors on wove paper.

BI *Baigneuses (Holland-Catania-Isen 297), 1926*, s., est. DM 4,000, (12-05-92, Bassenge, #7284, illus.), 21¼ x 17¹⁵⁄₁₆ in., (54 x 45.5 cm.), color etching on copper print paper.

$1840* *Baigneuses, (Bathers) (H., C. & I. 407), 1931*, s., blindstamp, (c), d. in margins, good condition, mat staining, light-staining, (03-31-93, Butterfield, #5217), 25½ x 17¾ in., (64.8 x 45.1 cm.), sheet 30⅛ x 21¾ in., (64.8 x 45.1 cm.), etching w/aquatint and drypoint printed in colors w/touches of hand-coloring on wove (BP 1217, DM 2960, FR 10,055, Y 211,592).

$935* *Baigneuses, 1926, Holland-Catania-Isen 297*, s., num. 279, (09-20-92, Hindman, #788), 21½ x 18⅛ in., (54.6 x 46 cm.), color aquatint and drypoint (BP 547, DM 1387, FR 4746, Y 115,560).

$773* *La Ballerine, 1939*, s., artist's (c), (06-28-93, Loudmer, #266), 19⁵⁄₁₆ x 22¹³⁄₁₆ in., (490 x 580 mm.), sh 24⁷⁄₁₆ x 27⅜ in., (490 x 580 mm.), color etching and aquatint on wove (BP 518, DM 1314, FR 4425, Y 82,016).

$2200* *Bathers (Baigneuses) (H., C. & I 297), 1931*, s., (c), plate d., blindstamp, margins, good cond.?, (10-28-92, Butterfield, #2656), 25½ x 17¾ in., (648 x 451 mm.), color etching w/aquatint and drypoint on wove (BP 1402, DM 3398, FR 11,536, Y 269,939).

BI *Bathers (Baigneuses) (H., C. and I. 297), 1926*, s., num. 182, (c)/d. in plate, pub. L'Estampe Moderne, blindstamp, margins, laid down, good cond., glue/paper remains, mat staining, pressure mark in image, est. $7/1000, (09-21-92, Butterfield, #807, illus.), sheet 21¹¹⁄₁₆ x 18³⁄₁₆ in., (550.3 x 461.2 mm.), 28¹⁄₁₆ x 24¹⁄₁₆ in., (550.3 x 461.2 mm.), etching w/aquatint in colors touches hand-coloring on wove.

$220* *"Battle"*, bears sig., blindstamp, (01-21-93, A. James, #11), 9½ x 7¼ in., (24.1 x 18.4 cm.), colored etching (BP 143, DM 353, FR 1193, Y 27,418).

$1265* *La Belle Au Bois Dormant, (Sleeping Beauty) (H., C. & I. 323), 1927*, s., blindstamp, (c), d. in plate, margins, glued in areas to overmat, good condition, mat and light-staining, (03-31-93, Butterfield, #5209), 15¼ x 19⅛ in., (38.7 x 48.6 cm.), sheet 19½ x 23⅝ in., (38.7 x 48.6 cm.), etching with aquatint and drypoint printed in colors w/touches of hand-coloring on wove paper (BP 836, DM 2035, FR 6913, Y 145,469).

$1495* *Belle Rose, 1933*, s., artist's blindstamp, (03-25-93, Christie-E, #214), 16¼ x 20⅞ in., (41.3 x 53 cm.), color etching and drypoint (BP 1015, DM 2456, FR 8352, Y 175,141).

$990* *Birds Of July, 1926*, s., windmill stamp, (03-12-93, DuMouchelle, #36, illus.), 18 x 11 in., (45.7 x 27.9 cm.), drypoint and etching (BP 691, DM 1648, FR 5603, Y 116,676).

BI *"The Black Shawl", 1925*, s., #98, est. $1,25/1,750, (02-12-93, DuMouchelle, #367, illus.), 16¼ x 11½ in., (41.3 x 29.2 cm.), drypoint and etching.

BI *"The Black Shawl", c. 1925*, s., est. $25/3000, (10-16-92, DuMouchelle, #1300), 16¼ x 11½ in., (41.3 x 29.2 cm.), color and drypoint etching.

BI *"The Black Shawl", c. 1925*, s., est. $2,5/3,000, (01-15-93, DuMouchelle, #1301), 16¼ x 11½ in., (41.3 x 29.2 cm.), color and drypoint etching.

$2070* *Blancheurs (Symphony In White)*, (c) 1932 by L. Icart Sty., s., w/artist's blindstamp, laid down, glue to mat, time darkened, mat burn, (06-09-93, Sotheby-Arcade, #252), 18⅞ x 15 in., (47.9 x 38.1 cm.), etching and drypoint in colors and touched w/hand-coloring (BP 1365, DM 3386, FR 11,386, Y 220,143).

$880* *Book Plate: Four*, bears sig. Louis Icart LD, (02-27-93, Dunning, #1083, illus.), 6½ x 4¾ in., (16.5 x 12.1 cm.), color lithograph (BP 619, DM 1447, FR 4916, Y 103,884).

BI *Les Cacatoes Indiscret, 1921*, s., pub. L'Estampe Moderne, blindstamp, margins, est. BP 4/600, (08-20-92, Bonhams-Chelsea, #136, illus.), plate 13¼ x 10¾ in., (33.7 x 27.3 cm.), etching and drypoint in colors laid down.

BI *La Cachette (The Hiding Place)*, (c) 1927 by Les Graveurs Modernes, s., blindstamp, annot. 118, good cond., laid down, time darkened, slight mat burning, est. $1,5/2,000, (06-09-93, Sotheby-Arcade, #269), 18⅛ x 14½ in., (46 x 36.8 cm.), etching and drypoint in colors touched w/hand-coloring.

$690* *La Cage Rouge (The Red Cage)*, (c) 1928 by L. Icart, s., blindstamp, annot. 111, laid down, glued to mat, time darkened, (06-09-93, Sotheby-Arcade, #270), 11¼ x 8⅞ in., (28.6 x 22.5 cm.), etching and drypoint in colors touched w/hand-coloring (BP 455, DM 1129, FR 3795, Y 73,381).

$1210* *Carmen*, (c) 1927 Les Graveurs Modernes, s., artist's blindstamp, generally good cond., darkening, laid down, glued to mat, (11-06-92, Sotheby-Arcade, #144, illus.), 21 x 14⅛ in., (53.3 x 35.9 cm.), etching/drypoint in colors/hand-coloring (BP 791, DM 1932, FR 6530, Y 149,346).

$690* *Carmen*, (c) 1927 by Les Graveurs Modernes, s., w/artist's blindstamp, annot.68, time darkened, mat stained, laid down, (06-09-93, Sotheby-Arcade, #253), 19⅞ x 13¼ in., (50.5 x 33.7 cm.), etching and drypoint in colors and touched w/hand-coloring (BP 455, DM 1129, FR 3795, Y 73,381).

BI *Carmen (H., C. and I. 315), 1927*, s., num. 412, (c)/d. in plate, pub. Les Graveurs Modernes, artist's blindstamp, margins, good cond., heavy staining, glue/paper remains, thinned spots, surface abrasions in image w/ink loss, creases, surface soiling, (09-21-92, Butterfield, #808), sheet 21¹⁄₁₆ x 14⅛ in., (534.4 x 359.4 mm.), 25³⁄₁₆ x 17⅞ in., (534.4 x 359.4 mm.), etching w/aquatint in colors, touches hand-coloring on wove.

$935* *Carmen, 1927*, s., windmill stamp, (03-12-93, DuMouchelle, #38, illus.), 20⅛ x 13½ in., (51.1 x 34.3 cm.), drypoint and etching (BP 652, DM 1556, FR 5291, Y 110,194).

BI *Casanova*, (c) 1928 by L. Icart, s., w/artist's blindstamp, annot. 340, laid down, glass glued to print, timed darkened, est. $1/1,500, (06-09-93, Sotheby-Arcade, #254), 20 x 13⅛ in., (50.8 x 33.3 cm.), etching and drypoint in colors touched w/hand-coloring.

$990* *Casanova, 1928,* s., #138, (03-12-93, DuMouchelle, #40, illus.), 20¼ x 13⅜ in., (51.4 x 34 cm.), drypoint and etching (BP 691, DM 1648, FR 5603, Y 116,676).

BI *"Champs Elysees",* s. Louis Icart, (c) 1918 Louis Icart, stamp, (06-16-93, Encans, #146, illus.), 14¾ x 21³⁄₁₆ in., (37.5 x 53.8 cm.), etching and aquatint.

BI *Cherry Blossoms,* s., num. illegibly, est. $2,5/3,000, (12-10-92, Sloan, #3056), oval 18 x 14¼ in., (45.7 x 36.2 cm.), color etching and aquatint.

$533* *Cinderella, 1927,* s., num. 111, blindstamp, pub. Les Graveurs Modernes, margins, (11-30-92, Phillips-London, #431), plate 15⅝ x 18⅞ in., (391 x 479 mm.), color etching and drypoint (BP 352, DM 849, FR 2883, Y 66,335).

BI *The Coach,* s., windmill stamp, est. $1/1,500, (03-12-93, DuMouchelle, #34, illus.), 21 x 14 in., (53.3 x 35.6 cm.), etching.

$990* *Coach (Holland/Catania/Isen fig. 265), 1926,* s., #454, bears artist's stamp, (05-16-93, Hindman, #463), 22 x 18⅛ in., (55.9 x 46 cm.), color drypoint and aquatint (BP 644, DM 1592, FR 5351, Y 109,744).

$1870* *"The Coach",* stamped, s., (05-15-93, Dunning, #1030, illus.), 21 x 17½ in., (53.3 x 44.5 cm.), aquatint and drypoint in color (BP 1216, DM 3008, FR 10,108, Y 207,294).

$770* *Coach, 1926, Holland-Catania-Isen 265,* s., num. 248, bears artist's stamp, (09-20-92, Hindman, #786), 22¼ x 18¼ in., (56.5 x 46.4 cm.), color aquatint and drypoint (BP 451, DM 1143, FR 3909, Y 95,167).

$1100* *The Coach, c. 1948,* s., artist's blindstamp, annotated 1198, full sheet, time darkened, glued to mat, (11-06-92, Sotheby-Arcade, #145), 21½ x 17½ in., (54.6 x 44.5 cm.), etching/drypoint in colors w/hand-coloring (BP 719, DM 1756, FR 5936, Y 135,769).

$4313* *Cocktail (Martini),* (c) 1932 by L. Icart Sty., s., good cond., loose sheet, margins trimmed slightly, (06-09-93, Sotheby-Arcade, #255, illus.), 12½ x 16⅝ in., (31.8 x 42.2 cm.), etching and drypoint in colors and touched w/ hand-coloring (BP 2845, DM 7054, FR 23,724, Y 458,683).

$605* *Color Etchings From Felicia, c. 1946: Three,* s., full margins, excellent cond., (10-10-92, Goldberg, #437), 7¼ x 5½ in., (18.4 x 14 cm.), color etching (BP 359, DM 899, FR 3017, Y 73,655).

BI *"Conchita", c. 1929,* s., windmill stamp, est. $2/2,500, (02-12-93, DuMouchelle, #1211, illus.), 20¼ x 13½ in., (51.4 x 34.3 cm.), color etching and drypoint.

BI *"Conchita", c. 1929,* s., windmill stamp, est. $22/2500, (10-16-92, DuMouchelle, #1303), 20¼ x 13½ in., (51.4 x 34.3 cm.), color etching and drypoint.

$1265* *"La Confidance" and "Venus": Two,* first, (c) 1926 by Les Graveurs Modernes, s., blindstamp; second, (c) 1928 by L. Icart, s., blindstamp, annot. 462/500, both laid down, glass gluedto print, glued to mat, (06-09-93, Sotheby-Arcade, #271), first 16 x 20¼ in., (40.6 x 51.4 cm.), second 13¼ x 18⅞ in., (40.6 x 51.4 cm.), etching and drypoint in colors touched w/hand-coloring (BP 834, DM 2069, FR 6958, Y 134,532).

$935* *Contentment (Holland-Cantania-Isen fig. 139), 1922,* s., #288, (03-14-93, Hindman, #272, illus.), 7¾ x 9¾ in., (19.7 x 24.8 cm.), color aquatint and drypoint (BP 652, DM 1556, FR 5291, Y 110,194).

$1650* *Le Coucher,* (c) 1925 Les Graveurs Modernes, s., annot. 45, good cond., time darkening, (11-06-92, Sotheby-Arcade, #146), 15½ x 15½ in., (39.4 x 39.4 cm.), etching/drypoint in colors w/hand-coloring (BP 1079, DM 2635, FR 8904, Y 203,653).

BI *Coursing II,* (c) 1929 L. Icart, s., artist's blindstamp, annot., extensive repairs, abraded, loose, est. $ 1/1500, (11-06-92, Sotheby-Arcade, #147), 16 x 25¾ in., (40.6 x 65.4 cm.), etching/drypoint in colors w/hand-coloring.

$3080* *Coursing II,* (c) 1929 L. Icart, s., artist's blindstamp, annot. 125/500, good cond., time-darkening, foxing, rubbed streak, laid down, glued to mat, (11-06-92, Sotheby-Arcade, #148), 16 x 25¼ in., (40.6 x 64.1 cm.), etching/drypoint in colors w/hand-coloring (BP 2014, DM 4918, FR 16,622, Y 380,153).

$2420* *Coursing II,* s., stamp, (01-15-93, DuMouchelle, #3, illus.), 15¼ x 25¼ in., (38.7 x 64.1 cm.), drypoint and etching (BP 1582, DM 3957, FR 13,378, Y 305,093).

$2013* *Coursing II,* (c) 1929 by L. Icart, s., w/artist's blindstamp, loose sheet, full margins, washed, minor abrasions to surface, (06-09-93, Sotheby-Arcade, #256), 15¼ x 25½ in., (38.7 x 64 cm.), etching and drypoint in colors touched w/hand-coloring (BP 1328, DM 3292, FR 11,073, Y 214,081).

BI *Coursing II,* (c) 1929 by L. Icart, s., w/artist's blindstamp, annot. indistinct, extensively repaired, abraded, loose sheet, loose sheet $800/1,200, (06-09-93, Sotheby-Arcade, #257), 16 x 25¾ in., (40.6 x 65.4 cm.), etching and drypoint in colors touched w/hand-coloring.

BI *Coursing II (H., C. and I. 371), 1929,* s., num. 302/500, artist's blind stamp, large margins, sealed in mat, good cond.?, est. $3/5000, (09-21-92, Butterfield, #813), sheet 16 x 25¹³⁄₁₆ in., (407.1 x 655.2 mm.), 21³⁄₁₆ x 30⁹⁄₁₆ in., (407.1 x 655.2 mm.), etching w/drypoint in colors on cream wove.

$2640* *Coursing II, 1929,* s., ded., annot. Epreuve d'artiste, bears artist's stamp, (12-13-92, Hindman, #291, illus.), 18½ x 28⅞ in., color etching and drypoint w/hand-coloring (BP 1688, DM 4149, FR 14,140, Y 326,611).

$660* *Coursing Lady With Greyhounds,* discoloration, laid down, torn in margin corner and missing, (11-12-92, Freemn/Fine Art, #95A), 21 x 17¼ in., (53.3 x 43.8 cm.), drypoint (BP 433, DM 1046, FR 3528, Y 81,835).

BI *Crying Ballerina,* s., time-darkened, repaired hole, waterstaining to edges, est. $1/1,500, (06-09-93, Sotheby-Arcade, #258), 17¾ x 13¾ in., (45.1 x 34.9 cm.), lithograph touched w/pastel.

$1035* *Dalila,* (c) 1929 by L. Icart, s., w/artist's blindstamp, annot. 163, time darkened, glued to mat, (06-09-93, Sotheby-Arcade, #259), 20⅛ x 13½ in., (51.1 x 34.3 cm.), etching and drypoint in colors and touched w/hand-coloring (BP 683, DM 1693, FR 5693, Y 110,071).

BI *La Dame Aux Camelias (Lady Of The Camelias),* (c) 1927 by Les Graveurs Modernes, s., artist's blindstamp, annot. A.339/500, good cond., time-darkened, margins trimmed, glued to mat, slight foxing, est. $1,5/2,000, (06-09-93, Sotheby-Arcade, #258A), 16¾ x 20¾ in., (42.5 x 52.7 cm.), etching and drypoint in colors and touched w/ hand-coloring.

$1380* *La Dame Aux Camerlias,* (c) 1927 by Les Graveurs Modernes, s., blindstamp, annot. 87, good cond., laid down, slight time darkening, (06-09-93, Sotheby-Arcade, #272), 16⅛ x 20¼ in., (41 x 51.4 cm.), etching and drypoint in colors touched w/hand-coloring (BP 910, DM 2257, FR 7591, Y 146,762).

$734* *La Dame En Rose (Schnessel et Carmel 209), 1933,* s., excellent cond., (11-16-92, Briest, #312), 8⁹⁄₁₆ x 11⁵⁄₁₆ in., (21.7 x 28.7 cm.), aquatint and drypoint in colors (BP 482, DM 1171, FR 3944, Y 91,601).

$438* *"La Dame Rose",* s. Louis Icart, (c) 1935, (05-18-93, Encans, #195), 8¹⁄₁₆ x 11 in., (20.5 x 28 cm.), eau-forte (etching) et pointe-seche (drypoint) maroufle sur carton (BP 285, DM 711, FR 2400, Y 48,813, C$ 555).

$1035* *La Dame Rose, (Pink Lady) (H., C. & I. 430), 1933,* s., blindstamp, (c), d. in plate, margins, good condition, mat and light-staining, paper remains, (03-31-93, Butterfield, #5220), 8¾ x 11½ in., (22.2 x 29.2 cm.), sheet 12¾ x 14⅞ in., (22.2 x 29.2 cm.), etching w/aquatint and drypoint printed in colors on wove (BP 684, DM 1665, FR 5656, Y 119,020).

$715* *La Dame Rose, 1933,* discoloration, (11-12-92, Freemn/Fine Art, #95), 8¼ x 10⅞ in., (21 x 27.6 cm.), colored etching (BP 470, DM 1133, FR 3821, Y 88,655).

$3520* *Dans Le Passe, Recollections, 1928,* s., bears blindstamp, (04-26-93, Selkirk, #158, illus.), 12½ x 17 in., (31.8 x 43.2 cm.), etching w/drypoint (BP 2222, DM 5517, FR 18,634, Y 388,435).

$880* *Dans Les Passes,* (c) 1928 L. Icart, s., artist's blindstamp, annot. A/238, time darkened, mat stained, laid down, abrasions, (11-06-92, Sotheby-Arcade, #149), 12½ x 17 in., (31.8 x 43.2 cm.), etching/drypoint in colors w/ hand-coloring (BP 575, DM 1405, FR 4749, Y 108,615).

$920* *Danse Apache,* (c) 1929 Louis Icart, s., w/artist's blindstamp, annot. 284, loose sheet, mat burn, glued margins, time darkened, margins trimmed, (06-09-93, Sotheby-Arcade, #260), 20¼ x 13⅛ in., (51.4 x 33.3 cm.), etching and drypoint in color, touched w/hand-coloring (BP 607, DM 1505, FR 5061, Y 97,841).

BI *Dessins Des Femmes, c. 1928,* s., est. $1/1500, (11-06-92, Sotheby-Arcade, #150), sight 16¼ x 13 in., (41.3 x 33 cm.), lithograph w/hand-coloring.

$700* *"Dom Juan",* s. Louis Icart, (c) 1928, (05-18-93, Encans, #197), 19¹¹⁄₁₆ x 13⅜ in., (50 x 34 cm.), eau-forte (etching) et pointe seche, marouflé sur carton (BP 456, DM 1136, FR 3836, Y 78,012, C$ 888).

$1210* *Don Juan,* s., stamp, (11-13-92, DuMouchelle, #197, illus.), 20¼ x 13¼ in., (51.4 x 33.7 cm.), drypoint and etching (BP 782, DM 1900, FR 6406, Y 150,180).

$863* *Don Juan (H., C. & I. 330), 1928,* s., #d212/500 in ink, blindstamp, (c), d. in plate, pub. Editions d'Art Devambez, margins trimmed unevenly, etched t., margin partially trimmed, good condition, tear, glue and paper remains, skinned areas, mat staining, foxing, (03-31-93, Butterfield, #5213, illus.), 21¼ x 14⅛ in., (54 x 35.9 cm.), sheet 26⅜ x 19 in., (54 x 35.9 cm.), etching w/ aquatint and drypoint printed in color on Rives BFK (BP 571, DM 1388, FR 4716, Y 99,241).

$825* *Don Juan (Holland/Catania/Isen fig. 300), 1928,* s., annot. EA, bears artist's stamp, (05-16-93, Hindman, #461), 21⅛ x 14¼ in., (53.7 x 36.2 cm.), color drypoint and aquatint w/hand-coloring (BP 536, DM 1327, FR 4459, Y 91,453).

$844* *"Don Juan",* Editions d'Art Devamber, Paris, stamp, s., (03-16-93, Encans, #192), 19¹¹⁄₁₆ x 12¹⁵⁄₁₆ in., (50 x 33 cm.), etching and aquatint (BP 583, DM 1403, FR 4768, Y 98,690, C$ 1055).

$1100* *"Dressing", c. 1926,* s., num. 270, blindstamp, lit., (01-21-93, A. James, #30), 18½ x 14¼ in., (47 x 36.2 cm.), drypoint and etching (BP 713, DM 1766, FR 5965, Y 137,089).

$920* *Les Elephants,* (c) 1925 Les Graveurs Modernes, s., annot. 168, laid down, glued to mat, time darkened, minor abrasions, (06-09-93, Sotheby-Arcade, #277), 16½ x 11¾ in., (41.9 x 29.8 cm.), etching and drpoint in colors, touched w/hand-coloring (BP 607, DM 1505, FR 5061, Y 97,841).

BI *Erotic Etchings: Six, 1946,* by George Guillot, s., est. $2/3000, (11-06-92, Sotheby-Arcade, #164), 6½ x 4½ in., (16.5 x 11.4 cm.), etching/drypoint in colors.

$1155* *Eve,* s., Schnessel no. 118, (11-01-92, Hanzel, #213), oval 19½ x 14 in., (49.5 x 35.6 cm.), colored etching (BP 755, DM 1822, FR 6140, Y 142,804).

$1210* *Eve,* s., stamp, (04-16-93, DuMouchelle, #11, illus.), 13¼ x 18⅞ in., (33.7 x 47.9 cm.), drypoint and etching (BP 794, DM 1954, FR 6605, Y 136,062).

BI *Eve (Schnessel 118), 1928,* s., L.I., Paris blindstamp, est. $1,500/2,000, (09-17-92, Sloan, #2598), 13⅜ x 18¾ in., (34 x 47.6 cm.), color etching and drypoint.

$1540* *Eve, 1928,* s., stamp, (01-15-93, DuMouchelle, #2, illus.), 13¼ x 18⅞ in., (33.7 x 47.9 cm.), drypoint and etching (BP 1007, DM 2518, FR 8513, Y 194,150).

$1093* *Eventail Noir, (Black Fan) (H., C. & I. 406), 1931,* s., blindtamp, d. and (c) in plate, margins trimmed unevenly, good condition, staining, thinned spots, paper loss, (03-31-93, Butterfield, #5218, illus.), 16¾ x 21¼ in., (42.5 x 54 cm.), sheet 22⅛ x 26¾ in., (42.5 x 54 cm.), etching w/aquatint and drypoint printed in colors w/touches of hand-coloring on Rives BFK (BP 723, DM 1758, FR 5973, Y 125,690).

$442* *"Fair Dancer, Music Hall",* s. Louis Icart, (c) 1939, (02-16-93, Encans, #119), 18⁹⁄₁₆ x 22⅛ in., (46.2 x 56.2 cm.), etching and aquatint (BP 306, DM 721, FR 2443, Y 52,953, C$ 555).

$1083* *Fair Dancer, c. 1939,* s., pub. by artist, full margins, excellent cond., mount-staining, (11-30-92, Phillips-London, #433), plate 19¼ x 22½ in., (489 x 572 mm.), drypoint w/aquatint in colors on wove (BP 715, DM 1725, FR 5857, Y 134,785).

$1150* *Fallen Nest, 1924,* s., Estampe Moderne seal, (03-25-93, Christie-E, #215), 14⅞ x 18¾ in., (37.8 x 47.6 cm.), color etching and drypoint (BP 781, DM 1889, FR 6425, Y 134,724).

$920* *La Falque (Wistfulness) (H., C. & I. 193), 1924,* s., d., (c) in plate, pub. Les Graveurs Modernes, margins, glued to overmat, mat staining, light staining, (03-31-93, Butterfield, #5202, illus.), 12½ x 17¾ in., (31.8 x 45.1 cm.), sheet 18 x 24 in., (31.8 x 45.1 cm.), (BP 608, DM 1480, FR 5027, Y 105,796).

BI *Fanny And Cat (H., C. and I. 260), 1926,* s., num. 168, artist's blindstamp, large margins, glued to overmat, good cond., mat staining, surface soiling, creases, est. $2/2500, (09-21-92, Butterfield, #801), sheet 15 x 13¾ in., (381.7 x 349.9 mm.), 22¼ x 19⅛ in., (381.7 x 349.9 mm.), etching/aquatint/drypoint in colors on cream wove.

$920* *Faust,* (c) 1928 by L. Icart, s., blindstamp, annot. 158, good cond., laid down, margins trimmed, (06-09-93, Sotheby-Arcade, #262), 20½ x 13 in., (52.1 x 33 cm.), etching and drypoint in colors touched w/hand-coloring (BP 607, DM 1505, FR 5061, Y 97,841).

$805* *Faust,* (c) 1928 by Louis Icart, s., blindstamp, good cond., margins trimmed, washed, loose sheet, (06-09-93, Sotheby-Arcade, #263), 20½ x 13 in., (52.1 x 33 cm.), etching and drypoint in colors, touched w/hand-coloring (BP 531, DM 1317, FR 4428, Y 85,611).

$2530* *Faust (Holland-Catania-Isen fig. 352), 1928,* s., #A 285/590, bears artist's blindstamp, (03-14-93, Hindman, #275), 21¼ x 13⅝ in., (54 x 34.6 cm.), color aquatint and drypoint (BP 1765, DM 4211, FR 14,318, Y 298,173).

$4313* *"Faust", "The Coach", "Les Hortensias" and "Pivones": Four,* various (c) years and pub., all s., w/artist's blindstamp, some annot., good cond., some time darkening, (06-09-93, Sotheby-Arcade, #249), largest 21¼ x 17½ in., (54 x 44.5 cm.), smallest 8½ x 11 in., (54 x 44.5 cm.), etching in colors and touched w/hand-coloring (BP 2845, DM 7054, FR 23,724, Y 458,683).

BI *Felicia Ou Mes Fredaines: Twenty,* est. $3/5,000, (06-09-93, Sotheby-Arcade, #264), 7½ x 5½ in., (19.1 x 14 cm.), etching, etching and drypoint in colors.

$6613* *La Fete (Mardi Gras),* (c) 1936, s., w/artist's blindstamp, good cond., laid down, glued toat, mat burned, (06-09-93, Sotheby-Arcade, #250, illus.), 18½ x 18¼ in., (47 x 46.4 cm.), etching and drypoint in colors and touched w/ hand-coloring (BP 4362, DM 10,816, FR 36,375, Y 703,286).

$733* *Flowerseller, 1928,* s., blindstamp, pub. Les Graveurs Modernes, full margins, good cond., (11-30-92, Phillips-London, #432), plate 19½ x 15 in., (495 x 381 mm.), etching and drypoint in colors (BP 484, DM 1168, FR 3964, Y 91,226).

$1045* *"Forbidden Fruit" (Holland, et al., 264), 1926,* s. Louis Icart, i. (c) and d., pub.'s blindstamp, stamped Gravure/Garantie/originale, watermark, very good cond., mount toning, annot., losses, (03-12-93, Skinner, #8, illus.), 17⅛ x 12⅝ in., (43.5 x 32.1 cm.), color aquatint on BFK Rives wove (BP 729, DM 1739, FR 5914, Y 123,159).

$1495* *Forsythia (H., C. & I. 295), 1925,* s., #211, (c), d. in plate, pub. Les Graveurs Modernes, full margins, margins glued to overmat, good condition, mat and light-staining, soiling, notations, (03-31-93, Butterfield, #5206, illus.), 19¼ x 15½ in., (48.9 x 39.4 cm.), sheet 25¾ x 20 in., (48.9 x 39.4 cm.), aquatint w/drypoint printed in colors w/touches of hand-coloring on BFK Rives paper (BP 988, DM 2405, FR 8169, Y 171,918).

$920* *Forsythia (H., C. & I. 295), 1925,* s., #59, large margins, good condition, surface soiling, abrasions, (03-31-93, Butterfield, #5204), 19¼ x 15½ in., (48.9 x 39.4 cm.), sheet 23½ x 18½ in., (48.9 x 39.4 cm.), etching w/drypoint printed in colors on BFK Rives paper (BP 608, DM 1480, FR 5027, Y 105,796).

BI *Forsythia (H., C. and I. 295), 1925,* s., num. 59, large margins, good cond., surface soiling, abrasions, est. $15/2000, (09-21-92, Butterfield, #803), sheet 19⁵⁄₁₆ x 15½ in., (489.8 x 394.4 mm.), 23⁹⁄₁₆ x 18⁹⁄₁₆ in., (489.8 x 394.4 mm.), etching w/drypoint in colors on BFK Rives.

$3600* *Fountain, 1936,* s., artist's blindstamp, sold after sale, (03-25-93, Christie-E, #216), 20⅛ x 8¼ in., (51.1 x 21 cm.), color etching and drypoint (BP 2445, DM 5914, FR 20,112, Y 421,743).

$1320* *Four Seasons: "Spring", #73 c. 1928,* s., (05-15-93, Dunning, #1032, illus.), 6½ x 9 in., (16.5 x 22.9 cm.), aquatint in color (BP 858, DM 2123, FR 7135, Y 146,325).

$330* *From "Gargantua",* s., (10-16-92, DuMouchelle, #1302), color book plate (BP 200, DM 487, FR 1656, Y 39,403).

BI *From Le Sopha, 1935: Six,* pub. Le Vasseur it Cie, est. $1/1,500, (03-25-93, Christie-E, #221), each plate 4½ x 6½ in., (11.4 x 16.5 cm.), etching.

$1495* *Fumee (Smoke),* (c) 1926 by Les Graveurs Modernes, s., blindstamp, glued to mat, time darkened, minor foxing, (06-09-93, Sotheby-Arcade, #266), 14 x 19½ in., (35.6 x 49.5 cm.), etching and drypoint in colors touched w/ hand-coloring (BP 986, DM 2445, FR 8223, Y 158,992).

$1495* *Gay Senorita, 1939,* s., artist's blindstamp, (06-08-93, Christie-E, #198), 17½ x 21½ in., (44.5 x 54.6 cm.), color etching and drypoint (BP 983, DM 2426, FR 8169, Y 158,789).

BI *Gitane,* (c) 1939 L. Icart Society, s., artist's blindstamp, good cond., abrasions, margins trimmed, soiled, est. $18/ 2500, (11-06-92, Sotheby-Arcade, #151, illus.), 18¼ x 22¼ in., (46.4 x 56.5 cm.), etching/drypoint in colors w/ hand-coloring.

BI *Golden Veil,* s., est. $3,25/3,750, (12-10-92, Sloan, #3054), 15½ x 19½ in., (39.4 x 49.5 cm.), color etching and aquatint.

BI *Gossip (Bavardage) (H., C. and I. 296), 1926,* s., num. 185/350, artist's blindstamp, good cond., mat staining, tape remains, est. $1/1500, (09-21-92, Butterfield, #804), sheet 17$\frac{9}{16}$ x 13¾ in., (445.3 x 349.9 mm.), 24$\frac{5}{16}$ x 18$\frac{5}{16}$ in., (445.3 x 349.9 mm.), etching w/aquatint/drypoint in colors on cream wove.

$1033* *Une Gravure Originale - Decoration Ideale, c. 1930,* (12-05-92, Bassenge, #7600), 19½ x 12⅝ in., (49.5 x 32 cm.), color lithograph (BP 647, DM 1611, FR 5489, Y 127,989).

$2090* *Green Screen or Intimacy,* d. 1928, s., artist's stamp, (11-28-92, Dunning, #1096), 16 x 18½ in., (40.6 x 47 cm.), color etching and drypoint (BP 1380, DM 3330, FR 11,303, Y 260,112).

BI *"Gust Of Wind" (Holland et al., 235), 1925,* s. Louis Icart, num. 125/500, i. (c)1925 by Les Graveurs Modernes, pub. dry stamp, very good cond., est. $1/2000, (09-11-92, Skinner, #8, illus.), 21⅝ x 18⅛ in., (54.9 x 46 cm.), color etching/aquatint, stencil color on cream paper.

BI *Happy Birthday,* (c) 1937 by L. Icart Society, s., blindstamp, good cond., slight foxing, laid down on board, (06-09-93, Sotheby-Arcade, #267, illus.), 14¼ x 18½ in., (36.2 x 47 cm.), etching and drypoint in colors and touched w/hand-coloring.

BI *"Le Hortenias", c. 1919,* s., (c), est. $3/3,500, (02-12-93, DuMouchelle, #1212, illus.), 16¼ x 20¼ in., (41.3 x 51.4 cm.), color etching and drypoint.

BI *"Le Hortenias", c. 1919,* s., (c), est. $3/3500, (10-16-92, DuMouchelle, #1304), 16¼ x 20¼ in., (41.3 x 51.4 cm.), color etching and drypoint.

$1100* *Les Hortensias,* (c) 1929 L. Icart, s., artist's blindstamp, annot. 169, good cond., foxing, darkening, glued to mat, (11-06-92, Sotheby-Arcade, #153, illus.), 16¾ x 21¼ in., (42.5 x 54 cm.), etching/drypoint in colors w/hand-coloring (BP 719, DM 1756, FR 5936, Y 135,769).

$1045* *Les Hortensias,* (c) 1929 L. Icart, s., artist's blindstamp, annot. B.61, laid down, margins trimmed, time darkened, abrasions, foxing, (11-06-92, Sotheby-Arcade, #154), 16¾ x 21¼ in., (42.5 x 54 cm.), etching/drypoint in colors w/hand-coloring (BP 683, DM 1669, FR 5640, Y 128,980).

BI *Les Hortensias (Holland/Catania/Isen fig. 373), 1929,* s., bears artist's stamp, est. $1/1,500, (05-16-93, Hindman, #465), 16½ x 21 in., (41.9 x 53.3 cm.), color drypoint.

$1150* *Les Hortensias (Hydrangeas),* (c) 1929 by L. Icart, s., blindstamp, good cond., glued to mat, slight time-darkening, (06-09-93, Sotheby-Arcade, #278), 16⅛ x 20½ in., (41 x 52.1 cm.), etching and drypoint in colors, touched w/hand-coloring (BP 759, DM 1881, FR 6326, Y 122,301).

$1150* *Les Hortensias, (Hydrangeas) (H., C. & I. 373), 1929,* s., blindstamp, (c), d. in plate, margins, laid down, good condition, mat and light-staining, glue, paper remains, paper loss, notation, (03-31-93, Butterfield, #5215), 17 x 21⅜ in., (43.2 x 54.3 cm.), sheet 21⅝ x 25$\frac{7}{16}$ in., (43.2 x 54.3 cm.), etching with aquatint and drypoint printed in colors w/touches of hand-coloring on Arches (BP 760, DM 1850, FR 6284, Y 132,245).

BI *Hydrangeas (Les Hortensias) (H., C. and I. 373), 1929,* s., artist's blindstamp, sealed in mat, trimmed margins, good cond.,mat/light/time-staining, est. $1/1500, (09-21-92, Butterfield, #814), sheet 16¾ x 21$\frac{1}{16}$ in., (426.2 x 534.4 mm.), 19$\frac{9}{16}$ x 23$\frac{13}{16}$ in., (426.2 x 534.4 mm.), etching w/aquatint/drypoint in colors on cream wove.

$1320* *Intimite,* (c) 1928 L. Icart, s., artist's blindstamp, annot. 165, generally good cond., time-darkening, glued to mat, (11-06-92, Sotheby-Arcade, #155, illus.), 15 x 18 in., (38.1 x 45.7 cm.), etching/drypoint in colors w/hand-coloring (BP 863, DM 2108, FR 7124, Y 162,923).

$1210* *Intimite, 1928,* s., laid down, (02-08-93, Selkirk, #570), image 16 x 18 in., (40.6 x 45.7 cm.), etching and drypoint (BP 842, DM 2004, FR 6779, Y 149,790).

$688* *Invitation (H. 206),* (c) 1924 by Les Graveurs Moderns, s., i. EP d'artiste, (06-11-93, Freemn/Fine Art, #110), 17$\frac{7}{16}$ x 11½ in., (44.3 x 29.2 cm.), drypoint and aquatint (BP 452, DM 1118, FR 3770, Y 72,997).

$825* *Japanese Goldfish, Interior With Two Women Admiring A Goldfish Bowl,1924,* s., pub. Les Graveurs Modernes, crackle, good cond.?, (12-08-92, Swann, #147, illus.), oval 14 x 18 in., (35.6 x 45.7 cm.), color drypoint (BP 517, DM 1284, FR 4379, Y 102,256).

$775* *La Jarretelle,* s. Louis Icart, (c) 1940, margins, (09-15-92, Encans, #153), 19$\frac{11}{16}$ x 17$\frac{11}{16}$ in., (50 x 45 cm.), etching and aquatint (BP 415, DM 1153, FR 3914, Y 96,214, C$ 944).

$821* *Jeunes Femmes Au Chat,* s., (c) 1924, margins, (09-15-92, Encans, #151), oval 16$\frac{15}{16}$ x 20½ in., (43 x 52 cm.), drypoint and aquatint (BP 439, DM 1222, FR 4146, Y 101,924, C$ 999).

$920* *Joan Of Arc, 1929,* s., artist's blindstamp, (03-25-93, Christie-E, #217), 19 x 14⅝ in., (48.3 x 37.1 cm.), color etching and drypoint (BP 625, DM 1511, FR 5140, Y 107,779).

BI *Joy Of Life (Joie De Vivre) (H., C. and I. 359), 1929,* s., artist's blindstamp, sealed in mat, surface soiling, mat/ light-staining, est. $2/3000, (09-21-92, Butterfield, #811, illus.), 24$\frac{9}{16}$ x 16 in., (623.4 x 407.1 mm.), etching w/ drypoint in colors on cream wove.

$2588* *Juenesse (Youth),* (c) 1930 by Louis Icart, s., blindstamp, laid down, time-darkened, soiling to margins, (06-09-93, Sotheby-Arcade, #268), 24 x 15⅜ in., (61 x 39.1 cm.), etching and drypoint in colors touched w/hand-coloring (BP 1707, DM 4233, FR 14,235, Y 275,231).

$1150* *L'Arbre, (Springtime) (H., C. & I. 196), 1924,* s., annot, Ep d'artiste, (c), d. in plate, pub. Les Graveurs Modernes, small margins, apparently good condition, foxing, water stain, rubbed spot, light staining, (03-31-93, Butterfield, #5203), 18⅞ x 15¼ in., (47.9 x 38.7 cm.), sheet 20 x 15¾ in., (47.9 x 38.7 cm.), aquatint and drypoint printed in colors w/a touch of hand-coloring on wove paper (BP 760, DM 1850, FR 6284, Y 132,245).

$1840* *L'Elan (Zest),* (c) 1928 by L. Icart, s., blindstamp, loose sheet, full margins, time darkened, soiled, (06-09-93, Sotheby-Arcade, #274), 19⅛ x 14 in., (48.6 x 35.6 cm.), etching and drypoint touched w/hand-coloring (BP 1214, DM 3009, FR 10,121, Y 195,682).

$1100* *"L'Elan",* s., embossed mark, (c) 1928, #307, (09-18-92, DuMouchelle, #2026), 19¼ x 14¼ in., (48.9 x 36.2 cm.), drypoint and etching (BP 633, DM 1647, FR 5641, Y 137,055).

$1650* *"L'Elan" (Zest) (Holland et al., 346), 1928,* s. Louis Icart, num. 307, printer's drystamp, i. w/(c) and d., good cond., wide margins, stain w/in image, mount staining, (03-12-93, Skinner, #10, illus.), 19¼ x 14¼ in., (48.9 x 36.2 cm.), color drypoint w/additional coloring (BP 1151, DM 2746, FR 9338, Y 194,461).

$2300* *L'Elan, (Zest) (H. C. & I. 346), 1928,* s., #364, blindstamp, (c), d. in plate, margins trimmed unevenly, good condition, mat staining, light-staining, foxing, paper remains, skinned areas, abrasions in image, notations, (03-31-93, Butterfield, #5212, illus.), 20 x 14⅞ in., (50.8 x 37.8 cm.), sheet 25⅜ x 19½ in., (50.8 x 37.8 cm.), drypoint printed in colors w/touches of hand-coloring on wove paper (BP 1521, DM 3700, FR 12,568, Y 264,489).

BI *L'Esarpolette (Swing),* (c) 1928 by L. Icart, s., blindstamp, annot. 380, good cond., loose sheet, full margins, time darkened, minor foxing, est. $6/9,000, (06-09-93, Sotheby-Arcade, #276, illus.), 19 x 13¼ in., (48.3 x 33.7 cm.), etching and drypoint in colors, touched w/hand-coloring.

BI *L'Essayage (Pink Slip),* (c) 1939 by L. Icart Sty., s., blindstamp, good cond., laid down, slightly mat burned, time darkened, est. $2,5/3,000, (06-09-93, Sotheby-Arcade, #282), 18⅞ x 11 in., (47.9 x 27.9 cm.), etching and drypoint in colors and touched w/hand-coloring.

$1035* *L'Eventail (Behind The Fan),* (c) 1922 by F.H. Bresler, s., annot. 262, good cond., laid down, slight soiling to margins, (06-09-93, Sotheby-Arcade, #283), 14¾ x 19 in., (37.5 x 48.3 cm.), etching and drypoint in colors, touched w/hand-coloring (BP 683, DM 1693, FR 5693, Y 110,071).

$2300* *L'Invitee (The Morning Cup),* (c) 1940 by L. Icart, s., blindstamp, good cond., full loose sheet, slight mat burn, (06-09-93, Sotheby-Arcade, #284, illus.), 19 x 17¼ in., (48.3 x 43.8 cm.), etching and drypoint in colors, touched w/hand-coloring (BP 1517, DM 3762, FR 12,651, Y 244,603).

$478* *Lady In Shawl,* s., num. 256, pub. Les Graveurs Modernes, margins, surface dirt, (12-10-92, Bonhams-Chelsea, #77), plate 17⅝ x 13 in., (44.8 x 33 cm.), color drypoint etching (BP 308, DM 756, FR 2582, Y 59,129).

BI *Lady Of The Camelias (La Dame Aux Camelias) (H., C. and I.), 1927,* s., num. 61, artist's blindstamp, large margins, sealed in mat, goodcond.?, time staining, est. $8/1200, (09-21-92, Butterfield, #809), 17$\frac{1}{16}$ x 21$\frac{1}{16}$ in., (432.6 x 534.4 mm.), etching w/aquatint/drypoint in colors on cream wove.

$1210* *"Lady Of The Camelias",* s. Louis Icart, artist's blindstamp, (c), (05-15-93, Wolf, #652, illus.), etching and drypoint (BP 787, DM 1946, FR 6541, Y 134,131).

$649* *Lady Picking Fruit, 1921,* s., num. 230, pub. L'Estampe Moderne, margins, spotting, (12-10-92, Bonhams-Chelsea, #78), plate 15½ x 11¾ in., (39.4 x 29.8 cm.), color drypoint etching (BP 418, DM 1027, FR 3506, Y 80,282).

$819* *Lady With Cat,* s., num. 210, pub. Les Graveurs Modernes, margins, surface dirt, (12-10-92, Bonhams-Chelsea, #76), plate 17¼ x 13⅞ in., (43.8 x 35.2 cm.), color drypoint etching (BP 528, DM 1295, FR 4425, Y 101,311).

$690* *La Lampe, (Lampshade) (H., C. & I. 494), 1948,* s., d., (c) in plate, pub. l'Estampe Moderne, margins possibly trimmed, good condition, staining, creases, skinned area, surface soiling, scuffing, (03-31-93, Butterfield, #5224), 15$\frac{9}{16}$ x 19$\frac{9}{16}$ in., (39.5 x 49.7 cm.), sheet 19⅞ x 25 in., (39.5 x 49.7 cm.), etching w/aquatint, drypoint and roulette printed in colors w/touches of hand-coloring on BFK Rives (BP 456, DM 1110, FR 3770, Y 79,347).

BI *Laughing (Rieuse) (H., C. and I. 394), 1930,* s., num. 82, artist's blindstamp, (c)/d. in plate, slightly trimmed,good cond., foxing, surface soiling, est. $15/2000, (09-21-92, Butterfield, #817), sheet 12⅛ x 17¼ in., (308.5 x 438.9 mm.), 19$\frac{9}{16}$ x 25$\frac{1}{16}$ in., (308.5 x 438.9 mm.), etching w/aquatint/drypoint in colors on Rives BFK.

$2640* *"Laziness", c. 1925,* s., (05-15-93, Dunning, #1029, illus.), 19 x 15 in., (48.3 x 38.1 cm.), etching and drypoint (BP 1717, DM 4246, FR 14,270, Y 292,650).

$1495* *Laziness, 1925,* s., (03-25-93, Christie-E, #218), 15 x 19 in., (38.1 x 48.3 cm.), color etching and drypoint (BP 1015, DM 2456, FR 8352, Y 175,141).

$9077* *Leda And The Swan (Holland 436), 1934,* s., blindstamp, full margins, good cond., light stain, foxing, tack holes, skinning, (10-14-92, Sotheby-Japan, #39, illus.), image 19⅝ x 30⅞ in., (498 x 784 mm.), colored etching and aquatint w/hand coloring and varnished on BFK Rives (BP 5328, DM 13,284, FR 45,047, Y 1,099,976).

$1980* *"Lesson Of Love", c. 1927,* s. artist's seal, (05-15-93, Dunning, #1028), 9½ x 10 in., (24.1 x 25.4 cm.), etching and drypoint in color (BP 1287, DM 3185, FR 10,703, Y 219,488).

$920* *Le Lettre (Letter),* (c) 1923 by Les Graveurs Modernes, s., annot. 256, laid down, slightly time darkened, foxing, (06-09-93, Sotheby-Arcade, #275), 17½ x 12⅝ in., (44.5 x 32.1 cm.), etching and drypoint in colors, touched w/hand-coloring (BP 607, DM 1505, FR 5061, Y 97,841).

$1265* *The Life Of Breasts, 1945,* from Le Vis Des Seins, bears sig., good condition, center fold, (03-31-93, Butterfield, #5223), 11 x 17$\frac{11}{16}$ in., (27.9 x 44.9 cm.), aquatint and roulette w/hand-coloring printed on Japan (BP 836, DM 2035, FR 6913, Y 145,469).

BI *Lilies (Les Lis) (H., C. and I. 468), 1934,* s., (c)/d. in plate, artist's blindstamp, sealed in mat, good cond.?, mat staining, glue/paper remains, thinned spots, est. $3/4000, (09-21-92, Butterfield, #818, illus.), sheet 28$\frac{7}{16}$ x 19$\frac{9}{16}$ in., (722 x 496.2 mm.), etching w/aquatint/drypoint in colors w/hand-coloring on wove.

$1980* *"Lilies" (Holland et al., 468), 1934,* s. Louis Icart, i. 1934 by L. Icart, fair cond., laid down between mats, (09-11-92, Skinner, #7, illus.), 28 x 18¼ in., (71.1 x 46.4 cm.), etching/aquatint w/hand coloring/varnish on paper (BP 1024, DM 2850, FR 9687, Y 245,323).

$1840* *Lilies, 1934,* s., artist's blindstamp, (06-08-93, Christie-E, #199), 27¾ x 18⅞ in., (70.5 x 47.9 cm.), color etching and drypoint (BP 1210, DM 2986, FR 10,055, Y 195,433).

$4304* *Lillies (H. 468), 1934,* s. artist's blindstamp, margins, generally good cond., (06-30-93, Sotheby-London, #466, illus.), sh c. 31⅞ x 23¼ in., (810 x 591 mm.), etching w/aquatint in color, finished by hand and varnished on BFK Rives (BP 2885, DM 7341, FR 24,764, Y 461,159).

$2415* *Les Lis (Lilies),* (c) 1934 by L. Icart, s., blindstamp, good cond., laid down, glued to mat, varnished, (06-09-93, Sotheby-Arcade, #279), 27⅞ x 18¾ in., (70.8 x 47.6 cm.), etching and drypoint in colors, touched w/hand-coloring (BP 1593, DM 3950, FR 13,284, Y 256,833).

$2588* *Les Lis, (Lilies) (H., C. & I. 468), 1934,* s., inkstamp, (c), d. in plate, margins, good condition, tears, water stain, mat staining, creases, surface soiling, notations, (03-31-93, Butterfield, #5221), 28$\frac{9}{16}$ x 19½ in., (72.5 x 49.5 cm.), sheet 35½ x 24 in., (72.5 x 49.5 cm.), aquatint and drypoint w/touches of hand-coloring printed on BFK Rives (BP 1711, DM 4163, FR 14,142, Y 297,608).

BI *Les Lis, c. 1934,* (c), s., artist's blindstamp, annot. 7/3, full sheet, cleaned, abrasions/scratches to image, est. $3/4000, (11-06-92, Sotheby-Arcade, #156, illus.), 27⅝ x 18¾ in., (70.2 x 47.6 cm.), etching/drypoint in colors w/hand-coloring.

$935* *Louise,* s., stamp, (11-13-92, DuMouchelle, #196, illus.), 20 x 13½ in., (50.8 x 34.3 cm.), drypoint and etching (BP 604, DM 1468, FR 4950, Y 116,048).

$1320* *Louise (Holland-Catania-Isen fig. 317), 1927,* s., #235, bears artist's blindstamp, (03-14-93, Hindman, #273), 20¾ x 14⅜ in., (52.7 x 36.5 cm.), color aquatint and drypoint (BP 921, DM 2197, FR 7470, Y 155,569).

BI *Love Letters (Lettres D'Amour) (H., C. and I. 289), 1926,* s., num. 153, t. (by another hand?), artist's blindstamp, inkstamp, good cond., staining, surface soiling, scuffing, est. $1/1500, (09-21-92, Butterfield, #802, illus.), sheet 14½ x 19 in., (369 x 483.5 mm.), 19⅜ x 24¾ in., (369 x 483.5 mm.), etching/drypoint w/aquatint in colors w/touches hand-coloring on BFKRives.

$743* *Love's Awakening,* s., blindstamp, (06-11-93, Freemn/Fine Art, #108, illus.), 8¼ x 10⅞ in., (21 x 27.6 cm.), etching and aquatint (BP 488, DM 1208, FR 4071, Y 78,833).

$2402* *Love's Blossom (H. 465), 1937,* s., #107, blindstamp, margins, scuffed areas w/in image, good cond., (06-30-93, Sotheby-London, #467, illus.), sh 21 x 29¾ in., (533 x 756 mm.), etching w/aquatint partly in color and finished by hand on wove (BP 1610, DM 4097, FR 13,820, Y 257,366).

BI *Love's Blossom (Parfum De Fleurs) (H., C. and I. 465), 1937,* s., artist's blindstamp, ink stamps, full margins, very good cond., handling creases, soiling, est. $15/2000,

(09-21-92, Butterfield, #819), sheet 17¹¹⁄₁₆ x 25⁵⁄₁₆ in., (448.5 x 642.5 mm.), 23⁹⁄₁₆ x 31¹³⁄₁₆ in., (448.5 x 642.5 mm.), etching w/aquatint/drypoint in colors on Rives BFK.

BI *Loves Blossom, 1937, Holland-Catania-Isen 465,* s., bears artist stamp, est. $1,5/2,000, (09-20-92, Hindman, #790), 17¼ x 25¼ in., (43.8 x 64.1 cm.), color aquatint and drypoint.

$990* *"Madame Bovary" (Holland et al., 390), 1929,* s. Louis Icart, i. w/(c) and d., pub.'s blindstamp, good cond., laid-down, loss, glue/residue, (03-12-93, Skinner, #9, illus.), oval 16⅝ x 21½ in., (42.2 x 54.6 cm.), color aquatint and etching on wove (BP 691, DM 1648, FR 5603, Y 116,676).

$805* *Madame Butterfly,* (c) 1927 by Les Graveurs Modernes, s. Epre d'arts, blindstamp, glued to mat, time darkened(06-09-93, Sotheby-Arcade, #285), 20 x 13¼ in., (50.8 x 33.7 cm.), etching and drypoint in colors, touched w/hand-coloring (BP 531, DM 1317, FR 4428, Y 85,611).

$1045* *"Madame Butterfly", c. 1927,* s., blindstamp, lit., (01-21-93, A. James, #151), 21 x 14 in., (53.3 x 35.6 cm.), drypoint and etching (BP 678, DM 1677, FR 5667, Y 130,234).

$690* *Manon (H., C. & I. 328), 1927,* s., annot. Epreuve d'Artiste, blindstamp, (c), d. in plate, pub. LesGraveurs Modernes, margins, good condition, mat staining, thinned spots, paperremains, light-staining, (03-31-93, Butterfield, #5210), 21 x 14 in., (53.3 x 35.6 cm.), sheet 24¾ x 17¾ in., (53.3 x 35.6 cm.), etching w/aquatint and drypoint printed in colors w/touches of hand-coloring on wove paper (BP 456, DM 1110, FR 3770, Y 79,347).

$990* *Manon (Holland-Catania-Isen fig. 328), 1927,* s., #174, bears artist's blindstamp, (03-14-93, Hindman, #274, illus.), 20¾ x 13¾ in., (52.7 x 34.9 cm.), (BP 691, DM 1648, FR 5603, Y 116,676).

$660* *"Manon", 1927,* s. Louis Icart, artist's blindstamp, (c), burn, glue, laid down, (04-17-93, Wolf, #596), 20⅛ x 13¼ in., (51.1 x 33.7 cm.), color etching and drypoint (BP 433, DM 1066, FR 3603, Y 74,216).

$1430* *"Manon", c. 1927,* s., (05-15-93, Dunning, #1031, illus.), 20½ x 13¼ in., (52.1 x 33.7 cm.), aquatint and drypoint in color (BP 930, DM 2300, FR 7730, Y 158,519).

$920* *Marchande De Fleurs, (Flower Seller) (H., C. & I. 336), 1928,* s., #A.206/500 ink, blindstamp, (c), d. in plate, pub. Graveurs Modernes, margins, good condition, thinned spots, tear, abrasions in image, creases, soiling, (03-31-93, Butterfield, #5214, illus.), 19½ x 15 in., (49.5 x 38.1 cm.), sheet 24⁹⁄₁₆ x 20⁹⁄₁₆ in., (49.5 x 38.1 cm.), etching w/aquatint and drypoint printed in colors on Rives BFK (BP 608, DM 1480, FR 5027, Y 105,796).

$880* *Marchande De Marrons (Holland/Catania/Isen fig. 335), 1928,* s., #E/426, bears artist's stamp, (05-16-93, Hindman, #462), 19½ x 14¾ in., (49.5 x 37.5 cm.), color drypoint and aquatint w/hand-coloring (BP 572, DM 1415, FR 4757, Y 97,550).

BI *Meditation (Dans Le Reve) (H., C. and I. 333), 1928,* s., num. 420, artist's blindstamp, large margins, good cond., extensive mat staining/foxing, est. $15/2000, (09-21-92, Butterfield, #810), sheet 12½ x 17¼ in., (318.1 x 438.9 mm.), 18⁹⁄₁₆ x 23¹⁄₁₆ in., (318.1 x 438.9 mm.), etching w/aquatint/drypoint in colors on cream wove.

$1320* *Milkmaid, 1928,* s., stamp, (01-15-93, DuMouchelle, #4, illus.), 19⅜ x 12¾ in., (49.2 x 32.4 cm.), drypoint and etching (BP 863, DM 2158, FR 7297, Y 166,415).

$990* *Milkmaid, 1928,* s., windmill stamp, (03-12-93, DuMouchelle, #32), 19⅜ x 12¾ in., (49.2 x 32.4 cm.), drypoint and etching (BP 691, DM 1648, FR 5603, Y 116,676).

$1495* *Mimi (H., C. & I. 318), 1927,* s., #200, blindstamp, (c), d. in plate, pub. Les Graveurs Modernes, margins, etched t., good condition, burning, light-staining, scuffing, skinned areas, tear, sticker, soiling, (03-31-93, Butterfield, #5208), 21⅛ x 14 in., (53.7 x 35.6 cm.), sheet 29⁵⁄₁₆ x 21⅜ in., (53.7 x 35.6 cm.), etching w/aquatint and drypoint printed in colors w/touches of hand-coloring on Rives paper (BP 988, DM 2405, FR 8169, Y 171,918).

$5110* *Mimi Pinson (S.M. Schnessel et M. Karmel, A 90), 1927,* yellowed, annot., stamped, s., cracks, creases, tears, staining, large untrimmed margins, (06-16-93, Ader Tajan, #109), 13¹⁵⁄₁₆ x 21¹⁄₁₆ in., (35.5 x 53.5 cm.), color etching and aquatint (BP 3407, DM 8483, FR 28,468, Y 545,009).

$1045* *Mimi, 1927,* s., windmill stamp, (03-12-93, DuMouchelle, #37, illus.), 20⅛ x 13¼ in., (51.1 x 33.7 cm.), drypoint and etching (BP 729, DM 1739, FR 5914, Y 123,159).

$1210* *Minuet (Holland-Catania-Isen fig. 363), 1929,* s., #183, bears artist's stamp, (03-14-93, Hindman, #278), 21⅛ x 14 in., (53.7 x 35.6 cm.), color aquatint and drypoint w/hand-coloring (BP 844, DM 2014, FR 6848, Y 142,605).

BI *Minuet (Menuet) (H., C. and I. 363), 1929,* s., num. 25, (c)/d. in plate, pub. David Ashley, Inc., laid down at edges, good cond., light-staining, surface soiling, est. $8/1200, (09-21-92, Butterfield, #812), sheet 21⁵⁄₁₆ x 14⅛ in., (540.7 x 359.4 mm.), 26⁷⁄₁₆ x 19⁹⁄₁₆ in., (540.7 x 359.4 mm.), etching in colors w/hand-coloring on wove.

$2090* *Minuet, 1929,* s., (11-28-92, Dunning, #1094), 21 x 13¾ in., (53.3 x 34.9 cm.), color etching and drypoint (BP 1380, DM 3330, FR 11,303, Y 260,112).

$1320* *"Minvet", c. 1929,* s., Icart seal, mint cond., (10-10-92, Goldberg, #436, illus.), 20½ x 13¼ in., (52.1 x 33.7 cm.), color drypoint etching (BP 783, DM 1961, FR 6584, Y 160,701).

$1100* *"Mischievious", 1927,* s., bearing blindstamp, (02-11-93, Boos, #412), oval, sight 16⅛ x 20½ in., (410 x 520 mm.), color etching and drypoint (BP 776, DM 1822, FR 6166, Y 132,610).

$1210* *"Montmarte", c. 1928,* s., blindstamp, lit., (01-21-93, A. James, #152), 21⅝ x 15 in., (54.9 x 38.1 cm.), drypoint and etching (BP 785, DM 1942, FR 6562, Y 150,798).

$990* *Montmartre, 1928,* s., windmill stamp, (03-12-93, DuMouchelle, #33, illus.), 20⅛ x 13⅛ in., (51.1 x 33.3 cm.), drypoint and etching (BP 691, DM 1648, FR 5603, Y 116,676).

BI *"Musetta", 1927,* s., sealed, #E/448, $800/1,200, (12-02-92, Boos, #454), 20 x 13¼ in., (50.8 x 33.7 cm.), color etching and aquatint.

$600* *Le Nid Tombe, 1924,* num. 182, s., (06-11-93, Picard, #76), 15⁹⁄₁₆ x 19½ in., (395 x 495 mm.), etching and aquatint (BP 394, DM 975, FR 3288, Y 63,660).

$1540* *"Nineteen Thirty", c. 1929,* s., bears blindstamp, (03-25-93, Boos, #624, illus.), sight 15³⁄₁₆ x 17½ in., (385 x 445 mm.), color etching and drypoint (BP 1046, DM 2530, FR 8603, Y 180,412).

$575* *Nude, c. 1930,* s., good cond., minor tears to margins, creasing, some soiling, foxing, (06-09-93, Sotheby-Arcade, #251), 19 x 15⅛ in., (48.3 x 38.4 cm.), lithograph in colors (BP 379, DM 940, FR 3163, Y 61,151).

$880* *Nurse, 1917,* s., #44/100, (03-12-93, DuMouchelle, #39), 19⅜ x 15⅜ in., (49.2 x 39.1 cm.), drypoint and etching (BP 614, DM 1465, FR 4980, Y 103,712).

$798* *On The Branches, 1922,* s., (06-11-93, Freemn/Fine Art, #109), 19 x 11¾ in., (48.3 x 29.8 cm.), drypoint and aquatint (BP 524, DM 1297, FR 4373, Y 84,668).

$805* *Les Oranges Renversees (Spilled Oranges),* (c) 1921 by F.H. Bresler Co., s., annot. 230, laid down, time darkened, foxing, (06-09-93, Sotheby-Arcade, #280), 15 x 11⅛ in., (38.1 x 28.3 cm.), etching and drypoint in colors, touched w/hand-coloring (BP 531, DM 1317, FR 4428, Y 85,611).

$3260* *Orchids (H. 466), 1934,* s. artist's blindstamp, margins, good cond., (06-30-93, Sotheby-London, #468, illus.), sh c. 31⅞ x 23¼ in., (810 x 591 mm.), etching w/aquatint in color, finished by hand and varnished on BFK Rives (BP 2185, DM 5560, FR 18,757, Y 349,298).

BI *Orchids (L'Orchides) (H., C. and I. 466), 1937,* s., full margins, good cond., creases, staining, surface soiling, est. $35/5500, (09-21-92, Butterfield, #820), sheet 28⁵⁄₁₆ x 19⁹⁄₁₆ in., (718.8 x 496.2 mm.), 35⁵⁄₁₆ x 25¹⁄₁₆ in., (718.8 x 496.2 mm.), etching w/aquatint/drypoint in colors on BFK Rives.

$1760* *Pals (Holland-Catania-Isen 188), 1923,* s., annot. Epr.d'-art, (10-18-92, Hindman, #467, illus.), 16⅞ x 21 in., (42.9 x 53.3 cm.), color drypoint and aquatint (BP 1077, DM 2620, FR 8884, Y 211,158).

$1035* *Panier De Pommes (Basket Of Apples), c. 1924,* s., annot. 126, good cond., loose sheet, mat glued at top, time darkened, mat burn, foxing, (06-09-93, Sotheby-

Arcade, #286), 16½ x 12 in., (41.9 x 30.5 cm.), etching and drypoint in colors, touched w/hand-coloring (BP 683, DM 1693, FR 5693, Y 110,071).

BI *"The Parasol", 1928,* s. Louis Icart, num. v/323, good/poor cond., est. $1,2/1,600, (11-21-92, Bakker, #102, illus.), image 17¼ x 14 in., (43.8 x 35.6 cm.), color etching and drypoint.

$1100* *"The Parasol", c. 1928,* s., blindstamp, lit., (01-21-93, A. James, #153, illus.), 18⅞ x 15½ in., (47.9 x 39.4 cm.), drypoint and etching (BP 713, DM 1766, FR 5965, Y 137,089).

$1210* *Paravent Rouge (Unmasked), 1933,* s., t.(11-08-92, Northeast, #807, illus.), sheet 20 x 14 in., (50.8 x 35.6 cm.), etching (BP 800, DM 1932, FR 6526, Y 150,161).

$1495* *Paresse (Laziness),* (c) 1925 by Les Graveurs Modernes, s., blindstamp, glued to mat, time darkened, (06-09-93, Sotheby-Arcade, #288), 14⅝ x 18½ in., (37.1 x 47 cm.), etching and drypoint in colors, touched w/hand-coloring (BP 986, DM 2445, FR 8223, Y 158,992).

$1760* *Parfum De Fleurs,* (c) 1937 L. Icart Society, s., good cond., laid down, (11-06-92, Sotheby-Arcade, #159), 17⅜ x 25¼ in., (44.1 x 64.1 cm.), etching/drypoint in colors w/hand-coloring (BP 1151, DM 2810, FR 9498, Y 217,230).

$2420* *Parfum De Fleurs,* (c) 1937 L. Icart Society, s., artist's blindstamp, good cond., margins trimmed, (11-06-92, Sotheby-Arcade, #158, illus.), 17⅜ x 25¼ in., (44.1 x 64.1 cm.), etching/drypoint in colors w/hand-coloring (BP 1582, DM 3864, FR 13,060, Y 298,692).

BI *"Parrots", c. 1925,* s., lit, est. $1,5/2,000, (12-12-92, A. James, #35), 14 x 18 in., (35.6 x 45.7 cm.), drypoint and etching.

$1320* *"Parrots", c. 1925,* s., num. 227, lit., (01-21-93, A. James, #29), 14 x 18 in., (35.6 x 45.7 cm.), drypoint and etching (BP 856, DM 2119, FR 7158, Y 164,506).

$770* *Pekinese Buddha (H. 278),* (06-11-93, Freemn/Fine Art, #111), 13¾ x 19¼ in., (34.9 x 48.9 cm.), drypoint (BP 506, DM 1251, FR 4219, Y 81,698).

$613* *"Peonies",* s. Louis Icart, (c) 1935, (05-18-93, Encans, #196), 8¼ x 11 in., (21 x 28 cm.), eau-forte (etching) et pointe seche, marroufle sur carton (BP 399, DM 995, FR 3359, Y 68,316, C$ 777).

$1150* *Perroquets (Parrots),* (c) 1925 by Les Graveurs Modernes, s., annot. 253, t., good cond., full loose sheet, formerly glued to mat, time darkened, slightly soiled, (06-09-93, Sotheby-Arcade, #289), 13⅝ x 18¼ in., (34.6 x 46.4 cm.), etching and drypoint in colors, touched w/hand-coloring (BP 759, DM 1881, FR 6326, Y 122,301).

$2415* *Persian Cat, c. 1923,* (c) by Les Graveurs Modernes, s., annot. 210, laid down, full sheet,minor foxing, (06-09-93, Sotheby-Arcade, #290), 16½ x 13¼ in., (41.9 x 33.7 cm.), etching and drypoint in colors, touched w/hand-coloring (BP 1593, DM 3950, FR 13,284, Y 256,833).

BI *Pierre Louys. "Chrysis" and "Leda": Two Books,* each w/ title-page, #65 and 84, pub. C.Meunier, 1940, good cond., est.BP 3,5/4,000, (06-30-93, Sotheby-London, #464, illus.), each c. 11⅝ x 9¼ in., (295 x 235 mm.), 15 and 16 color engravings in text.

$1150* *Les Pillards (Thieves),* (c) 1926 by Les Graveurs Modernes, s., blindstamp, annot. 193, laid down, margins trimmed, time darkened, foxing, (06-09-93, Sotheby-Arcade, #281), 16½ x 11⅞ in., (41.9 x 30.2 cm.), etching and drypoint in colors, touched w/hand-coloring (BP 759, DM 1881, FR 6326, Y 122,301).

$770* *Les Pillards, 1926, Holland-Catania-Isen 280,* s., num. 184, bears artist's stamp, (09-20-92, Hindman, #787), 17 x 12½ in., (43.2 x 31.8 cm.), color aquatint and drypoint (BP 451, DM 1143, FR 3909, Y 95,167).

$1840* *Pink Slip, 1939,* s., artist's blindstamp, (06-08-93, Christie-E, #200), 18⅞ x 11⅛ in., (47.9 x 28.3 cm.), color etching and drypoint (BP 1210, DM 2986, FR 10,055, Y 195,433).

$1725* *La Port Rouge (Red Gate),* (c) 1925 by Graveurs Modernes, s., annot. 38, good cond., loose sheet, full margins, slight soiling, (06-09-93, Sotheby-Arcade, #273), 17 x 12¼ in., (43.2 x 31.1 cm.), etching and drypoint in colors touched w/hand-coloring (BP 1138, DM 2821, FR 9488, Y 183,452).

BI *Poupee Moderne (French Doll) (Schnessel, fig. 17),* s., #6/350, pub. Les Gravures Modernes in 1926, prov., lit., est. C$1,2/1,800, (12-01-92, Ritchie, #13, illus.), oval 14 x 18 in., (35.6 x 45.7 cm.), color drypoint and etching.

$429* *Poupee Moderne, French Doll (Schnessel, Fig. 17),* s., #6/350, pub. Les Gravures Modernes, 1926, prov., lit., (06-08-93, Ritchie, #43, illus.), oval 14 x 18 in., (35.6 x 45.7 cm.), color drypoint and etching (BP 282, DM 696, FR 2344, Y 45,566, C$ 550).

BI *Praise (H., C. & I. 35), 1914,* s., annot. Epreuve d'Artiste, margins (trimmed unevenly), laid down, condition, glue remains, skinned areas, mat staining, creases in image, glue remains, surface soiling, est. $2/3000, (03-31-93, Butterfield, #5201, illus.), 19½ x 15⅝ in., (49.5 x 39.7 cm.), sheet 25¼ x 20¼ in., (49.5 x 39.7 cm.), drypoint printed in colors w/a touch of hend-coloring on wove paper.

$2663* *"Quelle Joie De Vivre L'Ete A Monte Carlo",* p. Monegasque Monte Carlo, s. in plate Louis Icart, (03-16-93, Encans, #132), 43⁵⁄₁₆ x 29½ in., (110 x 75 cm.), poster (BP 1839, DM 4428, FR 15,045, Y 311,389, C$ 3330).

$58* *Rain, 1928,* from Dessins de Femmes, s., (06-08-93, Christie-E, #202), 17¼ x 13¼ in., (43.8 x 33.7 cm.), lithograph and pastel on paper (BP 38, DM 94, FR 317, Y 6160).

$3300* *"Rainbow", 1930,* s., windmill stamp, (07-17-92, DuMouchelle, #51), 24¾ x 17 in., (62.9 x 43.2 cm.), drypoint and etching (BP 1693, DM 4810, FR 16,264, Y 410,244).

$440* *Reclining Nude,* s., (05-16-93, Hindman, #460), 11⅛ x 8¼ in., (28.3 x 21 cm.), color aquatint (BP 286, DM 708, FR 2378, Y 48,775).

$3850* *Resonance or Waltz Echoes,* (c) 1938, s., (11-28-92, Dunning, #1062), sight 19 x 19 in., (48.3 x 48.3 cm.), color etching and drypoint (BP 2541, DM 6134, FR 20,822, Y 479,154).

BI *Reve De Valse,* (c) 1940 L. Icart, s., mistitled, laid down, glued to mat, abrasions, trimmed, corner torn, est. $7/10,000, (11-06-92, Sotheby-Arcade, #160, illus.), 14¼ x 16¾ in., (36.2 x 42.5 cm.), etching/drypoint in colors w/hand-coloring.

$1610* *Rieuse, (Laughing) (H., C. & I. 394), 1930,* s., #A/153, blindstamp, (c), d. in plate, margins trimmed unevenly, good condition, mat staining, tape, (03-31-93, Butterfield, #5216, illus.), 12⅛ x 17¼ in., (30.8 x 43.8 cm.), sheet 16¾ x 21⅜ in., (30.8 x 43.8 cm.), etching w/aquatint and drypoint printed in colors w/a touch of hand-coloring on wove (BP 1064, DM 2590, FR 8798, Y 185,143).

BI *Salome,* (c) 1928 by L. Icart, s., blindstamp, good cond., full sheet, remains of glue in margin, slightly time darkened, small hole in margin, minor abrasions, est. $800/1,200, (06-09-93, Sotheby-Arcade, #292), 20½ x 13¼ in., (52.1 x 33.7 cm.), etching and drypoint in colors, touched w/hand-coloring.

$920* *Salome,* (c) 1928 by L. Icart, s., blindstamp, annot. 160, time darkened, glued to mat, (06-09-93, Sotheby-Arcade, #291), 20½ x 13¼ in., (52.1 x 33.7 cm.), etching and drypoint in colors, touched w/hand-coloring (BP 607, DM 1505, FR 5061, Y 97,841).

BI *Salome (H., C. and I. 388), 1928,* s., artist's blindstamp, (c)/d. in plate, laid down along edges, glued to overmat, small margins, good cond., time-staining, surface scuffing/soiling, est. $8/1000, (09-21-92, Butterfield, #816), sheet 21³⁄₁₆ x 14⅛ in., (537.5 x 359.4 mm.), 27¹³⁄₁₆ x 20¹⁄₁₆ in., (537.5 x 359.4 mm.), etching w/drypoint/aquatint in colors w/hand-coloring on wove.

$1840* *Scheherezade, 1927,* s., artist's blindstamp, (03-25-93, Christie-E, #219), 13⅜ x 20⅜ in., (34 x 51.8 cm.), color etching and drypoint (BP 1250, DM 3023, FR 10,279, Y 215,558).

$1980* *"Seagulls" (Les Mouettes) #A74, c. 1926,* s., (02-27-93, Dunning, #1030, illus.), pl 20½ x 16¼ in., (52.1 x 41.3 cm.), color etching drypoint (BP 1392, DM 3255, FR 11,061, Y 233,739).

$1100* *Seated Woman,* s. Louis Icart, (09-25-92, Wolf, #28), 17 x 23 in., (43.2 x 58.4 cm.), etching and drypoint (BP 642, DM 1631, FR 5514, Y 132,770).

BI   *Silk Robe,* s., #A.12H/500, pub. Les Graveur Modern Modernes, est. $2,6/2,800, (12-10-92, Sloan, #3053), 15¼ x 18½ in., (38.7 x 47 cm.), color etching and drypoint.

$2420* *Sleeping Beauty,* s., artist's device, (11-28-92, Dunning, #1064), 16½ x 19½ in., (41.9 x 49.5 cm.), color etching and drypoint (BP 1597, DM 3855, FR 13,088, Y 301,182).

BI   *Sleeping Beauty,* s., Schnessel no. 128, est. $1,5/2,000, (11-01-92, Hanzel, #214), 19½ x 15½ in., (49.5 x 39.4 cm.), colored etching.

$1210* *Sleeping Beauty (SK 128), 1927,* s., mar burn, darkening, some foxing, backboard burn, one skinned spot, (05-22-93, Weschler, #193, illus.), oval 18½ x 14¾ in., (47 x 37.5 cm.), hand-colored etching and drypoint w/mezzotint on wove (BP 784, DM 1967, FR 6619, Y 133,407).

$1495* *Sleeping Beauty, 1927,* s., artist's blindstamp, (03-25-93, Christie-E, #220), 14¾ x 18½ in., (37.5 x 47 cm.), color etching and drypoint (BP 1015, DM 2456, FR 8352, Y 175,141).

$1540* *Sleeping Beauty, 1927,* s., stamp, (01-15-93, DuMouchelle, #1, illus.), 14¾ x 18½ in., (37.5 x 47 cm.), drypoint and etching (BP 1007, DM 2518, FR 8513, Y 194,150).

$1035* *Sleeping Beauty, 1927,* s., artist's blindstamp, (06-08-93, Christie-E, #201), 14¾ x 18½ in., (37.5 x 47 cm.), color etching and drypoint (BP 680, DM 1679, FR 5656, Y 109,931).

$1210* *Sleeping Beauty, 1927,* s., windmill stamp, (03-12-93, DuMouchelle, #41, illus.), 14¾ x 18½ in., (37.5 x 47 cm.), drypoint and etching (BP 844, DM 2014, FR 6848, Y 142,605).

$671* *Le Sofa,* s., excellent cond., (11-16-92, Briest, #313), 8⅝ x 11⅜ in., (21.9 x 28.9 cm.), etching and drypoint in colors (BP 441, DM 1070, FR 3606, Y 83,739).

BI   *Sommeil-Repose,* est. $7,0/8,000, (12-10-92, Sloan, #3052, illus.), 18⅝ x 45½ in., (47.3 x 115.6 cm.), color etching and drypoint.

BI   *Speed (Vitesse) (H., C. and I. 311), 1927,* s., artist's blindstamp, margins, sealed in mat, good cond.?, mat staining, surface soiling, est. $4/6000, (09-21-92, Butterfield, #805), 15½ x 26¹⁄₁₆ in., (394.4 x 661.6 mm.), drypoint in colors on cream wove.

$1750* *Speed (Vitesse), c. 1933,* s., blindstamp, pub. Gravures Modernes, good cond., (11-30-92, Phillips-London, #437, illus.), plate 15¾ x 25½ in., (400 x 648 mm.), drypoint w/hand-coloring on wove (BP 1155, DM 2788, FR 9465, Y 217,797).

$3300* *"Study Of The Breast" La Vie Des Seins: Six,* Georges Duillot, Paris MCMXLV, (11-28-92, Dunning, #1065), 10½ x 8½ in., (26.7 x 21.6 cm.), lithograph (BP 2178, DM 5257, FR 17,847, Y 410,703).

$920* *Sur L'Herbe, (On The Green) (H., C. & I. 249), 1925,* s., blindstamp, (c), d. in plate, pub. Les Graveurs Modernes, GravureGarantie Originale inkstamp, full margins, good condition, toned, paper loss, staining, sticker, notations, creases, soiling, (03-31-93, Butterfield, #5205), 11³⁄₁₆ x 16⁷⁄₁₆ in., (28.4 x 41.8 cm.), sheet 19⅞ x 25⅞ in., (28.4 x 41.8 cm.), aquatint and drypoint printed in colors w/touches of hand-coloring on wove paper (BP 608, DM 1480, FR 5027, Y 105,796).

BI   *Sur Le Divan,* (c) 1925 Les Graveurs Modernes, s., annot. in ink A041/500, generally good cond., time darkening, margins trimmed, est. $2/3000, (11-06-92, Sotheby-Arcade, #161, illus.), 15¾ x 19¾ in., (40 x 50.2 cm.), etching/drypoint in colors w/hand-coloring.

$3775* *Swing (Holland 26), 1926,* s. artist's blindstamp, margins, good cond., tear, (06-30-93, Sotheby-London, #465, illus.), 25⅝ x 19½ in., (651 x 495 mm.), color drypoint and aquatint w/hand-coloring on BFK Rives (BP 2530, DM 6439, FR 21,720, Y 404,479).

$3300* *"The Swing" (Dans Les Branches),* pencil s. Louis Icart, 3.28, (02-27-93, Dunning, #1031, illus.), pl 19½ x 13½ in., (49.5 x 34.3 cm.), etching (BP 2320, DM 5425, FR 18,436, Y 389,564).

$358* *Swordsman,* s., (12-17-92, Mystic, #3, illus.), 21¼ x 14½ in., (54 x 36.8 cm.), color print (BP 227, DM 559, FR 1909, Y 43,997).

$1430* *Symphonie En Bleu (Hoffman/Cantania/Isen, fig. 461), 1936,* s., bears artist's stamp, (05-16-93, Hindman, #459),

22⅝ x 18⅞ in., (57.5 x 47.9 cm.), color drypoint and aquatint (BP 930, DM 2300, FR 7730, Y 158,519).

BI   *Symphonie En Bleu, (Symphony In Blue) (H., C. & I. 461), 1936,* s., (c), d. in plate, full margins, good condition, mat staining, creases, surface soiling, sticker, est. $7/900, (03-31-93, Butterfield, #5222), 23½ x 19⅝ in., (59.7 x 49.8 cm.), sheet 31¼ x 24⅞ in., (59.7 x 49.8 cm.), etching w/aquatint and drypoint printed in colors w/touches of drypoint on Arches.

BI   *Symphonie En Bleu, c. 1936,* s., good cond., loose full sheet, washed, slightly soiled, est. $1,2/1,800, (06-09-93, Sotheby-Arcade, #293), 23 x 19 in., (58.4 x 48.3 cm.), etching and drypoint in colors, touched w/hand-coloring.

$1200* *Symphony In Blue, 1936,* s., artist's blindstamp, pub. Icart, full margins, excellent cond., (11-30-92, Phillips-London, #436), plate 23¼ x 19½ in., (591 x 495 mm.), etching and drypoint in colors (BP 792, DM 1912, FR 6490, Y 149,347).

$1870* *The Tea,* (c), s., artist's device, (11-28-92, Dunning, #1063), sight 19 x 14½ in., (48.3 x 36.8 cm.), color etching and drypoint (BP 1234, DM 2979, FR 10,114, Y 232,732).

$880* *Tentation,* (c) 1926 Les Graveurs Modernes, s., artist's blindstamp, annot. 182,time-darkened, laid down, abrasions, (11-06-92, Sotheby-Arcade, #162), 19⅜ x 14⅛ in., (49.2 x 35.9 cm.), etching/drypoint in colors w/hand-coloring (BP 575, DM 1405, FR 4749, Y 108,615).

BI   *Thais (H., C. and I. 312), 1927,* s., num. A30, margins, restored tear in margins/image, paper loss, staining verso, surface soiling, est. $8/1200, (09-21-92, Butterfield, #806), sheet 16½ x 21¹⁄₁₆ in., (419.8 x 534.4 mm.), 21¹³⁄₁₆ x 26¹⁄₁₆ in., (419.8 x 534.4 mm.), etching w/aquatint in colors w/touches hand-coloring on wove.

BI   *Three Etchings,* from La Dame aux Camelias, pub. Francis Guillot, margins, apparentlygood condition, est. $1,2/1,800, (03-31-93, Butterfield, #5225), each 7⁹⁄₁₆ x 5⅜ in., (19.2 x 13.7 cm.), etchings printed in color on wove.

$1430* *Tosca (Holland/Catania/Isen, fig. 354), 1928,* s., #A139, bears artist's blindstamp, (03-14-93, Hindman, #276), 21¼ x 13⅝ in., (54 x 34.6 cm.), color aquatint and drypoint (BP 998, DM 2380, FR 8093, Y 168,533).

$1210* *Untitled,* s., (12-13-92, Hindman, #292, illus.), sight 17 x 12⅝ in., color drypoint w/hand-coloring (BP 774, DM 1902, FR 6481, Y 149,697).

BI   *Untitled, 1946,* from La Muit et le Moment, pub. Georges Guillot, est. $400/450, (07-03-92, Sloan, #1090), 7⅝ x 5⅜ in., (19.4 x 13.7 cm.), color etching and aquatint.

$1540* *Venus (Holland/Catania/Isen, fig. 355), 1928,* s., (03-14-93, Hindman, #277), 13⅞ x 19⅜ in., (35.2 x 49.2 cm.), color drypoint w/hand-coloring (BP 1074, DM 2563, FR 8715, Y 181,497).

$1430* *Venus, c. 1928,* s. Louis Icart, #204, Artist's Blind Stamp, lit., (03-25-93, A. James, #67), 13 x 18¾ in., (33 x 47.6 cm.), drypoint and etching (BP 971, DM 2349, FR 7989, Y 167,526).

BI   *Vitesse,* (c) 1927 L. Icart Society, s., artist's blindstamp, margins stained,cleaned, est. $2/3000, (11-06-92, Sotheby-Arcade, #163), 15½ x 25 in., (39.4 x 63.5 cm.), etching/drypoint w/hand-coloring.

$2070* *Vitesse (Speed),* (c) 1927 by L. Icart, s., blindstamp, laid down, cleaned, mat burn, minor foxing, (06-09-93, Sotheby-Arcade, #298), 14¼ x 24⅞ in., (36.2 x 63.2 cm.), etching and drypoint, touched w/hand coloring (BP 1365, DM 3386, FR 11,386, Y 220,143).

BI   *Vitesse (Speed),* (c) 1927 by Les Graveurs Modernes, s., blindstamp, annot. 32, abraded, washed, margins trimmed, est. $2/3,000, (06-09-93, Sotheby-Arcade, #297), 14⅝ x 24⅝ in., (37.1 x 62.5 cm.), etching and drypoint in colors touched w/hand-coloring.

$2875* *Vitesse II (Speed II),* (c) 1933 by L. Icart Society, s., blindstamp, annot. l/l 262, t., good cond., minor time darkening, minor foxing, laid down on board, (06-09-93, Sotheby-Arcade, #294, illus.), 16⅛ x 26 in., (41 x 66 cm.), etching and drypoint in colors, touched w/hand-coloring (BP 1896, DM 4702, FR 15,814, Y 305,753).

BI   *Vitesse, (Speed) (H., C. & I. 311), 1927,* s., #364, blindstamp, (c), d. in plate, pub. Les Graveurs Modernes, margins, sealed in mat, apparently good condition, mat staining, surface soiling, est. $3/5000, (03-31-93, Butter-field, #5211, illus.), 15½ x 26 in., (39.4 x 66 cm.), dry-point printed in colors w/touches of hand-coloring on wove paper.

$1200* *Vitesse, 1933*, s., num. 323, blindstamp, full margins, large repaired tear into image, (11-30-92, Phillips-London, #434), 15 x 24¾ in., (381 x 629 mm.), etching and dry-point in colors (BP 792, DM 1912, FR 6490, Y 149,347).

$2200* *Waltz Echoes, 1938*, s., windmill stamp, (03-12-93, DuMouchelle, #35, illus.), 19 x 19 in., (48.3 x 48.3 cm.), drypoint and etching (BP 1535, DM 3662, FR 12,450, Y 259,281).

$1150* *Welcome Companions*, (c) 1924 by Les Graveurs Mod-ernes, s., laid down, glued to mat, slight soiling, (06-09-93, Sotheby-Arcade, #299), 17 x 12½ in., (43.2 x 31.8 cm.), etching and drypoint in colors touched w/hand-col-oring (BP 759, DM 1881, FR 6326, Y 122,301).

BI *White Underwear*, s., A/166, full margins, est. $1,3/1,800, (12-11-92, DuMouchelle, #84, illus.), 14¾ x 19 in., (37.5 x 48.3 cm.), drypoint and etching mounted on board.

$990* *White Underwear*, s., A/166, full margins, (03-12-93, DuMouchelle, #31), 14¾ x 19 in., (37.5 x 48.3 cm.), drypoint and etching (BP 691, DM 1648, FR 5603, Y 116,676).

$2420* *"White Underwear"*, s., (05-15-93, Dunning, #1027, illus.), 15½ x 19½ in., (39.4 x 49.5 cm.), etching and drypoint (BP 1573, DM 3893, FR 13,081, Y 268,263).

$1430* *White Underwear, Sur Le Divan (Holland-Catania-Isen 247), 1925*, s., #A70/500, (10-18-92, Hindman, #468, illus.), 15 x 19⅜ in., (38.1 x 49.2 cm.), color drypoint and aquatint (BP 875, DM 2129, FR 7219, Y 171,566).

$1265* *Winter Bouquet*, (c) 1924, by Les Graveurs Modernes, s., laid down, glued to mat, time darkened, minor foxing, (06-09-93, Sotheby-Arcade, #295), 16½ x 11½ in., (41.9 x 29.2 cm.), etching and drypoint in colors touched w/ hand-coloring (BP 834, DM 2069, FR 6958, Y 134,532).

BI *"Wishing Well", c. 1925*, s., est. $2,5/3,000, (01-15-93, DuMouchelle, #1302), 16⅞ x 11¼ in., (42.9 x 28.6 cm.), color and drypoint etching.

BI *"Wishing Well", c. 1925*, s., $25/3000, (10-16-92, DuMouchelle, #1301), 16⅞ x 11¼ in., (42.9 x 28.6 cm.), color and drypoint etching.

BI *Wistfulness (La Falque) (H., C. and I. 193), 1924*, s., margins, glued to overmat, mat staining, est. $15/2500, (09-21-92, Butterfield, #800), sheet 12½ x 17¾ in., (318.1 x 451.7 mm.), 18 x 24 in., (318.1 x 451.7 mm.), etching/aquatint/drypoint in colors on cream wove.

$1430* *"Woman In Wings, Papillon III", 1936*, s. Louis Icart, varnished finish, (12-12-92, Wolf, #12), 6¾ x 8¾ in., (17.1 x 22.2 cm.), color etching and drypoint (BP 917, DM 2253, FR 7721, Y 176,958).

$650* *A Woman Picking Apples*, s., num. 41, margins, laid down on board, sig. rubbed, (11-30-92, Phillips-London, #435), plate 10⅞ x 7¾ in., (276 x 197 mm.), etching in colors (BP 429, DM 1036, FR 3515, Y 80,896).

BI *Woman With Doves, 1926*, s., i. 22, prov., est. $1,500/2,000, (09-17-92, Sloan, #2600), 19¼ x 11⅝ in., (48.9 x 29.5 cm.), color etching and drypoint.

BI *Woman With Jug*, s. on plate, time-darkened, margins trimmed, abrasions, water stains, est. $1/1,500, (06-09-93, Sotheby-Arcade, #296), 17¼ x 13¼ in., (43.8 x 33.7 cm.), lithograph touched w/pastel.

BI *Woman With Sparrows*, s., i. 60, prov., est. $1,500/2,000, (09-17-92, Sloan, #2599), 19¼ x 11½ in., (48.9 x 29.2 cm.), color etching and drypoint.

$1554* *"Zest, L'Elan"*, (c) Louis Icart 1928 Paris, s., repr. "The Etchings Of Louis Icart" by S. Michael Schnessed and Mel Karmel, (03-16-93, Encans, #191), 18¹¹⁄₁₆ x 13¾ in., (47.5 x 35 cm.), etching and aquatint (BP 1073, DM 2584, FR 8780, Y 181,712, C$ 1943).

$700* *"[The Performer]" and "[The Cat]": Two*, both s., (04-28-93, Doyle, #32), larger 18¼ x 22 in., (46.4 x 55.9 cm.), etchings w/color (BP 445, DM 1108, FR 3749, Y 78,449).

ICART, Louis   (after)

$83* *Le Panier De Pommes*, (06-11-93, DuMouchelle, #275), 16 x 13 in., (40.6 x 33 cm.), print (BP 55, DM 135, FR 455, Y 8806).

$33* *A Woman*, (05-14-93, DuMouchelle, #2541), photolitho-graph (BP 21, DM 53, FR 178, Y 3658).

ICART, Louis   (manner of)

BI *Lady In Pink Dress Reclining On A Chaise Longue*, mar-gins, est. BP 80/120, (04-22-93, Bonhams-Chelsea, #72), plate 11½ x 16½ in., (29.2 x 41.9 cm.), etching w/hand coloring.

IGNATOVICH, Boris   1899-1976

$8050* *Baths, 1938*, s., t., d.,; crayon s., t., various credit stamps, (04-08-93, Christie-NY, #146, illus.), 19⅛ x 12¼ in., (48.6 x 31.1 cm.), photograph, gelatin silver print (BP 5279, DM 12,932, FR 43,774, Y 913,527).

BI *"Khudozhnik I Natiurmort, 1965", Artist And Still Life*, ink s., t., d., Novosty press agency stamp, est. BP 4/600, (10-29-92, Christie-London, #143, illus.), 15 x 11¾ in., (38.1 x 29.8 cm.), photograph, gelatin silver print.

BI *"Konovod, 1944", Horse-Breeder*, contemp. retouching, s., t., d., press agency stamp, est. BP 8/1,200, (10-29-92, Christie-London, #142, illus.), 15¼ x 19⅝ in., (38.7 x 49.8 cm.), photograph, gelatin silver print.

BI *"Malodoi Kazak", Young Cossack, n.d., c. 1938*, ink s., t., press agency stamp, lit., est. BP 7/900, (10-29-92, Christie-London, #141, illus.), 15¾ x 11½ in., (40 x 29.2 cm.), photograph, gelatin silver print.

BI *Mother (1930s), c. 1946*, t., credit/exhib. stamps, label, est. $2/3,000, (04-08-93, Christie-NY, #147, illus.), 14¾ x 9¾ in., (37.5 x 24.8 cm.), photograph, gelatin silver print.

IGNATOVICH, Olga

$1725* *Two Runners*, s., photog. name stamp, 1920's, p.l., (04-06-93, Sotheby-NY, #317, illus.), 11⅞ x 15½ in., photo-graph (BP 1139, DM 2779, FR 9411, Y 196,738).

IKEMURA, Leiko   b. 1951

BI *Komposition*, 20/50, s., est. SF 400/500, (10-14-92, Ger-mann, #334), 16⅝ x 22¹⁵⁄₁₆ in., (423 x 584 mm.), color lithograph.

IKSIKTAARYUK   Inuit

BI *Dog And Caribou Fighting, 1975*, #18/50, est. C$2/350, (10-21-92, Maynard, #14), 18½ x 25 in., (47 x 63.5 cm.), stonecut.

ILIFF, Cynthia

$88* *"Christmas In Charlestown, S.C."*, s.; label verso, good/poor cond., (07-19-92, Bakker, #160), sheet 13¼ x 10½ in., (33.7 x 26.7 cm.), lithograph (BP 45, DM 128, FR 434, Y 10,940).

ILLIAN

$70 *Keep It Coming*, W.F. Powers Co., No. 14, edge loss, tear, (09-24-92, Alderfer, #308), 29 x 21 in., (73.7 x 53.3 cm.), (BP 41, DM 104, FR 352, Y 8421).

ILLION

$35 *"Cardinal Mercier"*, (03-04-93, Alderfer, #248), 28 x 20½ in., (71.1 x 52.1 cm.), poster (BP 24, DM 57, FR 195, Y 4075).

$15 *"Kosciuszko Pulawski"*, fold, (03-04-93, Alderfer, #246), 28 x 20½ in., (71.1 x 52.1 cm.), poster (BP 10, DM 25, FR 83, Y 1746).

$70 *"L. Italia"*, (03-04-93, Alderfer, #250), 28 x 20½ in., (71.1 x 52.1 cm.), poster (BP 48, DM 115, FR 390, Y 8150).

ILLORY

$189* *1er Salon De La France D'Outre-Mer. Grand Palais. 1935*, very good cond., (03-13-93, Laurin, #25), 39⅜ x 24⁷⁄₁₆ in., (100 x 62 cm.), (BP 132, DM 315, FR 1070, Y 22,275).

ILSTED, Peter   1861-1933

$978* *Courtyard Interior In Capri (O./S. 48), 1928*, i. by another hand, margins, good cond., skinned areas, foxing, crease, (05-19-93, Butterfield, #1918), 11⅝ x 8¾ in., (295 x 222 mm.), mezzotint in colors on wove (BP 635, DM 1590, FR 5356, Y 108,270).

$477* *Et Par Interiorer Med To Af Kunstnerens Dotre,* (10-20-92, B. Rasmussen, #366), mezzotint (BP 294, DM 725, FR 2454, Y 58,363, DK 2760).

$1265* *Evening (O./S. 47), 1904,* stamped s., margins, good cond., crease, notations, (05-19-93, Butterfield, #1917, illus.), 9 x 8 7/16 in., (229 x 214 mm.), etching and mezzotint in sepia on wove (BP 821, DM 2056, FR 6928, Y 140,042).

BI *Expecting A Guest (O./S. 6), 1911,* s., margins, good cond., foxing, creases, surface soiling, est. $3/4,000, (02-24-93, Butterfield, #2746, illus.), 13 1/8 x 15 1/4 in., (333 x 387 mm.), mezzotint on wove.

$139* *Gardexterior,* (10-20-92, B. Rasmussen, #368), mezzotint in colors (BP 86, DM 211, FR 715, Y 17,007, DK 805).

BI *Gate In A Wood (O./S. 68), 1930,* s., margins, good cond., paper split, stains, est. $1/1,200, (05-19-93, Butterfield, #1919), 7 5/8 x 9 3/4 in., (194 x 248 mm.), mezzotint in colors.

$1035* *Girl Sewing In Italian Villa, 1928,* stamped s., margins, good cond., surface soiling, notations, (05-19-93, Butterfield, #1920, illus.), 10 1/8 x 7 1/2 in., (257 x 191 mm.), mezzotint in sepia on wove (BP 672, DM 1682, FR 5668, Y 114,580).

$794* *Interior Med Aeldre Mand Der Laeser I En Bog,* s. Peter Ilsted, 27/200, (10-20-92, B. Rasmussen, #365), mezzotint (BP 489, DM 1206, FR 4084, Y 97,149, DK 4600).

$357* *Interior Med Kunstnerens Husfru Og Barn,* (10-20-92, B. Rasmussen, #367), mezzotint (BP 220, DM 542, FR 1836, Y 43,680, DK 2070).

$1412* *Junges Madchen An Einem Halbrunden Tisch (Olufsen-Svensson 1), 1904,* s., t., (06-10-93, Hauswedell/Nolt, #420, illus.), image 6 1/4 x 7 13/16 in., (15.8 x 19.8 cm.), color mezzotint on copper print (BP 924, DM 2299, FR 7741, Y 149,878).

$1650* *The Rainy Day (O./S. 71), 1930,* stamp s., margins, good cond., crease, rubbed spot, surface scuff, surface soiling, pencil notations, (02-24-93, Butterfield, #2747, illus.), 16 1/8 x 19 5/16 in., (410 x 491 mm.), mezzotint in colors on Chine applique attached to wove (BP 1151, DM 2679, FR 9081, Y 193,617).

BI *Der Regentag (O-S. 71, Donson 39),* est. DM 2,400, (12-05-92, Bassenge, #7290, illus.), 16 1/8 x 19 1/16 in., (41 x 48.4 cm.), color mezzotint.

$2090* *Sunshine (O. and S. 2), 1909,* s., large margins, good cond., creases in image, mat/glue staining, foxing, skinned areas, (10-28-92, Butterfield, #2657, illus.), 13 1/4 x 10 3/4 in., (337 x 273 mm.), color mezzotint on chine colle (pasted) attached to heavy wove (BP 1332, DM 3228, FR 10,960, Y 256,442).

$935* *Young Girl By A Semi-Circular Table (O./S. 1), 1909,* stamp s., margins, good cond., staining, pencil notations, (02-24-93, Butterfield, #2745), 6 1/8 x 7 1/16 in., (156 x 179 mm.), mezzotint on wove (BP 652, DM 1518, FR 5146, Y 109,716).

$2260* *Zwei Junge Madchen Im Turrahmen (Olufsen-Svensson 16), 1913,* s., #2/50, (06-10-93, Hauswedell/Nolt, #422, illus.), image 15 3/8 x 12 11/16 in., (39 x 32.2 cm.), color mezzotint on copper print (BP 1478, DM 3680, FR 12,390, Y 239,890).

$1766* *Zwei Spielende Kleine Madchen (Olufsen-Svensson 9), 1911,* s., #10/150, (06-10-93, Hauswedell/Nolt, #421, illus.), image 18 7/16 x 17 7/16 in., (46.8 x 44.3 cm.), mezzotint on copper print (BP 1155, DM 2876, FR 9682, Y 187,454).

IMBERT, Publisher, A.

$550* *U.S. Ship "Brandywine",* (11-07-92, Northeast, #172, illus.), 14 x 18 in., (35.6 x 45.7 cm.), lithograph (BP 360, DM 882, FR 2968, Y 67,884).

IMMENDORF, Jorg German b. 1945

BI *Adlerhalfte, 1984,* s., i., tear, est. DM 4,000, (10-07-92, Zeller, #873, illus.), sh approx. 24 7/16 x 34 7/16 in., (62 x 87.5 cm.), linocut.

BI *Angel Die, 1983,* s., t., d. in paint, unique, offset poster p. verso, paint overal crackling, est. $2/3,000, (11-09-92, Christie-NY, #315, illus.), 24 1/2 x 34 1/2 in., (622 x 876 mm.), colored linocut w/hand-painting in black on thin, smooth wove.

$1298* *Freudenmann Mit Kleiner Reise, 1990,* #53/60, d., (11-20-92, Lempertz, #606), sh 50 7/8 x 35 1/4 in., (129.3 x 89.5 cm.), color linocut on hand-made cardboard (BP 855, DM 2070, FR 6971, Y 161,423).

$679* *Maler, Mut, Rundum, 1980,* 6/30, s., d., 1285mm x 910mm, (10-14-92, Germann, #335), poster/color lithograph (BP 399, DM 994, FR 3370, Y 82,283, SF 885).

BI *Ohne Titel, 1988,* #12/50, pencil s., d., est. DM 1,800, (11-20-92, Lempertz, #605), sh 44 5/16 x 33 15/16 in., (112.5 x 86.3 cm.), serigraph in color on white cardboard.

BI *Richtigen Bringen, Rechnung Bringen, Richtung Bringen,* p. by artist as unique piece, good cond., prov., 1630 x 980 mm, est.G 3/5,000, (12-09-92, Sotheby-Amstrdm, #592, illus.), color linocut on wove.

BI *Standarte Darmstadt, 1984,* est. DM 12,000, (06-12-93, Hauswedell/Nolt, #144, illus.), 7 1/16 x 16 3/4 in., (18 x 42.5 cm.), linocut reworked w/oil and latex.

$361* *Tempel, 1986,* #45/45, pencil s., d., (11-20-92, Lempertz, #604), sh 25 7/8 x 18 3/4 in., (65.8 x 47.7 cm.), color lithograph on Velin (BP 238, DM 576, FR 1939, Y 44,895).

$776* *Temple, 1985,* s., d., stone t., num., (09-25-92, Granier, #2891), sheet 27 3/8 x 19 7/8 in., (69.5 x 50.5 cm.), color lithograph on copper print paper (BP 453, DM 1150, FR 3890, Y 93,663).

BI *Untitled, Pegasus Motiv, 1982,* s., d., est. DM 2,200-, (09-25-92, Granier, #2890), 25 9/16 x 19 11/16 in., (64.9 x 50 cm.), colored linocut on wove.

INAGAKI, Tomou

$605* *"Cat In The Moonlight",* s. T. Inagaki, t., #19/50, tate-e, (11-20-92, Skinner, #32), dai oban tate-e (BP 398, DM 965, FR 3249, Y 75,239).

INCANDELA, Gerald

$90* *"Empire State Building" and "Cactus", 1978: Two,* hand-developed, s., d. G. Incandela '78, each 609 x 507mm, (05-07-93, Sotheby-London, #292, illus.), photograph, silver print (BP 57, DM 142, FR 479, Y 9910).

INDIANA, Robert American b. 1928

$275* *Panel Love: Four, 1972,* (12-13-92, Hindman, #344), each 31 1/2 x 31 1/2 in., color serigraph (BP 176, DM 432, FR 1473, Y 34,022).

$413* *4 Square (Sheehan 86),* s., d. 75, #56/100, from series Polygons, prov., (05-16-93, Hindman, #633), 24 x 22 in., (61 x 55.9 cm.), color serigraph (BP 269, DM 664, FR 2232, Y 45,782).

BI *The American Dream #2 (S. 125), 1982: Four,* one plate s., d., i. 1 of 4, #54/100; 3 inits., i. 1 of 4, pub. Prestige Art Ltd., full margins, repair, creases, excell. cond., including Eat, Juke, Jack and The American Dream #2, est. $3,8/4,400, (05-11-93, Christie-NY, #455), each sheet 26 3/4 x 26 3/4 in., (679 x 679 mm.), color screenprint on Fabriano.

BI *The American Dream #2: Jack (S. 125), 1982,* s., init., annot. I of 4, pub. Prestige Art, blindstamp, full margins, good cond., from the suite of four, est. $4/600, (02-24-93, Butterfield, #3222), (610.7 x 610.7 mm.), silkscreen in colors on Fabriano.

$2070* *American Dream #5 (The Golden Five) (S. 113), 1980: Five,* one s., d., t., other four init., d., all i. P.P. 10/17, pub. Prestige Art Ltd., full margins, good cond., crease, soiling, (05-15-93, Sotheby-NY, #1016, illus.), each sheet 26 5/8 x 26 3/4 in., (67.6 x 67.9 cm.), silkscreen in colors on 5 sheets of Fabriano paper (BP 1346, DM 3330, FR 11,189, Y 229,465).

BI *American Dream #5, The Golden Five (S. 113), 1980: Five,* one plate s., t., d.; 4 inits., d.; each #97/100, pub. Prestige Art Ltd., full margins, crease, excell. cond., including Eat, Die, Hug, Err and American Dream 1928-1963, est. $4,5/5,000, (05-11-93, Christie-NY, #453), each sheet 26 3/4 x 26 3/4 in., (679 x 679 mm.), color screenprint on Fabriano.

$690* *American Dream (S. 136), 1986,* s., d., t., #3/10, pub. Vinalhaven Press, full margins, good cond., crease, (05-15-93, Sotheby-NY, #1018), 26 3/8 x 11 3/4 in., (67 x 29.8 cm.), etching, aquatint, drypoint and stencil (BP 449, DM 1110, FR 3730, Y 76,488).

$303* *An American Portrait 1778-1976: The Golden Future Of America (S. 92), 1976,* s., d., #XXX/L, pub. Trans World Art, blindstamp, full margins, original paper folder, good cond., surface soiling on paper folder, (02-24-93, Butterfield, #3220), 22⅜ x 17½ in., (56.8 x 44.5 cm.), silkscreen in colors on Arches 88 (BP 211, DM 492, FR 1668, Y 35,555).

$345* *An American Portrait 1778-1976: The Golden Future Of America (S. 92),1976*, s., d., #18/175, pub. Trans World Art, blindstamp printer, Simca Print Artists, full margins, very good cond., (05-19-93, Butterfield, #2197), 22⅜ x 17⅜ in., (568 x 441 mm.), silkscreen in colors on Arches (BP 224, DM 561, FR 1889, Y 38,193).

$920* *The Bowery Art (Sheehan 73), 1971*, s., d., #21/100, from portfolio On The Bowery, pub. Editions Domberger, full margins, good cond., (05-15-93, Sotheby-NY, #1014), 17¾ x 17¾ in., (45.1 x 45.1 cm.), silkscreen in colors (BP 598, DM 1480, FR 4973, Y 101,984).

$440* *The Bowery Art (Sheehan 73), 1971*, s., d. 71, #39/100, pub. Edition Domberger, (05-16-93, Hindman, #630), 17¾ x 17¾ in., (45.1 x 45.1 cm.), color serigraph (BP 286, DM 708, FR 2378, Y 48,775).

$330* *Decade, 1980*, s., d., #1/125, blindstamp pub. Multiples, Inc., good cond.?, smudge, prov., (12-12-92, Weschler, #129, illus.), sheet 26¾ x 26¾ in., (67.9 x 67.9 cm.), color silkscreen on Fabrino paper (BP 212, DM 520, FR 1782, Y 40,837).

$385* *Decade: Autoportrait 1969, V/H (S. 124), 1982*, s., d., t., #83/125, pub. William Farnsworth Library and Art Museum,full margins, good cond.?, shrink-wrapped, (10-28-92, Butterfield, #2984), 24 x 24 in., (610 x 610 mm.), silkscreen in white, yellow and black on BFK Rives (BP 245, DM 595, FR 2019, Y 47,239).

$460* *Decade: Autoportrait 1969, V/H (S. 124), 1982*, s., d., t., #102/125, pub. William A. Farnsworth Library and Art Museum, good cond., crease, (05-19-93, Butterfield, #2198), 24 x 24 in., (610 x 610 mm.), silkscreen in black, yellow and white on BFK Rives (BP 299, DM 748, FR 2519, Y 50,924).

$4025* *Decade: Autoportraits, Vinalhaven Suite (S. 114-23), 1980: Ten*, s., d., #118/125, Multiples, Inc. blindstamp, full margins, excell. cond., (05-11-93, Christie-NY, #454, illus.), each sheet 26¾ x 26¾ in., (679 x 679 mm.), color screenprint on Fabriano Classico (BP 2569, DM 6341, FR 21,364, Y 442,746).

$605* *Decade: Autoportraits, Vinalhaven Suite (S. 116; 119; 120; 121; 123), 1980: Five*, incomplete suite, s., d., #99/125, blindstamp pub. Multiples, full margins, good cond., surface scuffing; includes Penobscot; Carver's Pond; Coomb's Neck; Tiptoe Mt.; Brimstone, (10-28-92, Butterfield, #2983), each 24 x 24 in., (610 x 610 mm.), color silkscreen on white Fabriano Classico paper (BP 385, DM 934, FR 3173, Y 74,233).

BI *Decade: Autoportraits, Vinalhaven Suite (Sheehab 114-23), 1980: Set Of Ten*, s., d., #118/125, blindstamps, full margins, excellent cond., shrinkwrapped, est. $7/8,000, (11-09-92, Christie-NY, #316, illus.), 26¾ x 26¾ in., (679 x 679 mm.), colored screenprints on Fabriano Classico.

$1650* *Decade: Autoportraits, Vinalhaven Suite: "Coomb's Neck", "Tiptoe Mt."and "Star Of Hope" (S. 120; 121; 122): Three*, each s., d., num. 119/125, blindstamp of pub. Multiples, full margins, good cond., (02-24-93, Butterfield, #3059), each 24 x 24 in., (610 x 610 mm.), silkscreen in colors on Fabriano Classico (BP 1151, DM 2679, FR 9081, Y 193,617).

BI *Decade: Autoportraits, Vinalhaven Suite: "Crockett Cove", "Hurricane"and "Carver's Pond" (S. 117; 118; 119), 1980*, each s., d., num. 119/125, blindstamp of pub. Multiples, full margins, good cond., est. $1,5/2,000, (02-24-93, Butterfield, #3058), each 24 x 24 in., (610 x 610 mm.), silkscreen in colors on Fabriano Classico.

$1650* *Decade: Autoportraits, Vinalhaven Suite: "Vinalhaven", "Isle Au Haut" and "Penobscot" (S. 114; 115; 116), 1980: Three*, each s., d., num. 119/125, blindstamp of pub. Multiples, full margins, good cond., (02-24-93, Butterfield, #3057, illus.), each 24 x 24 in., (610 x 610 mm.), silkscreen in colors on Fabriano Classico (BP 1151, DM 2679, FR 9081, Y 193,617).

BI *Decade: The Brooklyn Bridge (S. 67), 1971*, s., d., num. 14/200, pub. Multiples, margins, apparently good cond.,-est. $1/2,000, (02-24-93, Butterfield, #3056), 22½ x 22½

in., (572 x 572 mm.), silkscreen in colors on Schoellers Parole.

BI *Decade: The Brooklyn Bridge (S. 67), 1971*, s., d., #14/200, pub. Multiples, margins, good cond.?, est. $5/700, (05-19-93, Butterfield, #2196), 22½ x 22½ in., (572 x 572 mm.), silkscreen in colors on Schoellers Parole.

$2200* *Denise Rene, 1972*, s., #95/150, good cond.?, creases, (10-28-92, Butterfield, #2979), 31½ x 31½ in., (800 x 800 mm.), silkscreen on wove (BP 1402, DM 3398, FR 11,536, Y 269,939).

$770* *Die Deutsche Liebe (S. 42), 1968*, s., d., num. 66/100, pub. Rolf-Gunter Deinst, margins, apparently good cond., (02-24-93, Butterfield, #3055), 22 x 22 in., (559 x 559 mm.), silkscreen in colors on wove (BP 537, DM 1250, FR 4238, Y 90,354).

$825* *Die Deutsche Liebe (S. 42), 1968*, s., d., #66/100, pub. Rolf-Gunter Deinst, margins, good cond.?, (10-28-92, Butterfield, #2978), 22 x 22 in., (559 x 559 mm.), color silkscreen on wove (BP 526, DM 1274, FR 4326, Y 101,227).

$770* *Eine Kleine Nachtmusik, 1971*, d., num., s., pub. Domberger, (05-27-93, Swann, #136, illus.), 23½ x 19½ in., (59.7 x 49.5 cm.), color serigraph (BP 493, DM 1236, FR 4164, Y 82,547).

$858* *The Figure 5, 1971*, s., #10/200, good cond., (06-30-93, Sotheby-London, #852), 35⅞ x 29⅞ in., (911 x 759 mm.), color silkscreen (BP 575, DM 1463, FR 4937, Y 91,932).

BI *A Garden Of Love (S. 126-131), 1982: Six*, complete suite, each s., d., t., i. PP II/V, pub. Prestige Art Ltd.,full margins, good cond., scuff mark, soiling, est. $8/10,000, (05-15-93, Sotheby-NY, #1015, illus.), each sheet 26¾ x 26¾ in., (67.9 x 67.9 cm.), six silkscreens in colors on Fabriano rag paper.

BI *A Garden Of Love: Lilac, 1982 (S. 131)*, s., d., t., #84/100, 15AP, blindstamp pub. Prestige Art, Ltd., full margins, very good cond.?, est. $1,2/1,400, (10-28-92, Butterfield, #2986), 26 x 26 in., (660 x 660 mm.), color silkscreen on Fabriano wove.

$805* *A Garden Of Love: Lily (Sheehan 127), 1982*, s., d., t., #61/100, pub. Prestige Art Ltd., full margins, good cond., (02-11-93, Sotheby-NY, #356), 24 x 24 in., (610 x 610 mm.), color silkscreen on Fabriano 100% rag (BP 568, DM 1333, FR 4512, Y 97,046).

BI *A Garden Of Love: Lily, 1982 (S. 127)*, s., d., t., #84/100, 15AP, blindstamp pub. Prestige Art, Ltd., full margins, very good cond.?, est. $1,2/1,400, (10-28-92, Butterfield, #2985), 26 x 26 in., (660 x 660 mm.), color silkscreen on Fabriano wove.

$1100* *A Garden Of Love: Phlox (S. 130), 1982*, s., d., t., num. 84/100, pub. Prestige Art, blindstamp, full margins,apparently very good cond., shrink-wrapped, (02-24-93, Butterfield, #3060), 24 x 24 in., (610 x 610 mm.), silkscreen in colors on Fabriano (BP 767, DM 1786, FR 6054, Y 129,078).

$3575* *"A Garden Of Love: Phlox" and "Lilac" (S. 130 and 131), 1982: Two*, s., d., t., #40/100, pub. Prestige Art Ltd., full margins, good cond., (11-07-92, Sotheby-NY, #593, illus.), 24 x 24 in., (610 x 610 mm.), silkscreens p. in colors on Fabriano 100% rag (BP 2337, DM 5708, FR 19,293, Y 441,249).

$920* *A Garden Of Love: Zinnia (S. 128), 1982*, s., d., t., #39/100, pub. Prestige Art Ltd., full margins, good cond., (05-15-93, Sotheby-NY, #1017), 24 x 24 in., (61 x 61 cm.), silkscreen in colors (BP 598, DM 1480, FR 4973, Y 101,984).

BI *The Golden Future Of America (S. 92), 1976*, s., d., #18/175, blindstamp p. Simca Print Artists, pub. Trans WorldArt, full margins, very good cond., est. $5/700, (10-28-92, Butterfield, #2980), 22⅜ x 17⅜ in., (568 x 441 mm.), color silkscreen on Arches 88.

BI *The Golden Future Of America, 1976*, s., #XIV/L, pub. Transworld Art, very good cond., est. $5/700, (06-11-93, Doyle, #95), 26 x 19½ in., (660 x 495 mm.), silkscreen.

$358* *Golden Love, 1973*, s., num. 93/150, (09-20-92, Hindman, #720), 30 x 30 in., (76.2 x 76.2 cm.), color serigraph (BP 210, DM 531, FR 1817, Y 44,247).

$358* *An Honest Man Has Been President, A Portrait Of Jimmy Carter (S. 112), 1980*, s., d., #38/150, from the

Presidential Portfolio, pub. Democratic National Committee, full margins, good cond.(10-28-92, Butterfield, #2982), 21 x 18 in., (533 x 457 mm.), color silkscreen on wove (BP 228, DM 553, FR 1877, Y 43,926).

BI *Indianapolis Museum Of Art Poster, 1970,* s., d., #58/100, pub. Indianapolis Museum and American Poster Co., est. $5/750, (12-08-92, Swann, #148, illus.), 45 x 32 in., (114.3 x 81.3 cm.), color serigraph.

BI *Indianapolis Museum Of Art Poster, 1970,* d., num., s., p. Domberger, nicks, est. $4/600, (05-27-93, Swann, #137), sh 45 x 32 in., (114.3 x 81.3 cm.), color serigraph.

BI *"Lillian Russel", (19)77,* s., d., num., est. DM 1000, (12-01-92, Karl/Faber, #764), 17¹⁵⁄₁₆ x 13¹⁵⁄₁₆ in., (45.5 x 35.5 cm.), color lithograph on Arches wove.

$3450* *"Lily" and "Zinnia" (S. 127 and 128), 1982: Two,* from A Garden of Love, s., t., d., #41/100 and 91/100, pub. PrestigeArt Ltd., full margins, time staining, excell. cond., (05-11-93, Christie-NY, #456, illus.), each sheet 26¾ x 26¾ in., (679 x 679 mm.), color screenprint on Fabriano (BP 2202, DM 5435, FR 18,312, Y 379,496).

$990* *Love,* s., num. 93/150, (11-12-92, Freemn/Fine Art, #95B), 30 x 30 in., (76.2 x 76.2 cm.), lithograph p. in color (BP 650, DM 1569, FR 5291, Y 122,753).

$193* *"Love",* s. R. Indiana '91, copyrighted inside plate (c) R. Indiana 1983 andLove 1966, excellent cond. (?), (04-25-93, Bakker, #55, illus.), image 13¾ x 13¾ in., (34.9 x 34.9 cm.), screenprint (BP 123, DM 305, FR 1031, Y 21,317).

$1980* *Mecca (Sheehan 93-95), 1977,* portfolio, each s., d., t., i. sequentially 'I-III', #19/50, pub. Posner Gallery, full margins, good cond., scuff marks, creases, (11-07-92, Sotheby-NY, #592, illus.), each image approx. 23⅜ x 12½ in., (594 x 318 mm.), three silkscreens on Arches 88 (BP 1295, DM 3161, FR 10,685, Y 244,384).

$1725* *"Mecca I", "Mecca II" and "Mecca III" (Sheehan 93-5), 1977: Three,* s., t., d., #28/50, pub. Posner Gallery, full margins, creasing, excell. cond., (05-11-93, Christie-NY, #452, illus.), each sheet 36 x 24⅞ in., (914 x 632 mm.), color screenprint on wove (BP 1101, DM 2717, FR 9156, Y 189,748).

$1732* *Mother Of Exiles (Black) (Sheehan 137, 1986,* t., s., d., (11-28-92, Schoppmann, #598), 35¹⁵⁄₁₆ x 24 in., (91.4 x 61 cm.), etching on Arches wove (BP 1143, DM 2759, FR 9367, Y 215,557).

BI *The Mother Of Us All (S. 96-108), 1977: Thirteen,* complete portfolio, s., d., #67/150, pub. Leon Amiel, full margins, good cond., discoloration, surface soiling; includes Susan B.; Gertrude S.; Gen. E.S. Grant; Indiana Elliot; Jo the Loiterer; Lillian Russell; Anthony Comstock; Anne; Henrietta M.; and 4 more, est. $2/3,000, (10-28-92, Butterfield, #2981), each 18 x 14 in., (457 x 356 mm.), color lithograph on Arches.

BI *The Mother Of Us All: Constance Fletcher (S. 107), 1977,* s., d., num. 147/150, full margins, good cond., yellow ink, surface soiling, est. $5/700, (02-24-93, Butterfield, #3221), 18 x 14 in., (457 x 356 mm.), silkscreen in colors on Arches.

$495* *The Neuberger Art, 1975(?),* t., num., s., (05-27-93, Swann, #139, illus.), 24 x 24 in., (61 x 61 cm.), color serigraph (BP 317, DM 794, FR 2677, Y 53,066).

$302* *"Octagon",* s., d. '75, #13/100, image scratches, good cond., (12-04-92, Doyle, #110), 24 x 22 in., (610 x 559 mm.), color silkscreen (BP 194, DM 481, FR 1632, Y 37,703).

$798* *"The Philadelphia Love, 1975",* s., t., #26/125, (06-11-93, Freemn/Fine Art, #111A), 24 x 24 in., (61 x 61 cm.), serigraph (BP 524, DM 1297, FR 4373, Y 84,668).

BI *Rose (Sheehan 129),* s., d. '82, i., #AP 13/15, from suite A Garden of Love, est. $1/2,000, (05-16-93, Hindman, #647), 24 x 24 in., (61 x 61 cm.), color serigraph.

BI *The Santa Fe Opera, 1976,* full margins, d., num., s., tears, paper scuffing, est. $6/900, (05-27-93, Swann, #138), 31 x 22 in., (78.7 x 55.9 cm.), color serigraph poster on heavy wove.

$866* *"Terre Haute No. 2" (Sheehan 72), 1971,* s., d., num., from the series "Decade", (11-28-92, Grisebach, #566, illus.), 35¾ x 29¹⁵⁄₁₆ in., (90.8 x 76 cm.), colored seri-

graph on cardboard (BP 572, DM 1380, FR 4684, Y 107,778).

$3080* *"Tulip", "Zinnia" and "Rose" (Sheehan 126, 128-9), 1982: Three,* from A Garden of Love, all s., t., d., num. 84.100, pub. Prestige Art, full margins, excell. cond., (09-19-92, Christie-E, #133, illus.), all sheet 26¾ x 26¾ in., (67.9 x 67.9 cm.), screenprint in colors on Fabriano (BP 1772, DM 4612, FR 15,795, Y 383,753).

INGRES, Jean Dominique   French 1780-1867
$1740* *Gabriel Cortois De Pressigny (D. 1), 1816,* oxidation, large margins, (02-24-93, Picard, #130), etching on strong wove (BP 1213, DM 2825, FR 9576, Y 204,177).

INNESS, George (after)
$275* *Evening Landscape,* (10-16-92, DuMouchelle, #2387), 20 x 36 in., (50.8 x 91.4 cm.), print on canvas (BP 167, DM 406, FR 1380, Y 32,836).

INTOURIST
$65 *Batumi,* tears, (09-24-92, Alderfer, #303), 39 x 24½ in., (99.1 x 62.2 cm.), (BP 38, DM 96, FR 327, Y 7819).
$195 *Summer Sports In USSR, Rowing,* minor edge loss, (09-24-92, Alderfer, #313, illus.), 40¼ x 20½ in., (102.2 x 52.1 cm.), (BP 114, DM 289, FR 981, Y 23,457).

INUIT PRINT, 20TH CENTURY
$138* *"Testing Her New Spear",* num., ident., d. 29/50, Elisapee Tshedutag/Josea Mancapek '84, blindstamp, very good cond., (06-26-93, Skinner, #62, illus.), 10½ x 15 in., (26.7 x 38.1 cm.), polychrome stencil (BP 92, DM 234, FR 790, Y 14,642).

INUIT SCHOOL
$17* *Chasseur En Kayac,* s., (06-16-93, Encans, #41), 12³⁄₁₆ x 12³⁄₁₆ in., (31 x 31 cm.), wood engraving (BP 11, DM 28, FR 95, Y 1813, C$ 22).

IONESCO, Irina
$1610* *Selected Portraits: "Eva In Front Of Mirror" and "Eva With Face Painted": Two,* each s. by photog. in ink, 1970's, p. 1986, (04-06-93, Sotheby-NY, #480, illus.), photograph (BP 1063, DM 2594, FR 8783, Y 183,622).

IPPITSUSAI BUNCHO   Japanese ac. c. 1765-1792
$1487* *Ichikawa Komazo I (II?) As Karigane Bunshichi Holding A Monkey Mask,And Arashi Otohachi I As Anbaiyoshi Rokubei Holding An Uchiwa (Fan),* Chuban, s. Ippitsusai Buncho ga, seal, d. Meiwa 5 (1768), gauffrages,faded, browned, fold mark, rubbed, frayed, Prof. H.R.W. Kuhne Coll., (06-11-93, Sotheby-London, #59, illus.), 10¾ x 8¹⁄₁₆ in., (27.3 x 20.5 cm.), woodblock (BP 977, DM 2417, FR 8148, Y 157,772).

$1925* *Ichikawa Komazo II As A Gallant Samurai And Ichikawa Kodanji II As ACourtesan,* Hosoban, s. Ippitsusai Buncho ga, seal, d. Meiwa 9 (1772), faded, rubbed, soiled, trimmed, paper added, repaired, Prof. H.R.W. Kuhne Coll., (06-11-93, Sotheby-London, #58, illus.), 11⅞ x 5¼ in., (30.2 x 13.3 cm.), woodblock (BP 1265, DM 3129, FR 10,548, Y 204,244).

$1137* *Ichikawa Monnosuke II As A Komuso (Mendicant Monk),* Hosoban, s. Ippitsusai Buncho ga seal, d. An'ei 1 (1772), faded, soiled, wormed, repaired, laid down, Prof. H.R.W. Kuhne Coll., (06-11-93, Sotheby-London, #55, illus.), 12½ x 6 in., (31.8 x 15.2 cm.), woodblock (BP 747, DM 1848, FR 6230, Y 120,637).

$2100* *Ichikawa Yaozo II As The Retainer Of Yoshida Family,* Hosoban, s. Ippitsusai Buncho ga, sea, d. Meiwa & (1770), faded, rubbed, trimmed, paper added, Prof. H.R.W. Kuhne Coll., (06-11-93, Sotheby-London, #57, illus.), 12¼ x 5½ in., (31.1 x 14 cm.), woodblock (BP 1380, DM 3413, FR 11,507, Y 222,812).

$5426* *Iwai Hanshiro IV As Shirabyoshi Dancer Mikumo,* Hosoban, s. Ippitsusai Buncho ga, seal, d. Meiwa 6 (1769), faded, soiled, rubbed, Prof. H.R.W. Kuhne Coll., (06-11-93, Sotheby-London, #60, illus.), 12¾ x 6 in., (32.4 x 15.2 cm.), woodlbock (BP 3565, DM 8818, FR 29,732, Y 575,703).

$1925* *Matsumoto Koshiro III As Musume Asagao,* Hosoban, s. Ippitsusai Buncho ga seal, d. Meiwa 5 (1768), faded, corner repaired, Prof. H.R.W. Kuhne Coll., (06-11-93, Sotheby-London, #56, illus.), 12¼ x 5¾ in., (31.1 x 14.6

cm.), woodblock (BP 1265, DM 3129, FR 10,548, Y 204,244).

$1750* *Sakata Hangoro II Holding A Closed Fan In His Mouth In The Role Of Takeami In The Play Shussei Taiheiki,* Hosoban, s. Ippitsusai Buncho ga, seal, d. Meiwa 5 (1768), faded, fold-mark, soiled, repaired, Prof. H.R.W. Kuhne Coll., (06-11-93, Sotheby-London, #53), 12¼ x 5½ in., (31.1 x 14 cm.), woodblock (BP 1150, DM 2844, FR 9589, Y 185,676).

BI *Two Fan-Prints In Monochrome: Two,* Chuban, fan-print, s. Ippitsusai Buncho ga, pub.'s mark, d. Kansei period?, fragile state, Prof. H.R.W. Kuhne Coll., est. BP 800/1,200, (06-11-93, Sotheby-London, #54), one 9½ x 12 in., (24.1 x 30.5 cm.), other 9¼ x 12¼ in., (24.1 x 30.5 cm.), woodblock.

IPPITSUSAI BUNCHO and KATSUKAWA SHUNSHO

BI *Ehon Butai Ogi "Picture Book Of Stage Fans",* Vol. 3, pub. Kariganeya, d. Meiwa 7 (1770), engraver Endo Matsugoro, pub. Kariganeya Ihei of Koishikawa Dentsuin mae, wormed, finger marked, ex-colls. Duret, Akagari, S. Sorimachi, H. Kaempher, collector's seals, lit., Prof. H.R.W. Kuhne Coll., est. BP 5/6,000, (06-11-93, Sotheby-London, #506, illus.), 11⅛ x 7⅛ in., (28.3 x 18.1 cm.), woodblock p. in color.

IPSEN, Poul Janus

$272* *"Koala Bear I" and "Koala Bear II": Two,* first s. 1982, a.p.; second s. 1982, 16/130, (09-29-92, B. Rasmussen, #325), serigraph in colors (BP 153, DM 384, FR 1311, Y 32,470, DK 1495).

$209* *"My Love I, II and III": Three,* s. 94/100, X/XV, and X/XV, (09-29-92, B. Rasmussen, #324), lithograph in colors (BP 117, DM 295, FR 1007, Y 24,949, DK 1150).

IPSEN, Poul Janus and Karl JACOBSEN

$367* *Mennesker I New York, 1976: Ten,* s. 96/150, portfolio, (03-24-93, Kunsthallen, #144), color offset lithograph (BP 249, DM 599, FR 2040, Y 43,121, DK 2300).

IRISH, E. B. J.   20th cent.

$748* *A Hunting Alphabet, c. 1930: Eight Plates,* margins, good cond., Anthony N. B. Garvan Coll., (06-05-93, Christie-NY, #79), all image 11⅝ x 8¼ in., (295 x 210 mm.), chromolithograph on wove (BP 492, DM 1213, FR 4087, Y 80,240).

IRRIERA, Roger

$199* *Ch. De Fer Algeriens De L'Etat: BISKRA. "Reine Des Zibans",* good cond., (03-13-93, Laurin, #50), 39⁹⁄₁₆ x 23¹³⁄₁₆ in., (100.5 x 60.5 cm.), (BP 139, DM 331, FR 1126, Y 23,453).

$189* *Chemins De Fer Algeriens, Touggourt, 1930,* p. Baconnier, cond. 1, corner repaired, laid on linen, (10-13-92, Phillips-London, #30, illus.), 39⅜ x 23⅝ in., (100 x 60 cm.), color lithograph (BP 110, DM 277, FR 941, Y 22,917).

ISABEY, Eugene   French 1803-1886

$440* *Radoub D'Une Barque A Maree Basse (L.D. 67), 1833,* second state of three, reddish stains, spots, large margins, yellowed, drystamp, (06-11-93, Picard, #79), 12⁵⁄₁₆ x 9⅝ in., (312 x 244 mm.), lithograph on chine fixe (BP 289, DM 715, FR 2411, Y 46,684).

$280* *Souvenir De Saint-Valery-Sur-Somme (L. Delteil 66), 1833,* second state of three before letter, reddish stains, drystamp, good margins, (06-11-93, Picard, #78), 11⅞ x 9⁹⁄₁₆ in., (302 x 243 mm.), lithograph on chine fixe (BP 184, DM 455, FR 1534, Y 29,708).

ISABEY, Jean Baptiste   French 1767-1855

$1870* *Voyage En Italie ... En 1822: Thirty,* folio, orig. wrapper bound in, foxing throughout, i. Isabey, (11-12-92, Swann, #112), 15¼ x 10¼ in., (388 x 260 mm.), lithograph, rebacked w/morocco (BP 1228, DM 2963, FR 9995, Y 231,866).

ISELI, Rolf   b. 1934

$453* *Amorphe Figur, 1987,* 44/49, s., d., (10-14-92, Germann, #554), 6¹⁵⁄₁₆ x 10 in., (177 x 254 mm.), etching (BP 266, DM 663, FR 2248, Y 54,896, SF 590).

$815* *Giftig, 1973,* 17/30, s., (10-14-92, Germann, #555), 30⅛ x 22¼ in., (765 x 565 mm.), lithograph (BP 478, DM 1193, FR 4045, Y 98,764, SF 1062).

$514* *Homme Cactusse, 1975,* #93/100, s., (04-21-93, Germann, #553), 6¹¹⁄₁₆ x 5⅞ in., (170 x 150 mm.), etching (BP 334, DM 822, FR 2778, Y 56,902, SF 748).

$328* *Liegende 5, 1970,* #179/200, s., d., (11-13-92, Koller, #5351), 19¹¹⁄₁₆ x 25⁹⁄₁₆ in., (50 x 65 cm.), lithograph on wove (BP 212, DM 515, FR 1736, Y 40,710, SF 464).

$514* *Mocken Rot (Iseli 29), 1969,* #33/55, s., d., (04-21-93, Germann, #552), 29¹⁵⁄₁₆ x 21⅞ in., (760 x 555 mm.), color lithograph (BP 334, DM 822, FR 2778, Y 56,902, SF 748).

ISHIGURO, Kenji

BI *Selected Images: Twenty-Nine, 1958-60,* each w/label w/t., d., est. $3,5/4,500, (10-13-92, Christie-NY, #461, illus.), each 9½ x 7 in., (24.1 x 17.8 cm.), photograph, gelatin silver prints.

ISHIKAWA, Toraji

$615* *A Nude Dancer,* large oban tate-e, t., s. Ishikawa w/ seal Tora, good cond., (06-10-93, Sotheby-London, #292), (BP 402, DM 1001, FR 3372, Y 65,280).

ISHIKAWA TOYONOBU   Japanese 1711-1785

BI *Nakamura Kiyosaburo As a Bikuni ("Nun"), A Disguise For A Prostitute,Talking To A Young Girl,* Hosoban, benizuri-e, sig. Ishikawa Toyonobu hitsu, pub.'s mark, d. c.Horeki 5 (1755), trimmed, rubbed, browned, tears, worm holes repaired, Prof. H.R.W. Kuhne Coll., est. BP 6/800, (06-11-93, Sotheby-London, #47), 11⅜ x 5¾ in., (28.9 x 14.6 cm.), woodblock.

$2100* *Sanogawa Ichimatsu Standing As A Mendicant Monk,* Hashira-e, benizuri-e, s. Tanjodo Ishikawa Shuha Toyonobu zu, w/seal,faded, creases, soiled, trimmed, Prof. H.R.W. Kuhne Coll., (06-11-93, Sotheby-London, #31, illus.), 21 x 6¾ in., (53.3 x 17.1 cm.), woodblock (BP 1380, DM 3413, FR 11,507, Y 222,812).

$2625* *Segawa Kikunojo I Dancing With A Harugoma (Hobby-Horse),* Hosoban benizuri-e, s. Ishikawa Toyonobu zu, w/ seal Toyonobu, d. c. Horeki 8-10 (1758-60), pub. Yama, rubbed, soiled, laid-down, extensively restored, Prof. H.R.W. Kuhne Coll., (06-11-93, Sotheby-London, #30, illus.), 15 x 6½ in., (38.1 x 16.5 cm.), woodblock (BP 1725, DM 4266, FR 14,384, Y 278,515).

ISODA KORYUSAI   Japanese ac. c. 1764-1788

$2450* *Kites Of The Actor Otani Hiroji: Two,* Hashira-e, s. Koryu/Koryusai ga, faded, darkened, soiled, one trimmed, both laid-down, Prof. H.R.W. Kuhne Coll., (06-11-93, Sotheby-London, #51, illus.), woodblock (BP 1610, DM 3982, FR 13,425, Y 259,947).

ISOZAKI, Arata

$275* *Moca Print (G. 977), 1981,* s., d., #262/500, blindstamp pub. Gemini G.E.L., full margins, very good cond.?, (10-28-92, Butterfield, #2988), 7⅛ x 8⅛ in., (181 x 206 mm.), etching w/aquatint on Somerset Satin paper (BP 175, DM 425, FR 1442, Y 33,742).

ISRAELS, Josef   Dutch 1824-1911

$303* *Woman Warming Her Hands,* by H. Koctsu, s., num. No. 146, (10-18-92, Hindman, #520), 28 x 17¾ in., (71.1 x 45.1 cm.), color etching and aquatint (BP 185, DM 451, FR 1530, Y 36,353).

ISRAELS, Jozef   Dutch 1824-1911

$93* *Avondstond (Hubert XX),* pub. in Zeitschrift fur bildende Kunst, neue Folge XII, Heft 7, April 1901 (Hubert XX), (11-18-92, Bubb Kuyper, #1537), 3¹⁵⁄₁₆ x 5¹⁵⁄₁₆ in., (10.1 x 15.1 cm.), etching (BP 61, DM 148, FR 499, Y 11,566, G 168).

BI *Bauernmadchen Mit Korb Am Strand Sitzend (Hubert 19), c. 1879,* est. DM 400, (12-01-92, Karl/Faber, #218), 5⅞ x 9¹⁄₁₆ in., (15 x 23 cm.), etching on handmade.

ITALIAN SCHOOL

BI *The Presentation In The Temple (B. XII, 31, 6),* after Parmigianino, trimmed, upper corners damaged, nicks, losses, glued down, est. BP 1,5/2,000, (06-30-93, Sotheby-London, #151), 16 x 11¾ in., (406 x 298 mm.), chiaroscuro woodcut from 4 blocks in black and shades of mushroom.

ITALIAN SCHOOL, 19TH CENTURY
$908* "Mythological Figures": A Group Of Six, (02-03-93, Doyle, #36), 14 x 10¾ in., (35.6 x 27.3 cm.), hand colored engraving (BP 634, DM 1495, FR 5070, Y 112,949).

ITALIAN SCHOOL, CIRCA 1525
$22,908* Portrait Kaiser Karl. V., watermark, (06-23-93, Kornfeld, #72, illus.), sh 8⅜ x 6¹¹⁄₁₆ in., (21.3 x 17 cm.), engraving (BP 15,563, DM 38,761, FR 130,381, Y 2,495,697, SF 34,500).

ITO, N.   Japanese 19th cent.
$198* "Pagoda Of Ninnaji Temple In Snow", pub. Uchida (seales), good cond., (10-31-92, Cleveland, #28), 15¾ x 10½ in., (40 x 26.7 cm.), color woodcut (BP 127, DM 305, FR 1033, Y 24,526).

ITTEN, Johannes   1888-1967
BI Landschaft Tirol (Itten 1978, 159), 1919, s., sheet 1 of portfolio "Johannes Itten, 10 Originallithographien",prov., est. DM 1,800, (12-05-92, Bassenge, #7291, illus.), 13⅞ x 11¹⁵⁄₁₆ in., (35.2 x 30.3 cm.), lithograph on thick paper.
$1083* "Linienrhythmus" (Itten 168), 1919, s., sheet 10 of "Lithographie-Mappe", (11-28-92, Grisebach, #567, illus.), 11⅝ x 12¹⁵⁄₁₆ in., (29.6 x 32.8 cm.), lithograph on copper print paper (BP 715, DM 1725, FR 5857, Y 134,785).

ITURBIDE, Graciela
$825* "Nina Del Peine", 1980, s., t., d., (11-16-92, Butterfield, #6023, illus.), 18⁹⁄₁₆ x 14⅞ in., (470.7 x 377.2 mm.), photograph, gelatin silver print (BP 543, DM 1315, FR 4431, Y 102,599).

ITURRINO, Francisco   Spanish 1864-1924
$921* "La Tablada La Veille Des Courses De Taureaux" and "Les Mendiants", c. 1900: Two, s., first, num.; second, t., dust, large margins, (02-24-93, Picard, #131), etching and aquatint in color on laid (BP 642, DM 1495, FR 5069, Y 108,073).

IZIS (Izis Bidermanas)
$690* Barge, c. 1950, credit/collection of Romeo Martinez stamps, prov., (04-08-93, Christie-NY, #192, illus.), 10⅞ x 8⅝ in., (27.6 x 21.9 cm.), photograph, gelatin silver print (BP 452, DM 1108, FR 3752, Y 78,302).
$2300* Double Portrait Of Paul Eluard, 1940s, ink s. recto; t., studio stamp, (04-08-93, Christie-NY, #190, illus.), 11⅝ x 9¼ in., (29.5 x 23.5 cm.), photograph, gelatin silver print (BP 1508, DM 3695, FR 12,507, Y 261,008).
BI Portrait Of Nusch Eluard, 1946, s., d., est. $2,5/3,500, (04-08-93, Christie-NY, #191, illus.), 11¾ x 8¼ in., (29.8 x 21 cm.), gelatin silver print.

IZZARD, Daniel
$52* "Lowtide Nova Scotia", artist proof, s., t., (05-12-93, Maynard, #271), 14²⁵ x 25⁵ in., (35.6 x 63.5 cm.), (BP 34, DM 84, FR 283, Y 5806, C$ 66).

JABLONSKY, Carol   American 20th cent.
BI Fish Or Fowl, s., t., #81/100, est. $3/400, (06-11-93, Freemn/Fine Art, #113), 4⅞ x 5¾ in., (12.4 x 14.6 cm.), color etching.

JACK
$24* Theatre Dejazet: Tous Criminels. Folie-Vaudeville, Imp. Gaillard & Berger, fairly good cond., (02-12-93, Cheval/Robert, #160), 50 x 36¹³⁄₁₆ in., (127 x 93.5 cm.), poster (BP 17, DM 40, FR 135, Y 2894).

JACK, Kenneth William   b. 1924
$29* Clunes-The Main Street, s. Kenneth Jack, i., #19/40, (08-11-92, L. Joel, #94G), 7¹⁵⁄₁₆ x 10½ in., (20.3 x 26.7 cm.), color linocut (BP 15, DM 43, FR 144, Y 3714, A$ 40).
$142* The Drovers, s. Kenneth Jack, i., #46/50, (08-11-92, L. Joel, #84G), 7½ x 9⅜ in., (19 x 23.8 cm.), engraving (BP 74, DM 208, FR 706, Y 18,184, A$ 192).
$81* The Farmer, s. Kenneth Jack, i. Artist Proof, (08-11-92, L. Joel, #8G), 9¹⁵⁄₁₆ x 12¹³⁄₁₆ in., (25.3 x 32.5 cm.), color lithograph (BP 42, DM 119, FR 403, Y 10,373, A$ 110).

$122* Flinders Street Facades, Melbourne, s. Kenneth Jack, i., #39/60, (08-11-92, L. Joel, #50G), 14³⁄₁₆ x 21¼ in., (36 x 54 cm.), color lithograph (BP 63, DM 179, FR 606, Y 15,623, A$ 165).
BI The Stockman, s. Kenneth Jack, i., #28/30, est. $150/250, (08-11-92, L. Joel, #21G), 7⅝ x 8⅜ in., (19.3 x 21.3 cm.), woodcut.

JACKLIN, Bill
$180* Bererun, 1971, s., #2/15, full margins, good cond.?, (10-15-92, Sotheby-London, #103, illus.), 17⅛ x 17⅜ in., (43.5 x 44.1 cm.), etching on wove (BP 110, DM 268, FR 909, Y 21,596).
$290* Composition In Black And White, 1965, s., d., t., #4/6, full margins, discoloration, creasing, (12-03-92, Sotheby-London, #748, illus.), overall size 15¾ x 41¼ in., (40 x 104.8 cm.), photo-etching, four plates p. on one sheet on wove (BP 187, DM 456, FR 1557, Y 36,083).
$180* "Gradition Suite: Gleaners A" and "Matter C", 1971: Two, s., d., first #5/15, second #9/15, full margins, apparently good cond., (10-15-92, Sotheby-London, #99, illus.), 6⅞ x 6⅞ in., (17.5 x 17.5 cm.), etching on wove (BP 110, DM 268, FR 909, Y 21,596).
BI The March Of 6th Avenue, 1987, s., d., i. A.P., artist's proof, pub. Marlborough Graphics, full margins, good cond., est. BP 4/600, (12-03-92, Sotheby-London, #750), 41¾ x 29 in., (106 x 73.7 cm.), lithograph in colors on wove.
$180* "Object" and "Shadow", 1968: A Pair, each s., d., #32/40, #9/10, margins, creasing, (10-15-92, Sotheby-London, #102, illus.), each sheet approx. 31 x 22¾ in., (78.7 x 57.8 cm.), screenprint in colors on white wove (BP 110, DM 268, FR 909, Y 21,596).
$90* "Weeny Rocker" and "Rocking Down The Line", 1973: Two, s., d., t., first #58/60, second i. A/P, full margins, good cond., (10-15-92, Sotheby-London, #100, illus.), each approx. 4¾ x 3¼ in., (12.1 x 8.3 cm.), etching on wove (BP 55, DM 134, FR 454, Y 10,798).
$90* "Weeny Rocker" and "Rocking Down The Line", 1973: Two, s., d., t., first #59/60, second i. A/P, full margins, good cond., (10-15-92, Sotheby-London, #101, illus.), each approx. 4¾ x 3¼ in., (12.1 x 8.3 cm.), etching on wove (BP 55, DM 134, FR 454, Y 10,798).

JACKSON, Alexander Young   Canadian b. 1882
$390* Georgian Bay, (05-18-93, Joyner, #284), 6¾ x 6½ in., (17.1 x 16.5 cm.), print (BP 254, DM 633, FR 2137, Y 43,464, C$ 495).
$194* Habitant Village (Coutt's No. 845), inits. in plate, t., pub.'s stamp support, pub. William E. Coutts Co., "Painters of Canada" series, 1931, prov., lit., (06-07-93, Ritchie, #54), 4¾ x 5¹¹⁄₁₆ in., (12.1 x 14.5 cm.), color serigraph (BP 128, DM 315, FR 1060, Y 20,811, C$ 248).
$151* Over The Hills (Coutt's no. 801), inits. in plate, t., pub.'s stamp support, pub. William E. Coutts Co., "Painters of Canada" series, 1931, prov., lit., (06-07-93, Ritchie, #55), 4¾ x 5¹¹⁄₁₆ in., (12 x 14.5 cm.), color serigraph (BP 99, DM 245, FR 825, Y 16,198, C$ 193).

JACKSON, Robert
$3520* The Shooting Of Lee Harvey Oswald, 1963, notations, (10-14-92, Swann, #320, illus.), 8 x 10 in., (20.3 x 25.4 cm.), photograph, silver print (BP 2066, DM 5151, FR 17,469, Y 426,563).

JACKSON, W.H.   American 1843-1942
$2179* "The Royal Gorge Grand Canyon Of The Arkansas", "Currecanti Needle, Black Canon Of The Ginnison", "Castle Gate D. & R.G.W.Ry", "The Grand Canon Of The Arkansas", "Cimarron Canon D. & R.G.Ry" and "Provo Falls Utah": Seven, 1870s, large format, credit in neg., mounted on folio card, eachapprox. 500 x 400mm, (05-07-93, Sotheby-London, #14), photograph, albumen print (BP 1380, DM 3445, FR 11,609, Y 239,925).

JACKSON, W.H. (attrib.)   American 1843-1942
$660* Grand Canon Of Arkansas River, Canon City, Colorado, With A Train Seen In The Distance, 1870's, (10-14-92, Swann, #200, illus.), 14 x 10½ in., (35.6 x 26.7 cm.),

photograph, albumen print (BP 387, DM 966, FR 3275, Y 79,981).

JACKSON, William Henry American 1843-1942

$165* *"Looking Down Teton Canyon",* (10-24-92, Dunning, #1457A, illus.), image 6 x 8 in., (15.2 x 20.3 cm.), albumen print (BP 105, DM 254, FR 863, Y 20,164).

$1380* *Rapids Of The Yellowstone Above The Falls,* 1880s, credit, t., num. 1120 in neg., re-mounted, (04-08-93, Christie-NY, #7, illus.), 16 x 19½ in., (40.6 x 49.5 cm.), photograph, mammoth albumen print (BP 905, DM 2217, FR 7504, Y 156,605).

$935* *"The Royal Gorge, Grand Canyon Of The Arkansas", 1880's,* attrib., t., neg. num., (11-16-92, Butterfield, #6024, illus.), 21⁹⁄₁₆ x 17¹⁄₁₆ in., (547.1 x 432.6 mm.), photograph, mammoth-plate albumen print (BP 616, DM 1491, FR 5021, Y 116,279).

$2200* *Selected Western Views (Era, fig. 185 and pls. 112, 116, 118, and 119; Newhall & Edkins, variants of pp. 63 and 75): Forty-Nine,* t. and/or num. in neg., i. in unidentified hand verso, 1870's, AlonzoBell Coll., (10-15-92, Sotheby-NY, #43, illus.), largest 10 x 13 in., (25.4 x 33 cm.), photograph, albumen prints (BP 1346, DM 3275, FR 11,106, Y 263,947).

$770* *View Of Vesta Pass, With The Denver & Rio Grande, "Kokomo" Locomotive, c. 1870,* photog. credit, t., num. in neg., (04-07-93, Swann, #226), 16 x 21 in., photograph, albumen print (BP 509, DM 1245, FR 4215, Y 87,480).

$11,000* *"Yellowstone Scenery, 1871", 1871: Ninety-Nine,* album, photog. credit, t., ex-coll. Col. Bernard John Dowling Irwin, (04-07-93, Swann, #225, illus.), each approx. 7 x 7¾ in., photograph, albumen print (BP 7269, DM 17,791, FR 60,208, Y 1,249,716).

$3300* *'Kokomo' On The Denver And Rio Grande,* mounted, photog.'s Denver credit, 1880's, (10-15-92, Sotheby-NY, #44, illus.), 17¼ x 21¼ in., (43.8 x 54 cm.), photograph, albumen print (BP 2019, DM 4912, FR 16,658, Y 395,921).

BI *'The Royal Gorge-Grand Canon Of The Arkansas',* photog.'s Denver credit, t., num. 1009 in neg., 1880's, mounted, est.$2/3,000, (10-15-92, Sotheby-NY, #43A, illus.), 21 x 16½ in., (53.3 x 41.9 cm.), photograph, albumen print.

JACOBI, Lotte b. Germany, d.U.S. 1896-1990

$1430* *Albert Einstein, c. 1938,* s. by photog. on image, p. 1970's, (10-15-92, Sotheby-NY, #400, illus.), 13¼ x 9⅞ in., (33.7 x 25.1 cm.), photograph, gelatin silver print (BP 875, DM 2129, FR 7219, Y 171,566).

$607* *Anna May Wong, 1931,* s., t., (11-12-92, Lempertz, #105, illus.), 9⅛ x 7⁷⁄₁₆ in., (23.1 x 17.9 cm.), photograph, gelatin silver print (BP 388, DM 954, FR 3251, Y 75,096).

BI *"German Square" and "Paul Strand": Two,* 1934, p.l., s., 2nd on image, est. $1,2/1,500, (05-23-93, Butterfield, #3470, illus.), one 4¾ x 7 in., other 10 x 8 in., photograph, gelatin silver print.

BI *Hanya Holm And Concert Group, 1950-55,* s. w/stylus recto, t. in ink, credit stamp, lit., est. $1500/2000, (10-13-92, Christie-NY, #463, illus.), 6¾ x 9¾ in., (17.1 x 24.8 cm.), photograph, gelatin silver print.

$455* *Herrenportrat, c. 1930,* s., (11-12-92, Lempertz, #104, illus.), 6¹¹⁄₁₆ x 6¹³⁄₁₆ in., (17 x 17.3 cm.), photograph, gelatin silver print (BP 291, DM 715, FR 2437, Y 56,291).

$2200* *Pauline Koner, Dancer, 1940,* s. by photog. in ink on image, credit stamp, (10-15-92, Sotheby-NY, #398, illus.), 9½ x 7⅝ in., (24.1 x 19.4 cm.), photograph, gelatin silver print (BP 1346, DM 3275, FR 11,106, Y 263,947).

$935* *Photogenic,* photog.'s sig., 1940s, (04-07-93, Swann, #491, illus.), 8 x 10 in., photograph, silver print (BP 618, DM 1512, FR 5118, Y 106,226).

$247* *Photogenic "Figure", 1977,* sig., i., (10-14-92, Swann, #482), 3¼ x 4 in., (8.3 x 10.2 cm.), photograph, silver print (BP 145, DM 361, FR 1226, Y 29,932).

BI *"Photogenic",* 1946, p.l., s. on image, est. $1/1,500, (05-23-93, Butterfield, #3471, illus.), 8⅜ x 6½ in., photograph, gelatin silver print.

$1380* *Photogenic, 1945-56,* s., lit., (04-08-93, Christie-NY, #301, illus.), 9⅞ x 7¾ in., (25.1 x 19.7 cm.), photograph, toned gelatin silver print (BP 905, DM 2217, FR 7504, Y 156,605).

$1210* *Photogenic, 1946-55,* s., t., annot., (10-13-92, Christie-NY, #462, illus.), 9½ x 5¾ in., (24.1 x 14.6 cm.), photograph, gelatin silver print (BP 705, DM 1773, FR 6023, Y 146,720).

$1840* *Self Portrait,* (1930s), c. 1950, s. recto, (04-08-93, Christie-NY, #302, illus.), 4½ x 6⅝ in., (11.4 x 16.8 cm.), photograph, gelatin silver print (BP 1207, DM 2956, FR 10,005, Y 208,806).

$1150* *Thomas Mann With His Wife, Katja, Princeton, N.J.,* c. 1936, p. 1960s, s. recto, lit., (04-08-93, Christie-NY, #303, illus.), 9¾ x 7½ in., (24.8 x 19.1 cm.), photograph, gelatin silver print (BP 754, DM 1847, FR 6253, Y 130,504).

JACOBSEN, Egill Danish b. 1910

$586* *Gron Maske,* s. 83, 53/125, (09-29-92, B. Rasmussen, #326), lithograph in colors (BP 329, DM 828, FR 2824, Y 69,953, DK 3220).

$147* *Gron Maske,* s. E.J., (03-24-93, Kunsthallen, #149), color lithograph (BP 100, DM 240, FR 817, Y 17,272, DK 920).

$211* *Gul Maske,* s. E.J., (09-30-92, Kunsthallen, #135), color lithograph (BP 119, DM 299, FR 1012, Y 25,321, DK 1150).

$92* *Gule Masker, 1969,* s. Egill Jacobsen 69, (03-24-93, Kunsthallen, #148), color lithograph (BP 62, DM 150, FR 511, Y 10,810, DK 575).

$202* *Kompositioner: Two,* s., (03-24-93, Kunsthallen, #151), color lithograph and lithograph (BP 137, DM 330, FR 1123, Y 23,734, DK 1265).

$230* *Maske,* s. 83, 121/150, (09-29-92, B. Rasmussen, #329), lithograph in colors (BP 129, DM 325, FR 1108, Y 27,456, DK 1265).

$119* *Maske,* s. E.J., (03-24-93, Kunsthallen, #150), color lithograph (BP 81, DM 194, FR 661, Y 13,982, DK 748).

$147* *Maske,* (09-30-92, Kunsthallen, #134), color lithograph (BP 83, DM 208, FR 705, Y 17,641, DK 805).

$73* *Maske, 1960,* s. E.J.60, (03-24-93, Kunsthallen, #146), color lithograph (BP 49, DM 119, FR 406, Y 8577, DK 460).

$184* *Maskekompositioner: Two,* s., (03-24-93, Kunsthallen, #147), color lithograph (BP 125, DM 301, FR 1023, Y 21,619, DK 1150).

$565* *Masker,* all s. e.j. Three, (09-29-92, B. Rasmussen, #328), lithograph in colors (BP 318, DM 798, FR 2723, Y 67,447, DK 3105).

$190* *Rod Maske, 1960,* s. E.J.60, (09-30-92, Kunsthallen, #137), color lithograph (BP 107, DM 269, FR 911, Y 22,801, DK 1035).

$349* *Rod Maske, 1972,* s. E.J.72, prov. 10/12, (03-24-93, Kunsthallen, #145), color lithograph (BP 236, DM 570, FR 1940, Y 41,006, DK 2185).

$469* *Rod Maske, 1972,* s. Egill Jacobsen 72, 37/150, (12-02-92, Kunsthallen, #252), lithograph in colors (BP 303, DM 738, FR 2517, Y 58,355, DK 2875).

$586* *Untitled: Three,* all s. e.j., (09-29-92, B. Rasmussen, #327), lithograph in colors (BP 329, DM 828, FR 2824, Y 69,953, DK 3220).

JACOBSEN, Robert Danish b. 1912

$750* *Composition,* s. Rob. Jacobsen, 15/25, (12-02-92, Kunsthallen, #254), etching in colors (BP 484, DM 1179, FR 4026, Y 93,318, DK 4600).

$126* *Composition,* s. Rob. Jacobsen, 10/60, (09-30-92, Kunsthallen, #140), color etching (BP 71, DM 179, FR 604, Y 15,121, DK 690).

$337* *Composition,* s. Rob. Jacobsen, E.A., (12-02-92, Kunsthallen, #255), lithograph in colors (BP 217, DM 530, FR 1809, Y 41,931, DK 2070).

$316* *Composition,* s. Rob. Jacobsen 1976, 87/90, (09-30-92, Kunsthallen, #141), color lithograph (BP 178, DM 448, FR 1516, Y 37,922, DK 1725).

$147* *Composition,* s. Rob. Jacobsen, (09-30-92, Kunsthallen, #142), color serigraph (BP 83, DM 208, FR 705, Y 17,641, DK 805).

$562* *Fem Kompositioner Fra Egtved-Mappen,* portfolio, s. Rob. Jacobsen, V/XX, (12-02-92, Kunsthallen, #253), etching (BP 363, DM 884, FR 3017, Y 69,927, DK 3450).

$251* *Komposition,* s., (09-29-92, B. Rasmussen, #330), etching and aquatint (BP 141, DM 355, FR 1210, Y 29,963, DK 1380).

$300* *Komposition,* s. Rob. Jacobsen, 57/80, (12-02-92, Kunsthallen, #259), etching in colors (BP 194, DM 472, FR 1610, Y 37,327, DK 1840).

$156* *Komposition,* s. Rob. Jacobsen, 13/100, (03-24-93, Kunsthallen, #152), color lithograph (BP 106, DM 255, FR 867, Y 18,329, DK 978).

BI *Komposition,* s. Rob. Jacobsen, 28/260, est. 1,500, (03-24-93, Kunsthallen, #153), color lithograph.

$184* *Komposition,* s. Rob. Jacobsen, 3/4, (03-24-93, Kunsthallen, #154), color lithograph (BP 125, DM 301, FR 1023, Y 21,619, DK 1150).

$202* *Komposition,* s. Rob. Jacobsen, (03-24-93, Kunsthallen, #155), color lithograph (BP 137, DM 330, FR 1123, Y 23,734, DK 1265).

$202* *Komposition,* s. Rob. Jacobsen, prov., (03-24-93, Kunsthallen, #156), color lithograph (BP 137, DM 330, FR 1123, Y 23,734, DK 1265).

BI *Komposition,* s. Rob. Jacobsen, 25/25, est. DK 1,500, (03-24-93, Kunsthallen, #157), lithograph.

$202* *Komposition,* s. Rob. Jacobsen 1963, 23/60, (03-24-93, Kunsthallen, #159), color lithograph (BP 137, DM 330, FR 1123, Y 23,734, DK 1265).

BI *Komposition, 1974,* s. Rob. Jacobsen, 35/150, est. DK 1,800, (09-30-92, Kunsthallen, #138), color etching.

$837* *Untitled,* s., 64/80, (09-29-92, B. Rasmussen, #331), etching in colors (BP 470, DM 1182, FR 4034, Y 99,916, DK 4600).

$208* *Untitled,* s., #40/40, full margins, good cond., (12-09-92, Sotheby-Amstrdm, #593), 18⅝ x 27³⁄₁₆ in., (473 x 690 mm.), color woodcut on Arches (BP 133, DM 326, FR 1114, Y 25,790, G 368).

BI *Untitled, 1962,* s., t. indistinctly, d., i. Provedryk, margins, good cond., handlingcreases, (05-27-93, Sotheby-Amstrdm, #634), sheet 17¹¹⁄₁₆ x 23⅞ in., (450 x 606 mm.), color lithograph on Japan.

JACONSEN, Robert

$165* *Ud Af Intet Kommer Du Blodt Gaende, 1979,* s. Rob. Jaconsen & Jorgen Gustava Brandt, portfolio, (03-24-93, Kunsthallen, #158), (BP 112, DM 269, FR 917, Y 19,387, DK 1035).

JACOULET, Paul b. Japan, French 1902-1960

$660* *Apres La Danse "Celebes",* (12-17-92, Mystic, #40A), 15½ x 12 in., (39.4 x 30.5 cm.), color woodblock (BP 419, DM 1030, FR 3520, Y 81,111).

$990* *Apres La Danse-Celebes, c. 1940,* image s., stamped w/ butterfly chop, seal, full margins, registrationholes, (12-08-92, Swann, #149, illus.), 15½ x 11⅞ in., (39.4 x 30.2 cm.), color woodcut on JP Japan Hosho type watermarked paper (BP 620, DM 1541, FR 5255, Y 122,707).

BI *Apres Le Pluie, Tarang, Yap [M48],* s., num. in Japanese verso, Ed. 150, est. $3/500, (12-10-92, Sloan, #3041), 15⅞ x 11⅞ in., (40.3 x 30.2 cm.), color woodcut.

BI *Apres Le Pluie, Tarang, Yap [M48],* s., num. verso in Japanese, est. $250/350, (02-04-93, Sloan, #2381), 15⅞ x 11⅞ in., (40.3 x 30.2 cm.), color woodcut.

BI *Une Averse A Metalanim, Ponape, Est Carolines (Miles 29),* pub. Oct. 1, 1935, s., bearing seal, stamp #205/350, 2nd printing, cut by Maeda, p. Honda and Ogawa, est. $2/2,500, (10-18-92, Hindman, #472, illus.), 15½ x 11¾ in., (39.4 x 29.8 cm.), color woodcut on paper, watermark.

BI *La Balance "Chinoise",* s., est. $6/800, (12-17-92, Mystic, #40C), 15½ x 12 in., (39.4 x 30.5 cm.), color woodblock.

$165* *Le Balance, Chinois [M54],* s., #197/250 verso, (12-10-92, Sloan, #3040), 15⅞ x 11⅞ in., (40.3 x 30.2 cm.), color woodcut (BP 106, DM 261, FR 891, Y 20,411).

$440* *"Le Bonze Errant Corez" and "Decembre, Japon": Two,* Christmas cards in orig. folders, (12-12-92, Wolf, #17, illus.), each 3¾ x 5¾ in., (9.5 x 14.6 cm.), color woodblock (BP 282, DM 693, FR 2376, Y 54,449).

$110* *"Chagrin D'Amour: Kusai",* Christmas card, orig. folder, good cond., (11-20-92, Skinner, #82), (BP 72, DM 175, FR 591, Y 13,680).

$764* *Le Chant Des Vagues,* dai oban, tate-e, s., w/seal, (12-01-92, Karl/Faber, #778), color woodblock (BP 505, DM 1218, FR 4150, Y 95,120).

$605* *"Le Chant Des Vagues. Ponape. Est. Carolinas", 1936,* seal, carver's seal Maeda, printer's seal Uchikawa, #268/350, (06-24-93, Boos, #620, illus.), image 15½ x 11¹³⁄₁₆ in., (393 x 300 mm.), sh 18¹¹⁄₁₆ x 14⅜ in., (393 x 300 mm.), color woodblock print (BP 412, DM 1033, FR 3479, Y 65,990).

BI *La Chenille Verte,* dai oban, tate-e, s., w/seal, d., est. DM 700, (12-01-92, Karl/Faber, #777), color woodblock.

BI *Chinese Mask Seller (C-67/M-72),* s., Butterfly seal, #19/350, very good cond., toning, tape, est. $5/700, (12-05-92, Eldred, #638), woodblock.

$550* *"Coucher De Soleil A Menado. Celebes", 1938,* seal, carver's seal Maeda, printer's seal Uchikawa, s., (06-24-93, Boos, #618, illus.), image, sight 15⅜ x 11⅝ in., (390 x 295 mm.), color woodblock print (BP 374, DM 939, FR 3163, Y 59,991).

$1115* *Les Deux Adversaires, Coree, "Gauche" and "Droite" (Miles 111 and 112), 1950: Two,* each s., stamp, p. Honda, margins, good cond., discoloration, defects, (06-30-93, Sotheby-London, #469, illus.), each sh c. 18⅝ x 13¾ in., (473 x 349 mm.), color woodcut on Japan (BP 747, DM 1902, FR 6415, Y 119,469).

BI *Ebisu, Dieu Du Bonheur Personnifie Par Une Courtisane Du Shimabara, Kyoto, Japan (Miles 122), 1952,* bears coin seal, carved by Maeda, est. $8/1,200, (12-13-92, Hindman, #288, illus.), 15½ x 11¾ in., color woodcut on Japan watermark.

BI *Ebisu, Dieu Du Bonheur Personnifie Par Une Courtisane Du Shimabara, Kyoto, Japan (Miles 122), 1952,* s., bears coin seal, carved by Maeda, (12-13-92, Hindman, #299, illus.), 15½ x 11¾ in., color woodcut on Japan watermark.

BI *"Fleurs Du Soir/Truck-Toloas",* s. Paul Jacoulet, seal, engraver Maeda Kentaro, printer Fujii Shunosuke; #314/350 verso, soiled, margins toned, tate-e, est. $800/1,200, (11-20-92, Skinner, #81, illus.), dai oban tate-e.

$550* *"Une Histoire Tres Drole Mongole",* s., Ivy Seal, (11-28-92, Young, #242, illus.), 15 x 12 in., (38.1 x 30.5 cm.), colored woodcut (BP 363, DM 876, FR 2975, Y 68,451).

$440* *"Hokkan Zan, Coree" and "Les Jades: Mandchoukuo": Two,* Christmas cards in orig. folders, (12-12-92, Wolf, #18), 3¾ x 5¾ in., (9.5 x 14.6 cm.), color woodblock (BP 282, DM 693, FR 2376, Y 54,449).

BI *Hokkan-Zan, Seoul, Coree (Miles 45), 1937,* s., bears Tea Jar seal, stamp, #94/150, carved by Maeda, est. $800/1,200, (12-13-92, Hindman, #279), 15½ x 11⅞ in., color woodcut on Japan watermark.

BI *Homme De Menado Et Mangoustans Celebes,* s., est. $6/800, (12-17-92, Mystic, #40D), 15½ x 12 in., (39.4 x 30.5 cm.), color woodblock.

$275* *"Un Homme De Yap. Ouest Carolines", 1936,* seal, carver's seal Maeda, printer's seal Honda, s., (06-24-93, Boos, #617, illus.), image 15½ x 11¹³⁄₁₆ in., (393 x 300 mm.), color woodblock print (BP 187, DM 470, FR 1581, Y 29,996).

$358* *"Un Homme De Yap/Ouest Carolines",* s. Paul Jacoulet, seal, engraver Maeda Kentaro, printer Ogawa Fusakichi, #264/350, toned, tate-e, (11-20-92, Skinner, #79), dai oban tate-e (BP 236, DM 571, FR 1923, Y 44,522).

$440* *Les Jades "Chinoise",* s., (12-17-92, Mystic, #40B, illus.), 15½ x 12 in., (39.4 x 30.5 cm.), color woodblock (BP 279, DM 687, FR 2347, Y 54,074).

$83* *"Les Jades: Mandchoukuo",* Christmas card, orig. folder, toned, (11-20-92, Skinner, #83), (BP 55, DM 132, FR 446, Y 10,322).

$3190* *"Jeune Fille De Polowat. Est Carolines", 1948,* carver's seal Maeda, printer's seal Fujii, s., #137/350, (06-24-93, Boos, #615, illus.), image 15½ x 11¹³⁄₁₆ in., (393 x 300 mm.), sh 18½ x 14 in., (393 x 300 mm.), color woodblock print (BP 2172, DM 5448, FR 18,344, Y 347,949).

$1029* *L'Etoile De Cobi. Mongole (M. 114), 1950,* s., stamp, p. Honda, margins, good cond., discoloration, defects, (06-

30-93, Sotheby-London, #470, illus.), sh 18⅝ x 14 in., (473 x 356 mm.), color woodcut on Japan (BP 690, DM 1755, FR 5921, Y 110,254).

BI *La Lettre Du Fils. Seoul, Coree (M49), 1938,* (04-02-93, Sloan, #1889), sight 11½ x 15 in., (292 x 381 mm.), color woodcut.

$358* *"La Lettre Du Fils/Seoul, Coree",* s. Paul Jacoulet, seal, engraver Maeda Kentaro, printer's seal; #172/350 verso, yoko-e, (11-20-92, Skinner, #80A), dai oban yoko-e (BP 236, DM 571, FR 1923, Y 44,522).

$55* *M. Keen Et M. Lee,* Dai oban tate-e, s., margins, mat burn, darkening, backboard burn, toning, (12-12-92, Weschler, #130), 15½ x 12 in., (39.4 x 30.5 cm.), color lithograph (BP 35, DM 87, FR 297, Y 6806).

$250* *"Le Mandarin Aux Lunettes Mandchouko" (Miles 106), 1950,* s., seals of carver Kentaro Maeda and printer Matashiro Uchikawa, #134/350, light struck, toning, tape hinges verso, (05-15-93, Cleveland, #393), 15½ x 12 in., (39.4 x 30.5 cm.), woodblock (BP 163, DM 402, FR 1351, Y 27,713).

BI *Le Mandarin Aux Lunettes-Mandchoukuo,* s., est. $5/700, (12-17-92, Mystic, #40DD), 15½ x 12 in., (39.4 x 30.5 cm.), color woodblock.

$110* *The Mandarin With Glasses (C-29/M-106),* s., Duck seal, #220/250, fair cond., faded, toned, (12-05-92, Eldred, #636), woodblock (BP 69, DM 171, FR 584, Y 13,629).

BI *"Mon Ami Francesco Ogarto, Marianes, Spaipan", 1935,* second printing, fan seal, carver's seal Yamagishi, printer seal, s., est. $800/1,200, (06-24-93, Boos, #611, illus.), image 15⅜ x 18½ in., (390 x 470 mm.), sh 18½ x 14½ in., (390 x 470 mm.), color woodblock print.

$248* *"Le Nid", "Les Jades", "Snowy Night" and "Sorrow Of Love": Set Of Four Christmas Cards,* toned, (12-05-92, Eldred, #615), (BP 155, DM 387, FR 1318, Y 30,727).

$165* *"Le Nid: Coree",* Christmas card, orig. folder, toning, (11-20-92, Skinner, #85), (BP 109, DM 263, FR 886, Y 20,520).

BI *"Le Nid: Coree": Christmas Card,* excell. cond, toning, est. $75/100, (12-05-92, Eldred, #616), .

$330* *"Le Nid: Coree"; "Le Bossu": Two,* (09-25-92, Wolf, #15), each 5¾ x 3¾ in., (14.6 x 9.5 cm.), colored woodblocks (BP 193, DM 489, FR 1654, Y 39,831).

$165* *"Nuit De Neige",* Christmas card, orig. folder, toning, (11-20-92, Skinner, #84), (BP 109, DM 263, FR 886, Y 20,520).

BI *"Nuit De Neige, Coree [M57]" and "Le Nid, Coree [M80]": Two,* Christmas cards, est. $150/200, (02-04-93, Sloan, #380), each 6 x 4 in., (15.2 x 10.2 cm.), color woodcut.

BI *"Nuit De Neige, Coree" and "Le Nid, Coree" [M57] [M80]: Two,* Christmas cards, est. $2/300, (12-10-92, Sloan, #3039), each 6 x 4 in., (15.2 x 10.2 cm.), color woodcut.

$1000* *Le Pacifique Mysterieux, Mers Du Sud,* s., blindstamp, full margins, time-staining, (11-30-92, Phillips-London, #438), border 15⅜ x 11¾ in., (391 x 298 mm.), woodcut in colors on japan (BP 660, DM 1593, FR 5408, Y 124,456).

$3960* *"Le Pacifique Mysterieux. Mers Du Sud", 1951,* seal, carver's seal Maeda, printer's seal Uchikawa, s., #18/350, (06-24-93, Boos, #616, illus.), image 15½ x 11¹³⁄₁₆ in., (393 x 300 mm.), sh 18½ x 13¹⁵⁄₁₆ in., (393 x 300 mm.), color woodblock print (BP 2696, DM 6763, FR 22,772, Y 431,937).

$303* *Les Papillions Tropiques (M 61),* s., (09-17-92, Sloan, #1647), 15½ x 11⅞ in., (39.4 x 30.2 cm.), woodblock (BP 170, DM 450, FR 1540, Y 37,724).

$1320* *"Les Papillons. Tropiques", 1939,* seal, carver's seal Maeda, printer's seal Fujii, s., #125/250, (06-24-93, Boos, #614, illus.), image 15½ x 11¹³⁄₁₆ in., (394 x 300 mm.), sh 18¹¹⁄₁₆ x 14⅜ in., (394 x 300 mm.), color woodblock print (BP 899, DM 2254, FR 7591, Y 143,979).

BI *Les Paradisiers, Birds of Paradise (C-41/M-48),* s., Tea Jar seal, seals of carver, Kentaro Maeda, p. Tetsunosuke Honda, pub. 25 December 1975, #212/350, good cond., crease, toning, previous tape,est. $1/1,500, (12-05-92, Eldred, #620, illus.), woodblock.

$425* *"Les Perles, Manchouko" (Miles 113), 1950,* s., peach seal, seals of carver Kentaro Maeda and p. Fusakichi Ogawa, #308/350, ded., light struck, old tape, (05-15-93, Cleveland, #394), 15½ x 11⅞ in., (39.4 x 30.2 cm.), woodblock (BP 276, DM 684, FR 2297, Y 47,112).

BI *Les Perles, The Pearls (C-101/M-113),* s., Peach seal, seals of carver, Kentaro Maeda, p. Matashiro Uchikawa, pub. 28 December 1950, #242/350, very good cond., toning, est. $2,5/3,500, (12-05-92, Eldred, #614, illus.), woodblock.

$468* *"Les Perls, Mandchoukuo", c. 1950,* s.; artist's peach seal verso, margins folded and tones, (10-10-92, Goldberg, #523, illus.), 15¼ x 11¾ in., (38.7 x 29.8 cm.), color woodcut (BP 278, DM 695, FR 2334, Y 56,976).

$3630* *"Premier Amour. Yap, Ouest Carolinas", 1937,* seal, carver's seal Maeda, printer's seal Fujii, s., #79/350, (06-24-93, Boos, #613, illus.), image 11⅞ x 15⅜ in., (302 x 390 mm.), sh 14⅜ x 18⅜ in., (302 x 390 mm.), color woodblock print (BP 2471, DM 6200, FR 20,874, Y 395,942).

$220* *Retour De La Jungle (C-79/M-90),* ded. General Douglas MacArthur, s., seal, #106/250, image within plate line darker due to smoke or dirt, margins, (12-05-92, Eldred, #640), woodblock (BP 138, DM 343, FR 1169, Y 27,258).

$660* *"Le Reveil. Saipan, Marianes", 1937,* seal, carver's seal Maeda, printer's seal Honda, s., (06-24-93, Boos, #619, illus.), image, sight 15⅜ x 11⅝ in., (390 x 295 mm.), color woodblock print (BP 449, DM 1127, FR 3795, Y 71,990).

BI *Le Sculpteur De Tokobuei, The Tokobuei Sculptor (C-140/M-136),* s., seals of the carver, Kentaro Maedo, p. Yoshizo Onotera, pub. May1954, seal, very good/excell. cond., evidence of tape, est. $1,5/2,000, (12-05-92, Eldred, #613, illus.), woodblock.

$220* *Snowy Night (C-52/M-57),* s., Boat seal, seals of p. and carver, #186/250, fair cond., toning,mat burn, (12-05-92, Eldred, #637), woodblock (BP 138, DM 343, FR 1169, Y 27,258).

$440* *"Souvenir D'Autrefois, Japon" and "Le Bossu Otaru, Hokkaido": Two,* Christmas cards in orig. folders, (12-12-92, Wolf, #16), 3¾ x 5¾ in., (9.5 x 14.6 cm.), color woodblock (BP 282, DM 693, FR 2376, Y 54,449).

$165* *Le Tabouret De Porcelaine, Mandchoukuo [M-38],* s., seal, #190/350 verso, (12-10-92, Sloan, #3042), 15⅞ x 11⅞ in., (40.3 x 30.2 cm.), woodblock (BP 106, DM 261, FR 891, Y 20,411).

BI *Tempest Of The Heart, Seoul, Korea (C-106/M-96),* s., seal, #159/250, fair cond., faded, toned, tape residue, est. $7/900, (12-05-92, Eldred, #635, illus.), woodblock.

$495* *"Vielle Aino, Chikabumi. Hokkaido. Japan", Mrs. Chikabumi, An Old Aino Woman, Hokkaido, Japan),* s. Paul Jacoulet, seal, watermark, (04-17-93, Wolf, #605), image 15½ x 12 in., (39.4 x 30.5 cm.), color woodblock (BP 325, DM 800, FR 2702, Y 55,662).

$220* *"Vielle Marchande De Carpes/Ibaraki...Japon",* s. Paul Jacoulet, seal, engraver Maeda Kentaro, printer Honda Tetsunosuke; #168/350 verso, toned, faded, tate-e, (11-20-92, Skinner, #80), dai oban tate-e (BP 145, DM 351, FR 1182, Y 27,360).

$110* *Waiting In Menado (C-77/M-86),* s., Sparrow seal, #182/250, poor to fair cond., toning, (12-05-92, Eldred, #639), woodblock (BP 69, DM 171, FR 584, Y 13,629).

$1430* *"Yagourah Et Mio. Yap, Ouest Carolines", 1938,* seal, carver's seal Maeda, printer's seal, s., (06-24-93, Boos, #612, illus.), image 15½ x 11¹³⁄₁₆ in., (393 x 300 mm.), sh 18½ x 14⅛ in., (393 x 300 mm.), color woodblock print (BP 973, DM 2442, FR 8223, Y 155,977).

JACQUE, Charles French 1813-1894

$90* *"Paysage Maison De Paysan" (Guiffrey 80) and "Premiere Lecon D'Equitation" (Guiffrey 178): Two,* proof before letters (Paysage), foxing, L. Valentin, Lugt 2498 and F. Mason, Lugt 1032 Colls., (05-15-93, Cleveland, #395), one 5⅞ x 8⅞ in., (14.9 x 22.5 cm.), other 6¼ x 7⅞ in., (14.9 x 22.5 cm.), etching (BP 59, DM 145, FR 486, Y 9977).

JACQUEMIN, A.

$262* *Soir De Fevrier (Inv. F.F. 661), 1955,* t., #2/62, s., large margins, (02-03-93, Ader Tajan, #166), 8⅛ x 15³⁄₁₆ in., (20.7 x 38.6 cm.), etching (BP 183, DM 431, FR 1463, Y 32,591).

JACQUES

$261* *Ligue Nationale Contre L'Alcoolisme: A Colombes,* good cond., (02-12-93, Cheval/Robert, #101), 33⁷⁄₁₆ x 23⅝ in., (85 x 60 cm.), poster (BP 184, DM 433, FR 1465, Y 31,476).

$181* *Ligue Nationale Contre L'Alcoolisme: A Quand La Greve?,* good cond., (02-12-93, Cheval/Robert, #102), 33⁷⁄₁₆ x 23⅝ in., (85 x 60 cm.), poster (BP 127, DM 300, FR 1016, Y 21,828).

JACQUES, Bertha

$990* *"Caleina-Venice", "Dogana-Venice", "Rio S. Cristoforo-Venice", and "Venice Waterway": Four,* each s., Dogana t., margins, good cond., tape, surface soiling, pencil notations, prop. Print Corner, Coll. of Elizabeth and Charles Whitmore, (02-24-93, Butterfield, #2838), from 5 x 3⁷⁄₁₆ in., (127 x 87 mm.), to 6¼ x 3⁷⁄₁₆ in., (127 x 87 mm.), etching on wove (BP 690, DM 1607, FR 5449, Y 116,170).

JACQUES and BROTHER, Publisher

$78* *Castle Garden 1850,* tears, (12-10-92, Bonhams-Chelsea, #81), image 15¼ x 20½ in., (38.7 x 52.1 cm.), color lithograph (BP 50, DM 123, FR 421, Y 9649).

JACQUET, Alain b. 1939

$165* *Composition, 1965,* s., d. 1965, creases, losses, (03-31-93, Briest, #E52), 29¾ x 20⅞ in., (75.5 x 53 cm.), serigraph (BP 109, DM 265, FR 902, Y 18,974).

$189* *Dejeuner Sur L'Herbe, 1964,* s., d. 64 verso, (11-16-92, Briest, #61), 25¹³⁄₁₆ x 33¹⁄₁₆ in., (5 x 5.5 cm.), quadrichrome (BP 124, DM 301, FR 1016, Y 23,587).

$126* *"Derriere Le Store",* #196/200, s., (01-28-93, Pescheteau, #162), 19¹¹⁄₁₆ x 25⁹⁄₁₆ in., (50 x 65 cm.), photolithograph and embossing on Lana (BP 83, DM 200, FR 676, Y 15,644).

BI *Marbel, c. 1970,* s., num., est. DM 650, (11-28-92, Schoppmann, #599), 35¼ x 35¼ in., (89.5 x 89.5 cm.), color serigraph on cardboard.

BI *Nature Morte, 1968,* s., #14/100, est. FF 2,5/3,000, (11-16-92, Briest, #314), 21⅝ x 29½ in., (55 x 75 cm.), serigraph.

BI *Olympia,* s., full margins, est. FF 6/7,000, (11-16-92, Briest, #315), 21¼ x 26¹⁵⁄₁₆ in., (54 x 68.5 cm.), etching in colors.

$227* *Silver Marble, The Geneva Project, 1971: Four,* originals, s., three #46/75, (03-31-93, Briest, #E171), serigraphs (BP 150, DM 365, FR 1240, Y 26,104).

JACQUIER, Marcel

BI *Femme A La Fontaine,* watermark, s., #10/50, full margins, good cond., staining, soiling, tear, handling creases, hinge remains, notations, est. $4/600, (05-19-93, Butterfield, #2062), 18 x 15⅝ in., (457 x 397 mm.), etching and aquatint in colors on laid.

JACQUOT, Pierre French b. 1929

$66* *Woman On Carousel,* s., #193/275, (06-11-93, Freemn/Fine Art, #115), 24 x 18 in., (61 x 45.7 cm.), lithograph in colors (BP 43, DM 107, FR 362, Y 7003).

JAECKEL, Willy 1888-1944

$177* *Selbstbildnis En Face (Stilijanov-Nedo 6),* s., artist's proof, (06-10-93, Hauswedell/Nolt, #427), image 7¹⁄₁₆ x 5⁵⁄₁₆ in., (17.9 x 13.5 cm.), etching on thick wove (BP 116, DM 288, FR 970, Y 18,788).

$166* *Weiblicher Akt,* s., margins, good cond., minor foxing, paper discoloration, soiling verso, upper margin glued to mount, Late Gerhard Brauer Coll., (05-27-93, Sotheby-Amstrdm, #739), 6¾ x 10⅜ in., (172 x 264 mm.), lithograph on Van Gelder laid (BP 106, DM 266, FR 898, Y 17,796, G 299).

JAHAN, Pierre French contemporary

$920* *Dolls, 1942,* s. by photog., d. in unident. hand, (c) stamp, 1942, p.l., (04-06-93, Sotheby-NY, #309, illus.), photograph (BP 608, DM 1482, FR 5019, Y 104,927).

BI *Foir Aux Puces (Paris), c. 1946,* s., t., credit & (c) stamps, est. $2,5/3,000, (10-13-92, Christie-NY, #244, illus.), 14 x 11 in., (35.6 x 27.9 cm.), photograph, gelatin silver print.

$4620* *Plongeur, 1935,* s., num. 1/20, d., annot., (10-13-92, Christie-NY, #243, illus.), 16¾ x 14¾ in., (42.5 x 37.5 cm.), photograph, gelatin silver prints (BP 2691, DM 6768, FR 22,997, Y 560,204).

BI *Pressure Gauge, 1939,* mounted, s., d. by photog. in ink, s., d., (c) stamp, est. $2/3,000, (10-15-92, Sotheby-NY, #309, illus.), 11¾ x 14 in., (29.8 x 35.6 cm.), photograph, gelatin silver print.

JAHN, Georg 1869-1941

$113* *Nacktes Junges Madchen,* i., s., d. Probedr., George Jahn 26, (03-24-93, Venator/Hansten, #4502), pl. 12³⁄₁₆ x 8¹⁵⁄₁₆ in., (31 x 22.7 cm.), mezzotint and roulette (BP 77, DM 185, FR 628, Y 13,277).

JAILLOT, Alexis Hubert French d. 1912

$154* *Royaume De Naples,* (04-02-93, Sloan, #1210), 19½ x 20½ in., (495 x 521 mm.), hand colored engraving (BP 101, DM 248, FR 841, Y 17,534).

JAMES, Clifford R.

$248* *"The New York And London Packet Ship Devonshire, 1300 Tons" and "TheNew York And London Packet Ship 'Victoria' 1000 Tons",* t., s. Clifford R. James, pub. James Connell and Sons, excell. cond., (02-13-93, Bourne, #104), image 12¾ x 19¾ in., (32.4 x 50.2 cm.), prints (BP 175, DM 411, FR 1392, Y 29,908).

JAMES, George P.

$82* *The Gower Children,* after George Romney, s., margins, foxing, (10-15-92, Bonhams-Chelsea, #60), plate 14¼ x 15 in., (36.2 x 38.1 cm.), color mezzotint (BP 50, DM 122, FR 414, Y 9838).

JANCO, Marcel Israeli b. 1895

BI *Amsterdam,* s., t., #155/200, full margins, good cond., occasional handling creases, est. Dfl. 6/800, (05-27-93, Sotheby-Amstrdm, #636), 13¹⁵⁄₁₆ x 20⅞ in., (355 x 530 mm.), silkscreen on BFK Rives.

BI *Arab Cafe,* s., t., #142/200, full margins, good cond., occasional handling creases, (05-27-93, Sotheby-Amstrdm, #635), 17⅜ x 21⁷⁄₁₆ in., (442 x 544 mm.), silkscreen on BFK Rives.

$332* *"Soldat Blesse", 1949,* s., d., t., Epreuve d'artiste, (12-01-92, Karl/Faber, #781), 23¹⁄₁₆ x 16⁵⁄₁₆ in., (58.5 x 41.5 cm.), color serigraph on BFK Rives wove (BP 219, DM 529, FR 1803, Y 41,335).

JANIN, J.

$200* *PLM. Divonne-Les-Bains "Station De Repos", 1934,* very good cond., (03-15-93, Arcole, #43), 39⁹⁄₁₆ x 24⅝ in., (100.5 x 62.5 cm.), (BP 139, DM 332, FR 1129, Y 23,691).

JANINET, Jean Francois 1752-1814

BI *Ah! Laisse-Moi Donc Voir! (Bocher 2; Inventaire 18e Siecle, XII, p. 18, no. 26), c. 1787,* 1st state of 3, pub. Janinet, margins, partly split, repaired, staining, very good cond., prov., est. BP 1,0/1,500(12-01-92, Christie-London, #251, illus.), plate 9⅝ x 7¹⁄₁₆ in., (245 x 180 mm.), etching w/engraving in colors (black, blue, brown, green, puple, redand yellow).

$4329* *"Colonade Et Jardins Du Palais Medicis" and "Restes Du Palais Du Pape Jules" (P. land B., II, p. 482, nos. 83-4; Inventaire 18e Siecle, XII, pp. 73-4, no. 172 and p. 73, no. 170), c. 1775: Two,* watermark, pub. Janinet, good cond., (12-01-92, Christie-London, #249, illus.), plate 15⁹⁄₁₆ x 19¹¹⁄₁₆ in., (396 x 500 mm.), etching w/ engraving in the lavis-manner in colors (BP 2860, DM 6900, FR 23,514, Y 538,969).

BI *"Les Comediens Comique" and "Le Rende-Vous Comique" (P. and B., II, p. 480, nos. 51-2, D. and V. 300-1; Inventaire 18e Siecle, XII, p. 9, nos. 3-4), 1774: A Pair,* after Jean-Antoine Watteau, pub. Janinet, trimmed, rubbing, staining, est. BP 3/4,000, (12-01-92, Christie-London, #248, illus.), sheet 10³⁄₁₆ x 7⅜ in., (258 x 187 mm.), etching w/engraving.

$2231* *"Les Comediens Comiques" (Portalis-Beraldi 51; Dacier 300) and "Le Rendez-Vous Comique" (P. B. 52; D. 301):*

Two, narrow, margins, paper discolored, defects, (06-30-93, Sotheby-London, #152), 10¼ x 7½ in., (260 x 191 mm.), etching w/aquatint in color (BP 1495, DM 3805, FR 12,837, Y 239,044).

$3538* *La Comparaison, 1786,* after N. Lavreince, creases, large margins, (06-16-93, Ader Tajan, #37, illus.), 14 3/16 x 11⅛ in., (36 x 28.2 cm.), tinted engraving aux outils (BP 2359, DM 5873, FR 19,710, Y 377,346).

$314* *Paysage, 1768,* after J.Houel, thin spots, staining, faults, w/out margins, (06-16-93, Ader Tajan, #36), 9 13/16 x 14¾ in., (25 x 37.5 cm.), wash manner engraving in sanguine (BP 209, DM 521, FR 1749, Y 33,490).

BI *"Reveil De Venus" and "Sommeil De Venus" (P. land B., II, p. 477, nos. 19-20), c. 1785: Two,* after Jacques Charlier, pub. Toulouze and Comp., staining, pinholes,foxing, est. BP 800/1,200, (12-01-92, Christie-London, #252, illus.), plate 5 3/16 x 5 3/16 in., (131 x 131 mm.), etching w/engraving in colors (black, blue, and red).

BI *La Toilette De Venus (P. and B., II, P. 476, no. 3; Inventaire 18e Siecle, XII, pp. 23-4, no. 39; J.-R. 1225), 1783,* watermark, pub. Chereau, trimmed, creases, foxing, surface dirt, estBP 10/15,000, (12-01-92, Christie-London, #250, illus.), sheet 16 15/16 x 12 3/16 in., (431 x 310 mm.), etching w/engraving in colors (black, blue, red and yellow) on laid paper.

$1211* *Les Trois Graces,* after Pellegrini, before t., good margins, (02-03-93, Ader Tajan, #63), 13 15/16 x 10 13/16 in., (35.5 x 27.5 cm.), tinted engraving (BP 845, DM 1994, FR 6762, Y 150,641).

JANINET, Jean Francois (attrib.) 1752-1814

$5896* *"Zephire Et Flore" and "Vertumne Et Pomone": Two,* after Coypel, first, stains, small margins, (06-16-93, Ader Tajan, #38, illus.), 10 7/16 x 13 3/16 in., (26.5 x 33.5 cm.), drawing manner engraving in color (BP 3931, DM 9788, FR 32,847, Y 628,840).

JANINET(?)

$152* *"Joseph Menier" (A Paris Chez Mondhare),* small margins, (03-22-93, Pescheteau, #20), color print (BP 102, DM 249, FR 847, Y 17,601).

JANSEM, Jean b. Armenia, French b. 1920

BI *Girl With Flowers,* s. 142/175, (09-21-92, Selkirk, #338), image 26 x 19 in., (66 x 48.3 cm.), colored lithograph.

$318* *Mere Et Enfant,* #63/100, s. Jansem, (10-20-92, Encans, #179), 15¾ x 10¼ in., (40 x 26 cm.), color lithograph (BP 178, DM 483, FR 1645, Y 39,860, C$ 389).

$165* *Mother And Child,* s., #94/200, blindstamp GG, good cond., time staining, rippling, (12-12-92, Weschler, #131), 13½ x 20¼ in., (34.3 x 51.4 cm.), color lithograph (BP 106, DM 260, FR 891, Y 20,418).

$116* *"La Muleta-1971",* #16/140, s., reddish stains, (01-28-93, Pescheteau, #163), 19 11/16 x 25 9/16 in., (50 x 65 cm.), color lithograph on Arches (BP 77, DM 184, FR 622, Y 14,403).

$1081* *Nu De Dos,* #56/120, good margins, (06-16-93, Ader Tajan, #110), 25 13/16 x 19 11/16 in., (65.5 x 50 cm.), color lithograph (BP 721, DM 1794, FR 6022, Y 115,294).

$110* *"Nude In Profile",* s. EA #1/20 Jansem, (02-27-93, Dunning, #1107), 25½ x 19¼ in., (64.8 x 48.9 cm.), print (BP 77, DM 181, FR 615, Y 12,985).

$83* *"Nude With Flowers",* s. 145/175 Jansem, (02-27-93, Dunning, #1125), 26¼ x 18¾ in., (66.7 x 47.6 cm.), lithograph (BP 58, DM 136, FR 464, Y 9798).

BI *Petite Veille Et La Porte Bleue,* s., #17/120, full margins, good cond., light-staining, glue, surfacesoiling, est. $3/500, (02-24-93, Butterfield, #2941), 7¼ x 6¾ in., (184.5 x 171.8 mm.), lithograph in colors on wove.

BI *Petite Veille Et La Porte Bleue,* s., #17/120, full margins, good cond., light/glue staining, surface soiling, est. $5/700, (10-28-92, Butterfield, #2825), 7¼ x 6¾ in., (184 x 171 mm.), color lithograph on cream wove.

BI *Seated Woman Wearing Kerchief,* s., i. E.A., est. $600/800, (09-17-92, Sloan, #2377), 25⅞ x 19 in., (65.7 x 48.3 cm.), color lithograph.

BI *Seated Woman With Kerchief,* s., i. E.A., very good cond., est. $700/1,000, (05-15-93, Cleveland, #469), 25⅛ x 19 in., (63.8 x 48.3 cm.), lithograph in colors.

$165* *"Les Semaphones", 1967,* s., num. 14/120, good cond., (10-31-92, Cleveland, #376, illus.), 14 x 20 in., (35.6 x 50.8 cm.), lithograph in colors (BP 106, DM 254, FR 861, Y 20,438).

$275* *Semi-Nude Lady Holding Flowers,* ed. #142/175, s., (02-12-93, DuMouchelle, #2119, illus.), 26¼ x 19 in., (66.7 x 48.3 cm.), color lithograph (BP 194, DM 456, FR 1543, Y 33,164).

$99* *Still Life With Bottle, Basket And Lemons,* #7/50, s., (05-14-93, DuMouchelle, #2377), 14½ x 10¼ in., (36.8 x 26 cm.), color lithograph (BP 64, DM 159, FR 535, Y 10,974).

BI *Untitled,* s., #7/10, est. $100/150, (06-11-93, Freemn/Fine Art, #116), 13½ x 7½ in., (34.3 x 19.1 cm.), etching.

JANSEN, Arno German b. 1938

$1213* *G.R. 1988,* s., t., from edit. of 5, lit., (11-12-92, Lempertz, #108, illus.), 19 15/16 x 15 13/16 in., (50.6 x 40.2 cm.), photograph, gelatin silver print (BP 776, DM 1906, FR 6497, Y 150,068).

JANSEN, Edwin 20th cent.

$521* *Kleider Machen Leute, 1990: Eight,* complete set, pub. Bebert, good cond.?, (12-09-92, Sotheby-Amstrdm, #594), each sheet 19 11/16 x 12 15/16 in., (500 x 330 mm.), silkscreen w/collage on wove (BP 332, DM 818, FR 2791, Y 64,600, G 920).

JANSEN, Franz Maria

$2090* *[8 UHR], c. 1920,* s., i., full margins, good cond., creases in image, (11-05-92, Sotheby-NY, #202, illus.), 11 x 15⅝ in., (278 x 396 mm.), woodcut on thin, soft (molle) Japan (BP 1359, DM 3305, FR 11,182, Y 256,410).

JANSONS, Ivars b. 1939

$101* *(Winter Landscape),* s. I Jansons, #50/350, (08-11-92, L. Joel, #184G), 15¾ x 22⅝ in., (40 x 57.5 cm.), color print (BP 52, DM 148, FR 502, Y 12,934, A$ 137).

$81* *(Winter Landscape),* s. I Jansons, #51/350, (08-11-92, L. Joel, #195G), 15¾ x 22⅝ in., (40 x 57.5 cm.), color print (BP 42, DM 119, FR 403, Y 10,373, A$ 110).

JANSSEN, Horst b. 1929

$707* *Ahab, 1957 (Vogel 101), 1957,* s., d., #3/10, stone s., d., t., watermark, (06-12-93, Hauswedell/Nolt, #227), 18½ x 13 3/16 in., (47 x 33.5 cm.), lithograph on paper (BP 463, DM 1151, FR 3868, Y 74,398).

$493* *Anagramm (Brockstedt R 87; Vogel 221), 1959,* s., d., num., (05-26-93, Dorling, #2737), 8 9/16 x 5 3/16 in., (21.7 x 13.1 cm.), etching on thick wove (BP 319, DM 804, FR 2707, Y 53,564).

BI *Der Angler, 1983/1984,* s.; edit. stamp verso, est. DM 150, (09-18-92, Schloss Ahlden, #1009), 8¼ x 11⅝ in., (20.9 x 29.5 cm.), etching on dark green.

$1413* *Ausstellung 25 Farbholzschnitte (Vogel 394; Meyer-Schomann I), 1957,* s., d., stone i., (06-12-93, Hauswedell/Nolt, #229), 27 3/16 x 16⅞ in., (69 x 42.8 cm.), poster, lithograph on smooth wove (BP 925, DM 2300, FR 7730, Y 148,690).

$848* *Ausstellung Kleine Radierungen (Vogel 400; Meyer-Schomann 9), 1959,* s., stone t., i., (06-12-93, Hauswedell/Nolt, #232), 22¼ x 12 3/16 in., (56.5 x 31 cm.), poster, lithograph on wove (BP 555, DM 1380, FR 4639, Y 89,235).

BI *Bar (Brockstedt 5), 1957,* s., d., i. ballpoint pen, #10/25, margins, tear, creasing, other minor defects, very good cond., est. BP 7/8,000, (05-20-93, Christie-London, #446, illus.), image 31¾ x 20¼ in., (80.6 x 51.4 cm.), sheet 33⅞ x 22⅛ in., (80.6 x 51.4 cm.), woodcut p. in colors on Japan w/wirelines.

$636* *Baume Und Kate, 1987,* s., d., #33/100, plate i., (06-12-93, Hauswedell/Nolt, #218, illus.), 23 7/16 x 19 9/16 in., (59.5 x 49.7 cm.), etching on 2 sh on natural color Japan (BP 416, DM 1035, FR 3479, Y 66,926).

$8479* *Beerdigung (Brockstedt H 32; Vogel 65), 1957,* s., d., #15/25, (06-12-93, Hauswedell/Nolt, #253, illus.), 18 11/16 x 21⅞ in., (47.5 x 55.5 cm.), color wood cut on handmade Japan (BP 5550, DM 13,800, FR 46,384, Y 892,245).

$120* *"Christoph August Vulpius", 1967,* s. Janssen, (03-24-93, Venator/Hansten, #4503), approx. 15¾ x 11⁷⁄₁₆ in., (40 x 29 cm.), etching (BP 81, DM 196, FR 667, Y 14,099).

$1413* *Cordula (Angelika Dessauer) (Vogel 15), 1952,* s., d., mono., (06-12-93, Hauswedell/Nolt, #219), 15¼ x 11⁷⁄₁₆ in., (38.8 x 29 cm.), lithograph on thin wove (BP 925, DM 2300, FR 7730, Y 148,690).

$565* *Cordula Dessauer Im Profil, 1952,* s., d., mono., (06-12-93, Hauswedell/Nolt, #221), 17³⁄₁₆ x 11 in., (43.7 x 28 cm.), lithograph on thin wove (BP 370, DM 920, FR 3091, Y 59,455).

$1413* *Dessauer Kind (Vogel 16), 1952,* s., d., mono., (06-12-93, Hauswedell/Nolt, #220), 17³⁄₁₆ x 11 in., (43.7 x 28 cm.), lithograph on thin wove (BP 925, DM 2300, FR 7730, Y 148,690).

$2261* *Don Quichotte (Brockstedt R 20; Vogel 164), 1958,* s., d., i. proof, (06-12-93, Hauswedell/Nolt, #177, illus.), 23⁷⁄₁₆ x 15⁹⁄₁₆ in., (59.5 x 39.5 cm.), etching on wove (BP 1480, DM 3680, FR 12,369, Y 237,925).

$159* *Dr. Med. Biedermeyer, 1966,* s., d., (11-28-92, Schoppmann, #602), 11 x 8¹⁄₁₆ in., (28 x 20.5 cm.), lithograph on wove (BP 105, DM 253, FR 860, Y 19,788).

$2473* *Edward (Brockstedt R 21; Vogel 162), 1958,* s., d., #2/20, (06-12-93, Hauswedell/Nolt, #178, illus.), 23¼ x 15½ in., (59 x 39.3 cm.), etching on copper print (BP 1619, DM 4025, FR 13,528, Y 260,234).

$1060* *Ein Eisbein, Bitte Fur Dr. Schmied (Ballhaus Jahnke) (Brockstedt R 308), 1965,* s., d., #22/40, plate t., (06-12-93, Hauswedell/Nolt, #201, illus.), 23⅜ x 15⅜ in., (59.3 x 39.1 cm.), etching on Lana watermark (BP 694, DM 1725, FR 5799, Y 111,544).

BI *Erotische Szene (Brockstedt R 198), 1962,* epreuve d'artiste, sheet 6 of 12 sheet complete series "L'Heure de Mylene", very rare, est. DM 1,500, (12-05-92, Bassenge, #7295), 10¹³⁄₁₆ x 7¹¹⁄₁₆ in., (27.5 x 19.5 cm.), etching on copper print paper.

$811* *Erotische Szene (Brockstedt R 201), 1962,* s., epreuve d'artiste, sheet 9 of 12-sheet complete series "L'Heure de Mylene", very rare, (12-05-92, Bassenge, #7296), 10¹³⁄₁₆ x 7¹¹⁄₁₆ in., (27.5 x 19.5 cm.), etching on wove (BP 508, DM 1264, FR 4309, Y 100,483).

$1696* *Die Erste Nacht (Vogel 26), 1954,* s., d., mono., stone s., d., (06-12-93, Hauswedell/Nolt, #225), 25¹¹⁄₁₆ x 34⅞ in., (65.3 x 88.6 cm.), lithograph on offset paper (BP 1110, DM 2760, FR 9278, Y 178,470).

$1130* *Die Erste Nacht (Vogel 27), 1954,* s., d., mono., stone s., d., (06-12-93, Hauswedell/Nolt, #226), 25¹¹⁄₁₆ x 34⅞ in., (65.3 x 88.6 cm.), color lithograph (BP 740, DM 1839, FR 6182, Y 118,910).

$5652* *Eulen (Brockstedt H 6; Vogel 51), 1957,* s., d., i. artist's proof, (06-12-93, Hauswedell/Nolt, #251, illus.), 31½ x 19¹¹⁄₁₆ in., (80 x 50 cm.), color wood cut on Japan (BP 3699, DM 9199, FR 30,919, Y 594,760).

$2126* *Flotenspielerin (Fr. IV/119), (19)73,* s., d., (06-08-93, Karl/Faber, #917), approx. 19⁵⁄₁₆ x 12³⁄₁₆ in., (49 x 31 cm.), etching on Arches wove (BP 1398, DM 3450, FR 11,617, Y 225,810).

$232* *Franzl, 2. Zustand, 1984,* s.; plate s., t., d., blindstamp, (09-18-92, Schloss Ahlden, #1015), 21¼ x 14¹⁵⁄₁₆ in., (54 x 38 cm.), etching in brown on hand-made (BP 136, DM 344, FR 1178, Y 28,674).

$10,598* *Fruhe Radierungen (Brockstedt R 7, 10, 16, 23, 29, 33, 48, 49, 52, 55, 56, 60, 61, 172, 244, 245,248, 249, 256, 281), 1957-1964: Twenty-Six,* s., d. 1989, num., (06-12-93, Hauswedell/Nolt, #258), each sh 30¹¹⁄₁₆ x 21¹⁄₁₆ in., (78 x 53.5 cm.), etching on handmade Hahnemuhle (BP 6937, DM 17,249, FR 57,976, Y 1,115,227).

$1844* *Fuchs Mit Fuchs (Brockstedt R 19), 1958,* artist's proof, s., (12-05-92, Bassenge, #7293, illus.), 23⁷⁄₁₆ x 15⁹⁄₁₆ in., (59.5 x 39.5 cm.), etching on thick copper print paper (BP 1155, DM 2875, FR 9798, Y 228,472).

$1762* *Galerie Sandner (Brockstedt R 38; Vogel 165), 1958,* s., d., artist's proof, i., (05-26-93, Dorling, #2735, illus.), 23⁷⁄₁₆ x 15⁹⁄₁₆ in., (59.5 x 39.5 cm.), etching on wove (BP 1140, DM 2875, FR 9676, Y 191,439).

$1756* *Gesche Irgendwo Hier In Der Gegend (Frielinghaus 1972.8), 1971-1972,* s., d., artist's proof, (06-23-93, Kornfeld, #416), Strich- und Flachenatzung on thick grey wove (BP 1193, DM 2971, FR 9994, Y 191,306, SF 2645).

BI *Gesellschaft Im Freien (Brockstedt, Nr. 74), 1959,* #4/50, d., s., est. DM 3,000, (11-13-92, Kunsthaus, #620, illus.), 23¼ x 15⁹⁄₁₆ in., (59 x 39.5 cm.), etching on thick Japan.

$532* *"Glucklich-Gemutlich 10oo" (Br. R 325), (19)69,* s., d., num., (06-08-93, Karl/Faber, #905), approx. 11⁷⁄₁₆ x 8¹⁄₁₆ in., (29 x 20.5 cm.), etching on hand-made (BP 350, DM 863, FR 2907, Y 56,506).

BI *Grosser Regen II (Vogel 88; Brockstedt H 42), 1961,* #21/100, pencil t., num., s., d., est. DM 18,000, (11-20-92, Lempertz, #611), sh 30¹⁵⁄₁₆ x 20¹⁵⁄₁₆ in., (78.7 x 53.3 cm.), color woodcut on machine-made.

$1413* *Guido Dessauer (Vogel 17), 1954,* s., d., mono., stone s., d., t., (06-12-93, Hauswedell/Nolt, #222, illus.), 18½ x 12³⁄₁₆ in., (47 x 30.9 cm.), lithograph on thick brownish wove (BP 925, DM 2300, FR 7730, Y 148,690).

BI *Heinrich Schwartz Nach Durer 1514, 1977,* s., d.; plate d., t.; edit. stamp verso, est. DM 300, (09-18-92, Schloss Ahlden, #1008), 13⁹⁄₁₆ x 10¹¹⁄₁₆ in., (34.5 x 27.1 cm.), etching on hand-made.

$565* *Hula-Hoop (Vogel 112), 1958,* s., d., #1/5, (06-12-93, Hauswedell/Nolt, #230), 15¾ x 12¹⁵⁄₁₆ in., (40 x 33 cm.), lithograph on wove (BP 370, DM 920, FR 3091, Y 59,455).

$387* *In Sich Selbst Verliebt, 1983,* s.; plate mono., d., t. d.; edit. stamp verso, (09-18-92, Schloss Ahlden, #1012), 11⅝ x 8¼ in., (29.5 x 21 cm.), etching in brown on Japan (BP 227, DM 574, FR 1964, Y 47,831).

BI *Janssen Und Ich ... Postma, 1968,* s., traces stains, est. DM 400-, (09-25-92, Granier, #2899), 19⁵⁄₁₆ x 24¹³⁄₁₆ in., (49 x 63 cm.), lithograph on hand-made.

$1837* *Judith, 1952,* s., d., (06-12-93, Hauswedell/Nolt, #175, illus.), 19¹¹⁄₁₆ x 13¾ in., (50 x 35 cm.), monotype on hand-made Japan (BP 1202, DM 2990, FR 10,049, Y 193,307).

$993* *Judith, Goltzius n. Spranger, Heut Eben War Birgit Hier, 15. 10. 76,1976,* s., num., (06-05-93, Bassenge, #6155), 21⁷⁄₁₆ x 13⁹⁄₁₆ in., (54.4 x 34.4 cm.), etching on copper print (BP 654, DM 1610, FR 5426, Y 106,522).

$496* *Karneval (Fr. V/99), (19)71,* after Gavarni, s., d., num., (06-08-93, Karl/Faber, #912), approx. 8¹⁄₁₆ x 5¹¹⁄₁₆ in., (20.5 x 14.5 cm.), etching w/drypoint on Auvergne hand-made (BP 326, DM 805, FR 2710, Y 52,682).

$806* *Katze (Vogel, Nr. 225), 1959,* d., s., (11-13-92, Kunsthaus, #619, illus.), 8⁹⁄₁₆ x 13¹⁵⁄₁₆ in., (21.8 x 35.5 cm.), etching, drypoint and aquatint on intaglio hand-made (BP 521, DM 1265, FR 4267, Y 100,037).

$3815* *Kleine Schlittschuhlaufer (Brockstedt H 7; Vogel 67), 1957,* s., d., #1/25, (06-12-93, Hauswedell/Nolt, #252, illus.), 11⅛ x 13⁹⁄₁₆ in., (28.3 x 34.5 cm.), color woodcut on hand-made Japan (BP 2497, DM 6209, FR 20,870, Y 401,452).

$1272* *Kleiner Traum (Brockstedt R 286; Vogel 304), 1964,* s., d., #2/15, plate i., (06-12-93, Hauswedell/Nolt, #194, illus.), 19⅜ x 15¾ in., (49.2 x 40 cm.), etching on wove (BP 833, DM 2070, FR 6958, Y 133,852).

$1272* *Krabbe (Frielinghaus 1976, 73), 1976,* s., d., i., artist's proof, (06-12-93, Hauswedell/Nolt, #208, illus.), 7 x 9¼ in., (17.8 x 23.5 cm.), etching worked over w/color chalk (BP 833, DM 2070, FR 6958, Y 133,852).

$564* *Krote Gustav (Janssen Griffelkunst 2; Vogel 94), 1957,* s., d., i., (05-26-93, Dorling, #2764, illus.), 13⅜ x 19³⁄₁₆ in., (33.9 x 48.8 cm.), lithograph on wove (BP 365, DM 920, FR 3097, Y 61,278).

$424* *Kruppelweide Und Gatter An Tumpel, 1970,* s., d., #2/22, (06-12-93, Hauswedell/Nolt, #202), 8¹⁵⁄₁₆ x 11¹³⁄₁₆ in., (22.8 x 30 cm.), etching on brownish thin hand-made Japan w/wide margin (BP 278, DM 690, FR 2319, Y 44,617).

$5017* *L'Heure De Mylene, Arrangee Par Mylene Pour Verena (Brockstedt 368),1962: Twelve,* s., d., #3/10, very good cond., loose in decorated paper board portfolio, verygood cond.(05-20-93, Christie-London, #447, illus.), overall sheet 15¾ x 21½ in., (40 x 54.6 cm.), etching on wove (BP 3220, DM 8095, FR 27,266, Y 553,997).

$938* *"Lammetime", 1986,* s., d., num., (11-28-92, Grisebach, #571, illus.), 16¹⁵⁄₁₆ x 22¹³⁄₁₆ in., (43 x 58 cm.), colored lithograph on handmade Japan (BP 619, DM 1494, FR 5073, Y 116,739).

$1011* *"Lammetoy", 1986,* s., d., (11-28-92, Grisebach, #570, illus.), 11½ x 13¾ in., (29.2 x 35 cm.), colored lithograph on handmade Japan (BP 667, DM 1611, FR 5468, Y 125,825).

$221* *Landschaft, 1970,* s., num., (12-05-92, Bassenge, #7297), 8⁷⁄₁₆ x 9½ in., (21.4 x 24.2 cm.), etching on handmade Japan (BP 138, DM 345, FR 1174, Y 27,382).

BI *Langenhorn: Kopie Ohne Vorlage, 1972,* s., d.; plate d., staining, est. DM 150, (09-18-92, Schloss Ahlden, #1007), 5⅞ x 8¾ in., (14.9 x 22.3 cm.), etching on hand-made.

$155* *Lever Dot As Sklav, 1983,* s.; plate t., d; edit. stamp verso, (09-18-92, Schloss Ahlden, #1011), 8¼ x 11⅝ in., (21 x 29.6 cm.), etching on slightly yellowed Japan (BP 91, DM 230, FR 787, Y 19,157).

BI *Liebe Gesche, So Liebt Mich Oskar-Ja, 1971,* s., stone s., d., t., (09-18-92, Schloss Ahlden, #1017), 25³⁄₁₆ x 19⁹⁄₁₆ in., (64 x 49.7 cm.), lithograph on wove.

$3153* *Melis Melis, Selbstbildnis 11.1.74 (Frielinghaus ff 165),* s., d., #12/80, (05-27-93, Lempertz, #817, illus.), 20⅞ x 29¹⁵⁄₁₆ in., (53 x 76 cm.), etching on wove (BP 2019, DM 5059, FR 17,052, Y 338,015).

BI *Memorial I, 1983,* s.; plate d.; edit. stamp verso, (09-18-92, Schloss Ahlden, #1010), 8¼ x 11⅝ in., (21 x 29.6 cm.), etching in green on hand-made Japan.

BI *Memorial II, 1983,* s.; plate s., d.; edit. stamp verso, est. DM 200, (09-18-92, Schloss Ahlden, #1014), 8³⁄₁₆ x 11⅝ in., (20.8 x 29.5 cm.), etching in reddish brown on hand-made.

BI *"Mit Frielinghaus" (Fr. VI/42), (19)70,* s., d., num., pub. der Galerie Brockstedt, est. DM 1600, (12-01-92, Karl/ Faber, #789), 5⅞ x 8¹¹⁄₁₆ in., (15 x 22 cm.), etching on hand-made Japan.

$2473* *Monckebergstrasse (Brockstedt H 41; Vogel 81), 1961,* s., d., #48/50, stamp, (06-12-93, Hauswedell/Nolt, #254), 22¼ x 19⁵⁄₁₆ in., (56.5 x 49 cm.), color wood cut on hand-made Japan (BP 1619, DM 4025, FR 13,528, Y 260,234).

$4564* *Monckebergstrasse (Vogel 81; Brockstedt H 41), (19)61/ (87),* s., d., num., (12-01-92, Karl/Faber, #783, illus.), 22¼ x 19⁵⁄₁₆ in., (56.5 x 49 cm.), color woodcut on hand-made Japan (BP 3016, DM 7274, FR 24,791, Y 568,227).

$707* *Monsieur Visat (Brockstedt R 307), 1965,* s., d., #28/40, blindstamp, Galerie Wolfgang Ketterer, (06-12-93, Hauswedell/Nolt, #200), 23⅝ x 17½ in., (60 x 44.4 cm.), etching on wove w/Lana watermark (BP 463, DM 1151, FR 3868, Y 74,398).

$2120* *Nachtwache (Brockstedt R 45; Vogel 169), 1958,* s., d., #9/20, (06-12-93, Hauswedell/Nolt, #181, illus.), 23⁵⁄₁₆ x 15½ in., (59.2 x 39.4 cm.), etching on thick wove (BP 1388, DM 3451, FR 11,597, Y 223,087).

$776* *Neunkopfe, 1990: Nine,* s., num., (09-25-92, Granier, #2898, illus.), 24¹³⁄₁₆ x 18⅛ in., (63 x 46 cm.), etching on Japan (BP 453, DM 1150, FR 3890, Y 93,663).

$794* *"Never More Poe", 1988,* s., d., num., (11-28-92, Grisebach, #572, illus.), 21¼ x 14³⁄₁₆ in., (53.9 x 36.1 cm.), colored aquatint on handmade Japan (BP 524, DM 1265, FR 4294, Y 98,818).

$14,131* *Oma (Brockstedt 3; Vogel 8), 1957,* s., d., i. artist's proof, (06-12-93, Hauswedell/Nolt, #250, illus.), 31¹¹⁄₁₆ x 20½ in., (80.5 x 52 cm.), color wood cut (BP 9249, DM 23,000, FR 77,303, Y 1,487,004).

$921* *Propylaen Mappe II (Fr. III/6 (ff. Nr. 315), 7 (316), 9 (318), 10 (139); IV/502, 68 (568), 69 (569), 91 (591), 123 (623), 127 (627); V/36 (509), (19)71-74: Eleven,* s., frontispiece, num., d., (06-08-93, Karl/Faber, #914, illus.), approx. 28¾ x 22¹³⁄₁₆ in., (73 x 58 cm.), etching and drypoint (BP 605, DM 1494, FR 5033, Y 97,823).

BI *Raufende Bettler, 1983,* after Bellange, #56/120, pencil s., d., tears, est. DM 1,500, (11-20-92, Lempertz, #617), sh 30¹³⁄₁₆ x 22¼ in., (78.2 x 56.5 cm.), etching on thick Velin.

$2339* *"Roswitha 2.10.72" (Fr. IV/63), (19)72,* s., d., num., watermark, (06-08-93, Karl/Faber, #915), approx. 15⅜ x 19½ in., (39 x 49.5 cm.), etching and drypoint in lilac

on tan (red color) Hahnemuhle hand-made (BP 1538, DM 3795, FR 12,781, Y 248,433).

BI *An Roswitha, 1972,* s., d.; plate t., edit. stamp verso, est. DM 550, (09-18-92, Schloss Ahlden, #1018), 8¾ x 5¹³⁄₁₆ in., (22.3 x 14.8 cm.), etching in brown on hand-made Arches.

BI *Schnorkellandschaft II, 1984,* s., edit. stamp verso, est. DM 150, (09-18-92, Schloss Ahlden, #1013), 1⅞ x 11⅝ in., (4.8 x 29.5 cm.), etching on Japan.

$1130* *Seestern (Frielinghaus 1976, 49), 1976,* s., d., plate i., artist's proof, (06-12-93, Hauswedell/Nolt, #206, illus.), 4¹¹⁄₁₆ x 7¹⁄₁₆ in., (11.9 x 17.9 cm.), etching w/color chalk (BP 740, DM 1839, FR 6182, Y 118,910).

$1097* *Selbst (Frielinghaus 1976), 1976,* s., d., num.; t., i. in plate, (12-02-92, Dorling, #2776, illus.), 11¹¹⁄₁₆ x 7⅜ in., (29.7 x 18.7 cm.), etching in red-brown on red ochre toned cardboard (BP 708, DM 1725, FR 5888, Y 136,494).

$775* *Selbst (Frielinhaus 1973, 195), 1973,* s., d., num., i., from series Caspar David Friedrich, (05-26-93, Dorling, #2742, illus.), 17⁹⁄₁₆ x 7¹¹⁄₁₆ in., (44.6 x 19.6 cm.), etching and line etching on handmade (BP 501, DM 1264, FR 4256, Y 84,203).

$1554* *Selbst Als Chess Addams (Brocksiedt R 265; Vogel 308), 1964,* s., d., num., #12/40, (06-12-93, Hauswedell/Nolt, #190), 13⅛ x 7⅝ in., (33.3 x 19.3 cm.), etching on copper print (BP 1017, DM 2529, FR 8501, Y 163,527).

$565* *Selbst Als Mozart (Vogel 396; Meyer-Schomann 4), 1958,* stone t., i., (06-12-93, Hauswedell/Nolt, #231), 20½ x 14¾ in., (52 x 37.5 cm.), poster, lithograph on wove (BP 370, DM 920, FR 3091, Y 59,455).

$424* *Selbst Am 15.12.1972, 1972,* mono., d., artist's proof, (06-12-93, Hauswedell/Nolt, #204), 8⁹⁄₁₆ x 5¹¹⁄₁₆ in., (21.8 x 14.5 cm.), etching on thick wove (BP 278, DM 690, FR 2319, Y 44,617).

$1272* *Selbst Am 29.3.65 (Brockstedt R 300; Vogel 334), 1965,* s., d., #19/65, (06-12-93, Hauswedell/Nolt, #197, illus.), 19⁵⁄₁₆ x 14⁹⁄₁₆ in., (49.1 x 37 cm.), etching on Arches (BP 833, DM 2070, FR 6958, Y 133,852).

$1766* *Selbst Dramatisch (Brockstedt R 302; Vogel 335),* s., d., artist's proof, portfolio Europaische Graphik, (06-12-93, Hauswedell/Nolt, #199), 14¹¹⁄₁₆ x 10¹⁄₁₆ in., (37.3 x 25.5 cm.), etching on Japan nacre (BP 1156, DM 2874, FR 9661, Y 185,836).

$1908* *Selbst Dramatisch (Brockstedt R 302; Vogel 335), 1965,* s., d., #42/65, portfolio Europaische Graphik IV, Galerie Wolfgang Kettere, blindstamp, (06-12-93, Hauswedell/ Nolt, #198), 15¹¹⁄₁₆ x 9⅞ in., (39.9 x 25.1 cm.), etching on thick wove (BP 1249, DM 3105, FR 10,438, Y 200,779).

$1272* *Selbst Elegisch (Brockstedt R 299; Vogel 333), 1965,* s., d., #21/65, blindstamp, Ketterer, crease, (06-12-93, Hauswedell/Nolt, #196), 18¹⁵⁄₁₆ x 15½ in., (48.2 x 39.3 cm.), etching on wove (BP 833, DM 2070, FR 6958, Y 133,852).

$565* *Selbst Im Profil Zu Birgit Jacobsen "Nocturno" (Frielinghaus 1976, 115), 1977,* s., d., #92/95, plate i., (06-12-93, Hauswedell/Nolt, #211, illus.), 8⅞ x 6⁷⁄₁₆ in., (22.5 x 16.3 cm.), etching (BP 370, DM 920, FR 3091, Y 59,455).

$638* *Selbst Mit 3 Nasenlochern (Fr. V/7), (19)71,* s., d., num., from 2nd portfolio Horst Janssen, 15 Etchings, pub. Propylaen Verlag, blindstamp, (06-08-93, Karl/Faber, #908), approx. 10¼ x 7½ in., (26 x 19 cm.), etching on wove (BP 419, DM 1035, FR 3486, Y 67,764).

$709* *Selbst Mit Gesche (Fr. V/22), (19)71,* s., d., i., artist proof, (06-08-93, Karl/Faber, #909), approx. 10⁷⁄₁₆ x 7⁵⁄₁₆ in., (26.5 x 18.5 cm.), etching on wove (BP 466, DM 1150, FR 3874, Y 75,305).

$878* *Selbst Nocturno (Frielinghaus 110), 1976,* plate s., d., t., (12-02-92, Dorling, #2773, illus.), 13⁵⁄₁₆ x 6 in., (33.8 x 15.3 cm.), etching in red on green toned hand-made (BP 566, DM 1381, FR 4713, Y 109,245).

$1097* *Selbst Nocturno (Frielinghaus 135), 1976,* s., d., t. in plate, (12-02-92, Dorling, #2775, illus.), 9¾ x 6¹⁵⁄₁₆ in., (24.7 x 17.7 cm.), etching in black-grey on grey handmade (BP 708, DM 1725, FR 5888, Y 136,494).

$1837* *Selbst Singend (25.3.65) (Vogel 141), 1965,* s., d., #52/ 100, Folie, d., t., i., blindstamp W. Ketterer, (06-12-93,

Hauswedell/Nolt, #236), 20¼ x 14¹⁵⁄₁₆ in., (51.5 x 38 cm.), zincograph on wove (BP 1202, DM 2990, FR 10,049, Y 193,307).

$1272* *Selbst Singend (25.3.65) (Vogel 1410, 1965,* s., d., #71/100, Folie, d., t., i., blindstamp, W. Ketterer, (06-12-93, Hauswedell/Nolt, #235), 20¼ x 15⅜ in., (51.5 x 39 cm.), zincograph on wove (BP 833, DM 2070, FR 6958, Y 133,852).

$2655* *Selbst Singend Am 25.3.65 (V. 141), (19)65,* s., d., num., (12-01-92, Karl/Faber, #786), 20¹⁄₁₆ x 14¾ in., (51 x 37.5 cm.), zincograph on hand-made Japan (BP 1754, DM 4232, FR 14,422, Y 330,553).

$989* *Selbst, Zwei Figuren Beobachtend (Brockstedt R 190), 1962,* s., i., plate d., (06-12-93, Hauswedell/Nolt, #187, illus.), 15⅝ x 10¹⁵⁄₁₆ in., (39.7 x 27.9 cm.), etching on hand-made rag (BP 647, DM 1610, FR 5410, Y 104,072).

$1130* *Selbst-Pinkus Plakat (Brockstedt R 264; Vogel 309), 1964,* d., ded., i., (06-12-93, Hauswedell/Nolt, #189), 15⁷⁄₁₆ x 12 in., (39.2 x 30.5 cm.), etching on wove (BP 740, DM 1839, FR 6182, Y 118,910).

$1554* *Selbst-Suff (Brockstedt R 266; Vogel 308), 1964,* s., d., #18/40, plate t., (06-12-93, Hauswedell/Nolt, #191), 15¾ x 11⁵⁄₁₆ in., (40 x 28.7 cm.), etching on thick wove (BP 1017, DM 2529, FR 8501, Y 163,527).

$1097* *Selbst. (Frielinghaus 1972), 1973,* s., d., num., from series Propylaen-Mappe I, (12-02-92, Dorling, #2771, illus.), 9⁵⁄₁₆ x 11¹¹⁄₁₆ in., (23.7 x 29.7 cm.), etching in grey on hand-made (BP 708, DM 1725, FR 5888, Y 136,494).

$1254* *Selbstbildnis - "Die Leute Reden + Reden + Reden", 1980,* s., num., 1st state, (12-05-92, Bassenge, #7307, illus.), 23⁷⁄₁₆ x 17⁷⁄₁₆ in., (59.5 x 44.3 cm.), etching on handmade Japan (BP 785, DM 1955, FR 6663, Y 155,371).

$885* *Selbstbildnis - "Ein Gruss Fur Alf Boe", 1980,* s., num., (12-05-92, Bassenge, #7306, illus.), 16¹⁵⁄₁₆ x 12¹¹⁄₁₆ in., (43.1 x 32.3 cm.), etching on handmade Japan (BP 554, DM 1380, FR 4702, Y 109,652).

$590* *Selbstbildnis - "Magdalenengrusse", 1982,* s., num., (12-05-92, Bassenge, #7308), 10¹³⁄₁₆ x 7½ in., (27.5 x 19 cm.), etching on Japan (BP 369, DM 920, FR 3135, Y 73,101).

$851* *Selbstbildnis Als 5-Jahriger Schuler, 1984,* s., num., (06-05-93, Bassenge, #6161), 19⁹⁄₁₆ x 15⅜ in., (49.7 x 39 cm.), etching in brick red on Japan (BP 560, DM 1380, FR 4650, Y 91,289).

$922* *Selbstbildnis En Face, "Gemutlich", 1970,* s., num., (06-05-93, Bassenge, #6149), 11⁹⁄₁₆ x 8¹⁄₁₆ in., (29.3 x 20.4 cm.), etching on thick paper (BP 607, DM 1495, FR 5038, Y 98,906).

$922* *Selbstbildnis Von Vorne, 1972,* ded., s., (06-05-93, Bassenge, #6152, illus.), 8⁹⁄₁₆ x 5¾ in., (21.8 x 14.6 cm.), etching on machine-made (BP 607, DM 1495, FR 5038, Y 98,906).

$2749* *Selbstbilnis "Melis Melis" (Friedlinghaus 1974, Nr. 10), 1974,* s.,d., num., (05-26-93, Dorling, #2743, illus.), 17¼ x 22¹⁵⁄₁₆ in., (43.8 x 58.4 cm.), etching on thick wove (BP 1778, DM 4485, FR 15,096, Y 298,674).

$369* *Stilleben Mit Wurfeln, 1974,* s., num., (12-05-92, Bassenge, #7300), 13⁹⁄₁₆ x 3¹³⁄₁₆ in., (34.5 x 9.7 cm.), etching on thick Japan (BP 231, DM 575, FR 1961, Y 45,719).

$1272* *Tierschadel (Frielinghaus 1976, 57), 1976,* s., d., plate i., artist's proof, (06-12-93, Hauswedell/Nolt, #207, illus.), 7 x 9⁵⁄₁₆ in., (17.8 x 23.7 cm.), etching worked over w/ color chalk (BP 833, DM 2070, FR 6958, Y 133,852).

$382* *Toter Vogel 22.5.81, 1981,* s., d., #5/100, plate i., (06-12-93, Hauswedell/Nolt, #213), 6⅝ x 9⅝ in., (16.9 x 24.4 cm.), etching on hand-made Japan (BP 250, DM 622, FR 2090, Y 40,198).

$369* *Um Sonst, 1976,* artist's proof, s., (12-05-92, Bassenge, #7305), 10¹⁄₁₆ x 14¹³⁄₁₆ in., etching on thick paper (BP 231, DM 575, FR 1961, Y 45,719).

$310* *Untitled, Korbweiden, 1975,* d., s., (09-25-92, Granier, #2893), sheet 13⁹⁄₁₆ x 9¹³⁄₁₆ in., (34.4 x 24.9 cm.), etching on thin cream hand-made (BP 181, DM 460, FR 1554, Y 37,417).

$474* *Veith Kind (Angelika Dessauer) (Vogel 23), 1954,* s., d., mono., stone s., d., (06-12-93, Hauswedell/Nolt, #223), 21⁷⁄₁₆ x 15½ in., (54.5 x 39.3 cm.), lithograph on smooth machine-made (BP 310, DM 771, FR 2593, Y 49,879).

$470* *Verlegenheitstanz 9Vogel 295, Brockstedt R 278), 1964,* s., (11-28-92, Schoppmann, #601), 15¹⁵⁄₁₆ x 19½ in., (40.5 x 49.5 cm.), etching on copper print (BP 310, DM 749, FR 2542, Y 58,494).

$1298* *Von Luigi Toninelli Bestellt, Von Bettina Gewunscht + Geliebt (Frielinghaus, Band 377), 1973,* artist's proof, pencil s., d., (11-20-92, Lempertz, #623), sh 19⁵⁄₁₆ x 12¹¹⁄₁₆ in., (49 x 32.3 cm.), etching on Velin (BP 855, DM 2070, FR 6971, Y 161,423).

BI *Vorgetauschtes Wissen, 1985,* plate t., d., s., est. DM 400-, (09-25-92, Granier, #2897), sheet 13½ x 9¹³⁄₁₆ in., (34.3 x 25 cm.), etching on blue thin machine hand-made.

$775* *Vorm Grimsel (Frielinghaus 1974/75, 18), 1974,* s., d., num., from series Caspar David Friedrich, (05-26-93, Dorling, #2744), 17⅜ x 23⁵⁄₁₆ in., (44.1 x 59.2 cm.), etching on copper print paper (BP 501, DM 1264, FR 4256, Y 84,203).

$2261* *Wolf (Brockstedt R 12; Vogel 157), 1957,* s., d., #9/20, (06-12-93, Hauswedell/Nolt, #176, illus.), 15¹³⁄₁₆ x 11¹¹⁄₁₆ in., (40.2 x 29.7 cm.), etching on thick wove (BP 1480, DM 3680, FR 12,369, Y 237,925).

$590* *Zehvogelkopf (Brockstedt R 49), 1958,* s., num., (12-05-92, Bassenge, #7294), 15⁹⁄₁₆ x 11³⁄₁₆ in., (39.5 x 28.4 cm.), etching on copper print paper (BP 369, DM 920, FR 3135, Y 73,101).

$254* *Zu "Brief An Mirjam", 1984,* s., d., #72/100, plate mono., t., (06-12-93, Hauswedell/Nolt, #217), 7¹⁵⁄₁₆ x 11⁵⁄₁₆ in., (20.3 x 28.8 cm.), etching on Japan (BP 166, DM 413, FR 1389, Y 26,728).

BI *Zu "Briefe An Roger Blin", 1980,* artist's proof, pencil s., d., est. DM 1,800, (11-20-92, Lempertz, #614), sh 26⅛ x 20⅜ in., (66.3 x 51.8 cm.), etching on thin Japan.

BI *Zu: Svanshall-Verkehrt ("Ich Bin So In Liebe"), 1986,* #6/20, plate t., d., pencil s., d., est. DM 1,300, (11-20-92, Lempertz, #620), sh 9¹⁄₁₆ x 12½ in., (23 x 31.7 cm.), etching on Japan.

$1010* *Zu: Svanshall-Verkehrt, 1986,* pencil s. and d., (11-20-92, Lempertz, #622), sh 8¾ x 12⅞ in., (22.2 x 32.7 cm.), etching on thin hand-made Japan, watercolor (BP 665, DM 1610, FR 5424, Y 125,606).

$3524* *Zwei Schwestern (Brockstedt 22 a; Vogel 68), 1957,* s., d., num., (05-26-93, Dorling, #2734, illus.), 31½ x 20¹⁄₁₆ in., (80 x 51 cm.), color woodcut on thick wove (BP 2280, DM 5750, FR 19,352, Y 382,877).

JANTHUR, Richard　　　　　　　　　　　　　1883-1956

BI *Die Bruder Karamasoff, 1919-22,* s., from the Mappe-Die Schaffenden, Jg. II, Mappe II, w/mount staining, est. DM 1400, (12-01-92, Karl/Faber, #796), 13⅜ x 10⁷⁄₁₆ in., (34 x 26.5 cm.), hand-colored lithograph.

JAPANESE SCHOOL

$143* *Battle Scene,* (10-11-92, Hanzel, #947), 14¼ x 9½ in., (36.2 x 24.1 cm.), color woodblock print (BP 85, DM 212, FR 713, Y 17,409).

$50* *Battle Scene,* (10-11-92, Hanzel, #956F), 14 x 9¾ in., (35.6 x 24.8 cm.), color woodblock print (BP 30, DM 74, FR 249, Y 6087).

$55* *Woman Eating Rice,* (10-11-92, Hanzel, #956C), 13¼ x 8¾ in., (33.7 x 22.2 cm.), color woodblock print (BP 33, DM 82, FR 274, Y 6696).

JAPANESE SCHOOL, 19TH CENTURY

$5121* *"Deux Personnages Traversant Un Pont Sous La Pluie" and "Hameau Lacustre Dans La Nuit": Two,* s., (02-16-93, Encans, #106), 6⅜ x 14⁹⁄₁₆ in., (16.2 x 37 cm.), woodcut (BP 3541, DM 8358, FR 28,308, Y 613,514, C$ 6438).

JAQUE, Louis (Louis Jacques BEAULIEU)　　　b. 1919

$221* *Sans Titre,* #2/90, s., d. Louis Jaque 76, (02-16-93, Encans, #47), 18⁵⁄₁₆ x 15¾ in., (46.5 x 40 cm.), serigraph (BP 153, DM 361, FR 1222, Y 26,477, C$ 278).

JARDIN, Karel du   Dutch 17th cent.
  BI *"Bebiendo En El Arroyo",* plate s., reserve P15,000, (02-03-93, Duran, #42, illus.), 7¹/₁₆ x 8¼ in., (18 x 21 cm.), engraving and etching.

JASIENSKI, Stefan   1899-1990
  BI *Still Life With Glass Fish And Ball,* early 1920s, s. verso; s., est. $2/3,000, (04-08-93, Christie-NY, #88, illus.), 8 x 11¾ in., (20.3 x 29.8 cm.), photograph, oil print.
  BI *Still Life With Vases And Perfume Bottle,* early 1920s, mono. insig. recto; s. verso, est. $2/3,000, (04-08-93, Christie-NY, #89, illus.), 9¼ x 11½ in., (23.5 x 29.2 cm.), photograph, oil print.

JAULMES, G.
  $294* *Salon D'Automne. Grand Palais, Ensemble Decoratifs, 1921,* p. B. Sirven, very good cond., (11-19-92, Ribeyre/Baron, #140), 62¹⁵/₁₆ x 47¼ in., (160 x 120 cm.), poster (BP 194, DM 469, FR 1579, Y 36,563).

JAWLENSKY, Alexej von   German 1864-1941
  $4149* *Kopf II (Rosenbach 19 A), 1922,* s., from the Mappe Kopfe, (12-01-92, Karl/Faber, #798, illus.), 11¹³/₁₆ x 7¹¹/₁₆ in., (30 x 19.5 cm.), lithograph on simili-Japan (BP 2741, DM 6613, FR 22,537, Y 516,150).
  $24,011* *Kopf VI (Rosenbach 23), 1922,* s., portfolio Kopfe, (06-10-93, Hauswedell/Nolt, #430, illus.), image 11⁹/₁₆ x 8¹⁵/₁₆ in., (29.3 x 22.7 cm.), lithograph worked over w/watercolor on imperial Japan (BP 15,706, DM 39,099, FR 131,639, Y 2,548,668).

JEAN-MORIN
  $140* *Batz, Plouharnel, St Jean De Monts, Etc.,: Eight,* s., num., full margins, (05-06-93, Laurin, #71), etchings (BP 89, DM 221, FR 742, Y 15,403).

JEAURAT, Etienne (after)   1699-1789
  $575* *Le Transport Des Filles De Joie A L'Hopital (P. and B. II, p. 692, no. 16), c. 1750,* proof, before t., trimmed, blank at left corner made up, staining, watermark, (05-11-93, Christie-NY, #74), sheet 17½ x 20¼ in., (445 x 514 mm.), engraving on laid (BP 367, DM 906, FR 3052, Y 63,249).

JEGHER, Christoffel   1596-1653
  $1300* *Der Liebesgarten Mit Den Sitzenden Frauen, Linker Teil (Wurzbach 14,Hollstein 17b),* after Rubens, (12-04-92, Bassenge, #6257, illus.), 18⅛ x 23¼ in., (46 x 59 cm.), woodcut (BP 834, DM 2070, FR 7023, Y 162,297).
  $5803* *Susanna Und Die Beiden Alten (Hollstein i/I (v. II)), c. 1630,* after Peter Paul Rubens, (06-23-93, Kornfeld, #59, illus.), woodcut (BP 3942, DM 9819, FR 33,028, Y 632,204, SF 8740).
  $3116* *The Temptation Of Christ By The Devil (Le Blanc 6 I, Hollstein II),* after Rubens, (06-04-93, Bassenge, #5217, illus.), 12¹³/₁₆ x 16¹⁵/₁₆ in., (32.5 x 43 cm.), woodcut (BP 2062, DM 5060, FR 17,055, Y 336,066).

JEGHER, Cristoffel   1596-1653
  BI *The Coronation Of The Virgin (Dut. VI, 96, 5; Holl. 10),* 1st state (of 2), watermark, trimmed, discolouration, residual backing, defects, est. BP 1,0/1,500, (12-01-92, Christie-London, #108), 13³/₁₆ x 17 in., (335 x 432 mm.), woodcut.
  $1364* *Silenus Accompanied By A Satyr And A Faun (Holl. 16),* after Rubens, first state, Rubens' address, trimmed to outer borderline, corner restored, minor defects, (12-03-92, Sotheby-London, #73), 17⅝ x 13⅜ in., (448 x 340 mm.), woodcut (BP 880, DM 2145, FR 7322, Y 169,715).
  $1840* *Susannah Surprised By The Elders (Holl. 1), c. 1632-40,* after Rubens, 1st state of 2, countermark, trimmed, restoration, tears, repaired tears, folds, discoloration, prop. Dora Jane Janson Coll. and H.W.Janson Estate, (05-13-93, Sotheby-NY, #161, illus.), 17⅜ x 22½ in., (440 x 572 mm.), woodcut (BP 1208, DM 2971, FR 10,022, Y 205,426).

JENICHEN, Baltasar   d. c. 1621
  $144* *Christus Am Kreuz (Hollstein 5),* prov., lit., after Jost Amman, (12-04-92, Bassenge, #6258), 5⁹/₁₆ x 4³/₁₆ in., (14.2 x 10.6 cm.), engraving (BP 92, DM 229, FR 778, Y 17,978).

JENKINS, Paul   American b. 1923
  $330* *Abstract,* s., d. 1965, num. 63/95, (09-20-92, Hindman, #727), 28¼ x 19½ in., (71.8 x 49.5 cm.), color lithograph (BP 193, DM 490, FR 1675, Y 40,786).
  $275* *Abstract,* s., d. '69, num., (06-11-93, Freemn/Fine Art, #118), 37 x 27½ in., (94 x 69.9 cm.), lithograph (BP 181, DM 447, FR 1507, Y 29,178).
  BI *Abstract,* s., est. $4/600, (09-24-92, Mystic, #45), 21 x 26 in., (53.3 x 66 cm.), colored lithograph.
  BI *Abstract,* s., est. $4/600, (09-24-92, Mystic, #46), 26 x 37 in., (66 x 94 cm.), colored lithograph.
  $138* *Abstract Arrangement With Purple And Yellow,* #36/40, good cond., (06-11-93, Freemn/Fine Art, #119), 15 x 10 in., (38.1 x 25.4 cm.), lithograph (BP 91, DM 224, FR 756, Y 14,642).
  $248* *Abstract Composition,* s., d. 1973, #48/60, (05-16-93, Hindman, #605), 28 x 19 in., (71.1 x 48.3 cm.), color serigraph (BP 161, DM 399, FR 1341, Y 27,491).
  BI *Composition,* s., d. 1980, est. $3/500, (12-13-92, Hindman, #351), 48 x 33 in., color lithograph w/etching.
  $1150* *"Four Winds (I)" and "West Winds (III)" (Tyler 288: PJ2 and T.290:PJ4), 1980:* Two, each s., d., one of 58 and 53 variations, blindstamp of pub., Tyler Graphics, Ltd., good cond., (02-11-93, Sotheby-NY, #357), sheet, one 48¹/₁₆ x 32¹/₁₆ in., (122 x 81.5 cm.), sheet, the other 50¹³/₁₆ x 37⅜ in., (122 x 81.5 cm.), hand-dyed monoprint p. in colors on hand-colored, handmade TGL paper- and hand-colored, Process Materials Corp. paper (BP 811, DM 1905, FR 6446, Y 138,638).
  $397* *Phenomena Brown And Blue, 1963,* s., d., num., (11-28-92, Schoppmann, #603), 22¼ x 13⁹/₁₆ in., (56.5 x 34.5 cm.), color lithograph on light brown handmade (BP 262, DM 632, FR 2147, Y 49,409).
  BI *Prism Zig-Zag, 1983,* s., d., num., est. DM 800, (12-01-92, Karl/Faber, #799), 34¼ x 22⁷/₁₆ in., (87 x 57 cm.), color lithograph on Arches France wove.
  $330* *Sinclair Red, 1981,* s., d., #46/150, blindstamps of pub. & printer, good cond., skinned areas, hinge removal, creases, (02-24-93, Butterfield, #3223), 38 x 29¼ in., (965 x 743 mm.), lithograph in colors on Somerset (BP 230, DM 536, FR 1816, Y 38,723).
  $247* *"Sound", 1972 and "Untitled Composition", 1969:* Two, s., annot. Unique Proof, creases, p. Triton Press, (05-27-93, Swann, #143), one, sh 27½ x 19½ in., (69.9 x 49.5 cm.), color lithograph (BP 158, DM 396, FR 1336, Y 26,479).
  $413* *Two Abstract Prints, 1973 and 1972,* former s., d., ded. Paul Jenkins, 1973 EA, latter Paul Jenkins Unique Proof 1972, very good cond., (03-12-93, Skinner, #107, illus.), sight 26 x 37 in., (66 x 94 cm.), lithograph in color (BP 288, DM 687, FR 2337, Y 48,674).
  $173* *Untitled (For Henry Abrams), 1971,* s., #72/100, good cond., hinge remains, (05-19-93, Butterfield, #2199), 30⅛ x 22⅜ in., (765 x 568 mm.), lithograph in colors on Arches (BP 112, DM 281, FR 947, Y 19,152).
  BI *Untitled, 1970,* artist proof, s., est. SF 900/1,300, (10-14-92, Germann, #338), 37³/₁₆ x 27⁹/₁₆ in., (945 x 700 mm.), color lithograph.

JENNINGS, Humphrey
  $726* *Table-Top Still Life, c. 1936,* 258 x 375mm, (05-07-93, Sotheby-London, #217, illus.), photograph, silver print (BP 460, DM 1148, FR 3868, Y 79,938).

JENSEN, Bill   American b. 1945
  BI *Etching For Denial,* s., d. 1987, #27/45, very good cond., est. $3/600, (06-11-93, Doyle, #97), 9¼ x 6¼ in., (235 x 159 mm.), color etching.
  $575* *Kepler, 1985-86,* s., d., #9/50, blindstamp, pub. ULAE, full margins, good cond., (05-15-93, Sotheby-NY, #1019, illus.), 5⅜ x 8½ in., (13.7 x 21.6 cm.), intaglio (BP 374, DM 925, FR 3108, Y 63,740).
  BI *"Sled" and "Lie-Light": Two,* s., d., t., num., very good cond., est. $6/800, (06-11-93, Doyle, #96), larger 9⅜ x 14⅝ in., (238 x 371 mm.), etching, 2nd w/color.
  $575* *Sled, 1987-89,* s., d., t., #19/40, blindstamp, pub. ULAE, full margins, good cond., (05-15-93, Sotheby-NY, #1020), 10¼ x 7¾ in., (26 x 19.7 cm.), intaglio (BP 374, DM 925, FR 3108, Y 63,740).

JENSEN, Julie

BI *Architectural Studies, 1976-1981: Eight,* t., s., d., annot., each approx. 353 x 276mm, est. BP 3/500, (05-07-93, Sotheby-London, #394), photograph, silver print.

JEUFFRAIN, Paul d. 1916

BI *View Of Tivoli,* 1851-52, lit., est. $3/4,000, (10-13-92, Christie-NY, #11, illus.), 8⅛ x 10⅜ in., (20.6 x 26.4 cm.), photograph, salt print.

JIMENEZ, Luis

BI *Border Crossing, 1987,* s., d., #10/90, blindstamp printer, Hand Graphics, margins, good cond., creases, soiling, est. $3/500, (05-19-93, Butterfield, #2202), 31⅛ x 23 1/16 in., (791 x 586 mm.), lithograph in colors on Japan colle.

$660* *The Howl, 1977,* s., d., $56/60, blindstamp of pub., Hand Graphics, very good cond. (?), (02-24-93, Butterfield, #3224), 36¼ x 26 in., (921 x 660 mm.), lithograph p. in colors on wove (BP 460, DM 1071, FR 3632, Y 77,447).

$880* *Southwest Pieta, 1983,* s., d., annot. hand colored trial proof, i., very good cond. (?), (02-24-93, Butterfield, #3225), 30¼ x 44¼ in., (76.8 x 112.4 cm.), lithograph in colors w/hand coloring on Rives BFK (BP 614, DM 1429, FR 4843, Y 103,262).

BI *Texas Waltz, 1979,* s., i., annot. A/P, blindstamp publisher, Hand Graphics, very good cond.?, est. $4/600, (05-19-93, Butterfield, #2200), 25⅛ x 19 in., (638 x 483 mm.), lithograph on wove.

$990* *Vaquero, 1981,* s., d., num. 31/50, blindstamp of pub. Landfall Press, apparently good cond., surface soiling, (02-24-93, Butterfield, #3061, illus.), 46 x 34 in., (116.8 x 86.4 cm.), lithograph in colors w/gold glitter on wove (BP 690, DM 1607, FR 5449, Y 116,170).

$1035* *Vaquero, 1981,* s., d., #48/50, blindstamp publisher, Landfall Press, good cond.?, handling creases, (05-19-93, Butterfield, #2201), 46 x 34 in., (116.8 x 86.4 cm.), lithograph in colors w/gold glitter on wove (BP 672, DM 1682, FR 5668, Y 114,580).

JIRLOW, Lennart b. 1936

$405* *Ateljen, 1975,* s., 16/380, Editions Linnaeus, blindstamp, (12-04-92, AB Stockholm, #7070), 18⅛ x 21⅝ in., (46 x 55 cm.), lithograph in colors on Arches (BP 260, DM 645, FR 2188, Y 50,562, SK 2750).

$730* *Blombukett, 1975,* from Portfolio I, Editions Linnaeus, Mourlot blindstamp, (12-04-92, AB Stockholm, #7071), 24 7/16 x 14 15/16 in., (62 x 38 cm.), lithograph in color on Arches (BP 468, DM 1163, FR 3944, Y 91,136, SK 4950).

$3925* *Den Gamla Restaurangen,* Portfolio III, 1978, s. 180/310, blindstamp Mourlot, (05-25-93, AB Stockholm, #29), 14¾ x 21¼ in., (37.5 x 54 cm.), lithograph in colors (BP 2544, DM 6393, FR 21,519, Y 429,009, SK 5720).

$1054* *Den Gamla Restaurangen, 1978,* from Portfolio III, s., E.A., Editions Linnaeus, Mourlot blindstamp, (12-04-92, AB Stockholm, #7075), 14 15/16 x 21¼ in., (38 x 54 cm.), lithograph in colors (BP 676, DM 1679, FR 5694, Y 131,586, SK 7150).

$3321* *Det Dagliga Brodet, 1986,* s., EA, (05-25-93, AB Stockholm, #33), 16 9/16 x 22⅝ in., (42 x 57.5 cm.), lithograph in colors (BP 2152, DM 5409, FR 18,207, Y 362,990, SK 4840).

$2868* *Grona Lund, 1983,* s. 94/210, blindstamp Mourlot, (05-25-93, AB Stockholm, #32), 43 5/16 x 29½ in., (110 x 75 cm.), lithograph in colors (BP 1859, DM 4671, FR 15,724, Y 313,477, SK 4180).

$535* *Huset Vid Boulevarden, 1978,* s., 116/310, from Portfolio III, Mourlot blindstamp, (12-04-92, AB Stockholm, #7076), 14 15/16 x 21¼ in., (38 x 54 cm.), lithograph in colors (BP 343, DM 852, FR 2890, Y 66,792, SK 3630).

$1378* *Koket, 1976,* s., 10/310, from Portfolio II, Editions Linnaeus, Mourlot blindstamp, (12-04-92, AB Stockholm, #7074), 18⅛ x 24 in., (46 x 61 cm.), lithograph in colors (BP 884, DM 2195, FR 7445, Y 172,035, SK 9350).

$3774* *Malaren, 1990,* s., 83/225, Mourlot blindstamp, (05-25-93, AB Stockholm, #35), 38 3/16 x 28¾ in., (97 x 73 cm.), lithograph in colors on Arches (BP 2446, DM 6147, FR 20,691, Y 412,504, SK 5500).

$1887* *Modellen, 1978,* Lennart, s. 27/310, Editions Linnaeus, Mourlot blindstamp, (05-25-93, AB Stockholm, #30), 17½ x 16 15/16 in., (44.5 x 43 cm.), lithograph in colors (BP 1223, DM 3073, FR 10,345, Y 206,252, SK 2750).

$715* *"Pa Stegen",* s., 243/310, (04-17-93, Falkkloos, #175, illus.), 21¼ x 14 15/16 in., (54 x 38 cm.), lithograph in colors (BP 464, DM 1143, FR 3863, Y 79,506, SK 5280).

$2340* *Paret I Graset,* from Portfolio IV, 1979, s. EA, (05-25-93, AB Stockholm, #31), 14 15/16 x 17 11/16 in., (38 x 45 cm.), lithograph in colors on Japan paper (BP 1517, DM 3811, FR 12,829, Y 255,766, SK 3410).

$3774* *Restaurant Interior,* from Portfolio I, 1975, Editions Linnaeus, blindstamp Mourlot, (05-25-93, AB Stockholm, #26), 18 5/16 x 21 7/16 in., (46.5 x 54.5 cm.), lithograph in colors on Arches (BP 2446, DM 6147, FR 20,691, Y 412,504, SK 5500).

$811* *"Souvenir- L'Exposition Paris", 1976,* Editions Linnaeus, s., 56/101, (12-04-92, AB Stockholm, #7073), 16 9/16 x 17 11/16 in., (42 x 45 cm.), lithograph in colors (BP 520, DM 1292, FR 4381, Y 101,248, SK 5500).

$1887* *Tradgardsmastarna,* from Portfolio II, 1976, Editions Linnaeus, blindstamp Mourlot, (05-25-93, AB Stockholm, #27), 18⅛ x 23 13/16 in., (46 x 60.5 cm.), lithograph in colors (BP 1223, DM 3073, FR 10,345, Y 206,252, SK 2750).

$2944* *Tradgardspaus, 1989,* s., 149/300, Mourlot blindstamp, (05-25-93, AB Stockholm, #34), 15¾ x 21¼ in., (40 x 54 cm.), lithograph in colors (BP 1908, DM 4795, FR 16,140, Y 321,784, SK 4290).

$715* *"Trubaduren",* s. EA, (04-17-93, Falkkloos, #174, illus.), 22 1/16 x 15⅜ in., (56 x 39 cm.), lithograph in colors (BP 464, DM 1143, FR 3863, Y 79,506, SK 5280).

JIRU, V. (Czechoslovakian)

$1320* *Women And Men Engaged In Eurythmic Activities: "Dancer", "Group Of Dancers in Sequined Costumes", "Legs", "Men And Women Excercising On Beach", "Smiling Woman", "Volleyball" and "Woman Doing Handstand On Beach": Seven,* most w/photog.'s handstamp, other handstamps, 1920s, (04-07-93, Swann, #518, illus.), largest 9 x 11 in., photograph, silver print (BP 872, DM 2135, FR 7225, Y 149,966).

JOB

BI *Prise De La Smala D'Abd El Kader,* good cond., (03-13-93, Laurin, #52), 35 1/16 x 41 5/16 in., (89 x 105 cm.), .

JOBERT, P.

$358* *PLM: Constantine,* very good cond., (03-13-93, Laurin, #53), 39 9/16 x 24 7/16 in., (100.5 x 62 cm.), (BP 250, DM 596, FR 2026, Y 42,192).

JODE, G. de

$505* *Icones Revelationum St Johs Evangeliste In Pathmos (Le B, nd; F.W.H.H., 50 to 74): Twenty-Five,* glued, w/out margins, (02-03-93, Ader Tajan, #26), etching and copper engraving (BP 353, DM 832, FR 2820, Y 62,819).

JODE I, P. de 1570-1634

$157* *"Germanicus Habitus" (Hollstein 237; Lipperheide Cg 69),* after S. Vrancx, (06-09-93, Bubb Kuyper, #2055, illus.), 8⅞ x 5 13/16 in., (22.6 x 14.8 cm.), copper engraving (BP 104, DM 257, FR 864, Y 16,697, G 288).

JOHN, Augustus British 1878-1961

BI *The Brook (C.D. 113),* 2nd final state, s., i. in ink, #13/25, full margins, 2 areas lacking, good cond., est. BP 150/200, (10-27-92, Phillips-London, #279), plate 3 x 4 in., (76 x 102 mm.), etching w/tone on laid.

$244* *Fruit Sellers D (C.D. 89), 1906,* s., i. Plate No 96 Fruit Sellers (D), #15/25 in pen and ink, full margins, good cond., (10-27-92, Phillips-London, #277), (127 x 102 mm.), etching on laid (BP 154, DM 374, FR 1269, Y 29,847).

$1650* *Head Of A Girl, c. 1905,* s., i., irregularly torn sheet as p., losses, creases, ripples, prop.Edith Schumann 1988 Trust, (11-05-92, Sotheby-NY, #203, illus.), sheet approx. 14⅜ x 9⅞ in., (365 x 250 mm.), monotype p. in colors on japon (Japan paper) pelure (very thin) laidon stiff wove (BP 1073, DM 2610, FR 8828, Y 202,429).

BI   *Little Grotto,* s., est. DM 600, (12-01-92, Karl/Faber, #800), 3⅛ x 2¹⁵⁄₁₆ in., (8 x 7.5 cm.), etching on handmade.

$261*   *Nude Girl Seated On The Ground (C.D. 103),* 2nd final state, s., #25/25, full margins, good cond., (10-27-92, Phillips-London, #278), plate 6⅜ x 5⅞ in., (162 x 149 mm.), etching (BP 165, DM 400, FR 1357, Y 31,927).

$487*   *Virginia (C.D. 75), 1906,* 2nd pub. state, s., i., #20/25, full margins, stained, (10-27-92, Phillips-London, #276), plate 5⅛ x 4 in., (130 x 102 mm.), etching on laid (BP 308, DM 746, FR 2533, Y 59,572).

$1788*   *William Butler Yeats,* s., margins, foxing, catalog back cover lot, (04-22-93, Bonhams-Chelsea, #149, illus.), plate 7 x 5 in., (17.8 x 12.7 cm.), etching (BP 1155, DM 2873, FR 9691, Y 196,592).

$1567*   *William Butler Yeats (CP. 28), 1907,* 4th and final state, s., #45/50, full margins, foxed, (10-27-92, Phillips-London, #274), plate 6⅞ x 5 in., (175 x 127 mm.), etching and drypoint on laid (BP 990, DM 2402, FR 8149, Y 191,682).

BI   *Woman Gathering Sticks (C.D. 81),* s., t., #8/25 in ink in a different hand w/tone, light staining, other defects, est. BP 150/250, (10-27-92, Phillips-London, #276A), sheet 8¼ x 11⅛ in., (210 x 283 mm.), etching on Van Gelder Zonen.

JOHN, Augustus (after)

$336*   *Figures By A Rock,* sig., (01-21-93, Bonhams-Chelsea, #29), subject 14¼ x 18⅞ in., (36.2 x 47.9 cm.), lithograph on laid paper (BP 220, DM 534, FR 1807, Y 42,053).

JOHNS, Jasper   American b. 1930

$6050*   *#2 (F. 250; Gemini 741), 1976,* after Untitled 1975, s., d., i. AP, num. 14/15, Gemini G.E.L. blindstamps, full margins, creases, excell. cond., (09-19-92, Christie-E, #137, illus.), sheet 30⅛ x 29¾ in., (76.5 x 75.6 cm.), lithograph in colors on gray Rives Newsprint (BP 3480, DM 9060, FR 31,026, Y 753,800).

$3575*   *#3, After Untitled 1975 (F. 251, G. 742), 1976,* s., d., #59/60, blindstamp pub. Gemini G.E.L., very good cond.?, (10-28-92, Butterfield, #2991, illus.), 28¾ x 28⅝ in., (730 x 727 mm.), color lithograph on Rives newsprint colored paper (BP 2278, DM 5521, FR 18,747, Y 438,650).

$3300*   *#4, After Untitled 1975 (F. 252, G. 743), 1976,* s., d., annot. PP II, blindstamp pub. Gemini G.E.L., full margins, very good cond.?, (10-28-92, Butterfield, #2992, illus.), 28⅝ x 28⅝ in., (727 x 727 mm.), color lithograph on Rives newsprint colored paper (BP 2103, DM 5097, FR 17,305, Y 404,908).

$14,300*   *0 Through 9 (F. 62; S. 70), 1967,* s., d., #15/50, blindstamp, pub. ULAE, full margins, good cond., foxing, Gertrude Kasle Coll., (11-07-92, Sotheby-NY, #601, illus.), 12⅛ x 9½ in., (308 x 241 mm.), lithograph p. in colors on black Japan paper laid down on handmade English Chatham (BP 9349, DM 22,833, FR 77,172, Y 1,764,996).

$44,000*   *0 Through 9 (Field 4; Sparks 4), 1960,* s., d., #30/35, blindstamp, pub. ULAE, full margins, good cond., creases, foxing, (11-07-92, Sotheby-NY, #594, illus.), 24⅛ x 18⅞ in., (613 x 479 mm.), lithograph on Arches (BP 28,768, DM 70,254, FR 237,453, Y 5,430,758).

BI   *0 Through 9, (Segal 2), 1977-8,* s., d. '77, num. 9/60, pub. Gemini GEL, good cond., est. BP 2,5/3,000, (12-01-92, Christie-London, #614, illus.), L. 6⁷⁄₁₆ x 5¹⁄₁₆ in., (164 x 128 mm.), lithograph p. in three shades of brown, on grey La Paloma handmade paper.

$3575*   *0-9 (A Set Of Ten Numerals): #8 (F. 207), 1975,* s., d., #37/100, pub. Petersburg Press, full margins, very good cond.(?), (02-24-93, Butterfield, #3063, illus.), 2½ x 2⅛ in., (63.6 x 54.1 mm.), etching w/lift-ground aquatint, soft-ground & open bite on Barcham Green handmade w/ watermark (BP 2493, DM 5804, FR 19,675, Y 419,502).

BI   *0-9 (F. 206), 1975,* s., d. #30/100, pub. Petersburg Press, full margins, good cond., tipped to mat, creases, est. $6/7,000, (05-15-93, Sotheby-NY, #1029, illus.), 4½ x 9¼ in., (11.4 x 23.5 cm.), etching and aquatint w/varnish stop-out printed from ten plates, on one sheet of Barcham Green handmade paper.

$77,000*   *0-9 (F. 27-36; S. 30-42), 1960-63,* complete suite, each s., d. '63, i. 'B/C', #10/10, blindstamp, pub. ULAE, full margins, good cond., (11-07-92, Sotheby-NY, #598, illus.), each sheet approx. 20⅛ x 15¾ in., (511 x 400 mm.), ten lithographs p. in gray on unbleached gray Angoumois a la main paper watermarked (BP 50,343, DM 122,944, FR 415,542, Y 9,503,826).

$3405*   *0-9 (Field 206), 1975,* s., 65/100, ed. Petersburg Press, (12-04-92, AB Stockholm, #7078), sh 16¹⁵⁄₁₆ x 13⁹⁄₁₆ in., (43 x 34.5 cm.), etching, torrnal (drypoint) and aquatint (BP 2184, DM 5423, FR 18,395, Y 425,094, SK 23,100).

$1201*   *Bent Blue (Field 143), 1971,* s., d., #25/240, pub. for portfolio Graphikmappe des SchweizerischenKunstvereins, 1975, good cond., (06-30-93, Sotheby-London, #854), sh 26 x 20⅛ in., (660 x 511 mm.), lithograph (BP 805, DM 2048, FR 6910, Y 128,683).

$39,600*   *Between The Clock And The Bed, 1989,* s., d., #18/32, blindstamp, pub. ULAE, full margins, good cond., (11-07-92, Sotheby-NY, #618, illus.), 19¾ x 34 in., (502 x 864 mm.), lithograph p. in colors on HMP paper custom watermarked (BP 25,891, DM 63,228, FR 213,708, Y 4,887,682).

$4400*   *Black And White Numerals: Figure 4 (F. 98; Gemini 91), 1968,* s., d., #4/70, blindstamp, pub. Gemini G.E.L., full margins, good cond., handling creases, soiling, pressure mark, (11-07-92, Sotheby-NY, #612, illus.), 27⅝ x 21¼ in., (702 x 540 mm.), lithograph p. in black and transparent gray (BP 2877, DM 7025, FR 23,745, Y 543,076).

$2645*   *Casts From Untitled: Leg (F. 187, Gemini 505), 1973-74,* s., d. '74, #17/50, blindstamp, pub. Gemini, G.E.L., full margins, good cond., (05-15-93, Sotheby-NY, #1028, illus.), 15¾ x 21⅜ in., (40 x 54.3 cm.), lithograph in colors on Laga Narcisse (BP 1720, DM 4254, FR 14,297, Y 293,205).

BI   *Cicada (S. 27; G. 923), 1981,* s., d., i. AP, #4/12, blindstamps, full margins, excellent cond., est. $20/25,000, (11-09-92, Christie-NY, #327, illus.), 35 x 26 in., (889 x 660 mm.), colored lithograph on wove.

$26,450*   *Cicada (Segal 18), 1979,* s., d., #11/100, blindstamp, pub. Simca Print Artists, Inc., full margins, good cond., (05-15-93, Sotheby-NY, #1032, illus.), 17½ x 13½ in., (44.5 x 34.3 cm.), silkscreen in colors on Kurotani Hosho paper (BP 17,198, DM 42,545, FR 142,973, Y 2,932,047).

BI   *Color Numerals: Figure 6 (Fiedl 110; Gemini 122), 1968-69,* crayon s., d., #3/40, blindstamp, pub. Gemini G.E.L., full margins, good cond., est. BP 8/10,000, (12-03-92, Sotheby-London, #752, illus.), 27½ x 21⅛ in., (700 x 535 mm.), lithograph in colors on Japanese Arjomari.

$37,400*   *Corpse And Mirror (F. 211), 1976,* s., d., #14/65, blindstamp, full margins, staining, excellent cond., (11-09-92, Christie-NY, #323, illus.), 42¼ x 53 in., (107.3 x 134.6 cm.), colored screenprint on Nishinouchi Kizuki Kozo (BP 24,727, DM 59,706, FR 201,726, Y 4,641,350).

BI   *Corpse And Mirror (Screenprint) (F. 211), 1976,* s., d., #58/65, pub. by artist and Simca Print Artists, full margins,excell. cond., est. $40/50,000, (11-07-92, Sotheby-NY, #617, illus.), 36⅝ x 47 in., (93 x 119.4 cm.), silkscreen p. in colors on ivory Nishinouchi Kizuki Kozo.

$42,550*   *Corpse And Mirror (Screenprint) (F. 211), 1976,* s., d., #58/65, pub. artist and Simca Print Artists, full margins, excell. cond., (05-15-93, Sotheby-NY, #1030, illus.), 36⅝ x 47 in., (93 x 119.4 cm.), silkscreen in colors on ivory Nishinouchi Kizuki Kozo paper (BP 27,666, DM 68,441, FR 230,000, Y 4,716,772).

$358*   *Cup 2 Picasso (F. 168, ULAE II3), 1973,* s. in stone, d., pub. special issue on American art in XXe Siecle, June 1973, prepared by ULAE, margins, good cond. (?), (02-24-93, Butterfield, #3227), 11 x 9¼ in., (279 x 235 mm.), lithograph in colors on wove (BP 250, DM 581, FR 1970, Y 42,009).

BI   *Decoy II (F. 169), 1971-73,* s., d., i. 2/2 Printer's Proof, blindstamp, pub. ULAE, full margins, good cond.. est. $90/110,000, (05-15-93, Sotheby-NY, #1025, illus.), sheet 41¼ x 29½ in., (104.8 x 74.9 cm.), lithograph in colors on BFK Rives.

$17,250* *Device (Field 12), 1962,* s., d., i. H.C. 6/8, blindstamp, pub. ULAE, full margins, good cond., discoloration recto, (05-15-93, Sotheby-NY, #1021, illus.), 29 x 19¾ in., (73.7 x 50.2 cm.), lithograph in brownish-black on English Crispbrook handmade paper (BP 11,216, DM 27,747, FR 93,243, Y 1,912,205).

$16,500* *The Dutch Wives (S. 10), 1978,* s., d., #14/53, blindstamp, full margins, excellent cond., (11-09-92, Christie-NY, #325, illus.), 43¼ x 56¼ in., (109.9 x 142.9 cm.), colored screenprint on Japanese (BP 10,909, DM 26,341, FR 88,997, Y 2,047,655).

$2760* *Embossed Alphabet (F. 116, G. 127), 1968-69,* s., d. 69, #33/70, Gemini G.E.L. blindstamps, full margins, surface soiling, creases, excell. cond., (05-11-93, Christie-NY, #459), sheet 29¾ x 37 in., (756 x 940 mm.), embossing on Arches (BP 1762, DM 4348, FR 14,650, Y 303,597).

BI *Embossed Alphabet (F. 116; G. 127), 1968-9,* s., d. 69, #33/70, blindstamps, full margins, soiling, crease, excellent cond., est. $4/4,500, (11-09-92, Christie-NY, #320, illus.), 29¾ x 37 in., (756 x 940 mm.), embossing on Arches.

$5720* *Evion (F. 160; G. 346), 1971-72,* s., d. '72, #32/64, blindstamp, pub. Gemini, G.E.L., good cond., (11-07-92, Sotheby-NY, #606, illus.), sheet 43½ x 29¼ in., (110.5 x 74.3 cm.), lithograph p. in colors on Angoumois a la main (BP 3740, DM 9133, FR 30,869, Y 705,999).

BI *Figure 4 (F. 98; Gemini 91), 1968,* from Black and White Numerals, s., d., #70/70, blindstamps, full margins, stains, crease, surface soiling, mat staining, est. $5/7,000, (11-09-92, Christie-NY, #319), 37 x 30 in., (940 x 762 mm.), gray and black lithograph on wove.

$5280* *Figure 4 (Field 67; Sparks 74), 1967,* s., d., #9/12, blindstamps, full margins, excellent cond., Gertrude Kasle Coll., (11-09-92, Christie-NY, #317, illus.), 17⅛ x 13⅜ in., (435 x 340 mm.), open-bite etching on Douglas Howell handmade (BP 3491, DM 8429, FR 28,479, Y 655,249).

$16,100* *Figure 8 (F. 112, Gemini 124), 1968-69,* from Color Numerals, s., d. 69, i. AP VII, Gemini G.E.L. blindstamps, full margins, excell. cond., (05-11-93, Christie-NY, #458, illus.), sheet 38⅛ x 31¼ in., (968 x 794 mm.), color lithograph on Arjomari (BP 10,278, DM 25,362, FR 85,456, Y 1,770,982).

BI *Fizzles (F. 215-248),* complete book, s. by artist and author, #37/250, p. Aldo Crommelynck,pub. Petersburg Press, 1975-76, pristine cond., off-setting, est. BP 12/14,000, (06-30-93, Sotheby-London, #853, illus.), eacg page c. 13⅛ x 9⅞ in., (333 x 251 mm.), 31 etchings in black, 2 colored, and 1 color lithograph, on Richard de Bas handmade.

$17,600* *Fizzles (Foirades) (F. 215-48), 1976: Set Of Thirty-Three,* Samuel Beckett, Petersburg Press, Inc., watermark, s. by artist and author, copy 160 of 250, (11-09-92, Christie-NY, #324, illus.), 13⅝/16 x 10⁷/16 in., (345 x 265 mm.), etchings and aquatints on Richard de Bas (BP 11,636, DM 28,097, FR 94,930, Y 2,184,165).

$29,700* *Flags (F. 70; S. 76), 1967-68,* pen s., d., #36/43, blindstamp, pub. ULAE, good cond., Gertrude KasleColl., (11-07-92, Sotheby-NY, #600, illus.), sheet 34 x 25⅝ in., (864 x 651 mm.), lithograph p. in colors on handmade Indian (BP 19,418, DM 47,421, FR 160,281, Y 3,665,762).

$6670* *Fragment-According To What-Bent "Blue" (F. 138, G. 286), 1971,* 2nd state, s., d., #10/66, Gemini G.E.L. blindstamps, excell. cond., (05-11-93, Christie-NY, #461, illus.), sheet 25⅝ x 28¾ in., (651 x 730 mm.), color lithograph on Arches (BP 4258, DM 10,507, FR 35,403, Y 733,693).

$4370* *Fragment-According To What-Bent "U" (F. 140, G. 291), 1971,* s., d., #20/69, Gemini G.E.L. blindstamps, excell. cond., (05-11-93, Christie-NY, #463), sheet 25⅛ x 20⅛ in., (638 x 511 mm.), color lithograph on Arches (BP 2790, DM 6884, FR 23,195, Y 480,695).

$1840* *Fragment-According To What-Bent Stencil (F. 141, G. 289), 1971,* s., d., #20/79, Gemini G.E.L. blindstamps, excell. cond., (05-11-93, Christie-NY, #464), sheet 27½ x 20 in., (699 x 508 mm.), color lithograph on Arches (BP 1175, DM 2899, FR 9766, Y 202,398).

$4025* *Fragment-According To What-Coathanger And Spoon (F. 142, G. 290), 1971,* s., d., #10/76, Gemini G.E.L. blindstamps, excell. cond., (05-11-93, Christie-NY, #465), sheet 34½ x 25½ in., (876 x 648 mm.), color lithograph on Arches (BP 2569, DM 6341, FR 21,364, Y 442,746).

$4600* *Fragment-According To What-Hinged Canvas (F. 139, G. 288), 1971,* s., d. 20/69, Gemini G.E.L. blindstamps, excell. cond., (05-11-93, Christie-NY, #462), sheet 36 x 29¾ in., (914 x 756 mm.), color lithograph on Arches (BP 2936, DM 7246, FR 24,416, Y 505,995).

$3220* *Fragment-According To What-Leg And Chair (F. 136, G. 287), 1971,* s., d., #10/68, Gemini G.E.L. blindstamps, excell. cond., (05-11-93, Christie-NY, #460, illus.), sheet 35½ x 29¾ in., (902 x 756 mm.), color lithograph on Arches (BP 2056, DM 5072, FR 17,091, Y 354,196).

$26,400* *Gray Alphabets (F. 114; G. 97), 1968,* s., d., #20/59, blindstamp, pub. Gemini, G.E.L., full margins, good cond., soiling, (11-07-92, Sotheby-NY, #603, illus.), 50¾ x 34½ in., (128.9 x 87.6 cm.), lithograph p. in grays on Special Rives (BP 17,261, DM 42,152, FR 142,472, Y 3,258,455).

BI *Harvey Gantt Portfolio: Untitled, 1990,* s., d., #216/250, blindstamp publisher, Gemini G.E.L., full margins,very good cond., rubbed, est. $2/3,000, (05-19-93, Butterfield, #2204, illus.), 6¹/16 x 4¹³/16 in., (154 x 122 mm.), lithograph in colors on Arches 88.

$7700* *Land's End (G. 831), 1979,* s., d., #55/70, blindstamp pub. Gemini G.E.L., full margins, very good cond., (10-28-92, Butterfield, #2993, illus.), sheet 52 x 36 in., (132.1 x 91.4 cm.), lithograph in black on Kurotani paper (BP 4906, DM 11,892, FR 40,378, Y 944,785).

BI *Land's End II (S. 19), 1979,* s., d., i. AP, #10/11, pub. Petersburg Press, full margins, crease, time staining, excellent cond., est. $6/7,000, (11-09-92, Christie-NY, #326, illus.), 41¾ x 29¾ in., (106 x 75.6 cm.), etching and aquatint on Arches.

$3680* *Land's End II (Se. 19), 1979,* s., d., i. AP, #10/11, pub. Petersburg Press, full margins, crease, time staining, excell. cond., (05-11-93, Christie-NY, #470, illus.), sheet 41¾ x 29¾ in., (106 x 75.6 cm.), etching and aquatint on Arches (BP 2349, DM 5797, FR 19,533, Y 404,796).

$3850* *Light Bulb (F. 128; S. 105), 1970,* s., d., #4/40, blindstamp, pub. ULAE, full margins, good cond., Gertrude Kasle Coll., (11-07-92, Sotheby-NY, #604, illus.), 10⅝ x 10⅜ in., (270 x 264 mm.), lithograph p. in black and silver on Fred Siegenthaler handmade (BP 2517, DM 6147, FR 20,777, Y 475,191).

$1540* *Moratorium, 1969,* s., #193/300, pub. by artist, margins, good cond.?, (10-28-92, Butterfield, #2990), 17⅛ x 26 in., (435 x 660 mm.), color offset lithograph on wove (BP 981, DM 2378, FR 8076, Y 188,957).

$1100* *Moratorium, 1969,* s., num. 98/300, pub. by artist, margins, mat staining, very good cond., (09-19-92, Christie-E, #134), sheet 20½ x 28⅝ in., (52.1 x 72.7 cm.), offset lithograph in colors on wove (BP 633, DM 1647, FR 5641, Y 137,055).

$16,100* *Numbers (F. 61, Sparks 69), 1967,* s., d., #7/35, blindstamp, pub. ULAE, full margins, good cond., (05-15-93, Sotheby-NY, #1023, illus.), 22¼ x 19¾ in., (56.5 x 50.2 cm.), lithograph on Angoumois handmade paper (BP 10,468, DM 25,897, FR 87,027, Y 1,784,725).

$30,800* *Painting With Two Balls I (F. 8; S. 8), 1962,* s., #25/39, blindstamp, pub. ULAE, full margins, good cond., (11-07-92, Sotheby-NY, #595, illus.), 20⅞ x 16½ in., (530 x 419 mm.), lithograph p. in colors on Kochi Japan (BP 20,137, DM 49,178, FR 166,217, Y 3,801,530).

$17,600* *Periscope I (Se. 14; G. 840), 1979,* s., d., #45/65, blindstamp, pub. Gemini G.E.L., good cond., (11-07-92, Sotheby-NY, #616, illus.), sheet 50¼ x 36⅜ in., (127.6 x 92.4 cm.), lithograph p. in colors on Kurotani (BP 11,507, DM 28,102, FR 94,981, Y 2,172,303).

BI *Periscope, 1981,* s., d., #66/88, pub. Petersburg Press, full margins, scuffs in image, nicks, excellent cond., est. $12/16,000, (11-09-92, Christie-NY, #328, illus.), 41½ x 29½ in., (105.4 x 74.9 cm.), etching and aquatint in colors on tan BFK Rives.

$11,000* *Pinion (F. 49; S. 58), 1963-66,* s., d., #5/36, blindstamp, pub. ULAE, full margins, good cond., crease, Gertrude Kasle Coll., (11-07-92, Sotheby-NY, #596, illus.), 38½ x

24¼ in., (978 x 616 mm.), lithograph p. in colors on handmade Italia (BP 7192, DM 17,563, FR 59,363, Y 1,357,689).

$468* *"Poems"*, copy No. 5 in edit. 326, pub. Arion Press, 1985, s. J. Johns, (12-12-92, Wolf, #39, illus.), etching (BP 300, DM 737, FR 2527, Y 57,914).

BI *Recent Still Life (F. 50), 1965-66,* s., d., #66/100, blindstamp pub. ULAE, full margins, very good cond.?, est. $3/4,000, (10-28-92, Butterfield, #2989, illus.), 35 x 20 in., (889 x 508 mm.), lithograph in grey w/black text on wove.

$2475* *Recent Still Life (F. 50, ULAE 59), 1965-66,* s., d., num. 66/100, pub. Rhode Island School of Design, blindstamp ULAE, full margins, apparently very good cond., (02-24-93, Butterfield, #3062), 35 x 20 in., (889 x 508 mm.), lithograph in gray w/black text on wove (BP 1726, DM 4018, FR 13,621, Y 290,425).

BI *Samuel Beckett, Fizzles (Foirades), London, New York, Petersburg Press, Inc. 1976 (F. 215-48): Thirty-Three,* watermark, s. by artist and author, copy 102 of 250, offsetting, creases, excell. cond., est. $18/22,000, (05-11-93, Christie-NY, #467, illus.), 13⁹⁄₁₆ x 10⁷⁄₁₆ in., (345 x 265 mm.), etching and aquatint, in- and hors-texte, including 2 double pages in colors on Richard de Bas.

$6800* *Savarin (Sp. 129), 1977-81,* s., d., #24/60, blindstamp, pub. ULAE, full margins, good cond., skinned spot, (05-15-93, Sotheby-NY, #1034, illus.), 39¾ x 29⅜ in., (101 x 74.6 cm.), lithograph in colors on BFK Rives (BP 4421, DM 10,938, FR 36,757, Y 753,797).

$6600* *Savarin 1 (Cookie) (Segal 5; S. 121), 1978,* s., d., #8/42, blindstamp, pub. ULAE, full margins, good cond., Gertrude Kasle Coll., (11-07-92, Sotheby-NY, #607, illus.), 15⅜ x 11 in., (391 x 279 mm.), lithograph p. in grays and black on Auvergne, Richard de Bas (BP 4315, DM 10,538, FR 35,618, Y 814,614).

$4950* *Savarin 2 (Wash And Line) (Se. 6; S. 122), 1978,* s., d., #8/42, blindstamp, pub. ULAE, full margins, good cond., Gertrude Kasle Coll., (11-07-92, Sotheby-NY, #608, illus.), 18½ x 13¼ in., (470 x 337 mm.), lithograph p. in gray and black on Auvergne, Richard de Bas (BP 3236, DM 7904, FR 26,713, Y 610,960).

$15,400* *Savarin 3 (Red) (Se. 7; S. 123), 1978,* s., d., #8/40, blindstamp, pub. ULAE, full margins, good cond., skinned spot, Gertrude Kasle Coll., (11-07-92, Sotheby-NY, #609, illus.), 21¼ x 14⅛ in., (540 x 359 mm.), lithograph p. in pink and red (rosso) on Auvergne, Richard de Bas (BP 10,069, DM 24,589, FR 83,108, Y 1,900,765).

$7700* *Savarin 4 (Oval) (Se. 8; S. 124), 1978,* s., d., #8/42, blindstamp, pub. ULAE, full margins, good cond., Gertrude Kasle Coll., (11-07-92, Sotheby-NY, #610, illus.), 16½ x 12 in., (419 x 305 mm.), lithograph p. in gray and black on Auvergne, Richard de Bas (BP 5034, DM 12,294, FR 41,554, Y 950,383).

$17,600* *Savarin 5 (Corpse And Mirror) (Se. 9; S. 125), 1978,* s., d., #8/42, blindstamp, pub. ULAE, full margins, good cond., Gertrude Kasle Coll., (11-07-92, Sotheby-NY, #611, illus.), 16½ x 13 in., (419 x 330 mm.), lithograph p. in colors on Auvergne, Richard de Bas (BP 11,507, DM 28,102, FR 94,981, Y 2,172,303).

$18,400* *Savarin 5, Corpse And Mirror (Segal 9, Sp. 125), 1978,* s., d., #11/42, ULAE blindstamp, full margins, excell. cond., (05-11-93, Christie-NY, #469, illus.), sheet 26 x 20 in., (660 x 508 mm.), color lithograph on Auvergne, Richard de Bas (BP 11,746, DM 28,986, FR 97,665, Y 2,023,980).

$4675* *Screen Piece (F. 146), 1972,* s., d., #38/67, pub. by artist and Simca Print Artists, blindstamp, full margins, good cond., (11-07-92, Sotheby-NY, #605, illus.), 31⅛ x 20⅛ in., (791 x 511 mm.), silkscreen p. in colors on BFK Rives (BP 3057, DM 7464, FR 25,229, Y 577,018).

$22,000* *The Seasons, 1989,* s., d., #36/59, blindstamp, pub. ULAE, full margins, good cond., (11-07-92, Sotheby-NY, #620, illus.), 38⅜ x 25½ in., (975 x 648 mm.), etching and aquating p. in tones of gray and black on Arches (BP 14,384, DM 35,127, FR 118,726, Y 2,715,379).

$39,600* *The Seasons, 1989,* s., d., #47/54, blindstamp, pub. ULAE, full margins, good cond., (11-07-92, Sotheby-NY, #619, illus.), 19⅛ x 51⅛ in., (48.6 x 129.9 cm.), etching and aquatint p. in tones of gray and black on Arches (BP 25,891, DM 63,228, FR 213,708, Y 4,887,682).

$20,700* *The Seasons, 1989,* s., d., #16/59, blindstamp, pub. ULAE, full margins, good cond., (05-15-93, Sotheby-NY, #1038, illus.), 38¼ x 25¼ in., (97.2 x 64.1 cm.), etching and aquatint in tones of gray and blacks on Arches (BP 13,459, DM 33,296, FR 111,892, Y 2,294,646).

$110* *Silver Cicada, 1982,* (11-12-92, Freemn/Fine Art, #98), 8¾ x 7¼ in., (22.2 x 18.4 cm.), lithograph (BP 72, DM 174, FR 588, Y 13,639).

$23,000* *Skin With O'Hara Poem (F. 48), 1963-65,* s., d., #30/30, blindstamp, pub. ULAE, full margins, very good cond., crease, ink mark showing through to recto, (05-15-93, Sotheby-NY, #1022, illus.), 20½ x 32⅝ in., (52.1 x 82.9 cm.), lithograph on KE Albanene Engineer Standard Form paper (BP 14,954, DM 36,995, FR 124,324, Y 2,549,606).

$20,900* *Souvenir (F. 127; S. 104), 1970,* s., d., i. 'AP 3/6', artist's proof, pub. blindstamp, ULAE, full margins, excell. cond., (11-07-92, Sotheby-NY, #602, illus.), 24⅛ x 17½ in., (613 x 445 mm.), lithograph p. in colors on handmade English (BP 13,665, DM 33,371, FR 112,790, Y 2,579,610).

BI *Souvenir (F. 156, G. 343), 1971-72,* s., d. 72, #40/63, Gemini G.E.L. blindstamps, full margins, excell. cond., est. $4/5,000, (05-11-93, Christie-NY, #466, illus.), sheet 38½ x 29⅛ in., (978 x 740 mm.), color lithograph on Angoumois a la main.

BI *Souvenir I (F. 156; G. 343), 1971-2,* s., d. 72, #40/63, blindstamps, full margins, excellent cond., est. $5/6,000, (11-09-92, Christie-NY, #321, illus.), 38½ x 29⅛ in., (978 x 740 mm.), colored lithograph on Angoumois a la main.

BI *Target (F. 135), 1971,* contained in Technics and Creativity: Gemini G.E.L., by Riva Castleman, est. $6/800, (02-24-93, Butterfield, #3226), 10½ x 8½ in., (267 x 216 mm.), offset lithograph w/collage of watercolor pads & paintbrush.

$75,900* *Target (F. 192), 1974,* s., d., #19/70, blindstamp, full margins, excellent cond., (11-09-92, Christie-NY, #322, illus.), 35 x 27⅜ in., (889 x 695 mm.), colored screenprint on J.B. Green (BP 50,182, DM 121,169, FR 409,385, Y 9,419,211).

$8625* *Target (Field 63, Sparks 71), 1967,* s., d., #12/28, ULAE blindstamp, full margins, colors faded, pressure marks, printer's ink, surface soiling, creases, good cond., (05-11-93, Christie-NY, #457, illus.), sheet 23 x 23 in., (584 x 584 mm.), color lithograph on J. Whatman 1956 (BP 5506, DM 13,587, FR 45,780, Y 948,741).

$8625* *Target With Four Faces (F. 92), 1968,* s., pen, d., #96/100, pub. by artist for Merce Cunningham Dance Company, p. Aetna Printing Company, full margins, good cond.?, creases, buckling, (05-19-93, Butterfield, #2203, illus.), sh 41 x 29½ in., (104.1 x 74.9 cm.), silkscreen in colors on Rives (BP 5599, DM 14,020, FR 47,234, Y 954,832).

$13,200* *Targets (F. 69; S. 75), 1967-68,* s., d., #41/42, blindstamp, pub. ULAE, good cond., (11-07-92, Sotheby-NY, #599, illus.), sheet 34½ x 25¾ in., (876 x 654 mm.), lithograph p. in colors on handmade Indian (BP 8630, DM 21,076, FR 71,236, Y 1,629,227).

$11,000* *Targets (F. 69; S. 75), 1967-8,* s., d., #12/42, blindstamp, colors slightly faded, foxmark, very good cond., (11-09-92, Christie-NY, #318, illus.), 34½ x 26¼ in., (876 x 667 mm.), colored lithograph on East Indian handmade (BP 7273, DM 17,561, FR 59,331, Y 1,365,103).

$440* *Technics And Creativity: Gemini G.E.L., Los Angeles, Gemini G.E.L. And The Museum Of Modern Art. 1971 (F. 135),* photographic sig., softbound catalogue, full sheets, excell. cond., offset lithograph glued to front cover, orig. white plastic cover/box w/minor soiling, (09-19-92, Christie-E, #135), 10⅝ x 8⅞ in., (270 x 225 mm.), offset lithograph in grey and black w/collage of red, yellow and blue watercolor pads and paintbrush on wove board (BP 253, DM 659, FR 2256, Y 54,822).

$4950* *Two Flags (Se. 24; G. 914), 1980,* s., d., #27/45, blindstamp, pub. Gemini G.E.L., full margins, good cond., paper tone, attenuated, (11-07-92, Sotheby-NY, #614), 39⅜ x 30⅛ in., (100 x 76.5 cm.), lithograph on Ivory Nishinouchi Kizuki (BP 3236, DM 7904, FR 26,713, Y 610,960).

$431* *Untitled (Catalogue Cover) (F.260), 1977,* pub. Brooke Alexander, complete cover, fold, good cond., tear, split,-time staining, (05-19-93, Butterfield, #2206), 9½ x 9⅜ in., (241 x 238 mm.), silkscreen in colors on Pataphar printing parchment (BP 280, DM 701, FR 2360, Y 47,714).

$37,950* *Untitled (F. 258), 1977,* s., d., #34/53, blindstamp, pub. ULAE, full margins, good cond., (05-15-93, Sotheby-NY, #1031, illus.), 24 x 37 in., (61 x 94 cm.), lithograph in colors on J.B. Green paper (BP 24,675, DM 61,042, FR 205,135, Y 4,206,851).

$660* *Untitled (F. 260), 1977,* catalog cover, pub. Brooke Alexander, full cover, folded as issued, orig. catalog, crease, pale offsetting, very good cond., (09-19-92, Christie-E, #138), borderline 9½ x 9¼ in., (24.1 x 23.5 cm.), screenprint in colors on Pataphar printing parchment (BP 380, DM 988, FR 3385, Y 82,233).

$4830* *Untitled (F. 260), 1977,* s., d., #85/130, Simca Print Artists blindstamp, full margins, repaired tear, paper losses, stains, excell. cond., (05-11-93, Christie-NY, #468, illus.), sheet 24 x 19 in., (610 x 483 mm.), color screenprint on Rives Moulin du Gue (BP 3083, DM 7609, FR 25,637, Y 531,295).

$6325* *Untitled (Ruler And Fork) II (F. 124, Sp. 101), 1969,* s., d., #8/9, blindstamp, pub. ULAE, full margins, good cond., foxing, Gertrude Kasle Coll., (05-15-93, Sotheby-NY, #1026, illus.), 29 x 19⅞ in., (73.7 x 50.5 cm.), etching and aquatint in gray on Barcham Green (BP 4112, DM 10,174, FR 34,189, Y 701,142).

$6900* *Untitled (Ruler) II (F. 126, Sp. 102), 1969,* s., d., #7/15, blindstamp, pub. ULAE, full margins, good cond., foxing, Gertrude Kasle Coll., (05-15-93, Sotheby-NY, #1027, illus.), 29 x 19¾ in., (73.7 x 50.2 cm.), etching and aquatint on Barcham Green paper (BP 4486, DM 11,099, FR 37,297, Y 764,882).

$3738* *Untitled (Shit) (Field 145; Gemini 293), 1971,* s., d., #8/20, blindstamp of pub., Gemini, G.E.L., full sheet, good cond., (02-11-93, Sotheby-NY, #358, illus.), sheet 18½ x 24⁷⁄₁₆ in., (470 x 620 mm.), colored silkscreen on handmade Waterleaf (BP 2638, DM 6192, FR 20,953, Y 450,633).

BI *Untitled II (Flagstones), 1976,* s., d., #AP x/x, p. Crommelynck, pub. Petersburg Press, full margins,good cond., creases, est. BP 2,5/3,500, (12-03-92, Sotheby-London, #751, illus.), 13 x 19¼ in., (330 x 490 mm.), aquatint in colors on Richard de Bas Auvergne a la main.

$2298* *Untitled, 1981,* s., 49/78, (05-12-93, AB Stockholm, #7028, illus.), approx. 16⁵⁄₁₆ x 12¹⁵⁄₁₆ in., (41.5 x 33 cm.), etching and aquatint (BP 1500, DM 3708, FR 12,489, Y 256,559, SK 17,050).

$4600* *Untitled, 1981,* s., d., #25/78, pub. Petersburg Press, full margins, good cond., crease, pressure mark, (05-15-93, Sotheby-NY, #1036, illus.), each plate 3⅜ x 2⅜ in., (8.6 x 6 cm.), etching and aquatint in colors from three plates, on one sheet of paper (BP 2991, DM 7399, FR 24,865, Y 509,921).

BI *Untitled, 1988,* s., d., i. AP, #7/8, pub. by artist, full margins, excellent cond., est. $12/15,000, (11-09-92, Christie-NY, #329, illus.), 29¾ x 22½ in., (756 x 572 mm.), colored carborundum etching on Somerset.

$33,000* *Untitled, 1988,* s., d., i. H.C., #8/9, pub. by artist, full margins, excellent cond., (11-09-92, Christie-NY, #330, illus.), 35½ x 49½ in., (90.2 x 125.7 cm.), colored carborundum etching on wove (BP 21,818, DM 52,682, FR 177,994, Y 4,095,309).

$295* *Untitled, Silver Cicada, 1982,* (11-13-92, Koller, #5356), 9¹⁄₁₆ x 7½ in., (23 x 19 cm.), lithograph on wove (BP 191, DM 463, FR 1562, Y 36,614, SF 417).

$1760* *Untitled, Skull, (F. 172), 1973,* from Reality and Paradoxes, NY, Multiples, Inc., s., d., num. 37/100, full sheet, dark spot, image scuffing, surface soiling, skinned patch, (09-19-92, Christie-E, #136, illus.), sheet 23³⁄₁₆ x 31¼ in., (58.9 x 79.4 cm.), screenprint in colors on J.B. Green (BP 1012, DM 2636, FR 9026, Y 219,287).

$1840* *Untitled-Red, 1981,* s., d., #8/25, pub. Petersburg Press, full margins, good cond., (02-11-93, Sotheby-NY, #359), 3¼ x 2⅜ in., (82 x 60 mm.), etching and aquatint (BP 1298, DM 3048, FR 10,314, Y 221,820).

$26,450* *Usuyuki (S. 26), 1980,* s., d., #24/57, blindstamp, pub. ULAE, full margins, good cond., (05-15-93, Sotheby-NY, #1033, illus.), 45⅝ x 14⅛ in., (115.9 x 35.9 cm.), lithograph in colors on BFK Rives (BP 17,198, DM 42,545, FR 142,973, Y 2,932,047).

$12,100* *Usuyuki (Se. 16), 1979,* s., d., #38/49, blindstamp, pub. ULAE, full margins, good cond., (11-07-92, Sotheby-NY, #615, illus.), 27½ x 44¼ in., (69.9 x 112.4 cm.), lithograph p. in colors on Arches (BP 7911, DM 19,320, FR 65,300, Y 1,493,458).

$20,700* *Usuyuki (Se. 25), 1980,* s., d., #68/90, Simca Print Artists blindstamp, full margins, excell. cond., (05-11-93, Christie-NY, #471, illus.), sheet 51¾ x 19¾ in., (131.4 x 50.2 cm.), color screenprint on Japan (BP 13,214, DM 32,609, FR 109,873, Y 2,276,977).

BI *Ventriloquist,* s., d., #34/70, blindstamp, pub. ULAE, full margins, good cond., est.$12/15,000, (11-07-92, Sotheby-NY, #613, illus.), 32¼ x 22 in., (819 x 559 mm.), lithograph on J. Whatman.

$63,000* *Voice II, 1982: Three,* s., annot. A/C, B/C, C/C, #25/54, blindstamp, pub. ULAE, full margins, good cond., (05-15-93, Sotheby-NY, #1035, illus.), 35⅞ x 24¼ in., (91.1 x 61.6 cm.), lithograph in colors on three sheets of Japanese Hanga paper (BP 40,962, DM 101,335, FR 340,541, Y 6,983,705).

BI *Wallace Stevens, Poems, 1985,* book, s., t. page and just., num. 265, pub. Arion Press, good cond.,bound, est. BP 2/2,500, (12-03-92, Sotheby-London, #753, illus.), etching w/aquatint on English mould-made T. Edmonds.

$20,900* *Watchman (F. 60), 1967,* s., d., i. 'Artists Proof 5/7', blindstamp, pub. ULAE, good cond., soiling, (11-07-92, Sotheby-NY, #597, illus.), sheet 36¼ x 24¼ in., (921 x 616 mm.), lithograph p. in colors on unbleached handmade Angoumois a la main (BP 13,665, DM 33,371, FR 112,790, Y 2,579,610).

$4600* *Winter, 1986-89,* s., d., #16/34, blindstamp, pub. ULAE, full margins, good cond., (05-15-93, Sotheby-NY, #1037, illus.), 9½ x 6⅜ in., (24.1 x 16.2 cm.), lithograph (BP 2991, DM 7399, FR 24,865, Y 509,921).

JOHNSON, Andrew

$2663* *Airmen Prefer Shell, 1930,* p. Chorley & Pickersgill, ref. #264, cond. 2, area missing right sheet edge, (10-13-92, Phillips-London, #88, illus.), 30¹⁄₁₆ x 44⅞ in., (76.3 x 114 cm.), color lithograph (BP 1551, DM 3901, FR 13,255, Y 322,905).

JOHNSON, C. Raymond

$110* *"Chicago Street Scene",* s., good cond.?, (03-28-93, Bakker, #191), 9¾ x 8 in., (24.8 x 20.3 cm.), etching (BP 74, DM 179, FR 610, Y 12,803).

JOHNSON, Clifton American 1865-1940

$2860* *George Washington Carver And Student, Tuskegee, Alabama, c. 1900,* credit, t., descrip. legend in pencil, prov., unique, (10-13-92, Christie-NY, #12, illus.), 6½ x 4⅝ in., (16.5 x 11.7 cm.), photograph, gelatin silver print (BP 1666, DM 4190, FR 14,236, Y 346,793).

$302* *Grandma Does The Churning, c. 1905,* notations, (10-14-92, Swann, #484, illus.), 10¾ x 7¾ in., (27.3 x 19.7 cm.), photograph, toned silver print (BP 177, DM 442, FR 1499, Y 36,597).

BI *Shaker Meeting House, New Lebanon, c. 1910,* t. verso of detached mount, est. $1/1,500, (04-08-93, Christie-NY, #57, illus.), 7⅛ x 5 in., (18.1 x 12.7 cm.), photograph, gelatin silver print.

JOHNSON, George

$13,200* *California Outdoor Scene, c. 1851,* sealed in leather case, (10-14-92, Swann, #129, illus.), photograph, half-plate daguerreotype (BP 7748, DM 19,318, FR 65,509, Y 1,599,612).

JOHNSON, Michael

$1540* *"Footbridge",* 1983/1985, s., t., d., edit. #19/250, photog. stamp, Dixon Collection, (11-16-92, Butterfield,

#6025, illus.), 33 9/16 x 24 9/16 in., (852.4 x 623.4 mm.), photograph, gelatin silver print (BP 1014, DM 2455, FR 8271, Y 191,518).

JOHNSON, Michael American 20th cent.

$33* *Church Door,* s., #12/77, (05-16-93, Hindman, #378), 9 x 12 in., photograph, silver print (BP 22, DM 53, FR 179, Y 3675).

JOHNSTON, Alfred Cheney 1884-1971

BI *Dorothy Fenron, c. 1925,* s., est. $1,2/1,800, (04-08-93, Christie-NY, #232, illus.), 12⅝ x 9¾ in., (32.1 x 24.8 cm.), photograph, gelatin silver print.

BI *Fanny Brice, c. 1918,* s. by photog., est. $1,5/2,500, (04-06-93, Sotheby-NY, #77, illus.), 12⅞ x 10 in., photograph, silver print on tissue mounted on deckle-edged Japan vellum.

BI *Gilda Gray, 1920s,* s. by photog.; s. and i. by photog., est. $1,5/2,500, (04-06-93, Sotheby-NY, #78, illus.), 13x9⅝ in., photograph, silver print on Old Masters Buff.

$1650* *Gloria Swanson, c. 1922,* t., (10-13-92, Christie-NY, #246, illus.), 12¾ x 9¾ in., (32.4 x 24.8 cm.), photograph, gelatin silver print (BP 961, DM 2417, FR 8213, Y 200,073).

$1980* *Hazel Forbes, Ziegfeld Girl, c. 1920,* s., t., (10-13-92, Christie-NY, #245, illus.), 13½ x 10⅜ in., (34.3 x 26.4 cm.), photograph, gelatin silver print (BP 1153, DM 2901, FR 9856, Y 240,087).

$880* *Jacqueline Schally,* photog.'s notations, handstamp, 1920s, (04-07-93, Swann, #492, illus.), 13¼ x 10⅜ in., photograph, silver print (BP 582, DM 1423, FR 4817, Y 99,977).

BI *Marion Davies, c. 1920,* credit stamp w/t., est. $1,2/1,800, (04-08-93, Christie-NY, #230, illus.), 13 x 10 in., (33 x 25.4 cm.), photograph, gelatin silver print.

$357* *New York City Buildings, c. 1927,* handstamp, (10-14-92, Swann, #485, illus.), 14 x 12 in., (35.6 x 30.5 cm.), photograph, silver print (BP 210, DM 522, FR 1772, Y 43,262).

$4830* *Norma Shearer, c. 1926,* credit stamp, t., (04-08-93, Christie-NY, #231, illus.), 12⅝ x 9 in., (32.1 x 22.9 cm.), photograph, gelatin silver print (BP 3167, DM 7759, FR 26,264, Y 548,116).

$1210* *Odalisques, c. 1920,* credit stamp, (10-13-92, Christie-NY, #247, illus.), photograph, gelatin silver print (BP 705, DM 1773, FR 6023, Y 146,720).

$1955* *"Peggy Shannon, Ziegfeld-Movie Star", 1920's,* s. by photog., (04-06-93, Sotheby-NY, #79, illus.), 13 x 9⅞ in., photograph, double-edged Japan vellum (BP 1291, DM 3150, FR 10,666, Y 222,970).

BI *Portrait Of Barbara Stanwyck,* handstamp, notations, 1920's, est. $7/1,000, (10-14-92, Swann, #486, illus.), 13½ x 10½ in., (34.3 x 26.7 cm.), photograph, silver print.

BI *Portrait Of John Barrymore,* handstamp, notations, 1920's, est. $7/1,000, (10-14-92, Swann, #487, illus.), 13½ x 10½ in., (34.3 x 26.7 cm.), photograph, toned silver print.

BI *Portrait Of Marion Bender,* photog.'s sig., 1920s, est. $700/1,000, (04-07-93, Swann, #493), 12½ x 9¼ in., photograph, toned silver print.

BI *Portrait Of Mary Pickford,* notations, 1920s, est. $800/1,200, (04-07-93, Swann, #494, illus.), 12¾ x 9¾ in., photograph, silver print.

$770* *Portrait Of Ziegfeld Girl Gladys Glad,* handstamp, 1920's, (10-14-92, Swann, #488, illus.), 13½ x 10½ in., (34.3 x 26.7 cm.), photograph, silver print (BP 452, DM 1127, FR 3821, Y 93,311).

$1320* *Ruth Etting, 1923,* mounted, s. by photog. in ink on mount, t., (10-15-92, Sotheby-NY, #126, illus.), 13 x 10⅛ in., (33 x 25.7 cm.), photograph, gelatin silver print (BP 808, DM 1965, FR 6663, Y 158,368).

BI *Study Of Legs,* double mounted, circular print, s. by photog. in ink, 1920s, est. $2/3,000, (10-15-92, Sotheby-NY, #127, illus.), photograph, gelatin silver print.

BI *Woman With Red Nails, c. 1930,* mounted, s. by photog. in ink, est. $3/5,000, (10-15-92, Sotheby-NY, #125, illus.), 7¼ x 6¼ in., (18.4 x 15.9 cm.), photograph, color carbro print.

JOHNSTON, Frank Hans Canadian 1888-1949

$86* *Shining Star,* "Greetings from Mr. and Mrs. Franz Johnston and Family", d. 1930 in plate, (06-07-93, Ritchie, #57, illus.), 8⅞ x 6 in., (22.5 x 15.3 cm.), color serigraph on card (BP 57, DM 139, FR 470, Y 9225, C$ 110).

$65* *Snow Covered Trees And Mountain Peak,* "The Season's Greetings from the Johnstons", d. 1929 in plate, (06-07-93, Ritchie, #56, illus.), 7 15/16 x 4¾ in., (20.3 x 12.1 cm.), color serigraph on card (BP 43, DM 105, FR 355, Y 6973, C$ 83).

JOHNSTON, John Dudley 1868-1955

BI *"Morning At Lezzeno, 1923", "Placid Avon's Stream, 1930" and "The Cart Shed, 1925": Three,* mounted on card, t., s., d., labels, each approx. 287 x 371mm, est. BP 3/500, (05-07-93, Sotheby-London, #165, illus.), photograph, chloro bromide print.

JOICHI, Hoshi

$605* *Milky Way (A),* s. Joichi Hoshi, artist's seal, d. '68, t., i. A.P., margins, good cond., folds along margins, (04-02-93, Weschler, #271, illus.), 10¾ x 15½ in., (27.3 x 39.4 cm.), wood engraving (BP 398, DM 972, FR 3302, Y 68,883).

$770* *Winter Grove,* s. Joichi Hoshi, d. '76, t., artist's seal, good cond.?, (04-02-93, Weschler, #270, illus.), 9½ x 9½ in., (24.1 x 24.1 cm.), wood engraving (BP 507, DM 1238, FR 4203, Y 87,669).

JOLIN, Einar 1890-1976

$746* *"5 Lithographs", 1957: Five,* s., 11/250, p. R. Jansson, (12-04-92, AB Stockholm, #7079), sh 21⅝ x 17 11/16 in., (55 x 45 cm.), lithograph (BP 479, DM 1188, FR 4030, Y 93,134, SK 5060).

$1438* *Einar Jolin, 1975-76,* portfolio, A.H. Grafik, 359/360, (05-12-93, AB Stockholm, #7030), 29 15/16 x 21¼ in., (76 x 54 cm.), color lithograph (BP 939, DM 2320, FR 7815, Y 160,545, SK 10,670).

JOLLY, Baron (after) French 19th cent.

$198* *Franklin At The Court Of France 1778,* by W.O. Geller, (09-20-92, Hindman, #675), 27¼ x 39½ in., (69.2 x 100.3 cm.), hand-colored engraving (BP 116, DM 294, FR 1005, Y 24,472).

JONAS, L.

$901* *PLM: Pougues Les Eaux, "A 3 Heures De Paris, Cure D'Air, Cure D'Eau Et De Repos", 1935,* p. Jules Simon, excell. cond., (01-23-93, Ribeyre/Baron, #165), 39⅜ x 24 in., (100 x 61 cm.), poster (BP 589, DM 1433, FR 4847, Y 112,766).

JONAS, Lucien Hector American/French 1880-1947

$55* *The Soul Of France: Four Portfolios,* (07-03-92, Sloan, #310), average 12 x 9 in., (30.5 x 22.9 cm.), twelve photogravures (BP 29, DM 83, FR 281, Y 6856).

JONCHEID, J.

$145* *Eden Voltaire Ouverture,* (01-31-93, Morelle/Marchan, #160), 34¼ x 48 1/16 in., (87 x 122 cm.), poster (BP 98, DM 234, FR 790, Y 18,089).

JONES, Allen British b. 1937

BI *Auffuhrung, 1982,* s., d., #28/75, est. DM 3,300-, (05-27-93, Lempertz, #825, illus.), 22 7/16 x 30⅛ in., (57 x 76.5 cm.), color lithograph on wove.

$707* *Bar, 1988,* s., d., #1/30, blindstamp, (06-12-93, Hauswedell/Nolt, #263), 39 3/16 x 27½ in., (99.6 x 69.8 cm.), lithograph on beige-brown BFK Rives (BP 463, DM 1151, FR 3868, Y 74,398).

$124* *Composition Aux Personnages, 1971,* s., d., #66/75, good cond., (03-31-93, Briest, #E173), 25 3/16 x 18⅞ in., (64 x 48 cm.), color lithograph on wove (BP 82, DM 199, FR 678, Y 14,259).

$597* *His Hers , 1966,* s., d., #1/20, good cond., staining, (12-03-92, Sotheby-London, #754, illus.), sheet 29½ x 22¼ in., (750 x 565 mm.), lithograph in colors on wove (BP 385, DM 939, FR 3205, Y 74,281).

BI *Memento, 1985,* #67/75, s., est. SF 1,5/1,800, 1080mm x 875mm, (04-21-93, Germann, #562), color lithograph.

BI *A New Perspective On Floors, 1966,* i., from the portfolio pub. Kelpra Press, very good cond., (10-27-92, Phillips-London, #205), image 21¼ x 18½ in., (540 x 470 mm.), lithograph in black, brown and grey on wove.

BI *Ohne Titel (Mutter Mit 2 Kindern), 1971,* pencil s., d., est. DM 1,000, (11-20-92, Lempertz, #630), sh 25¼ x 18⅞ in., (64.2 x 48 cm.), color lithograph on Velin.

$1463* *On The Beach,* s., d., num., (12-12-92, Wachholtz, #489, illus.), 25¹³⁄₁₆ x 37¹¹⁄₁₆ in., (65.5 x 95.8 cm.), color lithograph on copper print paper (BP 935, DM 2299, FR 7836, Y 180,997).

BI *Para Adultos, "Memento", "Table Talk" and "Party Time", 1985: Three,* from suite of 8, each s., d., num., good cond., est. BP 800/1,000, (06-30-93, Sotheby-London, #856), each sh c. 42⅞ x 34⅜ in., (108.9 x 87.3 cm.), color lithograph.

$1201* *Party Time, 1985,* s., d., #50/75, series para adultos, (06-12-93, Hauswedell/Nolt, #261), 42¹¹⁄₁₆ x 34⁷⁄₁₆ in., (108.5 x 87.5 cm.), color lithograph on thick wove in colors (BP 786, DM 1955, FR 6570, Y 126,381).

$948* *Party Time, 1985,* #67/75, s., 1080mm x 875mm, (04-21-93, Germann, #31, illus.), color lithograph (BP 615, DM 1515, FR 5124, Y 104,949, SF 1380).

$1027* *Party Time, 1985,* 67/75, s., 1080mm x 875mm, (06-24-93, Germann, #389, illus.), color lithograph (BP 676, DM 1665, FR 5612, Y 110,169, SF 1495).

$2749* *Shoe Box (Stunke 75-84), 1968: Seven,* London, Petersburg Press, 1968, s., d., num., (06-23-93, Kornfeld, #421), lithograph and embossed screenprint w/polished aluminum sculpture (BP 1868, DM 4651, FR 15,646, Y 299,488, SF 4140).

$1415* *Shoe Box, (Spiegel cat. 75), 1968,* Petersburg Press, s., num. 155/200, good cond., loose in sleeves in tray, sculpture w/ engraved sig. and num. 155/200, whole contained in box, screenprint in colors on inside of lid,s., num., t., defects, (12-01-92, Christie-London, #613), overall S. 15¾ x 12¹¹⁄₁₆ in., (400 x 323 mm.), mixed media works, set of 7 lithographs, screenprint in colors and sculpture, lithographs on BFK Rives (BP 935, DM 2255, FR 7686, Y 176,170).

BI *Shoes, 1968: Set Of Seven,* s., #73/200, est. FF 12/15,000, (11-16-92, Briest, #316, illus.), 13¾ x 10¼ in., (35 x 26 cm.), serigraph.

$866* *Three In One, 1971,* s., d., num., staubrandig, (11-28-92, Schoppmann, #605), 19⁵⁄₁₆ x 18⅛ in., (49 x 46 cm.), color serigraph on handmade board (BP 572, DM 1380, FR 4684, Y 107,778).

$707* *The Tree, 1988,* s., d., #42/60, portfolio Islands, (06-12-93, Hauswedell/Nolt, #262), 29½ x 41¹⁵⁄₁₆ in., (75 x 106.5 cm.), color lithograph on Arches (BP 463, DM 1151, FR 3868, Y 74,398).

BI *Untitled, 1971,* s., d., #4/75, full sheet p. to edges, good cond., est. Dfl. 800/1,200, (05-27-93, Sotheby-Amstrdm, #637), sh 25³⁄₁₆ x 18¹³⁄₁₆ in., (640 x 478 mm.), color lithograph on wove.

$993* *Untitled, 1988,* s., d., num., (06-05-93, Schoppmann, #899), 29½ x 41¾ in., (75 x 106 cm.), color lithograph on Arches wove (BP 654, DM 1610, FR 5426, Y 106,522).

$216* *Woman,* #4/75, s., d. 65, (10-15-92, Bonhams-Chelsea, #5), sheet 27½ x 22 in., (69.9 x 55.9 cm.), screenprint (BP 132, DM 322, FR 1090, Y 25,915).

JONES, Anthony Armstrong
$944* *Laurence Olivier As Archie Rice In "The Entertainer", 1959,* mounted on card, stamped photog.'s credit, 288 x 235mm, (05-07-93, Sotheby-London, #335, illus.), photograph, silver print (BP 598, DM 1492, FR 5029, Y 103,942).

JONES, Charles
$2906* *"Bean Longpod", c. 1900,* t., mono., 251 x 203mm, (05-07-93, Sotheby-London, #209, illus.), photograph, gelatin silver print (BP 1840, DM 4594, FR 15,482, Y 319,974).

$1180* *"Beans Ne Plus Ultra", c. 1900,* t., mono., 215 x 164mm, (05-07-93, Sotheby-London, #210, illus.), photograph, gelatin silver print (BP 747, DM 1866, FR 6287, Y 129,927).

$549* *"Oats White Winter", c. 1900,* t., mono. C.J., (10-29-92, Christie-London, #99, illus.), 9½ x 7½ in., (24.1 x 19.1 cm.), photograph, gelatin silver print mounted on card (BP 352, DM 845, FR 2865, Y 68,004).

$1816* *"Onion Ailsa Craig", c. 1900,* t., mono., 201 x 253mm, (05-07-93, Sotheby-London, #213, illus.), photograph, gelatin silver print (BP 1150, DM 2871, FR 9675, Y 199,956).

$1116* *"Parsnip Student", c. 1900,* mount i., (10-29-92, Christie-London, #98, illus.), 9⅞ x 7¾ in., (25.1 x 19.7 cm.), photograph, gelatin silver print mounted on card (BP 715, DM 1717, FR 5825, Y 138,239).

$1998* *"Parsnip Student", c. 1900,* t., mono., 201 x 255mm, (05-07-93, Sotheby-London, #212, illus.), photograph, gelatin silver print (BP 1265, DM 3159, FR 10,645, Y 219,996).

$1998* *"Potato Duke Of York", c. 1900,* t., mono., 202 x 254mm, (05-07-93, Sotheby-London, #214, illus.), photograph, gelatin silver print (BP 1265, DM 3159, FR 10,645, Y 219,996).

$618* *"Rammeya Caulteri (?)", c. 1900,* t., mono., 152 x 108mm, (05-07-93, Sotheby-London, #211, illus.), photograph, gelatin silver print (BP 391, DM 977, FR 3292, Y 68,047).

$1271* *"Turnip Snowball", c. 1900,* t., mono., 163 x 215mm, (05-07-93, Sotheby-London, #215, illus.), photograph, gelatin silver print (BP 805, DM 2009, FR 6771, Y 139,947).

JONES, Joe   American 1909-1963
$61* *Quiet Cove,* AAA, s., (02-12-93, DuMouchelle, #102), 14¼ x 20 in., (36.2 x 50.8 cm.), paintgraph (BP 43, DM 101, FR 342, Y 7356).

$25* *Reaching For The Sun,* s., (05-16-93, Hanzel, #466), 10½ x 14 in., (26.7 x 35.6 cm.), lithograph (BP 16, DM 40, FR 135, Y 2771).

$50* *Sailboats,* s., good cond., (10-31-92, Cleveland, #148), 11 x 14 in., (27.9 x 35.6 cm.), lithograph (BP 32, DM 77, FR 261, Y 6193).

JONES, John Lawrence
BI *Henson's Monsters From Labyrinth: Five, 1981,* pencil s., d., (c) stamp, est. BP 5/1,000, (12-17-92, Christie-S. Ken, #72, illus.), image, each approx. 15 x 15 in., (38.1 x 38.1 cm.), photograph, warm-toned gelatin silver print.

JONES, Philip Borne
$28* *Rudyard Kipling,* s., pub. Mendosa, (01-15-93, DuMouchelle, #200), 16 x 13 in., (40.6 x 33 cm.), etching (BP 18, DM 46, FR 155, Y 3530).

BI *Rudyard Kipling,* s., pub. Mendosa, est. $100/150, (11-13-92, DuMouchelle, #211), 16 x 13 in., (40.6 x 33 cm.), etching.

JONES, Pirkle
$770* *"Breaking Wave, Golden Gate, San Francisco" (Picturing California, p. 69), 1952,* s., i., (11-16-92, Butterfield, #6028, illus.), 9¼ x 13¼ in., (235.4 x 337.2 mm.), photograph, gelatin silver print (BP 507, DM 1228, FR 4135, Y 95,759).

$770* *Golden Gate Bridge From Baker's Beach, 1955,* s., i., (11-16-92, Butterfield, #6029, illus.), 9½ x 13⅜ in., (241.7 x 340.3 mm.), photograph, gelatin silver print (BP 507, DM 1228, FR 4135, Y 95,759).

$460* *"Leaf Study, Arboratium", 1948,* p.l., t., d., photog.'s stamp, (05-23-93, Butterfield, #3474, illus.), 9½ x 7¼ in., photograph, gelatin silver print (BP 300, DM 752, FR 2532, Y 50,846).

JONES, Reverend Calvert
$2361* *The Quayside, Naples, 1846,* 237 x 190mm, (05-07-93, Sotheby-London, #50), photograph, Talbotype (BP 1495, DM 3733, FR 12,579, Y 259,965).

JONES, Theodora Varnay
BI *Landscape-XI, 1986,* s., t., #2/50, blindstamp publisher, full margins, very good cond., est. $3/500, (05-19-93, Butterfield, #2207), 14⅞ x 17⅞ in., (378 x 454 mm.), etching and aquatint in colors on Rives BFK.

JONES, Tony Ray   1941-1972
$400* *Glyndebourne, 1967,* i. Printed by Tony Ray Jones, s. Anna Ray Jones, num. CRJ202 and V161, illus., 176 x 241mm, (05-07-93, Sotheby-London, #397), photograph, silver print (BP 253, DM 632, FR 2131, Y 44,043).

JONG, Jacqueline de

$96* *Eet Meer Aardappelen, 1975,* s., t., d., full margins, good cond., minor handling creases, minor soiling of lower margin, (05-27-93, Sotheby-Amstrdm, #427), 19 15/16 x 29 1/16 in., (507 x 738 mm.), colored lithograph on wove (BP 61, DM 154, FR 519, Y 10,292, G 173).

$141* *New Perfection Cookbook, 1975,* s., t., d., #150/190, full margins, good cond., minor handling creases, (05-27-93, Sotheby-Amstrdm, #428), 19 15/16 x 29 1/16 in., (507 x 738 mm.), colored lithograph on wove (BP 90, DM 226, FR 763, Y 15,116, G 253).

$141* *Les Pommes..., 1975,* s., t., d., #117/190, full margins, good cond., creases in lower margin, minor handling creases, (05-27-93, Sotheby-Amstrdm, #429), 19 15/16 x 29 1/16 in., (507 x 738 mm.), colored lithograph on wove (BP 90, DM 226, FR 763, Y 15,116, G 253).

JONGERT, Jacob

$3080* *Internationale Gastentoonstelling Amsterdam, 1912,* Paleis Voor Volksvlijt, A- cond., creasing, restoration, (08-06-92, Swann, #159, illus.), 57 x 28 in., (144.8 x 71.1 cm.), (BP 1609, DM 4551, FR 15,369, Y 392,857).

JONGH, Tinis de

$43* *Groot Constania, Capetown,* s., t., margins, (08-20-92, Bonhams-Chelsea, #159), plate 9 7/8 x 11 7/8 in., (25.1 x 30.2 cm.), etching on laid paper (BP 22, DM 62, FR 211, Y 5430).

JONGKIND, Johan Barthold Dutch 1819-1891

BI *Cahier De Six Eaux-Fortes, Vues De Hollande (Delteil 2-7), 1862:Le Canal (D. 2);Les Maisons Au Bord Du Canal (D. 3);La Nourrice (D. 4);Le Chemin de Halage (D. 5); La Barque Amarree (D. 6); & Les Deux Barques A Voile (D. 7),* lacking etched title piece, final states, large margins, good cond.,soiling, discoloration, fox marks, creases, est. $4/6,000, (11-05-92, Sotheby-NY, #204, illus.), sheets 14 3/4 x 21 1/8 in., (375 x 536 mm.), set of six etchings w/tone on laid w/watermarks.

$908* *Demolition De La Rue Des Francs-Bourgeois Saint-Marcel (L. Delteil 18), 1875,* second of four before i., stamped, d., ded., annot., large margins, creases, reddish stains, (02-03-93, Ader Tajan, #167), 6 5/16 x 9 7/16 in., (16 x 24 cm.), etching (BP 634, DM 1495, FR 5070, Y 112,949).

BI *Entree Du Port De Honfleur (Delteil 10 III), 1863,* est. DM 1,800, (12-04-92, Bassenge, #6837), 9 1/4 x 12 3/8 in., (23.5 x 31.5 cm.), êtching on handmade.

BI *Entree Du Port De Honfleur (L.D. 10), 1869,* definitive state, reddish stains, whole margins, (06-11-93, Picard, #81), 8 11/16 x 12 in., (220 x 305 mm.), etching on laid.

$385* *Jetee En Bois Dans Le Port De Honfleur (D. 12), 1865,* blindstamp pub. Cadart & Luquet, margins, good cond., paper losses, tears, surface soiling, foxing, mat staining, tape/glue remains, rubbed areas, creases, (10-28-92, Butterfield, #2826), 9 1/2 x 12 1/2 in., (241 x 318 mm.), etching on laid paper (BP 245, DM 595, FR 2019, Y 47,239).

$303* *Moulin En Hollande (D. 14), 1868,* margins, good cond., red ink, discoloration, surface soiling, (02-24-93, Butterfield, #2942), 5 11/16 x 7 5/8 in., (144 x 194 mm.), etching on laid (BP 211, DM 492, FR 1668, Y 35,555).

$55* *Sortie Du Port De Honfleur,* pub. Cadart & Luquet, Paris, foxing, (09-21-92, Selkirk, #563), 9 1/2 x 12 3/8 in., (24.1 x 31.4 cm.), copper engraving (BP 32, DM 82, FR 279, Y 6798).

$629* *Vue De La Ville De Maaslins (Hollande),* s., d. 1862 in plate, drystamp, Editions Cadart et Chevaliee, (11-16-92, Briest, #317), 14 3/8 x 21 1/4 in., (36.5 x 54 cm.), etching (BP 413, DM 1003, FR 3380, Y 78,497).

$1909* *Vue De La Ville De Maaslins En Hollande (Delteil 8/III), 1862,* Cadart & Luquet, (06-23-93, Kornfeld, #422), etching on thick wove (BP 1297, DM 3230, FR 10,865, Y 207,975, SF 2875).

JONK, Nic b. 1928

$117* *Untitled, 1980,* s., d., #128/200, margins, good cond., stain, (12-09-92, Sotheby-Amstrdm, #595), sheet 19 11/16 x 27 7/16 in., (500 x 697 mm.), color lithograph on wove (BP 75, DM 184, FR 627, Y 14,507, G 207).

JONSON, Sven 1902-1981

$3019* *Genombrutet Landskap,* s. 80/360, (05-25-93, AB Stockholm, #36), 23 5/8 x 35 7/16 in., (60 x 90 cm.), lithograph in colors (BP 1957, DM 4917, FR 16,552, Y 329,981, SK 4400).

$892* *Genombrutet Landskap,* s., 33/350, (12-04-92, AB Stockholm, #7080), 31 7/8 x 25 9/16 in., (81 x 65 cm.), lithograph in colors (BP 572, DM 1421, FR 4819, Y 111,361, SK 6050).

$2113* *Uppbrott, 1977,* s., 139/330, (05-25-93, AB Stockholm, #38), 17 15/16 x 22 5/8 in., (45.5 x 57.5 cm.), lithograph in colors (BP 1369, DM 3441, FR 11,584, Y 230,954, SK 3080).

JONSON, Sven (after) 1902-1981

$2642* *Aniarasviten: Five,* s. 203/390, blindstamp Galerie Borjeson, by R. Zurlinden, (05-25-93, AB Stockholm, #37), 12 15/16 x 16 1/8 in., (33 x 41 cm.), lithograph in color (BP 1712, DM 4303, FR 14,485, Y 288,775, SK 3850).

JONSSON, Lars b. 1952

$1434* *I Grongraset,* s. 275/360, (05-25-93, AB Stockholm, #39), 15 15/16 x 21 5/8 in., (40.5 x 55 cm.), lithograph in color (BP 929, DM 2336, FR 7862, Y 156,738, SK 2090).

$2189* *I Vila,* s., 220/250, (05-25-93, AB Stockholm, #42), 16 9/16 x 24 13/16 in., (42 x 63 cm.), lithograph in color (BP 1419, DM 3565, FR 12,001, Y 239,261, SK 3190).

$616* *Morkulla,* s., 205/250, (12-04-92, AB Stockholm, #7084), 19 1/8 x 26 3/16 in., (48.5 x 66.5 cm.), lithograph in colors (BP 395, DM 981, FR 3328, Y 76,904, SK 4180).

$1963* *Novemberapplen,* s. 106/310, (05-25-93, AB Stockholm, #40), 19 1/2 x 27 3/8 in., (49.5 x 69.5 cm.), lithograph in color (BP 1272, DM 3197, FR 10,762, Y 214,559, SK 2860).

$924* *Solig Utsikt,* 28/200, s., (12-04-92, AB Stockholm, #7081), 24 x 34 13/16 in., (61 x 88.5 cm.), lithograph in colors (BP 593, DM 1472, FR 4992, Y 115,356, SK 6270).

$486* *Tofsvipa,* s., 133/350, (12-04-92, AB Stockholm, #7082), 12 5/8 x 18 7/8 in., (32 x 48 cm.), lithograph in color (BP 312, DM 774, FR 2626, Y 60,674, SK 3300).

$1963* *Vid Havet,* s. 28/310, (05-25-93, AB Stockholm, #41), 18 5/16 x 24 13/16 in., (46.5 x 63 cm.), lithograph in color (BP 1272, DM 3197, FR 10,762, Y 214,559, SK 2860).

JONVELLE, Jean Francois b. 1943

BI *Portrait, 1984,* s., d., num. 4347, 607 x 470mm, est. BP 3/500, (05-07-93, Sotheby-London, #373, illus.), photograph, silver print.

JOPLING, Frederic Waistell

$26* *Court House Entrance,* s. twice in plate, s., (06-07-93, Ritchie, #18), 6 x 4 in., (15.3 x 10.2 cm.), drypoint etching w/tint (BP 17, DM 42, FR 142, Y 2789, C$ 33).

$94* *The Organ Grinder,* s., t., d. 1920, (11-30-92, Ritchie, #9), 7 1/2 x 4 3/8 in., (19 x 11.1 cm.), drypoint etching (BP 62, DM 150, FR 508, Y 11,699, C$ 121).

JORDAENS, Jacob Flemish 1593-1678

BI *Die Flucht Nach Agypten (Wurzbach 1), 1652,* plate t., center crease, trimmed, est. DM 750-, (09-25-92, Granier, #2648), 14 3/4 x 20 in., (37.5 x 50.8 cm.), color copper engraving.

$581* *Jupiter (Hollstein Bd. 9, 5), 1652,* 1st state, (09-14-92, Venator/Hansten, #1543), plate 8 7/16 x 11 3/4 in., (21.4 x 29.8 cm.), etching (BP 307, DM 864, FR 2927, Y 72,246).

JORDON, Allan 1898-1982

$41* *Banksia's Dromana,* s. Allan Jordon, i., #8/100, (08-11-92, L. Joel, #51G), 8 1/8 x 9 13/16 in., (20.7 x 25 cm.), etching (BP 21, DM 60, FR 204, Y 5250, A$ 55).

JORGENSEN, Erling

$73* *Seks Kompositioner, 1964,* s. Erling Jorgensen, (03-24-93, Kunsthallen, #202), color lithograph on ramme (frame) (BP 49, DM 119, FR 406, Y 8577, DK 460).

JORN, Asger Danish 1914-1973

$1125* *Au Pied Du Mur (Van de Loo 342), 1969,* s. Jorn 69, 42/75, (12-02-92, Kunsthallen, #262), lithograph in colors (BP 726, DM 1769, FR 6039, Y 139,978, DK 6900).

$1230* *Au Ventre Des Ames, (Van de Loo 274), 1966,* s. Jorn 66, 3/45, (03-24-93, Kunsthallen, #181), etching (BP 833, DM 2009, FR 6837, Y 144,519, DK 7705).

$514* *Le Beau Coup, (Van de Loo 289), 1966,* s. Jorn 66, (03-24-93, Kunsthallen, #183), etching (BP 348, DM 839, FR 2857, Y 60,392, DK 3220).

$940* *Le Chat Qui Rit (Van de Loo 110), 1953-1970,* s. Jorn 53-70, 7/100, from Silkeborg-Suiten, (06-03-93, Kunsthallen, #179), lithograph in colors (BP 609, DM 1504, FR 5070, Y 100,815, DK 5750).

$1978* *Clair-Obscur, 1961,* s., d., #92/100, blindstamp, Galerie Rive Gauche, (06-12-93, Hauswedell/Nolt, #265, illus.), 15¹⁵⁄₁₆ x 22¹⁵⁄₁₆ in., (40.5 x 58.4 cm.), color lithograph in color print on Arches (BP 1295, DM 3219, FR 10,821, Y 208,145).

$338* *Composition (Van de Loo 244), 1963,* s. Jorn 63, 29/50, (06-03-93, Kunsthallen, #187), lithograph in colors (BP 219, DM 541, FR 1823, Y 36,251, DK 2070).

$376* *Composition (Van de Loo 250), 1963,* s. Jorn 63, 12/50, from Jubilaeumsserien, (06-03-93, Kunsthallen, #182), lithograph in colors (BP 244, DM 602, FR 2028, Y 40,326, DK 2300).

$489* *Composition (Van de Loo 256), 1963,* s. Jorn 63, 12/50, from Jubilaeumsserien, (06-03-93, Kunsthallen, #183), lithograph in colors (BP 317, DM 783, FR 2638, Y 52,445, DK 2990).

$843* *Composition (Van de Loo 364), 1970,* s. Jorn 70, E.A., (09-30-92, Kunsthallen, #154), color lithograph (BP 476, DM 1195, FR 4043, Y 101,164, DK 4600).

$2067* *Composition (Van de Loo 89), 1945,* s. Jorn 45, (06-03-93, Kunsthallen, #77), 19¹¹⁄₁₆ x 14³⁄₁₆ in., (50 x 36 cm.), watercolor and lithograph (BP 1340, DM 3308, FR 11,149, Y 221,686, DK 12,650).

BI *Composition, 1969,* s., d., hors commerce IV/X, est. FF5/7,000, (06-28-93, Loudmer, #267), 24 x 16¾ in., (610 x 425 mm.), sh 25⁹⁄₁₆ x 18⅞ in., (610 x 425 mm.), color lithograph on wove.

$406* *Composition, 1969,* s., d., H.C. IV/X, (06-28-93, Loudmer, #268), 21⅝ x 15⅜ in., (550 x 390 mm.), sh 25⁹⁄₁₆ x 19⅛ in., (550 x 390 mm.), color lithograph on wove (BP 272, DM 690, FR 2324, Y 43,077).

$1101* *Creation Cosmique, (Van de Loo 161, Aflildet side 161), 1953,* s. Jorn 53, 41/50, (03-24-93, Kunsthallen, #168), etching (BP 746, DM 1798, FR 6120, Y 129,362, DK 6900).

$1377* *Dans Le Sillage D'Lf Aube, (Van de Loo 407), 1972,* s. Jorn 72, E.A., (03-24-93, Kunsthallen, #194), woodcut in colors (BP 932, DM 2249, FR 7654, Y 161,791, DK 8625).

$7342* *Den Rode Jorn, (Van de Loo 128, Afbildet side 23), 1953,* s. Jorn 53, (03-24-93, Kunsthallen, #160, illus.), color lithograph (BP 4972, DM 11,991, FR 40,812, Y 862,648, DK 46,000).

BI *Entree Secours, 1971,* s., artist's proof, est. DM 2,400, (12-05-92, Bassenge, #7313), 10⁹⁄₁₆ x 14⅜ in., (26.8 x 36.5 cm.), color etching on Arches.

$1101* *Etres Dans Le Ombre, (Van de Loo 64), 1945,* s. Jorn 45, from Occupations, epreuve d'artiste, (03-24-93, Kunsthallen, #163), etching (BP 746, DM 1798, FR 6120, Y 129,362, DK 6900).

$2386* *Euclide Coince, (Van de Loo 392, Afbildet side 37), 1971,* s. Jorn 71, 19/100, from Entree de Secours, (03-24-93, Kunsthallen, #189, illus.), color etching (BP 1616, DM 3897, FR 13,263, Y 280,343, DK 14,950).

$1875* *Fabeldyr (Jvf. Van de Loo 85), 1945,* s. Asger Jorn 45, (12-02-92, Kunsthallen, #261), lithograph (BP 1210, DM 2949, FR 10,064, Y 233,296, DK 11,500).

$422* *Farbige Komposition Mit Rot, 1973,* #6/150, relief sig./stamp, stamp, (03-24-93, Venator/Hansten, #4504), image approx. 20⅞ x 13⅜ in., (53 x 34 cm.), color lithograph on Arches (BP 286, DM 689, FR 2346, Y 49,583).

$918* *La Fete Des Mortes, (Van de Loo 351), 1969,* s. Jorn 69, 24/75, (03-24-93, Kunsthallen, #188), color lithograph (BP 622, DM 1499, FR 5103, Y 107,860, DK 5750).

$1264* *Le Foret Demivierge (Van de Loo 179), 1955,* s. Jorn 55, 105/300, (09-30-92, Kunsthallen, #155), color lithograph (BP 713, DM 1792, FR 6062, Y 151,686, DK 6900).

$551* *Le Foret Demivierge, (Van de Loo 179), 1957,* s. Jorn 57, (03-24-93, Kunsthallen, #170), color lithograph (BP 373, DM 900, FR 3063, Y 64,740, DK 3450).

BI *Friedhof Der Maulwurfe: Eight,* book, s., num. 62, pub. Edition Galerie van de Loo, very good cond.,est. BP 800/1,200, (11-30-92, Phillips-London, #536), plate and volume 5⅛ x 6⅛ in., (130 x 156 mm.), aquatint on wove.

$734* *Hautes Pyrenees, (Van de Loo 350), 1969,* s. Jorn 69, 35/75, (03-24-93, Kunsthallen, #187), color lithograph (BP 497, DM 1199, FR 4080, Y 86,241, DK 4600).

BI *Jadeflotjen (La Flute De Jade)(Van De Loo 17), 1940,* book, s., i. 15-3-43 Til Mari Modersen og frue med venleig hilsen and1940-43, p. Royal Academy of Fine arts, Copenhagen, good cond., discoloration,est. BP 2/2,500, (12-03-92, Sotheby-London, #756, illus.), overall size 7⅝ x 9 in., (195 x 230 mm.), 22 lithographs w/text on wove.

$3908* *Jadeflotjen, La Flute De Jade (Van De Loo 17), 1940: Twenty-Two,* book, ink s.; i. 15-3-43, good cond., discoloration, (12-09-92, Sotheby-Amstrdm, #596), lithograph on wove (BP 2494, DM 6134, FR 20,932, Y 484,563, G 6900).

$1264* *Jaune-Bleu (Van de Loo 315), 1970,* s. Jorn 70, E.A., (09-30-92, Kunsthallen, #149), color lithograph (BP 713, DM 1792, FR 6062, Y 151,686, DK 6900).

$632* *Je Suis Plein, (CRAS XXXVII 1984, Van de Loo 174), 1954,* s. Jorn 54, 9/15, (09-30-92, Kunsthallen, #150), etching (BP 357, DM 896, FR 3031, Y 75,843, DK 3450).

$734* *Jubilation Larmoyennageuse, (Van de Loo 338), 1969,* s. Jorn 69, 147/300, (03-24-93, Kunsthallen, #185), color lithograph (BP 497, DM 1199, FR 4080, Y 86,241, DK 4600).

BI *Jubilaumsserie (Van De Loo 239-262), 1963: Eighteen,* from set of 24, proofs, good cond., creases, soiling, corners papertaped, tear, prov., est. G 12/18,000, (12-09-92, Sotheby-Amstrdm, #597, illus.), each sheet approx. 24¼ x 18⅛ in., (616 x 460 mm.), color lithograph on wove.

$425* *Jubileumsserien (V.d.L. 262), (19)63,* s., d., num., (06-08-93, Karl/Faber, #934), approx. 24 x 18⅛ in., (61 x 46 cm.), color lithograph on wove (BP 279, DM 690, FR 2322, Y 45,141).

$3792* *Komiteen Til Udbredelse Af Dansk Skonhed I Udlandet (Van de Loo 124),1953,* s. Asger Jorn Paris 1956, w/dedication, (09-30-92, Kunsthallen, #147, illus.), color linocut (BP 2139, DM 5377, FR 18,187, Y 455,058, DK 20,700).

BI *Komposition (V. d. L. 252), 1963,* s., signs of wear, est. DM 3500, (12-01-92, Karl/Faber, #805, illus.), sh 18⅛ x 24³⁄₁₆ in., (46 x 61.5 cm.), color lithograph.

$1826* *Komposition (Van de Loo 243), 1963,* s., num., pub. Galerie Birch, creases, (12-01-92, Karl/Faber, #804, illus.), 24³⁄₁₆ x 18⅛ in., (61.5 x 46 cm.), color lithograph on wove (BP 1206, DM 2910, FR 9919, Y 227,341).

$244* *Komposition (Van de Loo 90), 1945,* s. Asger Jorn 45, (06-03-93, Kunsthallen, #184), lithograph (BP 158, DM 391, FR 1316, Y 26,169, DK 1495).

$586* *Komposition Fra Jubilaeumsserien, (Van de Loo 256),* s. 63, 32/50, (09-29-92, B. Rasmussen, #335), print (BP 329, DM 828, FR 2824, Y 69,953, DK 3220).

$460* *Komposition Fra Jubilaeumsserien, (Van de Loo 261),* s. 63, 21/50, (09-29-92, B. Rasmussen, #336), lithograph in colors (BP 259, DM 650, FR 2217, Y 54,912, DK 2530).

$1988* *Komposition Fra Von Kopf Bis Fuss, (Van de Loo 306),* s. 67, 23/75, (09-29-92, B. Rasmussen, #332), lithograph in colors (BP 1117, DM 2808, FR 9581, Y 237,316, DK 10,925).

$239* *Komposition, "Abstrakt Kunst", (Van de Loo 96), 1947,* s. Asger Jorn 47, (03-24-93, Kunsthallen, #166), lithograph (BP 162, DM 390, FR 1329, Y 28,081, DK 1495).

$1101* *Komposition, (Van de Loo 191), 1956,* s. Jorn 56, prov., (03-24-93, Kunsthallen, #198), color lithograph (BP 746, DM 1798, FR 6120, Y 129,362, DK 6900).

$642* *Komposition, (Van de Loo 192), 1957,* s. Jorn 57, (03-24-93, Kunsthallen, #171), color lithograph (BP 435, DM 1049, FR 3569, Y 75,432, DK 4025).

$367* *Komposition, (Van de Loo 201), 1959,* s. Jorn 59, 19/
35, (03-24-93, Kunsthallen, #175), color lithograph (BP
249, DM 599, FR 2040, Y 43,121, DK 2300).

$239* *Komposition, (Van de Loo 241), 1963,* s. Jorn 63, 6/50,
from Jubilaeumsserien, (03-24-93, Kunsthallen, #178),
lithograph (BP 162, DM 390, FR 1329, Y 28,081, DK
1495).

$367* *Komposition, (Van de Loo 244), 1963,* s. Jorn 63, 7/50,
from Jubilaeumsserien, (03-24-93, Kunsthallen, #179),
color lithograph (BP 249, DM 599, FR 2040, Y 43,121,
DK 2300).

$275* *Komposition, (Van de Loo 253), 1963,* s. Jorn 63, 8/50,
from Jubilaeumsserien, (03-24-93, Kunsthallen, #180),
color lithograph (BP 186, DM 449, FR 1529, Y 32,311,
DK 1725).

$1101* *Komposition, (Van de Loo 304), 1966,* s. Jorn 66,
epreuvre d'artiste, (03-24-93, Kunsthallen, #195), color
lithograph (BP 746, DM 1798, FR 6120, Y 129,362, DK
6900).

$275* *Komposition, (Van de Loo 428), 1972,* Kestner Gesell-
schaft, 133/150, (03-24-93, Kunsthallen, #193), color
lithograph (BP 186, DM 449, FR 1529, Y 32,311, DK
1725).

$1101* *Komposition, (Van de Loo 74), 1944,* s. Asger J.44, (03-
24-93, Kunsthallen, #199), color lithograph (BP 746, DM
1798, FR 6120, Y 129,362, DK 6900).

$330* *Komposition, (Van de Loo 91), 1945,* s. Asger Jorn 45,
from Ars portfolio, (03-24-93, Kunsthallen, #165), lithograph (BP 223, DM 539, FR 1834, Y 38,773, DK
2070).

$770* *Komposition, 1970,* 112/150, s., d., (10-14-92, Germann,
#339), 27¾ x 19⁹/₁₆ in., (705 x 497 mm.), color seri-
graph (BP 452, DM 1127, FR 3821, Y 93,311, SF
1003).

$367* *Komposition, Betegnet "Le Vieux Monde", (Van de Loo
200), 1959,* s. Jorn 59, 18/35, (03-24-93, Kunsthallen,
#174), color lithograph (BP 249, DM 599, FR 2040, Y
43,121, DK 2300).

$312* *Kompositions, (Van de Loo 269 and 271): Two,* (03-24-
93, Kunsthallen, #200), color lithographs (BP 211, DM
510, FR 1734, Y 36,658, DK 1955).

$2317* *L'Armure Desarmante (Van de Loo 124), 1971,* s. Jorn
71 E.A., (09-30-92, Kunsthallen, #148, illus.), color
woodcut (BP 1307, DM 3286, FR 11,113, Y 278,051,
DK 12,650).

$2291* *L'Enfer Des Jeux Clos (van de Loo 414), 1972,* s., d.,
num., (06-23-93, Kornfeld, #424), color woodcut on
wove (BP 1556, DM 3876, FR 13,039, Y 249,591, SF
3450).

$697* *L'Oubli, (Van de Loo 230), 1960-61,* s. Jorn 60-61, 20/
30, (03-24-93, Kunsthallen, #177), color lithograph (BP
472, DM 1138, FR 3874, Y 81,894, DK 4370).

$1680* *La Mere Ibis (van de Loo 410), 1972,* s., d., num., (06-
23-93, Kornfeld, #423), color woodcut on wove (BP
1141, DM 2843, FR 9562, Y 183,026, SF 2530).

$1138* *Mon Chateau D' Espagne, (Van de Loo 163, Afbildet
side 31), 1953,* s. Jorn 53, 41/50, (03-24-93, Kunsthallen,
#169, illus.), etching (BP 771, DM 1859, FR 6326, Y
133,709, DK 7130).

$459* *Le Monde Contraire, (Van de Loo 229), 1960-61,* s. Jorn
60-61, 29/30, (03-24-93, Kunsthallen, #176), color lithograph (BP 311, DM 750, FR 2551, Y 53,930, DK
2875).

$1560* *Nasobois La Laie Que Se Croit Un Sphinx, (Van de Loo
412), 1972,* s. jorn 72, E.A., (03-24-93, Kunsthallen,
#197), woodcut in colors (BP 1056, DM 2548, FR 8671,
Y 183,292, DK 9775).

BI *Nuit Dechiree (Van de Loo 354), 1969,* s. Jorn 69, 129/
300, est. DK 6,000, (09-30-92, Kunsthallen, #152), color
lithograph.

$628* *"Nuit Dechiree", (Van de Loo 354),* s. 69, 197/300, (09-
29-92, B. Rasmussen, #334), lithograph in colors (BP
353, DM 887, FR 3027, Y 74,967, DK 3450).

$1101* *Les Ondes Courtes, (Van de Loo 53, Afbildet side 25),
1943,* s. Jorn, epreuvre, (03-24-93, Kunsthallen, #162,
illus.), aquatint and etching (BP 746, DM 1798, FR
6120, Y 129,362, DK 6900).

$330* *Opus 4 A d'Une Mythe Muet, (Van de Loo 119), 1952,*
prov., (03-24-93, Kunsthallen, #167), color lithograph (BP
223, DM 539, FR 1834, Y 38,773, DK 2070).

$1101* *Panorama Des Prises De Bec, (Van de Loo 278), 1966,*
s. Jorn 66, 3/45, (03-24-93, Kunsthallen, #182), etching
(BP 746, DM 1798, FR 6120, Y 129,362, DK 6900).

$734* *Pensees En L'Air, (Van de Loo 399), 1971,* 39/100, from
Entree de Secours, (03-24-93, Kunsthallen, #191), color
etching (BP 497, DM 1199, FR 4080, Y 86,241, DK
4600).

BI *Personnages, 1950,* s., d. 50, #22/50, full margins, tear,
est. FF 5/6,000, (11-16-92, Briest, #318, illus.), 13⁹/₁₆ x
11¹⁵/₁₆ in., (34.5 x 30.4 cm.), etching.

$1101* *Pierre Qui Roule, (Van de Loo 408), 1971,* s. Jorn 71,
38/75, from Etudes Et Surprises, (03-24-93, Kunsthallen,
#192), woodcut in colors (BP 746, DM 1798, FR 6120,
Y 129,362, DK 6900).

$367* *Porca Miseria, (Van de Loo 197), 1958,* s. Jorn 58, 32/
35, (03-24-93, Kunsthallen, #172), color lithograph (BP
249, DM 599, FR 2040, Y 43,121, DK 2300).

$1256* *Posters Udfort I Forbindelse Med Ungdomsoproret I
Paris Maj 1968, (Van de Loo 320-323): Four,* p. Clot,
Bramsen and Georges, (09-29-92, B. Rasmussen, #333),
lithographic poster (BP 706, DM 1774, FR 6053, Y
149,934, DK 6900).

$587* *Provacation Ratee, (Van de Loo 338, Afbildet Side 29),
1969,* s. Jorn 69, 42/75, (03-24-93, Kunsthallen, #186,
illus.), color lithograph (BP 398, DM 959, FR 3263, Y
68,970, DK 3680).

$1101* *Ruckkehr, (Van de Loo 325), 1967,* s. Jorn 67, 46/50,
(03-24-93, Kunsthallen, #196), color lithograph (BP 746,
DM 1798, FR 6120, Y 129,362, DK 6900).

$1285* *Ruckkhehr, (Van de Loo 325, Afbildet side 27), 1967,* s.
Jorn 67, 30/50, (03-24-93, Kunsthallen, #184, illus.),
color lithograph (BP 870, DM 2099, FR 7143, Y
150,981, DK 8050).

$1801* *Sur Le Pont D'Or, 1969,* #31/75, s., d., (12-15-92,
Finarte-Milan, #27, illus.), 28¾ x 21¹/₁₆ in., (73 x 53.5
cm.), lithograph in colors (BP 1149, DM 2823, FR 9646,
Y 223,366, L 2530).

$1285* *Tarotaumagie Offusquee, (Van de Loo 395), 1971,* s. Jorn
71, 19/100, from Entree De Secours, (03-24-93, Kunsthallen, #190), color etching (BP 870, DM 2099, FR
7143, Y 150,981, DK 8050).

BI *Troldtoj (Van de Loo 181), 1955,* artist's proof, est. DK
8,000, (09-30-92, Kunsthallen, #153), color lithograph.

$866* *Untitled (Van de Loo 427), 1927,* num., blindstamp Kest-
ner-Gesellschaft, (11-28-92, Schoppmann, #606), 20⅞ x
12⅝ in., (53 x 32 cm.), color lithograph on Arches
wove (BP 572, DM 1380, FR 4684, Y 107,778).

$231* *Untitled, 1963,* crease, reddish stains, #14/50, d., s., (01-
28-93, Pescheteau, #166), 18⅛ x 24 in., (46 x 61 cm.),
color lithograph on wove (BP 153, DM 366, FR 1239,
Y 28,681).

$593* *Untitled, 1970,* #113/150, s., d., blindstamp, (04-21-93,
Germann, #563), 27⁹/₁₆ x 19⅝ in., (700 x 498 mm.),
color lithograph (BP 385, DM 948, FR 3205, Y 65,648,
SF 863).

$1556* *Untitled, 1972,* artist proof, s., d., (12-15-92, Finarte-
Milan, #86, illus.), 10⅝ x 14⁷/₁₆ in., (27 x 36.6 cm.),
etching in colors (BP 993, DM 2439, FR 8334, Y
192,980, L 2185).

$642* *Violon De Jorn, (Van de Loo 199), 1958,* s. Jorn 58,
prov., (03-24-93, Kunsthallen, #173), color lithograph (BP
435, DM 1049, FR 3569, Y 75,432, DK 4025).

BI *Vive La Revolution Pasione, (Van de Loo 322), 1968,* est.
DK 1,500, (03-24-93, Kunsthallen, #201), color lithograph.

BI *Die Zwei Elemente, (Van de Loo 360, Afbildet side 360),
1970,* s. Jorn 70, est. BI 45,000, (03-24-93, Kunsthallen,
#161), color lithograph.

JOSEPH, Antonio   Haitian 20th century
BI *African Market Scene,* s., #13/40 in red pen, est. $150/
200, (02-04-93, Sloan, #364), sight 17¾ x 25 in., (45.1
x 63.5 cm.), lithograph.

JOSSET, Lawrence
$115* *Mr. Powlett And His Hounds,* s., blindstamp, pub. Frost
and Reed, 1964, margins, (06-30-93, Bonhams-Chelsea,

#130), plate 20 x 23 in., (50.8 x 58.4 cm.), mezzotint in colors (BP 77, DM 196, FR 662, Y 12,322).

JOSSET, Lawrence, Engraver

$134* *Master James Sayer Fishing, 1955,* s., blindstamp, pub. Frost and Reed, margins, (11-12-92, Bonhams-Chelsea, #27, illus.), plate 21 x 15¾ in., (53.3 x 40 cm.), color mezzotint (BP 88, DM 212, FR 716, Y 16,615).

$268* *Master James Sayer Fishing, 1955,* s., blindstamp, pub. Frost and Reed, margins, (11-12-92, Bonhams-Chelsea, #69, illus.), plate 21 x 15¾ in., (53.3 x 40 cm.), color mezzotint (BP 176, DM 425, FR 1432, Y 33,230).

$167* *Master James Sayer Fishing, 1955,* s., blindstamp, pub. Frost and Reed, margins, (11-12-92, Bonhams-Chelsea, #70, illus.), plate 21 x 15¾ in., (53.3 x 40 cm.), color mezzotint (BP 110, DM 265, FR 893, Y 20,707).

$117* *La Tasse Chocolat, 1967,* s., blindstamp, pub. Frost and Reed, margins, (11-12-92, Bonhams-Chelsea, #7), plate 21¾ x 25 in., (55.2 x 63.5 cm.), color mezzotint (BP 77, DM 185, FR 625, Y 14,507).

$184* *William Inglis On The Gold Course, 1962,* s., blindstamp, pub. Frost and Reed, margins, (11-12-92, Bonhams-Chelsea, #30, illus.), plate 24¾ x 19 in., (62.9 x 48.3 cm.), color mezzotint (BP 121, DM 292, FR 983, Y 22,815).

$167* *William Inglis On The Gold Course, 1962,* s., blindstamp, pub. Frost and Reed, margins, (11-12-92, Bonhams-Chelsea, #29, illus.), plate 24¾ x 19 in., (62.9 x 48.3 cm.), color mezzotint (BP 110, DM 265, FR 893, Y 20,707).

$110* *William Inglis On The Golf Course, 1962,* s., blindstamp pub. Frost and Reed, margins, (11-12-92, Bonhams-Chelsea, #1, illus.), plate 24¾ x 19 in., (62.9 x 48.3 cm.), color mezzotint (BP 72, DM 174, FR 588, Y 13,639).

$234* *William Inglis On The Golf Course, 1962,* s., blindstamp, pub. Frost and Reed, margins, (11-12-92, Bonhams-Chelsea, #31, illus.), plate 24¾ x 19 in., (62.9 x 48.3 cm.), color mezzotint (BP 154, DM 371, FR 1251, Y 29,014).

$285* *William Inglis On The Golf Course, 1962,* s., blindstamp, pub. Frost and Reed, margins, (11-12-92, Bonhams-Chelsea, #77, illus.), plate 24¾ x 19 in., (62.9 x 48.3 cm.), color mezzotint (BP 187, DM 452, FR 1523, Y 35,338).

$201* *William Inglis On The Golf Course, 1962,* s., blindstamp pub. Frost and Reed, margins, (11-12-92, Bonhams-Chelsea, #74, illus.), plate 24¾ x 19 in., (62.9 x 48.3 cm.), color mezzotint (BP 132, DM 318, FR 1074, Y 24,923).

$218* *William Inglis On The Golf Course, 1962,* s., blindstamp, pub. Frost and Reed, margins, (11-12-92, Bonhams-Chelsea, #76, illus.), plate 24¾ x 19 in., (62.9 x 48.3 cm.), color mezzotint (BP 143, DM 345, FR 1165, Y 27,030).

$251* *William Inglis On The Golf Course, 1962,* s., blindstamp, pub. Frost and Reed, margins, (11-12-92, Bonhams-Chelsea, #75, illus.), plate 24¾ x 19 in., (62.9 x 48.3 cm.), color mezzotint (BP 165, DM 398, FR 1342, Y 31,122).

JOSSO, C.-P.

$538* *PLM and CTM: Tout Le Maroc Par La Cie Gle De Transport Et De Tourisme, 1929,* very good cond., (03-13-93, Laurin, #101, illus.), 38 15/16 x 24 7/16 in., (99 x 62 cm.), (BP 375, DM 895, FR 3045, Y 63,406).

JOSSOT

$261* *Amieux Freres. "Encore Une Qu'A La D'Vise", 1897,* Affiches Camis, good cond., (02-12-93, Cheval/Robert, #62), 55⅛ x 39⅜ in., (140 x 100 cm.), poster (BP 184, DM 433, FR 1465, Y 31,476).

$279* *PLM: Federation Des Syndicats D'Initiative De Tunisie,* very good cond., (03-13-93, Laurin, #69), 42 15/16 x 30⅞ in., (109 x 78.5 cm.), (BP 195, DM 464, FR 1579, Y 32,882).

JOSSOT, Henri 1886-1951

$439* *La Critique...Publie Des Dessins De Jossot, 1896,* cond. A, (03-16-93, Boisgirard, #130, illus.), 24 3/16 x 19 5/16 in., (61.5 x 49 cm.), poster (BP 303, DM 730, FR 2480, Y 51,333).

JOUVE, Paul French 1880-1973

$445* *Le Chat-Huant,* original, s. in plate, (05-27-93, Briest, #112), 29⅛ x 22 7/16 in., (74 x 57 cm.), lithograph (BP 285, DM 714, FR 2407, Y 47,706).

$720* *Famille De Tigres Au Bord D'Un Fleuve,* s., #38/60, artist's drystamp, full margins, (05-06-93, Laurin, #45), lithograph on Japan (BP 456, DM 1134, FR 3818, Y 79,217).

$347* *"Lionne Et Son Lionceau",* drystamp, (01-28-93, Peschet-eau, #168), 21⅝ x 29½ in., (55 x 75 cm.), black etching on Japan nacre (BP 229, DM 550, FR 1861, Y 43,084).

$627* *Paris, Maxime Cottet-Dumoulin, 1949: Sixteen,* from Une Passion Dans Le Desert by Honore de Balzac, s., (11-15-92, Christie-Geneva, #306, illus.), 13⅜ x 10⅝ in., (340 x 270 mm.), etching in black and in color on Arches wove (BP 412, DM 1000, FR 3369, Y 78,248, SF 904).

JOVE, Paul

BI *The Judgement Of Paris,* blindstamp, margins, staining, tear, est. BP 100/150, (02-17-93, Bonhams-Chelsea, #352), image 9¼ x 13½ in., (23.5 x 34.3 cm.), dark brown lithograph.

JOWETT, Ellen, engraver

BI *"Portrait Of A Lady", 1926,* blindstamp, pub. Frost and Reed, margins, est. BP 40/60, (11-19-92, Bonhams-Chelsea, #81), plate 20½ x 16½ in., (52.1 x 41.9 cm.), color mezzotint.

$26* *"Portrait Of A Lady", 1926,* blindstamp, pub. Frost & Reed, margins, (01-21-93, Bonhams-Chelsea, #90), plate 20½ x 16½ in., (52.1 x 41.9 cm.), mezzotint p. in colors (BP 17, DM 41, FR 140, Y 3254).

JOY, George (after)

$66* *Young Nelson,* (06-16-93, Bonhams-Chelsea, #447), image 20½ x 15⅜ in., (52.1 x 39.1 cm.), chromolithograph (BP 44, DM 110, FR 368, Y 7039).

JOY, Thomas Musgrove (after)

$76* *William Forbes Esq. Of Callendar,* by George Zobel, proof, trimmed, laid down, (11-12-92, Bonhams-Chelsea, #26), image 26 x 16 in., (66 x 40.6 cm.), hand-colored mezzotint (BP 50, DM 120, FR 406, Y 9423).

JUBIER, C.L. ac. 1760-1781

$1249* *Le Gouter Champetre (Herold 73; P. and B., II, p. 498; Inventaire 18e Siecle, XII, Pieces De Jubier Manquant A La B.LN., p. 207, no. 39), c. 1778,* after Jean-Baptiste Huet, pub. Bonnet, small to narrow margins, foxed, (12-01-92, Christie-London, #270), plate 9⅜ x 12⅛ in., (238 x 308 mm.), etching w/engraving in the lavis-manner in colors (BP 825, DM 1991, FR 6784, Y 155,503).

JUDD, Donald American b. 1928

$1840* *Aquatints, 1980: Six,* s., #44/150, #106/150, pub. Edition Schellmann, blindstamp printer, Styria Studio, full margins, good cond., (05-19-93, Butterfield, #2208, illus.), each sh 29⅜ x 34⅛ in., (746 x 867 mm.), aquatint on wove (BP 1194, DM 2991, FR 10,077, Y 203,698).

$1870* *Geometric Shapes: Seventeen,* (09-24-92, Mystic, #41), each 22 x 27 in., (55.9 x 68.6 cm.), engravings (BP 1095, DM 2771, FR 9411, Y 224,949).

BI *Untitled,* s., P(rinter's) P(roof) 4/6, est. DM 1200, (12-01-92, Karl/Faber, #807), 29 15/16 x 19⅞ in., (76 x 50.5 cm.), aquatint/etching on wove.

$632* *Untitled,* #55/150, blindstamp, (04-21-93, Germann, #564), 29 7/16 x 34½ in., (747 x 877 mm.), aquatint-etching (BP 410, DM 1010, FR 3416, Y 69,966, SF 920).

BI *Untitled Etchings, New York, Prestige Art Ltd., 1977-78: Sixteen,* s., d., num., copy 32 of 75, Styria Studio blindstamps, full margins, surface soiling, excell. cond., est. $4/6,000, (05-11-93, Christie-NY, #472), each sheet 30 x 35 in., (762 x 889 mm.), etching on German Etching.

$1840* *Untitled I-VI, 1980: Six,* complete suite, each s., #42/150, 124/150, 125/150, 122/150, 52/150,23/150, blindstamp, p. Stryria Studio, Ltd., released by Editions Schellmann, fll margins, good cond., discoloration, abrasions, skinned spots, (05-15-93, Sotheby-NY, #1041, illus.), each image 19⅞ x 24¾ in., (50.5 x 62.9 cm.), six aquatints (BP 1196, DM 2960, FR 9946, Y 203,969).

$990* *Untitled, 1961-69,* s., d. '61-69', #1/10, from suite of thirteen, pub. by artist, margins, good cond., repaired tear, (11-07-92, Sotheby-NY, #621, illus.), sheet 26 x 16½ in., (660 x 419 mm.), woodcut p. in cadmium orange on cartridge paper (BP 647, DM 1581, FR 5343, Y 122,192).

$3163* *Untitled, 1963,* s., d., #8/25, pub., full margins, good cond., discoloration, handling creases, (05-15-93, Sotheby-NY, #1039, illus.), 23⅜ x 14⅝ in., (59.4 x 37.1 cm.), woodcut in cadmium orange (BP 2057, DM 5088, FR 17,097, Y 350,626).

$565* *Untitled, 1980,* s., #4/6, printer's proof, blindstamp, (06-12-93, Hauswedell/Nolt, #267), 35³⁄₁₆ x 24⅝ in., (89.4 x 62.5 cm.), aquatint on thick wove (BP 370, DM 920, FR 3091, Y 59,455).

BI *Untitled, 1980,* #123/150, pencil s., est. DM 1,500, (11-20-92, Lempertz, #633), sh 29⅜ x 34⁵⁄₁₆ in., (74.6 x 87.2 cm.), etching on Velin.

$4180* *Untitled: Five Plates, c. 1980,* s., four i. P.P., num. 4/6; one num. 3/4; Styria Studio blindstamps,full margins, very good cond., (09-19-92, Christie-E, #139, illus.), all sheet 40 x 29½ in., (101.6 x 74.9 cm.), aquatint on wove (BP 2404, DM 6259, FR 21,436, Y 520,807).

$880* *Untitled: Two,* s., #18/150 and 58/150, from Woodcut Etching series, margins, blindstamp, (12-08-92, Swann, #151, illus.), each image 24 x 29½ in., (61 x 74.9 cm.), aquatint (BP 552, DM 1370, FR 4671, Y 109,073).

BI *Woodcut Etchings, 1974,* portfolio, s., #41/70, blindstamp, pub. Styria Studio, full margins,good cond., scuff mark, est. $2,5/3,500, (11-07-92, Sotheby-NY, #622, illus.), each sheet approx. 41⅞ x 29½ in., (106.4 x 74.9 cm.), three woodcut etchings p. in black.

JUGNARELLI, Marias

$521* *Felix Tarniquet, Beziers,* p. Casson Fils, folds, defects, backed on linen, laid on board, (05-07-93, Christie-S. Ken, #102, illus.), 42¾ x 56 in., (108.6 x 142.2 cm.), color lithograph (BP 330, DM 824, FR 2776, Y 57,366).

JUKES, Francis

BI *Hudsons River From Chambers Creek Looking Thro' The High Lands (S. &H. P.1795-1800-E-15; D. 207), 1795-1800,* after Alexander Robertson, pub. Jukes and Robertson 1802, small margins, image hole, soiling, skinning, tears, est. $3/3,500, (01-28-93, Sotheby-NY, #414, illus.), sheet 15¾ x 20⅛ in., (400 x 511 mm.), hand-colored aquatint.

BI *Mount Vernon In Virginia The Seat Of The Late Lieut. General George Washington... (S. & H. P.1799-E. 18); D. 236), c. 1799,* after Alexander Robertson, pub. Jukes and Robertson 1800, small margins, good cond., repaired image tears, scrapes, soiling, est. $3/4,000, (01-28-93, Sotheby-NY, #416, illus.), 14⅝ x 18⅞ in., (371 x 479 mm.), sheet 15⅛ x 19⅛ in., (371 x 479 mm.), hand-colored aquatint on wove.

$8050* *New York From Hobuck Ferry House New Jersey (S. & H. P.1796-E14; D. 216), 1796,* after Alexander Robertson, pub. F. Jukes and A. Robertson 1800, margins, good cond., image pin holes, repaired tears, skinning, soiling, mat stain,crease, (01-28-93, Sotheby-NY, #415, illus.), 14¼ x 18 in., (362 x 457 mm.), sheet 15⅝ x 20⅜ in., (362 x 457 mm.), hand-colored aquatint on cream wove (BP 5316, DM 12,756, FR 43,164, Y 999,503).

JULES, Mervin American b. 1912

BI *Boy With Flute,* s., proof, t., excell. cond., est. $200/250, (05-15-93, Cleveland, #171), 20 x 10 in., (50.8 x 25.4 cm.), woodcut in colors.

BI *"Crescendo", 1940,* pub. AAA, s. Jules, very good cond., light toning, est. $150/200, (09-11-92, Skinner, #27, illus.), 9 x 12 in., (22.9 x 30.5 cm.), lithograph on wove.

BI *Duo,* s., #149/150, est. $100/150, (10-30-92, Sloan, #826), 19⅞ x 8¾ in., (50.5 x 22.2 cm.), color wood engraving.

BI *Mozart,* s., t., proof, excell. cond., est. $150/200, (05-15-93, Cleveland, #170), 9 x 20 in., (22.9 x 50.8 cm.), woodcut in three colors.

$88* *"Trio",* #35/250, t., num., s. Jules, (12-11-92, Eldred, #322), sight 12 x 16 in., (30.5 x 40.6 cm.), lithograph (BP 56, DM 139, FR 475, Y 10,890).

BI *"Trio" and "Mexican Musicians", c. 1960: Two,* s., annot. Proof, est. $250/350, (12-08-92, Swann, #152), first 13 x 18 in., (33 x 45.7 cm.), second 12 x 20 in., (33 x 45.7 cm.), color woodcut on heavy Japan paper.

JULIEN, J.

$599* *PLM. Route D'Hiver Des Alpes. Aix-Les-Bains. Mont-Revard. "Services Automobiles PLM",* good cond., (03-15-93, Arcole, #44), 42½ x 30⅞ in., (108 x 78.5 cm.), (BP 417, DM 995, FR 3382, Y 70,955).

JULIUS, Kurt 1909-1986

BI *Mannequin In A Box, c. 1951,* exhib., est. $1,2/1,800, (04-08-93, Christie-NY, #440, illus.), 19⅛ x 15⅛ in., (48.6 x 38.4 cm.), photograph, gelatin silver print.

JUN'ICHIRO, Sekino

$248* *Owls,* s., d. 1958, #18/50, one seal, tape residue, (11-20-92, Skinner, #25, illus.), image 9½ x 21¾ in., (24.1 x 55.2 cm.), (BP 163, DM 395, FR 1332, Y 30,842).

JUNGNICKEL, Ludwig Heinrich 1881-1965

$4506* *Papageien,* s., (11-25-92, Dorotheum, #558, illus.), 11⅝ x 11¼ in., (29.5 x 28.5 cm.), color woodcut (BP 2946, DM 7165, FR 24,265, Y 557,811, SC 50,400).

JUNICHIRO, Sekino Japanese 1914-1988

$2860* *Portrait Of Koshiro Onchi (Jenkins #107), 1952,* s., num. 20/50, d., (11-28-92, Dunning, #1052), sight 24 x 19 in., (61 x 48.3 cm.), color woodblock (BP 1888, DM 4556, FR 15,468, Y 355,943).

JUNKERS, Adja American b. 1900

$110* *Summer In Venice I,* s., d. (19)66, edit. 250, The Print Club of Cleveland Publication number 43, 1966, (07-03-92, Sloan, #312), 13½ x 9⅛ in., (34.3 x 23.2 cm.), color lithograph (BP 57, DM 166, FR 561, Y 13,712).

JUNKIN, Marion Montague American 1905-1977

$55* *Mr. London At Work,* s., t., d. 1932, (11-01-92, Hanzel, #207), 10 x 13 in., (25.4 x 33 cm.), woodcut (BP 36, DM 87, FR 292, Y 6800).

JURY, Wilhelm 1763-1829

BI *Die Zwolf Monate: Twelve,* est. DM 1,200, (12-04-92, Bassenge, #6614), drypoint.

JYCEL

$336* *Royal-Moto. "A Ouvert L'Ere De La Moto Pour Tous", c. 1925,* p. Le Henaff, good cond., (11-19-92, Ribeyre/ Baron, #66), 45¹¹⁄₁₆ x 30⁵⁄₁₆ in., (116 x 77 cm.), poster (BP 221, DM 536, FR 1805, Y 41,786).

KAFHU, Clifton American/Japanese b. 1927

$220* *Lane In Gion-Kyoto,* s., d. '72, t., #48/80, (05-16-93, Hindman, #393), 22½ x 22 in., (57.2 x 55.9 cm.), color woodcut (BP 143, DM 354, FR 1189, Y 24,388).

KAHAN, Louis b. 1905

$122* *Two Dancers,* s. Louis Kahan, i., d. '86, #4/50, (08-11-92, L. Joel, #40G), 19½ x 12¹⁵⁄₁₆ in., (49.5 x 33 cm.), color etching (BP 63, DM 179, FR 606, Y 15,623, A$ 165).

KAHN, Max American 20th cent.

$143* *"Sea Bird",* s., 25/131, Seabird Max Kahn 53(?), (02-27-93, Dunning, #1045, illus.), 16 x 21 in., (40.6 x 53.3 cm.), color lithograph (BP 101, DM 235, FR 799, Y 16,881).

KAHN, Wolf German/American b. 1927

$138* *White Barn,* s., good cond., (06-11-93, Freemn/Fine Art, #120), 20 x 25 in., (50.8 x 63.5 cm.), lithograph in color (BP 91, DM 224, FR 756, Y 14,642).

KAIKO, Moti

$138* *"New Cats",* s., num., d. 1964 bottom image, (08-05-92, Boos, #689, illus.), approx. 25⁹⁄₁₆ x 19⁵⁄₁₆ in., (650 x 490 mm.), lithograph (BP 72, DM 204, FR 689, Y 17,575).

KAISER, Raffi Israeli contemporary

$220* *Espaces At Esprit D'Israel: Twenty,* each s., t., #200/250, (11-01-92, Hanzel, #277), each sheet 17 x²⁴in., lithograph (BP 144, DM 347, FR 1170, Y 27,201).

$248* *Espaces Et Esprit D'Israel: Twenty,* each s., t., #212/250, (11-01-92, Hanzel, #278), each sheet 17 x 24 in., (43.2 x 61 cm.), lithograph (BP 162, DM 391, FR 1318, Y 30,663).

KAISER, Wilder and RITZTULUHORN
$83* *Untitled: Two,* (11-13-92, DuMouchelle, #1396), one 8½ x 7 in., (21.6 x 17.8 cm.), other 11½ x 15¼ in., (21.6 x 17.8 cm.), colored engraving (BP 54, DM 130, FR 439, Y 10,302).

KAISHUNTEI SADAYOSHI   Japanese ac. c. 1837-1853
BI *Sawamura Tokiwa As Taruya Osen,* Oban, s. Kaishuntei Sadayoshi ga w/seal, pub.'s mark Wataki, d. Tenpo13 (1842), good state, Prof. H.R.W. Kuhne Coll., est. BP 6/800, (06-11-93, Sotheby-London, #483), 11 x 10⅛ in., (27.9 x 25.7 cm.), woodblock.

KAKS, Olle   b. 1941
$1661* *Guillaume Appolinaire,* s. EA XVI/XXV, Galerie Aix, 1989, (05-25-93, AB Stockholm, #43), 16¹⁵⁄₁₆ x 11⁷⁄₁₆ in., (43 x 29 cm.), serigraph in colors (BP 1076, DM 2705, FR 9106, Y 181,550, SK 2420).
$746* *Guillaume Appolinaire, Dikter Till Lou, 1989:* Fifteen, portfolio, 116/225, Galerie Aix, (12-04-92, AB Stockholm, #7086), sh, approx. 16¹⁵⁄₁₆ x 11⁷⁄₁₆ in., (43 x 29 cm.), serigraph in colors (BP 479, DM 1188, FR 4030, Y 93,134, SK 5060).

KALES, A.F.
BI *Portrait Of Jean Harlow,* photog.'s sig., notations recto, 1920s, est. 700/1,000, (04-07-93, Swann, #495, illus.), 14 x 12 in., photograph, bromoil print.
BI *Woman In Tree, c. 1918,* sig., est. $8/1,200, (10-14-92, Swann, #489, illus.), 9¾ x 7¾ in., (24.8 x 19.7 cm.), photograph, platinum print.

KALINOWSKI, Horst Egon   b. 1924
BI *"L'Oeil Arme", (19)69,* s., d., t., num., est. DM 400, (12-01-92, Karl/Faber, #812), 17⁵⁄₁₆ x 25⁹⁄₁₆ in., (44 x 65 cm.), color etching and drypoint on Arches wove.

KALISHER, Simpson   b. 1926
$1150* *Boy Pushing A Car, 1961,* s., d., credit stamp, lit., (04-08-93, Christie-NY, #493, illus.), 12½ x 8¼ in., (31.8 x 21 cm.), photograph, gelatin silver print (BP 754, DM 1847, FR 6253, Y 130,504).

KALLMORGEN, Friedrich   1856-1924
$171* *Ansicht Des Bremer Rathausplatzes Mit Markstanden,* stone s., (09-25-92, Granier, #2649), 21⅝ x 29½ in., (55 x 75 cm.), color lithograph (BP 100, DM 253, FR 857, Y 20,640).
$253* *Fischerfrauen Am Landungssteg,* s., (12-04-92, Bassenge, #6840), 6¹¹⁄₁₆ x 9⁷⁄₁₆ in., (17 x 24 cm.), color lithograph on Japan cardboard (BP 162, DM 403, FR 1367, Y 31,586).

KALMAN, Bohonkay
$920* *Portrait Of A Musician, c. 1930,* credit stamp, (04-08-93, Christie-NY, #193, illus.), 11½ x 8¼ in., (29.2 x 21 cm.), photograph, toned gelatin silver print (BP 603, DM 1478, FR 5003, Y 104,403).

KALNINS, Rheinhold   German 20th cent.
$10* *Parisian Street Scene,* s., good cond., thin spots, laid down, stained, (05-15-93, Cleveland, #396), 11 x 18 in., (27.9 x 45.7 cm.), etching (BP 7, DM 16, FR 54, Y 1109).

KALVAK, Helen   Eskimo b. 1901
$440* *"Nightmare",* d. 1967, t., s., #13/15, Holman Island Cooperative symbol, very goodcond., prov., (06-26-93, Skinner, #55, illus.), 17¾ x 23½ in., (45.1 x 59.7 cm.), crimson stone cut (BP 295, DM 748, FR 2519, Y 46,684).

KAMPF, Max   1912-1982
BI *Basler Umzug, 1974,* 14/25, s., d., est. SF 220/240, (10-14-92, Germann, #557), 14¹⁄₁₆ x 20¹⁄₁₆ in., (357 x 510 mm.), lithograph.
BI *Mummenschanz, 1965,* s., d., est. SF 170/200, (10-14-92, Germann, #556), 19¹¹⁄₁₆ x 13¾ in., (500 x 350 mm.), lithograph.

KAMPMANN, Gustav   German 1859-1917
$197* *"Eifellandschaft",* stone s., i., sig. G. Kampmann, (03-24-93, Venator/Hansten, #4506), image approx. 9⁷⁄₁₆ x 16⅛ in., (24 x 41 cm.), color lithograph on paper (BP 133, DM 322, FR 1095, Y 23,147).

$110* *Landscape At Dusk,* s. in stone, (09-17-92, Sloan, #619), sight 21 x 29 in., (53.3 x 73.7 cm.), color lithograph (BP 62, DM 163, FR 559, Y 13,695).

KAMURA, Kora
$25* *Adam And Eve,* s., d. 1958.3.30, num. 36/50, (10-11-92, Hanzel, #951), 13¾ x 22 in., (34.9 x 55.9 cm.), color woodblock print (BP 15, DM 37, FR 125, Y 3044).

KANANGINAK   Inuit 20th cent.
$165* *Sharks Near Our Boats,* s., t., num. 37/50, (09-20-92, Hindman, #737), 19 x 30 in., (48.3 x 76.2 cm.), color stone cut and stencil (BP 97, DM 245, FR 838, Y 20,393).

KANANGINAK, Pootoogook   b. 1935
$225* *Boats I Have Known, 1981,* #17/25, s., t., d. 1981, prov., (11-16-92, Hodgins, #111), 10 x 12 in., (25.4 x 30.5 cm.), etching and aquatint on paper (BP 148, DM 359, FR 1209, Y 28,079, C$ 286).
$130* *Camp From My Past, 1981,* #17/25, s., t., d. 1981, prov., (11-16-92, Hodgins, #112), 11⅜ x 13¾ in., (29.9 x 34.9 cm.), hand colored etching and aquatint on paper (BP 85, DM 207, FR 699, Y 16,224, C$ 165).
$238* *Caribou, 1977,* #88/200, s., t., d. 1977, prov., (11-16-92, Hodgins, #272), 27¼ x 20½ in., (69.2 x 52.1 cm.), stonecut on paper (BP 156, DM 380, FR 1279, Y 29,702, C$ 303).
$303* *Floe Edge Hunter, 1974,* #25/50, s., t., d. 1974, prov., (11-16-92, Hodgins, #269), 22¹⁵⁄₁₆ x 34¼ in., (58.4 x 87 cm.), stonecut on paper (BP 199, DM 483, FR 1628, Y 37,814, C$ 385).
$164* *Geese In Spring, 1981,* #17/25, s., t., d. 1981, prov., (11-16-92, Hodgins, #270), 10 x 11¾ in., (25.4 x 29.9 cm.), hand colored etching and aquatint on paper (BP 108, DM 262, FR 881, Y 20,467, C$ 209).
$239* *Metik,* #88/200 s. syllabics, t., d. 1977, prov., (05-10-93, Hodgins, #118, illus.), 27½ x 20½ in., (69.9 x 52.1 cm.), stonecut and stencil on paper (BP 156, DM 384, FR 1295, Y 26,707, C$ 303).
$225* *My Peoples World, 1981,* #17/25, s., t., d. 1981, prov., (11-16-92, Hodgins, #113), 9¾ x 11⅜ in., (24.8 x 29.9 cm.), hand colored etching on paper (BP 148, DM 359, FR 1209, Y 28,079, C$ 286).
$693* *Omingmungjuag (Musk Ox), 1977,* #88/200, s., t., d. 1977, prov., (11-16-92, Hodgins, #101, illus.), 27¼ x 20½ in., (69.2 x 52.1 cm.), stonecut on paper (BP 455, DM 1105, FR 3724, Y 86,484, C$ 880).
$325* *Walrus, 1977,* #88/200, s., t., d. 1977, prov., (11-16-92, Hodgins, #265, illus.), 19¾ x 27¼ in., (52.1 x 69.2 cm.), stonecut on paper (BP 214, DM 518, FR 1746, Y 40,559, C$ 413).

KANDINSKY, Wassily   Russian 1866-1944
BI *Composition,* mono. in plate, edit. of 100 impressions, est. FF2/3,000, (05-27-93, Briest, #114), 16⁹⁄₁₆ x 19⅞ in., (42 x 50.5 cm.), wood engraving.
$853* *"Composition", c. 1935,* p. posthumous, mono. in plate, (10-18-92, Pescheteau, #172), 9¹⁄₁₆ x 10⅝ in., (23 x 27 cm.), original wood engraving (BP 517, DM 1260, FR 4280, Y 101,851).
$105* *Compositions: Two,* (09-30-92, Kunsthallen, #165), offset print (BP 59, DM 149, FR 504, Y 12,601, DK 575).
$12,869* *Dame Mit Muff (Winter) (R. 3), 1903,* trimmed to or close to image, gouache s. on mount, i. HOLZSCHIN-ITT, good cond., foxing, (06-30-93, Sotheby-London, #472, illus.), 9¾ x 5¾ in., (248 x 146 mm.), woodcut, black ink on Japan (BP 8625, DM 21,950, FR 74,045, Y 1,378,871).
BI *Dame Mit Muff (Winter) (Roethel 3), 1903,* narrow margins, old hinges, skinning, good cond., est. BP 5/8,000, (05-20-93, Christie-London, #448, illus.), image 9¾ x 5⅞ in., (24.8 x 14.9 cm.), sheet 9⅞ x 6 in., (24.8 x 14.9 cm.), woodcut on firm grey-green wove.
$9200* *Frohlicher Aufsteig (R. 177), 1923,* s., included in Meistermappe Des Staatlichen Bauhauses, pub. BauhausVerlag G.M.H., full margins, good cond., faded, inconspicuous marks of ink, discoloration, mat stain, losses (backed w/ Japan), skinned spots, (02-11-93, Sotheby-NY, #153, illus.), 9⅜ x 7¹¹⁄₁₆ in., (238 x 195 mm.), color lithograph

on wove (BP 6492, DM 15,239, FR 51,570, Y 1,109,102).

$34,649* "Frohlicher Aufstieg" (Roethel 177; Sohn 210-2), 1923, s., sheet 2 of Meistermappe des Staatlichen Bauhauses Weimer, prov., (11-28-92, Grisebach, #232, illus.), 9¼ x 7¹¹⁄₁₆ in., (23.5 x 19.5 cm.), color lithograph on wove (BP 22,871, DM 55,200, FR 187,393, Y 4,312,259).

$1093* From Klange, 1913, bears sig. w/inits., #250/300, pub. R. Piper, p. Poechel and Trepte and F. Bruckmann, margins, good cond., staining, hinge remains, surface soiling,notations, (05-19-93, Butterfield, #2063), each sh. 12¼ x 9⅜ in., (311 x 238 mm.), woodcut on Arches (BP 710, DM 1777, FR 5986, Y 121,001).

$465* Heiliger Georg (Roethel 94), 1911, block mono., posthumous print, (09-25-92, Granier, #2902), sheet 6¹⁵⁄₁₆ x 9⅞ in., (17.7 x 25.1 cm.), woodcut on wove (BP 272, DM 689, FR 2331, Y 56,126).

BI Kleine Welten I (Roetnel 164), 1922, trimmed close to image, crease, foxing, est. BP 1/1,200, (11-30-92, Phillips-London, #439), sheet 13 x 7½ in., (330 x 191 mm.), color lithograph on heavy wove.

$8867* Kleine Welten VII (Roethel 170), 1922, s., pub. Propylaen-Verlag, margins, reduced at sides, good cond., light staining, mount staining, tape, (12-03-92, Sotheby-London, #353, illus.), 10⅝ x 9⅛ in., (270 x 232 mm.), lithograph in colors on wove (BP 5720, DM 13,944, FR 47,595, Y 1,103,272).

$9221* Kleine Welten VII (Roethel 170), 1922, s., (06-05-93, Bassenge, #6170, illus.), 10¹¹⁄₁₆ x 9³⁄₁₆ in., (27.1 x 23.3 cm.), color lithograph on machine-made (BP 6070, DM 14,950, FR 50,388, Y 989,165).

$5650* Kleine Welten VIII (Roethel 171), 1922, s., block mono., sheet 8 from Kleine Welten, (06-10-93, Hauswedell/Nolt, #434, illus.), image 10¾ x 9⅛ in., (27.3 x 23.2 cm.), woodcut on Japan (BP 3696, DM 9200, FR 30,976, Y 599,724).

$4600* Kleine Welten X (Roethel 173), 1922, s., pub. Propylaen Verlag, full margins, good cond., scrape in image,crease, (05-13-93, Sotheby-NY, #571, illus.), 9½ x 11¾ in., (240 x 300 mm.), etching on wove (BP 3020, DM 7428, FR 25,054, Y 513,565).

$5791* Kleine Welten XI (Roethel 174), 1922, s., plate mono., sheet 11 from Kleine Welten, (06-10-93, Hauswedell/Nolt, #435, illus.), image 9⁷⁄₁₆ x 7¹³⁄₁₆ in., (23.9 x 19.9 cm.), drypoint on Japan (BP 3788, DM 9430, FR 31,749, Y 614,691).

$5500* Kleine Welten XII (R. 175), 1922, s., full margins, good cond., foxing, light stain, loss, (11-05-92, Sotheby-NY, #206, illus.), 9⅜ x 7¾ in., (238 x 198 mm.), drypoint on wove (BP 3577, DM 8698, FR 29,428, Y 674,764).

$19,472* Kleine Welten. IV (Rothel 167), 1922, sheet 4 of series: Kleine Welten, s., (06-23-93, Kornfeld, #425, illus.), color lithograph on thick wove (BP 13,228, DM 32,948, FR 110,825, Y 2,121,364, SF 29,325).

$13,975* Kleine Welten: Plate I (Roethel 164), 1922, s., pub. Propylaen Verlag, margins, creasing, foxmarks, other minor defects, prov., (05-20-93, Christie-London, #449, illus.), image 10 x 8½ in., (25.4 x 21.6 cm.), sheet 14⅛ x 11 in., (25.4 x 21.6 cm.), lithograph p. in colors on Japan (BP 8970, DM 22,548, FR 75,951, Y 1,543,176).

BI Kleine Welten: Plate III (Roethel 166), 1922, s., pub. Propylaen Verlag, margins, mount-staining, tape, good cond., est. BP 6/8,000, (05-20-93, Christie-London, #450, illus.), image 11 x 9⅛ in., (27.9 x 23.2 cm.), sheet 14 x 11 in., (27.9 x 23.2 cm.), lithograph p. in colors.

$9317* Kleine Welten: Plate IV (Roethel 167), 1922, s., pub. Propylaen Verlag, margins, mount-staining, colors slightly attenuated, tape, good cond., (05-20-93, Christie-London, #451, illus.), image 10¾ x 10½ in., (27.3 x 26.7 cm.), sheet 13¼ x 11⅜ in., (27.3 x 26.7 cm.), lithograph in colors on wove (BP 5980, DM 15,032, FR 50,636, Y 1,028,821).

$17,050* Lithographie Fur Die Vierte Bauhausmappe (Roethel 162), 1922, s., probably a proof, margins, good cond., light staining, thin spots, (11-05-92, Sotheby-NY, #205, illus.), 10⅝ x 9¼ in., (270 x 235 mm.), sheet 13⅞ x 12⅜ in., (270 x 235 mm.), lithograph p. in colors on wove (BP 11,089, DM 26,965, FR 91,225, Y 2,091,768).

$2483* Postkarte Fur Die Bauhaus-Ausstellung (Roethel 179), 1923, stamp, (06-05-93, Bassenge, #6171, illus.), 4¹⁵⁄₁₆ x 3⁹⁄₁₆ in., (12.5 x 9 cm.), lithograph on board (BP 1635, DM 4026, FR 13,568, Y 266,359).

$1049* Promenade En Barque, yellowed, dust, #20/30, large margins, (02-03-93, Ader Tajan, #168), 8⅞ x 23⅛ in., (22.5 x 58.7 cm.), wood engraving (BP 732, DM 1727, FR 5857, Y 130,489).

$6005* Radierung Fur Den 'Kreis Der Freunde Des Bauhauses' (Roethel 197), 1932, s., full margins, good cond., nicks, skinned patch, creases, discoloration, (06-30-93, Sotheby-London, #471, illus.), 7⅞ x 9⅜ in., (200 x 238 mm.), drypoint on wove (BP 4025, DM 10,242, FR 34,551, Y 643,416).

$385* "Rouge Jaune Bleu", mono., d. in stone, (10-31-92, Litchfield, #89), 9½ x 14¾ in., (24.1 x 37.5 cm.), color lithograph (BP 252, DM 604, FR 2047, Y 47,601).

$3575* Schwarze Linien (R. 184), 1924, s., No 35/50, full margins, good cond., glue/mat staining, surface soiling, creases, catalog cover lot, (10-28-92, Butterfield, #2658, illus.), image 10 x 8½ in., (254 x 216 mm.), sheet 13½ x 10⅝ in., (254 x 216 mm.), lithograph on cream wove (BP 2278, DM 5521, FR 18,747, Y 438,650).

$116,848* "Der Spiegel" (Roethel 49/I), 1907, edit. 6, (06-04-93, Grisebach, #16, illus.), 12½ x 6⅛ in., (31.8 x 15.6 cm.), color linocut on Japan (BP 77,306, DM 189,750, FR 639,562, Y 12,602,243).

BI Tache Noire (Roethel 145), 1912, s., rare, excellent cond., fox marks, full margins, est. FF 50/60,000, (11-16-92, Briest, #319, illus.), 9¹³⁄₁₆ x 13¼ in., (25 x 33.6 cm.), wood engraving on Japan.

BI Violett (Roethel 178), 1923, i. Probedruck, pub. Staatliches Bauhaus, mount-staining, glue stains, short pen inscription, est. BP 15/20,000, (05-20-93, Christie-London, #452, illus.), image 11½ x 7¾ in., (29.2 x 19.7 cm.), sheet 13¼ x 10⅜ in., (29.2 x 19.7 cm.), lithograph in colors on wove.

BI "Xylographies" (Roethel 54, 55, 59-60, 65-66, 70-71), 1909: Eight, after Holzschnitten Kandinskys. Paris, Edition des Tendances Nouvelles, signs of wear, est. DM 4500, (12-01-92, Karl/Faber, #814), 12¹³⁄₁₆ x 12¹³⁄₁₆ in., (32.5 x 32.5 cm.), heliogravure (photoengraving).

BI "Xylographies", Paris 1909: Seven, Edition des Tendances Nouvelles, Paris, est. SC 30/40,000, (11-25-92, Dorotheum, #466, illus.), 12⅝ x 12¹¹⁄₁₆ in., (32 x 32.3 cm.), heliograph.

BI Xylographies, 1909: Series Of Five, tears, est. FF10/12,000, (05-27-93, Briest, #113), 12¹³⁄₁₆ x 12¹³⁄₁₆ in., (32.5 x 32.5 cm.), wood engravings.

KANDINSKY, Wassily (after)   1866-1944
$147* Composition, 1973, from Abstraction-Creation, Art Non-Figuratif 1932-1936, #6/150, sig.stamp, s. Nina Kandinsky, (11-16-92, Briest, #62), 25¹³⁄₁₆ x 33¹⁄₁₆ in., (65.5 x 84 cm.), serigraph in black (BP 97, DM 234, FR 790, Y 18,345).

KANEMITSU, Matsumi
BI Homage To Jules Langsner (T. 2719), 1969, s., d., #20/20, pub. Tamarind Lithography Workshop, good cond.?, est. $1/1,500, (10-28-92, Butterfield, #2994), 30 x 22 in., (762 x 559 mm.), color lithograph on wove.

BI Mickey Mouse Series (T. 2881-2889, 2923-2931, 2940), 1970: Nineteen, complete portfolio, s., d., #15/20, inks-tamp pub. Tamarind Lithography Workshop, full sheets, good cond., buckling, surface soiling, orig. mouse ear-shaped black leather case, est. $2,5/3,500, (10-28-92, Butterfield, #2995), each 9 x 10 in., (229 x 254 mm.), lithograph on BFK Rives.

KANNELY
$165* Ringling Bros. And Barnum And Bailey, B+ cond., fold marks, marginal damage, (08-06-92, Swann, #103, illus.), 41½ x 27½ in., (105.4 x 69.9 cm.), (BP 86, DM 244, FR 823, Y 21,046).

KANOLDT, Alexander   1881-1939
$738* Alba (Ammann 17), 1924, s., num., (12-05-92, Bassenge, #7317), 9⁵⁄₁₆ x 13⅛ in., (23.7 x 33.3 cm.), lithograph on imitation Japan (BP 462, DM 1151, FR 3921, Y 91,438).

$1299* *"Chiemsee I" (Amann L 47), 1937,* s., d., num., prov., (11-28-92, Grisebach, #579, illus.), 11 x 14 13/16 in., (28 x 37.6 cm.), lithograph on Japan (BP 857, DM 2069, FR 7025, Y 161,668).

$395* *Hiddensee II (Ammann 29), 1927,* s., d., t., #30/100, (06-10-93, Hauswedell/Nolt, #439), image 12 1/16 x 18¼ in., (30.7 x 46.4 cm.), lithograph on hand-made (BP 258, DM 643, FR 2166, Y 41,928).

BI *Hochgern (Ammann 5), 1922,* s., d., num., est. DM 2000, (12-01-92, Karl/Faber, #816), 10 13/16 x 16 9/16 in., (27.5 x 42 cm.), lithograph on hand-made.

$1180* *Olevano V, Hochformat (Ammann 24), 1925,* s., (12-05-92, Bassenge, #7318, illus.), 8 13/16 x 6⅞ in., (22.4 x 17.4 cm.), lithograph on Japan (BP 739, DM 1840, FR 6270, Y 146,202).

KANOVITZ, Howard

BI *Untitled, Fruhstuck Auf Der Farm,* s., est. DM 5,000-, (05-27-93, Lempertz, #834), 30 5/16 x 22 7/16 in., (77 x 57 cm.), color chalk on lithograph.

KAORU, Kawano Japanese 1916-1965

$198* *Untitled: Four,* s. w/seal, (03-25-93, Boos, #272), each image 10¼ x 15¼ in., (26 x 38.7 cm.), color woodblock print (BP 134, DM 325, FR 1106, Y 23,196).

$99* *Untitled: Three,* s. w/seal, (03-25-93, Boos, #270), each image 4¼ x 6 in., (10.8 x 15.2 cm.), color woodblock print (BP 67, DM 163, FR 553, Y 11,598).

KAPOOR, Anish Indian/American b. 1954

BI *Untitled, I, 1988,* s., d., i. (I), #4/20, Crown Point Press blindstamp, full margins, excell. cond., the Late M. Anwar Kamal, M.D. Coll., est. $1,5/2,000, (05-11-93, Christie-NY, #473), sheet 53 x 35 in., (134.6 x 88.9 cm.), color spit-bite aquatint on wove.

$1150* *Untitled, II, 1988,* s., d., i. (II), #3/20, Crown Point Press blindstamp, full margins, image scuffs, excell. cond., the Late M. Anwar Kamal, M.D. Coll., (05-11-93, Christie-NY, #474), sheet 53 x 42 in., (134.6 x 106.7 cm.), color spit-bite aquatint on wove (BP 734, DM 1812, FR 6104, Y 126,499).

KAPPEL, Philip American b. 1901

$22* *Frenchmans Bay, Bar Harbor, ME,* margins, s., (05-22-93, Collins, #6), 8⅞ x 6⅞ in., (22.5 x 17.5 cm.), etching (BP 14, DM 36, FR 120, Y 2426).

$17* *Mid Atlantic,* margins, s., (05-22-93, Collins, #7), 5 x 5¾ in., (12.7 x 14.6 cm.), etching (BP 11, DM 28, FR 93, Y 1874).

$10* *"Nile Boats", 1932,* s., t., good cond., tear, (05-15-93, Cleveland, #173), 8½ x 8 in., (21.6 x 20.3 cm.), etching (BP 7, DM 16, FR 54, Y 1109).

BI *"Off El Morro, Puerto Rico",* AAA edit., excell. cond., est. $80/120, (05-15-93, Cleveland, #172), 9⅞ x 7⅞ in., (25.1 x 20 cm.), etching and drypoint.

$88* *Star Class, Marblehead,* margins, s. Philip Kappel, d. 1929, (02-13-93, Collins, #70, illus.), 7⅜ x 9⅜ in., (18.7 x 23.8 cm.), etching (BP 62, DM 146, FR 494, Y 10,613).

KAR, Ida c. 1908-1974

$345* *"Cocteau" and "Foujita": Two,* 1920s, p.l., s. on image, photog.'s stamp, est. $7/900, (05-23-93, Butterfield, #3475), one 9⅛ x 9 in., other 9½ x 7½ in., photograph, gelatin silver print (BP 225, DM 564, FR 1899, Y 38,134).

BI *Colin McInnes, 1960,* crayon s., photog.'s ink (c) stamp, lit., est. BP 3/500, (05-06-93, Christie-London, #111, illus.), 9⅜ x 7½ in., photograph, gelatin silver print.

$907* *Georges Braques, 1960,* crayon s. recto, photog.'s ink (c) stamp, label, lit., (05-06-93, Christie-London, #112, illus.), 9⅜ x 9½ in., photograph, gloss gelatin silver print (BP 575, DM 1429, FR 4809, Y 99,791).

BI *Ivon Hitchens, c. 1960,* s. recto, est. BP 4/600, (05-06-93, Christie-London, #116, illus.), 10¾ x 9¾ in., photograph, gelatin silver print.

BI *Jean Dubuffet,* c. 1964, crayon s. recto, photog.'s ink (c) stamp, est. BP 3/500, (05-06-93, Christie-London, #115, illus.), 9¼ x 7 in., photograph, gloss gelatin silver print.

BI *Lynn Chadwick, 1954,* s. recto, photog.'s ink credit stamp, lit., est. BP 4/600, (05-06-93, Christie-London, #114, illus.), 11¾ x 9¼ in., photograph, gloss gelatin silver print.

$509* *Portrait Of Marc Chagall With Typography Advertising An Exhibition, 1954,* mounted on card, s. by photog. and Chagall, label, 365 x 487mm, (05-07-93, Sotheby-London, #195, illus.), photograph, silver print (BP 322, DM 805, FR 2712, Y 56,045).

$508* *Stanley Spencer, 1954,* crayon s. recto, photog.'s ink credit stamp, label, lit., (05-06-93, Christie-London, #113, illus.), 11¾ x 9 in., photograph, gloss gelatin silver print (BP 322, DM 800, FR 2694, Y 55,892).

KARASZ, Ilonka

$22* *"Homage D'Amour",* s., t., (06-11-93, DuMouchelle, #2270), 4 x 3 in., (10.2 x 7.6 cm.), etching (BP 14, DM 36, FR 121, Y 2334).

KAROLY, Andrew

$110* *"Mont St. Michel" and "Segovia, Spain", 1936 & 1938: Two,* s., pub. AAA, full margins, good cond., staining, surface soiling, (02-24-93, Butterfield, #2840), one 11 15/16 x 9¾ in., (303 x 248 mm.), other 12 15/16 x 9 7/16 in., (303 x 248 mm.), etching on wove (BP 77, DM 179, FR 605, Y 12,908).

KARSH, Yousuf b. 1908

$1213* *Albert Einstein, 1948,* ink s., t., lit., (11-12-92, Lempertz, #110, illus.), 11 x 10 11/16 in., (28 x 27.2 cm.), sheet 13¾ x 11⅛ in., (28 x 27.2 cm.), photograph, gelatin silver print (BP 776, DM 1906, FR 6497, Y 150,068).

BI *Canadian Prime Minister William Mackenzie King, 1947,* photog.'s sig., King's i., sig., (04-07-93, Swann, #322), 6½ x 4¾ in., photograph, silver print.

$433* *Cecil B. De Mille,* c. 1955, ink s., photog.'s credit stamp, mounted, (12-17-92, Christie-S. Ken, #64, illus.), 13 x 10¼ in., (33 x 26 cm.), photograph, matt gelatin silver print (BP 275, DM 676, FR 2309, Y 53,214).

$1150* *Ernest Hemingway,* 1957, p.l., ink s.; t., photog.'s credit stamp, sold after sale, (04-08-93, Christie-NY, #441, illus.), 19⅝ x 15⅞ in., (49.8 x 40.3 cm.), photograph, gelatin silver print (BP 754, DM 1847, FR 6253, Y 130,504).

$3300* *Georgia O'Keeffe, 1956 (Karsh, p. 111),* mounted, s. by photog. in ink, p. l., (10-15-92, Sotheby-NY, #452, illus.), 19¾ x 14¾ in., (50.2 x 37.5 cm.), photograph, gelatin silver print (BP 2019, DM 4912, FR 16,658, Y 395,921).

$1980* *Humphrey Bogart, 1946,* (c) credit stamp, lit., (10-13-92, Christie-NY, #249, illus.), 13½ x 10⅝ in., (34.3 x 27 cm.), photograph, gelatin silver print (BP 1153, DM 2901, FR 9856, Y 240,087).

$1150* *Jean Sibelius, 1949,* s., (c) by photog. in ink on image, (04-06-93, Sotheby-NY, #388, illus.), 19⅞ x 15⅞ in., photograph (BP 760, DM 1853, FR 6274, Y 131,159).

$2351* *Joan Miro, 1965,* ink s., t., lit., (11-12-92, Lempertz, #112, illus.), 13 15/16 x 11⅛ in., (35.5 x 28.2 cm.), photograph, gelatin silver print (BP 1503, DM 3695, FR 12,592, Y 290,857).

$1517* *Pablo Casals, 1954,* ink s., t., lit., (11-12-92, Lempertz, #111, illus.), 13 15/16 x 11⅛ in., (35.5 x 28.3 cm.), photograph, gelatin silver print (BP 970, DM 2384, FR 8125, Y 187,678).

$1045* *Portrait Of Albert Einstein,* sig., i., 1950's, p.l., (10-14-92, Swann, #490), photograph, silver print (BP 613, DM 1529, FR 5186, Y 126,636).

$2090* *Portrait Of Fidel Castro, 1971,* photog.'s ink sig. on notations, (04-07-93, Swann, #496, illus.), 19¾ x 15¾ in., photograph, silver print (BP 1381, DM 3380, FR 11,440, Y 237,446).

$935* *Portrait Of George Bernard Shaw, 1943,* s., handstamp, (10-14-92, Swann, #491, illus.), 9½ x 7½ in., (24.1 x 19.1 cm.), photograph, silver print (BP 549, DM 1368, FR 4640, Y 113,306).

$440* *Self-Portrait, 1971,* photog.'s sig., i., d. recto, (04-07-93, Swann, #497, illus.), 8 x 6 in., photograph, silver print (BP 291, DM 712, FR 2408, Y 49,989).

$358* *"Signore S. Landre",* s., i., photog. stamp, #10, (11-16-92, Butterfield, #6030, illus.), 9½ x 7½ in., (241.7 x 190.8 mm.), photograph, gelatin silver print (BP 236, DM 571, FR 1923, Y 44,522).

$3163* *Winston Churchill (Karsh, p. 38),* mounted, s. by photog., 1941, p.l., (04-06-93, Sotheby-NY, #389, illus.), 19¾ x

15¾ in., photograph (BP 2089, DM 5096, FR 17,256, Y 360,744).

$1725* *"Winston Churchill", 1941,* s., annot. Ottawa on image, photog.'s stamp, mount trimmed to print, (05-23-93, Butterfield, #3476, illus.), 17½ x 14 in., photograph, gelatin silver print (BP 1123, DM 2820, FR 9494, Y 190,671).

$3520* *Winston Churchill, 1941,* s., annot., (c) insig., lit., (10-13-92, Christie-NY, #248, illus.), 22 x 18 in., (55.9 x 45.7 cm.), photograph, gelatin silver print (BP 2050, DM 5157, FR 17,521, Y 426,822).

BI *Winston Churchill, 1941,* ink s., (c) Y. Karsh F.R.P.S., ded., good cond., est. $3/500, (03-12-93, Skinner, #118, illus.), sight 15⅛ x 13⅛ in., photograph, silver print on heavy paper.

$2475* *Winston Churchill, 1941 (Karsh, p. 38),* (c) credit in neg., s. by photog., (c) stamp, (10-15-92, Sotheby-NY, #451, illus.), 9⅛ x 6¾ in., (23.2 x 17.1 cm.), photograph, gelatin silver print (BP 1515, DM 3684, FR 12,494, Y 296,941).

KASAMATSU, Shiro Japanese b. 1898

$44* *Evening Village Scene,* p. sig., seals, (03-25-93, Boos, #267), image 14⅜ x 9⅝ in., (36.5 x 24.4 cm.), color woodblock print (BP 30, DM 72, FR 246, Y 5155).

BI *Pair Of Prints,* one t., both s. inside plate Shiro Kasamatsu, d. 1962, 1963, num.79/100, 30/100, very good cond. (?), est. $2/300, (04-25-93, Bakker, #145), image 14½ x 9¾ in., (36.8 x 24.8 cm.), color woodblock prints.

KASEBIER, Gertrude 1852-1934

BI *Baron De Meyer, 1903,* stamp num. 330, num. 450, est. $2/3,000, (04-06-93, Sotheby-NY, #69, illus.), 8⅝ x 5 in., photograph.

$1210* *Gertrude A. Herbert,* s. by photog. on image, mounted, i. in unidentified hand, early 1900's, (10-15-92, Sotheby-NY, #101, illus.), 8 x 6 in., (20.3 x 15.2 cm.), photograph, platinum print (BP 740, DM 1801, FR 6108, Y 145,171).

BI *Girl With White Bow, (Lunn, Photo-Secession, fig. 169),* mounted, early 1900's, (10-15-92, Sotheby-NY, #102, illus.), 8⅜ x 6⅞ in., (21.3 x 17.5 cm.), photograph, platinum print.

$3850* *Laborers,* early 1900's, (10-15-92, Sotheby-NY, #100, illus.), 6¼ x 8 in., (15.9 x 20.3 cm.), photograph, gum bichromate print (BP 2356, DM 5731, FR 19,435, Y 461,908).

$2530* *Mother And Child, 1906,* tipped to triple-mount, (04-06-93, Sotheby-NY, #70, illus.), 5½ x 7⅜ in., photograph, platinum print (BP 1671, DM 4076, FR 13,803, Y 288,549).

$1650* *Mother And Child, c. 1910,* (10-13-92, Christie-NY, #39, illus.), 7¾ x 5⅞ in., (19.7 x 14.9 cm.), photograph, platinum print (BP 961, DM 2417, FR 8213, Y 200,073).

$660* *Mr. O'Malley And Granddaughter, c. 1900,* sold after sale, (10-14-92, Swann, #492, illus.), 6⅛ x 4 in., (15.6 x 10.2 cm.), photograph, platinum print (BP 387, DM 966, FR 3275, Y 79,981).

BI *Portrait Of A Woman With Oriental Print, c. 1910,* prov., lit., est. $2,8/3,500, (10-13-92, Christie-NY, #40, illus.), 8⅛ x 6⅜ in., (20.6 x 16.2 cm.), photograph, gum-bichromate print.

$1210* *Self Portrait, c. 1905,* (10-14-92, Swann, #493, illus.), 8⅛ x 6⅛ in., (20.6 x 15.6 cm.), photograph, toned platinum print (BP 710, DM 1771, FR 6005, Y 146,631).

KASIMIR, Luigi Aus./American 1881-1962

$523* *Aggstein Castle (V. 32), 1915,* plate s., d., full margins, very good cond., foxing, surface soiling, creases, watermark, (10-28-92, Butterfield, #2830), 18⅛ x 23⅝ in., (460 x 600 mm.), color etching w/remarque on cream wove (BP 333, DM 808, FR 2743, Y 64,172).

$330* *"Arch Of Septimus Severus",* s. Luigi Kasimir, d. April 1923, Feb. 1924 in plate, (11-12-92, A. James, #36), 27¼ x 18½ in., (69.2 x 47 cm.), drypoint and etching (BP 217, DM 523, FR 1764, Y 40,918).

$138* *The Avenue,* s., i., (10-30-92, Sloan, #1787), 14⅞ x 13½ in., (37.8 x 34.3 cm.), color aquatint (BP 88, DM 212, FR 720, Y 17,094).

$225* *A Back Street,* (02-27-93, Young, #174, illus.), 10 x 8 in., (25.4 x 20.3 cm.), color etching (BP 158, DM 370, FR 1257, Y 26,561).

BI *Boats Along The Shore,* s., prov., est. $400/500, (09-17-92, Sloan, #2369), 9¹³⁄₁₆ x 9¼ in., (24.9 x 23.5 cm.), color etching.

BI *Bowling Green, New York City,* d. 1927, (c), i. in plate; s., i., est. $4/500, (09-17-92, Sloan, #1459), 17⅜ x 9⅜ in., (44.1 x 23.8 cm.), color etching.

BI *"Bowling Green, New York City", 1927,* s., i. Artist's Print, top mat glued margins, est. $6/800, (05-15-93, Cleveland, #400, illus.), 17⅜ x 9¾ in., (44.1 x 24.8 cm.), etching in color.

$935* *"Brooklyn Bridge",* s., slight mat stain, fold, (10-31-92, Cleveland, #299, illus.), 11¾ x 17 in., (29.8 x 43.2 cm.), color etching (BP 599, DM 1438, FR 4880, Y 115,818).

$33* *"Cathedral",* 9/150, s. L. Kasimir, (05-15-93, Dunning, #208), sh 17 x 12 in., (43.2 x 30.5 cm.), etching and aquatint in color laid down on board (BP 21, DM 53, FR 178, Y 3658).

$440* *Central Park South,* s., d. 28 Feb. 1927 in plate, (12-02-92, Boos, #467, illus.), image 17⅞ x 11 in., (454 x 280 mm.), color etching and aquatint (BP 284, DM 692, FR 2362, Y 54,747).

$385* *"Chartres Cathedral",* s.; plate t., (12-02-92, Boos, #465), image 17⅝ x 12¹¹⁄₁₆ in., (448 x 323 mm.), color etching and aquatint (BP 248, DM 605, FR 2067, Y 47,903).

BI *"Chicago University Chapel",* s., num. 1/100, good cond., est. $3-400, (10-31-92, Cleveland, #298), 17⅛ x 11¼ in., (43.5 x 28.6 cm.), color etching.

$220* *"Danzig",* s. Luigi Kasimir, i. Danzig, (11-12-92, A. James, #223), 16½ x 20 in., (41.9 x 50.8 cm.), drypoint and etching (BP 144, DM 349, FR 1176, Y 27,278).

BI *European Street Scene,* s., image scuff, laid down, burned, est. $30/40, (05-15-93, Cleveland, #399), 6¼ x 9¼ in., (15.9 x 23.5 cm.), etching.

$605* *"Gastein Springs, The Cascades" and "Gasten Springs": Two,* s., margins, good cond., extensive skinned areas, foxing, glue staining, creases, scratch, (10-28-92, Butterfield, #2832), one 18½ x 14½ in., (470 x 368 mm.), the other 18⅜ x 13⅝ in., (470 x 368 mm.), color etching on wove (BP 385, DM 934, FR 3173, Y 74,233).

$605* *Grinzing,* t., d. 1940 in plate; s., (10-30-92, Sloan, #1595), 18¼ x 23¼ in., (46.4 x 59.1 cm.), color etching and aquatint (BP 388, DM 931, FR 3158, Y 74,941).

$330* *Hamburg,* s., #146/300, (10-30-92, Sloan, #1594), 19⅛ x 23½ in., (48.6 x 59.7 cm.), color etching and aquatint (BP 211, DM 508, FR 1722, Y 40,877).

$248* *Independence Hall, Philadelphia (K. 522),* s., t. w/(c) in plate, full margins, mat burn, rippling, (12-12-92, Weschler, #132), 17½ x 13¾ in., (44.5 x 34.9 cm.), color etching, soft-ground etching and aquatint (BP 159, DM 391, FR 1339, Y 30,689).

$143* *"Janner" 1915,* s. Luigi Kasimir, good cond. (?), (04-25-93, Bakker, #62), image 16 x 22½ in., (40.6 x 57.2 cm.), etching w/hand coloring (BP 91, DM 226, FR 764, Y 15,794).

$385* *London, Fleet Street,* s., (11-12-92, Freemn/Fine Art, #101), 20¾ x 15⅛ in., (52.7 x 38.4 cm.), aquatint in color (BP 253, DM 610, FR 2058, Y 47,737).

$413* *"London, Fleet Street",* pencil s., (05-08-93, Young, #184, illus.), 21 x 15 in., (53.3 x 38.1 cm.), color etching (BP 262, DM 653, FR 2200, Y 45,475).

$770* *"Marienburg Castle",* s., num. 2/200, time staining, orig. cond., (10-31-92, Cleveland, #292, illus.), 18 x 23¼ in., (45.7 x 59.1 cm.), color etching and aquatint (BP 493, DM 1185, FR 4019, Y 95,380).

BI *Melk On The Danube,* estate sig., full margins, good cond., pressure marks, soiling, creases, est. $5/700, (05-19-93, Butterfield, #2065), 9¾ x 9¼ in., (248 x 235 mm.), etching and aquatint in colors on wove.

$523* *Michigan Avneue, Chicago,* s., #18/150, (05-16-93, Hindman, #458), 13¾ x 17¾ in., (34.9 x 45.1 cm.), color etching and aquatint (BP 340, DM 841, FR 2827, Y 57,976).

BI *"New York Stcok Exchange",* estate s., good cond., est. $5/700, (05-15-93, Cleveland, #401, illus.), 17⅛ x 10⅝ in., (43.5 x 27 cm.), color etching.

$413* *Notre Dame,* s., (09-17-92, Sloan, #2370), 17½ x 12¾ in., (44.5 x 32.4 cm.), color etching (BP 232, DM 613, FR 2099, Y 51,419).

BI *"Opera Invitation",* s., good cond., est. $50-100, (10-31-92, Cleveland, #297), 6¾ x 4¼ in., (17.1 x 10.8 cm.), etching.

$385* *Palace Gate,* (11-12-92, Freemn/Fine Art, #100), 13 x 11 in., (33 x 27.9 cm.), aquatint in color (BP 253, DM 610, FR 2058, Y 47,737).

$358* *"Paris, La Bourse",* pencil s., (05-08-93, Young, #183, illus.), 12 x 17 in., (30.5 x 43.2 cm.), color etching (BP 227, DM 566, FR 1907, Y 39,419).

$330* *"Philadelphia Independence Hall",* s., d. 23 Sept. 1941 in plate, (12-02-92, Boos, #466), image 18¹¹⁄₁₆ x 12⅝ in., (475 x 320 mm.), color etching and aquatint (BP 213, DM 519, FR 1771, Y 41,060).

$220* *Piazza San Marco,* s., #59/300, (11-01-92, Hanzel, #231), 17 x 23 in., (43.2 x 58.4 cm.), colored etching (BP 144, DM 347, FR 1170, Y 27,201).

$121* *Plaza With Fountain,* s., (02-14-93, Hanzel, #692), 12⅛ x 9⅞ in., (30.8 x 25.1 cm.), colored etching (BP 85, DM 201, FR 679, Y 14,592).

$275* *"Pottenbrunn",* s., very light struck, remnants, small tear, (10-31-92, Cleveland, #294), 14¾ x 12¾ in., (37.5 x 32.4 cm.), etching in colors (BP 176, DM 423, FR 1435, Y 34,064).

BI *"Prague", 1922,* s., fair cond.; staining verso, est. $75-125, (10-31-92, Cleveland, #293), 13½ x 9¾ in., (34.3 x 24.8 cm.), etching.

$303* *Roman Ruins, 1912,* s., pub. Grauert & Fink, margins, sealed in mat, skinned areas, foxing, surface soiling, (10-28-92, Butterfield, #2827), 19¾ x 26 in., (502 x 660 mm.), etching w/remarque on cream wove (BP 193, DM 468, FR 1589, Y 37,178).

$316* *Santa Fe, N.M.,* s., #33/150, full margins, very good cond., mat staining, (05-19-93, Butterfield, #2066), 13⅝ x 10⅜ in., (346 x 264 mm.), etching and aquatint in colors on wove (BP 205, DM 514, FR 1731, Y 34,983).

$460* *Seebenstein, 1915,* s., t., d. in plate, full margins, good cond., mat staining, tape remains, (05-19-93, Butterfield, #1921), 16⅜ x 22⅝ in., (416 x 575 mm.), etching and aquatint in colors on wove (BP 299, DM 748, FR 2519, Y 50,924).

$154* *"Street Scene",* #61/250; s., d. May 1923, (05-15-93, Dunning, #129), 19½ x 15½ in., (49.5 x 39.4 cm.), color etching (BP 100, DM 248, FR 832, Y 17,071).

$489* *"Thames And Tower Bridge, London" and "European City Scene", 1919-22: Two,* s., #134/CL, #63/100, first d. in plate, margins, good cond., mat/light-staining, handling creases, hinge remains, light-staining, (05-19-93, Butterfield, #2064), one 15⅛ x 20⅝ in., (384 x 524 mm.), the other 12¾ x 10⅜ in., (384 x 524 mm.), etching on wove and Van Gelder Zonen (BP 317, DM 795, FR 2678, Y 54,135).

$140* *"Trafalgar Square",* s., num. 46/100, blindstamp, margins, (08-20-92, Bonhams-Chelsea, #30), plate 13 x 14¼ in., (33 x 36.2 cm.), etching (BP 72, DM 203, FR 688, Y 17,679).

BI *Untitled,* s., good cond., est. $50-100, (10-31-92, Cleveland, #295), 6¼ x 4¾ in., (15.9 x 12.1 cm.), etching in black and white.

$605* *Venedig, Fischhalle,* s., full margins, very good cond., mat staining, creases, foxing, surface soiling, (10-28-92, Butterfield, #2833), 18⅛ x 23½ in., (460 x 597 mm.), color etching on cream wove, watermark (BP 385, DM 934, FR 3173, Y 74,233).

BI *"Vienna Belvede Palace", 1923,* s., num. 235/250, good cond., est. $75-125, (10-31-92, Cleveland, #296), 13 x 11½ in., (33 x 29.2 cm.), color etching.

BI *Vienna, Shubert's Birthplace (K. 25),* s., margins, good cond.?, est. $5/700, (12-12-92, Weschler, #133, illus.), 10 x 8 in., (25.4 x 20.3 cm.), etching, soft-ground etching and aquatint.

$550* *View Of The Walled City,* s., #26/100, (07-03-92, Sloan, #302), 12½ x 8 in., (31.8 x 20.3 cm.), color drypoint etching and aquatint (BP 287, DM 832, FR 2806, Y 68,561).

BI *Wien,* plate s., d., est. DM 1,500, (05-08-93, Schloss Ahlden, #2852), 18¼ x 15⁹⁄₁₆ in., (46.3 x 39.5 cm.), color etching on cardboard.

$132* *"Wien Am Hof" (Vienna In The Court),* s., (05-15-93, Dunning, #130), 11½ x 15 in., (29.2 x 38.1 cm.), etching (BP 86, DM 212, FR 714, Y 14,633).

KASIMIR, Robert   b. Vienna 1914

BI *Broad Street,* s. in plate, est. $350/450, (07-03-92, Sloan, #1083), 17½ x 12 in., (44.5 x 30.5 cm.), color lithograph.

BI *"Karlskirche",* s., good cond., est. $100-150, (10-31-92, Cleveland, #300), 12½ x 10 in., (31.8 x 25.4 cm.), color etching.

KASSAK, Lajos   Hungarian 20th cent.

$263* *"Composition", 1965,* s. Kassak Paderma, edit. of 130, (05-18-93, Encans, #198), 11¾ x 11⁷⁄₁₆ in., (29.8 x 29 cm.), linotype (BP 171, DM 427, FR 1441, Y 29,310, C$ 333).

KASSEK, Lajos   1887-1967

$363* *Kepeskonyv-Bilderbuch Heute, 1922,* s. stone, s. ink, (06-24-93, Germann, #393), 12⁷⁄₁₆ x 9¾ in., (316 x 248 mm.), color lithograph (BP 239, DM 589, FR 1984, Y 38,940, SF 529).

KASTEN, Barbara

BI *Construct 33, 1986,* s., t., d., num. 2/10 by photog., #2/10 ed., est. $3/5,000, (10-15-92, Sotheby-NY, #594A, illus.), 29⅝ x 37 in., (75.2 x 94 cm.), photograph, cibachrome print.

$3850* *Construct XI-A, 1982,* s., t., d., num. 6/6 by photog., #6/6 ed., (10-15-92, Sotheby-NY, #593, illus.), 37¼ x 29¼ in., (94.6 x 74.3 cm.), photograph, cibachrome print (BP 2356, DM 5731, FR 19,435, Y 461,908).

BI *Construct XIV, 1982,* s., t., d., num. 5/6 by photog., #5/6 ed., est. $3/5,000, (10-15-92, Sotheby-NY, #594, illus.), 37½ x 29¾ in., (95.3 x 75.6 cm.), photograph, cibachrome print.

$2750* *Construct XXI, 1983,* s., t., d., num. 2/6 by photog., #2/6 ed., (10-15-92, Sotheby-NY, #593A, illus.), 37 x 29½ in., (94 x 74.9 cm.), photograph, cibachrome print (BP 1683, DM 4093, FR 13,882, Y 329,934).

KATCHER, Adolf

BI *Winter, c. 1926,* orig. mount w/ t., credit stamp, est. $8/1,200, (10-13-92, Christie-NY, #250, illus.), 11½ x 9⅜ in., (29.2 x 23.8 cm.), photograph, blue-toned bromoil transfer print.

KATELHON, Hermann   1884-1940

BI *"Die Geisser", 1929,* i., s., est. DM 450-, (03-24-93, Venator/Hansten, #4505), pl. 24¹³⁄₁₆ x 20¹⁄₁₆ in., (63 x 51 cm.), etching.

KATO, Mikako

BI *Untitled (Teakettle), 1991,* s., d., edit. 1/5, Dixon Collection, est. $4/600, (11-16-92, Butterfield, #6031), 22¹⁄₁₆ x 32⁹⁄₁₆ in., (559.8 x 827 mm.), photograph, gelatin silver print.

KATORI, Susumu

$248* *"Space and Space: Sketch Book",* s., d. 88, excell. cond.?, (07-19-92, Bakker, #285), 17½ x 17½ in., (44.5 x 44.5 cm.), chromolithograph (BP 127, DM 361, FR 1222, Y 30,830).

KATSUKAWA SHUN'EI   Japanese 1762-1819

$1400* *Act III Of The Drama Chushingura,* Chuban, s. Shun'ei ga, pub.'s mark Eijudo, d. c. Kansei 1-2 (1789-90), wormage/restoration, rubbed, Prof. H.R.W. Kuhne Coll., (06-11-93, Sotheby-London, #211), 9⅞ x 7½ in., (25.1 x 19.1 cm.), woodblock (BP 920, DM 2275, FR 7671, Y 148,541).

$4201* *Bust-Portrait Of Ichikawa Komazo II,* oban, s. Shun'ei ga, censor's seal kiwame, pub.'s mark Tsuruya Kiemon, d. Kansei 6 (1794), faded, wormage restored, creased, Prof. H.R.W Kuhne Coll., (06-11-93, Sotheby-London, #184, illus.), 14¹⁄₁₆ x 9⅞ in., (35.7 x 25.1 cm.), woodblock (BP 2760, DM 6828, FR 23,019, Y 445,729).

$700* *Half-Length Of Ichikawa Ebizo IV In a Shibaraku Costume,* Hosoban, d. possibly Kansei 3 (1791), soiled, darkened, Prof. H.R.W.Kuhne Coll., (06-11-93, Sotheby-

London, #213), 12¾ x 6 in., (32.4 x 15.2 cm.), woodblock (BP 460, DM 1138, FR 3836, Y 74,271).

$7876* *Ichikawa Danzo IV In "Shibaraku" Attire,* Hosoban, s. Shun'ei ga, pub.'s mark, d. Kansei 10 (1798), soiled, rubbed, Prof. H.R.W. Kuhne Coll., (06-11-93, Sotheby-London, #195, illus.), 13 x 5⅝ in., (33 x 14.3 cm.), woodblock (BP 5175, DM 12,800, FR 43,156, Y 835,650).

$3501* *Ichikawa Komazo II And Arashi Ryuzo In A Combat With Swords,* oban, s. Shun'ei ga, d. Tenmei 7 (1787)?, faded, soiled, wormed, restored, Prof. H.R.W. Kuhne Coll., (06-11-93, Sotheby-London, #190, illus.), 14⅝ x 6⅛ in., (37.1 x 15.6 cm.), woodblock (BP 2300, DM 5690, FR 19,184, Y 371,459).

$1487* *Ichikawa Komazo II And Ichikawa Yaozo III In A "Mie" (Striking A Pose),* Aiban, s. Shun'ei ga, pub.'s mark, censor's seal Kiwame, d. Kansei 3(1791), trimmed, soiled, rubbed, new margin, Prof. H.R.W. Kuhne Coll., (06-11-93, Sotheby-London, #206, illus.), 9⅜ x 8 in., (23.8 x 20.3 cm.), woodblock, yellow ground (BP 977, DM 2417, FR 8148, Y 157,772).

$1225* *Ichikawa Komazo II As The Princess Nyosan-No-Miya (?),* Hosoban, s. Shun'ei ga, d. Kansei 3 (1791), collector's seal HayashiTadamasa, trimmed, wormed, repaired, Prof. H.R.W. Kuhne Coll., (06-11-93, Sotheby-London, #205, illus.), 12 x 5½ in., (30.5 x 14 cm.), woodblock (BP 805, DM 1991, FR 6712, Y 129,973).

BI *Ichikawa Komazo II As a Mendicant(?) Wrapped Up In A Straw Cape,* Hosoban, s. Shun'ei, d. c. Kansei 1 (1789), trimmed, Prof. H.R.W. Kuhne Coll., est. BP 800/1,100, (06-11-93, Sotheby-London, #203, illus.), 12¼ x 5½ in., (31.1 x 14 cm.), woodblock.

$962* *Ichikawa Monnosuke II As One Of The Gonnin Onna,* Hosoban, one panel of a pentatych, s. Shun'ei ga, pub.'s mark TsutayaJuzaburo, d. Kansei 5 (1793)?, faded, Prof. H.R.W. Kuhne Coll., (06-11-93, Sotheby-London, #210, illus.), 12¾ x 5⅝ in., (32.4 x 14.3 cm.), woodblock (BP 632, DM 1563, FR 5271, Y 102,069).

BI *"Ichikawa Monnosuke II As Soga No Juro" and "Ichikawa Yaozo III As Hachiman Taro Yoshiie": Two,* Hosoban, s. Shun'ei ga, pub.'s marks Kawaguchiya Uhei and YamaguchiyaChuemon, d. Kansei 6 (1794), faded, wormed, repaired, Prof. H.R.W. Kuhne Coll.,est. BP 800/1,100, (06-11-93, Sotheby-London, #215), one 11⅞ x 5¾ in., (30.2 x 14.6 cm.), other 12¾ x 5¾ in., (30.2 x 14.6 cm.), woodblock.

$2275* *Ichikawa Monnosuke II At A Fan Shop,* Hosoban, s. Shun'ei ga, pub.'s mark Kawaguchiya Uhei, collector's mark Deurasu, d. c. Kansei 5-6 (1793-94), color faded, Prof. H.R.W. Kuhne Coll., (06-11-93, Sotheby-London, #192, illus.), 12⅝ x 5⅞ in., (32.1 x 14.9 cm.), woodblock (BP 1495, DM 3697, FR 12,466, Y 241,379).

$1925* *Ichikawa Omezo As Soga No Goro,* hosoban, from triptych, s. Shun'ei ga, pub.'s mark, d. Kansei 9 (1797), soiled, good state, Prof. H.R.W. Kuhne Coll., (06-11-93, Sotheby-London, #189, illus.), 12½ x 5⅞ in., (31.8 x 14.9 cm.), woodblock (BP 1265, DM 3129, FR 10,548, Y 204,244).

$1487* *"Ichikawa Yaozo III As A Samurai Asahina", "Ichikawa Danjuro V As One Of The Seven Lucky Gods, Fukurokuju" and "Iwai Hanshiro IV As A Young Woman":-Three,* hosoban, s. Shun'ei, d. c. 1787-89, faded, trimmed, wormed, repaired, Prof. H.R.W. Kuhne Coll., (06-11-93, Sotheby-London, #185), each approx. 11⅜ x 5⅜ in., (28.9 x 13.7 cm.), woodblock (BP 977, DM 2417, FR 8148, Y 157,772).

BI *"Ichikawa Yaozo III" and "Nakamura Noshio II": Two,* Hosoban, left and center sh of a triptych(?), s. Shun'ei ga, pub.'s mark, d. Kansei 8 (1796), faded, new margin, soiled, rubbed, creased, Prof. H.R.W. Kuhne Coll., est. BP 4/6,500, (06-11-93, Sotheby-London, #198, illus.), one 12½ x 5¾ in., (31.8 x 14.6 cm.), other 12¾ x 5⅝ in., (31.8 x 14.6 cm.), woodblock.

$1750* *Iwai Hanshiro IV As The Pilgrim Otaki And Asano Tamejuro As Eji Matahei,* Aiban, s. Shun'ei ga, d. Tenmei 8 (1788), faded, worm holes, repaired, laid down, Prof. H.R.W. Kuhne Coll., (06-11-93, Sotheby-London, #219, illus.), 12⅝ x 8⅝ in., (32.1 x 21.9 cm.), woodblock (BP 1150, DM 2844, FR 9589, Y 185,676).

$2100* *Kataoka Nizaemon VII As Sasa No Sangobei,* Hosoban, right sh of a triptych, s. Shun'ei ga, pub.'s mark Enomoto Kichibei, repair, Prof. H.R.W. Kuhne Coll., (06-11-93, Sotheby-London, #193, illus.), 13 x 5⅞ in., (33 x 14.9 cm.), woodblock (BP 1380, DM 3413, FR 11,507, Y 222,812).

$875* *"Morita Kanzo?" and "Iwai Kiyotaro With Bando Zenji": Two,* Hosoban, parts of diptychs, s. Shun'ei ga, censor's seal, pub.'s markYamaguchiya Chuemon and Tsutaya Juzaburo, d. Kansei 6 (1794), faded, trimmed, rubbed, Prof. H.R.W. Kuhne Coll., (06-11-93, Sotheby-London, #212), one 12¼ x 5½ in., (31.1 x 14 cm.), other 11½ x 5⅜ in., (31.1 x 14 cm.), woodblock (BP 575, DM 1422, FR 4795, Y 92,838).

$962* *Nakamura Nakazo I As Ishikawa Goemon,* Hosoban, s. Shun'ei ga, d. Tenmei 8 (1788), faded, wormage, Prof. H.R. W. Kuhne Coll., (06-11-93, Sotheby-London, #202), 12⅝ x 5¾ in., (32.1 x 14.6 cm.), woodblock (BP 632, DM 1563, FR 5271, Y 102,069).

BI *Nakamura Nakazo I, Matsumoto Koshiro IV, Otani Hiroji III, Osagawa Tsuneyo II And Ichikawa Monnosuke II,* Oban, s. Shun'ei ga, pub.'s mark Igaya Kan'uemon, d. Tenmei 8 (1788),faded, worm holes, resotred, soiled, rubbed, creased, Prof. H.R.W. Kuhne Coll.,est. BP 1,2/1,800, (06-11-93, Sotheby-London, #220, illus.), 14⅝ x 9¾ in., (37.1 x 24.8 cm.), woodblock.

$9627* *Nakamura Noshio II As A Woman,* Aiban, s. Shun'ei ga, censor's seal kiwame, pub.'s mark Tsuruya Kiemon, d. Kansei 7 (1795), faded, fold mark, rubbed, Prof. H.R.W. Kuhne Coll., (06-11-93, Sotheby-London, #194, illus.), 12¾ x 8½ in., (32.4 x 21.6 cm.), woodblock (BP 6325, DM 15,646, FR 52,751, Y 1,021,432).

BI *"Osagawa Tsuneyo II" and "Sawamura Sojuro III": Two,* Hosoban, s. Shun'ei ga, d. c. Kansei 1-2 (1789-90) and c. Kansei 2 (1790), faded, trimmed, soiled, rubbed, Prof. H.R.W. Kuhne Coll., est. BP 1/1,200, (06-11-93, Sotheby-London, #214), one 12 x 5¾ in., (30.5 x 14.6 cm.), other 12½ x 5⅝ in., (30.5 x 14.6 cm.), woodblock.

$5951* *Otani Hiroji III And Bando Hikosaburo III,* Aiban, s. Shun'ei ga, pub.'s mark, d. Kansei 6 (1794), faded, worm holes, soiled, rubbed, Prof. H.R.W. Kuhne Coll., (06-11-93, Sotheby-London, #196, illus.), 12⅞ x 8¾ in., (32.7 x 22.2 cm.), woodblock (BP 3910, DM 9672, FR 32,608, Y 631,406).

$1137* *Otani Oniji III,* Hosoban, left sh of a triptych, s. Shun'ei ga, pub.'s mark Emiya Kichiemon, collector's mark Deurasu, d. Kansei 5 (1793), faded, worm hole, rubbed,- Prof. H.R.W. Kuhne Coll., (06-11-93, Sotheby-London, #209, illus.), 12⅝ x 5¾ in., (32.1 x 14.6 cm.), woodblock (BP 747, DM 1848, FR 6230, Y 120,637).

$962* *Otani Oniji III As An Elegantly Dressed Townsman,* Hosoban, part of a triptych, s. Shun'ei ga, censor's seal Kiwame, pub.'s mark, d. possibly Kansei 5 (1793), faded, wormed (repaired), Prof. H.R.W. Kuhne Coll., (06-11-93, Sotheby-London, #191, illus.), 12⅝ x 5¾ in., (32.1 x 14.6 cm.), woodblock (BP 632, DM 1563, FR 5271, Y 102,069).

BI *"Otani Oniji III" and "Segawa Kikunojo III": Two,* Hosoban part of a polyptych, s. Shun'ei ga, censor's seal, pub.'s mark, d. c. Kansei 3-5 (1791-93), faded, soiled, rubbed, Prof. H.R.W. Kuhne Coll.,est. BP 900/1,100, (06-11-93, Sotheby-London, #200), one 12⅜ x 5½ in., (31.4 x 14 cm.), other 12⅜ x 5⅝ in., (31.4 x 14 cm.), woodblock.

$1225* *Otani Tokuji As Kamei Rokuro,* Hosoban, part of a triptych, s. Shun'ei ga, censor's seal kiwame, pub.'s mark Tsutaya Juzaburo, collector's mark Deurasu, d. Kansei 4 (1792), trimmed, wormed, repaired, Prof. H.R.W. Kuhne Coll., (06-11-93, Sotheby-London, #208, illus.), 12 x 5¼ in., (30.5 x 13.3 cm.), woodblock (BP 805, DM 1991, FR 6712, Y 129,973).

$3676* *The Portrait Of A Sumo Wrestler,* Hosoban, s. Shun'ei ga, d. c. Tenmei 5 (1785), soiled, wormed, repaired, Prof. H.R.W. Kuhne Coll., (06-11-93, Sotheby-London, #218, illus.), 12⅜ x 5⅜ in., (31.4 x 13.7 cm.), woodblock (BP 2415, DM 5974, FR 20,142, Y 390,027).

$1225* *Portrait Of Segawa Kikunojo III,* Hosoban, s. Shun'ei ga, pub.'s mark Nishimura Yohachi, collector's mark Hayashi Tadamasa, d. c. Kansei 2 (1790), trimmed, wormage,

Prof. H.R.W. Kuhne Coll., (06-11-93, Sotheby-London, #217), 12 x 5⅜ in., (30.5 x 13.7 cm.), woodblock (BP 805, DM 1991, FR 6712, Y 129,973).

$962* *Portrait Of The Actor Nakayama Tatezo(?),* hosoban, part of diptych, s. Shun'ei, pub.'s mark Izutsuya Shokichi,d. c. Kansei 4 (1792), faded, wormed, trimmed, Prof. H.R.W. Kuhne Coll., (06-11-93, Sotheby-London, #183), 11⅞ x 5⅝ in., (30.2 x 14.3 cm.), woodblock (BP 632, DM 1563, FR 5271, Y 102,069).

$1312* *Sakata Hangoro III As A Pilgrim,* Hosoban, s. Shun'ei ga, d. Kansei 2 (1790), trimmed, rubbed, Prof. H.R.W. Kuhne Coll., (06-11-93, Sotheby-London, #204, illus.), 12 x 5⅜ in., (30.5 x 13.7 cm.), woodblock (BP 862, DM 2132, FR 7189, Y 139,204).

$1312* *"Sakata Hangoro III As Matagoro" and "Segawa Kikunojo III As A Courtier": Two,* Hosoban, s. Shun'ei ga, pub.'s mark, d. Kansei 3 (1791), faded, repaired, soiled, rubbed, Prof. H.R.W. Kuhne Coll., (06-11-93, Sotheby-London, #216), one 12⅛ x 5½ in., (30.8 x 14 cm.), other 11¾ x 5¾ in., (30.8 x 14 cm.), woodblock (BP 862, DM 2132, FR 7189, Y 139,204).

BI *Sawamura Sojuro III And Ichikawa Yaozo III About To Draw A Sword To Fight, With Osagawa Tsuneyo II As A Woman Intervening,* oban, s. Shun'ei ga, d. Tenmei 7 (1787), faded, fold-marks, trimmed,soiled, rubbed, Prof. H.R.W. Kuhne Coll., est. BP 800/1,200, (06-11-93, Sotheby-London, #186), 14½ x 9¾ in., (36.8 x 24.8 cm.), woodblock.

BI *Sawamura Sojuro III As Sukeroku,* hosoban, s. Shun'ei, censor's seal kiwame, pub.'s mark, coll.'s markDeurasu, d. Kansei 3 (1791), trimmed, soiled, rubbed, Prof. H.R.W. Kuhne Coll., est. BP 1/1,500, (06-11-93, Sotheby-London, #188, illus.), 12 x 5½ in., (30.5 x 14 cm.), woodblock.

$1662* *Sawamura Sojuro III As Taira No Kiyomori?,* Aiban, s. Shun'ei ga, censor's seal kiwame, pub.'s mark Tsuryuya Kiemon, d. c. Kansei 6, worm holes, repaired, soiled, rubbed, Prof. H.R.W. Kuhne Coll., (06-11-93, Sotheby-London, #207, illus.), 12⅝ x 8⅝ in., (32.1 x 21.9 cm.), woodblock (BP 1092, DM 2701, FR 9107, Y 176,340).

$1400* *Segawa Kikunojo III And Arashi Ryuzo,* Aiban, s. Shun'ei ga, pub.'s mark Iseji (Iseya Jisuke), d. c. Kansei2 (1790), wormed, trimmed, Prof. H.R.W. Kuhne Coll., (06-11-93, Sotheby-London, #221, illus.), 12⅜ x 8⅜ in., (31.4 x 21.3 cm.), woodblock (BP 920, DM 2275, FR 7671, Y 148,541).

BI *"Segawa Kikunojo III" and "Hanshiro IV": Two,* Hosoban, parts of polyptychs, s. Shun'ei ga, censor's seal, pub.'s mark, d. Kansei 7 (1795) (2nd print), faded, soiled, rubbed, Prof. H.R.W. Kuhne Coll., est. BP 950/ 1,200, (06-11-93, Sotheby-London, #201), one 12¾ x 5¾ in., (32.4 x 14.6 cm.), other 12⅝ x 5⅝ in., (32.4 x 14.6 cm.), woodblock.

$5251* *"Segawa Kikunojo III" and "Ichikawa Danjuro V": Two,* Hosoban, diptych (or 2 sh from a triptych?), s. Shun'ei ga, d. Tenmei6 (1786), trimmed, wormed, soiled, creased, Prof. H.R.W. Kuhne Coll., (06-11-93, Sotheby-London, #197, illus.), one 12⅜ x 5⅝ in., (31.4 x 14.3 cm.), other 12⅝ x 5⅝ in., (31.4 x 14.3 cm.), woodblock (BP 3450, DM 8534, FR 28,773, Y 557,135).

$1225* *"Yamashita Mangiku As A Young Manservant" and "Otani Oniji III": Two,* Hosoban, parts of polyptychs, s. Shun'ei ga, censor's seal Kiwame, pub.'s mark, d. Kansei 3 (1791) and c. 1791-92, rubbed, soiled, trimmed, Prof. H.R.W. Kuhne Coll., (06-11-93, Sotheby-London, #199), one 12¾ x 5⅝ in., (32.4 x 14.3 cm.), other 11⅞ x 5⅝ in., (32.4 x 14.3 cm.), woodblock (BP 805, DM 1991, FR 6712, Y 129,973).

KATSUKAWA SHUN'EN   Japanese ac. 1780-1800

$7001* *Okubi-e Of Ichikawa Komazo II,* Aiban, uchiwa-e, s. Shun'en ga, d. Kansei 6 (1794), pub. Kanochu, worm holes, soiled, rubbed, good state, Prof. H.R.W. Kuhne Coll., (06-11-93, Sotheby-London, #243, illus.), 9 x 9½ in., (22.9 x 24.1 cm.), woodblock (BP 4600, DM 11,378, FR 38,362, Y 742,812).

KATSUKAWA SHUNCHO   Japanese ac. late 1770s-late 1790s

$1487* *Ichikawa Yaozo III At Leisure Promenading With A Geisha,* Hosoban, beni-girai, s. Shuncho ga, d. c. Tenmei 5-

9 (1785-90), soile, rubbed, laid down, Prof. H.R.W. Kuhne Coll., (06-11-93, Sotheby-London, #248, illus.), 12¼ x 5¾ in., (31.1 x 14.6 cm.), woodblock (BP 977, DM 2417, FR 8148, Y 157,772).

$1662* *"Iwai Hanshiro IV As A Servant Woman" and "Ichikawa Monnosuke II As Usui Sadamitsu In A Shibaraku Costume": Two,* both hosoban, s. Shuncho ga, d. Tenmei 4 (1784) and Kansei 5 (1793),faded, wormed/repaired, laid down, Prof. H.R.W. Kuhne Coll., (06-11-93, Sotheby-London, #233), one 11⅞ x 5⅞ in., (30.2 x 14.9 cm.), other 12⅝ x 5⅞ in., (30.2 x 14.9 cm.), woodblock (BP 1092, DM 2701, FR 9107, Y 176,340).

KATSUKAWA SHUNDO   Japanese ac. c. 1780-1792

$2450* *Ichikawa Ebizo (Danjuro V),* Hosoban, s. Rantokusai Shundo hitsu, d. Tenmei 1 (1781), pub. faded,rubbed, soiled, Prof. H.R.W. Kuhne Coll., (06-11-93, Sotheby-London, #242, illus.), 11⅛ x 5¾ in., (28.3 x 14.6 cm.), woodblock (BP 1610, DM 3982, FR 13,425, Y 259,947).

KATSUKAWA SHUNJO   Japanese d. 1787

$1015* *Ichikawa Komazo In An Unidentified Role Standing Holding A Staff,* Hosoban, s. Shunjo ga, soiled, rubbed, Prof. H.R.W. Kuhne Coll., (06-11-93, Sotheby-London, #236), 12 x 5⅛ in., (30.5 x 13 cm.), woodblock (BP 667, DM 1650, FR 5562, Y 107,692).

$612* *Ichikawa Monnosuke II And Matsumoto Koshiro IV,* Hosoban, s. Shunjo ga, d. possibly An'ei 9 (1780), trimmed, rubbed, Prof. H.R.W. Kuhne Coll., (06-11-93, Sotheby-London, #225, illus.), 12 x 5½ in., (30.5 x 14 cm.), woodblock (BP 402, DM 995, FR 3353, Y 64,934).

$962* *Ichikawa Monnosuke II As Yoshitsune Standing Holding A Koto,* Hosoban, s. Shunjo ga, d. An'ei 9 (1780), soiled, rubbed, Prof. H.R.W. Kuhne Coll., (06-11-93, Sotheby-London, #234), 12¾ x 5⅞ in., (32.4 x 14.9 cm.), woodblock (BP 632, DM 1563, FR 5271, Y 102,069).

BI *Otani Tomoemon I And Bando Mitsugoro I,* Hosoban, s. Shunjo ga, d. probably An'ei 9-Tenmei 1 (1780/81), faded,wormed, Prof. H.R.W. Kuhne Coll., est. BP 7/900, (06-11-93, Sotheby-London, #226, illus.), 12½ x 5¾ in., (31.8 x 14.6 cm.), woodblock.

BI *"Sawamura Sojuro III In The Role Of Asahina Iwai" and "Hanshiro IV AsA Young Woman Dancing With A "Harugoma" (Hobby Horse)": Two,* Hosoban, s. Shunjo ga, d. c. 1780-1787, soiled, rubbed, wormed/repaired, laid down, Prof. H.R.W. Kuhne Coll., est. BP 1/1,400, (06-11-93, Sotheby-London, #235), one 11⅝ x 5¾ in., (29.5 x 14.6 cm.), other 11¾ x 5⅝ in., (29.5 x 14.6 cm.), woodblock.

KATSUKAWA SHUNKAKU   Japanese ac. 1790s

$2712* *"Segawa Kikunojo III" and "Otani Tokuji": Two,* Hosoban, a diptych, s. Shunkaku ga, censor's seal kiwame, pub.'s mark, d. c. Kansei 3 (1791), faded, soiled, wormed, restored, Prof. H.R.W. Kuhne Coll., (06-11-93, Sotheby-London, #228, illus.), each 12⅝ x 5⅜ in., (32.1 x 13.7 cm.), woodblock (BP 1782, DM 4408, FR 14,860, Y 287,745).

KATSUKAWA SHUNKO   Japanese 1743-1812

$1487* *"Bando Mitsugoro II As The Farmer Inasaku" and "Ichikawa Danjuro V As Lady Tsubone Iwafuji": Two,* hosoban, part of diptych, s. Shunko ga, d. Tenmei 6 (1786), faded, trimmed, rubbed, soiled, Prof. H.R.W. Kuhne Coll., (06-11-93, Sotheby-London, #180), one 12¾ x 5¾ in., (32.4 x 14.6 cm.), other 12⅛ x 5⅝ in., (32.4 x 14.6 cm.), woodblock (BP 977, DM 2417, FR 8148, Y 157,772).

$2625* *The Bust-Portrait Of Sakata Hangoro II Framed In A Fan,* hosoban, s. Shunko ga, d. An'ei 6 (1777), wormage, edge restored, soiled, rubbed, Prof. H.R.W. Kuhne Coll., (06-11-93, Sotheby-London, #171, illus.), 12¼ x 5½ in., (31.1 x 14 cm.), woodblock, pink ground (BP 1725, DM 4266, FR 14,384, Y 278,515).

$2100* *The Bust-Portraits Of Ichikawa Monnosuke II As A Young Samurai And Yamashita Kinsaku II In The Role Of A Young Woman,* hosoban, s. Katsukawa Shunko ga, pub. Sakaiya Kurobei, d. Tenmei 5 (1785), faded, wormed/torn/rubbed, restored, Prof. H.R.W. Kuhne Coll.,

(06-11-93, Sotheby-London, #172, illus.), 12½ x 5⅝ in., (31.8 x 14.3 cm.), woodblock (BP 1380, DM 3413, FR 11,507, Y 222,812).

$4901* *Head And Shoulder Portrait Of Ichikawa Monnosuke II*, hosoban, s. Shunko ga, d. c. Tenmei 5 (1785), soiled, good state, Prof. H.R.W. Kuhne Coll., (06-11-93, Sotheby-London, #157, illus.), 12¼ x 5⅝ in., (31.1 x 14.3 cm.), woodblock (BP 3220, DM 7965, FR 26,855, Y 520,000).

$2450* *"Ichikawa Danjuro V As Enya Hangan"* and *"Onoe Matsusuke I As Ko No Moronao"*: Two, hosoban, from polyptych, s. Shunko ga, d. An'ei 9 (1780), discolored, wormed, creases, soiled, rubbed, repaired, Prof. H.R.W. Kuhne Coll., (06-11-93, Sotheby-London, #167, illus.), one 12¾ x 5⅞ in., (32.4 x 14.9 cm.), other 12⅝ x 5¾ in., (32.4 x 14.9 cm.), woodblock (BP 1610, DM 3982, FR 13,425, Y 259,947).

$2625* *Ichikawa Danjuro V In Three Roles*, Hosoban, s. Shunko ga, d. An'ei 5 (1776), colors faded/oxidized, wormed, Prof. H.R.W. Kuhne Coll., (06-11-93, Sotheby-London, #154, illus.), 12 x 5½ in., (30.5 x 14 cm.), woodblock (BP 1725, DM 4266, FR 14,384, Y 278,515).

$3501* *"Ichikawa Danjuro V"* and *"Ichikawa Danzo IV"*: Two Bust-Portraits, hosoban, s. Shunko ga, d. c. An'ei 7-Tenmei 2 (1778-82), soiled, rubbed, wormed, trimmed, Prof. H.R.W. Kuhne Coll., (06-11-93, Sotheby-London, #164, illus.), one 12⅜ x 5½ in., (31.4 x 14 cm.), other 12³⁄₁₆ x 5⅜ in., (31.4 x 14 cm.), woodblock (BP 2300, DM 5690, FR 19,184, Y 371,459).

$3326* *Ichikawa Danjuro V, Sawamura Sojuro III And Iwai Hanshiro IV*, aiban, s. Shunk ga, d. Kensei 1 (1789), rubbed, creased, very good state, Prof. H.R.W. Kuhne Coll., (06-11-93, Sotheby-London, #152, illus.), 12⅞ x 8⅞ in., (32.7 x 22.5 cm.), woodblock (BP 2185, DM 5405, FR 18,225, Y 352,891).

$4901* *Ichikawa Danzo IV As Matsui Gengoro And Ichikawa Raizo II As Goro*, hosoban, s. Shunk ga, d. An'ei 4 (1775), wormage repaired, trimmed, Prof. H.R.W. Kuhne Coll., (06-11-93, Sotheby-London, #153, illus.), 12½ x 5¾ in., (31.8 x 14.6 cm.), woodblock (BP 3220, DM 7965, FR 26,855, Y 520,000).

$1487* *Ichikawa Danzo IV Dancing "Shakkyo"*, hosoban, s. Shunko ga, d. Tenmei 1 (1781), faded, trimmed, good state, Prof. H.R.W. Kuhne Coll., (06-11-93, Sotheby-London, #156, illus.), 12¼ x 5⅞ in., (31.1 x 14.9 cm.), woodblock (BP 977, DM 2417, FR 8148, Y 157,772).

BI *Ichikawa Kamazo II Posing, Standing In Front Of A Brushwood Fence And Bamboo Bush*, hosoban, s. Shunko ga, d. c. Tenmei 7 (1787), thinned part, wormage repaired, Prof. H.R.W. Kuhne Coll., est. BP 7/900, (06-11-93, Sotheby-London, #166, illus.), 12⅜ x 5⅜ in., (31.4 x 13.7 cm.), woodblock.

$1050* *Ichikawa Monnosuke II Dancing With A Fan*, hosoban, s. Shunko ga, pub.'s mark Nishimura Yohachi, d. c. Tenmei 3-4 (1783-84) or Tenmei 8 (1788), soiled, rubbed, trimmed, wormage, Prof. H.R.W.Kuhne Coll., (06-11-93, Sotheby-London, #182), 12⅛ x 6 in., (30.8 x 15.2 cm.), woodblock (BP 690, DM 1706, FR 5753, Y 111,406).

$7351* *"Ichikawa Monnosuke II", "Ichikawa Danjuro V" and "Onoe Matsusuke I"*: Three, hosoban triptych, s. Katsukawa Shunko ga, d. An'ei 8 (1779) or Tenmei (1783), soiled, rubbed, good state, Prof. H.R.W. Kuhne Coll., (06-11-93, Sotheby-London, #158, illus.), each sheet approx. 12¹⁵⁄₁₆ x 5⅝ in., (33 x 14.3 cm.), woodblock (BP 4830, DM 11,947, FR 40,279, Y 779,947).

$962* *"Ichikawa Monnosuke II, Possibly As Yoshitsune"* and *"The Twelve Characters"*: Two, hosoban, 2nd prob. cut-down from an aiban; s. Shunko ga, d. Tenmei 4(1784) and c. Tenmei 5-9 (1785-89), trimmed, faded, fold-mark, soiled, Prof. H.R.W. Kuhne Coll., (06-11-93, Sotheby-London, #169), one 12¾ x 5¾ in., (32.4 x 14.6 cm.), other 11⅝ x 5⅜ in., (32.4 x 14.6 cm.), woodblock (BP 632, DM 1563, FR 5271, Y 102,069).

BI *"Ichikawa Yaozo II As Goro With Sakata Hangoro II As Asahina"* and *"Otani Hiroemon III As Danschichi"*: Two, hosoban, part of triptych, s. Shunko ga, d. An'ei 4 (1775) and An'ei7 (1777), trimmed, soiled, rubbed, wormed, repaired, Prof. H.R.W. Kuhne Coll.,est. BP 1,2/1,600, (06-11-93, Sotheby-London, #174), one 12¹³⁄₁₆ x

5¹¹⁄₁₆ in., (32.5 x 14.5 cm.), other 11¹¹⁄₁₆ x 5⁷⁄₁₆ in., (32.5 x 14.5 cm.), woodblock.

$2275* *"Ichikawa Yaozo II As Sukeroku"* and *"Matsumoto Koshiro As A Pedlar Of Shirozake, Sweet Rice Wine"*: Two, hosoban, 2 sheets from polyptych, s. Shunko ga, d. An'ei 5 (1776), second trimmed, margin added, soiled, rubbed, Prof. H.R.W. Kuhne Coll., (06-11-93, Sotheby-London, #149, illus.), one 12⅞ x 5⅞ in., (32.7 x 14.9 cm.), other 12⁹⁄₁₆ x 5⅜ in., (32.7 x 14.9 cm.), woodblock (BP 1495, DM 3697, FR 12,466, Y 241,379).

$1487* *Ichikawa Yaozo III As A Samurai Carrying A Bow And Hunter's Hat OverHis Shoulder*, hosoban, s. Shunko ga, d. Tenmei 4 (1784), soiled, thinned parts, Prof. H.R.W. Kuhne Coll., (06-11-93, Sotheby-London, #165, illus.), 12⅝ x 5¾ in., (32.1 x 14.6 cm.), woodblock (BP 977, DM 2417, FR 8148, Y 157,772).

BI *"Nakamura Kumejiro As Kikuzono"* and *"Matsumoto Koshiro IV, Possibly In The Role Of Chubei"*: Two, hosoban, s. Katsukawa/Shunko ga, d. An'ei 9 (1780), faded, trimmed, soiled, rubbed, Prof. H.R.W. Kuhne Coll., est. BP 1/1,300, (06-11-93, Sotheby-London, #170), one 12¾ x 5¾ in., (32.4 x 14.6 cm.), other 12¼ x 5½ in., (32.4 x 14.6 cm.), woodblock.

BI *Nakamura Nakazo I As Yakko Holding A Tobacco Tray*, hosoban, panel of diptych, s. Shunko ga, d. Tenmei 3 (1783), faded, darkened, trimmed, wormed/soiled, Prof. H.R.W. Kuhne Coll., est. BP 7/900, (06-11-93, Sotheby-London, #163), 14⅜ x 5¾ in., (36.5 x 14.6 cm.), woodblock.

$1487* *"Nakamura Nakazo I"* and *"Sawamura Sojoro III"*: Two, hosoban, s. Shunko ga, d. possibly Tenmei 6 (1786) and Tenmei 7-8 (1787-88), faded, soiled, Prof. H.R.W. Kuhne Coll., (06-11-93, Sotheby-London, #181), one 11⅞ x 5⅝ in., (30.2 x 14.3 cm.), other 12⅛ x 5½ in., (30.2 x 14.3 cm.), woodblock (BP 977, DM 2417, FR 8148, Y 157,772).

BI *Nakamura Nazako I*, hosoban, part of triptych, s. Shunko ga, d. possibly An'ei 9 (1780),faded, wormed, soiled, Prof. H.R.W. Kuhne Coll., est. BP 6/800, (06-11-93, Sotheby-London, #160), 12¾ x 5⅞ in., (32.4 x 14.9 cm.), woodblock.

$1225* *Nakamura Nazako I As Danshichi Kurobei*, hosoban, part of diptych, s. Katsukawa Shunko ga, d. An'ei 8 (1779),faded, rubbed, soiled, Prof. H.R.W. Kuhne Coll., (06-11-93, Sotheby-London, #145, illus.), 12⅜ x 5¾ in., (31.4 x 14.6 cm.), woodblock (BP 805, DM 1991, FR 6712, Y 129,973).

$2800* *"Nakamura Shirogo"* and *"Segawa Kikunojo III"*: Two, hosoban, 2 sheets from polyptych, s. Shunko ga, d. c. An'ei 6-8 (1777-79), mica dust, wormed, trimmed, rubbed, Prof. H.R.W. Kuhne Coll., (06-11-93, Sotheby-London, #150, illus.), one 12¾ x 5⅞ in., (32.4 x 14.9 cm.), other 12⅝ x 5⅞ in., (32.4 x 14.9 cm.), woodblock (BP 1840, DM 4551, FR 15,342, Y 297,082).

$5251* *Okubi-e Of Ichikawa Ebizo In Shibaraku Costume*, oban, s. Shunko ga, d. Kensei 3 (1791), faded, browned, soiled, rubbed, Prof. H.R.W. Kuhne Coll., (06-11-93, Sotheby-London, #159, illus.), 15 x 9⅞ in., (38.1 x 25.1 cm.), woodblock (BP 3450, DM 8534, FR 28,773, Y 557,135).

BI *Okubi-e Of The Onnagata Actor Segawa Kikunojo III*, oban, sig. rubbed off, Shunko ga, d. c. Tenmei 7 (1787), faded, wormage repaired, soiled, rubbed, creased, Prof. H.R.W. Kuhne Coll., est. BP 12/18,000, (06-11-93, Sotheby-London, #148, illus.), 15 x 9⅞ in., (38.1 x 25.1 cm.), woodblock.

BI *Osagawa Tsuneyo II As A Woman Holding Up A Scent Bag"* and *"Iwai Hanshiro IV As A Courtesan(?)"*: Two, hosoban, part of triptych, s. Shunko ga, pub.'s mark Nishimura Yohachi, d. Tenmei 8 (1788), faded, soiled, rubbed, Prof. H.R.W. Kuhne Coll., est. BP 800/1,000, (06-11-93, Sotheby-London, #179), one 11¾ x 5⅝ in., (29.8 x 14.3 cm.), other 11¾ x 5¾ in., (29.8 x 14.3 cm.), woodblock.

$1050* *Otani Hiroji III And Nakamura Nakazo I*, hosoban, 1st is left-hand panel of a triptych, 2nd possibly right-hand panel of diptych; s. Katsukawa Shunko ga, d. possibly An'ei 8 (1779), faded,wormed, repaired, trimmed, new margin added, Prof. H.R.W. Kuhne Coll., (06-11-93,

Sotheby-London, #173), one 11¾ x 5⅝ in., (29.8 x 14.3 cm.), other 12 x 5⅜ in., (29.8 x 14.3 cm.), woodblock (BP 690, DM 1706, FR 5753, Y 111,406).

$1050* *Otani Tokuji As Igo,* hosoban, s. Katsukawa Shunko ga, d. Tenmei 1 (1781), rubbed, good state, Prof. H.R.W. Kuhne Coll., (06-11-93, Sotheby-London, #155, illus.), 12¾ x 5⅝ in., (32.4 x 14.3 cm.), woodblock (BP 690, DM 1706, FR 5753, Y 111,406).

$1225* *Otani Tomoemon I In An Unidentified Samurai Role,* hosoban, s. Shunko ga, seal i. Ki, d. c. Meiwa 8-9 (1771-72), faded,soiled, rubbed, Prof. H.R.W. Kuhne Coll., (06-11-93, Sotheby-London, #144, illus.), 12⅝ x 5⅞ in., (32.1 x 14.9 cm.), woodblock (BP 805, DM 1991, FR 6712, Y 129,973).

$1925* *"Sakata Hangoro II As A Chivalrous Man Of The Chushingura Play" and "Nakamura Tomijuro I As An Old Man": Two,* hosoban, s. Shunko ga, faded, trimmed, wormed, repaired, Prof. H.R.W. Kuhne Coll., (06-11-93, Sotheby-London, #175), one 11 7/16 x 5⅝ in., (29.1 x 14.3 cm.), other 12 5/16 x 5⅝ in., (29.1 x 14.3 cm.), woodblock (BP 1265, DM 3129, FR 10,548, Y 204,244).

$1050* *"Sakata Hangoro III(?)" and "Segawa Kikunojo III": Two,* hosoban, part of diptych, s. Shunko ga, d. c. An'ei 9 (1790) and Tenmei 7 (1787), latter faded, trimmed, soiled, rubbed, Prof. H.R.W. Kuhne Coll., (06-11-93, Sotheby-London, #161), one 12⅛ x 5¼ in., (30.8 x 13.3 cm.), other 11⅝ x 5⅜ in., (30.8 x 13.3 cm.), woodblock (BP 690, DM 1706, FR 5753, Y 111,406).

$2625* *Segawa Kikunojo III And Matsumoto Koshiro IV,* aiban, s. Shunko ga, pub.'s mark, d. c. Kensei 2 (1790), faded, rubbed, creased, soiled, Prof. H.R.W. Kuhne Coll., (06-11-93, Sotheby-London, #151, illus.), 12¾ x 8⅝ in., (32.4 x 21.9 cm.), woodblock (BP 1725, DM 4266, FR 14,384, Y 278,515).

$2100* *Yakusha Rokkasen, Portraits Of Three Actors As Immortal Poets,* chuban uchiwa-e (fan-print), s. Shunko ga, d. Kansei 1 (1789), wormed, repaired, soiled, Prof. H.R.W. Kuhne Coll., (06-11-93, Sotheby-London, #147), 8⅝ x 9⅞ in., (21.9 x 25.1 cm.), woodblock (BP 1380, DM 3413, FR 11,507, Y 222,812).

KATSUKAWA SHUNSEN Japanese ac. c. 1780-1800

BI *Asao Tamejuro Armour-Clad As Yamabushi Kiyomanin,* Hosoban, s. Shunsen ga, d. Tenmei 8 (1788), faded, trimmed, Prof. H.R.W. Kuhne Coll., est. BP 6/800, (06-11-93, Sotheby-London, #232), 12¼ x 5½ in., (31.1 x 14 cm.), woodblock.

BI *Otani Hiroji III As Shoemon(?),* Hosoban, s. Shunsen ga, d. Tenmei 7 (1787), soiled, repaired, Prof. H.R.W. Kuhne Coll., est. BP 6/800, (06-11-93, Sotheby-London, #227, illus.), 12⅛ x 5⅜ in., (30.8 x 13.7 cm.), woodblock.

KATSUKAWA SHUNSHO Japanese 1726-1792

$1662* *"Acts III And X Of The Drama Chushingura": Two,* from series Chushingura, chuban, s. Shunsho ga, d. c. An'ei 5-9 (1776-80), faded, Act X darkened, tears/thinned, parts restored, soiled, rubbed, Prof. H.R.W. Kuhne Coll., (06-11-93, Sotheby-London, #124, illus.), one 10¼ x 7¾ in., (26 x 19.7 cm.), other 9¾ x 7⅜ in., (26 x 19.7 cm.), woodblock (BP 1092, DM 2701, FR 9107, Y 176,340).

$962* *Arashi Sangoro II As Toriboshi Otaro,* hosoban, s. Shunsho ga, d. Meiwa 7 (1770), faded, wormed, (06-11-93, Sotheby-London, #97), 12⅔ x 5⅝ in., (32.2 x 14.3 cm.), woodblock (BP 632, DM 1563, FR 5271, Y 102,069).

$1312* *Arashi Sangoro II Holding A Naked Blade Standing Under A Wisteria Trellis,* Hosoban, s. Shunsho ga, d. c. An'ei 5-6 (1776-77), fold mark, faded,trimmed, laid down, Prof. H.R.W. Kuhne Coll., (06-11-93, Sotheby-London, #74, illus.), 12⅜ x 5¾ in., (31.4 x 14.6 cm.), woodblock (BP 862, DM 2132, FR 7189, Y 139,204).

$2625* *Arashi Sangoro II Possibly As Matano Goro? Brandishing A Naked Blade,* Hosoban, s. Shunsho ga, d. c. An'ei 3 (1774), fold-mark, binding hole, Prof. H.R.W. Kuhne Coll., (06-11-93, Sotheby-London, #63, illus.), 12¼ x 5⅞ in., (31.1 x 14.9 cm.), woodblock (BP 1725, DM 4266, FR 14,384, Y 278,515).

BI *Bando Mitsugoro I As Soga Juro,* hosoban, s. Shunsho ga, d. An'ei 5 (1776), coll.'s seal, faded, soiled, trimmed, Prof. H.R.W. Kuhne Coll., est. BP 6/800, (06-11-93, Sotheby-London, #137), 12¼ x 5½ in., (31.1 x 14 cm.), woodblock.

$1575* *"Bando Mitsugoro I" and "Ichikawa Monnosuke II In Menacing Confrontation": Two,* hosoban, s. Shunsho ga, coll.'s seal, d. c. An'ei 7 (1778), faded, soiled, trimmed, fold marks repaired, Prof. H.R.W. Kuhne Coll., (06-11-93, Sotheby-London, #140), one 12¼ x 5½ in., (31.1 x 14 cm.), other 11¾ x 5⅛ in., (31.1 x 14 cm.), woodblock (BP 1035, DM 2560, FR 8630, Y 167,109).

$2275* *Bust-Portrait Of Ichikawa Monnosuke II,* chuban, s. Shunsho ga, faded, rubbed, soiled, tear, repaired, Prof. H.R.W. Kuhne Coll., (06-11-93, Sotheby-London, #122, illus.), 10¼ x 7⅜ in., (26 x 18.7 cm.), woodblock (BP 1495, DM 3697, FR 12,466, Y 241,379).

$5251* *Danjuro IV Changing His Name To Ebizo III,* Hosoban, s. Shunsho ga, d. Meiwa ((1772), good state, Prof. H.R.W. Kuhne Coll., (06-11-93, Sotheby-London, #68, illus.), 12⅞ x 5⅞ in., (32.7 x 14.9 cm.), woodblock (BP 3450, DM 8534, FR 28,773, Y 557,135).

$3151* *The Gonin Otoko (Five Chivalrous Men): Three,* Hosoban, three sheets from pentatych, s. Shunsho ga, d. An'ei 9 (1780), faded, wormage repaired, trimmed, replaced margin, Prof. H.R.W. Kuhne Coll., (06-11-93, Sotheby-London, #70, illus.), smallest 12½ x 5⅞ in., (31.8 x 14.9 cm.), largest 12 13/16 x 5⅞ in., (31.8 x 14.9 cm.), woodblock (BP 2070, DM 5121, FR 17,266, Y 334,324).

$1225* *The Heads And Shoulders Of Iwai Hanshiro IV And Nakamura Sukegoro II,* aiban, s. Shunsho ga, d. Tenmei 1 (1781), wormage, restored, laid down, Prof. H.R.W. Kuhne Coll., (06-11-93, Sotheby-London, #123, illus.), 12⅝ x 8⅝ in., (32.1 x 21.9 cm.), woodblock (BP 805, DM 1991, FR 6712, Y 129,973).

$1050* *An Ichikawa Actor With A Sword,* hosoban, s. Shunsho ga, faded, wormed, repaired, Prof. H.R.W. Kuhne Coll., (06-11-93, Sotheby-London, #130), 12¾ x 5¾ in., (32.4 x 14.6 cm.), woodblock (BP 690, DM 1706, FR 5753, Y 111,406).

BI *Ichikawa Danjuro IV And Nakamura Nakazo I,* hosoban, s. Shunsho ga, seal, d. Meiwa 6 (1769), faded, trimmed, wormed, Prof. H.R.W. Kuhne Coll., est. BP 1,2/1,700, (06-11-93, Sotheby-London, #115, illus.), 11⅞ x 5⅜ in., (30.2 x 13.7 cm.), woodblock.

BI *Ichikawa Danjuro IV As Kagekiyo,* hosoban, seal, d. c. Meiwa 4-6 (1767-69), trimmed, soiled, Prof. H.R.W. Kuhne Coll., est. BP 7/900, (06-11-93, Sotheby-London, #116), 11⅜ x 5¼ in., (28.9 x 13.3 cm.), woodblock.

$1750* *"Ichikawa Danjuro V As A Monk" and "Bando Mitsugoro I and Segawa Kikunojo III": Two,* hosoban and aiban, s. Shunsho ga, d. An'ei 9 (1780) and Tenmei 1 (1781), tears, worm holes restored, later soiled, darkened, Prof. H.R.W. Kuhne Coll., (06-11-93, Sotheby-London, #102), one 11½ x 6 in., (29.2 x 15.2 cm.), other 12¾ x 8¾ in., (29.2 x 15.2 cm.), woodblock (BP 1150, DM 2844, FR 9589, Y 185,676).

$1225* *"Ichikawa Danjuro V As Fuwa Banzaemon In A Kamishimo With A Fan" and"Iwai Hanshiro IV As Osono Holding A Rosary": Two,* hosoban diptych, s. Shunsho ga, d. An'ei 8 (1780), faded, toned, soiled, rubbed, Prof. H.R.W. Kuhne Coll., (06-11-93, Sotheby-London, #100), each approx. 12 x 5½ in., (30.5 x 14 cm.), woodblock (BP 805, DM 1991, FR 6712, Y 129,973).

$3851* *Ichikawa Danjuro V In Shibaraku Costume,* Hosoban, kitsubushi, s. Shunsho ga, d. Meiwa 8 (1771), trimmed, creased, soiled, Prof. H.R.W. Kuhne Coll., (06-11-93, Sotheby-London, #61, illus.), 12½ x 5⅝ in., (31.8 x 14.3 cm.), woodblock (BP 2530, DM 6259, FR 21,101, Y 408,594).

$1487* *"Ichikawa Danjuro V" and "Ichikawa Yaozo III": Two,* hosoban, s. Shunsho ga, d. c. Tenmei 1 (1781) and Tenmei 4 (1784), faded, trimmed, soiled, thinned/restored parts, Prof. H.R.W. Kuhne Coll., (06-11-93, Sotheby-London, #106), one 12½ x 5¾ in., (31.8 x 14.6 cm.), other 12 x 5½ in., (31.8 x 14.6 cm.), woodblock (BP 977, DM 2417, FR 8148, Y 157,772).

$2976* *"Ichikawa Danjuro V" and "Nakamura Nakazo I": Two,* Hosoban, s. Shunsho ga, d. c. An'ei 7-8 (1778-79), trimmed, paper added, Prof. H.R.W. Kuhne Coll., (06-11-93, Sotheby-London, #78, illus.), one 11½ x 5¼ in.,

(29.2 x 13.3 cm.), other 12½ x 6 in., (29.2 x 13.3 cm.), woodblock (BP 1955, DM 4837, FR 16,307, Y 315,756).

$1575* *"Ichikawa Danjuro V" and "Nakamura Nakazo I": Two,* hosoban and chuban, s. Shunsho ga, d. An'ei 9 (1780) and Tenmei I (1781), faded, soiled, wormage repaired, Prof. H.R.W. Kuhne Coll., (06-11-93, Sotheby-London, #101), one 13 x 6 in., (33 x 15.2 cm.), other 10 x 7 in., (33 x 15.2 cm.), woodblock (BP 1035, DM 2560, FR 8630, Y 167,109).

BI *"Ichikawa Danjuro V" and "Segawa Kikunojo III": Two,* panels of triptych, hosoban, s. Shunsho ga, d. Tenmei 4 (1784), trimmed, wormage/tears restored, margin added, laid down, Prof. H.R.W. Kuhne Coll.,est. BP 800/1,300, (06-11-93, Sotheby-London, #94), each approx. 12½ x 5½ in., (31.8 x 14 cm.), woodblock.

$2100* *Ichikawa Danjuro VI As Kino Natora,* hosoban, kitsubushi, s. Shunsho ga, seal, d. Meiwa 2 (1765), faded, soiled, trimmed, Prof. H.R.W. Kuhne Coll., (06-11-93, Sotheby-London, #110), 12 x 5½ in., (30.5 x 14 cm.), woodblock (BP 1380, DM 3413, FR 11,507, Y 222,812).

$1312* *Ichikawa Danzo III In Shibaraku Costume,* hosoban, kitsubushi, seal, d. Meiwa 5 (1768), creased, soiled, rubbed, restoration, Prof. H.R.W. Kuhne Coll., (06-11-93, Sotheby-London, #90), 11⅝ x 5¾ in., (29.5 x 14.6 cm.), woodblock (BP 862, DM 2132, FR 7189, Y 139,204).

BI *Ichikawa Danzo IV And Otani Tokuji,* hosoban, s. Shunsho ga, d. Tenmei 1 (1781), faded, worm holes repaired, Prof. H.R.W. Kuhne Coll., est. BP 650/850, (06-11-93, Sotheby-London, #103), 11⅜ x 5¼ in., (28.9 x 13.3 cm.), woodblock.

$1662* *Ichikawa Danzo IV As Arakawa Taro,* Hosoban, s. Shunsho ga, d. Tenmei 2 (1782), faded, good state, Prof. H.R.W. Kuhne Coll., (06-11-93, Sotheby-London, #65), illus.), 12⅛ x 5⅝ in., (30.8 x 14.3 cm.), woodblock (BP 1092, DM 2701, FR 9107, Y 176,340).

BI *Ichikawa Ebizo II As A Samurai Official,* Hosoban, s. Shunsho ga, d. An'ei 4 (1775), trimmed, nick, very good state, Prof. H.R.W. Kuhne Coll., est. BP 1,5/2,000, (06-11-93, Sotheby-London, #75, illus.), 12¼ x 5¾ in., (31.1 x 14.6 cm.), woodblock.

$2100* *Ichikawa Monnosuke II,* hosoban, s. Shunsho ga, d. An'ei 7 (1778)-Tenmei 2 (1782), fold-mark, repair of wormage, good state, Prof. H.R.W. Kuhne Coll., (06-11-93, Sotheby-London, #135), 12¾ x 5⅞ in., (32.4 x 14.9 cm.), woodblock (BP 1380, DM 3413, FR 11,507, Y 222,812).

BI *Ichikawa Monnosuke II (?) As A Traveller: Two,* hosoban, one s. Shunsho ga, coll. seal; other sig. cut off, faded, wormage restored, trimmed, Prof. H.R.W. Kuhne Coll., est. BP 800/1,000, (06-11-93, Sotheby-London, #93), one 11½ x 4½ in., (29.2 x 11.4 cm.), other 11¼ x 5¼ in., (29.2 x 11.4 cm.), woodblock.

$1925* *Ichikawa Monnosuke II As A Fox-Hunter,* hosoban, s. Shunsho ga, d. An'ei 5 (1776), nick, good state, Prof. H.R.W. Kuhne Coll., (06-11-93, Sotheby-London, #120), 12¼ x 5¾ in., (31.1 x 14.6 cm.), woodblock (BP 1265, DM 3129, FR 10,548, Y 204,244).

$1312* *Ichikawa Monnosuke II Grappling With A Giant Carp,* hosoban, left sheet of triptych, s. Shunsho ga, d. An'ei 9 (1780), faded, trimmed, corner restored, Prof. H.R.W. Kuhne Coll., (06-11-93, Sotheby-London, #87, illus.), 12¼ x 5½ in., (31.1 x 14 cm.), woodblock (BP 862, DM 2132, FR 7189, Y 139,204).

$665* *Ichikawa Monnosuke II Standing Beside A New Year's Pine Decoration, Kadomatsu,* hosoban, s. Shunsho ga, d. An'ei 8 (1779), paper added to replace trimming, rubbed, soiled, Prof. H.R.W. Kuhne Coll.(06-11-93, Sotheby-London, #142), 12½ x 5½ in., (31.8 x 14 cm.), woodblock (BP 437, DM 1081, FR 3644, Y 70,557).

$3326* *Ichikawa Yaozo II As Farmer,* Hosoban, s. Shunsho ga, d. An'ei 1 (1772), faded, soiled, Prof. H.R.W. Kuhne Coll., (06-11-93, Sotheby-London, #67, illus.), 12⅞ x 5¾ in., (32.7 x 14.6 cm.), woodblock (BP 2185, DM 5405, FR 18,225, Y 352,891).

BI *Ichikawa Yaozo II As One Of The Gonin Otoko,* hosoban, seal, Coll.'s mark, d. Meiwa 5 (1768), soiled, rubbed, wormed, Prof. H.R.W. Kuhne Coll., est. BP 1,2/1,700, (06-11-93, Sotheby-London, #114, illus.), 12¼ x 5⅜ in., (31.1 x 13.7 cm.), woodblock.

BI *Ichikawa Yaozo II As Soga Juro?,* hosoban, s. Shunsho ga, seal, d. Meiwa 6 (1769), soiled, browned, worn, Prof. H.R.W. Kuhne Coll., est. BP 1,2/1,800, (06-11-93, Sotheby-London, #117), 12¾ x 6 in., (32.4 x 15.2 cm.), woodblock.

$2100* *Ichikawa Yaozo II As Sukeroku And Iwai Hanshiro IV As The Courtesan Agemaki,* oban, s. Shunsho ga, d. Am'ei 5 (1776), faded, browned, fold mark, Prof. H.R.W. Kuhne Coll., (06-11-93, Sotheby-London, #89, illus.), 14⅝ x 10 in., (37.1 x 25.4 cm.), woodblock (BP 1380, DM 3413, FR 11,507, Y 222,812).

$2100* *Ichimura Uzaemon IX And Nakajima Mihoemon,* Chuban, s. Shunsho ga, d. Meiwa 8 (1771), darkened, soiled, stained,Prof. H.R.W. Kuhne Coll., (06-11-93, Sotheby-London, #64, illus.), 10½ x 7 in., (26.7 x 17.8 cm.), woodblock (BP 1380, DM 3413, FR 11,507, Y 222,812).

$2450* *"Ichimura Uzaemon IX As A Wrestler", "Onoe Tamizo As A Wakashu" and "A Lady In The Service Of Court": Three,* hosoban, s. Shunsho ga, d. c. An'ei 2 (1773), faded, trimmed or soiled, wormage repaired, Prof. H.R.W. Kuhne Coll., (06-11-93, Sotheby-London, #129), largest 12⁵⁄₁₆ x 5¹¹⁄₁₆ in., (31.2 x 14.4 cm.), smallest 11⅞ x 5½ in., (31.2 x 14.4 cm.), woodblock (BP 1610, DM 3982, FR 13,425, Y 259,947).

$1137* *Iwai Hanshiro IV As A Young Woman,* hosoban, sheet from triptych, s. Shunsho ga, d. An'ei 9 (1780), faded, soiled, good state, Prof. H.R.W. Kuhne Coll., (06-11-93, Sotheby-London, #88, illus.), 13⅛ x 5¾ in., (33.3 x 14.6 cm.), woodblock (BP 747, DM 1848, FR 6230, Y 120,637).

$525* *"Iwai Hanshiro IV" and "Ichikawa Monnosuke II": Two,* hosoban, s. Shunsho ga, d. An'ei 7 (1778), browned, soiled, wormed, repaired, Prof. H.R.W. Kuhne Coll., (06-11-93, Sotheby-London, #118), one 12⅛ x 4⅛ in., (30.8 x 10.5 cm.), other 12 x 4¼ in., (30.8 x 10.5 cm.), woodblock (BP 345, DM 853, FR 2877, Y 55,703).

$1312* *Matsumoto Koshiro II (Danjuro IV) And Ichikawa Danzo III,* Hosoban, seal, d. Meiwa 7 (1770), trimmed, soiled, wormed, Prof. H.R.W. Kuhne Coll., (06-11-93, Sotheby-London, #80, illus.), 12 x 5½ in., (30.5 x 14 cm.), woodblock (BP 862, DM 2132, FR 7189, Y 139,204).

BI *"Morita Kanya IV (?) As A Samurai In An Agitated Pose In Front Of A Plum Tree" and "Mimasu Tokujiro In A Female Role And Ichikawa Yaozo III As A Duo": Two,* hosoban, s. Shunko ga, d. c. Tenmei 4 (1784), faded, trimmed, soiled, rubbed, Prof. H.R.W. Kuhne Coll., est. BP 900/1,200, (06-11-93, Sotheby-London, #108), one 12¼ x 5½ in., (31.1 x 14 cm.), other 11⅞ x 5⅜ in., (31.1 x 14 cm.), woodblock.

$875* *"Nakajima Mihoemon II And Ichikawa Ebizo III" and "Otani Hiroemon III": Two,* hosoban, second. s. Shunsho ga, both d. An'ei 5 (1776), faded, trimmed, paper added, Prof. H.R.W. Kuhne Coll., (06-11-93, Sotheby-London, #136), one 12 x 5¾ in., (30.5 x 14.6 cm.), other 11¼ x 5½ in., (30.5 x 14.6 cm.), woodblock (BP 575, DM 1422, FR 4795, Y 92,838).

$1137* *Nakamura Denkuro II And Nakamura Nakazo I,* hosoban, kitsubushi, seal, d. Meiwa 6 (1769), trimmed, laid down, Prof. H.R.W. Kuhne Coll., (06-11-93, Sotheby-London, #92), 11½ x 5¼ in., (29.2 x 13.3 cm.), woodblock (BP 747, DM 1848, FR 6230, Y 120,637).

$1400* *"Nakamura Juzo II As A Samurai Wearing A Formal Kamishimo Robe" and "Nakajima Mihoemon II As The Villain Court-Noble Tokihira": Two,* sheet from triptych, hosoban, s. Shunsho ga, d. An'ei 1 (1772) and An'ei 2 (1773), faded, darkened, soiled, Prof. H.R.W. Kuhne Coll., (06-11-93, Sotheby-London, #86), each approx. 12¼ x 5¾ in., (31.1 x 14.6 cm.), woodblock (BP 920, DM 2275, FR 7671, Y 148,541).

BI *Nakamura Nakazo I As A Warrior Holding A Spear,* hosoban, s. Shunsho ga, d. c. An'ei 5-6 (1776-'77), faded, trimmed, wormed, repaired, Prof. H.R.W. Kuhne Coll., est. BP 6/800, (06-11-93, Sotheby-London, #138), 11⅝ x 5½ in., (29.5 x 14 cm.), woodblock.

$3676* *Nakamura Nakazo I As Prince Koreaki,* Hosoban, s. Shunsho ga, d. An'ei 2 (1773), slightly soiled, rubbed, Prof. H.R.W. Kuhne Coll., (06-11-93, Sotheby-London,

#62, illus.), 12⅞ x 5¾ in., (32.7 x 14.6 cm.), woodblock (BP 2415, DM 5974, FR 20,142, Y 390,027).

$1312* *"Nakamura Nakazo I As Rokubu, Pilgrim" and "Kasaya Matakuro As SendoRokuzo": Two,* hosoban, s. Shunsho ga, seal, d. 1769 and 1770, browned, damage restored, second laid down, Prof. H.R.W. Kuhne Coll., (06-11-93, Sotheby-London, #126), one 12¼ x 5½ in., (31.1 x 14 cm.), other 12 x 5¾ in., (31.1 x 14 cm.), woodblock (BP 862, DM 2132, FR 7189, Y 139,204).

BI *Nakamura Nakazo I As Shishimai Dancer,* hosoban, s. Shunsho ga, d. c. An'ei 7 (1778), worm-holes, tear, corner restored, prof. H.R.W. Kuhne Coll., est. BP 1,2/1,800, (06-11-93, Sotheby-London, #84, illus.), 12⅞ x 6⅛ in., (32.7 x 15.6 cm.), woodblock.

BI *Nakamura Nakazo I As The Farmer Eisaku Holding A Sickle,* hosoban, s. Shunsho ga, d. An'ei 8 (1779), faded, soiled, restoration, good state, Prof. H.R.W. Kuhne Coll., est. BP 6/850, (06-11-93, Sotheby-London, #141), 12¾ x 5¾ in., (32.4 x 14.6 cm.), woodblock.

BI *Nakamura Nakazo I Possibly As Raigo Ajari,* Hosoban, s. Shunsho ga, seal, d. possibly Meiwa 7 (1770), good state,Prof. H.R.W. Kuhne Coll., est. BP 2,5/3,000, (06-11-93, Sotheby-London, #72, illus.), 11⅞ x 5⅞ in., (30.2 x 14.9 cm.), woodblock.

$1750* *"Nakamura Nakazo I" and "Ichikawa Danjuro V": Two,* Hosoban diptych, s. Shunsho ga, d. An'ei 8 (1779), faded, soiled, good state, Prof. H.R.W. Kuhne Coll., (06-11-93, Sotheby-London, #79, illus.), 12¾ x 5⅞ in., (32.4 x 14.9 cm.), woodblock (BP 1150, DM 2844, FR 9589, Y 185,676).

$1575* *"Nakamura Nakazo I" and "Ichikawa Yaozo III": Two,* hosoban, s. Shunsho ga, d. Tenmei 1 (1781) and c. Tenmei 3 (1783), faded, trimmed, soiled, repaired, Prof. H.R.W. Kuhne Coll., (06-11-93, Sotheby-London, #105), one 12¾ x 5⅞ in., (32.4 x 14.9 cm.), other 12 x 5½ in., (32.4 x 14.9 cm.), woodblock (BP 1035, DM 2560, FR 8630, Y 167,109).

$2450* *"Nakamura Riko I" and "Nakamura Nakazo I Standing In A Snowy Garden In Front Of A Brushwood Fence": Two,* hosoban, s. Shunsho ga, d. An'ei 9 (1780)?, faded, wormed, rubbed, Prof. H.R.W. Kuhne Coll., (06-11-93, Sotheby-London, #99, illus.), one 12⅞ x 5⅞ in., (32.7 x 14.9 cm.), other 12¾ x 6 in., (32.7 x 14.9 cm.), woodblock (BP 1610, DM 3982, FR 13,425, Y 259,947).

$1487* *"Nakamura Riko In The Roles Of Courtesan Wakamatsue" and "A Courtier": Two,* hosoban, s. Shunsho ga, d. c. An'ei 2 (1773), soiled or trimmed, faded, wormage repaired, Prof. H.R.W. Kuhne Coll., (06-11-93, Sotheby-London, #128), one 11½ x 5½ in., (29.2 x 14 cm.), other 12¼ x 5½ in., (29.2 x 14 cm.), woodblock (BP 977, DM 2417, FR 8148, Y 157,772).

$735* *Nakamura Schichisaburo II As A Samurai Official,* hosoban, seal, d. Meiwa 5 (1768), faded, creased, soiled, wormage restored, Prof. H.R.W. Kuhne Coll., (06-11-93, Sotheby-London, #91), 12 x 5¾ in., (30.5 x 14.6 cm.), woodblock (BP 483, DM 1195, FR 4027, Y 77,984).

$1225* *Nakamura Sukegoro II As A Yakko Holding A Wooden Tub,* hosoban, s. Shunsho ga, d. An'ei 2 (1773), faded, soiled, tear, repaired, Prof. H.R.W. Kuhne Coll., (06-11-93, Sotheby-London, #127), 12 x 5⅝ in., (30.5 x 14.3 cm.), woodblock (BP 805, DM 1991, FR 6712, Y 129,973).

BI *Nakamura Sukegoro II As Kennaya Goroemon?,* Hosoban, s. Shunsho ga, seal, d. Meiwa 7 (1770), trimmed, wormed, Prof. H.R.W. Kuhne Coll., est. BP 1,5/1,800, (06-11-93, Sotheby-London, #73, illus.), 11⅝ x 9½ in., (29.5 x 24.1 cm.), woodblock.

BI *Nakamura Sukegoro II As Matano Goro Hoisting Up A Large Temple Bell,* hosoban, s. Shunsho ga, d. c. An'ei 3 (1774), wormage restored, soiled, trimmed, Prof. H.R.W. Kuhne Coll., est. BP 800/1,200, (06-11-93, Sotheby-London, #83, illus.), 11⅞ x 5⅞ in., (30.2 x 14.9 cm.), woodblock.

$1312* *Nakamura Sukegoro II Pausing Stepping On A Fallen Fusuma,* hosoban, s. Shunsho ga, d. c. An'ei 3 (1774), browned, trimmed, soiled, Prof. H.R.W. Kuhne Coll., (06-11-93, Sotheby-London, #132), 12¼ x 5½ in., (31.1 x 14 cm.), woodblock (BP 862, DM 2132, FR 7189, Y 139,204).

$3851* *"Nakamura Sukegoro II", "Nakamura Noshio", and "Ichikawa Danjuro V?":Three,* Hosoban, triptych, s. Shunsho ga, d. An'ei 1 (1772), faded, trimmed,soiled, Prof. H.R.W. Kuhne Coll., (06-11-93, Sotheby-London, #71, illus.), approx. 11⅜ x 5¼ in., (28.9 x 13.3 cm.), woodblock (BP 2530, DM 6259, FR 21,101, Y 408,594).

$1050* *Nakamura Utaemon I Possibly As Taira No Kiyomori?,* hosoban, s. Shunsho ga, seal, d. c. Meiwa 7 (1770), faded, trimmed, Prof. H.R.W. Kuhne Coll., (06-11-93, Sotheby-London, #98), 12 x 5⅝ in., (30.5 x 14.3 cm.), woodblock (BP 690, DM 1706, FR 5753, Y 111,406).

$2800* *Nakayama Kojuro (Temporary Name Of Nakamura Nakazo I) As Osada No Taro,* Hosoban, seal, d. Tenmei 5 (1785), mica dust sprinkled over, faded, soiled, Prof. H.R.W. Kuhne Coll., (06-11-93, Sotheby-London, #66, illus.), 12⅞ x 5¾ in., (32.7 x 14.6 cm.), woodblock (BP 1840, DM 4551, FR 15,342, Y 297,082).

BI *Onoe Matsusuke I Standing Beside A Bench,* hosoban, s. Shunsho ga, s. An'ei 7 (1778), faded, trimmed, wormhole, good state, Prof. H.R.W. Kuhne Coll., est. BP 1,2/1,800, (06-11-93, Sotheby-London, #139), 12¼ x 5½ in., (31.1 x 14 cm.), woodblock.

$2800* *"Onoe Matsusuke I" and "Nakamura Nakazo I": Two,* hosoban diptych, s. Shunsho ga, d. An'ei 8 (1779), faded, margin trimmed, added margin, Prof. H.R.W. Kuhne Coll., (06-11-93, Sotheby-London, #85, illus.), each approx. 12¼ x 5¾ in., (31.1 x 14.6 cm.), woodblock (BP 1840, DM 4551, FR 15,342, Y 297,082).

$2275* *Osagawa Tsuneyo As A Courtesan,* Hosoban, seal, d. Tenmei 6 (1786), trimmed, good state, Prof. H.R.W.Kuhne Coll., (06-11-93, Sotheby-London, #77, illus.), 12¼ x 5⅝ in., (31.1 x 14.3 cm.), woodblock (BP 1495, DM 3697, FR 12,466, Y 241,379).

$1925* *Otani Hiroji III And Bando Matataro IV,* hosoban, kitsubushi, s. Shunsho ga, seal, d. Meiwa 6 (1769), soiled,stained, scuffed, Prof. H.R.W. Kuhne Coll., (06-11-93, Sotheby-London, #113, illus.), 12⅞ x 5⅞ in., (32.7 x 14.9 cm.), woodblock (BP 1265, DM 3129, FR 10,548, Y 204,244).

$2100* *Otani Hiroji III And Onoe Kikugoro I,* hosoban diptych, s. Shunsho ga, d. An'ei 2 (1773), one faded, wormed, soiled, repaired, Prof. H.R.W. Kuhne Coll., (06-11-93, Sotheby-London, #133), 12½ x 5¾ in., (31.8 x 14.6 cm.), woodblock (BP 1380, DM 3413, FR 11,507, Y 222,812).

$3851* *"Otani Hiroji III" and "Sakata Hangoro II In A Single Combat": Two,* hosoban, s. Shunsho ga, seal, d. An'ei 2 (1773), faded, trimmed, soiled, Prof. H.R.W. Kuhne Coll., (06-11-93, Sotheby-London, #95, illus.), each approx. 12 x 5⅜ in., (30.5 x 13.7 cm.), woodblock (BP 2530, DM 6259, FR 21,101, Y 408,594).

$5951* *Otani Hiroji III, Nakamura Sukegoro And Nakamura Nakazo I Dancing Suzume Odori (Sparrow Dance): Three,* Hosoban triptych, seal, d. either Meiwa 2 (1765) or An'ei 2 (1773), worm holes restored, soiled, Prof. H.R.W. Kuhne Coll., (06-11-93, Sotheby-London, #69, illus.), each sh approx. 12¾ x 5⅞ in., (32.4 x 14.9 cm.), woodblock (BP 3910, DM 9672, FR 32,608, Y 631,406).

BI *Otani Tomoemon I In The Role Of Yakko Orisuke,* hosoban, s. Shunsho ga, d. An'ei 3 (1774), wormage repaired, Prof. H.R.W. Kuhne Coll., est. BP 800/1,000, (06-11-93, Sotheby-London, #82, illus.), 12⅝ x 5⅞ in., (32.1 x 14.9 cm.), woodblock.

$2800* *Sakata Hangoro II And Ichikawa Danzo III,* hosoban, kitsubushi, s. Shunsho ga, seal, d. c. Meiwa 5-8 (1768-71),soiled, creased, Prof. H.R.W. Kuhne Coll., (06-11-93, Sotheby-London, #112, illus.), 12⅝ x 5⅞ in., (32.1 x 14.9 cm.), woodblock (BP 1840, DM 4551, FR 15,342, Y 297,082).

$1312* *Sakata Hangoro II And Ichikawa Yaozo II,* hosoban, s. Shunsho ga, d. c. An'ei 3 (1774), darkened, soiled, trimmed, Prof. H.R.W. Kuhne Coll., (06-11-93, Sotheby-London, #134), 11½ x 5⅜ in., (29.2 x 13.7 cm.), woodblock (BP 862, DM 2132, FR 7189, Y 139,204).

$1312* *Sawamura Sojuro II And Bando Matataro IV,* hosoban, kitsubushi, s. Shunsho ga, seal, d. Meiwa 5 (1768), faded, soiled, thinned parts, Prof. H.R.W. Kuhne Coll., (06-11-93, Sotheby-London, #111, illus.), 11⅞ x 5¾ in.,

(30.2 x 14.6 cm.), woodblock (BP 862, DM 2132, FR 7189, Y 139,204).

$1225* *Sawamura Sojuro III And Ichikawa Danjuro V,* chuban, s. Shunsho ga, d. Tenmei 1 (1781), wormage, restored, soiled, (06-11-93, Sotheby-London, #125, illus.), 9½ x 6⅞ in., (24.1 x 17.5 cm.), woodblock (BP 805, DM 1991, FR 6712, Y 129,973).

BI *"Sawamura Sojuro III As Kusunoki Masatsura", "Ichikawa Yaozo III As A Court-Gardener" and "Nakamura Nakazo I As Taira No Tokitada": Three,* hosoban, two sheets from diptych, seal, d. Tenmei 6 (1786), faded, soiled, trimmed, Prof. H.R.W. Kuhne Coll., est. BP 850/1,400, (06-11-93, Sotheby-London, #107), largest 12¼ x 5¾ in., (31.1 x 14.6 cm.), smallest 11¾ x 5½ in., (31.1 x 14.6 cm.), woodblock.

$1137* *"Sawamura Sojuro III As Sonobe Saemon" and "Segawa Kikunojo III As ANun": Two,* hosoban, s. Shunsho ga, d. An'ei 8 (1779) and An'ei 9 (1780), faded,rubbed, soiled, Prof. H.R.W. Kuhne Coll., (06-11-93, Sotheby-London, #143), one 12½ x 5¾ in., (31.8 x 14.6 cm.), other 12¾ x 6 in., (31.8 x 14.6 cm.), woodblock (BP 747, DM 1848, FR 6230, Y 120,637).

$5357* *Sawamura Sojuro III In His Dressing Room Backstage With Yamashita Mangiku,* oban, s. Shunsho ga, d. c. Tenmei 1 (1781), trimmed, tears, damages,restored, laid down, Prof. H.R.W. Kuhne Coll., (06-11-93, Sotheby-London, #81, illus.), 12¾ x 29⅞ in., (32.4 x 75.9 cm.), woodblock (BP 3520, DM 8706, FR 29,353, Y 568,382).

$1137* *"Sawamura Sojuro III" and "Onoe Matsusuke I", Both Holding A Naked Sword In A Night Scene: Two,* hosoban, diptych, s. Shunsho ga, d. Tenmei 1 (1781), faded, soiled, worn, Prof. H.R.W. Kuhne Coll., (06-11-93, Sotheby-London, #104), each approx. 12 x 5½ in., (30.5 x 14 cm.), woodblock (BP 747, DM 1848, FR 6230, Y 120,637).

$1312* *The Scene Of "Kuruma-Biki": Two,* hosoban, s. Shunsho ga, d. An'ei 9 (1779), faded, soiled, rubbed, trimmed, margins replaced, Prof. H.R.W. Kuhne Coll., (06-11-93, Sotheby-London, #109), one 13 x 5¾ in., (33 x 14.6 cm.), other 12¾ x 5¾ in., (33 x 14.6 cm.), woodblock (BP 862, DM 2132, FR 7189, Y 139,204).

$2100* *Segawa Kikunojo III As A Courtesan Standing Beside A Stream,* Hosoban, seal, d. possibly Tenmei 6 (1786), (06-11-93, Sotheby-London, #76, illus.), 12⅔ x 5⅝ in., (32.2 x 14.3 cm.), woodblock (BP 1380, DM 3413, FR 11,507, Y 222,812).

$2275* *"Segawa Kikunojo III" and "Ichikawa Danjuro V": Two,* hosoban triptych?, seal, d. Tenmei 6 (1786), faded, trimmed, soiled,Prof. H.R.W. Kuhne Coll., (06-11-93, Sotheby-London, #96, illus.), one 12 x 5¾ in., (30.5 x 14.6 cm.), other 11¼ x 5½ in., (30.5 x 14.6 cm.), woodblock (BP 1495, DM 3697, FR 12,466, Y 241,379).

$962* *Yamashita Kinsaku II As A Young Woman,* hosoban, s. Shunsho ga, d. c. An'ei 5 (1776), browned, soiled, Prof.-H.R.W. Kuhne Coll., (06-11-93, Sotheby-London, #121), 12⅝ x 5⅞ in., (32.1 x 14.9 cm.), woodblock (BP 632, DM 1563, FR 5271, Y 102,069).

KATSUKAWA SHUNTEI   Japanese 1770-1820

BI *Arashi Otokichi As Iwanaga Saemon, Onoe Monsaburo As Chichibu Moritada, And Ichikawa Dansaburo V As The Courtesan Akoya,* Oban, s. Shuntei ga, pub. Enomoto Kichibei, d. Kyowa 1 (1801)?, faded, wormage repaired, rubbed, soiled, Prof. H.R.W. Kuhne Coll., est. BP 1,2/1,600, (06-11-93, Sotheby-London, #258, illus.), 14½ x 9⅞ in., (36.8 x 25.1 cm.), woodblock.

BI *Scenes From The Drama Chushingura: Two,* Oban yoko-e and Aiban yoko-e, s. Shuntei ga, pub. Izumiya Ichibei (1st print), faded, soiled, browned, darkened, Prof. H.R.W. Kuhne Coll., est. BP 550/750, (06-11-93, Sotheby-London, #237), woodblock.

KATSUKAWA SHUNZAN   Japanese ac. c. 1782-1798

$1925* *Seiro Niwaka Zensei Asobi,* Aiban, s. Katsukawa Shunzan ga, censor's seal kiwame, pub. Eijudo Nishimura Yohachi, d. c. Tenmei 7 (1787), rubbed, laid down, Prof. H.R.W. Kuhne Coll., (06-11-93, Sotheby-London, #241, illus.), 14 x 8¾ in., (35.6 x 22.2 cm.), woodblock (BP 1265, DM 3129, FR 10,548, Y 204,244).

KATSUKAWA SHUNZAN and KATSUKAWA SHUNKAKU   18th cent.

BI *"Iwai Hanshiro IV In The Role Of O-Hana" and "Sawamura Sojuro III": Two,* Hosoban, s. Shunzan ga and Shunkaku ga, d. c. Kansei 3-4 (1791-2), faded, worn, wormed, Prof. H.R.W. Kuhne Coll., est. BP 800/1,100, (06-11-93, Sotheby-London, #238), one 12 x 5⅛ in., (30.5 x 13 cm.), other 11½ x 5¼ in., (30.5 x 13 cm.), woodblock.

KATSUSHIKA HOKUSAI   Japanese 1760-1849

$1400* *Degatari Scene,* Chuban, s. Hokusai, d. c. Kyowa 1-Bunka 7 (1801-10), pub. Iseya Rihei, censor's seal, worm holes, rubbed, Prof. H.R.W. Kuhne Coll., (06-11-93, Sotheby-London, #260, illus.), 9 x 6¾ in., (22.9 x 17.1 cm.), woodblock (BP 920, DM 2275, FR 7671, Y 148,541).

$1400* *(Ehon) Joruri Zekku "Picture Book Of Joruri Ballad Dramas", 1 Vol.,* pub. Kadomaruya Jinsuke and Yorozuya Tohei, d. Bunka 12 (1815), sumi-zuri, 28 num. sh., lit., Prof. H.R.W. Kuhne Coll., (06-11-93, Sotheby-London, #528, illus.), 9¹/₁₆ x 6¼ in., (23 x 15.9 cm.), woodblock (BP 920, DM 2275, FR 7671, Y 148,541).

$5951* *Fuji Seen From Soshu Umezawa,* from the series "The Thirty-six Views of Fuji", blue outline, oban yoko-e, s. Zen Hokusai Iitsu hitsu, d. c. Tenpo 2 (1831), rubbed, soiled, wormed, Prof. H.R.W. Kuhne Coll., (06-11-93, Sotheby-London, #269, illus.), 10¼ x 15⅛ in., (26 x 38.4 cm.), woodblock (BP 3910, DM 9672, FR 32,608, Y 631,406).

$1050* *"The Night-Raid Scene From The Play Chushingura" and "Komachi-ZakuraWith Three Actors": Two,* Oban yoko-e, d. c. Kyowa 1 (1801) and Bunka 3 (1806), rubbed, wormage, tears restored, center fold mark, trimmed, Prof. H.R.W. Kuhne Coll., (06-11-93, Sotheby-London, #262), one 9⅝ x 14½ in., (24.4 x 36.8 cm.), other 9½ x 14⅛ in., (24.4 x 36.8 cm.), woodblock (BP 690, DM 1706, FR 5753, Y 111,406).

$1750* *The Post-Stations Of Kuwana And Fukuroi: Three,* Chuban, trimmed, soiled, Prof. H.R.W. Kuhne Coll., (06-11-93, Sotheby-London, #261, illus.), woodblock (BP 1150, DM 2844, FR 9589, Y 185,676).

$5251* *Urashima Taro Visiting The Palace Of The King Of The Sea,* Oban yoko-e, s. Katsu Shunro ga, pub. Sanoya Kihei, early Kansei period, wormed, trimmed, laid down, Prof. H.R.W. Kuhne Coll., (06-11-93, Sotheby-London, #267, illus.), 9½ x 14⅝ in., (24.1 x 37.1 cm.), woodblock (BP 3450, DM 8534, FR 28,773, Y 557,135).

KATTAN, Vivienne   American School 20th cent.

$46* *Monotype,* num. Unique Print, s. Vivienne Kattan, (09-15-92, Encans, #154), 29½ x 20¹¹/₁₆ in., (75 x 52.5 cm.), lithograph (BP 25, DM 68, FR 232, Y 5711, C$ 56).

KATUSKAWA SHUNKO

$1487* *Onoe Matsusuke I In An Unidentified Role As A Recluse,* hosoban, s. Shunko ga, d. c. An'ei 9 (1780), worm holes, Prof. H.R.W. Kuhne Coll., (06-11-93, Sotheby-London, #146, illus.), 12⅝ x 5⅞ in., (32.1 x 14.9 cm.), woodblock (BP 977, DM 2417, FR 8148, Y 157,772).

KATZ, Alex   American b. 1927

$3025* *Ada And Alex, 1984,* s., i. '1/8 A.P.', proofs, pub. Styria Studio, good cond., scuffs, (11-07-92, Sotheby-NY, #627, illus.), sheet 29⅞ x 36 in., (759 x 914 mm.), silkscreen p. in colors (BP 1978, DM 4830, FR 16,325, Y 373,365).

$5500* *Ada With Flowers (M. 123), 1980,* s., #15/65, co-pub. by artist and Simca Print Artists, Inc., blindstamp, good cond., tear, creases, (11-07-92, Sotheby-NY, #624, illus.), sheet 48 x 36 in., (121.9 x 91.4 cm.), silkscreen p. in colors on Grammercy (BP 3596, DM 8782, FR 29,682, Y 678,845).

$1422* *Alex at Cheat Lake (Walker 7), 1969,* #10/50, s., West Virginia University, (04-21-93, Germann, #57, illus.), 38⁹/₁₆ x 24 in., (980 x 610 mm.), lithograph and photo-offset lithograph in color (BP 923, DM 2273, FR 7686, Y 157,423, SF 2070).

$1210* *Bicycling In Central Park, 1983,* s., #73/250, from the New York, New York portfolio, pub. New York Graphic Society, Ltd., printed to edges, good cond., (11-07-92,

Sotheby-NY, #626), sheet 21⅞ x 30 in., (556 x 762 mm.), lithograph p. in colors (BP 791, DM 1932, FR 6530, Y 149,346).

$2475* *Blue Umbrella (M. 121), 1979-80,* s., num. 28/120, pub. GHJ Graphics Inc., very good cond., creases, (02-24-93, Butterfield, #3064, illus.), 20 x 30¼ in., (508 x 768 mm.), lithograph in colors on Arches (BP 1726, DM 4018, FR 13,621, Y 290,425).

BI *Blue Umbrella (M. 121), 1979-80,* s., #28/120, very good cond., creases, est. $3,5/5,5,00, (10-28-92, Butterfield, #2997, illus.), 20 x 30¼ in., (508 x 768 mm.), color lithograph on Arches.

BI *Boy With Branch I (M. 77), 1975,* s., #49/90, co-pub. Bo Alveryd and Marlborough Graphics, good cond.,est. $1,5/2,000, (05-15-93, Sotheby-NY, #1044, illus.), sheet 23⅝ x 40¼ in., (60 x 102.2 cm.), aquatint in colors on Arches cover.

$220* *Frontal Portrait Of A Woman,* s., #48/175, (06-11-93, Freemn/Fine Art, #120A), 27 x 20 in., (68.6 x 50.8 cm.), lithograph in black (BP 145, DM 358, FR 1205, Y 23,342).

BI *Girl Bicycling In Central Park,* s., num. 159/200, est. $1000/1500, (11-12-92, Freemn/Fine Art, #102A), 22 x 30 in., (55.9 x 76.2 cm.), lithograph p. in color.

$4025* *Good Afternoon (M. 69), 1974,* s., #79/80, co-pub. Brooke Alexander Editions and Marlborough Graphics, good cond., crease, handling creases, stray dot of printer's ink, (05-15-93, Sotheby-NY, #1043, illus.), sheet 27½ x 36 in., (69.9 x 91.4 cm.), silkscreen and lithograph in colors on Arches Cover (BP 2617, DM 6474, FR 21,757, Y 446,181).

$1840* *Gray Interior (Maravell 17), 1968,* s., #12/50, pub. Fischbach Gallery, full margins, good cond., skinned spot, soiling, handling creases, (05-15-93, Sotheby-NY, #1042, illus.), 16¾ x 21⅝ in., (42.5 x 54.9 cm.), silkscreen in colors on Beckett paper (BP 1196, DM 2960, FR 9946, Y 203,969).

BI *Gray Umbrella (M. 122), 1979-80,* s., #20/120, pub. GHJ Graphics Inc., very good cond., est. $3/5,000, (10-28-92, Butterfield, #2998), 20 x 30¼ in., (508 x 768 mm.), lithograph in shades of gray on Arches.

BI *Gray Umbrella (M. 122), 1979-80,* s., #20/120, pub. GHJ Graphics, p. Styria Studio, very good cond., est. $1,8/2,000, (05-19-93, Butterfield, #2210), 20 x 30¾ in., (508 x 781 mm.), lithograph in shades of gray on Arches.

BI *Gray Umbrella (Maravell 122), 1979-80,* s., #51/120, pub. GHJ Graphics, excell. cond., the Late Anwar Kamal,M.D. Coll., est. $3/4,000, (05-11-93, Christie-NY, #475, illus.), sheet 20⅛ x 30⅛ in., (511 x 765 mm.), color lithograph on wove.

$990* *"Grey Ribbon",* s., num. Alex Katz 106/150, (03-06-93, Wolf, #187), 27 x 36 in., (68.6 x 91.4 cm.), silkscreen (BP 683, DM 1649, FR 5562, Y 116,361).

$6050* *Joan (Walker 44), 1986,* s., #42/65, pub. Crown Point Press, good cond., (11-07-92, Sotheby-NY, #628, illus.), sheet 31½ x 39⅜ in., (80 x 100 cm.), aquatint p. in colors on Somerset (BP 3956, DM 9660, FR 32,650, Y 746,729).

BI *Joan (Walker 44), 1986,* s., i. T.P.E., pub. Crown Point Press, good cond., tape hinges, mat-stain, handling creases, est. $4/5,000, (05-15-93, Sotheby-NY, #1045, illus.), sheet 31¼ x 39⅛ in., (79.4 x 99.4 cm.), aquatint in colors on Somerset paper.

BI *John Ashberry (Walker 43), 1986,* s., i. 8/12 A.P., blindstamp of pub., Crown Point Press, full margins, good cond., est. $2/2,500, (02-11-93, Sotheby-NY, #362, illus.), sheet 56⁹⁄₁₆ x 22¹⁄₁₆ in., (143.7 x 56 cm.), aquatint p. in tones of black and gray on Somerset.

BI *June Ekman's Class: Eleven Plates (Maravell 44-50, 52-55), 1972,* s., num. 2/50, co-pub. Brooke Alexander and Marlborough Graphics, full margins, excell. cond., est. $2/2,500, (09-19-92, Christie-E, #140, illus.), all sheet 11 x 15 in., (27.9 x 38.1 cm.), etching and aquatint on wove.

$688* *Man With Pipe, 1984,* 148/185, s., spot, (10-14-92, Germann, #114, illus.), 19¹¹⁄₁₆ x 25¹⁵⁄₁₆ in., (500 x 660 mm.), etching and aquatint in color (BP 404, DM 1007, FR 3414, Y 83,374, SF 897).

$2200* *Night: William Dunas Dance I-IV (M. 146-149), 1983,* suite, s., #31/100, 31/100, 31/100 and 31/125, pub. Jackie Fine Arts,good cond., (11-07-92, Sotheby-NY, #625), each sheet approx. 25 x 31¼ in., (635 x 794 mm.), four lithographs in colors on Arches Cover (BP 1438, DM 3513, FR 11,873, Y 271,538).

$1210* *Night: William Dunas Dance I-IV (M. 146-9), 1983: Set Of Four,* all s., num. 68/100, pub. Jackie Fine Arts, full sheets; M. 146 w/repaired tear; M. 147-8 w/creases, (09-19-92, Christie-E, #141), all, sheet 25 x 31¼ in., (635 x 794 mm.), lithograph in colors on Arches laid down (BP 696, DM 1812, FR 6205, Y 150,760).

$6325* *Red Cap, 1989-90,* s., #2/60, pub. Crown Point Press, full sheet, good cond., (02-11-93, Sotheby-NY, #363, illus.), 20⅞ x 69⅛ in., (53 x 175.5 cm.), etching and aquatint p. in colors (BP 4463, DM 10,477, FR 35,454, Y 762,508).

BI *Red Coat, 1983,* s., #67/73, co-pub. by artist and Simca Print Artists w/blindstamp, surface scuffs, excell. cond., the Late M. Anwar Kamal, M.D. Coll., est. $12/16,000, (05-11-93, Christie-NY, #476, illus.), sheet 58 x 29 in., (147.3 x 73.7 cm.), color screenprint on wove.

$825* *"Self-Portrait",* s., num. Alex Katz 106/150, (03-06-93, Wolf, #186), 32 x 36 in., (81.3 x 91.4 cm.), silkscreen (BP 569, DM 1375, FR 4635, Y 96,968).

$220* *Skowhegan Costume Ball, 1969,* s., full margins, good cond., crease, surface soiling, (10-28-92, Butterfield, #2996), 29⅜ x 20 in., (746 x 508 mm.), lithograph on wove (BP 140, DM 340, FR 1154, Y 26,994).

$2070* *Song (Maravell 126), 1980-81,* s., #38/99, pub. Brooke Alexander, Inc., full sheet, good cond., creases, (02-11-93, Sotheby-NY, #361, illus.), sheet 33¹⁄₁₆ x 43⅞ in., (84 x 111.5 cm.), lithograph and silkscreen p. in colors on Arches Rolled Cover (BP 1461, DM 3429, FR 11,603, Y 249,548).

BI *Still Life, 1974,* #12/62, s., prov., est. C$ 2/3,000, (11-16-92, Hodgins, #319), 22 x 30¹⁵⁄₁₆ in., (55.9 x 78.7 cm.), lithograph on paper.

BI *The Striped Shirt (M. 125), 1980,* s., num. 36/80, pub. The Metropolitan Museum Of Art, blindstamp, fullmargins, apparently good cond., shrink-wrapped, est. $800/1,000, (02-24-93, Butterfield, #3065), 40½ x 14¼ in., (102.9 x 36.2 cm.), aquatint in colors on Arches Cover.

$1588* *The Striped Shirt (Maravell 125),* s., num., (11-28-92, Schoppmann, #612), 45⁹⁄₁₆ x 20¹⁵⁄₁₆ in., (115.8 x 53.3 cm.), color etching on Arches (BP 1048, DM 2530, FR 8588, Y 197,635).

$379* *Sunset: Lake Wesserunsett I (Maravell 58; Walker 14), 1972,* #9/60, s., A, Brook Alexander and Marlborough Inc., (04-21-93, Germann, #58), 29¾ x 35¹³⁄₁₆ in., (755 x 910 mm.), color serigraph (BP 246, DM 606, FR 2049, Y 41,957, SF 552).

$550* *Susan, 1976,* ed. 175, s., num., (11-12-92, Freemn/Fine Art, #102), 26 x 16½ in., (66 x 41.9 cm.), silkscreen (BP 361, DM 871, FR 2940, Y 68,196).

BI *The Swimmer (Maravell 75), 1974,* s., #35/84, co-pub. by Brooke Alexander, Inc. and Marlborough Graphics, Inc., surface scuffs, creases, est. $1,5/1,800, (11-07-92, Sotheby-NY, #623, illus.), sheet 28⅛ x 35⅞ in., (714 x 911 mm.), aquatint on German Etching.

$880* *A Tremor In The Morning, 1986,* book, pub. Peter Blum, s., #29/45, (12-10-92, Sloan, #2724), 9¼ x 7⅝ in., (23.5 x 19.4 cm.), linocuts (BP 567, DM 1392, FR 4754, Y 108,857).

BI *A Tremor In The Morning, 1986: Two,* s., #29/45, appear very good ocnd., est. $7/900, (06-11-93, Doyle, #98), 12 x 12 in., (305 x 305 mm.), woodcut.

KATZ, Man   French 1894-1962
$55* *Fiesta,* s. in plate, (09-24-92, Mystic, #49), 19 x 25 in., (48.3 x 63.5 cm.), colored silk screen (BP 32, DM 82, FR 277, Y 6616).

KATZ, Renina
BI *"Elevation In Blue" and "Green Globe": Two,* each s., d. 1974, #15/17 and 6/30, est. C$ 250/400, (12-01-92, Ritchie, #47), largest 31 x 22½ in., (78.7 x 57.2 cm.), color lithograph.

KAUFFER, E. McKnight   American 1890-1954
$550* *Chesapeake And Ohio,* B+ cond., blistering, repairs, (08-06-92, Swann, #161, illus.), 37¼ x 27½ in., (94.6 x 69.9 cm.), (BP 287, DM 813, FR 2745, Y 70,153).

KAUFFER, Edward McKnight   American 1890-1954
$4105* *Actors Prefer Shell, 1935,* p. Waterlow and Sons, ref. #434, cond. 3, (10-13-92, Phillips-London, #98, illus.), 29¹⁵⁄₁₆ x 44⅞ in., (76 x 114 cm.), color lithograph (BP 2391, DM 6014, FR 20,433, Y 497,757).
$3886* *Aeroshell Lubricating Oil, The Aristocrat Of Lubrication, 1932,* p. Chorley & Pickersgill, ref. #317, cond. 4, (10-13-92, Phillips-London, #89, illus.), 29¹⁵⁄₁₆ x 44½ in., (76 x 113 cm.), color lithograph (BP 2263, DM 5693, FR 19,343, Y 471,202).
$2927* *Explorers Prefer Shell, 1935,* ref. #433, cond. 4, tears into image, foxing, (10-13-92, Phillips-London, #97, illus.), 29¹⁵⁄₁₆ x 45¹⁄₁₆ in., (76 x 114.5 cm.), color lithograph (BP 1705, DM 4288, FR 14,569, Y 354,917).
$1223* *For Pull Use Summer Shell, Rower, 1930,* ref. #262, cond. 3, (10-13-92, Phillips-London, #87, illus.), 29¹⁵⁄₁₆ x 45 in., (76 x 114.3 cm.), color lithograph (BP 712, DM 1792, FR 6088, Y 148,296).
$1775* *Imperial Airways Empire Flying Boat Canopus, 1937,* p. Waterlow and Sons, ref. #478, cond., 4, repaired tears, (10-13-92, Phillips-London, #117), 29¾ x 44⅞ in., (75.5 x 114 cm.), color lithograph w/half-tone (BP 1034, DM 2600, FR 8835, Y 215,230).
$1599* *New Shell Lubricating Oils, 1937,* p. Waterlow and Sons, ref. #483, cond. 1, tape stains, cover illus., (10-13-92, Phillips-London, #120, illus.), 29¹⁵⁄₁₆ x 45¹⁄₁₆ in., (76 x 114.4 cm.), color lithograph (BP 931, DM 2343, FR 7959, Y 193,889).
$1111* *Shell For Go, Go For Shell, 1938,* p. Waterlow and Sons, ref. #532, cond. 1, (10-13-92, Phillips-London, #148, illus.), 29¹³⁄₁₆ x 45¹⁄₁₆ in., (75.8 x 114.4 cm.), color lithograph (BP 647, DM 1628, FR 5530, Y 134,716).
$798* *Summer Shell, May To October, 1939,* p. Waterlow and Sons, ref. #537, cond. 3, (10-13-92, Phillips-London, #153, illus.), 29¹⁵⁄₁₆ x 45¹⁄₁₆ in., (76 x 114.4 cm.), color lithograph w/half-tone (BP 465, DM 1169, FR 3972, Y 96,762).
$1332* *To Visit Britain's Landmarks, Dinton Castle, Aylesbury, 1936,* p. Waterlow and Son, ref. #450, cond. 1, center fold, creased, (10-13-92, Phillips-London, #102, illus.), 29¹⁵⁄₁₆ x 44⅞ in., (76 x 114 cm.), color lithograph (BP 776, DM 1951, FR 6630, Y 161,513).

KAUFFER, Edward McNight
$845* *Winter Shell, From October To May, 1939,* p. Waterlow and Sons, ref. 547, cond. 1, creasing, (10-13-92, Phillips-London, #161, illus.), 29¹⁵⁄₁₆ x 45¹⁄₁₆ in., (76 x 114.4 cm.), color lithograph (BP 492, DM 1238, FR 4206, Y 102,462).

KAUFFMANN, Angelica   1741-1807
$275* *Classical Scenes: Pair,* (09-17-92, Sloan, #648), each 10⅞ x 14½ in., (27.6 x 36.8 cm.), stipple engravings (BP 154, DM 408, FR 1397, Y 34,238).
$1300* *Die Mutter Mit Dem Kind, Das Einen Apfel Halt (Andresen 32 II; Boerner 9 IV), 1763,* mono., (12-04-92, Bassenge, #6616), 5½ x 4⁵⁄₁₆ in., (14 x 11 cm.), etching w/aquatint in brown (BP 834, DM 2070, FR 7023, Y 162,297).
$850* *Nachdenkendes Madchen (Andresen 26 II, Le Blanc 22 II, Boerner 34 II),* pub. Oct. 1. 1780, (06-04-93, Bassenge, #5519), 8⁵⁄₁₆ x 5¹¹⁄₁₆ in., (21.1 x 14.4 cm.), etching w/aquatint (BP 562, DM 1380, FR 4652, Y 91,674).
$1083* *Sitzendes Nachdenkendes Madchen (Andresen 26 I; Nagler 21; Boerner 18), 1766,* (12-04-92, Bassenge, #6615), 7⅞ x 6⅛ in., (20 x 15.6 cm.), etching (BP 695, DM 1725, FR 5851, Y 135,206).

KAUFFMANN, Angelica   Swiss 1741-1807
BI *Classical Scenes: Pair,* est. $300/350, (07-03-92, Sloan, #670), 10⅞ x 14½ in., (27.6 x 36.8 cm.), stipple engraving.

KAUFFMANN, Angelica (after)
$66* *Attending The Maiden,* by Domer, (06-16-93, Bonhams-Chelsea, #485), image 10½ x 12 in., (26.7 x 30.5 cm.),

stipple engraving w/hand-coloring (BP 44, DM 110, FR 368, Y 7039).
$326* *"Blind Mans Buff" and "A Headdress For A Maiden": Two,* (08-14-92, G.A. Key, #106), hand colored stipple engraving (BP 170, DM 478, FR 1619, Y 41,110).
$250* *Lady Bingham, 1776,* engraved by James Watson, watermark, 3rd final state, small margins, crease through image, nick, good cond., (11-30-92, Phillips-London, #71, illus.), plate 19½ x 14¾ in., (495 x 375 mm.), mezzotint on laid (BP 165, DM 398, FR 1352, Y 31,114).
$99* *Two Women By A Pond,* by Thomas Burke, pub. J. Birchall, April 2nd, 1782, later strike, margins, (06-16-93, Bonhams-Chelsea, #487), pl. 13 x 11½ in., (33 x 29.2 cm.), stipple engraving w/hand-coloring (BP 66, DM 164, FR 552, Y 10,559).

KAUS, Max   1891-1977
BI *Badene An Bewaldeter Kuste, (19)22,* s., d., artist's proof 1st state, num., w/mount staining, est. DM 14/16,000, (12-01-92, Karl/Faber, #820, illus.), 21¼ x 14³⁄₁₆ in., (54 x 36 cm.), lithograph.
$5085* *Frauenkopf (Knupp 140), 1920,* s., d., t., watermark, collector's stamp, (06-10-93, Hauswedell/Nolt, #445, illus.), image 16⁹⁄₁₆ x 12¹⁵⁄₁₆ in., (42 x 33 cm.), woodcut on hand-made (BP 3326, DM 8280, FR 27,878, Y 539,752).
$2684* *Liegendes Madchen (Knupp 54 Oder 58), 1920,* s., d., #22/25, collector's stamp, (06-10-93, Hauswedell/Nolt, #443), image 14¹⁵⁄₁₆ x 19³⁄₁₆ in., (38 x 48.8 cm.), lithograph on Japan (BP 1756, DM 4371, FR 14,715, Y 284,895).
$1836* *Madchenkopf (Knupp 130), 1920,* s., d., from Die Schaffenden 1. year, portfolio 3., blindstamp, (06-10-93, Hauswedell/Nolt, #444), image 11⁵⁄₁₆ x 5 in., (28.7 x 12.7 cm.), woodcut on wove (BP 1201, DM 2990, FR 10,066, Y 194,884).
$194* *Mannerportrait, 1920,* block mono., (09-25-92, Granier, #2903), sheet 13⁷⁄₁₆ x 9⅞ in., (34.1 x 25.1 cm.), woodcut on wove (BP 113, DM 288, FR 972, Y 23,416).

KAWALSKI, Alfred Von Wierusz   Polish 1849-1915
$121* *The Return Home,* s. in plate, stamped sig., (05-28-93, Sloan, #189, illus.), 11⅞ x 8⅜ in., (30.2 x 21.3 cm.), etching on silk (BP 78, DM 192, FR 649, Y 12,974).

KAWANISHI, Ei   Japanese 20th cent.
BI *Coastal Village,* est. $250/350, (10-30-92, Sloan, #1898), sheet 15½ x 11⅜ in., (39.4 x 28.9 cm.), woodblock.

KAWANO
$275* *"Shell",* s. Kaoru Kawano, t., #48/50, seal, (11-20-92, Skinner, #17, illus.), 16 x 23 in., (40.6 x 58.4 cm.), (BP 181, DM 438, FR 1477, Y 34,200).

KAWANO   Japanese 1916-1965
BI *Girl,* s., red stamp, good cond., est. $100/150, (05-15-93, Cleveland, #25), 10¼ x 15¼ in., (26 x 38.7 cm.), color woodblock.
BI *"Owl",* s., red stamp, good cond., stains, est. $75/125, (05-15-93, Cleveland, #24), 15 x 10⅛ in., (38.1 x 25.7 cm.), color woodblock.
$55* *Two Ducks,* s. w/red stamp, image creases, good cond., (05-15-93, Cleveland, #25A), 9 x 15 in., (22.9 x 38.1 cm.), color woodblock print (BP 36, DM 88, FR 297, Y 6097).

KAWANO, Kaoru   Japanese 1916-1965
$65* *Dancing Figure, Mai Ogi,* stamped artist's character seal in plate, image s.; s., t., #149/300, stamped artist's label, prov., (06-08-93, Ritchie, #37), 22 x 15 in., (55.9 x 38.1 cm.), color woodcut on hand-made (BP 43, DM 105, FR 355, Y 6904, C$ 83).
$88* *"Dancing Figures", "Two Ducks" and "Two Birds": Three,* s., bears artist's stamp, (05-16-93, Hindman, #394), largest 22 x 15 in., (55.9 x 38.1 cm.), color woodcuts (BP 57, DM 142, FR 476, Y 9755).
BI *Little Flora (B),* stamped artist's character seal in plate, image gouache s.; s., t., #36/200, stamped artist's label, prov., est. C$ 5/700, (06-08-93, Ritchie, #38, illus.), image 22¼ x 11⅜ in., (56.5 x 28.9 cm.), color woodcut.
BI *Twilight (D),* s., t., #60/300, trimmed margins, ripplings, taped to mat, good cond., (04-02-93, Weschler, #275, illus.), 14¾ x 29½ in., (37.5 x 74.9 cm.), wood engraving.

BI *Young Child Emerging From A Seashell,* sealed, s., est. $3/400, (08-05-92, Boos, #691, illus.), image 10³⁄₁₆ x 14⅞ in., (258 x 378 mm.), wood block print.

KAY, J.
$33* *"Travells Eldest Son In Conversation With A Cherokee Chief",* badly stained, (10-03-92, Garth, #76), 13½ x 12 in., (34.3 x 30.5 cm.), handcolored engraving (BP 19, DM 47, FR 159, Y 3950).

KAYSER, Alex b. 1949
BI *Richard Lindner, 1976,* ink s., d., t., #7/20, est. DM 1,000, (11-12-92, Lempertz, #113, illus.), 5¾ x 8⅛ in., (14.6 x 20.7 cm.), photograph, gelatin silver print w/ hand-coloring.

KEAN, Kirby A. b. 1908
$880* *Boulder Dam, 1935,* partial credit label, (10-13-92, Christie-NY, #251, illus.), 14 x 11 in., (35.6 x 27.9 cm.), photograph, toned gelatin silver print (BP 513, DM 1289, FR 4380, Y 106,705).
BI *Loading Ship, Los Angeles, Ca., c. 1932,* s., est. $800/1,200, (04-08-93, Christie-NY, #312, illus.), 12⅞ x 10⅛ in., (32.7 x 25.7 cm.), photograph, gelatin silver print.

KEATING, Tom
$119* *John Constable At Flatford, 1977,* s., #707/850, pub. Frinton Gallery, (12-10-92, Bonhams-Chelsea, #15), image 17¼ x 22¼ in., (43.8 x 56.5 cm.), color reproduction (BP 77, DM 188, FR 643, Y 14,720).

KECK, William
BI *"Reflections And Mirroring" (New Bauhaus-50 Years, dust jacket and Vision in Motion, fig. 261, variant), 1939,* photog. stamp, est. $3/5,000, (04-06-93, Sotheby-NY, #331, illus.), 7⅝ x 9½ in., photograph.

KEELEEMEOMEE Inuit
$385* *"Hunter Chasing Geese",* #19/50, 1974, s., t., seal, blind-stamp, (05-14-93, DuMouchelle, #2031, illus.), 13¼ x 16½ in., (33.7 x 41.9 cm.), color stone cut (BP 250, DM 619, FR 2081, Y 42,678).

KEELY, Pat
BI *Southern Railway, 1932,* plate s., lined, est. $7/900, (03-25-93, Christie-E, #203), 39½ x 24½ in., (100.3 x 62.2 cm.), color lithograph.

KEENAN, Larry
BI *"City Lights Bookstore, The Last Gathering Of The Beat Poet/Artists,North Beach, S.F." and "Artist/Filmmaker Bruce Connor, Haight Ashbury, S.F.": Two,* 1965, p. 1967, s. twice, t., d., photog.'s stamp, est. $6/800, (05-23-93, Butterfield, #3478, illus.), one 12½ x 9½ in., other 9⅝ x 12½ in., photograph, gelatin silver print.
BI *"Poet/Playwrite Michael McClure Playing Autoharp, Haight Ashbury, S.F." and "Allen Ginsberg, Michael McClure, And Bruce Connor Chanting At Ginsberg's S.F. Apartment": Two,* 1965, p. 1967, s. twice, t., d., photog.'s stamp, est. $6/800, (05-23-93, Butterfield, #3477, illus.), one 11½ x 8½ in., other 9 x 13 in., photograph, gelatin silver print.

KEETMAN, Peter German b. 1916
BI *"Locomotive" and "Letzer Waggon": Train Studies, 1958 & 1953: Two,* each s., t., d. by photog., studio stamp, est. $3/4,000, (10-15-92, Sotheby-NY, #482, illus.), approx. 11½ x 9¼ in., (29.2 x 23.5 cm.), approx. 9¼ x 11½ in., (29.2 x 23.5 cm.), photograph, gelatin silver prints.
$1896* *Schraubenpumpe, 1960,* s., d., t., (11-12-92, Lempertz, #116, illus.), 11⁹⁄₁₆ x 9³⁄₁₆ in., (29.4 x 23.3 cm.), photograph, gelatin silver print (BP 1212, DM 2980, FR 10,155, Y 234,566).
$1289* *Sprudelndes Wasser, 1952,* s., d., (c) stamp, (11-12-92, Lempertz, #114, illus.), 9⁷⁄₁₆ x 7 in., (23.9 x 17.8 cm.), photograph, gelatin silver print (BP 824, DM 2026, FR 6904, Y 159,470).
$1289* *Tropfen Auf Glasplatte, 1956,* s., d., (11-12-92, Lempertz, #115, illus.), 9³⁄₁₆ x 6¾ in., (23.4 x 17.2 cm.), photograph, gelatin silver print (BP 824, DM 2026, FR 6904, Y 159,470).

KEIGHLEY, Alexander 1861-1947
BI *"Mountain Pass Algeria", "An Arab Funeral" and "The Potato Field", c. 1920: Three,* s., mounted on card, front s.; t., photog.'s labels, 475 x 360mm and480 x 280mm, est. BP 800/1,200, (05-07-93, Sotheby-London, #164, illus.), photograph, chromium bromide print.

KEIL, A. (Sandor Ek)
$259* *...La Fin De L'Allemagne Fasciste, 1944,* cond. B, (03-16-93, Boisgirard, #6), 21¼ x 15¹⁵⁄₁₆ in., (54 x 40.5 cm.), typolithograph poster (BP 179, DM 431, FR 1463, Y 30,285).

KEILEY, Joseph Turner
$605* *Zit-Kala-Sa, 1899,* (04-07-93, Swann, #498, illus.), 6¼ x 4½ in., photograph, platinum print (BP 400, DM 978, FR 3311, Y 68,734).

KEIMEL
$1129* *Pellicola, Perutz,* defects, creasing, (05-07-93, Christie-S. Ken, #80, illus.), 37½ x 54 in., (95.3 x 137.2 cm.), color lithograph (BP 715, DM 1785, FR 6015, Y 124,312).

KEIMEL, Hermann 1889-1948
BI *Carneval Im Wintergarten, 1926,* pierced plastic tape, sellotape marks, est. BP 4/600, (02-04-93, Christie-S. Ken, #168, illus.), 47 x 35 in., (119.4 x 88.9 cm.), color lithograph.

KEINEN, Imao Japanese 1845-1925
$260* *Sparrows, 1892,* s., t., d. in Japanese, prov., (05-10-93, Hodgins, #290, illus.), (31.8 x 47.6 cm.), color wood-block on paper (BP 170, DM 418, FR 1409, Y 29,054, C$ 330).

KEITH, Elizabeth British 1887-1956
$385* *Blue And White, Kyoto,* s., (09-17-92, Sloan, #1617), 14⅞ x 10⅞ in., (37.8 x 27.6 cm.), color woodcut (BP 216, DM 572, FR 1956, Y 47,933).
$176* *"Bridge Soochow", 1924,* t., image s., seal, (12-02-92, Boos, #522), image 10³⁄₁₆ x 14⅞ in., (258 x 378 mm.), color woodblock (BP 114, DM 277, FR 945, Y 21,899).
$715* *Camel Back Bridge, Soochow,* s., (09-17-92, Sloan, #1615, illus.), 12¾ x 11⅜ in., (32.4 x 28.9 cm.), color woodcut (BP 402, DM 1061, FR 3633, Y 89,019).
$468* *"Lama Temple Peking",* s. Elizabeth Keith, d. 1922, very good cond., (09-27-92, Bakker, #255, illus.), image 9¼ x 14¼ in., (23.5 x 36.2 cm.), color woodblock print (BP 273, DM 694, FR 2346, Y 56,488).
$495* *Lin Jung Monastary, Soochow,* s., (09-17-92, Sloan, #1616), 15½ x 10¾ in., (39.4 x 27.3 cm.), color wood-cut (BP 278, DM 735, FR 2515, Y 61,628).
$303* *Moro Umbrella,* s., (09-17-92, Sloan, #1611), 8⅝ x 6 in., (21.9 x 15.2 cm.), color woodcut (BP 170, DM 450, FR 1540, Y 37,724).
$550* *New Year's Lanterns,* s., (09-17-92, Sloan, #1618), 16⅝ x 11½ in., (42.2 x 29.2 cm.), color woodcut (BP 309, DM 817, FR 2795, Y 68,476).
$715* *Night Scene, Malacca,* s., (09-17-92, Sloan, #1613), 14⅞ x 9⅞ in., (37.8 x 25.1 cm.), color woodcut (BP 402, DM 1061, FR 3633, Y 89,019).
$715* *Old Chinese House, Malacca,* s., (09-17-92, Sloan, #1612), 14¾ x 10 in., (37.5 x 25.4 cm.), color woodcut (BP 402, DM 1061, FR 3633, Y 89,019).
$468* *Princess Of The House Of Min,* s., (09-17-92, Sloan, #1614), 14¾ x 9⅜ in., (37.5 x 23.8 cm.), color woodcut (BP 263, DM 695, FR 2378, Y 58,267).

KELLER, Ernst 1891-1968
$709* *Pferd Und Mensch, 1956,* fold mark, other minor defects, (02-04-93, Christie-S. Ken, #50, illus.), 50 x 35½ in., (127 x 90.2 cm.), color lithograph backed on linen (BP 495, DM 1167, FR 3959, Y 88,195).

KELLER, Henry G. American 1870-1949
$94* *"Circus", 1932,* s., mono., Print-A-Month Club Cleveland, June 1932, slightly toned, (10-31-92, Cleveland, #149), 14¾ x 19¼ in., (37.5 x 48.9 cm.), lithograph (BP 60, DM 145, FR 491, Y 11,644).
$60* *Circus, 1932,* s., plate No. 1, The Print-A-Month Club, very good cond.(05-15-93, Cleveland, #178), 14¾ x 19¼ in., (37.5 x 48.9 cm.), lithograph (BP 39, DM 97, FR 324, Y 6651).

$45* *"Fighting Horses", 1933,* s., plate 13 The Print-A-Month Club, very good cond., (05-15-93, Cleveland, #179), 14¼ x 20¼ in., (36.2 x 51.4 cm.), lithograph (BP 29, DM 72, FR 243, Y 4988).

BI *Floral Prints: Group Of Three,* all s. H. G. Keller, good cond., est. $1/200, (11-21-92, Bakker, #18), largest, plate 7¾ x 6½ in., (19.7 x 16.5 cm.), etching.

$20* *In The Fields,* s., paper toned, (05-15-93, Cleveland, #177), 8 x 8 in., (20.3 x 20.3 cm.), etching (BP 13, DM 32, FR 108, Y 2217).

$132* *"Mexican Wood Merchant", 1938,* Print Club of Cleveland Publication No. 16, very toned paper, (10-31-92, Cleveland, #150), 11½ x 15¾ in., (29.2 x 40 cm.), lithograph (BP 85, DM 203, FR 689, Y 16,351).

KELLEY, Tom

$770* *Marilyn Monroe,* proof for tonal quality, (04-26-93, Selkirk, #556), 16 x 12 in., (40.6 x 30.5 cm.), color photograph (BP 486, DM 1207, FR 4076, Y 84,970).

$5933* *Marilyn Monroe, Nude,* lifetime unique print, reprod. Marilyn Monroe Calendar, (10-10-92, Bonhams, #152, illus.), 10 x 8 in., (25.4 x 20.3 cm.), photograph (BP 3520, DM 8813, FR 29,591, Y 722,303).

KELLOGG

$105* *"Lucy",* stains, (09-04-92, Garth, #222, illus.), 11¾ x 10 in., (29.8 x 25.4 cm.), handcolored lithograph (BP 53, DM 147, FR 501, Y 12,925).

$22* *"The Sisters"* and *"Girl With Guitar": Two,* stained, (03-13-93, Garth, #432), 18½ x 14 in., (47 x 35.6 cm.), hand-colored lithograph (BP 15, DM 37, FR 125, Y 2593).

$39* *Untitled,* from a silhouette of Nathaniel Potter Tallmadge by Wm. H. Brown, (03-13-93, Garth, #454), 17½ x 13¾ in., (44.5 x 34.9 cm.), b/w lithograph (BP 27, DM 65, FR 221, Y 4596).

KELLOGG, D.W.   American 19th cent.

$77* *"The Declaration", "The Lover's Quarrel", "The Lover's Reconciliation"* and *"The Wedding Day": Four,* Ruth K. Flower Coll., (04-18-93, Hindman, #1675), each 12½ x 8½ in., (31.8 x 21.6 cm.), lithograph, 3 hand-colored (BP 51, DM 124, FR 420, Y 8658).

$121* *"The Life"* and *"Age Of Man And Woman": Two,* Ruth K. Flower Coll., (04-18-93, Hindman, #1709), each 9 x 13 in., (22.9 x 33 cm.), hand-colored lithograph (BP 79, DM 195, FR 660, Y 13,606).

$358* *Presidential Portraits: Four,* Ruth K. Flower Coll., (04-18-93, Hindman, #1680), each 13 x 10½ in., (33 x 26.7 cm.), hand-colored lithograph (BP 235, DM 578, FR 1954, Y 40,256).

KELLOGG & BULKELEY CO., Publishers

$550* *Chicago In Flames (Peters p. 247), 1871,* margins, creasing, light-staining, foxmarks, margins, staining, (01-22-93, Christie-NY, #320), borderline 8⅝ x 13½ in., (219 x 343 mm.), hand-colored lithograph and touches of gum arabic on wove (BP 360, DM 875, FR 2959, Y 68,836).

KELLOGG and COMSTOCK   American 19th cent.

$187* *"The Life"* and *"Age Of Man And Woman": Two,* (04-18-93, Hindman, #1710), each 9 x 13 in., (22.9 x 33 cm.), hand-colored lithograph (BP 123, DM 302, FR 1021, Y 21,028).

KELLY, Ellsworth   American b. 1923

$3850* *18 Colors, Cincinnati (A. 193, G. 978), 1982,* s., #24/57, blindstamp pub. Gemini G.E.L., full margins, very good cond.?, (10-28-92, Butterfield, #3002), sheet 16 x 90½ in., (40.6 x 229.9 cm.), color lithograph on Arches Cover paper (BP 2453, DM 5946, FR 20,189, Y 472,393).

$1588* *Algue (Axsom 53/1965-1966),* s., num., (11-28-92, Schoppmann, #613), 31⅛ x 13¾ in., (79 x 35 cm.), lithograph on BFK Rives (BP 1048, DM 2530, FR 8588, Y 197,635).

$2640* *Baie Rouge (Axsom 204; Gemini 1160), 1983-4,* s., i. RTP, Gemini G.E.L. blindstamps, full margins, excell. cond.?, (09-19-92, Christie-E, #142, illus.), sheet 52 x 51 in., (132.1 x 129.5 cm.), lithograph on Arches (BP 1519, DM 3953, FR 13,538, Y 328,931).

$4180* *Black Curve (G. 1335), 1988,* s., #9/25, blindstamps, full margins, excellent cond., (11-09-92, Christie-NY, #335,

illus.), 37½ x 84¼ in., (95.3 x 214 cm.), lithograph on wove (BP 2764, DM 6673, FR 22,546, Y 518,739).

$1100* *Black Variation V (A. 113, G. 593), 1973-75,* s., annot. A.P. IX, blindstamp of pub. Gemini G.E.L., full margins, apparently very good cond., (02-24-93, Butterfield, #3068), 29 x 29 in., (737 x 737 mm.), lithograph, intaglio, & debossing on Rives BFK (BP 767, DM 1786, FR 6054, Y 129,078).

$1840* *Blue With Black II (A. 98, G. 534), 1974,* s., #7/50, blindstamp publisher, Gemini G.E.L., full margins, good cond.?, staining, (05-19-93, Butterfield, #2219, illus.), 18½ x 15⅞ in., (470 x 403 mm.), silkscreen in blue/black on Arjomari (BP 1194, DM 2991, FR 10,077, Y 203,698).

$2300* *Blue/Red-Orange/Green (A. 75, G. 266), 1971,* s., #59/64, blindstamp publisher, Gemini G.E.L., p. Dan Freeman, fullmargins, good cond.?, (05-19-93, Butterfield, #2216, illus.), 32⅜ x 15½ in., (822 x 394 mm.), lithograph in colors on Special Arjomari (BP 1493, DM 3739, FR 12,596, Y 254,622).

BI *Blue/Yellow/Red (Untitled) (A. 91), 1970-73,* s., annot. P.P., pub. Harry N. Abrams, full margins, good cond., staining, surface scuffing in image, creases, discoloration, yellow stains, stain,est. $1,8/2,000, (02-24-93, Butterfield, #3067), 18 x 17½ in., (457 x 445 mm.), silkscreen in blue, yellow, & red on Strathmore Fairfield Opaque Number 8.

$690* *Blue/Yellow/Red (Untitled) (A. 91), 1970-73,* s., annot. P.P., pub. Harry N. Abrams, p. Maurel Studios, full margins, good cond., staining affecting sig., surface scuffing in image, creases, discoloration, stains, (05-19-93, Butterfield, #2218), 18 x 17½ in., (457 x 445 mm.), silkscreen in blue/yellow/red on Strathmore Fairfield Opague #8 (BP 448, DM 1122, FR 3779, Y 76,387).

$2588* *"Camellia I", "II"* and *"III" (A. 41-43), 1964-65: Three,* s., #52/75, 55/75, 52/75, pub. Maeght, p. Marcel Durassier, full margins, good cond., staining, handling creases, Albert Levinson Estate, (05-19-93, Butterfield, #2214), smallest 22½ x 18 in., (572 x 457 mm.), largest 26 x 16½ in., (572 x 457 mm.), lithograph on Rives BFK (BP 1680, DM 4207, FR 14,173, Y 286,505).

$12,075* *Colored Paper Image II (A. 142, Tyler 296:EK3), 1976,* s., #9/17, unique variations, blindstamp, pub. Tyler Graphics, Ltd.,full margins, good cond., (05-15-93, Sotheby-NY, #1047, illus.), sheet 46 x 31¾ in., (116.8 x 80.6 cm.), pressed paper pulp w/hand-coloring in green on HMP handmade paper (BP 7851, DM 19,423, FR 65,270, Y 1,338,543).

$7700* *Colored Paper Image IX (Four Grays With Black I) (A. 149; T. 304:EK11), 1976,* s., #5/18, blindstamp, pub. Tyler Graphics, Ltd., full margins, goodcond., (11-07-92, Sotheby-NY, #633, illus.), sheet 45⅞ x 31⅞ in., (116.5 x 81 cm.), colored and pressed paper pulp w/hand coloring on HMP handmade (BP 5034, DM 12,294, FR 41,554, Y 950,383).

$3080* *Colored Paper Image XVIII (Green Square With Dark Grey) (Axsom 158; Tyler 313), 1976,* s., #11/22, blindstamp, creases, excellent cond., (11-09-92, Christie-NY, #332), 31¾ x 30⅞ in., (806 x 784 mm.), colored pressed paper pulp (BP 2036, DM 4917, FR 16,613, Y 382,229).

$6900* *"Cyclamen I", "II", "III"* and *"IV" (A. 36-39), 1964-65: Four,* s., #51/75, 48/75, 48/75, 50/75, pub. Maeght, p. Marcel Durassier, full margins, good cond., staining, handling creases, Albert Levinson Estate, (05-19-93, Butterfield, #2213, illus.), smallest 26¼ x 15 in., (667 x 381 mm.), largest 29 x 17½ in., (667 x 381 mm.), lithograph on Rives BFK (BP 4479, DM 11,216, FR 37,788, Y 763,866).

BI *Dark Blue With Red (Axsom 10), 1964-1965,* s., est. SF 3/4,000, (04-21-93, Germann, #48, illus.), 35 1/16 x 23¼ in., (890 x 590 mm.), color lithograph.

$3300* *Dark Gray Curve (G. 1356), 1988,* s., #9/25, blindstamps, full margins, excellent cond., (11-09-92, Christie-NY, #336, illus.), 26 x 84¼ in., (66 x 214 cm.), lithograph on wove (BP 2182, DM 5268, FR 17,799, Y 409,531).

$1380* *Dracena II (A. 213, G. 1208), 1983-85,* s., #30/30, blindstamp publisher, Gemini G.E.L., p. James Reid and Alan

Holoubek, full margins, good cond.?, (05-19-93, Butterfield, #2223, illus.), 39 x 27 in., (99.1 x 68.6 cm.), lithograph on Rives BFK (BP 896, DM 2243, FR 7558, Y 152,773).

$577* *Ellsworth Kelly Munster, 1992,* pencil s., (11-20-92, Lempertz, #639), 33¼ x 26¾ in., (84.5 x 68 cm.), serigraph on hand-made cardboard (BP 380, DM 920, FR 3099, Y 71,757).

$7150* *Four Panels (A. 72, G. 263), 1970-71,* s., annot. A.P. VI, blindstamp pub. Gemini G.E.L., full margins, good cond.?, (10-28-92, Butterfield, #2999, illus.), 28¾ x 54 in., (73 x 137.2 cm.), color silkscreen on Special Arjomari paper (BP 4556, DM 11,042, FR 37,493, Y 877,301).

$4400* *Green Curve (G. 1352), 1988,* s., #8/25, blindstamps, full margins, excellent cond., (11-09-92, Christie, #334), 37½ x 84 in., (95.3 x 213.4 cm.), green lithograph on wove (BP 2909, DM 7024, FR 23,732, Y 546,041).

$2415* *Green Curve With Radius Of 20 Degrees (Axsom 101, Gemini 527), 1974,* s., #76/100, blindstamp, pub. Gemini, G.E.L., full margins, good cond., soiling, handling creases, (05-15-93, Sotheby-NY, #1046, illus.), 23⅞ x 24 in., (60.6 x 61 cm.), lithograph in colors on Arjomari (BP 1570, DM 3885, FR 13,054, Y 267,709).

BI *Jacmel (A. 181, G. 855), 1980,* s., annot. PP II, blindstamp publisher, Gemini G.E.L., p. Anthony Zepeda, full margins, very good cond.?, est. $1,2/1,500, (05-19-93, Butterfield, #2222), 22¾ x 24 in., (578 x 610 mm.), lithograph on Rives BFK.

$2588* *"Leaves", "Grapefruit", "Tangerine" and "Lemon" (A. 32-35), 1964-65:Four,* s., #17/75, 63/75, 64/75, 57/75, pub. Maeght, p. Marcel Durassier, full margins, good cond., staining, handling creases, surface soiling, Albert Levinson Estate, (05-19-93, Butterfield, #2212, illus.), smallest 35⅜ x 24¼ in., (899 x 616 mm.), largest 35⅜ x 25 in., (899 x 616 mm.), transfer lithograph on Rives BFK (BP 1680, DM 4207, FR 14,173, Y 286,505).

$660* *Lemon, Citron (Axsom 35), 1964-65,* s., num. 58/75, pub. Maeght Editeur, Paris, good cond., (05-22-93, Weschler, #195, illus.), 35½ x 24¼ in., (90.2 x 61.6 cm.), transfer lithograph on B.F.K. Rives (BP 428, DM 1073, FR 3611, Y 72,767).

$1045* *Olive, c. 1964,* s., #18/75, good cond.?, (12-08-92, Swann, #153, illus.), 35¼ x 23¾ in., (89.5 x 60.3 cm.), color lithograph on Rives (BP 655, DM 1627, FR 5547, Y 129,524).

$978* *Orange Over Green (A. 27), 1964-65,* s., #47/75, pub. Maeght, full margins, good cond.?, handling creases,soiling, (05-19-93, Butterfield, #2211), 20⅜ x 15⅝ in., (518 x 397 mm.), lithograph in colors on Rives BFK (BP 635, DM 1590, FR 5356, Y 108,270).

$770* *Orange Over Green (Axsom 27), 1964-65,* s., #59/75, (05-16-93, Hindman, #622), 20¼ x 15¾ in., (51.4 x 40 cm.), color lithograph (BP 501, DM 1239, FR 4162, Y 85,356).

$550* *"Orange Over Green", "Orange Over Blue", and "Green": Three (Axsom 27, 28), 1964-65,* s., # 17/75, (03-14-93, Hindman, #326), 20¼ x 15⅝ in., (51.4 x 39.7 cm.), color lithograph on Rives (BP 384, DM 915, FR 3113, Y 64,820).

$1980* *Orange/Green (A. 64, G. 233), 1970,* s., num. 56/75, blindstamp of pub Gemini G.E.L., full margins, apparently very good cond, (02-24-93, Butterfield, #3066, illus.), 31 x 19 in., (787 x 483 mm.), lithograph in orange & green on Special Arjomari (BP 1381, DM 3214, FR 10,897, Y 232,340).

$2860* *Orange/Green (Axom 64; Gemini 233), 1970,* s., #73/75, blindstamp, pub. Gemini, G.E.L., full margins, good cond., (11-07-92, Sotheby-NY, #630), sheet 41½ x 30¼ in., (105.4 x 76.8 cm.), lithograph p. in colors on Special Arjomari (BP 1870, DM 4567, FR 15,434, Y 352,999).

$2588* *"Pear 1", "II" and "III" (A. 45-47), 1965-66: Three,* s., #38/75, 40/75, 42/75, pub. Maeght, p. Imprimerie Arte, full margins, good cond., staining, crease, water staining, rubbed areas, (05-19-93, Butterfield, #2215), smallest 34⅝ x 23¼ in., (879 x 591 mm.), largest 35½ x 24¾ in., (879 x 591 mm.), lithograph on Rives BFK (BP 1680, DM 4207, FR 14,173, Y 286,505).

BI *Pear I, Poire I, (A. 45), 1965-1966,* s., num. 37/75, pub. Maeght Editeur, Paris, good cond., est. $8/1,200, (05-22-93, Weschler, #196, illus.), 35½ x 24½ in., (90.2 x 62.2 cm.), transfer lithograph on B.F.K. Rives.

BI *Portraits: Jack/Spectrum, 1989,* s., #17/35, blindstamp publisher, Gemini G.E.L., p. Michael Cascaddenand Mark Mahaffey, full margins, very good cond.?, est. $6/8,000, (05-19-93, Butterfield, #2225, illus.), 25⅛ x 92½ in., (63.8 x 235 cm.), lithograph in colors on wove.

$4313* *Red Curve (State II)(G. 1348), 1988,* s., #15/15, blindstamp publisher, Gemini G.E.L., p. Ken Farley, SergeLozingot and Claudio Stickar, full margins, very good cond.?, (05-19-93, Butterfield, #2224, illus.), sh 26 x 84 in., (66 x 213.4 cm.), lithograph in orange-red on Arches 88 (BP 2800, DM 7011, FR 23,620, Y 477,471).

BI *Saint Martin Landscape (A. 179, T. 324), 1979,* s., #24/39, Tyler Graphics blindstamp, full margins, excell. cond., est. $1,5/2,000, (05-11-93, Christie-NY, #478), sheet 26⅞ x 33½ in., (683 x 851 mm.), color lithograph, screenprint and collage on wove.

$1760* *Saint Martin Landscape (Tyler 324:EK31), 1979,* s., #23/39, blindstamp, pub. Tyler Graphics, full margins, good cond., crease, (11-07-92, Sotheby-NY, #632, illus.), 15¼ x 22 in., (387 x 559 mm.), silkscreen and lithograph p. in colors w/collage (BP 1151, DM 2810, FR 9498, Y 217,230).

$11,500* *Spectrum (A. 90, G. 465), 1973,* s., #30/34, blindstamp publisher, Gemini G.E.L., full margins, good cond.?, (05-19-93, Butterfield, #2217, illus.), sh 33⅞ x 83½ in., (86 x 212.1 cm.), silkscreen in colors on Arches (BP 7465, DM 18,693, FR 62,979, Y 1,273,110).

$13,200* *Spectrum (A. 90; G. 465), 1973,* s., #17/34, blindstamp, pub. Gemini G.E.L., full margins, good cond., (11-07-92, Sotheby-NY, #634, illus.), 17⅜ x 67⅛ in., (44.1 x 170.5 cm.), silkscreen p. in colors on Arches 88 (BP 8630, DM 21,076, FR 71,236, Y 1,629,227).

$1380* *Twelve Leaves: Leaf I (A. 166), G. 803), 1978,* s., t., annot. RTP, blindstamp publisher, Gemini G.E.L., full margins, good cond.?, crease, staining, (05-19-93, Butterfield, #2221), 18¼ x 24½ in., (464 x 622 mm.), lithograph on Arches 88 (BP 896, DM 2243, FR 7558, Y 152,773).

$248* *Twelve Leaves: Leaf VIII (A. 173, G. 810), 1978,* s., t., annot. S.P., blindstamp pub. Gemini G.E.L., full margins, good cond.?, stains, and in image, (10-28-92, Butterfield, #3001), sheet 30 x 42 in., (76.2 x 106.7 cm.), lithograph on Arches 88 (BP 158, DM 383, FR 1300, Y 30,429).

$468* *Twleve Leaves: Leaf II (A. 167, G. 804), 1978,* s., t., #5/20, blindstamp pub. Gemini G.E.L., full margins, good cond., creases, water stain, surface soiling, (10-28-92, Butterfield, #3000), 15 x 22 in., (381 x 559 mm.), lithograph on Arches 88 (BP 298, DM 723, FR 2454, Y 57,423).

$2090* *Untitled (A. 201; Gemini 1149), 1983,* from Eight by Eight to Celebrate the Temporary Contemporary, Los Angeles, Museum of Contemporary Art, s., #215/250, blindstamps, excellent cond., (11-09-92, Christie-NY, #333, illus.), 29 x 41 in., (73.7 x 104.1 cm.), blue lithograph on wove (BP 1382, DM 3337, FR 11,273, Y 259,370).

$1320* *Untitled (G. 1381), 1988,* s., #11/18, blindstamp, full margins, excellent cond., (11-09-92, Christie-NY, #337, illus.), 42½ x 46⅛ in., (108 x 117.2 cm.), gray lithograph on Arches (BP 873, DM 2107, FR 7120, Y 163,812).

$5750* *Wall (A. 177: T. 322:EK29), 1979,* s., #32/50, blindstamp, pub. Tyler Graphics, Ltd., full margins, good cond., soiling, (05-15-93, Sotheby-NY, #1048, illus.), 16⅛ x 13⅞ in., (41 x 35.2 cm.), etching and aquatint (BP 3739, DM 9249, FR 31,081, Y 637,402).

BI *White And Black, 1973,* s., #72/75, blindstamp pub. Gemini G.E.L., very good cond., est. $2/4,000, (12-12-92, Weschler, #134, illus.), sheet 23 x 35 in., (58.4 x 88.9 cm.), embossed point and silkscreen on Arjamari paper.

$2875* *Yellow (A. 107), G. 587), 1973-75,* s., #38/48, blindstamp publisher, Gemini G.E.L., p. Charly Ritt, fullmargins, good cond.?, (05-19-93, Butterfield, #2220), 29 x 29 in.,

(737 x 737 mm.), lithograph in yellow on Rives (BP 1866, DM 4673, FR 15,745, Y 318,277).

$938* *Yellow Over Yellow (Axsom 25), 1964-5,* s., #43/75, p., pub. Maeght, full margins, good cond., creases, (12-03-92, Sotheby-London, #757), 22½ x 15½ in., (571 x 395 mm.), lithograph in two shades of yellow on BFK Rives (BP 605, DM 1475, FR 5035, Y 116,710).

BI *"Yellow" and "Orange And Green" (A. 5 and 13), 1964-5,* each s., i. H.C., #v/vii, #iv/x, pub. Maeght, full margins, good cond., est. BP 9/1,200, (12-03-92, Sotheby-London, #758, illus.), each sheet 35½ x 23¾ in., (895 x 600 mm.), lithograph in colors on BFK Rives.

$2860* *Yellow/Red Orange (A. 66; G. 235), 1970,* s., #72/75, blindstamp, pub. Gemini, G.E.L., full margins, good cond., (11-07-92, Sotheby-NY, #631), sheet 35¼ x 36¼ in., (895 x 921 mm.), lithograph p. in colors on Special Arjomari (BP 1870, DM 4567, FR 15,434, Y 352,999).

KELLY, John   American early 20th cent.
$121* *Hawaiian Decoration,* s., t., (12-10-92, Sloan, #958), 14¾ x 10⅝ in., (37.5 x 27 cm.), etching and aquatint (BP 78, DM 191, FR 654, Y 14,968).

KELLY, Thomas
$220* *"American Hunting Scene, Light In The Woods",* folio, t., (02-06-93, Julia, #228), image 17½ x 24¾ in., (44.5 x 62.9 cm.), hand-colored print (BP 152, DM 365, FR 1233, Y 27,377).

KELLY, Wallace   American 20th cent.
$99* *I Remember Cincinnati,* s., t., num. 9/20, (09-20-92, Hindman, #709), 8 x 6 in., (20.3 x 15.2 cm.), wood engraving (BP 58, DM 147, FR 503, Y 12,236).

KEMP, Roger   1908-1987
BI *Cruciform,* s. Roger Kemp, i., d. '65, #26/97, est. $150/300, (08-11-92, L. Joel, #105G), 31⅛ x 22 1/16 in., (79 x 56 cm.), color screenprint.

KEMP-WELCH, L. (after)
$117 *"Timber Hauling",* etched by William Hole, 1st state, (12-11-92, G.A. Key, #145), 15 x 28 in., (38.1 x 71.1 cm.), black and white etching (BP 75, DM 184, FR 632, Y 14,478).

KEMPF, Franz   b. 1928
BI *Icon 1,* s. Franz Kempf, d. '69, #9/160, est. $1/200, (08-11-92, L. Joel, #141G), 19⅝ x 14 in., (49.8 x 35.6 cm.), color lithograph.

KENDRICK, John, Publisher
$57* *At The Races: A Pair,* (03-03-93, Bonhams-Chelsea, #191), image 4¼ x 13½ in., (10.8 x 34.3 cm.), etching (BP 39, DM 94, FR 318, Y 6660).

KENDRICK, Sydney (after)
$61 *"Loves Awakening" and "Wedded": A Pair,* (06-11-93, G.A. Key, #128), 21 x 11 in., (53.3 x 27.9 cm.), chromolithograph (BP 40, DM 99, FR 334, Y 6472).

KENICHI   Japanese 20th cent.
BI *Coastal Village,* est. $2/300, (10-30-92, Sloan, #1899), 9½ x 14½ in., (24.1 x 36.8 cm.), woodblock.

KENNA, Michael   American b. 1953
$770* *"Broadway Tower, Worcestershire, England," (Michael Kenna 1976-1986)1981,* s., d., t., photog. stamp, (11-16-92, Butterfield, #6034, illus.), 6¼ x 9 in., (159 x 229 mm.), photograph, toned gelatin silver print (BP 507, DM 1228, FR 4135, Y 95,759).

$978* *"Fountain Of Flora", Versailles, France",* 1988, p. 1989, s., #3/45, s., t., d., edit., photog.'s stamp, (05-23-93, Butterfield, #3479, illus.), 8½ x 6½ in., photograph, toned gelatin silver print (BP 637, DM 1599, FR 5382, Y 108,102).

$825* *"Golden Gate Bridge, Study 2, San Francisco",* s., d., edit. 10/45, t., photog. stamp, Dixon Collection, 1988/1990, (11-16-92, Butterfield, #6035, illus.), 7⅜ x 7½ in., (187.7 x 190.8 mm.), photograph, gelatin silver print (BP 543, DM 1315, FR 4431, Y 102,599).

BI *Prague, 1982,* mounted on card, s., d., #12/45, est. BP 2/400, (05-06-93, Christie-London, #117), 5½ x 9 in., photograph, toned gelatin silver print.

$990* *Reflection, Big Sur, California, USA (Picturing California, P. 125),* 1979/1981, s., d., t., photog. stamp, (11-16-92,

Butterfield, #6033, illus.), 6 x 9½ in., (152.7 x 241.7 mm.), photograph, toned gelatin silver print (BP 652, DM 1578, FR 5317, Y 123,119).

$715* *"River Thames, London, England",* s., #206, photog. name, 1983/1985, (11-16-92, Butterfield, #6037, illus.), 5¾ x 8⅝ in., (146.3 x 219.5 mm.), photograph, sepia and selenium toned gelatin silver print (BP 471, DM 1140, FR 3840, Y 88,919).

$2475* *"Swings, Catskill Mountains, New York" (Night Walk, pl. 13),* 1977/1981, s., d., t., photog. stamp, (11-16-92, Butterfield, #6032, illus.), 5¾ x 9 in., (146.3 x 229 mm.), photograph, toned gelatin silver print (BP 1630, DM 3946, FR 13,292, Y 307,798).

$1035* *"Tree, Kilkenny, Ireland",* 1982, p. 1984, #6/45, s., t., d., edit., photog.'s stamp, (05-23-93, Butterfield, #3480, illus.), 9½ x 6 in., photograph, toned gelatin silver print (BP 674, DM 1692, FR 5696, Y 114,403).

$715* *"Trees, Wimbledon Park, London, England",* s., d., edit. 23/45, t., photog. stamp, Dixon Collection, 1980/1986, (11-16-92, Butterfield, #6036, illus.), 8⅝ x 6⅛ in., (219.5 x 155.9 mm.), photograph, sepia and selenium toned gelatin silver print (BP 471, DM 1140, FR 3840, Y 88,919).

KENNY, Reginald
BI *Nazi Scientists Arraigned For War Crimes At Nuremburg, 1946,* handstamp, label, est. $4/500, (10-14-92, Swann, #354, illus.), 7 x 9 in., (17.8 x 22.9 cm.), photograph, silver print.

KENOJUAK
$302* *Owl Of The Sea,* #197/200, Dorset, s., d. 1977, (05-12-93, Maynard, #300A), sheet 21 x 27 in., (53.3 x 68.6 cm.), stonecut (BP 197, DM 487, FR 1641, Y 33,717, C$ 385).

KENOJUAK, Ashevak   b. 1927
$190* *The Owl With Bears, 1968,* #5/50, s., t., d. 1968, prov., (11-16-92, Hodgins, #271), 9½ x 11¾ in., (24.1 x 29.8 cm.), color etching on paper mounted on mat board (BP 125, DM 303, FR 1021, Y 23,711, C$ 242).

KENT, Norman   American 1903-1972
$248* *"Queer House", "The Book Shop" and "The Bentley-Kent House", 1831: Three,* 1st d. 1944; 3rd d. 1964, inits. in block; each s.,t., prov., (10-30-92, Sloan, #1743), largest 7¾ x 6 in., (19.7 x 15.2 cm.), woodblocks (BP 159, DM 382, FR 1294, Y 30,720).

KENT, Rockwell   American 1882-1971
$143* *"And Now Where?",* stamp s., t., (03-25-93, Boos, #614), 13¼ x 9 in., (33.7 x 22.9 cm.), lithograph (BP 97, DM 235, FR 799, Y 16,753).

BI *"Beowolf: Geneological Tree" (Jones, 71), 1931,* s. Rockwell Kent, very good cond., est. $4/600, (03-12-93, Skinner, #60, illus.), sight 23⅝ x 10 in., (60 x 25.4 cm.), lithograph on white paper.

$330* *"Beowulf: Beowulf And Grendel's Mother" (J. 74), 1931,* s., good cond., (10-31-92, Cleveland, #154), 13 9/16 x 9 5/16 in., (34.4 x 23.7 cm.), lithograph (BP 211, DM 508, FR 1722, Y 40,877).

$468* *Beowulf: Beowulf And The Dragon (B.J. 75), 1931,* s., margins, good cond., mat/glue staining, surface soiling, (10-28-92, Butterfield, #2528), 13½ x 10⅛ in., (343 x 257 mm.), lithograph on wove (BP 298, DM 723, FR 2454, Y 57,423).

$715* *Beowulf: Beowulf And The Dragon (B.J. 75), 1931,* s., large margins, good cond., glue remains, crease, stain, (02-24-93, Butterfield, #2636, illus.), 13½ x 10⅛ in., (343 x 257 mm.), lithograph on wove (BP 499, DM 1161, FR 3935, Y 83,900).

$385* *"Beowulf: Funeral Pyre" (B-J. 76), 1931,* s., mint cond., (10-31-92, Cleveland, #155), 13⅝ x 10¼ in., (34.6 x 26 cm.), lithograph (BP 247, DM 592, FR 2009, Y 47,690).

$319* *"Beowulf: Genealogical Tree (B-J. 71), 1931,* s., mint cond., (10-31-92, Cleveland, #153), 12⅝ x 10 in., (32.1 x 25.4 cm.), lithograph (BP 204, DM 491, FR 1665, Y 39,514).

$352* *"Beowulf: Genealogical Tree (B.J. 71), 1931" and "The Tree (B.J. 25), 1928": Two,* both s., margins, light-staining, very good cond., (09-19-92, Christie-E, #27), lithograph, first on wove, second on BFK (BP 202, DM 527, FR 1805, Y 43,857).

BI *Big Baby (Burne-Jones 101), 1933,* stamped estate stamp, est. $3/500, (03-24-93, Grogan, #90), 4½ x 6 in., (11.4 x 15.2 cm.), woodcut.

$460* *The Boatman (B.J. 37), 1929,* watermark, s., full margins, good cond., tear, paper loss, mat staining, skinned areas, surface soiling, (05-19-93, Butterfield, #1818), 13⅞ x 10¹⁄₁₆ in., (352 x 256 mm.), lithograph on wove (BP 299, DM 748, FR 2519, Y 50,924).

$1210* *Bowsprit (Burne Jones 56), 1930,* s., wide margins, excell. cond., (09-19-92, Christie-E, #26, illus.), borderline 5½ x 7 in., (140 x 178 mm.), woodcut on wove (BP 696, DM 1812, FR 6205, Y 150,760).

$28* *Casanova,* (02-19-93, Garth, #86), 13½ x 11½ in., (34.3 x 29.2 cm.), b/w woodcut (BP 19, DM 46, FR 155, Y 3322).

$248* *The Cheshire Academy (Bowden Hall, Cheshire School) (B.J. 142), 1947,* s., p. by George Miller, margins, good cond., light-staining, foxing,surface abrasions, tear in image, glue remains, thinned spots, creases, surface soiling, (02-24-93, Butterfield, #2841), 11 x 14⅞ in., (279 x 378 mm.), lithograph on wove (BP 173, DM 403, FR 1365, Y 29,101).

$200* *"Climbing The Bars" (Bourne-Jones 27), 1928,* s. w/ estate stamp, good cond., (05-15-93, Cleveland, #180, illus.), 11 x 8 in., (27.9 x 20.3 cm.), lithograph (BP 130, DM 322, FR 1081, Y 22,170).

$440* *Courtship,* s., t., (09-17-92, Sloan, #3124), 13⅞ x 9⅞ in., (35.2 x 25.1 cm.), lithograph (BP 247, DM 653, FR 2236, Y 54,781).

$825* *Deep Water (B.J. 87), 1931,* s., wide margins, tiny imperfection, very good cond., (09-19-92, Christie-E, #29), borderline 5⁵⁄₁₆ x 6⅞ in., (135 x 175 mm.), woodcut on wove (BP 475, DM 1235, FR 4231, Y 102,791).

$770* *"Diver" (Burne Jones 88), 1931,* s. Rockwell Kent, good cond., wide margins, light/mount staining, (09-11-92, Skinner, #76, illus.), 7¹³⁄₁₆ x 5⅜ in., (19.8 x 13.7 cm.), wood engraving on wove Japan (BP 398, DM 1108, FR 3767, Y 95,403).

$935* *The End (Burne Jones 17), 1927,* s., (12-08-92, Swann, #155, illus.), 4⅞ x 7¹⁄₁₆ in., (12.4 x 17.9 cm.), wood engraving on cream colored paper (BP 586, DM 1456, FR 4963, Y 115,890).

$2300* *End Of The World Series: "Lunar Disintegration", "Solar Fade Out", "SFlare-Up" and "Degravitation" (B.-J. 115-118), 1937: Suite Of Four,* s., p. George Miller, full margins, good cond., illus. Life magazine, Nov. 1, 1937, (02-11-93, Sotheby-NY, #22), each sheet approx. 15¹⁵⁄₁₆ x 11¾ in., lithograph (BP 1623, DM 3810, FR 12,892, Y 277,275).

$2090* *"The End" And "Twilight Of Man", 1927, 1926: Two,* both s. Rockwell Kent, latter ded., good cond., (03-12-93, Skinner, #63, illus.), sight 5½ x 8 in., (14 x 20.3 cm.), wood engraving on paper (BP 1458, DM 3479, FR 11,828, Y 246,317).

BI *"Eskimo Mother And Child" (B. 114), 1937,* s., light struck, tear, est. $4/500, (05-15-93, Cleveland, #185), 13¼ x 9½ in., (33.7 x 24.1 cm.), lithograph.

$330* *"Europe",* s. Rockwell Kent, (03-06-93, Wolf, #181), 13½ x 9½ in., (34.3 x 24.1 cm.), lithograph (BP 228, DM 550, FR 1854, Y 38,787).

$230* *Farewell (B.J. 61), 1931,* watermark, s., pub. City Child, full margins, staining, surface soiling, (05-19-93, Butterfield, #1820), 5¾ x 3¹⁵⁄₁₆ in., (146 x 100 mm.), lithograph on wove (BP 149, DM 374, FR 1260, Y 25,462).

BI *"Farewell", "Hero", "And Now Where?", "The Cheshire Academy", "Fire!"and "Merry Christmas" (B.-J. 61, 69, 110, 142, 143, and 146), 1931-51: Six,* s., 3rd estate stamp, 2 t., 5th i., full margins, 2nd and lstmargins trimmed, good cond., creases, masking tape stain, mat and light-stain, est. $1,5/2,000, (02-11-93, Sotheby-NY, #18), lithograph.

$550* *Fire (Burne-Jones 143), 1948,* s., hinged corners, (05-27-93, Swann, #146, illus.), 13¹¹⁄₁₆ x 10 in., (34.8 x 25.4 cm.), lithograph (BP 352, DM 883, FR 2975, Y 58,962).

$880* *Forest Pool (Burne Jones 14), 1927,* s., good cond.?, (12-08-92, Swann, #154, illus.), 5½ x 8¹⁄₁₆ in., (14 x

20.5 cm.), wood engraving (BP 552, DM 1370, FR 4671, Y 109,073).

BI *Genealogical Tree (Burne-Jones 71), 1931,* s., est. $4/600, (03-24-93, Grogan, #91), 12⅝ x 10 in., (32.1 x 25.4. cm.), lithograph.

BI *"Geneological Tree", "Beowulf", "Beowulf And Grendel's Mother", Beowuf And The Dragon", "Funeral Pyre" and "Colophon" (B.-J. 71, 72, 74-77), 1931:Six,* from Beowulf suite, s., p. George Miller, full margins, 3rd andlast trimmed, good cond., mat stain, est. $1,8/2,400, (02-11-93, Sotheby-NY, #19, illus.), lithograph.

$316* *Girl On A Cliff (B.J. 57), 1930,* s., margins, very good cond., glue remains, mat staining, handling creases, (05-19-93, Butterfield, #1819), 6½ x 4¾ in., (165 x 121 mm.), wood engraving on wove (BP 205, DM 514, FR 1731, Y 34,983).

$220* *Girl On Cliff (B.J. 57), 1930,* s., pub. for Literary Guild of America book club, margins, good cond., mat/light-staining, surface scuff, pressure mark, scuff w/ink loss, water stains, brown stain, surface soiling, (10-28-92, Butterfield, #2734), 6½ x 4¾ in., (165 x 121 mm.), wood engraving on Japan (BP 140, DM 340, FR 1154, Y 26,994).

$330* *Girl On Cliff (Jones 57), 1930,* s., (05-16-93, Hindman, #542), 6½ x 4¾ in., (16.5 x 12.1 cm.), wood engraving (BP 215, DM 531, FR 1784, Y 36,581).

$248* *Girl On Cliff (Jones 57), 1930,* s., (03-14-93, Hindman, #319), 6½ x 4¾ in., (16.5 x 12.1 cm.), wood engraving (BP 173, DM 413, FR 1404, Y 29,228).

$285* *"Girl On Cliff" (B. 57), 1930,* s., good cond., (05-15-93, Cleveland, #180A), 6½ x 4¾ in., (16.5 x 12.1 cm.), wood engraving (BP 185, DM 458, FR 1541, Y 31,593).

$850* *"Glory, Glory, Hallelujah" (B. 134), 1944,* ded., hand-coloring, very unique, good cond., (05-15-93, Cleveland, #186, illus.), 12 x 8⅝ in., (30.5 x 21.9 cm.), lithograph w/hand-coloring (BP 553, DM 1367, FR 4595, Y 94,225).

$275* *"Greenland Hunter" (Jones, 94), 1933,* s. Rockwell Kent, very good cond., (03-12-93, Skinner, #55, illus.), sight 8⅞ x 6⅝ in., (22.5 x 16.8 cm.), lithograph on paper (BP 192, DM 458, FR 1556, Y 32,410).

$275* *Greenland Mother Nursing Child,* s., (11-12-92, Freemn/ Fine Art, #103), mat 7¼ x 4½ in., (18.4 x 11.4 cm.), lithograph (BP 181, DM 436, FR 1470, Y 34,098).

BI *"Greenland Mother Nursing Child" (B-J. 108),* s., Print-A-Month Club, Cleveland December 1934, excellent cond., est. $3/400, (10-31-92, Cleveland, #157), 7⅛ x 4¹¹⁄₁₆ in., (18.1 x 11.9 cm.), lithograph.

$231* *"Greenland Mother Nursing Child" (B-J. 108),* s., Print-A-Month Club, Cleveland December 1934, excellent cond., (10-31-92, Cleveland, #158), 7⅛ x 4¹¹⁄₁₆ in., (18.1 x 11.9 cm.), lithograph (BP 148, DM 355, FR 1206, Y 28,614).

BI *"Greenland Mother Nursing Child" (B. 108), 1934,* pub., Print-A-Month Club Cleveland, s., good cond., creases, est. $3/400, (05-15-93, Cleveland, #184), 7⅛ x 4¹¹⁄₁₆ in., (18.1 x 11.9 cm.), lithograph.

$170* *"Greenland Mother Nursing" (B. 108), 1934,* s., Print-A-Month Club of Cleveland Publication October 1934, excell. cond., (05-15-93, Cleveland, #183), 4½ x 7 in., (11.4 x 17.8 cm.), lithograph (BP 111, DM 273, FR 919, Y 18,845).

$990* *Hail And Farewell (Burne-Jones 55), 1930,* s., (12-09-92, Grogan, #95), 8 x 5½ in., (20.3 x 14 cm.), woodcut (BP 632, DM 1554, FR 5303, Y 122,753).

$220* *"Heavy Hangs Over Thy Head" (Burne Jones, 137), 1946,* s. Rockwell Kent, ded., very good cond., (09-11-92, Skinner, #76A, illus.), 9⁹⁄₁₆ x 12 in., (23.3 x 30.5 cm.), lithograph on wove (BP 114, DM 317, FR 1076, Y 27,258).

$1210* *Home Port (Burne-Jones 62), 1931,* s., (12-09-92, Grogan, #96), 6½ x 7¼ in., (16.5 x 18.4 cm.), woodcut (BP 772, DM 1899, FR 6481, Y 150,031).

$743* *"Home Port" (Burne Jones, 62), 1931,* s. Rockwell Kent, fair cond., wide margins, light toning, mount staining, (09-11-92, Skinner, #79, illus.), 6½ x 7⅜ in., (16.5 x 18.7 cm.), wood engraving on wove Japan (BP 384, DM 1070, FR 3635, Y 92,058).

$165* *Image For Jewish Book Appeal,* s. Rockwell Kent in matrix, good cond., creasing, (03-12-93, Skinner, #64, illus.), 13¾ x 11½ in., (34.9 x 29.2 cm.), photo-offset on wove (BP 115, DM 275, FR 934, Y 19,446).

$2090* *The Lovers (Burne-Jones 23), 1928,* s., margins, good cond., scuffs, light stain, skinning, glued to backing sheet, (11-05-92, Sotheby-NY, #25, illus.), 6½ x 10⅛ in., (166 x 256 mm.), sheet 12⅛ x 15 in., (166 x 256 mm.), wood engraving (BP 1359, DM 3305, FR 11,182, Y 256,410).

$468* *"Merry Christmas" (B-J. 146), 1951,* s., excellent cond., (10-31-92, Cleveland, #159), 13 x 9¼ in., (33 x 23.5 cm.), lithograph (BP 300, DM 720, FR 2443, Y 57,971).

$220* *Minstrel Singer, c. 1936,* frontispiece from Complete Works of Shakespeare, s., full margins, good cond.?, (12-08-92, Swann, #160), 8¼ x 6⅛ in., (21 x 15.6 cm.), lithograph (BP 138, DM 343, FR 1168, Y 27,268).

$605* *Night Flight (Burne Jones 132), 1941,* s., good cond.?, (12-08-92, Swann, #162), 8½ x 6¼ in., (21.6 x 15.9 cm.), color chiaroscuro wood engraving (BP 379, DM 942, FR 3211, Y 74,988).

$2200* *"Night Watch" And "Home Port" (Jones, 34, 62), 1929, 1931: Twoo,* s. Rockwell Kent, s., ded., d. Rockwell 1930, good cond., mount staining, (03-12-93, Skinner, #56, illus.), sight 7⅞ x 5⅜ in., (20 x 13.7 cm.), wood engraving on paper (BP 1535, DM 3662, FR 12,450, Y 259,281).

$605* *Oarsman (B.J. 86), 1931,* s., wide margins, light/time staining, very good cond., (09-19-92, Christie-E, #28), borderline 5⅜ x 6^15/16 in., (137 x 176 mm.), woodcut on Japan (BP 348, DM 906, FR 3103, Y 75,380).

$825* *"Oarsman" (Burne Jones, 86), 1931,* s. Rockwell Kent, good cond., wide margins, light/mount staining, (09-11-92, Skinner, #77, illus.), 5⅜ x 6^15/16 in., (13.7 x 17.6 cm.), wood engraving on wove Japan (BP 427, DM 1188, FR 4036, Y 102,218).

$550* *"Portrait Of T. M. Cleland", "Beowulf And The Dragon", "Beowulf And Grendel's Mother", "Genealogical Tree" and "Merry Christmas" (Burne-Jones 39, 75, 74, 71, 146), 1929-51: Five,* s., wide or full margins, Merry Christmas creases, (05-27-93, Swann, #147), lithographs (BP 352, DM 883, FR 2975, Y 58,962).

BI *"Portrait Of T.M. Cleland" (B-J. 39), 1929,* s., good cond., est. $250-300, (10-31-92, Cleveland, #152), 9^11/16 x 7 in., (24.6 x 17.8 cm.), lithograph.

$715* *Sea And Sky (B.J. 85), 1931,* s., t., full margins, good cond., light-staining, water stain, tape remains, surface soiling, notations, (02-24-93, Butterfield, #2637), 10 x 6½ in., (254 x 165 mm.), wood engraving on Japan (BP 499, DM 1161, FR 3935, Y 83,900).

$5* *Shakespeare Themes: Ten,* after Kent drawings light struck, matt burn, corners glued, (05-15-93, Cleveland, #187), electrotypes (BP 3, DM 8, FR 27, Y 554).

$1210* *"Starlight" (Burne Jones, 52), 1930,* s. Rockwell Kent, very good cond., full margins, soiling, (09-11-92, Skinner, #80, illus.), 5^5/16 x 6⅞ in., (13.5 x 17.5 cm.), wood engraving on Japan wove (BP 626, DM 1742, FR 5920, Y 149,919).

$880* *"Starlight" (Burne Jones, 52), 1930,* s. Rockwell Kent, good cond., wide margin, light/mount staining, (09-11-92, Skinner, #75), 5^5/16 x 6⅞ in., (13.5 x 17.5 cm.), wood engraving on wove Japan (BP 455, DM 1267, FR 4305, Y 109,032).

$313* *Starry Night,* margins, s., (05-22-93, Collins, #26), 6⅞ x 4⅞ in., (17.5 x 12.4 cm.), wood engraving (BP 203, DM 509, FR 1712, Y 34,509).

$275* *Starry Night (BJ 103), 1933,* s., (12-10-92, Sloan, #1305), 7 x 4^15/16 in., (17.8 x 12.5 cm.), wood engraving (BP 177, DM 435, FR 1486, Y 34,018).

$275* *Starry Night (J. 103), 1933,* s., (06-11-93, Freemn/Fine Art, #121, illus.), 6⅝ x 5 in., (16.8 x 12.7 cm.), wood engraving (BP 181, DM 447, FR 1507, Y 29,178).

$880* *"Starry Night" (B-J. 103), 1933,* s., excellent cond., (10-31-92, Cleveland, #156), 7 x 4^15/16 in., (17.8 x 12.5 cm.), wood engraving (BP 564, DM 1354, FR 4593, Y 109,005).

BI *"Starry Night" (B. 103), 1933,* s., est. $5/700, (05-15-93, Cleveland, #182, illus.), 7 x 4^15/16 in., (17.8 x 12.5 cm.), wood engraving.

$248* *"Starry Night" (Jones, 103), 1933,* s. Rockwell Kent, annot., good cond., creasing, light-staining, (03-12-93, Skinner, #61, illus.), 7 x 4^15/16 in., (17.8 x 12.5 cm.), wood engraving on light wove (BP 173, DM 413, FR 1404, Y 29,228).

$440* *"Starry Night" And "Girl On The Cliff" or "The Abyss" (Jones, 103, 57), 1933, 1930: Two,* good cond., (03-12-93, Skinner, #59, illus.), sight 7 x 5 in., (17.8 x 12.7 cm.), wood engraving on paper (BP 307, DM 732, FR 2490, Y 51,856).

$83* *"The Tragedy Of King Lear", "The Merchant Of Venice" and "Untitled":Three Illustrations,* good cond., (03-28-93, Bakker, #280), largest, image 8½ x 6¼ in., (21.6 x 15.9 cm.), wood engraving (BP 56, DM 135, FR 460, Y 9660).

$133* *Untitled,* s., (10-21-92, Maynard, #201), 7¼ x 5¼ in., (18.4 x 13.3 cm.), b/w woodcut (BP 83, DM 201, FR 683, Y 16,200, C$ 165).

$149* *"Waldo Pierce" (Bourne-Jones 30),* s., excell. cond., (10-31-92, Cleveland, #151), 9⅞ x 7⅜ in., (25.1 x 18.7 cm.), lithograph (BP 95, DM 229, FR 778, Y 18,457).

$275* *Wayside Madonna,* s., excell. cond.?, (10-10-92, Litchfield, #117), image 10¼ x 5½ in., (26 x 14 cm.), color engraving (BP 163, DM 408, FR 1372, Y 33,479).

$220* *Wayside Madonna, 1927, Ed. 800,* inits. in plate, i.; label verso, (05-28-93, Sloan, #1911, illus.), 10¼ x 5⅜ in., (26 x 13.7 cm.), color wood engraving (BP 141, DM 349, FR 1180, Y 23,590).

$605* *Woman With Hands Clasped,* s., (03-12-93, DuMouchelle, #2151), 10½ x 7¼ in., (26.7 x 18.4 cm.), lithograph (BP 422, DM 1007, FR 3424, Y 71,302).

$440* *"Young Greenland Woman" And "Dirty Deborah" (Jones, 95,96), 1933: Two,* both s. Rockwell Kent, very good cond., (03-12-93, Skinner, #57, illus.), 8⅞ x 6⅝ in., (22.5 x 16.8 cm.), lithograph on paper (BP 307, DM 732, FR 2490, Y 51,856).

KEPES, Gyorgy American b. Hungary 1906

$1610* *Hand Imprint On Grid With Crystals, 1939,* s., d., annot, (04-08-93, Christie-NY, #305, illus.), 9¼ x 7½ in., (23.5 x 19.1 cm.), photograph, gelatin silver print (BP 1056, DM 2586, FR 8755, Y 182,705).

$2200* *Light Abstraction, 1941,* s., d., (10-13-92, Christie-NY, #253, illus.), 13½ x 10½ in., (34.3 x 26.7 cm.), photograph, gelatin silver print (BP 1281, DM 3223, FR 10,951, Y 266,764).

$2070* *Man With Cart, View From Berlin Window, 1928,* (04-08-93, Christie-NY, #304, illus.), 3 x 2¼ in., (7.6 x 5.7 cm.), photograph, gelatin silver print (BP 1357, DM 3325, FR 11,256, Y 234,907).

BI *Photogram, 1940's,* est. $1,5/2,000, (04-06-93, Sotheby-NY, #311, illus.), 10 x 8 in., photograph.

$2013* *Photogram, 1942,* s., d., annot. by photog., (04-06-93, Sotheby-NY, #310, illus.), 13⅞ x 10½ in., photograph (BP 1330, DM 3243, FR 10,982, Y 229,585).

$3220* *Shadow Picture With Drawings, 1938,* s., d., lit., (04-08-93, Christie-NY, #306, illus.), 9⅝ x 7⅝ in., (24.4 x 19.4 cm.), photograph, gelatin silver print (BP 2111, DM 5173, FR 17,510, Y 365,411).

$2860* *Shadow Picture With Drawings, 1938-39,* s., t., d., annot., (10-13-92, Christie-NY, #252, illus.), 9¼ x 7⅝ in., (23.5 x 19.4 cm.), photograph, gelatin silver print (BP 1666, DM 4190, FR 14,236, Y 346,793).

KERCHINE, Y.

$199* *Gloire A La Science Sovietique !, 1964,* cond. A, (03-16-93, Boisgirard, #7), 25^9/16 x 35^13/16 in., (65 x 91 cm.), offset and typograph (BP 137, DM 331, FR 1124, Y 23,269).

KERKOVIUS, Ida 1879-1970

$514* *Komposition, (19)47,* s., d., num., stains, (12-01-92, Karl/Faber, #822), approx. 11^13/16 x 16¾ in., (30 x 42.5 cm.), color lithograph on machine-made paper (BP 340, DM 819, FR 2792, Y 63,994).

$662* *Landschaft Mit Haus U. Leiterwagen, 1964,* s., #476/500, wrinkles, (11-03-92, Hartung, #2619), 10⅜ x 12⅝ in., (26.4 x 32.1 cm.), color serigraph (BP 427, DM 1036, FR 3510, Y 80,860).

BI *Mit Dem Bollerwagen Im Park, 1964,* s., num., est. DM 1,200-, (09-25-92, Granier, #2905), sheet 17⅛ x 22⅜ in., (43.5 x 56.8 cm.), color serigraph on wove.

KERMADEC, Eugene de 1899-1976

$253* *Composition,* s. E. de Kermadec, (09-30-92, Kunsthallen, #166), color lithograph (BP 143, DM 359, FR 1213, Y 30,361, DK 1380).

KERR, G.F.

$165* *New York Journal, Easter,* The Gillin Print, B cond., fold marks, creasing throughout, (08-06-92, Swann, #162, illus.), 30 x 40 in., (76.2 x 101.6 cm.), (BP 86, DM 244, FR 823, Y 21,046).

KERR, Illingworth Holey 1905-1989

$139* *Caribou Trek,* A/P s., t.; bears t. verso, prov., (05-10-93, Hodgins, #192), 6 x 9 in., (15.2 x 22.9 cm.), woodcut on paper (BP 91, DM 223, FR 753, Y 15,532, C$ 176).

$87* *Jack Rabbit,* #30/100 s., t., mono., prov., (05-10-93, Hodgins, #44), 5 x 9 in., (12.7 x 22.9 cm.), woodcut on paper (BP 57, DM 140, FR 472, Y 9722, C$ 110).

KERSCHBAUMER, Anton 1885-1931

BI *Schleuse, 1919,* s., d., est. DM 2,4/2,800, (11-28-92, Grisebach, #581, illus.), 14⅞ x 19³⁄₁₆ in., (37.8 x 48.7 cm.), colored lithograph on wove.

KERTESZ, Andre Hungarian 1894-1985

$5175* *"57th Street" (New York), 1942-45,* t. by photog., name stamp, (04-06-93, Sotheby-NY, #286, illus.), 10 x 7⅜ in., photograph (BP 3418, DM 8337, FR 28,232, Y 590,214).

BI *Apartment Of Valentine Hugo, c. 1927,* Rue de Vanves studio/reprod. limitation stamps, est. $3/4,000, (04-08-93, Christie-NY, #199, illus.), 6⅜ x 8¾ in., (16.2 x 22.2 cm.), photograph, gelatin silver print.

$1035* *"Aux Halles, Paris" (Sixty Years, p. 123),* d. by photog., 1928, p.l., (04-06-93, Sotheby-NY, #281, illus.), 9⅜ x 13⅝ in., photograph (BP 684, DM 1667, FR 5646, Y 118,043).

BI *Beekman Terrace, New York,* t., d. in unident. hand, 1946, p.l., est. $1/2,000, (04-06-93, Sotheby-NY, #284, illus.), 7¾ x 8¼ in., photograph.

BI *"Behind Notre Dame" (J'Aime Paris, p. 23),* s., d., i. by photog., 1963, p.l., est. $1/2,000, (04-06-93, Sotheby-NY, #291, illus.), 7¾ x 9¾ in., photograph.

BI *Billboard Silhouette,* (1930s), p. early 1950s, credit stamp, letterpress label w/reprod. limitation, est. $3,5/4,500, (04-08-93, Christie-NY, #206, illus.), 8¾ x 6½ in., (22.2 x 16.5 cm.), photograph, gelatin silver print.

$11,000* *Boulevard Des Invalides, Paris, 1926,* photog.'s studio & reprod. limit. stamps, (10-15-92, Sotheby-NY, #340A, illus.), 8½ x 6½ in., (21.6 x 16.5 cm.), photograph, gelatin silver print (BP 6731, DM 16,374, FR 55,528, Y 1,319,736).

$2070* *"Bridge Across The Seine",* 1928, p. 1970s, s., d., annot., (05-23-93, Butterfield, #3487, illus.), 9¾ x 7¾ in., photograph, gelatin silver print (BP 1348, DM 3385, FR 11,392, Y 228,805).

$2200* *"Broken Bench" (Sixty Years, p. 202),* 1962/1973, s., d., (11-16-92, Butterfield, #6044, illus.), 6½ x 9⅝ in., (165.4 x 244.9 mm.), photograph, gelatin silver print (BP 1449, DM 3508, FR 11,815, Y 273,598).

$2588* *"Broken Plate",* 1929, p. 1970s, s., t., d., illus., (05-23-93, Butterfield, #3485, illus.), 7¾ x 9½ in., photograph, gelatin silver print (BP 1685, DM 4232, FR 14,243, Y 286,062).

$1725* *"Broken Plate" (Sixty Years, p. 100),* s., d. by photog., 1929, p.l., (04-06-93, Sotheby-NY, #282, illus.), 7½ x 9¾ in., photograph (BP 1139, DM 2779, FR 9411, Y 196,738).

$2475* *Broken Plate, 1929 (Sixty Years, pl. 100),* s., t., d., i. by photog., p. l., (10-15-92, Sotheby-NY, #353, illus.), 7¾ x 9⅝ in., (19.7 x 24.4 cm.), photograph, gelatin silver print (BP 1515, DM 3684, FR 12,494, Y 296,941).

BI *Broken Plate, Paris,* 1929, p.l., s., d., lit., est. $2/2,500, (04-08-93, Christie-NY, #200, illus.), 10¾ x 13⅜ in., (27.3 x 34 cm.), photograph, gelatin silver print.

BI *Budapest,* 1920, p.l., s., t., d., est. $2/3,000, (04-08-93, Christie-NY, #195, illus.), 13⅝ x 10¾ in., (34.6 x 27.3 cm.), photograph, gelatin silver print.

$1650* *Budapest, 1920 (Sixty Years, pl. 33),* s., t., d. by photog., p. l., (10-15-92, Sotheby-NY, #342, illus.), 9¾ x 7¾ in., (24.8 x 19.7 cm.), photograph, gelatin silver print (BP 1010, DM 2456, FR 8329, Y 197,960).

$1320* *Cafe Du Dome, 1928,* s., t., d., i. by photog., p. early 1970's, (10-15-92, Sotheby-NY, #351, illus.), 7½ x 9¾ in., (19.1 x 24.8 cm.), photograph, gelatin silver print (BP 808, DM 1965, FR 6663, Y 158,368).

$2070* *"Cafe Du Dome, Paris" (Diary of Light, pl. 41),* tipped to mount, s. by photog., t., d. in unident. hand, 1928, p.l., (04-06-93, Sotheby-NY, #271, illus.), 7⅜ x 9¾ in., photograph (BP 1367, DM 3335, FR 11,293, Y 236,086).

$1179* *"Calder, Paris, 1929",* p. c. 1960s, t., d., photog.'s ink credit stamp, prov., (05-06-93, Christie-London, #130, illus.), 7¾ x 9¾ in., photograph, gloss gelatin silver print (BP 747, DM 1857, FR 6251, Y 129,717).

$1126* *"Carrefour Blois 1930",* p.l., t., s., d., matt stamped, 202 x 252mm, (05-07-93, Sotheby-London, #239, illus.), photograph, silver print (BP 713, DM 1780, FR 5999, Y 123,982).

$3520* *Carrefour, Blois,* (1930). frp, Portfolio Andre Kertesz: Photographs, Vol. II 1972, s.,lit., (10-13-92, Christie-NY, #262, illus.), 7⅛ x 9⅝ in., (18.1 x 24.4 cm.), photograph, gelatin silver print (BP 2050, DM 5157, FR 17,521, Y 426,822).

$2990* *Carrefour, Blois (1930),* from portfolio Andre Kertesz: Photographs, Vol. II. 1972, s., lit., (04-08-93, Christie-NY, #202, illus.), 7½ x 9⅝ in., (19.1 x 24.4 cm.), photograph, gelatin silver print (BP 1961, DM 4803, FR 16,259, Y 339,310).

$2300* *"Carrefour, Blois",* 1930, p.l., photog.'s estate stamp, illus., (05-23-93, Butterfield, #3491, illus.), 7½ x 10 in., photograph, gelatin silver print (BP 1498, DM 3761, FR 12,658, Y 254,228).

$2420* *Chairs Of Paris,* (1950), from portfolio Andre Kertesz: Photographs, Vol. I 1972, s., lit., (10-13-92, Christie-NY, #268, illus.), 7¾ x 9¾ in., (19.7 x 24.8 cm.), photograph, gelatin silver print (BP 1409, DM 3545, FR 12,046, Y 293,440).

$43,125* *"Chais, The Medici Fountain" (Of Paris and New York, cat. 17; Fixinga Shadow, dust jacket), 1926,* s. and i. by photog., (04-06-93, Sotheby-NY, #272A, illus.), 3⅛ x 3⅝ in., photograph, on carte-postale (BP 28,484, DM 69,478, FR 235,270, Y 4,918,453).

$2300* *Chat Noir, Paris,* 1926, mid 1960s, d., annot., credit stamp, lit., (04-08-93, Christie-NY, #197, illus.), 13½ x 10⅞ in., (34.3 x 27.6 cm.), photograph, gelatin silver print (BP 1508, DM 3695, FR 12,507, Y 261,008).

$3850* *Chez Mondrian,* (1926), p.l., s., t., d., lit., (10-13-92, Christie-NY, #264, illus.), 9¾ x 7¼ in., (24.8 x 18.4 cm.), photograph, gelatin silver print (BP 2242, DM 5640, FR 19,164, Y 466,836).

$3850* *Chez Mondrian, 1926 (Sixty Years, pl. 119),* s., d. by photog., p. l., (10-15-92, Sotheby-NY, #348, illus.), 13¾ x 10¼ in., (34.9 x 26 cm.), photograph, gelatin silver print (BP 2356, DM 5731, FR 19,435, Y 461,908).

$3850* *"Chez Mondrian, Paris" (Sixty Years, p. 118),* 1926/1970's, s., t., d., Dixon Collection, (11-16-92, Butterfield, #6041, illus.), 9¾ x 7⅛ in., (248.1 x 181.3 mm.), photograph, gelatin silver print (BP 2535, DM 6138, FR 20,677, Y 478,796).

$2300* *"Christopher Street, New York" (Sixty Years, p. 219),* s., d. 1930 (incorrectly) by photog., 1950, p.l., (04-06-93, Sotheby-NY, #287, illus.), 11⅛ x 10⅝ in., photograph (BP 1519, DM 3705, FR 12,548, Y 262,318).

$1725* *"Circus (Budapest)" (Diary of Light, pl. 27),* s., t., d. by photog.; 1920, p.l., (04-06-93, Sotheby-NY, #267, illus.), 9⅝ x 7¾ in., photograph (BP 1139, DM 2779, FR 9411, Y 196,738).

$3575* *Clock Of The Academy, Pont Des Arts And The Louvre, c. 1932 (Of Parisand New York, p. 171),* s., d. by photog., p. l., (10-15-92, Sotheby-NY, #350, illus.), 19½ x 14 in., (49.5 x 35.6 cm.), photograph, gelatin silver print (BP 2188, DM 5322, FR 18,046, Y 428,914).

$1840* *Colette, Paris,* 1930, p.l., s., d., annot., lit., (04-08-93, Christie-NY, #203, illus.), 10⅝ x 13⅝ in., (27 x 34.6 cm.), photograph, gelatin silver print (BP 1207, DM 2956, FR 10,005, Y 208,806).

$1100* *Demon From "Faust", 1929,* s., d. 3.8.82, studio & reprod. limit. stamps, prov., (10-13-92, Christie-NY, #257, illus.), 9¼ x 7 in., (23.5 x 17.8 cm.), photograph, gelatin silver print (BP 641, DM 1611, FR 5475, Y 133,382).

BI *Distortion #114 (Distortions, unpaginated), 1933,* num. by photog., studio (c) stamp, est. $6/9,000, (04-06-93, Sotheby-NY, #280, illus.), 8⅛ x 5⅞ in., photograph.

$1760* *Distortion #157, (1933),* p.l., s., t., d., annot., lit., (10-13-92, Christie-NY, #269, illus.), 9¾ x 6⅝ in., (24.8 x 16.8 cm.), photograph, gelatin silver print (BP 1025, DM 2578, FR 8761, Y 213,411).

$2185* *Distortion #45, 1933,* p.l., s., t., d., annot., lit., (04-08-93, Christie-NY, #208, illus.), 6¾ x 9¾ in., (17.1 x 24.8 cm.), photograph, gelatin silver print (BP 1433, DM 3510, FR 11,881, Y 247,957).

$5175* *Distortion #45, 1933,* s., d., i. #45 by photog., name stamp, (04-06-93, Sotheby-NY, #279, illus.), 6⅝ x 9½ in., photograph (BP 3418, DM 8337, FR 28,232, Y 590,214).

BI *Distortion #98 (1933), 1933,* p. early 1950s, d., num., credit stamp, lit., est. $3/4,000, (04-08-93, Christie-NY, #207, illus.), 9⅝ x 6¾ in., (24.4 x 17.1 cm.), photograph, gelatin silver print.

$880* *Dress Mannequins, New York, 1965,* d., credit stamp, (10-13-92, Christie-NY, #272, illus.), 9½ x 6⅞ in., (24.1 x 17.5 cm.), photograph, gelatin silver print (BP 513, DM 1289, FR 4380, Y 106,705).

$880* *Dubonnet Signs And Motorbike, 1934,* s., d. by photog., p. l., (10-15-92, Sotheby-NY, #349, illus.), 9⅝ x 7⅜ in., (24.4 x 18.7 cm.), photograph, gelatin silver print (BP 538, DM 1310, FR 4442, Y 105,579).

BI *East 10th Street, New York, 1960,* photog.'s inits., d., est. $1/1,500, (04-07-93, Swann, #499, illus.), 7¾ x 9½ in., photograph, silver print.

$2070* *Eiffel Tower, 1929,* p.l., s., t., d., lit., (04-08-93, Christie-NY, #201, illus.), 7¾ x 9¾ in., (19.7 x 24.8 cm.), photograph, gelatin silver print (BP 1357, DM 3325, FR 11,256, Y 234,907).

$2588* *"Eiffel Tower, Paris", 1929,* p.l., s., illus., (05-23-93, Butterfield, #3484, illus.), 7¾ x 9¾ in., photograph, gelatin silver print (BP 1685, DM 4232, FR 14,243, Y 286,062).

BI *"Esztergon", 1918,* p. 1970s, s., illus., est. $1,5/2,000, (05-23-93, Butterfield, #3490, illus.), 7¼ x 9½ in., photograph, gelatin silver print.

$935* *Fan, (1937),* p.l., s., d., annot., lit., (10-13-92, Christie-NY, #271, illus.), 9¼ x 7¾ in., (23.5 x 19.7 cm.), photograph, gelatin silver print (BP 545, DM 1370, FR 4654, Y 113,375).

$715* *Ferns, 1980,* s., d. by photog., handstamp, (04-07-93, Swann, #500, illus.), 7 x 9¼ in., photograph, silver print (BP 473, DM 1156, FR 3914, Y 81,232).

$990* *La Fete Foraine (Quai De L'Hotel De Ville) Paris, (1927),* 1970s, s., d., annot., lit., (10-13-92, Christie-NY, #267, illus.), 9¾ x 7¾ in., (24.8 x 19.7 cm.), photograph, gelain silver print (BP 577, DM 1450, FR 4928, Y 120,044).

$1100* *Garden Statue,* inits., 1960's, (10-14-92, Swann, #494, illus.), 4½ x 5½ in., (11.4 x 14 cm.), photograph, silver print (BP 646, DM 1610, FR 5459, Y 133,301).

BI *George Deininger, Stuttgart (Puppeteer) and Baden-Baden Theatre: Two,1929,* each s., t., studio & (c) stamps, prov., lit., est. $2,5/3,500, (10-13-92, Christie-NY, #256, illus.), 9⅜ x 7 in., (23.8 x 17.8 cm.), 6⅝ x 9 in., (23.8 x 17.8 cm.), photograph, gelatin silver prints.

$357* *Henri Deherain, 1936,* photog.'s (c) handstamp, news agency handstamp, label, penciled notations, (04-07-93, Swann, #324, illus.), 7 x 8¾ in., photograph, silver print (BP 236, DM 577, FR 1954, Y 40,559).

$2090* *Hoboes On The Bank Of The Seine,* sig., d., notations, 1926, p.l., (10-14-92, Swann, #495, illus.), 9½ x 7½ in., (24.1 x 19.1 cm.), photograph, silver print (BP 1227, DM 3059, FR 10,372, Y 253,272).

$1955* *"Homing Ship, New York", 1944,* p.l., s., d., illus., (05-23-93, Butterfield, #3483, illus.), 10 x 8 in., photograph, gelatin silver print (BP 1273, DM 3197, FR 10,759, Y 216,094).

$880* *Hungarian Boatmen,* photog.'s sig., 1920s, p.l., (04-07-93, Swann, #501, illus.), 7 x 9½ in., photograph, silver print (BP 582, DM 1423, FR 4817, Y 99,977).

$5175* *Hungarian Landscape (Hungarian Memories, p. 173), 1919,* d. by photog., (04-06-93, Sotheby-NY, #266, illus.), 1½ x 2 in., photograph (BP 3418, DM 8337, FR 28,232, Y 590,214).

$935* *Isamu Noguchi, 1945,* photog.'s handstamp, notations, (04-07-93, Swann, #502, illus.), 10 x 8 in., photograph, silver print (BP 618, DM 1512, FR 5118, Y 106,226).

$3105* *"Jardin Du Luxembourg" (Fixing A Shadow, dust jacket),* s., t., d., i. by photog., stamp, 1925, p. 1960's, (04-06-93, Sotheby-NY, #269, illus.), photograph (BP 2051, DM 5002, FR 16,939, Y 354,129).

$1150* *Kiki Of Montparnasse,* s., d. by photog., 1927, p.l., (04-06-93, Sotheby-NY, #275, illus.), 9¾ x 6¾ in., photograph (BP 760, DM 1853, FR 6274, Y 131,159).

$981* *"Kisling Paris 1931",* stamped photog.'s credit Photo by Andre Kertesz, t., 252 x 203mm, (05-07-93, Sotheby-London, #240, illus.), photograph, silver print (BP 621, DM 1551, FR 5226, Y 108,016).

$4140* *Landing Pigeon, New York, 1960,* t., d., credit stamp, lit., (04-08-93, Christie-NY, #212, illus.), 9⅝ x 7¾ in., (24.4 x 19.7 cm.), photograph, gelatin silver print (BP 2715, DM 6651, FR 22,512, Y 469,814).

$1438* *A Laundress In The Latin Quarter, Paris, 1928,* s. by photog., t., d. in unident. hand, (04-06-93, Sotheby-NY, #277, illus.), 9¾ x 6¾ in., photograph (BP 950, DM 2317, FR 7845, Y 164,005).

BI *Louis Tihanyi (1926),* from portfolio Andre Kertesz: Photographs, Vol. I 1972, s., d., blindstamped 5, lit., est. $1800/2200, (10-13-92, Christie-NY, #266, illus.), 9¼ x 6½ in., (23.5 x 16.5 cm.), photograph, gelatin silver print.

$1870* *"Lovers, Budapest" (Sixty Years, pl. 35),* 1915/1970's, s., d., Dixon Collection, (11-16-92, Butterfield, #6046, illus.), 7¾ x 9¾ in., (197.2 x 248.1 mm.), photograph, gelatin silver print (BP 1231, DM 2982, FR 10,043, Y 232,558).

BI *Magda Forstner And Etienne Boethy, 1926,* s., t., d., i. by photog., p. l., est. $1,5/2,000, (10-15-92, Sotheby-NY, #346, illus.), 9¾ x 7¾ in., (24.8 x 19.7 cm.), photograph, gelatin silver print.

BI *Magda Forstner, The Satiric Dancer, 1926,* prov., lit., est. $30/50,000, (10-13-92, Christie-NY, #258, illus.), 3½ x 1½ in., (8.9 x 3.8 cm.), photograph, gelatin silver print on section of carte-postale.

BI *March 20, 1978, No. 8,* s., t., d., est. $1,8/2,200, (10-13-92, Christie-NY, #274, illus.), 7¼ x 9¾ in., (18.4 x 24.8 cm.), photograph, gelatin silver print.

$2070* *Martinique, 1972,* p.l., s., t., d., lit., (04-08-93, Christie-NY, #210, illus.), 7⅜ x 9¾ in., (18.7 x 24.8 cm.), photograph, gelatin silver print (BP 1357, DM 3325, FR 11,256, Y 234,907).

$2875* *"Martinique" (Diary of Light, pl. 140),* s., t., d. by photog., 1972, p.l., (04-06-93, Sotheby-NY, #291A, illus.), 7½ x 9¾ in., photograph (BP 1899, DM 4632, FR 15,685, Y 327,897).

$3025* *Martinique, 1972 (Sixty Years, pl. 224),* s., t., d. by photog., (10-15-92, Sotheby-NY, #357, illus.), 10½ x 14 in., (26.7 x 35.6 cm.), photograph, gelatin silver print (BP 1851, DM 4503, FR 15,270, Y 362,927).

$2750* *Martinique, 1972 (Sixty Years, pl. 224),* s., t., d. by photog., p. l.(10-15-92, Sotheby-NY, #356, illus.), 7½ x 9⅝ in., (19.1 x 24.4 cm.), photograph, gelatin silver print (BP 1683, DM 4093, FR 13,882, Y 329,934).

$2200* *Mde. And M. Slivinsky, c. 1926,* s., i. by photog. on mount, i. in unidentified hand verso, (10-15-92, Sotheby-NY, #343, illus.), 3⅛ x 3⅝ in., (7.9 x 9.2 cm.), photograph, mounted on wove paper (BP 1346, DM 3275, FR 11,106, Y 263,947).

$4313* *"Melancholic Tulip",* s., d. by photog., 1939, p.l., (04-06-93, Sotheby-NY, #285, illus.), 19½ x 4½ in., photograph (BP 2849, DM 6949, FR 23,530, Y 491,902).

$2475* *"Melancholic Tulip" (Sixty Years, p. 78),* 1939/1970's, s., d., annot., (11-16-92, Butterfield, #6039, illus.), 13⅝ x 9⅞ in., (346.7 x 251.3 mm.), photograph, gelatin silver print (BP 1630, DM 3946, FR 13,292, Y 307,798).

$2200* *"Melancholic Tulip" (Sixty Years, p. 78),* 1939/1970's, s., d., (11-16-92, Butterfield, #6040, illus.), 9¾ x 7 in., (248.1 x 178.1 mm.), photograph, gelatin silver print (BP 1449, DM 3508, FR 11,815, Y 273,598).

$2420* *Melancholic Tulip, New York,* (1939), p.l., s., d., lit., (10-13-92, Christie-NY, #270, illus.), 23¾ x 17¾ in., (60.3 x 45.1 cm.), photograph, gelatin silver print (BP 1409, DM 3545, FR 12,046, Y 293,440).

BI *Melancholic Tulip-New York City,* 1939/printed later; s., d. Feb. 10 1939 verso, est. $2/2,500, (05-16-93, Hindman, #326, illus.), 6¾ x 9½ in., photograph, silver print.

$2475* *Meudon, 1928 (Sixty Years, pl. 141),* s., d. by photog., p. l., (10-15-92, Sotheby-NY, #347, illus.), 9⅝ x 6⅞ in., (24.4 x 17.5 cm.), photograph, gelatin silver print (BP 1515, DM 3684, FR 12,494, Y 296,941).

$2588* *"Mondrian's Pipe And Glasses" (Sixty Years, p. 116),* s., d., i. by photog., 1926, p.l., (04-06-93, Sotheby-NY, #270, illus.), 7¾ x 9⅝ in., photograph (BP 1709, DM 4169, FR 14,119, Y 295,164).

BI *Mt. Kisco, New York, 1939,* mounted, s. by photog., inits., d., name stamp, (10-15-92, Sotheby-NY, #354, illus.), 7⅜ x 9½ in., (18.7 x 24.1 cm.), photograph, gelatin silver print.

$1380* *My Friend Ernest, Paris,* 1931, p.l., s., t., d., lit., (04-08-93, Christie-NY, #204, illus.), 9¾ x 7¾ in., (24.8 x 19.7 cm.), photograph, gelatin silver print (BP 905, DM 2217, FR 7504, Y 156,605).

BI *My Mother's Hands, Hungary,* 1919, p.l., d., annot., lit., est. $1,5/2,000, (04-08-93, Christie-NY, #194, illus.), 7½ x 9¼ in., (19.1 x 23.5 cm.), photograph, gelatin silver print.

$920* *Near Pont De Grenelle, Paris,* s. by photog., t., d. in unident. hand, 1927, p.l., (04-06-93, Sotheby-NY, #276, illus.), 9¾ x 7 in., photograph (BP 608, DM 1482, FR 5019, Y 104,927).

BI *New York Ballet, 1938,* annot., lit., est. $8/12,000, (10-13-92, Christie-NY, #259, illus.), 2⅝ x 3⅜ in., (6.7 x 8.6 cm.), photograph, gelatin silver print.

$3450* *New York Sky, Rockefeller Center, 1936-37,* credit stamp, (04-08-93, Christie-NY, #209, illus.), 13⅜ x 9½ in., (34 x 24.1 cm.), photograph, gelatin silver print (BP 2262, DM 5542, FR 18,760, Y 391,512).

BI *New York, 1972,* t., d., notations, est. $1,5/2,000, (10-14-92, Swann, #496, illus.), 10 x 8 in., (25.4 x 20.3 cm.), photograph, silver print.

$2200* *"On The Quais, Paris" (Sixty Years, p. 130),* 1926/later, s., d., (11-16-92, Butterfield, #6043, illus.), 9½ x 7¾ in., (241.7 x 197.2 mm.), photograph, gelatin silver print (BP 1449, DM 3508, FR 11,815, Y 273,598).

BI *Paris Window, 1980,* d., annot., lit., est. $1,8/2,200, (10-13-92, Christie-NY, #273, illus.), 9¾ x 6¾ in., (24.8 x 17.1 cm.), photograph, gelatin silver print.

$2750* *"Paris, Magda-The Satiric Dancer" (Sixty Years, p. 70),* s., d., annot., 1926/1970's, (11-16-92, Butterfield, #6038, illus.), 13¾ x 10¾ in., (349.9 x 273.5 mm.), photograph, gelatin silver print (BP 1811, DM 4385, FR 14,769, Y 341,997).

$1320* *Passengers Getting On A Bus In Paris, c. 1928,* t., Paris credit stamp, reprod. limit. stamp, label, (10-13-92, Christie-NY, #255, illus.), 8¾ x 6⅜ in., (22.2 x 16.2 cm.), photograph, gelatin silver print (BP 769, DM 1934, FR 6570, Y 160,058).

$19,550* *Piet Mondrian (Of Paris and New York, cat. no. 24), 1926,* s., i. by photog., (04-06-93, Sotheby-NY, #272, illus.), 4⅛ x 3⅛ in., photograph, on carte-postale (BP 12,913, DM 31,497, FR 106,656, Y 2,229,699).

BI *"Pont De Solferino", 1963,* s., t., d. 11-13-63, num. 6A, i. by photog., est. $2/4,000, (10-15-92, Sotheby-NY, #355, illus.), 9½ x 7¾ in., (24.1 x 19.7 cm.), photograph, gelatin silver print.

BI *Pont Des Artes, Paris,* 1932, p.l., s., d., lit., est. $2,5/3,500, (04-08-93, Christie-NY, #205, illus.), 13⅝ x 9¾ in., (34.6 x 24.8 cm.), photograph, gelatin silver print.

$770* *"Ripples, Hungary",* 1913/1970's, s., t., d., (11-16-92, Butterfield, #6047, illus.), 6⅞ x 6¾ in., (174.9 x 171.8 mm.), photograph, gelatin silver print (BP 507, DM 1228, FR 4135, Y 95,759).

$2588* *"Satiric Dancer" (Sixty Years, p. 70),* s., d., i. by photog., 1926, p.l., (04-06-93, Sotheby-NY, #274, illus.), 9¾ x 7¾ in., photograph (BP 1709, DM 4169, FR 14,119, Y 295,164).

$3850* *Satiric Dancer, 1926 (Sixty Years, pl. 70),* s., d. by photog., p. 1979, (10-15-92, Sotheby-NY, #344, illus.), 4¼ x 3¼ in., (10.8 x 8.3 cm.), photograph, gelatin silver print (BP 2356, DM 5731, FR 19,435, Y 461,908).

$3025* *Satiric Dancer, 1926 (Sixty Years, pl. 70),* s., d. by photog., p. l., (10-15-92, Sotheby-NY, #345, illus.), 10 x 7¾ in., (25.4 x 19.7 cm.), photograph, gelatin silver print (BP 1851, DM 4503, FR 15,270, Y 362,927).

$2760* *Satiric Dancer, Paris,* 1926, p.l., s., d., lit., (04-08-93, Christie-NY, #196, illus.), 13⅝ x 10¾ in., (34.6 x 27.3 cm.), photograph, gelatin silver print (BP 1810, DM 4434, FR 15,008, Y 313,209).

$2200* *Satiric Dancer, Paris,* (1926), from portfoliio Andre Kertesz: Photographs, Vol. I 1972, s.,d., blindstamped 5, lit., est. $1,8/2,200, (10-13-92, Christie-NY, #265, illus.), 9⅝ x 7¾ in., (24.4 x 19.7 cm.), photograph, gelatin silver print (BP 1281, DM 3223, FR 10,951, Y 266,764).

BI *Sculpture Garden, Museum Of Modern Art, 1954,* d., credit stamp, est. $3/5,000, (10-13-92, Christie-NY, #260, illus.), 9¾ x 7⅞ in., (24.8 x 20 cm.), photograph, gelatin silver print.

$3450* *Sidewalk Conversation, 1924,* s., d., (05-23-93, Butterfield, #3481, illus.), 1½ x 2 in., photograph, gelatin silver contact print (BP 2247, DM 5641, FR 18,987, Y 381,342).

BI *Snake And Mouse, 1960,* tipped to heavy wove paper, initialled by photog., d. 1-12-60, num. 17, i. by photog., name stamp, est. $4/6,000, (10-15-92, Sotheby-NY, #358, illus.), 8½ x 6¼ in., (21.6 x 15.9 cm.), photograph, gelatin silver print.

$2090* *Stairs Of Montmartre,* (1926), 1970s, s., d., lit., (10-13-92, Christie-NY, #263, illus.), 7¾ x 9¾ in., (19.7 x 24.8 cm.), photograph, gelatin silver print (BP 1217, DM 3062, FR 10,403, Y 253,425).

$660* *Still Life With Glass Hearts And Bird, 1979,* s. by photog., d., num. 4/50, i. in unidentified hand, #4/50 ed., (10-15-92, Sotheby-NY, #359, illus.), photograph, cibachrome print of Polaroid print (BP 404, DM 982, FR 3332, Y 79,184).

$2200* *"Subway Stop, Paris",* 1928/1970's, s., d., (11-16-92, Butterfield, #6042, illus.), 9¾ x 7⅛ in., (248.1 x 181.3 mm.), photograph, gelatin silver print (BP 1449, DM 3508, FR 11,815, Y 273,598).

$1035* *"Swimming, Duna Hanastzi",* 1919, p. 1970s, s., d., illus., (05-23-93, Butterfield, #3488, illus.), 9¾ x 7¾ in., photograph, gelatin silver print (BP 674, DM 1692, FR 5696, Y 114,403).

$1760* *Three Chimneys, 1968,* handstamp, (10-14-92, Swann, #497, illus.), 6½ x 4 in., (16.5 x 10.2 cm.), photograph, silver print (BP 1033, DM 2576, FR 8734, Y 213,282).

BI *Tibor Harsanyi, late 1920's,* s. and i. by photog., est. $3/5,000, (04-06-93, Sotheby-NY, #273A, illus.), 4⅛ x 2½ in., photograph, on carte-postale.

$978* *"Tisza-Szalka, Hungary",* 1924, p. 1970s, s., illus., (05-23-93, Butterfield, #3489, illus.), 8 x 10 in., photograph, gelatin silver print (BP 637, DM 1599, FR 5382, Y 108,102).

BI *Two Friends, Paris,* 1926, p.l., d., annot., est. $1,8/2,200, (04-08-93, Christie-NY, #198, illus.), 6⅜ x 8⅜ in., (16.2 x 21.3 cm.), photograph, gelatin silver print.

$3163* *"Untitled, Meudon",* 1928, p.l., s., t., d., illus., (05-23-93, Butterfield, #3482, illus.), 19½ x 14¼ in., photograph, Gelatin silver print (BP 2060, DM 5172, FR 17,408, Y 349,619).

BI *"Washington Square #8A",* 1976, p.l., s., t., d., est. $2/2,500, (05-23-93, Butterfield, #3486, illus.), 6½ x 10 in., photograph, gelatin silver print.

$805* *Washington Square Park, 1970,* t., credit stamp, (04-08-93, Christie-NY, #211, illus.), 7¾ x 8¾ in., (19.7 x 22.2 cm.), photograph, gelatin silver print (BP 528, DM 1293, FR 4377, Y 91,353).

$3738* *Wassiliev Masks, 1929-31,* photog. studio and reprod. lim. stamps, i. in unident. hand, (04-06-93, Sotheby-NY, #273, illus.), 6⅜ x 7¼ in., photograph (BP 2469, DM 6022, FR 20,393, Y 426,323).

$880* *Window Dressing, Paris, 1925 (Sixty Years, pl. 152),* s., d., i. by photog. p. l., (10-15-92, Sotheby-NY, #348A, illus.), 9¾ x 7¾ in., (24.8 x 19.7 cm.), photograph, gelatin silver print (BP 538, DM 1310, FR 4442, Y 105,579).

BI *Wooden Horses,* (1929), 1960s, s., d., annot., credit stamp, lit., est. $4/6,000, (10-13-92, Christie-NY, #261, illus.), 13⅝ x 9¾ in., (34.6 x 24.8 cm.), photograph, gelatin silver print.

KESING, G.
$6 *Dutch Children Hearing A Story,* s., (04-16-93, G.A. Key, #38), 12 x 10 in., (30.5 x 25.4 cm.), etching (BP 4, DM 10, FR 33, Y 675).

KESSELS, Willy 1898-1974
BI *Industrial Photomontage, c. 1930,* credit stamp, lit., est. $4/6,000, (10-13-92, Christie-NY, #275, illus.), 13⅜ x 10⅜ in., (34 x 26.4 cm.), photograph, gelatin silver print.
$660* *Nude (Multiple Exposure), c. 1940,* handstamp, (10-14-92, Swann, #498, illus.), 3½ x 4½ in., (8.9 x 11.4 cm.), photograph, silver print (BP 387, DM 966, FR 3275, Y 79,981).
BI *Photocollage (With Mounted, Cut-Out Image), 1932,* handstamp, est. $1,5/2,000, (10-14-92, Swann, #499, illus.), photograph, silver prints.
BI *Photogram, c. 1935,* blindstamp, handstamp, est. $1/1,500, (10-14-92, Swann, #500, illus.), 6½ x 9 in., (16.5 x 22.9 cm.), photograph, silver print.

KESTING, Edmund German 1892-1970
$228* *Beim Baden,1926,* (11-12-92, Lempertz, #122a), 7½ x 4¹³⁄₁₆ in., (19 x 12.2 cm.), photograph, gelatin silver print (BP 146, DM 358, FR 1221, Y 28,207).
$455* *Bildnis Einer Jungen Frau, 1929,* t., (11-12-92, Lempertz, #122, illus.), 11¹³⁄₁₆ x 9½ in., (30 x 24.1 cm.), photograph, gelatin silver print (BP 291, DM 715, FR 2437, Y 56,291).
BI *Dresdner Zwinger, 30's,* s. in negative, est. DM 1,100, (11-12-92, Lempertz, #123a, illus.), 15⁷⁄₁₆ x 11⅝ in., (39.2 x 29.6 cm.), photograph, gelatin silver print.
$133* *Frauenbildnis (Lehmann 59), 1920,* s., (12-05-92, Bassenge, #7322), 6³⁄₁₆ x 4⅝ in., (15.7 x 11.7 cm.), drypoint on wove (BP 83, DM 207, FR 707, Y 16,479).
$948* *Gerda Mit Blume, 1930,* s., d., (c), (11-12-92, Lempertz, #123, illus.), 16¹⁄₁₆ x 11⅛ in., (40.8 x 28.2 cm.), photograph, gelatin silver print (BP 606, DM 1490, FR 5078, Y 117,283).
$379* *Hande, 1948,* ink s., d., (11-12-92, Lempertz, #124, illus.), 7¹³⁄₁₆ x 11¹⁵⁄₁₆ in., (19.8 x 30.3 cm.), photograph, gelatin silver print (BP 242, DM 596, FR 2030, Y 46,889).
$758* *Ohne Titel, 1926,* i., d., (11-12-92, Lempertz, #121, illus.), 8³⁄₁₆ x 6⅛ in., (20.8 x 15.5 cm.), photograph, gelatin silver print (BP 485, DM 1191, FR 4060, Y 93,777).
BI *Stretching Canvas, 1920s,* s. Kestingfoto, t., credit, est. $2/2,500, (10-13-92, Christie-NY, #276, illus.), 9 x 11½ in., (22.9 x 29.2 cm.), photograph, gelatin silver print.
$920* *Woman With Chrysanthemum (Avant-Garde Photography in Germany, pl. 86, solarized variant), 1930,* s., t., d., photog. name stamp, (04-06-93, Sotheby-NY, #328, illus.), 9⅜ x 7 in., photograph (BP 608, DM 1482, FR 5019, Y 104,927).

KEUHN, Gary American 20th cent.
BI *Another Of The Eternal Figures: Three,* est. $6/900, (11-12-92, Freemn/Fine Art, #104), sheet 27 x 22 in., (68.6 x 55.9 cm.), photo engravings.

KEULEN, Johannes van Dutch 17th cent.
$110* *Navigational Map, c. 1680,* (12-13-92, Hindman, #249), 20 x 23½ in., hand-colored engraving (BP 70, DM 173, FR 589, Y 13,609).

KEXYA, Algimatntus American contemporary
$44* *Lake Point Tower, Chicago, 1968,* t., s., (03-14-93, Hindman, #408), 15⅝ x 19⅝ in., photograph, silver gelatin print (BP 31, DM 73, FR 248, Y 5212).

KEY, Julian
BI *Waarborg Van Hoedanigheid,* Vanypeco, A- cond., marginal creasing, cracking, est. $2/300, (08-06-92, Swann, #163, illus.), 34½ x 50 in., (87.6 x 127 cm.), .

KEYSTONE VIEW CO.
$978* *Portraits Of Jack Dempsey: "Dempsey's Back Muscles", "Third Round OfThe Big Fight" and "Schemeling And*

Dempsey", 1920: Three, two t., stamps, (05-23-93, Butterfield, #3492, illus.), each approx. 6¼ x 8 in., photograph, gelatin silver print (BP 637, DM 1599, FR 5382, Y 108,102).

KIAKSHUK Inuit 1888-1965
$605* *"Summer Camp Scene", 1961,* #16/50, 1961, s., t., seal, (05-14-93, DuMouchelle, #2032, illus.), 16¼ x 21¼ in., (41.3 x 54 cm.), color sealskin stencil (BP 393, DM 973, FR 3270, Y 67,066).

KIDD, William (after)
BI *The Poacher Detected, 1820,* by Thomas Lupton, pub. Hurst, Robinson, and Co., trimmed inside plate, center crease, est. BP 1/150, (11-30-92, Phillips-London, #267), sheet 24¼ x 19⅛ in., (616 x 486 mm.), mixed-method engraving on laid.

KIECOL, Hubert b. 1950
$2308* *5 Holzschnitte, 1983,* #11/15, s., num., (11-20-92, Lempertz, #641), sh, approx. 19⅝ x 13¹³⁄₁₆ in., (49.8 x 35.1 cm.), woodcut on hand-made (BP 1520, DM 3680, FR 12,395, Y 287,029).

KIEFER, Anselm German b. 1945
$17,250* *Das Goldenes Haar, Margarete,* exec. 1987, prov., (05-04-93, Sotheby-NY, #161, illus.), 25 x 37 in., (63.5 x 94 cm.), b/w photograph w/straw (BP 11,012, DM 27,174, FR 91,561, Y 1,897,481).

KIEFF, Antonio Grediaga (called) Spanish School b. 1928
$186* *"Iris De Van Gogh",* #5/50, s., d. Kieff 87, (07-14-92, Encans, #224), 22¹⁄₁₆ x 29½ in., (56 x 75 cm.), serigraph (BP 97, DM 276, FR 930, Y 23,259, C$ 222).

KIENHOLZ, Edward American b. 1927
$863* *For A Mitre Saw, 1969,* s., d. w/thumb print, margins, good cond.?, Albert Levinson Estate, (05-19-93, Butterfield, #2226), 12 x 16 in., (305 x 406 mm.), inkstamp and watercolor on wove (BP 560, DM 1403, FR 4726, Y 95,539).
$217* *Kienholz 1960-1970,* ded., s., d., (11-28-92, Schoppmann, #614), 23¼ x 33¹⁄₁₆ in., (59 x 84 cm.), serigraph on silver paper (BP 143, DM 346, FR 1174, Y 27,007).
BI *Volchksempfanger With Mirror, 1983,* s., d., #74/100, good cond., est. BP 4/500, (06-30-93, Sotheby-London, #857, illus.), sh 24 x 18⅛ in., (610 x 460 mm.), etching and collage in color w/embossed metal on wove.
BI *Volsempfanger With Mirror, 1983,* s., d. 83, #69/100, est. FF3/4,000, (05-27-93, Briest, #115), 24 x 18⅛ in., (61 x 46 cm.), carborundum engraving, aluminum collage and paper.

KIES, Helmut German contemporary
$88* *Im Garten Der Venus: Ten,* each s., #36/100, (11-01-92, Hanzel, #232), 13 x 9½ in., (33 x 24.1 cm.), etching (BP 58, DM 139, FR 468, Y 10,880).

KIFFER, Ch.
$671* *Maurice Chevalier Au Canotier, c. 1950,* p. Bedos, very good cond., (11-19-92, Ribeyre/Baron, #179), 62¹⁵⁄₁₆ x 47¼ in., (160 x 120 cm.), lithograph poster (BP 442, DM 1070, FR 3604, Y 83,447).
$155* *Maurice Chevalier: Two,* ded., (01-31-93, Morelle/Marchan, #232), 15¾ x 23⅝ in., (40 x 60 cm.), poster (BP 104, DM 250, FR 844, Y 19,336).

KIJNO, Ladislas b. 1921
$116* *"Composition Noir, Rose, Rouge",* E.A., s., (01-28-93, Pescheteau, #169), a vue 19¹¹⁄₁₆ x 17⁵⁄₁₆ in., (50 x 44 cm.), lithograph on wove (BP 77, DM 184, FR 622, Y 14,403).
BI *"Humanite 72",* artist's proof, t., d., s., est. FF6/800, (04-04-93, Pescheteau, #227), 15³⁄₁₆ x 15³⁄₁₆ in., (38.5 x 38.5 cm.), color serigraph.
BI *Komposition,* #19/75, s., est. SF 450/500, (04-21-93, Germann, #573), 29⅛ x 22¹⁄₁₆ in., (740 x 560 mm.), color lithograph and collage.

KIKUMARO
BI *"A Boy Plays With Two Beaters",* block s., est. $100/150, (01-15-93, DuMouchelle, #2298, illus.), 8 x 5¾ in., (20.3 x 14.6 cm.), color woodblock print.

KILBOURNE
$1265* *Deep-Sea Fish: Three,* d. 1878, (04-07-93, Sotheby-Arcade, #160), sight 14 x 20¼ in., (35.6 x 51.4 cm.), chromolithograph (BP 836, DM 2046, FR 6924, Y 143,717).

KILIAN, Wolfgang 1581-1662
BI *XII Caesarum Qui Primi Rom. Imperarunt Effigies (Holl. 619-31), 1608: Title And Set Of Twelve,* after R. Schiaminossi, wide margins, 3 trimmed to subject and mounted, abrasion, staining, good cond., est. BP 400/600, (12-01-92, Christie-London, #106), 82³⁄₁₆ x 5⅜ in., (208.7 x 13.7 cm.), engraving.

KILIAN LE JEUNE, Bartholomaus 1630-1696
$302* *Portrait De Boebel (Leblanc II, p. 449),* after B. Hopffer, damp collector's stamp verso, (05-15-93, Loudmer, #80), 11⅛ x 7⅞ in., (282 x 200 mm.), copper engraving on laid w/2-headed bird on fleur-de-lis crown watermark (BP 196, DM 486, FR 1632, Y 33,477).
$302* *Portrait De Faber (Leblanc II, p. 449),* after B. Hopffer, damp collector's stamp verso, (05-15-93, Loudmer, #81, illus.), 9¹⁄₁₆ x 7½ in., (230 x 190 mm.), copper engraving w/2-headed bird on fleur-de-lis crown watermark (BP 196, DM 486, FR 1632, Y 33,477).

KILLAM, Walt American 1907-1979
$75* *Landscape, 1940,* s., excell. cond., (05-15-93, Cleveland, #188), 4 x 9½ in., (10.2 x 24.1 cm.), color monotype (BP 49, DM 121, FR 405, Y 8314).

KILLIE, Charles A.
BI *"50 Views Of Siege Of Peking", 1901,* est. BP 4/600, each approx. 190 x 240mm or 85 x 80mm, (05-07-93, Sotheby-London, #38), photograph, gelatin silver print.

KIMURA, Risaburo b. 1924
$109* *City Vision, 1974,* s., d., (09-25-92, Granier, #2907), sheet 22¹⁄₁₆ x 28¹¹⁄₁₆ in., (56.1 x 72.8 cm.), color serigraph on offset paper (BP 64, DM 162, FR 546, Y 13,156).
$109* *Metropolis,* s., d., (09-25-92, Granier, #2906), sheet 27 x 20¹³⁄₁₆ in., (68.6 x 52.9 cm.), color serigraph on black offset paper (BP 64, DM 162, FR 546, Y 13,156).

KIMURA, Shiero Japanese b. 1929
BI *Butterfly,* s., est. $150/250, (09-24-92, Mystic, #4A), 24 x 15 in., (61 x 38.1 cm.), colored lithograph.

KING, Charles Bird (after)
$1265* *Ap-Pa-Noo-Se, Saukie Chief, 1838,* pub. McKenney and Hall's History of the Indian Tribes of North America, by F.W. Greenough, margins, good cond., foxing, mat stain, offprint, (01-28-93, Sotheby-NY, #467), sheet 19¾ x 13½ in., (502 x 343 mm.), hand-colored lithograph w/touches gum arabic (BP 835, DM 2004, FR 6783, Y 157,065).
$2300* *"Ne. O. Mon-Ne, An Ioway Chief" and "Tah. Ro. Hon, An Ioway Warrior,1838: Two,* p. Bowen, pub. in McKenney and Hall's History of the Indian Tribes of North America, by F.W. Greenough, margins, good cond., soiling, (01-28-93, Sotheby-NY, #466), sheets 17⅞ x 12⅜ in., (454 x 314 mm.), hand-colored lithograph w/touches gum arabic (BP 1519, DM 3644, FR 12,332, Y 285,572).

KING, Edward
$1100* *"American Hunting Scenes": Set Of Four,* each s., (c) 1929 and 1930, pub. Derrydale Press, (09-18-92, DuMouchelle, #2055), image 9¼ x 17 in., (23.5 x 43.2 cm.), hand-colored aquatints (BP 633, DM 1647, FR 5641, Y 137,055).

KING, Edward American 20th cent.
$248* *"The First Flight," "The Check," "Full Cry," and "Wellaway", 1930: Four,* s., pub., (c) Derrydale Press, good cond., Janet-Lee Auchincloss Estate, (09-19-92, Weschler, #163), 12 x 18¼ in., (30.5 x 46.4 cm.), etching and aquatint (BP 145, DM 368, FR 1259, Y 30,651).

KING, James S. American 1852-1925
$35* *Young Girl,* (02-04-93, Sloan, #347), 13¾ x 11 in., (34.9 x 27.9 cm.), mezzotint (BP 24, DM 58, FR 195, Y 4354).

KING, Mark American 20th cent.
$220* *"Fox Hunt",* edit. #106/325, s., (09-18-92, DuMouchelle, #2297), 26 x 35 in., (66 x 88.9 cm.), silkscreen (BP 127, DM 329, FR 1128, Y 27,411).

KINGMAN, Dong American b. 1911
$193* *Hong Kong Port,* s., num. 66/250, (11-12-92, Freemn/Fine Art, #110), 22½ x 29½ in., (57.2 x 74.9 cm.), screen print (BP 127, DM 306, FR 1032, Y 23,931).
$193* *Shipyard,* very good cond., (09-27-92, Bakker, #130), sight 17¼ x 14¼ in., (18.4 x 36.2 cm.), screen print (BP 113, DM 286, FR 967, Y 23,295).

KINNEIR, Jock
$555* *To Visit Britain's Landmarks, Sham Ruins, Virginia Water, 1936,* p. Baynard Press, ref. #473, cond. 3, (10-13-92, Phillips-London, #115), 29¹⁵⁄₁₆ x 45¼ in., (76 x 115 cm.), color lithograph (BP 323, DM 813, FR 2763, Y 67,297).

KINNEY, Troy American 1871-1938
$110* *Girl Dancing: Pair,* s., (11-13-92, DuMouchelle, #2369), 6½ x 6½ in., (16.5 x 16.5 cm.), etching (BP 71, DM 173, FR 582, Y 13,653).
$1000* *"Impressions Of Great Dancer": "Fokinand Fokina In Le Spectre De La Rose", "Adolph Blom", "Lydia Lopokova And Waslay Nijinski In Les Sylphides", "Roshanara", "Adeline Genee" and others: Seven,* edit. 88, #5, s. in portfolio, very good cond., (05-15-93, Cleveland, #189), drypoint (six in color) (BP 650, DM 1608, FR 5405, Y 110,852).
BI *"Pan",* s., est. $1/150, (12-12-92, A. James, #495), 7½ x 8½ in., (19.1 x 21.6 cm.), etching.
BI *Untitled,* s., good cond., est. $1-150, (10-31-92, Cleveland, #160, illus.), 9 x 11¼ in., (22.9 x 28.6 cm.), etching.
BI *"Zephyr" (Kinney 30),* s., num. 36/120, tape staining, good cond., est. $1-150, (10-31-92, Cleveland, #161), 10 x 10 in., (25.4 x 25.4 cm.), etching and drypoint.

KINNIER, Jock
$1223* *Riders To Hounds Use Shell, 1938,* p. Waterlow and Sons, ref. #520, cond. 1, (10-13-92, Phillips-London, #139), 29¹⁵⁄₁₆ x 45 in., (76 x 114.3 cm.), color lithograph (BP 712, DM 1792, FR 6088, Y 148,296).

KINSEY, Darius
$1150* *"Stimson Mill Company, Seattle, Washington", c. 1900,* num. 5001A in unident. hand, (04-06-93, Sotheby-NY, #24, illus.), 19⅝ x 24 in., photograph (BP 760, DM 1853, FR 6274, Y 131,159).

KIP, Joannes
$578* *"Berkley Castle, The Seat Of The Earl Of Berkley" and "Battsford, TheSeat Of Richard Freeman, Esquire": Two,* (11-12-92, Freemn/Fine Art, #108), both, mat 14 x 17½ in., (35.6 x 43.8 cm.), hand colored engravings (BP 380, DM 916, FR 3089, Y 71,668).
$523* *"Cleeve Hill, The Seat Of William Player, Esquire" and "Knole, The Set Of Thomas Chester, Esquire", Brittania Illustrata, 1709: Two,* (11-12-92, Freemn/Fine Art, #106), both mat 14 x 17¼ in., (35.6 x 43.8 cm.), hand colored engravings (BP 344, DM 829, FR 2795, Y 64,848).
$275* *Leckhampton, The Seat Of The Reverend Thomas Norwood, Brittania Illustrata, 1709,* (11-12-92, Freemn/Fine Art, #105, illus.), mat 14 x 17¼ in., (35.6 x 43.8 cm.), hand colored engraving (BP 181, DM 436, FR 1470, Y 34,098).
$523* *"Little Compton, The Seat Of Sir Richard Howe Bar" and "Tortworth, The Seat Of Mathew Ducy Morton", Brittania Illustrata 1709: Two,* (11-12-92, Freemn/Fine Art, #107), both mat 14 x 17¼ in., (35.6 x 43.8 cm.), hand colored engravings (BP 344, DM 829, FR 2795, Y 64,848).
$770* *"The West Prospect Of Gloucester City", "Shipton Moyne, The Seat Of Messieurs Hodges", "Stoke, Gifford, The Seat Of John Berkeley", and "Sive, The Seat Of Sir Robert Atkyns": Four,* from Brittania Illustrata, 1790, (06-11-93, Freemn/Fine Art, #122), 14 x 17¾ in., (35.6 x 45.1 cm.), hand-colored engraving (BP 506, DM 1251, FR 4219, Y 81,698).

$578* *"Whitcomb Park, The Seat Of Sir Michael Hickes"* and *"Over, The Seat OJohn Dowell, Esquire", Brittania Illustrata, 1709:* Two, (11-12-92, Freemn/Fine Art, #109), both, mat 14 x 17¼ in., (35.6 x 43.8 cm.), hand colored engravings (BP 380, DM 916, FR 3089, Y 71,668).

$605* *"Wyck, The Seat Of Richard Haines", "Badminton, The Seat Of The Dukeof Beaufort", and "Henbury, The Seat Of Mr. John Sampson":* Three, from Brittania Illustrata, 1790, (06-11-93, Freemn/Fine Art, #123), 14 x 17¾ in., (35.6 x 45.1 cm.), hand-colored engraving (BP 398, DM 983, FR 3315, Y 64,191).

KIPNISS, Robert   American b. 1931

$231* *"Farm Scene",* s., #117/150, (02-27-93, Dunning, #6, illus.), 19¾ x 15¾ in., (50.2 x 40 cm.), lithograph (BP 162, DM 380, FR 1291, Y 27,270).

$70* *Fences And Steps,* s., #23/130, excell. cond., (05-15-93, Cleveland, #471), 14⅛ x 16⅛ in., (35.9 x 41 cm.), lithograph in colors (BP 46, DM 113, FR 378, Y 7760).

$220* *"Fences And Steps", "Window Pots", "Window With Road Wall" and "Window With Suspended Plant":* Four, each s., num. 19/130, 106/130, 44/120, 40/150, margins, smudging, soft handling creases, (05-22-93, Weschler, #197, illus.), lithograph in colors on Arches (BP 143, DM 358, FR 1204, Y 24,256).

BI *Hillside,* s., #198/260, est. $125/175, (02-04-93, Sloan, #371), 13½ x 9⅞ in., (34.3 x 25.1 cm.), lithograph.

$40* *"Interludes", 1981,* s., excell. cond., (05-15-93, Cleveland, #470), 13 x 14 in., (33 x 35.6 cm.), lithogrpah in colors (BP 26, DM 64, FR 216, Y 4434).

$275* *"Ohio Morning",* s., #83/120, excell. cond.?, (07-19-92, Bakker, #199), plate 8¾ x 9¾ in., (22.2 x 24.8 cm.), color lithograph (BP 141, DM 401, FR 1355, Y 34,187).

$68* *Scintilation II,* s., #76/150; t. label backing, prov., (12-01-92, Ritchie, #85), 16 x 13 in., (40.6 x 33 cm.), color lithograph (BP 45, DM 108, FR 369, Y 8466, C$ 88).

$165* *"View From A Window",* s., #XXXIV/L A/P, (02-27-93, Dunning, #5, illus.), 15¾ x 11¾ in., (40 x 29.8 cm.), lithograph (BP 116, DM 271, FR 922, Y 19,478).

BI *"The Window Box", c. 1975,* s., num. 94/130, excellent cond., est. $150-200, (10-31-92, Cleveland, #377), 16⅛ x 13¾ in., (41 x 34.9 cm.), color lithograph.

$65* *"The Window Box", c. 1975,* s., good cond., (05-15-93, Cleveland, #472), 16 x 13½ in., (40.6 x 34.3 cm.), color lithograph (BP 42, DM 105, FR 351, Y 7205).

$220* *"Winter" and "Autumn":* Two, s., num. 61/100, (11-12-92, Freemn/Fine Art, #112), both 17 x 13 in., (43.2 x 33 cm.), colored lithographs (BP 144, DM 349, FR 1176, Y 27,278).

KIRCHNER, Ernst Ludwig   German 1880-1938

$11,454* *Adam Und Eva (D. 472/III), 1923,* s. in ink, ded., (06-23-93, Kornfeld, #448, illus.), drypoint on wove (BP 7781, DM 19,381, FR 65,191, Y 1,247,848, SF 17,250).

$1165* *Alte Und Junge Frau (Sch. 386; D. 463 B), 1921,* 2nd state of 3, stamped sig.; stamp Fur Holz-Mappe verso, margins, tape, (12-01-92, Christie-London, #402), L. 13³⁄₁₆ x 9⁵⁄₁₆ in., (335 x 237 mm.), woodcut on Japan (BP 770, DM 1857, FR 6328, Y 145,045).

BI *Auf Dem Kasernenhof (D. 308), 1916,* num. 28/75, pub. in Der Bildermann, 2 lithographs by Grossman & Max Slevogt verso, margins, good cond., est. $6/800, (02-24-93, Butterfield, #2944), 10¹⁄₁₆ x 8½ in., (256 x 216 mm.), lithograph on wove.

BI *Ausstellung Ernst Ludwig Kirchner (Dube H 741-744, 751 and 843), 1933:* Six, est. DM 1000, (12-01-92, Karl/Faber, #830), 8⅞ x 6⅛ in., (22.5 x 15.5 cm.), woodcut.

$878* *Badende (Dube 111 II), 1938,* 1910, estate print 1979, estate E.L. Kirchner 15/30, (12-12-92, Bassenge, #8644), 6¹¹⁄₁₆ x 4¹¹⁄₁₆ in., (17 x 11.9 cm.), etching on copper print (BP 561, DM 1380, FR 4703, Y 108,623).

$42,373* *Badende Auf Steinen (Dube 164 III), 1913,* t., d., Basler estate stamp, (06-10-93, Hauswedell/Nolt, #456, illus.), image 8⅞ x 8⅞ in., (22.5 x 22.5 cm.), drypoint on Japan (BP 27,717, DM 69,000, FR 232,308, Y 4,497,718).

$10,946* *Badende In Hut (Dube 478 I), 1923,* s., t., d., Basler estate stamp, (06-10-93, Hauswedell/Nolt, #459, illus.), image 12³⁄₁₆ x 9⁹⁄₁₆ in., (31 x 24.3 cm.), drypoint on

Umdruck board (BP 7160, DM 17,824, FR 60,011, Y 1,161,872).

$12,262* *Badende Madchen In Hut (Dube 509), 1923,* s., ded., (11-21-92, Lempertz, #207, illus.), approx. 25¹³⁄₁₆ x 14⅝ in., (65.5 x 37.2 cm.), woodcut on hand-made Japan (BP 8073, DM 19,550, FR 65,854, Y 1,524,935).

BI *Bahnhof Konigstein Im Taunus (Schiefler 246; Dube H294), 1916,* margins, rubbing, crease, nick, tape, skinning, stain, lesser defects, very good cond., prov., est. BP 15/20,000, (05-20-93, Christie-London, #457, illus.), image 13⁹⁄₁₆ x 17³⁄₁₆ in., (34.4 x 43.7 cm.), sheet 16¼ x 22¹⁵⁄₁₆ in., (34.4 x 43.7 cm.), woodcut on firm wove w/ impressed stamp.

$24,011* *Bauerntanz (Dube 432), 1920,* s., (06-10-93, Hauswedell/ Nolt, #463, illus.), image 21⅞ x 16¹⁵⁄₁₆ in., (55.5 x 43 cm.), woodcut on Blotting (BP 15,706, DM 39,099, FR 131,639, Y 2,548,668).

$7093* *Der Berliner Strasse, Dresden (Dube 67), 1905,* i., s., (06-05-93, Bassenge, #6178, illus.), 4¹⁵⁄₁₆ x 7 in., (12.6 x 17.8 cm.), woodcut on Japan (BP 4669, DM 11,500, FR 38,760, Y 760,888).

$660* *Bildnis Carl Sternheims (D. 328, Sch. 291), 1916,* num. 3/75, pub. in Der Bilderman, margins, good cond., surface soiling, (02-24-93, Butterfield, #2945), 12⅛ x 8¼ in., (308 x 210 mm.), lithograph on wove (BP 460, DM 1071, FR 3632, Y 77,447).

$3319* *Bildnis David Muller (Dube H 409/II B, Peters V/6), 1919,* 5. Mappe Bauhaus Drucke, Neue Europaische Graphik, Deutsche Kunstler,Weimar, 1921, (12-01-92, Karl/Faber, #829, illus.), 13⅜ x 11⁷⁄₁₆ in., (34 x 29 cm.), woodcut on cardboard (BP 2193, DM 5290, FR 18,028, Y 413,222).

$901* *Bildnis Eines Jungen Mannes, Dr. Hans Butow, 1925,* s., (11-13-92, Koller, #5358), 11¹⁵⁄₁₆ x 9¹³⁄₁₆ in., (30.3 x 25 cm.), etching on wove (BP 582, DM 1414, FR 4770, Y 111,828, SF 1276).

$63,735* *"Bildnis Willem Van Vloten" (Dube 329), 1918,* mono., i. artist's proof, ded., (06-04-93, Grisebach, #26, illus.), 22½ x 10¾ in., (57.2 x 27.3 cm.), woodcut on light brown copper print paper (BP 42,167, DM 103,500, FR 348,851, Y 6,873,921).

$125,539* *Brucke Mappe 1910 - V. Mappe, Ernst Ludwig Kirchner, 1909-1910,* (06-25-93, Kornfeld, #22, illus.), portfolio 16⁹⁄₁₆ x 21¾ in., (42 x 55.2 cm.), 1 woodcut, 1 color woodcut, 1 drypoint, on thick wove (BP 84,910, DM 213,720, FR 719,834, Y 13,307,081, SF 189,750).

BI *Brustewaschendes Madchen (Dube L100), 1909,* margins, backed tear, associated tape-stain, creasing, other minor defects, prov., est. BP 14/18,000, (05-20-93, Christie-London, #454, illus.), image 13 x 16 in., (33 x 40.6 cm.), sheet 16½ x 20¾ in., (33 x 40.6 cm.), lithograph on smooth wove.

$31,955* *Dame Im Regen (Dube 248), 1914,* s. E.L. Kirchner, (06-25-93, Kornfeld, #66, illus.), image 16⅝ x 12⅜ in., (42.3 x 31.4 cm.), lithograph on thick vellum (BP 21,613, DM 54,401, FR 183,228, Y 3,387,216, SF 48,300).

$1680* *David Muller (Dube 409/II/B), 1919,* stamped sig., (06-23-93, Kornfeld, #443), woodcut on brown wove (BP 1141, DM 2843, FR 9562, Y 183,026, SF 2530).

$5660* *David Muller (Sch. 397; D. 409), 1919,* 1st state of 2, s., i., abrasion, glue-staining, rubbing, (12-01-92, Christie-London, #401), L. 13⅜ x 11⁹⁄₁₆ in., (339 x 293 mm.), sheet 15½ x 13⅜ in., (339 x 293 mm.), woodcut on Japan (BP 3740, DM 9021, FR 30,744, Y 704,681).

$6384* *Drei Badende An Den Moritzburger Seen (Dube 69), 1905,* s., V. Jahresmappe der Kunstlergruppe Brucke 1910, (06-05-93, Bassenge, #6180, illus.), 7¹⁄₁₆ x 8¹⁄₁₆ in., (17.9 x 20.4 cm.), drypoint on thick paper (BP 4202, DM 10,350, FR 34,885, Y 684,832).

$22,144* *Eingang Zum Sertig Im Winter, Mit Holzschlitten Und Der KnochenmuhleD. 570), 1926,* s., (06-23-93, Kornfeld, #444), woodcut on cream wove (BP 15,043, DM 37,469, FR 126,033, Y 2,412,463, SF 33,350).

$5968* *Fanny Wocke (Dube 275), 1916,* s., ded., i. margins, fairly good cond. within subject, damages, (12-03-92, Sotheby-London, #354, illus.), 11¾ x 15¾ in., (298 x 400 mm.), woodcut on soft wove (BP 3850, DM 9385, FR 32,034, Y 742,566).

$36,520* *Franzi, Stehend, Mit Langem Haar (Dube 172), 1910,* s. E.L. Kirchner, (06-25-93, Kornfeld, #64, illus.), sheet size 23⁷⁄₁₆ x 19¹³⁄₁₆ in., (59.6 x 50.3 cm.), lithograph on thick vellum (BP 24,701, DM 62,172, FR 209,404, Y 3,871,105, SF 55,200).

BI *Frau Julow (D. 219), 1916,* margins, good cond. within subject, tears, defects, est. BP 2,0/3,000, (12-03-92, Sotheby-London, #355, illus.), 10 x 8 in., (254 x 203 mm.), etching w/drypoint on wove.

$1373* *Frau Julow (Dube 219), 1916,* margins, good cond., w/in subject, tears, defects, (06-30-93, Sotheby-London, #473, illus.), 10 x 8 in., (254 x 203 mm.), etching w/drypoint on wove (BP 920, DM 2342, FR 7900, Y 147,112).

$4950* *Gewecke Und Erna (Dube 169), 1913,* i. by artist's wife, wide margins, scrapes, soiling, folds, i., goodcond., (11-05-92, Sotheby-NY, #207, illus.), 10 x 8⅛ in., (253 x 205 mm.), drypoint on thick wove (BP 3220, DM 7829, FR 26,485, Y 607,287).

$16,649* *Hugo Nach Dem Bade (Sch. 246; D. 279), 1915,* s., i. Handdruck, margins, repaired tears, crease, surface dirt, Chine-backed, (12-01-92, Christie-London, #399, illus.), L. 20¹⁄₁₆ x 23⁷⁄₁₆ in., (510 x 596 mm.), sheet 21¾ x 26⅝ in., (510 x 596 mm.), lithograph on wove (BP 11,000, DM 26,536, FR 90,435, Y 2,072,834).

BI *Josua Und Priska (Dube 823), c. 1922,* est. DM 400-, (09-25-92, Granier, #2909), sheet 3¹⁵⁄₁₆ x 5⅛ in., (10 x 13 cm.), woodcut on holzhaltigem factory print paper.

BI *Kopf Eines Jungen Mannes, Dr. Hannes Bulow (Dube R 532.II.B), 1925,* #109/(130), s., est. SF 1,5/1,800, (09-04-92, Germann, #71, illus.), 18⅞ x 13³⁄₁₆ in., (480 x 335 mm.), etching.

$1599* *Kopf Eines Junges Mannes (Dr. Hans Butow) (Dube 532), 1925,* s., full margins, good cond., minor creasing and rubbing in margins,Late Gerhard Brauer Coll., (05-27-93, Sotheby-Amstrdm, #740, illus.), 11⅞ x 9¾ in., drypoint w/tone on Japan (BP 1024, DM 2566, FR 8648, Y 171,419, G 2875).

$48,694* *Leipziger Strasse, Kreuzung (Dube 250/III), 1914,* estate stamp, artist's proof by Reiter im Grunewald, 1914 verso, light staining, (06-25-93, Kornfeld, #67, illus.), image 23⁷⁄₁₆ x 19¹⁵⁄₁₆ in., (59.5 x 50.6 cm.), lithograph on yellow paper (BP 32,935, DM 82,898, FR 279,209, Y 5,161,543, SF 73,600).

$32,455* *Leuchttrmzimmer (Dube 162 II), 1912,* s., (12-05-92, Bassenge, #7324, illus.), 9¹³⁄₁₆ x 8¹⁄₁₆ in., (25 x 20.5 cm.), drypoint and etching on copper print paper (BP 20,322, DM 50,600, FR 172,450, Y 4,021,187).

$10,690* *Liegende Frau Auf Teppich (Dube 286), 1919,* sig. stamp, (06-23-93, Kornfeld, #445, illus.), etching on thick wove (BP 7262, DM 18,088, FR 60,842, Y 1,164,615, SF 16,100).

BI *Madchen Mit Hut (Dube 61), 1908,* Erna Kirchner s., est. DM 26,000, (05-26-93, Lempertz, #251, illus.), 17⅜ x 21⁷⁄₁₆ in., (44.2 x 54.5 cm.), lithograph on Losch.

$11,654* *Milchmadchen (Sch. 425 II; D. 439 II), 1921,* 2nd (final) state, stamped sig., margins, creases, stain, very good cond., (12-01-92, Christie-London, #403, illus.), L. 24⅞ x 15⁹⁄₁₆ in., (632 x 395 mm.), sheet 25¹⁄₁₆ x 17¹⁄₁₆ in., (632 x 395 mm.), woodcut on soft, fibrous Japan (BP 7700, DM 18,575, FR 63,303, Y 1,450,946).

$2825* *Nackte Frau Am Fenster (Dube 147), 1912,* plate mono., estate stamp, num., 1970, (06-10-93, Hauswedell/Nolt, #455, illus.), image 6¼ x 4⅝ in., (15.9 x 11.8 cm.), drypoint on wove (BP 1848, DM 4600, FR 15,488, Y 299,862).

BI *Nackttanzerin (Dube 413 II), 1920,* est. DM 50,00, (05-26-93, Lempertz, #253, illus.), 25⅝ x 21⁹⁄₁₆ in., (65.1 x 54.7 cm.), lithograph on thin Japan.

$7062* *Portrait Frau Bluth (Dube 330 a I), 1916,* Basler estate stamp, (06-10-93, Hauswedell/Nolt, #461, illus.), image 16⅝ x 12⅜ in., (42.3 x 31.5 cm.), lithograph on wove (BP 4619, DM 11,500, FR 38,717, Y 749,602).

$10,750* *Portrat Alex (Schiefler 97; Dube H125), 1908,* margins, good cond., prov., (05-20-93, Christie-London, #453, illus.), image 19¼ x 13⅜ in., (48.9 x 34 cm.), sheet 23 x 16⅛ in., (48.9 x 34 cm.), woodcut on crisp Japan w/ wirelines (BP 6900, DM 17,344, FR 58,424, Y 1,187,058).

BI *Portrat Dr.Redslob (Dube R. 500 II), 1924,* s., i., est. DM 15,000, (06-05-93, Bassenge, #6182), 11¹³⁄₁₆ x 9¾ in., drypoint on thick board.

$28,667* *Sandberge (Schiefler 333; Dube H384), 1918,* recorded as unique by Schiefler, illus. by Dube, s. w/in subject, margins, re-attached patch, repaired tears, one extending into subject, short tears, creases, lesser defects, corners made-up, surface skinning, removal of tape, foxing, discoloration, #KFH 41, (05-20-93, Christie-London, #459, illus.), image 15¼ x 19 in., (38.7 x 48.3 cm.), sheet 16⅛ x 20¹¹⁄₁₆ in., (38.7 x 48.3 cm.), woodcut w/extensive hand-coloring in various washes of pink, blue, green, orange, yellow and red on soft wove blotting (BP 18,400, DM 46,252, FR 155,799, Y 3,165,526).

$3050* *Sandkarrer An Der Elbe (Dube 19), 1904,* (06-05-93, Bassenge, #6177, illus.), 3⁹⁄₁₆ x 5⅛ in., (9 x 13 cm.), woodcut on hand-made Japan (BP 2008, DM 4945, FR 16,667, Y 327,183).

BI *Schlankes Madchen Vor Offener Zimmertur (Edith Spengler) (Schiefler 290; Dube H304 III), 1917,* third (final) state, s., margins, laid, good cond., est. BP 7/9,000, (05-20-93, Christie-London, #458, illus.), image 13¼ x 10¼ in., (33.7 x 26 cm.), sheet 18¾ x 13¼ in., (33.7 x 26 cm.), woodcut on tan wove.

$54,780* *Segelboote Bei Fehmarn (Dube 243/a/I/II), 1914,* s. E.L. Kirchner, (06-25-93, Kornfeld, #65, illus.), image 16⁹⁄₁₆ x 15¹³⁄₁₆ in., (42 x 40.2 cm.), etching on blotting paper (BP 37,051, DM 93,258, FR 314,106, Y 5,806,657, SF 82,800).

$95,339* *Selbstbildnis (Zeichnend) (Dube 218 II), 1916,* artist's proof, prov., (06-10-93, Hauswedel/Nolt, #458, illus.), etching (BP 62,362, DM 155,250, FR 522,692, Y 10,119,839).

$53,259* *Selbstbildnis Mit Nacktem Madchen (Dube 275/I), 1915,* s. E.L. Kirchner, estate stamp, tears, (06-25-93, Kornfeld, #68, illus.), image 23⁷⁄₁₆ x 19¹⁵⁄₁₆ in., (59.6 x 50.6 cm.), lithograph on yellow paper (BP 36,022, DM 90,669, FR 305,384, Y 5,645,431, SF 80,500).

$2291* *Sitzende Bauerin (D. 410/III), 1922,* s. in ink, (06-23-93, Kornfeld, #447), drypoint on thick wove (BP 1556, DM 3876, FR 13,039, Y 249,591, SF 3450).

$2420* *Soldat Zu Hause, Schiefler 301; Dube 319,* s.; bears estate stamp verso (Lugt 1570 b.), i., stamp UnverkauflichE.L. Kirchner, (09-20-92, Hindman, #760, illus.), 6¾ x 8¼ in., (17.1 x 21 cm.), lithograph on smooth wove (BP 1417, DM 3591, FR 12,284, Y 299,098).

$8475* *Spielende Kinder Mit Begleiterinnen Im Grossen Garten (Dube 112), 1910,* s., Basler estate stamp, (06-10-93, Hauswedell/Nolt, #454, illus.), image 9¾ x 7¹³⁄₁₆ in., (24.8 x 19.9 cm.), drypoint on thick board (BP 5544, DM 13,801, FR 46,464, Y 899,586).

$25,108* *Stilleben Mit Krug Und Blumen (Dube 112), 1907,* s. and d. in pencil E.L. Kirchner 07, (06-25-93, Kornfeld, #20, illus.), image 7⅞ x 6⅝ in., (20 x 16.8 cm.), sheet size 12¹⁄₁₆ x 10¹⁄₁₆ in., (20 x 16.8 cm.), color woodcut (BP 16,982, DM 42,744, FR 143,968, Y 2,661,437, SF 37,950).

$853* *Strassenecke (Dube 66), 1905,* block mono., (09-25-92, Granier, #2908, illus.), sheet 8¹¹⁄₁₆ x 10¼ in., (22 x 26 cm.), woodcut on beige hand-made (BP 498, DM 1264, FR 4276, Y 102,957).

$60,606* *Strassenszene, Am Schaufenster (Schiefler 225; Dube H238), 1914,* s., i. Eigendruck, wide margins, repaired creases, tears, smaller repirs, other minor defects, prov., (05-20-93, Christie-London, #455, illus.), image 12½ x 9 in., (31.8 x 22.9 cm.), sheet 20½ x 15½ in., (31.8 x 22.9 cm.), woodcut on firm wove (BP 38,900, DM 97,783, FR 329,380, Y 6,692,359).

$851* *Der Tanz Zwischen Den Frauen (Dube 289 V), 1919,* (06-05-93, Bassenge, #6181), 6¹⁄₁₆ x 3⅜ in., (15.4 x 8.6 cm.), etching on Japan (BP 560, DM 1380, FR 4650, Y 91,289).

$8800* *Traumendes Madchen (D. 341), 1918,* third final state, full margins, touches of India ink, faded, creases, thin spots, estate stamp, (11-05-92, Sotheby-NY, #208, illus.), 15½ x 12¼ in., (393 x 310 mm.), woodcut on Japan (BP 5724, DM 13,917, FR 47,084, Y 1,079,622).

$23,305* *Traumendes Madchen (Dube 341 III), 1918,* s., Basler estate stamp, (06-10-93, Hauswedell/Nolt, #462, illus.), image 15½ x 12⅜ in., (39.3 x 31.5 cm.), woodcut on thick wove (BP 15,244, DM 37,950, FR 127,769, Y 2,473,729).

$34,999* *Van De Velde Als Architekt (Dube 311), 1917,* s. E.L. Kirchner, (06-25-93, Kornfeld, #69, illus.), 19¹¹⁄₁₆ x 15⅞ in., etching on blotting paper (BP 23,672, DM 59,583, FR 200,682, Y 3,709,879, SF 52,900).

$16,738* *Windmuhle Auf Fehmarn (Dube 48), 1908,* s. E.L. Kirchner, estate stamp, (06-25-93, Kornfeld, #63, illus.), plate 8⁹⁄₁₆ x 10¹⁵⁄₁₆ in., (21.8 x 27.8 cm.), etching on thick copper print paper (BP 11,321, DM 28,495, FR 95,975, Y 1,774,221, SF 25,300).

$53,751* *Zwei Akte Am Fenster (Schiefler 248; Dube 264), 1915,* s., i. Handdruck, margins, short tears, backed tape, creasing, old tape, excell. cond., prov., (05-20-93, Christie-London, #456, illus.), image 23½ x 20 in., (59.7 x 50.8 cm.), sheet 26 x 23⁹⁄₁₆ in., (59.7 x 50.8 cm.), lithograph on brilliant, unfaded, canary-yellow wove (BP 34,500, DM 86,723, FR 292,125, Y 5,935,402).

$5650* *Zwei Manner Im Bade (Botho Graf Und Hugo Biallowons In Jena) (Dube 201), 1915,* s., prov., (06-10-93, Hauswedell/Nolt, #457, illus.), image 9¾ x 7⁷⁄₁₆ in., (24.7 x 18.9 cm.), etching on copper print board (BP 3696, DM 9200, FR 30,976, Y 599,724).

BI *"Zwei Schnitter" (Dube R 585), 1928,* s., i., artist's proof, estate stamp, est. DM 7/8,000, (06-05-93, Grisebach, #278, illus.), 9¹⁵⁄₁₆ x 7½ in., (25.2 x 19 cm.), drypoint etching on chalked board.

BI *Zwei Schwestern (Sch. 26; D. 16), 1907,* s., margins, nicks, surface creases, foxmarks, prov., est. BP 10/15,000, (12-01-92, Christie-London, #400, illus.), plate 15⁹⁄₁₆ x 12³⁄₁₆ in., (396 x 310 mm.), sheet 17½ x 14³⁄₁₆ in., (396 x 310 mm.), etching w/aquatint in green-grey on thick wove.

KIRK, Eve 1900-1969

$445* *Everywhere You Go, The Liffey, Dublin, 1939,* p. Waterlow and Sons, ref. #546, cond. 1, foxing, (10-13-92, Phillips-London, #160), 29¾ x 44⅞ in., (75.5 x 114 cm.), color lithograph (BP 259, DM 652, FR 2215, Y 53,959).

KIRKALL, Elisha

$12,011* *Sea Pieces (Le Blanc 87-100), c. 1720: Fourteen,* 13 plates after William van de Velde and one after A. Vandiest, margins, surface dirt, staining, creases, very good cond., (06-30-93, Sotheby-London, #267), 17¾ x 12½ in., (451 x 318 mm.), mezzotint in green, some on paper w/a Dovecote watermark, and BCR w/Stars and Crescent watermark, etc. (BP 8050, DM 20,486, FR 69,108, Y 1,286,939).

KIRKEBY, Per Danish b. 1938

$316* *Composition (Hunov 57), 1980,* s. Per Kirkeby 80, E.A., (09-30-92, Kunsthallen, #176), color lithograph (BP 178, DM 448, FR 1516, Y 37,922, DK 1725).

BI *Composition (Hunov 58), 1981,* s. P.K. 81, est. DK 5,000, (09-30-92, Kunsthallen, #167), color lithograph.

$211* *Composition, 1984,* s. P.K. 84, 41/150, (09-30-92, Kunsthallen, #178), color lithograph (BP 119, DM 299, FR 1012, Y 25,321, DK 1150).

$990* *Composition, 1991,* s. P.K. 91, 42/100, (09-30-92, Kunsthallen, #172), color lithograph (BP 559, DM 1404, FR 4748, Y 118,805, DK 5405).

$312* *Engelbarnet; "Rebecca Med Turban", "Rebecca", "Prins Valiant", and "Engelbarnet, (Hunov 4-7): Four,* s. Per Kirkby 1970, 84/100, (03-24-93, Kunsthallen, #208), offset print in colors (BP 211, DM 510, FR 1734, Y 36,658, DK 1955).

$239* *Eurasphalt, 1984,* s. P.K.84, 92/120, (03-24-93, Kunsthallen, #205), color lithograph (BP 162, DM 390, FR 1329, Y 28,081, DK 1495).

$419* *Fem Kompositioner: Five,* all s. PK 84, (09-29-92, B. Rasmussen, #337), lithograph in colors (BP 236, DM 592, FR 2019, Y 50,018, DK 2300).

BI *Komposition, (Hunov 58), 1981,* s. P.K.81, est. DK 5,000, (03-24-93, Kunsthallen, #203), color lithograph.

$128* *Kompositioner: Two,* s. P.K. and P.K. 90, (03-24-93, Kunsthallen, #210), poster, offset in colors (BP 87, DM 209, FR 712, Y 15,039, DK 805).

$463* *Morgen Stilleben (Hunov 38), 1980,* s. Per Kirkeby 80, 83/100, (09-30-92, Kunsthallen, #169), color lithograph (BP 261, DM 657, FR 2221, Y 55,562, DK 2530).

BI *Per Kirkeby Skulpturer, 1985,* s. P.K.85, 22/50, est. DK 6,000, (03-24-93, Kunsthallen, #206), poster, offset in colors.

$734* *Rebecca Herbarium, (Hunov 19-23), 1975,* s. Per Kirkeby 75, 71/100, (03-24-93, Kunsthallen, #207), portfolio, offset prints in colors (BP 497, DM 1199, FR 4080, Y 86,241, DK 4600).

$1652* *Seks Kompositioner, 1980,* s. Per Kirkeby 80, 2/25, (03-24-93, Kunsthallen, #204), color woodcut (BP 1119, DM 2698, FR 9183, Y 194,102, DK 10,350).

$539* *Untitled, 1987,* init., d., #1/7, full margins, minor creasing, (10-15-92, Sotheby-London, #105, illus.), 31 x 46⅞ in., (78.7 x 119.1 cm.), etching p. in colours on wove (BP 330, DM 802, FR 2721, Y 64,667).

KIRMSE, Marguerite Anglo/American 1885-1954

$303* *Birds Ahead,* margins, s. Marguerite Kirmse, (02-13-93, Collins, #128, illus.), 5⅞ x 9¼ in., (14.9 x 23.5 cm.), etching (BP 213, DM 502, FR 1700, Y 36,541).

$110* *"Good Boy",* w/remarque, s., t., below image, (08-05-92, Boos, #688), 8¹⁄₁₆ x 5¹¹⁄₁₆ in., (205 x 145 mm.), etching (BP 58, DM 162, FR 549, Y 14,009).

$330* *Style,* first state, margins, s. Marguerite Kirmse, (02-13-93, Collins, #132, illus.), 7⅞ x 10 in., (20 x 25.4 cm.), etching (BP 232, DM 547, FR 1852, Y 39,797).

$55* *Vigilants,* margins, s. Marguerite Kirmse, t., (10-24-92, Collins, #15), 10½ x 7½ in., (26.7 x 19.1 cm.), etching (BP 34, DM 84, FR 285, Y 6707).

$303* *We,* margins, s. Marguerite Kirmse, t., (10-24-92, Collins, #14), 8¼ x 5¾ in., (21 x 14.6 cm.), etching (BP 187, DM 463, FR 1571, Y 36,951).

$275* *When We Were Very Young,* margins, s. Marguerite Kirmse, t., (10-24-92, Collins, #13, illus.), 5¾ x 8¼ in., (14.6 x 21 cm.), etching (BP 170, DM 420, FR 1426, Y 33,537).

KISLING, Moise Polish/French 1891-1953

$277* *Head And Shoulder Study Of A Young Woman With Long Hair,* artist's proof, s., i., margins, stained, (08-20-92, Bonhams-Chelsea, #167), plate 7⅜ x 5⅜ in., (18.7 x 13.7 cm.), etching (BP 143, DM 401, FR 1361, Y 34,979).

$225* *"Paysage Mediterraneen",* dry stamp, #42/150, s. Jean Kisling, (10-18-92, Pescheteau, #173), 22¹⁄₁₆ x 26⅜ in., (56 x 67 cm.), lithograph in colors on Arches (BP 136, DM 332, FR 1129, Y 26,866).

$660* *Young Woman,* s. Kisling, num. 28/100, good cond., soiling, handling creases, (09-11-92, Skinner, #15A, illus.), 16⅝ x 13⅝ in., (42.2 x 34.6 cm.), color etching/aquatint/roulette on wove (BP 341, DM 950, FR 3229, Y 81,774).

KISLING, Moise (after)

$420* *"Bouquet",* #181/250 verso, s. in plate, drystamp, (01-28-93, Pescheteau, #171), 27¹⁵⁄₁₆ x 21¼ in., (71 x 54 cm.), stencil print (BP 277, DM 666, FR 2252, Y 52,148).

KITAGAWA UTAMARO Japanese 1753-1806

$2800* *Iwai Kumesaburo As The Wife Of Shigetada,* Hosoban, s. Toyoaki ga, d. c. An'ei 5 (1776), pub.'s mark Ei ban, trimmed, rubbed, soiled, Prof. H.R.W. Kuhne Coll., (06-11-93, Sotheby-London, #255, illus.), 11⅝ x 5¼ in., (29.5 x 13.3 cm.), woodblock (BP 1840, DM 4551, FR 15,342, Y 297,082).

$787* *Nakayama Tomisaburo As An Onnagata,* Hosoban, s. Utamaro hitsu, d. Kansei 7 (1795), censor's seal kiwame,pub.'s mark Matsumura Tatsuemon, faded, soiled, rubbed, trimmed, restored, Prof. H.R.W. Kuhne Coll., (06-11-93, Sotheby-London, #251), 12¼ x 4½ in., (31.1 x 11.4 cm.), woodblock (BP 517, DM 1279, FR 4312, Y 83,501).

$1925* *"Puppeteers" and "Puppets Of The Lovers Of Umegawa And Chubei": Two,* Oban and aiban, s. Utamaro hitsu, pub. Moriya Jihei, d. late Kansei period, faded, trimmed, rubbed, soiled, wormage, repaired, Prof. H.R.W. Kuhne Coll., (06-11-93, Sotheby-London, #253), one 14½ x 9½ in., (36.8 x 24.1 cm.), other 12 x 8 in., (36.8 x 24.1

cm.), woodblock (BP 1265, DM 3129, FR 10,548, Y 204,244).

$2450* *Seiro Niwaka Ninokawari, Two Geisha In Disguise As Sukeroku And A Pedlar Of Shirozake*, Aiban, benigirai, s. Utamaro hitsu, d. c. 1801, pub. Yamaguchiya Chuemon, creased, tone, soiled, Prof. H.R.W. Kuhne Coll., (06-11-93, Sotheby-London, #256, illus.), 14¼ x 9 in., (36.2 x 22.9 cm.), woodblock (BP 1610, DM 3982, FR 13,425, Y 259,947).

KITAJ, R.B.   American b. 1933

$716* *Bullets Die Gute Alte Zeit (Museum Boymans-Van Beuningen 27B)*, 1972, s., #26/70, margins, scuffs, creasing, good cond., (12-03-92, Sotheby-London, #759, illus.), sheet 40¾ x 26⅝ in., (103.5 x 67.6 cm.), screenprint in colors w/collage (BP 462, DM 1126, FR 3843, Y 89,088).

BI *The Desire For Lunch Is A Bourgeois Obsessional Neurosis*, s., #31/70, good cond.?, est. BP 2/300, (06-30-93, Sotheby-London, #859), 27¾ x 18⅛ in., (705 x 460 mm.), color screenprint.

$128* *For Love, Robert Creeley*, plate t; s., #39/70, pub. Marlborough Graphics, 1966, (12-01-92, Ritchie, #82, illus.), 25½ x 18 in., (64.8 x 45.7 cm.), color serigraph (BP 85, DM 204, FR 695, Y 15,936, C$ 165).

$424* *Glue Words (Schmied 25 I)*, 1967, s., #46/70, series Mahler becomes political, Beisbol, (06-12-93, Hauswedell/Nolt, #270), 31⁵⁄₁₆ x 22¹³⁄₁₆ in., (79.5 x 58 cm.), color serigraph on brown board (BP 278, DM 690, FR 2319, Y 44,617).

$361* *Greetings Pablo Ruiz*, 1973, s., num., (11-28-92, Schoppmann, #615), 29¾ x 20⅞ in., (75.5 x 53 cm.), color serigraph on thick handmade Japan (BP 238, DM 575, FR 1952, Y 44,928).

$193* *Home Towns*, 1967, #44/70, crayon s., good cond., (06-11-93, Freemn/Fine Art, #125), 22¼ x 35¾ in., (56.5 x 90.8 cm.), screenprint (BP 127, DM 314, FR 1058, Y 20,477).

$88* *Kenneth Koch Peasant Print*, 1970, #9/70, s., good cond., (06-11-93, Freemn/Fine Art, #124), 36⅞ x 24½ in., (93.7 x 62.2 cm.), screenprint (BP 58, DM 143, FR 482, Y 9337).

$600* *Moderne Illustrat*, s., #5/75, full margins, good cond., discoloration, (06-30-93, Sotheby-London, #858), 23⅝ x 37⅜ in., (600 x 949 mm.), color screenprint on wove (BP 402, DM 1023, FR 3452, Y 64,288).

$325* *Performing Arts Center*, 1983, s., num., (11-28-92, Schoppmann, #616), 29½ x 22¹⁄₁₆ in., (75 x 56 cm.), color serigraph on Arches wove (BP 215, DM 518, FR 1758, Y 40,448).

$505* *Photographie (Greetings Pablo Ruiz)*, num. HC, pencil s., (11-20-92, Lempertz, #644), 29¹⁵⁄₁₆ x 21¹⁄₁₆ in., (76 x 53.5 cm.), serigraph in color on Japan (BP 332, DM 805, FR 2712, Y 62,803).

BI *"Photographie. Greetings To Pablo Ruiz"*, 1973, s., num., 2nd sheet from the series Hommage a Picasso, Propylaen Verlag, 1973, est. DM 800, (12-01-92, Karl/Faber, #832), 29¾ x 20⅞ in., (75.5 x 53 cm.), color serigraph on Japan.

BI *Sou-Wester*, s., num. 11/20, very good cond., est. BP 1/200, (11-30-92, Phillips-London, #542), sheet 18⅛ x 22¼ in., (460 x 565 mm.), silkscreen & lithograph on pink wove.

$356* *"Star Betelgeuse, Robert Duncan" and "Deerskin, John Weiner": Two*, s. 12/70, (09-29-92, B. Rasmussen, #338), photoserigraph (BP 200, DM 503, FR 1716, Y 42,497, DK 1955).

KITAO SHIGEMASA   Japanese 1739-1820

$3151* *(Shibai Fuzoku) Ehon Sakaegusa "Theatre Life, A Picture Book Of Three Theatres Prosperity", 3 Vols.*, engraver Nakamura Ryosuke, pub. Yamazaki Kinbei, Edo, 1771, soiled, stained, rubbed, lit., Prof. H.R.W. Kuhne Coll., (06-11-93, Sotheby-London, #516, illus.), 9 x 6⅜ in., (22.9 x 16.2 cm.), woodblock (BP 2070, DM 5121, FR 17,266, Y 334,324).

KITO, Akira   Japanese 20th century

$60* *Les Enfants*, s. stone, pub. Mourlot, (02-04-93, Sloan, #905), sight 10 x 7⅜ in., (25.4 x 18.7 cm.), color lithograph (BP 42, DM 99, FR 335, Y 7464).

KIYANAGA, Torii

$50* *"Three Women Enjoying Cool Evening Breeze By The Kamo River"*, block s., (01-15-93, DuMouchelle, #2301, illus.), 15½ x 10¼ in., (39.4 x 26 cm.), color woodblock print (BP 33, DM 82, FR 276, Y 6304).

KIYOCHIKA, Kobayaski

BI *"100 Battles, 100 Laughs"*, block s., est. $150/200, (01-15-93, DuMouchelle, #2303, illus.), 13¾ x 9⅜ in., (34.9 x 23.8 cm.), color woodblock print.

KIYOMASA, Torii   ac. 1690-1720

BI *Bildnis Eines Schauspielers In Einer Frauenrolle*, est. SC 5/6,000, (04-27-93, Dorotheum, #241), 6⁷⁄₁₆ x 13⁵⁄₁₆ in., (16.3 x 33.8 cm.), color woodcut.

KIYONAGA

$3868* *Princess Nyosan-No-Miya*, oban tate-e, collector's mark; Henri Vever, s. Kiyonaga ga, soiled, rubbed, laid-down, (06-10-93, Sotheby-London, #226, illus.), (BP 2530, DM 6299, FR 21,206, Y 410,572).

KLACKNET, C., Publisher

$43* *A Woman In A Wooded River Landscape*, 1892, foxed, (08-20-92, Bonhams-Chelsea, #64), image 19½ x 29¾ in., (49.5 x 75.6 cm.), etching (BP 22, DM 62, FR 211, Y 5430).

KLAPHECK, Konrad   German b. 1935

$415* *Sportschuh*, s., num., traces of old mounting, (12-01-92, Karl/Faber, #833), 11¼ x 13¾ in., (28.5 x 35 cm.), lithograph on wove (BP 274, DM 661, FR 2254, Y 51,668).

KLAPHEK, Konrad

$257* *"Patience" and "Question Du Sphynx"*, 1984 and 1985, s., #3/120 and 50/100, full margins, good cond., (06-30-93, Sotheby-London, #860, illus.), one 4¾ x 4 in., (121 x 102 mm.), the other 25¾ x 24⅜ in., (121 x 102 mm.), etching and lithograph in color on wove (BP 172, DM 438, FR 1479, Y 27,537).

KLASEN, Peter

$200* *"Age-Lock"*, #21/100, d., s., (04-04-93, Pescheteau, #229), 29¾ x 22¹⁄₁₆ in., (75.5 x 56 cm.), photolithograph on wove (BP 132, DM 321, FR 1092, Y 22,771).

$97* *Femme Et Interrupteur*, s., 50/200, (06-28-93, Loudmer, #62), 19⅛ x 25 in., (485 x 635 mm.), sh 19¹¹⁄₁₆ x 25⁹⁄₁₆ in., (485 x 635 mm.), offset color serigraph on papier glace (BP 65, DM 165, FR 555, Y 10,292).

KLASEN, Peter   b. 1935

$263* *Bache De Camion Z 87*, 1986, artist proof, s., (05-27-93, Briest, #116), 43¹¹⁄₁₆ x 31⅛ in., (111 x 79 cm.), color serigraph (BP 168, DM 422, FR 1422, Y 28,195).

$112* *"Serrure De Camion"*, #71/99, s., (10-18-92, Pescheteau, #174), 19¹¹⁄₁₆ x 27⁹⁄₁₆ in., (50 x 70 cm.), photolithograph on Fabriano (BP 68, DM 165, FR 562, Y 13,373).

$210* *Z 87*, 1986, epreuve d'artiste, s., ed. Agence Cintas, (11-16-92, Briest, #65), 43¹¹⁄₁₆ x 31⅛ in., (111 x 79 cm.), serigraph in colors (BP 138, DM 335, FR 1128, Y 26,207).

KLAUBER, Catharina   German 18th cent.

$158* *"Spes Jobi"*, (02-03-93, Duran, #39), 23¼ x 30¹¹⁄₁₆ in., (59 x 78 cm.), engraving (BP 110, DM 260, FR 882, Y 19,654, P 18,400).

KLAUKE, Jurgen   German b. 1943

$683* *Ohne Titel, 1972/73: Two*, s., d., #2/50, from portfolio "Selfperformance", edit. der Galerie Kochs, (11-12-92, Lempertz, #125, illus.), each 22⁷⁄₁₆ x 16⁹⁄₁₆ in., (57 x 42 cm.), photograph, gelatin silver print (BP 437, DM 1073, FR 3658, Y 84,498).

$115* *Schuhe*, 1974, s., d., num., (11-28-92, Schoppmann, #619), 15³⁄₁₆ x 19⁵⁄₁₆ in., (38.5 x 49 cm.), etching on wove (BP 76, DM 183, FR 622, Y 14,312).

KLAUKE, Jurgen and Stefan WEWERKA   20th cent.

$197* *Kopfe*, s., d. St. Wewerka 76 and J. Klauke 76, #71/115, (03-24-93, Venator/Hansten, #4510), pl. 25³⁄₁₆ x 19¼ in., (64 x 48.9 cm.), watercolor etching (BP 133, DM 322, FR 1095, Y 23,147).

KLEE, Paul Swiss 1879-1940

BI *Ausloeshendes Licht, 1919,* s. in plate, est. FF 2,5/2,800, (11-16-92, Briest, #320), 10⅞ x 8½ in., (27.7 x 21.6 cm.), drypoint.

BI *Blick Auf Einen Fluss (Kornfeld 42 B a), 1912,* s., d., t., num. 2, pub. Delphin, est. DM 10,000, (06-10-93, Hauswedell/Nolt, #465, illus.), image 7⅞ x 11¼ in., (20 x 28.5 cm.), lithograph on thick wove.

$4300* *Die Erhabene Seite (Postkarte Fur Die Bauhaus-Austellung Weimer 1923) (Kornfeld 88 IIIb), 1923,* third (final) state, narrow margins, colors somewhat attenuated, staining, tape, lesser defects, postcard text verso, (05-20-93, Christie-London, #462, illus.), image 5½ x 2⅞ in., (14 x 7.3 cm.), sheet 5⅞ x 4⅛ in., (14 x 7.3 cm.), lithograph in colors on wove (BP 2760, DM 6938, FR 23,370, Y 474,823).

$3666* *Esel (Kornfeld 7), 1925,* s., t., i. init., reduced margins, image in good cond., stains, creasing, (12-03-92, Sotheby-London, #356, illus.), sheet 10⅞ x 7½ in., (276 x 191 mm.), lithograph on simili-Japan (BP 2365, DM 5765, FR 19,678, Y 456,140).

BI *Die Heilige Vom Innern Licht (Kornfeld 81 II c), 1921,* s., pub. in Bauhuas-Drucke. Neue europaische Graphik. Erste Mappe. Mester des Staatlichen Bauhauses in Weimar, est. DM 35,000, (12-05-92, Bassenge, #7325, illus.), 12³⁄₁₆ x 6⅞ in., (31 x 17.5 cm.), color lithograph on thick wove.

BI *Die Hexe Mit Dem Kamm (K. 86 Bb), 1922,* s., pub. Kunstlerspende fur das Deutsche Buchmuseum, stains, excellent cond., est. BP 10/12,000, (12-01-92, Christie-London, #405, illus.), L. 12³⁄₁₆ x 8⅜ in., (310 x 213 mm.), lithograph on yellowish simili-Japan.

BI *Die Hexe Mit Dem Kamm (Kornfeld 86 Bb), 1922,* s., pub. Kunstlerspende fur das Deutche Buchmuseum, wide margins, foxing, creasing, mat staining, tape, taped to overmat w/masking tape, est. $12/15,000, (05-11-93, Christie-NY, #202, illus.), borderline 12¼ x 8⅜ in., (311 x 213 mm.), lithograph on smooth cream wove.

BI *Die Hexe Mit Dem Kamm (Kornfeld 86 Bb), 1922,* s., pub. in Kunstlerspende fur das Deutsche Buchmuseum, full margins, light/mat staining, very good cond., est. $20/25,000, (11-09-92, Christie-NY, #105, illus.), 311 x 212 in., (789.9 x 538.5 cm.), lithograph on smooth, cream wove.

$6109* *Insekten (Kornfeld 74/B, Werkverzeichnis), 1919,* blindstamp, (06-23-93, Kornfeld, #451), color lithograph on handmade (BP 4150, DM 10,337, FR 34,769, Y 665,541, SF 9200).

$6900* *Kleinwelt (Kornfeld 61 A/a), 1914,* s., t., d., i., full margins, good cond., soiling, crease through upper image, other creases, rubbing, (02-11-93, Sotheby-NY, #154, illus.), 5¹¹⁄₁₆ x 3¾ in., (144 x 95 mm.), etching on Japan (BP 4869, DM 11,430, FR 38,677, Y 831,826).

$10,459* *Kleinwelt (Kornfeld 61 B), 1914,* s., t., blindstamp, (11-21-92, Lempertz, #208, illus.), 5¹¹⁄₁₆ x 3¾ in., (14.4 x 9.5 cm.), etching on Japan (BP 6886, DM 16,676, FR 56,171, Y 1,300,709).

$3942* *Kleinwelt (Kornfeld 61 Ba), 1914,* s., t., pub. in Die Schaffenden 1. Jahrgang, 1. Mappe, by P. Westheim, 1919, their blindstamp, foxing, creasing, (05-20-93, Christie-London, #463, illus.), plate 5½ x 3¾ in., (14 x 9.5 cm.), sheet 16½ x 12¾ in., (14 x 9.5 cm.), etching on Japan (BP 2530, DM 6360, FR 21,424, Y 435,292).

BI *Kleinwelt (Kornfeld 61/A/a), 1914,* s., t., d., i. w/#120, proof, full margins, margin previously foldedback, good cond., soiling, creases, rubbing, est. $7/9,000, (11-05-92, Sotheby-NY, #209, illus.), 5⅝ x 3¾ in., (144 x 95 mm.), etching on Japan.

$9775* *Kleinwelt (Kornfeld 61/B/b), 1914,* s., t., pub. Die Schaffenden, pub. Gustav Kiepenhauer Verlag, 1919, full margins, good cond., (05-13-93, Sotheby-NY, #572, illus.), 5⅝ x 3¾ in., (142 x 95 mm.), etching on wove (BP 6417, DM 15,784, FR 53,241, Y 1,091,325).

$1950* *Kopf (E.Kornfeld 1963, Nr.98/Bb), 1925,* s., d., (10-21-92, Dobiaschofsky, #2086, illus.), 17¹⁵⁄₁₆ x 12⅝ in., (45.5 x 32 cm.), lithograph (BP 1210, DM 2951, FR 10,015, Y 237,515, SF 2640).

$15,229* *Laternenfest Bauhaus (Kornfeld 87b), 1922,* very good cond., (05-20-93, Christie-London, #461, illus.), sheet 3½ x 5⅝ in., (8.9 x 14.3 cm.), lithograph w/extensive hand-coloring in red, yellow and grey watercolor on firm wove (BP 9775, DM 24,571, FR 82,766, Y 1,681,648).

$304* *Musique Diurne, 1953,* from "d'art d'aujourd'hui" album, s. in plate, (05-27-93, Briest, #117), 19⁵⁄₁₆ x 25³⁄₁₆ in., (49 x 64 cm.), color serigraph (BP 195, DM 488, FR 1644, Y 32,590).

$19,854* *Rechnender Greis (Kornf. 104/b, Werkverzeichnis 1929.99), 1929,* s., num., (06-23-93, Kornfeld, #452, illus.), etching on Japan (BP 13,488, DM 33,594, FR 112,999, Y 2,162,981, SF 29,900).

$69,997* *Seiltanzer (Kornfeld 95/IV/c; Werkverzeichnis 1923.138), 1923,* s. Klee, oeuvre 1923.138, (06-25-93, Kornfeld, #73, illus.), image 17⁵⁄₁₆ x 10⁹⁄₁₆ in., (44 x 26.8 cm.), sheet 20¼ x 14½ in., (44 x 26.8 cm.), color lithograph on hand-made (BP 47,343, DM 119,164, FR 401,359, Y 7,419,652, SF 105,800).

$9854* *Der Verliebte (Kornfeld 941), 1923,* first state (of three), s., t., i., margins, deckle edge, tape, verygood cond., (05-20-93, Christie-London, #464, illus.), image 10½ x 7½ in., (26.7 x 19.1 cm.), sheet 11½ x 9 in., (26.7 x 19.1 cm.), lithograph on laid paper (BP 6325, DM 15,899, FR 53,554, Y 1,088,118).

$3330* *Vogelkomodie (K. 69 Bb), 1918,* pub. '25 Originallithographien der Munchener Neuen Secession', 1919,margins, light-staining, crease, foxmarks, tape, (12-01-92, Christie-London, #404, illus.), L. 16¾ x 8⁷⁄₁₆ in., (425 x 214 mm.), lithograph on van Gelder (BP 2200, DM 5308, FR 18,088, Y 414,592).

BI *Was Lauft Er (Kornfeld 109d), 1932,* s., pub. Editions Cahiers d'Art, wide margins, discoloration, foxingin margins, tape, good cond., est. BP 7/10,000, (05-20-93, Christie-London, #465, illus.), plate 9¼ x 11¾ in., (23.5 x 29.8 cm.), sheet 12⅝ x 15¾ in., (23.5 x 29.8 cm.), etching on firm wove.

$50,168* *Weib Und Tier-Inv. 1-II Fassung (Kornfeld 13a), 1904,* s., d., i. work #13, proof, wide margins, residual foxing, creasing,good cond., (05-20-93, Christie-London, #460, illus.), plate 7¾ x 9 in., (19.7 x 22.9 cm.), sheet 12½ x 16½ in., (19.7 x 22.9 cm.), etching on firm wove (BP 32,200, DM 80,942, FR 272,652, Y 5,539,753).

$930* *Zahlenbaum-Landschaft (Kornfeld 72 Ia (von II. Sohn HDO 33909-4), 1919,* stein mono., d., werknummer 112, (09-19-92, Wachholtz, #277, illus.), 6¹⁵⁄₁₆ x 5 in., (17.6 x 12.7 cm.), lithograph on wove (BP 544, DM 1380, FR 4721, Y 114,943).

$9023* *"Zerstorung Und Hoffnung" (Kornfeld 68/B Typ AB b), 1916,* discolored, (11-28-92, Grisebach, #231, illus.), 18½ x 12¹⁵⁄₁₆ in., (47 x 33 cm.), handcolored lithograph on handmade Van Gelder Zonen (BP 5956, DM 14,375, FR 48,799, Y 1,122,962).

KLEE, Paul (after)

$88* *Man With Blue Mouth,* num. 34/325, (11-12-92, Freemn/Fine Art, #113), 23 x 17 in., (58.4 x 43.2 cm.), litho in color (BP 58, DM 139, FR 470, Y 10,911).

$2083* *Park (Kornfeld A112), 1914,* s., #93/200, full margins, printing defect, mount stain, (11-30-92, Phillips-London, #441, illus.), sheet 10½ x 7¼ in., (267 x 184 mm.), color lithograph on wove (BP 1375, DM 3318, FR 11,266, Y 259,241).

KLEIBER, Hans American 1887-1967

$77* *"Ducks In Winter",* s., good cond., (10-31-92, Cleveland, #162), 3⅝ x 5⅜ in., (9.2 x 13.7 cm.), etching and aquatint (BP 49, DM 118, FR 402, Y 9538).

$133* *Geese Over The Marshes,* margins, s. Hans Kleiber, (02-13-93, Collins, #55, illus.), 11⅞ x 9¾ in., (30.2 x 24.8 cm.), etching (BP 94, DM 221, FR 746, Y 16,040).

$115* *Grand Teton,* s., t., margins, (06-30-93, Bonhams-Chelsea, #12), plate 12 x 8¾ in., (30.5 x 22.2 cm.), etching (BP 77, DM 196, FR 662, Y 12,322).

$99* *The Plume Hunter,* margins, s. Hans Kleiber, (02-13-93, Collins, #46, illus.), 11⅞ x 8¼ in., (30.2 x 21 cm.), etching (BP 70, DM 164, FR 556, Y 11,939).

$154* *Winter Residents,* margins, s. Hans Kleiber, (02-13-93, Collins, #52, illus.), 7⅞ x 10⅞ in., (20 x 27.6 cm.), etching (BP 108, DM 255, FR 864, Y 18,572).

KLEIN, Astrid   German b. 1951
$1289* *Ohne Titel, 1986: Six,* ink. s., d., (11-12-92, Lempertz, #128, illus.), each 15¹⁵⁄₁₆ x 12 in., (40.6 x 30.5 cm.), photograph, gelatin silver print (BP 824, DM 2026, FR 6904, Y 159,470).
   BI *Ohne Title, 1982,* unique, small tears, lit., est. DM 15,000, (11-12-92, Lempertz, #127, illus.), 101⅜ x 49½ in., (257.5 x 125.8 cm.), photograph, gelatin silver print.

KLEIN, Cesar   B. 1876
   BI *Austellung Cesar Klein, Fritz Gurlitt, c. 1909,* p. von H. Birkholtz, remains of tape staining, minor repaired tears,- est. BP 2/2,500, (05-20-93, Christie-London, #495, illus.), sheet 28½ x 19 in., (72.4 x 48.3 cm.), lithograph in black, red and yellow backed on Japan.

KLEIN, Deborah   b. 1951
   BI *Woman At A Window,* s. Deborah Klein, i., d. '91, #2/30, est. $1/200, (08-11-92, L. Joel, #120G), 3¹⁵⁄₁₆ x 3¹⁵⁄₁₆ in., (10 x 10 cm.), Chine Colle.
   BI *(Woman With Cat),* s. Deborah Klein, d. '89, #13/125, est. $100/150, (08-11-92, L. Joel, #99G), 3¹⁵⁄₁₆ x 3¹⁵⁄₁₆ in., (10 x 10 cm.), color acrylic over woodcut.

KLEIN, Erika Giovanni   1900-1957
$2450* *"Zwolf Original-Linolschnitte", 1933-1935: Twelve,* num., #19/50, stamp, Galerie Pabst, 1986, (05-19-93, Dorotheum, #434, illus.), linocut (BP 1590, DM 3982, FR 13,417, Y 271,228, SC 28,000).

KLEIN, G.
$110* *Comic Hunting Scene,* pub. Ducher and Mathieu, s., num., annot., (05-20-93, Boos, #578), plate 9 x 12½ in., (229 x 318 mm.), color etching and aquatint (BP 71, DM 177, FR 598, Y 12,147).

KLEIN, Johann Adam   1792-1875
$470* *Der Landschaftsmahler Auf Der Reise (Jahn 131 II), 1814,* (12-04-92, Bassenge, #6847), 5½ x 7⁹⁄₁₆ in., (13.9 x 19.2 cm.), etching (BP 301, DM 749, FR 2539, Y 58,677).
$1444* *Die Maler Auf Der Reise (Jahn 234 II), 1819,* (12-04-92, Bassenge, #6848, illus.), 9⅝ x 11¹³⁄₁₆ in., (24.4 x 30 cm.), etching (BP 926, DM 2300, FR 7801, Y 180,275).

KLEIN, William   American b. 1928
$1430* *"Four Heads, New York",* 1951/1981, s., t., d., print d., (11-16-92, Butterfield, #6048, illus.), 12¾ x 9⅝ in., (324.4 x 244.9 mm.), photograph, gelatin silver print (BP 942, DM 2280, FR 7680, Y 177,839).
   BI *"Hamburgers 40 Cents, New York",* 1955, p. 1981, s., t., d., est. $1/1,200, (05-23-93, Butterfield, #3493, illus.), 9 x 13⅜ in., photograph, gelatin silver print.
$690* *"New York", 1956,* Editions du Seuil, pub. in series Album Petite Planete, (05-07-93, Sotheby-London, #283), photograph (BP 437, DM 1091, FR 3676, Y 75,974).
   BI *Portrait 1964. William Klein + His Son + His Paintings, 1964,* s., t., d. by photog. in ink, studio stamp, est. $2/3,000, (10-15-92, Sotheby-NY, #569, illus.), 11¾ x 12 in., (29.8 x 30.5 cm.), photograph, gelatin silver print.

KLEIN, Yves   French 1928-1962
$4611* *Blau-Rosa-Gold, 1961: Two,* in Katalog Yves Klein, Haus Lange, (06-05-93, Schoppmann, #913), 12⅝ x 12⅝ in., (32 x 32 cm.), color serigraph (BP 3035, DM 7476, FR 25,197, Y 494,636).

KLEINHOLZ, Frank   American 20th cent.
$55* *In The Park,* s., t., i. Proof, (11-12-92, Freemn/Fine Art, #114), image 3¾ x 5¼ in., (9.5 x 13.3 cm.), etching (BP 36, DM 87, FR 294, Y 6820).
$110* *"The Readers",* s., t., AAA, (12-11-92, DuMouchelle, #1479, illus.), 6 x 14⅛ in., (15.2 x 35.9 cm.), serigraph (BP 71, DM 173, FR 594, Y 13,612).

KLEINSCHMIDT, Paul   German b. 1883
$439* *Hochzeit, 1923,* s., light-staining, (06-08-93, Karl/Faber, #961), approx. 9⅝ x 11⅝ in., (24.5 x 29.5 cm.), etching on wove (BP 289, DM 712, FR 2399, Y 46,628).

KLEINSHMIDT, Paul
   BI *(Bridge), 1930,* s., d., #2/6, margins, good cond., minor soiling and handling creases, Late Gerhard Brauer Coll., est. Dfl. 5/800, (05-27-93, Sotheby-Amstrdm, #741,

illus.), 9¾ x 7¹³⁄₁₆ in., (248 x 198 mm.), drypoint on laid paper.

KLEMM, Walter   Austrian 1883-1957
   BI *Ducks, c. 1917,* very good/good cond., est. $150/250, (11-21-92, Bakker, #124), image 5¼ x 6¼ in., (13.3 x 15.9 cm.), woodblock print.

KLEMM, Walther   German b. 1883
   BI *Don Quichotte Et Sancho Panza: Two,* one s. W. Klemm, (06-16-93, Encans, #147), one 8⅜ x 5⁷⁄₁₆ in., (21.3 x 13.8 cm.), other 8¹⁄₁₆ x 10⅜ in., (21.3 x 13.8 cm.), engraving.
$470* *"Neuschnee", (19)09,* s., d., foxing, (12-01-92, Karl/Faber, #837), sh 14¹⁵⁄₁₆ x 20¹¹⁄₁₆ in., (38 x 52.5 cm.), woodcut in olive and black on thin Japan (BP 311, DM 749, FR 2553, Y 58,516).
   BI *"Das Paradies", 1920,* s., sheet of the portfolio "Das Paradies", Weimer, Reiher-pub., est.DM 4/500, (11-28-92, Grisebach, #584, illus.), 17¹¹⁄₁₆ x 12⅞ in., (45 x 32.7 cm.), hand-colored lithograph on handmade.
   BI *Tauromachie,* s., crease, est. DM 1,200, (12-01-92, Karl/Faber, #836), 16⁵⁄₁₆ x 12⅜ in., (41.5 x 31.5 cm.), lithograph reworked w/water and chalk on cardboard.

KLEUKENS, Friedrich Wilhelm   1878-1956
$1733* *Hessische Landesausstellung, Darmstadt, 1908,* crease image center, other minor defects, lit., (02-04-93, Christie-S. Ken, #169, illus.), 35 x 24 in., (88.9 x 61 cm.), color lithograph (BP 1210, DM 2854, FR 9676, Y 215,574).

KLIEMANN, Carl Heinz   b. 1924
$516* *Bei Einer Kerze Lesender, c. 1947,* s., (12-05-92, Bassenge, #7326), 5⅞ x 8⅞ in., (14.9 x 22.6 cm.), color woodcut, watercolored on wove (BP 323, DM 804, FR 2742, Y 63,933).
$332* *Bei Einer Kerze Lesender, c. 1947,* s., (12-05-92, Bassenge, #7327), 5⅞ x 8⅞ in., (14.9 x 22.6 cm.), woodcut in red and orange watercolored on wove (BP 208, DM 518, FR 1764, Y 41,135).
$295* *Haus In Der Dammerung (Roters H79),1954,* s., num., (12-05-92, Bassenge, #7328), 21⅝ x 17¹¹⁄₁₆ in., (55 x 45 cm.), color woodcut (BP 185, DM 460, FR 1567, Y 36,551).
$403* *Kahler Baum (Roters H 27), 1947,* s., #VI/X, portfolio 7 color woodcuts, (06-10-93, Hauswedell/Nolt, #470, illus.), image 19½ x 15¾ in., (49.5 x 40 cm.), color woodcut on hand-made Japan (BP 264, DM 656, FR 2209, Y 42,777).
$155* *Sudlandische Stadt Mit Kettenbrucke,* s. C.h. Kliemann, (03-24-93, Venator/Hansten, #4511), pl. 3⅜ x 8¾ in., (8.5 x 22.2 cm.), drypoint (BP 105, DM 253, FR 862, Y 18,212).

KLINCKOWSTROM, Axel Leonhard
$1380* *Brodway-Gatan Och Radhuset I New York (S. & H. 1819-E-101; D. 310), 1819,* by Carl Fredrik Akrell, pub. in Bref om de Forenta Staterne 1824, 2 sides trimmed to platemark, small left margin, good cond., center fold, mat/light-staining, soiling, (01-28-93, Sotheby-NY, #419, illus.), image 8 x 15⅛ in., (203 x 384 mm.), sheet 12¼ x 18⅞ in., (203 x 384 mm.), hand-colored aquatint (BP 911, DM 2187, FR 7399, Y 171,343).
   BI *New Yorks Hamn Och Redd Fran Brooklyn Pa Long Island (S. & H. 1820-E-99; D. 322), 1820,* by Carl Fredrik Akrell, pub. in Bref om de Forenta Staterne 1824, margins, creases, center fold, filled-in image hole, tear just into subject, est.$1,5/2,000, (01-28-93, Sotheby-NY, #420), image 8⅝ x 18¾ in., (219 x 476 mm.), sheet 11¼ x 20 in., (219 x 476 mm.), hand-colored aquatint backed w/wove.

KLINE, Franz   American 1910-1962
$3163* *Untitled, 1960,* s., #42/50, from portfolio 21 Etchings and Poems, pub. Morris Gallery, full margins, good cond., handling creases, (05-15-93, Sotheby-NY, #1050, illus.), 8¼ x 14⅜ in., (21 x 36.5 cm.), etching and aquatint (BP 2057, DM 5088, FR 17,097, Y 350,626).

KLINGER

$95 *Wiener Internationale Messe, 1921,* folds, minor loss, (09-24-92, Alderfer, #251), 23⅝ x 18 in., (60 x 45.7 cm.), (BP 56, DM 141, FR 478, Y 11,428).

KLINGER, Max German 1857-1920

$1558* *"Accorde" (Singer 183/V-VII), c. 1894,* sheet 1 of series "Brahmsphantasie" (Opus XII), Georg Hirzel Coll., pov., (06-04-93, Grisebach, #145), 10¹⁵⁄₁₆ x 15¼ in., (27.8 x 38.8 cm.), engraving w/aquatint and mezzotint on imitation Japan (BP 1031, DM 2530, FR 8528, Y 168,033).

$1773* *"Amor Und Psyche, Ein Marchen Des Apulejus" (Opus V) (Singer 64-109), 1880: Forty-Six,* pub. Stroefers Kunstverlag, (06-05-93, Grisebach, #684, illus.), 13¾ x 9¹³⁄₁₆ in., (35 x 25 cm.), etching w/aquatint on copper print paper (BP 1167, DM 2875, FR 9689, Y 190,195).

$954* *"Amor Und Psyche, Opus V a" (Singer 64, 67, 73, 75, 81-82, 85, 91, 96-97, 100, 102, 104-105, and 107), 1880: Fifteen,* num., pub. Theo Stoefer, (06-19-93, Wachholtz, #195), each approx. 10¹⁄₁₆ x 6⅞ in., (25.5 x 17.5 cm.), etching on China (BP 641, DM 1610, FR 5414, Y 105,753).

$2974* *"Anerbieten" (Singer 132/II-IV), 1884,* s., sheet 6 of series "Ein Leben" (Opus VIII), Georg Hirzel Coll., prov., (06-04-93, Grisebach, #76, illus.), 7⁷⁄₁₆ x 11⅝ in., (18.9 x 29.5 cm.), etching on handmade Japan (BP 1968, DM 4829, FR 16,278, Y 320,751).

$991* *"Arme Familie" (Singer 179/III), c. 1888,* sheet 9 of series "Vom Tode. Erster Teil" (Opus XI), blindstamp, Georg Hirzel Coll., prov., (06-04-93, Grisebach, #105), 10⅞ x 7⅝ in., (27.7 x 19.4 cm.), aquatint in brown-black on imitation (BP 656, DM 1609, FR 5424, Y 106,881).

$3966* *"Atelierszene" (Singer 275), c. 1894,* mono., d., Georg Hirzel Coll., prov., (06-04-93, Grisebach, #146, illus.), 5¹⁄₁₆ x 7 in., (12.8 x 17.8 cm.), etching w/engraving on old handmade (BP 2624, DM 6440, FR 21,708, Y 427,739).

$202* *Bar Und Elfe (Intermezzi Opus IV) (Singer 52), 1880,* sheet 1 of series, (11-28-92, Grisebach, #591, illus.), 16⁷⁄₁₆ x 11⁷⁄₁₆ in., (41.8 x 29 cm.), aquatint on China (BP 133, DM 322, FR 1092, Y 25,140).

$637* *"Bar Und Elfe" (Singer 52/II), 1880,* sheet 1 of series "Intermezzi" (Opus IV), Georg Hirzel Coll., prov., (06-04-93, Grisebach, #28), 16⁵⁄₁₆ x 11¼ in., (41.5 x 28.5 cm.), aquatint laid down on China (BP 421, DM 1034, FR 3487, Y 68,701).

$765* *"Der Bauer, Dessen Saat In Unheil Aufgeht" (Singer 222/I-III), 1891,* sheet 40 of series "Brahmsphantasie" (Opus XII), blindstamp, Georg Hirzel Coll., prov., (06-04-93, Grisebach, #121, illus.), 11 x 2¹⁵⁄₁₆ in., (28 x 7.4 cm.), etching w/engraving on imitation Japan (BP 506, DM 1242, FR 4187, Y 82,506).

$1275* *"Der Befreite Prometheus" (Singer 223/II), 1892,* s., d., 2. Z.(ustand) 1. Dr.(uck), sheet 41 of series "Brahmsphantasie" (Opus XII), Georg Hirzel Coll., prov., (06-04-93, Grisebach, #128, illus.), 11 x 14¼ in., (28 x 36.2 cm.), aquatint w/mezzotint and engraving on imitation Japan (BP 844, DM 2070, FR 6979, Y 137,511).

$1416* *"Betender Greis (Der Heilige Antonius)" (Singer 269), 1885,* s., proof, blindstamp, Georg Hirzel Coll., prov., (06-04-93, Grisebach, #93), 6⁵⁄₁₆ x 4⅝ in., (16 x 11.8 cm.), aquatint on handmade (BP 937, DM 2299, FR 7750, Y 152,718).

$991* *Betender Greis (Singer 269), 1885,* s., (06-04-93, Bassenge, #5726), 6¼ x 4¾ in., (15.9 x 12 cm.), etching w/aquatint on Japan (BP 656, DM 1609, FR 5424, Y 106,881).

$269* *"Bildnis Des Kunsthandlers Louis Meder" (Beyer 410/I), 1912,* s., d., 1. Z.(ustand) 3. Dr.(uck), blindstamp, (06-04-93, Grisebach, #191), 9 x 6¹⁵⁄₁₆ in., (22.9 x 17.7 cm.), etching on old handmade (BP 178, DM 437, FR 1472, Y 29,012).

$127* *"Bildnis Geheimrat Prof. Dr. Lamprecht" (Beyer 422), 1915,* s., d., blindstamp, Georg Hirzel Coll., (06-04-93, Grisebach, #200), 6¼ x 4½ in., (15.9 x 11.5 cm.), etching and drypoint in Japan (BP 84, DM 206, FR 695, Y 13,697).

$127* *"Bildnis Geheimrat Prof. Dr. Lamprecht" (Beyer 423/III), 1915,* s., d., 3. Z.(ustand) 2. Dr.(uck), blindstamp, Georg Hirzel Coll., prov., (06-04-93, Grisebach, #201), 6⁵⁄₁₆ x 4⁵⁄₁₆ in., (16.1 x 11 cm.), aquatint on Japan (BP 84, DM 206, FR 695, Y 13,697).

$127* *"Bildnis Geheimrat Prof. Dr. Lamprecht" (Beyer 423/IV), 1915,* blindstamp, Georg Hirzel Coll., prov., (06-04-93, Grisebach, #202), 6⅜ x 4⁷⁄₁₆ in., (16.2 x 11.2 cm.), aquatint on beige Japan (BP 84, DM 206, FR 695, Y 13,697).

$4957* *"Blick Aus Dem Atelierfenster" (Singer 270), 1890,* s., blindstamp, Georg Hirzel Coll., prov., (06-04-93, Grisebach, #116, illus.), 8¼ x 12½ in., (21 x 31.8 cm.), drypoint w/engraving on old handmade (BP 3280, DM 8050, FR 27,132, Y 534,620).

$8498* *"Brahmsphantasie" (Opus XII) (Singer 183-223; Pommeranz-Liedtke S. 197), 1890-1891: Forty-One,* Georg Hirzel Coll., prov., (06-04-93, Grisebach, #118, illus.), 14¾ x 17⁵⁄₁₆ in., (37.5 x 44 cm.), 19 etchings, partly w/aquatint and engraving, 22 lithographs on imitation Japan (BP 5622, DM 13,800, FR 46,513, Y 916,523).

$5665* *"Die Burg Am Meer, Nach Bocklin" (Singer 329/III), c. 1883,* s., d., artist's proof, Georg Hirzel Coll., prov., (06-04-93, Grisebach, #73, illus.), 30 x 22¹⁄₁₆ in., (76.2 x 56 cm.), aquatint on China (BP 3748, DM 9199, FR 31,007, Y 610,979).

$867* *Burga-Ehrenurkunde (Beyer 421 II), 1915,* 2nd state, 8th print, s., d., (12-04-92, Bassenge, #6858, illus.), 22⅜ x 17¹⁵⁄₁₆ in., (56.8 x 45.6 cm.), etching on Japan (BP 556, DM 1381, FR 4684, Y 108,240).

$276* *"Burga-Ehrenurkunde" (Beyer 421/II), 1915,* s., d., 2. Zustand 7. Druck, Georg Hirzel Coll., prov., (06-04-93, Grisebach, #199), 22⅜ x 17⅞ in., (56.8 x 45.4 cm.), etching on copper print paper (BP 183, DM 448, FR 1511, Y 29,767).

$1558* *"Chaussee" (Singer 174/I), 1885-1889,* s., sheet 4 of series "Vom Tode. Erster Teil" (Opus XI), artist's proof, red mono. stamp, Georg Hirzel Coll., prov., (06-04-93, Grisebach, #97), 10¾ x 6⅝ in., (27.3 x 16.8 cm.), aquatint on China (BP 1031, DM 2530, FR 8528, Y 168,033).

$1204* *"Christus Und Die Sunderinnen" (Singer 139/I), 1884,* s., d., 1. Z.(ustand) 3. Dr.(uck), foxing, Georg Hirzel Coll., prov., (06-04-93, Grisebach, #79), 11¹¹⁄₁₆ x 16⅜ in., (29.7 x 41.6 cm.), etching and engraving on copper print paper (BP 797, DM 1955, FR 6590, Y 129,853).

$16,288* *"Dramen" (Opus IX) (Singer 147/VI, 154-156/III; Pommeranz-Liedtke S.197), 1882-1883: Ten,* num., Georg Hirzel Coll., prov., (06-04-93, Grisebach, #59, illus.), 25³⁄₁₆ x 18½ in., (64 x 47 cm.), etching, partly w/aquatint on imitation Japan (BP 10,776, DM 26,450, FR 89,152, Y 1,756,687).

$1155* *Ehrenbugerbrief Fur Oberburgermeister Dr. Otto Georgi (Singer 331 II), 1899,* s., d., 2nd state, 4th print, artist's proof, s., d., (12-04-92, Bassenge, #6855, illus.), 22⅝ x 18¾ in., (57.4 x 47.7 cm.), etching on Japan (BP 741, DM 1839, FR 6240, Y 144,195).

$1346* *"Ehrenburgerbrief Fur Oberburgermeister Dr. Otto Georgi" (Singer 331/IV), 1899,* s., artist's proof, Georg Hirzel Coll., prov., (06-04-93, Grisebach, #154), 22³⁄₁₆ x 18¼ in., (56.3 x 46.4 cm.), etching on Japan cardboard (BP 891, DM 2186, FR 7367, Y 145,168).

$354* *"Ehrenburgerbrief Fur Oberburgermeister Dr. Rudolf Dittrich" (Beyer 432/III), 1918,* s., d., 3 Zstd 5. Dr(uck), Georg Hirzel Coll., prov., (06-04-93, Grisebach, #214), 21³⁄₁₆ x 14¹⁵⁄₁₆ in., (53.8 x 38 cm.), etching on Japan (BP 234, DM 575, FR 1938, Y 38,179).

$361* *Ehrendiplom Fur Dr. Maercker (Singer 330 II), 1882,* artist's proof, (12-04-92, Bassenge, #6854), 20¾ x 15⁹⁄₁₆ in., (52.7 x 39.6 cm.), etching w/aquatint on China (BP 232, DM 575, FR 1950, Y 45,069).

$496* *"Ehrendiplom Fur Dr. Maercker" (Singer 330/III), 1882,* Georg Hanzel Coll., prov., (06-04-93, Grisebach, #56), 20¼ x 15¼ in., (51.5 x 38.7 cm.), aquatint on China (BP 328, DM 805, FR 2715, Y 53,494).

$1062* *"Ehrenurkunde Fur Wissenschaftliche Mitarbeit An Der InternationalenHygieneausstellung Dresden 1911" (Beyer 416/I-III), 1912,* s., d., 1. Z(ustand) 4. Dr(uck), ded., Georg Hirzel Coll., prov., (06-04-93, Grisebach, #192),

24⅛ x 14¹⁵⁄₁₆ in., (61.3 x 38 cm.), etching on imitation Japan (BP 703, DM 1725, FR 5813, Y 114,538).

$21,953* *"Eine Liebe" (Opus X) (Singer 157, 166), 1880-1887: Ten,* mono., d., Georg Hirzel Coll., prov., (06-04-93, Grisebach, #35, illus.), 33¼ x 23¹⁄₁₆ in., (84.5 x 58.5 cm.), aquatint, partly w/engraving, in brown-black on Japan (BP 14,524, DM 35,650, FR 120,159, Y 2,367,666).

$3225* *Eine Liebe, Opus X (Singer 157-66), c. 1887: Ten,* from Third Edition, p. W. Felsing, pub. by artist, 1903, full margins, t., creases, surface dirt, very good cond., loose in cloth-covered portfolio, very good cond., prov., (05-20-93, Christie-London, #467, illus.), overall sheet 26¼ x 19¾ in., (66.7 x 50.2 cm.), etching on Imperial Japan (BP 2070, DM 5203, FR 17,527, Y 356,117).

$708* *"Eine Mutter I" (Singer 149/VII), 1882-1883,* sheet 3 of series "Drasmen" (Opus IX), Georg Hirzel Coll., prov., (06-04-93, Grisebach, #60), 17¹³⁄₁₆ x 12⅝ in., (45.2 x 32 cm.), aquatint on China (BP 468, DM 1150, FR 3875, Y 76,359).

$1416* *"Eine Mutter II) (Singer 150/IX), 1882-1883,* sheet 4 of series "Dramen" (Opus IX), foxing, Georg Hirzel Coll., (06-04-93, Grisebach, #61), 17¹⁵⁄₁₆ x 12½ in., (45.5 x 31.8 cm.), aquatint on copper print paper (BP 937, DM 2299, FR 7750, Y 152,718).

$1275* *"Eine Mutter III" (Singer 151/II-IV), 1882-1883,* s., t., sheet 5 of series "Dramen" (Opus IX), artist's proof, Georg Hirzel Coll., prov., (06-04-93, Grisebach, #62), 18¹⁄₁₆ x 14³⁄₁₆ in., (45.8 x 36 cm.), etching in brown-black on light brown Japan (BP 844, DM 2070, FR 6979, Y 137,511).

$708* *"Elend" (Singer 236/III), 1892,* s., d., 4. Dr.(uck), sheet 7 of series "Vom Tode. Zweiter Teil" (Opus XIII), artist's proof, blindstamp, Georg Hirzel Coll., (06-04-93, Grisebach, #129), 17¹⁵⁄₁₆ x 13⅞ in., (45.7 x 35.3 cm.), etching w/engraving on copper print paper (BP 468, DM 1150, FR 3875, Y 76,359).

$602* *"Das Ende (Der Sterbende Greis)" (Singer 255/II), c. 1879,* mono., d., Georg Hirzel Coll., prov., (06-04-93, Grisebach, #20), 13⅛ x 10⅜ in., (33.3 x 26.3 cm.), aquatint on Japan (BP 398, DM 978, FR 3295, Y 64,927).

$1487* *"Entführung Des Prometheus" (Singer 206/IV-VI), 1894,* s., sheet 24 of series "Brahmsphantasie" (Opus XII), Georg Hirzel Coll., prov., (06-04-93, Grisebach, #143, illus.), 10¹³⁄₁₆ x 15⅜ in., (27.5 x 39.1 cm.), aquatint w/engraving on imitation Japan (BP 984, DM 2415, FR 8139, Y 160,375).

$1346* *"Erste Begegnung" (Singer 158/IV), 1881-1882,* sheet 2 of series "Eine Liebe" (Opus X), light-staining, Georg Hirzel Coll., prov., (06-04-93, Grisebach, #43, illus.), 17⅝ x 10⁹⁄₁₆ in., (44.8 x 26.8 cm.), aquatint w/engraving on copper print paper (BP 891, DM 2186, FR 7367, Y 145,168).

$5665* *"Eva Und Die Zukunft" (Opus III) (Singer; Pommeranz-Liedtke S. 197),1879-80: Six,* mono. stamp, Georg Hirzel Coll., prov., (06-04-93, Grisebach, #23, illus.), sheet 24³⁄₁₆ x 17¹¹⁄₁₆ in., (61.4 x 45 cm.), etching partly w/aquatint on China (BP 3748, DM 9199, FR 31,007, Y 610,979).

$2835* *"Eva Und Die Zukunft" (Singer 43-48), 1919: Six,* Amsler & Ruthardt, (06-08-93, Karl/Faber, #324, illus.), approx. 20½ x 14¹⁵⁄₁₆ in., (52 x 38 cm.), etching and aquatint on copper print paper (BP 1864, DM 4600, FR 15,492, Y 301,115).

$1766* *Evocation (Singer 201, II), 1890,* s., d., series Brahmsphantasie, (06-10-93, Hauswedell/Nolt, #476, illus.), image 11⁹⁄₁₆ x 14³⁄₁₆ in., (29.3 x 36 cm.), etching and mezzotint on Kaiserlich Japan (BP 1155, DM 2876, FR 9682, Y 187,454).

$2195* *"Evocation" (Singer 201/II-III), 1890,* s., d., sheet 19 of series "Brahmsphantasie" (Opus XII), artist's proof, collector's stamp, Georg Hirzel Coll., prov., (06-04-93, Grisebach, #112), 11⁷⁄₁₆ x 14³⁄₁₆ in., (29 x 36 cm.), aquatint w/engraving and mezzotint on imitation Japan (BP 1452, DM 3564, FR 12,014, Y 236,734).

$496* *"Ex Libris Dr. H. Klinger" (Singer 307/I-II), 1879,* s., d., blindstamp, Georg Hirzel Coll., prov., (06-04-93, Grisebach, #19), 3¹¹⁄₁₆ x 2⁹⁄₁₆ in., (9.4 x 6.5 cm.), etching on China (BP 328, DM 805, FR 2715, Y 53,494).

$496* *"Ex Libris Ernst Und Elisabeth Wiegandt" (Beyer 420/III), 1914,* s., d., 3. Z.(ustand) 16. Dr.(uck), blindstamp, Georg Hirzel Coll., prov., (06-04-93, Grisebach, #198), 5¹³⁄₁₆ x 3¹¹⁄₁₆ in., (14.7 x 9.4 cm.), etching on Japan (BP 328, DM 805, FR 2715, Y 53,494).

$354* *"Ex Libris Hildegard Heyne" (Beyer 433/II-III), 1918,* s., blindstamp, Georg Hirzel Coll., prov., (06-04-93, Grisebach, #215), 5¹⁄₁₆ x 3⁷⁄₁₆ in., (12.8 x 8.8 cm.), aquatint on strong Japan cardboard (BP 234, DM 575, FR 1938, Y 38,179).

$4957* *"Die Ferngeliebte (Erinnerung). Verworfene Platte" (Singer 226/II), 1894,* mono., d., 2. Z.(ustand 1. Dr.(uck), blindstamp, Georg Hirzel Coll.,prov., (06-04-93, Grisebach, #144, illus.), 10⅝ x 5¹³⁄₁₆ in., (27 x 14.8 cm.), mezzotint w/engraving on imitation Japan reworked w/pencil (BP 3280, DM 8050, FR 27,132, Y 534,620).

$1558* *"Fest" (Singer 205/IV), 1894,* s., sheet 23 of series "Brahmsphantasie" (Opus XII), Georg Hirzel Coll., prov., (06-04-93, Grisebach, #142, illus.), 9¹⁵⁄₁₆ x 13⅞ in., (25.3 x 35.3 cm.), aquatint and engraving on parchment (BP 1031, DM 2530, FR 8528, Y 168,033).

$4957* *"Festschrift Des Koniglichen Kunstgewerbemuseums Zu Berlin" (Singer 1to 14), 1881: Fourteen,* Berlin Selbstverlag, mono. stamp, Georg Hirzel Coll., prov., (06-04-93, Grisebach, #36, illus.), 17⁵⁄₁₆ x 11⁷⁄₁₆ in., (44 x 29 cm.), etching on handmade Japan (BP 3280, DM 8050, FR 27,132, Y 534,620).

$2549* *"Finis (Verworfene Platte)" (Singer 146/III), 1884,* s., d., artist's proof, Georg Hirzel Coll., prov., (06-04-93, Grisebach, #82, illus.), 22⅝ x 17¹⁄₁₆ in., (57.5 x 43.3 cm.), aquatint on handmade Japan (BP 1686, DM 4139, FR 13,952, Y 274,914).

$127* *"Frauengestalt In Faltiger Gewandung" (Beyer 395), 1909,* mono., d., blindstamp, Georg Hirzel Coll., prov., (06-04-93, Grisebach, #169), 13¾ x 9¹³⁄₁₆ in., (35 x 25 cm.), aquatint in brown-black on Japan (BP 84, DM 206, FR 695, Y 13,697).

$390* *"Gedenkblatt Fur Die Im Weltkrieg Gefallenen" (Beyer 419/III), 1914,* s., d., 3. Z.(ustand) 2. Dr.(uck), Georg Hirzel Coll., prov., (06-04-93, Grisebach, #197), 16¹⁄₁₆ x 14³⁄₁₆ in., (40.8 x 36 cm.), aquatint on beige Japan (BP 258, DM 633, FR 2135, Y 42,062).

$1841* *"Gefesselt" (Singer 137/I), 1884,* s., d., 1. Z.(ustand) 4. Dr.(uck), Berlin, sheet 11 of series "Ein Leben" (Opus VIII), Georg Hirzel Coll., prov., (06-04-93, Grisebach, #78, illus.), 22⁷⁄₁₆ x 17⁵⁄₁₆ in., (57 x 44 cm.), aquatint on handmade Japan (BP 1218, DM 2990, FR 10,077, Y 198,555).

$354* *"Generalfeldmarschall Von Hindenburg" (Beyer 431/II), 1917,* s., d., 2.Z.(ustand) 1. Dr.(uck), blindstamp, Georg Hirzel Coll., prov., (06-04-93, Grisebach, #209), 13½ x 9¾ in., (34.3 x 24.8 cm.), aquatint on Japan (BP 234, DM 575, FR 1938, Y 38,179).

$1083* *Genie (Singer 233 IV), 1903,* 4th state, 5th print, s., d., (12-04-92, Bassenge, #6852), 17¹¹⁄₁₆ x 13¹⁄₁₆ in., (45 x 33.2 cm.), etching w/aquatint on Japan (BP 695, DM 1725, FR 5851, Y 135,206).

$1275* *"Genie" (Singer 233/I), 1900-1903,* 1. Z.(ustand) 3. Dr.(uck), sheet 4 of series "Vom Tode Zweiter Teil"(Opus XIII), blindstamp, Georg Hirzel Coll., prov., (06-04-93, Grisebach, #156), 17⅝ x 13⁹⁄₁₆ in., (44.8 x 34.5 cm.), etching w/drypoint and engraving on imitation Japan (BP 844, DM 2070, FR 6979, Y 137,511).

$708* *"Die Gurlitt-Ausstellungskarte: Phantasie Und Kunstlerkind" (Singer 22 vor I), 1881,* s., d., Georg Hirzel Coll., prov., (06-04-93, Grisebach, #38), 9¾ x 8¹³⁄₁₆ in., (24.7 x 22.4 cm.), aquatint in red-brown on China (BP 468, DM 1150, FR 3875, Y 76,359).

$567* *"Die Gurlitt-Ausstellungskarte: Phantasie Und Kunstlerkind" (Singer 262/III), 1881,* Georg Hirzel Coll., prov., (06-04-93, Grisebach, #39), 9⅝ x 8⅞ in., (24.5 x 22.5 cm.), aquatint in red-brown on handmade (BP 375, DM 921, FR 3103, Y 61,152).

$12,747* *"Ein Handschuh" (Opus VI) (Singer 113/IV (v. V), 114-115/V, 116/VI (v. VII), 117-122/IV (v. V) (Pommerantz-Lieddtke S. 197), 1878-1881: Ten,* Georg Hirzel Coll., prov., (06-04-93, Grisebach, #12, illus.), 17⅝ x 24⁵⁄₁₆ in., (44.7 x 61.8 cm.), etching partly w/aquatint on China (BP 8433, DM 20,700, FR 69,770, Y 1,374,784).

$7803* *"Ein Handschuh", Opus VI (Singer 113-122; Pommeranz-Liedtke S. 197),1878-81: Ten,* estate stamp, (06-05-93, Grisebach, #256, illus.), plate each 12⅜ x 19⅛ in., (31.5 x 48.5 cm.), etching w/aquatint in beige Japan (BP 5137, DM 12,651, FR 42,639, Y 837,052).

BI *Herrscher (Singer 231 II), 1908,* from Vom Tode Zweiter Teil, Opus XIII, d., prov., est. DM 2,500, (12-04-92, Bassenge, #6851), etching on Japan.

$1275* *"Herrscher (Verworfene Platte)" (Singer 243/II), 1885-1888,* s., blindstamp, Georg Hirzel Coll., prov., (06-04-93, Grisebach, #95), 8⅛ x 13¹¹⁄₁₆ in., (20.6 x 34.8 cm.), etching w/engraving on old handmade (BP 844, DM 2070, FR 6979, Y 137,511).

$1133* *"Herrscher" (Singer 231), 1885-1910,* s., d., 3. Z.(ustand) 6. Dr.(uck), sheet 2 of series "Vom Tode. Zweiter Teil" (Opus XIII), Georg Hirzel Coll., prov., (06-04-93, Grisebach, #99), approx. 24 x 17⁹⁄₁₆ in., (61 x 44.6 cm.), etching and engraving on Japan (BP 750, DM 1840, FR 6201, Y 122,196).

$1841* *"Hexe Und Fledermaus" (Singer 259), 1880,* s., "Aquatintaprobe", blindstamp, Georg Hirzel Coll., prov., (06-04-93, Grisebach, #30), 4⅝ x 8¹⁵⁄₁₆ in., (11.8 x 22.8 cm.), aquatint on China (BP 1218, DM 2990, FR 10,077, Y 198,555).

$1700* *"Im Grase" (Singer 198/I), 1893,* mono., d., 1. Z.(ustand) 4 Dr.(uck), sheet 16 of series "Brahmsphantasie" (Opus XII), blindstamp, Georg Hirzel Coll., prov., (06-04-93, Grisebach, #132, illus.), 18½ x 12¹¹⁄₁₆ in., (47 x 32.3 cm.), color aquatint on Japan (BP 1125, DM 2761, FR 9305, Y 183,348).

$744* *"Im Unterstand. Sachsicher Ausschuss Fur Kunst Im Feld" (Beyer 429/I), 1917,* s., d., !. Z.(ustand) 4. (Dr.uck), blindstamp, Georg Hirzel Coll., prov., (06-04-93, Grisebach, #208), 9¾ x 7⅜ in., (24.8 x 18.7 cm.), aquatint on beige Japan (BP 492, DM 1208, FR 4072, Y 80,242).

$1594* *"In Die Gosse!" (Singer 136/III-V), 1884,* s., sheet 10 of series "Ein Leben" (Opus VIII), Georg Hirzel Coll., prov., (06-04-93, Grisebach, #77), 7¹⁵⁄₁₆ x 7⁵⁄₁₆ in., (20.3 x 18.5 cm.), aquatint on China (BP 1055, DM 2589, FR 8725, Y 171,915).

$2762* *"In Flagranti" (Singer 147/II), 1882,* s., d., deuxieme epreuve deuxieme etat, sheet 1 of series "Dramen" (Opus IX), Georg Hirzel Coll., prov., (06-04-93, Grisebach, #50), 18¹⁄₁₆ x 12⅝ in., (45.8 x 32 cm.), etching on Japan (BP 1827, DM 4485, FR 15,118, Y 297,886).

$283* *"Initial D" (Singer 295/I), 1889,* s., d., blindstamp, Georg Hirzel Coll., prov., (06-04-93, Grisebach, #107), 6¼ x 3¹⁄₁₆ in., (15.8 x 7.8 cm.), etching and engraving on imitation Japan (BP 187, DM 460, FR 1549, Y 30,522).

$1841* *"Ins Nichts Zuruck" (Singer 141/II), 1884,* s., d., 2. Zustand 4 Dr.(uck), sheet 15 of series "Ein Leben" (Opus VIII), Georg Hirzel Coll., prov., (06-04-93, Grisebach, #81, illus.), 11¾ x 9¹⁵⁄₁₆ in., (29.8 x 25.2 cm.), aquatint w/drypoint on handmade Japan (BP 1218, DM 2990, FR 10,077, Y 198,555).

$708* *"Integer Vitae (Verworfene Platte)" (Singer 242), 1885,* s., blindstamp, Georg Hirzel Coll., prov., (06-04-93, Grisebach, #92), 14¾ x 10⅞ in., (37.5 x 27.7 cm.), etching on Japan (BP 468, DM 1150, FR 3875, Y 76,359).

$602* *"Integer Vitae" (Singer 230/III-IV), 1885-1900,* sheet 1 of series "Vom Tode. Zweiter Teil" (Opus XIII), blindstamp, Georg Hirzel Coll., prov., (06-04-93, Grisebach, #98), 15¹⁵⁄₁₆ x 12½ in., (40.5 x 31.7 cm.), engraving on imitation Japan (BP 398, DM 978, FR 3295, Y 64,927).

$1695* *Intermezzi (Rad. Opus IV) (Singer 52-63), 1879-81: Twelve,* pub. Stroefer, wear, (06-10-93, Hauswedell/Nolt, #479), portfolio 25¹⁄₁₆ x 17⅞ in., (63.7 x 45.4 cm.), etching on China (BP 1109, DM 2760, FR 9293, Y 179,917).

$2444* *Intermezzi (Sing. 52-63), 1881: Twelve,* Stroefer's Kunstverlag Nurnberg, (06-23-93, Kornfeld, #459), etching (BP 1660, DM 4135, FR 13,910, Y 266,260, SF 3680).

$853* *Intermezzi (Singer 52-63): Twelve,* foxing, wear, (09-25-92, Granier, #2653), sheet 17¹¹⁄₁₆ x 24¹³⁄₁₆ in., (45 x 63 cm.), and 24¹³⁄₁₆ x 17¹¹⁄₁₆ in., (45 x 63 cm.), etching laid down on China (BP 498, DM 1264, FR 4276, Y 102,957).

$1197* *"Intermezzi Componirt, Radirt" (Singer 52-63), 1881: Twelve,* num., t., d., (03-24-93, Venator/Hansten, #4512), sh. approx. 24¹³⁄₁₆ x 17¹¹⁄₁₆ in., (63 x 45 cm.), etching and aquatint (BP 811, DM 1955, FR 6654, Y 140,642).

$2691* *"Intermezzi" (Opus IV) (Singer), c. 1879-1881: Twelve,* Georg Hirzel Coll., prov., (06-04-93, Grisebach, #24, illus.), 17⁵⁄₁₆ x 23¼ in., (44 x 59 cm.), etching, partly aquatint on China (BP 1780, DM 4370, FR 14,729, Y 290,229).

$992* *"Intermezzi" (S. 52-63/III),* Stroefers Kunstverlag, (06-08-93, Karl/Faber, #325), 25³⁄₁₆ x 18⅛ in., (64 x 46 cm.), etching and aquatint (BP 652, DM 1610, FR 5421, Y 105,364).

$830* *"Intermezzi" (Singer 52/II, 53/III, 54/II, 55/II, 56/III, 57/IV, 58/III, 59/IV, 60/II, 61-63/III), 1881: Twelve,* Theo Stroefers Kunstverlag, foxed, light-stained, (12-01-92, Karl/Faber, #224), 24¹³⁄₁₆ x 17¹¹⁄₁₆ in., (63 x 45 cm.), etching and aquatint on China (BP 548, DM 1323, FR 4508, Y 103,337).

$1841* *Intermezzi, Opus IV. 12 (Singer 52-63), 1881,* folio, orig. case J.B. Klein's Kunsthandlung, (06-04-93, Bassenge, #5724), etching on China (BP 1218, DM 2990, FR 10,077, Y 198,555).

$987* *Intermezzo (Singer 170 II), 1878,* s., d., in Eine Liebe, Opus 10, (05-26-93, Lempertz, #261), 14⅛ x 20⅜ in., (35.8 x 51.7 cm.), etching laid down on China (BP 639, DM 1610, FR 5420, Y 107,236).

$425* *"Die Kalte Hand" (Singer 193/IV-V), 1893,* sheet 11 of series "Brahmsphantasie" (Opus XII), Georg Hirzel Coll.,-prov., (06-04-93, Grisebach, #130), 6¹⁵⁄₁₆ x 5⅛ in., (17.7 x 13 cm.), etching and engraving on imitation Japan (BP 281, DM 690, FR 2326, Y 45,837).

$354* *"Kopf Felix Koenigs Auf Dem Totenbett" (Singer 278/IV), c. 1900,* s., blindstamp, Georg Hirzel Coll., prov., (06-04-93, Grisebach, #155), 14¹⁄₁₆ x 12¹⁵⁄₁₆ in., (35.7 x 33 cm.), mezzotint w/engraving on copper print paper (BP 234, DM 575, FR 1938, Y 38,179).

$1558* *"Krieg" (Singer 235), c. 1890,* s., d., 2. Z.(ustand) 6. Dr.(uck), sheet 6 of series "Vom Tode. Zweiter Teil" (Opus XIII), Georg Hirzel Coll., prov., (06-04-93, Grisebach, #117), 20½ x 13⁵⁄₁₆ in., (52 x 33.8 cm.), aquatint on Japan (BP 1031, DM 2530, FR 8528, Y 168,033).

$2266* *"Der Kunstler In Der Dachstube" (Singer 261), c. 1879,* s., blindstamp, Georg Hirzel Coll., prov., (06-04-93, Grisebach, #21), 6³⁄₁₆ x 2¹³⁄₁₆ in., (15.7 x 7.2 cm.), etching in brown on handmade (BP 1499, DM 3680, FR 12,403, Y 244,392).

$7167* *Ein Leben, Opus VIII (Singer 127-41), 1880-84: Fifteen,* t., from Third Edition, p. O. Felsing, pub. by artist, 1891, full margins, t. and list of contents foxed, very good cond., loose in covered portfolio, very good cond., prov., (05-20-93, Christie-London, #466, illus.), overall sheet 25¾ x 19 in., (65.4 x 48.3 cm.), etchings w/aquatint and engraving on firm cream wove (BP 4600, DM 11,563, FR 38,951, Y 791,409).

$991* *"Lecture Nocturne (Memphisto In Der Studierstube)", 1880,* s., Georg Hirzel Coll., prov., (06-04-93, Grisebach, #29), 4¹³⁄₁₆ x 7⅜ in., (12.3 x 18.7 cm.), etching brown-black on China (BP 656, DM 1609, FR 5424, Y 106,881).

$991* *"Leide!" (Singer 140/II), 1884,* s., d., 2. Z.(ustand) 4. Dr.(uck), sheet 14 of series "Ein Leben" (Opus VIII), Georg Hirzel Coll., prov., (06-04-93, Grisebach, #80), 22⅝ x 17⁵⁄₁₆ in., (57.4 x 43.9 cm.), etching w/aquatint on Japan (BP 656, DM 1609, FR 5424, Y 106,881).

$1300* *Leipzig Und Die Grossen Kriege (Beyer 432 I), 1917,* 1st state, 5th print, s., prov., (12-04-92, Bassenge, #6859), 21¹⁄₁₆ x 14¾ in., (53.5 x 37.5 cm.), etching on Japan (BP 834, DM 2070, FR 7023, Y 162,297).

$3895* *"Liebespaar Im Gemach (Verworfene Platte" (Singer 227), c. 1893,* s., blindstamp, Georg Hirzel Coll., prov., (06-04-93, Grisebach, #135, illus.), 10⅜ x 7 in., (26.3 x 17.8 cm.), aquatint w/engraving on old handmade (BP 2577, DM 6325, FR 21,319, Y 420,082).

$1770* *"Liebespaar Im Gemach" (Singer 195/II-IV), 1893,* mono., d., sheet 13 of series "Brahmsphantasie" (Opus XII), artist'sproof, Georg Hirzel Coll., prov., (06-04-93, Grisebach, #131), 10¹³⁄₁₆ x 7³⁄₁₆ in., (27.5 x 18.3 cm.), aquatint w/

engraving on copper print paper (BP 1171, DM 2874, FR 9688, Y 190,897).

$1062* *"Mannliches Bildnis Mit Halskrause" (Singer 264/II), 1882,* Georg Hirzel Coll., prov., (06-04-93, Grisebach, #54), 11 3/16 x 9 3/16 in., (28.4 x 23.3 cm.), aquatint in brown-black w/drypoint on copper print paper (BP 703, DM 1725, FR 5813, Y 114,538).

$1983* *"Marztage II" (Singer 155/VII), 1882,* sheet 9 of series "Dramen" (Opus IX), Georg Hirzel Coll., prov., (06-04-93, Grisebach, #53, illus.), 17 13/16 x 14 1/16 in., (45.3 x 35.7 cm.), aquatint on China (BP 1312, DM 3220, FR 10,854, Y 213,870).

$425* *"Menue Zum XVII. Kongress Der Association Litteraire" (Singer 277/III), 1895,* collector's stamp, Georg Hirzel Coll., prov., (06-04-93, Grisebach, #150), 12½ x 8 1/16 in., (31.8 x 20.4 cm.), aquatint w/engraving in brown on China (BP 281, DM 690, FR 2326, Y 45,837).

$1416* *"Das Menzelfestblatt" (Singer 268/I), 1884,* s., d., artist's proof, Georg Hirzel Coll., prov., (06-04-93, Grisebach, #83, illus.), 16 15/16 x 12¼ in., (43.1 x 31.1 cm.), etching on parchment (BP 937, DM 2299, FR 7750, Y 152,718).

$2125* *"Mittag" (Singer 123/II-III), c. 1881-1882,* sheet 1 of series "Vier Landschaften" (Opus VII), foxing, Georg Hirzel Coll., prov., (06-04-93, Grisebach, #44), 17 13/16 x 14¾ in., (45.3 x 37.5 cm.), aquatint on China (BP 1406, DM 3451, FR 11,631, Y 229,185).

$1700* *"Mondnacht" (Singer 125/II-III), 1881,* sheet 3 of series "Vier Landschaften", mono. stamp, #I/3, Georg Hirzel Coll., prov., (06-04-93, Grisebach, #37, illus.), 14 5/16 x 21 7/16 in., (36.3 x 54.5 cm.), aquatint on China (BP 1125, DM 2761, FR 9305, Y 183,348).

$1770* *"Ein Mord" (Singer 153/III), 1883,* s., d., 3. Zustand 3. Druck, sheet 7 of series "Dramen" (Opus IX), Georg Hirzel Coll., prov., (06-04-93, Grisebach, #71), 17 15/16 x 12½ in., (45.7 x 31.7 cm.), aquatint on copper print paper (BP 1171, DM 2874, FR 9688, Y 190,897).

$1133* *"Ein Mord" (Singer 153/IV-V), 1882-1883,* sheet 7 of series "Dramen" (Opus IX), Georg Hirzel Coll., prov., (06-04-93, Grisebach, #63), 17 13/16 x 12⅜ in., (45.3 x 31.5 cm.), aquatint on imitation Japan (BP 750, DM 1840, FR 6201, Y 122,196).

$1770* *"Nacht" (Singer 203/I), 1894,* mono., d., 1. Z.(ustand), 1. Dr.(uck), sheet 21 of series "Brahmsphantasie" (Opus XII), blindstamp, Georg Hirzel Coll., prov., (06-04-93, Grisebach, #140, illus.), 11 x 15¼ in., (28 x 38.7 cm.), aquatint w/drypoint on imitation Japan, reworked w/pencil and chalk (BP 1171, DM 2874, FR 9688, Y 190,897).

$1133* *"Nacht" (Singer 203/II), 1894,* mono., 2. Z.(ustand) 1. Dr.(uck), sheet 2 of series "Brahmsphantasie" (Opus XII), artist's proof, blindstamp, Georg Hirzel Coll., prov., (06-04-93, Grisebach, #141), 10 13/16 x 15 1/16 in., (27.5 x 38.3 cm.), aquatint w/drypoint on imitation Japan (BP 750, DM 1840, FR 6201, Y 122,196).

$3966* *"Nackte Frau Baum (Die Ferngeliebte)" (Singer 190/II), 1894,* mono., d., 1. Z.(ustand), sheet 8 of series "Brahmsphantasie" (Opus XII), artist's proof, blindstamp, Georg Hirzel Coll., prov., (06-04-93, Grisebach, #139, illus.), 10 5/16 x 5 3/16 in., (26.2 x 13.2 cm.), drypoint and engraving on light beige Japan (BP 2624, DM 6440, FR 21,708, Y 427,739).

$708* *"Opfer" (Singer 207/I), 1892,* s., d., sheet 25 of series "Brahmsphantasie" (Opus XII), artist's proof, collector's stamp, blindstamp, Georg Hirzel Coll., prov., (06-04-93, Grisebach, #127), 10⅝ x 14 5/16 in., (27 x 36.3 cm.), etching w/soft-ground etching and engraving on imitation Japan (BP 468, DM 1150, FR 3875, Y 76,359).

$6728* *"Philosoph" (Singer 232), 1910,* 3. Z.(ustand) 1. Dr.(uck), sheet 3 of series "Vom Tode. Zweiter Teil" (Opus XIII), blindstamp, Georg Hirzel Coll., prov., (06-04-93, Grisebach, #175, illus.), 19⅝ x 13 5/16 in., (49.8 x 33.8 cm.), aquatint w/engraving on Japan (BP 4451, DM 10,926, FR 36,825, Y 725,626).

$2125* *"Psyche Und Der Adler Jupiters" (Singer 263), c. 1882,* s., d., Georg Hirzel Coll., prov., (06-04-93, Grisebach, #58), 11⅝ x 5 11/16 in., (29.5 x 14.5 cm.), etching on Japan (BP 1406, DM 3451, FR 11,631, Y 229,185).

$921* *"Psyche Und Der Adler Jupiters" (Singer 263), c. 1882,* s., 1. Etat 4. Druck, blindstamp, Georg Hirzel Coll., prov., (06-04-93, Grisebach, #57, illus.), 11⅝ x 5⅝ in., (29.5 x 14.3 cm.), etching on Japan (BP 609, DM 1496, FR 5041, Y 99,331).

$1700* *"Die Quelle, Nach Bocklin" (Singer 325/III), 1889,* s., blindstamp, Georg Hirzel Coll., prov., (06-04-93, Grisebach, #109, illus.), 6 1/16 x 4½ in., (15.4 x 11.5 cm.), etching and engraving on beige handmade Japan (BP 1125, DM 2761, FR 9305, Y 183,348).

$921* *"Die Quelle, Nach Bocklin" (Singer 325/III), 1889,* s., blindstamp, Georg Hirzel Coll., prov., (06-04-93, Grisebach, #110), 14 3/16 x 9 1/16 in., (36 x 23 cm.), etching w/ engraving on handmade (BP 609, DM 1496, FR 5041, Y 99,331).

BI *"Radierte Skizzen" (Opus I) (Singer 16/IV, 17/V, 18/IV, 19-21/V, 22/VI, 23/V; Pommeranz-Liedtke S. 197, 1870: Eight,* est. DM 22/24,000, Georg Hirzel Coll., prov., (06-04-93, Grisebach, #1), 21¼ x 15 9/16 in., (54 x 39.5 cm.), aquatint on China.

$1558* *"Raub Des Lichtes" (Singer 204/III), 1890,* s., sheet 22 of series "Brahmsphantasie" (Opus XII), blindstamp, Georg Hirzel Coll., prov., (06-04-93, Grisebach, #113, illus.), 11 7/16 x 14 7/16 in., (29 x 36.7 cm.), mezzotint w/ etching on imitation Japan (BP 1031, DM 2530, FR 8528, Y 168,033).

$2444* *Rettung Ovidischer Opfer (Singer 25-39), 1898: Fifteen,* portfolio with traces of water, (06-23-93, Kornfeld, #458), etching (BP 1660, DM 4135, FR 13,910, Y 266,260, SF 3680).

$2524* *Rettungen Ovidischer Opfer (Singer 25-39, V): Fifteen,* (11-21-92, Lempertz, #214), 17 15/16 x 24 13/16 in., (45.5 x 63 cm.), etching on thick copper print paper (BP 1662, DM 4024, FR 13,555, Y 313,891).

BI *"Rettungen Ovidischer Opfer", Opus II (Singer 25-26/V-39; Pommeranz-Liedtke S. 197), 1879-82: Fifteen,* 3rd edit., mono. stamp, red stamped num., frontispiece num., estate stamp, est. DM 7/9,000, (06-05-93, Grisebach, #253, illus.), plate 21¼ x 15 9/16 in., (54 x 39.5 cm.), etching w/aquatint on Japan hand-made.

$7436* *"Rettungen Ovidischer Opfer. Sauvetage De Sacrifices D'Ovide" (Opus II) (Singer), 1879: Thirteen,* num., red mono. stamp, Georg Hirzel Coll., prov., (06-04-93, Grisebach, #17, illus.), 15 11/16 x 22 7/16 in., (39.8 x 57 cm.), etching partly w/aquatint on green China (BP 4920, DM 12,075, FR 40,701, Y 801,984).

$708* *"Ritter Tod" (Singer 220/III-V), 1891,* s., sheet 38 of series "Brahmsphantasie" (Opus XII), artist's proof,erso: "ZIERLEISTE MIT DEM BERGSTURZ" lithograph, Georg Hirzel Coll., prov., (06-04-93, Grisebach, #120), 10¾ x 6⅜ in., (27.3 x 16.2 cm.), etching w/engraving on copper print paper (BP 468, DM 1150, FR 3875, Y 76,359).

$2762* *"Rivalen" (Singer 133/II), 1883,* s., d., 2me etat 5ime epreuve, sheet 7 of series "Ein Leben" (Opus VIII), Georg Hirzel Coll., prov., (06-04-93, Grisebach, #70), 10½ x 6 9/16 in., (26.7 x 16.7 cm.), aquatint on handmade Japan (BP 1827, DM 4485, FR 15,118, Y 297,886).

$813* *Die Schlange (Singer 45, III), 1880,* sheet 3 of series Eva und die Zukunft, Opus III, artist's proof, num. III in plate, (10-09-92, Winterberg, #1197, illus.), 11⅝ x 6 5/16 in., (29.5 x 16 cm.), etching w/aquatint on handmade Japan (BP 482, DM 1208, FR 4055, Y 98,977).

$1204* *"Die Schonheit (Aphrodite)" (Singer 213/II-IV), 1891,* s., sheet 31 of series "Brahmsphantasie" (Opus XII), artist's proof,verso "ZIERLEIST E MIT DEM HERABFALL-ENDEN" lithograph, Georg Hirzel Coll., prov., (06-04-93, Grisebach, #119), 10¾ x 5 13/16 in., (27.3 x 14.7 cm.), engraving on copper print paper (BP 797, DM 1955, FR 6590, Y 129,853).

$2479* *"Ein Schritt" (Singer 148/I), 1882,* s., d., premiere etat premier epreuve, sheet 2 of series "Dramen" (Opus IX), Georg Hirzel Coll., prov., (06-04-93, Grisebach, #51, illus.), 17 15/16 x 10 15/16 in., (45.5 x 27.8 cm.), etching on Japan (BP 1640, DM 4026, FR 13,569, Y 267,364).

$2195* *"Ein Schritt" (Singer 148/I-II), 1882,* s., d., Duexieme etat Troisieme epreuve, sheet 2 of series "Dramen" (Opus IX), foxing, Georg Hirzel Coll., prov., (06-04-93, Grisebach, #52), 17 13/16 x 10 15/16 in., (45.3 x 27.8 cm.), etching on Japan (BP 1452, DM 3564, FR 12,014, Y 236,734).

$318* *Der Schuss (Beyer 341), 1914,* mono., d., series Zelt, (06-10-93, Hauswedell/Nolt, #477), image 8¹⁵⁄₁₆ x 7¹⁄₁₆ in., (22.8 x 18 cm.), etching worked over w/aquatint (BP 208, DM 518, FR 1743, Y 33,754).

$991* *"Der Schwan (Verworfene Platte)" (Beyer 378/I), c. 1915,* s., d., 1. Z.(ustand) 1. Dr.(uck), blindstamp, Georg Hirzel Coll., prov., (06-04-93, Grisebach, #205), 8¹⁵⁄₁₆ x 6⅞ in., (22.8 x 17.4 cm.), aquatint and engraving on imitation Japan (BP 656, DM 1609, FR 5424, Y 106,881).

$3895* *"Sehnsucht" (Beyer 396/II), 1909,* s., d., estate stamp, blindstamp, Georg Hirzel Coll., (06-04-93, Grisebach, #170, illus.), 24 x 17⁷⁄₁₆ in., (61 x 44.3 cm.), aquatint on Japan (BP 2577, DM 6325, FR 21,319, Y 420,082).

$847* *Selbstbildnis (Beyer-Singer 435 II), 1918,* s., d., (06-10-93, Hauswedell/Nolt, #478), image 9⅛ x 6³⁄₁₆ in., (23.1 x 15.7 cm.), aquatint on Japan (BP 554, DM 1379, FR 4644, Y 89,906).

$794* *Selbstbildnis Mit Brille (Beyer 398 I), 1909,* prov., (12-04-92, Bassenge, #6857), 8⅝ x 6⅝ in., (21.9 x 16.9 cm.), etching on Japan (BP 509, DM 1265, FR 4290, Y 99,126).

$850* *"Selbstbildnis Mit Brille" (Beyer 398/I), 1909,* s., d. in image, blindstamp, Georg Hirzel Coll., prov., (06-04-93, Grisebach, #172), 8⁹⁄₁₆ x 6½ in., (21.8 x 16.5 cm.), etching w/drypoint on old handmade (BP 562, DM 1380, FR 4652, Y 91,674).

$794* *Selbstbildnis Mit Zigarre (Beyer 397), 1909,* prov., (12-04-92, Bassenge, #6856), 9⁵⁄₁₆ x 5⅝ in., (23.6 x 14.3 cm.), aquatint on handmade (BP 509, DM 1265, FR 4290, Y 99,126).

$991* *"Selbstbildnis Mit Zigarre" (Beyer 397), 1909,* mono., artist's proof, d., 3 Dr.(uck), blindstamp, Georg Hirzel Coll., prov., (06-04-93, Grisebach, #171), 9¼ x 5¹¹⁄₁₆ in., (23.5 x 14.4 cm.), aquatint in brown-black on Japan (BP 656, DM 1609, FR 5424, Y 106,881).

$1558* *"Selbstbildnis Von Vorn Mit Auf Die Geballte Hand Gestutzem Kopf" (Beer 435/II), 1918,* s., d., 2. Z.(ustand) 2. Dr.(uck), blindstamp, Georg Hirzel Coll., prov., (06-04-93, Grisebach, #217), 9¹⁄₁₆ x 6¼ in., (23 x 15.8 cm.), aquatint on handmade Japan (BP 1031, DM 2530, FR 8528, Y 168,033).

$991* *"Selbstbildnis Von Vorn Mit Auf Die Geballte Hand Gestutztem Kopf" (Beyer 435/I), 1918,* s., d., 1. Z.(ustand) II. Dr.(uck), blindstamp, Georg Hirzel Coll., prov.(06-04-93, Grisebach, #216), 9¹⁄₁₆ x 6¹⁄₁₆ in., (23 x 15.4 cm.), aquatint on old handmade (BP 656, DM 1609, FR 5424, Y 106,881).

$850* *Selbstbildnis, Leicht Nach Links Gewendet (Beyer 436 II), 1918,* prov., (06-04-93, Bassenge, #5729), 9⅛ x 6⅞ in., (23.2 x 17.5 cm.), etching in brown on Japan (BP 562, DM 1380, FR 4652, Y 91,674).

$850* *"Selbstbildnis, Leicht Nach Links Gewendet" (Beyer 436/I), 1918,* s., d., 1. Z.(ustand) 1. Dr.(uck), blindstamp, Georg Hirzel Coll., prov., (06-04-93, Grisebach, #218), 9⅛ x 6⅞ in., (23.2 x 17.5 cm.), drypoint on handmade Japan (BP 562, DM 1380, FR 4652, Y 91,674).

$1487* *"Siesta II (Dolce Far Niente)" (Singer 23/I), 1879,* sheet 8 of series "Radierte Skizzen" (Opus I), artist's proof, GeorgHirzel Coll., prov., (06-04-93, Grisebach, #16), 12⅝ x 9⅜ in., (32 x 23.8 cm.), aquatint on copper print paper (BP 984, DM 2415, FR 8139, Y 160,375).

$673* *"Simplicius Am Grabe Des Einsiedlers" (Singer 59/IV), c. 1880,* s., sheet 8 of series "Intermezzi" (Opus IV), s., Georg Hirzel Coll., prov., (06-04-93, Grisebach, #31, illus.), 23⅝ x 17⅛ in., (60 x 43.5 cm.), etching on copper print paper (BP 445, DM 1093, FR 3684, Y 72,584).

$921* *"Sisyphus (Die Fakultaten)" (Beyer 385), 1914,* s., d., 1. Z.(ustand) 2. (Dr.(uck), blindstamp, Georg Hirzel Coll., prov., (06-04-93, Grisebach, #195), 9¾ x 6¹¹⁄₁₆ in., (24.8 x 17 cm.), aquatint on imitation Japan w/embossing (BP 609, DM 1496, FR 5041, Y 99,331).

$1770* *"Sommernachmittag" (Singer 126/II), c. 1883,* sheet 4 of series "Vier Landschaften" (Opus VII), artist's proof, monostamp, foxing, Georg Hirzel Coll., prov., (06-04-93, Grisebach, #72), 14½ x 21¹⁄₁₆ in., (36.8 x 53.5 cm.), aquatint on copper print cardboard (BP 1171, DM 2874, FR 9688, Y 190,897).

$155* *Sommertag (Singer 326 III), 1882,* after Bocklin, foxing, (09-25-92, Granier, #2654), 7½ x 5¾ in., (19.1 x 14.6 cm.), sheet 10⁷⁄₁₆ x 8⅞ in., (19.1 x 14.6 cm.), etching on hand-made (BP 91, DM 230, FR 777, Y 18,709).

$744* *"Sommertag, Nach Bocklin" (Singer 326/I), 1882,* artist's proof of first state, Georg Hirzel Coll., prov., (06-04-93, Grisebach, #55), 7½ x 5⅝ in., (19 x 14.3 cm.), aquatint on China (BP 492, DM 1208, FR 4072, Y 80,242).

$1204* *"Stehender Weiblicher Akt Im Profil" (Beyer 418/II), 1914,* s., d., 2. Z.(ustand) 6. Dr.(uck), blindstamp, Georg Hirzel Coll., prov., (06-04-93, Grisebach, #196, illus.), 16½ x 9¹³⁄₁₆ in., (41.9 x 24.9 cm.), drypoint w/light plate tone on Japan (BP 797, DM 1955, FR 6590, Y 129,853).

$2195* *"Titanen" (Singer 202/I), 1892,* sheet 20 of series "Brahmsphantasie" (Opus XII), artist's proof, blindstamp, Georg Hirzel Coll., prov., (06-04-93, Grisebach, #125), 10¾ x 14½ in., (27.3 x 36.8 cm.), etching w/engraving and mezzotint on copper print paper (BP 1452, DM 3564, FR 12,014, Y 236,734).

$1275* *"Titanen" (Singer 202/IV), 1892,* s., sheet 20 of series "Brahmsphantasie" (Opus XII), artist's proof,blindstamp, Georg Hirzel Coll., prov., (06-04-93, Grisebach, #126), 10¹³⁄₁₆ x 14⅜ in., (27.4 x 36.5 cm.), etching w/engraving and mezzotint on imitation Japan (BP 844, DM 2070, FR 6979, Y 137,511).

$850* *"Titelbild Zum Neuen Thannhauser" (Singer 285/I-II), 1885,* s., artist's proof, frontispiece for "Der neue Thannhauser", blindstamp, Georg Hirzel Coll., prov., (06-04-93, Grisebach, #94), 8⅜ x 6⅞ in., (21.3 x 17.5 cm.), etching in brown-black on imitation Japan (BP 562, DM 1380, FR 4652, Y 91,674).

$390* *"Titelblatt "Radierungen". Teich Mit Libellen", 1881,* s., d., artist's proof, blindstamp, Georg Hirzel Coll., prov., (06-04-93, Grisebach, #40), 6³⁄₁₆ x 3¹⁵⁄₁₆ in., (15.7 x 10 cm.), etching w/Roulette on China (BP 258, DM 633, FR 2135, Y 42,062).

$1416* *"Der Tod Als Heiland (Pax) (Singer 182), c. 1885-1888,* s., plate of series "Vom Tode. Erster Teil" (Opus XI), blindstamp, Georg Hirzel Coll., prov., (06-04-93, Grisebach, #96), 14³⁄₁₆ x 21⁹⁄₁₆ in., (36 x 54.7 cm.), etching w/plate tone on Japan (BP 937, DM 2299, FR 7750, Y 152,718).

$1416* *"Der Traum Des Kunstlers (Der Traumgott, Traume)" (Singer 260), c. 1880,* num., mono. stamp, num., Georg Hirzel Coll., prov., (06-04-93, Grisebach, #33, illus.), 9¾ x 16⁵⁄₁₆ in., (24.8 x 41.5 cm.), aquatint on China (BP 937, DM 2299, FR 7750, Y 152,718).

$4957* *"Traume" (Singer 129/wohl II), c. 1880,* s., sheet 3 of series "Ein Leben" (Opus VIII), artist's proof, GeorgHirzel Coll., prov., (06-04-93, Grisebach, #32, illus.), 20 x 14 in., (50.8 x 35.6 cm.), etching on copper print paper (BP 3280, DM 8050, FR 27,132, Y 534,620).

$297* *Umschlagtitel "Sezession" (Beyer 286/VI-VII), 1893,* blindstamp, Georg Hirzel Coll., prov., (06-04-93, Grisebach, #133), 11⅝ x 9¾ in., (29.5 x 24.7 cm.), aquatint w/engraving and mezzotint on copper print paper (BP 196, DM 482, FR 1626, Y 32,032).

$1416* *"Und Doch" (Singer 237/III), 1888,* s., d., III Zustand, sheet 8 of series "Vom Tode. Zweiter Teil" (OpusXIII), blindstamp, collector's stamp, Georg Hirzel Coll., prov., (06-04-93, Grisebach, #104), 16¼ x 12¹¹⁄₁₆ in., (41.3 x 32.3 cm.), aquatint w/engraving on Japan (BP 937, DM 2299, FR 7750, Y 152,718).

$637* *"Venus Anadyomene (Meereszug)" (Beyer 424/I), 1915,* s., d., 1.Z.(ustand) 7. Dr.(uck), blindstamp, Georg Hirzel Coll., prov., (06-04-93, Grisebach, #203), 18¹⁄₁₆ x 11¾ in., (45.8 x 29.8 cm.), aquatint in red on Japan (BP 421, DM 1034, FR 3487, Y 68,701).

$3895* *"Versuchung" (Singer 238/I), 1890,* s., d., 1. Z.(ustand) 1. Dr.(uck), sheet 9 of series "Vom Tode Zweite Teil (Opus XIII), artist proof of first state, Georg Hirzel Coll., prov., (06-04-93, Grisebach, #114), 17¹³⁄₁₆ x 14⅛ in., (45.3 x 35.8 cm.), engraving, partially w/Deckweiss, reworked on Japan (BP 2577, DM 6325, FR 21,319, Y 420,082).

$991* *"Versuchung" (Singer 238/IV), 1890,* s., d., sheet 9 of series "Vom Tode. Zweiter Teil" (Opus XIII), Georg Hirzel Coll., prov., (06-04-93, Grisebach, #115), 17¹⁵⁄₁₆ x 13⅞ in., (45.5 x 35.2 cm.), engraving on Japan (BP 656, DM 1609, FR 5424, Y 106,881).

$1346* *"Vision" (Beyer 387)*, blindstamp, Georg Hirzel Coll., prov., (06-04-93, Grisebach, #229), 10¹⁵⁄₁₆ x 5¹³⁄₁₆ in., (27.8 x 14.8 cm.), aquatint w/drypoint reworked on Japan (BP 891, DM 2186, FR 7367, Y 145,168).

$6576* *"Vom Tode II, Theil", 1898: Twelve*, blindstamp, Nr. 037, 1st edit., mono. MK, d., i., linen portfolio cover, (09-14-92, Venator/Hansten, #2463, illus.), sheet 24³⁄₁₆ x 18⁵⁄₁₆ in., (61.5 x 46.5 cm.), etching, parts w/aquatint on thick Japan (BP 3478, DM 9776, FR 33,128, Y 817,707).

$3547* *"Vom Tode, Erster Teil", (Opus XI (Singer 171-180, Pommeranz-LiedtkeS. 197), 1882-89: Ten*, 5th edit., pub. Amsler & Ruthardt, (06-05-93, Grisebach, #255, illus.), each 24³⁄₁₆ x 17¹¹⁄₁₆ in., (61.5 x 45 cm.), aquatint etching on thick beige Japan (BP 2335, DM 5751, FR 19,383, Y 380,498).

$5311* *"Vom Tode. Erster Teil" (Opus XI) (Singer 171-172/V; Pommeranz-Liedtke S. 197), 1882-1889: Ten*, Georg Hirzel Coll., prov., (06-04-93, Grisebach, #64, illus.), 23¹³⁄₁₆ x 17½ in., (60.5 x 44.5 cm.), aquatint on China (BP 3514, DM 8625, FR 29,070, Y 572,800).

BI *"Vom Tode. Zweiter Teil" (Opus XIII) (Singer), 1898-1909: Eight*, Georg Hirzel Coll., prov., est. DM 8/10,000, (06-04-93, Grisebach, #152, illus.), etching and engraving, partly w/aquatint, on imitation Japan.

$1416* *"Weiblicher Akt In Schabkunst" (Singer 271/II), 1891*, artist's proof, Georg Hirzel Coll., prov., (06-04-93, Grisebach, #122, illus.), 11¼ x 6⁹⁄₁₆ in., (28.6 x 16.7 cm.), etching and mezzotint on Japan (BP 937, DM 2299, FR 7750, Y 152,718).

$850* *"Weiblicher Kopf In Schabkunst" (Singer 272/II), c. 1891*, mono., d., rare Georg Hirzel Coll., prov., (06-04-93, Grisebach, #124), 7 x 5¹⁄₁₆ in., (17.8 x 12.8 cm.), etching and mezzotint on old handmade (BP 562, DM 1380, FR 4652, Y 91,674).

$1841* *"Zeit Und Ruhm" (Singer 240/III), c. 1888*, s., d., sheet 2 of series "Vom Tode. Zweiter Teil" (Opus XIII), 3. Zustand, artist's proof, Georg Hirzel Coll., prov., (06-04-93, Grisebach, #106), 17¹⁵⁄₁₆ x 10⅞ in., (45.5 x 27.7 cm.), engraving on Japan (BP 1218, DM 2990, FR 10,077, Y 198,555).

$7436* *"Zelt" (Beyer 322-377, 383 a-c), 1913-1915*, Berlin, Amsler + Ruthardt, num., Georg Hirzel Coll., prov., (06-04-93, Grisebach, #193, illus.), 23⅝ x 16⅛ in., (60 x 41 cm.), etching partly w/aquatint and engraving on China (BP 4920, DM 12,075, FR 40,701, Y 801,984).

$71* *"Zierleiste Mit Der Verschmachtenden" (Singer 229), c. 1891*, s., blindstamp, original sheet 27 of series "Brahmsphantasie" (Opus XII), Georg Hirzel Coll., prov., (06-04-93, Grisebach, #123), 10¼ x 2³⁄₁₆ in., (26 x 5.5 cm.), engraving in brown-black on copper print paper (BP 47, DM 115, FR 389, Y 7657).

$170* *"Zwei Figuren Aus Kompositionen Im Goldsaal" (Singer 8/III), c. 1881*, sheet 8 of series "Festschrift des Kgl. Kunstgewerbe-Museums zu Berlin", num., blindstamp, Georg Hirzel Coll., prov., (06-04-93, Grisebach, #42), 2¹⁵⁄₁₆ x 6¼ in., (7.5 x 15.8 cm.), etching on handmade Japan (BP 112, DM 276, FR 930, Y 18,335).

$6019* *"Zweites Intermezzo (Verworfene Platte)" (Singer 42/II), 1879*, artist's proof, mono. stamp, tear, Georg Hirzel Coll., prov., (06-04-93, Grisebach, #18, illus.), 11¹³⁄₁₆ x 16⁷⁄₁₆ in., (30 x 41.8 cm.), aquatint in red on copper print paper (BP 3982, DM 9774, FR 32,945, Y 649,159).

KLINKOWSTROM, Axel L.

$248* *"Bro Ofver Skuylkill Strommen"*, engraved by Carl Frederik Akrell, (06-11-93, Freemn/Fine Art, #2A), 9½ x 16½ in., (24.1 x 41.9 cm.), engraving (BP 163, DM 403, FR 1359, Y 26,313).

KLIPPER, Stuart   contemporary

$320* *Fog At The Antartic Convergence, Southern Ocean, 1987*, s., t. verso, (02-04-93, Sloan, #2912), 22 x 60¼ in., (55.9 x 153 cm.), photograph, color (BP 221, DM 531, FR 1794, Y 39,821).

$523* *Lightning Strike*, (12-10-92, Sloan, #2725), sight 13 x 39 in., (33 x 99.1 cm.), photograph, color (BP 337, DM 827, FR 2825, Y 64,696).

KLIPPER, Stuart   American contemporary

BI *Gates And Shed, Cobb Ranch, Near Choteau, Montana, 1981*, s., t., i. verso, est. $4/600, (02-04-93, Sloan, #2911), 16 x 44 in., (40.6 x 111.8 cm.), photograph, color.

KLOKIEN

$467* *International Automobile And Motorcycle Exhibition, Berlin, 1939*, Elsnerdruck, B cond., extensive repairs, chartex-backed, (08-06-92, Swann, #164, illus.), 39½ x 24½ in., (100.3 x 62.2 cm.), (BP 244, DM 690, FR 2330, Y 59,566).

KLOSS, Gene (Alice Geneva)   American b. 1903

$660* *Far Across The Rio Grande (K. 361), 1939*, s., t., annot. Artist's Proof, large margins, very good cond., mat staining, (10-28-92, Butterfield, #2529), 9⅞ x 13⅞ in., (251 x 352 mm.), etching on white wove (BP 421, DM 1019, FR 3461, Y 80,982).

$750* *"Indian Frienship Dance" (Kloss 450), 1953*, s., t., fine cond., tape, presentation print, (05-15-93, Cleveland, #193, illus.), 9 x 12 in., (22.9 x 30.5 cm.), etching and drypoint (BP 488, DM 1206, FR 4054, Y 83,139).

$308* *The Interpreter*, s., t., (02-14-93, Hanzel, #660), 7⅜ x 6⅜ in., (18.7 x 16.2 cm.), etching (BP 217, DM 511, FR 1728, Y 37,144).

$880* *Moonlight Circle Dance (K. 461), 1956*, s., margins, good cond., (02-24-93, Butterfield, #2640), 7¹⁵⁄₁₆ x 9¹⁵⁄₁₆ in., (202 x 252 mm.), aquatint & drypoint on wove (BP 614, DM 1429, FR 4843, Y 103,262).

$1320* *"Noonday Shadows" and "North House-Taos Pueblo (K. 46; 380), 1925, 1941: Two*, each s., t., margins, good cond., foxing, (02-24-93, Butterfield, #2638), one 7 x 8½ in., (178 x 216 mm.), other 6 x 8 in., (178 x 216 mm.), etchings on laid & wove (BP 921, DM 2143, FR 7265, Y 154,893).

$288* *On Windy Point (K. 544), 1973*, s., t., #1/25, annot. 2nd State, N.A., margins, good cond., staining, skinned area, remains, mat staining, (05-19-93, Butterfield, #1999), 12 x 14¹⁵⁄₁₆ in., (305 x 379 mm.), drypoint on wove (BP 187, DM 468, FR 1577, Y 31,883).

$935* *"Pueblo Feather Dance" (Kloss 543), 1973*, s., t., num. 3/25, good cond., (10-31-92, Cleveland, #163, illus.), 14⅞ x 11⅞ in., (37.8 x 30.2 cm.), drypoint (BP 599, DM 1438, FR 4880, Y 115,818).

$550* *Winter Woods (K. 378), 1941*, s., t., margins, good cond., (02-24-93, Butterfield, #2639), 6⅞ x 8⅜ in., (175 x 213 mm.), etching on laid (BP 384, DM 893, FR 3027, Y 64,539).

KLOTZ, Lenz   b. 1925

$1323* *Sehkarten, 1971: Six*, s., d., #50/70, (10-14-92, Germann, #558), 19¹¹⁄₁₆ x 25⁹⁄₁₆ in., (500 x 650 mm.), etching on Rives (BP 777, DM 1936, FR 6566, Y 160,325, SF 1725).

KLUCIS, Gustav   1895-1945

BI *Es Lebe Die Udssr, Das Vaterland Der Werktatigen Aller lander, 1931*, est. DM 4,000, (11-12-92, Lempertz, #130, illus.), 7⅞ x 5½ in., (20 x 14 cm.), photograph, gelatin silver print.

$2200* *Hoist The Flag Of Marx, Engels, Lenin, And Stalin, 1933*, ex-coll. Edouard Kulagin, (10-14-92, Swann, #325, illus.), 4½ x 9 in., (11.4 x 22.9 cm.), photograph, silver print (BP 1291, DM 3220, FR 10,918, Y 266,602).

BI *Metropolitain, 1390*, est. DM 14,000, (11-12-92, Lempertz, #129, illus.), 18⅛ x 13⅜ in., (46 x 34 cm.), retouched photocollage.

$13,200* *Poster For An Anti-Imperialist Exhibition, 1931*, 2 sheets mounted together & backed w/Japan paper, lit., (10-13-92, Christie-NY, #280, illus.), 54⅝ x 41⅜ in., (138.7 x 105.1 cm.), photograph, photo-offset lithography (BP 7688, DM 19,338, FR 65,704, Y 1,600,582).

BI *USSR-The Shock Brigade Of The World Proletariat, 1931*, credit, authenticated by artist's son, lit., est. $4/6,000, (10-13-92, Christie-NY, #281, illus.), 6½ x 4⅞ in., (16.5 x 12.4 cm.), photograph, gelatin silver print.

KLUG, Les   American 20th cent.

$66* *Self-Portrait With Wheelbarrow And Television*, (05-16-93, Hindman, #374), 7¾ x 7½ in., photograph, silver print (BP 43, DM 106, FR 359, Y 7350).

KLUGE, Gustav b. 1947

BI *Ballfangen, 1987,* s., d., #2/10, est. DM 2,500-, (05-27-93, Lempertz, #840, illus.), 27¹¹⁄₁₆ x 19⁷⁄₁₆ in., (70.3 x 49.3 cm.), woodcut on beige paper.

$1419* *Fuchsfalle, 1987,* i., s., d., num., (06-05-93, Schoppmann, #914, illus.), 43⁵⁄₁₆ x 27⁹⁄₁₆ in., (110 x 70 cm.), color woodcut on Pack (BP 934, DM 2301, FR 7754, Y 152,221).

$5414* *Junge Vor Der Fuchsfalle I,* t., s., d. 10-84, (11-28-92, Schoppmann, #625, illus.), 81½ x 17¹⁵⁄₁₆ in., (207 x 45.5 cm.), color woodcut on canvas (BP 3574, DM 8625, FR 29,281, Y 673,802).

KNAP, Joseph D.

$133* *Marsh Pools,* margins, s. J. D. Knap, (02-13-93, Collins, #62), 7 x 10⅞ in., (17.8 x 25.1 cm.), etching (BP 94, DM 221, FR 746, Y 16,040).

$121* *Redheads Alighting,* margins, s. J. D. Knap, (02-13-93, Collins, #43, illus.), 9⅞ x 11⅞ in., (25.1 x 30.2 cm.), etching (BP 85, DM 201, FR 679, Y 14,592).

$88* *Sailing In-Springtails,* margins, s. J. D. Knap, (02-13-93, Collins, #63), 7 x 9⅞ in., (17.8 x 25.1 cm.), etching (BP 62, DM 146, FR 494, Y 10,613).

$121* *Three Mallards,* margins, s. J. D. Knap, (02-13-93, Collins, #44, illus.), 7⅞ x 9⅞ in., (20 x 25.1 cm.), etching (BP 85, DM 201, FR 679, Y 14,592).

KNATHS, Karl American 1891-1971

$138* *Double Self Portrait,* ink s. Karl Knaths, #65/100, good cond., (03-12-93, Skinner, #78, illus.), 11¾ x 15 in., (29.8 x 38.1 cm.), lithograph on wove (BP 96, DM 230, FR 781, Y 16,264).

$140* *"Double Self Portrait",* s., num. ink, good cond., (05-15-93, Cleveland, #194, illus.), 12 x 15⅛ in., (30.5 x 38.4 cm.), lithograph (BP 91, DM 225, FR 757, Y 15,519).

KNAUPP, Werner b. 1936

BI *"Suizid", (19)75,* s., d., t., num., est. DM 500, (12-01-92, Karl/Faber, #848), 20⅞ x 19¹¹⁄₁₆ in., (53 x 50 cm.), lithograph on wove.

BI *Vernarbung, 1973,* s.., d., t., num., est. DM 250-, (09-25-92, Granier, #2911), sheet 19⅞ x 24½ in., (50.5 x 62.2 cm.), lithograph on wove.

KNAUS, E. (after)

$330* *Children And Landscape Settings: A Pair, 1868,* (10-16-92, DuMouchelle, #1352), 16 x 12 in., (40.6 x 30.5 cm.), engravings (BP 200, DM 487, FR 1656, Y 39,403).

KNIGHT, Dame Laura English 1877-1970

$597* *The Bareback Rider,* s., pub. Print Collector's Club, full margins, good cond., glued to mount, (12-03-92, Sotheby-London, #173, illus.), 10 x 4⅞ in., (254 x 124 mm.), etching on J. Whatman laid paper (BP 385, DM 939, FR 3205, Y 74,281).

$301* *Dressing Room No. 2,* s., i. Proof, margins, (11-19-92, Bonhams-Chelsea, #90), plate 6¾ x 8¾ in., (17.1 x 22.2 cm.), aquatint (BP 198, DM 480, FR 1617, Y 37,433).

$226* *A Quarrel,* s., i. 1st State, margin folded 1/2 in., good cond., (10-27-92, Phillips-London, #280), plate 8⅞ x 6⅝ in., (225 x 168 mm.), etching w/tone on wove (BP 143, DM 346, FR 1175, Y 27,645).

$605* *Zebras,* s., t., margins, front cover illus., (01-21-93, Bonhams-Chelsea, #6), plate 9¾ x 13¾ in., (24.8 x 34.9 cm.), drypoint etching (BP 396, DM 962, FR 3254, Y 75,720).

KNIGHT, Dame Laura (after)

$362* *Boys Bathing In A Cove,* s., pub. Frost and Reed Ltd, 1935, (07-16-92, Bonhams-Chelsea, #444), image 16⅛ x 25⅜ in., (41 x 64.5 cm.), reproduction in colors (BP 187, DM 535, FR 1805, Y 45,346).

KNIGHT, Laura

$1458* *"At The Footlights", "At The Folies Bergeres", "A Merry-Go-Round" and"A Chorus" (Bolling and Withington 5; 7; 12 and 17): Four,* each s., t., three i., full margins, good cond., (06-30-93, Sotheby-London, #310, illus.), etching, three w/aquatint on laid (BP 977, DM 2487, FR 8389, Y 156,220).

$2231* *"A Fair", "Dancing On Hampstead Heath", "Swing Boats", "Bank Holiday"and "A Box At The Theatre" (B./W. 9; 10; 22; 25 and 26): Five,* each s., t., i., full margins, good cond., creasing, (06-30-93, Sotheby-London, #311, illus.), etching, four w/aquatint all on laid (BP 1495, DM 3805, FR 12,837, Y 239,044).

$4118* *"Powder And Paint", "Youth And Age", "The Lipstick", "Putting On Rouge", "Mascots Make Up" and another (B./W. 30; 32; 34; 36 and 39): Ten,* s., i., t., latter i., good cond., creasing, (06-30-93, Sotheby-London, #313, illus.), six etchings, two w/aquatint on laid (BP 2760, DM 7024, FR 23,694, Y 441,230).

$943* *"Spanish Dancer No 1" and "Spanish Dancer No 2" (B./W. 8 and 19): Two,* s., t., i., full margins, good cond., marks, (06-30-93, Sotheby-London, #312), one 10⅜ x 8½ in., (264 x 216 mm.), the other 10½ x 8¼ in., (264 x 216 mm.), etching w/aquatint on laid (BP 632, DM 1608, FR 5426, Y 101,039).

KNIPP, Charles contemporary

$440* *Assisi Doorway,* s., d. 1970, #II EV 21/30, label verso, (12-10-92, Sloan, #2739), 10 x 20 in., (25.4 x 50.8 cm.), color etching (BP 284, DM 696, FR 2377, Y 54,429).

KNOEBEL, Imi German b. 1940

$12,136* *Ohne Titel, 1973: Eighty,* 16 series of 5, s., d., lit., (11-12-92, Lempertz, #131, illus.), each 9⁷⁄₁₆ x 12³⁄₁₆ in., (24 x 31 cm.), photograph, gelatin silver print (BP 7760, DM 19,073, FR 65,003, Y 1,501,423).

BI *Untitled, 1986,* s., for Fur Joseph Beuys, Edition Schellmann, #XXIII/XXX, d., s., num., est. DM 2,000-, (05-27-93, Lempertz, #842, illus.), 31½ x 23⅝ in., (80 x 60 cm.), collage color lithograph.

KNOPFF, Fernand 1858-1921

$430* *Sitzende Frau Mit Lorbeerkranz, Blumen Haltend,* s., (05-08-93, Schloss Ahlden, #2853), 7¹⁵⁄₁₆ x 5¹³⁄₁₆ in., (20.2 x 14.8 cm.), color etching on copper print paper (BP 281, DM 691, FR 2331, Y 48,050).

KNOX, Susan Ricker American 1875-1959

BI *"Chatter",* s., good cond., est. $75/125, (07-19-92, Bakker, #127), image 4¼ x 8 in., (10.8 x 20.3 cm.), woodblock print.

KNYFF, Leonard (after)

$118* *Somerset House,* by Jan Kip, margins, central fold, surface dirt, staining, (08-20-92, Bonhams-Chelsea, #65), plate 14 x 19 in., (35.6 x 48.3 cm.), etching w/hand coloring (BP 61, DM 171, FR 580, Y 14,901).

KOBAYASHI KIYOCHIKA Japanese 1847-1915

BI *Theatres Of Edo: Two,* from series Hana Moyo, Oban triptychs, s. Kiyochika w/seal Kobayashiand Kobayashi Kiyochika, pub.'s mark Kokkeido Akiyama Takeuemon, d. c. Meiji 29(1896), good state, Prof. H.R.W. Kuhne Coll., est. BP 1/1,200, (06-11-93, Sotheby-London, #484, illus.), each 14¾ x 28½ in., (37.5 x 72.4 cm.), woodblock.

KOBELL, Ferdinand German 1740-1799

$39* *Landscape With Travelers On A Road, c. 1780,* plate inits., (10-31-92, Cleveland, #14), 8½ x 6¾ in., (21.6 x 17.1 cm.), etching on chine colle (pasted) on wove (BP 25, DM 60, FR 204, Y 4831).

$75* *Travellers On A Road,* inits. in plate, (02-04-93, Sloan, #361), 8⅛ x 6½ in., (20.6 x 16.5 cm.), etching (BP 52, DM 123, FR 419, Y 9330).

$216* *Die Zwei Baume, Welche Sich Uber Eine Holzerne Brucke Kreuzen (Nagler60), 1769,* creased, stained, (12-01-92, Karl/Faber, #90A), etching (BP 143, DM 344, FR 1173, Y 26,892).

KOBELL, Wilhelm von 1766-1855

$2888* *Abendunterhaltung Am Lager (Lessing 104; Goedl-Roth 103), 1794,* after Ph. Wouverman, (12-04-92, Bassenge, #6863, illus.), 13⅜ x 17⁹⁄₁₆ in., (34 x 44.6 cm.), hand-colored aquatint (BP 1852, DM 4599, FR 15,602, Y 360,549).

$921* *Die Hirtin Mit Kind AnDer Brust Bei Der Ruhenden Herde (Lessing 67),1792,* after Th.v. Bergen, (06-04-93, Bassenge, #5733, illus.), 10⁹⁄₁₆ x 12¹³⁄₁₆ in., (26.8 x 32.6 cm.), watercolored aquatint/etching (BP 609, DM 1496, FR 5041, Y 99,331).

$850* *Die Spinnende Hirtin (Lessing 89, Goedl-Roth 127),* after A. Pynacker, (06-04-93, Bassenge, #5732), 14¾ x 13³⁄₁₆ in., (37.4 x 33.5 cm.), watercolored aquatint/etching (BP 562, DM 1380, FR 4652, Y 91,674).

$415* *Der Zeichner (Goedl-Roth 72), c. 1846,* signs of wear, (12-01-92, Karl/Faber, #227), 6⅛ x 5⅛ in., (15.5 x 13 cm.), etching (BP 274, DM 661, FR 2254, Y 51,668).

KOCH, Alex, Publisher

$25,300* *"Meister Der Innenkunst": "Meister Der Innen Kunst, 2, Charles RennieMackintosh", "Das Haus Eines Kunst-Freundes Ein Entwurf In Zwolf Tafeln Von Leopold Bauer" and "Meister Der Innen Kunst, 1, Baillie Scott": Three Portfolios,* pub. Alex Koch, 1902, 1st w/21 sheets, incl. 14 colored architecturalplates w/both English & German text; 2nd w/15 sheets, incl. 12 colored architectural plates; 3rd w/14 sheets, incl. 10 colored architectural plates, (06-12-93, Christie-NY, #36, illus.), 21 x 16 in., (53.3 x 40.6 cm.), (BP 16,560, DM 41,178, FR 138,403, Y 2,662,317).

KOCH, Joseph Anton 1768-1839

$4413* *Die Romischen Ansichten (Andresen 1-20), c. 1810: Twenty,* t., num. in plate, (10-09-92, Winterberg, #1216), each approx. 6¹¹⁄₁₆ x 8¹¹⁄₁₆ in., (17 x 22 cm.), etching on wove (BP 2618, DM 6555, FR 22,010, Y 537,253).

$318* *S. Francesco Di Civitella (Andresen 2 III), c. 1810,* plate i., t., sheet 2 of 20, series Romische Ansichten, (06-10-93, Hauswedell/Nolt, #258), etching (BP 208, DM 518, FR 1743, Y 33,754).

BI *Der Schwur Der 1500 Republikaner Bei Montenesimo (Andresen 28 III),* lit., est. DM 4,500, (12-04-92, Bassenge, #6865, illus.), 14½ x 26⅜ in., (36.8 x 67 cm.), etching.

KOCH, M. and O. Reith

$247* *Der Akt, Male And Female Nudes In Various Poses: Group of Twenty-Eight,* t.; photog.'s, printer's, pub.'s credit recto, (04-07-93, Swann, #80), each approx. 7½ x 5¾ in., (19.1 x 14.6 cm.), photograph, photogravures (BP 163, DM 399, FR 1352, Y 28,062).

KOCH, Walther 1875-1915

BI *Wintersport, 1915,* creases, folds, losses, est. BP 450/650, (02-04-93, Christie-S. Ken, #10, illus.), 37 x 49 in., (94 x 124.5 cm.), color lithograph backed on linen.

KODA, Kevin American 20th cent.

$44* *"Indian With Feather In His Hat",* blind stamp, s., #63/80, (02-27-93, Dunning, #23), 30 x 22½ in., (76.2 x 57.2 cm.), color lithograph (BP 31, DM 72, FR 246, Y 5194).

KOENIG, L.

$358* *Ch. De Fer Algeriens: ORAN. "La Porte D'Espagne", 1948,* good cond., restoration, (03-13-93, Laurin, #54), 38¹⁵⁄₁₆ x 23⅝ in., (99 x 60 cm.), (BP 250, DM 596, FR 2026, Y 42,192).

KOGAN, Moissej 1879-1943/44

$590* *Zwei Hockende Madchenakte, c. 1929/30,* s., (12-05-92, Bassenge, #7330), 9¾ x 7½ in., (24.7 x 19 cm.), linocut on Japan (BP 369, DM 920, FR 3135, Y 73,101).

KOGEVINAS, Lyc

$256* *Le Mont Athos: Plate II, III And VII,* s., margins, (08-20-92, Bonhams-Chelsea, #47), plate 7 x 10¼ in., (17.8 x 26 cm.), etching (BP 132, DM 371, FR 1258, Y 32,327).

KOHLHAGEN, Lisette 1890-1969

$263* *Bowl Of Flowers,* inits. L.K. in image, (08-11-92, L. Joel, #32G, illus.), 5½ x 6⁵⁄₁₆ in., (14 x 16 cm.), linocut (BP 137, DM 386, FR 1307, Y 33,679, A$ 357).

KOHN, Misch American b. 1916

$220* *Don Quixote,* s., #21/50, d. 1961, (05-16-93, Hindman, #640), 11¾ x 7¼ in., (29.8 x 18.4 cm.), aquatint w/color chine colle (BP 143, DM 354, FR 1189, Y 24,388).

KOHN, Mischa American b. 1916

BI *Pierron, 1963,* s., good cond., margins folded, est. $100/150, (05-15-93, Cleveland, #474), 4¹⁵⁄₁₆ x 2⁷⁄₁₆ in., (12.5 x 6.2 cm.), woodcut.

KOITSU, Tsuchiya Japanese 1870-1949

$11* *Mt. Fuji From Lake Hakone,* (10-11-92, Hanzel, #955), 9½ x 14¼ in., (24.1 x 36.2 cm.), color woodblock print (BP 7, DM 16, FR 55, Y 1339).

$113* *Pagoda,* s., (11-16-92, Hodgins, #339), 15¼ x 10 in., (38.7 x 25.4 cm.), color woodblock on paper (BP 74, DM 180, FR 607, Y 14,102, C$ 143).

BI *Two Snowscenes,* pub. Doi Sadaichi, p. Yokoi, 1939, 1940, both s. Koitsu, seal, one browned, rubbed spot, est. G 2/300, (11-18-92, Bubb Kuyper, #1589), print.

KOKA, Jay

$220* *312 T2,* limited edit., 11/249, s., (08-23-92, Christie-E, #23), color reproduction (BP 113, DM 315, FR 1070, Y 27,676).

$247* *Mondial III, 1989,* limited edit., 23/149, s., (08-23-92, Christie-E, #22), color reproduction (BP 127, DM 354, FR 1201, Y 31,073).

KOKOSCHKA, Oskar Austrian 1886-1980

$191* *The Action Painter (Wingler-Welz 212), 1959,* stone mono., d., watermark, (06-10-93, Hauswedell/Nolt, #493), image 17³⁄₁₆ x 15¾ in., (43.7 x 40 cm.), lithograph on wove (BP 125, DM 311, FR 1047, Y 20,274).

$776* *Allos Makar, (Wingler/Weiz 69-73), 1914: Five,* each stone mono., creases, (09-25-92, Granier, #2912), each sheet approx. 9⁷⁄₁₆ x 6⁵⁄₁₆ in., (24 x 16 cm.), lithograph on holzhaltigem factory print paper (BP 453, DM 1150, FR 3890, Y 93,663).

$660* *The Apple Of Eve, From Der Gefesselte Columbus, 1913,* s., margins, good cond., creases, tears, surface soiling, (10-28-92, Butterfield, #2834), 13½ x 11½ in., (343 x 292 mm.), lithograph on fine laid paper (BP 421, DM 1019, FR 3461, Y 80,982).

$6379* *"Apulia" (W./W. 268-287), 1964: Twenty,* Marlborough Fine Art Ltd., s., num., (06-08-93, Karl/Faber, #977), approx. 22¹⁄₁₆ x 27¹⁵⁄₁₆ in., (56 x 71 cm.), lithograph on Japon nacre (BP 4193, DM 10,350, FR 34,858, Y 677,536).

$783* *Autoritratto Con Bulino(Wingler/Welz 469), 1970-71,* proof, s., d., (05-20-93, Finarte-Milan, #82), 11⁹⁄₁₆ x 7⅞ in., (29.3 x 20 cm.), etching, bulino, on Giappone paper (BP 503, DM 1263, FR 4255, Y 86,462, L 1150).

BI *"Die Baumwollpfluckerin", 1908,* Kunstschau Wien poster, mono. in stone, artist's proof, lit., est. SC 180/190,000, (11-25-92, Dorotheum, #427, illus.), image 36¼ x 14¹⁵⁄₁₆ in., (92 x 38 cm.), color lithograph.

$565* *Bekenntnis (Wingler-Welz), 1961: Three,* from Bekenntnis for Hellas, pub. Marlborough Fine Art, (06-10-93, Hauswedell/Nolt, #504), each sh 26⁹⁄₁₆ x 20¹⁵⁄₁₆ in., (67.4 x 53.3 cm.), lithograph on Japan (BP 370, DM 920, FR 3098, Y 59,972).

$882* *"Der Beobachter" (Ich Und Meine Kritiker", 1970,* s. O. Kokoschka, #19/96, blindstamp, (05-19-93, Dorotheum, #468, illus.), plate 9¼ x 6¹⁵⁄₁₆ in., (23.5 x 17.6 cm.), sheet 15⅜ x 10⅝ in., (23.5 x 17.6 cm.), etching (BP 573, DM 1434, FR 4830, Y 97,642, SC 10,080).

BI *Bogenschutze, 1966,* from Odyssee, s., num., est. DM 1,800, (09-18-92, Schloss Ahlden, #1019), 22¼ x 15⁹⁄₁₆ in., (56.5 x 39.5 cm.), lithograph on hand-made.

$443* *Cathleen Und Der Dichter Aleel (Wingler-Welz 200), 1955,* s., from the series Irische Legende, (12-05-92, Bassenge, #7333), 10⅝ x 7⅞ in., (27 x 20 cm.), lithograph on vellum (BP 277, DM 691, FR 2354, Y 54,888).

$2164* *Comenius (Wingler/Welz 504-509 and 533-539), 1976: Twelve,* Meissner Edition, s., (11-21-92, Lempertz, #220), 26⅞ x 21³⁄₁₆ in., (68.2 x 53.8 cm.), 6 lithographs, 6 serigraphs (BP 1425, DM 3450, FR 11,622, Y 269,121).

$783* *Da: Irische Legende (Wingler/Welz 200 and 201 s.c.): Two,* s., (05-20-93, Finarte-Milan, #81), 12⅝ x 10¹⁄₁₆ in., (32 x 25.5 cm.), lithograph (BP 503, DM 1263, FR 4255, Y 86,462, L 1150).

BI *Delphi Mit Hirten (Wingler/Welz 245),* from Bekenntnis zu Hellasm sheet I, #37/65, s., creases, tears, est.SF 1/1,300, (09-04-92, Germann, #429), 20⅞ x 25⁹⁄₁₆ in., (530 x 650 mm.), lithograph.

$1568* *"Dr. Fritz Neuberger", 1917,* s. Oskar Kokoschka, (05-19-93, Dorotheum, #345, illus.), sheet 23¹⁄₁₆ x 15⁹⁄₁₆ in., (58.6 x 39.5 cm.), image 15³⁄₁₆ x 10¹³⁄₁₆ in., (58.6 x 39.5 cm.), lithograph (BP 1018, DM 2549, FR 8587, Y 173,586, SC 17,920).

$516* *"Dragon Au Dessus D'Une Flamme" (W.W. 59), 1914,* from Bachkantate, mono., creases, (10-18-92, Pescheteau,

#176), 21¼ x 15¾ in., (54 x 40 cm.), print on wove (BP 313, DM 762, FR 2589, Y 61,612).

$1176* *Erlebnis In Neapel (Wingler/W.214), 1960,* s., artist's proof, ded., wrinkles, (11-03-92, Hartung, #2621, illus.), color lithograph (BP 759, DM 1840, FR 6235, Y 143,642).

$1033* *Die Flehende (Wingler-Welz 62, 1), 1914,* mono., in the series O Ewigkeit - Du Donnerwort (Bachkantate), (12-05-92, Bassenge, #7332), 16⅛ x 10⅞ in., (41 x 27.7 cm.), lithograph on handmade (BP 647, DM 1611, FR 5489, Y 127,989).

$8121* *Der Gefesselte Kolumbus (Wingler-Welz 43-54; Arntz 23-34), 1913: Twelve,* s., stone mono., prov., (06-10-93, Hauswedell/Nolt, #498, illus.), portfolio 25⅞ x 1715/16 in., (65.8 x 45.5 cm.), lithograph on hand-made (BP 5312, DM 13,224, FR 44,523, Y 862,010).

$425* *Gitta (W./W. 199), 1953,* s., (06-08-93, Karl/Faber, #973), approx. 16⅛ x 20 11/16 in., (41 x 52.5 cm.), lithograph on copper print paper/board (BP 279, DM 690, FR 2322, Y 45,141).

$649* *Hamburger Hafen (Wingler/Welz 216), 1961,* stone mono., d., (11-21-92, Lempertz, #219), 18¼ x 24 in., (46.3 x 61 cm.), lithograph on wove (BP 427, DM 1035, FR 3485, Y 80,711).

$1277* *Hamburger Hafen (Winkler-Welz 216), 1961,* s., ded., (06-05-93, Bassenge, #6197), 18⅛ x 24 in., (46 x 61 cm.), chalk lithograph (BP 841, DM 2070, FR 6978, Y 136,988).

$2401* *Hefa (Wingler-Welz 155), 1922,* (06-10-93, Hauswedell/Nolt, #488, illus.), image 19 x 17⅛ in., (48.3 x 43.5 cm.), lithograph on hand-made (BP 1571, DM 3910, FR 13,163, Y 254,856).

$1299* *"Hefa" (Wingler/Welz 155), 1922,* s., num., (11-28-92, Grisebach, #598, illus.), 19 5/16 x 17⅛ in., (49 x 43.5 cm.), lithograph on handmade (BP 857, DM 2069, FR 7025, Y 161,668).

$793* *Kathe Richter (Wingler/Welz 112), 1917,* artist's proof, s., i., (11-21-92, Lempertz, #215), 10⅜ x 6 15/16 in., (26.4 x 17.7 cm.), lithograph on thick paper (BP 522, DM 1264, FR 4259, Y 98,620).

$4662* *Katia (Kathe Richter) (W.W. 133), 1918,* s., pub. P. Cassirer, margins, foxmarks, short tears and creases, staining, defects, (12-01-92, Christie-London, #406), L. 27 3/16 x 19⅛ in., (690 x 485 mm.), lithograph in blue on simili-Japan (BP 3080, DM 7431, FR 25,323, Y 580,428).

BI *Das Konzert I (Wingler/Welz 140), 1920,* s., num., est. DM 5,500, (05-26-93, Lempertz, #263, illus.), 27½ x 19¾ in., (69.8 x 50.1 cm.), lithograph on thick wove.

$2268* *Das Konzert IV (Wingler/Welz 143), 1920,* s., sheet 4 of 5 from the series Das Konzert, (06-08-93, Karl/Faber, #969), approx. 27 9/16 x 19 5/16 in., (70 x 49 cm.), lithograph on Zanders hand-made (BP 1491, DM 3680, FR 12,393, Y 240,892).

$709* *Kouros I (W./W. 449), 1968,* poster for Olympischen Spiele Munchen 1972, s., num., (06-08-93, Karl/Faber, #979), approx. 37 x 23 13/16 in., (94 x 60.5 cm.), color serigraph on Schoeller board (BP 466, DM 1150, FR 3874, Y 75,305).

$921* *Kouros II (W./W. 450), 1968/70,* s., num., (06-08-93, Karl/Faber, #980), approx. 34⅝ x 20 1/16 in., (88 x 51 cm.), lithograph on BFK Rives wove (BP 605, DM 1494, FR 5033, Y 97,823).

$706* *Madchen Mit Haarmasche (Wingler/Welz 156), 1922,* s., (06-10-93, Hauswedell/Nolt, #489), image 12⅜ x 8 15/16 in., (31.5 x 22.8 cm.), lithograph on hand-made (BP 462, DM 1150, FR 3871, Y 74,939).

$1134* *Madchen Mit Taube Und Totenkopf (W./W. 211), 1959,* s., d., i., num., (06-08-93, Karl/Faber, #976), approx. 25 3/16 x 17 15/16 in., (64 x 45.5 cm.), color lithograph on BFK Rives wove (BP 745, DM 1840, FR 6197, Y 120,446).

BI *"Der Mann Erhebt Seinen Kopf Aus Dem Grabe, Auf Dem Das Weib Sitz", 1914,* series "O Ewigkeit-Du Donnerwort", est. SC 20/24,000, (05-19-93, Dorotheum, #347, illus.), sheet 21 7/16 x 16⅛ in., (54.5 x 41 cm.), lithograph.

$377* *Olda (Wingler/Welz 207), 1956,* s., i. Proof Orig. Litho OK. 56, margins, (05-20-93, Bonhams-Chelsea, #71), image 16 x 12½ in., (40.6 x 31.8 cm.), lithograph (BP 242, DM 608, FR 2049, Y 41,630).

BI *Olympia (Wingler/Welz 257),* from Bekenntnis zu Hellas, sheet II, #37/65, s., creases, est. SF 1/1,300, (09-04-92, Germann, #428), 20 11/16 x 26⅛ in., (525 x 664 mm.), lithograph.

$1038* *"Olympische Spiele Munchen 1972" (W./W. 449), 1968,* s., num., (12-01-92, Karl/Faber, #857), 37 x 23 13/16 in., (94 x 60.5 cm.), color serigraph on Schoeller cardboard (BP 686, DM 1654, FR 5638, Y 129,233).

$706* *Paul Westheim (Kopf) (Wingler-Welz 162), 1923,* s., from Die Schaffenden, 4. Jahrgang, 3. portfolios, pub. Euphorion, (06-10-93, Hauswedell/Nolt, #490), image 10 3/16 x 11 15/16 in., (25.9 x 30.3 cm.), lithograph on hand-made (BP 462, DM 1150, FR 3871, Y 74,939).

$780* *Paul Westheim (W./W. 162), 1923,* s., (06-08-93, Karl/Faber, #971), approx. 10¼ x 11 13/16 in., (26 x 30 cm.), sh approx. 13 15/16 x 20⅞ in., (26 x 30 cm.), lithograph on J.W. Zanders hand-made (BP 513, DM 1266, FR 4262, Y 82,847).

$649* *Paul Westheim (Wingler/Welz 162), 1923,* s., embossed stamp, from Die Schaffenden, Jahrgang 4, 3, portfolio, (11-21-92, Lempertz, #216), 10 3/16 x 11 15/16 in., (25.9 x 30.3 cm.), lithograph on factory-made Van Gelder Zonen (BP 427, DM 1035, FR 3485, Y 80,711).

BI *"Penthesilea" (W./W. 454-63), (19)69: Ten,* Ars librorum, Edition de Beauclair, Frankfurt (1970), s., est. DM 10,000, (12-01-92, Karl/Faber, #858), 25 3/16 x 19⅛ in., (64 x 48.5 cm.), drypoint.

$546* *Portrait Of A Woman,* s., #36/50, margins, good cond., burning, 5/8" tear, staining, handling creases, surface soiling, notations, (05-19-93, Butterfield, #2067), 27 x 18½ in., (686 x 470 mm.), lithograph in greenish-yellow on JW Zanders laid (BP 354, DM 888, FR 2990, Y 60,445).

$1960* *"Das Prinzip", 1918,* s. O. Kokoschka, stone mono., blindstamp, Kiepenheuer, (05-19-93, Dorotheum, #344, illus.), sheet 16⅛ x 12 3/16 in., (41 x 31 cm.), lithograph in color (BP 1272, DM 3186, FR 10,734, Y 216,982, SC 22,400).

$2569* *"Ruth III" (Wingler/Welz 154), 1922,* s., t., num., w/ signs of wear, traces of old mounting, tears, (12-01-92, Karl/Faber, #854, illus.), 27 3/16 x 17 5/16 in., (69 x 44 cm.), lithograph on hand-made (BP 1697, DM 4095, FR 13,954, Y 319,846).

$674* *"Ruth V" (W.W. 219), 1961,* s., (10-18-92, Pescheteau, #175), 24⅝ x 19½ in., (62.5 x 49.5 cm.), lithograph in black on wove (BP 408, DM 996, FR 3382, Y 80,478).

$1939* *Selbstbildnis (Halbfigur) (Wingler/Welz 358 a), 1965,* s., num., block mono., (05-26-93, Dorling, #2798, illus.), 41 9/16 x 29¾ in., (105.5 x 75.5 cm.), lithograph on thick wove (BP 1254, DM 3164, FR 10,648, Y 210,669).

$709* *Selbstbildnis (W./W. 206), 1956,* s., num., Galerie Welz, (06-08-93, Karl/Faber, #974), approx. 22 7/16 x 16 9/16 in., (57 x 42 cm.), lithograph on wove (BP 466, DM 1150, FR 3874, Y 75,305).

$1328* *Selbstbildnis (Wingler-Welz 358a), 1965/66,* s., num., (12-05-92, Bassenge, #7335), 34 7/16 x 21¼ in., (87.5 x 54 cm.), chalk lithograph on copper print paper (BP 832, DM 2070, FR 7056, Y 164,540).

$21,186* *Selbstbildnis Von Zwei Seiten (Wingler-Welz 163), 1923,* s., #18/66, (06-10-93, Hauswedell/Nolt, #491, illus.), image 24¼ x 18⅜ in., (61.6 x 46.6 cm.), color lithograph on hand-made (BP 13,858, DM 34,499, FR 116,151, Y 2,248,806).

$550* *Statue Of Liberty,* s., inits in plate, num. XVII/XL, good cond., (12-12-92, Weschler, #136, illus.), sheet 29¾ x 35 in., (75.6 x 88.9 cm.), lithograph (BP 353, DM 867, FR 2970, Y 68,061).

$774* *Tiger (W.-W. 565), 1976,* #21/50 of Edit. A, s., d.; mono., d. in stone, (10-09-92, Winterberg, #2559), 14¾ x 18 5/16 in., (37.5 x 46.5 cm.), chalk lithograph on BFK Rives (BP 459, DM 1150, FR 3860, Y 94,229).

$234* *Tower Bridge,* #75/75, s., (11-19-92, Bonhams-Chelsea, #169), image 23 x 30¾ in., (58.4 x 78.1 cm.), lithograph (BP 154, DM 373, FR 1257, Y 29,101).

BI *"Die Traumenden Knaben" (Wingler/Welz 22-29, Pommeranz-Liedtke S. 197), 1908: Eleven,* est. DM 15/20,000, (11-28-92, Grisebach, #114, illus.), 9 9/16 x 11⅝ in., (24.3 x 29.6 cm.), 8 color lithographs and 3 line etchings on thick paper.

$247* *Urvater Der Fische (Wingler-Welz 217), 1961,* stone s., d., t., (06-10-93, Hauswedell/Nolt, #494), image 16 7/16 x 23 11/16 in., (41.8 x 60.1 cm.), color lithograph on wove (BP 162, DM 402, FR 1354, Y 26,218).

$590* *Urvater Der Fische (Wingler/Welz 217), 1961,* s., artist's proof, (12-05-92, Bassenge, #7334), 16 9/16 x 23 5/8 in., (42 x 60 cm.), color lithograph on vellum (BP 369, DM 920, FR 3135, Y 73,101).

BI *"Das WEib Triumphirt Uber Den Toten", 1913,* series "Der Gefesselte Kolumbus", s. O. Kokoschka, stone mono., est.SC 24/30,000, (05-19-93, Dorotheum, #346, illus.), sheet 19 1/8 x 13 15/16 in., (48.6 x 35.4 cm.), image 12 5/8 x 10 1/4 in., (48.6 x 35.4 cm.), lithograph.

$638* *Zwei Madchen Mit Taube (W./W. 208), 1956,* s., num., (06-08-93, Karl/Faber, #975), approx. 22 13/16 x 18 1/8 in., (58 x 46 cm.), color lithograph on wove (BP 419, DM 1035, FR 3486, Y 67,764).

$1271* *Zwei Madchen Mit Taube (Wingler/Welz 208), 1956,* s, #51/70, Beyeler Gallery, (06-10-93, Hauswedell/Nolt, #492, illus.), image 23 13/16 x 18 1/2 in., (60.5 x 47 cm.), color lithograph on wove (BP 831, DM 2070, FR 6968, Y 134,911).

$938* *Zwei Madchen Mit Taube (Wingler/Welz 208), 1956,* #60/70, s., (11-21-92, Lempertz, #218), 23 5/8 x 18 1/2 in., (60 x 47 cm.), lithograph on wove (BP 618, DM 1496, FR 5038, Y 116,652).

KOKYO 1864-1915

$550* *"Sea Battle During Russo-Japanese War": Triptych,* d. 1904, very good cond., (10-31-92, Goldberg, #658), (BP 360, DM 863, FR 2924, Y 68,002).

KOLAR, Jiri Czechoslovakian b. 1914

$67* *"Cavalerie Royale", 1986,* #12/75, s., (10-18-92, Pescheteau, #177), 22 13/16 x 31 1/2 in., (58 x 80 cm.), lithograph in colors on wove (BP 41, DM 99, FR 336, Y 8000).

BI *"Habipoticaire",* HC s., est. FF4/600, (04-04-93, Pescheteau, #230), 25 9/16 x 19 11/16 in., (65 x 50 cm.), color lithograph.

$1505* *La Malade, 1967,* mono., s., (05-27-93, Lempertz, #845, illus.), 41 1/2 x 26 3/4 in., (105.4 x 68 cm.), photo-lithograph on photo-canvas (BP 964, DM 2415, FR 8140, Y 161,342).

$126* *"Partitions 1982": Set Of Four,* d., s., (01-28-93, Pescheteau, #173), each 11 13/16 x 9 13/16 in., (30 x 25 cm.), serigraphs (BP 83, DM 200, FR 676, Y 15,644).

KOLBE, Carl Wilhelm 1759-1835

$217* *Die Heimkehrende Herde (Martens 275 IV),* foxed, (12-04-92, Bassenge, #6635), 17 11/16 x 20 15/16 in., (44.9 x 53.3 cm.), etching (BP 139, DM 346, FR 1172, Y 27,091).

$939* *Die Kuh Im Schilfe (Martens 88 III),* (12-04-92, Bassenge, #6629, illus.), 11 7/8 x 16 3/16 in., (30.2 x 41.1 cm.), etching (BP 602, DM 1495, FR 5073, Y 117,228).

$424* *Landschaft Mit Zwei Nymphen (Jentsch 61; Martens 208 II),* (06-10-93, Hauswedell/Nolt, #262), etching (BP 277, DM 690, FR 2325, Y 45,006).

BI *A Nude Youth Chasing A Nymph Round An Oak Tree (Martens 125),* small margins, creases, margins rubbed, est. BP 3/400, (06-30-93, Sotheby-London, #155), 10 1/4 x 6 3/4 in., (260 x 171 mm.), etching.

$614* *Ein Reiter Mit Lanze Und Einer Nackten Frau (Martens 173 III),* (12-04-92, Bassenge, #6633, illus.), 13 15/16 x 11 5/16 in., (35.5 x 28.7 cm.), etching (BP 394, DM 978, FR 3317, Y 76,654).

KOLBE, Carl Wilhelm (the elder) 1759-1835

$1056* *Grosses Krauterstuck Mit Nacktem Leierspieler (Martens 95), c. 1803,* water stains, i., (03-24-93, Venator/Hansten, #2607), pl. 16 1/8 x 20 1/2 in., (41 x 52 cm.), etching (BP 715, DM 1725, FR 5870, Y 124,075).

BI *Die Heimkehrende Herde,* foxed, trimmed, est. DM 800-, (09-14-92, Venator/Hansten, #1675), plate 16 1/4 x 20 15/16 in., (41.3 x 53.2 cm.), etching.

KOLBE, Georg German 1877-1947

$1277* *Nach Rechts Liegender Weiblicher Akt, c. 1920,* s., num., (06-05-93, Bassenge, #6203), 8 1/4 x 11 7/16 in., (21 x 29 cm.), lithgraph on hand-made (BP 841, DM 2070, FR 6978, Y 136,988).

KOLLAR, Francois 1904-1979

BI *Les Mains De Niedzielski, 1938,* s., t., d., (c) credit stamp, est. $2,2/2,800, (10-13-92, Christie-NY, #283, illus.), 3 3/4 x 8 5/8 in., (9.5 x 21.9 cm.), photograph, gelatin silver print.

BI *Pur Schiaparelli, 1939,* s., t., d., credit & reprod. limit. stamps, est. $2/3,000, (10-13-92, Christie-NY, #284, illus.), 10 7/8 x 8 5/8 in., (27.6 x 21.9 cm.), photograph, gelatin silver print.

KOLLWITZ, Kathe German 1867-1945

$2310* *Abschied Und Tod (K. 187/II), 1923-24,* second final state, s., margins, good cond., creases, glue stains, skinning, (11-05-92, Sotheby-NY, #213, illus.), 21 1/8 x 16 7/8 in., (536 x 430 mm.), sheet 23 1/8 x 19 in., (536 x 430 mm.), lithograph on thin wove (BP 1502, DM 3653, FR 12,360, Y 283,401).

$3971* *Abschied Und Tod (Kl. 187/II/a), 1923-1924,* s., (06-23-93, Kornfeld, #480, illus.), lithograph on cream handmade (BP 2698, DM 6719, FR 22,601, Y 432,618, SF 5980).

BI *"Abschied Und Tod" (Klipstein 187/II a), 1923-24,* s., est. DM 7/9,000, (06-05-93, Grisebach, #301, illus.), 21 1/16 x 17 1/8 in., (53.5 x 43.5 cm.), lithograph on wove.

$2128* *"Abschied Und Tod" (Klipstein 187/II), 1923/24,* s., pub. in Gerhart Hauptmann. Kathe Kollwitz, Abschied und Tod, Propylaen-Verlag, (06-05-93, Grisebach, #697, illus.), 21 1/16 x 16 7/8 in., (53.5 x 42.8 cm.), lithograph on wove (BP 1401, DM 3450, FR 11,628, Y 228,277).

$1844* *Der Agitationsredner (Klipstein 224 b), 1926,* s., (12-05-92, Bassenge, #7355), 12 3/16 x 8 7/16 in., (31 x 21.5 cm.), lithograph on handmade (BP 1155, DM 2875, FR 9798, Y 228,472).

$4600* *Arbeiterfrau Im Profil Nach Links (K. 67/II), 1903,* 2nd state of 3, margins, good cond., ink in image, scuffs, mat/light-stain, fox mark, (05-13-93, Sotheby-NY, #575, illus.), 17 1/2 x 12 5/8 in., (443 x 322 mm.), sh 23 3/8 x 18 in., (443 x 322 mm.), lithograph on heavy laid (BP 3020, DM 7428, FR 25,054, Y 513,565).

$9221* *"Arbeiterfrau Mit Schlafendem Jungen" (Klipstein 226 b), 1927,* s., pub. J.J. Ottens, (06-05-93, Grisebach, #307, illus.), 15 3/8 x 12 15/16 in., (39 x 33 cm.), lithograph on beige copper print paper (BP 6070, DM 14,950, FR 50,388, Y 989,165).

$1919* *Arbeitfrau (Mit Dem Ohrring) (Klipstein 105), 1910,* 4th state of 5, s. by artist and p. (Felsing), margins, tear in right margin, top 2 corners restored, Late Gerhard Brauer Coll., (05-27-93, Sotheby-Amstrdm, #747, illus.), 12 5/8 x 9 1/2 in., (321 x 242 mm.), etching on sturdy wove (BP 1229, DM 3079, FR 10,379, Y 205,725, G 3450).

$1773* *"Aufruhr" (Klipstein 44/V), 1899,* s., prov., (06-05-93, Grisebach, #690, illus.), 11 13/16 x 12 1/2 in., (30 x 31.7 cm.), aquatint in brownish-black on Japan (BP 1167, DM 2875, FR 9689, Y 190,195).

$599* *"Aus Vielen Wunden Blutest Du, Oh Volk" (Klipstein 29 III), 1896,* s., (05-26-93, Lempertz, #267), 12 3/8 x 17 11/16 in., (31.4 x 45 cm.), etching on thick wove (BP 388, DM 977, FR 3289, Y 65,080).

$2598* *Auto-Portrait (Klipstein 133), 1919,* whole margins, s., (06-11-93, Picard, #83), 13 3/8 x 11 7/16 in., (340 x 290 mm.), lithograph in black on Japan pelure laid (BP 1707, DM 4222, FR 14,236, Y 275,650).

$593* *"Bauernkrieg", 1921,* s., plate d.,, (09-05-92, Arnold, #2, illus.), 13 3/16 x 20 7/8 in., (33.5 x 53 cm.), etching (BP 296, DM 826, FR 2812, Y 72,788).

$2452* *Begrussung (Klipstein 10 II d), 1892,* s., (11-21-92, Lempertz, #225), 4 3/4 x 3 9/16 in., (12 x 9 cm.), etching on hand-made (BP 1614, DM 3909, FR 13,169, Y 304,937).

$989* *Beim Arzt (Klipstein 150 IIc), 1920,* s., stone mono., (06-10-93, Hauswedell/Nolt, #522), image 6 13/16 x 10 13/16 in., (17.3 x 27.5 cm.), lithograph on factory print (BP 647, DM 1610, FR 5422, Y 104,978).

$2655* *Beim Dengeln (Klipstein 90 X), 1905,* s., (12-05-92, Bassenge, #7340), 11 5/8 x 11 5/8 in., (29.6 x 29.6 cm.), etching and nature print on copper print paper (BP 1662, DM 4139, FR 14,107, Y 328,956).

$2020* *Beratung (Klipstein 36 c), 1898,* #7/50, s., plate 3 from Ein Weberaufstand, (11-21-92, Lempertz, #224, illus.), 10 11/16 x 6 9/16 in., (27.1 x 16.7 cm.), lithograph on copper print paper (BP 1330, DM 3221, FR 10,849, Y 251,213).

$1333* *Besuch Im Krakenhaus (K. 236 VI), 1929,* 6th final state, s., pub. Euphorian-Verlag, margins, trimmed, creasing, (11-30-92, Phillips-London, #445, illus.), border 10¾ x 14 in., (273 x 356 mm.), woodcut on japan (BP 880, DM 2124, FR 7209, Y 165,899).

$1333* *Betendes Madchen (K. 11IIb), 1920,* s., 2nd state of 4, full margins, mount-staining, (11-30-92, Phillips-London, #444), plate 7⅞ x 6 in., (200 x 152 mm.), etching on wove (BP 880, DM 2124, FR 7209, Y 165,899).

$2966* *Betendes Madchen (Klipstein 11 IIb), 1892,* s., #7/50, two states, (06-10-93, Hauswedell/Nolt, #507, illus.), image 7⁹⁄₁₆ x 5⅞ in., (19.2 x 14.9 cm.), etching and Vernis-mou on copper print (BP 1940, DM 4830, FR 16,261, Y 314,829).

$288* *Bettelnde (Klipstein 193), 1924,* 3rd final state, p. sig., pencil sig., margins, light-stained, shorttears, other defects at edges of sheet, Late Gerhard Bauer Coll., (05-27-93, Sotheby-Amstrdm, #751), sh 14¼ x 9¹⁄₁₆ in., lithograph on wove (BP 184, DM 462, FR 1558, Y 30,875, G 518).

BI *Bewaffnung In Einem Gewolbe (Kl. 95/VII (?)), 1906,* s., est. DM 5500, (12-01-92, Karl/Faber, #862, illus.), 18⅞ x 12³⁄₁₆ in., (48 x 31 cm.), etching and pressed print on copper print paper.

$2837* *"Brot" (Klipstein 196/III), 1924,* s., (06-05-93, Grise-bach, #698, illus.), 12 x 11 in., (30.5 x 28 cm.), litho-graph on copper print paper (BP 1868, DM 4600, FR 15,503, Y 304,334).

$5393* *Brustbild Einer Arbeiterfrau Mit Blauem Tuch (Kl. 68/II-III), 1903,* s., (12-01-92, Karl/Faber, #861, illus.), 13¹⁵⁄₁₆ x 9⁷⁄₁₆ in., (35.5 x 24 cm.), color lithograph on Kaiserli-chem Japan (BP 3563, DM 8596, FR 29,294, Y 671,439).

$709* *"Brustbild Einer Arbeiterfrau Mit Blauem Tuch" (Klip-stein 68/IIIb), 1903,* (06-05-93, Grisebach, #691, illus.), 13¹⁵⁄₁₆ x 9⅝ in., (35.5 x 24.5 cm.), color lithograph on copper print paper (BP 467, DM 1149, FR 3874, Y 76,057).

$6858* *"Brustbild Einer Arbeitfrau Mit Blauem Tuch" (Klipstein 68/II), 1903,* s., (11-28-92, Grisebach, #119, illus.), 13⅞ x 9¹¹⁄₁₆ in., (35.2 x 24.6 cm.), color lithograph on imita-tion Japan (BP 4527, DM 10,926, FR 37,090, Y 853,516).

$805* *Die Carmagnole (Klipstein 49 VIII), 1901,* tears, (12-12-92, Bassenge, #8665), 22¹⁵⁄₁₆ x 16¼ in., (58.2 x 41.3 cm.), etching on wove (BP 515, DM 1265, FR 4312, Y 99,592).

$475* *"Conspiracy" (Klipstein 25 v/vii), 1895,* pub. Emil Rich-ter, p. c. 1920, init. ER, good cond., (05-15-93, Cleve-land, #397, illus.), 11⅝ x 6⅞ in., (29.5 x 17.5 cm.), etching on heavy wove (BP 309, DM 764, FR 2568, Y 52,655).

$9163* *Dem Andenken Ludwig Franks (Kl. 127, Timm 719), 1914,* mono., (06-23-93, Kornfeld, #464, illus.), 19¹¹⁄₁₆ x 17⁷⁄₁₆ in., (50 x 44.3 cm.), lithograph on thin wove (BP 6225, DM 15,504, FR 52,151, Y 998,257, SF 13,800).

$1773* *"Die Eltern (III. Fassung)" (Klipstein 179 IVc), 1922/23,* s., sheet 4 of series Sieben Holzschnitte Zum Krieg, num., Edit. B, (06-05-93, Grisebach, #696, illus.), 13¹¹⁄₁₆ x 16⅝ in., (34.8 x 42.2 cm.), woodcut on thin beige copper print paper (BP 1167, DM 2875, FR 9689, Y 190,195).

$2749* *Die Eltern (Kl. 179/IV), 1923,* III Fassung, sheet 3 of series: Krieg, s., (06-23-93, Kornfeld, #479, illus.), wood-cut on cream wove (BP 1868, DM 4651, FR 15,646, Y 299,488, SF 4140).

$805* *Die Eltern Der Kunstlerin (K. 136/a), 1919,* s. (faint), margins, repaired tears, tear (repaired), soiling, abrasions, foxing, (05-13-93, Sotheby-NY, #577), 12⅜ x 18¼ in., (313 x 465 mm.), sh 15¼ x 21⅝ in., (313 x 465 mm.), lithograph on wove (BP 528, DM 1300, FR 4385, Y 89,874).

$1475* *Die Eltern Der Kunstlerin (Klipstein 136 c), 1919,* s., (12-05-92, Bassenge, #7343), 12⅝ x 18⅞ in., (32 x 48 cm.), lithograph on handmade (BP 924, DM 2300, FR 7837, Y 182,753).

$749* *Ende (K. 37 II), 1897,* 2nd state of 5, s., margins, minor creases, foxing, (12-01-92, Christie-London, #409), plate 9¹³⁄₁₆ x 12 in., (250 x 305 mm.), etching w/aquatint and punchwork (BP 495, DM 1194, FR 4068, Y 93,252).

BI *Ende (K. 37 II), 1897,* s., #46/50, sig., pub. E. Richter, margins, foxing, discoloration, est. BP 1,0/1,500, (12-01-92, Christie-London, #410), plate 9¾ x 12 in., (247 x 305 mm.), etching w/aquatint and punchwork on thick wove.

BI *Frau An Der Wiege (Klipstein 38 III c), 1897,* est. DM 1,200, (12-05-92, Bassenge, #7337), 10⅞ x 5¾ in., (27.6 x 14.6 cm.), etching on vellum.

$4950* *Frau Mit Totem Kind (K. 72/IX), 1903,* ninth state of ten, sig. stamp, pub. blindstamp, Emil Richter, unevenly cut margins, good cond., water stain, (11-05-92, Sotheby-NY, #211, illus.), 16⅝ x 19 in., (421 x 483 mm.), sheet 20⅞ x 22⅜ in., (421 x 483 mm.), etching and soft (molle) ground p. in brown on cream wove (BP 3220, DM 7829, FR 26,485, Y 607,287).

$640* *Frauenkopf (Klipstein 76), 1905,* 4th state of 5, pencil sig., margins, paper discoloration, minor creasing, small defects at edges of sheet, (05-27-93, Sotheby-Amstrdm, #745), 9¹⁄₁₆ x 5⁷⁄₁₆ in., (230 x 138 mm.), soft ground etching on wove (BP 410, DM 1027, FR 3461, Y 68,611, G 1150).

BI *Die Freiwilligen (Klipstein 178), 1922-23,* plate 2 from Krieg, s., proof, full margins, good cond., handling creases, est. BP 2/2,500, (06-30-93, Sotheby-London, #475, illus.), 13¾ x 19¼ in., (349 x 489 mm.), woodcut.

BI *Gedenkblatt Fur Karl Liebknecht (K. 137 V/A/b), 1919, 1945,* margins, good cond., staining, soiling, est. $6/800, (05-19-93, Butterfield, #2067A), 11 x 6¼ in., (279 x 159 mm.), etching and aquatint on wove.

$2750* *Gedenkblatt Fur Karl Liebknecht (K. 139/III), 1919-1920,* third state of four, s., i., #57, printer's sig., Voight, unevenly cut margins, good cond., scuffs, light stain, creases, tear, tape stains, rubbing, soiling, glue stain, (11-05-92, Sotheby-NY, #212, illus.), 13¾ x 19¾ in., (350 x 502 mm.), sheet 21¼ x 24½ in., (350 x 502 mm.), woodcut on cream wove (BP 1789, DM 4349, FR 14,714, Y 337,382).

$16,417* *Gedenkblatt Fur Karl Liebknecht (Kl. 139/II), 1919,* s., 2nd state, (06-23-93, Kornfeld, #474, illus.), woodcut (BP 11,153, DM 27,778, FR 93,438, Y 1,788,539, SF 24,725).

$3818* *Gedenkblatt Fur Karl Liebknecht (Kl. 139/IV/a), 1919-1920,* s., (06-23-93, Kornfeld, #475, illus.), woodcut on thick wove (BP 2594, DM 6460, FR 21,730, Y 415,949, SF 5750).

$3955* *Gedenkblatt Fur Karl Liebknecht (Klipstein 139 III), 1919/1920,* s., #89/100, (06-10-93, Hauswedell/Nolt, #517, illus.), image 13¹⁵⁄₁₆ x 19¹¹⁄₁₆ in., (35.5 x 50 cm.), wood-cut (BP 2587, DM 6440, FR 21,683, Y 419,807).

$4123* *Gefallen (Kl. 153/II/a), 1921,* s., artist's proof, (06-23-93, Kornfeld, #476, illus.), lithograph on handmade (BP 2801, DM 6976, FR 23,466, Y 449,177, SF 6210).

$1328* *Gefallen (Klipstein 153 II), 1921,* 2nd version, (12-05-92, Bassenge, #7347), 16⅛ x 15³⁄₁₆ in., (41 x 38.5 cm.), lithograph on thick wove (BP 832, DM 2070, FR 7056, Y 164,540).

$1554* *Gefallen (Klipstein 153 II), 1921,* (06-10-93, Hauswedell/Nolt, #523, illus.), image 16¼ x 14¹⁵⁄₁₆ in., (41.3 x 38 cm.), lithograph on wove (BP 1016, DM 2531, FR 8520, Y 164,951).

$6029* *"Gefallen, II Fassung" (Klipstein 153/Ib), 1921,* s., i., num., (06-05-93, Grisebach, #302, illus.), 15¹⁵⁄₁₆ x 14¹⁵⁄₁₆ in., (40.5 x 38 cm.), lithograph on thick Japan (BP 3969, DM 9775, FR 32,945, Y 646,750).

$2291* *Gefangene, Musik Horend (Kl. 203/II/a), 1925,* s., (06-23-93, Kornfeld, #481), lithograph on imperial Japan (BP 1556, DM 3876, FR 13,039, Y 249,591, SF 3450).

$3665* *Gefangene, Musik Horend (Klipstein 203 II a), 1925,* s., (05-26-93, Lempertz, #272, illus.), 21¹⁵⁄₁₆ x 15¹⁵⁄₁₆ in., (55.8 x 40.5 cm.), lithograph on Japan (BP 2371, DM 5980, FR 20,126, Y 398,196).

$3163* *Die Gefangenen (K. 98/VI), 1908,* plate 7 of Bauernkrieg, 6th state of 8, s., i., sig. printer, Felsing, p. 1921, mar-gins, good cond., pressure mark, discoloration, mat stain, creases, tape stain, skinning, (05-13-93, Sotheby-

NY, #576), 12¾ x 16⅝ in., (323 x 422 mm.), sh 17⅛ x 20⅛ in., (323 x 422 mm.), etching and soft-ground in dark brown on heavy wove (BP 2077, DM 5107, FR 17,228, Y 353,132).

$5040* *Die Gefangenen (Kl. 98/V), 1908,* sheet 7 of series: Bauernkrieg, s., (06-23-93, Kornfeld, #468, illus.), etching and Stoffdurchdruckverfahren on Japan (BP 3424, DM 8528, FR 28,685, Y 549,079, SF 7590).

$1265* *Gesenkter Frauenkopf (K. 77/IIIb), 1905,* bears sig., w/ Felsing and Richter info., 1920, margins, good cond., surface soiling, paper partially split, tears, hinges, notations, (05-19-93, Butterfield, #1922), 14¾ x 12¼ in., (375 x 311 mm.), soft-ground etching in sepia on heavy wove (BP 821, DM 2056, FR 6928, Y 140,042).

$4123* *Gesenkter Frauenkopf (Klipstein 77/III/a), 1905,* s., (06-23-93, Kornfeld, #466), soft-ground etching on thin Japan (BP 2801, DM 6976, FR 23,466, Y 449,177, SF 6210).

$1561* *"Gesenkter Frauenkopf" (Klipstein 77/IV), 1905,* s., (06-05-93, Grisebach, #692, illus.), 14⅞ x 12⅜ in., (37.8 x 31.5 cm.), soft-ground etching w/drypoint in brownish-black on copper print paper (BP 1028, DM 2531, FR 8530, Y 167,453).

$30,800* *Halbigur Einer Frau Mit Verscharankten Armen (Klipstein 85), 1905,* 2nd final state, s., i., wide margins, creasing, skinning, staining,very good cond., prop. R. Thornton Wilson, (11-09-92, Christie-NY, #106, illus.), 548 x 412 in., (x cm.), colored lithograph on heavy buff wove (BP 20,364, DM 49,170, FR 166,127, Y 3,822,288).

BI *Hamburger Kneipe (K./58/II/b), 1901,* 2nd state of 3, s., i. Fur Fraulein Helscher Taubler, margins, good cond., mat stain, foxing, skinned spot, staining, skinning, est. $1,5/2,000, (05-13-93, Sotheby-NY, #574), 7½ x 9¾ in., (192 x 247 mm.), sh 12¼ x 15¼ in., (192 x 247 mm.), soft-ground etching on heavy wove.

$1475* *Hamburger Kneipe (Klipstein 58 III a), 1901,* s., (12-05-92, Bassenge, #7339), 7⁹⁄₁₆ x 9¾ in., (19.2 x 24.7 cm.), soft-ground etching on thick copper print paper (BP 924, DM 2300, FR 7837, Y 182,753).

$1412* *Hamburger Kneipe (Klipstein 58 III a), 1910,* s., (06-10-93, Hauswedell/Nolt, #510), image 7⅞ x 9⅝ in., (20 x 24.5 cm.), Vernis-mou on copper print (BP 924, DM 2299, FR 7741, Y 149,878).

BI *"Hamburger Kneipe" (Klipstein 58/IIa), 1901,* s., est. DM 2,8/3,400, (11-28-92, Grisebach, #601, illus.), 7⅜ x 9⁷⁄₁₆ in., (18.7 x 24 cm.), soft ground with drypoint on copper print paper.

$160* *Hamburger Kneippe (Klipstein 58), 1901,* 3rd (final) state, w/Von Der Becke blindstamp, full margins, good cond., Late Gerhard Brauer Coll., (05-27-93, Sotheby-Amstrdm, #744), 7¹¹⁄₁₆ x 9⅝ in., (196 x 245 mm.), soft-ground etching on wove (BP 102, DM 257, FR 865, Y 17,153, G 288).

$1599* *Hanburger Kneippe (Klipstein 58), 1901,* 1st state of 3, s. by artist and p. (Felsing), #8/50, margins, foxing, Late Gerhard Brauer Coll., (05-27-93, Sotheby-Amstrdm, #743, illus.), 7¾ x 9¾ in., (197 x 247 mm.), soft-ground etching on sturdy wove (BP 1024, DM 2566, FR 8648, Y 171,419, G 2875).

$3319* *Heimarbeit (Klipstein 209 nach III), 1925,* s., (12-05-92, Bassenge, #7352), 13³⁄₁₆ x 16⁹⁄₁₆ in., (33.5 x 42 cm.), lithograph on copper print paper (BP 2078, DM 5175, FR 17,635, Y 411,225).

BI *"Heimarbeiterin", (K.93) 1906,* est. DK 5,000, (09-29-92, B. Rasmussen, #339), 15¹⁵⁄₁₆ x 21⅛ in., lithographic poster.

$2825* *Helft Russland (Klipstein 154 I), 1921,* (06-10-93, Hauswedell/Nolt, #524, illus.), image 26¹³⁄₁₆ x 18½ in., (68.1 x 47 cm.), lithograph on Japan (BP 1848, DM 4600, FR 15,488, Y 299,862).

$2582* *Helft Russland (Klipstein 154 III), 1921,* s., (12-05-92, Bassenge, #7348), 15¾ x 18½ in., (40 x 47 cm.), lithograph on handmade (BP 1617, DM 4026, FR 13,719, Y 319,911).

$1610* *Hockende Frau Von Vorne Mit Ubereinander Gelegten Handen (K. 156), 1921,* init., #70/100, in portfolio Freien Secession, full margins, good cond., mat stain, foxing, tape stains, (05-13-93, Sotheby-NY, #578, illus.), 11⅝ x 8¾ in., (295 x 223 mm.), lithograph on laid (BP 1057, DM 2600, FR 8769, Y 179,748).

$1150* *Hunger (K. 169/IV), 1923,* final state, full margins, good cond., creases, mat stain, masking tape, (05-13-93, Sotheby-NY, #579), 8¾ x 9 in., (223 x 228 mm.), woodcut on fibrous wove (BP 755, DM 1857, FR 6264, Y 128,391).

$1844* *Hunger (Klipstein 169 VI), 1923,* s., foxing, (12-05-92, Bassenge, #7349), 8¹³⁄₁₆ x 8¹⁵⁄₁₆ in., (22.4 x 22.7 cm.), woodcut on rough, thick handmade (BP 1155, DM 2875, FR 9798, Y 228,472).

$1980* *Hunger, 1923,* from the War cycle, s., full margins?, scuff marks, paper imperfections, time/mat stain, (12-08-92, Swann, #168), 11 x 10 in., (27.9 x 25.4 cm.), woodcut on soft (molle) laid paper (BP 1241, DM 3083, FR 10,510, Y 245,414).

$1695* *In Der Sprechstunde Des Kinderarztes (Klipstein 149 IIc), 1920,* s., stone mono., (06-10-93, Hauswedell/Nolt, #521), image 5⅛ x 10⅝ in., (13 x 27 cm.), lithograph on factory print (BP 1109, DM 2760, FR 9293, Y 179,917).

$1150* *Kie Pfluger (Kliptein 94/IX/b), 1906,* 9th (final) state, pub. von der Becke, blindstamp, full margins, good cond., mat/light stains, foxing, creases, masking tape, (02-11-93, Sotheby-NY, #155), 12½ x 17¹³⁄₁₆ in., (318 x 452 mm.), etching (BP 811, DM 1905, FR 6446, Y 138,638).

$4229* *Kinderkopf (Lotte) (Klipstein 213 a), 1925,* s., (05-26-93, Lempertz, #273, illus.), 10⁹⁄₁₆ x 7¹¹⁄₁₆ in., (26.8 x 19.5 cm.), lithograph on thin Japan (BP 2736, DM 6900, FR 23,224, Y 459,474).

$480* *Kinderkopf (Lotte) (Klipstein 213), 1925,* Von Der Becke blindstamp, margins, good cond., surface dirt in lower-margin, Late Gerhard Bauer Coll., (05-27-93, Sotheby-Amstrdm, #752), sh 11⅞ x 8¹¹⁄₁₆ in., (301 x 221 mm.), lithograph on wove (BP 307, DM 770, FR 2596, Y 51,458, G 863).

$1462* *Der Kirchenmauer (Klipstein 19 v (b)), 1893,* s., stamp, sig., (04-21-93, Germann, #578, illus.), 15¾ x 11¹³⁄₁₆ in., (400 x 300 mm.), etching (BP 949, DM 2337, FR 7903, Y 161,851, SF 2128).

$2216* *Der Kirchenmauer (Klipstein Nr.19. IVb),* s., #8/50, (10-21-92, Dobiaschofsky, #2091, illus.), 9¹³⁄₁₆ x 5³⁄₁₆ in., (24.9 x 13.2 cm.), etching (BP 1376, DM 3353, FR 11,382, Y 269,915, SF 3000).

$777* *Kleiner Mannerkopf Ohne Hande (Klipstein 163 VIb), 1922,* s., block mono., #77/150, (06-10-93, Hauswedell/ Nolt, #525), image 2¹³⁄₁₆ x 2⅝ in., (7.2 x 6.7 cm.), woodcut on factory print (BP 508, DM 1265, FR 4260, Y 82,475).

$416* *Kleiner Mannerkopf Ohne Hande (Klipstein 163), 1922,* 6th final state, s., #48/150, full margins, good cond., minor foxing, some paper discoloration, Late Gerhard Brauer Coll., (05-27-93, Sotheby-Amstrdm, #750), 2¾ x 2¹¹⁄₁₆ in., (70 x 68 mm.), woodcut on sturdy wove (BP 266, DM 668, FR 2250, Y 44,597, G 748).

$1985* *Kleines Selbstbildnis Nach Links (Kl. 159/a), 1922,* II Fassung, (06-23-93, Kornfeld, #478), lithograph on thick cream wove (BP 1349, DM 3359, FR 11,298, Y 216,254, SF 2990).

$2444* *Kleines Selbstbildnis Nach Links (Kl. 159/a), 1922,* II Fassung, (06-23-93, Kornfeld, #477), lithograph on thick wove (BP 1660, DM 4135, FR 13,910, Y 266,260, SF 3680).

$1023* *Mannerkopf Nach Rechts (Klipstein 78), 1905,* s., #36/50, s. by printer, margins, good cond., creases, tape stains, (12-03-92, Sotheby-London, #357), 13⅜ x 21 in., (340 x 533 mm.), soft-ground etching on wove (BP 660, DM 1609, FR 5491, Y 127,286).

$4229* *Maria Und Elisabeth (Klipstein 234 V a), 1928,* s., (05-26-93, Lempertz, #274, illus.), 15¹³⁄₁₆ x 18¹⁄₁₆ in., (40.2 x 45.9 cm.), wood engraving on Japan (BP 2736, DM 6900, FR 23,224, Y 459,474).

$99* *Mother And Child,* s. Kathe Kollwitz, sig. questionable, (04-02-93, Garth, #252), 25¾ x 19 in., (65.4 x 48.3 cm.), b/w lithograph (BP 65, DM 159, FR 540, Y 11,272).

$10,946* *Mutter Mit Jungen (Klipstein 246 II b), 1931,* s., foxed, (06-10-93, Hauswedell/Nolt, #529, illus.), image 13¾ x

8¼ in., (35 x 21 cm.), lithograph on wove (BP 7160, DM 17,824, FR 60,011, Y 1,161,872).

$1100* *"Mutter Mit Kind Auf Dem Arm (II. Fassung)" (Klipstein 110/IV), 1910,* blindstamp, (06-05-93, Grisebach, #695, illus.), 7¾ x 4¹⁵/₁₆ in., (19.7 x 12.6 cm.), etching in brownish black on copper print paper (BP 724, DM 1783, FR 6011, Y 118,000).

$968* *Mutter Mit Kind Auf Dem Arm (Kl. 132, II), 1916,* foxed, in Der Bildermann, (10-09-92, Winterberg, #2568, illus.), 11⁷/₁₆ x 7⅝ in., (29 x 19.3 cm.), lithograph on wove (BP 574, DM 1438, FR 4828, Y 117,848).

$1586* *Mutter Mit Kind Auf Dem Arm (Klipstein 110 V), 1910,* s., (05-26-93, Lempertz, #269, illus.), 14¹³/₁₆ x 10¹¹/₁₆ in., (37.7 x 27.2 cm.), etching on wove (BP 1026, DM 2588, FR 8710, Y 172,316).

$1171* *Mutter Mit Kind Auf Dem Arm (Klipstein 132 II (v. II)), 1916,* stein s., in Der Bildermann, (12-12-92, Wachholtz, #189), 10¹³/₁₆ x 7½ in., (27.5 x 19 cm.), lithograph (chalk) on machinemade paper (BP 749, DM 1840, FR 6272, Y 144,872).

BI *Die Mutter Und Der Tod,* pub. Emil Richter, Dresden, est. DM 2000, (09-05-92, Arnold, #1, illus.), 17⁹/₁₆ x 17⅜ in., (44.6 x 44.2 cm.), etching.

BI *Mutter Und Kind,* est. DK 1,000, (04-21-93, Kunsthallen, #158), lithograph.

$6638* *Mutter, II. Fassung (Klipstein 1351 I c), 1919,* s., (12-05-92, Bassenge, #7342), 17⅛ x 23¹/₁₆ in., (43.5 x 58.5 cm.), lithograph on JW Zanders-Papier (BP 4157, DM 10,349, FR 35,271, Y 822,451).

$6638* *Mutter, II. Fassung. (Kl. 135/I c), 1919,* s., signs of wear, glue stained, margin tears, (12-01-92, Karl/Faber, #867, illus.), 17⅛ x 22¹³/₁₆ in., (43.5 x 58 cm.), lithograph on wove (BP 4386, DM 10,580, FR 36,056, Y 826,444).

$7803* *Muttergluck (Klipstein 244), 1931,* s., (06-05-93, Bassenge, #6216, illus.), 8¼ x 12⅝ in., (21 x 32 cm.), lithograph on thin wove board (BP 5137, DM 12,651, FR 42,639, Y 837,052).

$7448* *Muttergluck (Klipstein 244), 1931,* s., (06-05-93, Bassenge, #6217, illus.), 8¼ x 12⅝ in., (21 x 32 cm.), lithograph on thin wove board (BP 4903, DM 12,075, FR 40,699, Y 798,970).

$169* *Muttergluck, 1931,* (04-21-93, Kunsthallen, #159), lithograph (BP 110, DM 270, FR 914, Y 18,709, DK 1035).

$5812* *Muttergluck, 1931,* s., creased, (09-18-92, Schloss Ahlden, #1020, illus.), 14¹³/₁₆ x 18⅝ in., (37.7 x 47.3 cm.), lithograph on light yellowish paper (BP 3403, DM 8624, FR 29,503, Y 718,329).

$1992* *Nachdenkende Frau (Klipstein 146 c), 1920,* 1st version, s., (12-05-92, Bassenge, #7346), 11⁷/₁₆ x 10¼ in., (29 x 26 cm.), lithograph on handmade (BP 1247, DM 3106, FR 10,584, Y 246,810).

$777* *Nachdenkende Frau (Klipstein 146 c), 1920,* s., (06-10-93, Hauswedell/Nolt, #518), image 11⁷/₁₆ x 10⁹/₁₆ in., (29.1 x 26.8 cm.), lithograph on hand-made (BP 508, DM 1265, FR 4260, Y 82,475).

$2467* *Nachdenkende Frau (Klipstein 147 II a), 1920,* s., (05-26-93, Lempertz, #271, illus.), 22⁷/₁₆ x 17 in., (57 x 43.2 cm.), lithograph on smooth wove (BP 1596, DM 4025, FR 13,548, Y 268,036).

$2260* *Nachdenkende Frau (Klipstein 147 II a), 1920,* 2nd version, s., from the Richter-portfolio Kathe Kollwitz, Handzeichnungen, edit. C., (06-10-93, Hauswedell/Nolt, #519, illus.), image 21¹/₁₆ x 14⁹/₁₆ in., (53.5 x 37 cm.), lithograph on wove (BP 1478, DM 3680, FR 12,390, Y 239,890).

$1981* *Nachdenkende Frau II (Klipstein 147 I c), 1920,* s., prov., (04-24-93, Kunsthaus, #660), 21¼ x 14¾ in., (54 x 37.5 cm.), lithograph on toned werkdruckkarton (BP 1250, DM 3105, FR 10,487, Y 218,605).

$193* *Nude Woman,* restrike, (11-12-92, Freemn/Fine Art, #115), plate 6½ x 5¼ in., (16.5 x 13.3 cm.), etching (BP 127, DM 306, FR 1032, Y 23,931).

$528* *Peasants March,* (03-20-93, Northeast, #738, illus.), sight 11 x 12 in., (27.9 x 30.5 cm.), etching (BP 354, DM 863, FR 2938, Y 61,246).

$206* *Le Penseur,* original, full margins, dirty, (03-31-93, Briest, #E58), sh 22¼ x 18⅛ in., (56.5 x 46 cm.), 10¹³/₁₆ x 5⅞

in., (56.5 x 46 cm.), etching (BP 136, DM 331, FR 1126, Y 23,689).

$4276* *Die Pfluger (Kl. 94/VI), 1906,* sheet 1 of series: Bauernkrieg, s., (06-23-93, Kornfeld, #467), line etching and aquatint on thick copper print paper (BP 2905, DM 7235, FR 24,337, Y 465,846, SF 6440).

$3107* *Die Pfluger (Klipstein 94 VII), 1906,* s., from Bauernkrieg, (06-10-93, Hauswedell/Nolt, #512, illus.), image 12⅜ x 17¹³/₁₆ in., (31.4 x 45.3 cm.), etching and aquatint on Japan (BP 2032, DM 5059, FR 17,034, Y 329,795).

$1582* *Die Pfluger, Plate 1 (K. 94 VIII), 1906,* 8th state of 9, s., pub. E. Richter, margins, surface dirt, good cond., (12-01-92, Christie-London, #411, illus.), plate 12⅜ x 17¹³/₁₆ in., (314 x 453 mm.), etching w/aquatint on wove (BP 1045, DM 2522, FR 8593, Y 196,962).

$2119* *Pflugzieher Und Weib (Klipstein 61 II b), 1902,* s., stone d., (06-10-93, Hauswedell/Nolt, #511, illus.), 14⁵/₁₆ x 19¹³/₁₆ in., (36.3 x 50.3 cm.), lithograph w/toneplate on hand-made (BP 1386, DM 3451, FR 11,617, Y 224,923).

$5675* *Plakat Zum Zille-Film (Klipstein 238), 1929/30,* s., ded., t., (06-05-93, Bassenge, #6215), 31¹¹/₁₆ x 34⅝ in., (80.5 x 88 cm.), sh 56⅜ x 37¹³/₁₆ in., (80.5 x 88 cm.), lithograph on wove (BP 3736, DM 9201, FR 31,011, Y 608,775).

$131* *Portraethoved,* (04-21-93, Kunsthallen, #160), lithograph (BP 85, DM 209, FR 708, Y 14,502, DK 805).

$550* *Return From The Market, 1932,* issued by Von der Beck, blindstamp, (05-27-93, Swann, #148, illus.), 7½ x 6 in., (19.1 x 15.2 cm.), etching (BP 352, DM 883, FR 2975, Y 58,962).

$5367* *Ruf Des Todes (Klipstein 263 b), 1934/35,* s., i. from Folge Tod, prov., (06-10-93, Hauswedell/Nolt, #531), image 14¹⁵/₁₆ x 15¹/₁₆ in., (38 x 38.3 cm.), lithograph on wove (BP 3511, DM 8740, FR 29,424, Y 569,685).

$878* *Ruf Des Todes (Klipstein 263 c), 1934/35,* (12-12-92, Bassenge, #8670, illus.), 14¹⁵/₁₆ x 15¹/₁₆ in., (38 x 38.3 cm.), lithograph on wove (BP 561, DM 1380, FR 4703, Y 108,623).

$1561* *Schlachtfeld (Klipstein 96 VIII), 1907,* s., (06-05-93, Bassenge, #6209), 16⅛ x 20⅞ in., (41 x 53 cm.), etching on thick copper print (BP 1028, DM 2531, FR 8530, Y 167,453).

$1443* *Schlachtfeld (Klipstein 96 X), 1921,* s., (11-21-92, Lempertz, #230), 15⅜ x 20¹/₁₆ in., (39 x 51 cm.), etching on wove (BP 950, DM 2301, FR 7750, Y 179,455).

$709* *"Schlachtfeld" (Klipstein 96/XII), 1907,* (06-05-93, Grisebach, #693, illus.), 16¼ x 20⁹/₁₆ in., (41.2 x 52.3 cm.), etching and soft-ground etching in greenish-black on copper print paper (BP 467, DM 1149, FR 3874, Y 76,057).

$4950* *Schlaffende Mit Kind (K. 235), 1929,* ninth state, pub. for Mitglieder des sachsischen Kunstverein., s., full margins, scuffs, foxing, mat staining, (11-05-92, Sotheby-NY, #216, illus.), 11⅞ x 14⅛ in., (301 x 360 mm.), woodcut on Japan (BP 3220, DM 7829, FR 26,485, Y 607,287).

$512* *Schwangere Frau (Klipstein 108), 1910,* 5th state of 6, pencil sig., some creasing w/in image and margins, Late Gerhard Brauer Coll., (05-27-93, Sotheby-Amstrdm, #746), 14¾ x 9⅜ in., (375 x 238 mm.), etching w/aquatint on wove (BP 328, DM 822, FR 2769, Y 54,889, G 920).

$1264* *Schwangers Frau (Klipstein 108 VI a), 1910-1931,* s., (06-24-93, Germann, #398, illus.), 20⁹/₁₆ x 13¾ in., (523 x 350 mm.), soft-ground etching and etching on wove (BP 832, DM 2049, FR 6907, Y 135,593, SF 1840).

$2750* *Selbstbildins Im Profil (K. 227), 1927,* s., t., d., pub. Kunstvereins Kassel, large margins, good cond., mat-stain, glue fleck, crease, (11-05-92, Sotheby-NY, #215, illus.), 12¾ x 11¾ in., (324 x 300 mm.), sheet 21¼ x 15⅛ in., (324 x 300 mm.), lithograph on wove (BP 1789, DM 4349, FR 14,714, Y 337,382).

BI *Selbstbildnis (K. 198), 1924,* s., d., i. Selbstbild, full margins, good cond., est. BP 3/4,000, (06-30-93, Sotheby-London, #476, illus.), 11½ x 8⅞ in., (292 x 225 mm.), lithograph on Butten.

$4123* *Selbstbildnis (Kl. 133/a), 1919,* s., (06-23-93, Kornfeld, #473), lithograph on thick Japan (BP 2801, DM 6976, FR 23,466, Y 449,177, SF 6210).

$3606* *Selbstbildnis (Klipstein 133 b), 1919,* s., (11-21-92, Lempertz, #228, illus.), 13⁹⁄₁₆ x 11½ in., (34.5 x 29.2 cm.), lithograph on factory-made paper (BP 2374, DM 5749, FR 19,366, Y 448,452).

$2467* *Selbstbildnis (Klipstein 133), 1919,* s., d., tears, (05-26-93, Lempertz, #270, illus.), 20¹⁵⁄₁₆ x 18⁵⁄₁₆ in., (53.2 x 46.5 cm.), lithograph on off-white hand-made (BP 1596, DM 4025, FR 13,548, Y 268,036).

$1836* *Selbstbildnis Am Tisch (Klipstein 14 III a), c. 1893,* 2nd version, s., (06-10-93, Hauswedell/Nolt, #508), image 7³⁄₁₆ x 5 in., (18.3 x 12.7 cm.), etching and aquatint on Japan (BP 1201, DM 2990, FR 10,066, Y 194,884).

$425* *Selbstbildnis Am Tisch II (Self-Portrait Seated At A Table, II) (K 14), 1893,* emb. pub. blindstamp, pub. A. Von Der Becke, (02-04-93, Sloan, #1243), 6¾ x 5 in., (17.1 x 12.7 cm.), etching, aquatint and roulette (BP 297, DM 700, FR 2373, Y 52,867).

$4256* *Selbstbildnis Im Profil (Klipstein 227 a), 1927,* s., d., (06-05-93, Bassenge, #6214, illus.), 12¹³⁄₁₆ x 11¹³⁄₁₆ in., (32.5 x 30 cm.), lithograph on thin China (BP 2802, DM 6900, FR 23,257, Y 456,554).

$2138* *Selbstbildnis Im Profil Nach Rechts (Kl. 265/III/b), 1938,* ded., (06-23-93, Kornfeld, #483), lithograph on cream wove (BP 1452, DM 3618, FR 12,168, Y 232,923, SF 3220).

BI *Selbstbildnis Im Profil Nach Rechts (Kl. 265/IIIb), 1938,* wrinkle, crease, est. DM 4000, (12-01-92, Karl/Faber, #871, illus.), 18½ x 11¹³⁄₁₆ in., (47 x 30 cm.), lithograph.

$1098* *Selbstbildnis Im Profil Nach Rechts (Klipstein 265 III b), 1938,* Hans Kollwitz, estate edit. 250, (12-12-92, Bassenge, #8671), 18¹¹⁄₁₆ x 11⁷⁄₁₆ in., (47.5 x 29 cm.), lithograph on imitation Japan (BP 702, DM 1726, FR 5881, Y 135,841).

$1299* "*Selbstbildnis Im Profil Nach Rechts*" *(Klipstein 265/III b.), 1938,* (11-28-92, Grisebach, #607, illus.), 18¹¹⁄₁₆ x 11⁷⁄₁₆ in., (47.5 x 29 cm.), lithograph on wove (BP 857, DM 2069, FR 7025, Y 161,668).

$5675* "*Selbstbildnis Im Profil*" *(Klipstein 227 b), 1927,* s., d., (06-05-93, Grisebach, #305, illus.), 12¹¹⁄₁₆ x 11⅝ in., (32.2 x 29.6 cm.), lithograph on Japan (BP 3736, DM 9201, FR 31,011, Y 608,775).

BI *Selbstbildnis Mit Der Hand An Der Stirn, 1910,* wrinkles, trimmed, est. DM 850, (05-08-93, Schloss Ahlden, #2856), 5⅞ x 5⅛ in., (15 x 13 cm.), etching on textured paper.

$6858* "*Selbstbildnis*" *(Klipstein 252 b), 1934,* s., d., foxed, (11-28-92, Grisebach, #120, illus.), 8⅛ x 7³⁄₁₆ in., (20.6 x 18.2 cm.), lithograph on handmade (BP 4527, DM 10,926, FR 37,090, Y 853,516).

$220* *Selbstbildnis, 1912,* (03-24-93, Kunsthallen, #213), etching (BP 149, DM 359, FR 1223, Y 25,849, DK 1380).

$1977* *Selbstbildnisse (Klipstein 106 IV b), 1910: Two,* s., sig. stamp, (06-10-93, Hauswedell/Nolt, #516), each approx. 6³⁄₁₆ x 5½ in., (15.7 x 13.9 cm.), etching on Simili-Japan (BP 1293, DM 3219, FR 10,839, Y 209,850).

$3025* *Self Portrait,* s., d. 1927, (05-14-93, DuMouchelle, #2034, illus.), image 12½ x 11½ in., (31.8 x 29.2 cm.), b/w lithograph (BP 1967, DM 4866, FR 16,351, Y 335,329).

$467* *Sharpening The Scynthe (Klipstein 90), 1905,* issued by Von der Beck, blindstamp, d. 1921, top and bottom margins folded back, (12-08-92, Swann, #167), 11¾ x 11¾ in., (29.8 x 29.8 cm.), etching w/drypoint and soft (molle) ground in dark brown ink (BP 293, DM 727, FR 2479, Y 57,883).

$10,593* *Sitzende Frau Mit Umschlagtuch (Selbstbildnis?) (Klipstein 191), 1924,* s., (06-10-93, Hauswedell/Nolt, #526, illus.), image 15¹⁵⁄₁₆ x 12⅝ in., (40.5 x 32 cm.), lithograph on thin wove (BP 6929, DM 17,250, FR 58,076, Y 1,124,403).

$992* *Sitzender Mannlicher Akt (Klipstien 108), 1891,* 2nd state of 2, s. by artist and p. (Felsing), margins, good cond., slight paper discoloration, glue staining at edges of sheet verso, Late Gerhard Brauer Coll., (05-27-93, Sotheby-Amstrdm, #742, illus.), 6¼ x 5¹⁄₁₆ in., (158 x 128 mm.),

etching on sturdy wove paper (BP 635, DM 1592, FR 5365, Y 106,346, G 1783).

$12,218* *Stadtisches Obdach (Kl. 219/a), 1926,* s., (06-23-93, Kornfeld, #482, illus.), lithograph on Japan (BP 8300, DM 20,673, FR 69,539, Y 1,331,082, SF 18,400).

$1549* *Stadtisches Obdach (Klipstein 219 B b), 1926,* (12-05-92, Bassenge, #7354), 16¹⁵⁄₁₆ x 21⁷⁄₁₆ in., (43 x 54.5 cm.), lithograph on machinemade paper (BP 970, DM 2415, FR 8231, Y 191,922).

$1217* *Stehende Mutter, Ihr Bublein Futternd,* blindstamp, (05-08-93, Schloss Ahlden, #2855, illus.), 7¹¹⁄₁₆ x 5⅞ in., (19.5 x 15 cm.), etching on handmade (BP 794, DM 1955, FR 6596, Y 135,993).

$851* "*Stehende Mutter, Ihr Bublein Futternd*" *(Klipstein 247/V), 1931,* sig. stamp, (06-05-93, Grisebach, #699, illus.), 7¾ x 5⅞ in., (19.7 x 15 cm.), etching in dark brown on copper print paper (BP 560, DM 1380, FR 4650, Y 91,289).

$1412* *Stehender Weiblicher Akt. (Klipstein 46 II c), 1900,* s., (06-10-93, Hauswedell/Nolt, #509), image 7¹⁄₁₆ x 5⁷⁄₁₆ in., (17.9 x 13.8 cm.), etching on copper print (BP 924, DM 2299, FR 7741, Y 149,878).

$2164* *Sturm (Klipstein 33 II a), 1897,* s., plate 5 from Ein Weberaufstand, (11-21-92, Lempertz, #226), 9⅛ x 11⁹⁄₁₆ in., (23.2 x 29.3 cm.), etching on thick wove (BP 1425, DM 3450, FR 11,622, Y 269,121).

$1490* *Der Sturm (Klipstein 33 III), 1897,* s., (06-05-93, Bassenge, #6206), 9⅛ x 11⁹⁄₁₆ in., (23.1 x 29.3 cm.), etching on thick wove (BP 981, DM 2416, FR 8142, Y 159,837).

BI *Szene Au Germinal (Klipstein 21 III), 1893,* s., est. SF 2,3/2,500, (04-21-93, Germann, #579, illus.), 16¹⁵⁄₁₆ x 28¾ in., (430 x 730 mm.), etching.

$26,726* *Tod Und Frau (Kl. 103/IV), 1910,* s., (06-23-93, Kornfeld, #469, illus.), line etching und Schmirgeldurchdruck-verfahren reworked on thick Japan (BP 18,156, DM 45,222, FR 152,112, Y 2,911,646, SF 40,250).

$6414* *Tod Und Frau (Kl. 103/V/a), 1910,* s., prov., (06-23-93, Kornfeld, #470), line etching und Schmirgeldurchdruck-verfahren (BP 4357, DM 10,853, FR 36,505, Y 698,769, SF 9660).

$1756* *Tod Und Frau (Kl. 103/VI), 1910,* s., (06-23-93, Kornfeld, #471), line etching und Schmirgeldurchdruckver-fahren on thick copper print paper (BP 1193, DM 2971, FR 9994, Y 191,306, SF 2645).

$2065* *Tod Und Frau (Klipstein 103 VII), 1910,* s., (12-05-92, Bassenge, #7341), 17⅝ x 17⁹⁄₁₆ in., (44.7 x 44.6 cm.), etching w/Schmirgeldruckverfahren on thick copper print pape (BP 1293, DM 3220, FR 10,972, Y 255,854).

$1271* *Tod Und Frau (Klipstein 103 VII), 1910,* s., (06-10-93, Hauswedell/Nolt, #514), image 17⅝ x 17⁹⁄₁₆ in., (44.7 x 44.6 cm.), etching on copper print (BP 831, DM 2070, FR 6968, Y 134,911).

$916* *Tod Und Frau Um Das Kind Ringend (K. 118 IX c), 1911,* 9th (final) state, s., pub. von der Becke, after 1931, s., margins, crease, good cond., (12-01-92, Christie-London, #412), plate 8¹³⁄₁₆ x 11 in., (224 x 280 mm.), etching (BP 605, DM 1460, FR 4976, Y 114,044).

BI *Tod, Frau Und Kind,* pub. Emil Richter, est. SF 2,8/3,500, (11-13-92, Koller, #5361), sheet 16¹⁵⁄₁₆ x 17⅛ in., (43 x 43.5 cm.), etching on wove.

BI *Tod, Frau Und Kind (Abschied) (Klippstein Nr. 113, Zustand XI), 1910,* #9/50, s., est. DM 8,000, (11-13-92, Kunsthaus, #656, illus.), 15¹⁵⁄₁₆ x 15⅞ in., (40.5 x 40.4 cm.), etching in brown on intaglio board.

$11,836* *Tod, Frau Und Kind (Kl. 113/IV), 1910,* s., (06-23-93, Kornfeld, #472), line etching und Durchdruckverfahren on soft copper print paper (BP 8041, DM 20,027, FR 67,365, Y 1,289,465, SF 17,825).

$722* "*Tod, Frau Und Kind*" *(Klipstein 113 XIII), 1910,* (11-28-92, Grisebach, #604, illus.), 15¾ x 16 in., (40 x 40.7 cm.), etching and soft-ground etching on copper print paper (BP 477, DM 1150, FR 3905, Y 89,857).

$2047* *Tot Im Wasser (Klipstein 262), 1934-1935,* portfolio tod, s., margins, good cond., small defects at edges of sheet, Late Gerhard Brauer Coll., (05-27-93, Sotheby-Amstrdm, #753, illus.), sheet 25 x 19¹¹⁄₁₆ in., (635 x 500 mm.), lithograph on wove (BP 1311, DM 3285, FR 11,071, Y 219,447, G 3680).

$990* *Verbrüderung (K. 199), 1924,* Klipstein's edit. b of e, s., full margins, creases, mat staining, tape, (11-05-92, Sotheby-NY, #214), 9¼ x 6⅞ in., (235 x 174 mm.), lithograph on warm toned laid (BP 644, DM 1566, FR 5297, Y 121,457).

$885* *Verbrüderung (Klipstein 199 b), 1924,* s., (12-05-92, Bassenge, #7351), 9¹/₁₆ x 6¹¹/₁₆ in., (23 x 17 cm.), lithograph on handmade (BP 554, DM 1380, FR 4702, Y 109,652).

$1695* *Verbrüderung (Klipstein 199 b), 1924,* s., (06-10-93, Hauswedell/Nolt, #527), image 8⅞ x 6¹¹/₁₆ in., (22.5 x 17 cm.), lithograph on hand-made (BP 1109, DM 2760, FR 9293, Y 179,917).

$4944* *Vergewaltigt (Klipstein 97 IV), 1907,* sheet 2 from Bauernkrieg, (06-10-93, Hauswedell/Nolt, #513, illus.), image 12¹/₁₆ x 20¹³/₁₆ in., (30.7 x 52.8 cm.), etching and nature print (BP 3234, DM 8051, FR 27,105, Y 524,785).

BI *Vier Manner In Der Kneipe (Kornfeld 12 IIIb), c. 1893,* from Von Der Becke ed., blindstamp, est. $100/150, (03-14-93, Hindman, #260), 5 x 6⅛ in., (12.7 x 15.6 cm.), etching.

$1407* *Das Warten (Klipstein 126), 1914,* 1st state of 2, s., #3/20, margins, minor water staining at edges ofsheet; papertape at left edge of sheet verso, Late Gerhard Brauer Coll., (05-27-93, Sotheby-Amstrdm, #748, illus.), sheet 16⁹/₁₆ x 12¼ in., (420 x 311 mm.), lithograph on Japan (BP 901, DM 2258, FR 7610, Y 150,836, G 2530).

$878* *Ein Weberaufstand (Klipstein 32 IV; 33 IV; 34 after II; 35 after II;36 after d; 37 IV): Six,* stamp sig., blindstamp, wear, (12-12-92, Bassenge, #8662), 3 etchings, 3 photolithographs (BP 561, DM 1380, FR 4703, Y 108,623).

BI *Ein Weberaufstand, 1897: Six,* s., est. DM 5,500, (05-08-93, Schloss Ahlden, #2854, illus.), 3 engravings, 3 lithographs.

$275* *Weberzug (Klipstein 32 IV b), 1897,* Plate 4 of Revolt of the Weavers, blindstamp von der Becke, (03-14-93, Hindman, #261), 8⅜ x 11¾ in., (21.3 x 29.8 cm.), etching (BP 192, DM 458, FR 1556, Y 32,410).

$1540* *Weberzug (Klipstein 32), 1897,* plate 4 from series Weberaufstand, third state of four, s., margins,paper loss, mat staining, foxing, notations, scotch tape, (11-05-92, Sotheby-NY, #210), 8¼ x 12⅛ in., (210 x 307 mm.), etching on thick wove (BP 1002, DM 2436, FR 8240, Y 188,934).

$1840* *Weberzug (Klipstein 32/II), 1897,* 2nd state of 4, s., good cond., stray red ink, mat stain, tape stains, masking tape, skinned spots, (05-13-93, Sotheby-NY, #573), 8⅛ x 11½ in., (206 x 293 mm.), sh 13¾ x 16¾ in., (206 x 293 mm.), etching on heavy wove (BP 1208, DM 2971, FR 10,022, Y 205,426).

BI *Zertretene,* good cond., est. $4/600, (06-11-93, Doyle, #53), 9 x 7¾ in., (229 x 197 mm.), etching.

$1064* *Zertretene (Klipstein 48 IV A 2), 1900,* s., (06-05-93, Bassenge, #6208), 9⅛ x 7⅞ in., (23.2 x 20 cm.), etching on wove (BP 700, DM 1725, FR 5814, Y 114,139).

$3967* *Zertretene (Klipstein 48 IV A 2a), 1900,* s., (11-21-92, Lempertz, #227, illus.), 9⁷/₁₆ x 8⅛ in., (23.9 x 20.6 cm.), etching on China on white copper print paper (BP 2612, DM 6325, FR 21,305, Y 493,347).

$1650* *Zuhörende, 1927,* s., one of 20, (06-13-93, Hindman, #399), sh 14¾ x 10 in., (37.5 x 25.4 cm.), lithograph (BP 1080, DM 2686, FR 9026, Y 173,629).

$6050* *Zwei Schwatzende Frauen Mit Zwei Kindern (K. 240), 1930,* margins, water stains, folds, creases, good cond., (11-05-92, Sotheby-NY, #217, illus.), 11⅝ x 10¼ in., (296 x 260 mm.), lithograph on stiff wove (BP 3935, DM 9568, FR 32,370, Y 742,240).

$256* *'Fragment' Gedenkblatt Fur Karl Liebknecht (Klipstein 193), 1919,* 5th (final) state, Von Der Becke blindstamp, full margins, good cond., Late Gerhard Brauer Coll., (05-27-93, Sotheby-Amstrdm, #749), sheet 10¹³/₁₆ x 6⁵/₁₆ in., (275 x 160 mm.), etching on wove (BP 164, DM 411, FR 1385, Y 27,444, G 460).

KOLSKI, Gan

$660* *"After Storm",* s.; i. verso, very good cond.?, (02-07-93, Bakker, #2, illus.), image 9 x 12 in., (22.9 x 30.5 cm.), wood engraving (BP 457, DM 1095, FR 3700, Y 82,130).

KOMORI   Japanese 19th cent.

$165* *Illustration Of Occupying At Weihaiwei: Triptych,* (09-17-92, Sloan, #1621), sight 13½ x 26½ in., (34.3 x 67.3 cm.), woodblock (BP 93, DM 245, FR 838, Y 20,543).

KONDOS, Greg

$1380* *"River Palms" and "Cathedral Hill", 1991, 1992: Two,* s., d., t., annot. 5/6 Pr.P., blindstamp publisher, Trillium Graphics, full margins, very good cond., (05-19-93, Butterfield, #2228), one 23 x 19½ in., (584 x 495 mm.), the other 26¼ x 21⅝ in., (584 x 495 mm.), lithograph in colors on Arches (BP 896, DM 2243, FR 7558, Y 152,773).

KONIG, Friedrich   1857-1941

BI *Secession XXXXI Ausstellung, 1912,* creases, repairs, est. BP 3,5/4,500, (02-04-93, Christie-S. Ken, #170, illus.), 19 x 25 in., (48.3 x 63.5 cm.), color lithograph backed on linen.

KONINGSBRUGGEN, Rob van   b. 1948

$115* *Untitled, 1978,* s., #136/190, full sheet p. to edges, good ocnd., minor soiling, (05-27-93, Sotheby-Amstrdm, #430), sh 21¹⁵/₁₆ x 29¹³/₁₆ in., (557 x 757 mm.), colored silkscreen on sturdy wove (BP 74, DM 185, FR 622, Y 12,328, G 207).

BI *Untitled, 1978,* s., full sheet p. to edges, good cond., small crease in right corner, est. Dfl. 3/400, (05-27-93, Sotheby-Amstrdm, #431), sh 21¹⁵/₁₆ x 29¹³/₁₆ in., (557 x 757 mm.), colored silkscreen on sturdy wove.

$115* *Untitled, 1978,* s., full sheet p. to edges, good cond., small crease in left corner(05-27-93, Sotheby-Amstrdm, #432), sh 21¹⁵/₁₆ x 29¹³/₁₆ in., (557 x 757 mm.), colored silkscreen on sturdy wove (BP 74, DM 185, FR 622, Y 12,328, G 207).

BI *Untitled, 1982: Diptych,* s., d., #49/50, good cond.?, est. G 800/1,000, (12-09-92, Sotheby-Amstrdm, #599), each sheet 22¼ x 29¹⁵/₁₆ in., (565 x 760 mm.), color lithograph on wove.

KONTZ

$12* *European Street Scene,* s., (03-12-93, DuMouchelle, #2438), 6¼ x 8¼ in., (15.9 x 21 cm.), etching (BP 8, DM 20, FR 68, Y 1414).

KOOKEEYOUT, Myra   Inuit b. 1929

$440* *"Dream",* t., num., d., s. 3/50, 1971 Kookieout, Aningnerk, Baker Lake (Sanavik) Cooperative symbol, very good cond., (06-26-93, Skinner, #57, illus.), 27 x 21¾ in., (68.6 x 55.2 cm.), color stencil (BP 295, DM 748, FR 2519, Y 46,684).

KOONS, Jeff   American b. 1955

BI *Luxury And Degradation, 1986: Three,* complete portfolio, each s., #23/60, pub. Editions Ilene Kurtz, fullsheets, good cond., est. $7/9,000, (02-11-93, Sotheby-NY, #365, illus.), each sheet approx. 24 x 31¹⁵/₁₆ in., (610 x 812 mm.), color photolithograph.

$9200* *Sir Sid,* exec. 1985, #2/2 edit., prov., exhib., lit., (05-05-93, Christie-NY, #139A, illus.), 45¾ x 31½ in., (116.2 x 80 cm.), color lithograph in artist's frame (BP 5874, DM 14,516, FR 48,910, Y 1,013,998).

KOOZUSKA   American 20th cent.

$55* *Artist And Model,* s., d. '65, num. 11/50, (11-12-92, Freemn/Fine Art, #116), 7½ x 8 in., (19.1 x 20.3 cm.), litho (BP 36, DM 87, FR 294, Y 6820).

KOPMAN, Benjamin   Russian/American 1887-1965

BI *"Doctor And Patient", 1945,* s., t., #8/20 ink, sun stain, tape residue, very good cond., est. $3/500, (05-15-93, Cleveland, #195), 14½ x 10½ in., (36.8 x 26.7 cm.), color lithograph.

KOPPITZ, Rudolf   1884-1936

$30,850* *Bewegungsstudie, Study Of Movement, 1926,* s., lit., (05-06-93, Christie-London, #122, illus.), 10¾ x 8 in., photograph, gelatin silver print (BP 19,550, DM 48,590, FR 163,574, Y 3,394,213).

KORAB, Karl   German b. 1937

$1360* *"Interieurs", 1979: Eight,* s., d., num., Edition E. Hilger, (05-08-93, Zeller, #899, illus.), 7⁵/₁₆ x 11¼ in., (18.5 x 28.5 cm.), 7¹¹/₁₆ x 9¼ in., (18.5 x 28.5 cm.), etching (BP 887, DM 2185, FR 7371, Y 151,972).

$348* *Stilleben Mit Profilkopf Und Zielscheibe, (19)72,* s., d., num., (12-01-92, Karl/Faber, #879), 15¾ x 17¹⁵⁄₁₆ in., (40 x 45.5 cm.), color lithograph on thick hand-made (BP 230, DM 555, FR 1890, Y 43,327).

KORBA, Joroslov

BI *Lokomotive Praha, 1935,* s., t., annot., s., est. $2/3,000, (04-08-93, Christie-NY, #130, illus.), 10⅝ x 14⅞ in., (27 x 37.8 cm.), photograph, gelatin silver print.

KORLING, Torkel

BI *Phosphorous Mine Worker In Tractor, Monsanto, Tennessee,* handstamps, 1930's, est. $5/750, (10-14-92, Swann, #501, illus.), 8 x 10 in., (20.3 x 25.4 cm.), photograph, silver print.

KORN, Marian

$11* *My Aquarium,* s., d. '74, num. 7/20, (10-11-92, Hanzel, #952), 15½ x 19 in., (39.4 x 48.3 cm.), color woodblock print (BP 7, DM 16, FR 55, Y 1339).

KORNIG, Hans b. 1905

$289* *"Otto Dix Und Ernst Bursche Im Atelier Kesselsdorfer Strasse", 1960,* s., d., t., (11-28-92, Grisebach, #595, illus.), 18⅜ x 14¹⁵⁄₁₆ in., (46.7 x 38 cm.), aquatint on copper print paper (BP 191, DM 460, FR 1563, Y 35,968).

KORTH, Fred

$1760* *Nude With Camera, 1936,* s., d. by photog. in ink on image, 1940s, (10-15-92, Sotheby-NY, #444, illus.), 13⅛ x 10⅜ in., (33.3 x 26.4 cm.), photograph, gelatin silver print (BP 1077, DM 2620, FR 8884, Y 211,158).

KORVIN, Lothar

BI *Man Fetching Water With Children And Horses Looking On,* plate d. 1959, s., i., est. C$ 2/300, (06-08-93, Ritchie, #27, illus.), plate 7⅞ x 11½ in., (20 x 29.2 cm.), etching.

KORYUSAI

$7032* *The Courtesan Kikunoe Of Wakamatsu-Ya,* oban tate-e, from series Hinagata Wakana no Hatsumoyo, pub. mark, Eijudo, collector's mark, s. Koryu ga, oxidized, binding holes, soiled, rubbed, (06-10-93, Sotheby-London, #225, illus.), (BP 4600, DM 11,451, FR 38,553, Y 746,418).

KOSEK, Ron

$11* *Grey Lines,* (09-18-92, DuMouchelle, #2509), 7 x 5 in., (17.8 x 12.7 cm.), graphic (BP 6, DM 16, FR 56, Y 1371).

KOSON

$193* *"Bird On A Flowering Branch", c. 1915,* OTANZUKA, excell. cond., (05-07-93, Goldberg, #1367), woodblock (BP 122, DM 305, FR 1028, Y 21,251).

BI *"Blackbird And Blossoms", c. 1915,* OTANZUKA, excell. cond., est. $250/350, (05-07-93, Goldberg, #1366), woodblock.

$303* *"Butterfly And Blossoms", c. 1915,* OTANZUKA, excell. cond., (05-07-93, Goldberg, #1368), woodblock (BP 192, DM 479, FR 1614, Y 33,363).

BI *"Cicada", c. 1915,* OTZNZUKA, excell. cond., est. $250/350, (05-07-93, Goldberg, #1361, illus.), woodblock.

$193* *"Duck Swimming", c. 1915,* OTANSUKA, excell. cond., (05-07-93, Goldberg, #1404), woodblock (BP 122, DM 305, FR 1028, Y 21,251).

BI *"Exotic Bird And Crescent Moon", c. 1915,* OZANTUKA, excell. cond., est. $250/350, (05-07-93, Goldberg, #1406), woodblock.

BI *"Flying Bird And Pawlania Leaves", c. 1915,* OTANZUKA, excell. cond., est. $250/350, (05-07-93, Goldberg, #1365), woodblock.

BI *"Flying Doves And Falling Leaves", c. 1915,* OTANZUKA, excell. cond., est. $230/350, (05-07-93, Goldberg, #1364, illus.), woodblock.

BI *"Flying Geese", c. 1915,* OTANZUKA, excell. cond., est. $250/350, (05-07-93, Goldberg, #1375), woodblock.

BI *"Four Flying Sparrows", c. 1915,* OTANZUKA, excell. cond., est. $250/350, (05-07-93, Goldberg, #1392), woodblock.

$242* *"Full Moon And Blossoms", c. 1915,* OTANZUKA, excell. cond., (05-07-93, Goldberg, #1370), woodblock (BP 153, DM 383, FR 1289, Y 26,646).

BI *"Goldfish", c. 1915,* OTANZUKA, excell. cond., est. $250/350, (05-07-93, Goldberg, #1369), woodblock.

BI *"Hawk On A Tree Branch", c. 1915,* OTANZUKA, excell. cond., est. $250/350, (05-07-93, Goldberg, #1371), woodblock.

BI *"Hawk On Branch", c. 1915,* OTANZULA, excell. cond., est. $250/350, (05-07-93, Goldberg, #1362), woodblock.

$275* *"Hen And Chicks", c. 1915,* OTANZUKA, excell. cond., (05-07-93, Goldberg, #1374), woodblock (BP 174, DM 435, FR 1465, Y 30,280).

BI *"Leaping Carp", c. 1915,* OTANZUKA, excell. cond., est. $250/350, (05-07-93, Goldberg, #1372, illus.), woodblock.

BI *"Mother Bird Flying To Baby Chicks", 1915,* OTANZUKA, excell. cond., est. $250/350, (05-07-93, Goldberg, #1405), woodblock.

$330* *"Pheasants On Branch", c. 1915,* OTANZUKA, excell. cond., (05-07-93, Goldberg, #1363), woodblock (BP 209, DM 522, FR 1758, Y 36,336).

$220* *"Tiger And Crescent Moon", c. 1915,* OTANZUKA, excell. cond., (05-07-93, Goldberg, #1373, illus.), woodblock (BP 139, DM 348, FR 1172, Y 24,224).

KOSON and OTANZUKA

BI *"Goldfish", c. 1915,* excell. cond., Koson print, est. $250/350, (05-07-93, Goldberg, #1360), woodblock.

KOSSOFF, Leon b. London 1926

BI *"The Booking Hall" and "The Letter", 1982: Two,* s., t., d., #17/100, Studio prints blindstamps, full margins, excell. cond., est. $1/1,500, (05-11-93, Christie-NY, #484, illus.), each sheet 16⅛ x 14½ in., (410 x 368 mm.), etching w/tone on T.H. Saunders.

$1115* *"Outside Kilburn Underground", "Father Asleep" and "Mother", 1982-83:Three,* each s., d., t., num., p. by Studio Prints, blindstamp, pub. BernardJacobson, full margins, good cond., (06-30-93, Sotheby-London, #861, illus.), etching on wove (BP 747, DM 1902, FR 6415, Y 119,469).

BI *"Resting" and "Mother", 1982: Two,* s., t., d., #17/60, Studio Prints blindstamps, full margins, excell.cond., (05-11-93, Christie-NY, #483, illus.), (508 x 594 mm.), other sheet 20⅜ x 19¾ in., (508 x 594 mm.), etching w/tone on T.H. Saunders.

KOSTABI, Mark American b. 1960

BI *Climbing, l985,* s., d., t., annot A/P, margins, good cond., surface soiling, creases, (02-24-93, Butterfield, #3228), 23¼ x 17⅞ in., (591 x 454 mm.), silkscreen in colors on Curtis Rag.

BI *Upheaval, 1988,* s., d., #TP 34/35, very good cond.?, est. $1/1,500, (10-28-92, Butterfield, #3007), sight 30 x 30 in., (762 x 762 mm.), color silkscreen.

$489* *Upheval, 1988,* s., d., #TP 34/35, p. Rupert Jasen Smith, very good cond.?, (05-19-93, Butterfield, #2232), sight 30 x 30 in., (762 x 762 mm.), silkscreen in colors (BP 317, DM 795, FR 2678, Y 54,135).

KOSTIA B., J. French b. 1928

BI *Beach View, Morning,* s., #209/275, est. $125/175, (10-30-92, Sloan, #845), 15¾ x 22¼ in., (40 x 56.5 cm.), color lithograph.

KOTHE, Fritz b. 1916

$1010* *Formel I, 1972: Five,* pub. Spiegel Gallery, #13/100, pencil s., (11-20-92, Lempertz, #657), 31¹¹⁄₁₆ x 26¹⁵⁄₁₆ in., (80.5 x 68.5 cm.), color serigraph on thin cardboard (BP 665, DM 1610, FR 5424, Y 125,606).

KOTONDO Japanese 20th cent.

$164* *Geisha,* s., (11-16-92, Hodgins, #340), 13¼ x 9¼ in., (33.7 x 23.5 cm.), color woodblock on paper (BP 108, DM 262, FR 881, Y 20,467, C$ 209).

KOTOZUKA, Eiichi Japanese b. 1906

BI *Cherry Blossoms,* stamped, est. $150/200, (04-02-93, Sloan, #1875), 15⅜ x 10⅝ in., (391 x 270 mm.), color woodcut.

$77* *"Cherry Blossoms", c. 1970,* pub. Uchida, stamped, good cond., (10-31-92, Cleveland, #42), 15⅜ x 10⅝ in., (39.1 x 27 cm.), color woodcut (BP 49, DM 118, FR 402, Y 9538).

$66* *"Drooping Cherry Blossoms", c. 1970,* pub. Uchida, stamped, good cond., (10-31-92, Cleveland, #41), 15⅜ x

10⅝ in., (39.1 x 27 cm.), color woodcut (BP 42, DM 102, FR 344, Y 8175).

$40* *"The Night Scene Of Kitano Shrine March In Kyoto"*, stamped by artist and pub., pub. Uchida, excellent cond., (05-15-93, Cleveland, #26), 15⅝ x 10½ in., (39.7 x 26.7 cm.), woodblock (BP 26, DM 64, FR 216, Y 4434).

$40* *"Street Scene In Kyoto On New Years Day"*, stamped by artist and pub., pub. Uchida, excellent cond., (05-15-93, Cleveland, #27), 15⅝ x 10½ in., (39.7 x 26.7 cm.), woodblock (BP 26, DM 64, FR 216, Y 4434).

KOUBO, Les
$55* *Cans On The Move*, margins, s. Les C. Koubo, (02-13-93, Collins, #47, illus.), 5⅛ x 7⅜ in., (13 x 18.7 cm.), etching (BP 39, DM 91, FR 309, Y 6633).

KOUDELKA, Josef   b. 1938
BI *"France"*, 1973, p.l., s., est. $1,5/2,000, (05-23-93, Butterfield, #3494, illus.), 13¾ x 21¾ in., photograph, gelatin silver print.

$1150* *Prisoner On His Way To His Execution (Looking At Photographs, p. 203)*, s. by photog., 1960's, p.l., (04-06-93, Sotheby-NY, #447A, illus.), 8¼ x 12⅞ in., photograph (BP 760, DM 1853, FR 6274, Y 131,159).

$2200* *Rumania*, s. by photog. in ink, 1968, p.l., (10-15-92, Sotheby-NY, #569A, illus.), 9⅛ x 14⅛ in., (23.2 x 35.9 cm.), photograph, gelatin silver print (BP 1346, DM 3275, FR 11,106, Y 263,947).

$690* *"Spisske Bystre"*, 1966, p.l., s., illus., (05-23-93, Butterfield, #3495, illus.), 9¼ x 14 in., photograph, gelatin silver print (BP 449, DM 1128, FR 3797, Y 76,268).

KOUNELLIS, Jannis   Greek/Italian b. 1936
$645* *Manifesto Per Un Teatro Utopistico (Schellmann 11)*, 1979, s., t., #7/35, blindstamp Crown Point Press, (05-27-93, Lempertz, #850), 35⁷⁄₁₆ x 25⅞ in., (90 x 65.7 cm.), color photo-lithograph on wove (BP 413, DM 1035, FR 3488, Y 69,147).

KOUTROULIS, Aris   Greek/American b. 1938
$248* *"Probable Dimensions 1-6": Six*, s., d. '91, #14/20, (05-20-93, Boos, #544), each image 21⅞ x 17¹¹⁄₁₆ in., (555 x 450 mm.), paper 30⅛ x 22⅝ in., (555 x 450 mm.), color etching (BP 159, DM 400, FR 1348, Y 27,385).

KOW, A.
$671* *Les Nouvelles Panhard. "4 Vitesses Silencieuses"*, very good cond., (11-19-92, Ribeyre/Baron, #67, illus.), 33⅞ x 24⁷⁄₁₆ in., (86 x 62 cm.), poster (BP 442, DM 1070, FR 3604, Y 83,447).

KOWANZ, Brigitte   b. 1957
$100* *Untitled*, s., d. B. Kowanz 87, (04-21-93, Dorotheum, #726), color screenprint (BP 65, DM 160, FR 541, Y 11,071, SC 1120).

KOZLOVSKY, Mikhail Ivanovich
$1029* *Russian Bath*, watermark, large margins, creases, paper split, defects, (06-30-93, Sotheby-London, #154, illus.), 17½ x 34⅛ in., (445 x 867 mm.), engraving on 2 joined sheets (BP 690, DM 1755, FR 5921, Y 110,254).

KOZMAN   American 20th cent.
$225* *"Abstraction #209"*, 1941, s., d., t., num., good overall cond., tear, (05-15-93, Cleveland, #196), 10 x 20 in., (25.4 x 50.8 cm.), silkscreen in colors (BP 146, DM 362, FR 1216, Y 24,942).

KRAFFT, P. (le jeune) (after)
BI *Der Sieg Bey Leipzig, 1820*, by J. Scott, pub. Artaria and Fontaine, Mannheim, Hurst, Robinson, and Co., margins, good cond., est. BP 150/200, (11-30-92, Phillips-London, #238), plate 20⅛ x 25 in., (511 x 635 mm.), mixed-method engraving on laid.

KRAININ, Ewing
$316* *Girl In Water, 1955*, from the Family of Man exhib., attrib., annot. LIFE, s. by printer, (05-23-93, Butterfield, #3496), 11⅜ x 10⅝ in., photograph, gelatin silver print (BP 206, DM 517, FR 1739, Y 34,929).

KRANZ, Kurt   b. 1910
BI *Augen, 1930-31: Sixteen*, 4 sets of 4, s., d., 1st version, lit., est. DM 8,000, (11-12-92, Lempertz, #132, illus.), each 2¹⁵⁄₁₆ x 4⅛ in., (7.4 x 10.4 cm.), photograph, gelatin silver print.

KRASNER, Lee   American 1912-1984
$528* *"Free Space (Green-Yellow), 1976" and "Free Space (Blue-Green), 1976": Two*, both s., Transworld Art ink stamp, full sheet; first i. H.C., num. 18/25, excell. cond.; second from An American Portrait, 1776-1976, NY, Transworld Art, num. 43/175, scuffs, ink stamp, very good cond., (09-19-92, Christie-E, #144), both, sheet 19½ x 26 in., (495 x 660 mm.), screenprint in colors; first w/collage on heavy wove; second on Arches (BP 304, DM 791, FR 2708, Y 65,786).

BI *Refractions, 1962*, s., t., d., num. 30/70, Pratt Graphic Arts Center blindstamp, margins, light-staining, staining, surface soiling, est. $1/1,500, (09-19-92, Christie-E, #143, illus.), sheet 20⅞ x 28⅞ in., (530 x 733 mm.), lithograph on Arches laid down.

KRAUS, Gustav   1804-1852
$1079* *Ansicht Der Wein-Und Theatinerstrasse*, foxing, stone s., t., (11-11-92, Ruef, #1629, illus.), 9¹⁄₁₆ x 15⅜ in., (23 x 39 cm.), color lithograph (BP 714, DM 1724, FR 5779, Y 134,171).

$2905* *Festzug Der Brautpaare (Pr. 492-494), 1842*, (04-27-93, Hartung, #2453, illus.), color lithograph (BP 1847, DM 4599, FR 15,560, Y 325,563).

$1525* *Vermaehlung Seiner Koen: Hoheit Des Kronprinzen Maximilian V. BayernMit Ihrer Koen: Hoheit Der Prinzessin Maria V. Preussen*, (04-27-93, Hartung, #2452, illus.), lithograph (BP 970, DM 2415, FR 8168, Y 170,907).

KRENEK, Carl   Austrian 1880-1948
$550* *"Couple In The Garden" and "Seated Woman": Two*, prov., (10-08-92, Grogan, #757), each 5¼ x 3¼ in., (13.3 x 8.3 cm.), woodcuts (BP 327, DM 813, FR 2761, Y 66,829).

KREPS, Ruth H.   American 20th cent.
$210* *Street Scene With Figures: A Pair*, excell. cond., (05-15-93, Cleveland, #197, illus.), each 7¼ x 6 in., (18.4 x 15.2 cm.), woodblock print (BP 137, DM 338, FR 1135, Y 23,279).

KRETZSCHMAR, Bernhard   1889-1972
$295* *Gostritz (Schmidt R 150 b)*, s., t., (12-05-92, Bassenge, #7359), 9⁷⁄₁₆ x 11¼ in., (24 x 28.5 cm.), etching on Japan (BP 185, DM 460, FR 1567, Y 36,551).

$1328* *Im Fleischerladen (Schmidt R 64 b), 1920*, s., for the I. Ganymed-Mappe der Marees-Gesellschaft, blindstamp, (12-05-92, Bassenge, #7356), 10½ x 11⅝ in., line and tone etching on wove (BP 832, DM 2070, FR 7056, Y 164,540).

$805* *Liebespaar (Schmidt 126 a (von b)), 1923*, sheet s., d., blindstamp Euphorion-pub., (12-12-92, Wachholtz, #195), 11⅛ x 7¹³⁄₁₆ in., (28.2 x 19.8 cm.), drypoint on machine-made (BP 515, DM 1265, FR 4312, Y 99,592).

$705* *Liebespaar, 1923*, s., (05-26-93, Lempertz, #276, illus.), 16¼ x 12⁷⁄₁₆ in., (41.2 x 31.6 cm.), etching (drypoint) on handmade (BP 456, DM 1150, FR 3871, Y 76,597).

$732* *Schlittenpartie (Schmidt R 126 b), 1923*, s., d., t., blindstamp Euphorion-pub., (12-12-92, Wachholtz, #196), 6¹¹⁄₁₆ x 10⅜ in., (17 x 26.4 cm.), drypoint on copper print paper (BP 468, DM 1150, FR 3921, Y 90,560).

$851* *Ungleiches Liebespaar (Schmidt R 126 a), 1923*, s., i. artist's proof, d., blindstamp, (06-05-93, Bassenge, #6226, illus.), 11 x 7¹³⁄₁₆ in., (28 x 19.8 cm.), drypoint on handmade (BP 560, DM 1380, FR 4650, Y 91,289).

BI *Ungleiches Liebespaar (Schmidt R 126 b, II), 1923*, s., est. DM 2,400, (12-05-92, Bassenge, #7357, illus.), 11 x 7¹³⁄₁₆ in., (28 x 19.8 cm.), drypoint on handmade.

$1238* *Zwangsversteigerung "1 Hose Fur Damen"*, trimmed, (09-14-92, Venator/Hansten, #2465, illus.), plate 13¹¹⁄₁₆ x 15½ in., (34.8 x 39.3 cm.), drypoint on strong paper (BP 655, DM 1840, FR 6237, Y 153,942).

KRIEGHOFF, C. (after)
$2185* *Indian Wigwam In Lower Canada, c. 1855*, by A. Borum, p. Th. Kammerer, small margins, good cond., soiling, skinning, (01-28-93, Sotheby-NY, #470, illus.), 13¾ x 19⅝ in., (349 x 498 mm.), sheet 15⅜ x 20¼ in., (349 x 498 mm.), lithograph (BP 1443, DM 3462, FR 11,716, Y 271,294).

KRIEGHOFF, Cornelius   Canadian 1815-1872
$875* *"Place D'Armes, Montreal",* (05-18-93, Encans, #86),
   12¹³/₁₆ x 17¹¹/₁₆ in., (32.5 x 45 cm.), color lithograph (BP
   570, DM 1420, FR 4795, Y 97,515, C$ 1110).

KRIKHAAR, Herman
$391* *Four Cobra Painters, 1977,* s., d., #4/100, i. van Herman
   voor Herman 30.04.'77, good cond.?, (12-09-92, Sotheby-
   Amstrdm, #600), sheet 20⅞ x 26⁹/₁₆ in., (530 x 675
   mm.), color lithograph on wove (BP 250, DM 614, FR
   2094, Y 48,481, G 690).

KRIMS, Les   b. 1943
   BI *From The Idea Group: "Classic Feminine Beauty,
   1977", 1977,* sig., notations, est. $4/600, (10-14-92,
   Swann, #502, illus.), 11 x 14 in., (27.9 x 35.6 cm.),
   photograph, toned silver print.
$986* *Ohne Titel, 1971,* s., d., (11-12-92, Lempertz, #134,
   illus.), 6¹³/₁₆ x 4⁷/₁₆ in., (17.3 x 11.2 cm.), sheet 9⁵/₁₆ x
   7⅛ in., (17.3 x 11.2 cm.), photograph, Kodalitho print
   (BP 630, DM 1550, FR 5281, Y 121,984).

KRINGS, Gunter   b. 1936
   BI *Malou Airaudo In Renate Wandert Aus,* 1977, 1992, ink
   s., d., t., #1/8, est. DM 500, (11-12-92, Lempertz, #135),
   15¹⁵/₁₆ x 11¹⁵/₁₆ in., (40.6 x 30.4 cm.), photograph, gelatin silver print.

KRIZ, Vilem
$220* *Untitled From "Seance" (Vilem Kriz, p. 51), 1977,* s., ink
   d. on image, photog. stamp, (11-16-92, Butterfield,
   #6050, illus.), 9⅝ x 7⅝ in., (244.9 x 194 mm.), photograph, gelaltin silver print (BP 145, DM 351, FR 1182,
   Y 27,360).
   BI *Untitled From "Sirague City" (Vilem Kriz, p. 45), 1973,*
   s., d., photog. stamp, est. $6/800, (11-16-92, Butterfield,
   #6049, illus.), 13½ x 10½ in., (343.5 x 267.2 mm.),
   photograph, toned gelatin silver print.
   BI *Woman's Hat On Styrofoam Head, 1980,* s. on image,
   photog.'s stamp, est. $5/700, (05-23-93, Butterfield,
   #3497, illus.), 13½ x 10½ in., photograph, toned gelatin
   silver print.

KROJER, Tom
$275* *Portrait, 1983,* s. Krojer, E.A., (03-24-93, Kunsthallen,
   #215), color serigraph (BP 186, DM 449, FR 1529, Y
   32,311, DK 1725).
$275* *Portrait, 1983,* s. Krojer E.A., (03-24-93, Kunsthallen,
   #216), color serigraph (BP 186, DM 449, FR 1529, Y
   32,311, DK 1725).
$312* *Portrait, 1983,* s. Krojer, e.a., (03-24-93, Kunsthallen,
   #214), color serigraph (BP 211, DM 510, FR 1734, Y
   36,658, DK 1955).

KROL, Abram   Polish b. 1919
$65* *"En Te Renversant Sur Le Lit-1948" (CR 3),* #54/180, s.,
   (01-28-93, Pescheteau, #174), 14¹⁵/₁₆ x 10¹³/₁₆ in., (38 x
   27.5 cm.), copperplate engraving on laid (BP 43, DM
   103, FR 349, Y 8071).

KRONENBERG, Fritz   1901-1960
   BI *Madchenkopf,* s. F. Kronenberg, est. DM 200-, (03-24-93,
   Venator/Hansten, #4518), 16¹⁵/₁₆ x 13⁹/₁₆ in., (43 x 34.5
   cm.), brush lithograph in brown.

KRONHEIM (after)
$55 *Genre Subjects: Three,* (12-11-92, G.A. Key, #66), 3 x 5
   in., (7.6 x 12.7 cm.), colored lithograph (BP 35, DM 87,
   FR 297, Y 6806).
$31 *Young Beauties: Two,* (12-11-92, G.A. Key, #64), 7 x 5
   in., (17.8 x 12.7 cm.), colored lithograph (BP 20, DM
   49, FR 167, Y 3836).

KRUG, Ludwig
$1389* *The Nativity (Holl. 3), 1516,* mono., trimmed outside bor-
   derline, repairs, damage, thin areas, defects, (06-29-93,
   Sotheby-London, #47, illus.), 6⅝ x 5 in., (16.8 x 12.7
   cm.), engraving (BP 920, DM 2345, FR 7906, Y
   147,860).

KRUG, Ludwig   c. 1488/90-1532
$619* *Memento Mori (Hollstein Bd. XIX, 18),* mono. LK,
   stained, prov., (09-14-92, Venator/Hansten, #1546, illus.),
   sh 4¹⁵/₁₆ x 3⅛ in., (12.5 x 8 cm.), engraving (BP 327,
   DM 920, FR 3118, Y 76,971).

KRUGER, Barbara   American b. 1945
   BI *Barbara Kruger And Stephen King, My Pretty Pony, New
   York, Library Fellows, Whitney Museum Of American
   Art, 1988,* livre d'artiste, s. by artist and author on just.,
   bound, orig. boards, excell. cond., est. $1,2/1,800, (05-11-
   93, Christie-NY, #486), 20³/₁₆ x 14¾ in., (513 x 374
   mm.), screenprint in black, blue and red w/text on wove.
$1380* *My Pretty Pony, 1988,* text by Stephen King, s. by artist
   and author, pub. Whitney Museum ofrt, overall size c.
   515 x 355 x 30mm, (02-11-93, Sotheby-NY, #366, illus.),
   book w/9 silkscreens & 9 lithographs in colors (BP 974,
   DM 2286, FR 7735, Y 166,365).
$1380* *Reach Out And Touch Someone, 1988-89,* s., #12/75,
   from portfolio Brooklyn Academy of Music II 1988-89
   Artist Print Portfolio, pub. Parasol Press, full margins,
   good cond., (05-15-93, Sotheby-NY, #1054, illus.), sheet
   26⅜ x 19⅝ in., (67 x 49.8 cm.), lithograph in red and
   black on pale wood veneer (BP 897, DM 2220, FR
   7459, Y 152,976).
$4400* *Untitled (Image D) Blue And White,* in artist's frame,
   exec. 1986, #2 edit. 6, prov., exhib., (10-08-92, Christie-
   NY, #181, illus.), 48 x 48 in., (121.9 x 121.9 cm.), len-
   ticular photograph (BP 2618, DM 6508, FR 22,088, Y
   534,629).
$16,500* *We Are Not Made For Each Other,* exec. 1983, prov.,
   (02-24-93, Christie-NY, #134, illus.), 73⅜ x 49⅛ in.,
   (186.4 x 124.8 cm.), photograph, b/w in artist's frame
   (BP 11,506, DM 26,786, FR 90,809, Y 1,936,165).
   BI *We Are Your Reservoir Of Poses,* exec. c. 1983, prov.,
   est. $15/20,000, (05-05-93, Christie-NY, #150, illus.), 47
   x 97½ in., (119.4 x 247.7 cm.), b/w photograph in artist's frame.

KRUGER, Dietrich   1575-1624
$181* *Die Taufe Christi (Nagler, Die Monogrammisten; Holl-
   stein 39), 1617,* from series Leben und Tod Johannes D.
   Taufers, (12-04-92, Bassenge, #6263), 11¹⁵/₁₆ x 13⅜ in.,
   (30.4 x 34 cm.), etching (BP 116, DM 288, FR 978, Y
   22,597).

KRULL, Germaine   1897-1985
   BI *Christian Berard, c. 1932,* (c) credit stamp, est. $1,5/
   2,000, (04-08-93, Christie-NY, #214, illus.), 10⅜ x 8¾
   in., (26.4 x 22.2 cm.), photograph, gelatin silver print.
   BI *Colette: Two: "Colette Leaning On A Pillow", and
   "Colette Crocheting",* 1st photog.'s stamp, 1920's, 2nd (c)
   stamp, t. in unidentified hand in French, label, 1930s,
   est. $2/2,500, (10-15-92, Sotheby-NY, #301, illus.), each
   approx. 8⅝ x 6½ in., (21.9 x 16.5 cm.), photograph, gelatin silver prints.
   BI *Hotel Alley, c. 1930,* (c) credit stamp, est. $1,5/1,800,
   (04-08-93, Christie-NY, #213, illus.), 8¼ x 5⅛ in., (21 x
   13 cm.), photograph, gelatin silver print.
   BI *Jean Cocteau,* 1929, 1978, s., t., d., #2/12, est. DM 500,
   (11-12-92, Lempertz, #137, illus.), 9⅜ x 7 in., (23.8 x
   17.8 cm.), photograph, gelatin silver print.
   BI *Varetha Albu,* 1930s, s., annot., est. $3/5,000, (10-13-92,
   Christie-NY, #285, illus.), 7¾ x 4⅝ in., (19.7 x 11.7
   cm.), photograph, gelatin silver print.

KRUSEMAN VAN ELTEN
$28* *On The Housatonic,* margins, plate s., (05-22-93, Collins,
   #1), 4⅞ x 8⅜ in., (12.4 x 21.3 cm.), etching (BP 18,
   DM 46, FR 153, Y 3087).

KRUSHENICK, Nicholas   American b. 1929
$55* *Composition,* (05-16-93, Hindman, #599), 72 x 41 in.,
   (182.9 x 104.1 cm.), color serigraph (BP 36, DM 88, FR
   297, Y 6097).

KRUSHENICK, Nicolas
$64* *Iron Butterfly,* s., num., t., d. 1908, num. print #9, 107/
   125, label, prov., exhib., (12-01-92, Ritchie, #53, illus.),
   35¼ x 27¼ in., (89.5 x 69.2 cm.), color serigraph (BP
   42, DM 102, FR 348, Y 7968, C$ 83).

KUBIK, Kamil   American 20th cent.
   BI *"Wall Street",* s., excell. cond., est. $2/300, (05-15-93,
   Cleveland, #473), 30 x 24 in., (76.2 x 61 cm.), serigraph
   in colors.

KUBIN, Alfred   Austrian 1877-1959

$601* *"Aschermittwoch" (Raabe 168), 1922,* s., foxing, (11-25-92, Dorotheum, #483, illus.), 14⁹⁄₁₆ x 12⅝ in., (37 x 32 cm.), lithograph (BP 393, DM 956, FR 3236, Y 74,400, SC 6720).

$177* *Blinder Lowe (Raabe 769), 1955,* s., (12-05-92, Bassenge, #7368), 12³⁄₁₆ x 15¾ in., (31 x 40 cm.), lithograph (BP 111, DM 276, FR 940, Y 21,930).

$954* *Friedhofsscene (R. 243), 1924,* s., (12-01-92, Karl/Faber, #892), 9¹³⁄₁₆ x 14¾ in., (25 x 37.5 cm.), lithograph (BP 630, DM 1521, FR 5182, Y 118,775).

$353* *Halluzination (Raabe 171 a), 1922,* s., (06-10-93, Hauswedell/Nolt, #537), image 10¹⁄₁₆ x 7¹¹⁄₁₆ in., (25.5 x 19.5 cm.), lithograph on wove (BP 231, DM 575, FR 1935, Y 37,469).

$217* *Ein Krebsartiges Traumwesen,* s., wear, (09-25-92, Granier, #2914), sheet 8¹⁵⁄₁₆ x 12⅜ in., (22.7 x 31.5 cm.), lithograph on hand-made (BP 127, DM 322, FR 1088, Y 26,192).

$4934* *Nach Damaskus (Raabe 167, Marks A 61, 731-749), 1920/21: Nineteen,* s., watermark, frontispiece XX, num., (05-26-93, Dorling, #2805, illus.), sh 13¹⁵⁄₁₆ x 10¾ in., (35.5 x 27.3 cm.), lithograph on handmade (BP 3192, DM 8050, FR 27,095, Y 536,071).

$1650* *"Nach Damaskus" (Strindberg), 1922: Eighteen,* portfolio, num. 70, pub. George Muller, time soiling, (12-08-92, Swann, #171, illus.), sheet 14¼ x 11 in., (36.2 x 27.9 cm.), lithograph w/lithographed title page and foreword, on untrimmed watermarked paper (BP 1034, DM 2569, FR 8758, Y 204,512).

$369* *Die Parzen (Raabe 379), 1929,* s., (12-05-92, Bassenge, #7365), 7¹⁄₁₆ x 9¹⁄₁₆ in., (18 x 23 cm.), lithograph on handmade (BP 231, DM 575, FR 1961, Y 45,719).

$325* *Pferdeschwemme (Raabe 127 b), 1920,* s., portfolio Alfred Kubin, pub. Neue Graphik, blindstamp, (06-10-93, Hauswedell/Nolt, #536), image 8¼ x 12¹³⁄₁₆ in., (21 x 32.5 cm.), lithograph on thick Japan-like paper (BP 213, DM 529, FR 1782, Y 34,497).

$587* *"Die Rauhnacht": Thirteen,* s., (04-24-93, Ruef, #981), each 14³⁄₁₆ x 17⁵⁄₁₆ in., (36 x 44 cm.), lithograph (BP 370, DM 920, FR 3107, Y 64,776).

$1123* *Der Sultan (R. 258), 1924,* #61/75, s., (10-09-92, Winterberg, #2590), 10¹⁵⁄₁₆ x 12⅝ in., (27.8 x 32 cm.), Federlithograph on Japan (BP 666, DM 1668, FR 5601, Y 136,718).

$516* *Tod Im Baum (Raabe 219), 1923,* s., blindstamp, (12-05-92, Bassenge, #7364), approx. 10⅝ x 13¹⁵⁄₁₆ in., (27 x 35.5 cm.), lithograph on handmade Japan (BP 323, DM 804, FR 2742, Y 63,933).

$295* *Transport Im Gebirge (Raabe 380), 1929,* s., (12-05-92, Bassenge, #7366), 13¾ x 11 in., (35 x 28 cm.), lithograph on Japan (BP 185, DM 460, FR 1567, Y 36,551).

$406* *Die Versuchung Des Hl. Antonius (Raabe 174), 1922,* s., (12-05-92, Bassenge, #7363), 12¹³⁄₁₆ x 10⁷⁄₁₆ in., (32.5 x 26.5 cm.), lithograph on imitation Japan (BP 254, DM 633, FR 2157, Y 50,304).

$244* *Winterlandschaft (Raabe 464), 1932,* s., (12-05-92, Bassenge, #7367), 8⅞ x 12⅝ in., (22.5 x 32 cm.), lithograph on handmade (BP 153, DM 380, FR 1296, Y 30,232).

KUBINYI, Kalman   American b. 1906

$160* *"A Cleveland Skyline": "The High Level Bridge", "Tom L. Johnson", "Old Stone Church", "The Fine Arts Garden": Four,* s., t., excell. cond.(05-15-93, Cleveland, #200), lithograph (BP 104, DM 257, FR 865, Y 17,736).

$70* *"Clifton Park",* s., t., very good cond., (05-15-93, Cleveland, #199), 11 x 9 in., (27.9 x 22.9 cm.), aquatint (BP 46, DM 113, FR 378, Y 7760).

$60* *"The Fisher's Bastion", 1934,* s., plate No. 2, Print-A-Month Club, very good cond., (05-15-93, Cleveland, #198), 9 x 7¼ in., (22.9 x 18.4 cm.), aquatint (BP 39, DM 97, FR 324, Y 6651).

$105* *"Saraband", 1932,* s., t., num. 75/225, Print-A-Month Club Cleveland, July 1932, (10-31-92, Cleveland, #164), 10¾ x 8¾ in., (27.3 x 22.2 cm.), mezzotint (BP 67, DM 162, FR 548, Y 13,006).

KUDO, Muramasa

BI *"Fireflies", c. 1988,* s., num. below image, est. $750/1,000, (08-05-92, Boos, #665), image 26 x 35½ in., (660 x 902 mm.), serigraphy w/hot stamping and embossing.

BI *"Ocean Breeze", c. 1989,* s., num. below image, est. $450/600, (08-05-92, Boos, #664), image 29⅜ x 40 in., (74.6 x 101.6 cm.), serigraphy w/hot stamping and embossing.

KUDRYASHOV, Oleg

BI *Diptyque 1981, 1981,* s., d., #1/1, full margins, good cond., est. BP 5/600, (12-03-92, Sotheby-London, #762), sheet 28¼ x 47½ in., (71.8 x 120.7 cm.), drypoint w/hand-coloring in gouache on Arches.

KUDYAROV, Boris   1903-1973

BI *Nevsky Prospect, St. Petersberg (1941),* p. 1940s, s., t., d., annot., est. $2,2/2,800, (04-08-93, Christie-NY, #148, illus.), 22¾ x 18 in., (57.8 x 45.7 cm.), photograph, gelatin silver print.

KUEHN, Heinrich   1866-1944

$6900* *Portrait Of A Young Man,* 1910s,, (04-08-93, Christie-NY, #70, illus.), 11 x 8 in., (27.9 x 20.3 cm.), photograph, bromoil transfer print (BP 4525, DM 11,084, FR 37,520, Y 783,023).

$9200* *Study Of Hands, 1915,* s., d., (04-08-93, Christie-NY, #71, illus.), 10⅞ x 13⅜ in., (27.6 x 34 cm.), gum biochromate print on hand-made laid paper (BP 6033, DM 14,779, FR 50,027, Y 1,044,031).

KUGLER, Rudolf   b. 1921

$183* *"Am Mer",* i., s., d. R. Kugler 62, #7/100, (03-24-93, Venator/Hansten, #4519), pl. approx. 15⁹⁄₁₆ x 19½ in., (39.5 x 49.5 cm.), color aquatint (BP 124, DM 299, FR 1017, Y 21,502).

$127* *"Rocca Massima",* i., s., d. R. Kugler 63, #57/100, (03-24-93, Venator/Hansten, #4520), pl. approx. 19½ x 15¹¹⁄₁₆ in., (49.5 x 39.9 cm.), color aquatint (BP 86, DM 207, FR 706, Y 14,922).

KUHLER, Otto

$77* *"Paddlewheeler On The Mississippi",* s., i. margins, plate mark, Groves' Coll., (10-16-92, Neal, #2), 7¼ x 11 in., (18.4 x 27.9 cm.), etching (BP 47, DM 114, FR 386, Y 9194).

KUHLER, Otto   German/American b. 1894

$50* *Street Scene With Cathedral,* s., light struck, mat glue, (05-15-93, Cleveland, #202), 7¾ x 5½ in., (19.7 x 14 cm.), etching (BP 33, DM 80, FR 270, Y 5543).

KUHN, Charles   b. 1903

$756* *Taxamater, Selnau, 1928,* wrinkling, excell. cond., (02-04-93, Christie-S. Ken, #51, illus.), 50 x 35½ in., (127 x 90.2 cm.), color lithograph backed on linen (BP 528, DM 1245, FR 4221, Y 94,042).

KUHN, Friedrich   1926-1972

BI *Figurenkomposition, 1971,* 87/100, s., d., est. DM 1/1,200, (06-24-93, Germann, #671), 3¹⁵⁄₁₆ x 27³⁄₁₆ in., (100 x 690 mm.), color serigraph.

$363* *Pinguin Unter Palme,* #129/150, s., signs of wear, (04-21-93, Germann, #583), 36⅝ x 26¾ in., (930 x 680 mm.), color serigraph (BP 236, DM 580, FR 1962, Y 40,186, SF 529).

KUHN, Heinrich

$4400* *Hanns Kuhn Posing For Walter Kuhn (Lunn Photo-Secession, fig. 126), c. 1910,* (10-15-92, Sotheby-NY, #110, illus.), 18 x 13¼ in., (45.7 x 33.7 cm.), photograph, platinum & gum bichromate print (BP 2692, DM 6550, FR 22,211, Y 527,894).

KUHN, Walt   American 1877/80-1949

$250* *Seated Nude,* (02-27-93, Young, #184, illus.), 9 x 6 in., (22.9 x 15.2 cm.), etching (BP 176, DM 411, FR 1397, Y 29,512).

KUHN, Walter Francis   American 1880-1949

$220* *Reclining Nude,* s., (10-30-92, Sloan, #1750), 5⅞ x 8⅞ in., (14.9 x 22.5 cm.), etching and drypoint (BP 141, DM 338, FR 1148, Y 27,251).

KUHNERT, Wilhelm   German 1865-1926
$514* *Giraffe, Von Einem Lowen Angefallen,* s., (04-24-93, Ruef, #982), 7⅞ x 6⁵⁄₁₆ in., (20 x 16 cm.), etching (BP 324, DM 806, FR 2721, Y 56,720).

KUHR, Friederich
BI *"Storm Birds", "Rising Wind"* and *"Glacier Region": Three,* s., num., very good cond., est. $2/300, (06-11-93, Doyle, #54), drypoint.

KUIK, William D.
BI *De Afbraak Van Het Zoutpaleis, 1978: Nine,* complete portfolio, each s., t., #1/20, just., p. Lonneke Uittenbogaard, full margins, good cond., in orig. portfolio, est. Dfl. 1/1,500, (05-27-93, Sotheby-Amstrdm, #639), each sheet 15¹¹⁄₁₆ x 22¹³⁄₁₆ in., (399 x 580 mm.), lithograph on wove.

KULAGINA, Valentina   1902-1987
$7150* *Studies For Workers' Posters: Two, c. 1930,* one: s., t., d.; second: w/applied gouache, (10-13-92, Christie-NY, #282, illus.), each 5⅝ x 3¾ in., (14.3 x 9.5 cm.), photograph, gelatin silver prints (BP 4164, DM 10,475, FR 35,590, Y 866,982).

KUMLER, Kipton   b. 1940
BI *A Portfolio Of Plants: Ten, c. 1977,* maquette for portfolio, unique, prov., est. $3/4,000, (10-13-92, Christie-NY, #554, illus.), each 13¼ x 10¼ in., (33.7 x 26 cm.), photograph, platinum palladium prints.

KUNC, Milan   Czechoslavakian b. 1944
$4600* *Seejungfrau, 1988/89,* s., d. in acrylic paint; gold leaf s., sold after sale, (04-08-93, Christie-NY, #529, illus.), 41 x 63 in., (104.1 x 160 cm.), photograph, gelatin silver print w/applied acrylic paint and gold leaf paper (BP 3016, DM 7390, FR 25,014, Y 522,015).

KUNICHIKA
$66* *Actor In Samurai Costume Under A Cherry Tree, Mid-19th Century,* (12-05-92, Eldred, #573), woodblock (BP 41, DM 103, FR 351, Y 8177).
$44* *Man With A Lantern, c. 1860,* (12-05-92, Eldred, #575), woodblock (BP 28, DM 69, FR 234, Y 5452).
$121* *Woman And Child, Mid-19th Century,* (12-05-92, Eldred, #572, illus.), woodblock (BP 76, DM 189, FR 643, Y 14,992).
$66* *Woman Under A Cherry Tree, Mid 19th-Century,* (12-05-92, Eldred, #574), wood block (BP 41, DM 103, FR 351, Y 8177).

KUNICHIKA   Japanese 1835-1900
$330* *"Man With Umbrella"* and *"Man With Sword",* prov., (05-16-93, Hindman, #387), each 14 x 9⅝ in., (35.6 x 24.4 cm.), color woodcuts (BP 215, DM 531, FR 1784, Y 36,581).

KUNICHIKA, Toyohara   Japanese 1835-1900
$101* *Brustportrait Eines Schauspielers In Frauenrolle,* Format Oban, (04-27-93, Dorotheum, #214, illus.), 9⁵⁄₁₆ x 13¹⁵⁄₁₆ in., (23.7 x 35.4 cm.), (BP 64, DM 160, FR 541, Y 11,319, SC 1120).

KUNICHIKA, Toyoharu   Japanese 1835-1900
BI *Figures In Interiors: Three,* est. $275/325, (09-17-92, Sloan, #1622), each, sight 13 x 8⅞ in., (33 x 22.5 cm.), woodblock.
BI *Rokusenya Kassen (The Battles of Loxinga): Triptych,* est. $300/350, (09-17-92, Sloan, #1629), sight 13½ x 28 in., (34.3 x 71.1 cm.), woodblock.

KUNIKAZU
BI *Two Men Present A Sword To A Third Figure: Diptych,* Osaka School, est. $150/200, (12-05-92, Eldred, #539), woodblock.

KUNIMASA, Utagawa   Japanese 1773-1810
$165* *Noshio II As Sakura-Maru,* (09-17-92, Sloan, #1625), sight 14¾ x 9½ in., (37.5 x 24.1 cm.), woodblock (BP 93, DM 245, FR 838, Y 20,543).
BI *Noshio II As Sakura-Maru,* est. $200/300, (07-03-92, Sloan, #890), sight 14¾ x 9½ in., (37.5 x 24.1 cm.), woodblock.

KUNISADA
$55* *Actors Preparing Calligraphy And Paintings,* pub. Yamamotoyo Heikichi, (10-08-92, Boos, #146), sight 14 x 10 in., (35.6 x 25.4 cm.), color wood block print (BP 33, DM 81, FR 276, Y 6683).
$44* *"Geisha Standing Beside A Folded Robe",* from Ukiyo Juroku Musashi, pub. Idzutsuia, (10-08-92, Boos, #149), 15½ x 10½ in., (39.4 x 26.7 cm.), color wood block print (BP 26, DM 65, FR 221, Y 5346).
BI *Gentleman In Landscape,* s., est. $150/250, (04-16-93, DuMouchelle, #2307, illus.), sight 12¾ x 8¾ in., (32.4 x 22.2 cm.), woodblock.
$80* *Maiden,* (05-16-93, Hanzel, #1111), 11¾ x 8 in., (29.8 x 20.3 cm.), color woodblock (BP 52, DM 129, FR 432, Y 8868).
$44* *"Memorial Portrait Of Bando Hikosaduro",* pub. Iseya Rihei, (10-08-92, Boos, #148), 15 x 10 in., (38.1 x 25.4 cm.), color wood block print (BP 26, DM 65, FR 221, Y 5346).
$88* *"Memorial Portrait Of Matsumoto Koshiro V Presenting Theatre Tickets To The Already Deceased Actors Iwia Hanshirio And Segawa Kikunojo",* pub. Kawaguchi Shozo, (10-08-92, Boos, #150), 10 x 15¼ in., (25.4 x 38.7 cm.), color wood block print (BP 52, DM 130, FR 442, Y 10,693).
$1870* *Oban Tate-E: Hayariso ("The Popular Type"),* from series Tosei sanjuniso, s. Gototei Kunisada ga, pub. Nishimiya Shinroku, (05-27-93, Swann, #152, illus.), (38.7 x 24.4 cm.), woodcut (BP 1198, DM 3001, FR 10,114, Y 200,472).
$1870* *Oban Tate-E: Rikoso ("The Clever Type"),* from series Tosei sanjuniso, s. Gotobei Kunisada ga, pub. Nishimiya Shinroku, (05-27-93, Swann, #153), woodcut (BP 1198, DM 3001, FR 10,114, Y 200,472).
$66* *"Onoe Kikugoro III As Oiwe",* pub. Joshuia Kinzo, (10-08-92, Boos, #147), 14½ x 10 in., (36.8 x 25.4 cm.), color wood block print (BP 39, DM 98, FR 331, Y 8019).
$1582* *Segawa Kikunojo As A Courtesan,* surimono, kakuban, s. Kochoro Kunisada ga w/seal, (06-10-93, Sotheby-London, #213), gold and silver details (BP 1035, DM 2576, FR 8673, Y 167,923).
BI *Warrior With Two Swords Wearing A Large Straw Hat, c. 1840,* rubbed, est. $1/150, (12-05-92, Eldred, #542), woodblock.
BI *"Yamamur Theatre",* triptych, laid down, tears, creasing, fair cond., est. $3/400, (05-07-93, Goldberg, #1389), woodblock.

KUNISADA   Japanese 1786-1865
$55* *"Bejin-Ga", c. 1830,* s. Kochoro Kunisada ga, pub. U-Yamaguchi-ya Tobei, made up voids, surface dirt, good cond., (10-31-92, Cleveland, #30), color woodblock (BP 35, DM 85, FR 287, Y 6813).
$110* *A Man Eating,* (03-14-93, Hindman, #369), 13⅝ x 9⅜ in., (34.6 x 23.8 cm.), color woodcut (BP 77, DM 183, FR 623, Y 12,964).
$385* *"Prince Genji And Attendants", c. 1860,* s. Toyokuni ga, cartouche, (10-31-92, Cleveland, #31), oban triptych (BP 247, DM 592, FR 2009, Y 47,690).
$209* *A Samurai,* s. in block, bearing censors seals, (10-18-92, Hindman, #528), 14 x 9⅜ in., (35.6 x 23.8 cm.), color woodcut (BP 128, DM 311, FR 1055, Y 25,075).
$132* *Tale Of Genji, c. 1860,* s. Toyokuni ga, cartouche, paper toned, corner voids, hinges, (10-31-92, Cleveland, #34), 14⅛ x 9⅞ in., (35.9 x 25.1 cm.), woodblock (BP 85, DM 203, FR 689, Y 16,351).
$132* *Two Women,* (03-14-93, Hindman, #370), 14¼ x 9¾ in., (36.2 x 24.8 cm.), color woodcut (BP 92, DM 220, FR 747, Y 15,557).

KUNISADA (Toyokuni III)   Japanese 1786-1865
$550* *Woman With Hawk: Diptych,* (10-18-92, Hindman, #530), overall 27½ x 9½ in., (69.9 x 24.1 cm.), color woodcut (BP 337, DM 819, FR 2776, Y 65,987).

KUNISADA (after)
BI *"Tales Of The Genji",* s., folded, est. $3/500, (12-11-92, DuMouchelle, #1127, illus.), approx. 13 x 8¾ in., (33 x 22.2 cm.), hand colored woodblock prints.

KUNISADA (attrib.)

$149* *Woman With An Umbrella In A Snow Storm,* (02-06-93, Julia, #1097), 9½ x 14 in., (24.1 x 35.6 cm.), woodblock print (BP 103, DM 247, FR 835, Y 18,542).

KUNISADA, Utagawa   Japanese 1786-1864

$150* *"Beauty With Fan", 1845,* from series Select Pictures to Match 100 Poets, pub. Sanoki, s. Kochoro Toyokuni ga, (05-15-93, Cleveland, #28), 14½ x 10¼ in., (36.8 x 26 cm.), color woodblock (BP 98, DM 241, FR 811, Y 16,628).

BI *Damen Auf Der Veranda Eines Schneebedeckten Hauses,* Format Aiban, est. SC 3/4,000, (04-27-93, Dorotheum, #231), 12¹³⁄₁₆ x 8¹⁄₁₆ in., (32.5 x 20.5 cm.), woodcut.

$248* *Elegantly Dressed Woman In An Interior,* 18th cent., s., Anita M. and Gerald A. Hamilton estate, (12-13-92, Hindman, #381), 13¾ x 9½ in., woodblock print (BP 159, DM 390, FR 1328, Y 30,682).

$204* *Family With Servant In Extensive Garden Landscape: Triptych,* (07-03-92, Sloan, #894), 14½ x 30 in., (36.8 x 76.2 cm.), woodblock (BP 107, DM 309, FR 1041, Y 25,430).

$303* *Garden Wedding Procession: A Pair,* (04-02-93, Sloan, #1885), each, sight 13½ x 9 in., (343 x 229 mm.), color woodcut (BP 200, DM 487, FR 1654, Y 34,498).

BI *Garden Wedding Procession: A Pair,* est. $300/350, (02-04-93, Sloan, #912), sight, each 13½ x 9 in., (34.3 x 22.9 cm.), color woodcut.

$100* *"Ichimura Kakitsu As Candyseller Sentaro", 1861,* binding holes, (05-15-93, Cleveland, #30), 13½ x 9⅛ in., (34.3 x 23.2 cm.), color woodblock (BP 65, DM 161, FR 541, Y 11,085).

$383* *Kabuki Scene,* diptych, (04-27-93, Dorotheum, #182, illus.), 19⁵⁄₁₆ x 14⁹⁄₁₆ in., (49 x 37 cm.), color woodcut (BP 244, DM 606, FR 2051, Y 42,923, SC 4256).

BI *Kneeling Samurai,* est. $175/225, (04-02-93, Sloan, #1878), 13½ x 10 in., (330 x 254 mm.), color woodcut.

BI *Kneeling Samurai,* est. $200/300, (02-04-93, Sloan, #921), 13½ x 10 in., (34.3 x 25.4 cm.), color woodcut.

BI *"Samurai With Fan Prepares For Festival",* oban tate-e, ukiyo-e style, block s., pub.'s seal, censor's seal, est. $150/250, (01-15-93, DuMouchelle, #2308, illus.), 14⅛ x 10⅛ in., (35.9 x 25.7 cm.), color woodblock print.

BI *Samurai Woman,* est. $175/225, (04-02-93, Sloan, #1881), 13¾ x 9½ in., (349 x 241 mm.), color woodcut.

BI *Samurai Woman,* est. $200/300, (02-04-93, Sloan, #920), 13¾ x 9½ in., (34.9 x 24.1 cm.), color woodcut.

BI *"Sawamura Tanosuke As Geisha", 1861,* from series Tosei Jihitsu Kagami, fine cond., binding holes, est. $2/300, (05-15-93, Cleveland, #29), 12⅞ x 9¼ in., (32.7 x 23.5 cm.), color woodblock.

$83* *"Traveller Receives Nice Wine From Women",* block s., pub.'s seal, seal, (01-15-93, DuMouchelle, #2305, illus.), 14¼ x 9⅞ in., (36.2 x 25.1 cm.), color woodblock print (BP 54, DM 136, FR 459, Y 10,464).

$66* *"Warrior In Snow"* and *"Two Kabuki Actors In Roles":* Two, (09-17-92, Sloan, #1649), each 14¾ x 10 in., (37.5 x 25.4 cm.), woodblock (BP 37, DM 98, FR 335, Y 8217).

KUNISADA, Utagawa (II)   Japanese 1823-1880

$110* *Geishas In Interior During Storm,* (02-04-93, Sloan, #913), sight 12¾ x 8¾ in., (32.4 x 22.2 cm.), color woodcut (BP 77, DM 181, FR 614, Y 13,683).

KUNISADA, Utagwa

$869* *Samurai Als "Komuso" (Pilgerer), c. 1835,* Oban, s., censure stamp, Kiwame, pub. Kawasho, (04-21-93, Germann, #252), color woodcut (BP 564, DM 1389, FR 4697, Y 96,203, SF 1265).

KUNIYOSHI

$110* *Chinese Hermit Cleaning His Ears,* from Women in Costumes with Striped Patterns Likened to Waterfalls, pub. Ibaya Sensaburo, trimmed, tate-e, (11-20-92, Skinner, #49), oban tate-e (BP 72, DM 175, FR 591, Y 13,680).

BI *Kabuki Actress Usugumo: Diptych,* s., Kuniyoshi, censor's, publisher's and d. 1852 seals, staining, creases, losses, est. $2/400, (04-02-93, Weschler, #260), .

$110* *"Omiwa And Two Court Ladies",* pub. Isekichi ?, sensor seal, (10-08-92, Boos, #153), 13¾ x 9 in. (34.9 x 22.9

cm.), color wood block print (BP 65, DM 163, FR 552, Y 13,366).

KUNIYOSHI   1797-1860

$220* *"Samurai",* d. 1852, trimmed, good cond., (01-23-93, Goldberg, #298, illus.), wood block (BP 144, DM 350, FR 1183, Y 27,534).

KUNIYOSHI   Japanese 1797-1861

$413* *Two Samurai And A Lady With A Lantern, c. 1847-1853: Triptych,* (03-14-93, Hindman, #372), each 14⅜ x 9⅜ in., (36.5 x 23.8 cm.), color woodcut (BP 288, DM 687, FR 2337, Y 48,674).

KUNIYOSHI   Japanese 19th cent.

$220* *Portrait Of An Actor,* (12-12-92, Wolf, #4), 10 x 14 in., (25.4 x 35.6 cm.), color woodblock print (BP 141, DM 347, FR 1188, Y 27,224).

KUNIYOSHI, Utagawa   Japanese 1797-1861

$237* *Bando Minosuke Als Samurai Date Tsukimi No Sangoro, c. 1840,* Oban, censure stamp, Kawasho, (04-21-93, Germann, #247, illus.), color woodcut (BP 154, DM 379, FR 1281, Y 26,237, SF 345).

$770* *From The Chushingura: Group Of Six,* (09-25-92, Wolf, #7), 6¼ x 8½ in., (15.9 x 21.6 cm.), woodblock (BP 450, DM 1141, FR 3860, Y 92,939).

$503* *Men By A Stream In A Rainstorm, 1861,* format Oban, (04-27-93, Dorotheum, #148, illus.), 14⁹⁄₁₆ x 9¹⁵⁄₁₆ in., (37 x 25.3 cm.), (BP 320, DM 796, FR 2694, Y 56,371, SC 5600).

$138* *"The True Stories Of The Faithful Samurai", "Fuwa Katsuemon ExaminingHis Sword",* from the series "Scichugishiden", t., block s., (01-15-93, DuMouchelle, #2307, illus.), 14¾ x 9¾ in., (37.5 x 24.8 cm.), color woodblock print (BP 90, DM 226, FR 763, Y 17,398).

$395* *Von Musashi Und Saganmi, 1852,* series: Szenen Aus Dem Heutigen Edo, Oban, censure, pub. Tsutaya Kichizo, (04-21-93, Germann, #246), color woodcut (BP 256, DM 631, FR 2135, Y 43,729, SF 575).

BI *"Yomogyu-Hisamatsu Holding Napkin, Yamazaki No Kyusaku Seated" (Robinson S45.15), 1845-6,* from series Genjii Kumo Ukiyoe Awase, pub. Iseibei, excell. cond., est. $3/400, (05-15-93, Cleveland, #31), color woodblock.

KUNIYOSHI, Yasuo   American 1893-1953

BI *Aerialist (D. L-50), 1930,* s., d., i., full margins, good cond., mat stain, foxing, crease through image, Harry R. Lea Estate, est. $4/5,000, (11-05-92, Sotheby-NY, #29), 9⅛ x 9¼ in., (233 x 235 mm.), lithograph.

$2185* *Aerialist (Davis L-50), 1930,* s., d., i. 30 proofs, full margins, good cond., mat stain, foxing,crease, tape hinge, stain, Harry R. Lea Estate, (02-11-93, Sotheby-NY, #24), 9³⁄₁₆ x 9¼ in., (233 x 235 mm.), lithograph (BP 1542, DM 3619, FR 12,248, Y 263,412).

BI *Before The Act (D. L-54), 1932,* s., d., i. 40 prints, full margins, good cond., crease in image,ink in image, mat and light stain, loss in corner, water stain, est. $3/4,000, (02-11-93, Sotheby-NY, #25, illus.), 13⅛ x 9½ in., (333 x 242 mm.), lithograph.

$2750* *Circus Performer Balanced On A Ball (Circus Ball Rider) (D. L-49), 1930,* s., d., i., p. George C. Miller, full margins, good cond., crease, soiling, stains, skinning, (11-05-92, Sotheby-NY, #28, illus.), 14⅛ x 9⅞ in., (360 x 250 mm.), lithograph on wove (BP 1789, DM 4349, FR 14,714, Y 337,382).

$3335* *Cyclist (D. L-77), 1939,* s., p., pub. by AAA, large margins, good cond., mat stain, bleaching, (02-11-93, Sotheby-NY, #26, illus.), 12½ x 8¾ in., (317 x 222 mm.), sheet 15¹⁵⁄₁₆ x 11⅞ in., (317 x 222 mm.), lithograph (BP 2353, DM 5524, FR 18,694, Y 402,049).

BI *Cyclist (D. L77), 1939,* s., full margins, staining, foxmarks, glue, good cond., est. $4/6,000, (11-09-92, Christie-NY, #20, illus.), border 12½ x 8¾ in., (318 x 222 mm.), lithograph on wove.

$1320* *Deserted Brickyard (D. L-76), 1939,* s., i., large margins, good cond., creases, tear, (11-05-92, Sotheby-NY, #31), 10¾ x 15⅝ in., (272 x 397 mm.), sheet 16 x 20½ in., (272 x 397 mm.), lithograph (BP 859, DM 2088, FR 7063, Y 161,943).

$6600* *Four Nudes (Cafe On The Boulevard Clichy) (D. L-28), 1928,* s., d., #34/41, large margins, good cond., mat staining, repaired tear, skinning, (11-05-92, Sotheby-NY, #27, illus.), chine 9½ x 13¼ in., (240 x 338 mm.), sheet 12⅝ x 17 in., (240 x 338 mm.), lithograph on chine applique (BP 4293, DM 10,438, FR 35,313, Y 809,717).

BI *Four Nudes, Cafe On The Blvd. Clichy (Davis 28), 1928,* s., d., num. 21/41, p. Desjobert, full margins on 3 sides, top margin cut, good cond., foxing, est. Y 1,5/1,800,000, (10-14-92, Sotheby-Japan, #43, illus.), 9⅜ x 13¼ in., (238 x 337 mm.), lithograph on chine applique.

$2750* *From The Boardwalk (Davis L70), 1936,* watermark, s., d., i. '45 pt', staining, (11-09-92, Christie-NY, #19), border 9¼ x 12½ in., (235 x 318 mm.), lithograph w/later (?) hand-coloring in red and green watercolor (BP 1818, DM 4390, FR 14,833, Y 341,276).

BI *Girl Putting On A Chemise (Davis 32), 1928,* s., d. 28, num. 21/32, p. Desjobert, margins, good cond., rubbed, mat stain, est. Y 7/800,000, (10-14-92, Sotheby-Japan, #44, illus.), 8½ x 5¼ in., (216 x 133 mm.), lithograph on cream chine applique.

BI *Girl With Cigarette (Davis 27), 1928,* s., num. 1/26, p. Desjobert, full margins, good cond., soiling, tapestain, skinning, est. Y 1,2/1,400,000, (10-14-92, Sotheby-Japan, #42, illus.), chine 9⅝ x 11⅝ in., (244 x 295 mm.), lithograph on chine applique.

$2723* *Landscape With Cow (Davis 22), 1927,* s., d., i. 50 print, p. George Miller, full margins, good cond., soiling, mat stain, skinned spots, (10-14-92, Sotheby-Japan, #41, illus.), 10⅜ x 14 in., (264 x 356 mm.), lithograph on wove (BP 1598, DM 3985, FR 13,514, Y 329,981).

$1100* *"New England Landscape", 1941,* s. Yasuo Kuniyoshi, good cond., thinning, pin hole, handling wrinkles, staining verso, (09-11-92, Skinner, #57, illus.), 9 x 12½ in., (22.9 x 31.8 cm.), lithograph on Rives BFK buff wove w/partial watermark (BP 569, DM 1583, FR 5382, Y 136,290).

BI *South Berwick, Maine (Davis 66), 1934,* s., est. $1/1,500, (03-24-93, Grogan, #92, illus.), 9 x 12⅜ in., (22.9 x 31.4 cm.), lithograph.

BI *"South Berwick, Maine" (Davis 66), 1934,* s., Print-A-Month Club, Cleveland, March, 1934, excellent cond., est.$2,5-3,500, (10-31-92, Cleveland, #165, illus.), 8⅞ x 12¼ in., (22.5 x 31.1 cm.), lithograph.

$800* *"South Berwick, Maine" (Davis 66), 1934,* s., Print-A-Month of Cleveland, March 1934, light struck, glued to mat, (05-15-93, Cleveland, #203), 8⅞ x 12¼ in., (22.5 x 31.1 cm.), lithograph (BP 520, DM 1287, FR 4324, Y 88,682).

$3300* *Tightrope Performer (D. L-72), 1936,* s., d., t., full margins, good cond., skinning, (11-05-92, Sotheby-NY, #30), 12⅞ x 9 in., (328 x 230 mm.), lithograph (BP 2146, DM 5219, FR 17,657, Y 404,858).

$5750* *Two Acrobats (Davis L33), 1928,* s., d. 28, #6/26, wide margins, skinned patches, tack holes, good cond., prov., (05-11-93, Christie-NY, #109, illus.), borderline 12¾ x 7½ in., (324 x 191 mm.), lithograph on Chine applique (BP 3671, DM 9058, FR 30,520, Y 632,494).

BI *Vaudeville (Davis L-16), 1927,* s., d., p. George C. Miller, full margins, good cond., traces light stain, creases, stains, skinned spots, est. $10/12,000, (11-05-92, Sotheby-NY, #26, illus.), 19⅛ x 11½ in., (486 x 291 mm.), lithograph.

KUNSHIRO, Goyama Kasane

$110* *The Attacker,* plate s., good/poor cond.?, (07-19-92, Bakker, #237), image 14⅝ x 10 in., (37.1 x 25.4 cm.), color woodblock (BP 56, DM 160, FR 542, Y 13,675).

KUNST, Carl   1884-1912

BI *Bilgeri-Ski-Ausrustung, c. 1910,* fold marks, excell. cond., est. BP 1/1,200, (02-04-93, Christie-S. Ken, #11, illus.), 20 x 29½ in., (50.8 x 74.9 cm.), color lithograph.

$1103* *Heinr. Schwaiger, 1905,* tear, repairs, lit., (02-04-93, Christie-S. Ken, #12, illus.), 36 x 48 in., (91.4 x 121.9 cm.), color lithograph backed on japan (BP 770, DM 1816, FR 6159, Y 137,206).

KUNSTLERGRUPPE BRUCKE

$13,975* *Ausstellung Von Kunstlergruppe Brucke Im Kunstsalon Fritz Gurlitt, Berlin W., Posdamerstr. 13, Villa 2, 1912: Nine,* foxmarks, central crease, excell. cond., nicks, creases(05-20-93, Christie-London, #426, illus.), overall

sheet 10 x 8 in., (25.4 x 20.3 cm.), woodcut on soft wove paper, cover woodcut on red paper collage on the blue paper wrapper (BP 8970, DM 22,548, FR 75,951, Y 1,543,176).

KUNSUNO, Tomoshige

BI *By 90,* s., t., d. '74, num. P.A., prov., est. C$ 2/300, (12-01-92, Ritchie, #24), 17⅜ x 25 in., (44.1 x 63.5 cm.), color serigraph.

KUNTZ, Karl   1770-1830

$15,871* *In Dem Churf. Schwetzinger Schlossgarten (Th.-B. XXII; S. 114; Nagler VIII, 16), c. 1795: Six,* (10-09-92, Winterberg, #1022, illus.), colored aquatint in red brown on wove (BP 9416, DM 23,575, FR 79,157, Y 1,932,189).

KUPCZYNSKI, S.

$332* *"Flute Player",* #56/60, s., t., num., (03-10-93, Maynard, #326), 28½ x 21 in., (72.4 x 53.3 cm.), silkscreen (BP 232, DM 553, FR 1876, Y 39,225, C$ 413).

$376* *"Her Toy",* #12/60, s., t., num., (03-10-93, Maynard, #325), 28½ x 21 in., (72.4 x 53.3 cm.), silkscreen (BP 262, DM 626, FR 2124, Y 44,423, C$ 468).

KUPER, Yuri   b. 1940

$206* *Vasque Neo-Classique,* artist's proof, s., crease, (03-31-93, Briest, #E61), 24⅝ x 32½ in., (62.5 x 82.5 cm.), color lithograph (BP 136, DM 331, FR 1126, Y 23,689).

KUPKA, Frantisek   Czechoslovakian 1871-1957

$405* *Oiseaux, c. 1923,* atelier drystamp, (05-27-93, Briest, #118), 9¹³⁄₁₆ x 15¾ in., (25 x 40 cm.), black wood engraving on Japan (BP 259, DM 650, FR 2190, Y 43,418).

$1165* *Untitled, 1913,* stamped s., margins, repaired tear, very good cond., (12-01-92, Christie-London, #413, illus.), plate 5⅞ x 13⁷⁄₁₆ in., (150 x 342 mm.), sheet 12¹³⁄₁₆ x 19⅞ in., (150 x 342 mm.), etching w/drypoint in colors on wove (BP 770, DM 1857, FR 6328, Y 145,045).

KUPKA, Frantisek (after)

$189* *Composition,* s., #71/300, soiling, (11-16-92, Briest, #68), 29½ x 22¹³⁄₁₆ in., (32.4 x 32.4 cm.), lithograph in colors (BP 124, DM 301, FR 1016, Y 23,587).

KURELEK, William   1927-1977

$171* *Map Of Canada,* s., #67/554, pub. Pagurian Press, (11-30-92, Ritchie, #35), image 20¹⁵⁄₁₆ x 22½ in., (53.3 x 57.2 cm.), color photo-lithograph (BP 113, DM 272, FR 925, Y 21,282, C$ 220).

KURHAJEC

$22* *Iguana,* s., d. 1970, edit. #3/120, (09-18-92, DuMouchelle, #2504), 18 x 10 in., (45.7 x 25.4 cm.), etching (BP 13, DM 33, FR 113, Y 2741).

KURICHIKA   Japanese 19th cent.

BI *Satsuma Rebellion: Two,* est. $3/500, (06-26-93, Wolf, #956), 13 x 15 in., (33 x 38.1 cm.), color woodblock.

KURODA, Aki

$223* *Femme, 1989,* artist proof, #3/3, (05-27-93, Briest, #119), 29½ x 22¹³⁄₁₆ in., (75 x 58 cm.), three-color serigraph (BP 143, DM 358, FR 1206, Y 23,907).

$210* *Femme, 1989,* artist's proof, s., #1/3, ed. Communications Carbure, (11-16-92, Briest, #69), 29½ x 22¹³⁄₁₆ in., (75 x 58 cm.), serigraph in colors (BP 138, DM 335, FR 1128, Y 26,207).

KUROSAKI, Akira   b. 1937

BI *"Lost Paradise 6", 1970,* t., s., est. SC 30/35,000, (04-27-93, Dorotheum, #236, illus.), 26⅜ x 37 in., (67 x 94 cm.), .

KURZ and ALLISON   American 1880-1899

$495* *"Assault On Fort Sanders", c. 1891,* toning, tear to margin, light soiling, (01-23-93, Goldberg, #727, illus.), 28¼ x 22 in., (71.8 x 55.9 cm.), color lithograph (BP 324, DM 787, FR 2663, Y 61,952).

$468* *"Battle Of Champion-Hills", c. 1887,* toning, minor nicks, (01-23-93, Goldberg, #720, illus.), 28¼ x 22 in., (71.8 x 55.9 cm.), color lithograph (BP 306, DM 744, FR 2517, Y 58,573).

$358* *"Battle Of Corinth", c. 1891,* toning, nicks, tears, loss right corner margins, (01-23-93, Goldberg, #721), 28¼ x 22 in., (71.8 x 55.9 cm.), color lithograph (BP 234, DM 569, FR 1926, Y 44,806).

$523* *"Battle Of Five Forks, V.A., c. 1886,* toning, nicks, splits to margins, abrasion paper loss, soiling, (01-23-93, Goldberg, #722, illus.), 28¼ x 22 in., (71.8 x 55.9 cm.), color lithograph (BP 342, DM 832, FR 2813, Y 65,457).

$385* *"Battle Of Fort Donelson", c. 1887,* toning, tears, splits to margins, (01-23-93, Goldberg, #719), 28¼ x 22 in., (71.8 x 55.9 cm.), color lithograph (BP 252, DM 612, FR 2071, Y 48,185).

BI *"Battle Of Fredericksburg",* est. $150/250, (12-05-92, Neal, #578), image 14½ x 20¾ in., (36.8 x 52.7 cm.), offset printing.

BI *"Battle Of New Orleans",* pub. 1890, est. $1/1500, (12-05-92, Neal, #555, illus.), image 17½ x 25 in., (44.5 x 63.5 cm.), color lithograph.

BI *"Battle Of New Orleans", c. 1890,* full margins, excellent cond., est. $750/1000, (11-21-92, Goldberg, #702, illus.), 17¼ x 24¾ in., (43.8 x 62.9 cm.), hand colored lithograph.

$550* *"Battle Of Opequan Or Winchester, VA", c. 1893,* toning, tear to margin, soiling, (01-23-93, Goldberg, #726, illus.), 28¼ x 22 in., (71.8 x 55.9 cm.), color lithograph (BP 360, DM 875, FR 2959, Y 68,836).

BI *"Battle Of Resaca",* est. $150/250, (12-05-92, Neal, #578A), image 14½ x 20½ in., (36.8 x 52.1 cm.), offset printing.

BI *"Battle Of Spotsylvania",* est. $150/250, (12-05-92, Neal, #576), image 14½ x 20½ in., (36.8 x 52.1 cm.), offset printing.

BI *"Battle Of Williamsburg",* est. $150/250, (12-05-92, Neal, #578B), image 14½ x 20¾ in., (36.8 x 52.7 cm.), offset printing.

$413* *"Battle Of Wilson's Creek", c. 1893,* toning, tear to upper margin, (01-23-93, Goldberg, #725), 28¼ x 22 in., (71.8 x 55.9 cm.), color lithograph (BP 270, DM 657, FR 2222, Y 51,690).

BI *"Capture Of Fort Fisher",* est. $150/250, (12-05-92, Neal, #577), image 14½ x 21 in., (36.8 x 53.3 cm.), offset printing.

$385* *"The Fort Pillow Massacre", c. 1892,* toning, tears, nicks, tear to image, (01-23-93, Goldberg, #723), 28¼ x 22 in., (71.8 x 55.9 cm.), color lithograph (BP 252, DM 612, FR 2071, Y 48,185).

BI *"The Fort Pillow Massacre", c. 1892,* toning, tears, nicks, abrasions to image, paper loss, est. $2/400, (01-23-93, Goldberg, #724, illus.), 28¼ x 22 in., (71.8 x 55.9 cm.), color lithograph.

$99* *George Washington,* (11-01-92, Hanzel, #230), 22 x 17 in., (55.9 x 43.2 cm.), lithograph (BP 65, DM 156, FR 526, Y 12,240).

BI *"George Washington Entering Trenton, 1789", 1907,* after Louis Kurz, margins, tears, hole in image, staining in image, est. $3/500, (09-19-92, Weschler, #150), 14½ x 19 in., (36.8 x 48.3 cm.), lithograph.

BI *"J.A. Garfield And Family",* (c) 1882, est. $2/300, (11-21-92, Goldberg, #715), 18 x 24 in., (45.7 x 61 cm.), lithograph.

$413* *"Siege Of Vicksburg", c. 1888,* toning, (01-23-93, Goldberg, #718), 28¼ x 22 in., (71.8 x 55.9 cm.), color lithograph (BP 270, DM 657, FR 2222, Y 51,690).

$275* *"William Penn's Treaty With The Indians",* (05-20-93, Boos, #543), image 17½ x 25 in., (445 x 635 mm.), paper 22¹⁄₁₆ x 28⅛ in., (445 x 635 mm.), color lithograph (BP 177, DM 444, FR 1495, Y 30,367).

KURZWEIL, Maximilian   1867-1916
$1001* *"Der Polster" (Novotny Adolph 428),* s., (11-25-92, Dorotheum, #426, illus.), image 11¼ x 10¼ in., (28.5 x 26 cm.), sh 21⅞ x 17¹¹⁄₁₆ in., (28.5 x 26 cm.), color woodcut (BP 654, DM 1592, FR 5390, Y 123,917, SC 11,200).

BI *Der Polster, 1903,* pub. Gesellschaft fur vervielfaltigende Kunst, margins, good cond., taped, creases, foxing, est. $1/2,000, (05-19-93, Butterfield, #1923), 11⁵⁄₁₆ x 10¼ in., (287 x 260 mm.), woodcut in colors on cream Japan.

KUSHNER, Robert   American b. 1949
$1760* *Another Question,* s., t., #6/20 within image, (12-10-92, Sloan, #2706, illus.), 60 x 31 in., (152.4 x 78.7 cm.), color lithograph (BP 1134, DM 2784, FR 9508, Y 217,714).

$55* *"Clothes-IV" and "Clothes V": Two,* s., (09-24-92, Mystic, #36A), each 24 x 18 in., (61 x 45.7 cm.), mixed medias (BP 32, DM 82, FR 277, Y 6616).

$528* *Flowered Mat For The Joy Of Ornament, 1980:* Four, and plates 2,5 and 19 from Joy of Ornament, mat s.; each s., num. 24/35, Crown Point Press ink stamps, full sheets, skinning, very good cond., (09-19-92, Christie-E, #145), overall sheet 18½ x 30¾ in., (470 x 781 mm.), mat w/etching in colors, three individual aquatints in black and grays on board and wove papers (BP 304, DM 791, FR 2708, Y 65,786).

$220* *"Tryst", 1987,* s. Robert Kushner in felt pen, num. 105/125, good cond., (09-11-92, Skinner, #107A, illus.), sight 11½ x 24¾ in., (29.2 x 62.9 cm.), photo-process on paper (BP 114, DM 317, FR 1076, Y 27,258).

BI *Tryst, 1987,* ed. 125, s., num. in pen, est. $3/400, (11-12-92, Freemn/Fine Art, #117), 11½ x 24¾ in., (29.2 x 62.9 cm.), colored print.

KUSUNO, Tomoshige
BI *Man That Goes And Returns,* s., d. '75, num. P.A., prov., est. C$ 2/300, (12-01-92, Ritchie, #22, illus.), 19 x 26 in., (48.3 x 66 cm.), color serigraph.

$64* *That's How I Created Perspective,* s., d. 74, num. P.A; t. label verso, prov., (12-01-92, Ritchie, #23, illus.), 17½ x 19⅝ in., (44.5 x 49.8 cm.), color serigraph (BP 42, DM 102, FR 348, Y 7968, C$ 83).

KUZNETSOV, Pavel
$583* *Turkestan Avtolitografi (Turkestan Autolithographs), Gosizdat, Moscow/Petrograd, 1923,* w/title pg., intro., set of 14 lihographs en suite, excell. cond., surface dirt, (12-01-92, Christie-London, #534, illus.), overall S. 9 x 6¾ in., (229 x 172 mm.), lithographs on cream wove (BP 385, DM 929, FR 3167, Y 72,585).

KUZNITSKY, Susan
$51 *Lady With Red Hat Seated In A Drawing Room,* s., limited edit., 348/600, (02-05-93, G.A. Key, #21), 19 x 23 in., (48.3 x 58.4 cm.), colored print (BP 35, DM 85, FR 286, Y 6346).

KUZWEIL, Maxmilian
BI *Der Polster,* tipped onto support, est. C$ 3/500, (12-01-92, Ritchie, #15), 17 x 15½ in., (43.2 x 39.4 cm.), color woodcut on japon.

KVAPIL, Charles (after)   1884-1957
$741* *"Bouquet De Roses",* ed. Carmen Guillard, #9/200, s., (10-18-92, Pescheteau, #178), sight 24⁷⁄₁₆ x 18½ in., (62 x 47 cm.), heliogravure (photoengraving) in colors (BP 449, DM 1095, FR 3718, Y 88,478).

KYOSAI
BI *Unusual Curling Tree With House Built Around Its Trunk, Mid-19th Century,* s. Chikamaro, est. $450/550, (12-05-92, Eldred, #570, illus.), woodblock.

KYOSAI, Kawanabe   Japanese 1831-1889
$88* *Ghost, 1891,* excell. cond., (10-31-92, Cleveland, #33), 7⅝ x 5⅛ in., (19.4 x 13 cm.), color woodcut (BP 56, DM 135, FR 459, Y 10,901).

L'ARCHEVEQUE, Andre   Canadian b. 1923
$35* *"Banque Nationale 1859",* t., s., d. Andre L'Archeveque 1984", (03-16-93, Encans, #73), 13¾ x 19¹¹⁄₁₆ in., (35 x 50 cm.), photolithograph (BP 24, DM 58, FR 198, Y 4093, C$ 44).

LA FRESNAYE, Roger de   French 1885-1925
$7593* *Nature Morte, 1914,* s., d. in stone, (06-11-93, Picard, #55, illus.), 11⁷⁄₁₆ x 14⁹⁄₁₆ in., (290 x 370 mm.), black lithograph on wove (BP 4989, DM 12,340, FR 41,605, Y 805,623).

LA HIRE, Laurent de   French 1606/16-1656/58
$217* *Die Heilige Familie (Nagler Bd. 6, 41, II), 1639,* ded., browning, (09-14-92, Venator/Hansten, #1548), sh 11¹¹⁄₁₆ x 16¼ in., (29.7 x 41.3 cm.), etching and engraving (BP 115, DM 323, FR 1093, Y 26,983).

LA MORE, Chet   American
BI *"Side Show",* s., t., excell. cond., est. $3/400, (05-15-93, Cleveland, #477, illus.), 14⅛ x 22⅝ in., (35.9 x 57.5 cm.), color serigraph.

BI *"Tiger Bug",* s., t., excell. cond., est. $2/300, (05-15-93, Cleveland, #476), 14¼ x 20⅛ in., (36.2 x 51.1 cm.), color silkscreen.

LAAGE, Wilhelm 1868-1930

$465* *Nachtstille (Hagenloscher 15 I), 1898,* s., (05-26-93, Dorling, #2810), 11⅛ x 8⅛ in., (28.3 x 20.7 cm.), woodcut on handmade (BP 301, DM 759, FR 2554, Y 50,522).

LABISSE, Felix

$72* *Femme Au Chale Noir,* s., #107/150, full margins, (05-06-93, Laurin, #46), color lithograph on Arches wove (BP 46, DM 113, FR 382, Y 7922).

LABORDE, Ernest

$93* *Rouen, Paris, Etc.: Fifteen,* s., 7 num., staining, large margins, (05-06-93, Laurin, #47), etchings (BP 59, DM 146, FR 493, Y 10,232).

LABOUREUR, Jean Emile French 1877-1943

$505* *5 Sujets Divers (S.L. 192, 413, 414, 456bis): Five,* large margins, (02-03-93, Ader Tajan, #170), etching and soft-ground etching, one on Japan, one in color (BP 353, DM 832, FR 2820, Y 62,819).

$825* *Bachelor's Faire (Laboureur 169), 1916,* s., #2/8 ep, first state, (10-18-92, Hindman, #459), 6 x 5 in., (15.2 x 12.7 cm.), engraving (BP 505, DM 1228, FR 4165, Y 98,980).

$132* *La Cafe, c. 1930,* frontspiece for Brillat-Savarin, Physiologic De Gout, good cond., (10-31-92, Cleveland, #303), 5¼ x 4⅜ in., (13.3 x 11.1 cm.), engraving (BP 85, DM 203, FR 689, Y 16,351).

$2200* *Cahier De Six Paysages (Laboureur 386-391), 1928,* third final state, s., i. epreuve d'artiste, full margins, good cond., scuffs, creases, stain, orig. portfolio, (11-05-92, Sotheby-NY, #218), each approx. 3⅝ x 5⅜ in., (92 x 135 mm.), set of six etchings on Japan (BP 1431, DM 3479, FR 11,771, Y 269,906).

$289* *Chez Le Patissier (S. Laboureur, 278), 1924,* definitive state, s., large margins, (04-02-93, Picard, #134), 4¹⁵⁄₁₆ x 4⅛ in., (12.5 x 10.5 cm.), copper engraving (BP 190, DM 464, FR 1578, Y 32,904).

$430* *Le Collectionneur Alphonse Lotz-Brissoneau (S.L. 700), 1913,* s., annot., oxidation, untrimmed margins, (02-24-93, Picard, #135), wood engraving on creme laid (BP 300, DM 698, FR 2367, Y 50,458).

$858* *Depart Pour La Chasse (L. 780), 1927,* s., #76/150, margins, good cond., foxing, (06-30-93, Sotheby-London, #478, illus.), sh 19¾ x 13½ in., (502 x 343 mm.), color lithograph on wove (BP 575, DM 1463, FR 4937, Y 91,932).

$1156* *Les Fraises (S.L., 286), 1924,* definitive state, #57/70, s., yellowed, good margins, drystamp, (04-02-93, Picard, #135), 7¹³⁄₁₆ x 6⅛ in., (19.8 x 15.6 cm.), copper engraving on old paper (BP 761, DM 1858, FR 6310, Y 131,618).

$537* *La Halte Des Bohemiens (S.L., 539), 1938,* definitive state, #97/108, Societe des Peintres Graveurs stamp, large margins, (04-02-93, Picard, #139), 12⅛ x 10⁹⁄₁₆ in., (30.8 x 26.8 cm.), copper engraving (BP 354, DM 863, FR 2931, Y 61,141).

BI *Jeune Homme A La Rose (S. Laboureur 620), 1905,* s., num. 1, full margins, (02-24-93, Picard, #132), wood engraving on old thin Japan laid.

$1299* *Le Jockey D'Epsom (S. Laboureur 125), 1913,* #5/30, s., frame trace, good margins, (06-11-93, Picard, #84), 8³⁄₁₆ x 8¾ in., (208 x 223 mm.), etching on wove (BP 853, DM 2111, FR 7118, Y 137,825).

$565* *L'Arrosoir (S. Laboureur 31), 1902,* num. 10, s., definitive state, large margins, (02-03-93, Ader Tajan, #169), 5³⁄₁₆ x 6¹⁵⁄₁₆ in., (13.1 x 17.7 cm.), etching (BP 394, DM 930, FR 3155, Y 70,282).

$759* *L'Auberge Au Bord De L'Eau (S.L. 310), 1925,* annot., #14/15, s., definitive state, reddish stains, good margins, (06-11-93, Picard, #89), 3⁷⁄₁₆ x 4¹³⁄₁₆ in., (87 x 122 mm.), etching on old greenish laid (BP 499, DM 1234, FR 4159, Y 80,531).

$2997* *L'Ile Deserte (S.L. 135), 1914,* #5/35, good margins, (06-11-93, Picard, #85, illus.), 11⅝ x 13¹¹⁄₁₆ in., (295 x 347 mm.), etching on wove (BP 1969, DM 4871, FR 16,422, Y 317,984).

$2252* *Marchande D'Oranges (S.L. 644), 1909,* s., num., full margins, (02-24-93, Picard, #134), color wood engraving on Japan (BP 1570, DM 3656, FR 12,394, Y 264,257).

$999* *Promenade A La Ferme (S.L. 330), 1926-27,* definitive state, #7/65, s., good margins, (06-11-93, Picard, #90), 6¹¹⁄₁₆ x 7³⁄₁₆ in., (170 x 183 mm.), copper engraving on greenish laid (BP 656, DM 1624, FR 5474, Y 105,995).

$1651* *Quatre Images Bretonnes (S.L., 681, 695, 698 et 706), 1912-1914: Four,* large margins, (04-02-93, Picard, #140), from 9¹³⁄₁₆ x 14³⁄₁₆ in., (25 x 36 cm.), to 13¾ x 13¾ in., (25 x 36 cm.), woodcuts au canif (BP 1087, DM 2653, FR 9012, Y 187,977).

BI *Suzanne Au Bain (Laboureur 699), 1913,* s., #2/3, 1st state, full margins, good cond., stains, est. BP 2/2,500, (06-30-93, Sotheby-London, #477, illus.), 13⅝ x 13⅝ in., (346 x 346 mm.), woodcut on Japan.

$799* *Le Tir Forain (S.L. 191), 1920,* second state of four, yellowed, good margins, (06-11-93, Picard, #86), 10⁹⁄₁₆ x 8⅞ in., (268 x 225 mm.), copper engraving on wove (BP 525, DM 1299, FR 4378, Y 84,775).

LABOUREY, L.

$189* *Comite Bougogne Dijon, "Fetes De La Vigne Pour La Bourgogne, Son Art, Ses Traditions,* good cond., (01-23-93, Ribeyre/Baron, #168), 33⁷⁄₁₆ x 23⅝ in., (85 x 60 cm.), poster (BP 124, DM 301, FR 1017, Y 23,655).

LACAZE, J.

$70* *Belgian Railway: Grottoes De Han. "The Finest Excursion",* good cond., (02-12-93, Cheval/Robert, #94), 39¾ x 24⁷⁄₁₆ in., (101 x 62 cm.), lithograph poster (BP 49, DM 116, FR 393, Y 8442).

$698* *PLM. Route Des Alpes De Nice A Chamonix Et A Evian, 1928-29,* very good cond., (03-15-93, Arcole, #47, illus.), 39³⁄₁₆ x 24⁷⁄₁₆ in., (99.5 x 62 cm.), (BP 486, DM 1159, FR 3941, Y 82,682).

$210* *PLM: Fontainebleau - Avon, Station Uvale, "La Treille Du Roy", c. 1980,* excell. cond., (01-23-93, Ribeyre/Baron, #39), 39⅜ x 24⅝ in., (100 x 62.5 cm.), poster (BP 137, DM 334, FR 1130, Y 26,283).

$210* *PLM: Fontainebleau - Avon, c. 1930,* excell. cond., (01-23-93, Ribeyre/Baron, #38), 39⅜ x 24⁷⁄₁₆ in., (100 x 62 cm.), poster (BP 137, DM 334, FR 1130, Y 26,283).

$272* *PLM: Services Automobiles De La Route Du Jura, "Mouthier, Haute-Pierre Et La Vallee De La Loue",* excell. cond., (01-23-93, Ribeyre/Baron, #171), 42⁵⁄₁₆ x 30¹¹⁄₁₆ in., (107.5 x 78 cm.), poster (BP 178, DM 433, FR 1463, Y 34,043).

LACAZE, Julien

BI *Paris, c. 1930,* p. Chaix, pub. French State Railways, cond. 1, repaired tears, laid on linen, est. BP 4/600, (10-13-92, Phillips-London, #34, illus.), 38¹⁵⁄₁₆ x 24⅝ in., (99 x 62.5 cm.), color lithograph.

LACHAPELLE, Edouard b. 1943

$133* *"Catinage", "Yvon L'Imprimeur", "A Tirer Sur Fond Ocre", "Eplilaco","Les Grands Savants" and "Orphee Chez Marie Calumet": Six,* #13/15, 6/10, E.A., 5/10, 6/10, E.A., 5/10, s., d. E. Lachapelle 72, (04-20-93, Encans, #64), 11¹³⁄₁₆ x 11¹³⁄₁₆ in., (30 x 30 cm.), woodcut (BP 86, DM 212, FR 715, Y 14,675, C$ 167).

$619* *"Otrae", "Chez Kepler", Sans Titre, "Orange-Alouette", "Nylonpie" and "Victoire": Six,* #2/10, 7/10, E.A., 4/10, 6/10, 13/25, s., d. E. Lachapelle 72, (04-20-93, Encans, #63), 11¹³⁄₁₆ x 11¹³⁄₁₆ in., (30 x 30 cm.), woodcut (BP 399, DM 986, FR 3328, Y 68,300, C$ 777).

LACHMAN

$9444* *A Series Of Studies Of Costumes Designed By Picasso For "Parade", 1917: Thirty-Seven,* illus., majority approx. 240 x 180mm, (05-07-93, Sotheby-London, #233, illus.), photograph, 11 silver prints, 26 glass plate negs. (BP 5980, DM 14,931, FR 50,314, Y 1,039,859).

LACHOU, W.

$159* *Mantalo,* s. in pl. Lachou, (04-20-93, Encans, #121), 45¹³⁄₁₆ x 29½ in., (116.3 x 75 cm.), affiche (poster) marfoule sur toile (BP 103, DM 253, FR 855, Y 17,544, C$ 200).

LACKERAY, L.

$378* *PLM Ch. De Fer De L'Etat Egyptien Et Cie Des Messageries Maritimes: Paris Marseille Alexandrie*, good cond., (03-13-93, Laurin, #123), 42¹⁵/₁₆ x 32⁵/₁₆ in., (109 x 82 cm.), (BP 264, DM 629, FR 2139, Y 44,549).

LACLOTTE, Jean Hyacinthe   French 1765-c. 1828/29

$5225* *The Battle Of New Orleans, With "Key of the Print", c. 1815-17,* pub. Philibert Louis Debucourt, text in English and French, (12-05-92, Neal, #551, illus.), plate 18½ x 25½ in., (47 x 64.8 cm.), aquatint engraving w/hand-coloring (BP 3272, DM 8146, FR 27,763, Y 647,380).

LACOURIERE, Roger   (after Georges Rouault)

$2588* *Pierrot, c. 1950,* s. in ink, i., #35/150, pub. Maeght, margins, good cond., light-stain, soiling, foxing, (02-11-93, Sotheby-NY, #263), 21³/₈ x 15³/₈ in., (543 x 390 mm.), sheet 23¹⁵/₁₆ x 17⅞ in., (543 x 390 mm.), color aquatint (BP 1826, DM 4287, FR 14,507, Y 311,995).

LACROIX, Richard   Canadian b. 1939

$168* *"Pointe A Diamant VI",* num. E.A. XII/120, s., d. Richard Lacroix 1970, (07-14-92, Encans, #53), 25¹⁵/₁₆ x 25¹⁵/₁₆ in., (66 x 66 cm.), serigraph (BP 88, DM 249, FR 840, Y 21,008, C$ 200).

$34* *"Variante 1-B",* #4/10, s., d. Richard Lacroix 1966, (06-16-93, Encans, #66), 22¹³/₁₆ x 22⁷/₁₆ in., (58 x 57 cm.), serigraph (BP 23, DM 56, FR 189, Y 3626, C$ 44).

LADBROOKE, J.B.

$76 *Ladbrooks Views Of The Churches In The County Of Norfolk: Fourteen,* (04-16-93, G.A. Key, #99), softground engraving (BP 50, DM 123, FR 415, Y 8546).

$6 *"Loddon Church",* (12-11-92, G.A. Key, #95), 8 x 11 in., (20.3 x 27.9 cm.), black and white engraving (BP 4, DM 9, FR 32, Y 742).

$122 *Norfolk Churches: Sixteen,* (04-16-93, G.A. Key, #119), 9 x 10 in., (22.9 x 25.4 cm.), b/w stone engravings (BP 80, DM 197, FR 666, Y 13,719).

LAFOSSE

$330* *"Young '76",* after C.G. Crehen, (06-02-93, Doyle, #47), 25 x 18½ in., (63.5 x 47 cm.), hand-colored lithograph (BP 214, DM 527, FR 1776, Y 35,408).

LAFRERI, Antoine

$81* *"La Visitation" and "Le Christ": Two,* w/out margins, glued, (02-03-93, Ader Tajan, #34), one 10⅝ x 7⅞ in., (27 x 20 cm.), other 12 x 8³/₈ in., (27 x 20 cm.), etching and copper engraving (BP 57, DM 133, FR 452, Y 10,076).

LAGE, Leif

$42* *Komposition, 1987,* s. Lage 87, VII/XXX, (09-30-92, Kunsthallen, #179), color lithograph (BP 24, DM 60, FR 201, Y 5040, DK 230).

LAGERFELD, Karl

$1453* *"Mistress Le Point", 1990,* mounted on card, s., 520 x 425mm, (05-07-93, Sotheby-London, #367, illus.), photograph, silver print (BP 920, DM 2297, FR 7741, Y 159,987).

$944* *Princess Caroline Of Monaco, 1990,* s., 500 x 405mm, (05-07-93, Sotheby-London, #368, illus.), photograph, silver print (BP 598, DM 1492, FR 5029, Y 103,942).

LAGHENY, F.

$715* *Cycles Omnium, 1895,* Des Gachons, B cond., extensive restoration, colors faded, (08-06-92, Swann, #165, illus.), 45 x 30 in., (114.3 x 76.2 cm.), (BP 373, DM 1056, FR 3568, Y 91,199).

LAGRENNE (le jeune) (after)

$109* *Enfants Che**s,* by Bonnet, trimmed, skinning, pen/ink repairs, good cond., (11-30-92, Phillips-London, #198), sheet 11¾ x 15¾ in., (298 x 400 mm.), color aquatint, finished by hand, on laid, laid on support (BP 72, DM 174, FR 590, Y 13,566).

LAIB, Wolfgang   German b. 1950

$430* *Die Reismahlzeiten Fur Die Neun Planeten, Fur Johannes Cladders, 1984,* s., #1/100, (05-27-93, Lempertz, #857), 16⅞ x 24 in., (42.9 x 61 cm.), color offset lithograph on half-board (BP 275, DM 690, FR 2326, Y 46,098).

LAIRESSE, Gerard de   Flemish 1641-1711

$422* *Bacchus,* (03-24-93, Venator/Hansten, #2538), pl. 16⁹/₁₆ x 11⁵/₁₆ in., (42 x 28.7 cm.), etching and engraving (BP 286, DM 689, FR 2346, Y 49,583).

$242* *Enee Allant Au Combat (Holl., vol. 10, 53; Leblanc II, p. 483),* annot. verso, (05-15-93, Loudmer, #84, illus.), 11¼ x 14¹⁵/₁₆ in., (285 x 380 mm.), sh 11⁵/₁₆ x 15¹/₁₆ in., (285 x 380 mm.), etching on laid w/Lys de Strasbourg watermark (BP 157, DM 389, FR 1308, Y 26,826).

$1415* *The Four Seasons (Holl. 80-83), c. 1670: Set Of Four,* 3rd state of 6, thin margins or trimmed, corners, prov., (12-01-92, Christie-London, #150), sheet 8⅝ x 11¹¹/₁₆ in., (219 x 297 mm.), etching (BP 935, DM 2255, FR 7686, Y 176,170).

LAM, Wifredo   Cuban 1902-1982

$316* *Abstrakte Figur,* #28/100, s., (04-21-93, Germann, #587), 29⅛ x 21⁷/₁₆ in., (740 x 545 mm.), color lithograph (BP 205, DM 505, FR 1708, Y 34,983, SF 460).

$3450* *Alain Jouffroy, L'Antichambre De La Nature, Paris, Odette Lazar-Vernet, 1966,* s., copy 50 of 60, excell. cond., original wrapper, sleeve and slipcase, (05-17-93, Christie-NY, #294), 14⁹/₁₆ x 9³/₁₆ in., (370 x 234 mm.), nine etchings in colors on Rives (BP 2250, DM 5566, FR 18,750, Y 384,187).

$4400* *Annonciation De Aime Cesaire, 1982,* s., #77/125, pub. Grafica Uno, Atelier Upiglio, full margins, good cond., yellowing, foxing, (11-23-92, Sotheby-NY, #262, illus.), image 19¼ x 25⅝ in., (490 x 650 mm.), etching and aquatint p. in colors (BP 2877, DM 7045, FR 23,900, Y 545,838).

$628* *"Barcelona",* s. hc, from El Ultimo Viaje, (09-29-92, B. Rasmussen, #341), lithograph in colors (BP 353, DM 887, FR 3027, Y 74,967, DK 3450).

$367* *Composition,* mono., 49/60, (03-24-93, Kunsthallen, #217), color etching (BP 249, DM 599, FR 2040, Y 43,121, DK 2300).

$419* *Composition Verte Et Rouge,* epreuve d'artiste, s., (11-16-92, Briest, #321), 29¾ x 22¹/₁₆ in., (75.5 x 56 cm.), lithograph in colors (BP 275, DM 668, FR 2251, Y 52,290).

$770* *Composition With Bird, 1977,* s., #79/99, (05-16-93, Hindman, #502), 12⅞ x 15½ in., (32.7 x 39.4 cm.), sheet 19⅝ x 25⅞ in., (32.7 x 39.4 cm.), color etching and aquatint on Arches wove (BP 501, DM 1239, FR 4162, Y 85,356).

$260* *"Composition",* HC s., (04-04-93, Pescheteau, #235), 22⁷/₁₆ x 14¹⁵/₁₆ in., (57 x 38 cm.), etching and aquatint on Japan nacre (BP 171, DM 418, FR 1419, Y 29,603).

$522* *Composition, 1967,* s., #79/250, from Flight portfolio, (12-08-92, Swann, #171A), 26 x 19 in., (66 x 48.3 cm.), color lithograph (BP 327, DM 813, FR 2771, Y 64,700).

$605* *Fantastic Landscape, 1977,* #58/99, s., (06-11-93, Freemn/Fine Art, #126), 12¾ x 15½ in., (32.4 x 39.4 cm.), color etching aquatint (BP 398, DM 983, FR 3315, Y 64,191).

$460* *Flight: Composition, 1971,* s., #79/250, full margins, apparently good cond., creases, (05-19-93, Butterfield, #1841), 24 x 17½ in., (610 x 445 mm.), lithograph in colors on wove (BP 299, DM 748, FR 2519, Y 50,924).

$715* *"Indian",* s., #155/262, very good cond.?, (10-28-92, Butterfield, #2565), 25½ x 19½ in., (648 x 495 mm.), color lithograph on cream wove paper (BP 456, DM 1104, FR 3749, Y 87,730).

$232* *J', 1966,* artist's proof, 135 edit., (06-28-93, Loudmer, #269), 10¹³/₁₆ x 5¾ in., (275 x 146 mm.), sh 15¹¹/₁₆ x 9¾ in., (275 x 146 mm.), color etching and aquatint on wove (BP 155, DM 394, FR 1328, Y 24,615).

$461* *Komposition Mit Maskenhaften Figuren,* s., num., (06-08-93, Karl/Faber, #1000), approx. 12 x 9⁷/₁₆ in., (30.5 x 24 cm.), color lithograph (BP 303, DM 748, FR 2519, Y 48,964).

$2415* *L'Annonciation,* s., #23/125, pub. Atelier Grafica Uno, full margins, excellent cond., handling creases, (05-18-93, Sotheby-NY, #258, illus.), image 19⅜ x 25⅝ in., (492 x 651 mm.), etching and aquatint p. in colors (BP 1573, DM 3919, FR 13,233, Y 269,141).

BI *L'Antichambre De La Nature: Nine,* book by Alain Jouffrey, in texte, s. in ink on just. page by artist and author, #52/85, pub. Collectiom Paroles Peintes, 1966, full sheets, good cond., est. $800/1,000, (02-11-93, Sotheby-NY, #156), 13⅝ x 8¹¹⁄₁₆ in., (346 x 220 mm.), color etching.

$8850* *Lames De Lam, 1977: Seven,* complete portfolio, s., #64/99, pub. Maeght, full margins, good cond., (10-28-92, Butterfield, #2566, illus.), each 12⅞ x 15⅞ in., (327 x 403 mm.), color etching w/aquatint on Arches paper (BP 5639, DM 13,668, FR 46,408, Y 1,085,890).

$4025* *Lames De Lam, 1977: Seven,* complete portfolio, each s., #74/99, pub. XXe Siecle, full margins, very good cond., (05-19-93, Butterfield, #1842, illus.), each 12⅞ x 15⅞ in., (327 x 403 mm.), etching on Arches (BP 2613, DM 6543, FR 22,043, Y 445,588).

BI *Lames De Lam: Two, 1977,* s. Wilf, num. 5/99, very good cond., full margins, handling crease, est. $12/1800, (09-11-92, Skinner, #104A, illus.), 12⅞ x 15½ in., (32.7 x 39.4 cm.), color etchings w/aquatint on Arches wove w/watermark.

$460* *"Paris",* s. 96/99, from El Ultimo Viaje..., (09-29-92, B. Rasmussen, #340), lithograph in colors (BP 259, DM 650, FR 2217, Y 54,912, DK 2530).

BI *Pleni Luna, Stockholm, A.H. Grafik, 1974: Eight Plates,* s., seven #170/262, one i. 'U/L', excell. cond., original linen-covered box, est. $6/8,000, (05-17-93, Christie-NY, #296, illus.), 25½ x 19¾ in., (648 x 502 mm.), lithograph in colors on Arches and Japan.

$3520* *Pleni Luna, Stockholm, A.H. Grafik, 1974: Four Plates,* all s., #236/262, full sheets, excell. cond., orig. folders/portfolio, (11-24-92, Christie-NY, #361, illus.), all sheet 25½ x 19¾ in., (648 x 502 mm.), color lithograph on Arches (BP 2319, DM 5636, FR 19,120, Y 436,670).

$4370* *Pleni Luna, Stockholm, A.H. Grafik, 1974: Four Plates,* s., #188/262; one, skinned spots, excell. cond., (05-17-93, Christie-NY, #297), 25½ x 19¾ in., (648 x 273 mm.), lithograph in colors on wove (BP 2851, DM 7051, FR 23,750, Y 486,637).

$231* *"Pour Joan Miro",* s., (01-28-93, Pescheteau, #175), 19¹¹⁄₁₆ x 15¾ in., (50 x 40 cm.), color lithograph on wove (BP 153, DM 366, FR 1239, Y 28,681).

$2738* *"Le Regard Vertical", 1973: Six,* Editions Agori/La Mata, s., num., (12-01-92, Karl/Faber, #897, illus.), 27³⁄₁₆ x 20⅞ in., (69 x 53 cm.), color lithograph on BFK Rives wove (BP 1809, DM 4364, FR 14,872, Y 340,886).

$434* *Sans Titre,* #79/99, s. Wilfredo, (06-16-93, Encans, #149), 12¹⁵⁄₁₆ x 15⅜ in., (33 x 39 cm.), color etching (BP 289, DM 720, FR 2418, Y 46,288, C$ 555).

$263* *Sans Titre,* #47/99, s. Wilfredo, (05-18-93, Encans, #205), 12³⁄₁₆ x 9⁷⁄₁₆ in., (31 x 24 cm.), color lithograph (BP 171, DM 427, FR 1441, Y 29,310, C$ 333).

$232* *"Sans Titre": Two,* both s., 35/50, 44/50, clear reddish stains, mount stains verso, (06-28-93, Loudmer, #63), 10⁹⁄₁₆ x 7¼ in., (268 x 184 mm.), sh 15⅜ x 11¼ in., (268 x 184 mm.), color etchings and aquatints on wove (BP 155, DM 394, FR 1328, Y 24,615).

$411* *Sans Titre, 1977,* #87/99, s., (09-15-92, Encans, #157), 12¹⁵⁄₁₆ x 15⁹⁄₁₆ in., (33 x 39.5 cm.), drypoint and aquatint (BP 220, DM 612, FR 2076, Y 51,024, C$ 500).

$4025* *Sans Titre, 1977: Set Of Seven,* s., #76/99, pub. Maeght Editeur; one, red mark center; one, foxmarks, excell. cond., (05-17-93, Christie-NY, #298, illus.), 13 x 15½ in., (330 x 394 mm.), etching w/aquatint in colors on Arches (BP 2626, DM 6494, FR 21,875, Y 448,218).

$1093* *Sans Titre, c. 1969,* s., #23/90, very good cond., creases, tape, (05-18-93, Sotheby-NY, #255, illus.), 29¾ x 21¾ in., (756 x 552 mm.), lithograph p. in colors (BP 712, DM 1773, FR 5989, Y 121,810).

BI *Sans Titre, c. 1970,* s., i., #XIV/XV, good condition, yellowing, mat burn, pinhole, est. $1,5/2,000, (05-18-93, Sotheby-NY, #254, illus.), 25½ x 19⅞ in., (648 x 505 mm.), lithograph p. in colors.

$1135* *Surrealistic Compositions: Five,* s., (12-04-92, AB Stockholm, #7087), 25⁹⁄₁₆ x 19¹¹⁄₁₆ in., (65 x 50 cm.), lithograph in colors (BP 728, DM 1808, FR 6132, Y 141,698, SK 7700).

$533* *Tenebre Lucenti, 1972,* #58/90, s., (12-15-92, Finarte-Milan, #29), 14⁹⁄₁₆ x 18¹¹⁄₁₆ in., (37 x 47.5 cm.), etching and aquatint in colors (BP 340, DM 835, FR 2855, Y 66,104, L 748).

$206* *Totem,* s., #68/80, good margins, (05-06-93, Laurin, #48), color lithograph (BP 131, DM 324, FR 1092, Y 22,665).

BI *"Totem",* s., HC s., est. FF1,000/1,500, (04-04-93, Pescheteau, #231), 12³⁄₁₆ x 9¼ in., (31 x 23.5 cm.), color lithograph.

$273* *"Totem",* s., (01-28-93, Pescheteau, #176), 12³⁄₁₆ x 9⁷⁄₁₆ in., (31 x 24 cm.), color lithograph on wove (BP 180, DM 433, FR 1464, Y 33,896).

$202* *"Totem",* H.C., s., (10-18-92, Pescheteau, #179), 12³⁄₁₆ x 9⁷⁄₁₆ in., (31 x 24 cm.), lithograph in colors on wove (BP 122, DM 298, FR 1014, Y 24,119).

$2300* *Trois Personnages, 1971,* s., #VII/XXX, p. Grafica Uno, very good cond., soiling, creases, (05-18-93, Sotheby-NY, #256, illus.), image 14¾ x 18⅝ in., (375 x 473 cm.), etching and aquatint p. in colors (BP 1498, DM 3732, FR 12,603, Y 256,325).

$550* *Untitled, 1972: A Pair,* s., (06-11-93, Freemn/Fine Art, #127), one 12⅛ x 9½ in., (30.8 x 24.1 cm.), other 12½ x 9¾ in., (30.8 x 24.1 cm.), lithograph (BP 361, DM 894, FR 3014, Y 58,355).

$825* *Untitled, 1972: Two,* s., num., (05-16-93, Hindman, #503), each 12½ x 9¾ in., (31.8 x 24.8 cm.), color lithograph (BP 536, DM 1327, FR 4459, Y 91,453).

$770* *Untitled, 1977,* s., #79/99, (05-16-93, Hindman, #501), sheet 19⅝ x 25⅞ in., (49.8 x 65.7 cm.), 13 x 15½ in., (49.8 x 65.7 cm.), color etching and aquatint on Arches wove (BP 501, DM 1239, FR 4162, Y 85,356).

BI *Untitled, 1982,* s., #91/125, pub. Grafica Uno, Atelier Upiglio, full margins, taped,unobtrusive flaw, excell. cond., from Annonciation de Aime Cesaire, est. $3,5/4,500, (05-17-93, Christie-NY, #300, illus.), 24 x 31½ in., (610 x 800 mm.), etching and aquatint in colors on wove.

BI *Untitled, 1982,* s., #91/125, pub. Grafica Uno, Atelier Upiglio, full margins, taped,excell. cond., from Annonciation de Aime Cesaire, est. $3,5/4,500, (05-17-93, Christie-NY, #301), 24 x 31½ in., (610 x 800 mm.), etching and aquatint in colors on wove.

$2300* *Untitled, 1982,* s., #23/125, pub. Grafica Uno, Atelier Upiglio, full margins, excell. cond., from Annonciation de Aime Cesaire, (05-17-93, Christie-NY, #299, illus.), 24 x 31½ in., (610 x 800 mm.), etching and aquatint in colors on wove (BP 1500, DM 3711, FR 12,500, Y 256,125).

$1136* *Untitled: Three,* #55/125, 77/125, 111/125, s., (05-20-93, Finarte-Milan, #84), 24 x 31¹¹⁄₁₆ in., (61 x 80.5 cm.), etching in colors (BP 729, DM 1833, FR 6174, Y 125,442, L 1668).

$1410* *Untitled: Two,* #55/125, foglio, s., (05-20-93, Finarte-Milan, #83), 23¹³⁄₁₆ x 31¹¹⁄₁₆ in., (60.5 x 80.5 cm.), etching in colors (BP 905, DM 2275, FR 7663, Y 155,698, L 2070).

$1840* *Visible.-Invisible,* #XXIV/XXX, pub. Grafica Uno, veru good cond., soiling, handling creases, (05-18-93, Sotheby-NY, #257, illus.), image 15 x 18⅝ in., (381 x 473 mm.), etching and aquatint p. in colors (BP 1198, DM 2986, FR 10,082, Y 205,060).

$4600* *Visible/Invisible, Milan, Edizioni Levi Art Center, 1972: Six Plates,* six s., watermark, #13/99, full margins, good cond., coll. of plates, (05-17-93, Christie-NY, #295), 28 x 20 in., (711 x 508 mm.), etching and aquatint in colors on wove (BP 3001, DM 7422, FR 25,000, Y 512,249).

BI *XX Siecle: Two,* both s. Wilf, num. 49/99 and 60/99, very good cond., full margins, est. $8/1200, (09-11-92, Skinner, #105A, illus.), 12⅛ x 9½ in., (30.8 x 24.1 cm.), color lithograph on Arches wove w/watermark.

$1100* *XXe Siecle: Untitled, 1972: Two,* s., num. 52/99 and 99/99, full margins, very good cond., (02-24-93, Butterfield, #2666), each 12⅝ x 9¹⁄₁₆ in., (321 x 230 mm.), lithographs in colors on Arches (BP 767, DM 1786, FR 6054, Y 129,078).

LAMAILLE, Adolphe

$1540* *Levy's Grave,* late 1840s, (04-07-93, Swann, #132, illus.), photograph, quarter-plate daguerreotype (BP 1018, DM 2491, FR 8429, Y 174,960).

LAMBERT, Georges   French b. 1919
  BI *"D'Arles"*, s., edit. #262/275, est. $1/200, (12-11-92,
     DuMouchelle, #1480), 15¾ x 21¾ in., (40 x 55.2 cm.),
     color lithograph.
  $88* *"D'Arles"*, s., #262/275, Collector's Guild, (03-12-93,
     DuMouchelle, #2274), 15¾ x 21¾ in., (40 x 55.2 cm.),
     color lithograph (BP 61, DM 146, FR 498, Y 10,371).

LAMBERT, Terence H.
  $62 *"A Norfolk Marsh" and "Heigham Sounds": Two,* d.
     1922/3, (12-11-92, G.A. Key, #5), one 6 x 9 in., (15.2 x
     22.9 cm.), the other 6 x 10 in., (15.2 x 22.9 cm.), black
     and white etching (BP 40, DM 98, FR 335, Y 7672).

LAMBERT, G.R. & CO.
  $4806* *Singapore, c. 1880s: Forty-Three,* majority negs. t., pho-
     tog.'s blindstamp, (10-29-92, Christie-London, #58, illus.),
     smallest 9 x 11 in., (22.9 x 27.9 cm.), largest 10 x 73½
     in., (22.9 x 27.9 cm.), photograph, albumen print (BP
     3080, DM 7394, FR 25,084, Y 595,318).

LAMPARE, G.
  $984* *Aerodrome De La Porte Maillot. Ballon Captif, c. 1900,*
     Asnieres, La lithographie nouvelle, cond. A-, (06-11-93,
     Boisgirard, #96, illus.), 31½ x 23⅝ in., (80 x 60 cm.),
     poster (BP 647, DM 1599, FR 5392, Y 104,403).

LAMPINKA, Tamara de
  $11,500* *Femme Bleu A La Guitar,* s., annot. 71/100, good cond.,
     loose sheet, conserved, (06-10-93, Sotheby-NY, #481,
     illus.), 29¾ x 20⅝ in., (75.6 x 52.4 cm.), color etching
     and drypoint (BP 7522, DM 18,727, FR 63,048, Y
     1,220,677).

LANCELEY, Colin   b. 1938
  BI *The Glass Of Haironymos Boach,* s. Lanceley, i., d. '65,
     #11/50, rondo, est. $250/350, (08-11-92, L. Joel, #57G),
     color lithograph.

LANCRET, N.   1690-1745
  BI *Le Maitre Galant,* tears, est. SC 6/9,000, (11-11-92, Dor-
     otheum, #331), 16⁹⁄₁₆ x 19½ in., (42 x 49.5 cm.), etching
     w/engraving.

LANCRET, Nicolas   French 1690-1743
  BI *"La Coquette De Village",* est. DM 300-, (03-24-93,
     Venator/Hansten, #2539), pl. approx. 12¹⁵⁄₁₆ x 14⅜ in.,
     (33 x 36.5 cm.), etching and engraving.

LANCRET, Nicolas (after)   French 1690-1743
  $225* *"Le Jeu De Pied De Beuf",* by Nicoleo de Larmessin,
     coll.'s stamp, (03-24-93, Venator/Hansten, #2540), pl.
     14⅞ x 18¹⁄₁₆ in., (37.8 x 45.9 cm.), etching (BP 152,
     DM 367, FR 1251, Y 26,436).

LAND, Eugenie de
  $138* *"Before Sunset",* 2nd Liberty Loan of 1917, fold creas-
     ing, margin repair, (09-12-92, Dunning, #98, illus.), 30
     x 20 in., (76.2 x 50.8 cm.), poster, laid on cloth (BP 71,
     DM 199, FR 675, Y 17,098).

LANDACRE, Paul   American 1893-1963
  $880* *Black Stallion, 1940,* s., t., annot. FTP, partially erased
     ded., trial proof, margins, good cond., mat staining, fox-
     ing, (10-28-92, Butterfield, #2531), 6 x 7 in., (152 x 178
     mm.), wood engraving on Japan paper (BP 561, DM
     1359, FR 4615, Y 107,975).
  $715* *Black Stallion, 1940,* s., t., pub. The Woodcut Society,
     full margins, good cond., crease, (02-24-93, Butterfield,
     #2642), 6 x 7 in., (152 x 178 mm.), wood engraving on
     laid Japan (BP 499, DM 1161, FR 3935, Y 83,900).
  $605* *Conflict,* s., t., #18/56, estate and Origins of Art stamps,
     full margins, goodcond., hinge remains, mat staining, (10-
     28-92, Butterfield, #2736), 8½ x 6 in., (216 x 152 mm.),
     wood engraving on Japan (BP 385, DM 934, FR 3173,
     Y 74,233).
  $1540* *Death Of A Forest,* s., #41/60, t., (12-09-92, Grogan,
     #90), 8¼ x 11⅛ in., (21 x 28.3 cm.), woodcut (BP 983,
     DM 2417, FR 8249, Y 190,949).
  BI *"Forest Girl", 1936,* AAG edit., good cond., est. $3-
     400, (10-31-92, Cleveland, #166, illus.), 8½ x 6 in.,
     (21.6 x 15.2 cm.), woodcut.
  $550* *Forest Girl, 1936,* s., t., #14/60, full margins, good
     cond., (10-28-92, Butterfield, #2735), 8⁷⁄₁₆ x 6 in., (214

x 152 mm.), wood engraving on Japan (BP 350, DM
     849, FR 2884, Y 67,485).
  $2200* *Growing Corn, 1938,* s., t., num. 29/60, margins, good
     cond., light-staining, taped, (02-24-93, Butterfield, #2641),
     8¹⁄₁₆ x 4⁷⁄₁₆ in., (205 x 113 mm.), wood engraving on
     Japan (BP 1534, DM 3571, FR 12,108, Y 258,155).
  BI *Johann Sebastian Bach, 1935,* s., t., #19/60, margins,
     very good cond., light-staining, pencil mark, est. $7/900,
     (05-19-93, Butterfield, #1823), 6¾ x 4⅝ in., (171 x 117
     mm.), wood engraving on thin laid Japan.
  $440* *Laguna Cove, 1935,* estate & Origins d'Art inkstamps,
     margins, good cond., crease, (02-24-93, Butterfield,
     #2643), 9⅜ x 12 in., (238 x 305 mm.), wood engraving
     on Japan (BP 307, DM 714, FR 2422, Y 51,631).
  BI *Ludwig Von Beethoven, 1935,* s., i., #22/60, margins, very
     good cond., light staining, est. $7/900, (05-19-93, Butter-
     field, #1822), 6⅞ x 4⅝ in., (175 x 117 mm.), wood
     engraving on thin laid Japan.
  $690* *Poachers, 1934,* s., t., #23/60, margins, good cond., light-
     staining, glue remains inimage, hinge remains, (05-19-
     93, Butterfield, #1821), 6 x 8½ in., (152 x 216 mm.),
     wood engraving on Kitakata (BP 448, DM 1122, FR
     3779, Y 76,387).
  $55* *"Reading" and "Tropical Paradise": Two,* s., d. 1936,
     (05-16-93, Hanzel, #462), each 8 x 6 in., (20.3 x 15.2
     cm.), woodblock (BP 36, DM 88, FR 297, Y 6097).
  BI *"Rima", 1936,* AAG edit., good cond., est. $3-400, (10-
     31-92, Cleveland, #167), 8½ x 6 in., (21.6 x 15.2 cm.),
     woodcut.
  $990* *Smoke Tree (L. of C.11),* c. 1953, s., t., i. FTP, wide
     margins, light-staining, old glue, good cond., (09-19-92,
     Christie-E, #30, illus.), borderline 7¹⁵⁄₁₆ x 6 in., (202 x
     152 mm.), woodcut on Japan (BP 569, DM 1482, FR
     5077, Y 123,349).
  $242* *Three Kids And A Horse (L. of C. 14), 1943,* wide mar-
     gins, estate stamp, creasing, good cond., (09-19-92,
     Christie-E, #31), borderline 7⁹⁄₁₆ x 10¹⁄₁₆ in., (192 x 256
     mm.), woodcut on Japan (BP 139, DM 362, FR 1241, Y
     30,152).

LANDAU, Jacob   American b. 1917
  $85* *"Cadillac", 1967,* s., excell. cond., (05-15-93, Cleveland,
     #479), 10½ x 7 in., (26.7 x 17.8 cm.), color lithograph
     (BP 55, DM 137, FR 459, Y 9422).
  $80* *Habethland And Schweddy,* AAA edit., s., excell. cond.,
     (05-15-93, Cleveland, #478), 10½ x 7 in., (26.7 x 17.8
     cm.), lithogrpah in colors (BP 52, DM 129, FR 432, Y
     8868).

LANDECK, Armin   b. 1905
  $1100* *Approaching Storm, Manhattan (K. 65), 1937,* s., d.,
     wide margins, foxing, old glue, (09-19-92, Christie-E,
     #33), plate 9 x 8⅜ in., (229 x 213 mm.), drypoint on
     wove (BP 633, DM 1647, FR 5641, Y 137,055).
  $495* *Approaching Storm, Manhattan (K. 65), 1937,* s., d.,
     num. Ed 100, margins, good cond., surface soiling, (02-
     24-93, Butterfield, #2842), 9¼ x 8½ in., (235 x 216
     mm.), drypoint on cream wove (BP 345, DM 804, FR
     2724, Y 58,085).
  $660* *Bantam Barns,* s., i., very good cond., (12-04-92, Doyle,
     #114), 5⅞ x 11¾ in., (149 x 298 mm.), lithograph (BP
     423, DM 1051, FR 3566, Y 82,397).
  $770* *Bedford Street, 1938,* s., very good cond., (12-04-92,
     Doyle, #111), 10½ x 8 in., (267 x 203 mm.), etching
     (BP 494, DM 1226, FR 4160, Y 96,130).
  $550* *City Lane (K. 96), 1945,* s., d., i. Ed 100, wide margins,
     mat staining, very good cond., (09-19-92, Christie-E,
     #34), plate 10 x 13⅜ in., (254 x 340 mm.), drypoint on
     wove (BP 316, DM 824, FR 2821, Y 68,527).
  BI *Corban's Silo, 1937,* s., printing creases, very good
     cond., est. $5/700, (12-04-92, Doyle, #113), 8 x 10 in.,
     (203 x 254 mm.), etching.
  $413* *"Cornwall Bridge Rail Road Station", 1936,* s., (12-12-
     92, Litchfield, #158), 5¾ x 9¾ in., (14.6 x 24.8 cm.),
     drypoint (BP 265, DM 651, FR 2230, Y 51,108).
  $467* *"Delmonico's Roof" (Kraeft 92), 1943, "Window On 14th
     Street" (Kraeft 103), 1949 and "Excavation Site, Manhat-
     tan" (Kraeft 138), 1933: Three,* s., full margins, d. 1983,
     (05-27-93, Swann, #155), smallest 9¾ x 7 in., (24.8 x

17.8 cm.), largest 12 x 9 in., (24.8 x 17.8 cm.), engravings (BP 299, DM 749, FR 2526, Y 50,064).

$920* *"Delmonico's Roof" and "Restaurant" (K. 92 and 109), 1943 and 1951: To,* s., d., i. Ed 100, margins, good cond., soiling, (02-11-93, Sotheby-NY, #30), 12⁵⁄₁₆ x 9⅛ in., (312 x 232 mm.), 12 x 15⅞ in., (312 x 232 mm.), engraving (BP 649, DM 1524, FR 5157, Y 110,910).

$303* *Demolition: Houston Street (K. 122), 1971,* s., d., num. Ed 100, margins, good cond., filled in holes, creases, (02-24-93, Butterfield, #2846), 16⅝ x 23⅞ in., (423 x 607.5 mm.), engraving on cream wove (BP 211, DM 492, FR 1668, Y 35,555).

$330* *Demolition: Houston Street (K. 122), 1971,* s., d., num. Ed 100, margins, good cond., light-staining, surface soiling, rubbed areas, notations, pinhole, (10-28-92, Butterfield, #2739), 16⅝ x 23⅞ in., (422 x 606 mm.), engraving on wove (BP 210, DM 510, FR 1730, Y 40,491).

$440* *Excavation Sight, Manhattan, 1983,* very good cond., (12-04-92, Doyle, #115), 9¾ x 6¾ in., (248 x 171 mm.), etching (BP 282, DM 701, FR 2377, Y 54,931).

BI *Fish, 1963,* s., smudging, tape residue, very good cond., est. $3/500, (12-04-92, Doyle, #112), 18 x 23½ in., (457 x 597 mm.), etching.

$575* *Locomotive (K. 61), 1936,* s., d., i. Ed 100, full margins, good cond., (05-13-93, Sotheby-NY, #427), 6⅜ x 4¾ in., (162 x 121 mm.), drypoint and aquatint (BP 377, DM 928, FR 3132, Y 64,196).

$2185* *Manhattan Canyon (Kraeft 46), 1934,* s., d., i. Ed 100, full margins, good cond., (02-11-93, Sotheby-NY, #27), 13¹⁵⁄₁₆ x 6¾ in., (355 x 172 mm.), drypoint (BP 1542, DM 3619, FR 12,248, Y 263,412).

$2860* *Manhattan Canyon (Kraeft 46), 1934,* s., wide margins, mat staining, taped, (09-19-92, Christie-E, #32, illus.), plate 13⅞ x 6¾ in., (352 x 171 mm.), drypoint on laid paper (BP 1645, DM 4283, FR 14,667, Y 356,342).

$2860* *"Manhattan Canyon" (Kraeft, 46), 1934,* s., d. Landeck 1934, num. ed., ident. label verso, very good cond., (03-12-93, Skinner, #30, illus.), 14 x 6¾ in., (35.6 x 17.1 cm.), drypoint on wove (BP 1995, DM 4760, FR 16,186, Y 337,065).

$303* *Manhattan Moonlight (K. 99), 1947,* s., d., num. Ed 100, full margins, very good cond., creases, surfacesoiling, (02-24-93, Butterfield, #2844), 11¾ x 14¾ in., (298 x 375 mm.), drypoint & engraving on wove (BP 211, DM 492, FR 1668, Y 35,555).

$358* *Manhattan Moonlight (K. 99), 1947,* s., d., num. Ed 100, full margins, good cond., surface soiling, staining, notation, (10-28-92, Butterfield, #2737), 11¾ x 14⅜ in., (298 x 365 mm.), drypoint and engraving in wove (BP 228, DM 553, FR 1877, Y 43,926).

$715* *"Manhattan Moonlight",* s. Landeck 1947, very good cond, (04-25-93, Bakker, #156, illus.), plate 12 x 14½ in., (30.5 x 36.8 cm.), etching (BP 454, DM 1131, FR 3819, Y 78,971).

$1000* *"Manhattan Nocturne" (Kraeft 70 i/ii), 1938,* s., excell. cond., hinges, presentation print, (05-15-93, Cleveland, #204, illus.), 7⅛ x 11⅞ in., (18.1 x 30.2 cm.), etching (BP 650, DM 1608, FR 5405, Y 110,852).

$1320* *Manhattan Vista (Kraeft 47), 1934,* s., d., i., full margins, good cond., fox mark, (11-05-92, Sotheby-NY, #32), 10 x 8½ in., (254 x 217 mm.), drypoint (BP 859, DM 2088, FR 7063, Y 161,943).

$920* *Manhattan Vista (Kraeft 47), 1934,* s., i. imp, margins, good cond., mat stain, glue, skinning, tear, losses, (05-13-93, Sotheby-NY, #426), 10⅛ x 8½ in., (258 x 217 mm.), sh 12⅞ x 10¾ in., (258 x 217 mm.), drypoint (BP 604, DM 1486, FR 5011, Y 102,713).

$1100* *Manhattan Vista [K47],* s., d. 1934, i. 100, (12-10-92, Sloan, #2695, illus.), 10 x 8½ in., (25.4 x 21.6 cm.), drypoint (BP 709, DM 1740, FR 5943, Y 136,071).

$935* *Manufacturer's Trust (Kraeft 127), 1974,* s., d. 1938-74, i., full margins, excell. cond., (11-09-92, Christie-NY, #21, illus.), plate 7¹⁄₁₆ x 11¹⁵⁄₁₆ in., (180 x 304 mm.), drypoint and engraving on white wove (BP 618, DM 1493, FR 5043, Y 116,034).

$385* *Newstand Manhattan, 1978,* s., very good cond., (12-04-92, Doyle, #116), 13⅞ x 7⅞ in., (352 x 200 mm.), etching (BP 247, DM 613, FR 2080, Y 48,065).

$413* *One Way Street (K. 106), 1950,* s., d., num. Ed 100, margins, good cond., surface soiling, creases, notation, (10-28-92, Butterfield, #2738), 10½ x 14 in., (267 x 356 mm.), engraving on wove (BP 263, DM 638, FR 2166, Y 50,675).

$385* *One Way Street (Kraeft 106), 1950,* s., (05-27-93, Swann, #154), 10½ x 14 in., (26.7 x 35.6 cm.), engraving and etching (BP 247, DM 618, FR 2082, Y 41,274).

$440* *"Paris Underground",* excell. cond., Mrs. Thelma B. Ingersoll Estate, (12-12-92, Litchfield, #157), 15 x 20 in., (38.1 x 50.8 cm.), engraving (BP 282, DM 693, FR 2376, Y 54,449).

$2300* *Pop's Tavern (Kraeft 45), 1934,* s., d., i. Ed 100, margins, light-staining, rubbing, very good cond., (05-11-93, Christie-NY, #110), plate 6⅛ x 10 in., (156 x 254 mm.), aquatint and drypoint on wove (BP 1468, DM 3623, FR 12,208, Y 252,997).

$440* *Rooftop (K. 84), 1941,* s., d., num. Ed 100, full margins, good cond., surface soiling, crease, (10-28-92, Butterfield, #2533), 4⅞ x 8¹⁵⁄₁₆ in., (124 x 227 mm.), engraving on wove (BP 280, DM 680, FR 2307, Y 53,988).

$600* *"Rooftop And Skylight" (K. 121), 1969,* s., d., excell. cond., (05-15-93, Cleveland, #205, illus.), 18 x 20⅞ in., (45.7 x 53 cm.), engraving (BP 390, DM 965, FR 3243, Y 66,511).

$413* *Rooftop And Skylights (K. 121), 1969,* s., d., num. Ed 100, margins, good cond., mat staining, stains, surface soiling, (10-28-92, Butterfield, #2536), 18 x 20¾ in., (457 x 527 mm.), engraving on heavy wove (BP 263, DM 638, FR 2166, Y 50,675).

$358* *Rooftop And Skylights (K. 121), 1969,* s., d., num. Ed 100, margins, very good cond., creases, skinned areas, (02-24-93, Butterfield, #2845), 18 x 20¾ in., (457 x 527 mm.), engraving on heavy wove (BP 250, DM 581, FR 1970, Y 42,009).

$1045* *"Rooftop, 14th Street (K. 97), 1946" and "Rooftop And Skylights (K. 121), 1969": Two,* both s., wide margins; first foxmark, very good cond.; second mat staining, paper losses, (09-19-92, Christie-E, #35), first drypoint and engraving on laid; second engraving on wove laid down (BP 601, DM 1565, FR 5359, Y 130,202).

$440* *Rooftop, 14th Street (K. 97), 1949,* s., d., num. Ed 100, margins, good cond., touched-in areas blue ink in image, creases, surface scuffing/soiling, notations, (10-28-92, Butterfield, #2534, illus.), 8⅜ x 14 in., (213 x 356 mm.), drypoint and engraving on wove (BP 280, DM 680, FR 2307, Y 53,988).

$248* *Self Portrait, 1942,* s., d., num. Ed 100, p. w/plate tone, good cond., surface soiling, hinge remains, creases, pressure mark, (02-24-93, Butterfield, #2843), 10 x 7 in., (254 x 178 mm.), etching on wove (BP 173, DM 403, FR 1365, Y 29,101).

$935* *Stairhall (K. 104), 1950,* s., wide margins, mat staining, foxmarks, (09-19-92, Christie-E, #36), plate 11⅜ x 14⅜ in., (289 x 365 mm.), drypoint and engraving on J. Whatman (BP 538, DM 1400, FR 4795, Y 116,496).

$863* *Studio Interior No. 1 (K. 57), 1935,* s., d., i. Ed 100, full margins, good cond., prop. Brooklyn Museum, (02-11-93, Sotheby-NY, #28), 7¹⁵⁄₁₆ x 10½ in., (203 x 267 mm.), drypoint (BP 609, DM 1430, FR 4837, Y 104,039).

$798* *"Studio Interior", 1935,* s., excell. cond., (08-08-92, Litchfield, #98), 7¾ x 10½ in., (19.7 x 26.7 cm.), etching and drypoint (BP 414, DM 1174, FR 3966, Y 101,851).

$385* *"West Cornwall Station",* s., d. 1936, very good cond., (03-28-93, Bakker, #211), plate 7 x 11 in., (17.8 x 27.9 cm.), etching (BP 259, DM 628, FR 2135, Y 44,809).

$690* *York Avenue Tenements (K. 74), 1938,* s., d., i. Ed 100, full margins, good cond., (02-11-93, Sotheby-NY, #29), 10¼ x 8¹⁵⁄₁₆ in., (261 x 227 mm.), drypoint (BP 487, DM 1143, FR 3868, Y 83,183).

$935* *York Avenue Tenements (K. 74), 1938,* s., d., num. Ed 100, margins, good cond., staining, surface soiling, (10-28-92, Butterfield, #2532, illus.), 10½ x 8⅞ in., (267 x 225 mm.), drypoint on wove (BP 596, DM 1444, FR 4903, Y 114,724).

LANDI, Juan

$825* *Inchauspe,* El Ministerio de Salud Publica, B+ cond., fold marks throughout, closed tears, (08-06-92, Swann, #166, illus.), 37½ x 52½ in., (95.3 x 133.4 cm.), (BP 431, DM 1219, FR 4117, Y 105,230).

LANDIS, John American 1805-c. 1851

$1650* *"Battle Of New Orleans",* pub. 1840 by Landis, (12-05-92, Neal, #552, illus.), image 15 x 24½ in., (38.1 x 62.2 cm.), lithograph (BP 1033, DM 2572, FR 8767, Y 204,436).

LANDOLT, Karl b. 1925

BI *Fischer An Der Verzasca, 1965,* 51/200, s., est. SF 80/120, (10-14-92, Germann, #559), 19¾ x 15⅝ in., (502 x 390 mm.), color woodcut.

LANDON, Edward

$44* *"Departure",* edit. of 50, (09-18-92, DuMouchelle, #2512), 12¼ x 14¼ in., (31.1 x 36.2 cm.), silkscreen (BP 25, DM 66, FR 226, Y 5482).

LANDSEER

$715* *The China Limodoron, 1802,* after Henderson, pub. Dr. Thornton, acid burn verso, discoloration, oxidized, good cond., Katherine Winn Estate, (12-04-92, Doyle, #6), 20⅞ x 16 in., (530 x 406 mm.), mixed method engraving (BP 459, DM 1139, FR 3863, Y 89,263).

LANDSEER, Sir Edwin (after)

$18 *"The Chieftan's Friends",* engraved by JC Armytage, water stained, (04-16-93, G.A. Key, #110), 8 x 9 in., (20.3 x 22.9 cm.), b/w engraving (BP 12, DM 29, FR 98, Y 2024).

$80* *"A Gamekeeper And His Dog By The Day's Bag",* (03-03-93, Bonhams-Chelsea, #78), image 13⅝ x 21½ in., (34.6 x 54.6 cm.), hand-colored engraving (BP 55, DM 132, FR 447, Y 9348).

$80* *A Gun Dog And Game,* blindstamp Print Sellers' Assoc., pub. G.P. McQueen, 1877, margins, (03-03-93, Bonhams-Chelsea, #79), plate 22¼ x 26 in., (56.5 x 66 cm.), engraving (BP 55, DM 132, FR 447, Y 9348).

$14 *"Head Of A Deerhound",* engraved by C.G. Lewis, (02-05-93, G.A. Key, #61), 5 x 7 in., (12.7 x 17.8 cm.), b/w engraving (BP 10, DM 23, FR 78, Y 1742).

$415* *Horse And Dogs By A Cottage,* indistinctly s., margins, staining, (03-03-93, Bonhams-Chelsea, #33), plate 28 x 34 in., (71.1 x 86.4 cm.), engraving (BP 286, DM 683, FR 2318, Y 48,493).

$53 *Inside The Blacksmiths Shops,* d. 1882, (04-16-93, G.A. Key, #63), 7 x 5 in., (17.8 x 12.7 cm.), b/w engraving (BP 35, DM 86, FR 289, Y 5960).

$253* *Laying Down The Law, 1843,* pub. Thomas McLean, foxing, staining, (01-18-93, Bonhams, #79), image 23¼ x 25 in., (59.1 x 63.5 cm.), mezzotint (BP 165, DM 414, FR 1379, Y 31,892).

$670* *The Lion Dog, From Malta, 1851,* by W.T. Davey, pub. Thomas McLean, margins, tear, front cover illus., (11-12-92, Bonhams-Chelsea, #81, illus.), plate 14¾ x 16¼ in., (37.5 x 41.3 cm.), hand-colored mezzotint (BP 440, DM 1062, FR 3581, Y 83,075).

$121* *A Piper And Pair Of Nutcrackers, 1897,* engraved by George Zobel, (02-14-93, Neal, #1141), image 18 x 15 in., (45.7 x 38.1 cm.), engraving (BP 85, DM 201, FR 679, Y 14,592).

$84* *Roebuck And Rough Hands, 1849,* pub. Thomas McLean, margins, foxing, staining, (01-18-93, Bonhams, #80), plate 24 x 18¾ in., (61 x 47.6 cm.), engraving (BP 55, DM 137, FR 458, Y 10,589).

LANE, Fitz Hugh (after)

$6050* *View Of Gloucester From Rocky Neck,* by Lane and Scott, (11-07-92, Northeast, #174, illus.), 15 x 25 in., (38.1 x 63.5 cm.), lithograph (BP 3956, DM 9706, FR 32,650, Y 746,729).

$8250* *View Of Gloucester, Massachusetts,* by L.H. Bradford, (11-07-92, Northeast, #169, illus.), 22 x 36 in., (55.9 x 91.4 cm.), hand colored lithograph (BP 5394, DM 13,236, FR 44,522, Y 1,018,267).

LANE, Lois American contemporary

$550* *"Bride", "Bull With Horn" and "Ski Mask", 1979: Three,* from Six Aquatints, s., t., d., num. 26/45, 39/45, 26/45, blindstamps of printer Aeropress, full margins; Bull w/ nick, crease; all excell. cond., (09-19-92, Christie-E, #146), each, sheet 29⅞ x 22¼ in., (759 x 565 mm.), aquatint, two w/colors, on BFK Rives Moulin du Gue (BP 316, DM 824, FR 2821, Y 68,527).

LANFAIR, Harriet Keese American b. 1900

$220* *"Race Point Light, Provincetown", "Backyard" and "Woman At The Fire": Three,* s.; first t., #4/5, (03-24-93, Grogan, #86), first 8⅛ x 11⅞ in., (20.6 x 30.2 cm.), lithograph (BP 149, DM 359, FR 1223, Y 25,849).

LANG, Daniel 20th cnet.

BI *"Kenya",* i., s., d. Daniel Lang 1974, #59/100, est. DM 300-, (03-24-93, Venator/Hansten, #4523), pl. approx. 16¾ x 24³⁄₁₆ in., (42.5 x 61.5 cm.), color aquatint.

LANGE, Dorothea American 1895-1965

$4400* *Argument In A Trailer Court, 1944,* photog.'s studio stamp, label, (10-15-92, Sotheby-NY, #186, illus.), 7⅝ x 9½ in., (19.4 x 24.1 cm.), photograph, gelatin silver print (BP 2692, DM 6550, FR 22,211, Y 527,894).

BI *Bessie, Daughter Of Zion, Mother Of Three, Toquerville, Utah, 1953,* authenticated, i., prov., lit., est. $3/4,000, (04-08-93, Christie-NY, #308, illus.), 10½ x 10⅜ in., (26.7 x 26.4 cm.), photograph, gelatin silver print.

$2070* *"Between Tulare And Fresno, California", "Mail Boxes Of The New Settlers On The Bench Lands" and "Mexicans Entering The United States At The U.S. Immigration Station", 1939: Three,* typed t., FSA stamp, est. $1,8/2,200, (05-23-93, Butterfield, #3498, illus.), each approx. 8 x 10 in., photograph, gelatin silver print (BP 1348, DM 3385, FR 11,392, Y 228,805).

BI *Black Maria, Oakland, 1955-57,* stamp, est. $6/8,000, (10-13-92, Christie-NY, #466, illus.), 11¼ x 10½ in., (28.6 x 26.7 cm.), photograph, gelatin silver print.

$1430* *"Dust Bowl Refugees Along Highway Near Bakersfield, California", 1935-1936,* t., num., photog. stamp, (11-16-92, Butterfield, #6053, illus.), 8 x 7¾ in., (203.6 x 197.2 mm.), photograph, gelatin silver print (BP 942, DM 2280, FR 7680, Y 177,839).

BI *Ex-Slave With A Long Memory, Alabama,* 1938, p. late 1940s-early 1950s, lit., est. $4/5,000, (04-08-93, Christie-NY, #310, illus.), 10¾ x 13¾ in., (27.3 x 34.9 cm.), photograph, gelatin silver print.

$3300* *Ex-Slave With A Long Memory, Alabama (Aperture, p. 92),* date stamp, 1937, p. before 1941, (10-15-92, Sotheby-NY, #185A, illus.), 7¼ x 9¼ in., (18.4 x 23.5 cm.), photograph, gelatin silver print (BP 2019, DM 4912, FR 16,658, Y 395,921).

$522* *Farmer, Hillhouse, Mississippi,* F.S.A., Pictures for Democracy handstamp, caption, 1930s, (04-07-93, Swann, #306, illus.), 9 x 7½ in., photograph, silver print (BP 345, DM 844, FR 2857, Y 59,305).

$3163* *"Girl From Tennessee, Outside Sacramento", 1930's,* photog. studio stamp, t. in unident. hand, (04-06-93, Sotheby-NY, #177, illus.), 9⅝ x 7⅝ in., photograph (BP 2089, DM 5096, FR 17,256, Y 360,744).

$2588* *"Jake Jones's Hands, Gunlock County, Utah" (Detail) (Aperture, p. 118, variant), 1953,* photog. studio stamp, (04-06-93, Sotheby-NY, #180, illus.), 11⅜ x 9 in., photograph (BP 1709, DM 4169, FR 14,119, Y 295,164).

$3300* *Landscape, New Mexico, 1937,* mounted, s., d. by photog., studio stamp, (10-15-92, Sotheby-NY, #185, illus.), 2⅞ x 9¼ in., (7.3 x 23.5 cm.), photograph, gelatin silver print (BP 2019, DM 4912, FR 16,658, Y 395,921).

$440* *McLennan County Court House, 1938,* handstamp, (10-14-92, Swann, #449, illus.), 10 x 8 in., (25.4 x 20.3 cm.), photograph, silver print (BP 258, DM 644, FR 2184, Y 53,320).

$8250* *Migrant Mother,* notations, handstamp, 1936, p. 1948, ex-coll. Charlotte Brooks, (10-14-92, Swann, #328, illus.), 9½ x 7½ in., (24.1 x 19.1 cm.), photograph, silver print (BP 4842, DM 12,074, FR 40,943, Y 999,758).

$3450* *Migrant Peapicker, 1936,* credit stamp, (04-08-93, Christie-NY, #311, illus.), 9 x 7¼ in., (22.9 x 18.4 cm.), photograph, toned gelatin silver print (BP 2262, DM 5542, FR 18,760, Y 391,512).

BI *"Migrant Workers In Lettuce Field, Califonia", 1935,* annot., FSA stamps, est. $800/1,000, (11-16-92, Butterfield, #6056, illus.), 7⅝ x 9½ in., (194 x 241.7 mm.), photograph, gelatin silver print.

$1430* *Portrait Of A Boy, 1930,* s., d., (10-13-92, Christie-NY, #287, illus.), 4¾ x 3⅝ in., (12.1 x 9.2 cm.), photograph, gelatin silver print (BP 833, DM 2095, FR 7118, Y 173,396).

$1430* *Portrait Of A Woman, 1920,* s., d., on image, (11-16-92, Butterfield, #6051, illus.), 7⅞ x 6 in., (200.4 x 152.7 mm.), photograph, gelatin silver print (BP 942, DM 2280, FR 7680, Y 177,839).

$2300* *Portrait Study,* 1930s, p. 1950s, credit stamp, (04-08-93, Christie-NY, #309, illus.), 3⅜ x 3¾ in., (8.6 x 9.5 cm.), photograph, gelatin silver print (BP 1508, DM 3695, FR 12,507, Y 261,008).

$2300* *"Shipyard Worker, Richmond" (MoMA, p. 60; Aperture, p. 127), c. 1942,* backed w/card, photog. studio stamp, (04-06-93, Sotheby-NY, #178, illus.), 13⅜ x 10¼ in., photograph (BP 1519, DM 3705, FR 12,548, Y 262,318).

$2300* *"Tenant Farmers Without Farms, Hardman County, Texas" (MoMA, p. 33; Aperture, p. 121),* photog. studio stamp, p. notations, (04-06-93, Sotheby-NY, #179A, illus.), 7½ x 9⅜ in., photograph (BP 1519, DM 3705, FR 12,548, Y 262,318).

$1540* *"Tom Collins, Manager Of The Kern Migrant Camp, California", 1935-1936,* t., num., photog. stamp, (11-16-92, Butterfield, #6052, illus.), 7½ x 9½ in., (190.8 x 241.7 mm.), photograph, gelatin silver print (BP 1014, DM 2455, FR 8271, Y 191,518).

$18,400* *Torso, San Francisco (1923),* 1930s, credit stamp, authenticated, i., lit., (04-08-93, Christie-NY, #307, illus.), 4⅝ x 3⅞ in., (11.7 x 9.8 cm.), photograph, gelatin silver contact print (BP 12,066, DM 29,558, FR 100,054, Y 2,088,062).

BI *Tourists In Small Highway Town, Utah, 1953,* backed w/ card, t., d. by photog. in ink, studio label, subjektive fotografie stamp, est. $3/5,000, (10-15-92, Sotheby-NY, #187, illus.), 96 x 11¼ in., (243.8 x 28.6 cm.), photograph, gelatin silver print.

BI *"Woman Called Queen, North Carolina" (Dorothea Lange, pl. 41),* crayon num., est. $1,0/1,500, 1939/later, (11-16-92, Butterfield, #6054, illus.), 10 x 7 in., (254.5 x 178.1 mm.), photograph, gelatin silver print.

$2588* *Woman On Bench, 1950's,* mounted, num. 38065-2 in unident. hand, (04-06-93, Sotheby-NY, #179, illus.), 9⅜ x 7⅜ in., photograph (BP 1709, DM 4169, FR 14,119, Y 295,164).

BI *Woman Sitting On Front Porch, 1930's,* p. notations in unidentified hand, est. #3/5,000, (10-15-92, Sotheby-NY, #184, illus.), 7½ x 7¾ in., (19.1 x 19.7 cm.), photograph, gelatin silver print.

$9350* *Young Girl In Torn Pinafore, 1930's,* photog.'s studio stamp, (10-15-92, Sotheby-NY, #183, illus.), 12¼ x 9½ in., (31.1 x 24.1 cm.), photograph, gelatin silver print (BP 5721, DM 13,918, FR 47,198, Y 1,121,776).

LANGE, Otto 1879-1944

$2128* *Kakteen Am Fenster, c. 1925,* s., i., (06-05-93, Bassenge, #6248), 20¹¹⁄₁₆ x 18⁷⁄₁₆ in., (52.5 x 46.8 cm.), color woodcut (BP 1401, DM 3450, FR 11,628, Y 228,277).

$5974* *Die Kartenspieler,* s., (12-01-92, Karl/Faber, #900, illus.), 16¹⁵⁄₁₆ x 11¹³⁄₁₆ in., (43 x 30 cm.), color monotype on simili-Japan (BP 3947, DM 9522, FR 32,450, Y 743,775).

$640* *(Reclining Figures),* s., margins, creasing, small defects at edges of sheet, soiling, foxing, minor handling creases, Late Gerhard Bauer Coll., (05-27-93, Sotheby-Amstrdm, #754, illus.), 15⅞ x 22¹⁄₁₆ in., (404 x 560 mm.), etching on sturdy wove (BP 410, DM 1027, FR 3461, Y 68,611, G 1150).

LANGENDIJK, P. 1683-1756

$432* *Depicting Fools, Beggars, Invalids: Set Of 5,* after P. BARBIERS THE ELDER, rare, (11-18-92, Bubb Kuyper, #1838, illus.), approx. 3⁹⁄₁₆ x 3⁹⁄₁₆ in., (9 x 9 cm.), etching (BP 284, DM 689, FR 2320, Y 53,725, G 780).

LANGENHEIM, Frederick and William

BI *Merchants' Exchange, Philadelphia (Taft, p. 108; Arnold, pl. 78; Buckland, p. 99), 1849,* i., s., d. by photogs. in neg., est. $40/60,000, (10-15-92, Sotheby-NY, #6, illus.), 9⅜ x 8⅞ in., (23.8 x 22.5 cm.), on paper 10⅜ x 9⅜ in., (23.8 x 22.5 cm.), photograph, talbotype.

LANGLOIS, Colonel Jean Charles and Leon MEHEDIN

BI *The Crimea, 1855-56: Four,* one s. Leon Mehedin, mounted on card, each approx. 250 x 300mm, est.BP 1/1,500, (05-07-93, Sotheby-London, #116), photograph, albumen print from waxed paper neg..

LANGMAID, Rowland

$319* *The Endeavour,* s., Academy Proof blindstamp, margins, (08-12-92, Bonhams, #196), plate 6½ x 13⅝ in., (16.5 x 34.6 cm.), drypoint etching (BP 165, DM 467, FR 1581, Y 40,658).

$234* *Fantome And Valhalla Off Cowes,* s., margins, staining, (08-12-92, Bonhams, #197), plate 6¾ x 13¾ in., (17.1 x 34.9 cm.), drypoint etching (BP 121, DM 342, FR 1160, Y 29,824).

BI *Fisherman Going To Sea,* s., margins, est. BP 80/120, (08-12-92, Bonhams, #198), plate 3½ x 10¼ in., (8.9 x 26 cm.), drypoint etching.

$185* *"Fishermen Going To Sea",* s., margins, (01-14-93, Bonhams, #114), plate 3½ x 10¼ in., (8.9 x 26 cm.), drypoint etching (BP 121, DM 302, FR 1023, Y 23,323).

$203* *H.M.S. Victory,* s., Academy Proof blindstamp, margins, foxing, (08-12-92, Bonhams, #199), plate 11¼ x 8⅜ in., (28.6 x 21.3 cm.), drypoint etching (BP 105, DM 297, FR 1006, Y 25,873).

$182* *H.M.S. Victory,* s., margins, slight foxing, (08-12-92, Bonhams, #200), image 8⅜ x 6½ in., (21.3 x 16.5 cm.), drypoint etching (BP 94, DM 266, FR 902, Y 23,197).

$319* *J-Class Yachts Racing,* s., Academy Proof blindstamp, margins, (08-12-92, Bonhams, #201), plate 6⅝ x 13¾ in., (16.8 x 34.9 cm.), drypoint etching (BP 165, DM 467, FR 1581, Y 40,658).

$106* *A Line Of Frigates And Other Shipping,* s., Academy Proof blindstamp, margins, stained, (08-12-92, Bonhams, #202), plate 6½ x 13¾ in., (16.5 x 34.9 cm.), drypoint etching (BP 55, DM 155, FR 525, Y 13,510).

BI *Newlyn And St. Michael's Mount,* s., blindstamp, margins, est. BP 1/150, (01-14-93, Bonhams, #115), plate 6¼ x 11¾ in., (15.9 x 29.8 cm.), drypoint etching.

$111* *Newlyn And St. Michaels Mount,* s., Academy Proof blindstamp, margins, (02-17-93, Bonhams-Chelsea, #332), plate 6¼ x 11¾ in., (15.9 x 29.8 cm.), drypoint etching (BP 77, DM 180, FR 611, Y 13,258).

BI *Sailing Boats Off A Lighthouse,* s., margins, est. BP 80/120, (08-12-92, Bonhams, #208), plate 6⅛ x 11¾ in., (15.6 x 29.8 cm.), drypoint etching.

$319* *Sailing Boats Off A Mountainous Coastline,* s., Academy Proof blindstamp, margins, (08-12-92, Bonhams, #203), plate 6¼ x 12⅛ in., (15.9 x 30.8 cm.), drypoint etching (BP 165, DM 467, FR 1581, Y 40,658).

$100* *Shipping In Lamlash Bay,* s., blindstamp, margins, surface dirt, (10-15-92, Bonhams-Chelsea, #54), plate 6½ x 12 in., (16.5 x 30.5 cm.), drypoint etching (BP 61, DM 149, FR 505, Y 11,998).

$168* *The Silver Serpent,* s., t., margins, (01-14-93, Bonhams, #116), plate 5¾ x 8¾ in., (14.6 x 22.2 cm.), drypoint etching (BP 110, DM 275, FR 929, Y 21,180).

BI *The Silver Solent,* s., t., margins est. BP 1/150, (08-12-92, Bonhams, #204), plate 5¾ x 8¾ in., (14.6 x 22.2 cm.), drypoint etching.

$101* *The Silver Solent,* s., t., margins, surface dirt, (01-14-93, Bonhams, #117), plate 5¾ x 8¾ in., (14.6 x 22.2 cm.), drypoint etching (BP 66, DM 165, FR 558, Y 12,733).

$185* *St. Ives,* s., blindstamp, margins, (01-14-93, Bonhams, #118), plate 6¼ x 11¾ in., (15.9 x 29.8 cm.), drypoint etching (BP 121, DM 302, FR 1023, Y 23,323).

$97* *St. Paul's From The River,* s., margins, (08-12-92, Bonhams, #205), plate 5¾ x 3⅞ in., (14.6 x 9.8 cm.), drypoint etching (BP 50, DM 142, FR 481, Y 12,363).

$182* *A Sunlit Sea (Spithead),* s., margins, (08-12-92, Bonhams, #206), plate 7¾ x 5⅞ in., (19.7 x 14.9 cm.), drypoint etching w/aquatint (BP 94, DM 266, FR 902, Y 23,197).

BI *The Thames At Billingsgate,* s., Academy Proof blindstamp, margins, est. BP 1/150, (08-12-92, Bonhams, #207), plate 11½ x 9 in., (29.2 x 22.9 cm.), drypoint etching.

$219* *The Thames At St. Pauls,* s., margins, (01-14-93, Bonhams, #119), plate 4¾ x 9⅝ in., (12.1 x 24.4 cm.), drypoint etching (BP 143, DM 358, FR 1211, Y 27,610).
$182* *Tower Bridge,* s., margins, wormhole, (08-12-92, Bonhams, #210), plate 7⅞ x 5⅞ in., (20 x 14.9 cm.), drypoint etching (BP 94, DM 266, FR 902, Y 23,197).
$99* *View On The Seine,* s., (05-20-93, Boos, #539), sight 11⅝ x 9¹⁄₁₆ in., (295 x 230 mm.), etching (BP 64, DM 160, FR 538, Y 10,932).
$99* *View On The Seine,* s., (05-20-93, Boos, #538), sight 11⅝ x 9¹⁄₁₆ in., (295 x 230 mm.), etching (BP 64, DM 160, FR 538, Y 10,932).
$319* *Westminster From The River,* s., Academy Proof blindstamp, margins, (08-12-92, Bonhams, #195, illus.), plate 7½ x 9¾ in., (19.1 x 24.8 cm.), drypoint etching (BP 165, DM 467, FR 1581, Y 40,658).
$297* *Yachts Racing,* s., Academy Proof blindstamp, margins, (08-12-92, Bonhams, #244), plate 6¼ x 12⅛ in., (15.9 x 30.8 cm.), drypoint etching (BP 154, DM 434, FR 1472, Y 37,854).

LANGMAID, Rowland English 1897-1956
$77* *London Bridge,* s., prov., (10-30-92, Sloan, #828), 3⅜ x 11⅝ in., (8.6 x 29.5 cm.), etching (BP 49, DM 118, FR 402, Y 9538).

LANSKOY, Andre Russian/French 1902-1976
BI *Composition,* s., i. E.A., margins, good cond., prov., est. Dfl. 6/800, (05-27-93, Sotheby-Amstrdm, #641), 25⅜ x 19⅝ in., (645 x 498 mm.), color lithograph on wove.
$367* *Composition,* s. Lanskoy, 56/150, (03-24-93, Kunsthallen, #220), color lithograph (BP 249, DM 599, FR 2040, Y 43,121, DK 2300).
$220* *Composition,* s. Lanskoy, (03-24-93, Kunsthallen, #218), color lithograph (BP 149, DM 359, FR 1223, Y 25,849, DK 1380).
$404* *Composition,* s. Lanskoy, 108/175, (03-24-93, Kunsthallen, #219), color lithograph (BP 274, DM 660, FR 2246, Y 47,468, DK 2530).
$516* *Composition,* s., #XXXI/L, (03-31-93, Briest, #E65), 30¹¹⁄₁₆ x 22¹³⁄₁₆ in., (78 x 58 cm.), color lithograph on Japan (BP 341, DM 830, FR 2820, Y 59,338).
$514* *Composition,* E.A., s., signs of wear, (04-21-93, Germann, #590), 30⅛ x 22¹⁄₁₆ in., (765 x 560 mm.), color lithograph on Japan (BP 334, DM 822, FR 2778, Y 56,902, SF 748).
$83* *Composition,* (01-31-93, Millon/Robert, #226), 14¹⁵⁄₁₆ x 21¼ in., (38 x 54 cm.), serigraph (BP 56, DM 134, FR 452, Y 10,354).
$144* *Composition A Fond Bleu,* s., #XXIV/L, full margins, (05-06-93, Laurin, #50), color lithograph (BP 91, DM 227, FR 764, Y 15,843).
BI *Composition En Vert, 1959,* s., d., #40/80, good margins, (05-06-93, Laurin, #49), color lithograph.
$269* *"Composition Fond Rouge",* #74/150, s., (10-18-92, Pescheteau, #180), 29¹⁵⁄₁₆ x 21⅝ in., (76 x 55 cm.), lithograph in colors on Arches (BP 163, DM 397, FR 1350, Y 32,119).
BI *"Composition Sur Fond Bleu",* EA s., est. FF1,000/1,500, (04-04-93, Pescheteau, #233), 25⁹⁄₁₆ x 19¹¹⁄₁₆ in., (65 x 50 cm.), color lithograph on Arches.
$155* *Composition Sur Fond Noir,* s., hors commerce, (06-28-93, Loudmer, #64), 21¼ x 15¾ in., (540 x 400 mm.), sh 25⁹⁄₁₆ x 19¹¹⁄₁₆ in., (540 x 400 mm.), color lithograph on Arches wove (BP 104, DM 263, FR 887, Y 16,446).
$116* *Composition Sur Fond Rouge,* s., artist's proof, crease, (06-28-93, Loudmer, #65), 20⅞ x 14³⁄₁₆ in., (530 x 360 mm.), sh 22⁷⁄₁₆ x 15⅜ in., (530 x 360 mm.), color lithograph on Rives wove (BP 78, DM 197, FR 664, Y 12,308).
BI *"Composition Sur Fond Rouge",* artist's proof, s., (04-04-93, Pescheteau, #232), 29½ x 22¹⁄₁₆ in., (75 x 56 cm.), color lithograph on Arches.
$422* *Composition, 1959,* s. Lanskoy 59, 39/80, (03-24-93, Kunsthallen, #221), color lithograph (BP 286, DM 689, FR 2346, Y 49,583, DK 2645).
$190* *Composition, 1959,* s. A. Lanskoy, 16/80, (09-30-92, Kunsthallen, #180), color lithograph (BP 107, DM 269, FR 911, Y 22,801, DK 1035).
BI *Composition-Brun, 1974,* 22/99, s., est. SF 400/600, (10-14-92, Germann, #341), 27⁷⁄₁₆ x 19¹³⁄₁₆ in., (697 x 503 mm.), color lithograph.
$332* *Composition-Brun, 1974,* #22/99, s., (09-04-92, Germann, #441), 27⁷⁄₁₆ x 19¹³⁄₁₆ in., (697 x 503 mm.), color lithograph (BP 166, DM 465, FR 1584, Y 40,867, SF 414).
BI *Composition-Rouge, 1974,* 22/99, s., tear, est. SF 400/600, (10-14-92, Germann, #340), 27⁹⁄₁₆ x 19⅞ in., (700 x 505 mm.), color lithograph.
$369* *Composition-Rouge, 1974,* #22/99, s., tear, (09-04-92, Germann, #440), 27⁹⁄₁₆ x 19⅞ in., (700 x 505 mm.), color lithograph (BP 185, DM 517, FR 1760, Y 45,421, SF 460).
$155* *Ensemble De Trois Lithographies: Three,* from "Journal D'Un Fou" series, s., XXIV/L, (06-28-93, Loudmer, #66), 26⁹⁄₁₆ x 17⁵⁄₁₆ in., (675 x 440 mm.), sh 37⅝ x 25¹³⁄₁₆ in., (675 x 440 mm.), color lithographs on Fabriano wove (BP 104, DM 263, FR 887, Y 16,446).
$116* *Sans Titre,* s., 6/150, (06-28-93, Loudmer, #270), 25⅜ x 19¹³⁄₁₆ in., (645 x 503 mm.), sh 6⅛ x 22¹⁄₁₆ in., (645 x 503 mm.), color lithograph on wove (BP 78, DM 197, FR 664, Y 12,308).
$97* *Sans Titre,* s., 94/197, (06-28-93, Loudmer, #272), 21⅜ x 15¾ in., (543 x 400 mm.), sh 25⁹⁄₁₆ x 19¹¹⁄₁₆ in., (543 x 400 mm.), color lithograph on Arches wove (BP 65, DM 165, FR 555, Y 10,292).
$160* *Untitled,* s., #XXIV/L, full margins, good cond., (05-27-93, Sotheby-Amstrdm, #640, illus.), 26¾ x 17¼ in., (680 x 438 mm.), color lithograph on Fabriano wove (BP 102, DM 257, FR 865, Y 17,153, G 288).
$160* *Untitled,* s., #XXIV/L, full margins, good cond., (05-27-93, Sotheby-Amstrdm, #643), 26¾ x 17¼ in., (680 x 438 mm.), color lithograph on Fabriano wove (BP 102, DM 257, FR 865, Y 17,153, G 288).
$160* *Untitled,* s., #XXIV/L, full margins, good cond., (05-27-93, Sotheby-Amstrdm, #646), 26¾ x 17¼ in., (680 x 438 mm.), color lithograph on Fabriano wove (BP 102, DM 257, FR 865, Y 17,153, G 288).
BI *Untitled,* s., #XXIV/L, full margins, good cond., est. Dfl. 5/700, (05-27-93, Sotheby-Amstrdm, #644), 26¾ x 17¼ in., (680 x 438 mm.), color lithograph on Fabriano wove.
$160* *Untitled,* s., #XXIV/L, full margins, good cond., (05-27-93, Sotheby-Amstrdm, #645), 26¾ x 17¼ in., (680 x 438 mm.), color lithograph on Fabriano wove (BP 102, DM 257, FR 865, Y 17,153, G 288).
BI *Untitled,* s., #XXIV/L, full margins, good cond., est. Dfl. 5/700, (05-27-93, Sotheby-Amstrdm, #642), 26¾ x 17¼ in., (680 x 438 mm.), color lithograph on Fabriano wove.
$284* *Untitled, 1973,* F 51/75, s., lit., (04-21-93, Germann, #592), 25¹⁄₁₆ x 18¾ in., (637 x 477 mm.), color lithograph (BP 184, DM 454, FR 1535, Y 31,440, SF 414).

LANSKOY, Andre, illus. and Pierre LECUIRE
$8625* *Cortege, 1959,* unbound as issued, offsetting, num., s. Lanskoy and Lecuire, (06-14-93, Sotheby-NY, #193), 17¾ x 13¼ in., (45.1 x 33.7 cm.), 24 superb puchoir plates (BP 5645, DM 14,038, FR 47,183, Y 907,608).

LANZ
$171* *PNT: Granada. Alhambra Y Sierra Nevada,* good cond., (02-12-93, Cheval/Robert, #95), 39⅜ x 24⁷⁄₁₆ in., (100 x 62 cm.), poster (BP 120, DM 284, FR 960, Y 20,622).

LAPICQUE, Charles French b. 1898
BI *Balises Et Rochers (B. et B. 423), 1970,* s., 39/50, edit. 125, est. FF600/800, (06-28-93, Loudmer, #273), 25⁹⁄₁₆ x 19½ in., (650 x 495 mm.), sh 34¾ x 24⅝ in., (650 x 495 mm.), color lithograph on wove.
BI *"Composition",* artist's proof, s., tear, crease, est. FF4/600, (04-04-93, Pescheteau, #236), 29¹⁵⁄₁₆ x 20¹⁄₁₆ in., (76 x 51 cm.), color lithograph on wove.
$135* *"Ete Breton - 1969" (B.B. 402),* H.C., #47/50, s., (10-18-92, Pescheteau, #184), 10¼ x 14⁹⁄₁₆ in., (26 x 37 cm.), lithograph in colors on Arches (BP 82, DM 199, FR 677, Y 16,119).
BI *Jean Follain: Appareil De La Terre,* book, s., w/title page, text & just., s. by artist & author, num. 23,pub. Editions Galanis, margins, good cond., orig. slipcase,

est. BP 7/900, (12-03-92, Sotheby-London, #358), 10 woodcuts in colors on Richard de Bas.

$68* *Oiseaux Dans Le Feuillage (B. and B 110), 1959,* s., 94/110, (06-28-93, Loudmer, #77), 20 11/16 x 13¾ in., (525 x 350 mm.), sh 25 15/16 x 19 11/16 in., (525 x 350 mm.), color aquatint on Arches wove (BP 46, DM 116, FR 389, Y 7215).

$105* *Olympische Spiele, 1972,* s. Lapicque, 136/200, (09-30-92, Kunsthallen, #181), color lithograph (BP 59, DM 149, FR 504, Y 12,601, DK 575).

$97* *Paysage,* s., 131/175, (06-28-93, Loudmer, #70), 20 1/16 x 27 3/16 in., (510 x 690 mm.), sh 23⅝ x 35 7/16 in., (510 x 690 mm.), color lithograph on BFK Rives (BP 65, DM 165, FR 555, Y 10,292).

$110* *"Riviere En Bretagne",* EA 22/30, s., (04-04-93, Peschet-eau, #237), 23⅝ x 35 7/16 in., (60 x 90 cm.), color lithograph on wove (BP 72, DM 177, FR 600, Y 12,524).

BI *La Route Mandarine, 1961,* E.A., s., light stains, est. SF 160/180, (10-14-92, Germann, #342), 14⅞ x 21⅛ in., (378 x 536 mm.), color lithograph.

LAPIERRE, Charles b. 1867

BI *Salon Des Cent (Brinckmann 255; Henriot 771; Wember 525), 1895,* rare, lit., est. DM 2,400, (12-05-92, Bassenge, #7603), 23⅝ x 16⅛ in., (60 x 41 cm.), color lithograph.

LAPINSKI, Tadeusz

$50* *"Reflections",* s., (01-15-93, DuMouchelle, #174), 24 x 17 in., (61 x 43.2 cm.), lithograph (BP 33, DM 82, FR 276, Y 6304).

LAPIQUE, Charles 1898-1988

BI *Personnage, 1959,* s., #20/75, est. FF6/800, (05-27-93, Briest, #120), 22 13/16 x 17 11/16 in., (58 x 45 cm.), lithograph.

BI *"Venise", (19)65,* s., d., t., num., est. DM 500, (12-01-92, Karl/Faber, #902), 18⅞ x 14 3/16 in., (48 x 36 cm.), color lithograph on Arches wove.

LAPORTE, George Henry (after)

$239* *Liverpool Grand Canal Steeple Chase, Plates I-IV: Four,* by R.G. and A.W. Reeve, pub. Messrs Fores, foxing, repaired tear to plate IV, (03-03-93, Bonhams-Chelsea, #192), image 14⅜ x 22¾ in., (36.5 x 57.8 cm.), hand-colored aquatint (BP 165, DM 394, FR 1335, Y 27,927).

LARAMET, H.

$521* *Monol En Plein Jour,* p. B. Chapellie jeune, creases, backed on linen, (05-07-93, Christie-S. Ken, #93), 52¾ x 47 in., (134 x 119.4 cm.), color lithograph (BP 330, DM 824, FR 2776, Y 57,366).

LARIONOV, Michel Russian/American 1881-1964

BI *Le Paon, 1970,* artist's proof, w/sig. stamp, est. FF4/600, (06-28-93, Loudmer, #78), 16⅛ x 9 7/16 in., (410 x 240 mm.), sh 20½ x 12 13/16 in., (410 x 240 mm.), color pochoir on wove.

$660* *Peacock,* stamped w/sig., #79-150, (10-09-92, Sotheby-Arcade, #68, illus.), 20 x 12¾ in., (50.8 x 32.4 cm.), color lithograph on paper (BP 392, DM 983, FR 3333, Y 80,488).

LARK PUBLICITE

$486* *Bauer Bosch 8MM,* p. Gaillard, folds, defects, backed on linen, (05-07-93, Christie-S. Ken, #89, illus.), 46¼ x 62½ in., (117.5 x 158.8 cm.), color lithograph (BP 308, DM 768, FR 2589, Y 53,512).

LARMESSIN, Nicolas de 1684-1756

BI *La Courtisanne Amoureuse (Le Blanc 49),* after Boucher, stained, est. DM 750, (12-04-92, Bassenge, #6637), 12 11/16 x 14 9/16 in., (32.3 x 37 cm.), etching w/engraving.

LAROCHE, R.

$90* *Epouse-La. Livret De Pierre Veber. Musique De Henri Hirchman, c. 1925,* Affiches Laroche, good cond., (02-12-93, Cheval/Robert, #159), 46 1/16 x 31⅛ in., (117 x 79 cm.), poster (BP 63, DM 149, FR 505, Y 10,854).

LARRAZ, Julio Cuban/American b. 1944

$2185* *Chambered Nautilus, 1989,* s., t., #51/100, excell. cond., (05-18-93, Sotheby-NY, #259, illus.), 18 x 35⅛ in., (457 x 892 mm.), etching and aquatint p. in colors (BP 1423, DM 3545, FR 11,973, Y 243,508).

$3850* *Magic Eye, 1989,* s., t., #4/35, p. Mohamed Khalil, full margins, excell. cond., (11-23-92, Sotheby-NY, #264, illus.), image 35¼ x 30¾ in., (895 x 780 mm.), etching, aquatint/spitbite p. in colors (BP 2517, DM 6164, FR 20,913, Y 477,608).

LARSON, Sally b. 1954

$2640* *Bamboo Grass, 1990,* mounted together, s., t., d., num. 1/10 in ink, #1/10, (10-13-92, Christie-NY, #555, illus.), sight 39¼ x 28¼ in., (99.7 x 71.8 cm.), photograph, 15 orotone panels (BP 1538, DM 3868, FR 13,141, Y 320,116).

$3575* *Chambord Forest,* s., t., d., num. 5/10 by photog. w/stylus, 1983, p. 1992, #5/10 ed., (10-15-92, Sotheby-NY, #610, illus.), each panel approx. 10 x 8 in., (25.4 x 20.3 cm.), frame 34 x 46 in., (25.4 x 20.3 cm.), photograph, 15 orotone panels mounted & framed together (BP 2188, DM 5322, FR 18,046, Y 428,914).

$3738* *"The Real White House", 1992,* s., t., d., #1/10 by photog. w/stylus, (04-06-93, Sotheby-NY, #497, illus.), each panel approx. 10 x 8 in., frame 35 x 46¼ in., photograph, 15 orotone panels mounted and framed together as single image (BP 2469, DM 6022, FR 20,393, Y 426,323).

LARSSON, Carl Swedish contemporary

$1167* *Kaj (Hjert & Hjert 65), 1909,* s., init., (12-04-92, AB Stockholm, #7088), 5½ x 4 5/16 in., (13.9 x 11 cm.), etching (BP 749, DM 1859, FR 6305, Y 145,693, SK 7920).

$722* *Lisbeth Spielt Theater (Brummer 69 I),* mono., (12-04-92, Bassenge, #6870), 4⅝ x 6⅜ in., (11.7 x 16.2 cm.), etching on copper print paper (BP 463, DM 1150, FR 3901, Y 90,137).

$2340* *Modellen Vid Kaminen, 1908,* inits., (05-25-93, AB Stockholm, #44, illus.), 16⅛ x 12 11/16 in., (40.9 x 32.2 cm.), etching (BP 1517, DM 3811, FR 12,829, Y 255,766, SK 3410).

$1112* *Suzanne Och Gunlog (Hjert & Hjert 104 i/ii), 1915,* s., init., (05-12-93, AB Stockholm, #7031, illus.), 17 7/16 x 12 13/16 in., (44.3 x 32.6 cm.), etching (BP 726, DM 1794, FR 6043, Y 124,149, SK 8250).

$486* *Ute Blaser Sommarvind (H & H 114),* (12-04-92, AB Stockholm, #7089), 11 x 39 3/16 in., (28 x 99.5 cm.), lithograph in colors (BP 312, DM 774, FR 2626, Y 60,674, SK 3300).

BI *Woman With A Flower,* margins, inits., sig. rubbed, foxing, damp stains, est. BP 4/600, (10-27-92, Phillips-London, #206), plate 11¾ x 9 in., (298 x 229 mm.), etching w/drypoint on wove.

LARTIGUE, Dany

BI *Enfant Et Animaux,* s., #54/75, margins, light-staining, laid down, est. BP 2/250, (06-30-93, Sotheby-London, #480), 17¾ x 24¾ in., (451 x 629 mm.), color lithograph on wove.

LARTIGUE, Jacques Henri 1894-1988

BI *At The Auteil Races: Two,* printed together, 1979, s. in ink, (1911), est. $2/3,000, (10-13-92, Christie-NY, #70, illus.), each 2¼ x 2½ in., (5.7 x 6.4 cm.), photograph, gelatin silver contact prints.

$1090* *"Biarritz",* 1927, p.l., s. J.H. Lartigue, sight 197 x 370mm, (05-07-93, Sotheby-London, #220, illus.), photograph, silver print (BP 690, DM 1723, FR 5807, Y 120,018).

$1100* *High Diver,* s. by photog. in ink, mono. blindstamp, early 1900's, p. later, (10-15-92, Sotheby-NY, #121, illus.), 14⅛ x 6¾ in., (35.9 x 17.1 cm.), photograph, gelatin silver print (BP 673, DM 1637, FR 5553, Y 131,974).

$920* *"J.H. Lartigue": Ten,* 1903-16, p. 1977, photog.'s blindstamp, #793/5000 US, each in presentation folder, pub. Time-Life, orig. portfolio case, (05-23-93, Butterfield, #3499, illus.), each approx. 6½ x 7½ in., photograph (BP 599, DM 1504, FR 5063, Y 101,691).

$460* *"Kite, Biarritz",* 1905, p.l., s., illus., est. $800/1,200, (05-23-93, Butterfield, #3500, illus.), 14 x 9½ in., photograph, gelatin silver print (BP 300, DM 752, FR 2532, Y 50,846).

$825* *Lady With Lorgnette,* c. 1900, oversized, 1975, s. in neg., lit., sold after sale, (10-13-92, Christie-NY, #71, illus.), 80 x 45 in., (203.2 x 114.3 cm.), photograph, gelatin silver print (BP 480, DM 1209, FR 4107, Y 100,036).

$835* *The Lipstick,* 1920s, p.l., s. J.H. Lartigue, blindstamped mono. J.H.L., 397 x 304mm, (05-07-93, Sotheby-London, #221, illus.), photograph, silver print (BP 529, DM 1320, FR 4449, Y 91,940).

$1725* *Little Equestrienne,* s. by photog., i. in unident. hand, c. 1912, p.l., (04-06-93, Sotheby-NY, #233, illus.), 10¼ x 14¼ in., photograph (BP 1139, DM 2779, FR 9411, Y 196,738).

$986* *Ohne Titel (Flugexperiment),* 20's, 70's, s., mono., stamp, (11-12-92, Lempertz, #139, illus.), 6⅛ x 13⁷⁄₁₆ in., (15.6 x 34.1 cm.), sheet 11¹⁵⁄₁₆ x 15⅞ in., (15.6 x 34.1 cm.), photograph, gelatin silver print (BP 630, DM 1550, FR 5281, Y 121,984).

$2300* *Playing Tennis,* s. by photog., mono., blindstamp, early 1900s, p.l., (04-06-93, Sotheby-NY, #232, illus.), 9¾ x 12⅞ in., photograph (BP 1519, DM 3705, FR 12,548, Y 262,318).

$2750* *"Renee",* 1930/later, s., photog. blindstamp, Dixon Collection, (11-16-92, Butterfield, #6058, illus.), 13⅜ x 10¾ in., (340.3 x 273.5 mm.), photograph, gelatin silver print (BP 1811, DM 4385, FR 14,769, Y 341,997).

$2200* *Woman Playing Tennis,* s. by photog. in ink, (c) stamp, early 1900s, p.l., (10-15-92, Sotheby-NY, #120, illus.), 10⅞ x 14 in., (27.6 x 35.6 cm.), photograph, gelatin silver print (BP 1346, DM 3275, FR 11,106, Y 263,947).

BI *Young Woman Gazing At Her Reflection,* 1920s, p.l., s. J.H. Lartigue, blindstamped mono. J.H.L., 403 x 304mm, (05-07-93, Sotheby-London, #222, illus.), photograph, silver print.

$2200* *"Zissou",* 1906/later, ink s., photog. blindstamp, Dixon Collection, (11-16-92, Butterfield, #6057, illus.), 12½ x 9¾ in., (318.1 x 248.1 mm.), photograph, gelatin silver print (BP 1449, DM 3508, FR 11,815, Y 273,598).

$3450* *"Zissou",* s. by photog., blindstamp, 1911, p.l., (04-06-93, Sotheby-NY, #231, illus.), 12⅛ x 9½ in., photograph (BP 2279, DM 5558, FR 18,822, Y 393,476).

LARTQUE, Jacques Henri   1894-1986
$1150* *M. Folletete And Tupy,* 1912, p.l., ink s., photog.'s inits. embossed, (04-08-93, Christie-NY, #47, illus.), 9½ x 11 in., (24.1 x 27.9 cm.), photograph, gelatin silver print (BP 754, DM 1847, FR 6253, Y 130,504).

$1035* *Paris Automobile Elegance Competition, The Rowe Twins,* c. 1911, p. 1979, ink s., (04-08-93, Christie-NY, #48, illus.), 2½ x 1⅝ in., (6.4 x 4.1 cm.), photograph, gelatin silver contact print (BP 679, DM 1663, FR 5628, Y 117,453).

BI *Promenade At Auteuil,* 1911, p. 1979, ink s., est. $2/3,000, (04-08-93, Christie-NY, #46, illus.), 3¼ x 4½ in., (8.3 x 11.4 cm.), photograph, gelatin silver contact print.

$1093* *Untitled,* early 1900s, p.l., ink s., (04-08-93, Christie-NY, #45, illus.), 10¼ x 11¼ in., (26 x 28.6 cm.), photograph, gelatin silver print (BP 717, DM 1756, FR 5943, Y 124,035).

LASANSKY, Mauricio   Argen./American b. 1914
$550* *Fall,* s., d. 47, t., (05-16-93, Hindman, #565), 23¾ x 8⅝ in., (60.3 x 21.9 cm.), color engraving, etching and aquatint (BP 358, DM 885, FR 2973, Y 60,969).

$660* *Spring,* s., d. 1947, t., annot. (Artists P.), (05-16-93, Hindman, #566), 23¾ x 8¾ in., (60.3 x 22.2 cm.), color enghraving, etching, soft ground and aquatint (BP 429, DM 1062, FR 3568, Y 73,163).

LASANSKY, Mauricio   Argentinian/Amer. b. 1914
$1000* *"Bodas De Sangre",* s., t., mat burn, tape, (05-15-93, Cleveland, #206), 20½ x 28¾ in., (52.1 x 73 cm.), etching and aquatint (BP 650, DM 1608, FR 5405, Y 110,852).

LASINIO, Carlo   1759-1838
$439* *"Il Trionfo Della Morte" (Nagler 21),* c. 1812, after A. Organga, (06-08-93, Karl/Faber, #99), engraving (BP 289, DM 712, FR 2399, Y 46,628).

LASKE, Oskar
$51* *Marche Aux Poissons, Bruges,* plate s., t., (06-08-93, Ritchie, #41, illus.), 4⅝ x 7 in., (11.7 x 17.8 cm.), etching (BP 34, DM 83, FR 279, Y 5417, C$ 66).

BI *Paradies,* laid down, sandwiched between front and back of the mat, good cond.,est. $3/500, (06-11-93, Doyle, #55), 15¼ x 17 in., (387 x 432 mm.), color lithograph.

LASKE, Oskar   1874-1951
$1302* *"Fischpredigt",* s. in stone O. Laske, (11-25-92, Dorotheum, #492, illus.), color lithograph (BP 851, DM 2070, FR 7011, Y 161,179, SC 14,560).

LASKER, Jonathan   American b. 1948
BI *Untitled, 1988-89,* s., d. 1989, #12/75, from portfolio Brooklyn Academy of Music II 1988-89 Artist Print Portfolio, pub. Parasol Press, Ltd., good cond., handling crease, est. $1/1,200, (05-15-93, Sotheby-NY, #1055, illus.), 22½ x 29¾ in., (57.2 x 75.6 cm.), etching and aquatint in colors.

LASSALLE, Emile   French 1813-1871
$1100* *Napoleon, 1814, c. 1852,* s. in stone, full margins, foxing, toning, (08-29-92, Goldberg, #366, illus.), image 24½ x 18½ in., (62.2 x 47 cm.), lithograph (BP 555, DM 1548, FR 5276, Y 135,635).

LASSNIG, Maria   b. 1919
$295* *Der Schrei, 1981,* s., num., (12-05-92, Bassenge, #7381), 18½ x 11⁷⁄₁₆ in., (47 x 29 cm.), color lithograph (BP 185, DM 460, FR 1567, Y 36,551).

LASTER, Paul and Edward STEICHEN
BI *Here Sir Fire Eat, 1990,* appropriated from an image by Edward Steichen, unique collage by artist, est. $2/3,000, (10-13-92, Christie-NY, #556, illus.), 4½ x 6⅛ in., (11.4 x 15.6 cm.), photograph, halftone print & colored transparent tape.

LASTER, Paul and MAN RAY
BI *Happy New Year, 1990,* appropriated from image by Man Ray, unique collage by artist, est. $2/3,000, (10-13-92, Christie-NY, #557, illus.), 5¼ x 4⅛ in., (13.3 x 10.5 cm.), photograph, halftone print w/colored transparent tape.

LATASTE, R.
$220* *Foire De Bordeaux, 1928,* Delteil Fils Freres, B cond., fold marks, (08-06-92, Swann, #167, illus.), 56 x 39¼ in., (142.2 x 99.7 cm.), (BP 115, DM 325, FR 1098, Y 28,061).

LATASTER, Ger   Dutch b. 1920
$228* *Untitled,* s., #76/200, good cond.?, (12-09-92, Sotheby-Amstrdm, #602), sheet 12 x 16¾ in., (305 x 426 mm.), color lithograph on wove (BP 146, DM 358, FR 1221, Y 28,270, G 403).

LATEGAN, Barry   b. 1935
BI *"Back View", c. 1985,* s., d., photog.'s credit, t., s., d., annot., ink stamped photog.'s credit, labels, 493 x 403mm, est. BP 2/300, (05-07-93, Sotheby-London, #197), photograph, silver print.

LATHAM, John   British b. 1921
$2200* *A General History Of Birds (Nissen Birds 532): 191,* 11 vols. in 10. 4to, foxing, offsetting; Vol. 1 i., (11-12-92, Swann, #138), hand-colored engraving (BP 1445, DM 3486, FR 11,758, Y 272,784).

LATHROP, Dorothy
$83* *"Goldfish",* s., very good cond., (07-19-92, Bakker, #283, illus.), image 6⅛ x 7⅛ in., (15.6 x 18.1 cm.), wood engraving (BP 43, DM 121, FR 409, Y 10,318).

$88* *"Kou Hsiung",* very good/good cond., (07-19-92, Bakker, #276, illus.), image 6⅛ x 7⅛ in., (15.6 x 18.1 cm.), wood engraving (BP 45, DM 128, FR 434, Y 10,940).

LAUBY
$77* *Ensemble De Quatre: Four,* three s. artist's proof; one s., 50/80, (06-28-93, Loudmer, #79), between 18⅛ x 16¹⁵⁄₁₆ in., (460 x 430 mm.), and 20¹⁄₁₆ x 26³⁄₁₆ in., (460 x 430 mm.), color lithographs on wove (BP 52, DM 131, FR 441, Y 8170).

LAUDAU, Jacob

$55* *"Ritual Happening",* (09-18-92, DuMouchelle, #2506), 20½ x 24¾ in., (52.1 x 62.9 cm.), lithograph (BP 32, DM 82, FR 282, Y 6853).

LAUGHLIN, Clarence John 1905-1985

$1035* *"Figment Of Desire" (Visionary Photography, pl. 32),* mounted on heavy black board, s., t., d. by photog., init., num. 6, (c) stamp, 1941, p. 1979, (04-06-93, Sotheby-NY, #366, illus.), 13¾ x 10⅝ in., photograph (BP 684, DM 1667, FR 5646, Y 118,043).

BI *Leg-A-Head And His Operating Device, 1961,* s., notations, est. $1,5/1,800, (04-08-93, Christie-NY, #495, illus.), 13⅛ x 10¼ in., (33.3 x 26 cm.), photograph, gelatin silver print.

$1150* *The Masquerade Of Fear And Hate, 1961,* t., d., credit stamp, (04-08-93, Christie-NY, #494, illus.), 13½ x 10¾ in., (34.3 x 27.3 cm.), photograph, gelatin silver print (BP 754, DM 1847, FR 6253, Y 130,504).

$374* *"The Paul Klee Cantaloupe", 1936,* pencil s., t., (c) stamp, (05-22-93, Neal, #595), 12 x 9 in., photograph, b/w (BP 244, DM 612, FR 2058, Y 41,340).

$1980* *We Cannot Retrieve Our Dead Hearts, 1941 (Visionary Photographer, fig. 15, there titled "We Reached For Our Dead Hearts"),* t., d., notations by photog. in ink, (c) stamp, (10-15-92, Sotheby-NY, #480, illus.), 13¾ x 10½ in., (34.9 x 26.7 cm.), photograph, gelatin silver print (BP 1212, DM 2947, FR 9995, Y 237,552).

LAUNAY, Nicolas de 1739-1792

BI *Le Billet Doux (Bocher 10; P. and B., II, p. 547, no. 23; L. and D. 95; Inventaire 18e Seicel, XII, pp. 518-19, no. 189), 1778,* after Nicolas Lavreince, 5th (final) state, pub. de Launay, margins,crease, prov., est. BP 3/500, (12-01-92, Christie-London, #242), plate 18⅜ x 13⁹⁄₁₆ in., (467 x 345 mm.), etching w/engraving.

$6992* *Les Hazards Heureux De L'Escarpolette (P. and B., II, p. 546, no. 12; L. and D. 85; Inventaire 18e Siecle, XII, ppo. 528-9, no. 223), 1782,* after Jean-Honore Fragonard, L. and D.'s 3rd state of 7, pub. de Launay, brown spot, creases, soiling, tape, (12-01-92, Christie-London, #243, illus.), sheet 23⅜ x 17⅜ in., (594 x 442 mm.), ethcing w/engraving (BP 4620, DM 11,144, FR 37,979, Y 870,518).

LAURENCIN, Marie French 1883-1956

$2483* *Alice Et Le Fiasco (Marchesseau 150 II), 1930,* s., num., (06-05-93, Bassenge, #6252, illus.), 14⁹⁄₁₆ x 11 in., (37 x 28 cm.), color lithograph on Van Gelder Zonen (BP 1635, DM 4026, FR 13,568, Y 266,359).

$1980* *Alice In Wonderland: Six,* Black Sun Press., Carroll, Lewis, 4to, 1930, 1 of 790 copies, (06-11-93, Doyle, #320), color lithograph (BP 1301, DM 3218, FR 10,849, Y 210,080).

BI *Autoportrait (M. 33), 1920,* inits., good cond., small patches at edges of sheet, right corner creases, prov., Late Gerhard Brauer Coll., est. Dfl. 2,2/2,800, (05-27-93, Sotheby-Amstrdm, #755, illus.), sheet 11⅞ x 9¹⁵⁄₁₆ in., lithograph in sanguine on wove.

BI *Les Aux Danse,* s., est. $1,5/2,500, (09-24-92, Mystic, #29), 13¼ x 17 in., (33.7 x 43.2 cm.), colored lithograph.

$4025* *Belle (M. 289), 1956,* s., #153/200, large (full?) margins, good cond., faded, mat/light-stain, discoloration, (05-13-93, Sotheby-NY, #585, illus.), 12⅞ x 10⅛ in., (327 x 258 mm.), sh 19⅛ x 14 in., (327 x 258 mm.), lithograph in colors (BP 2642, DM 6499, FR 21,923, Y 449,369).

$1278* *La Chanson De Bilitis (D. Marchesseau, 1), 1904,* #9/30, s., creases, pinholes, large margins, (06-16-93, Ader Tajan, #112), 9⁷⁄₁₆ x 5⅞ in., (23.9 x 14.9 cm.), etching and aquatint (BP 852, DM 2122, FR 7120, Y 136,305).

$2750* *Christine or L'Amazon (M. 153), 1930,* plate 5 of Pressentiments, s., #39/115, pub. Editions des Quatre Chemins, margins, good cond., mat stain, creases, tape stains, skinned spots, (11-05-92, Sotheby-NY, #221, illus.), 11⅝ x 15½ in., (294 x 394 mm.), sheet 12⅞ x 16⅛ in., (294 x 394 mm.), lithograph p. in colors (BP 1789, DM 4349, FR 14,714, Y 337,382).

$1320* *Columbine (M. 136),* s., glued to mat, John Walton Livermore Estate, (12-04-92, Doyle, #119), 14¾ x 10⅞ in., (375 x 276 mm.), lithograph (BP 847, DM 2102, FR 7131, Y 164,794).

$2420* *Le Concert (M 100),* s., i. H.C.X., light stained, laid down on cardboard, discoloration,soiling, good cond., (12-04-92, Doyle, #117), 9⅛ x 7⅛ in., (232 x 181 mm.), lithograph w/green highlights (BP 1552, DM 3854, FR 13,074, Y 302,122).

$1998* *La Creole (D.M. 72), 1924,* #26/100, s., untrimmed margins, (06-11-93, Picard, #95), 15⅜ x 12³⁄₁₆ in., (390 x 310 mm.), lithograph on Arches wove (BP 1313, DM 3247, FR 10,948, Y 211,989).

$2588* *Le Cygne (M. 102), 1926,* plate 3 of La Vie de chateau, s., #110/110, pub. Editions Quatre-Chemins, margins, good cond., tape stain, creases, backed w/wove, (05-13-93, Sotheby-NY, #582, illus.), 9¼ x 7¼ in., (235 x 183 mm.), sh 16¼ x 12⅜ in., (235 x 183 mm.), lithograph in colors on Chine (BP 1699, DM 4179, FR 14,096, Y 288,936).

$1100* *Le Cyne (M. 102),* s., i., abraded area in image, light stained, laid down on cardboard, discoloration, soiling, good cond., (12-04-92, Doyle, #118), 9¼ x 7⅛ in., (235 x 181 mm.), lithograph w/blue and green highlights (BP 706, DM 1752, FR 5943, Y 137,328).

$248* *Dancer With Black Ribbon,* mat s., very good cond.?, (07-19-92, Bakker, #38), plate 5 x 3 in., (12.7 x 7.6 cm.), etching (BP 127, DM 361, FR 1222, Y 30,830).

$1079* *La Danseuse Or Barbett (M. 125), 1926,* 3rd and final state, s., #64/80, pub. Jacquart, full margins, light stained, laid down, (10-27-92, Phillips-London, #207), plate 6¾ x 4⅝ in., (171 x 117 mm.), etching w/hand-coloring on wove (BP 682, DM 1654, FR 5611, Y 131,988).

$2598* *Les Deux Espagnoles (D. Marchesseau 70), 1924,* s., first state of two, good margins, (06-11-93, Picard, #94), 10⅝ x 7⅞ in., (270 x 200 mm.), etching on thick wove (BP 1707, DM 4222, FR 14,236, Y 275,650).

$1760* *Dinah (M. 166), 1931,* s., #87/125, blindstamp pub. Jacquart, margins, good cond., paper/glue remains, skinned area, water/light/basic staining, creases, hinge remains, (10-28-92, Butterfield, #2660, illus.), 15½ x 11½ in., (394 x 292 mm.), color lithograph on Japan (BP 1121, DM 2718, FR 9229, Y 215,951).

$1716* *Dinah (Marchesseau 166), 1931,* s., pub. Jacquart, margins, light-stained, colors, faded, laid down, (06-30-93, Sotheby-London, #481, illus.), 15⅛ x 10⅞ in., (384 x 276 mm.), color lithograph on wove (BP 1150, DM 2927, FR 9873, Y 183,864).

BI *Les Enfants De Chateau (M. 157), 1930,* s. twice, #55/125, blindstamp publisher, Jacquart, margins, red slightly faded, good cond., mat/light-staining, glue/paper remains, tape, surface soiling, notations, est. $3/4,00, (05-19-93, Butterfield, #1924), sh. 15 x 20⅛ in., (381 x 511 mm.), lithograph in colors on cream Japan.

BI *Les Enfants Du Chateau (M. 157),* s., #59/125, pub. blindstamp, margins, laid down, light stained, 2 areas lacking at top, est. BP 900/1,200, (10-27-92, Phillips-London, #208), sheet 14 x 18⅞ in., (356 x 479 mm.), color lithograph on simili japan.

BI *Les Enfants Du Chateau (M. 157), 1930,* s. twice, #46/125, pub. Nouvel Essor, margins, discoloration, est. $3/4,000, (11-05-92, Sotheby-NY, #222, illus.), 11 x 15⅜ in., (280 x 390 mm.), lithograph p. in colors on cream simili Japan.

$1083* *Femme Au Chien,* s. in stone, some reddish stains, (06-28-93, Loudmer, #280), 13⅜ x 9⅝ in., (340 x 245 mm.), color lithograph glued on cardboard of frame (BP 725, DM 1840, FR 6199, Y 114,907).

BI *Femme Au Guitare,* plate s., est. DM 2,500-, (11-21-92, Lempertz, #238), 7⅞ x 6¾ in., (20 x 17.1 cm.), etching on wove.

$7150* *Fillette A La Rose (M. 283), 1955,* faint s., #39/150, pub. Nouvel Essor, full margins, good cond., mat/light stain, tape stain, creases, glue stains, skinning, (11-05-92, Sotheby-NY, #225, illus.), 12¾ x 10⅜ in., (323 x 265 mm.), lithograph p. in colors (BP 4650, DM 11,308, FR 38,256, Y 877,193).

BI *Fillette A La Rose (M. 283), 1955,* s., num. 3/150, pub. Nouvel Essoir, margins trimmed, good cond., matstaining, light-staining, tape remains, est. $3,5/4,500, (02-24-93,

Butterfield, #2749), image 12¾ x 9⅝ in., (324 x 244 mm.), sheet 15½ x 11¹¹⁄₁₆ in., (324 x 244 mm.), lithograph in colors on cream wove.

$358* *Girl With Flowers*, s., #9/10, (04-26-93, Selkirk, #153), sight 10½ x 8 in., (26.7 x 20.3 cm.), lithograph (BP 226, DM 561, FR 1895, Y 39,506).

BI *La Gloire Des Bronte (M. 146), 1930*, 1st state prior to t., s., num. 6/30, large margins, light-stained, rubbed areas, est. BP 6/800, (11-30-92, Phillips-London, #447), sheet 15 x 11 in., (381 x 279 mm.), lithograph on chine japonais.

$1200* *Grande Tete De Femme (M. 19), 1910*, s., full margins, soft creases, good cond., (11-30-92, Phillips-London, #446, illus.), sheet 24⅛ x 16⅝ in., (613 x 422 mm.), woodcut on japan (BP 792, DM 1912, FR 6490, Y 149,347).

$908* *Head Of A Woman*, s., #4/10, trimmed, (11-30-92, Selkirk, #714), image 8¼ x 5½ in., (21 x 14 cm.), sepia lithograph (BP 599, DM 1447, FR 4911, Y 113,006).

BI *Head Of Woman*, s., est. $3/400, (09-20-92, Hindman, #768), 14½ x 10½ in., (36.8 x 26.7 cm.), pochoir.

$851* *Huit Filles Dans Un Pre (Marchesseau 96), 1926*, s., num., (06-05-93, Bassenge, #6249), 4¹⁵⁄₁₆ x 3⅛ in., (12.5 x 8 cm.), etching on wove (BP 560, DM 1380, FR 4650, Y 91,289).

BI *Jeune Fille A La Guitare (M. 238), 1946*, s., i. H.C., included in portfolio Alternance, full margins, good cond., soiling, est. $2/2,500, (11-05-92, Sotheby-NY, #224), 7⅞ x 6⅝ in., (200 x 168 mm.), etching w/hand coloring.

$590* *Jeune Fille A La Guitare (Marchesseau 238 II), 1946*, illus. for Alterance by Thierry Maulnier, (12-05-92, Bassenge, #7386), 7¹³⁄₁₆ x 6⅝ in., (19.8 x 16.8 cm.), etching and watercolor on copper print paper (BP 369, DM 920, FR 3135, Y 73,101).

$1898* *Jeune Fille Au Balcon (D.M. 84), 1925*, second state of three, s., large margins, (06-11-93, Picard, #97), 8¹⁄₁₆ x 5½ in., (204 x 139 mm.), etching on Arches wove (BP 1247, DM 3085, FR 10,400, Y 201,379).

$1199* *Jeune Fille Au Balcon (D.M. 84), 1925*, definitive state, illus. "Le Nouveau Langage Des Fleurs", large margins, (06-11-93, Picard, #98), 8¹⁄₁₆ x 5½ in., (204 x 139 mm.), etching in color on wove (BP 788, DM 1949, FR 6570, Y 127,215).

$511* *Jeune Fille Au Collier (D.M. 237)*, definitive state, #43/120, s., drystamp, untrimmed good margins, (06-16-93, Ader Tajan, #113), 9½ x 6⅜ in., (24.2 x 16.2 cm.), etching (BP 341, DM 848, FR 2847, Y 54,501).

$468* *"Jeune Fille"* and *"Girl With Mandolin": Two*, latter s. in plate, late impressions, (10-30-92, Sloan, #1605), larger 8 x 7 in., (20.3 x 17.8 cm.), color etching (BP 300, DM 720, FR 2443, Y 57,971).

$2200* *Jeune Filles Au Balcon*, s., num. 72/100, (09-20-92, Hindman, #762, illus.), 9½ x 7 in., (24.1 x 17.8 cm.), color etching and roulette (BP 1288, DM 3265, FR 11,168, Y 271,907).

BI *Jeunes Filles Au Balcon (M. 133), 1928*, s., #35/100, blindstamp pub. Jacquart, margins, good cond., mat staining, staining, glue remains, notations, surface soiling, est. $4/6,000, (10-28-92, Butterfield, #2659), 9½ x 7⅛ in., (241 x 181 mm.), color etching on wove.

$345* *L'Adolescente (M. 292), 1956*, 3rd final state, stamp inits., large margins, good cond., mat staining, handling creases, foxing, hinge remains, (05-19-93, Butterfield, #2068), 5¹³⁄₁₆ x 3⅞ in., (148 x 98 mm.), etching on wove (BP 224, DM 561, FR 1889, Y 38,193).

$3575* *L'Arlequine (Marchesseau 129), 1927*, second state of three, s., #1/2, i., full margins, good cond., lightstain, creases, scotch tape hinge, (11-05-92, Sotheby-NY, #219, illus.), 10¼ x 7⅛ in., (260 x 180 mm.), drypoint p. in brownish black w/hand coloring on BFK Rives wove (BP 2325, DM 5654, FR 19,128, Y 438,596).

$3080* *L'Endormie (M. 170), 1931*, s., #12/150, pub. blindstamp, H. Petiet, large margins, good cond., rubbed spots, creases, skinned area, (11-05-92, Sotheby-NY, #223), 9½ x 11¾ in., (240 x 297 mm.), sheet 15¾ x 19⅝ in., (240 x 297 mm.), etching in colors on simili Japan (BP 2003, DM 4871, FR 16,479, Y 377,868).

$770* *"L'Eternel Feminin"*, stone s., init. ML, (02-12-93, DuMouchelle, #2036, illus.), 8½ x 5¾ in., (21.6 x 14.6 cm.), lithograph w/colored crayon (BP 542, DM 1277, FR 4321, Y 92,861).

BI *L'Eventail Rose*, #24/100, s., est. DM 3,700-, (11-21-92, Lempertz, #239), 11¹³⁄₁₆ x 9⅝ in., (30 x 24.5 cm.), color etching on wove.

$3163* *L'Eventail Rose (M. 126), 1927*, s., #73/100, pub. Galerie Marcel Guiot, margins, discoloration, laiddown, (05-13-93, Sotheby-NY, #583), 11⅞ x 9⅞ in., (302 x 252 mm.), sh 17¼ x 13¾ in., (302 x 252 mm.), etching in colors on wove (BP 2077, DM 5107, FR 17,228, Y 353,132).

$1906* *Marie Laurencin Et Ses Deux Chiens (Marchesseau 167), 1931*, 4/15, s., signs of wear, (10-14-92, Germann, #347, illus.), 12¹³⁄₁₆ x 9¹³⁄₁₆ in., (325 x 249 mm.), etching (BP 1119, DM 2789, FR 9459, Y 230,974, SF 2484).

$750* *Miquette (M. 179), 1932*, inits. M.L., full margins, mount-stained, defects, (11-30-92, Phillips-London, #448, illus.), sheet 10¾ x 8⅝ in., (273 x 219 mm.), lithograph w/extensive hand-coloring on laid (BP 495, DM 1195, FR 4056, Y 93,342).

$1955* *La Mort D'Aimee (M. 151), 1930*, 2nd final state, s., #58/115, full margins, light-staining, laid down on board, Paul MacAlister Estate, (05-11-93, Christie-NY, #205, illus.), borderline 11¼ x 11⅝ in., (286 x 295 mm.), color lithograph on wove (BP 1248, DM 3080, FR 10,377, Y 215,048).

BI *La Mort D'Aimee (Marchesseau 151 I), 1930*, s., num., est. DM 6,000, (12-05-92, Bassenge, #7382, illus.), 11 x 12³⁄₁₆ in., (28 x 31 cm.), lithograph reworked in colored pencils on China.

$129* *Mother And Child*, plate s., paper blindstamped, (06-08-93, Ritchie, #44, illus.), image 12⅞ x 9⅜ in., (32.7 x 23.8 cm.), color aquatint w/hand-coloring (BP 85, DM 209, FR 705, Y 13,702, C$ 165).

$2530* *La Muse Couronnee (M. 282), 1954*, watermark, s., #67/220, full margins, staining, surface soiling, creasing, good cond., (05-11-93, Christie-NY, #206, illus.), borderline 11½ x 10 in., (292 x 254 mm.), color lithograph on wove (BP 1615, DM 3986, FR 13,429, Y 278,297).

$3086* *La Muse Couronnee (Marchesseau 282), 1954*, s., #55/220, pub. Guilde de la Gravure Internationale, large margins, good cond., laid down, (10-14-92, Sotheby-Japan, #45, illus.), 11⅝ x 9⅞ in., (295 x 251 mm.), lithograph in colors on white wove (BP 1811, DM 4516, FR 15,315, Y 373,970).

$1194* *La Petite Crinoline (Marchesseau 73), 1924*, second (final) state, s., #60/65, full margins, good cond., (12-03-92, Sotheby-London, #359), 5⅛ x 4 in., (130 x 102 mm.), etching w/roulette on Arches wove (BP 770, DM 1878, FR 6409, Y 148,563).

$1035* *La Petite Crinoline (Marchesseau 73), 1924*, s., #47/75, margins, good cond., mat stain, discolored, (05-13-93, Sotheby-NY, #580), 5⅛ x 4 in., (129 x 101 mm.), sh 8⅛ x 10⅝ in., (129 x 101 mm.), etching and aquatint (BP 679, DM 1671, FR 5637, Y 115,552).

$880* *"La Petite Crinoline" (M731)*, s., #47/65, (02-11-93, Boos, #420), image 5¹⁄₁₆ x 3¹⁵⁄₁₆ in., (129 x 100 mm.), paper 8¹⁄₁₆ x 6¹¹⁄₁₆ in., (129 x 100 mm.), etching, aquatint, and roulette (BP 621, DM 1458, FR 4933, Y 106,088).

$1925* *Petite Fille A La Rose (M. 140), 1926*, s., #02/110, plate 5 of La Vie de chateau, pub. Editions des Quatre Chemins, margins, good cond., fox marks, laid down, (11-05-92, Sotheby-NY, #220), 9½ x 7⅜ in., (241 x 187 mm.), sheet 12¾ x 10 in., (241 x 187 mm.), lithograph p. in colors (BP 1252, DM 3044, FR 10,300, Y 236,167).

$1610* *La Petite Loge Ou La Theatre (M. 79), 1925*, s., #63/65, full margins, good cond., foxing, mat stain, taped, (05-13-93, Sotheby-NY, #581, illus.), 6¾ x 4⅜ in., (170 x 111 mm.), etching on laid (BP 1057, DM 2600, FR 8769, Y 179,748).

$1760* *Portrait De L'Artiste (M. 130)*, s., num. 65/100, full margins, discoloration, tape, smudges, stains, image in good cond., (11-12-92, Freemn/Fine Art, #118, illus.), image 14¾ x 11⅛ in., (37.5 x 28.3 cm.), lithograph printed on heavy cream paper (BP 1156, DM 2789, FR 9407, Y 218,227).

BI *Portrait De L'Artiste (Marchesseau 130), 1927,* s., #17/100, wide margins, stain, glue showing through, very good cond., est. $4/6,000, (05-11-93, Christie-NY, #203, illus.), borderline 14½ x 11 in., (368 x 279 mm.), lithograph on Japan.

$2046* *La Premiere Voiture Renault 1898 (M. 180), 1936,* s., #33/100, pub. La Societe Renault, margins, good cond., rubbing, (12-03-92, Sotheby-London, #360, illus.), 19 x 14¾ in., (483 x 375 mm.), lithograph extensively hand-colored in blue, yellow and pink on Japan (BP 1320, DM 3217, FR 10,982, Y 254,573).

$3450* *La Promenade A Cheval (M. 135), 1928,* 4th final state, s., #16/100, blindstamp, full margins, light-staining, very good cond., prop. Montclair Art Museum, (05-11-93, Christie-NY, #204), plate 9⅜ x 7 in., (238 x 178 mm.), color etching on wove (BP 2202, DM 5435, FR 18,312, Y 379,496).

$1725* *La Ronde (Marchesseau 101), 1926,* plate 2 of La Vie de chateau, s., i., pub. Editions des Quatres-Chemins, full margins, good cond., margins folded, scotch-taped, (02-11-93, Sotheby-NY, #157), 7³⁄₁₆ x 9³⁄₁₆ in., (183 x 234 mm.), color lithograph on China (BP 1217, DM 2857, FR 9669, Y 207,957).

BI *Suzanne (Marchesseau 131), 1927,* s., #113/150, est. FF5/6,000, (05-27-93, Briest, #121, illus.), 14¹⁵⁄₁₆ x 13⅜ in., (38 x 34 cm.), black lithograph embellished w/mine de plomb and colored crayon.

$385* *Tete De Femme,* s., num. VIII/X, (11-01-92, Hanzel, #204), 10½ x 7 in., (26.7 x 17.8 cm.), lithograph (BP 252, DM 607, FR 2047, Y 47,601).

$1257* *Tete De Femme Au Noeud Noir (Marchesseau 140 I et II), 1928,* s., annot. first state and second state, small cracks, loss, small stain, (06-28-93, Loudmer, #276), 7¹³⁄₁₆ x 5¹³⁄₁₆ in., (198 x 148 mm.), sh 10¼ x 8¼ in., (198 x 148 mm.), black etchings on wove (BP 842, DM 2136, FR 7195, Y 133,369).

$1063* *Trois Femmes A La Guitare,* artist's proof, s. in stone, watercolor embellishments by artist, creases, hole, (06-28-93, Loudmer, #278), 9⅝ x 13⅜ in., (245 x 340 mm.), sh 13⅜ x 18⅞ in., (245 x 340 mm.), color lithograph on China (BP 712, DM 1806, FR 6085, Y 112,785).

BI *Les Trois Femmes Con Un Chien,* s., est. $2/4,000, (09-24-92, Mystic, #28), 21⅜ x 17¾ in., (54.3 x 45.1 cm.), colored aquatint.

BI *Trois Jeunes Filles (M. 220), 1944,* s., annot. 3e etat, full margins, good cond., mat/basic staining, surface soiling, foxing, est. $2/3,000, (10-28-92, Butterfield, #2661), 6¼ x 4½ in., (159 x 114 mm.), hand-colored etching on wove.

$330* *Les Trois Soeurs,* s., #47/115, (12-13-92, Hindman, #274), 6½ x 7⅛ in., color lithograph (BP 211, DM 519, FR 1768, Y 40,826).

$2059* *Les Trois Soeurs (M. 142), 1930,* 3rd final state, s., full margins, crease, mount/light-staining, foxing, handling marks, (06-30-93, Sotheby-London, #482, illus.), 6¼ x 7¼ in., (159 x 184 mm.), color lithograph on Van Gelder Zonen paper (BP 1380, DM 3512, FR 11,847, Y 220,615).

$990* *La Vie De Chateau: Le Cygne (M. 102), 1926,* s., num. 107/110, margins, laid down, good cond., inconspicuous restoration, paper loss, thinned spots, stain, foxing, surface soiling, (02-24-93, Butterfield, #2748, illus.), 9⅜ x 7½ in., (238 x 191 mm.), lithograph in colors on Chine volant (BP 690, DM 1607, FR 5449, Y 116,170).

$282* *La Voyageuse (Marchesseau 38), 1920,* mono., from Gedichtband Sommer, (06-10-93, Hauswedell/Nolt, #542), image 7⁹⁄₁₆ x 6⅞ in., (19.2 x 17.5 cm.), lithograph on hand-made (BP 184, DM 459, FR 1546, Y 29,933).

$3163* *[Deux Jeunes Filles A Chevaux Avec Un Chien] (not in Marchesseau), c.1930,* s., i. e.a., full margins, good cond., slightly faded, glued to backing, (05-13-93, Sotheby-NY, #584, illus.), 9⅞ x 13⅜ in., (251 x 341 mm.), sh 12 x 16 in., (251 x 341 mm.), lithograph in grey, green, blue and pink on chine volant (BP 2077, DM 5107, FR 17,228, Y 353,132).

LAURENCIN, Marie (after)

$230* *Three Ladies At A Table,* s., d. Marie Laurencin 1937 and Marie Laurencin, #90/100, (05-19-93, Christie-E, #157), plate 18½ x 12¼ in., (47 x 31.1 cm.), color reproduction in pastel tones (BP 149, DM 374, FR 1260, Y 25,462).

$165* *"Young Woman With Flower",* (03-24-93, Doyle, #42), 17¾ x 20½ in., (45.1 x 52.1 cm.), hand-painted lithograph (BP 112, DM 269, FR 917, Y 19,387).

LAURENS, Henri French 1885-1954

$1604* *Le Boxeur (V. 6), c. 1921,* s., num., pub. D.-H. Kahnweiler, (06-23-93, Kornfeld, #490), etching on thick wove (BP 1090, DM 2714, FR 9129, Y 174,747, SF 2415).

$1756* *La Femme A La Guitare (V. 5), Vor 1920,* s. in pencil, num., pub. D.-H. Kahnweiler, (06-23-93, Kornfeld, #489), etching on thick wove (BP 1193, DM 2971, FR 9994, Y 191,306, SF 2645).

BI *Femme Accroupie (Volker 27), 1950,* s., #28/75, pub. Galerie Louise Leiris, full margins, good cond., foxing, backboard staining, est. BP 6/800, (12-03-92, Sotheby-London, #361), 22½ x 14 in., (572 x 356 mm.), lithograph in colors on Arches.

$2164* *Femme Allongee Au Bras Leve (Volker 30), c. 1950,* #II/LX, s., blindstamp, (11-21-92, Lempertz, #241, illus.), 11⁵⁄₁₆ x 17½ in., (28.7 x 44.5 cm.), lithograph on wove (BP 1425, DM 3450, FR 11,622, Y 269,121).

$741* *Lucien De Samosate; Dialogues, 1951: Twenty-Four,* Teriade Editeur, 103/250, (05-12-93, AB Stockholm, #7032), color woodcut (BP 484, DM 1196, FR 4027, Y 82,729, SK 5500).

$1756* *Tete De Femme A L'Eventail (Volker 4),* before 1921, s., num., pub. D.-H. Kahnweiler, (06-23-93, Kornfeld, #488), etching on thick wove (BP 1193, DM 2971, FR 9994, Y 191,306, SF 2645).

$967* *Valencia (Brusberg Dokumente 9, 9), 1927,* mono., s., 49/100, (06-28-93, Loudmer, #281, illus.), 6⅝ x 8¹¹⁄₁₆ in., (168 x 220 mm.), sh 12¹³⁄₁₆ x 20¼ in., (168 x 220 mm.), black etching on Van Gelder Zonen (BP 647, DM 1643, FR 5535, Y 102,599).

$1373* *Valencia (Volker 9), before 1927,* d., #89/100, full margins, good cond., rubbed patch, creases, (06-30-93, Sotheby-London, #483), 6⅝ x 8⅝ in., (168 x 219 mm.), etching on Van Gelder laid (BP 920, DM 2342, FR 7900, Y 147,112).

LAURENT, J.

$2359* *"Spain H.H.B.": Two Albums,* 1880s, photog.'s credits, nums., t. in negs.; t., photog.'s credits on front covers, (05-06-93, Christie-London, #57, illus.), majority approx. 13 x 9¾ in., photograph, 155 albumen prints; morocco, ruled in gilt (BP 1495, DM 3716, FR 12,508, Y 259,545).

LAURIE, R. H., Publisher

$403* *Field Sports, Plate 2, The Stage Hunt, 1821,* watermark, d. 1819, small margins, light/mat/time staining, other defects, Anthony N. B. Garvan Coll., (06-05-93, Christie-NY, #60), pl 17½ x 13¾ in., (445 x 349 mm.), etching w/hand-coloring on laid (BP 265, DM 653, FR 2202, Y 43,231).

LAURITZ, Paul Norwegian/American 1889-1975

$248* *"A Song Of Spring",* s. Paul Lauritz, prov., (11-10-92, Moran, #154), 14½ x 17½ in., (36.8 x 44.5 cm.), serigraph on paper (BP 164, DM 398, FR 1343, Y 30,869).

LAUSEN, Uwe 1941-1970

BI *Raumpatrouille, (19)68,* s., d., num., est. DM 900, (12-01-92, Karl/Faber, #905), 17⅛ x 24 in., (43.5 x 61 cm.), color serigraph on cardboard.

LAUTENSACK, Hans German 1524-c 1560

$722* *Christus Erhort Das Kanaanaische Weib (B. 48; Schmitt 71 II; Hollstein 37 II), 1559,* prov., (12-04-92, Bassenge, #6268), 6⅛ x 8¹¹⁄₁₆ in., (15.6 x 22 cm.), etching (BP 463, DM 1150, FR 3901, Y 90,137).

$361* *Eine Reiterschlacht (B. 20; Schmitt 27, Hollstein 6), 1546,* (12-04-92, Bassenge, #6267), 7⅞ x 12⅜ in., (20 x 31.4 cm.), engraving (BP 232, DM 575, FR 1950, Y 45,069).

BI *Der Engel Trostet Hagar (B. 54, Schmitt 81, Hollstein 40),* prov., est. DM 15,000, (12-04-92, Bassenge, #6269), 7⅝ x 11⅝ in., (19.4 x 29.5 cm.), etching.

BI *Georg Roggenbach (B. 9; Holl. 65), 1554,* 1st state of 2, plate tone, watermark, trimmed, borderline w/false margin added, repairs, mark, glue, thin spots, discoloration, good cond., ex-coll. Friedrich August of Saxony, est. $6/8,000, (05-13-93, Sotheby-NY, #162, illus.), 13⅝ x 9⅝ in., (347 x 243 mm.), etching.

BI *Hieronymus Schurstab, Burgermeister Von Nurnberg (B. 7, Schmitt 8 I,Hollstein 68 I), 1554,* watermark, prov., est. DM 1,200, (12-04-92, Bassenge, #6266, illus.), 7¾ x 11⁷⁄₁₆ in., (19.7 x 29.1 cm.), etching.

$3399* *Landschaft Mit Bachlauf (B. 26, Hollstein 16 II), 1553,* prov., (06-04-93, Bassenge, #5227A, illus.), 6⅝ x 4⅜ in., (16.9 x 11.1 cm.), etching (BP 2249, DM 5520, FR 18,604, Y 366,588).

BI *Pankraz Von Freyberg-Hohenaschau (B. 5; Holl. 56), 1553,* watermark, trimmed, repaired tear, thin spots, foxing, good cond., est., $1,2/1,800, (05-13-93, Sotheby-NY, #163), 9⅛ x 6¾ in., (233 x 172 mm.), etching.

$3125* *Two Pines And A Church Across From A River Town (Holl. 32), 1533,* trimmed on borderline, stains, cockling, (06-29-93, Sotheby-London, #48, illus.), 4¼ x 6¾ in., (10.8 x 17.1 cm.), etching (BP 2070, DM 5277, FR 17,786, Y 332,659).

LAUTREC
$76 *Cafe Interior With Figures,* s., (04-16-93, G.A. Key, #154), 10 x 11 in., (25.4 x 27.9 cm.), colored lithograph (BP 50, DM 123, FR 415, Y 8546).

LAUVERGNE (after)
$328* *Voyage De La Botine - Uraguay: Five,* plates 9-13, p. Lemercier, pub. Ackermann, full margins, staining, (10-27-92, Phillips-London, #152A), sheet 12⅛ x 19⅛ in., (308 x 486 mm.), lithograph w/later hand coloring on chine applique (BP 207, DM 503, FR 1706, Y 40,122).

$367* *Voyage De La Botine Brasil: Six,* plates 3-8 from the series p. Lermercier, pub. Ackermann, full margins, staining, (10-27-92, Phillips-London, #153), sheet 12⅛ x 19⅛ in., (308 x 486 mm.), lithograph w/later hand-coloring on chine applique (BP 232, DM 562, FR 1908, Y 44,893).

LAUVERGNE and FISQUET (after)
BI *Voyage De La Botine India: Twelve,* plates 87-98 from the series, p. Lemercier, pub. Ackermann, full margins, foxing, staining, est. BP 4/500, (10-27-92, Phillips-London, #152), sheet 12⅛ x 19⅛ in., (308 x 486 mm.), lithograph w/later hand-coloring on chine applique.

LAVENSON, Alma   20th cent.
$950* *Carquinez Bridge, 1933,* s., d. verso, (02-04-93, Sloan, #2922, illus.), 10 x 8 in., (25.4 x 20.3 cm.), photograph, black and white (BP 657, DM 1575, FR 5325, Y 118,218).

$605* *"Eucalyptus Leaves",* s., Friends Of Photography's Collectors Print Program stamp, 1933/1987, (11-16-92, Butterfield, #6060, illus.), 8¾ x 12 in., (222.6 x 305.3 mm.), photograph, gelatin silver print (BP 398, DM 965, FR 3249, Y 75,239).

LAVOIE, Steve
$825* *Shirt On Clothesline, c. 1990,* Dixon Collection, (11-16-92, Butterfield, #6061, illus.), 36⁹⁄₁₆ x 48¹⁄₁₆ in., (92.8 x 122.1 cm.), photograph, gelatin silver print (BP 543, DM 1315, FR 4431, Y 102,599).

LAVREINCE, Nicholas (after)
BI *"L'Assemblee Au Concert"* and *"L'Assemblee Au Salon" (L. and D. 43-4), c. 1770: Two,* by F. Dequevauviller, proofs before letters, trimmed to platemark, folds, good cond., est. $6/10,000, (05-11-93, Christie-NY, #76, illus.), each sheet 13½ x 19¼ in., (343 x 489 mm.), engraving on laid.

BI *Le Mercure De France (L. and D. 68), c. 1760,* by H. Guttenberg, margins, surface loss, mat staining, est. $2/3,000, (05-11-93, Christie-NY, #77, illus.), plate 15 x 17¾ in., (381 x 451 mm.), engraving on laid.

BI *"Les Nymphes Scrupuleuses"* and *"La Balancoire Mysterieuse" (L. and D. 192-3), c. 1780,* 2nd final state and 5th state of 6, trimmed, taped to overmats, est.$2,5/3,500,

(05-11-93, Christie-NY, #79, illus.), each sheet 15¾ x 11¼ in., (400 x 286 mm.), engraving on laid.

LAVRIN, Nora (nee FRY)
BI *Weeding Women,* plate s.; s., t., est. C$ 1/150, (12-01-92, Ritchie, #8, illus.), 6⅜ x 7⅝ in., (16.2 x 19.4 cm.), etching on laid paper.

LAWRENCE, Sir Thomas (after)
$46 *"Charles Harvey Esquire",* by Charles Turner, (06-11-93, G.A. Key, #56), 23 x 15 in., (58.4 x 38.1 cm.), b/w mezzotint (BP 30, DM 75, FR 252, Y 4881).

$12 *George IV,* engr. by S. W. Reynolds, (12-11-92, G.A. Key, #122), 17 x 13 in., (43.2 x 33 cm.), black and white engraving (BP 8, DM 19, FR 65, Y 1485).

BI *His Excellency General The Marquis Of Anglesey, 1828,* engraved by Charles Turner, pub., est. $50/75, (02-14-93, Neal, #1142), image 24½ x 14½ in., (62.2 x 36.8 cm.), mezzotint.

BI *Miss Farren (De V. 1075), 1791,* by Francesco Bartolozzi, 4th state of 6, pub. Bull and Jeffryes, 1792, narrow to thread margins, foxing, thin spots, est. BP 250/350, (12-01-92, Christie-London, #292), plate 21⅞ x 14⅛ in., (555 x 358 mm.), stipple engraving in black on Auvergne laid paper.

LAWSON, Ernest   American 1873-1939
$4400* *Untitled (Spring), c. 1920,* s., full sheet, good cond., foxing, crease, soiling, (02-24-93, Butterfield, #2644, illus.), 8⅛ x 10 in., (206 x 254 mm.), monotype in colors on wove (BP 3068, DM 7143, FR 24,216, Y 516,311).

$2300* *[Landscape]. c. 1920,* margins, glue stains, remains glue, (05-13-93, Sotheby-NY, #428, illus.), 9 x 12 in., (230 x 305 mm.), monotype in colors on wove (BP 1510, DM 3714, FR 12,527, Y 256,782).

LAZI, Adolf   German 1884-1955
$531* *Portrat Dr. Ottomar Domnick, c. 1953,* photographer's stamp, (11-12-92, Lempertz, #140), 11¾ x 9⁷⁄₁₆ in., (29.9 x 24 cm.), photograph, gelatin silver print (BP 340, DM 835, FR 2844, Y 65,693).

$978* *Tea Pot Still Life,* 1950s, credit stamp, (04-08-93, Christie-NY, #442, illus.), 9¼ x 6¾ in., (23.5 x 17.1 cm.), photograph, gelatin silver print (BP 641, DM 1571, FR 5318, Y 110,985).

LAZZELL, Blanche   American 1878-1956
BI *Violet And Yellow [Flowers], 1939,* s., t., d., i. (M99) in ink, full margins, staining, taped to overmat, very good cond., est. $2,8/3,400, (11-09-92, Christie-NY, #22), border 8⅞ x 12⅞ in., (225 x 327 mm.), monotype in colors on laid Japan.

LE BAS, Jacques Phillippe
BI *The Four Elements: Four,* after David Teniers, narrow margins, good cond., est. BP 4/500, (12-03-92, Sotheby-London, #74), each approx. 8½ x 6 in., (215 x 150 mm.), etchings.

LE BOUL'CH, Jean Pierre   b. 1940
$60* *"Composition-1972",* #14/100, d., s., (04-04-93, Pescheteau, #238), 21¼ x 29½ in., (54 x 75 cm.), red serigraph (BP 40, DM 96, FR 328, Y 6831).

LE BRETON
$77* *Vue De Sacremento,* (06-11-93, Freemn/Fine Art, #129), 9½ x 14¼ in., (24.1 x 36.2 cm.), hand-colored engraving (BP 51, DM 125, FR 422, Y 8170).

LE BROCQUY, Louis   British b. 1916
BI *Child With Ball,* s., #8/20 in ink, defects, short tears into image, mounted, est. $150/250, (10-27-92, Phillips-London, #255), sheet 30⅞ x 20⅝ in., (784 x 524 mm.), color lithograph on wove.

LE BRUN, Christopher
$1978* *Seven Lithographs, 1988-89: Set Of Seven,* each s., #20/35, pub. Paragon Press, ful sheets, p. to edges, good cond., (10-15-92, Sotheby-London, #84, illus.), each approx. 35¾ x 29¾ in., (90.8 x 75.6 cm.), lithograph on mould made Zerkall wove (BP 1210, DM 2944, FR 9985, Y 237,313).

$503* *Untitled, 1984: Nine,* s., d., num. in sequence 54-62 of 100, full margins, good cond., (10-15-92, Sotheby-London, #89), each approx. 8¾ x 12¾ in., (22.2 x 32.4

cm.), etching on wove (BP 308, DM 749, FR 2539, Y 60,348).

$1169* *Untitled, 1984: Twenty-Two,* s., d., all num., from edit. of 100, full margins, good cond., (10-15-92, Sotheby-London, #90), each approx. 8¾ x 12¾ in., (22.2 x 32.4 cm.), etching on wove (BP 715, DM 1740, FR 5901, Y 140,252).

LE CLERC, J.

$137* *Saints Ermites: Twenty-Five,* yellowed, stained, good margins, (06-16-93, Ader Tajan, #13), copper engraving (BP 91, DM 227, FR 763, Y 14,612).

$354* *Solitudo Sive Vitae Foeminarum Anacoritum: Twenty-One,* frontispiece, yellowed, stained, color outline, good margins, (06-16-93, Ader Tajan, #12), copper engraving (BP 236, DM 588, FR 1972, Y 37,756).

LE CORBUSIER Swiss/French 1887-1965

$347* *Assise, 1940-1943,* mono., d., t. in stone, (06-24-93, Germann, #294), 22¹⁄₁₆ x 19¹¹⁄₁₆ in., (560 x 500 mm.), lithograph (BP 228, DM 563, FR 1896, Y 37,224, SF 506).

$922* *Chez Soi, 1960,* num., (06-05-93, Bassenge, #6253), 27¾ x 40½ in., (70.5 x 102.8 cm.), color lithograph (BP 607, DM 1495, FR 5038, Y 98,906).

$300* *Composition,* inits., image d. '54, creasing, good cond., (11-30-92, Phillips-London, #453), sheet 42¾ x 26¾ in., (108.6 x 67.9 cm.), color lithograph on wove (BP 198, DM 478, FR 1622, Y 37,337).

$400* *Composition, 1954,* (09-30-92, Kunsthallen, #67), color lithograph (BP 226, DM 567, FR 1918, Y 48,002, DK 2185).

$295* *Composition, 1955,* 107/125, (09-30-92, Kunsthallen, #68), color lithograph (BP 166, DM 418, FR 1415, Y 35,401, DK 1610).

$1311* *Femme Et Nature Morte, 1932,* s., d., stained, (11-13-92, Koller, #5364), sheet 25 x 17⅛ in., (63.5 x 43.5 cm.), lithograph on wove (BP 847, DM 2058, FR 6940, Y 162,716, SF 1856).

$2093* *Komposition Med Kvindehoved, 1953,* s. XXII/XXX, (09-29-92, B. Rasmussen, #293), aquatint in colors (BP 1177, DM 2956, FR 10,087, Y 249,851, DK 11,500).

$2126* *Komposition, (19)53,* s., num., light-staining, (06-08-93, Karl/Faber, #1015), approx. 16⅛ x 12³⁄₁₆ in., (41 x 31 cm.), colored aquatint on BFK Rives wove (BP 1398, DM 3450, FR 11,617, Y 225,810).

$363* *Komposition, Aus Petite "Confidences" (Heidi Weber 45), 1957,* stone mono., d., (06-24-93, Germann, #293), 17¹¹⁄₁₆ x 22¼ in., (450 x 565 mm.), lithograph (BP 239, DM 589, FR 1984, Y 38,940, SF 529).

$978* *La Main Ouverte, 1955,* s., #11/150, full margins, good cond., creases, skinned spots, label, foxing, (02-11-93, Sotheby-NY, #106), 21⁹⁄₁₆ x 15¾ in., (548 x 400 mm.), color lithograph on Arches wove (BP 690, DM 1620, FR 5482, Y 117,902).

BI *La Mer Est Toujours Presente: Ten,* portfolio, XXIV/XXX, in stone mono. or s., Editions Forces-Vives, est. SF 5/6,000, (04-21-93, Germann, #348), 22¹⁄₁₆ x 19¹¹⁄₁₆ in., (560 x 500 mm.), lithograph.

$253* *Personnages,* 53/185, stone mono., wrinkles, (06-24-93, Germann, #291), 17¹¹⁄₁₆ x 22¹⁄₁₆ in., (450 x 560 mm.), lithograph (BP 167, DM 410, FR 1383, Y 27,140, SF 368).

$1544* *Taureau, c. 1950,* s., #62/75, pub. Crommelynk, blindstamp, full margins, good cond., (06-30-93, Sotheby-London, #485, illus.), 25¼ x 19⅛ in., (641 x 486 mm.), etching on wove (BP 1035, DM 2633, FR 8884, Y 165,434).

$1064* *Totem, 1963,* stone s., (06-05-93, Bassenge, #6254), 27⁹⁄₁₆ x 30⅞ in., (70 x 78.5 cm.), color lithograph (BP 700, DM 1725, FR 5814, Y 114,139).

$3432* *Two Compositions, c. 1960,* each s., #90/130, full margins, good cond., (06-30-93, Sotheby-London, #484, illus.), each sh c. 17⅞ x 22⅜ in., (454 x 568 mm.), etching w/aquatint in color on BFK Rives (BP 2300, DM 5854, FR 19,747, Y 367,727).

$2904* *Unite "11", 1953,* s., num., stains verso, (12-01-92, Karl/Faber, #458, illus.), 16⁵⁄₁₆ x 12³⁄₁₆ in., (41.5 x 31 cm.), color aquatint/etching on wove (BP 1919, DM 4629, FR 15,774, Y 361,554).

$1210* *The Unite Series, 1953,* #14, s., num. 94/130, (11-12-92, Freemn/Fine Art, #53, illus.), 13½ x 18 in., (34.3 x 45.7 cm.), colored aquatint (BP 795, DM 1917, FR 6467, Y 150,031).

LE GAC, Jean b. 1936

$146* *"Odalisque", 1986,* #25/31, s., (10-18-92, Pescheteau, #187), 20⅞ x 29½ in., (53 x 75 cm.), lithograph in colors w/photo collage (BP 88, DM 216, FR 733, Y 17,433).

LE GRAY, Gustave 1820-1882

BI *Group Of Officers Seated At A Tent, Camp De Chalons, 1857,* notations on mount recto, est. $2/2,500, (04-07-93, Swann, #228, illus.), 8¾ x 13 in., photograph, albumen print.

LE LOSQUES, Daniel

$382* *Excelsior,* p. Daude Freres, fold marks, creases, paper back, laid on board, (05-07-93, Christie-S. Ken, #119), 23¾ x 31½ in., (60.3 x 80 cm.), color lithograph (BP 242, DM 604, FR 2035, Y 42,061).

LE MARESQUIER, Louis

$40* *Dix Jours Aux Pyrenees. Grande Operette. Musique De L. Varney, c. 1885,* cond. A, (03-16-93, Boisgirard, #143), 31½ x 23⅝ in., (80 x 60 cm.), poster (BP 28, DM 67, FR 226, Y 4677).

LE MEILLEUR, Georges

$103* *Paysage: Thirteen,* s., num., margins, (05-06-93, Laurin, #54), etchings (BP 65, DM 162, FR 546, Y 11,332).

LE MOUEL, Eugene 1859-1934

$100* *L'Olympienne, c. 1900,* Paris, Imp. Chaix, cond. A-, (06-11-93, Boisgirard, #104), 48¹⁄₁₆ x 32½ in., (122 x 82.5 cm.), poster (BP 66, DM 163, FR 548, Y 10,610).

LE PARC, Julio Argentinian b. 1928

BI *Circular Composition,* s., #81/200, 523 No. 1-3, pub. Denise Rene Editeur, blindstamped, prov., exhib., est. C$ 3/400, (12-01-92, Ritchie, #57, illus.), 24½ x 24½ in., (62.2 x 62.2 cm.), color serigraph.

BI *"Couleurs No. I": Album of Eight,* #118/125, s., ed. Denise Rene, est. FF 3/4,000, (10-18-92, Pescheteau, #192), serigraph in colors.

BI *Multi-Colored Circles,* s., #86/200, 523 No. 11.7, pub. Denise Rene Editeur, blindstamped, prov., exhib., est. C$ 3/400, (12-01-92, Ritchie, #58), 29½ x 29½ in., (74.9 x 74.9 cm.), color serigraph.

LE POITEVIN, G.

$119* *Ch. De Fer Algeriens: Algerie, Pays Du Soleil,* very good cond., (03-13-93, Laurin, #56), 39⅜ x 28¾ in., (100 x 73 cm.), (BP 83, DM 198, FR 673, Y 14,025).

LE PRINCE, J.B.

$91* *La Nourrice 1760,* good margins, (02-03-93, Ader Tajan, #66), 5⅝ x 7¹⁄₁₆ in., (14.3 x 17.9 cm.), tinted wash engraving (BP 64, DM 150, FR 508, Y 11,320).

LE QUESNE, F.

$239* *Cie Generale Transatlantique: Le Havre New-York "La Lorraine, La Savoie",* mediocre state, (03-13-93, Laurin, #164), 36 x 25¹⁵⁄₁₆ in., (91.5 x 66 cm.), (BP 167, DM 398, FR 1353, Y 28,167).

$309* *PLM and Cie Gle Transatlantique: Algerie Tunisie,* very good cond., (03-13-93, Laurin, #82, illus.), 42½ x 30¹¹⁄₁₆ in., (108 x 78 cm.), (BP 216, DM 514, FR 1749, Y 36,417).

LE SECQ, Henri

BI *South Facade, Church Of The Madeleine, Paris, c. 1850,* flush-mounted to heavy paper, mounted to album leaf, est. $2/3,000, (04-06-93, Sotheby-NY, #46, illus.), 9⅜ x 13⅛ in., photograph, salt print.

LE VASSEUR French School 19th cent.

$56* *"Le Frileux",* after David II Teniers, inits. D.T.F. in plate, (07-14-92, Encans, #230), 9¹⁄₁₆ x 7½ in., (23 x 19 cm.), drypoint (BP 29, DM 83, FR 280, Y 7003, C$ 67).

LE YAOUANC, Alain b. 1940

$67* *Untitled: Two,* s., (10-18-92, Pescheteau, #191), each 15¾ x 12⅝ in., (40 x 32 cm.), lithograph in colors on Arches (BP 41, DM 99, FR 336, Y 8000).

LEA, Henry, Publisher
$82* *Cricketing (Lord Cricket Ground, St. John's Wood, Match Of The Gentlemen And Players),* by T. Lorette, (06-30-93, Bonhams-Chelsea, #264), image 5¾ x 8½ in., (14.6 x 21.6 cm.), lithograph w/hand-coloring (BP 55, DM 140, FR 472, Y 8786).

LEADER, B.W. (after)
$39 *Wooded River Landscape With Figures And Dog On A Bank,* pub. 1887, (12-11-92, G.A. Key, #143), 14 x 21 in., (35.6 x 53.3 cm.), black and white engraving (BP 25, DM 61, FR 211, Y 4826).

LEANDRE, Charles
$17* *Couple Walking,* s., (10-16-92, DuMouchelle, #2494), lithograph (BP 10, DM 25, FR 85, Y 2030).
$171* *Panurge. De G. Spitzmuller Et M. Boukay. Musique De Massenet. Gaite Lyrique, 1913,* Imp. J. Minot, very good cond., (02-12-93, Cheval/Robert, #163), 35¼ x 25 in., (89.5 x 63.5 cm.), poster (BP 120, DM 284, FR 960, Y 20,622).

LEANDRE, G.
BI *Panurge Massener, 1913,* Imp. J. Minot, A cond., est. $6/900, (08-06-92, Swann, #168, illus.), 35½ x 25 in., (90.2 x 63.5 cm.), .

LEAR, Edward   English 1812-1888
BI *Rook Corvus Frugilegus (Linn), p.* by C Hallmandel, est. $3/400, (08-11-92, L. Joel, #60G), 19½ x 12¹⁵/₁₆ in., (49.5 x 33 cm.), color lithograph.

LEAR, John   American 20th cent.
$165* *Many Hands,* s., t., (11-12-92, Freemn/Fine Art, #118A), 11¾ x 17½ in., (29.8 x 44.5 cm.), lithograph (BP 108, DM 261, FR 882, Y 20,459).

LEATHERDALE, Marcus
$825* *"Sentry", 1985,* s., t., d., edit. 3/15, Dixon Collection, (11-16-92, Butterfield, #6062, illus.), 21¹⁵/₁₆ x 19⁵/₁₆ in., (556.6 x 489.8 mm.), photograph, platinum print (BP 543, DM 1315, FR 4431, Y 102,599).

LEBADANG   Vietnamese 20th cent.
$44* *Boats,* s., num. 129/200, (09-20-92, Hindman, #822), 14¾ x 21⅛ in., (37.5 x 53.7 cm.), color lithograph (BP 26, DM 65, FR 223, Y 5438).
$59* *"Composition",* #50/175, s., (01-28-93, Pescheteau, #184), 29¹⁵/₁₆ x 21¼ in., (76 x 54 cm.), color lithograph on Arches (BP 39, DM 93, FR 316, Y 7326).
$90* *Harlequins,* s., #5/120, (02-04-93, Sloan, #1866), 16¼ x 22¼ in., (41.3 x 56.5 cm.), color lithograph (BP 63, DM 148, FR 503, Y 11,195).
$99* *"Harlequins",* s., (06-11-93, Freemn/Fine Art, #128E), 24 x 18 in., (61 x 45.7 cm.), lithograph in colors (BP 65, DM 161, FR 542, Y 10,504).
$90* *Horse,* s. in plate; s., #10/120, (02-04-93, Sloan, #1867), 20¼ x 12 in., (51.4 x 30.5 cm.), embossed color litho-graph (BP 63, DM 148, FR 503, Y 11,195).
BI *Tabletop Still Life Of Flowers In Vase,* black pastel or charcoal s., #56/120 w/in image, est. $300/500, (09-17-92, Sloan, #1453), 19½ x 25½ in., (49.5 x 64.8 cm.), color lithograph.
$33* *Untitled,* artist's proof, s., (05-15-93, Dunning, #226), aquatint in color (BP 21, DM 53, FR 178, Y 3658).

LEBASQUE, Henri   French 1865-1937
$174* *L'Emprunt De La Paix,* s. in stone, trimmed, small tears, good cond., 1082 x 758mm, sh 1135x 795mm, (06-28-93, Loudmer, #282), color lithograph poster on wove (BP 117, DM 296, FR 996, Y 18,462).

LEBEAU
$142* *"L'Amant Victorieux",* after Touzet, (03-22-93, Pescheteau, #21), color print (BP 96, DM 233, FR 792, Y 16,443).

LEBRUN, Charles (after)
$341* *Battle Scenes: Three,* trimmed margins, (07-16-92, Bon-hams-Chelsea, #496), image 5⅛ x 3½ in., (13 x 8.9 cm.), etching w/hand wash (BP 176, DM 504, FR 1701, Y 42,374).

LEBRUN, Marcel   early 20th cent.
$247* *Cristille,* Prieure de Noiretable, A- cond., surface soil-ing, creasing, cracking, (08-06-92, Swann, #169, illus.),

54½ x 37¼ in., (138.4 x 94.6 cm.), (BP 129, DM 365, FR 1233, Y 31,505).

LEBRUN, Rico   Italian/American 1900-1964
BI *"Figure"; "Figure", 1963:* Two, each s., margins, laid down, good cond., paper losses, tears, glue remains, thinned spots, mat/light staining, surface soiling, est. $5/700, (02-24-93, Butterfield, #3229), one 10 x 10 in., (254 x 254 mm.), other 13½ x 7 in., (254 x 254 mm.), lithograph on wove.

LECK, Bart van der   1876-1958
BI *Fruitmand,* inits., good cond., discoloration, stains, burn hole center image, est. G 4/6,000, (12-09-92, Sotheby-Amstrdm, #603), sheet 11¹¹/₁₆ x 16⁷/₁₆ in., (297 x 418 mm.), color lithograph laid down on Japanese paper.

LECOMTE, Emile
BI *The Old Willow,* s., minor staining, light struck, est. $3/500, (05-22-93, Weschler, #198), 18 x 23½ in., (45.7 x 59.7 cm.), hand-colored etching.

LECORNU, Genevieve
$299* *5ieme Exposition De L'Habitation, 1938,* cond. A, (03-16-93, Boisgirard, #137, illus.), 47¼ x 31½ in., (120 x 80 cm.), poster (BP 206, DM 497, FR 1689, Y 34,963).

LEDUC, Fernand   b. 1916
$200* *S.G. 12,* #58/100, s., d. F. Leduc 72, (10-20-92, Encans, #108), 24 x 24 in., (61 x 61 cm.), serigraph (BP 112, DM 304, FR 1035, Y 25,069, C$ 244).
$200* *Untitled,* #51/100, s. F. Leduc, (10-20-92, Encans, #107), 11¹³/₁₆ x 20¹/₁₆ in., (30 x 51 cm.), serigraph (BP 112, DM 304, FR 1035, Y 25,069, C$ 244).

LEE, Doris   American b. 1905
BI *Cows In A Landscape,* s., margins, good cond., restored tear, surface soiling, est. $4/600, (10-28-92, Butterfield, #2740), 18 x 24⅛ in., (457 x 613 mm.), color lithograph on wove.
$275* *"Helicopter",* pub. AAA, s. Doris Lee, t. AAA label, very good cond., (09-11-92, Skinner, #59, illus.), 8⅞ x 12 in., (22.5 x 30.5 cm.), lithograph on wove (BP 142, DM 396, FR 1345, Y 34,073).
$248* *Skating On The River,* s. Doris Lee, good cond., taped to back, mount staining, (03-12-93, Skinner, #48, illus.), 9¼ x 12¾ in., (23.5 x 32.4 cm.), lithograph on wove (BP 173, DM 413, FR 1404, Y 29,228).
$173* *Still Life,* s., i., margins, good cond., masking tape, mat staining, surface soilng, (05-19-93, Butterfield, #2001), 9½ x 13¹⁵/₁₆ in., (241 x 354 mm.), lithograph on wove (BP 112, DM 281, FR 947, Y 19,152).

LEE, F*R* (after)
$25* *The Huntsman's Return,* by G.H. Every, pub. S. Hollyer, 1841, margins, surface defects, (06-30-93, Bonhams-Chelsea, #63), plate 14¼ x 16¼ in., (36.2 x 41.3 cm.), engraving (BP 17, DM 43, FR 144, Y 2679).

LEE, Russell   American 1903-1986
$1610* *Annual Replastering Of Adobe House, Chamisal, New Mexico, 1940,* p.l., s., t., d., lit., (04-08-93, Christie-NY, #315, illus.), 9½ x 12⅞ in., (24.1 x 32.7 cm.), photo-graph, gelatin silver print (BP 1056, DM 2586, FR 8755, Y 182,705).
$275* *Black Woman And Children,* notations, 1930's, (10-14-92, Swann, #450, illus.), 10 x 8 in., (25.4 x 20.3 cm.), photograph, silver print (BP 161, DM 402, FR 1365, Y 33,325).
BI *Children In Nursery School Receiving Cod Liver Oil, Lakeview Project, Arkansas, 1938,* t., d., F.S.A. stamps, est. $800/1,200, (04-08-93, Christie-NY, #314, illus.), 7⅛ x 9⅜ in., (18.1 x 23.8 cm.), photograph, gelatin sil-ver print.
$357* *County Meeting, San Augustine, Texas, 1939,* F.S.A., F.S.A. handstamp, typed caption, (04-07-93, Swann, #307, illus.), 8 x 10 in., photograph, silver print (BP 236, DM 577, FR 1954, Y 40,559).
BI *Dancing The Schottische At Party Given At Humble Camp, Hobbs, N.M., 1947,* credit, Standard Oil stamps, label, est. $7/900, (04-08-93, Christie-NY, #316, illus.), 9⅜ x 5¼ in., (23.8 x 13.3 cm.), photograph, gelatin sil-ver print.

BI *Fireplace And Mantel, Mount Vernon, Indiana,* late 1930s, t., credit stamp, est. $7/900, (04-08-93, Christie-NY, #313, illus.), 9½ x 7⅛ in., (24.1 x 18.1 cm.), photograph, gelatin silver print.

$2200* *Jigging Solo At Square Dance, Pictown, N.M.,* (1940), p.l., s., (10-13-92, Christie-NY, #289, illus.), 13¼ x 10 in., (33.7 x 25.4 cm.), photograph, gelatin silver print (BP 1281, DM 3223, FR 10,951, Y 266,764).

$357* *Kindergarten Children, 1939,* F.S.A., F.S.A. handstamps, notations, (04-07-93, Swann, #308, illus.), 7 x 9½ in., photograph, silver print (BP 236, DM 577, FR 1954, Y 40,559).

$1980* *School Children,* 1930's, s., (10-13-92, Christie-NY, #288, illus.), 10½ x 13½ in., (26.7 x 34.3 cm.), photograph, gelatin silver print (BP 1153, DM 2901, FR 9856, Y 240,087).

LEE, Sydney

BI *Limestone Rock,* d. 1904-1905, s., est. BP 6/90, (05-20-93, Bonhams-Chelsea, #16), image 13 x 16⅞ in., (33 x 42.9 cm.), woodcut.

LEE-HANKEY, William British 1869-1952

$143* *Peasant Girl At Rest,* s., annot. inv. et del, (09-20-92, Hindman, #793), 7 x 8⅞ in., (17.8 x 22.5 cm.), drypoint and aquatint (BP 84, DM 212, FR 726, Y 17,674).

LEFEBRE, Valentin 1642-1680/82

BI *Landschaft Mit Schlafenden Hirten Und Schafherde, Aufl. 1749,* after Tizian, trimmed, est. DM 500-, (09-25-92, Granier, #2662), 8¼ x 12$\frac{9}{16}$ in., (21 x 31.9 cm.), etching.

LEFEVRE, Lucien

BI *Cirage Jacquand, 1894,* Imp. Chaix, fairly good cond., creases, (02-12-93, Cheval/Robert, #63), 68⅛ x 47¼ in., (173 x 120 cm.), poster.

$171* *Cycle Rochet, 1891,* Imp. Chaix, good cond., (02-12-93, Cheval/Robert, #81), 48$\frac{13}{16}$ x 34⅝ in., (124 x 88 cm.), poster (BP 120, DM 284, FR 960, Y 20,622).

$130* *Exposition Internationale "Cycles Et Sport", 1892,* cond. B, (03-16-93, Boisgirard, #138), 47$\frac{7}{16}$ x 33$\frac{7}{16}$ in., (120.5 x 85 cm.), poster (BP 90, DM 216, FR 734, Y 15,201).

$36* *Lire Dans Le Radical: Dette De Haine Par G. Ohnet, 1891,* Imp. Chaix, mediocre state, (02-12-93, Cheval/Robert, #120), 48$\frac{7}{16}$ x 34¼ in., (123 x 87 cm.), poster (BP 25, DM 60, FR 202, Y 4342).

LEFRANC

$10* *Atelier De Delacroix,* s. artist's proof, (06-28-93, Loudmer, #80), 18½ x 13⅜ in., (470 x 340 mm.), sh 25$\frac{9}{16}$ x 19$\frac{11}{16}$ in., (470 x 340 mm.), color lithograph on Arches wove (BP 7, DM 17, FR 57, Y 1061).

LEGER, Fernand French 1881-1955

$920* *8 Lithographs Originales Pour Arthur Rimaud (S. 24, 25, 29, 30, 35, 36, and 38), 1949: Seven,* from set of 8, #23/99, s. pub. Grosclaude, Editions des Gaules, full sheets, good cond., hinge stains, loss, (02-11-93, Sotheby-NY, #160), each sheet 12$\frac{15}{16}$ x 9¾ in., (330 x 248 mm.), lithograph, 3 colored w/pochoir (BP 649, DM 1524, FR 5157, Y 110,910).

$72* *Abstract Design,* stamped F. Leger, 163/225, (02-19-93, Garth, #443), 21¼ x 29¾ in., (54 x 75.6 cm.), colored lithograph (BP 50, DM 118, FR 399, Y 8543).

$483* *Bonne Pensee Du Matin (Saphire, 25), c. 1949,* inits. in stone and crayon, illus., good cond., (06-28-93, Loudmer, #283), 10$\frac{7}{16}$ x 7½ in., (265 x 190 mm.), sh 12$\frac{15}{16}$ x 9$\frac{13}{16}$ in., (265 x 190 mm.), black lithograph w/gouache embellishments on wove (BP 323, DM 821, FR 2765, Y 51,247).

$3663* *Branches (Saphire Nr. 140), 1951-1955,* s., (11-13-92, Kunsthaus, #674, illus.), 19⅞ x 25$\frac{13}{16}$ in., (50.5 x 65.5 cm.), color lithograph on Arches handmade (BP 2367, DM 5750, FR 19,391, Y 454,636).

$1580* *Le Campeur,* epreuve d'artiste, #V/V, s., (04-21-93, Germann, #105, illus.), 30$\frac{5}{16}$ x 23¼ in., (770 x 590 mm.), color serigraph (BP 1025, DM 2526, FR 8541, Y 174,914, SF 2300).

$168* *"Chevreuse" (S E7),* d. 51, mono. in plate, (01-28-93, Pescheteau, #186), 21⅝ x 14$\frac{15}{16}$ in., (55 x 38 cm.), (BP 111, DM 266, FR 901, Y 20,859).

$17,600* *Cirque (Saphire 44-106), 1950,* book, pen s., num. 255, pub. Teriade, Les Editions Verve, good cond.,red ink bleeding through, (11-05-92, Sotheby-NY, #226, illus.), each sheet approx. 16½ x 12⅝ in., (420 x 320 mm.), 63 lithographs, 34 in colors (BP 11,447, DM 27,835, FR 94,168, Y 2,159,244).

$142* *"Le Cirque",* init., d. F.L. 53, (04-20-93, Encans, #124), 19$\frac{11}{16}$ x 25$\frac{9}{16}$ in., (50 x 65 cm.), lithograph on Rives (BP 92, DM 226, FR 763, Y 15,668, C$ 178).

$91* *"Le Cirque",* s., d. in plate F.L. 53, (09-15-92, Encans, #160), 13⅜ x 18⅛ in., (34 x 46 cm.), lithograph (BP 49, DM 135, FR 460, Y 11,297, C$ 111).

BI *Composition Aux Deux Oiseaux (S. 134), 1954,* pen s., #33/75, pub. Galerie Louise Leiris, full margins, colors faded, light/mount & backboard staining, glue staining, est. BP 1,0/1,500, (12-03-92, Sotheby-London, #363, illus.), 14¾ x 20½ in., (375 x 521 mm.), lithograph in colors on Arches.

$8867* *Composition Aux Deux Personnages (Saphire 2), 1920,* s., blindstamp, (06-05-93, Bassenge, #6256, illus.), 11$\frac{5}{16}$ x 9⅜ in., (28.8 x 23.8 cm.), lithograph on hand-made (BP 5837, DM 14,376, FR 48,454, Y 951,191).

$1214* *"Composition Mecanique", (Lawrence Saphire E 24),* s. 62/300, (09-29-92, B. Rasmussen, #342), serigraph in colors (BP 682, DM 1715, FR 5851, Y 144,921, DK 6670).

$3207* *Composition Murale (Saphire 107), 1951,* s. in ink, num., (06-23-93, Kornfeld, #503), color lithograph (BP 2179, DM 5426, FR 18,253, Y 349,384, SF 4830).

$191* *"Composition",* #185/300, s., wet stamp, (10-18-92, Pescheteau, #190), sight 14$\frac{9}{16}$ x 19$\frac{5}{16}$ in., (37 x 49 cm.), pochoir in colors on wove (BP 116, DM 282, FR 958, Y 22,806).

$459* *Composition, 1953,* stamped Musee Fernand Leger, Biot, 259/300, (03-24-93, Kunsthallen, #222), color lithograph (BP 311, DM 750, FR 2551, Y 53,930, DK 2875).

$1725* *Compositon Sur Fond Jaune (S. 138), 1954,* pen s. (faded), pub. Galerie Louise Leiris, full margins, good cond.,mat stain, foxing, discoloration, glue, (05-13-93, Sotheby-NY, #587), 16⅞ x 21½ in., (430 x 545 mm.), lithograph in colors (BP 1132, DM 2785, FR 9395, Y 192,587).

BI *"Le Compotier" (Maeght 1403),* #282/300, ink s., est. FF10,000/12,000, (04-04-93, Pescheteau, #239, illus.), 29$\frac{15}{16}$ x 22$\frac{1}{16}$ in., (76 x 56 cm.), color etching and aquatint on BFK Rives.

$304* *Country Outing, 1953,* init., prov., (05-10-93, Hodgins, #260, illus.), 13½ x 20½ in., (34.3 x 52.1 cm.), color lithograph on paper (BP 198, DM 488, FR 1648, Y 33,970, C$ 385).

$353* *"Le Cycliste",* inits., d. in plate F.L. 48, (02-16-93, Encans, #124), 29$\frac{15}{16}$ x 22$\frac{13}{16}$ in., (76 x 58 cm.), lithograph (BP 244, DM 576, FR 1951, Y 42,291, C$ 444).

$413* *"The Dancers", 1953,* artist's proof, s., d. in stone, (10-31-92, Litchfield, #104), 21½ x 17½ in., (54.6 x 44.5 cm.), color lithograph (BP 270, DM 648, FR 2196, Y 51,063).

$1194* *Les Deux Tournesols (S. 135), 1954,* s. (faded), #17/75, pub. Galerie Louise Leiris, rubbing, taped, (12-03-92, Sotheby-London, #364, illus.), sheet 23½ x 18½ in., (597 x 470 mm.), lithograph in colors on Arches (BP 770, DM 1878, FR 6409, Y 148,563).

$8140* *Femme Tenant Un Vase, 1928, Sapphire 13,* s., num. 1/50, pencil note on mat Proof#1 Ex-Stinnes Coll., by Teriad, Cahiers d'Art, 1928, (09-20-92, Hindman, #758, illus.), 9⅜ x 6¾ in., (23.8 x 17.1 cm.), lithograph on Imperial Japan (BP 4766, DM 12,079, FR 41,320, Y 1,006,056).

BI *Fetes De La Faim (Saphire, 29), c. 1949,* inits., annot., est. FF5/8,000, (06-28-93, Loudmer, #284, illus.), 10⅝ x 8$\frac{1}{16}$ in., (270 x 205 mm.), sh 12$\frac{15}{16}$ x 9$\frac{15}{16}$ in., (270 x 205 mm.), grey lithograph on wove.

$486* *Frontispiece, 1952,* mono. in stone, (05-27-93, Briest, #122), 12⅜ x 9$\frac{13}{16}$ in., (31.5 x 25 cm.), black lithograph on Chine (BP 311, DM 780, FR 2628, Y 52,101).

$3249* *La Grande Margot (Saphire 111), 1951,* s., #18/75, (06-10-93, Hauswedell/Nolt, #547, illus.), image 19⅛ x 14 in., (48.5 x 35.6 cm.), color lithograph on Arches (BP 2125, DM 5291, FR 17,813, Y 344,868).

$217* *"La Grande Parade"*, s., d. in plate F. Leger 53, (06-16-93, Encans, #150), 16⁹⁄₁₆ x 22¹⁄₁₆ in., (42 x 56 cm.), lithograph on Rives (BP 145, DM 360, FR 1209, Y 23,144, C$ 278).

$1038* *Komposition (Saphire E 8)*, s., num., wrinkle, crease, (12-01-92, Karl/Faber, #908), 10⅝ x 7⅞ in., (27 x 20 cm.), color serigraph on Arches wove (BP 686, DM 1654, FR 5638, Y 129,233).

$989* *Komposition Mit Vier Figuren (Saphire E 11)*, 1951, s., Form mono., d, #179/200, (06-10-93, Hauswedell/Nolt, #548), image 17¹¹⁄₁₆ x 13⅜ in., (45 x 34 cm.), color serigraph on Arches (BP 647, DM 1610, FR 5422, Y 104,978).

$3524* *L'Echafaudage Au Soleil (Saphire 112)*, 1951, #30/75, (05-26-93, Lempertz, #283), 15¹⁵⁄₁₆ x 21⁵⁄₁₆ in., (40.5 x 54.2 cm.), color lithograph on Arches wove (BP 2280, DM 5750, FR 19,352, Y 382,877).

$2875* *L'Enfant A L'Accordeon (Saphire 127)*, 1953, s. (faint), #48/75, margins, good cond., mat stain, creases, glue stains, laid-down, (05-13-93, Sotheby-NY, #586), 18⅝ x 22¼ in., (472 x 565 mm.), sh 21⅜ x 25¼ in., (472 x 565 mm.), aquatint and silkscreen in colors (BP 1887, DM 4642, FR 15,659, Y 320,978).

BI *L'Oiseau Magique (S. 129)*, 1953, pen and ink s., #64/75, pub. by artist, margins, pinholes, crease, est. BP 5/700, (12-01-92, Christie-London, #416), plate 21⅞ x 14⁷⁄₁₆ in., (555 x 366 mm.), aquatint w/screenprint in colors on BFK Rives.

$1756* *L'Oiseau Rouge Dans Le Bois (Saph. E 19)*, 1953, s. in ink, num., (06-23-93, Kornfeld, #504), color aquatint (BP 1193, DM 2971, FR 9994, Y 191,306, SF 2645).

BI *"Landscape"*, from the La Ville Suite 1959, p. Morlot, stamped sig., 1x/xx, est. $7/900, (06-11-93, Freemn/Fine Art, #131), 17 x 12¾ in., (43.2 x 32.4 cm.), lithograph.

$3685* *La Lecture (Saphire E 23)*, 1953, after Leger, s., num., (06-08-93, Karl/Faber, #1018, illus.), approx. 17⅛ x 21⁷⁄₁₆ in., (43.5 x 54.5 cm.), color lithograph (BP 2422, DM 5979, FR 20,137, Y 391,397).

$3031* *"La Lecture" (S.E. 23)*, 1924-25, stamp ed. Louis CARRE verso, #32/350, s., (10-18-92, Pescheteau, #188), 21⅝ x 27³⁄₁₆ in., (55 x 69 cm.), lithograph in colors on Arches (BP 1837, DM 4477, FR 15,208, Y 361,910).

$586* *Liberte*, pub. Editions Seghers, good cond.?, sheet 285 x 1115 mm, (12-09-92, Sotheby-Amstrdm, #604), color silkscreen on wove (BP 374, DM 920, FR 3139, Y 72,660, G 1035).

BI *Liberte, Paul Eluard, J'Ecris Ton Nom*, est. DK 2,500, (03-24-93, Kunsthallen, #223), color lithograph.

$440* *"A Man And A Woman"*, stamped sig., #169/350, embossed stamp, (05-24-93, Grogan, #377A), 21½ x 16½ in., (54.6 x 41.9 cm.), color lithograph (BP 287, DM 719, FR 2422, Y 48,635).

BI *"Man And Woman"*, from the La Ville Suite 1959, p. Morlot, stamped sig., 1x/xx, est. $7/900, (06-11-93, Freemn/Fine Art, #130), 17 x 12¾ in., (43.2 x 32.4 cm.), lithograph.

$2316* *Morceau De Gruyere (Saphire 15)*, 1935, s., #24/50, p. by J. Tanneur, full margins, paper tone darkened, foxed, good cond., (06-30-93, Sotheby-London, #486, illus.), 9⅛ x 7 in., (232 x 178 mm.), drypoint on wove (BP 1552, DM 3950, FR 13,326, Y 248,152).

$1621* *Morceau De Gryere (Saphire 15)*, 1935, s., num., from the series l'album 23 Gravures, Editions G. Orobitz &Cie, (05-26-93, Dorling, #2813, illus.), 9⅛ x 7 in., (23.1 x 17.8 cm.), etching on thick wove (BP 1049, DM 2645, FR 8902, Y 176,119).

$210* *"Nature Morte Aux Clefs"*, d. 29, mono. in plate, (01-28-93, Pescheteau, #187), 14¹⁵⁄₁₆ x 18½ in., (38 x 47 cm.), color lithograph (BP 139, DM 333, FR 1126, Y 26,074).

$1887* *Nature Morte Aux Fruits (S. 18)*, 1948, s., #52/75, pub. Galerie Louise Leiris, full margins, good cond., (06-30-93, Sotheby-London, #487, illus.), 14⅛ x 18⅛ in., (359 x 460 mm.), color lithograph on Arches (BP 1265, DM 3218, FR 10,857, Y 202,186).

$550* *Nature Morte Aux Pommes*, 1948, inits., d. in image, num. 231/300, pub. Maeght Editeur, Paris, blindstamp, wide margins, good cond., light staining, soft handling creases, toning, (05-22-93, Weschler, #199), 10¼ x 13¼

in., (26 x 33.7 cm.), screenprint in colors on wove (BP 356, DM 894, FR 3009, Y 60,639).

$220* *Nuages*, from the suite La Ville, stamped sig., #87/180, (06-13-93, Hindman, #390), 16 x 22¾ in., (40.6 x 57.8 cm.), color lithograph (BP 144, DM 358, FR 1204, Y 23,151).

$2970* *Le Port De Trouville (S. 117)*, 1951, faded ink s., #67/75, pub. Galerie Louise Leiris, full margins, goodcond., scratch, creases, skinned spot, (11-05-92, Sotheby-NY, #227), 14 x 17⅞ in., (357 x 454 mm.), lithograph p. in colors (BP 1932, DM 4697, FR 15,891, Y 364,372).

$880* *La Racine Grise*, ballpoint pen s. FLeger, #140/250, blindstamp, (03-24-93, Venator/Hansten, #4525), image 19⁵⁄₁₆ x 25³⁄₁₆ in., (49 x 64 cm.), color lithograph on Arches (BP 596, DM 1437, FR 4892, Y 103,396).

$1498* *La Racine Noire (S. 22)*, 1948, s., #39/75, pub. L. Leiris, margins, discoloration, mount-staining, good cond., (12-01-92, Christie-London, #415), L. 14¾ x 18⁵⁄₁₆ in., (375 x 465 mm.), lithograph in colors on Arches (BP 990, DM 2388, FR 8137, Y 186,504).

$716* *Sangerin Mit Rassel Am Mikrofon*, s., #60/180, (05-08-93, Schloss Ahlden, #2858, illus.), 15¾ x 11¹³⁄₁₆ in., (40 x 30 cm.), color Pochoir on handmade (BP 467, DM 1150, FR 3881, Y 80,009).

$853* *Tete De Femme (Saphire 131)*, 1953, #39/250, pub. Societe des Amateurs d'Art, full margins, good cond., (12-03-92, Sotheby-London, #362, illus.), sheet approx. 25¾ x 19¾ in., (654 x 502 mm.), lithograph in colors on Arches (BP 550, DM 1341, FR 4579, Y 106,134).

$1330* *Le Tournesol*, 1953, s., 118/120, (12-04-92, AB Stockholm, #7091), 15¾ x 13³⁄₁₆ in., (40 x 33.5 cm.), lithograph in colors on Arches (BP 853, DM 2118, FR 7185, Y 166,042, SK 9020).

LEGER, Fernand (after)

$77* *Composition*, bears stamped sig., #162225, blindstamp Musee Fernand Leger, (12-13-92, Hindman, #272), 21 x 16½ in., color lithograph (BP 49, DM 121, FR 412, Y 9526).

$733* *Composition Aux Dominos*, s., num. 43/50, light-staining, defects, (11-30-92, Phillips-London, #450), sheet 34¾ x 27½ in., (883 x 699 mm.), half-tone reprod. w/silkscreen coloring, finished by hand, on wove (BP 484, DM 1168, FR 3964, Y 91,226).

BI *"Composition"*, d. 24, s. in plate, #14/450, est. FF1,000/1,500, (04-04-93, Pescheteau, #241), 29½ x 39¾ in., (75 x 101 cm.), color lithograph.

$200* *"Composition"*, #259/300, s. verso, (04-04-93, Pescheteau, #240), a vue 17⅛ x 38⅜ in., (43.5 x 97.5 cm.), color lithograph on wove (BP 132, DM 321, FR 1092, Y 22,771).

BI *Le Compotier (S. E16)*, 1952, s., #285/300, pub. Maeght, margins, good cond., est. BP 7/900, (12-03-92, Sotheby-London, #365, illus.), sheet 22 x 29⅞ in., (559 x 759 mm.), etching & aquatint in colors.

$1801* *Le Compotier (S. E16)*, 1952, s., #285/300, pub. Maeght, margins, good cond., (06-30-93, Sotheby-London, #488, illus.), sh 22 x 29⅞ in., (559 x 759 mm.), color etching and aquatint (BP 1207, DM 3072, FR 10,362, Y 192,971).

$1411* *Les Dominos (S. Estampes 15, Maeght 1402)*, s., 103/150, blindstamp, Maeght Editeur, (12-04-92, AB Stockholm, #7092), 16¹⁵⁄₁₆ x 12¹³⁄₁₆ in., (43 x 32.5 cm.), etching and aquatint in colors on BFK Rives (BP 905, DM 2247, FR 7623, Y 176,155, SK 9570).

$1492* *La Lecture (Estampes 23)*, 1953, s., 103/350, (12-04-92, AB Stockholm, #7093), 16¹⁵⁄₁₆ x 21⅝ in., (43 x 55 cm.), lithograph in colors on Arches (BP 957, DM 2376, FR 8061, Y 186,267, SK 10,120).

BI *La Lecture (Saphire E 23)*, 1953, s., #106/350, est. DM 3,800, (05-26-93, Lempertz, #284), 19⅞ x 27⁹⁄₁₆ in., (50.5 x 70 cm.), color lithograph on Arches wove.

BI *Les Parapluies (S. p. 238)*, 1954-55, stamp s., #5/180, completed after artist's death by Fernand Mourlot and Nadia Leger, 1959, pub. Teriade, p. Mourlot Freres, full margins, good cond.?, crease, faint staining, est. $4/600, (05-19-93, Butterfield, #2071), 17⅛ x 12¼ in., (435 x 311 mm.), lithograph in colors on wove.

BI *Swimmers, 1948,* stamp s., d. by another hand, #47/180, blindstamp, full margins, goodcond.?, foxing, light-staining, surface soiling, est. $6/800, Albert Levinson Estate, (05-19-93, Butterfield, #2070), 24½ x 17 in., (622 x 432 mm.), lithograph in colors on wove.

$303* *Three Color Serigraphs,* bearing blindstamp Serigraphie F. Leger, (10-18-92, Hindman, #463), 12¾ x 10 in., (32.4 x 25.4 cm.), serigraph (BP 185, DM 451, FR 1530, Y 36,353).

$230* *Two Figures, 1933,* stamp s., d., num., watermark, full margins, good cond.?, light-staining, foxing, surface soiling, Albert Levinson Estate, (05-19-93, Butterfield, #2069), 18 x 13 in., (457 x 330 mm.), lithograph in colors on wove (BP 149, DM 374, FR 1260, Y 25,462).

$440* *(Untitled): Two,* stamped sig., num. 149/225 & 148/225, blindstamp of pub. Musee Fernand Leger, full margins, good cond., creases, (02-24-93, Butterfield, #2946), 21 x 16½ in., (533 x 419 mm.), lithograph in colors on BFK Rives (BP 307, DM 714, FR 2422, Y 51,631).

$1100* *La Ville (From) (S. p. 238), 1959: Four,* stamp s., #100/180, pub. Teriade, full margins, good cond., staining, foxing, notations, (10-28-92, Butterfield, #2662), each sheet 26 x 20 in., (660 x 508 mm.), color lithograph on Arches (BP 701, DM 1699, FR 5768, Y 134,969).

LEGRAIN, Pierre Emil 1888-1929

BI *The Typographic Treasures In Europe,* Bartlett Orr Press, for G.P. Putnam's Sons, 1925, large quarto, num.277, est. $8/12,000, (06-10-93, Sotheby-NY, #483, illus.), binding 16⅛ x 11⅞ in., (41 x 30.2 cm.), .

LEGRAND, Auguste Claude Simon 1766-c. 1815

BI *"Jamais D'Accord" and "Le Serin Cheri" (Bocher 32, 59; P. land B., II, p. 612; Inventaire 18e Siecle, XIII, p. 565, no. 31 and pp. 564-5, no. 30), 1787 and c. 1785: A Pair,* after Nicolas Lavreince, pub. Bonnet, staining, est. BP 2/3,000, (12-01-92, Christie-London, #272, illus.), sheet 9⅛ x 6³⁄₁₆ in., (232 x 157 mm.), stipple engraving in colors.

LEGRAND, Auguste and others (after Horace VERNET)

$1741* *The Life Of Louis XIV: Set Of Eight,* laid, trimmed close to platemark, defects, mould damage, skimming, broken paper, (10-27-92, Phillips-London, #72, illus.), each sheet 14⅓ x 17½ in., (364 x 445 mm.), stipple engraving w/hand-coloring on wove (BP 1100, DM 2668, FR 9054, Y 212,966).

LEGRAND, Louis French 1863-1951

$433* *Der Bar, c. 1900-1905,* s., num., (11-28-92, Grisebach, #616, illus.), 16¹³⁄₁₆ x 11⁵⁄₁₆ in., (42.7 x 28.8 cm.), drypoint on Japan (BP 286, DM 690, FR 2342, Y 53,889).

$191* *Le Chauffeur: Fifty,* s., #3/50, watermark, (06-10-93, Hauswedell/Nolt, #549), image 16⁵⁄₁₆ x 10¹³⁄₁₆ in., (41.4 x 27.5 cm.), etching on hand-made (BP 125, DM 311, FR 1047, Y 20,274).

$993* *Frio (Ramiro 20/I und 2 blatt Ram 20/IV), c. 1892: Three,* artist's proof, s., 4th state, (06-23-93, Kornfeld, #506), etching and drypoint on Japan (BP 675, DM 1680, FR 5652, Y 108,182, SF 1495).

BI *L'Amour,* 18/20, s., est. SF 350/450, (10-14-92, Germann, #348), 17⁵⁄₁₆ x 12⅜ in., (440 x 315 mm.), etching.

$3054* *Une Loge (Kat. Bibl. Nat. Paris, 161. XIII, 157), 1910,* s., mono. stamp, i. Epr. d'essai, (06-23-93, Kornfeld, #516, illus.), etching and drypoint, colored "a la poupee" (BP 2075, DM 5168, FR 17,382, Y 332,716, SF 4600).

BI *Mother And Child Seated With Dog,* s., pub. stamp Gustave Pellet, Lugt 1193, stains in image, good cond., est. $5-700, (10-31-92, Cleveland, #304, illus.), 12¼ x 12⅜ in., (31.1 x 31.4 cm.), drypoint.

$354* *"On Se Tourne" (Exsteens 73), 1893,* mono., from the series Les Petites du Ballet, Gustave Pellet, (06-08-93, Karl/Faber, #1018A), approx. 14⅜ x 8⁷⁄₁₆ in., (36.5 x 21.5 cm.), etching and aquatint on simili-Japan (BP 233, DM 574, FR 1934, Y 37,600).

$3272* *La Petite Classe (E. Exsteens, 247, 248, 251, 254, 256, 258 et 259),1908: Seven,* whole margins, #74/100, s., (04-02-93, Picard, #142), 23¼ x 16⅛ in., (59 x 41 cm.), etchings and aquatints in black on Arches laid (BP 2155, DM 5259, FR 17,860, Y 372,538).

$2138* *La Petite Classe (Kat. Bibl. Nat., Paris, Vol. XIII, 138), 1908: Twelve,* Ou: Jeunes Danseuses, Paris, Gustave Pellet, (06-23-93, Kornfeld, #514), 23¹⁄₁₆ x 16⅛ in., (58.5 x 41 cm.), etching and drypoint on handmade (BP 1452, DM 3618, FR 12,168, Y 232,923, SF 3220).

LEGRAND, Louis Auguste Mathieu French 1863-1951

BI *Dressing A Young Dancer,* s., margins, creasing, est. BP 2/300, (04-22-93, Bonhams-Chelsea, #57), plate 10⅜ x 5¾ in., (26.4 x 14.6 cm.), etching w/aquatint.

LEGRAND ?, Louis

$444* *Les Lutteuses: Suite Of Four,* (12-10-92, Christie-S. Ken, #59, illus.), subject 13⅜ x 24⅛ in., (339 x 613 mm.), lithograph (BP 286, DM 702, FR 2399, Y 54,923).

LEGROS, Alphonse French 1837-1911

$55* *"Le Arbe De Salut",* s., hinges, yellowed, fine cond., (10-31-92, Cleveland, #307), 10 x 8 in., (25.4 x 20.3 cm.), etching (BP 35, DM 85, FR 287, Y 6813).

$217* *Au Bord De L'Eau (Bliss 604),* s., (12-04-92, Bassenge, #6872), 8⅞ x 6⅞ in., (22.5 x 17.5 cm.), etching on handmade (BP 139, DM 346, FR 1172, Y 27,091).

$55* *"Coin D'Un Bois" (W. 229 VI/VI),* s., Printer's crease, good cond., (10-31-92, Cleveland, #306), 11½ x 9 in., (29.2 x 22.9 cm.), etching (BP 35, DM 85, FR 287, Y 6813).

$110* *"Fishing",* s. A. Legros verso, (02-27-93, Dunning, #1124), pl 11¼ x 8¾ in., (28.6 x 22.2 cm.), etching (BP 77, DM 181, FR 615, Y 12,985).

$361* *Landschaft Mit Baumen An Einem Bach,* s., (12-04-92, Bassenge, #6871), 6¹³⁄₁₆ x 6⅛ in., (17.3 x 15.5 cm.), etching on handmade (BP 232, DM 575, FR 1950, Y 45,069).

BI *"La Mort Et Le Bucheron" (Wright 142 XI/XII),* pub. L'Art, good cond., est. $150-200, (10-31-92, Cleveland, #305), 12⅜ x 9¼ in., (31.4 x 23.5 cm.), etching.

$184* *Portrait De Jules Dalou, 1877: Six,* mat-staining, staining, margins, 6 proof, (02-24-93, Picard, #139), etching and drypoint on thick laid (BP 128, DM 299, FR 1013, Y 21,591).

$92* *Trois Arbres,* s., (02-24-93, Picard, #142), etching on thick wove (BP 64, DM 149, FR 506, Y 10,796).

$110* *Untitled: A Pair,* both s., very good cond.?, (07-19-92, Bakker, #253), one 11¼ x 8¾ in., (28.6 x 22.2 cm.), the other 5½ x 10½ in., (28.6 x 22.2 cm.), etching (BP 56, DM 160, FR 542, Y 13,675).

$110* *Vieillard Au Repos (Beraldi/Cary 230 II/II),* Emmanuel Jacobson Estate, (03-14-93, Hindman, #245), 3⅞ x 5¼ in., (9.8 x 13.3 cm.), drypoint (BP 77, DM 183, FR 623, Y 12,964).

LEGROS, Charles

$80* *Arents. "Ses Malles, Ses Valises, Ses Sacs De Dames, Ses Portefeuilles",* Imp. Fr. Vermaelen, very good cond., (02-12-93, Cheval/Robert, #64), 39⅜ x 25¹³⁄₁₆ in., (100 x 65.5 cm.), poster (BP 56, DM 133, FR 449, Y 9648).

LEGUEY, Luc

$522* *Ne Toussez Plus! Prenez Le Delicieux Bonbon Rhumicide Au Miel De Pins,* Roubaix-Paris, Wallays, Nisse and Cie, cond. B-, restored, (06-11-93, Boisgirard, #99), 37⅜ x 50¹³⁄₁₆ in., (95 x 129 cm.), poster (BP 343, DM 848, FR 2860, Y 55,385).

LEHEUTRE, Gustave

$310* *Les Bords Du Durtint A Provins (M. Lecomte, 138),* second state, t., s., creases, large margins, (04-02-93, Picard, #143), 6¹⁵⁄₁₆ x 9⁵⁄₁₆ in., (17.6 x 23.6 cm.), etching on old paper (BP 204, DM 498, FR 1692, Y 35,295).

LEHMAN, George

$550* *The Great Elm Tree Of Shackamaxon (Now Kensington),* discoloration, foxing, pub. William Smith, (06-11-93, Freemn/Fine Art, #132), 12½ x 18½ in., (31.8 x 47 cm.), hand-colored engraving (BP 361, DM 894, FR 3014, Y 58,355).

LEHMBRUCK, Wilhelm German 1881-1919

BI *Junglings - Halbakt, Sich Umwendend (Petermann 15), 1911,* s. by Anita Lehmbruck, est. Dm 1,500, (12-05-92, Bassenge, #7393, illus.), 6⁵⁄₁₆ x 4⅝ in., (16 x 11.8 cm.), drypoint.

$496* *Junglings-Halbakt, Sich Umwendend (Petermann 15), 1911,* s. Anita Lehmbruck, (06-08-93, Karl/Faber, #1024), approx. 6⁵⁄₁₆ x 4¾ in., (16 x 12 cm.), etching, drypoint on Maschinen hand-made (BP 326, DM 805, FR 2710, Y 52,682).

$425* *Kleopatra I (P. 18), 1911,* s. Anita Lehmbruck, (06-08-93, Karl/Faber, #1025), approx. 6⅞ x 9¼ in., (17.5 x 23.5 cm.), etching on hand-made copper print board laid on hand-made board (BP 279, DM 690, FR 2322, Y 45,141).

$1038* *Kniende (Grosse) (Petermann 13/III), 1911,* estate stamp, s. von Anita Lehmbruck, brown stained, (12-01-92, Karl/Faber, #909, illus.), 13⁹⁄₁₆ x 9¹³⁄₁₆ in., (34.5 x 25 cm.), etching and drypoint (BP 686, DM 1654, FR 5638, Y 129,233).

$638* *Macbeth V (P. 182/II), 1918,* blindstamp, (06-08-93, Karl/Faber, #1026), blindstamp 15⅜ x 11¼ in., (39 x 28.5 cm.), etching on hand-made (BP 419, DM 1035, FR 3486, Y 67,764).

$709* *Macbeth V (Petermann 182 II), 1918,* (06-05-93, Bassenge, #6266), 15⅜ x 11⅝ in., (39.1 x 29.5 cm.), drypoint on hand-made (BP 467, DM 1149, FR 3874, Y 76,057).

$664* *Medea (Petermann 97 II), 1914/15,* s. by Anita Lehmbruck, estate stamp, (12-05-92, Bassenge, #7397), 11⅝ x 9⁵⁄₁₆ in., (29.5 x 23.7 cm.), etching (BP 416, DM 1035, FR 3528, Y 82,270).

$885* *Raub I, Weib Ganz (Petermann 9 III), 1911,* s. by Anita Lehmbruck, estate stamp, (12-05-92, Bassenge, #7391), 11⁹⁄₁₆ x 9⁵⁄₁₆ in., (29.3 x 23.7 cm.), etching on imitation Japan (BP 554, DM 1380, FR 4702, Y 109,652).

$5297* *Schlafendes Madchen (Petermann 80), 1913,* s., t., (06-10-93, Hauswedell/Nolt, #552, illus.), image 9³⁄₁₆ x 6¹⁵⁄₁₆ in., (23.3 x 17.6 cm.), drypoint on Arches (BP 3465, DM 8626, FR 29,041, Y 562,255).

$5932* *Schreitender Mann, Gross (Petermann 135), 1914,* s., tears, crease, (06-10-93, Hauswedell/Nolt, #553, illus.), image 19⁹⁄₁₆ x 12⁷⁄₁₆ in., (49.7 x 31.6 cm.), drypoint on wove (BP 3880, DM 9660, FR 32,522, Y 629,657).

$664* *Die Sklavin (Cassirer 68, Petermann 89),* estate stamp, s. by Anita Lehmbruck, (12-05-92, Bassenge, #7395), 9⁵⁄₁₆ x 7 in., (23.7 x 17.8 cm.), drypoint (BP 416, DM 1035, FR 3528, Y 82,270).

$738* *Der Taum Des Weibes (Petermann 94), 1914,* s. by Anita Lehmbruck, estate stamp, (12-05-92, Bassenge, #7396), 13⁵⁄₁₆ x 9¼ in., (33.8 x 23.5 cm.), etching (BP 462, DM 1151, FR 3921, Y 91,438).

LEHNERT, Rudolf and Ernest LANDROCK

$2300* *Tunis, c. 1904,* mono. insignia recto; reprod. limitation stamp verso, (04-08-93, Christie-NY, #44, illus.), 11½ x 23⅛ in., (29.2 x 58.7 cm.), photograph, toned gelatin silver print (BP 1508, DM 3695, FR 12,507, Y 261,008).

LEIBER, Tom

$440* *Untitled, 1986,* inits., d., pub. Garner Tullis Workshop, good cond., pinhole in image, hinge remains, skinned areas, est. $800/1,200, (02-24-93, Butterfield, #3073), (77.5 x 111.8 cm.), monotype in colors on Sommerset (BP 307, DM 714, FR 2422, Y 51,631).

$715* *Untitled, 1986,* inits., d., pub. Garner Tullis Workshop, very good cond., (10-28-92, Butterfield, #3009), 29⅛ x 43 in., (74 x 109.2 cm.), color monotype on Somerset wove (BP 456, DM 1104, FR 3749, Y 87,730).

LEIBL, Wilhelm German 1844-1900

$422* *Kopf Eines Knaben Von Vorn (Waldmann 11),* plate s. W. Leibl, (03-24-93, Venator/Hansten, #2610), 3¼ x 2⅝ in., (8.2 x 6.7 cm.), etching (BP 286, DM 689, FR 2346, Y 49,583).

LEIBOVITZ, Annie

$1650* *"Louis Armstrong, Greens, New York", 1971,* s., t., d., edit. 3/25, Dixon Collection, (11-16-92, Butterfield, #6063, illus.), 14¼ x 9½ in., (362.6 x 241.7 mm.), photograph, platinum print (BP 1086, DM 2631, FR 8861, Y 205,198).

LEIGHTON, Barbara (Barleigh) 1911-1986

$208* *Cool Water,* #21/100, s., t., prov., (11-16-92, Hodgins, #50), 12 x 15 in., (30.5 x 38.1 cm.), color block print on paper (BP 137, DM 332, FR 1118, Y 25,958, C$ 264).

$216* *Emerald Lake,* #30/100, s., t., prov., (11-16-92, Hodgins, #2), 11¼ x 14¾ in., (28.6 x 37.5 cm.), block print on paper (BP 142, DM 344, FR 1161, Y 26,956, C$ 275).

$216* *Emerald Lake,* #16/100, s., t., prov., (11-16-92, Hodgins, #98), 11¼ x 14¾ in., (28.6 x 37.5 cm.), block print on paper (BP 142, DM 344, FR 1161, Y 26,956, C$ 275).

LEIGHTON, Clare Anglo/American 1901-1988

$10* *"Fat Stock Market: December" (Boston Public Library 217), 1933,* from The Farmer's Year, Collins & Co., (05-15-93, Cleveland, #403), 8 x 10⁵⁄₁₆ in., (20.3 x 26.2 cm.), wood engraving (BP 7, DM 16, FR 54, Y 1109).

$715* *"Hop Pickers", 1930 and "Young Ferns": Two,* each s.; first #54/75, t.; second t., ded., (12-09-92, Grogan, #99), first 8½ x 10½ in., (21.6 x 26.7 cm.), second 3¾ x 3 in., (21.6 x 26.7 cm.), woodcut (BP 456, DM 1122, FR 3830, Y 88,655).

$715* *Landing (L. Of C. 19), 1931,* s., t., num. 74/100, margins, crease foxmark, very good cond., (09-19-92, Christie-E, #37), borderline 8⁵⁄₁₆ x 12½ in., (211 x 318 mm.), woodcut on Japan (BP 411, DM 1071, FR 3667, Y 89,085).

$550* *"Landing",* s., good cond., (08-08-92, Litchfield, #104), 8¼ x 12½ in., (21 x 31.8 cm.), woodcut (BP 286, DM 809, FR 2734, Y 70,198).

BI *New England Industries, Includ. "Maple Sugar", "Farming", "Logging","Ice Cutting", "Whaling", "Lobsters", "Ship Building", "Grist Mill", "Marble Quarry", "Cod Fishing", "Tobacco" and "Cranberry Gathering": Set Of Twelve,* orig. designs for a series of Wedgewood plates, s., t., i., from a broken set, 9 num., full margins, adhesive tape, excellent cond., catalog cover lot, est. BP 3,5/4,000, (10-27-92, Phillips-London, #282, illus.), woodcut on simili japan.

$220* *"Resting", 1931,* artists proof, i., very good/good cond., (02-07-93, Bakker, #158), image 9⅛ x 11⅛ in., (23.2 x 28.3 cm.), wood engraving (BP 152, DM 365, FR 1233, Y 27,377).

$696* *The Return Of The Native, 1929: Thirty-Two,* from the series of 61 illus., s., num., mounted, good cond., (10-27-92, Phillips-London, #283), sheet 6⅛ x 4½ in., (156 x 114 mm.), woodcut on laid japan (BP 440, DM 1067, FR 3619, Y 85,138).

$495* *"Sheep Shearing" and "Oyster Houses, Cape Cod": Two,* both s. Clare Leighton, num. 21/30, 161/200, very good cond.?, (11-21-92, Bakker, #25, illus.), image, one 8 x 10¼ in., (20.3 x 26 cm.), the other 8 x 9¾ in., (20.3 x 26 cm.), wood engraving (BP 326, DM 789, FR 2658, Y 61,560).

$880* *Stoving,* s., t., num. II/XX, residue of hinges, hinged to mat, very good cond., (12-04-92, Doyle, #120, illus.), 8 x 10¾ in., (203 x 273 mm.), wood engraving (BP 564, DM 1401, FR 4754, Y 109,863).

$165* *Turning The Plow, 1937,* s., t., #3/40, mint cond., designed for "Country Matter's", (05-15-93, Cleveland, #404), 3 x 5 in., (7.6 x 12.7 cm.), wood engraving on Japan (BP 107, DM 265, FR 892, Y 18,291).

LEIGHTON, Clare Veronica Hope Anglo/American 1901-1988

$205 *"Turning The Plough",* s., (06-11-93, G.A. Key, #79), 7 x 5 in., (17.8 x 12.7 cm.), woodblock engraving (BP 135, DM 333, FR 1123, Y 21,751).

LEIGHTON, Edmund Blair (after)

$174* *God Speed,* s., blindstamp, pub. I. P. Mendoza Ltd., 1901, margins, foxing, (06-16-93, Bonhams-Chelsea, #510), pl. 28½ x 20¾ in., (72.4 x 52.7 cm.), photogravure (BP 116, DM 289, FR 969, Y 18,558).

LEINARDI, Ermanno b. 1933

$332* *Afternoon Light, 1984,* #49/99, s., d., (04-21-93, Germann, #593), 23⅝ x 23⅝ in., (600 x 600 mm.), color lithograph (BP 215, DM 531, FR 1795, Y 36,754, SF 483).

LEISTIKOW, Walter 1865-1908

BI *Blick In Einem Dunklen Eichenwald,* s., est. DM 2,000, (12-04-92, Bassenge, #6875), 6¾ x 4⁹⁄₁₆ in., (17.2 x 11.6 cm.), etching on thick wove.

$708* *Markische Landschaft,* s., (06-04-93, Bassenge, #5742), 3⅜ x 3¼ in., (8.5 x 8.3 cm.), etching on copper print paper (BP 468, DM 1150, FR 3875, Y 76,359).

$197* *"Waldsee",* from Pan, (03-24-93, Venator/Hansten, #4526), pl. 6¾ x 8¹⁵⁄₁₆ in., (17.2 x 22.8 cm.), etching on hand-made (BP 133, DM 322, FR 1095, Y 23,147).

LEIZELT, Balth Frederic
$440* *"Vue De La Nouvelle New York",* (06-02-93, Doyle, #73), 10 x 15½ in., (25.4 x 39.4 cm.), hand-colored engraving (BP 286, DM 702, FR 2368, Y 47,210).

LELANDE, Jacques   French contemporary
BI   *Springtime Picnic,* s., #57/275, est. $250/350, (05-16-93, Hanzel, #485), 23 x 19 in., (58.4 x 48.3 cm.), color lithograph.

LELEE, C.
$755* *Au Depart De Nimes. "Autocars PLM Par Uzes, Le Pont Du Gard, Aigues-Mortes, Saint-Gilles",* p. Serre & Cie, very good cond., (11-19-92, Ribeyre/Baron, #112), 42⁵⁄₁₆ x 30⅞ in., (107.5 x 78.5 cm.), poster (BP 497, DM 1204, FR 4055, Y 93,894).

LELOIR, M.
BI   *Theatre National De L'Opera: La Cigalle. Musique De J. Massenet,* Imp. Devambez, good cond., (02-12-93, Cheval/Robert, #164), 34⅝ x 21⅝ in., (88 x 55 cm.), poster.

LELONG, B.
$1477* *...Offrez-Lui Un Kodak Pour Ses Entrennes,* p. Hachard & Cie, folds, repairs, backed on linen, (05-07-93, Christie-S. Ken, #57, illus.), 39 x 58½ in., (99.1 x 148.6 cm.), color lithograph (BP 935, DM 2335, FR 7869, Y 162,629).

$556* *Kodak Girl Looking At Friends,* defects, trimmed, laid on board, (05-07-93, Christie-S. Ken, #51, illus.), 16 x 23¾ in., (40.6 x 60.3 cm.), color lithograph (BP 352, DM 879, FR 2962, Y 61,220).

$556* *Kodak Girl With Friends In A Meadow,* tears, laid on board, (05-07-93, Christie-S. Ken, #52, illus.), 17 x 16 in., (43.2 x 40.6 cm.), color lithograph (BP 352, DM 879, FR 2962, Y 61,220).

$382* *Kodak, Chaque Saison A Ses Plaisirs Kodak,* p. Hachard & Cie, fold, tears, defects, laid on board, (05-07-93, Christie-S. Ken, #50, illus.), 16 x 23½ in., (40.6 x 59.7 cm.), color lithograph (BP 242, DM 604, FR 2035, Y 42,061).

$208* *Offrez Vous Un Kodak,* corners damaged, tears, water staining, backed on linen, (05-07-93, Christie-S. Ken, #49), 17 x 24 in., (43.2 x 61 cm.), color lithograph (BP 132, DM 329, FR 1108, Y 22,902).

$1564* *Revivex Dans Vos Photos Kodak,* p. Hachard & Cie, creases, tears, backed on linen, (05-07-93, Christie-S. Ken, #58, illus.), 38¼ x 58¼ in., (97.2 x 148 cm.), color lithograph (BP 990, DM 2473, FR 8332, Y 172,209).

$208* *Voulez-Vous Faire Du Cine? Venez Voir Le Cine-Kodak,* p. Hachard & Cie, creases, defects, laid on board, (05-07-93, Christie-S. Ken, #54, illus.), 38½ x 11¾ in., (97.8 x 29.8 cm.), color lithograph (BP 132, DM 329, FR 1108, Y 22,902).

LEM
$130* *La Belle Granero,* cond. A, (03-16-93, Boisgirard, #141), 47¼ x 34⁷⁄₁₆ in., (120 x 87.5 cm.), poster (BP 90, DM 216, FR 734, Y 15,201).

$1164* *Chemins De Fer De L'Ouest. Grand Casino Municipal De Saint-Malo, 1899,* Paris, Imp. Chaix, cond. A-, (06-11-93, Boisgirard, #100), 48¼ x 35⁷⁄₁₆ in., (122.5 x 90 cm.), poster (BP 765, DM 1892, FR 6378, Y 123,501).

$1064* *Dieppe(...) Transformation De La Plage, 1901,* Paris, Imp. Chaix, cond. B+, (06-11-93, Boisgirard, #103, illus.), 61⁷⁄₁₆ x 42⁵⁄₁₆ in., (156 x 107.5 cm.), poster (BP 699, DM 1729, FR 5830, Y 112,891).

$964* *Pierrot Absinthe. Garcon, Un Pierrot!!!, 1900,* Paris, Imp. Chaix, cond. B+, (06-11-93, Boisgirard, #102), 35⁷⁄₁₆ x 47¹³⁄₁₆ in., (90 x 121.5 cm.), poster (BP 633, DM 1567, FR 5282, Y 102,281).

$402* *La Place Clichy (...) Nouveautes De La Saison, 1899,* Paris, Imp. Chaix, cond. A-, (06-11-93, Boisgirard, #101),

---

63³⁄₁₆ x 43⁵⁄₁₆ in., (160.5 x 110 cm.), poster (BP 264, DM 653, FR 2203, Y 42,653).

LEMCKE, Dietmar   b. 1930
$256* *Hummer, 1966/1967,* s., d, #47/100, wear, (09-18-92, Schloss Ahlden, #1021), 21¼ x 27³⁄₁₆ in., (54 x 69 cm.), color etching on hand-made (BP 150, DM 380, FR 1299, Y 31,640).

LEMESLE, B.   French 18th cent.
$105* *Enee Porte Son Pere Anchise,* (12-10-92, Sloan, #2097), 12⅛ x 14¾ in., (30.8 x 37.5 cm.), engraving (BP 68, DM 166, FR 567, Y 12,989).

LEMIEUX, Annette   American b. 1957
BI   *"I Am", 1989,* d., num. on label verso, excellent cond., est. $3/500, (09-11-92, Skinner, #122, illus.), sight 12⅞ x 7¼ in., (32.7 x 18.4 cm.), photograph.

BI   *Mon Amour,* s., t., num. sc08, d. 1987, prov., est. $5/7,000, (05-04-93, Sotheby-NY, #272, illus.), 30 x 47¼ in., (76.2 x 120 cm.), b/w photograph.

LEMIEUX, F.   20th cent.
$133* *"Printemps D'Hiver",* #137/150, s., d. F. Lemieux 75, (04-20-93, Encans, #67), 16¾ x 23⅝ in., (42.5 x 60 cm.), serigraph (BP 86, DM 212, FR 715, Y 14,675, C$ 167).

LEMIEUX, Jean Paul   Canadian b. 1904
$109* *"Jean-Paul Lemieux Retrouve Maria Chapdelaine": Set of Ten,* s., d. Jean-Paul Lemieux 81, #30/125, (09-15-92, Encans, #69), lithograph (BP 58, DM 162, FR 551, Y 13,532, C$ 133).

$217* *"Jean-Paul Lemieux Retrouve Maria Chapdelaine": Ten,* s., d. 81 in plate, #3010/5000, (06-16-93, Encans, #70), photolithograph (BP 145, DM 360, FR 1209, Y 23,144, C$ 278).

$174* *La Petite Poule D'Eau,* #36/200, (11-17-92, Encans, #59), 3⁹⁄₁₆ x 4¾ in., (9 x 12 cm.), color lithograph (BP 115, DM 277, FR 934, Y 21,639, C$ 222).

$350* *"Le Porteur D'Eau",* #111/200, s. Jean Paul Lemieux, (05-18-93, Encans, #96), 10¹³⁄₁₆ x 8⅞ in., (27.5 x 22.5 cm.), lithograph (BP 228, DM 568, FR 1918, Y 39,006, C$ 444).

$1065* *"Saint-Francois",* #38/50, s. Jean-Paul Lemieux, s. in plate fecit, (03-16-93, Encans, #74), 39⅞ x 5⁷⁄₁₆ in., (101.3 x 13.8 cm.), lithograph (BP 735, DM 1771, FR 6017, Y 124,532, C$ 1332).

LEMKE, William   American 20th cent.
$121* *Joshua Tree,* s., (05-16-93, Hindman, #361), 15¼ x 19¼ in., photograph, silver print (BP 79, DM 195, FR 658, Y 13,474).

$121* *Old Barn,* s., (05-16-93, Hindman, #362), 13½ x 10¼ in., photograph, silver print (BP 79, DM 195, FR 658, Y 13,474).

$66* *Skunk Cabbage,* s., (05-16-93, Hindman, #363), 15⅛ x 18¼ in., photograph, silver print (BP 43, DM 106, FR 359, Y 7350).

LEMMEN, Georges   Belgian 1865-1916
$811* *L'Estampe, 1909,* Imp. Monnom, Bruxelles, (12-05-92, Bassenge, #7605), 13¹⁄₁₆ x 8¹⁵⁄₁₆ in., (33.2 x 22.7 cm.), color lithograph (BP 508, DM 1264, FR 4309, Y 100,483).

LEMMERT, C.
$33* *Nude Girl,* init., d. '99, (06-11-93, DuMouchelle, #2260), 13 x 7½ in., (33 x 19.1 cm.), lithograph (BP 22, DM 54, FR 181, Y 3501).

LEMORDANT
$273* *Finistere. "Ses Costumes, Ses Sites, Sa Mer",* very good cond., (11-19-92, Ribeyre/Baron, #113), 42⅛ x 30¹¹⁄₁₆ in., (107 x 78 cm.), poster (BP 180, DM 435, FR 1466, Y 33,951).

LEMOYNE, Serge   Canadian b. 1941
$219* *"Le 50eme But De Lafleur",* #2/35, s., d. Lemoyne 78, (05-18-93, Encans, #105), 23⅛ x 34⁷⁄₁₆ in., (58.8 x 87.5 cm.), lithograph (BP 143, DM 355, FR 1200, Y 24,407, C$ 278).

BI   *"Bleu, Blanc, Rouge",* #6/20, s., d. Lemoyne 78, (05-18-93, Encans, #103), 23⅛ x 34⁷⁄₁₆ in., (58.8 x 87.5 cm.), lithograph.

$105* *"Le Gros Bill"*, #4/30, s., d. Lemoyne 78, (05-18-93, Encans, #102), 23⅛ x 34⁷⁄₁₆ in., (58.8 x 87.5 cm.), lithograph (BP 68, DM 170, FR 575, Y 11,702, C$ 133).

LEMPICKA, Tamara de Polish 1898-1980
$248* *Lady In Lace,* s., t., #134/300, (12-13-92, Hindman, #301), 26 x 15¼ in., color lithograph (BP 159, DM 390, FR 1328, Y 30,682).
$6227* *Mandolinenspielerin,* #71/100, s., (11-13-92, Kunsthaus, #676, illus.), 24⁷⁄₁₆ x 15¹¹⁄₁₆ in., (62 x 39.8 cm.), color heliogravure (photoengraving) on wove (BP 4024, DM 9776, FR 32,965, Y 772,868).

LENFER
$622* *Chasseurs,* before letters, Paris, Imp. Camis, cond. B+, (06-11-93, Boisgirard, #105), 51³⁄₁₆ x 39⅜ in., (130 x 100 cm.), poster (BP 409, DM 1011, FR 3408, Y 65,995).

LENHART, Franz b. 1898
$1182* *Campionati Del Mondo Di Sci, Febraio 1941-XIX,* fold marks, tear, (02-04-93, Christie-S. Ken, #13, illus.), 55 x 39½ in., (139.7 x 100.3 cm.), color lithograph backed on linen (BP 825, DM 1946, FR 6600, Y 147,033).
$205* *Hutter, c. 1930,* creases, excell. cond., (02-04-93, Christie-S. Ken, #89, illus.), 37 x 24 in., (94 x 61 cm.), color lithograph (BP 143, DM 338, FR 1145, Y 25,501).
$504* *Internationales Tanzturnier, 1926: Six,* creasing, tears, (02-04-93, Christie-S. Ken, #88, illus.), 39½ x 29 in., (100.3 x 73.7 cm.), color lithograph (BP 352, DM 830, FR 2814, Y 62,694).
$158* *Spanel, c. 1930,* excell. cond., (02-04-93, Christie-S. Ken, #90), 39½ x 25½ in., (100.3 x 64.8 cm.), color lithograph (BP 110, DM 260, FR 882, Y 19,654).

LENK, Kaspar Thomas b. 1933
BI *Komposition Mit Silberflache, 1969,* artist's proof IV a, s., d., est. SF 120/150, (10-14-92, Germann, #349), 23⅜ x 23⅜ in., (593 x 593 mm.), color serigraph.

LENNON, John British 1940-1980
$18,400* *"Bag One", 1970: Thirteen,* num., poem, frontispiece and explanatory page, bears sig., (06-23-93, Sotheby-NY, #359, illus.), 23 x 30 in., (58.4 x 76.2 cm.), lithograph, reprods. in sepia and ink (BP 12,500, DM 31,134, FR 104,724, Y 2,004,576).
$22,000* *Bag One, 1970: Fourteen,* suite, edit. HCXXX 111/VL, (11-28-92, Dunning, #1106), 22½ x 30 in., (57.2 x 76.2 cm.), lithograph (BP 14,521, DM 35,049, FR 118,983, Y 2,738,021).
$5500* *From The "Bag One" Portfolio: Three,* plus the bag s. John Lennon, #213/300, s., pub. Cinnamon Press, (06-11-93, DuMouchelle, #2012, illus.), 22½ x 30 in., (57.2 x 76.2 cm.), lithograph (BP 3614, DM 8939, FR 30,137, Y 583,554).

LENOIR, Marcel
$403* *Portrait Of A Woman,* L'Estampe Moderne blindstamp, margins, good condition, light-staining, foxing, (03-31-93, Butterfield, #5242), 15¹⁄₁₆ x 10½ in., (38.3 x 26.7 cm.), lithograph printed in colors on wove (BP 266, DM 648, FR 2202, Y 46,343).
$1093* *Two Women Reading A Postcard,* s., #167/200, good condition, touched-in surface abrasions in image,linen-backed, (03-31-93, Butterfield, #5243, illus.), 13¾ x 28⅛ in., (34.9 x 71.4 cm.), lithograph printed in colors on wove (BP 723, DM 1758, FR 5973, Y 125,690).

LENTZ, Elizabeth
$66* *"Roof Patterns",* s., t., #2/50, (06-11-93, Freemn/Fine Art, #132A), 8⅞ x 6⅞ in., (22.5 x 17.5 cm.), etching (BP 43, DM 107, FR 362, Y 7003).

LENZ, M.
$195 *Kriegsanleihe, 1917,* J. Weiner, folds, edge damage, (09-24-92, Alderfer, #312), 37½ x 20¼ in., (95.3 x 51.4 cm.), (BP 114, DM 289, FR 981, Y 23,457).

LEONARD, Robert
$621* *Grammophon Tanz Orchester,* (01-31-93, Morelle/Marchan, #162, illus.), 37⅜ x 55⅛ in., (95 x 140 cm.), poster on Japan (BP 418, DM 1000, FR 3382, Y 77,470).

LEONCIO
$60 *Feria De Sevilla, 1954,* Jose MaVentura Hita, good cond., (09-24-92, Alderfer, #299), 36½ x 24½ in., (92.7 x 62.2 cm.), (BP 35, DM 89, FR 302, Y 7218).

LEOPOLD, Levy
$51* *"Montlery", "Normandie", "Provence" and "Picardie": Four,* s., num., full margins, (05-06-93, Laurin, #55), drypoint (BP 32, DM 80, FR 270, Y 5611).

LEPAULLE, Gabriel (after)
BI *L'Accompagne,* by F. Girard, trimmed, laid down, repaired tear, est. BP 70/100, (03-03-93, Bonhams-Chelsea, #138), image 14¼ x 25¼ in., (36.2 x 64.1 cm.), mezzotint.
BI *L'Accompagne,* by F. Girard, trimmed, laid down, repaired tear, est. BP 5/70, (06-30-93, Bonhams-Chelsea, #133), image 14¼ x 25¼ in., (36.2 x 64.1 cm.), mezzotint.

LEPERE, A.
$354* *Le Grand Marche Aux Pommes (A. Lotz Brissonneau, 35, Ch. Saulnier, 435), 1917,* #28/150, s., large untrimmed margins, (06-16-93, Ader Tajan, #114), 11⅛ x 17¹¹⁄₁₆ in., (28.3 x 45 cm.), etching on thin Japan (BP 236, DM 588, FR 1972, Y 37,756).
$182* *Scene De Rue,* s., small margins, (02-03-93, Ader Tajan, #174), 9¹³⁄₁₆ x 6¹¹⁄₁₆ in., (25 x 17 cm.), etching (BP 127, DM 300, FR 1016, Y 22,640).

LEPERE, August Louis
$357* *View Of Amsterdam From The Docks, c. 1900,* s., annot. 35 proofs, stamp, trimmed margins, time/mat stain, (12-08-92, Swann, #177), 10⅝ x 6¾ in., (27 x 17.1 cm.), etching (BP 224, DM 556, FR 1895, Y 44,249).

LEPERE, Auguste French 1849-1918
$560* *"La Foire De Saint Jean De Monts", "Le Dimanche Au Cabaret" and "Grandes Marees, Rochers De Sion" (Ch. Saunier 345, 346, 347), 1907: Three,* first two, s., num.; third, s., stamped, (06-11-93, Picard, #101), between 5¾ x 8⅜ in., (146 x 213 mm.), and 9⁷⁄₁₆ x 11¹⁵⁄₁₆ in., (146 x 213 mm.), etchings on Japan pelure (BP 368, DM 910, FR 3068, Y 59,416).
$115* *L'Ondee, 1900,* s., t., #1st st 4/8, margins, good cond., corner torn, mat stain, buckling, surface soiling, prov., inkstamp, (05-19-93, Butterfield, #2072), 5⅛ x 7¹⁄₁₆ in., (130 x 179 mm.), etching on tissue-thin laid (BP 75, DM 187, FR 630, Y 12,731).
BI *Outdoor Tavern Scene, "A L'Ami Jules",* s., i. A. Lepere, est. $8/1,200, (09-25-92, Wolf, #3, illus.), 12 x 18 in., (30.5 x 45.7 cm.), lithograph.
$2997* *Rouen Illustre (Lotz Brissonneau 166 a 177), 1913: Twenty-Three,* complete series, #1/50, stamped, s., reddish stains, (06-11-93, Picard, #100), 25¹⁵⁄₁₆ x 19¹¹⁄₁₆ in., (660 x 500 mm.), engravings (BP 1969, DM 4871, FR 16,422, Y 317,984).

LEPERE, Louis Auguste 1849-1918
BI *2e Exposition Des Peintres Lithographes, 1899,* lit., Impies Lemercier, Paris, est. DM 1,200, (12-05-92, Bassenge, #7606), 19⅝ x 25¼ in., (49.9 x 64.2 cm.), lithograph.

LEPICIE, Bernard Francois French 1698-1755
BI *La Gouvernante (Bocher 24), 1739,* est. DM 900, (12-04-92, Bassenge, #6639), 14⅝ x 10⁹⁄₁₆ in., (37.1 x 26.8 cm.), etching and engraving.
BI *L'Amour Oiseleur, c. 1734,* after F. Boucher, address, dust, (05-15-93, Loudmer, #157), 12⁷⁄₁₆ x 9¹¹⁄₁₆ in., (316 x 246 mm.), sh 15⁷⁄₁₆ x 11¹⁵⁄₁₆ in., (316 x 246 mm.), etching and copper engraving on laid w/T DUPUY FIN/ AUVERGNE watermark.
$4329* *"Le Toton" and "Le Chateau De Cartes" (Bocher 50, II; P. and B., II,p. 664, nos 13 and p. 663, no. 5; Inventaire 18e Siecle, XIV, pp.405-6, nos. 62, 64), 1742-3: Two,* after Jean-Baptiste Simeon Chardin, 1st state of 2, pub. L. Surugue,narrow to thread margins, trimmed, surface dirt, very good cond., (12-01-92, Christie-London, #246, illus.), plate 8⁹⁄₁₆ x 8¼ in., (218 x 209 mm.), engraving (BP 2860, DM 6900, FR 23,514, Y 538,969).

LEPPIEN, Jean 1910-1991
BI *7 U.F.O., 1971: Seven,* #43/75, s., est. DM 4,500, (11-13-92, Kunsthaus, #678), color screen print on wove.

LERFELDT, Hans Henrik

$169* *Composition,* s. Lerfeldt 1970, 15/20, (09-30-92, Kunsthallen, #182), color etching (BP 95, DM 240, FR 811, Y 20,281, DK 920).

$948* *Erotic Compositions: Five,* s., (09-30-92, Kunsthallen, #183), color etching and color lithograph (BP 535, DM 1344, FR 4547, Y 113,765, DK 5175).

$147* *Kompositioner, 1972: Two,* s., (03-24-93, Kunsthallen, #224), etching (BP 100, DM 240, FR 817, Y 17,272, DK 920).

LERICHE, Y.

BI *"Arch De Triomphe", c. 1920's,* s., est. $20/40, (08-14-92, DuMouchelle, #1397), 10¼ x 7½ in., (26 x 19.1 cm.), engraving.

BI *"La Concourse", c. 1920's,* s., est. $20/40, (08-14-92, DuMouchelle, #1393), 7 x 9¼ in., (17.8 x 23.5 cm.), engraving.

BI *"L'Opera", c. 1920's,* s., est. $20/40, (08-14-92, DuMouchelle, #1390), 6¾ x 9¾ in., (17.1 x 24.8 cm.), engraving.

BI *Notre Dame, c. 1920's,* s., est. $20/40, (08-14-92, DuMouchelle, #1400), 12¾ x 7½ in., (32.4 x 19.1 cm.), engraving.

BI *"Opera", c. 1920's,* s., est. $10/30, (08-14-92, DuMouchelle, #1395), 9 x 5 in., (22.9 x 12.7 cm.), engraving.

LEROUX, G.

BI *Art Nouveau Style Woman Holding A Luminous Globe With Fair PavilionsIn The Background, 1900,* linen-backed, Universal Exposition-Paris 1990, est. $1,5/2,500, (04-29-93, Swann, #134, illus.), 50 x 37 in., (127 x 94 cm.), color lithograph poster.

LERPINIERE, Daniel (after George ROBERTSON)

BI *"View Of London And Westminster From Highgate" and "View Of London And Westminster From Denmark Hill": A Pair,* pub. John Boydell, 1779, a scratched letter proof, narrow margins, repaired tear through sky, other trimmed to plate w/tears through titles, est. BP 1/1,500, (10-27-92, Phillips-London, #112, illus.), plate 18⅞ x 23¾ in., (479 x 603 mm.), etching w/engraving on laid.

LESLIE, George Dunlop (after)

$143* *Making Pot Pourri, 1881,* by F. Stacpoole, blindstamp, pub. Thomas Agnew and Sons, margins, (11-12-92, Bonhams-Chelsea, #32), plate 28 x 26½ in., (71.1 x 67.3 cm.), hand-colored mezzotint and gum arabic (BP 94, DM 227, FR 764, Y 17,731).

$126* *Showing Off The Ring,* (11-12-92, Bonhams-Chelsea, #8), image 13⅞ x 25⅞ in., (35.2 x 65.7 cm.), hand-colored reproduction (BP 83, DM 200, FR 673, Y 15,623).

LESOURD, J.-L.

$2550* *Montricine. Essence Pour Automobiles, c. 1900,* Paris, Imp. Courmont Freres, cond. A-, (06-11-93, Boisgirard, #106, illus.), 53¹⁵⁄₁₆ x 37¹³⁄₁₆ in., (137 x 96 cm.), poster (BP 1675, DM 4144, FR 13,973, Y 270,557).

LESQUES

$1737* *Excelsoir Illustre Quotidien,* p. Daude Freres, folds, tears, defects, backed on linen, laid on board, (05-07-93, Christie-S. Ken, #97, illus.), 51 x 78 in., (129.5 x 198.1 cm.), color lithograph (BP 1100, DM 2746, FR 9254, Y 191,257).

$434* *Man On A Telegraph Pole,* folds, repairs, defects, backed on linen, (05-07-93, Christie-S. Ken, #94, illus.), 39¾ x 45¾ in., (101 x 116.2 cm.), color lithograph (BP 275, DM 686, FR 2312, Y 47,787).

LESSER-URY German 1861-1931

$722* *Der Absinthtrinker,* s., artist's proof, (11-28-92, Grisebach, #812, illus.), 7¹³⁄₁₆ x 10¹³⁄₁₆ in., (19.8 x 27.4 cm.), woodcut on handmade (BP 477, DM 1150, FR 3905, Y 89,857).

$361* *Bauerngehoft, c. 1884,* s., num., (11-28-92, Grisebach, #804, illus.), 5⁹⁄₁₆ x 7¹⁵⁄₁₆ in., (14.2 x 20.2 cm.), woodcut on handmade (BP 238, DM 575, FR 1952, Y 44,928).

$542* *Bauerngehoft, c. 1884,* s., num., (11-28-92, Grisebach, #803, illus.), 5¹¹⁄₁₆ x 8¹⁄₁₆ in., (14.4 x 20.5 cm.), woodcut on handmade (BP 358, DM 863, FR 2931, Y 67,455).

$542* *Baumgruppen Am See, c. 1910,* s., (11-28-92, Grisebach, #807, illus.), 5⁹⁄₁₆ x 7¹⁵⁄₁₆ in., (14.2 x 20.3 cm.), woodcut and soft-ground etching on Japan (BP 358, DM 863, FR 2931, Y 67,455).

$2815* *Berliner Strassenszene Mit Passantin, c. 1920,* s., (11-28-92, Grisebach, #821, illus.), 9¹¹⁄₁₆ x 5¹³⁄₁₆ in., (24.6 x 14.8 cm.), woodcut on thin Japan (BP 1858, DM 4485, FR 15,224, Y 350,342).

$2599* *Berliner Strassenszene, c. 1920,* s., artist's proof, (11-28-92, Grisebach, #823, illus.), 7⅞ x 5⁹⁄₁₆ in., (20 x 14.2 cm.), woodcut on handmade (BP 1716, DM 4141, FR 14,056, Y 323,460).

$938* *"Birken Am See", c. 1920,* s., t., (11-28-92, Grisebach, #818, illus.), 7 x 5¹⁄₁₆ in., (17.8 x 12.8 cm.), aquatint on copper print paper (BP 619, DM 1494, FR 5073, Y 116,739).

$1155* *Birkengruppe Am See, c. 1920,* s., artist's proof, (11-28-92, Grisebach, #814, illus.), 4⅝ x 3⁷⁄₁₆ in., (11.8 x 8.8 cm.), drypoint on copper print paper (BP 762, DM 1840, FR 6247, Y 143,746).

$2166* *Blick Auf Die Strasse Mit Droschken,* s., num., (11-28-92, Grisebach, #820, illus.), 7⅝ x 10¹¹⁄₁₆ in., (19.3 x 27.1 cm.), lithograph on wove (BP 1430, DM 3451, FR 11,714, Y 269,571).

$2382* *Dame Auf Regennasser Strasse, c. 1920,* s., t., (11-28-92, Grisebach, #819, illus.), 15⅜ x 10⁷⁄₁₆ in., (39 x 26.5 cm.), lithograph on handmade (BP 1572, DM 3795, FR 12,883, Y 296,453).

$895* *Dame Im Cafe,* s., t., #24/100, full margins, good cond., occasional foxing, left corners of sheet glued to mount, Late Gerhard Brauer Coll., (05-27-93, Sotheby-Amstrdm, #792, illus.), 8⅛ x 5⅞ in., (207 x 149 mm.), etching on laid (BP 573, DM 1436, FR 4840, Y 95,948, G 1610).

$650* *Dame Mit Grossem Hut, c. 1915,* s., (11-28-92, Grisebach, #811, illus.), 6⁷⁄₁₆ x 4¾ in., (16.3 x 12 cm.), lithograph on handmade (BP 429, DM 1036, FR 3515, Y 80,896).

$794* *Dame Und Kind Im Tiergarten, c. 1920,* s., (11-28-92, Grisebach, #817, illus.), 9¹⁄₁₆ x 6⅝ in., (23 x 16.8 cm.), drypoint on copper print paper (BP 524, DM 1265, FR 4294, Y 98,818).

$1011* *Dame Und Kind Im Tiergarten, c. 1920,* s., num., (11-28-92, Grisebach, #816, illus.), 9¹⁄₁₆ x 6¹¹⁄₁₆ in., (23 x 17 cm.), woodcut with soft-ground etching on thin handmade Japan (BP 667, DM 1611, FR 5468, Y 125,825).

$2310* *Dame, Eine Droschke Rufend, c. 1920,* s., num., (11-28-92, Grisebach, #822, illus.), 8³⁄₁₆ x 6⅛ in., (20.8 x 15.6 cm.), woodcut on wove (BP 1525, DM 3680, FR 12,493, Y 287,492).

BI *Droschke Unter Bahnunterfuhrung, 1914,* s., blindstamp, est. DM 2,000, (05-26-93, Lempertz, #512), sh 13⁹⁄₁₆ x 10½ in., (34.5 x 26.7 cm.), etching on hand-made.

BI *Erntezeit: Beim Kornpuppenbinden, 1922,* s., est. DM 1200, (12-01-92, Karl/Faber, #1320), 7⅞ x 5¹¹⁄₁₆ in., (20 x 14.5 cm.), etching.

$325* *Grabender Mann,* s., (11-28-92, Grisebach, #805, illus.), 7 x 3¹⁵⁄₁₆ in., (17.8 x 10 cm.), woodcut on copper print paper (BP 215, DM 518, FR 1758, Y 40,448).

$706* *Gracht In Holland, 1922,* s., num., (12-01-92, Karl/Faber, #1319), 4⁵⁄₁₆ x 5½ in., (11 x 14 cm.), etching on handmade (BP 466, DM 1125, FR 3835, Y 87,898).

$505* *Grosse Birke, 1919,* s., d., (11-28-92, Grisebach, #813, illus.), 10½ x 7⁹⁄₁₆ in., (26.7 x 19.2 cm.), lithograph on wove (BP 333, DM 805, FR 2731, Y 62,850).

$577* *Grunewaldsee,* s., num., (11-28-92, Grisebach, #827, illus.), 6¹⁵⁄₁₆ x 4¹⁵⁄₁₆ in., (17.7 x 12.6 cm.), drypoint on handmade (BP 381, DM 919, FR 3121, Y 71,811).

$1083* *Grunewaldsee Bei Sonnenuntergang,* s., num., (11-28-92, Grisebach, #826, illus.), 8½ x 6⅛ in., (21.6 x 15.5 cm.), drypoint on handmade (BP 715, DM 1725, FR 5857, Y 134,785).

BI *Hollandische Fischerhauser, 1922,* s., light-staining, est. DM 1,200, (12-01-92, Karl/Faber, #1321), 4½ x 6⁵⁄₁₆ in., (11.5 x 16 cm.), etching.

$430* *Im Nachtlokal,* s., (05-08-93, Schloss Ahlden, #2898), 7⅝ x 10⁹⁄₁₆ in., (19.3 x 26.9 cm.), etching on handmade (BP 281, DM 691, FR 2331, Y 48,050).

$2021* *Im Tiergarten, c. 1914-1915,* s., num., (11-28-92, Grisebach, #810, illus.), 7¹⁵⁄₁₆ x 4⁵⁄₁₆ in., (20.1 x 11 cm.), woodcut on wove (BP 1334, DM 3220, FR 10,930, Y 251,525).

$650* *Die Kochin*, c. 1910, s., (11-28-92, Grisebach, #809, illus.), 15½ x 8⅜ in., (39.3 x 21.3 cm.), lithograph on machinemade paper (BP 429, DM 1036, FR 3515, Y 80,896).

$709* *Lesende Dame Im Cafe II*, c. 1920, s., num., (06-05-93, Bassenge, #6600), 11⁷⁄₁₆ x 7¹⁵⁄₁₆ in., (29 x 20.3 cm.), lithograph on hand-made (BP 467, DM 1149, FR 3874, Y 76,057).

$320* *(Man)*, s., stamped Nachl. L. Ury, margins, creasing, minor paper discoloration, soiling, Late Gerhard Brauer Coll., (05-27-93, Sotheby-Amstrdm, #795), sh 12¹¹⁄₁₆ x 18¹¹⁄₁₆ in., (323 x 475 mm.), lithograph on laid (BP 205, DM 513, FR 1731, Y 34,305, G 575).

$1011* *Mann Auf Einer Bank Im Tiergarten*, c. 1920, s., (11-28-92, Grisebach, #815, illus.), 5¹⁄₁₆ x 7¹⁄₁₆ in., (12.9 x 17.9 cm.), woodcut on Japan (BP 667, DM 1611, FR 5468, Y 125,825).

$745* *Portrait Einer Frau Mit Grossem Hut"*, c. 1915, s., (06-05-93, Grisebach, #910, illus.), 11 x 7¹¹⁄₁₆ in., (28 x 19.5 cm.), lithograph on handmade (BP 490, DM 1208, FR 4071, Y 79,918).

$1011* *Rauchender Zeitungleser Im Cafe*, c. 1910, s., (11-28-92, Grisebach, #806, illus.), 10⅝ x 7⅜ in., (27 x 18.8 cm.), lithograph on wove (BP 667, DM 1611, FR 5468, Y 125,825).

$1419* *Der Sammler*, s., num., (06-05-93, Bassenge, #6601, illus.), 10⅝ x 7¼ in., (27 x 18.4 cm.), lithograph on wove (BP 934, DM 2301, FR 7754, Y 152,221).

$704* *Schlafender Herr Im Cafe*, s., t., i. probedruck, full margin, good cond., very minor soiling, Late Gerhard Brauer Coll., (05-27-93, Sotheby-Amstrdm, #794, illus.), 5⁹⁄₁₆ x 4 in., (142 x 102 mm.), etching on laid (BP 451, DM 1130, FR 3807, Y 75,472, G 1265).

BI *Sitzender Weiblicher Akt*, s., #19/75, blindstamp, est. DM 1,200, (05-08-93, Schloss Ahlden, #2897, illus.), 8⅞ x 5¼ in., (22.5 x 13.3 cm.), etching on Japan.

$800* *(Walking Gentleman)*, s., indistinctly t., i. entgultigen probedruck, full margins, top corner of sheet glued to mount, soiling, Late Gerhard Brauer Coll., (05-27-93, Sotheby-Amstrdm, #793, illus.), 7 x 5½ in., (178 x 140 mm.), etching on laid (BP 512, DM 1284, FR 4327, Y 85,763, G 1438).

$1660* *Die Wartende*, c. 1910, s., (11-28-92, Grisebach, #808, illus.), 9¾ x 7 in., (24.7 x 17.8 cm.), lithograph on handmade (BP 1096, DM 2645, FR 8978, Y 206,596).

$1444* *Zeitungleser Im Leeren Cafe*, c. 1920, s., (11-28-92, Grisebach, #824, illus.), 10¹⁄₁₆ x 6⁹⁄₁₆ in., (25.6 x 16.7 cm.), lithograph on wove (BP 953, DM 2300, FR 7810, Y 179,714).

LESSIEUX
$1064* *De Dion-Bouton. "La France Presente Au Monde Le Plus Parfait ProduitDe Son Genie"*, c. 1920, glued to zinc, fairly good cond., (02-12-93, Cheval/Robert, #82, illus.), 72¹⁄₁₆ x 51³⁄₁₆ in., (183 x 130 cm.), poster (BP 749, DM 1765, FR 5971, Y 128,316).

LESSIEUX, L.   French b. 1874
$836* *PLM and Cie Gle Transatlantique: Algerie Tunisie. "Dans Le Sud Algerien"*, c. 1910, very good cond., (03-13-93, Laurin, #84, illus.), 41¾ x 29¹⁵⁄₁₆ in., (106 x 76 cm.), (BP 583, DM 1391, FR 4731, Y 98,527).

LESSING, Carl Friedrich   1808-1880
$211* *"Dusseldorf"*, trimmed, (03-24-93, Venator/Hansten, #2612), approx. 16¹⁵⁄₁₆ x 22¹⁄₁₆ in., (43 x 56 cm.), etching (BP 143, DM 345, FR 1173, Y 24,791).

LETE?, L.
$20 *"Food Will Win The War"*, tears, rips, (03-04-93, Alderfer, #271), 30 x 20 in., (76.2 x 50.8 cm.), poster (BP 14, DM 33, FR 111, Y 2329).

LETELLIER, Pierre   b. 1928
$63* *"Nu Au Boa Rose"*, #215/300, s., (01-28-93, Pescheteau, #189), 25⁹⁄₁₆ x 19¹¹⁄₁₆ in., (65 x 50 cm.), color lithograph on Arches (BP 42, DM 100, FR 338, Y 7822).

LETENDRE, Rita   b. 1929
$86* *Asor*, s., t., d. 79, #77/100, (06-07-93, Ritchie, #49), 15 x 20¹⁵⁄₁₆ in., (38.1 x 53.3 cm.), color serigraph (BP 57, DM 139, FR 470, Y 9225, C$ 110).

$140* *"Combustion"*, #3/50, s., t., d. R. Letendre 69, (07-14-92, Encans, #55), 20¹⁄₁₆ x 27¹⁵⁄₁₆ in., (51 x 71 cm.), serigraph (BP 73, DM 208, FR 700, Y 17,507, C$ 167).

$86* *Mistaken*, s., t., d. 77, #29/75, (11-30-92, Ritchie, #52), 28 x 40 in., (71.1 x 101.6 cm.), color serigraph (BP 57, DM 137, FR 465, Y 10,703, C$ 110).

LETY
$157* *PLM: Vienne Sur Le Rhone, "Monuments Romains Et Du Moyen-Age"*, excell. cond., (01-23-93, Ribeyre/Baron, #174), 42½ x 30¹¹⁄₁₆ in., (108 x 78 cm.), poster (BP 103, DM 250, FR 845, Y 19,650).

LEU, T. de
$197* *Solitudo Sive Vitae Patrum Cremicolarum: Thirty*, frontispice, yellowed, stained, losses, (06-16-93, Ader Tajan, #14), copper engraving (BP 131, DM 327, FR 1097, Y 21,011).

LEUBA
$690* *Mushrooms, 1890: Eight*, (04-07-93, Sotheby-Arcade, #285), sight 13 x 8½ in., (33 x 21.6 cm.), chromolithograph (BP 456, DM 1116, FR 3777, Y 78,391).

LEUPPI, Leo   1893-1972
$363* *Komposition, 1958*, #33/93, s., d., (04-21-93, Germann, #595), 25¹¹⁄₁₆ x 19⁹⁄₁₆ in., (652 x 497 mm.), color lithograph (BP 236, DM 580, FR 1962, Y 40,186, SF 529).

LEUTZE, Emmanuel Gottlieb (after)
$1495* *Washington Crossing The Delaware, 1853*, engraved Paul Girardet, pub. M. Knoedler, small margins, good cond.,time/light-staining, water-staining, thinned spots, surface soiling, foxing, (05-19-93, Butterfield, #1824), 22½ x 38¼ in., (572 x 972 mm.), engraving w/extensive hand-coloring on heavy wove (BP 970, DM 2430, FR 8187, Y 165,504).

LEUTZE, Emmanuel Gottlieb (after)   American 1816-1868
$187* *Washington Crossing The Delaware*, (04-02-93, Sloan, #1173), 24½ x 37½ in., (622 x 953 mm.), color engraving (BP 123, DM 301, FR 1021, Y 21,291).

LEUZINGER, G.
$1100* *Panorama Of Rio Harbor (Arsenal)*, 1860's, num., t., photog.'s credit in neg., (10-14-92, Swann, #204, illus.), 7½ x 26 in., (19.1 x 66 cm.), photograph, albumen print (BP 646, DM 1610, FR 5459, Y 133,301).

LEUZINGER, G., Publisher
$2200* *Rio De Janeiro*, c. 1850, p. Lemercier, margins, rubbed spot, nicks (touched), repaired splits affecting image, staining, defects, (01-22-93, Christie-NY, #313), borderline 19 x 28 in., (483 x 711 mm.), color lithograph w/hand-coloring on wove (BP 1439, DM 3498, FR 11,834, Y 275,344).

LEVAILLANT, Francois
BI *Histoire Naturelle Des Oiseaux D'Afrique*, Delachaussee, (1796-)1805-08 (reissued not before 1822), 6 vol. folio, plates after J. Lebrecht Reinhold by C. Fessard or J.L. Peree, first ed., large-paper issue, apparently John James Audobon's set, est. $20/30,000, (06-14-93, Sotheby-NY, #64), 19⅝ x 13 in., (49.8 x 33 cm.), 300 hand-colored engraved, finished by hand.

$16,100* *Histoire Naturelle Des Oiseaux De Paradis Et Des Rolliers; Suivie DeCelle Des Toucans Et Des Barbus (Fine Bird Books (1990) 118; Martin sale 2:144(part); Nissen IVB 559), 1801-06*, for Denne le jeune, and Perlet, 2 vol. folio, plates after Jacques Barraband by Peree, Gremillier, or Bouquet, foxed, light offsets, folds split w/out loss, first ed. apparently John James Audobon's copy, prov., catalog cover lot, (06-14-93, Sotheby-NY, #63, illus.), 20½ x 13¼ in., (52.1 x 33.7 cm.), 114 hand-colored engraved in colors finished by hand (BP 10,538, DM 26,204, FR 88,074, Y 1,694,202).

LEVENBERGER and LORENZI
$231* *Championnat Du Monde Des Conducteurs XVII Et XVIII. Grand Prix De Monaco 1959 Et 1960: Two*, p. Monegasque, good cond., (11-19-92, Ribeyre/Baron, #69), 12⅝

x 9¹³⁄₁₆ in., (32 x 25 cm.), poster (BP 152, DM 368, FR 1241, Y 28,728).

LEVENSTEIN, Leon   1913-1990
$1980* *East Harlem, N.Y. City, c. 1955,* s. in ink, stamped, (10-13-92, Christie-NY, #467, illus.), 13¾ x 10 in., (34.9 x 25.4 cm.), photograph, gelatin silver print (BP 1153, DM 2901, FR 9856, Y 240,087).
$2300* *Man Reading Newspaper, mid-1950's,* backed w/board, s. by photog., (04-06-93, Sotheby-NY, #420, illus.), 16½ x 13½ in., photograph (BP 1519, DM 3705, FR 12,548, Y 262,318).
$605* *New Orleans, 1976,* photog.'s handstamp, sig., notations, (04-07-93, Swann, #503, illus.), 14 x 11 in., photograph, silver print (BP 400, DM 978, FR 3311, Y 68,734).
$4025* *Rockefeller Center, 1952,* (04-08-93, Christie-NY, #443, illus.), 10½ x 12¾ in., (26.7 x 32.4 cm.), photograph, gelatin silver print (BP 2639, DM 6466, FR 21,887, Y 456,764).

LEVER, R. Hayley   American 1876-1958
BI *Doudtenez, 1928,* 3rd state, s., est. $2/400, (05-22-93, Collins, #111), 7 x 9¾ in., (17.8 x 24.8 cm.), etching.

LEVERD, Rene   b. 1872
$2891* *Chemin De Fer Du Nord Et De L'Etat Belge. Ostende. Fetes De 1902,* Paris, Imp. Eug. Marx, cond. A-, (06-11-93, Boisgirard, #107, illus.), 41¹⁵⁄₁₆ x 29½ in., (106.5 x 75 cm.), poster (BP 1899, DM 4699, FR 15,841, Y 306,737).

LEVI, Josef   American b. 1938
$303* *"K-RGbB", 1970,* s. Josef Levi verso, very good/good cond., (11-21-92, Bakker, #258), 35 x 35 in., (88.9 x 88.9 cm.), silkscreen on canvas (BP 199, DM 483, FR 1627, Y 37,682).

LEVICK, Eawin
$110* *Bi-Plane Open Airplane,* s. in ink Eawin Levick, (09-12-92, Dunning, #223, illus.), 10 x 13½ in., (25.4 x 34.3 cm.), photograph (BP 57, DM 158, FR 538, Y 13,629).
$110* *Single Wing Open Airplane,* s. in ink Eawin Levick, (09-12-92, Dunning, #224, illus.), 10 x 13½ in., (25.4 x 34.3 cm.), photograph (BP 57, DM 158, FR 538, Y 13,629).
$121* *Single Wing Open Airplane #16,* s. in ink Eawin Levick, (09-12-92, Dunning, #225, illus.), 10 x 13½ in., (25.4 x 34.3 cm.), photograph (BP 63, DM 174, FR 592, Y 14,992).
$121* *Single Wing Open Airplane Flying Close To The Ground,* s. in ink Eawin Levick, (09-12-92, Dunning, #221, illus.), 10 x 13½ in., (25.4 x 34.3 cm.), photograph (BP 63, DM 174, FR 592, Y 14,992).
$110* *Single Wing Open Airplane Landing Hard,* s. in ink Eawin Levick, (09-12-92, Dunning, #222, illus.), 10 x 13½ in., (25.4 x 34.3 cm.), photograph (BP 57, DM 158, FR 538, Y 13,629).
$121* *Two Men Flying In A Double Wing Open Airplane,* s. in ink Eawin Levick, (09-12-92, Dunning, #219, illus.), 10 x 13½ in., (25.4 x 34.3 cm.), photograph (BP 63, DM 174, FR 592, Y 14,992).

LEVINE, Jack   American b. 1915
BI *Ancient Scholar,* s., num. 199/200, full sheet, good cond., est. $5/700, (05-22-93, Weschler, #200), 10¾ x 7¾ in., (27.3 x 19.7 cm.), drypoint on Arches.
$1840* *"Apollo And Daphne", "Studies Of Heads", "Death's Head Hussar", "Volpone II", "Volpone III", "Venetian Lady", "The End Of The Weimar Republic", "ElGreco", "The Daley Gesture", "Vernisage" and Six Others: Group Of Sixteen,* 1964-69, s., full margins, good cond., mat/light stains, (02-11-93, Sotheby-NY, #31), 5 lithographs, 3 colored; 11 etchings (BP 1298, DM 3048, FR 10,314, Y 221,820).
$110* *Ashkenazi II, 1964, Prescott 16,* s., annot. Artist's Proof, (09-20-92, Hindman, #706), 9⅝ x 7¾ in., (24.4 x 19.7 cm.), etching and drypoint, on BFK Rives (BP 64, DM 163, FR 558, Y 13,595).
$385* *"Blue Angel",* pub. Lublin, excellent cond., (10-31-92, Cleveland, #378), 19¾ x 25½ in., (50.2 x 64.8 cm.), lithograph in five colors (BP 247, DM 592, FR 2009, Y 47,690).

$165* *Don Quixote,* s., #85/100, margins, (02-12-93, DuMouchelle, #353, illus.), 11¾ x 7¾ in., (29.8 x 19.7 cm.), etching (BP 116, DM 274, FR 926, Y 19,899).
BI *Dreigroschen Film, 1967: Twenty-Five,* complete portfolio, each s., num. 70/100, num. 70 justification page, pub. Touchstone Publishers, full margins, good cond., $2,5/3,000, (02-11-93, Sotheby-NY, #32), 17¹³⁄₁₆ x 13¹⁵⁄₁₆ in., (452 x 354 mm.), soft (molle) ground etching.
$715* *Facing East: Fifty-Eight,* portfolio, s. Jack Levine and James Michner, #729/2500, s. in stone, very good cond., (06-11-93, Doyle, #99), 19 x 12¼ in., (483 x 311 mm.), 4 lithograph, 54 drawing reproduced by phototypie (collotype) and pochoir processes and hand colored (BP 470, DM 1162, FR 3918, Y 75,862).
$220* *The Hairdresser,* #9/120, s., full margins, (02-12-93, DuMouchelle, #349, illus.), 3 x 3¾ in., (7.6 x 9.5 cm.), engraving (BP 155, DM 365, FR 1235, Y 26,532).
$358* *Hommage To Watteau, 1970,* crayon s., #53/100, good cond., surface soiling, (10-28-92, Butterfield, #3010), 19½ x 25¾ in., (495 x 654 mm.), color lithograph on wove (BP 228, DM 553, FR 1877, Y 43,926).
$193* *Judgement Of Paris, 1964,* s. J. Levine, annot. Artist's Proof, very good cond., (03-12-93, Skinner, #86, illus.), sight 5⅞ x 8¾ in., (14.9 x 22.2 cm.), etching on Rives BFK (BP 135, DM 321, FR 1092, Y 22,746).
$358* *Maimonides I (State Two), 1964, Presscott 14B,* s., annot. Printers' Proof, printer Letterio Calapai, pub. AAA, prov., (09-20-92, Hindman, #704), 9¾ x 7¾ in., (24.8 x 19.7 cm.), etching and aquatint (BP 210, DM 531, FR 1817, Y 44,247).
$259* *Musicians,* s., d., #40/120, full margins, good cond., mat staining, stains, notations, (05-19-93, Butterfield, #2002), 8¼ x 8¾ in., (210 x 222 mm.), etching on Rives (BP 168, DM 421, FR 1418, Y 28,673).
$83* *Portrait Of A General,* #92/120, s., (02-12-93, DuMouchelle, #351), 3⅞ x 3 in., (9.8 x 7.6 cm.), color engraving (BP 58, DM 138, FR 466, Y 10,010).
$77* *Portrait Of A man,* edit. A.P., (09-18-92, DuMouchelle, #2508), 22 x 17 in., (55.9 x 43.2 cm.), lithograph (BP 44, DM 115, FR 395, Y 9594).
$110* *Rape Of The Sabines,* first state, s., #57/100, margins, (02-12-93, DuMouchelle, #354), 8 x 10¾ in., (20.3 x 27.3 cm.), brown/white etching (BP 77, DM 182, FR 617, Y 13,266).

LEVINE, Kathy   American contemporary
BI *Compositional Device,* s., t., d. 1979, i., est. 125/175, (07-03-92, Sloan, #287), sheet 29 x 18 in., (73.7 x 45.7 cm.), color lithograph.

LEVINE, Les
BI *Presidential Ritual,* exec. 1974, prov., exhib., lit., box: 3 5/8 x 16 5/8 x 12 5/8; each photo: 11 7/8 x 15 3/4, est. $6/8,000, (02-23-93, Sotheby-NY, #312, illus.), photograph, 22 b/w mounted on board in paper box.

LEVINE, Sherrie   American b. 1947
$1980* *After Walker Evans,* s., t., num., d. Sherrie Levine, 1987 11/15 verso, prov., (11-17-92, Christie-E, #105, illus.), 9¹⁵⁄₁₆ x 7⅞ in., (25.2 x 20 cm.), b/w photograph (BP 1304, DM 3157, FR 10,634, Y 246,238).
$3025* *After Walker Evans, 1981,* s., t., d. by photog., (10-15-92, Sotheby-NY, #597, illus.), 7¾ x 9½ in., (19.7 x 24.1 cm.), photograph, gelatin silver print (BP 1851, DM 4503, FR 15,270, Y 362,927).
$2517* *Meltdown, 1989: Set of Four,* each s., t. verso, #16/35, w/page, explanation, justification, pub. Peter Blum Editions, full margins, good cond., orig. box, (10-15-92, Sotheby-London, #107, illus.), each approx. 36¾ x 25¾ in., (93.3 x 65.4 cm.), woodcut p. in colors on Korean Kozo (BP 1540, DM 3747, FR 12,706, Y 301,980).
$2420* *Untitled (After Karl Blossfeld: 12),* #12, stamped 12 566 verso, exec. 1990, unique, prov., (02-22-93, Christie-E, #227, illus.), 20 x 16 in., (50.8 x 40.6 cm.), photograph, b/w (BP 1662, DM 3932, FR 13,333, Y 280,710).

LEVINSON, Andre
$193* *"Bakst: The Story Of The Artist's Life", 1923,* Ltd. Ed. 167/315, orig. vellum, soiled, folio, (09-17-92, Sloan, #2654), 68 colored plates (BP 108, DM 287, FR 981, Y 24,029).

LEVINTHAL, David

$748* *Untitled, Toy Soldiers, c. 1987,* (05-23-93, Butterfield, #3501, illus.), 25½ x 20 in., photograph, polarois print (BP 487, DM 1223, FR 4117, Y 82,679).

LEVITSKY

$385* *Napoleon III, Emperor Of France, c. 1860's,* s. Napoleon in ink on image, (09-17-92, Swann, #214), photograph, sepia carte (BP 216, DM 572, FR 1956, Y 47,933).

LEVITT, Helen American b. 1918

$1045* *"Four Black Cats",* 1945/later, s., d., annot., Dixon Collection, (11-16-92, Butterfield, #6066, illus.), 9¾ x 6¾ in., (248.1 x 171.8 mm.), photograph, gelatin silver print (BP 688, DM 1666, FR 5612, Y 129,959).

$825* *Girl And Boy On Steps,* 1942/later, s., d., annot., Dixon Collection, (11-16-92, Butterfield, #6067, illus.), 9⅛ x 7⅜ in., (232.2 x 187.7 mm.), photograph, gelatin silver print (BP 543, DM 1315, FR 4431, Y 102,599).

BI *New York,* c. 1942, p.l., s., t., d., est. $1,2/1,500, (04-08-93, Christie-NY, #317, illus.), 8⅜ x 10¼ in., (21.3 x 26 cm.), photograph, gelatin silver print.

BI *New York,* c. 1945, p.l., ink s.; s., t., d., est. $1,5/1,800, (04-08-93, Christie-NY, #318, illus.), 9¾ x 6⅝ in., (24.8 x 16.2 cm.), photograph, gelatin silver print.

$1430* *New York,* (c. 1942), p.l., s., t., d., lit., (10-13-92, Christie-NY, #290, illus.), 11¾ x 7⅞ in., (29.8 x 20 cm.), photograph, gelatin silver print (BP 833, DM 2095, FR 7118, Y 173,396).

$690* *"New York City" (A Way Of Seeing, pl.36),* s. by photog., t., d. in unident. hand, 1942, p.l., (04-06-93, Sotheby-NY, #218, illus.), 9¼ x 6½ in., photograph (BP 456, DM 1112, FR 3764, Y 78,695).

BI *Untitled (Mexico), 1941,* est. $1,2/1,600, (11-16-92, Butterfield, #6065, illus.), 9⅝ x 6½ in., (244.9 x 165.4 mm.), photograph, gelatin silver print mounted on black board.

BI *Untitled (Two Women, New York), 1942,* s., d., annot., Dixon Collection, est. $2/3,000, (11-16-92, Butterfield, #6064, illus.), 6⅞ x 9⅞ in., (174.9 x 251.3 mm.), photograph, gelatin silver print.

LEVY, Alexander Oscar American 1881-1947

BI *"Hillside Village" and "Figures Crossing The Bridge": Two,* each s. in plate, prov., est. $150/200, (10-30-92, Sloan, #1728), each 4¼ x 4¼ in., (10.8 x 10.8 cm.), etching.

LEVY, Alphonse 1843-1918

$70* *Militaire Assis,* s., d. in pl., annot., (03-11-93, Ader Tajan, #115), 9$^{1}/_{16}$ x 5⅞ in., (23 x 15 cm.), intaglio (BP 49, DM 116, FR 395, Y 8232).

$639* *La Promenade Du Shabbat En Alsace,* original, s. in pl., (03-11-93, Ader Tajan, #116, illus.), 15$^{9}/_{16}$ x 21⅞ in., (39.5 x 55.5 cm.), lithograph on thin China (BP 446, DM 1061, FR 3604, Y 75,150).

$220* *Le Vieux Marcheur,* original, s., punctures, (03-11-93, Ader Tajan, #114), 13¾ x 11$^{7}/_{16}$ in., (35 x 29 cm.), lithograph on thin China (BP 153, DM 365, FR 1241, Y 25,873).

LEVY, Ch.

BI *Folies Bergere: La Belle Fatma. "Visible Sans Supplement, Tous Les Soirs Au Jardin",* good cond., (03-13-93, Laurin, #26), 48$^{13}/_{16}$ x 35$^{7}/_{16}$ in., (124 x 90 cm.), .

LEVY, Emile French 1826-1890

$130* *Theatre Du Chatelet: Germinal D'Emile Zola,* Imp. Em. Levy, good cond., (02-12-93, Cheval/Robert, #167), 50⅜ x 35$^{13}/_{16}$ in., (128 x 91 cm.), poster (BP 92, DM 216, FR 730, Y 15,678).

LEVY, Emile (studio of)

$171* *A Saint-Joseph (...) 6 Millions De Marchandises, Liquidation, c. 1895,* Paris, Imp. Emile Levy, cond. B+, (06-11-93, Boisgirard, #108), 51$^{3}/_{16}$ x 37$^{13}/_{16}$ in., (130 x 96 cm.), poster (BP 112, DM 278, FR 937, Y 18,143).

LEWINSKI, Jorge

BI *"Dame Barbara Hepworth, 1966",* t., s., d., stamped photog.'s credit, 500 x 405mm, est. BP 1/200, (05-07-93, Sotheby-London, #392, illus.), photograph, silver print.

BI *"Henry Moore", 1964,* mounted on card, t., labels, 455 x 580mm, est. BP 3/500, (05-07-93, Sotheby-London, #198, illus.), photograph, silver print.

BI *"Marcel Duchamp, 1966",* t., s., d., t., stamped photog.'s credit, 380 x 482mm, est. BP 1/200, (05-07-93, Sotheby-London, #393), photograph, silver print.

$690* *Selected Works: Portraits Of Artists, Including Francis Bacon, Marcel Duchamp, David Hockney, Henry Moore, And Man Ray: Eight,* 1960-70s, s., t., d., photog.'s stamp, est. $1,2/1,600, (05-23-93, Butterfield, #3502, illus.), from 14½ x 11¾ in., to 18½ x 15 in., photograph, gelatin silver print (BP 449, DM 1128, FR 3797, Y 76,268).

LEWIS, Allen

$248* *Prints: Six,* all s., very good/good cond., (03-28-93, Bakker, #13), each approx. 5 x 4 in., (12.7 x 10.2 cm.), color woodcuts (BP 167, DM 405, FR 1375, Y 28,864).

LEWIS, Charles G.

$247* *"The Melton Breakfast",* after F. Grant, (03-03-93, Doyle, #43), 18 x 28¼ in., (45.7 x 71.8 cm.), color engraving (BP 170, DM 407, FR 1380, Y 28,862).

LEWIS, Charles George

$639* *Napoleon At Bassano,* proof before t., s., i., blindstamp Print Sellers' Association, margins, staining, (07-16-92, Bonhams-Chelsea, #500, illus.), plate 28¼ x 47 in., (71.8 x 119.4 cm.), engraving (BP 330, DM 944, FR 3187, Y 80,045).

LEWIS, F.G.

$66* *"The Corn Hunt",* (05-15-93, Dunning, #219), 14½ x 21 in., (36.8 x 53.3 cm.), engraving (BP 43, DM 106, FR 357, Y 7316).

LEWIS, Henry English/German 1819-1904

$12,650* *Das Illustrirte Mississippithal ... Vom Wasserfalle Zu St. Anthony An Bis Zum Golf Von Mexico (Graff/Storm 2474, Howes L312, Sabin 40807, Streeter sale 3:1547), 1854-58,* in 4s, after Lewis, tears, repairs, foxing, browning, dampstaining, 1st edit., (05-21-93, Sotheby-NY, #84, illus.), 10⅝ x 7¼ in., (270 x 184 mm.), tinted lithographed half-title and 78 hand-finished color lithographed plates, one woodcut text illus. (BP 8196, DM 20,569, FR 69,201, Y 1,394,708).

LEWIS, James O.

$9775* *The Aboriginal Portfolio, Or, A Collection Of Portraits Of The Most Celebrated Chiefs Of The North American Indians (Bennett 68, Howes L315, Sabin 40812), 1835-36,* folio, after Lewis by T. Barincou, lithographed by Lehman & Duval, loss, repair, tears, 1st edit., (05-21-93, Sotheby-NY, #85, illus.), 15⅜ x 10¾ in., (391 x 273 mm.), 72 hand-colored lithographed plates (BP 6333, DM 15,894, FR 53,474, Y 1,077,729).

LEWIS, John F. 1805-1870

$5317* *La Alhambra En Los Anos 1833-34": Twenty-Six,* perfect cond., (03-17-93, Duran, #95, illus.), approx. 14$^{9}/_{16}$ x 10⅝ in., (37 x 27 cm.), hand-colored lithograph mounted on heavy cardboard, orig. portfolio (BP 3666, DM 8847, FR 30,074, Y 623,622, P 632,500).

LEWIS, Martin American 1881/83-1962

$1320* *Above The Yards, Weehawken (McC. 20), 1918,* #10/100, i. w/artist's name, inits., d. 1973 by wife, pub. Kennedy Galleries, full margins, crease, staining, very good cond., (09-19-92, Christie-E, #41), plate 17½ x 23¾ in., (44.5 x 60.3 cm.), sheet 26¼ x 40 in., (44.5 x 60.3 cm.), aquatint on wove (BP 759, DM 1977, FR 6769, Y 164,465).

$1045* *"Boss Of The Block (McC. 74), c. 1928" and "On The Roof (McC. 132), c. 1937": Two,* both s., wide margins, very good cond.; first i. imp, old hinges, (09-19-92, Christie-E, #45), first etching w/drypoint and aquatint on wove; second etching and aquatint w/roulette and drypoint on wove (BP 601, DM 1565, FR 5359, Y 130,202).

$4830* *Chance Meeting (McC. 138), 1941,* s., i., wide margins, mat staining, glue, very good cond., (05-11-93, Christie-NY, #116, illus.), plate 10½ x 7$^{7}/_{16}$ in., (267 x 189 mm.), drypoint on laid (BP 3083, DM 7609, FR 25,637, Y 531,295).

$8800* *Circus Night (M. 109), 1933,* s., hinged to mat, very good cond., (12-04-92, Doyle, #123, illus.), 11 x 14⅞ in., (279 x 378 mm.), drypoint (BP 5645, DM 14,015, FR 47,542, Y 1,098,627).

$3300* *Corner Shadows (M. 90), 1929,* s. Martin Lewis, label verso, (06-26-93, Wolf, #950A), 8⅜ x 8¹⁵⁄₁₆ in., (213 x 227 mm.), drypoint (BP 2210, DM 5607, FR 18,890, Y 350,133).

$1495* *Cronies (McC. 107), 1932,* s., wide margins, mat staining, good cond., (05-11-93, Christie-NY, #115, illus.), plate 9⅜ x 10⅞ in., (238 x 276 mm.), aquatint on laid (BP 954, DM 2355, FR 7935, Y 164,448).

$3300* *Derricks (McC. 58), 1927,* s., i. imp, wide margins, old glue, tape, good cond., (09-19-92, Christie-E, #44, illus.), plate 7⁵⁄₁₆ x 11⅞ in., (186 x 302 mm.), drypoint in brownish-black on laid paper (BP 1898, DM 4942, FR 16,923, Y 411,164).

$2640* *Derricks (McCarron 58), 1927,* s., i. 2nd state. 2nd trail proof, margins, excell. cond., (11-09-92, Christie-NY, #23, illus.), plate 7⅞ x 11⅞ in., (200 x 302 mm.), drypoint on wove (BP 1745, DM 4215, FR 14,239, Y 327,625).

$1430* *Dock Workers Under The Brooklyn Bridge (McCarron 6),* c. 1916, #25/100, i. w/artist's name, inits., d. 1973 by wife, pub. Kennedy Galleries, full margins, very good cond., (09-19-92, Christie-E, #38, illus.), plate 17½ x 23¾ in., (44.5 x 60.3 cm.), sheet 26¼ x 39⅞ in., (44.5 x 60.3 cm.), etching and aquatint on wove (BP 823, DM 2141, FR 7333, Y 178,171).

$3080* *From The River Front (McC. 7), 1916,* s., wide margins, very good cond., (09-19-92, Christie-E, #39, illus.), plate 14¾ x 11⅞ in., (375 x 302 mm.), etching and aquatint on wove (BP 1772, DM 4612, FR 15,795, Y 383,753).

BI *Glow Of The City (M. 87), 1929,* s., acid burn, discoloration, mat burn, very good cond., front coverlot, est. $12/18,000, (06-11-93, Doyle, #56), 11¼ x 14⅛ in., (286 x 359 mm.), drypoint.

$1430* *The Great Shadow (McC. 33), 1925,* s., i., margins, light-staining, old paper tape, (09-19-92, Christie-E, #42), plate 9⅞ x 6¾ in., (251 x 171 mm.), drypoint on wove (BP 823, DM 2141, FR 7333, Y 178,171).

BI *"The Great Shadow" (McCarron 33), 1925,* s., mint cond., old hinges, est. $4-5,000, (10-31-92, Cleveland, #170, illus.), 9⅞ x 6¾ in., (25.1 x 17.1 cm.), drypoint.

$660* *"Holocaust" and "Above The Yards, Wee-Hawken": Two,* first s. by artist; second by wife, hinged to mat, very good cond., (12-04-92, Doyle, #127), larger 17¼ x 23½ in., (438 x 597 mm.), etching (BP 423, DM 1051, FR 3566, Y 82,397).

$385* *"Homeward Bound",* s. Martin Lewis, good cond., (04-25-93, Bakker, #171, illus.), plate 7 x 12 in., (17.8 x 30.5 cm.), etching, matted (BP 245, DM 609, FR 2057, Y 42,523).

$2200* *Ice Cream Cones (M. 70), 1928,* collectors stamp, hinges, very good cond., (12-04-92, Doyle, #122, illus.), 9¼ x 14¾ in., (235 x 375 mm.), drypoint (BP 1411, DM 3504, FR 11,885, Y 274,657).

$7150* *Little Penthouse (McC. 101), 1931,* s., full margins, good cond., pub. American Etchers, Vol. XI, MartinLewis, Crafton Collection, Inc., num. 35, orig. boards and box, (11-05-92, Sotheby-NY, #35, illus.), 9⅞ x 6¾ in., (251 x 172 mm.), drypoint on laid (BP 4650, DM 11,308, FR 38,256, Y 877,193).

$7150* *Little Penthouse (McC. 101), 1931,* s., i. imp., 9th trail proof, wide margins, excell. cond., (11-09-92, Christie-NY, #25, illus.), plate 10¹⁄₁₆ x 6⅞ in., (255 x 175 mm.), drypoint on laid (BP 4727, DM 11,414, FR 38,565, Y 887,317).

$4180* *Lost Railroad (McC. 112), 1933,* s., wide margins, old glue, very good cond., (09-19-92, Christie-E, #48, illus.), plate 9⅞ x 16⅞ in., (251 x 429 mm.), drypoint and aquatint on wove (BP 2404, DM 6259, FR 21,436, Y 520,807).

$7700* *Misty Night, Danbury (McC. 122), 1936,* s., full margins, good cond., tape stain, soiling, (11-05-92, Sotheby-NY, #36, illus.), 11 x 15½ in., (280 x 394 mm.), lithograph on white wove (BP 5008, DM 12,178, FR 41,199, Y 944,669).

$4600* *Misty Night, Danbury (McC. 122), 1936,* s., full margins, good cond., (02-11-93, Sotheby-NY, #37, illus.), 11¹⁄₁₆ x 15⁹⁄₁₆ in., (281 x 395 mm.), lithograph on white wove (BP 3246, DM 7620, FR 25,785, Y 554,551).

$1650* *Neptunes Fountain, Yorkville (M. 126), c. 1936,* s., trial proof, tape residue, hinged to mat, very good cond., (12-04-92, Doyle, #125, illus.), 11¾ x 7¾ in., (298 x 197 mm.), drypoint (BP 1058, DM 2628, FR 8914, Y 205,993).

$2645* *Night In New York (McCarron 42), 1932,* s., pub. Chicago Society of Etchers, large margins, good cond., glueremains, (02-11-93, Sotheby-NY, #33, illus.), 8⁷⁄₁₆ x 8⅞ in., (214 x 226 mm.), sheet 13⅜ x 11¹⁵⁄₁₆ in., (214 x 226 mm.), drypoint on cream laid (BP 1866, DM 4381, FR 14,826, Y 318,867).

$5280* *Passing Freight (McC. 133), 1938,* s., wide margins, tape, excell. cond., (11-09-92, Christie-NY, #26, illus.), plate 8¹⁵⁄₁₆ x 14⁷⁄₁₆ in., (228 x 366 mm.), drypoint and sandpaper ground on laid (BP 3491, DM 8429, FR 28,479, Y 655,249).

$2640* *Politics (M. 125), 1936,* s., specks soiling, hinged to mat, very good cond., (12-04-92, Doyle, #124, illus.), 9¾ x 10½ in., (248 x 267 mm.), drypoint (BP 1693, DM 4204, FR 14,263, Y 329,588).

$3850* *Puffing Billys (McC. 10), 1916", "On The River (McC. 4), 1915" and "Trade Winds (McC. 23), c. 1918": Three,* each s., wide margins, very good cond.; first w/old paper tape; third w/crease, (09-19-92, Christie-E, #40), first etching on wove; second etching on laid paper; third drypoint on wove, watermark (BP 2215, DM 5765, FR 19,744, Y 479,691).

$7763* *Quarter Of Nine - Saturday's Children (McC. 88), 1929,* s., i. imp., margins, good cond., traces gold paint in margins,flecks in image, discoloration, (02-11-93, Sotheby-NY, #34, illus.), 9¹⁵⁄₁₆ x 12⅞ in., (253 x 327 mm.), sheet 12¹⁵⁄₁₆ x 15⅞ in., (253 x 327 mm.), drypoint on laid paper (BP 5478, DM 12,859, FR 43,515, Y 935,865).

$1210* *R.F.D. (McC. 110), 1933,* s., i., wide margins, light-staining, taped to overmat, staining, (09-19-92, Christie-E, #47), plate 9⅞ x 11¾ in., (251 x 298 mm.), drypoint and aquatint on wove (BP 696, DM 1812, FR 6205, Y 150,760).

$7700* *"Rain On Murray Hill" (McCarron, 66), 1928,* s. Martin Lewis-imp, very good cond., (03-12-93, Skinner, #24, illus.), 7¾ x 11¾ in., (19.7 x 29.8 cm.), drypoint on laid (BP 5371, DM 12,816, FR 43,577, Y 907,484).

$5463* *Rainy Day, Queens (McC. 100), 1931,* s., large margins, good cond., light-stain, glue stains, (02-11-93, Sotheby-NY, #36, illus.), 10¹¹⁄₁₆ x 11⅞ in., (272 x 301 mm.), sheet 13⁷⁄₁₆ x 15¹³⁄₁₆ in., (272 x 301 mm.), drypoint (BP 3855, DM 9049, FR 30,622, Y 658,590).

$8800* *Relics (McCarron 65), 1928,* s., large margins, good cond., white spots in image, scuff, mat stain, rust flecks, glue stains, soiling, handling creases, (11-05-92, Sotheby-NY, #33, illus.), 11⅞ x 10 in., (303 x 253 mm.), sheet 17⅝ x 13⅞ in., (303 x 253 mm.), drypoint on laid (BP 5724, DM 13,917, FR 47,084, Y 1,079,622).

$3520* *Route 6 (McC. 108), 1933,* s., margins, light-staining, taped to overmat, staining, (09-19-92, Christie-E, #46, illus.), plate 8⅞ x 14⅝ in., (225 x 371 mm.), drypoint on laid paper (BP 2025, DM 5271, FR 18,051, Y 438,575).

$11,550* *Shadow Dance (McC. 97), 1930,* s., margins, good cond., mat stain, repair, (11-05-92, Sotheby-NY, #34, illus.), 9⅜ x 10⅞ in., (237 x 276 mm.), sheet 12½ x 14½ in., (237 x 276 mm.), drypoint w/sandpaper ground on laid (BP 7512, DM 18,267, FR 61,798, Y 1,417,004).

BI *Shadow Dance (McC. 97), 1930,* s., wide margins, mat staining, excell. cond., est. $11/14,000, (05-11-93, Christie-NY, #114, illus.), plate 9¼ x 10¾ in., (235 x 273 mm.), drypoint and sandpaper-ground etching on laid.

$15,400* *Shadow Dance (McC. 97), 1930,* s., wide margins, mat staining , soiling, foxmark, excellent cond., (11-09-92, Christie-NY, #24, illus.), plate 9⅜ x 10⅞ in., (238 x 276 mm.), drypoint and sandpaper ground on laid (BP 10,182, DM 24,585, FR 83,064, Y 1,911,144).

$9775* *Stoops In Snow (McCarron 95), 1930,* 2nd final state, s., wide margins, very good cond., (05-11-93, Christie-NY, #113, illus.), plate 9¹⁵⁄₁₆ x 14⅞ in., (252 x 378 mm.), drypoint and sand paper-ground etching in bluish-black on laid (BP 6240, DM 15,399, FR 51,884, Y 1,075,239).

$10,925* *Stoops In The Snow (McC. 95), 1930,* first state of 2, s., i. trial proof No. 8, large margins, good cond., light-stain, labels, (02-11-93, Sotheby-NY, #35, illus.), 9¹⁵⁄₁₆ x 15 in., (253 x 381 mm.), sheet 13⅜ x 18⅜ in., (253 x 381 mm.), drypoint w/sandpaper ground (BP 7709, DM 18,097, FR 61,239, Y 1,317,058).

$1100* *Street Booth, Tokyo, New Year's Eve (McC. 57), 1927,* s., i., wide margins, light-staining, taped to overmat, (09-19-92, Christie-E, #43), plate 13⅞ x 10⅛ in., (352 x 257 mm.), drypoint on laid paper (BP 633, DM 1647, FR 5641, Y 137,055).

BI *Strength And Beauty (M. 135), 1935,* s., dirt smudges, tape residue, hinged to mat, very good cond., est.$1,5/2,000, (12-04-92, Doyle, #126, illus.), 9⅞ x 6¾ in., (251 x 171 mm.), drypoint.

$2420* *"Twin Silos (McC. 115), c. 1933"* and *"Angry Man (McC. 117), 1934":* Two, both s., very good cond.; first w/wide margins, foxmarks; second i. Trial Proof, margins, (09-19-92, Christie-E, #49), drypoint, first on wove; second on Rives (BP 1392, DM 3624, FR 12,410, Y 301,520).

$4840* *"Veterans" (McCarron, 113),* s. Martin Lewis, inits. M.L. in stone, good cond., light staining, foxing, (09-11-92, Skinner, #38, illus.), 9⅞ x 13½ in., (25.1 x 34.3 cm.), lithograph on Rives BFK wove w/partial watermark (BP 2503, DM 6967, FR 23,679, Y 599,678).

LEWITT, Sol   American b. 1928

BI *All Combinations Of Red, Yellow & Blue Straight, Not-Straight & Broken Lines On Red, Yellow And Blue (Tate Gallery S 19), 1976,* #33/50, pencil s., num., est. DM 1,200, (11-20-92, Lempertz, #668B), sh 30 x 29¹⁵⁄₁₆ in., (76.2 x 76 cm.), color serigraph on white Arches 88.

BI *All One-, Two-, Three-, Four-, Five-, & Six Part Combinations Of Geometric Figures (T. G. S33), 1980,* s., #21/33, pub. artist, full margins, good cond. ?, est. $2/2,500, (05-15-93, Sotheby-NY, #1057, illus.), sheet 65¾ x 38⅝ in., (167 x 98.1 cm.), silkscreen on BFK Rives.

$633* *Arcs (Large And Small), 1990:* Two, s., #PP1/4, full margins, very good cond., (05-19-93, Butterfield, #2235), one 31½ x 13¼ in., (800 x 337 mm.), the other 15¼ x 13⅜ in., (800 x 337 mm.), aquatint in colors on wove (BP 411, DM 1029, FR 3467, Y 70,076).

$1588* *Arcs From 4 Corners (WV W 4), 1986,* s., num., (11-28-92, Schoppmann, #634), 18½ x 28⁹⁄₁₆ in., (47 x 72.5 cm.), color woodcut on beige Japan (BP 1048, DM 2530, FR 8588, Y 197,635).

BI *Arcs, Circles & Grids (T. S16), 1972,* s., #63/144, pub. Lincoln Centre/List Art Posters for Lincoln Centre, full margins, good cond., est. $1,5/2,000, (05-19-93, Butterfield, #2233), sh 82¼ x 40⅛ in., (208.9 x 101.9 cm.), silkscreen on Strathmore backed by linen.

$330* *Black With White Lines, Vertical, Not Touching (T. L3), 1971,* s., d., annot. AP, inkstamps, pub. Chicago 7, good cond., (10-28-92, Butterfield, #3011), 17 x 23½ in., (432 x 597 mm.), lithograph on wove (BP 210, DM 510, FR 1730, Y 40,491).

$2475* *Complex Form, 1989:* Five, complete portfolio, s., num. 15/39, pub. Matsumura Editions, full margins, very good cond., 1 lightly rubbed area, est. $2/3,000, (02-24-93, Butterfield, #3075, illus.), each 19⅝ x 13⅝ in., (498 x 346 mm.), aquatint in colors on Arches 88 (BP 1726, DM 4018, FR 13,621, Y 290,425).

$2750* *Complex Form, 1989:* Five, complete portfolio, s., #16/39, pub. Matsumura Editions, full margins, very good cond., (10-28-92, Butterfield, #3013, illus.), each 19⅝ x 13⅝ in., (498 x 346 mm.), color aquatint on Arches 88 (BP 1752, DM 4247, FR 14,421, Y 337,423).

BI *Complex Form, 1989:* Five, complete portfolio, s., #37/39, pub. Matsumura Editions, full margins, very good cond., est. $2/3,000, (05-19-93, Butterfield, #2234, illus.), each 19⅝ x 13⅝ in., (498 x 346 mm.), aquatint in colors on Arches 88.

$3450* *Complex Forms, 1989:* Five, complete portfolio, each s., #17/39, pub. Tomoko Liguori Editions, full margins, good cond., (02-11-93, Sotheby-NY, #368, illus.), each sheet 30⅛ x 22½ in., (765 x 572 mm.), etching and aquatint

in colors on Arches 88 (BP 2434, DM 5715, FR 19,339, Y 415,913).

$3450* *Complex Forms, 1989:* Five, complete portfolio, s., #38/39, pub. Tomoko Ligouri Editions, full margins, good cond., (05-15-93, Sotheby-NY, #1059, illus.), each sheet 30⅛ x 22½ in., (76.5 x 57.2 cm.), five etching aquatints in colors on Arches 88 (BP 2243, DM 5549, FR 18,649, Y 382,441).

$1150* *Grids And Arcs, 1972,* s., #140/144, pub. Lincoln Center, List Art Posters and Prints, full margins, good cond., (02-11-93, Sotheby-NY, #367), 67¹¹⁄₁₆ x 36¼ in., (172 x 92 cm.), silkscreen (BP 811, DM 1905, FR 6446, Y 138,638).

$5500* *Lines In Color On Color To Points On A Grid (Tate S27), 1978:* Set Of Ten, all s., num. 21/25, pub. Multiples, Inc., full sheets, excell. cond.; one w/skinned spot; another w/crease, (09-19-92, Christie-E, #147, illus.), each, sheet 30 x 30 in., (762 x 762 mm.), screenprint in colors on heavy wove (BP 3164, DM 8236, FR 28,205, Y 685,273).

BI *The Location Of Lines (Tate Gallery E14), 1975:* Five, complete portfolio, s., #22/25, p. Crown Point Press, pub. Parasol Press, Ltd., good cond., est. $3/4,000, (05-15-93, Sotheby-NY, #1056, illus.), each sheet 17⅞ x 17⅞ in., (45.4 x 45.4 cm.), five etchings.

BI *Plate I Red, 1980,* from Four Part Combination Of Six Geometric Figures In Four Colors, s., num., appears very good cond., est. $4/600, (06-11-93, Doyle, #100), 5 x 14¼ in., (127 x 362 mm.), woodcut.

$5750* *Pyramids, 1987:* Six, complete suite, s., #14/19, pub. Parasol Press, Ltd., full margins, good cond., creases, handling creases, (05-15-93, Sotheby-NY, #1058, illus.), each sheet 23⅜ x 35⅜ in., (59.4 x 89.9 cm.), six aquatints in colors (BP 3739, DM 9249, FR 31,081, Y 637,402).

BI *Silk-Screen Prints In Four Colors, 1972:* Twenty-Four, s., num., lit., est. DM 15,000, (12-05-92, Bassenge, #7399), 13⅞ x 13⅞ in., (35.2 x 35.2 cm.), color screenprint.

BI *Six Geometric Figures In Three Colors On Three Colors & All Their Combinations (Tate Gallery S 29), 1978,* #7/60, pencil s., d., est. DM 1,200, (11-20-92, Lempertz, #668A), sh 29¹⁵⁄₁₆ x 29⅞ in., (76 x 75.9 cm.), color serigraph on thick white paper.

$303* *Six Geometric Figures In Three Colours On Three Colours & All Their Combinations (T. S29), 1978,* s., #5/60, pub. Multiples, margins, good cond.?, (10-28-92, Butterfield, #3012), 26¾ x 26¾ in., (679 x 679 mm.), silkscreen in red, yellow and blue on Arches 88 (BP 193, DM 468, FR 1589, Y 37,178).

BI *Stars-Black Center, 1983,* s., #10/10, full margins, est. FF4/5,000, (05-27-93, Briest, #123), 20⅞ x 20⅞ in., (53 x 53 cm.), aquatint and etching.

BI *Stars-Dark Centre, (Tate Gallery cat. E34), 1983:* Set Of Seven, num. 10/10, pub. Crown Point Press, margins, excell. cond., est. BP 1,0/1,500, (12-01-92, Christie-London, #615), averaging P. 17¹¹⁄₁₆ x 17¹¹⁄₁₆ in., (450 x 450 mm.), etchings w/aquatint on wove.

BI *Stars-Light Center (Tate E33), 1983:* Set Of Seven, s., #9/10, stamps verso, full margins, excellent cond., est. $6/7,000, (11-09-92, Christie-NY, #338, illus.), 19⅞ x 19⅞ in., (505 x 505 mm.), etchings and aquatints on wove.

BI *Twelve Forms Derived From A Cube (Tate S47), 1984:* Set Of Twenty-Four, New York and Bari, Multiples Inc. and Marilena Bonomo, s., num., copy PP 1 of 2, excellent cond., original box, est. $4/5,000, (11-09-92, Christie-NY, #339, illus.), 8 x 8 in., (203 x 203 mm.), colored black screenprint on Arches 88.

BI *Untitled (Wallpainting Graz):* Two, each s., num. 9/30, pub. Editions Atelier Graz, full margins, apparently very good cond., est. $1,2/1,400, (02-24-93, Butterfield, #3074), each sheet 22 x 30 in., (559 x 762 mm.), silk-screen in colors on cream wove.

$1083* *Untitled, 1991,* s., num., (11-28-92, Schoppmann, #632), 24 x 23¹³⁄₁₆ in., (61 x 60.5 cm.), color etching on handmade (BP 715, DM 1725, FR 5857, Y 134,785).

BI *Untitled, Wallpainting Graz:* Two, s., #9/30, pub. Editions Atelier Graz, full margins, very good cond.?, est. $2/

2,500, (10-28-92, Butterfield, #3014), each sheet 22 x 30 in., (559 x 762 mm.), color silkscreen on cream wove.

$325* *Vertical Lines Not Touching (Black) (Kornfeld L 3), 1971,* s., num., (11-28-92, Schoppmann, #633), 16 15/16 x 23 9/16 in., (43 x 59.9 cm.), lithograph on light cardboard (BP 215, DM 518, FR 1758, Y 40,448).

LEYDEN, Lucas van Dutch 1494-1533

BI *Alte Frau Mit Traube (B. 151; Volbehr 154; Hollstein 151), 1523,* prov., est. DM 2,400, (12-04-92, Bassenge, #6278), 4 7/16 x 3 1/4 in., (11.2 x 8.2 cm.), engraving.

BI *Apostel Johannes (B. 90; Volb. 87), 1510,* restored, prov., est. DM 800, (12-01-92, Karl/Faber, #96), engraving.

$248* *Christ Before Annias (B. 46),* mono., d. 1521 in plate, (10-30-92, Sloan, #2811, illus.), 4 1/2 x 3 in., (11.4 x 7.6 cm.), engraving (BP 159, DM 382, FR 1294, Y 30,720).

BI *Christi Gefangennahme (B. 45; Volb. 42), 1521,* trimmed, est. DM 2500, (12-01-92, Karl/Faber, #94), engraving.

$5777* *Christus Als Gartner Erscheint Maria Magdalena (B. 77; Volbehr 71 I;Hollstein 77 I),* (12-04-92, Bassenge, #6276, illus.), 5 3/16 x 6 1/2 in., (13.1 x 16.5 cm.), engraving (BP 3706, DM 9201, FR 31,210, Y 721,223).

$1300* *Christus Und Die Apostel (B. 86, 87, 89-94, 97; Volbehr u. Hollstein83, 84, 86-91, 94), c. 1511,* prov., (12-04-92, Bassenge, #6277), each approx. 4 5/8 x 2 13/16 in., (11.8 x 7.2 cm.), engraving (BP 834, DM 2070, FR 7023, Y 162,297).

BI *Die Dornenkronung (B. 49; Volb. 46), 1521,* num. 7 from the Passionsfolge, trimmed, est. DM 2500, (12-01-92, Karl/Faber, #95), engraving.

BI *Joseph Interpreting Pharoah's Dream, From The Story Of Joseph (B. 23),* grey impression, watermark, trimmed to plate and thread margins, glue glue stains, torn, repaired corners, tear into image, est. BP 3/500, (10-27-92, Phillips-London, #17), plate 5 x 6 1/2 in., (127 x 165 mm.), engraving on laid.

BI *The Last Supper (B. 43),* mono., d. 1521 in plate, est. $6/800, (10-30-92, Sloan, #2812, illus.), 4 1/2 x 3 in., (11.4 x 7.6 cm.), engraving.

$2166* *Potiphar's Frau Klagt Joseph An (B. 21, Volbehr 20; Hollstein 21), 1512,* from series Die Geschichte des Joseph, (12-04-92, Bassenge, #6275), 4 3/4 x 6 1/4 in., (12.1 x 15.9 cm.), engraving (BP 1389, DM 3450, FR 11,702, Y 270,412).

$867* *Die Vertreibung Aus Dem Paradies (B. 11; Volbehr 11; Hollstein 11), 1510,* (12-04-92, Bassenge, #6274), 6 7/16 x 4 3/4 in., (16.3 x 12.1 cm.), engraving (BP 556, DM 1381, FR 4684, Y 108,240).

$385* *Virgin And Child,* prov., (09-20-92, Hindman, #647), 4 3/4 x 3 in., (12.1 x 7.6 cm.), engraving (BP 225, DM 571, FR 1954, Y 47,584).

LEYENDECKER, Joseph Christian American 1874-1951

$77* *Get In The Game With Uncle Sam,* (02-14-93, Hanzel, #706), 24 1/2 x 18 1/2 in., (62.2 x 47 cm.), color lithographic poster (BP 54, DM 128, FR 432, Y 9286).

BI *The Inland Printer,* A- cond., marginal yellowing, abrasions, est. $6/900, (08-06-92, Swann, #175, illus.), 12 x 10 in., (30.5 x 25.4 cm.), .

$1210* *Order Coal Now,* Edwards and Deutsch Litho Co., B cond., creases, closed tears, (08-06-92, Swann, #174, illus.), 29 x 20 in., (73.7 x 50.8 cm.), (BP 632, DM 1788, FR 6038, Y 154,337).

$385* *"Order Coal Now - United States Fuel Administration",* repair, Edwards and Deutsch Litho Company, lit., (09-12-92, Dunning, #100, illus.), 29 1/4 x 20 in., (74.3 x 50.8 cm.), poster laid on cloth (BP 199, DM 554, FR 1884, Y 47,702).

$550* *U.S. Marines, "Soldiers Of The Sea",* B+ cond., repairs, creasing, (08-06-92, Swann, #173, illus.), 40 x 28 in., (101.6 x 71.1 cm.), (BP 287, DM 813, FR 2745, Y 70,153).

$248* *"U.S.A. Bonds/Third Liberty Loan Campaign, Boy Scouts Of America",* margin repair, lit., (09-12-92, Dunning, #99, illus.), 30 x 20 in., (76.2 x 50.8 cm.), poster laid down on cloth (BP 128, DM 357, FR 1213, Y 30,727).

LEYENDECKER(?), J.C.

$1045* *The Arrow Collar, 1915,* A- cond., restoration, (08-06-92, Swann, #172, illus.), 45 1/2 x 30 in., (115.6 x 76.2 cm.), (BP 546, DM 1544, FR 5215, Y 133,291).

LEYS, Hendrik Baron 1815-1869

$144* *Promenade Hors Les Murs (Delteil 11 I), 1869,* (12-04-92, Bassenge, #6879), 7 5/16 x 5 7/8 in., (18.6 x 15 cm.), etching on handmade (BP 92, DM 229, FR 778, Y 17,978).

LHOTE, Andre French 1885-1962

$767* *"Dhows Off African Coast" and "Harbour Scene", c. 1955: Two,* s., #Epreuve d'artiste 6/6, #136/200, pub. Guilde de la Gravure, fullmargins, good cond., (12-03-92, Sotheby-London, #367), one 10 1/2 x 17 1/8 in., (267 x 435 mm.), (267 x 435 mm.), (BP 495, DM 1206, FR 4117, Y 95,434).

BI *Femme Assise,* s., #12/150, est. DM 1,200, (05-26-93, Lempertz, #293), sh 22 1/2 x 15 1/16 in., (57.2 x 38.2 cm.), color lithograph on Arches wove.

$679* *Femme Assise, 1960,* 32/150., s., (10-14-92, Germann, #123, illus.), 20 1/16 x 13 3/16 in., (510 x 335 mm.), color lithograph on Japan (BP 399, DM 994, FR 3370, Y 82,283, SF 885).

$413* *"Harbour",* s. Andre Lhote, very good/good cond., (11-21-92, Bakker, #15), image 10 1/8 x 16 3/4 in., (25.7 x 42.5 cm.), color lithograph (BP 272, DM 658, FR 2218, Y 51,362).

$193* *Sans Titre,* s. in pl. and pen, 35/250, (06-28-93, Loudmer, #81), 22 7/16 x 17 5/16 in., (570 x 440 mm.), sh 27 9/16 x 19 1/2 in., (570 x 440 mm.), color lithograph on Arches wove (BP 129, DM 328, FR 1105, Y 20,477).

$660* *Seated Woman, c. 1956,* full margins, num., s., (05-27-93, Swann, #159), 11 1/4 x 15 3/4 in., (28.6 x 40 cm.), color lithograph (BP 423, DM 1059, FR 3569, Y 70,755).

LHUTER, L.

$439* *PLM. Concours De Saut Morez Du Jura. "Challenge Rhoptix", 1935,* very good cond., (03-15-93, Arcole, #98), 39 3/8 x 24 13/16 in., (100 x 63 cm.), (BP 306, DM 729, FR 2479, Y 52,002).

LIBBY, William Charles American b. 1919

$248* *Fantasy, 1959,* s., ed. 8/100, (11-12-92, Freemn/Fine Art, #120), mat 12 1/8 x 16 1/2 in., (30.8 x 41.9 cm.), lithograph (BP 163, DM 393, FR 1325, Y 30,750).

LICATA, Ricardo b. 1929

$70* *"Composition 1974",* EA d., s., (04-04-93, Pescheteau, #244), 27 9/16 x 27 9/16 in., (70 x 70 cm.), color serigraph (BP 46, DM 113, FR 382, Y 7970).

LICHFIELD, Lord

BI *"The Hand And Eye Of David Mlinaric",* 1980s, s., labels, 390 x 252mm, est. BP 2/300, (05-07-93, Sotheby-London, #204), photograph, silver print.

LICHTENSTEIN, Roy American b. 1923

$2640* *Against Apartheid, 1983,* s., d., #65/100, pub. Galerie Maeght, excellent cond., (11-09-92, Christie-NY, #349, illus.), 33 1/2 x 23 5/8 in., (851 x 600 mm.), lithograph and screenprint in colors on Arches (BP 1745, DM 4215, FR 14,239, Y 327,625).

$3850* *American Indian Theme III (Tyler 348), 1980,* s., d., #20/50, blindstamps, full margins, stain, foxmarks, very good cond., (11-09-92, Christie-NY, #348, illus.), 35 x 27 in., (889 x 686 mm.), colored woodcut on Suzuki handmade (BP 2545, DM 6146, FR 20,766, Y 477,786).

$4400* *American Indian Theme VI (Tyler 351:RL19), 1980,* s., d., #40/50, blindstamp, pub. Tyler Graphics, Ltd., full margins,good cond., (11-07-92, Sotheby-NY, #661, illus.), 29 5/8 x 42 3/8 in., (75.2 x 107.6 cm.), woodcut p. in colors on white handmade Suzuki (BP 2877, DM 7025, FR 23,745, Y 543,076).

$4025* *American Indian Theme VI (Tyler 351:RL19), 1980,* s., d., #37/50, blindstamp, pub. Tyler Graphics, Ltd., full margins,good cond., corners tipped to back mat, surface scuff, ink loss, (05-15-93, Sotheby-NY, #1072, illus.), 29 3/4 x 42 3/8 in., (75.6 x 107.6 cm.), woodcut in colors on white handmade Suzuki paper (BP 2617, DM 6474, FR 21,757, Y 446,181).

$3277* *"American Indian Theme",* s., 47/50, Tyler Graphics Ltd., 1980, (04-17-93, Falkkloos, #328), 31 1/2 x 41 5/16 in., (80 x 105 cm.), woodcut in colors (BP 2129, DM 5241, FR 17,704, Y 364,395, SK 24,200).

$1320* *Art Reflections, 1988,* s., pub. for The American Federation of Arts 80th Anniversary, margins, very good cond., surface scuffs, (02-24-93, Butterfield, #3081), 29¼ x 50 in., (74.3 x 127 cm.), silkscreen in colors on wove (BP 921, DM 2143, FR 7265, Y 154,893).

$590* *As I Opened Fire, The Enemy Would Have Been Warned That My Ship Was Below Them,* Stedelijk Museum, 1964, (09-30-92, Kunsthallen, #185), offset color lithograph (BP 333, DM 837, FR 2830, Y 70,803, DK 3220).

$404* *As I Opened Fire, The Enemy Would Have Been Warned, That My Ship WasBelow Them, 1964: Three,* (03-24-93, Kunsthallen, #225), offset lithograph in colors (BP 274, DM 660, FR 2246, Y 47,468, DK 2530).

$253* *As I Opened Fire...,* (11-01-92, Hanzel, #270), 24 x 19½ in., (61 x 49.5 cm.), lithograph (BP 165, DM 399, FR 1345, Y 31,281).

$293* *"As I Opened Fire...": Three,* pub. Stedelijk Museum, 1964, (09-29-92, B. Rasmussen, #344), offset print (BP 165, DM 414, FR 1412, Y 34,977, DK 1610).

$202* *As I Opened Fire...: Three,* from 3000 impressions, (05-27-93, Briest, #128), 25 x 20⅞ in., (63.5 x 53 cm.), color offsets (BP 129, DM 324, FR 1092, Y 21,655).

$110* *As I Opened Fire: Three,* pub. Coll. Stedelijk Museum Amesterdam, (02-14-93, Hanzel, #699), 25¼ x 21 in., (64.1 x 53.3 cm.), lithograph (BP 77, DM 182, FR 617, Y 13,266).

$176* *As I Opened Fire: Three,* pub. Coll. Stedelijk Museum Amsterdam, (02-14-93, Hanzel, #701), 25 x 20½ in., (63.5 x 52.1 cm.), lithograph (BP 124, DM 292, FR 988, Y 21,225).

BI *As I Opened Fire: Three,* #15/25, pencil s., est. DM 9,000, (11-20-92, Lempertz, #669, illus.), sh 25³⁄₁₆ x 20⅞ in., (64 x 53.1 cm.), offset print on cardboard.

$1255* *"Aspen Winter Jazz", 1967,* s., #152/300, (05-27-93, Briest, #127), 39¾ x 26¾ in., (101 x 68 cm.), offset color lithograph (BP 804, DM 2014, FR 6787, Y 134,541).

$4461* *Before The Mirror, 1975,* from portfolio Mirror of the Mind, s., d., #12/100, p. at Styria Studio, blindstamp, pub. Castelli Graphics, full margins, good cond., (06-30-93, Sotheby-London, #867, illus.), 35⅛ x 25⅛ in., (892 x 638 mm.), lithograph and silkscreen in color on wove (BP 2990, DM 7609, FR 25,667, Y 477,981).

$3850* *Before The Mirror, 1975,* s., d. '74, i. 'PP 3/3', printer's proofs, from suite Mirrors of theMind, co-pub. by Multiples, Inc. and Castelli Graphics, full margins, fading, water stain, discoloration, creases, soiling, good cond., (11-07-92, Sotheby-NY, #658, illus.), 32½ x 23⅞ in., (826 x 606 mm.), lithograph and silkscreen p. in colors w/embossing on BFK Rives (BP 2517, DM 6147, FR 20,777, Y 475,191).

$3300* *Before The Mirror, 1975,* from Mirrors of the Mind, Multiples Inc. and Castelli Graphics, s., d., #22/100, full margins, excellent cond., (11-09-92, Christie-NY, #347, illus.), 35⅛ x 25⅛ in., (892 x 638 mm.), lithograph and screeprint in colors on wove (BP 2182, DM 5268, FR 17,799, Y 409,531).

BI *Blue Face, 1987-9,* from Brushstroke Figures, s., d. 89, #25/60, pub. Waddington Graphics and GraphicStudio, blindstamp, full margins, excellent cond., est. $8/12,000, (11-09-92, Christie-NY, #352, illus.), 54¼ x 33½ in., (137.8 x 85.1 cm.), lithograph, woodcut, screenprint, encaustic and wax in colors on Cold Pressed Saunders Waterford.

$4125* *Brushstroke (B. 14), 1965,* s., #165/280, pub. Leo Castelli Gallery, full margins, good cond., (11-07-92, Sotheby-NY, #642, illus.), 22 x 28⅜ in., (559 x 721 mm.), silkscreen p. in colors (BP 2697, DM 6586, FR 22,261, Y 509,134).

$1870* *Brushstroke (B. 14), 1965,* s., #62/280, pub. Leo Castelli Gallery, small margins, good cond., light staining, rubbed areas, (10-28-92, Butterfield, #3018), 22 x 28 in., (559 x 711 mm.), color silkscreen on heavy cream wove (BP 1191, DM 2888, FR 9806, Y 229,448).

$4025* *Brushstroke (B. 14), 1965,* s., #249/280, pub. Leo Castelli Gallery, margins, good cond.?, light-staining, surface soiling, (05-19-93, Butterfield, #2237, illus.), sh 23 x 29 in., (584 x 737 mm.), silkscreen in yellow/blue/black on wove (BP 2613, DM 6543, FR 22,043, Y 445,588).

BI *Brushstroke Figures: Blonde, 1988-89,* s., d.'89, #34/60, pub. Waddington Graphics, Graphicstudio, full margins, good cond., est. BP 6/7,000, (06-30-93, Sotheby-London,

#871, illus.), sh 57⅝ x 37¼ in., (146.4 x 94.6 cm.), woodcut, lithograph, silkscreen and encaustic in color on Saunders Waterford.

BI *Brushstroke Figures: Blue Face, 1988-89,* s., d. '89, #34/60, pub. Waddington Graphics, w/Graphicstudio, full margins, good cond., est. BP 5/6,000, (06-30-93, Sotheby-London, #873, illus.), 54 x 33⅝ in., (137.2 x 85.4 cm.), woodcut, lithograph, silkscreen and encaustic in color on Saunders Waterford.

$10,925* *Brushstroke Figures: Blue Face, 1988-89,* s., d. '89, #3/60, pub. Waddington Graphics, Graphicstudio, University of South Florida, Tampa, full margins, good cond., (02-11-93, Sotheby-NY, #379, illus.), sheet 53¹⁵⁄₁₆ x 33⁷⁄₁₆ in., (137 x 85 cm.), woodcut, lithograph, silkscreen and encaustic p. in colors, on Saundes Waterford (BP 7709, DM 18,097, FR 61,239, Y 1,317,058).

BI *Brushstroke Figures: Grandpa, 1988-89,* s., d. '89, #34/60, pub. Waddington Graphics, w/Graphicstudio, full margins, good cond., est. BP 6/7,000, (06-30-93, Sotheby-London, #875, illus.), sh 56⅝ x 40¾ in., (143.8 x 103.5 cm.), woodcut, lithograph, silkscreen and encaustic in color on Saunders Waterford.

$16,100* *Brushstroke Figures: Grandpa, 1988-89,* s., d. '89, #3/60, pub. Waddington Graphics, full margins, good cond., (05-15-93, Sotheby-NY, #1078, illus.), sheet 56⅞ x 41 in., (144.5 x 104.1 cm.), woodcut, lithograph, silkscreen and encaustic in colors on Saunders Waterford paper (BP 10,468, DM 25,897, FR 87,027, Y 1,784,725).

BI *Brushstroke Figures: Green Face, 1988-89,* s., d. '89, #34/60, pub. Waddington Graphics, Graphicstudio, full margins, good cond., est. BP 6/7,000, (06-30-93, Sotheby-London, #872, illus.), 58⅝ x 40¾ in., (148.9 x 103.5 cm.), woodcut, lithograph, silkscreen and encaustic in color on Saunders Waterford.

$8050* *Brushstroke Figures: Green Face, 1988-89,* s., d. '89, #3/60, pub. Waddington Graphics, Graphicstudio, University of South Florida, full margins, good cond., (02-11-93, Sotheby-NY, #380, illus.), sheet 58¹¹⁄₁₆ x 40¹⁵⁄₁₆ in., (149 x 104 cm.), woodcut, lithograph, silkscreen and encaustic p. in colors on Saunders Waterford (BP 5680, DM 13,334, FR 45,123, Y 970,464).

BI *Brushstroke Figures: Portrait, 1988-89,* s., d. '89, #34/60, pub. Waddington Graphics, Graphicstudio, full margins, good cond., est. BP 6/7,000, (06-30-93, Sotheby-London, #870, illus.), 52⅜ x 34 in., (133 x 86.4 cm.), woodcut, lithograph, silkscreen and encaustic in color on Saunders Waterford.

$8800* *Brushstroke Figures: Portrait, 1988-89,* s., d., '89, #3/60, pub. Waddington Graphics, full margins, good cond., (11-07-92, Sotheby-NY, #670, illus.), sheet 52½ x 34¼ in., (133.4 x 87 cm.), woodcut, lithograph, silkscreen and encaustic p. in colors on Saunders Waterford (BP 5754, DM 14,051, FR 47,491, Y 1,086,152).

BI *Brushstroke Figures: The Mask, 1988-89,* s., d. '89, #34/60, pub. Waddington Graphics, w/Graphicstudio, full margins, good cond., est. BP 5/6,000, (06-30-93, Sotheby-London, #874, illus.), 46 x 31 in., (116.8 x 78.7 cm.), woodcut, lithograph, silkscreen and encaustic in color on Saunders Waterford.

$8800* *Brushstroke Figures: The Mask, 1988-89,* s., d. '89, #3/60, pub. Waddington Graphics, full margins, good cond., (11-07-92, Sotheby-NY, #671, illus.), sheet 46 x 31¼ in., (116.8 x 79.4 cm.), woodcut, lithograph, silkscreen and encaustic p. in colors on Saunders Waterford (BP 5754, DM 14,051, FR 47,491, Y 1,086,152).

$4950* *Brushstroke On Canvas, 1989,* s., d., num. 21/40, p. Tyler Graphics w/blindstamp, pub. Metro. Museum of Art, full margins, excell. cond., (09-19-92, Christie-E, #152, illus.), sheet 36 x 38 in., (914 x 965 mm.), lithograph in colors on BFK Rives (BP 2847, DM 7412, FR 25,385, Y 616,746).

$4125* *Brushstrokes (B. 20), 1967,* s., #235/300, pub. Pasadena Art Museum, full margins, good cond., stain, creases, surface scuffs, (11-07-92, Sotheby-NY, #654, illus.), 22 x 30 in., (559 x 762 mm.), silkscreen p. in colors (BP 2697, DM 6586, FR 22,261, Y 509,134).

BI *Brushstrokes (B. 20), 1967,* s., num. 264/300, s., num. 264/300, pub. Pasadena Art Museum, margins, skinned patches, very good cond., BP est. 2,0/3,000, (12-01-92,

Christie-London, #617), L. 21⅞ x 29¹⁵⁄₁₆ in., (555 x 760 mm.), screenprint in colors.

$3450* *Brushstrokes (B. 20), 1967,* s., #183/300, pub. Pasadena Art Museum, full margins, good cond., matstaining, surface soiling, (05-19-93, Butterfield, #2239, illus.), 21¹⁵⁄₁₆ x 30 in., (557 x 762 mm.), silkscreen in colors on wove (BP 2240, DM 5608, FR 18,894, Y 381,933).

BI *Brushtroke Figures: Nude, 1988-89,* s., d.'89, #34/60, pub. Waddington Graphics, w/Graphicstudio, full margins, good cond., est. BP 6/7,000, (06-30-93, Sotheby-London, #869, illus.), sh 56¼ x 32½ in., (142.9 x 82.6 cm.), woodcut, lithograph, silkscreen and encaustic in color on Saunders Waterford.

BI *Bull Profile Series: Bull I (G. 466), 1973,* s., d., #99/100, blindstamp, pub. Gemini G.E.L., full margins, good cond., crease, soiling, foxing, est. $4/5,000, (11-07-92, Sotheby-NY, #656, illus.), sheet 27 x 35 in., (686 x 889 mm.), linocut on Arjomari.

$2530* *Bull Profile Series: Bull I (G. 466), 1973,* s., d., #99/100, blindstamp, pub. Gemini, G.E.L., full margins, goodcond., crease, handling creases, soiling, foxing, (05-15-93, Sotheby-NY, #1070, illus.), sheet 27 x 35 in., (68.6 x 88.9 cm.), linocut on Arjomari paper (BP 1645, DM 4069, FR 13,676, Y 280,457).

BI *Bull Profile Series: Bull I-VI (G. 466-71), 1973,* complete series, s., d., annot. A/P X, blindstamp publisher, Gemini G.E.L., p. Ron McPherson, Bruce Porter, Dan Freeman, Jeff Wasserman, Ron Olds, Jim Webb and Serge Lozingot, full margins, very good cond.?, staining, est. $40/60,000, (05-19-93, Butterfield, #2250, illus.), each sh 27 x 35 in., (686 x 889 mm.), linecuts w/lithograph and silkscreen in colors on Arjomari.

$2750* *Cathedral Series: Cathedral #2 (G. 143), 1969,* s., d., num. 29/75, blindstamp of pub. Gemini G.E.L., full margins, apparently good cond., crease, buckling, (02-24-93, Butterfield, #3077, illus.), 41¾ x 27 in., (106 x 68.6 cm.), lithograph in blue & red on Special Arjomari (BP 1918, DM 4464, FR 15,135, Y 322,694).

$1610* *Cathedral Series: Cathedral #4 (G. 145), 1969,* s., d., annot. P.P. II, blindstamp publisher, Gemini G.E.L., p. Charles Ritt, full margins, good cond.?, Robert Tyler Estate, (05-19-93, Butterfield, #2242, illus.), 41⅞ x 27 in., (106.4 x 68.6 cm.), lithograph in red/blue on Special Arjomari (BP 1045, DM 2617, FR 8817, Y 178,235).

$1150* *Cathedral Series: Cathedral #6 (G. 147), 1969,* s., d., annot. T.P. II, blindstamp publisher, Gemini G.E.L., p. Dan Feeman, full margins, good cond.?, (05-19-93, Butterfield, #2243), 41⅞ x 27 in., (106.4 x 68.6 cm.), lithograph in blue/black on Special Arjomari (BP 747, DM 1869, FR 6298, Y 127,311).

$2200* *Cathedral Series: Cathedral #6 (G. 149), 1969,* s., d., annot. A/P VIII, blindstamp of pub., eeminii G.E.L., margins, apparently very good cond.?, (02-24-93, Butterfield, #3078, illus.), 41¾ x 27 in., (106 x 68.6 cm.), lithograph in blue & black on Special Arjomari (BP 1534, DM 3571, FR 12,108, Y 258,155).

$4400* *Chem IA (G. 248), 1970,* s., d., #52/100, blindstamp, pub. Gemini, G.E.L., full margins, goodcond., (11-07-92, Sotheby-NY, #652, illus.), 24 x 14⅜ in., (610 x 365 mm.), silkscreen p. in yellow and black on Special Arjomari (BP 2877, DM 7025, FR 23,745, Y 543,076).

$3850* *Chem IA (G. 248), 1970,* s., d., num. 35/100, blindstamp of pub. Gemini G.E.L, full margins, apparently good cond., (02-24-93, Butterfield, #3080, illus.), 24 x 14¼ in., (610 x 362 mm.), silkscreen in black & yellow on Special Arjomari (BP 2685, DM 6250, FR 21,189, Y 451,772).

$2875* *Chem IA (G. 248), 1970,* s., d., #25/100, blindstamp publisher, Gemini G.E.L., p. Jeff Wasserman, full margins, very good cond., creases, surface soiling, stain, (05-19-93, Butterfield, #2249), 30 x 20⅜ in., (762 x 518 mm.), silkscreen in yellow/black on Special Arjomari (BP 1866, DM 4673, FR 15,745, Y 318,277).

$5500* *Cow Goes Abstract, 1982: Three,* s., #105/150, pub. Fratelli Alinor, full margins, very good cond., creases, (10-28-92, Butterfield, #3022, illus.), each 23¹⁵⁄₁₆ x 28⁷⁄₁₆ in., (608 x 722 mm.), color silkscreen on white wove (BP 3504, DM 8494, FR 28,841, Y 674,847).

BI *"Cow Going Abstract": Three,* s. 1982, 149/150, est. DK 30,000, (09-29-92, B. Rasmussen, #343, illus.), serigraph.

$5735* *Cow Going Abstract, 1982: Three,* 63/150, s., (10-14-92, Germann, #54, illus.), 25¹⁵⁄₁₆ x 30¹¹⁄₁₆ in., (660 x 780 mm.), color serigraph (BP 3366, DM 8393, FR 28,462, Y 694,983, SF 7475).

BI *Cow Going Abstract, 1982: Triptych,* s., #33/150, creases, est. FF 12/15,000, (11-16-92, Briest, #323), 23⅝ x 20¼ in., (60 x 51.5 cm.), serigraph in colors.

$1316* *Cow Going Abstract, 1982: Triptyque,* s., #28/150, (05-27-93, Briest, #125), 23⅝ x 28⅛ in., (60 x 71.5 cm.), color serigraph (BP 843, DM 2112, FR 7117, Y 141,081).

$7700* *Crak! (B. 5), 1964,* s., d., #171/300, pub. Leo Castelli Gallery, full margins, good cond., tear, nick, scuff marks, creases, (11-07-92, Sotheby-NY, #640, illus.), 18⅝ x 26⅞ in., (473 x 683 mm.), offset lithograph p. in colors (BP 5034, DM 12,294, FR 41,554, Y 950,383).

$2185* *Crak! (B. 5), 1964,* s., d., i. H.C., pub. Leo Castelli Gallery, margins, tears, splits, losses, staining, light-staining, defects, (05-11-93, Christie-NY, #490), sheet 19¼ x 27⅝ in., (489 x 702 mm.), color offset lithograph on wove (BP 1395, DM 3442, FR 11,598, Y 240,348).

$3520* *Crak! (B. 5), 1964,* s., d., #42/300, pub. Leo Castelli Gallery, full margins, scrapes inimage, light/mat staining, colors faded, tear into image, remains of glue, (11-09-92, Christie-NY, #343, illus.), 19¼ x 27½ in., (489 x 699 mm.), offset colored lithograph (BP 2327, DM 5619, FR 18,986, Y 436,833).

BI *Crak! (Bianchini 5), 1964,* s., d., #117/300, est. DM 8,000-, (05-27-93, Lempertz, #860, illus.), 19⅞ x 28⁷⁄₁₆ in., (50.5 x 72.3 cm.), color offset lithograph on thin wove.

$2300* *Crying Girl (B. 4), 1963,* s., pub. Leo Castelli Gallery, full margins, colors faded, image splits/tears, foxing, laid down to board, defects, (05-11-93, Christie-NY, #489), sheet 18 x 24 in., (457 x 610 mm.), color offset lithograph on wove (BP 1468, DM 3623, FR 12,208, Y 252,997).

$9900* *Crying Girl (B. 4), 1963,* s., pub. Leo Castelli Gallery, full margins, excellent cond., (11-09-92, Christie-NY, #342, illus.), 18³⁄₁₆ x 24³⁄₁₆ in., (462 x 614 mm.), offset colored lithograph on wove (BP 6545, DM 15,805, FR 53,398, Y 1,228,593).

$4675* *Crying Girl (B. 4), 1963,* s., pub. Leo Castelli Gallery, full margins, red slightly faded, goodcond., discoloration, water staining, staining, (02-24-93, Butterfield, #3076, illus.), 17¼ x 23⅛ in., (438 x 587 mm.), offset lithograph in colors on wove (BP 3260, DM 7589, FR 25,729, Y 548,580).

$5225* *Crying Girl (B. 4), 1963,* s., pub. Leo Castelli Gallery, colors faded, margins, good cond., staining, creases, image surface scuff, surface soiling, (10-28-92, Butterfield, #3016, illus.), 17¼ x 23¼ in., (438 x 591 mm.), color offset lithograph on wove (BP 3329, DM 8069, FR 27,399, Y 641,104).

$2402* *Crying Girl (Bianchini 4), 1963,* s., pub. Leo Castelli Gallery, full margins, repaired tear into image, red faded, (06-30-93, Sotheby-London, #866, illus.), 17⅛ x 23¼ in., (435 x 591 mm.), offset color lithograph (BP 1610, DM 4097, FR 13,820, Y 257,366).

$9350* *Crying Girl (Bianchini 4), 1963,* s., pub. Leo Castelli Gallery, full margins, good cond., tear, pressure marks, creases, soiling, glue, (11-07-92, Sotheby-NY, #639, illus.), 17⅜ x 23¼ in., (441 x 591 mm.), offset lithograph p. in colors (BP 6113, DM 14,929, FR 50,459, Y 1,154,036).

$4950* *Crying Girl (Bianchini 4), 1963,* s., pub. Leo Castelli Gallery, full margins, splits, surface scrapes, creases, tiny tears, surface soiling, other minor defects, (09-19-92, Christie-E, #148, illus.), sheet 18¼ x 24⅛ in., (464 x 613 mm.), offset lithograph in colors on wove (BP 2847, DM 7412, FR 25,385, Y 616,746).

$5338* *Crying Girl, 1963,* s., Leo Castelli Gallery, (05-12-93, AB Stockholm, #7033, illus.), 17³⁄₁₆ x 23¼ in., (43.7 x 59 cm.), offset lithograph in colors (BP 3485, DM 8612, FR 29,011, Y 595,958, SK 39,600).

$8338* *Dr. Waldmann (G. 881), 1980,* s., d., #48/50, blindstamp, pub. Gemini, G.E.L., full margins, good cond. ?, (05-15-93, Sotheby-NY, #1073, illus.), 35⅛ x 27⅝ in., (89.2 x 70.2 cm.), woodcut in colors w/embossing on Arches Cover (BP 5421, DM 13,412, FR 45,070, Y 924,288).

BI *Entablature IX (Tyler 342), 1976,* s., d., num. 13/30, pub. Tyler Graphics, blindstamp, very good cond., est. BP 800/1,200, (12-01-92, Christie-London, #619), L. 21⁵⁄₁₆ x 37¹⁵⁄₁₆ in., (542 x 965 mm.), embossed screenprint in colors w/metallic foil collage.

$1840* *Entablature V (Tyler 338), 1976,* s., d., #8/30, Tyler Graphics blindstamp, full margins, excell. cond., the Late M. Anwar Kamal, M.D. Coll., (05-11-93, Christie-NY, #493), sheet 29¼ x 45 in., (74.3 x 114.3 cm.), color screenprint, lithograph, collage and embossing on wove (BP 1175, DM 2899, FR 9766, Y 202,398).

BI *Explosion (Bianchini 24), 1967,* s., embossed stamp, est. DM 7,000-, (05-27-93, Lempertz, #862, illus.), 22¹⁄₁₆ x 16¹⁵⁄₁₆ in., (56 x 43 cm.), color lithograph on white wove.

$1210* *Foot And Hand (B. 2), 1962,* s., d. 1964, #79/300, pub. Leo Castelli Gallery, margins, colors faded, good cond., tear, well-restored tears, discoloration, staining, (10-28-92, Butterfield, #3015), 16⅝ x 20⅞ in., (422 x 530 mm.), color offset lithograph on wove (BP 771, DM 1869, FR 6345, Y 148,466).

$1725* *Foot And Hand (Bianchini 2), 1962,* s., d. 1964, i. H.C., pub. Leo Castelli Gallery, full margins, colors faded, tears affecting image, light/time staining, foxing, (05-11-93, Christie-NY, #488), sheet 17¼ x 21½ in., (438 x 546 mm.), color offset lithograph on wove (BP 1101, DM 2717, FR 9156, Y 189,748).

$2420* *Foot And Hand (Bianchini 2), 1962,* s., d. 64, #105/300, pub. Leo Castelli Gallery, full margins, touched spots, short tears, defects, (11-09-92, Christie-NY, #341, illus.), 17¼ x 21⅜ in., (438 x 543 mm.), offset red, yellow and black lithograph on wove (BP 1600, DM 3863, FR 13,053, Y 300,323).

$2300* *Foot And Hand (Bianchini 2), 1962,* s., d. 1964, #36/300, pub. Leo Castelli Gallery, full margins, good cond., yellow attenuated, skinned spots, fox marks, soiling, creases, (02-11-93, Sotheby-NY, #369, illus.), 16⁹⁄₁₆ x 20⅞ in., (420 x 530 mm.), offset color lithograph (BP 1623, DM 3810, FR 12,892, Y 277,275).

BI *Foot And Hand (Waldman 2), 1962,* s., est. DM 7,500, (06-12-93, Hauswedell/Nolt, #278, illus.), 16⁹⁄₁₆ x 20¹⁵⁄₁₆ in., (42 x 53.2 cm.), offset lithograph on wove.

$1955* *Foot Medication, 1963,* s., pub. Leo Castelli Gallery, full margins, light stain, fold, discoloration, good cond., (05-15-93, Sotheby-NY, #1060, illus.), 15½ x 15¾ in., (39.4 x 40 cm.), offset lithograph in gray and black (BP 1271, DM 3145, FR 10,568, Y 216,717).

$3335* *For Meyer Schapiro: Still Life, 1973,* s., d. '74, #7/100, from portfolio pub. by The Committee to Endow a Chair in Honor of Meyer Schapiro at Columbia University, full margins, good cond., scratch, scuff marks, handling creases, (05-15-93, Sotheby-NY, #1071), 32½ x 23⅞ in., (82.6 x 60.6 cm.), lithograph and silkscreen in yellow and black (BP 2168, DM 5364, FR 18,027, Y 369,693).

$3520* *Forms In Space, 1985,* s., d., num. 57/125, pub. Institute of Contemp. Art, Univ. of Penn.,full margins, creasing, excell. cond., (09-19-92, Christie-E, #151), sheet 35¾ x 52 in., (90.8 x 132.1 cm.), screenprint in blue and red on wove (BP 2025, DM 5271, FR 18,051, Y 438,575).

$4539* *Goldfish Bowl (Tyler 362:RL30), 1981,* s., d., num. 4/30, blindstamp Tyler Graphics, full margins, good cond.?, (10-14-92, Sotheby-Japan, #49, illus.), 18¼ x 10⅞ in., (464 x 276 mm.), colored woodcut on Okawara handmade (BP 2664, DM 6643, FR 22,526, Y 550,048).

$863* *Haystack Series: Haystack #1, (G. 150), 1969,* s., d., annot. A/P I/X, blindstamp publisher, Gemini G.E.L., p. Stuart Henderson, full margins, good cond.?, (05-19-93, Butterfield, #2244), 13⅜ x 23½ in., (340 x 597 mm.), lithograph and silkscreen in yellow on Rives BFK (BP 560, DM 1403, FR 4726, Y 95,539).

$920* *Haystack Series: Haystack #5 (G. 154), 1969,* s., d., #A/P IX, blindstamp publisher, Gemini G.E.L., full margins, good cond., (05-19-93, Butterfield, #2246, illus.), 13⅞ x 23½ in., (352 x 597 mm.), lithograph and silkscreen in

red/blue on Rives BFK (BP 597, DM 1495, FR 5038, Y 101,849).

BI *Haystack Series: Haystack #6 (G. 155), 1969,* s., d. A/P IX, blindstamp publisher, Gemini G.E.L., p. Dan Gualdoni,full margins, good cond.?, est. $1,5/2,000, (05-19-93, Butterfield, #2247), 13½ x 23⅝ in., (343 x 600 mm.), lithograph in red/black on Rives BFK.

BI *Haystack Series: Haystack #7 (G. 159), 1969,* s., d., annot. A/P IX, blindstamp publisher, Gemini G.E.L., p. Charles Ritt, full margins, good cond.?, est. $1,5/2,000, (05-19-93, Butterfield, #2248, illus.), 13⅝ x 23⅝ in., (346 x 600 mm.), lithograph in black w/embossing on Special Arches.

BI *Haystack Series: Haytack #4 (G. 153), 1969,* s., d., #58/100, blindstamp publisher, Gemini G.E.L., p. Stuart Henderson, full margins, good cond., surface soiling, rubbed areas, est. $2/4,000, (05-19-93, Butterfield, #2245), 13⅜ x 23⅜ in., (340 x 594 mm.), lithograph and silkscreen in blue/red on Rives BFK.

$6050* *Head (G. 885), 1980,* s., d., #35/50, blindstamp, pub. Gemini G.E.L., full margins, good cond., discoloration, soiling, (11-07-92, Sotheby-NY, #668, illus.), 33¼ x 27¼ in., (845 x 692 mm.), woodcut p. in colors w/ embossing on Arches Cover (BP 3956, DM 9660, FR 32,650, Y 746,729).

$11,500* *Imperfect (G. 1361), 1988,* s., d., #19/45, blindstamp, pub. Gemini, G.E.L., full margins, good cond. ?, (05-15-93, Sotheby-NY, #1077, illus.), 40¾ x 92⅞ in., (103.5 x 235.9 cm.), woodcut and silkscreen in colors w/collage on Archivart Museum board (BP 7477, DM 18,498, FR 62,162, Y 1,274,803).

$8579* *Imperfect (G. 1365), 1988,* s., d., #17/45, pub. Gemini G.E.L., good cond., (06-30-93, Sotheby-London, #868, illus.), 54¼ x 81¾ in., (137.8 x 207.6 cm.), woodcut and screenprint in color on 3-ply Supra 100 (BP 5750, DM 14,632, FR 49,361, Y 919,211).

$11,500* *Imperfect (G. 1365), 1988,* s., d., #38/45, blindstamp publisher, Gemini G.E.L., full margins, very good cond.?, (05-19-93, Butterfield, #2251, illus.), 63⅜ x 88⅞ in., (161 x 225.7 cm.), woodcut and silkscreen in colors on Supra 100 (BP 7465, DM 18,693, FR 62,979, Y 1,273,110).

$9200* *Imperfect Diptych (G. 1360), 1988,* s., d., #24/45, blindstamp, pub. Gemini, G.E.L., full margins, good cond. ?, (05-15-93, Sotheby-NY, #1076, illus.), 45⅝ x 90½ in., (115.9 x 229.9 cm.), woodcut and silkscreen in colors w/ collage on Archivart Museum Board (BP 5982, DM 14,798, FR 49,730, Y 1,019,843).

BI *Imperfect Print For B.A.M. (G. 1359), 1988,* s., d. '87, #7/25, blindstamp, p. Gemini, G.E.L., from portfolio Brooklyn Academy of Music, I, pub. Parasol Press, Ltd., full margins, good cond. ?, est. $6/8,000, (05-15-93, Sotheby-NY, #1075, illus.), sheet 59⅛ x 31¼ in., (150.2 x 79.4 cm.), woodcut and silkscreen in colors on Arches Cover.

$2745* *Industry And Melody, 1969,* s., d. on remaining portion of original mount, #40/100, pub. MazzottaEditore, blindstamp, image in good cond., scuffs, scratches, foxing, glue remains, (06-30-93, Sotheby-London, #863, illus.), sh 25⅝ x 19 in., (651 x 483 mm.), color silkscreen on aluminum (BP 1840, DM 4682, FR 15,794, Y 294,118).

$3300* *Industry And Melody, 1969,* s., d., #135/250, blindstamp, pub. Editore Gabriele Mazzotta, full margins, good cond., tears, creases, (11-07-92, Sotheby-NY, #651), 17⅛ x 14¼ in., (435 x 362 mm.), silkscreen p. in colors on Fabriano (BP 2158, DM 5269, FR 17,809, Y 407,307).

$4400* *Industry and Melody, 1969,* s., d., #33/100, blindstamp, pub. Editore Gabriele Mazzotta, full margins, good cond., scratches, tape, (11-07-92, Sotheby-NY, #653, illus.), 17¼ x 14¼ in., (438 x 362 mm.), silkscreen p. in colors on aluminum, matted w/Fabriano (BP 2877, DM 7025, FR 23,745, Y 543,076).

$20,125* *Interior Series: La Sortie, 1991,* s., d. '90, #24/60, blindstamp, pub. Gemini, G.E.L., good cond. ?, (05-15-93, Sotheby-NY, #1081, illus.), sheet 58½ x 81 in., (148.6 x 205.7 cm.), woodcut in colors (BP 13,085, DM 32,371, FR 108,784, Y 2,230,906).

$1896* *Knock, Knock,* s., d., 1975, (04-21-93, Germann, #596, illus.), 21¹⁄₁₆ x 14⁹⁄₁₆ in., (535 x 370 mm.), lithograph (BP 1230, DM 3031, FR 10,249, Y 209,897, SF 2760).

$3575* *Lamp (T. 360:RL28), 1981,* s., d., #7/30, blindstamp, pub. Tyler Graphics, Ltd., full margins, good cond., (11-07-92, Sotheby-NY, #665, illus.), 19½ x 8⅛ in., (495 x 206 mm.), woodcut p. in colors on handmade Okawara (BP 2337, DM 5708, FR 19,293, Y 441,249).

$935* *Landscape 8 (B. 26H), 1967,* from Ten Landscapes, s., d., num. 35/100, pub. Original Editions, full sheet, scuffing, discoloration, good cond., (09-19-92, Christie-E, #150), sheet 19½ x 11⅛ in., (495 x 283 mm.), Rowlux and plastic collage in grey and white on composition board mounted as issued (BP 538, DM 1400, FR 4795, Y 116,496).

$330* *Lunch Counter, From Ten Works + Ten Painters), 1964,* portfolio num. 40/500, pub., full sheet, good cond., (05-22-93, Weschler, #201), 20 x 24 in., (50.8 x 61 cm.), silkscreen in colors (BP 214, DM 537, FR 1805, Y 36,384).

BI *The Melody Haunts My Reverie (B. 10), 1965,* s., #131/200, portfolio, 11 Pop Artists, Volume II, pub. Original Editions, full margins, good cond., soiling in image, scuffs, creases, est. $16/18,000, (11-07-92, Sotheby-NY, #645, illus.), 27¼ x 23 in., (692 x 584 mm.), silkscreen p. in colors.

$13,200* *The Melody Haunts My Reverie (B. 10), 1965,* from 11 Pop Artists, Volume II, Original Editions, s., #25/200, full margins, surface scuffing, excellent cond., (11-09-92, Christie-NY, #344, illus.), 30 x 24 in., (762 x 610 mm.), colored screenprint on wove (BP 8727, DM 21,073, FR 71,197, Y 1,638,124).

$11,500* *The Melody Haunts My Reverie, New York (B. 10),* from 11 Pop Artists Volume II, Original Editions, 1965, s., #68/200, full margins, light-staining, color attenuated, stains, image scuffs, printer's ink remains, very good cond., (05-11-93, Christie-NY, #491, illus.), sheet 30 x 24 in., (762 x 610 mm.), color screenprint on wove (BP 7341, DM 18,116, FR 61,040, Y 1,264,987).

BI *Merton Of The Movies, (B. 28), 1968,* s., num. 144/450, pub. List Art Poster, folded, defects, nicks, mount-staining, very good cond., est. BP 500/700, (12-01-92, Christie-London, #618), S. 30³⁄₁₆ x 20¹⁄₁₆ in., (766 x 510 mm.), screenprint in colors.

$2415* *Mirror #1 (G. 382), 1972,* s., d., #66/80, blindstamp, pub. Gemini, G.E.L., good cond., discoloration, (05-15-93, Sotheby-NY, #1069, illus.), sheet 28 x 28 in., (71.1 x 71.1 cm.), silkscreen and linocut w/embossing in colors on Arjomari paper (BP 1570, DM 3885, FR 13,054, Y 267,709).

BI *Mirror #3, 1972,* #63/80, pencil s., d., (11-20-92, Lempertz, #671, illus.), sh 27⁹⁄₁₆ x 27⁹⁄₁₆ in., (70 x 70 cm.), linocut and serigraph in color on Velin.

$1631* *Mirror #5 (Gemini 386),* s., 48/80, blindstamp Gemini, (05-12-93, AB Stockholm, #7035, illus.), 34¹⁄₁₆ x 24³⁄₁₆ in., (86.5 x 61.5 cm.), serigraph in colors (BP 1065, DM 2631, FR 8864, Y 182,092, SK 12,100).

$4620* *"Modern Art Poster (B. 21), 1967"* and *"The Solomon R. Guggenheim Museum Poster (B. 35), 1969": Two,* both s., full margins; first num. 115/300, pub. Leo Castelli Gallery, scuffing, time-staining; second d., num. 177/250, co-pub. Leo Castelli Gallery and Poster Originals Ltd., mat staining, very good cond., (09-19-92, Christie-E, #149), first, screenprint in colors on wove; second, lithograph in colors on Rives (BP 2657, DM 6918, FR 23,692, Y 575,629).

$4313* *Modern Head #1 (Gemini 242), 1970,* s., d., #72/100, blindstamp, pub. Gemini, G.E.L., full margins, good cond., (05-15-93, Sotheby-NY, #1063, illus.), sheet 24 x 19 in., (61 x 48.3 cm.), woodcut in colors on Hoshi paper (BP 2804, DM 6937, FR 23,314, Y 478,107).

BI *Modern Head #2 (G. 243), 1970,* s., d., #72/100, blindstamp, pub. Gemini, G.E.L., full margins, goodcond., est. $4,5/5,500, (05-15-93, Sotheby-NY, #1064, illus.), sheet 24½ x 18½ in., (62.2 x 47 cm.), lithograph and linocut w/embossing on handmade Waterleaf paper.

$3738* *Modern Head #3 (G. 244), 1970,* s., d., #72/100, blindstamp, pub. Gemini, G.E.L., full margins, goodcond., (05-15-93, Sotheby-NY, #1065, illus.), 24½ x 18½ in., (62.2

x 47 cm.), embossed linocut on handmade Waterleaf paper (BP 2430, DM 6013, FR 20,205, Y 414,366).

$4125* *Modern Head #4 (Gemini 245), 1970,* incised sig., d., #16/100, pub. Gemini G.E.L., good cond., scratches, (11-07-92, Sotheby-NY, #650, illus.), overall size 20¾ x 17⅜ in., (527 x 441 mm.), engraved, anodized aluminum p. in colors (BP 2697, DM 6586, FR 22,261, Y 509,134).

$3163* *Modern Head #5 (G. 246), 1970,* s., d., #72/100 on overlay, blindstamp, pub. Gemini, G.E.L., full margins, good cond., (05-15-93, Sotheby-NY, #1067, illus.), sheet 28 x 19½ in., (71.1 x 49.5 cm.), embossed graphite composition w/die-cut paper overlay (BP 2057, DM 5088, FR 17,097, Y 350,626).

$4313* *Modern Head #5 (Gemini 246), 1970,* s., d., #95/100, blindstamp of pub., Gemini G.E.L., full margins, good cond., (02-11-93, Sotheby-NY, #372, illus.), sheet 27¹⁵⁄₁₆ x 19½ in., (710 x 495 mm.), embossed graphite composition w/die-cut paper overlay on paper overlay (BP 3043, DM 7144, FR 24,176, Y 519,952).

$3025* *Modern Print (G. 277), 1971,* s., d., #137/200, blindstamp, pub. Gemini G.E.L., full margins, goodcond., soiling, rubbing, (11-07-92, Sotheby-NY, #655, illus.), 24 x 24 in., (610 x 610 mm.), lithograph and silkscreen p. in colors on Special Arjomari (BP 1978, DM 4830, FR 16,325, Y 373,365).

$1840* *Modern Print (G. 277), 1971,* s., d., #66/200, blindstamp of pub., Gemini G.E.L., full margins, good cond., crease, scuff marks, (02-11-93, Sotheby-NY, #374, illus.), 24 x 24 in., (610 x 610 mm.), silkscreen and lithograph p. in colors on Special Arjomari (BP 1298, DM 3048, FR 10,314, Y 221,820).

$967* *Modern Print, 1971,* s., #39/200, full margins, p. & pub. Gemini, excell. cond., (11-30-92, Phillips-London, #542A), sheet 24 x 24 in., (610 x 610 mm.), color lithograph and silkscreen on special Arjomari paper (BP 638, DM 1541, FR 5230, Y 120,348).

BI *Moonscape (B. 9), 1965,* s., #86/200, pub. Original Editions, from portfolio 11 Pop Artists I, good cond., est. BP 1,5/2,000, (12-03-92, Sotheby-London, #768, illus.), 20 x 24 in., (508 x 610 mm.), silkscreen in colors on metallic Rowlux.

$2970* *Morton A. Mort (G. 886), 1980,* s., d., #35/50, blindstamp, pub. Gemini G.E.L., full margins, good cond., light stain, soiling, crease, (11-07-92, Sotheby-NY, #662, illus.), 22⅞ x 32½ in., (581 x 826 mm.), woodcut p. in colors w/embossing on Arches Cover (BP 1942, DM 4742, FR 16,028, Y 366,576).

$522* *New Seascape (Bianchini 17), 1966,* s., pub. Leo Castelli Gallery, (05-27-93, Swann, #160), 12 x 8 in., (30.5 x 20.3 cm.), serigraph in black on optical plastic (BP 334, DM 838, FR 2823, Y 55,961).

$1955* *The New York Collection For Stockholm: Untitled, 1973,* copyright stamp, i. A.P. 10/25, pub. Experiments in Art and Technology, good cond., (02-11-93, Sotheby-NY, #375), sheet 11¹⁵⁄₁₆ x 8¹⁵⁄₁₆ in., (304 x 227 mm.), color silkscreen (BP 1379, DM 3238, FR 10,959, Y 235,684).

BI *Night Scene (T. 354), 1980,* s., d., #19/32, blindstamp pub. Tyler Graphics Ltd., full margins, very good cond., est. $4/5,000, (10-28-92, Butterfield, #3020, illus.), 7 x 9 in., (178 x 229 mm.), color etching w/aquatint and engraving on cream wove.

BI *Nude, 1987-9,* from Brushstroke Figures, s., d. 89, #39/60, pub. Waddington Graphics and GraphicStudio, blindstamp, full margins, excell. cond., est. $8/12,000, (11-09-92, Christie-NY, #351, illus.), 56½ x 32½ in., (143.5 x 82.6 cm.), lithograph, woodcut, screenprint, encaustic and wax in colors on Cold Pressed Saunders Waterford.

BI *The Oval Office,* s., d. '92, num. 91/175, est. $3/4000, (11-12-92, Freemn/Fine Art, #120A), 30 x 39 in., (76.2 x 99.1 cm.), screenprint.

$3300* *Oval Office, 1992,* s., d., num. 136/175, blindstamp, pub. for Democratic National Committee, full margins, apparently very good cond., (02-24-93, Butterfield, #3083, illus.), 29¾ x 39¼ in., (75.6 x 99.7 cm.), silkscreen in colors on wove (BP 2301, DM 5357, FR 18,162, Y 387,233).

BI *Oval Office, 1992,* s., d., #131/175, pub. for Democratic National Committee, blindstampprinter, Brand X Editions, full margins, very good cond., est. $2,5/3,500, (05-

19-93, Butterfield, #2254, illus.), 29¾ x 39¼ in., (75.6 x 99.7 cm.), silkscreen in colors on wove.

BI *Painting In A Gold Frame (G. 1145), 1984,* s., d., #35/60, blindstamp, pub. Gemini G.E.L., full margins, good cond., soiling, est. $8/10,000, (11-07-92, Sotheby-NY, #667), 43¼ x 33 in., (109.9 x 83.8 cm.), woodcut, lithograph and silkscreen p. in colors w/collage on Arches 88.

$5175* *Painting In A Gold Frame (G. 1145), 1984,* s., d., #35/60, blindstamp of pub., Gemini G.E.L., full margins, good cond., soiling, (02-11-93, Sotheby-NY, #378, illus.), 43¼ x 32¹⁵⁄₁₆ in., (109.9 x 83.6 cm.), woodcut, lithograph, and silkscreen p. in colors w/collage, on Arches 88 (BP 3652, DM 8572, FR 29,008, Y 623,870).

BI *Painting On Blue And Yellow Wall (G. 1147), 1984,* s., d., #15/60, blindstamp, pub. Gemini, G.E.L., full margins, good cond., skinned spots, est. $5/7,000, (11-07-92, Sotheby-NY, #663, illus.), 44⅛ x 28½ in., (112.1 x 72.4 cm.), woodcut and lithograph p. in colors on Arches 88.

$3738* *Painting On Blue And Yellow Wall (G. 1147), 1984,* s., d., #15/60, blindstamp of pub., Gemini, G.E.L., full margins, good cond., skinned spots, (02-11-93, Sotheby-NY, #381, illus.), 44⅛ x 28⁷⁄₁₆ in., (112 x 72.3 cm.), woodcut and lithograph p. in colors on Arches 88 (BP 2638, DM 6192, FR 20,953, Y 450,633).

$3450* *Painting On Canvas (G. 1141), 1984,* s., d., #10/60, blindstamp of Gemini, G.E.L., full margins, good cond., (02-11-93, Sotheby-NY, #376, illus.), 30⅞ x 25⅞ in., (785 x 657 mm.), woodcut, lithograph, and silkscreen p. in colors w/collage, on Arches 88 (BP 2434, DM 5715, FR 19,339, Y 415,913).

BI *Poetry Of Everyday Life, 1988,* s., full margins, very good cond., est. $1,5/2,000, (05-19-93, Butterfield, #2252, illus.), 40 x 26¾ in., (101.6 x 67.9 cm.), silkscreen in colors on wove.

BI *The Poetry Project 1988 Symposium,* pencil s., est. DM 1,500, (11-20-92, Lempertz, #673), sh 44⅛ x 31 in., (112 x 78.8 cm.), serigraph in color on hand-made cardboard.

$121* *The Poetry Project, 1988,* after painting of 1976, (09-20-92, Hindman, #719), 42¾ x 30 in., (108.6 x 76.2 cm.), color serigraph (BP 71, DM 180, FR 614, Y 14,955).

BI *Portrait (Fine and Corlett 140), 1987-89,* from Brushstroke Figures, s., d. 89, #16/60, pub. Waddington Graphics, Graphicstudio, USF blindstamp, full margins, excell. cond., est. $8/10,000, (05-11-93, Christie-NY, #494, illus.), sheet 52½ x 34¼ in., (133.4 x 87 cm.), color lithograph, woodcut, screenprint, encaustic and wax on Cold Pressed Saunders Waterford.

BI *Pyramid (B. 31), 1968,* folded in shape of pyramid, s., #99/300, pub. Leo Castelli Gallery, good cond., inkloss, creases, est. $2/4,000, (05-19-93, Butterfield, #2240, illus.), 19¾ x 19¾ in., (502 x 502 mm.), silkscreen in black/yellow on composition board.

BI *Pyramid (Bianchini 31), 1968,* #3/300, pencil s., est. DM 5,000, 50 x 50 x 50 cm., (11-20-92, Lempertz, #670, illus.), color serigraph on cardboard.

$3450* *Pyramids, 1969,* s., d., #85/101, pub. Mourlot, full margins, good cond., light-stain, handling crease, discoloration, soiling, (05-15-93, Sotheby-NY, #1062, illus.), 11⅝ x 35 in., (29.5 x 88.9 cm.), lithograph in yellow and black on Arches (BP 2243, DM 5549, FR 18,649, Y 382,441).

$2046* *Real Estate (B. 37), 1969,* s., d., #85/100, p. Mourlot, pub. IRL, full margins, good cond., (12-03-92, Sotheby-London, #766, illus.), 13¼ x 31⅞ in., (340 x 810 mm.), lithograph in blue on Arches (BP 1320, DM 3217, FR 10,982, Y 254,573).

$4180* *Real Estate (B. 37), 1969,* s., d., #72/100, pub. Publications IRL, full margins, good cond., creases, (11-07-92, Sotheby-NY, #648, illus.), 13½ x 31⅞ in., (343 x 810 mm.), lithograph p. in blue (BP 2733, DM 6674, FR 22,558, Y 515,922).

$2574* *Real Estate (Bianchini 37), 1969,* s., d., #2/100, p. by Mouriot, pub. Publications IRL, full margins, good cond., creasing, skinning, (06-30-93, Sotheby-London, #876), sh 19⅜ x 37¾ in., (492 x 959 mm.), lithograph in blue on Arches (BP 1725, DM 4390, FR 14,810, Y 275,796).

$1779* *Red Barn, 1969,* s., blindstamp Gabriele Mazzotta Editore, 240/250, (05-12-93, AB Stockholm, #7034, illus.), 14³⁄₁₆ x 17⅛ in., (36 x 43.5 cm.), serigraph in colors on Fabriano (BP 1162, DM 2870, FR 9668, Y 198,616, SK 13,200).

BI *Red Lamp And Table,* s., d. '92, num. 249/250, est. $1200/1500, (11-12-92, Freemn/Fine Art, #120B), 16 x 18½ in., (40.6 x 47 cm.), screenprint.

$1265* *Red Lamp, 1991,* s., d., #154/250, blindstamp, pub. Tyler Graphics, Ltd., good cond., (05-15-93, Sotheby-NY, #1082), sheet 21½ x 24 in., (54.6 x 61 cm.), lithograph in colors on BFK Rives (BP 822, DM 2035, FR 6838, Y 140,228).

BI *Reflection On Conversation, 1990,* from The Reflection Series, s., d., #5/68, blindstamps, full margins, excellent cond., est. $14/16,000, (11-09-92, Christie-NY, #354, illus.), 54 x 67¼ in., (137.2 x 170.8 cm.), lithograph, screenprint, woodcut, collage and embossing in colors onwove.

BI *Reflections On Brushstrokes, 1990,* from The Reflections Series, s., d., #5/68, blindstamp, full margins, excellent cond., est. $14/16,000, (11-09-92, Christie-NY, #353, illus.), 57½ x 71½ in., (146.1 x 181.6 cm.), lithograph, screenprint, woodcut, collage and embossing in colors onwove.

$22,000* *Reflections On Crash, 1990,* s., d., #5/68, blindstamp, pub. Tyler Graphics, Ltd., full margins, good cond., (11-07-92, Sotheby-NY, #674, illus.), 53 x 68⅞ in., (134.6 x 174.9 cm.), lithograph, silkscreen, woodcut, metalized PVC plastic film and embossing p. in colors w/collage on Somerset (BP 14,384, DM 35,127, FR 118,726, Y 2,715,379).

$19,550* *Reflections On Crash, 1990,* from The Reflections Series, s., d., #67/68, Tyler Graphics blindstamp, full margins, excell. cond., (05-11-93, Christie-NY, #496, illus.), sheet 59¼ x 75⅛ in., (150.5 x 190.8 cm.), color screenprint on wove (BP 12,480, DM 30,797, FR 103,769, Y 2,150,478).

$20,700* *Reflections On Crash, 1990,* s., d., #5/68, blindstamp, pub. Tyler Graphics, Ltd., full margins, good cond. ?, (05-15-93, Sotheby-NY, #1080, illus.), sheet 52½ x 68¾ in., (133.4 x 174.6 cm.), lithograph, silkscreen, woodcut, metalized PVC plastic film and embossing in colors, w/collage on Somerset paper (BP 13,459, DM 33,296, FR 111,892, Y 2,294,646).

$12,075* *Reflections On Girl, 1990,* s., d., #2/68, blindstamp, pub. Tyler Graphics, Ltd., full margins, good cond., catalog cover lot, (05-15-93, Sotheby-NY, #1079, illus.), 45⅛ x 54¾ in., (114.6 x 139.1 cm.), lithograph, silkscreen, woodcut, metalized PVC plastic film and embossing in colors w/collage on Somerset (BP 7851, DM 19,423, FR 65,270, Y 1,338,543).

$9900* *Reflections On Hair, 1990,* s., d., #5/68, blindstamp, pub. Tyler Graphics, Ltd., full margins, good cond., (11-07-92, Sotheby-NY, #673, illus.), 49¼ x 39 in., (125.1 x 99.1 cm.), lithograph, silkscreen, woodcut, metalized PVC plastic film and embossing p. in colors w/collage on Somerset (BP 6473, DM 15,807, FR 53,427, Y 1,221,921).

$8800* *Reflections On Minerva, 1990,* s., d., #5/68, blindstamp, pub. Tyler Graphics, Ltd., good cond., (11-07-92, Sotheby-NY, #672, illus.), 35¼ x 45⅝ in., (89.5 x 115.9 cm.), lithograph, silkscreen, woodcut, metalized PVC plastic film and embossing p. in colors w/collage on Somerset (BP 5754, DM 14,051, FR 47,491, Y 1,086,152).

$6326* *Reflections On Scream, 1990,* s., d., num. 21/68, blindstamp, margins, very good cond., L. 1074 x 1500 mm., (12-01-92, Christie-London, #621, illus.), woodcut, lithograph and screenprint in colors on wove (BP 4180, DM 10,083, FR 34,362, Y 787,600).

$17,600* *Reflections On The Scream, 1990,* from The Reflections Series, s., d., #5/68, blindstamp, full margins, excellent cond., (11-09-92, Christie-NY, #355, illus.), 49 x 65½ in., (124.5 x 166.4 cm.), lithograph, woodcut, screenprint, collage and embossing in colors onwove (BP 11,636, DM 28,097, FR 94,930, Y 2,184,165).

$3575* *Repeated Design (B. 36), 1969,* s., d., #47/100, pub. by artist, full maargins, good cond., (11-07-92, Sotheby-NY,

#647, illus.), 12 x 35⅞ in., (305 x 911 mm.), lithograph p. in black and yellow (BP 2337, DM 5708, FR 19,293, Y 441,249).

BI *Roads Collar (F. and C. 141), 1987-89,* s., d. 89, #23/30, Graphicstudio, USF blindstamp, full margins, excell. cond., the Late M. Anwar Kamal, M.D. Coll., est. $7/9,000, (05-11-93, Christie-NY, #495, illus.), sheet 52¼ x 28½ in., (132.7 x 72.4 cm.), color lithograph, woodcut, screenprint and wax on wove.

$1980* *Rouen Cathedral 6 (Waldman 34-F),* s., d. '69, #69/75, bearing chopmark Gemini G.E.L., (10-18-92, Hindman, #488, illus.), 48¼ x 32¼ in., (123.2 x 81.9 cm.), lithograph in black and blue (BP 1212, DM 2947, FR 9995, Y 237,552).

$1265* *Sandwich & Soda (Bianchini 7), 1964,* from Ten Works + Ten Painters portfolio, pub. Wadsworth Atheneum, full margins, good cond., scuffs, (05-15-93, Sotheby-NY, #1061, illus.), 19⅛ x 23 in., (48.6 x 58.4 cm.), silkscreen in blue and red on clear plastic (BP 822, DM 2035, FR 6838, Y 140,228).

$1320* *Sandwich And Soda (B. 7), 1964,* from the Ten Works + Ten Painters portfolio, pub. Wadsworth Atheneum,full margins, good cond., prop. Woodward Foundation, (11-07-92, Sotheby-NY, #641, illus.), 19⅛ x 23 in., (486 x 584 mm.), silkscreen p. in blue and red (rosso) on clear plastic (BP 863, DM 2108, FR 7124, Y 162,923).

$605* *Sandwich And Soda, 1964,* from 10 Works by 10 Painters, pub. Wadsworth Atheneum, (12-08-92, Swann, #180, illus.), 19 x 23 in., (48.3 x 58.4 cm.), color silkscreen on plexiglas (BP 379, DM 942, FR 3211, Y 74,988).

$6875* *Shipboard Girl (B. 12), 1965,* s., pub. Leo Castelli Gallery, full margins, good cond., creases, (11-07-92, Sotheby-NY, #644, illus.), 26 x 19⅛ in., (660 x 486 mm.), offset lithograph p. in colors (BP 4495, DM 10,977, FR 37,102, Y 848,556).

$5500* *Shipboard Girl (B. 12), 1965,* s., pub. Leo Castelli Gallery, full margins, colors faded, light-staining, creases, indentations, hinge remains, (10-28-92, Butterfield, #3017, illus.), 26 x 19¼ in., (660 x 489 mm.), color offset lithograph on cream wove (BP 3504, DM 8494, FR 28,841, Y 674,847).

$1840* *Shipboard Girl (B. 12), 1965,* s., pub. Leo Castelli Gallery, full margins, good cond., colors faded, (02-11-93, Sotheby-NY, #371), 25⅞ x 19$^{5}/_{16}$ in., (658 x 490 mm.), offset color lithograph (BP 1298, DM 3048, FR 10,314, Y 221,820).

$2300* *The Solomon R. Guggenheim Museum Poster (B. 35), 1969,* s., d., #85/250, co-pub. Leo Castelli Gallery and Poster Originals, full margins, colors faded, image scratches, mat staining, creases, good cond., (05-11-93, Christie-NY, #492), sheet 28⅜ x 28½ in., (721 x 724 mm.), color lithograph on wove (BP 1468, DM 3623, FR 12,208, Y 252,997).

$660* *Stedelijk Museum Poster (B. 23), 1967,* s., pub. Stedelijk Museum, good cond., water staining extending intoimage, creases, foxing, pressure marks in image, inkloss, (02-24-93, Butterfield, #3079), 30⅛ x 25⅛ in., (765 x 638 mm.), offset lithograph in red, yellow & black on wove (BP 460, DM 1071, FR 3632, Y 77,447).

$63* *Stedelijk Museum Poster (WVZ Bianchini 23), 1967,* (09-30-92, Kunsthallen, #184), offset in colors (BP 36, DM 89, FR 302, Y 7560, DK 345).

$4400* *Still Life With Crystal Bowl, 1976,* s., d., #31/45, co-pub. by Multiples, Inc. and Castelli Graphics, full margins, good cond., yellow, faded, skinned spot, (11-07-92, Sotheby-NY, #660, illus.), 31⅞ x 43¼ in., (81 x 109.9 cm.), lithograph and silkscreen p. in colors (BP 2877, DM 7025, FR 23,745, Y 543,076).

$7150* *Still Life With Lobster, 1974,* s., d., #41/100, from suite Six Still Lifes, co-pub. by Multiples, Inc. and Castelli Graphics, full margins, good cond., crease, scuff mark, (11-07-92, Sotheby-NY, #659, illus.), 32¼ x 31 in., (819 x 787 mm.), silkscreen and lithograph p. in colors on BFK Rives (BP 4675, DM 11,416, FR 38,586, Y 882,498).

BI *Still Life With Portrait, 1974,* s., d., #6/100, p. by Styria Studio, blindstamp, pub. Multiples, Inc., and Castelli Gallery, full margins, good cond., handling creases, est. BP 4/5,000, (06-30-93, Sotheby-London, #864, illus.), 38¼ x 28½ in., (972 x 724 mm.), lithograph and silkscreen in color on wove.

$6493* *Still Life With Portrait, 1974,* from Six Still Lifes, s., d., nnum. 24/100, pub. Multiples Inc. and Castelli Graphics, margins, apparently excell. cond., (12-01-92, Christie-London, #620, illus.), L. 37$^{15}/_{16}$ x 28$^{9}/_{16}$ in., (965 x 725 mm.), lithograph w/screen print in colors (BP 4290, DM 10,349, FR 35,269, Y 808,391).

$6600* *Still Life With Windmill, 1974,* s., d., i. 'PP 4/5', printer's proofs, from suite Six Still Lifes, co-pub. by Multiples, Inc. and Castelli Graphics, full margins, good cond., waterstain, (11-07-92, Sotheby-NY, #657, illus.), 29⅛ x 38⅛ in., (740 x 968 mm.), lithograph and silkscreen p. in colors w/embossing on BFK Rives (BP 4315, DM 10,538, FR 35,618, Y 814,614).

BI *Still Life With Windmill, 1974,* #30/100, pencil s., num., d., from series Six Still Lifes, Edition Castelli Graphics, est. DM 15,000, (11-20-92, Lempertz, #672, illus.), sh 35$^{1}/_{16}$ x 44⅛ in., (89 x 112 cm.), color lithograph and serigraph on thick Velin.

$1320* *Study For Red Lamp, 1991,* s., d. '92, num. 84/250, blindstamp, full margins, very good cond., (02-24-93, Butterfield, #3082), 15⅞ x 18½ in., (403 x 470 mm.), lithograph in colors on wove (BP 921, DM 2143, FR 7265, Y 154,893).

$1870* *Study For Red Lamp, 1991,* s., d. '92, #58/250, blindstamp pub. Tyler Graphics, full margins, very good cond., (10-28-92, Butterfield, #3023, illus.), 16 x 18½ in., (406 x 470 mm.), color lithograph on white wove (BP 1191, DM 2888, FR 9806, Y 229,448).

BI *Study For Red Lamp, 1991,* s., d. '92, #59/250, blindstamp printer, Tyler Graphics, full margins, very good cond., est. $1,5/2,000, (05-19-93, Butterfield, #2253), 16 x 18$^{12}/$ in., (406 x 457 mm.), lithograph in colors on wove.

$3025* *Study Of Hands, 1981,* s., d., i. 'AP 14/24', proofs, pub. Castelli Graphics, full margins,good cond., (11-07-92, Sotheby-NY, #664, illus.), sheet 31½ x 32⅝ in., (800 x 829 mm.), silkscreen p. in colors (BP 1978, DM 4830, FR 16,325, Y 373,365).

BI *Sunrise,* s., est. $1,5/2,500, (09-24-92, Mystic, #47), 18 x 25 in., (45.7 x 63.5 cm.), colored lithograph.

$1210* *Sunrise (B. 15), 1965,* s., pub. Leo Castelli Gallery, full margins, repaired tears, one extending into image, colors faded, discoloration, (11-07-92, Sotheby-NY, #649), 17¼ x 23¼ in., (438 x 591 mm.), offset lithograph p. in colors (BP 791, DM 1932, FR 6530, Y 149,346).

$2508* *Sunrise (Bianchini 15), 1965,* s., num., (05-27-93, Lempertz, #861, illus.), 18⅜ x 24$^{5}/_{16}$ in., (46.7 x 61.8 cm.), color offset lithograph on wove (BP 1606, DM 4024, FR 13,564, Y 268,868).

BI *Sweet Dreams Baby (Bianchini 11), 1965,* s., #152/200, from portfolio 11 Pop Artists, pub. Original Editions,margins, good cond., est. BP 10/12,000, (12-03-92, Sotheby-London, #764, illus.), sheet approx. 37⅝ x 27½ in., (956 x 700 mm.), silkscreen in colors.

$6600* *Sweet Dreams Baby! (B. 11), 1965,* from 11 Pop Artists, Volume III, Original Editions, s., #41/200, full margins, light-staining, foxing, surface scrapes, tears, creasing, patches, remains of glue, soiling, (11-09-92, Christie-NY, #345, illus.), 37½ x 27½ in., (953 x 699 mm.), colored screenprint on wove (BP 4364, DM 10,536, FR 35,599, Y 819,062).

BI *Sweet Dreams, Baby! (B. 11), 1965,* s., #159/200, from portfolio, 11 Pop Artists III, pub. Original Editions, full margins, good cond., yellow attenuated, discoloration, scuff marks, est. $15/20,000, (02-11-93, Sotheby-NY, #370, illus.), 35⅝ x 25$^{9}/_{16}$ in., (905 x 650 mm.), color silkscreen.

$13,200* *Tel Aviv Museum Print, 1989,* s., d., #58/60, printer's blindstamp, Tyler Graphics, Ltd., pub. Friends of the Tel Aviv Museum of Art, full margins, good cond., creases, (11-07-92, Sotheby-NY, #669, illus.), 20⅝ x 51½ in., (52.4 x 130.8 cm.), silkscreen p. in colors (BP 8630, DM 21,076, FR 71,236, Y 1,629,227).

$2090* *Temple (B. 6), 1964,* s., d., #74/300, pub. Leo Castelli Gallery, full margins, good cond.,nick, creases, (11-07-92, Sotheby-NY, #643, illus.), 23 x 17⅛ in., (584 x 435 mm.), offset lithograph p. in blue and black (BP 1366, DM 3337, FR 11,279, Y 257,961).

$2200* *This Must Be The Place (B. 13), 1965,* s., printed sig., pub. The Cartoonists Society, full margins, good cond., staining, creases, (11-07-92, Sotheby-NY, #646, illus.), 21¼ x 16 in., (540 x 406 mm.), offset lithograph p. in colors (BP 1438, DM 3513, FR 11,873, Y 271,538).

$1023* *Turkey Shopping Bag (B. 8), 1964,* s., pub. Bianchini Gallery, good cond., fox marks, (12-03-92, Sotheby-London, #765, illus.), overall size 23⅜ x 17 in., (595 x 433 mm.), silkscreen in yellow and red on shopping bag (BP 660, DM 1609, FR 5491, Y 127,286).

$920* *Twin Mirrors, 1970,* s., #15/250, pub. Solomon R. Guggenheim Museum, full margins, good cond., crease, (02-11-93, Sotheby-NY, #373), 33⅞ x 20¹⁵⁄₁₆ in., (860 x 532 mm.), silkscreen p. in black and blue (BP 649, DM 1524, FR 5157, Y 110,910).

$2200* *Twin Mirrors, 1970,* s., d., #233/250, pub. Solomon R. Guggenheim Museum, full margins, surface scuffs, excellent cond., (11-09-92, Christie-NY, #346, illus.), 39 x 26 in., (99.1 x 66 cm.), colored screenprint on wove (BP 1455, DM 3512, FR 11,866, Y 273,021).

BI *Two Figures With Teepee (T. 355), 1980,* s., d., #14/32, blindstamp pub. Tyler Graphics, Ltd., full margins, very good cond., est. $3,5/4,500, (10-28-92, Butterfield, #3021, illus.), 8 x 8 in., (203 x 203 mm.), color aquatint w/ engraving on cream wove.

$8800* *Two Paintings (G. 1144), 1984,* s., d., #35/60, blindstamp, pub. Gemini G.E.L., full margins, good cond., (11-07-92, Sotheby-NY, #666, illus.), 43 x 36 in., (109.2 x 91.4 cm.), woodcut, lithograph and silkscreen p. in colors w/collage on Arches 88 (BP 5754, DM 14,051, FR 47,491, Y 1,086,152).

$8050* *Two Paintings (G. 1144), 1984,* s., d., #50/60, blindstamp of pub., Gemini G.E.L., full margins, good cond., (02-11-93, Sotheby-NY, #377, illus.), 42¹⁵⁄₁₆ x 35¹⁵⁄₁₆ in., (109 x 91.3 cm.), woodcut, lithograph, and silkscreen p. in colors w/collage, on Arches 88 (BP 5680, DM 13,334, FR 45,123, Y 970,464).

BI *Two Paintings: Beach Ball (Gemini 1143), 1984,* s., d., #46/60, blindstamps, full margins, excellent cond., est. $7/9,000, (11-09-92, Christie-NY, #350, illus.), 40 x 39 in., (101.6 x 99.1 cm.), woodcut, lithograph and screenprint in colors on Arches.

BI *Two Paintings: Sleeping Muse (G. 1142), 1984,* s., d., #10/60, blindstamp, pub. Gemini, G.E.L., full margins, good cond., pressure mark in image, crease, soiling, est. $9/11,000, (05-15-93, Sotheby-NY, #1074, illus.), 34¾ x 45⅞ in., (88.3 x 116.5 cm.), woodcut, lithograph and silkscreen in colors on Arches 88.

$3069* *Untitled, 1987,* s., d., #18/75, from portfolio, pub. Parasol Press, margins, good cond., (12-03-92, Sotheby-London, #767, illus.), 45½ x 31½ in., (115.6 x 80 cm.), woodcut and silkscreen in colors (BP 1980, DM 4826, FR 16,473, Y 381,859).

$93* *"Whaam",* pub. Tate Gallery, (08-18-92, Encans, #126), 24⁷⁄₁₆ x 29⅛ in., (62 x 74 cm.), serigraph poster (BP 48, DM 135, FR 459, Y 11,725, C$ 111).

LICHTENSTEIN, Roy (after)

$235* *Wham!,* (01-21-93, Bonhams-Chelsea, #27), image 24¾ x 58 in., (62.9 x 147.3 cm.), reproduced in color (BP 154, DM 374, FR 1264, Y 29,412).

LIDNER, Richard   1901-1978

$130* *"Femme Et Oiseau",* s. in plate, (04-04-93, Pescheteau, #246), 12³⁄₁₆ x 9⁷⁄₁₆ in., (31 x 24 cm.), color lithograph (BP 86, DM 209, FR 710, Y 14,801).

$240* *"New-York City",* #14/175, s., (04-04-93, Pescheteau, #245), 25⁹⁄₁₆ x 19¹¹⁄₁₆ in., (65 x 50 cm.), photolithograph on wove (BP 158, DM 386, FR 1310, Y 27,326).

BI *Shoot, 1971,* s., #LXXIV/LXXV, est. FF2/2,500, (05-27-93, Briest, #131), 26⁹⁄₁₆ x 20¼ in., (67.5 x 51.5 cm.), color lithograph.

LIEBERMAN, Nathaniel   American contemporary

$140* *The East River,* s. on mat; stamped verso, (02-04-93, Sloan, #2907), 15¾ x 20 in., (40 x 50.8 cm.), photograph, (BP 97, DM 232, FR 785, Y 17,422).

$175* *Empire State Building; Evening,* s. on mat; stamped verso, (02-04-93, Sloan, #2910, illus.), 15¾ x 20 in., (40

x 50.8 cm.), photograph, (BP 121, DM 290, FR 981, Y 21,777).

$175* *Manhattan Skyline; Dusk,* s. on mat; stamped verso, (02-04-93, Sloan, #2906), 15¾ x 20 in., (40 x 50.8 cm.), photograph, (BP 121, DM 290, FR 981, Y 21,777).

$275* *Topographical View Above Central Park; Winter,* s. on mat; stamped verso, (02-04-93, Sloan, #2908), 15¾ x 20 in., (40 x 50.8 cm.), photograph, (BP 190, DM 456, FR 1541, Y 34,221).

$160* *View Of Manhattan; Dusk,* s. on mat; stamped verso, (02-04-93, Sloan, #2909), 15¾ x 20 in., (40 x 50.8 cm.), photograph, (BP 111, DM 265, FR 897, Y 19,910).

LIEBERMANN, Max   German 1847-1935

$3172* *Allee (Achenbach 110), 1926,* s., (12-05-92, Bassenge, #7429, illus.), 8¼ x 10¼ in., (21 x 26 cm.), lithograph on China (BP 1986, DM 4945, FR 16,854, Y 393,012).

$1106* *Aus Dem Judenviertel In Amsterdam: Der Fischmarkt (Klein), 1909,* s., num., (12-05-92, Bassenge, #7411), 5⅞ x 7 in., (14.9 x 17.8 cm.), etching on thick handmade (BP 693, DM 1724, FR 5877, Y 137,034).

$1986* *"Aus Dem Judenviertel In Amsterdam; der Fischmarkt An Der Strassenecke (Gross)" (Schiefler 77/IIa), 1908,* s., i., artist's proof, prov., (06-05-93, Grisebach, #734, illus.), etching w/chalk and Deckweiss ubergangen on Japan (BP 1307, DM 3220, FR 10,852, Y 213,044).

$406* *Badende (Achenbach 116), 1926,* s., (12-05-92, Bassenge, #7433), 9⁷⁄₁₆ x 7⅞ in., (24 x 20 cm.), lithograph on handmade China (BP 254, DM 633, FR 2157, Y 50,304).

$504* *Badende (Achenbach 116), 1926,* s., (11-27-92, Zeller, #637), 12³⁄₁₆ x 16⁹⁄₁₆ in., (31 x 42 cm.), lithograph (BP 332, DM 805, FR 2735, Y 62,726).

$959* *Badende Jungen (Schiefler 313 c), 1918,* s., num., (12-05-92, Bassenge, #7417), 7 x 9¼ in., (17.8 x 23.5 cm.), etching on copper print paper (BP 601, DM 1495, FR 5096, Y 118,820).

$660* *Badende Jungen (Schiefler 52), 1904,* s., large margins, good cond., repaired loss, skinned spots, glue stains, (11-05-92, Sotheby-NY, #228), 7⅛ x 9⅜ in., (181 x 237 mm.), etching on white wove (BP 429, DM 1044, FR 3531, Y 80,972).

$664* *Badende Knaben (Schiefler 85 c), 1909,* s., num., (12-05-92, Bassenge, #7412), 10¼ x 14³⁄₁₆ in., (26 x 36 cm.), lithograph on handmade (BP 416, DM 1035, FR 3528, Y 82,270).

$397* *"Badende" (Achenbach 116), 1926,* sheet 9 of series "9 Steinzeichnungen", Berlin, pub. Bruno Cassirer, (11-28-92, Grisebach, #628, illus.), 9⁷⁄₁₆ x 7¹¹⁄₁₆ in., (24 x 19.5 cm.), lithograph on China (BP 262, DM 632, FR 2147, Y 49,409).

$443* *Der Barmherzige Samariter (Schiefler 108 III b), 1910,* s., (12-05-92, Bassenge, #7414), 7⅞ x 9⁷⁄₁₆ in., (20 x 24 cm.), etching on wove (BP 277, DM 691, FR 2354, Y 54,888).

$738* *Bildnis Richard Strauss (Schiefler 320), 1919,* s., (12-05-92, Bassenge, #7418), 18⅞ x 15⅜ in., (48 x 39 cm.), lithograph on Japan (BP 462, DM 1151, FR 3921, Y 91,438).

$272* *Die Bootsfahrt (Schiefler LXV),* s., illus. for Der Mann von funfzig Jahren, staining, (09-25-92, Granier, #2917), sheet 5⅞ x 4¾ in., (15 x 12 cm.), lithograph on Japan (BP 159, DM 403, FR 1363, Y 32,830).

BI *Brustbild Eines Herrn Mit Ubereinander Gelegten Handen,* est. DM 1,800, (12-05-92, Bassenge, #7405), 12⅜ x 10¹³⁄₁₆ in., (31.5 x 27.5 cm.), etching.

$738* *Dackel Im Lehnstuhl (Schiefler 165), 1914,* s., red stain, creased, yellowed, (12-05-92, Bassenge, #7415), 11¹³⁄₁₆ x 7⅞ in., (30 x 20 cm.), lithograph on handmade Japan (BP 462, DM 1151, FR 3921, Y 91,438).

$325* *"Dame Im Pelz, Sitzend" (Achenbach 54 VI a), 1923,* s., num., (11-28-92, Grisebach, #623, illus.), 11¹¹⁄₁₆ x 9³⁄₁₆ in., (29.7 x 23.4 cm.), drypoint on handmade (BP 215, DM 518, FR 1758, Y 40,448).

$1145* *Damenreitpferd (Sch. 128/I), 1912,* s., i. I Etat, prov., (06-23-93, Kornfeld, #528), drypoint on Japan reworked in pencil (BP 778, DM 1937, FR 6517, Y 124,741, SF 1725).

$2138* *Einzug Der Konigin Von Holland In Einer Stadt (Sch. 146/I), 1913,* s. in pencil, i. I Etat, prov., (06-23-93, Kornfeld, #529, illus.), drypoint on Japan, reworked in charcoal (BP 1452, DM 3618, FR 12,168, Y 232,923, SF 3220).

$885* *Eislauf (Achenbach 59 c), 1923,* s., (12-05-92, Bassenge, #7426), 4¹⁵/₁₆ x 6⅞ in., (12.5 x 17.5 cm.), etching on wove (BP 554, DM 1380, FR 4702, Y 109,652).

$1588* *"Eislauf" (Achenbach 59 b), 1923,* s., num., (11-28-92, Grisebach, #624, illus.), 4¹³/₁₆ x 6¾ in., (12.2 x 17.1 cm.), etching with drypoint on copper print paper (BP 1048, DM 2530, FR 8588, Y 197,635).

$664* *Fischerdorf (Schiefler 37 II), 1896,* s., (12-05-92, Bassenge, #7408), 4¾ x 6¼ in., (12 x 15.8 cm.), etching on Japan w/drypoint work (BP 416, DM 1035, FR 3528, Y 82,270).

$1170* *Gartenszene (Schiefler 331 II d), 1921,* s., (12-02-92, Dorling, #2856, illus.), 4⁷/₁₆ x 6⅞ in., (11.2 x 17.5 cm.), drypoint on Japan (BP 755, DM 1840, FR 6280, Y 145,577).

$916* *Gartenszene (Warterin, Kind, Und Hund) (Schiefler 331 II), 1921,* s., (05-26-93, Lempertz, #298), 15⅜ x 13⅜ in., (39 x 34 cm.), etching on Zanders (BP 593, DM 1495, FR 5030, Y 99,522).

$1277* *"Die Gartenterrasse (Der Gehversuch)" (Schiefler 354 II b), 1922,* s., (06-05-93, Grisebach, #741, illus.), 7¹¹/₁₆ x 10³/₁₆ in., (19.5 x 25.8 cm.), drypoint on Japan (BP 841, DM 2070, FR 6978, Y 136,988).

$1291* *Gartenwirtschaft Am Wasser, 1911,* s., #32/50, (11-03-92, Fischer, #5137), 8¹⁵/₁₆ x 11⁵/₁₆ in., (22.8 x 28.8 cm.), drypoint on Van Gelder handmade (BP 833, DM 2020, FR 6845, Y 157,689, SF 1800).

$1121* *Goethe, Gedichte (A. 63, 64, 66, 67, 69, 73, 74 and 79), 1924: Nine,* s., pub. Paul Cassirer, (12-01-92, Karl/Faber, #928), smallest 4⁵/₁₆ x 6⅛ in., (11 x 15.5 cm.), largest 7½ x 8¹¹/₁₆ in., (11 x 15.5 cm.), lithograph on Japan (BP 741, DM 1787, FR 6089, Y 139,567).

$780* *"Jager Mit Hunden" (Schiefler 161 III b), 1914,* s., (06-05-93, Grisebach, #735, illus.), 6¹⁵/₁₆ x 9⁵/₁₆ in., (17.7 x 23.7 cm.), drypoint on copper print paper, aufgezogen (laid down) on board (BP 513, DM 1265, FR 4262, Y 83,673).

$667* *Jakob Departing From Isaac And Rebecca,* s., margins, (11-30-92, Phillips-London, #452), image 7½ x 6¼ in., (191 x 159 mm.), lithograph on wove (BP 440, DM 1063, FR 3607, Y 83,012).

$851* *Die Judengasse (Schiefler 136 b),* s., blindstamp, (06-05-93, Bassenge, #6288, illus.), 10¹³/₁₆ x 13¹⁵/₁₆ in., (27.5 x 35.5 cm.), lithograph on hand-made China (BP 560, DM 1380, FR 4650, Y 91,289).

$2128* *Die Judenstrasse In Amsterdam (Schiefler 57 b), 1906,* s., (06-05-93, Bassenge, #6272, illus.), 7⁹/₁₆ x 9¹³/₁₆ in., (19.2 x 24.9 cm.), etching on hand-made (BP 1401, DM 3450, FR 11,628, Y 228,277).

$1770* *Die Judenstrasse In Amsterdam (Schiefler 57 b), 1906,* s., (12-05-92, Bassenge, #7410), 8⅞ x 10¹³/₁₆ in., (22.5 x 27.5 cm.), etching on handmade (BP 1108, DM 2760, FR 9405, Y 219,304).

$738* *Junge Frau Im Pelz (Schiefler 365 II), 1922,* s., II/2, artist's proof, (12-05-92, Bassenge, #7422), 7⅞ x 5⁷/₁₆ in., (20 x 13.8 cm.), etching on wove (BP 462, DM 1151, FR 3921, Y 91,438).

$1011* *"Kaffeegarten" (Schiefler 358/II b), 1922,* s., (11-28-92, Grisebach, #622, illus.), 8½ x 12⁵/₁₆ in., (21.6 x 31.2 cm.), drypoint on handmade copper print paper (BP 667, DM 1611, FR 5468, Y 125,825).

$816* *"Kind Auf Dem SLofa Liegend" (Schiefler 334 III d), 1921,* s., (06-05-93, Grisebach, #738, illus.), 7⅞ x 11 in., (20 x 28 cm.), drypoint on Japan (BP 537, DM 1323, FR 4459, Y 87,535).

$443* *Kinder Am Strande (Schiefler 98), 1909,* s., (12-05-92, Bassenge, #7413), 4½ x 6½ in., (11.5 x 16.5 cm.), lithograph on wove (BP 277, DM 691, FR 2354, Y 54,888).

$443* *Kindervolkskuche (Schiefler 202), 1915,* s., (12-05-92, Bassenge, #7416), 9⁷/₁₆ x 11⁵/₁₆ in., (24 x 28.7 cm.), lithograph on handmade (BP 277, DM 691, FR 2354, Y 54,888).

$1057* *Das Konzert (Achenbach 112),* s., (05-26-93, Lempertz, #296), sh 15¹/₁₆ x 11⁹/₁₆ in., (38.3 x 29.3 cm.), lithograph on China (BP 684, DM 1725, FR 5805, Y 114,841).

$1135* *Das Konzert (Achenbach 112), 1926,* s., in Mappenwerk Max Liebermann/Neun Steinzeichnungen, pub. Cassirer, (06-05-93, Bassenge, #6292), 10⁷/₁₆ x 8⁷/₁₆ in., (26.5 x 21.5 cm.), chalk lithograph on hand-made China (BP 747, DM 1840, FR 6202, Y 121,755).

$866* *"Das Konzert" (Achenbach 112), 1926,* s., (11-28-92, Grisebach, #626, illus.), 10⁵/₁₆ x 8¼ in., (26.2 x 21 cm.), lithograph on China (BP 572, DM 1380, FR 4684, Y 107,778).

BI   *Die Kunstreiterin (Sch. 340 c), 1921,* s., est. DM 6000, (12-01-92, Karl/Faber, #924, illus.), 11⅝ x 10¹/₁₆ in., (29.5 x 25.5 cm.), lithograph on wove.

$1135* *Lesendes Madchen (Schiefler 41 a), 1896,* s., (06-05-93, Bassenge, #6284), 12 x 9⅝ in., (30.5 x 24.5 cm.), lithograph on hand-made (BP 747, DM 1840, FR 6202, Y 121,755).

$1130* *Lesendes Madchen (Schiefler 41 a), 1896,* s., blindstamp, (06-10-93, Hauswedell/Nolt, #578), image 12 x 9⅝ in., (30.5 x 24.5 cm.), lithograph on hand-made (BP 739, DM 1840, FR 6195, Y 119,945).

$369* *Liebesszene (Achenbach 114 b), 1926,* s., (12-05-92, Bassenge, #7431), 10¹/₁₆ x 7½ in., (25.5 x 19.1 cm.), lithograph on China (BP 231, DM 575, FR 1961, Y 45,719).

$903* *"Liebesszene" (Achenbach 114), 1926,* s., sheet 7 of series "9 Steinzeichnungen", Berlin, pub. Bruno Cassirer, (11-28-92, Grisebach, #627, illus.), 10⅛ x 7⅝ in., (25.7 x 19.3 cm.), lithograph on China (BP 596, DM 1439, FR 4884, Y 112,383).

$667* *Der Maler Josef Israels Am Strand (Sch. 151), 1912,* s., cockled, (11-30-92, Phillips-London, #451), image 3⅝ x 5⅜ in., (92 x 137 mm.), lithograph on japan (BP 440, DM 1063, FR 3607, Y 83,012).

$2624* *"Max Liebermann Radierungen" (Schiefler Seite 20), 1888/1892: Thirteen,* num., Verlag der Photographischen Gesellschaft, (06-05-93, Grisebach, #728, illus.), sh approx. 14⁹/₁₆ x 21¹/₁₆ in., (37 x 53.5 cm.), etching some w/aquatint on wide beige Japan (BP 1727, DM 4254, FR 14,339, Y 281,485).

$811* *Mein Landhaus In Wannsee (Schiefler 364), 1922,* (12-05-92, Bassenge, #7421), 2³/₁₆ x 3¼ in., (5.5 x 8.2 cm.), etching on wove (BP 508, DM 1264, FR 4309, Y 100,483).

$1271* *Netzflickerinnen (Schiefler 33 III a), 1894,* s., (06-10-93, Hauswedell/Nolt, #564), image 8¹⁵/₁₆ x 12⅜ in., (22.7 x 31.5 cm.), etching on hand-made (BP 831, DM 2070, FR 6968, Y 134,911).

$548* *Passeggiata,* s., (05-20-93, Finarte-Milan, #85), 8⅞ x 11⅝ in., (22.5 x 29.5 cm.), etching (BP 352, DM 884, FR 2978, Y 60,512, L 805).

$1773* *"Pferdebandigung" (Achenbach 107), c. 1926,* s., i., num., prov., (06-05-93, Grisebach, #744, illus.), 8³/₁₆ x 10½ in., (20.8 x 26.7 cm.), drypoint w/chalk uberzeichnet on thick copper print paper (BP 1167, DM 2875, FR 9689, Y 190,195).

$902* *Pferderennen (Schiefler 87), 1909,* s., (11-21-92, Lempertz, #246), 8¾ x 13⁷/₁₆ in., (22.2 x 34.2 cm.), lithograph on hand-made Japan (BP 594, DM 1438, FR 4844, Y 112,175).

$2128* *Polospiel (Schiefler 68 III), 1907,* s., (06-05-93, Bassenge, #6273, illus.), 11⁷/₁₆ x 15⁹/₁₆ in., (29.1 x 39.6 cm.), drypoint on hand-made (BP 1401, DM 3450, FR 11,628, Y 228,277).

BI   *"Portrait Of Karl Scheffler" (Achenbach 111), 1926,* s., sheet 4 of series "9 Steinzeichnungen", Berlin, pub. Bruno Cassirer, est. DM 5/600, (11-28-92, Grisebach, #625, illus.), 10¼ x 7½ in., (26 x 19 cm.), lithograph on China.

$1130* *Reiter Am Strande (Schiefler 112), 1910,* s., blindstamp, (06-10-93, Hauswedell/Nolt, #580), image 10¹¹/₁₆ x 13¾ in., (27.2 x 35 cm.), lithograph on hand-made (BP 739, DM 1840, FR 6195, Y 119,945).

$996* *Rindermarkt In Leiden (Sch. 51 c), 1900,* s., in der Mappe Max Liebermann. Sieben Radierungen, Bruno Cassirer, 1909, (12-01-92, Karl/Faber, #918), 8¹/₁₆ x 10¹³/₁₆ in., (20.5 x 27.5 cm.), etching on thick hand-made (BP 658, DM 1588, FR 5410, Y 124,004).

$1180* *Schafherde Unter Baumen (Schiefler 23 II), 1892,* etching on Japan, (12-05-92, Bassenge, #7406), 7 13/16 x 9 7/16 in., (19.8 x 24 cm.), etching on Japan (BP 739, DM 1840, FR 6270, Y 146,202).

$2291* *Selbstbildnis (Sch. 116/II), 1911,* s., prov., (06-23-93, Kornfeld, #527, illus.), etching and drypoint on thick Japan (BP 1556, DM 3876, FR 13,039, Y 249,591, SF 3450).

$1374* *Selbstbildnis Des Siebzigjahrigen, Von Vorn, Zeichnend (Sch. 222/VI), 1917,* s., i. VI/2, foxed, prov., (06-23-93, Kornfeld, #530), drypoint on thick Van Gelder Zonen (BP 933, DM 2325, FR 7820, Y 149,690, SF 2070).

$529* *Selbstbildnis Des Zeichnenden (Schiefler 141 III b), 1922,* s., (05-26-93, Dorling, #2828, illus.), 8 7/8 x 6 11/16 in., (22.6 x 17 cm.), etching on handmade (BP 342, DM 863, FR 2905, Y 57,475).

$443* *Selbstbildnis Des Zeichnenden (Schiefler 341 III b), 1922,* s., (12-05-92, Bassenge, #7420), 9 3/16 x 6 11/16 in., (23.3 x 17 cm.), etching on handmade (BP 277, DM 691, FR 2354, Y 54,888).

$851* *Selbstbildnis Mit Mutze (Achenbach 109), 1926,* s., (06-05-93, Bassenge, #6291, illus.), 10 7/16 x 7 7/8 in., (26.5 x 20 cm.), lithograph on hand-made China (BP 560, DM 1380, FR 4650, Y 91,289).

$664* *Selbstbildnis Mit Mutze (Achenbach 109), 1926,* s., (12-05-92, Bassenge, #7428), 10 7/16 x 7 7/8 in., (26.5 x 20 cm.), lithograph on China (BP 416, DM 1035, FR 3528, Y 82,270).

$686* *"Selbstbildnis Mit Mutze" (Achenbach 143 b), 1927,* s., (11-28-92, Grisebach, #629, illus.), 10 3/8 x 8 1/16 in., (26.3 x 20.5 cm.), lithograph on China (BP 453, DM 1093, FR 3710, Y 85,376).

$733* *Selbstbildnis Mit Pinsel In Der Hand (Schiefler, Nr. 342 V), 1922,* s., sheet 1 of series Selbstbildnisse Deutscher Graphiker, (11-13-92, Kunsthaus, #680), 8 15/16 x 6 7/16 in., (22.8 x 16.3 cm.), etching on handmade (BP 474, DM 1151, FR 3880, Y 90,977).

$567* *Selbstbildnis, Zeichnend (Sch. 330/IV c), 1921,* s., (06-08-93, Karl/Faber, #1036), approx. 9 13/16 x 7 5/16 in., (25 x 18.5 cm.), etching on thin J.W. Zanders paper (BP 373, DM 920, FR 3098, Y 60,223).

$565* *Selbstportrat (Schiefler 60 III b), 1906,* s., blindstamp, (06-10-93, Hauswedell/Nolt, #567), image 9 5/8 x 7 3/4 in., (24.4 x 19.7 cm.), etching on hand-made (BP 370, DM 920, FR 3098, Y 59,972).

$989* *Selbstportrat, Mit Zeichenblock (Schiefler 133 II b), 1912,* s., blindstamp, (06-10-93, Hauswedell/Nolt, #581), image 12 13/16 x 9 1/4 in., (32.5 x 23.5 cm.), lithograph on thick wove (BP 647, DM 1610, FR 5422, Y 104,978).

BI *Stehend Schreibendes Kind (Sch. 359/III b), 1922,* s., num., est. DM 1800, (12-01-92, Karl/Faber, #926), 11 5/8 x 9 1/16 in., (29.5 x 23 cm.), etching and drypoint on Van Gelder Zonen wove.

$1419* *Steindrucke Zu Heinrich Von Kleist (Sch. 227/I, 227/II, 282, 284-287, 289-304; A. 22), 1917: Twenty-Four,* s., mono., prov., (06-05-93, Grisebach, #737, illus.), sh 12 3/16 x 9 7/16 in., (31 x 24 cm.), lithograph on handmade Japan (BP 934, DM 2301, FR 7754, Y 152,221).

BI *Strandhauser (Schiefler 47 IV), 1896,* s., est. DM 1,200, (12-05-92, Bassenge, #7409), 5 1/8 x 7 1/16 in., (13 x 18 cm.), etching on Japan.

$1986* *"Theodor Fontane" (Schiefler 42/II b 1), 1896,* s., pub. in PAN II/I, blindstamp, (06-05-93, Grisebach, #730, illus.), 10 1/2 x 8 9/16 in., (26.6 x 21.8 cm.), lithograph on aufgewalztem (laid down) China on copper print paper (BP 1307, DM 3220, FR 10,852, Y 213,044).

$709* *Vor Der Bilderfibel,* s., (06-05-93, Bassenge, #6283), 10 15/16 x 8 5/8 in., (27.9 x 21.9 cm.), drypoint on hand-made (BP 467, DM 1149, FR 3874, Y 76,057).

$709* *Warterin Mit Kind (Achenbach 113), 1926,* s., (06-05-93, Bassenge, #6293), 8 1/8 x 9 1/8 in., (20.7 x 23.1 cm.), lithograph on China (BP 467, DM 1149, FR 3874, Y 76,057).

$1106* *Warterin Mit Kind (Achenbach 113), 1926,* s., (12-05-92, Bassenge, #7430, illus.), 8 1/8 x 9 1/8 in., (20.7 x 23.1 cm.), lithograph on China (BP 693, DM 1724, FR 5877, Y 137,034).

$494* *Wettrennen (Schiefler 352 b), 1922,* s., Cassirer, (06-10-93, Hauswedell/Nolt, #584), image 7 1/16 x 11 1/4 in., (18 x 28.5 cm.), lithograph on hand-made (BP 323, DM 804, FR 2708, Y 52,436).

$1155* *"Wettrennen" (Schiefler 352 b), 1922,* s., (11-28-92, Grisebach, #620, illus.), 7 1/16 x 11 1/4 in., (18 x 28.5 cm.), lithograph on handmade (BP 762, DM 1840, FR 6247, Y 143,746).

LIECHTENSTEIN, Princess Marie

BI *"Holland House", Vols. I-II, 1874,* Macmillan and Co., various sizes, est. BP 2/300, (05-07-93, Sotheby-London, #94), approx. 60 photographs and engravings, albumen print.

LIEVENS, Jan Dutch 1607-1672/74

BI *Bust Of A Young Man, Facing Right (B. 44; Holl. 65), c. 1640(?),* 1st state of 4, trimmed along platemark, wormholes, scrape in image,touches of grey wash, good cond., ex-coll. P. Davidsohn, est. $1,2/1,600, (05-13-93, Sotheby-NY, #164, illus.), 3 x 2 1/2 in., (76 x 62 mm.), etching.

$428* *"Bust Of An Old Woman, Facing Left" (Holl. 61) and "An Old Man" (Holl. 54): Two,* first, 1st state of 3, thread margins, thins spot, good cond., second, 2nd final state, repaired tear, (06-30-93, Sotheby-London, #159), 3 x 2 3/8 in., (76 x 60 mm.), etching (BP 287, DM 730, FR 2463, Y 45,859).

$1204* *Solomon Praying To False Idols (Hollstein 3),* (06-04-93, Bassenge, #5236, illus.), 2 7/8 x 2 1/16 in., (7.3 x 5.2 cm.), etching (BP 797, DM 1955, FR 6590, Y 129,853).

$1840* *St. Jerome (Holl. 15), c. 1650,* 3rd state of 5, trimmed, fold, good cond., (05-11-93, Christie-NY, #27A, illus.), sheet 9 5/8 x 8 1/4 in., (244 x 210 mm.), etching on laid (BP 1175, DM 2899, FR 9766, Y 202,398).

BI *St. Mark (Holl. 63 ii/ii), c. 1630,* from The Four Evangelists, margins, staining, left corner tip lacking, glue remains, skinning, est. $1/1,200, (05-11-93, Christie-NY, #28), plate 5 5/16 x 3 7/8 in., (135 x 98 mm.), etching on laid.

$1841* *Die Streitenden Spieler Und Der Tod (B., Wurzbach ll, Hollstein 19 II), c. 1638,* after Lievens, (06-04-93, Bassenge, #5237, illus.), 8 1/16 x 10 3/8 in., (20.4 x 26.4 cm.), etching (BP 1218, DM 2990, FR 10,077, Y 198,555).

LIGAUY, R.

BI *The Seine, c. 1920's,* s., est. $20/40, (08-14-92, DuMouchelle, #1391), 8 1/2 x 6 in., (21.6 x 15.2 cm.), engraving.

LIMBACH, Russell American 1904-1975

BI *"Approaching Storm",* s. Russell T. Limbach, pub. AAA, est. $1/150, (12-12-92, A. James, #323), sheet 12 1/8 x 15 in., (30.8 x 38.1 cm.), etching.

$40* *"Blessing The Hounds",* s., t., good cond., staining, (05-15-93, Cleveland, #210), 11 x 7 in., (27.9 x 17.8 cm.), etching (BP 26, DM 64, FR 216, Y 4434).

$50* *"Strictly Kosher", 1932,* s., plate 4, pub. Print-A-Month Club of Cleveland, (05-15-93, Cleveland, #208), 7 x 6 15/16 in., (17.8 x 17.6 cm.), etching (BP 33, DM 80, FR 270, Y 5543).

$40* *"Student & Master", 1934,* s., plate 20, Print-A-Month Club of Cleveland, very good cond., (05-15-93, Cleveland, #209), 9 7/8 x 12 1/8 in., (25.1 x 30.8 cm.), lithograph (BP 26, DM 64, FR 216, Y 4434).

BI *Student And Master,* s., circulated by Print-a-Month Club, est. $175/225, (09-17-92, Sloan, #643), 8 5/8 x 11 1/4 in., (21.9 x 28.6 cm.), lithograph.

$83* *Student And Master,* s., 1934, (04-02-93, Sloan, #811), 8 5/8 x 11 1/4 in., (219 x 286 mm.), lithograph (BP 55, DM 133, FR 453, Y 9450).

BI *Student And Master, 1934,* s., Print-a-Month-Club, est. $125/175, (10-30-92, Sloan, #855), 8 5/8 x 11 1/4 in., (21.9 x 28.6 cm.), lithograph.

BI *Student And Master, 1934,* s., edit. 250, circulated by Print-a-Month Club, est. $250/300, (07-03-92, Sloan, #1071), 8 5/8 x 11 1/4 in., (21.9 x 28.6 cm.), lithograph.

LINCK, Jean Antoine 1766-1843

$2763* *Ansicht Von Genf, Im Vordergrund Mundung Der Arve In Die Rhone,* (12-10-92, Ruef, #417, illus.), 14 3/16 x 18 7/8 in., (36 x 48 cm.), watercolored line etching (BP 1781, DM 4370, FR 14,927, Y 341,786).

LINCOLN, Edwin Hale

$302* *"Radicula Nasturtium-Aquaticum, True Water Cress" and "Cuscuta Gronovi, Dodder, Love-Vine", c. 1910: Two,* num., captioned, (10-14-92, Swann, #503), 9⅜ x 7⅜ in., (23.8 x 18.7 cm.), photograph, platinum prints (BP 177, DM 442, FR 1499, Y 36,597).

$2300* *Selected Flower Studies: "Indian Pipe", "Lady's Slipper", "Dutchman's Breeches And Squirrel Corn", "Buck Bean", "Red Bausberry" and "Dwarf Cornel",1905: Six,* each tipped, t. by photog., (04-06-93, Sotheby-NY, #73, illus.), each 9¼ x 7 in., photograph, platinum print (BP 1519, DM 3705, FR 12,548, Y 262,318).

LINDELL, Lage 1920-1980

$3623* *Betraktaren,* s. 25/36, (05-25-93, AB Stockholm, #46), 30⅞ x 41⁹⁄₁₆ in., (78.5 x 105.5 cm.), serigraph in colors (BP 2348, DM 5901, FR 19,863, Y 396,000, SK 5280).

$632* *Betraktaren,* s., 1/36, (12-04-92, AB Stockholm, #7096), 30⁵⁄₁₆ x 40⁹⁄₁₆ in., (77 x 103 cm.), serigraph in colors (BP 405, DM 1007, FR 3414, Y 78,901, SK 4290).

$1812* *Composition,* s. 26/175, (05-25-93, AB Stockholm, #47), 15³⁄₁₆ x 24⁷⁄₁₆ in., (38.5 x 62 cm.), serigraph in colors (BP 1174, DM 2951, FR 9934, Y 198,054, SK 2640).

$1208* *Composition,* s. 7/34, (05-25-93, AB Stockholm, #45), 9¹⁄₁₆ x 19¹¹⁄₁₆ in., (23 x 50 cm.), serigraph in colors (BP 783, DM 1967, FR 6623, Y 132,036, SK 1760).

$324* *Detta Ar En Bok Av Lage Lindell, Tv.4:0: Twenty-Two,* p. Ove Loof, s. on justification, 22/100, (12-04-92, AB Stockholm, #7098), serigraph in colors (BP 208, DM 516, FR 1750, Y 40,449, SK 2200).

$503* *Figurer I Rorelse,* s., 14/30, (12-04-92, AB Stockholm, #7097), 38³⁄₁₆ x 37 in., (97 x 94 cm.), serigraph in colors (BP 323, DM 801, FR 2717, Y 62,797, SK 3410).

$1248* *Tankaren,* s., 5/12, (12-04-92, AB Stockholm, #7094), 10¹³⁄₁₆ x 11¼ in., (27.5 x 28.5 cm.), serigraph in colors (BP 801, DM 1988, FR 6742, Y 155,805, SK 8470).

$681* *Vid Havet,* s., 10/18, (12-04-92, AB Stockholm, #7095), sh 10⁷⁄₁₆ x 25³⁄₁₆ in., (26.5 x 64 cm.), serigraph in colors (BP 437, DM 1085, FR 3679, Y 85,019, SK 4620).

LINDENMUTH, Tod American 1885-1976

BI *"Along Side",* s. Tod Lindenmuth, poor cond., est. $4/600, (11-21-92, Bakker, #73), 9 x 7¼ in., (22.9 x 18.4 cm.), color woodblock print.

$495* *"Along Side",* s. Tod Lindemuth, t., good cond., fox marks, (03-12-93, Skinner, #51, illus.), 9 x 7⅛ in., (22.9 x 18.1 cm.), block print in colors on paper (BP 345, DM 824, FR 2801, Y 58,338).

$550* *"Along Side",* s., (12-17-92, Mystic, #43), 9 x 7 in., (22.9 x 17.8 cm.), color woodblock (BP 349, DM 859, FR 2933, Y 67,592).

$715* *"The Fishing Fleet",* s. Tod Lindenmuth, poor cond., (11-21-92, Bakker, #64), image 10¾ x 14 in., (27.3 x 35.6 cm.), color woodblock print (BP 471, DM 1140, FR 3840, Y 88,919).

$1100* *"Fog Bound",* s. Tod Lindenmuth, very good cond., (09-27-92, Bakker, #259, illus.), image 14 x 11 in., (35.6 x 27.9 cm.), color woodblock print (BP 642, DM 1631, FR 5514, Y 132,770).

$110* *"The Home Port",* s. Tod Lindenmuth, poor cond., (11-21-92, Bakker, #71), image 8 x 6 in., (20.3 x 15.2 cm.), color woodblock print (BP 72, DM 175, FR 591, Y 13,680).

$770* *"Morning At The Weir",* s. Tod Lindenmuth, very good cond., (09-27-92, Bakker, #258, illus.), image 14 x 11 in., (35.6 x 27.9 cm.), color woodblock print (BP 450, DM 1141, FR 3860, Y 92,939).

$770* *"On The Mooring",* s., t., excellent cond., (10-31-92, Cleveland, #171, illus.), 6⅛ x 8 in., (15.6 x 20.3 cm.), color woodcut (BP 493, DM 1185, FR 4019, Y 95,380).

$230* *On The Mooring, 1915,* s., t., margins, good cond., foxing, hinge stains, (05-13-93, Sotheby-NY, #429), 6⅛ x 8⅛ in., (156 x 205 mm.), sh 9⅛ x 13¼ in., (156 x 205 mm.), linoleum cut in shades of lavender on Japan (BP 151, DM 371, FR 1253, Y 25,678).

LINDENSTAEDT, Hans b. 1874

BI *Blom's/ Engros- und/ Export-/ Adressbuch/ von Berlin, c. 1900,* Verlag Reklamekunst Curt Behrends & Co., Berlin-Wilmersdorf, wrinkles, tears, est. DM 450, (12-05-92, Bassenge, #7607), 13¹⁄₁₆ x 17¹⁵⁄₁₆ in., (33.1 x 45.7 cm.), color lithograph.

$315* *Maendl & Co., 1912,* tears, creases, hinged, lit., (02-04-93, Christie-S. Ken, #171), 27 x 18 in., (68.6 x 45.7 cm.), color lithograph (BP 220, DM 519, FR 1759, Y 39,184).

LINDGENS, Walter 1893-1978

BI *Ballspielende Nonne Mit Kindern,* i. Lindgens, est. DM 900-, (09-14-92, Venator/Hansten, #2466), approx. 9⁷⁄₁₆ x 8¹¹⁄₁₆ in., (24 x 22 cm.), color monotype over blk. chalk.

LINDIG, Otto German 1895-1966

BI *Selbstportrat Im Spiegel, c. 1929,* t., lit., est. DM 900, (11-12-92, Lempertz, #147, illus.), 5⅞ x 3⅞ in., (14.9 x 9.9 cm.), photograph, gelatin silver print w/brown tone.

LINDING, Lillian

$138* *"Village Street", 1931,* s., #10/24, d., very good cond.?, (07-19-92, Bakker, #175), image 13½ x 9¾ in., (34.3 x 24.8 cm.), lithograph (BP 71, DM 201, FR 680, Y 17,156).

LINDNER, Ernest 1897-1988

$282* *Untitled-Female Nude,* #38/150, s., prov., (05-10-93, Hodgins, #333), 29 x 21½ in., (73.7 x 54.6 cm.), lithograph on paper (BP 184, DM 453, FR 1528, Y 31,512, C$ 358).

LINDNER, Richard German/American 1901-1978

$882* *Ace Of Clubs, 1977,* 83/250, s., crease, (10-14-92, Germann, #113, illus.), 28¼ x 21¹⁵⁄₁₆ in., (718 x 558 mm.), color lithograph (BP 518, DM 1291, FR 4377, Y 106,883, SF 1150).

$3300* *Afternoon, 1976: Set Of Eight,* Shorewood Atelier, s., #2/250, full margins, time staining, (11-09-92, Christie-NY, #356, illus.), (711 x 552 mm.), colored lithograph on BFK Rives (BP 2182, DM 5268, FR 17,799, Y 409,531).

BI *An American Portrait, 1776-1876, 1976,* p. Mourlot, est. $125/175, (09-17-92, Sloan, #647), sheet 30 x 21 in., (76.2 x 53.3 cm.), lithograph poster.

$1154* *Aus: Fun City, 1970-71,* #148/175, pencil s., (11-20-92, Lempertz, #674), sh 26⅜ x 20⁵⁄₁₆ in., (67 x 51.6 cm.), color lithograph on Velin (BP 760, DM 1840, FR 6198, Y 143,514).

$349* *Ausstellung In Der Kestner-Gesellschaft (Hannover), 1968-1969,* s., #43/100, (09-18-92, Schloss Ahlden, #1022), 31⅜ x 23¹⁄₁₆ in., (79.7 x 58.5 cm.), color lithograph on hand-made (BP 204, DM 518, FR 1772, Y 43,134).

$1725* *Banner #3, 1968,* pub. Betsy Ross Flag and Banner Co., Inc., (02-11-93, Sotheby-NY, #382), 91⁹⁄₁₆ x 49¾ in., (232.5 x 126.3 cm.), mixed media banner w/vinyl and zipper (BP 1217, DM 2857, FR 9669, Y 207,957).

$330* *"Fantasy Composition", Man Walking A Rooster By A Crescent Moon,* from New York series, s., (10-10-92, Litchfield, #136), 25¼ x 19¾ in., (64.1 x 50.2 cm.), collage of color lithograph applied to silver material (BP 196, DM 490, FR 1646, Y 40,175).

BI *Fun City, 1971: Fourteen,* complete portfolio, s., #155/175, pub. Shorewood Publishers, good cond., tape/glue remains, skinned apots, creases, light-staining, surface soiling, est. $5/7,000, (10-28-92, Butterfield, #3024, illus.), each 26¼ x 19¾ in., (667 x 502 mm.), color lithograph on Arches, two collaged onto Rowlux.

$1311* *Girl With Hoop,* #108/175, s., (11-13-92, Koller, #5365, illus.), 24 x 16⁹⁄₁₆ in., (61 x 42 cm.), lithograph on wove (BP 847, DM 2058, FR 6940, Y 162,716, SF 1856).

$514* *Girl With Hoop, 1971,* s., num., from series of 13 Bll.: Fun City, Grafische Editionen HansHoeppner, Trittau, Hamburg, Munchen, trimmed, (12-01-92, Karl/Faber, #932), 24 x 19⅞ in., (61 x 50.5 cm.), color lithograph on wove (BP 340, DM 819, FR 2792, Y 63,994).

$495* *Lollipop, 1971,* s., #XIX/LXXV, (06-12-93, Hauswedell/Nolt, #283), 23⅞ x 19⅞ in., (60.7 x 50.5 cm.), color lithograph on thick wove (BP 324, DM 806, FR 2708, Y 52,089).

BI *Miss American Indian,* #13/250, s., creases, est. SF 1,2/1,800, (09-04-92, Germann, #11, illus.), 28¹⁄₁₆ x 21⅝ in., (713 x 550 mm.), color lithograph.

$711* *Miss American Indian*, #13/250, s., creases, (04-21-93, Germann, #599, illus.), 28¹/₁₆ x 21⅝ in., (713 x 550 mm.), color lithograph (BP 461, DM 1137, FR 3843, Y 78,711, SF 1035).

$315* *"New York City"*, #14/175, s., (01-28-93, Pescheteau, #190), 25⁹/₁₆ x 19¹¹/₁₆ in., (65 x 50 cm.), photolithograph on wove (BP 208, DM 499, FR 1689, Y 39,111).

$660* *Nude In An Armchair, 1975,* s. R. Lindner, num. 31/125, init. fm, i. X, good cond., indentations/marks in image, (09-11-92, Skinner, #102A, illus.), 20⅜ x 17 in., (51.8 x 43.2 cm.), lithograph in colors on Arches wove w/watermark (BP 341, DM 950, FR 3229, Y 81,774).

$588* *On,* #24/175, s., est. L 1,000, (05-20-93, Finarte-Milan, #86), 23⅞ x 19⅞ in., (60.7 x 50.5 cm.), lithograph in colors (BP 377, DM 949, FR 3196, Y 64,929, L 863).

$1393* *Piazza,* #105/175, s., (11-13-92, Koller, #5366, illus.), 24 x 16⁹/₁₆ in., (61 x 42 cm.), lithograph on wove (BP 900, DM 2187, FR 7374, Y 172,893, SF 1972).

BI *Plakat Vancouver 1964,* s., Vancouver Art Gallery, 3. - 20. 11. 1964, signs of wear, est. DM700, (12-01-92, Karl/Faber, #931), 24⁷/₁₆ x 15³/₁₆ in., (62 x 38.5 cm.), color photolithograph on BFK Rives wove.

$550* *Queen Of Hearts,* s. R. Lindner, good cond., thread margins, (10-09-92, Skinner, #230, illus.), 12⅛ x 9½ in., (30.8 x 24.1 cm.), lithograph in colors on wove (BP 326, DM 819, FR 2778, Y 67,073).

$1298* *Room For Rent,* #77/150, pencil s., (11-20-92, Lempertz, #675), sh 28⁹/₁₆ x 39¹⁵/₁₆ in., (72.5 x 101.5 cm.), serigraph in color on Velin (BP 855, DM 2070, FR 6971, Y 161,423).

$474* *St. Mark's Place, 1971,* s., #101/175, portfolio Fun City, (06-12-93, Hauswedell/Nolt, #284), 23⅞ x 19⅞ in., (60.7 x 50.5 cm.), color lithograph on Rowlux collage on Rowlux (BP 310, DM 771, FR 2593, Y 49,879).

$688* *Untitled, 1977,* s., #17/225, pub. Galerie Maeght, full margins, good cond.?, creases, rippling, foxing, prov., (12-12-92, Weschler, #137, illus.), 22¾ x 19½ in., (57.8 x 49.5 cm.), color lithograph (BP 441, DM 1084, FR 3715, Y 85,138).

$453* *Woman With A Parrot, 1969,* (10-14-92, Germann, #351), 21¼ x 14³/₁₆ in., (540 x 360 mm.), color lithograph (BP 266, DM 663, FR 2248, Y 54,896, SF 590).

LINDOE, Vivian   b. 1918
$65* *Dry Country II, 1973,* #7/9, s., t., d. '73, prov., (05-10-93, Hodgins, #357), 12 x 17¾ in., (30.5 x 45.1 cm.), serigraph on paper (BP 42, DM 104, FR 352, Y 7263, C$ 83).

LINDSAY, Lionel Arthur   1874-1961
$324* *Catch,* s. Lionel Lindsay, i. Artist Proof, lit., (08-11-92, L. Joel, #154G), 4 x 4⅛ in., (10.2 x 10.5 cm.), etching (BP 168, DM 475, FR 1610, Y 41,491, A$ 440).

$324* *Philosophy,* s. Lionel Lindsay, i. #100, lit., (08-11-92, L. Joel, #26G), 6¾ x 6¹/₁₆ in., (17.1 x 15.4 cm.), woodcut (BP 168, DM 475, FR 1610, Y 41,491, A$ 440).

BI *(The) Evening Ride,* s. Lionel Lindsay, i., #11 Ed. 35, lit. est. $450/550, (08-11-92, L. Joel, #56G, illus.), 8¹³/₁₆ x 13⁵/₁₆ in., (22.4 x 33.8 cm.), drypoint.

LINDSAY, Norman Alfred   1879-1969
$1054* *Adventure,* s. Norman Lindsay, i., d. '32, #33/50, (08-11-92, L. Joel, #24GA), 11⅛ x 10⅛ in., (28.3 x 25.7 cm.), etching (BP 548, DM 1547, FR 5239, Y 134,972, A$ 1430).

$973* *Beethoven,* s. Norman Lindsay, i., d. 1921, #20/50, (08-11-92, L. Joel, #47GA), 12⅞ x 11³/₁₆ in., (32.7 x 28.4 cm.), etching (BP 506, DM 1428, FR 4836, Y 124,600, A$ 1320).

$1784* *Desire,* s. Norman Lindsay, i., d. 1919, #34, lit., (08-11-92, L. Joel, #61G, illus.), 8¹⁵/₁₆ x 9³/₁₆ in., (22.7 x 23.3 cm.), etching (BP 927, DM 2618, FR 8867, Y 228,454, A$ 2420).

$730* *Dryad,* s. Norman Lindsay, i., d. 1923, #38/55, lit., (08-11-92, L. Joel, #92G), 4¾ x 3¹⁵/₁₆ in., (12 x 10 cm.), etching (BP 379, DM 1071, FR 3628, Y 93,482, A$ 990).

$1459* *Little Scandals,* s. Norman Lindsay, i., d. 1922, #34/55, lit., (08-11-92, L. Joel, #83G), 10⁵/₁₆ x 12¹¹/₁₆ in., (26.2 x 32.2 cm.), etching (BP 758, DM 2141, FR 7251, Y 186,836, A$ 1980).

BI *Madame Mystery,* s. Norman Lindsay, i., d. 1924, #22/50, lit., est. $1,6/2,000, (08-11-92, L. Joel, #17G), 12³/₁₆ x 10¹/₁₆ in., (31 x 25.5 cm.), etching.

$649* *Song Of The Faun,* s. Norman Lindsay, i., d. 1921, #24/50, (08-11-92, L. Joel, #76GA), 12¹¹/₁₆ x 11⁵/₁₆ in., (32.2 x 28.7 cm.), etching (BP 337, DM 952, FR 3226, Y 83,109, A$ 880).

$1135* *This Shrine,* s. Norman Lindsay, i., d. 1919, num. 31, lit., (08-11-92, L. Joel, #163G, illus.), 8⅜ x 8⅜ in., (21.3 x 21.3 cm.), etching (BP 590, DM 1666, FR 5641, Y 145,345, A$ 1540).

$1459* *Walpurgis,* s. Norman Lindsay, i., #15/40, lit., (08-11-92, L. Joel, #104G), 11⁷/₁₆ x 12½ in., (29.1 x 31.7 cm.), etching (BP 758, DM 2141, FR 7251, Y 186,836, A$ 1980).

LINDSAY, Norman and Jack
$3080* *A Homage To Sappho: 15,* 4to, s. Jack Lindsay, (11-12-92, Swann, #142, illus.), etching on Japan vellum (BP 2023, DM 4880, FR 16,462, Y 381,897).

LINDSTROM, Bengt   Swedish b. 1935
$190* *Composition,* s. Lindstrom, E.A., (09-30-92, Kunsthallen, #188), color lithograph (BP 107, DM 269, FR 911, Y 22,801, DK 1035).

$164* *Composition,* s., 58/150, (04-17-93, Falkkloos, #336), 29¹⁵/₁₆ x 22¹/₁₆ in., (76 x 56 cm.), lithograph in colors (BP 107, DM 262, FR 886, Y 18,236, SK 1210).

$194* *Composition,* s., 48/150, (04-17-93, Falkkloos, #337), 20⅞ x 29⅛ in., (53 x 74 cm.), lithograph in colors (BP 126, DM 310, FR 1048, Y 21,572, SK 1430).

BI *"Composition",* #8/100, s., est. FF800/1,000, (04-04-93, Pescheteau, #247), 29½ x 21¼ in., (75 x 54 cm.), color lithograph and embossing on wove.

BI *"Composition",* #31/100, s., est. FF800/1,000, (04-04-93, Pescheteau, #248), 29½ x 21¼ in., (75 x 54 cm.), lithograph and embossing on wove.

$1702* *De Sju Dodssynderna, 1976: Seven,* s., 72/90, ABCD, portfolio, (12-04-92, AB Stockholm, #7100), approx. 29¹⁵/₁₆ x 22¹/₁₆ in., (76 x 56 cm.), color engraving and carborundum (BP 1092, DM 2711, FR 9195, Y 212,484, SK 11,550).

$122* *Figures,* s., i. E.A., margins, good cond., minor handling creases, soiling inupper margin, (05-27-93, Sotheby-Amstrdm, #647), 25¾ x 19½ in., (654 x 495 mm.), color silkscreen on wove (BP 78, DM 196, FR 660, Y 13,079, G 219).

$362* *Hamlet, 1970,* 31/80, s., (10-14-92, Germann, #352), 29¹⁵/₁₆ x 22¼ in., (760 x 565 mm.), etching/aquatint w/ carborundum in color (BP 212, DM 530, FR 1797, Y 43,868, SF 472).

$2189* *Herakles, 1977: Twelve,* portfolio, ABCD, s., 26/99, (12-04-92, AB Stockholm, #7099), 29¾ x 22¼ in., (75.5 x 56.5 cm.), engravings w/carborundum (BP 1404, DM 3486, FR 11,826, Y 273,283, SK 14,850).

$110* *Komposition,* s. Lindstrom, E.A., (03-24-93, Kunsthallen, #228), etching (BP 74, DM 180, FR 611, Y 12,924, DK 690).

$184* *Komposition,* from the Shakespeare Series, s. Lindstrom, 31/80, (03-24-93, Kunsthallen, #226), color lithograph (BP 125, DM 301, FR 1023, Y 21,619, DK 1150).

$184* *Komposition,* from the Shakespeare series, s. Lindstrom, 31/80, (03-24-93, Kunsthallen, #227), color lithograph (BP 125, DM 301, FR 1023, Y 21,619, DK 1150).

$135* *Sans Titre,* s., 35/120, (06-28-93, Loudmer, #286), 21⅝ x 17⅛ in., (550 x 435 mm.), sh 26³/₁₆ x 20½ in., (550 x 435 mm.), color embossing on wove (BP 90, DM 229, FR 773, Y 14,324).

LINK, O. Winston   b. 1914
$2875* *Engineer Rumble Oils Bushing,* 1950s, ink s., reprod limitation stamp, (04-08-93, Christie-NY, #446, illus.), 3⅞ x 4¾ in., (9.8 x 12.1 cm.), photograph, gelatin silver print (BP 1885, DM 4618, FR 15,633, Y 326,260).

$1380* *"Entering Luray From The South, Time Freight 96 Crosses Over Top Of U.S. 340 And Hawksbill Creek"* and *"Class J At Max Meadows": Two,* 1950s, p. 1984 and 1983, each s., d., (c) and reprod. stamps, lit., (04-08-93, Christie-NY, #444, illus.), each approx. 19½ x 15⅜ in., (49.5 x 39.1 cm.), photograph, gelatin silver print (BP 905, DM 2217, FR 7504, Y 156,605).

$4600* *"From The Porch Of Their Victorian Home At Max Meadows, Mr. And Mrs.Ben Franklin Pope Bid Farewell To An Old Friend As Class J Pulls The Last Steam Train To Bristol"* (Steam Steel and Stars, p. 91), 1957, photog. (c) date stamp, (04-06-93, Sotheby-NY, #424, illus.), 4¾ x 3¾ in., photograph (BP 3038, DM 7411, FR 25,095, Y 524,635).

$2013* *"Hot Shot East Bound, Iaeger, West Virginia"* (Steam Steel and Stars,p. 124-25), 1956, s., d. by photog., studio (c) stamp, (04-06-93, Sotheby-NY, #429, illus.), 15⅜ x 19¼ in., photograph (BP 1330, DM 3243, FR 10,982, Y 229,585).

$2750* *Hot Shot East Bound, West Virginia (Steam, Steel & Stars, pp. 124-125)*, s., d. by photog., (c) stamp, 1956, p. 1987, (10-15-92, Sotheby-NY, #483, illus.), 15½ x 19½ in., (39.4 x 49.5 cm.), photograph, gelatin silver print (BP 1683, DM 4093, FR 13,882, Y 329,934).

$1980* *Hot Shot Eastbound, Iaeger, West Virginia*, (1956), p.l., s., (c) & reprod. limit. stamps, lit., (10-13-92, Christie-NY, #468, illus.), 15½ x 19⅜ in., (39.4 x 49.2 cm.), photograph, gelatin silver print (BP 1153, DM 2901, FR 9856, Y 240,087).

$2990* *Hot Shot Eastbound, West Virginia*, 1956, p.l., s., (c) and reprod. limitation stamps, lit., (04-08-93, Christie-NY, #445, illus.), 15½ x 19¼ in., (39.4 x 48.9 cm.), photograph, gelatin silver print (BP 1961, DM 4803, FR 16,259, Y 339,310).

$1955* *"Hot Shot Eastbound, West Virginia"*, 1956, p. 1987, s., neg. num., photog.'s stamp, illus., (05-23-93, Butterfield, #3503, illus.), 15½ x 19½ in., photograph, gelatin silver print (BP 1273, DM 3197, FR 10,759, Y 216,094).

$2750* *"Hot Shot Eastbound, West Virginia"* (Steam, Steel And Stars, pp. 124-5), 1956/1987, s., num. neg., photog. stamp, Dixon Collection, (11-16-92, Butterfield, #6068, illus.), 15½ x 19⁷⁄₁₆ in., (394.4 x 493 mm.), photograph, gelatin silver print (BP 1811, DM 4385, FR 14,769, Y 341,997).

$805* *"Main Line On Main Street"*, 1966, p. 1987, s., neg. num., photog.'s stamp, (05-23-93, Butterfield, #3504, illus.), 15½ x 19⅜ in., photograph, gelatin silver print (BP 524, DM 1316, FR 4430, Y 88,980).

$1045* *"Maud Bows To The Virginia Creeper"* (Steam, Steel, And Stars, p. 125), s., num. neg., photog. stamp, Dixon Collection, (11-16-92, Butterfield, #6071, illus.), 15½ x 19⁷⁄₁₆ in., (394.4 x 493 mm.), photograph, gelatin silver print (BP 688, DM 1666, FR 5612, Y 129,959).

BI *"Running Gear Of Class E2a 4-6-2 No. 578 In The Engine Service Building At Bluefield"* (Steam Steel and Stars, pp. 36-37), c. 1957, s. by photog., reprod. lim. stamp, est. $2,5/3,500, (04-06-93, Sotheby-NY, #426, illus.), 3¾ x 4¾ in., photograph.

$920* *"Rural Retreat"*, 1950s, p. 1987, s., annot. 1-91, neg. num., photog.'s stamp, illus., (05-23-93, Butterfield, #3505, illus.), 15½ x 19½ in., photograph, gelatin silver print (BP 599, DM 1504, FR 5063, Y 101,691).

$1210* *"Rural Retreat"* (Steam, Steel, And Stars, p. 87), 1950's/1988, s., num. neg., photog. stamp, Dixon Collection, (11-16-92, Butterfield, #6070, illus.), 15½ x 19⁷⁄₁₆ in., (394.4 x 493 mm.), photograph, gelatin silver print (BP 797, DM 1929, FR 6498, Y 150,479).

$770* *"Sometimes Electricity Fails"* (Steam, Steel, And Stars, p. 60), 1950's/1987, photog. stamp, printing notations, (11-16-92, Butterfield, #6069, illus.), 15½ x 19⁷⁄₁₆ in., (394.4 x 493 mm.), photograph, gelatin silver print (BP 507, DM 1228, FR 4135, Y 95,759).

$4600* *"W.A. Miller Mans The Old Gravity-Flow Gas Pump At The Vesuvius General Store"* (Steam Steel and Stars, pp. 60-61), 1950's, s. by photog., stamps, (04-06-93, Sotheby-NY, #425, illus.), 3¾ x 4¾ in., photograph (BP 3038, DM 7411, FR 25,095, Y 524,635).

LINN, Kenneth A.   1903-1979
$1100* *Calla Lily, c. 1929*, mounted, (10-15-92, Sotheby-NY, #130, illus.), 3⅜ x 4⅜ in., (8.6 x 11.1 cm.), photograph, toned gelatin silver print (BP 673, DM 1637, FR 5553, Y 131,974).

$1495* *Fruit Still-Life, late 1920's*, mounted, s. by photog., (04-06-93, Sotheby-NY, #93, illus.), photograph (BP 987, DM 2409, FR 8156, Y 170,506).

BI *Girders, c. 1928*, est. $1,2/1,500, (10-13-92, Christie-NY, #292, illus.), 3½ x 4⅝ in., (8.9 x 11.7 cm.), photograph, gelatin silver print.

$550* *Industrial Study, 1931*, s., sold after sale, (10-14-92, Swann, #504, illus.), 3½ x 4½ in., (8.9 x 11.4 cm.), photograph, toned silver print (BP 323, DM 805, FR 2730, Y 66,651).

BI *Industrial Study, c. 1930*, mounted, Kenneth A. Linn estate, est. $2/2,500, (04-06-93, Sotheby-NY, #94, illus.), 3⅝ x 4⅝ in., photograph.

$1760* *New York City, c. 1929*, mounted, (10-15-92, Sotheby-NY, #131, illus.), 4⅜ x 3½ in., (11.1 x 8.9 cm.), photograph, toned gelatin silver print (BP 1077, DM 2620, FR 8884, Y 211,158).

$440* *Potted Jade Plant*, 1930s, (04-07-93, Swann, #504, illus.), 3½ x 4½ in., photograph, silver print (BP 291, DM 712, FR 2408, Y 49,989).

$1150* *Pretzel Vendor, New York City, c. 1927*, mounted, (04-08-93, Christie-NY, #68, illus.), 6⅛ x 4⅛ in., (15.6 x 10.5 cm.), photograph, gelatin silver print (BP 754, DM 1847, FR 6253, Y 130,504).

$880* *Produce Market, Lower East Side, c. 1927*, (10-13-92, Christie-NY, #291, illus.), 3⅞ x 5¾ in., (9.8 x 14.6 cm.), photograph, gelatin silver print (BP 513, DM 1289, FR 4380, Y 106,705).

LION, Jules
$660* *"Bust Of A Gentleman Wearing Spectacles"*, 1847, s., d. in stone, (10-16-92, Neal, #971), image 7 x 6 in., (17.8 x 15.2 cm.), sheet 10 x 7½ in., (17.8 x 15.2 cm.), lithograph (BP 400, DM 975, FR 3312, Y 78,806).

$660* *"Portrait Of A Man With A Mustache"*, s. in stone, laid down, generally poor cond., illus., (10-16-92, Neal, #972), image 6 x 5 in., (15.2 x 12.7 cm.), sheet 10½ x 8½ in., (15.2 x 12.7 cm.), lithograph (BP 400, DM 975, FR 3312, Y 78,806).

LIPCHITZ, Jacques   French 1891-1973
$1380* *Le Chemin De L'Exile, c. 1945*, s., #1/33, i., full margins, good cond., mat stain, (02-11-93, Sotheby-NY, #162, illus.), 13¹³⁄₁₆ x 9¹³⁄₁₆ in., (351 x 250 mm.), etching and aquatint on Japan (BP 974, DM 2286, FR 7735, Y 166,365).

BI *Gelbe Figur*, from Hommage A Picasso, s., E.d'A, est DM 500, (09-18-92, Schloss Ahlden, #1023), 30¹¹⁄₁₆ x 22⅝ in., (78 x 57.4 cm.), color lithograph on hand-made.

BI *Promethee, c. 1940*, num., s., soiling, full margins, 50 proof, (02-24-93, Picard, #144), etching and aquatint in brown-black on ivory wove.

$412* *"Tree Of Life", 1972: Three*, complete portfolio, s., pub. Hadassah, (12-08-92, Swann, #181, illus.), 18¼ x 25¾ in., (46.4 x 65.4 cm.), color lithograph (BP 258, DM 641, FR 2187, Y 51,066).

$1840* *Tree Of Life, 1972: Suite Of Three*, two s., one s. white crayon, each #71/250, pub. Women's Zionist Organization of America, full sheets, good cond., (02-11-93, Sotheby-NY, #163), each sheet 25¹⁵⁄₁₆ x 18½ in., (660 x 470 mm.), lithograph (BP 1298, DM 3048, FR 10,314, Y 221,820).

$1380* *[Battle With Minotaur], 1945*, carefully wiped plate tone, s., #35/50, full margins, good cond., soiling, foxing, creases, handling traces, (05-13-93, Sotheby-NY, #588, illus.), 13⅞ x 11¼ in., (352 x 285 mm.), sh 25¼ x 15 in., (352 x 285 mm.), etching on wove (BP 906, DM 2228, FR 7516, Y 154,069).

LIPS, Johann Heinrich   Swiss 1758-1817
$67* *Henri Fuseli...A.M. Peintre, 1799*, margins, good cond., (11-30-92, Phillips-London, #134), plate 9¾ x 8 in., (248 x 203 mm.), engraving on laid (BP 44, DM 107, FR 362, Y 8339).

BI *Die Tageszeiten In Schaferszenen: Four*, foxing, wear, est. DM 3,300-, (09-25-92, Granier, #2663), plate 9⅝ x 11¾ in., (24.4 x 29.9 cm.), sheet 10⁹⁄₁₆ x 13⅜ in., (24.4 x 29.9 cm.), aquatint etching in brown.

LIRON, S.   20th cent.
$159* *"Quelle Bonne Mine A Votre Petit Garcon"*, s. S. Liron, (02-16-93, Encans, #125), 7⅞ x 6¹¹⁄₁₆ in., (20 x 17 cm.), engraving (BP 110, DM 260, FR 879, Y 19,049, C$ 200).

LISMER, Arthur   Canadian 1885-1911
  BI *Boats,* s., est. C$ 5/700, (05-18-93, Joyner, #288), 5 x
      6½ in., (12.7 x 16.5 cm.), print.
  BI *Isle Of Spruce,* s., est. C$ 5/700, (05-18-93, Joyner,
      #287), 5 x 6¾ in., (12.7 x 17.1 cm.), print.

LISSITZKY, El   b. Poland 1890 d. Moscow 1941
  BI *Chad Gadya (The Tale Of The Goat), 1919,* complete
      set, plates & ded. page, p. from black stones only, light
      staining, fox marks, creasing, nicks, est. BP 13/15,000,
      (12-03-92, Sotheby-London, #368, illus.), each sheet
      approx. 11¾ x 10¾ in., (298 x 273 mm.), lithographs on
      tan wove.
$6050* *Globetrotter-In Der Zeit (Globetrotter--in Time), 1920-1,*
      plate 5 from Die Plastische Gestaltung der Elektro-Mach-
      anischen Schau "Sieg Uber Die Sonne", s., pub. Rob.
      Leunis and Chapman GmbH, Hannover in 1923, wide
      margins, staining affecting image, mat staining, crease,
      very good cond., (11-09-92, Christie-NY, #108, illus.),
      520 x 445 in., (x cm.), colored lithograph on wove (BP
      4000, DM 9658, FR 32,632, Y 750,807).
$379* *Der Konstrukteur,* 1924, 1985, (11-12-92, Lempertz,
      #148), 7¹¹⁄₁₆ x 8⅝ in., (19.6 x 21.9 cm.), sheet 15⅞ x
      12 in., (19.6 x 21.9 cm.), photograph, gelatin silver print
      (BP 242, DM 596, FR 2030, Y 46,889).
  BI *Model Of The Meyerhold Theatre, 1929 (Thames and*
      Hudson, fig. 219, variant; Harvard, fig. 32, variant,
      Springrl Museum, fig. 137, variant), est. $7/9,000, (10-
      15-92, Sotheby-NY, #367A, illus.), 4¼ x 5½ in., (10.8 x
      14 cm.), photograph, gelatin silver print.
$7700* *Neuer (New Man), 1920-1,* plate 10 from Die Plastische
      Gestaltung der Elektro-Mechanischen Schau "Sieg uber
      die Sonne", s., pub. Rob. Leunis and Chapman GmbH,
      Hannover in 1923, wide margins, colors faded, rubbed
      spot at center, creases, tears, defects, (11-09-92, Christie-
      NY, #109, illus.), 521 x 443 in., (x cm.), colored litho-
      graph on wove (BP 5091, DM 12,292, FR 41,532, Y
      955,572).
$6050* *Self-Portrait With Propaganda Poster Of Lenin,* nota-
      tions in various hands, late 1920's-early 1930's, (10-15-
      92, Sotheby-NY, #368, illus.), 7⅛ x 6¾ in., (18.1 x 17.1
      cm.), photograph, gelatin silver print (BP 3702, DM
      9006, FR 30,540, Y 725,855).

LISSITZKY, El (after)   Russian 1890-1941
$165* *English Language Edition Of U.S.S.R. In Construction,*
      ident. in matrix; label verso, creases, wrinkles, tears, (05-
      22-93, Skinner, #263, illus.), sheet, sight 30 x 21½ in.,
      (76.2 x 54.6 cm.), photolithograph in black and red (BP
      107, DM 268, FR 903, Y 18,192).

LIST, Herbert   1903-1975
$1955* *Andrea Tagliabue, 1959-62: Two,* annot. in unident.
      hand, (04-06-93, Sotheby-NY, #340A, illus.), one 6¾ x 4½
      in., other 6¾ x 3¾ in., photograph (BP 1291, DM 3150,
      FR 10,666, Y 222,970).
$1980* *Andrea Tagliabue, 1960,* s., t., d. by photog. in ink, (10-
      15-92, Sotheby-NY, #420, illus.), 11¼ x 9 in., (28.6 x
      22.9 cm.), photograph, gelatin silver print (BP 1212, DM
      2947, FR 9995, Y 237,552).
  BI *"Die Begluckende Sonne Des Fruhen Morgens, San*
      Angelo Ischia", The Endearing Sun Of Early Morning,
      San Angelo, Ischia, 1937, ink t., photog.'s ink credit
      stamp Foto Herbert List, prov., est. BP1,5/2,000, (05-06-
      93, Christie-London, #133, illus.), 8⅞ x 10¾ in., photo-
      graph, gelatin silver print.
$607* *Curd Jurgens, 50's,* photographer's stamp, (11-12-92,
      Lempertz, #155, illus.), 9¼ x 11⁷⁄₁₆ in., (23.5 x 29 cm.),
      photograph, gelatin silver print (BP 388, DM 954, FR
      3251, Y 75,096).
$1380* *Dalmation And Friend, Portofino,* 1936, p.l., estate
      stamp, lit., (04-08-93, Christie-NY, #109, illus.), 8¼ x 7¼
      in., (21 x 18.4 cm.), photograph, gelatin silver print (BP
      905, DM 2217, FR 7504, Y 156,605).
$2013* *Footprints In The Sand (Baltic Sea), c. 1933,* mounted,
      s. by photog., (04-06-93, Sotheby-NY, #338, illus.), 4¾ x
      6¼ in., photograph (BP 1330, DM 3243, FR 10,982, Y
      229,585).
  BI *Franz Bauer As The Clown,* 1950s, t., credit stamp, est.
      $1,8/2,00, (04-08-93, Christie-NY, #110, illus.), 11⅝ x 9
      in., (29.5 x 22.9 cm.), photograph, gelatin silver print.

$2178* *Headstead, London,* 1936, p. c. 1950, Herbert List Estate
      vintage print ink stamp s. by Max Scheler, Executor,
      prov., (05-06-93, Christie-London, #132, illus.), 11½ x 9
      in., photograph, gelatin silver print (BP 1380, DM 3430,
      FR 11,548, Y 239,630).
  BI *Heinrich Kirchner, 1952,* photographer's stamp, lit., est.
      DM 600, (11-12-92, Lempertz, #158), 7¹³⁄₁₆ x 8¹⁵⁄₁₆ in.,
      (19.8 x 22.8 cm.), photograph, gelatin silver print.
$455* *Im Gangeviertel Hamburg,* 1932, 50's, lit., (11-12-92,
      Lempertz, #149, illus.), 10⁷⁄₁₆ x 7¹¹⁄₁₆ in., (26.5 x 19.6
      cm.), photograph, gelatin silver print (BP 291, DM 715,
      FR 2437, Y 56,291).
$1365* *In Den Kolonaden Des Bernini, 50's,* photographer's
      stamp, lit., (11-12-92, Lempertz, #151, illus.), 11¾ x 9³⁄₁₆
      in., (29.9 x 23.3 cm.), photograph, gelatin silver print
      (BP 873, DM 2145, FR 7311, Y 168,873).
$1265* *In The Shower, 1930's-40's,* photog. name stamp, (04-06-
      93, Sotheby-NY, #339, illus.), 11½ x 9¼ in., photograph
      (BP 836, DM 2038, FR 6901, Y 144,275).
$455* *Kunstgenuss Im Freien, 50's,* photographer's stamp, (11-
      12-92, Lempertz, #157), 11⁹⁄₁₆ x 7⅝ in., (29.3 x 19.3
      cm.), photograph, gelatin silver print (BP 291, DM 715,
      FR 2437, Y 56,291).
  BI *Kunstler, 50's,* photographer's stamp, est. DM 600, (11-
      12-92, Lempertz, #156), 7⅜ x 7⅞ in., (18.7 x 20 cm.),
      photograph, gelatin silver print.
$2013* *Lykabettos, Athens, Greece (The Draped Figure), c. 1936:*
      Two, 1 stamped twice, other mounted, (04-06-93,
      Sotheby-NY, #340, illus.), one 9⅝ x 8⅜ in., other 6¾ x
      3¾ in., photograph (BP 1330, DM 3243, FR 10,982, Y
      229,585).
  BI *Marino Marini, 1952,* ink t., Herbert List Estate vintage
      print ink stamp s. by Max Scheler, prov., est. BP 1,3/
      1,500, (05-06-93, Christie-London, #135, illus.), 10½ x
      9 in., photograph, gloss gelatin silver print.
  BI *Michaeliskirche Hamburg, 50's,* photographer's stamp, est.
      DM 900, (11-12-92, Lempertz, #154, illus.), 11³⁄₁₆ x 7³⁄₁₆
      in., (28.4 x 18.2 cm.), photograph, solarized print.
$834* *Monche, Rom, 50's,* (c), (11-12-92, Lempertz, #150,
      illus.), 11⁹⁄₁₆ x 9⅛ in., (29.4 x 23.1 cm.), photograph,
      gelatin silver print (BP 533, DM 1311, FR 4467, Y
      103,180).
$834* *Platz Mit Blick Auf Rom, 50's,* photographer's stamp,
      (11-12-92, Lempertz, #152, illus.), 9⁵⁄₁₆ x 11¹³⁄₁₆ in.,
      (23.6 x 30 cm.), photograph, gelatin silver print (BP 533,
      DM 1311, FR 4467, Y 103,180).
$748* *"Porto Ercole, Italy",* 1950s, photog.'s and Rohdruck
      stamps, (05-23-93, Butterfield, #3506, illus.), 11¾ x 9⅛
      in., photograph, gelatin silver print (BP 487, DM 1223,
      FR 4117, Y 82,679).
$345* *Reclining Male Nude,* 1950s, photog.'s stamp, (05-23-93,
      Butterfield, #3507, illus.), 8½ x 11¼ in., photograph, gel-
      atin silver print (BP 225, DM 564, FR 1899, Y 38,134).
  BI *Rome Fotomontage,* 1950s, credit stamp, est. $1,8/2,00,
      (04-08-93, Christie-NY, #111, illus.), 8 x 9 in., (20.3 x
      22.9 cm.), photograph, gelatin silver print.
  BI *Satyr Torso, Dionysos Theatre, Athens, 1937,* t., credit
      & reprod. limit. stamps, est. $4/5,000, (10-13-92,
      Christie-NY, #294, illus.), 11 x 9⅛ in., (27.9 x 23.2
      cm.), photograph, gelatin silver print.
$2860* *Ship's Funnel, c. 1935,* credit stamp, (10-13-92, Christie-
      NY, #293, illus.), 10⅛ x 8 in., (25.7 x 20.3 cm.), photo-
      graph, gelatin silver print (BP 1666, DM 4190, FR
      14,236, Y 346,793).
$607* *Strandstilleben, 50's,* photographer's stamp, (11-12-92,
      Lempertz, #153, illus.), 8⅛ x 11 in., (20.6 x 28 cm.),
      photograph, gelatin silver print (BP 388, DM 954, FR
      3251, Y 75,096).
  BI *Untitled, 1936,* stamp, est. $3/4,000, (10-15-92, Sotheby-
      NY, #419, illus.), 10⅞ x 9⅛ in., (27.6 x 23.2 cm.), pho-
      tograph, unique photocollage.
  BI *"W.H. Auden", 1953,* ink t., photog.'s ink (c) stamp and
      H L 57, prov., est. BP 1,8/2,200, (05-06-93, Christie-
      London, #136, illus.), 11½ x 8½ in., photograph, gloss
      gelatin silver print.
$3266* *William Somerset Maugham, Athens, 1950,* ink t., pho-
      tog.'s ink (c) stamp, ink stamp, prov., (05-06-93,
      Christie-London, #134, illus.), 9⅛ x 11⅝ in., photograph,

gloss gelatin silver print (BP 2070, DM 5144, FR 17,317, Y 359,335).
BI *"Zeitlupe Null"*, Galerie Gundlach, portfolio of 10, p. posthumously, each w/photog. blindstamp, estate portfolio stamp #23, s. by executor, 1931-37, p. c. 1980, #23/50, est. $3/4,000, (04-06-93, Sotheby-NY, #337, illus.), various sizes to 11 x 7 in., photograph.

LITTEN, Sidney M. English 1887-1949
$165* *"Guidecca Canal Venice", c. 1930,* s., num., glue residue, good cond., (10-31-92, Cleveland, #308), 9 x 11⅞ in., (22.9 x 30.2 cm.), etching (BP 106, DM 254, FR 861, Y 20,438).
$100* *"Il, Paradiso", c. 1930,* s., proof, good cond., (05-15-93, Cleveland, #405), 13¾ x 9¾ in., (34.9 x 24.8 cm.), etching on green paper (BP 65, DM 161, FR 541, Y 11,085).

LITTLE, William, Publishers
$95* *Rome MDCCCXLIX, Supplement To The Illustrated London News, May 4, 1850,* creasing, (02-17-93, Bonhams-Chelsea, #294), image 14 x 39 in., (35.6 x 99.1 cm.), engraving (BP 66, DM 154, FR 523, Y 11,347).

LITTLEFIELD, William H. American b. 1902
$193* *The Boxers,* s. Wm. H. Littlefield, d. 1928, num. 6/15, good cond., (09-27-92, Bakker, #193, illus.), sheet 23¼ x 15¼ in., (59.1 x 38.7 cm.), lithograph (BP 113, DM 286, FR 967, Y 23,295).

LIVEMONT, Privat 1852-1936
$3300* *Absinthe Robette, 1896,* Des Presses de Goffart, A cond., (08-06-92, Swann, #177, illus.), 43 x 32 in., (109.2 x 81.3 cm.), (BP 1724, DM 4876, FR 16,467, Y 420,918).
$1840* *Absinthe Robette, 1896,* p. J.L. Goffart, margins, good condition, creases, brown spot, linen-backed, (03-31-93, Butterfield, #5244, illus.), 41⁵⁄₁₆ x 29¾ in., (104.9 x 75.6 cm.), lithograph printed in colors on wove (BP 1217, DM 2960, FR 10,055, Y 211,592).
$412* *Ameublement,* Bruxelles, A cond., (08-06-92, Swann, #178, illus.), 4¾ x 10 in., (12.1 x 25.4 cm.), (BP 215, DM 609, FR 2056, Y 52,551).
$8450* *Michiels Freres, 1902,* proof before letters, margins, apparently good condition, handling creases, surface soiling, (03-31-93, Butterfield, #5245, illus.), 29⅛ x 16 in., (74 x 40.6 cm.), lithograph printed in colors on wove (BP 5587, DM 13,592, FR 46,175, Y 971,711).
$690* *Palais De La Femme, 1900,* plate s., (03-25-93, Christie-E, #204), sight 40 x 29 in., (101.6 x 73.7 cm.), color lithograph (BP 469, DM 1134, FR 3855, Y 80,834).
$3300* *"Woman Sculpting" and "Woman Painting", 1901: Two,* p. Privat Livemont Brux 1901, (12-12-92, Christie-NY, #438, illus.), lithograph in colors (BP 2116, DM 5199, FR 17,819, Y 408,365).

LIVINGSTON, Beulah
$302* *Portrait Of Bernhardt And Two Children, 1917,* notation, (04-07-93, Swann, #402, illus.), 7 x 9¼ in., photograph, toned silver print (BP 200, DM 488, FR 1653, Y 34,310).

LIVINGSTON, John
BI *"Michigan Bobcat",* s., d. '82, #505/1000, est. $10/20, (11-13-92, DuMouchelle, #2605), 18⅜ x 14⅜ in., (46.7 x 36.5 cm.), collotype.

LIXENBERG, Cyril
$460* *Untitled, 1980: Fifteen,* complete portfolio, s., num., good cond., handling creases, originalpaper portfolio, (05-19-93, Butterfield, #2255), each approx. 25⁹⁄₁₆ x 25⁹⁄₁₆ in., (649 x 649 mm.), silkscreen in colors on thick stock (BP 299, DM 748, FR 2519, Y 50,924).

LIZARS, William H. Scottish 1788-1859
$303* *Jardine Birds: Ten,* framed as 5 pairs, (05-28-93, Sloan, #232, illus.), each, sight 6 x 3¾ in., (15.2 x 9.5 cm.), color engravings (BP 194, DM 481, FR 1625, Y 32,490).

LJUNGBERG, Sven b. 1913
$179* *Asiatiska Kvinnor Och Man: Five,* s., V/XXV, (04-17-93, Falkkloos, #338), 18⅞ x 16¹⁵⁄₁₆ in., (48 x 43 cm.), lithograph (BP 116, DM 286, FR 967, Y 19,904, SK 1320).

LJUNGGREN, Reinhold b. 1920
$649* *Kvall, Vastra Langatan, Trosa,* s., 175/360, (12-04-92, AB Stockholm, #7101), 13⁹⁄₁₆ x 18⅞ in., (34.5 x 48 cm.), lithograph in colors (BP 416, DM 1034, FR 3506, Y 81,024, SK 4400).

LLOYD, John
$302* *Painter With Brush, Palette, And Human Skull,* 1850's, (10-14-92, Swann, #237, illus.), 4¾ x 3½ in., (12.1 x 8.9 cm.), photograph, albumenized salt print from paper neg. (BP 177, DM 442, FR 1499, Y 36,597).

LLUEWELLEN
$55* *Lone Yellowlegs,* margins, s. Lluewellen, (02-13-93, Collins, #39, illus.), 5 x 7⅜ in., (12.7 x 18.7 cm.), etching (BP 39, DM 91, FR 309, Y 6633).

LOAN, Dorothy van
$66* *"In The Order Of Bernadette",* s., (06-11-93, Freemn/Fine Art, #134A), 14½ x 10½ in., (36.8 x 26.7 cm.), lithograph (BP 43, DM 107, FR 362, Y 7003).
$66* *"In The Order Of Dominic",* s., (06-11-93, Freemn/Fine Art, #134B), 14½ x 10½ in., (36.8 x 26.7 cm.), lithograph (BP 43, DM 107, FR 362, Y 7003).

LOATES, (Martin) Glen b. 1945
$368* *Black-Capped Chickadee,* #38/125, s.; t. verso, (11-16-92, Hodgins, #6), 25½ x 19 in., (64.8 x 48.3 cm.), lithograph on paper (BP 242, DM 587, FR 1977, Y 45,925, C$ 468).
$152* *Blue Jay,* #38/125 s., t. verso, (05-10-93, Hodgins, #7, illus.), 25½ x 19 in., (64.8 x 48.3 cm.), lithograph on paper (BP 99, DM 244, FR 824, Y 16,985, C$ 193).
BI *Red Breasted Nuthatch,* #38/125, s., t., est. C$250/350, (05-10-93, Hodgins, #351), 255 x 19 in., (647.7 x 48.3 cm.), lithograph on paper.
$368* *Winter Wren,* #38/125, s., bears t., (11-16-92, Hodgins, #161), 25½ x 19 in., (64.8 x 48.3 cm.), lithograph on paper (BP 242, DM 587, FR 1977, Y 45,925, C$ 468).

LOATES, Glen
$88* *Ducks,* limited edit., d. 1978, s., #20/150, mint cond., (04-22-93, Guyette, #848, illus.), print (BP 57, DM 141, FR 477, Y 9676).

LOBE, W.
$55* *Face Of A Woman,* s., num. below image, (10-08-92, Boos, #692), 21¾ x 35 in., (552 x 889 mm.), serigraph (BP 33, DM 81, FR 276, Y 6683).

LOBEL-RICHE, Almery 1880-1950
$162* *La Promenade,* s., #16/60, restored, full margins, (05-27-93, Briest, #132), 25 x 18⅞ in., (63.5 x 48 cm.), color aquatint (BP 104, DM 260, FR 876, Y 17,367).

LOCCHI, Giuseppe (after)
BI *Veduta De Palazzi De Sig. March Corsi, E Vivani,* est. $4/600, (11-12-92, Freemn/Fine Art, #120C), 18½ x 26½ in., (47 x 67.3 cm.), engraving, hand colored.

LOCH, Joseph F. American 20th cent.
$25* *Mother And Daughter In Interior,* s., #5/100, (05-16-93, Hanzel, #467), 16 x 9¼ in., (40.6 x 23.5 cm.), lithograph (BP 16, DM 40, FR 135, Y 2771).

LOCHARD
$734* *Champignons De Paris, "Culture Et Mise En Conserves A Issy-Les-Moulineaux",* very good cond., (11-19-92, Ribeyre/Baron, #34), 61¹³⁄₁₆ x 44⅞ in., (157 x 114 cm.), poster (BP 483, DM 1170, FR 3942, Y 91,282).
$834* *Plaques & Papiers,* p. Lochard, folds, defects, backed on linen, laid on board, (05-07-93, Christie-S. Ken, #109, illus.), color lithograph (BP 528, DM 1319, FR 4443, Y 91,830).
$869* *Plaques & Papiers Tambour,* p. Lochard, tears, defects, backed on linen, laid on board, (05-07-93, Christie-S. Ken, #105, illus.), 39¼ x 39¼ in., (99.7 x 99.7 cm.), color lithograph (BP 550, DM 1374, FR 4630, Y 95,684).
$955* *Plaques, Papiers,* p. Lochard, defects, creases, backed on canvas, laid on board, (05-07-93, Christie-S. Ken, #108, illus.), 39 x 39 in., (99.1 x 99.1 cm.), color lithograph (BP 605, DM 1510, FR 5088, Y 105,153).

LOCKE, Charles American 1899-1953

$100* *Fountain Square, Cincinnati,* s., fine cond., mat stain, (05-15-93, Cleveland, #213), 6 x 7 in., (15.2 x 17.8 cm.), lithograph (BP 65, DM 161, FR 541, Y 11,085).

$176* *"Only One (Park Bench)", c. 1920,* init., t., good cond., fold, (10-31-92, Cleveland, #172), 8½ x 6⅞ in., (21.6 x 17.5 cm.), lithograph (BP 113, DM 271, FR 919, Y 21,801).

$180* *"Tramp Steamer",* pub. AAA, s., very fine cond., hinges, (05-15-93, Cleveland, #212, illus.), 9¼ x 12¼ in., (23.5 x 31.1 cm.), lithograph (BP 117, DM 290, FR 973, Y 19,953).

$230* *"Waterfront",* AAA edit., s., excell. cond., (05-15-93, Cleveland, #211, illus.), 8⅞ x 12⅛ in., (22.5 x 30.8 cm.), lithograph (BP 150, DM 370, FR 1243, Y 25,496).

LOCKE, Walter Ronald American b. 1883

$22* *Against The Wind,* W.R. Locke, '39, (10-03-92, Garth, #292, illus.), 22¾ x 26¾ in., (57.8 x 67.9 cm.), etching (BP 13, DM 31, FR 106, Y 2633).

$35* *"Against The Wind", 1939,* pub. AAA, s., excell. cond., (05-15-93, Cleveland, #214), 8 x 11⅞ in., (20.3 x 30.2 cm.), etching (BP 23, DM 56, FR 189, Y 3880).

$55* *"Along The Gulf Of Mexico, Fla.",* s., d. '35, AAA, (09-18-92, DuMouchelle, #2415), 11 x 8 in., (27.9 x 20.3 cm.), etching (BP 32, DM 82, FR 282, Y 6853).

$66* *"Changing Weather, Gulf Of Mexico, Fla.",* s., d. '36, (09-18-92, DuMouchelle, #2416), 9 x 11 in., (22.9 x 27.9 cm.), etching (BP 38, DM 99, FR 338, Y 8223).

BI *"Hickory Auclot River, Fl.",* s. W.R. Locke, d. '36, t., pub. AAA, est. $1/150, (12-12-92, A. James, #428), sight 12¼ x 9⅝ in., (31.1 x 24.4 cm.), etching.

BI *"Hickory Fla.",* s., d. 26, t., AAA print, est. $50/75, (04-16-93, DuMouchelle, #2173), 11½ x 8⅞ in., (29.2 x 22.5 cm.), etching.

BI *"In Beaufort, S.C.",* s. W.R. Locke, d. '37, t., pub. AAA, est. $1/150, (12-12-92, A. James, #349), sheet 16 x 13 in., (40.6 x 33 cm.), etching.

BI *"Peace On The Amelote, Florida",* s. W.R. Locke, d. '37, t., pub. AAA, est. $1/150, (12-12-92, A. James, #350), 12½ x 14⅞ in., (31.8 x 37.8 cm.), etching.

BI *"Trinity Church, St. Augustine, Fl.",* s. W.R. Locke, d. '36, t., pub. AAA, est. $1/150, (12-12-92, A. James, #429), sight 14 x 10 in., (35.6 x 25.4 cm.), etching.

LODEIZEN, Frank

$192* *Untitled, 1980,* s., d., #55/190, margins, good cond., (05-27-93, Sotheby-Amstrdm, #435), 15³⁄₁₆ x 15³⁄₁₆ in., colored silkscreen on wove (BP 123, DM 308, FR 1038, Y 20,583, G 345).

$64* *Untitled, 1980,* s., d., #15/190, full sheet p. to edges, good cond., (05-27-93, Sotheby-Amstrdm, #433), sh 22³⁄₁₆ x 26⁹⁄₁₆ in., (563 x 674 mm.), colored silkscreen on wove (BP 41, DM 103, FR 346, Y 6861, G 115).

$128* *Untitled, 1980,* s., d., #189/190, margins, good cond., (05-27-93, Sotheby-Amstrdm, #434), 23⅛ x 17⅝ in., (587 x 447 mm.), colored silkscreen on wove (BP 82, DM 205, FR 692, Y 13,722, G 230).

LOEB, Dr. Leonard B. 1891-1978

BI *The Bleachers, c. 1929,* layered mount, lit., est. $2,5/3,500, (04-08-93, Christie-NY, #390, illus.), 7¼ x 9½ in., (18.4 x 24.1 cm.), photograph, gelatin silver print.

BI *The Elevated, New York, c. 1926,* tipped to double-mount, p. num., est. $2/3,000, (04-06-93, Sotheby-NY, #88, illus.), 6⅝ x 8¼ in., photograph.

BI *Grand Central Station Skylight, 1925,* est. $3/5,000, (10-13-92, Christie-NY, #296, illus.), 6⅝ x 8⅝ in., (16.8 x 21.9 cm.), photograph, waxed platinum print.

$3850* *Grand Central Station, 1925,* lit., (10-13-92, Christie-NY, #295, illus.), 5¾ x 7½ in., (14.6 x 19.1 cm.), photograph, palladium print (BP 2242, DM 5640, FR 19,164, Y 466,836).

BI *Tree, Monterey, California, late 1920's,* tipped to double-mount, p. num. 20, photog. name stamp, est. $1,5/2,500, (04-06-93, Sotheby-NY, #89, illus.), 6¾ x 9 in., photograph.

LOEBER, Lou

$261* *Still Life Of Flowers, 1923: Four,* one s., d., 3 proofs for the same still life i. proefdruk I, II and IV, margins, good cond., discoloration, creases, soiling, tear, (12-09-92, Sotheby-Amstrdm, #605), each approx. 11¾ x 9⁷⁄₁₆ in., (298 x 240 mm.), etching w/aquatint on wove (BP 167, DM 410, FR 1398, Y 32,362, G 460).

LOEFFLER, Bertold 1874-1960

$10,640* *Internationale Kunstschau Wien 1909, Schwarzenbergplatz 9-7 (Reed 31), 1909,* stone mono., (06-05-93, Bassenge, #6452, illus.), sh 35⁵⁄₁₆ x 17¹¹⁄₁₆ in., (89.7 x 45 cm.), color lithograph (BP 7004, DM 17,250, FR 58,142, Y 1,141,386).

LOEWE, Von

$552* *Nsu.Motorrader,* tears, repairs, (02-04-93, Christie-S. Ken, #172), 35½ x 27 in., (90.2 x 68.6 cm.), color lithograph backed on linen (BP 385, DM 909, FR 3082, Y 68,665).

LOEWENSBERG, Verena 1912-1986

BI *Komposition Aus "9 x 5 Konkret", 1973,* #14/200, s., d.. est. SF 6/800, (04-21-93, Germann, #600), 23¹³⁄₁₆ x 23⅝ in., (605 x 600 mm.), color serigraph.

$3002* *"Vier Variationen Um Ein Quadrat", 1980: Four,* #10/50, s., d., (04-21-93, Germann, #39, illus.), 20¹⁄₁₆ x 14³⁄₁₆ in., (510 x 360 mm.), color serigraph (BP 1948, DM 4799, FR 16,227, Y 332,337, SF 4370).

LOEWIG, Roger b. 1930

$72* *Unter Dem Netz, 1972,* s., d., (11-28-92, Grisebach, #630, illus.), 7 x 10⁵⁄₁₆ in., (17.8 x 26.2 cm.), lithograph on copper print paper (BP 48, DM 115, FR 389, Y 8961).

LOEWY, Raymond

BI *Streamlined Train, c. 1940,* Loewy's assistant's name, "H. Poullier", in neg., vintage photo of original collage, est. $6/900, (10-14-92, Swann, #505, illus.), 10 x 15 in., (25.4 x 38.1 cm.), photograph, silver print.

LOGAN, Robert

$55* *"Harkness Tower, Yale" and "Dwight Chapel, Yale": Two,* (03-20-93, Northeast, #750), sight 16 x 9½ in., (40.6 x 24.1 cm.), etching (BP 37, DM 90, FR 306, Y 6380).

LOHAW

BI *Comic Book Characters,* s., 59/182, Frank Lohaw, est. $50/100, (03-12-93, DuMouchelle, #2326), 15 x 21 in., (38.1 x 53.3 cm.), lithograph.

LOHSE, Richard Paul 1902-1988

BI *"# Modulare Ordnungen 3 Serielle Ordnungen, 2",* A 9/35, s., Meissner Edition, est. SF 2/2,600, (04-21-93, Germann, #154, illus.), 23¹³⁄₁₆ x 23¹³⁄₁₆ in., (605 x 605 mm.), color serigraph.

$724* *2 X 2 Gleiche Farbgruppen, 1952-68/2,* 56/200, s., num., (10-14-92, Germann, #561), 23⅝ x 23⅝ in., (600 x 600 mm.), serigraph on fabric (BP 425, DM 1060, FR 3593, Y 87,736, SF 944).

$1014* *Bewegung Von Acht Farben Um Eine Achse,* #49/100, s., (09-04-92, Germann, #447, illus.), 28½ x 28⅜ in., (724 x 721 mm.), color serigraph (BP 508, DM 1421, FR 4838, Y 124,815, SF 1265).

$790* *Bewegung Von Acht Farben Um Eine Achse,* #37/100, s., (06-24-93, Germann, #679, illus.), 28½ x 28⅜ in., (724 x 721 mm.), color serigraph (BP 520, DM 1281, FR 4317, Y 84,746, SF 1150).

$790* *Komposition,* #32/200, s., (06-24-93, Germann, #680, illus.), 12⅝ x 31½ in., (320 x 800 mm.), color serigraph on Kunstoffplatte (BP 520, DM 1281, FR 4317, Y 84,746, SF 1150).

BI *"Vier Vertikale Serielle Strukturen", 1980: Four,* #10/50, s., Meissner Edition, est. SF 3/4,000, (04-21-93, Germann, #603), 19¹¹⁄₁₆ x 14¹⁄₁₆ in., (500 x 357 mm.), 10-color serigraph.

LOMAX, John A. (after)

BI *"The Reconcilliation",* (12-11-92, G.A. Key, #24), 16 x 22 in., (40.6 x 55.9 cm.), oleograph.

LOMBERS, Eckersley

$1554* *Scientists Prefer Shell, 1936,* ref. #446, cond. 1, creasing, (10-13-92, Phillips-London, #99, illus.), 29¹⁵⁄₁₆ x 45¹⁄₁₆ in., (76 x 114.5 cm.), color lithograph (BP 905, DM 2277, FR 7735, Y 188,432).

$798* *Time To Change To Winter Shell, 1938,* p. Waterlow and Sons, ref. #519, cond. 1, (10-13-92, Phillips-London, #138), 29¹⁵⁄₁₆ x 44⅞ in., (76 x 114 cm.), color lithograph (BP 465, DM 1169, FR 3972, Y 96,762).

LONDERSEEL, Jan van   1570/75-1624/25
$231* *Das Innere Einer Gotischen Kirche (Wurzbach 9; Le Blanc 32; Hollstein 75 II),* after Hendrick Arts, (12-04-92, Bassenge, #6282), 12¹⁄₁₆ x 16⁵⁄₁₆ in., (30.7 x 41.5 cm.), engraving (BP 148, DM 368, FR 1248, Y 28,839).

LONDON (after)
$450* *Representation Of The Defeat Of A Squadron Of French Ships... By A Sqadron Of English Ships Under The Command Of Admiral Nelson, 1st August 1798,* by Francis Weber, pub. S. Tessari & Francis Weber, staining, foxing, (11-30-92, Phillips-London, #233), plate 17¼ x 23 in., (438 x 584 mm.), hand-colored aquatint on laid (BP 297, DM 717, FR 2434, Y 56,005).

LONG, Edwin (after)
BI   *Anno Domini,* est. BP 1/150, (06-16-93, Bonhams-Chelsea, #511), image 19 x 39 in., (48.3 x 99.1 cm.), engraving.
$17* *Merab, 1890,* by Herbert Bourne, pub. Fairless and Beeforth, margins, (12-10-92, Bonhams-Chelsea, #60), plate 25½ x 16½ in., (64.8 x 41.9 cm.), engraving (BP 11, DM 27, FR 92, Y 2103).
$17* *Merab, 1890,* by Herbert Bourne, pub. Fairless and Beeforth, margins, (12-10-92, Bonhams-Chelsea, #59), plate 25½ x 16½ in., (64.8 x 41.9 cm.), engraving (BP 11, DM 27, FR 92, Y 2103).
$85* *Merab, 1890,* by Herbert Bourne, pub. Fairless and Beeforth, margins, (12-10-92, Bonhams-Chelsea, #101), plate 25½ x 16½ in., (64.8 x 41.9 cm.), engraving (BP 55, DM 134, FR 459, Y 10,515).

LONG, Richard   American b. 1945
$1083* *Dartmoor Walks, 1972,* s., d., num., (11-28-92, Schoppmann, #636), 23⅝ x 19¹¹⁄₁₆ in., (60 x 50 cm.), lithograph and offset on white wove (BP 715, DM 1725, FR 5857, Y 134,785).
$913* *A Line In Japan, 1979,* s., #43/50, margins, good cond., sh MM: 590 x 725, (05-27-93, Sotheby-Amstrdm, #648, illus.), xin., photograph, color on wove (BP 579, DM 1443, FR 4872, Y 101,648, G 1610).
BI   *Staight Miles And Meandering Miles, Dunkery Hill, 1985,* s., #63/80, pub. Galerie Media, full margins, good cond., est. $800/1,000, (02-11-93, Sotheby-NY, #383), 15¹⁵⁄₁₆ x 23⁷⁄₁₆ in., (405 x 595 mm.), silkscreen and offset lithograph p. in colors.
$9900* *Untitled,* s., d. 1969, prov., exhib., Sylvio Perlstein Coll., (11-18-92, Sotheby-NY, #222, illus.), 18½ x 23¾ in., (47 x 60.3 cm.), pencil and photograph mounted on paper (BP 6518, DM 15,784, FR 53,169, Y 1,231,190).

LONG, Sydney   1871-1955
$567* *Wilberforce Pastoral,* s. Sydney Long, i., #1/60, (08-11-92, L. Joel, #18G), 8¼ x 9⅝ in., (21 x 24.5 cm.), etching, blue ink (BP 295, DM 832, FR 2818, Y 72,609, A$ 770).

LONGO, Robert   American b. 1953
$1870* *Arena Brains, 1986,* s., d., #23/25, pub. Brooke Alexander, full margins, excell. cond., (11-09-92, Christie-NY, #357, illus.), 44½ x 29 in., (113 x 73.7 cm.), colored lithograph on BFK Rives (BP 1236, DM 2985, FR 10,086, Y 232,068).
$4313* *Frank And Glen, 1991,* s., d., #11/38, pub. Brooke Alexander, pub. Derriere l'Etoile Studios, full margins, excell. cond.?, (05-19-93, Butterfield, #2257, illus.), sh 37½ x 54 in., (95.3 x 137.2 cm.), lithograph in colors on Arches (BP 2800, DM 7011, FR 23,620, Y 477,471).
$7475* *"Frank" and "Gretchen", 1982-83 and 1984:* Two, s., d., #2/28 and 1/38, pub. Brooke Alexander, Inc., good cond., (05-15-93, Sotheby-NY, #1084, illus.), each sheet 67⅞ x 39 in., (172.4 x 99.1 cm.), lithograph on Arches 350 gm. (BP 4860, DM 12,023, FR 40,405, Y 828,622).
BI   *Heaven, 1983,* s., t., d., annot. A.P., full margins, good cond., glue residue, surface soiling, est. $4/600, (05-19-93, Butterfield, #2256), 8⅛ x 4½ in., (206 x 114 mm.), silkscreen in colors on heavy wove.

BI   *Jules, 1982-83,* s., d., #12/45, pub. Brooke Alexander, Inc., full margins, good cond., skinned spot, est. $2/3,000, (05-15-93, Sotheby-NY, #1083, illus.), 29⅞ x 15 in., (75.9 x 38.1 cm.), lithograph.
$8338* *Men In The Cities: "Larry" and "Joanna", 1983:* Two, s., d. #3/48, pub. Editions Schellmann, good cond. ?, (05-15-93, Sotheby-NY, #1085, illus.), each sheet 71¾ x 35⅞ in., (182.2 x 91.1 cm.), lithograph (BP 5421, DM 13,412, FR 45,070, Y 924,288).
$505* *Ohne Titel, 1986,* #XXVI/XXX, pencil s., d., (11-20-92, Lempertz, #676), sh 32¹⁄₁₆ x 24 in., (81.5 x 61 cm.), color lithograph on Velin (BP 332, DM 805, FR 2712, Y 62,803).

LONYN, Louis
$2258* *Plaques Jougla,* p. Minot, folds, defects, backed on linen, laid on board, back coverlot, (05-07-93, Christie-S. Ken, #101, illus.), 39 x 54¾ in., (99.1 x 139.1 cm.), color lithograph (BP 1430, DM 3570, FR 12,030, Y 248,624).

LORD, Elyse   English 1900-1971
$202* *"Geisha Girl Sitting On A Couch",* num. 81/100, margins, (01-21-93, Bonhams-Chelsea, #115), plate 8⅜ x 12 in., (21.3 x 30.5 cm.), hand-colored drypoint etching (BP 132, DM 321, FR 1087, Y 25,282).
$303* *"Lovers",* s., #40/63, (02-11-93, Boos, #419), plate 12¹³⁄₁₆ x 8⅞ in., (325 x 225 mm.), color drypoint and stencil on Japon (BP 214, DM 502, FR 1698, Y 36,528).
$220* *Untitled,* s., num. 55/75, good cond., (10-31-92, Cleveland, #309), 16¼ x 12¼ in., (41.3 x 31.1 cm.), hand-colored etching (BP 141, DM 338, FR 1148, Y 27,251).
$165* *Untitled,* s., num. 68/75, good cond., (10-31-92, Cleveland, #310), 16¼ x 12¼ in., (41.3 x 31.1 cm.), hand-colored etching (BP 106, DM 254, FR 861, Y 20,438).

LORENZI
$416* *Le Pays De Caux Et Ses Plages A La Mode, 1930,* pub. Comite Touristique du Pays de Caux, cond. 3, laid on linen, (10-13-92, Phillips-London, #35), 39³⁄₁₆ x 24⁷⁄₁₆ in., (99.5 x 62 cm.), color lithograph (BP 242, DM 609, FR 2071, Y 50,443).

LORENZI, Fabius
BI   *"Battle Scenes, World War I", 1920:* Seven, s., full margins, good cond., creasing, surface soiling, est. $1/1,500, (10-28-92, Butterfield, #2663), each image 11 x 11½ in., (279 x 292 mm.), color woodcut on Japan paper.

LORING, John   b. 1939
$200* *"Dial Tone First", 1972,* #16/100, d., s., (04-04-93, Pescheteau, #249), 45¹¹⁄₁₆ x 31½ in., (116 x 80 cm.), color serigraph (BP 132, DM 321, FR 1092, Y 22,771).
BI   *"New York", 1972,* #11/50, d., s., est. FF5/600, (04-04-93, Pescheteau, #250), 25⁹⁄₁₆ x 37¹³⁄₁₆ in., (65 x 96 cm.), color serigraph.
$73* *Untitled,* #11/50, d. 72, s., (01-28-93, Pescheteau, #192), 25¹⁵⁄₁₆ x 37¹³⁄₁₆ in., (66 x 96 cm.), serigraph (BP 48, DM 116, FR 391, Y 9064).

LORJOU, Bernard   French b. 1908
BI   *"Antinea-59",* red crayon HC s., est. FF1,000/1,500, (04-04-93, Pescheteau, #251), 25⁹⁄₁₆ x 17¹¹⁄₁₆ in., (65 x 45 cm.), color lithograph on Arches.
$257* *Clown Au Bonnet Jaune,* s., #36/50, good margins, (05-06-93, Laurin, #57), lithograph (BP 163, DM 405, FR 1363, Y 28,276).
$247* *Clown Sur Fond Bleu,* s., #35/50, good margins, (05-06-93, Laurin, #58), color lithograph (BP 157, DM 389, FR 1310, Y 27,176).
$116* *La Moto,* s. in stone, (06-28-93, Loudmer, #82), 18½ x 27⁹⁄₁₆ in., (470 x 700 mm.), sh 21⁷⁄₁₆ x 29¹⁵⁄₁₆ in., (470 x 700 mm.), color lithograph on Arches wove (BP 78, DM 197, FR 664, Y 12,308).

LORRAIN, Claude (Claude GELLEE)   French 1600-1682
$303* *Cattle In A Landscape,* margins trimmed, laid down, (11-12-92, Freemn/Fine Art, #121), 4¾ x 7½ in., (12.1 x 19.1 cm.), etching (BP 199, DM 480, FR 1619, Y 37,570).
$165* *Danse Sous Les Arbres (Country Dance)(Blum 35. Russell 28), c. 1651,* trimmed to plate mark, sixth state(?) of 6, #6 burnished out(?), (05-27-93, Swann, #162), 5½ x

7⅞ in., (14 x 20 cm.), etching (BP 106, DM 265, FR 892, Y 17,689).

BI *The Herd At The Watering-Place (M. 16),* 3rd state of 3, narrow margins, foxing, est. BP 80/120, (10-27-92, Phillips-London, #18), (124 x 191 mm.), etching on thin wove.

$380* *L'Enlevement D'Europe (Robert-Dumesnil 22),* trimmed, repaired tears, Late Sir Philip and Lady Hendy Coll., (06-16-93, Bonhams-Chelsea, #317, illus.), 7⅞ x 10⅛ in., (20 x 25.7 cm.), etching on laid (BP 253, DM 631, FR 2117, Y 40,529).

$165* *Le Passage Du Gue (The Ford) (Russell 18. Blum 8), 1634,* thread margins, third state of 3, d., plate s., (05-27-93, Swann, #161), 4⅛ x 6⅝ in., (10.5 x 16.8 cm.), etching (BP 106, DM 265, FR 892, Y 17,689).

$3410* *Le Pont De Mer Au Fanal (M. 37),* third state of five, narrow margins, paper loss, surface dirt, (12-03-92, Sotheby-London, #27, illus.), 5½ x 7¾ in., (140 x 197 mm.), etching (BP 2200, DM 5362, FR 18,304, Y 424,288).

$3751* *Le Port De Mer A La Grosse Tour (Mannocci 39),* third state of six, wide margins, foxing, (12-03-92, Sotheby-London, #25), 5 x 7¾ in., (127 x 197 mm.), etching (BP 2420, DM 5899, FR 20,134, Y 466,716).

$150* *Le Port De Mere Au Fanal (Bl. 13, R-D 11),* 4th final state, trimmed, laid down, nick, (11-30-92, Phillips-London, #293), sheet 5⅜ x 7⅝ in., (137 x 194 mm.), etching (BP 99, DM 239, FR 811, Y 18,668).

$920* *"Les Quatre Chevres" and "Les Trois Chevres" (M. 8, R, E19), 1630-34:Two,* watermark, double plate, final states, margins trimmed to or w/in image, good cond., possible restoration, staining, hinge remains, (05-19-93, Butterfield, #1859), one 7¹⁵⁄₁₆ x 5³⁄₁₆ in., (202 x 132 mm.), the other 7¹³⁄₁₆ x 5¹⁄₁₆ in., (202 x 132 mm.), etching on fine Japan and laid (BP 597, DM 1495, FR 5038, Y 101,849).

$108* *Shepherd With Four Goats (BL 6),* 2nd state, (06-08-93, Ritchie, #20), plate 7⅞ x 5⅛ in., (20 x 13 cm.), sheet 8 x 3¼ in., (20 x 13 cm.), etching (BP 71, DM 175, FR 590, Y 11,471, C$ 138).

$5457* *Le Soleil Levant (M. 15),* fourth state of eight, narrow margins, foxing, discoloration, (12-03-92, Sotheby-London, #26, illus.), 5¼ x 7¾ in., (133 x 197 mm.), etching on paper w/watermark (BP 3520, DM 8582, FR 29,291, Y 678,985).

$248* *"The Temple Of Apollo",* (12-11-92, DuMouchelle, #2280), 16 x 22½ in., (40.6 x 57.2 cm.), etching (BP 159, DM 391, FR 1339, Y 30,689).

LORRAIN, Claude (Claude GELLEE) (after)

$3399* *Coll. Of Prints, 1819: One Hundred,* after Claude Le Lorrain, by Richard Earlow, pub. Messrs. Boydell andCo. Chepside, (11-11-92, Dorotheum, #354, illus.), 16⁹⁄₁₆ x 11 in., (42 x 28 cm.), etching w/mezzotint (BP 2249, DM 5432, FR 18,206, Y 422,656, SC 17,920).

$220* *(Shepherds With Cows And Goats)" (No. 41), "(Sunrise With Cows)" (No. 39) and "The Port Of Ostia With The Embarkation Of St. Paula" (No. 84), 1774, 1803, 1817: Three,* by Richard Earlom, each pub. John Boydell, margins, good cond., papersplit, platemark, tears, foxing, staining, creases, surface soiling, pen & pencil notations, (02-24-93, Butterfield, #2920), from 5½ x 7¾ in., (140 x 197 mm.), to 8⅛ x 10¼ in., (140 x 197 mm.), engraving & mezzotint in sepia on wove & laid (BP 153, DM 357, FR 1211, Y 25,816).

LORY, Gabriel (after) (fils)

$383* *Chute Du Staubbach Prise A L'Entree Du Village De Lauterbrunne,* tears, crease, surface dirt, creasing, image good cond., (11-30-92, Phillips-London, #250), image 7⅝ x 11 in., (194 x 279 mm.), aquatint w/extensive hand-coloring & touches of gum arabic on J. Whatman 1826 (BP 253, DM 610, FR 2071, Y 47,666).

LOSQUES, Daniel de

$330* *Mistinguett,* Chacoin, B- cond., creasing, cracking, (08-06-92, Swann, #179, illus.), 75½ x 41½ in., (191.8 x 105.4 cm.), (BP 172, DM 488, FR 1647, Y 42,092).

$330* *Mistinguett,* Chacoin, A- cond., creasing, (08-06-92, Swann, #180, illus.), 75½ x 42½ in., (191.8 x 108 cm.), (BP 172, DM 488, FR 1647, Y 42,092).

LOTIRON, R.

$441* *Salon D'Automne, Grand Palais, 1935,* very good cond., (11-19-92, Ribeyre/Baron, #142), 62¹⁵⁄₁₆ x 47¼ in., (160 x 120 cm.), poster (BP 290, DM 703, FR 2368, Y 54,844).

LOTIRON, Robert 1886-1966

$162* *Le Port,* s., #7/20, (05-27-93, Briest, #133), 17¹⁵⁄₁₆ x 24 in., (45.5 x 61 cm.), color lithograph (BP 104, DM 260, FR 876, Y 17,367).

LOUIS

$90* *Pastilles Au Miel. Clermont-Ferrand, 1892,* Imp. Generale, very good cond., (02-12-93, Cheval/Robert, #66), 62¹⁵⁄₁₆ x 39¹⁵⁄₁₆ in., (160 x 101.5 cm.), poster (BP 63, DM 149, FR 505, Y 10,854).

LOUIS, G.

$1173* *Ch. De Fer Du Nord: Wimereux, "Casino, Golf, Tennis",* p. de Vaugirard, excell. cond., (01-23-93, Ribeyre/Baron, #41, illus.), 38⁹⁄₁₆ x 23⅝ in., (98 x 60 cm.), poster (BP 767, DM 1865, FR 6310, Y 146,809).

LOUPOT, Ch.

$1364* *Exposition Internationale Des Arts Decoratifs Et Industriels, 1925,* Les Belles Affiches, good cond., lit., (11-19-92, Ribeyre/Baron, #143, illus.), 47¼ x 31½ in., (120 x 80 cm.), poster (BP 898, DM 2175, FR 7325, Y 169,631).

$462* *Journee Nationale Pour Les Victimes De La Mer, 1930,* fair cond., lit., (11-19-92, Ribeyre/Baron, #144), 62¹⁵⁄₁₆ x 46⅞ in., (160 x 119 cm.), poster (BP 304, DM 737, FR 2481, Y 57,456).

$4030* *Mirus "Poele A Bois", 1928,* p. Chaix, good cond., lit., (11-19-92, Ribeyre/Baron, #35, illus.), 63⅜ x 47⅝ in., (161 x 121 cm.), poster (BP 2653, DM 6425, FR 21,643, Y 501,181).

LOUPOT, Charles 1892-1962

$1994* *Glaces Creme Ch. Gervais G I C, 1930,* cond. A, cover lot, (03-16-93, Boisgirard, #144, illus.), 18½ x 12⅝ in., (47 x 32 cm.), poster (BP 1377, DM 3316, FR 11,266, Y 233,162).

LOUPOT, D'Apres 1892-1960

$1891* *Fourrures Canton, c. 1950,* excell. cond., (02-04-93, Christie-S. Ken, #52, illus.), 50 x 35½ in., (127 x 90.2 cm.), color lithograph (BP 1320, DM 3114, FR 10,558, Y 235,228).

LOUPOT and CARLU

$525* *Monsavon, "Il Mousse, Il Sent Bon", c. 1925,* p. CFP, good cond., lit., (11-19-92, Ribeyre/Baron, #36, illus.), 24⅝ x 17¹⁵⁄₁₆ in., (62.5 x 45.5 cm.), poster (BP 346, DM 837, FR 2820, Y 65,290).

LOURDIN, R.

$140* *Automoto Saint-Etienne (Loire),* cond. A, (03-16-93, Boisgirard, #145), 47¼ x 30⅞ in., (120 x 78.5 cm.), poster (BP 97, DM 233, FR 791, Y 16,370).

LOUTHERBOURG, Jacques Philippe II 1740-1812

BI *Premiere Suite De Six (Leblanc II, p. 574),* narrow margins, good cond., (05-15-93, Loudmer, #160), 4¼ x 3⅛ in., (108 x 80 mm.), etching on laid.

LOUTHERBOURG, P.J. de (after)

$350* *The Battle Of Alexandria, 1806,* by Anthony Cardon, watermark, pub. Anthony Cardon, repaired tears, paper losses, foxing, creasing, (11-30-92, Phillips-London, #239), sheet 26⅓ x 34½ in., (669 x 876 mm.), stipple engraving on laid (BP 231, DM 558, FR 1893, Y 43,559).

LOVEJOY, Dr. Rupert 1885-1975

$357* *Night Landscape With Crescent Moon, c. 1925,* insignia, sig., (10-14-92, Swann, #506, illus.), 13½ x 10½ in., (34.3 x 26.7 cm.), photograph, multiple gum print (BP 210, DM 522, FR 1772, Y 43,262).

$385* *Nocturne, c. 1925,* s., label, (10-14-92, Swann, #507, illus.), 11½ x 7½ in., (29.2 x 19.1 cm.), photograph, multiple gum print (BP 226, DM 563, FR 1911, Y 46,655).

$1430* *Pillars Of Light, c. 1916,* s., t., exhib. stamps & labels, (10-13-92, Christie-NY, #297, illus.), 13⅜ x 10⅜ in., (34 x 26.4 cm.), photograph, gum bichromate print (BP 833, DM 2095, FR 7118, Y 173,396).

LOVEJOY, Dr. Rupert S.　　　　　　　　　1885-1975
$1380* *Nocturne, The Temple (Photograms of the Year 1921, pl. LVIII), c. 1918,* (04-08-93, Christie-NY, #63, illus.), 16 x 12 in., (40.6 x 30.5 cm.), photograph, green-toned gum bichromate print (BP 905, DM 2217, FR 7504, Y 156,605).

LOVET-LORSKI, Boris　　　　Lithuanian/Am. 1894-1973
BI *Nudes: Two,* s. Boris Lovet-Lorski, very good cond., soiling, tape verso, est. $5/700, (09-11-92, Skinner, #101), largest 10¼ x 6⅝ in., (26 x 16.8 cm.), lithograph on laid paper.

LOVING, Eugene E.　　　　　　　American 20th cent.
$55* *Green Shutter Patio, Old New Orleans,* margins, s., (05-22-93, Collins, #9), 7 x 4¾ in., (17.8 x 12.1 cm.), etching (BP 36, DM 89, FR 301, Y 6064).

LOVIS
$110* *Pastilles Au Miel. Ce Bonbon Delicieux...Previent Et Guerit Rhum, Toux...G. Darmond, Clermont-Ferrand, c. 1900,* cond. B, (03-16-93, Boisgirard, #146), 50 x 38¹⁵/₁₆ in., (127 x 99 cm.), poster (BP 76, DM 183, FR 621, Y 12,862).

LOVISA, Domenico　　　　　　ac. 1st half 18th cent.
$289* *Die Kirchen S. Nicolo Und S. Giuseppe Di Castello In Venedig, 1720,* (12-04-92, Bassenge, #6645), 12¹⁵/₁₆ x 18½ in., (33 x 47 cm.), etching (BP 185, DM 460, FR 1561, Y 36,080).

LOWELL, Nat
$220* *Tip Of Manhattan, 1936,* s., pub. AAA, margins, good cond., rubbed areas, surface soiling, (02-24-93, Butterfield, #2848), 10¹/₁₆ x 12⅛ in., (256 x 308 mm.), drypoint on wove (BP 153, DM 357, FR 1211, Y 25,816).

LOWERY, Lou
BI *"The Flag At Iwo Jima" and "Marines At Iwo Jima", 1945: Two,* est. $2,5/3,500, (04-07-93, Swann, #327, illus.), 10 x 8 in., photograph, silver print.

LOWERY, Louis
$3520* *The Flag At Iwo Jima, 1945,* label, caption, (10-14-92, Swann, #331, illus.), 8½ x 10 in., (21.6 x 25.4 cm.), photograph, silver print (BP 2066, DM 5151, FR 17,469, Y 426,563).
BI *Soldiers Preparing Flagpole, 1945: Two,* est. $6/900, (10-14-92, Swann, #330, illus.), 8 x 7 in., (20.3 x 17.8 cm.), photograph, silver prints.

LOWRY, Laurence Stephen　(after)
$152* *Burford Church,* #683/850, s., (03-17-93, Bonhams-Chelsea, #413), image 23¾ x 18 in., (60.3 x 45.7 cm.), reprod. in colors (BP 105, DM 253, FR 860, Y 17,828).
$255* *The Harbour,* s., blindstamp, (03-17-93, Bonhams-Chelsea, #411), image 16 x 22 in., (40.6 x 55.9 cm.), reprod. in colors (BP 176, DM 424, FR 1442, Y 29,909).
$175* *His Family,* num. 97, s., blindstamp, (03-17-93, Bonhams-Chelsea, #417), image 20¾ x 28 in., (52.7 x 71.1 cm.), reprod. in colors (BP 121, DM 291, FR 990, Y 20,525).
$383* *Industrial Scene,* s., blindstamp, front cover illus., (03-17-93, Bonhams-Chelsea, #419, illus.), image 13½ x 9¾ in., (34.3 x 24.8 cm.), reprod. in colors (BP 264, DM 637, FR 2166, Y 44,921).
$383* *The Level Crossing,* s., blindstamp, (03-17-93, Bonhams-Chelsea, #410), image 16 x 22½ in., (40.6 x 57.2 cm.), reprod. in colors (BP 264, DM 637, FR 2166, Y 44,921).
$191* *Man Lying On A Wall,* #464/500, s., (03-17-93, Bonhams-Chelsea, #415), image 16 x 20 in., (40.6 x 50.8 cm.), reprod. in colors (BP 132, DM 318, FR 1080, Y 22,402).
BI *"Man Taken III",* (12-11-92, G.A. Key, #36), 14 x 10 in., (35.6 x 25.4 cm.), black and white print.
$239* *Meeting Point,* num. 551, s., blindstamp, (03-17-93, Bonhams-Chelsea, #416), image 18½ x 28 in., (47 x 71.1 cm.), reprod. in colors (BP 165, DM 398, FR 1352, Y 28,032).
$255* *Mrs. Swindell's Picture,* num. 578, s., blindstamp, (03-17-93, Bonhams-Chelsea, #418), image 16 x 12 in., (40.6 x

30.5 cm.), reprod. in colors (BP 176, DM 424, FR 1442, Y 29,909).
$383* *Station Approach,* num. 265, s., blindstamp, (03-17-93, Bonhams-Chelsea, #412), image 15¾ x 20 in., (40 x 50.8 cm.), reprod. in colors (BP 264, DM 637, FR 2166, Y 44,921).
$207* *Two Brothers,* num. 440, s., blindstamp, (03-17-93, Bonhams-Chelsea, #414), image 23¾ x 12 in., (60.3 x 30.5 cm.), reprod. in colors (BP 143, DM 344, FR 1171, Y 24,279).

LOWRY, Lawrence Stephen　(after)
$137* *"The Playground",* s., #120/500, blindstamp, (12-10-92, Bonhams-Chelsea, #19), image 10½ x 14½ in., (26.7 x 36.8 cm.), reproduction (BP 88, DM 217, FR 740, Y 16,947).
BI *"Street Scene With Town Beyond",* s., blindstamp, est. BP 80/120, (11-19-92, Bonhams-Chelsea, #71), image 16¾ x 21¼ in., (42.5 x 54 cm.), color reproduction.

LOZOWICK, Louis　　　　　　American 1892-1973
BI *Above The City,* p. posthumously, good cond., s. Louis Lozowick, by artist's widow, i.AP, est. $2/300, (06-11-93, Freemn/Fine Art, #135), 17 7¾in., lithograph in black ink on white wove.
BI *"Above The City" (F. 88), 1932,* second printing 1982, s. by wife Adele, #195/200, excell. cond., est. $5/600, (05-15-93, Cleveland, #216, illus.), 17 x 7¾ in., (43.2 x 19.7 cm.), lithograph.
$12,100* *Allen Street (Under The El) (F. 14), 1929,* s., d., #17/20, p. George C. Miller, full margins, good cond., hinging defects, (11-05-92, Sotheby-NY, #38, illus.), 7⅝ x 11⅛ in., (193 x 284 mm.), lithograph on BFK Rives wove (BP 7870, DM 19,136, FR 64,741, Y 1,484,480).
$4620* *Backyards Of Broadway, Waterfront, No. 1 (Flint 7), 1926,* s., d., margins, (12-08-92, Swann, #183, illus.), 14⅜ x 9¼ in., (36.5 x 23.5 cm.), lithograph (BP 2896, DM 7193, FR 24,522, Y 572,633).
$90* *"Bangkok" Buddhist Monk Before The Temple (F. 270), 1966,* trial proof, s., d., very good cond., (05-15-93, Cleveland, #217), 12¼ x 12 in., (31.1 x 30.5 cm.), lithograph (BP 59, DM 145, FR 486, Y 9977).
$990* *"Bridges" (Flint 18), 1929 and "Central Park" (Flint 19), 1929: Two,* full margins, s., d. III/X; full margins, d., s., (05-27-93, Swann, #166), one 13¼ x 7¾ in., (33.7 x 19.7 cm.), other 12¾ x 8½ in., (33.7 x 19.7 cm.), lithographs (BP 634, DM 1589, FR 5354, Y 106,132).
$4125* *Checkerboard (Under The Elevated) (Flint 8), 1927-28,* s., d. '26', t., margins, scratch in image, soiling, discoloration, (11-05-92, Sotheby-NY, #37, illus.), 12 x 8¾ in., (305 x 222 mm.), sheet 14⅞ x 12 in., (305 x 222 mm.), lithograph on chine applique (BP 2683, DM 6524, FR 22,071, Y 506,073).
$374* *City On A Rock, Cohoes (F. 79), 1931,* s., d., pub. The Print Club of Cleveland, p. George C. Miller, full margins, good cond., light-staining, tape/glue remains, mat staining, (05-19-93, Butterfield, #2003, illus.), 8¼ x 13 in., (210 x 330 mm.), lithograph on cream wove (BP 243, DM 608, FR 2048, Y 41,404).
BI *"Fisherman's Widows, Portugal", 1968,* s., d., excell. cond., est. $2/300, (05-15-93, Cleveland, #218), 11⅜ x 13⅜ in., (28.9 x 34 cm.), lithograph.
$220* *Gate To Knesseth (F. 290), 1970,* s., d., full margins, good cond., mat staining, rubbed areas, pencilnotations, (02-24-93, Butterfield, #2849), 11¼ x 16¼ in., (286 x 413 mm.), lithograph on Rives (BP 153, DM 357, FR 1211, Y 25,816).
$13,200* *Hanover Square (F. 28), 1929,* s., d., #7/40, p. George C. Miller, full margins, good cond., handling creases, tear, remains tape stain, skinning, (11-05-92, Sotheby-NY, #39, illus.), 14¾ x 9 in., (376 x 227 mm.), lithograph (BP 8585, DM 20,876, FR 70,626, Y 1,619,433).
$1430* *Hudson Bridge (George Washington Bridge) (F. 30), 1929,* s., d., margins, good cond., light/mat stain, traces of glue, (11-05-92, Sotheby-NY, #40), 14½ x 8¾ in., (369 x 222 mm.), lithograph (BP 930, DM 2262, FR 7651, Y 175,439).
$990* *In The Park-No Job (Flint 31), 1929,* d., s., (05-27-93, Swann, #164), 14 x 9¹/₁₆ in., (35.6 x 23 cm.), lithograph (BP 634, DM 1589, FR 5354, Y 106,132).

$220* *"Light House"* (Flint, 285), *1969,* i., d. Louis Lozowick 69, mono. LL, crayon #65/130, watermark, good cond., wrinkling, (03-12-93, Skinner, #45, illus.), 10½ x 15¹³⁄₁₆ in., (26.7 x 40.2 cm.), lithograph on Rives wove (BP 153, DM 366, FR 1245, Y 25,928).

$165* *"Machu Picchu",* s. Louis Lozowick '63, num. 6/20, good cond.?, (11-21-92, Bakker, #6), image 15½ x 7 in., (39.4 x 17.8 cm.), lithograph (BP 109, DM 263, FR 886, Y 20,520).

BI *Minneapolis (Flint 5), 1925,* s., d., #6/40, full margins, good cond., soiling, discoloration,est. $16/20,000, (02-11-93, Sotheby-NY, #38, illus.), 11⁹⁄₁₆ x 8⅞ in., (294 x 225 mm.), lithograph on cream wove.

$660* *Oil Country (Flint 137), 1936,* full margins, pub. American Artists Group, tear, hinge remains, (12-08-92, Swann, #184, illus.), 12½ x 7⁷⁄₁₆ in., (31.8 x 18.9 cm.), lithograph (BP 414, DM 1028, FR 3503, Y 81,805).

BI *"Self Portrait" (Portrait Study) (Flint 64), 1930,* #IV/X, excell. cond., est. $2,5/3,500, (05-15-93, Cleveland, #215, illus.), 9⁹⁄₁₆ x 6⁵⁄₁₆ in., (24.3 x 16 cm.), lithograph.

$187* *"Shipbuilding" (Flint 138),* c. *1936,* s., excellent cond., (10-31-92, Cleveland, #174, illus.), 11³⁄₁₆ x 13¹³⁄₁₆ in., (28.4 x 35.1 cm.), lithograph (BP 120, DM 288, FR 976, Y 23,164).

BI *Skater's Island (F. 150), 1937,* s., ed. 1944, pub. AAA, margins, good cond., discoloration, soiling,est. $7/900, (02-24-93, Butterfield, #2645), 8¹⁄₁₆ x 13 in., (205 x 330 mm.), lithograph on wove.

$220* *Skater's Island (Flint 150), 1937,* s., pub. 1944 by AAA, (05-16-93, Hindman, #547), 8¾ x 13 in., (22.2 x 33 cm.), lithograph (BP 143, DM 354, FR 1189, Y 24,388).

$880* *"Storm Over Central Park",* s., mat burn, taped, good cond., (12-04-92, Doyle, #129), 9½ x 13½ in., (241 x 343 mm.), lithograph (BP 564, DM 1401, FR 4754, Y 109,863).

$1210* *"Storm Over Manhattan",* s., d. 1936, (05-20-93, Boos, #526, illus.), image 10³⁄₁₆ x 13⁵⁄₁₆ in., (258 x 338 mm.), paper 12¹⁵⁄₁₆ x 16¹⁄₁₆ in., (258 x 338 mm.), lithograph (BP 777, DM 1952, FR 6576, Y 133,613).

$3025* *Through Brooklyn Bridge Cables (Bridge Repairs; Repairing Brooklyn Bridge) (F. 158), 1938,* s., pub. AAA, 1939, p. George C. Miller, margins, good cond., light stain, foxing, (11-05-92, Sotheby-NY, #41, illus.), 9⅝ x 12⅞ in., (245 x 326 mm.), lithograph (BP 1967, DM 4784, FR 16,185, Y 371,120).

$4675* *Through Brooklyn Bridge Cables (F. 158), 1938,* s., d. '38, 1939, pub. AAA, p. by George Miller, full margins, taped,good cond., light-staining, mat staining, hinge remains, surface soiling, (02-24-93, Butterfield, #2646, illus.), 9⅝ x 12⅞ in., (244 x 327 mm.), lithograph on wove w/watermark (BP 3260, DM 7589, FR 25,729, Y 548,580).

BI *Winter Fun (F. 188), 1940,* s., pub. AAA, 1941, p. George C. Miller, margins, good cond., light stain, foxing, est. $1/1,200, (11-05-92, Sotheby-NY, #42), 9½ x 13 in., (241 x 329 mm.), lithograph.

$1210* *Winter Fun (Flint 188), 1940,* full margins, t., d. 42, s., i. A.P", (05-27-93, Swann, #165, illus.), 9½ x 12⅞ in., (24.1 x 32.7 cm.), lithograph (BP 775, DM 1942, FR 6544, Y 129,717).

BI *"Winter Fun", 1940,* pub. AAA, p. George C. Miller, s. Louis Lozowick, mono. in stone, good cond., light toning, taped, est. $15/3000, (09-11-92, Skinner, #22, illus.), 9½ x 13 in., (24.1 x 33 cm.), lithograph on wove.

LUBATTI

$251* *Raydo - Fur Sicheres Bremsen,* c. *1910,* Gros-Monti & Co., Torino, (12-05-92, Bassenge, #7608), 39⅜ x 27⁹⁄₁₆ in., (100 x 70 cm.), color lihograph (BP 157, DM 391, FR 1334, Y 31,099).

BI *Raydo. Fur Sicheres Bremsen,* c. *1920,* cond. B, (03-16-93, Boisgirard, #147), 38⁹⁄₁₆ x 26¹⁵⁄₁₆ in., (98 x 68.5 cm.), poster.

LUBLIN, Stephen

BI *Country Road II,* s., t., #23/155, prov., est. C$ 1/200, (12-01-92, Ritchie, #44), 23½ x 17¼ in., (59.7 x 43.8 cm.), color aquatint.

LUCAS, Ch.

$134* *Exposition Theatre De La Musique, 1896,* (01-31-93, Morelle/Marchan, #163), 32¹¹⁄₁₆ x 23⅝ in., (83 x 60 cm.), poster (BP 90, DM 216, FR 730, Y 16,717).

LUCAS, David (after CONSTABLE)

$362* *View On The Orwell,* margins, foxing, (08-20-92, Bonhams-Chelsea, #48), plate 6⅞ x 8⅝ in., (17.5 x 21.9 cm.), mezzotint (BP 187, DM 524, FR 1779, Y 45,713).

LUCAS, David (after Constable)

$231* *"A Summerland"* and *"Summer Afternoon, After A Shower": Two,* pub. Constable, 1831, foxing to latter, (06-16-93, Bonhams-Chelsea, #466), image 5¾ x 8¾ in., (14.6 x 22.2 cm.), mezzotint (BP 154, DM 383, FR 1287, Y 24,637).

LUCAS, H.F.

$28 *"Brooksby",* s., (12-11-92, G.A. Key, #53), 12 x 16 in., (30.5 x 40.6 cm.), photogravure (BP 18, DM 44, FR 151, Y 3465).

$47 *"The Dig",* engraved R. Wallace Hester, (12-11-92, G.A. Key, #6), 21 x 15 in., (53.3 x 38.1 cm.), photogravure (BP 30, DM 74, FR 254, Y 5816).

LUCAS, John

$318* *A Mill Near Brighton,* after Constable, engraver's proof, margins, surface dirt, (02-17-93, Bonhams-Chelsea, #324), plate 7¼ x 4¾ in., (18.4 x 12.1 cm.), mezzotint (BP 220, DM 516, FR 1749, Y 37,984).

LUCAS OF LEYDEN (after)

$119 *"The Poet Virgil Suspended From A Window In A Basket To The DerisionOf The Populace",* (04-16-93, G.A. Key, #72), 9 x 7 in., (22.9 x 17.8 cm.), b/w engraving (BP 78, DM 192, FR 650, Y 13,381).

LUCAS VAN LEYDEN   Dutch 1494-1553

$316* *Adoration Of The Kings, 1513,* watermark, margins trimmed to and w/in image, good cond., repaired losses, creases, tears, surface scuffing, staining, hinge, glue remains, prov., (05-19-93, Butterfield, #1860), 12 x 17³⁄₁₆ in., (305 x 437 mm.), etching on laid (BP 205, DM 514, FR 1731, Y 34,983).

$583* *The Adoration Of The Magi (B., Holl. 37), 1513,* 3rd (final) state, later, small to narrow margins, pen and ink i., staining, laid, (12-01-92, Christie-London, #1), 12 x 17⅛ in., (305 x 435 mm.), engraving (BP 385, DM 929, FR 3167, Y 72,585).

$3819* *The Annunciation (Holl. 35),* slightly light in printing, trimmed on borderline and w/in left edge, thin patch, nicks, ex. coll. Leonard Baskin, (06-29-93, Sotheby-London, #50, illus.), 3⅜ x 4¼ in., (8.6 x 10.8 cm.), engraving (BP 2530, DM 6449, FR 21,736, Y 406,536).

BI *The Beggars (Holl. 143),* trimmed outside borderline, surface dirt, repaired nick, nicks, abrasions, est. BP 2/3,000, (06-29-93, Sotheby-London, #53, illus.), 4¼ x 3 in., (10.8 x 7.6 cm.), engraving.

$3818* *Der Chirurg (Hollst. 156), 1524,* plate trimmed, (06-23-93, Kornfeld, #63, illus.), engraving (BP 2594, DM 6460, FR 21,730, Y 415,949, SF 5750).

$1389* *Christ On Gethsemane (Holl. 44), 1521,* from the Little Passion, narrow to thread margins, trimmed, paper thin, scrape, repairs, ex. coll. D.G. de Arozarena (L. 109), (06-29-93, Sotheby-London, #51, illus.), 4½ x 2⅞ in., (11.4 x 7.3 cm.), engraving (BP 920, DM 2345, FR 7906, Y 147,860).

$1527* *Christus Erscheint Maria Magdalena Als Gartner (Hollstein 77/I (v. II)), 1519,* (06-23-93, Kornfeld, #61), engraving (BP 1037, DM 2584, FR 8691, Y 166,358, SF 2300).

$5555* *The Dentist (Holl. 157), 1523,* narrow margins, paper loss, cockled, paper disturbances, good cond., (06-29-93, Sotheby-London, #54, illus.), 4½ x 3 in., (11.4 x 7.6 cm.), engraving (BP 3680, DM 9380, FR 31,616, Y 591,335).

BI *Esther Before Ahasuerus (Holl. 31), 1518,* 1st state of 3, trimmed, remargined, pen and ink border added, repaired tears, backed w/Japan, est. BP 1,5/2,000, (06-30-93, Sotheby-London, #158), 11⅞ x 8¾ in., (302 x 222 mm.), engraving.

BI *The Fall Of Man, (B., Holl. 10), 1530,* fourth (final) state, narrow margins, crease, repair, defects, prov., est.

BP 400/600, (12-01-92, Christie-London, #60), P. 31 x 9⁹⁄₁₆ in., (788 x 243 mm.), engraving.

BI *Joseph Interpreting His Dreams To Jacob (B., Holl. 19), 1512,* from The Story of Jacob, partly slipped in printing, trimmed along borderline, nicks, good cond., unidentified collector's mark, est. BP 1,5/2,000, (12-03-92, Sotheby-London, #75), 4⁷⁄₈ x 2⅝ in., (125 x 66 mm.), engraving on paper w/watermark.

$5803* *Mahomet Und Der Monch Sergius (Hollst. 126/I (v. II)), 1508,* (06-23-93, Kornfeld, #62, illus.), engraving (BP 3942, DM 9819, FR 33,028, Y 632,204, SF 8740).

$1665* *Mars, Venus And Cupid (B., Holl. 137), 1513,* third state (of four), 1513, (12-01-92, Christie-London, #62, illus.), S. 7⁵⁄₁₆ x 9⁷⁄₁₆ in., (186 x 240 mm.), engraving (BP 1100, DM 2654, FR 9044, Y 207,296).

$573* *Ornament Mit Dem Kopf Eines Soldaten (Hollst. 160), 1527,* (06-23-93, Kornfeld, #64), engraving (BP 389, DM 970, FR 3261, Y 62,425, SF 863).

$3829* *The Passion, (B., Holl. 43-55), 1521: Thirteen,* from the set of 14, first state (of 2), thread margins, crease, nicks, defects, (12-01-92, Christie-London, #61, illus.), average P. 4½ x 2¹⁵⁄₁₆ in., (115 x 75 mm.), engraving (BP 2530, DM 6103, FR 20,798, Y 476,718).

$7475* *The Poet Virgil Suspended In A Basket (B., Holl. 136), 1525,* 1st state of 3, trimmed, creasing, glue remains, good cond., watermark, prop. Akron Art Museum, (05-11-93, Christie-NY, #27, illus.), sheet 9⁹⁄₁₆ x 7⅜ in., (243 x 187 mm.), engraving on laid (BP 4772, DM 11,775, FR 39,676, Y 822,242).

BI *"Saint Mathew" (Bartsch 98),* good cond., collectors mark verso, est. $2/300, (10-31-92, Cleveland, #15), 4⅝ x 2⅞ in., (11.7 x 7.3 cm.), engraving.

$5956* *Samson Und Delila (Hollstein 5), 1517-1518,* early print, watermark, restored, prov., (06-23-93, Kornfeld, #60, illus.), woodcut (BP 4046, DM 10,078, FR 33,899, Y 648,872, SF 8970).

$3390* *Solomons Gotzendienst (Bartsch and Hollstein 30; Volbehr 28), 1514,* watermark, collector stamp, (06-10-93, Hauswedell/Nolt, #113), engraving on hand-made (BP 2217, DM 5520, FR 18,586, Y 359,834).

$4166* *The Standard Bearer (Holl. 140), 1510,* watermark, trimmed, narrow margin, stained, broken/repaired area, paper loss, (06-29-93, Sotheby-London, #52, illus.), 4¼ x 2¾ in., (10.8 x 7 cm.), engraving on paper (BP 2760, DM 7035, FR 23,711, Y 443,475).

$1760* *Susanna And The Two Elders (Bartsch 33, National Gallery, Washington15),* c. 1508, traces offset, ink loss, Dr. Gustave Seeligmann Coll., stamp verso, Lugt 1215, (12-08-92, Swann, #179, illus.), 7¾ x 5¾ in., (19.7 x 14.6 cm.), engraving on laid paper (BP 1103, DM 2740, FR 9342, Y 218,146).

$10,416* *The Triumph Of Mordecai (Holl. 32; Jacobowitz-Steparet 48), 1515,* Hollstein's 1st state of 3, Jacobowitz-Steparet's 2nd state of 4 w/reinforced outlines, watermark, trimmed outside border, paper loss, losses, repairs, repairs, tear, paper split, (06-29-93, Sotheby-London, #49, illus.), 8⅛ x 11¼ in., (20.6 x 28.6 cm.), engraving on paper (BP 6900, DM 17,589, FR 59,283, Y 1,108,793).

LUCAS-ROBIQUET

$378* *Tahadat and Khadidja,* very good cond., (03-13-93, Laurin, #8), 27¹⁵⁄₁₆ x 20¹¹⁄₁₆ in., (71 x 52.5 cm.), (BP 264, DM 629, FR 2139, Y 44,549).

LUCASSEN, Reinier   b. 1939

$288* *Is Art, 1979,* s., d., #49/190, margins, good cond., (05-27-93, Sotheby-Amstrdm, #436, illus.), 19¹¹⁄₁₆ x 15⅜ in., (500 x 390 mm.), colored lithograph on wove (BP 184, DM 462, FR 1558, Y 30,875, G 518).

$224* *Matisse In Spanje, 1979,* s., d., #154/190, margins, good cond., (05-27-93, Sotheby-Amstrdm, #437), 19¹¹⁄₁₆ x 15¾ in., (500 x 400 mm.), colored lithograph on wove (BP 143, DM 359, FR 1211, Y 24,014, G 403).

BI *Nicht Weinen Lieber Bird, 1979,* s., d., #12/190, full margins, good cond., minor handling creases, est. Dfl. 3/500, (05-27-93, Sotheby-Amstrdm, #650), 15⅞ x 20⅛ in., colored lithograph on wove.

$195* *Nicht Weinen Lieve Bird, 1978,* s., d., #131/190, pub. Prent 190, full margins, good cond., creases, (12-09-92, Sotheby-Amstrdm, #606), 15⅞ x 19⅞ in., (403 x 505

mm.), color lithograph on wove (BP 124, DM 306, FR 1044, Y 24,179, G 345).

$96* *Nicht Weinen Lieve Bird, 1979,* s., d., #36/190, margins, good cond., (05-27-93, Sotheby-Amstrdm, #438), 15¾ x 19⅞ in., (400 x 505 mm.), colored lithograph on wove (BP 61, DM 154, FR 519, Y 10,292, G 173).

$307* *Untitled, 1979,* s., #78/200, margins, good cond., slight foxing, (05-27-93, Sotheby-Amstrdm, #651), 17¹⁵⁄₁₆ x 15½ in., (457 x 393 mm.), colored lithograph on wove (BP 197, DM 493, FR 1660, Y 32,912, G 552).

LUCCHESE, Michele, Publisher   ac. 1553-1604

BI *The Dream Of Human Life, (Pass. VI, p. 168, no. 15),* c. 1560, after Michelangelo, margins, very good cond., est. BP 240/300, (12-01-92, Christie-London, #47), P. 17⅜ x 11¾ in., (441 x 298 mm.), engraving.

BI *The Martyrdom Of Saint Lawrence, (B. XIV, Raimondi, 104, copy c),* c. 1560, after Baccio Bandinelli, good but later impression, trimmed, good cond., laid, est. BP 240/280, (12-01-92, Christie-London, #48), S. 10¹¹⁄₁₆ x 13¾ in., (272 x 350 mm.), engraving.

LUCE, Maximilien   French 1858-1941

$1559* *La Mer A Camaret (I.F.F. 15), 1895,* whole margins, blue crayon s., num. 8, reddish stains, (06-11-93, Picard, #103), 12³⁄₁₆ x 17⁵⁄₁₆ in., (310 x 440 mm.), lithograph in color on chine applique on wove (BP 1024, DM 2534, FR 8542, Y 165,411).

BI *Montigny Pres Charleroi, 1895,* s. twice, margins, good cond., creases, foxing, discoloration, waterstain into image, repaired tears, est. $1,5/2,000, (11-05-92, Sotheby-NY, #229), 10 x 15⅝ in., (253 x 396 mm.), sheet 12⅞ x 17 in., (253 x 396 mm.), hand colored lithograph on cream wove.

BI *Rue Reaumur (I.F.F. 11), 1894,* whole margins, blue crayon s., num. 13, stamp, reddish stains, (06-11-93, Picard, #102), 12⅜ x 16⅛ in., (315 x 410 mm.), color lithograph on chine applique on wove.

$901* *Le Ruisseau Pres Gisors,* margins, foxing, (09-17-92, Bonhams-Chelsea, #90), image 8½ x 14 in., (21.6 x 35.6 cm.), color lithograph (BP 506, DM 1338, FR 4578, Y 112,176).

$143* *Usines A Charleroi, 1898,* staining, large margins, (02-24-93, Picard, #145), color lithograph on thin chine (BP 100, DM 232, FR 787, Y 16,780).

LUCEBERT   Dutch b. 1924

$295* *Composition,* s. Lucebert, 5/25, (09-30-92, Kunsthallen, #190), etching (BP 166, DM 418, FR 1415, Y 35,401, DK 1610).

$126* *Composition,* s. Lucebert, 58/75, (09-30-92, Kunsthallen, #189), color lithograph (BP 71, DM 179, FR 604, Y 15,121, DK 690).

$433* *Elephant, 1961,* s., d., num., (11-28-92, Schoppmann, #638), 15⅜ x 19½ in., (39 x 49.5 cm.), etching on handmade (BP 286, DM 690, FR 2342, Y 53,889).

LUCEBERT, Bengt   b. 1924

$165* *Composition,* s. Lucebert, (03-24-93, Kunsthallen, #229), color lithograph (BP 112, DM 269, FR 917, Y 19,387, DK 1035).

LUCEBERT, Jean   Dutch b. 1924

$170* *Mittelalterliche Szene, 1973,* s., (12-05-92, Bassenge, #7438), 15¹⁵⁄₁₆ x 23⅝ in., (40.5 x 60 cm.), color lithograph (BP 106, DM 265, FR 903, Y 21,063).

LUCIONI, Luigi   Italian/American 1900-1988?

$105* *"Between Birches",* s., pl. s., d. 1947, AAA, (12-11-92, DuMouchelle, #1481), 9 x 13 in., (22.9 x 33 cm.), etching (BP 67, DM 165, FR 567, Y 12,993).

$110* *"Beyond The Elm",* s.; plate s., d. '43, limited edit. AAA, (03-25-93, Boos, #606), image 7½ x 12¹³⁄₁₆ in., (190 x 325 mm.), etching (BP 75, DM 181, FR 615, Y 12,887).

$121* *"Big Elm",* s., hinges, (10-31-92, Cleveland, #176), 10 x 7¾ in., (25.4 x 19.7 cm.), etching (BP 78, DM 186, FR 632, Y 14,988).

$316* *Birches, 1977,* s., d., #8/50, publisher blindstamp, good cond., lightly rubbed, (05-19-93, Butterfield, #2004), 5⅝ x 4⁷⁄₁₆ in., (143 x 113 mm.), etching on wove (BP 205, DM 514, FR 1731, Y 34,983).

$143* *"The Edge Of The Birches" (Embury 117),* s., pub. AAA, good cond., (10-31-92, Cleveland, #175), 9⅜ x 12⅛ in., (23.8 x 30.8 cm.), etching (BP 92, DM 220, FR 746, Y 17,713).

$105* *"Elm On The Hill", 1948,* pub. AAA, s., ded., light staining, paper tape, (05-15-93, Cleveland, #226, illus.), 12¼ x 9⅞ in., (31.1 x 25.1 cm.), etching (BP 68, DM 169, FR 568, Y 11,640).

BI *"Elms By The Lake",* s. Luigi Lucioni, pub. AAA, est. $150/200, (12-12-92, A. James, #518), sheet 11⅛ x 15½ in., (28.3 x 39.4 cm.), etching.

$165* *"Elms By The Lake" (Embury 58),* pub. AAA, s., excell. cond., (05-15-93, Cleveland, #219), 7⅞ x 10⅞ in., (20 x 27.6 cm.), etching (BP 107, DM 265, FR 892, Y 18,291).

$165* *"Farm Scene": Two,* s., pub. AAA, margins, hood cond., surface scuff/soiling, image w/ink loss, mat/light-staining, (10-28-92, Butterfield, #2742), 6$^{9}/_{16}$ x 10$^{15}/_{16}$ in., (167 x 278 mm.), etching on wove (BP 105, DM 255, FR 865, Y 20,245).

$85* *"Late Shadows" (E. 91),* pub. AAA, ded., s., sun staining, paper tape, (05-15-93, Cleveland, #221), 9¾ x 13¼ in., (24.8 x 33.7 cm.), etching (BP 55, DM 137, FR 459, Y 9422).

$110* *"The Leaning Silo" (E. 69),* pub. AAA, s., ded., good cond., sun staining, tape, (05-15-93, Cleveland, #220), 7¼ x 10½ in., (18.4 x 26.7 cm.), etching (BP 72, DM 177, FR 595, Y 12,194).

$110* *"Pine In The Birches",* s.; plate s., d. '58, i., limited edit. AAA, (03-25-93, Boos, #605), image 8¼ x 11$^{13}/_{16}$ in., (210 x 300 mm.), etching (BP 75, DM 181, FR 615, Y 12,887).

BI *"Pomfret Church",* s. Luigi Lucioni, pub. AAA, est. $150/250, (12-12-92, A. James, #556), sheet 11¼ x 14 in., (28.6 x 35.6 cm.), etching.

$115* *"Route 7" (E. 97),* pub. AAA, good cond., tape, (05-15-93, Cleveland, #222), 8¾ x 1⅞ in., (22.2 x 4.8 cm.), etching (BP 75, DM 185, FR 622, Y 12,748).

$120* *"The Spreading Maple" (E. 103),* s., ded., good cond., skinning, tape, (05-15-93, Cleveland, #225), 10⅝ x 15⅝ in., (27 x 39.7 cm.), etching (BP 78, DM 193, FR 649, Y 13,302).

$105* *"The Steeple In The Mountains" (E. 98), 1946,* pub. AAA, s., light struck, taped to front mat, (05-15-93, Cleveland, #223), 11¾ x 8¾ in., (29.8 x 22.2 cm.), etching (BP 68, DM 169, FR 568, Y 11,640).

$130* *"Stones And Shadows" (E. 127), 1956,* pub. AAA, s., excell. cond., (05-15-93, Cleveland, #227), 10⅞ x 7¼ in., (27.6 x 18.4 cm.), etching (BP 85, DM 209, FR 703, Y 14,411).

$110* *"Stony Pasture",* plate s., d. '43; s., d. 1943, (03-25-93, Boos, #607), image 7⅞ x 11¼ in., (200 x 285 mm.), etching (BP 75, DM 181, FR 615, Y 12,887).

$85* *"Summer Shadows" (E. 99),* pub. AAA, excell. cond., (05-15-93, Cleveland, #224), 5⅞ x 12$^{1}/_{16}$ in., (14.9 x 30.6 cm.), etching (BP 55, DM 137, FR 459, Y 9422).

$110* *"Tree Rhythm",* s.; plate s., limited edit. AAA, (03-25-93, Boos, #604), image 11¾ x 9⅝ in., (298 x 245 mm.), etching (BP 75, DM 181, FR 615, Y 12,887).

$132* *"Trees And Mountains",* s., hinge stains, good cond., (10-31-92, Cleveland, #179), 8¾ x 10¾ in., (22.2 x 27.3 cm.), etching (BP 85, DM 203, FR 689, Y 16,351).

$132* *"Trees And Rocky Shore",* s., hinges, good cond., (10-31-92, Cleveland, #178), 7¾ x 10⅞ in., (19.7 x 27.6 cm.), etching (BP 85, DM 203, FR 689, Y 16,351).

$121* *"Vermont Castles",* s., good cond.; tape verso, (10-31-92, Cleveland, #177), 6 x 9 in., (15.2 x 22.9 cm.), etching (BP 78, DM 186, FR 632, Y 14,988).

LUCONI, Luigi American b. 1900

BI *"Vermont Pastoral",* s. Luigi Lucioni, pub. AAA, est. $150/250, (12-12-92, A. James, #555), sheet 11⅛ x 16⅛ in., (28.3 x 41 cm.), etching.

LUCUS, E. Charle

$1042* *Radiotint, Photographie En Couleurs,* p. Charles Verneau, folds, ink stamp, repaired edge tears, defects, backed on linen, (05-07-93, Christie-S. Ken, #135, illus.), 45¾ x 31 in., (116.2 x 78.7 cm.), color lithograph (BP 660, DM 1647, FR 5551, Y 114,732).

LUDLUM, Steven American contemporary

BI *Beacons: Nine,* each s., t., num. black chalk, 7 Artist's Proofs; 1 #3/8, 1 #5/8, est. $250/300, (02-04-93, Sloan, #2948), each 7$^{13}/_{16}$ x 7⅞ in., (19.8 x 20 cm.), woodcut, some on woven tissue.

$60* *Untitled,* s., t., d. (19)83, #21/22, (02-04-93, Sloan, #2949), 22¼ x 30 in., (56.5 x 76.2 cm.), lithograph on black paper (BP 42, DM 99, FR 335, Y 7464).

$60* *Untitled,* s., t., d. (19)83, #5/20, (02-04-93, Sloan, #2950), 22¼ x 30 in., (56.5 x 76.2 cm.), lithograph on black paper (BP 42, DM 99, FR 335, Y 7464).

$99* *Untitled,* s., t., #30/60, d. (19)80, (12-10-92, Sloan, #2747), 20 x 26 in., (50.8 x 66 cm.), silkscreen (BP 64, DM 157, FR 535, Y 12,246).

$121* *Untitled,* s., t., #4/20, d. (19)83 in image, (12-10-92, Sloan, #2748), 20 x 30 in., (50.8 x 76.2 cm.), silkscreen on black paper (BP 78, DM 191, FR 654, Y 14,968).

$99* *Untitled,* s., t., #4/20, d. (19)83 in image, (12-10-92, Sloan, #2740), 22 x 30 in., (55.9 x 76.2 cm.), silkscreen on black paper (BP 64, DM 157, FR 535, Y 12,246).

LUDOVICI (after)

$27 *"The Pickwickians On The Road To Dingley Dell" and "David CopperfieldOn His Way On School": A Pair,* (04-16-93, G.A. Key, #37), 12 x 19 in., (30.5 x 48.3 cm.), chromolithograph (BP 18, DM 44, FR 147, Y 3036).

LUDWIG, Wolfgang b. 1923

$289* *Kinematische Scheiben, 1966: Eight,* s., d., num., Berlin, Stolpe pub., (11-28-92, Grisebach, #631, illus.), 19$^{5}/_{16}$ x 19$^{5}/_{16}$ in., (49 x 49 cm.), serigraph on thin cardboard (BP 191, DM 460, FR 1563, Y 35,968).

LUGINBUHL, Bernhard b. 1929

$332* *Grosser Zyklop, 1967,* s., 700 x 1000mm, (09-04-92, Germann, #449), lithograph (BP 166, DM 465, FR 1584, Y 40,867, SF 414).

BI *Hammer Nr. 1, 1975,* s., #33/80; plate t., d., est. DM 300, (09-18-92, Schloss Ahlden, #1024), 16$^{13}/_{16}$ x 32$^{5}/_{16}$ in., (42.7 x 82 cm.), etching on hand-made.

$474* *Komposition 1985,* 59/75, s., (06-24-93, Germann, #682), 16$^{9}/_{16}$ x 23$^{7}/_{16}$ in., (420 x 595 mm.), woodcut (BP 312, DM 768, FR 2590, Y 50,847, SF 690).

$711* *Micky Maus, 1972,* A 36/50, s., (04-21-93, Germann, #166, illus.), 19$^{5}/_{16}$ x 25$^{3}/_{16}$ in., (490 x 640 mm.), color lithograph (BP 461, DM 1137, FR 3843, Y 78,711, SF 1035).

$573* *Strahler I (Kat. Luginbuhl 29), 1963,* s., d., num., (06-23-93, Kornfeld, #534), engraving (BP 389, DM 970, FR 3261, Y 62,425, SF 863).

$389* *Zellerstier,* #18/100, s., (11-13-92, Koller, #5369), 15$^{15}/_{16}$ x 21⅞ in., (40.5 x 55.5 cm.), engraving on Richard de Bas hand-made (BP 251, DM 611, FR 2059, Y 48,281, SF 550).

LUKAS, Jan b. 1915

BI *America, New York Harbor, 1964,* s., d., credit stamp, est. $1,2/1,500, (10-13-92, Christie-NY, #558, illus.), 13¾ x 9¾ in., (34.9 x 24.8 cm.), photograph, gelatin silver print.

LUM, Bertha American 1879-1954

$920* *O Yuki, The Frost Fairy (G., P. 49), 1916,* margins, good cond., thinned, area notations, (05-19-93, Butterfield, #1826, illus.), 17 x 10⅛ in., (432 x 257 mm.), woodcut in colors on tissue thin laid (BP 597, DM 1495, FR 5038, Y 101,849).

$1100* *Procession (Gravalos and Pulin 44), 1914,* i. copyright 1914 by Bertha Lum, num. 40, narrow margins, staining, foxing, (09-19-92, Christie-E, #50, illus.), borderline 13½ x 21⅛ in., (343 x 537 mm.), woodcut w/hand coloring and extensive ink and graphite additions on Japan (BP 633, DM 1647, FR 5641, Y 137,055).

$1540* *Rain, 1908,* s., t., d., small margins, good cond., time-staining, (10-28-92, Butterfield, #2537), 11⅛ x 6⅜ in., (283 x 162 mm.), color woodcut on tissue thin laid paper (BP 981, DM 2378, FR 8076, Y 188,957).

$358* *Sisters (G. & P. 14), 1907,* s., num. 220 48, annot. copy right - 07, small margins, good cond., glue remains, staining, hole, surface soiling, postage stamp remains, cream inkremains, (02-24-93, Butterfield, #2647), 15⅜ x

3 1/16 in., (391 x 78 mm.), woodcut in colors on tissue-thin Japan (BP 250, DM 581, FR 1970, Y 42,009).

$1035* *Tanabata (G., P. 36), 1912,* s., #99, annot. (c) 1913, small margins, good cond., light-staining, staining, (05-19-93, Butterfield, #1825, illus.), 15 x 7⅛ in., (381 x 181 mm.), woodcut in colors on thin laid Japan (BP 672, DM 1682, FR 5668, Y 114,580).

$440* *"Wedding Banners" (Gravalos and Pulin 88), 1924,* s. Bertha Lum, w/in image, i., d. 1924, no. 46, good cond., margins,soiling, (01-02-93, Skinner, #178), 8⅝ x 11¼ in., (21.9 x 28.6 cm.), color woodcut on paper (BP 293, DM 721, FR 2461, Y 55,165).

LUMSDEN, Ernest Stephen

BI *"The Alcantara Bridge", "Toledo", "Ragged Sails", "Miranda De Ebro" and "Central Flat", 1923-1929: Four,* s., i. imp, #50, 60 and 65, margins, good cond., handling marks, discoloration, est. BP 3/500, (06-30-93, Sotheby-London, #314), etching on cream laid.

$72* *Le Passage De Dragon, Paris,* s., num. 32, margins, (10-15-92, Bonhams-Chelsea, #144), plate 7½ x 5 in., (19.1 x 12.7 cm.), drypoint etching (BP 44, DM 107, FR 363, Y 8638).

LUNDSTROM, Vilhelm

BI *Opstilling,* s., 229/250, est. DK 2,000, (04-21-93, Kunsthallen, #175), lithograph in colors.

LUNOIS, Alexandre 1863-1916

BI *Le Colin-Maillard, 1897,* red crayon s., num., damp ring, soiling, 40 proof, (02-24-93, Picard, #151), color lithograph on thin wove.

$409* *Danae, 1894,* s., mat-staining, staining, (02-24-93, Picard, #149), color lithograph on old laid Japan (BP 285, DM 664, FR 2251, Y 47,993).

BI *Depart Pour La Chasse (Una Johnson 73), 1897,* creases, large margins, (02-24-93, Picard, #153), color lithograph on thin simili Japan.

BI *"Dernieres Prieres A La Fosse Commune" and "Evocations Chez Les Spirites", 1893 (L. 421): Two,* s., (02-24-93, Picard, #148), lithograph on chine volant and on Japan pelure.

BI *Interieur Hollandais,* s., #62/100, stains, yellowing, est. FF800/1,000, (05-27-93, Briest, #134), 18 5/16 x 23 1/16 in., (46.5 x 58.5 cm.), color lithograph.

$498* *L'Andalousie Au Temps Des Maures. Exposition Universelle Pris 1900,* good cond., (03-13-93, Laurin, #27), 102⅜ x 37 in., (260 x 94 cm.), (BP 347, DM 829, FR 2818, Y 58,692).

$123* *Reverie Devant La Mer, c. 1900,* full margins, staining, (05-06-93, Laurin, #60), lithograph on creme wove (BP 78, DM 194, FR 652, Y 13,533).

LUPERTZ, Markus German b. 1941

BI *Composition, 1989,* s., #10/125, full margins, good cond., est. BP 2/300, (06-30-93, Sotheby-London, #877, illus.), sh 30⅛ x 22 in., (765 x 559 mm.), color lithograph.

$275* *Komposition,* mono., (03-24-93, Kunsthallen, #230), color lithograph (BP 186, DM 449, FR 1529, Y 32,311, DK 1725).

BI *Ohne Titel (Hofmaier 111), c. 1981-1982,* pencil mono., est. DM 1,200, (11-20-92, Lempertz, #683), sh 27⅜ x 21 1/16 in., (69.6 x 53.5 cm.), etching on thick Velin.

$1075* *Rosa Linie (Hofmaier 215 B b), 1982,* mono., #VIII/VIII, from erste konzentration, Mappe 1, (05-27-93, Lempertz, #873), 38 1/16 x 30⅝ in., (96.7 x 77.8 cm.), color lithograph on wove (BP 688, DM 1725, FR 5814, Y 115,244).

$200* *"Sans Titre 89",* #6/125, s., (04-04-93, Pescheteau, #252), 29 15/16 x 22 1/16 in., (76 x 56 cm.), color lithograph on Arches (BP 132, DM 321, FR 1092, Y 22,771).

$289* *Untitled (WV 107), c. 1981-1982,* s., (11-28-92, Schoppmann, #641), 15 13/16 x 11⅛ in., (40.2 x 28.2 cm.), etching on wove (BP 191, DM 460, FR 1563, Y 35,968).

BI *Untitled, 1982,* s., i. probe, full margins, good cond., creases, prov., est. G 800/1,200, (12-09-92, Sotheby-Amstrdm, #608), 26 5/16 x 21⅛ in., (668 x 537 mm.), color lithograph on wove.

BI *Untitled, 1982,* s., i. probe, full margins, good cond., creases, prov., est. G 800/1,200, (12-09-92, Sotheby-Amstrdm, #607), 25 3/16 x 19 11/16 in., (640 x 500 mm.), color lithograph on wove.

LURCAT, Jean French 1892-1966

$95* *"Cheval Aile",* #36/50, s., wormholes, reddish stains, (01-28-93, Pescheteau, #194), 18⅞ x 14 15/16 in., (48 x 38 cm.), color lithograph (BP 63, DM 151, FR 509, Y 11,795).

$56* *"Composition Surrealiste",* s., stains, (10-18-92, Pescheteau, #197), 14 15/16 x 22 1/16 in., (38 x 56 cm.), dry point on wove (BP 34, DM 83, FR 281, Y 6687).

BI *Guerrier Vert Aux Lames, 1960,* 118/200, s., est. SF 120/150, (10-14-92, Germann, #353), 19 5/16 x 14 15/16 in., (490 x 380 mm.), color lithograph.

$202* *Hommes Et Femme,* #53/160, s., reddish stains, good margins, (02-03-93, Ader Tajan, #175), 19½ x 15⅜ in., (49.5 x 39 cm.), drystamp (BP 141, DM 333, FR 1128, Y 25,128).

$274* *Sans Titre,* s., #28/85, (09-15-92, Encans, #162), 19⅛ x 26 15/16 in., (48.5 x 68.5 cm.), lithograph (BP 147, DM 408, FR 1384, Y 34,016, C$ 333).

BI *"Solaire",* #208/300, s., est. FF6/800, (04-04-93, Pescheteau, #253), 29 15/16 x 22 1/16 in., (76 x 56 cm.), color lithograph on wove.

$19* *Le Soleil,* dust, small tear, (06-28-93, Loudmer, #84), 18⅛ x 13¾ in., (460 x 350 mm.), sh 22 7/16 x 17 15/16 in., (460 x 350 mm.), color lithograph on Arches wove (BP 13, DM 32, FR 109, Y 2016).

$82* *Le Soleil Et La Lune,* s., #31/40, full margins, (05-06-93, Laurin, #61), color lithograph on wove (BP 52, DM 129, FR 435, Y 9022).

BI *Tete Du Chevre Et Feuilles,* s., num., buckling, est. DM 800, (12-01-92, Karl/Faber, #939), 15¾ x 19 5/16 in., (40 x 49 cm.), watercolored lithograph on hand-made.

LUSSIER, Ann and Ernest

$55* *"Large Mouth Bass",* #3/20, excell. cond., (10-02-92, Guyette, #635, illus.), print (BP 32, DM 78, FR 262, Y 6567).

LUTHI, Urs Swiss b. 1947

BI *Champion III, 1976,* frame s., d., lit., est. DM 22,000, (11-12-92, Lempertz, #160, illus.), 45¼ x 161 13/16 in., (115 x 411 cm.), photograph.

BI *My Romance, 1975: Two,* s., d., #38/75, est. DM 1,000, (11-12-92, Lempertz, #159, illus.), each 7 5/16 x 17⅞ in., (18.6 x 45.4 cm.), photograph, gelatin silver print.

$379* *Ohne Titel, 1977: Two,* s., d., #3/10, (11-12-92, Lempertz, #162), each 3½ x 3 7/16 in., (8.9 x 8.7 cm.), color photograph (BP 242, DM 596, FR 2030, Y 46,889).

$3337* *Selfportrait, 1976,* frame s., d., t., lit., (11-12-92, Lempertz, #161, illus.), 27 11/16 x 37⅜ in., (70.3 x 95 cm.), photograph (BP 2134, DM 5244, FR 17,874, Y 412,842).

LUYTEN, Mark

BI *Intermezzo IV (From), 1989,* blindstamp pub. Echo Press, full margins, very good cond., est. $900/1,200, (10-28-92, Butterfield, #3025), sheet 42 x 30 in., (106.7 x 76.2 cm.), monoprint collograph w/collage on handmade paper.

LYCETT, Joseph 1774-c.1825

$527* *Ben Lomond From Arnolds Heights, A Part Of Tasman's Peak. Van Diemen's Land,* p. below image-J. Lycett. Delt. Et Execut. London Published Sept. 1st. 1824 by J Souter 73 St Pauls Church Yard, (08-11-92, L. Joel, #46G), 6½ x 10⅜ in., (16.5 x 26.4 cm.), color aquatint (BP 274, DM 773, FR 2619, Y 67,486, A$ 715).

$324* *View Of Lake George, New South Wales From The North East,* p. J Lycett Delt. Et Execut. London Pub. March 1. 1825 by J Souter, 7 St Pauls Church Yard, from Views in Australia of New South Wales & Van Diemens Land Delineated, in Fifty Views with Descriptive Letter Press by J Lycett, 1825, exhib., (08-11-92, L. Joel, #68G), 6⅞ x 11 in., (17.5 x 28 cm.), color aquatint (BP 168, DM 475, FR 1610, Y 41,491, A$ 440).

BI *View Of Roseneath Ferry (Taken From The East Side) Van Diemens Land,* p. below image-J Lycett Delt. Et Execut., pub. March 1 1825 by J Soutr, est. $6/900, (08-11-92, L. Joel, #16G, illus.), 6 11/16 x 10½ in., (17 x 26.7 cm.), color aquatint.

LYDIS, M. and J. MERCIER
$734* *Marie-Claire, "L'Hebdomadaire De La Femme", c. 1935,* p. Bedos & Cie, good cond., (11-19-92, Ribeyre/Baron, #37), 46⅞ x 62⅝ in., (119 x 159 cm.), poster (BP 483, DM 1170, FR 3942, Y 91,282).

LYDIS, Mariette   Austrian/Argent. 20th cent.
BI *Portrait Of A Girl,* s., good cond., est. $1/200, (05-15-93, Cleveland, #406A), 11 x 8½ in., (27.9 x 21.6 cm.), lithograph.

LYDON, A.F. (after)
$53 *"Minorca Cock, Black Prince",* (06-11-93, G.A. Key, #103), 10 x 7 in., (25.4 x 17.8 cm.), chromolithograph (BP 35, DM 86, FR 290, Y 5623).

LYNES, George Platt   American 1907-1955
BI *The Ballet "Orpheus" (Francisco Moncion And Nicholas Magallenes) (George Platt Lynes, pl. 111): Two,* studio stamp, est. $2/3,000, (04-06-93, Sotheby-NY, #379A, illus.), one 7 x 9½ in., other 9 x 7¾ in., photograph.
$1430* *Cyclops,* (1939), p.l., t., d., credit stamp, lit., (10-13-92, Christie-NY, #328, illus.), 9⅛ x 7¼ in., (23.2 x 18.4 cm.), photograph, gelatin silver print (BP 833, DM 2095, FR 7118, Y 173,396).
$1210* *"Figure Study (Ted Starkowski Walking" and "Ted Starkowski With Jared French's Drawings Of Him", c. 1949: Two,* photog.'s handstamp, (04-07-93, Swann, #508, illus.), one 9 x 7¼ in., other 9 x 7 in., photograph, silver print (BP 800, DM 1957, FR 6623, Y 137,469).
$880* *Male Nude,* handstamp, 1940's, (10-14-92, Swann, #508, illus.), 9½ x 7½ in., (24.1 x 19.1 cm.), photograph, silver print (BP 517, DM 1288, FR 4367, Y 106,641).
BI *Male Nude (Ted Stankowski),* notations in unident. hand, handstamp, 1940s, ex-coll. Paul Cadmus, est. $1/1,500, (04-07-93, Swann, #509, illus.), 9 x 7½ in., photograph, silver print.
BI *"Orpheus And Eros", 1948,* t., photog.'s stamp, est. $800/1,200, (05-23-93, Butterfield, #3508, illus.), 9¼ x 7½ in., photograph, gelatin silver print.
$1320* *Portrait Of Lincoln Kirstein In Uniform, c. 1941,* notations, (10-14-92, Swann, #509, illus.), 9½ x 7½ in., (24.1 x 19.1 cm.), photograph, silver print (BP 775, DM 1932, FR 6551, Y 159,961).
$935* *Reclining And Supporting Nudes,* photog.'s handstamp, 1940s, (04-07-93, Swann, #510, illus.), 9 x 7 in., photograph, silver print (BP 618, DM 1512, FR 5118, Y 106,226).
BI *Seated Male, Chair, And Columns,* 1940s, photog.'s stamp, est. $6/800, (05-23-93, Butterfield, #3509, illus.), 9 x 7¼ in., photograph, gelatin silver print.
$1380* *Selected Images: "Nude With Graffiti" and "Nude Back": Two,* 1st w/photog. name and Proof stamp, 2nd w/photog. studio stamp, 1940'-50's, p.l., (04-06-93, Sotheby-NY, #377, illus.), one 9¼ x 7½ in., other 9 x 7¼ in., photograph (BP 911, DM 2223, FR 7529, Y 157,391).
$715* *Self-Portrait In Studio,* collector's handstamp, 1940s, (04-07-93, Swann, #511, illus.), 9 x 7¾ in., photograph, silver print (BP 473, DM 1156, FR 3914, Y 81,232).
BI *"Ted Starkoskey",* 1940s, t., photog.'s stamp, est. $6/800, (05-23-93, Butterfield, #3510, illus.), 9 x 7¼ in., photograph, gelatin silver print.
$1540* *Two Male Nudes,* handstamp, notations, 1940's, (10-14-92, Swann, #510, illus.), 7¼ x 8¼ in., (18.4 x 21 cm.), photograph, silver print (BP 904, DM 2254, FR 7643, Y 186,621).
$1725* *Two Men With Nurse, c. 1943,* photog. studio stamp, (04-06-93, Sotheby-NY, #380, illus.), 9⅛ x 7⅜ in., photograph (BP 1139, DM 2779, FR 9411, Y 196,738).
$690* *Untitled (George Platt Lynes, p. 26),* 1930, p.l., (04-06-93, Sotheby-NY, #381, illus.), 9¼ x 7⅛ in., photograph (BP 456, DM 1112, FR 3764, Y 78,695).

LYON, Danny   b. 1942
$460* *"Clearing Land", 1967,* p. 1969, s., d., annot., (05-23-93, Butterfield, #3511, illus.), 8 x 11⅞ in., photograph, gelatin silver print (BP 300, DM 752, FR 2532, Y 50,846).
$605* *Columbia: Three,* (1972), p.l., s., t., d., include: Mary, Santa Marta; Santa Marta; Joselin, Santa Marta, (10-13-92, Christie-NY, #560, illus.), each 8⅝ x 13 in., (21.9 x

33 cm.), photograph, gelatin silver prints (BP 352, DM 886, FR 3011, Y 73,360).
$715* *"The Cornwagon, Ramsey Unit, Texas", 1967-1969,* s., t., d., num., Dixon Collection, (11-16-92, Butterfield, #6072, illus.), 8⅝ x 12⅞ in., (219.5 x 327.6 mm.), photograph, gelatin silver print (BP 471, DM 1140, FR 3840, Y 88,919).
$605* *Crossing The Ohio River, Louisville, Blue Rider Series, 1966,* s., prov., (05-16-93, Hindman, #345), 13 x 8¾ in., photograph, silver print (BP 395, DM 976, FR 3288, Y 67,372).
$605* *Mexico: Four,* (1975), p.l., s., t., d., include: Namequepa, Chihuahua; Morelia, Micigan; Bus Stop, Tehuantepec, Oaxaca; Truck In Nueva Casas Grandes, Chihuahua, (10-13-92, Christie-NY, #561, illus.), each 8¾ x 13 in., (22.2 x 33 cm.), photograph, gelatin silver prints (BP 352, DM 886, FR 3011, Y 73,360).
$605* *Namequepa, Mexico, 1973,* sig., notations, (10-14-92, Swann, #511, illus.), 14 x 11 in., (35.6 x 27.9 cm.), photograph, silver print (BP 355, DM 885, FR 3002, Y 73,316).
$575* *"Prison Rodeo, Walls",* s., d., i., t. in ink by photog., (c) stamp, 1967, p. 1978, (04-06-93, Sotheby-NY, #462, illus.), 9½ x 6½ in., photograph (BP 380, DM 926, FR 3137, Y 65,579).
$1760* *Prisoner Showering, 1968,* s., d. by photog. in ink, s. verso, (10-15-92, Sotheby-NY, #578, illus.), 13 x 8⅝ in., (33 x 21.9 cm.), photograph, gelatin silver print (BP 1077, DM 2620, FR 8884, Y 211,158).
$1980* *Selected Images, Ramsey, Texas,* (1967-69), p.l., each s., t., d., include: Showers, Diagnostic Unit;Clearing Land, Ellis Unit; Shakedown, Ramsey Unit; Heat Exhaustion, Ellis Unit, (10-13-92, Christie-NY, #559, illus.), each 8¾ x 13 in., (22.2 x 33 cm.), photograph, gelatin silver prints (BP 1153, DM 2901, FR 9856, Y 240,087).
BI *Selected Prison Studies: "Seven Years Flat On A 20-Year Sentence", "Hoe Squad" and "Schizophrenic Inmate, Imprisoned 20 Years" (Conversations, pp. 65, 111, and 175): Three,* each s. by photog., 1968, p.l., est. $2/2,500, (04-06-93, Sotheby-NY, #464, illus.), each approx. 8 x 12 in., photograph.
BI *Selected Prison Studies: "Six-Wing Cell Block", "Ramsey Unit" and "Building Shakedown" (Conversations, pp. 120 and 169): Two,* each s. by photog., 1968, p.l., est. $1,5/2,500, (04-06-93, Sotheby-NY, #463, illus.), each approx. 8 x 12 in., photograph.
$935* *Uptown Boys, Chicago, 1965,* photog.'s sig., d., news agency's handstamp, (04-07-93, Swann, #328, illus.), photograph, silver print (BP 618, DM 1512, FR 5118, Y 106,226).

LYTH, Harald   b. 1937
$1208* *Triptyk, 1978,* edition Galerie Olsson, s. 2/35, (05-25-93, AB Stockholm, #48), 25¹⁵⁄₁₆ x 14³⁄₁₆ in., (66 x 36 cm.), serigraph in colors (BP 783, DM 1967, FR 6623, Y 132,036, SK 1760).

LYTHGOE, Hermann C.
$1100* *"Afternoon Light", "The Armament Of Peace", "Cherry Blossoms", "In Yellowstone Canyon", "Low Tide", "The Push Cart Parade", "Souvenir Of The Opera 'Parsifal'", "Street Vendor, Nurnberg", "Under The Walls" and "Zurich": Ten,* photog.'s sig., t., exhib. labels, 1930s-40s, (04-07-93, Swann, #512, illus.), largest 13 x 10 in., photograph, bromide and toned bromide print (BP 727, DM 1779, FR 6021, Y 124,972).

MAAR, Dora   b. 1909
$22,000* *Le Simulateur, 1936 (Sam Wagstaff, pl. 128; Jaguer, p. 101),* mounted on tan card, s. by photog. in ink, (10-15-92, Sotheby-NY, #287, illus.), 10½ x 8⅝ in., (26.7 x 21.9 cm.), photograph, gelatin silver print (BP 13,462, DM 32,748, FR 111,055, Y 2,639,472).

MAAS, David
$83* *Late Migration-Bluebills,* excell cond., #180/480, (04-22-93, Guyette, #846E, illus.), image 15 x 25 in., (38.1 x 63.5 cm.), frame 25½ x 35 in., (38.1 x 63.5 cm.), print (BP 54, DM 133, FR 450, Y 9126).

MACBETH, Robert W.
$58 *"Figures And White Shire Horse Outside The Ferry Inn"*, (06-11-93, G.A. Key, #52), 13 x 21 in., (33 x 53.3 cm.), b/w etching (BP 38, DM 94, FR 318, Y 6154).

MACCARI, Mino Italian 1898-1989
$744* *Sonetti Lussuriosi Di Pietro L'Aretino, 1982,* #10/100, all s., ed. All'Insegna Del Lanzello, (05-20-93, Finarte-Milan, #88), 11¹³⁄₁₆ x 8¼ in., (30 x 21 cm.), book w/10 etchings (BP 478, DM 1200, FR 4043, Y 82,155, L 1093).
$1005* *Untitled: Five,* all s., (03-25-93, Finarte-Rome, #37), etching and aquatint (BP 683, DM 1651, FR 5615, Y 117,737, L 1610).

MACDHURHAJ(?), Robert American contemporary
$33* *The Thomas Wolfe Home; Ashville, North Carolina,* s., t., annot., (06-13-93, Hindman, #365), 17⅛ x 23½ in., (43.5 x 59.7 cm.), linocut (BP 22, DM 54, FR 181, Y 3473).

MACDONALD, J.E.H.
$449* *Western Tour Photographs: 3 Lake O'Hara Camp Depicting Mr. And Mrs. Peter White, Dr. Link And J.E.H. MacDonald; One Of Same Group At Oesa; One Of J.E.H. Bailing Water From A Boat, And J.E.H. With Browning Hooper: Six,* t., prov., (06-07-93, Ritchie, #1, illus.), each 2½ x 3⅝ in., black and white photographs (BP 296, DM 728, FR 2454, Y 48,166, C$ 575).

MACDONALD, James Edward Hervey Canadian 1873-1932
$477* *A Glacial Lake, Rocky Mountains,* s., (05-18-93, Joyner, #286), 6 x 6½ in., (15.2 x 16.5 cm.), print (BP 311, DM 774, FR 2614, Y 53,159, C$ 605).
$107* *The Red Canoe,* s. in plate, pub. William E. Coutts Co., Painters of Canada, series,1931, lit., (11-30-92, Ritchie, #28A), 4¾ x 5¾ in., (12 x 14.6 cm.), color serigraph (BP 71, DM 170, FR 579, Y 13,317, C$ 138).

MACDONALD, Leo
$50* *"Chelsea Warf, London",* s., d. 1932, (11-13-92, DuMouchelle, #2462), 7¼ x 11½ in., (18.4 x 29.2 cm.), etching (BP 32, DM 78, FR 265, Y 6206).

MACDONALD, Pirie American 1867-1942
$208* *Noel Coward, Autographed Portrait,* 1932, photog.'s stamps, ink s., i., d., mounted, (12-17-92, Christie-S. Ken, #85, illus.), 9 x 5⅞ in., (22.9 x 14.9 cm.), photograph, warm-toned gelatin silver print (BP 132, DM 325, FR 1109, Y 25,562).
$302* *Portrait Of Teddy Roosevelt, c. 1910,* credit, (c) in neg., (10-14-92, Swann, #512), 9 x 6 in., (22.9 x 15.2 cm.), photograph, silver print (BP 177, DM 442, FR 1499, Y 36,597).

MACDONALD, Thoreau
$150* *Tom Thomson Fishing,* s., (11-24-92, Joyner, #256), 7⅞ x 5⅞ in., (20 x 15 cm.), print (BP 99, DM 240, FR 815, Y 18,608, C$ 193).

MACK, Heinz b. 1931
BI *Aura I (Mack 174), 1972,* #XI/XV A. P., sig., est. DM 1,500, (11-20-92, Lempertz, #692), 28⅜ x 37¹⁄₁₆ in., (72 x 94.2 cm.), serigraph in 2 colors on folio.
$231* *Blauer Rotor (Mack 118), 1971,* s., d., num., (11-28-92, Schoppmann, #646), 23⅝ x 23⅝ in., (60 x 60 cm.), color serigraph on handmade cardboard (BP 152, DM 368, FR 1249, Y 28,749).
BI *Farbflugel (Mack 195.2), 1972,* #74/100, pencil s., d., est. DM 900, (11-20-92, Lempertz, #693), sh 23⅛ x 31⁵⁄₁₆ in., (58.8 x 79.5 cm.), multi-color screen print and embossing on aluminum board.
$427* *Flammenhand,* s., num., (09-25-92, Granier, #2923), sheet 41¾ x 30⅞ in., (106 x 78.5 cm.), color serigraph on hand-made (BP 249, DM 633, FR 2140, Y 51,539).
$233* *Lichtgitter,* s., num., (09-25-92, Granier, #2924), sheet 41¾ x 30⅞ in., (106 x 78.5 cm.), serigraph on hand-made (BP 136, DM 345, FR 1168, Y 28,123).
$155* *Lichtschraffur, 1971,* s, d., num., (09-25-92, Granier, #2921), 15¹³⁄₁₆ x 15⅝ in., (40.2 x 39.7 cm.), embossed aluminum (BP 91, DM 230, FR 777, Y 18,709).
BI *Lichtwirbel (Doppelblattmontage) (Mack 165), 1972,* pencil i., s., d., est. DM 1,000, (11-20-92, Lempertz, #691), 21⁷⁄₁₆ x 25⅛ in., (54.5 x 63.8 cm.), serigraph on tin foil.

$541* *Sahara-Edition: Station 1 Die Lichtstelen (Mack 208), 1972-1975,* #51/130, pencil s., num., 80.5 x 100.3 x 3.9 cm., (11-20-92, Lempertz, #694), color serigraph and collage (BP 356, DM 863, FR 2905, Y 67,280).
$433* *Trichter, 1968,* s., d., num., (11-28-92, Grisebach, #632, illus.), 23¹⁄₁₆ x 32³⁄₁₆ in., (58.6 x 81.7 cm.), serigraph in silver on black Chromoluxkarton (BP 286, DM 690, FR 2342, Y 53,889).

MACK, Heinze
$128* *Untitled,* s., #41/95, full margins, good cond., minor handling creases, (05-27-93, Sotheby-Amstrdm, #439), sh 41⁷⁄₁₆ x 30¹¹⁄₁₆ in., (105.3 x 78 cm.), colored lithograph on Hahnemuhle Butten (BP 82, DM 205, FR 692, Y 13,722, G 230).
$192* *Untitled,* s., full margins, good cond., crease lower edge of sheet, minor handling creases, (05-27-93, Sotheby-Amstrdm, #440), sh 41⁷⁄₁₆ x 30¹¹⁄₁₆ in., (105.3 x 78 cm.), colored lithograph on Hahnemuhle Butten (BP 123, DM 308, FR 1038, Y 20,583, G 345).
$224* *Untitled,* s., #50/190, full sheet p. to edges, good cond., minor defects in edges of sheet, minor handling creases, (05-27-93, Sotheby-Amstrdm, #441), sh 41⁵⁄₁₆ x 29¹¹⁄₁₆ in., (105 x 75.4 cm.), colored screenprint on wove (BP 143, DM 359, FR 1211, Y 24,014, G 403).

MACKE, August German 1887-1914
$1732* *""Begrussung", 1912,* s. Elisabeth Erdmann-Macke, No. 2 estate August Macke, (11-28-92, Grisebach, #633, illus.), 9½ x 7¹¹⁄₁₆ in., (24.2 x 19.6 cm.), linocut on cardboard (BP 1143, DM 2759, FR 9367, Y 215,557).
$2308* *Begrussung (Wingler III/8), 1912,* embossed stamp, i., plate 8 of III Bauhaus-portfolio Neue Europaische Graphik, (11-21-92, Lempertz, #249), 9⁹⁄₁₆ x 7¹¹⁄₁₆ in., (24.3 x 19.5 cm.), linocut on Japan (BP 1520, DM 3680, FR 12,395, Y 287,029).

MACKENZIE, F. (after)
$53 *Eastern View Of Oxford,* engraved by J Skelton, (04-16-93, G.A. Key, #129), 12 x 17 in., (30.5 x 43.2 cm.), b/w engraving (BP 35, DM 86, FR 289, Y 5960).
$39 *South West View Of Norwich Castle,* engr. by S. Rawle, (12-11-92, G.A. Key, #70), 6 x 8 in., (15.2 x 20.3 cm.), black and white engraving (BP 25, DM 61, FR 211, Y 4826).

MACKIE, Helen b. 1926
$43* *Mountains And Trees,* #5/50, s., t., prov., (05-10-93, Hodgins, #365), 8½ x 10¾ in., (21.6 x 27.3 cm.), etching on paper (BP 28, DM 69, FR 233, Y 4805, C$ 55).

MACKINTOSH, Charles Rennie 1868-1928
$97,697* *Glasgow Institute Of The Fine Arts, 1895,* bottom margins replaced, repaired tears, tears, other minor defects,lit., (02-04-93, Christie-S. Ken, #71, illus.), 89½ x 33½ in., (227.3 x 85.1 cm.), color lithograph on 4 sheets backed on linen (BP 68,200, DM 160,871, FR 545,489, Y 12,152,880).

MACLAUGHLAN, Donald Shaw Canadian/American 1876-1952
$160* *"Canal Venice" (R. 113) and "Great Dome" (R. 171), 1908: Two,* s., very good cond., edges trimmed, (05-15-93, Cleveland, #230), 9⅞ x 4 in., (25.1 x 10.2 cm.), etching (BP 104, DM 257, FR 865, Y 17,736).
$160* *"Chartes, Exterior", 1920,* s., excell. cond., (05-15-93, Cleveland, #228), 9¾ x 13¾ in., (24.8 x 34.9 cm.), etching (BP 104, DM 257, FR 865, Y 17,736).
$385* *"The Heart Of Chicago-Evening", 1931, "The Chapel, Chicago", 1931 and "Michigan Avenue-No. 2", 1931: Three,* s., (05-27-93, Swann, #169), smallest 10¼ x 14¾ in., (26 x 37.5 cm.), largest 15½ x 9 in., (26 x 37.5 cm.), etchings (BP 247, DM 618, FR 2082, Y 41,274).
$440* *Landscapes, 1914-19: Eight,* s., trimmed margins (as usual), t. by unknown hand, (05-27-93, Swann, #171), etchings (BP 282, DM 706, FR 2380, Y 47,170).
$220* *Michigan Avenue, Chicago-No. 2, 1931,* s., margins, (05-27-93, Swann, #168), 11 x 14¾ in., (27.9 x 37.5 cm.), etching on Van Gelder laid paper (BP 141, DM 353, FR 1190, Y 23,585).
$110* *"Song From Venice, No. 3" (Roullier 207) and "Portrait Of The Artist" (R. 238), 1913 and 1918: Two,* s., very good cond., (05-15-93, Cleveland, #229), one 7¾ x 11¾

in., (19.7 x 29.8 cm.), other 6½ x 4⅞ in., (19.7 x 29.8 cm.), engraving (BP 72, DM 177, FR 595, Y 12,194).

$309* *"St. Severini", "Le Vieux Fort D'Ambleteusee En 1902", "La Petite Loge", "Market Place", "Pavia Florence" and "A Dog": Six,* five s., margins, good cond., (06-30-93, Sotheby-London, #318), etching w/drypoint on laid and wove (BP 207, DM 527, FR 1778, Y 33,108).

$605* *Venice, c. 1912-32: Six,* s., Herman Armour Webster Estate, (05-27-93, Swann, #170), etchings (BP 387, DM 971, FR 3272, Y 64,858).

MACLEAN, William   American b. 1897
BI *"Vesper",* pub. AAA, good cond., est. $75-125, (10-31-92, Cleveland, #181), 9⅝ x 11¾ in., (24.4 x 29.8 cm.), etching and aquatint.
BI *"Winter Birch",* AAA edit., s., excell. cond., est. $120/150, (05-15-93, Cleveland, #231), 8¾ x 11⅞ in., (22.2 x 30.2 cm.), etching.

MACLEOD, William Douglas   British b. 1892
$55* *Sunrise, Tangiers,* s., num. XXXV A, (11-12-92, Freemn/Fine Art, #123), etching (BP 36, DM 87, FR 294, Y 6820).

MACLES, J.D.
$145* *Marie Bell,* (01-31-93, Morelle/Marchan, #233), 30⁵⁄₁₆ x 47¼ in., (77 x 120 cm.), poster (BP 98, DM 234, FR 790, Y 18,089).

MACOUILLARD
BI *American President Lines, 1937,* Velvetone, A- cond., marginal creasing, restoration, est. $1/1,500, (08-06-92, Swann, #181, illus.), 40 x 28 in., (101.6 x 71.1 cm.), silkscreen.

MACPHERSON, Marie R.   American 1879-1934
$330* *"Blond Satyr",* #34/45, num., s., (12-11-92, Eldred, #321), sight 19 x 24½ in., (48.3 x 62.2 cm.), lithograph (BP 212, DM 520, FR 1782, Y 40,837).

MACPHERSON, Robert   1811-1872
BI *Classical Architecture And Sculpture, 1850s-60s: Nine,* one trimmed to oval, each Macpherson blindstamp, num., ink t. label on mounts, est. BP 5/700, (10-29-92, Christie-London, #36), majority 11½ x 15½ in., (29.2 x 39.4 cm.), photograph, albumen print mounted on card.
BI *The Coliseum, Rome, c. 1859,* t. in ink, lit., est. $1,5/2,000, (10-13-92, Christie-NY, #14, illus.), 9½ x 15⅞ in., (24.1 x 40.3 cm.), photograph, albumen print.

MACPHERSON, Robert and ALII
$1361* *"Macpherson's Vatican Sculptures, 134 In All, Including Six Interiors Of The Vatica., 1st March, 1868",* mounted on card, (05-07-93, Sotheby-London, #29), photograph, albumen print (BP 862, DM 2152, FR 7251, Y 149,857).

MACPHERSON, Robert and James ANDERSON
$2232* *Italian Landscape, Architecture And Sculpture, 1850s: Eighteen,* one trimmed to oval, ink t., fifteen w/p. t. labels on mounts, lit., (10-29-92, Christie-London, #35), smallest 7¾ x 5¼ in., (19.7 x 13.3 cm.), largest 15½ x 12 in., (19.7 x 13.3 cm.), photograph, albumen prints mounted on album leaf (BP 1430, DM 3434, FR 11,649, Y 276,477).

MACRAE, Wendell
BI *Eternal Struggle, 1936,* sig., t., d., (c)limitation notice, est. $1/1,500, (10-14-92, Swann, #513, illus.), 9½ x 7½ in., (24.1 x 19.1 cm.), photograph, silver print.

MAETZEL, Emil   1877-1955
$1075* *Deutsche Lyrik Von Fr. Nietzsche, c. 1921,* p. Julius Pudbrese, repaired losses, losses, (05-20-93, Christie-London, #500, illus.), sheet 25 x 19 in., (63.5 x 48.3 cm.), lithograph in colors backed on Japan (BP 690, DM 1734, FR 5842, Y 118,706).
$1561* *Drei Knabenakte Am Strand, 1919,* s., i., (06-05-93, Bassenge, #6312), 5¹³⁄₁₆ x 7¹¹⁄₁₆ in., (14.7 x 19.6 cm.), watercolor on wove (BP 1028, DM 2531, FR 8530, Y 167,453).
BI *Die Gotzenpauke, c. 1921,* p. von Julius Pudbresse, tears, creases, est. BP 1,5/2,000, (05-20-93, Christie-London, #498, illus.), sheet 34 x 24 in., (86.4 x 61 cm.), lithograph in red and black.

$1075* *Hamburg Secession, Karl Lorenz, c. 1921,* p. Julius Pudbrese, repaired losses, (05-20-93, Christie-London, #499, illus.), sheet 24½ x 19½ in., (62.2 x 49.5 cm.), lithograph in colors backed on Japan (BP 690, DM 1734, FR 5842, Y 118,706).
$1106* *Landschaft Mit Haus, 1920,* s., (12-05-92, Bassenge, #7441), 9¾ x 13⅞ in., (24.8 x 35.2 cm.), woodcut and watercolor on imitation Japan (BP 693, DM 1724, FR 5877, Y 137,034).
$217* *(Maternite), 1912,* s., d., #10 blatt, margins, good cond., minor foxing, minor creasingt edges of sheet, Late Gerhard Brauer Coll., (05-27-93, Sotheby-Amstrdam, #756), sh 21³⁄₁₆ x 14⁷⁄₁₆ in., (538 x 367 mm.), lithograph on wove (BP 139, DM 348, FR 1174, Y 23,263, G 391).
$1702* *Nacktes Paar Am Fluss, 1918,* s., i., (06-05-93, Bassenge, #6311, illus.), 8¹⁄₁₆ x 9¹³⁄₁₆ in., (20.5 x 25 cm.), watercolored woodcut on hand-made Japan (BP 1120, DM 2759, FR 9301, Y 182,579).
$1770* *Sitzender Knabenakt, 1918,* s., (12-05-92, Bassenge, #7439, illus.), 10⅛ x 7⅜ in., (25.7 x 18.8 cm.), color linocut on machinemade paper (BP 1108, DM 2760, FR 9405, Y 219,304).
$886* *Stilleben Mit Negerplastik, 1920,* s., d., i., (06-19-93, Wachholtz, #239, illus.), 7 x 5³⁄₁₆ in., (17.8 x 13.1 cm.), watercolor woodcut on thick machine hand-made (BP 595, DM 1496, FR 5028, Y 98,215).
$369* *Stilleben Mit Negerplastik, 1920,* s., (12-05-92, Bassenge, #7440), 7 x 5⅛ in., (17.8 x 13 cm.), color woodcut on handmade machine paper (BP 231, DM 575, FR 1961, Y 45,719).
$680* *Zwei Knaben Am Waldteich, (19)19,* s., d., (12-01-92, Karl/Faber, #942), 9¹⁄₁₆ x 6⁵⁄₁₆ in., (23 x 16 cm.), watercolored woodcut on cardboard (BP 449, DM 1084, FR 3694, Y 84,661).

MAETZEL-JOHANNSEN, Dorothea   1886-1930
$2776* *Hamburg Secession, II Ausstellung, c. 1921,* p. Julius Pudbrese, excell. cond., (05-20-93, Christie-London, #497, illus.), sheet 22 x 17 in., (55.9 x 43.2 cm.), lithograph in black and cream (BP 1782, DM 4479, FR 15,087, Y 306,537).
$443* *Mutter Und Kind, 1920,* in Die Rote Erde, Heft 8/10, 1920, (12-05-92, Bassenge, #7444), 9¹⁵⁄₁₆ x 5¹¹⁄₁₆ in., (25.3 x 14.5 cm.), woodcut on machinemade paper (BP 277, DM 691, FR 2354, Y 54,888).
$1254* *Weiblicher Akt Mit Mondsichel, 1921,* s., (12-05-92, Bassenge, #7445, illus.), 8⁹⁄₁₆ x 6⅛ in., (21.7 x 15.5 cm.), watercolored etching on handmade (BP 785, DM 1955, FR 6663, Y 155,371).

MAGAFAN, Ethel   American b. 1916
$55* *November Leaves,* s., t., num. 69/250, (11-12-92, Freemn/Fine Art, #124), image 9½ x 11¾ in., (24.1 x 29.8 cm.), etching (BP 36, DM 87, FR 294, Y 6820).

MAGGIOTO, F. (after)
$283* *"L'Etude Des Gravures (sic) En Taille Douce" and "Le Maitre De La Peinture Apprend Le Dessin A Ses Ecoliers": Two,* restored tears, (03-22-93, Pescheteau, #23), (BP 191, DM 464, FR 1577, Y 32,770).

MAGLIONE
$64* *Untitled,* s., full sheet, good cond., (05-27-93, Sotheby-Amstrdm, #442), sh 21¹⁄₁₆ x 29½ in., (535 x 750 mm.), colored lithograph on Arches (BP 41, DM 103, FR 346, Y 6861, G 115).
BI *Untitled,* s., #111/190, good cond., est. Dfl. 2/300, (05-27-93, Sotheby-Amstrdm, #443), sh 21¹⁄₁₆ x 29½ in., (535 x 750 mm.), colored lithograph on Arches.
$64* *Untitled,* s., #111/190, full sheet, good cond., (05-27-93, Sotheby-Amstrdm, #444), sh 21¹⁄₁₆ x 29½ in., (535 x 750 mm.), colored lithograph on Arches (BP 41, DM 103, FR 346, Y 6861, G 115).

MAGNE, A.
$357* *Pinder Elephants, Les Elephants Savants,* Imp. Bedos, B-cond., fold marks, creasing, (08-06-92, Swann, #104, illus.), 48 x 62½ in., (121.9 x 158.8 cm.), (BP 186, DM 527, FR 1781, Y 45,536).

MAGNELLI, Alberto Italian 1888-1971

BI *Abstract,* s., #47/75, foxing, est. BP 3/500, (10-27-92, Phillips-London, #209), image 21⅝ x 16⅛ in., (549 x 410 mm.), color lithograph on wove.

$463* *Composition, 1950,* s. Magnelli 50, 15/30, (09-30-92, Kunsthallen, #191), color serigraph (BP 261, DM 657, FR 2221, Y 55,562, DK 2530).

BI *Composition, 1965,* s., #47/100, margins, good cond., est. BP 4/500, (06-30-93, Sotheby-London, #878, illus.), 7½ x 5¾ in., (191 x 146 mm.), color linocut on wove.

$278* *"La Magnanerie De La Ferrage",* epreuve d'artiste, s. Magnelli, d. 1970, (08-18-92, Encans, #128), 18⅞ x 16 5/16 in., (48 x 41.5 cm.), linogravure (linocut) (BP 144, DM 405, FR 1374, Y 35,048, C$ 333).

MAGNOLD, Robert

BI *Untitled, 1989: Four,* s., #9/40, pub. Brooke Alexander, full margins, very good cond., est. $3/4,000, (10-28-92, Butterfield, #3026), each sheet 14½ x 26 in., (368 x 660 mm.), color woodcut on Japan.

MAGRITTE, Rene Belgian 1898-1967

$5968* *Les Bijoux Indiscrets (Kaplan & Baum 3), 1963,* s., #54/75, deluxe edit., full margins, good cond., mount staining, (12-03-92, Sotheby-London, #369, illus.), 9⅛ x 11⅞ in., (232 x 302 mm.), lithograph in colors on Arches wove (BP 3850, DM 9385, FR 32,034, Y 742,566).

$337* *Compositions: Two,* stamped sig., 13/150 and 37/150, stamped Gravure originale Atelier Rene Magritte, (09-30-92, Kunsthallen, #192), etching in colors (BP 190, DM 478, FR 1616, Y 40,442, DK 1840).

$316* *Le Domaine Enchante, 1968,* sheet V of "Les enfants trouves", stone s., s. widow of Magritte, (06-24-93, Germann, #416), 17½ x 23⅝ in., (445 x 600 mm.), color lithograph (BP 208, DM 512, FR 1727, Y 33,898, SF 460).

BI *Le Double Autoportrait "La Clairvoyance", 1936,* in collaboration w/Jacqueline Nonkels, ink d. 4-10-36, i., exhib., lit., est. BP 4/6,000, (10-29-92, Christie-London, #144, illus.), image 2 3/16 x 3 3/16 in., (5.6 x 8.1 cm.), photograph, gelatin silver print.

BI *"Les Extra-Terrestres", I, II And III, 1936,* I d. 30-8-36, i.; II d. 30-8 by Georgette Magritte, i.; III i., w/annot., exhib., lit., est. BP 6/8,000, (10-29-92, Christie-London, #147, illus.), image, approx. 3⅛ x 2 3/16 in., (7.9 x 5.6 cm.), photograph, gelatin silver print.

$332* *Le Foret, 1968,* sheet 1 from "Les enfants trouves", Stein s. widow of Magritte, (06-24-93, Germann, #417), 17½ x 23⅝ in., (445 x 600 mm.), color lithograph (BP 219, DM 538, FR 1814, Y 35,615, SF 483).

BI *"Georgette A La Colombe", c. 1936,* ink i., exhib., lit., est. BP 2,5/4,000, (10-29-92, Christie-London, #146, illus.), 3 15/16 x 3 in., (10 x 7.6 cm.), photograph, gelatin silver print.

$1453* *"Georgette Et Ses Sauterelles...", 1937-38,* t., d., 110 x 86mm, (05-07-93, Sotheby-London, #245, illus.), photograph, silver print (BP 920, DM 2297, FR 7741, Y 159,987).

$2361* *Group Of Rene Magritte And A Young Woman,* 1930s, 90 x 92mm, (05-07-93, Sotheby-London, #244, illus.), photograph, silver print (BP 1495, DM 3733, FR 12,579, Y 259,965).

$1489* *Group Of Rene Magritte And Jacqueline Nonkels, Paris, 1927,* t., d. in later hand, 139 x 88mm, (05-07-93, Sotheby-London, #246, illus.), photograph, silver print (BP 943, DM 2354, FR 7933, Y 163,951).

$706* *L'Art De Vivre (Kaplan-Baum 16 A), 1968,* #33/150, sig. stamp, blindstamp, (06-10-93, Hauswedell/Nolt, #590), image 5 9/16 x 4 5/16 in., (14.2 x 11 cm.), color etching on BFK Rives (BP 462, DM 1150, FR 3871, Y 74,939).

$316* *Lion Et Homme Dans Un Cage,* sheet XII of "Les enfants trouves", stone s., s. widow of Magritte, (06-24-93, Germann, #418), 17½ x 23⅝ in., (445 x 600 mm.), color lithograph (BP 208, DM 512, FR 1727, Y 33,898, SF 460).

BI *"La Marchande D'Oubli", Georgette A La Pipe, 1937,* ink i., d., exhib., lit., est. BP 3/5,000, (10-29-92, Christie-London, #145, illus.), image 3 1/16 x 2⅛ in., (7.8 x 5.4 cm.), photograph, gelatin silver print.

$921* *Mondbaum, Le Seize Septembre (Kaplan 14), 1968,* #18/150, stamp sig., blindstamp, (09-04-92, Germann, #454), 10 13/16 x 8¾ in., (275 x 222 mm.), color etching on Japan (BP 462, DM 1291, FR 4394, Y 113,368, SF 1150).

$721* *Les Moyens D'Existence, 1967,* H.C., num., sig. stamp, (11-21-92, Lempertz, #250), 6 5/16 x 4 5/16 in., (16 x 11 cm.), color etching on wove (BP 475, DM 1150, FR 3872, Y 89,665).

$724* *Ohrglocke (Kaplan 15),* VII/XXV, estate stamp, (10-14-92, Germann, #357, illus.), 11 5/16 x 8 15/16 in., (288 x 228 mm.), color etching on Japan (BP 425, DM 1060, FR 3593, Y 87,736, SF 944).

$692* *Ohrglocke (Kaplan 15),* #XXIV/XXV, stamp sig., Atelier Rene Magritte blindstamp, lit., (09-04-92, Germann, #453, illus.), 10⅞ x 8¾ in., (277 x 222 mm.), etching (BP 347, DM 970, FR 3302, Y 85,180, SF 863).

$751* *Ohrglocke (Kaplan 15),* XXIV/XXV, stamp, blindstamp, (04-21-93, Germann, #156, illus.), 10 13/16 x 8 11/16 in., (275 x 220 mm.), color etching on Japan (BP 487, DM 1200, FR 4059, Y 83,140, SF 1093).

$5980* *Paysage De Baucis (Kaplan and Baum 5), 1966,* s., #72/100, full margins, mat staining, very good cond., (05-11-93, Christie-NY, #207, illus.), plate 8⅞ x 6½ in., (225 x 165 mm.), etching on BFK Rives (BP 3817, DM 9420, FR 31,741, Y 657,793).

$5750* *Paysage De Baucis (Kaplan/Baum 5), 1966,* s., #78/100, p., pub. George Visat, full margins, good cond., stain i image, creases, (02-11-93, Sotheby-NY, #164, illus.), 8¾ x 6⅝ in., (223 x 168 mm.), etching (BP 4057, DM 9525, FR 32,231, Y 693,189).

$7975* *Paysage De Baucis (Kaplan/Baum 5), 1966,* s., #10/100, p. and pub. by George Visat, full margins, good cond., mat stain, creases, skinned, soiling, (11-05-92, Sotheby-NY, #230, illus.), 8⅞ x 6¾ in., (226 x 170 mm.), etching (BP 5187, DM 12,613, FR 42,670, Y 978,408).

$4263* *Salon De Mai 1965 (K. & B.4), 1965,* s., d. 1965, #61/107, deluxe edit., p. Mourlot, pub. Musee d'Art Moderne de la Ville de Paris, full margins, good cond., (12-03-92, Sotheby-London, #370), 18⅞ x 14⅝ in., (479 x 371 mm.), lithograph in colors on Arches wove (BP 2750, DM 6704, FR 22,882, Y 530,422).

$3088* *Salon De Mai 1965 (Kaplan & Baum 4), 1965,* s., d. 1965, #61/70, from deluxe edit., p. by Mourlot, pub. Musee d'Art Moderne de la Ville de Paris, full margins, good cond., (06-30-93, Sotheby-London, #489, illus.), 18⅞ x 14⅝ in., (479 x 371 mm.), color lithograph on Arches wove (BP 2070, DM 5267, FR 17,768, Y 330,869).

MAGRITTE, Rene (after)

$3163* *Le Fils De L'Homme, c. 1965,* s. Georgette Magritte, i., #70/150, pub. Mourlot, blindstamp, full margins, good cond., mat stain, crease, verso discolored, (02-11-93, Sotheby-NY, #165, illus.), 30 9/16 x 23¼ in., (776 x 591 mm.), color lithograph (BP 2232, DM 5239, FR 17,730, Y 381,314).

$1840* *Le Fils De L'Homme, c. 1965,* s. by Georgette Magritte, i., #56/150, t., pub. Mourlot, blindstamp,good cond., scrape, scuffs, fox marks, mat/light-stain, tape hinges, (05-13-93, Sotheby-NY, #589), 30½ x 23⅜ in., (775 x 593 mm.), lithograph in colors (BP 1208, DM 2971, FR 10,022, Y 205,426).

$2530* *Le Fils De L'Homme, c. 1973,* s., t., i. Lithographie d'Apres l'oeuvre originale de mon mari Rene Magritte by artist's wife, i. E.A., pub. Mourlot, blindstamp, full margins, light-staining, surface soiling, mat staining, (05-11-93, Christie-NY, #208, illus.), borderline 30⅝ x 23½ in., (778 x 597 mm.), color lithograph on Arches (BP 1615, DM 3986, FR 13,429, Y 278,297).

$1201* *La Valise Hesitation Of Le Pretre Marie (K. & B. 13), 1968,* s. by Georgette Magritte, #58/150, p. Georges Visat, margins, good cond., (06-30-93, Sotheby-London, #490), 18 x 23 in., (457 x 584 mm.), color etching on wove (BP 805, DM 2048, FR 6910, Y 128,683).

MAHL, Claire Millman American 20th cent.

$220* *Street Accident,* s., t., tear, good cond., (11-12-92, Freemn/Fine Art, #125), image 13¼ x 16 in., (33.7 x

40.6 cm.), lithograph (BP 144, DM 349, FR 1176, Y 27,278).

MAHR, Mari b. 1941

$468* *"The Dreamers Birthday 2", 1981,* s., t., d., Dixon Collection, (11-16-92, Butterfield, #6074), 19 13/16 x 29 13/16 in., (502.5 x 757 mm.), photograph, gelatin silver print (BP 308, DM 746, FR 2513, Y 58,202).

$605* *"My Grandmother-Upon Her Return 2", 1991,* s., t., d., Dixon Collection, (11-16-92, Butterfield, #6073, illus.), 19 13/16 x 29 13/16 in., (502.5 x 757 mm.), photograph, gelatin silver print (BP 398, DM 965, FR 3249, Y 75,239).

MAHURIN, Matt

$460* *Children Holding Hands, 1990,* inits., #24/100, (05-23-93, Butterfield, #3512, illus.), 10 3/8 x 10 5/8 in., photograph, platinum print (BP 300, DM 752, FR 2532, Y 50,846).

MAIDEN, Joseph (after)

$48* *Sultan,* by C. Hunt, pub. Joseph Zanetti, 1838, laid down, (03-03-93, Bonhams-Chelsea, #54), image 12½ x 16½ in., (31.8 x 41.9 cm.), hand-colored aquatint (BP 33, DM 79, FR 268, Y 5609).

MAILAND, Eugene

BI *Fonderie D'Argent, Vallee De Luchon, France, 1856-58,* lit., est. $3/4,000, (10-13-92, Christie-NY, #15, illus.), 10¼ x 14⅛ in., (26 x 35.9 cm.), photograph, albumen print.

MAILLOL, Aristide French 1861-1944

$154* *"Baigneuse" (MG. 305),* (05-06-93, Laurin, #62B), lithograph (BP 98, DM 243, FR 817, Y 16,944).

$110* *"La Branche Du Poirier",* mono., (04-04-93, Pescheteau, #254), a vue 6 5/16 x 8⅞ in., (16 x 22.6 cm.), wood engraving on chine (BP 72, DM 177, FR 600, Y 12,524).

$716* *Deux Baigneues Nues Sous Un Arbre Au Bord De L'Eau (G. 263; A.A. B.-M. 284), 1895,* mono., 1 of 225, old mat verso, cracks, abrasion, (02-24-93, Picard, #157), zincograph on Japan (BP 499, DM 1162, FR 3941, Y 84,018).

$991* *Deux Baigneues Nues Sous Un Arbre Au Bord De L'Eau (G., 263), 1895,* whole margins, num., (04-02-93, Picard, #145), 9 15/16 x 12 in., (25.3 x 30.5 cm.), zincograph in black on wove (BP 653, DM 1593, FR 5409, Y 112,832).

$715* *Deux Femmes S'Etreignant, Two Women Wrestling (Gurein 288), 1898,* inits., num. 8, large margins, (12-08-92, Swann, #187, illus.), lithograph on Japan (BP 448, DM 1113, FR 3795, Y 88,622).

BI *Les Eglogues (Guerin 15-59): Forty-Three,* book by Virgil, in-texte, #221, just. page, pub. Galerie Druet, 1926, full sheets, good cond., est. $2/3,000, (02-11-93, Sotheby-NY, #166), 12 13/16 x 9 15/16 in., (325 x 252 mm.), woodcut.

$1328* *Femme Au Berceau, Bras Droit Leve (Guerin 267/I),* mono., artist proof print of 1st state, drystamp, (12-01-92, Karl/Faber, #945), 5 11/16 x 7½ in., (14.5 x 19 cm.), lithograph in red on kaiserlichem Japan (BP 877, DM 2117, FR 7213, Y 165,339).

$1475* *Femme En Berceau, Bras Droit Leve (Guerin 267 III),* mono., num., blindstamp, (12-05-92, Bassenge, #7446), 5¾ x 7⅝ in., (14.6 x 19.3 cm.), lithograph on handmade (BP 924, DM 2300, FR 7837, Y 182,753).

$522* *Femme En Berceau, Bras Gauche Releve, Bras Droite Abaisse, c. 1920s,* mono., #1/25, stamp, blindstamp, Lugt 1057b, full margins, discoloration, (12-08-92, Swann, #188), sight 6½ x 8 in., (16.5 x 20.3 cm.), lithograph (BP 327, DM 813, FR 2771, Y 64,700).

$1399* *Femme Etendue Sur Une Draperie (M.G. 6),c. 1893,* #23/75, mono., (06-11-93, Picard, #106), 3⅛ x 8¾ in., (80 x 222 mm.), wood engraving in black on thin chine (BP 919, DM 2274, FR 7666, Y 148,435).

$780* *"Femme Nu De Dos Demi-Redressee. Dian Sur Son Coude Droit" (Guerin 320), c. 1937,* num., blindstamp, (06-05-93, Grisebach, #751, illus.), 9 9/16 x 11⅝ in., (24.3 x 29.5 cm.), lithograph on thin wove (BP 513, DM 1265, FR 4262, Y 83,673).

$310* *Femme Nue Assise Sous Un Arbre (G., 264), 1895,* whole margins, num. verso, (04-02-93, Picard, #146), 8⅛ x 7 11/16 in., (20.7 x 19.5 cm.), zincograph in black on wove (BP 204, DM 498, FR 1692, Y 35,295).

BI *Femme Nue De Dos, 2e Planche (Guerin 278),* mono. in pencil, prov., est. DM 900, (12-05-92, Bassenge, #7447), 11¼ x 3 15/16 in., (28.5 x 10 cm.), lithograph on copper print paper.

$188* *Georgique: Untitled,* margins, good cond., mat staining, hinged to overmat w/masking tape,foxing, surface soiling, (10-28-92, Butterfield, #2836), 4⅜ x 4 15/16 in., (111 x 125 mm.), woodcut in sepia on laid paper, partial watermark (BP 120, DM 290, FR 986, Y 23,067).

$3300* *Les Georgiques (Guerin 159-215), 1937-50,* three volume set, each w/stamp, pub. Philippe Gonin, watermark, goodcond., incl. complimentary suites of woodcuts, (11-05-92, Sotheby-NY, #231, illus.), each sheet approx. 12⅝ x 9½ in., (320 x 240 mm.), 122 woodcuts, w/2 suites woodcuts, w/10 woodcuts, first state in sanguine on chine volant (BP 2146, DM 5219, FR 17,657, Y 404,858).

BI *Illustration Pour "Daphnis Et Chloe" (M. Guerin #111 et 115),* good margins, (03-22-93, Pescheteau, #76), on wove.

$993* *Jeune Femme Nue, Vue De Dos (Guerin 309), 1935,* mono. in stone, (06-23-93, Kornfeld, #536), lithograph on handmade (BP 675, DM 1680, FR 5652, Y 108,182, SF 1495).

$903* *Junon (Guerin 274/III), c. 1925,* num., (11-28-92, Grisebach, #639, illus.), 8 1/16 x 10 1/16 in., (20.5 x 25.5 cm.), lithograph in red chalk on handmade (BP 596, DM 1439, FR 4884, Y 112,383).

$1740* *Laveuse (Guerin 259; A. et A. Bonafous-Murat 312), 1895,* mono., num. 1 verso, 1 of 225, cracks, (02-24-93, Picard, #156), zincograph on simili-Japan (BP 1213, DM 2825, FR 9576, Y 204,177).

$354* *Laveuse (M. Guerin, 259), 1895,* faults, creases, good margins, (06-16-93, Ader Tajan, #115), 7½ x 11 13/16 in., (19 x 30 cm.), zincograph on simili-Japan (BP 236, DM 588, FR 1972, Y 37,756).

$523* *Nu Debout, De Dos,* s. w/mono., #4/100, (06-13-93, Hindman, #383), 12 x 4½ in., (30.5 x 11.4 cm.), lithograph (BP 342, DM 851, FR 2861, Y 55,035).

$220* *Nude,* from Dialogue des Courtesans, prov., (09-17-92, Sloan, #655), 7 x 4¾ in., (17.8 x 12.1 cm.), lithograph (BP 124, DM 327, FR 1118, Y 27,390).

$825* *"Nude Holding Her Arms In A Bent Position" and "Standing Nude With Arms Over Her Head": Two,* s., #42/50, time soiling, creases into image, red chalk init., (12-08-92, Swann, #190), each 15 x 11 in., (38.1 x 27.9 cm.), lithograph in sanguine (BP 517, DM 1284, FR 4379, Y 102,256).

$660* *Nude Standing With Her Back To The Viewer, c. 1925,* plate s., init., #43/50, time soiling, (12-08-92, Swann, #189), 15¼ x 11⅛ in., (38.7 x 28.3 cm.), lithograph in sanguine on laid paper (BP 414, DM 1028, FR 3503, Y 81,805).

$93* *Nymphe An Einer Quelle (Rewald 48),* mono. stamp, (09-25-92, Granier, #2929), sheet 8 7/16 x 6½ in., (21.5 x 16.5 cm.), woodcut on beige Japan (BP 54, DM 138, FR 466, Y 11,225).

$220* *Standing Nude,* init. M., #17/35, (05-28-93, Sloan, #1890, illus.), sight 15½ x 10½ in., (39.4 x 26.7 cm.), sepia lithograph (BP 141, DM 349, FR 1180, Y 23,590).

$210* *Untitled: Two,* mono. in pl., (01-28-93, Pescheteau, #195), each 12⅝ x 9⅝ in., (32 x 24.5 cm.), wood engravings on paper w/watermark (BP 139, DM 333, FR 1126, Y 26,074).

$1039* *La Vieille A La Jarre (M. Guerin 1), 1892,* mono., reddish stains, (06-11-93, Picard, #105), 6⅞ x 6 7/16 in., (175 x 164 mm.), wood engraving in black on thin Japan (BP 683, DM 1689, FR 5693, Y 110,239).

MAILLOL, Aristide (after)

BI *[Nude], c. 1930,* init., #21/75, full margins, good cond., mat/faint light-stain, discolored, est. $4/600, (05-13-93, Sotheby-NY, #590), 10½ x 14⅝ in., (268 x 370 mm.), lithograph in colors.

MAIMON, Isaac   American 20th cent.
$165* *Cafe Scene,* s., #89/250, (06-11-93, Freemn/Fine Art,
#136), 21 x 30 in., (53.3 x 76.2 cm.), lithograph (BP
108, DM 268, FR 904, Y 17,507).

MAINGOT, Rosalind
$1453* *"Chrysalis", c. 1930,* labels, exhib., sight 480 x 382mm,
(05-07-93, Sotheby-London, #173, illus.), photograph,
green toned silver print (BP 920, DM 2297, FR 7741, Y
159,987).
$1361* *"Chrysalis", c. 1930,* 501 x 402mm, (05-07-93, Sotheby-
London, #174), photograph, silver print (BP 862, DM
2152, FR 7251, Y 149,857).
$763* *Female Studies: Four,* 1930s and 1940s, three mounted
on card, s., t., labels, various sizes, (05-07-93, Sotheby-
London, #176, illus.), photograph, silver print (BP 483,
DM 1206, FR 4065, Y 84,012).
$654* *Five Flower Studies, 1940s,* mounted on card, s., t.,
labels, each approx. 470 x 380mm, (05-07-93, Sotheby-
London, #172), photograph, chromium bromide print
(BP 414, DM 1034, FR 3484, Y 72,011).
BI *Portrait Of F.J. Mortimer, c. 1943,* label, 350 x 260mm,
est. BP 100/150, (05-07-93, Sotheby-London, #175), pho-
tograph, silver print.

MAISEL, Steve
$460* *"Christine", 1990,* s., #24/100, (05-23-93, Butterfield,
#3513, illus.), 12¾ x 10¼ in., photograph, platinum/palla-
dium print (BP 300, DM 752, FR 2532, Y 50,846).

MAISON BONFILS (et alii)
$4675* *'Syria & The Lebanon' (Perez, pls. 30, 36 and 91): One
Hundred Two,* album, most s. and/or num. and/or t. in
neg. by BONFILS, few s. in neg. by DUMAS, t. in unidentified hand, (10-15-92, Sotheby-NY, #75, illus.), largest 8½ x 11 in., (21.6 x 27.9 cm.), photograph, albumen
prints (BP 2861, DM 6959, FR 23,599, Y 560,888).

MAITIN, Sam   American 20th cent.
$220* *First Psalm, Last Psalm,* s., #36/100, (06-11-93, Freemn/
Fine Art, #143), 25 x 19 in., (63.5 x 48.3 cm.), screenprint (BP 145, DM 358, FR 1205, Y 23,342).

MAJESKI, Thomas   American 20th cent.
$77* *Portrait Of Betty*s., t., num. 3/20(11-12-92, Freemn/Fine
Art, #132), 23 x 19½ in., etching (BP 51, DM 122, FR
412, Y 9547).
$110* *"The Artist"* and *"Self Portrait": Two,* first s., t., num. 7/
30; second s., d. '63, t., num. 2/5, (11-12-92, Freemn/
Fine Art, #128), first 15 x 13¾ in., (38.1 x 34.9 cm.),
second 13¾ x 15 in., (38.1 x 34.9 cm.), etching in color
(BP 72, DM 174, FR 588, Y 13,639).
$165* *Backside,* s., t., i., (11-12-92, Freemn/Fine Art, #126,
illus.), plate 35 x 23 in., (88.9 x 58.4 cm.), etching (BP
108, DM 261, FR 882, Y 20,459).
BI *Hooked,* s., t., d. 1974, i. AP, est. $100/150, (11-12-92,
Freemn/Fine Art, #133), 18 x 17½ in., (45.7 x 44.5
cm.), etching in color.
$83* *A Man,* t., i. AP, (11-12-92, Freemn/Fine Art, #129),
14½ x 12 in., (36.8 x 30.5 cm.), etching in color (BP
55, DM 132, FR 444, Y 10,291).
$83* *Mike,* s., t., d. '63, num. 5/30, (11-12-92, Freemn/Fine
Art, #130), plate 17½ x 16 in., (44.5 x 40.6 cm.), etching in color (BP 55, DM 132, FR 444, Y 10,291).
$55* *Portrait Of A Young Girl,* s., t., d. '63, num. 5/5, (11-
12-92, Freemn/Fine Art, #131), plate 14½ x 12 in., (36.8
x 30.5 cm.), etching in color (BP 36, DM 87, FR 294,
Y 6820).
$110* *Profile In Red,* s., t., d. '63, num. 4/20, (11-12-92,
Freemn/Fine Art, #127), 9½ x 12¾ in., (24.1 x 32.4
cm.), etching in color (BP 72, DM 174, FR 588, Y
13,639).
$83* *Self Portrait,* s., t., num. 2/10, (11-12-92, Freemn/Fine
Art, #134), plate 23½ x 21½ in., (59.7 x 54.6 cm.),
etching (BP 55, DM 132, FR 444, Y 10,291).
$83* *Self Portrait, 1965,* s., t., i. Artist's Proof, (11-12-92,
Freemn/Fine Art, #135), 29½ x 23½ in., (50.8 x 30.5
cm.), etching (BP 55, DM 132, FR 444, Y 10,291).

MAJOR, A., Publisher
$1725* *Bird's Eye View Of The Great Suspension Bridge, Con-
necting The Cities Of New York And Brooklyn, From
New York Looking South-East (R. 2744), 1883,* p. Frank-

lin Square Lithographic Co., margins, discolored, tears,
nicks, abraded area in image, backboard stain, ink
spots(?), reinforced areas, (01-28-93, Sotheby-NY,
#455B, illus.), 17⅞ x 36⅛ in., (454 x 918 mm.), sheet
22⅛ x 37¾ in., (454 x 918 mm.), hand-colored lithograph (BP 1139, DM 2733, FR 9249, Y 214,179).

MAJOR and KNAPP, Publisher
$11* *"Grand Reception Of The Notabilites Of The Nation",*
sample copy, fold creasing, slight damage, (09-12-92,
Dunning, #9), 19 x 24 in., (48.3 x 61 cm.), lithograph
(BP 6, DM 16, FR 54, Y 1363).

MAJORE, Frank   American b. 1948
$575* *Manhattan Lights, 1985,* s., t., d., #1/5, (04-08-93,
Christie-NY, #545, illus.), 19½ x 15⅞ in., (49.5 x 40.3
cm.), photograph, cibachrome print (BP 377, DM 924,
FR 3127, Y 65,252).

MAJORELLE, J.
$575* *Marrakech, 1926,* plate s., lined, (03-25-93, Christie-E,
#205), 42½ x 31 in., (108 x 78.7 cm.), color lithograph
(BP 390, DM 945, FR 3212, Y 67,362).
BI *Tanger. "Son Site, Son Climat". Syndicat D'Initiative Et
De TourismeDe Tanger, 1924,* fairly good cond.,
repainted, (02-12-93, Cheval/Robert, #96), 40¹⁵⁄₁₆ x 29⅛
in., (104 x 74 cm.), poster.

MAKI, Haku   Japanese b. 1924
BI *"Cell-1",* s., num., artist's red stamp, very good cond.,
est $225/300, (05-15-93, Cleveland, #32), 13½ x 13¾ in.,
(34.3 x 34.9 cm.), embossed print on thick wove.
$230* *"Cell-4",* s., num., artist's red chop, very good cond.,
(05-15-93, Cleveland, #33), 13⅝ x 13⅝ in., (34.6 x 34.6
cm.), embossed relief print on thick wove (BP 150, DM
370, FR 1243, Y 25,496).
BI *"Poems 71-72",* est. $175/225, (10-31-92, Cleveland,
#43), 15¼ x 10½ in., (38.7 x 26.7 cm.), color etching
and embossing.
$110* *Red Trees On A Silver Ground,* work 74-6, s. Haku
Maki, t., num., one seal, (11-20-92, Skinner, #4), (BP
72, DM 175, FR 591, Y 13,680).
BI *"Work 73-7-A",* est. $175/225, (10-31-92, Cleveland, #44),
9¾ x 9¾ in., (24.8 x 24.8 cm.), color etching and
embossing.

MAKIN, Jeffrey   b. 1943
BI *(Young Girl),* s. Makin on image, est. $150/250, (08-11-
92, L. Joel, #145G), 9¹³⁄₁₆ x 13¹⁵⁄₁₆ in., (25 x 35.5 cm.),
color lithograph and pencil.

MAKOS, Christopher   b. 1960
BI *Andy Warhol, 1981,* s., d., #2/5, lit., est. DM 1,200, (11-
12-92, Lempertz, #163, illus.), 7⅝ x 11¹¹⁄₁₆ in., (19.3 x
29.7 cm.), sheet 10⅞ x 14¹⁄₁₆ in., (19.3 x 29.7 cm.),
photograph, gelatin silver print.

MALAVAL, Robert   1937-1980
$315* *Homme De Dos,* s., #22/100, full margins, (11-16-92,
Briest, #72), 20³⁄₁₆ x 25¹⁵⁄₁₆ in., (51.2 x 66 cm.), etching
in 2 colors (BP 207, DM 502, FR 1693, Y 39,311).

MALCLES, Jean Denis   b. 1912
$239* *Les Freres Jacques, 1956,* cond. B, (03-16-93, Boisgirard,
#148), 46⅞ x 30¹¹⁄₁₆ in., (119 x 78 cm.), poster (BP
165, DM 397, FR 1350, Y 27,947).

MALEVICH, Kazimir   1878-1938
$3996* *A. Kruchenykh, Stikhi, Maiakovskogo (the Poems Of
Maiakovskii) (Karshan 8), 1914,* Petrograd, 1914, 29
pages of text, advertising page and lithograph, very good
cond., excellent cond., (12-01-92, Christie-London, #524,
illus.), overall sheet 8⅛ x 5⅞ in., (206 x 150 mm.),
lithograph on cream wove (BP 2640, DM 6369, FR
21,706, Y 497,510).
$2070* *O Novykh Sistemakh V Iskusstve (On New Systems Art)
(Compton 114, 127), 1919,* Vitebsk, in 32s, discoloration,
(06-14-93, Sotheby-NY, #258), 9 x 7⅜ in., (22.9 x 18.7
cm.), 3 leaves of lithograph (BP 1355, DM 3369, FR
11,324, Y 217,826).

MALEVICH, Kazimir, Pavel FILONOV, and Nikolai BURLIUK
BI *V. Khlebnikov, Izbornik Stikhov 1907-1914 (Selection Of
Poems 1907-1914), (Karshan 11; compton p. 126), 1914,*
Euy, St. Petersburg, 1914, 48 pages of typeset text w/one

letterpress design after Malevich, suite of 16 pages of lithographs and lithographic text by Filonov, good cond., est. BP 1,0/1,500, (12-01-92, Christie-London, #525, illus.), overall sheet 8³⁄₁₆ x 5¹⁵⁄₁₆ in., (208 x 152 mm.), letterpress design and lithograph on buff and orange wove.

MALINOVSKY, Lise
$295* *"Ben", 1988: Three,* portfolio, s., 42/100, (09-30-92, Kunsthallen, #193), three etchings (BP 166, DM 418, FR 1415, Y 35,401, DK 1610).
$110* *Komposition, 1988,* s. Lise Malinovsky 88, 396/985, (03-24-93, Kunsthallen, #231), color lithograph (BP 74, DM 180, FR 611, Y 12,924, DK 690).

MALPERN
BI *El Picador,* #12/25, s., t., margins, staining, est. BP 40/60, (02-17-93, Bonhams-Chelsea, #323), plate 10 x 11¼ in., (25.4 x 28.6 cm.), etching.

MALTESTE, Louis
$602* *Creme Bouttet, c. 1900,* Paris, Imp. de Vaugirard and Malherbe, cond. B, (06-11-93, Boisgirard, #109), 52⅜ x 41¾ in., (133 x 106 cm.), poster (BP 396, DM 978, FR 3299, Y 63,873).
$221* *J. Ferenczy Editeur (...) Les Apaches De Paris, c. 1900,* Paris, Imp. Bourgerie and Cie, cond. B+, (06-11-93, Boisgirard, #110), 50⅜ x 36⅝ in., (128 x 93 cm.), poster (BP 145, DM 359, FR 1211, Y 23,448).

MAN, Felix   b. 1893
BI *Czech Woman Spinning Yarn,* photog.'s and news agency's handstamps, notations in unident. hand, 1930s, est. $800/1,200, (04-07-93, Swann, #331, illus.), 9 x 7½ in., photograph, silver print.

MANCEAU, Alexandre Damien   French 1817-1865
$55* *Les Mysteres De Paris: A Pair,* (09-21-92, Selkirk, #188), sight 25 x 19 in., (63.5 x 48.3 cm.), hand colored lithograph (BP 32, DM 82, FR 279, Y 6798).

MANDELMAN, Beatrice   American b. 1912
$110* *Two Houses,* s., t., ink on image and margin, (11-12-92, Freemn/Fine Art, #136), image and margin 10¼ x 17¼ in., (26 x 43.8 cm.), lithograph (BP 72, DM 174, FR 588, Y 13,639).

MANE-KATZ   French/Israeli 1894-1962
$55* *Figures In A Horse Drawn Cart,* inits. in stone, (09-17-92, Sloan, #635), sight 8⅛ x 10¾ in., (20.6 x 27.3 cm.), lithograph (BP 31, DM 82, FR 279, Y 6848).
$110* *Five Musicians,* ink s., #40/50, (10-18-92, Hindman, #461), 18½ x 25 in., (47 x 63.5 cm.), color lithograph (BP 67, DM 164, FR 555, Y 13,197).

MANESSIER, Alfred   French b. 1941
$135* *"Boule De Neige I" and "Le Grand Nord": Two,* both s., 61/85 and 63/85, (06-28-93, Loudmer, #287), first 8¼ x 8¼ in., (210 x 210 mm.), second 9¹³⁄₁₆ x 13¾ in., (210 x 210 mm.), color lithographs on wove (BP 90, DM 229, FR 773, Y 14,324).
BI *Boule De Neige II,* s., i. Epreuve d'artiste 20/30, margins, good cond., est. Dfl. 250/350, (05-27-93, Sotheby-Amstrdm, #656), sheet 11¹⁵⁄₁₆ x 11⁷⁄₁₆ in., (303 x 290 mm.), color lithograph on wove.
BI *Les Cantiques Spirituels De Saint Jean De La Croix, 1958: Twelve,* #120/125, frontispiece s., est. DM 3,000-, (11-21-92, Lempertz, #255), 21¹⁄₁₆ x 16 in., (53.5 x 40.7 cm.), color lithograph on BFK Rives wove.
$275* *Composition,* s. Manessier 73/100, (03-24-93, Kunsthallen, #232), color lithograph (BP 186, DM 449, FR 1529, Y 32,311, DK 1725).
$184* *Composition,* s. Manessier, epreuve d'artiste, (03-24-93, Kunsthallen, #233), color lithograph (BP 125, DM 301, FR 1023, Y 21,619, DK 1150).
$565* *Composition,* s., #20/90, stamp Galerie de France, tears, crease, (06-12-93, Hauswedell/Nolt, #289), 21⁹⁄₁₆ x 32¹¹⁄₁₆ in., (54.7 x 83 cm.), color lithograph on BFK Rives (BP 370, DM 920, FR 3091, Y 59,455).
$126* *"Composition 26-1975",* #52/95, s., (01-28-93, Pescheteau, #196), 25⁹⁄₁₆ x 19¹¹⁄₁₆ in., (65 x 50 cm.), etching and aquatint on Arches (BP 83, DM 200, FR 676, Y 15,644).

$168* *"Composition B 20-1971",* E.A. 5/30, s., (01-28-93, Pescheteau, #197), 22¹⁄₁₆ x 29¹⁵⁄₁₆ in., (56 x 76 cm.), color lithograph on Arches (BP 111, DM 266, FR 901, Y 20,859).
$112* *"Composition", 1974,* ed. Galerie de France, #9/95, s., (10-18-92, Pescheteau, #198A), 19¹¹⁄₁₆ x 25⁹⁄₁₆ in., (50 x 65 cm.), etching and aquatint on Arches (BP 68, DM 165, FR 562, Y 13,373).
$213* *"Joie Champetre", 1975,* artist's proof, #23/30, s., (10-18-92, Pescheteau, #199), 34⅝ x 24 in., (88 x 61 cm.), lithograph in colors on wove (BP 129, DM 315, FR 1069, Y 25,433).
$390* *Komposition,* s., num., stamp, (12-01-92, Karl/Faber, #946), 13⅜ x 20¹⁄₁₆ in., (34 x 51 cm.), color lithograph on Arches wove (BP 258, DM 622, FR 2118, Y 48,556).
$375* *Komposition Blau-Turkis, c. 1955,* s., num., (11-28-92, Grisebach, #640, illus.), 15¹¹⁄₁₆ x 12¾ in., (39.8 x 32.4 cm.), colored lithograph on handmade (BP 248, DM 597, FR 2028, Y 46,671).
$167* *L'Eau Et La Purete,* s., t., num. 7/60, embossed B.F., full margins, good cond., light-staining; s., num. 49/75, (11-30-92, Phillips-London, #456), sheet 26⅜ x 19½ in., (670 x 495 mm.), lithograph in colors on wove; aquatint in colors (BP 110, DM 266, FR 903, Y 20,784).
BI *Neige,* s., #84/85, good margins, (05-06-93, Laurin, #64), color lithograph.
BI *Paques II,* #23/68, s., est. BP 1/200, (05-20-93, Bonhams-Chelsea, #162), sheet 21½ x 16¾ in., (54.6 x 42.5 cm.), lithograph in colors.
$77* *Printemps Precoce, 1966,* s., 635/700, (06-28-93, Loudmer, #86), 8¹¹⁄₁₆ x 8¹¹⁄₁₆ in., (220 x 220 mm.), sh 9¹³⁄₁₆ x 9¹³⁄₁₆ in., (220 x 220 mm.), color lithograph on wove (BP 52, DM 131, FR 441, Y 8170).
$189* *"Proces De Burgos",* E.A. 20/30, s., (01-28-93, Pescheteau, #198), 30¹¹⁄₁₆ x 47¼ in., (78 x 120 cm.), color lithograph on Arches (BP 125, DM 299, FR 1013, Y 23,467).
$58* *Sans Titre, 1953,* s., ded., 72/200, (06-28-93, Loudmer, #87), 8¹⁄₁₆ x 6⁵⁄₁₆ in., (205 x 160 mm.), sh 12¹³⁄₁₆ x 9¹³⁄₁₆ in., (205 x 160 mm.), color lithograph on wove (BP 39, DM 99, FR 332, Y 6154).
$2558* *Sept Lithographies De Manessier Sur Le Theme De Paques, 1949: Set OfSeven,* s., #7/68, margins, good cond., (12-03-92, Sotheby-London, #770, illus.), each sheet approx. 25¾ x 19¾ in., (655 x 503 mm.), lithographs in colors (BP 1650, DM 4023, FR 13,731, Y 318,278).
BI *Untitled,* s., #33/85, margins, good cond., minor paper discoloration along edges., est. Dfl. 250/350, (05-27-93, Sotheby-Amstrdm, #653), sheet 11¹³⁄₁₆ x 15¹⁵⁄₁₆ in., (300 x 405 mm.), color lithograph on wove.
BI *Untitled,* s., #59/85, full sheet, good cond., minor handling creases, minor paper discoloration, est. Dfl. 4/600, (05-27-93, Sotheby-Amstrdm, #655), sheet 255⅞ x 196⅞ in., (650 x 500 cm.), color lithograph on wove.
$128* *Untitled,* s., i. H.C., full margins, good cond., (05-27-93, Sotheby-Amstrdm, #652, illus.), sheet 22⅛ x 30 in., (562 x 762 mm.), color lithograph (BP 82, DM 205, FR 692, Y 13,722, G 230).
BI *Untitled,* s., #80/160, margins, good cond.?, est. G 5/700, (12-09-92, Sotheby-Amstrdm, #623), 25⅝ x 17⅝ in., (644 x 448 mm.), color lithograph on wove.
BI *Untitled, 1971,* s., #83/85, margins, good cond., minor paper discoloration along edges, est. Dfl. 4/600, (05-27-93, Sotheby-Amstrdm, #654), sheet 22⅛ x 30 in., (562 x 762 mm.), color lithograph on Arches.

MANET
$109 *Portrait Of Baudelaire,* (12-11-92, G.A. Key, #98A), 3 x 3 in., (7.6 x 7.6 cm.), black and white engraving (BP 70, DM 172, FR 589, Y 13,488).

MANET, Edouard   French 1832-1883
BI *Au Prado (Guerin 46; Beres-Wilson 53; Fisher 47), 1863,* second state, full margins, (02-24-93, Picard, #158), etching and aquatint in Japan thick laid.
$193* *"Baudelaire De Face",* s. in plate, full margins, excell. cond., (05-07-93, Goldberg, #428), 3½ x 3 in., (8.9 x

7.6 cm.), etching on arches (BP 122, DM 305, FR 1028, Y 21,251).

BI *"Baudelaire De Profil En Chapeau" (Guerine 31) and "Charles Baudelaire De Face" (G. 36), 1862 and 1865: Two,* posthumous impressions, excell. cond., est. $100/150, (05-15-93, Cleveland, #407), one 4 x 3¼ in., (10.2 x 8.3 cm.), other 3⅝ x 3⅛ in., (10.2 x 8.3 cm.), etching on MBM Arches.

BI *"Baudelaire De Profil En Chapeau" and "Baudelaire De Face" [G. 31,53], 1862, 1865: Two,* est. $325/375, (12-10-92, Sloan, #3023), larger 4 x 3 7/16 in., (10.2 x 8.7 cm.), etching.

$275* *"Baudelaire De Profile",* mono. plate, (05-07-93, Goldberg, #428A), 4 x 3½ in., (10.2 x 8.9 cm.), etching on arches (BP 174, DM 435, FR 1465, Y 30,280).

$440* *"Baudelaire De Profile", "Baudelaire De Face" and "Le Chat Et Les Flers" (Guerin 31, 38, 53), 1862, 1865, 1869: Three,* posthumous printings, (05-27-93, Swann, #173), etchings (BP 282, DM 706, FR 2380, Y 47,170).

$275* *Baudelaire En Profile (G. 30, H. 21), 1862,* only state, p. by A. Salmon, full margins, good cond., creases, hingeremains, (02-24-93, Butterfield, #2947), 4¼ x 3½ in., (108 x 89 mm.), etching on laid (BP 192, DM 446, FR 1513, Y 32,269).

BI *Berthe Morisot En Silhouette (G. 78; B.-W. 82; F. 58), 1872-1874,* first state before address, rubbing, staining, creases, cracks, (02-24-93, Picard, #159), 162 x 236 in., (411.5 x 599.4 cm.), lithograph on chine on thick creme wove.

BI *Berthe Morisot: Premiere Planche (G. 77; W., Ingl. 75; B. 81; cf. F.59-60; H. 73), 1872-4,* 2nd (final) state, wide margins, foxing, creases, patches, defects, prov., est. BP 8/12,000, (12-01-92, Christie-London, #418, illus.), L. 8 1/16 x 5⅝ in., (204 x 143 mm.), sheet 17½ x 11 9/16 in., (204 x 143 mm.), lithograph on Chine applique.

BI *Bildnis Berthe Morisot (Guerin 59, II), 1872,* reprint 1930, est. DM 250-, (09-25-92, Granier, #2665), 4⅝ x 3 1/16 in., (11.8 x 7.8 cm.), etching on hand-made.

$1159* *Le Buveur D'Absinthe (M.G. 9, J.C.H. 16), 1860,* third state, large margins, (06-11-93, Picard, #110), 9 11/16 x 5 11/16 in., (246 x 144 mm.), etching and aquatint on Japan (BP 761, DM 1884, FR 6351, Y 122,971).

BI *Chapeau Et Guitare (H. 39), 1874,* full margins, good cond., spot foxing, hinge remains, est. $8/1,000, (10-28-92, Butterfield, #2664), 9 x 8 in., (229 x 203 mm.), etching on cream laid paper, watermark.

$21,304* *Charles Cros. Le Fleuve (Harris 79, a-h; Guerin 63, a-h), 1874: Eight,* Paris, Librairie de l'Eau-forte, frontispiece in China ink, s. Ed. Manet, num., (06-25-93, Kornfeld, #80, illus.), sheet 11 x 9½ in., cover 10 13/16 x 8½ in., etching (BP 14,409, DM 36,268, FR 122,156, Y 2,258,215, SF 32,200).

$275* *Chat Et Les Fleurs (G. 53),* posthumous printing, appears very good cond., (06-11-93, Doyle, #58), 6⅝ x 5 in., (168 x 127 mm.), etching (BP 181, DM 447, FR 1507, Y 29,178).

BI *"Le Chat Et Les Fleurs",* posthumous p., s., est. $5/700, (10-10-92, Goldberg, #422), image 7 x 5 in., (17.8 x 12.7 cm.), etching.

$303* *"Le Chat Et Les Fleurs" and "Boudelaire En Face": Two,* late impressions, (10-30-92, Sloan, #1603), larger 6½ x 5 in., (16.5 x 12.7 cm.), etching (BP 194, DM 466, FR 1581, Y 37,533).

$358* *La Convalescente (G. 65, H. 85), 1876-8,* 3rd (final) state, pub. in Manet by Ed Bazire, 1884, margins, good cond, paper loss, sheet slightly toned, stains, foxing, hinge remains, pencil notations, (02-24-93, Butterfield, #2948), 5 x 3 15/16 in., (127 x 100 mm.), etching & drypoint on laid (BP 250, DM 581, FR 1970, Y 42,009).

$361* *La Convalescente (Guerin 65 III; Harris 85 III), 1867-80,* (12-04-92, Bassenge, #6883), 4 15/16 x 3 15/16 in., (12.6 x 10 cm.), etching w/aquatint in brown (BP 232, DM 575, FR 1950, Y 45,069).

$413* *"La Convalescente" (Guerin 65 III/III),* first issue, pub. Bazire 1884, good cond., foxing, (10-31-92, Cleveland, #313), 5 x 4 in., (12.7 x 10.2 cm.), etching (BP 265, DM 635, FR 2156, Y 51,158).

$107,000* *Les Courses (G. 72; H. 41; I.: W. 66; B. 76; F. 56), between 1865 and1878,* Fisher's 2nd state of 3, before letters and the printer's address, margins, good cond., scuff in image, mat stain, soiling, ex-coll. Maurice Loncle,stamp verso, (05-13-93, Sotheby-NY, #592, illus.), image 13¾ x 20⅛ in., (350 x 510 mm.), support 18⅞ x 24 in., (350 x 510 mm.), lithograph on chine applique (BP 70,247, DM 172,776, FR 582,789, Y 11,945,964).

$79,888* *Les Courses (Harris 41; Guerin 72/I), 1865-1869,* 1st state, (06-25-93, Kornfeld, #79, illus.), image 14⅜ x 20 3/16 in., (36.5 x 51.2 cm.), sheet 19 5/16 x 25 3/16 in., (36.5 x 51.2 cm.), lithograph on thick vellum (BP 54,033, DM 136,003, FR 458,073, Y 8,468,094, SF 120,750).

$999* *Enfant Portant Un Plateau (M.G. 15, J.C.H. 28), 1861,* second state of three, large margins, (06-11-93, Picard, #112), 8¾ x 5 11/16 in., (223 x 145 mm.), etching and aquatint on Japan (BP 656, DM 1624, FR 5474, Y 105,995).

$295* *Le Gamin (M. Guerin, 27), 1862,* second state, good margins, (06-16-93, Ader Tajan, #116), 8 1/16 x 5 11/16 in., (20.5 x 14.5 cm.), etching (BP 197, DM 490, FR 1643, Y 31,463).

$385* *Les Gitanos,* i. in plate, late impression, (10-30-92, Sloan, #1753), 11 x 8 in., (27.9 x 20.3 cm.), sepia etching (BP 247, DM 592, FR 2009, Y 47,690).

$1548* *Les Gitanos (E. Moreau Nelaton, 2; M. Guerin, 21), 1862,* yellowed, third state of four, drystamp, large margins, (04-02-93, Picard, #147), 11⅛ x 8⅛ in., (28.2 x 20.6 cm.), etching (BP 1020, DM 2488, FR 8450, Y 176,250).

$1048* *Les Gitanos (Harris 18, Guerin 23),* good cond., (11-16-92, Briest, #325, illus.), 14⅜ x 11 7/16 in., (36.5 x 29 cm.), etching in black on laid Arches (BP 689, DM 1671, FR 5631, Y 130,787).

$3767* *Le Guitarero or Le Chanteur Espagnol (E.M.N., 4, M.G., 16), 1861,* definitive state, large margins, (04-02-93, Picard, #149, illus.), 11 9/16 x 9 7/16 in., (29.4 x 23.9 cm.), etching (BP 2481, DM 6054, FR 20,562, Y 428,897).

$2831* *Le Guitariste Ou Le Chanteur Espagnol (Guerin 16),* full margins, (11-16-92, Briest, #326), 19 11/16 x 14 9/16 in., (50 x 37 cm.), etching in black on Chine applique (BP 1861, DM 4515, FR 15,212, Y 353,301).

$475* *"Jeanne-Le Printemps" (G. 39), 1882,* pub. in Gazette de Beaux-Arts, 1902, good cond., (05-15-93, Cleveland, #408), 7 x 9¼ in., (17.8 x 23.5 cm.), etching and aquatint (BP 309, DM 764, FR 2568, Y 52,655).

$10,990* *L'Enfant A L'Epee (M.G. 13, J.C.H. 26), 1861,* fourth state, creases, good margins, (06-11-93, Picard, #111, illus.), 10 11/16 x 7⅛ in., (271 x 181 mm.), etching and aquatint on thin wove (BP 7221, DM 17,861, FR 60,219, Y 1,166,048).

$636* *L'Enfant Aux Bulles De Savon (Moreau-Nelaton 36 III; Harris 63 III),1868/69,* pub. 1905, (06-10-93, Hauswedell/Nolt, #593, illus.), image 9 15/16 x 8 7/16 in., (25.3 x 21.5 cm.), etching and aquatint on hand-made (BP 416, DM 1036, FR 3487, Y 67,509).

$1961* *Lola De Valence (E.M.N., 3, M.G., 23), 1862,* definitive state, good margins, (04-02-93, Picard, #148), 9 1/16 x 6¼ in., (23 x 15.8 cm.), etching on Chine (BP 1292, DM 3152, FR 10,704, Y 223,272).

$1153* *Lola De Valence (Harris 33),* full margins, (11-16-92, Briest, #326A), 15¾ x 12 in., (40 x 30.5 cm.), etching in black on Chine applique on wove (BP 758, DM 1839, FR 6196, Y 143,891).

$884* *"Olympia", 1865 and "Jeanne", 1882 (M.G., 39 et 66): Two,* first, yellowed, holes, crease; second, yellowed, good margins, (06-16-93, Ader Tajan, #117), 6 1/16 x 4 3/16 in., (15.4 x 10.6 cm.), etching (BP 589, DM 1467, FR 4925, Y 94,283).

$1439* *Les Petits Cavaliers (M. Guerin 8, J.C. Harris 5), 1860,* third state of four, reddish stains verso, small margins, (06-11-93, Picard, #109), 9⅝ x 15¼ in., (245 x 387 mm.), etching on thin wove (BP 945, DM 2339, FR 7885, Y 152,679).

BI *Portrait De Beaudelaire,* init. M., (05-18-93, Encans, #206), 3 15/16 x 3 9/16 in., (10 x 9 cm.), etching.

$17,181* *Portrait De Berthe Morisot, En Noir (Harris 73; Guerin 77; Wilson-Bareau 81/II), 1872-1874,* (06-23-93, Kornfeld, #539, illus.), lithograph on Chine colle laid on wove (BP

11,672, DM 29,071, FR 97,786, Y 1,871,773, SF
25,875).

BI *"La Toilette" (Harris 20 ii/II), 1861,* from the Strolin
Edition, 1905, good cond., prov., est. $9/1,200, (05-15-93,
Cleveland, #409, illus.), 11⅛ x 8¾ in., (28.3 x 22.2
cm.), etching.

MANGOLD, Robert　　　American b. 1937
$1150* *Brooklyn Academy Of Music II: Untitled, 1988-89: Two,*
s.,. d. 1988, #26/75, pub. Parasol Press, full margins,
good cond., inconspicuous handling creases, (05-15-93,
Sotheby-NY, #1087, illus.), each sheet 22⅜ x 29⅞ in.,
(56.8 x 75.9 cm.), etching and aquatints in colors (BP
748, DM 1850, FR 6216, Y 127,480).

$523* *Five Color Frame, 1985,* s., num. 138/200, blindstamp of
pub. Crown Point Press, s., inkstampof printer, full margins, good cond., creases, (02-24-93, Butterfield, #3084),
21 x 17½ in., (533 x 445 mm.), woodcut in colors on
Japan (BP 365, DM 849, FR 2878, Y 61,371).

BI *"A Square Within Two Triangles", 1977,* s., num. 64/100,
full margins, image surface scrape, very good cond., est.
$8/1,000, (09-19-92, Christie-E, #153), sheet 16½ x
23⅜ in., (419 x 594 mm.), screenprint in brown and
blue on wove.

$1265* *Untitled Aquatint, 1978,* s., d., #6/20, blindstamp, pub.
Crown Point Press, full margins, good cond., handling
creases, soiling, (05-15-93, Sotheby-NY, #1086), sheet
22¼ x 20½ in., (56.5 x 52.1 cm.), etching and aquatint
in colors (BP 822, DM 2035, FR 6838, Y 140,228).

$660* *Untitled, 1973,* s., d., #22/50, pub. Parasol Press, full
margins, good cond., (11-07-92, Sotheby-NY, #676),
15¾ x 15¾ in., (400 x 400 mm.), aquatint p. in colors
(BP 432, DM 1054, FR 3562, Y 81,461).

$297* *Yellow Line, 1974,* s., d., num., t., i., (06-12-93,
Hauswedell/Nolt, #291), 21⅞ x 21⅞ in., (55.5 x 55.5
cm.), lithograph on thick wove (BP 194, DM 483, FR
1625, Y 31,253).

MANGOLD, Sylvia Plimack　　　American b. 1938
$440* *"The Pin Oak At The Pond", 1986,* s., d. Sylvia Plimack
Mangold 9/86, num. 16/50; t. verso, excellent cond., (09-
11-92, Skinner, #117, illus.), sight 17¾ x 22⅛ in., (45.1
x 56.2 cm.), color etching/drypoint w/aquatint on paper
(BP 228, DM 633, FR 2153, Y 54,516).

MANGRAVITE, Peppino　　　Italian/American b. 1896
BI *"Agony In The Garden Of The Gods-Colorado" After El
Greco's "Agony In The Garden",* s., t. ink, very good
cond., est. $125/175, (05-15-93, Cleveland, #234), 16⅞ x
20⅝ in., (42.9 x 52.4 cm.), serigraph in colors.

MANKES, Jan　　　1889-1920
$521* *Laan Bij Heerenveen, 1914,* margins, good cond., fox-
ing, taped, prov., (12-09-92, Sotheby-Amstrdm, #621), 7½
x 5¹¹⁄₁₆ in., (191 x 145 mm.), etching on wove (BP 332,
DM 818, FR 2791, Y 64,600, G 920).

$293* *Vader, 1914,* s., margins, good cond., creases, papertaped,
(12-09-92, Sotheby-Amstrdm, #617), 6⅞ x 6⅛ in., (174
x 155 mm.), woodcut on wove (BP 187, DM 460, FR
1569, Y 36,330, G 518).

$782* *Zelfportret Bij Het Raam, 1913,* reduced margins, discol-
oration, foxing, taped, prov., (12-09-92, Sotheby-Amstrdm,
#620), 6⅛ x 5⅜ in., (156 x 136 mm.), etching on wove
(BP 499, DM 1227, FR 4189, Y 96,962, G 1380).

BI *Zelfportret, Nestkuiken En Parelhoen, 1914-17: Five,*
proofs, p. Beint Mankes, margins, top margins stapled
to backboard, good cond., prov., est. G 5/700, (12-09-92,
Sotheby-Amstrdm, #619), woodcut on Japan.

MANLY, Elanor E., Engraver
BI *Portrait Of A Lady,* s., blindstamp, pub. McQueen and
Sons, 1887, margins, est. BP 5/70, (06-16-93, Bonhams-
Chelsea, #467), pl. 17¼ x 13½ in., (43.8 x 34.3 cm.),
mezzotint.

MANN, Cathleen　　　English 1896-1959
$644* *Everywhere You Go, West Wycombe, 1933,* p. Vincent
Brooks, Day & Son, ref. #367, cond. 2, (10-13-92, Phillips-London, #93), 29¹³⁄₁₆ x 45¹⁄₁₆ in., (75.7 x 114.4 cm.),
color lithograph (BP 375, DM 943, FR 3206, Y 78,089).

$1442* *Film Stars Use Shell, 1938,* p. Baynard Press, ref. #525,
cond. 3, (10-13-92, Phillips-London, #144, illus.), 29¹⁵⁄₁₆

x 44⅞ in., (76 x 114 cm.), color lithograph (BP 840,
DM 2113, FR 7178, Y 174,851).

MANN, H.C.　　　1866-1926
BI *Dunes, Virginia, c. 1914,* s., annot., est. $1/1,500, (10-13-
92, Christie-NY, #309, illus.), 4¾ x 6¾ in., (12.1 x 17.1
cm.), photograph, gelatin silver print.

MANN, Sally
$575* *Young Girl And Family, 1989,* s., (05-23-93, Butterfield,
#3514, illus.), 11 x 14 in., photograph, gelatin silver
print (BP 374, DM 940, FR 3165, Y 63,557).

MANNI, Marino　　　Italian 1901-1980
$303* *Figure On Horseback, 1955,* num. 35/200, (11-12-92,
Freemn/Fine Art, #137), 23½ x 19½ in., (59.7 x 49.5
cm.), screen print (BP 199, DM 480, FR 1619, Y
37,570).

MANNING, Jo　　　b. 1923
$43* *Woodlot VII, 1979,* s., t., d. '79, (11-16-92, Hodgins,
#313), 23½ x 17½ in., (59.7 x 44.5 cm.), etching on
paper (BP 28, DM 69, FR 231, Y 5366, C$ 55).

MANSEN, Mattias
$440* *Frau in Mannerwald, 1987: Two,* each s., #12/30, #18/
30, good cond., creases, tear, surface soiling,stray printing
ink, (02-24-93, Butterfield, #3230), each 31⅝ x 41¹⁄₁₆ in.,
(80.3 x 104.3 cm.), woodcut on wove (BP 307, DM
714, FR 2422, Y 51,631).

MANSOUROFF, Paul　　　Russian 1896-1983
$2129* *Diesegni Per Tessuti,(1929-1930), 1982: Eight,* album,
pub. F. Squattriti, #113/125, each s., (12-15-92, Finarte-
Milan, #102), 12¹⁵⁄₁₆ x 9¹³⁄₁₆ in., (33 x 25 cm.), serigraph
in colors (BP 1358, DM 3337, FR 11,403, Y 264,046, L
2990).

BI *Konstruktivistische Komposition, c. 1950,* s., E.A., est.
DM 280-, (09-25-92, Granier, #2930), sheet 25¹³⁄₁₆ x
13⁹⁄₁₆ in., (65.5 x 34.5 cm.), color lithograph on hand-
made.

MANTEGNA, Andrea　　　1431-1506
$4775* *Bacchanal With A Wine Vat (H. 4; Landau & Boorsch
74),* trimmed within platemark, repairs, discoloration,
minor defects, (12-03-92, Sotheby-London, #78), 11½ x
17¾ in., (295 x 450 mm.), engraving (BP 3080, DM
7509, FR 25,631, Y 594,127).

$10,690* *Hercules Und Antaeus (Hind II, 17; Borenius II), c.
1497,* (06-23-93, Kornfeld, #67, illus.), engraving (BP
7262, DM 18,088, FR 60,842, Y 1,164,615, SF 16,100).

$6325* *Risen Christ Between SS. Andrew And Longinus (Hind 5;
National Gallery Of Art 72; Royal Academy/Metropoli-
tan Museum Of Art 45),* watermark, trimmed, repaired
tear in image, crease, foxing, defects, (05-13-93, Sotheby-
NY, #329, illus.), 12½ x 9⅝ in., (317 x 245 mm.),
engraving (BP 4152, DM 10,213, FR 34,450, Y
706,152).

BI *The Risen Christ Between St. Andrew And St. Longinus,*
est. $6/800, (11-01-92, Hanzel, #246), 14¾ x 12 in.,
(37.5 x 30.5 cm.), engraving.

$23,873* *The Virgin And Child (Hind V, 1948; P. 10, No. 1; Lan-
dau & Boorsch 48),* cut to an arch above, surface dirt,
good cond., (12-03-92, Sotheby-London, #77, illus.),
approx. 9¼ x 10¼ in., (235 x 260 mm.), engraving on
paper w/watermark (BP 15,400, DM 37,542, FR 128,143,
Y 2,970,387).

MANTEGNA, Andrea (after)　　　Italian 1431-1506
BI *"The Daughter Of Herodeas",* t. verso, i., stamped 2365,
trimmed, toning, soiling, est. $6/900, (01-23-93, Gold-
berg, #487, illus.), 13⅛ x 8⅞ in., (33.3 x 22.5 cm.),
etching.

MANTEGNA, Andrea (attrib.)　　　1431-1506
$199,782* *The Flagellation: With The Pavement (B. XIII, p. 227,
no. 1; H. V, pp. 17-18, no. 8; R.A./M.M. cat., pp. 195-6,
no. 36), late 1460's,* small patch of missed printing,
watermark, trimmed, repaired tears, made-up loss, stain,
hole, ink spots, fine cond., (12-01-92, Christie-London,
#30, illus.), sheet 15⅞ x 12⅜ in., (404 x 315 mm.),
engraving (BP 132,000, DM 318,428, FR 1,085,182, Y
24,873,257).

MANTEGNA, Andrea (school of)   1431-1506
$361* *Der Triumph Des Caesar: Die Senatoren, Linke Untere Halfte (B. 11; Hind 16),* after Mantegna, (12-04-92, Bassenge, #6285), 5¹¹⁄₁₆ x 7¾ in., (14.5 x 19.7 cm.), engraving (BP 232, DM 575, FR 1950, Y 45,069).

MANTEGNA, Andrea and Robert van AUDENAERD
$1779* *"C. Iulii Caesaris Dictatoris Triumphi...", 1692: Ten,* staining, prov., (09-14-92, Venator/Hansten, #1552, illus.), plate approx. 15¾ x 17¹¹⁄₁₆ in., (40 x 45 cm.), engraving and etching (BP 941, DM 2645, FR 8962, Y 221,214).

MANTEL, J.G.
$839* *Un Bal A L'Ecole Des Beaux-Arts, Mai 1935,* good cond., (11-19-92, Ribeyre/Baron, #144bis), 47¼ x 31½ in., (120 x 80 cm.), poster (BP 552, DM 1338, FR 4506, Y 104,340).

MANTIN, K.N.
$33* *New Orleans Mardi Gras, 1981,* (08-05-92, Boos, #731), 21½ x 15½ in., (546 x 394 mm.), color serigraph (BP 17, DM 49, FR 165, Y 4203).

MANTZ, Werner   b. Germany 1901 d. 1983
$660* *"Architectural View Of Interior Of Department Store", "Interior Of Raio Store", and "Man Working At Desk In Fabric Warehouse", 1928-29: Three,* sig., notations, handstamp, (10-14-92, Swann, #515, illus.), each, approx. 6 x 9 in., (15.2 x 22.9 cm.), photograph, silver prints (BP 387, DM 966, FR 3275, Y 79,981).
BI *Lienberg, 1935,* photog.'s handstamp, notations, est. $1/1,500, (04-07-93, Swann, #514, illus.), 9 x 6¾ in., photograph, silver print.
BI *Limbourg, 1935,* s., t., d. by photog., (c) stamp, est. $2/3,000, (10-15-92, Sotheby-NY, #404A, illus.), 9 x 6½ in., (22.9 x 16.5 cm.), photograph, gelatin silver print.
BI *Viaduct, 1920s,* s., credit and reprod. limit. stamps, lit., est. $4/6,000, (10-13-92, Christie-NY, #310, illus.), 8⅝ x 6¾ in., (21.9 x 17.1 cm.), photograph, gelatin silver print.

MANUEL, G.L.
$990* *Josephine Baker In Costume,* photog.'s sig. in neg., address of Baker's agent, 1920s, (04-07-93, Swann, #398, illus.), 10½ x 8 in., photograph, silver print (BP 654, DM 1601, FR 5419, Y 112,474).

MANUEL, Henri
BI *Armistice Day, Paris, 1918,* handstamp, notations, est. $1/1,500, (10-14-92, Swann, #353, illus.), 7 x 9½ in., (17.8 x 24.1 cm.), photograph, silver print.
BI *The Salvation Army Feeding The Poor In The Streets Of Paris, c. 1919,* t., credit/picture agancy stamps, est. $800/1,200, (04-08-93, Christie-NY, #55, illus.), 6⅝ x 9 in., (16.8 x 22.9 cm.), photograph, gelatin silver print.

MANWOMAN   b. 1938
$113* *"Lion And Lamb" and "Happiness Tiger": Two,* s., t., artist's stamp, #28/49, #42/49, prov., (11-16-92, Hodgins, #352), serigraph on paper (BP 74, DM 180, FR 607, Y 14,102, C$ 143).

MANZANA PISSARRO, Georges
$512* *Orientale, c. 1910,* margins, (02-24-93, Picard, #160), color lithograph on wove (BP 357, DM 831, FR 2818, Y 60,080).

MANZU, Giacomo   Italian 1908-1990
$2741* *Autoritratto Con Modella Sulle Ginocchia (Ciranna 28), 1942,* #45/150, s., (05-20-93, Finarte-Milan, #92, illus.), 10⁵⁄₁₆ x 7¹³⁄₁₆ in., (26.2 x 19.9 cm.), etching and aquatint (BP 1759, DM 4422, FR 14,897, Y 302,672, L 4025).
$800* *Due Figure, # 29/30,* s., (11-09-92, Finarte-Milan, #58), 20¼ x 13³⁄₁₆ in., (51.5 x 33.5 cm.), etching (BP 529, DM 1277, FR 4315, Y 99,280, L 1093).
$3916* *Edipo Re (Ciranna 140-146), 1968: Seven,* #45, s. on colophon, (05-20-93, Finarte-Milan, #93), 14¹⁵⁄₁₆ x 11 in., (38 x 28 cm.), portfolio w/etching (BP 2513, DM 6318, FR 21,283, Y 432,420, L 5750).
$926* *Lezione Di Pittura, #29/30,* s., (11-09-92, Finarte-Milan, #35, illus.), 14³⁄₁₆ x 10⁷⁄₁₆ in., (36 x 26.5 cm.), etching (BP 612, DM 1478, FR 4995, Y 114,917, L 1265).
$850* *Liebespaar, 1973,* s., 1st portfolio of series Hommage a Picasso, pub. Propylaen Verlag, (06-08-93, Karl/Faber,

#1047), approx. 24³⁄₁₆ x 18½ in., (61.5 x 47 cm.), etching and aquatint on thick hand-made Japan (BP 559, DM 1379, FR 4645, Y 90,281).
$646* *Maternita, #17/25,* s., stamped, init., Edizioni 2RC, (03-25-93, Finarte-Rome, #48), etching and aquatint (BP 439, DM 1061, FR 3609, Y 75,679, L 1035).
$1723* *Maternita (Ciranna 3), 1929,* sig., (05-20-93, Finarte-Milan, #90, illus.), 7¾ x 6½ in., (19.7 x 16.5 cm.), etching and puntasecca (drypoint) (BP 1106, DM 2780, FR 9364, Y 190,261, L 2530).
$1566* *Orfeo E Euridice- La Danza, #4/6,* s., (05-20-93, Finarte-Milan, #95, illus.), 10⅝ x 8¼ in., (27 x 21 cm.), etching and calcografia a rilievo (BP 1005, DM 2527, FR 8511, Y 172,924, L 2300).
$1723* *Orfeo E Euridice-L'Amore, #6/6,* s., (05-20-93, Finarte-Milan, #94), 10⅝ x 8¼ in., (27 x 21 cm.), etching and calcografia a rilievo (BP 1106, DM 2780, FR 9364, Y 190,261, L 2530).
$1410* *Ragazzo Con Anatra (Ciranna 26), 1940, #12/12,* prima tirtura, s., (05-20-93, Finarte-Milan, #91, illus.), 11¹⁵⁄₁₆ x 9⅞ in., (30.4 x 25.1 cm.), etching (BP 905, DM 2275, FR 7663, Y 155,698, L 2070).
$357* *Vase Of Flowers, c. 1960,* s., #12/21, wide margins, label, (12-08-92, Swann, #192), 15 x 11¼ in., (38.1 x 28.6 cm.), etching, chine colle (BP 224, DM 556, FR 1895, Y 44,249).

MAPPIELLON
$1100* *"Pate Eclair",* s. Mappiellon, pub. in Paris, (09-18-92, DuMouchelle, #2057), 52 x 46 in., (132.1 x 116.8 cm.), lithograph (BP 633, DM 1647, FR 5641, Y 137,055).

MAPPLETHORPE, Robert   American 1946-1989
BI *Ajitto, 1981: Four,* each ink s., d., #10/15; each ink s., t., d., num., (c) stamp, lit.,est. $32/38,000, (04-08-93, Christie-NY, #537, illus.), each approx. 18 x 14 in., (45.7 x 35.6 cm.), photograph, gelatin silver print.
BI *America, 1988: Three,* photog.'s facsimile sig. stamp, s. by Michael Ward Stout #5/40 ed.,est. $4/6,000, (10-15-92, Sotheby-NY, #620, illus.), each, approx. 26 x 21¾ in., (66 x 55.2 cm.), photolithographs.
BI *Andy Warhol, 1986,* ink s., d., i.; i. A.P. 1/2 verso, lit., est. $20/30,000, (04-08-93, Christie-NY, #540, illus.), 15⅛ x 15⅛ in., (38.4 x 38.4 cm.), photograph, gelatin silver print.
BI *Antinous, 1987,* ink s., t., d., #2/10; (c) credit stamp, est. $6/8,000, (04-08-93, Christie-NY, #531, illus.), 23 x 19¼ in., (58.4 x 48.9 cm.), photograph, gelatin silver print.
$489* *Black Jack, 1984,* s., t.; i. proof, good cond., (12-09-92, Sotheby-Amstrdm, #622), sheet 12⅜ x 12⅜ in., (315 x 315 mm.), photograph (BP 312, DM 768, FR 2619, Y 60,632, G 863).
$2860* *Cactus, 1987,* s., d., num. 2/10 in ink in margin; s., d., num. (c) credit stamps, (10-13-92, Christie-NY, #570, illus.), 19 x 19¼ in., (48.3 x 48.9 cm.), photograph, gelatin silver print (BP 1666, DM 4190, FR 14,236, Y 346,793).
BI *"Calla Lily", 1988,* s., d., edit. 11/25, est. $5/7,000, (11-16-92, Butterfield, #6076, illus.), 19¹⁄₁₆ x 19⁵⁄₁₆ in., (483.5 x 489.8 mm.), photograph, blue-toned photogravure.
$63,250* *Calla Lily, 1987 (Whitney, pl. 181),* s., d. by photog., (10-15-92, Sotheby-NY, #611, illus.), photograph, unique platinum print on linen (BP 38,704, DM 94,150, FR 319,283, Y 7,588,482).
BI *Calla Lily, 1988,* s., d. in ink w/(c) insig., 1 of unnum. edit. of 2, est. $25/30,000, (10-13-92, Christie-NY, #572, illus.), 40 x 40 in., (101.6 x 101.6 cm.), photograph, gelatin silver print.
$3300* *Cedric, 1977 (The Black Book, pl. 1),* s., d., num. 1/5 by photog., backed w/card, #1/5 ed., (10-15-92, Sotheby-NY, #616A, illus.), 14 x 13¾ in., (35.6 x 34.9 cm.), photograph, gelatin silver print (BP 2019, DM 4912, FR 16,658, Y 395,921).
BI *Charles Bowman, 1980,* ink s., d., #4/15; ink s., (c)/reprod limitation stamps, lit., est. $6/8,000, (04-08-93, Christie-NY, #535, illus.), 14 x 14 in., (35.6 x 35.6 cm.), photograph, gelatin silver print.

$5812* *"Chest", 1987,* mounted on card, t., s., d., #3/10, stamped photog.'s credit and (c)info., 500 x 604mm, (05-07-93, Sotheby-London, #364, illus.), photograph, silver print (BP 3680, DM 9189, FR 30,964, Y 639,947).

BI *Chest, 1987,* unique, ink s., d. verso, est. $22/28,000, (04-08-93, Christie-NY, #538, illus.), 39¾ x 47½ in., (101 x 120.7 cm.), photograph, gelatin silver print.

$5493* *Chest, 1987,* s., stamped, num., edit. 10, (10-29-92, Christie-London, #200, illus.), 19½ x 23¼ in., (49.5 x 59.1 cm.), photograph, selenium-toned gelatin silver print (BP 3520, DM 8451, FR 28,669, Y 680,416).

$5750* *Continuous Profile Of Mussolini, 1988,* ink s., t., d., #2/10; (c) stamp, (04-08-93, Christie-NY, #530, illus.), 19¼ x 19¼ in., (48.9 x 48.9 cm.), photograph, gelatin silver print (BP 3770, DM 9237, FR 31,267, Y 652,519).

$4135* *The Dancer, John Reed, 1980,* edit. 3/15, s., d., num. in ink on border '3/15 Robert Mapplethorpe '80', (10-15-92, Sotheby-London, #50, illus.), 15⅛ x 14½ in., (38.4 x 36.8 cm.), photograph, gelatin silver print (BP 2530, DM 6155, FR 20,873, Y 496,101).

$3738* *Double Orchid, 1986: Two,* s., d., #47/60 by photog., (04-06-93, Sotheby-NY, #515, illus.), 21½ x 35⅛ in., photograph, photogravure p. on one sheet, one in color, one b/w; color gravure (intaglio) inset into silver glitter gro (BP 2469, DM 6022, FR 20,393, Y 426,323).

$9081* *Flag, 1987,* s., d., photog.'s ink stamped credit, sight 482 x 580mm, (05-07-93, Sotheby-London, #363, illus.), photograph, silver print (BP 5750, DM 14,357, FR 48,380, Y 999,890).

$7500* *Flower With Knife, 1985,* s., d., num. 2/3 by photog. in margin, s., d., by photog., (c) stamp,#2/3 ed., sold after sale, (10-15-92, Sotheby-NY, #611A, illus.), 19⅜ x 19⅝ in., (49.2 x 49.8 cm.), photograph, platinum-palladium print (BP 4589, DM 11,164, FR 37,860, Y 899,820).

$12,703* *"Flower", 1986,* s., t., d., #2/10, (05-06-93, Christie-London, #196, illus.), image 19¼ x 19¼ in., photograph, gelatin silver print (BP 8050, DM 20,008, FR 67,354, Y 1,397,624).

$23,000* *Flowers: Ten,* complete portfolio, s., #14/40, pub. by artist, Deli Sacilotto and Barbara Gladstone, full margins, good cond., scratches, retouched, mat-stain, (05-15-93, Sotheby-NY, #1089, illus.), each image 21½ x 17¾ in., (54.6 x 45.1 cm.), photogravures (BP 14,954, DM 36,995, FR 124,324, Y 2,549,606).

BI *Frank Diaz (Contact), 1979 (ICA, p. 35),* s., d., i. Artist's Proof, backed w/card, s., d. by photog. in ink, (c) stamp, est. $5/7,000, (10-15-92, Sotheby-NY, #616, illus.), photograph, gelatin silver print.

$5463* *"Iris", 1977,* backed w/card, s., d., t., #2/3 by photog., (c) stamp, (04-06-93, Sotheby-NY, #513, illus.), photograph (BP 3608, DM 8801, FR 29,804, Y 623,061).

$6351* *"Iris", 1982,* s. twice, d., #1/10, photog.'s (c) stamp, (05-06-93, Christie-London, #195, illus.), image 19¼ x 15¼ in., photograph, gelatin silver print (BP 4025, DM 10,003, FR 33,674, Y 698,757).

$4400* *Iris, 1982,* s. twice, d., num. 2/10 in ink, (c) credit stamp, (10-13-92, Christie-NY, #568, illus.), 19¼ x 15¼ in., (48.9 x 38.7 cm.), photograph, gelatin silver print (BP 2563, DM 6446, FR 21,901, Y 533,527).

$8050* *Ken And Lydia, 1985,* ink s., t., d., #1/2, annot For Bob-A.P.; (c) stamp, (04-08-93, Christie-NY, #533, illus.), 19 x 15 in., (48.3 x 38.1 cm.), photograph, gelatin silver print (BP 5279, DM 12,932, FR 43,774, Y 913,527).

$6600* *Ken Moody (The Black Book, pl. 87),* s., d., num. 1/3 by photog., s, d., (c) stamp, 1983, p. 1985, #1/3 ed., sold after sale, (10-15-92, Sotheby-NY, #618A, illus.), 19⅛ x 19⅜ in., (48.6 x 49.2 cm.), photograph, platinum-palladium print (BP 4039, DM 9824, FR 33,317, Y 791,842).

$2588* *Ken Moody, 1987,* s., #14/60 by photog., printer's blindstamp, (04-06-93, Sotheby-NY, #517, illus.), 21⅞ x 17⅞ in., photograph, photogravure (BP 1709, DM 4169, FR 14,119, Y 295,164).

$4600* *"Leaf", 1989,* backed w/card, photog. facsimile sig. stamp s. by Michael Ward Stout, executor, t., d., #3/10 in unident. hand., (04-06-93, Sotheby-NY, #524, illus.), photograph (BP 3038, DM 7411, FR 25,095, Y 524,635).

BI *"Lisa Lyon", 1981,* backed w/card, s. by photog., (c) date stamp, no. 6 in edit. of 10, est. $6/8,000, (04-06-93, Sotheby-NY, #519, illus.), 19⅛ x 15⅛ in., photograph.

$4888* *"Lisa Lyon", 1982,* s., d., #6/10 by photog., backed w/ card, s. by photog., (c) date stamp, (04-06-93, Sotheby-NY, #516, illus.), photograph (BP 3229, DM 7875, FR 26,667, Y 557,482).

BI *Lisa Lyon, 1981,* ink s., t., d., #3/10; (c) stamp, est. $6/8,000, (04-08-93, Christie-NY, #534, illus.), 19⅛ x 15¼ in., (48.6 x 38.7 cm.), photograph, gelatin silver print.

BI *Lisa Lyon, 1982,* ink s., t., d., #5/10; (c) stamp, est. $5/7,000, (04-08-93, Christie-NY, #541, illus.), 19¼ x 15¼ in., (48.9 x 38.7 cm.), photograph, gelatin silver print.

$6600* *Lisa Lyon, California, 1980,* s., d., num. 1/15 in ink in margin; s., d., t., (c) credit stamp, (10-13-92, Christie-NY, #565, illus.), 13¾ x 13¾ in., (34.9 x 34.9 cm.), photograph, gelatin silver print (BP 3844, DM 9669, FR 32,852, Y 800,291).

$8250* *Lydia, 1985,* backed w/card, s., t., d., num. 4/10 by photog. in ink, (c) d. stamp,#4/10 ed., (10-15-92, Sotheby-NY, #619, illus.), 19⅛ x 15¼ in., (48.6 x 38.7 cm.), photograph, gelatin silver print (BP 5048, DM 12,280, FR 41,646, Y 989,802).

$17,250* *Michael, 1987,* orig. frame, unique, lit., (04-08-93, Christie-NY, #539, illus.), 24 x 20 in., (61 x 50.8 cm.), photograph, platinum print on linen (BP 11,311, DM 27,711, FR 93,801, Y 1,957,558).

$7700* *Orchid, 1982 (Whitney, pl. 167),* s., d., num. 10/27 by photog., #10/27 ed., (10-15-92, Sotheby-NY, #613, illus.), 32½ x 32 in., (82.6 x 81.3 cm.), photogravure on chine colle (pasted) (BP 4712, DM 11,462, FR 38,869, Y 923,815).

$7130* *Orchid, 1988,* ink s., d., #6/10; ink s., t., d., num., (c) stamp, (04-08-93, Christie-NY, #544, illus.), 19¼ x 19¼ in., (48.9 x 48.9 cm.), photograph, gelatin silver print (BP 4675, DM 11,454, FR 38,771, Y 809,124).

$22,000* *Orchid; Hyacinth; and Vase Of Irises: Three, 1987,* large-format, each a., annot., (10-13-92, Christie-NY, #571, illus.), each 32½ x 32½ in., (82.6 x 82.6 cm.), photograph, photogravures (BP 12,813, DM 32,230, FR 109,507, Y 2,667,637).

$7150* *Parrot Tulip, 1987,* backed w/card, s., d., num. 4/10 by photog. in ink in margin, s., t.,d., num., (c) stamp, #4/10 ed., (10-15-92, Sotheby-NY, #614A, illus.), photograph, gelatin silver print (BP 4375, DM 10,643, FR 36,093, Y 857,828).

BI *Patti Smith With Dove, 1979,* s., d., num. 5/10 in margin; s., d. in ink (c) credit stamp, est. $7/9,000, (10-13-92, Christie-NY, #564, illus.), 13⅞ x 14 in., (35.2 x 35.6 cm.), photograph, gelatin silver print.

$4600* *"Patti Smith, N.Y.C." (Whitney, p. 72), 1976,* s., d., #3/10 by photog., backed w/card, s., d. by photog., (c) datestamp, (04-06-93, Sotheby-NY, #520, illus.), photograph (BP 3038, DM 7411, FR 25,095, Y 524,635).

BI *Peter Reed, 1979,* s., d., i. by photog., est. $1/2,000, (04-06-93, Sotheby-NY, #518, illus.), photograph.

$1760* *"Phyllis Tweel", 1979,* s., d., ink edit. 5/10, t., edit., photog. stamp, (11-16-92, Butterfield, #6077, illus.), 14 x 13⅞ in., (356.2 x 353.1 mm.), photograph, gelatin silver print (BP 1159, DM 2806, FR 9452, Y 218,878).

BI *Pillar, Rhinecliff, New York, 1979,* s., d., num. 1/10 in margin; s. in ink, t., d., num, (c) stamp, est.$6/8,000, (10-13-92, Christie-NY, #562, illus.), 14 x 13⅞ in., (35.6 x 35.2 cm.), photograph, gelatin silver print.

BI *Robert Sherman, 1983,* s., d., i. For Robert by photog., backed w/card, 1 aside from ed. of10, est. $5/7,000, (10-15-92, Sotheby-NY, #617, illus.), 15¼ x 15⅛ in., (38.7 x 38.4 cm.), photograph, gelatin silver print.

BI *Rose With Smoke, 1985,* s., d., num. 2/3 by photog., s., d., (c) stamp, #2/3 ed., est. $10/15,000, (10-15-92, Sotheby-NY, #612, illus.), 19⅜ x 19½ in., (49.2 x 49.5 cm.), photograph, platinum-palladium print.

BI *Rose, 1980,* s., est. $5/7,000, (05-23-93, Butterfield, #3517, illus.), 19¼ x 19¼ in., photograph, gelatin silver print.

BI *"A Season In Hell", 1986: Eight,* s., d., #20/40, pub. Limited Editions Club, orig. portfolio case, est. $4/6,000, (05-23-93, Butterfield, #3519, illus.), 4½ x 4½ in., photogravure.

BI *A Season In Hell, 1986,* s., #336, pub. The Limited Editions Club, est. $2/3,000, overall sizeapprox. 292 x 200 x 250 mm, (02-11-93, Sotheby-NY, #384, illus.), book w/ 8 photogravure etchings.

$6200* *A Season In Hell, 1986: Eight,* mono., s., num., Limited Editions Club, (09-19-92, Wachholtz, #864), dust-grain photogravure (BP 3630, DM 9200, FR 31,472, Y 766,284).

$1100* *Sebastian And Nda, 1981 (Certain People, unpaginated),* backed w/card, d., num. 2/15 by photog. in ink, s., d., (c) & reprod.stamps, #2/15 ed., (10-15-92, Sotheby-NY, #618, illus.), photograph, gelatin silver print (BP 673, DM 1637, FR 5553, Y 131,974).

BI *Self Portrait, 1972,* s., d., est. $6/8,000, (04-08-93, Christie-NY, #542, illus.), 22⅞ x 17⅜ in., (58.1 x 44.1 cm.), photograph, hand-colored photostat.

BI *Self-Portrait Triptych, 1972,* s., d., pub. by artist, tears, creases, ink loss, remains tape, surface scuffs, ink loss, est. $5/6,000, (05-15-93, Sotheby-NY, #1088, illus.), sheet 33½ x 22⅞ in., (85.1 x 58.1 cm.), photo-silkscreen.

$6538* *Self-Portrait With Knife, 1983,* sight 480 x 378mm, (05-07-93, Sotheby-London, #365, illus.), photograph, silver print (BP 4140, DM 10,337, FR 34,832, Y 719,885).

BI *Self-Portrait, 1988,* s., d., num. 2/10 in ink in margin; s., t., d., num., (c) credit stamp, est. $8/10,000, (10-13-92, Christie-NY, #573, illus.), 11 x 23 in., (27.9 x 58.4 cm.), photograph, gelatin silver print.

$5750* *Single Calla, 1980,* s., (05-23-93, Butterfield, #3518, illus.), 19¼ x 19¼ in., photograph, gelatin silver print (BP 3745, DM 9402, FR 31,646, Y 635,570).

$3450* *"Smitty" (Certain People, unpaginated), 1980,* s., d., #6/10 by photog. in ink, backed w/card, s., t., d., #6/10 byphotog., (c) stamp, (04-06-93, Sotheby-NY, #522, illus.), photograph (BP 2279, DM 5558, FR 18,822, Y 393,476).

$3163* *Smutty Smith (cf. Certain People, unpaginated), 1980,* s., .d, #3/15 by photog. in ink, backed w/card, s., d. by photog., (c) date stamp, (04-06-93, Sotheby-NY, #521, illus.), photograph (BP 2089, DM 5096, FR 17,256, Y 360,744).

$4600* *Still Life, 1980,* s., d., #8/15 by photog., s. by photog., (c) stamp, (04-06-93, Sotheby-NY, #514, illus.), photograph (BP 3038, DM 7411, FR 25,095, Y 524,635).

BI *Susan Breske, 1984,* ink s., d., annot.; ink s., d. verso, lit., est. $4/6,000, (04-08-93, Christie-NY, #532, illus.), 19¼ x 15¼ in., (48.9 x 38.7 cm.), photograph, gelatin silver print.

BI *Tampa, Orchid, 1986,* s., d., #43/60, est. $4/6,000, (04-08-93, Christie-NY, #543, illus.), 21½ x 35 in., (54.6 x 88.9 cm.), photograph, 3-color photogravure screen print.

BI *Tulip, 1985,* s., d., num. 1/10 in ink in margin; s., t., d., num., (c) credit stamp, est. $5/7,000, (10-13-92, Christie-NY, #569, illus.), 15⅛ x 15¼ in., (38.4 x 38.7 cm.), photograph, gelatin silver print.

$5225* *Tulips, 1985,* backed w/card, s., d., num. 1/10 by photog. in ink, s., d., (c) stamp, #1/10 ed., (10-15-92, Sotheby-NY, #614, illus.), photograph, gelatin silver print (BP 3197, DM 7778, FR 26,376, Y 626,875).

$7700* *Two Calla Lilies, 1988,* s., d., ink edit. 3/10, (11-16-92, Butterfield, #6075, illus.), 19³⁄₁₆ x 19⁵⁄₁₆ in., (486.6 x 489.8 mm.), photograph, gelatin silver print (BP 5070, DM 12,277, FR 41,353, Y 957,592).

BI *Untitled, 1980,* s., d., num 6/15 in ink in margin; s., d. i ink (c) credit stamp, lit., est. $8/10,000, (10-13-92, Christie-NY, #566, illus.), 18 x 14 in., (45.7 x 35.6 cm.), photograph, gelatin silver print.

BI *"Veronica", 1982,* s., d., i. For Veronica, by photog., est. $7/10,000, (04-06-93, Sotheby-NY, #515A, illus.), photograph.

BI *Victor Huston, NYC, 1979,* s., d., num. 3/10 in ink in margin; s., d., (c) credit stmap, est. $4/6,000, (10-13-92, Christie-NY, #563, illus.), 13⅞ x 13⅞ in., (35.2 x 35.2 cm.), photograph, gelatin silver print.

$1035* *"Vincent", 1984,* s., d., i. for Vincent by photog. on image, backed w/card, (04-06-93, Sotheby-NY, #523, illus.), 19⅛ x 15¼ in., photograph (BP 684, DM 1667, FR 5646, Y 118,043).

BI *William Burroughs, 1980,* s., d., num. 2/15 by photog., backed w/card, s., d., t. by photog. inink, (c) stamp, #2/15 ed., est. $4/6,000, (10-15-92, Sotheby-NY, #615, illus.), 13¾ x 14 in., (34.9 x 35.6 cm.), photograph, gelatin silver print.

$12,100* *X Portfolio: Thirteen,* (1977-1978), pub. by Henry Lunn, Robert Miller, and Robert Self, eachs., num. 5/25, #5/25, (10-13-92, Christie-NY, #567, illus.), each 7¾ x 7¾ in., (19.7 x 19.7 cm.), photograph, gelatin silver prints (BP 7047, DM 17,726, FR 60,229, Y 1,467,200).

MARATTA, Carlo Italian 1625-1713

$403* *L'Annonciation,* thin margins, before i., (05-15-93, Loudmer, #21, illus.), 8⁷⁄₁₆ x 5¹³⁄₁₆ in., (214 x 148 mm.), etching on laid (BP 262, DM 648, FR 2178, Y 44,674).

$242* *La Sainte Vierge, La Madeleine Et L'Enfant (Bartsch, vol. 21, 6),* oval, probably second state out of 4, stain verso, ink num., (05-15-93, Loudmer, #22, illus.), 6⅞ x 5¹⁄₁₆ in., (175 x 129 mm.), sh 7⅜ x 5⁹⁄₁₆ in., (175 x 129 mm.), etching on laid (BP 157, DM 389, FR 1308, Y 26,826).

MARATTI, Carlo Cavaliere (after) Italian 1625-1713

$110* *Sissera A Iaele Interemlus,* by Philipp Andreas Kilian, (12-10-92, Sloan, #2096), sight 7¾ x 5½ in., (19.7 x 14 cm.), engraving (BP 71, DM 174, FR 594, Y 13,607).

MARATTI, Ch.

$334* *Le Mariage De Sainte Catherine (Bartsch T 21, 10),* oval, staining, good margins, (06-16-93, Ader Tajan, #15), 6⅞ x 4¹⁵⁄₁₆ in., (17.5 x 12.5 cm.), etching (BP 223, DM 554, FR 1861, Y 35,623).

MARC

$239* *P.O. Midi and Cie De Navigation Mixte: Algeria Via Port Vendres. "The Shortest Sea Route", 1931,* good cond., (03-13-93, Laurin, #57), 39⅜ x 24⁷⁄₁₆ in., (100 x 62 cm.), (BP 167, DM 398, FR 1353, Y 28,167).

MARC, Franz German 1880-1916

BI *Aus Der Tierlegende (L. 831), 1912,* pub. in Genius, 1919, margins, good cond., staining, est. $5/700, (02-24-93, Butterfield, #2949), 9½ x 7¹⁄₁₆ in., (241 x 179 mm.), lithograph on wove.

BI *Ex Libris Bernhard Koehler (Postkarte An Herrn Paul Klee) (Lankheit 863), 1908,* margins, discolored, very good cond., prov., exhib., lit., est. BP 2,8/3,500, (05-20-93, Christie-London, #469, illus.), image 2 x 2 in., (5.1 x 5.1 cm.), sheet 2⅜ x 2⅜ in., (5.1 x 5.1 cm.), woodcut with handcoloring in red on fibrous Japan adhered to a postcard.

$11,500* *Geburt Der Pferde (L. 840), 1912,* s. by artist's wife, estate ink stamp, wide margins, taped to overmat, good cond., (05-11-93, Christie-NY, #210, illus.), borderline 8½ x 6 in., (216 x 152 mm.), color woodcut on tissue-thin Japan (BP 7341, DM 18,116, FR 61,040, Y 1,264,987).

$10,828* *"Geburt Der Pferde" (Lankheit 840), 1913,* s. Maria Marc, (11-28-92, Grisebach, #160, illus.), 8⁷⁄₁₆ x 5¾ in., (21.5 x 14.6 cm.), color woodcut on Japan (BP 7147, DM 17,250, FR 58,561, Y 1,347,604).

BI *Lowenjagd (Lankheit 838), 1913,* s. Maria Marc, estate stamp, wide margins, loss, rippling, very goodcond., est. BP 2,8/3,500, (05-20-93, Christie-London, #470, illus.), image 9½ x 10¾ in., (24.1 x 27.3 cm.), sheet 13¾ x 16½ in., (24.1 x 27.3 cm.), woodcut on tissue Japan w/ wirelines.

$42,525* *Pferde In Der Schwemme (Lankheit 822/2, Auflage), (19)08,* s., d., (06-08-93, Karl/Faber, #1065), approx. 13¹⁵⁄₁₆ x 11 in., (35.5 x 28 cm.), lithograph in colors w/ reworked white cover on hand-made (BP 27,955, DM 69,000, FR 232,377, Y 4,516,729).

$40,250* *Ruhende Pferde (Lankheit 825), 1911-12,* s. by artist's wife, estate ink stamp, margins, glued to overmat, tape, excell. cond., catalog cover lot, (05-11-93, Christie-NY, #209, illus.), borderline 6½ x 8⅞ in., (165 x 225 mm.), color woodcut on tissue-thin Japan (BP 25,694, DM 63,406, FR 213,641, Y 4,427,456).

$3754* *"Schopfungsgeschichte II" (Lankheit 843), 1914,* s., (11-28-92, Grisebach, #642, illus.), 9⁷⁄₁₆ x 7⅞ in., (24 x 20 cm.), colored woodcut on handmade (BP 2478, DM 5981, FR 20,303, Y 467,206).

$5827* *Tierlegende (L. 831 I), 1912,* s., num. No. 10, wide margins, foxmarks, creasing, tape, very good cond., (12-01-92, Christie-London, #420, illus.), L. 7¹³⁄₁₆ x 9½ in., (199 x 241 mm.), sheet 11¼ x 15½ in., (199 x 241 mm.), woodcut on thin Japan (BP 3850, DM 9288, FR 31,651, Y 725,473).

BI *Tierlegende (Lankheit 831 III), 1912,* block mono., from Genius, est. DM 800, (06-10-93, Hauswedell/Nolt, #594), image 7¾ x 9⁷⁄₁₆ in., (19.7 x 24 cm.), woodcut.

$724* *Tierlegende (Lankheit 831.3), 1912,* from "Genius", mono. in block; traces of mounting verso, (10-14-92, Germann, #365, illus.), 10¼ x 13⅝ in., (260 x 346 mm.), woodcut (BP 425, DM 1060, FR 3593, Y 87,736, SF 944).

BI *Versohnung (Lankheit 837), 1912,* from posthumous edit. s. by artist's widow, margins, good cond., foxmarks, paper losses, est. BP 1,5/2,000, (12-03-92, Sotheby-London, #372, illus.), 7⅞ x 10⅛ in., (200 x 257 mm.), woodcut on thin Japan.

$2326* *Versohnung (Lankheit 837), 1912,* s. Maria Marc, block mono., (05-26-93, Dorling, #2842, illus.), 7⅞ x 10³⁄₁₆ in., (20 x 25.8 cm.), woodcut on chamoisfarbenem Japan (BP 1505, DM 3795, FR 12,773, Y 252,716).

$11,825* *Wildpferdchen (Postkarte An Frau Lily Klee) (Lankheit 830), 1912,* discoloration, very good cond., prov., exhib., lit., (05-20-93, Christie-London, #468, illus.), image 2⅜ x 3⅛ in., (6 x 7.9 cm.), sheet 5½ x 3½ in., (6 x 7.9 cm.), woodcut on firm wove (BP 7590, DM 19,079, FR 64,266, Y 1,305,764).

BI *Zwei Fabeltier (Lankheit 845), 1914,* #13, wide margins, very good cond., est. BP 1,2/1,600, (05-20-93, Christie-London, #471, illus.), image 4 x 4⅞ in., (10.2 x 12.4 cm.), sheet 6 x 7⅞ in., (10.2 x 12.4 cm.), woodcut on tissue Japan w/wirelines.

BI *Zwei Fabeltiere (Lankheit 845), 1914,* stamped Bestatigung von Maria Marc, creased margin, est. DM 4500, (12-01-92, Karl/Faber, #964, illus.), 3¹⁵⁄₁₆ x 4¾ in., (10 x 12 cm.), woodcut on Japan.

MARC-LUC

$660* *Prochainement Ouverture, 1925,* Daude Freres, B cond., fold marks, cracking, surface soiling, discoloration, (08-06-92, Swann, #194, illus.), 63½ x 47½ in., (161.3 x 120.7 cm.), (BP 345, DM 975, FR 3293, Y 84,184).

MARCEAU, Marcel b. 1923

BI *"Le Troisieme Oeil",* #219/250, s., est. SF 5/600, (04-21-93, Germann, #609, illus.), 21⁷⁄₁₆ x 30¹⁄₁₆ in., (545 x 763 mm.), color lithograph.

MARCHAND, Andre

BI *Tete De Femme, 1945,* s., d., 12/28, creases, small tear, est. FF6/800, (06-28-93, Loudmer, #92), 3⅛ x 6¹¹⁄₁₆ in., (80 x 170 mm.), sh 9¹³⁄₁₆ x 11¹⁵⁄₁₆ in., (80 x 170 mm.), black lithograph on wove.

MARCHANT, L.

$40* *"Pears In Bowl",* s., t., #24/50, excell. cond., (05-15-93, Cleveland, #481), 14 x 15½ in., (35.6 x 39.4 cm.), mezzotint (BP 26, DM 64, FR 216, Y 4434).

$40* *Still Life And Bottle,* s., t., #44/50, excell. cond., (05-15-93, Cleveland, #480), 13¾ x 15⅝ in., (34.9 x 39.7 cm.), mezzotint (BP 26, DM 64, FR 216, Y 4434).

MARCKS, Gerhard German 1889-1981

$664* *Absage (Lammek H. 125), 1926,* s., (12-05-92, Bassenge, #7454), 10⁵⁄₁₆ x 8½ in., (26.2 x 21.6 cm.), woodcut on handmade Japan (BP 416, DM 1035, FR 3528, Y 82,270).

$503* *Adam Und Eva (Lammek H 341), 1960,* #38/50, s. G. Marcks, (09-14-92, Venator/Hansten, #2469), image 12⅝ x 9⁵⁄₁₆ in., (32.1 x 23.7 cm.), woodcut on Japan (BP 266, DM 748, FR 2534, Y 62,547).

$581* *"Almtanz" (Lammek H 118), 1926,* s., d., t., foxed, (12-01-92, Karl/Faber, #965), 11¼ x 15³⁄₁₆ in., (28.5 x 38.5 cm.), woodcut on hand-made Japan (BP 384, DM 926, FR 3156, Y 72,336).

$185* *Ariadne (Lammek H. 383), 1963,* s., num., (12-05-92, Bassenge, #7459), 12⅜ x 8¹⁄₁₆ in., (31.5 x 20.5 cm.), woodcut (BP 116, DM 288, FR 983, Y 22,922).

$369* *Fortuna I (Lammek H 239), 1954,* s., num., (12-05-92, Bassenge, #7455), 12⁷⁄₁₆ x 7¹⁵⁄₁₆ in., (31.6 x 20.3 cm.), woodcut on handmade Japan (BP 231, DM 575, FR 1961, Y 45,719).

$295* *Fortuna III (Lammek H 241), 1954,* s., num., (12-05-92, Bassenge, #7456), 12½ x 8¾ in., (31.8 x 22.2 cm.), woodcut on handmade Japan (BP 185, DM 460, FR 1567, Y 36,551).

BI *Frauenkopf (Lammek H 132), 1935,* s., #14/70, est. DM 900, (05-26-93, Lempertz, #326), 10¹¹⁄₁₆ x 8¹¹⁄₁₆ in., (27.2 x 22 cm.), woodcut on Japan.

BI *Ganse II (Lammek H 14), 1921,* est. DM 1,800, (12-05-92, Bassenge, #7452), 9¹³⁄₁₆ x 12⁷⁄₁₆ in., (25 x 31.6 cm.), woodcut on Japan.

$433* *"Ganse" (Lammek H 108), 1923,* s., d., t., (11-28-92, Grisebach, #643, illus.), 7¹⁵⁄₁₆ x 5¹³⁄₁₆ in., (20.1 x 14.8 cm.), woodcut on Japan (BP 286, DM 690, FR 2342, Y 53,889).

$332* *Hiob (Lammek H 375), 1963,* s., num., (12-05-92, Bassenge, #7458), 7³⁄₁₆ x 7¹⁵⁄₁₆ in., (18.2 x 20.1 cm.), woodcut on Japan (BP 208, DM 518, FR 1764, Y 41,135).

$465* *Im Kuhstall (Lammek H 5, I), 1920,* foxing, (09-25-92, Granier, #2933), sheet 7⅜ x 9⁵⁄₁₆ in., (18.7 x 23.6 cm.), woodcut on Japan (BP 272, DM 689, FR 2331, Y 56,126).

$325* *"Die Katze Von Aegina" (Lammek L 202), 1979,* num., (11-28-92, Grisebach, #644, illus.), lithograph on handmade (BP 215, DM 518, FR 1758, Y 40,448).

$529* *Die Katze Von Aigina (Lammek L 202; Hanstein 114), 1979,* s., num., watermark, (05-26-93, Dorling, #2849, illus.), 10⁵⁄₁₆ x 8⅛ in., (26.2 x 20.7 cm.), lithograph on wove (BP 342, DM 863, FR 2905, Y 57,475).

$125* *Noah Und Die Taube, 1948,* s., (12-01-92, Karl/Faber, #966), 7⅞ x 7⅞ in., (20 x 20 cm.), offset print on thick wove (BP 83, DM 199, FR 679, Y 15,563).

$2966* *Ovid. Orpheus (Lammek H 180), 1947: Ten,* s., d., Hauswedell & Co., (06-10-93, Hauswedell/Nolt, #595), portfolio 19⅜ x 16⅛ in., (49.2 x 41 cm.), woodcut (BP 1940, DM 4830, FR 16,261, Y 314,829).

$426* *Parisurteil I (Lammek H 325), 1959,* artist's proof, s. G Marcks, d. 15 Juli 1959, (09-14-92, Venator/Hansten, #2468, illus.), image 11⁹⁄₁₆ x 12³⁄₁₆ in., (29.3 x 31 cm.), woodcut on Japan (BP 225, DM 633, FR 2146, Y 52,972).

$275* *The Quartet,* s., d. '47, (11-12-92, Freemn/Fine Art, #138), image 6½ x 9½ in., (16.5 x 24.1 cm.), woodcut (BP 181, DM 436, FR 1470, Y 34,098).

$390* *Der Reiter,* s., light-staining, (06-08-93, Karl/Faber, #1083), approx. 8⅞ x 9¹³⁄₁₆ in., (22.5 x 25 cm.), woodcut on wove (BP 256, DM 633, FR 2131, Y 41,423).

BI *Reiter Bei Den Hirten (Lammek H 114), 1923,* s., t., est. DM 2,400, (12-05-92, Bassenge, #7453), 11¼ x 7⅞ in., (28.5 x 20 cm.), woodcut on imitation Japan.

$295* *Schnitter Tod (Lammek H. 352), 1961,* s., num., (12-05-92, Bassenge, #7457), 10¹⁄₁₆ x 6⅞ in., (25.5 x 17.5 cm.), woodcut (BP 185, DM 460, FR 1567, Y 36,551).

BI *Seated Figure,* s., #49/90, full margins, good cond.?, est. 4/600, (10-28-92, Butterfield, #2837), 10 x 7 in., (254 x 178 mm.), lithograph on wove.

$295* *Selbstbildnis II (Lammek L 85 I), 1973,* s., num., (12-05-92, Bassenge, #7460), 7¹⁄₁₆ x 7⁵⁄₁₆ in., (18 x 18.5 cm.), lithograph (BP 185, DM 460, FR 1567, Y 36,551).

$117* *Titelblatt Der Mappe "Orpheus" (Lammek H 180.2, 180.3), 1947,* s., foxing, (09-25-92, Granier, #2934), sheet 18⁵⁄₁₆ x 14⅞ in., (46.5 x 37.8 cm.), woodcut on handmade (BP 68, DM 173, FR 586, Y 14,122).

$438* *Zwei Pfluger, c. 1952/53,* (06-10-93, Hauswedell/Nolt, #596, illus.), image 6⁵⁄₁₆ x 14⁹⁄₁₆ in., (16 x 37 cm.), woodcut on wove (BP 286, DM 713, FR 2401, Y 46,492).

MARCOUSSIS, Louis French 1883-1941

$674* *"La Chanson Du Mal Aime" (G 118), 1934,* 5th from Alcool, s., (10-18-92, Pescheteau, #205), 17¹¹⁄₁₆ x 12⅜ in., (45 x 31.5 cm.), etching on Rives (BP 408, DM 996, FR 3382, Y 80,478).

$5651* *Le Comptoir (Milet 35/IV), 1920,* s., Die Schaffenden, III, Jahrgang, Heft 4, (06-23-93, Kornfeld, #549), Steich- und Flachenatzung on simili Japan, reworked w/drypoint (BP 3839, DM 9562, FR 32,163, Y 615,644, SF 8510).

$2213* *Komposition,* s., epreuve d'artiste, (12-05-92, Bassenge, #7462, illus.), 7¹³⁄₁₆ x 9⁷⁄₁₆ in., (19.9 x 24 cm.), etching on gewaltztem China (BP 1386, DM 3450, FR 11,759, Y 274,192).

BI   *Planches De Salut (Milet 66-78; Lafranchis G 67-77; Rauch 167; Boston186), 1931:* Ten, plate mono., #3/10, est. DM 60,000, (06-10-93, Hauswedell/Nolt, #603, illus.), image 7¹⁵⁄₁₆ x 9⁷⁄₁₆ in., (20.2 x 24 cm.), etching.

$273* *"Portrait De Rimbaud" (SM 184)*, #33/80, studio stamp, (01-28-93, Pescheteau, #202), 14⁹⁄₁₆ x 11 in., (37 x 28 cm.), drypoint and copper engraving on Rives (BP 180, DM 433, FR 1464, Y 33,896).

BI   *Serge Lifar (L. 106; Milet 97), 1933,* 12th state of 13, s., #27/50, light-staining, surface dirt, tape andsurface dirt, very good cond., est. BP 5/600, (12-01-92, Christie-London, #419), sheet 16⅞ x 9¼ in., (428 x 235 mm.), etching w/engraving in brown on Chine bistre applique sur Arches.

$5225* *La Table (Lafranchis 62; Milet 52), 1930,* s., #67/120, large margins, good cond., foxing, mat stain, (11-05-92, Sotheby-NY, #232, illus.), 9⅝ x 7 in., (243 x 178 mm.), sheet 19⅝ x 13¼ in., (243 x 178 mm.), etching and engraving p. in colors on cream wove (BP 3398, DM 8263, FR 27,956, Y 641,026).

$943* *"Zone - 1934" (G 115),* 2nd from "Alcool", artist's proof, #2/10, s., (10-18-92, Pescheteau, #204), 17¹¹⁄₁₆ x 12⅜ in., (45 x 31.5 cm.), etching on Rives (BP 571, DM 1393, FR 4732, Y 112,597).

MARDEN, Brice   American b. 1938

BI   *1, 2, 3, 4 (L. 38), 1983:* Four, s., t., d., i. pp, #2/2, co-pub. by artist and Simca Print Artists, blindstamp, excell. cond., est. $6/7,000, (05-11-93, Christie-NY, #501, illus.), each sheet 38¼ x 29 in., (972 x 737 mm.), screenprint in grey and black on Mino Kozo Kizuki hand-made.

$2300* *1, 2, 3, 4 (L. 38), 1983:* Four, complete portfolio, each s., d., t. 1-4, #22/32, co-pub. by artist and Simca Print Artists, blindstamp, good cond., (05-15-93, Sotheby-NY, #1095, illus.), each sheet 38¼ x 29 in., (97.2 x 73.7 cm.), silkscreen in tones of black and gray on Japanese handmade Mino KozoKizuki paper (BP 1495, DM 3700, FR 12,432, Y 254,961).

$6900* *12 Views For Caroline Tatyana (L. 29), 1989,* complete suite, s., #7/50, pub. Parasol Press, Ltd., full margins, good cond., original cardboard box, (05-15-93, Sotheby-NY, #1093, illus.), each sheet 26½ x 20½ in., (67.3 x 52.1 cm.), 12 etchings on handmade wove (BP 4486, DM 11,099, FR 37,297, Y 764,882).

BI   *12 Views For Caroline Tatyana (T. G. 29), 1989,* complete suite, s., #7/50, pub. Parasol Press, full margins, good cond., est. $12/15,000, (11-07-92, Sotheby-NY, #680, illus.), each sheet approx. 26½ x 20½ in., (673 x 521 mm.), twelve etchings on handmade wove.

BI   *Five Threes: (Untitled), 1976-1977,* s., d., #19/25, pub. Parasol Press, margins, very good cond.?, est. $8/1,000, (05-19-93, Butterfield, #2260), 20⅞ x 29¾ in., (530 x 756 mm.), etching in black on Stonehenge.

BI   *Focus I-V (L. 32), 1979,* complete, original portfolio, s., d., #39/75, pub. Brooke Alexander,Inc., full margins, good cond., est. $5,5/6,500, (02-11-93, Sotheby-NY, #386, illus.), each sheet approx. 15⅜ x 11 in., (390 x 280 mm.), 5 etchings w/aquatint in colors on handmade Twinrocker paper.

$6600* *Focus I-V, (L. 32), 1979:* Set Of Five, Brooke Alexander Editions, s., d., i. I-V, #61/75, blindstamps, fullmargins, excellent cond., (11-09-92, Christie-NY, #359, illus.), 15½ x 11 in., (394 x 279 mm.), etching and aquatint in greens on Twinrocker handmade (BP 4364, DM 10,536, FR 35,599, Y 819,062).

$3057* *Focus I-V, 1979:* Set of Five, each s., d., #9/75, pub. Brooke Alexander, full sheets, good cond., (10-15-92, Sotheby-London, #112, illus.), each approx. 4 x 4 in., (10.2 x 10.2 cm.), etching w/aquatint p. in colors on handmade Twinrocker (BP 1870, DM 4550, FR 15,432, Y 366,767).

$6900* *Focus I-V, New York, Brooke Alexander Editions, 1979 (L. 32):* Five, s., d., i. 'I'-'V', #73/75, Aeropress blindstamps, full margins, excell. cond., orig. just., (05-11-93, Christie-NY, #500, illus.), each sheet 15½ x 11 in., (394 x 279 mm.), etching and aquatint in greens on Twinrocker hand-made (BP 4405, DM 10,870, FR 36,624, Y 758,992).

$1495* *Gulf (Lewison 16), 1969,* s., d., #45/100, blindstamp, p. Chiron Press, blindstamp, pub. Tanglewood Editions, from portfolio, New York Ten, full margins, good cond., handling creases, (05-15-93, Sotheby-NY, #1091, illus.), 13½ x 20 in., (34.3 x 50.8 cm.), lithograph in gray and black (BP 972, DM 2405, FR 8081, Y 165,724).

$1100* *Gulf (Tate Gallery 16), 1969,* s., d., #89/100, blindstamp, Chiron Press, pub. Tanglewood Editions,from New York Ten portfolio, full margins, good cond., creases, scuff marks, (11-07-92, Sotheby-NY, #677, illus.), 13½ x 20 in., (343 x 508 mm.), lithograph p. in gray and black (BP 719, DM 1756, FR 5936, Y 135,769).

$2337* *"Painting Study I" and "Painting Study II", 1974:* Two, each s., d., #8/50, Styria Studios blindstamp, full margins, good cond., handling marks, (10-15-92, Sotheby-London, #114, illus.), each approx. 9⅝ x 6⅝ in., (24.4 x 16.8 cm.), silkscreen w/wax and graphite on wove (BP 1430, DM 3479, FR 11,797, Y 280,384).

BI   *The Skowhegan Print (L. 34), 1979,* s., d., #27/40, blindstamp of pub., Aeropress, released by SkowheganSchool, full margins, good cond., est. $2/3,000, (02-11-93, Sotheby-NY, #387, illus.), 5¹³⁄₁₆ x 4⅞ in., (148 x 124 mm.), etching and aquatint on BFK Rives.

$2200* *The Skowhegan Print (L. 34), 1979,* s., d., #9/40, pub. Skowhegan School of Painting and Sculpture, fullmargins, excellent cond., (11-09-92, Christie-NY, #360), 18 x 13⅞ in., (457 x 352 mm.), etching and aquatint on wove (BP 1455, DM 3512, FR 11,866, Y 273,021).

BI   *The Skowhegan Print (L. 34), 1979,* s., d., #27/40, blindstamp, pub. Aeropress, full margins, est. #1,5/2,000, (05-15-93, Sotheby-NY, #1094), 5⅞ x 4⅞ in., (14.9 x 12.4 cm.), etching and aquatint on BFK Rives.

BI   *The Skowhegan Print (T. G. 34), 1979,* s., d., #27/40, blindstamp, pub. Aeropress, full margins, good cond.,est. $2,5/3,000, (11-07-92, Sotheby-NY, #681, illus.), 5⅞ x 4⅞ in., (149 x 124 mm.), etching and aquatint on BFK Rives.

$2200* *Ten Days (T. G. 20 e), 1972,* s., d. '71, i. 'A.P.', pub. Parasol Press, full margins, good cond.,creases, (11-07-92, Sotheby-NY, #679), 12 x 15⅛ in., (305 x 384 mm.), etching and aquatint (BP 1438, DM 3513, FR 11,873, Y 271,538).

$1348* *The Ten Days Portfolio: Untitled, 1971,* s., d., #16/30, pub. Parasol Press, w/blindstamp Patricia Branstead,full margins, good cond., slight discoloration, slight soiling, (10-15-92, Sotheby-London, #110, illus.), 14½ x 23⅝ in., (36.8 x 60 cm.), etching on wove (BP 825, DM 2007, FR 6805, Y 161,728).

$1528* *Ten Days Portfolio: Untitled, 1971,* s., d., #16/30, pub. Parasol Press, blindstamp Patricia Branstead, full margins, good cond., slight discoloration, slight soiling, (10-15-92, Sotheby-London, #115, illus.), 14½ x 23⅝ in., (36.8 x 60 cm.), etching on wove (BP 935, DM 2274, FR 7713, Y 183,323).

$2860* *Tile I (L. 30), 1979,* s., d., i. AP, num. 5/10, pub. Crown Point Press, full margins, creases, pale time-staining, good cond., (09-19-92, Christie-E, #155, illus.), sheet 29¾ x 22¼ in., (756 x 565 mm.), aquatint on wove (BP 1645, DM 4283, FR 14,667, Y 356,342).

BI   *Tiles (Lewison 31), 1979,* complete, original portfolio, s., d., #17/50, pub. Parasol Press, Ltd., full margins, good cond., est. $7/9,000, (02-11-93, Sotheby-NY, #385, illus.), each sheet approx. 29⁹⁄₁₆ x 22⁹⁄₁₆ in., (751 x 573 mm.), 4 etchings w/aquatint on Somerset satin paper.

$8250* *Tiles (Lewison 31), 1979:* Set Of Four, Parasol Press, Ltd., s., d., num., copy 42 of 50, p. Crown Point Press, blindstamps, full margins, excellent cond., (11-09-92, Christie-NY, #358, illus.), 29½ x 22½ in., (749 x 572 mm.), etching and aquatint on Somerset Satin (BP 5455, DM 13,170, FR 44,498, Y 1,023,827).

$6325* *Tiles, New York, Parasol Press, Ltd., 1971 (L. 31):* Four, s., d., num. copy 25 of 50, full margins, excell. cond., orig. portfolio, (05-11-93, Christie-NY, #499, illus.), each sheet 29½ x 22½ in., (749 x 572 mm.), etching and aquatint and just. on Somerset (BP 4038, DM 9964, FR 33,572, Y 695,743).

$1840* *Untitled (L. 19), 1971,* s., d., i. AP, pub. Parasol Press, Ltd., full margins, good cond., skinned spot, (05-15-93, Sotheby-NY, #1092, illus.), 14¾ x 23⅜ in., (37.5 x

59.4 cm.), etching (BP 1196, DM 2960, FR 9946, Y 203,969).

$990* *Untitled (Lewison 19), 1971,* s., d., num. 1/50, pub. Parasol Press, full margins, very good cond.?, (09-19-92, Christie-E, #154), sheet 23 x 29 in., (584 x 737 mm.), etching on wove (BP 569, DM 1482, FR 5077, Y 123,349).

$1760* *Untitled (T. G. 19), 1971,* s., d., i. 'AP', proof, pub. Parasol Press, full margins, good cond., (11-07-92, Sotheby-NY, #678, illus.), 14⅝ x 23⅜ in., (371 x 594 mm.), etching (BP 1151, DM 2810, FR 9498, Y 217,230).

$1438* *Untitled 1971, 1971,* s., d., #9/30, margins, good cond., (10-15-92, Sotheby-London, #113, illus.), sheet approx. 29½ x 21⅞ in., (74.9 x 55.6 cm.), etching w/aquatint on wove (BP 880, DM 2141, FR 7259, Y 172,525).

BI *Untitled Press Series #1-6 (Lewison 21), 1972: Six,* s., d., num. 40/42, 41/48, 40/40, 33/46, 40/44 and 40/46, pub. Untitled Press, blindstamps, full margins, #1 stain, paper flaw, time staining, excell. cond., p. and pub. Untitled Press, est. $28/32,000, (05-11-93, Christie-NY, #497, illus.), each sheet 26¼ x 19¼ in., (667 x 489 mm.), lithographs, 1 w/screenprint in colors, on wove.

$14,437* *Untitled Press Series (Lewison 21), 1972: Six,* s., d., num., blindstamp United Press Inc., (11-28-92, Schoppmann, #655, illus.), 19⁵⁄₁₆ x 25¹⁵⁄₁₆ in., (49 x 66 cm.), color lithograph on Italia paper (BP 9529, DM 23,000, FR 78,080, Y 1,796,764).

BI *"Untitled" and "Untitled" (L. 22d-e), 1973: Two,* from Adriatics, s., d., #20/40, pub. Parasol Press, full margins, stain, excell. cond., est. $2,5/3,500, (05-11-93, Christie-NY, #498), each sheet 34 x 24 in., (864 x 610 mm.), etching on wove.

$1438* *Untitled, 1971,* s., d., #31/31, full margins, good cond., (10-15-92, Sotheby-London, #111, illus.), 14½ x 23⅝ in., (36.8 x 60 cm.), etching on wove (BP 880, DM 2141, FR 7259, Y 172,525).

$1265* *Untitled, 1979,* s., d., #35/40, blindstamp publisher, Aeropress, for The Skowhegan School, full margins, good cond., surface soiling, (05-19-93, Butterfield, #2261), 5⅞ x 4¹⁵⁄₁₆ in., (149 x 125 mm.), etching and aquatint on wove (BP 821, DM 2056, FR 6928, Y 140,042).

MARDEN, Luis
BI *Astronaut L. Gordon Cooper, 1963,* s., est. $1/1,500, (10-14-92, Swann, #332, illus.), 12½ x 19 in., (31.8 x 48.3 cm.), photograph, dye-transfer print.

BI *The Bounty, 1962,* s. in ink, stamp, est. $1/1,500, (10-13-92, Christie-NY, #574, illus.), 12 x 18⅝ in., (30.5 x 47.3 cm.), photograph, dye transfer print.

BI *Rocket In Flight, c. 1963,* credit, (c), s., handstamp, est. $1/1,500, (10-14-92, Swann, #333, illus.), 12¾ x 19 in., (32.4 x 48.3 cm.), photograph, dye-transfer print.

MARDER, David American 20th cent.
BI *Checkers,* s., num. 1/5, est. $175/225, (11-12-92, Freemn/ Fine Art, #138A), 15 x 20 in., (38.1 x 50.8 cm.), woodcut.

MARE, Pieter de (after) 1757-1796
$78* *Weinendes Kind,* by Christiana Chalon, (03-24-93, Venator/Hansten, #2543), pl. 4¼ x 3¹¹⁄₁₆ in., (10.8 x 9.4 cm.), engraving and etching (BP 53, DM 127, FR 434, Y 9165).

MARECHAL, Francois
BI *Les Boulevards, Soir, 1892,* s., annot., dust, mat traces verso, (02-24-93, Picard, #161), etching on ivory laid.

BI *"La Neige (St-Laurent et St-Gilles), 4 Mars 1895" and "Sous La Neige(Banlieue De Liege), 5 Mars 1895": Two,* s., annot., dust, glue traces, old mat verso, (02-24-93, Picard, #163), etching on laid.

MARESTE, Geo.
$955* *Portraits La Carte,* p. Affiches Pichot, backed on linen, (05-07-93, Christie-S. Ken, #114, illus.), 46 x 32 in., (116.8 x 81.3 cm.), color lithograph (BP 605, DM 1510, FR 5088, Y 105,153).

MARFURT, Leo 1894-1977
BI *Bruxelles Exposition Universelle 1935,* excell. cond., est. BP 1/200, (02-04-93, Christie-S. Ken, #129), 39 x 24½ in., (99.1 x 62.2 cm.), color lithograph backed on linen.

MARGO, Boris
BI *From "Meteorites", 1952,* full margins, num., s., pub. International Graphic Art Society (IGAS), est. $4/600, (05-27-93, Swann, #175), 11⅝ x 2⁷⁄₁₆ in., (29.5 x 6.2 cm.), color cellocut.

MARGOLIES, Samuel American b. 1897
BI *"Still As Night" and "Winter Solitude": Two,* pub. AAA, s., excell. cond., est. $2/300, (05-15-93, Cleveland, #235, illus.), one 8¾ x 11½ in., (22.2 x 29.2 cm.), other 8¼ x 11⅜ in., (22.2 x 29.2 cm.), aquatint.

BI *"White Fantasy" and "Slumbering Meadows": Two,* pub. AAA, s., good cond., toning, est. $2/300, (05-15-93, Cleveland, #236), one 11⅝ x 8⅞ in., (29.5 x 22.5 cm.), other 11¾ x 9⅞ in., (29.5 x 22.5 cm.), aquatint.

BI *Winter Wonderland,* s. S.L. Margolies, est. $3/500, (12-12-92, Wolf, #15), 8¾ x 11¼ in., (22.2 x 28.6 cm.), etching.

MARGULIES, Joseph Austrian/American 1896-1984
$22* *Rabbi Reading,* s., (06-11-93, DuMouchelle, #2518), 10½ x 7¾ in., (26.7 x 19.7 cm.), etching (BP 14, DM 36, FR 121, Y 2334).

$220* *Rabbinic Scenes: "Contemplation", "Reminiscences", "Scribes", "Meditations" and "Chasid": Five,* pub. AAA, s., num., very good cond., (09-11-92, Skinner, #38K, illus.), 12⅞ x 8⅞ in., (32.7 x 22.5 cm.), etchings (two w/aquatints w/sugar lift) on wove (BP 114, DM 317, FR 1076, Y 27,258).

$55* *"The Scholar",* pub. AAA, s., good cond., (05-15-93, Cleveland, #237), 10⅛ x 7¹³⁄₁₆ in., (25.7 x 19.8 cm.), etching w/aquatint (BP 36, DM 88, FR 297, Y 6097).

MARIANI, Carlos Maria
$449* *"Elaidi I" and "Castore", 1982: Two,* s., t., d., #79/90, #44/99, full margins, tape remains, hinges, (10-15-92, Sotheby-London, #116, illus.), one 24 x 35½ in., (61 x 90.2 cm.), other 24 x 17⅛ in., (61 x 90.2 cm.), lithograph on wove (BP 275, DM 668, FR 2267, Y 53,869).

MARIANI, Pompeo
$302* *(Sewing),* s., appears excellent cond., (06-11-93, Doyle, #59), 13¼ x 9¼ in., (337 x 235 mm.), monotype (BP 198, DM 491, FR 1655, Y 32,042).

MARIANI, Pompeo 1857-1927
$696* *Panfili Al Tramonto,* s., (12-15-92, Finarte-Milan, #99), 12³⁄₁₆ x 8⅞ in., (31 x 22.5 cm.), monotype in colors w/ pastel (BP 444, DM 1091, FR 3728, Y 86,320, L 978).

MARICHAL, Francisco
$99* *"Manos Quemadas",* s., t., d. 1974, artist's proof, X/X, (02-03-93, Duran, #220), 19¹¹⁄₁₆ x 16¾ in., (50 x 42.5 cm.), xylograph (BP 69, DM 163, FR 553, Y 12,315, P 11,500).

MARIE, G.
$155* *Olympia La Gran Via, c. 1900,* (01-31-93, Morelle/ Marchan, #202), 35⁷⁄₁₆ x 49⅝ in., (90 x 126 cm.), poster (BP 104, DM 250, FR 844, Y 19,336).

MARIE, G. ac. 1890s
BI *Edmond Sagot/ Affiches. Estampes. Dessins. Originaux, 1897,* rare, lit., est. DM 2,500, (12-05-92, Bassenge, #7609, illus.), 35¾ x 25⁹⁄₁₆ in., (90.8 x 65 cm.), color lithograph.

$1549* *F. Meyer Van Loo, 1897-98,* very rare, foxing, (12-05-92, Bassenge, #7610, illus.), 28¼ x 20¾ in., (71.8 x 52.7 cm.), color lithograph w/Golddruck (BP 970, DM 2415, FR 8231, Y 191,922).

MARIE, Gustave
$964* *Theatre De L'Athenee (...) Madame Flirt, c. 1905,* Paris, Atelier G. Marie, cond. B+, (06-11-93, Boisgirard, #113, illus.), 58⁷⁄₁₆ x 42¹⁵⁄₁₆ in., (148.5 x 109 cm.), poster (BP 633, DM 1567, FR 5282, Y 102,281).

MARIESCHI, Michele Italian 1696-1743
BI *Il Canal Grande Con Il Fondaco Dei Tedeschi (Mauroner 15; Succi 20),c. 1761,* from Magnificentiores Selectioresque Urbis Venetiarum, 1st state of 4, watermark, margins, crease, discoloration, tear, good cond., est. $2/3,000, (05-13-93, Sotheby-NY, #331, illus.), 12½ x 18½ in., (318 x 470 mm.), etching.

$8236* *"Veduta Di Venezia Con La Dedica", "Campo S. Maria Formosa", "L'Arsenale", "S. Giorgio Maggiore", "Piazza S. Marco Verso La Basilica", "La PiazzettaDi S. Basso" and "Ponte Di Rialto Da Sud" (Mauroner 2-5, 9, 14, 18): Seven*, 7 from the set of 23, 3rd state of 4, trimmed irregularly, wormhole,paper loss, corner, repaired, stains, (06-30-93, Sotheby-London, #161), 12⅜ x 18½ in., (314 x 470 mm.), etching on paper w/a Three Crescents and Armorial watermark (BP 5520, DM 14,047, FR 47,388, Y 882,460).

MARIESCHI, Michele (after)
$160* *A View From The Bridge Realto*, by J. Bowles, trimmed, scratched, defects, (01-21-93, Bonhams-Chelsea, #3), image 10⅞ x 14¾ in., (27.6 x 37.5 cm.), engraving w/ hand coloring (BP 105, DM 254, FR 861, Y 20,025).

MARIN, John   American 1870-1953
$4070* *Brooklyn Bridge, 1924*, s., crease, folds, pub. New Republic, (11-12-92, Freemn/Fine Art, #140), plate 10¾ x 8¾ in., (27.3 x 22.2 cm.), etching on wove paper (BP 2673, DM 6449, FR 21,753, Y 504,650).
$880* *Downtown New York, The El, 1921*, s., i. 1-30, laid down and sandwiched between mats, (05-27-93, Swann, #176, illus.), 6¹⁵⁄₁₆ x 8¹⁵⁄₁₆ in., (17.6 x 22.7 cm.), etching (BP 564, DM 1412, FR 4759, Y 94,340).
$853* *Downtown, NY, The El (Zegrosser 134), 1921*, from the New Republic portfolio, s., (06-11-93, Freemn/Fine Art, #137, illus.), 6⅞ x 8¾ in., (17.5 x 22.2 cm.), etching (BP 560, DM 1386, FR 4674, Y 90,504).
$385* *Place St. Jacques*, s., #20/30, light stain, small margins, laid down on cardboard, prov., (06-11-93, Doyle, #60), 5⅛ x 7 in., (130 x 178 mm.), etching (BP 253, DM 626, FR 2110, Y 40,849).
$330* *"Sail Boat", 1932*, pub. American Artists Group, s. d. Marin 32 in plate, t. AAA label, good cond., light toning in image, mount staining verso, (09-11-92, Skinner, #63), 7 x 9⅜ in., (17.8 x 23.8 cm.), etching on wove (BP 171, DM 475, FR 1614, Y 40,887).
$550* *"Sailboat" (Zigrosser 155)*, pub. AAG, light stain, paper hinge, fine cond., (10-31-92, Cleveland, #182, illus.), 7 x 9¼ in., (17.8 x 23.5 cm.), etching (BP 352, DM 846, FR 2871, Y 68,128).

MARINI, Marino   Italian 1901-1980
$1364* *Marino Marini Opera Grafica: "Gioco Felice" and "Tamburlano" (G. A93and 97), 1969*, s., #59/60 and 45/60, blindstamp, margins, good cond., (12-03-92, Sotheby-London, #375, illus.), sheets 27½ x 19½ in., (700 x 495 mm.), etching and an aquatint on Arches (BP 880, DM 2145, FR 7322, Y 169,715).
$1540* *2 Acrobats*, full margins, num., s., (05-27-93, Swann, #177, illus.), 19 x 13 in., (48.3 x 33 cm.), color aquatint (BP 986, DM 2471, FR 8329, Y 165,094).
BI *Abstract*, s., #XVIII/XL, est. $125/175, (06-11-93, Freemn/Fine Art, #138), 10 x 7¼ in., (25.4 x 18.4 cm.), etching and aquatint.
$638* *Acrobata (G.A 201), 1977*, ea, stamped sig., Edition Graphis Arte, (06-08-93, Karl/Faber, #1087), approx. 19½ x 14⅜ in., (49.5 x 36.5 cm.), color etching and aquatint on BFK Rives wove (BP 419, DM 1035, FR 3486, Y 67,764).
$566* *Adam Und Eva*, plate, mono., s., #XXIX/LXX, crease, (09-18-92, Schloss Ahlden, #1025), 26³⁄₁₆ x 18¾ in., (66.5 x 47.7 cm.), etching on Japan (BP 331, DM 840, FR 2873, Y 69,954).
BI *Animal Fantastique*, hors commerce, s., full margins, est. FF 5/6,000, (11-16-92, Briest, #328), 21⁷⁄₁₆ x 15⁵⁄₁₆ in., (54.5 x 38.5 cm.), etching and aquatint in colors.
$2885* *Apparizione*, #47/90, s., (11-21-92, Lempertz, #278), 15¹³⁄₁₆ x 11¹³⁄₁₆ in., (40.2 x 30 cm.), color etching on China (BP 1900, DM 4600, FR 15,494, Y 358,786).
BI *Aquarius (Guastalla L 130), 1978*, #61/100, mono., est. SF 1,8/2,200, (11-13-92, Koller, #5371), 20⅞ x 16⅝ in., (53 x 42.3 cm.), lithograph on Arches wove.
$1106* *Bagnanti, Badende (Guastalla 69), 1950*, #21/65, s., (09-04-92, Germann, #458), 20⅞ x 16¾ in., (530 x 425 mm.), etching (BP 554, DM 1550, FR 5277, Y 136,140, SF 1380).
$2387* *Ballerino (G. A177), 1974*, s., #28/75, pub. Albra, margins, good cond., (12-03-92, Sotheby-London, #378,

illus.), 26½ x 18⅞ in., (648 x 480 mm.), etching and aquatint in colors on wove (BP 1540, DM 3754, FR 12,813, Y 297,001).
$3812* *Ballerino (Guastalla A177), 1974*, s., num. 18/75, blindstamp, pub. Albra Turin, full margins, good cond., creases, (10-14-92, Sotheby-Japan, #51, illus.), 25¼ x 18¾ in., (641 x 476 mm.), etching and aquatint in colors (BP 2237, DM 5579, FR 18,918, Y 461,949).
$1705* *Bizarria (Exzentrizitat) (Guastalla 326), 1975*, s., num., blindstamp, (09-19-92, Wachholtz, #367), 14³⁄₁₆ x 19⁷⁄₁₆ in., (36 x 49.3 cm.), color etching on handmade (BP 998, DM 2530, FR 8655, Y 210,728).
BI *Bizzarria (Guastalla 326), 1975*, 80/175, s., pub. Trans World Art Corp., est. SF 1,5/2,000, (10-14-92, Germann, #366, illus.), 19¾ x 25⁹⁄₁₆ in., (502 x 650 mm.), color etching.
$2678* *Bunter Reiter I (Bruckmann L 122; Guastalla 332), 1976*, s., #XL, (05-26-93, Lempertz, #334, illus.), 37 x 26¾ in., (94 x 68 cm.), color lithograph on Arches wove (BP 1732, DM 4369, FR 14,706, Y 290,960).
$1417* *Bunter Reiter II (G.L 123), 1976*, s., num., (06-08-93, Karl/Faber, #1088, illus.), approx. 31½ x 22¹³⁄₁₆ in., (80 x 58 cm.), color lithograph on Arches wove (BP 932, DM 2299, FR 7743, Y 150,505).
BI *Bunter Reiter II (Guastalla 333), 1976*, s., #II/L, est. DM 4,000, (05-26-93, Lempertz, #336, illus.), 37 x 26¹¹⁄₁₆ in., (94 x 67.8 cm.), color lithograph on Arches wove.
BI *La Caduta (Guastalla A70), 1962*, s., i. e.a., pub. Propylaen, p. by Fetthauer & Loeding, full margins,good cond., est. BP 6/800, (06-30-93, Sotheby-London, #491), 16⅜ x 12¼ in., (416 x 311 mm.), etching on BFK Rives.
$940* *La Caduta Dell'Angelo (Toninelli, A 138; Guastalla, A 140), 1972*, #71/75, s., (05-20-93, Finarte-Milan, #102), 12¹⁵⁄₁₆ x 15⁹⁄₁₆ in., (33 x 39.5 cm.), etching, drypoint and aquatint in colors (BP 603, DM 1517, FR 5109, Y 103,799, L 1380).
$3220* *Cavalier Rouge (Guastalla 46), 1953*, s., #31/65, full margins, creases, foxmark, very good cond., (05-11-93, Christie-NY, #211, illus.), borderline 25¼ x 20 in., (641 x 508 mm.), color lithograph on wove (BP 2056, DM 5072, FR 17,091, Y 354,196).
BI *Cavallo*, s., i. epreuve d'artiste, full margins, excellent cond., est. BP 8/1,200, (11-30-92, Phillips-London, #459), image 26⅛ x 18½ in., (664 x 470 mm.), lithograph.
$2588* *Cavallo In Armonia (G./G. A-219), 1978*, s., #11/125, p. Grafica dei Greci, pub. Edizioni Grafica dei Greci, Tonninelli Arte Moderna, full margins, good cond., rolling creases, pen mark, (05-13-93, Sotheby-NY, #594), 19⅜ x 26⅝ in., (491 x 675 mm.), etching and aquatint in colors (BP 1699, DM 4179, FR 14,096, Y 288,936).
$2044* *Ceramica II (Katalog Bruckmann L 61; Guastalla 116), 1955*, s., #25/75, (05-26-93, Lempertz, #328), 25¹⁵⁄₁₆ x 19¹⁵⁄₁₆ in., (66 x 50.7 cm.), color lithograph on Arches wove (BP 1322, DM 3335, FR 11,225, Y 222,077).
$968* *Cheval Et Cavalier*, #38/150, sig. stamp, (10-09-92, Winterberg, #2698, illus.), 19⅝ x 14½ in., (49.8 x 36.8 cm.), color aquatint on BFK Rives (BP 574, DM 1438, FR 4828, Y 117,848).
$2524* *Chevaux Et Cavaliers (Bruckmann L 104)*, from Chevaux et Cavaliers, Paris/NY 1972, E.A. 4/10, s., (11-21-92, Lempertz, #275), approx. 15⅜ x 20¹⁄₁₆ in., (39 x 51 cm.), color lithograph on Arches wove (BP 1662, DM 4024, FR 13,555, Y 313,891).
$1947* *Chevaux Et Cavaliers (Bruckmann L 107)*, from Chevaux et Cavaliers, Paris/NY 1972, E.A. 4/10, s., (11-21-92, Lempertz, #276), approx. 15⅜ x 20¹⁄₁₆ in., (39 x 51 cm.), color lithograph on Arches wove (BP 1282, DM 3104, FR 10,456, Y 242,134).
$2236* *Chevaux Et Cavaliers (Bruckmann L 108)*, from Chevaux et Cavaliers, Paris/NY 1972, E.A. 4/10, s., (11-21-92, Lempertz, #277), approx. 15⅜ x 20¹⁄₁₆ in., (39 x 51 cm.), color lithograph on Arches wove (BP 1472, DM 3565, FR 12,009, Y 278,075).
$1023* *Chevaux Et Cavaliers, Plate III (Guastalla L106), 1972*, s., #31/50, p. Mourlot, pub. Societe International d'Art XXieme Siecle, & L.Amiel, full margins, good cond., handling crease, (12-03-92, Sotheby-London, #373, illus.),

15⅜ x 19⅝ in., (391 x 498 mm.), lithograph in colors on Arches (BP 660, DM 1609, FR 5491, Y 127,286).

$1194* *Chevaux Et Cavaliers, Plate V (G. L108), 1976*, s., #31/50, p. Mourlot, pub. Societe International d'Art XXe Siecle,and L. Amiel, full margins, good cond., (12-03-92, Sotheby-London, #380), 14⅞ x 20 in., (378 x 510 mm.), lithograph in colors on Arches (BP 770, DM 1878, FR 6409, Y 148,563).

$206* *Composition*, (12-02-92, Kunsthallen, #266), lithograph in colors (BP 133, DM 324, FR 1106, Y 25,631, DK 1265).

$649* *Composizione (Bruckmann R 48), 1956*, #43/65, s., plate 18 from Marino Marini Gravures, Paris 1970, (11-21-92, Lempertz, #273), 11¹³⁄₁₆ x 9¹⁵⁄₁₆ in., (30 x 25.2 cm.), etching on wove (BP 427, DM 1035, FR 3485, Y 80,711).

BI *Composizione (Guastalla 106), 1955*, #167/200, s., est. SF 3/3,500, (04-21-93, Germann, #613, illus.), 28¾ x 20½ in., (730 x 520 mm.), color lithograph.

BI *Danza Minima II (Toninelli II 167; Schulz-Hoffmann R. 170), 1973*, #24/25, s., est. DM 4,000, (04-24-93, Kunsthaus, #686, illus.), 25³⁄₁₆ x 19⁵⁄₁₆ in., (64 x 49 cm.), etching w/color aquatint on intaglio board.

BI *Danzatrice (G. A205), 1977*, crayon init., i. e.a., p. and pub. Crommelynck, 1981, margins, good cond., est. BP 800/1,200, (06-30-93, Sotheby-London, #492), 25½ x 19¾ in., (648 x 502 mm.), color aquatint on wove.

BI *Due Acrobati Con Cavallo (G. L54), 1955*, s., # 20/50, p. by Mourlot, pub. Berggruen & Cie, full margins, imagein good cond., discoloration, foxing, est. BP 800/1,000, (06-30-93, Sotheby-London, #495, illus.), color lithograph on wove.

$793* *Due Pomone (Bruckmann R 52), 1956*, #XXXIV/XL, s., plate 10 from Tout pres de Marino, Paris 1971, (11-21-92, Lempertz, #274), 10⅜ x 7½ in., (26.3 x 19 cm.), etching on Arches wove (BP 522, DM 1264, FR 4259, Y 98,620).

$2564* *Famiglia Di Acrobati (Toninelli, Nr. L. 55), 1955*, 1 (!)/50, s., (11-13-92, Kunsthaus, #695, illus.), 24⁷⁄₁₆ x 17¹¹⁄₁₆ in., (62 x 45 cm.), color lithograph on handmade (BP 1657, DM 4025, FR 13,573, Y 318,233).

$550* *Figure*, s., annot., (05-16-93, Hindman, #498), 15½ x 10⅝ in., (39.4 x 27 cm.), color etching and aquatint (BP 358, DM 885, FR 2973, Y 60,969).

$1419* *"Figuren Aus 'Le Sacre Du Printemps'" (Guastalla 315), 1974*, watermark, s., sheet 5 of series Le Sacre du Printemps, Leon Amiel, (06-05-93, Grisebach, #762, illus.), 20⅜ x 15⁷⁄₁₆ in., (51.8 x 39.2 cm.), color lithograph on wove (BP 934, DM 2301, FR 7754, Y 152,221).

$1566* *Fossile Equestre (Toninelli, A 74; Guastalla A 76), 1963*, #9/50, s., (05-20-93, Finarte-Milan, #98, illus.), 15⁹⁄₁₆ x 11¹³⁄₁₆ in., (39.5 x 30 cm.), etching in colors (BP 1005, DM 2527, FR 8511, Y 172,924, L 2300).

$21,980* *From Color To Form (Guastalla L. 92 a 101), 1969: Ten*, whole margins, #38/50, s., (06-11-93, Picard, #116), 19¹¹⁄₁₆ x 25⁹⁄₁₆ in., (500 x 650 mm.), lithographs in color on Arches wove (BP 14,442, DM 35,722, FR 120,438, Y 2,332,095).

$4600* *From Color To Form X (Guastallo and Guastallo L101), 1969*, s., #6/50, p. Mourlot, pub. XXe Siecle and Leon Amiel, full margins,good cond., scratch marks, paper adhering to surface, mat/light/masking tape stains, skinning, discoloration, Alan E. Paris, Jr. Estate, (02-11-93, Sotheby-NY, #167), 15⁷⁄₁₆ x 21¹⁄₁₆ in., (392 x 535 mm.), color lithograph (BP 3246, DM 7620, FR 25,785, Y 554,551).

$1323* *Gioco I (Guastalla 301), 1973*, P.A., s., (10-14-92, Germann, #140, illus.), 39³⁄₁₆ x 27⅜ in., (995 x 695 mm.), drypoint and etching (BP 777, DM 1936, FR 6566, Y 160,325, SF 1725).

$2185* *Giocolieri (G. 48), 1955*, s., #27/50, full margins, foxing, creasing, good cond., (05-11-93, Christie-NY, #212), borderline 25 x 17½ in., (635 x 445 mm.), color lithograph on Arches (BP 1395, DM 3442, FR 11,598, Y 240,348).

BI *Giocolieri (G.A. 135), 1971*, s., est. DM 2500, (12-01-92, Karl/Faber, #968), 16⁵⁄₁₆ x 10¼ in., (41.5 x 26 cm.), etching and color aquatint.

BI *Giocolieri (Guastalla 71), 1951*, 21/65, s., est. SF 1,5/2,500, (10-14-92, Germann, #367), 20⅞ x 16¹³⁄₁₆ in., (530 x 427 mm.), etching.

$1492* *Giocolieri (Guastalla L48), 1955*, s., 27/50, (12-04-92, AB Stockholm, #7102), 24¹³⁄₁₆ x 17⁵⁄₁₆ in., (63 x 44 cm.), color lithograph on Arches (BP 957, DM 2376, FR 8061, Y 186,267, SK 10,120).

$1057* *Giocolieri (Katalog Bruckmann 156; Guastalla 293), 1973*, s., num. P. A., (05-26-93, Lempertz, #330), 27³⁄₁₆ x 35¼ in., (69 x 89.5 cm.), etching on color Fabriano wove (BP 684, DM 1725, FR 5805, Y 114,841).

$3623* *Giocolieri, 1973*, s., A.P., blindstamp, (05-25-93, AB Stockholm, #49, illus.), 19⅛ x 25⅜ in., (48.5 x 64.5 cm.), etching on C.M. Fabriano (BP 2348, DM 5901, FR 19,863, Y 396,000, SK 5280).

$1290* *Giocolieri, Die Gaukler (Guastalla 71), 1951*, #21/65, s., (09-04-92, Germann, #457), 20⅞ x 16¹³⁄₁₆ in., (530 x 427 mm.), etching (BP 646, DM 1808, FR 6155, Y 158,789, SF 1610).

$1411* *Giocoliers (G. A206), 1977: Portfolio*, s., 14/100, (12-04-92, AB Stockholm, #7104), 10¹³⁄₁₆ x 7¾ in., (27.5 x 19.7 cm.), etching and aquatint in colors (BP 905, DM 2247, FR 7623, Y 176,155, SK 9570).

$1760* *Horse And Rider*, s., num. 22/75, (09-20-92, Hindman, #777), 31½ x 23½ in., (80 x 59.7 cm.), color lithograph (BP 1030, DM 2612, FR 8934, Y 217,526).

$1980* *Horse And Rider*, s., #25/50, full margins, good cond., skinned areas, creases, faded, (10-28-92, Butterfield, #2666), 16 x 20½ in., (406 x 521 mm.), color silkscreen on Japan (BP 1262, DM 3058, FR 10,383, Y 242,945).

$2860* *Horse And Two Figures*, s., num. XXXV/L, (09-20-92, Hindman, #776), 18½ x 15 in., (47 x 38.1 cm.), color aquatint (BP 1674, DM 4244, FR 14,518, Y 353,479).

$1100* *"Horse"*, s., #167/200, margins, good cond., light-staining, creases, hinge/glue remains, staining, soiling, (10-28-92, Butterfield, #2838), 25 x 13¾ in., (635 x 349 mm.), lithograph in orange and black on Arches (BP 701, DM 1699, FR 5768, Y 134,969).

$1106* *Il Grido (Guastalla-Schluz-Hoffmann R 66), 1962*, s., num., (12-05-92, Bassenge, #7463, illus.), 13⅞ x 11¾ in., (35.3 x 29.8 cm.), etching on thick copper print paper (BP 693, DM 1724, FR 5877, Y 137,034).

$1645* *Idea Del Cavaliere (Toninelli A 70; Guastalla A 72), 1963*, artist proof, (05-20-93, Finarte-Milan, #96), 13⅝ x 12⅛ in., (34.6 x 30.8 cm.), etching (BP 1056, DM 2654, FR 8940, Y 181,648, L 2415).

BI *Il Cavallo, 1976*, s., num. XXV III/L, p. by Crommelynck, pub. Transworld Art, full margins, creases, est. BP 8/1,000, (11-30-92, Phillips-London, #458), plate 14⅝ x 19½ in., (371 x 495 mm.), aquatint w/etching in colors on Arches.

$7468* *Il Grande Teatro Delle Maschere (G. L 133), 1979*, s., num., foxed, (12-01-92, Karl/Faber, #975, illus.), 23¼ x 25¹⁵⁄₁₆ in., (59 x 66 cm.), color lithograph on Arches wove (BP 4934, DM 11,903, FR 40,565, Y 929,781).

$3685* *Il Grande Teatro Delle Maschere (G. L 133), 1979*, s., num., (06-08-93, Karl/Faber, #1090, illus.), approx. 23¼ x 26³⁄₁₆ in., (59 x 66.5 cm.), color lithograph on Arches France wove (BP 2422, DM 5979, FR 20,137, Y 391,397).

$916* *Il Greco II (Guastalla 369), 1978*, s., #11/25, (05-26-93, Lempertz, #338), 29¹⁵⁄₁₆ x 22¼ in., (76 x 56.5 cm.), etching (aquatint) on Arches wove (BP 593, DM 1495, FR 5030, Y 99,522).

$1980* *Il Grido*, s., #28/50, blindstamp pub. l'Oeuvre Gravee, full margins, good cond., creases, soiling, rubbed areas, masking tape, mat staining, (10-28-92, Butterfield, #2665, illus.), 21 x 31 in., (533 x 787 mm.), color lithograph on BFK Rives (BP 1262, DM 3058, FR 10,383, Y 242,945).

$1253* *Il Grido (Toninelli, A 103; Guastalla, A 105), 1970*, #86/90, s., (05-20-93, Finarte-Milan, #100), 12³⁄₁₆ x 17⁵⁄₁₆ in., (31 x 44 cm.), etching in colors (BP 804, DM 2022, FR 6810, Y 138,361, L 1840).

$1263* *Il Grido, (Toninelli A 66), 1962*, #15/65, s., (11-09-92, Finarte-Milan, #96), 13¹⁵⁄₁₆ x 11¹³⁄₁₆ in., (35.5 x 30 cm.), etching (BP 835, DM 2016, FR 6812, Y 156,739, L 1725).

$1263* *Il Grido, (Toninelli, n. A 69), 1962,* #15/65, s., (11-09-92, Finarte-Milan, #9, illus.), 9 13/16 x 11 7/16 in., (25 x 29 cm.), etching and aquatint (BP 835, DM 2016, FR 6812, Y 156,739, L 1725).

$921* *Il Grido, Der Schrei (Guastalla 164), 1962,* #21/65, s., (09-04-92, Germann, #459), 21 1/16 x 16 9/16 in., (535 x 420 mm.), etching (BP 462, DM 1291, FR 4394, Y 113,368, SF 1150).

BI *Il Profondo II (Guastalla 298),* #24/25, series Il Teatro delle Maschere, blindstamp, est. DM 3,000, (06-10-93, Hauswedell/Nolt, #604, illus.), image 19 3/16 x 25 5/16 in., (48.7 x 64.3 cm.), color aquatint on wove.

$2875* *Immaginazione Di Colore (G./G. L-132), 1979,* s., #18/75, p., pub. Graphis Arte, full margins, good cond., rollingcreases, soiling, (05-13-93, Sotheby-NY, #595, illus.), 23 7/8 x 17 1/8 in., (605 x 435 mm.), lithograph in colors (BP 1887, DM 4642, FR 15,659, Y 320,978).

BI *Jongleur Et Deux Chevaux, Bleu, Jaune Et Noir (Guastalla 92), 1953,* s., est. SF 3/3,500, (04-21-93, Germann, #614, illus.), 25 13/16 x 19 11/16 in., (655 x 500 mm.), color lithograph.

BI *Komposition Fur "XXe Siecle" (Guastalla 178), 1963,* 32/50, s., est. SF 1,9/2,200, (10-14-92, Germann, #371), 17 1/4 x 12 15/16 in., (438 x 330 mm.), color lithograph on Rives.

$1527* *Lo Scudo (Guast. L20), 1943,* s., i. prova d'artista, num., (06-23-93, Kornfeld, #551), lithograph on wove (BP 1037, DM 2584, FR 8691, Y 166,358, SF 2300).

BI *Luci Di Danza (G. A157), 1973,* s., #59/75, pub. Albra, full margins, good cond., est. BP 8/1,200, (12-03-92, Sotheby-London, #377, illus.), 39 x 27 1/2 in., (990 x 700 mm.), etching, drypoint and aquatint in colors on wove.

$1373* *Magia (G. L131), 1979,* s., #19/75, p. and pub. Graphis Arte, full margins, good cond., (06-30-93, Sotheby-London, #493), 24 3/8 x 17 1/8 in., (619 x 435 mm.), color lithograph on wove (BP 920, DM 2342, FR 7900, Y 147,112).

$1006* *Malencontreuse Cavalcade,* hors commerce, s., full margins, (11-16-92, Briest, #327), 22 1/16 x 14 15/16 in., (56 x 38 cm.), etching and aquatint in colors (BP 661, DM 1604, FR 5406, Y 125,546).

$303* *Man On Horseback,* #95/200, (06-11-93, Freemn/Fine Art, #139), 24 x 19 in., (61 x 48.3 cm.), color lithograph (BP 199, DM 492, FR 1660, Y 32,149).

BI *Marino From Goethe (G. A225-228), 1979,* complete suite of four, init., #XXIV/L, stamp/sig. of artist's wife,-pub. ZWR, full margins, good cond., light stain, est. $8/12,000, (11-05-92, Sotheby-NY, #234, illus.), each sheet approx. 35 5/8 x 24 7/8 in., (904 x 632 mm.), aquatints p. in colors.

$1279* *Marino From Goethe IV (G. A228), 1979,* crayon init., pub. ZWR, 1980, full margins, good cond., (12-03-92, Sotheby-London, #379, illus.), 35 x 24 3/4 in., (890 x 630 mm.), etching and aquatint in colors on Velin Rives (BP 825, DM 2011, FR 6865, Y 159,139).

$6140* *Marino From Shakespeare I (G. A 189), 1971,* s., Bl. 3 from series Marino from Shakespeare, pub. Zwemmer, artist proof, (12-01-92, Karl/Faber, #970, illus.), 19 5/16 x 15 3/8 in., (49 x 39 cm.), color aquatint/etching on Arches wove (BP 4057, DM 9786, FR 33,351, Y 764,442).

BI *Marino From Shakespeare II (Guastallo A211 and A212), 1978,* plates I and II from suite of VIII, s., #XXXVI/L, pub. ZWR, 1979, full margins, good cond., mat/light stain, punctures, est. $8/12,000, (11-05-92, Sotheby-NY, #233, illus.), one 19 1/4 x 15 in., (488 x 381 mm.), other 19 3/8 x 15 1/8 in., (488 x 381 mm.), 2 etchings w/aquatint p. in colors.

$13,642* *"Marino To Stravinsky:Trovatore", "La Caduta Dell'Angelo", "I Giochi", "Gioco Perfetto", "Scomposizione", "Il Grido", "La Ribalta", "Fondale", "Immaginazione" and "Senso Lirico" (G. 139-148), 1972,* portfolio, s., i. P.A., title page & just., pub. Albra, full margins,good cond., loose, (12-03-92, Sotheby-London, #374, illus.), ten aquatints in colors on wove (BP 8800, DM 21,453, FR 73,226, Y 1,697,400).

BI *Miracolo (Guastalla 370), 1978,* s., #XII/XXV, est. DM 3,500, (05-26-93, Lempertz, #340, illus.), 29 13/16 x 22 1/4 in., (75.8 x 56.5 cm.), color lithograph (aquatint) on Arches wove.

BI *Miracolo (Guastalla A 55), 1957,* s., plate 9 from series Tout pres de Marino, EA, est. DM 2,500, (12-01-92, Karl/Faber, #967), 10 1/4 x 7 1/2 in., (26 x 19 cm.), etching and color aquatint on Arches wove.

$1410* *Miracolo (Toninelli, LQ 1970; Guastalla, LT 1970), 1970,* for XX Siecle, n. 35, #41/50, s., (05-20-93, Finarte-Milan, #101, illus.), 12 13/16 x 9 5/8 in., (32.5 x 24.5 cm.), lithograph in colors (BP 905, DM 2275, FR 7663, Y 155,698, L 2070).

$1527* *Nell 'Appartamento (Guastalla L9), 1943,* s., i. prova d'artista, num., (06-23-93, Kornfeld, #550), lithograph on wove (BP 1037, DM 2584, FR 8691, Y 166,358, SF 2300).

BI *Omaggio A Durer (Guastalla A 123), 1971,* Epreuve d'artiste, plate mono., s. MARINO, est. SF 2,8/3,600, (11-13-92, Koller, #5370), 17 5/8 x 14 1/2 in., (44.7 x 36.9 cm.), etching on wove.

$886* *Omaggio A Durer (Guastalla A 123), 1971,* s., num., (06-08-93, Karl/Faber, #1085), approx. 17 1/2 x 14 3/16 in., (44.5 x 36 cm.), etching on hand-made (BP 582, DM 1438, FR 4842, Y 94,105).

$4978* *Orfeo (G. L 135), 1979,* s., num., pub. Graphics Arte, (12-01-92, Karl/Faber, #976, illus.), 22 13/16 x 28 3/8 in., (58 x 72 cm.), color lithograph on Arches (BP 3289, DM 7934, FR 27,040, Y 619,771).

$1544* *Orfeo (G. L135), 1979,* s., #37/75, p. and pub. Graphis Arte, full margins, good cond., creasing, (06-30-93, Sotheby-London, #494), 22 7/8 x 28 1/8 in., (581 x 714 mm.), color lithograph on Arches (BP 1035, DM 2633, FR 8884, Y 165,434).

$280* *"Personnage",* EA, inits., (04-04-93, Pescheteau, #256), 28 3/8 x 22 1/4 in., (72 x 56.5 cm.), etching and aquatint on wove (BP 184, DM 450, FR 1528, Y 31,880).

$1762* *Personnages Du Sacre Du Printemps (Katalog Bruckmann L 118); Guastalla 315), 1974,* s., #40/75, (05-26-93, Lempertz, #331, illus.), 22 1/16 x 16 15/16 in., (56 x 43 cm.), color lithograph on wove (BP 1140, DM 2875, FR 9676, Y 191,439).

$1265* *Personnages Du Sacre Du Printemps I (Guastallo/Guastallo L-114), 1974,* s., #42/75, p. Mourlot, pub. XXe Siecle and Leon Amiel, full margins,good cond., lightstain, tape, discolored, (05-13-93, Sotheby-NY, #593), 20 1/2 x 15 3/8 in., (520 x 390 mm.), lithograph in colors (BP 830, DM 2043, FR 6890, Y 141,230).

$1059* *Presentazione II (Guastalla 296), 1973,* P.A., s., signs of wear, (10-14-92, Germann, #370), 27 9/16 x 39 1/8 in., (700 x 993 mm.), etching (BP 622, DM 1550, FR 5256, Y 128,333, SF 1380).

$783* *La Ribalta (Toninelli, A 83; Guastalla, A 58), 1964,* #III/XX, s., (05-20-93, Finarte-Milan, #99), 18 15/16 x 12 3/8 in., (48.2 x 31.4 cm.), etching (BP 503, DM 1263, FR 4255, Y 86,462, L 1150).

$642* *Rytter,* s. Marino, 26/50, (03-24-93, Kunsthallen, #234), lithograph (BP 435, DM 1049, FR 3569, Y 75,432, DK 4025).

BI *Scomposizioni,* s., #ES 30/60, pub. Liugi de Tullio, very good cond., est. BP 700/1,000, (10-27-92, Phillips-London, #210), (400 x 311 mm.), drypoint on wove.

BI *Scomposizioni, 1967,* s., num. E.S. 30/60, pub. Luigi De Tullio, good cond., est. BP 5/600, (11-30-92, Phillips-London, #457A), plate 15 3/4 x 12 1/4 in., (400 x 311 mm.), drypoint on wove.

$2245* *Senso Lirico (Schulz-Hoffmann R 146), 1972: Ten,* epreuve d'artiste, s., blindstamp, (10-09-92, Winterberg, #2697, illus.), 12 5/8 x 11 3/16 in., (32.1 x 28.4 cm.), drypoint w/color aquatint (BP 1332, DM 3335, FR 11,197, Y 273,314).

$1339* *La Sorpresa (Katalog Bruckmann 168; Guastalla 289), 1973,* s., #24/25, (05-26-93, Lempertz, #329), 39 3/16 x 27 9/16 in., (99.5 x 70 cm.), etching on wove (BP 866, DM 2185, FR 7353, Y 145,480).

$1431* *La Sorpresa I, (Toninelli A 166 s.c.), 1973,* #10/50, s., (11-09-92, Finarte-Milan, #39), 25 3/8 x 19 1/8 in., (64.5 x 48.5 cm.), etching, drypoint and aquatint in colors (BP 946, DM 2284, FR 7718, Y 177,587, L 1955).

BI *Sparticus (Grustella 326), 1975,* s., num. 80/175, p. Atelier Crommelyck, pub. Transworld Art Corp., full margins, good cond., est. BP 8/1,000, (11-30-92, Phillips-London, #458A), sheet 19⅞ x 25⅝ in., (505 x 651 mm.), etching aquatint in colors.

$2053* *Studio Di Cavaliere (Guastalla 83; L 125), 1952-1976,* 67/75, s., (06-24-93, Germann, #426, illus.), 29¼ x 21¹⁵⁄₁₆ in., (743 x 557 mm.), color lithograph (BP 1351, DM 3328, FR 11,219, Y 220,232, SF 2990).

$1194* *Teatrino (G. A155), c. 1970,* s., #7/75, p. Il Cigno, pub. Albra, full margins, good cond., (12-03-92, Sotheby-London, #376, illus.), 19 x 25 in., (485 x 633 mm.), etching, drypoint and aquatint in colors on Magnani wove (BP 770, DM 1878, FR 6409, Y 148,563).

$1650* *(Three Figures),* s., annot. E.A., full margins, good cond., tear, foxing, creases, staining, (02-24-93, Butterfield, #2750, illus.), 20½ x 15½ in., (521 x 394 mm.), lithograph in colors on Japon nacre (BP 1151, DM 2679, FR 9081, Y 193,617).

$825* *Three Standing Figures, c. 1970,* s., #36/75, good cond.?, (12-08-92, Swann, #194, illus.), image 20 x 15¼ in., (50.8 x 38.7 cm.), color lithograph (BP 517, DM 1284, FR 4379, Y 102,256).

$8625* *Tout Pres De Marino, Paris And New York, XXe Siecle And Leon Amiel, 1971 (G. 52-3, 55, 132-8): Ten,* text, just., s., num., copy 52 of 95, full margins, loose, excell. cond., orig. portfolio, (05-11-93, Christie-NY, #213, illus.), 23⅜ x 16⅛ in., (593 x 410 mm.), color etching, hors-texte, on Arches (BP 5506, DM 13,587, FR 45,780, Y 948,741).

$929* *Trois Chevaux,* #48/150, sig. stamp, (10-09-92, Winterberg, #2699, illus.), 19⅝ x 14½ in., (49.8 x 36.8 cm.), color aquatint on BFK Rives (BP 551, DM 1380, FR 4633, Y 113,100).

$990* *Untitled, Horse And Rider,* s., full margins, good cond., mat/time/water staining, foxing, (10-28-92, Butterfield, #2667), 23½ x 15¼ in., (597 x 387 mm.), color lithograph on Arches (BP 631, DM 1529, FR 5191, Y 121,472).

MARISOL, Escobar   American b. France 1930
$431* *The Kiss (ULAE M.5), 1965,* s., d., #19/26, blindstamp publisher, ULAE, p. Ben Berns and Mike Kuhno, full margins, good cond., hinge remains, skinned areas, (05-19-93, Butterfield, #2262), 11⅞ x 10¾ in., (302 x 273 mm.), lithograph in colors on Japan (BP 280, DM 701, FR 2360, Y 47,714).

$288* *Portrait Of Elizabeth C.P. Stanton And Lucretia P. Mott, 1975,* s., d., #82/125, blindstamp publisher, Styria Studio, good cond.?, (05-19-93, Butterfield, #2263), sh 41¾ x 29¹¹⁄₁₆ in., (106 x 75.4 cm.), lithograph in colors on wove (BP 187, DM 468, FR 1577, Y 31,883).

$385* *Progressive Color Variants, 1978: Suite of Six,* s., #71/100, pub. Prestige Art, (12-08-92, Swann, #196), each 52 x 38 in., (132.1 x 96.5 cm.), color lithograph (BP 241, DM 599, FR 2044, Y 47,719).

MARK, Mary Ellen   20th cent.
$1100* *Mother Teresa, Calcutta, 1980,* photog.'s sig., notations, (04-07-93, Swann, #332, illus.), 14 x 11 in., photograph, silver print (BP 727, DM 1779, FR 6021, Y 124,972).

$330* *Mother Teresa, Shishu Bhawan, Calcutta,* (05-16-93, Hindman, #347), 9 x 12 in., photograph, silver print (BP 215, DM 532, FR 1793, Y 36,748).

$690* *"Orega" and "Bars": Two,* one 1976, other 1977, s., t., d., (05-23-93, Butterfield, #3520, illus.), one 8 x 12 in., other 12 x 8 in., photograph, gelatin silver print (BP 449, DM 1128, FR 3797, Y 76,268).

MARKHAM, Kyra   American b. 1891
BI *Rewards Of A Virtuous Life,* s., t., #9/50, tape residue, very good cond., est. $5/700, (12-04-92, Doyle, #130), 9½ x 11⅞ in., (241 x 302 mm.), aquatint.

MARKOS, Andras
BI *Die Analyse Eines Fluzeuges, Analysis Of The Plane, 1988,* s., t., d., num. 18/60, w/margins, good cond., est. $6/800, (05-22-93, Weschler, #202, illus.), 25 x 36½ in., (63.5 x 92.7 cm.), aquatint in colors on Zirkal.

MARKS, Gerry
BI *'Beaver', 1977,* NWCIA guild, est. C$150/250, (10-21-92, Maynard, #52), approx. 22 x 30 in., (55.9 x 76.2 cm.), print.

BI *'Wolf',* NWCIA guild, est. C$150/250, (10-21-92, Maynard, #53), approx. 22 x 30 in., (55.9 x 76.2 cm.), print.

MARLBOROUGH, GOULD and CO., Publisher
$125 *"S.S. Iole",* (08-14-92, G.A. Key, #24), 10 x 17 in., (25.4 x 43.2 cm.), colored lithograph (BP 65, DM 183, FR 621, Y 15,763).

MARQUET, Albert   French 1875-1947
BI *Les Drapeaux,* mono., #80/100, wormholes, est. FF1,800/2,000, (05-27-93, Briest, #140), 29⁵⁄₁₆ x 20⅞ in., (74.5 x 53 cm.), color lithograph.

$1039* *Les Maitres De L'Estampe Francaise Contemporaine, 1947: Ten,* num., sig. stamp, (06-11-93, Picard, #117), 15⅜ x 11⁷⁄₁₆ in., (390 x 290 mm.), 7 black and color lithographs, 3 drypoints (BP 683, DM 1689, FR 5693, Y 110,239).

BI *Partie An Der Seine,* est. DM 150-, (09-25-92, Granier, #2935), sheet 17¹¹⁄₁₆ x 12¹⁵⁄₁₆ in., (45 x 33 cm.), etching on machine hand-made paper.

$403* *Port De Naples, 1925: Two,* 2 of same subject, 1st a proof, before removal of sig. in stone; 2nds., #17/35, from Album des Peintres lithographs, blindstamp pub., Galerie des Peintres-Graveurs, full margins, good cond., light-stain, tear, (02-11-93, Sotheby-NY, #168), each approx. 8¼ x 11⅝ in., (210 x 295 mm.), lithograph on chine volant (BP 284, DM 668, FR 2259, Y 48,583).

BI *Port De Naples, 1925: Two,* two impressions of the same subject, first a proof; second s., #17/35, pub. blindstamp, Galerie des Peintres Graveurs, full margins, good cond., light stain, est. $2/2,500, (11-05-92, Sotheby-NY, #235), each approx. 8¼ x 11⅝ in., (210 x 295 mm.), lithographs on chine volant.

BI *Smabade Udfor Kyst,* sig., est. DK 1,200, (12-02-92, Kunsthallen, #267), lithograph.

MARQUIS, Claude
$269* *Pierre Berezzi Danseur Et Choregraphe, c. 1950,* (01-31-93, Morelle/Marchan, #33), 39⅜ x 62¹⁵⁄₁₆ in., (100 x 160 cm.), poster (BP 181, DM 433, FR 1465, Y 33,558).

MARRIOTT, F.
$15 *Figures In A Lamp Lit Court Yard,* s., (04-16-93, G.A. Key, #49), 15 x 11 in., (38.1 x 27.9 cm.), colored mezzotint (BP 10, DM 24, FR 82, Y 1687).

MARSCHNER, Arthur
$55* *Seashore Scene, c. 1915,* s., (05-14-93, DuMouchelle, #2538), 7 x 4 in., (17.8 x 10.2 cm.), etching (BP 36, DM 88, FR 297, Y 6097).

MARSH, C.
$431* *Joni Mitchell Running,* s., #81/100, s., num. by Mitchell and artist, (06-23-93, Sotheby-NY, #400, illus.), 20½ x 26 in., (52.1 x 66 cm.), lithograph, blue tint (BP 293, DM 729, FR 2453, Y 46,955).

$403* *Joni Mitchell Running Through A Field,* s., #81/100, s., num. by Mitchell and artist, (06-23-93, Sotheby-NY, #401, illus.), 20½ x 26 in., (52.1 x 66 cm.), lithograph, green tint (BP 274, DM 682, FR 2294, Y 43,905).

$431* *Joni Mitchell With Outstretched Arms,* #81/100, s., num. by Mitchell and artist, (06-23-93, Sotheby-NY, #399, illus.), 20½ x 26 in., (52.1 x 66 cm.), lithograph, reddish tint (BP 293, DM 729, FR 2453, Y 46,955).

MARSH, Reginald   American 1898-1954
$2530* *"Box At The Metropolitan" (Sasowsky, 143), 1934,* s. Reginald Marsh, num. #3, ded., watermark, very good cond., mount staining, (03-12-93, Skinner, #20, illus.), 9⅞ x 7⅞ in., (25.1 x 20 cm.), etching and engraving on Rives wove (BP 1765, DM 4211, FR 14,318, Y 298,173).

BI *"Derrick Loaders" (Sasowsky 67 iii-iv/iv), 1929,* s. by artist's widow, very fine cond., annot., est. $2,5-3,500, (10-31-92, Cleveland, #184, illus.), 10 x 8 in., (25.4 x 20.3 cm.), etching.

$800* *"Erie R.R. Yards" (Sasowsky 18 i/i), 1928,* s., excell. cond., hinges, prov., (05-15-93, Cleveland, #238, illus.), 8¾ x 13⅛ in., (22.2 x 33.3 cm.), lithograph on Chine Colle (BP 520, DM 1287, FR 4324, Y 88,682).

BI *"Felecia" (S. 181 v/v), 1939,* Jones edit., 1956, s., init. by artist's widow, good cond., est. $350-450, (10-31-92,

Cleveland, #186), 3⅞ x 2⅞ in., (9.8 x 7.3 cm.), engraving.

$660* *Girl Walking, Elevated*, s., d. 45, very good cond., (07-19-92, Bakker, #39, illus.), image 10½ x 7¾ in., (26.7 x 19.7 cm.), lithograph (BP 339, DM 962, FR 3253, Y 82,049).

$220* *Grand Tier At The Met (S. 190), 1939*, embossed w/ inits., num. 55/100, pub. Whitney Museum of Art, margins, good cond., (02-24-93, Butterfield, #2850), 6¹/₁₆ x 9¹⁵/₁₆ in., (154 x 252 mm.), etching on wove (BP 153, DM 357, FR 1211, Y 25,816).

$248* *Irving Place Burlesque (Sasowsky 101), 1930*, p. Whitney Museum of American Art, 1969, #68/100, Whitney's stamp, (05-16-93, Hindman, #558), 9⅝ x 11¾ in., (24.4 x 29.8 cm.), etching (BP 161, DM 399, FR 1341, Y 27,491).

$220* *"Locomotive Going Through Jersey City" (Sasowsky, 89), 1930*, pub. Whitney Museum of American Art, 1969, s., d. Reginald Marsh 1930, pub. dry stamp, very good cond., wide margins, light toning, (09-11-92, Skinner, #35, illus.), 4⅞ x 9⅞ in., (12.4 x 25.1 cm.), etching on wove (BP 114, DM 317, FR 1076, Y 27,258).

BI *Merry-Go-Round (Sasowsky 99), 1930*, 6th final state, watermark, s., i. #17, margins, mat staining, taped to overmat, est. $3/3,500, (05-11-93, Christie-NY, #117, illus.), plate 7 x 9¾ in., (178 x 248 mm.), etching on wove.

$1725* *Minsky's Chorus (not in Sasowsky), 1935*, i. w/artist's name by his wife, t., annot. State II, #3/12, full margins, good cond., mat stain, staples holes, (05-13-93, Sotheby-NY, #430A, illus.), 9 x 11¾ in., (230 x 300 mm.), etching on wove (BP 1132, DM 2785, FR 9395, Y 192,587).

$3450* *Minsky's New Gotham Circus (S. 170), 1936*, s., i. 40 Proofs and erased, margins, good cond., mat stain, (05-13-93, Sotheby-NY, #431, illus.), 9 x 12 in., (229 x 304 mm.), etching extensively hand-colored on Rives wove (BP 2265, DM 5571, FR 18,791, Y 385,174).

$138* *"A Morning In May" (Sasowsky, 169), 1936*, pub. Whitney Museum of American Art, 1969, inits., d. R.M. 1936 in plate, pub. dry stamp, t., very good cond., wide margins, light staining, wrinkling, (09-11-92, Skinner, #33, illus.), 8¼ x 11⅜ in., (21 x 28.9 cm.), etching on wove (BP 71, DM 199, FR 675, Y 17,098).

$330* *New York Street Scene*, s., #9/25, (05-16-93, Hindman, #350), 7¼ x 5 in., photograph, silver print (BP 215, DM 532, FR 1793, Y 36,748).

$2090* *P.R.R. Loco Waiting To Be Junked (Sasowsky 130), 1932*, s., num. 17, margins, good cond., mat stain, nick, crease, (11-05-92, Sotheby-NY, #44), 5⅞ x 11¾ in., (150 x 300 mm.), etching (BP 1359, DM 3305, FR 11,182, Y 256,410).

$330* *Palm Tree (At) Ormond (S. 122)*, s.; s., located Ormond, d. 1931 in plate, (12-10-92, Sloan, #2727), 9¾ x 4⅞ in., (24.8 x 12.4 cm.), etching (BP 213, DM 522, FR 1783, Y 40,821).

$400* *"Palm Tree" (S. 122 ii/ii), 1931*, s., good cond., glue stain, (05-15-93, Cleveland, #240), etching (BP 260, DM 643, FR 2162, Y 44,341).

$275* *"Pickaback" (S. 180 ii/ii), 1938-9*, Whitney Museum, 1969, drystamp, num. 19/100, excellent cond., (10-31-92, Cleveland, #185), 9⅞ x 4⅞ in., (25.1 x 12.4 cm.), engraving (BP 176, DM 423, FR 1435, Y 34,064).

$193* *"Second Avenue El" (Sasowsky, 93), 1930*, pub. Whitney Museum of American Art, 1969, pub. dry stamp, t., very good cond., fox mark, light toning, soiling, (09-11-92, Skinner, #31, illus.), 6⅞ x 9 in., (17.5 x 22.9 cm.), etching on wove (BP 100, DM 278, FR 944, Y 23,913).

$220* *"Skyline From Pier 10 Brooklyn" (Sasowsky, 129), 1931*, pub. Whitney Museum of American Art, 1969, s., d. Reginald Marsh 1931 in plate, pub. dry stamp, very good cond., wide margins, light toning, soiling, (09-11-92, Skinner, #36, illus.), 6⅜ x 12 in., (16.2 x 30.5 cm.), etching on wove (BP 114, DM 317, FR 1076, Y 27,258).

$5500* *Smokehounds (S. 158), 1935*, s., mat burn, light stain, small margins, soiling, good cond., (06-11-93, Doyle, #62), 11¾ x 8⅞ in., (298 x 225 mm.), etching (BP 3614, DM 8939, FR 30,137, Y 583,554).

$660* *St. James De Luz (S. 12), 1928*, s., annot. 40 proofs, margins, good cond., surface soiling, glue remains, (10-28-92, Butterfield, #2538), 8¼ x 12⅝ in., (210 x 321 mm.), lithograph on chine colle (pasted) attached to wove (BP 421, DM 1019, FR 3461, Y 80,982).

$2415* *Star Burlesk (Sasowsky 142), 1933*, s., #14, margins, repaired tear through image, good cond., (02-11-93, Sotheby-NY, #39, illus.), 11⅞ x 8¹¹/₁₆ in., (302 x 221 mm.), sheet 14³/₁₆ x 10½ in., (302 x 221 mm.), etching (BP 1704, DM 4000, FR 13,537, Y 291,139).

$1320* *"Steeplechase","Flying Concellos", "Coney Island Beach #1", "Merry-Go-Round", "Bathers-in-the-Hudson", and "Two Girls Walking To Right" (S. 138; 163; 191; 210; 213; 226), 1932, 1936, 1939, 1940, 1941, 1943: Six*, each num. 30/100, embossed inits. of pub. Whitney Museum Of Art, 1969, full margins, very good cond., (02-24-93, Butterfield, #2648), etchings on wove (BP 921, DM 2143, FR 7265, Y 154,893).

BI *Striptease At New Gotham (S. 156), 1935*, 6th final state, s., t., d., i. State VI, #10/40, margins, mat staining, soiling, printer's ink, good cond., est. $4/4,500, (05-11-93, Christie-NY, #118, illus.), plate 12 x 9 in., (305 x 229 mm.), etching on wove.

$715* *"Switch Engines" (S. 232 ii/ii), 1948*, s. by artist's widow, init. F.M.M., (10-31-92, Cleveland, #187, illus.), 8 x 10 in., (20.3 x 25.4 cm.), engraving (BP 458, DM 1100, FR 3732, Y 88,567).

BI *"Switch Engines, Erie Yards" (S. 30), 1948*, s., The Print Club of Cleveland Publication No. 25, excell. cond., est. $1,250/1,750, (05-15-93, Cleveland, #239, illus.), 9⅛ x 13½ in., (23.2 x 34.3 cm.), lithograph.

$770* *Tank Car (S. 86), 1929*, s., #18, very good cond., prov., (06-11-93, Doyle, #61), 6 x 8⅞ in., (152 x 225 mm.), etching (BP 506, DM 1251, FR 4219, Y 81,698).

$3300* *Tattoo-Shave-Haircut (Sasowsky 140), 1932*, 10th final state, wide margins, hole, soiling, staining, good cond., (11-09-92, Christie-NY, #27, illus.), plate 9⅞ x 9¹³/₁₆ in., (251 x 249 mm.), etching on cream wove (BP 2182, DM 5268, FR 17,799, Y 409,531).

$690* *U.S. Marine (Sasowsky 144), 1934*, s., num. #5, p. by artist, margins, good cond., soiling, (05-13-93, Sotheby-NY, #430), 7⅞ x 5⅞ in., (201 x 150 mm.), sh 10⅝ x 7½ in., (201 x 150 mm.), etching (BP 453, DM 1114, FR 3758, Y 77,035).

MARSH, Reginald (after)   American 1898-1954

$110* *New York Harbor View*, s., (09-17-92, Sloan, #620), sight 15½ x 19¼ in., (39.4 x 48.9 cm.), color serigraph (BP 62, DM 163, FR 559, Y 13,695).

BI *New York harbor View*, s., est. $100/150, (07-03-92, Sloan, #284), sight 15½ x 19¼ in., (39.4 x 48.9 cm.), color serigraph.

MARSHALL, B.

$270 *"War" and "Peace": Two*, C. Turner, engraver, pub. W.C. Lee, (09-24-92, Alderfer, #248), image, both 17¾ x 14¼ in., (45.1 x 36.2 cm.), print (BP 158, DM 400, FR 1359, Y 32,479).

MARSHALL, B. (after)

$51 *"Sancho", 1835*, by T.B. Birkett, pub. W. Deeley, (10-09-92, G.A. Key, #75), 6½ x 9½ in., (16.5 x 24.1 cm.), hand colored etched print (BP 30, DM 76, FR 258, Y 6220).

MARSHALL, Jim

$1725* *Collection Of Vintage Photographs: Nine*, s. by artist, including The Grateful Dead Performing On Haight Street In S.F.; Brian Jones At Monterey Pop; Jimi Hendrix Jamming As Well As Janis Joplin At Pan Handel, 1967; several from Golden Gate Park "Be-In"; Grace Slick; The Charlatans; and group photo of various bands, (06-23-93, Sotheby-NY, #444), 8 b/w photographs, 1 color (BP 1172, DM 2919, FR 9818, Y 187,929).

MARSHALL, John Alexander   20th cent.

$33* *A Flea Market Scene*, s., num., ded. below image, (08-05-92, Boos, #684), 4½ x 5⅞ in., (115 x 150 mm.), soft ground etching (BP 17, DM 49, FR 165, Y 4203).

MARTELLY, John Stockton de American b. 1903

$330* *"Give Us This Day"*, s., good cond.?, ded., (02-07-93, Bakker, #44, illus.), plate 13 x 13½ in., (33 x 34.3 cm.), lithograph (BP 228, DM 547, FR 1850, Y 41,065).

$605* *"Mother And Child At Play" And "The Evangelist", 1941: Two,* both s. John S. de Martelly, latter t., num., d., very good cond., staining, (03-12-93, Skinner, #41, illus.), 9¼ x 12⅛ in., (23.5 x 30.8 cm.), lithograph on wove (BP 422, DM 1007, FR 3424, Y 71,302).

$413* *"Old Moon"*, pub. AAA, s. John S. de Martelly, t. AAA label, very good cond., orig. folder, (09-11-92, Skinner, #49, illus.), 10⅛ x 13¾ in., (25.7 x 34.9 cm.), lithograph on wove (BP 214, DM 595, FR 2021, Y 51,171).

$523* *"White Pastures"*, pub. AAA, s. John S. de Martelly, t. AAA label, very good cond., tape, orig. folder, (09-11-92, Skinner, #54, illus.), 101/16 x 13¾ in., (25.6 x 34.9 cm.), lithograph on wove (BP 270, DM 753, FR 2559, Y 64,800).

MARTEN, Frank

$97* *Queen Of All The Torch Singers,* num. 20/25, s., (08-20-92, Bonhams-Chelsea, #89), subject 25¾ x 19 in., (65.4 x 48.3 cm.), linocut in colors (BP 50, DM 140, FR 477, Y 12,249).

MARTEN, Jon

BI *Untitled, 1981,* s., full margins, good cond., est. Dfl. 150/250, (05-27-93, Sotheby-Amstrdm, #445), 18¾ x 16¼ in., (477 x 412 mm.), colored lithograph on wove.

$115* *Untitled, 1981,* s., #45/190, full margins, good cond., (05-27-93, Sotheby-Amstrdm, #446), 18¾ x 16¼ in., (477 x 412 mm.), colored lithograph on wove (BP 74, DM 185, FR 622, Y 12,328, G 207).

BI *Untitled, 1981,* s., full margins, good cond., est. Dfl. 150/250, (05-27-93, Sotheby-Amstrdm, #447), 22 1/16 x 14 3/16 in., (560 x 361 mm.), colored lithograph on wove.

MARTIALIS, Marci Valerii

$330* *Epigrammata Libri XIIII..., 1514,* Georgiumde Rufcanibus Mediolan, water staining, repair to CXLIX, (05-01-93, Skinner, #152), 12 x 8¼ in., (30.5 x 21 cm.), woodcut illustrations (BP 210, DM 522, FR 1762, Y 36,614).

MARTIN, A.

$279* *Regie Des Chemins De Fer De L'A.O.F.,* very good cond., (03-13-93, Laurin, #133, illus.), 39⅜ x 24 7/16 in., (100 x 62 cm.), (BP 195, DM 464, FR 1579, Y 32,882).

MARTIN, Agnes Canadian/American b. 1912

$2970* *On A Clear Day, 1973,* from the suite, each s., #19/50, #49/50, pub. Parasol Press, full margins, good cond., (11-07-92, Sotheby-NY, #682), each sheet approx. 12 x 12 in., (305 x 305 mm.), two silkscreens p. in gray on off-white Japanese Rag (BP 1942, DM 4742, FR 16,028, Y 366,576).

$1610* *On A Clear Day, 1973: Two,* from the suite, s., #19/50 and 44/50, pub. Parasol Press, full margins, good cond., (02-11-93, Sotheby-NY, #388, illus.), each sheet approx. 12⅛ x 12 1/16 in., (308 x 306 mm.), Gray silkscreens on off-white Japanese Rag (BP 1136, DM 2667, FR 9025, Y 194,093).

BI *On A Clear Day: Thirty,* complete portfolio, each s., i. H/A-N, artist's proofs, pub. ParasolPress, Ltd., good cond., original portfolio, est. $35/45,000, (05-15-93, Sotheby-NY, #1097, illus.), each sheet 12⅛ x 12⅛ in., (30.8 x 30.8 cm.), silkscreens in gray on off-white Japanese Rag.

MARTIN, Anson A. (after)

$80* *Famous Jockeys,* by G.B. Black, pub. Day and Haghe, margins, time-staining, (03-03-93, Bonhams-Chelsea, #193), image 14¼ x 20 in., (36.2 x 50.8 cm.), lithograph (BP 55, DM 132, FR 447, Y 9348).

MARTIN, Camille

$1474* *Couverture Decorative Pour La 2e Annee De L'Estampe Originale (Karshan 44), 1894,* s., num., center fold, staining, cracks, stamp, (02-24-93, Picard, #165), color lithograph on simili-Japan (BP 1028, DM 2393, FR 8112, Y 172,964).

MARTIN, Charles French 20th cent.

$110* *Four Paris Scenes,* each s., (10-18-92, Hindman, #474), each 8 x 11½ in., (20.3 x 29.2 cm.), color aquatints w/ etching (BP 67, DM 164, FR 555, Y 13,197).

MARTIN, David

$84* *Lord Mansfield, Chief Justice Of England, 1775, 1956,* by Lawrence Josset, s., blindstamp, pub. Frost and Reed, margins, (11-12-92, Bonhams-Chelsea, #35), plate 21¾ x 16¼ in., (55.2 x 41.3 cm.), color mezzotint (BP 55, DM 133, FR 449, Y 10,415).

MARTIN, David (after)

$76* *Lord Mansfield, Chief Justice Of England, 1775, 1956,* by Lawrence Josset, s., blindstamp, pub. Frost and Reed, margins, (11-12-92, Bonhams-Chelsea, #36), plate 21¾ x 16¼ in., (55.2 x 41.3 cm.), color mezzotint (BP 50, DM 120, FR 406, Y 9423).

$84* *Lord Mansfield, Chief Justice Of England, 1775, 1956,* by Lawrence Josset, s., blindstamp, pub. Frost and Reed, margins, (11-12-92, Bonhams-Chelsea, #33), plate 21¾ x 16¼ in., (55.2 x 41.3 cm.), color mezzotint (BP 55, DM 133, FR 449, Y 10,415).

$76* *Lord Mansfield, Chief Justice Of England, 1775, 1956,* by Lawrence Josset, s., blindstamp, pub. Frost and Reed, margins, (11-12-92, Bonhams-Chelsea, #34), plate 21¾ x 16¼ in., (55.2 x 41.3 cm.), color mezzotint (BP 50, DM 120, FR 406, Y 9423).

MARTIN, Fletcher American 1904-1979

BI *"Evening Song", "Arab Children" and "High, Wide And Handsome": Three,* lithograph, est. $2/400, (05-22-93, Weschler, #203), sight 10½ x 13½ in., (26.7 x 34.3 cm.), sight 13½ x 10½ in., (26.7 x 34.3 cm.), lithographs.

$210* *The Fight,* s., i., very fine cond., (05-15-93, Cleveland, #241), 8 x 12 in., (20.3 x 30.5 cm.), lithograph (BP 137, DM 338, FR 1135, Y 23,279).

BI *"Gesture", 1963,* s., excell. cond., est. $250/350, (05-15-93, Cleveland, #243), 23½ x 11¾ in., (59.7 x 29.8 cm.), serigraph in colors.

$413* *"Out At Home", 1943,* pub. Midtown Galleries, s., d. Fletcher Martin/1942 in matrix, ident., good cond., wrinkling, losses, (03-12-93, Skinner, #75, illus.), 21⅞ x 27⅞ in., (55.6 x 70.8 cm.), photographic screenprint in colors (BP 288, DM 687, FR 2337, Y 48,674).

BI *"The Picador",* s., very good cond., est. $50/100, (05-15-93, Cleveland, #242), 20 x 34 in., (50.8 x 86.4 cm.), color lithograph.

$308* *"Toe To Toe",* s., num., pub. AAA, excellent cond., (10-31-92, Cleveland, #188, illus.), 12½ x 9½ in., (31.8 x 24.1 cm.), lithograph (BP 197, DM 474, FR 1608, Y 38,152).

MARTIN, Ira

$357* *Plants And Rocks, 1931,* photog.'s sig., (04-07-93, Swann, #515, illus.), 9½ x 7½ in., photograph, silver print (BP 236, DM 577, FR 1954, Y 40,559).

MARTIN, John

$245* *Death Of The First Born,* proof w/scratched t., narrow margins, 3 sides, surface dirt, repairedtear, (10-07-92, Christie-S. Ken, #37), sh 22 x 31¾ in., (55.9 x 80.6 cm.), mezzotint w/line engraving (BP 143, DM 355, FR 1202, Y 29,465).

$10,364* *Paradise Lost: Sixteen,* margins, dirt, spotting, nine proofs before all letters, (10-07-92, Christie-S. Ken, #35), pl 9¾ x 14 in., (24.8 x 35.6 cm.), mezzotint on India (BP 6050, DM 14,996, FR 50,854, Y 1,246,422).

MARTIN, John English 1789-1854

BI *"Book 5, Line 136", 1825,* from John Milton's Paradise Lost, discoloration, est. $100-150, (10-31-92, Cleveland, #314), 9¾ x 14 in., (24.8 x 35.6 cm.), mezzotint and etching.

$2263* *Paradise Lost, 1825: Set Of Twenty-Four,* marked Proof, pub. Septimus Prowett, good cond., (10-27-92, Phillips-London, #45), plate 10½ x 14⅓ in., (267 x 364 mm.), mezzotint on laid (BP 1430, DM 3468, FR 11,768, Y 276,820).

MARTIN, John (after)

BI *"The Great Day Of His Wrath", "The Plains Of Heaven" and "The Last Judgement": Three,* by C. Mottram, posthumous publication, surface dirt and fading, laidon stretchers, est. BP 4/600, (10-07-92, Christie-S. Ken, #38), sh 28 x 41 in., (71.1 x 104.1 cm.), colored mezzotint w/line engraving.

$528* *"The Plains Of Heaven" and "The Last Judgement": Two,* by C.Mottram, pub. Thomas McLean, margins, discoloration on image, surface dirt, (10-07-92, Christie-S. Ken, #36), one, pl 28 x 40½ in., (71.1 x 102.9 cm.), the other, pl 32 x 45 in., (71.1 x 102.9 cm.), colored mezzotint w/line engraving (BP 308, DM 764, FR 2591, Y 63,500).

MARTIN, Knox Colombian/Amer. b. 1923

$176* *Untitled: Three,* all s., i. artist's proof, (06-13-93, Hindman, #329), each 33 x 31 in., (83.8 x 78.7 cm.), color serigraph (BP 115, DM 286, FR 963, Y 18,520).

MARTIN, L.

$251* *P.O.: Foret De Sainte-Genevieve Et Bois De Beausejour Pres De Juvisy, 1906,* tape, fair cond., (01-23-93, Ribeyre/Baron, #42), 40³⁄₁₆ x 29½ in., (102 x 75 cm.), poster (BP 164, DM 399, FR 1350, Y 31,414).

MARTINET (after)

$55* *"Fou Brun De Cayenne" and "Biboreau De Cayenne": Two,* discoloration, foxing, mat burn, John Walton Livermore Estate, (12-04-92, Doyle, #54), 8⅛ x 6¼ in., (206 x 159 mm.), hand colored etching (BP 35, DM 88, FR 297, Y 6866).

MARTINET, Francois Nicholas

$510* *Histoire Naturelle Des Oiseaux, c. 1770: Ten,* excellent cond., (10-27-92, Phillips-London, #178), plate 10 x 8⅛ in., (254 x 206 mm.), engraving w/hand-coloring on fine laid (BP 322, DM 782, FR 2652, Y 62,385).

MARTINET, Francois Nicolas

$452* *L'Histoire Des Oiseaux: Ten,* margins, surface dirt, (10-07-92, Christie-S. Ken, #30), pl 10 x 8¼ in., (25.4 x 21 cm.), colored etching (BP 264, DM 654, FR 2218, Y 54,360).

MARTINI, Alberto

$392* *La Famiglia Del Pescatore (Meloni 112), 1943,* s., i. Lit. originale su zinco rarissimo esemplare in nero A.M., (05-20-93, Finarte-Milan, #106, illus.), 9¹¹⁄₁₆ x 6 in., (24.6 x 15.3 cm.), lithograph in black (BP 252, DM 632, FR 2130, Y 43,286, L 575).

$627* *Il Bacio (F. Meloni 36), 1915,* s., d., (05-20-93, Finarte-Milan, #105, illus.), 14³⁄₁₆ x 10⅝ in., (36 x 27 cm.), lithograph (BP 402, DM 1012, FR 3408, Y 69,236, L 920).

$783* *Lacrime D'Amore (Meloni 37), 1915,* proof #IV/10, s., (05-20-93, Finarte-Milan, #103), 14³⁄₁₆ x 10¹¹⁄₁₆ in., (36 x 27.1 cm.), lithograph in bistro (BP 503, DM 1263, FR 4255, Y 86,462, L 1150).

MARTNER, William

$39* *"Farm",* #10/25, s., (10-16-92, DuMouchelle, #2477), 7 x 5 in., (17.8 x 12.7 cm.), aquatint (BP 24, DM 58, FR 196, Y 4657).

$17* *"Female Nude", 1970,* s., AP, (10-16-92, DuMouchelle, #2474), 7¾ x 13¾ in., (19.7 x 34.9 cm.), etching/aquatint (BP 10, DM 25, FR 85, Y 2030).

$39* *"Female Nude", 1974,* AP, (10-16-92, DuMouchelle, #2472), 7 x 7¾ in., (17.8 x 19.7 cm.), lithograph (BP 24, DM 58, FR 196, Y 4657).

$22* *"Life Study",* #19/25, (10-16-92, DuMouchelle, #2476), approx. 9¾ x 5¼ in., (24.8 x 13.3 cm.), etching/aquatint (BP 13, DM 32, FR 110, Y 2627).

$17* *"Male Nude",* AP, (10-16-92, DuMouchelle, #2473), 8½ x 9 in., (21.6 x 22.9 cm.), lithograph (BP 10, DM 25, FR 85, Y 2030).

$28* *Nudes: Three,* (10-16-92, DuMouchelle, #2475), smallest 7 x 6 in., (17.8 x 15.2 cm.), largest 10 x 7 in., (17.8 x 15.2 cm.), aquatint (BP 17, DM 41, FR 140, Y 3343).

MARTON

$1007* *Moto Peugeot, 1930,* very good cond., (11-19-92, Ribeyre/Baron, #71), 47¼ x 31½ in., (120 x 80 cm.), photo-montage (BP 663, DM 1606, FR 5408, Y 125,233).

$84* *Paris, "Ars Longa - Vita Brevis", 1936,* good cond., (01-23-93, Ribeyre/Baron, #43), 39³⁄₁₆ x 24⁷⁄₁₆ in., (99.5 x 62 cm.), poster (BP 55, DM 134, FR 452, Y 10,513).

MARTYN, Thomas

$4025* *Aranei, Or A Natural History Of Spiders (Freeman 2501; Nissen ZBI 2724), 1793,* folio, prov., (06-14-93, Sotheby-NY, #202, illus.), 13⅛ x 10½ in., (33.3 x 26.7 cm.), etched outline from frontispiece hand-colored, 28 hand-colored etched plates (BP 2635, DM 6551, FR 22,019, Y 423,550).

MARVAL, J.

$650* *2eme Bal De L'A.A.A.A., 1924,* before letter, good cond., (11-19-92, Ribeyre/Baron, #146, illus.), 47¼ x 31½ in., (120 x 80 cm.), poster (BP 428, DM 1036, FR 3491, Y 80,836).

$1301* *Salon D'Automne, Grand Palais, 1923,* p. J. Minot, good cond., (11-19-92, Ribeyre/Baron, #145, illus.), 61¹³⁄₁₆ x 45¹¹⁄₁₆ in., (157 x 116 cm.), poster (BP 857, DM 2074, FR 6987, Y 161,796).

MARVAL, Jacqueline

BI *Jeune Femme Regardant Une Estampe,* (02-24-93, Picard, #166), lithograph on thin chine.

MARVASI, Duccio

$1564* *Kodak 1937,* p. R A K Paris, creases, backed on linen, (05-07-93, Christie-S. Ken, #56, illus.), 29½ x 45½ in., (74.9 x 115.6 cm.), color lithograph (BP 990, DM 2473, FR 8332, Y 172,209).

MARVILLE, Charles 1816-c. 1879

$935* *Facade Of Church, Paris,* 1860s, (04-07-93, Swann, #231, illus.), 8½ x 6 in., photograph, albumen print (BP 618, DM 1512, FR 5118, Y 106,226).

MARWAN b. 1934

$317* *Selbstbildnis Mit Fruchtestilleben, 1975,* s., num., (12-05-92, Bassenge, #7467), 23¹³⁄₁₆ x 17¹⁄₁₆ in., (60.5 x 43.4 cm.), color etching (BP 198, DM 494, FR 1684, Y 39,276).

$280* *Stehender Mann Mit Stirntuch, Halbe Figur, 1972,* s., num., ded., (12-05-92, Bassenge, #7466), 24⅛ x 16¹⁄₁₆ in., (61.3 x 40.8 cm.), etching on copper print paper (BP 175, DM 437, FR 1488, Y 34,692).

$332* *Stilleben Mit Kaffeekanne, 1983,* unique print, s., (12-05-92, Bassenge, #7468), 11¹¹⁄₁₆ x 16⁷⁄₁₆ in., (29.7 x 41.8 cm.), color etching (BP 208, DM 518, FR 1764, Y 41,135).

MARYAN 1927-1977

$165* *Composition,* s. Maryan, 47/120, (03-24-93, Kunsthallen, #235), color lithograph (BP 112, DM 269, FR 917, Y 19,387, DK 1035).

MASANOBU, Okumura

$1055* *A Couple Walking Sharing An Umbrella,* hosoban benizuri-e, s. Hogetsudo okumura Masanobu, faded, rubbed, soiled, (06-10-93, Sotheby-London, #217), (BP 690, DM 1718, FR 5784, Y 111,984).

MASANOBU, Okumura 1686-1764

BI *Bildnis Des Schauspielers Nakamura Shichi Sa Buro,* est. SC 5/6,000, (04-27-93, Dorotheum, #242), 6⅛ x 13⅜ in., (15.6 x 33.9 cm.), color woodcut.

MASCII

$1241* *Le Prince Et La Danseuse (The Prince And The Showgirl), De L. Olivier, Avec Marilyn Monroe (French), 1957,* p. Bedos, (01-31-93, Morelle/Marchan, #78, illus.), 47¼ x 62¹⁵⁄₁₆ in., (120 x 160 cm.), poster (BP 835, DM 1999, FR 6759, Y 154,815).

MASEREEL, Frans Belgian 1889-1971

$811* *Ecce Homo, 1927,* s., t., num., (12-05-92, Bassenge, #7469), 15¾ x 11¹¹⁄₁₆ in., (40 x 29.7 cm.), woodcut on imitation Japan (BP 508, DM 1264, FR 4309, Y 100,483).

$274* *Ehepaar,* s., (11-28-92, Schoppmann, #659), 10⅝ x 8¼ in., (27 x 21 cm.), lithograph on wove (BP 181, DM 437, FR 1482, Y 34,101).

$776* *Liebespaar, 1967,* woodblock mono., pencil d., s., d., t., num. twice, (09-25-92, Granier, #2936, illus.), sheet 19¾ x 25¹¹⁄₁₆ in., (50.2 x 65.3 cm.), woodcut on cream board (BP 453, DM 1150, FR 3890, Y 93,663).

$217* *Nocturno, 1971,* s., d., #58/100; mono., d. in block, discolored, (09-18-92, Schloss Ahlden, #1026), 19⁹⁄₁₆ x 25½ in., (49.7 x 64.8 cm.), woodcut on hand-made (BP 127, DM 322, FR 1102, Y 26,820).

$880* *Skyscrapers, 1926,* s., t., i.; sig./i. faded, light stained, foxing, stains, missing corner, glued, good cond., (12-04-92, Doyle, #132, illus.), 21¾ x 14½ in., (552 x 368 mm.), woodcut (BP 564, DM 1401, FR 4754, Y 109,863).

MASI, Oliverio   Italian b. 1949
$61* *"After The Snow - Winter",* s., num. 78/125, excellent cond., (10-31-92, Cleveland, #379), 11¾ x 15½ in., (29.8 x 39.4 cm.), color lithograph (BP 39, DM 94, FR 318, Y 7556).

$50* *"Snow - Gennaio",* s., num. 109/150, excellent cond., (10-31-92, Cleveland, #380), 15¼ x 23¼ in., (38.7 x 59.1 cm.), color lithograph (BP 32, DM 77, FR 261, Y 6193).

MASIA, J.
$275* *Multi-Colored Stylized Boat At sea, 1944,* Exposition-Valencia 1944, linen-backed, (04-29-93, Swann, #146), 25½ x 17 in., (64.8 x 43.2 cm.), color lithograph poster (BP 175, DM 435, FR 1466, Y 30,593).

MASON, F.
$478* *British India Steam Navigation Co. "To And From London, Tanger, Marseille, Egypt, India And East Africa",* very good cond., (03-13-93, Laurin, #165), 39¾ x 25³⁄₁₆ in., (101 x 64 cm.), (BP 333, DM 796, FR 2705, Y 56,335).

MASON, Frank
$276* *Cowes In The Thirties,* s., blindstamp Fine Art Trade Guild, margins, (08-12-92, Bonhams, #209, illus.), plate 9¾ x 19½ in., (24.8 x 49.5 cm.), drypoint etching (BP 143, DM 404, FR 1368, Y 35,177).

MASON, Frank H.
$101* *A Clipper Off Whitby,* s., blindstamp, margins, scuffing, (01-14-93, Bonhams, #121), plate 6¾ x 13¾ in., (17.1 x 34.9 cm.), drypoint etching (BP 66, DM 165, FR 558, Y 12,733).

MASON, R.H.
BI *"Self Portrait", c. 1970,* mounted on card, s., t., i., stamped photog.'s credit, labels, 490 x355mm, est. BP 2/300, (05-07-93, Sotheby-London, #192), photograph, silver print.

MASON, W.H.
$4400* *Panorama Of Brighton,* continuous strip view, watermark, tears, repair, boxwood drum, lit.,drawn by H. Wilds, engr. A. Edington, (12-17-92, Sotheby-NY, #40, illus.), 4⁵⁄₁₆ x 18¼ in., (109 x 464 mm.), engraved, handcolored aquatint view of 6 panels (BP 2793, DM 6870, FR 23,467, Y 540,740).

MASON, W.H., Publisher
$17* *Cracks Of The North, A False Start, 1869,* (10-29-92, Bonhams-Chelsea, #157), image 5¼ x 11¼ in., (13.3 x 28.6 cm.), photographic print w/hand coloring (BP 11, DM 26, FR 89, Y 2106).

MASOUR, Sascha
BI *Ohne Titel, 1962,* d., (c), est. DM 600, (11-12-92, Lempertz, #168, illus.), 8¹¹⁄₁₆ x 6¾ in., (22.1 x 17.1 cm.), sheet 9⅜ x 6¾ in., (22.1 x 17.1 cm.), photograph, gelatin silver print.

MASQUIERIER, John James (after)
BI *La Diseuse De Bonne Aventure,* by A. Cardon, pub. by Tessari & Co., trimmed, laid on support, foxing, dirt, waterstains, est. BP 150/200, (11-30-92, Phillips-London, #146), sheet 20⅝ x 19¼ in., (524 x 489 mm.), color stipple engraving on wove.

MASSARA, Giovanni
BI *The Old Peasant Woman In Torazzo, Italy, c. 1948,* s., t., notations, credit stamp, est. $800/1,200, (04-08-93, Christie-NY, #188, illus.), 9⅝ x 7 in., (24.4 x 17.8 cm.), photograph, gelatin silver print.

MASSARD, Jean   French 18th/19th cent.
BI *Adam And Eve,* after Carlo Cegnani, est. $4/500, (04-02-93, Sloan, #2271), sight 22⅝ x 17½ in., (575 x 445 mm.), engraving.

MASSE, Zh.   ac. 1920
$1165* *V. Marta, Stroki, Zelenaia Koshka (Lines, The Green Cat)* c. 1920, 8 pages of woodcut text and illustrations, rust spots, stains, very ggood cond., surface dirt, (12-01-92, Christie-London, #526, illus.), overall sheet 7¹⁄₁₆ x 5¼ in., (180 x 134 mm.), woodcuts on cream wove (BP 770, DM 1857, FR 6328, Y 145,045).

MASSEAU, Pierre Fix
BI *Cote D'Azur Pullman-Express,* by L. Danel, Lille, 1929, good cond., creasing, est. $4/6,000, (06-10-93, Sotheby-NY, #475, illus.), 38¾ x 24 in., (98.4 x 61 cm.), color lithograph.

MASSICOTTE, Edmond Joseph   Canadian School 1875-1929
$233* *"Les Canadiens D'Autrefois": Set of Seven,* s., d. in plate Edmond J. Massicotte (1914 a 1928), (07-14-92, Encans, #144), 8⁷⁄₁₆ x 12 in., (21.5 x 30.5 cm.), print (BP 121, DM 346, FR 1166, Y 29,136, C$ 278).

MASSON, Andre   French 1896-1987
$138* *Abstract Figures,* plate s., very good cond.?, (07-19-92, Bakker, #192), sheet 13 x 17 in., (33 x 43.2 cm.), lithograph (BP 71, DM 201, FR 680, Y 17,156).

$341* *Adam Und Eva,* s., #61/80, (09-18-92, Schloss Ahlden, #1031), 25¹⁵⁄₁₆ x 19¹³⁄₁₆ in., (66 x 50.4 cm.), color etching on Arches wove (BP 200, DM 506, FR 1731, Y 42,146).

$3069* *Andre Maurois. Les Erophages, 1960: Sixteen,* book, three etchings on cover, title-page and text s. crayon by artist, author and pub., #1/145, pub. Felia Leon, full margins, good cond., creasing, (12-03-92, Sotheby-London, #391, illus.), etchings w/aquatint in colors on wove (BP 1980, DM 4826, FR 16,473, Y 381,859).

$426* *Baigneuse A L'Aube, 1955,* full margins, good cond., (12-03-92, Sotheby-London, #390), 12⅛ x 16⅛ in., (310 x 410 mm.), aquatint in colors on wove (BP 275, DM 670, FR 2287, Y 53,005).

$682* *Battements (S. 44), 1933,* s., num., pub. Blue Moon Gallery, p. Lacouriere-Frelaut, full margins, good cond., (12-03-92, Sotheby-London, #383, illus.), 5⅞ x 4½ in., (148 x 114 mm.), etching on wove (BP 440, DM 1072, FR 3661, Y 84,858).

$337* *Composition,* s. Andre Masson, 59/100, (09-30-92, Kunsthallen, #196), color etching (BP 190, DM 478, FR 1616, Y 40,442, DK 1840).

$268* *Composition,* s., 22/50, (04-17-93, Falkkloos, #346), 11 x 9¹⁄₁₆ in., (28 x 23 cm.), lithograph in colors (BP 174, DM 429, FR 1448, Y 29,801, SK 1980).

$577* *Composition,* s., artist's proof, (03-31-93, Briest, #E182), 16⁹⁄₁₆ x 20½ in., (42 x 52 cm.), color lithograph (BP 381, DM 928, FR 3153, Y 66,352).

$135* *Composition Sur Fond Beige,* s. artist's proof, good cond., (06-28-93, Loudmer, #303), 18⅞ x 24¹³⁄₁₆ in., (480 x 630 mm.), sh 22⁷⁄₁₆ x 29¹⁵⁄₁₆ in., (480 x 630 mm.), color lithograph on Arches wove (BP 90, DM 229, FR 773, Y 14,324).

$193* *Composition Sur Fond Marron,* s. artist's proof, (06-28-93, Loudmer, #301), 25¹⁵⁄₁₆ x 19¹⁵⁄₁₆ in., (660 x 507 mm.), sh 29¹⁵⁄₁₆ x 22¼ in., (660 x 507 mm.), color lithograph on Arches wove (BP 129, DM 328, FR 1105, Y 20,477).

$126* *Composition Sur Fond Noir,* s. artist's proof, (06-28-93, Loudmer, #302), 19½ x 24⁷⁄₁₆ in., (495 x 620 mm.), sh 22⁷⁄₁₆ x 29¹⁵⁄₁₆ in., (495 x 620 mm.), color lithograph on Arches wove (BP 84, DM 214, FR 721, Y 13,369).

$516* *Composition Surrealiste,* s., #8/10, full margins, good cond., (03-31-93, Briest, #E180), sh 20¹⁄₁₆ x 12¹⁵⁄₁₆ in., (51 x 33 cm.), 7½ x 7½ in., (51 x 33 cm.), etching and aquatint on Japan (BP 341, DM 830, FR 2820, Y 59,338).

BI *Compositions, c. 1960: Three,* each s., 2 #60/125 and 27/150, 1 i. E.A., full margins, good cond., creases, est. $1,4/1,800, (02-11-93, Sotheby-NY, #169), color lithograph.

BI *Compositions, c. 1960: Three,* s.; # 7/20, 11/74, 8/40; full margins, good cond., creases, soiling,skinned spot, est. $800/1,000, (02-11-93, Sotheby-NY, #171), lithograph, 2 in color.

BI *Compositions, c. 1960: Two,* each s., 1st #44/150, 2nd i. E.A., full margins, good cond., soiling, glue stains, est. $1/2,000, (02-11-93, Sotheby-NY, #170), 16⅛ x 22¹⁄₁₆ in., (410 x 560 mm.), 23⁷⁄₁₆ x 19⁵⁄₁₆ in., (410 x 560 mm.), color lithograph.

$248* *Conversation In Blue And Pink, 1968,* s., #130/200, (05-16-93, Hindman, #495), 22¼ x 14¾ in., (56.5 x 37.5 cm.), color lithograph (BP 161, DM 399, FR 1341, Y 27,491).

BI *"Corps",* s., num., est. DM 900, (12-01-92, Karl/Faber, #983), 11⅝ x 9⁷⁄₁₆ in., (29.5 x 24 cm.), etching on wove.

BI *Couple Enlace,* s., #3/47, est. FF2,000/2,500, (05-27-93, Briest, #144), 14¾ x 22¼ in., (37.5 x 56.5 cm.), color lithograph.

$330* *Couple, 1975,* s., #H.C. XXIV/XXV, from portfolio Je Reve, (03-14-93, Hindman, #287), 17 x 14¼ in., (43.2 x 36.2 cm.), color lithograph (BP 230, DM 549, FR 1868, Y 38,892).

$330* *Delila, 1975,* s., #H.C. XXIV/XXV, from portfolio Je Reve, (03-14-93, Hindman, #286), 24¾ x 18¾ in., (62.9 x 47.6 cm.), color lithograph (BP 230, DM 549, FR 1868, Y 38,892).

BI *"Dessins Erotiques": 20,* from 300 impressions, num., s., (05-18-93, Encans, #207), 25⁹⁄₁₆ x 19¹¹⁄₁₆ in., (65 x 50 cm.), lithographs, 5 in color, on Arches wove.

$1340* *Dessins Erotiques, 1971: Portfolio of Twenty,* s., #97/125, (03-31-93, Briest, #E179), 25¹⁵⁄₁₆ x 18⅞ in., (66 x 48 cm.), lithographs in black and in color (BP 886, DM 2155, FR 7322, Y 154,094).

$269* *"Erotique": Two,* s., (10-18-92, Pescheteau, #208), 21¼ x 29½ in., (54 x 75 cm.), lithograph in colors on Arches (BP 163, DM 397, FR 1350, Y 32,119).

$410* *Erotische Szene,* #11/125, s., blindstamp, studio blindstamp, (11-13-92, Koller, #5373), 16¹⁵⁄₁₆ x 22¹⁄₁₆ in., (43 x 56 cm.), color lithograph on Arches wove (BP 265, DM 644, FR 2170, Y 50,887, SF 580).

$330* *Exultation In Green,* s., annot. E.a., margins, apparently good cond., (02-24-93, Butterfield, #2951), 28¾ x 21½ in., (730 x 546 mm.), lithograph in colors on wove (BP 230, DM 536, FR 1816, Y 38,723).

$468* *Exultation Ronge,* s., num. 96/150, full margins, apparently good cond., (02-24-93, Butterfield, #2953), 29 x 21½ in., (737 x 546 mm.), lithograph in colors on wove (BP 326, DM 760, FR 2576, Y 54,917).

BI *Faune Et Femme En Armure, 1966,* s., num., est. DM 1,500, (12-01-92, Karl/Faber, #980), 12 x 9¼ in., (30.5 x 23.5 cm.), color etching and aquatint on BFK Rives wove.

$315* *Femme A La Colombe, 1956,* s., #145/150, (11-16-92, Briest, #329), 21⅝ x 14¹⁵⁄₁₆ in., (55 x 38 cm.), lithograph in colors (BP 207, DM 502, FR 1693, Y 39,311).

BI *Femme Attaquee Par Les Oiseaux (S. 245), 1947-56,* p. by Lacouriere, pub. Galerie Louise Leiris, full margins, good cond., creases, est. BP 4/500, (06-30-93, Sotheby-London, #499, illus.), 13⅞ x 9⅞ in., (352 x 251 mm.), drypoint w/engraving w/gold aquatint plage.

BI *Femme Attaquee Par Les Oiseaux (Saphire 245), 1947-56,* s., num., p. Lacouriere, pub. Galerie Louise Leiris, full margins, good cond., est. BP 5/700, (12-03-92, Sotheby-London, #381, illus.), 14 x 10⅛ in., (358 x 257 mm.), drypoint w/engraving w/gold aquatint plate on Arches.

$77* *Femme Nue De Dos,* s., annot., mat traces verso, tear, (06-28-93, Loudmer, #304), 6⅞ x 4¾ in., (175 x 120 mm.), sh 9¹³⁄₁₆ x 7½ in., (175 x 120 mm.), black lithograph on China (BP 52, DM 131, FR 441, Y 8170).

$240* *"Fertilite",* HC s., (04-04-93, Pescheteau, #258), 12³⁄₁₆ x 9⁷⁄₁₆ in., (31 x 24 cm.), color lithograph (BP 158, DM 386, FR 1310, Y 27,326).

$394* *Figurliche Komposition, 1973,* s., #61/75, (05-27-93, Lempertz, #892A), 12³⁄₁₆ x 9⅛ in., (31 x 23.1 cm.), color etching on wove (BP 252, DM 632, FR 2131, Y 42,238).

$361* *Frau Mit Herz, 1961,* s., (11-28-92, Grisebach, #646, illus.), 20½ x 16⅛ in., (52 x 41 cm.), colored lithograph on wove (BP 238, DM 575, FR 1952, Y 44,928).

$3575* *Je Reve Portefeuille: "Viviane", "Couple Alchimique", "Dalila", "Bacchanale", "Venise En Fleurs", "Le Philosophe Au Papillon", "Satan", "La Naissance D'Eve" and "Le Prince Iris", 1975: Ten,* complete portfolio, each s., #30/125, pub. Mourlot, very good cond., (02-24-93, Butterfield, #2751), each sheet 26 x 19⅞ in., (660 x 505 mm.), lithograph in colors on Arches (BP 2493, DM 5804, FR 19,675, Y 419,502).

$2185* *Je Reve: "Viviane", "Couple Alchimique", "Dalila", "Bacchanale", "Venise En Fleurs", "Le Philosophe Au Papillon", "Satan", "La Venitienne", "La Naissance D'Eve" and "Le Prince Iris", 1975: Ten,* complete portfolio, each s., #24/125, p. Mourlot, good cond., original portfolio, (05-19-93, Butterfield, #1927), each 25¾ x 19⅞ in., (654 x 505 mm.), lithograph in colors on Arches (BP 1418, DM 3552, FR 11,966, Y 241,891).

$618* *Jean Paulhan. Les Hain-Teny, 1956,* incomplete portfolio, 17 from set of 20, including 9 full page plates, double page cover, 7 vignettes on chapter headings, pub. Les Bibliophiles deL'Union Francaise, good cond., foxing, staining, (06-30-93, Sotheby-London, #500), color aquatint on Auvergne (BP 414, DM 1054, FR 3556, Y 66,217).

BI *Judith, c. 1974,* s., #148/150, est. $800/1,200, (12-08-92, Swann, #200), image 19½ x 24½ in., (49.5 x 62.2 cm.), color lithograph.

$369* *Komposition,* s., num., (12-05-92, Bassenge, #7474), 20¼ x 14³⁄₁₆ in., (51.5 x 36 cm.), color lithograph on Arches (BP 231, DM 575, FR 1961, Y 45,719).

BI *Komposition In Violett Auf Grun,* s., est. DM 850-, (09-25-92, Granier, #2938), sheet 11¾ x 9⅞ in., (29.8 x 25.1 cm.), color lithograph on hand-made.

$516* *Komposition Mit Flusslauf,* epreuve d'artiste, s., (12-05-92, Bassenge, #7471), 20¹⁄₁₆ x 15¾ in., (51 x 40 cm.), color lithograph on Arches (BP 323, DM 804, FR 2742, Y 63,933).

$480* *Komposition, c. 1960,* s., e.a., (12-05-92, Bassenge, #7472), 18¼ x 22½ in., (46.4 x 57.2 cm.), color lithograph (BP 301, DM 748, FR 2550, Y 59,472).

BI *L'Arbre Et Le Nid, 1964,* whole margins, #13/50, s., (06-11-93, Picard, #119), 10⅝ x 8¼ in., (270 x 210 mm.), etching in black-gray on wove.

BI *L'Arme Secrete (Saphire 146), 1946,* book, s., title page & reprods. of drawings, text & just., s. by author, num. 38, pub. Broder, full margins, good cond., orig. wrappers, est. BP 5/600, (12-03-92, Sotheby-London, #388, illus.), lithograph on wove.

BI *L'Arme Secrete (Saphire 146), 1946,* book, s., w/title-page and reprods. of drawings, text and justification, s. by author, #38, pub. Bordas, full margins, good cond., est. BP 3/400, (06-30-93, Sotheby-London, #496), lithograph on wove.

BI *L'Espagne Assassinee (Saphire 65), 1938,* s., plate mono., album Solidarite, est. DM 2,000, (06-10-93, Hauswedell/Nolt, #609, illus.), 3⅛ x 4⁵⁄₁₆ in., (8 x 11 cm.), etching on hand-made.

$597* *L'Homme Au Couteau (S. 42), c. 1933,* p. Lacouriere-Frelaut, pub. Blue Moon Gallery, 1972, full margins, good cond., (12-03-92, Sotheby-London, #385, illus.), 11½ x 9¼ in., (298 x 236 mm.), drypoint on wove (BP 385, DM 939, FR 3205, Y 74,281).

$495* *Marathon, Figure,* s., #38/75, full margins, good cond., surface soiling, creases, (10-28-92, Butterfield, #2839), 24¾ x 18½ in., (629 x 470 mm.), color lithograph on Arches (BP 315, DM 764, FR 2596, Y 60,736).

$193* *"Massacre" (Saphire #43), 1933,* #14/100, s., num., (02-13-93, Neal, #576), plate 4⅜ x 5¾ in., (11.1 x 14.6 cm.), drypoint etching (BP 136, DM 320, FR 1083, Y 23,275).

$360* *Mechoui, 1962,* whole margins, #15/50, s., (06-11-93, Picard, #118), 8¼ x 10⅝ in., (210 x 270 mm.), color etching and aquatint on wove (BP 237, DM 585, FR 1973, Y 38,196).

BI *Metamorphose,* epreuve d'artiste, s., full margins, est. FF 2,5/3,000, (11-16-92, Briest, #331), 19¹¹⁄₁₆ x 25¹⁵⁄₁₆ in., (50 x 66 cm.), etching and aquatint in colors.

BI   *"Metamorphose" and "Danse Des Tournesols" (Saphire E11, E16): Two,* pub. Art Conseil, est. $700/1,000, (05-27-93, Swann, #178), color lithograph.

$232* *Metamorphoses,* s., 39/50, losses, (06-28-93, Loudmer, #305), 8¾ x 11¹³⁄₁₆ in., (222 x 300 mm.), sh 12¹³⁄₁₆ x 17⅜ in., (222 x 300 mm.), black and gilded drypoint and aquatint on laid (BP 155, DM 394, FR 1328, Y 24,615).

$1540* *Le Misanthrope (Saphire 96), 1945,* s., #23/40, pub. Bucholz Gallery, full margins, good cond., (11-05-92, Sotheby-NY, #236, illus.), 8¾ x 7 in., (222 x 178 mm.), soft ground etching and aquatint (BP 1002, DM 2436, FR 8240, Y 188,934).

BI   *"Le Mort", 1964: Set of Nine,* each s., est. FF 20/25,000, (10-18-92, Pescheteau, #206, illus.), each 11 x 14¹⁵⁄₁₆ in., (28 x 38 cm.), etching and aquatint on Moulin Richard de Bas.

$597* *NU (S. 242), 1947,* p. Lacouriere, pub. Galerie Louise Leiris, full margins, good cond., (12-03-92, Sotheby-London, #382, illus.), 17⅝ x 13¾ in., (447 x 347 mm.), aquatint on Arches (BP 385, DM 939, FR 3205, Y 74,281).

$330* *La Naissance D'Ere, 1975,* s., #H.C. XXIV/XXV, from portfolio Je Reve, (03-14-93, Hindman, #290), 19¾ x 24⅞ in., (50.2 x 63.2 cm.), color lithograph (BP 230, DM 549, FR 1868, Y 38,892).

BI   *Nine Bookplates, c. 1960,* full margins, good cond., handling creases, est. BP 800/1,000, (06-30-93, Sotheby-London, #501), nine etchings, eight w/color aquatint, eight on wove, one on Japan.

$652* *Nu (S. 242), 1947,* pub. Galerie Louise Leiris, full margins, good cond., handling creases, discoloration, (06-30-93, Sotheby-London, #498, illus.), 17⅝ x 13¾ in., (448 x 349 mm.), aquatint on Arches (BP 437, DM 1112, FR 3751, Y 69,860).

BI   *Nude Woman,* s., annot. Epreuve d'Artist, full margins, good cond.?, staining, est. $3/500, (05-19-93, Butterfield, #2073), 25 x 19 in., (635 x 483 mm.), lithograph in colors on wove.

$272* *Ohne Titel (vierweibliche Akte),* from Die Welt des Klassizismus, s., #47/80, (09-18-92, Schloss Ahlden, #1028), 22⁵⁄₁₆ x 29¹¹⁄₁₆ in., (56.7 x 75.4 cm.), etching in colors on hand-made (BP 159, DM 404, FR 1381, Y 33,618).

$385* *Orphee,* s., annot. E.a., upper & left margin possibly trimmed, apparently good cond., creases, (02-24-93, Butterfield, #2952), 19 x 24 in., (483 x 610 mm.), lithograph in colors on Japon nacre (BP 268, DM 625, FR 2119, Y 45,177).

$597* *Orphee (S. 46), c. 1933,* s., num., p. Lacouriere-Frelaut, pub. Blue Moon Gallery, full margins, good cond., (12-03-92, Sotheby-London, #386, illus.), 11⅝ x 9¼ in., (296 x 235 mm.), etching and drypoint on wove (BP 385, DM 939, FR 3205, Y 74,281).

$387* *Orpheus,* s., #1/100, blindstamp, (09-18-92, Schloss Ahlden, #1027, illus.), 29⅝ x 21⅛ in., (75.3 x 53.6 cm.), color lithograph on Arches wove (BP 227, DM 574, FR 1964, Y 47,831).

$533* *Das Paar,* Epreuve d'artiste, s., (11-13-92, Koller, #5372), 19⁵⁄₁₆ x 25³⁄₁₆ in., (49 x 64 cm.), lithograph on Arches wove (BP 344, DM 837, FR 2822, Y 66,154, SF 754).

BI   *Paar, 1967,* s., #52/120, discolored, streaked, est. DM 350, (09-18-92, Schloss Ahlden, #1030), 25⁹⁄₁₆ x 19⅝ in., (65 x 49.9 cm.), color lithograph on Arches wove.

BI   *Paris, Au Vent D'Arles, 1964: Nine,* from Le Mort by Georges Bataille, num. XI to XXX, est. SF 6/7,000, (11-15-92, Christie-Geneva, #308, illus.), 12³⁄₁₆ x 16⅛ in., (310 x 410 mm.), color etching.

BI   *Penthesilee (Large Version) (S. 228), 1946,* p. by Lacouriere, pub. Galerie Louise Leiris, full margins, good cond., handling creases, discoloration, est. BP 5/700, (06-30-93, Sotheby-London, #497), 12 x 16 in., (305 x 406 mm.), drypoint on Arches.

BI   *Penthesilee (S. 228), 1946,* pub. Galerie Louise Leiris, full margins, good cond., est. BP 9/1,000, (12-03-92, Sotheby-London, #389), 12⅛ x 16 in., (308 x 407 mm.), drypoint on Arches.

$200* *"Personnages",* #XXXVII/XLV, s., (04-04-93, Pescheteau, #257), 14¹⁵⁄₁₆ x 11 in., (38 x 28 cm.), violet etching and

aquatint on wove (BP 132, DM 321, FR 1092, Y 22,771).

BI   *Un Peu D'Erotisme, 1974,* s., #6/60, est. BP 2/250, (10-27-92, Phillips-London, #211), plate 9¼ x 12¾ in., (235 x 340 mm.), etching w/aquatint in pink and black w/ touches of white heightening.

$303* *Le Philosophe Au Papillon, 1975,* s., #H.C.XXIV/XXV, from portfolio Je Reve, (03-14-93, Hindman, #285), 23⅛ x 18 in., (58.7 x 45.7 cm.), color lithograph (BP 211, DM 504, FR 1715, Y 35,710).

$500* *Portrait De Baudelaire,* full margins, s., num. 12/20, good cond., (11-30-92, Phillips-London, #543), plate 3 x 2 in., (76 x 51 mm.), etching on wove (BP 330, DM 797, FR 2704, Y 62,228).

$747* *Poursuite En Rouge, 1955,* s., num., restored tears, (12-01-92, Karl/Faber, #979), 17⁵⁄₁₆ x 22¹³⁄₁₆ in., (44 x 58 cm.), color lithograph on Arches wove (BP 494, DM 1191, FR 4058, Y 93,003).

$330* *Le Prince Iris, 1975,* s., #H.C. XXIV/XXV, from portfolio Je Reve, (03-14-93, Hindman, #289), 16 x 24 in., (40.6 x 61 cm.), color lithograph (BP 230, DM 549, FR 1868, Y 38,892).

$330* *Profile Portraits,* s., #176/200, (06-11-93, Freemn/Fine Art, #142), 22½ x 17¼ in., (57.2 x 43.8 cm.), lithograph in color (BP 217, DM 536, FR 1808, Y 35,013).

$440* *Ruisseau, c. 1974,* s., annot. E.A., (12-08-92, Swann, #201), 25¼ x 19½ in., (64.1 x 49.5 cm.), color lithograph (BP 276, DM 685, FR 2335, Y 54,536).

$2035* *Une Saison En Enfer, 1961,* portfolio, s., copy num. LXXXVII, pub. Les Cent Une, Societe Bibliophiles de Femmes, foxing, sold after sale, (11-05-92, Sotheby-NY, #237), each sheet approx. 15⅜ x 11⅜ in., (390 x 290 mm.), 9 etchings w/aquatint p. in colors on double pages, and 9 monochromeetchings w/aquatint (BP 1324, DM 3218, FR 10,888, Y 249,663).

$68* *"Sans Titre", 1969 and "Sans Titre", 1972: Two,* both pub. "XXe siecle", Paris, num. 32 and 38, (06-28-93, Loudmer, #94), 12³⁄₁₆ x 9⁷⁄₁₆ in., (310 x 240 mm.), color lithograph on wove (BP 46, DM 116, FR 389, Y 7215).

$330* *Satan, 1975,* s., #H.C. XXIV/XXV, from portfolio Je Reve, (03-14-93, Hindman, #288), 18⅛ x 23¾ in., (46 x 60.3 cm.), color lithograph (BP 230, DM 549, FR 1868, Y 38,892).

BI   *Le Septieme Chant, 1974: Four,* complete portfolio, s. by artist and author, #150, pub. Societe Internationale d'Art XXe, p. Freres Cromelynck, full margins, very good cond., original portfolio and slip case, (05-19-93, Butterfield, #1926), each sh 14¾ x 11³⁄₁₆ in., (375 x 284 mm.), etching w/aquatint on Arches.

BI   *Sisyphe (1st State) (Saphire 238), 1946,* s., i. 1 Etat, #10/10, margins, light/mat staining, creasing, surface soiling, tears, tips lacking, good cond., Ian Woodner Family Coll., est. $3/4,000, (05-11-93, Christie-NY, #214, illus.), plate 16¾ x 24⅞ in., (425 x 632 mm.), drypoint on wove.

BI   *Solidarite, 1938,* from portfolio Paul Eluard. Solidarite, s., #25/150, pub. G.L.M., reduced margins, good cond., est. BP 6/800, (12-03-92, Sotheby-London, #387), 3⅛ x 4¼ in., (80 x 110 mm.), etching.

BI   *Le Sommeil,* s., #92/99, margins, good cond.?, est. $4/600, (05-19-93, Butterfield, #2075), 19 x 25 in., (483 x 635 mm.), lithograph in colors on wove.

BI   *La Sorciere,* s., annot. Epreuve d'artiste, margins, good cond.?, est. $6/800, (05-19-93, Butterfield, #2074), 16 x 23¼ in., (406 x 591 mm.), lithograph in colors on Arches.

$597* *Sueur De Sang (S. 45), 1933,* s., num., pub. Blue Moon Gallery, p. Lacouriere-Frelaut, full margins, good cond., (12-03-92, Sotheby-London, #384, illus.), 7⅝ x 5½ in., (193 x 140 mm.), etching on wove (BP 385, DM 939, FR 3205, Y 74,281).

BI   *Terre Erotique,* 123/125, s., est. SF 700/800, (10-14-92, Germann, #374), 19⅛ x 25¹³⁄₁₆ in., (485 x 655 mm.), color lithograph.

$388* *Terre Erotique,* s., num., blindstamp, (05-26-93, Dorling, #2851), 8⅞ x 11⅞ in., (22.5 x 30.2 cm.), lithograph on Arches wove (BP 251, DM 633, FR 2131, Y 42,156).

BI *"Tortue D'Eau", #79/100, s.,* dry stamp Lacouriere, est. FF 6/8,000, (10-18-92, Pescheteau, #207), 25⁹⁄₁₆ x 19¹¹⁄₁₆ in., (65 x 50 cm.), etching and aquatint on Arches.

$220* *Two Standing Figures In Blue, c. 1970,* s., #170/200, mat burn, (12-08-92, Swann, #198), 22½ x 15 in., (57.2 x 38.1 cm.), color lithograph (BP 138, DM 343, FR 1168, Y 27,268).

$286* *Untitled,* s., (11-30-92, Selkirk, #713), image 29 x 22 in., (73.7 x 55.9 cm.), color lithograph (BP 189, DM 456, FR 1547, Y 35,594).

$1253* *Untitled: Four,* #29/50, 13/75, 49/150, 143/150, all s., (05-20-93, Finarte-Milan, #108), lithograph in colors (BP 804, DM 2022, FR 6810, Y 138,361, L 1840).

$1488* *Untitled: Four,* #14/75, 91/150, 106/150, proof, all s., (05-20-93, Finarte-Milan, #109), lithograph in colors (BP 955, DM 2401, FR 8087, Y 164,311, L 2185).

$440* *La Venitienne, 1975,* s., #H.C. XXIV/XXV, (03-14-93, Hindman, #291), 16 x 23 in., (40.6 x 58.4 cm.), color lithograph (BP 307, DM 732, FR 2490, Y 51,856).

$349* *Vogeldame,* s., #16/60, (09-18-92, Schloss Ahlden, #1029), 25¹⁵⁄₁₆ x 19¹¹⁄₁₆ in., (66 x 50 cm.), color etching on Arches wove (BP 204, DM 518, FR 1772, Y 43,134).

$325* *Wave Of The Future,* s., num., (11-28-92, Schoppmann, #660), 25⁹⁄₁₆ x 19¹¹⁄₁₆ in., (65 x 50 cm.), color lithograph on Arches wove (BP 215, DM 518, FR 1758, Y 40,448).

$358* *Wave Of The Future, 1972,* num., s., (11-12-92, Freemn/ Fine Art, #141), 19¾ x 25¾ in., (50.2 x 65.4 cm.), color lithograph (BP 235, DM 567, FR 1913, Y 44,389).

$247* *Wave Of The Future, 1975,* s., #17/50, pub. Trans World Art, (12-08-92, Swann, #202), 19¼ x 25¼ in., (48.9 x 64.1 cm.), color silkscreen on Japan (BP 155, DM 385, FR 1311, Y 30,615).

$395* *Wave Of The Future, 1975,* from portfolio "Bicentenial of USA", #41/175, s., (04-21-93, Germann, #624, illus.), 19⅞ x 25¹¹⁄₁₆ in., (505 x 653 mm.), color lithograph (BP 256, DM 631, FR 2135, Y 43,729, SF 575).

$465* *Weibliche Figur, c. 1960,* s., epreuve d'artiste, (12-05-92, Bassenge, #7473), color lithograph (BP 291, DM 725, FR 2471, Y 57,614).

$468* *Works Of Chance,* s., annot. EA., margins, apparently good cond., (02-24-93, Butterfield, #2950), 30 x 23¼ in., (762 x 591 mm.), lithograph in colors on wove (BP 326, DM 760, FR 2576, Y 54,917).

BI *Works Of Chance,* s., annot. E.A., margins, good cond.?, est. $4/600, (05-19-93, Butterfield, #2076), 30 x 23⅜ in., (762 x 594 mm.), lithograph in colors on Rives BFK.

MASSON, Andre (after)

BI *Lutte,* s., #91/125, full margins, (05-06-93, Laurin, #65), color lithograph.

$93* *Terre Erotique,* s., #113/125, full margins, (05-06-93, Laurin, #66), lithograph (BP 59, DM 146, FR 493, Y 10,232).

MASSON, Andre and Alain JOUFFROY

BI *Le Septieme Chant,* text, t., & just. page, s. by artist & author, num. page 149, p. Crommelynck, pub. Societe Interna- tionale d'Art XX Siecle, good cond., est. BP 7/800, (11- 30-92, Phillips-London, #544), sheet 15 x 11¼ in., (381 x 286 mm.), etchings, 1 in red, on Arches.

MASSON, Henri Leopold   Canadian b. 1907

$134* *"C'Est En Groupe Avec Le Christ Qu'On Est Fort",* #184/250, t., s. H. Masson, (03-16-93, Encans, #79), 15¾ x 11¹³⁄₁₆ in., (40 x 30 cm.), lithograph (BP 93, DM 223, FR 757, Y 15,669, C$ 167).

$134* *"Dis-Moi Le Donc Ovide Que Tu Me Desires",* #184/250, t., s. H. Masson, (03-16-93, Encans, #78), 15¾ x 11¹³⁄₁₆ in., (40 x 30 cm.), lithograph (BP 93, DM 223, FR 757, Y 15,669, C$ 167).

$186* *"Quand Les Humains Et La Nature Sont Freres. Pelo- quin"* and *"BonheurToujours Sur Place, Si Pres, Pas A L'Horizon. Peloquin": Two,* #86/250, s. Henri Masson, t., (07-14-92, Encans, #60), 15¹⁵⁄₁₆ x 20¹⁄₁₆ in., (40.5 x 51 cm.), lithograph (BP 97, DM 276, FR 930, Y 23,259, C$ 222).

$168* *"T'As Ri De Moi? Tu Vas Le Regretter Mon P'tit Gars! Roger Lemelin",* num. ex-auteur 22/30, s. Henri Masson, (07-14-92, Encans, #61), 15¹⁵⁄₁₆ x 12 in., (40.5 x 30.5

---

cm.), lithograph (BP 88, DM 249, FR 840, Y 21,008, C$ 200).

MASSONET, A.   Belgian b. 1892

$734* *VIeme Foire Commerciale. Bruxelles, 1925,* good cond., (11-19-92, Ribeyre/Baron, #147), 63⅜ x 47⁷⁄₁₆ in., (161 x 120.5 cm.), poster (BP 483, DM 1170, FR 3942, Y 91,282).

MASSYS, Cornelis   Flemish c. 1508-c. 1580

$325* *Der Streit Der Bettler (B. IX, 17; Hollstein 133 II), 1539,* (12-04-92, Bassenge, #6290, illus.), 2⅜ x 3⅝ in., (6.1 x 9.2 cm.), engraving (BP 208, DM 518, FR 1756, Y 40,574).

$2022* *Der Tanz Der Lahmen Bettler Und Bettlerinnen (B. IX, S. 91, 3-14; Hollstein 138-149 I): Twelve,* (12-04-92, Bassenge, #6289), each approx. 2⁵⁄₁₆ x 1⅝ in., (5.8 x 4.2 cm.), engraving (BP 1297, DM 3220, FR 10,924, Y 252,434).

MASTER, M.B.

BI *Anatomical Study Of Standing Male Nude,* inits. M.B. in plate, est. $250/350, (02-04-93, Sloan, #724), 8½ x 4¼ in., (21.6 x 10.8 cm.), engraving.

MASTER AG   German ac. 1480

BI *"The Death Of The Virgin" (Lehrs 5, Bartsch VI p. 121),* posthumous impression after Martin Schongauer, center fold, good cond., est. $8/1,200, (10-31-92, Cleveland, #16), 10⅛ x 6⅞ in., (25.7 x 17.5 cm.), engraving.

MASTER HFE

BI *Sea God Procession (Bartsch XV, 3),* watermark, narrow margins, trimmed, paper loss, stains, thin spots, defects, est. BP 2/3,000, (06-29-93, Sotheby-London, #55, illus.), 6½ x 15½ in., (16.5 x 39.4 cm.), engraving on paper.

MASTER I. O. V. (attrib.)

BI *Rebecca And Elisa (B. XVI, 81),* after Primaticcio, mar- gins, extensively stained, damaged, creases, defects, (06- 30-93, Sotheby-London, #162), 14¼ x 13 in., (362 x 330 mm.), etching.

MASTER I.B.   ac. c. 1525-1530

$1498* *The Seven Christian Virtues (B. 23-9): Set Of Seven,* thread margins or trimmed, loss, glue stains, very good cond., (12-01-92, Christie-London, #175, illus.), plate 3¹⁄₁₆ x 2 in., (78 x 51 mm.), engraving (BP 990, DM 2388, FR 8137, Y 186,504).

MASTER IV   ac. c. 1550

$11,654* *Apelle Peignant Alexandre Et Campaspe (B. XVI, p. 371, no. 2; Herbet, p. 201, no. 5), c. 1550,* after Primaticcio, narrow to thread margins, creases, very good cond., laid, (12-01-92, Christie-London, #25, illus.), sheet 17¾ x 12¹⁄₁₆ in., (451 x 307 mm.), etching (BP 7700, DM 18,575, FR 63,303, Y 1,450,946).

MASTER MZ   ac. 1500

$27,775* *The Embrace (Bartsch VI, 15), 1503,* polishing scratches, showing platemark, trimmed, foxing, thin spots,nicks, good cond., ex. coll. J.A. Boerner (d. 1809) (L. 270); and Fritz Rumpf (L. 2161), (06-29-93, Sotheby-London, #56, illus.), 6 x 4½ in., (15.2 x 11.4 cm.), engraving (BP 18,400, DM 46,901, FR 158,082, Y 2,956,674).

$2987* *Das Turnier (B. 14; Lehrs VIII, Nr. 18), 1500,* tears, (12- 01-92, Karl/Faber, #100, illus.), engraving (BP 1974, DM 4761, FR 16,225, Y 371,887).

$3895* *Das Tunier (B. 14, Lehrs VIII, Nr. 18, The Illustr. Bar- tsch 9, Commentary, Part 2, 018), 1500,* watermark, (06- 04-93, Bassenge, #5251, illus.), 8¾ x 12⅜ in., (22.2 x 31.4 cm.), engraving (BP 2577, DM 6325, FR 21,319, Y 420,082).

MASTER OF THE DIE

$334* *Putti Playing (Bartsch 30),* after Raphael, trimmed w/in margins, laid down on one side, (11-19-92, Bonhams- Chelsea, #148), sheet 7⅜ x 11 in., (18.7 x 27.9 cm.), engraving (BP 220, DM 533, FR 1794, Y 41,537).

$4461* *The Story Of Cupid And Psyche (B. XV. 39-70),* after Raphael, complete set, margins, glued down, cond., fine and good, ex coll. APF Robert Dumesnil (L. 2200), (06- 30-93, Sotheby-London, #163), (BP 2990, DM 7609, FR 25,667, Y 477,981).

MASTER W.H.G.
BI *Hillside, Pyrenees, 1854,* est. $6/8,000, (10-13-92, Christie-NY, #26, illus.), 9⅝ x 13⅜ in., (24.4 x 34 cm.), photograph, salt print.

MASTROIANNI, Umberto b. 1910
BI *Composizione,* s., num., w/traces of old mounting, est. DM 500, (12-01-92, Karl/Faber, #984), 17½ x 14⅜ in., (44.5 x 36.5 cm.), etching and relief print on thick wove.
BI *Energia, 1946,* 49/55, s., d., est. SF 210/270, (10-14-92, Germann, #377), 27⅜ x 19¹¹⁄₁₆ in., (695 x 500 mm.), color aquatint.
BI *Energia, 1976,* V/V, color proof, s., d., est. SF 150/210, (10-14-92, Germann, #376), 27⅜ x 19¹¹⁄₁₆ in., (695 x 500 mm.), color aquatint.

MASUROVSKY, Gregory b. 1929
BI *Plante, 1965,* 148/300, s., d., est. SF 60/80, (10-14-92, Germann, #378), 21⅞ x 17¹³⁄₁₆ in., (555 x 452 mm.), etching.

MATALONI
$1418* *Incandescenza, Lampada A Petrolio, 1896,* fold marks, (02-04-93, Christie-S. Ken, #91, illus.), 57 x 36 in., (144.8 x 91.4 cm.), color lithograph on two sheets (BP 990, DM 2335, FR 7917, Y 176,390).

MATARE, Ewald German 1887-1965
$3662* *"3 Gefiederte" (Matare/de Werd 411), 1963,* i., s., (03-24-93, Venator/Hansten, #4533), approx. 13⁵⁄₁₆ x 21¹⁵⁄₁₆ in., (33.8 x 55.7 cm.), color woodcut on Schoellers Hammer paper 4 R (BP 2480, DM 5981, FR 20,356, Y 430,267).
$3531* *Entsetzte, 1921,* s., d., t., collector's stamp, (06-10-93, Hauswedell/Nolt, #615, illus.), image 8¹¹⁄₁₆ x 10¹⁄₁₆ in., (22 x 25.5 cm.), woodcut on thin wove (BP 2310, DM 5750, FR 19,359, Y 374,801).
$4256* *Kuhe Im Mond (Peters 108, Matare-de Werd 156), 1928,* s., t., (06-05-93, Bassenge, #6334, illus.), 7¹⁄₁₆ x 10¾ in., (17.9 x 27.3 cm.), color woodcut on thick hand-made Japan (BP 2802, DM 6900, FR 23,257, Y 456,554).
$6921* *Kuhe Im November (Matare-Werd 401- Peters 249), 1955,* s., t., (06-10-93, Hauswedell/Nolt, #616, illus.), image 10½ x 11⅞ in., (26.6 x 30.1 cm.), color woodcut on wove (BP 4527, DM 11,270, FR 37,944, Y 734,635).
$3922* *Liegende Kuh, Plates I, II and III, 1958: Three,* s., two #65/125, #66/125, margins, good cond., (12-03-92, Sotheby-London, #394, illus.), 5¼ x 6¾ in., (135 x 170 mm.), woodcuts in colors on laid (BP 2530, DM 6168, FR 21,052, Y 487,993).
$6852* *Liegendes Pferd (Peters Band I 315), 1950,* s., t., (11-21-92, Lempertz, #285, illus.), 15¹¹⁄₁₆ x 16⁵⁄₁₆ in., (39.9 x 41.5 cm.), color woodcut on wove (BP 4511, DM 10,925, FR 36,799, Y 852,133).
$4229* *Liegendes Pferd (S. Matare 363), 1950,* s., i., (05-26-93, Lempertz, #353, illus.), 19¾ x 25⁹⁄₁₆ in., (50.2 x 65 cm.), wood engraving on wove (BP 2736, DM 6900, FR 23,224, Y 459,474).
$4929* *"Liegendes Pferd" (Matare/de Werd 363), 1950,* i., s., (03-24-93, Venator/Hansten, #4532), approx. 15⁹⁄₁₆ x 16⅛ in., (39.5 x 41 cm.), color woodcut on Schoelers Hammer paper 4 R (BP 3338, DM 8050, FR 27,399, Y 579,133).
$2537* *Madchen Mit Blume (S. Matare 75), 1921,* (05-26-93, Lempertz, #352, illus.), 25¹¹⁄₁₆ x 19¹¹⁄₁₆ in., (65.3 x 50 cm.), wood engraving on Fabriano (BP 1641, DM 4139, FR 13,932, Y 275,641).
$2213* *Stehende Kuh (Peters 13; Matare-de Werd 30), 1920,* s., t., num., (12-05-92, Bassenge, #7475), 2¹⁵⁄₁₆ x 5¹³⁄₁₆ in., (7.5 x 14.7 cm.), woodcut on handmade (BP 1386, DM 3450, FR 11,759, Y 274,192).

MATELET, A.
$100* *Theatre Moderne De L'Alcazar: Le Pardon,* Imp. Lemercier, good cond., (02-12-93, Cheval/Robert, #168), 59¹³⁄₁₆ x 39¾ in., (152 x 101 cm.), poster (BP 70, DM 166, FR 561, Y 12,060).

MATHAM, Jacob 1571-1631
BI *Eros And Antenor (Hollstein 242), 1588,* after H. GOLTZIUS, laid down, est. G 3/400, (11-18-92, Bubb Kuyper, #1839), 11⅝ x 8⅛ in., (29.5 x 20.7 cm.), engraving.
$2600* *Die Folgen Der Trunksucht (B. 55-58; Hollstein 312-315): Four,* prov., (12-04-92, Bassenge, #6291, illus.), 7¹⁄₁₆ x 7⅞ in., (18 x 20 cm.), engraving (BP 1668, DM 4141, FR 14,046, Y 324,594).
BI *Die Heilige Familie (Hollstein Bd. XI, 105),* est. DM 1,200-, (09-14-92, Venator/Hansten, #1553, illus.), plate 9¹⁵⁄₁₆ x 7⁵⁄₁₆ in., (25.3 x 18.6 cm.), engraving.
$1589* *Kuchenstuck Mit Biblischer Szene Im Hintergrund (B. 164, Hollstein 319),* after Pieter Aertsen, watermark, (12-04-92, Bassenge, #6294), 9³⁄₁₆ x 13⁵⁄₁₆ in., (23.4 x 33.8 cm.), engraving (BP 1019, DM 2531, FR 8585, Y 198,377).
$1733* *Kuchenstuck Mit Biblischer Szene Im Hintergrund: Christus In Emmaus (B. 165; Hollstein 320),* after Pieter Aertsen, watermark, prov., foxed, (12-04-92, Bassenge, #6295), 9⅝ x 12¹³⁄₁₆ in., (24.4 x 32.6 cm.), engraving (BP 1112, DM 2760, FR 9363, Y 216,355).
$2311* *Perseus Und Andromeda (B. 162; Hollstein 212 I), 1597,* after H. Goltzius, watermark, prov., (12-04-92, Bassenge, #6293, illus.), 10½ x 14⁹⁄₁₆ in., (26.7 x 37 cm.), engraving (BP 1482, DM 3681, FR 12,485, Y 288,514).
$1346* *Der Verlorene Sohn Beim Gelage (B. 196, Hollstein 63),* watermark, (06-04-93, Bassenge, #5247, illus.), 9¾ x 12½ in., (24.8 x 31.7 cm.), engraving (BP 891, DM 2186, FR 7367, Y 145,168).
$867* *Die Vier Jahreszeiten (B. 140-143; Hollstein 300-303 II), 1589,* round, after Goltzius, prov., (12-04-92, Bassenge, #6292), engraving (BP 556, DM 1381, FR 4684, Y 108,240).

MATHAM, Theodor 1605/06-1676
$144* *Maria Mit Dem Kinde Und Dem Johannesknaben (Wurzbach 2; Hollstein 5 II-III),* after Bassano, watermark, (12-04-92, Bassenge, #6297), 16⁵⁄₁₆ x 11½ in., (41.4 x 29.2 cm.), engraving (BP 92, DM 229, FR 778, Y 17,978).

MATHER, Margrethe 1885-1952
BI *Frayne Williams As "Anatol", 1926,* s., est. $25/30,000, (10-13-92, Christie-NY, #312, illus.), 9¾ x 7¼ in., (24.8 x 18.4 cm.), photograph, platinum print.
BI *Frayne Williams, 1926,* s., t., prov., (10-13-92, Christie-NY, #311, illus.), 9¼ x 7⅜ in., (23.5 x 18.7 cm.), photograph, platinum print.

MATHEUS, Georg c. 1554-1572
BI *Martha Geleitet Magdalena Zum Tempel (Bartsch XII, 37, 12; Hollstein7 I),* est. DM 3,000, (06-10-93, Hauswedell/Nolt, #114, illus.), chiaroscuro woodcut from 2 blocks.

MATHEWS, P. (after)
BI *The Trial Of "Bill Burn" Under Martins Act,* by C. Hunt, pub. Ackermann, trimmed, dirt, abrasions, est. BP 3/500, (10-07-92, Christie-S. Ken, #65), sh 20¼ x 26½ in., (51.4 x 67.3 cm.), colored aquatint.

MATHEY, Georg Alexander 1884-1968
$424* *Cirque De Paris, 1922,* s., from Die Schaffenden, III. Jahrg., portfolio 3, (06-10-93, Hauswedell/Nolt, #617, illus.), image 10¹⁄₁₆ x 8¹³⁄₁₆ in., (25.5 x 22.4 cm.), woodcut on hardernhaltigem wove (BP 277, DM 690, FR 2325, Y 45,006).

MATHIEU, Georges French b. 1921
$721* *Ohne Titel, 1959,* artist's proof, tears, (11-20-92, Lempertz, #705), sh 25¹³⁄₁₆ x 20 in., (65.5 x 50.8 cm.), color lithograph on Velin on BFK Rives (BP 475, DM 1150, FR 3872, Y 89,665).

MATHIEU, J. 18th cent.
BI *"Le Serment D'Amour",* after Fragonard, pub. Paris, est. $3/400, (12-06-92, Neal, #929), plate 22½ x 17 in., (57.2 x 43.2 cm.), engraving.

MATISSE, Henri French 1869-1954
$769* *Autoportrait (Duthuit 563), 1944,* damp stains, (05-27-93, Briest, #143), 18⅛ x 12⅝ in., (46 x 32 cm.), black lithograph on Arches (BP 492, DM 1234, FR 4159, Y 82,440).
$2750* *Buste De Jeune Fille, Bras Croises (Duthuit 450, Fribourg 407), 1925,* s., #45/50, plate 61, prov., (03-24-93,

Grogan, #106, illus.), 7⅛ x 5 in., (18.1 x 12.7 cm.), lithograph (BP 1862, DM 4491, FR 15,286, Y 323,111).

$4313* *Buste De Jeune Fille, Les Bras Croises (D. 450)*, 1925, s., #45/50, full margins, good cond., mat staining, rubbed areas, creases, glue stains, notations, (05-19-93, Butterfield, #1929, illus.), 7⅜ x 5⅛ in., (187 x 130 mm.), lithograph in Japan (BP 2800, DM 7011, FR 23,620, Y 477,471).

BI *Buste De Jeune Fille, Les Bras Croises (Duthuit-Matisse II, 250)*, 1925, s., 49/50, annot. PP61, creases, pinholes, tape remains, est. FF15/20,000, (06-28-93, Loudmer, #311), 7⁵⁄₁₆ x 5¹⁄₁₆ in., (186 x 128 mm.), sh 13¹⁵⁄₁₆ x 10⅞ in., (186 x 128 mm.), black lithograph on creme Japan.

$1135* *"Cirque"*, 1947, from Jazz, (12-04-92, AB Stockholm, #7105), 14³⁄₁₆ x 21⅝ in., (36 x 55 cm.), sh 16⁹⁄₁₆ x 25⁹⁄₁₆ in., (36 x 55 cm.), pochoir in colors on Arches w/ collage (BP 728, DM 1808, FR 6132, Y 141,698, SK 7700).

$325* *"La Cite-Notre Dame" (Duthuit-Matisse 248)*, s. in plate, (05-15-93, Cleveland, #410, illus.), 13¼ x 10⅜ in., (33.7 x 26.4 cm.), etching on cream laid on Ingres d'Arches MBM paper (BP 211, DM 523, FR 1757, Y 36,027).

$169* *Composition, 1950*, (09-30-92, Kunsthallen, #198), lithograph in colors (BP 95, DM 240, FR 811, Y 20,281, DK 920).

$184* *Composition, 1952*, (03-24-93, Kunsthallen, #237), color lithograph (BP 125, DM 301, FR 1023, Y 21,619, DK 1150).

$12,278* *La Danse (D. 247)*, 1936, s., ded., i. ep. artiste 3/5, margins, light/damp staining, scuffing, (12-03-92, Sotheby-London, #406, illus.), sheet 11¾ x 31⅜ in., (297 x 798 mm.), etching w/aquatint in colors on Arches (BP 7920, DM 19,308, FR 65,904, Y 1,527,684).

$68,200* *La Danse (Duthuit 247)*, 1935-6, s., #5/50, full margins, light-staining, very good cond., (11-09-92, Christie-NY, #110, illus.), 298 x 757 in., (756.9 x cm.), etching and aquatint in colors on Arches (BP 45,091, DM 108,876, FR 367,853, Y 8,463,639).

$9430* *Danseuse Au Divan, Pliee En Deux (D. 489)*, 1927, s., #8/15, margins, light/mat staining, creasing, good cond., (05-11-93, Christie-NY, #226, illus.), borderline 11 x 18 in., (279 x 457 mm.), lithograph on Japan (BP 6020, DM 14,855, FR 50,053, Y 1,037,290).

$11,000* *"Danseuse Au Fauteuil De Bois" (Fribourg #441)*, c. 1927, s., #102/130, from series Dix Danseuses, (03-12-93, DuMouchelle, #2016, illus.), 17½ x 9⅝ in., (44.5 x 24.4 cm.), lithograph (BP 7674, DM 18,309, FR 62,252, Y 1,296,405).

$6325* *Danseuse Au Fauteuil En Bois (D. 483)*, 1927, plate 95 or 97, s., #3/130, from portfolio Dix Danseuses, pub. Galerie d'Art Contemporain de Paris, full margins, good cond., fox marks, mat stain,crease, tape stains, (05-13-93, Sotheby-NY, #605, illus.), 17⅞ x 10⅜ in., (455 x 264 mm.), lithograph (BP 4152, DM 10,213, FR 34,450, Y 706,152).

$2798* *Danseuse Cambree Au Visage Coupe 9D. 491)*, 1927, whole margins, #42/50, s., (06-11-93, Picard, #132), 17¹¹⁄₁₆ x 10¹⁄₁₆ in., (450 x 255 mm.), lithograph in black on Japan (BP 1838, DM 4547, FR 15,332, Y 296,870).

$8625* *Danseuse Debout, Accoudee (D. 482)*, 1927, plate 99 or 91, s., #45/130, from Dix Danseuses, pub. Galerie d'Art Contemporain, full margins, good cond., foxing, mat stain, (05-13-93, Sotheby-NY, #604, illus.), 18⅛ x 11 in., (459 x 280 mm.), lithograph (BP 5662, DM 13,927, FR 46,977, Y 962,934).

$7150* *Danseuse Debout, Accoudee (D. 482)*, 1927, from Dix Danseuses, s., #26/130, full margins, light/mat staining, foxing, skinned patch, good cond., (11-09-92, Christie-NY, #115, illus.), 457 x 280 in., (x 711.2 cm.), lithograph on Arches (BP 4727, DM 11,414, FR 38,565, Y 887,317).

$3300* *Danseuse Debout, Accoudee, 1927*, from Dix Danseuses, s., #102/130, (06-13-93, Hindman, #386), 18 x 11 in., (45.7 x 27.9 cm.), lithograph (BP 2160, DM 5371, FR 18,053, Y 347,259).

$7150* *Danseuse Endormie (D. 479)*, 1926-27, plate 89, s., #19/50, full margins, good cond., crease, mat stain, scratch, soiling, (11-05-92, Sotheby-NY, #241, illus.), 8⅝ x 18

in., (218 x 457 mm.), lithograph on Arches wove (BP 4650, DM 11,308, FR 38,256, Y 877,193).

$8800* *Danseuse Endormie Au Divan (D. 485)*, 1927, plate 91 or 99, s., #130/130, pub. Galerie d'Art Contemporain, margins, good cond., mat/light stain, fox marks, water stain, (11-05-92, Sotheby-NY, #242, illus.), 11 x 18¼ in., (280 x 465 mm.), sheet 12¾ x 19½ in., (280 x 465 mm.), lithograph (BP 5724, DM 13,917, FR 47,084, Y 1,079,622).

$8800* *Danseuse Endormie Au Divan, Fribourg 438; Duthuit 485*, from Dix Danseuses, s., num. 15/15, prov., Emmanuel Jacobson Estate, (09-20-92, Hindman, #755, illus.), sheet 12¾ x 19⅝ in., (32.4 x 49.8 cm.), lithograph on Japan (BP 5152, DM 13,058, FR 44,670, Y 1,087,628).

$8050* *Danseuse Entendue (D. 488)*, 1927, plate 97 or 90, s., #79/130, from Dix Danseuses, pub. Galerie d'Art Contemporain, margins, good cond., mat stain, foxing, discoloration, tape stain,skinning, (05-13-93, Sotheby-NY, #606, illus.), 10 x 16½ in., (253 x 420 mm.), sh 12⅞ x 20 in., (253 x 420 mm.), lithograph on Arches wove (BP 5285, DM 12,999, FR 43,845, Y 898,738).

$7700* *Danseuse Etendue Au Divan (D. 484)*, 1927, (mains a la nuque), from Dix Danseuses, s., #107/130, full margins, light/mat staining, remains, glue, (11-09-92, Christie-NY, #116, illus.), 280 x 458 in., (711.2 x cm.), lithograph on wove (BP 5091, DM 12,292, FR 41,532, Y 955,572).

BI *Danseuse Etendue Au Divan (D.M. 484)*, 1927, from Dix Danseuses, s., #3/5, pub. Galerie d'Art, margins, thin spot, loss, tape, est. BP 3,5/4,500, (12-01-92, Christie-London, #432, illus.), L. 11⁷⁄₁₆ x 17⁷⁄₁₆ in., (290 x 443 mm.), lithograph on Chine volant.

$22,979* *Danseuse Refletee Dans La Glace (D. 490)*, 1927, whole margins, annot., s., (06-11-93, Picard, #131, illus.), 15¹¹⁄₁₆ x 11³⁄₁₆ in., (398 x 284 mm.), lithograph in black on thin chine (BP 15,098, DM 37,346, FR 125,912, Y 2,438,090).

$7941* *Danseuse Se Reposant (Dut.-Gar. 485, Pl. 91 or 99)*, 1925-1926, s., num., sheet 6 of later series: Dix Danseuses, (06-23-93, Kornfeld, #561), lithograph on Chine volant (BP 5395, DM 13,437, FR 45,196, Y 865,127, SF 11,960).

$839* *Deux Femmes En Costume De Ville (Duthuit 8)*, 1900-1903, whole margins, ink s., #4/30, (06-11-93, Picard, #121), 5⅞ x 3¹⁵⁄₁₆ in., (149 x 100 mm.), drypoint in black on wove (BP 551, DM 1364, FR 4597, Y 89,019).

$5968* *Dix Dandeuses: Danseuse Au Divan Pliee En Deux (D. 489)*, 1927, plate 98, s., #30/130, full margins, good cond., soiling, i. in another hand, prov., (12-03-92, Sotheby-London, #398, illus.), 11 x 17⅞ in., (280 x 455 mm.), lithograph on sturdy white wove (BP 3850, DM 9385, FR 32,034, Y 742,566).

$5968* *Dix Danseuses: Danseuse Allongee, Tete Accoudee (D. 486)*, 1927, plate 96, s., #30/130, full margins, good cond., foxing, i. in another hand, prov., (12-03-92, Sotheby-London, #400, illus.), 7 x 16½ in., (180 x 420 mm.), lithograph on sturdy white wove (BP 3850, DM 9385, FR 32,034, Y 742,566).

$5116* *Dix Danseuses: Danseuse Debout, Accoudee (D. 482)*, 1927, s., #30/130, full margins, good cond., crease, i. in another hand, prov., (12-03-92, Sotheby-London, #399, illus.), 18⅛ x 11 in., (460 x 280 mm.), lithograph on sturdy white wove (BP 3300, DM 8045, FR 27,461, Y 636,556).

BI *Etude D'Odalesque, 1948*, late impression, est. $4/450, (12-10-92, Sloan, #3021), 12 x 19⅜ in., (30.5 x 49.2 cm.), linocut.

$5345* *Etude De Jambes (Dut.-Gar. 460, Pl. 71)*, 1925, s., num., (06-23-93, Kornfeld, #559), lithograph on simili Japan (BP 3631, DM 9044, FR 30,421, Y 582,307, SF 8050).

$825* *Exposition De Dessins D'Etude Henri Matisse*, ink s. H. Matisse, foxing, discoloration, catalog back cover lot, (06-11-93, Freemn/Fine Art, #144, illus.), sh 22½ x 15 in., (57.2 x 38.1 cm.), lithographic poster in yellow, blue and red on cream paper (BP 542, DM 1341, FR 4521, Y 87,533).

$4600* *Fee Au Chapeau De Clarte, Souvenir Du Mallarme (D. 234)*, 1933, s., #18/25, full margins, creases, staining, good cond., (05-11-93, Christie-NY, #219, illus.), plate

14½ x 12⅛ in., (368 x 308 mm.), drypoint on Chine applique (BP 2936, DM 7246, FR 24,416, Y 505,995).

$10,309* *Femme Nue Couchee (Dut.-Gar. 462, Pl. 79), 1925,* s., num., (06-23-93, Kornfeld, #560, illus.), lithograph on simili-Japan (BP 7003, DM 17,443, FR 58,674, Y 1,123,107, SF 15,525).

$6821* *Figure Assise, Blouse Transparente (D. 519), 1929,* plate 129, s., #20/25, margins, good cond., discoloration, hinged tomount, (12-03-92, Sotheby-London, #403, illus.), sheet 25½ x 19⅝ in., (648 x 498 mm.), lithograph on Japan (BP 4400, DM 10,727, FR 36,613, Y 848,700).

$6991* *Figure Devant Tapa Africain (D. 515), 1929,* plate 126, s., #5/50, margins, good cond., paper discoloration, staining, (12-03-92, Sotheby-London, #402, illus.), 25¼ x 19½ in., (640 x 497 mm.), lithograph on Japan (BP 4510, DM 10,994, FR 37,525, Y 869,852).

BI *Figure Devant Tapa Africain (D. 515), 1929,* plate 126, s., #3/50, full margins, good cond., creases, rippling, est. $10/12,000, (11-05-92, Sotheby-NY, #248, illus.), 21 x 17⅛ in., (534 x 435 mm.), sheet 25½ x 19⅜ in., (534 x 435 mm.), lithograph on cream simili-Japan.

$7475* *Figure Endorme (D. 493), 1927,* plate 102, s., # 50/50, blindstamp of pub. Jacquart Editeur, margins, good cond., printer's crease, tape/light stains, razor cut, (02-11-93, Sotheby-NY, #173, illus.), 9⁵⁄₁₆ x 13¹⁄₁₆ in., (237 x 332 mm.), sheet 15¾ x 19¹³⁄₁₆ in., (237 x 332 mm.), lithograph on cream Japan (BP 5274, DM 12,382, FR 41,900, Y 901,145).

BI *Figure Endormie (D. 493), 1927,* plate 102, s., #39/50, margins, good cond., light stain, rubbed spot,est. $10/12,000, (11-05-92, Sotheby-NY, #243, illus.), 9⅜ x 13⅛ in., (237 x 332 mm.), sheet 15⅝ x 21¼ in., (237 x 332 mm.), lithograph on Japan paper.

$8050* *Figure Endormie (D. 493), 1927,* plate 102, s., #39/50, pub. Jacquart, (blindstamp partly cut away), margins, good cond., light-stain, rubbed spot, (05-13-93, Sotheby-NY, #607, illus.), 9⅜ x 13⅛ in., (237 x 332 mm.), sh 15⅝ x 21¼ in., (237 x 332 mm.), lithograph on Japan (BP 5285, DM 12,999, FR 43,845, Y 898,738).

$10,925* *Figure Endormie Aux Babouches (D. 512), 1929,* plate 111, s., #42/50, full margins, good cond., fox mark, light-stain, handling creases, discoloration, i., ex-coll. Blanche Adler, (05-13-93, Sotheby-NY, #612, illus.), 10¾ x 14⅞ in., (272 x 378 mm.), lithograph (BP 7172, DM 17,641, FR 59,504, Y 1,219,716).

$12,869* *Figure Endormie, Chale Sur Les Jambes (D. 511), 1929,* pl 110, s., i. Essai, full margins, good cond., mount-staining, (06-30-93, Sotheby-London, #514, illus.), 10¾ x 14¾ in., (273 x 375 mm.), lithograph on Arches (BP 8625, DM 21,950, FR 74,045, Y 1,378,871).

BI *Figure Endormie, Chale Sur Les Jambes (D. 511), 1929,* plate 110, s., i. Bon a tirer, full margins, good cond., fox marks, est. $20/25,000, (11-05-92, Sotheby-NY, #247, illus.), 10⅝ x 14⅞ in., (270 x 378 mm.), sheet 17⅝ x 24¾ in., (270 x 378 mm.), lithograph on Arches wove.

BI *Figure Endormie, Chale Sur Les Jambes (plate 110, Duthuit 51), 1929,* s., #33/50, full margins, prov., est. $15,/20,000, (03-14-93, Hindman, #283, illus.), 10⅝ x 14⅞ in., (27 x 37.8 cm.), lithograph on Arches.

BI *Florilege Des Amours De Ronsard (D. bk. 25), 1948,* deluxe edit. of book, i., s. by artist and publisher, num. 19, pub. Albert Skira, good cond., foxing, est. $28/32,000, (11-05-92, Sotheby-NY, #253A, illus.), each sheet 15⅛ x 11¼ in., (385 x 285 mm.), 126 lithographs p. in sanguine, in-texte and hors-texte on Arches, plus 20 lithographs in sanguine on japon.

BI *Grand Masque Massia (Duhuit 25), 1914,* s., i. tire a quinze ex, huitieme ep, full margins, foxing, time staining, good cond., est. $2,5/3,500, (05-11-93, Christie-NY, #217), plate 5¼ x 4 in., (133 x 102 mm.), etching on Chine applique.

$22,000* *Le Grand Nu (Duthuit 403), 1906,* plate 10 or 29, s., #31/50, full margins, good cond., tears, creases,soiling, creases, (11-05-92, Sotheby-NY, #238, illus.), 11⅜ x 10 in., (290 x 255 mm.), lithograph on chine volant (BP 14,309, DM 34,794, FR 117,710, Y 2,699,055).

BI *Grande Odalisque A La Culotte Bayadere (D. 455), 1925,* s., #29/50, trimmed margins, repaired splits, surface losses, tears into image, laid down on Japan, catalog cover lot, Sally and Harold Eisenman Coll., est. $100/140,000, (11-09-92, Christie-NY, #114, illus.), 543 x 445 in., (x cm.), lithograph on Chine.

$4600* *Hatienne (D. 567), 1945,* plate 273, s., #86/200, full margins, good cond., mat/light-stain, handling creases, scotch tape, (05-13-93, Sotheby-NY, #615), 14⅜ x 10¾ in., (366 x 273 mm.), lithograph (BP 3020, DM 7428, FR 25,054, Y 513,565).

$29,573* *Hindoue A La Jupe De Tulle (D. 510), 1929,* whole margins, #14/50, s., (06-11-93, Picard, #133, illus.), 11¼ x 14¹⁵⁄₁₆ in., (285 x 380 mm.), lithograph in black on thin chine (BP 19,430, DM 48,063, FR 162,044, Y 3,137,719).

$4834* *Interieur, La Lecture (Duthuit-Matisse, 457), 1925,* s., 50/50, losses, small stains, (06-28-93, Loudmer, #307), 10¹³⁄₁₆ x 7½ in., (275 x 190 mm.), sh 15¹⁵⁄₁₆ x 12½ in., (275 x 190 mm.), black lithograph on China (BP 3237, DM 8214, FR 27,670, Y 512,891).

$7492* *J. Joyce, Ulysses (D.M. 235-40; D. Books 6), 1934,* Limited Editions Club, s., #148/150, foxing, (12-01-92, Christie-London, #422), overall sheet 17⅜ x 13¹⁄₁₆ in., (442 x 332 mm.), soft-ground etching on Rives (BP 4950, DM 11,941, FR 40,695, Y 932,769).

$1665* *James Joyce, Ulysses (D.M. 235-40; D. Books 6), 1934,* The Limited Editions Club, t., text, just., set of 6, s., #267, staining, very good cond., (12-01-92, Christie-London, #423), overall sheet 11⅞ x 9⁵⁄₁₆ in., (302 x 236 mm.), soft-ground etchings on wove (BP 1100, DM 2654, FR 9044, Y 207,296).

$3300* *James Joyce: Ulysses (D.6), 1935,* pub. Limited Editions Club, full margins, s., num. 53/150, abrasions, repairs, (11-12-92, Freemn/Fine Art, #142), 16⅜ x 19½ in., (41.6 x 49.5 cm.), soft ground etching (BP 2167, DM 5229, FR 17,638, Y 409,175).

BI *Jazz (D. bk. no. 22; The Artist And The Book 200; Rauch 171),* complete book, facsimile text by the artist, s., num. 109, pub. Teriade, 1947, good cond., Plate I w/ scuffs, smudges cover sheets, fox marks, orig.paper wrapper and slipcase, est. $140/160,000, (05-13-93, Sotheby-NY, #619, illus.), each sh approx. 16⅝ x 12¾ in., (423 x 325 mm.), 20 stencils p. in colors after collages and cut paper designs.

$57,500* *Jazz (D. bk. no. 22; The Artist And The Book 200; Rauch 171),* portfolio edit., (lacking Plate X, L'Enterrement de Pierrot), t. page& just. page, s., num. 73, pub. Teriade, 1947, foxing, scuffs, creasing, orig.portfolio, (05-13-93, Sotheby-NY, #618, illus.), each sh approx. 25¾ x 16⅝ in., (655 x 423 mm.), 19 of the 20 unfolded stencils p. in colors after collages & cut paper designs on Arches wove (BP 37,749, DM 92,847, FR 313,181, Y 6,419,560).

BI *Jazz (D. bk. no. 22; The Artist And The Book 200; Rauch 171), 1947,* complete book, s., num. 12, pub. Teriade, pristine cond., orig. wrapper adn slipcase, est. $170/190,000, (11-05-92, Sotheby-NY, #253B, illus.), each page approx. 16⅝ x 12¾ in., (423 x 325 mm.), 20 stencils p. in colors after collages and cut paper designs.

$3088* *Jazz Plate 1 (Duthuit 22), 1947,* pub. Teriade, good cond., scuffs, (06-30-93, Sotheby-London, #502, illus.), sh 12⅝ x 25⅝ in., (321 x 651 mm.), color stencil after collage and cut out paper design (BP 2070, DM 5267, FR 17,768, Y 330,869).

$1380* *Jazz: Le Lagon No. 1 (D., Books 22 Bis), 1947,* pub. Teriade, good cond., center fold, foxing, (05-19-93, Butterfield, #1930, illus.), 16½ x 25½ in., (419 x 648 mm.), pochoir stencil in colors on Arches (BP 896, DM 2243, FR 7558, Y 152,773).

$20,900* *Jeune Fille Assise Au Bouquet De Fleurs (D. 438), 1923,* s., i. epreuve d'artiste, a Mlle Henriette Darnicarriere, #5/10, full margins, mat staining, very good cond., (11-09-92, Christie-NY, #113, illus.), 275 x 187 in., (698.5 x 475 cm.), lithograph on Japan (BP 13,818, DM 33,365, FR 112,729, Y 2,593,696).

$5297* *Jeune Fille Aux Boucles Brunes (Duthuit-Matisse 448; Planche 59), 1924,* s., #9/12, artist's proof, (06-10-93, Hauswedell/Nolt, #621, illus.), image 7⅜ x 5⅛ in., (18.8 x 13 cm.), lithograph (BP 3465, DM 8626, FR 29,041, Y 562,255).

BI *Jeune Fille De Face, Flot De Ruban Sur L'Epaule Gauche (D. 198), 1929,* plate 157, s., #10/25, full margins, good cond., glue stain, i., est.BP 3/3,500, (12-03-92, Sotheby-London, #404, illus.), 6½ x 4½ in., (165 x 114 mm.), etching on chine applique on Arches.

$12,650* *Jeune Hindoue (D. 508), 1929,* plate 106, s., #34/50, full margins, good cond., backboard stain, sold after sale, (11-05-92, Sotheby-NY, #246, illus.), 11⅜ x 14¼ in., (288 x 362 mm.), lithograph (BP 8228, DM 20,006, FR 67,683, Y 1,551,957).

$3450* *Josette Gris ("Seraphique") (D. 62), 1915,* plate 30, ink s., i. tirage a quinze exempl./troisieme epreuve, (#13/15), i. Pl. no. 9, full margins, good cond., stain, soiling, foxing, creases, discoloration, ex-coll. Eugene Mayer, (05-13-93, Sotheby-NY, #598), 5⅞ x 4⅜ in., (148 x 111 mm.), etching on chine applique (BP 2265, DM 5571, FR 18,791, Y 385,174).

BI *L'Homme Endormi (D.M. 771), 1936,* s., #136/150, margins, loss, mount-staining, very good cond., est. BP 5/7,000, (12-01-92, Christie-London, #431, illus.), plate 9¾ x 6⅞ in., (248 x 175 mm.), aquatint on laid.

$3797* *Loulou, Figure De Dos (D. 15), 1914-15,* ink s., #7/15, tears, (06-11-93, Picard, #122), 7¹⁄₁₆ x 5¹⁄₁₆ in., (179 x 128 mm.), etching in black on chine applique on wove (BP 2495, DM 6171, FR 20,805, Y 402,865).

BI *Marie-Jose En Robe Jaune (D. 817), 1950,* plate 362, s., i. Essai, i. H.C., full margins, good cond., mat stain, foxing, crease, est. $60/80,000, (05-13-93, Sotheby-NY, #616, illus.), 21⅛ x 16¼ in., (536 x 412 mm.), aquatint in colors.

$34,316* *Marie-Jose En Robe Jaune (D. 817), 1950,* pl 362, s., #46/100, p. by Lacouriere, full margins, very good cond.,yellow and red, attenuated, light-staining, stains, (06-30-93, Sotheby-London, #515, illus.), 21 x 16¼ in., (533 x 413 mm.), aquatint in black, red, yellow and green on Arches (BP 23,000, DM 58,530, FR 197,445, Y 3,676,846).

$5147* *Martiniquaise (D. 287), 1946,* pl 307, s., #10/25, full margins, good cond., mount-staining, (06-30-93, Sotheby-London, #512, illus.), 9¾ x 7½ in., (248 x 191 mm.), etching on annam applique (BP 3450, DM 8779, FR 29,614, Y 551,484).

$3531* *Martiniquaise (Duthuit-Matisse 283; Planche 301), 1946,* s., #20/25, from series of 14 sheets Martiniquaise, (06-10-93, Hauswedell/Nolt, #619), image 9¾ x 7⅝ in., (24.8 x 19.3 cm.), etching on thick wove (BP 2310, DM 5750, FR 19,359, Y 374,801).

BI *Massia Au Visage Allonge (G. 26), 1914,* ink s., annot. f.a quinze ex./cinquieme ep., plate tone, large margins, good cond., mat/glue staining, tape remain, est. $2,5/3,500, (10-28-92, Butterfield, #2668), 5⅜ x 4 in., (137 x 102 mm.), etching w/chine colle (pasted) on heavy wove.

$266* *"Mille Et Une Nuits",* s., d. H. Matisse juin 50, (03-16-93, Encans, #193), 16¾ x 35¹⁄₁₆ in., (42.5 x 89 cm.), lithograph (BP 184, DM 442, FR 1503, Y 31,104, C$ 333).

$14,300* *Nadia Au Menton Pointu (D. 807), 1948,* plate 356, s., #3/25, full margins, good cond., creases, mat stain, (11-05-92, Sotheby-NY, #249, illus.), 17⅛ x 13¾ in., (435 x 348 mm.), aquatint (BP 9301, DM 22,616, FR 76,512, Y 1,754,386).

$11,302* *Nadia Au Menton Pointu (D. 807). 1948,* pl 356, s., #14/25, full magins, good cond., mount-staining, crease, (06-30-93, Sotheby-London, #516, illus.), 17⅛ x 13¾ in., (435 x 349 mm.), aquatint on wove (BP 7575, DM 19,277, FR 65,029, Y 1,210,972).

$17,250* *Nadia Aux Cheveux Lisses (D. 805), 1948,* watermark, s., #9/25, full margins, mat staining, skinned patch, very good cond., Robert Motherwell/Dedalus Foundation estate, (05-11-93, Christie-NY, #228, illus.), plate 17 x 13⅝ in., (432 x 346 mm.), aquatint on wove (BP 11,012, DM 27,174, FR 91,561, Y 1,897,481).

BI *Nadia, Masque (D. 796), 1948,* plate 354, s., #9/25, margins, crease into image, mount staining, creases, est. BP 4/5,000, (12-03-92, Sotheby-London, #407, illus.), sheet 25¼ x 19½ in., (640 x 495 mm.), aquatint on Marais wove.

$459* *Nature Morte Aux Fruits De Mer, 1947,* (03-24-93, Kunsthallen, #236), lithographic poster (BP 311, DM 750, FR 2551, Y 53,930, DK 2875).

$550* *Notre Dame,* s. in plate, late impression, (10-30-92, Sloan, #1604), 13¼ x 10½ in., (33.7 x 26.7 cm.), etching (BP 352, DM 846, FR 2871, Y 68,128).

$220* *Notre Dame,* s. in plate, late impression, (05-28-93, Sloan, #1921, illus.), 13¼ x 10¼ in., (33.7 x 26 cm.), etching (BP 141, DM 349, FR 1180, Y 23,590).

BI *Notre Dame,* s. in plate, late impression, est. $375/425, (12-10-92, Sloan, #3022), 13¼ x 10¼ in., (33.7 x 26 cm.), etching.

$200* *Notre Dame,* (05-16-93, Hanzel, #481), 13¼ x 10¼ in., (33.7 x 26 cm.), etching (BP 130, DM 322, FR 1081, Y 22,170).

BI *"Notre Dame",* p.l., s. in plate, full margins, est. $6/800, (10-10-92, Goldberg, #424, illus.), image 13 x 10 in., (33 x 25.4 cm.), etching.

$1006* *Nu (Maeght Verz, Nr. 1505), c. 1950,* num. 300, (10-09-92, Winterberg, #2719, illus.), 18½ x 15⅜ in., (47 x 39 cm.), color lithograph on Arches (BP 597, DM 1494, FR 5017, Y 122,474).

$1559* *Nu Accroupi Sur Banquette Rayee (D. 209), 1929,* whole margins, annot., s., reddish stains, (06-11-93, Picard, #125), 4¹³⁄₁₆ x 3¹¹⁄₁₆ in., (123 x 94 mm.), etching in black on gray chine on wove (BP 1024, DM 2534, FR 8542, Y 165,411).

$5264* *Nu Accroupi, Une Cordeliere Autour Du Cou (Delteil 225), 1931,* #10/25, edit. from 25 impressions, num. E.E., margins, (05-27-93, Briest, #142, illus.), 47⅝ x 35¹³⁄₁₆ in., (121 x 91 cm.), black etching on Chine applied to wove (BP 3371, DM 8447, FR 28,469, Y 564,322).

$7475* *Nu Agenouille Et Cambre (D. 77), 1918,* plate 104, s., #10/15, pub. Petiet, full margins, good cond., light-stain, fox marks, discoloration, i., (05-13-93, Sotheby-NY, #599, illus.), 6¼ x 2⅜ in., (160 x 61 mm.), etching on chine applique (BP 4907, DM 12,070, FR 40,714, Y 834,543).

$1277* *Nu Allonge, Les Jambes Repliees, Avec Collier (Duthuit-Matisse 113),1929,* (06-05-93, Bassenge, #6336), 5 x 6¹⁵⁄₁₆ in., (12.7 x 17.7 cm.), etching on thick BFK-Rives (BP 841, DM 2070, FR 6978, Y 136,988).

$9775* *Nu Assis Dans Un Fauteuil Au Decor Fleuri (D. 445), 1924,* s., #134/250, trimmed margins, corner reattached, made-up loss, stain, (05-11-93, Christie-NY, #224, illus.), borderline 18¾ x 12½ in., (476 x 318 mm.), sheet 22 x 15½ in., (476 x 318 mm.), lithograph on Chine (BP 6240, DM 15,399, FR 51,884, Y 1,075,239).

$8050* *Nu Assis, Bras Gauche Sur La Tete (D. 497), 1929,* plate 108, s., #25/50, large margins, good cond., mat/light-stain, razor cut, rubbed spots, tape hinges, (05-13-93, Sotheby-NY, #609, illus.), 16⅛ x 16½ in., (410 x 420 mm.), sh 19⅝ x 25½ in., (410 x 420 mm.), lithograph on Japan (BP 5285, DM 12,999, FR 43,845, Y 898,738).

BI *Nu Assise Dans Un Fauteuil Au Decor Fleuri (D.M. 445), 1924,* s., #144/250, margins, crease, repaired split, nicks, surface dirt, mount-staining, est. BP 4/6,000, (12-01-92, Christie-London, #428, illus.), L. 18¾ x 12⅝ in., (477 x 320 mm.), lithograph on Chine volant.

$220* *Nu Au Bracelet,* Musee du Louvre Chalcographie blindstamp, late impression, (05-28-93, Sloan, #1920, illus.), 9⅝ x 7 in., (24.4 x 17.8 cm.), linocut (BP 141, DM 349, FR 1180, Y 23,590).

$413* *Nu Au Bracelet (D/G 725), 1940,* blindstamp, late impression, (12-10-92, Sloan, #3017), 9⅝ x 7 in., (24.4 x 17.8 cm.), linocut (BP 266, DM 653, FR 2231, Y 51,089).

$330* *"Nu Au Bracelet", c. 1940,* Musee du Louvre Chalcographie blind stamp, full margins, excell. cond., (05-07-93, Goldberg, #426, illus.), 9⅝ x 7 in., (24.4 x 17.8 cm.), linoleum cut (BP 209, DM 522, FR 1758, Y 36,336).

$2698* *Nu Au Collier (D. 90), 1926,* whole margins, s., #3/25, (06-11-93, Picard, #124), 4⅝ x 6⁹⁄₁₆ in., (118 x 166 mm.), etching in black on chine applique on wove (BP 1773, DM 4385, FR 14,784, Y 286,260).

BI *Nu Au Coussin Bleu (D. 442), 1924,* pl 55, s., full margins, good cond., w/in subject, tear, repaired tears, skinned areas, handling creases, est. BP 25/30,000, (06-30-93, Sotheby-London, #508, illus.), 24⅛ x 18⅝ in., (613 x 473 mm.), lithograph on wove.

BI *Nu Au Coussin Bleu (D. 442), 1924,* plate 55, s., #9/10, i. ep. d'artiste, full margins, good cond., handling creases, mat stain, est. $40/50,000, (05-13-93, Sotheby-NY, #603, illus.), 24¼ x 18⅞ in., (615 x 478 mm.), lithograph.

BI *Nu Au Coussin Bleu A Cote D'Une Cheminee (D. 454), 1925,* watermark, s., #36/50, margins, repaired splits in image, made-up patch, staining, tear, mat staining, skinning, good cond., est. $60/80,000, (05-11-93, Christie-NY, #225, illus.), borderline 26¹/₁₆ x 19 in., (662 x 483 mm.), lithograph on wove.

$5286* *Nu Au Fauteuil Sur Fond Moucharabieh (D. 470), 1925,* plate 103, trail proof, stamped w/mono. & essai, margins, good cond.,rubbing, creasing, discoloration, (12-03-92, Sotheby-London, #401, illus.), sheet 25½ x 19¾ in., (648 x 502 mm.), lithograph on Japan (BP 3410, DM 8313, FR 28,374, Y 657,708).

$15,950* *Nu Au Fauteuil Sur Fond Moucharabieh (D. 470), 1925,* plate 103, s., #3/50, margins, good cond., discoloration, stain, foxing, spot, (11-05-92, Sotheby-NY, #240, illus.), 21½ x 17½ in., (545 x 455 mm.), sheet 24¼ x 19⅜ in., (545 x 455 mm.), lithograph (BP 10,374, DM 25,225, FR 85,340, Y 1,956,815).

$3000* *Nu Au Rocking Chair (Duthuit-Matisse 410), 1913,* s., num. 50/50, paper scuffing, (11-30-92, Phillips-London, #460, illus.), sheet 19⅞ x 13 in., (505 x 330 mm.), lithograph on Imperial japan (BP 1980, DM 4779, FR 16,225, Y 373,367).

BI *Nu Couche Au Paravant Louis XIV (Dutuit 435), 1923,* s., num., est. DM 15,000, (12-05-92, Bassenge, #7477, illus.), 5⁵/₁₆ x 7⁹/₁₆ in., (13.2 x 19.2 cm.), lithograph on handmade China.

$7150* *Nu Couche Au Paravent Louis XIV (D. 435), 1923,* s., #14/50, margins slightly trimmed, good cond., repaired tear, tape, creases, (02-24-93, Butterfield, #2753, illus.), 5⁹/₁₆ x 7½ in., (141 x 191 mm.), sheet 10⅞ x 13¾ in., (141 x 191 mm.), lithograph on Chine (BP 4986, DM 11,607, FR 39,351, Y 839,005).

$9437* *Nu Couche De Dos (D. 496), 1929,* pl 113, s., #16/50, full margins, good cond., discoloration, (06-30-93, Sotheby-London, #509, illus.), 17⅞ x 22 in., (454 x 559 mm.), lithograph on Arches (BP 6325, DM 16,096, FR 54,298, Y 1,011,143).

$16,036* *Nu Couche Sur Sol Fleuri (Dut.-Gar. 502, Pl. 121), 1929,* s., num., (06-23-93, Kornfeld, #562, illus.), lithograph on thick wove (BP 10,894, DM 27,134, FR 91,269, Y 1,747,031, SF 24,150).

BI *Nu Mi-Allonge, Bras Replies Vers Les Yeux, Pl.2 Ter (D. 392), 1906,* pl 2, #8/25, good cond., rubbed, handling creases, pinholes, est. BP2/2,500, (06-30-93, Sotheby-London, #503), 17½ x 9¾ in., (445 x 248 mm.), lithograph on Japan.

$15,400* *Nu Sur Chaise De Repos Sur Fond Moucharabieh (D. 426), 1922,* s. in ink, num. 11/50, full margins, good cond., crease, hinge remains, (02-24-93, Butterfield, #2752, illus.), 19⅜ x 15⅞ in., (492 x 403 mm.), sheet 23½ x 17¾ in., (492 x 403 mm.), lithograph on Chine (BP 10,739, DM 25,000, FR 84,755, Y 1,807,088).

BI *Nu. Etude D'Un Mouvement De Jambes (D. 501), 1929,* plate 119, s., #22/50, full margins, good cond., light/masking tape stains, foxing, skinning, razor cut, est. $8/12,000, (02-11-93, Sotheby-NY, #175, illus.), 16¹⁵/₁₆ x 21⅝ in., (430 x 550 mm.), lithograph.

BI *Nu. Etude D'Un Mouvement De Jambes (D. 501), 1929,* plate 119, s., #22/50, good cond., foxing, skinning, razor cut, tapestain, est. $7/9,000, (05-13-93, Sotheby-NY, #610, illus.), 16⅞ x 21⅝ in., (430 x 550 mm.), lithograph.

$12,100* *La Nuit (D. 418), 1922,* s., #47/50, full margins, light staining, very good cond., (11-09-92, Christie-NY, #112, illus.), 250 x 295 in., (635 x 749.3 cm.), lithograph on Japan (BP 8000, DM 19,317, FR 65,264, Y 1,501,613).

BI *Odalisque Assise A La Jupe De Tulle (D.M. 443), 1924,* s., #(?)42/50, slightly rubbed, margins, tape adhesion, mount-staining, rubbing, foxmarks, defects, est. BP 12/16,000, (12-01-92, Christie-London, #424, illus.), L. 14³/₁₆ x 10⁷/₁₆ in., (360 x 265 mm.), lithograph on Chine volant.

$8050* *Odalisque Au Collier (D. 434), 1923,* plate 44, s., #38/50, large margins, good cond., fleck adhering to surface into image, printer's creases, repaired thin spot, (05-13-93, Sotheby-NY, #602, illus.), 9 x 12⅛ in., (228 x 307 mm.), sh 12⅞ x 17¼ in., (228 x 307 mm.), lithograph (BP 5285, DM 12,999, FR 43,845, Y 898,738).

$4396* *Odalisque Couchee (D. 86), 1923,* whole margins, (06-11-93, Picard, #123), 7¹³/₁₆ x 11¾ in., (199 x 299 mm.), black etching on wove (BP 2888, DM 7144, FR 24,088, Y 466,419).

$14,587* *Odalisque Debout Au Plateau De Fruits (D. 444), 1924,* whole margins, s., #3/50, (06-11-93, Picard, #128), 14¾ x 10¹³/₁₆ in., (375 x 275 mm.), lithograph in black on Japan (BP 9584, DM 23,707, FR 79,929, Y 1,547,692).

$3738* *Odalisque Sur Fond A Carreaux (D. 158), 1929,* plate 124, s., i., large margins, good cond., rubbed areas in subject, hinge stains, foxing, (02-11-93, Sotheby-NY, #174), 6³/₁₆ x 4¹⁵/₁₆ in., (157 x 125 mm.), sheet 14⁷/₁₆ x 10¹¹/₁₆ in., (157 x 125 mm.), drypoint on chine applique (BP 2638, DM 6192, FR 20,953, Y 450,633).

BI *Odalisque Sur Fond A Carreaux (D. 158), 1929,* plate 124, s., i. essai, large margins, good cond., rubbed areas, hinge stains, est. $4/6,000, (11-05-92, Sotheby-NY, #244), 6⅛ x 4⅞ in., (157 x 125 mm.), sheet 14⅜ x 10¾ in., (157 x 125 mm.), drypoint on chine applique.

BI *Odalisque Sur La Terrasse (GP 633, Duthuit: L'Oeuvre grave Tome II 1), 1922,* s. Henri Matisse, 71/200, est. DK 25,000, (09-30-92, Kunsthallen, #197), aquatint in colors.

$11,654* *Odalisque Voilee (D. M. 464), 1925,* s., i., trial proofs, full margins, very good cond., (12-01-92, Christie-London, #430), L. 21¼ x 17⅛ in., (540 x 435 mm.), lithograph on simili-Japan (BP 7700, DM 18,575, FR 63,303, Y 1,450,946).

$12,486* *Odalisque Voilee (D.M. 464), 1925,* s., #15/50, discoloration, very good cond., (12-01-92, Christie-London, #429, illus.), L. 21¼ x 17½ in., (540 x 445 mm.), lithograph on simili-Japan (BP 8250, DM 19,901, FR 67,822, Y 1,554,532).

$10,913* *Odalisque, Brasero Et Coupe De Fruits (D. 504), 1929,* plate 122, s., #93/100, full margins, good cond., (12-03-92, Sotheby-London, #405, illus.), 11 x 14⅞ in., (278 x 377 mm.), lithograph on Arches (BP 7040, DM 17,162, FR 58,578, Y 1,357,845).

$7636* *Orientale Sur Lit De Repos, Sol De Carreaux Rouges (Dut.-Gar. 513, Pl. 112), 1929,* s., num., (06-23-93, Kornfeld, #563), lithograph (BP 5188, DM 12,920, FR 43,460, Y 831,899, SF 11,500).

BI *Pasiphae (D. bk. 10), 1944,* book in- and hors-texte, s., #57, pub. Martin Fabriani, good cond., foxing, est. $18/24,000, (11-05-92, Sotheby-NY, #251, illus.), each sheet approx. 12⅝ x 9⅞ in., (320 x 250 mm.), 147 linoleum cuts.

$140,000* *Pasiphae (D. bk. 10): Folio,* printer's copy of deluxe edit. of bk. by Henry de Montherlant, incl.Portrait de Claude Duthuit, s., d. 45, t.; each proof init., num., ink s. on just., p. Fequet Baudier, pub. Martin Fabiani, good cond., rubbing, hole, imperfections, foxing, creases, tear, (05-13-93, Sotheby-NY, #617, illus.), each sh approx. 12⅝ x 9⅞ in., (320 x 250 mm.), 147 linoleum cuts, in-and hors-texte, 12 planches refusees on chine,18 linoleum cuts, , 12 planches refusees on wove (BP 91,912, DM 226,062, FR 762,527, Y 15,630,233).

$3088* *Patitcha Souriante (D. 785), 1947,* pl 365, margins, good cond., stray, crayon w/in image, spots, discoloration, (06-30-93, Sotheby-London, #517, illus.), sh 18⅛ x 13⅜ in., (460 x 340 mm.), aquatint on wove (BP 2070, DM 5267, FR 17,768, Y 330,869).

$66,000* *Le Persane (D. 507), 1929,* plate 100, s., #39/50, large margins, good cond., light/mat stain, rubbed streaks, (11-05-92, Sotheby-NY, #245, illus.), 17⅞ x 11⅜ in., (455 x 290 mm.), sheet 23⅞ x 16¾ in., (455 x 290 mm.), lithograph on white wove (BP 42,927, DM 104,381, FR 353,130, Y 8,097,166).

BI *La Persane (D. 507), 1929,* plate 100, s., #36/50, full margins, good cond., mat stain, skinned spots, est. $60/80,000, (05-13-93, Sotheby-NY, #611, illus.), 17⅝ x 11⅜ in., (448 x 290 mm.), lithograph on white wove.

$46,616* *La Persane (D. M. 507), 1929,* s., #50/50, pub. H. Petiet, blindstamp, margins, mount-staining, tape, very good cond., (12-01-92, Christie-London, #427, illus.), L. 18 1/16 x 11 7/16 in., (458 x 290 mm.), sheet 24 13/16 x 17 11/16 in., (458 x 290 mm.), lithograph on Arches (BP 30,800, DM 74,300, FR 253,210, Y 5,803,785).

$2875* *La Persane (Duthuit 27), 1914,* plate 12, s., i. t. a quinze exempl./dixieme epr., full margins, foxed, soiled, partly broken-through crease, pin hole, soiling, skinned spots, ex-coll. Eugene Mayer, (05-13-93, Sotheby-NY, #597, illus.), 6 3/8 x 2 3/8 in., (161 x 60 mm.), drypoint on chine applique (BP 1887, DM 4642, FR 15,659, Y 320,978).

$8185* *Personnage De Gauche De La Pl. 125 Bis (D. 533), 1930,* plate 124, s., #60/75, full margins, good cond., (12-03-92, Sotheby-London, #397, illus.), 17 3/4 x 12 1/4 in., (450 x 310 mm.), lithograph on Arches (BP 5280, DM 12,872, FR 43,935, Y 1,018,415).

BI *Petit Bois Clair (Duthuit 318), 1906,* num., s., staining, untrimmed margins, (02-24-93, Picard, #167, illus.), wood engraving on van Gelder laid.

$8625* *Petite Liseuse (D. 431), 1923,* plate 40, s., #43/50, full margins, good cond., scrape, pressure mark, creases, skinning, (05-13-93, Sotheby-NY, #601, illus.), 10 x 8 5/8 in., (255 x 220 mm.), lithograph (BP 5662, DM 13,927, FR 46,977, Y 962,934).

$2666* *Plate 97 From Dix Danseuses (D. 488), 1927,* s., num. 107/130, pub. Galerie d'art Contemporain de Paris, full margins, light-stained, glue stains, (11-30-92, Phillips-London, #461, illus.), sheet 13 x 19 1/4 in., (330 x 489 mm.), lithograph on Arches (BP 1760, DM 4247, FR 14,419, Y 331,798).

$6050* *Poemes De Charles D'Orleans (D., Books 28), 1950: Fifty-Four,* complete volume, hors-texte, s., copy 722/1200, pub. Teriade Editeur, p. Mourlot, good cond., (10-28-92, Butterfield, #2669, illus.), each sheet 16 1/8 x 10 3/8 in., (410 x 264 mm.), lithograph on specially-made Arches velin (BP 3855, DM 9344, FR 31,725, Y 742,331).

BI *Poesies (D. bk. 5), 1932,* book in- and hors-texte, #53, pub. Albert Skira, good cond., est. $25/30,000, (11-05-92, Sotheby-NY, #252, illus.), each sheet approx. 13 1/4 x 9 7/8 in., (335 x 250 mm.), 29 etchings.

BI *Poesies Antillaises (D. bk. 37), 1972,* deluxe edit. of book, #44, pub. Mourlot, good cond., est. $18/24,000, (11-05-92, Sotheby-NY, #253, illus.), each sheet approx. 14 5/8 x 11 1/4 in., (370 x 285 mm.), 28 lithographs and 27 ornamental vignettes p. in blue, plus suite oflithographs on japon nacre.

$825* *Poesies Antillaises: (Woman's Face) (D. bk. no. 37), 1972,* pub. Mourlot, full margins, apparently good cond., (02-24-93, Butterfield, #2755), 12 x 10 1/4 in., (305 x 260 mm.), lithograph in brown on Japon nacre (BP 575, DM 1339, FR 4540, Y 96,808).

$4934* *La Pompadour (Katalog Fribourg 543; Duthuit/Garnaud 664), 1951,* #96/200, (05-26-93, Lempertz, #354, illus.), 20 13/16 x 14 13/16 in., (52.8 x 37.7 cm.), lithograph on thin off-white paper (BP 3192, DM 8050, FR 27,095, Y 536,071).

BI *Portrait De Madame Matisse (D.M. 15), 1914,* s., #10/10, margins, very good cond., est. BP 3,5/4,500, (12-01-92, Christie-London, #421, illus.), plate 5 11/16 x 4 1/8 in., (145 x 105 mm.), drypoint on wove.

BI *Portrait De Mme Matisse (D. 15), 1914,* pl o, s., #10/10, full margins, good cond., est. BP 2,5/3,000, (06-30-93, Sotheby-London, #510, illus.), 5 7/8 x 4 1/4 in., (149 x 108 mm.), drypoint on wove.

$943* *"Portraits" (Pl. 670), 1951-54,* one of 15 artist's proofs, stamp, spots, (10-18-92, Pescheteau, #209), 12 3/16 x 9 1/2 in., (31 x 24.2 cm.), lithograph on Arches wove (BP 571, DM 1393, FR 4732, Y 112,597).

$2513* *Primavera (Duthuit 699), 1938,* inits. stamp, 24/25, (06-28-93, Loudmer, #309), 9 1/16 x 6 3/4 in., (230 x 171 mm.), sh 13 15/16 x 10 7/16 in., (230 x 171 mm.), black linocut on thin laid (BP 1683, DM 4270, FR 14,385, Y 266,631).

BI *Profil De Jeune Fille Coiffee A La Grecque (Duthuit-Matisse 241),* s., num., est. DM 8,000, (06-05-93, Bassenge, #6336A), etching on China.

$3916* *Une Religieuse A L'Expression Candide (Duthhuit-Matisse vol. 1 277),1945,* #10/25, s., num., (05-20-93, Finarte-Milan, #110, illus.), 6 1/4 x 4 11/16 in., (15.8 x 11.9 cm.), etching (BP 2513, DM 6318, FR 21,283, Y 432,420, L 5750).

BI *Le Renard Blanc (D. 514), 1929,* plate 123, s., #37/75, full margins, good cond., printer's creases inimage, foxing, mat stain, water stains, creases, est. $60/80,000, (05-13-93, Sotheby-NY, #613, illus.), 20 x 14 1/2 in., (515 x 368 mm.), lithograph.

BI *Le Renard Blanc (D. 514), 1929,* s., #33/75, full margins, light-mat staining, foxing, surface soiling, taped down in places, very good cond., est. $60/70,000, (05-11-93, Christie-NY, #227, illus.), borderline 20 x 14 1/2 in., (508 x 368 mm.), lithograph on Arches.

BI *Rene Leriche (G. 27), 1949,* s., #212/300, p. Mourlot, small margins, good cond., repaired holes,mat staining, surface soiling, est. $1/1,500, (10-28-92, Butterfield, #2671), 7 1/4 x 4 1/2 in., (184 x 114 mm.), lithograph on chine colle (pasted) attached to wove.

$1045* *Rene Leriche (G. 27), 1949,* s., num. 212/300, small margins, good cond., repaired holes, mat staining, surface soiling, (02-24-93, Butterfield, #2754, illus.), 7 1/4 x 4 1/2 in., (184 x 114 mm.), lithograph on Chine colle (BP 729, DM 1696, FR 5751, Y 122,624).

$3946* *Le Repos Du Modele (D. 416), 1922,* pl 29, i. ea, 1st state of 2, pub. Frapier, state stamps, margins, good cond., defects, (06-30-93, Sotheby-London, #504, illus.), sh 10 7/8 x 14 3/8 in., (276 x 365 mm.), lithograph on chine volant (BP 2645, DM 6730, FR 22,704, Y 422,801).

$4025* *Le Repos Du Modele (D. 416), 1922,* plate 29 bis, s., #40/50, pub. Galerie des Peintres-Graveurs, margins, good cond., light-stain, fox marks, (05-13-93, Sotheby-NY, #600), 8 3/4 x 12 in., (221 x 305 mm.), sh 12 3/4 x 17 1/4 in., (221 x 305 mm.), lithograph on smooth Japan (BP 2642, DM 6499, FR 21,923, Y 449,369).

BI *Le Repos Du Modele (D. 416), 1922,* 2nd final state, pub. Les Peintres-graveurs de Manet a Matisse, 1925, blindstamp, i. in another hand, staining, good cond., est. $3,2/3,600, (05-11-93, Christie-NY, #222), borderline 8 3/4 x 11 3/4 in., (222 x 298 mm.), lithograph on Chine applique.

$2760* *Le Repos Du Modele (D. 416), 1922,* 2nd final state, pub. Les Peintres-graveurs de Manet a Matisse, 1925, full margins, mat staining, foxing, crease, good cond., (05-11-93, Christie-NY, #223, illus.), borderline 8 3/4 x 11 3/4 in., (222 x 298 mm.), lithograph on Chine applique (BP 1762, DM 4348, FR 14,650, Y 303,597).

BI *Le Repos Du Modele (D. 416), 1929,* plate 29 bix, pub. Frapier, blindstamp Les peintres-graveurs, margins, good cond., paper tape, ext. BP 8/900, (12-03-92, Sotheby-London, #396), sheet 10 3/4 x 14 3/8 in., (275 x 365 mm.), lithograph on chine volant.

$9927* *Le Repos Du Modele (Dut.-Gar. 416, Pl. 29/bis), 1922,* s. in pencil, num., blindstamp, (06-23-93, Kornfeld, #556, illus.), lithograph on China (BP 6744, DM 16,797, FR 56,500, Y 1,081,490, SF 14,950).

$5628* *Le Repos Du Modele (Duthuit 416), 1922,* plate 29bis, 1st state of 2, s., pub. Galerie des Peintres-Graveurs,full margins, good cond., fox marks, (10-14-92, Sotheby-Japan, #50, illus.), 8 7/8 x 12 in., (225 x 305 mm.), lithograph on chine vollant (BP 3303, DM 8236, FR 27,931, Y 682,016).

$3069* *Le Repos Du Modele (Duthuit 416), 1922,* plate 29 bix, s., #14/50, pub. Frapier, blindstamp Galerie des Peintres-Graveurs, margins, tape, glue staining, tear, (12-03-92, Sotheby-London, #395, illus.), sheet 12 5/8 x 19 1/4 in., (322 x 490 mm.), lithograph on chine volant (BP 1980, DM 4826, FR 16,473, Y 381,859).

$884* *Le Repos Du Modele (M. Duthuit-Matisse, Cl. Duthuit 416), 1922,* second printing, staining, creases, good margins, drystamp, (06-16-93, Ader Tajan, #119), 8 11/16 x 11 3/4 in., (22 x 29.9 cm.), lithograph on chine volant (BP 589, DM 1467, FR 4925, Y 94,283).

$1430* *Le Repos Du Modele, Duthuit 416,* pub. Frapier in Album des Peintres-Graveurs, prov., (09-20-92, Hindman, #754), 8 5/8 x 11 3/4 in., (21.9 x 29.8 cm.), lithograph on chine volant (BP 837, DM 2122, FR 7259, Y 176,740).

$3520* *Le Repos Du Mosele (D. 416), 1922,* 2nd final state, pub. Les peintres-lithographies de Manet a Matisse,Galerie des Peintres-graveurs, 1925, blindstamp, full margins, mat staining, creasing, very good cond., prop. Steven and Ursula Schwartz, (11-09-92, Christie-NY, #111, illus.), 223 x 298 in., (566.4 x 756.9 cm.), lithograph on Chine (BP 2327, DM 5619, FR 18,986, Y 436,833).

$7150* *Repose Du Modele (Duthuit 416; Fribourg 375), 1922,* s., #21/50, 1st state, pub. Galerie des Peintres-Graveurs, blindstamp, Lugt 1057b, flawless cond., full margins, front cover lot, (12-08-92, Swann, #204, illus.), image 8¾ x 12 in., (22.2 x 30.5 cm.), lithograph (BP 4481, DM 11,132, FR 37,951, Y 886,217).

$10,690* *La Robe Jaune Au Ruban Noir (Dut.-Gar. 424, Pl. 34), 1922,* s. in ink, num., collector's stamp, (06-23-93, Kornfeld, #557, illus.), lithograph on China (BP 7262, DM 18,088, FR 60,842, Y 1,164,615, SF 16,100).

$5827* *La Sieste (D. M. 427), 1922,* pen and ink s., #25/50, margins, perforation, pinholes, mount stain,foxmarks, tape, good cond., (12-01-92, Christie-London, #425, illus.), L. 15¹⁵⁄₁₆ x 17¹⁄₁₆ in., (406 x 433 mm.), lithograph on Chine volant (BP 3850, DM 9288, FR 31,651, Y 725,473).

$5635* *La Sieste (Duthuit 427, Fribourg 385), 1922,* s., 42/50, (05-12-93, AB Stockholm, #7036, illus.), 17¹⁵⁄₁₆ x 21¹³⁄₁₆ in., (45.5 x 55.4 cm.), lithograph on chine (BP 3679, DM 9092, FR 30,625, Y 629,117, SK 41,800).

BI *"Sirena",* #16/25, plate s., reserve P40,000, (12-17-92, Duran, #181, illus.), 11 x 14¹⁵⁄₁₆ in., (28 x 38 cm.), lithograph.

$2150* *Small Blue Interior,* s. E.A., blindstamp Atelier Lacouriere, (05-12-93, AB Stockholm, #7037, illus.), 21¹⁄₁₆ x 17⅛ in., (53.5 x 43.5 cm.), color aquatint in colors on Arches (BP 1404, DM 3469, FR 11,685, Y 240,036, SK 15,950).

$2320* *Tahiti (Duthuit 715), 1938,* s., 12/30, losses, tears, good cond., (06-28-93, Loudmer, #308, illus.), 10¹⁵⁄₁₆ x 7¹¹⁄₁₆ in., (279 x 195 mm.), sh 19¹¹⁄₁₆ x 12⅝ in., (279 x 195 mm.), black linocut on wove (BP 1553, DM 3942, FR 13,280, Y 246,154).

$5147* *Tete De Jeune Fille Aux Sourcils Rectangulaires (D. 222), 1930,* pl 151, s., #3/25, full margins, good cond., (06-30-93, Sotheby-London, #511, illus.), 4¾ x 4 in., (121 x 102 mm.), etching on chine applique (BP 3450, DM 8779, FR 29,614, Y 551,484).

$3032* *"Tete De Marguerite II" (Hahnloser 29; Dutuit-Matisse S. 68), 1920,* s., (11-28-92, Grisebach, #647, illus.), 5½ x 3¾ in., (14 x 9.5 cm.), etching on laid down China (BP 2001, DM 4830, FR 16,398, Y 377,349).

BI *Tete Renversee (D. 397), 1906,* pl 5, #15/25 in ink, good cond., rubbed patches, marks, creases, pinholes, est. BP 2/3,000, (06-30-93, Sotheby-London, #506, illus.), 13¾ x 10¾ in., (349 x 273 mm.), lithograph on Japan.

BI *Torse A L'Aiguiere (D. 494), 1927,* plate 88, s., #16/50, full margins, good cond., printer's creases inimage, tear, est. $12/15,000, (05-13-93, Sotheby-NY, #608, illus.), 14¼ x 10¼ in., (363 x 261 mm.), lithograph.

$8400* *Torse De Face (Duthuit-Garneau 407, Planche 16), 1913,* s. in ink, num., (06-23-93, Kornfeld, #555), lithograph on thick wove (BP 5707, DM 14,213, FR 47,809, Y 915,132, SF 12,650).

$9437* *Torse Nu Au Collier D'Ambre (D. 502), 1929,* pl 116, s., #50/50, full margins, good cond., skinning, (06-30-93, Sotheby-London, #513, illus.), 22 x 17⅞ in., (559 x 454 mm.), lithograph on Arches (BP 6325, DM 16,096, FR 54,298, Y 1,011,143).

$3450* *Tristan Tzara, Le Signe De Vie, Paris, Bordas (D., Books 13), 1946,* s., watermark, t. page, just., text and 6 reprods. of drawings, s., copy 114 of 300, (05-11-93, Christie-NY, #216), 9¹⁵⁄₁₆ x 7¹⁄₁₆ in., (253 x 180 mm.), lithograph on BFK Rives (BP 2202, DM 5435, FR 18,312, Y 379,496).

BI *Trois Figures-Academies (D. 46), 1914,* pl 50, s., #3/12, full margins, good cond., foxing, rubbing, handlingcreases, est. BP 4/5,000, (06-30-93, Sotheby-London, #507, illus.), 5⅞ x 4 in., (149 x 102 mm.), drypoint on wove.

BI *Trois Nus, L'Un Appuye Sur Un Tabouret (D. 3), 1900-1903,* pl 57, s., #10/25, i., margins, light/mount/backboard-stained, est. BP 2/3,000, (06-30-93, Sotheby-London, #505, illus.), sh 10¼ x 6¾ in., (260 x 171 mm.), drypoint on C. H. (height) Wittman laid.

$2231* *Trois Tetes. A L'Amitie (D. 827), 1951-2,* pl 391, proofs, margins, good cond., handling marks, creases, (06-30-93, Sotheby-London, #518, illus.), sh 20⅞ x 15⅝ in., (530 x 397 mm.), aquatint on BFK Rives (BP 1495, DM 3805, FR 12,837, Y 239,044).

$19,800* *Ulysses (D. bk. 6), 1935,* complete suite, each s., #5/150, pub. The Limited Editions Club, 1935, full margins, good cond., orig. portfolio, (11-05-92, Sotheby-NY, #250, illus.), each sheet 16⅜ x 12½ in., (415 x 317 mm.), six soft (molle) ground etchings (BP 12,878, DM 31,314, FR 105,939, Y 2,429,150).

$12,650* *Ulysses, New York, The Print Club (D. 235-40), 1935: Six,* s., #57/150, full margins, surface soiling, stain, creases, very good cond., (05-11-93, Christie-NY, #220, illus.), each plate 11⅛ x 9 in., (283 x 229 mm.), softground etching on Arches (BP 8075, DM 19,928, FR 67,144, Y 1,391,486).

$314* *Untitled,* illus. Ulysse, (10-18-92, Pescheteau, #210), 16¾ x 12⅝ in., (42.5 x 32 cm.), etching in black on wove (BP 190, DM 464, FR 1576, Y 37,493).

$2185* *Untitled, Paris, (Duthuit, Books 8), 1939,* from Tristan Tzara, Midis Gagnes, Editions Denoel, s., #16/25, full margins, light/mat staining, (05-11-93, Christie-NY, #215), plate 7½ x 5¾ in., (191 x 146 mm.), drypoint on Chine applique (BP 1395, DM 3442, FR 11,598, Y 240,348).

$2200* *Vierge A L'Enfant Debout (D. 650), 1950-1,* s., #28/200, wide margins, light/mat staining, foxing, creasing, taped to overmat, (11-09-92, Christie-NY, #119), 285 x 140 in., (723.9 x 355.6 cm.), lithograph on Chine applique (BP 1455, DM 3512, FR 11,866, Y 273,021).

$4180* *Vierge Et Enfant Sur Fond De Fleurs Et D'Etoiles (D. 646), 1950-1,* s., #120/200, full margins, light/time staining, (11-09-92, Christie-NY, #117, illus.), 323 x 254 in., (820.4 x 645.2 cm.), lithograph on Chine applique (BP 2764, DM 6673, FR 22,546, Y 518,739).

$4125* *Vierge Et Enfant Sur Fond De Fleurs Et D'Etoiles (D. 646), 1950-51,* s., #53/200, annot., margins slightly trimmed, good cond., touched-in area in image, stains, light-staining, glue/paper remains, creases, foxing, surface soiling, (10-28-92, Butterfield, #2670, illus.), image 12 x 9⅛ in., (305 x 232 mm.), sheet 18¾ x 14⅛ in., (305 x 232 mm.), lithograph on chine colle (pasted) w/ Arches support paper (BP 2628, DM 6371, FR 21,631, Y 506,135).

$3850* *Vierge Et Enfant Sur Fond Etoile (D. 647), 1950-1,* s., #65/100, full margins, foxing, Japon lifting, remains of glue, (11-09-92, Christie-NY, #118), 325 x 252 in., (825.5 x 640.1 cm.), lithograph on Japon applique (BP 2545, DM 6146, FR 20,766, Y 477,786).

$3093* *Visage Au Collier De Perles (Duthuit-Matisse 136), 1929,* s., #7/15, frame traces, tears, (06-28-93, Loudmer, #310, illus.), 4¾ x 6⁵⁄₁₆ in., (120 x 161 mm.), sh 15³⁄₁₆ x 11³⁄₁₆ in., (120 x 161 mm.), black etching on China applique on wove (BP 2071, DM 5256, FR 17,705, Y 328,170).

BI *Visage De Femme,* from "Derriere le Miroir". 1951, est. $425/475, (12-10-92, Sloan, #3025), sheet 15¼ x 11¼ in., (38.7 x 28.6 cm.), lithograph.

$6670* *Visage De Jeune Femme Et Bocal Aux Trois Poissons (D. 169), 1929,* s., #8/10, full margins, staining, mat staining, good cond., Robert Motherwell/Dedalus Foundation Estate, (05-11-93, Christie-NY, #218, illus.), plate 3⅝ x 4¹⁵⁄₁₆ in., (92 x 125 mm.), etching on Chine applique (BP 4258, DM 10,507, FR 35,403, Y 733,693).

$12,599* *Visage De Profil, Reposant Sur Un Bras, Paravent Louis XIV (Dut.-Gar. 447, Pl. 57), 1924,* s., num., i. epr. d'artiste, (06-23-93, Kornfeld, #558, illus.), lithograph on Chine volant (BP 8559, DM 21,318, FR 71,707, Y 1,372,590, SF 18,975).

$4600* *Visage De Trois-Quarts (D. 273), 1945,* s., #9/25, full margins, good cond., printing crease, tear, staining,crease, (05-19-93, Butterfield, #1928, illus.), sh 15⅛ x 11 in., (384 x 279 mm.), etching on Chine applique (BP 2986, DM 7477, FR 25,192, Y 509,244).

$5750* *Visage Legerement Penche Vers La Gauche (D. 414), 1913,* ink s. partially erased, #50/50, repair, pin hole, rubbing, creasing, good cond., (05-11-93, Christie-NY, #221, illus.), sheet 19¾ x 13 in., (502 x 330 mm.), lithograph on Japan (BP 3671, DM 9058, FR 30,520, Y 632,494).

MATISSE, Henri (after)

$908* *Gueridon,* #131/200, s., large margins, (02-03-93, Ader Tajan, #178), 16⅝ x 19¹¹⁄₁₆ in., (42.2 x 50 cm.), color engraving (BP 634, DM 1495, FR 5070, Y 112,949).

$686* *Petit Interieur Bleu (D. IV), 1952,* pub. Lacouriere, full margins, foxing, discoloration, good cond., (06-30-93, Sotheby-London, #520), 30 x 22¼ in., (762 x 565 mm.), aquatint in color on Arches (BP 460, DM 1170, FR 3947, Y 73,503).

$2588* *Portrait De Femme, 1942,* s., #12/75, margins, good cond., light-stain, crease, scotch tape stain, (05-13-93, Sotheby-NY, #620), 11¼ x 8⅛ in., (285 x 206 mm.), lithograph (BP 1699, DM 4179, FR 14,096, Y 288,936).

$377* *Portrait Of A Young Girl Seated At A Table,* by Jacques Villon, blindstamp, margins, (05-20-93, Bonhams-Chelsea, #159), plate 15½ x 10¾ in., (39.4 x 27.3 cm.), aquatint in colors (BP 242, DM 608, FR 2049, Y 41,630).

MATISSE, Henri and James JOYCE

$1955* *Ulysses, 1935,* Limited EDitions Club, in 8s, dust-jacket slightly chipped, s. by artist, #124, (06-14-93, Sotheby-NY, #204), etched and lithographed plated (BP 1280, DM 3182, FR 10,695, Y 205,725).

MATSUBARA, Naoko

$55* *"Brick Workers",* ed. 25, s., red seal, (03-12-93, DuMouchelle, #2103), 9½ x 11½ in., (24.1 x 29.2 cm.), woodcut in b/w (BP 38, DM 92, FR 311, Y 6482).

$86* *"Horses And Monsters", "Tiger", "Temple" and "Flight Of Two Figures":Four,* s., t., i., prov., (11-30-92, Ritchie, #41), each 12⅜ x 18 in., (31.5 x 45.7 cm.), woodblock (BP 57, DM 137, FR 465, Y 10,703, C$ 110).

$470* *"Solitude", "Pine", "Wind", "Winter Pond", "Winter Serenity", "Rain", "Decaying Beauty", "Autumn Colour", "Spring Visitor", "Thoreau", and "Drop OfLife": Folio Of Eleven,* from Solitude, pub. Aquarius Press, 1971, #81, s., num., lit., (11-30-92, Ritchie, #7, illus.), woodblock prints (6 in color) on hand-made Hosho Mulberry (BP 310, DM 749, FR 2542, Y 58,494, C$ 605).

$65* *"Whale In A Gale", "Buffalo Jumping Over The Moon", "Poem B", "War God", "Kabuki Theatre House",* and *"Cherry At Daigo": Six,* s., t., two d. '77, one '78, 5 num., 3 artist's proofs, prov., (11-30-92, Ritchie, #39), largest 15¾ x 12¹⁵⁄₁₆ in., (40 x 33 cm.), woodblock on japon, 2 in color (BP 43, DM 104, FR 352, Y 8090, C$ 83).

MATSUGASCA, Hiroshigi

$160 *"Uyena Park, Tokyo",* (06-11-93, G.A. Key, #71), 13 x 9 in., (33 x 22.9 cm.), colored wood block print (BP 105, DM 260, FR 877, Y 16,976).

MATTA   Chilean b. 1911

BI *Le Verbo Hommerica, 1987: Six,* s., num., est. DM 4,500, (06-05-93, Bassenge, #6337), each 7⅞ x 20½ in., (20 x 52 cm.), gravures on Japan.

MATTA, Robert Sebastian

$577* *Untitled,* #60/100, s., (11-21-92, Lempertz, #286), 16⁵⁄₁₆ x 21¾ in., (41.5 x 55.3 cm.), color etching on Arches wove (BP 380, DM 920, FR 3099, Y 71,757).

MATTA, Roberto Echaurren   Chilean b. 1911

BI *Archistruttura,* s., #5/45, est. DM 500, (09-18-92, Schloss Ahlden, #1032, illus.), 22⅜ x 27 in., (56.8 x 70.6 cm.), color lithograph on hand-made.

$725* *Centre Noeuds,* s., #20/25, (05-16-93, Hanzel, #445), 14 x 10⅜ in., (35.6 x 26.4 cm.), aquatint (BP 471, DM 1166, FR 3919, Y 80,368).

$1980* *"Cherche Eve", "Untitled", and "Untitled", 1971: Three,* each s., num. E.A. 99/100 and H.C., w/L'Oeuvre Gravee blindstamp, p.Georges Visat, full margins, good cond., 2nd w/hinge remains, surface soiling, (02-24-93, Butterfield, #2667), smallest 19½ x 14⅞ in., (496.2 x 378.5 mm.), largest 22¾ x 16⅜ in., (496.2 x 378.5

mm.), etchings w/soft-ground & aquatint in colors on Japon nacre, Arches, &Lana paper (BP 1381, DM 3214, FR 10,897, Y 232,340).

$605* *Comic Strip,* (03-14-93, Hindman, #297), 15 x 19½ in., (38.1 x 49.5 cm.), color soft-ground and etching (BP 422, DM 1007, FR 3424, Y 71,302).

$220* *Composition,* mono., 89/100, (03-24-93, Kunsthallen, #238), color etching (BP 149, DM 359, FR 1223, Y 25,849, DK 1380).

$202* *Composition,* mono., 4/100, (03-24-93, Kunsthallen, #239), color etching (BP 137, DM 330, FR 1123, Y 23,734, DK 1265).

$379* *Composition,* mono., E.A., (09-30-92, Kunsthallen, #199), color etching (BP 214, DM 537, FR 1818, Y 45,482, DK 2070).

$421* *Composition,* mono., E.A., (09-30-92, Kunsthallen, #200), color etching (BP 238, DM 597, FR 2019, Y 50,522, DK 2300).

$250* *Composition,* s., #117/120, good cond., tear into image, (11-30-92, Phillips-London, #545), sheet 21¾ x 28 in., (552 x 711 mm.), color lithograph on Arches (BP 165, DM 398, FR 1352, Y 31,114).

$383* *Composition With Centaur,* s., #95/99, good cond., (10-27-92, Phillips-London, #212), sheet 33 x 24⅓ in., (838 x 618 mm.), colored lithograph on wove (BP 242, DM 587, FR 1992, Y 46,850).

BI *"Composition",* #37/100, s., est. FF1,500/2,000, (04-04-93, Pescheteau, #260), 17⁵⁄₁₆ x 12¹⁵⁄₁₆ in., (44 x 33 cm.), etching and aquatint on Arches.

$483* *"Composition",* XIII/XV, s., (01-28-93, Pescheteau, #206), 29¹⁵⁄₁₆ x 22¹⁄₁₆ in., (76 x 56 cm.), etching and aquatint on Arches (BP 319, DM 765, FR 2590, Y 59,970).

$674* *"Composition",* s., (10-18-92, Pescheteau, #213), 11¹³⁄₁₆ x 15⅜ in., (30 x 39 cm.), etching and aquatint in colors on Arches (BP 408, DM 996, FR 3382, Y 80,478).

$449* *"Composition",* #40/100, s., (10-18-92, Pescheteau, #212), 28¾ x 20¹¹⁄₁₆ in., (73 x 52.5 cm.), lithograph in colors on grey Canson (BP 272, DM 663, FR 2253, Y 53,612).

$211* *Composition, 1976,* s. Matta, 41/100, from Pour Jorn portfolio, (09-30-92, Kunsthallen, #201), lithograph in colors (BP 119, DM 299, FR 1012, Y 25,321, DK 1150).

$510* *Cosi Fan Tutte Nr. II (Sabatier 225), 1970,* s., num., (06-08-93, Karl/Faber, #1097), approx. 18½ x 14¹⁵⁄₁₆ in., (47 x 38 cm.), color etching and aquatint on Arches wove (BP 335, DM 828, FR 2787, Y 54,169).

$524* *Cosi Fan Tutte Nr. IV (S. 227), 1970,* s., (06-08-93, Karl/Faber, #1098), approx. 18½ x 14¹⁵⁄₁₆ in., (47 x 38 cm.), color etching and aquatint (BP 344, DM 850, FR 2863, Y 55,656).

$831* *"Le Cube",* #10/70, s., 15 x 15 x 15, (10-18-92, Pescheteau, #211), collage of prints on carton (BP 504, DM 1227, FR 4170, Y 99,224).

$4978* *La Danse De La Mort (S. 293-300), 1972: Eight,* s., HC, (12-01-92, Karl/Faber, #988, illus.), 19⅞ x 14⁹⁄₁₆ in., (50.5 x 37 cm.), color etching and aquatint on Arches wove (BP 3289, DM 7934, FR 27,040, Y 619,771).

$1045* *Droites Liberees (273, 277, 278 and 281): Four, 1971,* each mono. device, num. 96/100, very good cond., wide margins, (09-11-92, Skinner, #105, illus.), largest 10⅞ x 7¾ in., (27.6 x 19.7 cm.), color etching w/aquatint on wove (BP 540, DM 1504, FR 5113, Y 129,476).

$193* *Droites Liberees (Sabatier 280), 1971,* s., 37/100, (06-28-93, Loudmer, #318), 10¹³⁄₁₆ x 7⅞ in., (275 x 200 mm.), sh 17⅛ x 12⅜ in., (275 x 200 mm.), color etching and aquatint on Arches wove (BP 129, DM 328, FR 1105, Y 20,477).

BI *"Droites Liberees" (Ferrari 56), 1971,* s., #37/100, full margins, (05-06-93, Laurin, #67), color etching and aquatint on wove.

BI *"Droites Liberees-1958-71" (V272-273): Two,* illus., artist's proofs, s., est. FF2,500/3,000, (04-04-93, Pescheteau, #261), 17⅛ x 12¹³⁄₁₆ in., (43.5 x 32.5 cm.), etchings and aquatints on Japan nacre.

BI *"FMR-1971" (V.260).* #30/85, est. FF1,000/1,500, (04-04-93, Pescheteau, #262), 14¹⁵⁄₁₆ x 11 in., (38 x 28 cm.), color etchings and aquatint on Arches.

BI *"Fog, Gog, Magog" (S. 253), 1971,* pub. London Arts, s., num., est. $4-500, (10-31-92, Cleveland, #381, illus.), 19⅜ x 23⅝ in., (49.2 x 60 cm.), color lithograph.

$1265* *"Hecatombe De Toros", Plate 2, "Fog Gog Magog", Plates 4 and 5 (Sabatier 245, 254 and 255), 1971: Three,* s., #45/100, p. Atelier Michel Casse, pub. London Arts, blindstamp, full margins, good cond., light-stain, (02-11-93, Sotheby-NY, #177), color lithograph (BP 893, DM 2095, FR 7091, Y 152,502).

$638* *Hom'mere (Chaosmos) (S. 356), 1974,* s., num., Georges Visat, (06-08-93, Karl/Faber, #1103), approx. 19⁵⁄₁₆ x 14¾ in., (49 x 37.5 cm.), color etching and aquatint on Japon nacre (BP 419, DM 1035, FR 3486, Y 67,764).

$172* *"I Am A Gen", 1976,* #53/100, s., (01-28-93, Peschet-eau, #208), 14⁹⁄₁₆ x 9¹³⁄₁₆ in., (37 x 25 cm.), etching and aquatint on Arches (BP 114, DM 273, FR 922, Y 21,356).

$550* *Judgements (Sabatier 174-175), 1967: Two,* full margins, s., i. EA, p. Visat, pub. Blue Moon Gallery, (05-27-93, Swann, #179), 16¼ x 20⅜ in., (41.3 x 51.8 cm.), color soft ground etching (BP 352, DM 883, FR 2975, Y 58,962).

$514* *Komposition,* s., H(ors) C(ommerce), (12-01-92, Karl/ Faber, #996), 12 x 15⁹⁄₁₆ in., (30.5 x 39.5 cm.), color etching and aquatint on Arches wove (BP 340, DM 819, FR 2792, Y 63,994).

$443* *Komposition,* s., num., (12-05-92, Bassenge, #7478), 18¾ x 18⁹⁄₁₆ in., (47.7 x 47.2 cm.), etching and relief print on wove (BP 277, DM 691, FR 2354, Y 54,888).

$415* *Komposition III, 1976,* s., num., (12-01-92, Karl/Faber, #991), 15³⁄₁₆ x 11⅝ in., (38.5 x 29.5 cm.), color etching and aquatint on Japon nacre (BP 274, DM 661, FR 2254, Y 51,668).

$348* *Komposition V, 1976,* s., num., (12-01-92, Karl/Faber, #993), 15³⁄₁₆ x 11⅝ in., (38.5 x 29.5 cm.), color etching and aquatint (BP 230, DM 555, FR 1890, Y 43,327).

$290* *Kompositon IV, 1976,* s., num., (12-01-92, Karl/Faber, #992), 15³⁄₁₆ x 11⅝ in., (38.5 x 29.5 cm.), color etching and aquatint (BP 192, DM 462, FR 1575, Y 36,106).

$3795* *L'Arc, Obscure Des Heures, 1975: Ten,* portfolio, s., #86/ 125, (04-29-93, Bukowskis, #59, illus.), etching in colors (BP 2415, DM 6003, FR 20,229, Y 422,183, DK 23,000).

$498* *L'Eau Est Manna,* s., num., (12-01-92, Karl/Faber, #994), 21¼ x 30⅛ in., (54 x 76.5 cm.), color lithograph on wove (BP 329, DM 794, FR 2705, Y 62,002).

$715* *L'Excitateur,* s., #73/105, blindstamp pub. l'Oeuvre Gravee, large margins, good cond., staining, skinned areas, light-staining, surface soiling, notations, (10-28-92, Butterfield, #2672), 18 x 23½ in., (457 x 597 mm.), color lithograph on Rives BFK (BP 456, DM 1104, FR 3749, Y 87,730).

$419* *Mallarme L'Or (S. 370), 1974,* s., #I/XXV, full margins, (11-16-92, Briest, #332), 26¾ x 19¹¹⁄₁₆ in., (68 x 50 cm.), aquatint and engraving in colors (BP 275, DM 668, FR 2251, Y 52,290).

$290* *Les Mots Dans La Peinture (Sabatier 213), 1969,* s., hors commerce, tears, untrimmed margins, (06-28-93, Loudmer, #319), 10⅝ x 17⅛ in., (270 x 435 mm.), sh 19¹¹⁄₁₆ x 27⁹⁄₁₆ in., (270 x 435 mm.), color etching, aquatint and embossing on wove (BP 194, DM 493, FR 1660, Y 30,769).

BI *The New School, 1944/1980: Eleven,* #22/70, est. DM 12,000, (06-12-93, Hauswedell/Nolt, #293, illus.), ah 15⅛ x 11⅛ in., (38.4 x 28.2 cm.), 10 etchings w/one color etching.

$819* *"Nuremberg Judgment", (Sabatier 177), 1967 and "Cosi Fan Tutte", (Sabatier 124), 1970: Two,* first #11/100, s.; second #30/100, s., (12-15-92, Finarte-Milan, #92), 16⁵⁄₁₆ x 21⅝ in., (41.5 x 55 cm.), 18¾ x 14¾ in., (41.5 x 55 cm.), etching in colors (BP 522, DM 1284, FR 4387, Y 101,575, L 1150).

$747* *Les Oh! Tomobiles (S. 308), 1972,* s., num., Editions Georges Visat, streaked, (12-01-92, Karl/Faber, #989), 16⁵⁄₁₆ x 21⁷⁄₁₆ in., (41.5 x 54.5 cm.), color etching and aquatint w/relief print on Arches wove (BP 494, DM 1191, FR 4058, Y 93,003).

$3014* *Les Oh! Tomobiles, 1972: Ten,* # E/A6/10, all s., Edizioni G. Visat, portfolio, (03-25-93, Finarte-Rome, #17, illus.), 16⁵⁄₁₆ x 21¾ in., (41.5 x 55.3 cm.), etching and aquatint (BP 2047, DM 4952, FR 16,838, Y 353,093, L 4830).

$332* *Orbis Yeux (S. 332), 1973,* s., num., (12-01-92, Karl/ Faber, #990), 19¹¹⁄₁₆ x 23⅝ in., (50 x 60 cm.), lithograph on Arches wove (BP 219, DM 529, FR 1803, Y 41,335).

BI *Popol-Vuh,* s., #97/100, prov., est. $9/1,000, (05-16-93, Hanzel, #446), 22 x 30 in., (55.9 x 76.2 cm.), color lithograph.

$550* *Portrait Of Man Ray, 1976,* s., #72/100, good cond.?, (12-08-92, Swann, #205, illus.), sheet 20½ x 14 in., (52.1 x 35.6 cm.), color etching-aquatint (BP 345, DM 856, FR 2919, Y 68,171).

$379* *Premier Goal Au Chili,* #9/125, s., (04-21-93, Germann, #631), 21⅝ x 25⁹⁄₁₆ in., (550 x 650 mm.), color lithograph (BP 246, DM 606, FR 2049, Y 41,957, SF 552).

BI *"Requiem Pour La Fin Du Temps" Sex-Uberant (F. 246), 1979,* s., #38/100, full margins, (05-06-93, Laurin, #68), color etching and aquatint on wove.

$541* *Sans Titre,* s., XI/XXV, (06-28-93, Loudmer, #317), 19¹¹⁄₁₆ x 14¾ in., (500 x 375 mm.), sh 25¹⁵⁄₁₆ x 19¹¹⁄₁₆ in., (500 x 375 mm.), color etching and aquatint on Arches (BP 362, DM 919, FR 3097, Y 57,401).

$155* *Sans Titre,* s., 39/100, (06-28-93, Loudmer, #313), 8¹¹⁄₁₆ x 6⅛ in., (220 x 155 mm.), sh 17⅛ x 12⅜ in., (220 x 155 mm.), color aquatint on Japan (BP 104, DM 263, FR 887, Y 16,446).

$348* *Sans Titre,* s., hors commerce, pen and mat traces, good cond., (06-28-93, Loudmer, #315), 7⅜ x 5⁹⁄₁₆ in., (187 x 141 mm.), sh 20¹⁄₁₆ x 12¹⁵⁄₁₆ in., (187 x 141 mm.), color etchings and embossing on Lana wove (BP 233, DM 591, FR 1992, Y 36,923).

$271* *Sans Titre,* s., 38/100, (06-28-93, Loudmer, #316), 9⅝ x 7⁵⁄₁₆ in., (245 x 185 mm.), sh 17⁵⁄₁₆ x 12¹⁵⁄₁₆ in., (245 x 185 mm.), color etching and aquatint on wove (BP 181, DM 460, FR 1551, Y 28,753).

$77* *Sans Titre,* s., creases, (06-28-93, Loudmer, #95), 10⅝ x 8¹⁄₁₆ in., (270 x 205 mm.), sh 17⅝ x 12¹³⁄₁₆ in., (270 x 205 mm.), serigraph on gold paper on wove (BP 52, DM 131, FR 441, Y 8170).

$482* *Sans Titre, c. 1968,* artist proof, s. Matta, (05-18-93, Encans, #208), 16⅛ x 21⁷⁄₁₆ in., (41 x 54.5 cm.), color etching (BP 314, DM 782, FR 2641, Y 53,717, C$ 611).

$3300* *Scenes Familieres, Paris, Le Point Cardinale, 1964 (S. 86-93): Set Of Eight,* s., #24/50, full margins, foxing, good cond., orig. portfolio, (11-24-92, Christie-NY, #359, illus.), all sheet 19½ x 25½ in., (495 x 648 mm.), etching and aquatint in colors on Rives (BP 2174, DM 5283, FR 17,925, Y 409,378).

BI *Les Suissides (S. 221), 1970,* s., E/A, est. DM 1200, (12-01-92, Karl/Faber, #987), 16⁵⁄₁₆ x 21⅞ in., (41.5 x 55.5 cm.), color etching and aquatint on wove.

$622* *Les Suissides (Sabatier 221), 1970,* s., EA, (12-01-92, Karl/Faber, #986), 16⁵⁄₁₆ x 21⅞ in., (41.5 x 55.5 cm.), color etching and aquatint on Japon nacre (BP 411, DM 991, FR 3379, Y 77,440).

$348* *Sur Matta (Sabatier 135), 1970,* s., 75/150, mat traces, good cond., (06-28-93, Loudmer, #314), 10¹⁄₁₆ x 8⅛ in., (255 x 206 mm.), sh 14¹⁵⁄₁₆ x 11¼ in., (255 x 206 mm.), color etching and aquatint on wove (BP 233, DM 591, FR 1992, Y 36,923).

$571* *Surrealistische Komposition,* s., num., (05-26-93, Dorling, #2855), 19⁵⁄₁₆ x 26¹⁵⁄₁₆ in., (49 x 68.5 cm.), aquatint-etching on Japan (BP 369, DM 932, FR 3136, Y 62,038).

$1086* *Le Transesports (Cl. Kasett), 1977: Six,* s., 52/100, portfolio, (12-04-92, AB Stockholm, #7106), 17¹¹⁄₁₆ x 22¼ in., (45 x 56.5 cm.), etching in color on Japon nacre (BP 697, DM 1730, FR 5867, Y 135,581, SK 7370).

$448* *Untitled,* s., #41/100, pub. Georges Visat, w/their blindstamp, full margins, good cond., (05-27-93, Sotheby-Amstrdm, #658), 16¼ x 12⅝ in., (412 x 320 mm.), color etching on wove (BP 287, DM 719, FR 2423, Y 48,027, G 805).

$523* *Untitled,* s., #85/100, (10-30-92, Sloan, #2788), 14 x 11½ in., (35.6 x 29.2 cm.), etching and aquatint (BP 335, DM 805, FR 2730, Y 64,784).

$481* *Untitled*, s., num., (12-01-92, Karl/Faber, #995), 18⅞ x 18¹¹⁄₁₆ in., (48 x 47.5 cm.), color etching w/aquatint and relief print (BP 318, DM 767, FR 2613, Y 59,885).

$448* *Untitled*, s., #196/200, full margins, good cond., minor handling creases, (05-27-93, Sotheby-Amstrdm, #659), sheet 20 x 25⅞ in., (508 x 658 mm.), color lithograph on wove (BP 287, DM 719, FR 2423, Y 48,027, G 805).

$935* *"Untitled"*, s., #83/125, margins, very good cond.?, foxing, (10-28-92, Butterfield, #2673), 19⅜ x 27⅛ in., (492 x 689 mm.), color etching w/aquatint on Japan (BP 596, DM 1444, FR 4903, Y 114,724).

$1610* *(Untitled)", "Les Helvements" (S. 220), 1970 and "Affiche Pour L'Exposition Matta" (S. 207), 1968,* each s., #18/100, E.A., H.C., 2nd w/L'Oeuvre Gravee blindstamp, p. byAtelier Georges Visat, full margins, good cond., creases, surface soiling, (05-19-93, Butterfield, #1843, illus.), smallest 16⅜ x 22 in., (416 x 559 mm.), largest 19⅝ x 14¹⁵⁄₁₆ in., (416 x 559 mm.), aquatint w/soft-ground etching in color on Japan and Lana (BP 1045, DM 2617, FR 8817, Y 178,235).

$1880* *Untitled: Four*, #40/100, foglio, all s., (05-20-93, Finarte-Milan, #111), 26⅜ x 20½ in., (67 x 52 cm.), etching in colors on Japan (BP 1207, DM 3033, FR 10,217, Y 207,597, L 2760).

$1880* *Untitled: Four*, #12/100, foglio, all s., (05-20-93, Finarte-Milan, #112), 26⅜ x 20½ in., (67 x 52 cm.), etching in colors on Japan (BP 1207, DM 3033, FR 10,217, Y 207,597, L 2760).

$350* *Vaisseux Spatials*, hors commerce, s., full margins, (03-31-93, Briest, #E75), sh 19¹¹⁄₁₆ x 25¹⁵⁄₁₆ in., (50 x 66 cm.), 12³⁄₁₆ x 15¾ in., (50 x 66 cm.), etching and aquatint on Arches (BP 231, DM 563, FR 1913, Y 40,248).

$356* *Les Venusiennes (Sabatier 155, Silkeborg 128), 1967,* s., #157/300, pub. Prisunic, 1967, (11-16-92, Briest, #333), 19¹¹⁄₁₆ x 25⁹⁄₁₆ in., (50 x 65 cm.), lithograph in 4 colors on Arches (BP 234, DM 568, FR 1913, Y 44,428).

$293* *El Verbo America, 1986,* s., #65/100, full margins, (11-16-92, Briest, #335), 25⁹⁄₁₆ x 19¹¹⁄₁₆ in., (65 x 50 cm.), etching in colors (BP 193, DM 467, FR 1574, Y 36,566).

MATTA, Roberto Sebastian   b. 1911

$4300* *Sebastian Matta, L'Arc, Obscure Des Heures, 1975:* Ten, #119/125, s., (05-27-93, Lempertz, #894, illus.), 38¾ x 26¹⁵⁄₁₆ in., (98.5 x 68.5 cm.), color etching on Arches wove (BP 2754, DM 6900, FR 23,256, Y 460,978).

MATTA, Sebastian

BI *New School (Sabatier 1-7), 1943-44: Set Of Ten,* s., #30/70, pub. 1988 Sabatier-Satie, num., full margins, good cond.,original portfolio, est. BP 1,5/2,000, (06-30-93, Sotheby-London, #879, illus.), overall 15 x 11¼ in., (381 x 286 mm.), drypoint w/hand-colored etching made specially for this edit..

$2728* *New School (Sabatier 1-7), 1943: Seven,* s., #10/70, p. 1970, full margins, good cond., (12-03-92, Sotheby-London, #771, illus.), overall size approx. 15 x 11¼ in., (380 x 285 mm.), drypoints on wove (BP 1760, DM 4290, FR 14,643, Y 339,430).

$384* *Une Saison En Enfer-No 5. Damne Par L'Arc-En-Ciel, 1978,* s., #81/150, full margins, good cond., (05-27-93, Sotheby-Amstrdm, #661), 18¹³⁄₁₆ x 14¹⁄₁₆ in., (478 x 357 mm.), color etching on wove (BP 246, DM 616, FR 2077, Y 41,166, G 690).

MATTER, C.

$495* *Panorama Of New York And Brooklyn*, p. I. Schaerer, (08-08-92, Litchfield, #117), 22 x 30 in., (55.9 x 76.2 cm.), engraving (BP 257, DM 728, FR 2460, Y 63,178).

MATTER, Herbert   1907-1984

$1150* *Multiple Exposure Movement Study, 1942,* diagonal cropping, (04-08-93, Christie-NY, #319, illus.), 8⅛ x 10 in., (20.6 x 25.4 cm.), photograph, gelatin silver print (BP 754, DM 1847, FR 6253, Y 130,504).

MATTESON, T.H. (after)

$138* *The Spirit of '76,* p. Neal and Pate, (06-11-93, Freemn/ Fine Art, #145), 16 x 19½ in., (40.6 x 49.5 cm.), hand-colored engraving (BP 91, DM 224, FR 756, Y 14,642).

MATTHES, Ernst

$205* *Aux Courses (Scenes Parisiennes), 1909,* full margins, (02-24-93, Picard, #168), color lithograph on simili-Japan (BP 143, DM 333, FR 1128, Y 24,055).

MATTHEUER, Wolfgang   b. 1927

$469* *Horizont, 1968,* #18/25, pencil s., d., (11-20-92, Lempertz, #706), sh 13½ x 17¹¹⁄₁₆ in., (34.3 x 45 cm.), woodcut on red Japan (BP 309, DM 748, FR 2519, Y 58,326).

$428* *Spazierengehendes Paar Vor Einer Grossstadtsilhouette,* s., (12-05-92, Bassenge, #7479), 15¹⁄₁₆ x 14¹³⁄₁₆ in., (38.2 x 37.6 cm.), woodcut (BP 268, DM 667, FR 2274, Y 53,029).

$265* *Springender Mann, 1977,* s., num., (12-01-92, Karl/ Faber, #997), 25⅜ x 19⁵⁄₁₆ in., (64.5 x 49 cm.), lithograph on wove (BP 175, DM 422, FR 1439, Y 32,993).

MATTHEWS, George Bagby

$28* *"Lee And His Generals",* after a painting by G.B. Matthews, (c) 1907, holes, toning, (11-21-92, Goldberg, #716), 15 x 26½ in., (38.1 x 67.3 cm.), color lithograph (BP 18, DM 45, FR 150, Y 3482).

MATTHEY, L.

$100* *Favor Cycles, Velomoteurs, Motos. "Va Droit Au But", c. 1930,* good cond., (02-12-93, Cheval/Robert, #83), 62¹⁵⁄₁₆ x 47¼ in., (160 x 120 cm.), poster (BP 70, DM 166, FR 561, Y 12,060).

$252* *Favor. Cycles, Velomoteurs, Motos. "Va Droit Au But",* good cond., (11-19-92, Ribeyre/Baron, #70), 62¹⁵⁄₁₆ x 47¼ in., (160 x 120 cm.), poster (BP 166, DM 402, FR 1353, Y 31,339).

MAUER, Oscar

$489* *"Dawn",* 1930s, s., (05-23-93, Butterfield, #3521, illus.), 3¾ x 4½ in., photograph, gelatin silver print (BP 318, DM 800, FR 2691, Y 54,051).

MAUFRA, Maxime   French 1861/62-1918

$292* *"Bords De Seine", 1912,* s. in plate, (10-18-92, Pescheteau, #216), 8¼ x 11 in., (21 x 28 cm.), soft (molle) ground etching on Arches laid (BP 177, DM 431, FR 1465, Y 34,866).

$660* *Coastal View, 1894,* s. Maufra in blue pencil, s., d. in plate Maufra 1894, fair cond., ink losses, margin trimmed, losses, (09-11-92, Skinner, #14, illus.), 13¾ x 21¼ in., (34.9 x 54 cm.), aquatint/etching on wove (BP 341, DM 950, FR 3229, Y 81,774).

MAUNER, J. (after)

$269* *A View Of Chelsea, 1744,* by I. Viranez, pub. Thomas Bowles, margins, repaired tear, (01-21-93, Bonhams-Chelsea, #36), plate 10½ x 16 in., (26.7 x 40.6 cm.), etching (BP 176, DM 428, FR 1447, Y 33,667).

MAURICE, Denis   1870-1945

$286* *Maternite Devant La Mer Ou Maternite Au Pouldou, 1900,* mono. in stone, from the Insel portfolio, (05-08-93, Schloss Ahlden, #2838), 13⁹⁄₁₆ x 9¹³⁄₁₆ in., (34.5 x 25 cm.), color lithograph on wove (BP 187, DM 459, FR 1550, Y 31,959).

MAURIN, Charles

$201* *La Rose The, 1900,* mono. watermark, s., #23, full margins, good cond., staining, soiling, surface scuffing, hinge remains, pencil notations, (05-19-93, Butterfield, #2077), 16 x 11⅝ in., (406 x 295 mm.), aquatint w/drypoint and roulette in colors on laid (BP 130, DM 327, FR 1101, Y 22,252).

MAURON, P.

$17* *La Reine De Catulle Mendes, Musique De X. Leroux,* creased, (01-31-93, Morelle/Marchan, #165), 23⅝ x 32⁵⁄₁₆ in., (60 x 82 cm.), poster (BP 11, DM 27, FR 93, Y 2121).

MAURONER, Fabio

$345* *"Chioggia, 1906", "Traghetti", "Il Traghetto" and "Rio Ognissati": Four,* three w/watermarks, s., t., #31/50, 7/100, 29/30, and 30/50, margins,good cond., hinge remains, pencil notations, Elizabeth and Charles Whitmore Coll., (05-19-93, Butterfield, #2078), etching on laid (BP 224, DM 561, FR 1889, Y 38,193).

BI   *"Collina Di Montemaggiore, 1938", "Pianeastagnaio", "Tarquinia", "Tuscania" and "Venezia": Five*, s., first d., t., #2/75, 14/75, 7/50, 16/50, and 17/50, margins, good-cond., paper loss, hinge remains, notations, Elizabeth and Charles Whitmore Coll., est. $4/600, (05-19-93, Butterfield, #2083), etching on laid and wove.

BI   *Il Ghetto, Venice*, s., t., num. 6/30, margins, good cond., sheet toned, creases, hinge remains, surface soiling, prop. Print Corner Coll. of Elizabeth and Charles Whitmore, est. $2/300, (02-24-93, Butterfield, #2956), 8⅞ x 11⅞ in., (225 x 302 mm.), mezzotint on wove.

$330* *"Interior Of St. Mark, Venice", "St. Mark, Exterior", "Blessing WithThe Holy Relics In St. Mark, Venice, 1920" and "Corte Bottera, Venice": Four*, each s., t., d., num. 25/100, 59/100, 4/50, 17/50, margins, good cond., foxing, light-staining, paper stickers, creases, prop. Print Corner Coll. ofElizabeth and Charles Whitmore, est. $4/600, (02-24-93, Butterfield, #2954), from 10⅞ x 8⅞ in., (276 x 225 mm.), to 11¹⁵⁄₁₆ x 9⅞ in., (276 x 225 mm.), etching on laid (BP 230, DM 536, FR 1816, Y 38,723).

BI   *"Traguetto, Venice" (Two), "Ca Da Mosto" and "Madonna Di Gondoliera,1935": Four*, each s., last d., t., num. 8/100, 30/30, 18/100, 9/75, margins, goodcond., surface soiling, prop. Print Corner Coll. of Elizabeth and Charles Whitmore, est. $4/600, (02-24-93, Butterfield, #2955), from 2¾ x 4 in., (70 x 102 mm.), to 9¹⁵⁄₁₆ x 11¹⁄₁₆ in., (70 x 102 mm.), etching on laid.

$230* *"Venezia", 1931, "Venezia", 1934, "Venezia", 1935, "Venezia (Gondola)", "Venezia (Cannaregio)" and "Venezia (Canalarro)": Six*, four w/watermark, s., three d., t., #8/100, 10/75, 1/75, 3/100, 18/100, 38/100, margins, good cond., hinge remains, notations, Elizabeth and CharlesWhitmore Coll., (05-19-93, Butterfield, #2082), etching on laid (BP 149, DM 374, FR 1260, Y 25,462).

$403* *Venezia: Six*, s., t., #21/50, 31/100, 60/100, 12/50, 23/100, 7/100, full margins, good cond., surface soiling, hinge remains, handling creases, Elizabeth and Charles Whitmore Coll., (05-19-93, Butterfield, #2084), etching on laid (BP 262, DM 655, FR 2207, Y 44,614).

MAURUS

$241* *Le Ciel De Paris Sans Fumee Grace Au Coke De Gaz*, creased, (02-13-93, Morelle/Marchan, #52), 31½ x 47¼ in., (80 x 120 cm.), poster (BP 170, DM 400, FR 1352, Y 29,064).

BI   *PLM. La Lechere Les Bains. Savoie. "Station Thermale"*, very good cond., (03-15-93, Arcole, #49), 39⅜ x 24⁷⁄₁₆ in., (100 x 62 cm.), .

MAURUS, E.

BI   *Air France*, Goossens, A- cond., creasing, restoration, est. $5/700, (08-06-92, Swann, #195, illus.), 38½ x 24½ in., (97.8 x 62.2 cm.), .

$734* *C.I.D.N.A. Fleche D'Orient. "In The Same Day Paris Stamboul", c. 1935*, very good cond., (11-19-92, Ribeyre/Baron, #114, illus.), 39⁹⁄₁₆ x 24⅝ in., (100.5 x 62.5 cm.), poster (BP 483, DM 1170, FR 3942, Y 91,282).

MAUTIAUX?

$25   *Cathedral*, s., (05-20-93, Alderfer, #427), 15½ x 9 in., (39.4 x 22.9 cm.), etching (BP 16, DM 40, FR 136, Y 2761).

MAUZAN

$496* *Casa America Concertola 3450 Portatil Superfonica*, (01-31-93, Morelle/Marchan, #164), 40⁹⁄₁₆ x 61⁷⁄₁₆ in., (103 x 156 cm.), poster (BP 334, DM 799, FR 2702, Y 61,876).

MAUZAN, Achille

BI   *Parmigiano-Reggiano, Bertozzi, Parma, 1930*, plate s., Stampato in Italia, 4a Edizione 1930, Affissione Autorizzata dalla Regia Questura di Milano-15 Aprile 1930 (Anno VIII), est. $1,5/2,000, (06-08-93, Christie-E, #193, illus.), 55 x 39½ in., (139.7 x 100.3 cm.), color lithograph.

MAUZAN, Achille   1883-1952

$284* *Impermeabili, Ettore Moretti, c. 1930*, tears, excell. cond., (02-04-93, Christie-S. Ken, #92), 80 x 55 in., (203.2 x 139.7 cm.), color lithograph (BP 198, DM 468, FR 1586, Y 35,328).

MAVIGNIER, Almir da Silva   b. 1925

$830* *Permutation, (19)61: Forty-Eight*, s., d., num., (12-01-92, Karl/Faber, #998), 16⁹⁄₁₆ x 12⅝ in., (42 x 32 cm.), serigraph on wove (BP 548, DM 1323, FR 4508, Y 103,337).

MAX, Peter   German/American b. 1937

$688* *Blushing Beauty, 1988*, s., #136/300, (c) blindstamp, blindstamp p. Soma Fine Art Press, good cond., prov., (12-12-92, Weschler, #139), 40 x 30 in., (101.6 x 76.2 cm.), silkscreen on Arches (BP 441, DM 1084, FR 3715, Y 85,138).

$220* *"Christ"*, s., d. '71, (06-11-93, DuMouchelle, #2104), 20 x 28 in., (50.8 x 71.1 cm.), serigraph (BP 145, DM 358, FR 1205, Y 23,342).

$330* *Floral Still Life, 1978*, s., d., num., good cond., (10-31-92, Cleveland, #382), 21 x 16 in., (53.3 x 40.6 cm.), lithograph in colors (BP 211, DM 508, FR 1722, Y 40,877).

BI   *"Flower Garden"*, s. Max, d. 1987, #H/C 13, prov., est. $150/200, (12-12-92, A. James, #519), 10 x 14 in., (25.4 x 35.6 cm.), lithograph.

$550* *Hieroglyphic I*, s., d. '70, num. 84/100, (11-12-92, Freemn/Fine Art, #144), image 19½ x 23 in., (49.5 x 58.4 cm.), plate 22 x 30 in., (49.5 x 58.4 cm.), screen print (BP 361, DM 871, FR 2940, Y 68,196).

$138* *Max's City: Two*, s., d. 1979, i., (06-11-93, Freemn/Fine Art, #146), each 24¼ x 17 in., (61.6 x 43.2 cm.), poster (BP 91, DM 224, FR 756, Y 14,642).

$303* *Pegasus*, s. Max 1982, i. AP, (11-12-92, Freemn/Fine Art, #145), 27 x 37½ in., (68.6 x 95.3 cm.), offset litho (BP 199, DM 480, FR 1619, Y 37,570).

BI   *"Standing Nude"*, crayon s. Max, d. 1983, #21/75, artist's blindstamp, est. $700/1,000, (12-12-92, A. James, #38), 40¼ x 29 in., (102.2 x 73.7 cm.), lithograph.

MAXELL SMITH, Dina

$53* *"Street Cab. Corp."*, #25/200, s., (01-28-93, Pescheteau, #211), 19¹¹⁄₁₆ x 21¼ in., (50 x 54 cm.), color serigraph (BP 35, DM 84, FR 284, Y 6581).

MAXENT

$220* *"Regatta In Poulguen, France"*, s., t., #42/500, (12-02-92, Boos, #333), 8⁷⁄₁₆ x 20¹⁄₁₆ in., (215 x 510 mm.), color etching (BP 142, DM 346, FR 1181, Y 27,373).

MAXEY, Edward

$944* *"Annie Lennox", 1989*, mounted on card, s., d., num., photog.'s p. label, t., d., #7/10, 604 x 510mm, (05-07-93, Sotheby-London, #366, illus.), photograph, silver print (BP 598, DM 1492, FR 5029, Y 103,942).

$880* *"Maryanne", 1989*, s., d., ink edit. 3/10, photog. label, Dixon Collection, (11-16-92, Butterfield, #6078, illus.), 19⁵⁄₁₆ x 19⁵⁄₁₆ in., (489.8 x 489.8 mm.), photograph, gelatin silver print (BP 579, DM 1403, FR 4726, Y 109,439).

$495* *"Self Portrait With Mickey", 1991*, s., d., ink edit. 2/20, photog. label, Dixon Collection, (11-16-92, Butterfield, #6079, illus.), 19⁵⁄₁₆ x 19⁵⁄₁₆ in., (489.8 x 489.8 mm.), photograph, gelatin silver print (BP 326, DM 789, FR 2658, Y 61,560).

MAXIM, David   American contemporary

$55* *Composition*, s., i. 3/84, (03-14-93, Hindman, #340, illus.), height 29⅝ x 22½ in., (75.2 x 57.2 cm.), color soft-ground and aquatint (BP 38, DM 92, FR 311, Y 6482).

MAYER, Ferdinand, Publisher   19th cent.

$165* *The Canard Royal Mail Steamship, Brittania*, time discoloration, staining, tear, (11-12-92, Freemn/Fine Art, #143), 18½ x 24 in., (47 x 61 cm.), litho (BP 108, DM 261, FR 882, Y 20,459).

MAYER, L. (after)   19th cent.

BI   *"The Lover's Fountain With The Adjacent Mosque" and "Antique Fragements At Limisso": Pair*, est. $300/350, (09-17-92, Sloan, #1446), each, image 9 x 12¼ in., (22.9 x 31.1 cm.), color aquatints.

MAYER, L. (after)   Continental 19th cent.

$165* *"Lovers Fountain With Adjacent Mosque" and "Antique Fragments Of Limisso": A Pair*, (12-10-92, Sloan, #961), each, image 9 x 12¼ in., (22.9 x 31.1 cm.), color aquatint (BP 106, DM 261, FR 891, Y 20,411).

MAYER, Lou
$195 *Jewish War Sufferers,* Grinnell Litho. Co. NY, edge damage, (09-24-92, Alderfer, #263), 28 x 21 in., (71.1 x 53.3 cm.), (BP 114, DM 289, FR 981, Y 23,457).

MAYER and STETFIELD, Lithographers American 19th cent.
$468* *"Built By The Amoskeag Manufacturing Co., Manchester, N.H.",* ident. w/in matrix, staining, foxing, abrasions, (03-27-93, Skinner, #213, illus.), sight, sheet 19½ x 27½ in., (49.5 x 69.9 cm.), lithograph in black and tan on paper (BP 314, DM 763, FR 2596, Y 54,469).

MAYET, Leon and SCHUTZ-ROBERT
$120* *Caudieux. Horloge, c. 1900,* Paris, Lith G. Bataille, cond. B+, (06-11-93, Boisgirard, #114), 51³⁄₁₆ x 37 in., (130 x 94 cm.), poster (BP 79, DM 195, FR 658, Y 12,732).

MAYEUR, O.
$22* *Tavern Scene,* s., (10-16-92, DuMouchelle, #2495), 9½ x 12½ in., (24.1 x 31.8 cm.), etching (BP 13, DM 32, FR 110, Y 2627).

MAYUMI Japanese 20th cent.
$138* *"New Years Day, 1969", "The Evening Sun, 1968" and "Midsummer Dream,1969": Three,* s., t., num., (06-11-93, Freemn/Fine Art, #147), smallest 13½ x 11½ in., (34.3 x 29.2 cm.), largest 17 x 11½ in., (34.3 x 29.2 cm.), wood block (BP 91, DM 224, FR 756, Y 14,642).

MAYWALD, Wilhelm German 1907-1985
$1380* *Le Corbusier,* s. by photog., studio stamp, (c) stamp, c. 1948, p.l., (04-06-93, Sotheby-NY, #341, illus.), 13¾ x 12 in., photograph (BP 911, DM 2223, FR 7529, Y 157,391).
$341* *Florence Henri, 30's,* t., (11-12-92, Lempertz, #169, illus.), 9¾ x 9½ in., (24.8 x 24.2 cm.), photograph, gelatin silver print (BP 218, DM 536, FR 1826, Y 42,187).
$1438* *Portraits Of Artists: "Rufino Tamayo" and "Henry Moore": Two,* each s., one t. by photog., studio stamp, (c) stamp, 1948, p.l., (04-06-93, Sotheby-NY, #342, illus.), one 14⅜ x 12 in., other 12⅛ x 11⅞ in., photograph (BP 950, DM 2317, FR 7845, Y 164,005).

MAZUR, Michael American b. 1935
$468* *The Model, Her Shadow And Mine, 1968,* s., d., t., #29/50, good cond., creases, (12-12-92, Weschler, #140), sheet 36½ x 24 in., (92.7 x 61 cm.), etching and aquatint (BP 300, DM 737, FR 2527, Y 57,914).
BI *Two Untitled Prints,* s., num. 11/88, good cond., est. $4/600, (05-22-93, Weschler, #204, illus.), each 23 x 29 in., (58.4 x 73.7 cm.), lithographs, one in blue, one in black.

MCADOO, Donalo
BI *"Noah's Rhinos",* s., #79/100, est. $10/25, (03-12-93, DuMouchelle, #2437), 3½ x 5 in., (8.9 x 12.7 cm.), linocut.

MCARDELL, James
$690* *The Honble, Robert Monckton, Major General, Governor Of New York AndColonel Of His Majesty's 17th Regt. Of Foot, c. 1765,* after T. Hudson, margins, creases, light-stain, discoloration, soiling, (01-28-93, Sotheby-NY, #440, illus.), 15⅞ x 11 in., (403 x 279 mm.), sheet 16⅞ x 11⅞ in., (403 x 279 mm.), mezzotint on laid paper, laid down (BP 456, DM 1093, FR 3700, Y 85,672).

MCAVOY, Thomas D.
$1650* *Humorous Series Of Images Of F.D.R. At A State Dinner, 1938: Four,* photog.'s sig., exhib. label, (04-07-93, Swann, #351, illus.), each 6 x 9½ in., photograph, silver print (BP 1090, DM 2669, FR 9031, Y 187,457).

MCBEY, James English 1883-1959
BI *The Ebb Tide (Hardie 216), 1923,* s., ink, #XVI, margins, good cond., discoloration, est. BP 2/300, (06-30-93, Sotheby-London, #316), sh 10⅝ x 16¼ in., (270 x 413 mm.), etching on laid.
$226* *Foveran Burn, 1912,* s. in pen and ink, i. trial proof of Foveran Burne, full margins, foxing, staining, (10-27-92, Phillips-London, #284), plate 6⅛ x 10⅞ in., (156 x 276 mm.), etching on laid (BP 143, DM 346, FR 1175, Y 27,645).
$168 *"The Moray Firth",* s., first state, (04-16-93, G.A. Key, #128, illus.), 9 x 14 in., (22.9 x 35.6 cm.), b/w etching (BP 110, DM 271, FR 917, Y 18,891).
$825* *New York Harbour (H. 279), 1941,* ink s., num. XVI, ink i., margins, very good cond., prov., (09-19-92, Christie-E, #53), plate 10³⁄₁₆ x 14⅞ in., (259 x 378 mm.), etching on laid paper (BP 475, DM 1235, FR 4231, Y 102,791).
$858* *"Ransdor", "Monnickendam Sawmill", "Beggars Tetuan" (No. 2); "Penzance" and "A Norfolk Village" (H. 75; 77; 134; 144 and 158), 1910-1915: Five,* each s., num., full margins, good cond., discoloration, (06-30-93, Sotheby-London, #317, illus.), etching on laid (BP 575, DM 1463, FR 4937, Y 91,932).
$157* *Ras-El-Ain (G. 180), 1919,* s. in ink, #A13. light staining, (10-27-92, Phillips-London, #285), plate 7⅞ x 12¾ in., (200 x 324 mm.), drypoint on laid (BP 99, DM 241, FR 816, Y 19,205).
BI *Ras-El-Gin,* black ink s., num. XX, margins, est. BP 100/150, (09-17-92, Bonhams-Chelsea, #75), plate 8 x 12¾ in., (20.3 x 32.4 cm.), etching on laid paper.
$413* *Self Portrait, 1914,* ink s., #XXVII, (10-18-92, Hindman, #462), 6⅝ x 11 in., (16.8 x 27.9 cm.), etching (BP 253, DM 615, FR 2085, Y 49,550).
$550* *Venice, 1925,* s., num. L/V, good cond.?, (12-08-92, Swann, #209, illus.), 6⅜ x 14 in., (16.2 x 35.6 cm.), drypoint etching (BP 345, DM 856, FR 2919, Y 68,171).

MCCARTHY, Frank American b. 1924
$22* *"The Beaver Men",* num. 896/1000, s., (10-24-92, Dunning, #1531), 21 x 28½ in., (53.3 x 72.4 cm.), lithograph (BP 14, DM 34, FR 114, Y 2683).

MCCARTNEY, Michael
$345* *Portrait Of Paul McCartney,* 1960s, s., #18/250, (05-23-93, Butterfield, #3522, illus.), 12 x 10½ in., photograph, gelatin silver print (BP 225, DM 564, FR 1899, Y 38,134).

MCCLELLAN, John American 1908-1986
BI *"Chess Fantasies", 1948,* s., very good cond., est. $100/150, (05-15-93, Cleveland, #246), 16 x 13½ in., (40.6 x 34.3 cm.), lithograph.

MCCORMICK, Harry American b. 1942
BI *"Dawn",* s., t., num. 35/180, est. $70/100, (08-05-92, Boos, #562), image, sight 20¹¹⁄₁₆ x 14⁹⁄₁₆ in., (525 x 370 mm.), etching and aquatint.
BI *"Pablo",* s., t., num. 71/180, est. $70/100, (08-05-92, Boos, #563), etching and aquatint.

MCCORMICK, Jim American 20th cent.
$66* *Inside Out,* s., t., num. 49/50, (11-12-92, Freemn/Fine Art, #146), 10 x 14 in., (25.4 x 35.6 cm.), lithograph (BP 43, DM 105, FR 353, Y 8184).

MCCORMICK, Katherine Hood
$880* *"Ritterhouse Square",* s., very good cond., (07-19-92, Bakker, #279, illus.), image 10½ x 11½ in., (26.7 x 29.2 cm.), color woodblock print (BP 451, DM 1283, FR 4337, Y 109,398).

MCCOY, Guy American 1904-1983
$77* *"Kitten By Window",* s., d. '49, (11-10-92, Moran, #160), sight 11 x 14 in., (27.9 x 35.6 cm.), serigraph on paper (BP 51, DM 123, FR 417, Y 9584).

MCCRADY, John American 1911-1968
$160* *"Carnival In New Orleans",* s., t., very good cond., (05-15-93, Cleveland, #247), 8½ x 12⅛ in., (21.6 x 30.8 cm.), lithograph (BP 104, DM 257, FR 865, Y 17,736).
$358* *"Swing Low, Sweet Chariot",* s., t., pub. AAA, very good cond., (02-13-93, Neal, #587), image 10⅞ x 14¾ in., (27.6 x 37.5 cm.), lithograph (BP 252, DM 594, FR 2009, Y 43,174).

MCCRADY, John American b. 1911
$220* *"Steamboat Round The Bend",* s. John McCrady, very good cond., (11-21-92, Bakker, #3, illus.), image 9¾ x 14¾ in., (24.8 x 37.5 cm.), lithograph (BP 145, DM 351, FR 1182, Y 27,360).

MCCULLIN, Donald
$1210* *"Black Soldier With Ammunition And Equipment", "Portrait Of Soldier", "Soldier Holding Binoculars" and "Sol-*

diers Searching A Hut": Four, news agency handstamps, caption labels, 1960s, (04-07-93, Swann, #333, illus.), 12 x 8 in., photograph, silver print (BP 800, DM 1957, FR 6623, Y 137,469).

MCDARRAH, Fred W.

$1380* *Bob Dylan: Two,* s. by photog., (06-23-93, Sotheby-NY, #454, illus.), each approx. 21 x 16 in., b/w photograph (BP 938, DM 2335, FR 7854, Y 150,343).

$863* *Janis Joplin: Two,* s. by photog., (06-23-93, Sotheby-NY, #449, illus.), each 20 x 16 in., b/w photograph (BP 586, DM 1460, FR 4912, Y 94,019).

$690* *"Jim Morrison" and "His Grave": Two,* s. by photog., (06-23-93, Sotheby-NY, #450, illus.), each 20 x 16 in., b/w photograph (BP 469, DM 1168, FR 3927, Y 75,172).

$748* *Jimi Hendrix In Performance At Bill Graham's Fillmore East, 105 Second Ave., New York, May 11, 1968: Two,* s. by photog., (06-23-93, Sotheby-NY, #466, illus.), each 20 x 16 in., b/w photograph (BP 508, DM 1266, FR 4257, Y 81,490).

$460* *Mick Jagger: Two,* s. by photog., (06-23-93, Sotheby-NY, #415, illus.), each 20 x 16 in., b/w photograph (BP 313, DM 778, FR 2618, Y 50,114).

$1430* *"Robert Kennedy Visiting A Suffolk Street Tenement" and "Abbie Hoffman In A Show At The Judson Church", 1967, 1970: Two,* photog.'s caption, d., sig., (04-07-93, Swann, #334, illus.), one 12½ x 19 in., other 18 x 12 in., photograph, silver print (BP 945, DM 2313, FR 7827, Y 162,463).

MCDERMOTT, David and Peter MCGOUGH

$4888* *"Death Of Marat, 1907", 1989,* s., t., d., i. No. 3 from edit. of 3, in ink on label, (04-06-93, Sotheby-NY, #530, illus.), 10½ x 13½ in., photograph, cyanotype (BP 3229, DM 7875, FR 26,667, Y 557,482).

BI *The Essence Or Peculiarity Of Man Is To Comprehend A Whole, 1990,* ink s., t., d., fifteenth December 1858, #2/3 on credit label, est. $5/6,000, (04-08-93, Christie-NY, #546, illus.), 13½ x 10⅜ in., (34.3 x 26.4 cm.), photograph, palladium print.

MCDONALD, Joseph

$330* *"Stemware", 1990,* s., d., edit. 6/50, Dixon Collection, (11-16-92, Butterfield, #6080), 14¼ x 11¼ in., (362.6 x 286.3 mm.), photograph, platinum print (BP 217, DM 526, FR 1772, Y 41,040).

MCDOWELL, William

$495* *Cunard White Star, Queen Mary,* B+ cond., surface scratch, (08-06-92, Swann, #196, illus.), 18½ x 31½ in., (47 x 80 cm.), (BP 259, DM 731, FR 2470, Y 63,138).

MCGARRELL, James   American b. 1930

$11* *Wings II,* s., t., #2/20, pub. Tamarind, chop mark, (06-13-93, Hindman, #333), 22 x 29¾ in., (55.9 x 75.6 cm.), lithograph (BP 7, DM 18, FR 60, Y 1158).

MCGEE, Tony

BI *"Caroline From Monaco", 1977,* t., s., d., label, sight 295 x 420mm, est. BP 150/250, (05-07-93, Sotheby-London, #203), photograph, silver print.

MCGINNESS and SMITH

$660* *"View Of Nassau Hall, Princeton, N.J.", 1860,* poor cond.?, (02-07-93, Bakker, #257), oval 13 x 17½ in., (33 x 44.5 cm.), lithograph (BP 457, DM 1095, FR 3700, Y 82,130).

MCGOWAN, Maidie   b. 1906

$162* *Seated Nude,* s. Maidie McGowan, (08-11-92, L. Joel, #170G), 11½ x 9⅜ in., (29.2 x 23.8 cm.), monotype (BP 84, DM 238, FR 805, Y 20,745, A$ 220).

MCGRADY, John   American 1911-1968

BI *"Carnival In New Orleans",* s., t., full margins, good cond., est. $1,500/2000, (03-12-93, Goldberg, #1094, illus.), image 11½ x 16 in., (29.2 x 40.6 cm.), lithograph.

BI *"The Robert E. Lee And The Natchez",* s., t., full margins, good cond., est. $1,500/2000, (03-12-93, Goldberg, #1096, illus.), image 9½ x 14½ in., (24.1 x 36.8 cm.), lithograph.

MCIAN, Robert Ronald (after)

$193* *The Rev'D Charles Wesley, The Poet Of Methodism Preaching To The American Indians In 1736,* by Frank Bromley, pub. William Tegg, margins, tears/nicks, scrapes toimage, apparently laid down, (09-19-92, Weschler, #170), 17 x 23¾ in., (43.2 x 60.3 cm.), engraving (BP 113, DM 286, FR 980, Y 23,854).

MCKEE, Wm.

$40 *"The Spirit Of '18",* rip, water stains, (03-04-93, Alderfer, #252, illus.), 30 x 20 in., (76.2 x 50.8 cm.), poster (BP 28, DM 65, FR 223, Y 4657).

MCKENNEY and HALL

$55* *"Ong-Pa-Ton-Ga, Chief Of The Omahas*(10-24-92, Dunning, #1469, illus.), paper 17½ x 12¼ in., (44.5 x 31.1 cm.), (BP 34, DM 84, FR 285, Y 6707).

$55* *"Ahyouwaighs, Chief Of The Six Nations",* (10-24-92, Dunning, #1460, illus.), paper 10¼ x 6⅝ in., (26 x 16.8 cm.), colored lithograph (BP 34, DM 84, FR 285, Y 6707).

$1840* *American Indians, c. 1846: Eight,* (04-07-93, Sotheby-Arcade, #284), sight 10 x 6½ in., (25.4 x 16.5 cm.), hand-colored lithograph (BP 1216, DM 2976, FR 10,071, Y 209,043).

$825* *"Ap-Pa-Noo-Se", Sauke Chief, 1838,* folio edit., (05-22-93, Neal, #519), 18 x 13 in., (45.7 x 33 cm.), hand-colored lithograph (BP 534, DM 1341, FR 4513, Y 90,959).

$220* *"Chippeway Squaw And Child", 1836,* (10-24-92, Dunning, #1465, illus.), paper 17½ x 12¼ in., (44.5 x 31.1 cm.), (BP 136, DM 336, FR 1140, Y 26,829).

$495* *"Chou-Ca-Pe", 1837,* folio edit., (05-22-93, Neal, #518), 18 x 13 in., (45.7 x 33 cm.), hand-colored lithograph (BP 321, DM 805, FR 2708, Y 54,576).

$275* *Esh-Ta-Hum-Leah, 1838,* (10-18-92, Hindman, #481), 15½ x 10¾ in., (39.4 x 27.3 cm.), hand colored lithograph (BP 168, DM 409, FR 1388, Y 32,993).

$550* *"A Fox Brave", 1836,* pub. F.W. Greenough, (10-31-92, Litchfield, #115), 16 x 12 in., (40.6 x 30.5 cm.), hand colored lithograph (BP 360, DM 863, FR 2924, Y 68,002).

$550* *"A Fox Chief", 1837,* pub. E.C. Biddle, (10-31-92, Litchfield, #114), 17 x 13 in., (43.2 x 33 cm.), hand colored lithograph (BP 360, DM 863, FR 2924, Y 68,002).

$1610* *Indians: Nine, c. 1846,* (02-18-93, Sotheby-Arcade, #63), sight 10 x 6½ in., (25.4 x 16.5 cm.), hand-colored lithograph (BP 1112, DM 2626, FR 8890, Y 191,804).

$83* *"Itcho-Tustennuggee",* folded 1/2", (10-24-92, Dunning, #1459, illus.), paper 10¼ x 6⅝ in., (26 x 16.8 cm.), colored lithograph (BP 51, DM 127, FR 430, Y 10,122).

$1045* *"Ki-On-Twog-Ky", Or Cornplant, 1836,* folio edit., (05-22-93, Neal, #517, illus.), 18 x 13 in., (45.7 x 33 cm.), hand-colored lithograph (BP 677, DM 1699, FR 5717, Y 115,215).

$935* *"L'Ietan Or Chon-Mon-I-Case",* pub. 1836 E.C. Biddle, (12-05-92, Neal, #573), image 12½ x 9½ in., (31.8 x 24.1 cm.), hand-colored lithograph (BP 585, DM 1458, FR 4968, Y 115,847).

$28* *"Lap-Pa-Win-Soe, A Delaware Chief", 1837,* dirty, crease marks, (10-24-92, Dunning, #1462, illus.), paper 17½ x 12¼ in., (44.5 x 31.1 cm.), (BP 17, DM 43, FR 145, Y 3415).

$825* *"Ma-Has-Ka", Or White Cloud, An Ioway Chief, 1837,* folio edit., (05-22-93, Neal, #516), 18 x 13 in., (45.7 x 33 cm.), hand-colored lithograph (BP 534, DM 1341, FR 4513, Y 90,959).

$28* *"Meta-Koosega, A Chippeway Warrior",* (10-24-92, Dunning, #1470, illus.), paper 17½ x 12¼ in., (44.5 x 31.1 cm.), (BP 17, DM 43, FR 145, Y 3415).

$110* *"Ne-O-Mon-Ne, An Ioway Chief",* (10-24-92, Dunning, #1464, illus.), image 15½ x 11 in., (39.4 x 27.9 cm.), colored lithograph (BP 68, DM 168, FR 570, Y 13,415).

$2090* *"Ne-Sou-A-Quoit",* pub. 1837 E.C. Biddle, (12-05-92, Neal, #572, illus.), image 13½ x 10 in., (34.3 x 25.4 cm.), hand-colored lithograph (BP 1309, DM 3258, FR 11,105, Y 258,952).

$385* *"No-Way-Ke-Sug-Ga",* (10-24-92, Dunning, #1458, illus.), paper 17½ x 12¼ in., (44.5 x 31.1 cm.), colored lithograph (BP 238, DM 589, FR 1996, Y 46,951).

$1320* *"No-Way-Ke-Sug-Ga"*, pub. 1842 by Daniel, Rice and James G. Clark, (12-05-92, Neal, #575), image 13 x 9½ in., (33 x 24.1 cm.), hand-colored lithograph (BP 827, DM 2058, FR 7014, Y 163,549).

$1045* *"Okee-Maakee-Quid"*, after Charles Bird King, p. Lehman and Duvall Lithographers, pub. 1836 E.C. Biddle, (12-05-92, Neal, #571), image 13½ x 10 in., (34.3 x 25.4 cm.), hand-colored lithograph (BP 654, DM 1629, FR 5553, Y 129,476).

$385* *"An Ottawa Chief"*, 1842, (10-31-92, Litchfield, #116), 16 x 12 in., (40.6 x 30.5 cm.), hand colored lithograph (BP 252, DM 604, FR 2047, Y 47,601).

$935* *"PUSH-MA-TA-HA, A Choctaw Warrior"*, 1838, folio edit., (05-22-93, Neal, #520), 18 x 13 in., (45.7 x 33 cm.), hand-colored lithograph (BP 606, DM 1520, FR 5115, Y 103,087).

$193* *"Pa-She-Pa-Haw, A Sauk Chief"*, damage, (10-24-92, Dunning, #1466, illus.), paper 17½ x 12¼ in., (44.5 x 31.1 cm.), (BP 119, DM 295, FR 1001, Y 23,537).

$28* *"Peah-Mas-Ka, A Musquawkee Chief"*, 1837, damage, (10-24-92, Dunning, #1467, illus.), paper 17½ x 12¼ in., (44.5 x 31.1 cm.), (BP 17, DM 43, FR 145, Y 3415).

$935* *"Pow-A-Sheek"*, A Fox Chief, 1838, folio edit., (05-22-93, Neal, #514, illus.), 18 x 13 in., (45.7 x 33 cm.), hand-colored lithograph (BP 606, DM 1520, FR 5115, Y 103,087).

$1320* *"Red Jacket, A Seneca War Chief"*, 1837, folio edit., (05-22-93, Neal, #522, illus.), 18 x 13 in., (45.7 x 33 cm.), hand-colored lithograph (BP 855, DM 2146, FR 7221, Y 145,535).

$28* *"Sha-Ha-Ka-, A Mandan Chief"*, 1837, (10-24-92, Dunning, #1468, illus.), paper 17½ x 12¼ in., (44.5 x 31.1 cm.), (BP 17, DM 43, FR 145, Y 3415).

$165* *"Tish-Co-Han, A Delaware Chief"*, 1837, dirty, thin spots, (10-24-92, Dunning, #1461, illus.), paper 17½ x 12¼ in., (44.5 x 31.1 cm.), colored lithograph (BP 102, DM 252, FR 855, Y 20,122).

$467* *"To-Ka-Con"*, *"Kish-Kal-Wa"*, *"Apauly-Tustennuggee"* and *"Kee-She-Waa"*,1837-43: Group Of Four, from History of the Indian Tribes of North America, (12-08-92, Swann, #210), hand-colored lithograph (BP 293, DM 727, FR 2479, Y 57,883).

$1100* *"Wa-Pel-La"*, Chief Of The Musquakes, 1838, folio edit., (05-22-93, Neal, #513, illus.), 18 x 13 in., (45.7 x 33 cm.), hand-colored lithograph (BP 713, DM 1789, FR 6018, Y 121,279).

$33* *"Waa-Pa Shaw, A Sioux Chief"*, 1837, crease marks, thin spot, (10-24-92, Dunning, #1463, illus.), paper 17½ x 12¼ in., (44.5 x 31.1 cm.), (BP 20, DM 50, FR 171, Y 4024).

$935* *"War Dance Of Sauks And Foxes"*, 1834, folio edit., (05-22-93, Neal, #523, illus.), 13 x 18 in., (33 x 45.7 cm.), hand-colored lithograph (BP 606, DM 1520, FR 5115, Y 103,087).

MCLEAN, Bruce   b. 1944
BI *Ohne Titel*, 1986, #XXIII/XXX, s., d., (11-20-92, Lempertz, #709), sh 31½ x 23⁹⁄₁₆ in., (80 x 59.8 cm.), color serigraph on white board.

MCMANUS, Blanche   b. 1870
$100* *Scribner's Fiction Number (Golfeur)*, 1895, cond. C, tape, (03-16-93, Boisgirard, #152), 22⁷⁄₁₆ x 13⅜ in., (57 x 34 cm.), poster (BP 69, DM 166, FR 565, Y 11,693).

MCNAB, Allen   English b. 1901
$22* *Mediterranean Coast*, 1925, s., d., num. 5/75, (10-31-92, Cleveland, #315), 14½ x 14 in., (36.8 x 35.6 cm.), etching (BP 14, DM 34, FR 115, Y 2725).

MCNALLY, Bernie   American 20th cent.
$15* *"Tires Poplin"*, s., t., #46/200. excell. cond., (05-15-93, Cleveland, #248), 13¼ x 20¾ in., (33.7 x 52.7 cm.), lithograph (BP 10, DM 24, FR 81, Y 1663).

MCNALLY, John
$7 *"Northerly"*, s., num., (10-09-92, G.A. Key, #63), colored print (BP 4, DM 10, FR 35, Y 854).

MCNEILL, Angus (after)
$124* *The Melton Midnight Steeplechase: Four*, pub. Arthur Ackermann, 1894, margins, foxing, (06-30-93, Bonhams-Chelsea, #207), plate 12½ x 16 in., (31.8 x 40.6 cm.),

photogravure w/hand-coloring (BP 83, DM 211, FR 713, Y 13,286).

MCNULTY, William C.   American b. 1889
$358* *"Woolworth Bldg. - N.Y."*, 1929, s. Wm. C. McNulty Imp.; s., d. in plate, t., d., annot. 100 proofs, good cond.?, (09-11-92, Skinner, #20A, illus.), sight 13 x 9 in., (33 x 22.9 cm.), etching on paper (BP 185, DM 515, FR 1751, Y 44,356).

MCPHERSON, Craig
$4888* *Yankee Stadium At Night*, 1983, s., t., #5/75, pub. by artist, full margins, good cond., print hinged w/non-archival tape, scuff marks, (05-15-93, Sotheby-NY, #1096, illus.), 23⅝ x 35 in., (60 x 88.9 cm.), mezzotint on BFK Rives (BP 3178, DM 7862, FR 26,422, Y 541,847).

$4950 *Yankee Stadium At Night*, 1983, s., t., #10/75, p. by the artist, pub. John Szoke Graphics, full margins, good cond., tape remains, soiling, surface scuffs, (11-07-92, Sotheby-NY, #683, illus.), 23⅝ x 35⅛ in., (600 x 892 mm.), mezzotint on BFK Rives (BP 3236, DM 7904, FR 26,713, Y 610,960).

MCPHERSON & OLIVER
$715* *Farragut, Admiral D.G.*, 1864, s. D.G. Farragut/Rear Admiral, (09-17-92, Swann, #104), photograph, sepia carte (BP 402, DM 1061, FR 3633, Y 89,019).

MCRAE, John (engraved by)   19th cent.
$275* *The Marriage Of Pocahontas*, engraved, (11-13-92, DuMouchelle, #184, illus.), 39 x 29 in., (39 x 29 cm.), hand colored engraving (BP 178, DM 432, FR 1456, Y 34,132).

MCRAE, John C.
$182* *"The Marriage Of Pocahontas"*, c. 1855, after Henry Brueckner, pub. John C. McRae, (08-05-92, Boos, #669), image 34¼ x 34¾ in., (870 x 883 mm.), hand colored stiple engraving (BP 95, DM 269, FR 908, Y 23,179).

MCRAE, John C.   American ac. 1850
$165* *"Washington Family"* and *"The Prayer At Valley Forge"*: Two, (04-02-93, Sloan, #1171), larger 18 x 27¼ in., (457 x 692 mm.), engraving (BP 109, DM 265, FR 901, Y 18,786).

MEAKIN, Lewis Henry (attrib.)   Anglo/American 1850/53-1917
$77* *Collection Of Three Etchings*, (09-20-92, Hindman, #681), largest 6⅝ x 9¼ in., (16.8 x 23.5 cm.), etchings (BP 45, DM 114, FR 391, Y 9517).

MEAN, Roderick   American
BI *Untitled*, s. in block R.W. and in pencil, est. C$2/250, (10-21-92, Maynard, #200), 8 x 10 in., (20.3 x 25.4 cm.), b/w block print.

MEATYARD, Ralph Eugene   1925-1972
$2090* *Christopher*, 1961, (10-13-92, Christie-NY, #575, illus.), 7½ x 7⅝ in., (19.1 x 19.4 cm.), photograph, gelatin silver print (BP 1217, DM 3062, FR 10,403, Y 253,425).

BI *Untitled (Boy Sitting In Grass)*, 1960, s. by photog.'s widow, est. $1/2,000, (10-15-92, Sotheby-NY, #559, illus.), 5¾ x 8⅞ in., (14.6 x 22.5 cm.), photograph, gelatin silver print.

$920* *Untitled, Masked Adult With Children In Lap*, 1962, (c) credit, Witkin Gallery East 60th Street stamps, authen. by Madelyn Meatyard, lit., (04-08-93, Christie-NY, #498, illus.), 6¾ x 6¾ in., (17.1 x 17.1 cm.), photograph, gelatin silver print (BP 603, DM 1478, FR 5003, Y 104,403).

MECHAIN, Francis
BI *"Equivalence"*, 1980, s., t., d., est. $4/600, (05-23-93, Butterfield, #3523, illus.), 22 x 9½ in., photograph, gelatin silver print.

MECKENEM, Israhel van   German c. 1450-1503
$3450* *The Holy Family With The "Butterfly" (Dragonfly)* (B. 33; L., Holl. 219), c. 1495, after Albrecht Durer, watermark, trimmed, repaired tear, paper loss,center fold, creases, (05-13-93, Sotheby-NY, #167, illus.), 9⅝ x 7⅛ in., (243 x 182 mm.), engraving (BP 2265, DM 5571, FR 18,791, Y 385,174).

$51,157* *Judith With The Head Of Holofernes (Lehrs 8; Holl. 8),* fourth (final) state, trimmed enevenly on/within borderline into sig., central fold, creases, repairs, discoloration, ex-coll., (12-03-92, Sotheby-London, #79, illus.), 8½ x 12¼ in., (215 x 314 mm.), engraving on paper w/watermark (BP 33,000, DM 80,448, FR 274,595, Y 6,365,186).

$1665* *Saint Sebastian (B. 112; L., Holl. 381),* after M. Schongauer, 5th (final) state, watermark, trimmed, repairs, discoloration, prov., (12-01-92, Christie-London, #157), sheet 6⁵⁄₁₆ x 4¼ in., (161 x 108 mm.), engraving (BP 1100, DM 2654, FR 9044, Y 207,296).

BI *St Anthony (Lehrs IX, 309),* from divided plate, trimmed, stains, good cond., (06-30-93, Sotheby-London, #160, illus.), 6¼ x 2¾ in., (159 x 70 mm.), engraving.

$5457* *St. Anthony (Lehrs 310; Holl. 310),* sixth (final) state, trimmed outside borderline, surface dirt, collector's mark, ex-coll., (12-03-92, Sotheby-London, #80, illus.), 6¼ x 3½ in., (159 x 89 mm.), engraving on paper w/ watermark (BP 3520, DM 8582, FR 29,291, Y 678,985).

MECKSEPER, Friedrich   b. 1936

$318* *Birne (Cramer 155), 1974,* s., d., #XXVII/LXXXV, portfolio Naure morte, (06-12-93, Hauswedell/Nolt, #296), 13⁷⁄₁₆ x 17³⁄₁₆ in., (34.1 x 43.7 cm.), color etching on BFK Rives (BP 208, DM 518, FR 1740, Y 33,463).

$283* *Champos (Cramer 116), 1969,* s., blindstamp, (06-12-93, Hauswedell/Nolt, #295), 4⅝ x 6¼ in., (11.8 x 15.9 cm.), color etching on thick wove (BP 185, DM 461, FR 1548, Y 29,780).

BI *Elektrischer Friedhof, 1976,* s., d. #34/100, est. DM 850, (09-18-92, Schloss Ahlden, #1036), 29¹⁵⁄₁₆ x 22¹⁄₁₆ in., (76 x 56 cm.), color etching on BFK Rives.

$542* *Der Grosse Stein, 1976,* s., d., #84/100, (09-18-92, Schloss Ahlden, #1034), 22 x 29¾ in., (55.9 x 75.5 cm.), color etching on BFK Rives (BP 317, DM 804, FR 2751, Y 66,988).

$830* *Hans Christian Andersen (Cramer 218), (19)83,* s., d., num., (12-01-92, Karl/Faber, #1002), 14¹⁵⁄₁₆ x 18⁵⁄₁₆ in., (38 x 46.5 cm.), color etching and aquatint w/roulette on BFK Rives wove (BP 548, DM 1323, FR 4508, Y 103,337).

$968* *Hans Christian Anderson (Sch. 218), 1983,* #84/100, s., d., (10-09-92, Winterberg, #2732, illus.), 15¹⁄₁₆ x 18⁷⁄₁₆ in., (38.2 x 46.8 cm.), color aquatint on BFK Rives wove (BP 574, DM 1438, FR 4828, Y 117,848).

$339* *Insel (Cramer 247), 1987,* s., d., #53/75, (06-12-93, Hauswedell/Nolt, #298), 15⅜ x 19½ in., (39 x 49.5 cm.), color aquatint on BFK Rives (BP 222, DM 552, FR 1854, Y 35,673).

BI *Labyrinth, 1968,* s., d., #6/45, est. DM 600, (09-18-92, Schloss Ahlden, #1033), 30¹³⁄₁₆ x 25⁹⁄₁₆ in., (78.3 x 65 cm.), color etching on hand-made.

$464* *Sonnenuhr 1970 (Schmucking 126),* s., d. Meckseper 70, (09-14-92, Venator/Hansten, #2472), plate 6 x 5⁵⁄₁₆ in., (15.3 x 13.5 cm.), aquatint w/soft-ground etching and drypoint (BP 245, DM 690, FR 2338, Y 57,697).

$1348* *Stilleben (Cramer 67), 1965,* s., num., blindstamp, (06-05-93, Bassenge, #6345), 13¹¹⁄₁₆ x 19⅝ in., (34.8 x 49.8 cm.), color line etching w/aquatint on copper print (BP 887, DM 2185, FR 7366, Y 144,604).

$413* *Taschenausstellung, 1973: Six,* complete set, s., d., num. 166, pub. Galerie Schmucking, full margins, good cond., staining, tears, time-staining, (10-28-92, Butterfield, #3027), each sheet 4¼ x 5⅞ in., (108 x 149 mm.), etching w/aquatint on Rives BFK, two in colors (BP 263, DM 638, FR 2166, Y 50,675).

$1471* *Worpsweder Stilleben (Sch. 157), 1974,* sheet 4 of series Nature morte, s., d., (10-09-92, Winterberg, #2729, illus.), 15³⁄₁₆ x 19⅝ in., (38.5 x 49.9 cm.), color aquatint on BFK Rives (BP 873, DM 2185, FR 7337, Y 179,084).

MEDLEY, Samuel (after)

$109* *Abraham Goldsmid, Esq., 1802,* by Francesco Bartolozzi, pub. John Jeffreys, waterstain through image, dirt, defects, (11-30-92, Phillips-London, #100), sheet 18¾ x 14⅓ in., (476 x 364 mm.), stipple engraving on wove (BP 72, DM 174, FR 590, Y 13,566).

MEEKER, Dean   American 20th cent.

BI *Daedalus,* s., t., artist proof, est. $50/100, (05-16-93, Hanzel, #450), 27¾ x 19¾ in., (70.5 x 50.2 cm.), embossed lithograph.

MEES, F.   1887-1968

$120* *A Horseman And A Horsewoman,* (11-18-92, Bubb Kuyper, #1540), 14³⁄₁₆ x 10¼ in., (36 x 26 cm.), woodblock (BP 79, DM 191, FR 644, Y 14,924, G 216).

MEGERT, Christian

BI *Untitled, 1981,* s., #182/190, full margins, good cond., minor handling creases, est.Dfl. 150/250, (05-27-93, Sotheby-Amstrdm, #448), sh 27½ x 27½ in., (698 x 698 mm.), colored silkscreen on sturdy wove.

BI *Untitled, 1981,* s., #50/190, full margins, good cond., crease in lower left corner, minor handling creases, est. Dfl. 150/250, (05-27-93, Sotheby-Amstrdm, #449), sh 27½ x 27½ in., (698 x 698 mm.), colored silkscreen on sturdy wove.

BI *Untitled, 1981,* s., #163/190, full margins, good cond., minor handling creases, est.Dfl. 150/250, (05-27-93, Sotheby-Amstrdm, #450), sh 27½ x 27½ in., (698 x 698 mm.), colored silkscreen on sturdy wove.

MEID, Hans   1883-1957

$184* *Abschied (Sein Freund Der Turmer) (Jentsch 400), 1923,* s., Arno Holz-Mappe, Gurlitt, blindstamp, (06-10-93, Hauswedell/Nolt, #624), image 11⁹⁄₁₆ x 6⅝ in., (29.4 x 16.9 cm.), lithograph on Japan (BP 120, DM 300, FR 1009, Y 19,531).

$141* *"Albergo Costante" (Jentsch 552), c. 1929,* s. Hans Meid, (03-24-93, Venator/Hansten, #4534), pl. 7¹¹⁄₁₆ x 9⅝ in., (19.5 x 24.4 cm.), etching on Felsing paper (BP 95, DM 230, FR 784, Y 16,567).

BI *"Frankfurter Dom" (Jentsch 220/VII a), 1915,* s., d., artist's proof, est. DM 900/1,000, (11-28-92, Grisebach, #649, illus.), 12½ x 9⅛ in., (31.8 x 23.2 cm.), drypoint on handmade.

$458* *Lichtenthaler Allee In Baden-Baden (Jentsch 273 I/VI),* s., d., 1st state, prov., (05-26-93, Lempertz, #355), sh 13⅜ x 20³⁄₁₆ in., (34 x 51.2 cm.), etching (drypoint) on thick wove (BP 296, DM 747, FR 2515, Y 49,761).

$954* *Othello (Jensch 55-63), 1911: Nine,* pub. Jaques Casper, s., (04-24-93, Kunsthaus, #698), drypoint etching on hand-made (BP 602, DM 1495, FR 5050, Y 105,275).

BI *Der Rattenfanger (J. 511 a), 1925,* s., from the series Goethe, Gedichte, pub. Paul Cassirer, est. DM 600, (12-01-92, Karl/Faber, #1005), 10¼ x 7½ in., (26 x 19 cm.), lithograph on thin Japan.

BI *Tranke (Jentsch 381c), 1921,* s. Hans Meid, est. DM 300-, (09-14-92, Venator/Hansten, #2474), image 11¹³⁄₁₆ x 9⅜ in., (30 x 23.8 cm.), chalk lithograph on Holland hand-made.

MEIDNER, Else   b. 1927

$148* *Brustbild Des Schriftsteller Alfred Doblin, 1947,* s., (12-05-92, Bassenge, #7480), 6¹⁵⁄₁₆ x 5½ in., (17.6 x 14 cm.), etching on Japan (BP 93, DM 231, FR 786, Y 18,337).

MEIDNER, Hans   German 20th cent.

$55* *"Portrait",* d. 1917, good cond., (11-21-92, Bakker, #20), 7½ x 6 in., (19.1 x 15.2 cm.), lithograph (BP 36, DM 88, FR 295, Y 6840).

MEIDNER, Ludwig   German 1884-1966

$622* *Bildnis Des Pianisten Walter Kaempfer, 1922,* s., num., (12-01-92, Karl/Faber, #1006), 8¹¹⁄₁₆ x 7⅞ in., (22 x 20 cm.), etching on hand-made (BP 411, DM 991, FR 3379, Y 77,440).

$425* *Bildnis Max Tau II, 1921,* s., (06-08-93, Karl/Faber, #1108), approx. 9¼ x 7¹⁄₁₆ in., (23.5 x 18 cm.), etching on Japan (BP 279, DM 690, FR 2322, Y 45,141).

BI *Brustbild Einer Nach Links Blickenden Frau, Den Kopf Aufgestutzt,* s., est. DM 900, (12-05-92, Bassenge, #7482), 9⁵⁄₁₆ x 6¹⁵⁄₁₆ in., (23.6 x 17.6 cm.), etching on handmade.

$590* *Brustbild Eines Herrn, Den Kopf Auf Seine Linke Hand Gestutzt,* s., num., (12-05-92, Bassenge, #7483), 9¾ x 9⅝ in., (24.8 x 24.5 cm.), etching on handmade (BP 369, DM 920, FR 3135, Y 73,101).

$1033* *Brustbild Eines Jungen Mannes Nach Links, 1922,* s., artist's proof, 1st state, (12-05-92, Bassenge, #7489), 18⅞ x 17¹¹⁄₁₆ in., (48 x 45 cm.), lithograph on machinemade paper (BP 647, DM 1611, FR 5489, Y 127,989).

$4256* *"Ludwig Meidner September-Schrei, Hymnen, Gebete, Lasterungen", 1918/1920: Fourteen,* s., impr. num., pub. Paul Cassirer, (06-05-93, Grisebach, #772, illus.), 11⁷⁄₁₆ x 8¼ in., (29 x 21 cm.), lithograph and numerous text by Meidner (BP 2802, DM 6900, FR 23,257, Y 456,554).

$523* *Portrait Raoul Hausmann, 1914,* s., #21/40, (06-10-93, Hauswedell/Nolt, #626), image 16⁹⁄₁₆ x 10¼ in., (42 x 26 cm.), lithograph on hand-made (BP 342, DM 852, FR 2867, Y 55,514).

$608* *(Portrait), 1920,* s., d., i., full margins, good cond., diagonal crease in upper rightcorner of sheet, Late Gerhard Brauer Coll., (05-27-93, Sotheby-Amstrdm, #757, illus.), 8⁷⁄₁₆ x 6³⁄₁₆ in., (215 x 157 mm.), drypoint on wove (BP 389, DM 976, FR 3288, Y 65,180, G 1093).

$293* *Portrait, 1921,* s., d., (12-12-92, Wachholtz, #228), 8¹⁄₁₆ x 6⁵⁄₁₆ in., (20.5 x 16 cm.), etching on Werkdruckpapier (factory printed paper) (BP 187, DM 460, FR 1569, Y 36,249).

$851* *Selbstbildnis Mit Aufgestutztem Linken Arm, Eine Radiernadel Haltend, 1923,* s., (06-05-93, Bassenge, #6350, illus.), 10½ x 8³⁄₁₆ in., (26.7 x 20.8 cm.), etching on copper print (BP 560, DM 1380, FR 4650, Y 91,289).

$1419* *Selbstbildnis Mit Radiernadel In Der Linken Hand, 1921,* s., blindstamp, (06-05-93, Bassenge, #6348), 9³⁄₁₆ x 6¹⁵⁄₁₆ in., (23.4 x 17.7 cm.), etching on wove (BP 934, DM 2301, FR 7754, Y 152,221).

$885* *Selbstbildnis Mit Radiernadel In Der Linken Hand, 1921,* s., (12-05-92, Bassenge, #7481), 9³⁄₁₆ x 6¹⁵⁄₁₆ in., (23.3 x 17.7 cm.), etching on wove (BP 554, DM 1380, FR 4702, Y 109,652).

$505* *Selbstbildnis Mit Radiernadel In Der Linken Hand, 1921,* s., num., (11-28-92, Grisebach, #651, illus.), 8⅛ x 7½ in., (20.6 x 19 cm.), etching on handmade (BP 333, DM 805, FR 2731, Y 62,850).

$1098* *Selbstbildnis Mit Radiernadel, 1922,* s., d., 2. Zustand v. 2 (3 Druck), i. Gewidmet, artist's proof, (12-12-92, Wachholtz, #229), 8⅛ x 7⁹⁄₁₆ in., (20.7 x 19.2 cm.), etching on werkdruckpapier (BP 702, DM 1726, FR 5881, Y 135,841).

$686* *Selbstbildnis Radierend, c. 1922,* s., (11-28-92, Grisebach, #652, illus.), 10⅜ x 7¹⁵⁄₁₆ in., (26.4 x 20.2 cm.), drypoint on copper print paper (BP 453, DM 1093, FR 3710, Y 85,376).

$709* *Selbstbildnis Zeichnend, c. 1924,* s., (06-05-93, Grisebach, #776, illus.), 10⁷⁄₁₆ x 8⅛ in., (26.5 x 20.7 cm.), drypoint on copper print paper (BP 467, DM 1149, FR 3874, Y 76,057).

$532* *Sensemann Vor Apokalyptischer Stadt, 1918,* s., Probe II, artist's proof, sheet 2 of 12 from the series Septemberschrei, Paul Cassirer, (06-08-93, Karl/Faber, #1107), approx. 7⅞ x 5¹¹⁄₁₆ in., (20 x 14.5 cm.), lithograph on hand-made (BP 350, DM 863, FR 2907, Y 56,506).

$1986* *Strasse In Wilmersdorf, 1913,* s., (06-05-93, Bassenge, #6347, illus.), 6⁹⁄₁₆ x 5⁷⁄₁₆ in., (16.7 x 13.8 cm.), drypoint on imitation Japan (BP 1307, DM 3220, FR 10,852, Y 213,044).

$1098* *Victoria-Louise-Platz, 1922,* s., (12-12-92, Wachholtz, #231), 8¹⁵⁄₁₆ x 7¹¹⁄₁₆ in., (22.7 x 19.5 cm.), etching on thick copper print paper (BP 702, DM 1726, FR 5881, Y 135,841).

$2170* *Victoria-Louise-Platz, 1922,* s., (09-19-92, Wachholtz, #379, illus.), 8¹⁵⁄₁₆ x 7¹¹⁄₁₆ in., (22.7 x 19.5 cm.), drypoint on thick copper print paper (BP 1270, DM 3220, FR 11,015, Y 268,199).

$738* *Zwei Ekstatiker Vor Apokalyptischer Landschaft, 1918,* s., sheet 9 of series Septemberschrei, (12-05-92, Bassenge, #7487), 8¹⁄₁₆ x 5¹³⁄₁₆ in., (20.5 x 14.8 cm.), lithograph on thin cardboard (BP 462, DM 1151, FR 3921, Y 91,438).

MEIER, Melchor (ac. c. 1580)

$361* *Die Schindung Des Marsyas (Nagler, Die Monogrammisten IV, 2007), 1581,* (12-04-92, Bassenge, #6299), 8¹⁵⁄₁₆ x 12⁵⁄₁₆ in., (22.7 x 31.3 cm.), engraving (BP 232, DM 575, FR 1950, Y 45,069).

MEISSER, Leonhard 1902-1977

$236* *Landschaft In Der Nacht,* 22/120, s., (10-14-92, Germann, #564), 22⅛ x 17¹³⁄₁₆ in., (562 x 453 mm.), color lithograph (BP 139, DM 345, FR 1171, Y 28,599, SF 307).

$381* *Mondnacht, 1961,* 30/200, s., (10-14-92, Germann, #567), 19⁹⁄₁₆ x 15¼ in., (497 x 387 mm.), color lithograph (BP 224, DM 558, FR 1891, Y 46,171, SF 496).

$543* *Nachtlicher Garten, 1964,* 11/200, s., (10-14-92, Germann, #568), 19⅝ x 15⅜ in., (499 x 390 mm.), color lithograph (BP 319, DM 795, FR 2695, Y 65,802, SF 708).

$381* *Reiter Und Pferde,* X/XXV, s., tear, (10-14-92, Germann, #563), 19⅞ x 25⁹⁄₁₆ in., (505 x 650 mm.), color lithograph (BP 224, DM 558, FR 1891, Y 46,171, SF 496).

MEISSNER, Leo American 1895-1977

$55* *Submarine World,* s., t., i. child's proof, (11-12-92, Freemn/Fine Art, #148), image 8½ x 10⅞ in., (21.6 x 27.6 cm.), woodcut (BP 36, DM 87, FR 294, Y 6820).

MEISSONIER (after)

$29* *Les Joures Des Boules,* by Jules Jacquet, s., w/etched remarque, pub. Messrs Arthur Tooth and Sons, 1904, (03-03-93, Bonhams-Chelsea, #2), image 11 x 14 in., (27.9 x 35.6 cm.), etching (BP 20, DM 48, FR 162, Y 3389).

$54* *Napoleon's Retreat From Moscow, 1903,* indistinctly s., pub. Henry Graves and Co. Ltd., foxing, (08-20-92, Bonhams-Chelsea, #141), image 19 x 29½ in., (48.3 x 74.9 cm.), etching, etched remarque (BP 28, DM 78, FR 265, Y 6819).

MEISSONIER, Jean Louis French 1815-1891

$121* *"A Game Of Bowling" and "A Smoker": Two,* first by Jules Jacquet, s.; second by J. Rust, s., (10-18-92, Hindman, #523), larger 13½ x 15 in., (34.3 x 38.1 cm.), etchings (BP 74, DM 180, FR 611, Y 14,517).

MEISSONIER, Jean Louis (after) French 1815-1891

$33* *Monsieur Polichinelle,* by Paul Rajon after painting of 1850, prov., (09-20-92, Hindman, #738), 6¾ x 3⅞ in., (17.1 x 9.8 cm.), etching (BP 19, DM 49, FR 168, Y 4079).

MEISTER IB MIT DEM VOGEL ac. c. 1550-1506

BI *Leda Mit Dem Schwan (Bartsch XIII, 280, 46; Hind V, 257 9 II),* 2nd state, est. DM 18,000, (06-10-93, Hauswedell/Nolt, #115), engraving.

MEISTER LD ac. c. 1540-1550

BI *Christus In Der Vorholle (Bartsch XVI, 2; Zerner 84),* watermark, est. DM 6,000, (06-10-93, Hauswedell/Nolt, #116, illus.), etching on hand-made.

MEISTER MIT DEM WURFEL mid 16th cent.

BI *Der Triumph Des Amor In Friesform (Bartsch XV, 210, 37),* after Raphael, est. DM 2,000, (06-10-93, Hauswedell/Nolt, #118), engraving.

MEISTER P.M. (Pietro da MILANO)

$433* *Cloelia Fluchtet Aus Dem Lager Porsennas Uber Den Tiber (Robert-Dumesnil 19, Zerner P.M.6),* after Giulio Romano, (12-04-92, Bassenge, #6303), 15⁹⁄₁₆ x 21¼ in., (39.5 x 54 cm.), engraving (BP 278, DM 690, FR 2339, Y 54,057).

MEISTERMANN, Georg 1911-1990

$2524* *E. D. T. Lindner. Das Marchen Von Alinda Der Puppe: Seventeen,* ink mono., frontispiece, (11-20-92, Lempertz, #720), 20¹⁄₁₆ x 17⅜ in., (51 x 44.2 cm.), lithograph (BP 1662, DM 4024, FR 13,555, Y 313,891).

$735* *Komposition In Gelb, Schwarz Und Blau,* s. G. Meistermann, #57/100, (09-14-92, Venator/Hansten, #2475), approx. 9⁷⁄₁₆ x 13⅜ in., (24 x 34 cm.), color lithograph (BP 389, DM 1093, FR 3703, Y 91,395).

BI *Ohne Titel,* #20/70, pencil s., est. DM 1,000, (11-20-92, Lempertz, #719), sh 14¾ x 17⅛ in., (37.4 x 43.5 cm.), color offset lithograph on Velin.

BI *Ohne Titel, 1962,* ballpoint pen s., est. DM 1,000, (11-20-92, Lempertz, #717), sh 14¾ x 11⅞ in., (37.5 x 30.2 cm.), wood engraving in 6 colors.

MELIS, Roger
BI *Portrats Des Schriftstellers Hermann Kant, 60's: Three,* t., est. DM 400, (11-12-92, Lempertz, #172, illus.), each 11 15/16 x 9 7/16 in., (30.4 x 24 cm.), photograph, gelatin silver print.

MELNIK
$219* *Savon Blanche Leigh, c. 1900,* cond. C, (03-16-93, Boisgirard, #153), 97 1/16 x 62 in., (246.5 x 157.5 cm.), poster (BP 151, DM 364, FR 1237, Y 25,608).

MELZER, Moriz 1877-1966
$958* *Frauenraub, c. 1918,* s., (06-05-93, Grisebach, #780, illus.), 18 7/8 x 13 1/8 in., (48 x 33.3 cm.), monotype on light brown handmade Japan (BP 631, DM 1553, FR 5235, Y 102,768).
BI *Rauber, 1914,* s., d., est. DM 6,000, (05-26-93, Lempertz, #369, illus.), 51 3/16 x 35 13/16 in., (130 x 91 cm.), monotype on several pasted papers.
$1098* *Das Ufer Naht, 1918/20,* s., (12-12-92, Bassenge, #8733), 12 15/16 x 18 7/8 in., (33 x 48 cm.), color monotype on China (BP 702, DM 1726, FR 5881, Y 135,841).
$1215* *Weibliche Akte, Sturzend, c. 1914,* s., tears, foxed, (12-12-92, Bassenge, #8734, illus.), 12 13/16 x 18 11/16 in., (32.5 x 47.5 cm.), color monotype on China (BP 777, DM 1909, FR 6508, Y 150,315).

MENDEZ, Leopoldo b. Mexico 1902
$1035* *Fusilamiento,* s., d. 1950 Taller de Grafica Popular, full margins, good cond., handling creases, soiling, (05-18-93, Sotheby-NY, #261, illus.), image 11 7/8 x 16 1/2 in., (302 x 419 mm.), linoleum cut (BP 674, DM 1679, FR 5671, Y 115,346).
$690* *Prisionero,* s., d. 1950 Taller de Grafica Popular, full margins, good cond., handling creases, soiling, (05-18-93, Sotheby-NY, #260, illus.), image 11 7/8 x 16 3/8 in., (302 x 416 mm.), linoleum cut (BP 449, DM 1120, FR 3781, Y 76,897).
$690* *La Siembra,* s. Taller de Grafica Popular, fair cond., creases, soiling, yellow stains, tape, (05-18-93, Sotheby-NY, #262, illus.), image 11 7/8 x 15 7/8 in., (302 x 403 mm.), linoleum cut (BP 449, DM 1120, FR 3781, Y 76,897).
BI *El Tejedor, 1931,* crayon s.; inits. in pl., Taller de Grafica Popular, very good cond.,yellowing, paper loss, est. $1,5/2,000, (11-23-92, Sotheby-NY, #265, illus.), image 4 3/8 x 6 1/8 in., (112 x 156 mm.), linoleum cut.
BI *Twenty-Five Prints Of Leopoldo Mendez, 1943,* s., pub. La Estampa Mexicana, full margins, good cond., foxing, handling creases, est. $4/6,000, (11-23-92, Sotheby-NY, #266, illus.), smallest image 4 1/8 x 3 7/8 in., (105 x 97 mm.), largest image 9 3/4 x 7 3/4 in., (105 x 97 mm.), linoleum cuts.

MENDJINSKY, Serge French b. 1929
$88* *La Seine,* s., #CLXXXVIII/CCXXV, (12-13-92, Hindman, #331), 16 3/4 x 23 1/2 in., color lithograph (BP 56, DM 138, FR 471, Y 10,887).

MENDJISKY, S.
$69* *Rue De Montmartre,* #102/250, s., good margins, (06-16-93, Ader Tajan, #121), 14 9/16 x 21 7/16 in., (37 x 54.5 cm.), color lithograph (BP 46, DM 115, FR 384, Y 7359).

MENGUY, Frederic French b. 1927
$25* *"Jeune Femme Au Bouquet",* s., (01-28-93, Pescheteau, #212), 16 1/8 x 11 13/16 in., (41 x 30 cm.), color lithograph on Arches (BP 17, DM 40, FR 134, Y 3104).
BI *Two Women With Table Top,* s., edit. #163/200, est. $75/150, (10-16-92, DuMouchelle, #2399), 15 x 22 in., (38.1 x 55.9 cm.), color lithograph.
BI *Two Women With Table Top,* s., edit. #163/200, est. $75/150, (12-11-92, DuMouchelle, #2397), 15 x 22 in., (38.1 x 55.9 cm.), color lithograph.
$39* *Two Women With Table Top,* s., #163/200, (03-12-93, DuMouchelle, #2328), 15 x 22 in., (38.1 x 55.9 cm.), color lithograph (BP 27, DM 65, FR 221, Y 4596).

MENIN, PERICLE ac. 1935
$260* *"Case Del Cadore" and "Neve": Two,* s., t., (05-10-93, Hodgins, #353), etching on paper (BP 170, DM 418, FR 1409, Y 29,054, C$ 330).

MENPES, Mortimer
BI *Bronze Workers, Japan,* s., margins, est. BP 2/300, (03-17-93, Bonhams-Chelsea, #396), plate 7 3/4 x 7 7/8 in., (19.7 x 20 cm.), drypoint etching.
$171* *Bronze Workers, Japan,* s., margins, (05-20-93, Bonhams-Chelsea, #105), plate 7 3/4 x 7 7/8 in., (19.7 x 20 cm.), drypoint etching (BP 110, DM 276, FR 929, Y 18,883).
$54* *The Plaza, Madrid,* s., margins, (10-15-92, Bonhams-Chelsea, #137), plate 8 1/4 x 12 3/4 in., (21 x 32.4 cm.), color drypoint etching (BP 33, DM 80, FR 273, Y 6479).
$68* *A Street Corner, Damascus,* s., t., margins, (04-22-93, Bonhams-Chelsea, #122), plate 9 1/8 x 7 1/8 in., (23.2 x 18.1 cm.), etching (BP 44, DM 109, FR 369, Y 7477).

MENPES, Mortimer British 1860-1938
$187* *Tea Break,* s., annot. imp., (03-14-93, Hindman, #246), 5 7/8 x 9 5/8 in., (14.9 x 24.4 cm.), drypoint (BP 130, DM 311, FR 1058, Y 22,039).

MENTOR, Blasco b. 1918
$189* *"Toreador",* E.A., s., (01-28-93, Pescheteau, #213), 19 11/16 x 25 9/16 in., (50 x 65 cm.), color lithograph on wove (BP 125, DM 299, FR 1013, Y 23,467).

MENZ
BI *"Deutsche" and "Na Pomoc": Two,* creases, tears, losses, est. BP 3/500, (02-04-93, Christie-S. Ken, #173), 40 x 28 in., (101.6 x 71.1 cm.), color lithograph.

MENZEL, Adolf German 1815-1905
$1315* *Das Flotenkonzert Von Sanssouci,* pub. Dt. Kunst-Verein, (09-14-92, Venator/Hansten, #1685), engraving on China (BP 695, DM 1955, FR 6625, Y 163,517).
BI *Kunstlers Erdenwallen (Bloch 109-115), 1834: Eleven,* est. DM 3000, (06-04-93, Bassenge, #5751), lithograph on China.
$352* *Die Offiziere Friedrichs Des Grossen (Bock 1066, 1068-1076, d), 1888: Ten,* (03-24-93, Venator/Hansten, #2614), approx. 10 1/4 x 8 11/16 in., (26 x 22 cm.), woodcut (BP 238, DM 575, FR 1957, Y 41,358).
$249* *Die Zeitungsleserin (Bock 1152/IV), 1886,* brown stained, (12-01-92, Karl/Faber, #235), 10 13/16 x 9 1/16 in., (27.5 x 23 cm.), etching on simili-Japan (BP 165, DM 397, FR 1353, Y 31,001).

MERCERE, Gene
$303* *"En Memoriam",* s., i., d., slight creasing, toning, soiling, (06-25-93, Goldberg, #902A, illus.), 17 x 12 in., (43.2 x 30.5 cm.), etching (BP 205, DM 516, FR 1737, Y 32,118).

MERCIER, A.-L.
$159* *Ch. De Fer Algeriens: Algerie. "Pays De La Qualite",* very good cond., (03-13-93, Laurin, #58), 39 3/8 x 23 5/8 in., (100 x 60 cm.), (BP 111, DM 265, FR 900, Y 18,739).

MERCIER, J.A.
$357* *Le Sport "Cette Chevalerie Moderne", Education Generale Des Sports, c. 1939,* p. Bedos, very good cond., (11-19-92, Ribeyre/Baron, #148), 62 15/16 x 47 1/4 in., (160 x 120 cm.), poster (BP 235, DM 569, FR 1917, Y 44,397).

MERIAN, Matthaus Swiss 1593-1650
BI *Extensive Figural Scenes: Two,* after Sebastian Vranx, est. $3/400, (10-30-92, Sloan, #1330), each, sight 7 3/8 x 11 1/8 in., (18.7 x 28.3 cm.), engraving.
BI *Extensive Figural Scenes: Two,* after Sebastian Vrancx, est. $350/500, (09-17-92, Sloan, #1455), each, sight 7 3/8 x 11 1/8 in., (18.7 x 28.3 cm.), engraving.
BI *Extensive Figural Scenes: Two,* after Sebastian Vraux, est. $250/350, (12-10-92, Sloan, #1307), each, sight 7 3/8 x 11 1/8 in., (18.7 x 28.3 cm.), engravings.

MERIAN, Matthaus (the elder) 1593-1650
$123* *Talenge Mit Burgen (Wuthrich 583/II), 1620-22,* after A. Mirou, plate 1 from series Six Grossen Landschaften, (12-01-92, Karl/Faber, #101), etching (BP 81, DM 196, FR 668, Y 15,314).
$25,962* *Topographia Helvetiae, Rhaetiae Et Velesiae (Eckhardt pag. 48ff), 1642,* Merian, Frankfurt am Main, (06-23-93, Kornfeld, #71, illus.), (BP 17,637, DM 43,929, FR 147,763, Y 2,828,413, SF 39,100).

MERIDA, Carlos   Guatemalan 1891-1984
$4600* *Estampas Del Popol Vuh: Set of Ten,* s. ink on justifica-
tion, #251/1000; s., #15/50, time staining, very good
cond., Graphic Art Publications, 1943, (05-17-93,
Christie-NY, #302), 16¼ x 12¼ in., (412 x 311 mm.),
lithograph in colors on wove (BP 3001, DM 7422, FR
25,000, Y 512,249).
$805* *(Untitled), 1934: Four,* each s., d., #33/50, margins,
apparently good cond., water-staining,light-staining, foxing, surface soiling, (05-19-93, Butterfield, #1844), each
11¾ x 7⅞ in., (298 x 200 mm.), lithograph on wove
(BP 523, DM 1309, FR 4409, Y 89,118).
BI *(Untitled): Two,* s., #21/100, margins, good cond., mat/
light-staining, taped, est. $7/900, (05-19-93, Butterfield,
#1845), one 8¼ x 5⅝ in., (210 x 143 mm.), the other
8⅛ x 5½ in., (210 x 143 mm.), silkscreen in color on
wove.

MERIGOT, James
$2420* *A Select Collection Of Views And Ruins In Rome, And
Its Vicinity: 63,* English and French text, folio, some
plates watermarked, (11-12-92, Swann, #113), 19½ x
13⅜ in., (495 x 340 mm.), hand-colored aquatint (BP
1589, DM 3835, FR 12,934, Y 300,062).

MERISTERMANN, Georg   1911-1990
$794* *Das Marchen Von Alinda Der Puppe (BII), 1959,* text,
num., impress., (11-28-92, Schoppmann, #663), 20¹/₁₆ x
17⁵/₁₆ in., (51 x 44 cm.), lithograph on G. Meistermann
(BP 524, DM 1265, FR 4294, Y 98,818).

MERKE, Henri (after Samuel HOWITT)
BI *Oriental Field Sports, 1805: Four,* pub. Edward Orme,
est. BP 3/500, (10-27-92, Phillips-London, #145), image
12¼ x 17½ in., (311 x 445 mm.), aquatint w/hand-color-
ing on wove laid on card.

MERRY, Tom
BI *"The United American Nation Uncle Yank, (Log), "A
Pretty Derned Crowd!",* Tom Merry, Del et Lith, from
St. Stephen's Review Presentation Cartoon, April 11th,
1891, est. $2/300, (11-21-92, Goldberg, #719), 12 x 18½
in., (30.5 x 47 cm.), color lithograph.

MERSHIMER, Frederic W.   American 20th cent.
$358* *"New York Stock Exchange",* s. Frederic W. Mershimer
'89, num. 37/100, (04-25-93, Bakker, #50), plate 17½ x
13¼ in., (44.5 x 33.7 cm.), colored etching (BP 227,
DM 566, FR 1912, Y 39,541).

MERSON, L. Oliver
$115* *Salome,* L'Estampe Moderne blindstamp, full margins, tis-
sue paper t. page attached along sheet edge, good condition, tears, paper losses, staining, foxing, (03-31-93,
Butterfield, #5246), 13¹¹/₁₆ x 7⅝ in., (34.8 x 19.4 cm.),
lithograph printed in colors w/hand-coloring on wove (BP
76, DM 185, FR 628, Y 13,224).

MERYON, Charles   French 1821-1868
$330* *Armes Symboliques De La Ville De Paris (Delteil-Wright
21 III/III), 1864,* final state, (03-14-93, Hindman, #240),
5⅜ x 4⅜ in., (13.7 x 11.1 cm.), etching (BP 230, DM
549, FR 1868, Y 38,892).
BI *"Chateaux De Chenonceau (2e Planche) (D/W .58 III/
III),* posthumous impression, est. $1-150, (10-31-92,
Cleveland, #317), 4½ x 7¼ in., (11.4 x 18.4 cm.), etching.
BI *Entree Du Couvent Des Capucins Francais A Athenes
(L.D., W. 61), 1854,* 3rd final state, i., full margins, surface soiling, creasing, prov.,prop. Montclair Art
Museum, est. $800/1,200, (05-11-93, Christie-NY, #233),
plate 7½ x 4⅞ in., (191 x 124 mm.), etching on heavy
laid.
BI *Entree Du Couvent Des Capucins Francais A Athenes (S.
50; D./W. 61),1854,* 3rd final state, margins, light-staining, foxing, mount-staining, (06-30-93, Sotheby-London,
#525), sh 9⅞ x 5⅞ in., (251 x 149 mm.), etching on
laid.
$916* *Entree Du Couvent Des Capucins Francais A Athenes
(Schn. 50/III; D.-Wr. 61/III), 1854,* prov., (06-23-93,
Kornfeld, #577), etching and drypoint (BP 622, DM
1550, FR 5213, Y 99,793, SF 1380).

$2598* *La Galerie Notre-Dame (L. Delteil 26), 1853,* third state
of five, crease, good margins, (06-11-93, Picard, #134),
10⅝ x 6⁷/₁₆ in., (270 x 164 mm.), etching on greenish
paper (BP 1707, DM 4222, FR 14,236, Y 275,650).
$1604* *La Galerie Notre-Dame (Schn. 29/IV; D.-Wr. 26/III),
1853,* (06-23-93, Kornfeld, #573), etching and engraving
on wove (BP 1090, DM 2714, FR 9129, Y 174,747, SF
2415).
BI *L'Abside De Notre Dame De Paris (DW. 38), 1854,* plate
s., watermark, est. C$ 1,5/2,500, (06-08-93, Ritchie,
#23, illus.), plate 6⅝ x 11⅞ in., (16.8 x 30.2 cm.), sheet
10⅜ x 14½ in., (16.8 x 30.2 cm.), etching on laid.
$10,295* *L'Abside De Notre-Dame (S. 45; D./W. 38), 1854,*
Schneiderman's 3rd state of 9, i., ded., crease through
image, light-staining, foxing, defects, (06-30-93, Sotheby-
London, #527, illus.), sh 11¼ x 17¾ in., (286 x 451
mm.), etching on laid (BP 6900, DM 17,559, FR 59,235,
Y 1,103,075).
$4582* *L'Abside De Notre-Dame (Schn. 45/IV; D.-Wr. 38/IV),
1854,* (06-23-93, Kornfeld, #576, illus.), etching, engraving, and drypoint on handmade (BP 3113, DM 7753, FR
26,079, Y 499,183, SF 6900).
$2530* *L'Abside De Notre-Dame De Paris (L.D., W. 38), 1854,*
4th state of 8, wide margins, light/mat staining, defect,
foxing, glued down on wove, (05-11-93, Christie-NY,
#232), plate 6½ x 11¹³/₁₆ in., (165 x 300 mm.), etching
on laid (BP 1615, DM 3986, FR 13,429, Y 278,297).
$2331* *L'Abside De Notre-Dame De Paris (L.D., W. 38), 1854,*
4th state of 8, margins, light-stined, mount-stained,
prov., (12-01-92, Christie-London, #433), plate 6⁷/₁₆ x
11¹³/₁₆ in., (164 x 300 mm.), etching on laid paper (BP
1540, DM 3715, FR 12,662, Y 290,214).
BI *L'Ancien Louvre, D'Apres Zeeman (Delteil-Wright 53),
1866,* fifth state(?), inscription, wide margins, time soiling, mat burn, est. $6/900, (05-27-93, Swann, #180,
illus.), image 5½ x 9¾ in., (14 x 24.8 cm.), etching and
drypoint on old laid watermarked paper.
$1527* *Le Ministere De La Marine (Schn. 94/VI; D.-Wr. 45/V/
VI), 1865,* (06-23-93, Kornfeld, #578), etching on hand-
made (BP 1037, DM 2584, FR 8691, Y 166,358, SF
2300).
BI *La Morgue, 1854,* before letters, staining, full margins,
(02-24-93, Picard, #169), etching on thin laid.
$5345* *La Morgue, Paris (Schn. 42/IV; D.-Wr. 36/IV), 1854,*
watermark, prov., (06-23-93, Kornfeld, #575), etching on
handmade Japan (BP 3631, DM 9044, FR 30,421, Y
582,307, SF 8050).
BI *Partie De La Cite Vers La Fin Du XVIIe Siecle (Delteil/
Wright 51),* w/letter, eighth state, est. FF2/3,000, (03-31-
93, Briest, #E76), 8⁷/₁₆ x 13⅜ in., (21.5 x 34 cm.), etching.
$253* *Passerelle Du Pont-Au-Change Apres L'Incendie De 1621
(Delteil 50 VI; Wright 50 VII; Schneidermann 65 VII),
1860,* (12-04-92, Bassenge, #6891), 4⅝ x 8¹¹/₁₆ in., (11.7
x 22 cm.), etching on China (BP 162, DM 403, FR
1367, Y 31,586).
$75* *"Passerelle Du Pont-Au-Change, Paris" (D/W 50 vii/ix),
1860,* pub. in Gazette des Beaux-Arts, good cond., (05-
15-93, Cleveland, #413), 4¹¹/₁₆ x 9 in., (11.9 x 22.9 cm.),
etching (BP 49, DM 121, FR 405, Y 8314).
$880* *Le Petit Pont (Delteil-Wright 24), c. 1850,* fourth state of
seven, mono., paper fibers adhering to verso, good cond.,
(11-05-92, Sotheby-NY, #254), 9¾ x 7¼ in., (247 x 185
mm.), etching p. w/strong tone in brownish-black on
India paper removed from support sheet (BP 572, DM
1392, FR 4708, Y 107,962).
$505* *Le Petit Pont (L. Delteil 24),* fifth state of six, good
marges, (02-03-93, Ader Tajan, #179), 9⅝ x 7⁵/₁₆ in.,
(24.5 x 18.5 cm.), etching on fixed Chine (BP 353, DM
832, FR 2820, Y 62,819).
$5491* *Le Petit Pont (S. 20; D./W. 24), 1850,* Schneiderman's
1st state of 9, s. C. Meryon, d. 1850, narrow margin-
s,corner re-attached, glue stain, foxing, good cond., (06-
30-93, Sotheby-London, #522, illus.), sh 10½ x 7⅝ in.,
(267 x 194 mm.), etching on thin wove (BP 3680, DM
9366, FR 31,594, Y 588,342).
$2046* *Le Petit Pont Paris (LD. 24), 1850,* 3rd state of 7, inits.
C.M., narrow margins, flaw, (10-27-92, Phillips-London,
#213), plate 10⅛ x 7½ in., (257 x 191 mm.), etching on

japan paper (BP 1293, DM 3136, FR 10,640, Y 250,275).

$565* *La Pompe Notre Dame (L. Delteil 31),* seventh state of nine, good margins, (02-03-93, Ader Tajan, #180), 6 11/16 x 9 5/8 in., (17 x 24.5 cm.), etching on fixed Chine (BP 394, DM 930, FR 3155, Y 70,282).

$920* *La Pompe Notre-Dame (D./W. 31/VI), 1852,* 6th state of 9, watermark, margins, good cond., creases, (05-13-93, Sotheby-NY, #622), 6 3/4 x 10 in., (172 x 254 mm.), sh 9 x 12 3/8 in., (172 x 254 mm.), etching on laid (BP 604, DM 1486, FR 5011, Y 102,713).

$1680* *La Pompe Notre-Dame (Schn. 26/VII; D.-Wr. 31/VI), 1852,* (06-23-93, Kornfeld, #572), etching on tan (red color) handmade (BP 1141, DM 2843, FR 9562, Y 183,026, SF 2530).

BI *La Pompe Notre-Dame (Schneiderman 26), 1852,* pub. in l'Artiste, margins, good cond., (12-03-92, Sotheby-London, #408), 6 5/8 x 10 in., (168 x 254 mm.), etching on yellowish chine applique.

$1100* *La Pompe Notre-Dame, Paris (D./W. 31 vi/ix), 1852,* sixth state of nine, margins, good cond., fox marks, soiling, discoloration, stamped inventory number, repairs, spots, hinges, (11-05-92, Sotheby-NY, #254A), 6 3/4 x 10 in., (170 x 253 mm.), etching, p. in brown on laid (BP 715, DM 1740, FR 5886, Y 134,953).

BI *Le Pont Au Change, Paris (D/W 34), 1854,* mat stain, good cond., watermark, est. $1/1,500, (12-04-92, Doyle, #133), 5 1/2 x 12 5/8 in., (140 x 321 mm.), etching on paper.

$611* *Le Pont Neuf (Schn. 30/VII; D.-Wr. 33/VII), 1853,* (06-23-93, Kornfeld, #574), etching and drypoint on handmade (BP 415, DM 1034, FR 3478, Y 66,565, SF 920).

BI *"Le Pont Neuf Et La Samaritaine De Dessous La Premiere Arch De Pont-Au-Change, Paris" (D/W 46 v/v), 1855,* sun staining, tape, est. $6/800, (05-15-93, Cleveland, #412, illus.), 5 3/4 x 8 in., (14.6 x 20.3 cm.), etching on heavy laid.

$5175* *Le Pont Neuf, Paris (L.D., W. 33), 1852,* 6th state of 9, s., i., num. 17, margins, light-staining, foxing, laid down, (05-11-93, Christie-NY, #231, illus.), plate 7 x 7 1/4 in., (178 x 184 mm.), etching on verdatre (greenish) laid (BP 3304, DM 8152, FR 27,468, Y 569,244).

$210* *"Presqu'ile De Banks, Pointe Dite Des Charbonniers Akaroa: Peche A La Seine" (D/W 69 v/vii before removal of 2nd boat in the center), 1863,* mat staining, (05-15-93, Cleveland, #414, illus.), 6 1/8 x 12 13/16 in., (15.6 x 32.5 cm.), etching on heavy laid (BP 137, DM 338, FR 1135, Y 23,279).

$771* *La Rue Des Chantres (S. 85; D./W. 42), 1862,* 4th state of 5, watermark, margins, foxing, light-staining, crease, (06-30-93, Sotheby-London, #526), sh 18 x 7 1/4 in., (457 x 184 mm.), etching on laid (BP 517, DM 1315, FR 4436, Y 82,610).

BI *La Rue Des Toiles, A Bourges (D./W. 55/V), 1853,* 5th state of 9, large margins, good cond., creases, fox marks, loss,est. $3,5/4,500, (05-13-93, Sotheby-NY, #623, illus.), 8 1/2 x 4 3/4 in., (217 x 121 mm.), sh 17 x 12 5/8 in., (217 x 121 mm.), etching on laid.

$1150* *Saint-Etienne Du Mont, Paris (L.D., W. 30), 1852,* 4th state of 8, margins, light-staining, laid down on board, (05-11-93, Christie-NY, #230), plate 9 3/4 x 5 in., (248 x 127 mm.), etching on pale verdatre (greenish) laid (BP 734, DM 1812, FR 6104, Y 126,499).

BI *Saint-Etienne-Du-Mont (L.D. 30), 1852,* fourth state of eight, reddish stains, creases, drystamp, (06-11-93, Picard, #135), 9 5/8 x 5 1/8 in., (244 x 130 mm.), etching on greenish laid.

$825* *Le Stryge,* (11-01-92, Hanzel, #255), 7 x 5 1/8 in., (17.8 x 13 cm.), etching (BP 539, DM 1301, FR 4386, Y 102,003).

$686* *La Tour De L'Horloge (Delteil 28 VI; Wright 28 IV; Schneidermann 23 VI), 1852,* (12-04-92, Bassenge, #6889, illus.), 10 1/4 x 7 5/16 in., (26 x 18.5 cm.), etching on China (BP 440, DM 1093, FR 3706, Y 85,643).

BI *La Tour De L'Horloge, Paris (L.D., Wright 28), 1852,* watermark, 5th state of 10, wide margins, light/mat/time staining, good cond., prov., est. $1,5/2,000, (05-11-93, Christie-NY, #229), plate 10 1/4 x 7 1/4 in., (260 x 184 mm.), etching on laid.

BI *La Tour De L'Horloge, Paris (S. 23; D./W. 28), 1852,* 3rd state of 10, wide margins, foxing, light-staining, glue, good cond., est. BP 2/3,000, (06-30-93, Sotheby-London, #523, illus.), sh 14 5/8 x 10 in., (371 x 254 mm.), etching on pale green laid.

$1374* *La Tour De L'Horloge, Paris (Schneiderman 23/V; Delteil-Wright 28/V), 1852,* (06-23-93, Kornfeld, #570), etching and engraving on handmade (BP 933, DM 2325, FR 7820, Y 149,690, SF 2070).

$605* *"La Tour De L'Horloge, Paris" (Delteil/Wright 28 VI/X), 1852,* pub. L'Artiste, 1858, good cond., (10-31-92, Cleveland, #316), 10 3/8 x 7 1/2 in., (26.4 x 19.1 cm.), etching (BP 388, DM 931, FR 3158, Y 74,941).

$920* *Tourelle De La Rue De La Tixanderie (Delteil/Wright 29; Schneiderman24), 1852,* 3rd state of 5, margins, good cond., pin holes, ex-coll. R.L. Mayer, (05-13-93, Sotheby-NY, #621), 9 3/4 x 5 1/8 in., (246 x 130 mm.), etching in brown ink (BP 604, DM 1486, FR 5011, Y 102,713).

BI *Tourelle De La Rue De La Tixeranderie (Delteil-Wright 29), 1852,* second state of 5, trimmed, laid down onto a support, mat burn, est. $6/900, (05-27-93, Swann, #181), 9 3/4 x 5 1/4 in., (24.8 x 13.3 cm.), etching and drypoint.

$916* *Tourelle Rue De La Tixeranderie (Schn. 24/III; D.-Wr. 29/III), 1852,* (06-23-93, Kornfeld, #571), etching on handmade (BP 622, DM 1550, FR 5213, Y 99,793, SF 1380).

BI *"Tourelle, Rue De L'Ecolede Medecine" (Delteil/Wright 41 xii/xiii), 1861,* as pub. in Gazette des Beaux-Arts, 1863, good cond., est. $100/150, (05-15-93, Cleveland, #411), 8 5/16 x 5 1/8 in., (21.1 x 13 cm.), etching.

MESQUITA, Samuel Jesserun de 1868-1957

BI *Bird,* s., full sheet p. to edges, laid down on card, defects along edges of sheet, Late Gerhard Brauer Coll., est. Dfl. 6/900, (05-27-93, Sotheby-Amstrdm, #830), sheet 15 3/16 x 6 1/8 in., (385 x 155 mm.), etching on wove.

BI *(Figures), 1918,* s., #10/12, full margins, good cond., paper discoloration, minor creasing, Late Gerhard Brauer Coll., est. Dfl. 4/600, (05-27-93, Sotheby-Amstrdm, #826), 7 15/16 x 9 1/8 in., (201 x 231 mm.), etching w/tone on laid.

$256* *(Figures), 1918,* s., #5/12, full margins, good cond., paper discoloration, foxing, minor creasing, Late Gerhard Brauer Coll., (05-27-93, Sotheby-Amstrdm, #828), 7 7/8 x 9 1/16 in., (200 x 230 mm.), etching w/tone on laid (BP 164, DM 411, FR 1385, Y 27,444, G 460).

BI *(Figures), 1918,* s., #8/12, full margins, good cond., paper discoloration, minor soiling at edges of sheet, minor creasing, Late Gerhard Brauer Coll., est. Dfl. 4/600, (05-27-93, Sotheby-Amstrdm, #827), 8 1/16 x 10 3/16 in., (205 x 258 mm.), etching on tone on laid.

$230* *(Figures), 1918,* s., #8/12, full margins, good cond., paper discoloration, minor soiling at edges of sheet, minor handling creases, Late Gerhard Brauer Coll., (05-27-93, Sotheby-Amstrdm, #825), 13/16x9 3/16 in., (20 x 233 mm.), etching w/tone on laid (BP 147, DM 369, FR 1244, Y 24,657, G 414).

BI *Fish, 1914,* mount s., foxing, laid down, good cond., est. G 6/800, (12-09-92, Sotheby-Amstrdm, #609), sheet 8 3/16 x 9 5/8 in., (208 x 244 mm.), linocut on wove.

$192* *(Three Figures), 1918,* s., #1/12, full margins, good cond., minor paper discoloration, LateGerhard Brauer Coll., (05-27-93, Sotheby-Amstrdm, #824), 3 5/16 x 4 15/16 in., (84 x 125 mm.), etching w/aquatint on laid (BP 123, DM 308, FR 1038, Y 20,583, G 345).

BI *Zebu, 1916,* s., no. 14, margins, glued to backboard, foxing, Late Gerhard BrauerColl., est. Dfl. 6/900, (05-27-93, Sotheby-Amstrdm, #829), 9 x 10 7/8 in., (229 x 277 mm.), etching on wove.

MESS, George Jo American 1898-1962

$220* *"The Handy Pump" And "Rural Delivery": Two,* s. George Jo Mess, t., latter #81/100, very good cond., (03-12-93, Skinner, #52, illus.), approx. 7 1/2 x 8 in., (19.1 x 20.3 cm.), aquatints w/etching on wove (BP 153, DM 366, FR 1245, Y 25,928).

$99* *"The Locket," 1938,* (09-20-92, Jackson, #92), 6 x 8 in., (15.2 x 20.3 cm.), aquatint (BP 58, DM 147, FR 503, Y 12,236).

$132* *"Magnitude",* (09-20-92, Jackson, #91), 11 x 8 in., (27.9 x 20.3 cm.), aquatint (BP 77, DM 196, FR 670, Y 16,314).

MESSAGIER, Jean French b. 1920

$59* *"Avez-Vous Deja Trouve Cent Francs Dans Les Radis",* E.A., s., (01-28-93, Pescheteau, #214), 22⅟₁₆ x 29¹⁵⁄₁₆ in., (56 x 76 cm.), color lithograph on Arches (BP 39, DM 93, FR 316, Y 7326).

$48* *Composition En Rouge Et Vert,* s., 46/120, (06-28-93, Loudmer, #98), 17¹⁵⁄₁₆ x 24⅝ in., (455 x 625 mm.), sh 19⅛ x 25¹⁵⁄₁₆ in., (455 x 625 mm.), 2-color etching and aquatint on Arches wove (BP 32, DM 82, FR 275, Y 5093).

$58* *Composition En Vert Et Argente,* s., 40/120, (06-28-93, Loudmer, #96), 17⁷⁄₁₆ x 23⁷⁄₁₆ in., (443 x 596 mm.), sh 19⅛ x 25¹⁵⁄₁₆ in., (443 x 596 mm.), 2-color etching and aquatint on Arches wove (BP 39, DM 99, FR 332, Y 6154).

BI *Entre Ouies Et Coeur,* s., t., #57/75, full margins, good cond., paper discoloration of image, est. Dfl. 3/400, (05-27-93, Sotheby-Amstrdm, #662), 8⁹⁄₁₆ x 13⅞ in., (218 x 353 mm.), color etching on wove.

BI *Entre Ouies Et Coeur,* s., t., #57/75, full margins, good cond., est. Dfl. 3/400, (05-27-93, Sotheby-Amstrdm, #665), 8⁹⁄₁₆ x 13⅞ in., (218 x 353 mm.), color etching on wove.

$243* *Entre Ouies Et Coeur,* s., t., #57/75, full margins, good cond., (05-27-93, Sotheby-Amstrdm, #663), 8⁹⁄₁₆ x 13⅞ in., (218 x 353 mm.), color etching on wove (BP 156, DM 390, FR 1314, Y 26,051, G 437).

BI *Hommage A Bram Van Velde, 1979,* s., full sheet p. to edges, good cond., est. Dfl. 4/600, (05-27-93, Sotheby-Amstrdm, #453), sh 20½ x 29½ in., (520 x 749 mm.), colored lithograph on wove.

BI *Hommage A Hercule Seghers, 1979,* s., #85/190, full sheet p. to edges, good cond., est. Dfl. 4/600, (05-27-93, Sotheby-Amstrdm, #451, illus.), sh 21⅟₁₆ x 29⁷⁄₁₆ in., (535 x 748 mm.), colored lithograph on wove.

BI *Hommage A Van Gogh, 1979,* s., #112/190, full sheet p. to edges, good cond., est. Dfl. 4/600, (05-27-93, Sotheby-Amstrdm, #452), sh 20½ x 29½ in., (520 x 749 mm.), colored lithograph on wove.

$293* *Machine A Regarder,* s., t., i. E.A., margins, good cond., pinholes, creases, (12-09-92, Sotheby-Amstrdm, #610), sheet 25¹⁵⁄₁₆ x 18⅞ in., (660 x 480 mm.), color etching w/aquatint on Arches (BP 187, DM 460, FR 1569, Y 36,330, G 518).

$97* *Paysage Capture,* s., t., 134/300, dust, (06-28-93, Loudmer, #97), 17¹³⁄₁₆ x 25³⁄₁₆ in., (453 x 640 mm.), sh 19⅛ x 25¹⁵⁄₁₆ in., (453 x 640 mm.), etching and aquatint in pink on Arches wove (BP 65, DM 165, FR 555, Y 10,292).

BI *Paysage Sorbet,* s., t., #47/60, margins, good cond., creases, stain, est. Dfl. 250/350, (05-27-93, Sotheby-Amstrdm, #664), 17⅛ x 10¹³⁄₁₆ in., (435 x 275 mm.), etching and aquatint in colors on wove.

BI *Paysagesorbet,* s., t., #47/60, margins, good cond., creases, stain, est. G 4/600, (12-09-92, Sotheby-Amstrdm, #611), 17⅛ x 10¹³⁄₁₆ in., (435 x 275 mm.), color etching and aquatint on wove.

BI *Sous Le Mufle D'Une Genisse (Putman 188), 1971: Four,* s., #68/80, 54/80, 37/80 and 28/40, est. FF 4/5,000, (11-16-92, Briest, #337), each 24¹³⁄₁₆ x 35⁷⁄₁₆ in., (63 x 90 cm.), aquatint and drypoint on copper.

MESSER, Teall

$173* *La Carnival,* s., t., #11/40, Paris 2T, i., margins, laid down, good cond., water-staining affecting numbering, staining, soiling, (05-19-93, Butterfield, #2085), 8¹¹⁄₁₆ x 6⅝ in., (221 x 168 mm.), lithograph on Chine colle (BP 112, DM 281, FR 947, Y 19,152).

MESSICK, Ben American 1901-1981

$80* *"Nudist Cocktail Party", 1940,* excell. cond., (05-15-93, Cleveland, #251), 10 x 12 in., (25.4 x 30.5 cm.), lithograph (BP 52, DM 129, FR 432, Y 8868).

$80* *"Plantation Party", 1940,* excell. cond., (05-15-93, Cleveland, #252), 14½ x 18 in., (36.8 x 45.7 cm.), lithograph (BP 52, DM 129, FR 432, Y 8868).

$40* *"Polo Player",* excell. cond., (05-15-93, Cleveland, #253), 12 x 10 in., (30.5 x 25.4 cm.), lithograph (BP 26, DM 64, FR 216, Y 4434).

$80* *"Rainy Morning", 1939,* excell. cond., (05-15-93, Cleveland, #249), 11¾ x 8¾ in., (29.8 x 22.2 cm.), lithograph (BP 52, DM 129, FR 432, Y 8868).

MESSONIER

$88 *French Street Scene With Military Figures: Three,* (06-11-93, G.A. Key, #38), 16 x 13 in., (40.6 x 33 cm.), b/w engravings (BP 58, DM 143, FR 482, Y 9337).

MESSONIER (after)

$38 *"The Retreat From Moscow",* by J. Jauquet, (06-11-93, G.A. Key, #47), 14 x 22 in., (35.6 x 55.9 cm.), b/w engraving (BP 25, DM 62, FR 208, Y 4032).

MESSOZENIEC, J.

$25* *Giselle,* (01-31-93, Morelle/Marchan, #36), 29¹⁵⁄₁₆ x 37¹³⁄₁₆ in., (67 x 96 cm.), poster (BP 17, DM 40, FR 136, Y 3119).

METIVET, L.

$321* *Eugenie Buffet, 1895,* Imp. Charles-Verneau, good cond., (02-12-93, Cheval/Robert, #194A), 55⅛ x 21⅝ in., (140 x 55 cm.), poster (BP 226, DM 532, FR 1801, Y 38,712).

METIVET, Lucien Marie Francois French 1863-1930

$275* *Eugene Buffet,* toned, good cond., (03-12-93, Goldberg, #891B, illus.), 48 x 31 in., (121.9 x 78.7 cm.), lithograph (BP 192, DM 458, FR 1556, Y 32,410).

METLIKOVITZ

$495* *Impermeabili, Moretti,* G. Ricordi, B+ cond., edges browned, (08-06-92, Swann, #198, illus.), 54 x 38 in., (137.2 x 96.5 cm.), (BP 259, DM 731, FR 2470, Y 63,138).

METZ, C. (after)

BI *Thomas Johnson And Isaac Perrins,* by J. Grozer, pub. Nov. 5th, 1789, W. Richardson, margins, est. BP 80/120, (06-30-93, Bonhams-Chelsea, #41), plate 10¾ x 13¼ in., (27.3 x 33.7 cm.), etching w/hand-coloring.

METZAL, Olaf b. 1952

BI *Zeitungskomposition, 1985,* s., d., est. DM 300-, (09-25-92, Granier, #2941), sheet 28¾ x 20⅞ in., (73 x 53 cm.), mixed media on copper print paper.

METZGER, Charles

$867* *Standbad Lindau, 1934,* pierced plastic tape, sellotape marks, excell. cond., (02-04-93, Christie-S. Ken, #174, illus.), 31 x 43 in., (78.7 x 109.2 cm.), color lithograph (BP 605, DM 1428, FR 4841, Y 107,849).

METZKER, Ray b. 1931

$660* *Man And Woman On Train,* 1959/later, s., edit. 4/28, neg. num., Dixon Collection, (11-16-92, Butterfield, #6082, illus.), 5⅞ x 8¾ in., (149.5 x 222.6 mm.), photograph, gelatin silver print (BP 435, DM 1052, FR 3545, Y 82,079).

$3300* *Mykonos, Greece, 1979,* from series Pictus Interruptus, s., lit., (10-13-92, Christie-NY, #576, illus.), 12 x 16½ in., (30.5 x 41.9 cm.), photograph, gelatin silver print (BP 1922, DM 4834, FR 16,426, Y 400,146).

$660* *Untitled (City Whispers, Chicago), 1982,* s., edit. 3/25, Dixon Collection, (11-16-92, Butterfield, #6084, illus.), 7¾ x 12 in., (197.2 x 305.3 mm.), photograph, gelatin silver print (BP 435, DM 1052, FR 3545, Y 82,079).

$523* *Untitled (Empty Lobby), 1981,* s., edit. 5/30, Dixon Collection, (11-16-92, Butterfield, #6083, illus.), 11¾ x 17⁹⁄₁₆ in., (299 x 445.3 mm.), photograph, gelatin silver print (BP 344, DM 834, FR 2809, Y 65,042).

$1100* *Untitled (Philadelphia),* 1963/later, s., edit. 11/15, Dixon Collection, (11-16-92, Butterfield, #6081, illus.), 6⅛ x 8¾ in., (155.9 x 222.6 mm.), photograph, gelatin silver print (BP 724, DM 1754, FR 5908, Y 136,799).

METZKES, Harald b. 1929

$89* *Ein Dompteur An Einem Lowenkafig, 1977,* s., num., (12-05-92, Bassenge, #7490), 6⁵⁄₁₆ x 6⁹⁄₁₆ in., (16 x 16.6 cm.), lithograph on machinemade paper (BP 56, DM 139, FR 473, Y 11,027).

METZNER, Sheila American b. 1939

$1650* *"Ana Lucia", 1989,* s., t., d., ink edit., Dixon Collection, (11-16-92, Butterfield, #6085, illus.), 35⁵⁄₁₆ x 24³⁄₁₆ in., (896.9 x 613.9 mm.), photograph, fresson print (BP 1086, DM 2631, FR 8861, Y 205,198).

$978* *"Dianne B.", 1986,* inits., photog.'s blindstamp, s., d., annot., (05-23-93, Butterfield, #3524, illus.), 25 x 16½ in., photograph, fresson print (BP 637, DM 1599, FR 5382, Y 108,102).

$2300* *Joko Passion, 1984,* init., embossed credit; s., d., #18/20, annot., lit., (04-08-93, Christie-NY, #547, illus.), 7¾ x 11⅜ in., (19.7 x 28.9 cm.), photograph, fresson color print (BP 1508, DM 3695, FR 12,507, Y 261,008).

$3740* *Michal, Mermaid, 1980,* embossed credit, lit., (10-13-92, Christie-NY, #577, illus.), 11¾ x 7¾ in., (29.8 x 19.7 cm.), photograph, fresson print (BP 2178, DM 5479, FR 18,616, Y 453,498).

$1760* *"Rick (Dynamo Series)", 1989,* s., t., d., ink edit., Dixon Collection, (11-16-92, Butterfield, #6086, illus.), 35⁵⁄₁₆ x 24³⁄₁₆ in., (896.9 x 613.9 mm.), photograph, fresson print (BP 1159, DM 2806, FR 9452, Y 218,878).

$1150* *Stella By Starlight,* 1982, p. 1985, init., embossed credit; s., d., #46/50, annot., lit., (04-08-93, Christie-NY, #548, illus.), 11¾ x 7¾ in., (29.8 x 19.7 cm.), photograph, fresson color print (BP 754, DM 1847, FR 6253, Y 130,504).

$920* *"Vase, Bar, Sixth Floor", 1984,* inits., photog.'s blindstamp, s., d., #3/3, (05-23-93, Butterfield, #3525, illus.), 16 x 10¾ in., photograph, fresson print (BP 599, DM 1504, FR 5063, Y 101,691).

MEUNIER, Constantin Belgian 1831-1905

$246* *"Mineurs Borinage" and "Mineur", 1895: Two,* second, pen s., 1 of 100, stamp, tears, (02-24-93, Picard, #170), signature on laid (BP 172, DM 399, FR 1354, Y 28,866).

MEUNIER, Georges French 1869-1934

$275* *Escapades #1,* s., num. #1/100 in stone, p. Chaix, full margins, splits and nicks, image good cond., (03-12-93, Goldberg, #892A, illus.), 26¾ x 18¼ in., (67.9 x 46.4 cm.), color lithograph (BP 192, DM 458, FR 1556, Y 32,410).

BI *"Escapades #2",* s., #1/100 in stone, printed Chaix, full margins, tear, split and hole, image good condition, est. $4/600, (03-12-93, Goldberg, #892B, illus.), 26⅜ x 18¼ in., (66 x 46.4 cm.), color lithograph.

MEUNIER, Henri

BI *Rajah, 1897,* s. in stone, p. J.E. Goossens, Imprimerie Chaix, pub. blindstamp, Les Maitres de l'Affiche, margins, good cond., staining and on verso, tape, surface, est. $14/1600, (09-21-92, Butterfield, #828), 7¾ x 10⅛ in., (197.2 x 257.6 mm.), lithograph in colors on wove.

MEUNIER, Henry

BI *Waux Hall, 1897,* Lith. J.E. Goussens, B+ cond., fold marks, est. $8/1,200, (08-06-92, Swann, #197, illus.), 34½ x 23½ in., (87.6 x 59.7 cm.), .

MEURICE, Jean Michel

$64* *Deuxieme Element, 1978,* s., t., d., #34/190, full sheet p. to edges, good cond., (05-27-93, Sotheby-Amstrdm, #455), sh 18⅞ x 25¹¹⁄₁₆ in., (480 x 652 mm.), colored lithograph on wove (BP 41, DM 103, FR 346, Y 6861, G 115).

$64* *Le Peintre...,* s., i. E.A., full sheet p. to edges, good cond., (05-27-93, Sotheby-Amstrdm, #457), sh 21⁹⁄₁₆ x 30¾ in., (547 x 781 mm.), colored lithograph on sturdy wove (BP 41, DM 103, FR 346, Y 6861, G 115).

$64* *Premiere Element, 1978,* s., t., d., #124/190, full sheet p. to edges, good cond., (05-27-93, Sotheby-Amstrdm, #454), sh 18⅞ x 25¹¹⁄₁₆ in., (480 x 652 mm.), colored lithograph on wove (BP 41, DM 103, FR 346, Y 6861, G 115).

$64* *Troisieme Element, 1978,* s., t., d,. #124/190, full sheet p. to edges, good cond., (05-27-93, Sotheby-Amstrdm, #456), sh 18⅞ x 25¹¹⁄₁₆ in., (480 x 652 mm.), colored lithograph on wvoe (BP 41, DM 103, FR 346, Y 6861, G 115).

MEYER, Camille

$1405* *Huitres Cottat Et Porcher Ostreiculteurs A Locmariaquer (Morbihan),* Asnieres, La lithographie nouvelle, cond. A-, (06-11-93, Boisgirard, #115), 51³⁄₁₆ x 36⅝ in., (130 x 93 cm.), poster (BP 923, DM 2283, FR 7699, Y 149,072).

MEYER, Felix 1653-1713

$578* *Felsige Flusslandschaft Mit Zwei Wanderern, 1676,* artist's proof, unique, (12-04-92, Bassenge, #6304, illus.), 6⁵⁄₁₆ x 4⁹⁄₁₆ in., (16.1 x 11.6 cm.), etching (BP 371, DM 921, FR 3123, Y 72,160).

MEYER, Friedrich ac. 1802-1834, d. 1837

$886* *Die Saubachfalle Im Berner Oberland,* (06-08-93, Karl/Faber, #360), approx. 7⁵⁄₁₆ x 10¹³⁄₁₆ in., (18.5 x 27.5 cm.), watercolored aquatint/etching on board (BP 582, DM 1438, FR 4842, Y 94,105).

MEYER, Henry

$550* *Magpie And Others: Fifteen,* good cond., foxing, staining, (10-17-92, Weschler, #62, illus.), each 15 x 10½ in., (38 x 26.6 cm.), colored lithograph (BP 337, DM 819, FR 2776, Y 65,987).

BI *The Proposal,* after George Henry Harlow, margins, foxing, est. BP 60/80, (11-19-92, Bonhams-Chelsea, #88), plate 20½ x 15 in., (52.1 x 38.1 cm.), stipple engraving w/hand coloring.

MEYER, Johannes (the younger) 1655-1712

$1300* *Die Zwolf Monate (Nagler 14): Twelve,* (12-04-92, Bassenge, #6305, illus.), etching (BP 834, DM 2070, FR 7023, Y 162,297).

MEYER, Willi

$341* *"Willi Meyer Linolschnitte": Six,* pub. Galerie Brusberg, s., num., (12-01-92, Karl/Faber, #1011), color linocut on wove (BP 225, DM 544, FR 1852, Y 42,455).

MEYEROWITZ, Joel b. 1938

BI *French Portfolio: Twelve, 1980,* Grapestake Gallery, each s., num. 10/96 in ink, #10/96 edit., est. $6/8,000, (10-13-92, Christie-NY, #578, illus.), each 12¾ x 18½ in., (32.4 x 47 cm.), photograph, dye transfer prints.

MEYEROWITZ, Joel American contemporary

$165* *The Arch Riverboats,* edit. size 100, pub. Greenberg Gallery, St. Louis, 1979/82, (09-21-92, Selkirk, #336), 16 x 20 in., (40.6 x 50.8 cm.), dye transfer print (BP 97, DM 245, FR 838, Y 20,393).

$220* *The Arch, Pink Leg,* edit. size 100, pub. Greenberg Gallery, St. Louis, 1979/82, (09-21-92, Selkirk, #337), 16 x 20 in., (40.6 x 50.8 cm.), dye transfer print (BP 129, DM 326, FR 1117, Y 27,191).

MEYERS, Jerome American 1867-1940

BI *"Old Junk Shop At 43rd And 11th Ave.", c. 1930-35,* s., t., good cond., est. $175-225, (10-31-92, Cleveland, #189, illus.), 6½ x 10⅛ in., (16.5 x 25.7 cm.), etching.

MEYRON, Charles

$722* *La Galerie Notre Dame (L. Delteil, 26), 1853,* fourth state of five, large margins, (04-02-93, Picard, #152), 11 x 6¹¹⁄₁₆ in., (28 x 17 cm.), etching (BP 476, DM 1160, FR 3941, Y 82,204).

$660* *Le Pont Au Change (L.D., 34),* fifth state of nine, good margins, (04-02-93, Picard, #153), 6⅛ x 13¹⁄₁₆ in., (15.5 x 33.2 cm.), etching in bistre (BP 435, DM 1061, FR 3603, Y 75,145).

MICH

BI *Le Fakyr,* plate s., lined, est. $5/700, (03-25-93, Christie-E, #206), 62 x 47 in., (157.5 x 119.4 cm.), color lithograph.

$231* *Theatre Du Vaudeville: Monsieur Dumollet, Opera En 3 Actes,* good cond., (11-19-92, Ribeyre/Baron, #180), 61¹³⁄₁₆ x 46¹⁄₁₆ in., (157 x 117 cm.), poster (BP 152, DM 368, FR 1241, Y 28,728).

MICH (Michel LIEBEAUX) 1881-1923

$104* *Elle Grimpe Tout! La Bicyclette J.B. Louvet, c. 1925,* cond. A, (03-16-93, Boisgirard, #155), 44½ x 31⅛ in., (113 x 79 cm.), poster (BP 72, DM 173, FR 588, Y 12,161).

MICHALS, Duane American b. 1932

$1210* *Bride Holding Bouquet,* photog.'s sig., 1970s, (04-07-93, Swann, #516, illus.), 8 x 10 in., photograph, silver print (BP 800, DM 1957, FR 6623, Y 137,469).

$4600* *The Candy Kiss: Four,* a sequence, 1970s, first t.; second and third num.; fourth ink s., num., (04-08-93, Christie-NY, #499, illus.), each 3¼ x 5 in., (8.3 x 12.7 cm.), photograph, gelatin silver print (BP 3016, DM 7390, FR 25,014, Y 522,015).

$770* *"Homage To Cavafy (I Could...)", 1978,* s., edit. 24/25, ink captioned, Dixon Collection, (11-16-92, Butterfield, #6087, illus.), 3⅜ x 5⅛ in., (85.9 x 130.4 mm.), photograph, gelatin silver print (BP 507, DM 1228, FR 4135, Y 95,759).

$1540* *"Homage To Cavafy (The Son Returned Home...)", 1978,* s., edit. 24/25, ink captioned, Dixon Collection, (11-16-92, Butterfield, #6088, illus.), 3⅜ x 5 in., (85.9 x 127.2 mm.), photograph, gelatin silver print (BP 1014, DM 2455, FR 8271, Y 191,518).

$4400* *The Pleasures Of The Glove: Fourteen, 1974,* 1st t., 13 num., annot., last s., num. 9/25 in ink in margin, lit., (10-13-92, Christie-NY, #580, illus.), each 3¼ x 5 in., (8.3 x 12.7 cm.), photograph, gelatin silver prints (BP 2563, DM 6446, FR 21,901, Y 533,527).

$3185* *Portrait Of Andy Warhol, 1973: Three,* ink s., d., t., #2/25, (11-12-92, Lempertz, #174, illus.), each 3¹⁵⁄₁₆ x 5⅝ in., (10 x 14.3 cm.), photograph, gelatin silver print (BP 2036, DM 5006, FR 17,059, Y 394,037).

$772* *Restoration Of Worth Dress, c. 1982,* Jocelyn Kargere Coll., (10-29-92, Christie-London, #192, illus.), image 13⅝ x 9⅜ in., (34.6 x 23.5 cm.), photograph, gelatin silver print (BP 495, DM 1188, FR 4029, Y 95,627).

$715* *Study Of The Artist Rene Magritte, 1978,* photog.'s sig., notations VI/VII, (04-07-93, Swann, #517, illus.), 6½ x 10 in., photograph, silver print (BP 473, DM 1156, FR 3914, Y 81,232).

$5750* *Take One And See Mt. Fujiyama: Fifteen,* a sequence, 1970s, first t., annot; others num.; each annot. but one; last ink s., #2/25, (04-08-93, Christie-NY, #500, illus.), each approx. 3½ x 5⅛ in., (8.9 x 13 cm.), photograph, gelatin silver print (BP 3770, DM 9237, FR 31,267, Y 652,519).

$770* *"Violent Men",c. 1984,* s., t., ink edit. 6/25, Dixon Collection, (11-16-92, Butterfield, #6089, illus.), 8⅝ x 13⅛ in., (219.5 x 334 mm.), photograph, gelatin silver print (BP 507, DM 1228, FR 4135, Y 95,759).

$440* *"Violent Women" (Sleep And Dream, p. 27), c. 1984,* s., t., ink edit. 6/25, Dixon Collection, (11-16-92, Butterfield, #6090, illus.), 8⅞ x 13 in., (225.8 x 330.8 mm.), photograph, gelatin silver print (BP 290, DM 702, FR 2363, Y 54,720).

BI *Warren Beatty and Untitled (Woman With Skirt Lifted): Two, c. 1965,* one s., t., d., credit stamp, est. $2/2,500, (10-13-92, Christie-NY, #579, illus.), one 5⅞ x 7⅛ in., (14.9 x 18.1 cm.), other 3⅝ x 5¼ in., (14.9 x 18.1 cm.), photograph, gelatin silver prints.

$3641* *The Young Girl's Dream, 1970-1973: Five,* ink s., t., #2/25, (11-12-92, Lempertz, #173, illus.), each 4 x 5½ in., (10.2 x 14 cm.), photograph, gelatin silver print (BP 2328, DM 5722, FR 19,502, Y 450,452).

MICHAUD, R.

$1038* *De Megeve A Rochebrune. "Vers De Magnifiques Champs De Ski Par Le Telepherique",* very good cond., (03-15-93, Arcole, #50, illus.), 38⅜ x 31⅛ in., (97.5 x 79 cm.), (BP 723, DM 1724, FR 5861, Y 122,957).

MICHAUX, Henri Belgian b. 1899

$211* *Composition, 1976,* s. Michaux, 41/100, from Pour Jorn portfolio, (09-30-92, Kunsthallen, #204), lithograph (BP 119, DM 299, FR 1012, Y 25,321, DK 1150).

$389* *Composition, 1977,* s., #20/60, (06-12-93, Hauswedell/Nolt, #302), 9⅝ x 6¹¹⁄₁₆ in., (24.5 x 17 cm.), lithograph on Arches (BP 255, DM 633, FR 2128, Y 40,934).

BI *Compositions, 1974: Three Plates,* s., num. 20/60, XXIV/XXX and 57/100, blindstamp, surface dirt, est. BP 900/1,200, (12-01-92, Christie-London, #622), L. and smaller 9¹³⁄₁₆ x 7¹⁄₁₆ in., (250 x 180 mm.), lithographs on Arches.

$479* *Par La Voice Des Rythmes,* s., num., (05-26-93, Dorling, #2863), 7½ x 9¹³⁄₁₆ in., (19 x 25 cm.), lithograph on thick wove (BP 310, DM 782, FR 2630, Y 52,043).

BI *Voie Des Rythmes,* #74/90, s., est. SF 700/750, (04-21-93, Germann, #637), 14¹⁵⁄₁₆ x 12¹³⁄₁₆ in., (380 x 325 mm.), lithograph.

MICHEL, Geo. (after)

BI *Engagez-Vous Dans La Marine. "Vous Verrez Du Pays, Vous Apprendez UnMetier, Vous Gagnerez Une Retraite...",* good cond., (03-13-93, Laurin, #13, illus.), 46⅞ x 31¹¹⁄₁₆ in., (119 x 80.5 cm.), .

MICHEL, Jean Baptiste French 1748-1804

BI *"Venus And Cupid", 1779,* after Carlo Maratta, pub. John Boydell, margins, est. $1/150, (10-31-92, Cleveland, #17), 9¼ x 10⅞ in., (23.5 x 27.6 cm.), engraving.

MICHEL, P.

$1077* *Barcelonnette. Sports D'Hiver, 1928,* very good cond., (03-15-93, Arcole, #100), 41⁵⁄₁₆ x 29½ in., (105 x 75 cm.), (BP 750, DM 1789, FR 6081, Y 127,576).

MICHEL, Robert 1897-1983

BI *"Mez", 1919/20,* s., d., i. 20 sheet: 1, prov., est. DM 4000, (12-01-92, Karl/Faber, #1016, illus.), 18⅛ x 14¾ in., (46 x 37.5 cm.), woodcut on hand-made.

BI *Portfolio - "Yale", 1921-25/1965: Four,* s., Bl. 1-4 from the series Yale Versuchplatte, Yale Horizontalplatte, Yale Vertikalplatte, lit., est. DM 5000, (12-01-92, Karl/Faber, #1020, illus.), 15¹⁵⁄₁₆ x 14⁹⁄₁₆ in., (40.5 x 37 cm.), line etching on wove.

MICHELANGELO (after)

$162* *Details From The Sistine Chapel: Set Of Nine,* (10-15-92, Bonhams-Chelsea, #157), image 14½ x 20½ in., (36.8 x 52.1 cm.), color reproductions laid down on board (BP 99, DM 241, FR 818, Y 19,436).

MICHELE

$161* *Chocolat La Faveur. Montpellier, 1895,* Societe Generale De L'Imprimerie, good cond., (02-12-93, Cheval/Robert, #67), 59¹⁄₁₆ x 39⅜ in., (150 x 100 cm.), poster (BP 113, DM 267, FR 903, Y 19,416).

MICHELE, A.

$40* *Coquelicot. Opera Comique (...) Musique De Louis Varney, 1882,* cond. B, (03-16-93, Boisgirard, #156), 31¹¹⁄₁₆ x 23⅝ in., (80.5 x 60 cm.), poster (BP 28, DM 67, FR 226, Y 4677).

MICHL, Ferdinand Czecholslovakian b. 1877

$33* *Three Composers: Three,* each s., annot. Orig. Radierung, (09-20-92, Hindman, #807), each 8⅛ x 6½ in., (20.6 x 16.5 cm.), drypoints w/roulette (BP 19, DM 49, FR 168, Y 4079).

$33* *Oriental Scenes: Three,* s., t., very poor cond., (10-31-92, Cleveland, #318), 11 x 8¾ in., (27.9 x 22.2 cm.), etchings in color (BP 21, DM 51, FR 172, Y 4088).

MICHONZE, Gregoire 1902-1982

$73* *"Un Village En Galilee",* E.A., s., (01-28-93, Pescheteau, #215), 7½ x 11⁷⁄₁₆ in., (19 x 29 cm.), etching in bistre on wove (BP 48, DM 116, FR 391, Y 9064).

MIDDENDORF, Helmut German b. 1953

$860* *Grosser Stadtkopf, 1986,* s., #35/60, (05-27-93, Lempertz, #904), 39⁷⁄₁₆ x 39½ in., (100.2 x 100.3 cm.), color serigraph (BP 551, DM 1380, FR 4651, Y 92,196).

MIDDLETON, E.C.

$297* *"Washington", "Lincoln" and "Grant": Three,* all orig. labels E.C. Middleton, (03-13-93, Garth, #464, illus.), 21¾ x 18¾ in., (55.2 x 47.6 cm.), oil tinted lithographs on canvas (BP 207, DM 494, FR 1681, Y 35,003).

MIDDLETON, Sam b. 1927

$248* *Sun Dance, 1964,* s., t., d., #67/100, full margins, good cond.?, (12-09-92, Sotheby-Amstrdm, #612), 14⅜ x 10¼ in., (365 x 260 mm.), color lithograph on wove (BP 158, DM 389, FR 1328, Y 30,750, G 437).

MIDDLETON STROBRIDGE & CO., Lithographers

$330* *Encampent Views, Forts and A Siege, c. 1863: Five,* (12-02-92, Christie-E, #238, illus.), lithograph w/hand-coloring (BP 213, DM 519, FR 1771, Y 41,060).

MIEHLE, John
BI *Norma Talmadge, Autographed Portrait,* n.d. (1930s), photog.'s blindstamp, ink s., i., (12-17-92, Christie-S. Ken, #79), 13½ x 10½ in., (34.3 x 26.7 cm.), photograph, gelatin silver print on textured paper.

MIETH, Hansel b. 1909
$6600* *Mad Monkey, 1939,* s., d. by photog. in ink, (10-15-92, Sotheby-NY, #216, illus.), 13¼ x 10⅜ in., (33.7 x 26.4 cm.), photograph, gelatin silver print (BP 4039, DM 9824, FR 33,317, Y 791,842).

MIGDOLL, Herbert
$31* *Eliot Feld Ballet Christine Sarry Et Mikhael Baryshnikov, 1978,* (01-31-93, Morelle/Marchan, #34), 23⅝ x 34⅝ in., (60 x 88 cm.), poster (BP 21, DM 50, FR 169, Y 3867).
$114* *Joffrey Ballet City Center Astarte,* (01-31-93, Morelle/Marchan, #35), 29⅛ x 43 5/16 in., (74 x 110 cm.), poster (BP 77, DM 184, FR 621, Y 14,222).

MIGNON, Jean ac. 1537-1544
BI *Frauen Im Bade (B. 99, Zerner J.M. 46), c. 1544,* est. DM 5000, (06-04-93, Bassenge, #5255, illus.), 14 13/16 x 19 5/16 in., (37.6 x 49 cm.), engraving.

MIGNON, Jean ac. 1544
$19,978* *Bataille Sous Troie, (B. XVI, p. 414, no. 96, anonyme; Herbet, p. 34, no. 75, Davant; Zerner JM 42), c. 1545,* after Luca Penni, thread margins or trimmed, pencil (?) stroke in center, excellent cond., (12-01-92, Christie-London, #21, illus.), P. 12 13/16 x 17⅝ in., (325 x 447 mm.), etching in brownish-black, delicate tone, laid (BP 13,200, DM 31,843, FR 108,517, Y 2,487,301).
BI *Jesus-Christ Succombant Sous Le Poids De La Croix (B. XVI, p. 385, no. 23, anonyme; Herbet, p. 184, no. 6, Mignon; Zerner JM 29), 1544,* after Luca Penni, w/tone, margins, tear, surface loss, corner made-up, old pen and ink num., very good cond., laid, est. BP 12/16,000, (12-01-92, Christie-London, #23, illus.), plate 14½ x 19 5/16 in., (368 x 491 mm.), etching.
BI *Le Perfide Sinon Introduit Par Les Bergers Dans Le Camp Des Troyens,(B. XVI, p. 394, no.46, anonyme; Herbert, p. 185, Mignon; Zerner JM 43), c. 1544,* after Luca Penni, trimmed on or just inside platemark, scratches in image, very good cond., est. BP 8,5/10,000, (12-01-92, Christie-London, #22, illus.), S. 12⅝ x 17 5/16 in., (320 x 439 mm.), etching w/engraving.

MIGNOT, Victor 1872-1944
$1992* *La Maison N'A Pas De Succursale,* rare, before 1897, lit., (12-05-92, Bassenge, #7611, illus.), 33 15/16 x 24 in., (86.2 x 61 cm.), color lithograph (BP 1247, DM 3106, FR 10,584, Y 246,810).

MIKKIGAK, Ohotok b. 1936
$299* *Eskimo Fox Trapper,* s., t., d. 1961, #34/50, stamped w/ artist co-op, "namatuk" chop, (11-30-92, Ritchie, #77, illus.), 29¾ x 24¼ in., (75.5 x 61.6 cm.), color stonecut on japon (BP 197, DM 476, FR 1617, Y 37,212, C$ 385).

MIKPIGAK, Annie 1900-1984
$108* *E9-1389. Povungnituk. Walrus,* i. in syllabics, d. 1964, #29/30, t. label, (06-07-93, Ritchie, #72, illus.), image 9½ x 13 15/16 in., (24.1 x 35.5 cm.), sh 13 15/16 x 18¾ in., (24.1 x 35.5 cm.), color stone cut (BP 71, DM 175, FR 590, Y 11,585, C$ 138).

MILLAIS, J.E. (after)
$26 *"Little Mrs Gamp",* (02-05-93, G.A. Key, #5), 27 x 18 in., (68.6 x 45.7 cm.), chromolithograph (BP 18, DM 43, FR 146, Y 3235).

MILLAIS, Sir John Everett (after)
$76* *"A Courting Couple By A Stream", 1882,* by J. Oldham Barlow, pub. Thomas Agnew and Sons, blindstamp, margins, (11-12-92, Bonhams-Chelsea, #23), plate 31 x 23 in., (78.7 x 58.4 cm.), hand-colored mezzotint (BP 50, DM 120, FR 406, Y 9423).
$129 *"The Huguenot",* engraved by Thomas Oldham Barlow, d. 1857, (04-16-93, G.A. Key, #51), 22 x 16 in., (55.9 x 40.6 cm.), b/w engraving (BP 85, DM 208, FR 704, Y 14,506).
$118* *Little Flower Girl, 1885,* s., pub. Dowdeswell and Dowdeswell, (08-20-92, Bonhams-Chelsea, #56), image 19¾ x 14 in., (50.2 x 35.6 cm.), photogravure, printed on silk (BP 61, DM 171, FR 580, Y 14,901).

MILLAR, Fred
BI *Lady Hamilton,* after Sir Joshua Reynolds, #183/220, s., i., margins, est. BP 40/60, (11-19-92, Bonhams-Chelsea, #33), plate 12 x 10 in., (30.5 x 25.4 cm.), color mezzotint.

MILLARES, Manolo Spanish 1926-1972
$440* *Untitled Abstract Composition, c. 1965,* num., s., time stain, (05-27-93, Swann, #182, illus.), sh 22 x 29⅜ in., (55.9 x 74.6 cm.), intaglio etching (BP 282, DM 706, FR 2380, Y 47,170).

MILLEA, Tom
$575* *"Point Lobos", 1981 and "The Wave", 1985: Two,* s., t., d., t. w/notations, (05-23-93, Butterfield, #3526), each approx. 8 x 12 in., photograph, platinum/palladium print (BP 374, DM 940, FR 3165, Y 63,557).
$403* *"Redding",* 1969, p. c. 1985, s., t., d., (05-23-93, Butterfield, #3528), 3¾ x 4¾ in., photograph, palladium print (BP 262, DM 659, FR 2218, Y 44,545).
$385* *"Redding, Connecticut",* 1968/c. 1980, s., (11-16-92, Butterfield, #6091, illus.), 3¾ x 4⅝ in., (95.4 x 117.7 mm.), photograph, palladium print (BP 253, DM 614, FR 2068, Y 47,880).
$518* *Selected Works, Carmel Valley, 1979, 1980: Two,* s., t., d., (05-23-93, Butterfield, #3527, illus.), one 8¼ x 7½ in., other 9⅝ x 7½ in., photograph, platinum/palladium print (BP 337, DM 847, FR 2851, Y 57,257).

MILLER, Arthur
$110* *Administration Center, Los Angeles,* s., margins, good cond., mat & light-staining, creases, tears, (02-24-93, Butterfield, #2855), 9 x 14¾ in., (229 x 375 mm.), etching on hand-made F.J. Head & Co. laid (BP 77, DM 179, FR 605, Y 12,908).

MILLER, Frances St. Clair
$20* *"Cherry Path",* s., t., num., excell. cond., (05-15-93, Cleveland, #482), 15 x 21 in., (38.1 x 53.3 cm.), mezzotint (BP 13, DM 32, FR 108, Y 2217).
$10* *"Spring On River Wye I",* s., t., #53/150, excell. cond., (05-15-93, Cleveland, #483), 17¾ x 23⅜ in., (45.1 x 59.4 cm.), mezzotint and aquatint (BP 7, DM 16, FR 54, Y 1109).

MILLER, Henry
BI *Couple,* s., #32/100, blindstamp publisher, margins, very good cond.?, est. $150/250, (05-19-93, Butterfield, #2264), 16½ x 21½ in., (419 x 546 mm.), offset lithograph in colors on wove.

MILLER, Henry 1891-1980
$664* *Figurliche Szene Mit Weiblichen Akten,* s., num., (12-05-92, Bassenge, #7494, illus.), 6 3/16 x 8⅛ in., (15.7 x 20.7 cm.), etching on copper print paper (BP 416, DM 1035, FR 3528, Y 82,270).

MILLER, Henry American 20th cent.
$275* *"Insomnia Or The Devil At Large": Twelve,* each s., d. Henry Miller 10/15/70, (09-25-92, Wolf, #50), 12 x 16 in., (30.5 x 40.6 cm.), lithographs in color (BP 161, DM 408, FR 1378, Y 33,193).

MILLER, J.C.
$184* *Lower Yarra,* s. J.C. Miller, i., 21.5x29.7 cm., (08-11-92, L. Joel, #106G), photograph (BP 95, DM 272, FR 918, Y 22,980, A$ 247).

MILLER, Jan
$7206* *The Blind Fortune Distributing Her Presents (B. III, 33; Holl. 71), 1590,* after Cornelisz van Haarlem, 2nd state of 4, margins, trimmed irregularly, defects, staining, scratches, foxing, discoloration, wormholes, defects,laid down, (06-30-93, Sotheby-London, #169, illus.), 19½ x 35½ in., (495 x 902 mm.), engraving on 2 sheets of paper (BP 4830, DM 12,291, FR 41,461, Y 772,099).

MILLER, John ("Hack")
$660* *St. Valentine's Day Massacre, 1929,* handwritten notations, news agency handstamp, (04-07-93, Swann, #335, illus.),

13¼ x 9¾ in., photograph, silver print (BP 436, DM 1067, FR 3612, Y 74,983).

MILLER, Ken

$220* *"Andrew", 1985,* s., t., d., edit. 2/25, Dixon Collection, (11-16-92, Butterfield, #6092, illus.), 17³⁄₁₆ x 13⅜ in., (435.8 x 340.3 mm.), photograph, gelatin silver print (BP 145, DM 351, FR 1182, Y 27,360).

MILLER, Kenneth Hayes American 1876-1952

BI *"Bather", 1919,* s., d. Hayes Miller/19 in plate, t. on label, good cond., marks, annot., est. $3/500, (03-12-93, Skinner, #11, illus.), 8⅞ x 4¾ in., (22.5 x 12.1 cm.), etching on wove.

BI *"Bather", c. 1922,* s., annot., AAA catalog No. 20, very fine cond., est. $150-200, (10-31-92, Cleveland, #190), 8 x 6 in., (20.3 x 15.2 cm.), etching.

BI *"Couplet", c. 1923,* s., AAA catalog No. 21, very good cond., est. $150-200, (10-31-92, Cleveland, #192), 4⅝ x 4 in., (11.7 x 10.2 cm.), etching.

BI *"Head", c. 1923,* AAA catalog No. 70, marks verso, est. $150-200, (10-31-92, Cleveland, #191), 7⅞ x 5⅞ in., (20 x 14.9 cm.), etching.

$431* *Leaving The Shop,* s., margins, good cond., glue staining, rubbed areas, handling crease, surface soiling, (05-19-93, Butterfield, #2006), 8⅞ x 9¹⁵⁄₁₆ in., (225 x 252 mm.), etching on wove (BP 280, DM 701, FR 2360, Y 47,714).

$83* *Play,* s., foil margin, good cond., pub. New Republic, 1924, (11-12-92, Freemn/Fine Art, #151), plate 4¾ x 6 in., (12.1 x 15.2 cm.), etching on wove paper (BP 55, DM 132, FR 444, Y 10,291).

$412* *"Play", "Sun Bathers", "Washing Up" and "Three Ages Of Women", c. 1919-30: Group Of Four,* in 1924 New Republic magazine promo. Six American Etchings, s., (12-08-92, Swann, #211), etching (BP 258, DM 641, FR 2187, Y 51,066).

$605* *"Three Women Shoppers", "Shoppers", "The Dress Shop", "Woman With Umbrella" and "Two Women With Umbrellas Conversing", c. 1920-36: Five,* s., (05-27-93, Swann, #184, illus.), etchings (BP 387, DM 971, FR 3272, Y 64,858).

MILLER, Lee

BI *Selected Works: Portraits Of Picasso: Five,* 1937-56, p.l., photog.'s stamp, s. by artist's son Anthony Penrose, #3/30, est. $1,8/2,200, (05-23-93, Butterfield, #3529, illus.), from 10 x 10 in., to 11 x 7½ in., photograph, gelatin silver print.

$920* *Selected Works: Portraits Of Picasso: Five,* 1958-62, p.l., photog.'s stamp, s. by authenticator Anthony Penrose,#3/30, est. $1,8/2,200, (05-23-93, Butterfield, #3530, illus.), from 7 x 10 in., to 10½ x 10 in., photograph, gelatin silver print (BP 599, DM 1504, FR 5063, Y 101,691).

$920* *Selected Works: Portraits Of Picasso: Five,* 1937-59, p.l., photog.'s stamp, s. by authenticator Anthony Penrose,#3/30, est. $1,8/2,200, (05-23-93, Butterfield, #3531, illus.), from 6½ x 9¼ in., to 10 x 10 in., photograph, gelatin silver print (BP 599, DM 1504, FR 5063, Y 101,691).

BI *Selected Works: Portraits Of Picasso: Four,* 1950, p.l., photog.'s stamp, s. by authenticator Anthony Penrose, #3/30, est. $1,8/2,200, (05-23-93, Butterfield, #3532, illus.), from 6⅝ x 10 in., to 10⅝ x 10 in., photograph, gelatin silver print.

MILLER, Lilian

$385* *"East Mountain-Kyoto-Sunrise" and "East Mountain-Kyoto-Dusk": Two,* each s. in ink, t., small margins, good cond., foxing, buckling, prop. Print Corner, (02-24-93, Butterfield, #2854), 10⅞ x 9¾ in., (276 x 248 mm.), woodcut in colors on Japan (BP 268, DM 625, FR 2119, Y 45,177).

$358* *"Hong Kong Junk", "Sunrise and Festival Of Lanterns, Nara, Japan", 1928 & 1934: Two,* each s., d. in ink, 1st w/inkstamp, 2nd t., w/artist's monogram, small margins, good cond., staining, pencil notations, prop. Print Corner Coll. ofElizabeth and Charles Whitmore, (02-24-93, Butterfield, #2851), one 13⅝ x 9¹¹⁄₁₆ in., (346 x 246 mm.), other 14⁷⁄₁₆ x 6 in., (346 x 246 mm.), woodcut in colors on Japan (BP 250, DM 581, FR 1970, Y 42,009).

$460* *"Japanese Dwarf Berry Tree", "Japanese Dwarf Plum Tree" and "A Japanese Dwarf Plum Tree" (B, 1928): Three,* first two s., d., third s., d., #I/12, each w/inkstamp, margins, goodcond., stain, pin hole, notations, (05-19-93, Butterfield, #2012), smallest 11⅞ x 8⅜ in., (302 x 213 mm.), largest 14⅝ x 9⁹⁄₁₆ in., (302 x 213 mm.), woodcut in colors on Japan (BP 299, DM 748, FR 2519, Y 50,924).

$275* *"Lantern On A Hill, Nikko, Autumn" and "Lantern On A Hill, Nikko, Spring ", 1934: Two,* each s., d., t., small margins, good cond., printing creases, paper tape, foxing, prop. Print Corner, (02-24-93, Butterfield, #2852), each 10 x 10 in., (254 x 254 mm.), woodcut in colors on laid Japan (BP 192, DM 446, FR 1513, Y 32,269).

$460* *"Lantern On A Hill, Nikko, Autumn, 1934", "Lantern On A Hill, Nikko,Spring, 1934" and "The Nikko Gateway, Japan, 1928": Three,* s., d., first two t., third t. inkstamp, mono., margins, good cond.,pin holes, third w/pin hole, pencil notations, (05-19-93, Butterfield, #2011), smallest 9¹⁵⁄₁₆ x 9¹⁵⁄₁₆ in., (252 x 252 mm.), largest 14⅝ x 9½ in., (252 x 252 mm.), woodcut in colors on Japan (BP 299, DM 748, FR 2519, Y 50,924).

$468* *"Moonlight On Mt. Fuji" and "Pagoda At Dusk": Two,* each s. in ink, t., annot. Edition B, mono. stamp, small margins, good cond., surface scuffing, pencil notation, prop. Print Corner, (02-24-93, Butterfield, #2853), one 9⁹⁄₁₆ x 14⅞ in., (243 x 378 mm.), other 5⅞ x 13¹⁄₁₆ in., (243 x 378 mm.), woodcut in colors on Japan (BP 326, DM 760, FR 2576, Y 54,917).

$288* *"Mountain Lake At Dawn" and "Moonlight On Mount Fuji": Two,* each s., t., margins, good cond., pencil notations, (05-19-93, Butterfield, #2013), one 11¹³⁄₁₆ x 17⅜ in., (300 x 441 mm.), the other 9½ x 14⅜ in., (300 x 441 mm.), woodcut in colors on Japan (BP 187, DM 468, FR 1577, Y 31,883).

BI *"Tokyo Coolie Boy A" and "Tokyo Coolie Boy B", 1920, 1928: Two,* each s., d., #No. 217, No.12, second w/inkstamp, artist's mono. stamp, small margins, good cond., mat staining, surface scuffing, stray printing ink, notations, est. $3/500, (05-19-93, Butterfield, #2008), each 10⅞ x 4⅝ in., (276 x 121 mm.), woodcut in colors on Japan.

MILLER, Lowell

$1430* *Blue Crystal, 1950,* s., t. in ink on mount, labels, stamps, prov., (10-13-92, Christie-NY, #473, illus.), 16½ x 13⅝ in., (41.9 x 34.6 cm.), photograph, gelatin silver print (BP 833, DM 2095, FR 7118, Y 173,396).

MILLER, Paul Continental 19th/20th cent.

$220* *Art Nouveau Designs: Three,* (03-14-93, Hindman, #247), 8⅜ x 14½ in., (21.3 x 36.8 cm.), color lithographs (BP 153, DM 366, FR 1245, Y 25,928).

MILLER, Robert

$579* *To Visit Britain's Landmarks, Devil's Elbow, Braemar, 1936,* p. Waterlow and Sons, ref. #464, cond. 1, (10-13-92, Phillips-London, #108), 29¹⁵⁄₁₆ x 45¹⁄₁₆ in., (76 x 114.4 cm.), color lithograph (BP 337, DM 848, FR 2882, Y 70,207).

MILLER, Vernon

$715* *Orchids, 1990,* s., d., edit. 6/15, num. 11078, Dixon Collection, (11-16-92, Butterfield, #6093), 13⅜ x 10½ in., (340.3 x 267.2 mm.), photograph, platinum print (BP 471, DM 1140, FR 3840, Y 88,919).

MILLER, William (after)

$362* *King Henry The Sixth, Act IV, Scene V, 1797,* by Michel and Leney, pub. J. and J. Boydell, margins, (08-20-92, Bonhams-Chelsea, #19), plate 19¾ x 25 in., (50.2 x 63.5 cm.), stipple engraving, verre eglomise mount (BP 187, DM 524, FR 1779, Y 45,713).

BI *You Can't Spell, 1801,* by R. Cooper, pub. G. Testolini, replaced corner, repaired tear through image, thread margins, defects, est. BP 1/150, (11-30-92, Phillips-London, #161), sheet 20¼ x 14⅛ in., (514 x 359 mm.), color stipple engraving, finished by hand, on wove.

MILLER, William, Publisher

$550* *Seashells, 1810: Set Of Six,* heavy mat burn, notations, discoloration, foxing, hinged to mat, (12-04-92, Doyle,

#55), 12½ x 9 in., (318 x 229 mm.), aquatint (BP 353, DM 876, FR 2971, Y 68,664).

MILLET, Clarence American 1897-1959

$440* *"St. Louis Cathedral" and "Pirate's Alley": A Pair,* s., t., (05-22-93, Neal, #606, illus.), each image 6½ x 5½ in., (16.5 x 14 cm.), hand-colored linocut (BP 285, DM 715, FR 2407, Y 48,512).

$44* *St. Loun Cathedral, Jackson Square, New Orleans,* s. Clarence Millet, (06-26-93, Wolf, #977), 10 x 8 in., (25.4 x 20.3 cm.), woodblock (BP 29, DM 75, FR 252, Y 4668).

MILLET, Jean Francois French 1814-1875

$1898* *La Baratteuse (L. Delteil 10), 1855,* large margins, (06-11-93, Picard, #138), 6½ x 4 3/16 in., (165 x 107 mm.), etching on chine fixe (BP 1247, DM 3085, FR 10,400, Y 201,379).

$3450* *Les Becheurs (D., M. 13), c. 1855-56,* 4th (final) state, margins, good cond., foxing, scrape, rubbed spot, (02-11-93, Sotheby-NY, #180, illus.), 9¼ x 13¼ in., (235 x 336 mm.), sheet 9¾ x 13 9/16 in., (235 x 336 mm.), etching on laid (BP 2434, DM 5715, FR 19,339, Y 415,913).

$5225* *Les Becheurs (Delteil, Melot 13), c. 1855-56,* fourth (final) state, good cond., folds, thin spot, (11-05-92, Sotheby-NY, #255), 9¼ x 13⅛ in., (235 x 333 mm.), etching p. in brown on thin laid (BP 3398, DM 8263, FR 27,956, Y 641,026).

$4996* *Les Becheurs (L.D. 13),* definitive state, good margins, (06-11-93, Picard, #139), 8 13/16 x 12 13/16 in., (224 x 325 mm.), etching in bistre on laid (BP 3283, DM 8120, FR 27,375, Y 530,080).

$1527* *La Bouillie (D. 17/IV), 1861,* (06-23-93, Kornfeld, #585), etching on Chine colle (BP 1037, DM 2584, FR 8691, Y 166,358, SF 2300).

$690* *La Bouillie (D., M. 17), 1861,* 4th state of 5, p. A. Delatre, pub. in Gazette des Beaux-Arts, margins, good cond., foxing, (02-11-93, Sotheby-NY, #181, illus.), 7 15/16 x 6¼ in., (202 x 158 mm.), sheet 11 x 7 9/16 in., (202 x 158 mm.), etching on chine applique (BP 487, DM 1143, FR 3868, Y 83,183).

$2300* *La Bouillie (D., M. 17), 1861,* 4th state of 5, p. A. Delatre, pub. in Gazette des Beaux-Arts, margins, good cond., foxing, (05-13-93, Sotheby-NY, #626, illus.), 8⅜ x 6¼ in., (213 x 159 mm.), sh 10⅜ x 7⅛ in., (213 x 159 mm.), etching on chine applique (BP 1510, DM 3714, FR 12,527, Y 256,782).

$920* *Bouillie (D., M. 17), 1861,* final state, s., d. in plate, from Etudes sur l'Ecole Francaise, 1903, or L'Imprimerie et les Procedes de Gravure au XXe Siecle, 1906, margins, goodcond., toned, paper loss, glue/hinge remains, pinhole, surface soiling, notation, (05-19-93, Butterfield, #1931), 7 5/16 x 6¼ in., (186 x 159 mm.), etching on laid (BP 597, DM 1495, FR 5038, Y 101,849).

BI *La Bouillie (Delteil 17 IV), 1861,* trimmed, est. DM 3000, (06-04-93, Bassenge, #5758, illus.), image 6⅛ x 5 1/16 in., (15.6 x 12.9 cm.), sh 8 7/16 x 6¼ in., (15.6 x 12.9 cm.), etching on China.

$3994* *La Bouillie (Delteil 17), 1861,* 3rd state of 5, margins, good cond., (10-14-92, Sotheby-Japan, #52, illus.), plate 8¼ x 6¼ in., (210 x 159 mm.), image 6 x 5 in., (210 x 159 mm.), etching (BP 2344, DM 5845, FR 19,821, Y 484,004).

BI *La Bouillie (Delteil 17), 1861,* 5th final state, est. $1/1,500, (12-09-92, Grogan, #71), 7⅜ x 6¼ in., (18.7 x 15.9 cm.), etching.

$1488* *La Bouillie (Delteil 17/V), 1861,* (06-08-93, Karl/Faber, #362), approx. 6⅛ x 5⅛ in., (15.5 x 13 cm.), etching on hand-made (BP 978, DM 2414, FR 8131, Y 158,046).

$1769* *La Bouillie (L. Delteil, 17), 1861,* fourth state of five, creases, stains, good margins, (06-16-93, Ader Tajan, #122), 8⅜ x 6¼ in., (21.2 x 15.8 cm.), etching on creme Chine fixe (BP 1179, DM 2937, FR 9855, Y 188,673).

$358* *"La Bouillie" (Lebrun/Keppel 18, 3/3),* very good cond., (09-27-92, Bakker, #235), plate 6 x 5 in., (15.2 x 12.7 cm.), etching (BP 209, DM 531, FR 1794, Y 43,211).

BI *La Cardeuse (D., M. 15), 1855-56,* margins, good cond., mat stain, loss, crease, masking tape stain, est. $2,5/3,500, (05-13-93, Sotheby-NY, #625A), 10⅛ x 6⅞ in., (257 x 176 mm.), sh 13⅛ x 8⅛ in., (257 x 176 mm.), etching in dark brown on laid.

BI *La Cardeuse (D., M. 15), 1855-56,* margins, good cond., rubbed spot in image, rubbed ink, glue stains, scuff, fox marks in image, est. $2,5/3,500, (05-13-93, Sotheby-NY, #625, illus.), 10⅛ x 7 in., (258 x 178 mm.), sh 12 x 8⅝ in., (258 x 178 mm.), etching in dark brown on Japan.

$3797* *La Cardeuse (L.D. 15),* large margins, (06-11-93, Picard, #140), 9 7/16 x 6 7/16 in., (240 x 164 mm.), print in bistre on thick laid (BP 2495, DM 6171, FR 20,805, Y 402,865).

BI *Cardeuse (L.D. 15), c. 1860,* watermark, margins, staining, paper losses, good cond., est. $2/3,000, (05-11-93, Christie-NY, #235), plate 9⅞ x 6¾ in., (251 x 171 mm.), etching on laid.

$2200* *La Cardeuse (Melot 15), c. 1858,* margins, (12-08-92, Swann, #212, illus.), 10⅛ x 7 in., (25.7 x 17.8 cm.), sepia etching on thin Japan paper (BP 1379, DM 3425, FR 11,677, Y 272,682).

$920* *La Couseuse (Delteil, Melot 9), c. 1855-56,* 3rd (final) state, margins, good cond., tape stains, foxmarks, (02-11-93, Sotheby-NY, #179), 4 3/16 x 2 15/16 in., (106 x 74 mm.), etching p. in brown, on antique laid (BP 649, DM 1524, FR 5157, Y 110,910).

BI *Le Depart Pour Le Travail (Delteil 19; Melot 19), 1863,* slipped printing at the top, fifth state of seven, full margins, goodcond., foxing, discoloration, est. BP 5/8,000, (12-03-92, Sotheby-London, #409, illus.), sheet 20 x 13⅝ in., (508 x 346 mm.), etching on fibrous laid.

BI *La Fileuse Auvergnate (D. 20),* s. in plate, prov., est. $1,500/2,000, (09-17-92, Sloan, #3085, illus.), 7⅞ x 5 in., (20 x 12.7 cm.), etching.

$1222* *La Fileuse Auvergnate (D. 20/V),* before 1869, (06-23-93, Kornfeld, #586), etching on handmade (BP 830, DM 2068, FR 6955, Y 133,130, SF 1840).

$3300* *Grand Bergere (Delteil 18), 1862,* only state, (05-24-93, Grogan, #303), 12½ x 9¼ in., (31.8 x 23.5 cm.), etching (BP 2149, DM 5396, FR 18,162, Y 364,762).

$614* *"La Grande Bergere Assise" and Becheur Au Repos" (D., M. 33 et 34), 1873-74: Two,* (02-24-93, Picard, #174), wood engraving on thin wove (BP 428, DM 997, FR 3379, Y 72,049).

$7260* *La Grande Bergere, Delteil 18,* c. 1862, i., prov., (09-20-92, Hindman, #744), sheet 15⅛ x 11¼ in., (32.1 x 23.8 cm.), etching on thin laid Japan (BP 4251, DM 10,773, FR 36,853, Y 897,293).

$2300* *Le Paysan Rentrant Du Fumier (Delteil, Melot 11), 1855,* final state, full margins, good cond., light-stain, glued to backing, (05-13-93, Sotheby-NY, #624, illus.), 6⅜ x 5⅜ in., (161 x 135 mm.), etching on japon pelure (BP 1510, DM 3714, FR 12,527, Y 256,782).

BI *Le Paysan Rentrant Du Fumier (L.D. 11), 1855,* watermark, 3rd state of 4, wide margins, mat staining, glue patch, very good cond., est. $4/5,000, (05-11-93, Christie-NY, #234, illus.), plate 6½ x 5 in., (165 x 127 mm.), etching on laid.

BI *La Planche Aux Trois Sujets (Melot 2), c. 1847,* staining, margins, (02-24-93, Picard, #171), etching and roulette in brown on old laid.

$6109* *Le Semeur (D. 22/II), 1851,* (06-23-93, Kornfeld, #587), lithograph on handmade (BP 4150, DM 10,337, FR 34,769, Y 665,541, SF 9200).

$3054* *Le Semeur (D. 22/II), 1851,* prov., (06-23-93, Kornfeld, #588), lithograph on strong handmade (BP 2075, DM 5168, FR 17,382, Y 332,716, SF 4600).

$11,550* *Le Semeur (D., M. 22), 1851,* final state, stain, losses, glued to backing, (11-05-92, Sotheby-NY, #256), 7½ x 6¼ in., (190 x 158 mm.), sheet 8⅞ x 8⅜ in., (190 x 158 mm.), lithograph on japon pelure (BP 7512, DM 18,267, FR 61,798, Y 1,417,004).

MILLET, Jean Francois (after)

$5015* *Les Glaneuses (D., M. 12), c. 1855,* small margins, (02-24-93, Picard, #173), etching in brown bistre on thin old laid (BP 3497, DM 8141, FR 27,600, Y 588,477).

$901* *L'Homme Appuye Sur Sa Beche (D., M. 3), c. 1847,* staining, margins, (02-24-93, Picard, #172), on thin laid (BP 628, DM 1463, FR 4959, Y 105,726).

MILLET, Jean Francoise
$1100* *Fileuse Auvergnate (D. 20), 1869,* pub. in Sonnets et eau-fortes, by Alphonse Lemerre, margins, good cond., tear, repaired tear, paper loss, mat staining, tape, creases, Muriel F. Kahn Estate, (02-24-93, Butterfield, #2756), 7⅞ x 5¹/₁₆ in., (200 x 129 mm.), etching on laid w/watermark (BP 767, DM 1786, FR 6054, Y 129,078).

MILLIERE, Maurice   French b. 1871
BI *Woman With Two Masks,* s., num. 127, full margins, good cond., est. BP 100/150, (11-30-92, Phillips-London, #464), plate 15 x 19¼ in., (381 x 489 mm.), drypoint in colors on wove.

MILLSPAUGH, J.H.
$66* *Harbor,* (11-13-92, DuMouchelle, #370), 5 x 11 in., (12.7 x 27.9 cm.), etching on silk (BP 43, DM 104, FR 349, Y 8192).

MILNE, David Brown   Canadian 1882-1953
BI *Painting Place (The Colophon Edition) (Tovell, Cat. no. 63),* s., pub. 1930-1931, lit., est. $7/900, (11-30-92, Ritchie, #38), 4¹³/₁₆ x 6⅞ in., (12.3 x 17.5 cm.), color drypoint on Fabriano wove.
$516* *Painting Place (Tovell Cat. no. 63), 1930-1931,* The Colophon Edition, State II, s. twice in plate, s., lit., (06-07-93, Ritchie, #43), 4¹³/₁₆ x 6⅞ in., (12.3 x 17.5 cm.), color drypoint on Fabriano wove (BP 340, DM 837, FR 2820, Y 55,353, C$ 660).
$660* *Painting Place (large plate) (Tovell 63), 1929-30,* state 2 of 6, w/o plate sig., trimmed margins, (05-27-93, Swann, #185), 4⅞ x 6⅞ in., (12.4 x 17.5 cm.), two-plate color drypoint (BP 423, DM 1059, FR 3569, Y 70,755).

MILOW, Keith
$126* *Untitled, 1969: Four Plates,* crayon s., d., one #9/75; three i. Artist's Proof, margins, minor creasing, (10-15-92, Sotheby-London, #120, illus.), each sheet approx. 27⅛ x 39⅞ in., (68.9 x 101.3 cm.), screenprint in colors on wove (BP 77, DM 188, FR 636, Y 15,117).
$126* *Untitled, 1969: Four Plates,* crayon s., d., one #2/70, three i. Artist's Proof, margins, creasing, (10-15-92, Sotheby-London, #119, illus.), each sheet approx. 27⅛ x 39⅞ in., (68.9 x 101.3 cm.), screenprint in colors on wove (BP 77, DM 188, FR 636, Y 15,117).

MILTON, Peter   American b. 1930
$1430* *American Interior I: Family Reunion, 1984,* s., d., t., #109/175, full margins, good cond., surface soiling, (10-28-92, Butterfield, #3032, illus.), 20 x 35½ in., (508 x 902 mm.), photo-sensitive ground etching, aquatint and engraving on BFK Rives (BP 911, DM 2208, FR 7499, Y 175,460).
$440* *April's August, 1975,* s., t., d., #58/160, full margins, hinge tape remains, (12-08-92, Swann, #214), 32 x 20 in., (81.3 x 50.8 cm.), photo-sensitive ground etching w/ aquatint (BP 276, DM 685, FR 2335, Y 54,536).
$1155* *Before The Hunt (Les Belles Et Le Bete),* s., t., num. 21/160, d. '78, (11-12-92, Freemn/Fine Art, #153, illus.), mat 23¾ x 40½ in., (60.3 x 102.9 cm.), photo sensitive etching (BP 759, DM 1830, FR 6173, Y 143,211).
$825* *Les Belles Et La Bete I: The Rehearsal, 1977,* s., d., t., num. 123/160, blindstamp of pub. Impressions Workshop, full margins, good cond., (02-24-93, Butterfield, #3086), 19¾ x 35¾ in., (502 x 908 mm.), photosensitive-ground etching & engraving on wove (BP 575, DM 1339, FR 4540, Y 96,808).
$990* *Les Belles Et La Bete II: Before The Hunt, 1978,* s., d., t., #33/160, blindstamp pub. Impressions Workshop, full margins, good cond., mat staining, surface soiling, (10-28-92, Butterfield, #3030), 21½ x 28⅝ in., (546 x 727 mm.), photo-sensitive etching, aquatint and engraving on wove (BP 631, DM 1529, FR 5191, Y 121,472).
$715* *The Card House, 1975,* full margins, t., num., s., (05-27-93, Swann, #186), 22 x 27½ in., (55.9 x 69.9 cm.), etching w/stipple work (BP 458, DM 1147, FR 3867, Y 76,651).
$1100* *Collecting With Rudy,* s., t., num. 45/140, (11-12-92, Freemn/Fine Art, #154, illus.), mat 29¼ x 19½ in., (74.3 x 49.5 cm.), photo sensitive etching (BP 722, DM 1743, FR 5879, Y 136,392).

$358* *"Country Pieces I: The Couple" and "Country Pieces II: In The Park",1979: Two,* s., d., t., #63/170, blindstamp pub., full margins, very good cond., (10-28-92, Butterfield, #3031), each 18¾ x 25¾ in., (476 x 654 mm.), etching on Somerset wove (BP 228, DM 553, FR 1877, Y 43,926).
BI *"Country Pieces II, In The Park", 1979,* s., d., t., num. 114/170, good cond., est. $7-900, (10-31-92, Cleveland, #383), 17½ x 23½ in., (44.5 x 59.7 cm.), engraving.
$467* *From "The Jolly Corner Suite", 1971,* s., d., #67/90, full margins, plate III.7, pub. Ferdinand Roten Gallery, (12-08-92, Swann, #213, illus.), stipple etching w/photo engraving (BP 293, DM 727, FR 2479, Y 57,883).
$1540* *Interiors I: Family Reunion, 1984,* s., d., t., annot. Trial Proof, full margins, very good cond., creases, surface soiling, (02-24-93, Butterfield, #3087), 20 x 35¾ in., (508 x 908 mm.), mezzotint on Rives BFK (BP 1074, DM 2500, FR 8476, Y 180,709).
$275* *The Jolly Corner,* s., num., (06-11-93, Freemn/Fine Art, #149), 10 x 14¾ in., (25.4 x 37.5 cm.), etching and engraving (BP 181, DM 447, FR 1507, Y 29,178).
$2200* *The Jolly Corner (Mc N. 62-82), 1971: Twenty-One,* complete portfolio, t., s., #59/150, blindstamp pub. Impressions Workshop, full margins, very good cond., orig. portfolio, (10-28-92, Butterfield, #3028, illus.), each sheet 19½ x 15⅝ in., (495 x 391 mm.), photo-sensitive ground etching w/engraving, aquatint and direct photographic transfer on Rives (BP 1402, DM 3398, FR 11,536, Y 269,939).
$3520* *The Jolly Corner By Henry James: Twenty-One,* Aquarius Press, 1971, complete folio w/case, (11-12-92, Freemn/Fine Art, #154A), sheet 19½ x 15½ in., (49.5 x 39.4 cm.), etchings (BP 2312, DM 5578, FR 18,813, Y 436,454).
$468* *The Jolly Corner II: Plate 3; Plate 7 (McN. 71; 75), 1971: Two,* each s., t., d., #88/90 & #6/90, pub. Aquarius Press, margins, good cond. (?), mat staining, (02-24-93, Butterfield, #3231), each 10 x 15 in., (254 x 381 mm.), photosensitive-ground etching and engraving on Arches (BP 326, DM 760, FR 2576, Y 54,917).
$550* *Passage 1 (McNulty 85), 1971,* full margins, num., s., creases, (05-27-93, Swann, #187), 18 x 24 in., (45.7 x 61 cm.), photosensitive ground etching and engraving (BP 352, DM 883, FR 2975, Y 58,962).
$358* *Second Opinion (McN. 91), 1974,* s., d., t., #44/140, blindstamp pub., Impressions Workshop, full margins, good cond., glue remains, surface soiling, creases, (02-24-93, Butterfield, #3232), 21¾ x 28 in., (552 x 711 mm.), photosensitive-ground etching and engraving p. on Murillo (BP 250, DM 581, FR 1970, Y 42,009).
$715* *Second Opinion, 1974,* s., pub. Impressions Workshop, (06-11-93, Freemn/Fine Art, #150), 22 x 28 in., (55.9 x 71.1 cm.), photo-sensitive engraving and etching (BP 470, DM 1162, FR 3918, Y 75,862).
$990* *A Sky-Blue Life (Mc N. 97), 1976,* s., d., t., #133/160, blindstamp pub. Impressions Workshop, full margins, good cond.?, (10-28-92, Butterfield, #3029), 25⅝ x 32¾ in., (651 x 832 mm.), photo-senstive ground etching and engraving on Copperplate Deluxe paper (BP 631, DM 1529, FR 5191, Y 121,472).
$690* *A Sky-Blue Life (Mc N. 97), 1976,* s., d., t., #21/160, margins, good cond.?, (05-19-93, Butterfield, #2265), 25½ x 32¾ in., (648 x 832 mm.), photosensitive-ground etching and engraving on wove (BP 448, DM 1122, FR 3779, Y 76,387).
$825* *Street Scene, 1965,* s., t., num. 43/50, (11-12-92, Freemn/Fine Art, #152, illus.), mat 24 x 18 in., (61 x 45.7 cm.), etching (BP 542, DM 1307, FR 4409, Y 102,294).
$908* *Time With Celia,* artist's proof, (06-11-93, Freemn/Fine Art, #151), 29⅝ x 23⅞ in., (75.2 x 60.6 cm.), photo-sensitive etching and intaglio (BP 597, DM 1476, FR 4975, Y 96,340).
$880* *Victoria'a Children, 1967,* s., d., t., num. 61/100, good cond., (05-22-93, Weschler, #205, illus.), 17½ x 23¾ in., (44.5 x 60.3 cm.), lift ground etching and engraving (BP 570, DM 1431, FR 4814, Y 97,023).

MINAMI, Keiko Japanese contemporary

$303* *A Bird In A Winter Landscape,* s., num., (03-25-93, Boos, #631), 13½ x 11½ in., (34.3 x 29.2 cm.), color etching (BP 206, DM 498, FR 1693, Y 35,497).

MINAUX, Andre French b. 1923

BI *Femme Assise,* epreuve d'artiste, #2/5, s., est. BP 5/70, (05-20-93, Bonhams-Chelsea, #161), sheet 25¾ x 19½ in., (65.4 x 49.5 cm.), lithograph.

$103* *L'Attente (Ch. Sorlier 264), 1972,* s., #90/140, large margins, drystamp, (05-06-93, Laurin, #70), color lithograph on wove (BP 65, DM 162, FR 546, Y 11,332).

$29* *Nu Dans Un Interieur,* s., 125/125, (06-28-93, Loudmer, #99), 22⁷⁄₁₆ x 16⁹⁄₁₆ in., (570 x 420 mm.), sh 26⅜ x 20¹⁄₁₆ in., (570 x 420 mm.), color lithograph on Arches wove (BP 19, DM 49, FR 166, Y 3077).

$129* *Tete,* s., d. 49, (05-20-93, Bonhams-Chelsea, #160), sheet 18¼ x 14 in., (46.4 x 35.6 cm.), lithograph (BP 83, DM 208, FR 701, Y 14,245).

$248* *"Woman And Still-Life",* s., num. 2/150, good cond., (10-31-92, Cleveland, #384), 22½ x 17¼ in., (57.2 x 43.8 cm.), lithograph in colors (BP 159, DM 382, FR 1294, Y 30,720).

MINICK, Roger American 20th cent.

$88* *Country Store,* s., d., studio stamp (c) Robert Minick 1972, (05-16-93, Hindman, #357), 12 x 10¾ in., photograph, silver print (BP 57, DM 142, FR 478, Y 9800).

MINNIS and COWELL (attrib.)

$2420* *General Lee In The Field, 1862,* (04-07-93, Swann, #186, illus.), oval 6¾ x 4¾ in., photograph, Albumen print (BP 1599, DM 3914, FR 13,246, Y 274,938).

MINUZZI, Maurilio b. 1937

$141* *"LandschaftsAusbruch",* s., d. Minuzzi 77, #15/100, (03-24-93, Venator/Hansten, #4535), pl. 11¼ x 14¹¹⁄₁₆ in., (28.5 x 37.3 cm.), etching and aquatint on 2 color plates (BP 95, DM 230, FR 784, Y 16,567).

MIOTTE, Jean b. 1926

$200* *"Composition",* #53/120, s., (04-04-93, Pescheteau, #264), 29⅛ x 21⅝ in., (74 x 55 cm.), color lithograph on wove (BP 132, DM 321, FR 1092, Y 22,771).

MIRER, Rudolf b. 1937

$2027* *Clown Mit Pferd, 1986,* #125/150, s., d., (09-04-92, Germann, #475), 29¹⁵⁄₁₆ x 22¹⁄₁₆ in., (760 x 560 mm.), color lithograph (BP 1016, DM 2841, FR 9671, Y 249,508, SF 2530).

MIRO, Joan Spanish 1893-1983

$11,000* *23 Gravures (Dupin 16; Cramer 3), 1935,* s., #24/50, pub. Orobitz, good cond., mat stain, tape stain in image,creases, (11-05-92, Sotheby-NY, #257, illus.), 12¼ x 9¼ in., (311 x 235 mm.), sheet 12¾ x 9⅞ in., (311 x 235 mm.), etching (BP 7154, DM 17,397, FR 58,855, Y 1,349,528).

$16,649* *A. Jouffroy, Hommage A San Lazzaro (Cr. 229), 1977,* Editions Gerald Cramer, 1977, 2 t., just., text, set of 8 plates, s., #13/60, excellent cond., (12-01-92, Christie-London, #441, illus.), overall sheet 22³⁄₁₆ x 15¹⁵⁄₁₆ in., (563 x 405 mm.), etching w/aquatint in colors on Rives (BP 11,000, DM 26,536, FR 90,435, Y 2,072,834).

$2562* *Abstract,* s., #18/55, pub. Maeght, c. 1974, (12-01-92, Ritchie, #98, illus.), sheet 17½ x 24⅝ in., (44.5 x 62.5 cm.), color lithograph (BP 1693, DM 4084, FR 13,916, Y 318,974, C$ 3300).

$2750* *Abstract Faces,* ed. H.C., s., (03-12-93, DuMouchelle, #2018, illus.), 29¾ x 22 in., (75.6 x 55.9 cm.), color lithograph (BP 1918, DM 4577, FR 15,563, Y 324,101).

BI *"Adonides" (Cramer 203), 1975: Forty-Five,* text Jacques Prevert, s., Maeght Editeur, est. DM 20/22,000, (12-01-92, Karl/Faber, #1026, illus.), color aquatint/etching on Arches.

$372* *Affiche D'Exposition De La Galerie Maeght,* s. Miro, (07-14-92, Encans, #234), 23¹⁄₁₆ x 16¹⁵⁄₁₆ in., (58.5 x 43 cm.), lithograph (BP 194, DM 552, FR 1861, Y 46,517, C$ 444).

$1194* *Affiche Perun Teatre Catalunya, c. 1970,* s., #36/50, watermark, full margins, good cond., (12-03-92, Sotheby-London, #436, illus.), 23 x 19½ in., (585 x 495 mm.), lithograph in colors on wove (BP 770, DM 1878, FR 6409, Y 148,563).

$262* *Affiche Pour L'Exposition "Joan Miro, Oeuvre Grave Et Lithographie" (Maeght 627), 1969,* small margins, (02-03-93, Ader Tajan, #181), 25⁹⁄₁₆ x 19¹¹⁄₁₆ in., (65 x 50 cm.), color lithograph (BP 183, DM 431, FR 1463, Y 32,591).

$20,900* *Album 13 (Cramer 18; Mourlot 72-86), 1948: Set Of Thirteen,* Maeght Editeur, s., d., num., watermark, full margins, staining, skinning, good cond., (11-09-92, Christie-NY, #122, illus.), all 559 x 450 in., (x cm.), lithograph on wove (BP 13,818, DM 33,365, FR 112,729, Y 2,593,696).

$1588* *"Album 19 Lamina 6" (Mourlot 249), 1961,* mono., num., from series: Raymond Queneau, Album 19, (11-28-92, Grisebach, #654, illus.), 19¹³⁄₁₆ x 25⅜ in., (50.3 x 64.5 cm.), colored lithograph on wove (BP 1048, DM 2530, FR 8588, Y 197,635).

BI *Album 19: Plate 12 (Mourlot 323), 1961,* init., #50/75, pub. Maeght, good cond., est. BP 1,6/2,000, (06-30-93, Sotheby-London, #537, illus.), 20 x 26⅛ in., (508 x 664 mm.), color lithograph on Rives.

$1540* *Album 19: Plate 16 (M. 327), 1961,* init., #29/75, pub. & p. Maeght, good cond., creases, surface soiling, (02-24-93, Butterfield, #2759), 20 x 26¼ in., (508 x 667 mm.), lithograph in colors on Rives (BP 1074, DM 2500, FR 8476, Y 180,709).

$2420* *Album 19: Plate 8 (M. 319; C. 70), 1961,* init., #68/75, p. and pub. by Maeght, full margins, good cond., crease, skinning, (11-05-92, Sotheby-NY, #270), 23⅜ x 26 in., (595 x 660 mm.), lithograph p. in colors (BP 1574, DM 3827, FR 12,948, Y 296,896).

BI *Andre Frenaud. Le Miroir De L'Homme Par Les Betes (C. 159): Three,* album w/title-page and text, s., justification by author and artist,an Exemplair de Collaborateur, pub. Maeght, 1972, good cond., original paper covers, est. BP 1,6/2,000, (06-30-93, Sotheby-London, #550, illus.), 17½ x 13 in., (445 x 330 mm.), etching w/aquatint in color and one carborundum etching.

$968* *Anti-Platon (D. 312 and 315), 1962: Two,* (10-09-92, Winterberg, #2771), one 5⅛ x 3⁹⁄₁₆ in., (13 x 9 cm.), the other 5⅞ x 4¹⁵⁄₁₆ in., (13 x 9 cm.), one aquatint w/relief print and one color aquatint on Japan (BP 574, DM 1438, FR 4828, Y 117,848).

BI *Archipel Sauvage,* s. Miro, num. 14/35, est. $5/7,000, (09-25-92, Wolf, #34, illus.), 23 x 36 in., (58.4 x 91.4 cm.), colored aquatint w/embossing.

$3069* *Arlequin Crepusculaire (MA. 738), 1975,* s., i. HC XII/XV, an Hors Commerce, p. Morsang, pub. Maeght, full margins, good cond., crease, (12-03-92, Sotheby-London, #447, illus.), sheet 21⅝ x 13 in., (550 x 330 mm.), etching and aquatint in colors on Arches (BP 1980, DM 4826, FR 16,473, Y 381,859).

$3850* *Astre Et Fumee (D. 424), 1967,* s., #15/75, p. and pub. by Maeght, full margins, good cond., foxing,creases, rubbed spots, (11-05-92, Sotheby-NY, #275), 27½ x 20½ in., (700 x 520 mm.), etching, aquatint and carborundum p. in colors (BP 2504, DM 6089, FR 20,599, Y 472,335).

$2402* *Astrologie I (Maeght 201), 1953,* s., #79/100, pub. Maeght, margins, good cond., (06-30-93, Sotheby-London, #530, illus.), sh 15⅝ x 11¼ in., (397 x 286 mm.), color lithograph on Arches (BP 1610, DM 4097, FR 13,820, Y 257,366).

$2487* *Astrologie II (MA. 202), 1953,* s., #67/100, pub. Maeght, margins, good cond., (06-30-93, Sotheby-London, #532, illus.), sh 15⅝ x 11⅜ in., (397 x 289 mm.), color lithograph on Arches (BP 1667, DM 4242, FR 14,310, Y 266,474).

$2487* *Astrologie III (Ma. 195), 1953,* s., #70/100, pub. Maeght, margins, good cond., (06-30-93, Sotheby-London, #531, illus.), sh 15⅝ x 11⅝ in., (397 x 295 mm.), color lithograph on Arches (BP 1667, DM 4242, FR 14,310, Y 266,474).

BI *Astrology I (M. 201), 1953,* s., i. HC, pub. Maeght, full margins, good cond., crease, loss, backed w/masking tape, skinning, est. $1/1,500, (05-13-93, Sotheby-NY, #634), 14⅝ x 10⅝ in., (372 x 270 mm.), lithograph in black and red.

BI *Astrology III (M. 195), 1960*, s., #65/100, pub. Maeght, margins, sealed in mat, good cond., est.$2/4,000, (05-19-93, Butterfield, #1933, illus.), 14½ x 10¾ in., (368 x 273 mm.), lithograph in black and yellow on wove.

$94* *Atelier Mourlot*, s. Miro, (06-26-93, Wolf, #974), 28 x 21 in., (71.1 x 53.3 cm.), color poster (BP 63, DM 160, FR 538, Y 9973).

$2574* *Atmosphera Miro (MA. 258), 1959*, s., #128/160, p. by Mourlot, pub. R.M., margins, good cond., (06-30-93, Sotheby-London, #534, illus.), sh 13 x 9⅞ in., (330 x 251 mm.), color lithograph on wove (BP 1725, DM 4390, FR 14,810, Y 275,796).

BI *Le Bagnard Et Sa Compagne (D. 749), 1975*, s., i. HC, p. Morsang, pub. Maeght, good cond., printer's creases, discoloration, soiling, est. $8/10,000, (05-13-93, Sotheby-NY, #662, illus.), sh 47¼ x 63 in., (120 x 160 cm.), etching and aquatint in colors.

$6325* *La Bague D'Aurore*, text by Rene Crevel, Louis Broder, 1957, p. Robert Dutrou, original wrappers, hors commece copies, s. by Miro, (06-14-93, Sotheby-NY, #219), 6½ x 5⅜ in., (16.5 x 13.7 cm.), 5 etchings w/aquatint in colors (BP 4140, DM 10,295, FR 34,601, Y 665,579).

$1760* *La Bague D'Aurore (D. 140; C. 45), 1957*, s., #III/XV, pub. Louis Broder, full margins, good cond., light stain, margins folded back, creases, foxing, hinges, (11-05-92, Sotheby-NY, #264), 4½ x 5½ in., (115 x 140 mm.), etching w/aquatint p. in colors on japon nacre (BP 1145, DM 2783, FR 9417, Y 215,924).

$3659* *La Bague D'Aurore (Dupin 122), 1957*, s., num., from la bague d'aurore, (12-12-92, Wachholtz, #236, illus.), 10¾ x 9⁹⁄₁₆ in., (27.3 x 24.3 cm.), etching on Rives hand-made reworked w/color chalk (BP 2340, DM 5750, FR 19,598, Y 452,678).

$6900* *Barbare Dans La Nuit, 1976*, s., i. H.C., good cond., scuffs, touched-in, repaired tears, printer's creases, creases, skinning, foxing, (05-13-93, Sotheby-NY, #664, illus.), 42 x 29⅝ in., (106.7 x 75.2 cm.), etching and aquatint in colors (BP 4530, DM 11,142, FR 37,582, Y 770,347).

$9775* *Barcelona 1972-1973: Plate I (D. 592), 1973*, s., #32/50, p. J. Torralba, pub. Sala Gaspar, good cond.?, creases, (05-13-93, Sotheby-NY, #659, illus.), sh 27½ x 41¼ in., (69.9 x 104.8 cm.), etching & carborundum in colors (BP 6417, DM 15,784, FR 53,241, Y 1,091,325).

$7150* *Barcelona Series: Plate II (Mourlot 7), 1944*, s., d., #3/5, margins (full?), good cond., discoloration, water stain, repaired tear, foxing, (11-05-92, Sotheby-NY, #259, illus.), 24¾ x 17 in., (630 x 432 mm.), sheet 27⅝ x 19¾ in., (630 x 432 mm.), lithograph (BP 4650, DM 11,308, FR 38,256, Y 877,193).

$5500* *Barnabe, 1979*, s., #2/50, pub. Maeght, full margins, good cond., light stain, (11-05-92, Sotheby-NY, #309, illus.), 35 x 24 in., (890 x 610 mm.), lithograph p. in colors (BP 3577, DM 8698, FR 29,428, Y 674,764).

$2574* *Betelgeuse (MA. 387), 1965*, s., #47/75, pub. Maeght, margins, good cond., rubbing, (06-30-93, Sotheby-London, #541, illus.), sh 31¾ x 23⅛ in., (806 x 587 mm.), color lithograph on BFK Rives (BP 1725, DM 4390, FR 14,810, Y 275,796).

BI *Betelgeuse (Maeght 387), 1965*, s., #47/75, pub. Maeght, margins, good cond., rubbing, margins, tipped, est. BP 2,5/3,000, (12-03-92, Sotheby-London, #423, illus.), sheet 31¾ x 23⅛ in., (807 x 587 mm.), lithograph in colors on BFK Rives.

$3029* *Bleu, Jaune Et Rouge, 1974*, s., i. H.C., (11-21-92, Schloss Ahlden, #2135, illus.), 12⅝ x 19⅞ in., (32 x 50.5 cm.), colored etching on Arches (BP 1994, DM 4829, FR 16,267, Y 376,694).

$4950* *Bon Cop...De Lluna, 1979*, s., #47/75, pub. Maeght, full margins, good cond., creases, skinned spots, (11-05-92, Sotheby-NY, #307, illus.), 35 x 24 in., (890 x 610 mm.), lithograph p. in colors (BP 3220, DM 7829, FR 26,485, Y 607,287).

$2741* *Bronzes (Maeght Vol. IV 846), 1972*, #142/150, s., foglio, (05-20-93, Finarte-Milan, #113, illus.), 34¹³⁄₁₆ x 24⁷⁄₁₆ in., (88.5 x 62 cm.), lithograph in colors (BP 1759, DM 4422, FR 14,897, Y 302,672, L 4025).

$33,350* *Cahiers D'Art (D. 14; see C. bk. III), 1934*, ink s., d., #26/48, p. Crete, pub. Cahiers d'Art, good cond., scuffs,- discoloration, (05-13-93, Sotheby-NY, #628, illus.), sh 15 x 11 in., (380 x 280 mm.), pochoir in blue and black on wove (BP 21,895, DM 53,851, FR 181,645, Y 3,723,345).

$27,600* *Cahiers D'Art (Dupin 14; see Cramer bk. III), 1934*, ink s., d., #2/48, p. Crete, pub. Cahiers d'Art, good cond., scuffs,discoloration, (05-13-93, Sotheby-NY, #627, illus.), sh 15 x 11 in., (380 x 280 mm.), pochoir in orange-red and black on wove (BP 18,120, DM 44,566, FR 150,327, Y 3,081,389).

$7673* *Le Caissier (D. 487), 1969*, s., #53/75, p., pub. Maeght, good cond., tipped to back board, (12-03-92, Sotheby-London, #434), 35½ x 27 in., (900 x 685 mm.), etching, aquatint and carborundum in colors on wove (BP 4950, DM 12,066, FR 41,186, Y 954,709).

$8800* *La Calebasse (D. 488), 1969*, s., #7/75, pub. Maeght, good cond., soiling, (11-05-92, Sotheby-NY, #284, illus.), sheet 40 x 27¾ in., (101.6 x 70.5 cm.), etching, aquatint and carborundum p. in colors on Arches (BP 5724, DM 13,917, FR 47,084, Y 1,079,622).

$7188* *La Calebasse (D. 488), 1969*, s., #7/75, pub. Maeght, good cond., soiling, tipped to backing, (05-13-93, Sotheby-NY, #651, illus.), sh 40 x 27¾ in., (101.6 x 70.5 cm.), etching, aquatint & carborundum in colors on Arches (BP 4719, DM 11,607, FR 39,150, Y 802,501).

$1535* *Camillo Jose Cela. Joan Miro Drawings And Lithographs From...(C. 56)*, book, one s., w/text and reprods., num. 546, pub. New York Graphic Society, 1959, good cond., orig. binding, (12-03-92, Sotheby-London, #419, illus.), overall size 13⅜ x 9½ in., (340 x 240 mm.), three lithographs joined together (BP 990, DM 2414, FR 8239, Y 190,992).

$3476* *Cap I Cua (Cramer/Mourlot 1182), 1979*, #60/75, s., creases, (04-21-93, Germann, #643, illus.), 38¾ x 28⁷⁄₁₆ in., (985 x 723 mm.), color lithograph (BP 2255, DM 5556, FR 18,789, Y 384,811, SF 5060).

$7475* *La Captive (D. 489), 1969*, s., annot. HC, pub. Maeght, p. Arte Adrien Maeght, very good cond.?,staining, (05-19-93, Butterfield, #1940, illus.), sh 37¼ x 28½ in., (946 x 724 mm.), etching, aquatint and carborundum in colorson wove (BP 4852, DM 12,151, FR 40,936, Y 827,521).

$290* *Catalonia (Mourlot 667), 1970*, stone s., (10-14-92, Germann, #388), 19¹¹⁄₁₆ x 25¹³⁄₁₆ in., (500 x 655 mm.), color lithograph (BP 170, DM 424, FR 1439, Y 35,143, SF 378).

$660* *Ceramiques, c. 1975*, s. in stone, watermark of pub. Galerie Maeght, full sheet, (05-22-93, Weschler, #206, illus.), sheet 21½ x 30 in., (54.6 x 76.2 cm.), lithograph in colors (BP 428, DM 1073, FR 3611, Y 72,767).

$2834* *Chanteur Des Rues IV, 1981*, s., #25/80, full margins, (05-27-93, Briest, #146), 22¼ x 16¾ in., (56.5 x 42.5 cm.), color etching and aquatint (BP 1815, DM 4547, FR 15,327, Y 303,816).

$3432* *Chanteurs Des Rues: Plates IV and V, 1981: Two*, s., #9/80, 54/80, full margins, good cond., (06-30-93, Sotheby-London, #552, illus.), each sh c. 22⅜ x 16⅝ in., (568 x 422 mm.), etching w/aquatint in color on wove (BP 2300, DM 5854, FR 19,747, Y 367,727).

$3850* *La Chasse Aux Papillons, 1975*, s., num. 32/50, pub. Maeght, full margins, very good cond., creases,glued, (02-24-93, Butterfield, #2762, illus.), 26¼ x 19⅞ in., (667 x 505 mm.), soft varnish, etching & aquatint in colors on wove (BP 2685, DM 6250, FR 21,189, Y 451,772).

BI *Le Chasseur De Pieuvres (D. 490), 1969*, s., #10/75, pub. Maeght, good cond., discoloration, rubbing, est. BP5/7,000, (12-03-92, Sotheby-London, #430, illus.), 41⅛ x 26¼ in., (104.5 x 66.7 cm.), etching w/aquatint and carborundum in colors on wove.

$1045* *Le Chemin De Ronde I (Dupin 411), 1966*, s., num. 46/50, pub. Maeght, Paris, prov., Tamara Strickland Estate, (05-22-93, Weschler, #208, illus.), 13½ x 10¼ in., (34.3 x 26 cm.), etching and aquatint in colors (BP 677, DM 1699, FR 5717, Y 115,215).

$2749* *Chevauchee - Brun (M. 540), 1969*, s. in violet, num., (06-23-93, Kornfeld, #591), color lithograph (BP 1868, DM 4651, FR 15,646, Y 299,488, SF 4140).

$2596* *Chevauchee - Rouge Et Brun (M. 541), 1969,* s., num., (06-23-93, Kornfeld, #592), color lithograph (BP 1764, DM 4393, FR 14,775, Y 282,819, SF 3910).

BI *"Chevauchee Rouge Et Brun-1969" (M 541), #62/75,* est. FF12,000/15,000, (04-04-93, Pescheteau, #266), 33¹⁄₁₆ x 23¼ in., (84 x 59 cm.), color lithograph on Rives.

$2105* *Chevauchee-bleu, (Maeght, vol. III, n.539), 1969, #30/75,* s., (11-09-92, Finarte-Milan, #6, illus.), 33¼ x 23¹³⁄₁₆ in., (84.5 x 60.5 cm.), lithograph in colors (BP 1392, DM 3360, FR 11,354, Y 261,231, L 2875).

BI *Le Ciel Du Forgeron (D. 364), 1964,* s., #32/75, pub. Maeght, good cond., est. BP 1,6/2,000, (06-30-93, Sotheby-London, #536, illus.), 22¾ x 18¾ in., (578 x 476 mm.), drypoint, aquatint and embossing in color on Arches.

BI *A Collection Of Posters (Corredor-Matheos 13; 24; 40X3; 41; 64; 67; 78; 80; 95; 102; 107; 108 and Another), 1970-1978: Sixteen,* good cond., (06-30-93, Sotheby-London, #549), color lithograph poster.

$3268* *Colombine Au Saut Du Lit, c. 1980,* s., num. 31/50, pub. Maeght, full margins, good cond., (10-14-92, Sotheby-Japan, #55, illus.), approx. 25⅝ x 19⅞ in., (651 x 505 mm.), colored lithograph (BP 1918, DM 4783, FR 16,218, Y 396,025).

BI *Commedia Dell'Arte, No. 63, 1980,* s., #16/30, pub. Maeght, good cond., est. BP 1,2/1,400, (12-03-92, Sotheby-London, #450), sheet 22¼ x 30 in., (565 x 760 mm.), etching w/aquatint in colors on wove.

$220* *Composition,* s. Miro 29/200, (03-24-93, Kunsthallen, #245), color lithograph w/relief print (BP 149, DM 359, FR 1223, Y 25,849, DK 1380).

$202* *Composition,* s. Miro, 29/200, (03-24-93, Kunsthallen, #246), color lithograph w/relief print (BP 137, DM 330, FR 1123, Y 23,734, DK 1265).

$147* *Composition,* from Derriere Le Miroir, (09-30-92, Kunsthallen, #209), color lithograph (BP 83, DM 208, FR 705, Y 17,641, DK 805).

$1100* *Composition,* s., #19/150, (05-16-93, Hindman, #483), 16 x 23 in., (40.6 x 58.4 cm.), color lithograph (BP 715, DM 1769, FR 5946, Y 121,938).

$2070* *Composition (M. 384: see C. bk. 84), 1963,* s., #4/125, p., pub. Mourlot, full margins, good cond., (05-13-93, Sotheby-NY, #643), 18¼ x 15¾ in., (464 x 400 mm.), lithograph in colors (BP 1359, DM 3342, FR 11,275, Y 231,104).

$1150* *Composition (M. 384; see Cramer bk. 84), 1963,* s., #109/125, p., pub. Mourlot, 1963, full margins, good cond., light stain, hinged to mat, (02-11-93, Sotheby-NY, #188, illus.), 18½ x 15¾ in., (470 x 400 mm.), color lithograph (BP 811, DM 1905, FR 6446, Y 138,638).

$3531* *Composition (Serie III) (Dupin 90), 1953,* s., d., #10/50, series Serie III, (06-10-93, Hauswedell/Nolt, #642, illus.), image 9½ x 11¹³⁄₁₆ in., (24.1 x 30 cm.), color etching on Arches (BP 2310, DM 5750, FR 19,359, Y 374,801).

$248* *Composition - Centerfold,* s. Miro, (06-26-93, Wolf, #975), 15 x 22 in., (38.1 x 55.9 cm.), lithograph (BP 166, DM 421, FR 1420, Y 26,313).

$2294* *Composition 15 From "Fissures" (Dupin 477, Cramer 130), 1969,* 54/75, s., (10-14-92, Germann, #384, illus.), 19⅛ x 22⅝ in., (485 x 575 mm.), color aquatint (BP 1346, DM 3357, FR 11,385, Y 277,993, SF 2990).

$1250* *Composition From Album 21, 1972,* s., num. 72/75, full margins, excellent cond., (11-30-92, Phillips-London, #466), sheet 14 x 11¾ in., (356 x 298 mm.), lithograph in colors on Arches (BP 825, DM 1991, FR 6760, Y 155,569).

BI *Composition XIV, 1961,* from Album 19, mono., #65/75, discolored, (09-18-92, Schloss Ahlden, #1039), 26⅛ x 20¹⁄₁₆ in., (66.4 x 50.9 cm.), color lithograph on Rives wove.

$1498* *Composition for Catalogue "Maitres-Graveurs Contemporains 1970" (M. 682), 1970,* s., #63/100, pub. Berggruen, margins, mount-stained, tape, (12-01-92, Christie-London, #443), L. 9¹⁄₁₆ x 9¹³⁄₁₆ in., (230 x 250 mm.), lithograph in colors on Arches (BP 990, DM 2388, FR 8137, Y 186,504).

$210* *"Composition",* s. in pl., (01-28-93, Pescheteau, #216), 19¹¹⁄₁₆ x 27⁹⁄₁₆ in., (50 x 70 cm.), color lithograph on wove (BP 139, DM 333, FR 1126, Y 26,074).

$292* *"Composition",* s. in plate, water stains in margin, (10-18-92, Pescheteau, #218), 21¼ x 29¹⁵⁄₁₆ in., (54 x 76 cm.), lithograph in colors on Arches (BP 177, DM 431, FR 1465, Y 34,866).

$1082* *Composition, From Album 21 (cf. Cr. 241), 1978,* s., #50/75, pub. Maeght, margins, surface dirt, very good cond., (12-01-92, Christie-London, #444), L. 25⁹⁄₁₆ x 18⅛ in., (640 x 460 mm.), lithograph on Arches (BP 715, DM 1725, FR 5877, Y 134,711).

BI *Composition, Miro, Obra Inedita Recent, (Mourlot 356E), 1964,* s. M., 21/100, est. DK 5,000, (03-24-93, Kunsthallen, #241), color lithograph.

$1205* *Composition, c. 1965,* s., num., blindstamp, (06-08-93, Karl/Faber, #1123, illus.), approx. 15⅜ x 33⁷⁄₁₆ in., (39 x 85 cm.), color lithograph on wove (BP 792, DM 1955, FR 6585, Y 127,987).

$642* *Compositions, Miro, Obra Inedita Recent, (Mourlot 356C and 356J), 1964,* s. M., 71/100 and 53/100, (03-24-93, Kunsthallen, #242), color lithograph on ramme (frame) (BP 435, DM 1049, FR 3569, Y 75,432, DK 4025).

$2119* *Constellation (Mourlot 191), 1959,* s., d., #69/150, Berggruen, (06-10-93, Hauswedell/Nolt, #643, illus.), image 21¼ x 18⁵⁄₁₆ in., (54 x 46.5 cm.), color lithograph on Arches (BP 1386, DM 3451, FR 11,617, Y 224,923).

BI *Constellations (M. 261; see C. Bk. 58), 1959: Two,* working proof impressions, p. Mourlot, full margins, good cond., soiling, est. $1,8/2,400, (05-13-93, Sotheby-NY, #642), each 11¾ x 9½ in., (298 x 240 mm.), lithograph in blk/green, w/yellow/red crayon w/collage; lithograph inred/green/yellow w/graphite/crayon on Arches wove.

$7150* *Le Courtesan Grotesque: Plate III; And Plate VI (D. 663 and 666; C. 182), 1974,* s., #12/12, pub. Iliazd, good cond., (11-05-92, Sotheby-NY, #302), sheet, one 16⅛ x 23⅛ in., (410 x 587 mm.), sheet, other 16⅛ x 23 in., (410 x 587 mm.), two drypoints w/aquatint p. in colors on japon (Japan paper) ancien (BP 4650, DM 11,308, FR 38,256, Y 877,193).

$3581* *Croc A Phynances I (MA. 688), 1971,* s., Hors Commerce, p., pub. Maeght, full margins, good cond., discolooration, handling creases, (12-03-92, Sotheby-London, #438, illus.), sheet 36¼ x 49 in., (92.1 x 124.5 cm.), lithograph in colors on Arches (BP 2310, DM 5631, FR 19,222, Y 445,564).

$3581* *Croc A Phynances II (MA. 689), 1971,* s. Hors Comerce, p., pub. Maeght, margins, good cond., discoloration,creases, (12-03-92, Sotheby-London, #439, illus.), sheet 49 x 36¼ in., (124.5 x 92.1 cm.), lithograph in colors on Arches (BP 2310, DM 5631, FR 19,222, Y 445,564).

$3581* *Croc A Phynances III (MA. 690), 1971,* s., Hors Commerce, p., pub. Maeght, full margins, good cond., discoloration, (12-03-92, Sotheby-London, #440, illus.), sheet 49 x 36¼ in., (124.5 x 92.1 cm.), lithograph in colors on Arches (BP 2310, DM 5631, FR 19,222, Y 445,564).

$10,925* *Le Dandy (D. 492), 1969,* s., i. HC, p., pub. Maeght, full margins, good cond., mat stain, creases, (05-13-93, Sotheby-NY, #652, illus.), 16¼ x 17¼ in., (413 x 437 mm.), etching, aquatint & carborundum in colors (BP 7172, DM 17,641, FR 59,504, Y 1,219,716).

BI *Daphnis And Chloe (Dupin 9), 1933,* s., d., #4/100, wide margins, light/mat staining, remains of glue, very good cond., est. $11/13,000, (11-09-92, Christie-NY, #120, illus.), 268 x 326 in., (680.7 x 828 cm.), drypoint on wove.

BI *Demi-Mondaine A Sa Fenetre (D. 742), 1975,* s., #44/50, p. Morsang, blindstamp pub. Maeght, good cond.?, creases, est. $2,5/3,000, (10-28-92, Butterfield, #2684, illus.), 36¼ x 25 in., (921 x 635 mm.), etching w/aquatint and color wash on wove.

$5500* *La Demoiselle A Bascule (D. 486), 1969,* s., #37/75, rubbed spots, good cond., (11-09-92, Christie-NY, #131, illus.), 22¹¹⁄₁₆ x 18¹¹⁄₁₆ in., (577 x 475 mm.), etching, aquatint, and carborundum in colors on wove (BP 3636, DM 8780, FR 29,666, Y 682,552).

$3360* *La Dentelliere (Maeght 525), 1969,* s., num., (06-23-93, Kornfeld, #590), color lithograph (BP 2283, DM 5685, FR 19,124, Y 366,053, SF 5060).

$14,300* *Les Deux Amis (D. 493), 1969,* s., #70/75, pub. Maeght, full margins, good cond., mat stain, soiling, fox marks, (11-05-92, Sotheby-NY, #285, illus.), 28⅜ x 41⅞ in., (72.1 x 106.4 cm.), etching, aquatint and carborundum p. in colors (BP 9301, DM 22,616, FR 76,512, Y 1,754,386).

BI *Les Deux Amis (Dupin Band II 493), 1969,* watermark, H.C. XXIV/XXIV, s., est. DM 52,000-, (11-21-92, Lempertz, #292, illus.), 28⅛ x 42⅛ in., (71.5 x 107 cm.), color etching on wove.

$9900* *Dog Barking At The Moon (M. 189), 1952,* crayon s., d., #19/80, pub. Teriade, faded, foxing, discoloration, glued to back, skinned spots, (11-05-92, Sotheby-NY, #261, illus.), 14⅜ x 21½ in., (365 x 546 mm.), lithograph p. in colors (BP 6439, DM 15,657, FR 52,970, Y 1,214,575).

$660* *Dog Barking At The Moon (M. 189), 1952,* pub. in Verve, Vol. VII, NO 27-28, pub. Teriade, apparently good cond., (02-24-93, Butterfield, #2958), (356 x 533 mm.), lithograph in colors on wove (BP 460, DM 1071, FR 3632, Y 77,447).

BI *Dog Barking At The Moon (Mourlot 189), 1952,* s., d., #19/80 in crayon, pub. Teriade, faded, foxing, discoloration,glued to back mat, skinned spots, est. $10/14,000, (05-13-93, Sotheby-NY, #631, illus.), 14⅜ x 21½ in., (365 x 546 mm.), lithograph in colors.

BI *Edition 1973,* s., num. 67/75, full sheet, good cond., minor rippling, est. $3/4,000, (05-22-93, Weschler, #209, illus.), 32½ x 23 in., (82.6 x 58.4 cm.), lithograph in colors.

$6863* *Egyptienne, 1979,* s., #38/50, pub. Maefght, full margins, good cond., (06-30-93, Sotheby-London, #556, illus.), sh c. 55⅛ x 37¾ in., (140 x 95.9 cm.), etching and aquatint and carborundum in color on wove (BP 4600, DM 11,706, FR 39,488, Y 735,348).

$1840* *The Empress (M. 396), 1964,* s., #13/75, p., pub. Maeght, full sheet, good cond., foxing, Harry R. Lea Estate, (02-11-93, Sotheby-NY, #189), sheet 35³⁄₁₆ x 24⅛ in., (893 x 612 mm.), color lithograph (BP 1298, DM 3048, FR 10,314, Y 221,820).

$2387* *Engance D'Ubu: Plate 16 (C. 204), 1975,* s., i. e.a., pub. Teriade, full margins, good cond., light staining, (12-03-92, Sotheby-London, #451), sheet 12¾ x 19⅞ in., (325 x 504 mm.), lithograph in colors on wove (BP 1540, DM 3754, FR 12,813, Y 297,001).

$1721* *Eros, 1964,* #I/X, s., (11-13-92, Koller, #5379), lithograph (BP 1112, DM 2702, FR 9111, Y 213,603, SF 2436).

$5500* *Escalade (D. 494), 1969,* s., num. 18/75, pub. Maeght, apparently good cond., light-staining, (02-24-93, Butterfield, #2761, illus.), 26 x 19⅝ in., (660 x 498 mm.), etching w/aquatint & carborundum in colors on Arches (BP 3835, DM 8929, FR 30,270, Y 645,388).

BI *Espiru-Miro (D. 869-877; C. 197), 1975,* from portfolio, s., i. H.C., pub. Sala Gaspar, good cond., foxing, est. $40/50,000, (11-05-92, Sotheby-NY, #305, illus.), each sheet approx. 35¼ x 28⅜ in., (895 x 720 mm.), nine etchings, eight w/aquatint p. in colors.

$3738* *Les Essencies De La Terra (M. 576), 1968,* s., pub. Poligrafa, full sheet, good cond., repaired punctures, creases, scrapes, masking tape stain, (02-11-93, Sotheby-NY, #193, illus.), sheet 19⅝ x 14⅛ in., (498 x 359 mm.), color lithograph w/hand coloring in black, orange and yellow wash on japon (Japan paper) nacre (BP 2638, DM 6192, FR 20,953, Y 450,633).

$3025* *Les Essencies De La Terra (M. 577; C. 123), 1968,* s., pub. Poligrafa, full margins, good cond., mat stain, (11-05-92, Sotheby-NY, #280), 12¼ x 11⅝ in., (310 x 295 mm.), lithograph w/hand coloring in red wash on japon nacre (BP 1967, DM 4784, FR 16,185, Y 371,120).

$3025* *Les Essencies De La Terra (M. 580; C. 123), 1968,* s., pub. Poligrafa, full margins, good cond., mat stain, creases, inktraces, soiling, Julie Andrews and Blake Edwards Coll., (11-05-92, Sotheby-NY, #281), 15⅜ x 12⅜ in., (390 x 315 mm.), lithograph p. in colors w/ hand coloring in black crayon on japon nacre (BP 1967, DM 4784, FR 16,185, Y 371,120).

$1725* *Exhibition "Miro-Artigas, Monumental Ceramics" (M. 338), 1963,* s., #13/200, p., pub. Maeght, full sheet, good cond., mat stain, foxing, masking tape hinge remains, related skin spots, backboard, (02-11-93, Sotheby-NY, #187), sheet 33⅜ x 22⅜ in., (848 x 569 mm.), color lithograph (BP 1217, DM 2857, FR 9669, Y 207,957).

BI *Exhibition Poster For "A Toute Epreuve" (Duplin 235), c. 1958,* s., #1/125, p. Fequet et Baudier, full margins, good cond., creases,hinged w/scotch tape, est. $1,5/2,000, (02-11-93, Sotheby-NY, #184), 14¾ x 12¹⁵⁄₁₆ in., (375 x 330 mm.), color woodcut.

$2588* *Exhibition Poster For "Constellations" (M. 259), 1959,* s., d., #128/150, p. Mourlot, pub. Berggruen, full margins, good cond., faded, light-stain, crease, glued to backing, (05-13-93, Sotheby-NY, #641), 21⅝ x 19 in., (548 x 482 mm.), lithograph in colors (BP 1699, DM 4179, FR 14,096, Y 288,936).

$4370* *Exhibition Poster For "Museu De La Resistencia-Salvador Allende" (C.1227), 1980,* s., #65/75, p. Litografias artisticas, Damia Caus, pub. Ajuntament de Palma, full sheet, good cond., light/masking tape stain, foxing, skinning, discolored, (02-11-93, Sotheby-NY, #199, illus.), sheet 34¾ x 23⅜ in., (883 x 593 mm.), color lithograph (BP 3084, DM 7239, FR 24,496, Y 526,823).

$2475* *Exhibition Poster For Sobreteixims (Picazo 64), 1973,* s., #93/150, pub. Maeght, good cond., creases, water stain, (11-05-92, Sotheby-NY, #296), sheet 33¾ x 23¼ in., (857 x 591 mm.), lithograph p. in colors (BP 1610, DM 3914, FR 13,242, Y 303,644).

$3850* *Exhibition Poster For 'Foundation Maeght' (P. 112), 1979,* s., #73/75, pub. Maeght, full margins, good cond., (11-05-92, Sotheby-NY, #308), 29½ x 19⅝ in., (750 x 497 mm.), lithograph p. in colors (BP 2504, DM 6089, FR 20,599, Y 472,335).

$62* *Exposicion Homenaje A Josep-Lluis Sert ... (Corredor-Matheos 55), 1972,* (09-25-92, Granier, #2945), 29¹⁵⁄₁₆ x 22⅝ in., (76 x 57.5 cm.), color lithograph poster on wove (BP 36, DM 92, FR 311, Y 7483).

$8800* *La Femme Angora (D. 499), 1969,* s., #45/75, pub. Maeght, good cond., light stain, skinned spot, (11-05-92, Sotheby-NY, #286, illus.), sheet 41⅜ x 27½ in., (105.1 x 69.9 cm.), etching, aquatint and carborundum p. in colors (BP 5724, DM 13,917, FR 47,084, Y 1,079,622).

$35,200* *Femme Au Miroir (M. 242), 1956,* s., #43/150, pub. Maeght, good cond., creases, soiling, (11-05-92, Sotheby-NY, #263, illus.), sheet 15⅜ x 22¼ in., (390 x 565 mm.), lithograph p. in colors (BP 22,894, DM 55,670, FR 188,336, Y 4,318,489).

$23,601* *Femme Au Miroir (Mourlot 242), 1956,* s., num. 81/150, pub. Maeght, full sheet, blue attenuated, touched-in surface scuffs, discoloration, good cond., (10-14-92, Sotheby-Japan, #53, illus.), sheet 15⅜ x 22¼ in., (391 x 565 mm.), colored lithograph on Rives wove (BP 13,853, DM 34,540, FR 117,127, Y 2,860,034).

$7162* *La Femme Des Sables (D. 500), 1969,* s., #22/75, p., pub. Maeght, good cond., soiling, (12-03-92, Sotheby-London, #433, illus.), sheet 41⅜ x 26¼ in., (105.1 x 66.7 cm.), etching, aquatint and carborundum in colors (BP 4620, DM 11,263, FR 38,443, Y 891,129).

$6177* *La Femme Des Sables (D. 500), 1969,* s., #72/75, p. and pub. by Maeght, margins, good cond., (06-30-93, Sotheby-London, #542, illus.), 36 x 23 in., (914 x 584 mm.), etching and aquatint and carborundum in color on Arches (BP 4140, DM 10,536, FR 35,541, Y 661,845).

$4263* *Femme En Colere (D. 148), 1958,* s., #30/75, pub. Maeght, full margins, good cond., (paper tone darkened), (12-03-92, Sotheby-London, #416, illus.), 4⅞ x 3¼ in., (123 x 83 mm.), etching and aquatint in colors on BFK Rives (BP 2750, DM 6704, FR 22,882, Y 530,422).

$7700* *Femme En Colere (D. 148), 1958,* s., #39/75, pub. Maeght, full margins, good cond., mat stain, marginsfolded back, (11-05-92, Sotheby-NY, #265, illus.), 4⅞ x 3¼ in., (125 x 84 mm.), etching and aquatint (BP 5008, DM 12,178, FR 41,199, Y 944,669).

$2300* *Femme Et Oiseau Devant La Lune (Dupin 51), 1947,* from Laurels Number One, Laurels Gallery, s., d., #257/300, full margins, remains, glue patches, very good cond., (05-11-93, Christie-NY, #237, illus.), plate 4⁵⁄₁₆ x

5¾ in., (110 x 146 mm.), etching on wove (BP 1468, DM 3623, FR 12,208, Y 252,997).

$89* *"Femme Et Oiseaux", 1964,* s. Miro, (03-16-93, Encans, #198), 22³⁄₁₆ x 17¹¹⁄₁₆ in., (56.3 x 45 cm.), poster before No F 62 (BP 61, DM 148, FR 503, Y 10,407, C$ 111).

BI *La Femme Toupie (D. 652), 1974,* s., #46/50, pub. Maeght, full margins, good cond., mat stain, est. $20/25,000, (11-05-92, Sotheby-NY, #299, illus.), 46½ x 29⅜ in., (118.1 x 74.6 cm.), etching and aquatint p. in colors.

$3450* *Fissures: Plate 12 (D. 476), 1969,* s., #26/75, p., pub. Maeght, good cond., (05-13-93, Sotheby-NY, #650), sh 19⅛ x 22⅞ in., (486 x 581 mm.), aquatint w/soft varnish & wash tint in colors (BP 2265, DM 5571, FR 18,791, Y 385,174).

$660* *Flux De L'Aimant: Ohne Titel (D. 373), 1964,* init., #20/75, pub. Maeght, full margins, good cond., restored, toucheduched-in tear in image, mat staining, creases, staining, (02-24-93, Butterfield, #2760), sheet 19¹⁄₁₆ x 23 in., (484 x 584 mm.), drypoint on BFK Rives (BP 460, DM 1071, FR 3632, Y 77,447).

$1760* *"Flying Figure",* s. Miro, ident. and designated artist's proof, Kanegis Gallery label, very good cond., (03-12-93, Skinner, #83, illus.), sight 5¾ x 6⅜ in., (14.6 x 16.2 cm.), etching in color on paper (BP 1228, DM 2929, FR 9960, Y 207,425).

BI *Fondation Maeght. Saint-Paul-De-Vence (Mourlot 502), 1968,* wrinkles, est. SF 100/150, (10-14-92, Germann, #386), 29³⁄₁₆ x 20¹⁄₁₆ in., (742 x 510 mm.), color lithograph/poster.

$11,000* *Les Forestiers (blue) (D. 150), 1958,* s., #59/75, wide margins, skinned spot, time staining, spots of glue, (11-09-92, Christie-NY, #125, illus.), 12¾ x 19⁵⁄₁₆ in., colored aquatint on BFK Rives (BP 7273, DM 17,561, FR 59,331, Y 1,365,103).

$1840* *Fotoscop (C. 938; see bk. 209), 1974,* s., i., p. La Poligrafa, pub. Galierie Borjeson, full margins, good cond., mat stain, (02-11-93, Sotheby-NY, #195), 7¹¹⁄₁₆ x 15³⁄₁₆ in., (195 x 385 mm.), color lithograph (BP 1298, DM 3048, FR 10,314, Y 221,820).

BI *Fotoscop (Cramer 939), 1974,* #36/100, s., est. DM 4,000-, (11-21-92, Lempertz, #294), 8⁷⁄₁₆ x 15⅝ in., (21.5 x 39.7 cm.), color lithograph on Guarro wove.

$3319* *Fotoscope Danes, 1975,* s., num., Edition der Galerie Borjeson, (12-01-92, Karl/Faber, #1023, illus.), 8¼ x 15¾ in., (21 x 40 cm.), color lithograph on thick wove (BP 2193, DM 5290, FR 18,028, Y 413,222).

$2622* *Le Frelon, 1978,* s., watermark, lit., (06-08-93, Karl/Faber, #1122, illus.), sh approx. 19⅞ x 26³⁄₁₆ in., (50.5 x 66.5 cm.), color etching and aquatint on Arches France wove (BP 1724, DM 4254, FR 14,328, Y 278,492).

$706* *From Hai-Ku (Mourlot 492), 1967,* s., #17/25, for Haiku, (06-10-93, Hauswedell/Nolt, #644), image 10¹⁄₁₆ x 7⅜ in., (25.5 x 18.8 cm.), lithograph on Japan nacre (BP 462, DM 1150, FR 3871, Y 74,939).

$2825* *From Jacques Dupin. Miro Escultor (Cramer 935; Cramer 192), 1974,* s., #16/100, (06-10-93, Hauswedell/Nolt, #646), image 13¾ x 20½ in., (35 x 52 cm.), color lithograph on wove (BP 1848, DM 4600, FR 15,488, Y 299,862).

$1760* *From Les Essencies De La Terra (Mourlot 510), 1970,* s., i. 10F/100 in a different hand, pub. Poligrafa, (12-13-92, Hindman, #276), 19½ x 12½ in., color lithograph on Japan nacre w/ink wash additions by the artist (BP 1125, DM 2766, FR 9427, Y 217,741).

$1495* *From Sans Le Soleil, Malgre Les Autres Astres, Il Ferait Nuit (D. 402), 1965,* bears sig., #31/75, pub. Adrien Maeght, p. Levallois-Perret, Maeght,margins, good cond., mat staining, hinge remains, surface scuff affecting sig.-foxing, (05-19-93, Butterfield, #1937, illus.), sh. 8⅝ x 11³⁄₁₆ in., (219 x 284 mm.), soft-ground etching and aquatint in colors on wove (BP 970, DM 2430, FR 8187, Y 165,504).

$2684* *From Strindberg Mappen (Cramer 1104), 1976,* s., i. E.A., (06-10-93, Hauswedell/Nolt, #648, illus.), image 29¾ x 22¹⁄₁₆ in., (75.5 x 56 cm.), color lithograph on Japan nacre (BP 1756, DM 4371, FR 14,715, Y 284,895).

$4229* *From: Le Marteau Sans Maitre (Cramer Illustr. Books 216), 1976,* (05-26-93, Lempertz, #375, illus.), 17½ x 13³⁄₁₆ in., (44.5 x 33.5 cm.), aquatint-etching on Japan nacre (BP 2736, DM 6900, FR 23,224, Y 459,474).

$4400* *Fueses (D. 253; C. 54), 1959,* s., #49/50, pub. Louis Broder, full margins, good cond., prop. Woodward Foundation, (11-05-92, Sotheby-NY, #266), 5⅝ x 16¼ in., (142 x 412 mm.), etching and aquatint p. in colors on BFK Rives wove (BP 2862, DM 6959, FR 23,542, Y 539,811).

$58* *Fundacio Joan Miro Barcelona 1976 (Corredor-Matheos 90), 1984,* (09-25-92, Granier, #2947), 27⁹⁄₁₆ x 19¹¹⁄₁₆ in., (70 x 50 cm.), color lithograph poster on wove (BP 34, DM 86, FR 291, Y 7001).

$2520* *Fur: Graphikmappe Hochschule St. Gallen (Cramer, Nachtrag In Bd. VI,357/a), 1964,* s., i. HC, (06-23-93, Kornfeld, #589), color lithograph (BP 1712, DM 4264, FR 14,343, Y 274,540, SF 3795).

$2875* *Fusees (D. 249), 1959,* s., #7/50, p. Crommelynck et Dutrou, pub. Louis Broder, full margins, (05-13-93, Sotheby-NY, #635), 5⅛ x 7 in., (129 x 179 mm.), aquatint in black and red w/touches of hand-coloring (BP 1887, DM 4642, FR 15,659, Y 320,978).

$3738* *Fusees (D. 252), 1959,* s., #7/50, p. Crommelynck et Dutrou, pub. Louis Broder, full margins,good cond., (05-13-93, Sotheby-NY, #636, illus.), 5⅛ x 7 in., (130 x 178 mm.), etching and aquatint in red and yellow w/touches of hand-coloring (BP 2454, DM 6036, FR 20,359, Y 417,327).

$4025* *Fusees (D. 253), 1959,* s., #7/50, p. Crommelynck et Dutrou, pub. Louis Broder, full margins,good cond., (05-13-93, Sotheby-NY, #637, illus.), 5⅝ x 16¼ in., (144 x 413 mm.), aquatint w/touches of hand-coloring (BP 2642, DM 6499, FR 21,923, Y 449,369).

$2875* *Fusees (D. 254), 1959,* s., #7/50, p. Crommelynck et Dutrou, pub. Louis Broder, full margins,good cond., (05-13-93, Sotheby-NY, #638), 5⅝ x 16¼ in., (143 x 413 mm.), aquatint in blue and black (BP 1887, DM 4642, FR 15,659, Y 320,978).

$2875* *Fusees (D. 255), 1959,* s., #7/50, p. Crommelynck et Dutrou, pub. Louis Broder, full margins,good cond., (05-13-93, Sotheby-NY, #639, illus.), 5⅝ x 16¼ in., (144 x 413 mm.), aquatint in red and black (BP 1887, DM 4642, FR 15,659, Y 320,978).

$3450* *Fusees (D. 256), 1959,* s., #7/50, p. Crommelynck et Dutrou, pub. Louis Broder, full margins,good cond., (05-13-93, Sotheby-NY, #640, illus.), 5⅝ x 16¼ in., (143 x 412 mm.), aquatint in red, blue and black (BP 2265, DM 5571, FR 18,791, Y 385,174).

$3160* *Fusees-Nousm Avons (Rene Char) (Dupin 257; Cramer 54), 1959,* #VI/XV, s., (04-21-93, Germann, #640, illus.), 11¼ x 14¹⁵⁄₁₆ in., (285 x 380 mm.), color aquatint (BP 2050, DM 5051, FR 17,081, Y 349,828, SF 4600).

$1870* *Fusees: Untitled (D. 261), 1959,* s., annot. II/V, pub. Louis Broder, margins possibly trimmed, good cond. (/), foxing, (02-24-93, Butterfield, #2758, illus.), 5⅛ x 7 in., (130 x 178 mm.), etching & aquatint in colors on Japan (BP 1304, DM 3036, FR 10,292, Y 219,432).

$12,650* *Galatee, 1976,* s., #32/50, full margins?, good cond., (05-13-93, Sotheby-NY, #663, illus.), 45¼ x 29⅛ in., (114.9 x 74 cm.), etching, aquatint & carborundum in colors (BP 8305, DM 20,426, FR 68,900, Y 1,412,303).

$193* *"Galerie Maeght",* s. Miro, (05-15-93, Wolf, #678), 30 x 19½ in., (76.2 x 49.5 cm.), poster (BP 125, DM 310, FR 1043, Y 21,395).

$10,231* *La Geante (Dupin 27), 1938,* s., i. 2ieme etat 1/1 tiree par moi-meme 3 mars 1938, full margins, mount-staining and soiling, foxing, staining, scuffing, rubbing, tipped to mountat top, prov., (12-03-92, Sotheby-London, #410, illus.), 13¾ x 9⅜ in., (350 x 236 mm.), drypoint w/thone on wove (BP 6600, DM 16,089, FR 54,917, Y 1,272,987).

$5661* *Les Geants (Dupin 280), 1960,* ed. Maeght, s., 23/50, (05-25-93, AB Stockholm, #50), 22¹³⁄₁₆ x 36 in., (58 x 91.5 cm.), aquatint on BFK Rives (BP 3669, DM 9220, FR 31,036, Y 618,756, SK 8250).

BI *Les Geants: Plate V (D. 280), 1960,* s., #27/50, pub. Maeght, handling creases, discoloration, good cond., est. BP 1,5/2,000, (12-01-92, Christie-London, #435), plate 23¼ x 36¼ in., (590 x 920 mm.), aquatint on BFK Rives.

$919* *Germination Nocturne (Mourlot 145), 1955,* s., 2/50, (05-12-93, AB Stockholm, #7038), 26³⁄₁₆ x 19⅞ in., (66.5 x 50.5 cm.), color lithograph (BP 600, DM 1483, FR 4995, Y 102,601, SK 6820).

BI *Giboulees (D. 282), 1960,* s., #16/90, p. Crommelynck et Dutrou, pub. Maeght, full margins, goodcond., creases, staining, est. BP 1,6/2,000, (06-30-93, Sotheby-London, #538, illus.), 13½ x 18¼ in., (343 x 464 mm.), soft-ground etching and aquatint in color, on BRK Rives.

BI *"Gran Rupestre 22",* s. Miro, num. 14/30, est. $3/5,000, (09-25-92, Wolf, #35, illus.), 27 x 35 in., (68.6 x 88.9 cm.), color aquatint w/embossing.

$6821* *Le Grand Carnassier (D. 502), 1969,* s., #37/75, p., pub. Maeght, good cond., soiling, (12-03-92, Sotheby-London, #431, illus.), sheet 41⅝ x 26¼ in., (105.7 x 66.7 cm.), etching, aquatint and carborundum in colors (BP 4400, DM 10,727, FR 36,613, Y 848,700).

$5491* *Le Grand Carnassier (D. 502), 1969,* s., #37/75, p. and pub. Maeght, good cond., soiling, (06-30-93, Sotheby-London, #546, illus.), sh 41⅝ x 26¼ in., (105.7 x 66.7 cm.), etching, aquatint and carborundum in color (BP 3680, DM 9366, FR 31,594, Y 588,342).

$3300* *Grand Duc II (D. 395), 1965,* s., #46/75, p. and pub. by Maeght, full margins, good cond., rubbed spots, scuffs, light stain, foxing, Julie Andrews and Blake Edwards Coll., (11-05-92, Sotheby-NY, #273, illus.), 26⅞ x 20⅞ in., (683 x 530 mm.), etching p. in colors (BP 2146, DM 5219, FR 17,657, Y 404,858).

BI *Le Grand Ordinateur (D. 503), 1969,* s., #60/75, p. Morsang, pub. Maeght, good cond., mat stain, scotch tape, est. $10/12,000, (05-13-93, Sotheby-NY, #653, illus.), 41⅛ x 26¾ in., (104.5 x 67.9 cm.), etching, aquatint & carborundum in colors.

$13,200* *Le Grand Ordinateur (Dupin 503), 1969,* s., #23/75, (03-14-93, Hindman, #301, illus.), 39⅝ x 25⅛ in., (100.6 x 63.8 cm.), color etching, aquatint and carborundum (BP 9208, DM 21,971, FR 74,703, Y 1,555,687).

$25,300* *La Grand Sorcier (D. 453), 1968,* s., #24/75, pub. Maeght, good cond., (11-05-92, Sotheby-NY, #279, illus.), sheet 35⅛ x 26⅝ in., (892 x 675 mm.), etching, aquatint, drypoint and carborundum p. in colors (BP 16,455, DM 40,013, FR 135,367, Y 3,103,914).

$20,700* *La Grand Sorcier (D. 453), 1968,* s., i. H.C., pub. Maeght, good cond., scuffs, creases, (05-13-93, Sotheby-NY, #649, illus.), 35⅛ x 26⅜ in., (891 x 670 mm.), etching, aquatint, drypoint and carborundum in colors (BP 13,590, DM 33,425, FR 112,745, Y 2,311,042).

$20,700* *Grand Triptyque Noir (D. 504), 1969,* watermark, s., #19/50, staining, surface soiling, creases, skinned patches, good cond., (05-11-93, Christie-NY, #241, illus.), sheet 63¼ x 47½ in., (160.7 x 120.7 cm.), color etching, aquatint and carborundum on thick wove (BP 13,214, DM 32,609, FR 109,873, Y 2,276,977).

$4025* *Grans Rupestres, 1979,* s., #4/30, p. Joan Barbara, pub. Maeght, good cond., foxing, maskingtape stain, (05-13-93, Sotheby-NY, #665, illus.), sh 35¼ x 26¾ in., (894 x 680 mm.), aquatint in colors (BP 2642, DM 6499, FR 21,923, Y 449,369).

$2300* *Graphikmappe Hochschule St. Gallen (M. 425a), 1964,* s., #88/150, pub. Hochschule, p. Atelier Maeght, good cond.?, (05-19-93, Butterfield, #1936, illus.), 25¾ x 19¹¹⁄₁₆ in., (654 x 500 mm.), lithograph in colors on wove (BP 1493, DM 3739, FR 12,596, Y 254,622).

$8185* *Le Greve Noir (D. 576; B. 199), 1973,* s., i. H.C., pub. Maeght, good cond., (12-03-92, Sotheby-London, #448, illus.), sheet 54 x 23⅝ in., (137.2 x 60 cm.), etching and carborundum in colors (BP 5280, DM 12,872, FR 43,935, Y 1,018,415).

$1716* *Hai-Ku: La Lune Pres De Paraitre... (M. 485), 1967,* s., #97/100, pub. Maeght, margins, good cond., back-board staining, (06-30-93, Sotheby-London, #544, illus.), 12¼ x 9 in., (311 x 229 mm.), color on wove (BP 1150, DM 2927, FR 9873, Y 183,864).

$2059* *Hai-Ku: Silence...(M. 487), 1967,* s., #20/100, pub. Maeght, margins, good cond., back-board staining, (06-30-93, Sotheby-London, #543, illus.), sh 12¼ x 9 in., (311 x 229 mm.), color lithograph on wove (BP 1380, DM 3512, FR 11,847, Y 220,615).

$1650* *"Hibou X",* s., #119/120, prov., (06-11-93, DuMouchelle, #2094, illus.), 20 x 26 in., (50.8 x 66 cm.), lithograph (BP 1084, DM 2682, FR 9041, Y 175,066).

$4950* *Homenatge A Joan Prats: Pl. XIII (M. 729; C. 153), 1971,* s., #22/75, pub. Poligrafa, margins, good cond., discoloration, (11-05-92, Sotheby-NY, #291), 21⅝ x 29½ in., (550 x 748 mm.), lithograph p. in colors (BP 3220, DM 7829, FR 26,485, Y 607,287).

$3300* *Homenatge A Joan Prats: Pl. XV (M. 733; C. 153), 1971,* s., #XVI/XV, pub. Poligrafa, full margins, good cond., creases, (11-05-92, Sotheby-NY, #292), 21⅜ x 29½ in., (544 x 748 mm.), lithograph p. in colors (BP 2146, DM 5219, FR 17,657, Y 404,858).

$4313* *Homenatge A Joan Prats: Plate I (M. 705), 1971,* s., #59/75, p., pub. Poligrafa, full margins, good cond., handling creases, tape hinges, (05-13-93, Sotheby-NY, #656), 21⅜ x 29¼ in., (543 x 742 mm.), lithograph in colors (BP 2832, DM 6964, FR 23,491, Y 481,523).

$5175* *Homenatge A Joan Prats: Plate XIII (M. 729), 1971,* s., #XVI/XXV, pub. Poligrafa, full margins, good cond., handling creases, creases, skinning, (05-13-93, Sotheby-NY, #657, illus.), 21⅝ x 29⅜ in., (548 x 745 mm.), lithograph in colors (BP 3397, DM 8356, FR 28,186, Y 577,760).

$3392* *Homentage A Joan Prats (M. 709), 1971,* from set of 15, #21/75, s., large margins, (02-03-93, Ader Tajan, #183), 21¼ x 29⅛ in., (54 x 74 cm.), color lithograph (BP 2368, DM 5585, FR 18,939, Y 421,943).

$3005* *Homentage A Joan Prats (M. 713), 1971,* from set of 15, s., #21/75, large margins, (02-03-93, Ader Tajan, #184), 21¼ x 29⅛ in., (54 x 74 cm.), color lithographs (BP 2098, DM 4948, FR 16,778, Y 373,803).

$3105* *Hommage A Miro (M. 868), 1972,* s., #13/75, p. Maeght, full margins, good cond., light stain, creases, Alan E. Paris, Jr. Estate, (02-11-93, Sotheby-NY, #194, illus.), 12¹³⁄₁₆ x 19¹¹⁄₁₆ in., (325 x 500 mm.), color lithograph (BP 2191, DM 5143, FR 17,405, Y 374,322).

$4600* *Hommage A Picasso (D. 565; see C. bk. 172), 1972,* s., i. HC, p. Maeght, pub. Propylaen, 1973, good cond., crease, (05-13-93, Sotheby-NY, #658), sh 22½ x 30 in., (571 x 762 mm.), etching and aquatint in colors (BP 3020, DM 7428, FR 25,054, Y 513,565).

BI *Hommenatge A Joan Prats (M. 714), 1971,* s., #xxii/xxv, pub. Poligrafa, full margins, good cond., creasing, est. BP 2/2,500, (06-30-93, Sotheby-London, #540, illus.), 21¼ x 29¼ in., (540 x 743 mm.), lithograph on Guarro paper.

$1985* *Illustration Pour: Jean Leymarie - Jacques Dupin. Joan Miro. Paris 194 (Cramer, Livres illustres, 186), 1974,* s., num., (06-23-93, Kornfeld, #595), color lithograph (BP 1349, DM 3359, FR 11,298, Y 216,254, SF 2990).

BI *Issue Derobee (D. 711), 1974,* s., #36/50, p. and pub. Maeght, good cond., est. BP 1,2/1,800, (06-30-93, Sotheby-London, #557), sh 13 x 19⅝ in., (330 x 498 mm.), drypoint w/aquatint in color on wove.

$7673* *Jacques Prevert.Adonides (C. 203),* portfolio, s. by Miro, num.; s., num. on just. by artist and pub. andin facsimile by author, pub. Maeght Editeur, 1975, full margins, good cond., orig. paper wrappers and cloth covered box, (12-03-92, Sotheby-London, #446), each sheet approx. 15⅝ x 13 in., (397 x 330 mm.), 45 etchings w/ aquatint in colors, 44 in texte, the hors-texte etching (BP 4950, DM 12,066, FR 41,186, Y 954,709).

$1201* *Jaillie Du Calcaire (Mourlot 850), 1974,* s., #28/50, (06-10-93, Hauswedell/Nolt, #645), image 12¹⁵⁄₁₆ x 9¹³⁄₁₆ in., (33 x 25 cm.), color lithograph on Arches (BP 786, DM 1956, FR 6584, Y 127,481).

$2200* *Japanese Woman (M. 829), 1971,* s., #17/150, good cond.?, (10-28-92, Butterfield, #2677), 14 x 19¾ in., (356 x 502 mm.), color lithograph on Rives vellum w/ artist's watermark (BP 1402, DM 3398, FR 11,536, Y 269,939).

BI *Je Travaille Comme Un Jardinier (Miro Lithograph II, 283-313), 1963:Nine,* num., est. DM 12,000, (12-05-92, Bassenge, #7495), color lithograph.

$2420* *Jeune Fille Aux Deux Oiseaux (Benhoura 92, Dupin 190), 1967,* s., i. H.C., (03-24-93, Grogan, #112, illus.), 13⁹⁄₁₆ x 12⅜ in., (34.4 x 31.4 cm.), etching and aquatint (BP 1639, DM 3952, FR 13,452, Y 284,338).

BI *Joan Brossa, Tres Joans (Cramer 244), 1978,* #168/500, frontispiece, s., est. SF 3/4,000, (09-04-92, Germann, #476), color lithograph.

$181* *Joan Miro Graphics (Philadelphia Museum of Art 1966) (Picazo 26),* (11-28-92, Schoppmann, #665), 29¹⁵⁄₁₆ x 22¹⁄₁₆ in., (76 x 56 cm.), color lithograph on wove (BP 119, DM 288, FR 979, Y 22,526).

$1716* *Joan Miro Lithographs IV (MA. 1259), 1981,* s., #XLVIII/LXXX, p. by Mourlot, pub. Maeght, full margins, good cond., (06-30-93, Sotheby-London, #558), 11⅝ x 9¼ in., (295 x 235 mm.), color lithograph on wove (BP 1150, DM 2927, FR 9873, Y 183,864).

$1870* *Joan Miro Lithographs, Volumes I-IV, 1972-81,* catalogues raisonnes, pub. Tudor Publishing Company, good cond., (11-05-92, Sotheby-NY, #310), 32 orig. lithographs in colors (BP 1216, DM 2957, FR 10,005, Y 229,420).

$2300* *Joan Miro Lithographs, Volumes I-IV: Four,* text in English, pub. Tudor Publishing Company, Leon Amiel and Maeght, 1972-81, all w/orig. lithographic jackets, good cond., (05-13-93, Sotheby-NY, #666), catalogues raisonne, incl. 32 orig. lithographs in colors (BP 1510, DM 3714, FR 12,527, Y 256,782).

$1084* *Joan Miro. Samlade Litografier II (C. 198; C. L 1036-1047), 1975: Twelve,* Malmo, Galerie Borjeson, #25/300, (10-09-92, Winterberg, #2811), color lithograph (BP 643, DM 1610, FR 5406, Y 131,970).

$3080* *Jose-Miguel Ullan (C. 256), 1985: Set Of Six,* Almario, Robert Lydie Dutrou, s., num., s. by Emilio Miro, copy 28, very good cond., (11-09-92, Christie-NY, #139, illus.), 13³⁄₁₆ x 10⁷⁄₁₆ in., (335 x 265 mm.), etching and aquatint in colors; 5 drypoints on wove (BP 2036, DM 4917, FR 16,613, Y 382,229).

$1264* *"Journal D'Un Graveur" (Cramer 200), 1975: Four,* #40/75, s., (04-21-93, Germann, #642), 22¹⁄₁₆ x 17½ in., (560 x 445 mm.), lithograph (BP 820, DM 2020, FR 6832, Y 139,931, SF 1840).

$790* *"Journal D'Un Graveur" (Cramer 200), 1975: Four,* #40/75, s., (04-21-93, Germann, #644), 22¹⁄₁₆ x 17½ in., (560 x 445 mm.), lithograph (BP 513, DM 1263, FR 4270, Y 87,457, SF 1150).

$4734* *Komposition,* s., #18/75, (05-08-93, Dobiaschofsky, #2129, illus.), 34¹³⁄₁₆ x 23⅝ in., (88.5 x 60 cm.), color lithograph (BP 3089, DM 7605, FR 25,659, Y 528,998, SF 6900).

$632* *Komposition,* 53/100, mono., (06-24-93, Germann, #440), 12 x 8¾ in., (305 x 223 mm.), color lithograph (BP 416, DM 1025, FR 3454, Y 67,797, SF 920).

$1692* *Komposition (Cramer 154), 1972,* s., num., from series Mois Mondial du coeur, (05-26-93, Dorling, #2865, illus.), 21⁷⁄₁₆ x 21¹⁄₁₆ in., (54.5 x 53.5 cm.), color lithograph on BFK Rives wove (BP 1095, DM 2761, FR 9292, Y 183,833).

$2212* *Komposition (Cramer 204), 1975,* from L'enfance d'Ubu, s., (09-04-92, Germann, #12), 12³⁄₁₆ x 19⅛ in., (310 x 485 mm.), color lithograph on Japan (BP 1108, DM 3100, FR 10,553, Y 272,280, SF 2760).

BI *Komposition (Cramer 204), 1975,* from L'enfance d'Ubu, #XI/XX, s., est. SF 2,8/3,500, (09-04-92, Germann, #13), 12³⁄₁₆ x 19⅛ in., (310 x 485 mm.), color lithograph.

BI *Komposition Mit Drei Kugeln,* gold s., est. DM 10,000, (09-18-92, Schloss Ahlden, #1038, illus.), 29⅞ x 22⅛ in., (75.9 x 56.2 cm.), colored etching w/carborundum on Velin Arches.

$642* *Kompositioner, Miro, Obra Inedita Recent, (Mourlot 356F and 356G), 1964: Two,* s. M. 49/100 and 53/100, (03-24-93, Kunsthallen, #243), color lithograph on ramme (frame) (BP 435, DM 1049, FR 3569, Y 75,432, DK 4025).

$367* *Kompositioner: Three,* from Derriere Le Miroir, (03-24-93, Kunsthallen, #247), color lithograph (BP 249, DM 599, FR 2040, Y 43,121, DK 2300).

$858* *Kronenhalle 1862-1922-1962 (M. 337A), 1962,* s., p. by Maeght, crease, soiling, tape stains, ink inscription, (06-30-93, Sotheby-London, #553), sh 12¼ x 10 in., (311 x 254 mm.), color lithograph on BFK Rives (BP 575, DM 1463, FR 4937, Y 91,932).

$7700* *L'Adorateur Du Soleil (D. 483), 1969,* s., #9/75, light staining, creasing, good cond., (11-09-92, Christie-NY, #130, illus.), 41¾ x 26¾ in., (106 x 68 cm.), etching, aquatint, and carborundum in colors on Arches (BP 5091, DM 12,292, FR 41,532, Y 955,572).

$7475* *L'Adorateur Du Soleil (D. 484), 1969,* s., #51/75, time staining, very good cond., (05-11-93, Christie-NY, #240, illus.), sheet 41½ x 26¾ in., (105.4 x 67.9 cm.), color aquatint w/carborundum on Arches (BP 4772, DM 11,775, FR 39,676, Y 822,242).

$9900* *L'Aieule Devant La Mer (D. 484), 1969,* s., #43/75, pub. Maeght, good cond., soiling, foxing, (11-05-92, Sotheby-NY, #283, illus.), sheet 41¾ x 27¾ in., (106 x 70.5 cm.), aquatint and carborundum p. in colors on Arches (BP 6439, DM 15,657, FR 52,970, Y 1,214,575).

BI *L'Antitete Volume 3, Le Desesperanto Plate II (D. 63; C. 20), 1949,* from negative printing, pub. Bordas, est. $10/12,000, (11-05-92, Sotheby-NY, #260, illus.), 5⅝ x 4½ in., (144 x 113 mm.), etching w/watercolor on Van Gelder laid.

$4400* *L'Archipel Sauvage III (D. 529), 1970,* s., #6/35, pub. Maeght, full margins, good cond., crease, Julie Andrews and Blake Edwards Coll., (11-05-92, Sotheby-NY, #288), 23 x 36 in., (585 x 914 mm.), etching and aquatint p. in colors (BP 2862, DM 6959, FR 23,542, Y 539,811).

$9200* *L'Astre Du Labyrinthe (D. 425), 1967,* s., #58/75, full margins, staining, image scrape, platemarks partially broken through, skinned patch, defects, (05-11-93, Christie-NY, #239, illus.), plate 36⅜ x 23⅛ in., (924 x 587 mm.), color etching, drypoint, aquatint and carborundum on wove (BP 5873, DM 14,493, FR 48,832, Y 1,011,990).

$4162* *L'Astre Du Marecage (D. 426), 1967,* s., #46/75, Maeght, trimmed, crease, good cond., laid, (12-01-92, Christie-London, #436), sheet 40¹⁵⁄₁₆ x 27½ in., (104 x 69.8 cm.), aquatint on wove (BP 2750, DM 6634, FR 22,607, Y 518,177).

$1430* *L'Enfance D'Ubu (C. 204), 1975,* s., #24/120, pub. Teriade, full margins, good cond.?, (10-28-92, Butterfield, #2685), 11½ x 18¼ in., (292 x 464 mm.), color lithograph on wove (BP 911, DM 2208, FR 7499, Y 175,460).

$1974* *L'Enfance D'Ubu (Cramer 1019; Cramer, Illustr. Books 204), 1975,* s., sheet 22 of series, #IX/XX, num., (05-26-93, Lempertz, #374), color lithograph (BP 1277, DM 3221, FR 10,840, Y 214,472).

$2902* *L'Entraineuse (M. 546), 1969,* s. in violet, num., (06-23-93, Kornfeld, #593), color lithograph (BP 1971, DM 4910, FR 16,517, Y 316,156, SF 4370).

$5750* *L'Homme Au Balancier (D. 507), 1969,* s., i. H.C., p., pub. Maeght, good cond., (05-13-93, Sotheby-NY, #654, illus.), 26⅝ x 19½ in., (677 x 494 mm.), etching, aquatint & carborundum in colors (BP 3775, DM 9285, FR 31,318, Y 641,956).

$3931* *L'Homme Au Balancier (J. Dupin, 507), 1969,* annot. H.C., s., cracks, good untrimmed margins, (06-16-93, Ader Tajan, #123), 16¹⁵⁄₁₆ x 10⅝ in., (43 x 27 cm.), etching, aquatint and carborundum on Japan nacre (BP 2621, DM 6526, FR 21,900, Y 419,262).

$2825* *L'Illettre - Vert. (M. 552), 1969,* s. in white chalk, num., (06-23-93, Kornfeld, #594), color lithograph (BP 1919, DM 4780, FR 16,079, Y 307,768, SF 4255).

BI *L'Inhibe (D. 508), 1969,* s., #39/75, foxmarks, good cond., est. $8/10,000, (11-09-92, Christie-NY, #132, illus.), 27⅜ x 21¼ in., (695 x 540 mm.), etching, aquatint, and carborundum in colors on wove.

$2310* *L'Invention Du Feu (M. 267; D. 284), 1960,* s., #40/90, pub. Maeght, full margins, good cond., creases, light stain, taped to backmat, (11-05-92, Sotheby-NY, #267), 14⅝ x 21 in., (372 x 535 mm.), lithograph and aquatint (BP 1502, DM 3653, FR 12,360, Y 283,401).

BI *L'Ogre Enjoue (D. 511), 1969,* s., #42/75, p. and pub. Maeght, full margins, good cond., mount-staining, est. BP 8/10,000, (06-30-93, Sotheby-London, #548, illus.), 28½ x 41⅜ in., (72.4 x 105.1 cm.), etching and aquatint and carborundum in color on wove.

$6236* *L'Oiseau - Fusee, 1952,* #176/200, t., d., s., (04-24-93, Kunsthaus, #711, illus.), 13¹¹⁄₁₆ x 17¾ in., (34.7 x 45.1 cm.), color etching and aquatint on hand-made Arches (BP 3936, DM 9774, FR 33,012, Y 688,148).

$2990* *"L'Oiseau Destructeur" (Ed Maeght M 512), 1969,* s. 32/75, (11-07-92, Falkkloos, #330, illus.), etching, aquatint and carborundum (BP 1955, DM 4797, FR 16,136, Y 369,045, SK 17,820).

$1760* *L'Oiseau Du Feu (D. 360), 1967,* s., #9/75, large margins, good cond.?, (10-28-92, Butterfield, #2675), 22¼ x 31 in., (565 x 787 mm.), color lithograph on cream wove (BP 1121, DM 2718, FR 9229, Y 215,951).

$4331* *"L'Oiseau Du Paradis" (Dupin 361), 1963,* s., num., (11-28-92, Grisebach, #252, illus.), 22⁵⁄₁₆ x 31 in., (56.6 x 78.8 cm.), color aquatint on copper print paper (BP 2859, DM 6900, FR 23,423, Y 539,017).

$2664* *L. Aragon, Je N'Ai Jamais Appris A Ecrire On Les Incitip (Cr. 129), 1969,* Editions Skira, t., text illus. and one orig. p., copy num. 111, s.,#111/175, folded sheet, fine cond., (12-01-92, Christie-London, #437), overall sheet 11¹³⁄₁₆ x 9⁷⁄₁₆ in., (300 x 240 mm.), etching w/ aquatint in colors on wove (BP 1760, DM 4246, FR 14,470, Y 331,673).

BI *"Las Esencias De La Tierra",* s., #41/F/100 verso, lit., reserve P450,000, (10-15-92, Duran, #174, illus.), 19¹¹⁄₁₆ x 14³⁄₁₆ in., (50 x 36 cm.), color lithograph and drawing in tint and brush on Japan nacre.

$6384* *"Las Mujeres" (Mourlot 60), 1948,* s., d., num., (06-05-93, Grisebach, #367, illus.), 22⁹⁄₁₆ x 16⅛ in., (57.3 x 41 cm.), lithograph on copper print paper (BP 4202, DM 10,350, FR 34,885, Y 684,832).

BI *Latido (Cramer 154; Mourlot 500), 1972,* from Mois Mondial du Coeur, s., #52/75, est. SF 2,5/3,000, (04-21-93, Germann, #190), 25⅞ x 25 in., (658 x 635 mm.), color lithograph.

$2860* *Laurels Number One, 1947: Set Of Six,* Laurel Gallery, s., #27/300, full margins, very good cond., includ. Joan Miro, Femmes et oiseau devant la lune (D. 51; C. 10)-etching; Anne Ryan, Now ever alake, My Master Dear, I fear a deadly storm-colored wood engraving; Stanley William Hayter, Night Moth, (11-09-92, Christie-NY, #192, illus.), 425 x 330 in., (x 838.2 cm.), print (BP 1891, DM 4566, FR 15,426, Y 354,927).

$3300* *Le Lezard Aux Plume D'Or (M. 524), 1967,* s., i. E.A., good cond., skinned spot, (11-05-92, Sotheby-NY, #278), sheet 15⅞ x 22⅛ in., (404 x 562 mm.), lithograph p. in colors (BP 2146, DM 5219, FR 17,657, Y 404,858).

$5750* *Le Lezard Aux Plumes D'Or (M. 514), 1967,* s., d. 6/XI/65, full margins, good cond., (02-11-93, Sotheby-NY, #191, illus.), 13¾ x 19⁵⁄₁₆ in., (350 x 490 mm.), color lithograph (BP 4057, DM 9525, FR 32,231, Y 693,189).

BI *Le Lezard Aux Plumes D'Or (M. 517), 1967,* s., #37/50, full margins, good cond., creases, est. $1,2/1,500, (02-11-93, Sotheby-NY, #192), 13⁷⁄₁₆ x 19⁷⁄₁₆ in., (341 x 493 mm.), color lithograph on japon (Japan paper) nacre.

$4313* *Le Lezard Aux Plumes D'Or (M. 525), 1967,* s., #9/100, good cond., pink slightly faded, crease, discoloration, skinning, (05-13-93, Sotheby-NY, #647), sh 14 x 39 in., (355 x 992 mm.), lithograph in colors on wove (BP 2832, DM 6964, FR 23,491, Y 481,523).

$7475* *Le Lezard Aux Plumes D'Or (M. 526), 1967,* s., #1/20, good cond., (05-13-93, Sotheby-NY, #648, illus.), (350 x 496 mm.), lithograph in colors on vellum (BP 4907, DM 12,070, FR 40,714, Y 834,543).

$3922* *Le Lezard Aux Plumes D'Or (MA 461), 1971,* s., i. Epreuve d'artiste, pub. Louis Broder, margins, good cond., (12-03-92, Sotheby-London, #427, illus.), sheet 16 x 22 in., (408 x 560 mm.), lithograph in colors on wove (BP 2530, DM 6168, FR 21,052, Y 487,993).

$3410* *Le Lezard Aux Plumes D'Or (MA. 818), 1971,* s., #49/50, pub. Louis Broder, margins, good cond., creasing, (12-03-92, Sotheby-London, #444, illus.), sheet 14 x 19⅝ in., (356 x 500 mm.), lithograph in colors on Japan (BP 2200, DM 5362, FR 18,304, Y 424,288).

$3410* *Le Lezard Aux Plumes D'Or (MA. 824), 1971,* s., #49/50, pub. Louis Broder, margins, good cond., creasing, (12-03-92, Sotheby-London, #445, illus.), sheet 14 x 19¾ in., (355 x 500 mm.), lithograph in colors on Japan (BP 2200, DM 5362, FR 18,304, Y 424,288).

$3922* *Le Lezard Aux Plumes D'Or (Ma. 447), 1969,* s., i. E.A., pub. Louis Broder, margins, good cond., (12-03-92, Sotheby-London, #428, illus.), sheet 16⅛ x 21⅞ in., (408 x 555 mm.), lithograph in colors on Arches (BP 2530, DM 6168, FR 21,052, Y 487,993).

$3673* *"Le Lezard Aux Plumes D'Or" (Mourlot 800 and 812), 1971 and "Le Lezard Aux Plumes D'Or" (Mourlot 450), 1967: Two,* first, s., hors commerce, illus., (06-28-93, Loudmer, #322), first, approx. 13¾ x 19¹¹⁄₁₆ in., (350 x 500 mm.), second, approx. 12⅝ x 18⅞ in., (350 x 500 mm.), lithographs, first, in color on parchment; second, in black on parchment (BP 2459, DM 6241, FR 21,025, Y 389,708).

$3575* *Le Lezard Aux Plumes D'Or: Plate VIII (M. 809; C. 148), 1971,* s., #33/40, pub. Broder, full margins, good cond., creases, (11-05-92, Sotheby-NY, #293), 13⅛ x 18⅞ in., (334 x 480 mm.), lithograph p. in colors on japon nacre (BP 2325, DM 5654, FR 19,128, Y 438,596).

$2750* *Lithograph I (M. I), 1930,* s., num. 50/75, pub. Zervos, good cond., thinned area, glue remains,creases, Miro's 1st lithograph, (02-24-93, Butterfield, #2757, illus.), 9⅝ x 12⅞ in., (244 x 327 mm.), lithograph on Chine volant (BP 1918, DM 4464, FR 15,135, Y 322,694).

$1610* *Lithographer I (Mourlot 1), 1930,* s., #47/75, pinholes, creasing, staining, good cond., Dian Woodner and Andrea Woodner Coll., (05-11-93, Christie-NY, #236, illus.), sheet 9¾ x 12⅞ in., (248 x 327 mm.), lithograph on Chine volant (BP 1028, DM 2536, FR 8546, Y 177,098).

$1179* *Lithographie Originale II, (Maeght, vol. II p. 18, vol. III p. 28 s.c), 1974,* H.C., s., (11-09-92, Finarte-Milan, #60), 11¹³⁄₁₆ x 9¹³⁄₁₆ in., (30 x 25 cm.), lithograph in colors (BP 780, DM 1882, FR 6359, Y 146,314, L 1610).

$1320* *Lithographie Pour La Revue XXe Siecle (Mourlot 515), 1968,* s., #H.C. 5/25, (05-16-93, Hindman, #484), sheet 22 x 29¾ in., (55.9 x 75.6 cm.), 13¼ x 29 in., (55.9 x 75.6 cm.), color lithograph on Arches wove (BP 858, DM 2123, FR 7135, Y 146,325).

$23,873* *Lithographie Pour Le Centenaire De L'Imprimerie Mourlot (M. 190), 1953,* s., i. Epreuve d'artist, p., pub. Mourlot, good cond., tipped to mount, (12-03-92, Sotheby-London, #429, illus.), 19⅞ x 25¾ in., (505 x 655 mm.), lithograph in colors on Arches (BP 15,400, DM 37,542, FR 128,143, Y 2,970,387).

$14,950* *Lithographie Pour Le Centennaire De L'Imprimerie Mourlot (Mourlot 190), 1953,* s. ink (slightly faded), #44/75, p. and pub. Mourlot, full sheet, good cond., faded, (02-11-93, Sotheby-NY, #182, illus.), sheet 19⅞ x 26¹⁄₁₆ in., (505 x 662 mm.), color lithograph (BP 10,549, DM 24,764, FR 83,800, Y 1,802,291).

$1650* *Lithographs Volumes I; II; III; IV, 1972; 1975; 1977; 1981: Four,* complete volumes, pub. Tudor Publishing Co., Leon Amiel, and Maeght Editeur, Vol. I & IV num. 2868/5000 & 1117/5000, good cond., surface soiling, scuffing of covers, (02-24-93, Butterfield, #2763), orig. lithograph (BP 1151, DM 2679, FR 9081, Y 193,617).

$1210* *Livres Illustres Et Lithographies Exhibition (B./G. 588), 1973,* s., #39/100, p. Ediciones Poligrafia, S.A., pub. Galeries Gerald Cramer, good cond.?, (10-28-92, Butterfield, #2682), 25½ x 19⅝ in., (648 x 498 mm.), color lithograph on wove (BP 771, DM 1869, FR 6345, Y 148,466).

$4934* *Lune Etoile (Mourlot 146), 1955,* s., #15/50, (05-26-93, Lempertz, #371, illus.), 29⅝ x 22³⁄₁₆ in., (75.2 x 56.3 cm.), color lithograph on Arches wove (BP 3192, DM 8050, FR 27,095, Y 536,071).

$4640* *La Magie Quotidienne (Dupin 271), 1959,* s., 54/70, (06-28-93, Loudmer, #321, illus.), 6⁵⁄₁₆ x 16⁷⁄₁₆ in., (160 x 417 mm.), sh 12¹⁵⁄₁₆ x 20¼ in., (160 x 417 mm.), color etching and aquatint on handmade French laid (BP 3107, DM 7884, FR 26,560, Y 492,308).

$13,319* *La Main (D. 100), 1953,* s., d., #44/75, pub. Maeght, margins, stain, surface dirt, tape, very good cond., (12-01-92, Christie-London, #434, illus.), plate 13¹⁵⁄₁₆ x 18¹⁵⁄₁₆ in., (354 x 482 mm.), sheet 19¹⁄₁₆ x 25⅜ in., (354 x 482 mm.), aquatint in colors on Rives (BP 8800, DM 21,229, FR 72,347, Y 1,658,242).

$46,000* *Makemono, Paris, Aime Maeght, 1956 (Wember 183),* s. in paint, #18/50, staining, fixed w/nails to 2 wood batons (as pub.), very good cond., orig. box, (05-11-93, Christie-NY, #238, illus.), sheet 15¾ x 383⅞ in., (40 x 975 cm.), color lithograph on natural Canton silk (BP 29,365, DM 72,464, FR 244,161, Y 5,059,949).

BI *Mambo, 1978,* s., #32/50, pub. Maeght, full margins, good cond., scuffs, fiber adhering to surface, creases in image, foxing, est. $12/15,000, (11-05-92, Sotheby-NY, #306, illus.), 44⅞ x 29 in., (114 x 73.7 cm.), etching and aquatint p. in colors.

$3968* *"Maravillas Acrosticas En El Jardin",* #49/75, s., (12-17-92, Duran, #166, illus.), 29½ x 21¼ in., (75 x 54 cm.), lithograph (BP 2518, DM 6195, FR 21,163, Y 487,649, P 437,000).

$3025* *Maravillas Con Variaciones Acrosticas En El Jardin De Miro (C. 211),1975,* portfolio, s. by Miro and Alberti, num. 81, pub. Ediciones Poligrafa,good cond., crease, orig. slipcase and box, (11-05-92, Sotheby-NY, #303), each sheet approx. 19¾ x 14⅛ in., (500 x 360 mm.), 20 lithographs p. in colors (BP 1967, DM 4784, FR 16,185, Y 371,120).

$4698* *"Maravillas Con Variaciones Acrosticas En El Jardin De Miro": Twenty,* text by Rafael Alberti, #49/75, plate s., s. by poet and artist, (12-17-92, Duran, #167, illus.), 19⁵⁄₁₆ x 13¹⁵⁄₁₆ in., (49 x 35.5 cm.), lithograph (BP 2982, DM 7335, FR 25,056, Y 577,363, P 517,500).

BI *Le Marteau Sans Maitre VI,* num. 81/125, full sheet, good cond., some foxing, est. $1/1,500, (05-22-93, Weschler, #207, illus.), 5¾ x 8¼ in., (14.6 x 21 cm.), etching and aquatint in colors on Arches.

BI *"La Melodie Acide Mod 3",* outside regular edit., s. Miro, prov., (05-18-93, Encans, #209), 13⅜ x 10¹⁄₁₆ in., (34 x 25.5 cm.), color lithograph on Japan.

$1100* *The Mesmerizer-Orange (M. 600), 1969,* s., #12/75, p. Arte Adrien Maeght, pub. Maeght editions, good cond., (10-28-92, Butterfield, #2676), 33¼ x 23¾ in., (845 x 603 mm.), lithograph in orange and black on Rives (BP 701, DM 1699, FR 5768, Y 134,969).

$2516* *Miro - Grand Palais (Maeght 945), 1974,* s., (11-16-92, Briest, #339), 33¼ x 23⅝ in., (84.5 x 60 cm.), lithograph in colors on Arches wove (BP 1654, DM 4013, FR 13,520, Y 313,990).

$3029* *Miro Escultor (Cramer Band V 935), 1974,* #26/100, s., (11-21-92, Lempertz, #293), 13¾ x 20½ in., (34.9 x 52 cm.), color lithograph on Guarro wove (BP 1994, DM 4829, FR 16,267, Y 376,694).

BI *Miro Fotoscope Danes, (Patrick Cramer, The Illustrated Book, 209), 1975,* #185 edit. of 500, est. DK 1,500, (03-24-93, Kunsthallen, #248), original lithograph in colors.

BI *Miro Juiol, 1975,* #XXIV/XXV, s., est. DM 6,000-, (11-21-92, Lempertz, #295), image, sheet 29¹³⁄₁₆ x 22¼ in., (75.7 x 56.5 cm.), color lithograph on Japan.

BI *Miro Juliol 1975, 1975,* s., num., Edition der Galerie Borjeson, est. DM 7000, (12-01-92, Karl/Faber, #1022, illus.), sh 29¹⁵⁄₁₆ x 22¹⁄₁₆ in., (76 x 56 cm.), color lithograph on Japon nacre.

BI *Miro Lithographe: Vols. I-IV, vol. I A.C., 1972-81,* Mazo and Cie, 1972, vols. II-IV, Maeght, est. BP 1,2/1,600, (12-01-92, Christie-London, #445), sheet 12¹⁵⁄₁₆ x 10¼ in., (330 x 260 mm.), lithograph in colors.

$2070* *Miro Lithographs, Volume II; Composition (see M. Vol. III, p. 31), 1974,* s., #VX/LXXX, apparently w/margins, good cond., (02-11-93, Sotheby-NY, #197), 12³⁄₁₆ x 18⅞ in., (310 x 480 mm.), color lithograph on large format paper on white wove (BP 1461, DM 3429, FR 11,603, Y 249,548).

$3910* *Miro Lithographs, Volume II; Compositions (see M. vol. III, pp. 29 and 32), 1974: Three,* s., i., full margins, good cond., (02-11-93, Sotheby-NY, #196), color lithograph on Arches wove (BP 2759, DM 6477, FR 21,917, Y 471,368).

$825* *Miro, L'Oeuvre Graphique Exhibition, 1974,* s., #34/100, pub. Musee d'Art Moderne, good cond.?, image creases, light-staining, (10-28-92, Butterfield, #2683), 30½ x 22⅜ in., (775 x 568 mm.), color lithograph on wove (BP 526, DM 1274, FR 4326, Y 101,227).

$3491* *"Miro-Grand-Palais" (Picazo 76), 1974,* s., num., (09-25-92, Granier, #2944, illus.), sheet 27³⁄₁₆ x 20⅞ in., (69 x 53 cm.), color lithograph on hand-made Arches (BP 2039, DM 5175, FR 17,499, Y 421,364).

$3738* *Mon Chemin (D. 103; C. bk. 29), 1953,* s., d. 9/3/54, p., pub. Pierre Andre Benoit (PAB), good cond., (05-13-93,

Sotheby-NY, #633, illus.), 2 x 2 in., (50 x 50 mm.), sh 3⅝ x 6¾ in., (50 x 50 mm.), hand-colored drypoint on laid (BP 2454, DM 6036, FR 20,359, Y 417,327).

$4370* *Montroig 4 (Cramer 956), 1974,* s., #IV/XX, (05-26-93, Lempertz, #372, illus.), 22¹⁄₁₆ x 22⁷⁄₁₆ in., (56 x 57 cm.), color lithograph on Guarro (BP 2827, DM 7130, FR 23,998, Y 474,794).

BI *Montroig II (M. 954), 1974,* s., annot. H.C., pub. p. Ediciones Poligrafa S.A., good cond.?, light-staining, est. $4/6,000, (05-19-93, Butterfield, #1939, illus.), sh. 30 x 22½ in., (762 x 572 mm.), lithograph in colors on Guarro.

$1980* *Murale (M. 297), 1961,* s., #32/90, pub. Maeght, good cond., light stain, creases, glued to back mat, (11-05-92, Sotheby-NY, #269), 17⅜ x 22¾ in., (440 x 579 mm.), lithograph p. in colors (BP 1288, DM 3131, FR 10,594, Y 242,915).

BI *Murale (M. 297), 1964,* s., #89/90, pub.and p. Maeght, slightly trimmed, red faded, good cond., glue staining, skinned, est. $2/3,000, (05-19-93, Butterfield, #1935, illus.), 17⅜ x 22¾ in., (441 x 578 mm.), lithograph in colorson Rives.

BI *Musee D'Art Moderne, 1977,* wrinkles, est. SF 100/150, (10-14-92, Germann, #387), 30¹⁄₁₆ x 21⁹⁄₁₆ in., (763 x 548 mm.), color lithograph/poster.

$2153* *Nebulosa, 1958,* #52/100, s., stamp edit. A. Maeght, lit., (03-25-93, Finarte-Rome, #53, illus.), lithograph in colors (BP 1462, DM 3537, FR 12,028, Y 252,226, L 3450).

BI *Obscur Laurier (Cramer 75), 1962,* text by Marsye Lafont, Guy Levis Mano, unbound as issued, num., s. Miro, est. $3/5,000, (06-14-93, Sotheby-NY, #220, illus.), 9⅜ x 6⅜ in., (23.8 x 16.2 cm.), frontispiece etching w/aquatint.

$4950* *Oda A Joan Miro (B. 506), C. 175), 1973,* s., #27/75, pub. Ediciones Poligrafia, S.A., margins, good cond.?, light-staining, (10-28-92, Butterfield, #2681), 31¼ x 23 in., (794 x 584 mm.), color lithograph on Guarro paper (BP 3154, DM 7645, FR 25,957, Y 607,362).

BI *Oda A Joan Miro (B. 506, C. 175), 1973,* s., #61/75, pub. Ediciones Poligrafia, S.A., good cond.?, light-staining, creases, est. $2/4,000, (10-28-92, Butterfield, #2680), 34½ x 24 in., (876 x 610 mm.), color lithograph on Guarro paper.

$3850* *Oda A Joan Miro (B. 506, C. 175), 1973,* s., #39/75, pub. Ediciones Poligrafia, S.A., good cond.?, light-staining, image crease, (10-28-92, Butterfield, #2679), 34½ x 24 in., (876 x 610 mm.), color lithograph on Guarro paper (BP 2453, DM 5946, FR 20,189, Y 472,393).

$6600* *Oda A Joan Miro (C. 175), 1973,* s., #11/75, pub. Poligrafa, good cond., scuff in image, (11-05-92, Sotheby-NY, #297, illus.), sheet 34⅝ x 24 in., (880 x 610 mm.), lithograph p. in colors (BP 4293, DM 10,438, FR 35,313, Y 809,717).

$3300* *Oda A Joan Miro (C. 175), 1973,* s., i. H.C., pub. Poligrafa, good cond., crease, (11-05-92, Sotheby-NY, #298, illus.), sheet 34¼ x 24 in., (869 x 609 mm.), lithograph p. in colors (BP 2146, DM 5219, FR 17,657, Y 404,858).

$4313* *Oda A Joan Miro (C. 906), 1973,* s., i. H.C., p., pub. Poligrafa, good cond., mat/light-stain, (05-13-93, Sotheby-NY, #660), sh 34½ x 24 in., (875 x 608 mm.), lithograph in colors (BP 2832, DM 6964, FR 23,491, Y 481,523).

$2727* *Oda A Joan Miro, 1973,* #56/75, s., stamped La Poligrafa S.A., lit., (03-25-93, Finarte-Rome, #44, illus.), lithograph in colors (BP 1852, DM 4480, FR 15,235, Y 319,470, L 4370).

$66* *Omnium Cultural (Corredor-Matheos 81), 1974,* (09-25-92, Granier, #2946), 28¾ x 21¼ in., (73 x 54 cm.), color lithograph poster on wove (BP 39, DM 98, FR 331, Y 7966).

$1574* *Osaka, 1970,* #34/75, s., creases, large margins, (02-03-93, Ader Tajan, #182), 19¹¹⁄₁₆ x 27⁹⁄₁₆ in., (50 x 70 cm.), color lithograph (BP 1099, DM 2592, FR 8788, Y 195,795).

$2046* *Ouvrage Du Vent (D. 344), 1963,* s., #63/75, pub. Maeght, full margins, good cond., rubbed fox marks,discoloration, (12-03-92, Sotheby-London, #425, illus.), 8½ x 23 in., (215 x 582 mm.), aquatint in colors on wove (BP 1320, DM 3217, FR 10,982, Y 254,573).

BI   *Palotin Giron (M. 215), 1955,* s., d., #22/50, pub. Maeght, full margins, good cond., foxing, creases, water stain, glued to backing, est. $10/15,000, (11-05-92, Sotheby-NY, #262, illus.), 28½ x 18⅞ in., (723 x 480 mm.), lithograph p. in colors.

BI   *La Paludeenne (Dupin 737), 1975,* s., blindstamp, #37/50, est. DM 6,000, (05-26-93, Lempertz, #373, illus.), 25¹³⁄₁₆ x 17¹¹⁄₁₆ in., (65.5 x 45 cm.), etching on Arches wove.

$2046*   *La Paludeenne (MA. 737), 1975,* s., i. HC XVII/XXIV, p. Morsang, pub. Maeght, full margins, good cond., creases, surface dirt, (12-03-92, Sotheby-London, #432), sheet 26 x 17¾ in., (660 x 451 mm.), etching and aquatint in colors on Arches (BP 1320, DM 3217, FR 10,982, Y 254,573).

BI   *Paris, Jean Hugues, 1960,* from La Rame Et La Roue by Rene Cazelles, hors-commerce, s., marked H.C., includes 1 watercolor by Miro, envoi-autographe, est. SF35/45,000, (11-15-92, Christie-Geneva, #322, illus.), 7¹¹⁄₁₆ x 5⅝ in., (195 x 143 mm.), lithograph on Arches wove.

BI   *Paris, Librairie Jose Corti (Cramer 65), 1961,* from Chemin Faisant by Pierre Andre Benoit, s., num. by Miro, est. SF 6/8,000, book, (11-15-92, Christie-Geneva, #311, illus.), 7⁵⁄₁₆ x 4⅝ in., (185 x 118 mm.), drypoint on celluloid on pur fil Lafuma.

$9350*   *Partie De Campagne II (D. 431), 1967,* s., #63/75, p. and pub. by Maeght, full margins, good cond., creases,-mat stain, foxing, (11-05-92, Sotheby-NY, #276, illus.), 23¼ x 36⅜ in., (589 x 925 mm.), etching and aquatint p. in colors (BP 6081, DM 14,787, FR 50,027, Y 1,147,099).

BI   *Partie De Campagne IV (D. 433), 1967,* s., i. HC, Hors Commerce, p. and pub. Maeght, full margins, good cond., est. BP 4/5,000, (06-30-93, Sotheby-London, #539, illus.), 23 x 36⅜ in., (584 x 924 mm.), etching w/aquatint in color on chiffon de Mandeure.

$16,100*   *Paysage Meurtrier (D. 30), 1938,* tone, s., i. Bon a tirer, full (large) margins, good cond., (05-13-93, Sotheby-NY, #629, illus.), 4¼ x 3⅛ in., (109 x 79 mm.), soft-ground etching (BP 10,570, DM 25,997, FR 87,691, Y 1,797,477).

$4410*   *"Peinture", c. 1965,* s. Miro, #225/300, blindstamp, (05-19-93, Dorotheum, #461, illus.), plate 24 x 18½ in., (61 x 47 cm.), sheet 33¹⁄₁₆ x 24¹³⁄₁₆ in., (61 x 47 cm.), mixed media in color (BP 2863, DM 7168, FR 24,151, Y 488,210, SC 50,400).

BI   *Le Permissionaire (B. 215), 1974,* s., #18/50, pub. Maeght, margins, discoloration, very good cond., est. BP 8/12,000, (12-01-92, Christie-London, #439, illus.), plate 28¹⁵⁄₁₆ x 44⅞ in., (73.5 x 114 cm.), etching w/aquatint and carborundum in colors on wove.

BI   *Le Permissionnaire (D. 655), 1974,* s., #34/50, pub. Maeght, full margins, good cond., scuffs, discoloration, creases, est. $20/25,000, (11-05-92, Sotheby-NY, #301, illus.), 44⅞ x 29 in., (114 x 73.7 cm.), etching and aquatint.

$8655*   *Personage (Mourlot Band II 144), 1955,* #39/50, s., d., (11-21-92, Lempertz, #290, illus.), 21⁹⁄₁₆ x 28⅞ in., (54.7 x 73.3 cm.), color lithograph on Arches wove (BP 5699, DM 13,799, FR 46,482, Y 1,076,359).

BI   *Personage Dans Le Soleil (Mourlot Band I 61), 1948,* #10/50, num., s., d., est. DM 5,500-, (11-21-92, Lempertz, #289, illus.), 12¹⁵⁄₁₆ x 12 in., (33 x 30.5 cm.), lithograph on wove.

$605*   *Personnage Au Soleil (Benhoura 397), 1938,* pub. as supplement to XXe Siecle, no. 4, Paris, Noel, 1938, (10-18-92, Hindman, #470), 11¾ x 9⅛ in., (29.8 x 23.2 cm.), linocut in blue on red paper (BP 370, DM 901, FR 3054, Y 72,585).

BI   *Personnage Dans le Soleil (M. 61), 1948,* s., d., #37/50, p. Mourlot, margins, good cond., est. BP 1,5/2,500, (12-01-92, Christie-London, #440), L. 9¹⁄₁₆ x 11⅞ in., (230 x 302 mm.), lithograph on Pur Fil du Marais.

$6139*   *Petite Fille Devant La Mer (D. 435), 1967,* s., #66/75, p., pub. Maeght, full margins, good cond., (12-03-92, Sotheby-London, #422, illus.), 22⅞ x 36⅜ in., (580 x

925 mm.), etching and aquatint in colors (BP 3960, DM 9654, FR 32,952, Y 763,842).

$8250*   *Pic De La Mirandole (D. 761), 1975,* s., #43/50, pub. Maeght, good cond., discoloration, (11-05-92, Sotheby-NY, #304, illus.), sheet 41½ x 29⅜ in., (105.4 x 74.6 cm.), etching, aquatint and collotype p. in colors (BP 5366, DM 13,048, FR 44,141, Y 1,012,146).

$3618*   *Pierrot Le Fou (MA. 324), 1964,* s., #47/75, p. and pub. Maeght, good cond., mount-staining, crease, (06-30-93, Sotheby-London, #535, illus.), sh 35⅝ x 23¾ in., (899 x 603 mm.), color lithograph on Arches (BP 2425, DM 6171, FR 20,817, Y 387,657).

$20,900*   *Le Pitre Rose (D. 653), 1974,* s., #37/50, pub. Maeght, full margins, good cond., tear, creases, foxing, soiling, (11-05-92, Sotheby-NY, #300, illus.), 45½ x 29⅛ in., (115.6 x 74 cm.), etching and aquatint p. in colors (BP 13,593, DM 33,054, FR 111,825, Y 2,564,103).

$1373*   *Le Polyglotte-Sable (M. 536), 1969,* s., #54/75, p. and pub. Maeght, margins, good cond., (06-30-93, Sotheby-London, #545, illus.), sh 33¼ x 23¾ in., (845 x 603 mm.), color lithograph on Rives (BP 920, DM 2342, FR 7900, Y 147,112).

$3069*   *"Le Polyglotte-Sable" and "L'Illetre-Vert" (M. 536 and 552), 1969: Two,* each s., #54/75, #64/75, p., pub. Maeght, margins, good cond., (12-03-92, Sotheby-London, #437, illus.), each sheet 33¼ x 23¾ in., (845 x 605 mm.), lithograph in colors on Rives (BP 1980, DM 4826, FR 16,473, Y 381,859).

BI   *Le Porteur D'Eau I (D. 341), 1962,* s., #61/75, p. and pub. Maeght, margins, good cond., est. BP 2/2,500, (12-03-92, Sotheby-London, #421, illus.), 22 x 29½ in., (560 x 750 mm.), aquatint in colors on Rives.

$3738*   *Poster For "II Congres De Pediatres De LLengna Catalana" (C. 1228), 1980,* s., #13/75, p. Litografias artisticas, Damia Caus, pub. Congres de Pediatres de Llengua Catalana, full margins, good cond., light/masking tape stain, foxing, skinning, (02-11-93, Sotheby-NY, #200, illus.), 29¾ x 21¹⁵⁄₁₆ in., (756 x 557 mm.), color lithograph (BP 2638, DM 6192, FR 20,953, Y 450,633).

$2745*   *Poster For The Exhibition 'Miro' Fondation Maeght, Saint-Paul-De-Vence (MA. 1190), 1979,* s., #33/75, pub. Fondation Maeght, p. by Les Artisans Lithographes, margins, good cond., creasing, light-staining, (06-30-93, Sotheby-London, #559, illus.), 35½ x 23⅞ in., (902 x 606 mm.), color lithograph on wove (BP 1840, DM 4682, FR 15,794, Y 294,118).

$2046*   *Poster For The Exhibition 'Miro' Louisiana, Humelbaek (Denmark) (MA 944),* s., #16/75, full margins, good cond., handling marks, creases, (12-03-92, Sotheby-London, #435), sheet 30¼ x 21¾ in., (768 x 552 mm.), lithograph in colors (BP 1320, DM 3217, FR 10,982, Y 254,573).

$2231*   *Poster For The Quiriquibu Barcelona, 1976,* s., #92/99, from unsigned poster edit., pub. Ediciones Poligrafa, sheet reduced, discoloration, tape, backboard-stained, (06-30-93, Sotheby-London, #551, illus.), 29⅝ x 21⅞ in., (752 x 556 mm.), color lithograph on Guarro (BP 1495, DM 3805, FR 12,837, Y 239,044).

$3088*   *Poster For Unesco, 'Human Rights' (C. 930), 1974,* before letters, s., #6/75, p. by Maeght, pub. UNESCO, good cond., (06-30-93, Sotheby-London, #547, illus.), sh 31⅜ x 23½ in., (797 x 597 mm.), color lithograph on wove (BP 2070, DM 5267, FR 17,768, Y 330,869).

$1705*   *Poster: Exhibition Of Mural Paintings At The Gallerie Maeght, Paris 1961, 1961,* s., #80/100, pub. Maeght, full margins, good cond., tape stains, (12-03-92, Sotheby-London, #420), 26⅜ x 19 in., (670 x 482 mm.), lithograph in colors (BP 1100, DM 2681, FR 9152, Y 212,144).

$2295*   *Pour Matarasso, 1957,* #106/125, s., d., (11-13-92, Koller, #5380), 21⅝ x 18⅛ in., (55 x 46 cm.), lithograph on wove (BP 1483, DM 3603, FR 12,149, Y 284,845, SF 3248).

$6050*   *Pour Paul Eluard (D. 587), 1973,* s., #85/100, pub. Le Cercle d'Art Editeur, good cond., scuff in image, (11-05-92, Sotheby-NY, #294, illus.), sheet 26 x 19¾ in., (660 x 503 mm.), etching and aquatint p. in colors (BP 3935, DM 9568, FR 32,370, Y 742,240).

$4125*   *Preparatifs D'Oiseaux I (D. 365), 1963,* s., #29/75, pub. by Maeght, full margins, good cond., hinge stains, (11-

05-92, Sotheby-NY, #271, illus.), 8⅛ x 10⅜ in., (205 x 264 mm.), soft ground etching and aquatint p. in colors (BP 2683, DM 6524, FR 22,071, Y 506,073).

$3025* *Preparatifs D'Oiseaux II (D. 366), 1963,* s., #70/75, pub. Maeght, full margins, good cond., mat stain, skinning, (11-05-92, Sotheby-NY, #272, illus.), 16¼ x 17⅜ in., (413 x 440 mm.), aqautint p. in colors (BP 1967, DM 4784, FR 16,185, Y 371,120).

BI *La Presidente,* s., #34/75, est. $5/7,000, (05-16-93, Hanzel, #79A, illus.), 24¾ x 18¼ in., (62.9 x 46.4 cm.), color etching and aquatint.

$4675* *Le Prophete Encercle (D. 396), 1965,* s., #22/75, pub.-Maeght, good cond., soiling, creases, (11-05-92, Sotheby-NY, #274, illus.), sheet 35⅜ x 25⅛ in., (900 x 637 mm.), etching and aquatint p. in colors (BP 3041, DM 7394, FR 25,013, Y 573,549).

$3410* *Le Prophete La Nuit (D. 397), 1965,* s., #66/75, pub. Maeght, full margins, good cond., (12-03-92, Sotheby-London, #424, illus.), 26¾ x 20⅞ in., (680 x 530 mm.), etching in colors on Arches (BP 2200, DM 5362, FR 18,304, Y 424,288).

$2475* *Proverbes A La Main (M. 675; C. bk. 139), 1970,* s., i. 51/75, pub. Ediciones Poligrafa, full margins, good cond., matstain, (11-05-92, Sotheby-NY, #290), 21⅝ x 29¾ in., (550 x 755 mm.), lithograph p. in colors (BP 1610, DM 3914, FR 13,242, Y 303,644).

$9775* *La Rebelle (D. 439), 1967,* s., #18/75, p., pub. Maeght, full margins, good cond., foxing, creasing, (05-13-93, Sotheby-NY, #646, illus.), 36¾ x 25 in., (935 x 635 mm.), etching, aquatint & carborundum in colors (BP 6417, DM 15,784, FR 53,241, Y 1,091,325).

$2640* *Red And Blue (M. 269), 1960,* s., #50/100, pub. Maeght, full margins, good cond., creases, glued tobackmat, (11-05-92, Sotheby-NY, #268), 22⅞ x 16 in., (582 x 405 mm.), lithograph p. in colors (BP 1717, DM 4175, FR 14,125, Y 323,887).

$2387* *Red Bird II (M. 99), 1950,* s., d., full margins, good cond., foxmarks, (12-03-92, Sotheby-London, #414), 10½ x 17¼ in., (265 x 440 mm.), lithograph in colors on BFK Rives wove (BP 1540, DM 3754, FR 12,813, Y 297,001).

BI *Red Bird II (Mourlot 99), 1950,* s., d., #35/75, full margins, good cond., est. BP 2/3,000, (12-03-92, Sotheby-London, #413, illus.), 10½ x 17¼ in., (265 x 440 mm.), lithograph in colors on BFK Rives.

BI *Red Sky (MA. 268), 1968,* s., #27/100, p. and pub. Maeght, margins, good cond., light-staining,scuff, est. BP 1,5/2,000, (06-30-93, Sotheby-London, #533, illus.), sh 18⅛ x 26 in., (460 x 660 mm.), color lithograph on Arches.

$935* *Red Sky, 1960,* full margins, s., i., collector's stamp, p., pub. Galerie Maeght, time soiling, (05-27-93, Swann, #189), 18⅛ x 26 in., (46 x 66 cm.), color lithograph on Arches vellum (BP 599, DM 1500, FR 5057, Y 100,236).

$3631* *"Retour A La Position Primitive" and "La Destruction Du Miroir" (Cramer 229), 1977: Two,* each s., num. 3/60, from Hommage a San Lazzaro, pub. Gerald Cramer, full margins, good cond., (10-14-92, Sotheby-Japan, #54, illus.), each 13⅝ x 9 in., (346 x 229 mm.), etching w/ aquatint in colors (BP 2131, DM 5314, FR 18,020, Y 440,015).

$4029* *Le Roi David (Dupin, Nr. 555), 1972,* hors commerce, s., (11-13-92, Kunsthaus, #712, illus.), 26¾ x 21¹⁄₁₆ in., (68 x 53.5 cm.), color etching and aquatint on Arches handmade (BP 2604, DM 6325, FR 21,329, Y 500,062).

$1358* *"La Rosee Matinale Au Clair De Lune" (M1713), 1958,* #226/300, s., (04-04-93, Pescheteau, #267, illus.), 21⅝ x 25⁹⁄₁₆ in., (55 x 65 cm.), etching and aquatint on Rives (BP 894, DM 2183, FR 7413, Y 154,617).

$3967* *La Rosee Matinale, 1958,* watermark, HC, s., blindstamp, (11-21-92, Lempertz, #296, illus.), 15¹¹⁄₁₆ x 19⁵⁄₁₆ in., (39.8 x 49 cm.), color etching on wove (BP 2612, DM 6325, FR 21,305, Y 493,347).

BI *La Ruisselante Solaire, 1976,* s., i., full sheet, scuffs, inconspicuous printer's crease, skinned spots, est. $6/8,000, (02-11-93, Sotheby-NY, #198, illus.), sheet 61¹³⁄₁₆ x 45¹¹⁄₁₆ in., (157 x 116 cm.), color lithograph.

$2004* *Rupestres XVII, 1978,* s., #27/30, full margins, (05-27-93, Briest, #148), 30⅛ x 22¼ in., (76.5 x 56.5 cm.), two-color etching and aquatint (BP 1283, DM 3216, FR 10,838, Y 214,837).

BI *Les Saltimbanques VIII, 1975,* s., num., est. DM 2500, (12-01-92, Karl/Faber, #1024), 6¹¹⁄₁₆ x 4½ in., (17 x 11.5 cm.), aquatint/etching on wove.

$2490* *Les Saltimbanques XIII, 1975,* s., (12-01-92, Karl/Faber, #1025), 6¹¹⁄₁₆ x 5⁵⁄₁₆ in., (17 x 13.5 cm.), aquatint/etching (BP 1645, DM 3969, FR 13,525, Y 310,010).

$9163* *Salvat Papasseit. V (Dupin 716), 1974,* s., num., (06-23-93, Kornfeld, #596), color etching (BP 6225, DM 15,504, FR 52,151, Y 998,257, SF 13,800).

BI *Sans Titre,* #33/75, s. Miro, (06-16-93, Encans, #151, illus.), 33¹⁵⁄₁₆ x 24 in., (86.3 x 61 cm.), lithograph on canvas.

$1914* *Les Scarabees, 1978,* s., lit., (06-08-93, Karl/Faber, #1121, illus.), sh approx. 17¹⁵⁄₁₆ x 25 in., (45.5 x 63.5 cm.), color etching and aquatint on Arches France wove (BP 1258, DM 3106, FR 10,459, Y 203,293).

$3450* *Sculptures II (C. bk. 181), 1974,* s., i. H.C., p. Maeght, full margins, good cond., light-stain, fox mark, handling crease, (05-13-93, Sotheby-NY, #661), 11⅜ x 22⅝ in., (290 x 574 mm.), lithograph in colors (BP 2265, DM 5571, FR 18,791, Y 385,174).

$66* *"Sculptures-Art Graphique",* s., for Galerie Maeght, (12-02-92, Boos, #525), 28¾ x 20¼ in., (730 x 514 mm.), color lithograph (BP 43, DM 104, FR 354, Y 8212).

$3738* *Sea Shells (M. 641), 1969,* s., #9/75, p., pub. Maeght, good cond., discoloration, foxing, handling creases, water stain, repaired tear, soiling, (05-13-93, Sotheby-NY, #655, illus.), sh 30⅛ x 44¼ in., (76.5 x 112.4 cm.), lithograph in colors (BP 2454, DM 6036, FR 20,359, Y 417,327).

$3548* *Serie II, Bleu (Mourlot 219), 1961,* s., 24/30, ed. Maeght, (05-25-93, AB Stockholm, #51), 17¹¹⁄₁₆ x 23⅝ in., (45 x 60 cm.), lithograph in colors on BFK Rives (BP 2299, DM 5779, FR 19,452, Y 387,802, SK 5170).

$1135* *Serie II, Bleu Et Rouge, 1961,* s., 14/30, ed. Maeght, (12-04-92, AB Stockholm, #7108), 17¹¹⁄₁₆ x 23⅝ in., (45 x 60 cm.), lithograph in colors on BFK Rives (BP 728, DM 1808, FR 6132, Y 141,698, SK 7700).

BI *Serie II, Rojo (M. 289), 1961,* s., #17/30, p. Maeght, margins, very good cond.?, est. $1,8/2,200, (05-19-93, Butterfield, #1934), sight 17 x 23⅛ in., (432 x 587 mm.), lithograph in red and black on BFK Rives.

$14,584* *Serie II: Plate II (Dupin 84), 1952-53,* s., d., #3/13, pub. Maeght, full margins, good cond., creases, foxingdiscoloration, (06-30-93, Sotheby-London, #529, illus.), 14⅞ x 17⅞ in., (378 x 454 mm.), color etching on Arches (BP 9775, DM 24,875, FR 83,913, Y 1,562,627).

$3300* *Serie III,* s., d. 1953, num. 32/50, (09-20-92, Hindman, #761, illus.), sheet 14⅞ x 20¼ in., (24.4 x 31.8 cm.), color etching and aquatint on wove, watermark (BP 1932, DM 4897, FR 16,751, Y 407,861).

BI *Serie III (D. 88), 1952-53,* ink s., #V/XIII, pub. Maeght, p. Lacouriere, full margins, good cond., discoloration, buckling, est. $20/30,000, (05-19-93, Butterfield, #1932, illus.), pl. 9½ x 12¼ in., (241 x 311 mm.), image 15¼ x 16 in., (241 x 311 mm.), etching and aquatitn w/ hand-coloring in gouache on parchment.

BI *Serie III: Plate V (D. 92), 1953,* s., d., #15/50, p. Lacouriere, pub. Maeght, full margins, good cond.,-creases, skinned spots, est. $5/7,000, (05-13-93, Sotheby-NY, #632, illus.), 9⅛ x 11¾ in., (231 x 298 mm.), etching and aquatint.

BI *Serie Mallorca (D. 613), 1973,* s., #33/50, pub. Sala Pelaires, margins, good cond., foxing, glued tomount, est. BP 2,5/3,500, (12-03-92, Sotheby-London, #443, illus.), sheet 27½ x 34 in., (700 x 863 mm.), etching w/aquatint in colors on wove.

BI *Serie Mallorca (D. 613), 1973,* pencil s., #33/50, pub. Sala Pelaires, margins, good cond., foxing, glued to mount, est. BP 2/2,500, (06-30-93, Sotheby-London, #555, illus.), sh 27½ x 34 in., (699 x 864 mm.), etching w/aquatint in color on wove.

BI *Serie Mallorca (D. 617), 1972,* proof impression, i. V 26/xii, pub. Sala Pelaires, full margins, goodcond., est. BP 9/11,000, (12-03-92, Sotheby-London, #442, illus.), 21½ x 27⅛ in., (545 x 690 mm.), etching w/tone w/

hand-coloring in yellow & blue on thick fibrous hand-made.

$3300* *Serie Mallorca (D. 618; C. 177), 1973,* s., #11/50, pub. Sala Pelaires, full margins, good cond., foxing, (11-05-92, Sotheby-NY, #295), 21½ x 27¼ in., (545 x 692 mm.), etching w/aquatint p. in colors (BP 2146, DM 5219, FR 17,657, Y 404,858).

$28,302* *Serie Mallorca: Portfolios I-II (Cr. 177 1-2), 1973,* portfolio I just., set. of 27, s., #2/50; portfolio II just., set of 9, s., #IX/XXV, foxmarks, good cond., (12-01-92, Christie-London, #438, illus.), overall sheet 35⁷⁄₁₆ x 28¾ in., (900 x 730 mm.), aquatint on Guarro wove (BP 18,700, DM 45,110, FR 153,732, Y 3,523,655).

$29,700* *Serie Noir Et Rouge (D. 38), 1938,* s., #15/30, pub. Pierre Loeb, and Pierre Matisse, full margins, good cond., light stain, tape stain, skinned spots, (11-05-92, Sotheby-NY, #258, illus.), 6¾ x 10¼ in., (170 x 260 mm.), etching p. in black and red (BP 19,317, DM 46,971, FR 158,909, Y 3,643,725).

$1725* *Series I, Blue And Red Graphisms (M. 277), 1961,* s., #19/30, p., pub. Maeght, full margins, good cond., scratches, discoloration, tear, creases, skinned spots, (02-11-93, Sotheby-NY, #186), 28¾ x 39⅜ in., (73 x 100 cm.), color lithograph (BP 1217, DM 2857, FR 9669, Y 207,957).

$825* *Series II: Blue And Red Wash (M. 286), 1961,* s., #10/30, pub. Maeght, good cond., water/light staining, skinned in image, creases, surface soiling, (10-28-92, Butterfield, #2674), 17¾ x 23¾ in., (451 x 603 mm.), color lithograph on BFK Rives (BP 526, DM 1274, FR 4326, Y 101,227).

BI *Solidarite (D. 42), 1938,* from portfolio Paul Eluard. Solidarite, s., #25/150, pub. G.L.M., reduced margins, good cond., est. BP 3,5/4,000, (12-03-92, Sotheby-London, #411, illus.), 4 x 3 in., (100 x 78 mm.), etching.

BI *Le Souffre-Douleur (D. 539), 1970,* s., #32/75, pub. Maeght, p. Arte Adrien, good cond.?, crease, est. $6/8,000, (05-19-93, Butterfield, #1938, illus.), 25 x 19⅝ in., (635 x 498 mm.), etching w/aquatint and carborundum in colors on wove.

$551* *Sourire Aux Ailes Flamboyantes,* s. Miro 1954, 175/400, (03-24-93, Kunsthallen, #244), offset in colors (BP 373, DM 900, FR 3063, Y 64,740, DK 3450).

$2977* *Spirale II (Aus Cramer 245), 1974/79,* s., from series Spirale, (06-08-93, Karl/Faber, #1119, illus.), approx. 9¹⁄₁₆ x 5⅛ in., (23 x 13 cm.), color etching and aquatint on wove (BP 1957, DM 4830, FR 16,268, Y 316,198).

$5968* *Le Styx (D. 159), 1958,* s., #65/75, pub. Maeght, full margins, good cond., (12-03-92, Sotheby-London, #415, illus.), 7 x 9¾ in., (178 x 237 mm.), etching and aquatint in colors on BFK Rives (BP 3850, DM 9385, FR 32,034, Y 742,566).

$5188* *Le Styx (Dupin 159), 1958,* s., 44/75, prov., (12-04-92, AB Stockholm, #7107), 7¹⁄₁₆ x 9⁷⁄₁₆ in., (17.9 x 23.9 cm.), etching and aquatint in colors on BFK Rives (BP 3328, DM 8262, FR 28,028, Y 647,690, SK 35,200).

$2558* *Sur Le Fleuve Jaune, 1978,* s., #VII/XV, good cond., (12-03-92, Sotheby-London, #449), sheet 29¾ x 21½ in., (756 x 545 mm.), lithograph in colors on wove (BP 1650, DM 4023, FR 13,731, Y 318,278).

$4400* *"The Taciturn Majorcan" and "Woman With Dove" (M. 595 and 597), 1969:Two,* s., i. H.C., pub. Maeght, good cond., creases, discoloration, soiling, (11-05-92, Sotheby-NY, #287), sheet, one 33⅜ x 23¾ in., (848 x 604 mm.), sheet, other 37⅜ x 23¾ in., (848 x 604 mm.), 2 lithographs p. in colors (BP 2862, DM 6959, FR 23,542, Y 539,811).

$6821* *Tete Au Soleil Couchant (D. 437), 1967,* s., #37/75, full margins, good cond., (12-03-92, Sotheby-London, #426, illus.), 10⅞ x 14¾ in., (287 x 375 mm.), aquatint and carborundum in colors on Chiffon de Mandeure (BP 4400, DM 10,727, FR 36,613, Y 848,700).

$4180* *Tete Fleche, 1968,(Dupin 460),* s., annot. H.C., (09-20-92, Hindman, #764), sheet 26 x 19⅜ in., (39.4 x 29.5 cm.), color aquatint and carboundum on wove w/watermark (BP 2447, DM 6203, FR 21,218, Y 516,623).

$19,800* *Trace Sur La Paroi IV (D. 443), 1967,* s., #62/75, p. and pub. Maeght, full margins, good cond., discoloration into image, (11-05-92, Sotheby-NY, #277, illus.), 23 x

36⅜ in., (585 x 925 mm.), etching, aquatint and carborundum p. in colors (BP 12,878, DM 31,314, FR 105,939, Y 2,429,150).

$4041* *La Traversee Du Miroir, (Maeght vol. II, 276), 1963,* #26/90, s., from the series Derriere le miroir, (11-09-92, Finarte-Milan, #85, illus.), 23⅝ x 35⁷⁄₁₆ in., (60 x 90 cm.), lithograph in colors (BP 2672, DM 6451, FR 21,796, Y 501,489, L 5520).

BI *Tristan Tzara. L'Arbre Des Voyageurs (Mourlot 2-5; Cramer 1), 1930: Set Of Four,* book w/title-page, text and justification, s. by artist and author, #68, pub. Editions de la Montaigne, good cond., discoloration, est. BP 2,5/3,000, (06-30-93, Sotheby-London, #528), overall 10⅛ x 6¾ in., (257 x 171 mm.), lithograph on Arches wove.

BI *Tristan Tzara. Parler Seul (Cramer 17),* book, full page and in text, s. by author and artist, pub. Maeght, 1950, good cond., orig. covers w/color lithogrph and collage on uppers, slipcasebox w/color lithograph, est. BP 7,5/8,500, (12-03-92, Sotheby-London, #412, illus.), overall size approx. 15½ x 12 in., (392 x 302 mm.), 72 lithograph in black and in colors on Arches.

BI *Ubu Aux Baleares (Cramer 146, Mourlot 767), 1971,* #84/120, s., est. SF 3/3,800, (09-04-92, Germann, #86, illus.), 19⁵⁄₁₆ x 24¹³⁄₁₆ in., (490 x 630 mm.), color lithograph.

$31,955* *Ubu Aux Baleares (Maeght 757-788), 1963: Twenty-Three,* s. Miro, num., (06-25-93, Kornfeld, #81, illus.), portfolio 20½ x 26⅜ in., color lithograph (BP 21,613, DM 54,401, FR 183,228, Y 3,387,216, SF 48,300).

$2304* *Ubu Aux Baleares, 1971,* s., (10-21-92, Dobiaschofsky, #2171, illus.), 19¹¹⁄₁₆ x 26¹⁄₁₆ in., (50 x 66.2 cm.), color lithograph (BP 1430, DM 3486, FR 11,834, Y 280,633, SF 3120).

BI *Ubu Roi (Cramer 108, Mourlot 408), 1966,* 4/75, light staining, est. SF 1/1,500, (10-14-92, Germann, #389), 21¼ x 29½ in., (540 x 750 mm.), color lithograph.

$51,474* *Ubu Roi (MA. 397-430), 1966,* s., p. by Mourlot, pub. Teriade, good cond., light-staining, (06-30-93, Sotheby-London, #554, illus.), each sh 21¼ x 29½ in., (540 x 749 mm.), color lithograph on Arches (BP 34,500, DM 87,795, FR 296,168, Y 5,515,268).

$5750* *Ubu Roi: Plate IV (M. 471), 1966,* s., #31/75, p. Mourlot, pub. Teriade, full margins, good cond., light stain, foxing, skinned spots, discoloration, (02-11-93, Sotheby-NY, #190, illus.), 16¼ x 24⅞ in., (412 x 632 mm.), color lithograph (BP 4057, DM 9525, FR 32,231, Y 693,189).

$4888* *Ubu Roi: Plate X (M. 489), 1966,* s., #21/75, p. Mourlot, pub. Teriade, full margins, good cond., (05-13-93, Sotheby-NY, #644, illus.), 16⅛ x 24⅝ in., (411 x 626 mm.), lithograph in colors (BP 3209, DM 7893, FR 26,623, Y 545,718).

$5750* *Ubu Roi: Plate XI (M. 492), 1966,* s., #22/75, p. Mourlot, pub. Teriade, full margins, good cond., (05-13-93, Sotheby-NY, #645, illus.), 16¼ x 24⅝ in., (412 x 625 mm.), lithograph in colors (BP 3775, DM 9285, FR 31,318, Y 641,956).

BI *Untitled,* HC s. verso, est. FF10,000/12,000, (04-04-93, Pescheteau, #265, illus.), 19¹¹⁄₁₆ x 12¹³⁄₁₆ in., (50 x 32.5 cm.), etching and aquatint and embossing on wove.

$2090* *Untitled,* s., i. E.A., (10-18-92, Hindman, #471, illus.), 25½ x 18¾ in., (64.8 x 47.6 cm.), color lithograph (BP 1279, DM 3111, FR 10,550, Y 250,750).

$1320* *Untitled,* s., #14/50, (05-16-93, Hindman, #482), 8⅛ x 6⅝ in., (20.6 x 16.8 cm.), sheet 14¾ x 11 in., (20.6 x 16.8 cm.), color aquatint and etching on BFK Rives (BP 858, DM 2123, FR 7135, Y 146,325).

$660* *Untitled (C. III, D. 14), 1934,* pub. in Cahiers d'Art 1-4, p. by Crete, margins, apparently good cond., (02-24-93, Butterfield, #2959), 10¾ x 9 in., (273 x 229 mm.), pochoir in colors on wove (BP 460, DM 1071, FR 3632, Y 77,447).

$4620* *Untitled (Corredor-Matheos 70), 1973,* for Homage to Miro Exhib. 1973, s., #91/150, time staining, excell. cond., (11-09-92, Christie-NY, #134), 35½ x 24 in., (901 x 610 mm.), colored lithograph on wove (BP 3055, DM 7375, FR 24,919, Y 573,343).

$1760* *Untitled (D. 249), 1959,* from Fusees, s., #21/50, wide margins, light/mat staining, remains of tape, glue, good cond., (11-09-92, Christie-NY, #126), 5 x 7 in., (127 x 178 mm.), colored aquatint on wove (BP 1164, DM 2810, FR 9493, Y 218,416).

$2860* *Untitled (D. 253), 1959,* from Fusees, s., #4/50, full margins, excell. cond., (11-09-92, Christie-NY, #127), 5¾ x 16¾ in., (146 x 425 mm.), colored aquatint on BFK Rives (BP 1891, DM 4566, FR 15,426, Y 354,927).

$5500* *Untitled (D. 47), 1947,* from The Prints of Joan Miro, s., d., #84/100, full margins, light staining, nick, glue remains, (11-09-92, Christie-NY, #121, illus.), 128 x 149 in., (325.1 x 378.5 cm.), etching and aquatint in black and orange on wove (BP 3636, DM 8780, FR 29,666, Y 682,552).

$1887* *Untitled (Kramer 209),* from "Joan Miro" by James Johnson Sweeney, s., #87/100, p. La Poligrafa S.A, 1975, (11-16-92, Briest, #338), 13¾ x 20¼ in., (35 x 51.5 cm.), lithograph in colors on Guarro (BP 1240, DM 3010, FR 10,140, Y 235,492).

$2200* *Untitled (M. 191), 1953,* for Oeuvres recentes, s., #28/150, full margins, colors faded, good cond., (11-09-92, Christie-NY, #123), 686 x 520 in., (x cm.), colored lithograph on Arches (BP 1455, DM 3512, FR 11,866, Y 273,021).

$2420* *Untitled (M. 247), 1957,* Exhib. at Gallery Matarasso, s., d., #73/125, full margins, light staining, nicks, skinning, foxing, (11-09-92, Christie-NY, #124, illus.), 604 x 482 in., (x cm.), colored lithograph on wove (BP 1600, DM 3863, FR 13,053, Y 300,323).

$5280* *Untitled (M. 834), 1971,* for the International Plastic Arts Association, Unesco, s., #33/75, blindstamp, time staining, good cond., (11-09-92, Christie-NY, #133, illus.), 30¹⁄₁₆ x 22¹⁄₁₆ in., (763 x 560 mm.), colored lithograph on Arches (BP 3491, DM 8429, FR 28,479, Y 655,249).

BI *Untitled (Mourlot 211), 1975,* from Maravillas Con Varaciones Arosticas En El Jardin de Miro, s. instone, est. $4/600, (05-15-93, Cleveland, #415), 18 x 13 in., (45.7 x 33 cm.), color lithograph.

$4400* *Untitled (see C. 217), 1976,* plate 4 from El Pi de Formentor, s., #37/50, full margins, very goodcond., (11-09-92, Christie-NY, #135), 41⁵⁄₁₆ x 35⁹⁄₁₆ in., (105 x 90.3 cm.), etching, aquatint and carborundum in colors on wove (BP 2909, DM 7024, FR 23,732, Y 546,041).

BI *Untitled (see C. 217), 1976,* plate 6 from El Pi de Formentor, s., #39/50, full margins, creases, very good cond., est. $5/7,000, (11-09-92, Christie-NY, #137, illus.), 41¼ x 35⁹⁄₁₆ in., (104.8 x 90.3 cm.), etching and aquatint in colors w/embossing on wove.

$4180* *Untitled (see C. 217), 1976,* s., #39/50, full margins, staining, very good cond., (11-09-92, Christie-NY, #136, illus.), 41⁷⁄₁₆ x 16¹⁄₁₆ in., (105.3 x 40.8 cm.), etching and aquatint in colors on wove (BP 2764, DM 6673, FR 22,546, Y 518,739).

$7130* *Untitled, 1976,* plate 6 from El Pi de Formentor, s., #39/50, full margins, creases, very good cond., (05-11-93, Christie-NY, #242), sheet 41¼ x 35½ in., (104.8 x 90.2 cm.), color etching and aquatint w/embossing on wove (BP 4552, DM 11,232, FR 37,845, Y 784,292).

$880* *Untitled, 1978,* from Album 21, full margins, num., s., (05-27-93, Swann, #190, illus.), 25½ x 19½ in., (64.8 x 49.5 cm.), color lithograph (BP 564, DM 1412, FR 4759, Y 94,340).

BI *Untitled, 1979,* from Els Gossos, s., #14/30, very good cond., est. $2,5/3,500, (11-09-92, Christie-NY, #138, illus.), 45½ x 29 in., (115.6 x 73.7 cm.), etching and aquatint in colors on wove.

$1540* *Untitled, c. 1972,* s., annot. H.C., good cond.?, (12-08-92, Swann, #215, illus.), sight 17 x 23 in., (43.2 x 58.4 cm.), color lithograph (BP 965, DM 2398, FR 8174, Y 190,878).

$13,200* *Vers La Gauche (D. 461), 1968,* s., #26/75, pub. Maeght, good cond., defects, foxing, creases, waterstains, (11-05-92, Sotheby-NY, #282, illus.), sheet 28¾ x 41 in., (73 x 104.1 cm.), etching, aquatint and carborundum p. in colors (BP 8585, DM 20,876, FR 70,626, Y 1,619,433).

$4400* *Village D'Oiseaux (Benhoura 168, Dupin 526), 1969,* annot. e.a., pub. Maeght, (12-13-92, Hindman, #275, illus.), 36¼ x 25 in., color etching, aquatint and carborundum on Arches wove paper (BP 2813, DM 6915, FR 23,567, Y 544,352).

$5225* *Les Voyants III (M. 663), 1970,* s., #41/75, full margins, good cond., tape stains, (11-05-92, Sotheby-NY, #289, illus.), 25⅜ x 19¾ in., (643 x 500 mm.), lithograph p. in colors (BP 3398, DM 8263, FR 27,956, Y 641,026).

BI *William Butler Yeats. Le Vent Parmi Les Roseaux (C. 149),* book w/additional suite of 2 etchings in 3 states, all s., #I/X, s.,num., pub. Collection Paroles Peintes, 1971, p. Maeght, good cond., orig. binding, est. BP 7/8,000, (12-03-92, Sotheby-London, #441, illus.), each sheet approx. 13¼ x 10 in., (335 x 255 mm.), etchings w/aquatint in colors on japon nacre.

$3623* *XXe Siecle No. 46 (M. 1106), 1976,* s. 52/75, (05-25-93, AB Stockholm, #52), 12³⁄₁₆ x 9⁷⁄₁₆ in., (31 x 24 cm.), lithograph in colors (BP 2348, DM 5901, FR 19,863, Y 396,000, SK 5280).

BI *Zephirvogel, 1960,* s., #59/100, est. DM 5,500, (09-18-92, Schloss Ahlden, #1037, illus.), 15¾ x 22¹³⁄₁₆ in., (40 x 57.9 cm.), color lithograph on handmade.

BI *from Quatre Colors Aparien El Mon (D. 825), 1975,* s., #42/50, appears good cond., est. $6/8,000, (06-11-93, Doyle, #65, illus.), sight 34½ x 24 in., (876 x 610 mm.), color aquatint.

$275* *from Sans Le Soleil (D. 408),* s., #18/25, soiling, glued down, good cond., (06-11-93, Doyle, #64), 2⅜ x 5½ in., (60 x 140 mm.), b&w aquatint (BP 181, DM 447, FR 1507, Y 29,178).

MIRO, Joan (after)

$1320* *Composition,* s. by Miro, #92/300, pub. Atelier Crommelynck, (05-16-93, Hindman, #485), 15½ x 19 in., (39.4 x 48.3 cm.), color intaglio w/relief elements (BP 858, DM 2123, FR 7135, Y 146,325).

$1320* *Composition,* s. by Miro, #27/300, pub. Maeght, (05-16-93, Hindman, #487), 15½ x 21½ in., (39.4 x 54.6 cm.), color lithograph (BP 858, DM 2123, FR 7135, Y 146,325).

$2300* *Composition Sur Fond Vert (Maeght 1703), 1950,* s., d., #213/400, pub. Maeght, margins, good cond., light-stain, creases in image, tear into image, repaired tears and creases, water stain, (05-13-93, Sotheby-NY, #667), 13⅝ x 18¼ in., (347 x 465 mm.), sh 19⅛ x 23⅛ in., (347 x 465 mm.), lithograph in colors on Arches wove (BP 1510, DM 3714, FR 12,527, Y 256,782).

$3000* *Composition Sur Fond Vert (Maeght Nr. 1703), 1950,* 387/400, s., d., trimmed, traces of glue, (10-14-92, Germann, #385, illus.), 20 x 25½ in., (508 x 648 mm.), color lithograph (BP 1761, DM 4390, FR 14,888, Y 363,548, SF 3910).

$2760* *Femmes, Oiseaux, Etoile, 1960,* s., #178/300, pub. Maeght Editeur, blindstamp, margins, time staining, staining, good cond., (05-11-93, Christie-NY, #244, illus.), borderline 23½ x 18¾ in., (597 x 476 mm.), color lithograph on Rives (BP 1762, DM 4348, FR 14,650, Y 303,597).

$825* *Figures,* s. by Miro, #251/300, pub. Maeght, (05-16-93, Hindman, #486), 18 x 20¾ in., (45.7 x 52.7 cm.), color lithograph (BP 536, DM 1327, FR 4459, Y 91,453).

BI *Untitled,* bears sig., est. $80/120, (12-02-92, Boos, #313), sight 17½ x 14 in., (44.5 x 35.6 cm.), lithograph.

MIRO, Joan and Louis MARCOUSSIS

$49,450* *Portrait De Miro (D. 31; Milet 193), 1938,* s. by Miro w/both artists' names, d., #13/50, exec., pub. Pierre Loeb, & Pierre Matisse, full margins, good cond., crease in image, mat stain, crease, discolored, skinned spots, (05-13-93, Sotheby-NY, #630, illus.), 13¼ x 11 in., (335 x 280 mm.), drypoint and engraving on Arches wove (BP 32,465, DM 79,848, FR 269,336, Y 5,520,822).

MIRRI, Lodovico and Francesco SMUGLIEWICZ

$9900* *Vestigia Delle Terme Di Tito E Loro Interne Pitture: 59,* t., ded., many double-page, folio, some foxed, (11-12-92, Swann, #114, illus.), 24½ x 16⁷⁄₁₆ in., (622 x 418 mm.), engraving (BP 6502, DM 15,687, FR 52,913, Y 1,227,526).

MISHAAN

BI *The Wounded Quetzall,* from The Palladium Series, s., #11/50, est. $150/250, (02-12-93, DuMouchelle, #366), 23½ x 29½ in., (59.7 x 74.9 cm.), lithograph.

$138* *The Wounded Quetzall,* from the palladium series, s. #11/50, (04-16-93, DuMouchelle, #1452), 23½ x 29½ in., (59.7 x 74.9 cm.), lithograph (BP 91, DM 223, FR 753, Y 15,518).

MISHKIN, C.

$1100* *Caruso, Enrico, May 1917,* subscribed, d., remnants of tape,, (09-17-92, Swann, #57), approx. 4½ x 7½ in., (11.4 x 19.1 cm.), photograph (BP 618, DM 1633, FR 5589, Y 136,952).

MISRACH, Richard b. 1949

$1265* *Desert Cactus, 1976,* s., d., est. $1,2/1,600, (05-23-93, Butterfield, #3533, illus.), 14½ x 14½ in., photograph, toned gelatin silver print (BP 824, DM 2068, FR 6962, Y 139,825).

$2300* *"Desert Fire #249" and "Pyramid, Pyramid Lake": Two,* 1985 and 1986, p. 1987, s., t., d., #17/25 and #7/25 in ink, (04-08-93, Christie-NY, #550, illus.), each 18¼ x 23 in., (46.4 x 58.4 cm.), photograph, color coupler print (BP 1508, DM 3695, FR 12,507, Y 261,008).

$605* *"Road Blockade and Pyramids", 1989,* s., t., d., (11-16-92, Butterfield, #6096, illus.), 10¼ x 13 in., (260.8 x 330.8 mm.), photograph, c-print (BP 398, DM 965, FR 3249, Y 75,239).

$3220* *Sandstorm, Ground Sky Transition, 1976,* s., t., d., (c) insig., annot., (04-08-93, Christie-NY, #549, illus.), 14¼ x 14⅛ in., (36.2 x 35.9 cm.), photograph, toned gelatin silver print (BP 2111, DM 5173, FR 17,510, Y 365,411).

$440* *Untitled (Two Palm Trees In The Desert), 1979,* s., d., inventory num., (11-16-92, Butterfield, #6097, illus.), 10⅜ x 10⅜ in., (264 x 264 mm.), photograph, c-print (BP 290, DM 702, FR 2363, Y 54,720).

$316* *Untitled, Santa Barbara, Oil Derricks And Sand,* 1984, p. 1987, s., t., d., #16/25, (05-23-93, Butterfield, #3534, illus.), 18¼ x 23 in., photograph, C-print (BP 206, DM 517, FR 1739, Y 34,929).

$460* *"White Man Contemplating Pyramids", 1989,* s., t., d., #9/30, illus., (05-23-93, Butterfield, #3535, illus.), 9½ x 12 in., photograph, C-print (BP 300, DM 752, FR 2532, Y 50,846).

MISTI

$695* *Demaria Fres Photographiques,* p. Kossuth, defects, backed on linen, laid on board, (05-07-93, Christie-S. Ken, #106, illus.), 27 x 39 in., (68.6 x 99.1 cm.), color lithograph (BP 440, DM 1099, FR 3703, Y 76,525).

MISTI (Ferdinand MIFLIEZ) 1865-1923

$1104* *Cleveland Car. Automobiles Electriques, c. 1900,* Paris, Imp. Vercasson, cond. B, (06-11-93, Boisgirard, #116), 118⅛ x 43⁵⁄₁₆ in., (300 x 110 cm.), poster (BP 725, DM 1794, FR 6049, Y 117,135).

$1144* *Fetes De Neuilly Sur Seine Du 15 Juin Au 7 Juillet, 1902,* Neuilly, Imp. Duchateau, cond. B, (06-11-93, Boisgirard, #117), 62¹⁵⁄₁₆ x 45¼ in., (160 x 115 cm.), poster (BP 752, DM 1859, FR 6268, Y 121,379).

MISTI (after)

BI *Le Velo, Lisez Tous Les Jours, 1898,* fold marks, tears, losses, repairs, est. BP 1/200, (02-04-93, Christie-S. Ken, #131), 51 x 37 in., (129.5 x 94 cm.), color lithograph backed on linen.

MITCHELL, Joan American b. 1926

$1650* *"Bedford II" and "Bedford III" (Tyler 364:JM2; & Tyler 365:JM3), 1981:Two,* s., #48/70 and 64/70, blindstamp, pub. Tyler Graphics, Ltd., full margins, good cond., (11-07-92, Sotheby-NY, #684), each sheet approx. 42½ x 32½ in., (108 x 82.6 cm.), two lithographs p. in colors on Arches 88 (BP 1079, DM 2635, FR 8904, Y 203,653).

$1980* *"Brush"; and "Brush, State I" (T. 372:JM10 & T. 373:JM11), 1981: Two,* s., #20/70, #20/35, good cond., creases, (11-07-92, Sotheby-NY, #687), each sheet approx. 42½ x 32½ in., (108 x 82.6 cm.), two lithographs p. in colors (BP 1295, DM 3161, FR 10,685, Y 244,384).

$3575* *"Flower I"; "Flower II"; and "Flowers III" (T. 369:JM7; T. 370:JM8; and T. 371:JM9), 1981: Three,* s., #55/70, blindstamp, pub. Tyler Graphics, Ltd., full margins, goodcond., (11-07-92, Sotheby-NY, #686, illus.), each sheet approx. 42½ x 32½ in., (108 x 82.6 cm.), three lithographs p. in colors (BP 2337, DM 5708, FR 19,293, Y 441,249).

$4125* *"Sides Of A River I"; "Sides Of A River II"; and "Sides Of A River III" (T. 366:JM4; T.367:JM5; and T. 368:JM6), 1981: Three,* s., #52/70, blindstamp, pub. Tyler Graphics, Ltd., full margins, goodcond., (11-07-92, Sotheby-NY, #685, illus.), each sheet approx. 42½ x 32½ in., (108 x 82.6 cm.), three lithographs p. in colors (BP 2697, DM 6586, FR 22,261, Y 509,134).

MITELLI, Agostino

$2640* *Capricci Incisi In Rame ... Nel 1628: 23,* mono., oblong 4to, (11-12-92, Swann, #155, illus.), engraving (BP 1734, DM 4183, FR 14,110, Y 327,340).

MIYOSHIN-JI

BI *Kyoto(a), 1961,* s., t., #45/200, est. $100/150, (06-11-93, Freemn/Fine Art, #148), 20½ x 15 in., (52.1 x 38.1 cm.), lithograph.

MOCHETTI, G. (after)

$234 *Religious Subjects: A Set Of Six,* one d. 1816, (12-11-92, G.A. Key, #4), 13 x 19 in., (33 x 48.3 cm.), black and white engraving (BP 150, DM 369, FR 1263, Y 28,957).

MODEL, Lisette 1901-1983

BI *"Blind Man In Front Of Billboard",* 1935, p. 1977, s., #74/75, photog.'s stamp, from portfolio Twelve Photographs, illus., est. $7/900, (05-23-93, Butterfield, #3541, illus.), 19¼ x 15½ in., photograph, gelatin silver print.

$403* *"Cafe Metropole",* 1946, p. 1977, s., #74/75, photog.'s stamp, from portfolio Twelve Photographs, illus., (05-23-93, Butterfield, #3538, illus.), 19⅜ x 15⅝ in., photograph, gelatin silver print (BP 262, DM 659, FR 2218, Y 44,545).

BI *Coney Island, New York,* (1940s), 1960s, ink s., flush-mounted, est. $2,5/3,500, (04-08-93, Christie-NY, #321, illus.), 15¾ x 19⅞ in., (40 x 50.5 cm.), photograph, gelatin silver print.

$990* *"Coney Island, Standing" (Lisette Model, Cover),* 1942/1977, s., edit. 21/75, photog. stamp, (11-16-92, Butterfield, #6098, illus.), 19⁹⁄₁₆ x 15⅜ in., (496.2 x 391.2 mm.), photograph, gelatin silver print (BP 652, DM 1578, FR 5317, Y 123,119).

BI *Fashion Show, Pierre Hotel,* (1940-46), 1976, s., num. 21/75, (c) credit & date stamp, lit., est.$1,5/2,000, (10-13-92, Christie-NY, #315, illus.), 15⅜ x 19½ in., (39.1 x 49.5 cm.), photograph, gelatin silver print.

$450* *Fashion Show, Pierre Hotel (1940-46),* s., #74/75 verso; stamped (c), Lisette Model, 1977, (02-04-93, Sloan, #2913, illus.), photograph, silver gelatin print (BP 311, DM 746, FR 2522, Y 55,998).

$690* *"Fifth Avenue",* 1945, p. 1977, s., #74/75, photog.'s stamp, from portfolio Twelve Photographs, (05-23-93, Butterfield, #3542, illus.), 15⅜ x 19⅜ in., photograph, gelatin silver print (BP 449, DM 1128, FR 3797, Y 76,268).

$770* *"Fifth Avenue",* 1930's/1977, s., edit. 21/75, photog. stamp, (11-16-92, Butterfield, #6100, illus.), 15¾ x 19⁹⁄₁₆ in., (400.8 x 496.2 mm.), photograph, gelatin silver print (BP 507, DM 1228, FR 4135, Y 95,759).

$1320* *French Gambler, Promendade Des Anglais, Nice, France,* (1934), 1976, s., num. 21/75, (c) credit & date stamp, lit., (10-13-92, Christie-NY, #314, illus.), 19¾ x 15¼ in., (50.2 x 38.7 cm.), photograph, gelatin silver print (BP 769, DM 1934, FR 6570, Y 160,058).

BI *"Greed",* 1937, p. 1977, s., #74/75, photog.'s stamp, from portfolio Twelve Photographs, est. $7/900, (05-23-93, Butterfield, #3537, illus.), 19½ x 15¾ in., photograph, gelatin silver print.

$2588* *"Greed", 1937,* s., cropping notations, pub. in PM magazine, 1941, t., (05-23-93, Butterfield, #3536, illus.), 13½ x 11 in., photograph, gelatin silver print (BP 1685, DM 4232, FR 14,243, Y 286,062).

$403* *"Lower East Side",* 1942, p. 1977, s., #74/75, photog.'s stamp, from portfolio Twelve Photographs, illus., (05-23-93, Butterfield, #3540, illus.), 19¼ x 15½ in., photograph, gelatin silver print (BP 262, DM 659, FR 2218, Y 44,545).

$770* *"Lower East Side, New York" (Lisette Model, p. 63),* 1940's/1977, s., edit. 21/75, photog. stamp, (11-16-92,

Butterfield, #6099, illus.), 19⁹⁄₁₆ x 15¼ in., (496.2 x 388 mm.), photograph, gelatin silver print (BP 507, DM 1228, FR 4135, Y 95,759).

$489* *"Promenade Des Anglais"*, 1934, p. 1977, s., #74/75, photog.'s stamp, from portfolio Twelve Photographs, illus., (05-23-93, Butterfield, #3539, illus.), 19⅝ x 15⅜ in., photograph, gelatin silver print (BP 318, DM 800, FR 2691, Y 54,051).

$7150* *Running Legs, Wall Street, New York City, 1940-41*, s. in ink, t., lit., (10-13-92, Christie-NY, #313, illus.), 10⅜ x 13½ in., (26.4 x 34.3 cm.), photograph, gelatin silver print (BP 4164, DM 10,475, FR 35,590, Y 866,982).

BI *Seated Lady*, s., #74/75 verso; stamped (c) Lisette Model, 1977, est. $1/1,500, (02-04-93, Sloan, #2914), 19½ x 15½ in., (49.5 x 39.4 cm.), photograph, gelatin silver print.

BI *"Woman With Hat And Veil", "Woman With Shawl", "Woman In Flowered Dress", "French Gamble", Fashion Show", "Newspaper Salesman", "Woman At Coney Island", "Blind Man", "Singer At The Cafe", "Metropole" and Two Others: Twelve*, 1930's-40's, Graphics International Ltd., 1976, p. under photog.'s supervision, s., num. XI/IV, (c) limitation stamp, this was given to Berenice Abbott for her contribution of the essay p. on just. page, Berenice Abbott Coll.,est. $6/8,000, (04-08-93, Christie-NY, #320, illus.), each approx. 19½ x 15¾ in., (49.5 x 40 cm.), photograph, gelatin silver print.

MODENA, Nicoleto da
$6597* *St. Roch (B. 49; Hind V, P. 126, No. 56)*, trimmed into subject, made up holes, paper discolored, (06-29-93, Sotheby-London, #57, illus.), 5¾ x 4⅛ in., (14.6 x 10.5 cm.), engraving (BP 4370, DM 11,140, FR 37,547, Y 702,257).

MODERSOHN-BECKER, Paula   1876-1907
BI *Die Frau Mit Der Gans, Frau Mit Gans, Ein Nebelbild (Werner 5)*, 1902, 3rd state of 4, i.; s. by artist's husband, full margins, mat staining, excell. cond., prov., est. $6/10,000, (05-11-93, Christie-NY, #245, illus.), plate 4¾ x 6¾ in., (121 x 171 mm.), etching, aquatint and roulette on wove.

$1380* *Sitzende Alte (Werner 3/III), c. 1900*, i. be printer Felsing, full (large) margins, good cond., tape stains, soiling, (02-11-93, Sotheby-NY, #202), 7⁹⁄₁₆ x 5¹³⁄₁₆ in., (192 x 147 mm.), etching and aquatint p. in dark green on cream wove (BP 974, DM 2286, FR 7735, Y 166,365)

$4276* *Sitzende Alte, c. 1905*, (06-23-93, Kornfeld, #599), strich- und Flachenatzung on thick wove (BP 2905, DM 7235, FR 24,337, Y 465,846, SF 6440).

MODIGLIANI, Amedeo   Italian 1884-1920
$282* *Bildnis Einer Jungen Frau Von Vorn*, s. Modigliani, (03-24-93, Venator/Hansten, #4536), image 23¹⁵⁄₁₆ x 18⁵⁄₁₆ in., (60.8 x 46.5 cm.), color screenprint (BP 191, DM 461, FR 1568, Y 33,134).

$825* *"Hebuterne"*, s. in stone, #73/375, (05-07-93, Goldberg, #423A, illus.), 23 x 16½ in., (58.4 x 41.9 cm.), color lithograph (BP 522, DM 1304, FR 4395, Y 90,839).

$825* *"Reclining Nude"*, plate s., large margins, good cond., surface soiling, notations, (10-28-92, Butterfield, #2842), 3¹⁵⁄₁₆ x 5⅞ in., (100 x 149 mm.), etching on cream wove (BP 526, DM 1274, FR 4326, Y 101,227).

MODOTTI, Tina   Italian 1896-1942
$2750* *Architectural Study, Mexico*, stamp, mid-1920's, (10-15-92, Sotheby-NY, #263, illus.), 3⅝ x 4¾ in., (9.2 x 12.1 cm.), photograph, platinum print (BP 1683, DM 4093, FR 13,882, Y 329,934).

$29,700* *Corn, Guitar, Cartridge, 1928, (A Fragile Life, p. 92; Photographien& Dokumente, p. 111)*, mounted, stamp & reduction notations in unidentified hand, (10-15-92, Sotheby-NY, #262, illus.), 9½ x 7½ in., (24.1 x 19.1 cm.), photograph, gelatin silver print (BP 18,174, DM 44,210, FR 149,924, Y 3,563,287).

$6900* *Hands Of The Puppeteer, Louis Bunin (Agostinis, p. 124), c. 1926*, (04-06-93, Sotheby-NY, #158A, illus.), 8⅝ x 5½ in., photograph (BP 4557, DM 11,116, FR 37,643, Y 786,953).

$4125* *Jose Clemente Orozco At Work On A Mural, c. 1925 (A Fragile Life, p.100)*, credit stamp, (10-15-92, Sotheby-NY,

#265, illus.), 7½ x 9½ in., (19.1 x 24.1 cm.), photograph, gelatin silver print (BP 2524, DM 6140, FR 20,823, Y 494,901).

BI *Maria Marin De Orozco, 1925*, prov., est. $12/15,000, (04-08-93, Christie-NY, #393, illus.), 13⅜ x 9⅛ in., (34 x 23.2 cm.), photograph, gelatin silver print.

$1650* *Marionette, 1926 (Photographien & Dokumente, p. 42)*, (10-15-92, Sotheby-NY, #264, illus.), 9½ x 7¼ in., (24.1 x 18.4 cm.), photograph, gelatin silver print (BP 1010, DM 2456, FR 8329, Y 197,960).

$26,450* *"Mella's Typewriter" (A Fragile Life, p. 52; Photographien and Dokumente, p. 96), 1928*, tipped to double-mount, s., d. by photog., stamp, Tina Modotti Collection, (04-06-93, Sotheby-NY, #158, illus.), 9½ x 7½ in., photograph (BP 17,470, DM 42,613, FR 144,299, Y 3,016,651).

$40,700* *Mella's Typewriter, 1928 (A Fragile Life, p. 152; Photographien & Dokumente, p. 96)*, s., d., i. by photog. in ink, (10-15-92, Sotheby-NY, #266, illus.), 9½ x 7½ in., (24.1 x 19.1 cm.), photograph, gelatin silver print (BP 24,905, DM 60,584, FR 205,452, Y 4,883,023).

$33,000* *Untitled, Mexico, 1924*, sig., d., ex-coll. Caroline "Carry" Wagner, (10-14-92, Swann, #517, illus.), 3½ x 4⅝ in., (8.9 x 11.7 cm.), photograph, platinum print (BP 19,370, DM 48,295, FR 163,772, Y 3,999,031).

MOE, Louis
$179* *"Alf Og Ugle"*, s. Louis Moe, ded., (10-20-92, B. Rasmussen, #369), etching (BP 110, DM 272, FR 921, Y 21,901, DK 1035).

MOHLWEIN, Ludwig
$869* *Oka Eisenberger*, p. O & P Leroi GmbH, creases, (05-07-93, Christie-S. Ken, #77, illus.), 15¾ x 24 in., (40 x 61 cm.), color lithograph (BP 550, DM 1374, FR 4630, Y 95,684).

MOHOLY-NAGY, Laszlo   Hungarian 1895-1946
BI *Sailors Rolling Gangplank Into Position, Scandinavia, 1930*, handstamps, est. $25/35,000, (10-14-92, Swann, #378, illus.), 9¼ x 6¾ in., (23.5 x 17.1 cm.), photograph, silver print.

$28,750* *"Decorating Work" (Switzerland) (Haus, pl. 7; roh, no. 59, cropped variant), 1925*, photog. stamp, (04-06-93, Sotheby-NY, #329A, illus.), 15½ x 11¾ in., photograph (BP 18,989, DM 46,319, FR 156,847, Y 3,278,969).

$8351* *Konstruktion, 1923*, s., ded., full margins, good cond., (10-14-92, Sotheby-Japan, #56, illus.), 12 x 9⅛ in., (305 x 232 mm.), linoleum cut on thin Japan (BP 4902, DM 12,222, FR 41,444, Y 1,011,997).

$148,364* *Konstruktionen. - VI. Kestnermappe, 1923*, pub. Ludwig Ey, s. Maholy-Nagy, num., (06-25-93, Kornfeld, #82, illus.), portfolio 23⅞ x 17¹³⁄₁₆ in., (60.6 x 45.2 cm.), (BP 100,348, DM 252,577, FR 850,711, Y 15,726,521, SF 224,250).

$1168* *Laszlo Moholy-Nagy Ten Fotogramme, 1922-1926, 1973: Portfolio, 1922-1926, 1973*, p. Hattula Moholy-Nagy, missing num. 7 and 9, reprinted, each blind stamped 'Fotorepro 1973', each stamped 'Nachlass Moholy-Nagy, 1873, Fotorepro, Exemplar 1 von 50' verso, i. 'Hattula Moholy-Nagy', edit. 1/60,pub. Galerie Heiner Friedrich, (10-15-92, Sotheby-London, #52), photogram (BP 715, DM 1739, FR 5896, Y 140,132).

BI *"Pont Transbordeur...Marseille", c. 1925-30*, t., stamped photog.'s credit foto moholy-nagy, 274 x 182mm, est. BP 5/8,000, (05-07-93, Sotheby-London, #229, illus.), photograph, silver print.

$6600* *Ship Scene, Scandinavia*, handstamp, 1930, p. c. 1946, (10-14-92, Swann, #379, illus.), 9½ x 7 in., (24.1 x 17.8 cm.), photograph, silver print (BP 3874, DM 9659, FR 32,754, Y 799,806).

$44,850* *Untitled (View From The Berlin Radio Tower In Winter) (Haus, pl. 40;Art of Photography, pl. 236)*, s., d. by photog., label, t., d. in unident. hand, 1928, p. c. 1941, (04-06-93, Sotheby-NY, #330, illus.), 9⅝ x 7½ in., photograph, mounted on Hi-Art Illustration board (BP 29,624, DM 72,257, FR 244,681, Y 5,115,192).

$7162* *(Untitled-Construction), c. 1920*, s., full margins, good cond. within subject, necks, tears, handling marks, creases, (12-03-92, Sotheby-London, #452, illus.), 4¾ x

5⅞ in., (121 x 150 mm.), wood engraving on soft wove (BP 4620, DM 11,263, FR 38,443, Y 891,129).

$9890* *(Untitled-Construction), c. 1920,* s., full margins, good cond. within subject, tears, marks, creases, (12-03-92, Sotheby-London, #453, illus.), 3⅞ x 4¾ in., (99 x 119 mm.), wood engraving on soft wove (BP 6380, DM 15,553, FR 53,086, Y 1,230,559).

$1079* *'Laszlo Moholy-Nagy Ten Fotoplastiken 1925-1927', 1973: Portfolio,* p. Hattula Moholy-Nagy, missing num. 1 and 10, each nmounted on mat,reprinted from origs., blind stamped 'Fotorepro 1973', stamped 'Nachlass Moholy-Nagy, 1973, Fotorepro, Exemplar, 1 von 50' verso, i., edit. 1/60, pub. GalerieHeiner Freidrich und Edizione o Milano, (10-15-92, Sotheby-London, #53, illus.), photograph, portfolio of fotoplastiken (BP 660, DM 1606, FR 5447, Y 129,454).

MOHOLY-NAGY, Lucia b. Chechoslovakia 1894-1989

$399* *"The Countess Of Oxford And Asquith",* early 1940s, t., photog.'s credit Copyright LUCIA MOHOLY A.R.P.S., (05-06-93, Christie-London, #139, illus.), 5½ x 4½ in., photograph, gelatin silver print (BP 253, DM 628, FR 2116, Y 43,899).

BI *Moholy-Nagy Dining Room In One Of The Bahaus Master's Houses, Dessau,1925-26,* credit and reprod. limit. stamp, lit., est. $1,2/1,500, (10-13-92, Christie-NY, #316, illus.), photograph, gelatin silver print.

BI *Mutter Margen, c. 1930,* photog.'s t., handstamp, notations in unidentified hand, est. $1,5/2,000, (10-14-92, Swann, #380, illus.), 9 x 7 in., (22.9 x 17.8 cm.), photograph, silver print.

BI *"Theo Van Doesburg",* 1924, p.l., cropping notations, attrib., est. $1,2/1,600, (05-23-93, Butterfield, #3543, illus.), 10½ x 8½ in., photograph, gelatin silver print.

MOLA, Giovanni Battista 1616-1661

$867* *Cupido Auf Einem Triumphwagen (B. 6),* stained, (12-04-92, Bassenge, #6307, illus.), 6³⁄₁₆ x 7⅝ in., (15.7 x 19.4 cm.), etching (BP 556, DM 1381, FR 4684, Y 108,240).

MOLE and THOMAS

$275* *The Human American Eagle, 2500 Officers, Nurses, And Men, Camp Gordon, Atlanta, Georgia, 1918,* names, t., (c), d. in neg., (10-14-92, Swann, #518), 9½ x 11½ in., (24.1 x 29.2 cm.), photograph, silver print (BP 161, DM 402, FR 1365, Y 33,325).

$715* *Y.M.C.A. Emblem Formed By Officers, Men And Camp Activity Workers AtCamp Wheeler, Georgia, c. 1918,* w/ photog. names, t., (c) in neg., (04-07-93, Swann, #519), 10¼ x 13 in., photograph, silver print (BP 473, DM 1156, FR 3914, Y 81,232).

MOLENKAMP, Nico

$1279* *Untitled: Four,* complete set, each s., #17/20 HC, pub. Galerie Willy Schoots, p. Peter Wilms, full sheets p. to edges, good cond., in orig. cloth-covered portfoliobox, (05-27-93, Sotheby-Amstrdm, #666), each sheet 34¼ x 31⅛ in., (870 x 790 mm.), color silkscreen on Museum Karton (cardboard) (BP 819, DM 2052, FR 6917, Y 137,114, G 2300).

MOLES

$83* *Festival International De Musique Et De Danse, Bordeaux, 1950,* (01-31-93, Morelle/Marchan, #37), 15¾ x 23⅝ in., (40 x 60 cm.), poster (BP 56, DM 134, FR 452, Y 10,354).

MOLEU

BI *Quartet In The Garden,* #139/318, s., est. $100/200, (12-11-92, DuMouchelle, #162), 24 x 36 in., (61 x 91.4 cm.), serigraph.

MOLIN, Brita Swedish b. 1919

BI *"Open Doors",* s., The Print Club of Cleveland Publication, good cond., est. $2-300, (10-31-92, Cleveland, #385), 8⅛ x 10⅞ in., (20.6 x 27.6 cm.), inkless embossed intaglio.

$121* *"Southern Eye", 1967,* s., d., t., good cond., (10-31-92, Cleveland, #384A), 7¾ x 9¾ in., (19.7 x 24.8 cm.), monoprint (BP 78, DM 186, FR 632, Y 14,988).

MOLIN, Verner b. 1907

$21* *Composition,* s. V. Molin, (09-30-92, Kunsthallen, #214), color etching (BP 12, DM 30, FR 101, Y 2520, DK 115).

MOLINARI, Guido

$516* *Noir-Blanc,* s., d. 1965-67, #Epreuve d'artiste 9/10/90, prov., (06-07-93, Ritchie, #51, illus.), 26¾ x 25 in., (67.9 x 63.5 cm.), color serigraph (BP 340, DM 837, FR 2820, Y 55,353, C$ 660).

MOLINIER, Pierre 1900-1976

$834* *Godemiche A Deux, 1968,* prov., lit., (11-12-92, Lempertz, #176, illus.), 6⁹⁄₁₆ x 4¹³⁄₁₆ in., (16.6 x 12.3 cm.), photograph, gelatin silver print (BP 533, DM 1311, FR 4467, Y 103,180).

MOLINS, Pompeo and Fratelli ALINARI

$772* *"Monte Pincio Roma", c. 1862 and "Logia Firenze Perse Michel Angelo", 1860s: Two,* both ink t. on mount; second num. 21 in neg., blindstamp Alinari, (10-29-92, Christie-London, #37, illus.), first 9⅞ x 14³⁄₁₆ in., (25.1 x 36 cm.), second 13⅝ x 10³⁄₁₆ in., (25.1 x 36 cm.), photograph, albumen print mounted on card (BP 495, DM 1188, FR 4029, Y 95,627).

MOLL, Carl Austrian 1861-1945

$2970* *Beethoven Hauser, 1916,* Weinerwerkstatte portfolio, group of 11 views of Beethoven's homes, 1802-1827, plus title page, s., d. fruhling 1916, Carl Moll, each indent. on mat, individual folders, original box, very good cond., (09-11-92, Skinner, #17B, illus.), 8¼ x 8¼ in., (21 x 21 cm.), color woodcut on fine laid paper (BP 1536, DM 4275, FR 14,530, Y 367,984).

$1078* *"Therese Krones Haus", c. 1902,* lit., (05-19-93, Dorotheum, #305, illus.), 16¹¹⁄₁₆ x 16¹¹⁄₁₆ in., (42.4 x 42.4 cm.), woodcut in color (BP 700, DM 1752, FR 5904, Y 119,340, SC 12,320).

$2744* *"Verschneite Villa In Dobling", 1903,* lit., (05-19-93, Dorotheum, #306, illus.), 17¹⁄₁₆ x 16¾ in., (43.3 x 42.5 cm.), woodcut in color (BP 1781, DM 4460, FR 15,027, Y 303,775, SC 31,360).

$1960* *"Winter", 1903,* s. Carl Moll, lit., (05-19-93, Dorotheum, #304, illus.), 16¹⁵⁄₁₆ x 16¹⁵⁄₁₆ in., (43 x 43 cm.), woodcut in colors on Japan (BP 1272, DM 3186, FR 10,734, Y 216,982, SC 22,400).

MOLLER, Gunnar

$84* *Composition, 1989,* s. G.M. 89, 13/75, (09-30-92, Kunsthallen, #225), color lithograph (BP 47, DM 119, FR 403, Y 10,080, DK 460).

MOLUSSON, A.

$199* *Vittel Delices. Le Premier Soda De France, c. 1960,* cond. B, (03-16-93, Boisgirard, #160), 47¼ x 62¹⁵⁄₁₆ in., (120 x 160 cm.), poster (BP 137, DM 331, FR 1124, Y 23,269).

MOLYN, Pieter 1595-1661

$867* *Drei Bauern Und Eine Frau (B. 1, Hollstein 1 I), 1626,* (12-04-92, Bassenge, #6308, illus.), 6¹⁄₁₆ x 7⁷⁄₁₆ in., (15.4 x 18.9 cm.), etching (BP 556, DM 1381, FR 4684, Y 108,240).

$939* *Ein Soldat Erhalt Befehle Von Einem Sitzenden Offizier (B. 4; Hollstein 4 I), 1626,* watermark, (12-04-92, Bassenge, #6309, illus.), 5¹⁵⁄₁₆ x 7⁵⁄₁₆ in., (15.1 x 18.5 cm.), etching (BP 602, DM 1495, FR 5073, Y 117,228).

MOLZAHN, Johannes German 1892-1965

BI *Mysterium (Salzmann-Guse 19; Molzahn Verzeichnis 16), 1919,* s., d., est. DM 12,000, (06-10-93, Hauswedell/Nolt, #656, illus.), image 13⁹⁄₁₆ x 10⅝ in., (34.5 x 27 cm.), woodcut worked over w/watercolor.

$959* *Summa Summarum,* s., i., margins, paper discoloration, soiling, some foxing, Late Gerhard Brauer Coll., (05-27-93, Sotheby-Amstrdm, #759), 9⅛ x 13¹³⁄₁₆ in., (232 x 351 mm.), woodcut on wove (BP 614, DM 1539, FR 5187, Y 102,809, G 1725).

$1023* *Summa Summarum, 1921,* s., d., i., margins, defects in margins, paper discoloration, soiling, some foxing, Late Gerhard Brauer Coll., (05-27-93, Sotheby-Amstrdm, #758, illus.), 11¼ x 13½ in., woodcut on laid (BP 655, DM 1642, FR 5533, Y 109,670, G 1840).

MONCORNET, Baltazar c. 1600-1668
$4188* *Le Manifique Carousel Fait Sur Le Fleuve De L'Arne A Florence Pour Le Mariage Du Grand Duc: Ninteen,* (12-04-92, Bassenge, #6310, illus.), 3 15/16 x 5 3/16 in., (10 x 13.2 cm.), etching (BP 2686, DM 6670, FR 22,626, Y 522,846).

MONDRIAN, Piet (after)
BI *Album, 1957: Twelve,* album #162/200, est. FF 18/20,000, (11-16-92, Briest, #340), 25 9/16 x 19 11/16 in., (65 x 50 cm.), serigraph in colors on San Francisco bristol.
$165* *Composition With Red, Blue And Yellow, 1930,* inits., d. in screen, pub. Spadem, 1980, margins, laid down, good cond., (10-28-92, Butterfield, #3033), 24½ x 24½ in., (622 x 622 mm.), color silkscreen on wove (BP 105, DM 255, FR 865, Y 20,245).

MONET, Claude (after) 1840-1926
BI *"Port Coton" (W. 1092),* dry stamp, mono. stamp G.W.T., sig. of 2 artists, est. FF 8/10,000, cover lot, (10-18-92, Pescheteau, #220), 15 9/16 x 22 1/16 in., (39.5 x 56 cm.), lithograph on green China applique.
BI *"Vetheuil Dans Le Brouillard",* dry stamp, mono. stamp G.W.T., sig. of 2 artists, est. FF 8/10,000, (10-18-92, Pescheteau, #219, illus.), 15¾ x 22⅜ in., (40 x 56.8 cm.), lithograph in pencil on blue China applique.

MONKS, John Austin Sands American 1850-1917
$220* *Sheep Grazing In Pasture,* s. in plate, (09-17-92, Sloan, #664), 8¼ x 11⅛ in., (21 x 28.3 cm.), etching (BP 124, DM 327, FR 1118, Y 27,390).

MONNIER, Henri le French 1805-1877
$192* *Cordial-Medoc,* Bedos and Cie, A cond., (08-06-92, Swann, #171, illus.), 30 x 32 in., (76.2 x 81.3 cm.), (BP 100, DM 284, FR 958, Y 24,490).
$247* *Valmya, 1937,* Joseph-Charles, A- cond., marginal soiling, (08-06-92, Swann, #170, illus.), 61½ x 47 in., (156.2 x 119.4 cm.), (BP 129, DM 365, FR 1233, Y 31,505).

MONNOYER, Baptiste
$127* *Floral,* (11-13-92, DuMouchelle, #2456), 18½ x 16½ in., (47 x 41.9 cm.), hand-colored engraving (BP 82, DM 199, FR 672, Y 15,763).

MONOGRAMIST PVL
BI *Drei Manner Beim Wurfelspiel (Bartsch VIII, 1; Hollstein 7),* prov., est. DM 1,200, (06-10-93, Hauswedell/Nolt, #119, illus.), engraving.

MONOGRAMMIST CC
BI *L'Assomption De La Vierge,* after Rubens, annot., damp stains, (05-15-93, Loudmer, #163), 10 7/16 x 7⅝ in., (265 x 193 mm.), sh 12 1/16 x 7 15/16 in., (265 x 193 mm.), copper engraving on laid w/partiel watermark.

MONOGRAMMIST I. F.
BI *The Wedding Of Vertumnus And Pomona (B. XV, 1), 1542,* narrow margins, trimmed, tear, foxing, laid down, est. BP 2/3,000, (06-30-93, Sotheby-London, #166), 10 x 15¾ in., (254 x 400 mm.), engraving.

MONOGRAMMIST I.O.B.B.I.F.
$565* *Diane Et Mercure: In Amore Et In Eloquentia Fraus (Brulliot 1622),* pinholes, glue traces and annot. verso, (05-15-93, Loudmer, #23, illus.), 7 15/16 x 6 3/16 in., (203 x 157 mm.), copper engraving on trimmed laid (BP 367, DM 909, FR 3054, Y 62,632).

MONOGRAMMIST NBSE, ACTIVE 1570
BI *The Adoration Of The Shepherds, c. 1570,* after Taddeo Zuccaro, narrow margins, trimmed, very good cond., laid, BP est. 360/500, (12-01-92, Christie-London, #51), P. 15⅞ x 11 9/16 in., (403 x 293 mm.), engraving.

MONOGRAMMIST Z. B. M.
BI *Pandora Opening The Box Or An Allegory Of Enlightenment (Passavant, Vol. 6, P. 173),* narrow margin, trimmed, paper thin, est. BP 1/1,500, (06-30-93, Sotheby-London, #167), 14¼ x 9½ in., (362 x 241 mm.), etching and engraving on paper w/a Letter P in Circle watermark.

MONORY, Jacques b. 1924
$60* *"Adieu Ma Jolie", 1984,* #13/75, s., (04-04-93, Pescheteau, #269), 22 1/16 x 29 15/16 in., (56 x 76 cm.), color serigraph (BP 40, DM 96, FR 328, Y 6831).

BI *U.S.A. 76, 1976: Seven,* s., ed. Philippe Liband, est. FF 2,5/3,000, (11-16-92, Briest, #343), each 14 15/16 x 11 in., (38 x 28 cm.), serigraph.

MONSEN, Frederick 1865-1929
BI *"Hopi Children, Arizona", 1903,* t., est. $1,0/1,500, (11-16-92, Butterfield, #6102, illus.), 13¾ x 10⅜ in., (349.9 x 264 mm.), photograph, gelatin silver print.
BI *Navaho Children,* estate stamp, early 1900s, est. 2/2,500, (10-13-92, Christie-NY, #53, illus.), 18⅞ x 13 in., (47.9 x 33 cm.), photograph, gelatin silver print.
BI *"Navajo Man, Northeast Arizona", 1900,* t. on mount, est. $1,0/1,500, (11-16-92, Butterfield, #6101, illus.), 16 x 11¾ in., (407.1 x 299 mm.), photograph, albumen print.

MONTAGNA, Benedetto ac. 1510
BI *Madonna And Child With The Bird (H. 5),* later impression, 2nd state of 4, borderlines partially removed, trimmed, pinhole, good cond., ex-coll. Gilhofer & Ranschburg, est. $4,5/5,500, (05-13-93, Sotheby-NY, #332), 8⅛ x 6½ in., (205 x 165 mm.), engraving on laid.
BI *Die Madonna Mit Dem Kinde, Das Einen Vogel In Den Handen Halt (B. 7,Hind 14 IV, Tafel 749),* watermark, prov., est. DM 2400, (06-04-93, Bassenge, #5258), 7 15/16 x 6¼ in., (20.2 x 15.8 cm.), engraving.
BI *Man Seated By A Palm Tree (B. 44; Hind V, P. 183, No. 31),* 1st state of 2, trimmed w/in platemark, crease, repair, est. BP 2/3,000, (06-29-93, Sotheby-London, #58, illus.), 4⅜ x 3 in., (11.1 x 7.6 cm.), engraving.
BI *The Nativity (Hind V, 182.23),* thread margins, trimmed on platemark, stain, abrasions, dirt, est. BP2/3,000, (12-03-92, Sotheby-London, #81), 6½ x 4¼ in., (165 x 110 mm.), engraving.
$1716* *The Virgin And Child (H. 14), c. 1502,* 3rd state of 4, trimmed, good cond., (06-30-93, Sotheby-London, #168), 8½ x 6⅜ in., (216 x 162 mm.), engraving (BP 1150, DM 2927, FR 9873, Y 183,864).

MONTANUS, Arnoldus 1625?-1683
$55* *Untitled: Five,* from Atlas Chinensis, London, 1671, (09-17-92, Sloan, #628), approx. 5 x 6⅜ in., (12.7 x 16.2 cm.), engraved (BP 31, DM 82, FR 279, Y 6848).

MONTGOMERY, A. American
$110* *"Game Birds",* s., d. 1892, (02-12-93, DuMouchelle, #2325), 17 x 25 in., (43.2 x 63.5 cm.), colored lithograph (BP 77, DM 182, FR 617, Y 13,266).

MONTIJN, Jan contemporary
$895* *Des Seaux Des Planetes, 1969-1970: Seven,* complete portfolio, each s., d., #14/50, just., p. Piet Clement, full-margins, good cond., discoloration, in orig. cloth-covered portfolio box, (05-27-93, Sotheby-Amstrdm, #667), etching w/aquatint in colors on Hahnemule (BP 573, DM 1436, FR 4840, Y 95,948, G 1610).
$288* *Untitled, 1975,* s., d., #177/190, margins, good cond., (05-27-93, Sotheby-Amstrdm, #458), etching w/tone on wove (BP 184, DM 462, FR 1558, Y 30,875, G 518).
$192* *Untitled, 1975,* s., d., #177/190, margins, good cond., (05-27-93, Sotheby-Amstrdm, #459), 15 9/16 x 19½ in., (396 x 495 mm.), colored etching on wove (BP 123, DM 308, FR 1038, Y 20,583, G 345).
$352* *Untitled, 1975,* s., d., margins, good cond., (05-27-93, Sotheby-Amstrdm, #460), 13 15/16 x 19⅜ in., colored etching on wove (BP 225, DM 565, FR 1904, Y 37,736, G 633).
$192* *Untitled, 1985,* s., d., #E.A. III/III, full margins, good cond., minor handling creases, (05-27-93, Sotheby-Amstrdm, #668), 13⅞ x 18½ in., (352 x 470 mm.), etching w/aquatint in colors on wove (BP 123, DM 308, FR 1038, Y 20,583, G 345).

MONTPEZAT, de (after)
$1089* *"Cheveaux A Voitures": Plates 4 and 9: Two,* (02-03-93, Doyle, #45), sight 20 x 26 in., (50.8 x 66 cm.), hand colored print (BP 760, DM 1793, FR 6080, Y 135,465).

MOODY, C., Lithographer
$61 *"Cromer",* (04-16-93, G.A. Key, #71), 9 x 12 in., (22.9 x 30.5 cm.), tinted lithograph (BP 40, DM 99, FR 333, Y 6859).

MOON, Karl   1879-1948

$3220* *The Flute Player, 1908,* s., (c) blindstamp, (04-08-93, Christie-NY, #16, illus.), 21 x 13⅛ in., (53.3 x 33.3 cm.), photograph, toned gelatin silver print on heavy paper (BP 2111, DM 5173, FR 17,510, Y 365,411).

BI *Last Of The Council, 1910,* est. $1,5/2,000, (04-08-93, Christie-NY, #17, illus.), 14⅞ x 11 in., (37.8 x 27.9 cm.), photograph, toned gelatin silver print textured paper.

$715* *Portrait Of Native American Elder, 1912,* photog.'s sig., blindstamp, (c), d., (04-07-93, Swann, #520, illus.), 9½ x 7½ in., (photograph, toned silver print (BP 473, DM 1156, FR 3914, Y 81,232).

$1650* *'Last Of His People' (Argonaut Book Shop, cover), 1914,* s., t. by photog. in ink, blindstamp, (c) date blindstamp, (10-15-92, Sotheby-NY, #58, illus.), 7⅝ x 9¾ in., (19.4 x 24.8 cm.), photograph, toned silver print (BP 1010, DM 2456, FR 8329, Y 197,960).

MOON, Karl (attrib.)   1879-1948

$330* *Isleta Pueblo Woman,* good cond., (06-26-93, Skinner, #43, illus.), 19 x 11½ in., photograph, sepia toned silver print (BP 221, DM 561, FR 1889, Y 35,013).

MOORE, Henry   English 1898-1986

BI *Abstract Composition, #XX/XXXV,* s., d. '63, est. BP 150/250, (05-20-93, Bonhams-Chelsea, #2), image 20¼ x 19 in., (51.4 x 48.3 cm.), lithograph in colors.

$683* *Abstracted Reclining Figure, #15/50,* s., (10-15-92, Bonhams-Chelsea, #115, illus.), sheet 29½ x 23½ in., (74.9 x 59.7 cm.), lithograph on wove (BP 418, DM 1017, FR 3448, Y 81,944).

$633* *Adam (C. 574), 1980,* s., #I/XV, pub. Raymond Spencer Co., Lts., margins, excellent cond., (12-01-92, Christie-London, #457), L. 10⁷⁄₁₆ x 13³⁄₁₆ in., (265 x 335 mm.), lithograph in colors on T H Saunders wove (BP 418, DM 1009, FR 3438, Y 78,810).

BI *Animals In The Zoo (C. 631-645): Set Of Ten,* portfolio, s., i. w/plate nos., #40/65, s., num., p. by J. C. Editions, blindstamp, pub. Raymond Spencer Company, good cond., original portfolio box, est. BP 5/7,000, (06-30-93, Sotheby-London, #561, illus.), etching.

$431* *Animals In The Zoo: Rhinoceros (Pl. I) (C. 634), 1981,* s., annot. PL. I, #17/65, pub. Raymond Spencer Company for The HenryMoore Foundation Much Hadam, 1983,, blindstamp printer, Cames Collyer and JohnCrossley of J.C. Editions, very good cond., (05-19-93, Butterfield, #2087), 8⅜ x 10⅞ in., (213 x 276 mm.), etching on Arches (BP 280, DM 701, FR 2360, Y 47,714).

$2750* *Auden Poems (C. 245, 246, 248, 250, 253, 254, 256, 260, 262, 265-273), 1973,* complete portfolio, each s., #P.P. 5/10, pub. Petersburg Press, goodcond., (11-05-92, Sotheby-NY, #313), each sheet approx. 25 x 20¼ in., (635 x 515 mm.), 18 lithographs (BP 1789, DM 4349, FR 14,714, Y 337,382).

$425* *Black Figure On Pink Background (C./G./M. 96), (19)66/(67),* s., num., (06-08-93, Karl/Faber, #1130), approx. 4⅛ x 4⅛ in., (10.5 x 10.5 cm.), color lithograph on Japon nacre (BP 279, DM 690, FR 2322, Y 45,141).

$2200* *Eight Reclining Figures II (C. 75), 1967,* s., d., num. III/X, pub. Marlborough Fine Art Ltd., num. 10 in portfolio Meditations on the Effigy, full margins, good cond.?, mat staining, (10-28-92, Butterfield, #2687, illus.), 11¾ x 9½ in., (298 x 241 mm.), color lithograph on Japan nacre paper (BP 1402, DM 3398, FR 11,536, Y 269,939).

$851* *Eight Reclining Figures On Rock Background (Cramer 43), 1963,* s., num., sheet of 2 series Nudes, (06-05-93, Bassenge, #6356), 20½ x 16⅜ in., (52.1 x 41.6 cm.), color lithograph on Arches (BP 560, DM 1380, FR 4650, Y 91,289).

$545* *Elephant, #32/50,* s., catalog front cover lot, (04-22-93, Bonhams-Chelsea, #123, illus.), image 9 x 9 in., (22.9 x 22.9 cm.), lithograph (BP 352, DM 876, FR 2954, Y 59,923).

$8526* *Elephant Skull Album (Cramer 109-146), 1970: Set Of Twenty-Eight,* portfolio, s., i.w/plate num., #77/100, w/title page and text, s., num. 77, pub. Cramer, excell. cond., (12-03-92, Sotheby-London, #454, illus.), etchings, w/four unsigned etchings in text on wove (BP 5500, DM 13,408, FR 45,765, Y 1,060,844).

BI *Elephant Skull Plate IX (C.R. 122), 1969,* s., annot. Pl. IX, #51/100, pub. Gerald Cramer, full margins, good cond., est. $6/800, (10-28-92, Butterfield, #2843), 10¹⁵⁄₁₆ x 9⁵⁄₁₆ in., (278 x 237 mm.), etching on Rives.

$686* *"Elephant Skull Plate XVII", "Hommage A Seghers Plate II" and "Log Pile I" (C. 130; 172 and 189): 1960-72,* s., #50/100, 4/5 and 46/50, margins, good cond., (06-30-93, Sotheby-London, #566, illus.), etching, two w/drypoint on wove (BP 460, DM 1170, FR 3947, Y 73,503).

$1879* *Fat Lambs (Cramer No. 227),* Sheep Album series, Plate V, s., num. PL. V, 39/80, exec. 1974, p. Atelier Lacouriere et Frelaut, pub. Gerald Cramer, 1975, prov., lit., (12-01-92, Ritchie, #102, illus.), plate 7½ x 10 in., (19.1 x 25.4 cm.), sheet 12 x 15¼ in., (19.1 x 25.4 cm.), etching and drypoint on Rives paper w/Moore symbol (BP 1241, DM 2995, FR 10,206, Y 233,939, C$ 2420).

$600* *Feet On Holiday I (C. 562), 1979,* s., #2/50, pub. Raymond Spencer Company, good cond., handling creases, (06-30-93, Sotheby-London, #562), 8½ x 10 in., (216 x 254 mm.), color lithograph (BP 402, DM 1023, FR 3452, Y 64,288).

$605* *Figure Studies,* s., edit. #108/200, (10-16-92, DuMouchelle, #2014, illus.), approx. 12 x 9¼ in., (30.5 x 23.5 cm.), etching in black and white (BP 367, DM 894, FR 3036, Y 72,239).

$2542* *Five Ideas For Sculpture (Cramer 610), 1981,* s., num. 49/50, pub. Raymond Spencer Co., Ltd., for the Henry Moore Foundation, full margins, good cond., (10-14-92, Sotheby-Japan, #57, illus.), 13⅞ x 9⅞ in., (352 x 251 mm.), colored lithograph (BP 1492, DM 3720, FR 12,615, Y 308,047).

$972* *Five Reclining Figures (Cramer III, 536), 1979,* s., #32/50, (05-27-93, Briest, #151), 18½ x 25³⁄₁₆ in., (47 x 64 cm.), six-color lithograph (BP 622, DM 1560, FR 5257, Y 104,202).

$2875* *Four Ideas For Sculpture (C. 649), 1982,* s., #49/50, p. by J.E. Wolfensberger, pub. Raymond Spencer Company Ltd., 1984, full margins, good cond., creases, Alan E. Paris, Jr. Estate, (02-11-93, Sotheby-NY, #207, illus.), 9¼ x 12¹⁄₁₆ in., (235 x 306 mm.), color lithograph (BP 2029, DM 4762, FR 16,115, Y 346,594).

$1100* *Girl 2, 1976,* full margins, s., from Nudes portfolio, pub. by artist, (05-27-93, Swann, #193, illus.), (22.9 x 18.1 cm.), lithograph in colors w/tinted background on J. Green (BP 704, DM 1765, FR 5949, Y 117,925).

$749* *Girl Doing Homework II (C. 327), 1974,* s., #II/X, pub. G. Cramer, margins, excellent cond., (12-01-92, Christie-London, #455), plate 6⅞ x 6⅞ in., (175 x 175 mm.), etching w/aquatint on Rives (BP 495, DM 1194, FR 4068, Y 93,252).

$1708* *Girl Doing Homework III (Cramer No. 328),* s., #37/50, exec. 1974, p. Atelier Lacouriere et Frelaut, pub. Gerald Cramer, prov., lit., (12-01-92, Ritchie, #101, illus.), plate 8⅞ x 7 in., (22.5 x 17.8 cm.), sheet 18½ x 14½ in., (22.5 x 17.8 cm.), etching w/aquatint on Rives paper w/ Moore symbol (BP 1129, DM 2722, FR 9278, Y 212,649, C$ 2200).

BI *Girl Seated At Desk IV (C. 340), 1974,* s., #43/50, pub. by artist, margins, excellent cond., est. BP 450/650, (12-01-92, Christie-London, #456), L. 9¹⁄₁₆ x 7¹⁄₁₆ in., (230 x 180 mm.), lithograph in colors on J Whatman wove.

$749* *Girl Seated At Desk VII (C. 384), 1974,* s., #25/50, pub. Henry Moore Foundation, 1977, margins, excellent cond., (12-01-92, Christie-London, #460), L. 9⅝ x 6⅞ in., (245 x 175 mm.), lithograph in colors on J Green wove (BP 495, DM 1194, FR 4068, Y 93,252).

$11,982* *Goethe. Promethee (Cramer 18-32), 1950: Fifteen,* (05-26-93, Lempertz, #382, illus.), case 16¹⁄₁₆ x 12³⁄₁₆ in., (40.8 x 31 cm.), color lithograph on wove (BP 7751, DM 19,550, FR 65,799, Y 1,301,825).

$1115* *"Head Of A Girl I" and "Head Of A Girl II" (C. 504 and 505), 1979: Two,* s., #37/50, 12/50, full margins, good cond., skinned areas, (06-30-93, Sotheby-London, #563, illus.), one 8¾ x 6¼ in., (222 x 159 mm.), the other 10 x 7¼ in., (222 x 159 mm.), etching w/drypoint on Rives on wove (BP 747, DM 1902, FR 6415, Y 119,469).

$468* *Heads And Figures (C. 41), 1958,* artist's proof, pub. George Rainbird & New York Graphic Society, p. by

Curwen Prints, margins, apparently good cond., (02-24-93, Butterfield, #2960), 12 x 9⅞ in., (305 x 251 mm.), lithograph in colors on English handmade w/watermark (BP 326, DM 760, FR 2576, Y 54,917).

$2997* *Helmet Head Lithographs (C. 356-60), 1974: Set Of Five,* s., i., #11/50, pub. G. Cramer, margins, good cond., (12-01-92, Christie-London, #459), averaging L. 12⅝ x 14⁹⁄₁₆ in., (320 x 370 mm.), lithograph in colors on T H Saunders wove (BP 1980, DM 4777, FR 16,279, Y 373,132).

$990* *Idea For Metal Sculpture V (C.R. 615), 1981,* s., num. VIII/XV, pub. Raymond Spencer Co., Ltd., for Henry Moore Foundation, full margins, good cond., (10-28-92, Butterfield, #2688), 8¾ x 9⅝ in., (222 x 244 mm.), color lithograph on T.H. Saunders paper (BP 631, DM 1529, FR 5191, Y 121,472).

$1535* *Ideas For Sculpture (C. 103), 1969,* s., #53/100, pub. Arted Editions d'Art, full margins, good cond., (12-03-92, Sotheby-London, #457, illus.), 12⅛ x 9⅜ in., (308 x 238 mm.), etching on Arches (BP 990, DM 2414, FR 8239, Y 190,992).

$686* *Ideas For Sculpture In Landscape (C. 104), 1969,* s., #xv/xxxv, p. by Frelaut and Lacouriere, pub. Arted Editions d'Art, full margins, good cond., (06-30-93, Sotheby-London, #565, illus.), 12⅛ x 9⅜ in., (308 x 238 mm.), etching on Arches (BP 460, DM 1170, FR 3947, Y 73,503).

$735* *"Ideas For Sculpture In Landscape, 1969" (C. 104),* #XV/XXV, s., (01-28-93, Pescheteau, #219), 14¹⁵⁄₁₆ x 11¹³⁄₁₆ in., (38 x 30 cm.), etching on Arches (BP 485, DM 1165, FR 3941, Y 91,259).

BI *Landscape (C. 287), 1973,* s., i. AP 2/4, pub. Petersburg Press, 1975, margins, very good cond., est. BP 250/350, (12-01-92, Christie-London, #452), L. 8½ x 11⁷⁄₁₆ in., (216 x 290 mm.), lithograph on wove.

BI *Landscape, 1974,* s., #3/75, est. $3/500, (06-11-93, Freemn/Fine Art, #153), 17 x 13 in., (43.2 x 33 cm.), lithograph.

$2459* *Large Reclining Figure And Small Motifs, 1967,* #8/50, s., d., lit., (11-13-92, Koller, #5381), 10¹⁵⁄₁₆ x 14½ in., (27.9 x 36.8 cm.), lithograph on Barcham Green (BP 1589, DM 3860, FR 13,017, Y 305,200, SF 3480).

BI *Lullaby Sleeping Head (C. 250), 1973,* from Auden Poems, s., #16/75, full margins, excellent cond., est. BP500/800, (12-01-92, Christie-London, #451), L. 10¹³⁄₁₆ x 11⅝ in., (275 x 295 mm.), lithograph on wove.

BI *Male Figure In Landscape (C. 470), 1977-78,* s., num. 31/50, pub. Raymond Spencer Co. for Henry Moore Foundation,margins, apparently very good cond., est. $1/2,000, (02-24-93, Butterfield, #2766, illus.), 9¼ x 11⅜ in., (235 x 289 mm.), lithograph in colors on TH Saunders.

$1320* *Man And Woman,* s., #12/50, (12-13-92, Hindman, #277), 9 x 13 in., lithograph in black and green (BP 844, DM 2074, FR 7070, Y 163,306).

$1488* *Maternita Della Terra, 1981,* #I/XV, s., est. L 1,2/2,500, (05-20-93, Finarte-Milan, #115, illus.), 11¹³⁄₁₆ x 16⅛ in., (30 x 41 cm.), lithograph (BP 955, DM 2401, FR 8087, Y 164,311, L 2185).

$2825* *Mother And Child XI (Cramer 681), 1983,* s., #18/65, series Mother and Child, (06-10-93, Hauswedell/Nolt, #660, illus.), image 13⅝ x 10⅜ in., (34.6 x 26.4 cm.), color etching on thick wove (BP 1848, DM 4600, FR 15,488, Y 299,862).

$1201* *Mother And Child XXVI (C. 696), 1983,* s., i. pl xxvi 18/65, pub. Raymond Spencer, full margins, good cond., (06-30-93, Sotheby-London, #564), 8⅞ x 6⅜ in., (225 x 162 mm.), etching w/aquatint and roulette in color on wove (BP 805, DM 2048, FR 6910, Y 128,683).

$425* *Nude (C./G./M. 344), 1974,* s., num., (06-08-93, Karl/Faber, #1131), approx. 10¹³⁄₁₆ x 9⁷⁄₁₆ in., (27.5 x 24 cm.), lithograph in dark brown on wove (BP 279, DM 690, FR 2322, Y 45,141).

$420* *"Personnages",* H.C., s., (01-28-93, Pescheteau, #220), 12³⁄₁₆ x 9¼ in., (31 x 23.5 cm.), color lithograph on wove (BP 277, DM 666, FR 2252, Y 52,148).

$922* *Reclining Figure (Cramer 399), 1974,* s., num., sheet 3 of series Nudes, (06-05-93, Bassenge, #6358), 4¾ x 6⅞ in., (12 x 17.5 cm.), color lithograph on thick wove (BP 607, DM 1495, FR 5038, Y 98,906).

$880* *Reclining Figure Interior Setting II (C. 459), 1978,* s., num. 53/60, pub. The Friends of the Tate Gallery, 1978, full margins, good cond., mat & light-staining, (02-24-93, Butterfield, #2768), 9⅜ x 12¹⁄₁₆ in., (238 x 306 mm.), lithograph in colors on TH Saunders (BP 614, DM 1429, FR 4843, Y 103,262).

BI *Reclining Figure, Architectural Background IV (Cramer 457), 1977,* s., #11/100, est. FF4,000/4,500, (05-27-93, Briest, #153), 22⁷⁄₁₆ x 29¹⁵⁄₁₆ in., (57 x 76 cm.), five-color lithograph.

$2899* *Reclining Woman On Beach (C. 595), 1980-81,* s., #5/50, pub. Raymond Spencer Co. Ltd., full margins, good cond., (12-03-92, Sotheby-London, #458, illus.), 21¼ x 29 in., (540 x 735 mm.), lithograph in colors on T H Saunders (BP 1870, DM 4559, FR 15,561, Y 360,707).

$1540* *Sculptural Ideas Portfolio, 1981,* s., num. 37/50, (09-20-92, Hindman, #792, illus.), 9¾ x 13¼ in., (24.8 x 33.7 cm.), color etching and aquatint (BP 902, DM 2285, FR 7817, Y 190,335).

$440* *Sculptural Objects (Cramer 11), 1949,* stone s., d. '49, p. W.S. Cowell Ltd., pub. School Arts Prints, goodcond.?, (12-08-92, Swann, #216), 19½ x 30 in., (49.5 x 76.2 cm.), color lithograph (BP 276, DM 685, FR 2335, Y 54,536).

BI *Sculptural Objects, 1949,* pub. School Arts Prints Limited, est. $4/600, (05-27-93, Swann, #195), 19½ x 30 in., (49.5 x 76.2 cm.), lithograph in six colors.

$1265* *Seated Figure (Cramer 13), 1950,* s., #40/50, p. W.S. Cowell Ltd., pub. School Prints, Ltd., margins, good cond., thin line of masking tape stain, (02-11-93, Sotheby-NY, #203), 11⁵⁄₁₆ x 8¹¹⁄₁₆ in., (287 x 220 mm.), sheet 15¼ x 11¹⁵⁄₁₆ in., (287 x 220 mm.), color lithograph (BP 893, DM 2095, FR 7091, Y 152,502).

$3300* *Seated Figures (C. 37), 1957,* s., #151/200, pub. Berggruen & Cie, small margins, good cond., tears, creases, light-staining, (10-28-92, Butterfield, #2686, illus.), image 21 x 14½ in., (533 x 368 mm.), sheet 22 x 15⅜ in., (533 x 368 mm.), color lithograph on Arches (BP 2103, DM 5097, FR 17,305, Y 404,908).

$3450* *Seated Figures (C. 407-412), 1974: Suite Of Six,* each s., #38/50, s., num. on just. page, p. Curwen Prints, pub. by arst, 1976, full sheets, good cond., (02-11-93, Sotheby-NY, #204), each sheet approx. 19⁵⁄₁₆ x 16¾ in., (490 x 425 mm.), lithograph, 4 in color (BP 2434, DM 5715, FR 19,339, Y 415,913).

$6875* *Seated Figures (Cramer 37), 1957,* s., i. Epreuve d'artiste, pub. Berggruen, full margins, good cond., discoloration, (11-05-92, Sotheby-NY, #311, illus.), 21¼ x 14⅜ in., (540 x 365 mm.), lithograph p. in colors (BP 4472, DM 10,873, FR 36,784, Y 843,455).

BI *Seated Girl On Bed, 1976,* full margins, num., s., from "Nudes" portfolio pub. by artist, est. $1/1,500, (05-27-93, Swann, #194), 6¼ x 6¾ in., (15.9 x 17.1 cm.), lithograph in two colors.

$3955* *Seated Mother And Child (Cramer 588), 1980/81,* s., #15/50, blindstamp, (06-10-93, Hauswedell/Nolt, #659, illus.), image 13⅝ x 10¼ in., (34.6 x 26.1 cm.), color etching w/aquatint and roulette on Arches (BP 2587, DM 6440, FR 21,683, Y 419,807).

$767* *Seated Woman (C. 520), 1979,* s., #39/50, pub. Raymond Spencer Company Ltd, 1980, full margins, good cond., (12-03-92, Sotheby-London, #455), 8⅞ x 6½ in., (225 x 165 mm.), etching on Barcham Green (BP 495, DM 1206, FR 4117, Y 95,434).

BI *Seated Woman (C. 520), 1979,* s., #38/50, pub. Raymond Spencer Company Ltd., 1980, margins, very good cond., est. 5/700, (12-01-92, Christie-London, #463), plate 8⅞ x 6⅛ in., (225 x 155 mm.), etching on Barcham Green Penshurst.

$2310* *Seven Reclining Figures (C. 495), 1978,* s., #XIII/XV, pub. Raymond Spencer Company, 1980, margins, good cond., (11-05-92, Sotheby-NY, #314), 12¼ x 15⅛ in., (312 x 385 mm.), sheet 20¾ x 23⅞ in., (312 x 385 mm.), lithograph p. in colors (BP 1502, DM 3653, FR 12,360, Y 283,401).

$749* *Seventeen Reclining Figures (C. 46), 1963,* 2nd (final) state, s., d., #(?)9/50, pub. by artist, 1969, margins, mount-staining, tape-staining, (12-01-92, Christie-London, #448), L. 16¹⁵⁄₁₆ x 21¼ in., (430 x 540 mm.), lithograph on Barcham Green wove (BP 495, DM 1194, FR 4068, Y 93,252).

$832* *Shelter Sketchbook (C. 80), 1966,* English Edition A, Marlborough Fine Art Ltd., and Rembrandt Verlag GmbH, t., text, 80 facsimile collotypes, one orig., s., #176/180, staining, goodcond., (12-01-92, Christie-London, #449), lithograph in colors on Japon nacre (BP 550, DM 1326, FR 4519, Y 103,586).

BI *Shorn Sheep (Cramer No. 231),* Sheep Album series, Plate XI, s., num. PL XI 51/80, exec. 1974, p. Atelier Lacouriere et Frelaut, pub. Gerald Cramer, 1975, prov., lit., est. C$ 3/4,000, (12-01-92, Ritchie, #103, illus.), plate 7½ x 10½ in., (19.1 x 26.7 cm.), sheet 18½ x 14½ in., (19.1 x 26.7 cm.), etching and drypoint on Rives paper w/Moore symbol.

$633* *Silhouette Figures With Border Design (C. 297), 1973,* s., d., #IX/X, pub. Penwith Galleries Ltd., margins, surface dirt, handling creases, good cond., (12-01-92, Christie-London, #453, illus.), L. 18⅞ x 17⅝ in., (480 x 448 mm.), lithograph in colors on T H Saunders wove (BP 418, DM 1009, FR 3438, Y 78,810).

BI *Six Reclining Figures (C. 38), 1957,* s., i. Artist's Proof. For Hans. June 15th '57, pub. Berggruen and Cie, full margins, good cond., mat/light stain, handling creases, est. $4/5,000, (11-05-92, Sotheby-NY, #312, illus.), 17⅛ x 14⅛ in., (435 x 358 mm.), lithograph p. in colors.

$1348* *"Six Sculpture Motives" (Cramer 154), 1970,* s., blindstamp, (06-05-93, Grisebach, #789, illus.), 11⁹⁄₁₆ x 7¹¹⁄₁₆ in., (29.3 x 19.6 cm.), etching on handmade copper print paper (BP 887, DM 2185, FR 7366, Y 144,604).

$277* *Sketches Of Auden, Aus "Auden Poems-Moore Lithographs" (Cramer 265),1973,* 1/75, s., (06-24-93, Germann, #445), 25⅜ x 20¼ in., (645 x 515 mm.), lithograph (BP 182, DM 449, FR 1514, Y 29,715, SF 403).

$1320* *Sleeping Child (Cramer 499), 1979,* s., num. 5/50, tape hinges, full sheet, good cond., (05-22-93, Weschler, #210, illus.), 7¼ x 9¾ in., (18.4 x 24.8 cm.), etching (BP 855, DM 2146, FR 7221, Y 145,535).

$275* *Sleeping Head,* s., #10/25, (06-11-93, Freemn/Fine Art, #152), 10¾ x 11½ in., (27.3 x 29.2 cm.), lithograph (BP 181, DM 447, FR 1507, Y 29,178).

BI *Split Stone (C.R. 259), 1973,* s., num. XLIV/CL, from Auden Poems-Moore Lithographs, pub. Petersburg Press, full margins, good cond., est. $4/600, (10-28-92, Butterfield, #2844), 12 x 5⅞ in., (305 x 149 mm.), lithograph on Hodgkinson paper.

$1980* *Standing And Reclining Figures (Cramer, Grant and Mitchinson 15), 1950,* watermark, i. Revised Proof 24/10/50, S.E. Sepia, Picture BI Golden Yellow, Coates Intense Black, proof, crease, repaired tears, good cond., (11-09-92, Christie-NY, #140, illus.), 11⁹⁄₁₆ x 9¼ in., (293 x 235 mm.), colored lithograph on wove (BP 1309, DM 3161, FR 10,680, Y 245,719).

BI *"Three Reclining Figures On Pedestals" C. 62,* s., num., d. Moore '66, 60/75, est. $2/3,000, (09-25-92, Wolf, #33, illus.), 12 x 10½ in., (30.5 x 26.7 cm.), lithograph in colors.

BI *Three Reclining Figures With Water Background (C. 303), 1973,* s., #23/75, pub. Fischer Fine Art, Ltd., tape, very good cond., est.BP 5/700, (12-01-92, Christie-London, #454), L. 14¹³⁄₁₆ x 19 in., (377 x 483 mm.), lithograph in colors on T H Saunders wove.

BI *Three Reclining Figures, 1972,* #61/90, s., d. '72, prov., est. C$ 1,5/2,000, (11-16-92, Hodgins, #114, illus.), 12 x 9 in., (30.5 x 22.9 cm.), lithograph on paper.

$1791* *Three Seated Figures With Children (Cramer 305), 1973,* s. Moore, 6/75, (09-30-92, Kunsthallen, #215), color lithograph (BP 1010, DM 2540, FR 8590, Y 214,929, DK 9775).

BI *Three Seated Figures With Children , (Cramer 305), 1973,* s. Moore 38/75, est. DK 8,000, (03-24-93, Kunsthallen, #249, illus.), lithograph.

$858* *"Turning Figure No. 2", "Two Seated Figures", "Reclining Figure IV","Two Reclining Figures" and "Head Of Girl And Reclining Figure" (Cramer 176, 177, 195, 204 and 506), 1971-1979: Five,* watermark, full margins, good

cond., (06-30-93, Sotheby-London, #560), etching, first in black and grey, second w/aquatint in black and brown on wove (BP 575, DM 1463, FR 4937, Y 91,932).

$1082* *Two Reclining Figures (C. 240), 1973,* from Reclining Figures Portfolio, s., d., i., pub. Societe Internationale d'Art XXe Siecle, excell. cond., (12-01-92, Christie-London, #450), L. 16¹³⁄₁₆ x 13¹⁄₁₆ in., (427 x 332 mm.), lithograph in colors on wove (BP 715, DM 1725, FR 5877, Y 134,711).

$1227* *Two Reclining Figures (Cramer 205), 1971-1972,* s., num., (11-28-92, Schoppmann, #666), 7⅞ x 6⁹⁄₁₆ in., (20 x 16.6 cm.), etching on handmade (BP 810, DM 1955, FR 6636, Y 152,707).

$1650* *Two Reclining Figures (Cramer 440), 1977,* s., #27/75, pub. Ediciones Poligraphie, (12-08-92, Swann, #217, illus.), sheet 15¾ x 19¾ in., (40 x 50.2 cm.), color lithograph (BP 1034, DM 2569, FR 8758, Y 204,512).

$1443* *Two Reclining Figures (Cramer/Grant/Mitchinson Band III 467), 1977-78,* #X/XLVI, s., (11-21-92, Lempertz, #298, illus.), 11⅞ x 8¹⁵⁄₁₆ in., (30.2 x 22.7 cm.), etching on wove (BP 950, DM 2301, FR 7750, Y 179,455).

$880* *Two Seated Figures I (C. 35), 1951,* s., num. 37/50, pub. Gerald Cramer, 1970, good cond., creases, pencilnotations, light-staining, glue staining, (02-24-93, Butterfield, #2765, illus.), 2⅞ x 4⅞ in., (73 x 124 mm.), drypoint on laid (BP 614, DM 1429, FR 4843, Y 103,262).

$1150* *Two Seated Figures With Children (C. 441), 1976,* s., #30/50, p. Curwen Prints Ltd., pub. Universite Libre de Bruxelles, 1977, full margins, good cond., Alan E. Paris, Jr. Estate, (02-11-93, Sotheby-NY, #205), 8⅜ x 10½ in., (213 x 267 mm.), lithograph p. in black and 2 shades of grey (BP 811, DM 1905, FR 6446, Y 138,638).

$636* *Two Tall Figures (Cramer 179), 1970/71,* (06-10-93, Hauswedell/Nolt, #658), image 11⅝ x 7¹³⁄₁₆ in., (29.5 x 19.8 cm.), etching on wove (BP 416, DM 1036, FR 3487, Y 67,509).

$987* *Two Women Bathing Child II (Cramer 310 A), 1973,* s., #87/175, (05-26-93, Lempertz, #380), 19¹¹⁄₁₆ x 25½ in., (50 x 64.8 cm.), color lithograph on wove (BP 639, DM 1610, FR 5420, Y 107,236).

$738* *Violet Torso On Orange Stripes (Cramer 86), 1967,* s., num., (12-05-92, Bassenge, #7497), 6½ x 7¾ in., (16.5 x 19.7 cm.), color lithograph on Japan (BP 462, DM 1151, FR 3921, Y 91,438).

$4675* *Wystan H. Auden Portfolio: "Sketches Of Auden", "Windswept Landscape", "Cavern", "Multitude I", "Multitude II", "Thin-Lipped Armourer I", "Two Heads", "Thin-Lipped Armourer II", and Others (C. 243-265), 1974: Eighteen,* complete portfolio, artist's inits. watermark, s., num. 66/75, pub. Petersburg Press, p. by Curwen Studios & Petersburg Press, full margins, very good cond., foxing, stain, orig. portfolio, (02-24-93, Butterfield, #2767, illus.), each sheet 25¼ x 20¼ in., (641 x 514 mm.), lithograph on handmade paper (BP 3260, DM 7589, FR 25,729, Y 548,580).

MOORE, Henry and Marc CHAGALL

$3996* *Georges Pompidou, La Poesie, Art Et Poesie (Moore, C. 312-3, 315, 317-25; Chagall M. 898), 1974-5: Two Albums,* 1975-6, t., text, just., set of 12 by Moore in one, one by Chagall in 2ns vol., each s., #63/110, good cond., (12-01-92, Christie-London, #458, illus.), overall sheet 19½ x 15¹³⁄₁₆ in., (495 x 402 mm.), lithograph in colors on wove (BP 2640, DM 6369, FR 21,706, Y 497,510).

MOORE, J., Publisher

$83* *The Age, Brighton Coach At The Bull And Mouth, Regent Circus, Piccadilly,* discoloration, good condition(11-12-92, Freemn/Fine Art, #155), Hogarth mat 11½ x 16¼ in., (29.2 x 41.3 cm.), hand colored engraving (BP 55, DM 132, FR 444, Y 10,291).

$96* *Charles Westhall, The Pedestrian Champion,* by N. Ploszcynski, tear into image, foxing, (03-03-93, Bonhams-Chelsea, #16), image 19¾ x 14¾ in., (50.2 x 37.5 cm.), hand-colored lithograph (BP 66, DM 158, FR 536, Y 11,218).

MOORE, Raymond
  $654* *"Alderney", 1965-1966,* illus., 302 x 402mm, (05-07-93, Sotheby-London, #418, illus.), photograph, silver print (BP 414, DM 1034, FR 3484, Y 72,011).
  $654* *"Allonby, 1977",* illus., 302 x 382mm, (05-07-93, Sotheby-London, #421, illus.), photograph, silver print (BP 414, DM 1034, FR 3484, Y 72,011).
  BI *"Allonby, 1982",* illus., 301 x 402mm, est. BP 800/1,200, (05-07-93, Sotheby-London, #422, illus.), photograph, silver print.
  $472* *"Ayr, 1979",* 302 x 405mm, (05-07-93, Sotheby-London, #425, illus.), photograph, silver print (BP 299, DM 746, FR 2515, Y 51,971).
  $472* *"Cumbria, 1977",* 298 x 280mm, (05-07-93, Sotheby-London, #429, illus.), photograph, silver print (BP 299, DM 746, FR 2515, Y 51,971).
  BI *"Galloway, 1979",* t., s., illus., 242 x 298mm, est. BP 4/600, (05-07-93, Sotheby-London, #426, illus.), photograph, silver print.
  $654* *"Harrington, 1982",* illus., 302 x 403mm, (05-07-93, Sotheby-London, #420, illus.), photograph, silver print (BP 414, DM 1034, FR 3484, Y 72,011).
  $545* *"Maryport, 1977",* illus., 238 x 302mm, (05-07-93, Sotheby-London, #424, illus.), photograph, silver print (BP 345, DM 862, FR 2904, Y 60,009).
  $545* *"Porthgain, 1964-65",* mounted on card, t., s., illus., 165 x 252mm, (05-07-93, Sotheby-London, #427, illus.), photograph, silver print (BP 345, DM 862, FR 2904, Y 60,009).
  $654* *"Raes Knowes, 1980",* illus., 303 x 402mm, (05-07-93, Sotheby-London, #423, illus.), photograph, silver print (BP 414, DM 1034, FR 3484, Y 72,011).
  BI *"Scene At Felixstowe Ferry",* c. 1965, 258 x 334mm, est. BP 5/800, (05-07-93, Sotheby-London, #417, illus.), photograph, silver print.
  $872* *"Silloth, 1982",* illus., 302 x 403mm, (05-07-93, Sotheby-London, #419, illus.), photograph, silver print (BP 552, DM 1379, FR 4646, Y 96,014).
  BI *"Workington, 1977",* illus., 302 x 386mm, est. BP 5/800, (05-07-93, Sotheby-London, #428, illus.), photograph, silver print.

MOORE, Wayland
  $88* *"Golf Tee Shot",* s., #295/300, (02-27-93, Dunning, #58), 21¾ x 29½ in., (55.2 x 74.9 cm.), lithograph (BP 62, DM 145, FR 492, Y 10,388).
  $220* *"Jumpers",* edit. #203/300, (09-18-92, DuMouchelle, #2304), 30 x 29½ in., (76.2 x 74.9 cm.), silkscreen (BP 127, DM 329, FR 1128, Y 27,411).

MOORE, Waylon   American contemporary
  $77* *Grand Prix,* s., #206/300, (12-13-92, Hindman, #355), 21½ x 27 in., color serigraph (BP 49, DM 121, FR 412, Y 9526).

MOOS, Carl   1879-1959
  $630* *Pontresina, c. 1910,* nicks at edges, (02-04-93, Christie-S. Ken, #15, illus.), 40 x 25 in., (101.6 x 63.5 cm.), b/w lithograph backed on japan (BP 440, DM 1037, FR 3518, Y 78,368).
  $867* *Pontresina, c. 1910,* tears, (02-04-93, Christie-S. Ken, #14, illus.), 40 x 25 in., (101.6 x 63.5 cm.), b/w lithograph backed on japan (BP 605, DM 1428, FR 4841, Y 107,849).

MORA, Francisco Luis   American b. 1922
  $83* *"Antonia",* s.; glue residue verso, good cond., (10-31-92, Cleveland, #193), 6⅞ x 5½ in., (17.5 x 14 cm.), etching (BP 53, DM 128, FR 433, Y 10,281).

MORALES, Armando   Nicaraguan/Amer. b. 1927
  $2760* *Despedida,* s., d. 80, i., very good cond., creases, (05-18-93, Sotheby-NY, #263, illus.), 22¼ x 30⅛ in., (565 x 765 mm.), lithograph p. in colors (BP 1798, DM 4478, FR 15,123, Y 307,589).
  $3575* *Dos Banistas, 1980,* s., d. 80, #FGII, printer blindstamp, Kyron Press, full sheet, excell. cond., (11-23-92, Sotheby-NY, #268, illus.), 30⅛ x 22½ in., (765 x 570 mm.), lithograph in colors (BP 2337, DM 5724, FR 19,419, Y 443,493).

MORAN, Edward
  BI *Barren Trees By A Lake,* bears sig., foxing, toning, est. $2/400, (01-05-93, Bourne, #236), image 9 x 12 in., (22.9 x 30.5 cm.), etching.

MORAN, Mary N.   American 1842-1899
  $140* *"A California Forest",* after Thomas Moran, excell. cond., (05-15-93, Cleveland, #254), 11⅞ x 8⅛ in., (30.2 x 20.6 cm.), etching on ivory satin cloth (BP 91, DM 225, FR 757, Y 15,519).
  $330* *Gardiner's Bay From Fresh Ponds,* margins, s., (05-22-93, Collins, #5), 7¾ x 11½ in., (19.7 x 29.2 cm.), etching (BP 214, DM 537, FR 1805, Y 36,384).
  $143* *Interior Of California Forest,* margins, plate s., (05-22-93, Collins, #49), 12 x 8 in., (30.5 x 20.3 cm.), etching (BP 93, DM 233, FR 782, Y 15,766).

MORAN, Peter   American 1841-1914
  $55* *Lily Pond,* margins, s. P. Morgan, (10-24-92, Collins, #12), 7½ x 5½ in., (19.1 x 14 cm.), etching (BP 34, DM 84, FR 285, Y 6707).
  $210* *Marsh With Heron, c. 1890,* s., excell. cond., (05-15-93, Cleveland, #255), 11¾ x 8⅝ in., (29.8 x 21.9 cm.), etching (BP 137, DM 338, FR 1135, Y 23,279).
  $22* *Noonday Rest,* margins, plate s., (05-22-93, Collins, #125), 3⅝ x 5⅝ in., (9.2 x 14.3 cm.), etching (BP 14, DM 36, FR 120, Y 2426).
  $99* *"Sunlight And Shadows",* s., (02-27-93, Dunning, #46), 15½ x 23¾ in., (39.4 x 60.3 cm.), etching (BP 70, DM 163, FR 553, Y 11,687).

MORAN, Thomas   American 1837-1926
  BI *An American Sunset,* est. $75/150, (05-22-93, Collins, #124), 5 x 7 in., (12.7 x 17.8 cm.), etching.
  $1870* *The Gate Of Venice (K. 61), 1888,* s., d. in plate, pub. C. Klackner, stamped B13619, good cond., light-staining, mat staining, surface abrasions in image, (02-24-93, Butterfield, #2649, illus.), 21⅝ x 34⅞ in., (549 x 886 mm.), sheet 25¾ x 37½ in., (549 x 886 mm.), etching on heavy Japan (BP 1304, DM 3036, FR 10,292, Y 219,432).
  $55* *Glencoe,* margins, plate s. T, Moran, (10-24-92, Collins, #7), 9¼ x 11½ in., (23.5 x 29.2 cm.), etching (BP 34, DM 84, FR 285, Y 6707).
  $880* *"Grand Canyon From Hermit Rim Road",* (02-27-93, Dunning, #1025, illus.), 25 x 34 in., (63.5 x 86.4 cm.), color lithograph (BP 619, DM 1447, FR 4916, Y 103,884).
  $375* *"The Half Dome-View From Moran Point" (K. 60), 1887,* good cond., toning, pub. in Picturesque California, (05-15-93, Cleveland, #257, illus.), 13 x 9 in., (33 x 22.9 cm.), etching (BP 244, DM 603, FR 2027, Y 41,570).
  $248* *Half Done View From Moran Point,* margins, plate s., (05-22-93, Collins, #48), 11¾ x 8 in., (29.8 x 20.3 cm.), etching (BP 161, DM 403, FR 1357, Y 27,343).
  BI *Landscape On The River Marne,* after Daubigny, s. T. Moran, est. $6/900, (10-24-92, Collins, #8, illus.), 4½ x 8½ in., (11.4 x 21.6 cm.), etching.
  $22* *Morning,* margins, plate s., (05-22-93, Collins, #47, illus.), 4½ x 7⅛ in., (11.4 x 18.1 cm.), etching (BP 14, DM 36, FR 120, Y 2426).
  $350* *"Morning On The St. John's, Florida",* s., excell. cond., (05-15-93, Cleveland, #256), 5⅝ x 8⅝ in., (14.3 x 21.9 cm.), etching and drypoint on thin Japan vellum (BP 228, DM 563, FR 1892, Y 38,798).
  $66* *Passaic Meadows,* margins, plate s., (05-22-93, Collins, #52), 5½ x 8½ in., (14 x 21.6 cm.), etching (BP 43, DM 107, FR 361, Y 7277).
  $605* *Sailing Ships,* s. T. Moran, scuffs in image, discoloration, re-mark, (04-22-93, Freemn/Fine Art, #1301), 14¼ x 23½ in., (36.2 x 59.7 cm.), engraving (BP 391, DM 972, FR 3279, Y 66,520).
  BI *Ships At Sea, 1894,* s., time discoloration, est. $6/900, (11-12-92, Freemn/Fine Art, #156A), plate 14½ x 23¾ in., (36.8 x 60.3 cm.), engraving.
  $1320* *Venetian Port Scene,* s., d. 1885, (c) 1886 by C. Klackner, good cond.?, (03-28-93, Bakker, #8), image 11¾ x 26¾ in., (29.8 x 67.9 cm.), engraving (BP 887, DM 2153, FR 7321, Y 153,631).

$90* *Wolf At Night,* (05-16-93, Hanzel, #482), 6 x 8⅝ in., (15.2 x 21.9 cm.), etching (BP 59, DM 145, FR 486, Y 9977).

MORAN, Thomas (after) American 1837-1926

$935* *Grand Canyon Of Arizona, 1913,* pub. Atchison, Topeka and Santa Fe Railway System, (12-13-92, Hindman, #306), 26½ x 35 in., chromolithograph (BP 598, DM 1469, FR 5008, Y 115,675).

MORANDI, Giorgio Italian 1890-1964

$16,446* *Cornetto Con Fiori Di Campo (Vitali 22), 1924,* #40/50, s., d., est. L 26/34,000, (05-20-93, Finarte-Milan, #117, illus.), 8 1/16 x 6 7/16 in., (20.5 x 16.3 cm.), etching (BP 10,556, DM 26,534, FR 89,380, Y 1,816,034, L 24,150).

BI *Fiori In Un Cornetto Su Fondo Ovoidale (Vitali 63), 1929,* s., d., #31/40, wide margins, mat staining, repaired tear, very goodcond., est. $15/18,000, (05-11-93, Christie-NY, #246, illus.), plate 11¾ x 7¾ in., (298 x 197 mm.), etching on thick wove.

$29,463* *Gruppo Di Zinnie, (Vitali 86), 1931,* # 5/30, s., (11-09-92, Finarte-Milan, #80, illus.), 8 15/16 x 7½ in., (22.7 x 19.1 cm.), etching on zinc (BP 19,480, DM 47,035, FR 158,916, Y 3,656,366, L 40,250).

$26,096* *Il Poggio Di Sera (Vitali 42) 1928,* proof, s., d. Morandi 1928, (11-09-92, Finarte-Milan, #63, illus.), 5½ x 9⅝ in., (14 x 24.5 cm.), etching on zinc (BP 17,254, DM 41,660, FR 140,755, Y 3,238,521, L 35,650).

$22,729* *Natura Morta Con La Statuina, (Vitali 17), 1922,* #12/30, s., d. Morandi 1922, (11-09-92, Finarte-Milan, #47, illus.), 2⅜ x 2 15/16 in., (6 x 7.4 cm.), etching on rame (BP 15,027, DM 36,285, FR 122,594, Y 2,820,675, L 31,050).

$30,296* *Natura Morta Con La Tazzina Bianca A Sinistra, (Vitali 70), 1930,* artist proof, s. Morandi, (12-15-92, Finarte-Milan, #51, illus.), 7⅜ x 10⅝ in., (18.7 x 27 cm.), etching (BP 19,328, DM 47,486, FR 162,271, Y 3,757,410, L 42,550).

$55,539* *Natura Morta Con Oggetti Bianchi Su Fondo Scuro, 1931,* #20/30, s., d. Morandi 1931, lit., (10-10-92, Finarte S.A., #232, illus.), 9⅝ x 11 7/16 in., (244 x 290 mm.), etching (BP 32,951, DM 82,500, FR 277,002, Y 6,761,505, SF 72,600).

$11,747* *Natura Morta Con Pigna E Frammento Di Vaso (Vitali 18), 1922,* #19/30, s., d., (05-20-93, Finarte-Milan, #116, illus.), 2 15/16 x 4 3/16 in., (7.5 x 10.7 cm.), etching (BP 7540, DM 18,953, FR 63,842, Y 1,297,151, L 17,250).

$26,450* *Natura Morta Con Sette Oggetti In Un Tondo (Vitali 111), 1945,* 1st state of 2, s., d. 1946, i. prova di stampa, full margins, good cond., crease, stray ink mark, (05-13-93, Sotheby-NY, #668, illus.), 10½ x 11¾ in., (266 x 299 mm.), etching on cream wove (BP 17,365, DM 42,710, FR 144,063, Y 2,952,998).

$10,994* *"Natura Morta Con Vaso, Conchiglie E Chitarra" (Vitali 7/II; Cordaro1921,2), 1921,* s., (06-05-93, Grisebach, #375, illus.), 3 15/16 x 4 9/16 in., (10 x 11.6 cm.), etching and drypoint in thick imitation Japan (BP 7237, DM 17,824, FR 60,077, Y 1,179,361).

$6600* *Natura Morta Con Zucceriera, Conchiglie E Frutto (Vitali *), 1921,* s., d., #2/50, margins, light/mat staining, skinning, good cond., (11-09-92, Christie-NY, #142, illus.), 4 3/16 x 5⅛ in., (107 x 130 mm.), etching on simili Japan (BP 4364, DM 10,536, FR 35,599, Y 819,062).

BI *Natura Morta Di Vasi, Bottiglie Ecc. Su Un Tavalo (V. 67), c. 1929,* 1st state of 2, #44/62, margins, mat/time/glue staining, crease, skinning, good cond., est. $10/14,000, (11-09-92, Christie-NY, #143, illus.), 5⅝ x 7¾ in., (143 x 197 mm.), etching on India colle.

$18,520* *Paesaggio (I Camini Dell'Arsenale Nei Dintorni Di Bologna), (Vitali 12), 1921,* s., d., (11-09-92, Finarte-Milan, #32, illus.), 3⅛ x 3¾ in., (8 x 9.5 cm.), etching on rame paper (BP 12,245, DM 29,566, FR 99,892, Y 2,298,337, L 25,300).

$24,669* *Paesaggio Del Poggio (Vitali 33), 1927,* #46/50, s., d., (05-20-93, Finarte-Milan, #120, illus.), 9 3/16 x 11 7/16 in., (23.4 x 29 cm.), etching (BP 15,834, DM 39,802, FR 134,071, Y 2,724,050, L 36,225).

$18,796* *Piante Di Gerani E Rete Di Filo Di Ferro (Vitali 45), 1928,* #39/50, s., d., est. L 30/40,000, (05-20-93, Finarte-Milan, #121, illus.), 9¾ x 5½ in., (24.8 x 13.9 cm.), etching (BP 12,064, DM 30,326, FR 102,152, Y 2,075,530, L 27,600).

$16,500* *Piccola Natura Morta Con Tre Oggetti (V. 131), 1961,* s., #97/100, pub. Lamberto Vitali, Giorgio Morandi pittore, Editore del Milione, 1964, full margins, light staining, skinned patch, very good cond., (11-09-92, Christie-NY, #144, illus.), 4 13/16 x 6¼ in., (123 x 158 mm.), etching on wove (BP 10,909, DM 26,341, FR 88,997, Y 2,047,655).

$23,103* *Rose In Boccio In Un Vaso (Vitali 88), 1929,* #36/50, s., d., (05-20-93, Finarte-Milan, #119, illus.), 12½ x 9 13/16 in., (31.7 x 25 cm.), etching (BP 14,829, DM 37,275, FR 125,560, Y 2,551,126, L 33,925).

MORE, Chet la American

BI *"Boxing Kangaroos", 1943,* s., num., light struck, est. $100/150, (05-15-93, Cleveland, #475), 10 x 16 in., (25.4 x 40.6 cm.), color silkscreen.

MOREAU, Jean Michel

$690* *Decoration Du Sacre De Louis XVI Roi De France...(P. and B. III, p. 461, no. 34), 1775,* margins, fold, creasing, surface soiling, (05-11-93, Christie-NY, #81), plate 22½ x 32½ in., (572 x 826 mm.), engraving on laid (BP 440, DM 1087, FR 3662, Y 75,899).

$690* *"Le Festin Royal" and "Le Bal Masque" (P. and B. III, p. 461, nos. 37-8), 1782: Two,* blindstamps, margins, staining, (05-11-93, Christie-NY, #82), each plate 20½ x 15½ in., (521 x 394 mm.), engraving on wove (BP 440, DM 1087, FR 3662, Y 75,899).

MOREAU, Jean Michel (after) French 1741-1814

$330* *"Madamouselle's Escorts" and "Offering After The Hunt": Two,* (10-30-92, Sloan, #1749), each 7⅝ x 6⅛ in., (19.4 x 15.6 cm.), handcolored engraving (BP 211, DM 508, FR 1722, Y 40,877).

MOREAU, Jean Michel (called the younger) 1741-1814

$578* *Le Couche De La Mariee (Portalis-Beraldi 1), 1768,* after P.A. Baudouin, (12-04-92, Bassenge, #6652), 18 7/16 x 13 3/16 in., (46.8 x 33.5 cm.), etching w/engraving (BP 371, DM 921, FR 3123, Y 72,160).

MOREAU, Jean Michel and Jean Baptiste SIMONET 1742-c. 1813

$999* *Le Couche De la Mariee (Bocher 16; P. and B., III, p. 456, no. 1; L.and D. 186), 1768,* after Pierre-Antoine Baudouin, 3re (final) state, pub. Moreau, wide margins, crease, discoloration, mounting, tape, good cond., (12-01-92, Christie-London, #241, illus.), plate 18 7/16 x 13 3/16 in., (468 x 335 mm.), etching w/engraving on Auvergne laid (BP 660, DM 1592, FR 5426, Y 124,377).

MOREAU, Jean Michel and Sigmund FREUDENBERG (after)

$2530* *Le Monument Du Costume, 1774: Eight Plates,* includ. N'ayez pas peur, ma bonne amie, by Helman (L. and D. 222 v/v), Les Petites parrains, by Bagnoy and Patas (224 iv/iv), La Dame du Palais de la Reine, by Martini (230 iii/iv), La Course des Cheveaux, by Guttenberg, and four others; 235 and 215 trimmed; margins, stains, (05-11-93, Christie-NY, #80, illus.), each plate 16 x 12¾ in., (406 x 324 mm.), engraving on laid (BP 1615, DM 3986, FR 13,429, Y 278,297).

MOREAU, Pierre Louis

$246* *"Sisteron", "Le Port De Cassis" and "Sisteron Vu De La Baume": Three,* s., num., margins, (02-24-93, Picard, #175), etching on old laid (BP 172, DM 399, FR 1354, Y 28,866).

MOREAU-NELATON French 19th cent.

BI *La Nativite,* from Les Maitres de l'Affiche, PL. 118, est. $150/200, (02-14-93, Hanzel, #680), 8 x 11 in., (20.3 x 27.9 cm.), lithograph.

MOREELSE, Paulus Dutch 1571-1638

BI *Cupido Mit Zwei Allegorischen Frauengestalten Tanzend (Hollstein 2 II), 1612,* est. DM 600, (06-10-93, Hauswedell/Nolt, #121), chiaroscuro woodcut in 2 blocks.

MOREL, Francois French 1768-1830

$55* *"Veduta Del'Arco Di Tito",* (12-02-92, Boos, #523), plate 14½ x 18⅝ in., (368 x 473 mm.), hand colored engraving (BP 35, DM 86, FR 295, Y 6843).

MORELAND, George (after)

$181* *The Lucky Sportsman,* by Francois Davide Soiron, (06-30-93, Bonhams-Chelsea, #65), image 12 x 10 in., (30.5 x 25.4 cm.), stipple engraving (BP 121, DM 309, FR 1041, Y 19,394).

MORELL

$482* *Exposicion Conmemorativa Del Primer Centenario Del Ferrocarril En Espana, Barcelona, 1948,* p. Seix y Barrl, very good cond., (11-19-92, Ribeyre/Baron, #149), 38 15/16 x 24 3/16 in., (99 x 61.5 cm.), poster (BP 317, DM 768, FR 2589, Y 59,943).

MORELLET, Francois b. 1926

BI *Komposition In Orange-Rot Und Violett,* s., num., est. DM 500-, (09-25-92, Granier, #2948), 31 9/16 x 31 5/8 in., (80.2 x 80.3 cm.), color serigraph on offset board.

$1805* *Trames, 1965: Eight,* Galerie der Spiegel, s., num., (11-28-92, Schoppmann, #667), 24 13/16 x 24 5/8 in., (63 x 62.5 cm.), serigraph (BP 1191, DM 2876, FR 9762, Y 224,642).

MORELLI, Francesco

$192 *Classical Landscapes With Figures And Animals: Two,* (08-14-92, G.A. Key, #77), 11 x 16 in., (27.9 x 40.6 cm.), engraving (BP 100, DM 282, FR 954, Y 24,212).

MORENO

$420* *Chemin De Fer D'Orleans: Bretagne. "Feux De La Saint Jean Aux Menhirs Du Moulin De Saint-Pierre De Quiberon", 1902,* p. Moderne M. de Brunoff, very good cond., (11-19-92, Ribeyre/Baron, #115bis), 42 1/8 x 28 3/4 in., (107 x 73 cm.), poster (BP 277, DM 670, FR 2256, Y 52,232).

MORET, Jean Baptiste ac. 1790-1820

BI *Bonaparte 1er. Consul, c. 1803,* after Andrea Appiani, pub. Drouhin, trimmed, surface dirt, est. BP 5/800, (12-01-92, Christie-London, #279), sheet 16 13/16 x 12 11/16 in., (427 x 322 mm.), etching w/engraving in colors.

MORETTI

$141* *Portrait D'Homme A La Guitare,* annot., #60/100, s., good margins, (02-03-93, Ader Tajan, #185), 22 1/4 x 17 15/16 in., (56.5 x 45.5 cm.), color lithograph (BP 98, DM 232, FR 787, Y 17,539).

MORETTI, Lucien Philippe b. 1922

$135* *"Mere Et Enfant", 1975,* illus "un sac de billes", #186/270, s., (10-18-92, Pescheteau, #225), 16 9/16 x 11 13/16 in., (42 x 30 cm.), lithograph in colors on wove (BP 82, DM 199, FR 677, Y 16,119).

$77* *Sans Titre,* artist's proof, annot., (06-28-93, Loudmer, #323), 21 1/4 x 28 9/16 in., (540 x 725 mm.), black lithograph embellished w/watercolor on Arches wove (BP 52, DM 131, FR 441, Y 8170).

MORGAN, Barbara 1900-1992

BI *Cadenza,* (1940), 1973, s., t., d. on mount; s., t., d., i. in ink, (c) & credit stamps, lit., est. $1,5/1,800, (10-13-92, Christie-NY, #317, illus.), 11 7/8 x 10 1/4 in., (30.2 x 26 cm.), photograph, gelatin silver print.

BI *Funkia Leaf (Solarized),* (1950), 1971, s., t., d. on mount; s., t., d., i in ink w/(c) & credit stamp, lit., est. $1,5/1,800, (10-13-92, Christie-NY, #474, illus.), 12 3/4 x 10 5/8 in., (32.4 x 27 cm.), photograph, gelatin silver print.

$920* *"Martha Graham, American Document",* 1938, p. 1979, s., t., d., photog.' stamp, (05-23-93, Butterfield, #3545, illus.), 7 1/2 x 9 1/2 in., photograph, gelatin silver print (BP 599, DM 1504, FR 5063, Y 101,691).

$546* *"Martha Graham, Letter To The World, Kick",* 1940, p. 1986, s., d. twice, t., (05-23-93, Butterfield, #3546, illus.), 9 3/8 x 12 3/4 in., photograph, gelatin silver print (BP 356, DM 893, FR 3005, Y 60,351).

BI *Martha Graham-Lamentation,* sig., notations, handstamp, 1935, p.l., est. $5/750, (10-14-92, Swann, #519), 13 1/4 x 10 1/2 in., (33.7 x 26.7 cm.), photograph, silver print.

$990* *"Martha Graham-Letter To The World (Kick)" and "Martha Graham, Sixteen Dances In Photographs.": Two,* photog.'s sig., d.; sig., t., neg., print, d. verso, 1940; p.l., (04-07-93, Swann, #521, illus.), 9 1/4 x 13 3/4 in., photograph, silver print (BP 654, DM 1601, FR 5419, Y 112,474).

$1380* *Spring On Madison Avenue,* 1938, p. 1980, ink s., t., d.,; ink s., t., d., annot., lit., (04-08-93, Christie-NY, #322, illus.), 18 1/8 x 22 1/8 in., (46 x 56.2 cm.), photograph, gelatin silver print (BP 905, DM 2217, FR 7504, Y 156,605).

$302* *U.F.O. Visits New York,* sig., notations, handstamp, sig. verso, 1965, p.l., (10-14-92, Swann, #520, illus.), 11 x 10 1/4 in., (27.9 x 26 cm.), photograph, silver print (BP 177, DM 442, FR 1499, Y 36,597).

MORGAN, Fred (after)

$107 *"Little Lady Bountiful",* (06-11-93, G.A. Key, #28), 19 x 27 in., (48.3 x 68.6 cm.), b/w photogravure (BP 70, DM 174, FR 586, Y 11,353).

$84 *"Over The Garden Wall", Circa 1910,* (10-09-92, G.A. Key, #9), 19 x 12 in., (48.3 x 30.5 cm.), chromolithograph (BP 50, DM 125, FR 424, Y 10,244).

MORGAN, William Evan Charles

BI *Young Love Birds,* margins, est. BP 30/50, (09-17-92, Bonhams-Chelsea, #69), plate 5 3/8 x 5 1/4 in., (13.7 x 13.3 cm.), etching w/drypoint on laid paper.

MORGNER, Wilhelm 1891-1917

$1705* *Fressende Holzarbeiter (Lempertz 28; Tappert 31), 1912,* ink s., d., t., i. Holzchnitt Handdruck Nu. 9, full margins, good cond., defects, (12-03-92, Sotheby-London, #459, illus.), 11 3/4 x 14 1/4 in., (300 x 362 mm.), woodcut on thin Japan (BP 1100, DM 2681, FR 9152, Y 212,144).

$2255* *Grosse Brucke Bei Soest (Witte 14), c. 1911,* s., d., (05-26-93, Lempertz, #387, illus.), 15 3/8 x 21 15/16 in., (39 x 55.8 cm.), wood cut on thin paper (BP 1459, DM 3679, FR 12,383, Y 245,002).

$2115* *Grosse Kreuzigung (A. Witte 44), c. 1913,* by mother of artist, #8/50, (05-26-93, Lempertz, #384), 18 5/16 x 25 1/2 in., (46.5 x 64.7 cm.), wood engraving on fibrous paper (BP 1368, DM 3451, FR 11,614, Y 229,791).

BI *Der Holzhacker (Witte 34; Tappert 20; Arntz 18), 1912,* #38/50, Mutter des Kunstlers, num., est. DM 3,500, (06-10-93, Hauswedell/Nolt, #663, illus.), image 14 5/8 x 22 5/16 in., (37.2 x 56.6 cm.), woodcut on wove.

$738* *Kartoffelernte (Witte 12), c. 1911,* s., num., (12-05-92, Bassenge, #7500), 16 1/4 x 20 1/2 in., (41.2 x 52 cm.), linocut on copper print paper (BP 462, DM 1151, FR 3921, Y 91,438).

BI *Krankenhauskaspar (Tappert 8, Arntz 7, Witte 1), 1909/10,* s. by artist's mother, num., est. DM 1,500, (12-05-92, Bassenge, #7499), 9 5/8 x 6 15/16 in., (24.5 x 17.6 cm.), woodcut on handmade machine paper.

$1471* *Kreuzigung (Witte 43; Tappert 41), 1913,* s., t., stained, (10-09-92, Winterberg, #2827, illus.), 11 7/8 x 14 13/16 in., (30.2 x 37.6 cm.), woodcut on China (BP 873, DM 2185, FR 7337, Y 179,084).

$155* *Patroklidom In Soest,* posthumous, block mono., mount s., wear, (09-25-92, Granier, #2952), sheet 12 15/16 x 8 11/16 in., (32.8 x 22 cm.), woodcut on cream Japan (BP 91, DM 230, FR 777, Y 18,709).

$1082* *Tierdresseur (Witte 39), 1912,* #2/50, s. by mother of artist, num., t., (11-21-92, Lempertz, #299), 14 5/8 x 22 1/2 in., (37.2 x 57.2 cm.), woodcut on thick paper (BP 712, DM 1725, FR 5811, Y 134,560).

MORI, Yoshitoshi

$110* *"Tanabata Festival",* s., very good cond.?, (07-19-92, Bakker, #226, illus.), sheet 12 1/4 x 8 3/4 in., (31.1 x 22.2 cm.), color woodblock print (BP 56, DM 160, FR 542, Y 13,675).

MORILLON

$132* *RTL Presente, "Comedie Rock",* St. Martin, A cond., (08-06-92, Swann, #201, illus.), 59 x 39 in., (149.9 x 99.1 cm.), (BP 69, DM 195, FR 659, Y 16,837).

MORIMURA, Yasumasa b. 1951

$6050* *Dublonnage: Dancer II,* s., num. Yasumasa Morimura 2/5 verso, exec. 1988, prov., (02-24-93, Christie-NY, #133, illus.), 94 x 46 7/8 in., (238.8 x 119.1 cm.), photograph, varnished color mounted on panel (BP 4219, DM 9821, FR 33,297, Y 709,927).

MORIS

$279* *SNCF. Les Gets. Haute-Savoie. "Une Symphonie Neige Et Soleil", c. 1930,* very good cond., (03-15-93, Arcole, #51), 39⅜ x 24⁷⁄₁₆ in., (100 x 62 cm.), (BP 194, DM 463, FR 1575, Y 33,049).

MORISOT, Berthe French 1841-1895

BI *"Fillette Au Chat (Julie Manet)", c. 1880,* t., verso/ mount, good cond., registration, other marks, toning, foxing; tape verso, est. $3/500, (09-11-92, Skinner, #9, illus.), 6 x 4¾ in., (15.2 x 12.1 cm.), drypoint on wove.

MORLAND, G. (after)

$79 *"The Corn Bin",* (04-16-93, G.A. Key, #66), 16 x 20 in., (40.6 x 50.8 cm.), colored aquatint (BP 52, DM 128, FR 431, Y 8883).

BI *Figures And Horses In A Stable,* (12-11-92, G.A. Key, #39), 12 x 15 in., (30.5 x 38.1 cm.), colored print.

$43 *Figures In Side A Stable With Horse And Dogs,* (02-05-93, G.A. Key, #59), 12 x 17 in., (30.5 x 43.2 cm.), colored print (BP 30, DM 71, FR 241, Y 5351).

$50 *Hunting Scenes: Four,* (12-11-92, G.A. Key, #58), 11 x 15 in., (27.9 x 38.1 cm.), black and white print (BP 32, DM 79, FR 270, Y 6187).

$61 *"Inside Of A Country Ale House" and "The First Of September, Evening" Two,* (04-16-93, G.A. Key, #41), 16 x 19 in., (40.6 x 48.3 cm.), colored print (BP 40, DM 99, FR 333, Y 6859).

$140 *"A Lady Feeding Poultry" and "A Lady Watering The Garden": A Pair,* engraved by J R Smith, (04-16-93, G.A. Key, #52), 12 x 9 in., (30.5 x 22.9 cm.), colored stipple engraving (BP 92, DM 226, FR 764, Y 15,743).

$44 *"Morning On The Benevolent Sportsman",* engraved J. Grozer, (12-11-92, G.A. Key, #21), 18 x 22 in., (45.7 x 55.9 cm.), colored print (BP 28, DM 69, FR 238, Y 5445).

$227 *"Returning Home After A Days Shooting" and "Thatching The Public House": Two,* (10-09-92, G.A. Key, #18), 15 x 19 in., (38.1 x 48.3 cm.), colored print (BP 135, DM 338, FR 1146, Y 27,683).

$34 *Two Figures Seated On A Settee With Child,* (04-16-93, G.A. Key, #23), colored print (BP 22, DM 55, FR 186, Y 3823).

$76 *"The Wreckers",* (10-09-92, G.A. Key, #39), 15 x 18 in., (38.1 x 45.7 cm.), colored aquatint (BP 45, DM 113, FR 384, Y 9268).

MORLAND, George (after)

$76 *"The Country Stable",* (04-16-93, G.A. Key, #67), 16 x 20 in., (40.6 x 50.8 cm.), colored print (BP 50, DM 123, FR 415, Y 8546).

$63* *Cow House,* by William Ward, tear, some scuffing, (06-16-93, Bonhams-Chelsea, #432), image 17¾ x 23¼ in., (45.1 x 59.1 cm.), reprod. w./hand-coloring (BP 42, DM 105, FR 351, Y 6719).

$215* *Dancing Dogs,* by T. Gaugain, (09-17-92, Bonhams-Chelsea, #103), image 20¼ x 16 in., (51.4 x 40.6 cm.), stipple engraving (BP 121, DM 319, FR 1092, Y 26,768).

$193* *"The Effects Of Extravagance And Idleness" and "The Fruits Of Early Industry And Economy": Two,* each engraved by William Ward, margins, foxing, staining, surface scuffs, May and Howard Joynt Coll., (01-30-93, Weschler, #46), each 23½ x 19 in., (59.7 x 48.3 cm.), mezzotint (BP 130, DM 311, FR 1051, Y 24,077).

$144* *Fishermen Going Out, 1805,* by Samuel William Reynolds, pub. J.R. Smith, trimmed, foxing, (01-21-93, Bonhams-Chelsea, #81), image 17¼ x 22 in., (43.8 x 55.9 cm.), mezzotint (BP 94, DM 229, FR 775, Y 18,023).

$118* *The Furze Cutter,* trimmed, staining, (10-15-92, Bonhams-Chelsea, #22), image 22¾ x 16 in., (57.8 x 40.6 cm.), engraving w/hand coloring (BP 72, DM 176, FR 596, Y 14,157).

$754* *Hunting (S.p 190): Six Plates,* trimmed, losses, abrasions, repairs, hinged, (10-07-92, Christie-S. Ken, #62), sh 13¼ x 15¾ in., (33.7 x 40 cm.), colored soft-ground etching (BP 440, DM 1091, FR 3700, Y 90,679).

$791* *Juvenile Navigators,* by W. Ward, pub. J. R. Smith, staining along subject, creasing, repaired tear, dirt, (10-07-92, Christie-S. Ken, #9), pl 17¾ x 21½ in., (45.1 x 54.6 cm.), colored mezzotint in color (BP 462, DM 1145, FR 3881, Y 95,129).

$517* *Milk Maid & Cow Herd,* by J. R. Smith, pub. J. R. Smith, margins, staining, creasing, tear,dirt, (10-07-92, Christie-S. Ken, #8), pl 18 x 22 in., (45.7 x 55.9 cm.), colored mezzotint (BP 302, DM 748, FR 2537, Y 62,177).

$117* *Morland's Woodman, 1805,* engraved & pub. by Thomas Williamson, time-stained, mounted on stretcher, (11-30-92, Phillips-London, #217), image 20⅛ x 16¾ in., (511 x 425 mm.), color stipple engraving (BP 77, DM 186, FR 633, Y 14,561).

$76 *"Number 5 The Farmyard",* engaved by W Ward, pub. July 1795, (04-16-93, G.A. Key, #4), 17 x 20 in., (43.2 x 50.8 cm.), mezzotint (BP 50, DM 123, FR 415, Y 8546).

BI *"Outside The Alehouse" and "Hanging Up The Washing": Two,* trimmed, dirt, staining, abrasion, laid, est. BP 150/ 250, (10-07-92, Christie-S. Ken, #14), sh 20 x 15 in., (50.8 x 38.1 cm.), colored soft-ground etching.

$1567* *"A Party, Angling" and "The Anglers Repast", 1789: A Pair,* by G. Keating, pub. I.R. Smith, margins, stained, (09-17-92, Bonhams-Chelsea, #102, illus.), plate 18 x 21¾ in., (45.7 x 55.2 cm.), mezzotint (BP 880, DM 2326, FR 7962, Y 195,095).

$1498* *The Pleasures Of Retirement (Frankau 221), 1789,* by William Ward, watermark, pub. J.T. Smith, margins, platemark partly split and repaired, very good cond., prov., (12-01-92, Christie-London, #295, illus.), plate 14⅝ x 11⅛ in., (371 x 283 mm.), mezzotint in colors finished by hand (BP 990, DM 2388, FR 8137, Y 186,504).

$46 *River Scene With Figures Taking Break Upon A Boat,* (04-16-93, G.A. Key, #36), 13 x 17 in., (33 x 43.2 cm.), hand-colored engraving (BP 30, DM 74, FR 251, Y 5173).

$91 *Rustic Scene With Figure Returning Home With Faggots, Family By A Cottage Door,* (04-16-93, G.A. Key, #29), 25 x 21 in., (63.5 x 53.3 cm.), colored mezzotint (BP 60, DM 147, FR 497, Y 10,233).

$99* *Shepherd's Meal,* by John Raphael Smith, (06-16-93, Bonhams-Chelsea, #429), image 20 x 16 in., (50.8 x 40.6 cm.), mezzotint w/hand-coloring (BP 66, DM 164, FR 552, Y 10,559).

$221* *Summer Amusement,* by Thomas Williamson, pub. R. Lambe, 1812, w/margins, time-staining, (04-22-93, Bonhams-Chelsea, #6), plate 20 x 23½ in., (50.8 x 59.7 cm.), stipple engraving w/hand coloring (BP 143, DM 355, FR 1198, Y 24,299).

$223* *Summer Amusement,* by Thomas Williamson, (10-29-92, Bonhams-Chelsea, #79), image 17¼ x 22¾ in., (43.8 x 57.8 cm.), stipple engraving w/hand coloring, in verre eglomise mount (BP 143, DM 343, FR 1164, Y 27,623).

BI *"The Thatcher" and "The Warrner": Two,* by William Ward, est. BP 1/200, (06-16-93, Bonhams-Chelsea, #434), image 18 x 23¼ in., (45.7 x 59.1 cm.), reprod. w/hand-coloring.

BI *"The Warrner" and "The Shepherds": Two,* by William Ward, pub. R. Lambe, 1813, margins, staining, est. BP 3/ 500, (06-16-93, Bonhams-Chelsea, #431, illus.), pl. 18½ x 23¾ in., (47 x 60.3 cm.), mezzotint w/hand-coloring.

$565* *"The Weary Sportsman" and "Shepherds Reposing": A Pair,* by W. Bond, pub. H. Macklin, margins, staining, dirt, foxing on image, repairs, laid, (10-07-92, Christie-S. Ken, #47), stipple engraving in color (BP 330, DM 818, FR 2772, Y 67,949).

MORLEY, Malcolm American b. 1931

$3520* *Beach Scene (Tyler 374), 1982,* s., #46/58, blindstamp, excellent cond., (11-09-92, Christie-NY, #361, illus.), 38¼ x 51⅛ in., (97.2 x 129.9 cm.), colored lithograph on wove (BP 2327, DM 5619, FR 18,986, Y 436,833).

$805* *Beach Scene, 1969,* from Six New York Artists, Brooke Alexander, s., num. XXXI/XL, Chiron Press blindstamp, margins, excell. cond., (05-11-93, Christie-NY, #502), sheet 29¾ x 21¾ in., (756 x 552 mm.), color offset lithograph and screen on BFK Rives (BP 514, DM 1268, FR 4273, Y 88,549).

$605* *Black Rainbow Over Oedipus At Thebes II (G. 1391), 1988,* s., num. 21/32, Gemini G.E.L. blindstamps, margins, (09-19-92, Christie-E, #161), borderline 46 x 56 in., (116.8 x 142.2 cm.), lithograph and screenprint in colors on wove (BP 348, DM 906, FR 3103, Y 75,380).

$288* *Coconut Grove (G. 1335), 1987,* s., annot. PP II, pub. Gemini G.E.L., p. Serge Lozingot and MichelleRies, margins, very good cond.?, (05-19-93, Butterfield, #2266), 28¾ x 22 in., (730 x 559 mm.), lithograph in colors on Arches 88 (BP 187, DM 468, FR 1577, Y 31,883).

$1150* *Devonshire Bullocks (Tyler 376:MM3), 1982,* s., #14/58, blindstamp, pub. Tyler Graphics, Ltd., good cond., (05-15-93, Sotheby-NY, #1098), sheet 47⅝ x 35 in., (121 x 88.9 cm.), lithograph in colors on BFK Rives (BP 748, DM 1850, FR 6216, Y 127,480).

$220* *"Down",* s., (09-24-92, Mystic, #36), 23 x 33 in., (58.4 x 83.8 cm.), colored lithograph (BP 129, DM 326, FR 1107, Y 26,465).

$352* *Eve Born Of Adam (Gemini 1342), 1987,* s., num. 21/35, Gemini G.E.L. blindstamps, full sheet, scuffing, very good cond., (09-19-92, Christie-E, #160), sheet 22¼ x 26½ in., (565 x 673 mm.), etching, aquatint and engraving in colors on Barcham Green Crisbrook (BP 202, DM 527, FR 1805, Y 43,857).

BI *"Fish" (Tyler 378), 1982 and "Goat" (T. 379), 1982: Two,* both s., num. 27/30, 15/30, Tyler Graphics blindstamps, full sheet, excell. cond., shrink-wrapped, est. $1/1,500, (09-19-92, Christie-E, #157), lithograph, first in blue on tissue-thin Japan; second on grey handmade paper.

$330* *Horses (Tyler 380:MM7), 1982,* s., i. ~PP 2', blindstamp, pub. Tyler Graphics, Ltd., good cond., (11-07-92, Sotheby-NY, #688), sheet 38⅝ x 28½ in., (981 x 724 mm.), lithograph p. in red-black on TGL handmade (BP 216, DM 527, FR 1781, Y 40,731).

BI *"Horses" (T. 380), 1982 and "Goat And Shed" (T. 381), 1982: Two,* both s., num. 30/35, 12/30, Tyler Graphics blindstamp, full sheet, excell. cond., shrink-wrapped, est. $1/1,500, (09-19-92, Christie-E, #158), lithograph on Japan, first in aubergine.

BI *Horses, 1969,* s., t., d., i. A/P, p. Kelpra Studios, stamp, full margins, good cond., marks, creases, est. BP 4/600, (12-03-92, Sotheby-London, #772), 23¾ x 26¾ in., (605 x 681 mm.), screenprint in colors on wove.

$352* *Jazz (Gemini 1341), 1987,* s., num. 21/47, Gemini G.E.L. blindstamps, full margins, excell. cond., (09-19-92, Christie-E, #159, illus.), sheet 31⅝ x 37⅝ in., (803 x 956 mm.), photo-etching and aquatint in black and yellowish gray on wove (BP 202, DM 527, FR 1805, Y 43,857).

$220* *"Mini Masters",* s., (09-24-92, Mystic, #37), 24 x 34 in., (61 x 86.4 cm.), colored lithograph (BP 129, DM 326, FR 1107, Y 26,465).

$3300* *Odesseys Of Enoch,* complete suite, s., #65/69, blindstamp, pub. Novack Graphics, full margins, good cond., (11-07-92, Sotheby-NY, #689), each sheet approx. 29½ x 41¾ in., (74.9 x 106 cm.), six etchings and aquatints p. in colors (BP 2158, DM 5269, FR 17,809, Y 407,307).

$2875* *Odyssey Of Enoch, 1986: Six,* complete suite, s., #58/69, blindstamp, pub. Novak Graphics, full margins, good cond., handling creases, (05-15-93, Sotheby-NY, #1099), each sheet 29½ x 41½ in., (74.9 x 105.4 cm.), etching and aquatints in colors (BP 1869, DM 4624, FR 15,541, Y 318,701).

$220* *"Parrot Jungle",* s., (09-24-92, Mystic, #38), 24 x 34 in., (61 x 86.4 cm.), colored lithograph (BP 129, DM 326, FR 1107, Y 26,465).

BI *"Skaters",* s., est. $4/600, (09-24-92, Mystic, #35), 24 x 34 in., (61 x 86.4 cm.), colored lithograph.

$660* *Untitled, 1983: Two,* from Fallacies of Enoch, full margins, num., s., pub. Novak Graphics, (05-27-93, Swann, #196, illus.), each 20 x 32⅞ in., (50.8 x 83.5 cm.), color aquatint (BP 423, DM 1059, FR 3569, Y 70,755).

$495* *Untitled, Arch With American Flag Bearer, c. 1970s,* s., i. A.P, full margins, excell. cond., (09-19-92, Christie-E, #156, illus.), sheet 29⅝ x 21¾ in., (752 x 552 mm.), screenprint and offset lithograph in colors on BFK Rives (BP 285, DM 741, FR 2538, Y 61,675).

MORNAS

$522* *Nuits De Theatre, Danse,* Ateliers Brugier, A cond., (08-06-92, Swann, #202, illus.), 23 x 15 in., (58.4 x 38.1 cm.), (BP 273, DM 771, FR 2605, Y 66,582).

MORONOBU, Hishikawa   Japanese 1618-1695
BI *"Drei Schonheiten In Yoshiwara",* est. SC 6/9,000, (04-27-93, Dorotheum, #162, illus.), 5¹⁵⁄₁₆ x 10⅜ in., (15.2 x 26.4 cm.), colored woodcut.

MORRICE, James Wilson   Canadian 1865-1924
$83* *Effet De Neige,* s. print, Markgraff screenprint, (05-10-93, Hodgins, #177), 20 x 24 in., (50.8 x 61 cm.), serigraph on paper (BP 54, DM 133, FR 450, Y 9275, C$ 105).

MORRIS, Cedric   b. 1889
$798* *Summer Shell, On Sale Until Next October, 1938,* p. Baynard Press, ref. #510, cond. 1, (10-13-92, Phillips-London, #134, illus.), 29¹³⁄₁₆ x 44¹¹⁄₁₆ in., (75.8 x 113.5 cm.), color lithograph (BP 465, DM 1169, FR 3972, Y 96,762).

MORRIS, Francis Orpen   1810-1893
$105* *Ornithological Prints: Six,* w/text, (05-28-93, Sloan, #233, illus.), each 10 x 6¾ in., (25.4 x 17.1 cm.), hand colored print (BP 67, DM 167, FR 563, Y 11,259).

$132* *Untitled: Six,* from A History Of British Birds, London, 1870, (09-17-92, Sloan, #641), handcolored engraving (BP 74, DM 196, FR 671, Y 16,434).

BI *Untitled: Six,* from "A History Of British Birds", London, 1870, est. $200/250, (07-03-92, Sloan, #1066), handcolored etching.

$121* *"White Wagtail", "Coletint", "Grey Shrike" and "Pied Flycatcher": Four,* from "A History Of British Birds", London, 1851-1857, (07-03-92, Sloan, #329), hand colored engraving (BP 63, DM 183, FR 617, Y 15,084).

MORRIS, Rev. F.O. (after)
$19 *British Birds: Three,* (12-11-92, G.A. Key, #84), each, approx. 4 x 6 in., (10.2 x 15.2 cm.), hand colored engraving (BP 12, DM 30, FR 103, Y 2351).

MORRIS, Robert   American b. 1931
BI *In The Realm Of The Caceral, 1979: Set Of Five,* s., d., pub. John Nichols, est. $1,8/2,200, (12-08-92, Swann, #221, illus.), each 33 x 43¾ in., (83.8 x 111.1 cm.), aquatint.

BI *Observatory, 1971,* s., d., #93/150, est. $2/300, (06-11-93, Freemn/Fine Art, #154), 17½ x 23¾ in., (44.5 x 60.3 cm.), lithograph.

MORRIS, Wright   1910-1992
$605* *"Barber Shop Interior, Cahow's Barber Shop" (Photographs And Words, pl. 36),* s., 1942/1975, (11-16-92, Butterfield, #6106, illus.), 7⅜ x 9¼ in., (187.7 x 235.4 mm.), photograph, gelatin silver print (BP 398, DM 965, FR 3249, Y 75,239).

$920* *Drawer With Silverware, Home Place, 1947,* p. 1970s, s., lit., (04-08-93, Christie-NY, #323, illus.), 7⅜ x 9¾ in., (18.7 x 24.8 cm.), photograph, gelatin silver print (BP 603, DM 1478, FR 5003, Y 104,403).

$715* *"Gano Grain Elevator, Western Kansas" (Photographs And Work, pl. 30),* s., 1940/1945, (11-16-92, Butterfield, #6104, illus.), 9⅜ x 7½ in., (238.5 x 190.8 mm.), photograph, gelatin silver print (BP 471, DM 1140, FR 3840, Y 88,919).

$880* *"Model T In Shed, Home Place" (Photographs And Words, pl. 22),* s., (11-16-92, Butterfield, #6105, illus.), 9⅜ x 7½ in., (238.5 x 190.8 mm.), photograph, gelatin silver print (BP 579, DM 1403, FR 4726, Y 109,439).

BI *"Ranchos De Taos", 1940,* ink s., t., d., est. $1,5/2,000, (11-16-92, Butterfield, #6103, illus.), 7¾ x 9½ in., (197.2 x 241.7 mm.), photograph, gelatin silver print.

$413* *Reflections In Oval Mirror-Home Place, 1947,* (05-16-93, Hindman, #333), 7¼ x 9¼ in., photograph, silver print (BP 269, DM 666, FR 2245, Y 45,991).

MORRISON, Phillipe
BI *Distances,* s., #115/175; labels verso, prov., est. C$ 1/200, (12-01-92, Ritchie, #73), 21¼ x 26¼ in., (54 x 66.7 cm.), color serigraph.

MORRISSEAU, Norval   b. 1930
$95* *"Bear Spirit"*, #5/500, s., t., num., (05-12-93, Maynard, #301), print (BP 62, DM 153, FR 516, Y 10,606, C$ 121).
$726* *"Children Of Light And Sound", "Bird Speaks To These Children", "Woodland Creatures", "Fish And Loons Of Lake Nipigan", "Sermon To The Birds" and "We Are God Within Ourselves": Set Of Six*, #31/150, s. N. Morrisseau, (10-20-92, Encans, #113), 25¹⁵/₁₆ x 19¹¹/₁₆ in., (66 x 50 cm.), lithograph (BP 406, DM 1104, FR 3756, Y 91,000, C$ 888).
$121* *Fish Spirit, 1970,* A/P s., t., prov., (11-16-92, Hodgins, #110), 20 x 24¼ in., (50.8 x 61.6 cm.), serigraph on paper (BP 80, DM 193, FR 650, Y 15,100, C$ 154).
$412* *Manifestation,* #1/55, s., t., prov., (11-16-92, Hodgins, #109, illus.), 35 x 23½ in., (88.9 x 59.7 cm.), serigraph on paper (BP 271, DM 657, FR 2214, Y 51,416, C$ 523).
$172* *Shaman Thunderbird,* s., t., #57/75, blindstamped Norval Morrisseau Edition, prov., (06-07-93, Ritchie, #74, illus.), image 24 x 14⁵/₁₆ in., (61 x 36.3 cm.), sh 30 x 20 in., (61 x 36.3 cm.), color serigraph (BP 113, DM 279, FR 940, Y 18,451, C$ 220).
BI *Vision To Its Soul,* #123/195, s., t., prov., lit., est. C$ 3/500, (11-16-92, Hodgins, #266, illus.), 22 x 17 in., (55.9 x 43.2 cm.), serigraph on paper.

MORSE   American 20th cent.
$77* *Figures In Front Of The Players Club,* plate s., d. '33, (03-25-93, Boos, #612), 11 x 6¾ in., (27.9 x 17.1 cm.), etching (BP 52, DM 126, FR 430, Y 9021).

MORSE, Ralph
$770* *The Future, 1954,* handstamp, (10-14-92, Swann, #335, illus.), 14 x 11 in., (35.6 x 27.9 cm.), photograph, silver print (BP 452, DM 1127, FR 3821, Y 93,311).

MORTENSEN, Richard
$211* *Composition, 1972,* s. Mortensen 72, 35/75, (09-30-92, Kunsthallen, #223), color serigraph (BP 119, DM 299, FR 1012, Y 25,321, DK 1150).
$316* *Composition, 1972,* s. Mortensen 72, 27/75, (09-30-92, Kunsthallen, #221), color serigraph (BP 178, DM 448, FR 1516, Y 37,922, DK 1725).
$92* *Hons I Gronkal,* s. R.M.47, 290/410, (03-24-93, Kunsthallen, #260), color lithograph (BP 62, DM 150, FR 511, Y 10,810, DK 575).
$239* *Komposition,* s. Mortensen, 23/100, (03-24-93, Kunsthallen, #253), color serigraph (BP 162, DM 390, FR 1329, Y 28,081, DK 1495).
$184* *Komposition V., 1965,* s. Mortensen 65, 46/75, (03-24-93, Kunsthallen, #257), color serigraph (BP 125, DM 301, FR 1023, Y 21,619, DK 1150).
$1046* *Komposition, 1955,* s. Mortensen 55, 75/100, (03-24-93, Kunsthallen, #256), color serigraph (BP 708, DM 1708, FR 5814, Y 122,900, DK 6555).
$274* *Komposition, 1961,* s. Mortensen 61, 72/300, (09-30-92, Kunsthallen, #220), color serigraph (BP 155, DM 389, FR 1314, Y 32,881, DK 1495).
BI *Komposition, 1963,* s. Mortensen 63, est. DK 1,000, (03-24-93, Kunsthallen, #250), offset in colors.
BI *Komposition, 1966,* 30/75, est. DK 1,500, (03-24-93, Kunsthallen, #258), color lithograph.
BI *Komposition, 1966,* s. Richard Mortensen, 31/75, est. DK 31/75, (03-24-93, Kunsthallen, #259), color lithograph.
$257* *Komposition, 1970,* s. Mortensen 70, 40/75, (03-24-93, Kunsthallen, #251), color serigraph (BP 174, DM 420, FR 1429, Y 30,196, DK 1610).
$147* *Komposition, 1972,* s. Mortensen 72, 72/200, (03-24-93, Kunsthallen, #252), color serigraph (BP 100, DM 240, FR 817, Y 17,272, DK 920).
BI *Komposition, 1972,* s. Mortensen 72, 112/200, est. DK 1,200, (03-24-93, Kunsthallen, #254), color serigraph.
BI *Komposition, 1981,* s. Mortensen 81, 41/100, est. DK 1,200, (03-24-93, Kunsthallen, #255), color serigraph.
$126* *Untitled,* s. 1965, 45/150, (09-29-92, B. Rasmussen, #348), serigraph in colors (BP 71, DM 178, FR 607, Y 15,041, DK 690).
$126* *Untitled,* s. 76, 159/270, (09-29-92, B. Rasmussen, #349), serigraph in colors (BP 71, DM 178, FR 607, Y 15,041, DK 690).

$251* *Untitled,* s. 62, 23/75, (09-29-92, B. Rasmussen, #347), serigraph in colors (BP 141, DM 355, FR 1210, Y 29,963, DK 1380).
$209* *Untitled,* s. 1969, 30/75, (09-29-92, B. Rasmussen, #350), serigraph in colors (BP 117, DM 295, FR 1007, Y 24,949, DK 1150).

MORTENSEN, William   1897-1965
$799* *"The Bandit", c. 1948,* mounted on card, t., s., annot., labels, 395 x 310mm, (05-07-93, Sotheby-London, #191), photograph, Mortensen metal krome process color print (BP 506, DM 1263, FR 4257, Y 87,976).
$1955* *An Evening Song, c. 1932,* s., t., mono. credit stamp, (04-08-93, Christie-NY, #227, illus.), 13 x 9⅛ in., (33 x 23.2 cm.), photograph, gelatin silver print (BP 1282, DM 3141, FR 10,631, Y 221,857).
BI *June Collyer, c. 1928,* s., d. 8/15/28, est. BP 2/250, (12-17-92, Christie-S. Ken, #13, illus.), 9½ x 7½ in., (24.1 x 19.1 cm.), photograph, matt gelatin silver print.
$431* *"Miss June Storey" and "Barbara", 1930: Two,* first s., t., mono.; second s. on image, t., (05-23-93, Butterfield, #3548, illus.), each approx. 10 x 13½ in., photograph, first hand colored gelatin silver print; second bromoil transfer print in red chalk (BP 281, DM 705, FR 2372, Y 47,640).
$546* *"Obsession", 1927,* t., photog.'s mono. stamp, (05-23-93, Butterfield, #3547, illus.), 7¼ x 5¾ in., photograph, gelatin silver print (BP 356, DM 893, FR 3005, Y 60,351).
$1430* *Tarde, c. 1928,* mono. insig., credit stamp recto, (10-13-92, Christie-NY, #318, illus.), 13½ x 9⅜ in., (34.3 x 23.8 cm.), photograph, gelatin silver print (BP 833, DM 2095, FR 7118, Y 173,396).
$495* *"Thunder" (Monsters And Madonnas), 1930,* s., t., (11-16-92, Butterfield, #6107, illus.), 7⅝ x 6⅛ in., (194 x 155.9 mm.), photograph, gelatin silver print (BP 326, DM 789, FR 2658, Y 61,560).
$2640* *Youth, c. 1927,* s., blindstamped credit, lit., (10-13-92, Christie-NY, #319, illus.), 7¼ x 4¾ in., (18.4 x 12.1 cm.), photograph, gelatin silver print (BP 1538, DM 3868, FR 13,141, Y 320,116).

MORTIMER, F.J.
$1361* *Angry Seas: Five,* 1930s, majority mounted on paper or card, t., s., labels, each approx. sight 350 x 450mm, (05-07-93, Sotheby-London, #141, illus.), photograph, silver print (BP 862, DM 2152, FR 7251, Y 149,857).
$3996* *"Britannia Becalmed", c. 1930: Two,* mounted on paper, labels, sight 325 x 435mm and 417 x 411mm, (05-07-93, Sotheby-London, #136, illus.), photograph, silver print (BP 2530, DM 6318, FR 21,289, Y 439,991).
$1271* *"Channel Roll", c. 1935,* mounted on paper, t., s., label, 349 x 456mm, (05-07-93, Sotheby-London, #137, illus.), photograph, silver print (BP 805, DM 2009, FR 6771, Y 139,947).
BI *Coastal Scenes, "Christmas Dinner At Sea", "The Wild West Coast" and"Bringing The Boat In": Three,* 1930s, mounted on card, s., t., stamps, label, smallest sight 370 x 357mm, largest sight 480 x 480mm, est. BP 4/600, (05-07-93, Sotheby-London, #142), photograph, toned matt silver print.
$1998* *"The Gate Of Goodbye", An Allegorical Composite Image, With Preparatory Images, 1917: Six,* mounted on card, labels verso, various sizes, (05-07-93, Sotheby-London, #131, illus.), photograph, albumen prints and half-toned reprods. (BP 1265, DM 3159, FR 10,645, Y 219,996).
$136* *"A Nude" and "A War Photograph", c. 1920: Two,* mounted on card, 238 x 187mm and 349 x 270mm, (05-07-93, Sotheby-London, #133), photograph, silver print (BP 86, DM 215, FR 725, Y 14,975).
$1816* *"A Reminiscence Of The Hereford Convention", 1907,* mounted on card, label, 340 x 264mm, (05-07-93, Sotheby-London, #134, illus.), photograph, toned silver print (BP 1150, DM 2871, FR 9675, Y 199,956).
BI *Seascape, c. 1935,* mounted on paper, verso s., label, sight 452 x 350mm, est. BP 4/600, (05-07-93, Sotheby-London, #135, illus.), photograph, silver print.
$1271* *"Stowing The Jib", c. 1935,* mounted on paper, t., s., label, sight 483 x 370mm, (05-07-93, Sotheby-London,

#139, illus.), photograph, silver print (BP 805, DM 2009, FR 6771, Y 139,947).

BI *War Portraits And Images, c. 1914-19:* Twenty-Three, majority t., s., annots., smallest 106 x 132mm, largest 442 x 298mm,est. BP 3/500, (05-07-93, Sotheby-London, #132), silver prints, half-tone and gravure (intaglio) reprods..

$1635* *Yachts At Sea: Nine,* 1920s, several mounted on card, annot., labels, each approx. sight 370 x 475mm, (05-07-93, Sotheby-London, #140), photograph, toned silver print (BP 1035, DM 2585, FR 8711, Y 180,026).

$1725* *Yachts On Calm Seas, c. 1930: Two,* mounted on card, label, each approx. sight 450 x 350mm, (05-07-93, Sotheby-London, #138, illus.), photograph, gelatin silver print (BP 1092, DM 2727, FR 9190, Y 189,936).

BI *Yachts Under Sail: Four,* 1930s, two mounted on card, label, t., s., smallest sight 302 x 370mm, largest sight 370 x 477mm, est. BP 600/1,000, (05-07-93, Sotheby-London, #143), photograph, toned gelatin silver print.

MORTON, G. (after)

$48* *A Coaching Scene,* by Henry Alken, margins, (03-03-93, Bonhams-Chelsea, #218), plate 8½ x 12½ in., (21.6 x 31.8 cm.), etching w/aquatint (BP 33, DM 79, FR 268, Y 5609).

MOSBACHER, Alois

$149* *Untitled,* s., #34/50, (04-21-93, Dorotheum, #720), etching (BP 97, DM 238, FR 805, Y 16,495, SC 1680).

MOSCHLIN, Walter   1902-1961

BI *Vogel Gryf,* 1955, 6/50, s., d., est. SF 60/70, (10-14-92, Germann, #571), 19¹¹⁄₁₆ x 13¾ in., (500 x 350 mm.), lithograph.

BI *Vogel Gryf,* 1955, s., d., est. SF 40/50, (10-14-92, Germann, #572), 19¹¹⁄₁₆ x 13¾ in., (500 x 350 mm.), lithograph.

MOSER, Carl   1873-1939

$5642* *Bauerin Am Feldweg In Einer Gebirgslandschaft,* (19)28, s., d., i., (12-01-92, Karl/Faber, #1032, illus.), 11¼ x 16¾ in., (28.5 x 42.5 cm.), color woodcut on Japan (BP 3728, DM 8993, FR 30,646, Y 702,440).

MOSER, Koloman

BI *Ver Sacrum,* s., margins, foxing, est. BP 50/80, (02-17-93, Bonhams-Chelsea, #346), sheet 11¾ x 11¼ in., (29.8 x 28.6 cm.), chromolithograph.

$446* *Ver Sacrum,* s., blindstamp, margins, foxing, back cover lot, (05-20-93, Bonhams-Chelsea, #137, illus.), sheet 11¾ x 11⅛ in., (29.8 x 28.3 cm.), lithograph in colors (BP 286, DM 720, FR 2424, Y 49,249).

MOSES, Ed   American b. 1926

$275* *Broken Wedge Series: Wedge 4, 1973,* inits., t., d., #30/50, pub. Cirrus, very good cond.?, (10-28-92, Butterfield, #3036), 24 x 18 in., (610 x 457 mm.), lithograph on tissue, wove and Japan paper (BP 175, DM 425, FR 1442, Y 33,742).

$460* *Untitled, 1982,* inits., d., #18/100, blindstamp publisher, 3EP Editions and printer,Ikuru Kuwahara, full margins, good cond., handling creases, surface soiling, (05-19-93, Butterfield, #2267), 35½ x 25½ in., (902 x 648 mm.), lithograph in colors on BFK Rives (BP 299, DM 748, FR 2519, Y 50,924).

$385* *"Wedge I" and "Wedge 7", 1973: Two,* each s., inits., d., #3/50 & 23/50, blindstamp pub., Cirrus, good cond., creases, (02-24-93, Butterfield, #3233), one 24¼ x 18⅝ in., (616 x 473 mm.), other 23⅞ x 17⅞ in., (616 x 473 mm.), lithograph in colors on tissue and wove (BP 268, DM 625, FR 2119, Y 45,177).

MOSKOWITZ, Ira   Polish/American b. 1912

$88* *"Golden Jerusalem",* s., num., annot. 69 below image, (10-08-92, Boos, #670), 13½ x 11¾ in., (343 x 298 mm.), hand colored etching (BP 52, DM 130, FR 442, Y 10,693).

MOSKOWITZ, Robert   American b. 1935

BI *The Red And The Black, 1988,* s., d., #31/75, s. by p., blindstamp pub. Crown Point Press, full margins, very good cond., est. $1,5/2,000, (10-28-92, Butterfield, #3037), 8⅝ x 20¼ in., (219 x 514 mm.), color woodcut on Japan.

MOTHERWELL, Robert   American 1915-1991

$1870* *Africa Suite #4 (B. 43), 1970,* inits., num. 106/150, artist's blindstamp, pub. Marlborough Graphics,inkstamp, full margins, good cond., (02-24-93, Butterfield, #3089), 32 x 23¾ in., (813 x 603 mm.), silkscreen in black & cream on J. B. (width) Green (BP 1304, DM 3036, FR 10,292, Y 219,432).

$14,950* *Alphabet Series (B. 343U), 1986,* s., i. U, unique, pub. by artist, blindstamp, full margins, excell. cond., (05-11-93, Christie-NY, #511, illus.), sheet 37 x 28 in., (940 x 711 mm.), aquatint in red, brown and black w/collage on wove (BP 9544, DM 23,551, FR 79,352, Y 1,644,484).

BI *America Cup II,* init., d. July '77; i., init., prov., est. C$5/700, (05-10-93, Hodgins, #66), (50.8 x 33.7 cm.), lithograph on paper.

$3300* *America-La France VIII (Belknap 304), 1984,* s., #56/69, (05-16-93, Hindman, #522), 43⅜ x 15⅜ in., (110.2 x 39.1 cm.), sheet 50 x 29½ in., (110.2 x 39.1 cm.), color lithograph w/collage (BP 2146, DM 5308, FR 17,838, Y 365,813).

$3850* *America-La France Variations II (B. 298), 1983-84,* s., i. 'PP I', pub. blindstamp, Tyler Graphics, Ltd., full margins, good cond., (11-07-92, Sotheby-NY, #696, illus.), 42⅛ x 26 in., (107 x 66 cm.), lithograph p. in colors w/ collage on TGL handmade (BP 2517, DM 6147, FR 20,777, Y 475,191).

$2875* *America-La France Variations III (B. 299, T. 445), 1984,* s., #30/70, Tyler Graphics blindstamp, excell. cond.?, in a passe-partout, (05-11-93, Christie-NY, #507, illus.), sheet 48¼ x 30¾ in., (122.6 x 78.1 cm.), color lithograph w/ collage on Arches (BP 1835, DM 4529, FR 15,260, Y 316,247).

$3738* *America-La France Variations VI (B. 302), 1983-84,* s., #22/60, blindstamp pub. Tyler Graphics, Ltd., good cond., crease, (05-15-93, Sotheby-NY, #1105, illus.), sheet 45⅞ x 31¼ in., (116.5 x 79.4 cm.), lithograph in colors w/ collage on Arches Cover (BP 2430, DM 6013, FR 20,205, Y 414,366).

BI *American-La France Variations IX (B. 305, T. 451), 1984,* s., #32/60, Tyler Graphics blindstamp, excell. cond., est. $3/3,500, (05-11-93, Christie-NY, #509), sheet 28¾ x 21¾ in., (730 x 552 mm.), color lithograph w/ collage on tan mottled Bemboka hand-made.

BI *American-La France Variations V (B. 301, T. 447), 1984,* s., #22/60, Tyler Graphics blindstamp, excell. cond., est. $3/3,500, (05-11-93, Christie-NY, #508), sheet 46 x 31½ in., (116.8 x 80 cm.), color lithograph w/collage on TGL hand-made.

$935* *Automatism Elegy, State II Buff (B. 239), 1979-80,* inits., #36/50, blindstamp, full margins, very good cond.?, (10-28-92, Butterfield, #3042), 4⅞ x 10 in., (124 x 254 mm.), lithograph on buff Arches Cover paper (BP 596, DM 1444, FR 4903, Y 114,724).

$1150* *Beige Open (B. 245), 1981,* inits., #72/80, blindstamp, pub. Petersburg Press, p. Catherine Mousley, very good cond.?, handling creases, (05-19-93, Butterfield, #2272), 19⅞ x 26¼ in., (505 x 667 mm.), soft-ground on beige Auvergne a la Main handmade (BP 747, DM 1869, FR 6298, Y 127,311).

$935* *Black And Two Blues,* s., #81/100, (05-16-93, Hindman, #519), 21½ x 15⅝ in., (54.6 x 39.7 cm.), color lithograph (BP 608, DM 1504, FR 5054, Y 103,647).

BI *Black For Mozart, 1991,* s., #12/40, blindstamp, pub. Tyler Graphics, Ltd., full margins, good cond. ?, est. $16/18,000, (05-15-93, Sotheby-NY, #1113, illus.), sheet 64 x 41 in., (162.6 x 104.1 cm.), lithograph in colors w/ collage on hand-colored, handmade TGL paper.

$2875* *Black Gesture On Copper Ground (B. 243). 1980-81,* inits., i. PP II/II, artist's proofs, pub. Petersburg Press, full margins, good cond., creases, skinned spot, (02-11-93, Sotheby-NY, #394), 27⁹⁄₁₆ x 10⅝ in., (700 x 270 mm.), aquatint p. in ochre and black on German Etching (BP 2029, DM 4762, FR 16,115, Y 346,594).

BI *Black Rumble (B. 308; T. 460), 1983-4,* s., #30/65, blindstamp, glued down, excellent cond., est. $2,5/3,500, (11-09-92, Christie-NY, #369, illus.), 38 x 29 in., (965 x 737 mm.), red, yellow and black lithograph on wove.

$7475* *Black With No Way Out (B. 285), 1983,* s., #33/98, blindstamp, pub. Tyler Graphics, Ltd., good cond., printpoint-tipped to back mat, (05-15-93, Sotheby-NY, #1107, illus.), sheet 15 x 37⅝ in., (38.1 x 95.6 cm.), lithograph in red and black (BP 4860, DM 12,023, FR 40,405, Y 828,622).

$8050* *Black With No Way Out (B. 285, T. 434), 1983,* s., #10/98, Tyler Graphics blindstamp, excell. cond., (05-11-93, Christie-NY, #506, illus.), sheet 15⅛ x 38 in., (384 x 965 mm.), lithograph in black and red on TGL handmade (BP 5139, DM 12,681, FR 42,728, Y 885,491).

$6050* *Black With No Way Out (B. 285; T. 434), 1983,* s., i. ppII, blindstamp, excellent cond., (11-09-92, Christie-NY, #368, illus.), 15¼ x 38 in., (387 x 965 mm.), black and red lithograph on TGL handmade (BP 4000, DM 9658, FR 32,632, Y 750,807).

$882* *Black, Yellow And White (Belknap 66), 1972,* 34/150, s., pub. Marlborough Graphics, 715mm x 1040mm, (10-14-92, Germann, #52, illus.), color serigraph (BP 518, DM 1291, FR 4377, Y 106,883, SF 1150).

$23,100* *Burning Elegy, 1991,* init., #28/36, pub. blindstamp, Tyler Graphics, Ltd., full margins, good cond., (11-07-92, Sotheby-NY, #703, illus.), 42½ x 53⅛ in., (108 x 134.9 cm.), lithograph p. in colors on handcolored TGL handmade (BP 15,103, DM 36,883, FR 124,663, Y 2,851,148).

$23,000* *Burning Elegy, 1991,* init., #26/36, blindstamp, pub. Tyler Graphics, Ltd., full margins, good cond. ?, (05-15-93, Sotheby-NY, #1112, illus.), 42½ x 53⅛ in., (108 x 134.9 cm.), lithograph in colors on hand-colored handmade TGL (BP 14,954, DM 36,995, FR 124,324, Y 2,549,606).

BI *Calligraphy (Belknap 8), 1965-66,* s., #63/80, pub. Hollander Workshop, full margins, excell. cond., est. $1,2/1,800, (05-11-93, Christie-NY, #503), sheet 19⅛ x 26 in., (486 x 660 mm.), lithograph on BFK Rives.

$433* *Calligraphy 1965-66,* blindstamp, s., num. 63/80, very good cond., (11-30-92, Phillips-London, #547), sheet 19 x 26 in., (483 x 660 mm.), lithograph in black on Irwin Hollander wove (BP 286, DM 690, FR 2342, Y 53,889).

$575* *Capriccio (B. 1 app.), 1961,* s., #72/200, pub. Berggruen & Cie, p. Daniel Jacomet, margins, sealedin mat, good cond., mat staining, (05-19-93, Butterfield, #2268), 20⁷⁄₁₆ x 15¹¹⁄₁₆ in., (519 x 398 mm.), collotype and photo silkscreen in colors on Arches (BP 373, DM 935, FR 3149, Y 63,655).

$3080* *The Celtic Stone (Belknap 72), 1970-1,* s., i. artists proof, #IV/IV, blindstamp, full margins, glued down, excellent cond., (11-09-92, Christie-NY, #362, illus.), 41½ x 29½ in., (105.4 x 74.9 cm.), yellow and purple lithograph on Rives (BP 2036, DM 4917, FR 16,613, Y 382,229).

$1003* *Chair (Belknap 79), 1972,* s., #221/300, (05-27-93, Lempertz, #908), 37¹¹⁄₁₆ x 27 in., (95.7 x 68.6 cm.), color lithograph on wove (BP 642, DM 1609, FR 5425, Y 107,526).

$450* *Composition,* s., #5/150, artist's blindstamp, surface soiling, creasing, (11-30-92, Phillips-London, #550), sheet 40½ x 28 in., (102.9 x 71.1 cm.), lithograph in orange on wove (BP 297, DM 717, FR 2434, Y 56,005).

BI *Composition,* s., num. 30/45, good cond., est. BP 4/600, (11-30-92, Phillips-London, #552), sheet 30¼ x 22 in., (768 x 559 mm.), lithograph in blue & black on wove.

$440* *Cultural Institutions,* s., num. 18/250, (11-12-92, Freemn/Fine Art, #155A), 28 x 21½ in., (71.1 x 54.6 cm.), lithograph p. in color (BP 289, DM 697, FR 2352, Y 54,557).

BI *Cultural Institutions, 1983,* s., num., a p, traces of old mounting, est. DM 1800, (12-01-92, Karl/Faber, #1033), sh 29¹⁵⁄₁₆ x 22⁷⁄₁₆ in., (76 x 57 cm.), color offset and relief print on wove.

$2200* *Dance II (B. 200), 1978,* inits., num. 13/30, pub. Brooke Alexander, full margins, foxing, oldglue, excell. cond., (09-19-92, Christie-E, #164), sheet 25½ x 41 in., (64.8 x 104.1 cm.), etching and aquatint on J.B. Green (BP 1265, DM 3294, FR 11,282, Y 274,109).

$13,200* *Elegy Black Black (B. 274; T. 423), 1982-3,* s., #35/98, blindstamp, excellent cond., (11-09-92, Christie-NY, #367, illus.), 15 x 37¾ in., (381 x 959 mm.), colored lithograph on TGL handmade (BP 8727, DM 21,073, FR 71,197, Y 1,638,124).

$8800* *Elegy Study I (B. 425), 1989,* s., #5/50, blindstamp, full margins, excellent cond., (11-09-92, Christie-NY, #374, illus.), 39½ x 61½ in., (100.3 x 156.2 cm.), black and white lithograph on light brown TGL handmade (BP 5818, DM 14,049, FR 47,465, Y 1,092,082).

$9200* *Elegy Study I (B. 425), 1989,* s., #32/50, blindstamp, pub. Tyler Graphics, Ltd., full margins, good cond. ?, (05-15-93, Sotheby-NY, #1111, illus.), sheet 39 x 61 in., (99.1 x 154.9 cm.), lithograph in black and white on light brown TGL handmade (BP 5982, DM 14,798, FR 49,730, Y 1,019,843).

$5520* *Flags (B. 408), 1989,* inits., #13/68, Tyler Graphics blindstamp, full margins, creases, excell. cond., (05-11-93, Christie-NY, #512, illus.), sheet 36½ x 30⅛ in., (927 x 765 mm.), lithograph on red Moriki hand-made applique (BP 3524, DM 8696, FR 29,299, Y 607,194).

$6600* *Flags (B. 408), 1989,* inits., #5/68, blindstasmp, full margins, excellent cond., (11-09-92, Christie-NY, #373, illus.), 36¼ x 30 in., (921 x 762 mm.), lithograph on red Moriki handmade applique (BP 4364, DM 10,536, FR 35,599, Y 819,062).

$7188* *Flags (B. 408), 1989,* init., #45/68, blindstamp, pub. Tyler Graphics, Ltd., full margins, good cond., (05-15-93, Sotheby-NY, #1109, illus.), 28 x 25 in., (71.1 x 63.5 cm.), lithograph in black on handmade red Moriki paper, Chine applique to cream BFK Rives (BP 4674, DM 11,562, FR 38,854, Y 796,807).

$1320* *From Africa Suite (B. 48), 1970,* inits., #66/150, pub. Marlborough Graphics, full margins, good cond., thinned spot, (10-28-92, Butterfield, #3038), 31⅝ x 23¾ in., (803 x 603 mm.), silkscreen in black and cream on J.B. Green paper (BP 841, DM 2039, FR 6922, Y 161,963).

BI *From Africa Suite (B. 49), 1970,* inits., #144/150, pub. Marlborough Graphics, full margins, good cond., est. $1,5/2,000, (10-28-92, Butterfield, #3039, illus.), 32 x 23⅝ in., (813 x 600 mm.), silkscreen in black and cream on J.B. Green paper.

BI *Game Of Chance (B. 345), 1987,* s., #54/100, pub. blindstamp, Tyler Graphics, Ltd., full margins, good cond., est. $5/7,000, (11-07-92, Sotheby-NY, #697, illus.), 22¾ x 16⅜ in., (578 x 416 mm.), aquatint and lithograph p. in colors w/collage.

$4180* *Game Of Chance (B. 345), 1987,* s., #28/100, blindstamp, full margins, excellent cond., (11-09-92, Christie-NY, #371, illus.), 34½ x 27½ in., (876 x 699 mm.), lithograph, aquatint and collage in colors w/hand-coloring on HMP handmade (BP 2764, DM 6673, FR 22,546, Y 518,739).

BI *Gestural Presence, 1979,* inits., d., annot., artist's blindstamp, full margins, apparently good cond., light-brown stains in image, creases pin hole, est. $10/15,000, (02-24-93, Butterfield, #3092, illus.), 24 x 20 in., (610 x 508 mm.), monotype on wove.

$715* *Gray Open With White Paint (B. 246), 1981,* inits., num. 54/79, artist's blindstamp, pub. Petersburg Press, apparently very good cond., (02-24-93, Butterfield, #3095), 13¼ x 11⅝ in., (337 x 295 mm.), soft-ground etching & pochoir on gray Auvergne a la Main handmade (BP 499, DM 1161, FR 3935, Y 83,900).

BI *La Guerra I (B. 219), 1979-80,* init., #42/50, blindstamp, pub. Tyler Graphics, Ltd., good cond., est. $2/3,000, (05-15-93, Sotheby-NY, #1104), sheet 37¼ x 48⅝ in., (94.6 x 123.5 cm.), lithograph on Japanese Suzuki handmade paper.

$1650* *Gypsy Curse (B. 286), 1983,* s., #82/98, pub. blindstamp, Tyler Graphics, Ltd., full margins, good cond., (11-07-92, Sotheby-NY, #695, illus.), 8½ x 5¾ in., (216 x 146 mm.), lithograph in black on red Chine applique (BP 1079, DM 2635, FR 8904, Y 203,653).

$7700* *Hollow Men Suite (B. 336-342), 1985-86: Seven,* complete suite, inits., #6/49, blindstamp pub. Waddington Graphics, full margins, very good cond., (10-28-92, Butterfield, #3044, illus.), 3¾ x 4¹⁵⁄₁₆ in., (95 x 125 mm.), lift-ground etching w/aquatint and Chine colle (pasted) on Rives BFK (BP 4906, DM 11,892, FR 40,378, Y 944,785).

$3080* *In White With Green Stripe (B. 346), 1987,* s., #56/75, blindstamp, full margins, excellent cond., (11-09-92, Christie-NY, #372, illus.), 34 x 24 in., (864 x 610 mm.), etching and lithograph w/collage in green and black on Arches laid down on handmade paper (BP 2036, DM 4917, FR 16,613, Y 382,229).

BI *James Joyce, Ulysses (Belknap 384-405), 1988: Forty,* Arion Press, #135/150, frontispiece s., est. DM 18,000-, (05-27-93, Lempertz, #910, illus.), 13⁹⁄₁₆ x 11 in., (34.5 x 28 cm.), etching.

BI *Lament For Lorca (B. 254), 1981-82,* init., i. 'ap VIII/XVII', pub. blindstamp, Tyler Graphics, Ltd., full margins, good cond., est. $10/12,000, (11-07-92, Sotheby-NY, #698, illus.), 40½ x 56¾ in., (102.9 x 144.1 cm.), lithograph p. in black and red (rosso) sienna.

BI *Lament For Lorca (B. 254, Tyler 413), 1981-82,* inits., #10/52, Tyler Graphics blindstamp, full margins, excell. cond.?, the Late M. Anwar Kamal, M.D. Coll., est. $7/8,000, (05-11-93, Christie-NY, #505, illus.), sheet 44 x 60¾ in., (111.8 x 154.3 cm.), color lithograph on TGL hand-made.

$7700* *Lament For Lorca (B. 254; T. 413), 1981-2,* inits., i. ap, #X/XVII, pub. Tyler Graphics, rubbing, very good cond., (11-09-92, Christie-NY, #366, illus.), 44 x 61 in., (111.8 x 154.9 cm.), colored lithograph on TGL handmade (BP 5091, DM 12,292, FR 41,532, Y 955,572).

BI *London Series I: Orange (B. 60), 1970-71,* s., #121/150, pub. Marlborough Graphics, full margins, good cond., est. $1/2,000, (10-28-92, Butterfield, #3040), 36 x 24 in., (914 x 610 mm.), silkscreen in orange on J.B. Green paper.

$1320* *London Series II: Open Series No. 1, (B. 65), 1970,* init., num. 30/150, artist's blindstamp, inkstamp, pub. Marlborough Graphics, very good cond., creases, foxing, (02-24-93, Butterfield, #3090), 28½ x 41 in., (72.4 x 104.1 cm.), silkscreen in colors on wove paper w/watermark (BP 921, DM 2143, FR 7265, Y 154,893).

$1320* *London Series II: Open Series No. 2 (B. 66), 1970-1971,* init., num. 29/150, inkstamp, pub. Marlborough Graphics, very good cond., surface soiling, crease, (02-24-93, Butterfield, #3091), 28½ x 41 in., (72.4 x 104.1 cm.), silkscreen in colors on wove w/watermark (BP 921, DM 2143, FR 7265, Y 154,893).

$920* *London Series II: Untitled (B. 66), 1970-71,* s. in screen, i., #82/150, pub. Marlborough Graphics, Inc., good cond., foxing, creases, (02-11-93, Sotheby-NY, #393), sheet 28¼ x 41⁳⁄₁₆ in., (71.8 x 104.6 cm.), colored silkscreen on J.B. Green (BP 649, DM 1524, FR 5157, Y 110,910).

$3794* *M. Pleynet. Beau Geste: Six,* 38/150, mono., stamped, Trestle, (10-14-92, Germann, #66, illus.), 22¹⁄₁₆ x 14⅞ in., (560 x 378 mm.), color lithograph (BP 2227, DM 5552, FR 18,829, Y 459,767, SF 4945).

$13,200* *Mask (For Ingmar Bergman) (B. 412), 1989,* s., #9/62, pub. blindstamp, Tyler Graphics, Ltd., good cond., (11-07-92, Sotheby-NY, #702, illus.), sheet 52¼ x 40¾ in., (132.7 x 103.5 cm.), lithograph p. in colors on handmade, hand-colored TGL (BP 8630, DM 21,076, FR 71,236, Y 1,629,227).

BI *Mediterranean (B. 147; T. 392), 1975,* s., i. State I, #13/26, Tyler Graphic, blindstamps, staining, good cond., est. $1,5/2,000, (11-09-92, Christie-NY, #365, illus.), 46½ x 31¾ in., (118.1 x 80.6 cm.), lithograph and screenprint in colors on Arches.

$13,200* *Mexican Night II (B. 318), 1984,* s., i. 'h.c.', hors commerce impressions, artist blindstamp, pub. Tyler Graphics, Ltd., full margins, good cond., (11-07-92, Sotheby-NY, #699, illus.), 17½ x 17¾ in., (445 x 451 mm.), aquatint and etching p. in red and black (BP 8630, DM 21,076, FR 71,236, Y 1,629,227).

$13,800* *Mexican Night II (B. 318), 1984,* s., #63/70, pub. Tyler Graphics, artist's blindstamp, full margins, very good cond., (05-11-93, Christie-NY, #510, illus.), sheet 25 x 24 in., (635 x 610 mm.), etching and aquatint in red and black on Whatman (BP 8809, DM 21,739, FR 73,248, Y 1,517,985).

BI *Mexican Night II (Belknap-Terenzio 318), 1984,* s., i., est. DM 25,000, (06-12-93, Hauswedell/Nolt, #307, illus.), 17¹¹⁄₁₆ x 17¹¹⁄₁₆ in., (45 x 45 cm.), color lithograph on wove.

BI *Monster (B. 139), 1974-75,* init., #18/26, blindstamp, pub. Tyler Graphics, Ltd., good cond., est. $6/8,000, (11-07-92, Sotheby-NY, #692, illus.), sheet 41¾ x 30⅞ in., (106 x 78.4 cm.), lithograph on speckled gray HMP handmade.

BI *Monster (B. 139), 1974-75,* inits., #18/26, blindstamp of pub., Tyler Graphics, Ltd., good cond., est. $3,5/4,500, (02-11-93, Sotheby-NY, #391, illus.), sheet 41¾ x 30⅞ in., (106 x 78.5 cm.), lithograph on speckled gray HMP handmade.

BI *New York Portfolio: Untitled (B. 260), 1982,* s., #64/250, pub. New York Graphic Society, good cond.?, est. $7/900, (10-28-92, Butterfield, #3043), 28 x 22⅜ in., (711 x 568 mm.), color lithograph on Arches Cover paper.

BI *Octavio Paz Suite: Black Sun (B. 377), 1987-88,* inits., annot. trial, pub. The Limited Editions Club, margins, very good cond., creases, est. $2/4,000, (10-28-92, Butterfield, #3045, illus.), 10¾ x 13⅞ in., (273 x 352 mm.), lithograph in black and ochre on Masa Dose Chine colle (pasted) attached to Arches.

$3850* *Orange Lyric (B. 415), 1989,* inits. #11/30, blindstamp pub. Waddington Graphics, full margins, very good cond., (10-28-92, Butterfield, #3046, illus.), 18 x 24 in., (457 x 610 mm.), color aquatint w/carborundum on cream wove (BP 2453, DM 5946, FR 20,189, Y 472,393).

BI *Paris Review (B. 9 app.), 1965,* s., #114/150, pub. Chiron Press, good cond., surfacing scuffing, abrasions, creases, inkloss, creases, surface soiling, est. $1/2,000, (05-19-93, Butterfield, #2269), sight 40³⁄₁₆ x 26¼ in., (102.1 x 66.7 cm.), silkscreen in colors on Beckett Cartridge.

BI *Paris Suite I-IV (Spring, Summer, Autumn & Winter) (B.231-4): Four,* init., #30/60, pub. Brooke Alexander, Inc., full margins, good cond., discoloration, soiling, est. $5/7,000, (05-15-93, Sotheby-NY, #1106, illus.), lithograph in colors on J.B. Green Hot Press handmade.

$1760* *Paris Suite III (Autumn) (B. 233) 1979-80,* inits., num. 54/60, pub. Brooke Alexander, margins, apparently very good cond., (02-24-93, Butterfield, #3093, illus.), 9⅞ x 13⅝ in., (251 x 346 mm.), lithograph in blue, sienna, & black on Green Hot Press handmade (BP 1227, DM 2857, FR 9686, Y 206,524).

$1650* *Paris Suite IV (Winter) (B. 234), 1979-80,* inits., num. 52/60, pub. Brooke Alexander, margins, apparently very good cond., (02-24-93, Butterfield, #3094, illus.), 9¾ x 9⅛ in., (248 x 232 mm.), lithograph in blue. gray, & black on Green Hot Press handmade (BP 1151, DM 2679, FR 9081, Y 193,617).

$660* *Peace Portfolio I: Untitled (B. 39), 1970,* s., num. 51/175, pub. Academic & Professional Action Committee for aResponsible Congress, apparently very good cond., (02-24-93, Butterfield, #3088), sheet 26 x 21 in., (660 x 533 mm.), silkscreen on Rives BFK (BP 460, DM 1071, FR 3632, Y 77,447).

$4620* *The Poet's Eye (B. 429), 1989-90,* inits., num. 18/35, artist's and Waddington Graphics blindstamps, full margins, excell. cond., (09-19-92, Christie-E, #165, illus.), sheet 25¼ x 31 in., (641 x 787 mm.), aquatint and carborundum in pale blue and black on Whatman (BP 2657, DM 6918, FR 23,692, Y 575,629).

$2372* *Red Open With White Line (Belknap 207), 1979,* s. ap V/X, Brooke Alexander Inc., blindstamp Motherwell, (05-12-93, AB Stockholm, #7040, illus.), approx. 18⅛ x 35¹⁄₁₆ in., (46 x 89 cm.), color aquatint and etching (BP 1549, DM 3827, FR 12,891, Y 264,821, SK 17,600).

$4600* *Red Sea II (B. 211), 1979,* s., #55/100, pub. Harry N. Abrams, Inc., full margins, good cond., handling creases, (05-15-93, Sotheby-NY, #1102, illus.), 23⅝ x 19⅞ in., (60 x 50.5 cm.), etching and aquatint in red and black on German Etching paper (BP 2991, DM 7399, FR 24,865, Y 509,921).

$12,100* *Redness Of Red (B. 324), 1984-85,* init., #28/100, pub. blindstamp, Tyler Graphics, Ltd., good cond., (11-07-92, Sotheby-NY, #701, illus.), sheet 24 x 16⅛ in., (610 x 410 mm.), silkscreen and lithograph p. in red w/collage on Arches Cover (BP 7911, DM 19,320, FR 65,300, Y 1,493,458).

$11,000* *Redness Of Red (B. 326; T. 458), 1985,* inits., i. h.c., blindstamp, excellent cond., (11-09-92, Christie-NY, #370, illus.), 24 x 16 in., (610 x 406 mm.), lithograph, screenprint and collage in colors on Arches (BP 7273, DM 17,561, FR 59,331, Y 1,365,103).

$4950* *Rite Of Passage II (B. 216), 1979-80,* s., #3/51, pub. blindstamp, Tyler Graphics, Ltd., full margins, good cond., (11-07-92, Sotheby-NY, #704, illus.), 23 x 28½ in., (584 x 724 mm.), lithograph on red and white duplex handmade TGL (BP 3236, DM 7904, FR 26,713, Y 610,960).

BI *Roth-Handle (B. 137),* inits., num. 30/53, pub. Brooke Alexander Inc., full margins, good cond., est. BP 1/1,200, (11-30-92, Phillips-London, #551), sheet 19½ x 15½ in., (495 x 394 mm.), aquatint in black w/collage on Auvergne a la Main paper.

$2475* *Roth-Handle II (B. 153), 1975,* s., i. 'proof', pub. John Berggruen Gallery, full margins, good cond., (11-07-92, Sotheby-NY, #693, illus.), 8⅝ x 12¾ in., (219 x 324 mm.), aquatint and linocut p. in rust and black, w/hand painting of blue tempera paint by artist on buff Dewint handmade (BP 1618, DM 3952, FR 13,357, Y 305,480).

BI *Samurai (B. 75), 1971,* s., annot. Proof L, blindstamp publisher, ULAE, p. Ben Berns, full margins, good cond.?, buckling, creases, est. $5/7,000, (05-19-93, Butterfield, #2270), sh 73½ x 37 in., (186.7 x 94 cm.), lithograph on Japanese Suzuki handmade.

$4400* *Samurai (Belknap 75), 1971,* s., i. 'Proof P', blindstamp, pub. ULAE, full margins, good cond., (11-07-92, Sotheby-NY, #690, illus.), sheet 72½ x 36¾ in., (184.2 x 93.3 cm.), lithograph on Japanese Suzuki handmade (BP 2877, DM 7025, FR 23,745, Y 543,076).

BI *Samurai II (B. 213), 1979-80,* init., i. ap XV/XVI, blindstamp, pub. Tyler Graphics, Ltd., good cond., est. $4/5,000, (05-15-93, Sotheby-NY, #1103, illus.), overall 56½ x 24⅝ in., (143.5 x 62.5 cm.), lithograph w/Chine applique on handmade Napal paper.

$324* *Sans Titre (Belknap 165), 1976,* mono., d. 76 in plate, s., #30/70, (05-27-93, Briest, #154), 29¹³/₁₆ x 35⅛ in., (75.7 x 89.2 cm.), black lithograph on Arches (BP 207, DM 520, FR 1752, Y 34,734).

$605* *Soot Black Stone, No. 2 (Belknap 114), 1973,* full margins, s., #12.47, pub. Gemini G.E.L., (12-08-92, Swann, #222), 10 x 18⅛ in., (25.4 x 46 cm.), lithograph (BP 379, DM 942, FR 3211, Y 74,988).

$460* *Soot-Black Stone #4 (B. 116, G. 599), 1973,* s., #3/50, artist's blindstamp, Gemini G.E.L., p. Serge Lozingot, full margins, good cond., (05-19-93, Butterfield, #2271), 30 x 18 in., (762 x 457 mm.), lithograph on Hawthorne Of Larroque handmade (BP 299, DM 748, FR 2519, Y 50,924).

BI *Soot-Black Stone #5 (Belknap 117), 1973,* mono., pencil s., est. DM 2,500, (11-20-92, Lempertz, #723, illus.), sh 35¾ x 24¾ in., (90.8 x 62.8 cm.), lithograph on handmade Velin.

$1433* *Soot-Black Stone #5 (Belknap 117), 1973,* s., #41/53, watermark, mono., blindstamp Gemini G.E.L., (05-27-93, Lempertz, #909, illus.), 35¾ x 24¾ in., (90.8 x 62.8 cm.), lithograph on hand-stamped wove (BP 918, DM 2299, FR 7750, Y 153,623).

$686* *St. Marks (Belknap 240), 1979-80,* s., #26/50, full margins, good cond., soiling, (06-30-93, Sotheby-London, #882, illus.), 9⅝ x 7⅜ in., (244 x 187 mm.), color lithograph on wove (BP 460, DM 1170, FR 3947, Y 73,503).

BI *St. Michael (State II) (B. 204), 1975-79,* init., #4/34, blindstamp, pub. Tyler Graphics, Ltd., good cond., scuff marks, est. $3/4,000, (05-15-93, Sotheby-NY, #1101, illus.), sheet 62¾ x 25⅜ in., (159.4 x 64.5 cm.), lithograph, silkscreen and monotype in colors.

$6600* *St. Michael I (State II); and St. Michael II (B. 204 & 205), 1975-79,* init., #7/34, #6/46, blindstamp, pub. Tyler Graphics, Ltd., good cond., light staining, (11-07-92, Sotheby-NY, #694, illus.), sheet 62¾ x 25⅜ in., (159.4 x 64.5 cm.), sheet 60¼ x 17¾ in., (159.4 x 64.5 cm.), two lithographs p. in colors on Arches Cover (BP 4315, DM 10,538, FR 35,618, Y 814,614).

$3850* *Summer Light Series: Harvest, With Blue Bottom (B. 124), 1973,* s., num. 8/55, pub. Gemini G.E.L., wide margins, excell. cond.?, (09-19-92, Christie-E, #163), borderline 30 x 12 in., (762 x 305 mm.), lithograph in orange and blue w/collage on wove (BP 2215, DM 5765, FR 19,744, Y 479,691).

$2475* *Summer Light Series: Harvest, With Leaf (B. 123), 1973,* s., #37/54, blindstamp, pub. Gemini, G.E.L., full margins, good cond., skinned spots, (11-07-92, Sotheby-NY, #691, illus.), 30 x 11⅞ in., (762 x 302 mm.), lithograph p. in orange w/collage on Hawthorne of Larroque handmade (BP 1618, DM 3952, FR 13,357, Y 305,480).

BI *Summer Light Series: Harvest, With Two White Stripes (B. 126), 1973,* s., #27/55, blindstamp of pub., Gemini, G.E.L., full margins, good cond., est. $2/3,000, (02-11-93, Sotheby-NY, #392, illus.), 29¹⁵/₁₆ x 11⅞ in., (760 x 302 mm.), lithograph p. in orange, blue and white pochoir, w/collage on Hawthorne of Larroque handmade.

BI *Summer Light Series: Pauillac (B. 121; Gemini 474), 1973,* s., #5/53, blindstamps, full margins, crease, stain, excellent cond., est. $2/3,000, (11-09-92, Christie-NY, #363), 35½ x 18½ in., (902 x 470 mm.), lithograph, screenprint and pochoir in colors w/collage on Hawthorne of Larroque handmade.

BI *Summer Light Series: The Highlands (B. 128; G. 482), 1973,* s., #33/56, blindstamps, full margins, rubbed spot (touched) in image, rubbing, soiling, creasing, est. $1,5/2,000, (11-09-92, Christie-NY, #364), 35⅞ x 18¾ in., (911 x 476 mm.), colored lithograph w/collage on Hawthorne of Larroque handmade.

$3575* *Summer Sign (B. 430), 1990,* init., #27/38, pub. blindstamp, Waddington Graphics, Ltd., full margins, good cond., (11-07-92, Sotheby-NY, #706, illus.), 17¾ x 23½ in., (451 x 597 mm.), carborundum p. in colors on Whatman (BP 2337, DM 5708, FR 19,293, Y 441,249).

$2750* *Summerlight Series: Pauillac #1 (B. 119, G. 472), 1973,* s., #76/92, blindstamp pub. Gemini G.E.L., full margins, very good cond.?, (10-28-92, Butterfield, #3041), 32¼ x 18 in., (819 x 457 mm.), lithograph w/collage and embossing in colors on Arjomari paper (BP 1752, DM 4247, FR 14,421, Y 337,423).

$1650* *Summertime In Italy,* s., #64/150, (05-16-93, Hindman, #520), 28 x 22 in., (71.1 x 55.9 cm.), lithograph (BP 1073, DM 2654, FR 8919, Y 182,907).

$333* *Summertime, Italy 1971,* blindstamp, s., num. 67/100, very good cond., (11-30-92, Phillips-London, #549), sheet 29⅞ x 22½ in., (759 x 572 mm.), lithograph in black on Irwin Hollander wove (BP 220, DM 531, FR 1801, Y 41,444).

$7150* *Three Figures (B. 426), 1989,* s., #45/80, blindstamp, excellent cond., (11-09-92, Christie-NY, #375, illus.), 55¾ x 40 in., (141.6 x 101.6 cm.), red and black lithograph on wove (BP 4727, DM 11,414, FR 38,565, Y 887,317).

BI *Three Forms (B. 407), 1988,* init., #25/50, pub. blindstamp, Waddington Graphics Ltd., full margins, good cond., est. $5/6,000, (11-07-92, Sotheby-NY, #705, illus.), 11¾ x 23¾ in., (298 x 603 mm.), etching and aquatint p. in red (rosso) and black on German Etching.

$3163* *Three Forms (B. 407), 1988,* inits., #25/50, blindstamp of pub., Waddington Graphics Ltd., full margins, good cond., (02-11-93, Sotheby-NY, #395), 11¹³/₁₆ x 23¹¹/₁₆ in., (300 x 602 mm.), etching and aquatint p. in red and black on German Etching (BP 2232, DM 5239, FR 17,730, Y 381,314).

BI *Untitled,* plate s., est. $800/1,200, (06-11-93, Freemn/Fine Art, #155), 28¼ x 41 in., (71.8 x 104.1 cm.), relief print.

BI *Untitled (A La Pintura) (Belknap 82), 1968-72,* init., i. trial, unique trial proof from livre d'artiste A LA PINTURA, trimmed to plate edge by artist, blindstamp, pub. ULAE, good cond., pinholes, est. $1,5/2,000, (05-15-93, Sotheby-NY, #1100), 17¾ x 23½ in., (45.1 x 59.7 cm.), aquatint in colors on handmade J.B. Green paper.

$3740* *Untitled (Belknap 106), 1973,* s., #3/50, prov., (05-16-93, Hindman, #624), 23¾ x 35½ in., (60.3 x 90.2 cm.), aquatint (BP 2432, DM 6016, FR 20,216, Y 414,588).

$1430* *Untitled (Belknap 19), 1965-6,* s., num. 23/25, pub. Hollander Workshop, full margins, excell. cond., (09-19-92, Christie-E, #162, illus.), sheet 29¾ x 22 in., (756 x 559 mm.), etching on BFK Rives (BP 823, DM 2141, FR 7333, Y 178,171).

$1955* *Untitled (Belknap 28), 1966,* s., #149/225, pub. Tanglewood Press, full margins, good cond., remains of hinges, creases, (02-11-93, Sotheby-NY, #389, illus.), 18¹⁵/₁₆ x

13 15/16 in., (482 x 355 mm.), lithograph (BP 1379, DM 3238, FR 10,959, Y 235,684).

BI *Untitled (Belknap, 250), 1982,* from New York Portfolio, s., num. Motherwell 20/250, pub.'s drystamp, very good cond., est. $8/1,200, (03-12-93, Skinner, #112, illus.), sight, sheet 30 x 22½ in., (76.2 x 57.2 cm.), photo-screenprint, screenprint and embossing on wove.

BI *Untitled (Belknap, 5), 1964,* from Ten Works by Ten Painters, for the Wadsworth Atheneum, shrink wrapped, very good cond., est. $4/600, (03-12-93, Skinner, #106, illus.), sheet 23⅜ x 19½ in., (59.4 x 49.5 cm.), screen-print and collage on paper.

$333* *Untitled 1966,* blindstamp, s., num. 23/30, pastel, very good cond., (11-30-92, Phillips-London, #546), sheet 22¼ x 17⅛ in., (565 x 435 mm.), lithograph in black on Irwin Hollander wove (BP 220, DM 531, FR 1801, Y 41,444).

$1870* *Untitled From The Africa Suite (Belknap 40), 1970,* init., #144/150, s. ink, prov., (05-16-93, Hindman, #623), 31¼ x 23½ in., (79.4 x 59.7 cm.), color serigraph (BP 1216, DM 3008, FR 10,108, Y 207,294).

$2090* *Untitled From The Basque Suite (Belknap 54), 1970,* init., #129/150, pub. Marlborough Graphics, prov., (05-16-93, Hindman, #625), 22 x 17 in., (55.9 x 43.2 cm.), color serigraph (BP 1359, DM 3362, FR 11,297, Y 231,682).

$358* *Untitled, 1964,* from Ten Works + Ten Painters, #40/500, pub. Ives-Sillman, blindstamp, margins, good cond.?, prop. Woodward Foundation, (12-12-92, Weschler, #142, illus.), sight 21½ x 15¼ in., (54.6 x 38.7 cm.), silk-screen and collage (BP 230, DM 564, FR 1933, Y 44,301).

$500* *Untitled, 1966,* blindstamp, s., #35/100 in pastel, very good cond., (11-30-92, Phillips-London, #548), sheet 22¼ x 17⅛ in., (565 x 435 mm.), color lithograph on Irwin Hollander wove (BP 330, DM 797, FR 2704, Y 62,228).

$1320* *Untitled, 1966,* Belknap No. 28, pub. Tanglewood Press, excellent cond., (10-31-92, Cleveland, #386), 19 x 14 in., (48.3 x 35.6 cm.), lithograph (BP 846, DM 2031, FR 6889, Y 163,508).

$221* *Untitled, Gauloise Caporal,* (11-13-92, Koller, #5383), 11 9/16 x 9 7/16 in., (29.3 x 24 cm.), lithograph w/collage (BP 143, DM 347, FR 1170, Y 27,430, SF 313).

$3450* *Water's Edge (B. 307), 1983-84,* s., i. A.P. X/XII, blinds-tamp, pub. Tyler Graphics, Ltd., full margins, good cond., (05-15-93, Sotheby-NY, #1108), 27¾ x 22⅞ in., (70.5 x 58.1 cm.), lithograph in colors w/collage on TGL handmade paper (BP 2243, DM 5549, FR 18,649, Y 382,441).

$13,200* *Wave (B. 413), 1989,* s., #4/92, pub. blindstamp, Tyler Graphics, Ltd., full margins, good cond., (11-07-92, Sotheby-NY, #700, illus.), 39 x 54½ in., (99.1 x 138.4 cm.), lithograph p. in red and black on Somerset (BP 8630, DM 21,076, FR 71,236, Y 1,629,227).

$14,950* *The Wave (B. 413), 1989,* s., #2/92, Tyler Graohics blindstamp, full margins, excell. cond., (05-11-93, Christie-NY, #513, illus.), sheet 41 x 56½ in., (104.1 x 143.5 cm.), lithograph in red and black on Somerset (BP 9544, DM 23,551, FR 79,352, Y 1,644,484).

$10,925* *Wave (B. 413), 1989,* s., #30/92, blindstamp, pub. Tyler Graphics, Ltd., full margins, good cond. ?, (05-15-93, Sotheby-NY, #1110, illus.), sheet 41 x 56⅜ in., (104.1 x 143.2 cm.), lithograph in red and black on Somerset (BP 7103, DM 17,573, FR 59,054, Y 1,211,063).

$1840* *West Islip (B. 36), 1965-70,* s., #18/20, blindstamp of pub., ULAE, good cond., creases, (02-11-93, Sotheby-NY, #390), sheet 29 9/16 x 41 5/16 in., (75.1 x 105 cm.), color lithograph w/handcoloring in acrylic on BFK Rives (BP 1298, DM 3048, FR 10,314, Y 221,820).

MOTHERWELL, Robert (after) American 1915-1991

$880* *Capriccio (Belknap App. 1), 1961,* s., (03-14-93, Hindman, #330), 20⅜ x 15⅝ in., (51.8 x 39.7 cm.), color collotype and silkscreen (BP 614, DM 1465, FR 4980, Y 103,712).

MOTI, Kaiko Indian b. 1921

BI *"Return From The Journey",* excellent cond., est. $4-500, (10-31-92, Cleveland, #387, illus.), 11½ x 15½ in., (29.2 x 39.4 cm.), color etching.

$165* *"School Of Fish",* s., #85/120, (03-12-93, Goldberg, #896, illus.), image 22 x 16½ in., (55.9 x 41.9 cm.), color lithograph (BP 115, DM 275, FR 934, Y 19,446).

MOTTE, Jean

$77* *Sans Titre,* s., 28/75, 785 x 595mm, sh 1000 x 750mm, (06-28-93, Loudmer, #320), color aquatint and collage on Arches wove (BP 52, DM 131, FR 441, Y 8170).

MOTTI, Giuseppe

BI *"Dinamica Del Desnudo",* s., d. 1975, #32/60, reserve P20,000, (02-03-93, Duran, #229), 19 11/16 x 27 9/16 in., (50 x 70 cm.), lithograph.

MOTTRAM, C. (after)

$1760* *Boston,* (03-20-93, Northeast, #739, illus.), 27 x 40½ in., (68.6 x 102.9 cm.), hand-colored engraving (BP 1180, DM 2878, FR 9794, Y 204,153).

MOTTRAM, C. (after) American 19th cent.

$1045* *"Boston", 1857,* after John William Hill, ident. in plate, very good cond., (10-31-92, Skinner, #48, illus.), 28¾ x 41¾ in., (73 x 106 cm.), collotype w/hand coloring on paper (BP 683, DM 1641, FR 5556, Y 129,204).

MOTTRAM, Charles

$1035* *Boston, c. 1855,* after John W. Hill, p. McQueen, pub. Colnaghi and Smith Bros. & Co. 1857, small margins, good cond., scrapes, foxing, scuffs, streaks, discoloration, water stains, backboard stain, (01-28-93, Sotheby-NY, #455), sheet 29 x 41⅞ in., (73.7 x 106.4 cm.), engraving on applique (BP 683, DM 1640, FR 5550, Y 128,508).

MOULIN STUDIOS

$440* *Cliff House, San Francisco, 1930,* (11-16-92, Butterfield, #6108, illus.), 7½ x 9½ in., (190.8 x 241.7 mm.), photograph, gelatin silver print (BP 290, DM 702, FR 2363, Y 54,720).

MOULY, Marcel French b. 1918

$413* *La Grande Voile Jaune,* s., num. 19/300, (11-12-92, Freemn/Fine Art, #156), 11¼ x 15¼ in., (28.6 x 38.7 cm.), screen print (BP 271, DM 654, FR 2207, Y 51,209).

$110* *Marine Bleue No.2,* s., #224/300, (05-16-93, Hanzel, #489), 27½ x 21 in., (69.9 x 53.3 cm.), color lithograph (BP 72, DM 177, FR 595, Y 12,194).

$70* *"Port",* #94/150, s., ink s. verso, (04-04-93, Pescheteau, #270), 16 9/16 x 5½ in., (42 x 14 cm.), color lithograph (BP 46, DM 113, FR 382, Y 7970).

MOUNERAT, P.

$945* *Davos Parsenn, 1947,* excell. cond., (02-04-93, Christie-S. Ken, #16, illus.), 40 x 25½ in., (101.6 x 64.8 cm.), color lithograph backed on linen (BP 660, DM 1556, FR 5276, Y 117,552).

MOUNT, William Sidney (after)

$330* *Coming To The Point, 1855,* by Soulange Teissier, pub. W. Schaus, margins, stains, scratches in image, paper losses, splits, tears affecting image, laid down on board, defects, (01-22-93, Christie-NY, #316, illus.), borderline 20¾ x 24½ in., (527 x 622 mm.), lithograph on India applique (BP 216, DM 525, FR 1775, Y 41,302).

$220* *Music Is Contagious,* (05-29-93, Northeast, #624, illus.), colored engraving (BP 141, DM 349, FR 1180, Y 23,590).

MOURGUE, Pierre

$2276* *Jean Borlin,* p. H. Chachoin, (01-31-93, Morelle/Marchan, #38, illus.), 44⅞ x 59 7/16 in., (114 x 151 cm.), poster (BP 1531, DM 3667, FR 12,397, Y 283,932).

MOURGUE and SONS

$462* *Chocolat Felix Potin, c. 1900,* Paris, Lith. Deymarie and Jouet, (06-11-93, Boisgirard, #118), poster (BP 304, DM 751, FR 2532, Y 49,019).

MOURLAT

$75 *Belard, 1950,* good cond., (09-24-92, Alderfer, #309), 28½ x 20½ in., (72.4 x 52.1 cm.), (BP 44, DM 111, FR 377, Y 9022).

MOURLOT
$90 *Le Dessin Francais, 1950,* foxing, (09-24-92, Alderfer, #271), 28⅝ x 20⅜ in., (72.7 x 51.8 cm.), (BP 53, DM 133, FR 453, Y 10,826).

MOURLOT (after MANE KATZ)   French/ Israeli 1894-1962
BI *Fiddler On The Roof,* est. $2/300, (02-04-93, Sloan, #1863), 19½ x 25½ in., (49.5 x 64.8 cm.), color lithograph.

MOURLOT, Fernand
$640* *Souvenirs Et Portraits D'Artistes: Twenty-Five,* folio, w/ text, pub. Mourlot, 1972, #260/800, (12-01-92, Ritchie, #109, illus.), lithograph, most in color (BP 423, DM 1020, FR 3476, Y 79,681, C$ 825).

MOWATT, Ken   American 20th cent.
$55* *The Whale Hunt,* s., t., d. '77, i. AP, num. 5/9, (11-12-92, Freemn/Fine Art, #157), 22 x 19 in., (55.9 x 48.3 cm.), block print (BP 36, DM 87, FR 294, Y 6820).

MOY, Seong   b. 1921
$468* *"Lovers In Flight", 1952: Ten,* s., t., num. A.E. 6/15, excellent cond., (10-31-92, Cleveland, #194, illus.), 19⅛ x 14¼ in., (48.6 x 36.2 cm.), color woodcut (BP 300, DM 720, FR 2443, Y 57,971).
BI *"The Mystical Garden", 1955,* s., d., t., num., ded., regis. holes, mat stain, very good cond., est. $5-700, (10-31-92, Cleveland, #195), 14½ x 14⅞ in., (36.8 x 37.8 cm.), color lithograph.
$660* *Portfolio, 1952: Five,* each tipped to a support sheet, t., num., s., pub. Ted Gotthelf, 195, (05-27-93, Swann, #197), average sh 20 x 10½ in., (50.8 x 26.7 cm.), color woodcuts w/2-6 blocks (BP 423, DM 1059, FR 3569, Y 70,755).
$468* *"The Yellow Chamber",* s. S. Moy '53, very good cond.?, (11-21-92, Bakker, #173, illus.), 15 x 13 in., (38.1 x 33 cm.), woodcut (BP 308, DM 746, FR 2513, Y 58,202).

MOYREAU, Jean   1690-1762
$433* *L'Alliance De La Musique Et De La Comedie (Portalis-Beraldi S. 210; Le Blanc 16),* after Watteau, (12-04-92, Bassenge, #6653, illus.), 17¹¹⁄₁₆ x 12⁷⁄₁₆ in., (45 x 31.6 cm.), etching w/engraving (BP 278, DM 690, FR 2339, Y 54,057).

MOZLEY, Charles
$335* *Everywhere You Go, Box Hill, 1952,* p. Vincent Brooks, Day and Son, ref. P 51, cond. 3, (10-13-92, Phillips-London, #180), 30¹⁄₁₆ x 39¾ in., (76.3 x 101 cm.), color lithograph (BP 195, DM 491, FR 1667, Y 40,621).
$1554* *Mobile Police Use Shell, 1938,* p. Waterlow and Sons, ref. #526, cond. 1, (10-13-92, Phillips-London, #145), 30¹⁄₁₆ x 45¹⁄₁₆ in., (76.3 x 114.5 cm.), color lithograph (BP 905, DM 2277, FR 7735, Y 188,432).
$1509* *These Men Use Shell, Sightseers, 1938,* p. Waterlow and Sons, ref. #522, cond. 1, creased, (10-13-92, Phillips-London, #141), 29¹⁵⁄₁₆ x 44⅞ in., (76 x 114 cm.), color lithograph (BP 879, DM 2211, FR 7511, Y 182,976).
$1442* *These People Use Shell, Blondes & Brunettes, 1939,* p. Waterlow and Sons, ref. #544, cond. 1, creasing, (10-13-92, Phillips-London, #159, illus.), 29¹⁵⁄₁₆ x 44⅞ in., (76 x 114 cm.), color lithograph (BP 840, DM 2113, FR 7178, Y 174,851).

MUCHA, Alphonse   Czechoslovakian 1860-1939
$2200* *1918-1928 (Rennert/Weill 112), 1928,* by K. Kriz, good cond., Rod Stewart Collection, 1.16m x 78.1m, (11-07-92, Sotheby-NY, #259, illus.), sight 45¾ x 30¾ in., lithograph in colors (BP 1438, DM 3530, FR 11,873, Y 271,538).
$660* *Art Et Decoration, 1902,* cover, A- cond., (08-06-92, Swann, #206, illus.), 15 x 9 in., (38.1 x 22.9 cm.), (BP 345, DM 975, FR 3293, Y 84,184).
$13,800* *The Arts (Rennert/Weill 54), 1898: Four,* time darkened, good cond.?, (03-19-93, Sotheby-NY, #297, illus.), 30 x 20½ in., (76.2 x 52.1 cm.), color lithograph (BP 9249, DM 22,564, FR 76,795, Y 1,600,742).
$20,900* *The Arts, (Les Arts) (Rennert/Weill 54), 1898: Four,* by F. Champenois, good cond., water staining to Poetry, minor losses, Rod Stewart Collection, (11-07-92, Sotheby-NY, #257, illus.), sight 22⅜ x 13¾ in., (56.8 x 34.9 ï),

lithographs in colors (BP 13,665, DM 33,531, FR 112,790, Y 2,579,610).
BI *Les Arts: Danse (Rennert/Weill 54), 1898,* p. by Champenois, good cond.?, est. $4/5,000, (03-19-93, Sotheby-NY, #301, illus.), 22 x 13¾ in., (55.9 x 34.9 cm.), color lithograph.
BI *Aurore, 1899,* Imp. F. Champenois, fairly good cond., restored, (02-12-93, Cheval/Robert, #122, illus.), 21⅝ x 38³⁄₁₆ in., (55 x 97 cm.), poster.
BI *Automne,* est. $5,0/5,500, (12-10-92, Sloan, #3055), 34½ x 21 in., (87.6 x 53.3 cm.), lithograph on linen.
$1430* *"Automne",* s. Alphonse Mucho, (09-12-92, Dunning, #176, illus.), 19 x 29 in., (48.3 x 73.7 cm.), poster (BP 740, DM 2058, FR 6996, Y 177,178).
$3575* *Benedictine (Rennert/Weill 58), 1898,* by F. Champenois, good cond., repaired tears, creases, Rod Stewart Collection, 2.07m x 74.9cm, (11-07-92, Sotheby-NY, #265, illus.), 81⅜ x 29½ in., lithograph in colors (BP 2337, DM 5736, FR 19,293, Y 441,249).
$8250* *Bieres De La Meuse (Rennert/Weill 27), 1897,* by F. Champenois, good cond., minor creasing, repaired tears, Rod Stewart Collection, 1.45m x 95.9cm, (11-07-92, Sotheby-NY, #258, illus.), 57¼ x 37¾ in., lithograph in colors (BP 5394, DM 13,236, FR 44,522, Y 1,018,267).
$4675* *"Biscuits Lefevre Utile" (Jm 126),* F. Champenois Printer 1897, s. S. Stone; Merrill Chase Certificate verso, (02-27-93, Dunning, #1170, illus.), 23½ x 17 in., (59.7 x 43.2 cm.), lithograph in colors (BP 3287, DM 7685, FR 26,117, Y 551,883).
BI *Biscuits Lefevre-Utile (Ennert/Weill 22), 1896,* est. $7/8,000, (05-16-93, Hindman, #448, illus.), 23¾ x 17⅛ in., (60.3 x 43.5 cm.), color lithograph.
BI *Biscuits Lefevre-Utile (R./W.22), 1896,* stone s., p. F. Champenois, small margins, good cond., 1 1/4" tear, tears, staining, creases, soiling, est. $4/6,000, (05-19-93, Butterfield, #1941, illus.), 23¾ x 17⅛ in., (603 x 435 mm.), lithograph in colors on wove.
$247* *Biscuits Madere, Lefevre-Utile,* label, A cond., (08-06-92, Swann, #207, illus.), 11½ x 8½ in., (29.2 x 21.6 cm.), on stiff board (BP 129, DM 365, FR 1233, Y 31,505).
$3300* *Cassan Fils, Variant 1 (Rennert/Weill 11), 1896,* by Cassan Fils, good cond., full loose sheet, (11-07-92, Sotheby-NY, #271, illus.), 21½ x 11½ in., lithograph in colors (BP 2158, DM 5294, FR 17,809, Y 407,307).
$4400* *Champagne Ruinart (Rennert/Weill 16), 1896,* by F. Champenois, good cond., several repairs, Rod Stewart Collection, 1.73m x 58.4cm, (11-07-92, Sotheby-NY, #262, illus.), sight 68¼ x 23 in., lithograph in colors (BP 2877, DM 7059, FR 23,745, Y 543,076).
$15,400* *La Dame Aux Camelias (Camille) (Rennert/Weill 13), 1896,* by F.Champenois, good cond., losses, repairs, minor creasing, staining, holes, rolled, 2.07m x 77.5cm, (11-07-92, Sotheby-NY, #269, illus.), 81½ x 30½ in., lithograph in colors (BP 10,069, DM 24,707, FR 83,108, Y 1,900,765).
$3152* *Ete, 1896,* tear, good cond., lit., (02-04-93, Christie-S. Ken, #134, illus.), 41 x 22 in., (104.1 x 55.9 cm.), color lithograph backed on linen (BP 2200, DM 5190, FR 17,599, Y 392,089).
$5988* *F. Champenois, 1898,* repaired tear, all corners repaired, lit., (02-04-93, Christie-S. Ken, #133, illus.), 29 x 23 in., (73.7 x 58.4 cm.), color lithograph backed on japan (BP 4180, DM 9860, FR 33,434, Y 744,869).
BI *Flirt (R./W. 72), 1900,* s. in stone, p. Champenois, margins, good cond., holes, staining, surface scuffing, linen-backed, est. $2/4000, (09-21-92, Butterfield, #829, illus.), 23⁷⁄₁₆ x 10 in., (594.8 x 254.5 mm.), lithograph in colors on wove.
$2475* *Flirt Bisquits (Rennert/Weill 72), 1899,* by F. Champenois, good cond., Rod Stewart Collection, (11-07-92, Sotheby-NY, #261, illus.), 24¾ x 10¾ in., (62.9 x 27.3 ï), lithograph in colors (BP 1618, DM 3971, FR 13,357, Y 305,480).
$2640* *Flirt, Biscuits Lefevre-Utile, 1900,* Imp. F. Champenois, A cond., (08-06-92, Swann, #205, illus.), sight 24 x 11 in., (61 x 27.9 cm.), (BP 1379, DM 3901, FR 13,174, Y 336,735).

$3520* *Four Seasons, Fall, 1897,* small format, A- cond., (08-06-92, Swann, #203, illus.), sight 12¼ x 5¾ in., (31.1 x 14.6 cm.), (BP 1839, DM 5201, FR 17,565, Y 448,980).

$7700* *Hamlet (Rennert/Weill 63), 1899,* by F. Champenois, good cond., creasing, repaired tears, Rod Stewart Collection, 2.08m x 74.6cm, (11-07-92, Sotheby-NY, #263, illus.), sight 82 x 29⅜ in., lithograph in colors (BP 5034, DM 12,354, FR 41,554, Y 950,383).

$20,900* *Heures Du Jour (The Times Of The Day) (Rennert/Weill 62), 1899: Four,* by F. Champenois, good cond., Rod Stewart Collection, 1.04m x 37.5cm, (11-07-92, Sotheby-NY, #264, illus.), each 41 x 14¾ in., lithographs in colors (BP 13,665, DM 33,531, FR 112,790, Y 2,579,610).

$6900* *Heures Du Jour, The Times Of The Day (Rennert/Weill 62), 1899: SuiteOf Four,* p. by F. Champenois, (03-19-93, Sotheby-NY, #298, illus.), 44½ x 33¼ in., (113 x 84.5 cm.), color lithograph (BP 4625, DM 11,282, FR 38,397, Y 800,371).

$1373* *Imprimerie Cassan Fils (Bridges A24), 1897,* p. Cassan Fils, margins, damp-staining, soiling, discoloration, creased, (06-30-93, Sotheby-London, #567, illus.), 63¾ x 23½ in., (161.9 x 59.7 cm.), color lithograph on two sheets (BP 920, DM 2342, FR 7900, Y 147,112).

BI *Job (R./W. 51), 1898,* s. in stone, p. F. Champenois, margins, good cond.?, paper loss in image, light-staining, crease in image, linen-backed, est. $4/6000, (09-21-92, Butterfield, #831, illus.), 55½ x 37¼ in., (141 x 94.6 cm.), lithograph in colors on wove.

$5225* *Job (Rennert/Weill 51), 1898,* by F. Champenois, good cond., minor creasing, repaired tears, Rod Stewart Collection, (11-07-92, Sotheby-NY, #260, illus.), 59¼ x 39¼ in., lithograph in colors (BP 3416, DM 8383, FR 28,198, Y 644,902).

BI *"Job", 1898,* est. $8/10,000, (12-12-92, Christie-NY, #439, illus.), 53 x 37½ in., (134.6 x 95.3 cm.), lithograph in colors.

$5212* *L'Art Enseigne Au Peuple Par Les Projections,* p. F. Champebois, creases, (05-07-93, Christie-S. Ken, #137, illus.), 17½ x 24 in., (44.5 x 61 cm.), color lithograph (BP 3300, DM 8240, FR 27,768, Y 573,882).

$695* *L'Art Photographique, Mars 1900,* magazine cover design, creases, (05-07-93, Christie-S. Ken, #136, illus.), 12½ x 18 in., (31.8 x 45.7 cm.), color lithograph (BP 440, DM 1099, FR 3703, Y 76,525).

$1606* *L'Ete. Un Des 4 Panneaux Des Saisons 1896,* Imp. F. Champenois, fairly good cond., repainted, (02-12-93, Cheval/Robert, #121), 39⅜ x 20¹⁄₁₆ in., (100 x 51 cm.), poster (BP 1131, DM 2663, FR 9012, Y 193,681).

$605* *Lefevre-Utile, Gaufrettes Vanille,* label, A cond., (08-06-92, Swann, #208, illus.), 7 x 7 in., (17.8 x 17.8 cm.), (BP 316, DM 894, FR 3019, Y 77,168).

$3782* *Lefevre-Utile, Sarah Bernhardt, 1904,* repaired tears, creases, nicks, losses, lit., (02-04-93, Christie-S. Ken, #136, illus.), 27 x 20 in., (68.6 x 50.8 cm.), color lithograph backed on linen (BP 2640, DM 6228, FR 21,117, Y 470,457).

BI *Lorenzaccio (R./W. 20), 1896,* s. in stone, p. Champenois, margins, repaired tears, handling creases, time/light-staining, est. $15/2000, (09-21-92, Butterfield, #830), 38¹¹⁄₁₆ x 14¼ in., (982.8 x 362.6 mm.), lithograph in colors on cream wove backed w/Japan.

$4675* *Lorenzaccio (Rennert/Weill 20, Variant 1), 1896,* good cond., repaired tears, creasing, abrasions, Rod Stewart Collection, 2.04m x 70.5cm, (11-07-92, Sotheby-NY, #267, illus.), 80¼ x 27¾ in., lithograph in colors (BP 3057, DM 7500, FR 25,229, Y 577,018).

$3782* *Lorenzaccio, 1896,* tears, repairs, nicks, lit., (02-04-93, Christie-S. Ken, #135, illus.), 39 x 15 in., (99.1 x 38.1 cm.), color lithograph backed on linen (BP 2640, DM 6228, FR 21,117, Y 470,457).

$8250* *Medee (Rennert/Weill 53), 1898,* by F. Champenois, good cond., repaired tears, soiling, Rod Stewart Collection, 2.07m x 73cm, (11-07-92, Sotheby-NY, #268, illus.), 81⅝ x 28¾ in., lithograph in colors (BP 5394, DM 13,236, FR 44,522, Y 1,018,267).

$2588* *Menus Publies Par Moet & Chandon (M./H. Pl. 29-31), 1900: Ten,* complete suite, p. F. Champenois, each in good cond., light-staining,includes title page/envelope framed together, (05-19-93, Butterfield, #1942, illus.), each 5½ x 3½ in., (140 x 89 mm.), postcard lithographs in color (BP 1680, DM 4207, FR 14,173, Y 286,505).

$5750* *Monaco Monte-Carlo (Rennart-Weill 31), 1897,* by F. Champenois, good cond., loose, time darkening, tears, losses, (06-10-93, Sotheby-NY, #469, illus.), 43⅝ x 30 in., (110.8 x 76.2 cm.), color lithograph (BP 3761, DM 9363, FR 31,524, Y 610,339).

BI *Monaco, Monte-Carlo, 1897,* plate s., est. $10/15,000, (03-25-93, Christie-E, #207, illus.), overall 44 x 30½ in., (111.8 x 77.5 cm.), color lithograph.

$2841* *"Monaco-Monte-Carlo" (Mucha Graphics, 70; Brno. 29, Rizzoli, 6 et Fruhe Plakat 11, 639),* s. Mucha 1897, (03-16-93, Encans, #133), 43⁵⁄₁₆ x 29¹⁵⁄₁₆ in., (110 x 76 cm.), color lithograph (BP 1962, DM 4724, FR 16,051, Y 332,203, C$ 3552).

BI *Monaco. Monte-Carlo (Mucha-Henderson 1973, Abb. S. 54), 1897,* est. DM 2,500, (12-05-92, Bassenge, #7612A), 43⁵⁄₁₆ x 29¹⁵⁄₁₆ in., (110 x 76 cm.), color lithograph.

$2750* *Monaco/Montecarlo (Rennert Weill 31), 1897,* by F. Champenois, creases, folds, restorations, laid down on canvas, (11-06-92, Sotheby-Arcade, #140, illus.), 42⅜ x 27⅝ in., (107.6 x 70.2 cm.), lithograph in colors (BP 1798, DM 4391, FR 14,841, Y 339,422).

$1760* *"Paris 1900",* (09-09-92, Doyle, #64A), 38 x 24 in., (96.5 x 61 cm.), color lithograph and poster (BP 889, DM 2489, FR 8457, Y 216,349).

$330* *La Plume, 1898,* cover, Vaugirard G. de M & Cie, A-cond., (08-06-92, Swann, #204, illus.), 10 x 7 in., (25.4 x 17.8 cm.), (BP 172, DM 488, FR 1647, Y 42,092).

$1330* *Poetry (Renneart/Weill 54), 1898,* from Les Arts, imp. A. Champenois, (12-04-92, AB Stockholm, #7109, illus.), 22⁵⁄₁₆ x 13½ in., (56.7 x 34.3 cm.), sh 23⅛ x 15¹⁄₁₆ in., (56.7 x 34.3 cm.), lithograph in colors (BP 853, DM 2118, FR 7185, Y 166,042, SK 9020).

$2200* *"La Primavera, Polyanthus", 1899,* p. by F. Champenois, s., d. Mucha 99, good cond., (10-09-92, Skinner, #197, illus.), 28¼ x 11⅛ in., (71.8 x 28.3 cm.), lithographic poster in colors on paper (BP 1306, DM 3277, FR 11,111, Y 268,293).

$880* *La Primevere Et La Plume (The Primrose And The Quill) (Rennert/Weill 64, Variant 2), Paris, 1899,* by J. Royer, margins trimmed, losses, staining, Rod Stewart Collection, (11-07-92, Sotheby-NY, #266, illus.), 21¼ x 9⅛ in., (54 x 23.2 ï), lithograph in colors (BP 575, DM 1412, FR 4749, Y 108,615).

$7700* *"Reverie", c. 1896,* p. by F. Champenois, (12-11-92, DuMouchelle, #1303, illus.), 25¼ x 18¾ in., (64.1 x 47.6 cm.), color lithograph (BP 4937, DM 12,132, FR 41,577, Y 952,852).

$3575* *Le Rubis (Ruby) (Rennert/Weill 73), 1900,* by F. Champenois, slight staining, losses, laid down on paper, trimmed, (11-07-92, Sotheby-NY, #273, illus.), 38¾ x 15¼ in., (98.4 x 38.7 ï), lithograph in colors (BP 2337, DM 5736, FR 19,293, Y 441,249).

$4255* *Les Saisons, "Spring", "Summer" and "Winter" (Rennart-Weill 74, Variant 1), 1900: Three,* by F. Champenois, good cond., laid down, faded, tears, (06-10-93, Sotheby-NY, #470, illus.), 27½ x 12¼ in., (69.9 x 31.1 cm.), color lithograph on satin (BP 2783, DM 6929, FR 23,328, Y 451,651).

$2750* *Salonbo,* margins trimmed, stains on border, (11-07-92, Sotheby-NY, #270, illus.), 15½ x 11¾ in., lithograph in colors, loose sheet (BP 1798, DM 4412, FR 14,841, Y 339,422).

$863* *La Samaritaine,* Maitres de l'Affiche blindstamp, p. Chaix, margins, apparently good condition, light-staining, (03-31-93, Butterfield, #5247), 14¾ x 5⅜ in., (37.5 x 13.7 cm.), lithograph printed in colors on wove (BP 571, DM 1388, FR 4716, Y 99,241).

$7475* *"La Samaritaine", Sarah Bernhardt As Photina, 1897,* plate s., (03-27-93, Christie-NY, #106, illus.), 68½ x 22½ in., (174 x 57.2 cm.), color lithograph (BP 5022, DM 12,194, FR 41,459, Y 869,995).

$2530* *Sarah Bernhardt (Rennart-Weill 21, Variant 2), 1897,* by F. Champenois, good cond., loose, time darkened, (06-10-93, Sotheby-NY, #471, illus.), 30³⁄₁₆ x 20⅞ in., (76.7 x 53 cm.), color lithograph (BP 1655, DM 4120, FR 13,871, Y 268,549).

$4025* *Summer (Rennert/Weill 18), 1898,* edit. F. Champenois, laid down, time darkened, margins trimmed, staining, (03-19-93, Sotheby-NY, #300, illus.), 43 x 22¾ in., (109.2 x 57.8 cm.), (BP 2698, DM 6581, FR 22,398, Y 466,883).

$3575* *La Topaze (Topaz) (Rennert/Weill 73), 1900,* by F. Champenois, staining, minor creases, small hole, (11-07-92, Sotheby-NY, #272, illus.), 38¾ x 15¼ in., (98.4 x 38.7 ï), lithograph in colors (BP 2337, DM 5736, FR 19,293, Y 441,249).

$2420* *Voluptuous Woman, c. 1900,* (04-07-93, Swann, #522, illus.), 4½ x 3¼ in., photograph, gold chloride printing-out paper (BP 1599, DM 3914, FR 13,246, Y 274,938).

MUCHA, Alphonse (attrib.) Czechoslovakian 1860-1939

$301* *Tournee Sarah Bernhardt: L'Aiglon, 1900,* Imp. F. Champenais, good cond., (02-12-93, Cheval/Robert, #172), 40⁹⁄₁₆ x 27¹⁵⁄₁₆ in., (103 x 71 cm.), poster (BP 212, DM 499, FR 1689, Y 36,300).

MUDD, James

$230* *"Alfred Lord Tennyson", 1857,* (05-23-93, Butterfield, #3549, illus.), 3½ x 2¼ in., photograph, albumen print, remounted to a modern mount (BP 150, DM 376, FR 1266, Y 25,423).

MUDD, John P. 1888-1955

BI *Locomotive Study, Philadelphia, c. 1931,* s., t., credit stamp, exhib. labels, est. $1,2/1,500, (10-13-92, Christie-NY, #320, illus.), 12¼ x 9¾ in., (31.1 x 24.8 cm.), photograph, gelatin silver print.

MUEHL, Otto b. 1925

$3465* *12 Aktionen, 1971-1972: Twelve,* s., (11-28-92, Schoppmann, #670), 40⁹⁄₁₆ x 28¾ in., (103 x 73 cm.), color serigraph (BP 2287, DM 5520, FR 18,740, Y 431,238).

$2887* *Aktionen 1964-1966, 1984: Eight,* s., (11-28-92, Schoppmann, #668, illus.), 32½ x 26⁹⁄₁₆ in., (82.5 x 67.5 cm.), color serigraph and photograph (BP 1906, DM 4599, FR 15,614, Y 359,303).

$2887* *Aktionen 1966-1970, 1984: Eight,* s., num., (11-28-92, Schoppmann, #669), 32½ x 26⁹⁄₁₆ in., (82.5 x 67.5 cm.), 1 serigraph, 7 photograph (BP 1906, DM 4599, FR 15,614, Y 359,303).

MUELLER

BI *Le Livre Prefere,* s., #5/50, full margins, good cond., mat staining, paper partially split, tears, surface soiling, tape remains, notations, est. $5/700, (05-19-93, Butterfield, #2086), 16⅛ x 21¼ in., (410 x 540 mm.), aquatint and roulette in colors on Arches laid.

MUELLER, Otto German 1874-1930

$5642* *Drei Madchen Im Profil (K. 111 c), 1921,* pub. Arndt Beyer, (12-01-92, Karl/Faber, #1038, illus.), 11⁵⁄₁₆ x 15⅜ in., (28.7 x 39 cm.), lithograph on simili-Japan (BP 3728, DM 8993, FR 30,646, Y 702,440).

$17,655* *Drei Madchen Im Profil (Karsch 111 b), 1920,* blue chalk s., Kreis graphischer Kunstler und Sammler, portfolio 1, Beyer, (06-10-93, Hauswedell/Nolt, #667), image 11¼ x 15⁵⁄₁₆ in., (28.6 x 38.9 cm.), lithograph on handmade (BP 11,548, DM 28,749, FR 96,793, Y 1,874,005).

$9384* *"Drei Madchen Vor Dem Spiegel" (Karsch 124), c. 1922,* s., num., (11-28-92, Grisebach, #157, illus.), 13⅞ x 10¹⁄₁₆ in., (35.3 x 25.5 cm.), lithograph on soft thick handmade (BP 6194, DM 14,950, FR 50,752, Y 1,167,890).

$21,262* *Funf Gelbe Akte Am Wasser (K. 156 c), 1921,* mono., pub. Hyperion Verlag, (06-08-93, Karl/Faber, #1137, illus.), approx. 13³⁄₁₆ x 17⁵⁄₁₆ in., (33.5 x 44 cm.), color lithograph (BP 13,977, DM 34,499, FR 116,186, Y 2,258,311).

BI *Funf Gelbe Akte Am Wasser (Karsch 156a), 1921,* s., margins, creases, other minor defects, very good cond., est. BP 20/30,000, (05-20-93, Christie-London, #472, illus.), image 13⅛ x 17¼ in., (33.3 x 43.8 cm.), lithograph in colors on Japan w/wirelines.

$15,765* *Gegabelter Baum Und Badendes Madchen (K. 77), c. 1919,* s., stained, creases, old mounting traces, (12-01-92, Karl/Faber, #1036, illus.), 12 x 16¾ in., (30.5 x 42.5 cm.), lithograph on smooth paper (BP 10,416, DM 25,128, FR 85,633, Y 1,962,774).

$4379* *Knabe Zwischen Blattpflanzen (Karsch 2, II), 1912,* estate stamp, prov., (06-10-93, Hauswedell/Nolt, #671, illus.), image 11 x 14¾ in., (28 x 37.5 cm.), woodcut on Japan-like paper (BP 2864, DM 7131, FR 24,008, Y 464,813).

$14,935* *Madchen Auf Der Liege (K. 93 b), 1919: Three,* black chalk s., num., (12-01-92, Karl/Faber, #1037, illus.), 9⅝ x 13¾ in., (24.5 x 35 cm.), lithograph on copper print cardboard (BP 9868, DM 23,805, FR 81,124, Y 1,859,437).

$1415* *Madchen Zwischen Blattpflanzen (K. 3IIA), 1912,* 2nd (final) state, p. Maschka Mueller, Eugen Meyerhofer after 1945; stamp, i. verso, margins, tape, backed, (12-01-92, Christie-London, #465), L. 10¹⁵⁄₁₆ x 14⁹⁄₁₆ in., (278 x 370 mm.), woodcut on simili Japan (BP 935, DM 2255, FR 7686, Y 176,170).

$9887* *Madchen-Halbakt Im Profil (Karsch 129), 1922,* s., (06-10-93, Hauswedell/Nolt, #670, illus.), image 8¹¹⁄₁₆ x 6⅞ in., (22 x 17.5 cm.), lithograph on Japan-like paper (BP 6467, DM 16,100, FR 54,205, Y 1,049,464).

$3225* *Polnische Familie (Judenfamilie, Polen) (Karsch 114c), 1920-21,* second (final) state, inits., pub. in Die Schaffenden 3. Jahrgang, 1. Mappe, by P. Westheim, blindstamp, creasing, good cond., (05-20-93, Christie-London, #475, illus.), image 10¼ x 7½ in., (26 x 19.1 cm.), sheet 16 x 12¼ in., (26 x 19.1 cm.), lithograph on wove (BP 2070, DM 5203, FR 17,527, Y 356,117).

$2825* *Polnische Familie (Karsch 114 II c), 1920-1921,* mono., from Die Schaffenden, III. Jahrg., portfolio I, Westheim, blindstamp, (06-10-93, Hauswedell/Nolt, #669, illus.), image 10¼ x 7½ in., (26 x 19 cm.), lithograph on wove (BP 1848, DM 4600, FR 15,488, Y 299,862).

BI *Polnische Familie (Karsch 114/II c), 1920-21,* mono., blindstamp, est. DM 12,000, (12-05-92, Bassenge, #7503, illus.), 10¼ x 7½ in., (26 x 19 cm.), lithograph on copper print paper.

$18,313* *Selbstbildnis Nach Rechts (2) (K. 140b), 1921-2,* crayon s., #XXX/XXX, pub. Otto Mueller-Zehn Lithographien, 1922, margins, foxing, discoloration, very good cond., (12-01-92, Christie-London, #464, illus.), L. 15½ x 11⅞ in., (393 x 302 mm.), lithograph on simili-Japan (BP 12,100, DM 29,189, FR 99,473, Y 2,280,005).

$1463* *Ein Sitzendes Und Ein Knieendes Unter Blattern (Karsch 110 c. Sohn HDO 108-13), 1920,* (12-12-92, Wachholtz, #241), 6⅞ x 9¼ in., (17.5 x 23.5 cm.), lithograph on wove cardboard (BP 935, DM 2299, FR 7836, Y 180,997).

$3249* *Stehender Knabe Mit Zwei Madchen (Drei Akte) (Karsch 67), 1917,* 2nd version, (06-10-93, Hauswedell/Nolt, #665, illus.), image 12¹¹⁄₁₆ x 9¹³⁄₁₆ in., (32.3 x 25 cm.), lithograph on wove (BP 2125, DM 5291, FR 17,813, Y 344,868).

$5675* *Stehendes, Sitzendes Und Badendes Madchen Am Baum (Karsch 106), 1920,* s., (06-05-93, Bassenge, #6366), 10¹⁄₁₆ x 7⅜ in., (25.6 x 18.7 cm.), lithograph on handmade (BP 3736, DM 9201, FR 31,011, Y 608,775).

BI *Stehendes, Sitzendes Und Badendes Madchen Am Baum (Karsch 106), 1920/21,* i., est. DM 7,000, (05-26-93, Lempertz, #388A), 13¹⁵⁄₁₆ x 10⁷⁄₁₆ in., (35.5 x 26.5 cm.), lithograph on machine-made.

$4611* *Van Zantens Gluckliche Zeit (Karsch 1), c. 1912,* s., (06-05-93, Bassenge, #6364, illus.), 6¾ x 4³⁄₁₆ in., (17.1 x 10.7 cm.), woodcut (BP 3035, DM 7476, FR 25,197, Y 494,636).

$8458* *Waldsee Mit Drei Badenden Und Einem Sitzenden Madchen (Karsch 112 b),1918,* relief stamp, (05-26-93, Lempertz, #388, illus.), 16⁹⁄₁₆ x 12⅝ in., (42 x 32 cm.), lithograph on wove (BP 5472, DM 13,800, FR 46,447, Y 918,948).

$21,500* *Waldsee Mit Drei Badenden Und Einem Sitzenden Madchen 2 (Landschaft Mit Vier Badenden) (Karsch 112a), 1918,* s., pub. in Die Schaffenden 1. Jahrgang, 1. Mappe, by P. Westheim, 1919, blindstamp, margins, deckle edge, foxmarks, creasing, tape, (05-20-93, Christie-London, #473, illus.), image 13 x 10¾ in., (33 x 27.3 cm.), sheet 16¼ x 12 in., (33 x 27.3 cm.), lithograph w/extensive hand-coloring in yellow crayon and green watercolor on Japan (BP 13,800, DM 34,689, FR 116,848, Y 2,374,117).

BI *"Zigeunerfamilie Am Planwagen" (Karsch 167/III), 1926-1927,* sheet 8 of "Zigeunermappe", est. DM 50/60,000,

(11-27-92, Grisebach, #20, illus.), 26¹⁵⁄₁₆ x 19¾ in., (68.5 x 50.2 cm.), color lithograph w/colored chalk overworked, on machinemade.

$24,892* *Zigeunermadonna (K. 168 A), 1926-27,* s., (12-01-92, Karl/Faber, #1040, illus.), sh 27³⁄₁₆ x 20¼ in., (69 x 51.5 cm.), lithograph (BP 16,447, DM 39,675, FR 135,209, Y 3,099,104).

$4300* *Zirkuspaar (Karsch 113c), 1920-21,* inits., pub. Die Schaffenden 3. Jahrgang, 1. Mappe, by P. Westheim, 1921, blindstamp, creases, good cond., (05-20-93, Christie-London, #474, illus.), image 10¼ x 7¼ in., (26 x 18.4 cm.), sheet 16 x 12¼ in., (26 x 18.4 cm.), lithograph on wove (BP 2760, DM 6938, FR 23,370, Y 474,823).

$13,418* *Zirkuspaar (Variete) (Karsch 113 b), 1920-21,* s., from Die Schaffenden, III. Jahrg., portfolio 1, blindstamp, (06-10-93, Hauswedell/Nolt, #668, illus.), image 10⁵⁄₁₆ x 7³⁄₈ in., (26.2 x 18.8 cm.), lithograph worked over w/color chalk and watercolor (BP 8777, DM 21,850, FR 73,564, Y 1,424,265).

BI *Zwei Badende Im Bach (Karsch 151), c. 1922,* s., pub. Galerie Nierendorf, margins, mount/backboard-stained, tear,tape, est. 6/8,000, (06-30-93, Sotheby-London, #572, illus.), 9⁷⁄₈ x 6¾ in., (251 x 171 mm.), lithograph in black and ochre on a fibrous wove.

$18,032* *Zwei Madchen-Halbakte (Karsch 121 b), 1920,* num., mono., (11-21-92, Lempertz, #303, illus.), 17⅛ x 13⅜ in., (43.5 x 34 cm.), lithograph on factory-made paper (BP 11,873, DM 28,750, FR 96,842, Y 2,242,507).

$10,372* *Zwei Sitzende Madchen (K. 147, Variante A), 1921-22: Two,* s., num., mount stained, glue, prov., (12-01-92, Karl/Faber, #1039, illus.), 11⁷⁄₁₆ x 15⅜ in., (29 x 39 cm.), lithograph (BP 6853, DM 16,532, FR 56,339, Y 1,291,335).

$6271* *Zwei Stehende Und Ein Sitzendes Madchen (Zwei Stehende Und Ein Hockender Akt) (Karsch 128), 1922-5,* wide margins, excell. cond., (05-20-93, Christie-London, #476, illus.), image 15⅛ x 11⅞ in., (38.4 x 30.2 cm.), sheet 21 x 17 in., (38.4 x 30.2 cm.), lithograph on beige wove (BP 4025, DM 10,118, FR 34,082, Y 692,469).

BI *"Zwei Zigeunermadchen Im Wohnraum" (Karsch 163/III), 1926-1927,* s., sheet 4 of series "Zigeunermappe", est. DM 65/80,000, (11-27-92, Grisebach, #19, illus.), 27¹¹⁄₁₆ x 19⅜ in., (70.3 x 49.2 cm.), color lithograph on Japan.

MUELLER, R.   German 19th/20th cent.
$138* *Post Mortem,* s. illegibly, num. 11/17, good cond., (11-21-92, Bakker, #159), plate 6⅜ x 16⅜ in., (16.2 x 41.6 cm.), etching (BP 91, DM 220, FR 741, Y 17,162).

MUHL, Roger   French b. 1929
$60* *"Paysage",* #54/150, s., (04-04-93, Pescheteau, #271), 26¾ x 21¼ in., (68 x 54 cm.), color lithograph on Arches (BP 40, DM 96, FR 328, Y 6831).

MUKY
$440* *Cagney And Jean Cramer Dancing In Western Gear In The Film "The Oklahoma Kid", 1938: Six,* James Cagney Estate, (09-30-92, Doyle, #610), photograph (BP 248, DM 624, FR 2110, Y 52,802).

MULDERS, Marc   20th cent.
$169* *Geseling, 1989,* s., t., d., #I/IV, good cond.?, prov., (12-09-92, Sotheby-Amstrdm, #614), sheet 15⅞ x 23⅜ in., (403 x 593 mm.), photograph, on photographic paper (BP 108, DM 265, FR 905, Y 20,955, G 299).

$248* *Handschoen Met Corpus, 1989,* s., t., d., #II/IV, good cond.?, prov., (12-09-92, Sotheby-Amstrdm, #615, illus.), sheet 14¾ x 23¼ in., (375 x 590 mm.), photograph, on photographic paper (BP 158, DM 389, FR 1328, Y 30,750, G 437).

MULLER
$412* *Two Peacocks,* A cond., (08-06-92, Swann, #209, illus.), 25¼ x 61½ in., (64.1 x 156.2 cm.), (BP 215, DM 609, FR 2056, Y 52,551).

MULLER, Albert   1897-1926
$1985* *Eingang Zum Sertigtal, Mit Der Alten Knochenmuhle (M. Kornfeld 39/c),1925,* num., 1968, estate stamp, (06-23-93, Kornfeld, #606), color woodcut on Japan (BP 1349, DM 3359, FR 11,298, Y 216,254, SF 2990).

MULLER, Alfredo
$1887* *Can-Can Dancer,* crayon s., full margins, good cond., discoloration, tear, (06-30-93, Sotheby-London, #574, illus.), 15½ x 11¾ in., (394 x 298 mm.), etching and hand-coloring on Auvergne a la main laid (BP 1265, DM 3218, FR 10,857, Y 202,186).

BI *Fillettes Au Piano (Cat. Livorno 6), 1897,* whole margins, (06-11-93, Picard, #141), 25¹⁵⁄₁₆ x 19⁵⁄₁₆ in., (660 x 490 mm.), etching and aquatint in brown-black on Hollande laid.

$721* *Girl With Cat, 1897,* s., margins, good cond., creases, (06-30-93, Sotheby-London, #575, illus.), sh 19⅞ x 19⅛ in., (505 x 486 mm.), etching w/hand-coloring on wove (BP 483, DM 1230, FR 4148, Y 77,253).

BI *Interior (Q. 3), 1897,* watermark, s., margins, good cond., staining, soiling, surface scuffing, creases, est. $8/1,000, (05-19-93, Butterfield, #1943), 15⁹⁄₁₆ x 15½ in., (395 x 394 mm.), etching and drypoint in colors on wove.

$858* *Ladies Opposite Moulin Rouge,* s., margins, good cond., discoloration, scuff marks w/in image, (06-30-93, Sotheby-London, #576, illus.), sh 19⅞ x 19⅛ in., (505 x 486 mm.), etching w/aquatint and hand-coloring (BP 575, DM 1463, FR 4937, Y 91,932).

BI *Peacocks, 1899,* s. in stone, margins trimmed unevenly/ into image, good cond., tears,staining, handling creases, surface soiling, est. $7/900, (09-21-92, Butterfield, #832), 23 x 58½ in., (58.4 x 148.6 cm.), lithograph in colors on wove.

BI *Place Blanche (Q. 47), 1904,* s., margins, good cond., staining, tears, paper losses, creases, scuffing, surface soiling, est. $1,2/1,400, (05-19-93, Butterfield, #1944), 26⅛ x 16⅛ in., (664 x 410 mm.), etching and aquatint in colors on wove.

MULLER, Alfredo   French 1869-1939
$176* *"La Grande Cascade De Saint Cloud", 1905,* s., pub. Sagot, drystamp, very good cond., (10-31-92, Cleveland, #319), 33¼ x 17½ in., (84.5 x 44.5 cm.), color aquatint (BP 113, DM 271, FR 919, Y 21,801).

BI *"La Viosne A Pontoise" (Wutzer 16), 1903,* s., red stamp, excell. cond., est. $4/600, (05-15-93, Cleveland, #416), 17½ x 11⅜ in., (44.5 x 28.9 cm.), color aquatint.

MULLER, Herman Jansz   c. 1540-1617
$438* *Die Zehn Gebote (Hollstein 17-26 III),* after M. van Heemskerck, (06-10-93, Hauswedell/Nolt, #122), engraving on hand-made (BP 286, DM 713, FR 2401, Y 46,492).

MULLER, J.   1571-1628
$125* *Theodorus Coornhertius Amstelredamus (McGee, Corn. Corneliszoon van Haarlem, p.330. Hollstein 83),* after Cornelis Corneliszoon van Haarlem, backed, 2nd state of 5, (06-09-93, Bubb Kuyper, #2060, illus.), 7³⁄₁₆ x 5 in., (18.3 x 12.7 cm.), copper engraving (BP 82, DM 204, FR 688, Y 13,294, G 230).

MULLER, J.F.
BI *Vallee De Joux, c. 1920,* folds, staining, est. BP 7/900, (02-04-93, Christie-S. Ken, #17, illus.), 39½ x 27½ in., (100.3 x 69.9 cm.), color lithograph backed on linen.

MULLER, J.G.
$660* *The Battle At Bunker's Hill Near Boston, 1798,* after John Trumbell, thread margins, discoloration, multiple repairs, good cond., (06-11-93, Doyle, #66), 20 x 30 in., (508 x 762 mm.), engraving (BP 434, DM 1073, FR 3616, Y 70,027).

MULLER, J.J.
$1955* *Albert Einstein,* s., inits. J.J.M., pristine cond., (06-14-93, Sotheby-NY, #149, illus.), 10 x 7¾ in., (25.4 x 19.7 cm.), etching in sepia (BP 1280, DM 3182, FR 10,695, Y 205,725).

MULLER, Jan
$16,711* *The Creation Of The World (Holl. 1-7): Set Of Seven,* second (final) state, margins, rustmark, surface dirt, good cond., (12-03-92, Sotheby-London, #83, illus.), engravings on paper w/watermark (BP 10,780, DM 26,279, FR 89,699, Y 2,079,258).

MULLER, Jan Harmensz.   1571-1628
BI *"Die Schopfung" (B./Strauss 35, 37, 38 and 40): Four,*
    partially laid down, est. SC 12/13,000, (11-11-92, Dor-
    otheum, #310, illus.), engraving.

MULLER, Otto   German 1874-1930
$2291* *Polnische Familie (Karsch 114/II/c), 1920-1921,* pencil
    mono., (06-23-93, Kornfeld, #610), lithograph on wove
    (BP 1556, DM 3876, FR 13,039, Y 249,591, SF 3450).

MULLER, Richard   1874-1954
$166* *Maus, Eine Nuss Knabbernd, 1910,* s., (12-01-92, Karl/
    Faber, #1041), 2¾ x 7⅞ in., (7 x 20 cm.), etching on
    simili-Japan (BP 110, DM 265, FR 902, Y 20,667).

MULLER, Z.
$28* *Hunter Blowing Horn,* s., (10-16-92, DuMouchelle,
    #2497), 11½ x 17½ in., (29.2 x 44.5 cm.), etching (BP
    17, DM 41, FR 140, Y 3343).

MULLERS, Rims
$110* *Various Scenes Of Frankfurt: Three,* s., wide, good cond.,
    (05-22-93, Weschler, #211), first and second 6¾ x 5 in.,
    (17.1 x 12.7 cm.), third 5 x 7 in., (17.1 x 12.7 cm.),
    etching and drypoint on laid (BP 71, DM 179, FR 602,
    Y 12,128).

MULLICAN, Matt   American b. 1951
BI *Untitled, 1988: Sixteen,* complete suite, first s., d., #45/
    64, rest init., d., #45/64, pub. Cal Solway Gallery, full
    margins, good cond., crease, orginal portfolio box, est.
    $6/7,000, (05-15-93, Sotheby-NY, #1114, illus.), each
    sheet 22 x 15⅛ in., (55.9 x 38.4 cm.), etching and aqua-
    tints in colors on Magnani Incisioni paper.

MULLINS, William J.   1860-1917
BI *The River Road, c. 1900,* stamped mono., est. $8/1,200,
    (10-13-92, Christie-NY, #41, illus.), 2½ x 4¾ in., (6.4 x
    12.1 cm.), photograph, gelatin silver print.
BI *Tree Study, 1895,* sig., photog.'s handstamp, est. $8/1,200,
    (10-14-92, Swann, #212, illus.), 6 x 3¾ in., (15.2 x 9.5
    cm.), photograph, carbon print.

MULVANEY, John   American 1844-1906
$825* *Famous American Frontiersman, 1877,* proof before let-
    ters, losses, water staining, (11-28-92, Dunning, #1014),
    22 x 29 in., (55.9 x 73.7 cm.), chromolithograph (BP
    545, DM 1314, FR 4462, Y 102,676).

MUMPRECHT, Walter Rudolf   b. 1918
$362* *Murten, 1476,* 15/15, s., d., (10-14-92, Germann, #576),
    14⅝ x 22¹⁄₁₆ in., (372 x 560 mm.), color etching (BP
    212, DM 530, FR 1797, Y 43,868, SF 472).

MUNAKATA, Shiko   Japanese b. 1903
$605* *Bust Of A Woman,* s., sealed, (03-25-93, Boos, #264,
    illus.), 3½ x 5¾ in., (8.9 x 14.6 cm.), woodblock print
    (BP 411, DM 994, FR 3380, Y 70,876).
$495* *A Man Walking With A Cane Wearing A Hat And
    Glasses,* s., sealed, (03-25-93, Boos, #263, illus.), 5¾ x 3
    in., (14.6 x 7.6 cm.), woodblock print, monochrome (BP
    336, DM 813, FR 2765, Y 57,990).

MUNCH, Edvard   Norwegian 1863-1944
BI *Abend (An Strand; Melancholie) (Sch. 144 bII), 1901,*
    margins, creases, stains, est. BP 25/35,000, (12-01-92,
    Christie-London, #466, illus.), L. 17⅛ x 23⁷⁄₁₆ in., (435
    x 595 mm.), sheet 17⅛ x 23⁷⁄₁₆ in., (435 x 595 mm.),
    woodcut in colors (black, pale brown, green and grey)
    on thin Japan.
BI *Abend (Melancholie Am Strand) (S. 144), 1901,* s., good
    but damaged impression, paper splits, restorations at
    edgesof image and in margins, est. BP 10/12,000, (12-
    03-92, Sotheby-London, #466, illus.), 14½ x 17¾ in.,
    (367 x 452 mm.), woodcut in 5 colors from 2 blocks (2
    blues, grey, indigo and flesh) on thin Japan.
BI *Der Alte Schiffer (Schiefler 124 II), 1899,* s., t., very
    rare, est. DM 18,000, (12-05-92, Bassenge, #7504), 17⅛
    x 13¹⁵⁄₁₆ in., (43.5 x 35.5 cm.), woodcut on paper.
$17,905* *Anziehung (S. 65), 1896,* full margins, good cond.,
    rubbed patch, stain, marks, prov., (12-03-92, Sotheby-
    London, #465, illus.), 18½ x 14¼ in., (472 x 362 mm.),
    lithograph on soft wove (BP 11,550, DM 28,157, FR
    96,108, Y 2,227,821).

$32,486* *Anziehung Von Mann Und Weib (Schiefler 66), 1896,*
    (06-10-93, Hauswedell/Nolt, #679, illus.), image 15⅞ x
    25¼ in., (40.4 x 64.2 cm.), color lithograph (BP 21,249,
    DM 52,900, FR 178,103, Y 3,448,254).
BI *"Asche (Nach Dem Sundenfall)" (Schiefler 120), 1899,* s.,
    est. DM 30/40,000, (06-04-93, Grisebach, #17, illus.),
    13⅞ x 17⅞ in., (35.3 x 45.4 cm.), lithograph on grey
    wove, laid down on cardboard.
$167,112* *Auf Der Brucke (S. 380), 1912,* s., i. Handkolert Tryk
    1913, watermark, margins, good cond., staining, defects,
    pinholes, (12-03-92, Sotheby-London, #463, illus.), 15½ x
    20⅞ in., (394 x 530 mm.), lithograph in black, exten-
    sively hand-colored w/watercolor on wove (BP 107,800,
    DM 262,796, FR 897,005, Y 20,792,833).
$5040* *Die Beiden Madchen Und Das Gerippe (Sch. 44, Will.
    36/II), 1896,* s., (06-23-93, Kornfeld, #612, illus.), dry-
    point on cream wove (BP 3424, DM 8528, FR 28,685,
    Y 549,079, SF 7590).
$4775* *Christiania-Boheme I (S. 10; Willoch 9), 1895,* w/
    platetone, Willoch's third (final) state, s., i. a., s. and p.
    Felsing, margins, fold in center, split in border, discolora-
    tion, crease, paper tape, (12-03-92, Sotheby-London,
    #461, illus.), 8⅝ x 11⅝ in., (218 x 296 mm.), etching
    w/drypoint on wove (BP 3080, DM 7509, FR 25,631, Y
    594,127).
$7376* *Christiania-Boheme I (Schiefler 10 II d, Willoch 9 III),
    1895,* s., (12-05-92, Bassenge, #7505), 8⁹⁄₁₆ x 11⅝ in.,
    (21.7 x 29.6 cm.), drypoint w/aquatint on copper print
    paper (BP 4619, DM 11,500, FR 39,192, Y 913,889).
$9887* *Christiania-Boheme II (Schiefler 11 b III; Willoch 10 V),
    1895,* s., (06-10-93, Hauswedell/Nolt, #674, illus.),
    image 11⅝ x 15⁷⁄₁₆ in., (29.6 x 39.2 cm.), drypoint
    worked over w/aquatint (BP 6467, DM 16,100, FR
    54,205, Y 1,049,464).
$36,885* *Eifersucht (Grosse Fassung) (Schiefler 58), 1896,* s., (06-
    05-93, Bassenge, #6372, illus.), 18⅝ x 22¹¹⁄₁₆ in., (47.3 x
    57.7 cm.), lithograph on fine China (BP 24,281, DM
    59,801, FR 201,557, Y 3,956,769).
$9720* *Eifersucht (S. 58), 1896,* p. Clot, margins, good cond.
    within subject, nicks, repaired tears, one extending into
    image, (12-03-92, Sotheby-London, #462, illus.), 18¼ x
    22½ in., (468 x 574 mm.), lithograph on stiff wove (BP
    6270, DM 15,285, FR 52,174, Y 1,209,406).
$6600* *Der Garten Bei Nacht (Schiefler 189), 1902,* from portfo-
    lio Aus dem Hause Max Linde, s., s. by printer, Felsing,
    full margins, good cond., mat/light staining, creases, (11-
    05-92, Sotheby-NY, #315, illus.), 19½ x 25⅜ in., (495 x
    644 mm.), etching, drypoint and aquatint p. in brown
    (BP 4293, DM 10,438, FR 35,313, Y 809,717).
$5457* *Gebet Des Alten Mannes (S. 173), 1902,* s., margins,
    good cond., defects, (12-03-92, Sotheby-London, #469,
    illus.), 18 x 12¾ in., (457 x 324 mm.), woodcut in
    black and ochre on Japan (BP 3520, DM 8582, FR
    29,291, Y 678,985).
BI *Head Of A Bearded Gentleman,* est. $2/400, (02-11-93,
    Boos, #414), image, sight 4½ x 3⅜ in., (115 x 85 mm.),
    drypoint.
$7803* *Im Cirkus, 1930,* s., t., i. artist's proof, (06-05-93, Bas-
    senge, #6368, illus.), 14⁹⁄₁₆ x 17¹⁵⁄₁₆ in., (37 x 45.6 cm.),
    woodcut on hand-made (BP 5137, DM 12,651, FR
    42,639, Y 837,052).
$464* *Kopfbild Eines Alteren Bartigen Mannes Mit Mit-
    telscheitel (Schiefler243), 1906,* i. sig. E Munch, (09-14-
    92, Venator/Hansten, #2477), plate 4½ x 3⅜ in., (11.5 x
    8.5 cm.), drypoint etching (BP 245, DM 690, FR 2338,
    Y 57,697).
$46,610* *Das Kranke Madchen (Schiefler 7 V b; Willoch 7 V),
    1894,* s., (06-10-93, Hauswedell/Nolt, #673, illus.),
    image 15⁵⁄₁₆ x 11⁷⁄₁₆ in., (38.9 x 29 cm.), drypoint on
    hand-made Japan (BP 30,488, DM 75,900, FR 255,537,
    Y 4,947,458).
$250* *Landschaft,* prov., (02-04-93, Sloan, #2938), 3⅜ x 4⅞
    in., (8.6 x 12.4 cm.), drypoint (BP 175, DM 412, FR
    1396, Y 31,098).
BI *Die Letzte Stunde (Sch. 491), 1920,* s., t., wide margins,
    fold, staining, very good cond., est. BP 5/7,000, (12-01-
    92, Christie-London, #467, illus.), plate 16⅞ x 22¾ in.,
    (428 x 578 mm.), sheet 21¼ x 27⅜ in., (428 x 578
    mm.), woodcut on wove.

$4597* *Die Letzte Stunde (Schiefler 491), 1920,* s., (05-12-93, AB Stockholm, #7041, illus.), 21¹⁄₁₆ x 27⅜ in., (53.5 x 69.5 cm.), woodcut (BP 3002, DM 7417, FR 24,984, Y 513,230, SK 34,100).

$8475* *Die Letzte Stunde (Schiefler 491), 1920,* s., blindstamp, (06-10-93, Hauswedell/Nolt, #688, illus.), image 17 x 22¹³⁄₁₆ in., (43.2 x 58 cm.), woodcut on copper print (BP 5544, DM 13,801, FR 46,464, Y 899,586).

$21,186* *Madchenakt (Schiefler 40 a), 1896,* s., (06-10-93, Hauswedell/Nolt, #676, illus.), image 5⅞ x 5⅛ in., (14.9 x 13 cm.), mezzotint and drypoint on copper print (BP 13,858, DM 34,499, FR 116,151, Y 2,248,806).

BI *Madonna (Eva Mudocci) (S. 212), 1903,* first state, margins, good cond., handlingmarks, stains, prov., est.BP 35/40,000, (12-03-92, Sotheby-London, #467, illus.), 23⅝ x 18⅜ in., (600 x 467 mm.), lithograph on sturdy Japan.

BI *Madonna (Eva Mudocci) (S. 212), 1903,* s., second state, margins, restored hole in image, stain, good cond.,est. BP 30/35,000, (12-03-92, Sotheby-London, #468, illus.), 23¾ x 18⅛ in., (605 x 465 mm.), lithograph on thin laid Japan.

$54,567* *Madonna (Liebendes Weib) (S. 33AB1), 1896-1902,* p. Lassally, large margins, good cond., prov., (12-03-92, Sotheby-London, #464, illus.), 21¾ x 13¾ in., (552 x 349 mm.), lithograph and woodcut in 3 colors (blue, red and black), w/later additions to the drawing stone on stiff wove (BP 35,200, DM 85,811, FR 292,899, Y 6,789,474).

$48,694* *Madonna (Schiefler 33/A/a/I), 1895,* (06-25-93, Kornfeld, #84, illus.), image 23⁹⁄₁₆ x 17⁵⁄₁₆ in., (59.8 x 44 cm.), sheet 24¾ x 18³⁄₁₆ in., (59.8 x 44 cm.), lithograph on thin vellum (BP 32,935, DM 82,898, FR 279,209, Y 5,161,543, SF 73,600).

$28,600* *Madonna (Schiefler 33B), 1896-1902,* final state, margins partially made-up, repaired splits/tears, uninked crease, laid down on laid, defects, (11-09-92, Christie-NY, #145, illus.), 21½ x 13¼ in., (546 x 337 mm.), black, rust, blue, and buff lithograph on thin Japan (BP 18,909, DM 45,658, FR 154,261, Y 3,549,268).

BI *Madonna-Liebendes Weib (Schiefler 33AB1), 1895-1902,* s., i., good cond., thin spot, creases, est. BP 70/90,000, (06-30-93, Sotheby-London, #568, illus.), 23¾ x 17½ in., (603 x 445 mm.), lithograph in black/red/blue on a thin greyish-white Japan?, laid onto a thickish brown fibrous support sheet.

BI *Mannerportrat (S. 201; W. 105), 1903,* s.; s. by p. Felsing, plate tone, large margins, good cond., defects,est. BP 3,5/4,500, (12-03-92, Sotheby-London, #470, illus.), 19½ x 12¾ in., (495 x 324 mm.), etching on sturdy cream wove.

$155,367* *Melancholie (Schiefler 116), 1898,* s., (06-10-93, Hauswedell/Nolt, #685, illus.), approx. 12⅝ x 16⁹⁄₁₆ in., (32 x 42.1 cm.), color woodcut worked over w/watercolor and chalk (BP 101,627, DM 253,000, FR 851,793, Y 16,491,561).

$4965* *Mondschein (Schiefler 13 IIId), 1895,* s., (06-05-93, Bassenge, #6369, illus.), 13¹⁵⁄₁₆ x 10½ in., (35.4 x 26.6 cm.), drypoint and aquatint on copper print (BP 3268, DM 8050, FR 27,131, Y 532,611).

$5727* *Nachtcafe (Sch. 138; Will. 57), 1901,* s., (06-23-93, Kornfeld, #614), etching on cream simili Japan (BP 3891, DM 9690, FR 32,595, Y 623,924, SF 8625).

$211* *Omega Weint (Schiefler 322), 1909,* from Alfa & Omega, (09-30-92, Kunsthallen, #224), lithograph (BP 119, DM 299, FR 1012, Y 25,321, DK 1150).

$1059* *Omega Weint (Schiefler 497), 1908-09,* s., from Alfa og Omega, (06-10-93, Hauswedell/Nolt, #682, illus.), image 10¹¹⁄₁₆ x 7⅜ in., (27.2 x 18.8 cm.), lithograph on board (BP 693, DM 1724, FR 5806, Y 112,408).

BI *"Portraet Af Ludwig Justi", 1927,* s., est. DK 10,000, (09-29-92, B. Rasmussen, #353, illus.), lithograph.

BI *Selbstbildnis Mit Weinflasche (Munch Museet Inventory No. OKK G-L 492), 1925-26,* margins, creasing, good cond., est. BP 3/4,000, (06-30-93, Sotheby-London, #569, illus.), 16¾ x 20 in., (425 x 508 mm.), lithograph.

$26,836* *Selbstportrait (Schiefler 31), 1895,* s., d., num., (06-10-93, Hauswedell/Nolt, #678, illus.), image 18⅛ x 12⅝ in., (46 x 32 cm.), lithograph (BP 17,554, DM 43,700, FR 147,127, Y 2,848,530).

$10,350* *Sterbezimmer (Schiefler 73), 1896,* s., p. August Clot, unevenly cut margins, stained pinhole, staining,graphite, good cond., (05-11-93, Christie-NY, #248, illus.), sheet 15¾ x 22¼ in., (400 x 565 mm.), lithograph on ivory tissue-thin laid Japan (BP 6607, DM 16,304, FR 54,936, Y 1,138,489).

$4123* *Strassentype (Sch. 163; Will. 78), 1902,* s., (06-23-93, Kornfeld, #616), etching on cream simili Japan (BP 2801, DM 6976, FR 23,466, Y 449,177, SF 6210).

BI *Studienkopfe (Schiefler 242), 1906,* s., est. DM 5,000, (06-05-93, Bassenge, #6370), 4½ x 6¼ in., (11.5 x 15.8 cm.), drypoint.

$10,593* *Der Tag Danach (Schiefler 15 IV; Willoch 14 V), 1895,* (06-10-93, Hauswedell/Nolt, #675, illus.), image 6⅝ x 8⅞ in., (16.8 x 22.6 cm.), drypoint on copper print (BP 6929, DM 17,250, FR 58,076, Y 1,124,403).

$8781* *Der Tag Darnach (Schiefler 15/IV/c; Willoch 14/V), 1895,* (06-23-93, Kornfeld, #611), etching and drypoint on thick wove (BP 5965, DM 14,858, FR 49,977, Y 956,640, SF 13,225).

$27,453* *Todeskampf (S. 72), 1896,* s., #?4, margins, very good cond., touched-in areas, back-board staining, handling creases, spots, (06-30-93, Sotheby-London, #570, illus.), sh 17¾ x 21½ in., (451 x 546 mm.), lithograph in black on olive green MBM laid (BP 18,400, DM 46,824, FR 157,957, Y 2,941,498).

BI *"Todeskampf" (Schiefler 72), 1896,* light-staining, est. DM 50/60,000, (06-04-93, Grisebach, #18, illus.), 15⁹⁄₁₆ x 19¹¹⁄₁₆ in., (39.5 x 50 cm.), lithograph on light beige copper print paper.

$7636* *Totes Liebespaar (Sch. 139; Will. 58), 1901,* s., (06-23-93, Kornfeld, #615), etching on wove (BP 5188, DM 12,920, FR 43,460, Y 831,899, SF 11,500).

BI *Trauermarsch (Schiefler 94), 1897,* ink s., p. Lemercier, margins, good cond., tear, image tear, est. Y 1/1,200,000, (10-14-92, Sotheby-Japan, #58, illus.), 21⅞ x 15 in., (556 x 381 mm.), lithograph on chine volant.

BI *Vampyr (S. 34), 1895,* s., d. 1895, good cond., light/mount-staining, est. BP 80/120,000, (06-30-93, Sotheby-London, #571, illus.), 15⅛ x 21½ in., (384 x 546 mm.), lithograph in black and extensively hand-colored w/red and blue watercolor and gouache on cream wove.

BI *"Der Vampyr" (Schiefler 34 II b), 1895-1902,* s., est. DM 160/180,000, (11-27-92, Grisebach, #10, illus.), 15¹⁄₁₆ x 21⅞ in., (38.3 x 55.5 cm.), color woodcut and color lithograph on copper print paper.

BI *Der Vershucher (Schieffer 407),* s. in stone, collector's stamp verso, est. FF1,000/1,200, (06-28-93, Loudmer, #324, illus.), 17⁵⁄₁₆ x 24⁷⁄₁₆ in., (440 x 620 mm.), sh 19 x 26 in., (440 x 620 mm.), black lithograph on China.

$3410* *Der Versucher (Schiefler 407), 1913,* s., margins, good cond., creases, defects, (12-03-92, Sotheby-London, #460, illus.), 17¾ x 24⅜ in., (450 x 620 mm.), lithograph on wove (BP 2200, DM 5362, FR 18,304, Y 424,288).

$3818* *Zeichnung Zu: Peer Gynt (Sch. 74), 1896,* 1st state, tear, (06-23-93, Kornfeld, #613), lithograph on grey paper (BP 2594, DM 6460, FR 21,730, Y 415,949, SF 5750).

BI *Zwei Menschen (Schiefler 504), 1920,* s., large margins, good cond., mat/light-stain, handling creases, repaired tear, loss, est. $25/35,000, (05-13-93, Sotheby-NY, #669, illus.), 25⅝ x 23⅞ in., (650 x 605 mm.), sh 35¼ x 29⅛ in., (650 x 605 mm.), lithograph in sanguine on wove.

MUNKACSI, Martin   1896-1963
$23,000* *Berlin, c. 1933,* photog. (c) stamp, catalog cover lot, (04-06-93, Sotheby-NY, #333, illus.), 11⅝ x 9¼ in., photograph, silver print (BP 15,192, DM 37,055, FR 125,477, Y 2,623,175).

MUNNINGS, Sir A.J. (after)
$62 *Fox Hunters And Hounds,* (12-11-92, G.A. Key, #7), 15 x 18 in., (38.1 x 45.7 cm.), colored print (BP 40, DM 98, FR 335, Y 7672).

MUNNINGS, Sir Alfred   English 1878-1959
$311 *"Belvoir Hounds Exercising In The Park", 1956,* s., artists proof, pub. Frost and Reed, faded, (02-05-93, G.A. Key, #94), 19 x 26 in., (48.3 x 66 cm.), colored print (BP 215, DM 516, FR 1743, Y 38,701).

$1035* *Pictures Of Horses And English Life, 1927,* Eyre and Spottiswoode, in 4s, num., s., (06-14-93, Sotheby-NY, #404), 13⅝ x 10¼ in., (34.6 x 26 cm.), 28 mounted color plates (BP 677, DM 1685, FR 5662, Y 108,913).

$548 *"The Saddling Paddock, Cheltenham, March Meeting",* s., artist's proof, pub. 1952 by Frost and Reed, (06-11-93, G.A. Key, #141, illus.), 15 x 25 in., (38.1 x 63.5 cm.), colored print (BP 360, DM 891, FR 3003, Y 58,143).

MUNNINGS, Sir Alfred (after)

$460* *"The Belvoir Hounds Exercising In The Park"* and *"After The Race",* 1956 and 1951: *Two,* full margins, good cond., Anthony N. B. Garvan Coll., (06-05-93, Christie-NY, #81), both, sh 24½ x 29½ in., (622 x 749 mm.), reprod. in color on wove (BP 303, DM 746, FR 2514, Y 49,346).

$144 *"Collecting The Fox Hounds"* and *"Horse Rider And Hounds In Landscape": Two,* (08-14-92, G.A. Key, #35), one 15 x 17 in., (38.1 x 43.2 cm.), the other 14 x 16 in., (38.1 x 43.2 cm.), colored print (BP 75, DM 211, FR 715, Y 18,159).

$510* *Going Out At Epsom,* s., blindstamp, pub. Frost and Reed, 1932, scuffing, (03-03-93, Bonhams-Chelsea, #194), image 19 x 19 in., (48.3 x 48.3 cm.), color reproduction (BP 352, DM 840, FR 2849, Y 59,593).

$558* *The Paddock At Epsom, Spring Meeting,* s., pub. Frost and Reed, 1932, (03-03-93, Bonhams-Chelsea, #195), image 15¾ x 20½ in., (40 x 52.1 cm.), color reproduction (BP 385, DM 919, FR 3117, Y 65,202).

$64* *Portrait Of Major T. Booch, M.F.H. With The Belvoir Hounds,* trimmed to image, (07-16-92, Bonhams-Chelsea, #529), image 19½ x 23½ in., (49.5 x 59.7 cm.), reproduction in colors (BP 33, DM 95, FR 319, Y 8017).

$220* *Unsaddling At Epsom, Summer Meeting,* s., (09-17-92, Sloan, #1440), 15½ x 20¼ in., (39.4 x 51.4 cm.), chromolithograph (BP 124, DM 327, FR 1118, Y 27,390).

MUNTZ, J. H. (after)

$132* *A View Of Twickenham,* by J. Green, repaired tears, other defects, (06-16-93, Bonhams-Chelsea, #390), image 15 x 20 in., (38.1 x 50.8 cm.), etching w/hand-coloring (BP 88, DM 219, FR 735, Y 14,078).

MURAY, Nickolas

BI *Dancer Leon Barte In Costume, 1921: Three,* s., d., handstamp, est. $7/1,000, (10-14-92, Swann, #521, illus.), 9½ x 7½ in., (24.1 x 19.1 cm.), photograph, silver prints.

$1925* *Gloria Swanson, (Sobies-zek, fig. 87),* mounted on black board, photog.'s studio stamp, pub. stamp, 1920s, (10-15-92, Sotheby-NY, #128, illus.), 13¼ x 10½ in., (33.7 x 26.7 cm.), photograph, gelatin silver print (BP 1178, DM 2865, FR 9717, Y 230,954).

MURAY, Nickolas   Am., b. Hungary 1892-1965

$4600* *"Mikhail Mordkin"* and *"Diaghilev's Ballet Russe Dancer", 1922: Two,* each s., d., presentation folder w/ embossed inits., lit., (04-08-93, Christie-NY, #229, illus.), each approx. 7⅛ x 9 in., (18.1 x 22.9 cm.), photograph, gelatin silver print (BP 3016, DM 7390, FR 25,014, Y 522,015).

MURCH, Arthur James   1902-1989

BI *Alpulurgna, Pentu Pui Tribe, Central Australia,* s. A.J Murch, i. on image, lit., est. $2/300, (08-11-92, L. Joel, #162G), 14⅜ x 8¼ in., (36.5 x 21 cm.), hand-color screenprint.

MURPHY, Gladys Wilkins   American b. 1907

$165* *"By A Lake",* s., #1/50, very good cond.?, (02-07-93, Bakker, #160), image 9 x 7 in., (22.9 x 17.8 cm.), color woodblock print (BP 114, DM 274, FR 925, Y 20,533).

$220* *"Harrie",* s. Gladys M. Wilkins, d. 2/10, (09-27-92, Bakker, #245), image 10 x 6 in., (25.4 x 15.2 cm.), color woodblock print (BP 128, DM 326, FR 1103, Y 26,554).

$165* *"Shadows",* s., #4/50, good cond.?, (02-07-93, Bakker, #161), image 8½ x 6¼ in., (21.6 x 15.9 cm.), color woodblock print (BP 114, DM 274, FR 925, Y 20,533).

MURPHY, Henry Dudley

$193* *Group Of Four,* three s., good/poor cond.?, each i., (02-07-93, Bakker, #245), largest plate 7 x 5 in., (17.8 x

12.7 cm.), etching (BP 134, DM 320, FR 1082, Y 24,017).

MURPHY, John J. A.

$412* *"A Family"* and *"Family Group", 1922: Two,* s., wide margins, mat burn, (05-27-93, Swann, #200, illus.), one 7 x 5 in., (17.8 x 12.7 cm.), other 5¾ x 5½ in., (17.8 x 12.7 cm.), woodcut (BP 264, DM 661, FR 2228, Y 44,168).

MURPHY, John J.A.

$1980* *Wrestlers, c. 1925-30,* s., full margins, good cond., (11-05-92, Sotheby-NY, #45, illus.), 11⅛ x 14¼ in., (284 x 361 mm.), woodcut on wove (BP 1288, DM 3131, FR 10,594, Y 242,915).

MURPHY, Joseph J.A.   American 1888-1967

$1650* *"Wrestlers", c. 1925-30,* s., excellent cond., (10-31-92, Cleveland, #196, illus.), 11⅛ x 14⅛ in., (28.3 x 35.9 cm.), woodcut (BP 1057, DM 2538, FR 8612, Y 204,385).

MURPHY, Minny Lois   American b. 1863

$55* *Bayside Cottage, 1931,* s., t., d. '31, s., good cond., foxing, (11-12-92, Freemn/Fine Art, #158), image 8⅛ x 10 in., (20.6 x 25.4 cm.), woodcut (BP 36, DM 87, FR 294, Y 6820).

MURPHY, Rowley Walter

$43* *Winter Scene,* s., t., (06-07-93, Ritchie, #22, illus.), 3⅞ x 4⅞ in., (9.8 x 12.4 cm.), etching (BP 28, DM 70, FR 235, Y 4613, C$ 55).

MURRAY, Amelia

$51 *"Kranberg"* and *"Waldlienegen": Two,* (10-09-92, G.A. Key, #1), 13 x 19 in., (33 x 48.3 cm.), colored print (BP 30, DM 76, FR 258, Y 6220).

MURRAY, Charles Oliver

BI *The Convent Garden, 1893,* after John Everett Millais, s. by both artists, pub. J.S. Virtue, margins, est. BP 100/ 150, (11-19-92, Bonhams-Chelsea, #76), 10⅛ x 13½ in., (25.7 x 34.3 cm.), etching.

MURRAY, Charles Oliver (after John Everett MILLAIS)

$17* *The Convent Garden, 1893,* s., pub. J.S. Virtue, margins, (01-21-93, Bonhams-Chelsea, #162), plate 10⅛ x 13½ in., (25.7 x 34.3 cm.), etching (BP 11, DM 27, FR 91, Y 2128).

MURRAY, E. Douglas

BI *"On The La De Lan Glacier", "The Pique D'Arolla"* and *"The Matterhorn", 1912: Three,* p. exhib. labels, i. w/t., est. BP 2/300, (10-29-92, Christie-London, #94), approx. 8¼ x 11¼ in., (21 x 28.6 cm.), photograph, gelatin silver print mounted on 2 layers of card.

MURRAY, Elizabeth   American b. 1940

BI *Blue Body (K. 16), 1986-87,* s., d., #35/70, ULAE blindstamp, excell. cond.?, the Late M. Anwar Kamal, M.D. Coll., est. $3/4,000, (05-11-93, Christie-NY, #515, illus.), sheet 48 x 31½ in., (121.9 x 80 cm.), color lithograph on wove.

BI *Down Dog (K. 17), 1988,* s., t., d., #35/65, ULAE blindstamp, excell. cond., the Late M. Anwar Kamal, M.D. Coll., est. $8/10,000, (05-11-93, Christie-NY, #516, illus.), overall 42 x 50 in., (106.7 x 127 cm.), color lithograph on 12 hand-torn collaged pieces of wove.

BI *Down Dog (K. 17), 1989,* s., d., t., #18/65, handtorn into 12 pieces and attached w/Japanese paper verso, blindstamp, pub. ULAE, good cond., est. $7/9,000, (05-15-93, Sotheby-NY, #1116, illus.), overall 41⅛ x 50¼ in., (104.5 x 127.6 cm.), lithograph in colors on Arches.

$1725* *Hand On Head (Krakow 10), 1983-84,* s., t., d. 84, #16/ 40, pub. District 1199 Cultural center, Inc., Bread and Roses Cultural Project for Amnesty International, excell. cond., (05-11-93, Christie-NY, #514), sheet 30 x 22⅜ in., (762 x 568 mm.), color lithograph on Arches (BP 1101, DM 2717, FR 9156, Y 189,748).

$3300* *Undoing, 1989-90,* s. verso, d., t., #42/60, pub. blindstamp, ULAE, good cond., (11-07-92, Sotheby-NY, #709, illus.), overall size 28⅞ x 23 in., (733 x 584 mm.), lithograph w/etching p. in colors on 3 sheets of Somerset paper, hand-torn assembled in layers w/cut-out (BP 2158, DM 5269, FR 17,809, Y 407,307).

$3300* *Untitled (Krakow 9), 1982,* s., #11/50, co-pub. Simca Print Artists and the artist, good cond., (11-07-92, Sotheby-NY, #708, illus.), overall size 49 x 32¼ in., (124.5 x 81.9 cm.), silkscreen p. in colors on three sheets, on handmade Kurotani Kozo (BP 2158, DM 5269, FR 17,809, Y 407,307).

$2530* *Untitled (Krakow 9), 1982,* s., #37/50, co-pub. Simca Print Artists and artist, good cond., (05-15-93, Sotheby-NY, #1115, illus.), overall 48¼ x 31½ in., (122.6 x 80 cm.), silkscreen in colors on three sheets on handmade Kurotani Kozo paper (BP 1645, DM 4069, FR 13,676, Y 280,457).

$330* *Untitled (Mostly Mozart Festival), 1979,* s., d., annot. AP, chop mark Charles Cardivale, (09-20-92, Hindman, #718), color serigraph (BP 193, DM 490, FR 1675, Y 40,786).

BI *Up Dog (K. 18), 1987-88,* s., d., #40/62, hand-torn into 14 pieces and attached w/ Japanese paper verso, blindstamp, pub. ULAE, good cond., est. $7/9,000, (05-15-93, Sotheby-NY, #1117, illus.), overall 45⅝ x 46 in., (115.9 x 116.8 cm.), lithograph in colors on Arches.

MURRAY, Joan

BI *"Ruth Bernhard In Her Studio" and "Elizabeth": Two,* one 1968, other 1972, both p. 1990, s., t., d., second photog.'s stamp, est. $6/800, (05-23-93, Butterfield, #3550, illus.), each approx. 13½ x 10½ in., photograph, gelatin silver print.

MURRAY, Nicholas 1892-1965

BI *Theatrical Portrait and Female Nude Torso: Two,* 1920s, est. $1,8/2,000, (10-13-92, Christie-NY, #321, illus.), each 7½ x 9⅜ in., (19.1 x 23.8 cm.), photograph, gelatin silver prints.

MUSCHAMP, Sidney (after)

$28 *A Game Of Badminton,* modern, (12-11-92, G.A. Key, #48), 16 x 23 in., (40.6 x 58.4 cm.), colored print (BP 18, DM 44, FR 151, Y 3465).

MUSI, Agostino Dei (called Veneziano) ac. 1514-1536

BI *The Blinding Of Elymas (B. XIV, 43 copy), c. 1520,* after Raphael, narrow margin, trimmed, abrasion, laid, est. BP 240/300, (12-01-92, Christie-London, #33), sheet 10⅛ x 13¹⁄₁₆ in., (257 x 332 mm.), engraving.

MUSIC, Zoran Antonio Italian 1909-1952

$1639* *Le Bac (Schmucking 27), 1950,* artist's proof, s., (11-13-92, Koller, #5386), 12¹⁵⁄₁₆ x 17⅜ in., (33 x 44.2 cm.), lithograph on wove (BP 1059, DM 2573, FR 8677, Y 203,426, SF 2320).

$275* *"Le Bac", 1950,* artist's proof, s., t., annot., (02-11-93, Boos, #404), 15³⁄₁₆ x 19½ in., (385 x 495 mm.), color lithograph (BP 194, DM 456, FR 1541, Y 33,153).

$1500* *Cavallino Azzurro (Schmucking), 1952,* artist's proof, (06-24-93, Germann, #449), 14⅝ x 18⅞ in., (372 x 480 mm.), color lithograph (BP 987, DM 2432, FR 8197, Y 160,910, SF 2185).

$866* *Cinque Torri (Schmucking 159), 1975,* s., num., (11-28-92, Schoppmann, #673), 11 x 14¾ in., (28 x 37.5 cm.), color etching on BFK Rives (BP 572, DM 1380, FR 4684, Y 107,778).

$1421* *Donne Delle Isole (Schmucking 53), 1955,* 74/90, s., (06-24-93, Germann, #451), 19⁵⁄₁₆ x 26¹⁄₁₆ in., (490 x 662 mm.), color lithograph (BP 935, DM 2304, FR 7765, Y 152,435, SF 2070).

$1106* *Fische (Schmucking 37), 1951,* #34/200, s., (09-04-92, Germann, #498), 14⅝ x 19⅛ in., (372 x 485 mm.), color lithograph (BP 554, DM 1550, FR 5277, Y 136,140, SF 1380).

$715* *Horses,* s., #71/140, prov., (10-18-92, Hindman, #817), 13 x 19¾ in., (33 x 50.2 cm.), color lithograph (BP 438, DM 1064, FR 3609, Y 85,783).

$498* *Komposition Mit Gelb, (19)64,* s., d., num., light-stained, (12-01-92, Karl/Faber, #1047), 8¹¹⁄₁₆ x 11⅝ in., (22 x 29.5 cm.), etching on Arches wove (BP 329, DM 794, FR 2705, Y 62,002).

$789* *Komposition, (19)67,* s., num., mount-staining, (12-01-92, Karl/Faber, #1048), 8⁷⁄₁₆ x 11⁷⁄₁₆ in., (21.5 x 29 cm.), color aquatint/etching on Rives wove (BP 521, DM 1258, FR 4286, Y 98,232).

$465* *Komposition, 1964,* s, d., num., (05-26-93, Dorling, #2876, illus.), 8⁵⁄₁₆ x 11⁵⁄₁₆ in., (21.1 x 28.8 cm.), color etching on thick wove (BP 301, DM 759, FR 2554, Y 50,522).

$866* *Motif Vegetal I (Schmucking 152), 1973,* i. E.A., s., d., (11-28-92, Schoppmann, #671), 18⁵⁄₁₆ x 14⅜ in., (46.5 x 36.5 cm.), color etching on BFK Rives (BP 572, DM 1380, FR 4684, Y 107,778).

$866* *Motif Vegetal II (Schmucking 153), 1973,* s., d., num., (11-28-92, Schoppmann, #672), 18⁵⁄₁₆ x 14³⁄₁₆ in., (46.5 x 36 cm.), color etching on BFK Rives (BP 572, DM 1380, FR 4684, Y 107,778).

$1342* *Motivo Carsico (Schmucking 121), 1966-1967,* 33/200, s., d., (06-24-93, Germann, #452, illus.), 12¹⁵⁄₁₆ x 16¼ in., (330 x 412 mm.), color aquatint (BP 883, DM 2176, FR 7333, Y 143,961, SF 1955).

$1895* *Paysage Siennois (Schmucking 59), 1956,* 19/90, s., blindstamp, (06-24-93, Germann, #450), 19¹³⁄₁₆ x 26⅛ in., (503 x 664 mm.), etching (BP 1247, DM 3072, FR 10,355, Y 203,283, SF 2760).

$1647* *Pferd Vor Hugellandschaft,* s., (05-08-93, Dobiaschofsky, #2155, illus.), 14¾ x 19⅛ in., (37.5 x 48.5 cm.), color lithograph (BP 1075, DM 2646, FR 8927, Y 184,043, SF 2400).

$2295* *Pferde (Schmucking 23), 1949,* artist's proof, s., (11-13-92, Koller, #5384), 13⅜ x 12³⁄₁₆ in., (34 x 31 cm.), lithograph on wove (BP 1483, DM 3603, FR 12,149, Y 284,845, SF 3248).

$2470* *Pferde In Hugeliger Landschaft,* s., edit. Arta, (05-08-93, Dobiaschofsky, #2156, illus.), 15⅜ x 19¹¹⁄₁₆ in., (39 x 50 cm.), color lithograph (BP 1612, DM 3968, FR 13,388, Y 276,008, SF 3600).

$210* *"Sauche D'Arbre-1972",* E.A., d., s., (01-28-93, Peschetteau, #222)), 11⁷⁄₁₆ x 8¼ in., (29 x 21 cm.), etching on wove (BP 139, DM 333, FR 1126, Y 26,074).

$3723* *Steppenpferde,* s., #135/140, (10-21-92, Dobiaschofsky, #2209, illus.), 15⅜ x 22⁷⁄₁₆ in., (39 x 57 cm.), color lithograph (BP 2311, DM 5633, FR 19,122, Y 453,471, SF 5040).

$921* *Terre D'Istrie II (Schmucking 73), (19)59,* s., d., num., blindstamp, (06-08-93, Karl/Faber, #1144), approx. 16⅛ x 22⁷⁄₁₆ in., (41 x 57 cm.), color etching on Arches wove (BP 605, DM 1494, FR 5033, Y 97,823).

$892* *Terres Dalmates (Schmucking 79), 1959,* s., d., #16/95, p. by Atelier Lacouriere, pub. L'Oeuvre Gravee, blindstamp, margins, good cond., mount-staining, creases, (06-30-93, Sotheby-London, #883, illus.), 19¼ x 24 in., (489 x 610 mm.), aquatint in brown and black on BFK Rives (BP 598, DM 1521, FR 5132, Y 95,575).

$983* *Umbrische, Landschaft (Schmucking 33), 1952,* artist's proof, s., (11-13-92, Koller, #5385), 12⁷⁄₁₆ x 16⅞ in., (31.6 x 42.8 cm.), lithograph on wove (BP 635, DM 1543, FR 5204, Y 122,006, SF 1392).

MUYBRIDGE, Eadweard English 1830-1904

$3520* *Animal And Human Locomotion, 1872-1885,* 10 from Animal Locomotion, pub. 1887, credit, plate num., (c) d., reprod. limitation printed, (10-13-92, Christie-NY, #16, illus.), each 8½ x 12¼ in., (21.6 x 31.1 cm.), photograph, collotype plates (BP 2050, DM 5157, FR 17,521, Y 426,822).

$5520* *Animal And Human Locomotion, 1887: Fifteen,* from Animal Locomotion, An Electro-Photographic Investigation of Consecutive Phases of Animal Movements, 1872-85, credit, t., plate num., (c), reprod. limitation , plate nums. 43, 276, 332, 421, 597, 602, 670, 693, 705, 727, 740, 750, 755, 773 and 778, (04-08-93, Christie-NY, #9, illus.), smallest 8⅜ x 13¾ in., (21.3 x 34.9 cm.), largest 10⅜ x 11⅜ in., (21.3 x 34.9 cm.), photograph, collotype plates (BP 3620, DM 8867, FR 30,016, Y 626,419).

$5940* *Animal Locomotion Series: Group Of Twenty-two Plates,* soiling, Philadelphia: University of Pennsylvania, 1887, (04-07-93, Swann, #76, illus.), 18½ x 23¾ in., (47 x 60.3 cm.), photograph, collotypes, various sizes on two-toned leaves (BP 3925, DM 9607, FR 32,512, Y 674,847).

$358* *"Animal Locomotion, Plate 133", 1887,* i. w/t., plate num., (c), d., good cond., water stain, handling marks, (03-12-93, Skinner, #123, illus.), 9⅛ x 12¼ in., (23.2 x 31.1 cm.), collotype on album (BP 250, DM 596, FR 2026, Y 42,192).

$5175* *Human Locomotion, 1887: Ten,* from Animal Locomotion, An Electro-Photographic Investigation of Consecutive Phases of Animal Movements, 1872-85, stamp, credit, t., plate num., (c), reprod. limitation, plate nums. 180, 322, 368, 441, 468, 470, 475, 501, 502 and 513, (04-08-93, Christie-NY, #10, illus.), smallest 5⅛ x 17⅞ in., (13 x 45.4 cm.), largest 8½ x 14 in., (13 x 45.4 cm.), photograph, collotype plates (BP 3393, DM 8313, FR 28,140, Y 587,267).

$550* *Plate 29 From "Animal Locomotion", 1887,* attrib., t., d. printed, ink stamp, Dixon Collection, (11-16-92, Butterfield, #6109), 6⅛ x 18⁹⁄₁₆ in., (155.9 x 470.7 mm.), photograph, collotype (BP 362, DM 877, FR 2954, Y 68,399).

$374* *Plate 587 From "Animal Locomotion", 1887,* attrib., t., d. p., stamp num. 377, (05-23-93, Butterfield, #3551, illus.), 13⅝ x 19½ in., photograph, collotype (BP 244, DM 612, FR 2058, Y 41,340).

BI *Selected Animal Locomotion Studies, 1887: Eighteen,* 18 plates from Animal Locomotion, all but 1 p. w/series t., plate num., photog.'s (c), plate num. includ. in lot: 81, 97, 123, 158, 167, 176, 314, 346, 355, 385, 412, 467, 568, 646, 681 and 682, est. $5/7,000, (04-06-93, Sotheby-NY, #23a, illus.), various sizes 19 x 24 in., photograph, collotypes.

BI *Selected Animal Locomotion Studies, 1887: Six,* 6 plates from "Animal Locomotion", all but 1 p. w/series t., plate num., photog. (c), plate num. includ. in lot: 274, 289, 321, 359, 517, and 557,est. $1,5/2,500, (04-06-93, Sotheby-NY, #23, illus.), photograph, collotypes.

$1610* *"Valley Of The Yosemite" (Base Of A Giant Sequoia And Cabin), c. 1872,* photog. credit, series t., (04-06-93, Sotheby-NY, #20, illus.), 16⅞ x 21⅜ in., photograph, albumen print (BP 1063, DM 2594, FR 8783, Y 183,622).

$3450* *"Valley Of The Yosemite, From Union Point", 1872,* p. w/ t., photog. and pub. credits, num. 33, (04-06-93, Sotheby-NY, #21, illus.), 16⅞ x 21½ in., photograph, albumen print (BP 2279, DM 5558, FR 18,822, Y 393,476).

$1725* *Wild Cat Fall. Valley Of The Yosemite, 1872,* mount trimmed to image, (04-06-93, Sotheby-NY, #22, illus.), 16¾ x 21⅛ in., photograph, albumen print (BP 1139, DM 2779, FR 9411, Y 196,738).

$2475* *'Mirror Lake-Valley Of The Yosemite' (Era, pl. 70), 1872,* mounted, photog.'s credit, t., credit pub. Bradley & Rulofson, (10-15-92, Sotheby-NY, #23, illus.), 17 x 21¼ in., (43.2 x 54 cm.), photograph, albumen print (BP 1515, DM 3684, FR 12,494, Y 296,941).

MUYBRIDGE, Eadweard (attrib.) English 1830-1904

$2200* *'North And South Dome, Yosemite Valley. No. 40', c. 1872,* mounted, t. in ink, pub. credit Thomas Houseworth & Co. Photographers, (10-15-92, Sotheby-NY, #24, illus.), 15⅞ x 20⅜ in., (40.3 x 51.8 cm.), photograph, albumen print (BP 1346, DM 3275, FR 11,106, Y 263,947).

MYDANS, Carl

$1210* *"Roosevelt And Garner", "Tenement Kitchen, Cincinnati", and "Bed Sitting Room, Cincinnati": Three,* F.S.A., R.A. handstamp, 1930s, (04-07-93, Swann, #309, illus.), each approx. 8 x 10 in., photograph, silver print (BP 800, DM 1957, FR 6623, Y 137,469).

MYERS, Frances

BI *Great Sands: The Ascent,* s., t., #32/100, prov., est. C$ 1/200, (12-01-92, Ritchie, #49), 15⅞ x 22 in., (40.3 x 55.9 cm.), color etching and aquatint.

MYERS, Jerome American 1867-1940/41

$110* *Old City Corner,* s. Jerome Myers, mono. JM, good cond., light tonong, water stain, wrinkling, soil, (09-11-92, Skinner, #19A), 8⅜ x 10⅛ in., (21.3 x 25.7 cm.), soft ground etching w/plate tone on fine laid paper (BP 57, DM 158, FR 538, Y 13,629).

$55* *Teacher With Children,* s., (12-17-92, Mystic, #21A), 7 x 8 in., (17.8 x 20.3 cm.), color etching (BP 35, DM 86, FR 293, Y 6759).

NABOKOV, Dominque

BI *Azzedine Alaia With Poupouf In Front Of His New Store, Paris, c. 1980,* photog.'s (c) stamp, Jocelyn Kargere Coll., est. BP 250/300, (10-29-92, Christie-London, #186), image 9½ x 6⅜ in., (24.1 x 16.2 cm.), photograph, gelatin silver print.

NACHIPEIN, A.

$763* *Grande Brasserie De La Loire, c. 1895,* St-Chamond, Lith. A. Pomeon and Fils, cond. A-, (06-11-93, Boisgirard, #119, illus.), 50⅜ x 37¹⁵⁄₁₆ in., (128 x 96.5 cm.), poster (BP 501, DM 1240, FR 4181, Y 80,955).

NADAR

BI *Portrait Of Victor Hugo, c. 1880,* est. $6/900, (10-14-92, Swann, #190, illus.), 9½ x 7½ in., (24.1 x 19.1 cm.), photograph, Woodburytype.

$935* *"Victor Hugo", "Emil Zola" and "Honore Balzac": Three,* reprod. of daguerreotype, photog.'s red imprint, 1880s, (04-07-93, Swann, #238, illus.), photograph, cabinet cards (BP 618, DM 1512, FR 5118, Y 106,226).

NADAR French 1844-1923

$522* *"Sarah Bernhardt On The Stage" and "Portrait Of Sarah Bernhardt": Two,* photog.'s imprint on mounts, 1880s, (04-07-93, Swann, #109, illus.), photograph, albumen cabinet cards (BP 345, DM 844, FR 2857, Y 59,305).

NADEAU, Marc Antoine Canadian b. 1943

$17* *"De Liegende Hollander",* #5/15, s., d. Nadeau 71, (06-16-93, Encans, #77), 9⅜ x 12³⁄₁₆ in., (23.8 x 31 cm.), serigraph (BP 11, DM 28, FR 95, Y 1813, C$ 22).

$46* *"St-Eustache, Ete 47",* #e/a 5/5, s., d. Nadeau 73, (09-15-92, Encans, #79), 17¹⁵⁄₁₆ x 24 in., (45.5 x 61 cm.), etching (BP 25, DM 68, FR 232, Y 5711, C$ 56).

NADELMAN, Elie American, b.Poland 1882-1946

BI *"Female Head, Draped", "Female Figure" and "Female Head" (Kirstein 2; 8; and 18): Three,* 1920, K.8 2nd final state, p. Charles S. White in 1951, margins trimmed, very good cond., est $3/4,000, (11-09-92, Christie-NY, #28, illus.), drypoint on simili Japan.

NAGAO, Yasushi

$1320* *The Assassination Of Inejiro Asanuma (Great News Photos And The Stories Behind Them, p. 127), 1960,* (04-07-93, Swann, #338, illus.), 7¼ x 9 in., photograph, silver print (BP 872, DM 2135, FR 7225, Y 149,966).

NAGAOKA, Kunito b. 1940

$563* *"Horizonte", 1976: Six,* s., d., num., Berlin, Galerie Lietzow, (11-28-92, Grisebach, #660, illus.), 10⁹⁄₁₆ x 8⅜ in., (26.8 x 21.3 cm.), colored etching on copper print paper (BP 372, DM 897, FR 3045, Y 70,068).

NAGASAKI-E SCHOOL

BI *"Foreign Boat",* faded, est. $250/350, (05-07-93, Goldberg, #1377), stenciled print.

NAGATANI, Patrick

$468* *"Fin De Siecle', Bat Flight Amphitheater, Carlsbad Caverns, New Mexico", 1989,* ink s., t., d., edit. 7/50, Dixon Collection(11-16-92, Butterfield, #6111), 15 x 19¹⁄₁₆ in., (381.7 x 483.5 mm.), photograph, cibachrome print (BP 308, DM 746, FR 2513, Y 58,202).

$230* *"Fin De Siecle, Bat Flight Amphitheater, Carlsbad Caverns, N.M.", 1989,* s., t., d., #22/50, (05-23-93, Butterfield, #3552, illus.), 15 x 19 in., photograph, cibachrome print (BP 150, DM 376, FR 1266, Y 25,423).

$275* *"Japanese Children's Day Carp Banners, Paguate Village, Jackpile Mine Uranium Tailings, Laguna Pueblo Reservation, New Mexico", 1990,* ink s., t., d., Dixon Collection, (11-16-92, Butterfield, #6110, illus.), 14⅞ x 18⁹⁄₁₆ in., (378.5 x 470.7 mm.), photograph, cibachrome print (BP 181, DM 438, FR 1477, Y 34,200).

NAGATANI, Patrick/Andree TRACEY

$1150* *"Alamogordo Blues", diptych, 1986-89,* s., t., d., #18/25 by photog., (04-06-93, Sotheby-NY, #225, illus.), image 18½ x 29¼ in., photograph, 2 dye-transfer prints (BP 760, DM 1853, FR 6274, Y 131,159).

NAGEL, Peter b. 1941

BI *Ballonblaser Am Fenster,* plate s., d. Peter Nagel 72, est. DM 300-, (03-24-93, Venator/Hansten, #4538), pl. 19⅝ x 15⅜ in., (49.9 x 39.1 cm.), colored color etching w/mezzotint and roulette.

NAILOR, Gerald (Toh Yah)   Native American 1917-1952
$44* *Two Works On Paper,* each ident. Gerald Nailor, (06-26-93, Skinner, #37), sight 11¼ x 9½ in., (28.6 x 24.1 cm.), silkscreen (BP 29, DM 75, FR 252, Y 4668).

NAIN, Louis le (after)
$138* *The Darling Children, 1767,* by Alexander Bannerman, (04-02-93, Sloan, #2266), sight 11¾ x 14⅝ in., (298 x 371 mm.), engraving (BP 91, DM 222, FR 753, Y 15,712).

NAIWINCX, Herman   c. 1624-c. 1651
$1629* *Landschaften (B. 9-16, Dutuit, Hollstein 9-16 II): Eight,* watermark, prov., (06-04-93, Bassenge, #5264), each approx. 5⅛ x 4¾ in., (13 x 12 cm.), etching (BP 1078, DM 2645, FR 8916, Y 175,690).

NAKAYAMA, Tadashi   Japanese b. 1927
$440* *Abstraction,* s., d. T. Nakayama 1963, num. 51/55, (09-25-92, Wolf, #46), 36 x 22 in., (91.4 x 55.9 cm.), colored woodcut (BP 257, DM 652, FR 2206, Y 53,108).
$303* *Two Zebras,* s., d. 1967, #35/65, (05-16-93, Hindman, #392), 24¾ x 22½ in., (62.9 x 57.2 cm.), color woodcut (BP 197, DM 487, FR 1638, Y 33,588).
$125* *Untitled, 1959,* s., d., num., burned, (05-15-93, Cleveland, #34, illus.), 9½ x 9½ in., (24.1 x 24.1 cm.), woodcut (BP 81, DM 201, FR 676, Y 13,857).

NAKIAN, Reuben   American 1897-1986
$357* *Untitled, c. 1979,* from the Leda series, s., annot. HC, pub. International Images, crease, tear, (12-08-92, Swann, #223), 19¾ x 31½ in., (50.2 x 80 cm.), drypoint, chine colle on heavy wove (BP 224, DM 556, FR 1895, Y 44,249).

NALIER, L.G.
$33* *Lincoln, 1908,* s. L.G. Nalier, (09-12-92, Dunning, #1179), 13½ x 19½ in., (34.3 x 49.5 cm.), print (BP 17, DM 48, FR 161, Y 4089).

NAMUTH, Hans
$935* *Jackson Pollack In His Studio,* handstamps, 1950's, (10-14-92, Swann, #522, illus.), 10 x 8 in., (25.4 x 20.3 cm.), photograph, silver print (BP 549, DM 1368, FR 4640, Y 113,306).
BI *Portrait Of A Woman,* 1950s, photog.'s stamp, est. $5/700, (05-23-93, Butterfield, #3553, illus.), 16½ x 13 in., photograph, gelatin silver print.

NANOGAK, Agnes   b. 1925
$208* *Dance, 1975,* #41/50 s., t., prov., (05-10-93, Hodgins, #117), 19 x 28½ in., (48.3 x 72.4 cm.), stonecut on paper (BP 136, DM 334, FR 1127, Y 23,243, C$ 264).
$173* *Hunger, 1974,* #13/50 s., t., d. 1974, prov., (05-10-93, Hodgins, #116), 19 x 29 in., (48.3 x 73.7 cm.), stonecut on paper (BP 113, DM 278, FR 938, Y 19,332, C$ 220).
$243* *Shaman, 1973,* #23/50, s. in print, t., d. 1973, prov., (05-10-93, Hodgins, #319, illus.), 28 x 18½ in., (71.1 x 47 cm.), stonecut on paper (BP 159, DM 390, FR 1317, Y 27,154, C$ 308).

NANTEUIL, Robert   French 1623-1678
$358* *"Francois Guenault" and "Jean Antoine De Mesmes": Two, Petitjean & Wickert 83, P&W 172 I or II/VII,* 1664 and 1665, ex-coll., Lugt 636, (09-20-92, Hindman, #662), larger 13½ x 10⅝ in., (34.3 x 27 cm.), engravings (BP 210, DM 531, FR 1817, Y 44,247).
BI *Pierre Poncet (P-W 197), 1673,* 4th state, narrow margins, foxing, staining, est. $2/300, (12-12-92, Weschler, #143), 12 x 10 in., (30.5 x 25.4 cm.), engraving.
BI *Pierre Poncet (P-W 197), 1673,* fourth state, narrow margins, foxing, staining, est. $2/400, (06-11-93, Weschler, #42), 12 x 10 in., (30.5 x 25.4 cm.), engraving.

NAPOLETANO, Filippo (called Teodoro Filippo di LIAGNO)
BI *St. John The Baptist Preaching In The Wilderness (B. XVII, 1),* trimmed into subject, title i. in old hand, crease, dirt staining, laid down, est. BP 3/4,000, (06-30-93, Sotheby-London, #170), 19¾ x 15½ in., (502 x 394 mm.), etching.

NAPPELBAUM, Ida   b. 1900
BI *Ballerina Nina Molodzinskaja, 1925,* est. DM 2,500, (11-12-92, Lempertz, #181, illus.), 6⁵⁄₁₆ x 4½ in., (16 x 11.5 cm.), photograph, gelatin silver print.
BI *Die Kunsthistorikerin Antonina Isergina, 1927,* est. DM 4,000, (11-12-92, Lempertz, #182, illus.), 6¼ x 4⅛ in., (15.8 x 10.5 cm.), photograph, gelatin silver print (brown).

NAPPELBAUM, Moisei   1869-1958
BI *Ein Sommernachmittag, 20's,* est. DM 4,000, (11-12-92, Lempertz, #183, illus.), 8¼ x 12 in., (21 x 30.5 cm.), photograph, gum bichromate print.

NARANJO, Eduardo
BI *"Poeta En Nueva York", 1929-30: Thirteen,* text by Federico Garcia Lorca, #93/250, s., d. 88, w/box, reserve P1,150,000, (12-17-92, Duran, #165, illus.), 24⁷⁄₁₆ x 20¹⁄₁₆ in., (62 x 51 cm.), engraving.

NARDOIS, Jean Galioth
BI *Flusslandschaft Mit Figurlicher Staffage (Nagler, Die MonogrammistenIII, 2460),* est. DM 1,200, (12-04-92, Bassenge, #6318, illus.), 7¾ x 9¹⁵⁄₁₆ in., (19.7 x 25.2 cm.), etching.

NARIKAWA, Shigenu   Japanese 20th cent.
$61* *"Flower And Pot", 1983,* s., d., num. 96/150, excell. cond., (10-31-92, Cleveland, #46), 15½ x 19½ in., (39.4 x 49.5 cm.), mezzotint (BP 39, DM 94, FR 318, Y 7556).
$83* *"Gladiola",* s., num. 66/100, excell. cond., (10-31-92, Cleveland, #45), 19½ x 14 in., (49.5 x 35.6 cm.), mezzotint (BP 53, DM 128, FR 433, Y 10,281).
$72* *"Thistle", 1981,* s., d., num. 29/50, excell. cond., (10-31-92, Cleveland, #47), 5¾ x 7 in., (14.6 x 17.8 cm.), mezzotint (BP 46, DM 111, FR 376, Y 8919).

NAROUF, F.
BI *Fight Carbon With The Anti-Carbon Pair, Horses & Imps, 1926,* p. EVP, ref. #153, cond. 3, est. BP 4/600, (10-13-92, Phillips-London, #60, illus.), 29¹⁵⁄₁₆ x 44¹¹⁄₁₆ in., (76 x 113.5 cm.), color lithograph.

NARTINS, D.
$76* *Untitled,* (03-10-93, Maynard, #645), 13 x 15½ in., (33 x 39.4 cm.), engraving (BP 53, DM 126, FR 429, Y 8979, C$ 94).

NASH, John
$348* *Cat On Cushion,* s., margins, 1 p. w/3 wood engravings, all proof impressions, good cond., (10-27-92, Phillips-London, #286), borderline 1¾ x 2 in., (44 x 51 mm.), woodcut on japan (BP 220, DM 533, FR 1810, Y 42,569).

NASH, Paul   English 1889-1946
$313* *Promenade No. 1 (Postan W9),* s., d. 1921 in ink, i., time stained, tear to image, defects, prov., (10-27-92, Phillips-London, #287), sheet 5½ x 6⅞ in., (140 x 175 mm.), woocut on laid japan (BP 198, DM 480, FR 1628, Y 38,287).
$1732* *To Visit Britain's Landmarks, Kimmeridge Folly, Dorset, 1937,* p. Waterlow and Sons, ref. #505, cond. 1, creases, (10-13-92, Phillips-London, #129, illus.), 29¹⁵⁄₁₆ x 44⅞ in., (76 x 114 cm.), color lithograph (BP 1009, DM 2537, FR 8621, Y 210,016).
$550* *Winter Wood, 1922,* s., t., d., num. from edition 50, (12-09-92, Grogan, #93, illus.), 5¾ x 4½ in., (14.6 x 11.4 cm.), woodcut (BP 351, DM 863, FR 2946, Y 68,196).

NASINI, J.N.
$565* *Vierge Avec L'Enfant Jesus Et Saint Jean (Bartsch 1),* thin margins, (02-03-93, Ader Tajan, #35), 6¾ x 4¹⁵⁄₁₆ in., (17.2 x 12.6 cm.), etching (BP 394, DM 930, FR 3155, Y 70,282).

NASON, Thomas   American 1889-1971
BI *"The Little Farm" and "Upland Pastures", 1955, 1934: Two,* 1st AAA edit., s., d., excell. cond; second The Woodcut Society edit., time staining, discoloration, tape, est. $3/400, (05-15-93, Cleveland, #258), one 5½ x 8⅞ in., (14 x 22.5 cm.), other 3⅝ x 7½ in., (14 x 22.5 cm.), wood engraving.

$523* *"Winter Sunlight", "Feeding The Chickens", and "Spring Landscape", 1940, 1945: Three,* each s., 1st 2 d., p. by artist, margins, good cond., Winter Sunlightw/light-staining, surface soiling, pencil notations, prop. Print Corner Coll. of Elizabeth and Charles Whitmore, (02-24-93, Butterfield, #2857), from 4¾ x 7¾ in., (121 x 197 mm.), to 5¹⁄₁₆ x 9⅞ in., (121 x 197 mm.), engraving on wove (BP 365, DM 849, FR 2878, Y 61,371).

$385* *"Wooded Shore", "Summer Evening", and "Evening Mists", 1933, 1940, &1943: Three,* each s., last 2 d., num. 10/100, Ed. 100 and Ed. 75, margins, good cond., prop. Print Corner, (02-24-93, Butterfield, #2856), from 2¼ x 4⅜ in., (57 x 111 mm.), to 4⁷⁄₁₆ x 6⁵⁄₁₆ in., (57 x 111 mm.), engraving & wood engraving on wove, laid & Japan (BP 268, DM 625, FR 2119, Y 45,177).

NASON, Thomas W. American 1889-1971

$99* *"Eggemogg Reach",* s., d. 1940, AAA label, (05-20-93, Boos, #525), image 6⅛ x 10³⁄₁₆ in., (155 x 258 mm.), paper 9⁵⁄₁₆ x 12³⁄₁₆ in., (155 x 258 mm.), wood engraving (BP 64, DM 160, FR 538, Y 10,932).

NATHE, Christoph Friedrich 1753-1806

$217* *Ansicht Von Lauban In Schlesien (Rumann 73), 1805,* (12-04-92, Bassenge, #6657), 6¼ x 7¾ in., (15.8 x 19.7 cm.), etching (BP 139, DM 346, FR 1172, Y 27,091).

$87* *Landschaft Mit Personen (Rumann 64),* (12-04-92, Bassenge, #6656), 6⁹⁄₁₆ x 8¹⁵⁄₁₆ in., (16.7 x 22.8 cm.), etching (BP 56, DM 139, FR 470, Y 10,861).

$116* *Die Teufelsbrucke Am S. Gotthard (Nagler 9; Rumann 40 I),* foxed, (12-04-92, Bassenge, #6655), 6⅛ x 4⅝ in., (15.6 x 11.7 cm.), etching (BP 74, DM 185, FR 627, Y 14,482).

NATKIN, Robert American b. 1930

$605* *Composition,* s., d. 1973, #63/70, (05-16-93, Hindman, #628), 33 x 55 in., (83.8 x 139.7 cm.), color serigraph (BP 393, DM 973, FR 3270, Y 67,066).

BI *Untitled Abstract Composition, 1979,* s., #7/75, full margins, est. $5/750, (12-08-92, Swann, #225), 26¾ x 36 in., (67.9 x 91.4 cm.), color serigraph on black paper.

$193* *Untitled, 1971,* s., d., #16/125, good cond., (02-24-93, Butterfield, #3234), 23¹³⁄₁₆ x 35½ in., (605 x 902 mm.), lithograph in colors on Arches (BP 135, DM 313, FR 1062, Y 22,647).

BI *Untitled, 1978: Two,* s., #7/75 and #71/75, margins, stamp, est. $700/1,000, (12-08-92, Swann, #224), each 26¼ x 36 in., (66.7 x 91.4 cm.), color serigraph.

NATORI SHUNSEN Japanese 1886-1960

$1575* *"Okubi-e Of Ichikawa Uzaemon XV" and "Nakamura Tomijuro IV As A Dancing Kamuro": Two,* Oban, s. Shunsen hitsu and Bichosai Shunsen w/seals, pub. Watanabe, d. c. 1920s; second d. Showa 27 (1952), good state, Prof. H.R.W. Kuhne Coll., (06-11-93, Sotheby-London, #491), one 15½ x 10½ in., (39.4 x 26.7 cm.), other 15¾ x 10½ in., (39.4 x 26.7 cm.), woodblock, mica ground, and pale pink ground (BP 1035, DM 2560, FR 8630, Y 167,109).

NATTES, John Claude (after) British 1765-1822

$176* *Marlborough Street, Bath, 1805,* by I. Hill, pub. William Miller, (10-18-92, Hindman, #515), 10¾ x 14½ in., (27.3 x 36.8 cm.), hand colored etching and aquatint (BP 108, DM 262, FR 888, Y 21,116).

NAUDET, Th. Ch. (after)

$49* *Cortege De Sa Majeste L'Empereur Napoleon 1er,* engraved by Le Beau, crack, tears, large margins, (06-16-93, Ader Tajan, #42), 16⁹⁄₁₆ x 20¹¹⁄₁₆ in., (42 x 52.5 cm.), etching and copper engraving (BP 33, DM 81, FR 273, Y 5226).

NAUEN, Heinrich 1880-1949

BI *In Memoriam Paul A. Seehavs, c. 1915,* s., repaired, tear, repaired tears, est. BP 800/1,000, (05-20-93, Christie-London, #501, illus.), sheet 24½ x 18 in., (62.2 x 45.7 cm.), lithograph in black and red.

$1106* *Ein Karren Auf Dem Feld, c. 1920,* s., (12-05-92, Bassenge, #7510), 13¼ x 18⅜ in., (33.6 x 46.6 cm.), drypoint on thick Arches (BP 693, DM 1724, FR 5877, Y 137,034).

$1106* *Landschaft Mit Seeufer, c. 1920,* s., wrinkled, (12-05-92, Bassenge, #7509), 15⅜ x 12½ in., (39 x 31.8 cm.), drypoint on thick handmade Arches (BP 693, DM 1724, FR 5877, Y 137,034).

$530* *Sudliche Landschaft, 1922,* s., d., (06-10-93, Hauswedell/Nolt, #690), image 13⅛ x 18½ in., (33.3 x 47 cm.), etching and drypoint on JW Zanders (BP 347, DM 863, FR 2906, Y 56,257).

NAUMAN, Bruce American b. 1941

$5750* *Clown Taking A Shit (C., L.-M. & Y. 56), 1988,* s., d., #13/35, pub. Brooke Alexander Editions, full margins, good cond., (05-15-93, Sotheby-NY, #1126, illus.), 40 x 27¾ in., (101.6 x 70.5 cm.), lithograph in colors on Transpagra paper (BP 3739, DM 9249, FR 31,081, Y 637,402).

$16,100* *Cold Coffee Thrown Away,* s., t., num., d. 1966 5/8 B. Nauman verso, prov., lit., (05-05-93, Christie-NY, #109, illus.), 20 x 23¾ in., (50.8 x 60.3 cm.), color photograph mounted on foamcore (BP 10,280, DM 25,402, FR 85,593, Y 1,774,496).

BI *Dead (C. L.-M. & Y. 30), 1975,* s., d., i. 'VI/VII AP', artist's proof, pub. blindstamp, Gemini G.E.L., full margins, good cond., staining, est. $4/5,000, (11-07-92, Sotheby-NY, #716, illus.), sheet 33⅞ x 49 in., (86 x 124.5 cm.), lithograph.

$1955* *Dead (C., L.-M. & Y. 30), 1975,* s., d., i. VI/VII AP, artist's proofs, blindstamp, pub. Gemini, G.E.L., full margins, good cond., (05-15-93, Sotheby-NY, #1121, illus.), sheet 33⅞ x 49 in., (86 x 124.5 cm.), lithograph (BP 1271, DM 3145, FR 10,568, Y 216,717).

$2070* *Double Face (C., L.-M. & Y. 43, Gemini 943), 1981,* s., d., #6/50, blindstamp, pub. Gemini, G.E.L., full margins, good cond., (05-15-93, Sotheby-NY, #1122, illus.), 24¼ x 34⅛ in., (61.6 x 86.7 cm.), lithograph on Arches Cover (BP 1346, DM 3330, FR 11,189, Y 229,465).

BI *Earth-World (C., L-M. & Y. 54), 1985,* s., #7/25, co-pub. by artist and Arber and Son Editions, full margins, good cond., est. $2/3,000, (11-07-92, Sotheby-NY, #718, illus.), 28¾ x 43⅞ in., (73 x 111.4 cm.), lithograph on BFK Rives.

$1610* *Earth-World (C., L.-M. & Y. 54), 1985,* s., #7/25, co-pub. artist and Arber and Son Editions, full margins, good cond., (05-15-93, Sotheby-NY, #1124), 28¾ x 43⅞ in., (73 x 111.4 cm.), lithograph on BFK Rives (BP 1047, DM 2590, FR 8703, Y 178,472).

BI *Eat Death (C., L.-M. & Y. 13), 1973,* s., d., #67/68, blindstamp, pub. Gemini, G.E.L., good cond., creases, soiling, handling creases, est. $3/4,000, (05-15-93, Sotheby-NY, #1119, illus.), sheet 42½ x 31 in., (108 x 78.7 cm.), lithograph on Arjomari paper.

$2530* *Life Mask (C. 41, G. 941), 1981,* s., d., #32/50, Gemini G.E.L. blindstamps, full margins, excell. cond., (05-11-93, Christie-NY, #518, illus.), sheet 28 x 38 in., (711 x 965 mm.), lithograph on Arches (BP 1615, DM 3986, FR 13,429, Y 278,297).

BI *Life Mask (C., L.-M. & Y. 41; G. 941), 1981,* s., d., #33/50, pub. blindstamp, Gemini, G.E.L., full margins, good cond., est. $2/3,000, (11-07-92, Sotheby-NY, #717, illus.), 25¼ x 34⅞ in., (641 x 886 mm.), lithograph.

BI *Life Mask (G. 941), 1981,* s., d., #5/50, blindstamp pub. Gemini G.E.L., full margins, very good cond., est. $2,5/3,500, (10-28-92, Butterfield, #3047, illus.), 25 x 34 in., (635 x 864 mm.), lithograph on Arches Cover paper.

$1438* *M.Ampere, 1973,* s., d., #22/58, margins, minor creasing, good cond., (10-15-92, Sotheby-London, #123, illus.), sheet 31 x 45¼ in., (78.7 x 114.9 cm.), lithograph p. in colors on wove (BP 880, DM 2141, FR 7259, Y 172,525).

$1210* *No Sweat (C., L.-M. & Y. 35), 1975,* s., d., #24/25, pub. blindstamp, Gemini G.E.L., full margins, good cond., rubbing, (11-07-92, Sotheby-NY, #715, illus.), sheet 39¾ x 31⅞ in., (101 x 81 cm.), silkscreen on Arches 88 (BP 791, DM 1932, FR 6530, Y 149,346).

$4025* *Raw War, 1971,* s., d., #54/100, pub. Castelli Graphics and Nicholas Wilder Gallery,blindstamp printer, Cirrus, very good cond.?, (05-19-93, Butterfield, #2273, illus.), 22½ x 28¼ in., (572 x 718 mm.), lithograph in colors on Arches (BP 2613, DM 6543, FR 22,043, Y 445,588).

$7700* *Raw-War (Castelli, Lorence-Monk & Young 7), 1971,* s., d., #49/100, co-pub. Castelli Graphics and Nicholas Wilder Gallery, good cond., (11-07-92, Sotheby-NY, #710, illus.), sheet 22½ x 28⅛ in., (572 x 714 mm.), lithograph p. in colors on white Arches (BP 5034, DM 12,294, FR 41,554, Y 950,383).

BI *Raw-War (Castelli, Lorence-Monk & Young 7), 1971,* s., d., #38/100, co-pub. Castelli Graphics and Nicholas Wilder Gallery, good cond. est. $8/10,000, (05-15-93, Sotheby-NY, #1118, illus.), sheet 22½ x 28⅜ in., (57.2 x 72.1 cm.), lithograph in colors on white Arches.

BI *Shit And Die (C., L.-M. & Y. 51, G. 1241), 1985,* s., d. '83, #13/38, blindstamp, pub. Gemini, G.E.L., full margins, good cond., est. $5/6,000, (05-15-93, Sotheby-NY, #1123, illus.), 6 x 9⅜ in., (15.2 x 23.8 cm.), drypoint etching on J. Barcham Green Crisbrook paper.

BI *Small Carousel (Cordes 58), 1988,* s., d., #7/35, pub. Brooke Alexander Editions, full margins, excellent cond., est. $2,5/3,000, (11-09-92, Christie-NY, #376, illus.), 15⅜ x 17¾ in., (391 x 451 mm.), drypoint on Somerset Satin.

$1438* *Sugar (G. 432), 1973,* s., d., #13/57, pub. Gemini GEL w/workshop blindstamp, margins, goodcond., (10-15-92, Sotheby-London, #122, illus.), 25⅞ x 34½ in., (65.7 x 87.6 cm.), lithograph and silkscreen p. in colors (BP 880, DM 2141, FR 7259, Y 172,525).

BI *Sugar/Ragus (C. L.-M. & Y. 14), 1973,* s., d., #35/57, pub. blindstamp, Gemini G.E.L., full margins, good cond., est. $2,5/3,500, (11-07-92, Sotheby-NY, #713, illus.), sheet 27¾ x 36 in., (705 x 914 mm.), lithograph and silkscreen p. in colors on Arjomari.

$1495* *Sugar/Ragus (C., L.-M. & Y. 14), 1973,* s., d., #35/57, blindstamp, pub. Gemini, G.E.L., full margins, good cond., (05-15-93, Sotheby-NY, #1120), sheet 27¾ x 36 in., (70.5 x 91.4 cm.), lithograph and silkscreen in colors in Arjomari paper (BP 972, DM 2405, FR 8081, Y 165,724).

$1840* *Sugar/Ragus (Cordes 14, Gemini 432), 1973,* s., d., #44/57, Gemini G.E.L. blindstamps, full margins, stain, skinned patches, very good cond., (05-11-93, Christie-NY, #517, illus.), sheet 27¾ x 35⅞ in., (705 x 911 mm.), color lithograph and screenprint on wove (BP 1175, DM 2899, FR 9766, Y 202,398).

$990* *Suposter (C., L.-M. & Y. 12), 1973,* s., d., #40/72, pub. blindstamp, Gemini G.E.L., good cond., (11-07-92, Sotheby-NY, #712, illus.), sheet 36 x 29¾ in., (914 x 756 mm.), lithograph and silkscreen p. in colors on Arjomari (BP 647, DM 1581, FR 5343, Y 122,192).

BI *TV Clown (C., L.-M. & Y. 55), 1988,* s., d., #32/35, pub. Brooke Alexander Editions, full margins, good cond., est. $4/5,000, (05-15-93, Sotheby-NY, #1125, illus.), 27⅝ x 41½ in., (70.2 x 105.4 cm.), lithograph on Transpagra paper.

BI *Tone Mirror (C. L.-M. & Y. 26), 1974,* s., d., #71/100, co-pub. Multiples, Inc. and Castelli Graphics, fullmargins, good cond., est. $3/3,500, (11-07-92, Sotheby-NY, #714, illus.), 28½ x 38⅝ in., (724 x 981 mm.), lithograph p. in brown.

$750* *Tone Mirror, 1974,* s., num. 70/100, d. '74, pub. Castelli Graphics, from series MirrorsOf The Mind, p. by Cirrus Editions, good cond., (11-30-92, Phillips-London, #553), sheet 30 x 40⅛ in., (76.2 x 101.9 cm.), lithograph in colors (BP 495, DM 1195, FR 4056, Y 93,342).

$660* *Untitled (Gray) (C. 9), 1971,* s., d., #58/75, pub. Castelli Graphics, Nicholas Wilder Gallery and Cirrus, blindstamp Cirrus, good cond., creases, (02-24-93, Butterfield, #3235), 30 x 42 in., (76.2 x 106.7 cm.), lithograph in colors on wove (BP 460, DM 1071, FR 3632, Y 77,447).

$880* *Untitled (Gray) (C., L-M. & Y. 9), 1971,* s., d., #11/75, co-pub. Castelli Graphics, Nicholas Wilder Gallery and Cirrus Editions, good cond., creases, glue, skinned spot, rubbed spots, (11-07-92, Sotheby-NY, #711), sheet 29⅞ x 41⅞ in., (75.9 x 106.4 cm.), lithograph p. in colors on Rives (BP 575, DM 1405, FR 4749, Y 108,615).

$2200* *Use Me (C. 59), 1988,* s., d., #7/35, pub. Brooke Alexander Editions, full margins, excellent cond., (11-09-92, Christie-NY, #377, illus.), 15⁷⁄₁₆ x 17⅞ in., (392 x 454 mm.), etching on Somerset Satin (BP 1455, DM 3512, FR 11,866, Y 273,021).

NAURAC, J.R.

$2409* *Nord Wagons-Lits: Londres Vichy Pullmann, 1927,* p. L. Serre And Cie, excell. cond., (01-23-93, Ribeyre/Baron, #7, illus.), 42⅛ x 30⅛ in., (107 x 76.5 cm.), poster (BP 1576, DM 3830, FR 12,959, Y 301,502).

$738* *PLM. Sports De Neige Des Alpes Et Du Jura, 1930,* very good cond., (03-15-93, Arcole, #101, illus.), 39⅜ x 24⁷⁄₁₆ in., (100 x 62 cm.), (BP 514, DM 1226, FR 4167, Y 87,420).

NAY, Ernst Wilhelm German 1902-1968

BI *"Dominant Blau", Farblitho (Gabler 72), 1964-2,* pencil s., d., from Europaische Graphik II portfolio, est. DM 6,500, (11-20-92, Lempertz, #733, illus.), sh 25¹⁵⁄₁₆ x 20¹⁄₁₆ in., (66 x 51 cm.), color lithograph on Velin on BFK Rives.

BI *Farbaquatinta (NOR) (Gabler 70), 1964,* #34/100, pencil s., d., est. DM 7000, (11-20-92, Lempertz, #732, illus.), sh 16⅜ x 14⅝ in., (41.6 x 37.2 cm.), color aquatint on Velin.

$2599* *Farbaquatinta 1957-6,* s., num., (11-28-92, Schoppmann, #676), 8⅛ x 7¹¹⁄₁₆ in., (20.7 x 19.6 cm.), color etching on handmade (BP 1716, DM 4141, FR 14,056, Y 323,460).

$2007* *Farbaquatinta 1965-2(Gabler 75), 1965,* s., d., #36/100, plate 2 from E.W. Nay, Uber den Menschen, blindstamp, (05-27-93, Lempertz, #922, illus.), 25¹⁵⁄₁₆ x 19¹³⁄₁₆ in., (66 x 50.3 cm.), color etching on wove (BP 1285, DM 3220, FR 10,855, Y 215,159).

BI *Farbaquatinta 1965-5, Spiele Des Menschen (Gabler 78), 1965,* s., d., #47/100, plate 5 from E.W. Nay, Uber den Menschen, est. DM 3,500-, (05-27-93, Lempertz, #923, illus.), 26⅛ x 19⅞ in., (66.3 x 50.5 cm.), color etching on Arches wove.

$1226* *Farbholzschnitt "C. G. Heise Zum Geburtstag" (Gabler 80 B), 1965,* #67/200, pencil s., (11-20-92, Lempertz, #734), sh 30⅛ x 22⁵⁄₁₆ in., (76.5 x 56.7 cm.), color wood cut on Arches-Velin (BP 807, DM 1955, FR 6584, Y 152,469).

$2693* *Farbholzschnitt 1959 (Gabler 62), (19)59,* s., d., num., (06-08-93, Karl/Faber, #1149, illus.), approx. 8¼ x 8¼ in., (21 x 21 cm.), color woodcut on wove (BP 1770, DM 4370, FR 14,716, Y 286,033).

$1154* *Farblitho (NOR) (Gabler 64), 1961,* (11-20-92, Lempertz, #731), sh 19⁵⁄₁₆ x 26¼ in., (49 x 66.7 cm.), color lithograph on offset paper (BP 760, DM 1840, FR 6198, Y 143,514).

BI *Farblitho (NOR) (Gabler 83), 1966-1,* #77/100, pencil s., est. DM 3,000, (11-20-92, Lempertz, #735), sh 38½ x 25¹¹⁄₁₆ in., (97.8 x 65.2 cm.), lithograph in color on Velin.

BI *Figures With Boats: Two,* s., i. Epreuve d'Etat, s., #21/50, margins, good cond., est. BP 6/800, (06-30-93, Sotheby-London, #573, illus.), one 10 x 15½ in., (254 x 394 mm.), the other 15¼ x 10 in., (254 x 394 mm.), etching w/aquatint in color on japon nacre.

$928* *Komposition,* #6/300, s. Nachlass Nay: Elizabeth Nay, (09-14-92, Venator/Hansten, #2479), color screenprint on Rives (BP 491, DM 1380, FR 4675, Y 115,394).

BI *Komposition (NOR) (Gabler 46), 1955,* s., num., est. DM 9,000, (12-05-92, Bassenge, #7513), 14³⁄₁₆ x 20¹¹⁄₁₆ in., (36 x 52.5 cm.), lithograph in 9 colors on copper print paper.

BI *Komposition Weiss-Rot-Blau, (19)67,* est. DM 1800, (12-01-92, Karl/Faber, #1051), 51⁹⁄₁₆ x 47¼ in., (131 x 120 cm.), color serigraph on cardboard.

$1226* *Siebdruck (NOR) (Gabler 85), 1966-1,* #17/200, pencil s., d., (11-20-92, Lempertz, #736), sh 25¹⁵⁄₁₆ x 17½ in., (66 x 44.5 cm.), serigraph in color on Velin (BP 807, DM 1955, FR 6584, Y 152,469).

BI *Untitled,* s. Nachlass Nay: Elizabeth Nay, #214/300, pub. Kunstverein, 1968, full margins, good cond., minor handling creases, creasing in margins, minor soiling, Late Gerhard Brauer Coll., est. Dfl. 1/1,500, (05-27-93, Sotheby-Amstrdm, #760), 19⅝ x 18¹⁄₁₆ in., colored silkscreen on wove.

$2560* *Untitled (Gabler 46), 1955,* stone s.; s., d., artist's proof, water stains, (09-25-92, Granier, #2955, illus.), sheet 19³⁄₁₆ x 25¹³⁄₁₆ in., (48.7 x 65.6 cm.), color lithograph on cream hand-made Arches (BP 1495, DM 3795, FR 12,832, Y 308,992).

$1158* *Untitled (Gabler 66), 1962,* s., d., num., (06-19-93, Wachholtz, #529), 6¹⁵⁄₁₆ x 5½ in., (17.6 x 13.9 cm.), color aquatint etching in copper print paper (BP 777, DM 1955, FR 6572, Y 128,367).

$1844* *Vernis Mou III (Gabler 60), 1959,* (06-05-93, Bassenge, #6378), 13¹¹⁄₁₆ x 18⅛ in., (34.7 x 46 cm.), soft-ground on copper print (BP 1214, DM 2990, FR 10,077, Y 197,812).

NAYA

$472* *Venetian Palazzo, c. 1860-65,* mounted on card, photog.'s blindstamped credit Naya Photografo Venezia, 420 x 530mm, (05-07-93, Sotheby-London, #27, illus.), photograph, albumen print (BP 299, DM 746, FR 2515, Y 51,971).

NAYA, Carlo

$288* *Selected Works: Views Of Venice", 1866: Three,* attrib., third t. in neg., (05-23-93, Butterfield, #3554, illus.), from 9½ x 7¼ in., to 10⅝ x 14¼ in., photograph, albumen prints, third blue-toned (BP 188, DM 471, FR 1585, Y 31,834).

NEBEL, Otto 1892-1975

BI *Komposition L. 556, 1963,* est. SF 140/160, (10-14-92, Germann, #579), 8⁷⁄₁₆ x 6³⁄₁₆ in., (215 x 157 mm.), linocut.

$1065* *Konnen Ist Hochstes Wissen, 1973: Ten,* s., (11-13-92, Koller, #5387), 19¹¹⁄₁₆ x 13¾ in., (50 x 35 cm.), color linocut on print paper (BP 688, DM 1672, FR 5638, Y 132,183, SF 1508).

$1991* *Sinnesgefuge, 1973: Ten,* s., d., 1 Edition, (12-01-92, Karl/Faber, #1052), sh 19¹¹⁄₁₆ x 13¾ in., (50 x 35 cm.), color linocut w/silver bzw. gold on cardboard (BP 1315, DM 3173, FR 10,815, Y 247,883).

NEDELEC 20th cent.

$10* *"Composition",* G/7, s., (01-28-93, Pescheteau, #223), 20¹⁄₁₆ x 25⁹⁄₁₆ in., (51 x 65 cm.), etching and aquatin on Auvergne (BP 7, DM 16, FR 54, Y 1242).

NEEFS, Jacob 1610-after 1660

$390* *Nosce Te Ipsum (Wurzbach 27; Hollstein 27),* after J. Jordaens, (12-04-92, Bassenge, #6320), 10¹³⁄₁₆ x 13⅜ in., (27.5 x 34 cm.), etching (BP 250, DM 621, FR 2107, Y 48,689).

NEEL, Alice American 1900-1984

BI *Barnaby Rube, 1981,* s., d., blindstamp pub., good cond.?, surface soiling, est. $4/600, (10-28-92, Butterfield, #3048), 20 x 19 in., (508 x 483 mm.), silkscreen on white wove.

$193* *Seated Man, 1981,* s., d., annot. A.P. 10/16, full margins, good cond., creases, surface soiling, (10-28-92, Butterfield, #3049), 26½ x 22⅛ in., (673 x 562 mm.), color lithograph on wove (BP 123, DM 298, FR 1012, Y 23,681).

$165* *Untitled (Seated Youth), 1980,* s., d., num. Neel '80 3/100, pub.'s chop, watermark, very good cond., foxing, inclusion, (03-12-93, Skinner, #104, illus.), sight, sheet 36¼ x 27½ in., (92.1 x 69.9 cm.), lithograph in colors on Arches wove (BP 115, DM 275, FR 934, Y 19,446).

NEGRE, Charles 1820-1880

BI *Imperial Asylum At Vincennes, c. 1859,* s. in ink, lit., est. $6/8,000, (10-13-92, Christie-NY, #17, illus.), 17 x 13¼ in., (43.2 x 33.7 cm.), photograph, albumen print.

NEGRETTI & ZAMBRA

BI *The Crystal Palace With Train And Telegraph Wires, c. 1853-55,* w/orig. edging, label, est. $10/15,000, (10-15-92, Sotheby-NY, #83, illus.), overall 3¼ x 6¾ in., (8.3 x 17.1 cm.), photograph, stereo daguerreotype.

NEIL, A. (after)

BI *The Noble Game Of Cricket As Played In The Celebrated Cricket Field Near White Conduit House, 1787,* by Noble, pub. Alexander Hogg, 1787, est. BP 250/350, (03-03-93, Bonhams-Chelsea, #247), image 5¾ x 7½ in., (14.6 x 19.1 cm.), hand-colored etching.

NEIL, Jan

$142* *MacDonnell Ranges,* s. Jan Neil, i., d. '91, #8/25, (08-11-92, L. Joel, #147G), 11¹³⁄₁₆ x 14⁹⁄₁₆ in., (30 x 37 cm.), color screenprint (BP 74, DM 208, FR 706, Y 18,184, A$ 192).

NEIMAN, Leroy American b. 1927

$165* *"Bullfighting",* s., #46/300, (02-27-93, Dunning, #1121), pl 18¼ x 22¼ in., (46.4 x 56.5 cm.), screenprint (BP 116, DM 271, FR 922, Y 19,478).

BI *"F.X. McCrory's Whiskey Bar",* s., #186/300, Styria studio blindstamp, full margins, est. $5,0/10,000, (01-23-93, Goldberg, #485, illus.), image 22½ x 45 in., (57.2 x 114.3 cm.), color lithograph.

$935* *Football Game,* pencil s., num. 239/300, (09-21-92, Selkirk, #189), 26 x 37 in., (66 x 94 cm.), color silkscreen (BP 547, DM 1387, FR 4746, Y 115,560).

BI *"Grand Prix De Monaco",* edit. #182/300, s., est. $1,8/3,500, (09-18-92, DuMouchelle, #2032), 24 x 36¼ in., (61 x 92.1 cm.), color silkscreen.

$275* *"Lincoln",* s., AP, (12-11-92, DuMouchelle, #1160), approx. 18 x 18 in., (45.7 x 45.7 cm.), serigraph (BP 176, DM 433, FR 1485, Y 34,030).

$193* *"Match Point",* s., #177/300, (02-27-93, Dunning, #1038, illus.), sh 48 x 36 in., (121.9 x 91.4 cm.), screenprint (BP 136, DM 317, FR 1078, Y 22,784).

$180* *Mixed Doubles,* s., (05-16-93, Hanzel, #451), 19 x 18¾ in., (48.3 x 47.6 cm.), lithograph (BP 117, DM 290, FR 973, Y 19,953).

$121* *Sailing,* s., (02-14-93, Hanzel, #697), 19¾ x 24½ in., (50.2 x 62.2 cm.), photolithograph (BP 85, DM 201, FR 679, Y 14,592).

$187* *Self Portrait,* s., #299/500, (12-13-92, Hindman, #356), 9¼ x 9¼ in., color serigraph (BP 120, DM 294, FR 1002, Y 23,135).

BI *Self-Portrait,* s., #459/500, est. $5/700, (05-16-93, Hanzel, #453), 9¼ x 9¼ in., (23.5 x 23.5 cm.), serigraph.

$275* *Showgirls,* s., num. 240/1000, (11-12-92, Freemn/Fine Art, #159), 14 x 10 in., (35.6 x 25.4 cm.), serigraph (BP 181, DM 436, FR 1470, Y 34,098).

$1430* *"Zebra Family",* edit. A.P., s., (09-18-92, DuMouchelle, #2031), 28 x 37¾ in., (71.1 x 95.9 cm.), color silkscreen (BP 823, DM 2141, FR 7333, Y 178,171).

NELSON, Joan American b. 1958

BI *Untitled, 1990: Two,* s., d., #42/45, blindstamp, pub. Cirrus Editions, full margins, goodcond., est. $1,2/1,800, (05-15-93, Sotheby-NY, #1127, illus.), each 16 x 16 in., (40.6 x 40.6 cm.), lithograph in colors w/silkscreen varnish on BFK Rives.

NELSON, William

BI *"Bruce Jenner Decathalon Suite": Ten, 1976,* portfolio, limited edit., s., est. $6/800, (07-10-92, Skinner, #411), lithograph.

NESBITT, Jackson Lee American b. 1913

$330* *Auction Barn, 1989,* s., d., t., num. 131/250, pub. Rolling Stone Press blindstamp, full margins, excellent cond., (02-24-93, Butterfield, #2859), 12⅝ x 17¼ in., (321 x 451 mm.), lithograph on buff wove (BP 230, DM 536, FR 1816, Y 38,723).

$440* *Evening In March, 1942,* s., t., pub. AAA, full margins, very good cond., fingerprints, (02-24-93, Butterfield, #2858), 11⅞ x 9 in., (302 x 229 mm.), lithograph on wove (BP 307, DM 714, FR 2422, Y 51,631).

$220* *Making Ingots, 1938,* s., num. 46/60, smudging, tear, (11-12-92, Freemn/Fine Art, #160), image 12 x 9¼ in., (30.5 x 23.5 cm.), etching (BP 144, DM 349, FR 1176, Y 27,278).

$132* *"Ozark Farmer",* s., t., num. 15/250, excellent cond., (10-31-92, Cleveland, #197), 12¾ x 10¼ in., (32.4 x 26 cm.), lithograph (BP 85, DM 203, FR 689, Y 16,351).

NESBITT, Lowell American b. 1933

$176* *From The Andy Warhol Suite,* s., d. 1974, #20/50, prop. Price Waterhouse Corporate Coll., (05-16-93, Hindman, #652), 26½ x 37 in., (67.3 x 94 cm.), color aquatint (BP 114, DM 283, FR 951, Y 19,510).

$110* *Iris,* s., num. 74/200, d. 1981, (11-12-92, Freemn/Fine Art, #160C), 24 x 24 in., (61 x 61 cm.), screenprint (BP 72, DM 174, FR 588, Y 13,639).

$165* *Irises,* s., d. 1973, #27/100, (05-16-93, Hindman, #616), 19¾ x 33¼ in., (50.2 x 84.5 cm.), color etching and aquatint (BP 107, DM 265, FR 892, Y 18,291).

$165* *Lily,* s., d. 1980, num. 135/200, (11-12-92, Freemn/Fine Art, #160A), 25½ x 25½ in., (64.8 x 64.8 cm.), screenprint (BP 108, DM 261, FR 882, Y 20,459).

BI   *Moving White,* s., d. 1963, t., #8/10, est. $200/250, (09-17-92, Sloan, #663), 16¾ x 33¾ in., (42.5 x 85.7 cm.), color woodcut on wove paper.

BI   *Red Rose,* d. 1981, est. $150/250, (06-13-93, Hindman, #363), 19¾ x 17⅞ in., (50.2 x 45.4 cm.), color lithograph.

$165* *Three Floral Lithographs,* s., num., (06-13-93, Hindman, #364), each 31½ x 31½ in., (80 x 80 cm.), lithograph (BP 108, DM 269, FR 903, Y 17,363).

$187* *Tiger Lily,* s., d. 1981, (06-13-93, Hindman, #361), 19¾ x 17⅞ in., (50.2 x 45.4 cm.), color lithograph (BP 122, DM 304, FR 1023, Y 19,678).

$165* *Tiger Spotted Lily,* s., d. '78, num. 54/175, (11-12-92, Freemn/Fine Art, #160B), 24 x 20 in., (61 x 50.8 cm.), screenprint (BP 108, DM 261, FR 882, Y 20,459).

$110* *Tulip,* s., #82/20, very good cond., (02-07-93, Bakker, #258), 24½ x 28 in., (62.2 x 71.1 cm.), color lithograph (BP 76, DM 182, FR 617, Y 13,688).

$110* *Tulip,* s., d. 1974, num. 50/200, (11-12-92, Freemn/Fine Art, #160D), 26 x 18 in., (66 x 45.7 cm.), screenprint (BP 72, DM 174, FR 588, Y 13,639).

$358* *Yellow Flower,* s., d. '78, #119/175, (06-11-93, Freemn/Fine Art, #156), 24 x 24 in., (61 x 61 cm.), screenprint (BP 235, DM 582, FR 1962, Y 37,984).

NESCH, Irma   1894-1970
BI   *Figurliche Darstellungen, 1930/31: Twenty-Five,* s., d., t., artist's proof, est. DM 9,000, (06-10-93, Hauswedell/Nolt, #718A), etching.

NESCH, Rolf   1893-1975
$3390* *Abschied, 1932,* s., t., series Hamburger Brucken, lit., (06-10-93, Hauswedell/Nolt, #711, illus.), image 17¹¹⁄₁₆ x 23⁹⁄₁₆ in., (45 x 59.9 cm.), color etching on wove (BP 2217, DM 5520, FR 18,586, Y 359,834).

$3319* *"Bernadette",* s., i., tire par l'artiste, (12-01-92, Karl/Faber, #1054, illus.), 17¹⁄₁₆ x 15¾ in., (43.4 x 40 cm.), color metal print on heavy wove (BP 2193, DM 5290, FR 18,028, Y 413,222).

$155* *Dr. M. Fischer,* s., num., light staining, (09-25-92, Granier, #2957), sheet 14¾ x 11³⁄₁₆ in., (37.5 x 28.4 cm.), drypoint on copper print paper (BP 91, DM 230, FR 777, Y 18,709).

$8324* *Elbbrucke, Gelb, Plate II (Detroit cat. p. 25, no. 52, p. 74, no. 11), 1932,* from Hamburger Brucken, s., i., t., brown spots, staining, (12-01-92, Christie-London, #468, illus.), plate 13¹⁄₁₆ x 23⅜ in., (331 x 593 mm.), sheet 18⅝ x 25¹⁵⁄₁₆ in., (331 x 593 mm.), metal print in black, grey and yellow on thick wove (BP 5500, DM 13,267, FR 45,215, Y 1,036,355).

$565* *Er Und Sie, 1960,* s., #210/300, (06-10-93, Hauswedell/Nolt, #717), image 21¹⁵⁄₁₆ x 14¹³⁄₁₆ in., (55.8 x 37.6 cm.), color lithograph and metal print (BP 370, DM 920, FR 3098, Y 59,972).

$1833* *Erzengel Gabriel, 1952-1953,* s., (06-23-93, Kornfeld, #626), 18½ x 14⅜ in., (47 x 36.5 cm.), color lithograph on cream handmade (BP 1245, DM 3102, FR 10,433, Y 199,695, SF 2760).

$1271* *Eselreiter, 1968,* s., #209/300, (06-10-93, Hauswedell/Nolt, #718), image 19½ x 12½ in., (49.5 x 31.7 cm.), color metal print on Johannot (BP 831, DM 2070, FR 6968, Y 134,911).

BI   *Eselreiter, 1968,* watermark, s., #209/300, pub. Jahresgabe 1968; stamp verso, margins, surface dirt, good cond., est. BP 1,0/1,200, (12-01-92, Christie-London, #469), L. 19⅜ x 12½ in., (492 x 317 mm.), relief etching w/metal cut in colors on wove.

$4732* *Fagottisten, 1931,* s., t., series Karl Muck und sein Orchester, lit., (06-10-93, Hauswedell/Nolt, #710, illus.), image 17⅝ x 11⅞ in., (44.8 x 30.1 cm.), etching on Umdruck paper (BP 3095, DM 7706, FR 25,943, Y 502,282).

$3814* *Fjord, 1933-34,* s., t., from series Schnee, lit., (06-10-93, Hauswedell/Nolt, #716, illus.), image 17 x 22¹¹⁄₁₆ in.,

(43.2 x 57.6 cm.), metal print on wove (BP 2495, DM 6211, FR 20,910, Y 404,840).

$310* *Frauenportrait,* s., num., creases, staining, (09-25-92, Granier, #2956), sheet 15⅞ x 12⅝ in., (40.4 x 32.1 cm.), etching on cream wove (BP 181, DM 460, FR 1554, Y 37,417).

$1985* *Gespenster (Erlkonig?), c. 1955,* s. in chalk, num., (06-23-93, Kornfeld, #627), 15⁹⁄₁₆ x 19⅛ in., (39.5 x 48.5 cm.), color lithograph on cream handmade (BP 1349, DM 3359, FR 11,298, Y 216,254, SF 2990).

$2825* *Karl Muck Dirigierend, 1931,* s., t., sheet 1 of series Karl Muck und sein Orchester, lit., (06-10-93, Hauswedell/Nolt, #709, illus.), image 19¾ x 13⅞ in., (50.1 x 35.2 cm.), etching on transfer paper (BP 1848, DM 4600, FR 15,488, Y 299,862).

$3107* *Kiefer Und Tannen, 1933-34,* s., t., from series Schnee, lit., (06-10-93, Hauswedell/Nolt, #715, illus.), image 22¾ x 16¹⁵⁄₁₆ in., (57.8 x 43.1 cm.), metal print on hand-made (BP 2032, DM 5059, FR 17,034, Y 329,795).

BI   *Kneipenszene, 1929,* s., est. DM 900, (12-05-92, Bassenge, #7516), 5⁹⁄₁₆ x 5¹³⁄₁₆ in., (14.2 x 14.7 cm.), drypoint on copper print paper.

$1680* *Kobold Und Vogel, c. 1950,* s., artist's proof, (06-23-93, Kornfeld, #624), image 19⅛ x 15⁹⁄₁₆ in., (48.5 x 39.5 cm.), color lithograph on thick wove (BP 1141, DM 2843, FR 9562, Y 183,026, SF 2530).

$4802* *Landungsbrucken, 1932,* s., t., series Hamburger Brucken, lit., (06-10-93, Hauswedell/Nolt, #713, illus.), image 23⅜ x 17¹³⁄₁₆ in., (59.8 x 45.2 cm.), metal print on thick wove (BP 3141, DM 7820, FR 26,327, Y 509,712).

$366* *Mannerportrat,* i., s. Probedruck, Nesch, #1/5, (03-24-93, Venator/Hansten, #4540), pl. approx. 8⁹⁄₁₆ x 6¹¹⁄₁₆ in., (21.8 x 17 cm.), drypoint on thin tracing paper (BP 248, DM 598, FR 2034, Y 43,003).

$2291* *Musiker, c. 1948,* s., 1st state, ded., very rare, (06-23-93, Kornfeld, #623), 16¾ x 9⅝ in., (42.5 x 24.5 cm.), color etching on thick wove (BP 1556, DM 3876, FR 13,039, Y 249,591, SF 3450).

$847* *Nachtwache, 1926,* s., prov., lit., (06-10-93, Hauswedell/Nolt, #703, illus.), image 9¾ x 11⅞ in., (24.8 x 30.1 cm.), drypoint on wove (BP 554, DM 1379, FR 4644, Y 89,906).

$2596* *Negersanger, c. 1952,* s. in chalk, num. 2/2, (06-23-93, Kornfeld, #625), 19³⁄₁₆ x 15½ in., (48.7 x 39.4 cm.), color lithograph (BP 1764, DM 4393, FR 14,775, Y 282,819, SF 3910).

$2966* *Schichtwechsel, 1929,* s., t., (06-10-93, Hauswedell/Nolt, #705, illus.), image 10¹⁵⁄₁₆ x 14³⁄₁₆ in., (27.8 x 36 cm.), etching on wove (BP 1940, DM 4830, FR 16,261, Y 314,829).

$2401* *Selbstbildnis Im Profil Nach Links, 1933,* s., t., artist's proof, lit., prov., (06-10-93, Hauswedell/Nolt, #714, illus.), image 13⅛ x 7¹³⁄₁₆ in., (33.4 x 19.8 cm.), metal print on wove (BP 1571, DM 3910, FR 13,163, Y 254,856).

$3390* *Selbstbildnis Mit Weichem Hut, 1923-24,* s., lit., ded., (06-10-93, Hauswedell/Nolt, #702, illus.), image 9 x 6¹¹⁄₁₆ in., (22.9 x 17 cm.), drypoint (BP 2217, DM 5520, FR 18,586, Y 359,834).

$3672* *Stimmungssangerin, 1931,* s., t., series St. Pauli, lit., (06-10-93, Hauswedell/Nolt, #708, illus.), image 19¹¹⁄₁₆ x 12⅞ in., (50 x 32.7 cm.), color etching on transfer paper (BP 2402, DM 5979, FR 20,132, Y 389,768).

$2119* *Treppe Am Hafen, c. 1923,* (06-10-93, Hauswedell/Nolt, #701, illus.), image 12¹⁵⁄₁₆ x 17½ in., (33 x 44.5 cm.), etching on hand-made Japan (BP 1386, DM 3451, FR 11,617, Y 224,923).

$4965* *"Tschingis Khan", c. 1960,* s., i., t., (06-05-93, Grisebach, #391, illus.), 23⁹⁄₁₆ x 12¹⁄₁₆ in., (59.8 x 30.6 cm.), color metal print on thin copper print hand-made (BP 3268, DM 8050, FR 27,131, Y 532,611).

NESENSOHN, Carl   1898-1970
$357* *Charles Lindbergh Testifying At Kidnapping Trial, 1936,* label, (10-14-92, Swann, #336, illus.), 6½ x 9½ in., (16.5 x 24.1 cm.), photograph, silver print (BP 210, DM 522, FR 1772, Y 43,262).

$770* *The New Wright Plane, c. 1910,* t., (10-13-92, Christie-NY, #68, illus.), 6¾ x 8⅞ in., (17.1 x 22.5 cm.), photograph, gelatin silver print (BP 448, DM 1128, FR 3833, Y 93,367).

BI *President And Mrs. Calvin Coolidge In The Reception Room Of The Willard Hotel,* 1923, p. 1930s, unique, est. $800/1,200, (04-07-93, Swann, #340, illus.), 8 x 6½ in., photograph, silver print.

NETO, Mario Cravo

$880* *"Lord Of The Head", 1988,* s., d., edit. 7/25, Dixon Collection, (11-16-92, Butterfield, #5913, illus.), 15¾ x 15¾ in., (400.8 x 400.8 mm.), photograph, gelatin silver print (BP 579, DM 1403, FR 4726, Y 109,439).

$990* *"Tinho With Bone, Brasil",* 1990/1992, s., d., edit. 7/25, (11-16-92, Butterfield, #5912, illus.), 15¾ x 15¾ in., (400.8 x 400.8 mm.), photograph, gelatin silver print (BP 652, DM 1578, FR 5317, Y 123,119).

NEUENBORN, Paul 1866-1913

BI *Ausstellung Das Tier In Der Kunst, 1904,* pierced plastic tape, sellotape marks, tape, lit., est. BP 3/500, (02-04-93, Christie-S. Ken, #175), 38 x 27 in., (96.5 x 68.6 cm.), color lithograph.

NEUENHAUSEN, Siegfried b. 1931

$78* *Hurra! Schon Wieder Ein Krankenhaus In Hanoi Getroffen, 1973,* s., d., num., staining, (09-25-92, Granier, #2958), sheet 27⅝ x 19¹³⁄₁₆ in., (70.2 x 50.4 cm.), color lithograph on offset board (BP 46, DM 116, FR 391, Y 9415).

NEUGASS, Fritz

$357* *"City Buildings Reflected In Hood Of Car" and "Empire State BuildingReflected In A Puddle", c. 1946: Two,* handstamps, (10-14-92, Swann, #525, illus.), 7¾ x 8¾ in., (19.7 x 22.2 cm.), photograph (BP 210, DM 522, FR 1772, Y 43,262).

NEUHAUS, Ervin

$51* *Composition Marine,* s., #1/1, (05-06-93, Laurin, #72), color monotype (BP 32, DM 80, FR 270, Y 5611).

NEUHAUS, Eugene

$220* *"Girl By The Lake", 1920,* ink inits., trimmed to image, laid down, time staining, good cond., scuffing, (10-28-92, Butterfield, #2746), image 8 x 10 in., (203 x 254 mm.), color monotype on laid paper (BP 140, DM 340, FR 1154, Y 26,994).

NEUMANN, Ernest

$642* *"The Accused" and "Lawyers And Client": Two,* d. 42, latter '49 in plate, s., t., (11-30-92, Ritchie, #16, illus.), each 10½ x 8¾ in., (26.7 x 22.2 cm.), etching (BP 424, DM 1023, FR 3472, Y 79,900, C$ 825).

NEUMANN, Hans

BI *Winter Landscape,* s., t. illegibly, good cond., est. $3/500, (07-19-92, Bakker, #5), image 14¾ x 11¾ in., (37.5 x 29.8 cm.), color woodblock print.

NEUMANN, Robert von American 1888-1976

$165* *"Hauling The Net",* s. Robert von Neumann, very good cond., (11-21-92, Bakker, #10), image 10¼ x 14¾ in., (26 x 37.5 cm.), lithograph (BP 109, DM 263, FR 886, Y 20,520).

NEUQELMAN, Lucien French 1909-1988

$332* *Fransk Hamn Med Segelbatar,* s. 15/250, (11-07-92, Falkkloos, #342), lithograph in colors (BP 217, DM 533, FR 1792, Y 40,978, SK 1980).

$369* *Franskt Kustmotiv,* s. 19/250, (11-07-92, Falkkloos, #341), lithograph in color (BP 241, DM 592, FR 1991, Y 45,544, SK 2200).

$209* *Kvinnor I Franskt Landskap,* s., LXIV/CL, (04-17-93, Falkkloos, #357), 15¾ x 22⁷⁄₁₆ in., (40 x 57 cm.), lithograph in colors (BP 136, DM 334, FR 1129, Y 23,240, SK 1540).

$332* *Picnic Vid Franska Kusten,* s. V/XXXX, (11-07-92, Falkkloos, #340), lithograph in colors (BP 217, DM 533, FR 1792, Y 40,978, SK 1980).

$238* *Utflykt Vid Kusten,* s., IX/XXXX, (04-17-93, Falkkloos, #356), 18⅛ x 25³⁄₁₆ in., (46 x 64 cm.), lithograph in colors (BP 155, DM 381, FR 1286, Y 26,465, SK 1760).

NEUSUSS, Floris M. b. 1937

$569* *Hannah Hoch Im Atelier, 1962,* mono., d., t., photographer's stamp, (11-12-92, Lempertz, #187, illus.), 11½ x 11⅞ in., (29.2 x 30.2 cm.), photograph, gelatin silver print (BP 364, DM 894, FR 3048, Y 70,395).

$379* *Heinz Hajek-Halke, 1983: Two,* felt pen mono., d., t., photographer's stamp, (11-12-92, Lempertz, #189), each 11¹⁵⁄₁₆ x 9⁷⁄₁₆ in., (30.3 x 24 cm.), photograph, gelatin silver print (BP 242, DM 596, FR 2030, Y 46,889).

$379* *Katwijk, 1959,* ink s., d., t., photographer's stamp, (11-12-92, Lempertz, #186), 11¹⁵⁄₁₆ x 14⁵⁄₁₆ in., (30.3 x 36.3 cm.), photograph, gelatin silver print (BP 242, DM 596, FR 2030, Y 46,889).

$455* *Prinzip Fotogramm, 1972,* felt pen s., d., t., (11-12-92, Lempertz, #188), 15⅞ x 12 in., (40.4 x 30.5 cm.), photograph, gelatin silver print (BP 291, DM 715, FR 2437, Y 56,291).

BI *Studie, 1958,* s., d., est. DM 600, (11-12-92, Lempertz, #184), 15¼ x 11 in., (38.8 x 28 cm.), photograph, gelatin silver print.

$531* *Traumbild, 1958,* mono., d., (11-12-92, Lempertz, #185, illus.), 15⁷⁄₁₆ x 11⁹⁄₁₆ in., (39.2 x 29.4 cm.), photograph, gelatin silver print (BP 340, DM 835, FR 2844, Y 65,693).

NEVELSON, Louise Russian/American 1900-1988

BI *Abstraction, 1973,* s., d. Louise Nevelson-73, #64/90, very good cond., est. $1/1,500, (03-12-93, Skinner, #109, illus.), sight 27¾ x 23½ in., (70.5 x 59.7 cm.), aquatint and gold leaf collage on wove.

BI *American Jewish Congress Print (B. 107), 1973,* s., d. '74, pub. Pace Editions, margins, good cond., staining, est. $1,5/2,000, (02-24-93, Butterfield, #3096), 28 x 22⅛ in., (711 x 562 mm.), silkscreen in colors on Arches.

$690* *American Jewish Congress Print (B. 107), 1973,* s., pub. Pace Editions New York, p. Sheila and Carl MarGain at MaurelStudios, margins, good cond., staining, (05-19-93, Butterfield, #2274), 28 x 22⅛ in., (711 x 562 mm.), silkscreen in colors on Arches (BP 448, DM 1122, FR 3779, Y 76,387).

$495* *American Jewish Congress Print (B. 107), 1974,* inits., d., num. 26/100, pub. Pace Editions, full margins, printer'sink, mat staining, (09-19-92, Christie-E, #167), sheet 32½ x 26 in., (826 x 660 mm.), screenprint in colors on wove (BP 285, DM 741, FR 2538, Y 61,675).

BI *Aquatint & Collage Series: Untitled III (B. 117) 1973,* s., d., num. 10/90, pub. Pace Editions, margins, apparently good cond., est. $2/3,000, (02-24-93, Butterfield, #3097), 29¾ x 19½ in., (756 x 495 mm.), aquatint in colors w/ collage on C.M. Fabriano Rosapina.

$252* *"Composition 1973",* #61/150, s., (01-28-93, Pescheteau, #224), 35⁷⁄₁₆ x 24¹³⁄₁₆ in., (90 x 63 cm.), color lithograph on wove (BP 166, DM 399, FR 1351, Y 31,289).

BI *Composition With Collage, 1966,* s., d., est. DM 800, (12-01-92, Karl/Faber, #1058), sh 23¹⁄₁₆ x 17½ in., (58.5 x 44.5 cm.), serigraph and collage on blue cardboard.

$825* *Double Imagery,* s., d. 67, #3/20, part of a diptych, prov., (05-16-93, Hindman, #601), 26¼ x 51¾ in., (66.7 x 131.4 cm.), color lithograph (BP 536, DM 1327, FR 4459, Y 91,453).

$2860* *"Facade-Homage To Edith Sitwell", 1966: Suite Of 12,* num., s., pub. Harry N. Abrams in collaboration w/Pace Gallery, 1966, (05-27-93, Swann, #201, illus.), sh 23 x 17¾ in., (58.4 x 45.1 cm.), serigraphs p. on acetate and paper collage on colored papers (BP 1832, DM 4589, FR 15,468, Y 306,604).

BI *Flower Queen (Baro 7), 1953-55,* s., t., #10/20, edit. pub. 1965-66, blindstamp of p. Emiliano Sorini, full margins, stain, excell. cond., est. $1/1,500, (05-11-93, Christie-NY, #519), sheet 29¾ x 22 in., (756 x 559 mm.), etching on wove.

BI *Flower Queen (Brooklyn Museum Catalogue 7), c. 1953-55,* full margins, t., num., s., est. $800/1,200, (05-27-93, Swann, #202), 19⅞ x 15½ in., (50.5 x 39.4 cm.), etching and soft ground.

$770* *Jungle Figures (Baro 10), 1953-5,* s., t., i. Artist Proof, p. 1965-6, w/Emiliano Sorini blindstamp, full margins, time staining, skinned spot, (09-19-92, Christie-E, #166, illus.), plate 23⁷⁄₁₆ x 19½ in., (595 x 495 mm.), etching and aquatint on Rives (BP 443, DM 1153, FR 3949, Y 95,938).

BI *Komposition,* #59/150, s., est. SF 1/1,500, (04-21-93, Germann, #657), 35¾ x 24⅞ in., (908 x 632 mm.), color serigraph.

$275* *Lullaby For Jumbo, 1966,* from Facade suite portfolio, i. A.P., s., pub. Harry Abrams/Pace Gallry, (05-27-93, Swann, #203), sh 23 x 18 in., (58.4 x 45.7 cm.), color photo-screen print w/collage (BP 176, DM 441, FR 1487, Y 29,481).

$357* *Lullaby For Jumbo, 1966,* artist's proof, s., d., p. Chiron Press, embossed chop mark, also called Facade, (12-08-92, Swann, #226), 23 x 18¼ in., (58.4 x 46.4 cm.), photo-lithograph w/photo collage on stiff yellow paper (BP 224, DM 556, FR 1895, Y 44,249).

$770* *Magic Garden (Baro 12), c. 1955,* s., t., i., #1/30, wide margins, tears, split, creasing, staining, (11-09-92, Christie-NY, #378, illus.), 5¾ x 8⅞ in., (146 x 225 mm.), etching on laid (BP 509, DM 1229, FR 4153, Y 95,557).

BI *One Ancient Figure (B. 20), 1953-55,* s., t., #16/20, edit. pub. 1965-66, blindstamp of p. Emiliano Sorini, full margins, mat staining, excell. cond., est. $1/1,500, (05-11-93, Christie-NY, #520), sheet 22 x 29¾ in., (559 x 756 mm.), etching on Rives.

$825* *Untitled,* s., d. 86, #115/125, (12-13-92, Hindman, #342), 36 x 23¾ in., color lithograph and collage (BP 527, DM 1297, FR 4419, Y 102,066).

$4180* *Untitled (B. 115-120), 1973: Set Of Six,* s., d., num., pub. Pace Editions, blindstamp, full margins, very good cond., orig. portfolio, (11-09-92, Christie-NY, #379, illus.), 39 x 27¾ in., (99.1 x 70.5 cm.), aquatints w/collage in colors on C.M. Fabriano (BP 2764, DM 6673, FR 22,546, Y 518,739).

$605* *Untitled Composition, 1971,* d., num., s., (05-27-93, Swann, #204), sh 25 x 18 in., (63.5 x 45.7 cm.), mixed media (etching,aquatint, and soft ground) on heavy wove w/printer/publisher's chop marks embossed (BP 387, DM 971, FR 3272, Y 64,858).

BI *(Untitled), 1974,* s., d. '74, annot. P.P., margins, good cond., brown stain, est. $1,2/1,400, (02-24-93, Butterfield, #3098), 25¾ x 16³⁄₁₆ in., (654 x 411 mm.), silkscreen in colors on wove.

$1210* *Untitled, 1973,* s., d., #6/90, blindstamp pub. 2RC, full margins, very good cond., (10-28-92, Butterfield, #3050), 29¾ x 19¹¹⁄₁₆ in., (756 x 500 mm.), color aquatint w/collage on C.M. Fabriano paper (BP 771, DM 1869, FR 6345, Y 148,466).

BI *Untitled, 1974,* s., d., annot. P.P., margins, good cond., stain, est. $1/1,200, (05-19-93, Butterfield, #2275), 25¾ x 16³⁄₁₆ in., (654 x 411 mm.), silkscreen in colors on wove.

NEVINSON, Christopher Richard Wynne 1889-1946

BI *Anemones In A Jug On A Table,* David Strang impression, margins, prov., back cover illus., est. BP 5/600, (08-20-92, Bonhams-Chelsea, #119, illus.), 12¾ x 10⅞ in., (32.4 x 27.6 cm.), drypoint etching on Arches, watermark.

$86* *Badger Moody,* Strang impression, margins, (05-20-93, Bonhams-Chelsea, #150), plate 9⅞ x 6⅞ in., (25.1 x 17.5 cm.), etching on laid (BP 55, DM 139, FR 467, Y 9496).

BI *Couple In A Cafe,* watermarked, margins, s., 1 in. tear, soft creasing, surface dirt, est. BP 2/250, (10-27-92, Phillips-London, #288), plate 8⅞ x 5⅞ in., (225 x 149 mm.), drypoint on laid.

BI *Ebb Tide, Rye,* s., margins, est. BP 3/400, (10-15-92, Bonhams-Chelsea, #4), plate 10¼ x 14¼ in., (26 x 36.2 cm.), drypoint etching.

$404* *"An Embracing Couple",* s., margins, (01-21-93, Bonhams-Chelsea, #137), plate 10¾ x 6¾ in., (27.3 x 17.1 cm.), etching on laid paper (BP 264, DM 642, FR 2173, Y 50,563).

$84* *The Louvre,* margins, (01-21-93, Bonhams-Chelsea, #136), plate 10¾ x 6¾ in., (27.3 x 17.1 cm.), etching (BP 55, DM 134, FR 452, Y 10,513).

$469* *A Man Working In Front Of A Thatched Cottage,* s., margins, (08-20-92, Bonhams-Chelsea, #104), plate 5½ x 7½ in., (14 x 19.1 cm.), drypoint etching on laid paper (BP 242, DM 679, FR 2305, Y 59,225).

$51* *Manette Street,* Strang impression, margins, (05-20-93, Bonhams-Chelsea, #86), plate 7 x 5⅜ in., (17.8 x 13.7 cm.), etching on laid (BP 33, DM 82, FR 277, Y 5632).

$286* *Pont Des Arts,* margins, back cover illus., (01-21-93, Bonhams-Chelsea, #135), plate 12¼ x 10 in., (31.1 x 25.4 cm.), etching on laid paper (BP 187, DM 455, FR 1538, Y 35,795).

$146* *Pont Neuf,* Strang impression, margins, (05-20-93, Bonhams-Chelsea, #84), plate 7¼ x 11¾ in., (18.4 x 29.8 cm.), etching on laid (BP 94, DM 236, FR 793, Y 16,122).

$696* *The Pool (G. 77),* s., excellent cond., full margins, (10-27-92, Phillips-London, #289), plate 8⅞ x 6 in., (225 x 152 mm.), etching and drypoint on laid (BP 440, DM 1067, FR 3619, Y 85,138).

$160* *The Rising City,* margins, (01-21-93, Bonhams-Chelsea, #138), plate 13⅞ x 9⅜ in., (35.2 x 23.8 cm.), etching on laid paper (BP 105, DM 254, FR 861, Y 20,025).

$129* *Sevres,* Strang impression, margins, (05-20-93, Bonhams-Chelsea, #83), plate 10⅞ x 13¾ in., (27.6 x 34.9 cm.), etching (BP 83, DM 208, FR 701, Y 14,245).

$274* *Silvery Estuary, Rye,* s., margins, foxing, (05-20-93, Bonhams-Chelsea, #81), plate 6⅞ x 9¾ in., (17.5 x 24.8 cm.), etching on laid (BP 176, DM 442, FR 1489, Y 30,256).

$34* *Trees,* Strang impression, margins, (05-20-93, Bonhams-Chelsea, #87), plate 7⅛ x 5⅜ in., (18.1 x 13.7 cm.), etching on laid (BP 22, DM 55, FR 185, Y 3754).

$137* *A Valley In The South Downs,* Strang impression, margins, (05-20-93, Bonhams-Chelsea, #82), plate 9¾ x 13⅞ in., (24.8 x 35.2 cm.), etching on laid (BP 88, DM 221, FR 745, Y 15,128).

$326* *Venice, Night,* Strang impression, margins, (05-20-93, Bonhams-Chelsea, #85), plate 5½ x 6⅞ in., (14 x 17.5 cm.), etching on laid (BP 209, DM 526, FR 1772, Y 35,998).

$298* *The Willows,* s., margins, (08-20-92, Bonhams-Chelsea, #103), plate 6¾ x 5¼ in., (17.1 x 13.3 cm.), drypoint etching on laid paper (BP 154, DM 432, FR 1464, Y 37,631).

NEWBOULD, Frank

$770* *East Coast Frolics,* Chorley and Pickersgill Ltd., B cond., creasing, abrasions, surface soiling, (08-06-92, Swann, #210, illus.), 39½ x 25 in., (100.3 x 63.5 cm.), (BP 402, DM 1138, FR 3842, Y 98,214).

$1210* *"Shopping" and "Amusement": Two,* for London Transport, J. Weiner Ltd., B cond., (08-06-92, Swann, #211, illus.), 39½ x 25 in., (100.3 x 63.5 cm.), (BP 632, DM 1788, FR 6038, Y 154,337).

NEWHALL, Beaumont b. 1908

BI *Beaumont Newhall Photographs: Twelve, 1981,* Lunn Gallery, each s., label w/t., portfolio num., #36/50, images include: Chase National Bank, New York, 1928; Edward Weston, Carmel, California, 1940; Charis Weston's Typewriter, 1940; On The Square Rigger, Pacific Queen, Fife Rail, 1940; est. $4/6,000, (10-13-92, Christie-NY, #476, illus.), each 11 x 8¾ in., (27.9 x 22.2 cm.), photograph, gelatin silver prints, 1 dye transfer print.

$1725* *"Photographs": Twelve,* Lunn Gallery, portfolio, mounted, each s. by photog., label, num. inunident. hand, 1940-80, p. 1981, num. 36 in unident. hand, (04-06-93, Sotheby-NY, #159, illus.), various sizes to 8½ x 11 in., photograph, 11 silver prints, 1 Ektachrome print (BP 1139, DM 2779, FR 9411, Y 196,738).

NEWHOUSE, C.B. (after)

$140 *"A False Alarm On The Road To Gretna" and "One Mile From Gretna": A Pair,* engraved R. Reeves, (12-11-92, G.A. Key, #19), 10 x 15 in., (25.4 x 38.1 cm.), colored aquatint (BP 90, DM 221, FR 756, Y 17,325).

NEWMAN, Arnold b. 1918

BI *"The Art Students Alumni",* 1950, p. 1982, s., t., d., i., photog.'s stamp, illus., est. $2/3,000, (05-23-93, Butterfield, #3555, illus.), 10⅛ x 18½ in., photograph, gelatin silver print.

BI *Edward And Jo Hopper, 1960*, photog.'s sig., t., d., est. $1/1,500, (04-07-93, Swann, #525, illus.), 13 x 10½ in., photograph, silver print.

BI *"Germaine Richier" and "Nadine Effron", Portraits of Artists: Two*, mounted, s., 1st t., d. by photog., (c) stamp, 1956 & c. 1955, p. early 1970's, est. $1,8/2,200, (10-15-92, Sotheby-NY, #458, illus.), each, approx. 9½ x 6½ in., (24.1 x 16.5 cm.), photograph, gelatin silver prints.

$581* *"I.M. Pei, 1967"*, p.l., mounted on card, t., s., d., #5/25, stamped photog.'s credit and (c) limitation, 309 x 254mm, (05-07-93, Sotheby-London, #302, illus.), photograph, silver print (BP 368, DM 919, FR 3095, Y 63,973).

$1955* *"Igor Stravinsky"*, s., t., d. by photog., photog. studio stamp, 1946, p.l., (04-06-93, Sotheby-NY, #387, illus.), 7 x 12⅞ in., photograph (BP 1291, DM 3150, FR 10,666, Y 222,970).

BI *"Kim Stanley, 1963"*, p.l., mounted on card, t., s., d., #5/25, stamped photog.'s credit and (c) limitation, 312 x 245mm, est. BP 3/400, (05-07-93, Sotheby-London, #301, illus.), photograph, silver print.

$1100* *Piet Mondrian, New York City, 1942 (Five Decades, pl. 17)*, s., t., d., (c) by photog., (c) & reprod. limit. stamps, p. l., (10-15-92, Sotheby-NY, #456, illus.), 12¾ x 7½ in., (32.4 x 19.1 cm.), photograph, gelatin silver print (BP 673, DM 1637, FR 5553, Y 131,974).

BI *"Portrait Of David Rockefeller" and "Portrait Of Winthrop Rockefeller", 1963: Two*, magazine's handstamp, identifying info. verso, est. $4/600, (04-07-93, Swann, #341), each 9 x 8½ in., photograph, silver print.

$1980* *Portraits Of Artists: Two: "Georges Rouault, Paris" and "Jacques Villon, Paris", 1957 (Five Decades, pl. 35)*, mounted, s., d., i. by photog., (c) stamp, p. early 1970's, (10-15-92, Sotheby-NY, #457, illus.), each approx. 9½ x 7½ in., (24.1 x 19.1 cm.), photograph, gelatin silver print (BP 1212, DM 2947, FR 9995, Y 237,552).

$2200* *Portraits Of Artists: Two: "Max Ernst, N.Y.C.", and "Matta", 1942 & 1959 (Five Decades, pl. 20)*, mounted, s., t., d. by photog., (c) stamp, p. early 1970's, (10-15-92, Sotheby-NY, #459, illus.), each approx. 9½ x 6½ in., (24.1 x 16.5 cm.), photograph, gelatin silver print (BP 1346, DM 3275, FR 11,106, Y 263,947).

NEWMAN, Barnett American 1905-1970

$17,600* *18 Cantos: Canto VI (S. 8), 1963-64*, s., d. '11/63', t., #3/18, pub. blindstamp, ULAE, good cond., Gertrude Kasle Coll., (11-07-92, Sotheby-NY, #720, illus.), sheet 16½ x 12⅝ in., (419 x 321 mm.), lithograph on grayish white wove (BP 11,507, DM 28,102, FR 94,981, Y 2,172,303).

BI *18 Cantos: Canto XI (Sparks 13), 1964*, s., d., #3/18, blindstamp, pub. ULAE, full margins, good cond., repaired puncture and small tear, foxing, Gertrude Kasle Coll., est. $15/20,000, (05-15-93, Sotheby-NY, #1134, illus.), 14⅝ x 13 in., (37.1 x 33 cm.), lithograph in colors on white wove Shogun.

BI *18 Cantos: Canto XII (S. 14), 1964*, s., d., #3/18, blindstamp, pub. ULAE, full margins, good cond., crease, Gertrude Kasle Coll., est. $15/20,000, (05-15-93, Sotheby-NY, #1136, illus.), 14¾ x 13⅛ in., (37.5 x 33.3 cm.), lithograph in colors on white wove Shogun paper.

BI *18 Cantos: Canto XIII (S. 15), 1964*, s., d., #3/18, blindstamp, pub. ULAE, full margins, good cond., creases, Gertrude Kasle Coll., est. 15/20,000, (05-15-93, Sotheby-NY, #1135, illus.), 14⅝ x 13¼ in., (37.1 x 33.7 cm.), lithograph in colors on white wove shogun.

$17,600* *18 Cantos: Canto XIV (S. 16), 1963-64*, s., d. '4/64', t., #3/18, pub. blindstamp, ULAE, full margins, good cond., Gertrude Kasle Coll., (11-07-92, Sotheby-NY, #721, illus.), 14½ x 12¼ in., (368 x 311 mm.), lithograph p. in tones of red, on grayish white laid (BP 11,507, DM 28,102, FR 94,981, Y 2,172,303).

$1650* *18 Cantos: Title Page (Sparks 1), 1963-64*, s., d. '4/64', #3/18, pub. blindstamp, ULAE, full margins, good cond., Gertrude Kasle Coll., (11-07-92, Sotheby-NY, #719, illus.), 15¾ x 12 in., (400 x 305 mm.), lithograph

p. in red and black on white wove (BP 1079, DM 2635, FR 8904, Y 203,653).

BI *Untitled, 1961*, s., d., #5/30, pub. by artist, full margins, excell. cond., est. $15/20,000, (05-11-93, Christie-NY, #521, illus.), sheet 30 x 22 in., (762 x 559 mm.), lithograph on Arches.

BI *Untitled, 1961*, s., d., #21/30, pub. by artist, full margins, stain, excell. cond., est. $30/35,000, (05-11-93, Christie-NY, #522, illus.), sheet 30 x 22 in., (762 x 559 mm.), lithograph on Arches.

NEWMAN, John b. 1952

$1100* *Fold-Out, 1985*, s., d., num. 29/60, Vermillion Editions blindstamp, full sheet, excell. cond., (09-19-92, Christie-E, #168, illus.), sheet 40 x 30 in., (101.6 x 76.2 cm.), lithograph w/etching, drypoint and rubber stamping in colors on wove (BP 633, DM 1647, FR 5641, Y 137,055).

$825* *Grande Romano Blu, 1988*, s., d., #11/58, pub. Editions Ilene Kurtz, full margins, skillfully repaired tear, printer's ink, rubbing, creases, very good cond., shrink-wrapped, (09-19-92, Christie-E, #170), sheet 60½ x 29 in., (153.7 x 73.7 cm.), soft-ground etching and aquatint in colors on wove (BP 475, DM 1235, FR 4231, Y 102,791).

$86 *"Norwich Castle"*, (12-11-92, G.A. Key, #52, illus.), 9 x 12 in., (22.9 x 30.5 cm.), black and white lithograph (BP 55, DM 135, FR 464, Y 10,642).

$550* *Piccolo Romano Rosso, 1988*, s., d., #11/58, Editions Ilene Kurtz blindstamps, full margins, rubbed spots, excell. cond., (09-19-92, Christie-E, #169), sheet 19⅝ x 27¼ in., (498 x 692 mm.), hard and soft-ground etching in colors w/touches of hand-coloring onJapan applique (BP 316, DM 824, FR 2821, Y 68,527).

NEWMAN, John American 20th cent.

$413* *"Two Pulls", 1986*, t., d. num. 12/39 on label, excellent cond., (09-11-92, Skinner, #108, illus.), sight 44¾ x 25⅛ in., (113.7 x 63.8 cm.), etching/aquatint/drypoint on paper (BP 214, DM 595, FR 2021, Y 51,171).

NEWTON, Alison Houston Lockerbie

$65* *Mount Robson*, s., t., #24/100, prov., exhib., lit., (06-07-93, Ritchie, #31, illus.), image 5¼ x 6⅜ in., (13.3 x 16.2 cm.), color woodcut (BP 43, DM 105, FR 355, Y 6973, C$ 83).

NEWTON, Helmut German b. 1920

$863* *"Andy Warhol In Paris", 1977*, p.l., s., t., d., (05-23-93, Butterfield, #3556, illus.), 12½ x 8¼ in., photograph, gelatin silver print (BP 562, DM 1411, FR 4750, Y 95,391).

$1100* *Berlin Nude, 1977 (Pantheon, pl. 22)*, s., d., i. by photog. in ink, (c) stamp, (10-15-92, Sotheby-NY, #572, illus.), 11¾ x 17¼ in., (29.8 x 43.8 cm.), photograph, gelatin silver print (BP 673, DM 1637, FR 5553, Y 131,974).

$1725* *"Cannes Film Festival 1981"*, t., s.,d., #4/10, pub., 508 x 607mm, (05-07-93, Sotheby-London, #352, illus.), photograph, silver print (BP 1092, DM 2727, FR 9190, Y 189,936).

$1650* *Lisa Lyon In Paris III, (1980), 1982*, s., t., d., num. 1/27, (c) & reprod. limit. stamps, (10-13-92, Christie-NY, #582, illus.), 53½ x 39 in., (135.9 x 99.1 cm.), photograph, gelatin silver print (BP 961, DM 2417, FR 8213, Y 200,073).

$4722* *"Paloma Picasso, Saint-Tropez 1973"*, t., s., d., #3/10, 402 x 302mm, (05-07-93, Sotheby-London, #349, illus.), photograph, silver print (BP 2990, DM 7466, FR 25,157, Y 519,930).

$1725* *"Piscine Deligny, Paris", 1978*, s., t., d. by photog., (04-06-93, Sotheby-NY, #483, illus.), 23 x 15¼ in., photograph (BP 1139, DM 2779, FR 9411, Y 196,738).

$13,800* *"Private Property, Suite II": Fifteen*, self-pub., 1984, portfolio, each s., #6/75 by photog., portfolio (c)stamp, 1972-83, p. 1984, #6/75 II in unident. hand, (04-06-93, Sotheby-NY, #484, illus.), various sizes 14¼ x 9½ in., photograph (BP 9115, DM 22,233, FR 75,286, Y 1,573,905).

$24,150* *"Private Property, Suite III": Fifteen*, self-pub., 1984, #6/75 by photog., (c) stamp, 1975-81, p. 1984, #6/75 III in unident. hand, (04-06-93, Sotheby-NY, #484A, illus.), various sizes to 14¼ x 9½ in., photograph (BP 15,951, DM 38,908, FR 131,751, Y 2,754,334).

$14,950* *"Private Property, Suite III": Fifteen,* self-pub., 1984, #6/75 by photog., (c) stamp, 1975-81, p. 1984, #6/75 III in unident. hand, (04-06-93, Sotheby-NY, #483A, illus.), various sizes to 14¼ x 9½ in., photograph (BP 9875, DM 24,086, FR 81,560, Y 1,705,064).

$2185* *"Saddle I", Paris, 1976,* s., t., d., #1/10, (04-08-93, Christie-NY, #503, illus.), 15⅛ x 23 in., (38.4 x 58.4 cm.), photograph, gelatin silver print (BP 1433, DM 3510, FR 11,881, Y 247,957).

$7210* *The School Teacher, Lake Como, 1990,* s., d., num. 1/3, (10-29-92, Christie-London, #205, illus.), image approx. 60 x 20 in., (152.4 x 50.8 cm.), photograph, gelatin silver print (BP 4620, DM 11,092, FR 37,630, Y 893,100).

$6175* *"Sie Kommen, Dressed" and "Sie Kommen, Paris, 1981":* Two, t., s., d., num. 4365/8, 4436/6, pub., each approx. 502 x 404mm, (05-07-93, Sotheby-London, #351, illus.), photograph, silver print (BP 3910, DM 9763, FR 32,898, Y 679,916).

BI *Sylvia Reclining Nude Inside The House and Sylvia Reclining Dressed Inside The House, Boescia, Italy: Two, 1981,* each s., t., d., num. 3/10, est. $4/5,000, (10-13-92, Christie-NY, #581, illus.), each 19 x 23 in., (48.3 x 58.4 cm.), photograph, gelatin silver prints.

$726* *"Viviane F. Hotel Volney", New York, 1972,* print 8, suite II, edit. no. 22 from Private Property portfolio, stamped photog.'s credit, s., matt #22/75, stamped, 402 x 302mm, (05-07-93, Sotheby-London, #353, illus.), photograph, silver print (BP 460, DM 1148, FR 3868, Y 79,938).

$1093* *"Winnie Off The Coast Of Cannes", 1975,* p.l., s., t., d., photog.'s stamp, (05-23-93, Butterfield, #3557, illus.), 13½ x 9 in., photograph, gelatin silver print (BP 712, DM 1787, FR 6015, Y 120,814).

$1816* *"'Mannequins At Patou', Paris 1977",* s., t., d., #2/10, pub., 605 x 502mm, (05-07-93, Sotheby-London, #350, illus.), photograph, silver print (BP 1150, DM 2871, FR 9675, Y 199,956).

NEWTOWN

$75 *"Stock Farm Of Thos. B. Scott",* (09-24-92, Alderfer, #254), 12 x 15 in., (30.5 x 38.1 cm.), lithograph (BP 44, DM 111, FR 377, Y 9022).

NEZIERE, J. de la

$239* *PLM and Ch. De Fer Tunisiens: Visitez La Tunisie. Dougga, 1929,* very good cond., (03-13-93, Laurin, #70), 39⅜ x 25⅜ in., (100 x 64.5 cm.), (BP 167, DM 398, FR 1353, Y 28,167).

$359* *PLM. La Grotte De Lamartine. "Environs D'Aix-Les-Bains, Le Lac Du Bourget Et La Chaine Du Mont-Blanc", 1927,* very good cond., (03-15-93, Arcole, #48), 42½ x 30¹¹⁄₁₆ in., (108 x 78 cm.), (BP 250, DM 596, FR 2027, Y 42,525).

$378* *Simplon Orient-Express: ALEP. "Grande-Bretagne, France, Suisse, Italie, Serbie, Croatie, Slovenie, Bulgarie, Roumanie, Grece, Turquie, Syrie", 1927,* very good cond., (03-13-93, Laurin, #124, illus.), 42½ x 30⅞ in., (108 x 78.5 cm.), (BP 264, DM 629, FR 2139, Y 44,549).

NIAL, Jack Levine

$86* *Watteau,* s., #83/100, t., (06-08-93, Ritchie, #46, illus.), 19¾ x 26 in., (50.2 x 66 cm.), color lithograph on Arches (BP 57, DM 140, FR 470, Y 9134, C$ 110).

NICHOLLS, John

$240* *Bantry Hill, c. 1930,* s., full margins, good cond., remains, tape, (06-30-93, Sotheby-London, #319), 4⅛ x 5 in., (105 x 127 mm.), etching on laid (BP 161, DM 409, FR 1381, Y 25,715).

NICHOLS (after)

$205* *A View Of Stocks Market, 1753,* by Fletcher, pub. J. Boydell, (12-10-92, Bonhams-Chelsea, #56), image 11¾ x 17½ in., (29.8 x 44.5 cm.), hand-colored engraving (BP 132, DM 324, FR 1108, Y 25,359).

NICHOLS, C.M.

$47 *"A Norwich By-Way",* s., (12-11-92, G.A. Key, #34), 11 x 7 in., (27.9 x 17.8 cm.), black and white etching (BP 30, DM 74, FR 254, Y 5816).

NICHOLS, Dale   American b. 1904

$248* *Company For Supper,* time discoloration, mat burns, good cond., s., (06-11-93, Freemn/Fine Art, #157), 10½ x 14¼ in., (26.7 x 36.2 cm.), lithograph in black (BP 163, DM 403, FR 1359, Y 26,313).

$193* *September Morning,* s., margins, good cond., mat & light-staining, glue remains, (02-24-93, Butterfield, #2860), 9½ x 12½ in., (241 x 318 mm.), lithograph on wove (BP 135, DM 313, FR 1062, Y 22,647).

NICHOLS, Jack

$278* *Clown And Assistant,* s., #28/50; t. labels verso, c. 1965, prov., exhib., (11-30-92, Ritchie, #42), 30 x 22 in., (76.2 x 55.9 cm.), lithograph (BP 183, DM 443, FR 1504, Y 34,599, C$ 358).

NICHOLS, Joseph

$330* *Puffin Shooting,* painted by P. Reinagle, crease, small margins, (04-02-93, Picard, #19), 14⁹⁄₁₆ x 19¹¹⁄₁₆ in., (37 x 50 cm.), 2-tone aquatint (BP 217, DM 530, FR 1801, Y 37,573).

NICHOLSON

$29 *Cambridge College,* s., (02-05-93, G.A. Key, #40), 11 x 14 in., (27.9 x 35.6 cm.), sepia print (BP 20, DM 48, FR 163, Y 3609).

NICHOLSON, Ben   British 1894-1982

$1583* *5 Circles (Lewison 14E), 1934,* s., margins, creases, rust spots, (11-30-92, Phillips-London, #467), border 6¼ x 7⅞ in., (159 x 200 mm.), woodcut in black on thick simili japan (BP 1045, DM 2522, FR 8561, Y 197,013).

$8781* *Ben Nicholson, 1965: Six,* s., d., num., printer's blindstamp, (06-23-93, Kornfeld, #628), 20¼ x 18½ in., (51.5 x 47 cm.), etching (BP 5965, DM 14,858, FR 49,977, Y 956,640, SF 13,225).

$2144* *Complicated Forms (La Franca 48), 1967,* s., d., #42/50, pub. by artist, full margins, good cond., (06-30-93, Sotheby-London, #577, illus.), 10¼ x 4⅞ in., (260 x 124 mm.), etching and drypoint w/tone on wove (BP 1437, DM 3657, FR 12,336, Y 229,722).

$836* *Composition Of Circles And Squares,* inits., d. 1939, time stained, fox mark, good cond., (10-27-92, Phillips-London, #214), sheet 9⅝ x 7¼ in., (244 x 184 mm.), lithograph in black, greys and browns on wove (BP 528, DM 1281, FR 4347, Y 102,263).

$199* *Siena (Large Version), 1965,* #45/50, s., d., num., blindstamp, Edition Lafranca, lit., (06-15-93, Schuler, #3372, illus.), 16¹⁵⁄₁₆ x 14¾ in., (43 x 37.5 cm.), sh 12⅝ x 11 in., (43 x 37.5 cm.), etching (BP 131, DM 327, FR 1101, Y 21,012, SF 2300).

$500* *Tenement,* s., d. '57, full margins, good cond., (11-30-92, Phillips-London, #468), plate 6⅞ x 5¼ in., (175 x 133 mm.), drypoint on B.F.K. Rives (BP 330, DM 797, FR 2704, Y 62,228).

$1306* *Tenement,* s., d. '57, together w/an etched poem by Herbert Read, p. on same sheeys, light staining, (10-27-92, Phillips-London, #215), sheet 17 x 19⅞ in., (432 x 505 mm.), drypoint on B.F.K. Rives (BP 825, DM 2002, FR 6791, Y 159,755).

$1154* *These Men Use Shell, Guardsmen, 1938,* p. Waterlow and Sons, ref. #515, cond. 1, (10-13-92, Phillips-London, #137, illus.), 29¹⁵⁄₁₆ x 44⅞ in., (76 x 114 cm.), color lithograph (BP 672, DM 1691, FR 5744, Y 139,930).

$2640* *Two And A Half Goblets (see Lafranca 94), 1967,* s., d., i., pub. Ganymed and Marlborough Graphics, full margins, creasing, foxing, skinned patches, good cond., (11-09-92, Christie-NY, #380, illus.), 14⅞ x 12¾ in., (378 x 324 mm.), etching w/graphit and pale grey watercolor additions on wove (BP 1745, DM 4215, FR 14,239, Y 327,625).

$6262* *Two Sculptural Forms (Lafranca 89), 1967,* s., d., (06-23-93, Kornfeld, #629), 11⁷⁄₁₆ x 11 in., (29.1 x 28 cm.), etching reworked w/watercolor and pencil on thick wove (BP 4254, DM 10,596, FR 35,640, Y 682,209, SF 9430).

$2898* *Untitled, 1967,* #43/50, s., d., (05-20-93, Finarte-Milan, #122, illus.), 17½ x 16¾ in., (44.5 x 42.5 cm.), etching (BP 1860, DM 4676, FR 15,750, Y 320,009, L 4255).

NICHOLSON, Sir William English 1872-1949
$200* *Sarah Bernhardt, c. 1898,* (02-04-93, Sloan, #1834), sight 9¼ x 9 in., (23.5 x 22.9 cm.), color woodcut (BP 140, DM 329, FR 1117, Y 24,879).

NICHOLSON, William
$748* *An Almanac Of Sports, 1898: Twelve,* margins, sealed in mat, good cond.?, light-staining, (05-19-93, Butterfield, #2089), each 7¾ x 7⅞ in., (197 x 200 mm.), woodcut in colors on wove (BP 486, DM 1216, FR 4096, Y 82,807).
$309* *An Alphabet, 1898: Twenty-Six,* book, complete set, bound as plates, good cond., (06-30-93, Sotheby-London, #320), overall 12⅜ x 10 in., (314 x 254 mm.), colored lithograph on wove (BP 207, DM 527, FR 1778, Y 33,108).
$302* *Her Ladyship's Elephant,* Henry Holt, A cond., (08-06-92, Swann, #212, illus.), 20 x 12½ in., (50.8 x 31.8 cm.), (BP 158, DM 446, FR 1507, Y 38,520).
$2728* *Queen Victoria, 1897,* pen s. within borderline, trimmed to borderline, mounted, i. in ink on card, (12-03-92, Sotheby-London, #174, illus.), 9¼ x 8¾ in., (235 x 222 mm.), hand colored woodcut on tan paper (BP 1760, DM 4290, FR 14,643, Y 339,430).
BI *Twelve Portraits: H.M. The Queen, 1897,* s. in block, margins, good cond., surface scuffing, est. $3/500, (05-19-93, Butterfield, #2088), 9⁹⁄₁₆ x 9 in., (243 x 229 mm.), lithograph transfer from a woodcut w/hand-coloring on wove.
$303* *Twelve Portraits: Rudyard Kipling, 1899,* Auchenbach coll. stamp, margins, good cond., surface soiling, creases, scuffs, mat staining, (02-24-93, Butterfield, #2961), 11 x 8¾ in., (279 x 222 mm.), lithograph in colors on thin wove (BP 211, DM 492, FR 1668, Y 35,555).
$660* *V Is For Villian, 1898,* ink s., pub. W. Heinemann, full margins, good cond., discoloration, surface soiling, crease, (10-28-92, Butterfield, #2845), 9⅞ x 7¹³⁄₁₆ in., (251 x 198 mm.), hand-colored wood engraving on chine colle (pasted) attached to board (BP 421, DM 1019, FR 3461, Y 80,982).

NICHOLSON, William 1872-1949
$1475* *An Alphabet By William Nicholson, 1898,* very rare, pub. R.H. Russell, New York, lit., (12-05-92, Bassenge, #7613), 28¹⁵⁄₁₆ x 21⅝ in., (73.5 x 55 cm.), color lithograph (BP 924, DM 2300, FR 7837, Y 182,753).
BI *"An Alphabet" (Thieme-Becker XXV, S. 442): Twenty-Six,* William Heinemann, London, 1899, est. DM 1500, (12-01-92, Karl/Faber, #1059), 12³⁄₁₆ x 9¹³⁄₁₆ in., (31 x 25 cm.), woodcut.

NICHOLSON, William (after)
$66* *"February", "May", "July" and "November": Four,* (06-30-93, Bonhams-Chelsea, #9A), sheet 11½ x 9½ in., (29.2 x 24.1 cm.), lithograph in colors (BP 44, DM 113, FR 380, Y 7072).

NICOLL, James (Jim) 1892-1986
$130* *Chinese Courtyard, 1979,* #60/65, s., t., d. '79; s. block, prov., (05-10-93, Hodgins, #182, illus.), 8½ x 9½ in., (21.6 x 24.1 cm.), woodcut on paper (BP 85, DM 209, FR 705, Y 14,527, C$ 165).

NICOLL, Marion 1909-1985
$196* *Self Portrait,* A/P s., t., d. 1979, prov., (05-10-93, Hodgins, #42, illus.), 9½ x 7½ in., (24.1 x 19.1 cm.), clay print on paper (BP 128, DM 315, FR 1062, Y 21,902, C$ 248).
$304* *Self Portrait, 1979,* A/P s., t., d. 1979, prov., (05-10-93, Hodgins, #234), 9¼ x 7 in., (23.5 x 17.8 cm.), clay print on paper (BP 198, DM 488, FR 1648, Y 33,970, C$ 385).

NICOSIA, Nic b. 1951
$1955* *Near Modern Disaster #6, 1983,* #1/15, (04-08-93, Christie-NY, #551, illus.), 40 x 60 in., (101.6 x 152.4 cm.), photograph, cibachrome print (BP 1282, DM 3141, FR 10,631, Y 221,857).

NIE, Eric de b. 1944
$91* *Untitled, 1977,* s., d., #10/70, margins, good cond.?, (12-09-92, Sotheby-Amstrdm, #624), 16⁹⁄₁₆ x 29¹⁵⁄₁₆ in., (420 x 760 mm.), color lithograph on wove (BP 58, DM 143, FR 487, Y 11,283, G 161).

NIERMAN, Leonardo M. Mexican b. 1932
$110* *Untitled: Three,* each s., num., (09-17-92, Sloan, #2358), largest 24¼ x 18¼ in., (61.6 x 46.4 cm.), color lithograph (BP 62, DM 163, FR 559, Y 13,695).

NIESLONY, Boris b. 1945
$834* *Studie Su Einer Hamburger Liebe, 1980/91: Two,* unique, felt pen s., d., t., (11-12-92, Lempertz, #190, illus.), one 10⅝ x 12³⁄₁₆ in., (27 x 30.9 cm.), other 10⅝ x 15¹¹⁄₁₆ in., (27 x 30.9 cm.), photograph, gelatin silver print (BP 533, DM 1311, FR 4467, Y 103,180).
$834* *Wer Sind Die Beiden Anderen, 1989/91: Five,* ink s., d., t., (11-12-92, Lempertz, #191, illus.), each 11⅝ x 8¼ in., (29.5 x 21 cm.), photograph, 4 gelatin silver prints, 1 2-color Malerei (painting) (BP 533, DM 1311, FR 4467, Y 103,180).

NIETO, John American 20th cent.
$303* *Figure With Blanket,* s. Nieto, #25/25, very good cond., (06-26-93, Skinner, #30, illus.), sheet 28 x 22 in., (71.1 x 55.9 cm.), color silkscreen on paper (BP 203, DM 515, FR 1734, Y 32,149).

NIEUWENKAMP, W.O.J. 1874-1950
$266* *Aan De Zaan (Hubert E12), 1896,* s., (11-18-92, Bubb Kuyper, #1549), 3¼ x 12⁹⁄₁₆ in., (8.2 x 31.9 cm.), etching (BP 175, DM 424, FR 1429, Y 33,080, G 480).
$66* *Benares,* s., t., 25 Ex. No 17, (11-18-92, Bubb Kuyper, #1552), 15¹⁵⁄₁₆ x 13⁵⁄₁₆ in., (40.5 x 33.8 cm.), lithograph (BP 43, DM 105, FR 354, Y 8208, G 120).
BI *Benares, "Een Tempel Aan De Ganges" and "De Laatste Zonnestralen" (Hubert 10): Two,* s., t., artist's proof, #E163/E165, est. G 4/600, (11-18-92, Bubb Kuyper, #1551), etching on Japan.
$100* *Benares. Aam De Ganges (wasvrouwen),* s., t., artist's proof, #E180, only state, rare, (11-18-92, Bubb Kuyper, #1553), 9⅝ x 7¹¹⁄₁₆ in., (24.5 x 19.5 cm.), etching (BP 66, DM 159, FR 537, Y 12,436, G 180).
$60* *Ex Libris Koninklijke Vereeniging Indisch Instituut, 1947,* s., (11-18-92, Bubb Kuyper, #1554), approx. 5⅛ x 3⁹⁄₁₆ in., (13 x 9 cm.), woodcut on Japanese (BP 40, DM 96, FR 322, Y 7462, G 108).
BI *Fontein In De Tuin Van De Villa Dei Vescovi In Florence, 1936,* s., #20ex-no5; lithograph verso, est. G 1/200, (11-18-92, Bubb Kuyper, #1555), 19¹³⁄₁₆ x 17⁷⁄₁₆ in., (50.3 x 44.3 cm.), lithograph.
$93* *Gezicht Op Brugge (Hubert H21), 1900,* s., t., #H21, (11-18-92, Bubb Kuyper, #1556), 6⁵⁄₁₆ x 12½ in., (16.1 x 31.7 cm.), woodcut (BP 61, DM 148, FR 499, Y 11,566, G 168).
$399* *Het Aardige Sluisje, Edam (Hubert E141), 1913,* s., t., artist's proof, 3rd final state, fine cond., (11-18-92, Bubb Kuyper, #1550, illus.), 18½ x 14¹⁵⁄₁₆ in., (47 x 38 cm.), etching (BP 263, DM 636, FR 2143, Y 49,621, G 720).
$66* *Het Paleis Van De Goeverneur Generaal Te Buitenzorg,* (11-18-92, Bubb Kuyper, #1561), 18½ x 22⅝ in., (47 x 57.5 cm.), lithograph (BP 43, DM 105, FR 354, Y 8208, G 120).
$140* *Het Visschertje, Edam (Hubert E134), 1914,* s., artist's proof, 4th state of 4, (11-18-92, Bubb Kuyper, #1565), 4⅛ x 6⁵⁄₁₆ in., (10.5 x 16 cm.), etching in sanguine (BP 92, DM 223, FR 752, Y 17,411, G 252).
$80* *Het Wachthuisje (Hubert H66), 1908,* s., (11-18-92, Bubb Kuyper, #1567), 8⅛ x 5⅞ in., (20.7 x 15 cm.), woodcut (BP 53, DM 128, FR 430, Y 9949, G 144).
BI *Houtsneden Van Nieuwenkamp Aan Boord Van "De Zwerver" (Hubert 8), 1912: Seven,* all s., t., est. G 6/800, (11-18-92, Bubb Kuyper, #1557), woodcut.
$80* *In Semarang (Hubert E35), 1908/1909,* s., #E35, 2nd or 3rd state, (11-18-92, Bubb Kuyper, #1559), 7⅜ x 7¹⁵⁄₁₆ in., (18.7 x 20.2 cm.), etching (BP 53, DM 128, FR 430, Y 9949, G 144).
$73* *Neurenberg (Hubert H68), 1909,* s., t., Proefdruk 1910, #H68, (11-18-92, Bubb Kuyper, #1560), 6⅞ x 6⁷⁄₁₆ in., (17.5 x 16.3 cm.), woodcut (BP 48, DM 116, FR 392, Y 9078, G 132).
$73* *Le Puy-En-Velay (Hubert H22), 1901,* s., t., #H22, (11-18-92, Bubb Kuyper, #1562), 8½ x 6¼ in., (21.6 x 15.9

cm.), woodcut (BP 48, DM 116, FR 392, Y 9078, G 132).

BI *Spelevaren, Benares (Hubert E143), 1914*, s., t., artist's proof, #E143, 2nd state, rare, est. G 2/300, (11-18-92, Bubb Kuyper, #1563), 3⁷⁄₁₆ x 5¹¹⁄₁₆ in., (8.7 x 14.5 cm.), etching in sanguine mounterd on board.

$199* *Vallende Bladeren (Amersfoort) (Hubert E88), 1914*, 4th state of 4, rare, (11-18-92, Bubb Kuyper, #1564), 12¹⁵⁄₁₆ x 14¹⁵⁄₁₆ in., (33 x 37.9 cm.), etching (BP 131, DM 317, FR 1069, Y 24,748, G 360).

BI *Voorplein Van De Villa Dei Vescovi In Florence In De Sneeuw, 1936*, s., est. G 1/150, (11-18-92, Bubb Kuyper, #1566), 20¹⁵⁄₁₆ x 17½ in., (53.3 x 44.5 cm.), lithograph.

$166* *Weltevreden, 1918*, oval lithograph below, s., t., litho no. 8 1ste staat, proefdruk, 11exemplaren, fine cond., (11-18-92, Bubb Kuyper, #1568, illus.), 18⁵⁄₁₆ x 22⁷⁄₁₆ in., (46.5 x 57 cm.), lithograph (BP 109, DM 265, FR 892, Y 20,644, G 300).

NIKUTOWSKI, Erich   1872-1921
BI *Burg Gutenfels Und Die Pfalz Bei Caub*, stone s. E. Nikutowski, est. DM 400-, (03-24-93, Venator/Hansten, #4541), approx. 14¹⁵⁄₁₆ x 33⅞ in., (38 x 86 cm.), color lithograph.

NILSON, Johann Esaias   German 1721-1788
$650* *Kupferstichfolge Nach Fresken Johannes Holzers An Augsburger Gebauden (Schuster 1, 3, 4, 5, 7-14, 20-25, 30): Twenty-Two*, (12-04-92, Bassenge, #6661), engraving (BP 417, DM 1035, FR 3512, Y 81,149).

$113* *Symbole Der 4 Jahreszeiten (Schuster 77)*, (03-24-93, Venator/Hansten, #2548), pl. 10⁷⁄₁₆ x 7¹¹⁄₁₆ in., (26.5 x 19.5 cm.), etching and engraving (BP 77, DM 185, FR 628, Y 13,277).

NILSSON, Bert Johnny   b. 1934
$277* *Gront Klot Pa Pelarbord*, s. 209/250, (11-07-92, Falkkloos, #345), lithograph in colors (BP 181, DM 444, FR 1495, Y 34,189, SK 1650).

$185* *Surrealistic Composition*, s. 66/150, (11-07-92, Falkkloos, #346), woodcut in colors (BP 121, DM 297, FR 998, Y 22,834, SK 1100).

NILSSON, Nils   1901-1949
BI *Kvinna*, s., est. SK 1,000, (11-07-92, Falkkloos, #348), etching.

NINAS, Paul   American 20th cent.
$110* *"Mardi Gras", "Brennan's Patio" and "Yacht Harbor": Three*, (11-21-92, Goldberg, #708), 20 x 14½ in., (50.8 x 36.8 cm.), color lithograph (BP 72, DM 175, FR 591, Y 13,680).

NINHAM, Henry
$28 *Norwich Houses: Two*, d. 1842, (12-11-92, G.A. Key, #67), 8 x 6 in., (20.3 x 15.2 cm.), black and white engraving (BP 18, DM 44, FR 151, Y 3465).

NISHIMURA SHIGENAGA   Japanese c. 1697-1756
$2100* *Armour-Clad Warrior Grappling With A Tiger: Ichikawa Danjuro II As Ishiyama Genta In The Play Ishiyama Genta Kimonya(?)*, Hosoban, tan-e, s. Nihon Gako, Nishimura Shigenaga hitsu, pub.'s mark, d. Shotoku 3 (1713), wormed, soiled, rubbed, darkened, laid-down, restored, Prof. H.R.W. Kuhne Coll., (06-11-93, Sotheby-London, #23, illus.), 12⅝ x 6⅛ in., (32.1 x 15.6 cm.), hand-colored woodblock (BP 1380, DM 3413, FR 11,507, Y 222,812).

NITSCH, Hermann   b. 1938
$5775* *Das Abendmahl, 1983*, s., d., num., (11-28-92, Schoppmann, #680), 84⅝ x 193¹¹⁄₁₆ in., (215 x 492 cm.), serigraph on canvas w/reworked Blut (BP 3812, DM 9200, FR 31,233, Y 718,731).

BI *Anatomie*, s., i. proof, est. DM 2,400-, (05-27-93, Lempertz, #930, illus.), 30⁵⁄₁₆ x 22¹³⁄₁₆ in., (77 x 58 cm.), color lithograph on wove.

BI *Architektur Des Orgien-Mysterien-Theaters, 1979-80*, est. DM 12,000-, (05-27-93, Lempertz, #926, illus.), 62¹⁵⁄₁₆ x 156⅞ in., (160 x 398.5 cm.), screenprint.

BI *Untitled, 1984-1988*, s., artist's proof, (06-12-93, Hauswedell/Nolt, #313), 11⁷⁄₁₆ x 8⅛ in., (29 x 20.7 cm.), color etching on thick wove w/Hahnemuhle.

NITTIS, Giuseppe de   Italian 1846-1884
$983* *"Etude Dans Mon Jardin", "Vue Prise A Londres" and "Femme Vue De DosA L'Eventail" (Ber. 7,9 et 10): Three*, large margins, (02-24-93, Picard, #178), etching or drypoint on laid (BP 685, DM 1596, FR 5410, Y 115,349).

$1802* *Femme Nue Couchee De Dos, c. 1875*, studio drystamp, fingerprints, margins, (02-24-93, Picard, #177), etching and drypoint on white laid (BP 1257, DM 2925, FR 9917, Y 211,453).

$110* *Portrait Of Edgar Degas*, plate cancelled, (03-24-93, Grogan, #109), 3⅜ x 2¾ in., (8.6 x 7 cm.), etching (BP 74, DM 180, FR 611, Y 12,924).

$289* *Vue De Londres, Sous Un Pont De Chemin De Fer (H. Beraldi, 9)*, reddish stains, good margins, (04-02-93, Picard, #155), 5½ x 8⁹⁄₁₆ in., (14 x 21.8 cm.), etching (BP 190, DM 464, FR 1578, Y 32,904).

NIXON, Job
$51 *Continental River Scene With Figures And Buildings*, s., (10-09-92, G.A. Key, #94), 10 x 8¼ in., (25.4 x 21 cm.), etching (BP 30, DM 76, FR 258, Y 6220).

NIXON, Nicholas   American b. 1947
$1100* *The Brown Sisters, Brighton, Mass. and The Brown Sisters, Woodstock,Vt.: Two, 1985 & 1990*, each s., t., d., num. 7/50 and 24/50, (10-13-92, Christie-NY, #583, illus.), each 7⅝ x 9⅝ in., (19.4 x 24.4 cm.), photograph, gelatin silver prints (BP 641, DM 1611, FR 5475, Y 133,382).

$1760* *The Brown Sisters, Cambridge, 1986*, s., t., d., num. (25) by photog., (10-15-92, Sotheby-NY, #595, illus.), 18⅛ x 22¾ in., (46 x 57.8 cm.), photograph, gelatin silver print (BP 1077, DM 2620, FR 8884, Y 211,158).

BI *"The Brown Sisters, Watertown, Massachusetts", 1991*, s., t., d., edit. 12/50, inventory num., Dixon Collection, est. $800/1,000, (11-16-92, Butterfield, #6114, illus.), 7¾ x 9¾ in., (197.2 x 248.1 mm.), photograph, gelatin silver print.

BI *Cambridge, 1985*, s., t., d., num. 20/50 (No. 3 of 3 enlargements) by photog., #3/3 ed., est. $1,5/2,000, (10-15-92, Sotheby-NY, #596, illus.), 18⅛ x 22¾ in., (46 x 57.8 cm.), photograph, gelatin silver print.

BI *"Heather Brown McCann, Mimi Brown, Bebe Brown Nixon, Laurie Brown, Hartford, Connecticut", 1976*, s., t., d., inventory num., Dixon Collection, est. $1,0/1,500, (11-16-92, Butterfield, #6113, illus.), 7¾ x 9⅝ in., (197.2 x 244.9 mm.), photograph, gelatin silver print.

BI *South Boulevard, Houston, Texas and West Springfield, Massachusetts:Two, 1977 & 1978*, s., t.,d., est. $1200/1500, (10-13-92, Christie-NY, #585, illus.), each 7¾ x 9¾ in., (19.7 x 24.8 cm.), photograph, gelatin silver prints.

$440* *View Of Mother Church And Christian Science Center, Boston, (1977), 1979-80*, s., t., d., annot., (10-13-92, Christie-NY, #584, illus.), 14¼ x 18 in., (36.2 x 45.7 cm.), photograph, gelatin silver print (BP 256, DM 645, FR 2190, Y 53,353).

BI *Yazoo City, Mississippi, 1979*, t., d., sig., est. $2/3,000, (10-14-92, Swann, #526, illus.), 18 x 23 in., (45.7 x 58.4 cm.), photograph, silver print.

NOBEL, Pierre
BI *Abstraction With Glass Ball, 1920's*, est. $800/1,200, (04-06-93, Sotheby-NY, #87A, illus.), 12¾ x 10⅛ in., photograph.

NOCKOLDS, Roy
BI *"The Angler"*, s., d. 1971, (12-11-92, G.A. Key, #29), 18 x 31 in., (45.7 x 78.7 cm.), colored print.

BI *Duck Shooting, Early Morning*, s., d. 1971, (12-11-92, G.A. Key, #28), 18 x 31 in., (45.7 x 78.7 cm.), colored print.

BI *"The Salmon Fisherman"*, s., d. 1971, (12-11-92, G.A. Key, #30), 18 x 31 in., (45.7 x 78.7 cm.), colored print.

NOHLWEIN, Ludwig
$1477* *Kleinfilmkamera Leica*, tears, (05-07-93, Christie-S. Ken, #72, illus.), 8½ x 11 in., (21.6 x 27.9 cm.), color lithograph (BP 935, DM 2335, FR 7869, Y 162,629).

NOLAN, Sidney Robert Australian b. 1917

$81* *Paradise Gardens,* s. Nolan, #6/70, (08-11-92, L. Joel, #55G), 21⅝ x 17¹⁵⁄₁₆ in., (55 x 45.5 cm.), color screen-print (BP 42, DM 119, FR 403, Y 10,373, A$ 110).

NOLAND, Kenneth American b. 1924

$2875* *Handmade Paper Project: Circle II (See Tyler 465:KN121), 1978,* s., d., blindstamp of pub., Tyler Graphics, Ltd., good cond., (02-11-93, Sotheby-NY, #396), sheet 20¹¹⁄₁₆ x 31¹⁵⁄₁₆ in., (525 x 812 mm.), 5 layers of colored pulp w/one lithographic monoprinting (BP 2029, DM 4762, FR 16,115, Y 346,594).

BI *Handmade Paper Project: Circle II (Tyler 465:KN121), 1978,* s., d., pub. blindstamp, Tyler Graphics, Ltd., good cond., est. $2,5/3,500, (11-07-92, Sotheby-NY, #722), sheet 20⅝ x 32 in., (524 x 813 mm.), five layers of colored pulp w/one lithographic monoprinting.

BI *Horizontal Stripes Series: I-29 (Tyler 466:KN229), 1978,* s., d., unique, blindstamp, pub. Tyler Graphics, Ltd., good cond., est. $4,5/5,000, (05-15-93, Sotheby-NY, #1132, illus.), sheet 50⅜ x 33⅞ in., (128 x 86 cm.), four layers of pressed colored pulp.

$825* *Linear Abstraction,* (05-16-93, Hindman, #632), 6¼ x 58¾ in., (15.9 x 149.2 cm.), color serigraph (BP 536, DM 1327, FR 4459, Y 91,453).

$1725* *Palimpsest (PA-87-15), 1987,* s., t., d., full margins, crease, excell. cond., (05-11-93, Christie-NY, #525, illus.), sheet 35¾ x 24⅜ in., (908 x 619 mm.), color monotype on hand-made (BP 1101, DM 2717, FR 9156, Y 189,748).

BI *Palimpsest (PA-87-15), 1987,* s., t., d. verso, full margins, crease, excellent cond., est. $3,5/5,500, (11-09-92, Christie-NY, #381, illus.), 35¾ x 24⅜ in., (908 x 619 mm.), mono. in colors on handmade.

$2070* *Palimpsest, 1987,* s. verso, d., t., pub. artist, good cond., prop. African Arts Fund, Inc., (05-15-93, Sotheby-NY, #1133, illus.), sheet 24¼ x 35⅝ in., (61.6 x 90.5 cm.), monotype in colors w/additional hand-painting (BP 1346, DM 3330, FR 11,189, Y 229,465).

BI *Shadow Line, 1968,* s., d., #92/150, pub. for Dokumenta IV, excell. cond.?, est. $2/2,500, (05-11-93, Christie-NY, #523), sheet 16⅞ x 47½ in., (42.9 x 120.7 cm.), color screenprint on canvas laid down on board.

$1955* *Twin Planes, 1969,* s., d., #179/200, Sarah Lawrence Art Press and Chiron Press ink stamps, excell. cond., (05-11-93, Christie-NY, #524), sheet 6¼ x 59 in., (15.9 x 149.9 cm.), color screenprint on canvas laid down on board (BP 1248, DM 3080, FR 10,377, Y 215,048).

$3163* *Twin Planes, 1969,* s., d. 5/5/69, #144/200, stamp, pub. Chiron Press and Sarah LawrenceArt Press, good cond. ?, (05-15-93, Sotheby-NY, #1130, illus.), 6¼ x 58¼ in., (15.9 x 148 cm.), silkscreen in colors on canvas laminated to board (BP 2057, DM 5088, FR 17,097, Y 350,626).

$2875* *Untitled, 1981,* s., d., pub. by artist, good cond., (02-11-93, Sotheby-NY, #397, illus.), sheet 25⅜ x 29¾ in., (645 x 755 mm.), monotype, handcolored, handmade cotton rag paper (BP 2029, DM 4762, FR 16,115, Y 346,594).

$1150* *Yellow, Blue, Green Stripe, 1978,* s. verso, d., erased sig., d., pub., blindstamp artist, good cond., (05-15-93, Sotheby-NY, #1131, illus.), sheet 22⅞ x 18⅛ in., (58.1 x 46 cm.), monotype, hand-colored, handmade cotton rag paper (BP 748, DM 1850, FR 6216, Y 127,480).

NOLDE, Emil German 1867-1956

$1840* *Abschied (Schiefler E20), 1906,* s., d., i. by printer O. Felsing, margins, light/mat staining, crease, good cond., prop. Francesca Robinson Sanchez, (05-11-93, Christie-NY, #249, illus.), plate 6⅝ x 4¾ in., (168 x 121 mm.), etching in blue and black on wove (BP 1175, DM 2899, FR 9766, Y 202,398).

$2291* *Altere Herren (Schiefler-Mosel 71/II), 1926,* (06-23-93, Kornfeld, #635), color lithograph on thick Japan (BP 1556, DM 3876, FR 13,039, Y 249,591, SF 3450).

BI *"Altere Herren" (Schiefler/Mosel 71/II), 1926,* est. DM 1,4/1,800, (06-05-93, Grisebach, #799, illus.), 6⁷⁄₁₆ x 4⁷⁄₁₆ in., (16.3 x 11.2 cm.), color lithograph on handmade Japan.

BI *"Altere Herren" (Schiefler/Mosel 71/II), 1926,* est. DM 1,7/1,900, (11-28-92, Grisebach, #670, illus.), 6⅜ x 4⁷⁄₁₆ in., (16.2 x 11.2 cm.), colred lithograph on handmade Japan.

BI *Angetrunkene (Sch., M.R. 201), 1918,* 1st state of 2, s., t., num. I.3, wide margins, light-staining, tape, good cond., est. BP 2/3,000, (12-01-92, Christie-London, #473), plate 12¹⁄₁₆ x 8¹³⁄₁₆ in., (306 x 224 mm.), sheet 22⅜ x 17¹³⁄₁₆ in., (306 x 224 mm.), etching w/aquatint on van Gelder.

$1884* *"Beim Absinth", (Schiefler, E.175), 1911,* s., (09-29-92, B. Rasmussen, #354, illus.), aquatint (BP 1059, DM 2661, FR 9080, Y 224,902, DK 10,350).

$2331* *Boot (Sch., M. L24), 1907,* s., d., ded., margins, creasing, tape, skinning, (12-01-92, Christie-London, #471), L. 12⅝ x 18¹⁵⁄₁₆ in., (320 x 482 mm.), lithograph on tan wove (BP 1540, DM 3715, FR 12,662, Y 290,214).

BI *Boote (Sch., M.L. 18), 1907-15,* s., t., i., margins, light-staining, creases, very good cond., est. BP 8/12,000, (12-01-92, Christie-London, #470, illus.), L. 12¹⁵⁄₁₆ x 19¾ in., (328 x 502 mm.), sheet 17¹⁄₁₆ x 24³⁄₁₆ in., (328 x 502 mm.), lithograph in black, grey and green on smooth buff wove.

BI *Boote (Schiefler/Mosel 18 II/II), 1907/1915,* s., i., artist's proof, est. DM 35,000, (05-26-93, Lempertz, #393, illus.), 17 x 24³⁄₁₆ in., (43.2 x 61.4 cm.), lithograph on smooth thick paper.

$24,892* *Boote (Schiefler/Mosel L 18/II), 1907,* s., artist's proof, i., (12-01-92, Karl/Faber, #1061, illus.), 12¹⁵⁄₁₆ x 19⁵⁄₁₆ in., (33 x 49 cm.), color lithograph on cardboard (BP 16,447, DM 39,675, FR 135,209, Y 3,099,104).

$7062* *Christus Und Die Sunderin (Schiefler-Mosel 155 IV), 1911,* s., t., i. III. 3, (06-10-93, Hauswedell/Nolt, #734, illus.), image 11¹³⁄₁₆ x 9¹³⁄₁₆ in., (30 x 25 cm.), etching on hand-made Van Gelder Zonen (BP 4619, DM 11,500, FR 38,717, Y 749,602).

$6050* *The Conversation,* s. Emile Nolde, very good cond.(09-27-92, Bakker, #269, illus.), image 10½ x 11¾ in., (26.7 x 29.8 cm.), lithograph (BP 3533, DM 8968, FR 30,326, Y 730,235).

$14,896* *Dampfer (Schiefler-Mosel 135 IV), 1910,* s., watermark, (06-05-93, Bassenge, #6383, illus.), 11¹¹⁄₁₆ x 15¹¹⁄₁₆ in., (29.7 x 39.8 cm.), etching (BP 9806, DM 24,150, FR 81,399, Y 1,597,940).

$25,424* *Dusterer Mannerkopf (Schiefler-Mosel 17 III), 1907/15,* s., t., (06-10-93, Hauswedell/Nolt, #740, illus.), image 22 x 16¹⁵⁄₁₆ in., (55.9 x 43.1 cm.), color lithograph on wove (BP 16,630, DM 41,400, FR 139,386, Y 2,698,652).

$9930* *"E.N., Selbstportrat", (Schiefler/Mosel 89/II), 1908,* s., (06-05-93, Grisebach, #279, illus.), 12⅛ x 9⁵⁄₁₆ in., (30.8 x 23.7 cm.), aquatint etching on copper print paper (BP 6537, DM 16,099, FR 54,262, Y 1,065,222).

$1298* *Fabelwesen (Sch.-M. 77/II), 1926,* (06-23-93, Kornfeld, #636), color lithograph on thick Japan (BP 882, DM 2196, FR 7388, Y 141,410, SF 1955).

$2508* *Fabelwesen (Schiefler-Mosel 77 II), 1926,* s., (12-05-92, Bassenge, #7518), 6⁷⁄₁₆ x 4⁷⁄₁₆ in., (16.3 x 11.2 cm.), lithograph on Japan (BP 1570, DM 3910, FR 13,326, Y 310,742).

$3967* *Faust (Schiefler/Mosel 34 III), 1911,* #17/20, s., (11-21-92, Lempertz, #312, illus.), 6³⁄₁₆ x 4¼ in., (15.7 x 10.8 cm.), lithograph on thin hand-made Japan (BP 2612, DM 6325, FR 21,305, Y 493,347).

$10,994* *Frau Mit Dunklem Haar (Schiefler-Mosel 86 II), 1907,* s., t., (06-05-93, Bassenge, #6382A), 12 x 9⁵⁄₁₆ in., (30.5 x 23.7 cm.), drypoint (BP 7237, DM 17,824, FR 60,077, Y 1,179,361).

$8679* *"Frauenkopf I",* s., num. II/4, i., (05-08-93, Dobiaschofsky, #2169, illus.), 15¾ x 12¹⁵⁄₁₆ in., (40 x 33 cm.), woodcut (BP 5663, DM 13,942, FR 47,041, Y 969,829, SF 12,650).

$13,832* *"Frauenkopf I" (Schiefler/Mosel 114/II), 1912,* s., t., i., (06-05-93, Grisebach, #283, illus.), 11½ x 9⅛ in., (29.2 x 23.2 cm.), woodcut on copper print paper (BP 9105, DM 22,425, FR 75,585, Y 1,483,802).

$7150* *Frauenprofil (S./M. 136 III/III), 1917,* s., t., num. III.9, margins, good cond., creasing, mat stain, skinnedspots, (11-05-92, Sotheby-NY, #318, illus.), 8⅜ x 6 in., (212 x 152 mm.), woodcut on heavy white wove (BP 4650, DM 11,308, FR 38,256, Y 877,193).

$2902* *Der Graf (Sch.-M. 206), 1918,* s., t., ded., (06-23-93, Kornfeld, #633), etching on thick copper print paper (BP 1971, DM 4910, FR 16,517, Y 316,156, SF 4370).

$6900* *Grosse Muhle (S. L23), 1907,* s., i. Grosse Muhle, num. Aufl. Nr. 16, wide margins, colors faded, foxing, crease, skinning, good cond., sold after sale, (05-11-93, Christie-NY, #250, illus.), borderline 20⅛ x 13¼ in., (511 x 337 mm.), color lithograph on wove (BP 4405, DM 10,870, FR 36,624, Y 758,992).

BI *Grosse Muhle (Schiefler, Mosel L23II), 1907,* s., t., #Aufl. Nr. 2, margins, very good cond., est. BP 15/20,000, (05-20-93, Christie-London, #481, illus.), image 19½ x 13¾ in., (49.5 x 34.9 cm.), sheet 24 x 17 in., (49.5 x 34.9 cm.), lithograph in black and blue on smooth cream wove.

$16,484* *Hamburg, Binnenhafen (Schiefler, Mosel R144), 1910,* second (final) state, s., #II.2, ded., margins, deckle edge three sides, mount-staining, very good cond., prov., (05-20-93, Christie-London, #478, illus.), plate 12¼ x 16¼ in., (31.1 x 41.3 cm.), sheet 17½ x 23¾ in., (31.1 x 41.3 cm.), etching on fine van Gelder laid paper (BP 10,580, DM 26,596, FR 89,587, Y 1,820,230).

BI *Hamburg, Reiherstiegdock (S. E145), 1910,* 2nd final state, s., margins, staining, good cond., est. $6/8,000, (05-11-93, Christie-NY, #253, illus.), plate 12¼ x 16 in., (311 x 406 mm.), etching on wove.

$8475* *Hamburg, Reiherstiegdock (Schiefler-Mosel 145 II), 1910,* s., #II. 4, (06-10-93, Hauswedell/Nolt, #731, illus.), image 12⁵⁄₁₆ x 16¼ in., (31.2 x 41.3 cm.), etching on hand-made (BP 5544, DM 13,801, FR 46,464, Y 899,586).

$6356* *Hamburg, Reiherstiegdock (Schiefler-Mosel 145 II), 1910,* s., (06-10-93, Hauswedell/Nolt, #732, illus.), image 12³⁄₁₆ x 16⅛ in., (30.9 x 41 cm.), etching on copper print (BP 4158, DM 10,350, FR 34,846, Y 674,663).

BI *Handler (Schiefler, Mosel L50), 1913,* s., t., i. Aufl. Nr 12, wide margins, good cond., light-staining, paper discoloration, creases, est. BP 32/36,000, (06-30-93, Sotheby-London, #578, illus.), sh 27¾ x 22¼ in., (705 x 565 mm.), lithograph in black, rose and brown on fibrous wove.

$14,437* *"Die Heiligen Drei Konige" (Schiefler-Mosel 49), 1913,* (11-28-92, Grisebach, #159, illus.), 25⁹⁄₁₆ x 21¼ in., (65 x 54 cm.), color lithograph on handmade Japan (BP 9529, DM 23,000, FR 78,080, Y 1,796,764).

$1980* *Hugo Del Caril (S./M. 88/II), 1908,* second (final) state, s., d., s. by printer, Felsing, large margins,good cond., creases, foxing, discoloration, creases, tears, (11-05-92, Sotheby-NY, #317), 12 x 9½ in., (306 x 240 mm.), sheet 23⅝ x 17⅜ in., (306 x 240 mm.), etching and aquatint on heavy wove (BP 1288, DM 3131, FR 10,594, Y 242,915).

$1210* *Jorgensby (Schiefler/Mosel 62/II), 1907,* second (final) state, s., d., large margins, good cond., creases, tack holes, tear, creases, (11-05-92, Sotheby-NY, #316), 7½ x 5¾ in., (190 x 145 mm.), sheet 17¾ x 12½ in., (190 x 145 mm.), drypoint on wove (BP 787, DM 1914, FR 6474, Y 148,448).

$5500* *Junger Furst Und Tanzerinnen (Schiefler 196), 1918,* 2nd final state, s., wide margins, mat/staining, surface soiling, good cond., (11-09-92, Christie-NY, #146, illus.), 10⅜ x 8⁹⁄₁₆ in., (263 x 218 mm.), etching, drypoint and aquatint on wove (BP 3636, DM 8780, FR 29,666, Y 682,552).

BI *Junges Madchen (Schiefler-Mosel 106 II), 1912,* s., num., est. DM 20,000, (06-05-93, Bassenge, #6381, illus.), 8¹¹⁄₁₆ x 12⅝ in., (22 x 32 cm.), woodcut on Japan.

BI *Jungle Madchen (Schiefler/Mosel 15 II by II), 1907,* est. DM 70,000, (05-26-93, Lempertz, #392, illus.), 23⅛ x 18¹¹⁄₁₆ in., (58.7 x 47.4 cm.), lithograph, watercolor on smooth thick paper.

$10,256* *"Kind U. Grosser Vogel-Kommen Ihnen, Von Emil Nolde" (Schiefler/Mosel Nr. 9, I), 1906,* t., s., 1. state, (11-13-92, Kunsthaus, #730A, illus.), 6¼ x 8¼ in., (15.8 x 21 cm.), sh 8¹¹⁄₁₆ x 10⅝ in., (15.8 x 21 cm.), woodcut on board (BP 6627, DM 16,100, FR 54,293, Y 1,272,930).

$2542* *Kinder Und Strassenmusikant (Schiefler-Mosel 128), 1909,* s., t., (06-10-93, Hauswedell/Nolt, #728, illus.), image 4⁹⁄₁₆ x 3¹⁄₁₆ in., (11.6 x 7.8 cm.), etching on strong paper (BP 1663, DM 4139, FR 13,936, Y 269,823).

BI *Kirche Und Schiff, Sonderburg (Sch./M. L 21/II), 1907,* s., i., mount-staining, est. DM 35/40,000, (12-01-92, Karl/Faber, #1062, illus.), 18⅞ x 12¹³⁄₁₆ in., (48 x 32.5 cm.), color lithograph on cardboard.

$12,712* *Kniendes Madchen (Schiefler-Mosel 76 IV), 1907,* s., (06-10-93, Hauswedell/Nolt, #727, illus.), image 11⅞ x 8⅞ in., (30.1 x 22.5 cm.), drypoint and etching on copper print board (BP 8315, DM 20,700, FR 69,693, Y 1,349,326).

$5932* *Kopf Mit Pfeife, E. N. (Schiefler-Mosel 5), 1907,* s., d., (06-10-93, Hauswedell/Nolt, #738, illus.), image 15¾ x 11¼ in., (40 x 28.5 cm.), lithograph on wove (BP 3880, DM 9660, FR 32,522, Y 629,657).

$2444* *Madchenbildnis (Sch.-M. 230/II), 1924,* (06-23-93, Kornfeld, #634), etching on thick Japan (BP 1660, DM 4135, FR 13,910, Y 266,260, SF 3680).

$1836* *Madchenprofil (Schiefler-Mosel 169), 1911,* s., t., (06-10-93, Hauswedell/Nolt, #735, illus.), image 3¹⁄₁₆ x 4⁵⁄₁₆ in., (7.8 x 11 cm.), etching (BP 1201, DM 2990, FR 10,066, Y 194,884).

$1398* *Muhle (Schiefler 22), 1907,* margins, repaired tear, creases, paper discoloration, (12-03-92, Sotheby-London, #471, illus.), sheet 23¾ x 16¾ in., (603 x 425 mm.), lithograph on wove (BP 902, DM 2198, FR 7504, Y 173,946).

$91,455* *Muhle Am Wasser (Schiefler, Mosel L82), 1926,* s., i., small margin at bottom, printer's crease, printer's creases and perforations, nicks, excell. cond., (05-20-93, Christie-London, #480, illus.), sheet 24¼ x 30¾ in., (61.6 x 78.1 cm.), lithograph in black, red, orange-pink and grey on fine Japan w/wirelines (BP 58,700, DM 147,556, FR 497,038, Y 10,098,830).

$3910* *Mutter Und Kind (S. W142), 1917,* s., wide margins, light-stained, laid down on board, (05-11-93, Christie-NY, #254, illus.), borderline 8⅜ x 6 in., (213 x 152 mm.), woodcut on wove (BP 2496, DM 6159, FR 20,754, Y 430,096).

$3531* *Nelly (Schiefler-Mosel 4), 1907,* s., d., (06-10-93, Hauswedell/Nolt, #737, illus.), image 12¹⁄₁₆ x 9¹⁄₁₆ in., (30.7 x 23 cm.), lithograph on wove (BP 2310, DM 5750, FR 19,359, Y 374,801).

$45,080* *Prophet (Schiefler/Mosel Band II 110), 1912,* s., (11-21-92, Lempertz, #313, illus.), 12½ x 8⁹⁄₁₆ in., (31.7 x 21.7 cm.), woodcut on thick copper print paper (BP 29,681, DM 71,875, FR 242,105, Y 5,606,268).

BI *"Prophet" (Schiefler/Mosel 110), 1912,* s., t., est. DM 60/70,000, (06-04-93, Grisebach, #25, illus.), 12½ x 8⅜ in., (31.8 x 21.3 cm.), woodcut on light brown Japan.

BI *"Prophet" (Schiefler/Mosel 110), 1912,* s., est. DM 50/60,000, (11-27-92, Grisebach, #11, illus.), 12½ x 8⅞ in., (31.7 x 22.6 cm.), woodcut on thick copper print paper.

$7062* *Salomo Und Seine Frauen (Schiefler-Mosel 153 II), 1911,* s., (06-10-93, Hauswedell/Nolt, #733, illus.), image 11¹³⁄₁₆ x 9¹³⁄₁₆ in., (30 x 25 cm.), etching on wove (BP 4619, DM 11,500, FR 38,717, Y 749,602).

$5639* *Schiffe Bei Alsen (Schiefler/Mosel 72), 1907,* s., (05-26-93, Lempertz, #394, illus.), 17¼ x 13¾ in., (43.8 x 34.9 cm.), etching on thick copper print (BP 3648, DM 9201, FR 30,967, Y 612,668).

BI *Schiffe Bei Windstille (S. E71), 1907,* 2nd final state, s., d., i. by printer O. Felsing, wide margins, stains, very good cond., est. $3/5,000, (05-11-93, Christie-NY, #251), plate 8⅝ x 11¾ in., (219 x 298 mm.), drypoint in green on owve.

$8475* *Schlepper (MTL.) (Schiefler-Mosel 139 III), 1910,* s., num., t., (06-10-93, Hauswedell/Nolt, #729, illus.), image 12⁵⁄₁₆ x 16¼ in., (31.3 x 41.3 cm.), etching on hand-made Van Gelder Zonen (BP 5544, DM 13,801, FR 46,464, Y 899,586).

BI *Schlepper, Mtl. (S. E132), 1910,* s., t., wide margins, staining, very good cond., est. $5/7,000, (05-11-93, Christie-NY, #252, illus.), plate 7¾ x 10⅞ in., (197 x 276 mm.), etching and drypoint on laid.

$10,690* *Schriftgelehter (Sch.-M. 154/II), 1911,* s., 2nd state, (06-23-93, Kornfeld, #631, illus.), etching on handmade (BP 7262, DM 18,088, FR 60,842, Y 1,164,615, SF 16,100).

$8600* *Segler Und Drei Kleine Dampfer (Schiefler, Mosel R140), 1910,* second (final) state, s., margins (trimmed unevenly), mount-staining, (05-20-93, Christie-London,

#479, illus.), plate 12 x 16 in., (30.5 x 40.6 cm.), sheet 15¼ x 19 in., (30.5 x 40.6 cm.), etching on wove (BP 5520, DM 13,875, FR 46,739, Y 949,647).

$8781* *Segler Und Drei Kleine Dampfer (Schiefler-Mosel 140/II), 1910,* s., (06-23-93, Kornfeld, #630, illus.), etching on wove (BP 5965, DM 14,858, FR 49,977, Y 956,640, SF 13,225).

$6344* *Spazierende (Schiefler/Mosel 115), 1908,* s., i., (05-26-93, Lempertz, #395, illus.), 23¾ x 17⁹⁄₁₆ in., (60.3 x 44.6 cm.), etching on van Geldern Zonen (BP 4104, DM 10,351, FR 34,838, Y 689,266).

$2401* *Stehende Frau (Klein((Schiefler-Mosel 47), 1911,* s., #6/ 20, collector's stamp, (06-10-93, Hauswedell/Nolt, #741, illus.), image 6¹¹⁄₁₆ x 1¹⁵⁄₁₆ in., (17 x 5 cm.), lithograph on hand-made Japan (BP 1571, DM 3910, FR 13,163, Y 254,856).

$233,700* *Tanzerin (Schiefler, Mosel L56), 1913,* s., i. Probedruck Tanzerin, narrow margins, repaired tear extending into subjects, other small repairs, lesser defects, (05-20-93, Christie-London, #477, illus.), image 20¾ x 26⅞ in., (52.7 x 68.3 cm.), sheet 21¼ x 27⅛ in., (52.7 x 68.3 cm.), lithograph in black, ochre, pink and violet, w/pencil additions on tan wove (BP 150,000, DM 377,057, FR 1,270,109, Y 25,806,095).

$5345* *Der Tierfreund (Sch.-M. 203/I), 1918,* s., 1st print of 1st state, d., ded., (06-23-93, Kornfeld, #632), etching (BP 3631, DM 9044, FR 30,421, Y 582,307, SF 8050).

$6709* *Der Tierfreund (Schiefler-Mosel 203 II), 1918,* s., t., (06-10-93, Hauswedell/Nolt, #736, illus.), image 11⅞ x 8¾ in., (30.2 x 22.3 cm.), etching on wove (BP 4388, DM 10,925, FR 36,782, Y 712,132).

$1831* *Waldkinder (Sch., M. R161), 1911,* 4th (final) state, s., t., wide margins, mount-staining, foxmarks, creasing, tears, defects, (12-01-92, Christie-London, #472), plate 9¾ x 11⅝ in., (247 x 295 mm.), sheet 24¹³⁄₁₆ x 18¹³⁄₁₆ in., (247 x 295 mm.), drypoint w/aquatint on van Gelder (BP 1210, DM 2918, FR 9946, Y 227,963).

NOLPE, Pieter   Dutch 1613/14-1652/53
$853* *Ladies And Gentlemen In Fashionable Costumes (Holl. 274-279): Four,* after Quast, small margins, one plate crumpled at edge, (12-03-92, Sotheby-London, #85), 7½ x 5½ in., (192 x 133 mm.), etching (BP 550, DM 1341, FR 4579, Y 106,134).

BI *Two Dancing Couples,* plate s., rare, est. G 350/450, (11-18-92, Bubb Kuyper, #1840), 3¹¹⁄₁₆ x 4⅝ in., (9.3 x 11.7 cm.), engraving.

NORBLIN, Jean Pierre   1745-1830
$1275* *Selbstbildnis (Franke 1 a),* artist's proof, (06-04-93, Bassenge, #5533, illus.), 5⅜ x 5¹³⁄₁₆ in., (13.7 x 14.7 cm.), etching (BP 844, DM 2070, FR 6979, Y 137,511).

NORDELL, Carl   American b. 1885
$220* *Mending The Nets: A Pair,* s. Carl Nordell imp., very good cond., (11-21-92, Bakker, #155, illus.), each, plate 10 x 6 in., (25.4 x 15.2 cm.), etching (BP 145, DM 351, FR 1182, Y 27,360).

NORDELL, Carl Johan David   Danish/American b. 1885
BI *Trees Surrounding Quiet Lake,* plate inits., s., d. 1925, num. Trial Proof-5 impressions, prov., est. C$ 2/300, (06-08-93, Ritchie, #30), 7½ x 9⅝ in., (19.1 x 24.4 cm.), etching and drypoint.

NORDFELDT, B.J.O.   Swedish/American 1878-1955
BI *"Christmas Subjects": Five,* s. by Emily Nordfeldt, margins, good cond., thinned spots, surface soiling, light-staining, creases, est. $3/400, (10-28-92, Butterfield, #2747), color linoleum cut on various papers.

NORDFELDT, Bjor Julius Olsson   Swedish/American 1878-1955
$220* *Group Of Three Lithographs,* good cond. (?), prov., (04-25-93, Bakker, #157, illus.), image 12½ x 16 in., (31.8 x 40.6 cm.), lithographs (BP 140, DM 348, FR 1175, Y 24,299).

$110* *Venice,* margins, s., (05-22-93, Collins, #4), 4¾ x 6½ in., (12.1 x 16.5 cm.), etching (BP 71, DM 179, FR 602, Y 12,128).

$1320* *"Windmill In Skane" (Catalogue Raisonne #5), 1903,* ded., good cond.?, (03-28-93, Bakker, #44), 10 x 5¾ in., (25.4 x 14.6 cm.), color woodblock (BP 887, DM 2153, FR 7321, Y 153,631).

NORGAARD, Bjorn Julius Olsson
$169* *Gentagelser 3, 1976,* portfolio, s., 18/100, (09-30-92, Kunsthallen, #226), lithograph (BP 95, DM 240, FR 811, Y 20,281, DK 920).

BI *Komposition, 1981,* s. Bjorn Norgaard 81, 8/50, est. DK 1,500, (03-24-93, Kunsthallen, #263), color lithograph.

NORGARD, Lars
$147* *Kompositioner, 1988: Two,* s. Lars Norgard 88, 48/125, 51/125, (03-24-93, Kunsthallen, #264), color lithograph (BP 100, DM 240, FR 817, Y 17,272, DK 920).

NORMAN, Dorothy   b. 1905
$770* *An American Place, O'Keeffe Painting And Light Bulb,* (1930s), p.l., s. in ink, t., d., credit stamp, (10-13-92, Christie-NY, #322, illus.), 3¾ x 2½ in., (9.5 x 6.4 cm.), photograph, gelatin silver print (BP 448, DM 1128, FR 3833, Y 93,367).

$805* *An American Place-Phone, Shadow And Stieglitz Equivalent In Background,* 1930s, p.l., ink s.; t., d., credit stamp, (04-08-93, Christie-NY, #324, illus.), 4¼ x 2¾ in., (10.8 x 7 cm.), photograph, gelatin silver print (BP 528, DM 1293, FR 4377, Y 91,353).

NORO, M.   **(after)**
$791* *Venice, Plates 1-10, "Palazzo Ducale", "Palazzo Grimani", "Palazzo Trevisan", "Palazzo Pesaro", "Vendramin Calergi", "Palazzo Corner Della Regina","Palazzo Grassi", "Palazzo Corner Ca' Grande" and others: Eleven,* pub. Joseph Kier, margins, creasing, spotting, (10-07-92, Christie-S. Ken., #83), 7½ x 12 in., (19.1 x 30.5 cm.), lithograph (BP 462, DM 1145, FR 3881, Y 95,129).

NORTH, Arthur
$55* *Down Come,* margins, s. Arthur North, (02-13-93, Collins, #58), 10⅞ x 8⅞ in., (27.6 x 22.5 cm.), etching (BP 39, DM 91, FR 309, Y 6633).

NORTHCOTE, I.   (after)
$235* *Country Girl Of Tuscany: Pair,* by T. Gaugin, (01-21-93, Bonhams-Chelsea, #26), image 9½ x 7¾ in., (24.1 x 19.7 cm.), hand-colored stipple engravings (BP 154, DM 374, FR 1264, Y 29,412).

NORTHCOTE, James   (after)
$770* *Tigress,* margins trimmed, image crease, repaired areas, discoloration, hingedto mat, (12-04-92, Doyle, #56), 13 x 18⅞ in., (330 x 479 mm.), mixed method engraving (BP 494, DM 1226, FR 4160, Y 96,130).

$639* *"A Visit To Grandmother" and "A Visit To Grandfather": A Pair,* by John R. Smith, trimmed, (01-21-93, Bonhams-Chelsea, #75), image 20 x 15¼ in., (50.8 x 38.7 cm.), hand-colored mezzotints (BP 418, DM 1016, FR 3437, Y 79,975).

NORTHCOTE, James   (after)   English 1746-1831
$88* *Country Girl Of Tuscany,* by Thomas Gaugain, pub. 1794, (12-10-92, Sloan, #2084), 11 x 8½ in., (27.9 x 21.6 cm.), color engraving (BP 57, DM 139, FR 475, Y 10,886).

NORTON, Elizabeth
$259* *"Goldfish No. I" and Goldfish No. II, 1924": Two,* s., d., t., #44/100, #48/100, annot. del A.C. et imp., deline et imp,mono. inkstamp, margins, good cond., notations, tear, creases, light-staining,staining, (05-19-93, Butterfield, #2014), one 8¼ x 5¾ in., (210 x 146 mm.), the other 8⁹⁄₁₆ x 6¾ in., (210 x 146 mm.), woodcut in colors on tissue-thin Japan (BP 168, DM 421, FR 1418, Y 28,673).

NORWICH, C.
$357* *Canadian National Railways, 1924,* Johnson, Riddle & Co., A- cond., surface soiling, marginal creasing, (08-06-92, Swann, #213, illus.), 40 x 25 in., (101.6 x 63.5 cm.), (BP 186, DM 527, FR 1781, Y 45,536).

NOSKOWIAK, Sonya   1900-1975
$3520* *Bark Detail-Point Lobos, 1933,* sig., (10-14-92, Swann, #527, illus.), 4 x 3 in., (10.2 x 7.6 cm.), photograph, silver print (BP 2066, DM 5151, FR 17,469, Y 426,563).

BI *Carlos Dyer, 1937,* est. $2/3,000, (04-08-93, Christie-NY, #391, illus.), 8¾ x 7⅛ in., (22.2 x 18.1 cm.), photograph, gelatin silver print.

BI *Elyse Armitage, Mrs. Merle, c. 1935,* s., est. $2,5/3,500, (04-08-93, Christie-NY, #392, illus.), 8⅜ x 7⅝ in., (21.3 x 19.4 cm.), photograph, gelatin silver print.

BI *From Telegraph Hill, (Noskowiak Archive, p. 16, 76:009:186),* mounted, 1930's, est. $2,5/3,500, (10-15-92, Sotheby-NY, #283, illus.), 9½ x 7½ in., (24.1 x 19.1 cm.), photograph, gelatin silver print.

BI *Industrial Study (Noskowiak Archive, p. 10, 76:009:231, variant),* mounted, est. $2,5/3,500, (10-15-92, Sotheby-NY, #282, illus.), 7½ x 9½ in., (19.1 x 24.1 cm.), photograph, gelatin silver print.

BI *Martha Graham, c. 1936,* mounted, s. by photog., est. $3/5,000, (04-06-93, Sotheby-NY, #175, illus.), 8⅝ x 6½ in., photograph.

$1980* *Rooms, 1933,* s., d. by photog., notations, (04-07-93, Swann, #528, illus.), 3¾ x 2⅞ in., photograph, silver print (BP 1308, DM 3202, FR 10,837, Y 224,949).

$4888* *Study Of Reflections, 1937,* mounted, s., d. by photog., (04-06-93, Sotheby-NY, #176, illus.), 9⅜ x 7½ in., photograph (BP 3229, DM 7875, FR 26,667, Y 557,482).

NOTMAN, William
$550* *Snoeshow Club, 1897,* photog.'s sig., d. in neg., (04-07-93, Swann, #242), 12 x 18 in., photograph, albumen composite print (BP 363, DM 890, FR 3010, Y 62,486).

NOTMAN, William and Henry SANDHAM (after KRIEGHOFF)
$385* *Lorette Indians Camping At The Big Rock Of Lake Lagon Near Valcartier,* s. NOTMAN & SANDHAM, lit., (11-30-92, Ritchie, #57, illus.), 6 x 9½ in., (15.3 x 24 cm.), photograph, b/w by Notman, hand-colored in watercolor by Sandham (BP 254, DM 613, FR 2082, Y 47,915, C$ 495).

NOTMAN, William and Henry SANDHAM (after Krieghoff)
$321* *Tracking The Moose On Lake Famine South Of Quebec, 1863,* s. NOTMAN & SANDHAM, lit., (11-30-92, Ritchie, #58, illus.), 5¾ x 8½ in., (14.5 x 21.5 cm.), photograph, b/w after Krieghoff by Notman, hand-colored in watercolorby Sandham (BP 212, DM 511, FR 1736, Y 39,950, C$ 413).

NOURY, Gaston b. 1866
BI *Le Pere Didier/ Affiches Et Bouquins, c. 1900,* rare, Imp. Bourgerie, Paris, est. DM 1,800, (12-05-92, Bassenge, #7614), 24 x 15⅞ in., (61 x 40.3 cm.), color lithograph.

NOVAK, Louis American 1903-1988
$55* *Old State House, Hartford,* #4/100, s., (12-17-92, Mystic, #16), 8½ x 10 in., (21.6 x 25.4 cm.), color woodblock (BP 35, DM 86, FR 293, Y 6759).

NOVELLI, Gastone b. 1923
$166* *Composizione, (19)65,* s., d., num., (12-01-92, Karl/Faber, #1065), 15⅜ x 15¾ in., (39 x 40 cm.), color lithograph on Arches wove (BP 110, DM 265, FR 902, Y 20,667).

NOWAK?, Otto
$60 *Schubert And Strauss,* folds, (03-04-93, Alderfer, #256), 34¼ x 20 in., (87 x 50.8 cm.), poster (BP 41, DM 98, FR 334, Y 6986).

NOWINSKI, Ira
$345* *"Luciano Pavarotti, La Giocanda", 1979,* s., t., d., num., photog.'s stamp, (05-23-93, Butterfield, #3558, illus.), 12 x 17¾ in., photograph, gelatin silver print (BP 225, DM 564, FR 1899, Y 38,134).

NOYEZ, Ph. H.
$880* *Limonade Brault, 1938,* Joel Bellon, A cond., (08-06-92, Swann, #214, illus.), 63 x 46 in., (160 x 116.8 cm.), (BP 460, DM 1300, FR 4391, Y 112,245).

NOZAL, Alexandre 1852-1929
BI *Saint Briac,* p. Affiche Gaillard, for Chemins de Fer de l'Etat, cond. 2, laid on linen, est. BP 2/300, (10-13-92, Phillips-London, #38), 39⅜ x 24⁷⁄₁₆ in., (100 x 62 cm.), color lithograph.

NUNEZ, Guillermo
BI *Figure In A Box,* s., d. 73, #35/50, prov., est. C$ 150/200, (12-01-92, Ritchie, #21), 21 x 30 in., (53.3 x 76.2 cm.), color serigraph.

BI *"Figure" and "Abstract In Green & Rose": Two,* s., d. 73, #43/50 and 35/40, est. C$ 3/400, (12-01-92, Ritchie,

#20), each approx. 30⅜ x 21¾ in., (77.2 x 55.2 cm.), color serigraph.

NUNNEY
$1288* *The Perfect Power Pair, Oarsmen, 1926,* p. Waterlow & Sons, ref. #141, cond. 4, (10-13-92, Phillips-London, #57, illus.), 29¹⁵⁄₁₆ x 44¹¹⁄₁₆ in., (76 x 113.5 cm.), color lithograph (BP 750, DM 1887, FR 6411, Y 156,178).

NUREMBERG WORLD CHRONICLE
$30* *"Folio CCXII" and "Folio CLXXVI": Two,* by Wogleniut and Pleydenwurff, set in text, very good cond., repaired tear on folio, (05-15-93, Cleveland, #14, illus.), 17 x 11¾ in., (43.2 x 29.8 cm.), woodcut (BP 20, DM 48, FR 162, Y 3326).

NURNBERG, Walter
BI *Portrait Of A Welder, c. 1935,* mounted on card, stamped photog.'s credit, label, 579 x 464mm, est. BP 3/500, (05-07-93, Sotheby-London, #170, illus.), photograph, silver print.

NUTTALL, Charles 1872-c.1950
$130* *(Dutch Windmill),* s. Nuttall, d. '26, (08-11-92, L. Joel, #80G), 7¹¹⁄₁₆ x 4¾ in., (19.5 x 12.1 cm.), etching (BP 68, DM 191, FR 646, Y 16,647, A$ 176).

NUTTING, Wallace American b. 1861
$99* *Among The Birches,* (07-17-92, DuMouchelle, #314), 9⅜ x 7⅝ in., (23.8 x 19.4 cm.), colored print (BP 51, DM 144, FR 488, Y 12,307).

$99* *Among The Birches,* (07-17-92, DuMouchelle, #315), 9⅜ x 7⅝ in., (23.8 x 19.4 cm.), print (BP 51, DM 144, FR 488, Y 12,307).

$165* *"Avenue",* (11-13-92, DuMouchelle, #128), photograph (BP 107, DM 259, FR 873, Y 20,479).

$55* *Birches,* s., (09-18-92, DuMouchelle, #248), 6¼ x 3 in., (15.9 x 7.6 cm.), print (BP 32, DM 82, FR 282, Y 6853).

$138* *"Blossoms",* (11-13-92, DuMouchelle, #130), photograph (BP 89, DM 217, FR 731, Y 17,128).

$110* *A Bonnie Brook,* (07-17-92, DuMouchelle, #316), 12⅜ x 7⅛ in., (31.4 x 18.1 cm.), print (BP 56, DM 160, FR 542, Y 13,675).

$121* *"Country Road" and "In Woerden": Two,* one s., other bears sig., (06-13-93, Hindman, #420), larger 9½ x 4¼ in., photograph, hand-colored (BP 79, DM 197, FR 662, Y 12,733).

$77* *Elm Beach,* (07-17-92, DuMouchelle, #317), 7¼ x 9½ in., (18.4 x 24.1 cm.), print (BP 39, DM 112, FR 379, Y 9572).

$99* *Highland Blossoms,* (07-17-92, DuMouchelle, #318), 12¾ x 4¾ in., (32.4 x 12.1 cm.), print (BP 51, DM 144, FR 488, Y 12,307).

$88* *Honeymoon Drive,* (07-17-92, DuMouchelle, #313), 9 x 7½ in., (22.9 x 19.1 cm.), colored print (BP 45, DM 128, FR 434, Y 10,940).

$110* *Patti's Favorite Walk,* (07-17-92, DuMouchelle, #312), 6½ x 4½ in., (16.5 x 11.4 cm.), colored print (BP 56, DM 160, FR 542, Y 13,675).

$132* *Patti's Favorite Walk,* (07-17-92, DuMouchelle, #319), 9⅜ x 7⅝ in., (23.8 x 19.4 cm.), print (BP 68, DM 192, FR 651, Y 16,410).

$110* *"Settle",* (11-13-92, DuMouchelle, #129), photograph (BP 71, DM 173, FR 582, Y 13,653).

$55* *Trees And Stream,* s., (09-18-92, DuMouchelle, #247), 3¾ x 3 in., (9.5 x 7.6 cm.), print (BP 32, DM 82, FR 282, Y 6853).

$83* *Untitled,* s., (11-13-92, DuMouchelle, #386), 6 x 3 in., (15.2 x 7.6 cm.), photograph (BP 54, DM 130, FR 439, Y 10,302).

$110* *"Wentworth Gardens Lower Hall",* s., t., (02-27-93, Dunning, #107), 9½ x 7 in., (24.1 x 17.8 cm.), print (BP 77, DM 181, FR 615, Y 12,985).

NUYTTENS, Josef Pierre Amrerican b. 1885
$187* *Exotic Dancer,* s., (11-01-92, Hanzel, #205), 19 x 12 in., (48.3 x 30.5 cm.), color lithograph (BP 122, DM 295, FR 994, Y 23,121).

NYBORG, Peter
  $335* *Untitled*, s. 84, 92/96, (09-29-92, B. Rasmussen, #355), lithograph in colors (BP 188, DM 473, FR 1614, Y 39,990, DK 1840).

O'GORMAN, Juan   Mexican 1905-1982
  $3575* *Autorretrato, 1963*, t., s., #28/50, d. handling creases, stain, foxing, (11-23-92, Sotheby-NY, #269, illus.), image 13⅝ x 9¼ in., (345 x 235 mm.), lithograph (BP 2337, DM 5724, FR 19,419, Y 443,493).
  BI *Flores Imaginarias, c. 1955*, s., #21/100, full margins, very good cond., tears, handling creases,yellowing, est. $1,5/2,500, (11-23-92, Sotheby-NY, #270, illus.), image 21⅞ x 17⅜ in., (555 x 440 mm.), lithograph.
  BI *Pocker De Ases Con Gorila, 1963*, s., #32/50, d., full margins, good cond., handling creases, t. verso,s., est. $2/4,000, (11-23-92, Sotheby-NY, #271, illus.), image 16⅞ x 20¾ in., (430 x 528 mm.), lithograph.

O'HIGGINS, Pablo   Mexican b. 1904
  $165* *Mexican Man Freeing Bird*, s., d. Pablo O'Higgins, #47/50, (12-12-92, Wolf, #30), 18¼ x 12 in., (46.4 x 30.5 cm.), lithograph (BP 106, DM 260, FR 891, Y 20,418).
  $275* *"Mujer De Vera Cruz"*, s., num. 39/50, good cond., (10-31-92, Cleveland, #320), 14½ x 24½ in., (36.8 x 62.2 cm.), lithograph (BP 176, DM 423, FR 1435, Y 34,064).

O'SULLIVAN, Timothy
  $1100* *"Aboriginal Life Among The Navajoe Indians", 1873*, #26 in neg., photog's credit., t., #7, Wheeler Survey info., s. AlsoBell, i., sold after sale, (10-15-92, Sotheby-NY, #29, illus.), 10¾ x 7⅞ in., (27.3 x 20 cm.), photograph, albumen print (BP 673, DM 1637, FR 5553, Y 131,974).
  $550* *Appache Lake, Sierra Blanca Range, Arizona, 1874*, letterpress t., series t., photog. credit, series #7, (04-07-93, Swann, #244, illus.), 8 x 10¾ in., photograph, albumen print on toned Wheeler Survey mount (BP 363, DM 890, FR 3010, Y 62,486).
  $1760* *Astronomical Observatory, South Ruby Valley, Nevada, 1868*, photog. credit, (04-07-93, Swann, #245, illus.), 7 x 10½ in., photograph, albumen print (BP 1163, DM 2847, FR 9633, Y 199,955).
  $1760* *"Black Canon, Colorado River, Looking Above From Camp 7", 1871*, #5 in neg., photog's credit., t., #5, Wheeler Survey info., Alonzo Bell Coll., (10-15-92, Sotheby-NY, #28, illus.), 8 x 10 in., (20.3 x 25.4 cm.), photograph, albumen print (BP 1077, DM 2620, FR 8884, Y 211,158).
  BI *"View On Apache Lake, Sierra Blanca Range, Arizona" (Snyder, p. 36),1873*, #2 in neg., photog.'s credit, t., #2, Wheeler Survey info., est. $2/3,000, (10-15-92, Sotheby-NY, #30, illus.), 7⅞ x 10⅞ in., (20 x 27.6 cm.), photograph, albumen print.
  $3520* *'Field Where General Reynolds Fell, Gettysburg'(Fixing A Shadow, p. 94)*, photog./printer credits, (c), t., #37, d., 1863, p. 1866, (10-15-92, Sotheby-NY, #11, illus.), 7 x 9 in., (17.8 x 22.9 cm.), photograph, albumen print, on 2-toned 'Sketch Book' mount (BP 2154, DM 5240, FR 17,769, Y 422,316).
  $1320* *'Indian Pueblo, Zuni, N.M.: View From The South' (Horan, pp. 298-299), 1873*, #17 in neg., p. w/photog's credit, t., #17, Wheeler Survey info., (10-15-92, Sotheby-NY, #26, illus.), 8 x 10⅞ in., (20.3 x 27.6 cm.), photograph, albumen print (BP 808, DM 1965, FR 6663, Y 158,368).
  BI *'Section Of South Side Of Zuni Pueblo, N.M.' (Photography and Architecture, pl. 101), 1873*, p. w/photog's credit, t., #15, Wheeler Survey info., est. $1/2,000, (10-15-92, Sotheby-NY, #25, illus.), 7⅞ x 10⅞ in., (20 x 27.6 cm.), photograph, albumen print.

O'SULLIVAN, Timothy and William BELL
  $935* *Entrance To Black Canon, Colorado River, From Above; and Grand CanonOf The Colorado River, Mouth Of Kanab Wash, Looking West: Two, 1871*, credit, t., d., plate num. 10, 11, (10-13-92, Christie-NY, #25, illus.), 8 x 10¾ in., (20.3 x 27.3 cm.), photograph, albumen prints (BP 545, DM 1370, FR 4654, Y 113,375).
  $14,300* *The Wheeler Survey: One Hundred Forty-Five*, from the United States Geographical and Geological Explorations and Surveys West of the 100th Meridian, 63 w/credit

recto or p. label w/credit of TIMOTHY O'SULLIVAN verso, 55 w/credit recto or label w/credit of WILLIAM BELL verso, 27 w/no p. credit or label, few annot., (10-15-92, Sotheby-NY, #27, illus.), on mounts 4 x 7 in., (10.2 x 17.8 cm.), photograph, stereographs (BP 8750, DM 21,286, FR 72,186, Y 1,715,657).

O'SULLIVAN, T. PYWELL, W. GARDNER, ALEXANDER
  $1100* *Sketchbook Of The Civil War: "High Bridge, Crossing The Appomattox","Interior View Of The Confederate Line", "Old Capitol Prison, Washington" and "Popular Grove Church": Four*, imprinted w/photog. and printer's credits, t., each w/accompanying caption leaf, 1860s, (04-07-93, Swann, #187, illus.), approx. 7 x 9 in., photograph, albumen print (BP 727, DM 1779, FR 6021, Y 124,972).

OCHOA, Rafael de   b. 1858
  $341* *Cie. Int. Le Des Wagons-Lits Et Des Grands Express Europeens. Rome Express. Train De Luxe. Hiver, 1901-1902*, Paris, Imp. Lemercier, cond. B+, (06-11-93, Boisgirard, #120), 42⅛ x 30⁵⁄₁₆ in., (107 x 77 cm.), poster (BP 224, DM 554, FR 1868, Y 36,180).

ODJIG, Daphne   b. 1928
  $304* *Bad Medicine Woman, 1974*, #40/60, s., t., d. '74, prov., (05-10-93, Hodgins, #322, illus.), 41 x 31 in., (104.1 x 78.7 cm.), serigraph on paper (BP 198, DM 488, FR 1648, Y 33,970, C$ 385).
  $369* *The Evil Spell*, #28/60, s., t., d. '75, prov., (05-10-93, Hodgins, #323), 30 x 40 in., (76.2 x 101.6 cm.), serigraph on paper (BP 241, DM 593, FR 2000, Y 41,234, C$ 468).

OEHM, Herbert
  $43* *Swing Portfolio #8*, s., #40/75; t. label verso, pub. Edition Denis Rene Hans Mayer, blindstamped, prov., (12-01-92, Ritchie, #75), 24⅜ x 28½ in., (61.9 x 72.4 cm.), color serigraph (BP 28, DM 69, FR 234, Y 5354, C$ 55).

OELENHEINZ, Friedrich (after)
  BI *Prince Charles De Schwarzenburg (Leblanc 88), c. 1800*, by Johann Peter Pichler, proof, trimmed, repaired, defects, good cond., est. BP 100/150, (11-30-92, Phillips-London, #92), sheet 19¼ x 13¼ in., (489 x 337 mm.), mezzotint on wove.

OELMAN, Paul H.   1890-1957
  $990* *Pinhole Photo - G.E., c. 1940*, s., t., prov., (10-13-92, Christie-NY, #323, illus.), 12¾ x 9½ in., (32.4 x 24.1 cm.), photograph, gelatin silver print (BP 577, DM 1450, FR 4928, Y 120,044).

OFFICER, Robert
  BI *Don Quixote, c. 1930*, s., lit., est. $1/1,500, (04-08-93, Christie-NY, #228, illus.), 8½ x 8⅛ in., (21.6 x 20.6 cm.), photograph, gelatin silver print.

OFFICER, Robert Ambler
  BI *"Glamour Gal (Linda Darnell)", 1930's*, s., t., d., annot. #4, est. $4/600, (11-16-92, Butterfield, #6116, illus.), 14¹³⁄₁₆ x 13⅝ in., (376.7 x 346.7 mm.), photograph, gelatin silver print.
  $220* *"Situation Wanted", 1930's*, s., t., d., annot. #2, (11-16-92, Butterfield, #6117, illus.), 13¾ x 11 in., (349.9 x 279.9 mm.), photograph, gelatin silver print (BP 145, DM 351, FR 1182, Y 27,360).

OGBORNE, John
  $117* *L'Allegro, 1798*, pub. John Ogborne, waterstain, crease, (11-30-92, Phillips-London, #156), plate 16½ x 12¼ in., (419 x 311 mm.), stipple engraving in colors on wove (BP 77, DM 186, FR 633, Y 14,561).

OGDEN, H.A. (after)
  BI *18th Century Style Scene With Couple Walking On A Street: With Soldiers*, est. $40/60, (03-12-93, DuMouchelle, #2464), 13 x 8½ in., (33 x 21.6 cm.), color lithograph.

OGE, Eugene   French 1861-1936
  BI *Allegorie Relative Au Suicide Du General Boulanger", 1894*, staining, cracks, (02-24-93, Picard, #179), sanguine lithograph on creme wove.

$93* *Apotheose De La Femme, c. 1900,* full margins, (05-06-93, Laurin, #73), lithograph on creme wove (BP 59, DM 146, FR 493, Y 10,232).

$201* *Brillant Russe Pour Nettoyer Et Polir Tous Les Metaux, c. 1900,* Paris, Imp. Caby and Chardin, cond. B+, (06-11-93, Boisgirard, #121), 59¹/₁₆ x 37 in., (150 x 94 cm.), poster (BP 132, DM 327, FR 1101, Y 21,326).

$134* *"Le Journal Public-Les Memoires De Kruger",* s. in plate Oge #25, (03-16-93, Encans, #134), approx. 73⅜ x 25⁹/₁₆ in., (186.3 x 65 cm.), poster (BP 93, DM 223, FR 757, Y 15,669, C$ 167).

OGUISS
$161* *Venice,* s., num. 13/175, (07-16-92, Bonhams-Chelsea, #407), image 17½ x 21¼ in., (44.4 x 54 cm.), lithograph in colors (BP 83, DM 238, FR 803, Y 20,168).

OHE, Katie   b. 1937
BI *Javo Way Swing, 1959,* #31/40, s., t., d. '69, est. C$1/150, (05-10-93, Hodgins, #188), 11 x 18 in., (27.9 x 45.7 cm.), serigraph on paper.

OKIIE, Hashimoto   Japanese b. 1899
BI *Temple Rooftops Through The Trees,* est. $3/400, (10-30-92, Sloan, #1894), sheet 12⅞ x 16¾ in., (32.7 x 42.5 cm.), woodblock.

OKLEY
$550* *Casino De Paris, 1950,* Ets. Saint-Martin, A cond., (08-06-92, Swann, #215, illus.), 57 x 39 in., (144.8 x 99.1 cm.), (BP 287, DM 813, FR 2745, Y 70,153).

$41* *Holiday On Ice U.S.A. Arenes De Nimes, 1966,* (01-31-93, Morelle/Marchan, #203), 32¹¹/₁₆ x 45¹¹/₁₆ in., (83 x 116 cm.), poster (BP 28, DM 66, FR 223, Y 5115).

OKUMURA MASANOBU   Japanese 1686-1764
BI *Ebisu-Ko Party In Progress In The Room Of A Tea-House,* Oban yoko-e, d. c. Kyoho 15 (1730), fold, soiled, rubbed, tears restored, laid-down, Prof. H.R.W. Kuhne Coll., est. BP 3/4,000, (06-11-93, Sotheby-London, #33, illus.), 10⅜ x 14¼ in., (26.4 x 36.2 cm.), hand-colored woodblock.

$2100* *Nakamura Tomijuro I As Oiso No Tora Holding Up A Puppet Of Soga JuroSukenari Playing A Flute In The Play Otodate Hatsugai Soga,* Hosoban, benizuri-e, s. Hogetsudo Okumura Bunkaku Masanobu ga, seal, d. Horeki3 (1753), rubbed, soiled, browned, repaired, Prof. H.R.W. Kuhne Coll.(06-11-93, Sotheby-London, #15, illus.), 11½ x 5⅝ in., (29.2 x 14.3 cm.), woodblock (BP 1380, DM 3413, FR 11,507, Y 222,812).

$1050* *Onoe Kikugoro I And Nakamura Tomijuro In The Roles Of Benkei(?) And Ushiwakamaru(?) (On The Gojo Bridge),* Hosoban, benizuri-e, s. Okumura Bunkaku Masanobu ga, d. c. Horeki 10(1760), trimmed, rubbed, wormed, laid down, Prof. H.R.W. Kuhne Coll., (06-11-93, Sotheby-London, #14), 11⅞ x 5½ in., (30.2 x 14 cm.), woodblock (BP 690, DM 1706, FR 5753, Y 111,406).

OKUMURA MASANOBU (follower of)
$10,852* *The Interior Of The Nakamura-za Theatre,* t., Dai-oban yoko-e, uki-e sumizuri-e, d. c. Enkyo 2-Kan'en 3 (1754-50), darkened, rubbed, soiled, restored, Prof. H.R.W. Kuhne Coll., (06-11-93, Sotheby-London, #34, illus.), 13⅛ x 17¾ in., (33.3 x 45.1 cm.), hand-colored woodblock (BP 7130, DM 17,637, FR 59,463, Y 1,151,406).

OKUMURA TOSHINOBU   Japanese ac. 1717-1750
$1662* *Ichikawa Danjuro II And Ichikawa Monnosuke I,* Hosoban, urushi-e, s. Yamato gako Okumura Toshinobu hitsu, d. c. Kyoho 5-12 (1720-27), pub. Soshu-ya, soiled, rubbed, restored, Prof. H.R.W. Kuhne Coll., (06-11-93, Sotheby-London, #40, illus.), 12¼ x 6 in., (31.1 x 15.2 cm.), hand-colored woodblock (BP 1092, DM 2701, FR 9107, Y 176,340).

$2800* *(Shinpan Kitano No Yashiro) Sakiwake No Ume "Plum Blossom Of Kitano Shrine", Three Vols.,* sumizuri illus., s. Kakugetsudo Okumura Bunsen Toshinobu ga; c. 1720/30(?), (06-11-93, Sotheby-London, #499, illus.), 7¹/₁₆ x 5¼ in., (17.9 x 13.3 cm.), hand-colored woodblock (BP 1840, DM 4551, FR 15,342, Y 297,082).

OKUYAMA, Gihachiro   Japanese 1907-1981
BI *"Geese" and "Winter Scene": Two,* s., i., bears artist stamp, est. $100/150, (05-16-93, Hindman, #395), largest 8¼ x 18 in., (21 x 45.7 cm.), woodcuts.

OKUYAMA, Gihachiro   Japanese 20th cent.
$70* *Winter Landscape,* s., mat burn, (05-15-93, Cleveland, #35), 11⅛ x 17½ in., (28.3 x 44.5 cm.), woodblock print (BP 46, DM 113, FR 378, Y 7760).

OLBRICHT, Alexander   1876-1942
$346* *"Weimer" Im Schnee, c. 1920,* s., t., (11-28-92, Grisebach, #672, illus.), 6⅜ x 6¹⁵/₁₆ in., (16.2 x 17.7 cm.), woodcut on Japan (BP 228, DM 551, FR 1871, Y 43,062).

OLDENBURG, Claes   Swedish/American b. 1929
$605* *Alphabet In The Form Of A Good Humor Bar, Levin 19,* init., d. 70, num. 211/250, pub. Paul Bianchini, (09-20-92, Hindman, #724, illus.), sheet 29 x 20 in., (73.7 x 50.8 cm.), color offset lithograph (BP 354, DM 898, FR 3071, Y 74,774).

BI *Ashtray And Fag Ends,* pub. Crown Point Press, s. Oldenburg, num. 37/50, pub. dry stamp, very good cond., full sheet, est. $15/2500, (09-11-92, Skinner, #125, illus.), sight 21⅞ x 25 in., (55.6 x 63.5 cm.), etching/aquatint in four colors on Arches paper.

$825* *Baked Potato With Butter,* s., d. 72, #96/100, (05-16-93, Hindman, #608), 26½ x 33 in., (67.3 x 83.8 cm.), color lithograph (BP 536, DM 1327, FR 4459, Y 91,453).

$3850* *Broken Button (Platzker 19), 1981,* inits., d., num. 60/100, pub. Multiples, Inc., excell. cond., orig. plexiglas box, overall 16 x 14 1/4 x 6 1/4in., (09-19-92, Christie-E, #179, illus.), cast paper relief in colors mounted on a faux-bois screenprinted foamcore base (BP 2215, DM 5765, FR 19,744, Y 479,691).

BI *Butter Pat In Berkeley Hills, 1976,* s., num. 5/35, pub. Multiples, Inc., full margins, excell. cond., est. $750/850, (09-19-92, Christie-E, #177), sheet 25¾ x 20 in., (654 x 508 mm.), soft-ground etching on Auvergue a la Main.

$1380* *Coffee Cup, 1973,* s., d., #46/50, pub. Landfall Press, Inc., full margins, good cond., (02-11-93, Sotheby-NY, #399, illus.), sheet 18⅛ x 22⅞ in., (460 x 581 mm.), color lithograph (BP 974, DM 2286, FR 7735, Y 166,365).

$935* *Colossal Baked Potato In A Landscape, 1971,* inits., d. '72, num. 44/75, pub. Petersburg Press, full margins, verygood cond., staining, (02-24-93, Butterfield, #3101), 7 x 10¾ in., (178 x 273 mm.), lithograph in colors on wove (BP 652, DM 1518, FR 5146, Y 109,716).

BI *Colossal Flashlight In Place Of Hoover Dam, 1982,* s., #64/100, pub. Multiples, Inc., full margins, good cond., crease,est. $1/1,200, (02-11-93, Sotheby-NY, #402, illus.), sheet 32¹⁵/₁₆ x 23⅞ in., (838 x 606 mm.), color offset lithograph.

$3450* *Colossal Screw In Landscape, Type 2 (G. 704), 1976,* s., # 17/35, artist's blindstamp, blindstamp publisher, Gemini G.E.L., p. Charly Ritt and Anthony Zepeda, good cond.?, (05-19-93, Butterfield, #2280, illus.), 67½ x 40½ in., (171.5 x 102.9 cm.), lithograph on Arches (BP 2240, DM 5608, FR 18,894, Y 381,933).

BI *Double-Nose/Purse/Punching Bag/Ashtray (G. 259), 1970,* inits., d., num. 48/50, Gemini G.E.L. blindstamps, full margins, rubbed spot, excell. cond., est. $2,5/3,500, (09-19-92, Christie-E, #174, illus.), sheet 21 x 19 in., (533 x 483 mm.), lithograph on wove.

$7150* *Floating Three Way Plug, 1976,* s., d., #34/60, printer's blindstamp Crown Point Press, pub. Multiples, Inc., full margins, good cond., (11-07-92, Sotheby-NY, #727, illus.), 42⅛ x 32⅛ in., (107 x 81.6 cm.), aquatint and etching p. in colors (BP 4675, DM 11,416, FR 38,586, Y 882,498).

$181* *Der Gartenschlauch, 1983,* s., (11-28-92, Schoppmann, #682), 16⁵/₁₆ x 23¼ in., (41.5 x 59 cm.), offset on light cardboard (BP 119, DM 288, FR 979, Y 22,526).

BI *Ice Cream Deserts - Praline, 1976,* s., d., num. 45/60, pub. Petersburg Press, full margins, good cond.,hinge remains, surface soiling, est. $8/1,000, (02-24-93, Butterfield, #3103), 9¾ x 7¾ in., (248 x 197 mm.), etching & aquatint in colors on handmade w/watermark.

$1130* *Ice Cream Dessert Pralines, 1976,* s., d., plate t., (06-12-93, Hauswedell/Nolt, #316, illus.), 9¾ x 7¹¹⁄₁₆ in., (24.8 x 19.6 cm.), color lithograph on copper print (BP 740, DM 1839, FR 6182, Y 118,910).

BI *Ice Cream Desserts - Praline, 1976,* s., d., #1/60, pub. Petersburg Press, full margins, good cond., soiling, creases, est. $7/800, (02-11-93, Sotheby-NY, #400), 9¹³⁄₁₆ x 7⅞ in., (250 x 200 mm.), etching and aquatint p. in colors.

BI *Ice Cream Desserts, Praline, 1976,* s., d., num. 37/60, pub. Petersburg Press, full margins, rubbing, very good cond., est. $1,2/1,400, (09-19-92, Christie-E, #178), sheet 24⅞ x 20¼ in., (632 x 514 mm.), hard and soft-ground etching and aquatint in colors on wove, watermark.

$1650* *Knife Ship Superimposed On The Guggenheim Museum, 1986,* s., num. 70/75, pub. Multiples, full margins, very good cond., (02-24-93, Butterfield, #3106, illus.), 21½ x 28¾ in., (546 x 730 mm.), silkscreen in colors on T.H. Saunders (BP 1151, DM 2679, FR 9081, Y 193,617).

BI *The Letter Q As A Beach House, With Sailboat (Gemini 416), 1972,* inits., i. C, #27/100, blindstamps, full margins, excellent cond., est. $3/3,500, (11-09-92, Christie-NY, #383, illus.), 39⅛ x 29½ in., (99.4 x 74.9 cm.), colored lithograph on wove.

BI *The Letter Q As Beach House, With Sailboat (Gemini 416), 1972,* inits., i. (c), #27/100, Gemini G.E.L. blindstamps, full margins, excell. cond., est. $2,5/3,000, (05-11-93, Christie-NY, #526), sheet 39⅛ x 29½ in., (99.4 x 74.9 cm.), color lithograph on wove.

$660* *Lipstick (Ascending) On Catepillar Track, 1972,* s., #55/100, pub. Styria Studio, Ltd., (06-13-93, Hindman, #330), sh 30 x 23¼ in., (76.2 x 59.1 cm.), color lithograph (BP 432, DM 1074, FR 3611, Y 69,452).

$523* *London Drums,* s., #281/300, (06-13-93, Hindman, #331, illus.), 24 x 35 in., (61 x 88.9 cm.), color offset lithograph (BP 342, DM 851, FR 2861, Y 55,035).

$1364* *Nose, 1968,* s., d., #99/150, good cond., (12-03-92, Sotheby-London, #773, illus.), 19 x 6½ in., (485 x 165 mm.), lithograph on silk (BP 880, DM 2145, FR 7322, Y 169,715).

BI *Nose, 1968,* s., d., #36/150, pub. Documenta, good cond., foxing, est. 1,2/1,500, (05-15-93, Sotheby-NY, #1137), overall 18⅞ x 18¼ in., (47.9 x 46.4 cm.), silkscreen on silk handkerchief.

$6050* *Notes (Gemini 104-15), 1968: Set Of Twelve,* s., d., d. just., all num. 73/100, Gemini G.E.L. blindstamps, full sheets, excell. cond., orig. letterpress paper folder, t., intro. and text, black linen-covered box, gray slipcase, (09-19-92, Christie-E, #172, illus.), each, sheet 22⅝ x 15⅝ in., (575 x 397 mm.), lithograph in colors on BFK Rives (BP 3480, DM 9060, FR 31,026, Y 753,800).

BI *Notes: Untitled (G. 112), 1968,* s., d., #95/100, blindstamp publisher Gemini G.E.L., p. James Webb, full margins, very good cond.?, est. $2,5/3,500, (05-19-93, Butterfield, #2276), 22¹¹⁄₁₆ x 15¾ in., (576 x 400 mm.), lithograph in colors on Rives BFK.

$990* *Orpheum Sign, 1962,* from International Anthology of Contemporary Engraving: the International Avant Garde: America Discovered, Volume 5, Galleria Schwartz, Milan, 1962, s., d., num. 10/60, margins, light/mat staining, split, thinned patches, goodcond., (09-19-92, Christie-E, #171), plate 5⅞ x 4³⁄₁₆ in., (149 x 106 mm.), aquatint on wove (BP 569, DM 1482, FR 5077, Y 123,349).

$489* *Pick-Axe Superimposed On A Drawing By Ludwig Grimm, 1982,* s., d. by another hand?, #21/100, pub. Multiples, blindstamp printer,Aeropress, p. Patricia Branstead, full margins, good cond.?, (05-19-93, Butterfield, #2282), sh 26 x 20¼ in., (660 x 514 mm.), etching and aquatint in colors on wove (BP 317, DM 795, FR 2678, Y 54,135).

BI *Proposal For A Broome Street Expressway In The Form Of A Cigarette And Smoke, 1972,* from Reality and Paradoxes, NY, Multiples, Inc., 1973, s., i. A.P., num. XXII, full margins, very good cond., est. $8/1,200, (09-19-92, Christie-E, #175), sheet 30 x 22½ in., (762 x 572 mm.), lithograph in colors on CM Fabriano.

$1650* *Proposed Colossal Monument For Battersea Park, London, Drum Set, 1966, 1969,* s., num. 44/300, full sheet, surface scrapes, good cond., (09-19-92, Christie-E, #173, illus.), sheet 23⅞ x 35¼ in., (606 x 895 mm.), offset lithograph on wove (BP 949, DM 2471, FR 8462, Y 205,582).

$523* *Sailboat Thinking Of Q, 1976,* inits., annot. T.P., very good cond., (10-28-92, Butterfield, #3057), sheet 15¾ x 12 in., (400 x 305 mm.), color offset lithograph on white wove (BP 333, DM 808, FR 2743, Y 64,172).

$715* *Scissors To Cut Out, 1967,* pub. List Art Program, full margins, good cond., (10-28-92, Butterfield, #3052), 26 x 18 in., (660 x 457 mm.), color lithograph on Arches (BP 456, DM 1104, FR 3749, Y 87,730).

BI *Sketch Of A 3-Way Plag, 1965,* s., #232/250, 1972, good cond., skinned spots, creases, (02-24-93, Butterfield, #3236), 32 x 24¼ in., (813 x 616 mm.), offset lithograph in colors on wove.

BI *Soft Drum Set (G. 417), 1972,* s., d., #66/68, Gemini G.E.L. blindstamps, full margins, rubbed spot, image stains, good cond., est. $2,5/3,000, (05-11-93, Christie-NY, #527, illus.), sheet 29 x 40⅛ in., (73.7 x 101.9 cm.), lithograph on pale yellow Angoumois a la main.

$880* *Soft Fire Plug Inverted, 1973,* s., d., num. 88/100, pub. Petersburg Press, full margins, creasing, excell. cond.?, shrink-wrapped, (09-19-92, Christie-E, #176), sheet 40¼ x 30½ in., (102.2 x 77.5 cm.), lithograph in colors on wove (BP 506, DM 1318, FR 4513, Y 109,644).

BI *Soft Picasso Cufflink, 1973,* from Hommage to Picasso, Propylaen Verlag, s., d. 1974, #88/90, fullmargins, light/mat staining, good cond., est. $2,5/3,000, (11-09-92, Christie-NY, #384, illus.), 29 x 23 in., (737 x 584 mm.), colored lithograph on wove.

BI *Soft Picasso Cufflink, 1973,* s., d. 1974, #88/90, from Hommage to Picasso portfolio, blindstamp publisher, Landfall Press, margins, good cond.?, mat staining, handling creases,est. $1,5/2,000, (05-19-93, Butterfield, #2279, illus.), 33 x 25 in., (838 x 635 mm.), lithograph in colors on wove.

$1650* *Soft Toilet #3 - On Chalkboard (G. 415), 1972,* s., num. 63/70, blindstamps of pub. Gemini G.E.L. & artist, full margins, apparently good cond., creases, shrink-wrapped, (02-24-93, Butterfield, #3102), 18½ x 14¼ in., (470 x 368 mm.), silkscreen in colors on Special Arjomari (BP 1151, DM 2679, FR 9081, Y 193,617).

BI *Soft Toilet #3, On Chalkboard (G. 415), 1972,* s., #63/70, blindstamp pub. Gemini G.E.L., full margins, good cond.?, creases, shrink-wrapped, est. $2,5/3,500, (10-28-92, Butterfield, #3055, illus.), 18½ x 14¼ in., (470 x 362 mm.), color silkscreen on Special Arjomari paper.

$770* *Study For Steel And Lead Ashtray, 1976,* s., #39/50, blindstamp pub. Multiples, full margins, very good cond.?, (10-28-92, Butterfield, #3058), 22 x 25½ in., (559 x 648 mm.), color etching w/aquatint on wove (BP 491, DM 1189, FR 4038, Y 94,479).

$805* *Study For Steel And Lead Ashtray, 1976,* s., #31/50, pub. Multiples, blindstamp printer, Crown Point Press, margins, very good cond.?, (05-19-93, Butterfield, #2281), 22 x 25½ in., (559 x 648 mm.), etching and aquatint in colors on wove (BP 523, DM 1309, FR 4409, Y 89,118).

BI *Study For Stel And Lead Ashtray, 1976,* s., num. 31/50, pub. Multiples, blindstamp, margins, apparently verygood cond., est. $1,5/2,500, (02-24-93, Butterfield, #3104), 22 x 25½ in., (559 x 648 mm.), etching & aquatint in colors on wove.

BI *Symbolic Self-Portrait With "Equals", 1971,* s., #23/300, pub. Sidney Janis Gallery, full margins, good cond., creases, soiling, est. $1,5/2,500, (11-07-92, Sotheby-NY, #726), 19⅞ x 15 in., (505 x 381 mm.), offset lithograph.

$978* *System Of Iconography, Plug, Mouse, Good Humor, Lipstick, Switches, 1970-71,* s., #101/250, pub. Margo Leavin Gallery, p. Imprimieries Reunies Lausanne, margins, good cond.?, staining, crease, (05-19-93, Butterfield, #2277), 20 x 15⁵⁄₁₆ in., (508 x 389 mm.), offset lithograph in colors on wove (BP 635, DM 1590, FR 5356, Y 108,270).

BI *Tar Pits, 1968,* #95/100, pencil s., d., est. DM 1,500, (11-20-92, Lempertz, #742), sh 22¾ x 15¾ in., (57.8 x 40 cm.), lithograph on thick Velin.

$920* *Tea Bag, 1972,* inits., d., i. AP, num. II, pub. Petersburg Press, artist's blindstamp, full margins, rubbed spot, creasing, light/mat staining, (05-11-93, Christie-NY, #528, illus.), sheet 31 x 22½ in., (787 x 572 mm.), color lithograph on Richard de Bas Auvergne a la main (BP 587, DM 1449, FR 4883, Y 101,199).

$938* *Tea Bag, 1972,* #82/100, pencil mono., d., (11-20-92, Lempertz, #743), sh 30¹³⁄₁₆ x 22⅝ in., (78.3 x 57.5 cm.), color lithograph on Velin (BP 618, DM 1496, FR 5038, Y 116,652).

$825* *Teabag,* init., d. 72, #71/100, (05-16-93, Hindman, #607), 24 x 18¾ in., (61 x 47.6 cm.), color lithograph (BP 536, DM 1327, FR 4459, Y 91,453).

$861* *"Thea Bag, 1972" and "La Colonna Rossa, 1973": Two,* first #79/100, s., d., second #78/100, (05-20-93, Finarte-Milan, #123), first 24 x 18⅛ in., (61 x 46 cm.), second 29½ x 24⁷⁄₁₆ in., (61 x 46 cm.), lithograph in colors (BP 553, DM 1389, FR 4679, Y 95,075, L 1265).

$748* *Three Hats, 1974,* from For Meyer Schapiro, The Committee to Endow a Chair in Honor of Meyer Schapiro at Columbia University, inits., i. (c) 1974, H.C. 3, full margins, image scuff, skinned patches, excell. cond., (05-11-93, Christie-NY, #529, illus.), sheet 35⅝ x 23⅜ in., (905 x 594 mm.), color lithograph on Twinrocker (BP 477, DM 1178, FR 3970, Y 82,279).

$523* *Typewriter Eraser,* s., #100/100, (05-16-93, Hindman, #638, illus.), 4¼ x 5¾ in., (10.8 x 14.6 cm.), lithograph (BP 340, DM 841, FR 2827, Y 57,976).

$374* *Typewriter Eraser As Tornado, 1972,* s., #77/200, pub. Multiples, p. Patricia Branstead, margins, good cond., glue remains, (05-19-93, Butterfield, #2278), 20 x 14⅛ in., (508 x 359 mm.), offset lithograph in colors on BFK Rives (BP 243, DM 608, FR 2048, Y 41,404).

$920* *Untitled, 1988-9,* s., d. '89, #12/75, from portfolio Brooklyn Academy of Music II 1988-89 Artist Print Portfolio, pub. Parasol Press, full margins, good cond., (05-15-93, Sotheby-NY, #1142), sheet 31½ x 41⅛ in., (80 x 104.5 cm.), lithograph (BP 598, DM 1480, FR 4973, Y 101,984).

$681* *Weiblicher Akt,* s., num., (06-19-93, Wachholtz, #532), 31⁹⁄₁₆ x 21⅛ in., (80.2 x 53.6 cm.), color lithograph on white copper print paper (BP 457, DM 1150, FR 3865, Y 75,491).

BI *Woman Entwined In Giant Electric Cord, Ed. B, 1976,* s., d., annot. A.P. XI/XII, full margins, good cond., est. $1,2/1,400, (02-24-93, Butterfield, #3105), 30¼ x 21¾ in., (768 x 552 mm.), soft-ground etching & aquatint on BFK Rives.

OLDES, Elizabeth

$247* *Bootleg Mine, Pennsylvania,* s., creases, taped, (12-04-92, Doyle, #137), 9¾ x 13¾ in., (248 x 349 mm.), lithograph (BP 158, DM 393, FR 1334, Y 30,836).

OLEY, Moses   American 20th cent.

$248* *Bridges Over Harlem River,* s., t., oil stains, discoloration, (11-12-92, Freemn/Fine Art, #161), image, unframed 11½ x 17 in., (29.2 x 43.2 cm.), litho (BP 163, DM 393, FR 1325, Y 30,750).

OLITSKI, Jules   American b. 1922

$935* *Graphics Suite No. 2, 1970: Five,* d., num., s., one i. A.P./23, closed tear, (05-27-93, Swann, #209), (66 x 88.9 cm.), color serigraphs (BP 599, DM 1500, FR 5057, Y 100,236).

$176* *Untitled, From Graphics Suite,* s., #44/150, prov., (05-16-93, Hindman, #603), 35 x 26 in., (88.9 x 66 cm.), color serigraph (BP 114, DM 283, FR 951, Y 19,510).

OLIVEIRA, Nathan   American b. 1928

$523* *Emerson Site I, 1979,* s., d., t., annot. To Modesto, with love, Nathan, 2.20.85, blindstamp pub. 3EP, Ltd., full margins, very good cond., Modesto Lanzone Coll., (10-28-92, Butterfield, #3063), 4 x 7 in., (102 x 178 mm.), monotype on white wove (BP 333, DM 808, FR 2743, Y 64,172).

BI *Miramar II, 1969,* s., d., t., #10/75, blindstamp pub. Collector's Press, very good cond.?, est. $6/800, (10-28-92, Butterfield, #3059), 25 x 22 in., (635 x 559 mm.), color lithograph on cream wove.

$660* *Seated Nude, 1973,* s., d., t., annot. To Modesto/ Love Nathan, 10.8.81, full margins, very good cond., Modesto Lanzone Coll., (10-28-92, Butterfield, #2060), 13¹³⁄₁₆ x

10⅞ in., (351 x 276 mm.), color monotype on cream wove (BP 421, DM 1019, FR 3461, Y 80,982).

$1210* *Standing Nude, 1973,* s., d., t., annot. To Modesto/ Affectionately Nathan, 10.8.81, full margins, very good cond.?, Modesto Lanzone Coll., (10-28-92, Butterfield, #3061), 13¾ x 10¾ in., (349 x 273 mm.), monotype in black and brown on cream wove (BP 771, DM 1869, FR 6345, Y 148,466).

$770* *Tauromaquia 21, 1973,* s., t., d., annot. To Modesto Lanzoni/ Affectionately/ N. Oliveira 12.2.77, full margins, very good cond., Modesto Lanzone Coll., (10-28-92, Butterfield, #3062, illus.), 10⅝ x 13¾ in., (270 x 349 mm.), monotype on laid paper (BP 491, DM 1189, FR 4038, Y 94,479).

$2875* *Untitled (Standing Female Figure), 1989,* s., crayon, d., annot. Pr.P1/4, blindstamp publisher, Trillium Graphics, very good cond.?, (05-19-93, Butterfield, #2284, illus.), sh 40 x 27 in., (101.6 x 68.6 cm.), monoprint in colors on wove (BP 1866, DM 4673, FR 15,745, Y 318,277).

BI *Untitled (Standing Man Seen From The Front), 1989,* crayon s., d., annot. Pr.P.1/4, blindstamp publisher, Trillium Graphics, very good cond.?, est. $2,5/3,500, (05-19-93, Butterfield, #2285), 40 x 27 in., (101.6 x 68.6 cm.), monoprint in colors on wove.

$1725* *Untitled (Standing Man), 1989,* s., d., annot. P.P. 4/4, blindstamp publisher, Trillium Graphics, good cond., stray ink, (05-19-93, Butterfield, #2283, illus.), 40 x 27⅜ in., (101.6 x 69.5 cm.), monoprint in colors on wove (BP 1120, DM 2804, FR 9447, Y 190,966).

OLIVER, E.

$154* *Scenes Of Williamsburg, VA: Three,* s., (12-06-92, Neal, #829), hand-colored etching (BP 96, DM 240, FR 818, Y 19,081).

OLIVER, Elizabeth Paxton

BI *"Wood Thrush In Pines",* est. $40/60, (01-15-93, DuMouchelle, #1568), approx. 28 x 20½ in., (71.1 x 52.1 cm.), print.

OLIVIER, Ferdinand   1785-1841

$3632* *Dienstag. Bergveste Salzburg Von Der Mittagseite (Th.-B. XXVI,2), 1823,* series v. 9 Bll. Sieben Gegenden aus Salzburg u. Berchtesgaden, collector's stamp, (04-27-93, Hartung, #2460, illus.), 7⅝ x 10⁹⁄₁₆ in., (19.4 x 26.8 cm.), toned lithograph (BP 2310, DM 5750, FR 19,454, Y 407,038).

$9922* *"Montag. Rosenecker Garten Vor Salzburg" (Thieme/ Becker XXVI, S. 2; Grote 219, Abb. 219: H. Schwarz (1926), Abb. S. 17; Rumann 1504), 1818-1823,* series Sieben Gegenden aus Salzburg und Berchtesgaden, (06-08-93, Karl/Faber, #367, illus.), approx. 7¹¹⁄₁₆ x 10¹³⁄₁₆ in., (19.5 x 27.5 cm.), toned lithograph on wove (BP 6522, DM 16,099, FR 54,219, Y 1,053,850).

OLSEN, John   b. 1928

$689* *Albert Tucker,* s. John Olsen, i. A.P., d. '73, lit., (08-11-92, L. Joel, #19G), 26¾ x 20⅞ in., (68 x 53 cm.), lithograph (BP 358, DM 1011, FR 3424, Y 88,232, A$ 935).

$405* *Brett Whiteley,* s. John Olsen, d.'79, #64/100, lit., (08-11-92, L. Joel, #10G), 25⁹⁄₁₆ x 19¹¹⁄₁₆ in., (65 x 50 cm.), lithograph on stone (BP 210, DM 594, FR 2013, Y 51,863, A$ 550).

OLSEN, Wiliam Skotte

$293* *Untitled: Ten,* s. 1991, (09-29-92, B. Rasmussen, #361), etching and aquatint (BP 165, DM 414, FR 1412, Y 34,977, DK 1610).

OLSON, Axel   1899-1986

$185* *"Liljan",* s. EA, (11-07-92, Falkkloos, #408), color lithograph (BP 121, DM 297, FR 998, Y 22,834, SK 1100).

BI *"Rosornas Flykt",* s. 121/260, est. SK 1,500, (11-07-92, Falkkloos, #406), lithograph in colors.

BI *"Stenig Strand",* s. 21/260, est. SK 1,500, (11-07-92, Falkkloos, #407), 14⁹⁄₁₆ x 18⅛ in., (37 x 46 cm.), color lithograph.

OLSON, Erik   1901-1986

$221* *"Den Vackra TV-Reportern, 1972",* s. 91/350, (11-07-92, Falkkloos, #417, illus.), color lithograph (BP 144, DM 355, FR 1193, Y 27,277, SK 1320).

OLSSON HAGALUND, Olle Swedish b. 1904
$1812* *Hagalundstorg, Gul Skylt, 1967,* s., 75/75, (05-25-93, AB Stockholm, #54), 14 15/16 x 16 15/16 in., (38 x 43 cm.), lithograph in colors (BP 1174, DM 2951, FR 9934, Y 198,054, SK 2640).
$2491* *Kolutkoraren, 1949,* s., 23/260, (05-25-93, AB Stockholm, #53), 15 9/16 x 18 5/16 in., (39.5 x 46.5 cm.), lithograph in colors (BP 1614, DM 4057, FR 13,657, Y 272,270, SK 3630).
$1297* *Modisten, 1953,* s., ded., 236/360, (12-04-92, AB Stockholm, #7111), 26 9/16 x 20½ in., (67.5 x 52 cm.), lithograph in colors (BP 832, DM 2066, FR 7007, Y 161,923, SK 8800).

OMICCIOLI, Giovanni Italian 1901-1975
BI *Conchiglia, 1965,* #16/40, s., d., est. L 6/700, (03-25-93, Finarte-Rome, #1), etching.

ONCELIN, Charles
$522* *Equestrian Pursuits: Set Of Ten,* very good cond., (10-27-92, Phillips-London, #216), image 11¾ x 18⅞ in., (298 x 479 mm.), colored woodcut, heightened w/ gouache on wove (BP 330, DM 800, FR 2715, Y 63,853).

ONGANIA, Ferdinand, Publisher
$627* *Calli E Canali In Venezia (Parts 1-10): Approximately Eighty,* pub. 1894, margins, foxing, (06-16-93, Bonhams-Chelsea, #369), pl. 15½ x 10½ in., (39.4 x 26.7 cm.), heliogravure (photoengraving) (BP 418, DM 1041, FR 3493, Y 66,873).
$270* *Calli E Canali In Venezia: Collection,* folios, pub. 1894, margins, foxing, (02-17-93, Bonhams-Chelsea, #335), plate 15½ x 10½ in., (39.4 x 26.7 cm.), approx. 80 heliogravures (BP 187, DM 438, FR 1485, Y 32,250).
$871* *"Streets And Canals In Venice", 1890-91: Book,* english edit., p. credit, folio, (05-06-93, Christie-London, #21, illus.), each approx. 13¼ x 9 in., photograph, 100 photogravures (BP 552, DM 1372, FR 4618, Y 95,830).

ONGANIA, Ferdinando, Publisher
$1100* *Calli E Canali In Venezia, 1890-91,* Ferd. Ongania, (10-15-92, Sotheby-NY, #92, illus.), each approx. 13 x 9 in., (33 x 22.9 cm.), book of 100 large format photogravures (BP 673, DM 1637, FR 5553, Y 131,974).

ONLEY, Toni b. 1928
$222* *Darkening Land,* #5/28, s., (10-21-92, Maynard, #183), 11¼ x 15¼ in., (28.6 x 38.7 cm.), color silkscreen (BP 138, DM 336, FR 1140, Y 27,040, C$ 275).
$364* *Silent Coast,* #4/18, s., t., prov., (11-16-92, Hodgins, #343, illus.), 11¼ x 15¼ in., (28.6 x 38.7 cm.), serigraph on paper (BP 239, DM 581, FR 1956, Y 45,426, C$ 462).
$89* *Strange Place,* #5/28, s., (10-21-92, Maynard, #182), 11¼ x 15¼ in., (28.6 x 38.7 cm.), color silkscreen (BP 55, DM 135, FR 457, Y 10,840, C$ 110).

ONO, Tadashige
$143* *A Lighthouse,* s., (03-25-93, Boos, #212), 8¾ x 11¼ in., (22.2 x 28.6 cm.), color woodblock print (BP 97, DM 235, FR 799, Y 16,753).

ONOFRIO, Crescenzio di 1632-after 1712
BI *Die Landschaft Mit Mars Und Adonis,* est. DM 1,200, (12-04-92, Bassenge, #6333, illus.), 12⅜ x 17 7/16 in., (31.4 x 44.3 cm.), etching.

OONARK, Jessie Inuit b. 1906
$1210* *"A Shaman's Helping Spirits", 1971,* t., num., s., ident. 1/40, Baker Lake (Sanavik) cooperative symbol, very good cond., prov., (06-26-93, Skinner, #53, illus.), 32 x 23 in., (81.3 x 58.4 cm.), stone cut and stencil in colors (BP 810, DM 2056, FR 6926, Y 128,382).

OOSTANEN, Jacob Cornelisz. van
BI *Christ Carrying The Corss (B. 9; Holl. 75), 1514,* from Passion, date removed, lacking p. frame, trimmed to borderline,repairs, thin spots, soiling, minor stains, ex-coll., est. BP 1,2/1,800, (12-03-92, Sotheby-London, #87), woodcut on paper w/watermark.

OPIE, J. (after)
$15 *Pretty Ladies Of The Age: Two,* (04-16-93, G.A. Key, #96), 9 x 7 in., (22.9 x 17.8 cm.), colored prints (BP 10, DM 24, FR 82, Y 1687).

OPIE, James (after)
BI *Henry And Emma, 1796,* by Francesco Bartolozzi, pub. Thomas Macklin, taped, creased, defects, est. BP 150/200, (11-30-92, Phillips-London, #173), plate 20⅝ x 15¾ in., (524 x 400 mm.), color stipple engraving, finished by hand, on wove.

OPIE, John (after)
$633* *A Winter's Tale (C.S. 157), 1785,* scratch-letter proof, engraved by Valentine Green, 1st state, pub. byGreen, margins, good cond., (11-30-92, Phillips-London, #76, illus.), plate 20⅞ x 24¼ in., (530 x 616 mm.), mezzotint on laid (BP 418, DM 1008, FR 3423, Y 78,780).
BI *Winter's Tale, Act. II, Scene III,* by J. P. Simon, time stained, est. BP 7/100, (06-16-93, Bonhams-Chelsea, #435), image 17¼ x 23½ in., (43.8 x 59.7 cm.), stipple engraving w/hand-coloring.

OPPENHEIM, Dennis American b. 1938
$6325* *Reading Position For Second-Degree Burn: Stage 1 And Stage 2 Photo Documentation Of Action At Jones Beach, New York, 1970,* s., d. 70, prov., lit., (02-23-93, Sotheby-NY, #319, illus.), 22 x 13 in., (55.9 x 33 cm.), photograph, color w/typed descriptions mounted on paperboard (BP 4333, DM 10,218, FR 34,658, Y 738,729).

OPPENHEIM, Meret 1913-1985
$53* *"D'Apres La Photo De Man Ray 1936",* #86/190, d. 71, s., water stains, (01-28-93, Pescheteau, #225), 21¼ x 29 15/16 in., (54 x 76 cm.), color lithograph on Arches (BP 35, DM 84, FR 284, Y 6581).
BI *Komposition, 1985,* 61/75., s., est. SF 7/900, (10-14-92, Germann, #168), 16⅝ x 11⅝ in., (422 x 296 mm.), woodcut.
$2127* *Parapapillonneries, 1976: Six,* s., #57/100, (10-21-92, Dobiaschofsky, #2231), 22 13/16 x 18⅛ in., (58 x 46 cm.), color lithograph (BP 1320, DM 3218, FR 10,924, Y 259,074, SF 2880).
BI *Die Seidenmotte Und Die Stolze Rosamunde (Curiger Y 298), 1976,* from portfolio "Parapapillonneries", #57/100, s., d., est. SF 1/1,300, (04-21-93, Germann, #664), 17 15/16 x 22¾ in., (457 x 578 mm.), color lithograph.
$993* *Zwei, Sich Kussend (Curiger K 11), 1961,* mono., d., num., (06-23-93, Kornfeld, #637), color lithograph, reworked, on gray wove (BP 675, DM 1680, FR 5652, Y 108,182, SF 1495).

OPPENHEIMER, Max (called Mopp) German 1895-1954
BI *Max Oppenheimer, Kunstsalon Pisko, c. 1920,* p. Pan Presse, von Cassirer, s., creases, tears, repairs, some losses, est. BP 3/5,000, (05-20-93, Christie-London, #502, illus.), sheet 33 x 21 in., (83.8 x 53.3 cm.), lithograph in colors backed on linen.
$1960* *"Musikstilleben": Thirty-Two,* stone s., d. Mopp 32, (05-19-93, Dorotheum, #418, illus.), 26¾ x 21⅝ in., (68 x 55 cm.), lithograph in color (BP 1272, DM 3186, FR 10,734, Y 216,982, SC 22,400).
$1602* *"Quartett",* s., d. in stone Mopp 32, trimmed, (11-25-92, Dorotheum, #486, illus.), sh 37 3/16 x 27 3/16 in., (94.5 x 69 cm.), image 26¾ x 22 1/16 in., (94.5 x 69 cm.), color lithograph (BP 1047, DM 2547, FR 8627, Y 198,316, SC 17,920).
$352* *Schauspieler Ernst Deutsch (Goldstein Seite 541),* i. proof, stone s., d. MOPP 32, s. MOPP, (03-24-93, Venator/Hansten, #4543), approx. 10⅝ x 9 13/16 in., (27 x 25 cm.), chalk lithograph on Japan (BP 238, DM 575, FR 1957, Y 41,358).

OPPLER, Ernst German 1867-1929
BI *The Ballerina (Der Sterbende Schioan),* s., margins, repaired tear into image, laid down, est. BP 150/200, (10-27-92, Phillips-London, #217), plate 5⅜ x 7¼ in., (137 x 184 mm.), etching w/drypoint on laid.
BI *Ballettszenen, 1922: Six,* s., est. DM 600, (12-01-92, Karl/Faber, #1068), smallest 5⅞ x 3¾ in., (15 x 9.5 cm.), largest 5 11/16 x 8 11/16 in., (15 x 9.5 cm.), etching.
BI *Tanzerinnen Und Tanzende Paare, 1921/22: Eight,* s., num., stained, est. DM 1,200, (12-01-92, Karl/Faber,

#1067), smallest 4¹⁵⁄₁₆ x 3⁹⁄₁₆ in., (12.5 x 9 cm.), largest 12³⁄₁₆ x 9¹⁄₁₆ in., (12.5 x 9 cm.), etching.

ORAZI, Manuel

BI   *L'Hippodrome, 1905,* p. Imressions d'Art Industriel, margins, good cond., creases throughimage, toned, surface soiling, linen-backed, est. $6/900, (09-21-92, Butterfield, #833), 22⁵⁄₁₆ x 14½ in., (566.2 x 369 mm.), lithograph in colors/gold on wove.

$805*   *L'Hippodrome, 1905,* p. Impressions d'Art Industriel, margins, good condition, creases through image, tears, creases, toned, surface soiling, linen-backed, (03-31-93, Butterfield, #5248), 22¼ x 14½ in., (56.5 x 36.8 cm.), lithograph printed in colors and gold on wove (BP 532, DM 1295, FR 4399, Y 92,571).

$641*   *Reve De Noel - Olympia, Avec Liane De Pougy, 1899,* (01-31-93, Morelle/Marchan, #181, illus.), 42⅛ x 59¹³⁄₁₆ in., (107 x 152 cm.), poster (BP 431, DM 1033, FR 3491, Y 79,965).

ORAZI, Manuel (after)

$110*   *"La Maison Moderne",* plate s., very good cond.?, (07-19-92, Bakker, #153), image 20 x 29½ in., (50.8 x 74.9 cm.), color lithograph (BP 56, DM 160, FR 542, Y 13,675).

ORDNER, Paul

$778*   *Combloux. Teleski. "L'Hotel PLM Du Mont-Blanc Et Les Aiguilles De Warrens", 1935,* very good cond., (03-15-93, Arcole, #105), 39⅜ x 24³⁄₁₆ in., (100 x 61.5 cm.), (BP 542, DM 1292, FR 4393, Y 92,158).

$918*   *PLM. Mont-Revard Par Aix-Les-Bains. "Sport, Confort, Repos", c. 1935,* very good cond., (03-15-93, Arcole, #102, illus.), 39⅜ x 24⁷⁄₁₆ in., (100 x 62 cm.), (BP 639, DM 1525, FR 5184, Y 108,742).

$907*   *Teleski Combloux, 1940,* pub. M. Dechaux, for French State Railways PLM, cond. 1, laid on linen, (10-13-92, Phillips-London, #39, illus.), 38⁹⁄₁₆ x 24⁷⁄₁₆ in., (98 x 62 cm.), color lithograph (BP 528, DM 1329, FR 4515, Y 109,979).

ORELLANO, Gaston   Spanish 20th cent.

BI   *"Moonchild",* s., artist's proof, est. $2/300, (10-10-92, Goldberg, #536), 10 x 8¼ in., (25.4 x 21 cm.), etching.

ORGAN, Brian

$263*   *Six British Jockeys: Six,* folio, #106/150, s., d. 1974, pub. Arthur Ackermann and Son Ltd., (06-30-93, Bonhams-Chelsea, #210), sheet 20¾ x 16¾ in., (52.7 x 42.5 cm.), lithograph (BP 176, DM 449, FR 1513, Y 28,180).

ORGAN, Bryan   b. 1935

$68*   *Beggars,* #13/25, d. 1968, (12-10-92, Bonhams-Chelsea, #87), image 24½ x 18½ in., (62.2 x 47 cm.), screenprint (BP 44, DM 108, FR 367, Y 8412).

BI   *Beggars,* #13/25, s., d. 1968, est. BP 50/70, (10-15-92, Bonhams-Chelsea, #25), image 24½ x 18½ in., (62.2 x 47 cm.), screenprint.

$43*   *Head And Shoulder Portrait Of A Gentleman,* #45/100, s., (04-22-93, Bonhams-Chelsea, #19), image 22 x 30¾ in., (55.9 x 78.1 cm.), lithograph (BP 28, DM 69, FR 233, Y 4728).

BI   *Six British Jockeys, 1974: Set Of Six,* A. Ackermann and Son, incl. title, text, justification, each s. by artist and sitter, margins, very good cond., tape, skinning, portfolio, est. BP 3/400, (12-01-92, Christie-London, #623), overall S. 21⅞ x 17¹³⁄₁₆ in., (555 x 452 mm.), lithographs p. in colors on wove.

ORKIN, Ruth   1921-1985

$2990*   *"American Girl In Italy",* s., t., d. by photog., 1951, p. 1980's, (04-06-93, Sotheby-NY, #421, illus.), 12 x 18 in., photograph (BP 1975, DM 4817, FR 16,312, Y 341,013).

BI   *Drunken Women, Greenwich Village, NY,* c. 1948, p.l., ink s., t., d.; s., t., d., lit., est. $1,5/2,000, (04-08-93, Christie-NY, #325, illus.), 10¼ x 13⅜ in., (26 x 34 cm.), photograph, gelatin silver print.

BI   *Photographers At World's Fair, 1963,* sig., i., handstamp, est. $600/900, (10-14-92, Swann, #531, illus.), 8 x 10 in., (20.3 x 25.4 cm.), photograph, silver print.

ORLIK, Emil   German 1870-1932

$1130*   *Am Meer,* s., (06-10-93, Hauswedell/Nolt, #749), image 10¹³⁄₁₆ x 10 in., (27.5 x 25.4 cm.), color etching on wove (BP 739, DM 1840, FR 6195, Y 119,945).

$1986*   *"Aus Agypten" (Pommeranz-Liedtke S. 207),* 1922: Fifteen, s., Propylaen-Verlag, (06-05-93, Grisebach, #812, illus.), sh largest approx. 7⅞ x 11 in., (20 x 28 cm.), drypoint on hand-made (BP 1307, DM 3220, FR 10,852, Y 213,044).

$201*   *Bernhard Pankok, Portrat Des Malers, 1901,* s. E. Orlik, (09-14-92, Venator/Hansten, #2487), image 5 x 3⅞ in., (12.7 x 9.8 cm.), woodcut in gold on brown paper (BP 106, DM 299, FR 1013, Y 24,994).

$295*   *Blumenbouquet,* s., light-staining, (12-05-92, Bassenge, #7529), 15⅜ x 10⅝ in., (39 x 27 cm.), colored etching (BP 185, DM 460, FR 1567, Y 36,551).

$1064*   *Der Dichter Gerhart Hauptmann, c. 1924,* s., (06-05-93, Grisebach, #813, illus.), 8³⁄₁₆ x 6¼ in., (20.8 x 15.8 cm.), etching on Japan (BP 700, DM 1725, FR 5814, Y 114,139).

$959*   *Feluke Auf Dem Nil,* s., (12-05-92, Bassenge, #7525), 11⅝ x 7¹³⁄₁₆ in., (29.5 x 19.8 cm.), color etching (BP 601, DM 1495, FR 5096, Y 118,820).

$738*   *Feluke Auf Dem Nil,* s., small tear and spots, (12-05-92, Bassenge, #7526), 11⁹⁄₁₆ x 7¹³⁄₁₆ in., (29.4 x 19.8 cm.), color etching (BP 462, DM 1151, FR 3921, Y 91,438).

BI   *Head Of A Woman, 1916,* s., d., margins, good cond., foxing, prov., Late Gerhard Brauer Coll., est. Dfl. 5/600, (05-27-93, Sotheby-Amstrdm, #831), 11⅛ x 7⅝ in., (283 x 194 mm.), etching on sturdy wove.

$851*   *Heimkehr Vom Felde,* s., (06-05-93, Bassenge, #6394, illus.), 7½ x 12⅜ in., (19 x 31.5 cm.), etching w/Roulette on yellowish wove (BP 560, DM 1380, FR 4650, Y 91,289).

$139*   *Hugelige Wustenlandschaft Mit Hausern,* s. Emil Orlik, ded., artist's proof, (09-14-92, Venator/Hansten, #2483), plate 4¹¹⁄₁₆ x 7¹³⁄₁₆ in., (11.9 x 19.8 cm.), drypoint and emery (BP 74, DM 207, FR 700, Y 17,284).

$309*   *Im Atelier, 1899,* from Kleine Holzschnitte, s. Orlik, (09-14-92, Venator/Hansten, #2480), image 5¼ x 6⅛ in., (13.4 x 15.6 cm.), color woodcut on thin Japan (BP 163, DM 459, FR 1557, Y 38,423).

$253*   *Im Nachtzug, c. 1920,* s., (11-28-92, Grisebach, #681, illus.), 4¹⁵⁄₁₆ x 7¹⁄₁₆ in., (12.6 x 17.9 cm.), aquatint on handmade (BP 167, DM 403, FR 1368, Y 31,487).

BI   *Italienische Fahrt,* s., num., est. DM 4/600, (11-28-92, Grisebach, #683, illus.), 11⁷⁄₁₆ x 11½ in., (29 x 29.2 cm.), etching on handmade Japan.

$88*   *Japanese Figures At A Window,* s., num., (12-02-92, Boos, #521), 8¼ x 13⅜ in., (210 x 340 mm.), color etching and drypoint (BP 57, DM 138, FR 472, Y 10,949).

$120*   *The Japanese Screen,* watermark, mat stain, light struck, hinges, tape, (05-15-93, Cleveland, #417), 4½ x 6½ in., (11.4 x 16.5 cm.), etching and roulette on wove (BP 78, DM 193, FR 649, Y 13,302).

$1419*   *Japanische Kinder Als Zuschauer Bei Einem Umzug, 1902,* (06-05-93, Bassenge, #6388, illus.), 8¼ x 13⅜ in., (21 x 34 cm.), color etching on Japan (BP 934, DM 2301, FR 7754, Y 152,221).

$2260*   *Japanische Kinder Als Zuschauer Bei Einem Umzug, 1902,* s., artist's proof, (06-10-93, Hauswedell/Nolt, #748), image 8⅜ x 13⅜ in., (21.3 x 33.9 cm.), color etching on wove (BP 1478, DM 3680, FR 12,390, Y 239,890).

$516*   *Junge Frau In Der Eisenbahn,* (12-05-92, Bassenge, #7522, illus.), 6³⁄₁₆ x 3⅞ in., (15.7 x 9.8 cm.), woodcut on China (BP 323, DM 804, FR 2742, Y 63,933).

$354*   *Junge Frau Mit Einem Lilienstrauss, 1898,* s., num., 3 corners torn, (12-05-92, Bassenge, #7530), color lithograph on handmade (BP 222, DM 552, FR 1881, Y 43,861).

$110*   *"Landscape",* s., #38/50, large margins, mat staining, (10-28-92, Butterfield, #2846), 11¾ x 17³⁄₁₆ in., (298 x 437 mm.), drypoint in sepia on cream wove (BP 70, DM 170, FR 577, Y 13,497).

BI   *Der Maler Ferdinand Hodler (G. 92; 209), 1904,* s., d., margins, good cond., est. BP 8/1,000, (12-03-92,

Sotheby-London, #474, illus.), 13¾ x 8⅞ in., (350 x 225 mm.), woodcut on Japan.

$258* *Marktweib, 1898,* s., (12-05-92, Bassenge, #7521), 4⅛ x 2⅞ in., (10.4 x 7.3 cm.), color woodcut on China (BP 162, DM 402, FR 1371, Y 31,966).

$139* *Nubisches Madchen, 1925,* artist's proof, from series aus Agypten, i., s., foxing, (09-14-92, Venator/Hansten, #2482), plate 7¹¹⁄₁₆ x 4½ in., (19.5 x 11.5 cm.), drypoint etching (BP 74, DM 207, FR 700, Y 17,284).

$433* *Portrait Gerhart Hauptmann, 1909,* s., d., (11-28-92, Grisebach, #677, illus.), 11¹¹⁄₁₆ x 7¹¹⁄₁₆ in., (29.7 x 19.6 cm.), etching with Roulette on China (BP 286, DM 690, FR 2342, Y 53,889).

$60* *Portrait Of Thomas Masaryk,* s., i., (12-01-92, Ritchie, #12), 11¾ x 8½ in., (29.8 x 21.6 cm.), etching and drypoint on wove (BP 40, DM 96, FR 326, Y 7470, C$ 77).

BI *Portrat Des Malers Max Klinger (Voigtlander-Tetzner 212), 1902,* s., num., est. DM 1,200, (12-05-92, Bassenge, #7523), 11⁷⁄₁₆ x 7¹⁵⁄₁₆ in., (29 x 20.1 cm.), etching on simili Japan.

BI *Reclinig Nude,* s., annot. probedruck, est. $5/700, (12-13-92, Hindman, #266), 8½ x 12¼ in., etching.

$2401* *Die Reise Nach Japan, 1921: Twelve,* s., #15/100, pub. Bruckmann, (06-10-93, Hauswedell/Nolt, #753), etching on hand-made Van Gelder Zonen (BP 1571, DM 3910, FR 13,163, Y 254,856).

$248* *Die Sangerin Und Schauspielerin Fritzi Massary, Pallenberg,* artist's proof, s. Emil Orlik, (09-14-92, Venator/Hansten, #2484), plate 10⅝ x 8¼ in., (27 x 21 cm.), etching, drypoint and roulette (BP 131, DM 369, FR 1249, Y 30,838).

$477* *Ein Sommertag (Schutte 36), 1893,* s., d., full margins, foxed, good cond., (12-03-92, Sotheby-London, #472, illus.), 7¾ x 7 in., (198 x 176 mm.), etching w/aquatint, drypoint and roulette on laid (BP 308, DM 750, FR 2560, Y 59,351).

$1419* *Sonntagmorgen In Brotzen, 1902,* s., (06-05-93, Bassenge, #6403), 9⁷⁄₁₆ x 18⅛ in., (24 x 46 cm.), color lithograph on Japan (BP 934, DM 2301, FR 7754, Y 152,221).

$330* *Study Of A Girl,* s., annot. Probedruck, (03-14-93, Hindman, #258), 8½ x 12¼ in., (21.6 x 31.1 cm.), etching (BP 230, DM 549, FR 1868, Y 38,892).

$253* *Die Sykomore Von Aniba,* s., (11-28-92, Grisebach, #682, illus.), 7¹⁵⁄₁₆ x 12 in., (20.2 x 30.5 cm.), etching and soft-ground etching on handmade (BP 167, DM 403, FR 1368, Y 31,487).

$1535* *Tempelgarten In Kioto (G. 92; 94), 1901,* s., d., margins, good cond., (12-03-92, Sotheby-London, #473, illus.), 4⅞ x 7½ in., (125 x 186 mm.), woodcut in colors on Japan (BP 990, DM 2414, FR 8239, Y 190,992).

$289* *Treppenhaus Am Quai Voltaire, 1913,* s., d., in: "Zeitschrift fur bildende Kunst", ded., (11-28-92, Grisebach, #678, illus.), 8³⁄₁₆ x 4¹⁵⁄₁₆ in., (20.8 x 12.5 cm.), etching and soft-ground etching on handmade (BP 191, DM 460, FR 1563, Y 35,968).

$340* *Trois Paysannes Assises, 1905,* whole margins, s., d., reddish stains, (06-11-93, Picard, #142), 8⅞ x 8⁷⁄₁₆ in., (225 x 215 mm.), etching and softground etching in black brown on laid (BP 223, DM 553, FR 1863, Y 36,074).

$253* *Verschleierte Araberin, c. 1915,* s., (11-28-92, Grisebach, #680, illus.), 7 x 5¹⁄₁₆ in., (17.8 x 12.8 cm.), etching and soft-ground etching on handmade (BP 167, DM 403, FR 1368, Y 31,487).

$664* *Weiblicher Akt, Sich Die Haare Flechtend, 1911,* s., artist's proof, (12-05-92, Bassenge, #7527), 9⅛ x 7 in., (23.2 x 17.8 cm.), etching on wove (BP 416, DM 1035, FR 3528, Y 82,270).

$959* *Zimmerleute Am Flussufer In Japan, 1901,* s., (12-05-92, Bassenge, #7531), 8¹⁵⁄₁₆ x 6⁵⁄₁₆ in., (22.7 x 16 cm.), color lithograph on handmade (BP 601, DM 1495, FR 5096, Y 118,820).

BI *"Zuhorer Und Zuschauer", 1911/23: Eight,* s., num., Amsler & Ruthardt, est. DM 3/4,000, (06-05-93, Grisebach, #809), 14⅜ x 12⅝ in., (36.5 x 32 cm.), etching on handmade Japan.

$253* *Zuschauer Im Zirkus, 1913,* s., d., (11-28-92, Grisebach, #679, illus.), 6¹⁵⁄₁₆ x 5¹⁄₁₆ in., (17.7 x 12.8 cm.), etching

and soft-ground etching on handmade (BP 167, DM 403, FR 1368, Y 31,487).

ORLOWSKI, Alexander

BI *Oriental Horsemen, 1820,* blindstamp, margins, paper loss, tear, stains, discoloration, defects, ex coll. Baron Paul von Schilling, est. BP 5/700, (06-30-93, Sotheby-London, #172), 25 x 19⅜ in., (635 x 492 mm.), lithograph on wove.

BI *Troika With A Courier, 1819,* artist's blindstamp, pub. in St. Petersburg, margins, stains, discoloration, stains, defects, (06-30-93, Sotheby-London, #171, illus.), 19⅜ x 25 in., (492 x 635 mm.), lithograph on heavy laid paper.

ORME, Edward   English 18th/19th cent.

$225* *View From The Summit Of Monte Carlo, 1809,* after Dubourg, (02-04-93, Sloan, #1234), 14¹⁵⁄₁₆ x 47½ in., (37.9 x 120.7 cm.), handcolored aquatint (BP 157, DM 370, FR 1256, Y 27,989).

BI *View From The Summit Of Monte Cavo, 1809,* after Dubourg, est. $400/600, (12-10-92, Sloan, #1651, illus.), 14¹⁵⁄₁₆ x 47½ in., (37.9 x 120.7 cm.), handcolored aquatint.

OROZCO, Jose Clemente   Mexican 1883-1949

BI *20 Dibujos De Jose Clemente Orozco, 1945,* stamp #135, pub. Los Talleres Graficos de la Nacion, good cond., staining, Albert Levinson Estate, est. $9/1,000, (05-19-93, Butterfield, #1846), 21¾ x 15½ in., (552 x 394 mm.), facsimile on De Fortuin Pannekoek laid.

BI *Casa Arruinada (Hopkins 8), 1928,* s., full margins, good cond., 1" repaired tear, tape remains, mat staining, yellowing, est. $2/3,000, (11-23-92, Sotheby-NY, #277, illus.), image 12⅝ x 17¾ in., (320 x 450 mm.), lithograph.

$805* *Casa Arruinada: Hopkins 8 (1928),* s., full margins, good cond., repaired tear, tape remains, yellowing, mat-staining, (05-18-93, Sotheby-NY, #264, illus.), image 12⅝ x 17¾ in., (321 x 451 mm.), lithograph (BP 524, DM 1306, FR 4411, Y 89,714).

$2640* *Dead Woman (Hopkins 28), 1935,* full margins, good cond., yellowing, (11-23-92, Sotheby-NY, #278, illus.), image 12¼ x 17 in., (311 x 432 mm.), lithograph (BP 1726, DM 4227, FR 14,340, Y 327,503).

$1100* *Dead Woman, 1935, Hopkins 28,* s., num. 33/140, Emmanuel Jacobson Estate, (09-20-92, Hindman, #797, illus.), 12¼ x 17 in., (31.1 x 43.2 cm.), lithograph (BP 644, DM 1632, FR 5584, Y 135,954).

$1980* *Desocupados (Hopkins 22), 1932,* s., pub. Delphic Studios, full margins, good cond., pencil notations, tape stains verso, (11-23-92, Sotheby-NY, #275, illus.), image 14⅛ x 10¼ in., (360 x 260 mm.), lithograph (BP 1295, DM 3170, FR 10,755, Y 245,627).

$1650* *Fin De Fiesta (H. 26), 1935,* s., #24/50, full margins, surface soiling, good cond., (11-24-92, Christie-NY, #356, illus.), borderline 12 x 15⁹⁄₁₆ in., (305 x 395 mm.), lithograph on wove paper (BP 1087, DM 2642, FR 8963, Y 204,689).

$2640* *The Franciscan, 1930,* s., narrow margins, also called The Franciscan and the Indian, (12-08-92, Swann, #230, illus.), 12⅜ x 10⅜ in., (31.4 x 26.4 cm.), lithograph on Rives watermarked paper (BP 1655, DM 4110, FR 14,013, Y 327,219).

$2200* *Las Masas (Hopkins 24), 1935,* s., d. on stone Sep.1935., full margins, good cond., water stains, yellowing, pin hole, (11-23-92, Sotheby-NY, #276, illus.), image 13¼ x 17⅛ in., (335 x 435 mm.), lithograph (BP 1438, DM 3522, FR 11,950, Y 272,919).

BI *Los Turistas (Hopkins 12), 1928,* s., full margins, good cond., yellowing, handling creases, est. $1,5/2,500, (11-23-92, Sotheby-NY, #274, illus.), image 12 x 16½ in., (305 x 420 mm.), lithograph.

$330* *Numeral Twenty, Drawings By Jose Clemente Orozco From The Exhibition Of August 1945: Twelve,* (09-21-92, Selkirk, #192, illus.), 21½ x 15¾ in., (54.6 x 40 cm.), lithograph (BP 193, DM 490, FR 1675, Y 40,786).

BI *Pedregal (Hopkins 14), 1928,* s., d., wide margins, staining, tears, surface soiling, est. $2/3,000, (05-17-93, Christie-NY, #303, illus.), 12¼ x 16⅜ in., (311 x 416 mm.), lithograph on wove.

$3025* *Pueblo Mexicano (H. 20), 1930,* s., num. 1/100, large margins, good cond., creases, surface soiling,mat staining, repaired area of paper loss, (02-24-93, Butterfield, #2668, illus.), 10¾ x 15½ in., (273 x 394 mm.), lithograph on wove (BP 2109, DM 4911, FR 16,648, Y 354,964).

$2200* *Pulqueria (Hopkins 11), 1928,* s., #67, full margins, excell. cond., yellowing, (11-23-92, Sotheby-NY, #273, illus.), image 13 x 16⅛ in., (330 x 410 mm.), lithograph (BP 1438, DM 3522, FR 11,950, Y 272,919).

BI *The Revolution (H. 19), c. 1929,* s., margins, foxing, staining, holes (backed) just affecting image, tears (some backed); staining verso, est. $5/7,000, (05-17-93, Christie-NY, #304, illus.), 11¾ x 15⅞ in., (298 x 403 mm.), lithograph on wove.

$4400* *Zapatistas (Hopkins 29), 1936,* s., #20/130, full margins, good cond., yellowing, (11-23-92, Sotheby-NY, #272, illus.), image 13 x 16½ in., (330 x 420 mm.), lithograph (BP 2877, DM 7045, FR 23,900, Y 545,838).

ORR, Alfred Everit
$65 *For Home And Country, 1918,* American Lithographic Co. NY, fold, (09-24-92, Alderfer, #285), 30 x 20 in., (76.2 x 50.8 cm.), (BP 38, DM 96, FR 327, Y 7819).

ORR, Louis   Franco/American 1879-1961
BI *Boston, c. 1940,* s., t., very good cond., est. $2/250, (05-15-93, Cleveland, #259), 9⁵⁄₁₆ x 12 in., (23.7 x 30.5 cm.), etching.

$17* *"En Camaigne",* s., (10-16-92, DuMouchelle, #2486), approx. 9 x 13¾ in., (22.9 x 34.9 cm.), etching (BP 10, DM 25, FR 85, Y 2030).

BI *"Interior Of Rheims Cathedral, Bombed Out", "Side View Of Rheims Cathedral, Bombed" and "Entrance To Rheims Cathedral With Red Cross Truck": Three,* two s., d. Aout 1917, i. in plate; each s.; second num. Artist Proof, est. C$ 2/300, (12-01-92, Ritchie, #10A), largest 27 x 20¾ in., (68.6 x 52.7 cm.), etching.

$28* *"La Maison Du Berger",* (10-16-92, DuMouchelle, #2488), 14 x 12 in., (35.6 x 30.5 cm.), etching (BP 17, DM 41, FR 140, Y 3343).

BI *Paris Street Scene, 1916: Two,* s., d., t. in plate, margins, good cond., mat/light-staining, tears,skinned spots in image, est. $6/800, (05-19-93, Butterfield, #2015), one 16½ x 9¾ in., (419 x 248 mm.), the other 16¼ x 9⅞ in., (419 x 248 mm.), etching on wove.

$17* *"Pont Marie, Pairs",* (10-16-92, DuMouchelle, #2487), 11 x 7¾ in., (27.9 x 19.7 cm.), etching (BP 10, DM 25, FR 85, Y 2030).

$220* *Port Saint Denis, 1923,* s., discoloration, laid down on cardboard, good cond., (06-11-93, Doyle, #67), 19¼ x 15¼ in., (489 x 387 mm.), etching (BP 145, DM 358, FR 1205, Y 23,342).

$55* *"Le Port St. Denis",* s., (10-16-92, DuMouchelle, #2491), 19 x 15 in., (48.3 x 38.1 cm.), etching (BP 33, DM 81, FR 276, Y 6567).

$50* *"St. Germain Des Pres",* s., (10-16-92, DuMouchelle, #2492), 17¾ x 13¼ in., (45.1 x 33.7 cm.), etching (BP 30, DM 74, FR 251, Y 5970).

$44* *"Theatre De L'Odion",* s., (10-16-92, DuMouchelle, #2490), 16 x 9½ in., (40.6 x 24.1 cm.), etching (BP 27, DM 65, FR 221, Y 5254).

$44* *"Tour Philip Le Bel",* s., (10-16-92, DuMouchelle, #2489), 15¾ x 13¼ in., (40 x 33.7 cm.), etching (BP 27, DM 65, FR 221, Y 5254).

$11* *"Village Of Generac",* s., (10-16-92, DuMouchelle, #2485), 8¼ x 13 in., (21 x 33 cm.), etching (BP 7, DM 16, FR 55, Y 1313).

ORTEGA, Jose   Spanish
$385* *"Composition",* s., #57/120, large margins, good cond., glue/tape remains, mat staining, (10-28-92, Butterfield, #2567), 15½ x 20¾ in., (394 x 527 mm.), color aquatint w/intaglio on Rives BFK (BP 245, DM 595, FR 2019, Y 47,239).

$116* *"Composition",* E.A., s., (01-28-93, Pescheteau, #226), 7¹¹⁄₁₆ x 6⁵⁄₁₆ in., (19.5 x 16 cm.), etching and aquatint on Arches (BP 77, DM 184, FR 622, Y 14,403).

$330* *Rebellion, 1970,* s. artist's proof, #20 from The Segadores series, pub. Bank Street Atelier and M. Casse, appears very good cond., (06-11-93, Doyle, #101), 22½ x

25 in., (572 x 635 mm.), lithograph w/inaglio and soft ground etching (BP 217, DM 536, FR 1808, Y 35,013).

$1220* *Untitled: Six,* all s., (03-25-93, Finarte-Rome, #7), etching and aquatint (BP 829, DM 2004, FR 6816, Y 142,924, L 1955).

ORTELIUS
BI *Hispanica Novae Sine Magnae Vera Descripto, 1599,* est. $200/300, (09-17-92, Sloan, #2691), 8⅛ x 11⅜ in., (20.6 x 28.9 cm.), handcolored.

$165* *Persici Sive Sophorum Regnu Typus, 1572,* (09-17-92, Sloan, #2693), 13¾ x 19½ in., (34.9 x 49.5 cm.), hand-colored (BP 93, DM 245, FR 838, Y 20,543).

ORTH
$90* *Banco Di Roma. Emprunt Du Tresor Francais, 1920,* good cond., (02-12-93, Cheval/Robert, #112), 30⁵⁄₁₆ x 46⅞ in., (77 x 119 cm.), poster (BP 63, DM 149, FR 505, Y 10,854).

ORTMAN, George
BI *Yellow Crosses, 1964,* from Ten Works + Ten Painters, pub. Ives-Sillman, bearing blindstamp, good cond.?, est. $2/300, (12-12-92, Weschler, #146), sheet 24 x 20 in., (61 x 50.8 cm.), color silkscreen.

BI *Yellow Crosses, 1964,* from Ten Works + Ten Painters, from portfolio #40/500, pub. Ives-Sillman, bearing blindstamp, good cond.?, est. $2/300, (12-12-92, Weschler, #145), sheet 24 x 20 in., (61 x 50.8 cm.), color silkscreen.

ORTNER, Joerg
$677* *Tholos IV, 1983-1986: Six,* s., t., d., 30 edit., editor's drystamp, (06-28-93, Loudmer, #102), 20¹⁄₁₆ x 13¾ in., (510 x 350 mm.), sh 24¹³⁄₁₆ x 17¹¹⁄₁₆ in., (510 x 350 mm.), softgound etchings, aquatints, copper engravings, etchings, manieresnoires on Japan applique on Arches wove (BP 453, DM 1150, FR 3875, Y 71,830).

ORUP, Bengt   b. 1916
$166* *Composition,* s., 184/290, (11-07-92, Falkkloos, #430), color lithograph (BP 109, DM 266, FR 896, Y 20,489, SK 990).

OS, Pieter Gerardus van   Dutch 1776-1839
BI *Rinder (Wurzbach 1), 1878: Six,* s., d. P.G. ram Os fec. A. 1798, staining, est. SC 4/5,000, (11-11-92, Dorotheum, #345), 7¹⁄₁₆ x 9¹⁄₁₆ in., (18 x 23 cm.), etching.

OS, Pim Van   1910-1954
$1540* *Photograms, c. 1950: Two,* each w/credit stamp, (10-13-92, Christie-NY, #477, illus.), each 9¼ x 7 in., (23.5 x 17.8 cm.), photograph, gelatin silver prints (BP 897, DM 2256, FR 7666, Y 186,735).

OS, Ton van
$64* *Untitled, 1972,* s., d., i. Eigen Druk 1/35, margins, good cond., (05-27-93, Sotheby-Amstrdm, #461), 19½ x 23⁷⁄₁₆ in., (495 x 595 mm.), etching w/tone on wove (BP 41, DM 103, FR 346, Y 6861, G 115).

$64* *Untitled, 1972,* s., d., i. Eigen Druk, #2/35, full margins, good cond., minor handling creases, crease in upper and lower margin, (05-27-93, Sotheby-Amstrdm, #462), 19½ x 20¹⁄₁₆ in., (495 x 509 mm.), etching on wove (BP 41, DM 103, FR 346, Y 6861, G 115).

$64* *Untitled, 1973,* s., d., i. eigen druk, #9/35, good cond., crease in upper margin, (05-27-93, Sotheby-Amstrdm, #463), 19½ x 20¹⁄₁₆ in., etching on wove (BP 41, DM 103, FR 346, Y 6861, G 115).

OSAKA, Hiroshi
$1760* *Nude, 1990: Diptych,* s., d., num. 6/8 by photog., #6/8 ed., (10-15-92, Sotheby-NY, #609A, illus.), each 13⅝ x 17¼ in., (34.6 x 43.8 cm.), framed 30 x 40 in., (34.6 x 43.8 cm.), photograph of 2 toned gelatin silver prints mounted together (BP 1077, DM 2620, FR 8884, Y 211,158).

OSBORNE, Elizabeth   American 20th cent.
$193* *Saba Bank,* s., t., #62/100, d. '73, (06-11-93, Freemn/ Fine Art, #161), 22¼ x 26¾ in., (56.5 x 67.9 cm.), screenprint (BP 127, DM 314, FR 1058, Y 20,477).

OSBORNE, Malcolm
$60* *"Figures Outside A Fortified Building, River Landscape Beyond",* s., margins, (01-21-93, Bonhams-Chelsea, #121),

plate 7¾ x 13 in., (19.7 x 33 cm.), etching (BP 39, DM 95, FR 323, Y 7509).

$135* *The Goose Fair, Albi*, s., t., margins, (01-21-93, Bonhams-Chelsea, #120), plate 10½ x 13¾ in., (26.7 x 34.9 cm.), etching w/aquatint (BP 88, DM 215, FR 726, Y 16,896).

$50* *"Riverside Washing, A Continental Town"*, s., margins, (01-21-93, Bonhams-Chelsea, #130), plate 8⅛ x 14½ in., (20.6 x 36.8 cm.), etching (BP 33, DM 80, FR 269, Y 6258).

$59* *The Veil Of Spring, Windermere*, s., margins, (11-19-92, Bonhams-Chelsea, #13), plate 8⅛ x 15½ in., (20.6 x 39.4 cm.), aquatint (BP 39, DM 94, FR 317, Y 7337).

OSGOOD, George

$85* *Earth Rhythms I*, s., t., #50/65, prov., (12-01-92, Ritchie, #86), 42 x 30¾ in., (106.7 x 78.1 cm.), embossed aquatint (BP 56, DM 135, FR 462, Y 10,583, C$ 110).

OSTADE, Adriaen van   Dutch 1610-1685

BI *The Barn (B., Dut., God., Holl. 23)*, *1647*, 9th state of 10, thread margins or trimmed on platemark, good cond.,prov., est. BP 7/900, (12-01-92, Christie-London, #147), sheet 6⁵⁄₁₆ x 7⁹⁄₁₆ in., (160 x 192 mm.), etching.

$6325* *The Barn (G., Holl. 23)*, *1647*, Godefroy's 5th state of 10, thread margins or trimmed, printer's crease, good cond., ex-coll. V. Weisbach, W. Weisbach and another FPM, (05-13-93, Sotheby-NY, #171, illus.), 6¼ x 7⅝ in., (159 x 193 mm.), etching (BP 4152, DM 10,213, FR 34,450, Y 706,152).

$850* *Der Bauer In Der Haustur (B. 9, Dutuit I, Davidsohn, Godefroy, Hollstein II)*, (06-04-93, Bassenge, #5278, illus.), 4⅛ x 3½ in., (10.5 x 8.9 cm.), etching (BP 562, DM 1380, FR 4652, Y 91,674).

$225* *Bauer, In Der Tur Lehnend (Hollstein Bd. 15, 9)*, *c. 1672*, later print, (03-24-93, Venator/Hansten, #2551), pl. 4³⁄₁₆ x 3⁹⁄₁₆ in., (10.6 x 9 cm.), (BP 152, DM 367, FR 1251, Y 26,436).

$220* *Die Brettspieler (The Checker Players) (C. 1682. (3.39)*, (12-10-92, Sloan, #2094), 3¼ x 2⅞ in., (8.3 x 7.3 cm.), etching (BP 142, DM 348, FR 1189, Y 27,214).

$2816* *Der Bucklige Violinspieler (B. 44; Dutuit II; Davidsohn II; Godefroy, Hollstein III)*, *1654*, prov., watermark, (12-04-92, Bassenge, #6342, illus.), 6¹⁄₁₆ x 4¼ in., (15.4 x 10.8 cm.), etching (BP 1806, DM 4485, FR 15,213, Y 351,561).

$220* *Dance At The Inn*, very good/good cond., (11-21-92, Bakker, #83, illus.), image 9½ x 12½ in., (24.1 x 31.8 cm.), etching (BP 145, DM 351, FR 1182, Y 27,360).

$303* *The Dance In The Inn (Godefroy, Hollstein 49)*, *1652*, (10-08-92, Grogan, #649), sheet 10 x 12⅝ in., (25.4 x 32.1 cm.), etching (BP 180, DM 448, FR 1521, Y 36,817).

$3249* *Die Familie (B. 46; Dutuit, Davidsohn V; Godefroy V; Hollstein V)*, *1647*, prov., (12-04-92, Bassenge, #6343, illus.), 6¹⁵⁄₁₆ x 6³⁄₁₆ in., (17.7 x 15.7 cm.), etching (BP 2084, DM 5174, FR 17,553, Y 405,618).

$5956* *Die Familie (Godefr. Und Hollst. 46/IV (v. VII)*, *1647*, fourth state, watermark, prov., (06-23-93, Kornfeld, #74, illus.), etching (BP 4046, DM 10,078, FR 33,899, Y 648,872, SF 8970).

$498* *Der Familienvater (B. 33 und Dav. 33/IV)*, *1648*, (12-01-92, Karl/Faber, #114), etching (BP 329, DM 794, FR 2705, Y 62,002).

$1150* *The Fiddler And The Hurdy-Gurdy Player (B., Dut., God., Holl. 45)*, *c. 1660*, 3rd state of 6, wear, trimmed on or inside platemark, foxmarks, watermark, prop. Montclair Art Museum, (05-11-93, Christie-NY, #29), sheet 6 x 5⅛ in., (152 x 130 mm.), etching on laid (BP 734, DM 1812, FR 6104, Y 126,499).

$1372* *Das Fruhstuck (B. 50, Dutuit, Davidsohn XI; Godefroy und Hollstein XII)*, *c. 1664*, (12-04-92, Bassenge, #6345), 8⁹⁄₁₆ x 10⁵⁄₁₆ in., (21.7 x 26.2 cm.), red etching (BP 880, DM 2185, FR 7412, Y 171,286).

$166* *Die Garnweiferin (B. und Dav. 25/IV)*, *c. 1684*, (12-01-92, Karl/Faber, #111), etching (BP 110, DM 265, FR 902, Y 20,667).

$2125* *Die Gevatterinnen (B. 40, Dutuit II, Davidsohn, Godefroy und Hollstein IV I*, *c. 1642*, prov., (06-04-93, Bassenge, #5288), 3¹⁵⁄₁₆ x 3½ in., (10.1 x 8.9 cm.), etching (BP 1406, DM 3451, FR 11,631, Y 229,185).

$466* *The Hunchbacked Fiddler (B., Dut., God., Holl. 44)*, *1654*, 4th state of 6, narrow to thread margins, repaired tear, good cond.,prov., (12-01-92, Christie-London, #149), plate 6⁵⁄₁₆ x 4½ in., (161 x 114 mm.), etching (BP 308, DM 743, FR 2531, Y 58,018).

$197* *Der Jahrmarkt (Hollstein 48)*, *c. 1660*, later print, (03-24-93, Venator/Hansten, #2555), 4¾ x 8¾ in., (12.1 x 22.3 cm.), colored etching on thick paper (BP 133, DM 322, FR 1095, Y 23,147).

$1498* *The Knifegrinder (B., Dut., God., Holl. 36)*, *c. 1682*, 1st state of 3, watermark, margins, repaired nicks, thin spots, foxing, good cond., (12-01-92, Christie-London, #148), plate 3⁵⁄₁₆ x 2⅞ in., (84 x 73 mm.), etching on fine laid paper (BP 990, DM 2388, FR 8137, Y 186,504).

$1228* *Die Landliche Zartlichkeit (B. 11; Dutuit 11 VII, Davidsohn 11 IX, Godefroy, Hollstein 11 X)*, *1667*, (12-04-92, Bassenge, #6336, illus.), 6⁹⁄₁₆ x 5¹⁄₁₆ in., (16.7 x 12.8 cm.), etching (BP 788, DM 1956, FR 6634, Y 153,308).

BI *Der Leere Krug (B. und Davidsohn 15/VIII)*, *1653*, margins, foxing, prov., est. DM 1000, (12-01-92, Karl/Faber, #110), etching.

$66* *"Paysan Avec Une Petit Tagge Noir" (Bartsch 1)*, late 18th/early 19th cent. impression, plate mark visible, good cond., (10-31-92, Cleveland, #20), 1³⁄₁₆ x 1³⁄₁₆ in., (3 x 3 cm.), etching (BP 42, DM 102, FR 344, Y 8175).

BI *Peasant Leaning On His Doorway (Godefroy, Holl. 9)*, *1672*, 2nd state of 4, narrow margins, tear, paper loss, defects, good cond., est. $3/5,000, (05-13-93, Sotheby-NY, #168, illus.), 4⅛ x 3⅜ in., (104 x 87 mm.), etching.

BI *The Peasant Settling His Debt (G., Holl. 42)*, seventh state of twelve, small margins, thin spots, good cond., ex-coll., est. BP 3/4,000, (12-03-92, Sotheby-London, #90, illus.), 4⅛ x 3½ in., (106 x 88 mm.), etching.

BI *The Pig Killers (Godefroy 41 VI/VIII and VIII/VIII)*: Two Impressions, *c. 1642*, Godefroy's 6th and 8th states (of 8), 2nd trimmed to circular borderline, framed together, est. $1,8/2,400, (10-18-92, Hindman, #497, illus.), 4⅜ x 4⅜ in., (11.1 x 11.1 cm.), etchings w/drypoint.

$466* *Der Raucher (Bartsch 5; Davidson 5 V; Godefroy and Boon-Verbeek 5 VI)*, *1640 (?)*, (06-10-93, Hauswedell/Nolt, #127, illus.), etching (BP 305, DM 759, FR 2555, Y 49,464).

BI *Die Scheune, Innen, (Godefroy 23)*, *c. 1710*, plate s., d. A v ostade 1647, est. DM 900-, (09-14-92, Venator/Hansten, #1579), plate 6³⁄₁₆ x 7½ in., (15.7 x 19.1 cm.), etching.

BI *The Schoolmaster (Holl. 17; Godefroy 17)*, third (final) state, margins, good cond., est. BP 1,2/1,800, (12-03-92, Sotheby-London, #88), 3½ x 3¼ in., (92 x 83 mm.), etching.

$433* *Der Schuhflicker (B. 27; Dutuit IX; Davidsohn, Godefroy, Hollstein X)*, *1671*, foxed, (12-04-92, Bassenge, #6338), 7⅜ x 5⅞ in., (18.7 x 14.9 cm.), etching (BP 278, DM 690, FR 2339, Y 54,057).

$374* *Der Schuhflicker (B. und Dav. 27/X)*, *1671*, trimmed, (12-01-92, Karl/Faber, #112), etching (BP 247, DM 596, FR 2032, Y 46,564).

$381* *Das Schweineschlachten (Bartsch 41; Davidson, Godefroy and Boon-Verbeek 41 VIII)*, *1642(?)*, prov., (06-10-93, Hauswedell/Nolt, #136, illus.), etching (BP 249, DM 620, FR 2089, Y 40,442).

$176* *The Singers (B. 19)*, 7th final state, margins, tear w/in platemark, (09-17-92, Bonhams-Chelsea, #94), plate 9½ x 7½ in., (24.1 x 19.1 cm.), etching on laid paper (BP 99, DM 261, FR 894, Y 21,912).

BI *Die Spinnerin (B. 31 und Dav. 31/VII)*, *1652*, crease, stained, est. DM 900, (12-01-92, Karl/Faber, #113), etching.

BI *Three Figures Conversing*, est. $175/225, (05-16-93, Hanzel, #447), 3 x 2⅜ in., (7.6 x 6 cm.), etching.

$2455* *Das Tischgebet (B. 34; Dutuit, IV; Davidsohn V; Godefroy VI; Hollstein VII)*, *1653*, (12-04-92, Bassenge, #6340), 6⅛ x 5⅛ in., (15.5 x 13 cm.), red etching (BP 1575, DM 3910, FR 13,263, Y 306,492).

$636* *Die Unterhaltung (Bartsch 37; Davidson, Godefroy and Boon-Verbeek 37V), 1650 (?)*, (06-10-93, Hauswedel/Nolt, #134, illus.), etching (BP 416, DM 1036, FR 3487, Y 67,509).

$918* *Die Unterhaltung (Bartsch 37; Dutuit 37 I; Davidson, Godefroy, and Bon-Verbeek 37 II), 1650?*, collector stamp, (06-10-93, Hauswedel/Nolt, #133, illus.), etching on hand-made (BP 600, DM 1495, FR 5033, Y 97,442).

$2974* *Der Violinspieler Und Der Kleine Leiermann (B. 45, Dutuit III, Davidsohn, Godefroy IV, Hollstein V), c. 1660*, watermark, prov., (06-04-93, Bassenge, #5291, illus.), 6⅛ x 5¹⁄₁₆ in., (15.5 x 12.9 cm.), etching (BP 1968, DM 4829, FR 16,278, Y 320,751).

$410* *Das Wandernde Paar (Bartsch 24; Davidson, Godefroy and Boon-Verbeek 24 V), 1638 (?)*, (06-10-93, Hauswedell/Nolt, #130, illus.), etching (BP 268, DM 668, FR 2248, Y 43,520).

OSTERLIND, Allan
$115* *Spanish Women And A Man Sitting On Stone Steps, 1896*, s., #No. 23/50, remarque, margins, good cond., crease, surface scuffs surface soiling, (05-19-93, Butterfield, #2090), 27½ x 19⅜ in., (699 x 492 mm.), etching and aquatint in colors on wove (BP 75, DM 187, FR 630, Y 12,731).

OSTERLIND, Allan Anders
$39* *Paysage*, s., (06-28-93, Loudmer, #325), 11⅝ x 15⁹⁄₁₆ in., (295 x 395 mm.), sh 17⅛ x 24 in., (295 x 395 mm.), color aquatint on Arches wove (BP 26, DM 66, FR 223, Y 4138).

OSTHAUS, Edmund H. (after)
$295* *Three Gun Dogs Amongst The Brambles*, s., pub. R. Dudensing & Sons, 1894, staining, (06-30-93, Bonhams-Chelsea, #66), image 19 x 29¾ in., (48.3 x 75.6 cm.), photogravure w/photographic remarque (BP 198, DM 503, FR 1697, Y 31,608).

OSTROWSKY, Abbo   American b. 1889
BI *"Backyard", 1925*, s., annot. in plate New York, 1925, tear to plate mark, est. $150-200, (10-31-92, Cleveland, #200), 11⅞ x 9 in., (30.2 x 22.9 cm.), etching.

$88* *"Roofs", 1934*, pencil corrections drawn on print by artist, s., annot. Trial Proof;skinning, hinges verso, (10-31-92, Cleveland, #201), 9⅞ x 12⅜ in., (25.1 x 31.4 cm.), etching (BP 56, DM 135, FR 459, Y 10,901).

OTHON-FRIESZ, Emile   1879-1949
$339* *Bal Aide Amicale Des Artistes. A. Bullier, 1923*, cond. B, (03-16-93, Boisgirard, #164, illus.), 46¼ x 30¹¹⁄₁₆ in., (117.5 x 78 cm.), poster (BP 234, DM 564, FR 1915, Y 39,640).

$336* *Bal De L'A.A.A.A.*, half t., very good cond., (11-19-92, Ribeyre/Baron, #150), 47¼ x 31½ in., (120 x 80 cm.), poster on wove (BP 221, DM 536, FR 1805, Y 41,786).

OUDE, Crispijn de Passe de   c. 1565-1637
$709* *Christus Und Die Apostel (Hollstein 240-253), 1594: Fourteen*, (06-08-93, Karl/Faber, #122), engraving (BP 466, DM 1150, FR 3874, Y 75,305).

OUDOT, R.
$141* *Le Vieux Moulin A Eygalieres (F.D. 210), 1973*, artist proof, #X/XX, s., margins not trimmed, (02-03-93, Ader Tajan, #187), 12⅝ x 20¹⁄₁₆ in., (32 x 51 cm.), color lithograph (BP 98, DM 232, FR 787, Y 17,539).

OUDRY, J.B.   French 1686-1755
$2522* *Chasses (R. Portalis and H. Beraldi p. 243), 1725: Four*, original, reddish stains, good margins, (02-03-93, Ader Tajan, #67), etching (BP 1761, DM 4153, FR 14,082, Y 313,721).

OUTERBRIDGE, Paul   American 1896-1958
$31,050* *"Beauty" (Dines, pl. 73; Photographing in Color, pl. 14), c. 1936*, photog. Estate stamp num. 821 in unident. hand in ink, (04-06-93, Sotheby-NY, #136, illus.), 16¾ x 10⅛ in., photograph, color carbro print (BP 20,509, DM 50,024, FR 169,394, Y 3,541,286).

BI *From My Window (Dines, fig. 168), 1923*, mounted, est. $5/8,000, (10-15-92, Sotheby-NY, #123A, illus.), 4⅛ x 4⅝ in., (10.5 x 11.7 cm.), photograph, gelatin silver print.

$3300* *Horseless Carriage (Dines, fig. 239), 1926*, mounted, photog.'s estate stamp num. 420 in unidentified hand, (10-15-92, Sotheby-NY, #124, illus.), 4⅛ x 9⅜ in., (10.5 x 23.8 cm.), photograph, platinum print (BP 2019, DM 4912, FR 16,658, Y 395,921).

BI *Laguna Beach, California, c. 1950: Nineteen*, 19 photos, comprising essay on Life In Laguna Beach, California, in the 1950's, each w/typed caption label, est. $5/8,000, (10-15-92, Sotheby-NY, #504, illus.), each, approx. 9½ x 7½ in., (24.1 x 19.1 cm.), photograph, gelatin silver print.

$38,500* *Nude, 1928*, s., d. by photog., (10-15-92, Sotheby-NY, #123, illus.), 4¾ x 3⅜ in., (12.1 x 8.6 cm.), photograph, waxed platinum print (BP 23,559, DM 57,309, FR 194,346, Y 4,619,076).

BI *Siegel Mannequin, 1928*, s., d., annot.; s., d., annot. in ink on mount verso, lit., est. $22/28,000, (10-13-92, Christie-NY, #324, illus.), 8½ x 6¼ in., (21.6 x 15.9 cm.), photograph, gelatin silver print.

$10,925* *Wine Glass On Checkerboard, 1922*, lit., (04-08-93, Christie-NY, #327, illus.), 8 x 6 in., (20.3 x 15.2 cm.), photograph, gelatin silver print (BP 7164, DM 17,550, FR 59,407, Y 1,239,787).

OWEN, Frederick L.   20th cent.
BI *"Australian Wheat Race"*, s. Frederick L. Owen, t., stamped, d. '32 in pl., est. $1/150, (12-12-92, A. James, #427), sight 13½ x 11⅛ in., (34.3 x 28.3 cm.), etching.

$121* *Full And By*, margins, s. Frederick L. Owen, (02-13-93, Collins, #76, illus.), 11¾ x 8⅞ in., (29.8 x 22.5 cm.), etching (BP 85, DM 201, FR 679, Y 14,592).

OWEN, William (after)
$165* *Captain Sir Christopher Cole, R.N.*, by George H. Phillips, staining, (06-16-93, Bonhams-Chelsea, #469), pl. 17 x 13¼ in., (43.2 x 33.7 cm.), mezzotint (BP 110, DM 274, FR 919, Y 17,598).

OXMAN, Katja   German/American b. 1942
BI *"Seal On Kandinsky", 1985*, s., t., excell. cond., est. $4/600, (05-15-93, Cleveland, #484), 12 x 16 in., (30.5 x 40.6 cm.), aquatint in color.

OZANNE, J.F. and M.J.
$491* *Paysages Et Marines (J. Vichot, C1c. D14): Four*, 2 w/ margins, yellowed, (06-16-93, Ader Tajan, #43), 6⁵⁄₁₆ x 7½ in., (16 x 19 cm.), etching and copper (BP 327, DM 815, FR 2735, Y 52,368).

OZANNE, Nicolas (after)
$141* *Le Port D'Antibes, Vu De La Campagne Du Cote De L'Ouest*, by Gouaz, (06-16-93, Bonhams-Chelsea, #370), image 5½ x 8⅝ in., (14 x 21.9 cm.), engraving w/hand-coloring on laid (BP 94, DM 234, FR 786, Y 15,038).

PACKARD, Emmy Lou
BI *Artichoke Picker Near Half Moon Bay*, s., t., margins, good cond.?, est. $4/600, (05-19-93, Butterfield, #2016), 23 x 17⅛ in., (584 x 435 mm.), linoleum cut on Japan.

$275* *Front Street - 5 AM*, s., t., 3 margins folded, hinged to overmat, good cond., light-staining, (10-28-92, Butterfield, #2748), 18⅛ x 14¼ in., (460 x 362 mm.), color woodcut on fine laid paper (BP 175, DM 425, FR 1442, Y 33,742).

PACKER, Thomas
$26 *Battle Maps Of The Crimea War: Two*, (02-05-93, G.A. Key, #24), 17 x 24 in., (43.2 x 61 cm.), colored lithograph (BP 18, DM 43, FR 146, Y 3235).

PADEN, Bernard   American
BI *'Aoshima'*, #14/50, s., t., est. C$2/250, (10-21-92, Maynard, #199), 10¾ x 15 in., (27.3 x 38.1 cm.), color woodblock.

PAI-HUNG
BI *L'Annam. Bureau Officiel Du Tourisme De HUE. 1928*, fairly good cond., (03-13-93, Laurin, #139), 42⅛ x 29½ in., (107 x 75 cm.), .

PAIK, Nam June   Korean/American b. 1932
BI *July 20*, #85/120, pencil s., est. DM 1,200, (11-20-92, Lempertz, #748), sh 27⁹⁄₁₆ x 19¹¹⁄₁₆ in., (70 x 50 cm.), serigraph in color on Velin.

PAL French 19th cent.

$341* *Arista. La Meilleure Eau De Table, 1894,* Imp. P. Dupont, good cond., (02-12-93, Cheval/Robert, #68, illus.), 58¼ x 43 5/16 in., (148 x 110 cm.), poster (BP 240, DM 566, FR 1914, Y 41,124).

$382* *A Bas L'Intermediaire. Pour Avoir Votre Vin Pur, Achetez DirectementAu Producteur,* Imp. P. Dupont, good cond., (02-12-93, Cheval/Robert, #69), 108¼ x 59 1/16 in., (275 x 150 cm.), 3 sheets (BP 269, DM 633, FR 2144, Y 46,068).

$422* *Cleo De Merode,* before letters, good cond., (02-12-93, Cheval/Robert, #193), 50 13/16 x 37 in., (129 x 94 cm.), poster (BP 297, DM 700, FR 2368, Y 50,892).

$517* *Danses Renaissance, Les Soeurs De Belval,* (01-31-93, Morelle/Marchan, #39), 31½ x 47¼ in., (80 x 120 cm.), poster (BP 348, DM 833, FR 2816, Y 64,496).

$341* *Domaine Du Chateau De Villette,* good cond., loss, (02-12-93, Cheval/Robert, #70), 59 1/16 x 43 5/16 in., (150 x 110 cm.), poster (BP 240, DM 566, FR 1914, Y 41,124).

$1339* *Enghien Les Bains, 1899,* tears, repairs, (02-04-93, Christie-S. Ken, #139, illus.), 84 x 43 in., (213.4 x 109.2 cm.), color lithograph on two sheets backed on linen (BP 935, DM 2205, FR 7476, Y 166,563).

$301* *Exposition Universelle, 1889,* w/out text, Imp. Canning & Cie, good cond., (02-12-93, Cheval/Robert, #132), 78¾ x 51 3/16 in., (200 x 130 cm.), poster (BP 212, DM 499, FR 1689, Y 36,300).

$372* *Folies Bergere (Danseuse Classique),* (01-31-93, Morelle/Marchan, #40), 37 13/16 x 50 in., (96 x 127 cm.), poster (BP 250, DM 599, FR 2026, Y 46,407).

$315* *La Francaise, c. 1898,* creases, repairs, (02-04-93, Christie-S. Ken, #138), 62 x 45 in., (157.5 x 114.3 cm.), color lithograph backed on linen (BP 220, DM 519, FR 1759, Y 39,184).

$248* *Theatre Des Bouffes Parisiens, L'Enlevement De La Toledad,* (01-31-93, Morelle/Marchan, #182), 43 5/16 x 59 1/16 in., (110 x 150 cm.), poster (BP 167, DM 400, FR 1351, Y 30,938).

PAL (Jean de PALEOLOGUE) French 1860-1942

$642* *Affichage National Dufayel. 8, Rue Montesquieu Paris, c. 1898,* Paris, Imp. Chardin, cond. A-, (06-11-93, Boisgirard, #126, illus.), 62 15/16 x 43⅞ in., (160 x 111.5 cm.), poster (BP 422, DM 1043, FR 3518, Y 68,117).

$462* *Bock-Orbec, Boisson Gazeuse A La Mode, c. 1900,* Paris, Imp. Caby and Chardin, cond. B+, (06-11-93, Boisgirard, #128, illus.), 62 15/16 x 45¼ in., (160 x 115 cm.), poster (BP 304, DM 751, FR 2532, Y 49,019).

$462* *Cycles Clement Paris. Pneu Dunlop, av. 1900,* Paris, Affiches artistiques Caby and Chardin, cond. B+, (06-11-93, Boisgirard, #129), 62 15/16 x 45¼ in., (160 x 115 cm.), poster (BP 304, DM 751, FR 2532, Y 49,019).

$1907* *Fernand Clement And Cie. Usine Et Bureaux 130 Rue Du Bois, LevalloisPerret, 1895,* Paris, Imp. P. Dupont, cond. A-, (06-11-93, Boisgirard, #124), 58¼ x 41 5/16 in., (148 x 105 cm.), poster (BP 1253, DM 3099, FR 10,449, Y 202,334).

$683* *Hygiene Beaute Icilma, c. 1895,* Paris, Affiches artistiques Chardin, cond. B+, (06-11-93, Boisgirard, #125), 51 3/16 x 37 in., (130 x 94 cm.), poster (BP 449, DM 1110, FR 3742, Y 72,467).

$279* *Mi-Careme 1896. La Vache Enragee,* cond. B, (03-16-93, Boisgirard, #165), 56½ x 42 5/16 in., (143.5 x 107.5 cm.), poster (BP 193, DM 464, FR 1576, Y 32,624).

$1144* *Patin Bicyclette. Richard Choubersky, c. 1900,* Paris, Imp. P. Dupont (atelier de l'affiche Pal), cond. B+, (06-11-93, Boisgirard, #133), 51 15/16 x 37 13/16 in., (132 x 96 cm.), poster (BP 752, DM 1859, FR 6268, Y 121,379).

$1004* *La Peoria. Bicyclette Americaine De Luxe, c. 1900,* Asnieres, Imp. P. Lemenil, cond. A-, (06-11-93, Boisgirard, #131, illus.), 63 15/16 x 42 15/16 in., (162.5 x 109 cm.), poster (BP 660, DM 1632, FR 5501, Y 106,525).

$301* *Quinquina Dubonnet,* Paris, Imp. Charles Verneau, cond. A-, (06-11-93, Boisgirard, #122), 27⅜ x 77 15/16 in., (69.5 x 198 cm.), poster (BP 198, DM 489, FR 1649, Y 31,936).

$321* *La Republique (...) Journal Des Republicains Progressistes, 1898,* Paris, Imp. Chardin, cond. B+, (06-11-93, Boisgirard, #127), 63 3/16 x 45¼ in., (160.5 x 115 cm.), poster (BP 211, DM 522, FR 1759, Y 34,058).

$1044* *Republique Francaise (...) Exposition Universelle de 1900 (...) Concours Internationaux D'Escrime,* Paris, Imp. Chardin, cond. A-, (06-11-93, Boisgirard, #130, illus.), 61 7/16 x 44⅛ in., (156 x 112 cm.), poster (BP 686, DM 1697, FR 5721, Y 110,769).

$522* *Visitez Le Palais Royal, Maisons Notables Et Recommandees, c. 1900,* Paris, Imp. Chardin, cond. A-, (06-11-93, Boisgirard, #132), 55⅛ x 43 5/16 in., (140 x 110 cm.), poster (BP 343, DM 848, FR 2860, Y 55,385).

$201* *Yves Sans Peur,* Paris, Imp. Caby and Chardin, cond. B+, (06-11-93, Boisgirard, #123), 78¾ x 55⅛ in., (200 x 140 cm.), poster (BP 132, DM 327, FR 1101, Y 21,326).

PAL (Jean de Paleologue) French 1860-1942

$605* *Loterie, 1900,* Imp. Chardin Pas. Daudin, A- cond., creasing, (08-06-92, Swann, #217, illus.), 60 x 40 in., (152.4 x 101.6 cm.), (BP 316, DM 894, FR 3019, Y 77,168).

$467* *Societe La Francaise,* Affiches Artistiques Chardin, B cond., fold marks, repairs, (08-06-92, Swann, #219, illus.), 61 x 42½ in., (154.9 x 108 cm.), (BP 244, DM 690, FR 2330, Y 59,566).

$357* *Theatre Des Bouffes,* Paul Dupont, B+ cond., surface soiling, chipping, (08-06-92, Swann, #218, illus.), 59 x 42½ in., (149.9 x 108 cm.), (BP 186, DM 527, FR 1781, Y 45,536).

PALADINO, Mimmo Italian b. 1948

BI *Atlantico, 1987,* s., d., #7/27, full margins, good cond., prov., 1880 x 580 mm, est. G 4/6,000, (12-09-92, Sotheby-Amstrdm, #627, illus.), linocut on wove.

BI *Come In Uno Specchio, 1990,* s., d., #18/60, blindstamp pub. Waddington Graphics, full margins, good cond., creases, surface soiling, est. $1,5/2,000, (10-28-92, Butterfield, #3068), 22¾ x 19⅜ in., (578 x 492 mm.), color lithograph on laid.

$3450* *Essere Portato In Carro, 1990,* s., d., #33/50, left side of a triptych, pub. Waddington Graphics, good cond. ?, (05-15-93, Sotheby-NY, #1143, illus.), 69½ x 49¼ in., (176.5 x 125.1 cm.), etching, drypoint, woodcut, and silkscreen in colors (BP 2243, DM 5549, FR 18,649, Y 382,441).

$858* *Figure With Glass, 1985,* s., d., #21/60, pub. Waddington, blindstamp, full margins, good cond., tape hinges, (06-30-93, Sotheby-London, #885, illus.), 22¼ x 19⅝ in., (565 x 498 mm.), color lithograph on laid (BP 575, DM 1463, FR 4937, Y 91,932).

$470* *Geflugeltes Wesen, 1982,* s., d., (11-28-92, Grisebach, #687, illus.), 17⅝ x 13⅜ in., (44.8 x 34 cm.), colored serigraph on wove (BP 310, DM 749, FR 2542, Y 58,494).

$8800* *Le Immagini Sono Riflessi Bruciati,* s., d. 75 verso, prov., lit., Sylvio Perlstein Coll., (11-18-92, Sotheby-NY, #225, illus.), 41¼ x 37¾ in., (104.8 x 95.9 cm.), nine photographs mounted in wood frame (BP 5794, DM 14,031, FR 47,261, Y 1,094,391).

BI *Lacrimose, 1986,* s., d., #35/42, i. D., pub. Waddington Graphics, good cond., est. BP1,2/1,500, (06-30-93, Sotheby-London, #886, illus.), overall sh 30⅞ x 62½ in., (78.4 x 158.8 cm.), woodcut and etching in color on double sh.

$1082* *Nudo Azurro, 1983,* #117/150, pencil s., (11-20-92, Lempertz, #751), sh 31⅛ x 23 7/16 in., (79 x 59.5 cm.), color lithograph on Velin (BP 712, DM 1725, FR 5811, Y 134,560).

$2166* *Ohne Titel, 1982: Four,* series, s., d., blindstamp Edit. Schellmann & Kluser, (11-28-92, Schoppmann, #684), largest 19 3/16 x 25 15/16 in., (48.8 x 66 cm.), smallest 13¾ x 27¾ in., (48.8 x 66 cm.), color lithograph, etching on Arches wove (BP 1430, DM 3451, FR 11,714, Y 269,571).

BI *Self-Portrait, 1989,* s., d. Mimmo Paladino 89, num. 10/35, p. dry stamp inits. H.W., pub.dry stamp, very good cond., est. $3/5000, (09-11-92, Skinner, #113, illus.), sight 52⅝ x 38½ in., (133.7 x 97.8 cm.), etching/aquatint and chine colle (pasted) on wove.

BI *The Skater, 1984,* s., d., #7/35, very good cond., est. $1,4/1,800, (10-28-92, Butterfield, #3067), 38 x 30½ in.,

(965 x 775 mm.), color etching w/aquatint on cream wove.

BI *The Skater, 1984,* s., d., #7/35, very good cond.?, est. $1/1,500, (05-19-93, Butterfield, #2286), 38 x 30½ in., (965 x 775 mm.), etching w/aquatint in color on wove.

BI *Solo Du Pesci, 1980,* s., d., #11/35, blindstamp pub. Multiples, full margins, good cond.,surface soiling, creases, skinned area, glue stain, est. $1,2/1,400, (10-28-92, Butterfield, #3065), 9¾ x 19¹³⁄₁₆ in., (248 x 503 mm.), color etching w/aquatint on cream wove.

$1320* *Tane De Napoli, 1983: Four,* complete portfolio, s., d., #16/33, pub. Figura Editions, full margins, good cond., orig. portfolio, (10-28-92, Butterfield, #3066, illus.), each sheet 19½ x 23 in., (495 x 584 mm.), etching w/ drypoint on Sant'Ilario wove paper, cover w/Chine colle, watermark (BP 841, DM 2039, FR 6922, Y 161,963).

BI *Untitled (Sarajevo), 1984,* s., d. 1983, num. 131/150, pub. Visconti ARt Spectrum, full margins,good cond., surface soiling, est. $1/1,500, (02-24-93, Butterfield, #3107), 28¼ x 20½ in., (718 x 521 mm.), lithograph in colors on Arches.

PALAZUELO, Pablo Spanish b. 1916

$50* *"Composition En Vert",* HC s., (04-04-93, Pescheteau, #272), 19¹¹⁄₁₆ x 15¾ in., (50 x 40 cm.), color lithograph (BP 33, DM 80, FR 273, Y 5693).

$415* *"Sigilla IV",* i. b.a. meaning bon a tirer, proof, (02-03-93, Duran, #231, illus.), 36¼ x 24¹³⁄₁₆ in., (92 x 63 cm.), lithograph (BP 290, DM 683, FR 2317, Y 51,623, P 48,300).

PALENCIA, Benjamin Spanish b. 1902

BI *"Desde Mi Rincon", 1977: Ten,* Antonio Machado, s., in portfolio, #11/25, Ediciones de Arte y Bibliofilia, reserve P300,000, (12-17-92, Duran, #168, illus.), 20¹⁄₁₆ x 15⅜ in., (51 x 39 cm.), lithograph.

PALENSKE, R.H. American 1884-1954

BI *"The Intruder",* s., est. $40/60, (02-12-93, DuMouchelle, #363), approx. 10 x 14 in., (25.4 x 35.6 cm.), engraving.

$198* *"Moving To New Hunting Grounds",* s., t., (02-27-93, Dunning, #118), 8¼ x 11¼ in., (21 x 28.6 cm.), etching (BP 139, DM 325, FR 1106, Y 23,374).

$165* *"My Name Is Polly" and "My Name Is Max": Two,* s., t., large margins, good cond., mat/light-staining, hinged to overmet w/tape, (10-28-92, Butterfield, #2847), each 9⅞ x 7⅞ in., (251 x 200 mm.), color etching on cream wove (BP 105, DM 255, FR 865, Y 20,245).

$44* *"Pretty Soft" and "In Conference": Two,* (02-27-93, Dunning, #118A), first 8 x 10½ in., (20.3 x 26.7 cm.), second 7½ x 10½ in., (20.3 x 26.7 cm.), print (BP 31, DM 72, FR 246, Y 5194).

PALERMO, Blinky German? 1943-1977

$7167* *12 Original Lithographien Zur Ausstellung Wandzeichnungen 1968 In Der Galerie Heiner Friedrich Munchen (Jahn 10), 1970: Twelve,* Edition Galerie Heiner Friedrich, #47/50, s., d., num., (05-27-93, Lempertz, #938, illus.), 20¹⁄₁₆ x 19⁵⁄₁₆ in., (51 x 49 cm.), lithograph on wove (BP 4590, DM 11,500, FR 38,761, Y 768,332).

$10,828* *12 Original-Lithographien (Jahn 10), 1970: Twelve,* Wamdzeichnungen in der Gsalerie Heiner Friedrich 1968 in Munchen, num., s., d., (11-28-92, Schoppmann, #686, illus.), 20¹⁄₁₆ x 19⁵⁄₁₆ in., (51 x 49 cm.), lithograph (BP 7147, DM 17,250, FR 58,561, Y 1,347,604).

$1299* *Dreiteilige Miniatur (Jahn 32), 1972,* s., d., num., (11-28-92, Schoppmann, #690), 2⅞ x 4⅝ in., (7.3 x 11.7 cm.), color folio relief print on handmade Aquarell (BP 857, DM 2069, FR 7025, Y 161,668).

$9023* *Funf Miniaturen. 5 (Wedewer S. 66/67),* s., num., impress., (11-28-92, Schoppmann, #687), 29⅛ x 1⁷⁄₁₆ in., (74 x 3.6 cm.), color print on handmade Aquarell (BP 5956, DM 14,375, FR 48,799, Y 1,122,962).

$1588* *Ohne Titel "Mit Komma" (Jahn 18), 1971,* s., d., num., (11-28-92, Grisebach, #688, illus.), 13¹⁄₁₆ x 21⅞ in., (33.2 x 55.5 cm.), colored serigraph on thin cardboard (BP 1048, DM 2530, FR 8588, Y 197,635).

$1154* *Ohne Titel (Oliv/Silbergrau) (Jahn 25), 1971,* #92/100, pencil s., d., num., (11-20-92, Lempertz, #752), sh 28¹⁵⁄₁₆ x 25¾ in., (73.5 x 65.4 cm.), color serigraph on white cardboard (BP 760, DM 1840, FR 6198, Y 143,514).

$866* *Projektion (1971) (Jahn 24), 1971,* s., d., num., (11-28-92, Schoppmann, #689), 7¹¹⁄₁₆ x 10¹⁄₁₆ in., (19.5 x 25.5 cm.), color offset on light cardboard (BP 572, DM 1380, FR 4684, Y 107,778).

$3032* *Untiled (Jahn 35), 1974,* s., d., num., from portfolio Amerikas Homage A Picasso, blindstamp v. Matthieu, mount staining, (11-28-92, Schoppmann, #688), 18⅞ x 13³⁄₁₆ in., (48 x 33.5 cm.), color granolithograph on handmade (BP 2001, DM 4830, FR 16,398, Y 377,349).

BI *Untitled, 1971,* s., d., #54/110, crease, est. DM 2,200, (09-18-92, Schloss Ahlden, #1040, illus.), 20¹³⁄₁₆ x 28¾ in., (52.9 x 73 cm.), color screen print on white board.

PALLANDRE, M.

$165* *"Thermes De Cauterets",* p. Camis, (08-05-92, Boos, #585), 39½ x 29½ in., (100.3 x 74.9 cm.), color lithograph (BP 86, DM 244, FR 823, Y 21,014).

PALMER, Samuel British 1805-1881

$905* *Christmas Or Folding The Last Sheep (Lister 4),* 4th state of 5, foxing, (10-27-92, Phillips-London, #46), sheet 8⅝ x 5¾ in., (219 x 146 mm.), etching on laid (BP 572, DM 1387, FR 4706, Y 110,703).

$4434* *Harvest,* edit. 50, privately p. Temple Sheen Press, January 1932, creased at center, damaged area, ex-coll., (12-03-92, Sotheby-London, #159, illus.), 1 x 3 in., (25 x 76 mm.), wood engraving on Japan (BP 2860, DM 6973, FR 23,800, Y 551,698).

BI *The Herdsman's Cottage (Lister 3),* second (final) state, margins, trimmed unevenly, paper flaw, surfacedirt, est. BP 2/300, (12-03-92, Sotheby-London, #160), 5 x 4 in., (127 x 102 mm.), etching.

$83* *"The Herdsman's Cottage",* good cond., (09-27-92, Bakker, #236), plate 4⅞ x 4 in., (12.4 x 10.2 cm.), etching (BP 48, DM 123, FR 416, Y 10,018).

$1219* *The Lonely Tower (L. 12), 1880,* 8th state, pub. R. Ansdell, full margins, foxed, waterstain, scuffed, cracking, (10-27-92, Phillips-London, #49), plate 7⅝ x 9½ in., (194 x 241 mm.), etching on japan (BP 770, DM 1868, FR 6339, Y 149,113).

$3240* *The Lonely Tower (Lister 12), 1879,* sixth state of seven, margins, defects, laid down, (12-03-92, Sotheby-London, #161), 7½ x 9¾ in., (191 x 248 mm.), etching (BP 2090, DM 5095, FR 17,391, Y 403,135).

BI *The Morning Of Life (L. 10), 1860,* 2nd state, stain, glue stains, est. BP 2/250, (10-27-92, Phillips-London, #48), image 5¼ x 8¼ in., (133 x 210 mm.), etching on chine applique on thick wove.

$990* *The Morning Of Life (Lister 10 VIII), 1869,* narrow margins, prov., ex-coll. Goulding (Lugt 999) and Edward G. Kennedy (Lugt 857), (12-08-92, Swann, #233, illus.), 5⁹⁄₁₆ x 8¹³⁄₁₆ in., (14.1 x 22.4 cm.), sepia etching on Japan (BP 620, DM 1541, FR 5255, Y 122,707).

$870* *Opening The Fold (Early Morning) (L. 13), 1880,* 5th state of 8, s., full margins, mounted at sheet edges, (10-27-92, Phillips-London, #47), plate 6½ x 9 in., (165 x 229 mm.), etching on wove (BP 550, DM 1333, FR 4524, Y 106,422).

$25* *"The Weary Poughman" (Lister 8 viii/viii), 1858,* pub. by the Etching Club, sun staining, plate mark broken through, paper remnant, (05-15-93, Cleveland, #418), 5³⁄₁₆ x 7¹⁵⁄₁₆ in., (13.2 x 20.2 cm.), etching on chine colle (BP 16, DM 40, FR 135, Y 2771).

PALMORE, Tom American 20th cent.

$385* *Cockatoo,* s., d., num. 45/120, (11-12-92, Freemn/Fine Art, #162), 34 x 25 in., (86.4 x 63.5 cm.), color litho (BP 253, DM 610, FR 2058, Y 47,737).

$248* *Cockatoo,* s., d. '80, #36/50, (06-11-93, Freemn/Fine Art, #162), 33¾ x 24¾ in., (85.7 x 62.9 cm.), lithograph (BP 163, DM 403, FR 1359, Y 26,313).

$330* *Massa,* s., (06-11-93, Freemn/Fine Art, #163), 25 x 19¾ in., (63.5 x 50.2 cm.), lithograph (BP 217, DM 536, FR 1808, Y 35,013).

PANAMARENKO b. 1940

$1731* *The Aeromodel, 1973-1976,* pencil s., d., artist proof, (11-20-92, Lempertz, #753), 39⁹⁄₁₆ x 32½ in., (100.5 x 82.5 cm.), color offset lithograph on board (BP 1140, DM 2760, FR 9296, Y 215,272).

$433* *Atom And Manpower (Van de Velde), 1975,* i. E.A., s., (11-28-92, Schoppmann, #693), 39⁹⁄₁₆ x 24⅞ in., (100.5 x 63.2 cm.), color offset on wove laid down on cardboard (BP 286, DM 690, FR 2342, Y 53,889).

BI *Atom And Manpower, 1975,* s., i., artist's proof, est. DM 1,000, (06-12-93, Hauswedell/Nolt, #322), 4⅛ x 25 in., (10.5 x 63.5 cm.), color offset on board.

PANKOK, Otto 1893-1966

$1127* *Angler Im Schilf (Zimmermann WH 632), 1960,* s. Otto Pankok, #1/9, (03-24-93, Venator/Hansten, #4546), image 14⅜ x 13⁹⁄₁₆ in., (36.5 x 34.5 cm.), color woodcut on hand-made (BP 763, DM 1841, FR 6265, Y 132,417).

$1623* *Blume (Zigeunermadchen) (Zimmermann-Jager WH 181), 1944,* s., (12-05-92, Bassenge, #7537), 4¼ x 3¹¹⁄₁₆ in., (10.8 x 9.3 cm.), color woodcut on handmade (BP 1016, DM 2530, FR 8624, Y 201,090).

$437* *Dahlien Und Sommerblumen In Vase (Zimmermann WH 546), 1958,* s., Otto Pankok, (03-24-93, Venator/Hansten, #4545), 11 x 4⁵⁄₁₆ in., (28 x 11 cm.), woodcut (BP 296, DM 714, FR 2429, Y 51,345).

$660* *Ehra Im Wind (Zimmermann WH 208), 1947,* block mono., s., light staining, (09-25-92, Granier, #2964), sheet 18¹⁵⁄₁₆ x 14³⁄₁₆ in., (48.2 x 36 cm.), woodcut on hand-made (BP 385, DM 978, FR 3308, Y 79,662).

$452* *Gorki (Zimmermann WH 235), 1947,* s., blindstamp, (06-10-93, Hauswedell/Nolt, #755), image 11¹³⁄₁₆ x 5¹³⁄₁₆ in., (30 x 14.8 cm.), woodcut on wove (BP 296, DM 736, FR 2478, Y 47,978).

$3541* *Herteli, Kopf (Jager WR 562), 1932,* s., (12-05-92, Bassenge, #7540, illus.), 13⁹⁄₁₆ x 9¾ in., (34.5 x 24.7 cm.), etching on handmade (BP 2217, DM 5521, FR 18,815, Y 438,731).

$705* *Katze,* (05-26-93, Lempertz, #402), 27¹⁄₁₆ x 12³⁄₁₆ in., (68.8 x 31 cm.), color lithograph on wove (BP 456, DM 1150, FR 3871, Y 76,597).

$986* *Lauschende Kinder (Zimmermann WH 213), 1947,* s. Otto Pankok, (03-24-93, Venator/Hansten, #4544), 11¾ x 5⅞ in., (29.8 x 15 cm.), color woodcut (BP 668, DM 1610, FR 5481, Y 115,850).

$530* *Lauschende Kinder (Zimmermann WH 213), 1947,* s., (06-10-93, Hauswedell/Nolt, #754), image 11¹³⁄₁₆ x 5¹⁵⁄₁₆ in., (30 x 15.1 cm.), color woodcut on wove (BP 347, DM 863, FR 2906, Y 56,257).

$1106* *Leuchtturm (Jager WR 228), 1921,* s., Die Schaffenden, III. Jg., 3. Mappe, (12-05-92, Bassenge, #7539), 9¹⁄₁₆ x 12⅜ in., (23 x 31.4 cm.), etching on handmade (BP 693, DM 1724, FR 5877, Y 137,034).

BI *Leuchtturm (Jager-Zimmermann WR 228), 1921,* s., est. DM 3,500, (06-05-93, Bassenge, #6413, illus.), 9¹⁄₁₆ x 12⅜ in., (23 x 31.4 cm.), etching on imitation Japan.

$1026* *Marabu (Zimmermann WH 232), 1942,* s., (11-13-92, Kunsthaus, #740), 11 x 5⅞ in., (28 x 15 cm.), woodcut on wove (BP 663, DM 1611, FR 5431, Y 127,343).

$279* *Mowe (Zimmermann WH 226), 1947,* s., (09-25-92, Granier, #2965), sheet 14⅛ x 18⅞ in., (35.8 x 48 cm.), woodcut on hand-made (BP 163, DM 414, FR 1398, Y 33,675).

$505* *"Die Nova-Mahala" (Zimmermann/Jager WH 537), 1957,* s., Kunstverein fur die Rheinlande und Westfalen, Dusseldorf, (11-28-92, Grisebach, #689, illus.), 23¹³⁄₁₆ x 16¼ in., (60.5 x 41.2 cm.), woodcut on handmade (BP 333, DM 805, FR 2731, Y 62,850).

$409* *Punxken (Zimmermann 260), 1948,* s., t. in plate, watermark, (05-26-93, Dorling, #2895), 5⅞ x 11⅞ in., (15 x 30.2 cm.), woodcut on wove (BP 265, DM 667, FR 2246, Y 44,437).

$210* *Rohlfs (Zimmermann WH 187), 1946,* block mono., (09-25-92, Granier, #2963), sheet 19½ x 13⁵⁄₁₆ in., (49.5 x 33.8 cm.), woodcut on Japan paper (BP 123, DM 311, FR 1053, Y 25,347).

$5901* *Strassenecke (Jager WR 215), 1921,* t., s., (12-05-92, Bassenge, #7538, illus.), 13⁵⁄₁₆ x 12½ in., (33.8 x 31.7 cm.), etching on wove (BP 3695, DM 9200, FR 31,355, Y 731,136).

$1026* *Wanderer Am Gebirgssee,* #19/60, s., (11-13-92, Kunsthaus, #741A), 21⅝ x 29¹⁵⁄₁₆ in., (55 x 76 cm.), lithograph on wove (BP 663, DM 1611, FR 5431, Y 127,343).

PANN, Arthur (after)

$80* *Sir Winston Churchill,* s., blindstamp, (03-17-93, Bonhams-Chelsea, #402), image 22½ x 30 in., (57.2 x 76.2 cm.), reprod. in colors (BP 55, DM 133, FR 452, Y 9383).

PANNAGGI, Ivo b. 1901

$861* *Potenza Della Moto,* #32/100, s., (03-25-93, Finarte-Rome, #34, illus.), lithograph in colors (BP 585, DM 1414, FR 4810, Y 100,867, L 1380).

PANNINI, J.P. (after) Italian

$220* *Rrine D'Un Aqueduc Antique,* by J. Moyreau, (05-16-93, Hindman, #426), 17 x 13½ in., (43.2 x 34.3 cm.), etching (BP 143, DM 354, FR 1189, Y 24,388).

PANUNZI, Benito

BI *Una Pulperia A La Frontera, c. 1865,* photog.'s credit, t., est. $7/1,000, (10-14-92, Swann, #221, illus.), 8½ x 11½ in., (21.6 x 29.2 cm.), photograph, albumen print.

BI *Toldos De Indios En La Pampa, c. 1865,* t., photog.'s credit, est. $7/1,000, (10-14-92, Swann, #220, illus.), 8½ x 12 in., (21.6 x 30.5 cm.), photograph, albumen print.

PAOLINI, Giulio Italian b. 1940

$926* *Belvedere, 1990,* artist's proof, s., d., (11-09-92, Finarte-Milan, #74), 17½ x 16¾ in., (44.5 x 42.5 cm.), photolithograph in colors (BP 612, DM 1478, FR 4995, Y 114,917, L 1265).

$1566* *Les Fausses Confidences: Twelve,* #XV/XX, s. on the colophon, ed. Einaudi, 1983, est. L. 2/3,000, (05-20-93, Finarte-Milan, #124), 18¹¹⁄₁₆ x 13⅜ in., (47.5 x 34 cm.), portfolio of 12 lithographs in colors (BP 1005, DM 2527, FR 8511, Y 172,924, L 2300).

$515* *Flora, 1985,* s., d., i. p.a. artist's proof, full margins, good cond., (06-30-93, Sotheby-London, #890), sh 27⅝ x 19⅞ in., (702 x 505 mm.), offset lithograph and collage in color on wove (BP 345, DM 878, FR 2963, Y 55,181).

$1347* *Il Modello Del Tempio Il Tempio Del Modello, 1986,* #XXVI/XXX, s., (11-09-92, Finarte-Milan, #66), 14¹⁵⁄₁₆ x 33⅞ in., (38 x 86 cm.), lithograph (BP 891, DM 2150, FR 7265, Y 167,163, L 1840).

$1431* *Il Tempio Della Sibilla, 1984,* #XXV/L, s., d., (11-09-92, Finarte-Milan, #81), 20½ x 33⁷⁄₁₆ in., (52 x 85 cm.), lithograph (BP 946, DM 2284, FR 7718, Y 177,587, L 1955).

$1263* *Osservatorio, 1988,* #XXI/XXX, s., d., (11-09-92, Finarte-Milan, #93), 10⅝ x 27¹⁵⁄₁₆ in., (27 x 71 cm.), lithograph (BP 835, DM 2016, FR 6812, Y 156,739, L 1725).

$2778* *Untitled,* #17/99, s., (11-09-92, Finarte-Milan, #84, illus.), 38¹⁵⁄₁₆ x 53⅜ in., (99 x 135.5 cm.), lithograph and photolithograph in colors (BP 1837, DM 4435, FR 14,984, Y 344,751, L 3795).

PAOLOZZI, Eduardo Italian/British b. 1924

$1320* *As Is When, 1965: Ten,* portfolio, each s., d., num. 52/65, pub. Editions Electo, London, each bears chop mark, (09-20-92, Hindman, #796, illus.), overall 39 x 27 in., (99.1 x 68.6 cm.), color serigraphs (BP 773, DM 1959, FR 6701, Y 163,144).

$581* *"Colour Theory Experiment", 1979,* s., d., num., (12-01-92, Karl/Faber, #1076), 14⁹⁄₁₆ x 10¹⁄₁₆ in., (37 x 25.5 cm.), color offset print on rough wove (BP 384, DM 926, FR 3156, Y 72,336).

BI *Hors Concours (Miles 162), 1974,* s., d. 1974, num. 13/70, pub. Marlborough Graphics, good cond., est.BP 1/200, (11-30-92, Phillips-London, #556), sheet 39½ x 30 in., (100.3 x 76.2 cm.), screenprint in colors on Vellin Arches.

$597* *Pop Art Redefined, 1971,* s., #46/100, full margins, good cond., (12-03-92, Sotheby-London, #774, illus.), 14½ x 7½ in., (370 x 190 mm.), screenprint in colors w/collage on wove (BP 385, DM 939, FR 3205, Y 74,281).

$158* *Quadrum Dax, 1973,* s., d., num., (12-01-92, Karl/Faber, #1074), 34¼ x 26¾ in., (87 x 68 cm.), color serigraph on rough wove (BP 104, DM 252, FR 858, Y 19,671).

$216* *Who's Afraid Of Sugar Pink And Lime Green, (V. & A. Museum, cat. 100), 1971,* s., d., i. A.P., artist proof, pub. by Jacobson Ltd., margins, creases, surface dirt, scratches, L. 1443 x 1040 mm, (12-01-92, Christie-London, #624), screenprint in colors on Hollingsworth mouldmade paper (BP 143, DM 344, FR 1173, Y 26,892).

BI *Who's Afraid Of Sugar Pink And Lime Green? (Miles 100), 1971,* s., d., num. 73/100, from series 14 Big Prints, p. by Advanced Graphics, pub. Bernard Jacobson, time-stained, est. BP 2/300, (11-30-92, Phillips-London, #555), sheet 60¼ x 43¾ in., (153 x 111.1 cm.), screenprint in colors on Hollingsworth wove.

PAONE, Peter American 20th cent.

$88* *Ms. Dutchmaster,* s., num. 31/100, (11-12-92, Freemn/Fine Art, #164), 28 x 20 in., (71.1 x 50.8 cm.), color litho (BP 58, DM 139, FR 470, Y 10,911).

PAPART, Max French b. 1911

$268* *Composition,* s., (04-17-93, Falkkloos, #446), 23¼ x 19¹¹⁄₁₆ in., (59 x 50 cm.), etching in colors (BP 174, DM 429, FR 1448, Y 29,801, SK 1980).

$179* *Composition,* s., 18/99, (04-17-93, Falkkloos, #445), 26⅜ x 19⁵⁄₁₆ in., (67 x 49 cm.), color etching w/relief (BP 116, DM 286, FR 967, Y 19,904, SK 1320).

$145* *"Composition Ovale": Two,* s. artist's proof, (06-28-93, Loudmer, #326), larger 27³⁄₁₆ x 18⅞ in., (690 x 480 mm.), smaller 22¹³⁄₁₆ x 17⅛ in., (690 x 480 mm.), color lithographs on Arches wove (BP 97, DM 246, FR 830, Y 15,385).

BI *Composition, c. 1956,* s., #72/180, est. FF1,800/2,000, (05-27-93, Briest, #155), 28¹⁵⁄₁₆ x 20½ in., (73.5 x 52 cm.), color lithograph.

BI *Manhattan In Red,* s., #49/95, full margins, good cond., est. Dfl. 700/1,000, (05-27-93, Sotheby-Amstrdm, #670), 19 x 23¾ in., color etching w/embossing on wove.

BI *"Moonlight",* s. Max Papart, #33/95, prov., est. $1/1,500, (12-12-92, A. James, #150), 27¼ x 24¼ in., (69.2 x 61.6 cm.), aquatint.

BI *Morning,* s., #70/75, margins, good cond., est. Dfl. 700/1,000, (05-27-93, Sotheby-Amstrdm, #671), 17³⁄₁₆ x 21⁹⁄₁₆ in., (437 x 547 mm.), color etching w/embossing on wove.

$280* *"Personnage Avec Chien" and "Pianiste": Two,* s. artist's proof, (06-28-93, Loudmer, #327), first 19⅛ x 19⅛ in., (485 x 485 mm.), second 19¹¹⁄₁₆ x 25¹³⁄₁₆ in., (485 x 485 mm.), color lithograph, first, on Japan; second, BFK Rives wove (BP 187, DM 476, FR 1603, Y 29,708).

$248* *Specimen,* s., t., (05-16-93, Hindman, #507), 23¼ x 19⅝ in., (59.1 x 49.8 cm.), color lithograph (BP 161, DM 399, FR 1341, Y 27,491).

$88* *Untitled,* s., num. 94/150, (09-20-92, Hindman, #817), 20 x 26 in., (50.8 x 66 cm.), lithograph (BP 52, DM 131, FR 447, Y 10,876).

PAPPE, Carl American 20th cent.

$330* *"Mexican Stone Cutter", "La Concepcion-Coyoacan" and "Tepetates-Cuernavaca", 1936: Three,* each s., Mexican Stone Cutter d. 1936, num. 9/18, i., La Conception &Tepetates annot. Imp, i., each mono. in plate, full margins, good cond., staining, Tepetates laid down, Mexican Stone Cutter & La Concepcion glued down, (02-24-93, Butterfield, #2864), from 13¼ x 11½ in., (337 x 292 mm.), to 15⅜ x 11½ in., (337 x 292 mm.), woodcut on tissue (BP 230, DM 536, FR 1816, Y 38,723).

$110* *Portfolio "Taxco": Six,* s. Carl Pappe in matrix, t., annot., creases, handling marks, water stains, edges torn, (06-26-93, Skinner, #131), sh. 13⅜ x 16 in., (34 x 40.6 cm.), screenprint in black on wove, portfolio cover w/additional screenprint (BP 74, DM 187, FR 630, Y 11,671).

PAPPRILL, Henry A.

$11,500* *New York From The Steeple Of St. Paul's Church, Looking East, South And West (S. & H. P. 1848-E-119; D. 578), c. 1848,* 2nd state of 3, after J.W. Hill, pub. Henry J. Megarey 1849, small margins, good cond., repaired tear into image, mat/water stain, tape hinge, skinning, (01-28-93, Sotheby-NY, #434, illus.), 26⅜ x 40⅛ in., (67 x 101.9 cm.), sheet 27 x 40¾ in., (67 x 101.9 cm.), color aquatint w/additional hand-coloring (BP 7594, DM 18,222, FR 61,662, Y 1,427,862).

$5175* *New York, Taken From The North West Angle Of Fort Columbus, Governor's Island (S. & H. 1846-E-121; D. 531), 1844,* 1st state of 2, after Frederick Catherwood, pub. Henry J. Megarey 1846, margins, good cond., tears, 1 extending into image, light-stain, soiling, remnants tape, skinning, soiling, (01-28-93, Sotheby-NY, #433, illus.), image 16⅝ x 26¾ in., (422 x 679 mm.), sheet 20¼ x 28⅜ in., (422 x 679 mm.), hand-colored aquatint in white wove (BP 3417, DM 8200, FR 27,748, Y 642,538).

PARADISE, Phil American b. 1905

BI *"Thomas" and "Maria",* AAA edit., s., est. $4/600, (05-15-93, Cleveland, #260, illus.), 13 x 8½ in., (33 x 21.6 cm.), lithograph.

PARC, Julio le Argentinian b. 1928

$784* *Couleurs No. 1, 1971: Eight,* #44/200, s., Edition Denise Rene, (09-04-92, Germann, #507), each 29⅛ x 29⅛ in., (740 x 740 mm.), color serigraph (BP 393, DM 1099, FR 3740, Y 96,504, SF 978).

PARDES, A. de and H. ALKEN (after)

$358* *Untitled: Two Pairs,* (09-21-92, Selkirk, #187), 10½ x 14¾ in., (26.7 x 37.5 cm.), (26.7 x 37.5 cm.), colored lithograph (BP 210, DM 531, FR 1817, Y 44,247).

PAREDES, V. de (after)

$125 *Military Figures And Their Ladies By A River,* (12-11-92, G.A. Key, #18), 18 x 29 in., (45.7 x 73.7 cm.), photogravure (BP 80, DM 197, FR 675, Y 15,468).

PARENT, A.

$201* *Les Chansons De Beranger. "Publiees Pour La Premiere Fois",* Imp. P. Dupont, good cond., (02-12-93, Cheval/Robert, #123), 57⅞ x 42¹¹⁄₁₆ in., (147 x 108.5 cm.), poster (BP 142, DM 333, FR 1128, Y 24,240).

PARK, Bertram 1883-1972

BI *"Breton Fishing Boats, Newlyn", c. 1930,* mounted on card, front s.; t., label, (c) limitation, 357 x 260mm, est. BP 800/1,200, (05-07-93, Sotheby-London, #158, illus.), photograph, silver print.

$2179* *C.R.W. Nevinson, 1919,* labels, exhib., sight 285 x 225mm, (05-07-93, Sotheby-London, #150, illus.), photograph, silver print (BP 1380, DM 3445, FR 11,609, Y 239,925).

BI *Corsica And France, Landscapes: Twenty-Three,* 1920s and 1930s, majority mounted on paper and card, s., labels, some t., majority approx. 270 x 360mm, est. BP 800/1,200, (05-07-93, Sotheby-London, #156, illus.), photograph, matt warm toned silver print.

BI *English Scenes: Five,* 1930s-40s, majority mounted on card and paper, front s.; t., labels,approx. 270 x 350mm, est. BP 3/400, (05-07-93, Sotheby-London, #159, illus.), photograph, matt warm toned silver print.

$1453* *"An Impression Of Oxford", 1906,* mounted on paper, 221 x 292mm, (05-07-93, Sotheby-London, #145, illus.), photograph, platinum print (BP 920, DM 2297, FR 7741, Y 159,987).

$453* *A Male And A Female Nude, c. 1930: Seven Studio Studies,* mounted on paper, each front s., labels, (c) limitation stamps, eachapprox. 369 x 255mm, (05-07-93, Sotheby-London, #155), photograph, matt warm toned silver print (BP 287, DM 716, FR 2413, Y 49,879).

$763* *Male Nudes: Three,* 1930s, mounted on card, s., label, each approx. 360 x 272mm, (05-07-93, Sotheby-London, #151), photograph, matt warm toned silver print (BP 483, DM 1206, FR 4065, Y 84,012).

$1453* *"Mesopotamia, Oxford, 1906",* mounted on card, t., d., annot., exhib., label, 224 x 300mm, (05-07-93, Sotheby-London, #144), photograph, platinum print (BP 920, DM 2297, FR 7741, Y 159,987).

$654* *Montage Nudes: Six,* 1930s, majority mounted on paper, front s.; t., labels, each approx.380 x 270mm, (05-07-93, Sotheby-London, #161), photograph, matt warm toned silver print (BP 414, DM 1034, FR 3484, Y 72,011).

$327* *Mountain Scenes, c. 1925: Eleven,* mounted on paper and card, majority t., s., labels, majority approx.350 x 260mm, (05-07-93, Sotheby-London, #147), photograph, matt warm toned silver print (BP 207, DM 517, FR 1742, Y 36,005).

$3088* *Nude Studies, c. 1930: Four,* mounted on card, one front s., labels, various sizes, (05-07-93, Sotheby-London, #157), photograph, color process print (BP 1955, DM 4882, FR 16,452, Y 340,013).

$1361* *Nude Studies: Fourteen,* 1930s, majority mounted on card or paper, s., t., labels, (c) limitation, various sizes, (05-07-93, Sotheby-London, #153), photograph, matt warm toned silver print (BP 862, DM 2152, FR 7251, Y 149,857).

$453* *Nudes In Nature, c. 1930: Four,* mounted on card, front s., photog.'s label, labels, each approx. 365x 265mm, (05-07-93, Sotheby-London, #162), photograph, matt warm toned silver print (BP 287, DM 716, FR 2413, Y 49,879).

BI *Portrait Of A Woman, c. 1920,* mounted on card, blindstamp, label, 385 x 341mm, est. BP 4/600, (05-07-93, Sotheby-London, #148), photograph, gelatin silver print.

$908* *Portrait Of Ward Muir, 1920,* labels, exhib., sight 287 x 225mm, (05-07-93, Sotheby-London, #152, illus.), photograph, silver print (BP 575, DM 1436, FR 4838, Y 99,978).

$327* *Siena: Seven,* 1930s, majority mounted on card, front s., labels, majority approx. 360 x 270mm, (05-07-93, Sotheby-London, #146), photograph, matt warm toned silver print (BP 207, DM 517, FR 1742, Y 36,005).

$1361* *Ten Montage Nudes And Three Friezes,* 1930s, majority mounted on card, s., t., labels verso, photog.'s limitation stamp, from 365 x 290mm to 76 x 375mm, (05-07-93, Sotheby-London, #154, illus.), photograph, matt warm toned silver print (BP 862, DM 2152, FR 7251, Y 149,857).

$1090* *"Torso Design No. 1", c. 1935,* mounted on paper, front s.; t., label, 361 x 285mm, (05-07-93, Sotheby-London, #160, illus.), photograph, matt warm toned silver print (BP 690, DM 1723, FR 5807, Y 120,018).

$1361* *Views Of French Chateaux: Twenty-Nine,* 1930s, mounted on paper and card, several t., s., labels, annots., each approx. 360 x 270mm, (05-07-93, Sotheby-London, #149, illus.), photograph, matt warm toned silver print (BP 862, DM 2152, FR 7251, Y 149,857).

PARKER, Cushman

$35 *Little Americans Do Your Bit,* for U.S. Food Administration, No. 21, (09-24-92, Alderfer, #247), 21 x 14 in., (53.3 x 35.6 cm.), (BP 20, DM 52, FR 176, Y 4210).

PARKER, Olivia

$805* *"After The Barn Door",* 1980, p. 1982, s., d., (05-23-93, Butterfield, #3561, illus.), 9½ x 7½ in., photograph, dye-transfer print (BP 524, DM 1316, FR 4430, Y 88,980).

$468* *"Hiatus", 1982/1989,* s., t., d., edit. 18/50, ink neg. num., Dixon Collection, (11-16-92, Butterfield, #6118, illus.), 9¾ x 7¾ in., (248.1 x 197.2 mm.), photograph, split-toned gelatin silver print (BP 308, DM 746, FR 2513, Y 58,202).

PARKINSON, Norman   1913-1990

$2746* *British Airways Electra, n.d. c. 1937,* (10-29-92, Christie-London, #158, illus.), 12 x 16½ in., (30.5 x 41.9 cm.), photograph, gelatin silver print (BP 1760, DM 4225, FR 14,332, Y 340,146).

$1373* *"Changing Of The Guard", Late 1970s,* ink s. recto, Jocelyn Kargere Coll., (10-29-92, Christie-London, #169, illus.), image 14 x 11½ in., (35.6 x 29.2 cm.), photograph, gelatin silver print (BP 880, DM 2112, FR 7166, Y 170,073).

$1925* *Country Picnic, 1949 (Fifty Years of Style and Fashion, p. 9),* s., d. by photog. in ink on image, p. l., (10-15-92, Sotheby-NY, #435A, illus.), 19⅝ x 15½ in., (49.8 x 39.4 cm.), photograph, gelatin silver print (BP 1178, DM 2865, FR 9717, Y 230,954).

$1542* *Fashion Study, Striped Jacket, 1937-38,* mounted on card, s., ink stamp, only vintage print known to exist, (05-06-93, Christie-London, #103, illus.), 11½ x 4½ in., photograph, gelatin silver print (BP 977, DM 2429, FR 8176, Y 169,656).

$1816* *"The Headless Tulip Dress 1938",* mounted on card, t., s., d., stamped photog.'s credit Can-Can Limited, Ref. NPV 0150, 340 x 280mm, (05-07-93, Sotheby-London, #322, illus.), photograph, silver print (BP 1150, DM 2871, FR 9675, Y 199,956).

$2300* *"The New Mayfair Edwardians, Savile Row" (Style and Fashion, p. 67),* s., d. by photog., 1948, p.l., (04-06-93, Sotheby-NY, #365, illus.), 19⅜ x 15⅜ in., photograph (BP 1519, DM 3705, FR 12,548, Y 262,318).

BI *"Under The Influenece Of Charles James", 1938,* mounted on card, s., t., d., ink stamp, only vintage print known to exist, est. BP 1/1,500, (05-06-93, Christie-London, #104, illus.), 13 x 10 in., photograph, gelatin silver print.

BI *Wenda And Dog, 1949,* p.l., s., d. '49, Jocelyn Kargere Coll., est. BP 8/1,000, (10-29-92, Christie-London, #168, illus.), image 11½ x 9 in., (29.2 x 22.9 cm.), photograph, gelatin silver print.

$1725* *Wenda In London,* s., d. by photog., 1948, p.l., (04-06-93, Sotheby-NY, #364, illus.), photograph (BP 1139, DM 2779, FR 9411, Y 196,738).

$1452* *"Wenda In Portugal", 1946,* s., t., d., (05-06-93, Christie-London, #105, illus.), 15 x 12 in., photograph, gelatin silver print (BP 920, DM 2287, FR 7699, Y 159,754).

PARKINSON, Thomas (after)

$350* *Mr. Shutter, Mr. Quick & Mrs. Green In She Stoops To Conquer, 1776,* by Robert Laurie, from the series, proof, trimmed to image, repairedtears, (11-30-92, Phillips-London, #120), sheet 17½ x 21⅞ in., (445 x 556 mm.), mezzotint on laid (BP 231, DM 558, FR 1893, Y 43,559).

PARKS, Gordon   American b. 1912

BI *Hosiery Studies, c. 1950: Two,* stamps, est. $1/1,500, (10-13-92, Christie-NY, #478, illus.), one 9½ x 7⅝ in., (24.1 x 19.4 cm.), other 7¾ x 7⅝ in., (24.1 x 19.4 cm.), photograph, gelatin silver prints.

PARLOSKY, Vladimir

$43* *Two Peacocks By A Fountain,* s., margins, surface dirt, (08-20-92, Bonhams-Chelsea, #161), plate 10¾ x 13¾ in., (27.3 x 34.9 cm.), etching (BP 22, DM 62, FR 211, Y 5430).

PARRISH, Maxfield   American 1870-1966

$275* *Arcadian Musicians, c. 1920,* Rod Stewart Coll., (11-06-92, Sotheby-Arcade, #141), 18 x 30 in., (45.7 x 76.2 cm.), lithograph in colors (BP 180, DM 439, FR 1484, Y 33,942).

$165* *Daybreak, 1923,* pub. House of Art, (06-11-93, Freemn/Fine Art, #164), 17¼ x 29½ in., (43.8 x 74.9 cm.), offset lithograph (BP 108, DM 268, FR 904, Y 17,507).

$275* *Garden Of Allah,* (07-17-92, DuMouchelle, #50), 15¼ x 30 in., (38.7 x 76.2 cm.), print (BP 141, DM 401, FR 1355, Y 34,187).

BI *"Poster Show Perma. Fine Arts",* est. $2/300, (10-16-92, DuMouchelle, #1305, illus.), 13¼ x 10¼ in., (33.7 x 26 cm.), poster.

$193* *"Poster Show Perma.Fine Arts",* (01-15-93, DuMouchelle, #1303), 13¼ x 10¼ in., (33.7 x 26 cm.), poster (BP 126, DM 316, FR 1067, Y 24,332).

BI *Stars,* est. BP 80/120, (02-17-93, Bonhams-Chelsea, #360), image 9¾ x 6 in., (24.8 x 15.2 cm.), color photolithograph.

PARRISH, Stephen   American 1846-1938

$17* *November,* margins, plate s., (05-22-93, Collins, #3), 5½ x 10½ in., (14 x 26.7 cm.), etching (BP 11, DM 28, FR 93, Y 1874).

PARROTT, William

$3053* *London From The Thames: Twelve,* pub. Henry Brooks, 1841, margins, staining, (06-16-93, Bonhams-Chelsea, #393, illus.), 14 x 20 in., (35.6 x 50.8 cm.), hand-colored lithograph (BP 2035, DM 5068, FR 17,008, Y 325,619).

PARRY, Roger   1905-1977

$1725* *Photogram With Feather, 1928-30,* s., d. by Madeline Parry, (04-08-93, Christie-NY, #220, illus.), 9½ x 7⅛ in., (24.1 x 18.1 cm.), photograph, gelatin silver print (BP 1131, DM 2771, FR 9380, Y 195,756).

PARSONS, C.

$330* *Steamer Herman,* discoloration, staining, foxing in image, creasing, (11-12-92, Freemn/Fine Art, #166), mat 24 x 34 in., (61 x 86.4 cm.), litho (BP 217, DM 523, FR 1764, Y 40,918).

PARTEOUS, R.H.

$75 *Women! Help America's Sons,* Edwards and Deutsch, No. 11, edge damage, (09-24-92, Alderfer, #307, illus.),

30 x 20 in., (76.2 x 50.8 cm.), (BP 44, DM 111, FR 377, Y 9022).

PARTRIDGE, Roi   American 1888-1984

$858* *Al Bordo Del Campo (W. 127), 1922*, s., t., margins, good cond., mat staining, hinge remains, surface soiling, (10-28-92, Butterfield, #2540), 7 x 8⅝ in., (178 x 219 mm.), etching on laid paper, watermark (BP 547, DM 1325, FR 4499, Y 105,276).

$330* *Born In Cedarville (W. 261), 1946-48)*, s., full margins, good cond., (02-24-93, Butterfield, #2653), 7¹⁵⁄₁₆ x 10¹⁄₁₆ in., (202 x 256 mm.), etching of F.J. Head & Co. laid (BP 230, DM 536, FR 1816, Y 38,723).

BI *"Curvilinear Contrast", 1935*, s., t., d. by photog., est. $2/3,000, (04-06-93, Sotheby-NY, #190, illus.), 13¾ x 10¾ in., photograph.

$385* *Dancing Water (W. 19), 1911*, s., margins, good cond., (02-24-93, Butterfield, #2650), 13 x 9⁹⁄₁₆ in., (330 x 243 mm.), etching on wove (BP 268, DM 625, FR 2119, Y 45,177).

$275* *Grupos De Arboles (W. 128), 1922*, s., full margins, very good cond., creases, surface soiling, (10-28-92, Butterfield, #2541), 5 x 6⅝ in., (127 x 168 mm.), etching on laid paper, watermark (BP 175, DM 425, FR 1442, Y 33,742).

BI *Mesembrianthemum, c. 1935*, s., t., est. $1,2/1,800, (04-08-93, Christie-NY, #394, illus.), 9¾ x 8⅛ in., (24.8 x 20.6 cm.), photograph, gelatin silver print.

$220* *Northcoast (W. 169), 1926*, margins, glued along edges, very good cond., (10-28-92, Butterfield, #2543), 10 x 11¹⁵⁄₁₆ in., (254 x 303 mm.), etching on cream wove (BP 140, DM 340, FR 1154, Y 26,994).

$275* *On The Range (W. 223), 1932-34*, s., margins, good cond., mat staining, staining, (02-24-93, Butterfield, #2652), 9⅞ x 13⅞ in., (251 x 352 mm.), etching on laid (BP 192, DM 446, FR 1513, Y 32,269).

BI *Organization Of Interpenetrating Geometric Planes, 1938*, s., t., d., credit stamp, est. $2/3,000, (04-08-93, Christie-NY, #395, illus.), 10⅞ x 9⅝ in., (27.6 x 24.4 cm.), photograph, gelatin silver print.

$2070* *"Rhythmic Forms", c. 1935*, mounted, s., t. by photog., (04-06-93, Sotheby-NY, #189, illus.), 10¾ x 8⅝ in., photograph (BP 1367, DM 3335, FR 11,293, Y 236,086).

$880* *Sierra Slopes (W. 134), 1922-23*, s., t., d., large margins, good cond., light/glue staining, (10-28-92, Butterfield, #2542), 4¹⁵⁄₁₆ x 5⅞ in., (125 x 149 mm.), etching on oatmeal laid paper, watermark (BP 561, DM 1359, FR 4615, Y 107,975).

$303* *Snowfields (W. 182), 1927*, s., d. in plate, Roi Partridge, Mills College sticker, good cond., tears, surface soiling, mat staining, taped to backboard, (02-24-93, Butterfield, #2651), 15 x 12 in., (381 x 305 mm.), etching on handmade laid paper (BP 211, DM 492, FR 1668, Y 35,555).

BI *Two Of A Kind, 1930s*, s., t., est., $3/5,000, (10-13-92, Christie-NY, #325, illus.), 9¾ x 7¾ in., (24.8 x 19.7 cm.), photograph, gelatin silver print.

$495* *Up North (W. 180), 1927*, s., full margins, good cond., mat staining, glue remains, (10-28-92, Butterfield, #2544, illus.), 7 x 8⅜ in., (178 x 213 mm.), etching on laid paper (BP 315, DM 764, FR 2596, Y 60,736).

PASCHKE, Ed   American b. 1939

$1100* *Hairy Shoes (Adrian/Born 236), 1971*, s., t., #16/30, chop mark, stamp, (03-14-93, Hindman, #338), 10⅛ x 13¼ in., (25.7 x 33.7 cm.), color lithograph on BFK Rives (BP 767, DM 1831, FR 6225, Y 129,641).

BI *Hubert (Adrian/Born 240), 1976-77*, s., d. '76, t., #21/35, pub. Landfall Press, est. $800/1,200, (05-16-93, Hindman, #644), 29 x 23 in., (73.7 x 58.4 cm.), color lithograph on Arches Cover white.

BI *Klaus (Adrian/Born 242), 1976*, s., d. 76, t., #6/35, pub. Landfall Press, est. $800/1,200, (05-16-93, Hindman, #643), 28¾ x 23 in., (73 x 58.4 cm.), color lithograph on Arches cover white.

BI *Tudor (Adrian/Born 244), 1976-77*, s., d. '76, t., #6/35, pub. Landfall Press, est. $800/1,200, (05-16-93, Hindman, #645), 28¾ x 23 in., (73 x 58.4 cm.), color lithograph on Arches cover white.

PASCIN, F.   French 20th cent.

BI *Le Divan*, est. $2/400, (02-14-93, Hanzel, #673), 6 x 7⅜ in., (15.2 x 18.7 cm.), restrike etching.

BI *Le Divan*, restrike, est. $2/300, (11-01-92, Hanzel, #223), 6 x 7⅜ in., (15.2 x 18.7 cm.), etching.

PASCIN, Jules   French/American 1885-1930

$759* *Charmante Soiree (H. 154), 1929*, whole margins, #69/100, s., (06-11-93, Picard, #144), 12¹³⁄₁₆ x 9⅝ in., (325 x 245 mm.), drypoint and aquatint in black on wove (BP 499, DM 1234, FR 4159, Y 80,531).

$333* *Cinderella*, plate s., stains, (11-30-92, Phillips-London, #470), plate 9⅞ x 13⅞ in., (251 x 352 mm.), color etching w/aquatint on wove (BP 220, DM 531, FR 1801, Y 41,444).

$600* *Cubains (Hemin/Krohg/Perls/Rambert 76), 1917*, stamped, sig., #13/100, full margins, good cond., tape, (06-30-93, Sotheby-London, #579), 7 x 7⅞ in., (178 x 200 mm.), drypoint on wove (BP 402, DM 1023, FR 3452, Y 64,288).

BI *Dans Le Parc (Rigal 43), 1910*, s., ded., est. DM 1,200, (12-05-92, Bassenge, #7541), 2¹⁵⁄₁₆ x 3¹⁵⁄₁₆ in., (7.5 x 10 cm.), drypoint and soft-ground etching on handmade.

$165* *"Le Divan"*, atelier stamp, full margins, excell. cond., (05-07-93, Goldberg, #427), 6 x 7½ in., (15.2 x 19.1 cm.), color etching (BP 104, DM 261, FR 879, Y 18,168).

$294* *"Le Lever", 1925*, s. in pl., drystamp, annot., (01-28-93, Pescheteau, #229), 14³⁄₁₆ x 11 in., (36 x 28 cm.), black lithograph on Japan (BP 194, DM 466, FR 1576, Y 36,504).

BI *Salome, Salome (Hemin, Krohg, Perls and Rambert III, 145), 1927*, t., sig. stamp, 17/100, est. FF4/6,000, (06-28-93, Loudmer, #328), 9⁷⁄₁₆ x 12⅜ in., (240 x 315 mm.), sh 14⅞ x 22⁵⁄₁₆ in., (240 x 315 mm.), etching and champleve on Arches wove.

$500* *Two Nudes*, s., num. 23/60, good cond., (11-30-92, Phillips-London, #469), plate 7 x 7⅛ in., (178 x 181 mm.), aquatint w/etching (BP 330, DM 797, FR 2704, Y 62,228).

$1210* *Two Women In A Brothel, c. 1920*, s., margins, paper flaws, (05-27-93, Swann, #211, illus.), 7 x 7 in., (17.8 x 17.8 cm.), drypoint and soft ground(?) on time-stained cream wove (BP 775, DM 1942, FR 6544, Y 129,717).

$639* *Une, Deux, Trois, Quatre Dames (Hemin 118), 1924*, whole margins, #60/100, s., (06-11-93, Picard, #143), 7¹⁄₁₆ x 7¼ in., (180 x 184 mm.), drypoint in black on wove (BP 420, DM 1039, FR 3501, Y 67,798).

PASGRIMAUD, Daniel

$19* *"Bogart", 1983 and "Platine", 1983*, s., t.; first, 34/40; second, DL, (06-28-93, Loudmer, #103), first 9⁷⁄₁₆ x 7 in., (239 x 178 mm.), second 5⅛ x 5⅞ in., (239 x 178 mm.), mezzotints in black on wove (BP 13, DM 32, FR 109, Y 2016).

PASMORE, Victor   English b. 1908

$880* *3 Images*, s., d. 75, #55/90, prov., (05-16-93, Hindman, #577), 25¾ x 20 in., (65.4 x 50.8 cm.), etching and aquatint (BP 572, DM 1415, FR 4757, Y 97,550).

$604* *"Abstract Study"*, #40/70, s., d. '84, (02-17-93, Bonhams-Chelsea, #309), image 17½ x 16½ in., (44.5 x 41.9 cm.), screenprint on wove (BP 418, DM 981, FR 3322, Y 72,145).

$375* *Apollo 2*, s., d. '85, (04-22-93, Bonhams-Chelsea, #148), subject 26 x 34¾ in., (66 x 88.3 cm.), screenprint (BP 242, DM 603, FR 2033, Y 41,231).

$375* *Apollo I*, s., d. '85, (04-22-93, Bonhams-Chelsea, #147), subject 26 x 34¾ in., (66 x 88.3 cm.), screenprint (BP 242, DM 603, FR 2033, Y 41,231).

BI *Black Tiger*, #59/70, s., d. '79, est. BP 250/350, (12-10-92, Bonhams-Chelsea, #124), sheet 31¼ x 47½ in., (79.4 x 120.7 cm.), screenprint.

$613* *Blue Fantasy II*, #70/70, s., d. '86, (04-22-93, Bonhams-Chelsea, #145), (87.6 x 102.9 cm.), screenprint (BP 396, DM 985, FR 3322, Y 67,400).

BI *"Cave Of Calypso II", 1978*, init., d. VP 78, #90/90, very good cond., est. $7/900, (03-12-93, Skinner, #108, illus.), sight 39 x 38⅝ in., (99.1 x 98.1 cm.), etching and aquatint on wove.

$67* *Composition,* inits., d. '66, num. 8/70, very good cond., (11-30-92, Phillips-London, #558), sheet 30⅞ x 23¼ in., (784 x 591 mm.), lithograph in black on J. Green wove (BP 44, DM 107, FR 362, Y 8339).

BI *Composition,* inits., good cond., est. BP 150/250, (10-27-92, Phillips-London, #218), sheet 23⅝ x 28⅞ in., (600 x 733 mm.), color screenprint on wove.

$512* *The Dance Of Modern Man, 1972,* portfolio, text and just., pub. 2RC, (12-03-92, Sotheby-London, #775, illus.), nine aquatints in colors on C.M. Fabriano wove (BP 330, DM 805, FR 2748, Y 63,705).

$1212* *Owl Of Mirerva, 1978,* #11/90, s., mono., d. '78, prov., (11-16-92, Hodgins, #116), 39 x 38½ in., (99.1 x 97.8 cm.), color etching on paper (BP 797, DM 1933, FR 6513, Y 151,254, C$ 1540).

BI *Points Of Contact No. 1 (Pasmore Werkverzeichnis G 2), 1965,* #11/70, mono., signs of wear, 680mm x 1010mm, est. SF 9/1,200, (04-21-93, Germann, #669, illus.), color serigraph.

$1544* *The Pulse, 1985,* init., d., #44/90, pub. 2RC, margins, good cond., (06-30-93, Sotheby-London, #887, illus.), sh c. 15¾ x 99¾ in., (40 x 253.4 cm.), color aquatint on wove (BP 1035, DM 2633, FR 8884, Y 165,434).

$1286* *Senza Titolo 10, 1989,* init., d., #46/90, pub. 2RC, margins, good cond., (06-30-93, Sotheby-London, #889), sh c. 35½ x 100¾ in., (90.2 x 255.9 cm.), color aquatint (BP 862, DM 2193, FR 7399, Y 137,791).

$195* *Unititled (Kelpra 7826),* inits., d. '71, num. 74/75, full margins, surface soiling, tape, (11-30-92, Phillips-London, #557), sheet 28 x 27¾ in., (711 x 705 mm.), lithograph in colors (BP 129, DM 311, FR 1055, Y 24,269).

$440* *Untitled,* s., d. '82, #41/90, (05-16-93, Hindman, #509), 24¼ x 30 in., (61.6 x 76.2 cm.), color lithograph (BP 286, DM 708, FR 2378, Y 48,775).

$307* *Untitled III,* #XII/XXI, s., d. '88, (04-22-93, Bonhams-Chelsea, #146), subject 33 x 44 in., (83.8 x 111.8 cm.), screenprint (BP 198, DM 493, FR 1664, Y 33,755).

$1716* *Untitled, 1986,* init., d., #36/90, margins, good cond., (06-30-93, Sotheby-London, #888), sh c. 30¼ x 90 in., (76.8 x 228.6 cm.), color aquatint on wove (BP 1150, DM 2927, FR 9873, Y 183,864).

PASSARI

$345* *Urns, 1787: Eight,* (04-07-93, Sotheby-Arcade, #281), sight 11½ x 7½ in., (29.2 x 19.1 cm.), copper engraving (BP 228, DM 558, FR 1888, Y 39,196).

PASSAROTTI, Bartolommeo (after) c. 1530-1592

$499* *A Man In Pain, 1580,* margins, abrasions, staining, laid, (12-01-92, Christie-London, #56), P. 17⅛ x 11⅝ in., (435 x 296 mm.), engraving (BP 330, DM 795, FR 2710, Y 62,126).

PASSE, Crispijn (the elder) 1564-1637

$249* *The Good Samaritan Binding The Traveller's Wounds (Hollstein 108),* after H. BOL, #4 of 6, brown stain, collector's stamp, (11-18-92, Bubb Kuyper, #1841), 7¹³⁄₁₆ x 9¹³⁄₁₆ in., (19.8 x 25 cm.), engraving (BP 164, DM 397, FR 1337, Y 30,966, G 450).

BI *Die Sieben Tugenden (Franken 1006-1012, Hollstein 426-432): Seven,* after Marten de Vos, watermark, est. DM 3500, (06-04-93, Bassenge, #5295, illus.), each approx. 6⅛ x 3⁹⁄₁₆ in., (15.6 x 9 cm.), engraving.

PASSE, Crispijn (the elder) Dutch 1564-1637

$614* *Die Erzengel (Franken 269-277; Hollstein 305-313): Nine,* prov., after Marten de Vos, (12-04-92, Bassenge, #6349), 6⁵⁄₁₆ x 3⁹⁄₁₆ in., (16 x 9 cm.), engraving (BP 394, DM 978, FR 3317, Y 76,654).

$2311* *Die Funf Sinne (Franken 1098-1102; Hollstein 499-504): Five,* (12-04-92, Bassenge, #6350, illus.), engraving (BP 1482, DM 3681, FR 12,485, Y 288,514).

$1155* *Susanna Und Die Alten (Franken 58; Hollstein 44),* after G. Goltzius, prov., watermark, (12-04-92, Bassenge, #6348, illus.), 6⅜ x 7¹³⁄₁₆ in., (16.2 x 19.8 cm.), engraving (BP 741, DM 1839, FR 6240, Y 144,195).

PASSE, Magdalena de 1600-1638

$231* *Fruhling (Hollstein 9 I),* (12-04-92, Bassenge, #6353), 9⁵⁄₁₆ x 6⁵⁄₁₆ in., (23.7 x 16 cm.), engraving (BP 148, DM 368, FR 1248, Y 28,839).

PASSE, Magdalena de 1600-before 1640

$399* *Latona (Hollstein 6),* after A. ELSHEIMER, only state, (11-18-92, Bubb Kuyper, #1842), 8⁷⁄₁₆ x 10¼ in., (21.4 x 26 cm.), etching and engraving (BP 263, DM 636, FR 2143, Y 49,621, G 720).

PASSE, W. de 1598-c. 1637

BI *Tactus (Feeling). Loving Couple Near A Bed. Armor With A Parrot (Hollstein 31),* 4th of 5, the five senses, 3rd state?, sig. Wil pas fe erased, est. G5/700, (11-18-92, Bubb Kuyper, #1843), 8¹³⁄₁₆ x 6⁹⁄₁₆ in., (22.4 x 16.6 cm.), engraving.

PASSE, Willem (after)

$36* *Portrait Of Charles Villiers, First Duke Of Buckingham,* (04-22-93, Bonhams-Chelsea, #135), image 14½ x 10¼ in., (36.8 x 26 cm.), engraving (BP 23, DM 58, FR 195, Y 3958).

PATER, Jean Baptiste (after)

$66* *"The Dance",* (02-12-93, DuMouchelle, #1191), approx. 25 x 34 in., (63.5 x 86.4 cm.), print (BP 46, DM 109, FR 370, Y 7959).

PATHE

$217* *Charles Trenet Dans Romance De Paris De J. Boyer (Belgian), 1941,* (01-31-93, Morelle/Marchan, #216), 11 x 14³⁄₁₆ in., (28 x 36 cm.), poster (BP 146, DM 350, FR 1182, Y 27,071).

PATON, Frank English 1856-1909

$168* *"Coming Events Cast Their Shadows Before", "Gone Away" and "British Interests", 1899: A Set Of Three,* all s., foxed, (01-18-93, Bonhams, #82), image 8⅛ x 10¼ in., (20.6 x 26 cm.), etching (BP 110, DM 275, FR 916, Y 21,177).

$152 *Sporting Subjects: Three,* s., (02-05-93, G.A. Key, #84), 4 x 6 in., (10.2 x 15.2 cm.), b/w engraving (BP 105, DM 252, FR 852, Y 18,915).

PATON, Frank (after)

$44* *"Royal And Ancient (St. Andrews 1798)",* (10-29-92, Bonhams-Chelsea, #36), image 15½ x 19½ in., (39.4 x 49.5 cm.), reproduction w/hand coloring (BP 28, DM 68, FR 230, Y 5450).

PATON, H.

$40* *Madame La Presidente. Operette...Musique D'Edmond Diet, c. 1905,* cond. A, (03-16-93, Boisgirard, #168), 35⅝ x 36⁷⁄₁₆ in., (90.5 x 92.5 cm.), poster (BP 28, DM 67, FR 226, Y 4677).

PATON, Richard (after)

$317* *The Burning Of The Prudent In Louisbourgh Harbour, 1771,* by P.C. Canot, pub. John Boydell, skinning, thin spots, mounting, unevenly trimmed, (11-30-92, Phillips-London, #234), sheet 17 x 24 in., (432 x 610 mm.), engraving on laid (BP 209, DM 505, FR 1714, Y 39,452).

$402* *The Defence Of Gibraltar Against The United Force Of Spain And France On The 14th September, 1782, 1784,* by James Fittler, pub. John Boydell, (11-12-92, Bonhams-Chelsea, #49), image 17¾ x 25½ in., (45.1 x 64.8 cm.), hand-colored engraving (BP 264, DM 637, FR 2149, Y 49,845).

$333* *The Defence Of Gibraltar, 1785,* by James Fittler, scratch-letter proof, pub. John Boydell, tears/defects, some into image, surface scuffs, creasing, (11-30-92, Phillips-London, #232), sheet 21⅞ x 28¾ in., (556 x 730 mm.), engraving on laid (BP 220, DM 531, FR 1801, Y 41,444).

PATRICE

$12* *Two Lithographs,* damp stains, (03-31-93, Briest, #E86), color lithograph (BP 8, DM 19, FR 66, Y 1380).

PATTERSON, Malcolm

$510* *St. Andrews From The Links, 1920,* s., margins, (03-03-93, Bonhams-Chelsea, #271), plate 6¾ x 9¾ in., (17.1 x 24.8 cm.), drypoint etching (BP 352, DM 840, FR 2849, Y 59,593).

PATTERSON, Margaret Jordan American 1867-1950

$990* *"Bleeding Heart",* very good cond., (02-07-93, Bakker, #87, illus.), image 6¾ x 9¾ in., (17.1 x 24.8 cm.), color woodblock print (BP 685, DM 1642, FR 5549, Y 123,196).

$55* "The Brook - Pine Manor", s., very good cond.?, (03-28-93, Bakker, #250), 10½ x 7¼ in., (26.7 x 18.4 cm.), woodblock (BP 37, DM 90, FR 305, Y 6401).

$220* "The Brook In Spring, Pine Manor", s. Margaret J. Patterson, num. 50/100, very good cond., (09-27-92, Bakker, #166), image 9½ x 7¼ in., (24.1 x 18.4 cm.), lithograph (BP 128, DM 326, FR 1103, Y 26,554).

$138* "The Cathedral, Anacapri", s. Margaret Patterson, num. 11/50, very good cond., (09-27-92, Bakker, #180), image 7⅜ x 10½ in., (18.7 x 26.7 cm.), woodblock print (BP 81, DM 205, FR 692, Y 16,657).

$468* "Coast Cedars, Winter", s., #39/100, good cond.?, (02-07-93, Bakker, #163), image 7 x 10 in., (17.8 x 25.4 cm.), color woodblock print (BP 324, DM 776, FR 2623, Y 58,238).

$358* "A Dutch Canal", s., good cond., (07-19-92, Bakker, #1), image 6¾ x 5⅛ in., (17.1 x 13 cm.), color woodblock print (BP 184, DM 522, FR 1764, Y 44,505).

$1870* "Garden Flowers", s. Margaret J. Patterson, very good cond.?, (11-21-92, Bakker, #69, illus.), image 10¼ x 7¼ in., (26 x 18.4 cm.), color woodblock print (BP 1231, DM 2982, FR 10,043, Y 232,558).

$440* "The Guinea Boat", s. Margaret Patterson, good cond., (09-27-92, Bakker, #243, illus.), image 7¼ x 10¼ in., (18.4 x 26 cm.), color woodblock print (BP 257, DM 652, FR 2206, Y 53,108).

$935* "Heartsease", s. Margaret J. Patterson, very good cond., (09-27-92, Bakker, #239, illus.), image 7 x 9⅞ in., (17.8 x 25.1 cm.), color woodblock print (BP 546, DM 1386, FR 4687, Y 112,855).

$110* "Little House Sluis", good/poor cond., (07-19-92, Bakker, #27), image 8¼ x 6 in., (21 x 15.2 cm.), color woodblock print (BP 56, DM 160, FR 542, Y 13,675).

$1980* "Main Street, Nantucket", s., very good cond.?, (07-19-92, Bakker, #200, illus.), sheet 7 x 10 in., (17.8 x 25.4 cm.), color woodblock print (BP 1016, DM 2886, FR 9759, Y 246,146).

$1320* "Morning Glories", s., #66/100, ded., very good cond., (07-19-92, Bakker, #126, illus.), image 10 x 7⅛ in., (25.4 x 18.1 cm.), color woodblock print (BP 677, DM 1924, FR 6506, Y 164,097).

$1870* "Petunias", s. Margaret J. Patterson, very good cond., (09-27-92, Bakker, #240, illus.), sight 6¾ x 9½ in., (17.1 x 24.1 cm.), color woodblock print (BP 1092, DM 2772, FR 9373, Y 225,709).

$330* "Pink Dogwood", fair cond., water damage, (03-12-93, Skinner, #49, illus.), 7⅛ x 10¼ in., (18.1 x 26 cm.), color woodblock print on soft wove (BP 230, DM 549, FR 1868, Y 38,892).

$1430* "Pink Dogwood", s. Margaret J. Patterson, very good cond., (09-27-92, Bakker, #238, illus.), image 7 x 10⅜ in., (17.8 x 26.4 cm.), color woodblock print (BP 835, DM 2120, FR 7168, Y 172,601).

$385* "Surf And Rocks" (Bakker, 47), c. 1918, s. Margaret Patterson, good cond., trimmed, creasing, misinking of green block, (03-12-93, Skinner, #54, illus.), 7⅜ x 10⅝ in., (18.7 x 27 cm.), color woodblock on soft wove (BP 269, DM 641, FR 2179, Y 45,374).

$358* "The Swan", very good cond., (09-27-92, Bakker, #244, illus.), sight 8¼ x 6 in., (21 x 15.2 cm.), color woodblock print (BP 209, DM 531, FR 1794, Y 43,211).

$1540* "Water Lily", s. Margaret J. Patterson, very good/good cond., (09-27-92, Bakker, #242, illus.), image 10¼ x 7¼ in., (26 x 18.4 cm.), color woodblock print (BP 899, DM 2283, FR 7719, Y 185,878).

$1210* "White Dogwood", s. Margaret J. Patterson, i., very good cond., (09-27-92, Bakker, #237, illus.), image 7 x 10¼ in., (17.8 x 26 cm.), color woodblock print (BP 707, DM 1794, FR 6065, Y 146,047).

$1045* "Windblown Trees", s., very good cond., (02-07-93, Bakker, #6, illus.), sight 6¾ x 9¾ in., (17.1 x 24.8 cm.), color woodblock print (BP 723, DM 1733, FR 5858, Y 130,040).

PATTISON, Edgar L.

$80* "Figures And A Carriage On A Bridge, Church Beyond", s., margins, (02-17-93, Bonhams-Chelsea, #233), plate 11 x 13¾ in., (27.9 x 34.9 cm.), drypoint etching (BP 55, DM 130, FR 440, Y 9556).

PATTON, Frank

$44 "Rough And Ready", s., (12-11-92, G.A. Key, #124), 4 x 6 in., (10.2 x 15.2 cm.), etching (BP 28, DM 69, FR 238, Y 5445).

PAUL, John Dean (after)

$246* Hunting Scenes: Four, trimmed, laid down, defects, (06-30-93, Bonhams-Chelsea, #140), image 8½ x 22 in., (21.6 x 55.9 cm.), aquatint w/hand-coloring (BP 165, DM 420, FR 1415, Y 26,358).

BI Leicestershire (Siltzer p. 193), 1825: Set Of Four, later impressions, foxing, laid, est. BP 5/700, (10-27-92, Phillips-London, #99), image 8⅝ x 21⅞ in., (219 x 556 mm.), aquatint w/hand-coloring, touches of gum arabic on wove.

BI Leicestershire, Gaudet Equis Canibusque, Plates 1-4: Four, pub. w/George Rees, margins, surface defects, est. BP 2/300, (10-29-92, Bonhams-Chelsea, #135), plate 12¾ x 25 in., (32.4 x 63.5 cm.), aquatint w/hand coloring.

$394* Leicestershire. Gardet Equis Canibusque: Four, staining, defects, (06-30-93, Bonhams-Chelsea, #141), image 9 x 21¾ in., (22.9 x 55.2 cm.), aquatint w/hand-coloring (BP 264, DM 672, FR 2267, Y 42,216).

$223* A Trip To Brighton, Plates 1-4: Four, margins, (03-03-93, Bonhams-Chelsea, #219), image 4 x 21½ in., (10.2 x 54.6 cm.), hand-colored lithographic reproductions (BP 154, DM 367, FR 1246, Y 26,057).

PAUL, Peter   b. 1943

BI Was Boullee Befurchtet Hat, 1972, s., #37/75, est. DM 350, (09-18-92, Schloss Ahlden, #1041), 25¹⁵⁄₁₆ x 19¹⁵⁄₁₆ in., (66 x 50.6 cm.), lithograph on Arches wove.

PAULEMILE-PISSARRO   French 1884-1972

$301* Bal De L'A.A.A.A., c. 1925, poster before letters, (02-12-93, Cheval/Robert, #134), 41¹⁵⁄₁₆ x 30⅞ in., (106.5 x 78.5 cm.), poster (BP 212, DM 499, FR 1689, Y 36,300).

PAULI, Fritz   Swiss b. 1891

BI 4 Manner In Betrachtung, 1924, s., t., d., i. 2.probedruck, margins, good cond., minor creasing, minor soiling of margins, minor paper discoloration, Late Gerhard Brauer Coll., est. Dfl. 6/900, (05-27-93, Sotheby-Amstrdm, #771), 22¹¹⁄₁₆ x 14⅞ in., (577 x 378 mm.), etching on laid.

BI Engel Am Ostermorgen, 1922, s., d., #9/20, margins, minor creasing, minor paper discoloration, foxing, crease along top of sheet, Late Gerhard Brauer Coll., est. Dfl. 6/900, (05-27-93, Sotheby-Amstrdm, #766), 21 x 15⅞ in., (534 x 404 mm.), etching on wove.

$576* Erinnerung An M., 1924, s., t., d., num. indistinctly, margins, creasing, minor paper discoloration, minor soiling, foxing, tape staining in upper margins, Late Gerhard Brauer Coll., (05-27-93, Sotheby-Amstrdm, #763, illus.), 25¹⁄₁₆ x 22³⁄₁₆ in., (637 x 563 mm.), etching on laid (BP 369, DM 924, FR 3115, Y 61,750, G 1035).

BI (Figure In A Landscape), s., i. Herrn Dr. W. Minnich, mai 1924, margins, soiling, small defects in margins, minor creasing, some foxing, Late Gerhard Brauer Coll., est. Dfl. 6/900, (05-27-93, Sotheby-Amstrdm, #762, illus.), 22¹¹⁄₁₆ x 19½ in., (577 x 495 mm.), etching w/ aquatint on laid.

$344* Notturno O Der Nachtliche Erscheinung (Freiburghaus 316), 1948, s., d., t., (10-14-92, Germann, #583), 22¹⁄₁₆ x 24⁷⁄₁₆ in., (560 x 620 mm.), aquatint (BP 202, DM 503, FR 1707, Y 41,687, SF 448).

BI (Portrait Of A Man), s., i. Dr. W. Minnich dankbar zugeeignet, #5/30, margins, some creasing, minor soiling of margins, occasional foxing, minor paper discoloration, good cond., Late Gerhard Brauer Coll., est. Dfl. 700/1,000, (05-27-93, Sotheby-Amstrdm, #767, illus.), 27¼ x 15⁹⁄₁₆ in., (692 x 396 mm.), etching on wove.

$448* (Portrait), 1918, s., d., i. Ad. Frey, margins, good cond., minor foxing, paper discoloration, minor creasing, Late Gerhard Brauer Coll., (05-27-93, Sotheby-Amstrdm, #761, illus.), 17⅛ x 13⁹⁄₁₆ in., (435 x 345 mm.), etching on laid (BP 287, DM 719, FR 2423, Y 48,027, G 805).

$320* *(Two Men In An Interior)*, 1925, s.,d., i. indistinctly, margins, minor paper discoloration, foxing, margins w/ soiling, creasing, small defects, Late Gerhard Brauer Coll., (05-27-93, Sotheby-Amstrdm, #764), 23⁷⁄₁₆ x 18⁷⁄₁₆ in., (595 x 469 mm.), etching on laid (BP 205, DM 513, FR 1731, Y 34,305, G 575).

PAULL, Grace   American b. 1898
$149* *"Winter Sunday In Washington Square"*, c. 1947, s., t., (03-25-93, Boos, #613), 13¾ x 9⁷⁄₈ in., (34.9 x 25.1 cm.), lithograph (BP 101, DM 245, FR 832, Y 17,455).

PAULY, Erhardt   American 20th cent.
$55* *Collage*, s., d. 1971, num. 535/3000, (09-20-92, Hindman, #726), 29 x 19¾ in., (73.7 x 50.2 cm.), print (BP 32, DM 82, FR 279, Y 6798).

PAXTON, William
$385* *"Portrait Of A Young Woman"*, s., very good cond., (03-28-93, Bakker, #19), 5 x 4 in., (12.7 x 10.2 cm.), drypoint (BP 259, DM 628, FR 2135, Y 44,809).

PAYE, Richard Morton
$111* *"The Boy Discovering The Golden Eggs"* and *"The Boy Disappointed Of His Treasure": A Pair*, by John Young, pub. John Jeffryes, January, 1796, trimmed, laid down,- some surface defects, (04-22-93, Bonhams-Chelsea, #24), (57.2 x 44.5 cm.), mezzotints hand coloring (BP 72, DM 178, FR 602, Y 12,205).

PAYNE, Charles Johnson (Snaffles)
$386* *The Bender*, blindstamped w/interlocking snafflebits, s., t. in w/c, lit., (06-08-93, Ritchie, #4, illus.), image 10⅛ x 13 in., (25.7 x 33 cm.), sheet 16 x 18½ in., (25.7 x 33 cm.), photographic lithograph w/remarque, hand-colored w/watercolor and gouache on paper (BP 254, DM 626, FR 2109, Y 40,998, C$ 495).
BI *Le Poilu*, blindstamped w/interlocking snafflebits, s., t., d. 15 in plate, est. C$ 2/300, (06-08-93, Ritchie, #6), plate 11¼ x 8 in., (28.6 x 20.3 cm.), sheet 17½ x 13½ in., (28.6 x 20.3 cm.), photographic color lithograph w/ remarque, heightened w/white on board.
$386* *Swagger, But A Workman, Captain Bert Of Berkley*, blindstamped w/interlocking snafflebits, s., t. in plate, s., i., (06-08-93, Ritchie, #5, illus.), plate 12⅜ x 11⅜ in., (31.4 x 28.9 cm.), sheet 18 x 15¾ in., (31.4 x 28.9 cm.), photographic color lithograph w/remarque, hand-colored w/watercolor and gouache on paper (BP 254, DM 626, FR 2109, Y 40,998, C$ 495).

PAYNE, Charles Johnson ('Snaffles')   British 1884-1947
BI *Infantryman W.W.I.*, s., tear, staining, est. C$150/250, (10-21-92, Maynard, #234), 10 x 8 in., (25.4 x 20.3 cm.), hand colored lithograph.

PAYNE, Edgar   American 1882-1947
$605* *Brittany Boats*, s. Edgar Payne, (02-16-93, Moran, #145), 20 x 24 in., (50.8 x 61 cm.), oil serigraph on artist board (BP 418, DM 987, FR 3344, Y 72,481).

PAYNE, R. W. (after)
BI *"Boys Playing At Marbles"* and *"Boys Playing At Peg Top": Two*, by Robert Pollard, est. BP 2/300, (06-16-93, Bonhams-Chelsea, #436, illus.), image 15 x 20 in., (38.1 x 50.8 cm.), aquatint.

PEABODY, Dr. Charles
$825* *Mother And Child*, c. 1910, credit, (10-13-92, Christie-NY, #42, illus.), 7⅛ x 5¾ in., (18.1 x 14.6 cm.), photograph, platinum print (BP 480, DM 1209, FR 4107, Y 100,036).

PEAH-MUS-KA
BI *"A Musquakee Chief"*, pub. Greenough, 1838, est. $4/600, (12-11-92, DuMouchelle, #2219), 18 x 12½ in., (45.7 x 31.8 cm.), hand colored lithograph.

PEALSTEIN, Philip   American b. 1924
$303* *Girl On Empire Sofa*, s., #42/75, pub. Landfall Press, (05-16-93, Hindman, #635), 32⅛ x 24 in., (81.6 x 61 cm.), lithograph (BP 197, DM 487, FR 1638, Y 33,588).

PEAN
$161* *Revolution Et Empire. Panorama De La Bataille De Iena. Exposition DeParis 1900*, Imp. Chaix, good cond., (02-12-93, Cheval/Robert, #133), 51³⁄₁₆ x 37 in., (130 x 94 cm.), poster (BP 113, DM 267, FR 903, Y 19,416).

PEAN, R.
BI *La Veuve Soyeuse*, before letters, good cond., (02-12-93, Cheval/Robert, #173), poster.

PEAN, Rene   French 1875-1945
$763* *Belle Jardiniere (...) Exposition Et Grande Mise En Vente De Chemises Et Linge Confectionne*, 1903, Paris, Imp. Chaix, cond. B-, restored in text, (06-11-93, Boisgirard, #136), 62¹⁵⁄₁₆ x 43⁵⁄₁₆ in., (160 x 110 cm.), poster (BP 501, DM 1240, FR 4181, Y 80,955).
$440* *Le Fiance De Thylda Theatre Cluny*, (05-16-93, Hindman, #446), 32 x 22½ in., (81.3 x 57.2 cm.), (BP 286, DM 708, FR 2378, Y 48,775).
$241* *Folies Dramatiques. Le Billet De Logement*, 1901, Paris, Imp. Chaix, cond. B+, (06-11-93, Boisgirard, #135), 62¹⁵⁄₁₆ x 43½ in., (160 x 110.5 cm.), poster (BP 158, DM 392, FR 1321, Y 25,570).
$201* *Le Sanitor. Desinfectant Sans Odeur*, 1895, Paris, Imp. Chaix, cond. B+, (06-11-93, Boisgirard, #134), 48¹³⁄₁₆ x 34⅝ in., (124 x 88 cm.), poster (BP 132, DM 327, FR 1101, Y 21,326).

PEARCE, Stephen (after)
BI *Richard Foley Onslow Esq.*, by William Giller, foxed, est. BP 150/250, (03-03-93, Bonhams-Chelsea, #141), image 20 x 25½ in., (50.8 x 64.8 cm.), engraving.
$246* *Richard Foley Onslow, Esq.*, by William Giller, foxed, (06-30-93, Bonhams-Chelsea, #142), image 20 x 25½ in., (50.8 x 64.8 cm.), engraving (BP 165, DM 420, FR 1415, Y 26,358).

PEARLSTEIN, Philip   American b. 1924
$413* *Girl On Blue Coverlet*, s., #10/50, (05-16-93, Hindman, #637), 22¼ x 27 in., (56.5 x 68.6 cm.), color lithograph (BP 269, DM 664, FR 2232, Y 45,782).
$770* *Machu Picchu*, 1979, s., d., t., #10/41, blindstamp pub., very good cond. (?), (02-24-93, Butterfield, #3238), 28½ x 40 in., (72.4 x 101.6 cm.), lithograph in colors on wove (BP 537, DM 1250, FR 4238, Y 90,354).
$330* *Nude Lying On Black And Red Blanket (F. 58)*, 1974, s., d., t., #24/50, pub. by artist, margins, faded, good cond. (?), (02-24-93, Butterfield, #3237), 22⅜ x 29½ in., (568 x 749 mm.), etching and aquatint in colors on German Etching (BP 230, DM 536, FR 1816, Y 38,723).
$275* *Nude On A Couch*, s. Philip Pearlstein, num. XXIV/XL, very good cond., (11-21-92, Bakker, #150), sheet 22 x 30 in., (55.9 x 76.2 cm.), color lithograph (BP 181, DM 438, FR 1477, Y 34,200).
$440* *Nude On A Navaho Rug*, s. Pearlstein, num. 9/75, very good cond., (11-21-92, Bakker, #147), sheet 24½ x 34 in., (62.2 x 86.4 cm.), color lithograph (BP 290, DM 702, FR 2363, Y 54,720).
$440* *Nude On A Silver Bench*, 1972, s., t., #66/75, pub. by artist, full margins, good cond.?, pressure marks, prov., (12-12-92, Weschler, #147, illus.), 21¾ x 29¼ in., (55.2 x 74.3 cm.), etching and aquatint (BP 282, DM 693, FR 2376, Y 54,449).
$330* *Nude On Couch, Arms Outstretched*, 1972, s., t., num. 23/50, pub. by artist, full margins, old paper tape, very good cond., (09-19-92, Christie-E, #180), sheet 22 x 29¼ in., (559 x 743 mm.), etching and aquatint on Arches (BP 190, DM 494, FR 1692, Y 41,116).
$358* *Nude On The Couch*, s., num. 23/60, (09-20-92, Hindman, #713), 22½ x 29 in., (57.2 x 73.7 cm.), color lithograph (BP 210, DM 531, FR 1817, Y 44,247).
$468* *Reclining Nude On Green Couch (F. 20)*, 1971, s., d., #18/72, blindstamp pub. Landfall Press, good cond., hinge remains, surface soiling, creases, (10-28-92, Butterfield, #3069), 27 x 22⅜ in., (686 x 568 mm.), color lithograph on Arches (BP 298, DM 723, FR 2454, Y 57,423).
$330* *Reclining Nude With Head On Elbow*, 1968, s., #2/20, (05-16-93, Hindman, #636), 18⅛ x 23 in., (46 x 58.4 cm.), lithograph (BP 215, DM 531, FR 1784, Y 36,581).
$825* *The Sphinx*, 1979, s., d., t., #15/41, blindstamp pub., good cond. (?), (02-24-93, Butterfield, #3239), 28½ x 40⅜ in., (72.4 x 102.6 cm.), lithograph in colors on wove (BP 575, DM 1339, FR 4540, Y 96,808).
$550* *Two Nudes With Oak Stool And Canvas*, 1976, s., d., #14/100, pub. Landfall Press, (12-08-92, Swann, #234),

29⅛ x 36⅞ in., (74 x 93.7 cm.), lithograph (BP 345, DM 856, FR 2919, Y 68,171).

PEARS, Charles 1873-1958

$299* *The Isle Of Man, British Railways, c. 1949,* fold marks w/corresponding defects, nicks, losses, (02-04-93, Christie-S. Ken, #74), 40 x 50 in., (101.6 x 127 cm.), color lithograph (BP 209, DM 492, FR 1669, Y 37,194).

PEARY, Admiral Robert Edwin 1856-1920

BI *Eskimo Portraits, 1894: Two,* prov., est. $1/1,500, (04-08-93, Christie-NY, #11, illus.), each approx. 4⅝ x 3¾ in., (11.7 x 9.5 cm.), photograph, albumen prints.

PEARY, Robert American 1856-1920

$1210* *Arctic Studies (New York, 1898): Two,* incl. Digging Out and Sunrise Camp: Dr. Cook, Astrup & the Flags, t.,num., annot. by photog. in red ink, (10-15-92, Sotheby-NY, #67, illus.), each, approx. 3½ x 4½ in., (8.9 x 11.4 cm.), photograph, gelatin silver prints (BP 740, DM 1801, FR 6108, Y 145,171).

PEASE, H.M.

$174* *The American Annual Of Photography, c. 1898,* crease, tears, (05-07-93, Christie-S. Ken, #70, illus.), 14 x 19 in., (35.6 x 48.3 cm.), color lithograph (BP 110, DM 275, FR 927, Y 19,159).

PEATTIE, Margaret Rhodes

$302* *Carmel-By-The-Sea, c. 1900,* sig., notations, (10-14-92, Swann, #533, illus.), 6½ x 9¾ in., (16.5 x 24.8 cm.), photograph, bromoil print (BP 177, DM 442, FR 1499, Y 36,597).

PECHAUBES, Eugene French 1890-1967

$198* *Jockeys On Horseback,* s., #242/200, (10-18-92, Hindman, #460A), 14¾ x 20½ in., (37.5 x 52.1 cm.), hand colored lithograph (BP 121, DM 295, FR 999, Y 23,755).

$44* *"Safely Over The Last",* num. 189/300, s., (10-29-92, Bonhams-Chelsea, #158), subject 17¾ x 24¼ in., (45.1 x 61.6 cm.), lithograph finished by hand (BP 28, DM 68, FR 230, Y 5450).

PECHSTEIN, Max German 1881-1955

$3531* *Alfred Hess (Kruger H 216 I), 1919,* s., d., 3. artist's proof, (06-10-93, Hauswedell/Nolt, #766), image 13¹⁄₁₆ x 17⅝ in., (33.2 x 44.7 cm.), woodcut (BP 2310, DM 5750, FR 19,359, Y 374,801).

$356* *"Aod" (Kruger H 174), 1919,* Berlin, Gurlitt, (09-14-92, Venator/Hansten, #2488), image approx. 9¹³⁄₁₆ x 7¹¹⁄₁₆ in., (25 x 19.5 cm.), woodcut on paper (BP 188, DM 529, FR 1793, Y 44,268).

BI *Ausstellung Der Gurlitt Presse, c. 1918,* p. H. Birkholz, skimming, vertical fold, tears, repairs, est. BP 2/4,000, (05-20-93, Christie-London, #503, illus.), sheet 28 x 38 in., (71.1 x 96.5 cm.), lithograph in colors backed on Japan.

BI *Ausstellung H.M. Pechstein, Fritz Gurlitt (Kruger L 298), 1919,* p. H. Birkholz, vertical fold marks, brown tape, staining, creases, est. BP 2/4,000, (05-20-93, Christie-London, #504, illus.), sheet 28 x 37½ in., (71.1 x 95.3 cm.), lithograph in colors.

$851* *Bacchuskopf (Kruger L 420), 1948,* s., num., pub. Dr. Heinrich Mock, (06-05-93, Bassenge, #6428), 15¾ x 11 in., (40 x 28 cm.), lithograph on machine-made (BP 560, DM 1380, FR 4650, Y 91,289).

$847* *Bacchuskopf (Kruger L 420), 1948,* s., d., collector's stamp, (06-10-93, Hauswedell/Nolt, #764), image 15¾ x 11 in., (40 x 28 cm.), color lithograph (BP 554, DM 1379, FR 4644, Y 89,906).

$6659* *Badende IX (K. H104), 1911,* s., d. 1912, wide margins, very good cond., (12-01-92, Christie-London, #478, illus.), L. 12½ x 15½ in., (318 x 394 mm.), woodcut on Japan (BP 4400, DM 10,614, FR 36,171, Y 829,059).

$1623* *Badende Mit Kind (Kruger H 227 II), 1920,* s., num., (12-05-92, Bassenge, #7544), 15¾ x 12⅜ in., (40 x 31.5 cm.), woodcut on copper print paper (BP 1016, DM 2530, FR 8624, Y 201,090).

$1419* *Badende Mit Kind (Kruger H 227 II), 1920,* s., num., (06-05-93, Bassenge, #6417), 15¾ x 12⅜ in., (40 x 31.5 cm.), woodcut on copper print (BP 934, DM 2301, FR 7754, Y 152,221).

$988* *Bartiger Mannerkopf (Kruger H 191), 1917,* s., d., (12-12-92, Wachholtz, #255, illus.), 4⅛ x 3¹⁄₁₆ in., (10.4 x 7.8 cm.), woodcut on Simili Japan (BP 632, DM 1553, FR 5292, Y 122,232).

$440* *"Bathers",* s., good cond., (07-19-92, Bakker, #3), sheet 11 x 8 in., (27.9 x 20.3 cm.), lithograph (BP 226, DM 641, FR 2169, Y 54,699).

BI *Bildnis Dr. Freundlich (F H 142/Kruger H 206), 1918,* s., full margins, good cond., occasional foxing, paper discoloration, creasing at edges of sheet, Late Gerhard Brauer Coll., est. Dfl. 2,2/2,800, (05-27-93, Sotheby-Amstrdm, #776, illus.), 14¹⁄₁₆ x 9⁵⁄₁₆ in., (357 x 237 mm.), woodcut on sturdy wove.

BI *Bildnis Dr. Freundlich (Fechter 142; Kruger H 206), 1918,* mono., "wood engraving 1919" series, d., est. DM 3,000, (05-26-93, Lempertz, #411, illus.), 20¹⁄₁₆ x 14⅝ in., (51 x 37.2 cm.), wood engraving on thick cardboard.

$715* *Boats At Harbor,* s., good cond.?, (07-19-92, Bakker, #183), 7 x 8½ in., (17.8 x 21.6 cm.), woodblock print (BP 367, DM 1042, FR 3524, Y 88,886).

$687* *Boot An Der Brucke (Kr. H 311), 1948,* sheet 7 of Boettcher Portfolio, s., d., num., (06-23-93, Kornfeld, #641), woodcut on tan (red color) wove (BP 467, DM 1162, FR 3910, Y 74,845, SF 1035).

BI *Deutsche Graphiker Der Gegenwart: Weib Vom Manne Begehrt (F. 157), 1919,* pub. in Pfister, blindstamp, margin, good cond., surface soiling, est. $6/800, (02-24-93, Butterfield, #2963), 9⅞ x 6¼ in., (251 x 159 mm.), woodcut on wove.

BI *Deutsche Kunstgemeinschaft Berlin 23. Marz 1929 (Kruger H 298),* s., est. DM 3,500, (12-05-92, Bassenge, #7543), 12¹⁵⁄₁₆ x 17¹⁵⁄₁₆ in., (33 x 45.5 cm.), woodcut on copper print paper.

$11,277* *Ein Dorf (Fechter 124-130; Kruger H 193-199), 1918,* s., #52/75, d., (05-26-93, Lempertz, #407, illus.), portfolio 20⅞ x 25³⁄₁₆ in., (53.1 x 64 cm.), wood engraving on JWZanders (BP 7295, DM 18,399, FR 61,928, Y 1,225,228).

$989* *Drei Kopfe (Kruger 291), 1923,* s., #35/51, (06-10-93, Hauswedell/Nolt, #770), image 19½ x 15¾ in., (49.5 x 40 cm.), woodcut on wove (BP 647, DM 1610, FR 5422, Y 104,978).

$1444* *"Fischer Am Strand, Italienische Fischer XI" (Kruger L 189), 1917,* s., d., sheet 11 of series Ital Fischer, in 1st series Neue Mappenwerke,Berlin, Gurlitt-Presse, (11-28-92, Grisebach, #692, illus.), 14³⁄₁₆ x 18¹¹⁄₁₆ in., (36 x 47.5 cm.), lithograph on wove (BP 953, DM 2300, FR 7810, Y 179,714).

$5410* *Fischer Mit Fang Im Netz (Kruger H 287), 1923,* #45/51, s., (11-21-92, Lempertz, #316A, illus.), 15¹¹⁄₁₆ x 12⁹⁄₁₆ in., (39.9 x 31.9 cm.), woodcut on cream copper print paper (BP 3562, DM 8626, FR 29,055, Y 672,802).

$1165* *Fischerkopf IV (K. H120), 1911,* s., d., t., creases, tears, tape-staining, dirt, very good cond., (12-01-92, Christie-London, #479), L. 8⅞ x 7¹⁵⁄₁₆ in., (225 x 203 mm.), sheet 18¹⁄₁₆ x 14⅝ in., (225 x 203 mm.), woodcut on wove (BP 770, DM 1857, FR 6328, Y 145,045).

BI *Fischerkopf IX (Kr. H 245; Peters V/10), 1921,* s., 5. portfolio Bauhaus Drucke, Neue Europaische Graphik, Deutsche Kunstler, Weimer, 1921, est. DM 6000, (12-01-92, Karl/Faber, #1087, illus.), 15¾ x 12⅝ in., (40 x 32 cm.), woodcut on hand-made.

$1599* *Fischerkopf VII (F H 79/Kruger H 123), 1911,* s., d., #14/100, margins, good cond, some minor foxing, paper discoloration, glued to mount at corners verso, Late Gerhard Brauer Coll., (05-27-93, Sotheby-Amstrdm, #774, illus.), 11⁷⁄₁₆ x 9⁹⁄₁₆ in., (290 x 243 mm.), woodcut on wove (BP 1024, DM 2566, FR 8648, Y 171,419, G 2875).

$5226* *Fischerkopf VII (Kruger H 123; Fechter H 79), 1911,* s., d., from Reihe der Fischerkopfe, from VII. Jahresmappe of Brucke, (06-10-93, Hauswedell/Nolt, #765), image 11½ x 9⁷⁄₁₆ in., (29.2 x 24 cm.), woodcut on wove (BP 3418, DM 8510, FR 28,651, Y 554,718).

BI *Gesprach (Fechter 13; Kruger L 19 I), 1908,* est. DM 12,000, prov., (05-26-93, Lempertz, #406, illus.), 16¾ x 22¹³⁄₁₆ in., (42.5 x 57.9 cm.), lithograph on smooth wove.

$5827* *Getandel (K. R159), 1923,* s., d., #42/51, wide margins, crease, tears, defects, (12-01-92, Christie-London, #481, illus.), plate 12 15/16 x 15 11/16 in., (329 x 398 mm.), sheet 19⅝ x 27 15/16 in., (329 x 398 mm.), drypoint w/aquatint on firm wove (BP 3850, DM 9288, FR 31,651, Y 725,473).

$1465* *Heilige Familie (Kruger H. 162), 1913,* d., mono., wear, (11-13-92, Kunsthaus, #743), 7 3/16 x 5 in., (18.2 x 12.7 cm.), woodcut on handmade (BP 947, DM 2300, FR 7755, Y 181,829).

$1773* *Heimkehrende Fischer II (Kruger L. 386), 1923,* s., i. artist's proof, (06-05-93, Bassenge, #6424), 11 13/16 x 9 11/16 in., (30 x 24.6 cm.), lithograph on machine-made (BP 1167, DM 2875, FR 9689, Y 190,195).

BI *Illustrationen Zu Carl Sternheims "Heidenstamm" (Fe. R 84-87/II; Kr.R. 92-95/II), 1918: Four,* s., pub. Heinrich Hochstim, crease, brown stained, est. DM 10,000s., pub, (12-01-92, Karl/Faber, #1085, illus.), 8⅞ x 6 11/16 in., (22.5 x 17 cm.), drypoint on Strathmore-Japan.

BI *"Im Harem" (Kruger L73/I; Fechter L66/I), 1909,* blindstamp, mono., d., t., est. DM 50/60,000, (06-04-93, Grisebach, #24, illus.), 14⅜ x 19 5/16 in., (36.5 x 49 cm.), color lithograph on thick Japan.

$989* *Im Wasser (Kruger L 372), 1921,* s., stone mono., #24/100, portfolio Freie Secession, 17 Steinzeichnungen, (06-10-93, Hauswedell/Nolt, #762), image 12⅜ x 9 7/16 in., (31.4 x 24 cm.), lithograph on hand-made (BP 647, DM 1610, FR 5422, Y 104,978).

$1998* *Indische Scene (K. H27), 1906,* 1st state of 2, margins, trimmed, foxing, discoloration, good cond., (12-01-92, Christie-London, #475), L. 6⅞ x 8⅜ in., (174 x 212 mm.), sheet 8⅜ x 8⅜ in., (174 x 212 mm.), woodcut w/ hand-coloring in grey wash on figures and in border on soft wove (BP 1320, DM 3185, FR 10,853, Y 248,755).

$516* *Italienerinnen (Kruger L 412), 1945,* s., artist's proof, (12-05-92, Bassenge, #7547), 16 9/16 x 11 7/16 in., (42 x 29.1 cm.), lithograph on wove (BP 323, DM 804, FR 2742, Y 63,933).

$551* *Italienerinnen (Kruger L 412), 1945,* s., d., stone mono., collector's stamp, (06-10-93, Hauswedell/Nolt, #763), image 15 15/16 x 10 13/16 in., (40.5 x 27.5 cm.), lithograph (BP 360, DM 897, FR 3021, Y 58,486).

$3153* *"Jungling Mit Frauen" (Fe. L 141; Kr. L 157), 1912,* mono., d., i., artist's proof, (12-01-92, Karl/Faber, #1082, illus.), 15 3/16 x 13 9/16 in., (38.5 x 34.5 cm.), lithograph (BP 2083, DM 5026, FR 17,127, Y 392,555).

$13,745* *Kind Auf Der Bank (Druger L 37), 1908,* mono., i., (06-23-93, Kornfeld, #642, illus.), color lithograph on thin wove (BP 9338, DM 23,257, FR 78,230, Y 1,497,440, SF 20,700).

$3583* *Kniender Akt Mit Schale (Kruger H132; Bolliger & Kornfeld 21), 1911,* as the wrapper for VI. Jahresmappe der Kunstlergruppe Brucke, margins stain, tear, creases, tape, (05-20-93, Christie-London, #484, illus.), image 14½ x 11¾ in., (36.8 x 29.8 cm.), sheet 23 x 34½ in., (36.8 x 29.8 cm.), woodcut on blue wove (BP 2300, DM 5781, FR 19,473, Y 395,649).

$780* *"Kommen Und Gehen (Kindheit Und Alter)" (Kruger H 1), 1905,* s., d., (06-05-93, Grisebach, #819, illus.), 7 x 7 3/16 in., (17.8 x 18.2 cm.), color woodcut on green wove (BP 513, DM 1265, FR 4262, Y 83,673).

$832* *Der Kritiker (Dr. Paul Fechter) (Kruger R 124), 1921,* sig., margins, good cond., slight foxing, corners glued to mount, staining and restoration at lower right corner, Late Gerhard Brauer Coll., (05-27-93, Sotheby-Amstrdm, #777, illus.), 15½ x 12⅜ in., (394 x 315 mm.), drypoint w/tone on laid (BP 533, DM 1335, FR 4500, Y 89,194, G 1495).

BI *Kurenkahne In Schwerer See (K. L 421), 1948,* s., d., margins, good cond., light-staining, tape, creases, notations, est. $8/1,000, (05-19-93, Butterfield, #1945), 5¾ x 3¾ in., (146 x 95 mm.), lithograph on wove.

$148* *Lesende Auf Einer Parkbank (Kruger L 178), 1917,* (09-25-92, Granier, #2968), sheet 5⅞ x 8¼ in., (15 x 21 cm.), lithograph on machine made paper (BP 86, DM 219, FR 742, Y 17,864).

$4662* *Madchen (K. H26), 1906,* s., d., t., margins, ink and wash additions, loss, creases, tape, (12-01-92, Christie-London, #474), L. 10 3/16 x 7 3/16 in., (258 x 182 mm.), woodcut on soft wove (BP 3080, DM 7431, FR 25,323, Y 580,428).

BI *Madchenbildnisse IX - Kopfe II (Kr. L 215), 1917,* s., d., pub. Fritz Gurlitt, tears, est. DM 2400, (12-01-92, Karl/Faber, #1083), 14 15/16 x 14 15/16 in., (38 x 38 cm.), lithograph on hand-made.

$1831* *Madchenkopf (K. L50), 1908,* s., d., num. I, wide margins, creasing, tear, dirt, tape, very good cond., (12-01-92, Christie-London, #477), L. 16 15/16 x 12 13/16 in., (431 x 325 mm.), lithograph on smooth wove (BP 1210, DM 2918, FR 9946, Y 227,963).

$2904* *Nach Dem Bade (Kr. R. 135), 1923,* s., d., (12-01-92, Karl/Faber, #1088, illus.), 11 13/16 x 7½ in., (30 x 19 cm.), drypoint on simili-Japan (BP 1919, DM 4629, FR 15,774, Y 361,554).

$1106* *Das Netz (Kruger L 182), 1917,* sheet IV of series Italienische Fischer, s., (12-05-92, Bassenge, #7546), 10 1/16 x 16 9/16 in., (25.5 x 42 cm.), lithograph on handmade J.W. Zanders (BP 693, DM 1724, FR 5877, Y 137,034).

BI *Palaumadchen (K. R87), 1917,* s., margins, crease, very good cond., est. BP 4/500, (12-01-92, Christie-London, #480), plate 6 11/16 x 5 7/16 in., (170 x 138 mm.), drypoint w/roulette on laid paper.

BI *Raucher (F L 155/Kruger L 173), 1916,* s., margins, creases, short tear at lower edge of sheet; skinned areas at corners of sheet verso, Late Gerhard Brauer Coll., est. Dfl. 1,8/2,500, (05-27-93, Sotheby-Amstrdm, #775, illus.), sheet 22 13/16 x 16 7/16 in., (580 x 418 mm.), lithograph on Japan.

BI *Reiter I (Kreiger H87), 1910,* inits., d., i., wide margins, discoloration, skillful repairs, otherminor defects, good cond., est. BP 14/18,000, (05-20-93, Christie-London, #482, illus.), image 8¼ x 11¾ in., (21 x 29.8 cm.), sheet 14½ x 18¾ in., (21 x 29.8 cm.), woodcut in brick-red, olive-green and blue-black on thin pale green wove.

$1701* *"Samlandische Ode" (Kruger L230-250), 1918: Twenty-One,* text by H. Lautensack, s., frontispiece num., d., (06-08-93, Karl/Faber, #1172), approx. 20½ x 15¾ in., (52 x 40 cm.), lithograph on double hand-made (BP 1118, DM 2760, FR 9295, Y 180,669).

$4149* *Schneiderin (Fechter L 34/I; Kruger L 40/I), (19)09,* mono., d., (12-01-92, Karl/Faber, #1081, illus.), 13⅜ x 14 15/16 in., (34 x 38 cm.), lithograph on brown toned paper (BP 2741, DM 6613, FR 22,537, Y 516,559).

$3249* *Seenebel Am Strom (Kruger R 145 II), 1923,* s., d., #46/51, two states, (06-10-93, Hauswedell/Nolt, #761), image 12 13/16 x 15 9/16 in., (32.6 x 39.6 cm.), etching on wove (BP 2125, DM 5291, FR 17,813, Y 344,868).

$11,299* *Selbstbildnis Im Atelier (Kruger H 251), 1921,* s., d., #2/5, (06-10-93, Hauswedell/Nolt, #768, illus.), image 19 9/16 x 15¾ in., (49.7 x 40 cm.), woodcut (BP 7391, DM 18,399, FR 61,946, Y 1,199,342).

$2046* *Selbstbildnis Mit Pfeife (Kruger H250), 1921,* s., pub. Die Schaffenden, 1924, reduced margins, good cond., (12-03-92, Sotheby-London, #478, illus.), 13½ x 11⅛ in., (341 x 282 mm.), woodcut on wove (BP 1320, DM 3217, FR 10,982, Y 254,573).

$14,334* *Sitzender Weiblicher Akt (Kruger L69), 1909,* s., d., i., small margins, minor defects, excell. cond., (05-20-93, Christie-London, #483, illus.), image 20½ x 16⅛ in., (52.1 x 41 cm.), sheet 23 x 16⅞ in., (52.1 x 41 cm.), lithograph in black and grey on smooth wove (BP 9200, DM 23,127, FR 77,902, Y 1,582,818).

$2452* *Uberlegende (Kruger L 390), 1923,* num., s., d., (11-21-92, Lempertz, #316B), 18⅝ x 12⅜ in., (47.3 x 31.5 cm.), lithograph on cream factory-made paper (BP 1614, DM 3909, FR 13,169, Y 304,937).

$709* *Das Vater Unser (Kruger H 258, Ausgabe B), 1921,* s., from series Das Vater Unser, (06-05-93, Bassenge, #6418), 15 11/16 x 11⅝ in., (39.8 x 29.6 cm.), woodcut on imitation Japan (BP 467, DM 1149, FR 3874, Y 76,057).

$2128* *Vergramt (Kruger R 114), 1920,* s., artist's proof, (06-05-93, Bassenge, #6421, illus.), 10 7/16 x 8 1/16 in., (26.5 x 20.5 cm.), etching on thin copper print (BP 1401, DM 3450, FR 11,628, Y 228,277).

$2128* *Vergramt (Kruger R 114I), 1920,* s., artist's proof, (06-05-93, Bassenge, #6420, illus.), 10 7/16 x 8 1/16 in., (26.5 x 20.5 cm.), etching on thin copper print (BP 1401, DM 3450, FR 11,628, Y 228,277).

$709* *Wartende (Kruger L 413), 1946,* s., num., stamp, (06-05-93, Bassenge, #6426), 13⁹⁄₁₆ x 10¹⁄₁₆ in., (34.5 x 25.5 cm.), lithograph on machine-made (BP 467, DM 1149, FR 3874, Y 76,057).

$554* *Wartende (Kruger L. 413), 1946,* s., d., (12-05-92, Bassenge, #7548), 17½ x 10¹⁄₁₆ in., (44.5 x 25.5 cm.), lithograph (BP 347, DM 864, FR 2944, Y 68,641).

$6491* *Die Wolke (Kruger H 150/II), 1912,* s., d., ded., (06-23-93, Kornfeld, #640, illus.), woodcut on thin cream handmade Japan (BP 4410, DM 10,983, FR 36,944, Y 707,158, SF 9775).

$381* *Yali VII (Gewitter) (Kruger R 142), 1923,* s., series Yali und sein weisses Weib, Gurlitt, (06-10-93, Hauswedell/Nolt, #760), image 9⁷⁄₁₆ x 7¹⁄₁₆ in., (23.9 x 18 cm.), drypoint on wove (BP 249, DM 620, FR 2089, Y 40,442).

$3970* *"Zwei Boote" (Fechter H 97, Kruger H 145), 1912,* s., d., (11-28-92, Grisebach, #153, illus.), 6¹¹⁄₁₆ x 8½ in., (17 x 21.6 cm.), woodcut on hand-made Japan (BP 2620, DM 6325, FR 21,471, Y 494,088).

$774* *Zwei Liegende (Kr. L 248; Ausgabe A), 1917,* sheet 19 from H. Lautensacks Paraphrasen zur Samlandischen Ode, mono., (10-09-92, Winterberg, #2894), 12¹⁵⁄₁₆ x 11⁷⁄₁₆ in., (32.8 x 29 cm.), lithograph on van Gelder-Zonen handmade (BP 459, DM 1150, FR 3860, Y 94,229).

$15,859* *Zweisprache (Kruger H 228), 1920,* s., (12-05-92, Bassenge, #7545, illus.), 15¹³⁄₁₆ x 12½ in., (40.2 x 31.8 cm.), color woodcut on handmade (BP 9930, DM 24,726, FR 84,267, Y 1,964,936).

BI *Zweisprachen (K.H. 228), 1920,* s., d., num. 6/50, margins, good cond., repaired tears, thinned spot,mat staining, est. $10/12,000, (02-24-93, Butterfield, #2770, illus.), 15⅞ x 12½ in., (403 x 318 mm.), woodcut in 3 colors on fine laid.

$9384* *Zwiesprache (Kruger H 228), 1920,* s., d., gebraunt, papierverlust, (11-28-92, Schoppmann, #695, illus.), 15¹⁵⁄₁₆ x 12¹¹⁄₁₆ in., (40.5 x 32.2 cm.), color woodcut on wove (BP 6194, DM 14,950, FR 50,752, Y 1,167,890).

$12,006* *Zwiesprache (Kruger H 228; Fechter H 162), 1920,* s., d., (06-10-93, Hauswedell/Nolt, #767, illus.), image 15⅞ x 12¹¹⁄₁₆ in., (40.4 x 32.3 cm.), color woodcut on handmade (BP 7853, DM 19,551, FR 65,822, Y 1,274,387).

PECK and CO., S.
$726* *"The Landing Of Columbus", c. 1858,* lit., (05-06-93, Christie-London, #6), photograph, whole-plate thermoplastic union case, containing two hand-tinted albumen prints (BP 460, DM 1143, FR 3849, Y 79,877).

PECKHAM, Charles
$491* *Imperial Airways, Egypt To India, 1929,* cond. 3, creasing, nicks, (10-13-92, Phillips-London, #40), 29¹⁵⁄₁₆ x 20¹⁄₁₆ in., (76 x 51 cm.), color lithograph (BP 286, DM 719, FR 2444, Y 59,537).

PEDERSEN, Carl Henning   Danish b. 1913
BI *"Barbizon Suite, Numbers 2 And 3": Two,* s. 1976, est. DK 4,000, (09-29-92, B. Rasmussen, #351), lithograph.

$527* *Barbizon-Suite #1,* s. Carl-Henning Pedersen Paris 1976, 127/150, (09-30-92, Kunsthallen, #229), color lithograph (BP 297, DM 747, FR 2528, Y 63,243, DK 2875).

$590* *Barbizon-Suite #2,* s. Carl-Henning Pedersen Paris 1976, 127/150, (09-30-92, Kunsthallen, #230), color lithograph (BP 333, DM 837, FR 2830, Y 70,803, DK 3220).

$421* *Barbizon-Suite #3,* Carl-Henning Pedersen Paris 1976, 127/150, (09-30-92, Kunsthallen, #231), lithograph in colors (BP 238, DM 597, FR 2019, Y 50,522, DK 2300).

$379* *Composition,* from H.C. Andersen Suite, s. Carl-Henning Pedersen 1985, 92/250, (09-30-92, Kunsthallen, #238), color lithograph (BP 214, DM 537, FR 1818, Y 45,482, DK 2070).

$485* *Dage I Barbizon Nr. 1,* s. Carl-Henning Pedersen Paris 1976, 30/150, (09-30-92, Kunsthallen, #232), color lithograph (BP 274, DM 688, FR 2326, Y 58,202, DK 2645).

$442* *Dage I Barbizon Nr. 2,* s. Carl-Henning Pedersen Paris 1976, 30/150, (09-30-92, Kunsthallen, #233), color lithograph (BP 249, DM 627, FR 2120, Y 53,042, DK 2415).

$843* *Den Himmelske Drage V, VI, VII. Kinarejsen: Three,* portfolio, s. Carl-Henning Pedersen Paris 1978, 34/150,

(09-30-92, Kunsthallen, #228), woodcut in colors (BP 476, DM 1195, FR 4043, Y 101,164, DK 4600).

$404* *Eventyrets Univers Nr. 2,* s. Carl Henning Pedersen Paris 1974, 48/150, (03-24-93, Kunsthallen, #269), color lithograph (BP 274, DM 660, FR 2246, Y 47,468, DK 2530).

$442* *Eventyrets Univers Nr. 3,* s. Carl-Henning Pedersen Paris 1974, 48/150, (09-30-92, Kunsthallen, #240), color lithograph (BP 249, DM 627, FR 2120, Y 53,042, DK 2415).

$312* *Fugl Foniks I,* s. Carl Henning Pedersen Paris 1975, 51/150, (03-24-93, Kunsthallen, #267), color lithograph (BP 211, DM 510, FR 1734, Y 36,658, DK 1955).

BI *H.C. Andersens Fairytales, 1985: Twenty-Four,* s., d., #176/250, full margins, good cond., est. G 8/12,000, (12-09-92, Sotheby-Amstrdm, #628, illus.), each approx. 20½ x 15¾ in., (520 x 400 mm.), color lithograph on Arches.

$514* *Jerusalems Syv Porte Nr. 1,* s. Carl Henning Pedersen 1975, 102/150, (03-24-93, Kunsthallen, #270), color lithograph (BP 348, DM 839, FR 2857, Y 60,392, DK 3220).

$514* *Jerusalems Syv Porte Nr. 4,* s. Carl Henning Pedersen 1975, 102/150, (03-24-93, Kunsthallen, #271), color lithograph (BP 348, DM 839, FR 2857, Y 60,392, DK 3220).

$184* *Komposition,* s. Carl Henning Pedersen Paris 1985, ded., (03-24-93, Kunsthallen, #268), color lithograph (BP 125, DM 301, FR 1023, Y 21,619, DK 1150).

$367* *Louisiana, Suite 1,* s. Carl Henning Pedersen 1973, 80/125, (03-24-93, Kunsthallen, #265), color lithograph (BP 249, DM 599, FR 2040, Y 43,121, DK 2300).

$385* *Louisiana, Suite Nr. 2,* s. Carl Henning Pedersen 1973, 75/150, (03-24-93, Kunsthallen, #272), color lithograph (BP 261, DM 629, FR 2140, Y 45,236, DK 2415).

$379* *Louisiana-Suite #1,* s. Carl-Henning Pedersen 1973, 84/150, (09-30-92, Kunsthallen, #239), color lithograph (BP 214, DM 537, FR 1818, Y 45,482, DK 2070).

$330* *Rod Og Gron,* s. Carl Henning Pedersen Paris 1975, 54/150, (03-24-93, Kunsthallen, #266), color lithograph (BP 223, DM 539, FR 1834, Y 38,773, DK 2070).

$514* *Skabelsens 5 Dag-Morgen,* s. Carl Henning Pedersen Paris 1983, 148/150, (03-24-93, Kunsthallen, #273), color lithograph (BP 348, DM 839, FR 2857, Y 60,392, DK 3220).

PEEL, Fred P.
BI *Cider, 1931,* sig., notations, C.P.S.P. Merit Award affixed recto; handstamp, notatations, label verso, est. $500/750, (10-14-92, Swann, #534, illus.), 9⅝ x 6½ in., (24.4 x 16.5 cm.), photograph, bromide print.

PEEREBOOM, Peter
BI *Il Viaggio, 1985,* each s., d., text by artist, t. sheets., just., #7 of 40, pub. Bebert, good cond., in orig. wooden box, Dfl. 800/1,200, (05-27-93, Sotheby-Amstrdm, #672), overall size 19½ x 21⅛ in., (496 x 537 mm.), polaroid, 2 collages, drawing, video tape.

PEETERS, Henk and K. SCHIPPERS
$977* *Niet, 1986: Five,* complete portfolio, s., d. '86, i. E.A., i. H.C., pub. Bebert, good cond., (12-09-92, Sotheby-Amstrdm, #629, illus.), each sheet approx. 19⅞ x 13³⁄₁₆ in., (505 x 335 mm.), color silkscreen and 4 multiples in different techniques (BP 623, DM 1534, FR 5233, Y 121,141, G 1725).

PEETS, Orville Houghton   American 1884-1968
BI *The Embankment Of The _____ Chartres,* s., t., est. $100/150, (02-04-93, Sloan, #367), 16 x 11½ in., (40.6 x 29.2 cm.), etching.

$154* *The Embarkment Of The...Chartres,* s., t., (04-02-93, Sloan, #806), 16 x 11½ in., (406 x 292 mm.), etching (BP 101, DM 248, FR 841, Y 17,534).

PEHRSON, Karl Axel   b. 1921
$2189* *Attoittisk Ranka,* s. 1988, 183/385, (05-25-93, AB Stockholm, #55), 22¹³⁄₁₆ x 15⅜ in., (58 x 39 cm.), lithograph in colors (BP 1419, DM 3565, FR 12,001, Y 239,261, SK 3190).

$185* *Fantastic Landscape,* s., d. 73, 174/350, (11-07-92, Falkkloos, #437), color lithograph (BP 121, DM 297, FR 998, Y 22,834, SK 1100).

$519* *Mansken Over Tropiska Vaxter, 1983,* s., 102/385, (12-04-92, AB Stockholm, #7112), 19⁵⁄₁₆ x 24 in., (49 x 61 cm.), lithograph in colors (BP 333, DM 827, FR 2804, Y 64,794, SK 3520).

$185* *Tropiska Vaxter,* s., d. 76, 88/140, (11-07-92, Falkkloos, #436), color lithograph (BP 121, DM 297, FR 998, Y 22,834, SK 1100).

$665* *Tropiska Vaxter Vid Vatten, 1982,* s., 160/385, (12-04-92, AB Stockholm, #7113), 16⁹⁄₁₆ x 21¼ in., (42 x 54 cm.), lithograph in colors (BP 427, DM 1059, FR 3593, Y 83,021, SK 4510).

PEIFFER-WATENPHUL, Max 1896-1976

$1011* *Annemonen, Veilchen Und Mimosen, c. 1970,* s., num., (11-28-92, Grisebach, #695, illus.), 11⁵⁄₁₆ x 22⅝ in., (28.7 x 57.5 cm.), colored lithograph on handmade (BP 667, DM 1611, FR 5468, Y 125,825).

$1056* *Blick Auf Sudlandische Meeresbucht Von Villen-Terrasse Aus,* s. Max Peiffer Watenphul, #79/100, creases, (03-24-93, Venator/Hansten, #4548), approx. 31⅛ x 39⅜ in., (79 x 100 cm.), color lithograph (BP 715, DM 1725, FR 5870, Y 124,075).

$845* *Blick Durch Pinien Und Zypressen Auf Das Meer,* s. Max Peiffer Watenphul, #76/80, (03-24-93, Venator/Hansten, #4549), approx. 13¹⁵⁄₁₆ x 18⅞ in., (35.5 x 48 cm.), color lithograph (BP 572, DM 1380, FR 4697, Y 99,283).

$1086* *Garten In Venedig,* s., num., (09-25-92, Granier, #2969), sheet 19¹¹⁄₁₆ x 27¹⁵⁄₁₆ in., (50 x 71 cm.), color lithograph on hand-made (BP 634, DM 1610, FR 5444, Y 131,080).

$371* *Salzburg Im Herbst, 1955,* s., num., (10-14-92, Germann, #394), 15¼ x 19⁹⁄₁₆ in., (387 x 497 mm.), color lithograph (BP 218, DM 543, FR 1841, Y 44,959, SF 484).

BI *Segelboote Von Chioggia, c. 1955,* s., est. DM 2/3,000, (11-28-92, Grisebach, #693, illus.), 29⅛ x 27⅜ in., (74 x 69.6 cm.), colored lithograph on wove.

$1408* *Sudlandische Meerekuste, Sizilien,* s. Max Peiffer Watenphul, #1/100, (03-24-93, Venator/Hansten, #4547), approx. 10⁷⁄₁₆ x 23⅝ in., (26.5 x 60 cm.), color lithograph (BP 953, DM 2300, FR 7827, Y 165,433).

$1011* *Sudliche Kuste, 1957,* s., d., num., (11-28-92, Grisebach, #694, illus.), 10½ x 23¹⁄₁₆ in., (26.7 x 58.5 cm.), colored lithograph on handmade (BP 667, DM 1611, FR 5468, Y 125,825).

$794* *Venedig, c. 1970,* s., num., (11-28-92, Grisebach, #696, illus.), 17¹³⁄₁₆ x 11⅛ in., (45.2 x 28.3 cm.), colored lithograph on copper print paper (BP 524, DM 1265, FR 4294, Y 98,818).

PEIHUNG, Xu (after) Chinese 1895-1953

$50* *Running Horse,* (12-10-92, Sloan, #1255), 8 x 11¼ in., (20.3 x 28.6 cm.), woodblock (BP 32, DM 79, FR 270, Y 6185).

PEIKERT, Martin 1901-1975

BI *Le Pays Du Soleil, Adelboden 1400m, c. 1930,* p. Otto Schaefli, cond. 3, image tear, est. BP 2/300, (10-13-92, Phillips-London, #41, illus.), 39³⁄₁₆ x 25 in., (99.5 x 63.5 cm.), color lithograph.

PELAYO, Orlando Spanish 1920-1947

$835* *"El Lazarillo De Tormes", 1975: Eleven,* #177/195, s., Ediciones de Arte y Bibliofilia, (12-17-92, Duran, #176, illus.), 20½ x 15⅜ in., (52 x 39 cm.), etching (BP 530, DM 1304, FR 4453, Y 102,618, P 92,000).

PELLAN, Alfred Canadian b. 1906

$205* *"Andante",* #5/150, s., d. Pellan 74, t., Guilde Graphique stamp, (07-14-92, Encans, #70), 16¹⁵⁄₁₆ x 20¹⁄₁₆ in., (43 x 51 cm.), serigraph (BP 107, DM 304, FR 1026, Y 25,635, C$ 244).

$174* *Chute,* #47/80, s., d. Pellan 80, (11-17-92, Encans, #66), 8⁷⁄₁₆ x 7½ in., (21.5 x 19 cm.), color etching (BP 115, DM 277, FR 934, Y 21,639, C$ 222).

$131* *"Chute",* #76/80, s., d. Pellan 80, (06-16-93, Encans, #80), 8⅜ x 7⅜ in., (21.3 x 18.8 cm.), color etching (BP 87, DM 217, FR 730, Y 13,972, C$ 167).

BI *Le Cirque Sacre: Six,* Folio, Studio 7 blindstamp, s., d., #80/80, illus. text, pub. M. Pierre Guillaume and M. Paul Machnik, autographed by artist and author, est. C$3,500/4,000, (06-07-93, Ritchie, #52, illus.), each image approx. 9¹³⁄₁₆ x 7¹³⁄₁₆ in., (25 x 19.8 cm.), color etchings on Arches.

$233* *"Crepuscule",* #29/150, s., d. Pellan 74, t., Guilde Graphique stamp, (07-14-92, Encans, #67), 21¹⁄₁₆ x 16⅛ in., (53.5 x 41 cm.), serigraph (BP 121, DM 346, FR 1166, Y 29,136, C$ 278).

$205* *"Crepuscule",* #51/150, s., d. Pellan 74, t., Guilde Graphique stamp, (07-14-92, Encans, #69), 21¹⁄₁₆ x 16⅛ in., (53.5 x 41 cm.), serigraph (BP 107, DM 304, FR 1026, Y 25,635, C$ 244).

$205* *"Crepuscule",* #26/150, s., d. Pellan 74, t., Guilde Graphique stamp, (07-14-92, Encans, #68), 21¹⁄₁₆ x 16⅛ in., (53.5 x 41 cm.), serigraph (BP 107, DM 304, FR 1026, Y 25,635, C$ 244).

$195* *"Evolution",* #76/80, s., d. Pellan 81, (03-16-93, Encans, #89), 9⅝ x 7⅜ in., (24.5 x 18.8 cm.), etching (BP 135, DM 324, FR 1102, Y 22,802, C$ 244).

$438* *"Faconnage",* t., #99/100, s., d. Pellan 73, (05-18-93, Encans, #118), 21³⁄₁₆ x 18¹¹⁄₁₆ in., (53.8 x 47.5 cm.), serigraph (BP 285, DM 711, FR 2400, Y 48,813, C$ 555).

$1061* *"Fleuron",* #33/100, s., d. Pellan 75, t., (04-20-93, Encans, #74), 23⅝ x 35⁷⁄₁₆ in., (60 x 90 cm.), serigraph (BP 685, DM 1690, FR 5704, Y 117,069, C$ 1332).

$263* *"Incredulite",* #76/80, s., d. Pellan 81, (05-18-93, Encans, #117), 8⅞ x 7⅞ in., (22.5 x 20 cm.), etching (BP 171, DM 427, FR 1441, Y 29,310, C$ 333).

$137* *"Incredulite",* #47/80, s., d. Pellan 81, (09-15-92, Encans, #84), 9⁷⁄₁₆ x 7⅞ in., (24 x 20 cm.), etching and aquatint (BP 73, DM 204, FR 692, Y 17,008, C$ 167).

$309* *"Positions",* #76/80, s., d. Pellan 80, (02-16-93, Encans, #59), 10¹⁄₁₆ x 7⅞ in., (25.5 x 20 cm.), etching in color (BP 214, DM 504, FR 1708, Y 37,019, C$ 389).

$156* *"La Vie",* #76/80, s., d. Pellan 81, (06-16-93, Encans, #79), 9⅝ x 8⅜ in., (24.5 x 21.3 cm.), color etching (BP 104, DM 259, FR 869, Y 16,638, C$ 200).

$227* *"La Vie",* #47/80, s., d. Pellan 81, (10-20-92, Encans, #117), 8⁷⁄₁₆ x 7¹⁄₁₆ in., (21.5 x 18 cm.), etching (BP 127, DM 345, FR 1174, Y 28,453, C$ 278).

$261* *"Viola",* #93/100, s., d. Pellan 71, (11-17-92, Encans, #67), 25⁹⁄₁₆ x 19¹¹⁄₁₆ in., (65 x 50 cm.), color lithograph (BP 172, DM 416, FR 1402, Y 32,459, C$ 333).

PELLEGRINO, Domenico (called Tibaldi) c. 1532- c. 1582

$999* *Peace (B. XVIII, 6), c. 1570,* thread margins or trimmed, rust spot, very good cond., laid., (12-01-92, Christie-London, #54, illus.), S. 15¹³⁄₁₆ x 10⁹⁄₁₆ in., (401 x 269 mm.), engraving (BP 660, DM 1592, FR 5426, Y 124,377).

PELLIGRINI, Alfred Heinrich 1881-1958

$114* *Bauern Mit Holzschlitten,* #125/130, s., creases, (11-13-92, Koller, #5390), 24 x 18⁵⁄₁₆ in., (61 x 46.5 cm.), lithograph on wove (BP 74, DM 179, FR 603, Y 14,149, SF 162).

PEMBERTON, H.M.

$17 *"Low Water",* s., (10-09-92, G.A. Key, #86), 5¾ x 8¾ in., (14.6 x 22.2 cm.), etching (BP 10, DM 25, FR 86, Y 2073).

PEN, Rene

$3301* *The Royal Biograph,* p. Chaix, folds, repairs, edge defects, backed on linen, (05-07-93, Christie-S. Ken, #134, illus.), 42 x 61½ in., (106.7 x 156.2 cm.), color lithograph (BP 2090, DM 5219, FR 17,587, Y 363,466).

PENALBA, Alicia Argentinian b. 1918

BI *Champ Aile,* 117/150, s., est. SF 100/130, (10-14-92, Germann, #395), 19¹¹⁄₁₆ x 25¹³⁄₁₆ in., (500 x 655 mm.), lithograph.

BI *Sonate,* s., 37/95, est. FF6/800, (06-28-93, Loudmer, #330), 26⅜ x 21¼ in., (670 x 540 mm.), sh 29⅛ x 21¼ in., (670 x 540 mm.), black lithograph on Arches wove.

PENCK, A.R. (Ralf WINKLER) German b. 1939

$289* *"Am Lit. Neue Literatur Aus Den USA",* s., num., poster, (11-28-92, Grisebach, #705, illus.), 29⅝ x 23⁹⁄₁₆ in., (75.3 x 59.8 cm.), colored serigraph on offset paper (BP 191, DM 460, FR 1563, Y 35,968).

$239* *"Amalyse Einer Situation", 1992,* posters Ausstellung Staatliche Kunstsammlungen Albertinum, Dresden, num., (11-28-92, Grisebach, #706, illus.), 32¹⁄₁₆ x 22¹³⁄₁₆ in., (81.5 x 58 cm.), lithograph on handmade (BP 158, DM 381, FR 1293, Y 29,745).

$443* *Analyse Einer Situation, 1992,* Staatliche Kunstsammlungen Albertinum, Dresden, s., (12-05-92, Bassenge, #7616), lithograph (BP 277, DM 691, FR 2354, Y 54,888).

BI *Die Arbeit Geht Weiter, 1982,* s., num., est. DM 3,000-, (09-25-92, Granier, #2970, illus.), sheet 39¼ x 30¹³⁄₁₆ in., (99.7 x 78.3 cm.), woodcut w/oil color on copper print paper.

$5116* *Banana Elephant, 1990,* s., #12/50, pub. Aschenbach Editions, full margins, good cond., creases, (12-03-92, Sotheby-London, #776, illus.), approx. 51¼ x 98½ in., (130.2 x 250.2 cm.), lithograph in colors on wove (BP 3300, DM 8045, FR 27,461, Y 636,556).

BI *"Das Blaue Huhn", 1990: Nine,* Edition Galerie Aschenbach, s., num., est. DM 3000, (12-01-92, Karl/Faber, #1090, illus.), 19½ x 16¾ in., (49.5 x 42.5 cm.), color serigraph on thick, smooth cardboard.

BI *Das Blaue Huhn, Gedichte Und Siebdrucke, 1990: Sixteen,* num., last page s., num., Edition Galerie Aschenbach, Amsterdam, est. DM 2,500, (12-05-92, Bassenge, #7554), color screen print, bound.

$1135* *Dani Und Kinder, 1985,* s., num., (06-05-93, Bassenge, #6431), 25³⁄₁₆ x 36⅝ in., (64 x 93 cm.), drypoint on thick paper (BP 747, DM 1840, FR 6202, Y 121,755).

BI *Drei Figuren, 1985,* 3rd state, s., #5/V, est. DM 4,500-, (05-27-93, Lempertz, #943, illus.), 25⁹⁄₁₆ x 36⅞ in., (65 x 93.7 cm.), etching on wove.

BI *Drei Figuren, 1989,* s, num., est. DM 1,8/2,000, (11-28-92, Grisebach, #700, illus.), 29¹⁵⁄₁₆ x 21¼ in., (76 x 54 cm.), colored serigraph on copper print paper.

BI *Die Dunkelheit Der Macht,* s., #62/100, est. DM 1,400, (06-12-93, Hauswedell/Nolt, #325), 23¹³⁄₁₆ x 35⁷⁄₁₆ in., (60.5 x 90 cm.), linocut on thick wove.

$542* *Gruppe, 1961,* i. a.p., mono., (11-28-92, Schoppmann, #703), 11⅝ x 15¹⁵⁄₁₆ in., (29.5 x 40.5 cm.), linocut in brown on light cardboard (BP 358, DM 863, FR 2931, Y 67,455).

BI *Hamlet - AM LIT Neue Literatur Aus Den USA, 1992,* s., num., Druckhaus Galrev, Berlin, est. DM 600, (12-05-92, Bassenge, #7615), color screen print in red on turquoise ground.

BI *"Keramik", 1990,* #29/66, s., est. SF 2,2/2,800, (11-13-92, Koller, #5391), 32⁵⁄₁₆ x 23¼ in., (82 x 59 cm.), serigraph on wove.

$709* *Komposition Mit Figuren, c. 1980,* s., i. epreuve d'artiste, (06-05-93, Grisebach, #823, illus.), 22¹³⁄₁₆ x 30¹⁵⁄₁₆ in., (58 x 78.7 cm.), lithograph on imitation Japan (BP 467, DM 1149, FR 3874, Y 76,057).

$1765* *Komposition, 1986,* E.A., s., 882mm x 1242mm, (10-14-92, Germann, #40, illus.), serigraph (BP 1036, DM 2583, FR 8759, Y 213,888, SF 2300).

$794* *Liegender Schwarzer Akt,* s., artist's proof, (11-28-92, Grisebach, #699, illus.), 11⁹⁄₁₆ x 19⅜ in., (29.4 x 49.2 cm.), aquatint on copper print paper (BP 524, DM 1265, FR 4294, Y 98,818).

$1082* *Lowe I, 1988,* #15/20, pencil s., (11-20-92, Lempertz, #763, illus.), sh 18³⁄₁₆ x 22⁵⁄₁₆ in., (46.2 x 56.7 cm.), etching on Velin (BP 712, DM 1725, FR 5811, Y 134,560).

$575* *Lyrik, 1988,* text by Sarah Kirsch, s. by artist and author, #26, pub. Edition Malebucher, original slipcase, overall size approx. 337 x 240 x 102 mm, (02-11-93, Sotheby-NY, #404), book, color silkscreen (BP 406, DM 952, FR 3223, Y 69,319).

BI *O.A.T.M.I., 1986,* #9/35, s., (11-20-92, Lempertz, #769), sh 24⅞ x 31⅞ in., (63.2 x 81 cm.), color lithograph on Arches wove.

BI *Ohne Titel,* #1/10, pencil s., est. DM 2,000, (11-20-92, Lempertz, #767), sh 39¹³⁄₁₆ x 27¹¹⁄₁₆ in., (101.1 x 70.3 cm.), serigraph on hand-made cardboard.

$1587* *Ohne Titel,* #10/10, pencil s., (11-20-92, Lempertz, #765, illus.), sh 27¹¹⁄₁₆ x 39⁷⁄₁₆ in., (70.3 x 100.2 cm.), serigraph on hand-made cardboard (BP 1045, DM 2530, FR 8523, Y 197,364).

$1443* *Ohne Titel,* e.a., pencil s., (11-20-92, Lempertz, #766, illus.), sh 48⅛ x 33¹⁵⁄₁₆ in., (122.3 x 86.3 cm.), serigraph on hand-mdae cardboard (BP 950, DM 2301, FR 7750, Y 179,455).

BI *Ohne Titel,* #XX/X, pencil s., est. DM 2,000, (11-20-92, Lempertz, #768, illus.), sh 48⅛ x 33¹⁵⁄₁₆ in., (122.3 x 86.3 cm.), serigraph on white handmade cardboard.

$8242* *Quo Vadis Germania, 1985,* s., #13/30, (05-27-93, Lempertz, #942, illus.), 34¹⁵⁄₁₆ x 64¹⁵⁄₁₆ in., (88.8 x 165 cm.), color etching on thick wove (BP 5278, DM 13,225, FR 44,575, Y 883,576).

$1805* *Romantischer Streit, 1989,* s., num., (11-28-92, Grisebach, #698, illus.), 25³⁄₁₆ x 39⅛ in., (64 x 99.3 cm.), colored aquatint on copper print paper (BP 1191, DM 2876, FR 9762, Y 224,642).

$2200* *Roted Flugzeug, 1985,* s., d. 4/10, (12-13-92, Hindman, #333, illus.), 25 x 36¾ in., drypoint (BP 1407, DM 3457, FR 11,784, Y 272,176).

BI *Situation 1979,* #17/30, pencil s., d., est. DM 1,800, (11-20-92, Lempertz, #762), sh 15⅝ x 21³⁄₁₆ in., (39.7 x 53.8 cm.), etching on thick Hahnemuhle-Velin.

$577* *Sitzende, 1989,* s., epreuve d'artiste, (11-28-92, Grisebach, #701, illus.), 16¹⁵⁄₁₆ x 13⅜ in., (43 x 34 cm.), colored serigraph on copper print paper (BP 381, DM 919, FR 3121, Y 71,811).

BI *Untitled,* s., #247/250, margins, good cond.?, light-staining, handling creases,est. $1/2,000, (05-19-93, Butterfield, #2287, illus.), 33½ x 48 in., (85.1 x 121.9 cm.), silkscreen in black/red/blue on wove.

BI *(Untitled) From The Lausanne Suite, 1989,* s., #46/70, full margins, good cond., est. BP 5/700, (06-30-93, Sotheby-London, #891, illus.), 27½ x 29½ in., (699 x 749 mm.), color lithograph on wove.

$2280* *Untitled, 1989,* s., #4/30, good cond., 2510 x 1285 mm, (12-09-92, Sotheby-Amstrdm, #630), color silkscreen on wove (BP 1455, DM 3579, FR 12,212, Y 282,703, G 4025).

$502* *Untitled, Lowe Und Figur, 1988,* s., #32/50, (05-27-93, Lempertz, #944), 4 x 5¹³⁄₁₆ in., (10.2 x 14.7 cm.), color woodcut (BP 321, DM 806, FR 2715, Y 53,816).

BI *Untitled, c. 1970,* est. DM 500, (12-01-92, Karl/Faber, #1089), 11⅝ x 15¹⁵⁄₁₆ in., (29.5 x 40.5 cm.), serigraph in brown on smooth, thin board.

BI *Zone D, 1991,* #24/35, pencil s., est. DM 1,800, (11-20-92, Lempertz, #764), sh 48⁷⁄₁₆ x 34¼ in., (123 x 87 cm.), serigraph in color on paper.

PENCZ, Georg German c. 1500-c.1550

$169* *"Dialectia", Mit Waage (Hollstein 83),* sheet 2 from series Kunste, mono. PG, trimmed, (03-24-93, Venator/Hansten, #2558), sh. 2¹⁵⁄₁₆ x 2¹⁄₁₆ in., (7.5 x 5.2 cm.), engraving (BP 114, DM 276, FR 939, Y 19,857).

$916* *The Five Senses (B. 105-9; L. 104-8; Holl. 103-7): Set Of Five,* thread margins or trimmed, defects, prov., (12-01-92, Christie-London, #174), plate 3⅛ x 2 in., (79 x 51 mm.), engraving (BP 605, DM 1460, FR 4976, Y 114,044).

$1275* *Die Harfenspielerin (B. 96, Landau 96, Hollstein 81), 1544,* (06-04-93, Bassenge, #5305), diameter 1¹⁵⁄₁₆ xin., (5.5 x cm.), round engraving (BP 844, DM 2070, FR 6979, Y 137,511).

$1300* *Joseph Wird An Die Handler Verkauft (B. 11; Landau 10), 1546,* prov., (12-04-92, Bassenge, #6354, illus.), engraving (BP 834, DM 2070, FR 7023, Y 162,297).

BI *"Marcus Curtius" (Bartsch 75 i/i), c. 1535,* platemark visible, mounted, est. $4/500, (10-31-92, Cleveland, #19), 4⅝ x 3⅛ in., (11.7 x 7.9 cm.), engraving.

$1831* *Medea And Jason (B. 71; L. 74; Holl. 121),* 1st state of 2, light tone, watermark, small margins, good cond., (12-01-92, Christie-London, #169), plate 4⁹⁄₁₆ x 2¹⁵⁄₁₆ in., (116 x 74 mm.), engraving (BP 1210, DM 2918, FR 9946, Y 227,963).

$709* *Salomons Urteil (B. 23; Landau 24), c. 1531,* prov., (06-08-93, Karl/Faber, #123), engraving (BP 466, DM 1150, FR 3874, Y 75,305).

$1249* *The Seven Deadly Sins (B. 98-104; L. 97-103; Holl. 108-114),* 1st state of 2, rest only state, repair, defects, prov., (12-01-92, Christie-London, #173, illus.), plate, largest 3¼ x 2¹⁄₁₆ in., (83 x 53 mm.), engraving (BP 825, DM 1991, FR 6784, Y 155,503).

$1912* *Die Sieben Todsunden (B. 98-99, 100 I, 101-104, Landau 97-103, Hollstein 108-114), c. 1541: Seven,* (06-04-93, Bassenge, #5306, illus.), each approx. 3¼ x 2¹⁄₁₆ in., (8.3 x 5.3 cm.), engraving (BP 1265, DM 3105, FR 10,465, Y 206,212).

BI *The Story Of Tobias (B. 13-19; L. 12-18; Holl. 26-32): Set Of Seven,* repaired tear, defects, prov., est. BP 700/ 1,000, (12-01-92, Christie-London, #170, illus.), plate, largest 2¹¹⁄₁₆ x 4³⁄₁₆ in., (69 x 107 mm.), engraving.

$155* *"Titus Manlius" (Hollstein Bd. 31, 128),* mono. PG, (03-24-93, Venator/Hansten, #2557), pl. 4⁹⁄₁₆ x 2¹⁵⁄₁₆ in., (11.6 x 7.4 cm.), engraving (BP 105, DM 253, FR 862, Y 18,212).

PENFIELD, Edward   American 1866-1925

$302* *"Harper's April" and "Harper's February": Two,* B-cond., restored, (08-06-92, Swann, #222, illus.), approx. 9 x 13 in., (22.9 x 33 cm.), (BP 158, DM 446, FR 1507, Y 38,520).

$504* *"Harper's April", 1897 and "Harper's February", 1896: Two,* creases, loss, other small defects, lit., (02-04-93, Christie-S. Ken., #75, illus.), 20 x 14½ in., (50.8 x 36.8 cm.), color lithograph backed on card (BP 352, DM 830, FR 2814, Y 62,694).

$880* *"Harper's February", 1897 (American Posters of the 90's, 193),* s. Edward Penfield, ident., good cond., nicks, tears; thinning to corners verso, (10-09-92, Skinner, #134, illus.), 19 x 14 in., (48.3 x 35.6 cm.), lithographic poster in color on paper (BP 522, DM 1311, FR 4444, Y 107,317).

$523* *"Harper's July" and "Harper's March", 1897: Two Posters (American Posters of the 90's, 197 and 194),* s. Edward Penfield, both matrix ident., good cond.?, staining, (10-09-92, Skinner, #48), sight 18¹⁄₃ x 13½ in., (46.6 x 34.3 cm.), lithographic poster in color on paper (BP 310, DM 779, FR 2641, Y 63,780).

$440* *Harper's March, 1896,* B+ cond., restoration, (08-06-92, Swann, #220, illus.), 18 x 10½ in., (45.7 x 26.7 cm.), (BP 230, DM 650, FR 2196, Y 56,122).

$1100* *Harper's November, 1896,* A cond., back cover illus., (08-06-92, Swann, #221, illus.), 18 x 13½ in., (45.7 x 34.3 cm.), Japan paper backed (BP 575, DM 1625, FR 5489, Y 140,306).

BI *"Harper's/February, Man & Cat, 1898", "Harper's/February, 1897, Group Reading" and "Harper's/August, 1897, Lady By A Beach Chair": Three,* plate s., est. $2/3,000, (06-08-93, Christie-E, #194), each sight 17¾ x 12¾ in., (45.1 x 32.4 cm.), color lithograph.

BI *Lady In Horse Carriage,* mono., est. $300/400, (12-10-92, Sloan, #1310), sight 14¾ x 21½ in., (37.5 x 54.6 cm.), color lithograph.

PENMAN, Edith

BI *Beagles In Pursuit,* after John M. Tracy, s. Edith Penman and John M. Tracy, est. $1/300, (02-13-93, Collins, #133, illus.), 9 x 26½ in., (22.9 x 67.3 cm.), etching.

PENN, Irving   American b. 1917

$3088* *"3 New Guinea Men, 2 With Pipes, Photographed 1970",* p. 1983, t., s., num. 3120, 1/7, annot., stamped, 586 x 507mm, (05-07-93, Sotheby-London, #342, illus.), photograph, platinum palladium print (BP 1955, DM 4882, FR 16,452, Y 340,013).

$12,100* *Ballet Society (MoMA, dust jacket and pl. 19),* s., t., d., num. 9/15, i. w/technical info by photog., (c) & ed. limit. stamps, 1948 p. 1976, #9/15 ed., (10-15-92, Sotheby-NY, #544, illus.), 18 x 22¼ in., (45.7 x 56.5 cm.), photograph, platinum-palladium print, mounted on aluminum (BP 7404, DM 18,011, FR 61,080, Y 1,451,710).

$4600* *"Ballet Society, New York",* mounted, s., t., d., num. by photog., (c), edit. lim. stamps, 1948, p. 1984, (04-06-93, Sotheby-NY, #450, illus.), 9½ x 7½ in., photograph (BP 3038, DM 7411, FR 25,095, Y 524,635).

$6600* *"Ballet Theatre" (Moments Preserved, p. 146),* 1948/1977, s., t., d., edit. 8/25, photog. name, edit., Conde Nast stamps, (11-16-92, Butterfield, #6119, illus.), 15½ x 21⁹⁄₁₆ in., (394.4 x 547.1 mm.), photograph, platinum/pal-

ladium print mounted on aluminum (BP 4346, DM 10,523, FR 35,446, Y 820,793).

$6600* *Ballet Theatre, 1947 (MoMA, pl. 15),* s., t., d., num., printing notations by photog., (c) & printing info.stamps verso, (10-15-92, Sotheby-NY, #545, illus.), 14 x 19 in., (35.6 x 48.3 cm.), photograph, gelatin silver print (BP 4039, DM 9824, FR 33,317, Y 791,842).

$12,100* *Black And White Vogue Cover,* (1950), 1968, s., t., d., num., exhib. data, (c) credit stamp, #11/34in platinum metals, exhib., lit., (10-13-92, Christie-NY, #483, illus.), 17 x 13⅝ in., (43.2 x 34.6 cm.), photograph, platinum-palladium print on Arches paper (BP 7047, DM 17,726, FR 60,229, Y 1,467,200).

$10,299* *Black And White Vogue Cover, Jean Patchett, New York, 1950,* p. 1976, s., stamped #23/24, lit., (10-29-92, Christie-London, #167, illus.), 17 x 13¾ in., (43.2 x 34.9 cm.), photograph, platinum palladium print (BP 6600, DM 15,845, FR 53,753, Y 1,275,734).

$4400* *Cecil Beaton,* (1950), 1980, s., t., d., edit. #, (c) stamp, #9/15, lit., (10-13-92, Christie-NY, #482, illus.), 15 x 14⅝ in., (38.1 x 37.1 cm.), photograph, multiple-printed, multiple-coated platinum-palladium print on Rives paper (BP 2563, DM 6446, FR 21,901, Y 533,527).

$5290* *Cigarette 37,* 1972, p. 1975, s., t., d., num., (c) credit/ reprod. limitation stamps; #30/71 in platinum metals, lit., (04-08-93, Christie-NY, #511, illus.), 23 x 17 in., (58.4 x 43.2 cm.), photograph, multiple-coated and multiple-printed platinum-palladium print on Arches w/aluminum backing (BP 3469, DM 8498, FR 28,766, Y 600,318).

$5775* *Cigarette 37 (MoMA, pl. 18),* s., d., num. 35/70, printing notations by photog., (c) stamp, 1974, p. 1975, #35/70 ed., (10-15-92, Sotheby-NY, #551, illus.), 23¼ x 17¼ in., (59.1 x 43.8 cm.), photograph, platinum-palladium print (BP 3534, DM 8596, FR 29,152, Y 692,861).

$15,400* *Cigarette 37, New York: Four,* (1972), mounted together, 1977, s., t., d., num., (c) & reprod. limitstamps, #1/11 edit., lit., (10-13-92, Christie-NY, #590, illus.), 50½ x 40½ in., (128.3 x 102.9 cm.), photograph, hand-coated platinum-palladium prints on Arches paper (BP 8969, DM 22,561, FR 76,655, Y 1,867,346).

$2906* *Cigarettes, c. 1975,* s., annot. edit., credit and (c) limitation stamps, 630 x 558mm, (05-07-93, Sotheby-London, #336, illus.), photograph, platinum paladium print on aluminium (BP 1840, DM 4594, FR 15,482, Y 319,974).

$9350* *Colette (MoMA, pl. 35),* s., t., d., num. 21/50 by photog., (c) & ed. info. stamps, 1951, p. 1978, #21/50 ed., (10-15-92, Sotheby-NY, #540A, illus.), 19¾ x 19⅝ in., (50.2 x 49.8 cm.), photograph, platinum-palladium print, mounted on aluminum (BP 5721, DM 13,918, FR 47,198, Y 1,121,776).

$11,500* *Colette, Paris, 1951,* credit stamp, reprod. limitation stamps, labels; 1954 (c) d./reprod.limitation, lit., (04-08-93, Christie-NY, #508, illus.), 13½ x 13⅜ in., (34.3 x 34 cm.), photograph, gelatin silver print (BP 7541, DM 18,474, FR 62,534, Y 1,305,039).

$2760* *"Croissant",* s., t., d. by photog., name, edit., date, (c) stamps, 1982, p. 1992, (04-06-93, Sotheby-NY, #223A, illus.), 21 x 16¼ in., photograph, dye-transfer print (BP 1823, DM 4447, FR 15,057, Y 314,781).

$4125* *Duchess Of Windsor (MoMA, pl. 19),* s., t., d., num. 5/9, i. w/technical info. by photog., photog.'s ed.limit. stamp & label, 1949, p. 1970, #5/9 ed., (10-15-92, Sotheby-NY, #542, illus.), 19 x 12¼ in., (48.3 x 31.1 cm.), photograph, gelatin silver print (BP 2524, DM 6140, FR 20,823, Y 494,901).

$3575* *Dusek Brothers (MoMA, pl. 20),* s., t., d., printing notations by photog. in ink, (c) & printing info. stamps, 1948, p. c. 1948, (10-15-92, Sotheby-NY, #547, illus.), 7⅝ x 9⅝ in., (19.4 x 24.4 cm.), photograph, gelatin silver print (BP 2188, DM 5322, FR 18,046, Y 428,914).

$5750* *Father And Son With Eggs, Cuzco,* 1948, p. 1978, s., t., d., num., credit/(c) reprod. limitation stamps, #13/14 in platinum metals, lit., (04-08-93, Christie-NY, #506, illus.), 11¾ x 11⅜ in., (29.8 x 28.9 cm.), photograph, hand-coated platinum-palladium print on Rives w/aluminum-backing (BP 3770, DM 9237, FR 31,267, Y 652,519).

$8800* *Four Guedras, Morocco,* (1971), 1985, s., t., d., num., (c) credit stamp, #17/18 in platinummetals, (10-13-92,

Christie-NY, #589, illus.), 23 x 19¾ in., (58.4 x 50.2 cm.), photograph, multiple-printed platinum-palladium, print on Rives paperw/aluminum backing (BP 5125, DM 12,892, FR 43,803, Y 1,067,055).

$8970* *Gorilla (Male), Prague, 1986,* ink s., t.; edit. (c), printing and neg. info. stamps, lit., (04-08-93, Christie-NY, #513, illus.), 23¼ x 18½ in., (59.1 x 47 cm.), photograph, gelatin silver print (BP 5882, DM 14,410, FR 48,777, Y 1,017,930).

$9900* *Harlequin Dress-Lisa Fonssagrives Penn (MoMA, pl. 49),* s., t., d. by photog., (c) & printing info. stamps, 1950, p. 1983, (10-15-92, Sotheby-NY, #546A, illus.), 19⅝ x 18¾ in., (49.8 x 47.6 cm.), photograph, gelatin silver print (BP 6058, DM 14,737, FR 49,975, Y 1,187,762).

$3450* *Hippie Family (K), San Francisco,* 1967, p. 1976, s., t., d., edit. #4/25, (c) credit stamp, lit., soldafter sale, (04-08-93, Christie-NY, #507, illus.), 16¾ x 14¼ in., (42.5 x 36.2 cm.), photograph, hand-coated platinum-palladium print on Arches (BP 2262, DM 5542, FR 18,760, Y 391,512).

$1870* *Igor Stravinsky,* (1948), 1984, s., t., d. in ink, (c) credit & reprod. limit. stamps,#1/25, lit., (10-13-92, Christie-NY, #480, illus.), 9½ x 7½ in., (24.1 x 19.1 cm.), photograph, selenium-toned gelatin silver print (BP 1089, DM 2740, FR 9308, Y 226,749).

$7475* *Italian Still Life, New York,* 1981, p. 1984, ink s., t., d., credit (c) stamp, lit., (04-08-93, Christie-NY, #512, illus.), 19½ x 15¼ in., (49.5 x 38.7 cm.), photograph, dye-transfer print (BP 4902, DM 12,008, FR 40,647, Y 848,275).

$8250* *Man With Pink Face, New Guinea,* (1970), 1978, s., t., d., num., (c) credit stamp, #36/49 in platinummetals, lit., (10-13-92, Christie-NY, #587, illus.), 20x19¼ in., (x 48.9 cm.), photograph, multiple-printed platinum-palladium print on Rives paperw/aluminum backing (BP 4805, DM 12,086, FR 41,065, Y 1,000,364).

$1725* *"Marchand De Concombres, Paris", 1950,* s., t., d., #17/41, p. nototations by photog., (c) stamps, p. 1967, (04-06-93, Sotheby-NY, #451A, illus.), 16⅛ x 12½ in., photograph, platinum-palladium print (BP 1139, DM 2779, FR 9411, Y 196,738).

$3300* *Marlene Dietrich, 1948,* s., t., d. by photog., (c), print info, (c) stamp, (10-15-92, Sotheby-NY, #541, illus.), 10 x 8 in., (25.4 x 20.3 cm.), photograph, gelatin silver print (BP 2019, DM 4912, FR 16,658, Y 395,921).

$4620* *Marlene Dietrich, New York, 1948,* s., t., d., annot., ltd. edit. of 39, (c) credit & reprod. limit. stamps, #1/39, lit., (10-13-92, Christie-NY, #481, illus.), 9⅝ x 7⅝ in., (24.4 x 19.4 cm.), photograph, gelatin silver print (BP 2691, DM 6768, FR 22,997, Y 560,204).

$6050* *"Miles Davis", 1986,* s., t., d., annot. New York, edit. of 12, photog. edit. stamps, Dixon Collection, (11-16-92, Butterfield, #6120, illus.), 14⅞ x 14⅞ in., (378.5 x 378.5 mm.), photograph, gelatin silver print (BP 3983, DM 9646, FR 32,492, Y 752,394).

$1998* *"Mother And Child With Tweed Overall (Cuzco, Peru, 1948)",* p. 1949, t., s., annot. Print made 1949 IP, stamped signed, silver prints of this negative not exceeding 13, Photograph by Irving Penn copyright 1985, (c) limitation stamps, 352 x 279mm, (05-07-93, Sotheby-London, #337, illus.), photograph, silver print (BP 1265, DM 3159, FR 10,645, Y 219,996).

$1725* *"Mrs. Lewis Amory And Son" (Moments Preserved, p. 108, variant cropping),* s., t., d., i. Early Print, I.P. by photog., (c), edit. info stamp, 1948, p. before 1970's, (04-06-93, Sotheby-NY, #450A, illus.), 13½ x 10½ in., photograph (BP 1139, DM 2779, FR 9411, Y 196,738).

$3910* *New York Still Life, 1947,* ink s., t., d., annot. Print made near to date of photograph, I.P., various stamps, lit., (04-08-93, Christie-NY, #504, illus.), 7¾ x 9⅝ in., (19.7 x 24.4 cm.), photograph, gelatin silver print (BP 2564, DM 6281, FR 21,262, Y 443,713).

$3300* *New York Still Life, 1947,* s., t., d., annot. in ink, (c) credit & reprod. limit. stamps, lit., (10-13-92, Christie-NY, #479, illus.), 7¾ x 9⅝ in., (19.7 x 24.4 cm.), photograph, gelatin silver print (BP 1922, DM 4834, FR 16,426, Y 400,146).

$11,550* *New York Still-Life, (MoMA, pl. 73),* s., t., d., num. 18/65, i. w/printing notations by photog., (c) & ed.stamps, 1947, p. 1978, #18/65 ed., (10-15-92, Sotheby-NY, #539, illus.), 17¾ x 22½ in., (45.1 x 57.2 cm.), photograph, platinum-palladium print, mounted on aluminum (BP 7068, DM 17,193, FR 58,304, Y 1,385,723).

$4313* *"Nude 150" (MoMA, pl. 79), c. 1950,* s., t., d., #16/57, p. notations by photog., edit. and (c) stamps, p. 1976, (04-06-93, Sotheby-NY, #452, illus.), 18⅛ x 17⅜ in., photograph, platinum-palladium print (BP 2849, DM 6949, FR 23,530, Y 491,902).

$3776* *Opticians Window, New York, 1939,* p.l., s., stamped, lit., (10-29-92, Christie-London, #166, illus.), 13 x 9½ in., (33 x 24.1 cm.), photograph, gelatin silver print (BP 2420, DM 5809, FR 19,708, Y 467,732).

$8050* *"Rock Groups (Big Brother And The Holding Company And The Grateful Dead)" (Worlds, p. 57), 1967,* s., t., d., #43/50, printing notations, edit. and (c) stamps, (04-06-93, Sotheby-NY, #453, illus.), 19 x 19¾ in., photograph, platinum-palladium print (BP 5317, DM 12,969, FR 43,917, Y 918,111).

$9900* *Saul Steinberg In Nose Mask, New York,* (1966), 1976, s., t., d., num. (c) credit stamp, #17/36 in platinum metals, lit., (10-13-92, Christie-NY, #586, illus.), 25½ x 22¼ in., (64.8 x 56.5 cm.), photograph, platinum-palladium print (BP 5766, DM 14,503, FR 49,278, Y 1,200,437).

$3451* *"Scarred Dahomey Girl",* 1967, p. 1984, s., t., num. 3204, 20/21, annot., stamped Photograph by Irving Penn. Copyright 1974 by Irving Penn, 610 x 509mm, (05-07-93, Sotheby-London, #340, illus.), photograph, platinum palladium print (BP 2185, DM 5456, FR 18,386, Y 379,982).

$7700* *Seated Warrior, Reclining Girl (Worlds, p. 45),* s., t., d., num. 13/14, printing notations by photog., name, ed., (c)stamps, 1974, p. 1982, #13/14 ed., (10-15-92, Sotheby-NY, #550, illus.), 20¼ x 19½ in., (51.4 x 49.5 cm.), photograph, platinum-palladium print, mounted on aluminum (BP 4712, DM 11,462, FR 38,869, Y 923,815).

$8338* *"Sitting Man With Pink Face",* s., t., d., #22/50, i. by photog., photog. (c) and edit. lim. stamps, 1970, p. 1979, (04-06-93, Sotheby-NY, #452A, illus.), 20¾ x 19⅜ in., photograph, platinum-palladium print, mounted on aluminum (BP 5507, DM 13,433, FR 45,488, Y 950,958).

$2200* *Six Dahomey Girls (Worlds, p. 40),* s., t., d., num. 2/30 by photog., (c) & ed. info. stamps, 1967, p. 1968, #2/30 ed., (10-15-92, Sotheby-NY, #547A, illus.), 19⅞ x 19⅝ in., (50.5 x 49.8 cm.), photograph, platinum-palladium print (BP 1346, DM 3275, FR 11,106, Y 263,947).

BI *(Small) Flat Grove, 1975 (MoMA, pl. 125),* s., t., d., num. 18/53, i. by photog., (c) stamp, #18/53 ed., est. $4/6,000, (10-15-92, Sotheby-NY, #552, illus.), 29½ x 22½ in., (74.9 x 57.2 cm.), photograph, platinum-palladium print.

BI *Still LIfe (With Mouse), (MoMA, pl. 74),* mounted, s., t., d., printing notations by photog., (c) and info stamps, 1947, p. c. 1947, est. $2,5/4,000, (10-15-92, Sotheby-NY, #540, illus.), 13⅛ x 10¼ in., (33.3 x 26 cm.), photograph, gelatin silver print.

$3996* *"The Tarot Reader Jean Patchett And Bridget Tichenor, New York, 1949",* p. 1984, t., s., stamped signed, silver prints of this negative not exceeding 26, annot. Print made 1984 IP mtd on Strathmore Paper, (c) stamp, pub., 431 x 400mm, (05-07-93, Sotheby-London, #338, illus.), photograph, selenium toned silver print (BP 2530, DM 6318, FR 21,289, Y 439,991).

$3910* *Three Sitting Masked Men, Cuzco, Peru, 1948,* ink s., t., d., various stamps, lit., (04-08-93, Christie-NY, #505, illus.), 10⅛ x 10⅜ in., (25.7 x 26.4 cm.), photograph, gelatin silver print (BP 2564, DM 6281, FR 21,262, Y 443,713).

$3632* *Two Cuzco Children, 1948,* mounted on card, t., ded., s., i., stamped photog.'s credit, (c) limitation stamp, 293 x 263mm, (05-07-93, Sotheby-London, #343, illus.), photograph, silver print (BP 2300, DM 5742, FR 19,350, Y 399,912).

$3220* *Two New Guinea Warriors Holding Hands,* 1970, p. 1979, s., t., d., edit. num., (c) stamp; #2/31 in platinum metals, (04-08-93, Christie-NY, #510, illus.), 15⅝ x 15⅝ in., (39.7 x 39.7 cm.), photograph, multiple-printed and multiple-coated platinum-palladium print on Rives w/aluminum backing (BP 2111, DM 5173, FR 17,510, Y 365,411).

BI *Two New Guinea Young Women With Feathers (cf. Worlds, p. 70),* s., t., d., (c) & d. stamps, 1970, p. 1990, est. $4/6,000, (10-15-92, Sotheby-NY, #548, illus.), 19 x 18¾ in., (48.3 x 47.6 cm.), photograph, dye transfer print.

$4025* *"Two Standing Men In White Masks (Cuzco, Peru)" (Moments Preserved, p. 96, color variant),* s., t., d. by photog., (c), edit. lim. stamps, p. 1949, (04-06-93, Sotheby-NY, #451, illus.), 10¾ x 10 in., photograph, mounted on Artmar illus. board (BP 2659, DM 6485, FR 21,959, Y 459,056).

$3575* *Two Women Both With Nose Rings (Nepal), (Worlds, p. 59),* s., d., num. 5/15, i. w/printing notations by photog., t./(c) label,ed. stamp, 1967, p. 1972, #5/15 ed., (10-15-92, Sotheby-NY, #546, illus.), photograph, gelatin silver print (BP 2188, DM 5322, FR 18,046, Y 428,914).

$6050* *Two Women In Black With Bread, Morocco,* (1971), 1986, s., t., d., num., (c) credit stamp, #15/21 in platinummetals, (10-13-92, Christie-NY, #588, illus.), 19¾ x 19½ in., (50.2 x 49.5 cm.), photograph, multiple-printed, multiple-coated platinum-palladium print on Rives paper w/aluminum backing (BP 3524, DM 8863, FR 30,114, Y 733,600).

$8625* *Two Young Nondugl Girls, New Guinea,* 1970, p. 1972, ink s., d., num.; (c) credit label, #2/3 in platinum metals, lit., (04-08-93, Christie-NY, #509, illus.), 19⅝ x 20 in., (49.8 x 50.8 cm.), photograph, multiple-printed and multipl coated platinum-palladium print on wiggins w/aluminum backing (BP 5656, DM 13,855, FR 46,900, Y 978,779).

$1635* *Woman In Green Balenciaga Coat, 1950,* mounted on card, i. in neg. Penn copy, neg. num. 20462M-12, pub., 252 x 203mm, (05-07-93, Sotheby-London, #341, illus.), photograph, silver contact print (BP 1035, DM 2585, FR 8711, Y 180,026).

$3996* *"Woman With Umbrella (Lisa Fonssagrives-Penn) New York, 1950",* p. 1984, s., t., d., i. Print made 1984, I.P., signed, silver printsof this negative not exceeding 14, (c) c. 1950, annot., 398 x 482mm, (05-07-93, Sotheby-London, #339, illus.), photograph, selenium toned silver print (BP 2530, DM 6318, FR 21,289, Y 439,991).

$9900* *Young Berber Shepherdess, Morocco (Worlds, p. 85),* mounted, s., t., d. by photog. in ink, (c) stamp, 1971, p. 1984, (10-15-92, Sotheby-NY, #549, illus.), 19⅛ x 18⅞ in., (48.6 x 47.9 cm.), photograph, gelatin silver print (BP 6058, DM 14,737, FR 49,975, Y 1,187,762).

$1320* *[H.L.] Mencken and [George Jean] Nathan (MoMA, pl. 7),* s., d., num. 13/17, i. w/technical info. by photog., photog.'s ed. limit. stamp, label verso, 1948, p. 1969, #13/17 ed., (10-15-92, Sotheby-NY, #543, illus.), 21¾ x 17¾ in., (55.2 x 45.1 cm.), photograph, platinum-palladium print, mounted on aluminum (BP 808, DM 1965, FR 6663, Y 158,368).

PENNANT, Thomas

BI *The British Zoology, 1761: Twelve,* engraved Peter Mazell after Peter Paillouion, watermark, full margins, light stained, est. BP 6/700, (10-27-92, Phillips-London, #174), sheet 20½ x 14 in., (521 x 356 mm.), hand-colored engraving on laid.

PENNELL, Joseph American 1860-1926

$99* *The Bridge,* (11-12-92, Freemn/Fine Art, #167), 10 x 8 in., (24.1 x 31.8 cm.), etching (BP 65, DM 157, FR 529, Y 12,275).

$440* *The Bridges From Brooklyn (W 782),* s., (09-17-92, Sloan, #1458), 10 x 7 in., (25.4 x 17.8 cm.), etching (BP 247, DM 653, FR 2236, Y 54,781).

$715* *"The Bridges From Brooklyn (Wuerth 782), 1921", "St. Martins Bridge,Toledo (W. 312), 1904" and "Cafe Orientale, Venice (W. 618), 1911": Three,* each s., margins; first and second light/mat staining; first and third i. imp.; first taped to overmat; third paper losses, (09-19-92, Christie-E, #54), etching on laid paper; first in dark brown, watermark; second and third laid down (BP 411, DM 1071, FR 3667, Y 89,085).

$1150* *Brooklyn Bridge At Night (Wuerth 790), 1922,* s., i. imp, full margins, good cond., mat stain, printer's crease, tape remains, (05-13-93, Sotheby-NY, #432), 7½ x 8⅞ in., (189 x 224 mm.), aquatint in brownish-black on laid (BP 755, DM 1857, FR 6264, Y 128,391).

$165* *"Charing Cross Station" (W. 165),* (06-11-93, Freemn/Fine Art, #172), 6¾ x 9⅞ in., (17.1 x 25.1 cm.), lithograph (BP 108, DM 268, FR 904, Y 17,507).

$1430* *The City, Evening (W. 506), 1909,* good cond.?, s., (06-11-93, Freemn/Fine Art, #170), 10 x 14⅞ in., (25.4 x 37.8 cm.), mezzotint (BP 940, DM 2324, FR 7836, Y 151,724).

BI *Cityscape,* s., i., d. 1912, est. $2/300, (06-11-93, DuMouchelle, #2255), 8½ x 11 in., (21.6 x 27.9 cm.), lithograph.

$330* *Coal And Coke, 1909,* s., foxing, smudging, tears, good cond., (11-12-92, Freemn/Fine Art, #168), image 9½ x 12½ in., (24.1 x 31.8 cm.), etching (BP 217, DM 523, FR 1764, Y 40,918).

$495* *The Golden Cornice, No. 1 (Wuerth 349), 1904,* (05-27-93, Swann, #213), 10¾ x 7¼ in., (27.3 x 18.4 cm.), etching (BP 317, DM 794, FR 2677, Y 53,066).

$275* *The Horseshoe Curve, 1919,* good cond.?, s., (06-11-93, Freemn/Fine Art, #171), 9⅞ x 11¾ in., (25.1 x 29.8 cm.), etching (BP 181, DM 447, FR 1507, Y 29,178).

$225* *"Interieur De Fonderie" and "Le Marteau Pilon", c. 1910: Two,* dust, untrimmed margins, (02-24-93, Picard, #180), lithograph on laid (BP 157, DM 365, FR 1238, Y 26,402).

$193* *Interior View,* s., i. in plate, (07-03-92, Sloan, #307), 22½ x 16¾ in., (57.2 x 42.5 cm.), lithograph (BP 101, DM 292, FR 985, Y 24,059).

$385* *Liberty Bonds, "That Liberty Shall Not Perish...",* Heywood Strasser & Voight, A cond., chartex-backed, (08-06-92, Swann, #223, illus.), 40½ x 28 in., (102.9 x 71.1 cm.), (BP 201, DM 569, FR 1921, Y 49,107).

$110* *Morris House, Germantown,* s., (06-11-93, Freemn/Fine Art, #169), 16½ x 22 in., (41.9 x 55.9 cm.), lithograph (BP 72, DM 179, FR 603, Y 11,671).

$275* *N.Y. Street Scene With Street Cars,* s. J. Pennell, (02-16-93, Moran, #143), image 12 x 7¾ in., (30.5 x 19.7 cm.), etching on paper (BP 190, DM 449, FR 1520, Y 32,946).

$165* *Old And New Rome (W. 622),* s., mat burn, hinged to mat, (12-04-92, Doyle, #139), 12¼ x 9⅛ in., (311 x 232 mm.), etching (BP 106, DM 263, FR 891, Y 20,599).

$550* *"Park Row" and "The Times Building" (Wuerth 326, 339), 1904: Two,* s., (05-27-93, Swann, #217, illus.), one 11⅞ x 7 in., (30.2 x 17.8 cm.), the other 11⅞ x 8⅜ in., (30.2 x 17.8 cm.), etching (BP 352, DM 883, FR 2975, Y 58,962).

$220* *Philadelphia, From Belmont,* s., (06-11-93, Freemn/Fine Art, #165), 16¾ x 21 in., (42.5 x 53.3 cm.), lithograph (BP 145, DM 358, FR 1205, Y 23,342).

$110* *Pineapple Street, 1924,* s., good cond., (06-11-93, Freemn/Fine Art, #168), 9⅞ x 6¾ in., (25.1 x 17.1 cm.), etching (BP 72, DM 179, FR 603, Y 11,671).

$138* *Pineapple Street, 1924,* good cond., s., (06-11-93, Freemn/Fine Art, #167), 9⅞ x 6⅞ in., (25.1 x 17.5 cm.), etching (BP 91, DM 224, FR 756, Y 14,642).

BI *"Porch Gate, St. Mary, The Virgin",* s., d. September, 1884, t., est. $2/300, (06-11-93, DuMouchelle, #2254), 9½ x 8¾ in., (24.1 x 22.2 cm.), lithograph.

$138* *The Portico, 1923,* good cond., s., (06-11-93, Freemn/Fine Art, #166), 12¼ x 9⅛ in., (31.1 x 23.2 cm.), etching (BP 91, DM 224, FR 756, Y 14,642).

$193* *Saint Paul's,* s., i. imp, t., i. indistinctly, (11-12-92, Freemn/Fine Art, #170), plate 10⅞ x 8⅜ in., (27.6 x 21.3 cm.), etching (BP 127, DM 306, FR 1032, Y 23,931).

$193* *The Shot Tower (W. 414), 1906,* s., small margins, laid down, good cond., (10-28-92, Butterfield, #2750), 8⅝ x 10¾ in., (219 x 273 mm.), etching on wove (BP 123, DM 298, FR 1012, Y 23,681).

$660* *Sunset, From Williamsburg Bridge (W. 674), 1915,* s., p. by artist, margins, good cond., surface soiling, surface scuffing, crease, staining, (10-28-92, Butterfield, #2751), 8⁵⁄₁₆ x 10⅞ in., (211 x 276 mm.), etching w/aquatint on laid paper (BP 421, DM 1019, FR 3461, Y 80,982).

$220* *The Tribune And The Sun (Wuerth 346), 1904,* wide margins, s., (05-27-93, Swann, #214), 11¾ x 7 in., (29.8 x

17.8 cm.), etching (BP 141, DM 353, FR 1190, Y 23,585).

BI *When Storms Gather Beyond The Parthenon,* s., t., margins, laid down, good cond., creases, surface soiling, mat staining, est. $4/600, (10-28-92, Butterfield, #2749), 16¾ x 21½ in., (425 x 546 mm.), lithograph on laid paper, watermark.

PEPPER, Beverly American b. 1924

$330* *Untitled,* s., #22/45 , prop. Price Waterhouse Corp. Coll., (05-16-93, Hindman, #649), 36½ x 36½ in., (92.7 x 92.7 cm.), color etching and aquatint (BP 215, DM 531, FR 1784, Y 36,581).

PEREE French 1767-1809

BI *"Le Grand Oiseau De Paradis Emeraude, No. 1" and "Le Grand Oiseau DeParadis Emeraude, No. 4": A Pair,* taken from Jacques Barraband, est. $1/2000, (09-25-92, Wolf, #12), each 18 x 12 in., (45.7 x 30.5 cm.), lithographs in colors.

PEREHUDOFF, William b. 1919

$347* *La Plonge #9,* #37/75, s., t., prov., (05-10-93, Hodgins, #258), (54.6 x 74.9 cm.), serigraph on paper (BP 226, DM 557, FR 1881, Y 38,775, C$ 440).

PERELLE, Adam French 1638-1696

$28* *Figures In A Topographical Landscape,* (09-17-92, Sloan, #1991), 4⅝ x 8¼ in., (11.7 x 21 cm.), engraving (BP 16, DM 42, FR 142, Y 3486).

PERELLE, Gabriel French 1603-1677

BI *Loading The Ship,* i. in plate, est. $200/300, (09-17-92, Sloan, #657), 3½ x 3⅜ in., (8.9 x 8.6 cm.), engraving.

BI *Loading The Ship,* i. in plate, est. $175/225, (12-10-92, Sloan, #594), 3½ x 3⅜ in., (8.9 x 8.6 cm.), engraving.

$468* *Three Landscapes,* prov., (09-20-92, Hindman, #661), larger 6½ x 9 in., (16.5 x 22.9 cm.), etchings (BP 274, DM 694, FR 2376, Y 57,842).

PEREZ, Ricardo James

BI *"Blossom",* 1980, p. 1982, s., t., d., annot., est. $4/600, (05-23-93, Butterfield, #3562), 8½ x 12⅝ in., photograph, gelatin silver print.

PEREZ VILLAAMIL, Jenaro

$290* *"Gate Of San Martin In Toledo",* (03-17-93, Duran, #21, illus.), 15³⁄₁₆ x 21¼ in., (38.6 x 54 cm.), two color lithograph (BP 200, DM 483, FR 1640, Y 34,014, P 34,500).

$271* *"Gate Of The Hospital Of Santa Cruz",* (03-17-93, Duran, #22, illus.), 15³⁄₁₆ x 21¼ in., (38.6 x 54 cm.), two color lithograph (BP 187, DM 451, FR 1533, Y 31,785, P 32,200).

$406* *"Parroquia De Santo Tome",* (03-17-93, Duran, #26, illus.), 21¼ x 15³⁄₁₆ in., (54 x 38.6 cm.), two color lithograph (BP 280, DM 676, FR 2296, Y 47,619, P 48,300).

PERFLAUDIN

$261* *Musee Cognacq-Jay 1942,* p. Mourlot, repaired, backed on linen, (05-07-93, Christie-S. Ken, #115, illus.), 18 x 46 in., (45.7 x 116.8 cm.), color lithograph (BP 165, DM 413, FR 1391, Y 28,738).

PERI

$439* *Evian Les Bains, c. 1930,* very good cond., (03-15-93, Arcole, #106, illus.), 39⅜ x 24⁷⁄₁₆ in., (100 x 62 cm.), (BP 306, DM 729, FR 2479, Y 52,002).

PERICLES, Leon b. 1949

BI *Last Ride Of The Gold Leaf Camel,* s. Leon Pericles, i., #38/70, est. $2/300, (08-11-92, L. Joel, #161G), 9⁷⁄₁₆ x 19¹¹⁄₁₆ in., (24 x 50 cm.), color etching.

PERIGNON, Alexis Nicolas French 1726-1782

$202* *Ensemble De Cinq Paysages, c. 1771: Five,* small margins, wormholes, (05-15-93, Loudmer, #169), smallest 3⅞ x 4½ in., (98 x 114 mm.), largest 5¹⁵⁄₁₆ x 7¹⁄₁₆ in., (98 x 114 mm.), etching on laid (BP 131, DM 325, FR 1092, Y 22,392).

PERILLI, Achille Italian b. 1927

BI *Komposition Mit Blau Und Turkis, (19)66,* s., d., num., est. DM 400, (12-01-92, Karl/Faber, #1093), 20½ x 14¹⁵⁄₁₆ in., (52 x 38 cm.), color lithograph on hand-made.

PERINESE, Francesco Italian 1758-1810

$330* *"Veduta...Fontanadi Trevi...Fountain Scene",* (05-15-93, Dunning, #1000, illus.), 16 x 22 in., (40.6 x 55.9 cm.), engraving (BP 215, DM 531, FR 1784, Y 36,581).

PERINI, Antonio 1830-1879

$363* *"Ricordo Di Venezia": Twelve,* 1870s, album, mounted one-per-page on card, p. series t., credit, (05-06-93, Christie-London, #53), each approx. 10¼ x 13⅜ in., photograph, albumen print (BP 230, DM 572, FR 1925, Y 39,938).

PERNET, Percival

$1024* *Grand-Prix 1948, Canots, Automobiles Et Hors-Bords, 1948,* excell. cond., (02-04-93, Christie-S. Ken, #53, illus.), 39 x 25 in., (99.1 x 63.5 cm.), color lithograph (BP 715, DM 1686, FR 5717, Y 127,379).

PERON, P.

$301* *Un Pote. Anis Breton Surfin, 1936,* Imp. Depeche, good cond., (02-12-93, Cheval/Robert, #71), 62¹⁵⁄₁₆ x 47¼ in., (160 x 120 cm.), poster (BP 212, DM 499, FR 1689, Y 36,300).

PERON, R.

$321* *L'Equipage. D'Apres J. Kessel. Lutece Film,* Imp. Baudin, good cond., (02-12-93, Cheval/Robert, #203), 62¹⁵⁄₁₆ x 47¼ in., (160 x 120 cm.), poster (BP 226, DM 532, FR 1801, Y 38,712).

PEROT, R.

$587* *Le Blanc A La Maison Dore, Paris, 1929,* p. Hachard, very good cond., (11-19-92, Ribeyre/Baron, #38), 59¹⁄₁₆ x 82¹¹⁄₁₆ in., (150 x 210 cm.), poster (BP 386, DM 936, FR 3153, Y 73,001).

$482* *La Cuisine Au Gaz, "Economie", c. 1930,* p. Bedos, good cond., (11-19-92, Ribeyre/Baron, #39), 62⅝ x 46⅞ in., (159 x 119 cm.), poster (BP 317, DM 768, FR 2589, Y 59,943).

$797* *Pernod, "Quand Un Ami Rencontre Un Autre Ami",* p. Bacque de Plas, very good cond., (11-19-92, Ribeyre/Baron, #40), 47¼ x 122¹⁄₁₆ in., (120 x 310 cm.), poster (BP 525, DM 1271, FR 4280, Y 99,117).

PERROT, Ferd

BI *"Laule Toner",* est. $30/50, (04-16-93, DuMouchelle, #2346), 11¼ x 16¾ in., (28.6 x 42.5 cm.), lithograph.

PERRY, Roy (after)

$67 *"Village Cricket",* #123/500, s., (10-09-92, G.A. Key, #36, illus.), 14¾ x 22¼ in., (37.5 x 56.5 cm.), colored print (BP 40, DM 100, FR 338, Y 8171).

PERRY, William

$1725* *Shells, 1816: Six,* (04-07-93, Sotheby-Arcade, #279), sight 14 x 10 in., (35.6 x 25.4 cm.), hand-colored aquatint (BP 1140, DM 2790, FR 9442, Y 195,978).

PESCHERET, Leon R. Anglo/American 1892-1961

$105* *The Chicago Watertower,* s., (11-01-92, Hanzel, #268), 12 x 9¾ in., (30.5 x 24.8 cm.), drypoint etching (BP 69, DM 166, FR 558, Y 12,982).

$85* *"Into The West" and "Snow Bound": Two,* s., t., tape, staining, foxing, (05-15-93, Cleveland, #262), 13 x 17⅜ in., (33 x 44.1 cm.), engraving in color (BP 55, DM 137, FR 459, Y 9422).

$11* *Watertower,* (09-20-92, Hindman, #708), 8¾ x 6¾ in., (22.2 x 17.1 cm.), etching (BP 6, DM 16, FR 56, Y 1360).

PESKE, H.

$219* *Le Hulla. Opera Comique D'Andre Rivoire Et M. Samuel Rousseau. 1923,* very good cond., (03-13-93, Laurin, #28), 47¼ x 31½ in., (120 x 80 cm.), (BP 153, DM 365, FR 1239, Y 25,810).

PESKIN, David

$209* *Marilyn Monroe, Negligee,* (12-11-92, DuMouchelle, #1173), approx. 3⅝ x 4¾ in., (9.2 x 12.1 cm.), photograph, color (BP 134, DM 481, FR 1129, Y 25,863).

PESNE, Antoine (after)

$33* *Frederic II, Roi De Prusse, c. 1750,* engraved by Wille, full margins, time/water-stained, hole, defect, (11-30-92, Phillips-London, #89), plate 15¾ x 11¼ in., (400 x 286 mm.), engraving on laid (BP 22, DM 53, FR 178, Y 4107).

PETERDI, Gabor   Hungarian/American b. 1915
$303* *Angry Waves,* s., (09-24-92, Mystic, #15), 20 x 24 in., (50.8 x 61 cm.), 9 x 11 in., (50.8 x 61 cm.), woodcut and colored etching (BP 177, DM 449, FR 1525, Y 36,449).
$110* *Blue Rock, 1962,* #1/50, s., (05-14-93, DuMouchelle, #2380), 17¾ x 11½ in., (45.1 x 29.2 cm.), color etching and aquatint (BP 72, DM 177, FR 595, Y 12,194).
$220* *Desert II,* #1/50, s., d. 1961, (05-14-93, DuMouchelle, #2379), 19¾ x 23¾ in., (50.2 x 60.3 cm.), color etching and aquatint (BP 143, DM 354, FR 1189, Y 24,388).
BI *"First Day Of Spring", 1961,* s., t., d., very good cond., est. $3/400, (05-15-93, Cleveland, #485), 16 x 12 in., (40.6 x 30.5 cm.), etching.
BI *Genesis Portfolio: Aquarium, 1966,* s., d., annot. A-CCCVII-L, full margins, good cond., staining, hingeremains, est. $250/450, (05-19-93, Butterfield, #2288), 13⅞ x 10¾ in., (352 x 273 mm.), relief etching w/soft-ground and embossing in colors on Auvergne a laMain.
$358* *A Genesis, 1967: Twelve,* incomplete portfolio, two s., d. '66 and annot. AP, num. 68 on justification page, pub. Touchstone Publishers, full margins, good cond., pencil notations, in orig. portfolio, (02-24-93, Butterfield, #3240), 20 x 15 in., (508 x 381 mm.), etching in colors on Arches (BP 250, DM 581, FR 1970, Y 42,009).
$275* *"Red Blue Sunset" and "Red Blue Eclipse": Two,* s., d. 67, #105/150 and #128/150, very good/good cond., (02-07-93, Bakker, #128), one image 17¼ x 23½ in., (43.8 x 59.7 cm.), other image 23½ x 17½ in., (43.8 x 59.7 cm.), etching and aquatint (BP 190, DM 456, FR 1541, Y 34,221).
$193* *Still Life No. 1, 1955,* s., t., d. 5-25-56, (06-11-93, Freemn/Fine Art, #174), 22 x 26 in., (55.9 x 66 cm.), etching and engraving, stenciled colors (BP 127, DM 314, FR 1058, Y 20,477).
$143* *Untitled,* s., d. 66, num. XXVI-L, prov., (09-20-92, Hindman, #695), 13¾ x 11 in., (34.9 x 27.9 cm.), color etching, aquatint and soft-ground (BP 84, DM 212, FR 726, Y 17,674).
$468* *Untitled,* s., d. 51, #7/35, (05-16-93, Hindman, #564), 12¾ x 7½ in., (32.4 x 19.1 cm.), etching (BP 304, DM 753, FR 2530, Y 51,879).
$20* *Untitled, 1957,* s., d., #145+, light toned, mat burn, (05-15-93, Cleveland, #486), 17½ x 13½ in., (44.5 x 34.3 cm.), etching (BP 13, DM 32, FR 108, Y 2217).
$55* *"Wisteria", 1962,* num. 250 plus 10, Print Club of Cleveland Publication No. 48, s. Peterdi, (12-12-92, Wolf, #31), 9⅞ x 14 in., (25.1 x 35.6 cm.), etching and engraving on Arches wove (BP 35, DM 87, FR 297, Y 6806).

PETERSEN, Hans Meyer
$502* *Untitled: Two,* s. 87, 25/50 and 1/50, (09-29-92, B. Rasmussen, #345), serigraph in colors (BP 282, DM 709, FR 2419, Y 59,926, DK 2760).

PETERSEN, Martin   Danish/American 1870-1956
$193* *"Sunset, New Hampshire",* s., AAA, (12-11-92, DuMouchelle, #1483, illus.), 8⅞ x 8¾ in., (22.5 x 22.2 cm.), etching (BP 124, DM 304, FR 1042, Y 23,883).

PETERSEN, Will   American contemporary
$77* *Untitled,* s., d. Jan. 80, num. 31/35, (09-20-92, Hindman, #728), 17 x 24 in., (43.2 x 61 cm.), lithograph (BP 45, DM 114, FR 391, Y 9517).

PETERSON, Gosta
$509* *Fashion Study For Harper's Bazaar, c. 1964,* t., d., s., Harper's Bazaar 64 Gosta Peterson, 505 x 346mm, (05-07-93, Sotheby-London, #344, illus.), photograph, silver print (BP 322, DM 805, FR 2712, Y 56,045).

PETICOV, Antonio   Brazilian b. 1946
$50* *"Morning Song",* s., t., num. 16/195, excellent cond., (10-31-92, Cleveland, #388), 21½ x 32½ in., (54.6 x 82.6 cm.), silkscreen in colors (BP 32, DM 77, FR 261, Y 6193).

PETIT, M.
BI *Sakharoff. Clotilde Et Alexandre, 1923,* fold marks, tears, losses, brown tape, est. BP 1/200, (02-04-93, Christie-S. Ken, #140), 55 x 39 in., (139.7 x 99.1 cm.), color lithograph.

PETIT, Pierre
BI *"Chamfleury", "Alphonse Karr", "Mlle. Castellan, Violoncelliste", Mr.Delangle, Ministre De La Justice" and "Derriet [?] (de Charivari)": Five Portraits,* 1 s. by photog. in ink, photog.'s credit, t. in unidentified hand, est. $2/3,000, (10-15-92, Sotheby-NY, #81, illus.), largest 9⅞ x 7⅜ in., (25.1 x 18.7 cm.), photograph, albumen prints.

PETITJEAN, Edmond Marie, Engraver
BI *Blind Man's Buff,* s., foxing, est. BP 80/120, (02-17-93, Bonhams-Chelsea, #252), image 18 x 14¼ in., (45.7 x 36.2 cm.), hand-colored mezzotint.

PETITOT, Enneamond Alexandre (after)
$13,726* *Mascarades A La Greque (Guilmard PP. 225-226): Set Of Nine,* by Benigno Bossi, w/titlepage, 1st Parma edit., margins, surface dirt, stain, (06-30-93, Sotheby-London, #178, illus.), 10½ x 7¼ in., (267 x 184 mm.), etching, 4 and 5 on paper w/a large Fleur-de-Lys watermark (BP 9200, DM 23,411, FR 78,976, Y 1,470,695).

PEZZO, Lucio del
$96* *Untitled,* s., #159/190, full margins, good cond., minor handling creases in margin, (05-27-93, Sotheby-Amstrdm, #464), 27⅛ x 20⁹/₁₆ in., (689 x 522 mm.), colored lithograph on wove (BP 61, DM 154, FR 519, Y 10,292, G 173).
$96* *Untitled,* s., #40/190, full margins, good cond., (05-27-93, Sotheby-Amstrdm, #465), 26¼ x 19⁵/₁₆ in., (667 x 490 mm.), colored lithograph on wove (BP 61, DM 154, FR 519, Y 10,292, G 173).
$96* *Untitled,* s, #111/190, full margins, good cond., (05-27-93, Sotheby-Amstrdm, #466), 18⅛ x 26⅞ in., (460 x 683 mm.), colored lithograph on wove (BP 61, DM 154, FR 519, Y 10,292, G 173).

PFAFF, Judy   American b. 1946
$2300* *Six Of One, Melone, 1987,* s., t., d., #17/25, pub. Crown Point Press, full margins, excell. cond.?, the Late M. Anwar Kamal, M.D. Coll., (05-11-93, Christie-NY, #532, illus.), sheet 55 x 63 in., (139.7 x 160 cm.), color woodcut on Japan (BP 1468, DM 3623, FR 12,208, Y 252,997).

PFAHL, John   b. 1939
$690* *"Mangrove Swamp Lightning, Matheson Hammock, Florida", "Bamboo Lightning, Penland, North Carolina", "Snow Creek Lightning, Wing, North Carolina", "Slanting Orange Lines, Route 17, New York" and "Untitled": Five,* 1977, 1975 and 1974, each ink s., d., (c) insig., lit., (04-08-93, Christie-NY, #514, illus.), each approx. 7¾ x 10 in., (19.7 x 25.4 cm.), photograph, dye-transfer print (BP 452, DM 1108, FR 3752, Y 78,302).
$1320* *Selected Images: Five, 1975, 1977, 1978,* includes: Great Salt Lake Angles, Great Salt Lake, Utah; Triangle, Bermuda; Australian Pines, Fort DeSoto, Florida; Bamboo Lightning, Penland, NorthCarolina; Coconut Palm Horizon, Kona Coast, Hawaii; s., d., (c) insig. in ink,lit., (10-13-92, Christie-NY, #591, illus.), each 7¾ x 10 in., (19.7 x 25.4 cm.), photograph, dye transfer prints (BP 769, DM 1934, FR 6570, Y 160,058).

PFAHLER, Georg Karl   b. 1926
$860* *Untitled (Rottloff 34, 70, 95, 134), 1966-71: Six,* s., num., (05-27-93, Lempertz, #946), each approx. 27⁹/₁₆ x 27⁹/₁₆ in., (70 x 70 cm.), color serigraph on thick paper (BP 551, DM 1380, FR 4651, Y 92,196).
BI *Untitled, 1960,* s., d., printers mark, creases, papertape, good cond., est. G 4/600, (12-09-92, Sotheby-Amstrdm, #631), sheet 23⁷/₁₆ x 16¾ in., (595 x 425 mm.), color lithograph on wove.

PFAU, G.
$385* *"Encampment At Neponset-Dorchester",* after S. Rowse, (06-02-93, Doyle, #82), 19¼ x 29 in., (48.9 x 73.7 cm.), hand-colored lithograph (BP 250, DM 615, FR 2072, Y 41,309).

PFEIFFER, Frits   1815-1960
$385* *Provincetown,* s., d. 1936, (09-24-92, Mystic, #24), 13½ x 16 in., (34.3 x 40.6 cm.), monotype (BP 225, DM 571, FR 1938, Y 46,313).

PFEIFFER-WATENPHUL, Max 1896-1976

$361* *Frau Mit Fruchtschale, 1922,* s., d., from Die Schaffenden 3. Jg., 3 portfolio, (11-28-92, Schoppmann, #697), 11³⁄₁₆ x 7¹³⁄₁₆ in., (28.4 x 19.8 cm.), etching on wove (BP 238, DM 575, FR 1952, Y 44,928).

$433* *Stilleben Mit Feigen, 1966,* s., num., (11-28-92, Schoppmann, #696), 15¾ x 10⁷⁄₁₆ in., (40 x 26.5 cm.), color lithograph (BP 286, DM 690, FR 2342, Y 53,889).

PHILI (Pierre GRACH) 1898-1987

$279* *Le Parisien,* cond. A, (03-16-93, Boisgirard, #173), 62¹⁵⁄₁₆ x 45¼ in., (160 x 115 cm.), poster (BP 193, DM 464, FR 1576, Y 32,624).

PHILIPOTEAUX, Barry di apres (after)

BI *"Ste. Anne", c. 1883,* est. $7/900, (04-16-93, DuMouchelle, #1047, illus.), approx. 30½ x 40 in., (77.5 x 101.6 cm.), colored lithograph.

PHILIPP, Robert American 1895-1981

$66* *"Julia", c. 1950,* s., pub. AAA, good cond., (10-31-92, Cleveland, #202), 12⅞ x 8¾ in., (32.7 x 22.2 cm.), lithograph (BP 42, DM 102, FR 344, Y 8175).

PHILLIPS, George Henry (after William DRUMMOND) (and Charles BASEBEE)

$435* *The Cricket Match Between Sussex And Kent At Brighton, 1849,* margins, pub. E. Gambart, mould damage, (10-27-92, Phillips-London, #106), image 23⅓ x 35¾ in., (593 x 908 mm.), mixed method engraving w/touches of white bodycolor on wove (BP 275, DM 667, FR 2262, Y 53,211).

PHILLIPS, Matt American b. 1927

BI *Suite Of Seven: Seven,* each s., d. '84, #18/20, (12-13-92, Hindman, #343), sheet size 29¾ x 22¼ in., hand-colored etchings.

$495* *Untitled,* s., d. (19)78 in image, (12-10-92, Sloan, #2720), 17½ x 9 in., (44.5 x 22.9 cm.), color monotype (BP 319, DM 783, FR 2674, Y 61,232).

BI *Untitled, 1989,* s., d., pub. Graphic Arts Council of the Achenbach Foundation, full margins, very good cond., shrink-wrapped, est. $6/700, (10-28-92, Butterfield, #3071), 14½ x 8¾ in., (368 x 222 mm.), color monotype w/collage on wove.

BI *Untitled, 1989,* s., d., full margins, good cond., crease, stray printing ink, est. $3/500, (05-19-93, Butterfield, #2289), 17⅛ x 10½ in., (435 x 267 mm.), monotype in colors w/collage and hand-coloring on Arches.

PHILLIPS, Peter b. 1939

$217* *Custom Print I, 1965,* s., d., from: 11 Pop Artists. Vol. New York 1965, (11-28-92, Schoppmann, #705), 24 x 20 in., (61 x 50.8 cm.), color serigraph (BP 143, DM 346, FR 1174, Y 27,007).

PHILLIPS, Thomas (after)

$150* *Sir Joseph Banks, 1812,* scratch-letter proof prior to t., engraved Nicolas Schiavonetti, small margins, defects, repair, (11-30-92, Phillips-London, #102), plate 20⅛ x 15¼ in., (511 x 387 mm.), mixed-method engraving on laid (BP 99, DM 239, FR 811, Y 18,668).

PHILLIPS, Tom

BI *Dante Alighieri. The Divine Comedy: Inferno,* complete portfolio (2 volumes), each init., w/ artist's translation text, p. by Nick Tite and artist, good cond., est. BP 3/4,000, (06-30-93, Sotheby-London, #893, illus.), overall 17⅛ x 13⅜ in., (435 x 340 mm.), 139 etchings, lithographs and silkscreens, mostly in color.

PHILLIPS, Walter

$193* *Offshore Island,* good cond.?, (02-07-93, Bakker, #108, illus.), 6½ x 7¼ in., (16.5 x 18.4 cm.), color woodblock print (BP 134, DM 320, FR 1082, Y 24,017).

PHILLIPS, Walter Joseph Canadian 1884-1963

$412* *Alpine Meadow (MBL #91), 1926,* mono. in block, s., prov., (11-16-92, Hodgins, #96), 3¼ x 4 in., (8.2 x 10.2 cm.), color woodcut on paper (BP 271, DM 657, FR 2214, Y 51,416, C$ 523).

$326* *Elevators At La Salle,* s., mono. block, (05-10-93, Hodgins, #200, illus.), 4¼ x 4½ in., (10.8 x 11.4 cm.), color woodcut on paper (BP 213, DM 524, FR 1767, Y 36,429, C$ 413).

$172* *Engineer's House And South Wall, 1931,* s., lit., (06-07-93, Ritchie, #30), 3¾ x 5¼ in., (9.5 x 13.4 cm.), wood engraving (BP 113, DM 279, FR 940, Y 18,451, C$ 220).

$1041* *Fall,* #44/50, s., mono. in block, t., (05-10-93, Hodgins, #241, illus.), 5¾ x 7¼ in., (14.6 x 18.4 cm.), color woodcut on paper (BP 679, DM 1672, FR 5642, Y 116,326, C$ 1320).

$954* *A Gloucester Village, 1926: MBL #88,* #50/100, mono., d. 1926; s., t., (05-10-93, Hodgins, #125, illus.), 8½ x 9¾ in., (21.6 x 24.8 cm.), color woodblock on paper (BP 623, DM 1533, FR 5171, Y 106,604, C$ 1210).

$996* *Lake Macarthur, Canadian Rockies (MBL #151), 1931,* s., mono., prov., (11-16-92, Hodgins, #60), 7½ x 9¼ in., (19.1 x 23.5 cm.), color woodcut on paper (BP 655, DM 1589, FR 5352, Y 124,298, C$ 1265).

$390* *Margaret (MBL. #38), 1918,* s., mono. in block, i., (11-16-92, Hodgins, #95), 4¼ x 4¼ in., (10.8 x 10.8 cm.), color woodblock on paper (BP 256, DM 622, FR 2096, Y 48,671, C$ 495).

$866* *Mount Cathedral From Lake O'Hara, British Columbia (MBL #98), 1927,* #19 edit. of 250, s., mono. in block, prov., (11-16-92, Hodgins, #326, illus.), 7 x 8⅝ in., (17.8 x 22.9 cm.), color woodblock on paper (BP 569, DM 1381, FR 4653, Y 108,074, C$ 1100).

$952* *Mount Rundle (MBL #246A), 1950,* #8/100, s., prov., (11-16-92, Hodgins, #335), 8¼ x 12¼ in., (21 x 31.1 cm.), color woodcut on paper (BP 626, DM 1518, FR 5116, Y 118,807, C$ 1210).

$220* *Mountain Torrent, 1926,* s., t., i. 1st state, #3/8, (03-24-93, Grogan, #83), 8¾ x 12 in., (22.2 x 30.5 cm.), color woodcut (BP 149, DM 359, FR 1223, Y 25,849).

$813* *Norman Bay - 2,* mono., d. Oct. 1923 in plate, s., t., #97/100, lit., (11-30-92, Ritchie, #36, illus.), 8⅞ x 9¾ in., (22.5 x 24.8 cm.), color woodcut (BP 537, DM 1295, FR 4397, Y 101,182, C$ 1045).

$801* *Rain, Lake of The Woods, (MBL #106), 1927,* #31/250, s., mono. in block, prov., (11-16-92, Hodgins, #258), 5¼ x 8¾ in., (13.3 x 22.2 cm.), color woodcut on paper (BP 526, DM 1278, FR 4304, Y 99,963, C$ 1018).

$390* *Rosie (MBL #34A), 1918,* s., t., mono. in block, (11-16-92, Hodgins, #92), 5½ x 4½ in., (14 x 11.4 cm.), color woodcut on paper (BP 256, DM 622, FR 2096, Y 48,671, C$ 495).

$470* *Rundle In Winter (Boulet, No. MBL244), 1949,* s., issued 1949, lit., (11-30-92, Ritchie, #37, illus.), 5 x 6⅞ in., (12.7 x 17.5 cm.), color woodcut (BP 310, DM 749, FR 2542, Y 58,494, C$ 605).

$564* *Rushing River, 1920: MBL # 52,* s., (05-10-93, Hodgins, #338), 4¼ x 7½ in., (10.8 x 19.1 cm.), woodcut on paper (BP 368, DM 906, FR 3057, Y 63,024, C$ 715).

$519* *Snow Bank (MBL #74), 1923,* s., mono. in block, prov., (11-16-92, Hodgins, #255), 4¼ x 3¹⁵⁄₁₆ in., (10.8 x 10.2 cm.), color woodcut on paper (BP 341, DM 828, FR 2789, Y 64,770, C$ 660).

$194* *Stockton, Manitoba, 1932,* s., t., lit., (06-07-93, Ritchie, #29, illus.), 3¹¹⁄₁₆ x 6¹⁵⁄₁₆ in., (9.3 x 17.7 cm.), wood engraving (BP 128, DM 315, FR 1060, Y 20,811, C$ 248).

$736* *The Stump (MBL #116), 1928,* #199/300, mono. in block, num., prov., (11-16-92, Hodgins, #30, illus.), 6¾ x 9 in., (17.2 x 22.9 cm.), color woodcut on paper (BP 484, DM 1174, FR 3955, Y 91,851, C$ 935).

$325* *Suburban Street (MBL #55), 1920,* s.; mono. in block, prov., (11-16-92, Hodgins, #52), 3½ x 5¹⁵⁄₁₆ in., (8.9 x 15.2 cm.), color woodcut on paper (BP 214, DM 518, FR 1746, Y 40,559, C$ 413).

$563* *Summer Night (Lake Of The Woods) (MBL #153), 1931,* s., prov., (11-16-92, Hodgins, #224), 7 x 9½ in., (17.8 x 24.1 cm.), color woodcut on paper (BP 370, DM 898, FR 3025, Y 70,261, C$ 715).

$651* *Sunset-Whitefish Bay, 1919,* s., t., prov., (05-10-93, Hodgins, #28, illus.), 5½ x 8 in., (14 x 20.3 cm.), color woodcut on paper (BP 425, DM 1046, FR 3528, Y 72,746, C$ 825).

BI *"Tulips", 1928,* s., num., faint stains, est. $1-1,500, (10-31-92, Cleveland, #203, illus.), 9¼ x 12¼ in., (23.5 x 31.1 cm.), color woodcut.

$911* *Warren's Landing: MBL#154,* s., prov., (05-10-93, Hodgins, #20), 6¾ x 9½ in., (17.1 x 24.1 cm.), color woodblock on paper (BP 594, DM 1463, FR 4938, Y 101,799, C$ 1155).

$266* *Winter Evening,* s., (10-21-92, Maynard, #203), 3 x 3 in., (7.6 x 7.6 cm.), color woodcut (BP 165, DM 402, FR 1366, Y 32,400, C$ 330).

$477* *Winter Woods: MBL#93,* s., mono. block, prov., (05-10-93, Hodgins, #170), 3½ x 3¾ in., (8.9 x 9.5 cm.), color woodblock on paper (BP 311, DM 766, FR 2585, Y 53,302, C$ 605).

$781* *Winter, 1917: MBL# 30,* #39/50, s., prov., (05-10-93, Hodgins, #339), 5½ x 9½ in., (14 x 24.1 cm.), color woodcut on paper (BP 510, DM 1255, FR 4233, Y 87,272, C$ 990).

$606* *Wylie Mill Bridge (MBL #80), 1925,* s., t., mono. in block, prov., (11-16-92, Hodgins, #225, illus.), 8¼ x 9¾ in., (21 x 24.8 cm.), color woodcut on paper (BP 398, DM 967, FR 3256, Y 75,627, C$ 770).

PIA

$856* *L'Indochine Francaise. TONKIN. "Le Delta", 1930,* fairly good cond., (03-13-93, Laurin, #140), 42⅛ x 29½ in., (107 x 75 cm.), (BP 597, DM 1425, FR 4844, Y 100,884).

PIAUBERT, Jean French b. 1900

BI *Composition,* s. Piaubert, 38/120, est. DK 1,000, (03-24-93, Kunsthallen, #276), color lithograph.

BI *Composition,* s. Piaubert, est. DK 1,000, (03-24-93, Kunsthallen, #274), color lithograph.

BI *Composition,* s. Piaubert 92/150, est. DK 1,200, (03-24-93, Kunsthallen, #275), color lithograph.

PIAZ, Teddy

$442* *Esmeralda (Spectacle),* stamp, (04-20-93, Encans, #128), 44$^{5}/_{16}$ x 30$^{1}/_{16}$ in., (112.5 x 76.3 cm.), photo-affiche (BP 285, DM 704, FR 2376, Y 48,770, C$ 555).

BI *"Esmeralda" (Spectacle),* Teddy Diaz stamp, (03-16-93, Encans, #145), approx. 4½ x 30$^{1}/_{16}$ in., (11.5 x 76.3 cm.), photo-poster.

$579* *Serge Lifar,* (01-31-93, Morelle/Marchan, #41), 47¼ x 62$^{15}/_{16}$ in., (120 x 160 cm.), poster (BP 389, DM 933, FR 3154, Y 72,231).

PICART, B. American 19th cent.

$165* *Lifestyles Of Native Virginians: Six,* (12-10-92, Sloan, #608), each 13½ x 8⅝ in., (34.3 x 21.9 cm.), engravings (BP 106, DM 261, FR 891, Y 20,411).

PICART LE DOUX, Jean French 1902-1982

BI *"Coquillage Etoile",* t., s., est. FF6/800, (04-04-93, Pescheteau, #273), 25$^{9}/_{16}$ x 19$^{11}/_{16}$ in., (65 x 50 cm.), color lithograph.

BI *Le Phenix, 1972,* artist's proof, s., t., d., est. FF6/800, (06-28-93, Loudmer, #105), 13⅜ x 14¾ in., (340 x 375 mm.), sh 29½ x 21$^{1}/_{16}$ in., (340 x 375 mm.), color lithograph on Arches wove.

PICASSO, Pablo b. Spain 1881 d. France 1973

$1716* *156 Series (B. 1864), 1970,* stamped sig., #41/50, full margins, good cond., (06-30-93, Sotheby-London, #651, illus.), 6 x 8 in., (152 x 203 mm.), etching and drypoint on wove (BP 1150, DM 2927, FR 9873, Y 183,864).

$2059* *156 Series (B. 1874), 1970,* stamped sig., #41/50, full margins, good cond., (06-30-93, Sotheby-London, #650, illus.), 12⅜ x 16¼ in., (314 x 413 mm.), etching on wove (BP 1380, DM 3512, FR 11,847, Y 220,615).

$2917* *156 Series (B. 1964), 1971,* stamped sig., #40/50, full margins, good cond., (06-30-93, Sotheby-London, #655, illus.), 14⅜ x 19¼ in., (365 x 489 mm.), etching on wove (BP 1955, DM 4975, FR 16,784, Y 312,547).

BI *156 Series (B. 1967), 1971,* stamped sig., #41/50, full margins, good cond., est. BP 1,2/1,800, (06-30-93, Sotheby-London, #654, illus.), 14⅜ x 19⅜ in., (365 x 492 mm.), etching on wove.

$3775* *156 Series (B. 2010), 1972,* sig. stamp, #48/50, full margins, good cond., (06-30-93, Sotheby-London, #656, illus.), 14½ x 19⅝ in., (368 x 498 mm.), etching and aquatint on wove (BP 2530, DM 6439, FR 21,720, Y 404,479).

$3738* *156 Series: No. 108 (B. 1963), 1971,* stamped sig., #21/50, full margins, good cond., (05-13-93, Sotheby-NY, #749, illus.), 14⅝ x 19¾ in., (370 x 500 mm.), etching (BP 2454, DM 6036, FR 20,359, Y 417,327).

$4400* *156 Series: No. 112 (B. 1967), 1971,* stamped sig., #17/50, full margins, mat staining, excellent cond., (11-09-92, Christie-NY, #174, illus.), 14½ x 19$^{7}/_{16}$ in., (368 x 493 mm.), etching on wove (BP 2909, DM 7024, FR 23,732, Y 546,041).

$3910* *156 Series: No. 3 (B. 1858), 1970,* stamped sig., #29/50, full margins, excell. cond., (05-11-93, Christie-NY, #312, illus.), plate 12⅜ x 16½ in., (314 x 419 mm.), etching and drypoint on wove (BP 2496, DM 6159, FR 20,754, Y 430,096).

$3680* *156 Series: No. 47 (B. 1902), 1970,* stamped sig., #29/50, full margins, tape, (05-11-93, Christie-NY, #313), plate 10¾ x 13¾ in., (273 x 349 mm.), etching on wove (BP 2349, DM 5797, FR 19,533, Y 404,796).

$4600* *156 Series: Nos. 101; and 109 (B. 1957 and 1964), 1971: Two,* stamped sig., #21/50, full margins, good cond., soiling, (05-13-93, Sotheby-NY, #748, illus.), one 12⅝ x 16½ in., (320 x 420 mm.), other 14⅝ x 19¾ in., (320 x 420 mm.), mezzotint, and etching (BP 3020, DM 7428, FR 25,054, Y 513,565).

$1610* *156 Series: Nos. 138; and 139 (B. 1992 and 1993), 1971: Two,* stamped sig., #21/50, full margins, good cond., soiling, (05-13-93, Sotheby-NY, #750), one 12⅝ x 16½ in., (320 x 420 mm.), other 14⅝ x 19¾ in., (320 x 420 mm.), drypoint, and etching (BP 1057, DM 2600, FR 8769, Y 179,748).

$5750* *156 Series: Nos. 17; and 23 (B. 1872 and 1878), 1970: Two,* stamped sig., #21/50, full margins, good cond., soiling, (05-13-93, Sotheby-NY, #745, illus.), each 12⅝ x 16½ in., (320 x 420 mm.), etching (BP 3775, DM 9285, FR 31,318, Y 641,956).

$4600* *156 Series: Nos. 89; and 95 (B. 1944 and 1950), 1971: Two,* stamped sig., #21/50, full margins, good cond., soiling, (05-13-93, Sotheby-NY, #746, illus.), one 14⅝ x 19½ in., (370 x 495 mm.), other 9 x 12¼ in., (370 x 495 mm.), etching (BP 3020, DM 7428, FR 25,054, Y 513,565).

$6325* *156 Series: Nos. 91; and 100 (B. 1946 and 1956), 1971: Two,* stamped sig., #21/50, full margins, good cond., soiling, (05-13-93, Sotheby-NY, #747, illus.), each 14⅝ x 19½ in., (370 x 495 mm.), etching (BP 4152, DM 10,213, FR 34,450, Y 706,152).

BI *156 Series: Untitled (B. 1944), 1971,* stamp s., num. 34/50, full margins, good cond., mat staining, taped,pencil notations, est. $2/4,000, (02-24-93, Butterfield, #2779), 14½ x 19¼ in., (368 x 489 mm.), etching on wove.

$2185* *156 Series: Untitled (B. 1944), 1971,* stamp s., #34/50, full margins, good cond., mat staining, tape, notations, (05-19-93, Butterfield, #1952), 14½ x 19¼ in., (368 x 489 mm.), etching on wove (BP 1418, DM 3552, FR 11,966, Y 241,891).

$677* *17.7.70 I., 1970,* s., 2/100, 1160 x 1520mm, (06-28-93, Loudmer, #106), offset color poster (BP 453, DM 1150, FR 3875, Y 71,830).

$580* *25.7.61, 1961,* s., d., 36/200, (06-28-93, Loudmer, #339), 19½ x 18⅛ in., (495 x 460 mm.), sh 25$^{13}/_{16}$ x 19$^{11}/_{16}$ in., (495 x 460 mm.), color lithograph on Arches wove (BP 388, DM 986, FR 3320, Y 61,538).

$2401* *26 Juin 1968 III (Bloch 1670), 1968,* s., plate d., #8/50, series 347 gravures, (06-10-93, Hauswedell/Nolt, #787), image 3⅞ x 4$^{13}/_{16}$ in., (9.8 x 12.3 cm.), aquatint on thick wove (BP 1571, DM 3910, FR 13,163, Y 254,856).

$3367* *347 Gravures 9.9.68.I, (Bloch 1799),* #37/50, s., (11-09-92, Finarte-Milan, #48, illus.), 5⅞ x 8¼ in., (15 x 21 cm.), etching (BP 2226, DM 5375, FR 18,161, Y 417,846, L 4600).

$2420* *"347 Gravures",* plate 36 #27/50 by Picasso, (04-23-93, Clearing House, #228, illus.), 12¼ x 16 in., (31.1 x 40.6 cm.), aquatint etching (BP 1537, DM 3829, FR 12,927, Y 267,285).

$2035* *"347 Gravures",* plate 39 #27/50 by Picasso, (04-23-93, Clearing House, #229, illus.), 10¾ x 15 in., (27.3 x 38.1 cm.), aquatint etching (BP 1293, DM 3219, FR 10,871, Y 224,763).

$3759* *347 Gravures- 1.8.1968 III (Bloch 1710),* #37/50, s., (05-20-93, Finarte-Milan, #131, illus.), 6¾ x 10$^{5}/_{16}$ in., (17.2

x 26.2 cm.), etching and aquatint (BP 2413, DM 6065, FR 20,429, Y 415,084, L 5520).

$2620* *347 Gravures- 15 Juillet 1968, (Bloch 1684)*, #4/50, s. Picasso, (12-15-92, Finarte-Milan, #44, illus.), 16⅛ x 19½ in., (41 x 49.5 cm.), etching (BP 1671, DM 4107, FR 14,033, Y 324,941, L 3680).

$3133* *347 Gravures- 18.8.1968 VI, (Bloch 1767)*, #37/50, s., (05-20-93, Finarte-Milan, #133, illus.), 6 x 8³⁄₁₆ in., (15.3 x 20.8 cm.), etching (BP 2011, DM 5055, FR 17,027, Y 345,958, L 4600).

$2819* *347 Gravures- 4.7.1968 I (Bloch 1679)*, # 37/50, s., (05-20-93, Finarte-Milan, #130, illus.), 5¹³⁄₁₆ x 8³⁄₁₆ in., (14.8 x 20.8 cm.), aquatint (BP 1809, DM 4548, FR 15,321, Y 311,285, L 4140).

$2819* *347 Gravures-3.7.1968 I (Bloch 1678)*, #37/50, s., (05-20-93, Finarte-Milan, #129, illus.), 5¹³⁄₁₆ x 8¼ in., (14.8 x 20.9 cm.), aquatint (BP 1809, DM 4548, FR 15,321, Y 311,285, L 4140).

BI *347 Series Number 96 (Bloch 1576; Livre #147)*, *1971*, num. 172/350, w/margins, good cond., est. $6/800, (05-22-93, Weschler, #212, illus.), 3½ x 4¾ in., (8.9 x 12.1 cm.), etching.

BI *347 Series Untitled (B. 1808)*, *1968*, s., #48/50, full margins, good cond., est. BP 2,5/3,000, (12-03-92, Sotheby-London, #564, illus.), 8⅛ x 10⅜ in., (207 x 265 mm.), aquatint on wove.

$6650* *347 Series Untitled (B. 1827)*, *1968*, s., #23/50, full margins, good cond., (12-03-92, Sotheby-London, #568, illus.), 9 x 12¾ in., (228 x 325 mm.), aquatint on BFK Rives (BP 4290, DM 10,458, FR 35,695, Y 827,423).

$1650* *"347 Series" (Bloch, 1786)*, *1968*, s. Picasso, #47/50, d. 2.9.68.II in plate, watermark, very good cond., mount toning, tape residue, annot., (03-12-93, Skinner, #82, illus.), 5¾ x 8⅛ in., (14.6 x 20.6 cm.), etching on Rives BFK (BP 1151, DM 2746, FR 9338, Y 194,461).

$4604* *347 Series: No 152 (B. 1633)*, *1968*, s., #26/50, full margins, good cond., (12-03-92, Sotheby-London, #557, illus.), 14¾ x 10⅝ in., (375 x 270 mm.), etching on BFK Rives (BP 2970, DM 7240, FR 24,713, Y 572,851).

$2046* *347 Series: No 239 (B. 1719)*, *1968*, s., #8/50, full margins, good cond., (12-03-92, Sotheby-London, #556, illus.), 6¾ x 10½ in., (172 x 268 mm.), etching (BP 1320, DM 3217, FR 10,982, Y 254,573).

$3581* *347 Series: No 243 (B. 1723)*, *1968*, s., #45/50, full margins, good cond., (12-03-92, Sotheby-London, #562, illus.), 11¾ x 12¾ in., (298 x 325 mm.), etching (BP 2310, DM 5631, FR 19,222, Y 445,564).

$2558* *347 Series: No 45 (B. 1525)*, *1968*, s., #23/50, full margins, good cond., (12-03-92, Sotheby-London, #551, illus.), 12½ x 15⅜ in., (318 x 392 mm.), aquatint and drypoint (BP 1650, DM 4023, FR 13,731, Y 318,278).

$2530* *347 Series: No. 104 (B. 1584)*, *1968*, s., #24/50, full margins, mat staining, excell. cond., (05-11-93, Christie-NY, #306), plate 12⅜ x 16⅜ in., (314 x 416 mm.), aquatint on BFK (BP 1615, DM 3986, FR 13,429, Y 278,297).

$7378* *347 Series: No. 111 (B. 1591)*, *1968*, s., #23/50, full margins, good cond., mount-staining, (06-30-93, Sotheby-London, #648, illus.), 9⅛ x 13 in., (232 x 330 mm.), aquatint on wove (BP 4945, DM 12,584, FR 42,451, Y 790,528).

$7975* *347 Series: No. 120; No. 162; and No. 193 (B. 1602; 1642 and 1673)*, *1968*, s., #45/50, 23/50, 45/50, full margins, good cond., soiling, (11-05-92, Sotheby-NY, #381), two aquatints, and aquatint and drypoint (BP 5187, DM 12,613, FR 42,670, Y 978,408).

$7700* *347 Series: No. 134 (B. 1614)*, *1968*, s., #18/50, full margins, good cond., (11-05-92, Sotheby-NY, #382, illus.), 13¼ x 19⅜ in., (337 x 492 mm.), aquatint (BP 5008, DM 12,178, FR 41,199, Y 944,669).

$3450* *347 Series: No. 14 (B. 1494)*, *1968*, s., #45/50, full margins, good cond., crease into image, (05-13-93, Sotheby-NY, #736, illus.), 16⅜ x 12⅜ in., (415 x 315 mm.), etching (BP 2265, DM 5571, FR 18,791, Y 385,174).

$6600* *347 Series: No. 140; and No. 254 (B. 1620 and 1734)*, *1968*, s., #18/50 and #20/50, full margins, good cond., discoloration, straymark, (11-05-92, Sotheby-NY, #383), one 8¾ x 11½ in., (222 x 291 mm.), other 8⅛ x 10½

in., (222 x 291 mm.), two etchings (BP 4293, DM 10,438, FR 35,313, Y 809,717).

$4400* *347 Series: No. 153 (B. 1633)*, *1968*, s., #4/50, full margins, good cond., abrasions, (11-05-92, Sotheby-NY, #384, illus.), 14¾ x 10¾ in., (374 x 273 mm.), etching (BP 2862, DM 6959, FR 23,542, Y 539,811).

$2990* *347 Series: No. 165 (B. 1645)*, *1968*, s., #21/50, full margins, mat staining, excell. cond., (05-11-93, Christie-NY, #307, illus.), plate 8¼ x 5⅞ in., (210 x 149 mm.), etching on wove (BP 1909, DM 4710, FR 15,870, Y 328,897).

$12,650* *347 Series: No. 180 (B. 1660)*, *1968*, s., #23/50, full margins, good cond., creases, discoloration, (11-05-92, Sotheby-NY, #385, illus.), 19½ x 16¾ in., (495 x 425 mm.), aquatint and drypoint (BP 8228, DM 20,006, FR 67,683, Y 1,551,957).

$3410* *347 Series: No. 196 (B. 1676)*, *1968*, s., #32/50, full margins, good cond., (12-03-92, Sotheby-London, #555, illus.), 11 x 15⅛ in., (280 x 385 mm.), etching on BFK Rives (BP 2200, DM 5362, FR 18,304, Y 424,288).

$2530* *347 Series: No. 204 (B. 1684)*, *1968*, s., #21/50, full margins, very good cond., (05-11-93, Christie-NY, #308), plate 16¼ x 19½ in., (413 x 495 mm.), etching on wove (BP 1615, DM 3986, FR 13,429, Y 278,297).

$2300* *347 Series: No. 217 (B. 1697)*, *1968*, s., #20/50, full margins, good cond., creases, (02-11-93, Sotheby-NY, #225, illus.), 12⅜ x 12⅜ in., (315 x 315 mm.), etching (BP 1623, DM 3810, FR 12,892, Y 277,275).

$7700* *347 Series: No. 21; And No. 82 (B. 1501 and B. 1562)*, *1968*, s., #20/50 and 23/50, full margins, good cond., (11-05-92, Sotheby-NY, #377), one 12⅜ x 16⅜ in., (313 x 415 mm.), other 10¾ x 14¾ in., (313 x 415 mm.), etching (BP 5008, DM 12,178, FR 41,199, Y 944,669).

$4085* *347 Series: No. 230 (Bloch 1710)*, *1968*, s., num. 45/50, full margins, good cond., mat stain, (10-14-92, Sotheby-Japan, #74, illus.), 16¾ x 10¼ in., (425 x 260 mm.), etching and aquatint (BP 2398, DM 5978, FR 20,273, Y 495,032).

BI *347 Series: No. 232 (B. 1713)*, *1968*, s., #45/50, full margins, good cond., creases, est. $4/6,000, (05-13-93, Sotheby-NY, #744, illus.), 12⅜ x 12⅜ in., (315 x 315 mm.), etching and drypoint.

$3812* *347 Series: No. 236 (Bloch 1716)*, *1968*, s., num. 23/50, full margins, good cond., (10-14-92, Sotheby-Japan, #75, illus.), 16¾ x 10¼ in., (425 x 260 mm.), etching (BP 2237, DM 5579, FR 18,918, Y 461,949).

BI *347 Series: No. 241 (B. 1721)*, *1968*, s., #47/50, full margins, good cond., est. $3/3,500, (02-11-93, Sotheby-NY, #226), 6¾ x 10⁵⁄₁₆ in., (171 x 262 mm.), etching.

$4400* *347 Series: No. 262 (B. 1742)*, *1968*, s., #18/50, full margins, good cond., (11-05-92, Sotheby-NY, #386), 10⅜ x 8¼ in., (263 x 208 mm.), etching (BP 2862, DM 6959, FR 23,542, Y 539,811).

$2728* *347 Series: No. 296 (B. 1776)*, *1968*, s., #18/50, full margins, good cond., (12-03-92, Sotheby-London, #563, illus.), 11 x 15⅜ in., (280 x 389 mm.), etching (BP 1760, DM 4290, FR 14,643, Y 339,430).

$2905* *347 Series: No. 324 (Bloch 1804)*, *1968*, s., num. 23/50, full margins, good cond., (10-14-92, Sotheby-Japan, #76, illus.), 8¼ x 10½ in., (210 x 267 mm.), etching (BP 1705, DM 4251, FR 14,417, Y 352,036).

$2875* *347 Series: No. 326 (B. 1806)*, *1968*, s., #45/50, full margins, good cond., (02-11-93, Sotheby-NY, #227), 8⅛ x 10½ in., (207 x 267 mm.), etching (BP 2029, DM 4762, FR 16,115, Y 346,594).

BI *347 Series: No. 334 (B. 1814)*, *1968*, s., #18/50, full margins, good cond., est. $3/3,500, (02-11-93, Sotheby-NY, #228), 8³⁄₁₆ x 10½ in., (208 x 267 mm.), etching.

$2760* *347 Series: No. 336 (B. 1816)*, *1968*, s., #20/50, full margins, surface scuff, staining, creasing, good cond., (05-11-93, Christie-NY, #309, illus.), plate 9 x 12¾ in., (229 x 324 mm.), aquatint on wove (BP 1762, DM 4348, FR 14,650, Y 303,597).

$2530* *347 Series: No. 340 (B. 1820)*, *1968*, s., #21/50, full margins, mat staining, excell. cond., (05-11-93, Christie-NY, #310), plate 8⅛ x 10 in., (206 x 254 mm.), aquatint on wove (BP 1615, DM 3986, FR 13,429, Y 278,297).

$3631* *347 Series: No. 37 (Bloch 1517)*, *1968*, s., num. 45/50, full margins, good cond., (10-14-92, Sotheby-Japan, #72, illus.), 12½ x 15⅜ in., (318 x 391 mm.), aquatint (BP 2131, DM 5314, FR 18,020, Y 440,015).

$4675* *347 Series: No. 4 (B. 1484), 1968,* s., #23/50, full margins, good cond., (11-05-92, Sotheby-NY, #375), 11⅝ x 20⅜ in., (294 x 516 mm.), etching (BP 3041, DM 7394, FR 25,013, Y 573,549).

$3631* *347 Series: No. 43 (Bloch 1523), 1968,* s., num. 18/50, full margins, good cond., indentations, (10-14-92, Sotheby-Japan, #73, illus.), 12½ x 15⅜ in., (318 x 391 mm.), etching (BP 2131, DM 5314, FR 18,020, Y 440,015).

$4629* *347 Series: No. 5 (Bloch 1485), 1968,* s., num. 27/50, full margins, good cond., soiling, (10-14-92, Sotheby-Japan, #71, illus.), 16½ x 12⅜ in., (419 x 314 mm.), etching (BP 2717, DM 6774, FR 22,973, Y 560,955).

$4600* *347 Series: No. 51 (B. 1531), 1968,* s., #45/50, full margins, good cond., (02-11-93, Sotheby-NY, #223), 12⅜ x 15⁷⁄₁₆ in., (315 x 392 mm.), etching w/drypoint and aquatint (BP 3246, DM 7620, FR 25,785, Y 554,551).

$6050* *347 Series: No. 54 (B. 1534), 1968,* s., #45/50, full margins, good cond., creases, remains of hinges, (11-05-92, Sotheby-NY, #378, illus.), 11⅛ x 15⅜ in., (282 x 389 mm.), etching (BP 3935, DM 9568, FR 32,370, Y 742,240).

$4675* *347 Series: No. 59 (B. 1539), 1968,* s., #23/50, full margins, good cond., crease, (11-05-92, Sotheby-NY, #379), 12½ x 15½ in., (318 x 395 mm.), etching (BP 3041, DM 7394, FR 25,013, Y 573,549).

$5225* *347 Series: No. 6 (B. 1486), 1968,* s., #23/50, full margins, good cond., (11-05-92, Sotheby-NY, #376), 16⅝ x 13⅝ in., (423 x 346 mm.), etching (BP 3398, DM 8263, FR 27,956, Y 641,026).

$3922* *347 Series: No. 69 (B. 1549), 1968,* s., #45/50, full margins, good cond., (12-03-92, Sotheby-London, #552), 12⅜ x 16⅜ in., (315 x 415 mm.), etching (BP 2530, DM 6168, FR 21,052, Y 487,993).

$6050* *347 Series: No. 69 (B. 1549), 1968,* s., #17/50, full margins, good cond., graphite line, (11-05-92, Sotheby-NY, #380, illus.), 12⅜ x 16⅜ in., (313 x 416 mm.), etching (BP 3935, DM 9568, FR 32,370, Y 742,240).

$4370* *347 Series: No. 71 (B. 1551), 1968,* s., #4/50, full margins, excell. cond., (05-11-93, Christie-NY, #305, illus.), plate 12¼ x 16¼ in., (311 x 413 mm.), etching on wove (BP 2790, DM 6884, FR 23,195, Y 480,695).

$4600* *347 Series: No. 80 (B. 1560), 1968,* s., #18/50, full margins, good cond., (05-13-93, Sotheby-NY, #739, illus.), 10⅞ x 14¾ in., (275 x 375 mm.), etching (BP 3020, DM 7428, FR 25,054, Y 513,565).

$2588* *347 Series: No. 89 (B. 1569), 1968,* s., #34/50, full margins, good cond., (05-13-93, Sotheby-NY, #740), 6⅝ x 8⅛ in., (168 x 207 mm.), aquatint (BP 1699, DM 4179, FR 14,096, Y 288,936).

$3069* *347 Series: Nos. 100 and 263 (B. 1580 and 1743), 1968: Two,* s., #18/50, #23/50, full margins, good cond., crease, (12-03-92, Sotheby-London, #554), one 11⅝ x 13¾ in., (296 x 348 mm.), other 12¾ x 7⅞ in., (296 x 348 mm.), aquatint and etching, and an aquatint and drypoint (BP 1980, DM 4826, FR 16,473, Y 381,859).

BI *347 Series: Nos. 139; and 154 (B. 1619 and 1634), 1968: Two,* s., #45/50, full margins, good cond., glue stain, (05-13-93, Sotheby-NY, #742), one 8⅝ x 11⅜ in., (220 x 290 mm.), other 8⅞ x 11⅜ in., (220 x 290 mm.), etching and aquatint, and etching.

$9200* *347 Series: Nos. 17; and 20 (B. 1497 and 1500), 1968: Two,* s., #18/50 and #22/50, full margins, good cond., skinning, glue stain, (05-13-93, Sotheby-NY, #737), one 14¾ x 10¾ in., (375 x 272 mm.), other 12½ x 14½ in., (375 x 272 mm.), etching and aquatint (BP 6040, DM 14,855, FR 50,109, Y 1,027,130).

$3410* *347 Series: Nos. 241 and 320 (B. 1721 and 1800), 1968: Two,* s., #8/50, #23/50, full margins, good cond., (12-03-92, Sotheby-London, #558), one 6⅞ x 10⅜ in., (175 x 263 mm.), other 5⅞ x 8¼ in., (175 x 263 mm.), etchings (BP 2200, DM 5362, FR 18,304, Y 424,288).

BI *347 Series: Nos. 337 and 340 (B. 1817 and 1820), 1968: Two,* s., #48/50, #18/50, full margins, good cond., stray red pencil mark,est. BP 2/2,500, (12-03-92, Sotheby-London, #565), each 8¼ x 10½ in., (209 x 266 mm.), aquatint and drypoint, and an aquatint.

$7475* *347 Series: Nos. 58; and 76 (B. 1538 and 1556), 1968: Two,* s., #18/50 and #45/50, full margins, good cond., soiling, skinning, (05-13-93, Sotheby-NY, #738), one 12⅜ x 15½ in., (315 x 395 mm.), other 7½ x 4½ in., (315 x 395 mm.), etching (BP 4907, DM 12,070, FR 40,714, Y 834,543).

$8625* *347 Series: Nos. 6; and 13 (B. 1486 and 1493), 1968: Two,* s., #21/50, #17/50, full margins, good cond., crease, skinning, (05-13-93, Sotheby-NY, #735), one 16½ x 13⅝ in., (420 x 345 mm.), other 16⅜ x 12⅜ in., (420 x 345 mm.), etching (BP 5662, DM 13,927, FR 46,977, Y 962,934).

$2387* *347 Series: Nos. 77; and 268 (B. 1557 and 1748), 1968: Two,* s., #45/50, #18/50, full margins, good cond., (12-03-92, Sotheby-London, #553), one 7½ x 4⅝ in., (189 x 117 mm.), other 5⅜ x 4⅜ in., (189 x 117 mm.), etchings (BP 1540, DM 3754, FR 12,813, Y 297,001).

$2997* *347 Series: Plate 217 (Bl. 1697), 1968,* s., #17/50, margins, discoloration, good cond., (12-01-92, Christie-London, #503), plate 12⅜ x 12⅜ in., (315 x 314 mm.), ethcing on BFK Rives (BP 1980, DM 4777, FR 16,279, Y 373,132).

$1998* *347 Series: Plate 280 (Bl. 1760), 1968,* s., #48/50, margins, (12-01-92, Christie-London, #504), plate 6¹⁄₁₆ x 8¼ in., (154 x 209 mm.), etching on wove (BP 1320, DM 3185, FR 10,853, Y 248,755).

$1998* *347 Series: Plate 322 (Bl. 1802), 1968,* s., #48/50, margins, excellent cond., (12-01-92, Christie-London, #505), plate 5⅞ x 7⅞ in., (150 x 200 mm.), etching on wove (BP 1320, DM 3185, FR 10,853, Y 248,755).

$3850* *347 Series: Untitled (B. 1533), 1968,* s., num. 23/50, full margins, apparently very good cond., (02-24-93, Butterfield, #2778, illus.), 11⅛ x 15½ in., (283 x 394 mm.), etching on wove (BP 2685, DM 6250, FR 21,189, Y 451,772).

$3751* *4 Mai 1945 (B. 371; Baer 700), 1945,* Baer's 2nd state of 3, s., i. 1er etat no 33 of 50, margins, light staining, fox marks, creases, skinned areas, tape remains, (12-03-92, Sotheby-London, #499, illus.), sheet 10¼ x 15⅞ in., (262 x 403 mm.), engraving on wove (BP 2420, DM 5899, FR 20,134, Y 466,716).

$2048* *5 Aout 1968 III (Bloch 1728), 1968,* s., plate d., #18/50, series from 347 gravures, (06-10-93, Hauswedell/Nolt, #788), image 2⅜ x 3⅜ in., (6 x 8.5 cm.), etching on thick wove (BP 1340, DM 3335, FR 11,228, Y 217,387).

$132* *60 Years Of Graphic Works,* s., (11-01-92, Hanzel, #284), 28 x 18½ in., (71.1 x 47 cm.), color lithograph poster (BP 86, DM 208, FR 702, Y 16,320).

$715* *60 Years Of Graphic Works, Los Angeles County Museum Of Art (B. 1302), 1966,* s., #68/100, full margins, good cond.?, image creases, light-staining creases, staining, (10-28-92, Butterfield, #2697), 29½ x 22 in., (749 x 559 mm.), color lithograph on wove (BP 456, DM 1104, FR 3749, Y 87,730).

$354* *60 Years Of Graphik Works (Bloch 1302, Czwiklitzer 53), 1966,* Los Angeles County Museum Of Art, p. by Mourlot-Paris, (12-05-92, Bassenge, #7618), 29⅛ x 20³⁄₁₆ in., (74 x 51.2 cm.), color lithograph (BP 222, DM 552, FR 1881, Y 43,861).

$2291* *Accouplement I (G.-Baer 340/II/B/d; Bl. 181), 1933,* sheet 29 of Suite Vollard, (06-23-93, Kornfeld, #671), etching on handmade (BP 1556, DM 3876, FR 13,039, Y 249,591, SF 3450).

$20,700* *Afat; Soixante Sonnets (Cramer 33), 1940,* text by Ilia Zdanevitch, Le Degre Quarante et Un, unbound and attached w/string as issued, d. May and June 1939, num., s. Picasso and Iliazd, (06-14-93, Sotheby-NY, #241, illus.), 8 x 11⅞ in., (20.3 x 30.2 cm.), 4 engravings w/ burin and 2 aquatints of arabesques on Montval wove ala cuve (BP 13,549, DM 33,691, FR 113,239, Y 2,178,259).

$938* *Affiche Exposition De Ceramiques (B. 1281; C31), 1958,* s., from poster edit., full margins, good cond., (12-03-92, Sotheby-London, #544), 23¼ x 16⅜ in., (590 x 415 mm.), lithograph in colors (BP 605, DM 1475, FR 5035, Y 116,710).

$819* *Affiche Pour Le Musee De Ceret (Manolo Huguet)(B. 1278; Czwiklitzer 26), 1957,* crayon s., full margins, good cond., handling marks, creases, (12-03-92, Sotheby-London, #543), 25½ x 18¾ in., (650 x 475 mm.), lithograph on Arches wove (BP 528, DM 1288, FR 4396, Y 101,904).

$686* *Affiche, Exposition 1960 (B. 1288), 1968,* crayon s., d. ler 12 60, i. pour ami..., full margins, good cond., discoloration, handling creases, (06-30-93, Sotheby-London, #640), 21⅝ x 16½ in., (549 x 419 mm.), lithographic poster in black and brown on wove (BP 460, DM 1170, FR 3947, Y 73,503).

BI *Affiche, Exposition De Ceramiques (B. 1280), 1958,* crayon s., p. by Mourlot, good cond., creasing, (06-30-93, Sotheby-London, #638), sh 25⅜ x 18¾ in., (645 x 476 mm.), lithograph in black and brown on wove.

$15,525* *Apres La Pique (Taureau Et Picador) (B. 910; Baer 1230), 1959,* s., #41/50, p. Arnera, pub. Galerie Louise Leiris, 1960, full margins, good cond., (05-13-93, Sotheby-NY, #708, illus.), 21 x 25¼ in., (533 x 641 mm.), linoleum cut in colors (BP 10,192, DM 25,069, FR 84,559, Y 1,733,281).

BI *Aquatinte 7 Juin 1968 II (Bloch Band II 1624),* #7/50, s., est. DM 11,000-, (11-21-92, Lempertz, #329, illus.), 16¼ x 19½ in., (41.2 x 49.5 cm.), etching on wove.

$2749* *Au Bain (G.-Baer 201/B/d; Bl. 136), 1930,* sheet 3 of Suite Vollard, (06-23-93, Kornfeld, #651), etching on handmade (BP 1868, DM 4651, FR 15,646, Y 299,488, SF 4140).

$4582* *Au Bain (G.-Baer 408/B/d; Bl. 210), 1934,* sheet 79 of Suite Vollard, (06-23-93, Kornfeld, #674), etching on handmade (BP 3113, DM 7753, FR 26,079, Y 499,183, SF 6900).

$1374* *Au Cirque, Cavaliere Sur Cheval (Bl. 1455), 1967,* sig. stamp, num., (06-23-93, Kornfeld, #695), drypoint (BP 933, DM 2325, FR 7820, Y 149,690, SF 2070).

$121* *Bacchanal,* after 1959, from Bacchanals, Women and Bullfights, Abrams 1962, s. Picasso, (06-26-93, Wolf, #961), linoleum cut (BP 81, DM 206, FR 693, Y 12,838).

$9058* *Bacchanale,* s. 143/250, blindstamp Editeur Atelier Crommelynck, (05-25-93, AB Stockholm, #56, illus.), 18¹¹⁄₁₆ x 22¹⁄₁₆ in., (47.5 x 56 cm.), aquatint (BP 5870, DM 14,752, FR 49,660, Y 990,054, SK 13,200).

BI *Bacchanale (B. 927), 1959,* s., #30/50, full margins, stain, excell. cond., est. $7/9,000, (05-11-93, Christie-NY, #278, illus.), borderline 20⅞ x 25¼ in., (530 x 641 mm.), linocut in brown and black on Arches.

$23,000* *Bacchanale (B. 930), 1959,* s., #13/50, wide margins, light-staining, good cond., (05-11-93, Christie-NY, #279, illus.), borderline 20¾ x 25 in., (527 x 635 mm.), color linocut on Arches (BP 14,682, DM 36,232, FR 122,081, Y 2,529,975).

$1298* *Bacchanale Au Flutiste (Baer 959/B/b/1; Bl. 773), 1955,* p. 1961, pub. 1981, sig. stamp, num., (06-23-93, Kornfeld, #689), etching (BP 882, DM 2196, FR 7388, Y 141,410, SF 1955).

$110* *Bacchanale Au Hibou,* after 1959, from Bacchanals, Women and Bullfights, Abrams, 1962, s. Picasso, (06-26-93, Wolf, #964), color linoleum cut (BP 74, DM 187, FR 630, Y 11,671).

$8407* *Bacchanale Au Taureau (B. 932), 1959,* s., #32/50, full margins, good cond., discoloration, (06-30-93, Sotheby-London, #620, illus.), 20½ x 25⅛ in., (521 x 638 mm.), color linocut on Arches (BP 5635, DM 14,339, FR 48,372, Y 900,782).

$1985* *Bacchanale Avec Enfant Aux Cymbales (Baer 947/B/b/1; Bl. 772), 1955,* p. 1961, pub. 1981, sig. stamp, num., (06-23-93, Kornfeld, #685), etching on handmade (BP 1349, DM 3359, FR 11,298, Y 216,254, SF 2990).

$1527* *Bacchanale Avec Eros En Haut A Gauche (Baer 951/B/b/1; Bl. 776), 1955,* p. 1961, pub. 1981, num., (06-23-93, Kornfeld, #688), etching (BP 1037, DM 2584, FR 8691, Y 166,358, SF 2300).

$1298* *Bacchanale Avec Jeune Homme Au Masque (Baer 948/B/b/1; Bl. 774), 1955,* p. 1961, pub. 1981, sig. stamp, num., (06-23-93, Kornfeld, #686), etching on handmade (BP 882, DM 2196, FR 7388, Y 141,410, SF 1955).

$9163* *Bacchanale Avec Une Femme Assise Tenant Un Bebe (Baer 1254/III/B/b; Bl. 929), 1959,* s., (06-23-93, Kornfeld, #724), color linocut on wove (BP 6225, DM 15,504, FR 52,151, Y 998,257, SF 13,800).

$3884* *Bacchanale II (Bloch 902; Mourlot 329), 1959,* s., plate d., #18/50, (06-10-93, Hauswedell/Nolt, #797, illus.), image 16⁹⁄₁₆ x 24 in., (42 x 61 cm.), lithograph on Arches (BP 2541, DM 6325, FR 21,294, Y 412,270).

$1985* *Baigneuses En Maillot De Bain Par Temps Nuageux (G.-Baer 276/C/1; Bl.247), 1932,* p. 1961, pub. 1981, sig. stamp, num., (06-23-93, Kornfeld, #657), etching on handmade (BP 1349, DM 3359, FR 11,298, Y 216,254, SF 2990).

$3960* *Les Baigneuses Suprises (Geiser 355 III/III, Bloch 194), 1933,* s., Plate 14 of Suite de 100 eaux-fortes originales (Suite Vollard), (05-16-93, Hindman, #470), 7½ x 10½ in., (19.1 x 26.7 cm.), etching and drypoint (BP 2575, DM 6370, FR 21,405, Y 438,976).

$5750* *Le Bain (B. 12), 1905,* from La Suite des Saltimbanques, pub. Vollard 1913 after plate was steel-faced, wide margins, staining, repaired tear, creases, margin edges previously folded back, (05-11-93, Christie-NY, #257, illus.), plate 13⅜ x 11¼ in., (340 x 286 mm.), drypoint on Van Gelder Zonen (BP 3671, DM 9058, FR 30,520, Y 632,494).

$10,098* *Le Bain (Geiser Band I 14 b, Bloch Band I 12), 1905,* watermark, plate s., d., (11-21-92, Lempertz, #322, illus.), 13½ x 11⅜ in., (34.3 x 28.9 cm.), etching on thick wove (BP 6649, DM 16,100, FR 54,232, Y 1,255,814).

BI *Le Bain (g. 14; Bl. 12), 1905,* margins, foxmarks, mount-staining, est. BP 2,5/3,500, (12-01-92, Christie-London, #482), plate 13⅜ x 11⁵⁄₁₆ in., (339 x 288 mm.), drypoint on wove.

BI *Balzac (Bloch 723), 1952,* d., s., 10/25, frame trace, reddish stains, est. FF5/6,000, (06-28-93, Loudmer, #333), 26¾ x 20½ in., (680 x 520 mm.), sh 29¹⁵⁄₁₆ x 22¼ in., (680 x 520 mm.), black lithograph on wove.

$1909* *Balzac, D'Apres Rodin (Baer 899/B/b/1; Bl. 713), 1952,* p. 1961, pub. 1981, sig. stamp, (06-23-93, Kornfeld, #683), etching (BP 1297, DM 3230, FR 10,865, Y 207,975, SF 2875).

$3922* *Les Banderilles (B. 610), 1949,* crayon s., #15/50, full margins, good cond., (12-03-92, Sotheby-London, #502, illus.), 18⅛ x 19¼ in., (460 x 490 mm.), lithograph (BP 2530, DM 6168, FR 21,052, Y 487,993).

$4256* *Bathseba Im Bade, 1966,* s., num., blindstamp, (06-05-93, Bassenge, #6441), 10⁵⁄₁₆ x 14⁵⁄₁₆ in., (26.2 x 36.4 cm.), color etching on BFK Rives (BP 2802, DM 6900, FR 23,257, Y 456,554).

$4400* *"Bathsheba",* s., stamped, edit. #57/300, (12-11-92, DuMouchelle, #2030, illus.), 10¼ x 14½ in., (26 x 36.8 cm.), colored etching (BP 2821, DM 6932, FR 23,758, Y 544,487).

$4394* *Les Bleus De Barcelone (Bloch 1130; Bl. Bucher 117), (19)63,* s., Les Belus de Barcelone, watermark, (06-08-93, Karl/Faber, #1183, illus.), approx. 9¹⁄₁₆ x 12¹⁵⁄₁₆ in., (23 x 33 cm.), etching and aquatint on wove (BP 2889, DM 7130, FR 24,011, Y 466,702).

$593* *Buch. James Sabartes. "A Los Toros" Mit Picasso (Cramer 113): Four,* Andre Sauret, (06-24-93, Germann, #476), 4 lithographs, one in color (BP 390, DM 961, FR 3240, Y 63,613, SF 863).

$9927* *Buste Au Corsage A Carreaux (Mourl. 308; Bl. 849), 1957,* s. in red pencil, i. Epreuve d'artiste, (06-23-93, Kornfeld, #716, illus.), lithograph on wove (BP 6744, DM 16,797, FR 56,500, Y 1,081,490, SF 14,950).

$10,690* *Buste Au Fond Etoile (Mourl. 163; Bl. 594), 1949,* s. in red pencil, artist's proof, (06-23-93, Kornfeld, #706), lithograph on wove (BP 7262, DM 18,088, FR 60,842, Y 1,164,615, SF 16,100).

$1705* *Buste D'Homme (B. 4), 1905,* from the Saltimbanques Suite, pub. Vollard 1913, full margins, severelight/backboard staining, surface abrasions lower left of image, (12-03-92, Sotheby-London, #480, illus.), 4½ x 3½ in., (115 x 90 mm.), drypoint on Van Gelder Zonen wove (BP 1100, DM 2681, FR 9152, Y 212,144).

BI *Buste De Femme Au Chapeau (Portrait De Femme Au Chapeau A Pompons EtAu Corsage Imprime) (B. 1072; Baer 1318), 1962,* s., #4/50, p. Arnera, pub. Galerie Louise Leiris, 1963, full margins,good cond., mat stain, crease into image, est. $100/140,000, (05-13-93, Sotheby-NY, #716, illus.), 24⅝ x 20¾ in., (625 x 527 mm.), linoleum cut in colors.

BI *Buste De Femme Au Corsage Blanc (B. 848; M. 311), 1957,* s., #41/50, full margins, good cond., crease, light-stain, spots ink(?), est. $25/30,000, (05-13-93, Sotheby-NY, #705, illus.), 27¾ x 19⅞ in., (705 x 505 mm.), lithograph on wove.

$7700* *Buste De Jeaune Fille (B. 405), 1946,* s., #37/50, full margins, light staining, creasing, taped to overmat, (11-09-92, Christie-NY, #160, illus.), 21⅝ x 18⅞ in., (550 x 480 mm.), lithograph on Arches (BP 5091, DM 12,292, FR 41,532, Y 955,572).

$14,508* *Buste De Profil (Mourl. 306/I; Bl. 845), 1957,* s. in red pencil, num., (06-23-93, Kornfeld, #714, illus.), lithograph on wove (BP 9856, DM 24,548, FR 82,573, Y 1,580,564, SF 21,850).

$1286* *Buveur Sur Un Ane Et Femme (B. 980), 1960,* sig. stamp, #18/50, p. by Atelier Lacouriere et Frelaut 1961, margins, good cond., discoloration, (06-30-93, Sotheby-London, #621), 7 x 10⅝ in., (178 x 270 mm.), drypoint on laid (BP 862, DM 2193, FR 7399, Y 137,791).

$1876* *Carmen (B. 531), 1949: Seventeen,* from the set, bearing pencil numbering 50/289, w/title page, text andjust. s. by the artist, num. 50, pub. La Bibliotheque Francais, (12-03-92, Sotheby-London, #501), overall size 13 x 10¼ in., (330 x 260 mm.), drypoint on Montval wove (BP 1210, DM 2950, FR 10,070, Y 233,420).

$3575* *Carnaval (B. 1193), 1965,* s., #76/160, margins, good cond., mat/light-staining, creases, soiling, (10-28-92, Butterfield, #2696, illus.), 25¼ x 20¾ in., (641 x 527 mm.), color linoleum cut on Arches (BP 2278, DM 5521, FR 18,747, Y 438,650).

$5500* *Carnaval 1967 (B. 1242), 1967,* s., #62/160, full margins, good cond., scuffs, light stain, crease, printer's ink, tape stains, (11-05-92, Sotheby-NY, #371), 25¼ x 20⅞ in., (641 x 529 mm.), sheet 17⅞ x 24½ in., (641 x 529 mm.), linoleum cut p. in brown and beige (BP 3577, DM 8698, FR 29,428, Y 674,764).

$6808* *Carnaval 1967, Clown Et Danseurs (Bloch 1242), 1967,* s., num. 63/160, full margins, good cond., light stain, skinned area, (10-14-92, Sotheby-Japan, #70, illus.), 25¼ x 20⅞ in., (641 x 530 mm.), linoleum cut in brown and beige (BP 3996, DM 9963, FR 33,787, Y 825,012).

$2058* *"Carnaval 61", 1961,* s., #167/200, d. 20.1.1961, (05-08-93, Dobiaschofsky, #2199, illus.), 25³⁄₁₆ x 19¹¹⁄₁₆ in., (64 x 50 cm.), color lithograph (BP 1343, DM 3306, FR 11,154, Y 229,970, SF 3000).

$2919* *Carnaval, 1967,* s., 155/160, (12-04-92, AB Stockholm, #7118), 25³⁄₁₆ x 20⅞ in., (64 x 53 cm.), linoleum print in two colors on Arches (BP 1872, DM 4649, FR 15,770, Y 364,419, SK 19,800).

$2728* *Carnet De La Californie (B. 900), 1959,* s., #64/100, good cond., rubbed areas, (12-03-92, Sotheby-London, #512, illus.), sheet 18⅜ x 12⅝ in., (466 x 320 mm.), lithograph on Arches (BP 1760, DM 4290, FR 14,643, Y 339,430).

$3088* *Carnet De La Californie (B. 900; C. 101), 1959,* album, s., pub. Editions Cercle d'Art, good cond., (06-30-93, Sotheby-London, #616, illus.), overall 19 x 13 in., (483 x 330 mm.), lithographic (BP 2070, DM 5267, FR 17,768, Y 330,869).

$4263* *La Celestine (B. 1597, 1602, 1605-1607, 1616, 1617, 1626-1629, 1631,and 1635), 1971: Thirteen,* thirteen plates from the set of 66, bearing #142/350, w/t. page, just., s., num. 142, pub. Galerie Louie Leiris, good cond., (12-03-92, Sotheby-London, #559, illus.), each sheet approx. 8¼ x 6¾ in., (210 x 172 mm.), aquatints on Richard de Bas laid (BP 2750, DM 6704, FR 22,882, Y 530,422).

$820* *"La Celestine", 19.6.1968. V (Bloch 1648),* stamp s., (11-13-92, Koller, #5392), 4¹⁵⁄₁₆ x 3⁹⁄₁₆ in., (12.5 x 9 cm.), etching on wove (BP 530, DM 1287, FR 4341, Y 101,775, SF 1160).

$561* *"Le Chat" (Cramer #37), 1942,* 6th plate illus Buffon, (10-18-92, Pescheteau, #236), 14½ x 11 in., (36.8 x 28 cm.), etching and sugar aquatint on laid Vollard (BP 340, DM 829, FR 2815, Y 66,985).

$1265* *La Chevre-Feuille (B. 361; bk. no. 37; Goeppert/Cramer 38): Six,* book by Georges Hugnet, p. Lacouriere, #320, pub. Robert-J. Godet, 1943, full sheets, good cond., discoloration, (02-11-93, Sotheby-NY, #211), each sheet 11⅛

x 8¹⁵⁄₁₆ in., (283 x 228 mm.), zincograph on wove (BP 893, DM 2095, FR 7091, Y 152,502).

$220* *La Colombe,* for La Paix, s., d. in plate 28-12-61, s. Picasso, pub. blindstamp, (06-26-93, Wolf, #970), 19½ x 25 in., (49.5 x 63.5 cm.), lithograph (BP 147, DM 374, FR 1259, Y 23,342).

$48,694* *La Colombe (Moulot 141; Bloch 583), 1949,* s. Picasso, epreuve d'artiste, (06-25-93, Kornfeld, #100, illus.), 21½ x 27⁹⁄₁₆ in., (54.6 x 70 cm.), lithograph on vellum (BP 32,935, DM 82,898, FR 279,209, Y 5,161,543, SF 73,600).

$898* *"Colombe Voland (A L'Arc En Ciel" (BI 172),* 1 of 238, d. 10.10.52, s. in plate, (10-18-92, Pescheteau, #234), 21⅝ x 29¹⁵⁄₁₆ in., (55 x 76 cm.), lithograph in colors on wove (BP 544, DM 1326, FR 4506, Y 107,224).

$323* *Colombe Volant (A L'Arc En Ciel) (G. Bloch 712, Mourlot 214), 1952,* dirt spots, good margins, (02-03-93, Ader Tajan, #188), 19¹¹⁄₁₆ x 25⁹⁄₁₆ in., (50 x 65 cm.), lithograph (BP 225, DM 532, FR 1803, Y 40,179).

BI *Colombe Volant (A L'Arc-En-Ciel) (B. 712), 1952,* full margins, good cond., handling marks, creases, est. BP 6/800, (12-03-92, Sotheby-London, #508), 20 x 25½ in., (510 x 650 mm.), lithograph in colors on Arches.

$771* *Colombe Volant (A L'Arc-En-Ciel) (B. 712), 1952,* full marginsk good cond., handling marks, creases, (06-30-93, Sotheby-London, #590), 20 x 25½ in., (508 x 648 mm.), color lithograph on Arches (BP 517, DM 1315, FR 4436, Y 82,610).

$5500* *Colombe Volant (A l'Arc-En-Ciel) (B. 712), 1952,* s., #20/38, full margins, creasing, good cond., (11-09-92, Christie-NY, #163, illus.), 17¹¹⁄₁₆ x 24⁷⁄₁₆ in., (450 x 620 mm.), colored lithograph on Japon nacre (BP 3636, DM 8780, FR 29,666, Y 682,552).

$2200* *Colombe Volant (A l'Arc-En-Ciel) (B. 712), 1952,* s., #161/200, wide margins, colors faded, light staining, foxmarks, vertical margin edges folded back 1/2 inch, taped to overmat, (11-09-92, Christie-NY, #164), 19¾ x 26 in., (502 x 661 mm.), colored lithograph on Arches (BP 1455, DM 3512, FR 11,866, Y 273,021).

$9200* *Le Combat (B. 301), 1937,* watermark, s., #47/50, full margins, light/mat staining, foxing, stain, surface soiling, (05-11-93, Christie-NY, #269, illus.), plate 15¾ x 19⅜ in., (400 x 492 mm.), etching on Montval (BP 5873, DM 14,493, FR 48,832, Y 1,011,990).

BI *Combat De Centaures IV (B. 904), 1959,* s., #41/50, full margins, good cond., est. BP 2,5/3,500, (12-03-92, Sotheby-London, #513, illus.), sheet 19⅝ x 25¾ in., (500 x 655 mm.), lithograph on Arches.

$2917* *Combat De Centaures IV (B. 904), 1959,* s., #41/50, full margins, good cond., (06-30-93, Sotheby-London, #618, illus.), sh 19⅝ x 25¾ in., (498 x 654 mm.), lithograph on Arches (BP 1955, DM 4975, FR 16,784, Y 312,547).

$2837* *"Combat De Centaures" (Bloch 904; Mourlot 331), 1959,* watermark, s., num., (06-05-93, Grisebach, #368, illus.), 17¹⁵⁄₁₆ x 24¹³⁄₁₆ in., (45.5 x 63 cm.), lithograph on wove (BP 1868, DM 4600, FR 15,503, Y 304,334).

$2300* *Composition (B. 1415), 1966,* sig. stamp, #12/50, full margins, good cond., (05-13-93, Sotheby-NY, #733), 8¾ x 12⅝ in., (223 x 320 mm.), etching and aqaquatint (BP 1510, DM 3714, FR 12,527, Y 256,782).

$3300* *Composition (B. 1424), 1966,* sig. stamp, #12/50, full margins, good cond., crease, (11-05-92, Sotheby-NY, #372), 8⅞ x 12⅝ in., (224 x 321 mm.), etching and aquatint (BP 2146, DM 5219, FR 17,657, Y 404,858).

$3575* *Composition (B. 1438), 1966,* sig. stamp, #12/50, full margins, good cond., (11-05-92, Sotheby-NY, #373), 8¾ x 12⅝ in., (223 x 320 mm.), etching and aquatint (BP 2325, DM 5654, FR 19,128, Y 438,596).

BI *Composition (B. 1446), 1967,* s. stamp, #33/50, full margins, good cond., est. $4/5,000, (02-11-93, Sotheby-NY, #221, illus.), 13¹¹⁄₁₆ x 11⅝ in., (348 x 295 mm.), drypoint.

$2875* *Composition (B. 1447), 1967,* s. stamp, #35/50, full margins, good cond., skinning, (02-11-93, Sotheby-NY, #222, illus.), 13¹¹⁄₁₆ x 11⅝ in., (348 x 295 mm.), drypoint (BP 2029, DM 4762, FR 16,115, Y 346,594).

$2200* *Composition (B. 1451), 1967,* stamp sig., #32/50, full margins, good cond., (11-05-92, Sotheby-NY, #374), 8⅞ x 12⅝ in., (224 x 321 mm.), etching (BP 1431, DM 3479, FR 11,771, Y 269,906).

$2402* *Composition (B. 838), 1957,* crayon s., #103/250, margins, good cond., discoloration, (06-30-93, Sotheby-London, #614, illus.), sh 25½ x 19⅞ in., (648 x 505 mm.), color lithograph on wove (BP 1610, DM 4097, FR 13,820, Y 257,366).

$1249* *Composition (Bl. 1420), 1966,* stamped sig., #34/50, margins, tape, stitch marks, excellent cond., (12-01-92, Christie-London, #501), plate 8¹¹⁄₁₆ x 12⅝ in., (220 x 320 mm.), etching on wove (BP 825, DM 1991, FR 6784, Y 155,503).

BI *Composition Au Vase De Fleures (B. 426; M. 74), 1947,* s., #15/50, full margins, good cond., scuffs, touched-in printing defects, light/glue stains, est. $3/5,000, (02-11-93, Sotheby-NY, #214, illus.), 17¹¹⁄₁₆ x 23¹¹⁄₁₆ in., (450 x 602 mm.), color lithograph.

BI *Composition Au Vase De Fleurs (B. 426; M. 74), 1947,* s., #15/50, full margins, good cond., scuffs, touched in printing defects, light stain, stains, est. $8/10,000, (11-05-92, Sotheby-NY, #345, illus.), 17¾ x 23¾ in., (450 x 602 mm.), lithograph p. in colors.

$948* *Compositions From Verve, 1954: Three,* (09-30-92, Kunsthallen, #247), lithograph in color (BP 535, DM 1344, FR 4547, Y 113,765, DK 5175).

BI *Corps Perdu, 1950,* est. FF 6/7,000, (11-16-92, Briest, #345, illus.), 15¾ x 11¼ in., (40 x 28.5 cm.), etching in black.

$21,448* *Corrida En Arles (Baer 887 BB), 1952,* rare proof from Baer's 2nd state of 3, p. Frelaut at Lacouriere, fullmargins, good cond., water-stain, creases, ex coll. Marina Picasso, (06-30-93, Sotheby-London, #634, illus.), aquatint and scraper in color on Arches (BP 14,375, DM 36,582, FR 123,406, Y 2,298,082).

$21,315* *Corrida En Arles (Baer 887 CC), 1952,* unrecorded proof from Baer's third state, p. 1955, by Frelaut at Lacouriere, full margins, good cond., (12-03-92, Sotheby-London, #550, illus.), 16⅜ x 21⅜ in., (415 x 545 mm.), aquatint and scraper in colors on wove (BP 13,750, DM 33,519, FR 114,412, Y 2,652,109).

BI *Corrida, Le Picador (B. 599), 1949,* s., #13/50, full margins, light staining, foxing, creasing, good cond., est. $5/7,000, (11-09-92, Christie-NY, #162, illus.), 21¾ x 25¾ in., (553 x 654 mm.), lithograph on Arches.

$253* *Cote D'Azur,* s., (10-14-92, Germann, #400), 39³⁄₁₆ x 25⅞ in., (996 x 658 mm.), poster (BP 149, DM 370, FR 1256, Y 30,659, SF 330).

$225* *"Couverture Mourlot III" (Bl 795),* (10-18-92, Pescheteau, #235), 20¹⁄₁₆ x 25⁹⁄₁₆ in., (51 x 65 cm.), lithograph in black on cream (BP 136, DM 332, FR 1129, Y 26,866).

BI *"Le Crane De Chevre" (Bloch 691; Baer 890/Ba), 1952,* s., num., est. DM 13/15,000, (11-28-92, Grisebach, #245, illus.), 18¾ x 25³⁄₁₆ in., (47.6 x 64 cm.), aquatint on hand-made copper print paper.

$550* *The Dance With The Dove,* from La Paix, s., pub. blindstamp, (06-26-93, Wolf, #971), 25 x 19 in., (63.5 x 48.3 cm.), lithograph (BP 368, DM 935, FR 3148, Y 58,355).

$110* *Dancing Figures,* s. in stone, d. 17-11-59, #997/2000, (06-11-93, Freemn/Fine Art, #178), 16 x 20 in., (40.6 x 50.8 cm.), lithograph in black (BP 72, DM 179, FR 603, Y 11,671).

$4140* *Dans L'Atelier (B. 1162), 1964,* s., #38/50, full margins, excell. cond., (05-11-93, Christie-NY, #287, illus.), plate 9¼ x 13 in., (235 x 330 mm.), etching and aquatint on wove (BP 2643, DM 6522, FR 21,975, Y 455,395).

$3922* *Dans L'Atelier (B. 1219), 1965,* s., #41/50, full margins, good cond., (12-03-92, Sotheby-London, #538, illus.), 12¾ x 18¾ in., (325 x 475 mm.), (BP 2530, DM 6168, FR 21,052, Y 487,993).

$7162* *Dans L'Atelier (B. 1220), 1965,* s., #41/50, full margins, good cond., fox marks, (12-03-92, Sotheby-London, #539, illus.), 12⅝ x 18¼ in., (320 x 465 mm.), drypoint w/ aquatint on wove (BP 4620, DM 11,263, FR 38,443, Y 891,129).

$3581* *Dans L'Atelier (B. 1226), 1965,* s., num., full margins, good cond., (12-03-92, Sotheby-London, #540, illus.), 10⅞ x 15 in., (275 x 380 mm.), aquatint on Richard de Bas wove (BP 2310, DM 5631, FR 19,222, Y 445,564).

$3220* *Dans L'Atelier (B. 1226), 1965,* s., #21/50, full margins, foxmarks, creasing, light/mat staining, surface soiling, (05-11-93, Christie-NY, #292), plate 10¾ x 14⅞ in., (273 x 378 mm.), aquatint on Auvergne (BP 2056, DM 5072, FR 17,091, Y 354,196).

$4025* *Dans L'Atelier (B. 1228), 1965,* s., #24/50, full margins, mat staining, linen tape, good cond., (05-11-93, Christie-NY, #293), plate 9⅝ x 15⅛ in., (244 x 384 mm.), etching and aquatint on Auvergne a la main (BP 2569, DM 6341, FR 21,364, Y 442,746).

$2990* *Dans L'Atelier (B. 1399), 1966,* s., #24/50, full margins, excell. cond., (05-11-93, Christie-NY, #304), plate 12½ x 18½ in., (318 x 470 mm.), etching and aquatint in BFK (BP 1909, DM 4710, FR 15,870, Y 328,897).

$3360* *Dans L'Atelier (Bl. 1399), 1966,* s., num., (06-23-93, Kornfeld, #694), line etching and aquatint on wove (BP 2283, DM 5685, FR 19,124, Y 366,053, SF 5060).

$3996* *Dans L'Atelier (bl. 1371), 1966,* s., #38/50, margins, abrasions, (12-01-92, Christie-London, #498), plate 15½ x 22³⁄₁₆ in., (394 x 564 mm.), etching w/aquatint on BFK Rives (BP 2640, DM 6369, FR 21,706, Y 497,510).

$5175* *"Dans L'Atelier" and "Dans L'Atelier" (B. 1217 and 1226; Baer 1199 and 1209), 1965: Two,* s., #12/50, #27/50, full margins, good cond., light-stain, fox marks, (05-13-93, Sotheby-NY, #724), one 8⅞ x 12¾ in., (225 x 325 mm.), other 10⅞ x 15 in., (225 x 325 mm.), aquatint and drypoint, and aquatint (BP 3397, DM 8356, FR 28,186, Y 577,760).

$6900* *"Dans L'Atelier" and "Peintre Et Modele" (B. 1223 and 1373), 1965: Two,* s., #38/50, #24/50, full margins, good cond., mat stain, light-stain,fox mark, (05-13-93, Sotheby-NY, #725), one 9¾ x 15 in., (247 x 382 mm.), other 11 x 15⅜ in., (247 x 382 mm.), etching and aquatint (BP 4530, DM 11,142, FR 37,582, Y 770,347).

$2217* *La Danse (B. 15), 1905,* from the Saltimbanques Suite, pub. Vollard 1913, margins, good cond.,light staining, foxing, (12-03-92, Sotheby-London, #484), sheet 12⅞ x 17 in., (325 x 432 mm.), etching on Van Gelder Zonen (BP 1430, DM 3486, FR 11,900, Y 275,849).

BI *La Danse (B. 15), 1905,* from the Saltimbanques Suite, pub. Vollard 1913, full margins, foxing, mount staining, est. BP 2,2/2,500, (12-03-92, Sotheby-London, #483, illus.), 7¼ x 9 in., (186 x 230 mm.), drypoint on Van Gelder Zonen.

$3163* *La Danse (B. 15; G. 18), 1905,* from Saltimbanques suite, pub. Vollard, 1913, full margins, good cond., repaired rubbed spot, tear, nick, crease, foxing, (05-13-93, Sotheby-NY, #675), 7¼ x 9⅛ in., (185 x 231 mm.), drypoint (BP 2077, DM 5107, FR 17,228, Y 353,132).

$3054* *La Danse Barbare Devant Salome Et Hesiode (G.-Baer 18/b/2, kBl. 15),1905,* p. 1913, (06-23-93, Kornfeld, #646), drypoint on wove (BP 2075, DM 5168, FR 17,382, Y 332,716, SF 4600).

$98,909* *La Danse De Salome (Geiser-Baer 17/III/a; Bloch 14), 1905,* s. Picasso in black chalk, fruhdruck, (06-25-93, Kornfeld, #91, illus.), plate 15¾ x 13¹¹⁄₁₆ in., (40 x 34.8 cm.), sheet 23⅛ x 17⁷⁄₁₆ in., (40 x 34.8 cm.), drypoint on handmade (BP 66,898, DM 168,384, FR 567,139, Y 10,484,312, SF 149,500).

$2046* *La Danse Des Faunes (B. 830), 1957,* full margins, good cond,. handling creases, (12-03-92, Sotheby-London, #505), 16⅛ x 20¾ in., (410 x 530 mm.), lithograph on Arches (BP 1320, DM 3217, FR 10,982, Y 254,573).

$500* *La Danse Des Faunes (B. 830), 1957,* stamped sig., margins, trimmed, foxed, (11-30-92, Phillips-London, #472), sheet 18¾ x 22¾ in., (476 x 578 mm.), lithograph on Arches (BP 330, DM 797, FR 2704, Y 62,228).

$1839* *La Danse Des Faunes (Bloch 830; Mourlot 291), 1957,* watermark, stone s., d., (06-19-93, Wachholtz, #289, illus.), 16¼ x 20¹³⁄₁₆ in., (41.2 x 52.8 cm.), lithograph on wove (BP 1235, DM 3104, FR 10,437, Y 203,858).

$2166* *"La Danse Des Faunes" (Bloch 830; Mourlot 291), 1957,* (11-28-92, Grisebach, #708, illus.), 16⅛ x 20¾ in., (41 x 52.7 cm.), lithograph on wove (BP 1430, DM 3451, FR 11,714, Y 269,571).

$11,072* *Danses (Mourl. 246; Bl. 750), 1954,* s. in green pencil, num., (06-23-93, Kornfeld, #710), lithograph on wove (BP 7522, DM 18,734, FR 63,017, Y 1,206,232, SF 16,675).

$3946* *Le Danseur (B. 1849), 1965,* s., #14/200, full margins, good cond., crease in center of image, light/backboard-staining, tape, (06-30-93, Sotheby-London, #657, illus.), sh 29½ x 24⅜ in., (749 x 619 mm.), linocut in black and brown on Arches (BP 2645, DM 6730, FR 22,704, Y 422,801).

$3450* *Le Danseur (B. 1849), 1965,* s., #89/200, full margins, surface scuffs, creases, very good cond., (05-11-93, Christie-NY, #311, illus.), borderline 25 x 20¾ in., (635 x 527 mm.), linocut in brown and black on Arches (BP 2202, DM 5435, FR 18,312, Y 379,496).

$4620* *Le Danseur (B. 1849), 1965,* s., #151/200, wide margins, light/mat staining, taped to overmat, (11-09-92, Christie-NY, #173, illus.), 25⅛ x 20¹¹⁄₁₆ in., (638 x 525 mm.), black and brown linocut on wove (BP 3055, DM 7375, FR 24,919, Y 573,343).

$5175* *Le Danseur (Tete D'Histrion) (B. 1849; Baer 1360), 1965,* s., #102/200, full margins, good cond., light/mat stain, (05-13-93, Sotheby-NY, #727), 21½ x 17½ in., (546 x 443 mm.), linoleum cut in black and reddish-brown (BP 3397, DM 8356, FR 28,186, Y 577,760).

$6325* *Les Danseurs Au Hibou (Danse Nocturne Avec Un Hibou) (B. 936; Baer 1256), 1959,* s., p. Arnera, pub. Galerie Louise Leiris, 1960, full margins, good cond., creases, skinned spots, ex-coll. Marina Picasso (stamp verso), (05-13-93, Sotheby-NY, #710, illus.), 21 x 25¼ in., (535 x 642 mm.), linoleum cut in black and brown (BP 4152, DM 10,213, FR 34,450, Y 706,152).

BI *Danseurs Et Musicien (B. 939), 1959,* s., #30/50, full margins, staining, crease, mat staining, very good cond., est. $9/11,000, (05-11-93, Christie-NY, #280, illus.), borderline 20⅞ x 25⅛ in., (530 x 638 mm.), linocut in beige and black on Arches.

BI *Les Danseuses,* s. in plate, #II/XX, est. DM 3,800, (11-21-92, Schloss Ahlden, #2136), 10¹⁵⁄₁₆ x 7¹¹⁄₁₆ in., (27.8 x 19.5 cm.), etching on copper print paper.

$1150* *De Memoire D'Homme (B. 665-673), 1950: Nine,* complete portfolio, init. by author, #322, p. Mourlot, pub. Bordas, very good cond., (05-19-93, Butterfield, #1948, illus.), 12¾ x 9⅞ in., (324 x 251 mm.), lithograph on Arches (BP 747, DM 1869, FR 6298, Y 127,311).

$3910* *Le Dejeuner Sur L'Herbe (B. 1024), 1962,* s., #105/125, pub. in Les Dejeuners, Editions Cercle d'Art, 1962, full margins, staining, good cond., (05-11-93, Christie-NY, #281, illus.), borderline 10 x 12¾ in., (254 x 324 mm.), lithograph on wove (BP 2496, DM 6159, FR 20,754, Y 430,096).

BI *Dejeuner Sur L'Herbe (B. 1097), 1962,* s., #6/50, full margins, mat staining, creasing, good cond., est. $18/22,000, (05-11-93, Christie-NY, #283, illus.), borderline 20¾ x 25⅛ in., (527 x 638 mm.), color linocut on Arches.

BI *Dejeuner Sur L'Herbe (B. 1097), 1962,* s., #6/50, full margins, mat staining, creasing, good cond., est. $22/28,000, (11-09-92, Christie-NY, #167, illus.), 20¾ x 25³⁄₁₆ in., (527 x 640 mm.), colored linocut on Arches.

BI *"Dejeuner Sur L'Herbe" (Block 1096), 1962,* #8/50, s., prov., est. $12/15,000, (07-17-92, DuMouchelle, #2013, illus.), image 13¾ x 10½ in., (34.9 x 26.7 cm.), linocut.

$68,476* *Le Dejeuner Sur L'Herbe, D'Apres Manet. I (Baer 1287/V/B/b; Bloch 1027), 1962,* s. Picasso, epreuve d'artiste, (06-25-93, Kornfeld, #112, illus.), image 20¹³⁄₁₆ x 25³⁄₁₆ in., (52.8 x 64 cm.), sheet 24⁵⁄₁₆ x 29½ in., (52.8 x 64 cm.), color linocut (BP 46,315, DM 116,575, FR 392,638, Y 7,258,427, SF 103,500).

$2490* *Deux Clowns (Bl. 766; M. 264), 1954,* s., num., w/traces of old mounting, (12-01-92, Karl/Faber, #1097, illus.), sh 29⁵⁄₁₆ x 21¼ in., (74.5 x 54 cm.), color lithograph on Arches wove (BP 1645, DM 3969, FR 13,525, Y 310,010).

$4600* *Deux Femmes Accroupies (B. 790), 1956,* s., mat/time staining, creasing, label, (05-11-93, Christie-NY, #273, illus.), borderline 17 x 21 in., (432 x 533 mm.), lithograph on tan wove (BP 2936, DM 7246, FR 24,416, Y 505,995).

$22,825* *Deux Femmes Avec Un Vase A Fleurs (Baer 1239/IV/B/b, Bloch 915), 1959,* s. Picasso, artist's proof, (06-25-93, Kornfeld, #110, illus.), 21 x 25⅜ in., (53.4 x 64.5 cm.), color linocut on vellum (BP 15,438, DM 38,858, FR 130,877, Y 2,419,440, SF 34,500).

$5175* *Deux Femmes Nues (see M. 16), 1946,* trial proof of 2nd stone made for 5th state of 18, margins, good cond., soiling, discoloration, creases, (02-11-93, Sotheby-NY, #213, illus.), 10¹³⁄₁₆ x 14¹⁵⁄₁₆ in., (275 x 380 mm.), sheet 12¹⁵⁄₁₆ x 17¹³⁄₁₆ in., (275 x 380 mm.), lithograph p. in bistre on wove (BP 3652, DM 8572, FR 29,008, Y 623,870).

$8526* *Deux Femmes Pres De La Fenetre (B. 924), 1959,* s., #28/50, margins, good cond., scuff in image, (12-03-92, Sotheby-London, #516, illus.), sheet 24⅜ x 29⅝ in., (620 x 753 mm.), linocut in colors on Arches (BP 5500, DM 13,408, FR 45,765, Y 1,060,844).

BI *Deux Figures Nues (Geiser 21 III b; Bloch 17), 1909,* s., est. DM 20,000, (06-05-93, Bassenge, #6437, illus.), 5⅛ x 4⁵⁄₁₆ in., (13 x 10.9 cm.), drypoint on hand-made Arches.

$17,499* *Deux Figures Nues: Femme A La Guitare Et Garcon A La Coupe (Geiser-Baer 21/III/b; Bloch 17), 1909,* s. Picasso, num., (06-25-93, Kornfeld, #92, illus.), plate 5⅛ x 4⁵⁄₁₆ in., (13 x 11 cm.), sheet 23⅞ x 17⁵⁄₁₆ in., (13 x 11 cm.), engraving on handmade Arches (BP 11,836, DM 29,791, FR 100,338, Y 1,854,887, SF 26,450).

$4600* *Deux Hommes Sculptes (B. 161; G. 314; S.V. 52), 1933,* from Vollard suite, s., full margins, good cond., mat/light-stain, discoloration, skinned areas, (05-13-93, Sotheby-NY, #687), 10⅝ x 7⅝ in., (269 x 194 mm.), etching (BP 3020, DM 7428, FR 25,054, Y 513,565).

$6325* *Deux Modeles Se Regardant (B. 209), 1934,* plate 80 for Suite Vollard, s., #3/3, wide margins, tack holes, mat staining, glue, laid down, Dian Woodner and Andrea Woodner Coll., (05-11-93, Christie-NY, #263, illus.), plate 10⅝ x 7⅜ in., (270 x 187 mm.), etching on parchment (BP 4038, DM 9964, FR 33,572, Y 695,743).

$4775* *Deux Saltimbanques (B. 5), 1905,* from the Saltimbanques Suite, pub. Vollard 1913, reduced margins, light staining, backboard stained, (12-03-92, Sotheby-London, #481, illus.), sheet 9¾ x 7¼ in., (250 x 186 mm.), drypoint on Van Gelder Zonen (BP 3080, DM 7509, FR 25,631, Y 594,127).

$7475* *Les Deux Saltimbanques (B. 5; G. 6), 1905,* from Saltimbanques suite, pub. Vollard, 1913, full margins, good cond., fox marks, (05-13-93, Sotheby-NY, #671, illus.), 4¾ x 3⅝ in., (121 x 91 mm.), drypoint on Van Gelder Zonen wove (BP 4907, DM 12,070, FR 40,714, Y 834,543).

$2444* *Deux Sculptures Devant Une Statue (G.-Baer 208/7/B/d; Bl. 140), 1931,* sheet 7 of Suite Vollard, (06-23-93, Kornfeld, #653), etching on handmade (BP 1660, DM 4135, FR 13,910, Y 266,260, SF 3680).

$1194* *Les Deux Tourterelles Double (B. 407), 1946,* s., #37/50, full margins, good cond., creases, rubbed patch, skinned, (12-03-92, Sotheby-London, #500, illus.), 13¾ x 17¼ in., (350 x 440 mm.), lithograph in colors on Arches (BP 770, DM 1878, FR 6409, Y 148,563).

$2640* *les Deux Tourterelles, I (B. 405), 1946,* s., #7/25, full margins, light staining, foxing, glue, good cond., (11-09-92, Christie-NY, #159), 13⁹⁄₁₆ x 19 in., (344 x 483 mm.), red lithograph on Arches (BP 1745, DM 4215, FR 14,239, Y 327,625).

$4400* *Diurnes (Femme Assise En Pyjama De Plage II) (B. 1062; Baer 1276), 1961,* s., i. Epreuve d'artiste, full margins, good cond., creases, touched-in printing defect, soiling in image, fox mark, tape, (11-05-92, Sotheby-NY, #357, illus.), 15⅜ x 11¾ in., (391 x 299 mm.), linoleum cut p. in brown and beige (BP 2862, DM 6959, FR 23,542, Y 539,811).

$15,400* *La Dormeuse (B. 435; M. 81), 1947,* s., #20/50, full margins, good cond., crease, light stain, skinned spots, glue stains, (11-05-92, Sotheby-NY, #346, illus.), sheet 19½ x 25½ in., (495 x 647 mm.), lithograph (BP 10,016, DM 24,356, FR 82,397, Y 1,889,339).

$4582* *Dormeuse Et Sculptures (G.-Baer 306/IV/C/b/1; Bl. 158), 1933,* s., num., (06-23-93, Kornfeld, #664), etching on handmade (BP 3113, DM 7753, FR 26,079, Y 499,183, SF 6900).

BI *Eau-Forte 10 Aout 1968 IV (Bloch 1746),* s., #27/50, est. DM 4,500, (05-26-93, Lempertz, #447, illus.), 15$\frac{3}{16}$ x 11⅛ in., (38.5 x 28.3 cm.), etching on copper print.

BI *Eau-Forte 14 Mai 1968 (Bloch Band II 1565),* #7/50, s., est. DM 8,000-, (11-21-92, Lempertz, #327, illus.), 15$\frac{9}{16}$ x 13$\frac{11}{16}$ in., (39.6 x 34.8 cm.), etching on wove.

$2596* *Eau-Forte 16 Mai 1968. III (Bl. 1574), 1968,* s., num., from the series 347 gravures, (06-23-93, Kornfeld, #696), etching (BP 1764, DM 4393, FR 14,775, Y 282,819, SF 3910).

$1773* *Eau-Forte 1er Avril 1971 III (Bloch 1961),* stamp sig., (06-05-93, Bassenge, #6440), 14$\frac{9}{16}$ x 19$\frac{11}{16}$ in., (37 x 50 cm.), drypoint on wove (BP 1167, DM 2875, FR 9689, Y 190,195).

$1985* *Eau-Forte 22 Mai 1970 (Bl. 1908), 1970,* sig. stamp, num., from the series 156 gravures, (06-23-93, Kornfeld, #699), etching (BP 1349, DM 3359, FR 11,298, Y 216,254, SF 2990).

$2291* *Eau-Forte 28 Septembre 1968. I (Bl 1822), 1968,* s., num., from the series 347 gravures, (06-23-93, Kornfeld, #697), etching (BP 1556, DM 3876, FR 13,039, Y 249,591, SF 3450).

$7213* *Eau-Forte 5 Mai 1968 II (Bloch Band II 1545),* #38/50, s., (11-21-92, Lempertz, #326, illus.), 12$\frac{13}{16}$ x 15$\frac{13}{16}$ in., (32.5 x 40.1 cm.), etching on wove (BP 4749, DM 11,500, FR 38,738, Y 897,028).

$1760* *Ecuyere (Mourlot 333, Bloch 999), 1960,* s., #146/200, (12-13-92, Hindman, #268), 19¾ x 25 in., lithograph (BP 1125, DM 2766, FR 9427, Y 217,741).

$3922* *El Entiero Del Conde De Orgaz (B. 1476), 1966,* s., #5/12, pub. Gustavo Gili, full margins, good cond., creasing, foxmarks, (12-03-92, Sotheby-London, #547, illus.), 8⅞ x 12¾ in., (225 x 325 mm.), etching w/drypoint on Japan (BP 2530, DM 6168, FR 21,052, Y 487,993).

$3114* *Etreinte II (Bloch 1150, Baer-Geiser 1344 Ba), 1963,* s., 18/50, edition galerie Louise Leiris, prov., (05-12-93, AB Stockholm, #7042, illus.), 24$\frac{7}{16}$ x 29½ in., (62 x 75 cm.), linoleum print on Arches (BP 2033, DM 5024, FR 16,924, Y 347,661, SK 23,100).

$632* *"Exposition (19)55 Vallauris (Bloch 1268),* (09-30-92, Kunsthallen, #244), linoprint (BP 357, DM 896, FR 3031, Y 75,843, DK 3450).

BI *Exposition 1958 Vallauris (B. 1284), 1958,* s., #69/175 twice, full margins, light/mat staining, bottom edge folded back, good cond., est. $3/3,500, (05-11-93, Christie-NY, #297), borderline 25 x 20⅞ in., (635 x 530 mm.), color linocut on Arches.

$1725* *Exposition Ceramique Vallauris 1959 (B. 1286; Baer 1216), 1959,* s., #90/175, pub. Association des Potiers de Vallauris, full margins,good cond., creases, soiling, (05-13-93, Sotheby-NY, #711), 25¼ x 20¾ in., (640 x 528 mm.), linoleum cut in light brown and black (BP 1132, DM 2785, FR 9395, Y 192,587).

BI *Exposition Ceramique, Vallauris 1959 (B. 1286), 1959,* s., #120/175, full margins, light-staining, creasing, skinned spot, good cond., est. $2/2,500, (05-11-93, Christie-NY, #298), borderline 25¼ x 20¾ in., (641 x 527 mm.), linocut in brown and black on Arches.

$916* *Exposition De Vallauris 1955 (Baer 1031/B; Bl. 1267), 1955,* poster, (06-23-93, Kornfeld, #718), linocut (BP 622, DM 1550, FR 5213, Y 99,793, SF 1380).

$880* *Exposition Vakavris 1964,* s. in crayon, 70/168, (11-12-92, Freemn/Fine Art, #173), 25⅛ x 20¾ in., (63.8 x 52.7 cm.), linocut in brown (BP 578, DM 1394, FR 4703, Y 109,113).

$1059* *Exposition Vallauris 1962 (Bloch 1299), 1962,* s., plate t., #90/175, (06-10-93, Hauswedell/Nolt, #800), image 25⅛ x 20⅞ in., (63.8 x 53 cm.), color linocut on Arches (BP 693, DM 1724, FR 5806, Y 112,408).

$7025* *Farol (Baer 1223/II/B/a; Bl. 945), 1959,* s., num., (06-23-93, Kornfeld, #721), color linocut on wove (BP 4772, DM 11,887, FR 39,983, Y 765,334, SF 10,580).

$31,780* *Faune Devoilant Une Dormeuse (Jupiter Et Antiope D'Apres Rembrandt) (Bloch 230; Baer 609 VI B d), 1936,* s., (06-10-93, Hauswedell/Nolt, #784, illus.), image 12$\frac{7}{16}$ x 16⅜ in., (31.6 x 41.6 cm.), aquatint on hand-made (BP 20,788, DM 51,751, FR 174,232, Y 3,373,315).

BI *Faune Devoilant Une Femme (B. 230), 1936,* from Vollard Suite, s., full margins, good cond., mount-staining, est. BP 25/30,000, (06-30-93, Sotheby-London, #593, illus.), 12½ x 16¼ in., (318 x 413 mm.), aquatint on Montval laid.

$52,250* *Faune Devoilant Une Femme (B. 230; Baer 609; S.V. 27), 1936,* from Vollard suite, s., full margins, good cond., (11-05-92, Sotheby-NY, #340, illus.), 12½ x 16½ in., (318 x 419 mm.), aquatint (BP 33,984, DM 82,635, FR 279,561, Y 6,410,256).

BI *Faune Devoilant Une Femme (B. 230; Baer 609; S.V. 27), 1936,* from Vollard suite, s., full margins, good cond., glue stains, est. $35/45,000, (05-13-93, Sotheby-NY, #696, illus.), 12⅜ x 16⅜ in., (313 x 415 mm.), etching and aquatint.

$39,658* *"Faune Devoilent Une Femme" (Bloch 230; Baer 609/Bd.), 1936,* s., sheet 27 from Suite Vollard, (06-04-93, Grisebach, #45, illus.), 12⅜ x 16$\frac{7}{16}$ in., (31.5 x 41.7 cm.), aquatint on copper print hand-made (BP 26,238, DM 64,401, FR 217,066, Y 4,277,179).

$1955* *Faune Et Chevre (Flutiste Et Chevre Savante) (B. 949; Baer 1267), 1959,* s., #38/50, margins, good cond., light/backboard stain, skinned spot, masking tape hinge, (02-11-93, Sotheby-NY, #216), 8¼ x 4½ in., (209 x 114 mm.), sheet 13$\frac{9}{16}$ x 9$\frac{3}{16}$ in., (209 x 114 mm.), linoleum cut p. in brown (BP 1379, DM 3238, FR 10,959, Y 235,684).

$6600* *Faune Musicien No. 4 (B. 522; M. 515), 1948,* s., (numbering trimmed away), large margins, good cond., mat stain, foxing, (11-05-92, Sotheby-NY, #349, illus.), 26½ x 20⅞ in., (672 x 529 mm.), sheet 28 x 21⅝ in., (672 x 529 mm.), lithograph (BP 4293, DM 10,438, FR 35,313, Y 809,717).

$9460* *Faune Souriant (Bloch 519, Mourlot 112), 1948,* s., #24/50, prov., (05-16-93, Hindman, #472, illus.), sheet 30 x 22¼ in., (76.2 x 56.5 cm.), 26 x 21⅛ in., (76.2 x 56.5 cm.), lithograph on wove (BP 6151, DM 15,216, FR 51,135, Y 1,048,664).

$22,599* *Faune Souriant (Bloch 519; Mourlot 112), 1948,* (06-10-93, Hauswedell/Nolt, #791, illus.), image 25$\frac{9}{16}$ x 21$\frac{1}{16}$ in., (65 x 53.5 cm.), lithograph on Arches (BP 14,782, DM 36,800, FR 123,898, Y 2,398,790).

$28,912* *Faunes Et Chevre (Baer 1263/B/h/2/beta; Bloch 934), 1959,* s. Picasso, (06-25-93, Kornfeld, #111, illus.), image 20$\frac{13}{16}$ x 25$\frac{3}{16}$ in., (52.8 x 64 cm.), color linocut on vellum (BP 19,555, DM 49,220, FR 165,780, Y 3,064,660, SF 43,700).

$40,960* *Faunes Et Chevre (Bloch 934; Baer 1263 B h 2 a), 1959,* s., #27/50, (06-10-93, Hauswedell/Nolt, #798, illus.), image 20⅞ x 25$\frac{3}{16}$ in., (53 x 64 cm.), color linocut (BP 26,792, DM 66,699, FR 224,561, Y 4,347,734).

BI *Les Faunes Et La Centauresse (B. 413), 1947,* s., #5/50, good cond., hinged to mount, est. BP 6/7,000, (06-30-93, Sotheby-London, #597, illus.), sh 19½ x 25⅝ in., (495 x 651 mm.), lithograph on wove.

$7974* *Les Faunes Et La Centauresse (Bl. 413; Mourlot 59), 1947,* #39/50, s.; sig., d. in stone, (10-09-92, Winterberg, #2908, illus.), 19½ x 25$\frac{3}{16}$ in., (49.5 x 64 cm.), lithograph on wove (BP 4731, DM 11,845, FR 39,771, Y 970,782).

$1775* *Les Faunes, 1961,* #277/300, (10-21-92, Maynard, #308), 22 x 30 in., (55.9 x 76.2 cm.), color lithograph (BP 1102, DM 2686, FR 9117, Y 216,200, C$ 2200).

$550* *Female Figure, Holding A Broom In One Hand And A Robe In The Other (Bloch 704, Bloch book 62), 1952,* from Le Maigre, small margins, working proof, annot., Francoise Gilot Coll., (12-08-92, Swann, #242, illus.), 7 x 2 in., (17.8 x 5.1 cm.), drypoint etching (BP 345, DM 856, FR 2919, Y 68,171).

BI *Femme A L'Oiseau (B. 1391), 1966,* s., #17/50, full margins, good cond., mount-staining, est. BP 2/2,500, (06-30-93, Sotheby-London, #644, illus.), 10¼ x 14¾ in., (260 x 375 mm.), etching and aquatint on BFK Rives.

$38,500* *Femme Accoudee (B. 922; Baer 1240), 1959,* s., #30/50, full margins, good cond., (11-05-92, Sotheby-NY, #353A, illus.), 25¼ x 20⅞ in., (640 x 530 mm.), sheet 29⅝ x 24¼ in., (640 x 530 mm.), linoleum cut p. in colors (BP 25,041, DM 60,889, FR 205,993, Y 4,723,347).

$7673* *Femme Accoudee, Sculpture De Dos Et Tete Barbue (B. 184), 1933,* from Vollard Suite, s., full margins, good cond., discoloration, (12-03-92, Sotheby-London, #488, illus.), 14¾ x 11⅛ in., (375 x 283 mm.), etching on Montval laid (BP 4950, DM 12,066, FR 41,186, Y 954,709).

$6005* *Femme Assise Au Chapeau Et Femme Debout Drapee (B. 210), 1934,* from Vollard Suite, s., margins, good cond., (06-30-93, Sotheby-London, #594, illus.), 10⅞ x 7¾ in., (276 x 197 mm.), etching on Montval laid (BP 4025, DM 10,242, FR 34,551, Y 643,416).

$2530* *Femme Assise Dans Un Fauteuil (B. 1393), 1966,* s., #11/50, full margins, good cond., ink mark, (stray graphite marks, glue stains), (05-13-93, Sotheby-NY, #731), 15 x 10⅞ in., (380 x 275 mm.), aquatint (BP 1661, DM 4085, FR 13,780, Y 282,461).

$4370* *Femme Assise Dans Un Fauteuil (B. 1393), 1966,* s., #24/50, full margins, excell. cond., (05-11-93, Christie-NY, #302, illus.), plate 14¾ x 10⅝ in., (375 x 270 mm.), aquatint on wove (BP 2790, DM 6884, FR 23,195, Y 480,695).

$858* *"Femme Au Balcon, Affiche Oeuvre Grave", "Sala Gaspar Pintura De Picasso" and "Sala Gaspar, Pintura-Dibujo-Grabado" (CZ. 39; CZ. 40 and CZ. 324), 1960-68:* Three, good cond., handling creases, discoloration, (06-30-93, Sotheby-London, #639), lithographic poster, last in black and brown on wove (BP 575, DM 1463, FR 4937, Y 91,932).

$49,500* *La Femme Au Chapeau (B. 1145), 1963,* s., #50/50, full margins, light/mat staining, very good cond., (11-09-92, Christie-NY, #169, illus.), 20¹⁵⁄₁₆ x 15¹⁵⁄₁₆ in., (533 x 406 mm.), colored linocut on Arches (BP 32,727, DM 79,023, FR 266,990, Y 6,142,964).

BI *Femme Au Chapeau (Portrait De Femme A La Fraise Et Au Chapeau) (B. 1145; Baer 1323), 1962,* s., #12/50, pub. by Galerie Louise Leiris, 1963, full margins, good cond., discoloration, est. $60/80,000, (11-05-92, Sotheby-NY, #361, illus.), 21 x 15½ in., (532 x 395 mm.), linoleum cut p. in colors.

BI *Femme Au Chignon (Bloch Band I 853), 1957,* #7/50, s., est. DM 28,000, (11-21-92, Lempertz, #325, illus.), 21¾ x 17⁵⁄₁₆ in., (55.3 x 43.9 cm.), color zincograph on wove.

$19,782* *Femme Au Chignon (Mourlot 310/I; Bloch 853), 1957,* s. Picasso, epreuve d'artiste, 1st state, (06-25-93, Kornfeld, #106, illus.), 21⅞ x 17⁵⁄₁₆ in., (55.5 x 44 cm.), lithograph on Arches vellum (BP 13,380, DM 33,677, FR 113,429, Y 2,096,884, SF 29,900).

$11,500* *Femme Au Collier (Portrait De Jacqueline Accoudee, Au Collier) (B. 928; Baer 1258), 1959,* s., #15/50, p. Arnera, pub. Galerie Louise Leiris, 1960, full margins, good cond., crease, scuffs, mat stain, creases, skinned spots, hinge stains, (05-13-93, Sotheby-NY, #709, illus.), 25 x 20¾ in., (635 x 527 ï), linoleum cut in brown, beige and black (BP 7550, DM 18,569, FR 62,636, Y 1,283,912).

BI *Femme Au Corsage A Fleurs (M. 307), 1957-58,* second state of three, full margins, good cond., discoloration, creases, est. $25/30,000, (11-05-92, Sotheby-NY, #354, illus.), 24⅛ x 19 in., (633 x 482 mm.), sheet 26⅛ x 20⅛ in., (633 x 482 mm.), lithograph on Arches.

$15,525* *Femme Au Corsage A Fleurs (M. 307), 1957-58,* full margins, good cond., discoloration, creases, thin spot, (05-13-93, Sotheby-NY, #704, illus.), 24⅞ x 19 in., (633 x 482 mm.), sh 26⅛ x 20⅛ in., (633 x 482 mm.), lithograph on Arches (BP 10,192, DM 25,069, FR 84,559, Y 1,733,281).

$24,435* *Femme Au Corsage A Fleurs (Mourl. 307/I; Bl. 846), 1957,* s. in red pencil, num., (06-23-93, Kornfeld, #715, illus.), lithograph (BP 16,600, DM 41,345, FR 139,072, Y 2,662,055, SF 36,800).

$41,085* *Femme Au Corsage A Fleurs (Mourlot 307/III; Bloch 847), 1957-1958,* s. Picasso, epreuve d'artiste, (06-25-93, Kornfeld, #105, illus.), 25 x 19⅛ in., (63.5 x 48.5 cm.), lithograph on Arches vellum (BP 27,788, DM 69,944, FR 235,579, Y 4,354,993, SF 62,100).

BI *La Femme Au Fauteuil (Bl. 422; Mourlot 69), (19)74,* red pen s., num., Edition Galerie Louise Leiris, est. DM 24/26,000, (12-01-92, Karl/Faber, #1096, illus.), 18½ x 12³⁄₁₆ in., (47 x 31 cm.), color lithograph on thick wove.

$11,454* *La Femme Au Fauteuil (Mourl. 69; Bl. 422), 1947,* s. in red pencil, i. Epreuve d'artiste, (06-23-93, Kornfeld, #703), color lithograph on wove (BP 7781, DM 19,381, FR 65,191, Y 1,247,848, SF 17,250).

$27,390* *Femme Au Fauteuil No. 1 (Mourlot 134/III; Bloch 586.4), 1948-1949,* s. Picasso, num., 3rd state, (06-25-93, Kornfeld, #99, illus.), 27⅜ x 21⁹⁄₁₆ in., (69.5 x 54.7 cm.), lithograph (BP 18,526, DM 46,629, FR 157,053, Y 2,903,328, SF 41,400).

BI *La Femme Au Singe (B. 747), 1954,* s., #30/50, full margins, good cond., mount-stain, tape, est. BP 3,5/4,500, (06-30-93, Sotheby-London, #605, illus.), 9⅞ x 12½ in., (251 x 318 mm.), lithograph.

$4429* *Femme Au Voile, Modele Assis Et Tete De Rembrandt (G.-Baer 414/B/d; Bl. 215), 1934,* sheet 35 of Suite Vollard, (06-23-93, Kornfeld, #676), etching on handmade (BP 3009, DM 7494, FR 25,208, Y 482,514, SF 6670).

$9350* *Femme Aux Cheveux Flous, Jacqueline Au Bandeau II (B. 1080), 1962,* s., #41/50, large margins, good cond., mat/light-staining, creases, surface soiling, notations, (10-28-92, Butterfield, #2693, illus.), 13⅞ x 10¹¹⁄₁₆ in., (352 x 271 mm.), sheet 24¾ x 17½ in., (352 x 271 mm.), color linoleum cut on Arches (BP 5957, DM 14,440, FR 49,030, Y 1,147,239).

$6863* *Femme Couchee Et Guitariste (B. 918), 1959,* s., #30/50, full margins, colors faded, glass scratch, good cond., (06-30-93, Sotheby-London, #619, illus.), 20⅞ x 25⅛ in., (530 x 638 mm.), color linocut on Arches (BP 4600, DM 11,706, FR 39,488, Y 735,348).

$6325* *Femme Dans Un Fauteuil Et Guitariste (B. 917), 1959,* s., #30/50, full margins, staining, mat staining, very good cond., (05-11-93, Christie-NY, #277, illus.), borderline 20⅞ x 25¼ in., (530 x 641 mm.), linocut in browns and black on Arches (BP 4038, DM 9964, FR 33,572, Y 695,743).

$2291* *Femme Nue A La Jamnbe Pliee (G.-Baer 208/B/d; Bl. 141), 1931,* sheet 8 of Suite Vollard, (06-23-93, Kornfeld, #654), etching on handmade (BP 1556, DM 3876, FR 13,039, Y 249,591, SF 3450).

$7503* *Femme Nue Cueillant Des Fleurs (B. 1092), 1962,* s., #18/50, full margins, good cond., (12-03-92, Sotheby-London, #521, illus.), sheet 24⅝ x 17½ in., (625 x 445 mm.), linocut in colors on Arches (BP 4840, DM 11,799, FR 40,274, Y 933,557).

$3054* *Femme Nue Devant Une Statue (G.-Baer 201/B/d; Bl. 139), 1931,* sheet 6 of Suite Vollard, (06-23-93, Kornfeld, #652), etching on handmade (BP 2075, DM 5168, FR 17,382, Y 332,716, SF 4600).

BI *Femme Nue Se Couronnant De Fleurs (Bloch 135), 1930,* from Suite Vollard, s., est. SF 9/11,000, (11-13-92, Koller, #5393), 12¼ x 8¾ in., (31.1 x 22.3 cm.), etching on petit paper verge de Montval.

BI *Femme Toredo II (B. 220), 1933,* from Vollard Suite, s., watermarked, full margins, good cond., est. BP 5/7,000, (06-30-93, Sotheby-London, #588, illus.), 11⅝ x 9¼ in., (295 x 235 mm.), etching on Montval laid.

BI *Femme Torero V,* #13/50 stamped sig., posthumous restrike, prov., est. C$1,5/2,000, (05-10-93, Hodgins, #70), 9¼ x 11¾ in., (23.5 x 29.8 cm.), etching on paper.

$2291* *Femme Torero, Cheval Et Taureau, Mourant. I (G.-Baer 428/A/b/1; Bl. 280), 1934,* p. 1961, pub. 1981, sig. stamp, num., (06-23-93, Kornfeld, #677), etching (BP 1556, DM 3876, FR 13,039, Y 249,591, SF 3450).

$11,802* *Femme Torero, II (Bloch 22, Geiser 426 II c), 1934,* s., (12-05-92, Bassenge, #7556), 11⅝ x 9¼ in., (29.6 x 23.5 cm.), etching on handmade (BP 7390, DM 18,400, FR 62,710, Y 1,462,272).

$2475* *Femme Vue De Dos (B. 822), 1956,* s. in red crayon, num. 45/125, from Temoignage by Jean Cocteau, pub.Pierre Bertrand, large margins, good cond., mat staining, foxing, tape remains,surface soiling, (02-24-93, Butterfield, #2776), 14¹⁄₁₆ x 11¹⁄₁₆ in., (357 x 281 mm.), etching on wove w/watermark (BP 1726, DM 4018, FR 13,621, Y 290,425).

$1985* *Femmes Au Bain (G.-Baer 404/B/d; Bl. 206), 1934,* sheet 78 of Suite Vollard, (06-23-93, Kornfeld, #673), etching on handmade (BP 1349, DM 3359, FR 11,298, Y 216,254, SF 2990).

$28,912* *Femmes D'Alger, D'Apres Delacroix (Baer 917/IV), 1955,* 4e etat, (06-25-93, Kornfeld, #103, illus.), plate 10¹³⁄₁₆ x 13¹¹⁄₁₆ in., (27.5 x 34.7 cm.), sheet 12¹³⁄₁₆ x 16⅛ in., (27.5 x 34.7 cm.), aquatint, stipple engraving (BP 19,555, DM 49,220, FR 165,780, Y 3,064,660, SF 43,700).

$3922* *Femmes Nues Au Miroir (B. 1199), 1964,* s., #41/50, full margins, good cond., tipped to mount, (12-03-92, Sotheby-London, #537, illus.), 12½ x 10⅞ in., (318 x 275 mm.), aquatint w/etching on Richard de Bas Auvergne a la main wove (BP 2530, DM 6168, FR 21,052, Y 487,993).

BI *Fernand Crommelynck, Le Cocu Magnifique (C. 140; B. 1244-55), 1968: Seven,* s. by artist and author, #65/200, full margins, loose, est. $14/18,000, (11-09-92, Christie-NY, #172, illus.), 12³⁄₁₆ x 16 in., (310 x 407 mm.), 7 etchings, 4 aquatints, etching and one aquatint, drypoint and etching on wove.

$13,800* *Fernand Crommelynck, Le Cocu Magnifique, Paris, Editions Crommelynck, 1968 (B. 1244-55, B., books 134, C. 140): Twelve,* s. by artist and authorm copy 65 of 200, full margins, loose, (05-11-93, Christie-NY, #295, illus.), 12³⁄₁₆ x 16 in., (310 x 407 mm.), 7 etchings, 4 aquatints and etchings, 1 aquatint, drypoint and etching, t. page, page de numerotation, just., text (BP 8809, DM 21,739, FR 73,248, Y 1,517,985).

$248* *Figural Composition,* s. Picasso, d. in plate 7-25-40, (06-26-93, Wolf, #967), 16 x 11 in., (40.6 x 27.9 cm.), lithograph (BP 166, DM 421, FR 1420, Y 26,313).

$9200* *Figure (B. 593), 1949,* s., #13/50, foxing, staining, skinned, creases, (05-19-93, Butterfield, #1947, illus.), 26 x 19¾ in., (660 x 502 mm.), lithograph on Arches (BP 5972, DM 14,954, FR 50,383, Y 1,018,488).

$3220* *Figure (B. 96; G. 246; M. XXVI), 1929,* s., p. Atelier Duchatel, pub. Auguste Blaizot & Fils, Libraires Editeurs, margins, good cond., (handling creases), (05-13-93, Sotheby-NY, #680), 9 x 5½ in., (230 x 139 mm.), sh 11 x 8⅞ in., (230 x 139 mm.), lithograph (BP 2114, DM 5199, FR 17,538, Y 359,495).

BI *Figure Au Corsage Raye (B. 604; M. 179), 1949,* s., #19/50, good cond., scuffed, skinned patches, ex. coll. HeinrichNeuerburg (L. 1344a), est. BP 55/65,000, (06-30-93, Sotheby-London, #624, illus.), sh 26 x 19¾ in., (660 x 502 mm.), color linocut on Arches.

BI *Figures Surrealistes, I (B. 1323; G. 353), 1935,* full margins, good cond., mat stain, discoloration, fox mark, crease, skinning, ex-coll. Marina Picasso (stamp verso), est. $30/40,000, (05-13-93, Sotheby-NY, #698, illus.), 7⅝ x 10⅝ in., (194 x 269 mm.), sh 17¾ x 12½ in., (194 x 269 mm.), etching on Arches wove.

$4093* *La Fille Au Chapeau (B. 872), 1959,* s., num., full margins, good cond., tear, (12-03-92, Sotheby-London, #510, illus.), 25¼ x 19¼ in., (640 x 490 mm.), lithograph on Arches (BP 2640, DM 6437, FR 21,970, Y 509,270).

$83* *Les Fleurs,* s. in plate, (06-26-93, Wolf, #966), 14½ x 15 in., (36.8 x 38.1 cm.), lithograph (BP 56, DM 141, FR 475, Y 8806).

$2200* *Fleurs (For U.C.L.A.) (B. 1297), 1961,* s., num. 14/100, full margins, apparently good cond., light-staining, (02-24-93, Butterfield, #2777), 22¾ x 18¼ in., (578 x 464 mm.), lithograph in colors on Arches (BP 1534, DM 3571, FR 12,108, Y 258,155).

$1100* *Les Fleurs En Mains,* for La Paix, d. in plate 21-4-58, s. Picasso, #189/400, (06-26-93, Wolf, #969), 25 x 19½ in., (63.5 x 49.5 cm.), lithograph (BP 737, DM 1869, FR 6297, Y 116,711).

$332* *Fleurs For U.C.L.A. (Cwiklitzer 47), 1961,* s. in stone, d., (12-05-92, Bassenge, #7617), 22¹³⁄₁₆ x 18⅛ in., (58 x 46 cm.), lithograph in seven colors (BP 208, DM 518, FR 1764, Y 41,135).

$550* *Flutist And Young Girl With Tambourine (B. 213), 1934,* s., margins trimmed, glued to board, (06-11-93, Freemn/Fine Art, #176, illus.), 10¹³⁄₁₆ x 7¾ in., (27.5 x 19.7 cm.), etching (BP 361, DM 894, FR 3014, Y 58,355).

$22,693* *Flutiste Assise Et Dormeuse, VI (Geiser 469), 1933,* p. by artist, full margins, good cond., (10-14-92, Sotheby-Japan, #65, illus.), 5⅞ x 7¼ in., (149 x 184 mm.),

monotype on Arches a la Main laid paper (BP 13,320, DM 33,211, FR 112,620, Y 2,750,000).

$22,825* *Flutiste Et Dormeuse (Geiser-Baer 485), 1933,* (06-25-93, Kornfeld, #89, illus.), image 5⅞ x 7⅜ in., (14.9 x 18.8 cm.), sheet 6⅞ x 10¹⁄₁₆ in., (14.9 x 18.8 cm.), copper monotype on handmade (BP 15,438, DM 38,858, FR 130,877, Y 2,419,440, SF 34,500).

$4600* *Flutiste Et Dormeuse, II (G. 292/II), 1933,* tone, p. Lacouriere, full margins, good cond., printer's crease in image, handling creases, (05-13-93, Sotheby-NY, #683, illus.), 3½ x 3⅛ in., (88 x 80 mm.), etching on laid (BP 3020, DM 7428, FR 25,054, Y 513,565).

$4950* *Flutiste Et Trois Femmes Nues (B. 144), 1932,* plate 11 from the Suite Vollard, watermark, s., full margins, mat staining, very good cond., (11-09-92, Christie-NY, #150, illus.), 11⁹⁄₁₆ x 14⅜ in., (294 x 365 mm.), drypoint on Montval (BP 3273, DM 7902, FR 26,699, Y 614,296).

$4429* *Flutiste Et Trois Femmes Nues (G.-Baer 258/B/d, Bl. 144), 1932,* sheet 11 of Suite Vollard, (06-23-93, Kornfeld, #656), drypoint on handmade (BP 3009, DM 7494, FR 25,208, Y 482,514, SF 6670).

$3450* *Football (B. 1019; M. 356), 1961,* s., #17/200, full margins, good cond., sheet discolored, crease, water stain, (05-13-93, Sotheby-NY, #712), 18¼ x 24⅝ in., (465 x 625 mm.), lithograph in colors (BP 2265, DM 5571, FR 18,791, Y 385,174).

$2271* *Football- 3.6.61 (Bloch 1019),* 42/200, s., (05-20-93, Finarte-Milan, #132), 18⅛ x 24⁷⁄₁₆ in., (46 x 62 cm.), lithograph in colors (BP 1458, DM 3664, FR 12,342, Y 250,773, L 3335).

$27,500* *Francoise (B. 401; M. 45), 1946,* s., #23/50, full margins, good cond., soiling, (11-05-92, Sotheby-NY, #344, illus.), 24¾ x 19 in., (628 x 484 mm.), lithograph (BP 17,886, DM 43,492, FR 147,138, Y 3,373,819).

$16,649* *Francoise (M. 40; Bl. 396), 1946,* s., #3/50, full margins, stamp, discoloration, good cond., (12-01-92, Christie-London, #488, illus.), L. 23½ x 19⁵⁄₁₆ in., (597 x 490 mm.), lithograph on Arches (BP 11,000, DM 26,536, FR 90,435, Y 2,072,834).

BI *Francoise Au Noeud Dans Les Cheveux (M. 41; Bl. 397), 1946,* s., #28/50, margins, stain, discoloration, good cond., est. BP 12/16,000, (12-01-92, Christie-London, #489, illus.), L. 24⅝ x 18⁵⁄₁₆ in., (625 x 465 mm.), lithograph on Arches.

$15,537* *Francoise Aux Cheveux Ondules (Bloch 403; Mourlot 47), 1946,* s., stone d., #19/50, (06-10-93, Hauswedell/Nolt, #789, illus.), image 25½ x 19⁷⁄₁₆ in., (64.7 x 49.4 cm.), lithograph on Arches (BP 10,163, DM 25,300, FR 85,181, Y 1,649,188).

$6050* *Francoise En Soleil (B. 4040), 1946,* s., #28/50, full margins, light staining, taped to overmat, defects, (11-09-92, Christie-NY, #158, illus.), 21¼ x 17¹¹⁄₁₆ in., (540 x 450 mm.), lithograph on wove (BP 4000, DM 9658, FR 32,632, Y 750,807).

BI *Francoise Sur Fond Gris (B. 681), 1950,* s., #2/50 re-traced, full margins, good cond., est. BP 25/30,000, (06-30-93, Sotheby-London, #603, illus.), 24½ x 18½ in., (622 x 470 mm.), lithograph on Ingres Cansor. sized blue-gray paper applied to Arches.

BI *Francoise Sur Fond Gris (B. 681; M. 195), 1951,* watermark, 2nd (final) state, s., i. Epreuve d'artiste, full margins, applique lifting slightly in places, mat/time staining, support sheet, very good cond., est. $45/55,000, (11-09-92, Christie-NY, #162A, illus.), 24½ x 18½ in., (622 x 470 mm.), lithograph on blue-grey wove paper applique.

BI *Francoise Sur Fond Gris (Bloch 681; Mourlot 195), 1950,* s., num. 19/50, full margins, good cond., foxing, est. Y 10/14,000,000, (10-14-92, Sotheby-Japan, #66, illus.), 24½ x 18⅛ in., (622 x 460 mm.), lithograph on Ingres Canson sized blue-gray paper applied to Arches paper.

$39,564* *Francoise Sur Fond Gris (Mourlot 195/II; Bloch 681), 1950,* s. Picasso, epreuve d'artiste, (06-25-93, Kornfeld, #101, illus.), 24¹³⁄₁₆ x 18⁹⁄₁₆ in., (63 x 47.2 cm.), lithograph on grey blue China (BP 26,760, DM 67,354, FR 226,858, Y 4,193,767, SF 59,800).

$2291* *Francoise, Claude Et Paloma: La Lecture Et Les Jeux. I (Baer 900/B/b/1; Bl. 735), 1953,* p. 1961, pub. 1981, num., (06-23-93, Kornfeld, #684), etching on handmade (BP 1556, DM 3876, FR 13,039, Y 249,591, SF 3450).

$715* *From A Los Toros Avec Picasso: Four (1014-1017, Mourlot 346, 348, 349, 250), 1961,* from the book ed., framed together, (03-14-93, Hindman, #267), larger 8⅛ x 10¼ in., (20.6 x 26 cm.), lithographs, one in color (BP 499, DM 1190, FR 4046, Y 84,266).

BI *Fumeur (B. 1166), 1964,* s., #40/50, full margins, good cond., est. BP 4/5,000, (12-03-92, Sotheby-London, #534, illus.), 16½ x 12½ in., (418 x 315 mm.), soft-ground etching in colors on Auvergne laid.

$5750* *Fumeur (B. 1166), 1964,* s., #25/50, full margins, fox-marks, tape, very good cond., (05-11-93, Christie-NY, #289, illus.), plate 16⅜ x 12⅜ in., (416 x 314 mm.), color soft-ground etching on Richard de Bas Auvergne a la main (BP 3671, DM 9058, FR 30,520, Y 632,494).

$3240* *Fumeur (B. 1173), 1964,* s., #41/50, full margins, good cond., light-staining, (12-03-92, Sotheby-London, #535, illus.), 16¾ x 12¼ in., (410 x 310 mm.), aquatint and etching on Richard de Bas Auvergne a la main wove (BP 2090, DM 5095, FR 17,391, Y 403,135).

$3680* *Fumeur (B. 1175), 1964,* s., #6/50, full margins, stains, foxmarks, very good cond., (05-11-93, Christie-NY, #290, illus.), plate 16½ x 12½ in., (419 x 318 mm.), etching and aquatint on Richard de Bas Auvergne a la main (BP 2349, DM 5797, FR 19,533, Y 404,796).

$10,450* *Fumeur (Fumeur A La Cigarette Verte) (B., Baer 1168), 1964,* s., #14/50, large margins, good cond., light stain, creases into image, Julie Andrews and Blake Edwards Coll., (11-05-92, Sotheby-NY, #366, illus.), 23½ x 16¾ in., (597 x 427 mm.), sheet 30⅞ x 22⅝ in., (597 x 427 mm.), soft ground etching p. in colors (BP 6797, DM 16,527, FR 55,912, Y 1,282,051).

$7150* *Fumeur I (B., Baer 1165), 1964,* s., #24/50, full margins, good cond., light stain, discoloration, hinges, (11-05-92, Sotheby-NY, #364, illus.), 16⅜ x 12½ in., (416 x 318 mm.), soft ground etching p. in colors on Auvergne a la main (BP 4650, DM 11,308, FR 38,256, Y 877,193).

BI *Fumeur II (B., Baer 1166), 1964,* s., #25/50, full margins, good cond., foxing, hinges, est. $8/12,000, (11-05-92, Sotheby-NY, #365, illus.), 16¼ x 12⅞ in., (413 x 317 mm.), soft ground etching p. in colors on Auvergne a la main.

$4675* *Fumeur V (B., Baer 1176), 1964,* s., #31/50, full margins, good cond., trace of printer's ink, soiling, (11-05-92, Sotheby-NY, #367), 16⅜ x 12⅜ in., (415 x 315 mm.), aquatint on Auvergne a la main (BP 3041, DM 7394, FR 25,013, Y 573,549).

$5175* *Fumeur V (B., Baer 1176), 1964,* s., #25/50, p. Crommelynck, full margins, good cond., (05-13-93, Sotheby-NY, #721, illus.), 16¼ x 12⅜ in., (413 x 315 mm.), aquatint (BP 3397, DM 8356, FR 28,186, Y 577,760).

BI *"Fumeur",* est. $5/700, (10-10-92, Goldberg, #430, illus.), 15 x 22 in., (38.1 x 55.9 cm.), color lithograph.

$19,782* *Garcon Et Dormeuse (Geiser-Baer 440 III/B/d; Bloch 226), 1934,* s. Picasso, (06-25-93, Kornfeld, #96, illus.), sheet 13⅜ x 17½ in., etching and aquatint on handmade (BP 13,380, DM 33,677, FR 113,429, Y 2,096,884, SF 29,900).

$20,463* *Garcon Et Dormeuse A La Chandelle (B. 226), 1934,* from Vollard Suite, s., watermark, full margins, good cond., discoloration, (12-03-92, Sotheby-London, #492, illus.), 9¼ x 11½ in., (235 x 292 mm.), aquatint on Montval laid (BP 13,200, DM 32,180, FR 109,839, Y 2,546,099).

$17,600* *Garcon Et Dormeuse A La Chandelle (B. 226), 1934,* plate 26 from the Suite Vollard, watermark, s., full margins, foxmarks, very good cond., prop. Steven and Ursula Schwartz, (11-09-92, Christie-NY, #155, illus.), 9⁵⁄₁₆ x 11¹¹⁄₁₆ in., (237 x 297 mm.), etching and aquatint on Montval (BP 11,636, DM 28,097, FR 94,930, Y 2,184,165).

BI *Georges Hugnet. Pablo Picasso (Cramer 35), 1941: Six,* title & text ink s. by artist, s. by author and artist, p. Grou-Radenez, folded into four, good cond., est. BP 2/2,500, (12-03-92, Sotheby-London, #495, illus.), sheet approx. 7½ x 11⅝ in., (190 x 295 mm.), zincographs, 3 reworked w/engraving by artist, p. on 1 folded sheet, on Rives wove.

BI *Georges Louis Leclerc, Comte De Buffon. Histoire Naturelle (B. 328-358, C. 37, BAER 575-606), 1941-2: Set Of Thirty-Two,* complete, p. afer plates cancelled in 1964, full margins, good cond., est. BP 4/6,000, (06-30-93, Sotheby-London, #599, illus.), each sh c. 23 x 17½ in., (584 x 445 mm.), etching w/aquatint on large format Arches wove.

BI *Georges Louis Leclerc, Comte De Buffon. Histoire Naturelle (B. 328-358, C. 37, BAER 575-606), 1942,* portfolio w/text and justification, copy #11, p. by Lacouriere, pub.Martin Fabiani, good cond., creases, est. BP 16/18,000, (06-30-93, Sotheby-London, #598, illus.), each sh c. 14½ x 11 in., (368 x 279 mm.), etching w/aquatint.

$4093* *Georges Louis Leclerc, Comte De Buffon. Histoire Naturelle (Textes DeBuffon) (Bloch 330; 331; 337; 339-342; 346; 352-354; 356; and 358), 1942: Fourteen,* from the set of 31, bearing pencil numbering, w/title page, text andjust., num. 209, good cond., (12-03-92, Sotheby-London, #496), etchings and aquatint on wove (BP 2640, DM 6437, FR 21,970, Y 509,270).

$2530* *Gilbert Seldes, Lysistrata, Westport, Connecticut, Limited Editions Club, 1934 (B. 267-72, Bloch, Books 22, Cramer 24): Six,* s., copy 709 of 1500, foxing, good cond., (05-11-93, Christie-NY, #267), 11¹³⁄₁₆ x 9⁹⁄₁₆ in., (300 x 243 mm.), etching on BFK Rives (BP 1615, DM 3986, FR 13,429, Y 278,297).

$3603* *Gongora. Vingt Poemes (See C. 51), 1948,* 19 pl from the group of 41, p. by Lacouriere, pub. by Les Grands Peintres Modernes et le Livre, good cond., minor discoloration, stains, (06-30-93, Sotheby-London, #601, illus.), etching w/aquatint on wove (BP 2415, DM 6145, FR 20,731, Y 386,050).

$6038* *Grande Nature Morte Au Compotier (B. 425; M. 73), 1947,* crayon s., #27/50, full margins, margin corners re-attached (into image, loss, tear), discoloration, skinning, glue stains, Dora Jane Janson and theLate H.W. Janson Coll., (05-13-93, Sotheby-NY, #702, illus.), 18⅝ x 24 in., (472 x 611 mm.), lithograph (BP 3964, DM 9750, FR 32,887, Y 674,110).

$40,250* *Grande Tete De Femme Au Chapeau Orne (Grande Tete De Jacqueline Au Chapeau) (B. 1077; Baer 1317), 1962,* s., #38/50, p. Arnera, pub. Galerie Louise Leiris, 1963, full margins, good cond., light-stain, handling crease, skinning, (05-13-93, Sotheby-NY, #717, illus.), 25⅛ x 20¾ in., (638 x 527 mm.), linoleum cut in tan (red color) and black (BP 26,425, DM 64,993, FR 219,227, Y 4,493,692).

$22,908* *Grande Tete De Jacqueline Au Chapeau (Baer 1317/II/B/b/2; Bl. 1077),1962,* s., i. Epreuve d'artiste, (06-23-93, Kornfeld, #729), color linocut on wove (BP 15,563, DM 38,761, FR 130,381, Y 2,495,697, SF 34,500).

$3663* *Le Gros Pigeon (M. 66; Bl. 419), 1947,* crayon s., #50/50, margins, crease, tape, mount-staining, defects, (12-01-92, Christie-London, #490), L. 15¾ x 20¼ in., (400 x 514 mm.), lithograph on wove (BP 2420, DM 5838, FR 19,897, Y 456,051).

BI *Groupe De Trois Femmes (B. 57), 1922-3,* s., #99/100, wide margins, good cond., est. $14/16,000, (05-11-93, Christie-NY, #259, illus.), plate 6⅞ x 5 in., (175 x 127 mm.), drypoint and etching on laid.

$13,983* *Groupe De Trois Femmes (B. 57; G. 102V), 1922-23,* s., #66/100, p. Leblanc & Trautmann, 1929, pub. Marcel Guiot, full margins, good cond., light/mount staining, paper loss, tape, (12-03-92, Sotheby-London, #485, illus.), 6⅞ x 5 in., (174 x 126 mm.), drypoint and etching on laid (BP 9020, DM 21,989, FR 75,056, Y 1,739,828).

$43* *Guernica (C. 76 (II)),* pub. Offsetdruk Smeets Weert, 1956, lit., (12-01-92, Ritchie, #17), 36⅞ x 54¼ in., (93.7 x 137.8 cm.), grisaille lithograph (BP 28, DM 69, FR 234, Y 5354, C$ 55).

BI *"La Guitare Sur La Table" (Bloch, 54),* after 1922, pub. 1961 in suite Caisse A Remords, estate s. Picasso, num. 29/50, good cond., wide margins, wrinkle, soiling, taped, est. $15/2500, (09-11-92, Skinner, #94, illus.), 3⅛ x 4¹¹⁄₁₆ in., (7.9 x 11.9 cm.), etching/drypoint w/plate tone on wove.

$514* *Head Of A Man, c. 1970,* Atelier Crommelynck, Editeur blindstamp, s., #177/200, (06-08-93, Ritchie, #57, illus.), plate 11⅞ x 10 in., (30.2 x 25.4 cm.), sheet 21⅜ x 16⅞ in., (30.2 x 25.4 cm.), engraving on japon (BP 338, DM 834, FR 2809, Y 54,594, C$ 660).

$1650* *Head Of Dora Maar (Bloch 55), c. 1949-50,* from Corps Perdu, num., s., pub. Editions Fragrance, foxing, paper rippled, (05-27-93, Swann, #219, illus.), sh 15⅜ x 11¼ in., (39.1 x 28.6 cm.), line engraving (BP 1057, DM 2648, FR 8924, Y 176,887).

$1907* *Hercule Tue Le Centaure Nessus (Bloch 116; Geiser 160 II b; Goeppert-Cramer 19, 18), 1930,* artist's proof, from Ovide, Les Metamorphoses, Livre IX, (06-10-93, Hauswedell/Nolt, #778, illus.), image 12⁵⁄₁₆ x 8¹³⁄₁₆ in., (31.3 x 22.4 cm.), etching (BP 1247, DM 3105, FR 10,455, Y 202,420).

$10,231* *Hommage A Bacchus (B. 1006), 1960,* s., #31/50, margins, good cond., rust mark, (12-03-92, Sotheby-London, #519, illus.), 19½ x 25¼ in., (495 x 645 mm.), lithograph on wove (BP 6600, DM 16,089, FR 54,917, Y 1,272,987).

$20,590* *Homme A La Fraise (B. 1148), 1963,* proof impression, s., i., full margins, good cond., back-board staining, (06-30-93, Sotheby-London, #635, illus.), 20⅞ x 15¾ in., (530 x 400 mm.), color linocut on Arches (BP 13,800, DM 35,119, FR 118,470, Y 2,206,150).

$394* *"Homme A La Pipe", c. 1965: Two,* (05-18-93, Encans, #216), 18⅛ x 11¹³⁄₁₆ in., (46 x 30 cm.), color lithograph (BP 257, DM 639, FR 2159, Y 43,910, C$ 500).

$6109* *Homme Barbu Couronne De Feuilles De Vigne (Baer 1308/V/B/b; Bl. 1088), 1962,* s., i. Epreuve de passe, (06-23-93, Kornfeld, #727), color linocut on wove (BP 4150, DM 10,337, FR 34,769, Y 665,541, SF 9200).

$16,799* *Homme Barbu Couronne De Vigne (Baer 1310/VI/B/a; Bl. 1089), 1962,* s., num., (06-23-93, Kornfeld, #728, illus.), color linocut on wove (BP 11,412, DM 28,425, FR 95,612, Y 1,830,156, SF 25,300).

$2402* *Homme Couche Et Femme Accroupie (B. 797), 1956,* s., #38/50, full margins, good cond., handling creases, foxing, discoloration of sheet, (06-30-93, Sotheby-London, #609, illus.), 16¾ x 20¾ in., (425 x 527 mm.), lithograph on Arches (BP 1610, DM 4097, FR 13,820, Y 257,366).

$1540* *Homme Et Femme (B. 77; G. 118), 1927,* brushpoint s., #137/250 (faded), margins, light stain, loss w/tears,soiling, foxing, discolored, (11-05-92, Sotheby-NY, #325), 7⅝ x 11 in., (195 x 280 mm.), sheet 11⅛ x 14 in., (195 x 280 mm.), etching on stiff wove (BP 1002, DM 2436, FR 8240, Y 188,934).

$3513* *Homme Et Femme (Bl. 1385), 1966,* s., num., (06-23-93, Kornfeld, #693), etching on heavy wove (BP 2387, DM 5944, FR 19,994, Y 382,721, SF 5290).

$5345* *Homme Et Femme (G.-Baer 118/b/2; Bl. 77, Johnson, 1977, 91), 1927,* s. in brush in dark grey, num., (06-23-93, Kornfeld, #649), etching on thick wove (BP 3631, DM 9044, FR 30,421, Y 582,307, SF 8050).

$4000* *"Homme Et Femme" (Bloch 77), 1927,* pub. Ambrose Vollard, s., num. ink, excell. cond., (05-15-93, Cleveland, #420, illus.), 7⅝ x 11 in., (19.4 x 27.9 cm.), etching (BP 2601, DM 6434, FR 21,622, Y 443,410).

BI *Homme Nu Assis Avec Femme Nue Sur Les Genoux (B. 775), 1955,* sig. stamp, #2/50, p. by Lacouriere, 1961, full margins, good cond.,est. BP 1,4/1,800, (06-30-93, Sotheby-London, #611, illus.), 10 x 12⅛ in., (254 x 308 mm.), etching on Richard de Bas laid.

$1716* *Homme Nu Avec Femme Ivre Et Jeune Flutiste (B. 773), 1955,* sig. stamp, #2/50, p. by Atelier Lacouriere et Frelaut in 1961, margins, good cond., (06-30-93, Sotheby-London, #610, illus.), 10 x 12⅛ in., (254 x 308 mm.), etching on laid (BP 1150, DM 2927, FR 9873, Y 183,864).

$2860* *Huit Silhouettes (B. 388), 1946,* s., #5/50, shaved, light staining, skinned patches, remains of glue,defects, (11-09-92, Christie-NY, #157), 12¹⁵⁄₁₆ x 17⅜ in., (330 x 442 mm.), lithograph on wove (BP 1891, DM 4566, FR 15,426, Y 354,927).

$1740* *Huit Silhouettes (Bloch 338), 1946,* s., 2/50, d., colophon trace, (06-28-93, Loudmer, #331), 12¹³⁄₁₆ x 17⁷⁄₁₆ in., (325 x 443 mm.), sh 12¹⁵⁄₁₆ x 17⁷⁄₁₆ in., (325 x 443 mm.), black lithograph on wove (BP 1165, DM 2957, FR 9960, Y 184,615).

$605* *Illustration From Balzac's Le Cocu Magnifique, Plate 10, 1966 (Bloch, 1253),* d. 8,12,66 (reversed) in plate, num. 29/180; annot. B/1253 verso, very good cond., (09-11-92, Skinner, #92, illus.), 8¾ x 12⅝ in., (22.2 x 32.1 cm.), sugar-lift etching on wove (BP 313, DM 871, FR 2960, Y 74,960).

$11,454* *Jacqueline Au Bandeau. II (Baer 1297/III/A/b/2; Bl. 1980), 1962,* s., (06-23-93, Kornfeld, #726), color linocut on wove (BP 7781, DM 19,381, FR 65,191, Y 1,247,848, SF 17,250).

$22,825* *Jacqueline Au Chapeau A Fleurs. II (Baer 1304/B/b/2; Bloch 1149), 1963,* s. Picasso, epreuve d'artiste, (06-25-93, Kornfeld, #116, illus.), image 21¹⁄₁₆ x 15⅜ in., (53.5 x 39 cm.), sheet 24¾ x 17⁷⁄₁₆ in., (53.5 x 39 cm.), color linocut on thick vellum Arches (BP 15,438, DM 38,858, FR 130,877, Y 2,419,440, SF 34,500).

$12,075* *Jacqueline Au Mouchoir Noir (B. 873; M. 316), 1958,* s., #41/50, full margins, good cond., pressure marks, discoloration,handling creases, (05-13-93, Sotheby-NY, #706, illus.), 25⅜ x 19¼ in., (643 x 490 mm.), lithograph (BP 7927, DM 19,498, FR 65,768, Y 1,348,108).

$4859* *Jacqueline De Profil (Bloch 833, Mourlot 294), 1957,* s., d. 24.5.57 in stone, #48/50, (05-27-93, Briest, #156, illus.), 29½ x 21⅝ in., (75 x 55 cm.), lithograph on Arches (BP 3112, DM 7797, FR 26,279, Y 520,905).

$5035* *Jacqueline De Profil (Bloch 833, Mourlot 294), 1957,* s., d. in stone, #48/50, (11-16-92, Briest, #344, illus.), 29½ x 21⅝ in., (75 x 55 cm.), lithograph on Arches (BP 3309, DM 8030, FR 27,055, Y 628,354).

BI *Jacqueline De Profil A Droite (B. 854), 1958,* s., #28/50, full margins, good cond., handling creases, discoloration, est. BP 18/22,000, (06-30-93, Sotheby-London, #617, illus.), 21¾ x 17⅜ in., (552 x 441 mm.), lithograph on Arches.

$27,390* *Jacqueline De Profil A Droite (Mourlot 310/III; Bloch 854), 1958,* s. Picasso, num., (06-25-93, Kornfeld, #107, illus.), 21⅞ x 17⁵⁄₁₆ in., (55.5 x 44 cm.), lithograph on Arches vellum (BP 18,526, DM 46,629, FR 157,053, Y 2,903,328, SF 41,400).

$600* *Jaime Sabartes. A Los Toros Avec Picasso (B. 1014-1017; B. 108; C. 113),* book, text and numerous reprods. of drawings, pub. Andre Sauret, (06-30-93, Sotheby-London, #633), four lithographs, one in color (BP 402, DM 1023, FR 3452, Y 64,288).

$7035* *Jaime Sabartes. Dans L'Atelier De Picasso (C. 88; M. 32; 75-79; 91; 92; 97; 269-271), 1957: Set Of Six,* book, w/title-page and text, crayon s., #7, each #7/50, s. by FernandMourlot, publisher, #7/50, full margins, good cond., foxing, loose, original box, (06-30-93, Sotheby-London, #613, illus.), lithograph, 3 colored, w/a separate suite of 13 lithographs on JaponHodumara paper in color (BP 4715, DM 11,999, FR 40,478, Y 753,777).

$3971* *Jeune Bacchus Au Tambourin Avec Une Bacchante (G.-Baer 411/B/d; Bl. 212), 1934,* sheet 19 of Suite Vollard, (06-23-93, Kornfeld, #675), etching on handmade (BP 2698, DM 6719, FR 22,601, Y 432,618, SF 5980).

$7162* *Jeune Couple Accroupi, L'Homme Avec Un Tambourin (B. 212), 1933,* from Vollard Suite, s., watermark, full margins, good cond., (12-03-92, Sotheby-London, #491, illus.), 17½ x 13⅜ in., (445 x 340 mm.), etching on Montval laid (BP 4620, DM 11,263, FR 38,443, Y 891,129).

$2387* *Jeune Femme (B. 1836), 1949,* #28/75, pub. 1968, full margins, good cond., foxing, creases, (12-03-92, Sotheby-London, #569, illus.), 15⅛ x 11¾ in., (395 x 300 mm.), lithograph on chine applique (BP 1540, DM 3754, FR 12,813, Y 297,001).

BI *"Jeune Garcon Buste",* est. $5/700, (10-10-92, Goldberg, #429, illus.), 14¾ x 11 in., (37.5 x 27.9 cm.), color lithograph.

BI *Jeune Homme Couronne De Feuillage (Bloch 1087, Baer, Bd. V, S. 224),1962,* #49/50, s., est. SF 22/24,000, (11-13-92, Koller, #5394), 13¾ x 14⁹⁄₁₆ in., (35 x 37 cm.), color linocut on wove.

$6050* *Jeune Sculpteur Au Travail (B. 156), 1933,* plate 46 from the Suite Vollard, watermark, s., full margins, light/mat staining, very good cond., (11-09-92, Christie-NY, #151, illus.), 10½ x 7⅝ in., (267 x 193 mm.), etching on Montval (BP 4000, DM 9658, FR 32,632, Y 750,807).

$22,908* *Jeunesse (Mourl. 188/II; Bl. 675), 1950,* s., i. Epreuve d'artiste, (06-23-93, Kornfeld, #707, illus.), lithograph on wove (BP 15,563, DM 38,761, FR 130,381, Y 2,495,697, SF 34,500).

$22,305* *Jose Delgado Alias Pepe Illo. La Tauromaquia (C. 100), 1959,* complete book, w/text and justification page, #151, pub. Gustavo Gili, good cond., creasing, (06-30-93, Sotheby-London, #622, illus.), each sh c. 13¾ x 19½ in., (349 x 495 mm.), 1 drypoint, 26 aquatints, on wove w/a bull's head watermark (BP 14,950, DM 38,044, FR 128,337, Y 2,389,907).

$2300* *Jours De Gloire (B. 372), 1945,* s., margins, light-stained, i. num. X/XX, mat staining, good cond., (05-11-93, Christie-NY, #270, illus.), plate 7½ x 5¼ in., (191 x 133 mm.), engraving on wove (BP 1468, DM 3623, FR 12,208, Y 252,997).

$48,694* *Jupiter Et Antiope, D'Apres Rembrandt (Baer 609/VI/B/ d.; Bloch 230),1936,* s. Picasso, (06-25-93, Kornfeld, #97, illus.), sheet 13⅜ x 17¹¹⁄₁₆ in., (34 x 44.9 cm.), line etching, aquatint, and engraving on handmade (BP 32,935, DM 82,898, FR 279,209, Y 5,161,543, SF 73,600).

$3759* *Knabe Mit Maske, 1953,* s., (06-05-93, Bassenge, #6435, illus.), 18¹¹⁄₁₆ x 14⅝ in., (47.5 x 37.1 cm.), offset-lithograph painted over w/Deckfarben on wove (BP 2474, DM 6094, FR 20,541, Y 403,240).

$550* *Kneeling Female Figure (Bloch 704), c. 1952-53,* from Le Maigre, margins, printer's working proof, Francois Gilot Coll., (05-27-93, Swann, #218, illus.), sight 9½ x 7 in., (24.1 x 17.8 cm.), drypoint etching (BP 352, DM 883, FR 2975, Y 58,962).

$2490* *Komposition Mit Liegestuhl Und Palmen,* s., num., margin w/light-staining, (12-01-92, Karl/Faber, #1100, illus.), 15¹⁵⁄₁₆ x 12¹⁵⁄₁₆ in., (40.5 x 33 cm.), color etching on BFK Rives wove (BP 1645, DM 3969, FR 13,525, Y 310,010).

$642* *Kompositioner, 1954,* from Verve, (03-24-93, Kunst-hallen, #278), color lithograph (BP 435, DM 1049, FR 3569, Y 75,432, DK 4025).

$257* *Kompositioner, 1954: Three,* from Verve, (03-24-93, Kunsthallen, #277), photolithograph on ramme (frame) (BP 174, DM 420, FR 1429, Y 30,196, DK 1610).

$202* *Kompositioner, 1964: Three,* 107/666, (03-24-93, Kunst-hallen, #279), lithograph (BP 137, DM 330, FR 1123, Y 23,734, DK 1265).

$3300* *L'Abreuvoir (B. 8), 1905,* discoloration, pencil notations, very good cond., (06-11-93, Doyle, #69, illus.), 4¾ x 7¼ in., (121 x 184 mm.), etching (BP 2168, DM 5363, FR 18,082, Y 350,133).

$2875* *L'Abreuvoir (B. 8; G. 10), 1905,* from Saltimbanques suite, pub. Vollard 1913, full margins, good cond., foxing, (05-13-93, Sotheby-NY, #673), 4¾ x 7⅜ in., (121 x 187 mm.), drypoint on Van Gelder Zonen wove (BP 1887, DM 4642, FR 15,659, Y 320,978).

$2090* *L'Age De Soleil (B. 680), 1950,* s. in red crayon, full margins, good cond., mat staining, creases, surface soiling, skinned areas, tape remains, (02-24-93, Butterfield, #2775), 9¼ x 7⅛ in., (235 x 181 mm.), etching on Rives (BP 1457, DM 3393, FR 11,502, Y 245,248).

$1907* *L'Ane (Bloch 329; Baer 576 IV B a; Goeppert-Cramer 37.2), 1936,* red chalk s., plate t., d., from Buffon, Histoire Naturelle, (06-10-93, Hauswedell/Nolt, #786, illus.), image 16⁷⁄₁₆ x 12⁷⁄₁₆ in., (41.7 x 31.6 cm.), etching on hand-made (BP 1247, DM 3105, FR 10,455, Y 202,420).

BI *L'Artiste Et L'Enfant (B. 590; M. 156), 1949,* s., #14/50, full margins, good cond., est. $7/9,000, (11-05-92, Sotheby-NY, #350, illus.), 24⅜ x 18½ in., (620 x 470 mm.), lithograph.

$9163* *L'Aubade, Avec Guitariste (Baer 1235/III/B/a; Bl. 918), 1959,* s., num., (06-23-93, Kornfeld, #723, illus.), color linocut on thick wove (BP 6225, DM 15,504, FR 52,151, Y 998,257, SF 13,800).

$794* *"L'Autruche" (Bloch 343; Block livre 35; Goeppert/ Cramer 37), 1941-42,* sheet 16 of series G.L. Leclerc, C. Buffon "Histoire naturelle".Paris, estate stamp, (11-28-92, Grisebach, #707, illus.), 16⁷⁄₁₆ x 12⅜ in., (41.7 x 31.5 cm.), aquatint w/drypoint on thick copper print paper (BP 524, DM 1265, FR 4294, Y 98,818).

BI *L'Ecuyere (B. 999), 1960,* s., #142/200, full margins, good cond., est. BP 2/2,500, (12-03-92, Sotheby-London, #518, illus.), 19⅝ x 25½ in., (500 x 650 mm.), lithograph on Arches.

$515* *L'Ecuyere (B. 999), 1960,* good cond., light staining, creasing, soiling, paper tape, (06-30-93, Sotheby-London, #626), sh 21⅝ x 27⅛ in., (549 x 689 mm.), lithograph on wove (BP 345, DM 878, FR 2963, Y 55,181).

$2497* *L'Ecuyere (Bl. 999; M. 333), 1960,* s., #165/200, full margins, crease, discoloration, (12-01-92, Christie-London, #495), L. 19¹¹⁄₁₆ x 25⅜ in., (500 x 645 mm.), lithograph on Arches (BP 1650, DM 3980, FR 13,563, Y 310,881).

$42,607* *L'Egyptienne - Torse De Femme (Baer 906/II/B/b; Bloch 746), 1953,* (06-25-93, Kornfeld, #102, illus.), plate 32¹¹⁄₁₆ x 18½ in., (83 x 47 cm.), sheet 35⅞ x 24¹⁵⁄₁₆ in., (83 x 47 cm.), aquatint on thick Arches vellum (BP 28,818, DM 72,535, FR 244,306, Y 4,516,324, SF 64,400).

$4093* *L'Entreinte (B. 1110), 1963,* s., #31/50, full margins, good cond., creasing, (12-03-92, Sotheby-London, #525, illus.), 16¾ x 22⅜ in., (425 x 568 mm.), etching and drypoint w/tone on BFK Rives (BP 2640, DM 6437, FR 21,970, Y 509,270).

BI *L'Entreinte (B. 1116), 1963,* s., #43/50, full margins, good cond., handling marks, est. BP 2,5/3,000, (12-03-92, Sotheby-London, #526, illus.), 13½ x 16½ in., (345 x 420 mm.), aquatint on wove.

BI *L'Entreinte (B. 1116), 1963,* s., #43/50, full margins, good cond., handling marks, est. BP 1,8/2,200, (06-30-93, Sotheby-London, #636), 13½ x 16½ in., (343 x 419 mm.), aquatint on wove.

$4995* *L'Etreinte I (Bl. 1150; Baer 1344), 1963,* s., #15/50, pub. L. Leiris, margins, light-staining, indentations, very good cond., (12-01-92, Christie-London, #496), L. 20⅞ x 25⅛ in., (530 x 638 mm.), linocut rince in colors on Arches (BP 3300, DM 7961, FR 27,132, Y 621,887).

$3163* *L'Etreinte I (Bl. 1150; Baer 1344), 1963,* s., #48/50, excellent cond., (12-01-92, Christie-London, #507), L. 20¹¹⁄₁₆ x 24¹⁵⁄₁₆ in., (526 x 634 mm.), linocut rince in colors on Arches (BP 2090, DM 5041, FR 17,181, Y 393,800).

$6325* *L'Etreinte, I (B. 1150), 1963,* s., #2/50, pub. A. Leiris, margins, partially glued to undermat, goodcond., mat/ light-staining, glue, surface soiling, (05-19-93, Butter-field, #1949, illus.), sh. 24½ x 29⁹⁄₁₆ in., (622 x 751 mm.), linoleum cut rince in colors on Arches (BP 4106, DM 10,281, FR 34,639, Y 700,210).

$15,946* *L'Homme A La Guitare (G. Bloch, 30, B. Geiser, 51), 1915,* definitive state, #1/100, s., good margins, (04-02-93, Picard, #157), 6 x 4½ in., (15.3 x 11.5 cm.), etching on Japan (BP 10,503, DM 25,628, FR 87,041, Y 1,815,553).

$22,599* *L'Homme A La Guitarre (Bloch 30; Geiser 51 IX), 1915,* s., num., (06-10-93, Hauswedell/Nolt, #777A, illus.), engraving on hand-made Japan (BP 14,782, DM 36,800, FR 123,898, Y 2,398,790).

$10,295* *L'Homme A La Pipe (G. 45/V), 1914-15,* Geiser's 5th state of 8, discoloration, (06-30-93, Sotheby-London, #587, illus.), sh 4¾ x 6 in., (121 x 152 mm.), etching and aquatint on laid (BP 6900, DM 17,559, FR 59,235, Y 1,103,075).

BI *L'Homme Au Baton (B. 1106), 1963,* s., #41/50, full margins, good cond., light staining, creases, est. BP 4/ 6,000, (12-03-92, Sotheby-London, #523, illus.), 25¼ x 20⅝ in., (641 x 526 mm.), linocut in colors on Arches.

BI *L'Italienne (B. 740), 1953,* s., #41/50, pub. 1955, full margins, good cond., creases, discoloration, skinning, est. BP 17/20,000, (06-30-93, Sotheby-London, #608, illus.), 17⅝ x 14⅞ in., (448 x 378 mm.), lithograph on Arches.

$19,854* *L'Italienne (Mourl. 238/II; Bl. 740), 1953,* s., artist's proof, (06-23-93, Kornfeld, #709, illus.), lithograph on wove (BP 13,488, DM 33,594, FR 112,999, Y 2,162,981, SF 29,900).

$193* *"A Los Toros - La Pique", c. 1961,* Mourlot impression, excellent cond., (10-10-92, Goldberg, #428), image 9¾ x 12½ in., (24.8 x 31.8 cm.), lithograph (BP 115, DM 287, FR 963, Y 23,496).

$220* *"A Los Toros-La Pique III" and "IV": Two,* late impressions, (05-28-93, Sloan, #1919, illus.), each, sight 9 x 11¾ in., (22.9 x 29.8 cm.), lithograph (BP 141, DM 349, FR 1180, Y 23,590).

BI *"A Los Toros-Mit Picasso" (Bloch 1014-1017), 1961: Four,* pub. A. Savret, est. 20/25,000, (05-19-93, Dorotheum, #437, illus.), lithograph.

$19,800* *Lysistrata (B. 267-72), 1934: Set Of Six,* Westport, Connecticut, Limited Editions Club, s., #150/34, full margins, foxing, staining, good cond., (11-09-92, Christie-NY, #156, illus.), etching on Arches (BP 13,091, DM 31,609, FR 106,796, Y 2,457,185).

BI *Lysistrata D'Aristophane (B. 267-274; book no. 22; C. 387-392; G./C.24), 1934: Six,* each s., #150/123, from separate portfolio edit., pub. Limited Editions Club, full margins, good cond., fox marks, creases, orig. portfolio, est. $15/25,000, (05-13-93, Sotheby-NY, #699, illus.), each sh approx. 15⅛ x 11¼ in., (385 x 285 mm.), etching.

$14,300* *Lysistrata D'Aristophanes, 1934: Set of Six,* s., #150/72, pub. The Limited Editions Club, each w/full margins, good cond., prop. Christopher Brown, prov., (02-10-93, Barridoff, #1, illus.), pl. size 8½ x 4¾ in., (21.6 x 12.1 cm.), etchings on Arches wove (BP 10,037, DM 23,723, FR 80,247, Y 1,733,123).

$2415* *Lysistrata, 1934,* text by Aristophanes, new version by Gilbert Seldes, Limited Editions Club, in 4s, s., #124, (06-14-93, Sotheby-NY, #239, illus.), etched plates (BP 1581, DM 3931, FR 13,211, Y 254,130).

$2310* *Lysistrata, 1934,* illus. Aristophanes, #1389/1500, s. Pablo Picasso, (05-01-93, Skinner, #175), 11¹³⁄₁₆ x 9⁷⁄₁₆ in., (30 x 24 cm.), six etched plates (BP 1469, DM 3657, FR 12,333, Y 256,296).

$20,700* *Lysistrata, Westport, Connecticut, Limited Editions Club, 1934 (B. 267-72): Six,* s., #150/34, full margins, foxing, staining, good cond., orig. wrapper, (05-11-93, Christie-NY, #266, illus.), each sheet 15½ x 11⅝ in., (394 x 295 mm.), etching on Arches (BP 13,214, DM 32,609, FR 109,873, Y 2,276,977).

$17,600* *Mademoiselle Leonie Dans Une Chaise Longue (Bloch 21), 1910,* tone, touches burr, full margins, light/mat staining, left margin edge folded, very good cond., (11-09-92, Christie-NY, #147, illus.), 7¾ x 5⅝ in., etching and drypoint on laid (BP 11,636, DM 28,097, FR 94,930, Y 2,184,165).

$2875* *Madoura (B. 1021; Baer 1270), 1961,* s., #77/100, margins, good cond., mat stain, foxing, skinning, (05-13-93, Sotheby-NY, #713), 4 x 8⅝ in., (100 x 220 mm.), sh 12⅛ x 13 in., (100 x 220 mm.), linoleum cut in colors (BP 1887, DM 4642, FR 15,659, Y 320,978).

$2745* *La Magie Quotidienne (B. 1460), 1968,* s., #xiii/xv, full margins, good cond., handling creases, pressure mark, discoloration, (06-30-93, Sotheby-London, #642, illus.), 8¾ x 12¾ in., (222 x 324 mm.), etching on pale green Japan (BP 1840, DM 4682, FR 15,794, Y 294,118).

$1702* *Les Mains Liees, IV (Bl. 711, Mourlot 213), 1952,* s., 45/50, (12-04-92, AB Stockholm, #7117), 18⅛ x 23⅝ in., (46 x 60 cm.), lithograph (BP 1092, DM 2711, FR 9195, Y 212,484, SK 11,550).

$1373* *Maison De La Pensee Francaise Dessins Et Gravures De Maitres Contemporains (CZ. 168), 1959,* proof before letters, bearing numbering 12/30, full margins, good cond., creases, (06-30-93, Sotheby-London, #612), 16 x 12¼ in., (406 x 311 mm.), offset lithograph on Arches (BP 920, DM 2342, FR 7900, Y 147,112).

$496* *Mann Mit Rotem Mund, (19)69,* num., blindstamp, (06-08-93, Karl/Faber, #1190), approx. 20⅞ x 15¾ in., (53 x 40 cm.), color lithograph on wove (BP 326, DM 805, FR 2710, Y 52,682).

$60,867* *Le Manteau Polonais (Mourlot 134/III/etat definitif; Bloch 587), 19481949,* s. Picasso, epreuve d'artiste, (06-25-93, Kornfeld, #98, illus.), drawing 27⁷⁄₁₆ x 20³⁄₁₆ in., (69.7 x 51.2 cm.), sheet 29¹⁵⁄₁₆ x 22¼ in., (69.7 x 51.2 cm.), lithograph on thick vellum (BP 41,168, DM 103,621, FR 349,008, Y 6,451,876, SF 92,000).

$385* *March Against Death-March On Washington. November 13-15, 1969,* (04-29-93, Swann, #312), 15 x 23 in., (38.1 x 58.4 cm.), poster (BP 245, DM 609, FR 2052, Y 42,830).

$5994* *Marie-Therese Regardant Son Corps Sculpte Ou Modele Et Grande Sculpture De Dos (Baer II, 345 IVB; Bloch 186), 1933,* fourth and final state, s., 3/3, d., 1 of 3 of edit. 300 on parchment, scored plate, pinholes, good cond., (06-28-93, Loudmer, #336, illus.), 10¼ x 7½ in., (260 x 190 mm.), sh 20⅞ x 16⁵⁄₁₆ in., (260 x 190 mm.), black etching and grattoir on parchment (BP 4013, DM 10,185, FR 34,310, Y 635,968).

$2902* *Marie-Therese, Sculpteur Au Travail Et Sculpture Representant Un Athlete Grec (G.-Baer 332/B/d; Bl. 179), 1933,* sheet 70 of Suite Vollard, (06-23-93, Kornfeld, #670), etching on handmade (BP 1971, DM 4910, FR 16,517, Y 316,156, SF 4370).

BI *"Maternite",* #36/200, s., d. in pl. Picasso, 29/4/63, s. Picasso, (10-20-92, Encans, #188), 35¹⁄₁₆ x 24⁷⁄₁₆ in., (89 x 62 cm.), lithograph.

BI *"La Mere Poule" (Cramer No. 37), 1942,* plate 18 illus Buffon, est. FF 2,5/3,000, (10-18-92, Pescheteau, #237), 14½ x 11 in., (36.8 x 28 cm.), etching and aquatint on laid Vollard.

BI *Merimee-Aragon Le Carmen Des Carmen (See C. 126; B. 1001), 1960,* s., p. by Lacouriere-Frelaut and Aldo Crommeylnck, pub. 1969 EditeursFrancais Reunis, wide margins, good cond., est. BP 1,5/2,000, (06-30-93, Sotheby-London, #628, illus.), 13¾ x 10 in., (349 x 254 mm.), drypoint on wove.

BI *Merimee-Aragon. Le Carmen Des Carmen (See C. 126; B. 1000), 1960,* s., p. by Lacouriere-Frelaut and Aldo Crommelynck, pub. 1969 by Editeurs Francais Reunis, wide margins, good cond., est. BP 1/1,300, (06-30-93, Sotheby-London, #627, illus.), 13¾ x 10 in., (349 x 254 mm.), drypoint on wove.

$343* *Merimee-Aragon. Le Carmen Des Carmen (See C. 126; B. 1002), 1949,* s., p. by Lacouriere-Frelaut and Aldo Crommelynck, pub. 1969 EditeursFrancais Reunis, wide margins, good cond., (06-30-93, Sotheby-London, #629, illus.), 13¼ x 10 in., (337 x 254 mm.), aquatint on wove (BP 230, DM 585, FR 1974, Y 36,751).

$428* *Merimee-Aragon. Le Carmen Des Carmen (See C. 126; B. 1003), 1960,* s., p. by Lacouriere-Frelaut and Aldo Crommelynck, pub. 1969 EditeursFrancais Reunis, wide margins, good cond., (06-30-93, Sotheby-London, #630, illus.), 14⅛ x 10 in., (359 x 254 mm.), aquatint (BP 287, DM 730, FR 2463, Y 45,859).

$600* *Merimee-Aragon. Le Carmen Des Carmen (See C. 126; B. 1005), 1960,* s, p. by Lacouriere-Frelaut and Aldo Crommelynck, pub. 1969 EditeursFrancais Reunis, wide margins, good cond., (06-30-93, Sotheby-London, #631, illus.), 14 x 9⅞ in., (356 x 251 mm.), color lithograph on wove (BP 402, DM 1023, FR 3452, Y 64,288).

$4640* *Metamorphoses D'Ovide: Twenty-Eight,* s. by editor, reddish stains, (06-28-93, Loudmer, #341), approx. 12¹⁵⁄₁₆ x 10¹⁄₁₆ in., (330 x 255 mm.), black etchings on China (BP 3107, DM 7884, FR 26,560, Y 492,308).

$1265* *Les Metamorphoses: Combat Pour Andromede Entre Persee Et Phinee (B. 108; G. 152), 1930,* remarque, proof, margins, good cond., mat stain, (05-13-93, Sotheby-NY, #682), 12¼ x 8½ in., (310 x 215 mm.), sh 13⅝ x 10¼ in., (310 x 215 mm.), etching on vellum (BP 830, DM 2043, FR 6890, Y 141,230).

$63,000* *Minotaure Aveugle Guide Par Une Fillette Dans La Nuit (B. 225), 1934,* plate 97 from Suite Vollard, watermark, s., full margins, excell. cond., prop. Steven and Ursula Schwartz, (05-11-93, Christie-NY, #264, illus.), plate 9¹¹⁄₁₆ x 13⅝ in., (246 x 346 mm.), aquatint on Montval (BP 40,217, DM 99,244, FR 334,395, Y 6,929,931).

$29,661* *Minotaure Aveugle Guide Par Une Fillette Dans La Nuit (Bloch 225; Geiser 473 IV c), 1934,* s., watermark, sheet 97 of Suite Vollard, (06-10-93, Hauswedell/Nolt, #783, illus.), image 9¾ x 13¹¹⁄₁₆ in., (24.7 x 34.7 cm.), aquatint (BP 19,401, DM 48,300, FR 162,615, Y 3,148,392).

$46,616* *Minotaure Aveugle Guide Par Une Fillette Dans la Nuite (G. 437; Bl. 225), 1934,* watermark, s., mount-staining, margins, good cond., (12-01-92, Christie-London, #486, illus.), plate 9⅝ x 13⁹⁄₁₆ in., (245 x 345 mm.), aquatint on Montval (BP 30,800, DM 74,300, FR 253,210, Y 5,803,785).

BI *Minotaure Aveugle Guide Par Une Fillette, Dans La Nuit (B. 225; G. 437; S.V. 97), 1934,* from Vollard suite, s., full margins, good cond., scuff, hinge stains, est. $40/50,000, (11-05-92, Sotheby-NY, #338, illus.), 9¾ x 13¾ in., (248 x 350 mm.), aquatint.

BI *Minotaure Aveugle Guide Par Une Fillette, II (B. 223), 1934,* from Vollard Suite, s., watermarked, margins, good cond., light/mount-staining, (06-30-93, Sotheby-London, #592, illus.), sh 13⅜ x 17⅜ in., (340 x 441 mm.), etching on Montval laid.

BI *Minotaure Blesse VI (B. 196), 1933,* plate 88 from the Suite Vollard, watermark, full margins, foxmark, ink mark, staining, est. $4/6,000, (11-09-92, Christie-NY, #153, illus.), 7⅝ x 10½ in., (193 x 266 mm.), etching on Montval.

$2596* *Minotaure Blesse. VI (G.-Baer 363/A/b; Bl. 196), 1933,* sheet 88 of Suite Vollard, (06-23-93, Kornfeld, #672), etching on wove (BP 1764, DM 4393, FR 14,775, Y 282,819, SF 3910).

BI *Minotaure Caressant Une Dormeuse (B. 201; G. 369; S.V. 93), 1933,* from Vollard suite, s., full margins, good cond., stains, est. $30/35,000, (11-05-92, Sotheby-NY, #334, illus.), 11¾ x 14⅜ in., (297 x 365 mm.), drypoint.

$18,400* *Minotaure Caressant Une Dormeuse (B. 201; G. 369; S.V. 93), 1933,* from Vollard Suite, s., full margins, good cond., Vitya Vronsky BabinColl., (05-13-93, Sotheby-NY, #693, illus.), 11¾ x 14⅝ in., (300 x 370 mm.), etching and drypoint (BP 12,080, DM 29,711, FR 100,218, Y 2,054,259).

BI *Minotaure Caressant Une Femme (B. 1919), 1933,* plate 84 from Suite Vollard, watermark, s., full margins, mat staining, very good cond., est. $11/14,000, (05-11-93, Christie-NY, #262, illus.), plate 11⅞ x 14½ in., (302 x 368 mm.), etching on Montval.

BI *Minotaure Caressant Une Femme (B. 191; S.V. 84), 1933,* from Vollard Suite, s., watermark, full margins, good cond., mount staining, est. BP 7/9,000, (12-03-92, Sotheby-London, #489, illus.), 11¾ x 14½ in., (298 x 368 mm.), etching on Montval laid.

$6325* *Minotaure Endormi Contemple Par Une Femme (B. 193; G. 352; S.V. 86),1933,* from Vollard suite, s., full margins, good cond., mat stain, foxing,gold paint, discoloration, (05-13-93, Sotheby-NY, #690, illus.), 7⅝ x 10½ in., (193 x 267 mm.), etching (BP 4152, DM 10,213, FR 34,450, Y 706,152).

$4732* *Minotaure Mourant (Bloch 198; Geiser 366 IIc), 1933,* s., plate d., Bl. 90 from series Suite Vollard, watermark, (06-10-93, Hauswedell/Nolt, #782, illus.), image 7⅝ x 10⁹⁄₁₆ in., (19.4 x 26.9 cm.), etching on hand-made (BP 3095, DM 7706, FR 25,943, Y 502,282).

$5750* *Minotaure Vaincu (B. 197; G. 365; S.V. 89), 1933,* from Vollard suite, s., full margins, good cond., (discoloration), (05-13-93, Sotheby-NY, #691, illus.), 7⅝ x 10⅝ in., (193 x 269 mm.), etching (BP 3775, DM 9285, FR 31,318, Y 641,956).

$16,500* *Minotaure, Buveur Et Femmes (B. 200; G. 368; S.V. 92), 1933,* from Vollard suite, s., full margins, good cond., (11-05-92, Sotheby-NY, #333, illus.), 11¾ x 14½ in., (298 x 367 mm.), etching (BP 10,732, DM 26,095, FR 88,283, Y 2,024,291).

$14,950* *Minotaure, Buveur Et Femmes (B. 200; G. 368; S.V. 92), 1933,* from Vollard suite, s., full margins, good cond., (05-13-93, Sotheby-NY, #692, illus.), 11¾ x 14⅜ in., (297 x 365 mm.), etching (BP 9815, DM 24,140, FR 81,427, Y 1,669,086).

$5457* *Minotaure, Une Coupe A La Main Et Jeune Femme (B. 190), 1933,* from Vollard Suite, s., watermarked Picasso, full margins, good cond., (12-03-92, Sotheby-London, #487, illus.), 7½ x 10⅝ in., (190 x 270 mm.), etching on Montval laid (BP 3520, DM 8582, FR 29,291, Y 678,985).

$7700* *Minotaure, Une Coupe A La Main, Et Jeune Fille (B. 190; G. 349; S.V.83), 1933,* from Vollard suite, s., full margins, good cond., discoloration, (11-05-92, Sotheby-NY, #332, illus.), 7½ x 10½ in., (190 x 267 mm.), etching (BP 5008, DM 12,178, FR 41,199, Y 944,669).

$4834* *"Minotauro",* #34/50, s., (03-17-93, Duran, #175, illus.), 27⁹⁄₁₆ x 22¹⁄₁₆ in., (70 x 56 cm.), linocut (BP 3333, DM 8043, FR 27,342, Y 566,972, P 575,000).

$4582* *Modele Au Repose, Avec Statue Equestre A L'Arriere-Plan (Baer 1183/B/b/1; Bl. 1204), 1965,* s., num., (06-23-93, Kornfeld, #691), aquatint and drypoint on wove (BP 3113, DM 7753, FR 26,079, Y 499,183, SF 6900).

BI *Modele Contemplant Un Groupe Sculpte (B. 175), 1933,* from Vollard Suite, s., full margins, good cond., est. BP 4/5,000, (06-30-93, Sotheby-London, #591, illus.), 11⅝ x 14⅜ in., (295 x 365 mm.), etching on Montval laid.

$5827* *Modele Contemplant Un Groupe Sculpte, Plate 66 (G. 328 II; Bl. 175),1933,* watermark, s., margins, mount-staining, very good cond., (12-01-92, Christie-London, #485, illus.), plate 11¾ x 14⅜ in., (298 x 365 mm.), etching on Montval (BP 3850, DM 9288, FR 31,651, Y 725,473).

$6497* *Modele Et Grande Tete Sculptee (Bloch 170; Geiser 232 Ii), 1933,* s., plate d., sheet 61 of Suite Vollard, watermark, (06-10-93, Hauswedell/Nolt, #779, illus.), image 10½ x 7⁹⁄₁₆ in., (26.7 x 19.2 cm.), etching (BP 4250, DM 10,580, FR 35,620, Y 689,630).

$5320* *Le Modele Nu (Geiser 119 II; Bloch 78), 1927,* s., num., (06-05-93, Bassenge, #6438), 10⅞ x 7⅜ in., (27.6 x 18.8 cm.), etching on fine imitation Japan (BP 3502, DM 8625, FR 29,071, Y 570,693).

$9350* *Modele Nu Et Sculptures (B. 185; G. 344; S.V. 72), 1933,* from Vollard suite, s., full margins, good cond., (11-05-92, Sotheby-NY, #331, illus.), 15 x 11¾ in., (380 x 300 mm.), etching (BP 6081, DM 14,787, FR 50,027, Y 1,147,099).

$4434* *Modele Posant Et Peintre (B. 1389), 1966,* s., #37/50, full margins, good cond., creases, (12-03-92, Sotheby-London, #548, illus.), 10⅝ x 14¾ in., (270 x 375 mm.), etching and aquatint on BFK Rives (BP 2860, DM 6973, FR 23,800, Y 551,698).

$2596* *Modele, Tableau Et Sculpture (G.-Baer 303/A/b; Bl. 151), 1933,* sheet 43 of Suite Vollard, (06-23-93, Kornfeld, #661), etching on wove (BP 1764, DM 4393, FR 14,775, Y 282,819, SF 3910).

$2444* *Modele, Tableau Et Sculpture (G.-Baer 303/B/d; Bl. 151), 1933,* sheet 32 of Suite Vollard, (06-23-93, Kornfeld, #662), etching on handmade (BP 1660, DM 4135, FR 13,910, Y 266,260, SF 3680).

$5490* *Monaco, Editions Du Rocher, 1962: Twenty-Four,* from Picasso de 1916 a 1961 by Jean Cocteau, includes other illus., orig. drawing by Cocteau s. and ded., (11-15-92, Christie-Geneva, #331, illus.), 14¹⁵⁄₁₆ x 11 in., (380 x 280 mm.), lithograph on pur chiffon (BP 3608, DM 8756, FR 29,500, Y 685,137, SF 7910).

$4400* *Morte Au Soleil, IV (B. 204; G. 384; S.V. 16), 1933,* from Vollard suite, s., full margins, good cond., mat stain, foxing, (11-05-92, Sotheby-NY, #335), 7⅞ x 11 in., (199 x 278 mm.), drypoint and aquatint (BP 2862, DM 6959, FR 23,542, Y 539,811).

$5320* *Mousquetaire (Bloch 1623), 1968,* s., num., (06-05-93, Bassenge, #6439), 19⅜ x 16⅛ in., (49.2 x 41 cm.), etching w/aquatint on copper print (BP 3502, DM 8625, FR 29,071, Y 570,693).

BI *Nature Mort Au Pot De Gres (B. 443; M. 86), 1947,* crayon s., #13/50, full margins, good cond., fox marks, creases, tear, skinned spots, est. $4/4,500, (11-05-92, Sotheby-NY, #347), 16¾ x 23⅝ in., (425 x 600 mm.), lithograph.

$12,650* *Nature Morte A La Bouteille (B. 1100), 1962,* s., proof, printer stamp, margins, image scuffs, foxing, skinning, good cond., (05-11-93, Christie-NY, #284, illus.), borderline 25¼ x 20⅞ in., (641 x 530 mm.), linocut in browm, grey and black on Arches (BP 8075, DM 19,928, FR 67,144, Y 1,391,486).

$12,712* *Nature Morte A La Bouteille (Bloch 1100; Baer 1315 I B b), 1962,* s., #7/50, (06-10-93, Hauswedell/Nolt, #799, illus.), color linocut on Arches (BP 8315, DM 20,700, FR 69,693, Y 1,349,326).

$17,600* *Nature Morte A La Pasteque (B. 1098), 1962,* s., #136/160, full margins, mat staining, good cond., (11-09-92, Christie-NY, #168, illus.), 23⁷⁄₁₆ x 28¾ in., (595 x 730 mm.), colored linocut on Arches (BP 11,636, DM 28,097, FR 94,930, Y 2,184,165).

$16,500* *Nature Morte A La Pasteque (B. 1098; Baer 1301), 1962,* s., #76/160, pub. Galerie Louise Leiris, 1963, full margins, good cond., handling crease, scuff in image, glue stains, (11-05-92, Sotheby-NY, #359, illus.), 23¼ x

28½ in., (592 x 725 mm.), linoleum cut p. in colors (BP 10,732, DM 26,095, FR 88,283, Y 2,024,291).

$63,911* *Nature Morte A La Suspension (Baer 1313/B/g/2/beta; Bloch 1102), 1962,* s. Picasso, epreuve d'artiste, (06-25-93, Kornfeld, #115, illus.), image 25³⁄₁₆ x 20⅞ in., (64 x 53 cm.), sheet 29⅝ x 24½ in., (64 x 53 cm.), color linocut on thick Arches vellum (BP 43,227, DM 108,803, FR 366,462, Y 6,774,539, SF 96,600).

BI *Nature Morte Au Casse-Croute I, 1962,* s., prov., est. DM 16/18,000, (12-01-92, Karl/Faber, #1098, illus.), 25³⁄₁₆ x 20¹³⁄₁₆ in., (64 x 52.8 cm.), color linocut on Arches wove.

$22,064* *Nature Morte Au Compotier (Geiser-Baer 22/III/b, Bloch 18), 1908-1909,* s. Picasso, num., (06-25-93, Kornfeld, #93, illus.), plate 5⅛ x 4⁵⁄₁₆ in., (13 x 11 cm.), sheet 23⅞ x 17⁵⁄₁₆ in., (13 x 11 cm.), engraving (BP 14,923, DM 37,562, FR 126,514, Y 2,338,775, SF 33,350).

$9469* *Nature Morte Au Crane (G.-Baer 36/II/b/e; Bl. 26), 1913,* s., prov., (06-23-93, Kornfeld, #648, illus.), drypoint on handmade (BP 6433, DM 16,022, FR 53,893, Y 1,031,594, SF 14,260).

$391* *Nature Morte Au Pichet,* num. A.P. 4/39, Marina Picasso coll., stamp, (06-16-93, Encans, #154), 17¹¹⁄₁₆ x 28⁹⁄₁₆ in., (45 x 72.5 cm.), lithograph (BP 261, DM 649, FR 2178, Y 41,702, C$ 391).

BI *Nature Morte Sous La Lampe (B. 1102; Baer 1313), 1962,* s., num., full margins, good cond., catalog cover lot, est. BP 60/80,000, (12-03-92, Sotheby-London, #561, illus.), sheet 29⅝ x 24⅜ in., (750 x 620 mm.), linocut in colors on Arches.

BI *Nature Morte Sous La Lampe (Nature Morte A La Suspension) (B. 1102; Baer 1313), 1962,* s., #34/50, pub. Galerie Louise Leiris, 1963, full margins, good cond., mat stain, scuff, foxing, est. $120/150,000, (11-05-92, Sotheby-NY, #360, illus.), 25¼ x 20⅞ in., (640 x 530 mm.), sheet 29½ x 24½ in., (640 x 530 mm.), linoleum cut p. in colors.

$20,590* *Nature Morte, Bouteille (B. 24; 33/B), 1912,* p. by Delatre, pub. Kahnweiller, full margins, sig., numbering erased, tears, good cond., (06-30-93, Sotheby-London, #586, illus.), 19¾ x 12 in., (502 x 305 mm.), drypoint on Arches laid (BP 13,800, DM 35,119, FR 118,470, Y 2,206,150).

$10,350* *Nature Morte, Compotier (B. 18; G. 22), 1909,* s., p. Delatre, pub. Kahweiler, 1912, margins, good cond., (05-13-93, Sotheby-NY, #676, illus.), 5⅛ x 4⅜ in., (130 x 110 mm.), sh 11½ x 9 in., (130 x 110 mm.), drypoint on laid (BP 6795, DM 16,712, FR 56,373, Y 1,155,521).

$15,442* *Nature Morte, Compotier (B. 18; G. 22/III/B), 1909,* pub. Kahweiler, 1911, full margins, trimmed, creases, folded, good cond., discoloration, (06-30-93, Sotheby-London, #584, illus.), 5⅛ x 4¼ in., (130 x 108 mm.), drypoint on Arches laid (BP 10,350, DM 26,338, FR 88,849, Y 1,654,559).

$2574* *Nu A La Chaise (B. 763), 1954,* s., # 16/50, margins, mount-staining, backboard-staining, tape stains, (06-30-93, Sotheby-London, #641, illus.), sh 19⅞ x 15 in., (505 x 381 mm.), color lithograph on Arches (BP 1725, DM 4390, FR 14,810, Y 275,796).

$4434* *Nu Assis Entoure D'Esquisses De Betes Et D'Hommes (B. 91), 1927,* from Le Chef d'Oeuvre Inconnu, brush s. in ink, margins, mount/backboard staining, good cond., (12-03-92, Sotheby-London, #486, illus.), 7⅝ x 11 in., (194 x 278 mm.), etching (BP 2860, DM 6973, FR 23,800, Y 551,698).

$7608* *Orphee. - Le Poete. I (Geiser-Baer 540), 1933,* (06-25-93, Kornfeld, #88, illus.), image 5½ x 4⁷⁄₁₆ in., (14 x 11.3 cm.), sheet 10³⁄₁₆ x 6¾ in., (14 x 11.3 cm.), copper monotype on handmade (BP 5146, DM 12,952, FR 43,624, Y 806,445, SF 11,500).

$858* *Paix Desarmement Pour Le Succes De La Conference Au Sommet (Czwiklitzer 169, See Bloch 712), 1960,* p. by Mourlot, folds, tear, defects, (06-30-93, Sotheby-London, #604, illus.), sh 47¼ x 31½ in., (120 x 80 cm.), color lithographic poster on wove (BP 575, DM 1463, FR 4937, Y 91,932).

$1100* *Paloma Et Claude (Rechter Teil) (Bloch 664; Mourlot 186), 1959,* (06-05-93, Grisebach, #826, illus.), 12⅝ x

9⁹⁄₁₆ in., (32.1 x 24.3 cm.), lithograph on wove (BP 724, DM 1783, FR 6011, Y 118,000).

$19,090* *Paloma Et Sa Poupee (Mourl. 229; Bl. 727), 1952,* s., num., (06-23-93, Kornfeld, #708, illus.), lithograph on wove (BP 12,969, DM 32,301, FR 108,651, Y 2,079,747, SF 28,750).

$34,493* *Paloma Et Sa Poupee Sur Fond Noir (Bloch 727; Mourlot 229), 1952,* crayon s., num. 6/50, full sheet, good cond., time staining, tipped to backing, (10-14-92, Sotheby-Japan, #67, illus.), sheet 30 x 22½ in., (762 x 572 mm.), lithograph (BP 20,246, DM 50,480, FR 171,181, Y 4,179,956).

BI *Paloma Et Sa Poupee, Fond Blanc (M. 228; Bl. 726), 1952,* crayon s., #11/50, foxmarks, discoloration, good cond., est. BP 7/9,000, (12-01-92, Christie-London, #493, illus.), L. 28⅛ x 21⁹⁄₁₆ in., (714 x 547 mm.), lithograph on Arches.

$16,799* *Pan (Mourl. 111; Bl. 518), 1948,* s., artist's proof, (06-23-93, Kornfeld, #705, illus.), lithograph on wove (BP 11,412, DM 28,425, FR 95,612, Y 1,830,156, SF 25,300).

BI *Les Pauvres (B. 3; G. 4), 1905,* pub. Vollard, 1913, w/ complimentary sig. in ink c. 1930, margins, good cond., staining, crease, cellophane tape, est. BP 12/15,000, (06-30-93, Sotheby-London, #581, illus.), sh 15⅛ x 12½ in., (384 x 318 mm.), etching on vieux Japon on Van Gelder Zonen.

$4400* *Les Pauvres (B. 3; G. 4), 1905,* from Saltimbanques suite, pub. Vollard, 1913, full margins, good cond., glue, speck, creases, glue, sold after sale, (11-05-92, Sotheby-NY, #320, illus.), 9¼ x 7 in., (235 x 179 mm.), etching on Van Gelder Zonen wove (BP 2862, DM 6959, FR 23,542, Y 539,811).

$11,072* *Les Pauvres (Geiser-Baer 4/II/b/2; Bloch 3), 1905,* prov., (06-23-93, Kornfeld, #644), etching on thick wove (BP 7522, DM 18,734, FR 63,017, Y 1,206,232, SF 16,675).

$3922* *Paysage A Vallauris (B. 734), 1953,* s., #2/50, full margins, good cond., light staining, taped to mount, (12-03-92, Sotheby-London, #504, illus.), 19½ x 25⅝ in., (495 x 650 mm.), lithograph on Arches (BP 2530, DM 6168, FR 21,052, Y 487,993).

$23,873* *Le Peintre A La Palette (B. 1153), 1963,* s., margins, good cond., paper discoloration, soiling, backboard staining, prov., (12-03-92, Sotheby-London, #560, illus.), sheet 29½ x 24⅜ in., (750 x 620 mm.), extensively hand-colored linocut in red, blue, green, white, brown and mauve crayon on Arches (BP 15,400, DM 37,542, FR 128,143, Y 2,970,387).

$8236* *Le Peintre A La Palette (B. 1153), 1963,* s., #28/150, margins, good cond., light/mount-staining, handling creases, (06-30-93, Sotheby-London, #637, illus.), sh 29½ x 14½ in., (749 x 368 mm.), linocut on Arches (BP 5520, DM 14,047, FR 47,388, Y 882,460).

$7700* *Le Peintre A La Palette (B. 1153), 1963,* s. #113/150, wide margins, mat/time staining, very good cond., (11-09-92, Christie-NY, #170, illus.), 25⁵⁄₁₆ x 20⅞ in., (643 x 530 mm.), linocut on Arches (BP 5091, DM 12,292, FR 41,532, Y 955,572).

$7150* *Le Peintre A La Palette (Peintre Et Sa Toile) (B. 1153; Baer 1342), 1963,* s., #101/150, margins, good cond., light stain, discolored, rubbed, soiling, (11-05-92, Sotheby-NY, #362, illus.), 25¼ x 20⅞ in., (640 x 530 mm.), linoleum cut (BP 4650, DM 11,308, FR 38,256, Y 877,193).

$3922* *Peintre Au Travail (B. 1117), 1963,* s., #26/50, full margins, good cond., crease within image, paper discloration, (12-03-92, Sotheby-London, #530, illus.), 12½ x 16½ in., (320 x 420 mm.), etching on BFK Rives (BP 2530, DM 6168, FR 21,052, Y 487,993).

$4263* *Peintre Au Travail (B. 1117), 1963,* s., #29/50, full margins, good cond., tape hinges, (12-03-92, Sotheby-London, #529, illus.), 12⅜ x 16⅜ in., (313 x 415 mm.), etching and drypoint on BFK Rives (BP 2750, DM 6704, FR 22,882, Y 530,422).

$3410* *Peintre Au Travail (B. 1126), 1963,* s., #26/50, full margins, good cond., (12-03-92, Sotheby-London, #532), 12½ x 16½ in., (315 x 420 mm.), etching on Rives (BP 2200, DM 5362, FR 18,304, Y 424,288).

$2902* *Peintre Avec Modele Barbu Assis Sur Une Chaise (Baer 1133/B/b/1; Bl.1136), 1963,* s., num., (06-23-93, Kornfeld, #690), aquatint (BP 1971, DM 4910, FR 16,517, Y 316,156, SF 4370).

$4123* *Peintre Entre Deux Modeles Regardant Une Toile (G.-Baer 124/b/2; Bl.83), 1927,* s. in brown ink, num., (06-23-93, Kornfeld, #650), etching on wove (BP 2801, DM 6976, FR 23,466, Y 449,177, SF 6210).

$4263* *Peintre Et Modele (B. 1132), 1963,* s., #26/50, full margins, good cond., (12-03-92, Sotheby-London, #531, illus.), 12⅜ x 16⅛ in., (313 x 410 mm.), etching on wove (BP 2750, DM 6704, FR 22,882, Y 530,422).

$3410* *Peintre Et Modele (B. 1161), 1964,* s., #14/50, full margins, good cond., (12-03-92, Sotheby-London, #528, illus.), 10⅞ x 15½ in., (275 x 386 mm.), aquatint and etching on Arches (BP 2200, DM 5362, FR 18,304, Y 424,288).

$3910* *Peintre Et Modele (B. 1161), 1964,* s., #30/50, full margins, mat staining, linen tape, skinned spot, tape, good cond., (05-11-93, Christie-NY, #286), plate 10⅝ x 15⅛ in., (270 x 384 mm.), etching and aquatint on BFK Rives (BP 2496, DM 6159, FR 20,754, Y 430,096).

$2875* *Peintre Et Modele (B. 1212), 1965,* s., #5/50, full margins, good cond., light stain, (02-11-93, Sotheby-NY, #217), 8¾ x 12⅝ in., (222 x 321 mm.), aquatint and drypoint (BP 2029, DM 4762, FR 16,115, Y 346,594).

$2300* *Peintre Et Modele (B. 1376), 1966,* s., #17/50, full margins, crease, tape, very good cond., (05-11-93, Christie-NY, #299), plate 10¾ x 15¼ in., (273 x 387 mm.), etching and aquatint on BFK Rives (BP 1468, DM 3623, FR 12,208, Y 252,997).

$4093* *Peintre Et Modele (B. 1381), 1966,* s., #47/50, full margins, good cond., (12-03-92, Sotheby-London, #533, illus.), 10¾ x 15 in., (275 x 380 mm.), etching and aquatint on BFK Rives (BP 2640, DM 6437, FR 21,970, Y 509,270).

$2875* *Peintre Et Modele (B. 1387), 1966,* s., #24/50, full margins, excell. cond., (05-11-93, Christie-NY, #301, illus.), plate 12½ x 18½ in., (318 x 470 mm.), etching and aquatint on Rives (BP 1835, DM 4529, FR 15,260, Y 316,247).

$2432* *Peintre Et Modele (Bl. 1374), 1966,* s., 30/50, (12-04-92, AB Stockholm, #7115), 10¹³⁄₁₆ x 15¼ in., (27.5 x 38.7 cm.), engraving on BFK Rives (BP 1560, DM 3873, FR 13,139, Y 303,620, SK 16,500).

$1915* *Peintre Et Modele (Bl. 1375), 1966,* s., #32/50, margins, surface dirt, good cond., (12-01-92, Christie-London, #499), plate 10¹³⁄₁₆ x 15¼ in., (275 x 387 mm.), etching w/aquatint on BFK Rives (BP 1265, DM 3052, FR 10,402, Y 238,421).

$3971* *Peintre Et Modele (Bloch 1375), 1966,* s., num., (06-23-93, Kornfeld, #692), etching on wove (BP 2698, DM 6719, FR 22,601, Y 432,618, SF 5980).

$5750* *Peintre Et Modele Au Fauteuil A Bascule (B. 1852; Baer 1359), 1966,* s., #47/50, full margins, good cond., repaired tear, related crease, (02-11-93, Sotheby-NY, #218, illus.), 20¹³⁄₁₆ x 25⅛ in., (528 x 638 mm.), sheet 24⁷⁄₁₆ x 29½ in., (528 x 638 mm.), linoleum cut (BP 4057, DM 9525, FR 32,231, Y 693,189).

$2300* *Le Peintre Et Son Modele (B. 1156), 1964,* s., #38/50, full margins, foxmarks, taped to overmat, very good cond., (05-11-93, Christie-NY, #285), plate 9⅛ x 13 in., (232 x 330 mm.), aquatint on Auvergne a la main (BP 1468, DM 3623, FR 12,208, Y 252,997).

$6613* *Le Peintre Et Son Modele (B. 765; M. 262), 1954,* s., #5/50, full margins, good cond., faded, creased, foxing, mat stain, skinning, small label, (02-11-93, Sotheby-NY, #215, illus.), 19¹¹⁄₁₆ x 25⅜ in., (500 x 645 mm.), color lithograph (BP 4666, DM 10,954, FR 37,068, Y 797,227).

BI   *Le Peintre Et Son Modele (B. 765; M. 262), 1954,* s., #5/50, full margins, good cond., faded, creases, foxing, mat stain, skinning, label, est. $15/20,000, (11-05-92, Sotheby-NY, #353, illus.), 19¾ x 25⅜ in., (500 x 645 mm.), lithograph p. in colors.

BI   *Le Peintre Et Son Modele (B. 98; G. 247; M. XXVII; G./C. 18), 1930,* s., p. L'Atelier Desjobert, pub. XXe Siecle, full margins, good cond., mat stain, soiling, est.

$6/8,000, (05-13-93, Sotheby-NY, #681, illus.), 9¼ x 11½ in., (235 x 291 mm.), lithograph on chine colle.

$2580* *Peintre Et Son Modele (G.B., 1188, P. Cramer, 136), 1966,* from 50 impressions, #8/50, s., large margins, (04-02-93, Picard, #158), aquatint on large paper w/Auvergne watermark (BP 1699, DM 4147, FR 14,083, Y 293,749).

$13,363* *Le Peintre Et Son Modele (Mourl. 262; Bl. 765), 1954,* s., num., (06-23-93, Kornfeld, #712), color lithograph on light cream wove (BP 9078, DM 22,611, FR 76,056, Y 1,455,823, SF 20,125).

$6600* *Le Peintre Et Son Modele (Peintre Dessinant Et Modele Nu Au Chapeau)(B. 1194; Baer 1357), 1956,* s., #14/160, large margins, good cond., light/mat stain, scuffs in image, (11-05-92, Sotheby-NY, #370, illus.), 20⅝ x 24⅞ in., (523 x 633 mm.), linoleum cut on Arches (BP 4293, DM 10,438, FR 35,313, Y 809,717).

BI   *Le Peintre Et la Modele (Bl. 1404), 1966,* stamped sig., #37/50, margins, excellent cond., est. BP 800/1,200, (12-01-92, Christie-London, #500), plate 8¹¹⁄₁₆ x 12½ in., (220 x 318 mm.), etching w/aquatint on wove.

$4400* *Le Peintre Son Modele (B. 1133, 1963,* s., #9/50, full margins, good cond., foxing, notations, hinge remains, (10-28-92, Butterfield, #2694, illus.), 9⅛ x 13 in., (232 x 330 mm.), aquatint w/burin on laid Auvergne a la Main hand made paper (BP 2803, DM 6795, FR 23,073, Y 539,877).

$12,934* *Le Peintre Sur La Plage (Baer 919/B/b; Bloch 769), 1955,* s. Picasso, epreuve d'artiste, (06-25-93, Kornfeld, #104, illus.), plate 18⁹⁄₁₆ x 32¾ in., (47.2 x 83.2 cm.), aquatint on vellum (BP 8748, DM 22,019, FR 74,163, Y 1,370,999, SF 19,550).

$3895* *Personnage Assis Et Personnage Couche (Mourlot 278, Bloch Band I 798), 1956,* #10/50, s., (11-21-92, Lempertz, #323, illus.), 17⅛ x 20¹³⁄₁₆ in., (43.5 x 52.8 cm.), lithograph on Arches wove (BP 2565, DM 6210, FR 20,918, Y 484,392).

$3450* *Personnages (B. 1241), 1966,* watermark, s., #94/125, full margins, mat staining, stain, very goodcond., (05-11-93, Christie-NY, #294), plate 12¾ x 8¾ in., (324 x 222 mm.), etching on wove (BP 2202, DM 5435, FR 18,312, Y 379,496).

BI   *Le Petit Dessinateur (B. 768), 1954,* s., #16/50, good cond., creasing, paper discoloration, tipped to mount, est. BP 6/8,000, (12-03-92, Sotheby-London, #511, illus.), 26 x 19¾ in., (660 x 505 mm.), transfer lithograph in colors.

BI   *Le Petit Dessinateur (B. 768), 1954,* s., #28/50, trimmed into subject, glue traces, good cond., est. BP 3/4,000, (06-30-93, Sotheby-London, #607, illus.), sh 25½ x 19¾ in., (648 x 502 mm.), color lithograph on Arches.

$13,363* *Le Petit Dessinateur (Mourl. 263; Bl. 768), 1954,* s., i. Epreuve d'artiste, (06-23-93, Kornfeld, #713), color lithograph (BP 9078, DM 22,611, FR 76,056, Y 1,455,823, SF 20,125).

$10,572* *Petite Buste De Femme (B. 1082), 1962,* s., #18/50, full margins, good cond., light staining, glue stain, (12-03-92, Sotheby-London, #522, illus.), sheet 24¾ x 17½ in., (630 x 443 mm.), linocut in colors on Arches (BP 6820, DM 16,625, FR 56,747, Y 1,315,416).

$579* *"La Petite Corrida" (Bl.839),* d. 23.II.57, s. in plate, (04-04-93, Pescheteau, #274), 12⅜⁄₁₆ x 9⁷⁄₁₆ in., (31 x 24 cm.), color lithograph (BP 381, DM 931, FR 3160, Y 65,923).

$330* *La Petite Corrida, Cannes (Bloch 839, Mourlot 302), 1957,* stone s., d., p. for XXe Siecle, (12-08-92, Swann, #243), 13 x 10 in., (33 x 25.4 cm.), color lithograph (BP 207, DM 514, FR 1752, Y 40,902).

$275* *La Petite Corrida-Cannes (Bloch 839. Mourlot 302), 1957,* d., s. in stone, (05-27-93, Swann, #220), sh 13 x 10 in., (33 x 25.4 cm.), color lithograph (BP 176, DM 441, FR 1487, Y 29,481).

$12,981* *Le Picador (Baer 894/b/2; Bl. 692), 1952,* s., i. epreuve d'artiste, num., (06-23-93, Kornfeld, #682, illus.), aquatint on wove (BP 8819, DM 21,964, FR 73,882, Y 1,414,206, SF 19,550).

$7636* *Picador Entrant Dans L'Arene (Baer 1221/II/B/a; Bl. 942), 1959,* s., num., (06-23-93, Kornfeld, #720), color linocut on thick wove (BP 5188, DM 12,920, FR 43,460, Y 831,899, SF 11,500).

$5968* *Picador Et Cheval (B. 912), 1959,* s., #26/50, full margins, good cond., (12-03-92, Sotheby-London, #515, illus.), 25⅛ x 21⅛ in., (640 x 535 mm.), linocut in black and brown on Arches (BP 3850, DM 9385, FR 32,034, Y 742,566).

BI *Picador Et Cheval (B. 912), 1959,* s., #41/50, full margins, good cond., creases, discoloration, est. BP3,5/4,500, (06-30-93, Sotheby-London, #625, illus.), 25¼ x 21 in., (641 x 533 mm.), linocut in black and browns on Arches.

$143* *Picador Et Toreso,* after 1959, from Bacchanals, Women and Bullfights, Abrams, 1962, s. Picasso, (06-26-93, Wolf, #963), color linoleum cut (BP 96, DM 243, FR 819, Y 15,172).

$2090* *Le Picador II (Bloch 1017), 1961,* red crayon s., #27/50, prov., (09-17-92, Sloan, #3084, illus.), 8 x 10⅜ in., (20.3 x 26.4 cm.), color lithograph (BP 1174, DM 3103, FR 10,620, Y 260,209).

$688* *Picasso "Toros" 15 Lavis,* s., 1 of 300, faults, tears, creases, (06-16-93, Ader Tajan, #127), 25⁹⁄₁₆ x 19¹¹⁄₁₆ in., (65 x 50 cm.), lithograph poster (BP 459, DM 1142, FR 3833, Y 73,379).

$385* *"Picasso Dessins (1959-1960)", 1960,* exhib. poster, s., d. in stone, (10-31-92, Litchfield, #133), 25 x 19 in., (63.5 x 48.3 cm.), lithograph (BP 252, DM 604, FR 2047, Y 47,601).

BI *Pigeon Au Fond Gris (B. 418), 1947,* s., crayon, #12/50, full margins, 3 sides, good cond., paper discoloration, rubbed spot, skinning, ex coll. Heinrich Neurerburg (L. 1344a), est. BP10/12,000, (06-30-93, Sotheby-London, #596, illus.), sh 13 x 19⅝ in., (330 x 498 mm.), lithograph on Arches.

$7062* *Pigeon Au Fond Gris (Bloch 418; Mourlot 64), 1947,* s., stone d., #39/50, red s., (06-10-93, Hauswedell/Nolt, #790, illus.), image 10⅝ x 17¹³⁄₁₆ in., (27 x 45.2 cm.), lithograph on Arches (BP 4619, DM 11,500, FR 38,717, Y 749,602).

$1870* *Pigeonneau (B. 326), 1939,* s. in brown crayon, num. 71/226, from vol. 40 Dessins de Picasso en Marge du Buffon, 1957, pub. Jonquieres, margin possibly trimmed, good cond., mat& light-staining, glue remains, skinned area, crease, surface soiling, pencil notations, (02-24-93, Butterfield, #2774, illus.), 6¼ x 7⅞ in., (159 x 200 mm.), linoleum cut on wove (BP 1304, DM 3036, FR 10,292, Y 219,432).

$1985* *Le Pigeonneau (Baer 1028/B/a; Bloch 326), 1954-1957,* s. in red chalk, num., (06-23-93, Kornfeld, #717), linocut (BP 1349, DM 3359, FR 11,298, Y 216,254, SF 2990).

BI *Pigeonneau (Bl. 326; cf. C. and G. 84), c. 1939,* crayon s., #45/226, pub. in 40 Dessins de Picasso en Marge du Buffon, Galerie Berggruen, 1957, margins, creases, est. BP 1,8/2,200, (12-01-92, Christie-London, #487), L. 6⁵⁄₁₆ x 7⅞ in., (160 x 200 mm.), woodcut on BFK Rives.

$110* *La Pique,* after 1959, from Bacchanals, Women and Bullfights, Abrams 1962, s. Picasso, (06-26-93, Wolf, #962), linoleum cut (BP 74, DM 187, FR 630, Y 11,671).

$12,650* *Pique (B. 911), 1959,* s., #30/50, full margins, light/mat staining, excell. cond., (05-11-93, Christie-NY, #276, illus.), borderline 20⅞ x 25⅛ in., (530 x 638 mm.), linocut in browns and black on Arches (BP 8075, DM 19,928, FR 67,144, Y 1,391,486).

$8623* *Pique (Bloch 944; Baer 1219 II/B/a), 1959,* s., num. 3/50, full margins, good cond., (10-14-92, Sotheby-Japan, #68, illus.), 6½ x 8⅞ in., (165 x 225 mm.), linoleum cut in beige, brown and black (BP 5061, DM 12,620, FR 42,794, Y 1,044,959).

$10,450* *Pique (Rouge Et Jaune) (B. 908), 1959,* s., #19/50, wide margins, mat staining, very good cond., (11-09-92, Christie-NY, #165, illus.), 20¹⁵⁄₁₆ x 25 in., (532 x 635 mm.), colored linocut on Arches (BP 6909, DM 16,683, FR 56,365, Y 1,296,848).

BI *Pique 1 (G.B. 944, B.G. 1219), 1959,* s., good margins, est. FF15,000, (06-16-93, Ader Tajan, #126, illus.), 6½ x 8⅞ in., (16.5 x 22.5 cm.), 2-tone linocut.

$12,100* *La Pique Cassee (B. 921), 1959,* s., #17/50, full margins, light/mat staining, very good cond., (11-09-92, Christie-NY, #166, illus.), 21¹⁄₁₆ x 25¼ in., (535 x 642 mm.), colored linocut on Arches (BP 8000, DM 19,317, FR 65,264, Y 1,501,613).

$3450* *La Pique I (B. 898), 1959,* s., #30/50, full margins, creases, foxing, stains, good cond., (05-11-93, Christie-NY, #275), borderline 16½ x 22 in., (419 x 559 mm.), lithograph on Arches (BP 2202, DM 5435, FR 18,312, Y 379,496).

$2819* *La Pique I- 2.9.59 (Bloch 898),* #40/50, s., d., (05-20-93, Finarte-Milan, #126, illus.), 16⁹⁄₁₆ x 22¹⁄₁₆ in., (42 x 56 cm.), lithograph (BP 1809, DM 4548, FR 15,321, Y 311,285, L 4140).

$11,454* *Pique II (Baer 1228/B/b/2/beta; Bl. 911), 1959,* s., une vingtaine d'epreuves d'artiste, (06-23-93, Kornfeld, #722, illus.), color linocut on thick wove (BP 7781, DM 19,381, FR 65,191, Y 1,247,848, SF 17,250).

$7254* *Pique. I (Baer 1219/II/B/b; Bl. 944), 1959,* s., num., (06-23-93, Kornfeld, #719, illus.), color linocut on wove (BP 4928, DM 12,274, FR 41,286, Y 790,282, SF 10,925).

$5345* *La Plongeuse (G.-Baer 277/B/b; B. 1322), 1932,* s., (06-23-93, Kornfeld, #658), etching on collage (BP 3631, DM 9044, FR 30,421, Y 582,307, SF 8050).

$993* *Pointe Seche 11 Avril 1970 (Bl. 1885), 1970,* sig. stamp, num., from the series 156 gravures, (06-23-93, Kornfeld, #698), drypoint (BP 675, DM 1680, FR 5652, Y 108,182, SF 1495).

$2902* *Pointe Seche 31 Mai 1971 (Bl. 1991), 1971,* sig. stamp, num., from the series 156 gravures, (06-23-93, Kornfeld, #701), drypoint (BP 1971, DM 4910, FR 16,517, Y 316,156, SF 4370).

$4229* *Pointe-Seche 31 Mai 1971 (Bolch 1991),* s., #18/50, sig. stamp, (05-26-93, Lempertz, #448, illus.), approx. 17¹³⁄₁₆ x 22⁵⁄₁₆ in., (45.2 x 56.6 cm.), etching on light textured copper print (BP 2736, DM 6900, FR 23,224, Y 459,474).

$385* *Portfolio #347,* (04-23-93, Clearing House, #267), (BP 245, DM 609, FR 2057, Y 42,523).

$75* *Portrait,* pub. Mourlot, s. Picasso in plate, (07-14-92, Encans, #239), 17¹¹⁄₁₆ x 11¹³⁄₁₆ in., (45 x 30 cm.), lithograph (BP 39, DM 111, FR 375, Y 9379, C$ 89).

$3103* *Portrait "Pour Daniel-Henry Kahnweiler" (Bloch 1179), 1964,* s., d., (09-25-92, Granier, #2975, illus.), sheet 11¹³⁄₁₆ x 9¹³⁄₁₆ in., (30 x 25 cm.), lithograph on handmade BFK (BP 1812, DM 4600, FR 15,554, Y 374,532).

$9163* *Portrait D'Homme A La Fraise. Variation D'Apres El Greco (Baer 1320/B/b/2; Bl. 1148), 1962,* s., i. Epreuve d'artiste, (06-23-93, Kornfeld, #730), color linocut on wove (BP 6225, DM 15,504, FR 52,151, Y 998,257, SF 13,800).

$2090* *Portrait De D.H. Kahnweiler, I (B. 834), 1957,* red crayon s., #4/50, good cond.?, foxing, stain, creases, (10-28-92, Butterfield, #2691, illus.), 25¾ x 19⅞ in., (654 x 505 mm.), lithograph on Arches (BP 1332, DM 3228, FR 10,960, Y 256,442).

$2749* *Portrait De Dora Maar Au Chignon. II (Baer 612/C/b; Bl. 292), 1936,* p. 1961, pub. 1981, num., (06-23-93, Kornfeld, #678), drypoint on handmade (BP 1868, DM 4651, FR 15,646, Y 299,488, SF 4140).

$5345* *Portrait De Famille Ingresque. IV (Baer 1337/B/b; Bl. 1146), 1962,* s., num., epreuve de passe, (06-23-93, Kornfeld, #732), color linocut on wove (BP 3631, DM 9044, FR 30,421, Y 582,307, SF 8050).

$47,172* *Portrait De Femme A La Frise Et Au Chapeau (Baer 1323/B/b/2; Bloch 1145), 1962,* s. Picasso, epreuve d'artiste, (06-25-93, Kornfeld, #117, illus.), image 21¹⁄₁₆ x 15⅜ in., (53.5 x 39 cm.), sheet 24⁹⁄₁₆ x 17⁵⁄₁₆ in., (53.5 x 39 cm.), color linocut on thick Arches vellum (BP 31,905, DM 80,306, FR 270,482, Y 5,000,212, SF 71,300).

$5040* *Portrait De Femme Au Col En Ruche: Marie-Therese (Baer 671/B/b; Bl. 323), 1939,* num., (06-23-93, Kornfeld, #680, illus.), aquatint (BP 3424, DM 8528, FR 28,685, Y 549,079, SF 7590).

$28,750* *Portrait De Femme De Profil, Epreuve Rincee (Baer 1361), 1965,* wide margins, good cond., prov., (05-11-93, Christie-NY, #291, illus.), sheet 29½ x 24¼ in., (749 x 616 mm.), linocut in cream w/encre de Chine on Arches (BP 18,353, DM 45,290, FR 152,601, Y 3,162,468).

$16,799* *Portrait De Francoise Aux Cheveux Flous (Baer 791 B/b/2; Bl. 457), 1947,* s., i. epreuve d'artiste, (06-23-93,

Kornfeld, #681, illus.), aquatint on wove (BP 11,412, DM 28,425, FR 95,612, Y 1,830,156, SF 25,300).

$10,350* *Portrait De Jacqueline (B. 827), 1956,* s., #48/100, full margins, mat staining, good cond., (05-11-93, Christie-NY, #274, illus.), borderline 20½ x 15¾ in., (521 x 400 mm.), lithograph black and brown on Arches (BP 6607, DM 16,304, FR 54,936, Y 1,138,489).

$30,434* *Portrait De Jacqueline (Baer 1245/B/b; Bloch 923), 1959,* s. Picasso, artist's proof, (06-25-93, Kornfeld, #109, illus.), 25⅛ x 20¹¹⁄₁₆ in., (63.8 x 52.5 cm.), color linocut on vellum (BP 20,584, DM 51,811, FR 174,507, Y 3,225,991, SF 46,000).

$1867* *Portrait De Jacqueline (G.B. 827, Mourlot 289), 1956,* from 500, trimmed, s., cracks, small margins, (06-16-93, Ader Tajan, #125), 20½ x 14⁹⁄₁₆ in., (52 x 37 cm.), color lithograph (BP 1245, DM 3099, FR 10,401, Y 199,125).

$33,477* *Portrait De Jacqueline Aux Cheveux Lisses (Baer 1302/IV/B/b; Bloch 1066), 1962,* s., (06-25-93, Kornfeld, #114, illus.), 24¹⁵⁄₁₆ x 20¾ in., (63.4 x 52.7 cm.), color linocut on Arches vellum (BP 22,643, DM 56,992, FR 191,955, Y 3,548,548, SF 50,600).

$21,381* *Portrait De Jacqueline De Face. II (Baer 1278/III/B/b; Bl. 1064), 1961,* s., i. une vingtaine d'epreuves d'artiste, (06-23-93, Kornfeld, #725), color linocut on wove (BP 14,525, DM 36,178, FR 121,690, Y 2,329,339, SF 32,200).

$14,508* *Portrait De Jacqueline En Carmen (Baer 1324/IV/B/b; Bl. 1095), 1962,* s., num., epreuve de passe, (06-23-93, Kornfeld, #731, illus.), color linocut on wove (BP 9856, DM 24,548, FR 82,573, Y 1,580,564, SF 21,850).

$228,252* *Portrait De Jeune Fille, D'Apres Cranach Le Jeune. II (Baer 1053/B/i; Bloch 859), 1958,* s., d. Picasso, le 11.12/58, ded., (06-25-93, Kornfeld, #108, illus.), image 25½ x 21¹⁄₁₆ in., (64.7 x 53.5 cm.), sheet 30⁹⁄₁₆ x 22⁷⁄₁₆ in., (64.7 x 53.5 cm.), color linocut on thick vellum (BP 154,381, DM 388,580, FR 1,308,784, Y 24,194,615, SF 345,000).

$884* *Portrait De Paul Valery I (G. Bloch, 39; P. Cramer, 9), 1920,* s. after edit., crack, yellowed, small margins, (06-16-93, Ader Tajan, #124), 3¾ x 3¹⁄₁₆ in., (9.6 x 7.7 cm.), lithograph (BP 589, DM 1467, FR 4925, Y 94,283).

$2420* *Portrait De Pierre Crommelynck (Bloch 1378), 1966,* num., s., (05-27-93, Swann, #221, illus.), 22 x 15⅜ in., (55.9 x 39.1 cm.), soft ground etching and aquatint (BP 1550, DM 3883, FR 13,088, Y 259,434).

$2447* *Portrait De Vollard Au Chat,* s. E.A., (05-12-93, AB Stockholm, #7043, illus.), 23⅝ x 17¹⁵⁄₁₆ in., (60 x 45.5 cm.), color aquatint on BFK (BP 1598, DM 3948, FR 13,299, Y 273,194, SK 18,150).

$5750* *"Portrait De Vollard II" and "Portrait De Vollard IV" (B. 231 and 233; S.V. 98 and 100), c. 1937: Two,* from Vollard suite, crayon s., full margins, good cond., mat stain, fox marks, (05-13-93, Sotheby-NY, #697), one 13¾ x 9¾ in., (348 x 248 mm.), other 13⅝ x 9¾ in., (348 x 248 mm.), aquatint (BP 3775, DM 9285, FR 31,318, Y 641,956).

$2860* *Portrait De Vollard, III (B. 232; Baer 617; S.V. 98), c. 1937,* from Vollard suite, s., full margins, good cond., mat stain, (11-05-92, Sotheby-NY, #341), 13⅝ x 9¾ in., (347 x 248 mm.), aquatint (BP 1860, DM 4523, FR 15,302, Y 350,877).

$295* *Portrait Of A Man,* s. 158/200, (11-07-92, Falkkloos, #441), lithograph in colors (BP 193, DM 473, FR 1592, Y 36,411, SK 1760).

$24,347* *Portrait Stylise De Jacqueline (Baer 1285/IV/B/b; Bloch 1065), 1962,* s. Picasso, artist's proof, (06-25-93, Kornfeld, #113, illus.), 25⅛ x 20¹³⁄₁₆ in., (63.8 x 52.8 cm.), color linocut on Arches vellum (BP 16,467, DM 41,449, FR 139,604, Y 2,580,772, SF 36,800).

$818* *Portraits Imaginaires (Czwiklitzer 407), 1971,* watermark, stone s., d., (06-19-93, Wachholtz, #677), plate 30⅛ x 22¹⁄₁₆ in., (76.5 x 56 cm.), color lithograph on copper print paper (BP 549, DM 1381, FR 4642, Y 90,677).

BI *La Pose Nue (M. 255; B. 761), 1954,* s., #27/50, full margins, staining, creases, good cond., est. BP 2,5/3,000, (12-01-92, Christie-London, #491), L. 25⁹⁄₁₆ x 19¹¹⁄₁₆ in., (650 x 500 mm.), lithograph on Arches.

BI *Poteries, Fleurs, Parfums, Vallauris (Czwiklitzer 1, Bloch 1258, Mourlot 118), 1948,* pub. Mourlot, est. FF 3/4,000, (11-16-92, Briest, #347), 23¹³⁄₁₆ x 15¾ in., (60.5 x 40 cm.), lithograph poster.

$928* *Poteries, Fleurs, Parfums, Valluaris (Czwilklitzer 1, Bloch 1258, Mourlot 118), 1948,* (03-31-93, Briest, #E188), 23¹³⁄₁₆ x 15¾ in., (60.5 x 40 cm.), lithograph poster (BP 614, DM 1493, FR 5071, Y 106,716).

$495* *Potteries De Picasso,* pen s., foxing, time discoloration, (06-11-93, Freemn/Fine Art, #177, illus.), 23¾ x 15¾ in., (60.3 x 40 cm.), lithographic poster (BP 325, DM 804, FR 2712, Y 52,520).

BI *La Poule (B. 694), 1952,* s., $36/50, margins, light/mat staining, creasing, good cond., est. $7/9,000, (05-11-93, Christie-NY, #272, illus.), plate 20¼ x 26 in., (514 x 660 mm.), drypoint and aquatint on Arches.

BI *"Pour Jacqueline", 1960,* plate s., d., est. DM 3,000, (09-05-92, Arnold, #6, illus.), 16⅛ x 21⅛ in., (41 x 53.7 cm.), lithograph.

BI *Pour Toby,* est. $3/500, (05-16-93, Hanzel, #484), 8½ x 6 in., (21.6 x 15.2 cm.), etching.

$11,454* *Profil Au Fond Noir (Mourl. 83; Bl. 437), 1947,* s., i. Epreuve d'artiste, (06-23-93, Kornfeld, #704), lithograph on wove (BP 7781, DM 19,381, FR 65,191, Y 1,247,848, SF 17,250).

BI *Profil De Femme (B. 436), 1947,* s., #36/50, margins, mount/light-stained, tear, skinning, est. BP 4/6,000, (06-30-93, Sotheby-London, #600, illus.), sh 22¼ x 15 in., (565 x 381 mm.), lithograph on Arches.

BI *Profil Et Femme (B. 1195), 1965,* s., #26/50, full margins, good cond., est. BP 1,6/2,000, (12-03-92, Sotheby-London, #541, illus.), 15⅝ x 10¾ in., (385 x 274 mm.), aquatint on BFK Rives.

$2596* *Profil Scuptural De Marie-Therese (G.-Baer 294/III/C; Bl. 255), 1933,* (06-23-93, Kornfeld, #659), etching and drypoint on handmade (BP 1764, DM 4393, FR 14,775, Y 282,819, SF 3910).

$2530* *Profils (B. 1379), 1966,* s., #11/50, full margins, tape, excell. cond., (05-11-93, Christie-NY, #300), plate 10⅞ x 15¼ in., (276 x 387 mm.), etching and aquatint on BFK Rives (BP 1615, DM 3986, FR 13,429, Y 278,297).

$19,250* *Quatre Femmes Nue Et Tete Sculptee (B. 219), 1934,* plate 82 from the Suite Vollard, watermark, s., full margins, excellent cond., (11-09-92, Christie-NY, #154, illus.), 8¾ x 12⅜ in., (222 x 314 mm.), etching on Montval (BP 12,727, DM 30,731, FR 103,830, Y 2,388,930).

$16,500* *Quatre Femmes Nues Et Tete Sculptee (B. 219; G. 424; S.V. 82), 1934,* from Vollard suite, s., full margins, good cond., (11-05-92, Sotheby-NY, #337, illus.), 8¾ x 12⅜ in., (221 x 313 mm.), etching w/burin (BP 10,732, DM 26,095, FR 88,283, Y 2,024,291).

$1069* *Radierung Vom 25. Marz 1971. IV (Bl. 1950), 1971,* sig. stamp, num., sheet from series 156 Gravures, (06-23-93, Kornfeld, #700), etching (BP 726, DM 1809, FR 6084, Y 116,461, SF 1610).

$1756* *Le Rapt (Baer 950/B/b/1; Bl. 775), 1955,* p. 1961, pub. 1981, sig. stamp, num., (06-23-93, Kornfeld, #687), etching (BP 1193, DM 2971, FR 9994, Y 191,306, SF 2645).

BI *Reclining Nude,* s. Picasso, i., est. $4/600, (06-26-93, Wolf, #965), 15 x 22 in., (38.1 x 55.9 cm.), lithograph.

$9163* *Rembrandt Tenant Par La Main Une Jeune Femme Au Voile (Bloch 214; Baer 413 B d), 1934,* sheet 36 of Suite Vollard, (05-26-93, Lempertz, #446, illus.), 17⁷⁄₁₆ x 15¼ in., (44.3 x 38.8 cm.), etching on Montval (BP 5928, DM 14,950, FR 50,319, Y 995,545).

$1495* *La Rentree Du Taureau (B. 386; Mourlot 167), 1945,* s., #22/50, full margins, good cond., creases, glued to backing, (02-11-93, Sotheby-NY, #212), 6¼ x 11¹⁵⁄₁₆ in., (158 x 303 mm.), lithograph (BP 1055, DM 2476, FR 8380, Y 180,229).

$444* *"Le Repas Du Sculpteur Devant Un Centaure Et Une Femme-1933-Be 167",* Paris 31 mars XXXIII, s. Picasso, t., d., (03-16-93, Encans, #200), 7⅞ x 10¹³⁄₁₆ in., (20 x 27.5 cm.), etching on Arches (BP 307, DM 738, FR 2508, Y 51,918, C$ 555).

$101,500* *Le Repas Frugal (Bloch 1), 1904,* from La Suite des Saltimbanques, pub. Vollard 1913 after plate was steel-faced, wide (full?) margins, staining, surface scuffs (some touched), verygood cond., (05-11-93, Christie-NY, #255, illus.), plate 18¼ x 14¾ in., (464 x 375 mm.), etching on Van Gelder Zonen (BP 64,794, DM 159,893, FR 538,747, Y 11,164,888).

$122,542* *Le Repas Frugal (Bloch 1; Geiser 2), 1904,* from Saltimbanques, pub. Vollard, 1913, full margins, good cond., (10-14-92, Sotheby-Japan, #59, illus.), 18⅛ x 14⅞ in., (460 x 378 mm.), etching on Van Gelder Zonen paper (BP 71,927, DM 179,339, FR 608,149, Y 14,849,976).

BI *Le Repas Frugal (Bloch 1; Geiser 2), 1904,* from the Saltimbanques suite, margins, discoloration, creases throughimage, scuffs, losses, tack holes, repaired tears, est. $20/40,000, (02-11-93, Sotheby-NY, #208, illus.), 18⅛ x 14⅞ in., (461 x 378 mm.), sheet 21¹³⁄₁₆ x 16⁷⁄₁₆ in., (461 x 378 mm.), etching.

$93,500* *Le Repas Frugal (Bloch 1; Geiser 2), 1904,* from Saltimbanques suite, plate tone, pub. Vollard, 1913, full margins, good cond., light staining, foxing, creases, soiling in margin edges, previously folded back, thin spots, (11-05-92, Sotheby-NY, #319, illus.), 18¼ x 14¾ in., (462 x 375 mm.), etching on cream Van Gelder Zonen wove (BP 60,813, DM 147,873, FR 500,268, Y 11,470,985).

$96,000* *Le Repas Frugal (Bloch 1; Geiser 2), 1904,* from Saltimbanques suite, pub. Vollard, 1913, full margins, good cond., tears, mat stain, foxing, glue, handling creases, (05-13-93, Sotheby-NY, #670, illus.), 18⅛ x 14⅞ in., (461 x 377 mm.), etching on Van Gelder Zonen wove (BP 63,025, DM 155,014, FR 522,876, Y 10,717,874).

BI *Le Repas Frugal (Bloch 1; Geiser 2), 1905,* from Saltimbanques Suite, pub. Vollard, 1913, margins, good cond., staining, skinned, est. BP 55/60,000, (06-30-93, Sotheby-London, #580, illus.), sh 25 x 20 in., (635 x 508 mm.), etching on Van Gelder Zonen.

$104,235* *Le Repas Frugal (Geiser-Baer 2/II/b/2; Bloch 1; Johnson 1977, 85.1),* (06-25-93, Kornfeld, #90, illus.), plate 18¼ x 14¹³⁄₁₆ in., (46.3 x 37.7 cm.), sheet 25¹³⁄₁₆ x 20¹⁄₁₆ in., (46.3 x 37.7 cm.), zinc etching on thick vellum (BP 70,501, DM 177,451, FR 597,678, Y 11,048,866, SF 157,550).

$12,100* *La Repetition (B. 756; M. 252), 1954,* s., #49/50, good cond., mat stain, creases, foxing, stamp, (11-05-92, Sotheby-NY, #352, illus.), 19¾ x 25⅝ in., (500 x 652 mm.), lithograph (BP 7870, DM 19,136, FR 64,741, Y 1,484,480).

$11,000* *Le Repos De Sculpteur (B. 171; G. 324; S.V. 62), 1933,* from Vollard suite, brushpoint s., #3/3, large margins, foxing, mat staining, tape stains, good cond., (rippling, tack holes), (11-05-92, Sotheby-NY, #329, illus.), 7½ x 10⅛ in., (190 x 257 mm.), sheet 16¼ x 20⅝ in., (190 x 257 mm.), etching on parchment (BP 7154, DM 17,397, FR 58,855, Y 1,349,528).

BI *Le Repos De Sculpteur Devant Une Bacchanale Au Taureau, Plate 56 (G.318; Bl. 165), 1933,* watermark, s., margins, discoloration, very good cond., est. BP 3,8/4,000, (12-01-92, Christie-London, #484), plate 7⅝ x 10½ in., (194 x 266 mm.), etching on Montval.

$5940* *Le Repos Du Sculpteur Devant Le Jeune Cavalier, 1933,* s., plate 55 of Suite Vollard, w/Picasso watermark, (06-13-93, Hindman, #377, illus.), sh 7½ x 13¼ in., (19.1 x 33.7 cm.), etching (BP 3888, DM 9668, FR 32,495, Y 625,066).

$5999* *Le Repos Du Sculpteur Devant Un Centauer Et Une Femme (Bloch 167, Geiser 320 IIc), 1933,* s., sheet 58 from Vollard Suite, watermark, (12-04-92, AB Stockholm, #7114), 7⅝ x 10½ in., (19.4 x 26.7 cm.), etching on Montval (BP 3848, DM 9554, FR 32,410, Y 748,939, SK 40,700).

BI *Le Repos Du Sculpteur Devant Un Centaur Et Une Femme (B. 167), 1933,* bears sig., watermark, full margins, staining, remains of glue, goodcond., est. $7/9,000, (11-09-92, Christie-NY, #152, illus.), 7⁹⁄₁₆ x 10½ in., (192 x 266 mm.), etching on Montval.

BI *Le Repos Du Sculpteur Devant Un Centaure Et Une Femme (B. 167; G. 320; S.V. 58), 1933,* from Vollard suite, s., full margins, good cond., discoloration, est.$7/9,000, (05-13-93, Sotheby-NY, #688, illus.), 7⅝ x 10½ in., (194 x 268 mm.), etching.

$7475* *La Repos Du Sculpteur Devant Un Nu A La Draperie (B. 160; G. 313; S.V. 51), 1933,* from Vollard suite, s., full margins, good cond., fox marks, (05-13-93, Sotheby-NY, #686, illus.), 10½ x 7⅝ in., (267 x 193 mm.), etching (BP 4907, DM 12,070, FR 40,714, Y 834,543).

BI *Le Repos Du Sculpteur Et La Sculpture Surrealiste (B. 169; G. 322; S.V. 60), 1933,* from Vollard suite, s., large margins, (trimmed), good cond., est. $8/10,000, (05-13-93, Sotheby-NY, #689, illus.), 7⅝ x 10½ in., (194 x 268 mm.), etching.

$6863* *Le Repos Du Sculpteur I (b. 171), 1933,* from Vollard Suite, s., watermarked, full margins, good cond., (06-30-93, Sotheby-London, #589, illus.), 7½ x 10⅝ in., (191 x 270 mm.), etching on Montval laid (BP 4600, DM 11,706, FR 39,488, Y 735,348).

$7475* *Les Repos Du Sculpteur, IV (B. 174; G. 327; S.V. 65), 1933,* from the Vollard suite, s., full margins, good cond., light-stain, foxing, (02-11-93, Sotheby-NY, #210, illus.), 7⅝ x 10⁹⁄₁₆ in., (193 x 268 mm.), etching (BP 5274, DM 12,382, FR 41,900, Y 901,145).

$6600* *Le Repos Su Sculpteur Devant Un Nu A La Draperie (B. 160; G. 313; S.V. 51), 1933,* from Vollard Suite, s., full margins, good cond., discoloration, (11-05-92, Sotheby-NY, #328, illus.), 10⅜ x 7½ in., (264 x 192 mm.), etching (BP 4293, DM 10,438, FR 35,313, Y 809,717).

$3069* *Robert Desnos. Contree (B. 362), 1943,* #147/200, p. Lacouriere, margins, good cond., (skinned patch), (12-03-92, Sotheby-London, #498, illus.), 14⅜ x 15⅞ in., (365 x 405 mm.), etching (BP 1980, DM 4826, FR 16,473, Y 381,859).

$440* *La Ronde,* for La Paix, s., d. in plate 25-7-61, s. Picasso, pub. blindstamp, (06-26-93, Wolf, #968), (BP 295, DM 748, FR 2519, Y 46,684).

$8800* *Sable Mouvant (B. 1183-1192, bk. no. 129; Goeppert/Cramer 136), 1966,* book, s. by artist, num., pub. Louis Broder, good cond., stains, (11-05-92, Sotheby-NY, #368, illus.), each sheet approx. 18⅞ x 15 in., (480 x 380 mm.), ten aquatints (BP 5724, DM 13,917, FR 47,084, Y 1,079,622).

$4093* *Sable Mouvant (B. 1185), 1965,* s., #6/50, pub. Louis Broder, watermarked, full margins, good cond., (12-03-92, Sotheby-London, #536, illus.), 15 x 10⅞ in., (380 x 275 mm.), aquatint on wove (BP 2640, DM 6437, FR 21,970, Y 509,270).

$2750* *Sable Mouvant (B. 1187; Baer 1156; G./C. 136), 1965,* s., #VIII/X, pub. Louis Broder, 1966, full margins, good cond., mat/light stain, loss, (11-05-92, Sotheby-NY, #369), 15 x 10⅞ in., (381 x 276 mm.), aquatint (BP 1789, DM 4349, FR 14,714, Y 337,382).

BI *Sable Mouvant: Plates II; And IV (B. 1184 and 1188; Baer 1153 and 1157; see G./C. 136), 1964: Two,* separate suite, s., #14/50, #12/50, p. Crommelynck, pub. Louis Broder, 1966, full margins, good cond., fox mark, traces glue, soiling, glue stain, est. $6/7,000, (05-13-93, Sotheby-NY, #723), each 15⅛ x 11 in., (385 x 280 mm.), xin., (385 x 280 mm.), aquatint.

$4775* *Salome (B. 14), 1905,* from the Saltimbanques Suite, pub. Vollard 1913, full margins, severely mount stained, light stained, (12-03-92, Sotheby-London, #482, illus.), 15¾ x 13¾ in., (401 x 346 mm.), drypoint on Van Gelder Zonen (BP 3080, DM 7509, FR 25,631, Y 594,127).

BI *Salome (B. 14), 1905,* from the Saltimbanques Suite, pub. Vollard, 1913, full margins, goodcond., discoloration, skinned, est. BP 10/12,000, (06-30-93, Sotheby-London, #583, illus.), 15¾ x 13¾ in., (400 x 349 mm.), drypoint on Van Gelder Zonen.

$7150* *Salome (B. 14; G. 17), 1905,* from Saltimbanques suite, pub. Vollard, 1913, large margins, good cond., foxing, mat stain, skinned spots, repaired tears, (11-05-92, Sotheby-NY, #323, illus.), 15⅞ x 13¾ in., (402 x 348 mm.), sheet 22½ x 19¾ in., (402 x 348 mm.), drypoint on Van Gelder Zonen wove (BP 4650, DM 11,308, FR 38,256, Y 877,193).

$18,442* *Salome (Geiser 17 b; Bloch 14), 1905,* Vollard, (06-05-93, Bassenge, #6436, illus.), 15¾ x 13⅝ in., (40 x 34.6 cm.), drypoint on Van-Gelder-Zonen (BP 12,140, DM 29,899, FR 100,776, Y 1,978,331).

$3220* *Le Saltimbanque En Repos (B. 10), 1905,* from La Suite des Saltimbanques, pub. Vollard 1913 after plate was steel-faced, wide margins, light/mat staining, good cond., (05-11-93, Christie-NY, #256, illus.), plate 4¾ x 3⅜ in., (121 x 86 mm.), etching on wove (BP 2056, DM 5072, FR 17,091, Y 354,196).

$1364* *La Sauterelle (B. 358), 1936,* from Georges Luis Leclerc, comte de Buffon. Histoire Naturelle, s., margins, p. Lacouriere, pub. Martin Fabiani, 1942, full margins, good cond., (12-03-92, Sotheby-London, #497, illus.), 17¼ x 13 in., (438 x 330 mm.), aquatint, scraper and drypoint, on Montval laid (BP 880, DM 2145, FR 7322, Y 169,715).

$3410* *Le Sauvetage II (B. 245; G. 273), 1932,* s., #18/50, 1961, Galerie Louise Leiris, full margins, good cond., creases, (12-03-92, Sotheby-London, #494, illus.), 6¼ x 7⅞ in., (160 x 200 mm.), etching w/tone on laid Arches (BP 2200, DM 5362, FR 18,304, Y 424,288).

$2875* *Scene Antique (B. 801; M. 286), 1956,* s., #38/50, full margins, good cond., light-stain, foxing, skinned spot, (05-13-93, Sotheby-NY, #703), 17¾ x 13¾ in., (450 x 350 mm.), lithograph (BP 1887, DM 4642, FR 15,659, Y 320,978).

$11,084* *Scene Bacchique Au Minotaure (B. 192), 1933,* from Vollard Suite, s., watermark, margins, good cond., mount staining, (12-03-92, Sotheby-London, #490, illus.), 13⅜ x 17¾ in., (341 x 450 mm.), etching on Montval laid (BP 7150, DM 17,430, FR 59,495, Y 1,379,122).

$1716* *Scene Buccolique Avec Amour Aux Castagnetes (B. 772), 1955,* sig. stamp, #2/50, p. by Atelier Lacouriere et Frelaut, margins, goodcond., discoloration, (06-30-93, Sotheby-London, #606, illus.), 10 x 12⅛ in., (254 x 308 mm.), etching on wove (BP 1150, DM 2927, FR 9873, Y 183,864).

$2899* *Scene D'Atelier (B. 1124), 1963,* s., #41/50, full margins, good cond., creasing, (12-03-92, Sotheby-London, #527, illus.), 12¼ x 16⅜ in., (312 x 415 mm.), etching on Rives (BP 1870, DM 4559, FR 15,561, Y 360,707).

$2530* *Scene De Theatre (B. 1397), 1966,* s., #19/50, full margins, creases, surface soiling, tape, good cond., (05-11-93, Christie-NY, #303), plate 12½ x 18½ in., (318 x 470 mm.), etching and aquatint on BFK (BP 1615, DM 3986, FR 13,429, Y 278,297).

$3581* *Scene Mythologique (B. 1398), 1966,* s., num., full margins, good cond., (12-03-92, Sotheby-London, #546, illus.), 10½ x 14¾ in., (268 x 375 mm.), drypoint on BFK Rives (BP 2310, DM 5631, FR 19,222, Y 445,564).

$4400* *Sculpteur A Mi-Corps Au Travail, 1933,* s., plate 49 of Suite Vollard, Picasso watermark, (06-13-93, Hindman, #376), sh 17½ x 13¼ in., (19.1 x 33.7 cm.), etching (BP 2880, DM 7161, FR 24,070, Y 463,012).

$3054* *Sculpteur Au Repos Avec Son Modele, Anemones Et Petit Torse (G.-Baer315/A/b; Bl. 152), 1933,* sheet 53 of Suite Vollard, (06-23-93, Kornfeld, #668), etching on wove (BP 2075, DM 5168, FR 17,382, Y 332,716, SF 4600).

$3818* *Sculpteur Avec Son Modele, Sa Sculpture Et Un Bol D'Anemones (G.-Baer 308/II/B/d; Bl. 155), 1933,* sheet 39 of Suite Vollard, (06-23-93, Kornfeld, #665), etching on handmade (BP 2594, DM 6460, FR 21,730, Y 415,949, SF 5750).

$24,078* *"Sculpteur Et Modele Agenouille (Bloch 178; Geiser 331/ IIc), 1933,* watermark, sheet 69 from Suite Vollard, (06-04-93, Grisebach, #46, illus.), 14½ x 11⅝ in., (36.8 x 29.6 cm.), woodcut on handmade copper print paper (BP 15,930, DM 39,100, FR 131,790, Y 2,596,851).

$2749* *Sculpteur Et Son Autoportrait Sculpte Servant De Socle A Une Tete DeMarie-Therese (G.-Baer 310/B/d; Bl. 157), 1933,* sheet 48 of Suite Vollard, (06-23-93, Kornfeld, #666), etching on handmade (BP 1868, DM 4651, FR 15,646, Y 299,488, SF 4140).

$337* *"Sculpteur Et Son Modele Devant Une Fenetre-1933-Be 168",* Paris 31 mars XXIII, s. Picasso, t., d. verso, (03-16-93, Encans, #199), 7⅞ x 10¹³⁄16 in., (20 x 27.5 cm.), etching on Arches (BP 233, DM 560, FR 1904, Y 39,406, C$ 422).

$7700* *Sculpteur Et Trois Danseuses Sculptees (B. 217; G. 421; S.V. 81), 1934,* from Vollard suite, s., full margins, good cond., rubbed fox mark, (11-05-92, Sotheby-NY, #336, illus.), 8⅞ x 12⅜ in., (224 x 314 mm.), etching (BP 5008, DM 12,178, FR 41,199, Y 944,669).

$7475* *Sculpteur Et Trois Danseuses Sculptees (B. 217; G. 421; S.V. 81), 1934,* from Vollard suite, s., full margins, good cond., foxing in image, mat stain, (05-13-93, Sotheby-NY, #695, illus.), 8¾ x 12¼ in., (223 x 312 mm.), etching (BP 4907, DM 12,070, FR 40,714, Y 834,543).

BI *Sculpteur Et Trois Danseuses Sculptees (Bloch 217, Geiser 421 II c),1934,* s., staining, est. SF 8/12,000, (09-04-92, Germann, #93, illus.), 13⁹⁄16 x 17⅝ in., (345 x 448 mm.), etching.

$3207* *Sculpteur, Garcon Et Modele Avec Un Groupe Sculpte Representant Le Rapt D'Europe (G.-Baer 318/A/b; Bl. 165), 1933,* sheet 56 of Suite Vollard, (06-23-93, Kornfeld, #669), etching on wove (BP 2179, DM 5426, FR 18,253, Y 349,384, SF 4830).

$6325* *Sculpteur, Modele Et Buste Sculpte (B. 148; G. 300; S.V. 38), 1933,* from Vollard suite, s., full margins, good cond., scratch through subject, mat staining, (11-05-92, Sotheby-NY, #327, illus.), 10½ x 7⅝ in., (268 x 194 mm.), etching (BP 4114, DM 10,003, FR 33,842, Y 775,978).

$2825* *Sculpture D'Un Jeune Homme A La Coupe (Bloch 179; Geiser 332 II c), 1933,* s., plate d., watermark, sheet 28 of Suite Vollard, (06-10-93, Hauswedell/Nolt, #780, illus.), image 10½ x 7⅝ in., (26.7 x 19.3 cm.), etching (BP 1848, DM 4600, FR 15,488, Y 299,862).

$4600* *Sculptures Et Vase De Fleurs (B. 189), 1933,* plate 76 from Suite Vollard, watermark, s., full margins, excell. cond., (05-11-93, Christie-NY, #261, illus.), plate 10⁷⁄16 x 7½ in., (265 x 191 mm.), etching and aquatint on Montval (BP 2936, DM 7246, FR 24,416, Y 505,995).

$1216* *Series 347:146 (Bl. 1626),* s., 22/50, from La Celestine, (12-04-92, AB Stockholm, #7116), 2⅜ x 3¼ in., (6 x 8.3 cm.), aquatint (BP 780, DM 1937, FR 6569, Y 151,810, SK 8250).

$1980* *Soldier Facing A Woman, Resting On Top Of A Horse, 1968,* s., #11/50, good cond.?, (12-08-92, Swann, #244, illus.), 3½ x 4¾ in., (8.9 x 12.1 cm.), etching (BP 1241, DM 3083, FR 10,510, Y 245,414).

BI *La Source (B. 45), 1921,* s., #63/100, wide margins, foxing, mat staining, repaired tears, paper losses, good cond., est. $8/12,000, (05-11-93, Christie-NY, #258, illus.), plate 6¾ x 9⅛ in., (171 x 232 mm.), drypoint and engraving in laid.

$6050* *Stylized Figure (M. 131), 1948,* 3rd final state, proof, s., num., surface losses, 1 touched, staining, good cond., (11-09-92, Christie-NY, #161, illus.), 25½ x 19½ in., (648 x 495 mm.), lithograph on Arches (BP 4000, DM 9658, FR 32,632, Y 750,807).

$3300* *Sueno Y Mentira De Franco (B. 297 and 298, book no. 28; Baer 615 and616; G./C. 28), 1937,* complete portfolio, stamp s., #324/850, full margins, good cond., discoloration, in orig. wrappers, (11-05-92, Sotheby-NY, #343), each sheet approx. 15⅜ x 22½ in., (389 x 570 mm.), two etchings w/aquatint (BP 2146, DM 5219, FR 17,657, Y 404,858).

$3220* *Sueno Y Mentira De Franco (B. 297-8, B. Books 28, Cramer 28), 1937: A Pair,* traces atmped sigs., #537/850, margins, mat staining, tears, surfacerubbing, staining, (05-11-93, Christie-NY, #268), each plate 12½ x 16½ in., (318 x 419 mm.), etching and aquatint on Montval (BP 2056, DM 5072, FR 17,091, Y 354,196).

BI *Sueno Y Mentira De Franco (Cramer 28; Manet to Hockney 106),* pub. by author, 1937, unbound as issued, each d. 8 janvier 1937, second etching also d. 9 janvier 1937-7 juin 37, est. $5/8,000, (06-14-93, Sotheby-NY, #240, illus.), 22⅛ x 14⅞ in., (56.2 x 37.8 cm.), 4 unnumbered leaves from 1 sheet folded and 2 single leaves, 2 etchings and aquatint on Montval laid.

$1210* *"Sueno Y Mentira De Franco" (Bloch 297), 1937,* stamp sig., excellent cond., (10-31-92, Cleveland, #321, illus.), 12⅜ x 16⅝ in., (31.4 x 42.2 cm.), engraving and aquatint on Arches (BP 775, DM 1862, FR 6315, Y 149,882).

BI *La Suite 156 (Bl. 1857-1861, 1863-2011), 1968-72,* complete set of 155, each w/sig. stamp, #21/50, excellent cond., est. BP 90/120,000, (12-01-92, Christie-London,

#508, illus.), plate 20 1/16 x 25 3/16 in., (510 x 640 mm.), etching and aquatint on wove.

$3444* *Suite 156, 1970,* #37/50, cachet s., d., lit., (03-25-93, Finarte-Rome, #29, illus.), etching (BP 2339, DM 5658, FR 19,240, Y 403,468, L 5520).

$30,800* *Suite Sable Mouvant (B. 1183-92; see Cramer 1360), 1966: Set Of Ten,* s., num., copy III of XX, full margins, good cond., orig. folders, (11-09-92, Christie-NY, #171, illus.), 15 3/16 x 10 7/8 in., (385 x 277 mm.), aquatint on old Japan (BP 20,364, DM 49,170, FR 166,127, Y 3,822,288).

$998,910* *La Suite Vollard (Bl. 134-233), including "Femme Nue Couronnee De Fleurs", "Femme Nue, Se Couronnant De Fleurs", "Au Bain", "Femme Nue Assise, Devant Un Rideau", "Homme Devoilant Une Femme", etc., 1930-1937,* watermark, complete set of 100, plates 1-97 s., margins, discoloration, very good cond., (12-01-92, Christie-London, #483, illus.), largest plate 14 9/16 x 11 13/16 in., (370 x 300 mm.), etchings, engravings, drypoints and aquatints on Montval (BP 660,000, DM 1,592,142, FR 5,425,910, Y 124,366,285).

BI *La Suite Vollard: Faune Devoilant Une Femme (B. 230), 1936,* full margins, good cond., well-restored tear, creases, surface soiling, hinge remains, est. $40/50,000, (10-28-92, Butterfield, #2689, illus.), 12½ x 16½ in., (318 x 419 mm.), sheet 13½ x 17½ in., (318 x 419 mm.), etching and aquatint on Montval paper w/watermark.

$4400* *La Suite Vollard: Le Viol Sous La Fenetre (B. 183), 1933,* s., pub. Ambroise Vollard, 1939, margin slightly trimmed, good cond.,light-staining, pencil notations, (02-24-93, Butterfield, #2773, illus.), 10 7/8 x 7¾ in., (276 x 197 mm.), sheet 17¾ x 13 9/16 in., (276 x 197 mm.), aquatint, etching & drypoint on Montval w/watermark (BP 3068, DM 7143, FR 24,216, Y 516,311).

BI *La Suite Vollard: Modele Et Grande Tete Sculptee (B. 170), 1933,* s., pub. Ambroise Vollard, 1939, full margins, right margin slightlytrimmed, good cond., crease, pencil notations, ex-coll. Marina Picasso, est. $6/8,000, (02-24-93, Butterfield, #2772, illus.), 10½ x 7 5/8 in., (267 x 194 mm.), sheet 17½ x 13 9/16 in., (267 x 194 mm.), etching on Montval w/watermark.

$3575* *La Suite Vollard: Vieux Sculpteur Au Travail (B. 153), 1933,* s., plate tone, pub. Ambroise Vollard, 1939, left margin trimmed, good cond., mat staining, (02-24-93, Butterfield, #2771, illus.), 10½ x 7½ in., (267 x 191 mm.), sheet 17¾ x 13 7/16 in., (267 x 191 mm.), etching & scraper on Montval w/watermark (BP 2493, DM 5804, FR 19,675, Y 419,502).

$6325* *"Susanne Et Les Vieillards" and "Buste De Femme" (B. 1390 and 1392),1966: Two,* s., #36/50, #38/50, full margins, good cond., skinned spots, (05-13-93, Sotheby-NY, #730), one 10 7/8 x 15 in., (275 x 380 mm.), other 14¾ x 10½ in., (275 x 380 mm.), etching and aquatint, and aquatint (BP 4152, DM 10,213, FR 34,450, Y 706,152).

$21,381* *La Table (G.-Baer 24/b/4; Bl. 20), 1910,* s. in red pencil, prov., (06-23-93, Kornfeld, #647, illus.), etching on cream Japan (BP 14,525, DM 36,178, FR 121,690, Y 2,329,339, SF 32,200).

$189,500* *Le Taureau (B. 389; M. 17), 1945-46: Ten,* 2nd through the 11th (final) states, from the set of proof impressions reserved for artist, good cond., (05-13-93, Sotheby-NY, #701, illus.), sh approx. 13 x 17¾ in., (330 x 450 mm.), lithograph on wove (BP 124,409, DM 305,991, FR 1,032,135, Y 21,156,637).

$12,100* *Taureau Aile Contemple Par Quatre Enfants (B. 229; G. 444; S.V. 13),1934,* from Vollard suite, s., full margins, good cond., (11-05-92, Sotheby-NY, #339, illus.), 9 3/8 x 11¾ in., (237 x 298 mm.), etching (BP 7870, DM 19,136, FR 64,741, Y 1,484,480).

$771* *Taureau De Profil (Mourlot 27), 1945,* proofs, full margins, good cond., ex coll. Marina Picasso, (06-30-93, Sotheby-London, #595, illus.), 11 7/8 x 16 5/8 in., (302 x 422 mm.), lithograph on Arches (BP 517, DM 1315, FR 4436, Y 82,610).

$3163* *Taureau Et Chevaux Dans L'Arene)B. 203; G. 380; S.V. 15), 1933,* from Vollard suite, s., full margins, good cond., foxing, mat stain, (05-13-93, Sotheby-NY, #694), 7 5/8 x 10½ in., (193 x 267 mm.), etching (BP 2077, DM 5107, FR 17,228, Y 353,132).

$5750* *Tete (B. 1164), 1964,* s., #14/50, full margins, light staining, stains, good cond., (05-11-93, Christie-NY, #288), plate 16 3/8 x 12½ in., (416 x 318 mm.), color aquatint and soft-ground etching on Richard de Bas Auvergne a la main (BP 3671, DM 9058, FR 30,520, Y 632,494).

$2728* *Tete (B. 256; G. 295), 1933,* s., #26/50, pub. 1961, Galerie Louise Leiris, full margins, good cond., creases, light staining, (12-03-92, Sotheby-London, #493, illus.), 6 7/8 x 6 1/8 in., (175 x 155 mm.), etching w/tone on Auvergne Richard de Bas laid (BP 1760, DM 4290, FR 14,643, Y 339,430).

BI *Tete (Tete D'Homme Au Maillot Raye) (B., Baer 1164), 1964,* s., #14/50, full margins, good cond., light stain, discoloration, est. $5/6,000, (11-05-92, Sotheby-NY, #363), 16 3/8 x 12¼ in., (417 x 312 mm.), soft ground etching and aquatint p. in colors on Auvergne a la main.

BI *Tete D'Homme (Geiser 32, Bloch 23), 1912,* s., est. DM 18,000, (12-05-92, Bassenge, #7555, illus.), 5 1/16 x 4 5/16 in., (12.9 x 10.9 cm.), etching on handmade.

$11,800* *Tete D'Homme A La Pipe (Bloch 23; Geiser/Baer 32b), 1912,* s., pub. Edition Henry Kahnweiler, full margins, good cond., fox marks, foxing, (10-14-92, Sotheby-Japan, #61, illus.), 5 1/8 x 4 3/8 in., (130 x 111 mm.), etching (BP 6926, DM 17,269, FR 58,561, Y 1,429,956).

$28,912* *Tete D'Homme A La Pipe (Geiser-Baer 32/b; Bloch 23), 1912,* s. Picasso, num., (06-25-93, Kornfeld, #94, illus.), plate 5 1/8 x 4 5/16 in., (13 x 11 cm.), sheet 23¾ x 17 5/16 in., (13 x 11 cm.), etching on handmade Arches (BP 19,555, DM 49,220, FR 165,780, Y 3,064,660, SF 43,700).

$6821* *Tete De Faune (B. 1094; Baer 1291), 1962,* s., num., full margins, good cond., handling creases, paper tone darkened, (12-03-92, Sotheby-London, #524, illus.), 25¼ x 20 5/8 in., (640 x 530 mm.), linocut in colors on Arches (BP 4400, DM 10,727, FR 36,613, Y 848,700).

$6600* *Tete De Faune (B. 1094; Baer 1291), 1962,* s., #24/50, pub. Galerie Louise Leiris, full margins, good cond., mat/light stain, (11-05-92, Sotheby-NY, #358), 25¼ x 20 5/8 in., (640 x 525 mm.), linoleum cut p. in brown and black (BP 4293, DM 10,438, FR 35,313, Y 809,717).

$6309* *Tete De Faune (B. 1370), 1964,* s., #5/50, full margins, good cond., mount-staining, (12-03-92, Sotheby-London, #542, illus.), 21¼ x 15½ in., (540 x 395 mm.), drypoint on wove (BP 4070, DM 9921, FR 33,865, Y 784,994).

$6992* *Tete De Faune (Bl. 1094; Baer 1291), 1962,* s., #30/50, margins, surface dirt, very good cond., (12-01-92, Christie-London, #506), L. 25 3/8 x 20 13/16 in., (644 x 528 mm.), sheet 29 7/8 x 24 5/8 in., (644 x 528 mm.), linocut in colors on Arches (BP 4620, DM 11,144, FR 37,979, Y 870,518).

$43,700* *Tete De Femme (B. 1067), 1962,* s., #1/50, full margins, time staining, very good cond., (05-11-93, Christie-NY, #282, illus.), borderline 25 3/16 x 20 7/8 in., (640 x 530 mm.), color linocut on Arches (BP 27,897, DM 68,841, FR 231,953, Y 4,806,952).

$8250* *Tete De Femme (B. 73), 1926,* s., annot. XI/XXV, from book Picasso Dessins, pub. Editions des Quatre Chemins, full margins, good cond., crease through image, creases, mat staining, tape, (10-28-92, Butterfield, #2688A, illus.), image 5 1/16 x 4¾ in., (129 x 121 mm.), sheet 10 1/8 x 8 3/16 in., (129 x 121 mm.), lithograph on Imperial Japan paper (BP 5256, DM 12,741, FR 43,262, Y 1,012,270).

BI *Tete De Femme (B. 73; Mourlot XX; Goeppart/Cramer 14), 1925,* s., pub. Editions des Quatre Chemins, 1926, full margins, good cond.,discoloration, creases, fox marks, est. $15/18,000, (05-13-93, Sotheby-NY, #678, illus.), 9 x 4 5/8 in., (230 x 118 mm.), lithograph on japon imperiale.

BI *Tete De Femme (Bloch 1064), 1962,* s., num. 21/50, full margins, good cond., mat stain, est. Y 5/6,000,000, (10-14-92, Sotheby-Japan, #69, illus.), 25¼ x 20 7/8 in., (641 x 530 mm.), linoleum cut in beige, brown and black.

BI *Tete De Femme (Bloch; Bucher 14; Bloch 73; Geiser 240; Mourlot 20; Goeppert/Cramer 14), 1925,* s., est. DM 20,000, (06-05-93, Bassenge, #6442, illus.), 10¼ x 8 3/8 in., (26 x 21.2 cm.), lithograph on imperial Japan.

$9689* *Tete De Femme (De Profil) (B. 905), 1959*, s., #2/50, full margins, good cond., light/mount staining, staining,repaired tear, (12-03-92, Sotheby-London, #514, illus.), 25¼ x 21 in., (640 x 532 mm.), linocut in colors (BP 6250, DM 15,237, FR 52,008, Y 1,205,549).

BI *Tete De Femme (Jacqueline Au Chapeau Noir) (B. 1028; Baer 1311), 1962*, s., #2/50, pub. Galerie Louise Leiris, 1963, full margins, good cond., creases, est. $50/60,000, (11-05-92, Sotheby-NY, #356, illus.), 25¼ x 20¾ in., (640 x 526 mm.), sheet 25⅝ x 24½ in., (640 x 526 mm.), linoleum cut p. in colors.

$39,100* *Tete De Femme (Jacqueline Au Chapeau Noir) (B. 1028; Baer 1311), 1962*, s., #2/50, p. Arnera, pub. Galerie Louise Leiris, 1963, full margins,good cond., handling creases, (05-13-93, Sotheby-NY, #714, illus.), 25¼ x 20¾ in., (640 x 526 mm.), sh 25⅝ x 24½ in., (640 x 526 mm.), linoleum cut in colors (BP 25,670, DM 63,136, FR 212,963, Y 4,365,301).

$51,474* *Tete De Femme (Portrait De Jacqueline De Face. I (B. 1064), 1962*, s., #16/50, margins, good cond., creases, skinned areas, (06-30-93, Sotheby-London, #647, illus.), sh 29½ x 24½ in., (749 x 622 mm.), color linocut on Arches (BP 34,500, DM 87,795, FR 296,168, Y 5,515,268).

BI *Tete De Femme (Portrait Stylise De Jacqueline) (B. 1065; Baer 1285),1962*, s., #10/50, p. Arnera, pub. Galerie Louise Leiris, 1963, full margins, good cond., mat stain, tape stains, discolored verso, est. $30/40,000, (05-13-93, Sotheby-NY, #715, illus.), 25¼ x 20¾ in., (640 x 526 mm.), linoleum cut in colors.

$35,810* *Tetes De Femme (Portrait Styliste De Jacqueline) (B. 1065; Baer 1285),1962*, s., #30/50, margins, good cond., light staining, creasing, nicks, abrasions, (12-03-92, Sotheby-London, #520, illus.), sheet 29½ x 24¼ in., (752 x 618 mm.), linocut in colors on Arches (BP 23,100, DM 56,314, FR 192,217, Y 4,455,643).

BI *Tete De Femme A Droite (B. 252), 1933*, watermark, stamped sig., #30/50, margins, crease, mat staining, tape, est. $3/4,000, (05-11-93, Christie-NY, #265), plate 2⅞ x 2⁷⁄₁₆ in., (73 x 62 mm.), soft-ground etching on laid.

$18,700* *Tete De Femme Aux Cheveux Flous (B. 457; Baer 791), 1947*, s., #7/50, pub. Galerie Louise Leiris, full margins, good cond., water stain, foxing, creases, skinning, (11-05-92, Sotheby-NY, #348, illus.), 24⅛ x 17¾ in., (614 x 451 mm.), aquatint (BP 12,163, DM 29,575, FR 100,054, Y 2,294,197).

$11,500* *Tete De Femme De Profil (B. 6; G. 7), 1905*, from Saltimbanques suite, pub. Vollard, 1913, large margins, good cond., pressure marks in plate, foxing, (05-13-93, Sotheby-NY, #672, illus.), 11½ x 9¾ in., (292 x 249 mm.), sh 25¼ x 19½ in., (292 x 249 mm.), etching on cream Van Gelder Zonen wove (BP 7550, DM 18,569, FR 62,636, Y 1,283,912).

$17,250* *Tete De Femme De Profil (B. 905; Baer 1246), 1959*, s., #15/50, p. Arnera, pub. Galerie Louise Leiris, 1960, full margins, good cond., mat/light-stain, discolored, Late Vitya Vronsky Babin Coll., (05-13-93, Sotheby-NY, #707, illus.), 25¼ x 21 in., (640 x 535 mm.), linoleum cut in colors (BP 11,325, DM 27,854, FR 93,954, Y 1,925,868).

$12,100* *Tete De Femme De Profil (B. g; G. 7), 1905*, from Saltimbanques suite, pub. Vollard, 1913, full (large) margins, good cond., light stain, fox marks, touched in rubbed spot, repaired tear, discolored verso, (11-05-92, Sotheby-NY, #321, illus.), 11½ x 9⅞ in., (292 x 251 mm.), etching on cream Van Gelder Zonen wove (BP 7870, DM 19,136, FR 64,741, Y 1,484,480).

$69,914* *Tete De Femme De Profil (Bloch 6; Geiser 7A), 1905*, s., strong burr, plate tone, wiped, p. before steelfacing, full margins, areas of missed printing at top of image, pinhole, mount staining, very good cond., (12-03-92, Sotheby-London, #479, illus.), sheet 20½ x 17¼ in., (520 x 440 mm.), drypoint on Arches (BP 45,100, DM 109,945, FR 375,276, Y 8,699,017).

$19,090* *Tete De Femme No. 4 - Portrait De Dora Maar (Baer 652/D; Bl. 1121), 11939*, s., num., (06-23-93, Kornfeld, #679), color aquatint from 5 plates (BP 12,969, DM 32,301, FR 108,651, Y 2,079,747, SF 28,750).

BI *Tete De Femme No. 6 (Portrait De dora Maar) (bl. 1338; Baer 654D), 1939*, watermark, #4/80, p. Lacouriere, margins, very good cond., est. BP 8/12,000, (12-01-92, Christie-London, #497, illus.), plate 11¹¹⁄₁₆ x 9¼ in., (297 x 235 mm.), aquatint in colors on Montval laid paper.

BI *Tete De Femme Profil (B. 6; G. 7), 1905*, from the Saltimbanques Suite, pub. Vollard, 1913, margins, good cond., discoloration, rubbed, handling mark, est. BP 8/10,000, (06-30-93, Sotheby-London, #582, illus.), sh 21¾ x 20⅛ in., (552 x 511 mm.), drypoint on Van Gelder Zonen.

$939* *Tete De Femme Tournee A Droit (Block 252), #30/50*, 1 of 66 pulled in 1961, black ink s., margins, (12-10-92, Bonhams-Chelsea, #113, illus.), plate 2⅞ x 2⅜ in., (7.3 x 6 cm.), etching on laid paper, maker's watermark (BP 605, DM 1485, FR 5073, Y 116,155).

$19,854* *Tete De Jeune Fille (Mourlot 68/IV; Bloch 423), 1947*, s., i. Epreuve d'artisted, (06-23-93, Kornfeld, #702, illus.), lithograph on wove (BP 13,488, DM 33,594, FR 112,999, Y 2,162,981, SF 29,900).

BI *Tete De Jeune Garcon (B. 378), 1945*, s., $35/50, margins, mat staining, good cond., est. $7/10,000, (05-11-93, Christie-NY, #271, illus.), borderline 12½ x 9½ in., (318 x 241 mm.), lithograph on Arches.

$1380* *Tetes De Beliers (B. 382; M. 19), 1945*, impressions reserved for artist, full margins, good cond., glue stain, (05-13-93, Sotheby-NY, #700, illus.), 9½ x 13⅝ in., (240 x 345 mm.), lithograph on Arches wove (BP 906, DM 2228, FR 7516, Y 154,069).

$3850* *Tetes Et Pierre (B. 682; M. 194), 1950*, s., #39/50, full margins, good cond., foxing, creases, (11-05-92, Sotheby-NY, #351), 18¼ x 23½ in., (465 x 597 mm.), lithograph (BP 2504, DM 6089, FR 20,599, Y 472,335).

$3239* *La Toilette (Bloch 65, Mourlot XV, Geiser 235)*, s. 43/50, tear, (05-27-93, Briest, #157), 14¹⁵⁄₁₆ x 10⅝ in., (38 x 27 cm.), crayon lithograph on Hollande van Gelder (BP 2074, DM 5197, FR 17,518, Y 347,234).

$5750* *La Toilette De La Mer (B. 13; G. 15), 1905*, from Saltimbanques suite, pub. Vollard, 1913, full margins, good cond., thin spot in image, foxing, (05-13-93, Sotheby-NY, #674, illus.), 9⅜ x 7 in., (237 x 178 mm.), etching on Van Gelder Zonen wove (BP 3775, DM 9285, FR 31,318, Y 641,956).

$6600* *La Toilette De La Mere (B. 13; G. 15), 1905*, from Saltimbanques suite, pub. Vollard, 1913, margins, good cond., mat/light stain, fox marks, creases, tear, soiling, (11-05-92, Sotheby-NY, #322, illus.), 9⅜ x 7 in., (237 x 179 mm.), sheet 16 x 12½ in., (237 x 179 mm.), etching (BP 4293, DM 10,438, FR 35,313, Y 809,717).

$9927* *La Toilette De La Mere (G.-Baer 15/b/2; Bl. 13), 1905*, from the series Les Saltimbangues, (06-23-93, Kornfeld, #645, illus.), etching on thick wove (BP 6744, DM 16,797, FR 56,500, Y 1,081,490, SF 14,950).

$1933* *Le Torero Blesse (Bloch 799), 1956*, s., artist's proof, d., oxidation, (06-28-93, Loudmer, #332), 13¹⁵⁄₁₆ x 18¹¹⁄₁₆ in., (355 x 475 mm.), sh 19¹³⁄₁₆ x 25¹⁵⁄₁₆ in., (355 x 475 mm.), black lithograph on Arches wove (BP 1294, DM 3285, FR 11,065, Y 205,093).

$1650* *Toros En Vallauris (B. 1291), 1960*, s., #36/185, full margins, good cond., skinned areas, foxing, mat staining, (10-28-92, Butterfield, #2692), 25 x 20¾ in., (635 x 527 mm.), color linoleum cut on Arches (BP 1051, DM 2548, FR 8652, Y 202,454).

$2300* *Toros En Vallauris 1955 (B. 1265), 1955*, s., proof, wide margins, creasing, bottom folded back, taped down w/masking tape, (05-11-93, Christie-NY, #296, illus.), borderline 25⅝ x 20⅛ in., (651 x 511 mm.), color linocut on wove (BP 1468, DM 3623, FR 12,208, Y 252,997).

$8800* *"Le Tricorne": 32*, 4to, (11-12-92, Swann, #165, illus.), color reproduction (BP 5780, DM 13,944, FR 47,034, Y 1,091,135).

$4025* *Trois Acteurs (B. 145; G. 296; Suite Vollard 77), 1933*, from Vollard suite, s., full margins, good cond., printer's crease inimage, soiling, creases, (05-13-93, Sotheby-NY, #684, illus.), 11 x 7¼ in., (278 x 183 mm.), drypoint (BP 2642, DM 6499, FR 21,923, Y 449,369).

$6900* *Les Trois Amies (B. 76; G. 117), 1927,* s. in red brushpoint, num., p. Fort, pub. Vollard, margins, good cond-specks of foxing, mat stain, discoloration, adhesive tape, (02-11-93, Sotheby-NY, #209, illus.), 16⁵⁄₁₆ x 11¹¹⁄₁₆ in., (414 x 297 mm.), sheet 24¼ x 17⅝ in., (414 x 297 mm.), etching on Arches wove (BP 4869, DM 11,430, FR 38,677, Y 831,826).

$8132* *Les Trois Amies (Bloch 76; Geiser/Baer Bd. I, 117/II b 1), c. 1923/1927,* s., (12-01-92, Karl/Faber, #1095, illus.), 16⁵⁄₁₆ x 11⅝ in., (41.5 x 29.5 cm.), etching on Japan (BP 5373, DM 12,961, FR 44,172, Y 1,012,450).

$6508* *"Les Trois Baigneuses III" (Bloch 62), 1922-23,* s., #73/100, handling traces, (11-25-92, Dorotheum, #468, illus.), plate size 7¹⁄₁₆ x 5⅛ in., (18 x 13 cm.), sh 15¹⁄₁₆ x 15¹⁄₁₆ in., (18 x 13 cm.), etching (BP 4255, DM 10,348, FR 35,046, Y 805,645, SC 72,800).

BI *Les Trois Baigneuses, I (B. 60), 1922-3,* s., full margins, light/mat staining, very good cond., est. $14/16,000, (11-09-92, Christie-NY, #148, illus.), 7 x 5⅛ in., (178 x 130 mm.), drypoint on wove.

$9200* *Les Trois Baigneuses, III (B. 62), 1922-3,* s., #44/100, wide margins, foxing, mat staining, very good cond., (05-11-93, Christie-NY, #260, illus.), plate 7 x 5⅛ in., (178 x 130 mm.), etching on wove (BP 5873, DM 14,493, FR 48,832, Y 1,011,990).

$2596* *Trois Comediens Avec Buste De Marie-Therese (G.-Baer 296/II/B/d; Bl.145), 1933,* sheet 77 of Suite Vollard, (06-23-93, Kornfeld, #660), drypoint on handmade (BP 1764, DM 4393, FR 14,775, Y 282,819, SF 3910).

BI *Trois Femmes Nues Pres D'Une Fenetre (B. 176; G. 329; S.V. 67), 1933,* from Vollard suite, brushpoint s., #3/3, large margins, good cond., rubbed spot, soiling, mat stain, creases, tack holes, est. $15/20,000, (11-05-92, Sotheby-NY, #330, illus.), 14⅛ x 11⅝ in., (358 x 295 mm.), sheet 21 x 16⅛ in., (358 x 295 mm.), etching on parchment.

$3410* *Trois Figures Sur La Plage, I (B. 241; G. 268; C. bk. 25), 1932,* s., in portfolio 23 Gravures, pub. Orobitz, Paris, 1935, full margins, good cond., discoloration, repaired tear, pin holes, crease, (11-05-92, Sotheby-NY, #342), 4⅞ x 3⅝ in., (125 x 92 mm.), sheet 12¾ x 9¾ in., (125 x 92 mm.), etching (BP 2218, DM 5393, FR 18,245, Y 418,354).

$3740* *Trois Nus Debout, Avec Esquisses De Visage, Geiser/Baer 131b.2; Bloch90,* s. ink, num. 18/99, plate 9 of Le Chef-d'Oeuvre Inconnu, by Balzac, pub. Vollard, 1931, (09-20-92, Hindman, #757, illus.), sheet 14¾ x 17⅞ in., (19.4 x 27.6 cm.), etching on heavy wove (BP 2190, DM 5550, FR 18,985, Y 462,242).

BI *Trois Personnages (B. 384), 1966,* s., #32/50, full margins, good cond., est. BP 2,2/2,800, (12-03-92, Sotheby-London, #549, illus.), 10¾ x 15 in., (273 x 382 mm.), etching w/aquatint.

$4600* *"Trois Personnages" and "Peintre Et Modele" (B. 1384 and 1387), 1966:Two,* s., #36/50, full margins, good cond., (05-13-93, Sotheby-NY, #729), one 11 x 15⅜ in., (280 x 390 mm.), other 12¾ x 18¾ in., (280 x 390 mm.), etching w/aquatint (BP 3020, DM 7428, FR 25,054, Y 513,565).

$421* *Trois Visages, 1964: Three,* VII, IX, X, (09-30-92, Kunsthallen, #248), lithograph in color (BP 238, DM 597, FR 2019, Y 50,522, DK 2300).

$3818* *Troupe D'Acteurs (Mourl. 250; Bl. 754), 1954,* d., s. in pen, num., (06-23-93, Kornfeld, #711), lithograph on thick wove (BP 2594, DM 6460, FR 21,730, Y 415,949, SF 5750).

BI *Two Compositions (B. 1405 and 1442), 1966,* sig. stamp, #12/50, full margins, good cond., printer's crease in image, est. $5/7,000, (05-13-93, Sotheby-NY, #732), one 9¾ x 15 in., (248 x 380 mm.), other 8¾ x 8⅝ in., (248 x 380 mm.), aquatint and drypoint, and etching, aquatint and drypoint.

$1495* *Two Compostions (B. 1413 and 1417), 1966: Two,* s. stamp, #12/50, full margins, good cond., creases, (02-11-93, Sotheby-NY, #220), each 8¹³⁄₁₆ x 12⅝ in., (224 x 321 mm.), xin., (224 x 321 mm.), etching w/aquatint, and aquatint (BP 1055, DM 2476, FR 8380, Y 180,229).

$4025* *Untitled (4 Mai 1945) (B. 371), 1945,* s., annot., #Ier etat no. 43 2/50, full margins, good cond., light-staining, crease, paper remains, soiling, (05-19-93, Butterfield, #1946, illus.), 8⁹⁄₁₆ x 13½ in., (217 x 343 mm.), engraving on wove (BP 2613, DM 6543, FR 22,043, Y 445,588).

$2231* *Untitled (B. 1418), 1966,* sig. stamp, #15/50, full margins, good cond., (06-30-93, Sotheby-London, #643, illus.), 8¾ x 12⅝ in., (222 x 321 mm.), etching and aquatint on wove (BP 1495, DM 3805, FR 12,837, Y 239,044).

$3080* *Untitled (Bloch 1634), 1968,* s., #8/50, plate 154, (05-16-93, Hindman, #471), 8⅝ x 11¼ in., (21.9 x 28.6 cm.), etching (BP 2003, DM 4954, FR 16,649, Y 341,426).

BI *Vallauris Exposition 1956 (B. 1271), 1956,* s. w/red crayon, paper lightly toned, appears good cond., prov., est. $4/5,000, (06-11-93, Doyle, #70, illus.), 21 x 26 in., (533 x 660 mm.), color linoleum cut and poster.

$2059* *Vallauris Exposition 1960 (B. 1290), 1960,* s., #136/170, full margins, good cond., handling creases, tear, (06-30-93, Sotheby-London, #645), 29½ x 24½ in., (749 x 622 mm.), linocut in black and blue on Arches (BP 1380, DM 3512, FR 11,847, Y 220,615).

$1650* *Vallauris Peinture Et Lumiere, XE Anniversaire (B. 1850, 1964,* crayon s., #90/185, p. Arnera, margins, good cond., mat/light-staining, creases, soiling, (10-28-92, Butterfield, #2695), 25¼ x 20⅞ in., (641 x 530 mm.), color linoleum cut on Arches (BP 1051, DM 2548, FR 8652, Y 202,454).

BI *Vallauris. Peinture Et Lumiere. Xe Anniversaire, 1964,* green crayon s.; s., d. in image, water-stained, est. DM 5,500, (09-18-92, Schloss Ahlden, #1042, illus.), 29⁵⁄₁₆ x 23⅞ in., (74.5 x 60.7 cm.), linocut on Arches wove.

$6863* *Venus Foraine (B. 1232), 1966,* s., #32/50, full margins, good cond., (06-30-93, Sotheby-London, #632, illus.), 12⅜ x 16⅜ in., (314 x 416 mm.), etching w/drypoint on wove (BP 4600, DM 11,706, FR 39,488, Y 735,348).

$4600* *Venus Foraine (B. 1232), 1966,* s., #11/50, full margins, good cond., creases, skinned spots, (05-13-93, Sotheby-NY, #728, illus.), 12⅜ x 16⅜ in., (314 x 415 mm.), etching and drypoint (BP 3020, DM 7428, FR 25,054, Y 513,565).

$3069* *Le Vieux Roi (B. 869), 1959,* crayon s., #143/200, full margins, good cond., creases, tear, (12-03-92, Sotheby-London, #506, illus.), 24⅜ x 19½ in., (645 x 495 mm.), lithograph on Arches (BP 1980, DM 4826, FR 16,473, Y 381,859).

$2950* *Le Vieux Roi (Bloch 869), 1959,* s. Picasso, 194/200, (09-30-92, Kunsthallen, #242, illus.), lithograph (BP 1664, DM 4183, FR 14,149, Y 354,014, DK 16,100).

$605* *Le Vieux Roi (Bloch 869), 1959,* red sig., (12-08-92, Swann, #245), 26⅜ x 20⅛ in., (67 x 51.1 cm.), lithograph (BP 379, DM 942, FR 3211, Y 74,988).

$412* *Le Vieux Roi (Bloch 869), 1959,* p. red sig., masking tape, (05-27-93, Swann, #223), sh 26⅜ x 20⅛ in., (67 x 51.1 cm.), lithograph (BP 264, DM 661, FR 2228, Y 44,168).

$1412* *Le Vieux Roi (Bloch 869; Mourlot 317), 1959,* stone d., red s., (06-10-93, Hauswedell/Nolt, #796, illus.), image 25⁹⁄₁₆ x 19⅝ in., (65 x 49.9 cm.), lithograph on Arches (BP 924, DM 2299, FR 7741, Y 149,878).

$12,075* *Le Vieux Roi (Le Vieux Bouffon) (B. 1152; Baer 1338), 1963,* s., #91/160, full margins, good cond., creases, foxing, (05-13-93, Sotheby-NY, #720, illus.), 25¼ x 20⅞ in., (642 x 530 mm.), linoleum cut in colors (BP 7927, DM 19,498, FR 65,768, Y 1,348,108).

$2024* *Le Vieux Roi (Mourlot 317), 1959,* s., d on stone 6.1.59, (05-27-93, Briest, #160), 26³⁄₁₆ x 20¹⁄₁₆ in., (66.5 x 51 cm.), lithograph on Arches (BP 1296, DM 3248, FR 10,946, Y 216,981).

$440* *"Le Vieux Roi" (Bloch, 869),* ident. Picasso, d. 6.1.59 in stone, bears sig., H.C., watermark Mourlot, good cond., light toning, (09-11-92, Skinner, #96A, illus.), 25¾ x 19¾ in., (65.4 x 50.2 cm.), lithograph on Arches wove (BP 228, DM 633, FR 2153, Y 54,516).

$1029* *"Le Vieux Roi" and "L'Ecuyere" (B. 869 and 999), 1959 and 1960: Two,* full margins, good cond., (06-30-93, Sotheby-London, #615), one 26⅛ x 20⅛ in., (664 x 511 mm.), the other 26⅞ x 21⅜ in., (664 x 511 mm.), lithograph (BP 690, DM 1755, FR 5921, Y 110,254).

$3558* *"Le Vieux Roi", (Mourlot 317 and Block 869)*, s. 197/200, (09-29-92, B. Rasmussen, #352, illus.), lithograph (BP 2000, DM 5025, FR 17,147, Y 424,734, DK 19,550).

$4630* *Le Vieux Roi- 6.1.59 (Bloch 869)*, #29/200, s., (11-09-92, Finarte-Milan, #59, illus.), 25⅜ x 19½ in., (64.5 x 49.5 cm.), lithograph (BP 3061, DM 7391, FR 24,973, Y 574,584, L 6325).

$5750* *"Vieux Sculpteur Au Travail" and "Rembrandt A La Palette" (B. 153 and208; G. 305 and 405; S.V. 47 and 34), 1933 and 1934: Two,* from the Vollard suite, s., full margins, good cond., mat stain, foxing, i.; foxing, light-stain, (05-13-93, Sotheby-NY, #685), one 10½ x 7½ in., (266 x 192 mm.), other 11 x 7¾ in., (266 x 192 mm.), etching (BP 3775, DM 9285, FR 31,318, Y 641,956).

$2138* *Vieux Sculpteur Au Travail. I. (G.-Baer 305/B/d; Bl. 153), 1933,* sheet 47 of Suite Vollard, (06-23-93, Kornfeld, #663), etching on handmade (BP 1452, DM 3618, FR 12,168, Y 232,923, SF 3220).

$2749* *Vieux Sculpteur Au Travail. II (G.-Baer 311/B/d; Bl. 158), 1933,* sheet 49 of Suite Vollard, (06-23-93, Kornfeld, #667), etching on handmade (BP 1868, DM 4651, FR 15,646, Y 299,488, SF 4140).

$1833* *Le Viol (G.-Baer 209/B/d; Bl. 142), 1931,* sheet 9 of Suite Vollard, (06-23-93, Kornfeld, #655), etching on handmade (BP 1245, DM 3102, FR 10,433, Y 199,695, SF 2760).

$1320* *"Le Viol I" (Bloch, 239),* after 1932, pub. 1961 in suite Caisse A Remords, estate s. Picasso, num. 29/50, good cond., wide margins, light toning, foxing, (09-11-92, Skinner, #90, illus.), 4¹⁵⁄₁₆ x 3⅝ in., (12.5 x 9.2 cm.), drypoint on pale gray laid paper (BP 683, DM 1900, FR 6458, Y 163,549).

$28,600* *Visage (B. 95; Mourlot XXIII), 1928,* s., #3/25, wide margins, Chine lifting slightly, glue stains, good cond., (11-09-92, Christie-NY, #149, illus.), L. 8⅛ x 5½ in., (206 x 139 mm.), S. 18⅛ x 14⁵⁄₁₆ in., (206 x 139 mm.), lithograph on Chine applique (BP 18,909, DM 45,658, FR 154,261, Y 3,549,268).

$38,124* *Visage (Bloch 95; Geiser 243; Mourlot XXIII; Goeppert/Cramer 16), 1928,* s., num. 57/75, full margins, good cond., scrape, staining, erased pencil marks, rubbed, (10-14-92, Sotheby-Japan, #64, illus.), 8⅛ x 5½ in., (206 x 140 mm.), sheet 16¾ x 12¼ in., (206 x 140 mm.), lithograph on Japan (BP 22,377, DM 55,794, FR 189,201, Y 4,619,971).

BI *Young Man With A Crown Of Vines (B. 1087, K. 66), 1962,* s., num. 450, full margins, p. by Arnera, Vallauris, pub. Louise Leiris, light-staining, margin folded, est. BP 4/6,000, (11-30-92, Phillips-London, #471, illus.), image 13⅞ x 10⅝ in., (352 x 270 mm.), linocut in black, dark brown, light brown & beige on Arches.

$1950* *Zwei Kopf,* prov., (10-21-92, Dobiaschofsky, #2268, illus.), 3⅛ x 3⁹⁄₁₆ in., (8 x 9 cm.), woodcut in red (BP 1210, DM 2951, FR 10,015, Y 237,515, SF 2640).

PICASSO, Pablo (after)

$44* *Abstract Portrait,* p. Mourlot, (06-11-93, Freemn/Fine Art, #175), 18 x 11½ in., (45.7 x 29.2 cm.), lithograph (BP 29, DM 72, FR 241, Y 4668).

$2432* *Bacchanale,* by Crommelynck, s., 143/250, blindstamp, Editeur Atelier Crommelynck, (12-04-92, AB Stockholm, #7119, illus.), 18¹¹⁄₁₆ x 22¹⁄₁₆ in., (47.5 x 56 cm.), aquatint on Crommelynck (BP 1560, DM 3873, FR 13,139, Y 303,620, SK 16,500).

$1725* *Bacchanale, 1959: Two,* progressive color proofs, annot. III passage and IV passage, full margins, good cond., full toned, hinge remains, creases, surface soiling, notions, (05-19-93, Butterfield, #1953, illus.), each 18¾ x 22¼ in., (476 x 565 mm.), aquatint in colors on Rives BFK (BP 1120, DM 2804, FR 9447, Y 190,966).

$2990* *Bethsabee, 1966,* by Aldo Crommelynck, s. Picasso, #248/300, pub. Atelier Crommelynck, blindstamp, full margins, good cond., light-stain, handling crease, (05-13-93, Sotheby-NY, #751), 10⅜ x 10¾ in., (263 x 272 mm.), aquatint in colors (BP 1963, DM 4828, FR 16,285, Y 333,817).

$3058* *Corrida,* s. by Picasso; sig. of Crommelynck in plate; by Aldo Crommelynck after 1950's gouache by Picasso, (10-

09-92, Winterberg, #2921, illus.), 19 x 25⅞ in., (48.3 x 65.7 cm.), aquatint/etching on Arches (BP 1814, DM 4542, FR 15,252, Y 372,291).

$248* *Cote D'Azur,* p. Henri Deschamps, (11-12-92, Freemn/Fine Art, #174), 30½ x 25 in., (77.5 x 63.5 cm.), lithograph (BP 163, DM 393, FR 1325, Y 30,750).

$107* *Couple With Child,* d. 27 April XXXVI in plate, stamped sig., (12-01-92, Ritchie, #100), 21½ x 16½ in., (54.6 x 41.9 cm.), lithograph (BP 71, DM 171, FR 581, Y 13,322, C$ 138).

$880* *Le Faune, 1958,* s., annot. H.C., blindstamp of p. & pub. Atelier Crommelynck, full margins, good cond., creasing, light-staining, tape, surface soiling, (02-24-93, Butterfield, #2780), 11⅞ x 10 in., (302 x 254 mm.), aquatint w/touches of roulette on Japon nacre (BP 614, DM 1429, FR 4843, Y 103,262).

$2308* *Le Faune, 1958,* H.C., s., blindstamp, (11-21-92, Lempertz, #330), 11⅞ x 9¹⁵⁄₁₆ in., (30.2 x 25.2 cm.), aquatint etching on Japon nacre (BP 1520, DM 3680, FR 12,395, Y 287,029).

$3005* *L'Arene,* #143/200, s., (02-03-93, Ader Tajan, #189), 25⅜ x 18¹¹⁄₁₆ in., (64.5 x 47.5 cm.), color engraving (BP 2098, DM 4948, FR 16,778, Y 373,803).

$2675* *L'Entente,* by Guy Spitzer, s., 11/125, (12-04-92, AB Stockholm, #7121), 20¼ x 21⅝ in., (51.5 x 55 cm.), collotype and pochoir on Arches (BP 1716, DM 4260, FR 14,452, Y 333,958, SK 18,150).

$143* *Lover's Engaged,* i. 8.10.64 XIII in stone, (12-10-92, Sloan, #583), 12⅝ x 9¾ in., (32.1 x 24.8 cm.), chromolithograph (BP 92, DM 226, FR 773, Y 17,689).

BI *"Mere Et Enfant",* d. 3.6.69, s. in plate, est. FF800/1,000, (04-04-93, Pescheteau, #275), 14¹⁵⁄₁₆ x 19⁵⁄₁₆ in., (38 x 49 cm.), color lithograph.

$51* *Le Modele,* (12-10-92, Bonhams-Chelsea, #7), image 8½ x 6¾ in., (21.6 x 17.1 cm.), reproduction (BP 33, DM 81, FR 276, Y 6309).

$1650* *Nature Morte Au Citron Et Aux Oranges,* s., #254/325, inkstamp pub. Guy Spitzer, margins, good cond., mat/light-staining, crease, buckling, surface soiling, (10-28-92, Butterfield, #2712), 18¹³⁄₁₆ x 22¾ in., (478 x 578 mm.), hand-colored lithograph on wove (BP 1051, DM 2548, FR 8652, Y 202,454).

$3575* *Nature Morte Aux Poires Et Au Pichet,* s., #270/300, blindstamp pub. Aldo Crommelynck, full margins, good cond., mat/light-staining, staining, foxing, tape remains, surface soiling, (10-28-92, Butterfield, #2711, illus.), 12¾ x 17¼ in., (324 x 438 mm.), color aquatint on Arches (BP 2278, DM 5521, FR 18,747, Y 438,650).

$2185* *Nature Morte Aux Poires, 1961,* s., #290/300, blindstamp, pub. Atelier Crommelynck, p. Aldo Crommelynck, good cond., mat staining, surface soiling, creases, (05-19-93, Butterfield, #1954), 19½ x 23⅝ in., (495 x 600 mm.), etching and aquatint in colors on Arches (BP 1418, DM 3552, FR 11,966, Y 241,891).

$5177* *"Nature Morte a La Charlotte",* d. 24, s. in plate, dry stamp ed. Spitzer, #225/350, s., (10-18-92, Pescheteau, #233), sight 22⁷⁄₁₆ x 26¾ in., (57 x 68 cm.), pochoir in colors on wove (BP 3137, DM 7647, FR 25,976, Y 618,149).

$419* *Picasso Les Dejeuners (Czwiklitzer 218), 1962,* s., d. 6.12.69, (11-16-92, Briest, #85), 20½ x 14¾ in., (52 x 37.5 cm.), poster in colors on Arches (BP 275, DM 668, FR 2251, Y 52,290).

$90* *"Portrait Imaginaire",* s. in plate, d. 12.3.69, (10-18-92, Pescheteau, #238), 29¹⁵⁄₁₆ x 22¹⁄₁₆ in., (76 x 56 cm.), lithograph in colors on Arches (BP 55, DM 133, FR 452, Y 10,746).

$1100* *(Poster For Cannes Festival), 1951,* s., #399, appears good cond., prov., (06-11-93, Doyle, #68), 16 x 20½ in., (406 x 521 mm.), color lithograph (BP 723, DM 1788, FR 6027, Y 116,711).

$771* *Tete De Roi, c. 1951,* s., p. by Imp. de la Victoire, good cond., tear, creases, (06-30-93, Sotheby-London, #659), 19¼ x 15⅜ in., (489 x 391 mm.), color lithographic poster on wove (BP 517, DM 1315, FR 4436, Y 82,610).

$1784* *Vanitas,* s., EA, blindstamp Atelier Lacouriere, (12-04-92, AB Stockholm, #7120, illus.), 16¾ x 24⅝ in., (42.5

x 62.5 cm.), aquatint in colors on Arches (BP 1144, DM 2841, FR 9638, Y 222,722, SK 12,100).

$3775* *Verve Nos 29-30, 1954: Four,* s., three #50/75, one #45/75, pub. Verve, blindstamp, margins, good cond., discoloration, (06-30-93, Sotheby-London, #658), color lithograph (BP 2530, DM 6439, FR 21,720, Y 404,479).

$4950* *[Bacchanale], c. 1959,* s., #112/300, pub. Crommelynck, full margins, good cond., scuffs, printer's crease, handling creases, light stain, tape stain, (11-05-92, Sotheby-NY, #387), 18¾ x 22¼ in., (475 x 565 mm.), aquatint p. in colors on BFK Rives wove (BP 3220, DM 7829, FR 26,485, Y 607,287).

PICELJI, Ivan   20th cent.
$166* *Oeuvre Programme No. 1, 1966: Twelve,* #15/50, s., (09-04-92, Germann, #520), each 25⁹⁄₁₆ x 17¹¹⁄₁₆ in., (650 x 449 mm.), serigraph (BP 83, DM 233, FR 792, Y 20,433, SF 207).

PICHAT
$90* *Cycles Rochet,* good cond., (02-12-93, Cheval/Robert, #84), 49⅝ x 37⅜ in., (126 x 95 cm.), poster (BP 63, DM 149, FR 505, Y 10,854).

PICHET, Roland   Canadian b. 1936
$233* *"Gaspesienne",* s. Pichet, t., (07-14-92, Encans, #73), 22¹⁄₁₆ x 27¾ in., (56 x 70.5 cm.), lithograph (BP 121, DM 346, FR 1166, Y 29,136, C$ 278).
$78* *Lightning, 1980,* #35/75, s., t., d. '80; bears t. verso, (05-10-93, Hodgins, #189), 7¾ x 5¾ in., (19.7 x 14.6 cm.), etching on paper (BP 51, DM 125, FR 423, Y 8716, C$ 99).
BI *"Spatiale No 6",* from Apatrides series, t., #20/50, s., d. Pichet 65-66, (06-16-93, Encans, #85), 7⅞ x 9¹³⁄₁₆ in., (20 x 25 cm.), color etching.

PICHETTE, James
BI *"En Son-1971",* #2/100, s., est. FF800/1,000, (04-04-93, Pescheteau, #276), 25³⁄₁₆ x 18⅞ in., (64 x 48 cm.), color lithograph on wove.

PICHLER, Johann
$100* *Le Prince Antoine D'Esterhasy,* pub. Artaria, margins, good cond., (11-30-92, Phillips-London, #90), plate 14¾ x 10½ in., (375 x 267 mm.), mezzotint on laid (BP 66, DM 159, FR 541, Y 12,446).

PICKEN, Thomas   (after F. Le B. BEDWELL)
$226* *Attack And Capture Of The Forts At The Entrance Of The River Pei-Ho,China,* pub. Day and Son, good cond., (10-27-92, Phillips-London, #161), image 13⅓ x 23¼ in., (339 x 591 mm.), lithograph w/hand-coloring on wove (BP 143, DM 346, FR 1175, Y 27,645).

PICKHARDT, Carl   American b. 1908
$550* *"Wrestlers", "Mid Morning", "Barroom", "Hanging Out The Wash", "The Soloist" and "Street Scene", 1939, 1935: Six,* each s. Pickhardt, some annot., good cond., wrinkling of corners, (03-12-93, Skinner, #40, illus.), sheet 23 x 16½ in., (58.4 x 41.9 cm.), various media including lithograph on wove (BP 384, DM 915, FR 3113, Y 64,820).

PICOT, V.M.
$217* *A View Of The Bay And Mountain Of Rosstrevor In The Harbour Of Carlingford, 1772,* after J. Fisher, pub. T. Mayor, margins, (11-19-92, Bonhams-Chelsea, #29), plate 15½ x 21 in., (39.4 x 53.3 cm.), engraving (BP 143, DM 346, FR 1165, Y 26,987).

PIECK, A.   1895-1987
$382* *Kerkvenster Te Amersfoor (Hallema E62; Vogelesang p. 71), 1917,* s. Anton Pieck, (11-18-92, Bubb Kuyper, #1576), 7¹¹⁄₁₆ x 13³⁄₁₆ in., (19.6 x 33.5 cm.), etching (BP 252, DM 609, FR 2052, Y 47,507, G 690).

PIENE, Otto   German/American b. 1928
$109* *Ausstellung Rixdorfer Werkstattdrucke, 1964,* Galerie von der Hoh, s., (11-28-92, Schoppmann, #712), 27⁹⁄₁₆ x 19¹¹⁄₁₆ in., (70 x 50 cm.), color woodcut on wove (BP 72, DM 174, FR 590, Y 13,566).
BI *"Blaue Feuerblume",* s., d. Piene 67, #7/100, restored, est. DM 600-, (09-14-92, Venator/Hansten, #2489), 27⁹⁄₁₆ x 19⅛ in., (70 x 48.5 cm.), screenprint on thin red board.

$339* *Feuerblume, 1967,* s., d., #44/200, (06-12-93, Hauswedell/Nolt, #327), 24⁷⁄₁₆ x 18⅛ in., (62 x 46 cm.), color serigraph on red board (BP 222, DM 552, FR 1854, Y 35,673).
BI *Untitled, 1966,* s., d., num., wear, est. DM 900-, (09-25-92, Granier, #2977), sheet 21¹⁄₁₆ x 25¹⁄₁₆ in., (53.5 x 63.6 cm.), relief print, watercolor and serigraph on offset board.

PIERCE, Elijah   American 1892-1982
$72* *"Kids Don't Care About Race?",* s., (10-03-92, Garth, #376), 23½ x 16¼ in., (59.7 x 41.3 cm.), poster w/ woodcut (BP 42, DM 102, FR 346, Y 8619).

PIERCE, Waldo   American 1884-1970
$138* *Old Absinthe House,* s., t., (03-06-93, LA Auction Ex., #79), 6 x 7¾ in., (15.2 x 19.7 cm.), etching (BP 95, DM 230, FR 775, Y 16,220).

PIETRI, Alberto de
$28* *Surrealistic Horse,* s. A. De Pietri, (02-19-93, Garth, #445), 22 x 30 in., (55.9 x 76.2 cm.), colored lithograph (BP 19, DM 46, FR 155, Y 3322).

PIFFARD, Harold
$871* *Nudes, c. 1895-99: Fifteen,* majority num. in negs., (05-06-93, Christie-London, #69), smallest 5½ x 3½ in., largest 6 x 4¼ in., photograph, warm toned gelatin silver print (BP 552, DM 1372, FR 4618, Y 95,830).

PIGNON, Edouard   French b. 1905
$112* *"Combat De Coqs - 1969",* H.C., d., s., (10-18-92, Pescheteau, #243), 11 x 15³⁄₁₆ in., (28 x 38.5 cm.), lithograph in colors on wove (BP 68, DM 165, FR 562, Y 13,373).
$247* *"Combat De Coqs", 1977,* #72/100, s., d., (10-18-92, Pescheteau, #241), 26⅜ x 40³⁄₁₆ in., (67 x 102 cm.), lithograph in colors on grey paper (BP 150, DM 365, FR 1239, Y 29,493).
$225* *"Grand Nu Rouge", 1979,* #32/75, d., s., (10-18-92, Pescheteau, #240), 27³⁄₁₆ x 38³⁄₁₆ in., (69 x 97 cm.), lithograph in colors on wove (BP 136, DM 332, FR 1129, Y 26,866).
BI *"Nu Allonge", 1986 and "Combat De Coqs": Two,* s., #13/110, H.C., est. FF2,000/2,500, (03-31-93, Briest, #E88), one 18¹¹⁄₁₆ x 25⁹⁄₁₆ in., (47.5 x 65 cm.), other 22¹⁄₁₆ x 29¹⁵⁄₁₆ in., (47.5 x 65 cm.), color lithographs.
$77* *Nu, 1979,* s., d., 60/110, (06-28-93, Loudmer, #107), 15¾ x 23⁷⁄₁₆ in., (400 x 595 mm.), sh 18⅞ x 25⁹⁄₁₆ in., (400 x 595 mm.), red lithograph on BBFK Rives wove (BP 52, DM 131, FR 441, Y 8170).
BI *Personnage, 1972,* from "Pour Paul Eluard" portfolio, s., #4/100, est. FF800/1,000, (05-27-93, Briest, #164), 25⁹⁄₁₆ x 19¹¹⁄₁₆ in., (65 x 50 cm.), color lithograph.
$192* *Untitled, 1979,* s., d., #43/75, full margins, good cond., (05-27-93, Sotheby-Amstrdm, #673, illus.), 25 x 35 in., (635 x 889 mm.), color lithograph on wove (BP 123, DM 308, FR 1038, Y 20,583, G 345).

PIGNORIA, Lorenzo
$715* *Characteres Aegyptii; Hoc Est, Sacrorum Quibus Aegyptii Utuntur, Simulachrorum Accurata Delineatio Et Explicatio: Nine,* small 4to, (11-12-92, Swann, #166), engraving (BP 470, DM 1133, FR 3821, Y 88,655).

PILGRIM, Hubertus von   b. 1931
$332* *"Twelve Kupferstiche Zu Heinrich Von Kleist Das Erdbeben In Chili", (19)61/62: Thirteen,* Edition Rothe, Heidelberg, s., d., (12-01-92, Karl/Faber, #1101), 17⁵⁄₁₆ x 13⁹⁄₁₆ in., (44 x 34.5 cm.), engraving on wove (BP 219, DM 529, FR 1803, Y 41,335).

PILLSBURY PICTURES
$1650* *"Bridal Veil Falls" and "El Capitan Yosemite", 1907,* t., d., neg. num., attrib., (11-16-92, Butterfield, #6121, illus.), 33⁹⁄₁₆ x 9½ in., (852.4 x 241.7 mm.), photograph, gelatin silver print (BP 1086, DM 2631, FR 8861, Y 205,198).

PILLSBURY PICTURES (attrib.)
$1320* *View Down The Valley, Yosemite, c. 1900,* (10-14-92, Swann, #224, illus.), 12 x 16 in., (30.5 x 40.6 cm.), photograph, orotone (BP 775, DM 1932, FR 6551, Y 159,961).

$605* *View Of Yosemite Valley, 1900's,* (11-16-92, Butterfield, #6122, illus.), 11 x 14 in., (279.9 x 356.2 mm.), photograph, orotone (BP 398, DM 965, FR 3249, Y 75,239).

PILLSBURY'S PICTURES

$770* *El Capitan, c. 1900,* letterpress studio label, (04-07-93, Swann, #535), approx. 8½ x 3¼ in., photograph, orotone (BP 509, DM 1245, FR 4215, Y 87,480).

$1380* *"The Gates Of Yosemite",* 1920s, t., label, (05-23-93, Butterfield, #3563, illus.), 20 x 24 in., photograph, orotone in orig. studio frame (BP 899, DM 2256, FR 7595, Y 152,537).

$978* *"Half Dome, Yosemite", 1923,* t., d., label, (05-23-93, Butterfield, #3564, illus.), 14 x 11 in., photograph, orotone in orig. studio from (BP 637, DM 1599, FR 5382, Y 108,102).

PILLSBURY'S PICTURES (attrib.)

$990* *Landscape Scene Of Yosemite, c. 1900,* fragment of label verso, (04-07-93, Swann, #532), approx. 17 x 13½ in., photograph, orotone (BP 654, DM 1601, FR 5419, Y 112,474).

PILOT, Robert Wakeham Canadian 1898-1967/68

$172* *Caleches, Lower Town, Quebec,* s. in plate, (06-07-93, Ritchie, #15, illus.), plate 7¹³⁄₁₆ x 8⅜ in., (19.8 x 21.3 cm.), sh 11 x 13⅜ in., (19.8 x 21.3 cm.), etching (BP 113, DM 279, FR 940, Y 18,451, C$ 220).

$108* *View Of Quebec, c. 1920s-30s,* s. in plate, (06-07-93, Ritchie, #17), plate 7¾ x 4⅞ in., (19.7 x 12.4 cm.), sh 11¼ x 8⁷⁄₁₆ in., (19.7 x 12.4 cm.), etching (BP 71, DM 175, FR 590, Y 11,585, C$ 138).

$215* *View Of Quebec, c. 1925-1926,* s. in plate, lit., (06-07-93, Ritchie, #16, illus.), plate 7¹⁄₁₆ x 11¾ in., (18 x 29.9 cm.), sh 13⅜ x 16⅞ in., (18 x 29.9 cm.), etching (BP 142, DM 349, FR 1175, Y 23,064, C$ 275).

PINCHON, J.P.

$60* *Chemins De Fer Du Nord. Ou Aller? A Compiegne, c. 1925,* cond. B, (03-16-93, Boisgirard, #174), 38¹⁵⁄₁₆ x 28¹⁵⁄₁₆ in., (99 x 73.5 cm.), poster (BP 41, DM 100, FR 339, Y 7016).

PINELLI, Bartolomeo Italian 1781-1835

$825* *Nuova Raccolta Di Ventiquattro Vedute De' Contorni Di Napoli: Twenty-Four,* oblong 8vo, wrappers, some foxed, (11-12-92, Swann, #115), etching (BP 542, DM 1307, FR 4409, Y 102,294).

PINGRET, Edouard Henri Theophile (after)

$110* *The State Visit To Britain By King Louis Philippe Of France: Five,* margins, (11-12-92, Bonhams-Chelsea, #55), image, each approx. 11 x 16 in., (27.9 x 40.6 cm.), hand-colored lithograph (BP 72, DM 174, FR 588, Y 13,639).

$67* *The State Visit To Britain By King Louis Philippe Of France: Four,* margins, (11-12-92, Bonhams-Chelsea, #55B), image, each approx. 11 x 16 in., (27.9 x 40.6 cm.), hand-colored lithograph (BP 44, DM 106, FR 358, Y 8308).

$160* *The State Visit To Britain By King Louis Philippe Of France: Four,* margins, (11-12-92, Bonhams-Chelsea, #55C), image, each apprx. 11 x 16 in., (27.9 x 40.6 cm.), hand-colored lithograph (BP 105, DM 254, FR 855, Y 19,839).

$59* *The State Visit To Britain By King Louis Philippe Of France: Four,* margins, (11-12-92, Bonhams-Chelsea, #55A), image, each approx. 11 x 16 in., (27.9 x 40.6 cm.), hand-colored lithograph (BP 39, DM 93, FR 315, Y 7316).

PINKERTON, John Scottish early 19th cent.

$220* *United States Of America Northern Part, 1810,* (04-02-93, Sloan, #1212), 20¼ x 27½ in., (514 x 699 mm.), color engraving (BP 145, DM 354, FR 1201, Y 25,048).

PINS, Jacob

BI *Self Portrait With Japanese Print, 1957,* s., d., #3/12, margins, Japan-backed, repaired tears/creases in image, surface soiling, est. $4/600, (10-28-92, Butterfield, #2848), 20 x 15½ in., (508 x 394 mm.), color woodcut on Japan.

BI *Self-Portrait With Japanese Print, 1957,* s., d., num. 3/12, margins, repaired tears & creases in image, surface soiling, est. $3/500, (02-24-93, Butterfield, #2964), 20 x 15½ in., (508 x 394 mm.), woodcut in colors on wove backed by Japan.

PINTO, Salvatore American 20th cent.

$110* *"City Hall Tower From Spruce Street", "15th And Market Street", and "Independence Hall": Three,* (11-12-92, Freemn/Fine Art, #175), first, second 9½ x 7½ in., (24.1 x 19.1 cm.), third 8¾ x 11½ in., (24.1 x 19.1 cm.), etchings (BP 72, DM 174, FR 588, Y 13,639).

PIPER, John English b. 1903

BI *Bethesda Baptist Chapel, Swansea, 1966,* s., #27/75, p. Curwen Studio, pub. Marlborough Fine Art, good cond.,- est. BP 250/300, (10-27-92, Phillips-London, #293), sheet 23¼ x 32 in., (591 x 813 mm.), black, blue and green lithograph on wove.

BI *Church Series,* s., #60/70, good cond., (12-12-92, Weschler, #150), 19¼ x 25 in., (48.9 x 63.5 cm.), lithograph on heavy wove.

BI *Crug Glas, Swansea (L. 173), 1966,* s., #41/95, p. Curwen Studio, pub. Marlborough Fine Art, creasing, good cond., est. BP 250/300, (10-27-92, Phillips-London, #294), sheet 23¼ x 32 in., (591 x 813 mm.), black and green lithograph on wove.

$853* *Dahlias And Ferns (L. 390), 1987,* s., i. A/P, artist's proof, p. Kelpra Studios, their blindstamp, pub.Marlborough Graphics, full margins, good cond., (12-03-92, Sotheby-London, #177, illus.), 16 x 21⅝ in., (406 x 549 mm.), aquatint in colors on wove (BP 550, DM 1341, FR 4579, Y 106,134).

$447* *The Dovecote,* #63/120, s., blindstamped, (03-17-93, Bonhams-Chelsea, #458), subject 22¾ x 30½ in., (57.8 x 77.5 cm.), screenprint (BP 308, DM 744, FR 2528, Y 52,428).

$251* *"Four Reclining Figures",* #24/70, s., (11-19-92, Bonhams-Chelsea, #162), image 19 x 25¾ in., (48.3 x 65.4 cm.), screenprint (BP 165, DM 400, FR 1348, Y 31,215).

$308* *Inglesham, Wilts.,* #49/70, s., time-staining, (05-20-93, Bonhams-Chelsea, #128), sheet 23½ x 32½ in., (59.7 x 82.6 cm.), screenprint (BP 198, DM 497, FR 1674, Y 34,011).

BI *King's College, Cambridge, From Trinity (L. 86), c. 1954,* s., #56/75, pub., good cond., est. BP 5/700, (10-27-92, Phillips-London, #290), image 16⅛ x 21½ in., (410 x 546 mm.), blue and black lithograph on T.H. Saunders.

$287* *Leckhampstead,* #44/70, s., margins, (03-17-93, Bonhams-Chelsea, #340), subject 32 x 23¼ in., (81.3 x 59.1 cm.), lithograph in colors (BP 198, DM 478, FR 1623, Y 33,662).

$200* *Lewknor, Oxfordshire (L. 133),* s., num. 63/70, plate XII form A Retrospect Of Churches, p. by CurwenStudio, pub. Marlborough Fine Art, 1964, good cond., (11-30-92, Phillips-London, #560), sheet 23⅝ x 32¼ in., (600 x 819 mm.), lithograph in blue & black on wove (BP 132, DM 319, FR 1082, Y 24,891).

$425* *Llangloffan, Pembrokeshire: The Baptist Chapel (Levinson 140), 1964,* s., num., sheet 19 from portfolio Churches, watermark, (06-08-93, Karl/Faber, #1201), approx. 20½ x 27⅜ in., (52 x 69.5 cm.), color lithograph on Crisbrook paper (BP 279, DM 690, FR 2322, Y 45,141).

BI *North Grimstone, Yorkshire (L. 138), 1964,* s., #51/70, plate XVII from A Retrospect Of Churches, pub. Marlborough Fine Art, good cond., est. BP 2/250, (10-27-92, Phillips-London, #292), (819 x 600 mm.), orange and black lithograph on wove.

$200* *Rudbaxton, Pembrokeshire (L. 131),* s., num. 30/70, plate X from A RETROSPECT OF CHURCHES, p. by Curwen Studio, pub. Marlborough Fine Art 1964, good cond., (11-30-92, Phillips-London, #561), sheet 23⅜ x 32¼ in., (594 x 819 mm.), lithograph in colors on wove (BP 132, DM 319, FR 1082, Y 24,891).

$398* *Spring,* s., #99/100, margins, (02-17-93, Bonhams-Chelsea, #234), plate 15¾ x 12¾ in., (40 x 32.4 cm.), color aquatint (BP 275, DM 646, FR 2189, Y 47,539).

$1194* *Summer Garden, Fawley Bottom (Levinson 369), 1984,* s., i. P/P, printer's proof, p. Kelpra Studio, their blindstamp, pub.Marlborough Graphics, full margins, good cond., (12-03-92, Sotheby-London, #175, illus.), 15⅛ x 22⅜ in., (384 x 568 mm.), aquatint in colors on wove (BP 770, DM 1878, FR 6409, Y 148,563).

BI *Swansea Chapel (O.L. 175), 1966,* s., #52/75, p. Curwen Studio, pub. Marlborough Fine Art, full margins, stained, creased, tape stains, est. BP 150/200, (10-27-92, Phillips-London, #291), sheet 31½ x 23½ in., (800 x 597 mm.), black and blue lithograph on Barcham green.

$251* *"Three Abstract Studies",* #12/70, s., (11-19-92, Bonhams-Chelsea, #163), image 20 x 30 in., (50.8 x 76.2 cm.), screenprint (BP 165, DM 400, FR 1348, Y 31,215).

$307* *Tickencote, Rutland,* #50/70, s., laid down, (04-22-93, Bonhams-Chelsea, #20), subject 23¼ x 32 in., (59.1 x 81.3 cm.), lithograph in colors (BP 198, DM 493, FR 1664, Y 33,755).

$238* *Venetian Scene,* #41/70, (04-22-93, Bonhams-Chelsea, #92, illus.), subject 30½ x 26¾ in., (77.5 x 67.9 cm.), screenprint (BP 154, DM 382, FR 1290, Y 26,168).

$682* *Venetian Scene,* num. 41/70, (08-20-92, Bonhams-Chelsea, #74), subject 30½ x 26¾ in., (77.5 x 67.9 cm.), screenprint (BP 352, DM 988, FR 3351, Y 86,122).

$133* *Warkton, Northamptonshire (L. 125),* s., num. 32/70, plate IV from A Retrospect Of Churches, p. by CurwenStudio, pub. Marlborough Fine Art, 1964, good cond., (11-30-92, Phillips-London, #559), sheet 32¼ x 23⅝ in., (819 x 600 mm.), lithograph in blue, brown & black on wove (BP 88, DM 212, FR 719, Y 16,553).

$943* *"Westminster School I"* and *"Westminster School II" (Levinson I; II):Two,* each s., #27/100, pub. on behalf of school, margins, good cond., paper discoloration, (06-30-93, Sotheby-London, #321), 16¾ x 23 in., (425 x 584 mm.), colored lithograph on wove (BP 632, DM 1608, FR 5426, Y 101,039).

$351* *Winter,* #100/100, s., margins, (03-17-93, Bonhams-Chelsea, #354), plate 15½ x 13 in., (39.4 x 33 cm.), aquatint in colors (BP 242, DM 584, FR 1985, Y 41,168).

$853* *Yellow Flowers (L. 391), 1987,* s., i. A.P., p. Kelpra and C.C. A. Galleries, full margins, good cond., (12-03-92, Sotheby-London, #178), 16 x 21⅝ in., (406 x 549 mm.), etching w/aquatint in colors on wove (BP 550, DM 1341, FR 4579, Y 106,134).

PIPER, John   (after)

$111* *Llangloffan,* s., blindstamp, (02-17-93, Bonhams-Chelsea, #361), image 15½ x 22⅝ in., (39.4 x 57.5 cm.), color reproduction (BP 77, DM 180, FR 611, Y 13,258).

BI *Llangloffan, 1980,* s., stamped F.A.T.G., pub. Cavendish Collection, good cond., est. BP1/150, (10-27-92, Phillips-London, #295), image 20½ x 26¾ in., (521 x 679 mm.), colored reproduction.

PIPPAL, Hans Robert   b. 1915

$686* *"Theater In Der Josefstadt",* s., H. Rob. Pippal, #93/100, (05-19-93, Dorotheum, #476, illus.), screen print in color, watercolor (BP 445, DM 1115, FR 3757, Y 75,944, SC 7840).

PIRANESE, Jean Baptiste

$137* *Antiquita D'Albano E Di Castel Gandolfo...Deuxieme Frontispice (H.F., 506),* ded., crease, large margins, (06-16-93, Ader Tajan, #45), 17¹⁵⁄₁₆ x 25¹⁵⁄₁₆ in., (45.5 x 66 cm.), etching and copper (BP 91, DM 227, FR 763, Y 14,612).

$846* *Veduta Di Campo Vaccino (J.B. Hind, num. 40),* 3 out of 6, reddish stains, crease, dirt spots, tears, good margins, (04-02-93, Picard, #20), 16⅛ x 21⁷⁄₁₆ in., (41 x 54.5 cm.), etching and copperplate (BP 557, DM 1360, FR 4618, Y 96,322).

PIRANESI

$2475* *Classical Figures: A Pair,* neoclassical style, after designs by Piranesi, (09-26-92, Sotheby-NY, #126), frame 29 x 37½ in., (73.7 x 95.3 cm.), print (BP 1433, DM 3593, FR 12,115, Y 296,443).

$660* *Landscape Scene Of Tivoli,* pl. s., (12-11-92, DuMouchelle, #2168, illus.), 18 x 24¼ in., (45.7 x 61.6 cm.), etching (BP 423, DM 1040, FR 3564, Y 81,673).

$4125* *Ornaments: Set Of Seven,* neoclassical style, after designs by Piranesi, (09-26-92, Sotheby-NY, #127, illus.), 24½ x

19½ in., (62.2 x 49.5 cm.), print (BP 2388, DM 5989, FR 20,191, Y 494,071).

PIRANESI   (after)

$385* *"Basilica", "Castle St. Angelo"* and *"View Of The Colisseum": Three,* (09-18-92, DuMouchelle, #79, illus.), 15 x 21¼ in., (38.1 x 54 cm.), engraving (BP 221, DM 577, FR 1974, Y 47,969).

$55* *European City Scenes: A Pair,* (06-24-93, Boos, #610), sight 14¹⁵⁄₁₆ x 21¼ in., (380 x 540 mm.), engraving (BP 37, DM 94, FR 316, Y 5999).

PIRANESI, Francesco   Italian 1754-1810

$22 *From The Prison Series I.Carceri,* (02-05-93, G.A. Key, #9), 15 x 21 in., (38.1 x 53.3 cm.), b/w etching (BP 15, DM 36, FR 123, Y 2738).

$303* *Niche Dans Le Temple D'Isis, A Pompeia, 1806,* full margins, center binding fold, good cond., staining, surface soiling, tears, foxing, creases, 2 purple inkstamps, (02-24-93, Butterfield, #2696), 29¼ x 21 in., (743 x 533 mm.), engraving in sepia on wove (BP 211, DM 492, FR 1668, Y 35,555).

$220* *"Orestes And Electra"* and *"Niobe And Her Daughter": Two,* good cond.?, rippling, smudging, (06-11-93, Weschler, #43), 19 x 12½ in., (48.3 x 31.8 cm.), engraving (BP 145, DM 358, FR 1205, Y 23,342).

PIRANESI, Giovanni Battista   Italian 1720-1778

BI *Alcune Vedute Di Archi Trionfali... (F. 41-71), c. 1745: Thirty-Two,* t., later edit. pub. 1778-92, margins, t. sheet stained, other sheets w/staining, loose, lacking spine, watermarks, est. $5/7,000, (05-11-93, Christie-NY, #30, illus.), each sheet 12½ x 18⅝ in., (318 x 473 mm.), etching on laid.

$880* *Altra Veduta Del Tempio Della Sibella In Tivoli (Focillon 766, Hind 63 II/III), 1761,* (03-14-93, Hindman, #361), 24½ x 17⅜ in., (62.2 x 44.1 cm.), etching (BP 614, DM 1465, FR 4980, Y 103,712).

$358* *Altra Veduta Del Tempio Della Sibilla In Tivoli (H. 62),* fold, margins, good cond., foxing, old tape/paper remains, staining,notations, surface soiling, (10-28-92, Butterfield, #2602), 24¼ x 17¼ in., (616 x 438 mm.), engraving on heavy laid paper (BP 228, DM 553, FR 1877, Y 43,926).

$220* *Altro Spaccato Per Longo,* (09-17-92, Sloan, #2345), 9½ x 12 in., (24.1 x 30.5 cm.), etching (BP 124, DM 327, FR 1118, Y 27,390).

$1700* *Ansichten Aus Rom "Tempio Antico Volgarmente Detto Della Salute" (Hind 71,2),* stained, restored, (11-11-92, Dorotheum, #327), 28⅛ x 29¹¹⁄₁₆ in., (71.5 x 75.4 cm.), etching (BP 1125, DM 2717, FR 9106, Y 211,390, SC 8960).

$1275* *Ansichten Aus Rom, Colonna Antonia (Hind 52,3),* (11-11-92, Dorotheum, #339), 29⅝ x 20¼ in., (75.3 x 51.4 cm.), etching (BP 844, DM 2038, FR 6829, Y 158,543, SC 6720).

$956* *Ansichten Aus Rom, Sepolcio Di Cecilia Metella (Hind 67,2),* restored, (11-11-92, Dorotheum, #329), 20¼ x 29⅝ in., (51.5 x 75.2 cm.), etching (BP 633, DM 1528, FR 5121, Y 118,876, SC 5040).

BI *Ansichten Aus Rom, Veduta Del Palazzo Farnese (Hind 107, 1),* residue, est. SC 10/12,000, (11-11-92, Dorotheum, #335), 20³⁄₁₆ x 29⁷⁄₁₆ in., (51.3 x 74.7 cm.), etching.

$1487* *Ansichten Aus Rom, Veduta Del Palazzo Odelscalchi (Hind 26,2),* (11-11-92, Dorotheum, #340), 19¹⁵⁄₁₆ x 29⅝ in., (50.7 x 75.3 cm.), etching (BP 984, DM 2377, FR 7965, Y 184,904, SC 7840).

$1275* *Ansichten Aus Rom, Veduta Del Palazzo Stopani (Hind 128,1),* (11-11-92, Dorotheum, #341), 20¹⁄₁₆ x 29⁷⁄₁₆ in., (51 x 74.7 cm.), etching (BP 844, DM 2038, FR 6829, Y 158,543, SC 6720).

$2550* *Ansichten Aus Rom, Veduta Del Pantheon D'Agrippa (Hind 60,1 or 2),* tears, (11-11-92, Dorotheum, #337), 20⅜ x 29¹¹⁄₁₆ in., (51.7 x 75.4 cm.), etching (BP 1687, DM 4075, FR 13,658, Y 317,085, SC 13,440).

$1700* *Ansichten Aus Rom, Veduta Dell Tempio Delle Camene (Hind 106,1),* (11-11-92, Dorotheum, #336), 20³⁄₁₆ x 29¾ in., (51.3 x 75.5 cm.), etching (BP 1125, DM 2717, FR 9106, Y 211,390, SC 8960).

BI *Ansichten Aus Rom, Veduta Della Gran Curia Innocenzi-ana, Monte Citorio (Hind 23,1)*, est. SC 10/12,000, (11-11-92, Dorotheum, #338), 20¹⁄₁₆ x 29⁵⁄₈ in., (51 x 75.2 cm.), etching.

BI *Ansichten Aus Rom, Veduta Di Piazza Navona (Hind 108,1)*, (11-11-92, Dorotheum, #326, illus.), 20³⁄₁₆ x 29⁵⁄₈ in., (51.2 x 75.2 cm.), etching.

BI *Le Antichita Romane*, est. $1/200, (02-14-93, Hanzel, #684), 17¾ x 11½ in., (45.1 x 29.2 cm.), etching.

$19,854* *Antichita Romane De Tempi Della Repubblica E De'P-rimi Imperatori...Parte Prima E Seconda (pag. 75 ff)*, 1748: Twenty-Five, watermark, (06-23-93, Kornfeld, #83, illus.), sheet approx. 15⁷⁄₁₆ x 21¼ in., (BP 13,488, DM 33,594, FR 112,999, Y 2,162,981, SF 29,900).

$3466* *Antichita Romane De'Tempi Della Republica (Focillon 41-71; Giesecke 8)*, 1748: Twenty-Nine, (12-04-92, Bassenge, #6666), etching (BP 2223, DM 5520, FR 18,725, Y 432,709).

$110* *The Arch Of Constantine-Vedut Dell'Arco Di Constantino (H. 97)*, embossed stamp, (06-11-93, Freemn/Fine Art, #182), 18⁷⁄₈ x 28¼ in., (47.9 x 71.8 cm.), engraving (BP 72, DM 179, FR 603, Y 11,671).

$110* *The Arch Of Septimius Severus-Vedut A Dell'Arco Di Settimio Severo (Holland 99)*, embossed stamp, repaired, (06-11-93, Freemn/Fine Art, #180), 18¾ x 28¼ in., (47.6 x 71.8 cm.), engraving (BP 72, DM 179, FR 603, Y 11,671).

$550* *"The Arch Of Titus", 1760, "The So-Called Villa Of Maecenas At Tivoli, Interior, With Two Figures In The Opening Of An Arch Above", 1764 and "The So-Called Villa Of Maecenas At Tivoli, Interior", 1767 (Hind 55, 73 & 84): Three*, first, 5th final state; second, 4th final state; third, 1st state of3; from Vedute di Roma, (03-24-93, Grogan, #30), first 15⁷⁄₈ x 24 in., (40.3 x 61 cm.), etching (BP 372, DM 898, FR 3057, Y 64,622).

$248* *Architectural Fragments: Three*, (06-13-93, Hindman, #392), larger 26 x 16 in., (66 x 40.6 cm.), etching (BP 162, DM 404, FR 1357, Y 26,097).

$770* *Avanzi Del Tempio Del Dio Canopo (Focillon 844, Hind 90 II/IV)*, 1768, (05-16-93, Hindman, #422), 17⁷⁄₈ x 23 in., (45.4 x 58.4 cm.), etching (BP 501, DM 1239, FR 4162, Y 85,356).

$496* *"Avanzi Del Tempio Del Dio Canopo Nella Villa Adriana In Tivoli" (H.90/I/II)*, 1768, early print, (06-08-93, Karl/Faber, #151), etching (BP 326, DM 805, FR 2710, Y 52,682).

$764* *Avanzi Del Tempio Detto Di Apollo Nella Villa Adriana Vicino A Tivoli (H. 85/II (v. IV))*, 1768, early print, (06-23-93, Kornfeld, #80), etching (BP 519, DM 1293, FR 4348, Y 83,233, SF 1150).

$1540* *Avanzi Della Villa Di Mecenate A Tivoli (Focillon 768, Hind 65 I/III)*, 1763, (03-14-93, Hindman, #362), 17⁷⁄₈ x 26⁵⁄₈ in., (45.4 x 67.6 cm.), etching (BP 1074, DM 2563, FR 8715, Y 181,497).

$1063* *"Avanzi Della Villa Di Mecenate A Tivoli, Costruita Di Travertini A Opera Incerta" (H. 65/I)*, 1. Pariser Ausgabe, (06-08-93, Karl/Faber, #146), etching on hand-made (BP 699, DM 1725, FR 5809, Y 112,905).

$425* *"Avanzi Di Una Sala Appartenente Al Castro Pretorio Nella Villa Adriana In Tivoli" (H. 112/I)*, 1774, 1. Pariser Ausgabe, (06-08-93, Karl/Faber, #153), etching (BP 279, DM 690, FR 2322, Y 45,141).

$248* *The Batheon Exterior*, from ed. of Fermin-Didot (Paris 1835-9), discoloration, buckling, (11-12-92, Freemn/Fine Art, #176), 18½ x 27⅛ in., (47 x 68.9 cm.), etching (BP 163, DM 393, FR 1325, Y 30,750).

BI *Beatissime Pater*, est. $100/150, (05-16-93, Hanzel, #454), 18 x 12½ in., (45.7 x 31.8 cm.), etching.

$722* *Bildnis Des Giovanni Battista Piranesi, 1779*, (12-04-92, Bassenge, #6682), 16⁵⁄₈ x 12⁵⁄₁₆ in., (42.3 x 31.2 cm.), etching (BP 463, DM 1150, FR 3901, Y 90,137).

$1300* *Das Capriccio Mit Dem Skelett Und Dem Faun (Focillon 20; Robinson 21IV)*, from Caprici decorative, foxed, (12-04-92, Bassenge, #6665, illus.), 15⅜ x 21½ in., (39.1 x 54.6 cm.), etching (BP 834, DM 2070, FR 7023, Y 162,297).

BI *Carcere Oscura (Focillon 4; Robinson 3 III), 1743*, from Prima parte di architettura, est. DM 1,500, (12-04-92,

Bassenge, #6664), 15¼ x 9⁷⁄₁₆ in., (38.8 x 24 cm.), etching.

$31,664* *Carceri D'Invenzione (Focillon 24-39, Robinson 29-44), c. 1778-1799:Sixteen*, 3rd issue, full margins, large stain image center, soiling, foxing, waterstain, wormhole, tear, (11-30-92, Phillips-London, #294), plate 21¼ x 16¼ in., (540 x 413 mm.), etchings on laid (BP 20,900, DM 50,444, FR 171,249, Y 3,940,759).

$1029* *Carceri II (Hind 2), 1761*, tears, (11-03-92, Hartung, #4070), etching on handmade (BP 664, DM 1610, FR 5456, Y 125,687).

$2750* *Carceri: The Drawbridge (An Immense Interior) (H. 7), 1749*, large margins, good cond., repaired tears, creases, foxing, mat staining, surface soiling, (10-28-92, Butterfield, #2597, illus.), 21⅛ x 16 in., (537 x 406 mm.), etching on wove, watermark (BP 1752, DM 4247, FR 14,421, Y 337,423).

$3450* *Catalogo Delle Opere Date Finora Alla Luce Da Gio-Battista Piranesi (Focillon 1), c. 1743-57*, 60 plates from the Vedute di Roma, watermark, wide margins, repairedtears, water stains, foxing, laid down, i., (05-13-93, Sotheby-NY, #333, illus.), 15⅝ x 11⅝ in., (397 x 294 mm.), etching (BP 2265, DM 5571, FR 18,791, Y 385,174).

$850* *"Colonna Antonia" (H. 52/V; V.S.D 16/V), 1758*, 1. Pariser Ausgabe, (06-08-93, Karl/Faber, #143), etching (BP 559, DM 1379, FR 4645, Y 90,281).

$231* *Colonna Antonina*, (02-14-93, Hanzel, #686), 17½ x 13⅛ in., (44.5 x 33.3 cm.), etching (BP 163, DM 383, FR 1296, Y 27,858).

$2974* *Colonna Trajana (Hind 3 (VII))*, (11-11-92, Dorotheum, #334, illus.), 29½ x 20⅜ in., (75 x 51.7 cm.), etching (BP 1968, DM 4753, FR 15,929, Y 369,809, SC 15,680).

$165* *The Colosseum-Veduta Dell Anfiteatro Falvio Dettoil Colosseo (H. 57)*, (06-11-93, Freemn/Fine Art, #184), 17⅜ x 27⅝ in., (44.1 x 70.2 cm.), engraving (BP 108, DM 268, FR 904, Y 17,507).

$110* *Della Magnificenza*, (02-14-93, Hanzel, #682), 18⅜ x 12⅛ in., (46.7 x 30.8 cm.), etching (BP 77, DM 182, FR 617, Y 13,266).

$557* *The Egyptian Obelisk In The Piazza Di S. Giovanni Laterano (Hind 53), 1759*, 2nd state of 5, watermark, full margins, good cond., (10-27-92, Phillips-London, #24), plate 21⅜ x 15⅞ in., (543 x 403 mm.), etching on laid (BP 352, DM 854, FR 2897, Y 68,135).

$132* *"Fantastic Scene With Architectural Elements, Skulls, Weapons Etc..."*, num. 348 in plate, (12-05-92, Neal, #143), plate 15½ x 20½ in., (39.4 x 52.1 cm.), etching (BP 83, DM 206, FR 701, Y 16,355).

$193* *Figures At The Ruins*, (12-17-92, Mystic, #39), 24½ x 17½ in., (62.2 x 44.5 cm.), engraving (BP 122, DM 301, FR 1029, Y 23,719).

$297,654* *A Fine Collection In Nineteen Volumes: "Vedute Di Roma" (Hind 1-135),1744-77, "Differentes Vues De Quelques Restes" (F. 583-599), 1778-79, "Plans And Elevations For The Pantheon", 1786 and others*, (06-30-93, Sotheby-London, #179, illus.), etching on paper w/Fleur-de-Lys in Double Circle watermark w/Serafinicountermark, others on a thin paper w/Fleur-de-Lys (BP 199,500, DM 507,682, FR 1,712,624, Y 31,892,639).

$330* *Frontispice Du Della Magnificenze De Architettura De'Romani (Focillon 927), 1761*, (03-14-93, Hindman, #366), 17¾ x 11⅜ in., (45.1 x 28.9 cm.), etching (BP 230, DM 549, FR 1868, Y 38,892).

$314* *Galleria Grande Di Statue (H. Focillon 3)*, yellowed, staining, creases, large margins, (06-16-93, Ader Tajan, #44), 13¾ x 9⅝ in., (35 x 24.5 cm.), etching (BP 209, DM 521, FR 1749, Y 33,490).

$220* *Hadrian's Villa, A Hall In The So Called Academia (H.134)*, (11-12-92, Freemn/Fine Art, #177), 17¼ x 22⅝ in., (43.8 x 57.5 cm.), etching (BP 144, DM 349, FR 1176, Y 27,278).

$1152* *Hirten Mit Kuhherde Im Poseiden-Tempel Von Paestum*, sheet i., (11-27-92, Zeller, #494), 19¹¹⁄₁₆ x 26¾ in., (50 x 68 cm.), engraving, etching on handmade (BP 759, DM 1840, FR 6251, Y 143,373).

$1080* *Hirten Mit Tieren In Ruinen Des Juno-Tempels In Paestum*, (11-27-92, Zeller, #495), 19¹¹⁄₁₆ x 26¾ in., (50 x 68 cm.), print (BP 712, DM 1725, FR 5860, Y 134,412).

$110* *Il Campo*, s. in plate, (11-01-92, Hanzel, #235), 18½ x 12 in., (47 x 30.5 cm.), engraving (BP 72, DM 174, FR 585, Y 13,600).

$458* *"Il Castel Dell' Acqua Marcia" (Hind 34, I)*, 1753, stained, (03-24-93, Venator/Hansten, #2560), pl. 15¾ x 23¹³⁄₁₆ in., (40 x 60.5 cm.), etching w/engraving (BP 310, DM 748, FR 2546, Y 53,813).

$440* *Interior Of The So-Called Temple Of Neptune*, from Views of Paestum, (03-24-93, Grogan, #27), 19½ x 26½ in., (49.5 x 67.3 cm.), etching (BP 298, DM 719, FR 2446, Y 51,698).

$385* *Listesso Sepolcro Delineato (Focillon 514)*, 1764, plate VIa of Antichita d'Abano e di Castel Gandofo, (05-16-93, Hindman, #417), 7½ x 11¼ in., (19.1 x 28.6 cm.), etching (BP 250, DM 619, FR 2081, Y 42,678).

$550* *Mausoleo Antico (Focillon 14, Robinson 5 V/VI)*, 1743, plate 3 of Prima Parte, (05-16-93, Hindman, #411), 14 x 9⅞ in., (35.6 x 25.1 cm.), etching (BP 358, DM 885, FR 2973, Y 60,969).

BI *Methods Of Raising Travertine (F. 335)*, 1756, margins, laid down, good cond., foxing, surface abrasions in image, est. $5/700, (02-24-93, Butterfield, #2692), 15 x 20⅜ in., (381 x 518 mm.), engraving on heavy laid.

$567* *"Obelisco Egizio" (H. 53/III; V.S.D 18/IV)*, 1759, 1. Pariser Ausgabe, (06-08-93, Karl/Faber, #144), etching (BP 373, DM 920, FR 3098, Y 60,223).

$248* *"Obelisco Eglizo"*, 1764, from Vedute di Roma, (12-12-92, Wolf, #2), 15½ x 21 in., (39.4 x 53.3 cm.), etching (BP 159, DM 391, FR 1339, Y 30,689).

$2300* *"Piazza Di Monte Cavallo" and "Fontana Dell'Acqua Felice" (Hind 15 and 20)*, c. 1760: Two, from Vedute di Roma, Hinds's state B-3, H. 15, watermark, margins, center fold, foxing, (05-13-93, Sotheby-NY, #334), one 15¼ x 21⅜ in., (390 x 540 mm.), other 15⅞ x 26⅞ in., (390 x 540 mm.), etching (BP 1510, DM 3714, FR 12,527, Y 256,782).

$1133* *Rovine D'Una Galleria Di Statue Nella Villa Adriana A Tivoli (Hind 931)*, 1770, (06-04-93, Bassenge, #5549), 17¹⁵⁄₁₆ x 22¹³⁄₁₆ in., (45.5 x 58 cm.), etching (BP 750, DM 1840, FR 6201, Y 122,196).

BI *Le Rovine Del Castello*, est. $100/150, (05-16-93, Hanzel, #456), 18½ x 12 in., (47 x 30.5 cm.), etching.

$1100* *Rovine Del Sisto, O Sia Delle Terme Antoniniane*, 1765, Focillon 851; Hind 77 II/IV, prov., (09-20-92, Hindman, #667), 17 x 26 in., (43.2 x 66 cm.), etching (BP 644, DM 1632, FR 5584, Y 135,954).

$1276* *"Rovine Delle Terme Antoniniane" (H. 77/II)*, 1765, (06-08-93, Karl/Faber, #150), etching (BP 839, DM 2070, FR 6973, Y 135,528).

$2291* *The Sawhorse (Robison 38/V (v.VI)*, sheet 12 of series: Carceri, 1745, reworked 1760, (06-23-93, Kornfeld, #84, illus.), etching and engraving (BP 1556, DM 3876, FR 13,039, Y 249,591, SF 3450).

$413* *Scenographia Insulae Tiberinae (Focillon 441)*, 1762, Plate XI of Ie Campo Marzio Dell'Antica Roma, (03-14-93, Hindman, #365), 8 x 17½ in., (20.3 x 44.5 cm.), etching (BP 288, DM 687, FR 2337, Y 48,674).

$303* *Schemata Emissarii Lacus Albani*, margins, good cond.?, (10-28-92, Butterfield, #2850), 16 x 44½ in., (40.6 x 113 cm.), etching on wove (BP 193, DM 468, FR 1589, Y 37,178).

$770* *Sepolcro Di Cecilia Metella (Focillon 772, Hind 67 I/III)*, 1762, (03-14-93, Hindman, #363), 18 x 25 in., (45.7 x 63.5 cm.), etching (BP 537, DM 1282, FR 4358, Y 90,748).

BI *Sepolcro Di Cecilia Metella (Hind 67)*, margins, water staining, mat burn, some foxing, darkening, backboard-burn, est. $4/600, (05-22-93, Weschler, #213), 18 x 25 in., (45.7 x 63.5 cm.), etching.

$110* *The So Called Temple Of Minerva Medica-Veduta Del Tempio OttangolareDi Minerva Medica (H. 74)*, embossed stamp, (06-11-93, Freemn/Fine Art, #183), 18½ x 27⅞ in., (47 x 70.8 cm.), engraving (BP 72, DM 179, FR 603, Y 11,671).

BI *"The So-Called Villa Of Maecenas At Tivoli" and "The Piazza Del Campidoglio" (H. 84 and 111)*, c. 1770: Two,

from Vedute di Roma, posthumous impressions, watermark, margins, crease, staining, est. $7/900, (05-13-93, Sotheby-NY, #335), one 16⅞ x 23¾ in., (430 x 600 mm.), other 17⅞ x 27 in., (430 x 600 mm.), etching.

$567* *"Spaccato Interno Della Basilica Di S. Paolo Fuori Delle Mura" (H. 7/IV; V.S.D 5/V)*, 1749, early print, (06-08-93, Karl/Faber, #130), etching (BP 373, DM 920, FR 3098, Y 60,223).

BI *Statue Design*, margins, central fold, est. BP 8/120, (06-16-93, Bonhams-Chelsea, #347), pl. 25¾ x 16¼ in., (65.4 x 41.3 cm.), etching on wove.

$648* *Der Sybillen-Tempel In Tivoli*, from Vedute di Roma, (11-27-92, Zeller, #496), 16⁹⁄₁₆ x 25³⁄₁₆ in., (42 x 64 cm.), etching (BP 427, DM 1035, FR 3516, Y 80,647).

$880* *Tempi Del Sole E Della Luna (Focillon 812; Hind 50 I or II/VI)*, 1759, (05-16-93, Hindman, #419), 16⅛ x 21⅝ in., (41 x 54.9 cm.), etching (BP 572, DM 1415, FR 4757, Y 97,550).

$2383* *Temple De Neptune A Pesto (Focillon 593)*, 1778, from Differentes Vues De Quelques Restes...De Pesto, (12-04-92, Bassenge, #6667), 18⅛ x 26¾ in., (46 x 68 cm.), etching (BP 1529, DM 3795, FR 12,874, Y 297,503).

$487* *The Temple Of Antoninus And Faustina (Hind 49)*, 1758, 3rd state of 6, full margins, watermark, good cond., central fold, tears, water staining, (10-27-92, Phillips-London, #23), plate 16 x 21⅜ in., (406 x 543 mm.), etching on laid (BP 308, DM 746, FR 2533, Y 59,572).

BI *Tomb Design*, margins, central fold, est. BP 150/200, (03-17-93, Bonhams-Chelsea, #422), plate 19 x 28¼ in., (48.3 x 71.8 cm.), etching on wove.

$231* *Tomb Design*, margins, central fold, (06-16-93, Bonhams-Chelsea, #346), pl. 25¾ x 16¼ in., (65.4 x 41.3 cm.), etching on wove (BP 154, DM 383, FR 1287, Y 24,637).

$165* *The Tomb Of Caecilia Metella-Sepolcro Di Cecila Metella (H. 67)*, embossed stamp, (06-11-93, Freemn/Fine Art, #181), 17⅞ x 24⅞ in., (45.4 x 63.2 cm.), engraving (BP 108, DM 268, FR 904, Y 17,507).

$385* *Various Group Of Architectural Details: Six*, full margins, good cond., staining, surface soiling, creases, tears,binding holes, pencil notations, five w/inkstamp, (02-24-93, Butterfield, #2693), each sheet 20⅛ x 29⅝ in., (511 x 752 mm.), engraving on wove (BP 268, DM 625, FR 2119, Y 45,177).

$10,231* *Vasi, Candelabri, Cippi...(F. 601-718): Large Folio*, a nearly complete set, w/frontispiece, lacking F. 602, 603, 613 and 718, all w/margins, torn and damaged, tear, central fold, stains, other defects,bound, (12-03-92, Sotheby-London, #91, illus.), etching (BP 6600, DM 16,089, FR 54,917, Y 1,272,987).

$690* *Veduta De Campo Vaccino (H. 40)*, 1757, watermark, margins, good cond., mat/glue staining, glue remains, crease, glue remains, surface soiling, (05-19-93, Butterfield, #1864), 16⅛ x 21¾ in., (410 x 552 mm.), etching on heavy laid (BP 448, DM 1122, FR 3779, Y 76,387).

$880* *Veduta Degli Avanzi Del Foro Di Nerva (Hind 95 II/IV)*, 1770, from 1st Paris Edition, 1800-1807, (10-18-92, Hindman, #500), 18⅝ x 28 in., (47.3 x 71.1 cm.), etching (BP 538, DM 1310, FR 4442, Y 105,579).

$248* *Veduta Degli Avanzi Del Sepolero Della Famiglia Plavzia*, (12-10-92, Sloan, #1320), 18 x 24 in., (45.7 x 61 cm.), etching (BP 160, DM 392, FR 1340, Y 30,678).

$515* *Veduta Degli Avanzi Delle Fabbriche Del Secondo Piano Delle Terme DiTito (Hind 127)*, 1st state of 4, from contemporary Roman edit., margins, rubbed, defects, discoloration, laid down, (06-30-93, Sotheby-London, #184), 19¼ x 28 in., (489 x 711 mm.), etching (BP 345, DM 878, FR 2963, Y 55,181).

$385* *Veduta Degli Avanzi Di Antiche Fabbriche*, 1756, Focillon 187, plate XXIIa of Tome I of Le Antichita Romane, prov., (09-20-92, Hindman, #666), 5⅛ x 8¼ in., (13 x 21 cm.), etching (BP 225, DM 571, FR 1954, Y 47,584).

BI *Veduta Degli Avanzi Di Fabbrica Magnifica Sepolcrale Co'Fue Rovine,... (F. 282)*, 1756, large margins, center fold split, yellow staining, staining, surfacesoiling, tear, est. $8/1,000, (05-19-93, Butterfield, #1863), 16 x 20⅞ in., (406 x 530 mm.), engraving on laid.

$939* *Veduta Degli Avanzi Di due Triclini Che Appartenevano Alla Casa Aurea Di Nerone (Hind 50 IV), 1759,* (12-04-92, Bassenge, #6676), 16⅛ x 21¾ in., (41 x 55.3 cm.), etching (BP 602, DM 1495, FR 5073, Y 117,228).

$709* *"Veduta Degli Avanzi Superiori Delle Terme Di Diocleziano" (H. 116/I), 1774,* 1. Pariser Ausgabe, watermark, (06-08-93, Karl/Faber, #154), etching (BP 466, DM 1150, FR 3874, Y 75,305).

$303* *Veduta Del Avanzo De Mayfoleo De S. Elena,* (10-30-92, Sloan, #897), 15¾ x 25⅝ in., (40 x 65.1 cm.), etching (BP 194, DM 466, FR 1581, Y 37,533).

$638* *"Veduta Del Campidoglio Di Fianco" (H. 39/IV; V.S.D 55/II), 1775,* 1. Pariser Ausgabe, (06-08-93, Karl/Faber, #139), etching (BP 419, DM 1035, FR 3486, Y 67,764).

$1228* *Veduta Del Castello Dell' Acqua Felice (Hind 20 II), 1751,* (12-04-92, Bassenge, #6673), 15¾ x 26¾ in., (40 x 68 cm.), etching (BP 788, DM 1956, FR 6634, Y 153,308).

$605* *Veduta Del Castello Dell'Acqua Paola Sul Monte Aurco (Focillon 736, Hind 21 II/V), 1751,* (03-14-93, Hindman, #349), 15¾ x 24⅛ in., (40 x 61.3 cm.), etching (BP 422, DM 1007, FR 3424, Y 71,302).

$535* *Veduta Del Castello Dell'Aqua Paola Sul Monte Aureo (H. 21/III (v.V)), 1751,* (06-23-93, Kornfeld, #79), etching (BP 363, DM 905, FR 3045, Y 58,285, SF 805).

$660* *Veduta Del Mausoleo D'Elio Adriano (Focillon 743, Hind 30 I/IV), 1754,* (03-14-93, Hindman, #353), 17¼ x 22 in., (43.8 x 55.9 cm.), etching (BP 460, DM 1099, FR 3735, Y 77,784).

$1300* *Veduta Del Mausoleo D'Elio Adriano (Hind 30 I), 1754,* (12-04-92, Bassenge, #6674), 17½ x 22½ in., (44.5 x 57.2 cm.), etching (BP 834, DM 2070, FR 7023, Y 162,297).

$201* *Veduta Del Palazzo Farnese (H. 107), 1773,* center fold, good cond., toned, surface soiling, tape remains, foxing, notations, (05-19-93, Butterfield, #1865), 15⁵⁄₁₆ x 25¹⁵⁄₁₆ in., (389 x 659 mm.), engraving on laid (BP 130, DM 327, FR 1101, Y 22,252).

$425* *"Veduta Del Palazzo Odeschalchi" (H. 26/III; V.S.D 35/IV), 1753,* 1. Pariser Ausgabe, (06-08-93, Karl/Faber, #135), etching (BP 279, DM 690, FR 2322, Y 45,141).

$354* *"Veduta Del Palazzo Stopani" (H. 128/I), 1776,* 1. Pariser Ausgabe, (06-08-93, Karl/Faber, #155), etching (BP 233, DM 574, FR 1934, Y 37,600).

$425* *"Veduta Del Piano Superiore Del Serraglio Delle Fiere Fabbricato Da Domiziano A Uso Dell'Anfiteatro Flavio" (H. 43/III; V.S.D 30/V), 1757,* (06-08-93, Karl/Faber, #140), etching (BP 279, DM 690, FR 2322, Y 45,141).

$443* *Veduta Del Ponte E Castello Sant 'Angelo,* laid down, margins, (04-22-93, Bonhams-Chelsea, #156), plate 15 x 23¼ in., (38.1 x 59.1 cm.), engraving on wove (BP 286, DM 712, FR 2401, Y 48,708).

$143* *Veduta Del Ponte E Castello Sant' Angelo,* (02-14-93, Hanzel, #683), 11½ x 17⅜ in., (29.2 x 44.1 cm.), etching (BP 101, DM 237, FR 802, Y 17,246).

$275* *Veduta Del Ponte Molle (H. 64),* repaired tears, crease, damp staining, tape hinges, foxing, darkening, (05-22-93, Weschler, #214), 17¼ x 26½ in., (43.8 x 67.3 cm.), etching w/margins on laid (BP 178, DM 447, FR 1504, Y 30,320).

$1045* *Veduta Del Ponte Salario (Focillon 744, Hind 31 II/V), 1754,* (03-14-93, Hindman, #354), 16 x 24 in., (40.6 x 61 cm.), etching (BP 729, DM 1739, FR 5914, Y 123,159).

$1412* *Veduta Del Porto Di Ripa Grande (Hind 27 III; Focillon 742), 1753,* from series Vedute di Roma, 3rd state, (06-10-93, Hauswedell/Nolt, #204, illus.), etching (BP 924, DM 2299, FR 7741, Y 149,878).

$605* *Veduta Del Porto Di Ripetta (Focillon 814, Hind 28 IV/VII), 1753,* (03-14-93, Hindman, #352), 15⅝ x 23½ in., (39.7 x 59.7 cm.), etching (BP 422, DM 1007, FR 3424, Y 71,302).

$770* *Veduta Del Tempio Della Fortuna Virile (Focillon 817, Hind 46 III/VII), 1758,* (03-14-93, Hindman, #357), 15 x 23 in., (38.1 x 58.4 cm.), etching (BP 537, DM 1282, FR 4358, Y 90,748).

$850* *Veduta Del Tempio Della Sibilla In Tivoli (Hind 61 III), 1761,* (06-04-93, Bassenge, #5544), 16¾ x 25¹⁄₁₆ in., (42.5 x 63.7 cm.), etching (BP 562, DM 1380, FR 4652, Y 91,674).

$916* *Veduta Del Tempio Detto Della Concordia. Arco Di Settimio Severo (H.109/I), 1774,* 1st state, (06-23-93, Kornfeld, #81), etching (BP 622, DM 1550, FR 5213, Y 99,793, SF 1380).

$880* *Veduta Del Tempio Di Bacco (Focillon 753, Hind 48 III/V), 1758,* (05-16-93, Hindman, #418), 16 x 24½ in., (40.6 x 61 cm.), etching (BP 572, DM 1415, FR 4757, Y 97,550).

$1100* *Veduta Del Tempio Di Bacco (Focillon 753, Hind II/V), 1753,* (03-14-93, Hindman, #351), 16 x 24¼ in., (40.6 x 61 cm.), etching (BP 767, DM 1831, FR 6225, Y 129,641).

$935* *Veduta Del Tempio Di Cibele A Piazza Bocca Della Verita (Focillon 820, Hind 47 II/V), 1758,* (03-14-93, Hindman, #358), 15⅝ x 23½ in., (39.7 x 59.7 cm.), etching (BP 652, DM 1556, FR 5291, Y 110,194).

$722* *Veduta Del Tempio Ottangolare Di Minerva Medica (Hind 74 I-II), 1764,* (12-04-92, Bassenge, #6678), 18½ x 27¾ in., (47 x 70.5 cm.), etching (BP 463, DM 1150, FR 3901, Y 90,137).

$880* *Veduta Del Tempio, Detto Della Tosse (Focillon 774, Hind 69 I/IV), 1763,* (03-14-93, Hindman, #364), 17⅜ x 22½ in., (44.1 x 57.2 cm.), etching (BP 614, DM 1465, FR 4980, Y 103,712).

$2089* *"Veduta Dell' Anfiteatro Flavio Detto Il Colosseo" (Hind 126), 1776,* 1st state, tears, (09-14-92, Venator/Hansten, #1580), plate 19⁹⁄₁₆ x 27¹⁵⁄₁₆ in., (49.7 x 71 cm.), etching (BP 1105, DM 3105, FR 10,524, Y 259,761).

$770* *Veduta Dell'Anfiteatro Flavio Detto Il Colosseo (Focillon 215), 1757,* Plate XXXVIIa of Le Antichita Romane, (05-16-93, Hindman, #416), 5½ x 10⅝ in., (14 x 27 cm.), etching (BP 501, DM 1239, FR 4162, Y 85,356).

$143* *Veduta Dell'Anfiteatro Flavio, Detto Il Colosseo,* (11-01-92, Hanzel, #236), 11 x 17¼ in., (27.9 x 43.8 cm.), engraving (BP 93, DM 226, FR 760, Y 17,681).

$660* *Veduta Dell'Anfiteatro Flavio, Detto Il Colosseo (Focillon 758; Hind7 IV/IV), 1757,* from the Edition Firmin-Didot, (05-16-93, Hindman, #421), 17¼ x 27⅝ in., (43.8 x 70.2 cm.), etching (BP 429, DM 1062, FR 3568, Y 73,163).

$303* *Veduta Dell'Arco De Costantino (H. 97, F. 757), 1771,* p.l., margins, laid down, good cond., staining, surface soiling, (10-28-92, Butterfield, #2849), 15¼ x 22⅝ in., (387 x 575 mm.), engraving on wove (BP 193, DM 468, FR 1589, Y 37,178).

$1062* *Veduta Dell'Arco Di Benevento (Hind 135 II), 1778,* watermark, (06-04-93, Bassenge, #5552, illus.), 18¹¹⁄₁₆ x 27¹⁵⁄₁₆ in., (47.4 x 71.1 cm.), etching (BP 703, DM 1725, FR 5813, Y 114,538).

$450* *Veduta Dell'Arco Di Constantino [H97],* (02-04-93, Sloan, #2029), 18¾ x 28¼ in., (47.6 x 71.8 cm.), etching (BP 314, DM 741, FR 2513, Y 55,977).

$1540* *Veduta Dell'Arco Di Costantino, E Dell'Anfiteatro Flavio Detto Il Colosseo (Focillon 805; Hind 56 I/VI), 1760,* (05-16-93, Hindman, #420), 16 x 21⅜ in., (40.6 x 54.3 cm.), etching (BP 1001, DM 2477, FR 8324, Y 170,713).

$424* *Veduta Dell'Arco Di Settimio Severo (Hind 99 I; Focillon 754), 1772,* 1st state, (06-10-93, Hauswedell/Nolt, #206), etching (BP 277, DM 690, FR 2325, Y 45,006).

$770* *Veduta Dell'Atrio Del Ottavia (Focillon 815, Hind 58 IV/VII), 1760,* (03-14-93, Hindman, #360), 15¾ x 23⅜ in., (40 x 59.4 cm.), etching (BP 537, DM 1282, FR 4358, Y 90,748).

$496* *"Veduta Dell'Atrio Del Portico Di Ottavia" (H. 58/V; V.S.D 28/VI), 1760,* 1. Pariser Ausgabe, (06-08-93, Karl/Faber, #145), etching (BP 326, DM 805, FR 2710, Y 52,682).

$425* *"Veduta Dell'Avanzo Del Castello (H. 34/III; V.S.D 36/V), 1753,* early print, (06-08-93, Karl/Faber, #137), etching (BP 279, DM 690, FR 2322, Y 45,141).

BI *Veduta Dell'Esterno Della Gran Basilica Di S. Pietro In Vaticano (Focillon Hind 5 III/VII), 1748,* est. $550/650, (03-14-93, Hindman, #344), 15¾ x 23¾ in., (40 x 60.3 cm.), etching.

$880* *Veduta Della Arco Di Constantino, E Dell' Anfiteatro Flavio Detto IlColoseo (Focillon 805, Hind 56 III/VI), 1760,* (03-14-93, Hindman, #359), 16 x 21¼ in., (40.6 x

54 cm.), etching (BP 614, DM 1465, FR 4980, Y 103,712).

$578* *Veduta Della Basilica Di S. Giovanni In Laterano (Hind 8 III), 1749*, watermark, (12-04-92, Bassenge, #6671), 15⁷⁄₁₆ x 21⁹⁄₁₆ in., (39.2 x 54.8 cm.), etching (BP 371, DM 921, FR 3123, Y 72,160).

BI *Veduta Della Basilica Di S. Giovanni Laterano*, est. $6/800, (10-30-92, Sloan, #1593), 15½ x 22 in., (39.4 x 55.9 cm.), etching.

BI *Veduta Della Basilica Di S. Giovanni Laterano (H. 8), 1749*, margins, good cond., glue remains, rubbed areas, soiling, est. $9/1,200, (05-19-93, Butterfield, #1861), 17⅜ x 27½ in., (441 x 699 mm.), engraving on laid backed by heavy wove.

$916* *Veduta Della Basilica Di S. Giovanni Laterano (Hind 8/II (v. VI), 1749*, (06-23-93, Kornfeld, #77), etching (BP 622, DM 1550, FR 5213, Y 99,793, SF 1380).

$275* *Veduta Della Basilica Di S. Giovanni Laterano 1749 (Hind 8)*, (11-12-92, Freemn/Fine Art, #179), plate 15¼ x 21¼ in., (38.7 x 54 cm.), etching laid down on cardboard (BP 181, DM 436, FR 1470, Y 34,098).

$425* *Veduta Della Basilica Di S. Giovanni Laterano; (H8; F790)*, (02-04-93, Sloan, #1493), 15½ x 22 in., (39.4 x 55.9 cm.), etching (BP 297, DM 700, FR 2373, Y 52,867).

BI *Veduta Della Basilica Di S. Giovanni Laterno (Focillon 790, Hind 8 III/VI), 1749*, est. $550/650, (03-14-93, Hindman, #345), 15½ x 21⅜ in., (39.4 x 54.3 cm.), etching.

$939* *Veduta Della Basilica Di S. Lorenzo Fuor Della Mura (Hind 12 II), 1750*, (12-04-92, Bassenge, #6672), 14¹³⁄₁₆ x 25¹⁵⁄₁₆ in., (37.7 x 66 cm.), etching (BP 602, DM 1495, FR 5073, Y 117,228).

$433* *Veduta Della Basilica Di S. Paolo Fuor Delle Mura (Focillon 723; Hind 6 IV), 1748*, from Veduti Di Roma, (12-04-92, Bassenge, #6670), 16¹⁄₁₆ x 24½ in., (40.8 x 62.2 cm.), etching (BP 278, DM 690, FR 2339, Y 54,057).

BI *"Veduta Della Basilica Di S. Paolo Fuor Delle Mura, Eretto Da Costantino Magno" and "Veduta Della Gran Curia Innocenziana" (H. 4; H. 23), 1748; 1752*, trimmed margins, laid down, mat or light-staining, foxing, creasing,tear into image, est. $1,5/2,000, (10-28-92, Butterfield, #2603), one 16 x 24⅝ in., (406 x 625 mm.), the other 16⅛ x 24⅝ in., (406 x 625 mm.), engraving on laid paper.

$425* *"Veduta Della Basilica Di S. Paolo Fuor Delle Mura..." (H. 6/V; V.S.D51/V), 1748*, 1. Pariser Ausgabe, watermark, (06-08-93, Karl/Faber, #129), etching (BP 279, DM 690, FR 2322, Y 45,141).

$605* *Veduta Della Basilica Di S. Sebastiano (Focillon 731, Hind 13 I/IV),1750*, (03-14-93, Hindman, #348), 16½ x 26 in., (41.9 x 66 cm.), etching (BP 422, DM 1007, FR 3424, Y 71,302).

$567* *"Veduta Della Basilica Di S. Sebastiano Fuori Delle Mura..." (H. 13/II; V.S.D 59/II), 1750*, 1. Pariser Ausgabe, (06-08-93, Karl/Faber, #133), etching (BP 373, DM 920, FR 3098, Y 60,223).

$528* *Veduta Della Basilica Di San Sebastiano Fuori Delle Mura Di Roma Su La Via Appia (H. 13)*, 1st state of 4, margins, dirt, creasing, prop. Lady Manning, (10-07-92, Christie-S. Ken, #4), pl 16½ x 26¼ in., (41.9 x 66.7 cm.), etching (BP 308, DM 764, FR 2591, Y 63,500).

$690* *Veduta Della Basilica Di Sta. Maria Maggiore Con Le Due Fabbriche Laterali Di Detta Basilica (H. 9), 1749*, watermark, margins, good cond., restoration, thinned spots, mat staining glue, remains, (05-19-93, Butterfield, #1862), 16 x 21¾ in., (406 x 552 mm.), etching on laid (BP 448, DM 1122, FR 3779, Y 76,387).

$1238* *"Veduta Della Basilica Di Sta. Maria Maggiore" (Hind 9), 1749*, 1st state, watermark, (09-14-92, Venator/Hansten, #1581), plate 15¹¹⁄₁₆ x 21⁵⁄₁₆ in., (39.9 x 54.2 cm.), etching (BP 655, DM 1840, FR 6237, Y 153,942).

$605* *Veduta Della Basilica di S. Lorenzo Fuor Della Mura (Focillon 730, Hi12 II/V), 1750*, (03-14-93, Hindman, #347), 15 x 26 in., (38.1 x 66 cm.), etching (BP 422, DM 1007, FR 3424, Y 71,302).

$605* *Veduta Della Dogana Di Terra A Piazza A Pietra (Focillon 821, Hind 32 III/VI), 1753*, (03-14-93, Hindman,

#355), 15⅞ x 23¼ in., (40.3 x 59.1 cm.), etching (BP 422, DM 1007, FR 3424, Y 71,302).

$1083* *Veduta Della Dogana Di Terra A Piazza Die Pietra (Hind 32 III)*, (12-04-92, Bassenge, #6675), image 15¾ x 23¹³⁄₁₆ in., (40 x 60.5 cm.), etching (BP 695, DM 1725, FR 5851, Y 135,206).

$605* *Veduta Della Facciata Della Basilica Di S. Croce In Gerusalemme (Focillon 729, Hind II III/IV), 1750*, (03-14-93, Hindman, #346), 15¾ x 24⅛ in., (40 x 61.3 cm.), etching (BP 422, DM 1007, FR 3424, Y 71,302).

$2835* *"Veduta Della Gran Piazza E Basilica Di S. Pietro" (H. 101/I)*, 1. Pariser Ausgabe, watermark, (06-08-93, Karl/Faber, #152, illus.), etching on thick hand-made (BP 1864, DM 4600, FR 15,492, Y 301,115).

$764* *Veduta Della Piazza E Basilica Di S. Giovanni In Laterno (H. 117/I (v IV)), 1775*, very rare, early print, (06-23-93, Kornfeld, #82), etching (BP 519, DM 1293, FR 4348, Y 83,233, SF 1150).

$605* *Veduta Della Villa Estiuse In Tivoli (H. 105), 1773*, plate s., t., large margins, laid down, good cond., surface soiling,creases, one in image, (10-28-92, Butterfield, #2601), 18⅝ x 28 in., (473 x 711 mm.), engraving on laid paper (BP 385, DM 934, FR 3173, Y 74,233).

$498* *"Veduta Della Villa Estnse In Tivoli" (H. 105/nach III)*, tears, (12-01-92, Karl/Faber, #120), etching on thick hand made (BP 329, DM 794, FR 2705, Y 62,002).

$1133* *Veduta Delle Antiche Sostruzioni...Dette Il Bel Lido (Hind 125 I), 1776*, (06-04-93, Bassenge, #5550), 17⅝ x 26½ in., (44.8 x 67.3 cm.), etching (BP 750, DM 1840, FR 6201, Y 122,196).

$708* *Veduta Delle Cascatelle A Tivoli (Hind 92 II), 1769*, (06-04-93, Bassenge, #5548, illus.), 18¹¹⁄₁₆ x 27¹⁵⁄₁₆ in., (47.5 x 71 cm.), etching (BP 468, DM 1150, FR 3875, Y 76,359).

$913* *"Veduta Delle Cascatelle A Tivoli" (H. 92/I)*, small margins, (12-01-92, Karl/Faber, #118), etching on thick hand made (BP 603, DM 1455, FR 4959, Y 113,670).

$791* *Veduta Delle Due Chiese, L'Una Detta Delle Maddona Di Loreto L'AltraDel Nome Di Maria Presso La Colonna Trajana (H. 66)*, 1st state of 4, margins, dirt, cockling, laid, prop. Lady Manning, (10-07-92, Christie-S. Ken, #5, illus.), pl 16¾ x 27½ in., (42.5 x 69.9 cm.), etching (BP 462, DM 1145, FR 3881, Y 95,129).

$622* *Veduta Delle Gran Curia Innocenziana (Hind 23/III; Villa-Salamon D 52/VI)*, from the series Vedute di Roma, foxed, (12-01-92, Karl/Faber, #115), etching (BP 411, DM 991, FR 3379, Y 77,440).

$1210* *Veduta Di Altra Parte Della Camera Sepolcrale Di L. Arrunzio (Focillon 232), 1756*, pl. X, Tome II of Le Antichita Romane, (10-18-92, Hindman, #501), 17 x 23½ in., (43.2 x 59.7 cm.), etching (BP 740, DM 1801, FR 6108, Y 145,171).

$605* *Veduta Di Campo Vaccino (Focillon 803, Hind 40 III/VI), 1757*, (03-14-93, Hindman, #356), 16 x 21⅜ in., (40.6 x 54.3 cm.), etching (BP 422, DM 1007, FR 3424, Y 71,302).

$1554* *Veduta Di Campo Vaccino (Hind 100 I; Focillon 748), 1772*, 1st state, (06-10-93, Hauswedell/Nolt, #207, illus.), etching (BP 1016, DM 2531, FR 8520, Y 164,951).

$880* *Veduta Di Pesto, Planche II, 1778, Focillon 584*, (09-20-92, Hindman, #668), 19¾ x 26⅞ in., (50.2 x 68.3 cm.), etching (BP 515, DM 1306, FR 4467, Y 108,763).

$825* *Veduta Di Pesto, Planche III, 1778, Focillon 585*, (09-20-92, Hindman, #669), 20 x 26⅞ in., (50.8 x 68.3 cm.), etching (BP 483, DM 1224, FR 4188, Y 101,965).

$990* *Veduta Di Pesto, Planche V, 1778, Focillon 587*, (09-20-92, Hindman, #670), 19¾ x 26⅞ in., (49.5 x 68.3 cm.), etching (BP 580, DM 1469, FR 5025, Y 122,358).

$935* *Veduta Di Pesto, Planche VIII, 1778, Focillon 590*, (09-20-92, Hindman, #671), 19½ x 26⅜ in., (49.5 x 67 cm.), etching (BP 547, DM 1387, FR 4746, Y 115,560).

$935* *Veduta Di Pesto, Planche X, 1778, Focillon 592*, (09-20-92, Hindman, #672), 20¾ x 28 in., (52.7 x 71.1 cm.), etching (BP 547, DM 1387, FR 4746, Y 115,560).

$1045* *Veduta Di Pesto, Planche XIII, 1778, Focillon 595*, (09-20-92, Hindman, #673), 19¾ x 26¾ in., (50.2 x 67.9 cm.), etching (BP 612, DM 1551, FR 5305, Y 129,156).

$1045* *Veduta Di Pesto, Planche XV, 1778, Focillon 598*, (09-20-92, Hindman, #674), 20 x 27 in., (50.8 x 68.6 cm.), etching (BP 612, DM 1551, FR 5305, Y 129,156).

$2673* *Veduta Di Piazza Navona Sopra Le Rovine Del Circo Agonale (H. 16/II (v. VI), 1751*, early print, (06-23-93, Kornfeld, #78), etching (BP 1816, DM 4523, FR 15,213, Y 291,208, SF 4025).

BI *Veduta Di Piazza Navona...*, est. $100/150, (05-16-93, Hanzel, #457), 13 x 17¼ in., (33 x 43.8 cm.), etching.

$1328* *"Veduta In Perspettiva Della Gran Fontana Dell'Acqua Vergine Detta DiTrevi..." (H. 104/I)*, browning, (12-01-92, Karl/Faber, #119, illus.), etching on thick hand made (BP 877, DM 2117, FR 7213, Y 165,339).

$1540* *Veduta Interna Del Pronao Del Panteon (H. 82), 1769*, plate s., large margins, fold, good cond., staining, surface soiling, tears, (10-28-92, Butterfield, #2604, illus.), 15¼ x 21 in., (387 x 533 mm.), engraving on heavy laid paper (BP 981, DM 2378, FR 8076, Y 188,957).

BI *Veduta Interna Dell'Antico Tempio De Bacco (F. 752, H. 81), 1767*, margins, good cond., tears, thinned spot, light-staining, mat staining, surface soiling, est. $7/900, (02-24-93, Butterfield, #2694), 16¾ x 24 in., (425 x 610 mm.), engraving on wove.

$468* *Veduta Interna Dell'Atrio Portico Di Ottavia (Hind 59)*, (11-12-92, Freemn/Fine Art, #178), plate 16⅛ x 21⅝ in., (41 x 54.9 cm.), etching laid down on cardboard (BP 307, DM 742, FR 2501, Y 58,029).

$708* *Veduta Interna Della Basilica Di S. Maria Maggiore (Hind 87 I-II), 1768*, (06-04-93, Bassenge, #5546), 17¹/₁₆ x 26⁹/₁₆ in., (43.3 x 67.5 cm.), etching (BP 468, DM 1150, FR 3875, Y 76,359).

$706* *Veduta Sul Monte Quirinale Del Palazzo Dell'Eccellentissima Casa Barberini...(H. 25/II; V.S. D 56/III), 1760*, (12-01-92, Karl/Faber, #116), etching on thick hand made (BP 466, DM 1125, FR 3835, Y 87,898).

$1155* *Veduta delle Due Chies, L'Una Detta Della Madonna Di Loreto, L'Abra Del Nome Di Maria (Hind 66 II), 1762*, (12-04-92, Bassenge, #6677), 16¹⁵/₁₆ x 27⅜ in., (43 x 69.5 cm.), etching (BP 741, DM 1839, FR 6240, Y 144,195).

$605* *Veduta, Nella Via Del Corso, Del Palazzo Dell'Accademia (Focillon 739, Hind 24 II/V), 1852*, (03-14-93, Hindman, #350), 16 x 24½ in., (40.6 x 62.2 cm.), etching (BP 422, DM 1007, FR 3424, Y 71,302).

BI *"Vedute Della Fonte E Delle Spelonche D'Egeria Fuor Della Porta CapenOr Di S. Seb.", and "Avanzi Del Tempie Detto Di Appollo Nella Villa Adriana Vicino A Tivoli"*: Two, margins, center creases, tears, binding holes, surface soiling, goodcond. (?), est. $1,5/2,000, (02-24-93, Butterfield, #2695), one 15⅞ x 27⅛ in., (403 x 689 mm.), other 18½ x 24⅜ in., (403 x 689 mm.), engraving on thick laid.

$330* *Veduto Dell'Arco Di Gallieno (Focillon 84), 1748*, from Varie vedute di Roma, (05-16-93, Hindman, #413), 5¼ x 7¾ in., (13.3 x 19.7 cm.), etching (BP 215, DM 531, FR 1784, Y 36,581).

$766* *The Villa D'Este, Tivoli (H. 105), 1773*, 1st state of 4, laid on card, foxing, (10-27-92, Phillips-London, #26), plate 18½ x 27½ in., (470 x 699 mm.), etching on laid (BP 484, DM 1174, FR 3983, Y 93,700).

$10,831* *Die Ziehbrucke (Hind 7; Robison 33 1)*, first state, (12-04-92, Bassenge, #6668A, illus.), 22¹/₁₆ x 16⁵/₁₆ in., (56.1 x 41.5 cm.), etching (BP 6947, DM 17,250, FR 58,514, Y 1,352,185).

PIRANESI, Giovanni Battista (after)

$220* *Architectural Detail Prints: A Pair*, good/poor cond., (03-28-93, Bakker, #18), largest, plate 16 x 20½ in., (40.6 x 52.1 cm.), etching (BP 148, DM 359, FR 1220, Y 25,605).

$33* *Pont Triomphal Erige Par Un Empereur Romain*, (05-28-93, Sloan, #209, illus.), image area 9 x 13⅞ in., (22.9 x 35.2 cm.), color engraving (BP 21, DM 52, FR 177, Y 3538).

BI *Pont Triomphal Erige Par Un Empereur Romain*, by Emile-Florentin Daumont, est. $150/250, (12-10-92, Sloan, #587), image 9 x 13⅞ in., (22.9 x 35.2 cm.), color engraving.

PISSARO, H. Claude   French b. 1935

$770* *Winter Landscape*, s., #191/200, (06-11-93, Freemn/Fine Art, #185), 14 x 19 in., (35.6 x 48.3 cm.), color etching (BP 506, DM 1251, FR 4219, Y 81,698).

PISSARRO, Camille   French 1830-1903

BI *Baigneuse Aux Oies (D. 115), 1895*, i. 2e etat no. 1, unique impression of 2nd state, margins, good cond., smudges, glue stain, est. $8/10,000, (05-13-93, Sotheby-NY, #779, illus.), 5⅛ x 7⅛ in., (129 x 180 mm.), etching and aquatint on wove.

$7475* *Baigneuses (Le Jour) (D., C. 151), c. 1895*, s., t., no. 14, watermark, large margins, good cond., foxing, (05-13-93, Sotheby-NY, #786, illus.), 5¼ x 8 in., (132 x 203 mm.), sh 10⅜ x 14¼ in., (132 x 203 mm.), lithograph on greenish-blue applique on white wove (BP 4907, DM 12,070, FR 40,714, Y 834,543).

BI *Baigneuses A L'Ombre Des Berges Boisees (D. 142), 1895*, 2nd (final) state, s., pub. in L'Estampe originale, blindstamp, fullmargins, good cond., foxing, soiling, est. $2/3,000, (05-13-93, Sotheby-NY, #783), 6⅛ x 8⅝ in., (156 x 219 mm.), zincograph on chine applique.

BI *Baigneuses A L'Ombre Des Berges Boisees (L.D. 142), 1895*, 2nd final state, s., t., i. Ep defininitive no 4, proof, margins, light/mat staining, foxing, skinned patches, glue, good cond., est. $7/10,000, (11-09-92, Christie-NY, #191, illus.), 6⅛ x 8⁹/₁₆ in., (155 x 217 mm.), lithograph on Chine applique.

BI *Baigneuses Gardeuses D'Oies (D., C. 119), c. 1895*, 2nd state (of 9), i. no. 1., 2 etat, couleur Prusse/Rouge Venise, full margins, good cond., printer's crease, foxing, est. $10/15,000, (05-13-93, Sotheby-NY, #780, illus.), 5 x 7⅛ in., (128 x 181 mm.), etching in colors on white wove.

$1535* *La Bonne Faisant Son Marche (D. 74), 1888*, first of definitive state, (02-24-93, Picard, #181), etching and drypoint on laid (BP 1070, DM 2492, FR 8448, Y 180,122).

$4025* *Bucheronnes (D., C. 164), c. 1896*, s., t., no. 2, good cond., soiling, fox marks, (05-13-93, Sotheby-NY, #788), 5⅛ x 4¼ in., (130 x 108 mm.), sh 14⅞ x 10⅞ in., (130 x 108 mm.), lithograph on chine applique (BP 2642, DM 6499, FR 21,923, Y 449,369).

BI *Camille Pissaro Par Lui-Meme (Delteil 90II), c. 1890*, s., i. a mon fils Lucien C.P. and Ier Etat No. 9 Portrait, laid downmargins, mount-stained, defects, tear, prov., est. BP 12/18,000, (11-30-92, Phillips-London, #477, illus.), sheet 12½ x 10¾ in., (318 x 273 mm.), etching and drypoint on japan.

BI *La Charrue (D. 194), 1901*, first state, annot., margins, (02-24-93, Picard, #184), lithograph in black-green on glace creme wove.

$3450* *La Charrue (D., C. 194), 1901*, Cailac's 2nd state (of 3), s., t. Frontispiece pour les temps nouveaux, i. no. 2 ep. def. en trait, margins, foxed, light-stained, discolored, (05-13-93, Sotheby-NY, #796, illus.), 8⅞ x 6 in., (225 x 151 mm.), sh 10⅞ x 7¼ in., (225 x 151 mm.), lithograph in green on wove (BP 2265, DM 5571, FR 18,791, Y 385,174).

$4025* *La Charrue (D., C. 194), 1901*, Cailac's 3rd (final) state, full margins, good cond., light-stain, soiling, discoloration, handling creases, skinning, (05-13-93, Sotheby-NY, #797, illus.), 8⅞ x 6 in., (225 x 153 mm.), lithograph in colors on smooth wove (BP 2642, DM 6499, FR 21,923, Y 449,369).

$4485* *La Charrue (L.D. 194), 1901*, 2nd final state, stone s., from edit. pub. in Les Temps Nouveaux, wide margins, light-staining, soiling, very good cond., (05-11-93, Christie-NY, #326, illus.), borderline 8⅞ x 6 in., (225 x 152 mm.), color lithograph on smooth wove (BP 2863, DM 7065, FR 23,806, Y 493,345).

$929* *Chemin Sous Bois A Pontoise (L. Delteil, 19), 1879*, sixth and final state, stamped, #3/18, good margins, (04-02-93, Picard, #159), 6⁵/₁₆ x 8⅜ in., (16 x 21.2 cm.), etching (BP 612, DM 1493, FR 5071, Y 105,773).

$3025* *Convalescence: Lucien Pissaro, c. 1930*, inits. stamp, from edit. of 11, perfect cond., (05-15-93, Loudmer, #312), 12⅝ x 9¹/₁₆ in., (320 x 230 mm.), sh 12¹¹/₁₆ x

9⅛ in., (320 x 230 mm.), lithograph on very thin China paper (BP 1967, DM 4866, FR 16,351, Y 335,329).

BI *Couple De Paysans (D., C. 125), c. 1899,* No. 5/6, from posthumous edit., p. in 1923, full margins, good cond.,-paper tone darkened, foxing, soiling, est. $1/1,200, (05-13-93, Sotheby-NY, #782), 4¾ x 3¼ in., (120 x 81 mm.), etching and soft-ground on Arches laid.

$4379* *Eglise D'Osny, Pres Pontoise (Delteil 62 VI), 1885,* s., i. 4e etat no 6, (06-10-93, Hauswedell/Nolt, #804, illus.), image 4¾ x 6⁵⁄₁₆ in., (12 x 16.1 cm.), drypoint w/aquatint (BP 2864, DM 7131, FR 24,008, Y 464,813).

BI *"Faneuses" (Delteil 94 XII/XII, Melot 94), 1890,* pub. Duret 1906, excell. cond., est. $6/800, (10-31-92, Cleveland, #322, illus.), 7¾ x 5¼ in., (19.7 x 13.3 cm.), etching in brown ink.

BI *Femme A La Barriere (D., C. 84), 1889,* 10th (final) state, i. epreuve d'etat, 3e no. 1, full margins, good cond., creases, foxing, soiling, holes, est. $7/9,000, (05-13-93, Sotheby-NY, #773, illus.), 6⅜ x 4½ in., (162 x 113 mm.), etching, drypoint and aquatint on laid.

$4600* *Femme Cueillant Des Choux (D. 77), 1888,* i. 4e et., 4th state of 7, full margins, good cond., soiling, only one impression p. in this state, (05-13-93, Sotheby-NY, #772, illus.), 2⅜ x 4 in., (60 x 100 mm.), etching on laid (BP 3020, DM 7428, FR 25,054, Y 513,565).

$3450* *Femme Gardant Des Vaches (D. 88), 1889,* 2nd state of 2, s., t., i. no. 1, 2e etat no. 1, margins, good cond.,soiling, skinning, tape remains, (05-13-93, Sotheby-NY, #775), 2⅜ x 3⅞ in., (61 x 99 mm.), drypoint w/a light veil of tone on wove (BP 2265, DM 5571, FR 18,791, Y 385,174).

BI *Gardeuse D'Oies (D. 187), c. 1898,* atelier stamp, margins, good cond., soiling, staining, creases, est.$3/4,000, (05-13-93, Sotheby-NY, #794, illus.), 5⅜ x 6¾ in., (135 x 170 mm.), sh 8¼ x 11¼ in., (135 x 170 mm.), lithograph on chine applique.

BI *Grand'Mere (La Femme De L'Artiste) (D. 143), c. 1895,* s., No. 9, large margins, good cond., fox marks, creases, skinning, est. $3/4,000, (05-13-93, Sotheby-NY, #784, illus.), 9⅜ x 4⅞ in., (237 x 125 mm.), lithograph on heavy wove.

$2866* *Grand'mere (La Femme De L'Artiste) (D. 143), c. 1895,* 1 of 10, num., s., dust, full margins, (02-24-93, Picard, #183), lithograph on white wove (BP 1999, DM 4653, FR 15,773, Y 336,306).

$1933* *Grand'mere (La Femme De L'Artiste) (Delteil XVII, 143), c. 1895,* mono. stamp, 3/6, reddish stains, light stains, (06-28-93, Loudmer, #342, illus.), 5⅞ x 4⁷⁄₁₆ in., (150 x 112 mm.), avec remarque 2¾ x 3¹⁵⁄₁₆ in., (150 x 112 mm.), black lithograph on zinc on beige China, applique on wove (BP 1294, DM 3285, FR 11,065, Y 205,093).

BI *Groupe De Paysannes (D., C. 165), c. 1896,* s., t., no. 4, large margins, good cond., foxing, soiling, creases, est. $6/8,000, (05-13-93, Sotheby-NY, #789, illus.), 5⅜ x 4½ in., (135 x 115 mm.), sh 14⅞ x 10¾ in., (135 x 115 mm.), lithograph on white wove.

$3450* *Groupe De Paysans: 2e Planche, Variante (L.D. 189), c. 1899,* s., t., i. no 14, wide margins, staining, surface soiling, tape, very good cond., (05-11-93, Christie-NY, #325, illus.), borderline 5 x 4⅛ in., (127 x 105 mm.), lithograph on Chine applique (BP 2202, DM 5435, FR 18,312, Y 379,496).

BI *L'Eglise Et Ferme D'Eragny (D. 96), 1894-95,* i., 6th final state, full margins, registration holes, stains, good cond., ex. coll. H. Neuerburg (L. 1344a), est. BP 30/35,000, (06-30-93, Sotheby-London, #660, illus.), 6 x 9⅝ in., (152 x 244 mm.), color etching from 4 pl on bluish laid.

BI *Marchande De Marrons (Delteil 15), 1878,* 1st state of 2, annot. 7 (retraced), full margins, good cond., foxing, discoloration, est. $6/7,000, (05-13-93, Sotheby-NY, #762, illus.), 8¼ x 6½ in., (210 x 165 mm.), etching on laid Van Gelder.

BI *Marchande Et Clientele Dans Un Magasin, c. 1895,* mono. stamp, laid down on linen, stretch-mounted, est. $20/30,000, (05-13-93, Sotheby-NY, #781, illus.), sh 8⅜ x 6 in., (212 x 154 mm.), monotype on laid.

$1650* *Marche Aux Legumes, A Pontoise (L.D. 97), 1891,* mono., #14/18, p.l., margins, good cond., tear, mat stain-

ing, foxing, creases, surface soiling, (10-28-92, Butterfield, #2713, illus.), 8¼ x 6⅜ in., (210 x 162 mm.), etching w/aquatint on pinkish-gray paper (BP 1051, DM 2548, FR 8652, Y 202,454).

$20,700* *Marche De Gisors (Rue Cappeville) (D., C. 112), c. 1894,* s., t., i. no. 9 ep.d'art, full margins, good cond., printer's crease, soiling, discoloration, glue stains, (05-13-93, Sotheby-NY, #778, illus.), 7⅞ x 5½ in., (201 x 141 mm.), etching in colors on laid (BP 13,590, DM 33,425, FR 112,745, Y 2,311,042).

$38,500* *Marche De Gisors (Rue Cappeville) (Delteil 112), c. 1894-95,* first state of seven, i. No. 2, mat staining, foxing, stains, good cond., prop. Edith Schumann 1988 Trust, (11-05-92, Sotheby-NY, #410, illus.), 7⅞ x 5½ in., (200 x 140 mm.), etching w/extensive hand coloring on laid (BP 25,041, DM 60,889, FR 205,993, Y 4,723,347).

$23,000* *Mendiant Et Paysanne (D., C. 183), c. 1897,* 2nd state (of 2), s., t., i. Ep. d'essai no. 3, watermark, large margins, good cond., soiling, foxing, creases, skinning, tape remains, (05-13-93, Sotheby-NY, #792, illus.), 11⅝ x 8½ in., (296 x 215 mm.), sh 17¾ x 12½ in., (296 x 215 mm.), lithograph on pale grey-green applique on white wove (BP 15,100, DM 37,139, FR 125,272, Y 2,567,824).

BI *Mendiantes (D. 110), c. 1894,* just., t., soiling, crack, creases, large margins, (02-24-93, Picard, #182), drypoint in black bistre on thin laid Japan.

BI *Mendiantes (D., C. 110), c. 1894,* 2nd (final) state, init., i. No 1, full margins, good cond., mat stain, soiling, stains, creased, est. $10/14,000, (05-13-93, Sotheby-NY, #777, illus.), 7⅞ x 6 in., (200 x 151 mm.), etching, drypoint and aquatint on laid Japan.

BI *Mendiantes (Delteil 110 II; Melot 111), c. 1894,* num., mono. stamp, est. DM 15,000, (12-04-92, Bassenge, #6903, illus.), 7¹⁵⁄₁₆ x 5¹⁵⁄₁₆ in., (20.1 x 15.1 cm.), color etching on handmade.

BI *Paysage A L'Hermitage (Pontoise) (D., C. 28), 1880,* 1st state of 3, s., t., i. 1er etat, full margins, good cond., crease, fox marks, soiling, ex-coll. D. G. de Arozarena, est. $8/12,000, (05-13-93, Sotheby-NY, #764, illus.), 4¼ x 4⅞ in., (108 x 125 mm.), drypoint on laid.

$2398* *Paysage A Osny (L.D. 70), 1887,* num. 62, s., drystamp, frame traces, large margins, (06-11-93, Picard, #148), 6³⁄₁₆ x 4½ in., (157 x 114 mm.), etching on laid (BP 1576, DM 3897, FR 13,140, Y 254,430).

BI *Paysage Avec Berger Et Moutons, Osny (D. 40), 1883,* 6th (final) state, t., num. no. 11, large margins, good cond., light-stain, glue stains, soiling, creases, backboard stained, est. $2,5/3,500, (05-13-93, Sotheby-NY, #765), 4 x 5½ in., (100 x 140 mm.), etching and aquatint on laid.

$2070* *Paysage En Long (D., Cailac 17), 1879,* Cailac's 3rd (final) state, mono. stamp, from posthumous edit., p. 1923, full margins, good cond., soiling, creases, (05-13-93, Sotheby-NY, #763), 4⅝ x 15½ in., (116 x 395 mm.), etching and aquatint on laid (BP 1359, DM 3342, FR 11,275, Y 231,104).

$21,315* *Paysage Sous-Bois, A L'Hermitage (Pontoise) (Delteil 16), 1879,* s., proof impression, good cond., mount staining, discoloration, prov., (12-03-92, Sotheby-London, #571, illus.), 8½ x 10½ in., (215 x 266 mm.), etching and aquatint on laid (BP 13,750, DM 33,519, FR 114,412, Y 2,652,109).

BI *Paysanne A La Fourche (D. 87), 1889,* 4th state (of 5), t., i. 4e etat no. 1, full margins, good cond., soiling, mat stain, est. $3/5,000, (05-13-93, Sotheby-NY, #774), 4¾ x 2⅞ in., (119 x 74 mm.), etching and aquatint on laid.

$24,150* *Paysanne Au Puits (D. 101), 1891,* w/tone, 2nd state of 3, s., t., i. 2e etat no. 2, (full?) margins, good cond., discoloration, handling creases, (05-13-93, Sotheby-NY, #776, illus.), 9¼ x 7¾ in., (235 x 197 mm.), sh 12½ x 8⅛ in., (235 x 197 mm.), etching on fine laid (BP 15,855, DM 38,996, FR 131,536, Y 2,696,215).

BI *Paysanne Dans Les Choux (D., C. 61), 1885,* Cailac's undescribed 1st state (of three), s., trimmed to image, laiddown on card, est. $40/50,000, (05-13-93, Sotheby-NY, #769, illus.), sh 5½ x 4 in., (139 x 102 mm.), etching, w/elaborate hand-coloring.

$393* *Paysanne Portant Du Foin (L. Delteil, 126), 1900,* definitive state, good margins, (06-16-93, Ader Tajan, #128),

4¹¹⁄₁₆ x 3⅛ in., (11.9 x 8 cm.), etching and drypoint (BP 262, DM 652, FR 2189, Y 41,916).

$722* *Paysans Dans Les Champs (L.D., 104), 1891,* #2/35, large margins, (04-02-93, Picard, #160), 2¹³⁄₁₆ x 5⅞ in., (7.2 x 15 cm.), etching on Japan (BP 476, DM 1160, FR 3941, Y 82,204).

$208* *Paysans Portant Du Foin (Delteil 126/7),* mount staining, (12-01-92, Karl/Faber, #246), 4⁵⁄₁₆ x 2¹⁵⁄₁₆ in., (11 x 7.5 cm.), etching on hand-made (BP 137, DM 332, FR 1130, Y 25,896).

$3738* *Place Du Havre, A Paris (D., C. 185), c. 1897,* 2nd state (of 2), large margins, good cond., pressure marks, soiling,puckering, ex-coll. Otto Gerstenberg, (05-13-93, Sotheby-NY, #793, illus.), 5¾ x 8⅜ in., (145 x 214 mm.), support sh 9¾ x 12¾ in., (145 x 214 mm.), zincograph on pinkish-beige Ingres applique (BP 2454, DM 6036, FR 20,359, Y 417,327).

$5750* *Le Pont De Pierre, A Rouen (D. 66), 1887,* 2nd state (of 2), s., t., i. 2e etat/imprime par F. Jacques, Ep. d'art-no. 25, large (full?) margins, good cond., paper tone darkened, soiling, gluestains, loss, tear, (05-13-93, Sotheby-NY, #768, illus.), 5⅞ x 7⅞ in., (150 x 200 mm.), etching and aquatint on laid Van Gelder (BP 3775, DM 9285, FR 31,318, Y 641,956).

$1265* *Porteuses De Fagots (D., C. 153), 1896,* pub. in Les Temps nouveaux, full (large) margins, generally good cond., mat/light-stain, creases, tape stain, foxing, (05-13-93, Sotheby-NY, #787), 8⅞ x 12 in., (225 x 305 mm.), lithograph on laid Van Gelder Zonen (BP 830, DM 2043, FR 6890, Y 141,230).

$4025* *Portrait De Jeanne Pissarro (D. 144), c. 1895,* one of only two known impressions, margins on 3 sides, possibly trimmed into subject, good cond., soiling, (05-13-93, Sotheby-NY, #785, illus.), 10⅞ x 9½ in., (275 x 242 mm.), sh 12⅞ x 9⅞ in., (275 x 242 mm.), lithograph on wove (BP 2642, DM 6499, FR 21,923, Y 449,369).

BI *Quai Boielvieu, A Rouen (D., C. 169), c. 1896,* s., t., no. 1, Cailac's 1st edit. of 6, large margins, good cond., foxing, soiling, creases, ex-coll. A.T. Tallent, est. $3,5/5,000, (05-13-93, Sotheby-NY, #790), 7 x 8⅞ in., (177 x 225 mm.), sh 10¾ x 15 in., (177 x 225 mm.), lithograph on white wove.

BI *Quai De Paris A Rouen (D. 123), 1896,* watermark, stamp inits., #I/13, margins, good cond., mat/light-staini-ing, foxing, hinge remains, surface soiling, notations, est. $1,8/2,200, (05-19-93, Butterfield, #1960, illus.), 7¹⁄₁₆ x 6¹⁵⁄₁₆ in., (179 x 176 mm.), etching on laid paper.

$2030* *Quai De Rouen (Grand Pont) (Delteil XVII, 172), 1896,* mono. stamp, 10/12, reddish stains, (06-28-93, Loudmer, #343), 8⅜ x 11¾ in., (212 x 298 mm.), sh 12⁷⁄₁₆ x 17⁵⁄₁₆ in., (212 x 298 mm.), black lithograph on zinc, on greyish paper contrecolle on wove (BP 1359, DM 3449, FR 11,620, Y 215,385).

$3163* *Une Rue A Rouen (Rue Des Arpents) (D. 68), 1887,* 3rd (final) state, s., d. 1883, t., i. 3e Etat, full margins, good cond., foxing, mat/light-stain, stains, (05-13-93, Sotheby-NY, #770, illus.), 4⅜ x 6¼ in., (110 x 160 mm.), etching and drypoint in dark brown on laid Van Gelder (BP 2077, DM 5107, FR 17,228, Y 353,132).

BI *Rue Saint-Romain, A Rouen, 1Re Planche (D. 176), 1896,* 1st state (of 2), i. No 1, large margins, good cond., foxing, mat stain, creases, tack holes, soiling, discoloration, est. $2,5/3,500, (05-13-93, Sotheby-NY, #791, illus.), 7½ x 5½ in., (190 x 141 mm.), lithograph on smooth wove.

BI *Sente Des Pouilleux A Pontoise (L. Delteil 32), 1880,* definitive state, #17/30, stamped, good margins, (06-11-93, Picard, #147), etching on laid.

$1840* *La Vache (D. 58), 1885,* 3rd (final) state, large margins, good cond., soiling, losses, repaired tear, platemark reinforced w/Japan, (05-13-93, Sotheby-NY, #766), 4⅜ x 4⅝ in., (111 x 117 mm.), sh 7⅛ x 10⅞ in., (111 x 117 mm.), etching, drypoint and aquatint on cream wove (BP 1208, DM 2971, FR 10,022, Y 205,426).

BI *Vachere (D. 190), c. 1899,* s., t., No 11, full margins, good cond., foxing, pressure marks, est. $2,5/3,500, (05-13-93, Sotheby-NY, #795), 4⅜ x 4½ in., (110 x 114 mm.), zincograph on pink Ingres applique on white wove.

$825* *Vachere Au Bord De L'Eau (Delteil 93), 1890,* full(?) margins, state 8, pub. Gazette des Beaux-Arts in 1904, (05-27-93, Swann, #224), 7⅞ x 5½ in., (20 x 14 cm.), etching (BP 528, DM 1324, FR 4462, Y 88,443).

$807* *Vachere Au Bord De L'Eau (L. Delteil 93), 1890,* definitive state, large margins, (02-03-93, Ader Tajan, #191), 7¹³⁄₁₆ x 5¼ in., (19.8 x 13.4 cm.), etching (BP 563, DM 1329, FR 4506, Y 100,386).

$2070* *Vue De Pontoise (D. 60), 1885,* 7th (final) state, mono. stamp, num., from posthumous edit., watermark, full margins, good cond., stain in image, soiling, mat stain, handling creases, tape stain, (05-13-93, Sotheby-NY, #767), 6¼ x 9⅝ in., (160 x 245 mm.), etching, drypoint and aquatint on laid (BP 1359, DM 3342, FR 11,275, Y 231,104).

$1985* *Vue De Pontoise (Delteil 60/VII), 1885,* (06-23-93, Kornfeld, #740), etching on Japan (BP 1349, DM 3359, FR 11,298, Y 216,254, SF 2990).

PISSARRO, Jean Baptiste Camille

BI *Le Dome Florentin (Delteil 13), 1869-1870,* Delteil's 1st state of 3, (06-30-93, Sotheby-London, #414), sh 13¼ x 9⅝ in., (337 x 244 mm.), etching on laid Japan.

PISSARRO, Orovida French 1893-1968

$351* *The Calf,* s., t., d. 1949, margins, (11-19-92, Bonhams-Chelsea, #91), plate 7 x 9 in., (17.8 x 22.9 cm.), etching on Arches (BP 231, DM 560, FR 1885, Y 43,651).

$549* *"Tiger And A Python" and "An Interrupted Meal", 1917 and 1930: Two,* each s., d., t., first i., 2nd #4/50, margins, good cond., soiling, handling marks, (06-30-93, Sotheby-London, #322, illus.), one 4⅜ x 5⅞ in., (111 x 149 mm.), the other 10⅞ x 6⅞ in., (111 x 149 mm.), etching, first p. w/tone, on laid and wove (BP 368, DM 936, FR 3159, Y 58,824).

PISTOLETTO, Michelangelo Italian b. 1933

BI *Art Assumes Religion, 1980,* s., d., est. SF 330/370, (10-14-92, Germann, #403), 5¹³⁄₁₆ x 29½ in., (148 x 750 mm.), lithograph in color.

$6314* *Dettaglio Di Un Uomo Che Si Gira, 1981,* s., t., d., (11-09-92, Finarte-Milan, #148, illus.), 15¾ x 15¾ in., (40 x 40 cm.), seigraph (BP 4175, DM 10,080, FR 34,056, Y 783,569, L 8625).

BI *I Am Third, 1980,* #100/100, s., d., creases, est. SF 6/700, 1048mm x 750mm, (04-21-93, Germann, #690), color lithograph.

$2948* *L'Uovo, 1987,* #27/50, s., (12-15-92, Finarte-Milan, #75), 19¹¹⁄₁₆ x 15¾ in., (50 x 40 cm.), serigraph in colors (BP 1881, DM 4621, FR 15,790, Y 365,621, L 4140).

$583* *Untitled,* #4/100, (05-18-93, Auction Phila, #135), 19¹¹⁄₁₆ x 13¾ in., (50 x 35 cm.), serigraph on rame (BP 380, DM 946, FR 3195, Y 64,973, L 863).

PITSEOLAK, Peter b. Alaska 1904 d. 1973

$238* *Hawk, 1977,* #88/100, s., t., d. 1977, prov., (11-16-92, Hodgins, #103), 20½ x 27¼ in., (52.1 x 69.2 cm.), stonecut and stencil on paper (BP 156, DM 380, FR 1279, Y 29,702, C$ 303).

$550* *"Igloos At Ikerusak", 1975,* #19/50, (05-14-93, DuMouchelle, #2033, illus.), 25 x 19 in., (63.5 x 48.3 cm.), color stone cut (BP 358, DM 885, FR 2973, Y 60,969).

PITTONI, Giovanni Battista (the elder) (Battista VICENTINO) Italian 1687-1767

$505* *Romische Ruinen (Passavant VI), 1561: Five,* from series Praecipua Aliquot Romanae Antiquitatis Suinarum Monimenta, (12-04-92, Bassenge, #6362), etching (BP 324, DM 804, FR 2728, Y 63,046).

PITZ, Henry

$28* *Swamp Land,* s., AAA label, (05-14-93, DuMouchelle, #350), 9¾ x 12¼ in., (24.8 x 31.1 cm.), lithograph (BP 18, DM 45, FR 151, Y 3104).

PIVIDOR Y VIOLA, Cecchini

$1450* *"Monuments Of Venice": Thirteen,* orig. portfolio, prov., excell. cond., (03-17-93, Duran, #96, illus.), 12⅝ x 18⅛ in., (32.1 x 46 cm.), color lithograph (BP 1000, DM 2413, FR 8201, Y 170,068, P 172,500).

PIZA, Arthur Luiz   b. 1928
$55* *Composition,* s. Piza, (03-24-93, Kunsthallen, #281), etching in colors (BP 37, DM 90, FR 306, Y 6462, DK 345).
$55* *Composition,* s. Piza, (03-24-93, Kunsthallen, #282), color etching (BP 37, DM 90, FR 306, Y 6462, DK 345).
$55* *Composition,* s. Piza, (03-24-93, Kunsthallen, #280), etching in colors (BP 37, DM 90, FR 306, Y 6462, DK 345).
$309* *Compositions: Two,* s., #85/99, 81/99, full margins, (03-31-93, Briest, #E90), sh one 29^{15}/₁₆ x 22¼ in., (76 x 56.5 cm.), sh other 29^{15}/₁₆ x 22¼ in., (76 x 56.5 cm.), carborundum engraving and drypoint (BP 204, DM 497, FR 1689, Y 35,534).
$199* *Mai, c. 1968,* s., num., (12-01-92, Karl/Faber, #1102), 28^{15}/₁₆ x 21⁷/₁₆ in., (73.5 x 54.5 cm.), color aquatint/etching w/relief print on Arches wove (BP 131, DM 317, FR 1081, Y 24,776).

PLANGG, Warner   b. 1934
$78* *Near Cochrane,* #7/20, s., t.; t. verso, prov., (05-10-93, Hodgins, #364), 6 x 8 in., (15.2 x 20.3 cm.), etching on paper (BP 51, DM 125, FR 423, Y 8716, C$ 99).

PLATT, Charles A.
$275* *"Coal Barge And Wharf"* and *"Covered Bridge, Hartford": Two,* (03-20-93, Northeast, #749), etching (BP 184, DM 450, FR 1530, Y 31,899).
$358* *"Harbor Scene With Tugboats"* and *"Two Sloops", 1890: Two,* (03-20-93, Northeast, #746, illus.), etching (BP 240, DM 585, FR 1992, Y 41,527).
$193* *"Park River, Hartford", 1881* and *"Winter Landscape": Two,* (03-20-93, Northeast, #752), 8 x 13½ in., (20.3 x 34.3 cm.), etching (BP 129, DM 316, FR 1074, Y 22,387).
$138* *"River At Low Tide"* and *"Windmill", 1883: Two,* (03-20-93, Northeast, #754), etching (BP 92, DM 226, FR 768, Y 16,007).
$220* *"Spars Boat Yard"* and *"Interior Of Fish Houses": Two,* (03-20-93, Northeast, #748), etching (BP 147, DM 360, FR 1224, Y 25,519).
$138* *"Westminster Abbey", "Oxford"* and *"Larmor": Three,* (03-20-93, Northeast, #756), etching (BP 92, DM 226, FR 768, Y 16,007).

PLEISSNER, Ogden M.   American 1905-1983
$264* *Blue Boat On The Saint Anne,* s. Ogden M. Pleissner, (02-13-93, Collins, #92, illus.), 5 x 9 in., (12.7 x 22.9 cm.), color offset lithograph (BP 186, DM 438, FR 1481, Y 31,838).
$550* *Dry Fly Fishing For Salmon,* pub. for Theodore Gordon Flyfishers, s. Ogden M. Pleissner, (02-13-93, Collins, #82, illus.), 15 x 24⅝ in., (38.1 x 62.5 cm.), color offset lithograph (BP 387, DM 912, FR 3086, Y 66,329).
$275* *Hendrickson's Pool,* s. Ogden M. Pleissner, (02-13-93, Collins, #94, illus.), 5 x 9 in., (12.7 x 22.9 cm.), color offset lithograph (BP 194, DM 456, FR 1543, Y 33,164).
$220* *Marsh Gunners,* s. Ogden M. Pleissner, (02-13-93, Collins, #64, illus.), 5 x 9 in., (12.7 x 22.9 cm.), color offset lithograph (BP 155, DM 365, FR 1235, Y 26,532).
$138* *Pheasant Hunter,* issued for Hercules Powder Co., 1951, discoloration, excell. cond., (10-02-92, Guyette, #635B, illus.), lithograph (BP 80, DM 196, FR 657, Y 16,478).
$908* *Salmon Fishing In A Canoe,* s., (12-17-92, Mystic, #14), 14½ x 23½ in., (36.8 x 59.7 cm.), color lithograph (BP 576, DM 1418, FR 4843, Y 111,589).
$440* *"Woodcock Cover",* s., excell. cond., (04-13-93, Bourne, #80, illus.), image size 16 x 25½ in., (40.6 x 64.8 cm.), print (BP 283, DM 695, FR 2352, Y 49,921).

PLESSEN, Hans Wilhelm   b. 1868
BI *Germania, Paradiso Invernali, c. 1930,* p. RDV, cond. 4, paper losses, est. BP 2/300, (10-13-92, Phillips-London, #42, illus.), 39¾ x 25 in., (101 x 63.5 cm.), color lithograph.

PLOOS VAN AMSTEL, Cornelis   1726-1798
$3971* *Collections D'Imitations De Dessins D'Apres Les Principaux Maitres Hollandais Et Flamands: Thirty-Seven,* lit., (12-04-92, Bassenge, #6684), etching w/aquatint (BP 2547, DM 6324, FR 21,453, Y 495,755).

$341* *Die Lautenspielerin (Wurzbach 31),* after G. Netscher, (12-01-92, Karl/Faber, #121), aquatint and etching (BP 225, DM 544, FR 1852, Y 42,455).
$283* *Uferlandschaft (Wurzb. 41),* after J. v. Esselens, artist stamp, (06-08-93, Karl/Faber, #164), aquatint/etching (BP 186, DM 459, FR 1546, Y 30,058).
$8163* *The Wandering Musicians (Laurentius 17), c. 1766,* after Adriaen van Ostade, Laurentius' 4th state, Ploos' stamp, trimmed to borderline, good cond., thin spots, (05-13-93, Sotheby-NY, #172), 13⅝ x 11¾ in., (346 x 300 mm.), etching in colors (BP 5359, DM 13,181, FR 44,461, Y 911,354).

PLOWDEN, David   b. 1932
$187* *From Bridge Series,* s., (05-16-93, Hindman, #349), 11¾ x 10¼ in., photograph, silver print (BP 122, DM 302, FR 1016, Y 20,824).
$165* *"Reading Co. Steam Locomotive #2100, Port Clinton, Pennsylvania" (A Time Of Trains, p. 42), 1963,* s., t., d., neg. num., Dixon Collection, (11-16-92, Butterfield, #6123, illus.), 12½ x 10⅛ in., (318.1 x 257.6 mm.), photograph, gelatin silver print (BP 109, DM 263, FR 886, Y 20,520).

PLUSCHOW, Guglielmo
$531* *Madchen Halbakt, c. 1900,* (11-12-92, Lempertz, #192, illus.), 8^{13}/₁₆ x 6⁷/₁₆ in., (22.4 x 16.4 cm.), sheet 13¾ x 10⅝ in., (22.4 x 16.4 cm.), photograph, gelatin silver print (BP 340, DM 835, FR 2844, Y 65,693).
$605* *"Nude Boy With Horn", "Male Nude Lying On Animal Skin"* and *"Innocence": Three,* photog. handstamp, last w/ Paul Cava's handstamp, 1890s, ex-coll. Paul Cava and Michael Simon, (04-07-93, Swann, #246, illus.), largest 8¾ x 6½ in., photograph, albumen and printing-out prints (BP 400, DM 978, FR 3311, Y 68,734).
$690* *Study Of A Nude Boy, c. 1900,* num. 10233 in unident. hand, photog. studio stamp, (04-06-93, Sotheby-NY, #230, illus.), 8¾ x 6½ in., photograph, albumen print (BP 456, DM 1112, FR 3764, Y 78,695).

POCCI, Franz Graf von   1807-1876
BI *"Todtentanz" (Bernhard 483-91 und 493-94), 1862: Eleven,* E.A. Fleischmanns Buchhandlung, est. DM 300, (12-01-92, Karl/Faber, #247), 4⅛ x 6⁵/₁₆ in., (10.5 x 16 cm.), woodcut.

POCOCK, Nicholas (after)
$469* *The Conflict Between Frigate "Java" And Frigate "Constitution", Plates I-IV: Four,* by Denis Wreford, #16/200, s., margins, (11-12-92, Bonhams-Chelsea, #48), image 11 x 18⅛ in., (27.9 x 46 cm.), hand-colored lithograph (BP 308, DM 743, FR 2507, Y 58,153).
$318* *The Conflict Between Frigate "Java"* and *Frigate "Constitution", Plates I-IV: Four,* by Denis Wreford, #14/200, s., margins, (11-12-92, Bonhams-Chelsea, #47), image 11 x 18⅛ in., (27.9 x 46 cm.), hand-colored lithograph (BP 209, DM 504, FR 1700, Y 39,430).

POCOCK, Philip   b. 1954
BI *Day Of Judgement,* s., t., d. 1984 PHILIP POCOCK verso, prov., Fredrik Roos Estate, est. $1/1500, (11-17-92, Christie-E, #111, illus.), 40 x 31¼ in., (101.6 x 79.4 cm.), dye-deconstruction photograph.
BI *Egg,* exec. 1986, prov., est. $2/3000, (11-17-92, Christie-E, #113, illus.), 79¾ x 29¾ in., (202.6 x 75.6 cm.), dye-destruction photograph.

POGANY, Willy   Hungarian/American 1882-1955
$108* *Sleeping Nudes Under Watchful Figure,* s., (06-08-93, Ritchie, #29, illus.), 11¾ x 8⅞ in., (29.8 x 22.5 cm.), etching (BP 71, DM 175, FR 590, Y 11,471, C$ 138).

POILPOT, T. (after)
$935* *Panorama De La Compagnie Generale Transatalique, 1889,* Universal Exposition-Paris 1889, linen-backed, (04-29-93, Swann, #130, illus.), 48 x 34 in., (121.9 x 86.4 cm.), color lithographed poster (BP 595, DM 1479, FR 4984, Y 104,016).

POIRIER
$167* *Cannes, 2 Projets,* good cond., (01-23-93, Ribeyre/Baron, #138), 42⅛ x 25^{15}/₁₆ in., (107 x 66 cm.), poster (BP 109, DM 266, FR 898, Y 20,901).

POLEO, Hector Venezuelan b. 1918

BI *Untitled,* A/P s., prov., est. C$3/400, (05-10-93, Hodgins, #34), 17 x 17 in., (43.2 x 43.2 cm.), color lithograph on paper.

POLIAKOFF, Serge French 1900-1969

$165* *Composition,* Charles Sorlier Imp., (03-24-93, Kunsthallen, #287), color lithograph (BP 112, DM 269, FR 917, Y 19,387, DK 1035).

$2326* *Composition (Riviere 11), 1956,* s., epreuve d'artiste, i., (05-26-93, Dorling, #2906, illus.), 17⅛ x 23½₁₆ in., (43.5 x 58.5 cm.), color lithograph on BFK Rives wove (BP 1505, DM 3795, FR 12,773, Y 252,716).

$4029* *Composition Avec Rouge, Grise Et Noire (Poliakoff, Nr. 29), 1960,* s., (11-13-92, Kunsthaus, #763, illus.), 25³⁄₁₆ x 19⁵⁄₁₆ in., (64 x 49 cm.), color lithograph on Arches hand-made (BP 2604, DM 6325, FR 21,329, Y 500,062).

$3663* *Composition Avec Rouge, Jaune Et Bleu (Poliakoff, Nr. 13), 1957,* #134/200, s., (11-13-92, Kunsthaus, #762, illus.), 22¹³⁄₁₆ x 17⁵⁄₁₆ in., (58 x 44 cm.), color lithograph on Arches hand-made (BP 2367, DM 5750, FR 19,391, Y 454,636).

$583* *Composition Bleu, Jaune Et Verte, (R. 40), 1963,* i. E.d.'a, artist proof, pub. Galerie Cavalero, margins, mount-staining, good cond., (12-01-92, Christie-London, #625), L. 10⁷⁄₁₆ x 7⅝ in., (265 x 193 mm.), lithograph in colors on BFK Rives (BP 385, DM 929, FR 3167, Y 72,585).

$1705* *Composition Bleue (R. 21), 1958-59,* s., #101/110, pub. Nesto Jacometti, l'Oeuvre Gravee, full margins, good cond., (12-03-92, Sotheby-London, #778), 19⅞ x 25½ in., (505 x 650 mm.), lithograph in colors on BFK Rives (BP 1100, DM 2681, FR 9152, Y 212,144).

$1887* *Composition Bleue (R. 50), 1966,* s., #44/49, pub. La Guilde de la Lithographie, margins, blue faded, foxed, creases, tear, water-stain, (06-30-93, Sotheby-London, #898, illus.), sh 30 x 22 in., (762 x 559 mm.), color lithograph on wove (BP 1265, DM 3218, FR 10,857, Y 202,186).

$2624* *Composition Bleue (Riviere 21),* 1958-59, s. Serge Poliakoff, 23/110, (12-02-92, Kunsthallen, #271), lithograph in colors (BP 1693, DM 4126, FR 14,085, Y 326,490, DK 16,100).

$3792* *Composition Bleue (Riviere 21), 1958-59,* 56/110, s. Serge Poliakoff, (09-30-92, Kunsthallen, #253, illus.), color lithograph (BP 2139, DM 5377, FR 18,187, Y 455,058, DK 20,700).

$4934* *Composition Bleue (Riviere 21), 1958/59,* s., #23/110, (05-26-93, Lempertz, #451, illus.), 22⅜ x 30⅛ in., (56.8 x 76.5 cm.), lithograph on wove (BP 3192, DM 8050, FR 27,095, Y 536,071).

$445* *Composition Bleue (Riviere 82), 1973,* s. in stone, #72/180, (05-27-93, Briest, #166), 29¹⁵⁄₁₆ x 21⁷⁄₁₆ in., (76 x 54.5 cm.), ten-color lithograph (BP 285, DM 714, FR 2407, Y 47,706).

$3432* *Composition Bleue Et Brune (R. XXVIII),* by S. Esmeraldo, s., #15/75, p. Leblanc, pub. XXe siecle, margins, good cond., mount-staining, creases, (06-30-93, Sotheby-London, #896, illus.), 25⅜ x 19½ in., (645 x 495 mm.), aquatint, etching and drypoint in color on wove (BP 2300, DM 5854, FR 19,747, Y 367,727).

$3967* *Composition Bleue Et Rouge (Riviere 57), 1966,* #58/75, s., plate 3 from 10 Lithographies, (11-21-92, Lempertz, #335), 25³⁄₁₆ x 19 in., (64 x 48.3 cm.), color lithograph on BFK Rives wove (BP 2612, DM 6325, FR 21,305, Y 493,347).

$2999* *Composition Bleue Et Verte (Riviere 36), 1962,* s. Serge Poliakoff, 20/65, est. DK 20,000, (12-02-92, Kunsthallen, #258), lithograph in colors (BP 1935, DM 4716, FR 16,098, Y 373,149, DK 18,400).

$3533* *Composition Bleue Et Verte (Riviere 36), 1962,* s., artist's proof, blindstamp, (06-12-93, Hauswedell/Nolt, #336, illus.), 25 x 18½ in., (63.5 x 47 cm.), color lithograph in color print on BFK Rives (BP 2312, DM 5750, FR 19,327, Y 371,777).

$3246* *Composition Bleue Et Verte (Riviere 52), 1966,* #3/75, s., (11-21-92, Lempertz, #334, illus.), 18⁵⁄₁₆ x 26⁹⁄₁₆ in., (46.5 x 67.5 cm.), color lithograph on wove (BP 2137, DM 5175, FR 17,433, Y 403,681).

$3484* *Composition Bleue, Jaune Et Rouge (Riviere 18), 1958,* #16/110, s., blindstamp, (10-09-92, Winterberg, #2932, illus.), 23⁷⁄₁₆ x 17½ in., (59.5 x 44.5 cm.), color lithograph on Arches (BP 2067, DM 5175, FR 17,377, Y 424,154).

$1468* *Composition Bleue, Jaune Et Rouge, (Riviere 47), 1964,* s. Serge Poliakoff, 46/75, (03-24-93, Kunsthallen, #285, illus.), color lithograph (BP 994, DM 2398, FR 8160, Y 172,483, DK 9200).

$2367* *Composition Bleue, Noire Et Jaune (Alexis Poliakoff 17), 1957,* s., num., (06-23-93, Kornfeld, #741), color lithograph (BP 1608, DM 4005, FR 13,472, Y 257,871, SF 3565).

$3792* *Composition Bleue, Noire Et Jaune (Riviere 15), 1957,* s. Serge Poliakoff, E.A., (09-30-92, Kunsthallen, #252), lithograph in colors (BP 2139, DM 5377, FR 18,187, Y 455,058, DK 20,700).

$853* *Composition Bleue, Rose Et Grise (R. 30), 1960-61,* s., bearing inscription, p. Pons, margins, discoloration, soiling, creasing, (12-03-92, Sotheby-London, #779), 10¾ x 7⅞ in., (275 x 197 mm.), lithograph in colors on Arches (BP 550, DM 1341, FR 4579, Y 106,134).

BI *Composition Bleue, Rose Et Grise (Rivere 30), 1960-61,* Epreuve d'artiste, s., est. DM 4,500, (11-21-92, Lempertz, #333), 10¹³⁄₁₆ x 7¾ in., (27.5 x 19.7 cm.), color lithograph on wove.

$1413* *Composition Bleue, Rose Et Grise (Riviere 30), 1960-61,* s., i. artist's proof, (06-12-93, Hauswedell/Nolt, #335), 10⅝ x 7¹¹⁄₁₆ in., (27 x 19.5 cm.), color lithograph in color print on thick wove (BP 925, DM 2300, FR 7730, Y 148,690).

$983* *Composition Bleue, Rose Et Grise, (Poliakoff 30), 1960-1961,* artist proof, s., (12-15-92, Finarte-Milan, #65), 10¹³⁄₁₆ x 7⅞ in., (27.5 x 20 cm.), lithograph in colors (BP 627, DM 1541, FR 5265, Y 121,915, L 1380).

$983* *Composition Bleue, Rouge Et Rose, (Poliakoff 34), 1961,* proof, ded., s., (12-15-92, Finarte-Milan, #26, illus.), 10¹³⁄₁₆ x 7¹³⁄₁₆ in., (27.5 x 19.8 cm.), lithograph in colors (BP 627, DM 1541, FR 5265, Y 121,915, L 1380).

$2599* *"Composition Bleue, Verte Et Grise" (Riviere 8), 1954-1956,* s., num., (11-28-92, Grisebach, #709, illus.), 16¾ x 19¹³⁄₁₆ in., (42.5 x 50.3 cm.), colored serigraph on hand-made (BP 1716, DM 4141, FR 14,056, Y 323,460).

$4290* *Composition Bleue, Verte Et Rouge (R. XXXIV), 1967-68,* by J. David, #24/75, pub. XXeme Siecle, full margins, good cond., light-staining, creases, (06-30-93, Sotheby-London, #899, illus.), 16½ x 25¼ in., (419 x 641 mm.), color aquatint on Arches (BP 2875, DM 7317, FR 24,684, Y 459,659).

$2574* *Composition Brune Et Rouge (R. XV), 1964,* by S. Esmeraldo, s., #H.C.II/X, pub. XXe Siecle, full margins, creasing, foxing, soiling, (06-30-93, Sotheby-London, #894, illus.), 25 x 19½ in., (635 x 495 mm.), aquatint and burin in black and red on Arches (BP 1725, DM 4390, FR 14,810, Y 275,796).

$2217* *Composition Brune Et Rouge (R. XV), 1964,* s., #75/75, engraved S. Esmeraldo, pub. XXe Siecle, full margins, good cond., tape, (12-03-92, Sotheby-London, #780, illus.), 25⅛ x 19½ in., (638 x 495 mm.), aquatint in brown and red on Arches (BP 1430, DM 3486, FR 11,900, Y 275,849).

$1887* *Composition Grise, Brune Et Jaune (R. IX), 1962,* s., #HC/VII/XXV, full margins, crease through image, creasing, rubbing, prov., (06-30-93, Sotheby-London, #895, illus.), 25⅜ x 19¼ in., (645 x 489 mm.), etching and aquatint by Jean Signovert in color on Arches (BP 1265, DM 3218, FR 10,857, Y 202,186).

$6742* *Composition Grise, Brune Et Jaune (Riviere IX), 1962,* s. Serge Poliakoff, 12/75, (09-30-92, Kunsthallen, #251, illus.), etching and aquatint in colors (BP 3804, DM 9560, FR 32,336, Y 809,072, DK 36,800).

$2402* *Composition Grise, Brune Et Jaune (Riviere IX), 1962,* s., #34/75, (06-12-93, Hauswedell/Nolt, #330, illus.), 25¼ x 19⁷⁄₁₆ in., (64.2 x 49.4 cm.), color etching on BFK Rives (BP 1572, DM 3910, FR 13,140, Y 252,762).

$4276* *Composition Grise, Rouge Et Jaune (Alex. Pol. 27), 1960,* s., num., (06-23-93, Kornfeld, #743), color lithograph (BP 2905, DM 7235, FR 24,337, Y 465,846, SF 6440).

$2819* *Composition Grise, Rouge Et Verte (Riviere 6), 1954,* s. Serge Poliakoff, #70/75, (06-03-93, Kunsthallen, #173, illus.), lithograph in colors (BP 1828, DM 4512, FR 15,205, Y 302,338, DK 17,250).

$2673* *Composition Grise, Verte Et Bleue (Alex. Pol. 54), 1966,* s., num., (06-23-93, Kornfeld, #744), color lithograph (BP 1816, DM 4523, FR 15,213, Y 291,208, SF 4025).

$3688* *"Composition Grise, Verte Et Bleue" (Riviere 54), 1966,* s., num., blindstamp, (06-05-93, Grisebach, #829, illus.), 19⅛ x 24⅝ in., (48.5 x 62.5 cm.), color lithograph on wove (BP 2428, DM 5979, FR 20,153, Y 395,623).

$2120* *Composition Jaune Et Verte (Riviere 14), 1957,* s., #98/150, blindstamp, (06-12-93, Hauswedell/Nolt, #334, illus.), 15⁹⁄₁₆ x 21⅝ in., (39.5 x 55 cm.), color lithograph on BFK Rives (BP 1388, DM 3451, FR 11,597, Y 223,087).

BI *Composition Jaune, Bleue Et Rouge (Riviere 73), 1969,* #11/80, s., blindstamp, est. DM 12,000-, (11-21-92, Lempertz, #338, illus.), 25¹³⁄₁₆ x 38⁹⁄₁₆ in., (65.5 x 98 cm.), color lithograph on BFK Rives wove.

$2059* *Composition Jaune, Orange Et Verte (R. 14), 1957,* s., p. by Pons, pub. L'Oeuvre Gravee, full margins, good cond., discoloration, (06-30-93, Sotheby-London, #900, illus.), 15½ x 21⅞ in., (394 x 556 mm.), color lithograph on BFK Rives (BP 1380, DM 3512, FR 11,847, Y 220,615).

$2826* *Composition Jaune, Orange Et Verte (Riviere 14), 1957,* s., #125/50, blindstamp, (06-12-93, Hauswedell/Nolt, #332), 15½ x 21⁹⁄₁₆ in., (39.4 x 54.7 cm.), color lithograph on BFK Rives (BP 1850, DM 4600, FR 15,460, Y 297,380).

$4328* *Composition Jaune, Rouge Et Grise (Rivere 9), 1954-56,* #51/101, s., (11-21-92, Lempertz, #332), 15³⁄₁₆ x 21⁹⁄₁₆ in., (38.5 x 54.8 cm.), color lithograph on BFK Rives wove (BP 2850, DM 6901, FR 23,244, Y 538,242).

$3606* *Composition Jaune, Verte, Bleue Et Rouge (Rivere 10), 1954-56,* #185/220, s., blindstamp, (11-21-92, Lempertz, #332A), 13⅛ x 20 in., (33.4 x 50.8 cm.), color lithograph on BFK Rives wove (BP 2374, DM 5749, FR 19,366, Y 448,452).

$3180* *Composition Lie-De-Vin Et Bleue (Riviere 63), 1966,* s., #49/75, blindstamp, (06-12-93, Hauswedell/Nolt, #337, illus.), 18⅞ x 25³⁄₁₆ in., (47.9 x 64 cm.), color lithograph in color print on BFK Rives (BP 2081, DM 5176, FR 17,396, Y 334,631).

BI *Composition Lie-De-Vin Et Bleue (Riviere 63), 1966,* #1/75, s., watermark, est. DM 10,000-, (11-21-92, Lempertz, #336, illus.), 18⅞ x 25³⁄₁₆ in., (48 x 64 cm.), color lithograph on wove.

$2166* *Composition Lie-De-Vin Et Orange (Riviere 39/1963),* s., num., Edit. Kestner-Gesellschaft, gegilbt, walfatig, (11-28-92, Schoppmann, #715), 18½ x 24 in., (47 x 61 cm.), color lithograph on BFK Rives (BP 1430, DM 3451, FR 11,714, Y 269,571).

$4328* *Composition Lie-De-Vin, Jaune Et Noire (Riviere 33), 1961,* #10/50, s., (11-21-92, Lempertz, #333A, illus.), 18¾ x 23¹⁵⁄₁₆ in., (47.7 x 60.8 cm.), color lithograph on Arches wove (BP 2850, DM 6901, FR 23,244, Y 538,242).

$5049* *Composition Noire, Jaune, Bleue Et Rouge (Riviere XXX), 1966,* #48/75, s., (11-21-92, Lempertz, #337, illus.), 18¹¹⁄₁₆ x 25½ in., (47.5 x 64.7 cm.), color etching on Arches wove (BP 3324, DM 8050, FR 27,116, Y 627,907).

BI *Composition Orange (Riviere 23), 1959,* s., i. H.C., p. Pons, pub. XXe Siecle, full margins, good cond. mat/light-stain, printer's creases in image, repaired nicks, tape remains, skinned spots, discolored verso, est. $2,5/3,500, (05-13-93, Sotheby-NY, #798, illus.), 17⅞ x 24¼ in., (455 x 616 mm.), lithograph in colors.

$5735* *Composition Orange (Riviere 23), 1959,* 12/95, s., light stain, (10-14-92, Germann, #61, illus.), 19⁵⁄₁₆ x 25³⁄₁₆ in., (490 x 640 mm.), lithograph in colors (BP 3366, DM 8393, FR 28,462, Y 694,983, SF 7475).

BI *Composition Orange (Riviere 23), 1959,* #4/95, est. SF 5/6,000, (04-21-93, Germann, #691, illus.), 19⅞ x 26³⁄₁₆ in., (505 x 665 mm.), lithograph in 5 colors.

$2527* *Composition Rouge Et Bleue (Riviere XXXII), 1967,* #19/75, s., (06-24-93, Germann, #484, illus.), 29⅝ x 21¾ in., (752 x 552 mm.), color aquatint (BP 1663, DM 4097, FR 13,809, Y 271,079, SF 3680).

$2837* *"Composition Rouge Et Bleue" (Riviere 49), 1965,* s., num., blindstamp, (06-05-93, Grisebach, #828, illus.), 23¹⁵⁄₁₆ x 17⅞ in., (60.8 x 45.4 cm.), color lithograph on copper print paper (BP 1868, DM 4600, FR 15,503, Y 304,334).

$3131* *Composition Rouge, Carmin Et Jaune (Alex. Pol. 19), 1958,* s., num., (06-23-93, Kornfeld, #742), color lithograph (BP 2127, DM 5298, FR 17,820, Y 341,105, SF 4715).

$4413* *Composition Rouge, Carmin Et Jaune (R. 19), 1958,* epreuve d'artiste, s., (10-09-92, Winterberg, #2933, illus.), 25⁵⁄₁₆ x 19⁵⁄₁₆ in., (64.3 x 49 cm.), color lithograph on Rives (BP 2618, DM 6555, FR 22,010, Y 537,253).

$2558* *Composition Rouge, Carmin Et Jaune (Riviere 19), 1958,* s., #72/125, p. Pons, pub. Nesto Jacometti, L'Oeuvre Gravee, reducedmargins, good cond., (12-03-92, Sotheby-London, #777, illus.), 25¼ x 19⅛ in., (642 x 487 mm.), lithograph in colors on Rives (BP 1650, DM 4023, FR 13,731, Y 318,278).

BI *Composition Rouge, Carmin Et Jaune, (Riviere 19), 1958,* s. Serge Poliakoff, Epr. d'artiste, est. DK 20,000, (03-24-93, Kunsthallen, #283, illus.), color lithograph.

$4581* *Composition Rouge, Carmine Et Jaune (Riviere 19), 1958,* s., #61/125, (05-26-93, Lempertz, #450, illus.), 29¾ x 22¹⁄₁₆ in., (75.6 x 56 cm.), color lithograph on Rives wove (BP 2964, DM 7474, FR 25,157, Y 497,718).

$4098* *Composition Rouge, Jaune Et Noir (Poliakoff 3),* #16/100, s., (11-13-92, Koller, #5396), sheet 14³⁄₁₆ x 11¼ in., (36 x 28.5 cm.), lithograph on wove (BP 2648, DM 6433, FR 21,694, Y 508,626, SF 5800).

$3391* *Composition Rouge, Verte, Jaune Et Bleue (Riviere XVI), 1964,* s., artist's proof, (06-12-93, Hauswedell/Nolt, #331, illus.), 24½ x 19¹¹⁄₁₆ in., (62.2 x 50 cm.), color etching on Arches (BP 2220, DM 5519, FR 18,550, Y 356,835).

$2270* *Composition Rouge, verte, Bleu Et Jaune (Riviere 12), 1956-57,* s., 105/150, ed. Nesto Jacometti, L'Oeuvre Gravee, (12-04-92, AB Stockholm, #7122), 22⁷⁄₁₆ x 16¹⁵⁄₁₆ in., (57 x 43 cm.), lithograph in colors (BP 1456, DM 3615, FR 12,264, Y 283,396, SK 15,400).

$862* *Composition Verte, Beige, Rouge, Et Brune (R. 43),* s., num. 39/200, p. by Pons, pub. Calcographia de Louvre, full margins, surface soiling, (11-30-92, Phillips-London, #562), sheet 13¾ x 15¾ in., (349 x 400 mm.), lithograph in 4 colors on B.F.K. Rives (BP 569, DM 1373, FR 4662, Y 107,281).

$4461* *Composition Verte, Bleue, Rouge Et Jaune (R. XXXV), 1968,* by J. David, s., #73/75, pub. XXeme Siecle, full margins, good cond.,discoloration, (06-30-93, Sotheby-London, #901, illus.), 19¼ x 25¼ in., (489 x 641 mm.), etching and aquatint in color on Arches (BP 2990, DM 7609, FR 25,667, Y 477,981).

$8605* *Composition Verte, Bleue, Rouge Et Jaune (Riviere XXXV), 1968,* H.C., s., (11-13-92, Koller, #5397, illus.), sheet 19½ x 25⅜ in., (49.5 x 64.5 cm.), aquatint and etching w/three p. plates on Arches wove (BP 5561, DM 13,509, FR 45,553, Y 1,068,015, SF 12,180).

$2997* *Composition Verte, Rouge Et Bleue (Riviere 64), 1966,* s. artist's proof, (06-28-93, Loudmer, #344), 19½ x 25 in., (495 x 635 mm.), sh 25¹⁄₁₆ x 31½ in., (495 x 635 mm.), 8-color lithograph on Rives wove (BP 2007, DM 5093, FR 17,155, Y 317,984).

$2614* *Composition Verte, Rouge Et Orange (Riviere V), 1959-60,* s., #14/100, (06-12-93, Hauswedell/Nolt, #329), 7⁷⁄₁₆ x 10 in., (18.9 x 25.4 cm.), color etching w/aquatint and drypoint on BFK Rives (BP 1711, DM 4255, FR 14,300, Y 275,071).

BI *Composition, 1960,* Knoedler-Berggruen, s. Serge Poliakoff 19-1-60, est. DK 2,500, (03-24-93, Kunsthallen, #286), poster.

$6236* *Komposition (Poliakoff 9), 1954/56,* s., (04-24-93, Kunsthaus, #746, illus.), 14¹⁵⁄₁₆ x 21⅝ in., (38 x 55 cm.), color lithograph by 6 stones on wove (BP 3936, DM 9774, FR 33,012, Y 688,148).

$4441* *"Komposition In Rot, Blau, Gelb, Grau Und Schwarz",* s., E.A., (11-21-92, Arnold, #4, illus.), 22¹⁄₁₆ x 27¹⁵⁄₁₆ in., (56 x 71 cm.), color lithograph (BP 2924, DM 7081, FR 23,851, Y 552,294).

POLIAKOFF, Serge (after)

$929* *Composition Verte (A.P., XXXVIII), 1968-69,* engraved by Signovert, #47/75, creases, dirt stains, drystamp, large-margins, (04-02-93, Picard, #163), 8⁹⁄₁₆ x 13⁵⁄₁₆ in., (21.8 x 33.8 cm.), etching and aquatint in color (BP 612, DM 1493, FR 5071, Y 105,773).

POLK, Prentice Hall

$330* *A Very Gracious Smile From First Lady Eleanor Roosevelt Just Before Chief Anderson Takes Off, Tuskegee, Alabama,* photog.'s sig., typewritten caption, 1930s, (04-07-93, Swann, #346), 7½ x 9½ in., photograph, silver print (BP 218, DM 534, FR 1806, Y 37,491).

POLKE, Sigmar German b. 1941

$993* *Blaue Linie, 1989,* s., (06-05-93, Grisebach, #830, illus.), 38¹¹⁄₁₆ x 23¹¹⁄₁₆ in., (98.3 x 60.2 cm.), color offset serigraph on handmade board (BP 654, DM 1610, FR 5426, Y 106,522).

$912* *Desastres Und Andere Bare Wunder, 1984,* pen s., d. verso, unique, (12-09-92, Sotheby-Amstrdm, #632), sheet 12 x 15¹⁵⁄₁₆ in., (305 x 405 mm.), photograph (BP 582, DM 1431, FR 4885, Y 113,081, G 1610).

$354* *Fernsehbild Eishockey ("Rauwolfiaalkaloide") (Vogel/Freitag 19), 1973,* s., (06-08-93, Karl/Faber, #1207), approx. 24¹³⁄₁₆ x 21⁷⁄₁₆ in., (63 x 54.5 cm.), offset print on chromolux (BP 233, DM 574, FR 1934, Y 37,600).

$343* *Fernsehbild Eishockey (Rauwolfia Alkoloide), 1973,* s., margins, good cond., (06-30-93, Sotheby-London, #902), 24⅝ x 18 in., (625 x 457 mm.), offset lithograph (BP 230, DM 585, FR 1974, Y 36,751).

BI *Fernsehbild Eishockey (Rauwolfia Alkoloide), 1973,* s., margins, good cond. est. BP 3/400, (12-03-92, Sotheby-London, #781), 24⅝ x 18 in., (625 x 455 mm.), offset lithograph.

$424* *Fernsehbild, 1971,* s., d., (06-12-93, Hauswedell/Nolt, #338), 25³⁄₁₆ x 32¹³⁄₁₆ in., (64 x 83.4 cm.), offset print on marbleized thin board (BP 278, DM 690, FR 2319, Y 44,617).

BI *Freundinnen (Vogel/Freitag 1), 1967,* #53/150, pencil s., d., est. DM 5,500, (11-20-92, Lempertz, #780, illus.), sh 18⅞ x 24 in., (48 x 61 cm.), offset print on smooth board.

BI *Hauserfront (Wer Hier Nichts Erkennen Kann...) (Vigel/Freitag 22), 1973,* s., est. DM 700, (11-20-92, Lempertz, #783), sh 17¹³⁄₁₆ x 24¾ in., (45.3 x 62.8 cm.), offset print on Buchungs transparent paper.

$553* *Hauserfront. Wer Hier Nichts Erkennen Kann, Muss Selber Pendeln (Block/Vogel P17; Vogel/Freitag 22), 1972-1973,* s., (06-24-93, Germann, #488), 17⅞ x 24¹¹⁄₁₆ in., (454 x 627 mm.), 4 color photo offset lithograph on transparent paper (BP 364, DM 897, FR 3022, Y 59,322, SF 805).

$354* *In Der Oper (V./F. 23), 1973,* s., (06-08-93, Karl/Faber, #1208), approx. 24¹³⁄₁₆ x 17¹⁵⁄₁₆ in., (63 x 45.5 cm.), offset print (BP 233, DM 574, FR 1934, Y 37,600).

$339* *Metamorphosen, 1987,* s., (12-05-92, Bassenge, #7644), 19¹¹⁄₁₆ x 15¹¹⁄₁₆ in., (50 x 39.8 cm.), color offsetlithograph on smooth paper (BP 212, DM 529, FR 1801, Y 42,002).

$794* *New Yorker Bettler, 1974,* s., num. V/30, (11-28-92, Schoppmann, #718), 16¹⁵⁄₁₆ x 23¹⁵⁄₁₆ in., (43 x 60.8 cm.), color offset print on light cardboard (BP 524, DM 1265, FR 4294, Y 98,818).

BI *Punktraster Mit Grossem Weissem Farbklecks,* s., d., est. DM 1,200-, (09-25-92, Granier, #2978), 38⅞ x 26½ in., (98.8 x 67.3 cm.), b/w serigraph on black velour.

$84,700* *Quetta 74,* s. S. Polke; s., d. 74, 75 and 78 verso, exec. 1978, prov., (11-19-92, Christie-NY, #168, illus.), 23¾ x 37⅜ in., (60.3 x 94.9 cm.), photograph, oil tint on b/w (BP 55,768, DM 135,045, FR 454,887, Y 10,533,516).

$2597* *Schuldruck (Vogel/Freitag 10), 1972,* #193/250, pencil s., d., (11-20-92, Lempertz, #781), 19⁹⁄₁₆ x 25½ in., (49.7 x 64.8 cm.), serigraph and blind embossing on Bristol board (BP 1710, DM 4141, FR 13,947, Y 322,970).

$805* *Untitled, 1987,* s. in pen, d., pub. Erhardt Klein, full margins, good cond., creases, (02-11-93, Sotheby-NY, #405), 19¹¹⁄₁₆ x 15¾ in., (500 x 400 mm.), color offset lithograph (BP 568, DM 1333, FR 4512, Y 97,046).

$474* *Untitled, 1989,* s., d., (06-12-93, Hauswedell/Nolt, #341), 38⁹⁄₁₆ x 26⅜ in., (98 x 67 cm.), serigraph on black Samt (BP 310, DM 771, FR 2593, Y 49,879).

BI *Untitled, 1989,* s. pen, #168, blindstamp, pub. Griffelkunst, good cond., est. $2/2,500, (05-15-93, Sotheby-NY, #1144), sheet 38⅝ x 26⅛ in., (98.1 x 66.4 cm.), silkscreen in black velour.

BI *Untitled, 1990,* felt tip pen s., pub. Staatliche Kunsthalle Baden-Baden, good cond.?, est. G 6/800, (12-09-92, Sotheby-Amstrdm, #633, illus.), sheet 27¹⁄₁₆ x 33¹⁄₁₆ in., (688 x 840 mm.), color offset lithograph and collage.

BI *Untitled, 1992,* s., d., #26/70, blindstamp printer, full margins, good cond., stain,surface soiling, est. $1,2/1,400, (05-19-93, Butterfield, #2290), 21¾ x 15³⁄₁₆ in., (552 x 386 mm.), silkscreen in colors on wove.

$1419* *Weisser Klecks, 1989,* s., d., (06-05-93, Grisebach, #831, illus.), 38¹⁵⁄₁₆ x 26⁵⁄₁₆ in., (99 x 66.8 cm.), white serigraph on black Samtpapier (BP 934, DM 2301, FR 7754, Y 152,221).

POLLACK, Max Austrian b. 1886

BI *"Guatemala, Fiesta San Pedro",* s., t., #35/100, excell. cond., est. $100/200, (05-15-93, Cleveland, #263), 8¼ x 8½ in., (21 x 21.6 cm.), color etching and aquatint.

$248* *"New York: Battery",* s. Max Pollack, t., num. 66/150, good cond., toning, (09-11-92, Skinner, #34, illus.), 12¼ x 16 in., (31.1 x 40.6 cm.), color etching/aquatint on paper (BP 128, DM 357, FR 1213, Y 30,727).

POLLAK, Max

BI *"Gathering Of People" and "Village": Two,* sealed in mat, good cond., water staining, foxing in image, foxing, est. $4/600, (05-19-93, Butterfield, #2017), one 16½ x 21⅛ in., (419 x 537 mm.), the other 21½ x 19 in., (419 x 537 mm.), etching w/aquatint and drypoint on wove.

POLLARD, J. (after)

$33* *Arrival Of The Stage Coach,* (11-12-92, Freemn/Fine Art, #181), 11 x 16 in., (27.9 x 40.6 cm.), hand colored engraving (BP 22, DM 52, FR 176, Y 4092).

$125 *"The Birmingham Tally-Ho! Coaches" and "The Age, Brighton Coach At The Bull and Mouth, Regent Circus, Piccadilly": A Pair,* modern, (12-11-92, G.A. Key, #37), 11 x 17 in., (27.9 x 43.2 cm.), colored print (BP 80, DM 197, FR 675, Y 15,468).

$77* *Doncaster Races,* engraved by Smart & Hunt, discoloration, foxing, (11-12-92, Freemn/Fine Art, #180), 13½ x 24 in., (34.3 x 61 cm.), colored engraving (BP 51, DM 122, FR 412, Y 9547).

$96 *"The Jolly Old Squire": A Set Of Four,* engraved H. Papprill, (08-14-92, G.A. Key, #96), 15 x 20 in., (38.1 x 50.8 cm.), hand colored aquatint (BP 50, DM 141, FR 477, Y 12,106).

POLLARD, James English 1797-1859/67

BI *Coursing, The Death,* pub. Dean and Munday, Sept. 14, 1825, est. C$ 1/150, (06-08-93, Ritchie, #8), 5½ x 15¾ in., (14 x 40 cm.), hand-colored aquatint.

POLLARD, James (after)

$9045* *Epsom Races (S. p 222): Six Plates,* by C. Hunt, pub. Ackermann, watermarked, discoloration, spotting, damage, (10-07-92, Christie-S. Ken, #61, illus.), pl 14¾ x 21¼ in., (37.5 x 54 cm.), colored aquatint (BP 5280, DM 13,088, FR 44,382, Y 1,087,793).

$292* *Epsom, Plates I-VI: A Set Of Six,* margins, (10-29-92, Bonhams-Chelsea, #159), plate 15¼ x 21½ in., (38.7 x 54.6 cm.), aquatint, restrike w/hand coloring (BP 187, DM 449, FR 1524, Y 36,170).

BI *Four In Hand,* foxing, est. BP 150/200, (03-03-93, Bonhams-Chelsea, #220), image 14 x 17¾ in., (35.6 x 45.1 cm.), hand-colored aquatint.

BI *Four In Hand,* foxing, est. BP 1/150, (06-30-93, Bonhams-Chelsea, #247), image 14 x 17¾ in., (35.6 x 45.1 cm.), aquatint w/hand-coloring.

BI *The Four-In-Hand Club, Hyde Park,* by J. Harris, est. BP 1/150, (06-30-93, Bonhams-Chelsea, #248), image 14 x 21¾ in., (35.6 x 55.2 cm.), aquatint w/hand-coloring.

$358* *The Mail Coach Changing Horses,* engraved by G. Reeves, very good cond.?, (06-11-93, Weschler, #53), 13¾ x 18 in., (34.9 x 45.7 cm.), colored engraving (BP 235, DM 582, FR 1962, Y 37,984).

BI *A North East View Of The New General Post Office,* by H. Pyall, pub. Messer Fores, trimmed, staining, laid, est. BP 3/500, (10-07-92, Christie-S. Ken, #63), sh 18 x 24 in., (45.7 x 61 cm.), colored aquatint part p. in color.

$230* *The Royal Mail's Departure From The General Post Office, London,* by R.G. Reeves, pub. J. Watson, February 1830, foxing, defects, (06-30-93, Bonhams-Chelsea, #250), image 16¾ x 24½ in., (42.5 x 62.2 cm.), aquatint w/hand-coloring (BP 154, DM 392, FR 1323, Y 24,644).

BI *The Royal Mails Starting From The Central Post Office, London,* by R.G. Reeves, pub. Thomas McLean, 1830, repaired tears, est. BP 150/250, (03-03-93, Bonhams-Chelsea, #223), image 16½ x 24¼ in., (41.9 x 61.6 cm.), hand-colored aquatint.

$164* *The Royal Mails Starting From The Central Post Office, London,* by. R.G. Reeves, pub. Thomas McLean, 1830, repaired tears, (06-30-93, Bonhams-Chelsea, #251), image 16½ x 24¼ in., (41.9 x 61.6 cm.), aquatint w/ hand-coloring (BP 110, DM 280, FR 944, Y 17,572).

BI *Scenes From The Road To Epsom (S.p 222): Four,* by J. Harris, trimmed, fading, trimmed, dirt, repaired tears, est. BP75/900, (10-07-92, Christie-S. Ken, #46), sh 16½ x 22½ in., (41.9 x 57.2 cm.), colored aquatint.

$264* *York And Edinboro' Mail, Plate 1 Mail Coach In A Drift Of Snow (S.p 217),* spotting, abrasion, (10-07-92, Christie-S. Ken, #40), sh 10½ x 15½ in., (26.7 x 39.4 cm.), colored aquatint part p. in color (BP 154, DM 382, FR 1295, Y 31,750).

POLLARD, R.

$1840* *The Representation Of His Majesty's Ship Mediator: Plates 2 And 3, 1782: Two,* after D. Serres, pub. R. Wilkinson and R. Pollard 1784, trimmed nearly to platemark, good cond., soiling, discoloration, foxing, tear or crease into lettering, (01-28-93, Sotheby-NY, #456), sheets approx. 19⅞ x 25 in., (505 x 635 mm.), engraving on laid (BP 1215, DM 2916, FR 9866, Y 228,458).

POLLARD and BROWN, Publishers

$34* *Portrait Of A Lady Collecting Flowers,* pub. 1884, (01-21-93, Bonhams-Chelsea, #93), image 14 x 11½ in., (35.6 x 29.2 cm.), mezzotint (BP 22, DM 54, FR 183, Y 4255).

BI *Portrait Of A Lady Collecting Flowers, 1884,* foxing, est. BP 60/80, (11-19-92, Bonhams-Chelsea, #80), image 14 x 11½ in., (35.6 x 29.2 cm.), mezzotint.

POLLOCK, Jackson American 1912-1956

BI *Untitled (Silkscreens I-VI) (P. 27-32), 1951: Six,* #39/50, from posthumous edit. p. 1964, Estate of Jackson Pollock, 1964 blindstamp, full margins, excell. cond., est. $24/28,000, (05-11-93, Christie-NY, #533, illus.), each sheet 23 x 29 in., (584 x 737 mm.), or 29 x 23 in., (584 x 737 mm.), screenprint on Strathmore.

POLLOCK, Reginald

BI *Theatrical Scenes: Five,* s., num., good cond., creases, smudges, est. $6/800, (12-12-92, Weschler, #151, illus.), sheets, approx. 29 x 23 in., (73.7 x 58.4 cm.), lithograph.

POMARDI, Simone

$825* *Antichita Di Roma Recentemente Scavate Fino All' Antico Piano: Twelve,* oblong folio, (11-12-92, Swann, #116, illus.), 13¹⁵⁄₁₆ x 20⁵⁄₁₆ in., (354 x 516 mm.), etching (BP 542, DM 1307, FR 4409, Y 102,294).

POMI, A.

$357* *Luxardo, 1938,* Arti Grafiche Navarra, A- cond., marginal creasing, (08-06-92, Swann, #224, illus.), 55 x 39 in., (139.7 x 99.1 cm.), (BP 186, DM 527, FR 1781, Y 45,536).

BI *Posters And Publicity, 1928 Annual Of Commercial Art,* B+ cond., est. $2/300, (08-06-92, Swann, #225, illus.), 11¼ x 8¼ in., (28.6 x 21 cm.), .

POMODORO, Arnaldo Italian b. 1926

BI *De-Cantare Urbino Portfolio, 1985: Eight,* complete portfolio, s., annot. XV/XXV, title page, colophon, pub. Edizioni Della Pergola, very good cond., in orig. portfolio, est. $2,5/3,000, (02-24-93, Butterfield, #3108, illus.), 17¾ x 13½ in., (451 x 343 mm.), etching & engraving in relief w/aquatint in colors on Magnani paperboard.

POMODORO, Gio Italian b. 1930

$404* *"Ariannaurea...", 1984,* s., num., watermark, blindstamp, (06-08-93, Karl/Faber, #1209), approx. 23⅟₁₆ x 15⁹⁄₁₆ in., (58.5 x 39.5 cm.), color etching and aquatint on thick wove (BP 266, DM 656, FR 2208, Y 42,910).

PONCE, Nicolas 1746-1831

$2164* *L'Enlevement Nocturne (Bocher 20; P. and B., III, p. 336, no. 1; L. and D. 171), 1780,* after Pierre-Antoine Baudouin, Bocher's 2nd state of 4, pub. Ponce, margins, staining, repaired tear, very good cond., (12-01-92, Christie-London, #240, illus.), plate 18⁹⁄₁₆ x 13⅟₁₆ in., (471 x 331 mm.), etching w/engraving on Auvergne laid paper (BP 1430, DM 3449, FR 11,754, Y 269,422).

PONCHIN, J.-H.

$358* *L'Indochine Francaise. Cambodge. "Angkor", 1931,* fairly good cond., (03-13-93, Laurin, #142, illus.), 44⅛ x 28¾ in., (112 x 73 cm.), (BP 250, DM 596, FR 2026, Y 42,192).

BI *L'Indochine Francaise. Cochinchine. "Arroyo",* fairly good cond., (03-13-93, Laurin, #141), 43¹¹⁄₁₆ x 27¹⁵⁄₁₆ in., (111 x 71 cm.), .

PONTI, Carlo

$908* *"Ricordo De Venezia": Twenty-One,* album, 1870s, 18 neg. t., blindstamped, (05-07-93, Sotheby-London, #23), photograph, albumen print (BP 575, DM 1436, FR 4838, Y 99,978).

PONTING, Herbert G.

$453* *The Alhambra, Early 20th Century,* blindstamped facsimile sig. H.G. Ponting, sight 555 x 405, (05-07-93, Sotheby-London, #205), photograph, warm toned silver print (BP 287, DM 716, FR 2413, Y 49,879).

PONTING, Herbert George 1871-1935

BI *"The 'Terra Nova' In A Gale, Scott's Last Expedition", 1910,* s., t., lit., est. BP 3/500, (10-29-92, Christie-London, #93), image 18 x 13¾ in., (45.7 x 34.9 cm.), photograph, blue-toned gelatin silver print.

PONTY, Max

$503* *Ch. De Fer Francais: Plages De France, c. 1935,* excell. cond., (01-23-93, Ribeyre/Baron, #8, illus.), 39⅜ x 24⁷⁄₁₆ in., (100 x 62 cm.), poster (BP 329, DM 800, FR 2706, Y 62,954).

$869* *Chamonix, Mont Blanc, 1935,* pub. Agence Francaise de Propagande for PLM, cond. 1, laid on linen, (10-13-92, Phillips-London, #44), 39⅜ x 24³⁄₁₆ in., (100 x 61.5 cm.), color lithograph (BP 506, DM 1273, FR 4326, Y 105,372).

BI *Chemins De Fer Francais, Montagnes De France, 1930,* pub. Agence France de Propagande, cond. 2, laid on linen, est. BP 3/400, (10-13-92, Phillips-London, #45), 39³⁄₁₆ x 24⁷⁄₁₆ in., (99.5 x 62 cm.), color lithograph.

BI *Chemins De Fer Francais, Plages De France, 1930,* pub. Agence Francaise de Propagande, cond. 1, laid on linen, est. BP3/500, (10-13-92, Phillips-London, #43, illus.), 39³⁄₁₆ x 24⁷⁄₁₆ in., (99.5 x 62 cm.), color lithograph.

$499* *PLM. Routes Ferrees Des Alpes. "De Grenoble A Nice, Autorail Par Digne Et Puget-Theniers", 1930,* very good cond., (03-15-93, Arcole, #52), 39⅜ x 24⁷⁄₁₆ in., (100 x 62 cm.), (BP 347, DM 829, FR 2818, Y 59,109).

POONS, Larry American b. 1937

$176* *Linear Composition,* init., #94/95, (05-16-93, Hindman, #604), 27 x 17 in., (68.6 x 43.2 cm.), color serigraph (BP 114, DM 283, FR 951, Y 19,510).

BI *Untitled, 1964,* from Ten Works + Ten Painters, from portfolio #40/500, pub. Ives-Sillman, blindstamp, good cond.?, prop. Woodward Foundation, est. $2/400, (12-12-92, Weschler, #154), sheet 24 x 20 in., (61 x 50.8 cm.), color silkscreen.

BI *Untitled: Two,* s., #28/100, margins, very good cond., est. $6/800, (12-12-92, Weschler, #153, illus.), each 34 x 24 in., (86.4 x 61 cm.), color silkscreen.

BI *Untitled: Two,* s., #28/100, margins, very good cond., est. $6/800, (12-12-92, Weschler, #152), each 34 x 24 in., (86.4 x 61 cm.), color silkscreen.

POPE, Alexander   American 1849-1924
$2420* *The Rape Of The Lock (Griffith 29; Foxon P941; Rothschild 1570): Six,* 8vo, (11-12-92, Swann, #168), engraving (BP 1589, DM 3835, FR 12,934, Y 300,062).

POPE, Alexander (Jr.)
$660* *Game Birds: Six,* each plate s., pub. Armstrong and Co., very good cond.?, (07-19-92, Bakker, #102), each approx. 13½ x 19½ in., (34.3 x 49.5 cm.), chromolithograph (BP 339, DM 962, FR 3253, Y 82,049).

POPE, Alexander (after)
$33* *Two Grouse,* (02-12-93, DuMouchelle, #2407), 13½ x 19¾ in., (34.3 x 50.2 cm.), chromolithograph (BP 23, DM 55, FR 185, Y 3980).

POPHILLAT, Jean Pierre   b. 1937
BI *"Nature Morte Devant La Fenetre",* #112/150, est. FF6/800, (04-04-93, Pescheteau, #277), 18½ x 25⅜ in., (47 x 64.5 cm.), color lithograph on wove.

POPKINS, Samuel K.   American 20th cent.
$30* *"Cathedral-Seville", 1934,* plate No. 27 for Print-A-Month Club of Cleveland, s., t., excell. cond., (05-15-93, Cleveland, #264), 8½ x 5¼ in., (21.6 x 13.3 cm.), drypoint (BP 20, DM 48, FR 162, Y 3326).

PORCELLIS, Jan   1585-1632
$340* *"Verscheyden Stranden En Water" (Hollstein Bd. XVII, 1-17), 1645: Twelve,* 2nd state, trimmed, (09-14-92, Venator/Hansten, #1583), each approx. 2⅜ x 3⅜ in., (6 x 8.5 cm.), etching (BP 180, DM 505, FR 1713, Y 42,278).

PORTER, Elliot   American contemporary
$385* *Path In The Woods, c. 1972,* s., label verso, (12-10-92, Sloan, #2721), 15½ x 12½ in., (39.4 x 31.8 cm.), dye transfer print (BP 248, DM 609, FR 2080, Y 47,625).

PORTER, Fairfield   American 1907-1975
$1210* *"Interior With Christmas Tree",* s. Fairfield Porter, num. 7/100, very good cond.?, (11-21-92, Bakker, #169, illus.), image 26 x 20 in., (66 x 50.8 cm.), color lithograph (BP 797, DM 1929, FR 6498, Y 150,479).

BI *"Sixth Avenue II",* s. Fairfield Porter, num. 3/60, very good cond.?, est. $8/1,200, (11-21-92, Bakker, #170, illus.), 21 x 28 in., (53.3 x 71.1 cm.), color lithograph.

PORTER, Katherine   American b. 1941
$440* *Perpetuum Mobile: The City, 1987,* s., num. 17/30, pub. Joe Fawbush Editions, full margins, excell. cond., (09-19-92, Christie-E, #181), sheet 26 x 38½ in., (660 x 978 mm.), woodcut in colors w/hand-coloring on Japan (BP 253, DM 659, FR 2256, Y 54,822).

PORTERFIELD, Wilbur
$715* *Night's Curtain, 1906,* t., d. by photog., notations, gallery handstamp, (04-07-93, Swann, #536, illus.), 10¼ x 13½ in., photograph, gum print (BP 473, DM 1156, FR 3914, Y 81,232).

PORTFOLIO
$2200* *1 Cent Life, 1964,* portfolio, text by Walasse Ting, ed. by Sam Francis, num. 105, pub. E.W. Kornfeld, good cond., incl. Pierre Alechinsky, Karel Appel, Enrico Baj, Alan Davie, Jim Dine, Oyvind Fahlstrom, Sam Francis, Robert Indiana, Alfred Jensen, Asger Jorn, (11-07-92, Sotheby-NY, #730), each sheet approx. 16¼ x 11⅝ in., (413 x 295 mm.), 62 lithographs, nearly all p. in colors (BP 1438, DM 3513, FR 11,873, Y 271,538).

$2070* *1 Cent Life, 1964,* text by Walasse Ting, edit. Sam Francis, pub. E.W. Kornfeld, good cond., including works by Alechinsky, Appel, Baj, Davie, Dine, Fahlstrom, Francis, Indiana, Jensen, Jorn, O.K., Kaprow, Leslie, Lichtenstein, Mitchell, and Oldenburg, Gertrude Kasle Coll., (05-15-93, Sotheby-NY, #1145), each single sheet 16¼ x 11⅝ in., (41.3 x 29.5 cm.), 62 lithographs in colors (BP 1346, DM 3330, FR 11,189, Y 229,465).

$2530* *1 Cent Life, Berne, E.W. Kornfeld, 1964: Sixty-Two,* copy 1631 of 2000, excell. cond., orig. sleeve and dustjacket,

worksby Alechinsky, Appel, Baj, Davie, Dine, Fahlstrom, Francis, Indiana, Jensen, Jorn, Kiki O.K., Kaprow, Leslie, Lichtenstein, Mitchell, Oldenburg, Ramos, Rauschenberg, Reinhoud, Riopelle, and 8 others, (05-11-93, Christie-NY, #535), 16⁵⁄₁₆ x 11¹⁵⁄₁₆ in., (414 x 303 mm.), color lithograph, in- and hors-texte, numerous reprods. and text on wove (BP 1615, DM 3986, FR 13,429, Y 278,297).

$7475* *11 Pop Artists, Volume I, New York, Original Editions, 1965: Eleven,* s., num., copy 122 of 200, creases, scuff, very good cond., orig. portfolio, damaged, works by D'Arcangelo, Dine, Jones, Laing, Lichtenstein, Phillips, Ramos, Rosenquist, Warhol, Wesley, and Wesselmann, (05-11-93, Christie-NY, #536, illus.), 24 x 20 in., (610 x 508 mm.), screenprints, screenprints w/collage and lithograph in colors on various papers (BP 4772, DM 11,775, FR 39,676, Y 822,242).

$17,250* *11 Pop Artists, Volume III, 1965: "Landscape III", "Calico", "Janet Is Wearing...", "Triple", "Sweet Dreams, Baby!", "Custom Print III", "Miss Comfort Creme", "For Love", "Jaqueline Kennedy III", "Dream Of Unicorns", and others,* complete portfolio, each s., #181/200, pub. Original Editions, creasing, soiling, tears, (05-15-93, Sotheby-NY, #1146, illus.), silkscreen in colors, lithograph in colors, silkscreen printed in colors on Alufoil (BP 11,216, DM 27,747, FR 93,243, Y 1,912,205).

$3520* *20th Century Photographers, 1982,* portfolio, pub. Anthology Film Archives, most contain photographer's-sig., t., d., num., images by Siskind, Levitt, Meyerowitz, Parker, Van Dyke, Steiner, Snow, Shore, Mayes, Beard, Greenfield, Frampton, and Burckhardt, (04-07-93, Swann, #569, illus.), each image 20 x 16 in., print, largest 13 x 10 in., photograph, 13 silver, dye transfer, and chromogenic prints (BP 2326, DM 5693, FR 19,267, Y 399,909).

BI *21 Etching And Poems: Thirteen Plates, New York, Morris Gallery, 1960 (Boston 145): Thirteen,* 8 s.; i., full margins, tear, very good cond., orig. portfolio, works by Becker, Ben-Zion, Grippe, Hayter, Martinelli, Nicholson, Pereira, Phillips, Roesch, Salemme, Schanker, Schrag and Vicente, est. $5/7,000, (05-11-93, Christie-NY, #534, illus.), etching and text on BFK Rives.

$690* *4x4x4x4, 1990: Four,* s., #1/100, Bochner and LeVa, d., full margins, very good cond., MelBochner, Barry LeVa, Sol Lewitt and Robert Mangold, (05-19-93, Butterfield, #2291), each 48 x 48 in., (121.9 x 121.9 cm.), silkscreen in colors on wove (BP 448, DM 1122, FR 3779, Y 76,387).

BI *Allan D'Arcangelo, "Landscape 1", Allen Jones, "Miss America", Gerald Laing, "Compact", Peter Phillips, "Custom Print 1" and John Wesley, "Maiden": Five, 1965,* from Eleven Pop Artists Volume I, s., d., #28/200, pub. Original Editions, good cond., soiling, wear, est. $2,5/3,500, (12-12-92, Weschler, #155, illus.), each approx. 24 x 20 in., (61 x 50.8 cm.), 4 silkscreens, 1 lithograph.

BI *Allan D'Arcangleo, Landscape 1; Allen Jones, Miss America; Gerald Laing, Compact; Peter Phillips, Custom Print 1; John Wesley, Maiden, 1965: ElevenPop Artists Volume I,* s., d., #28/200, by Original Editions, U.S.A., est. $1/1,500, (05-22-93, Weschler, #217, illus.), approx. 24 x 20 in., (61 x 50.8 cm.), .

BI *Andy Warhol, "Birmingham Race Riot", Roy Lichtenstein, "Lunch Counter", Robert Indiana, "Eternal Hexagon" and Ad Reinhardt, "Untitled": Four, 1964,* from Ten Works + Ten Painters, from portfolio #40/500, pub. Ives-Sillman, bearing blindstamp, good cond., orig. portfolio case, prop. Woodward Foundation, est. $3/5,000, (12-12-92, Weschler, #156, illus.), each approx. 24 x 20 in., (61 x 50.8 cm.), color silkscreen.

BI *Ars Viva Edition, 1973,* incl. works by Niki de St. Phalle, Rotella, Villegle, Hains, Arman, Dufrene, Christo, Cesar, Restany and Spoerri, example 512, est. DK 6,000, (06-03-93, Kunsthallen, #174), .

$825* *Art In America Graphics '70: Six,* includ. Richard Anuszkiewicz, Alexander Calder, Peter Dechar, Paul Jenkins, Ray Parker and Robert Rauschenberg, s., #91/100, excellent cond., orig.portfolio, (06-11-93, Doyle, #102), (BP 542, DM 1341, FR 4521, Y 87,533).

$2185* *Blacks During Or After The Civil War, 1860's: Six,* one w/imprint of J. CREMER & CO., Philadelphia, one w/ imprint of W.P. KENDALL, Woodstock, Vt., label, (04-06-93, Sotheby-NY, #9, illus.), photograph, tintype (BP 1443, DM 3520, FR 11,920, Y 249,202).

BI *Brasenose College And Exeter College, University Life, 1903-1907: One Hundred And Five,* album, compiled by R.B. Halfield, by J.S. Came, H. de Blois Leach, Lafayette et alii, majority w/manuscript t., d., various sizes, est. BP 3/400, (05-07-93, Sotheby-London, #208, illus.), photograph, platinum and albumen prints.

$1265* *Camera Work: Selected Works, 1905: Seven,* including images by J. Craig Annan, George Davison, Hill and Adamsonand Eduard Steichen, (05-23-93, Butterfield, #3365, illus.), from 5½ x 4½ in., to 8 x 6 in., photogravure (BP 824, DM 2068, FR 6962, Y 139,825).

$1725* *Chefs D'Oeuvre, 1900: Six Volumes,* from the Paris Exposition, #29/100, pub. George Barrie and Son, (06-10-93, Sotheby-NY, #467), leather bound, on Whatman drawing paper (BP 1128, DM 2809, FR 9457, Y 183,102).

$173* *A Collection Of Fourteen Sporting Subjects, c. 1830: Fourteen,* margins, good cond., Anthony N. B. Garvan Coll., (06-05-93, Christie-NY, #62), etchings, aquatint and lithograph w/hand-coloring, various papers (BP 114, DM 280, FR 945, Y 18,558).

$460* *A Collection Of Hunting And Sporting Scenes, c. 1900: Eleven,* minor defects, Anthony N. B. Garvan Coll., (06-05-93, Christie-NY, #75), lithograph, chromolithograph, etching, engraving and photograph on various papers (BP 303, DM 746, FR 2514, Y 49,346).

BI *Derrier Le Miroir,* 10 ans d'edition 1946-1956, Maeght Editeur, Paris 1956, containing original lithographs by Chagall, Miro and Bazaine, and etchings by Miro and Giacometti, est. DK 8,000, (11-14-92, Bukowskis, #19), .

BI *Derriere Le Miroir,* from the series Derriere le Miroir, including Bazaine, Braque, Calder, Giacometti and Tapies, est. DK 2,000, (09-30-92, Kunsthallen, #89), color lithograph.

BI *Derriere Le Miroir, 10 Ans D'Edition, 1956,* complete anniversary edit., incl. Miro's Femme au Miroir (Mourlot 242), and five other orig. prints by Bazain, Chagall, Giacometti, Miro, and Ubac,good cond., creasing, est. $1,8/2,200, (11-05-92, Sotheby-NY, #412), 14¾ x 11 in., (375 x 280 mm.), print.

BI *Derriere Le Miroir-10 Ans, 1956,* Edit. 1946-1956, Maeght, portfolio w/original lithographs of Chagall, Miro and Bazaine, and w/etchings of Miro and Giacometti, est. DK 8,000, (09-30-92, Kunsthallen, #90), etching.

$4722* *Early Italian Views, Nineteen Studies, 1860s,* by Fratelli Alinari, Cuccioni, Pozzi, Ningi and Anon., blindstamped w/photog.'s credit, from 312 x 226mm to 427 x 320mm, (05-07-93, Sotheby-London, #28, illus.), photograph, 3 salt prints, remainder albumen print (BP 2990, DM 7466, FR 25,157, Y 519,930).

$4093* *Eddy Batache. La Mysticite Charnelle De Rene Crevel,* portfolio incl. Francis Bacon, Max Ernst, Andre Masson, Sonia Delaunay and others, all s., #40/100, w/t. page and text, s. by author, num. 40, pub.Georges Visat, 1976, full margins, good cond., (12-03-92, Sotheby-London, #782, illus.), 14 prints, various media on Arches (BP 2640, DM 6437, FR 21,970, Y 509,270).

$13,200* *Eight By Eight To Benefit The Temporary Contemporary, 1983,* complete portfolio, s., #207/250, pub. Mus. of Cont. Art, good cond.,orig. box; Richard Diebenkorn, Sam Francis, David Hockney, Ellsworth Kelly, Robert Rauschenberg, Niki de Saint Phalle, Jean Tinguely, and Andy Warhol, (11-07-92, Sotheby-NY, #728, illus.), overall size 42 x 29 in., (106.7 x 73.7 cm.), 8 prints by various artists incl. lithograph, etching and aquatint p.in colors; silkscreen p. in colors (BP 8630, DM 21,076, FR 71,236, Y 1,629,227).

$16,100* *Eight By Eight To Celebrate The Temporary Contemporary, Los Angeles,The Museum Of Contemporary Art, 1983: Eight,* #38/250, rubbed spot, excell. cond., orig. portfolio box designed byJoseph Kosuth, works by Diebenkorn, Francis, Hockney, Kelly, Rauschenberg, Saint Phalle, Tinguely and Warhol, (05-11-93, Christie-NY, #539, illus.), each approx. sheet 42 x 29 in., (106.7 x

73.7 cm.), lithographs, screenprints and etching w/aquatint in colors on just. on various papers (BP 10,278, DM 25,362, FR 85,456, Y 1,770,982).

$4400* *Experiments In Art And Technology, Inc., 1973: Set Of Thirty,* The New York Collection for Stockholm, NY, s., #195/300, excell. cond., includ. Lee Bontecou, Robert Breer, John Chamberlain, Walter de Maria, Markdi Suvero, Jim Dine, Oyvind Fahlstrom, Dan Flavin, Red Grooms, Hans Haacke, Alex Hay, Donald Judd, (11-09-92, Christie-NY, #387, illus.), (305 x 229 mm.), print, multiple, photograph, some in colors on various paper (BP 2909, DM 7024, FR 23,732, Y 546,041).

$1495* *Fernand Mourlot, Souvenirs Et Portraits D'Artistes, Paris And New York, A.A.C. Mazo And L. Amiel, 1972: Twenty-Five,* copy 403 of 800, full margins, excell. cond., loose, orig. portfolio, includes works by Brianchon, Masson, Baudin, Apel les Fenosa, Esteve, Matisse, Guiramand, Terechkovitch, Braque, Derain, Picasso, Jenkins, Miro, Cocteau, Minaux, Villon, Chagall, Giacometti and 7 others, (05-11-93, Christie-NY, #329), 12¹⁵⁄₁₆ x 11 in., (330 x 280 mm.), 19 color lithographs, 6 lithographs in black, t. page, text and just., on Arches (BP 954, DM 2355, FR 7935, Y 164,448).

$1635* *Fighter Planes, c. 1940: Ten Studies,* by Hensser, Bellamy, Devon, Crouch. and Anon., mounted on card, labels, each approx. 370 x 300mm, (05-07-93, Sotheby-London, #193, illus.), photograph, silver print (BP 1035, DM 2585, FR 8711, Y 180,026).

BI *Five Studies, 1930s,* by Pecsi, Pollier, Staples and Anon., s., stamped photog.'s credit, from 228 x 165mm to 367 x 296mm, est. BP 1/200, (05-07-93, Sotheby-London, #227), photograph, silver print.

$3300* *Flight, 1971: Twelve,* pub. International Rescue Committee, includ. Berman, Calder, Chagall, da Silva, Gottlieb, Lam, Lipchitz, Masson, Miro, Motherwell, Pignon, Wotruba,all but Chagall s., #50/250, good cond., smudging, creases, (06-11-93, Doyle, #103), 11 lithograph, 1 serigraph (BP 2168, DM 5363, FR 18,082, Y 350,133).

$19,550* *For Joseph Beuys, 1986-87,* complete portfolio, each s., #18/90, co-pub. Galerie Bernd Kluser and Editions Schellmann, good cond., original portfolio box, including Arakawa: "Portrait Of Hellen Keller Or Joseph Beuys", Brown "The Whitewater", Chia "Non Come Figli Di Genitori", and others, (05-15-93, Sotheby-NY, #1149, illus.), overall 31⅞ x 23⅝ in., (81 x 60 cm.), 28 prints and 2 multiples (BP 12,711, DM 31,446, FR 105,676, Y 2,167,166).

$400* *French Architectural Studies, c. 1860: Eleven,* by Blanquart-Evrard, Cundall, Downes and Co., Bisson Freres and Thompson & Co., photog.'s credit, pencil annots., smallest 171 x 207mm, largest 442x 368mm, (05-07-93, Sotheby-London, #105, illus.), photograph, albumen prints, two Blanquart-Evrard process prints, onegravure (intaglio) (BP 253, DM 632, FR 2131, Y 44,043).

$431* *Girls And Women: Six Cased Images,* 1860s, (05-23-93, Butterfield, #3374, illus.), photograph, 1 1/4-plate daguerreotype, 1 1/4-plate tintype, 3 1/4-plate and 1 1/6-plate ambrotype, 5 w/gilt preservers (BP 281, DM 705, FR 2372, Y 47,640).

BI *Graphikmappe Des Schweizerischen Kunstvereins: Plates 1; 3; 6; 19; 22and 24, 1970-75: Six,* s., num., pub. Swiss Society for the Arts, full margins, good cond.,includes Valerio Adami, Shusaku Arakawa, Robert Cottingham, Peter Phillips, Dieter Roth and Pierre Tal Coat, est. BP 900/1,100, (06-30-93, Sotheby-London, #905, illus.), 3 silkscreens, 2 lithographs, all in color, 1 aquatint and drypoint in orange.

BI *Helhesten, 1 Arg. Nr. 1-6; 2 Arg Nr. 1-3: A Portfolio,* containing works by Asger Jorn, Else Alfet, Ejler Bille, Egill Jacobsen and others, est. DK 5,000, (09-30-92, Kunsthallen, #125), lithograph.

$248* *Homme Dans La Ville: Three,* portfolio, s., #42/60, num. in ink 42/60 on justification page, fullmargins, good cond. (?), light staining, orig. portfolio, (02-24-93, Butterfield, #3241), each sheet 16 x 13 in., (406 x 330 mm.), etching and aquatint in colors on Arches (BP 173, DM 403, FR 1365, Y 29,101).

BI *In Memory Of My Feeling, 1967: Forty-Four,* complete portfolio, just., #1206 of 2500, p. Crafton Graphic Company, good cond., orig. cloth covered box, lit., incl.de Kooning, de Saint Phaller,Guston, Johns, Lichtenstein, Motherwell, Newman, Oldenburg, and others, est. Dffl. 2/2,500, (05-27-93, Sotheby-Amstrdm, #638, illus.), lithograph on Mohawk Superfine Smooth paper.

$1303* *In Memory Of My Feelings, 1967: Forty-Four,* complete portfolio by de Kooning, Saint Phalle, Guston, Johns, Lichtenstein, Motherwell, Newman, Oldenburg, Rauschenberg and others, pub. Museum ofModern Art, good cond., in orig. box, lit., (12-09-92, Sotheby-Amstrdm, #601), lithograph on Mohawk Superfine Smooth paper (BP 832, DM 2045, FR 6979, Y 161,562, G 2300).

BI *Inaugural Impressions, 1977,* each s., num. 84/100, good cond., slight rippling, est. $5/7,000, (05-22-93, Weschler, #215, illus.), 23 x 20 in., (58.4 x 50.8 cm.), to 30 x 20 in., (58.4 x 50.8 cm.), four screenprints, one lithograph, three in colors.

$518* *Issue 22, 1908: Three,* by Eduard Steichen, photographic quarterly edit./pub. by Alfred Steiglitz, arranged/p. Fleming Press, binding damaged, covers torn, (05-23-93, Butterfield, #3366, illus.), 12 x 8½ in., color gravure (intaglio) (BP 337, DM 847, FR 2851, Y 57,257).

$581* *"Italia": Eight-Eight,* album, 1880s, by Van Lint, Achille Mauri, G. Sommer et alii, some t., num., various photog.'s credits, each approx. 250 x 390mm or 260 x 200mm, (05-07-93, Sotheby-London, #30), photograph, albumen print (BP 368, DM 919, FR 3095, Y 63,973).

$944* *Japan, Hong Kong And Egypt,* Carte de Visite album, 1860s, by Felice Beato, Afong, Pun-Lun, Ngha-Chan, F. Schoenke et alii, (05-07-93, Sotheby-London, #41), photograph, albumen print, some hand-colored (BP 598, DM 1492, FR 5029, Y 103,942).

$1610* *John Ashbery, Self-Portrait In A Convex Mirror, San Francisco, ArionPress, 1984: Eight,* s., num., y., text, num. just., colophon, s., by pub. on colophon, copy 39 of 150, loose, excell. cond., works by Avedon, Elaine de Kooning, de Kooning, Dine, Freilicher, Katz, Kitaj and Rivers, (05-11-93, Christie-NY, #540, illus.), lithographs, offset lithographs, etchings, photogravures and woodcut, 1 in colors, on circular Twinrocker hand-made (BP 1028, DM 2536, FR 8546, Y 177,098).

$3088* *L'Emerveile Merveilleux Hommage A Joan Miro, 1973,* portfolio, #42, pub. Le Vent d'Arles, good cond., marks, (06-30-93, Sotheby-London, #906), 20 x 16⅛ in., (508 x 410 mm.), color photograph, print, and music tape, wrapped in scarf w/Catalan colors, in plexiglass box w/8 track cassette (BP 2070, DM 5267, FR 17,768, Y 330,869).

$3680* *Metrolpitan Opera Fine Art: A Collection Of Original Graphic WorksBy Eight Renowned Contemporary Artists, New York, Metropolitan Opera Association And Circle Gallery, Ltd., 1978: Eight,* s., num., copy 17 of 250, pub. MET blindstamps, excell. cond., orig.portfolio, soiled, works by Clave, Fini, Lindner, Marini, Masson, Rivers, Wundelich and Wyeth, (05-11-93, Christie-NY, #538, illus.), each sheet 23 x 30½ in., (584 x 775 mm.), or 30½ x 23 in., (584 x 775 mm.), lithographs, offset lithographs and etching in colors, t. and colophon on wove (BP 2349, DM 5797, FR 19,533, Y 404,796).

BI *New Years Wishes: Ten,* collection by Jaap Wagemaker, Yasse Tabuchi and others, good cond., est. G 4/600, (12-09-92, Sotheby-Amstrdm, #671), prints in various techniques.

$8050* *The New York Collection For Stockholm, 1973,* complete portfolio, each s., #162/300, pub. Experiments in Art and Technology, good cond., original portfolio box, including works by Bontecou, Breer, Chamberlain, Maria, Dine, Suvero, Fahlstrom, Flavin, Grooms, Haacke, Hay, Judd, Kelly, Lewitt and Lichtenstein, (05-15-93, Sotheby-NY, #1148, illus.), each sheet 12 x 9 in., (30.5 x 22.9 cm.), 30 prints by various artists (BP 5234, DM 12,948, FR 43,514, Y 892,362).

BI *The New York Collection For Stockholm/ 30 Artists, 1973: Thirty,* complete portfolio, most init. or s., each d., #23/30 AC, p. by Styria Studio, pub. Experiments in Art And Technology, good cond., est. BP 3/4,000, (06-30-93, Sotheby-London, #904), overall 12 x 9 in., (305 x 229 mm.), print.

BI *The New York Collection For Stockholm/30 Artists, 1973: Thirty,* complete portfolio, most init. or s., #202/300, pub. Experiments in Art and Technology, good cond., including Lee Bontecou, Robert Breer, John Chamberlain, Walter de Maria, Jim Dine, Mark de Suvero, Oyvind Fahlstrom, Dan Flavin, Red Grooms and other, est. BP 3/3,500, (06-30-93, Sotheby-London, #903, illus.), overall 12 x 9 in., (305 x 229 mm.), print.

$4950* *New York, New York, 1983,* complete portfolio, s., #177/250, pub. New York Graphic Society, goodcond.; Robert Indiana, Larry Rivers, Robert Rauschenberg, R.B. Kitaj, James Rosenquist, Alex Katz, Robert Motherwell, and Red Grooms, (11-07-92, Sotheby-NY, #729), 8 prints by various artists incl. silkscreen/lithograph p. in colors, lithograph (BP 3236, DM 7904, FR 26,713, Y 610,960).

$5968* *Paroles Peintes V, 1975,* portfolio incl. Joan Miro, Sebastiano Matta, Eduardo Chillida, AntoniTapies and others, s. by pub. O. Lazar-Vernet, num. 42, w/additional suite of the plates, all s., #42/75, good cond., orig. boards and slipcase, (12-03-92, Sotheby-London, #784, illus.), overall size 15⅜ x 11¾ in., (390 x 300 mm.), nine aquatints in colors on Arches (BP 3850, DM 9385, FR 32,034, Y 742,566).

$4355* *"Pleasant Memories Of Pleasant Lands": Album,* F.M. Good and others, p. by Frith, 1860s, mounted two-per-page, t., folio, lit., (05-06-93, Christie-London, #76, illus.), each approx. 6 x 8 in., photograph, 363 albumen prints (BP 2760, DM 6859, FR 23,091, Y 479,151).

BI *Portfolio,* including the works of Merete Barker, Margarethe Sorenson, Thomas Bang, and Toben Ebbsen, est. DK 4,000, (03-24-93, Kunsthallen, #116), .

BI *Pour Jorn, 1976: Fourteen,* portfolio, each pl s., #63/100, #63, pub. Asger Jorn Foundation, fullmargins, good cond., including Pierre Alechinsky, Karel Appel, Enrico Baj, Constant, Corneille, Dotremont, Wifredo Lam, Sebastian Matta, Antonio Saura, HenriMichaux and others, est. BP 2,5/3,000, (06-30-93, Sotheby-London, #908, illus.), each sh c. 29½ x 21¼ in., (749 x 540 mm.), color lithograph w/photographic pl on Arches.

$3946* *Pour Jorn, 1976: Fourteen,* portfolio, #62/100, full margins, good cond., original box, includingPierre Alechinsky, Karel Appel, Enrico Baj, Constant, Corneille, Dotremont, Wifredo Lam, Sebastian Matta, Antonio Saura, Henri Michaux, Saura, Ting, Bram VanVelde, Wemaere and Wyckaert, (06-30-93, Sotheby-London, #909, illus.), each sh c. 29½ x 21¼ in., (749 x 540 mm.), color lithograph on Arches (BP 2645, DM 6730, FR 22,704, Y 422,801).

BI *Rene Char. Le Monde De L'Art N'Est Pas Le Monde Du Pardon (Cramer 178),* portfolio incl. Joan Miro, Wilfredo Lam, Zao Wou-ki and others, s., pub. Maeght, 1974, loose, orig. folder, est. BP 2/2,500, (12-03-92, Sotheby-London, #783, illus.), lithographs and intaglios on Arches.

$220* *Robert Indiana, Eternal Hexagon; Adreinhardt, Untitled, 1964: Ten Works + Ten Painters,* portfolio 40/50, blindstamp, full sheets, good cond., soiling, surface scuffs, (05-22-93, Weschler, #216, illus.), 20 x 24 in., (50.8 x 61 cm.), colored silkscreen (BP 143, DM 358, FR 1204, Y 24,256).

$15,425* *Rome And Other Views, Parc St. Cloud, c. 1850-1870s: Thirty-Seven,* few possibly also from paper negs., 4 num. in negs., t., num., one w/photog.'s credit, one w/blindstamp, (05-06-93, Christie-London, #49, illus.), largest approx. 8 x 10 in., photograph, 2 salt prints from paper negs., others albumen prints orlight albumen prints (BP 9775, DM 24,295, FR 81,787, Y 1,697,106).

$508* *Royalty And Aristocracy: Forty-Eight,* Mayer & Pierson, Disderi & Co., London Stereoscopic Co., ink t., sitters ident., (05-06-93, Christie-London, #7, illus.), cartes-de-visite (BP 322, DM 800, FR 2694, Y 55,892).

$784* *S.l., Aux Nourritures Terrestres, 1950: Ten,* works by Jean Arp, Sonia Delaunay, Alberto Magnelli, Sophie Taeuber-Arp, hors commerce, num., s. by all artists, sig. stamp of Sophie Taeuber-Arp, (11-15-92, Christie-Geneva, #304, illus.), 14¹⁵⁄₁₆ x 11¼ in., (380 x 285 mm.), lithograph in color on Arches (BP 515, DM 1250, FR 4213, Y 97,841, SF 1130).

$1045* *"San Lazzaro Et Ses Amis": Fifteen,* by BRAQUE, BILL, CALDER, CHAGALL, FONTANA, ERNST, MIRO, MOORE, MAGNELLI, PICASSO, POLIAKOFF, SUTHERLAND, ZAO WOU-KI, HARTUNG, and MAGRITTE, Folio, num, pub. XXe Siecle, 1975, (05-27-93, Swann, #226), 14 x 10⅝ in., (35.6 x 27 cm.), color lithographs (BP 669, DM 1677, FR 5652, Y 112,028).

$3775* *Die Schaffenden: 5-8 Jahrgang, c. 1924, 54: A Collection,* from series, pub. Paul Westheim, margins, good cond., including KurtBeyerlin, Bernhard Kretzschmar, Wilhelm Rudolph, Carl Mense, Charles Crodel, Paul Gangolf, Otto Herbig, Moissey Kogan, Else Meidner, Edouard Gunzinger, WernerLaves, Hermann Huber, Walter Heisig and others, (06-30-93, Sotheby-London, #661, illus.), etching, lithograph and woodcut (BP 2530, DM 6439, FR 21,720, Y 404,479).

BI *Schweizer Gruppe 'Moderner Bund' 1913, 2. Mappe, 1913,* complete portfolio, comprising Paul Klee's Garten des Leidenschaft (K. 56), good cond., orig. cover, est. $12/16,000, (11-05-92, Sotheby-NY, #411, illus.), each sheet approx. 12⅝ x 9⅞ in., (320 x 250 mm.), etching and prints by Gimmi, Helbig, Huber, and Luthy.

$12,650* *Sema, 15 Originale Steinzeichnungen, Munich, Delphin Verlag, 1912: Fifteen,* s., t. page, num. just., text sheet and list of contents, copy 200 of 280, full margins, loose, creases, excell. cond., orig. portfolio, includes works by Caspar, Caspar-Filser, Fricke, Genin, Hermann, Hofman-Juan, Jagerspacher, Klee, Kubin, Oppenheimer and 5 others, (05-11-93, Christie-NY, #327, illus.), 19⅛ x 16⅛ in., (485 x 410 mm.), lithograph on buff wove (BP 8075, DM 19,928, FR 67,144, Y 1,391,486).

BI *Ships: Collection Of One Hundred And Twenty Six,* 1880s-1905, by West & Son, White, Waterlow & Co., Symonds & Co., W. Fred Mitchell et Alii, photog.'s blindstamped credit, annots., mounted on blackcard, est. BP 3/500, (05-07-93, Sotheby-London, #206, illus.), photograph, albumen print, cyanotypes, silver print, platinum print.

$293* *The Situationist Times No. 6, 1967: Thirty,* by Alechinsky, Jorn, Lam, Roberto Matta, Saura, Segui, Tabuchi and others, p. Clot, Bramsen and Georges, pub. Jacqueline de Jong, good cond., creases, (12-09-92, Sotheby-Amstrdm, #459), each sheet 11 x 8⅞ in., (280 x 225 mm.), color lithograph (BP 187, DM 460, FR 1569, Y 36,330, G 518).

BI *Solto Arte, 1975,* including Pour Journal, Wrapped (S. 90), by Christo, SOLTO ARTE (S. 133) by Beuys, mostly s., #40/100, good cond., including Joseph Beuys, Christo,Immendorf, Sol Lewitt, Yoko Ono, A. R. Penck, Polke and others, est. BP 2/3,000, (06-30-93, Sotheby-London, #907, illus.), overall 14½ x 11¾ in., (368 x 298 mm.), 30 multiples.

$1870* *"Souvenir Et Portraits D'Artistes", 1925: Twenty-Five,* complete portfolio, first state, p. Mourlot, pub. Alain Mazo and LeonAmiel, artists: BRIANCHON, MASSON, BAUDIN, FENOSA, ESTEVE, MATISSE,GUIRAMAND, TERECHKOVITCH, BRAQUE, DERAIN, PICASSO, JENKINS, MIRO, COCTEAU, MINAUX, VILLON,CHAGALL, BUFFET, GIACOMETTI, and six others, (05-27-93, Swann, #227), sh 13 x 10 in., (33 x 25.4 cm.), lithographs, 19 in color (BP 1198, DM 3001, FR 10,114, Y 200,472).

BI *Souvenirs Et Portraits D'Artistes, 1972,* A. C. Mazo and L. Amilel, #257/800, p. Mourlot, very good cond., est. BP 1,0/1,500, (12-01-92, Christie-London, #307), lithograph on wove.

$1210* *Souvenirs Et Portraits D'Artistes, 1972: Set Of Nineteen,* Ferdinand Mourlot, A.A.C. Mazo and L. Amiel, #362/800, full margins,very good cond., includ. works by Briancon; Masson; Baudin; Apel les Fenosa; Esteve; Matisse; Guiramand; Terechkovitch; Braque, Bahgall; Buffet; Delvaux; andSutherland, (11-09-92, Christie-NY, #193), 12¹⁵⁄₁₆ x 11 in., (330 x 280 mm.), 19 colored lithographs, 6 black lithographs on Arches (BP 800, DM 1932, FR 6526, Y 150,161).

$1840* *Souvenirs Et Portraits D'Artistes, 1972: Twenty-Five,* complete vol., #186, p. Fernand Mourlot, pub. Leon Amiel,, good cond., time staining, offsetting on each image, original box, including works by: Andre Baudin; Georges Braque; Maurice Brianchon; Bernard Buffet; Marc Chagall; Jean Cocteau; Paul Delvaux; and others, (05-19-93, Butterfield, #1971), each sh. 12¾ x 9¹⁵⁄₁₆ in., (324 x 252 mm.), lithograph on Arches (BP 1194, DM 2991, FR 10,077, Y 203,698).

$2200* *Stamped Indelibly, 1967,* complete album, by various artists and poets, bound together, s., d.,#112/225, pub. William Katz, good cond., (11-07-92, Sotheby-NY, #731, illus.), each sheet approx. 9½ x 6½ in., (241 x 165 mm.), 15 rubberstamp prints (BP 1438, DM 3513, FR 11,873, Y 271,538).

$977* *Stillevens, 1982: Ten,* by Pat Andrea, Constant, Marlene Dumas, Mareike Geus, Klaas Gubbels,Jeroen Henneman, Mart Kempers, Walter Nobbe, Hannes Postma and Elisabeth de Vaal, complete portfolio, s., d., #XV/XV, pub. Uitgeverij Polychrome, good cond., (12-09-92, Sotheby-Amstrdm, #460), each sheet 29³⁄₁₆ x 21³⁄₁₆ in., (742 x 538 mm.), color lithograph on BFK Rives (BP 623, DM 1534, FR 5233, Y 121,141, G 1725).

$634* *"Sun Artists", 1890-91: Book,* by H.P. Robinson, J.B.B. Wellington, L. Sawyer, B. Gay Wilkinson andJ. Gale, orig. series edit. W. Arthur Boord, 6 parts, by Annan & Swan, 12 s., folio, (05-06-93, Christie-London, #19, illus.), photograph, 22 of 24 photogravures (BP 402, DM 999, FR 3362, Y 69,755).

$1996* *"Sun Artists", Nos. 1-8, 1889-91: Book,* by J. Gale, H.P. Robinson, J.B.B. Wellington, L. Sawyer, J.M. Cameron, B. Gay Wilkinson, E. Myers and F.M. Sutcliffe, orig. series, edit. W. ArthurBoord, 8 parts, by Annan & Swan, t., 24 s., part 1 w/half-title, folio, (05-06-93, Christie-London, #18, illus.), photograph, 30 of 32 photogravures (BP 1265, DM 3144, FR 10,583, Y 219,606).

BI *Surface Of The Moon, Day 321, Survey Q, Sectors 11 & 12: 100,* assembled to Cartographer's specifications as a lunar map, 1966-68, each ink s. recto; credit, t., vectors, est. $4/6,000, (04-08-93, Christie-NY, #502, illus.), each approx. 1⅞ x 1⅞ in., (4.8 x 4.8 cm.), overall 31 x 14½ in., (4.8 x 4.8 cm.), photograph, gelatin silver prints, stapled on U.S. Geological Surveyblueprinted grid paper mount.

$4025* *Surface Of The Moon, Day 321, Survey S, Sectors 15 & 16: 114,* by U.S. Geological Survey and NASA, Surveyor III, assembled to cartographer's specifications as a lunar map, 1966-68, each ink d. recto; credit, t.and vectors, lit., (04-08-93, Christie-NY, #501, illus.), each approx. 1⅞ x 1⅞ in., (4.8 x 4.8 cm.), overall 30½ x 14⅝ in., (4.8 x 4.8 cm.), photograph, gelatin silver prints, stapled on U.S. Geological Surveyblueprinted grid paper mount (BP 2639, DM 6466, FR 21,887, Y 456,764).

$220* *Syv Unge Danske Kunstnere 1973,* including prints by Erik Clausen, Niels Borch Jensen, and Erik Rasmussen, s., (03-24-93, Kunsthallen, #316), portfolio (BP 149, DM 359, FR 1223, Y 25,849, DK 1380).

BI *TV-KUNSTMAPPE 1966,* including prints by Svend Wiig Hansen and Frede Christoffersen, p. Danmarks Radio-TV-Kulturafdeling, est. DK 800, (03-24-93, Kunsthallen, #322), .

$895* *Vita Brevis Ars Longa, 1984,* complete portfolio, each s., t. sheets, just., #61 of 75, pub. Bebert, good cond., in orig. portfolio box, incl. Mapplethorpe, van der Kaap, van deKlashorst, Longo, Pieck, (05-27-93, Sotheby-Amstrdm, #657), overall size 12¹⁵⁄₁₆ x 12¹⁵⁄₁₆ in., (328 x 328 mm.), 2 photographs, drawing, silkscreen, 12" record (BP 573, DM 1436, FR 4840, Y 95,948, G 1610).

POSADA, Jose Guadalupe Mexican 1852-1913

$3300* *Revoltillo De Calaveras De Muchachos Papeleros, c. 1900,* margins, excell. cond., (11-24-92, Christie-NY, #353, illus.), borderline 5⅞ x 9⅛ in., (150 x 231 mm.), metalcut on tissue thin Japan (BP 2174, DM 5283, FR 17,925, Y 409,378).

BI *Small Collection Of Seventeen Broadsides, c. 1900: "Senora Su Conejito, La Terrible Granizada, Murio Valentin Mancera, Divertidos Fabulosos, Misteriosos Fantasmas, Que Les Gusta En-Amorar, Mi Grandota, Corrido De La Vida, et al,* margins, losses, tears, staining, good cond., est. $2/3,000, (05-17-93, Christie-NY, #305), woodcut on variously colored tissue-thin wove.

POSSOZ, Mily   Portuguese b. 1896
   BI *Preparing A Bouquet*, s., good cond., est. $150/250, (05-15-93, Cleveland, #422), 12 x 9¼ in., (30.5 x 23.5 cm.), drypoint and roulette in colors.
$210* *"Les Tulipes"*, 1936, The Print Club of Cleveland Publication No. 15 for 1937, s., light struck, tape, (05-15-93, Cleveland, #421), 18⅞ x 13¼ in., (47.9 x 33.7 cm.), drypoint and roulette in colors (BP 137, DM 338, FR 1135, Y 23,279).
$133* *Woman With Cat By A Wimdow*, s., i. Epreuve d'Artiste, pub. Marcel Giout, very good cond., (11-30-92, Phillips-London, #476), plate 10¾ x 9⅝ in., (273 x 244 mm.), drypoint on wove (BP 88, DM 212, FR 719, Y 16,553).

POST, William B.
$1650* *"Chrysanthemums", "Flowering Tree", "Seascape" and "The Morning After", c. 1905: Four*, fourth w/photographer's notations, label, (04-07-93, Swann, #537, illus.), largest 7½ x 9½ in., photograph, platinum prints (BP 1090, DM 2669, FR 9031, Y 187,457).
$690* *"Portrait"*, 1894, s., t., (05-23-93, Butterfield, #3565, illus.), 6¼ x 4¼ in., photograph, platinum print (BP 449, DM 1128, FR 3797, Y 76,268).
$1210* *"Tracks In Snow", "Snowy Scene With Fence", and "Landscape View WithPine Trees": Three*, sig., 1900-10, (10-14-92, Swann, #536, illus.), 8 x 10 in., (20.3 x 25.4 cm.), photograph, platinum prints (BP 710, DM 1771, FR 6005, Y 146,631).

POSTMA, Hannes
   BI *Untitled*, 1975, s., #117/190, full sheet p. to edges, good cond., handling creases, est. Dfl. 2/300, (05-27-93, Sotheby-Amstrdm, #467), sh 22⅜ x 30¼ in., (568 x 768 mm.), colored lithograph on wove.
$77* *Untitled*, 1975, s., #151/190, full sheet p. to edges, good cond., handling creases, (05-27-93, Sotheby-Amstrdm, #468), sh 22⅜ x 30¼ in., (568 x 768 mm.), colored lithograph on wove (BP 49, DM 124, FR 416, Y 8255, G 138).
$64* *Untitled*, 1975, s., full sheet p. to edges, good cond., minor handling creases, (05-27-93, Sotheby-Amstrdm, #469), sh 22⅜ x 30¼ in., (568 x 768 mm.), colored lithograph on wove (BP 41, DM 103, FR 346, Y 6861, G 115).

POTEMONT, Adolphe Martial   1828-1883
   BI *Elegante Junge Frau Mit 2 Kavalieren In Palais-Innenraum (Goldstein S. 46)*, artist's proof, mono. APM, est. DM 300-, (09-14-92, Venator/Hansten, #1687), plate 6⁷⁄₁₆ x 4¹³⁄₁₆ in., (16.3 x 12.2 cm.), etching on thin handmade Japan.

POTTER, Frank
   BI *Demolition Of The Old G.P.O. Building*, s., margins, est. BP 60/80, (11-19-92, Bonhams-Chelsea, #79), plate 14 x 12 in., (35.6 x 30.5 cm.), drypoint etching.
$17* *Demolition Of The Old G.P.O. Building*, s., margins, (01-21-93, Bonhams-Chelsea, #98), plate 14 x 12 in., (35.6 x 30.5 cm.), drypoint etching (BP 11, DM 27, FR 91, Y 2128).

POTTER, Paulus   Dutch 1625-1654
   BI *Die Schafherde (Hollstein Bd. 17, 15), 1644*, 5th state, browning, est. DM 240-, (09-14-92, Venator/Hansten, #1586), plate approx. 7 x 10⁷⁄₁₆ in., (17.8 x 26.5 cm.), etching.

POTTHAST, Edward Henry   American 1857-1927
$738* *The July Number/The Century*, 1896, lit., (12-05-92, Bassenge, #7619, illus.), 20⅞ x 14¾ in., (53 x 37.5 cm.), color lithograph (BP 462, DM 1151, FR 3921, Y 91,438).

POUGNY, Jean   French 1894-1956
$231* *"Arlequin"*, E.A., s. in pl., (01-28-93, Pescheteau, #235), a vue 16⅛ x 12¹⁵⁄₁₆ in., (41 x 33 cm.), color lithograph on wove (BP 153, DM 366, FR 1239, Y 28,681).
   BI *Scene D'Interieur*, s., #180/220, drystamp, est. FF1,2/1,500, (05-27-93, Briest, #168), 14¹⁵⁄₁₆ x 20¹⁄₁₆ in., (38 x 51 cm.), color lithograph.
$180* *"Scene De Plage"*, #111/180, s., creases, (10-18-92, Pescheteau, #244), 17⁵⁄₁₆ x 21⅝ in., (44 x 55 cm.), litho-

graph in colors on Rives (BP 109, DM 266, FR 903, Y 21,493).

POULBOT
$432* *Soldat Et Fillette Au Tambour: Vive La Nation*, #29/200, s., creases, cracks, (06-16-93, Ader Tajan, #129), 27⁹⁄₁₆ x 32⁵⁄₁₆ in., (70 x 82 cm.), color lithograph poster (BP 288, DM 717, FR 2407, Y 46,075).

POULBOT, F.
$441* *Republique De Montmartre, Arbre De Noel Des Petits Poulbot*, 1927, p. H. Chachouin, good cond., (11-19-92, Ribeyre/Baron, #152), 62¹⁵⁄₁₆ x 47¼ in., (160 x 120 cm.), poster (BP 290, DM 703, FR 2368, Y 54,844).

POULBOT, F.   French 1879-1946
$839* *Fete Du Printemps De Paris "Au Profit Des Petits Enfants De France"*,1927, p. H. Chachouin, good cond., (11-19-92, Ribeyre/Baron, #151), 62¹⁵⁄₁₆ x 47¼ in., (160 x 120 cm.), poster (BP 552, DM 1338, FR 4506, Y 104,340).

POUSIN, Nicolas (after)
   BI *Cupids Hunting*, by William Baillie, oval image, large margins, trimmed to plate, est.BP 60/100, (11-30-92, Phillips-London, #197), image 11¾ x 13⅝ in., (298 x 346 mm.), stipple engraving.

POUSSIN, Nicolas   French 1594-1665
$121* *Landscape*, s. in plate, (02-14-93, Hanzel, #672), 7⅛ x 9⅞ in., (18.1 x 25.1 cm.), etching (BP 85, DM 201, FR 679, Y 14,592).

POUWELSZOON, Claes   early 17th cent.
$815* *Landschaft Mit Der Flucht Nach Agypten (Wurzbach und Hollstein I/II)*, (06-08-93, Karl/Faber, #166), etching (BP 536, DM 1322, FR 4454, Y 86,564).

POWELL, P.
$660* *Untitled Architectural Poster/Prints: Group Of Four*, A cond., each num., (08-06-92, Swann, #226, illus.), 19 x 25 in., (48.3 x 63.5 cm.), (BP 345, DM 975, FR 3293, Y 84,184).

POWELL, W.E. (after)
   BI *"Shore Birds" and "A Frosty Morning": A Pair*, (12-11-92, G.A. Key, #51), 13 x 19 in., (33 x 48.3 cm.), colored print.

POWER, Cyril   1872-1951
$3775* *The Escalator (Redfern XII), c. 1929*, s., t., #13/50. good cond., creasing, (06-30-93, Sotheby-London, #323, illus.), 14½ x 16⅛ in., (368 x 410 mm.), linocut in red-orange, green and yellow on thin cream oriental laid (BP 2530, DM 6439, FR 21,720, Y 404,479).
$2217* *Hockey (Redfern Gallery Catalogue 16), c. 1930*, s., t., #9/50, margins, good cond., glued to mount, (12-03-92, Sotheby-London, #179, illus.), sheet 7⅞ x 13⅜ in., (200 x 340 mm.), linocut in colors on very fine Japan (BP 1430, DM 3486, FR 11,900, Y 275,849).
$2217* *Skaters (Redfern Gall. Cat. 30), c. 1932*, s., t., #51/60, margins, good cond., taped to mount, (12-03-92, Sotheby-London, #180, illus.), sheet 10⅜ x 15 in., (264 x 381 mm.), linocut in colors on fine Japan (BP 1430, DM 3486, FR 11,900, Y 275,849).
$2664* *Speed Trail (Redfern Gallery cat. 31), c. 1932*, s., t., i. E.P. no. 2, 1st state, annot., margins, loss, excellent cond., (12-01-92, Christie-London, #510, illus.), sheet 10¹⁄₁₆ x 17¹⁄₁₆ in., (255 x 433 mm.), linocut in green, red, blue on tissue Japan (BP 1760, DM 4246, FR 14,470, Y 331,673).
$1998* *Tennis (Redfern Gallery cat. 38), c. 1934*, s., t., i., margins, fold, very good cond., (12-01-92, Christie-London, #511), sheet 7⅞ x 14¾ in., (200 x 375 mm.), linocut in orange, blue and yellow on tissue Japan (BP 1320, DM 3185, FR 10,853, Y 248,755).
$666* *The Tow Path*, s., i., very good cond., (12-01-92, Christie-London, #512), plate 7¹⁵⁄₁₆ x 11¹³⁄₁₆ in., (202 x 300 mm.), monotype in colors on firm wove (BP 440, DM 1062, FR 3618, Y 82,918).

POWNALL, Governor Thomas and Captain Hervey SMYTH (after)
$1320* *"A View Of Miramichi, A French Settlement In The Gulf Of St. Laurence", "A View Of Gaspe Bay, In The*

Gulf Of St. Laurence" and "A View Of The FallsOn The Passaick" (Deak, c. 1768): Three, two by Paul Sanby, one by Peter Mazell, from Scenographia Americana,pub. John Bowles, Robert Sayer, Thomas Jefferys, Carington Bowles and Henry Parker, margins, staining, soiling, defects, after drawings by Thomas Pownall, (01-22-93, Christie-NY, #301, illus.), each plate 14¼ x 20⅞ in., (362 x 530 mm.), engraving on laid paper (BP 864, DM 2099, FR 7101, Y 165,207).

POYNTER, Edward   (after)
$100* *Diadumene, The Bather,* s., pub. Berlin Photographic Co., 1887, margins, (11-19-92, Bonhams-Chelsea, #17), plate 23¾ x 14½ in., (60.3 x 36.8 cm.), photogravure (BP 66, DM 159, FR 537, Y 12,436).
$165* *Horae Serenae,* by J. Dobic, pub. Art Union of London, 1896, surface tears, margins, (06-16-93, Bonhams-Chelsea, #512), pl. 15¾ x 36¾ in., (40 x 93.3 cm.), etching on laid India (BP 110, DM 274, FR 919, Y 17,598).

PRADIER, Raoul
$82* *Paysage A Coudes,* s., #4/50, good margins, (05-06-93, Laurin, #74), color lithograph on Arches wove (BP 52, DM 129, FR 435, Y 9022).

PRANDONI
$170* *Nice-La Colmiane,* very good cond., (03-15-93, Arcole, #54), 39⅜ x 24⁷⁄₁₆ in., (100 x 62 cm.), (BP 118, DM 282, FR 960, Y 20,137).

PRANG, Louis and Co.   American 1860-1899
$550* *"Old Warehouse-Dock Square, Boston. Built 1680, Taken Down 1860",* ident. in i., good cond., margins 1 1/4 in. or more, toning, fading, (10-31-92, Skinner, #117, illus.), 10½ x 14¾ in., (26.7 x 37.5 cm.), lithograph printed in colors on paper (BP 360, DM 863, FR 2924, Y 68,002).

PRASSINOS, Mario   Greek 1916-1965
BI *Composition Verticale, c. 1950,* s., #6/40, full margins, est. FF700/1,000, (05-27-93, Briest, #169), 15⅜ x 10⅝ in., (39 x 27 cm.), etching.
$67* *"Composition",* s. in plate, (10-18-92, Pescheteau, #246), 12⅝ x 9⁷⁄₁₆ in., (32 x 24 cm.), lithograph in black on Auvergne (BP 41, DM 99, FR 336, Y 8000).
$67* *"Composition",* #40/60, s., (10-18-92, Pescheteau, #245), 15⅜ x 21¼ in., (39 x 54 cm.), drypoint on Arches (BP 41, DM 99, FR 336, Y 8000).
$77* *Pretextat,* s., 33/100, (06-28-93, Loudmer, #108), 23¹⁄₁₆ x 18¹¹⁄₁₆ in., (585 x 475 mm.), sh 25¹⁵⁄₁₆ x 19⅞ in., (585 x 475 mm.), color lithograph on BFK Rives (BP 52, DM 131, FR 441, Y 8170).
$96* *Untitled,* s., #XVII/XXV, margins, good cond., creases, (05-27-93, Sotheby-Amstrdm, #674), 14¾ x 21¼ in., (375 x 540 mm.), etching w/aquatint in colors on BFK Rives (BP 61, DM 154, FR 519, Y 10,292, G 173).

PRATT
$105* *Colorful Red Peony,* (03-13-93, Garth, #142, illus.), 12⅞ x 9⅞ in., (32.7 x 25.1 cm.), chromolithograph (BP 73, DM 175, FR 594, Y 12,375).

PRATT, Christopher   Canadian b. 1935
$1735* *Night Trestle,* s., t., d. Aug '83, #4/48, (05-18-93, Joyner, #114), 20 x 20 in., (50.8 x 50.8 cm.), serigraph in colors (BP 1130, DM 2815, FR 9507, Y 193,358, C$ 2200).
$1474* *Spring At My Place,* s., t., d. March '85, #16/47, prov., lit., (05-18-93, Joyner, #115), 14½ x 33 in., (36.8 x 83.8 cm.), serigraph in colors (BP 960, DM 2392, FR 8077, Y 164,271, C$ 1870).
BI *Summer In The South East,* s., t., d. Feb. '87, #15/70, prov., est. C$2,5/3,000, (05-18-93, Joyner, #34, illus.), 15 x 33¾ in., (38.1 x 85.7 cm.), serigraph in colors.
$2389* *Two Houses In The Spring,* s., t., d. 1968, #5/25, lit., (11-24-92, Joyner, #264), 10⁹⁄₁₆ x 28⁹⁄₁₆ in., (26.9 x 72.5 cm.), serigraph p. in colors (BP 1574, DM 3825, FR 12,977, Y 296,365, C$ 3080).

PRATT, Frederick Haven
BI *Mother And Child On Rocks, 1906,* init. by photog., est. $500/750, (04-07-93, Swann, #538, illus.), 6 x 8 in., photograph, platinum print.

PREISLER, J.M. and O.H. LODE
$278* *Portraetter Af Danske Konger Af Den Oldenborgske Slaegt: Thirteen,* (10-20-92, B. Rasmussen, #371), copperplate etching (BP 171, DM 422, FR 1430, Y 34,014, DK 1610).

PREISSIG, Vojtech   Czech./American died 1944
$1320* *"Arts And Crafts Of The Homelands",* mono. of printer in matrix, good cond., nicks, tears, toning, (05-22-93, Skinner, #52, illus.), sheet 38 x 25 in., (96.5 x 63.5 cm.), lithograph printed in colors on paper (BP 855, DM 2146, FR 7221, Y 145,535).

PREM, Heimrad   1934-1978
$84* *Vertropfter Tropfen, 1966,* s. H. Prem 66, (09-30-92, Kunsthallen, #257), lithograph (BP 47, DM 119, FR 403, Y 10,080, DK 460).

PRENDERGAST, Maurice   American 1859-1924
BI *Children In The Park (Clark, Mathews, Owens 1652), c. 1895,* wide margins, good cond., faint mat stain, exhib., prov., est. $120/150,000, (11-05-92, Sotheby-NY, #45A, illus.), 6⅞ x 5 in., (174 x 127 mm.), sheet 11⅝ x 9¾ in., (174 x 127 mm.), monotype p. in colors w/touches of graphite on soft, thin Japan affixed to a card.

PRENNER, Anton Joseph von   1683-1761
$169* *Junge Frau Von Einem Affen An Reich Gedeckter Tafel Bedient,* after Hans Jordaens III, (03-24-93, Venator/Hansten, #2562), image approx. 6⅛ x 9¹⁄₁₆ in., (15.5 x 23 cm.), etching (BP 114, DM 276, FR 939, Y 19,857).

PRENTICE   20th cent.
$159* *Sans Titre, #78/225,* s., d. Prentice 81, (04-20-93, Encans, #80), 56⅛ x 31 in., (142.5 x 78.8 cm.), serigraph (BP 103, DM 253, FR 855, Y 17,544, C$ 200).

PRESTON, Rick   American 20th cent.
$88* *Boat,* s., (05-16-93, Hindman, #364), 6½ x 4½ in., photograph, silver print (BP 57, DM 142, FR 478, Y 9800).
$66* *Shore Bird,* s., (05-16-93, Hindman, #365), 6½ x 5½ in., photograph, silver print (BP 43, DM 106, FR 359, Y 7350).

PRIETO, Gregorio
$178* *"El Amor Florece",* s., #89/100, (02-03-93, Duran, #227), 27⁹⁄₁₆ x 19¹¹⁄₁₆ in., (70 x 50 cm.), lithograph (BP 124, DM 293, FR 994, Y 22,142, P 20,700).
$1566* *"La Biblia", 1982: Twenty-Two,* #153/195, (12-17-92, Duran, #171, illus.), 20¹⁄₁₆ x 15³⁄₁₆ in., (51 x 38.5 cm.), etching (BP 994, DM 2445, FR 8352, Y 192,454, P 172,500).

PRIKING, Franz   1927-1979
$674* *"Bouquet De Fleurs",* #94/120, s., (10-18-92, Pescheteau, #247), 25⁹⁄₁₆ x 19¹¹⁄₁₆ in., (65 x 50 cm.), lithograph in colors on Rives (BP 408, DM 996, FR 3382, Y 80,478).
BI *Portrait De Sa Femme,* s., #109/200, est. FF2,000/2,500, (05-27-93, Briest, #171), 31⅞ x 25³⁄₁₆ in., (81 x 64 cm.), 2-color lithograph.

PRINCE, Doug   American 20th cent.
$132* *Boy In Boat,* (05-16-93, Hindman, #352), 6¾ x 8¾ in., photograph, silver print (BP 86, DM 213, FR 717, Y 14,699).

PRINCE, Len
$805* *"Niles With Elephant Mask", 1990,* photog.'s stamp, s., t., d., #5/10, (05-23-93, Butterfield, #3566, illus.), 18½ x 15 in., photograph, toned gelatin silver print (BP 524, DM 1316, FR 4430, Y 88,980).

PRINCE, Richard   American b. 1949
$8050* *Cowboys,* s., #1/2, d. 1986, prov., (05-04-93, Sotheby-NY, #271, illus.), 22¾ x 15¼ in., (57.8 x 38.7 cm.), color photograph (BP 5139, DM 12,681, FR 42,728, Y 885,491).
$14,950* *Three Girlfiends, One With Motorcycle,* exec. 1987-88, #2/2, prov., (05-04-93, Sotheby-NY, #278, illus.), 86 x 47 in., (218.4 x 119.4 cm.), color photograph (BP 9544, DM 23,551, FR 79,352, Y 1,644,484).
BI *Three Untitled Photographs,* each s., num., d. R Prince '78 3/10 verso, prov., est. $15/20,000, (05-05-93, Christie-NY, #151, illus.), each 19¾ x 23¾ in., (50.2 x 60.3 cm.), color photographs.

$31,900* *Untitled,* artist's frame, exec. 1987, prov., (11-19-92, Christie-NY, #109, illus.), 86¾ x 47¾ in., (220.3 x 121.2 cm.), photograph, color (BP 21,003, DM 50,861, FR 171,321, Y 3,967,168).

$2640* *Untitled,* s., num., d. R Prince 86 2/5, #2 edit. 5, prov., (10-08-92, Christie-NY, #179, illus.), 24 x 20 in., (61 x 50.8 cm.), color photograph (BP 1571, DM 3905, FR 13,253, Y 320,778).

$2300* *Untitled,* s., d. 1983, i. A.P., prov., (05-04-93, Sotheby-NY, #272A, illus.), 23¼ x 16¼ in., (59.1 x 41.3 cm.), color photograph (BP 1468, DM 3623, FR 12,208, Y 252,997).

BI *Untitled,* s., num., d. R. Prince 4/10 80 verso, prov., est. $7/10,000, (02-24-93, Christie-NY, #110, illus.), 20 x 24¼ in., (50.8 x 61.6 cm.), photograph, color.

$16,500* *Untitled (Cowboys),* s., num., d. R Prince 1986 2/2 verso, prov., (10-08-92, Christie-NY, #237, illus.), 24 x 20 in., (61 x 50.8 cm.), color photograph (BP 9819, DM 24,405, FR 82,831, Y 2,004,860).

BI *Untitled (Teddy, Elizabeth, Marlene, Astrid),* s., num., d. R. Prince 1987 1/2 om cardboard backing, prov., est.10/15,000, (02-24-93, Christie-NY, #104, illus.), 86¾ x 48 in., (220.3 x 121.9 cm.), photograph, color in artist's frame.

$60,500* *Untitled (Three Man's Hands With Watches),* three panels, s., num., d. R. Prince 1980 1/1 on backing of first panel, unique, prov., exhib., lit., (11-19-92, Christie-NY, #140, illus.), each 38¹⁵⁄₁₆ x 56 in., (99 x 142.3 cm.), photograph, color in artist's frames (BP 39,834, DM 96,460, FR 324,919, Y 7,523,940).

PRINKING

$343* *Composition,* #25/45, s., large margins, (02-03-93, Ader Tajan, #192), 10⅝ x 13¾ in., (27 x 35 cm.), color lithograph (BP 239, DM 565, FR 1915, Y 42,667).

PRINSEP, Val C. (after)

$220* *"The Proposal",* (10-11-92, Dunning, #1250, illus.), 26 x 21¾ in., (66 x 55.2 cm.), chromolithograph enhanced w/ oil (BP 131, DM 327, FR 1097, Y 26,784).

PRITTS, J.

$770* *"The Hunters Of Kentucky, Or The Battle Of New Orleans",* p. c. 1815 by J. Pritts, (12-05-92, Neal, #555A), sheet 16¼ x 9¾ in., (41.3 x 24.8 cm.), (BP 482, DM 1200, FR 4091, Y 95,403).

PRIVAT-LIVEMONT

$181* *Absinthe Robette, 1896,* Planche des Maitres de l'Affiche no. 104, good cond., (02-12-93, Cheval/Robert, #17), 12 x 8⅞ in., (30.5 x 22.5 cm.), poster (BP 127, DM 300, FR 1016, Y 21,828).

PRIVAT-LIVEMONT, Antoine 1861-1936

$2108* *Automobile Club De France. 5e Salon De L'Automobile Du Cycle Et Des Sports, 1902,* Paris, Imp. J. Barreau, cond. B, restored, (06-11-93, Boisgirard, #137), 78¾ x 50 in., (200 x 127 cm.), poster (BP 1385, DM 3426, FR 11,551, Y 223,660).

PROCKTOR, Partick

BI *Vineyard,* #21/180, s., est. BP 70/100, (04-22-93, Bonhams-Chelsea, #5), image 20 x 28¾ in., (50.8 x 73 cm.), photolithograph in colors.

PRONTI, Domenico

$330* *Nuova Raccolta Di 100 Vedute Antiche Della Citta Di Roma E Sue Vicinanze: 85,* small 4to, stiff wrappers, cover stain, scattered foxing, (11-12-92, Swann, #117), engraving (BP 217, DM 523, FR 1764, Y 40,918).

PROUST, Marcel and Eugene ATGET

BI *"Paris Du Temps Perdu", 1963,* Edita Lausanne, pub., est. BP 100/150, (05-07-93, Sotheby-London, #125), photograph.

PROUT, John Skinner 1806-1876

$486* *Hobart Town From The Newtown Road,* s. J.S. Prout in image, from Tasmania Illustrated by J.S. Prout, (08-11-92, L. Joel, #6G, illus.), 10³⁄₁₆ x 14¹³⁄₁₆ in., (25.8 x 37.6 cm.), hand-color lithograph (BP 253, DM 713, FR 2416, Y 62,236, A$ 660).

PROUT, Samuel English 1783-1852

BI *Sketches In The Thames Estuary And On The South Coast, "Under Convoy", "Prison Ships", "Sandgate Beach", "On The Tamar" and "On The Thames": Five,* pub. T. Palser, margins, staining, foxing, est. BP 1/200, (10-07-92, Christie-S. Ken, #74), pl 9¾ x 13¾ in., (24.8 x 34.9 cm.), soft-ground etching.

PRUD'HON, Pierre Paul French 1758-1823

$655* *Amours De Phrosine Et Melidore,* third state of 6, staining, good margins, (02-24-93, Picard, #193), etching and copper engraving (BP 457, DM 1063, FR 3605, Y 76,860).

$282* *L'Enfant Au Chien (E. de Goncourt 8),* first state of three before i., small margins, (02-03-93, Ader Tajan, #193), 7⅞ x 5¹¹⁄₁₆ in., (20 x 14.5 cm.), lithograph (BP 197, DM 464, FR 1575, Y 35,079).

$430* *Mme. Navier, c. 1820-22,* hole, untrimmed margins, (02-24-93, Picard, #194), lithograph on thin creme wove (BP 300, DM 698, FR 2367, Y 50,458).

PRUDHON, Pierre Paul (after) French 1758-1823

$55* *The Awakening Of Psyche,* by Leopold Flameng, pub. George Barrie, (09-17-92, Sloan, #629), 6¼ x 8⅜ in., (15.9 x 21.3 cm.), engraving (BP 31, DM 82, FR 279, Y 6848).

PRUITT-EARLY b. 1964/b. 1963

$1100* *The Artists In Their Studio: Two Photographs,* one s. Robert Pruitt John Early, exec. c. 1991, #5/[5], prov., (11-17-92, Christie-E, #107, illus.), each 12⅜₁₆ x 8¼ in., (78.8 x 53.3 cm.), color photograph (BP 724, DM 1754, FR 5908, Y 136,799).

PUGH, Clifton Ernest 1924-1991

$142* *Mirage,* s. Clifton, #17/30, (08-11-92, L. Joel, #45G), 15⅜ x 19½ in., (39 x 49.5 cm.), color etching (BP 74, DM 208, FR 706, Y 18,184, A$ 192).

PULSIFER, Mina Schutz American 1899-1989

BI *The Day's Catch,* s. Mina Pulsifer, very good cond., est. $2/300, (11-21-92, Bakker, #39), 13 x 9¾ in., (33 x 24.8 cm.), lithograph.

PURCELL, Richard (R. Corbutt)

BI *Miss Greville And Brother As Hebe And Cupid,* after Joshua Reynolds, p. for Robert Sayer, margins, prov., Lugt. 2535, est. BP 2/300, (06-16-93, Bonhams-Chelsea, #471, illus.), pl. 13¾ x 9¾ in., (34.9 x 24.8 cm.), mezzotint.

PURRMANN, Hans German 1880-1966

$1623* *Interieur Porto D'Ischia (Heilmann 89), 1921/22,* s., (12-05-92, Bassenge, #7646, illus.), 9¾ x 7¹¹⁄₁₆ in., (24.8 x 19.5 cm.), drypoint on copper print paper (BP 1016, DM 2530, FR 8624, Y 201,090).

$1064* *Interieur Porto D'Ischia (Heilmann 89), 1921/22,* s., (06-05-93, Bassenge, #6465), 9½ x 7⅝ in., (24.2 x 19.3 cm.), drypoint on copper print (BP 700, DM 1725, FR 5814, Y 114,139).

BI *Landschaft (Heilmann 22), 1915,* after Matisse, s., num., est. DM 3000, (12-01-92, Karl/Faber, #1109, illus.), 4¾ x 3⁹⁄₁₆ in., (12 x 9 cm.), drypoint on hand-made.

$332* *Landschaft Mit Schloss Montfort (H. 97 b), c. 1924,* s., num., II state, brown stained, drystamp, (12-01-92, Karl/Faber, #1110), 4½ x 6⅛ in., (11.5 x 15.5 cm.), drypoint on hand-made (BP 219, DM 529, FR 1803, Y 41,335).

$1064* *Sechs Badende Frauen Am Strand (Heilmann 61), 1918,* s., (06-05-93, Bassenge, #6464, illus.), 6¾ x 9³⁄₁₆ in., (17.1 x 23.3 cm.), drypoint on imitation Japan (BP 700, DM 1725, FR 5814, Y 114,139).

$1328* *Sudlicher Hafen (Heilmann 90), 1921,* s., (12-05-92, Bassenge, #7647), 7⅞ x 5¹³⁄₁₆ in., (20 x 14.8 cm.), drypoint on Japan (BP 832, DM 2070, FR 7056, Y 164,540).

$1059* *Vier Badende Frauen (Heilmann 60), 1918,* s., Die Schaffenden, 1. Jahrg. 1918, 2. portfolio, blindstamp, (06-10-93, Hauswedell/Nolt, #807), image 6¹⁵⁄₁₆ x 8⅛ in., (17.7 x 20.6 cm.), drypoint (BP 693, DM 1724, FR 5806, Y 112,408).

$1206* *"Vier Badende Frauen (Sommer)" (Heilmann 60; Jahn-Berger 16), 1918,* s., blindstamp, (06-05-93, Grisebach, #833, illus.), 6¾ x 8¹⁄₁₆ in., (17.2 x 20.5 cm.), drypoint on copper print paper (BP 794, DM 1955, FR 6590, Y 129,371).

PURSELL, Weimer
BI *Winchester, 1955,* A cond., chartex-backed, est. $2/300, (08-06-92, Swann, #227, illus.), 42 x 28 in., (106.7 x 71.1 cm.), .

PURVIS, Tom   1888-1959
BI *British Industries Fair, 1932,* Jarrold and Sons Ltd., B cond., pinholes, fold marks, est. $3/500, (08-06-92, Swann, #228, illus.), 29½ x 20 in., (74.9 x 50.8 cm.), .
BI *No Points Overdeveloped, 1928,* ref. #208, cond. 5, est. BP 2/300, (10-13-92, Phillips-London, #70), 29¹⁵⁄₁₆ x 45¹⁄₁₆ in., (76 x 114.5 cm.), color lithograph.
BI *No Unbalanced Features In Shell, 1929,* ref. #214, cond. 4, image hole, est. BP 3/500, (10-13-92, Phillips-London, #73, illus.), 29¾ x 45¹⁄₁₆ in., (75.5 x 114.5 cm.), color lithograph.

PUSHMAN, Hovsep   American 1877-1966
$715* *"Daughter Of The Pain God", "Summer Twilight" and "Untitled": Three,* s., Margaret Nagel Estate, (01-06-93, Doyle, #53), largest 17½ x 25 in., (44.5 x 63.5 cm.), colored lithograph (BP 466, DM 1171, FR 3990, Y 89,464).

PUSHMAN, Hovsep (after)
$77* *Fire Worshipper,* pub. Frost and Reed, (06-11-93, Freemn/Fine Art, #187), 24 x 14¼ in., (61 x 36.2 cm.), lithograph in color (BP 51, DM 125, FR 422, Y 8170).
$110* *Oriental Still Life,* s., (05-16-93, Hanzel, #469), 18 x 23 in., (45.7 x 58.4 cm.), lithograph (BP 72, DM 177, FR 595, Y 12,194).

PUVIS DE CHAVANNES, Pierre   French 1824-1898
$999* *Normandie (Karshan 57), 1893,* whole margins, s., num. 6, drystamp, (06-11-93, Picard, #150), 18¹⁄₁₆ x 15¹⁄₁₆ in., (459 x 382 mm.), lithograph in brown on chine applique on laid (BP 656, DM 1624, FR 5474, Y 105,995).
$1392* *Pauvre Pecheur (Una Johnson 98; Druick 11), 1897,* sig., small margins, 1 of 100, (02-24-93, Picard, #195), lithograph in mauve on gray laid (BP 971, DM 2260, FR 7661, Y 163,342).

PYK, Madeleine   b. 1934
$762* *Barndomen, 1977: Six,* s., 215/250, portfolio, Editions Linnaeus, blindstamp Mourlot, (12-04-92, AB Stockholm, #7123), 15¾ x 19¹¹⁄₁₆ in., (40 x 50 cm.), lithograph in colors (BP 489, DM 1214, FR 4117, Y 95,131, SK 5170).

PYNE, William
$920* *Royal Residences, 1819: Eight,* (03-03-93, Sotheby-Arcade, #144), sight 12¾ x 10½ in., (32.4 x 26.7 cm.), hand-colored aquatint (BP 635, DM 1515, FR 5140, Y 107,502).

PYTLAK, Leonard   American b. 1910
BI *"Dock Wallopers", c. 1920,* s., t., made for W.P.A. but not stamped, good cond., ink, creases, est. $3/400, (05-15-93, Cleveland, #266), 11¾ x 14 in., (29.8 x 35.6 cm.), color woodcut.
BI *They Serve On All Fronts, Floral Arrangement: Two,* s., scratches, creases, est. $7/900, (05-15-93, Cleveland, #265), silkscreen.

QUADRI, Antonio
$1100* *La Piazza Di San Marco In Venezia Considerata Come Monumento D'Arte E Di Storia: Seventeen,* oblong small folio, orig. p. boards, soiled, rebacked w/morocco, (11-12-92, Swann, #118), hand-colored engraving (BP 722, DM 1743, FR 5879, Y 136,392).

QUANANAAPIK, Timothy   b. 1938
$108* *E9-1445. Povungnituk. Seal Hunting,* i. in syllabics, #23/30, d. 1967, t., (06-07-93, Ritchie, #71), image 8½ x 6 in., (21.6 x 15.3 cm.), sh 11¾ x 9¼ in., (21.6 x 15.3 cm.), stonecut (BP 71, DM 175, FR 590, Y 11,585, C$ 138).

QUANRUD, John
BI *Come Up'n See Me Sometime,* s., num. AP, init. mono. stamp; t. label, pub. Olympus Graphics, label verso, prov., est. C$ 150/250, (12-01-92, Ritchie, #32), 39¾ x 30¾ in., (101 x 78.1 cm.), color serigraph.

QUAST, Pieter Jansz   Dutch 1605/06-1647
$217* *Eine Spinnerin Und Ein Bauer, Dem Ein Teufel Beim Aufwickeln Des Fadens Hilft (Wurzbach 1; Hollstein 7 II), 1652,* from series Bettler und Bauern, glue remains, (12-04-92, Bassenge, #6365), 8⁷⁄₁₆ x 6½ in., (21.4 x 16.5 cm.), etching (BP 139, DM 346, FR 1172, Y 27,091).

QUAYTMAN, Harvey   American b. 1937
$385* *"Red And Black", "Blue And Yellow", and "Diamond", 1988: Three,* each s., #17/20, full margins, good cond., (02-24-93, Butterfield, #3242), smallest 19⅞ x 19⅞ in., (505 x 505 mm.), largest 25⅜ x 25⅜ in., (505 x 505 mm.), aquatint in colors on heavy wove (BP 268, DM 625, FR 2119, Y 45,177).

QUEEN, James   American 19th cent.
$88* *Buildings Of The Great Central Fair, In Aid Of The U.S. Sanitary Commission, Philadephia, Duvall And Son, 1864,* poor cond., (06-11-93, Freemn/Fine Art, #188), 12⅛ x 26¼ in., (30.8 x 66.7 cm.), chromolithograph (BP 58, DM 143, FR 482, Y 9337).

QUENTIN, Bernard   b. 1923
BI *"Composition",* #46/50, est. FF800/1,000, (04-04-93, Pescheteau, #278), 18⅞ x 25⁹⁄₁₆ in., (48 x 65 cm.), color lithograph.

QUESNEL, Auguste
$61* *Crucifixion,* trimmed to composition, yellowed, glued, oxydation, (02-03-93, Ader Tajan, #37, illus.), 9⁷⁄₁₆ x 11⅝ in., (24 x 29.5 cm.), etching and copper engraving (BP 43, DM 100, FR 341, Y 7588).

QUIGLEY, Edward   1898-1977
BI *Abstraction, 1930's,* mounted, est. $2/3,000, (10-15-92, Sotheby-NY, #438, illus.), 13¾ x 10⅝ in., (34.9 x 27 cm.), photograph, gelatin silver print.
$1045* *Airplane Being Refueled, c. 1939,* w/photog.'s address label, (04-07-93, Swann, #348, illus.), 11 x 13¾ in., photograph, silver print (BP 691, DM 1690, FR 5720, Y 118,723).
$990* *Branches With Snow, 1938,* s., d., credit label, lit., (10-13-92, Christie-NY, #329, illus.), 13⅝ x 10⅞ in., (34.6 x 27.6 cm.), photograph, gelatin silver print (BP 577, DM 1450, FR 4928, Y 120,044).
BI *Frozen Branches, 1945,* s., d., handstamp., notations., est. $1,2/1,800, (10-14-92, Swann, #538, illus.), 13½ x 10¾ in., (34.3 x 27.3 cm.), photograph, silver print.
BI *Light,* mounted, s. by photog., t., studio stamp, c. 1930, p.l., est. $1,5/2,500, (10-15-92, Sotheby-NY, #440, illus.), 13½ x 10½ in., (34.3 x 26.7 cm.), photograph, gelatin silver print.
BI *Light Abstraction,* handstamp, label, 1930's, est. $1,5/2,500, (10-14-92, Swann, #539, illus.), 13½ x 10 in., (34.3 x 25.4 cm.), photograph, silver print.
BI *Light Abstraction, c. 1931,* notation, est. $1,8/2,200, (04-08-93, Christie-NY, #329, illus.), 13⅞ x 10¾ in., (35.2 x 27.3 cm.), photograph, gelatin silver print.
$1320* *Light Abstraction, c. 1944,* mounted on board, studio label, (10-15-92, Sotheby-NY, #439, illus.), 13⅛ x 9¾ in., (33.3 x 24.8 cm.), photograph, gelatin silver print (BP 808, DM 1965, FR 6663, Y 158,368).
$1380* *"Motion", 1931,* photog. name stamp, t. in unident. hand, exhib., (04-06-93, Sotheby-NY, #86A, illus.), 6½ x 4⅝ in., photograph (BP 911, DM 2223, FR 7529, Y 157,391).
$1035* *Philadelphia Street Scene, late 1920's,* photog. name stamp, (04-06-93, Sotheby-NY, #86, illus.), 6⅛ x 4⅛ in., photograph (BP 684, DM 1667, FR 5646, Y 118,043).
BI *Self-Portrait Distortion, 1930s,* est. $1,2/1,800, (04-08-93, Christie-NY, #328, illus.), 5¼ x 3⅜ in., (13.3 x 8.6 cm.), photograph, gelatin silver print on carte-postale.
BI *Spire, Princeton Presbyterian Church,* handstamp, notations, 1930's, est. $1,2/1,800, (10-14-92, Swann, #540, illus.), 13½ x 10½ in., (34.3 x 26.7 cm.), photograph, silver print.

QUINTANILLA, Alberto   b. 1934
$169* *Compositions: Three,* s. Quintanilla 1971-1973, (09-30-92, Kunsthallen, #258), color lithograph (BP 95, DM 240, FR 811, Y 20,281, DK 920).

QUINTANILLA, Luis   American b. 1895
BI   *"Deer And Fawn" and "Paulette", 1939: Two,* each s., pub. AAA, margins, good cond. (?), mat/light staining, est.$5/700, (02-24-93, Butterfield, #2669), each 13⅜ x 9¾ in., (340 x 248 mm.), etchings on wove.
$10*   *"Deer And Fawn", 1939,* pub. AAA, s., excell. cond., (05-15-93, Cleveland, #267), 13¼ x 9¾ in., (33.7 x 24.8 cm.), etching (BP 7, DM 16, FR 54, Y 1109).

QUIRIN, E.
$275*   *Various Scenes Of Frankfurt And The Environs Circa 1900: Six,* each s., smudges, wear, nicks throughout images, est. $3/500, (12-12-92, Weschler, #157), each approx. 8½ x 6½ in., (21.6 x 16.5 cm.), etching (BP 176, DM 433, FR 1485, Y 34,030).

QUIROS, Antonio
BI   *"La Vida Del Busca Vida De Francisco De Quevedo", 1984: Fifteen,* #120/170, s., reserve P150,000, (12-17-92, Duran, #170, illus.), 24⁷⁄₁₆ x 18½ in., (62 x 47 cm.), etching.

QUMULAK, Leah   Inuit
$133*   *Woman With A Bird, 1968,* s., #3/50, (10-21-92, Maynard, #13), sheet 15 x 11½ in., (38.1 x 29.2 cm.), stonecut (BP 83, DM 201, FR 683, Y 16,200, C$ 165).

R.B. STUDIOS
$2330*   *The Quick-Starting Pair, Shell Oil & Shell Petrol, Eagles And Cars, 1928,* p. Waterlow & Sons, ref. #170, cond. 3, (10-13-92, Phillips-London, #64, illus.), 29¾ x 44¾ in., (75.5 x 113.7 cm.), color lithograph (BP 1357, DM 3413, FR 11,598, Y 282,527).

RAAB, George   b. 1948
$173*   *I Know A Dark Secluded Place, 1980,* #29/50, s., t., d. '83, prov., (05-10-93, Hodgins, #190), 10½ x 21½ in., (26.7 x 54.6 cm.), etching on paper (BP 113, DM 278, FR 938, Y 19,332, C$ 220).

RAALTE, Henri van   1881-1929
$446*   *The Madonna Of The Pool,* s. H Van Raalte, i., #10/25, reprod., lit., (08-11-92, L. Joel, #12G, illus.), 10 x 11¾ in., (25.4 x 29.8 cm.), drypoint (BP 232, DM 655, FR 2217, Y 57,114, A$ 605).

RABIER, Benjamin   French 1869-1939
$329*   *Le Corbeau Et Le Renard. Librairie Delgrave, 15 Rue Soufflot, Paris,* cond. B, (03-16-93, Boisgirard, #177), 36⅝ x 16⅛ in., (93 x 41 cm.), poster (BP 227, DM 547, FR 1859, Y 38,471).
$839*   *La Vache Qui Rit "Est La Creme De Gruyere De Luxe", 1927,* very good cond., (11-19-92, Ribeyre/Baron, #41), 62¹⁵⁄₁₆ x 47¼ in., (160 x 120 cm.), poster (BP 552, DM 1338, FR 4506, Y 104,340).

RABINOVITCH, Ben   1884-1964
BI   *Harlequin, 1923,* s., d., (c) insig., label, legend, est. $1/1,500, (10-13-92, Christie-NY, #330, illus.), 13 x 10 in., (33 x 25.4 cm.), photograph, photogravure.
$1265*   *Nude Studies, early 1930's: Two,* variants of the same neg., (04-06-93, Sotheby-NY, #142, illus.), one 13½ x 10⅝ in., photograph (BP 836, DM 2038, FR 6901, Y 144,275).

RACHOU, Henri   French 1856-1944
$2661*   *Panneau Decoratif (Capucines Et Tortues) (Karshan 59), 1893,* s., num., staining, untrimmed margins, 1 of 100, (02-24-93, Picard, #196), color lithograph on creme wove (BP 1856, DM 4320, FR 14,645, Y 312,251).

RACINET
$288*   *Costumes, c. 1880: Eight,* (03-03-93, Sotheby-Arcade, #121), sight 7 x 8 in., (17.8 x 20.3 cm.), chromolithograph (BP 199, DM 474, FR 1609, Y 33,653).
$805*   *Costumes: Eight, 1880,* (02-18-93, Sotheby-Arcade, #65), sight smallest 6½ x 8 in., (16.5 x 20.3 cm.), sight largest 8 x 13 in., (16.5 x 20.3 cm.), lithographs (BP 556, DM 1313, FR 4445, Y 95,902).
$518*   *Ornamental Designs, 1868: Eight,* (04-07-93, Sotheby-Arcade, #282), sight 13 x 9 in., (33 x 22.9 cm.), chromolithograph (BP 342, DM 838, FR 2835, Y 58,850).

RACZ, Andre   b. 1916 Romanian/American
$413*   *"Mother And Child", 1944,* s., d., t., num. 4/35, excellent cond., (10-31-92, Cleveland, #323), 11¾ x 17⅞ in., (29.8

x 45.4 cm.), etching and engraving (BP 265, DM 635, FR 2156, Y 51,158).
$880*   *Perseus Beheading Medusa V., 1945,* d., num., s., exec. Stanley William Hayler's Atelier 17 workshop, (05-27-93, Swann, #230, illus.), 21½ x 14⅞ in., (54.6 x 37.8 cm.), color intaglio etching, engraving, and soft ground (BP 564, DM 1412, FR 4759, Y 94,340).

RADINSKI, Emmanuel (called MAN-RAY)   American 1890-1976
$413*   *"The Rope Dancer Accompanies Herself With Her Shadow",* s. Man Ray, num. 86/99, fair cond., light toning, water stains, (09-11-92, Skinner, #100A, illus.), sight 19¾ x 27¹¹⁄₁₆ in., (50.2 x 70.3 cm.), color screenprint on paper (BP 214, DM 595, FR 2021, Y 51,171).

RADNAY, Charles T.
BI   *Hothouse Shadow,* s. Charles T Radnay, i., d. '85, 18.8x18.8 cm., est. $250/300, (08-11-92, L. Joel, #107G), photograph, hand-colored.

RADZIWILL, Franz   1895-1983
$7048*   *Etchings, 1922: Ten,* s., (05-26-93, Lempertz, #456, illus.), portfolio 19¹¹⁄₁₆ x 13⁹⁄₁₆ in., (50 x 34.5 cm.), etching on thick wove (BP 4559, DM 11,499, FR 38,704, Y 765,754).
$3046*   *Mutter Mit Kind, 1920,* s., d., t., i., wide margins, discoloration, very good cond., (05-20-93, Christie-London, #485, illus.), image 11¼ x 8 in., (28.6 x 20.3 cm.), sheet 25¾ x 19¾ in., (28.6 x 20.3 cm.), woodcut on wove (BP 1955, DM 4914, FR 16,554, Y 336,352).

RAE, Henrietta (after)
$143*   *Psyche Before The Throne Of Venus, 1895,* pub. Arthur Tooth and Sons, margins, time stained, (11-19-92, Bonhams-Chelsea, #38), plate 23¼ x 34 in., (59.1 x 86.4 cm.), photogravure (BP 94, DM 228, FR 768, Y 17,784).

RAE, M. Oliver
$125   *Views Of Cambridge And One Of Ely: Nine,* s., (08-14-92, G.A. Key, #86), etching (BP 65, DM 183, FR 621, Y 15,763).

RAEBURN, Henry Macbeth
$167*   *James Alexander Simpson, 1936,* pub. by artist, margins, scratch to image, (09-17-92, Bonhams-Chelsea, #168), plate 24½ x 16⅜ in., (62.2 x 41.6 cm.), mezzotint w/ hand-coloring (BP 94, DM 248, FR 849, Y 20,792).
BI   *Portrait Of James Alexander Simpson, 1936,* s., blindstamp, margins, scratch, est. BP 1/150, (07-16-92, Bonhams-Chelsea, #446), plate 24½ x 16⅜ in., (62.2 x 41.6 cm.), mezzotint w/hand coloring.

RAEBURN, Sir Henry (after)   English 1756-1823
BI   *"Honourable Mrs. Wilson Wharton" and "The Honourable Mrs. Spiers": Two,* est. $150/250, (02-04-93, Sloan, #397), each 22½ x 18¼ in., (57.2 x 46.4 cm.), color mezzotint.

RAEBURN, Sir Henry (after)   English 1756-1823
BI   *"Honourable Mrs. William Wharton" and "Honourable Mrs. Spiers": Two,* est. $200/300, (12-10-92, Sloan, #1306), each 22½ x 18¼ in., (57.2 x 46.4 cm.), color mezzotints.
BI   *"Honourable Mrs. Wilson" and "The Honourable Mrs. Speirs": Two,* est. $1/200, (04-02-93, Sloan, #808), 8¼ x 9¼ in., (210 x 235 mm.), color mezzotint.

RAETZ, Markus   b. 1941
$553*   *"Anne"-Trilogie II (Masone 140), 1970,* 135/150, mono., (04-21-93, Germann, #703), 27⅜ x 19½ in., (695 x 495 mm.), etching (BP 359, DM 884, FR 2989, Y 61,220, SF 805).
$553*   *Tori, 1968,* s., #4/120, (09-04-92, Germann, #530), approx. 19¹¹⁄₁₆ x 15⅜ in., (500 x 390 mm.), color screenprint on wood (BP 277, DM 775, FR 2638, Y 68,070, SF 690).
BI   *Zucker Und Salz, 1969,* s., d., est. DM 400-, (09-25-92, Granier, #2981), 19⅝ x 27½ in., (49.8 x 69.8 cm.), serigraph on offset board.

RAFFAEL, Joseph   American b. 1933
$1650*   *Celebration-Koi Fish, 1980,* s., d., #10/44, blindstamp p. Archer Press, very good cond.?, (10-28-92, Butterfield, #3074), 30 x 23¾ in., (762 x 603 mm.), color lithograph

on heavy wove (BP 1051, DM 2548, FR 8652, Y 202,454).

$920* *Luxembourg Gardens: Summer, 1982,* s., d., #23/77, pub. artist, blindstamp Trillium Graphics, good cond., tears, hinge remains, skinned areas, (05-19-93, Butterfield, #2293, illus.), 40 x 29¾ in., (101.6 x 75.6 cm.), lithograph on Arches (BP 597, DM 1495, FR 5038, Y 101,849).

$1540* *Pink Lily With Dragonfly, 1981,* s., d., annot. P.P. 3/3, blindstamp, very good cond.?, (10-28-92, Butterfield, #3075), 41 x 30 in., (104.1 x 76.2 cm.), color lithograph on Arches (BP 981, DM 2378, FR 8076, Y 188,957).

BI *Untitled, 1974,* s., d., #IV/7, blindstamp publisher, very good cond., est. $8/1,000, (05-19-93, Butterfield, #2292), 20¾ x 30⅛ in., (527 x 765 mm.), lithograph in colors on Rives.

$1100* *Winter Moon Lily, 1978,* s., d., num. 30/72, blindstamp, full margins, apparently very good cond., (02-24-93, Butterfield, #3111), 20 x 26 in., (508 x 660 mm.), lithograph in colors on wove (BP 767, DM 1786, FR 6054, Y 129,078).

RAFFAELLE (after)

$222* *An Analysis Of The Picture Of The Transfiguration, 1817: Twenty,* volume, by James Godby, staining, (12-10-92, Bonhams-Chelsea, #100A), stipple engraving (BP 143, DM 351, FR 1199, Y 27,462).

RAFFAELLI, Jean Francois French 1850-1924

$1535* *Le Demenagement (Delteil 12/I (von III), 1894,* s., Ep. d'etat I. Zustand, light-staining, prov., (12-01-92, Karl/Faber, #251, illus.), 7⅞ x 6⅛ in., (20 x 15.5 cm.), reworked etching and watercolor on hand-made (BP 1014, DM 2447, FR 8338, Y 191,111).

$237* *La Fumee Du Bateau (L.D. 98), 1911,* second state of 3, inits. verso, full margins, (05-06-93, Laurin, #75), etching and aquatint on paper w/Imprimerie Ch. Wittman watermark (BP 150, DM 373, FR 1257, Y 26,075).

$328* *L'Homme A La Pipe (D. 132), c. 1896,* creases, cracks, tears, soiling, (02-24-93, Picard, #199), lithograph au pinceau, pochoir on white laid (BP 229, DM 532, FR 1805, Y 38,489).

$1961* *La Neige (L.D., 68), 1906,* defintive state, num. 20, s., dirt stains, drystamp, large margins, (04-02-93, Picard, #165), 17¹¹⁄₁₆ x 22⁵⁄₁₆ in., (45 x 56.7 cm.), color etching, drypoint and aquatint (BP 1292, DM 3152, FR 10,704, Y 223,272).

$744* *La Neige, Soleil Couchant (Delteil 77), 1907,* fourth state of five, s., num. Ep. n#20, crayons marks, good cond., (06-28-93, Loudmer, #345), 8⁹⁄₁₆ x 18⅜ in., (218 x 466 mm.), sh 14¾ x 24⅛ in., (218 x 466 mm.), color etching and drypoint on Japan (BP 498, DM 1264, FR 4259, Y 78,939).

$177* *"The Old Lady's Garden" (L. Delteil 19), 1894,* rare, 1 of 3 or 4, stamped and after glycerine, s., good margins, (06-16-93, Ader Tajan, #130), 2¾ x 7¹⁵⁄₁₆ in., (7 x 20.2 cm.), 3-color etching on Japan (BP 118, DM 294, FR 986, Y 18,878).

$660* *La Route Ensoleillee (L.D., 99), 1912,* definitive state, num. 108, s., large margins, (04-02-93, Picard, #166), 8¹⁄₁₆ x 10½ in., (20.5 x 26.6 cm.), color etching and aquatint on Japan (BP 435, DM 1061, FR 3603, Y 75,145).

BI *A Sa Toilette (D. 49), 1898,* annot., num., s., good margins, (02-24-93, Picard, #198), drypoint in color on simili-Japan.

$516* *Le Village Sur La Colline (L. Delteil, 64), 1905,* definitive state, num. 33, s., creases, dirt stains, holes, large margins, (04-02-93, Picard, #164), 8⁹⁄₁₆ x 11³⁄₁₆ in., (20.8 x 28.4 cm.), color etching, drypoint and aquatint (BP 340, DM 829, FR 2817, Y 58,750).

RAFFET, Auguste

$134* *"Combat D'Oeud Alleg.", 1839 and "Infanterie Polonaise Marchant A L'Ennemi", 1813 (H. Giacomelli, 82, 161): Two,* tears, large margins, (04-02-93, Picard, #167), one 9⁷⁄₁₆ x 14½ in., (24 x 36.9 cm.), other 8⁹⁄₁₆ x 12⅝ in., (24 x 36.9 cm.), lithographs on Chine fixe (BP 88, DM 215, FR 731, Y 15,257).

$114* *"Le Drapeau Du 17e Leger", 1841 and "Le Reveil", 1848 (H.G., 83 et 85): Two,* reddish stains, large margins, (04-02-93, Picard, #168), one 14³⁄₁₆ x 10¹⁄₁₆ in., (36 x 25.5 cm.), other 74¹³⁄₁₆ x 90⁹⁄₁₆ in., (36 x 25.5 cm.), lithographs on Chine fixe (BP 75, DM 183, FR 622, Y 12,980).

RAGAN, Leslie American b. 1897

BI *The New Union Terminal, Cleveland, c. 1930,* tears, creases, losses, est. BP 3/500, (02-04-93, Christie-S. Ken, #76, illus.), 41 x 27 in., (104.1 x 68.6 cm.), color lithograph dry mounted on linen.

RAIMONDI, Marcantonio c. 1480-1527

BI *Birth Of The Virgin,* after Albrecht Durer, trimmed, good cond., surface soiling, repairedtear, hinge remains, skinned areas, wear, printing creases, notations, est. $3/400, (10-28-92, Butterfield, #2852), 11⁷⁄₁₆ x 8¼ in., (302 x 210 mm.), engraving on laid paper, watermark.

$1725* *The Climbers (B. 487), 1510,* after Michelangelo, watermark, trimmed, creases, chalk marks, repairs, stains, soiling, (05-13-93, Sotheby-NY, #337), 10½ x 8¼ in., (267 x 208 mm.), engraving (BP 1132, DM 2785, FR 9395, Y 192,587).

BI *The Death Of Dido (B. XIV, 187),* after Raphael, platetone, margins, surface dirt, good cond., (06-30-93, Sotheby-London, #185), 6¼ x 5 in., (159 x 127 mm.), engraving.

$383* *Die Entfuhrung Der Hele (B. 209 I),* (12-04-92, Bassenge, #6367), 11⁷⁄₁₆ x 16⁷⁄₁₆ in., (29.1 x 41.8 cm.), engraving (BP 246, DM 610, FR 2069, Y 47,815).

$478* *Die Jungfrau Mit Dem Langen Schenkel (B. 57),* stain, tear, prov., (11-03-92, Hartung, #4071, illus.), 15¾ x 10⁹⁄₁₆ in., (40 x 26.8 cm.), engraving (BP 308, DM 748, FR 2534, Y 58,385).

$244* *Mars, Venus And Eros (B. 345), 1508,* 2nd state, grey impression, trimmed to image, repairs, defects, (10-27-92, Phillips-London, #28), sheet 11⅝ x 8¼ in., (295 x 210 mm.), engraving (BP 154, DM 374, FR 1269, Y 29,847).

$722* *Schule. Die Hochzeit Der Psyche (B. XV, V, 141),* in 2 parts put together, (12-04-92, Bassenge, #6373), 13¾ x 28⅜ in., (35 x 72 cm.), engraving (BP 463, DM 1150, FR 3901, Y 90,137).

$208* *Der Trunkene Silen Auf Einem Esel Von Zwei Satyren Gestutzt (B. 222),* from series Les bas-reliefs antiques, (12-01-92, Karl/Faber, #124), etching (BP 137, DM 332, FR 1130, Y 25,896).

$779* *Das Urteil Des Paris (B. XIV, 245 II),* (06-04-93, Bassenge, #5316), 11⁷⁄₁₆ x 17¹⁄₁₆ in., (29.1 x 43.3 cm.), engraving (BP 515, DM 1265, FR 4264, Y 84,016).

$989* *Venus, Mars Und Amor (Bartsch XIV, 257, 345), 1508,* (06-10-93, Hauswedell/Nolt, #143, illus.), engraving (BP 647, DM 1610, FR 5422, Y 104,978).

RAIMONDI, Marcantonio (after Raphael SANZIO) Italian 1480-1534

$138* *"The Judgement Of Paris", c. 1540,* mono., i., ident., fair cond., laid down, glued to mat face, abrasions, foxing, soiling, (03-12-93, Skinner, #1, illus.), 11⅝ x 17⅜ in., (29.5 x 44.1 cm.), engraving on wove (BP 96, DM 230, FR 781, Y 16,264).

RAINER, Arnulf German b. 1929

$300* *"Comosition 1986",* #26/99, s., (04-04-93, Pescheteau, #279), 36¼ x 24⁷⁄₁₆ in., (92 x 62 cm.), color lithograph on wove (BP 198, DM 482, FR 1638, Y 34,157).

$686* *"Composition" and "Self-Portrait", 1985 and 1987: Two,* s., #10/99 and 20/25, good cond., (06-30-93, Sotheby-London, #910, illus.), one sh 36⅛ x 24¼ in., (918 x 616 mm.), the other sh 18 x 20⅞ in., (918 x 616 mm.), color lithograph and photo-etching w/drypoint in black and brown on wove (BP 460, DM 1170, FR 3947, Y 73,503).

$805* *Deep Red Cross, 1987,* s., #2/35, full margins, good cond., skinned spot, soiling, (02-11-93, Sotheby-NY, #408, illus.), 11½ x 7¹¹⁄₁₆ in., (292 x 195 mm.), red etching (BP 568, DM 1333, FR 4512, Y 97,046).

$425* *"Dencke Dein!", 1969,* s., num., blindstamp, (06-08-93, Karl/Faber, #1229), approx. 17⁵⁄₁₆ x 24⅝ in., (44 x 62.5 cm.), color serigraph on wove (BP 279, DM 690, FR 2322, Y 45,141).

$738* *Grimassierender Kopf, Uberarbeitet,* s., num., (12-05-92, Bassenge, #7650), 11¹⁵⁄₁₆ x 15¹¹⁄₁₆ in., (30.3 x 39.9 cm.), etching over aquatint on copper print paper (BP 462, DM 1151, FR 3921, Y 91,438).

$1083* *Hugel (Breicha R 37), 1963,* s., num., (11-28-92, Schoppmann, #720), 11¾ x 16⁹⁄₁₆ in., (29.8 x 42 cm.), etching on copper print paper (BP 715, DM 1725, FR 5857, Y 134,785).

$2120* *Kreuz, c. 1979,* s., i., artist's proof, (06-12-93, Hauswedell/Nolt, #347, illus.), 45¼ x 19½ in., (115 x 49.5 cm.), drypoint on thick wove (BP 1388, DM 3451, FR 11,597, Y 223,087).

$649* *Maske 6 (Breicha R 123), 1971,* pencil s., artist proof, (11-20-92, Lempertz, #793), sh 22⁵⁄₁₆ x 14¹⁵⁄₁₆ in., (56.7 x 38 cm.), drypoint on copper print paper (BP 427, DM 1035, FR 3485, Y 80,711).

$1803* *Ohne Titel (Selbst Im Profil Nach Links), 1972-1974,* #35/50, pencil s., (11-20-92, Lempertz, #788), sh 21¹⁄₁₆ x 14⅞ in., (53.5 x 37.8 cm.), drypoint on photogravure overworked w/black Olkreide on Velin (BP 1187, DM 2875, FR 9683, Y 224,226).

$1517* *Ohne Titel (Selbstbildnisse), 70's: Three,* s., #23/80, 43/80, 75/80, (11-12-92, Lempertz, #193, illus.), two 18¹⁵⁄₁₆ x 23¹¹⁄₁₆ in., (48.1 x 60.2 cm.), one 23⅝ x 19⅛ in., (48.1 x 60.2 cm.), photograph, gelatin silver print (BP 970, DM 2384, FR 8125, Y 187,678).

$938* *Otto Breicha, Arnulf Rainer, Uberdeckungen (Breicha R 124, 125, 127 and 166): Four,* (11-20-92, Lempertz, #797), 9¹⁵⁄₁₆ x 8¹⁵⁄₁₆ in., (25.2 x 22.8 cm.), etching (BP 618, DM 1496, FR 5038, Y 116,652).

$354* *"Projekt Herrenhelm",* s., num., (06-08-93, Karl/Faber, #1230), approx. 16⁹⁄₁₆ x 11⅝ in., (42 x 29.5 cm.), offset lithograph on wove (BP 233, DM 574, FR 1934, Y 37,600).

BI *Selbstbildnis, 1970,* red s. ARainer, i., est. DM 15,000-, (05-27-93, Lempertz, #958, illus.), 23⅝ x 19⁵⁄₁₆ in., (60 x 49 cm.), Fotoubermalung.

$294* *Selbstportrait Glatzkopf, 1972,* s., #3/20, pub. Bonner Kunstverein, good cond., sheet MM: 250 x 191, (05-27-93, Sotheby-Amstrdm, #675), xin., photograph (BP 186, DM 465, FR 1569, Y 32,732, G 518).

$326* *Selbstportrait Glatzkopf, 1972,* s., #3/20, pub. Bonner Kunstverein, good cond., sheet MM: 250 x 191, (05-27-93, Sotheby-Amstrdm, #676), xin., photograph (BP 207, DM 515, FR 1740, Y 36,295, G 575).

$3850* *Stirnstrandwand, 1971,* complete suite, s., #7/50, pub. blindstamp, Galerie Ariadne, full margins, good cond., orig. folder, (11-07-92, Sotheby-NY, #732), each sheet approx. 25¾ x 19¾ in., (654 x 502 mm.), 12 etchings (BP 2517, DM 6147, FR 20,777, Y 475,191).

$430* *Tuchent (Breicha 32), 1961-63,* s., #31/98, (05-27-93, Lempertz, #960), 14¾ x 21¼ in., (37.5 x 53.9 cm.), drypoint etching on wove (BP 275, DM 690, FR 2326, Y 46,098).

$352* *Uberdeckung, c. 1974,* s., num., blindstamp, (05-26-93, Dorling, #2917), 11¹¹⁄₁₆ x 16⅜ in., (29.7 x 41.6 cm.), color etching on BFK Rives wove (BP 228, DM 574, FR 1933, Y 38,244).

BI *Untitled, 1987,* s., #4/40, blindstamp publisher Radierwerkstatt Kurt Zein, good cond., soft handling creases, surface soiling, est. $1/1,200, (05-19-93, Butterfield, #2294), 12½ x 17³⁄₁₆ in., (318 x 437 mm.), etching in colors on Arches.

$2887* *"Wasserwelt I (Die Gesturzten Stehen Auf)" (Breicha L 3), 1950-1951,* s., d., from portfolio Cave Canem, (11-28-92, Grisebach, #253, illus.), 17¹³⁄₁₆ x 27½ in., (45.2 x 69.8 cm.), lithograph on imitation Japan (BP 1906, DM 4599, FR 15,614, Y 359,303).

$425* *Wasserwelt II, 1951,* s., d., creases, (06-28-93, Loudmer, #347), 16⅝ x 25¹¹⁄₁₆ in., (423 x 653 mm.), sh 18⅞ x 28⅜ in., (423 x 653 mm.), black lithograph on trimmed wove (BP 285, DM 722, FR 2433, Y 45,093).

RAINER, Arnulf and Dieter ROTH

$860* *Doppelportrait Oder Stirnsplat (Roth 379), 1972,* s., d., (05-27-93, Lempertz, #963), 24½ x 30⅞ in., (62.3 x 78.5 cm.), etching on wove (BP 551, DM 1380, FR 4651, Y 92,196).

BI *"Durre" (Rainer) and "Heh, Gebeine!!" (Roth) (Roth 389), 1975: Two,* #4/4, s., d., est. DM 1,800-, (05-27-93, Lempertz, #965), 19¹¹⁄₁₆ x 25¹⁵⁄₁₆ in., (50 x 66 cm.), etching on 1 sheet Rives wove.

BI *"An Kopf" (Rainer) and "Ah, Gestalten!!" (Roth) (Roth 395), 1975: Two,* #4/4, s., d., est. DM 1,800-, (05-27-93, Lempertz, #966), 19¹¹⁄₁₆ x 25¹⁵⁄₁₆ in., (50 x 66 cm.), etching on 1 sheet Rives wove.

RALEIGA

$75 *Hun Or Home?,* Edwards and Deutsch Litho. Co., folds, (09-24-92, Alderfer, #287), 30 x 20 in., (76.2 x 50.8 cm.), (BP 44, DM 111, FR 377, Y 9022).

$30 *"Hun Or Home?",* tear, (03-04-93, Alderfer, #244), 30 x 20 in., (76.2 x 50.8 cm.), poster (BP 21, DM 49, FR 167, Y 3493).

RALPH, Lestor

$35 *Girl Scouts Campaign, 1919,* minor loss, (09-24-92, Alderfer, #245), 23¼ x 16½ in., (59.1 x 41.9 cm.), (BP 20, DM 52, FR 176, Y 4210).

RAMBERG, Johann Heinrich 1763-1840

$1239* *Die Nachtigall (N. 13; Bl. 29), 1799,* d. in plate, (10-09-92, Winterberg, #1327, illus.), 17½ x 22¹⁄₁₆ in., (44.5 x 56 cm.), color etching on wove (BP 735, DM 1840, FR 6180, Y 150,840).

RAMBOUX, Johann Anton Alban 1790-1866

$1805* *Aeussere Anischt Der Roemischen Baeder Zu Trier, 1826,* (12-04-92, Bassenge, #6908), 16¼ x 19¹¹⁄₁₆ in., (41.3 x 50 cm.), lithograph (BP 1158, DM 2875, FR 9751, Y 225,343).

RAMBURG, H. English 18th/19th cent.

$330* *The Exhibition Of The Royal Academy, 1787,* engraved by P.A. Martini, good cond., light staining, repaired tear?, (01-30-93, Weschler, #299), sight 14 x 20 in., (35.6 x 50.8 cm.), hand-colored engraving (BP 222, DM 532, FR 1797, Y 41,168).

RAMEL, J.

$199* *Principaute De Monaco (...) Monte Carlo, 1951,* cond. A, (03-16-93, Boisgirard, #178), 46¹⁄₁₆ x 30½ in., (117 x 77.5 cm.), poster (BP 137, DM 331, FR 1124, Y 23,269).

RAMOS, Mel American b. 1935

$358* *Coca Cola, 1972,* s., d., good cond. (?), (02-24-93, Butterfield, #3243), 30½ x 25 in., (775 x 635 mm.), offset lithograph in colors on wove (BP 250, DM 581, FR 1970, Y 42,009).

$230* *From Leta And The Swan, 1969: Two,* s., d., #5/100, blindstamp publisher Collector Press, blindstamp printer, Ernest de Soto, full margins, good cond., light-staining, creases, (05-19-93, Butterfield, #2297), one 26 x 20 in., (660 x 508 mm.), the other 21⅛ x 26 in., (660 x 508 mm.), lithograph in colors on Arches (BP 149, DM 374, FR 1260, Y 25,462).

BI *Leta And The Swan, 1969,* complete portfolio, s., d., variously num.; s., d., #21/25, blindstamp pub., Collectors Press, p. Ernest de Soto, Kenjilo Nanao & David Folkman, full margins, full sheet, good cond., crease (through image), orig. portfolio, est. $2/3,000, (02-24-93, Butterfield, #3112A), each 22½ x 28 in., (572.5 x 712.5 mm.), 11 lithographs in colors (2 w/embossing & 1 in silver) on Arches, (1on Fabriano).

BI *Leta And The Swan, 1969: Eleven,* complete portfolio, s., d., num.; s., d., #21/25 on title page, blindstamp publisher, Collectors Press and printers, Ernest de Soto, Kenjilo Nanao and David Folkman, full margins, good cond., one w/crease through image, original portfolio, est. $2/3,000, (05-19-93, Butterfield, #2296, illus.), each sh 22½ x 28 in., (562 x 711 mm.), lithograph in colors (two w/embossing and one in silver) on Arches (one on Fabriano).

BI *Leta And The Swan, 1969: Ten,* incomplete portfolio, each s., d., variously num. out of 100, blindstamp of pub. Collectors Press, full margins, good cond., light-staining, est. $1,2/1,400, (02-24-93, Butterfield, #3112), 22½ x 28 in., (572 x 711 mm.), 28 x 22½ in., (572 x 711 mm.), lithograph in colors on Arches.

$880* *"Manet's Olympia", "You Get More Salami With Modigliani", "Touche Boucher" and "Navajo Nudo", 1974: Four,* s., d., annot. AP 2/20, blindstamp p. Matthieu Litho, full margins, good cond., creases, (10-28-92, Butterfield, #3077), each sheet 20⅛ x 26½ in., (511 x 673 mm.), color collotype on BFK Rives (BP 561, DM 1359, FR 4615, Y 107,975).

$1535* *Tobacco Rose, 1965,* s., d., #30/200, from portfolio 11 Pop Artists II, full margins, goodcond., creasing, (12-03-92, Sotheby-London, #785, illus.), sheet 30 x 24 in., (762 x 612 mm.), screenprint in colors on wove (BP 990, DM 2414, FR 8239, Y 190,992).

$413* *Vantage Cigarettes, 1972,* s., d., margins, good cond. (?), (02-24-93, Butterfield, #3244), 26½ x 20¼ in., (673 x 514 mm.), lithograph in colors on wove (BP 288, DM 670, FR 2273, Y 48,463).

$505* *Weibl, Liegender Akt Beim Sonnenbaden, 1974,* s., d., num., (09-25-92, Granier, #2982), sheet 20¹/₁₆ x 26⅜ in., (51 x 67 cm.), color lithograph on BFK Rives (BP 295, DM 749, FR 2531, Y 60,954).

$413* *Woman With A Bottle Of Coca-Cola,* s., d. '72, (11-12-92, Freemn/Fine Art, #182), offset lithograph (BP 271, DM 654, FR 2207, Y 51,209).

$489* *Wonder Woman No. 2, 1963,* s., #20/60, blindstamp publisher, Plura Edizioni, margins, good cond.?, staining, (05-19-93, Butterfield, #2295), 23½ x 21¾ in., (597 x 552 mm.), offset lithograph in colors on Fabriano (BP 317, DM 795, FR 2678, Y 54,135).

RANFT, Richard   Swiss 1862-1931
$860* *Au Bal A L'Opera, 1899,* annot., ded., s., crease, small margins, stamp, (02-24-93, Picard, #201), color etching and aquatint a la poupee on thin wove (BP 600, DM 1396, FR 4733, Y 100,915).

$1499* *Trottins (Karshan 61), 1894,* whole margins, num. 7, s., drystamp, (06-11-93, Picard, #151), 15¹¹/₁₆ x 10⅛ in., (398 x 257 mm.), etching and aquatint in brown on wove (BP 985, DM 2436, FR 8214, Y 159,045).

RANKIN, David   b. 1946
BI *Aqua Lily,* s. Rankin, i., d. '90, #64/90, est. $2/300, (08-11-92, L. Joel, #157G), 29⅛ x 21¼ in., (74 x 54 cm.), color lithograph.

RANSHU
BI *Iwai Hanshiro IV, Matsumoto Koshiro IV And Otani Tokuji,* Aiban uchiwa-e (fan print), sumizuri-e, s. Ranshu ga, d. Tenmei 2 (1782), pub. Hayakawa Matabei?, fold mark, hole, Prof. H.R.W. Kuhne Coll., est. BP4/600, (06-11-93, Sotheby-London, #274), 9¾ x 13½ in., (24.8 x 34.3 cm.), woodblock.

RANSOM, Sidney
$315* *The Poster, 1898,* fold marks, tears, stains, lit., (02-04-93, Christie-S. Ken, #77, illus.), 30 x 19½ in., (76.2 x 49.5 cm.), color lithograph backed on linen (BP 220, DM 519, FR 1759, Y 39,184).

RANSON, Paul   French 1864-1909
$8872* *Tigre Dans Les Jungles (Karshan 62), 1893,* s., num., staining, untrimmed margins, 1 of 100, stamp, (02-24-93, Picard, #202), pinceau lithograph in color (BP 6187, DM 14,403, FR 48,828, Y 1,041,070).

$6374* *Tigre Dans Les Jungles (Vicaire III, S. 595, Nr. 6), 1893,* s., num., pub. L'Estampe originale, blindstamp, (06-04-93, Bassenge, #5769, illus.), 14⁷/₁₆ x 11⅛ in., (36.6 x 28.3 cm.), lithograph in colors (BP 4217, DM 10,351, FR 34,888, Y 687,446).

RANSON, Paul Elie
$220* *Dancing Woman, 1894,* from Revue Blanche, margins, apparently good cond., tear, est. $4/600, (02-24-93, Butterfield, #2965), 6⅞ x 3⅜ in., (175 x 86 mm.), lithograph on wove (BP 153, DM 357, FR 1211, Y 25,816).

BI *Tigre Dans Les Jungles (Stein & Karshan 62), 1893,* s., num. no 58, blindstamp pub. L'Estampe Originale, Album 1, full margins, foxing, soiling, creases, good cond., est. $10/12,000, (11-05-92, Sotheby-NY, #413, illus.), 14⅝ x 11¼ in., (371 x 286 mm.), lithograph p. in yellow, black and grey on wove.

RAPHAEL (after)
$171* *Madonna Of The Chair,* c. 1910, (01-15-93, DuMouchelle, #121), print (BP 112, DM 280, FR 945, Y 21,558).

$858* *Sibyl Reading A Book (B. XII, 89, 6): Two,* trimmed, repairs, good cond., (06-30-93, Sotheby-London, #190), one 10½ x 8¾ in., (267 x 222 mm.), the other 11 x 8⅞ in., (267 x 222 mm.), chiaroscuro woodcut from 2 blocks in black and tan (BP 575, DM 1463, FR 4937, Y 91,932).

$121* *The Transfiguration,* (02-14-93, Hanzel, #685), plate 31½ x 21½ in., (80 x 54.6 cm.), engraving (BP 85, DM 201, FR 679, Y 14,592).

BI *Urbis Leonin,* est. $225/275, (04-02-93, Sloan, #2264), sight 16¾ x 22¼ in., (425 x 565 mm.), engraving.

$619* *Vogel Strauss (Illus. Bartsch Bd. 29, S. 190), 1602,* by Monogrammist B w/the Wurfel, (09-14-92, Venator/Hansten, #1589, illus.), plate 8¼ x 10⅞ in., (21 x 27.7 cm.), engraving (BP 327, DM 920, FR 3118, Y 76,971).

RAPHAEL, Joseph   American 1869/72-1950
BI *Place De La Bourse, Bruxelles,* s., rich plate tone, margins slightly trimmed, good cond., crease, surface soiling, est. $3/500, (10-28-92, Butterfield, #2752), 4¾ x 6⅞ in., (121 x 175 mm.), etching on cream wove.

RAPHAELO   Italain 1483-1520
$16,500* *Loggie Di Rafaele Nel Vaticano: 45,* parts 1-3 of 4 in one vol., leaf of letterpress text, folio, blind-tooled russia by Staggemeier & Welcher, (11-12-92, Swann, #121, illus.), 25¹⁵/₁₆ x 20¹/₁₆ in., (660 x 510 mm.), engraving (BP 10,837, DM 26,145, FR 88,188, Y 2,045,877).

RASSENFOSSE, Andre Louis Armand   1862-1934
BI *1896/L'ART INDEPENDANT,* lit., est. DM 2,500, (12-05-92, Bassenge, #7621, illus.), 23¹³/₁₆ x 16¼ in., (60.5 x 41.3 cm.), color lithograph.

RASSENFOSSE, Armand   1862-1934
BI *Salon Des Cents, 1896,* loss, creases, tears, lit., est. BP 4/600, (02-04-93, Christie-S. Ken, #141, illus.), 24 x 16½ in., (61 x 41.9 cm.), color lithograph backed on linen.

RAU, William H.   1855-1920
$1955* *"Nanticoke, From Wilkesbarre Mountain, L.V.R.R.", c. 1895,* credited, t., num. 576 in neg., (04-06-93, Sotheby-NY, #25, illus.), 17 x 20½ in., (43.2 x 52.1 cm.), photograph, albumen print (BP 1291, DM 3150, FR 10,666, Y 222,970).

$1760* *Pennsylvania Railroad, Central Pa., c. 1890,* credit in neg., (10-13-92, Christie-NY, #18, illus.), 17 x 20½ in., (43.2 x 52.1 cm.), photograph, albumen print (BP 1025, DM 2578, FR 8761, Y 213,411).

RAUSCHEHBERG, Robert
BI *White Walk, (MIA cat. 95), 1970,* s., d., num. 30/53, pub. Gemini G.E.L., blindstamp, good cond., S. 1,073 x 747 mm., est. BP 1,8/2,500, (12-01-92, Christie-London, #626, illus.), lithograph in colors on Arjomari wove.

RAUSCHENBERG, Robert   American b. 1925
$2310* *Airport Series: Cat Paws (Baro 83), 1974,* s., d., i. 'VI/XX', pub. University of South Florida, good cond., (11-07-92, Sotheby-NY, #739, illus.), overall size approx. 33⅞ x 35⅝ in., (860 x 905 mm.), relief and intaglio p. in colors on fabric w/collage (BP 1510, DM 3688, FR 12,466, Y 285,115).

BI *Airport Series: Cat Paws (Fine and Corlett 193), 1974,* ink s., d., #XX/XX, pub. GraphicStudio, excell. cond., est. $3/4,000, (11-09-92, Christie-NY, #391, illus.), 33¼ x 35¾ in., (845 x 908 mm.), colored etching w/collage in bottled caps on cotton and satin fabric.

$2750* *Airport Series: Platter (B. 84), 1974,* s., d., i. 'VI/XX', pub. University of South Florida, good cond., (11-07-92, Sotheby-NY, #737, illus.), overall size approx. 45¼ x 28⅜ in., (114.9 x 72.1 cm.), relief and intaglio p. in colors on fabric (BP 1798, DM 4391, FR 14,841, Y 339,422).

$1955* *Airport Series: Room Service (B. 86), 1974,* s., d., i. XV/XX, pub. University of South Florida, (02-11-93, Sotheby-NY, #416, illus.), overall size 53¹/₁₆ x 57½ in., (134.7 x 146 cm.), relief and intaglio p. in colors on fabric w/collage (BP 1379, DM 3238, FR 10,959, Y 235,684).

$2200* *Airport Series: Sheephead (B. 87), 1974,* s., d., i. 'AP', artist's proofs, pub. University of South Florida, good cond., (11-07-92, Sotheby-NY, #740), overall size approx. 35 x 42⅛ in., (88.9 x 107 cm.), relief and intaglio p. in colors on fabric w/collage (BP 1438, DM 3513, FR 11,873, Y 271,538).

$1610* *Airport Series: Sheephead (B. 87), 1974,* s., d., i. XV/XX, pub. University of South Florida, good cond., (02-11-93, Sotheby-NY, #417, illus.), overall size 34¹³⁄₁₆ x 50¹⁵⁄₁₆ in., (88.5 x 129.5 cm.), relief and intaglio p. in colors on fabric w/collage (BP 1136, DM 2667, FR 9025, Y 194,093).

$4313* *Airport Series: Switchboard (B. 85), 1974,* s., d., i. XV/XX, pub. University of South Florida, good cond., (02-11-93, Sotheby-NY, #415, illus.), overall size 35¹⁄₁₆ x 36¼ in., (890 x 920 mm.), relief and intaglio p. in colors on fabric w/collage (BP 3043, DM 7144, FR 24,176, Y 519,952).

BI *American Pewter With Burroughs VI (G. 951), 1981,* s., d., #18/43, pub. Gemini, G.E.L., blindstamp, good cond., est. BP1,2/1,500, (06-30-93, Sotheby-London, #914, illus.), sh 31¾ x 23¼ in., (806 x 591 mm.), lithograph and embossing in color.

$1540* *Arcanum IX, 1981,* s., d., num. 80/85, Styria Studio blindstamp, full sheet, excell. cond., (09-19-92, Christie-E, #184), sheet 23 x 16 in., (584 x 406 mm.), screenprint in colors w/collage in silk and paper in colors on handmade paper (BP 886, DM 2306, FR 7897, Y 191,876).

$1650* *Ark, Minneapolis 18,* s., d. 1964, annot. A.P., pub. U.L.A.E., their chop, (09-20-92, Hindman, #729, illus.), sheet 15⅝ x 16¼ in., (33.7 x 41.3 cm.), lithograph on Angoumois a la main paper (BP 966, DM 2448, FR 8376, Y 203,930).

$805* *Aus "Hommage A Picasso", 1973,* #27/90, s., d., num., (12-05-92, Mangisch, #672, illus.), 29½ x 21⅝ in., (75 x 55 cm.), color screenprint (BP 504, DM 1255, FR 4277, Y 99,740, SF 1150).

$2685* *Backout, 1979,* s., d., #81/100, blindstamp, (06-12-93, Hauswedell/Nolt, #356), 30½ x 23¹⁄₁₆ in., (77.5 x 58.5 cm.), color serigraph on copper print w/red rectangle (BP 1757, DM 4370, FR 14,688, Y 282,542).

$7700* *Bellini #4, 1988,* s., d., i. 'H.C. 1/12', pub. blindstamp, ULAE, good cond., (11-07-92, Sotheby-NY, #742, illus.), sheet 60 x 38⅝ in., (152.4 x 98.1 cm.), intaglio etching p. in colors (BP 5034, DM 12,294, FR 41,554, Y 950,383).

BI *Bellini #4, 1988,* s., d., #4/47, blindstamp pub. ULAE, full margins, very good cond., est. $6/8,000, (10-28-92, Butterfield, #3085, illus.), 60⅛ x 38½ in., (152.7 x 97.8 cm.), color intaglio etching on Arches.

BI *Bones And Unions: Little Joe (G. 637), 1975,* s., d., num., pub. Gemini G.E.L., good cond., in orig. plexi case, est., 3,5/4,500, (10-28-92, Butterfield, #3080), 24 x 28½ in., (610 x 724 mm.), handmade paper w/bamboo and fabric.

$3300* *"Bottle Cap", 1974,* from "Airport Series", pen s., d. 74, edit. A.P., prov., (11-13-92, DuMouchelle, #2015, illus.), 42¼ x 66¼ in., (107.3 x 168.3 cm.), color mixed media and collage (BP 2132, DM 5181, FR 17,470, Y 409,582).

$33,350* *Breakthrough II (F. 27, S. 23), 1965,* s., d., #13/43, blindstamp, pub. ULAE, full margins, good cond., (05-15-93, Sotheby-NY, #1151, illus.), 44 x 30⅞ in., (111.8 x 78.4 cm.), lithograph in colors (BP 21,684, DM 53,643, FR 180,270, Y 3,696,929).

$1760* *Cage, 1983,* s., d., num. 112/125, Styria Studio blindstamp, full sheet, creasing, skinning, (09-19-92, Christie-E, #185, illus.), sheet 41½ x 29½ in., (105.4 x 74.9 cm.), screenprint in colors w/collage in silk and plastic on wove (BP 1012, DM 2636, FR 9026, Y 219,287).

$1029* *Cardbird Box I (G. 560), 1971,* s., d., #10/20, pub. Gemini G.E.L., stamp, good cond., (06-30-93, Sotheby-London, #913), height by width 8 x 6¼ in., (203 x 159 mm.), offset lithograph and collage mounted on wooden and cardboard box (BP 690, DM 1755, FR 5921, Y 110,254).

$1115* *Cardbird VII (Gemini 309), 1971,* s., num., pub. Gemini G.E.L., good cond., creases, (06-30-93, Sotheby-London, #912, illus.), 33 x 33½ in., (838 x 851 mm.), offset lithograph and collage mountd on cardboard (BP 747, DM 1902, FR 6415, Y 119,469).

BI *"Ceiling + Lightbulb, 1950 #5",* p.l., t., s., d., 500 x 401mm, est. BP 800/1,000, (05-07-93, Sotheby-London, #289, illus.), photograph, silver print.

$3080* *Centennial Certificate MMA (F. 71), 1969,* s. Metropolitian Museum of Art, d., #10/45, blindstamp, excell. cond., (11-09-92, Christie-NY, #389, illus.), 36 x 24⅜ in., (914 x 619 mm.), colored lithograph on Angoumois a la main (BP 2036, DM 4917, FR 16,613, Y 382,229).

$825* *Centennial Certificate MMA (Foster 71), 1969,* s., pub. U.L.A.E., full margins, excell. cond., (09-19-92, Christie-E, #182), sheet 40⅝ x 26 in., (103.2 x 66 cm.), lithograph on handmade paper (BP 475, DM 1235, FR 4231, Y 102,791).

$2310* *Chow Bag Series: Six,* s., (09-24-92, Mystic, #31), 48 x 36 in., (121.9 x 91.4 cm.), colored lithograph (BP 1352, DM 3423, FR 11,626, Y 277,878).

$1650* *Chow Bag Series: Six,* s., (09-24-92, Mystic, #30), each 48 x 36 in., (121.9 x 91.4 cm.), colored lithograph (BP 966, DM 2445, FR 8304, Y 198,484).

$2420* *Chow Bag Series: Six,* s., (09-24-92, Mystic, #32), each 48 x 36 in., (121.9 x 91.4 cm.), colored lithograph (BP 1416, DM 3586, FR 12,179, Y 291,110).

$1540* *Chow Bags: "Goat Chow" and "Monkey Chow", 1977: Two,* s., d., num. 94/100, blindstamp of pub. Untitled Press, apparently good cond., (02-24-93, Butterfield, #3117, illus.), each 48¼ x 36½ in., (122.6 x 92.7 cm.), silkscreen in colors w/collage on wove (BP 1074, DM 2500, FR 8476, Y 180,709).

$575* *Chow Bags: Monkey Chow, 1977,* s., #AP 8/20, blindstamp publisher, Untitled Press and printer, Styria Studio, good cond.?, (05-19-93, Butterfield, #2306), 48¼ x 36½ in., (122.6 x 92.7 cm.), silkscreen in colors w/collage on wove (BP 373, DM 935, FR 3149, Y 63,655).

$169* *Composition,* s. Rauschenberg, (09-30-92, Kunsthallen, #259), offset in colors (BP 95, DM 240, FR 811, Y 20,281, DK 920).

$5175* *Crops: "Mangrove", "Coconut", "Peanuts", "Cactus" and "Watermelon" (B. 78-82), 1973: Five,* complete suite, each unique, s., d., i. USF XV/XX, blindstamp of pub., University of South Florida, Tampa, good cond., (02-11-93, Sotheby-NY, #414, illus.), each sheet approx. 59¹⁵⁄₁₆ x 37¹⁵⁄₁₆ in., (152.3 x 96.5 cm.), 5 silkscreens w/solvent transfers on BFK Rives (BP 3652, DM 8572, FR 29,008, Y 623,870).

$2185* *Dante's Inferno (Foster 19; Sparks 15), 1965,* complete, original portfolio, KAR, s., d. 1964, t., #31/44, blindstamp of pub., ULAE, pub. Harry N. Abrams, #201, good cond., staining, foxing, (02-11-93, Sotheby-NY, #409, illus.), lithograph 16¼ x 15¹¹⁄₁₆ in., (413 x 398 mm.), 1 lithograph and 34 facsimile drawings (BP 1542, DM 3619, FR 12,248, Y 263,412).

$2750* *Earth Day (G. 256), 1970,* s., d., num. 11/50, blindstamp of pub. Gemini G.E.L., margins, good cond., discoloration, creases, (02-24-93, Butterfield, #3115, illus.), 48 x 34¼ in., (121.9 x 87 cm.), lithograph in colors w/collage on Rives (BP 1918, DM 4464, FR 15,135, Y 322,694).

$343* *Earth Day 1990,* s., blindstamp, good cond., (06-30-93, Sotheby-London, #915), sh 15⅞ x 39⅞ in., (40.3 x 101.3 cm.), photo-lithograph on white wove (BP 230, DM 585, FR 1974, Y 36,751).

$56* *"Earth Day April 22", 1970,* s., d. 70, (08-18-92, Encans, #131), 33⁷⁄₁₆ x 25³⁄₁₆ in., (85 x 64 cm.), offset poster (BP 29, DM 82, FR 277, Y 7060, C$ 67).

$82* *Earth Summit '92, Rio De Janiero,* s., d. 91, pub. Robert Rauschenberg Foundation, 1991, (06-08-93, Ritchie, #48), 26 x 26 in., (66 x 66 cm.), offset color lithograph (BP 54, DM 133, FR 448, Y 8710, C$ 105).

$1413* *Features From Currents (Fosters 129), 1970,* s., d., #13/50, series Features from Currents, Castelli Graphics, (06-12-93, Hauswedell/Nolt, #350, illus.), 34¹³⁄₁₆ x 34¹³⁄₁₆ in., (88.5 x 88.5 cm.), serigraph on wove (BP 925, DM 2300, FR 7730, Y 148,690).

$2078* *From Currents (Foster 109), 1970,* s., d., #13/100, (05-27-93, Lempertz, #967, illus.), 35¹⁄₁₆ x 35¹⁄₁₆ in., (89 x 89 cm.), color serigraph on hand-made board (BP 1331, DM 3334, FR 11,239, Y 222,770).

$2200* *From The Seat Of Authority, 1979,* s., d., #87/100, blindstamp of printer Styria Studio, pub. Multiples,Inc., good cond., creases, (11-07-92, Sotheby-NY, #738, illus.), sheet

30½ x 23 in., (775 x 584 mm.), offset lithograph p. in colors w/collage (BP 1438, DM 3513, FR 11,873, Y 271,538).

BI *Fuse (G. 187), 1970,* s., d. 69, #62/63, Gemini G.E.L. blindstamps, skinned spots, excell.cond., est. $1,5/2,500, (05-11-93, Christie-NY, #543), sheet 38 x 26 in., (965 x 660 mm.), lithograph on wove.

$6050* *Gamble (F. 49; S. 31), 1968,* s., d., #31/41, pub. blindstamp, ULAE, full margins, good cond., (11-07-92, Sotheby-NY, #735, illus.), 36⅝ x 22⅝ in., (930 x 575 mm.), lithograph p. in colors on England J. Whatman (BP 3956, DM 9660, FR 32,650, Y 746,729).

$13,200* *Gondolas (From the Bleacher Series, Venice): Four,* (1952), 1990, s., d. in ink, attached aluminum frame, (10-13-92, Christie-NY, #592, illus.), 50½ x 44 in., (128.3 x 111.8 cm.), photograph, toned & bleached polaroid prints mounted together on aluminum (BP 7688, DM 19,338, FR 65,704, Y 1,600,582).

BI *Guardian (F. 58; S. 33), 1968,* s., d., #27/44, pub. blindstamp, ULAE, good cond., creases, pressuremarks, est. $6/8,000, (11-07-92, Sotheby-NY, #736, illus.), sheet 42½ x 30⅛ in., (108 x 76.5 cm.), lithograph p. in colors on German Copperplate.

BI *Hoarfrost Editions: Plus Fours (G. 573), 1974,* s., d., #28/28, pub. Gemini G.E.L., good cond., est. $4/6,000, (10-28-92, Butterfield, #3079, illus.), 67 x 95 in., (170.2 x 241.3 cm.), offset lithograph and newspaper images transferred to silk satin andsilk chiffon.

$11,500* *Hoarfrost Editions: Plus Fours (G. 573), 1974,* s., d., i. A.P. VI, pub. Gemini, G.E.L., (05-15-93, Sotheby-NY, #1158, illus.), overall 66⅞ x 95 in., (169.9 x 241.3 cm.), offset lithograph and newspaper image transfer in colors on silk satin and silk chiffon (BP 7477, DM 18,498, FR 62,162, Y 1,274,803).

$2310* *Hommage A Picasso, 1973,* num., (11-28-92, Schoppmann, #721), 29¾ x 22¼ in., (75.5 x 56.5 cm.), color serigraph on handmade (BP 1525, DM 3680, FR 12,493, Y 287,492).

$1100* *Horsefeathers Thirteen - XI (G. 729), 1976,* s., d. '72, annot. AP V, blindstamp pub. Gemini G.E.L., full margins, good cond., (10-28-92, Butterfield, #3081), 21½ x 15¼ in., (546 x 387 mm.), offset lithograph w/silkscreen, collage and embossing in colors on Arches (BP 701, DM 1699, FR 5768, Y 134,969).

$682* *Horsefeathers Thirteen-IV (Gemini 424), 1972,* s., d., #XI, blindstamp, pub. Gemini; full margins, good cond., creases, (12-03-92, Sotheby-London, #786), 17¾ x 14¾ in., (450 x 376 mm.), lithograph in colors w/collage and embossing on Amgoumois (BP 440, DM 1072, FR 3661, Y 84,858).

BI *Horsefeathers Thirteen-VIII (G. 728), 1976,* s., d., num. 70/79, blindstamp of pub. Gemini G.E.L., full margins, apparently very good cond., creases, est. $2,5/3,500, (02-24-93, Butterfield, #3116, illus.), 24 x 17⅝ in., (356 x 448 mm.), offset lithograph, screenprint, pochoir, collage, & embossing in colors on Jeff Goodman pencil buff handmade.

BI *International Very Special Arts Festival, Washington D.C., 1989,* s., d., #153/275, very good cond., est. $1/2,000, (05-19-93, Butterfield, #2308), 36¾ x 26½ in., (933 x 673 mm.), offset lithograph and silkscreen on wove.

$3575* *Lawn (F. 31; S. 27), 1965,* s., d., i. '2/9 HC', pub. blindstamp, ULAE, full margins, good cond., (11-07-92, Sotheby-NY, #734, illus.), 31¾ x 23⅝ in., (806 x 600 mm.), lithograph p. in colors on BFK Rives (BP 2337, DM 5708, FR 19,293, Y 441,249).

$3738* *Made In Tampa: "Tampa 1", "Tampa 2" and "Tampa 3" (Baro 58; 59 and 60, 1972: Three,* s., d., i. USF XII/XX, blindstamp of pub., University of South Florida, good cond., (02-11-93, Sotheby-NY, #412, illus.), 3 color lithographs, last w/collage (BP 2638, DM 6192, FR 20,953, Y 450,633).

BI *Made In Tampa: "Tampa 8", "Tampa 9", Tampa 11" and "Tampa 12" (B. 65; 66; 68 and 69), 1972: Four,* s., d., i. USF XII/XX, blindstamp of pub., University of South Florida, good cond., est. $6/8,000, (02-11-93, Sotheby-NY, #413), 4 color lithographs, 1st w/collage.

$770* *Merce Cunningham, 1984,* s., artist's proof, (05-16-93, Hindman, #527), 29 x 8½ in., (73.7 x 21.6 cm.), silkscreen and collage, pochoir and graphite drawing (BP 501, DM 1239, FR 4162, Y 85,356).

$1843* *Mink Chow, 1977,* #86/100, s., d., Styria Studio and Untitled Press Inc. stamps, 1215 x 920mm, (09-04-92, Germann, #14, illus.), color serigraph w/collage (BP 924, DM 2583, FR 8793, Y 226,859, SF 2300).

$1650* *Moon Rose (F. 80; Gemini 170), 1969,* s., d., num. 38/47, Gemini G.E.L. blindstamps, full sheet, light/time/brown/mat staining, shrink-wrapped, (09-19-92, Christie-E, #183), sheet 51 x 35 in., (129.5 x 88.9 cm.), lithograph on Arches (BP 949, DM 2471, FR 8462, Y 205,582).

$665* *More Distant Visible Part Of the Sea, 1979,* s., 19/100, blindstamp, Styria Studio, (12-04-92, AB Stockholm, #7125), 30⁵⁄₁₆ x 21⅝ in., (77 x 55 cm.), offset lithograph in colors (BP 427, DM 1059, FR 3593, Y 83,021, SK 4510).

$2475* *Morocco, 1989,* s., d., #28/38, pub. blindstamp, ULAE, good cond., (11-07-92, Sotheby-NY, #743, illus.), sheet 41¾ x 29½ in., (106 x 74.9 cm.), intalgio p. in colors on Arches (BP 1618, DM 3952, FR 13,357, Y 305,480).

$1150* *New York Philharmonic 150th Anniversary, 1991,* s., d., #51/102, pub. New York Philharmonic, p. Jim Goldston at ULAE,excell. cond.?, (05-19-93, Butterfield, #2309), 45⅜ x 36 in., (115.3 x 91.4 cm.), lithograph and silkscreen in colors on rag (BP 747, DM 1869, FR 6298, Y 127,311).

$1650* *"One More And We Will Be More Than Halfway There" and "More Distant Visible Part Of The Sea", 1979: Two,* s., d., num. 48/100 & 39/100, pub. Multiples, blindstamp, good cond.,More Distant... w/creases, (02-24-93, Butterfield, #3118), each sheet 30¾ x 23 in., (781 x 584 mm.), silkscreen in colors w/collage on wove (BP 1151, DM 2679, FR 9081, Y 193,617).

BI *Peace Portfolio I: Untitled, 1970,* s., d., #51/175, pub. Academic and Professional Action Committee fora Responsible Congress, blindstamp printer, very good cond.?, creases, buckling, est. $1/1,500, (05-19-93, Butterfield, #2301), 24¼ x 21 in., (616 x 533 mm.), mixed media on Rives BFK.

BI *Peace Portfolio I: Untitled, 1970,* s. in crayon, d., num. 51/175, pub. Academic and Professional ActionCommittee for a Responsible Congress, blindstamp, apparently very good cond., creases, buckling, est. $1,5/2,000, (02-24-93, Butterfield, #3114), 24¼ x 21 in., (616 x 533 mm.), mixed media on Rives BFK.

$880* *People Have Enough Trouble Without Being Intimidated By An Artichoke,1979,* s., d., num. 81/100, pub. Multiples, blindstamp, good cond., surface soiling(02-24-93, Butterfield, #3119), 30¾ x 23 in., (781 x 584 mm.), offset lithograph in colors on fabric collaged to wove (BP 614, DM 1429, FR 4843, Y 103,262).

$681* *People Have Enough Trouble Without Being Intimidated By An Artichoke,1979,* s., 19/100, blindstamp, Styria Studio, (12-04-92, AB Stockholm, #7124), 29⅛ x 22⁷⁄₁₆ in., (74 x 57 cm.), offset lithograph in colors (BP 437, DM 1085, FR 3679, Y 85,019, SK 4620).

$1395* *Poster For Peace, 1970,* s., #237/250; t., s., d., blindstamp, (09-18-92, Schloss Ahlden, #1043, illus.), 28¹¹⁄₁₆ x 21⁹⁄₁₆ in., (72.9 x 54.7 cm.), color offsett print on handmade (BP 817, DM 2070, FR 7081, Y 172,414).

BI *Poster For Peace, 1970,* s., d., #144/250, blindstamp, rippling, good cond.?, est. $1/1,500, (12-12-92, Weschler, #158, illus.), 28 x 21 in., (71.1 x 53.3 cm.), color silkscreen.

BI *Pre-Morocco, Los Angeles, 1983,* from Eight By Eight To Celebrate the Temporary Contemporary, Museum of Contemporary Art, s., d., #123/250, ULAE blindstamp, full margins, crease, excell. cond., est. $1,5/2,500, (05-11-93, Christie-NY, #544), sheet 42⅛ x 29¾ in., (107 x 75.6 cm.), color lithograph on BFK Rives.

$935* *Rabbit Chow, 1977,* from the Chow Bag series, s., d., #86/100, full margins, (12-08-92, Swann, #253, illus.), 48 x 36½ in., (121.9 x 92.7 cm.), color silkscreen w/photo collage and twine (BP 586, DM 1456, FR 4963, Y 115,890).

$1588* *Rack, 1969,* s., d., (11-28-92, Schoppmann, #721A), 27⁹⁄₁₆ x 21⁷⁄₁₆ in., (70 x 54.5 cm.), lithograph on BFK Rives (BP 1048, DM 2530, FR 8588, Y 197,635).

$6325* *"Rauschenberg Photographs" (Rauschenberg Photographs, pls. 1, 3, 12,13, 15, 24), 1979:* Twelve, Sonnabend Editions, portfolio, each s., d., #48/50 by photog., 1949-61, p. 1979, large square 4to, (04-06-93, Sotheby-NY, #457, illus.), photograph (BP 4178, DM 10,190, FR 34,506, Y 721,373).

BI *The Razorback Bunch: Etching II (S. 107), 1980,* s., d., #6/24, blindstamp, pub. ULAE, full margins, good cond., Gertrude Kasle Coll., est. $3/4,000, (05-15-93, Sotheby-NY, #1159), 37¾ x 18½ in., (95.9 x 47 cm.), photoetching on 3 sheets of cream Japanese Kitakata wove tissue chine colle on Arches.

$863* *Reality And Paradoxes: Plot, 1973,* s., d., #25/25, pub. Multiples, blindstamp printer, Styria Studio, good cond.?, (05-19-93, Butterfield, #2303), 32 x 23½ in., (813 x 597 mm.), silkscreen w/collage and embossing in colors on India rag (BP 560, DM 1403, FR 4726, Y 95,539).

BI *Reels (B+C): Flower Re-Run (F. 56, G. 102), 1968,* s., d., #39/52, blindstamp, pub. Gemini, G.E.L., excell. cond., est.$3/4,000, (05-15-93, Sotheby-NY, #1156, illus.), sheet 23⅜ x 18¼ in., (59.4 x 46.4 cm.), lithograph in purple on BFK Rives.

BI *Reels (B+C): Love-Zone (F. 55, G. 101), 1968,* s., d., #56/100, blindstamp, pub. Gemini, G.E.L., good cond., est. $3/4,000, (05-15-93, Sotheby-NY, #1155, illus.), sheet 26¾ x 23 in., (67.9 x 58.4 cm.), lithograph in colors on BFK Rives.

$3565* *Reels (B+C): Storyline I (F. 52, Gemini 98), 1968,* s., d., #58/62, blindstamp, pub. Gemini, G.E.L., good cond., soiling, crease, (05-15-93, Sotheby-NY, #1152, illus.), sheet 21⅝ x 16¾ in., (54.9 x 42.5 cm.), lithograph in colors on BFK Rives (BP 2318, DM 5734, FR 19,270, Y 395,189).

$3450* *Reels (B+C): Storyline II (F. 53, G. 99), 1968,* s., d., #55/59, blindstamp, pub. Gemini, G.E.L., good cond., creases, (05-15-93, Sotheby-NY, #1153, illus.), sheet 22 x 17⅞ in., (55.9 x 45.4 cm.), lithograph in colors on BFK Rives (BP 2243, DM 5549, FR 18,649, Y 382,441).

$2760* *Reels (B+C): Storyline III (F. 54, G. 100), 1968,* s., d., #55/72, blindstamp, pub. Gemini, G.E.L., good cond., pressure mark, (05-15-93, Sotheby-NY, #1154, illus.), sheet 21⅝ x 17½ in., (54.9 x 44.5 cm.), lithograph in colors on BFK Rives (BP 1795, DM 4439, FR 14,919, Y 305,953).

$1650* *Rookery Mounds: Grape Levee (G. 844), 1979,* s., d., #40/52, blindstamp pub. Gemini G.E.L., full margins, very good cond.?, (10-28-92, Butterfield, #3083, illus.), 37 x 29¾ in., (940 x 756 mm.), lithograph in shades of purple on Twinrocker paper (BP 1051, DM 2548, FR 8652, Y 202,454).

$3220* *Samarkand Sticthes VII (G. 1405), 1988,* sticthed sig., d., num. #11, pub.'s label, 1 of approx. 77 unique fabric variants, pub. Gemini G.E.L., excell. cond., (05-11-93, Christie-NY, #546, illus.), sheet 48½ x 43 in., (123.2 x 109.2 cm.), color screenprint and collage on fabric in colors (BP 2056, DM 5072, FR 17,091, Y 354,196).

$11,500* *Samarkand Stitches I-VII (G. 1401-1407), 1988:* Seven, stctiched sigs., d., num. #41, pub.'s labels, from edits. approx. 76, 78, 79, 81, 78, 75 and 77 unique fabric variants, pub. Gemini G.E.L., II and III fraying, good cond., sold after sale, (05-11-93, Christie-NY, #545, illus.), color screenprint and collages on fabric in colors (BP 7341, DM 18,116, FR 61,040, Y 1,264,987).

$4600* *Signs, 1970,* s., d., #33/250, pub. Castelli Graphics, margins, good cond.?, (05-19-93, Butterfield, #2300, illus.), sh 43 x 34 in., (109.2 x 86.4 cm.), silkscreen in colors on Arjomari (BP 2986, DM 7477, FR 25,192, Y 509,244).

$6050* *Sling-Shots Lit #1 (Gemini 1169), 1985,* stamped sig., #2/25 on plaque affixed to box, pub. Gemini G.E.L., (11-07-92, Sotheby-NY, #741, illus.), overall size approx. 84½ x 38¼ in., (214.6 x 97.2 cm.), (214.6 x 97.2 cm.), wood light box assemblage w/color lithographs p. on mylar and sailcloth (BP 3956, DM 9660, FR 32,650, Y 746,729).

$550* *Sneakers, 1979,* plate from Rauschenberg Photographs portfolio, s., d., num. 36/50 byphotog. in ink, #36/50 ed., (10-15-92, Sotheby-NY, #574, illus.), photograph, gelatin silver print (BP 337, DM 819, FR 2776, Y 65,987).

$11,000* *Soviet American Array I, 1988-89,* s., d., #46/55, pub. blindstamp, ULAE, good cond., (11-07-92, Sotheby-NY, #744, illus.), sheet 88½ x 53⅛ in., (224.8 x 134.9 cm.), intaglio p. in colors w/collage (BP 7192, DM 17,563, FR 59,363, Y 1,357,689).

$8050* *Soviet American Array I, 1988-89,* s., d., #36/55, blindstamp, pub. ULAE, good cond. ?, (05-15-93, Sotheby-NY, #1160), sheet 92⅜ x 53⅛ in., (234.6 x 134.9 cm.), intaglio in colors w/collage (BP 5234, DM 12,948, FR 43,514, Y 892,362).

$11,000* *Soviet American Array II, 1988-89,* s., d. '88-90', #3/55, pub. blindstamp, ULAE, good cond., (11-07-92, Sotheby-NY, #745, illus.), sheet 87¾ x 54¼ in., (222.9 x 137.8 cm.), intaglio p. in colors w/collage (BP 7192, DM 17,563, FR 59,363, Y 1,357,689).

BI *Soviet American Array II, 1988-89,* s., d. 88-90, #36/55, blindstamp, pub. ULAE, good cond. ?, est. $10/12,000, (05-15-93, Sotheby-NY, #1161, illus.), sheet 87½ x 52⅜ in., (222.3 x 133 cm.), intaglio in colors w/collage.

$15,525* *Soviet American Array III, 1988-89,* s., d. 89-90, #36/57, blindstamp, pub. ULAE, good cond. ?, (05-15-93, Sotheby-NY, #1162, illus.), sheet 86⅝ x 51⅝ in., (220 x 131.1 cm.), intaglio in colors w/collage (BP 10,094, DM 24,972, FR 83,919, Y 1,720,984).

$10,350* *Spot (Foster 24, Sparks 20), 1964,* s., d., #4/37, ULAE blindstamp, excell. cond., (05-11-93, Christie-NY, #541, illus.), sheet 41¼ x 29½ in., (104.8 x 74.9 cm.), lithograph on BFK Rives (BP 6607, DM 16,304, FR 54,936, Y 1,138,489).

$93* *"St-Louis Symphony Orchestra Powell Symphony Hall Opening Jan. 24, 1968",* poster original 1968 #72, (08-18-92, Encans, #132), 29¹⁵⁄₁₆ x 25 in., (76 x 63.5 cm.), offset poster (BP 48, DM 135, FR 459, Y 11,725, C$ 111).

$2875* *Star Quarters Panel III, 1971,* incised sig., i. HC 4/6, pub. Multiples, Inc., good cond., scratches, (02-11-93, Sotheby-NY, #411, illus.), sheet 47¹⁵⁄₁₆ x 47¹⁵⁄₁₆ in., (121.8 x 121.8 cm.), color silkscreen on mirrored plexiglas (BP 2029, DM 4762, FR 16,115, Y 346,594).

$1154* *Statue Of Liberty, 1983,* #162/250, pencil s., d., (11-20-92, Lempertz, #799), 35¹¹⁄₁₆ x 24 in., (90.7 x 61 cm.), color serigraph and collage on Japan (BP 760, DM 1840, FR 6198, Y 143,514).

BI *Stoned Moon Series: Rack (G. 172), 1969,* s., d., #38/54, blindstamp publisher, Gemini G.E.L., p. Charles Ritt,good cond.?, staining, soiling, est. $2/3,000, (05-19-93, Butterfield, #2299), sh 30 x 24⁷⁄₁₆ in., (762 x 621 mm.), lithograph on wove.

BI *Stoned Moon Series: Shell (G. 161),1969,* s., d., num. 53/70, blindstamp of pub. Gemini G.E.L., full margins, apparently very good cond., staining, est. $3,5/4,500, (02-24-93, Butterfield, #3113, illus.), 23¾ x 19⅜ in., (603 x 492 mm.), lithograph in colors on Special Arches.

$10,925* *"Stuntman I", "Stuntman II" and "Stuntman III" (Foster 9-11, Sparks 6-8), 1962:* Three, complete suite, s., d., #34/37, 27/35, and 24/36, blindstamp, pub. ULAE, full margins, good cond., skinned spots, Gertrude Kasle Coll., (05-15-93, Sotheby-NY, #1150, illus.), each sheet 22½ x 17½ in., (57.2 x 44.5 cm.), 3 lithographs in tones of blue, yellow and red on Japan paper (BP 7103, DM 17,573, FR 59,054, Y 1,211,063).

$14,300* *"Stuntman I", "Stuntman II" and "Stuntman III" (Foster 9-11; Sparks 6-8), 1962:* Suite Of Three, suite, s., d., #20/37, 20/35, 10/36, blindstamps, full margins, excellent cond., (11-09-92, Christie-NY, #388, illus.), 22¾ x 17¾ in., (578 x 451 mm.), 3 lithographs in blues, light greens or oranges on Japan (BP 9455, DM 22,829, FR 77,131, Y 1,774,634).

BI *Sub-Total (Gemini 429), 1972,* s., d. 71, #259/500, blindstamps, excellent cond., est. $1,2/1,800, (11-09-92, Christie-NY, #390, illus.), 8⅛ x 12⅝ in., (206 x 321 mm.), colored lithograph on wove.

$863* *Subtotal (G. 429), 1971,* s., d., #338/500, blindstamp publisher, Gemini G.E.L., p. Ron Olds, Dan Freeman and Stuart Henderson, very good cond.?, (05-19-93, Butterfield, #2302), 8¼ x 12½ in., (210 x 318 mm.), lithograph in color on Rives BFK (BP 560, DM 1403, FR 4726, Y 95,539).

$2185* *Test Stone i (F. 40, Gemini 26), 1967,* s., d., #22/77, Gemini G.E.L. blindstamps, full margins, light-staining, skinned patches, very good cond., (05-11-93, Christie-NY, #542, illus.), sheet 20¼ x 14¾ in., (514 x 375 mm.), lithograph on wove (BP 1395, DM 3442, FR 11,598, Y 240,348).

$4680* *Two Reasons Birds Sing, "One More" and "We Will Be More Than Half Way There": Two,* s., 1979, 19/100, blindstamp, Styria Studio, (05-25-93, AB Stockholm, #57), 30⁵⁄₁₆ x 22¹³⁄₁₆ in., (77 x 58 cm.), offset lithograph in colors (BP 3033, DM 7622, FR 25,658, Y 511,531, SK 6820).

$578* *Untitled (Elephant), 1973,* s., i. AP XII/XIII, (06-11-93, Freemn/Fine Art, #189), 28 x 20 in., (71.1 x 50.8 cm.), screenprint w/embossing and gesso (BP 380, DM 939, FR 3167, Y 61,326).

$660* *"Untitled",* U.N. Series, s. Rauschenberg '84, (04-17-93, Wolf, #610), 18½ x 16½ in., (47 x 41.9 cm.), offset color lithograph (BP 433, DM 1066, FR 3603, Y 74,216).

$1100* *Untitled, 1983,* s., d., num. 122/125, pub. Ruth Eckered Hall, good cond., surface soiling, (02-24-93, Butterfield, #3120), 28¼ x 20½ in., (718 x 521 mm.), offset lithograph in colors w/collage, pencil additions & embossing (BP 767, DM 1786, FR 6054, Y 129,078).

$1540* *Untitled, 1983,* s., i. printer's proof, pub. Galerie Maeght, (05-16-93, Hindman, #526), 23 x 18¼ in., (58.4 x 46.4 cm.), silkscreen (BP 1001, DM 2477, FR 8324, Y 170,713).

$920* *Untitled, 1984,* s., d., #39/120, pub. to benefit Gary Hart, Presidential Candidate, good cond., (02-11-93, Sotheby-NY, #419), sheet 22¹⁵⁄₁₆ x 18⁵⁄₁₆ in., (583 x 465 mm.), offset lithograph and silkscreen p. in colors (BP 649, DM 1524, FR 5157, Y 110,910).

$3850* *Visitation II (Foster 30; Sparks 26), 1965,* s., d., #3/44, pub. blindstamp, ULAE, good cond., (11-07-92, Sotheby-NY, #733, illus.), sheet 30 x 22 in., (762 x 559 mm.), lithograph on BFK Rives (BP 2517, DM 6147, FR 20,777, Y 475,191).

$1147* *Week In Review, 1973,* 71/250, s., (10-14-92, Germann, #405, illus.), 29¹⁵⁄₁₆ x 22¹⁄₁₆ in., (760 x 560 mm.), offset serigraph in color (BP 673, DM 1679, FR 5692, Y 138,997, SF 1495).

BI *Why You Can't Tell II, 1979,* s., d., #35/100, pub. Multiples, Inc., good cond., est. $1,5/2,000, (02-11-93, Sotheby-NY, #418), sheet 30½ x 23¹⁄₁₆ in., (775 x 586 mm.), color silkscreen w/collage.

$550* *With Liberty And Justice For All, 1976,* s., d., #66/125, blindstamp pub. Styria Studio, good cond., creasing, surface soiling, glue staining, hinge remains, (10-28-92, Butterfield, #3082), 30¼ x 22¾ in., (768 x 578 mm.), color offset lithograph w/silkscreen on smooth wove (BP 350, DM 849, FR 2884, Y 67,485).

BI *"Words Appearing In A Dream Of William Burroughs",* s., d. '72, est. $2/400, (11-13-92, DuMouchelle, #2375), 30 x 20½ in., (76.2 x 52.1 cm.), color photo lithograph poster.

BI *"Words Appearing In A Dream Of William Burroughs",* s., d. '72, est. $2/400, (03-12-93, DuMouchelle, #2273), 30 x 20½ in., (76.2 x 52.1 cm.), color lithograph poster.

RAVANESI, Gil contemporary

$330* *"High Street" and "1980-1982": A Pair,* s., t., d., (12-10-92, Sloan, #2717), each 16 x 20 in., (40.6 x 50.8 cm.), photograph, color (BP 213, DM 522, FR 1783, Y 40,821).

RAVEEL, Roger

$416* *Picknick, 1976,* s., #79/190, full sheet p. to edges, good cond., (05-27-93, Sotheby-Amstrdm, #472), sh 30¹¹⁄₁₆ x 22¼ in., (780 x 565 mm.), colored lithograph on wove (BP 266, DM 668, FR 2250, Y 44,597, G 748).

$544* *Untitled, 1976,* s., #43/190, full sheet p. to edges, good cond., creases in upper and lower edge of sheet, (05-27-93, Sotheby-Amstrdm, #470, illus.), sh 30¹⁄₁₆ x 22⁵⁄₁₆ in., (764 x 567 mm.), colored lithograph on wove (BP 348, DM 873, FR 2942, Y 58,319, G 978).

$192* *Untitled, 1976,* s., #109/190, full sheet p. to edges, good cond., crease in right corner, (05-27-93, Sotheby-Amstrdm, #471), sh 20¹⁄₁₆ x 25¹¹⁄₁₆ in., (510 x 653 mm.), colored lithograph on wove (BP 123, DM 308, FR 1038, Y 20,583, G 345).

RAVENET (after R. DALTON)

$495* *"Faunus Saltans", "Mercurnis" and "Antinous": A Set Of Three,* Louis Bonadio Estate, (10-14-92, Doyle, #69), 21¼ x 12¼ in., (54 x 31.1 cm.), engraving (BP 291, DM 724, FR 2457, Y 59,985).

RAVENNA, Marco da (Marco DENTE) d. 1527

$390* *L'Annunciazione (B. 15, Le Blanc 2),* after Raphael, torn margins, (12-01-92, Karl/Faber, #44), engraving (BP 258, DM 622, FR 2118, Y 48,556).

RAY

$150* *Valda, Barre La Route A La Rhume,* cond. B, (03-16-93, Boisgirard, #179), 59⁷⁄₁₆ x 78¾ in., (151 x 200 cm.), poster (BP 104, DM 249, FR 847, Y 17,540).

RAY, Man American 1890-1976

$193* *Abstract Composition With Spoons, c. 1972,* s., #5/150, full margins, good cond., (03-12-93, Goldberg, #895A, illus.), image 7¼ x 5¼ in., (18.4 x 13.3 cm.), aquatint etching (BP 135, DM 321, FR 1092, Y 22,746).

$1150* *Adam And Even,* s., annot. Experimental Proof VII, i., t. in stone, good cond.?, (05-19-93, Butterfield, #2311), 22¼ x 30 in., (565 x 762 mm.), lithograph in colors on wove (BP 747, DM 1869, FR 6298, Y 127,311).

BI *Ady,* late 1930s, stamp, est. $9/12,000, (10-13-92, Christie-NY, #308, illus.), 5¼ x 3½ in., (13.3 x 8.9 cm.), photograph, gelatin silver print.

BI *Les Anatomes (Anselmini 70 B), 1970,* 17/100, s., wrinkles, est. SF 450/550, (10-14-92, Germann, #360), 26¹⁄₁₆ x 20¹⁄₁₆ in., (662 x 510 mm.), color lithograph.

$362* *Les Anatomes (Anselmini 70 H), 1970,* 17/100, s., wrinkles, (10-14-92, Germann, #359), 26⅛ x 20¹⁄₁₆ in., (663 x 510 mm.), color lithograph (BP 212, DM 530, FR 1797, Y 43,868, SF 472).

$1500* *Les Anatomes (Anselmino 70), 1970: Five,* s., num., 87/100, (10-14-92, Germann, #18), 26³⁄₁₆ x 20¹⁄₁₆ in., (665 x 510 mm.), color aquatint (BP 880, DM 2195, FR 7444, Y 181,774, SF 1955).

$2294* *Les Anatomes (Anselmino 70), 1970: Six,* s., 87/100, (10-14-92, Germann, #16, illus.), 26³⁄₁₆ x 20¹⁄₁₆ in., (665 x 510 mm.), color acquatint (BP 1346, DM 3357, FR 11,385, Y 277,993, SF 2990).

$3680* *Les Anatoms, 1970: Ten,* s., #5/100, t., pub. George Visat, full margins, surface soiling, crease, excell. cond., (05-11-93, Christie-NY, #330, illus.), each plate 16⅞ x 12½ in., (429 x 318 mm.), color aquatint on Lana wove (BP 2349, DM 5797, FR 19,533, Y 404,796).

$362* *Aus "Les Anatomes" (Anselmini 70 I), 1971,* 17/100, s., (10-14-92, Germann, #362), 25¹⁵⁄₁₆ x 20¹⁄₁₆ in., (660 x 510 mm.), color aquatint (BP 212, DM 530, FR 1797, Y 43,868, SF 472).

$362* *Aus "Les Anatomes" (Anselmini 70 M), 1971,* 17/100, s., (10-14-92, Germann, #361), 25¹⁵⁄₁₆ x 19⅞ in., (660 x 505 mm.), color aquatint (BP 212, DM 530, FR 1797, Y 43,868, SF 472).

$38,500* *Bird Of Paradise, c. 1928,* i. in Man Ray's hand, stamp, lit., (10-13-92, Christie-NY, #304, illus.), 11½ x 9 in., (29.2 x 22.9 cm.), photograph, gelatin silver print (BP 22,423, DM 56,402, FR 191,638, Y 4,668,364).

BI *"Cactus Suite, Transfiguration D'Un Cactus" (Anselmini 29 D and 29 H), 1969: Two,* #74/90, s., est. SF 1/1,400, (04-21-93, Germann, #607, illus.), 30⅛ x 22⁷⁄₁₆ in., (765 x 570 mm.), color aquatint.

$440* *"Composition",* s., #23/75, prov., (02-11-93, Boos, #417), sight 22¹³⁄₁₆ x 17⁵⁄₁₆ in., (580 x 440 mm.), color lithograph (BP 310, DM 729, FR 2466, Y 53,044).

$3850* *Distortion (Adrienne),* studio stamp, 1930's, (10-15-92, Sotheby-NY, #295, illus.), 5¼ x 3⅜ in., (13.3 x 8.6 cm.), photograph, gelatin silver print (BP 2356, DM 5731, FR 19,435, Y 461,908).

$793* *Donna (Anselmino Band I 49), 1968,* #62/99, mono., (11-21-92, Lempertz, #260), 7 x 5³⁄₁₆ in., (17.8 x 13.1 cm.), etching on wove (BP 522, DM 1264, FR 4259, Y 98,620).

$1138* *Drei Rayographien: Three,* 1921-23, 1978, (11-12-92, Lempertz, #164), smallest 11⁹⁄₁₆ x 8¹¹⁄₁₆ in., (29.3 x 22.1 cm.), largest 11¹³⁄₁₆ x 9⁹⁄₁₆ in., (29.3 x 22.1 cm.), photograph, gelatin silver print (BP 728, DM 1788, FR 6095, Y 140,789).

$19,800* *Duchamp's Rotative Demisphere (Point De Vue A 1m Dans L'Axe), c. 1926,* crop marks recto, stamp in unidentified hand, notations, lit., (10-13-92, Christie-NY, #303, illus.), 9 x 6⅛ in., (22.9 x 15.6 cm.), photograph, gelatin silver print (BP 11,532, DM 29,007, FR 98,556, Y 2,400,873).

BI *Electricite, 1931: Ten,* La Compagnie Parisienne De Distribution D'Electricite, each s. in neg., num. on colophon, #323/500 edit., lit., est. $22/28,000, (10-13-92, Christie-NY, #305, illus.), each 10¼ x 8 in., (26 x 20.3 cm.), photograph, photogravures of orig. rayographs.

BI *Electricite: Ten (Perpetual Motif, pl. 183), 1931,* La Compagnie Parisienne de Distribution d'Electricite, 1931, portfolio of 10 photogravures of rayographs, s. in neg., mounted, edit. #186/500, est.$25/35,000, (10-15-92, Sotheby-NY, #289, illus.), each plate, approx. 10¼ x 8 in., (26 x 20.3 cm.), photogravure.

BI *"Electro)Magie", c. 1972,* s., #65/150, good cond. est. $4/600, (03-12-93, Goldberg, #895, illus.), image 7¼ x 5¼ in., (18.4 x 13.3 cm.), aquatint etching.

BI *Electro-Magie (A. 40 F), 1972,* s., num., light-stained, est. DM 1200, (12-01-92, Karl/Faber, #1129), 7$\frac{1}{16}$ x 5$\frac{5}{16}$ in., (18 x 13.5 cm.), color etching and aquatint on BFK Rives wove.

$2200* *Electro-Magie (Anselmino 40), 1969,* book by Gui Rosey, s., #81/150, pub. Editions Georges Visat, good cond., stain, (11-07-92, Sotheby-NY, #675, illus.), each sheet approx. 11¼ x 8⅞ in., (286 x 225 mm.), book including six orig. etchings w/aquatint p. in colors on Rives (BP 1438, DM 3513, FR 11,873, Y 271,538).

$590* *Electro-Magie (Anselmino 40), 1969: Three,* s. Man Ray, XI/XXV, (09-30-92, Kunsthallen, #194), color etching (BP 333, DM 837, FR 2830, Y 70,803, DK 3220).

BI *"Emak Bakia", 1926-27: Eleven,* one stamped; one i., lit., est. BP 22/25,000, (10-29-92, Christie-London, #105, illus.), each approx. 5¼ x 7¼ in., (13.3 x 18.4 cm.), photograph, gelatin silver print.

$1801* *Enigma II, 1935,* #4/23, sig., (12-15-92, Finarte-Milan, #88, illus.), 19$\frac{5}{16}$ x 23$\frac{7}{16}$ in., (49 x 59.5 cm.), photograph (BP 1149, DM 2823, FR 9646, Y 223,366, L 2530).

$387* *Figur Aus "Les Anatomes" (Anselmini 70 B), 1971,* #17/100, s., creases, (09-04-92, Germann, #455), 26$\frac{1}{16}$ x 20$\frac{1}{16}$ in., (662 x 510 mm.), color aquatint (BP 194, DM 542, FR 1846, Y 47,637, SF 483).

BI *Gertrude Stein, 1926,* s., stamped twice, lit., est. $8/10,000, (10-13-92, Christie-NY, #300, illus.), 7 x 5 in., (17.8 x 12.7 cm.), photograph, gelatin silver print.

$193,464* *Glass Tears, c. 1930,* mono. MR, stamped photog.'s credits Man Ray Paris and Photograph ManRay, 228 x 298mm, catalog cover lot, (05-07-93, Sotheby-London, #235, illus.), photograph, silver print (BP 122,500, DM 305,872, FR 1,030,709, Y 21,301,916).

$1320* *Harbor Study,* studio stamp, 1930's, (10-15-92, Sotheby-NY, #293A, illus.), 4⅞ x 6½ in., (12.4 x 16.5 cm.), photograph, gelatin silver print (BP 808, DM 1965, FR 6663, Y 158,368).

BI *Henri Matisse, 1926,* t., annot., stamp, prov., lit., est. $24/28,000, (10-13-92, Christie-NY, #302, illus.), 11¼ x 8¼ in., (28.6 x 21 cm.), photograph, gelatin silver print.

$8250* *Hildegarde Lasell Watson,* tipped to mount, s., i. by photog., studio stamp, 1920's, (10-15-92, Sotheby-NY, #294A, illus.), 9 x 6⅞ in., (22.9 x 17.5 cm.), photograph, gelatin silver print (BP 5048, DM 12,280, FR 41,646, Y 989,802).

$425* *Image A Deux Faces (Studio Marconi I, 31), 1971,* artist's proof, mono., (06-28-93, Loudmer, #290), 25$\frac{13}{16}$ x 19½ in., (655 x 495 mm.), sh 29$\frac{13}{16}$ x 22$\frac{5}{16}$ in., (655 x 495 mm.), color lithograph on Arches wove (BP 285, DM 722, FR 2433, Y 45,093).

$337* *"Images A Deux Faces" (OG 31), 1971,* #XIII/XXX, mono., (10-18-92, Pescheteau, #201), 29$\frac{15}{16}$ x 22$\frac{1}{16}$ in., (76 x 56 cm.), lithograph in colors on Arches (BP 204, DM 498, FR 1691, Y 40,239).

$77* *In Cima Al Mondo (Studio Marconi I, 35), 1972,* mono. artist's proof, edit. 100, (06-28-93, Loudmer, #90), 19⅛ x 16⅛ in., (485 x 410 mm.), sh 25⅜ x 19½ in., (485 x 410 mm.), color lithograph on Arches wove (BP 52, DM 131, FR 441, Y 8170).

$116* *In Cima Al Mondo (Studio Marconi I, 35), 1972,* mono., (06-28-93, Loudmer, #292), 19⅛ x 16¼ in., (485 x 412 mm.), sh 25$\frac{9}{16}$ x 19$\frac{11}{16}$ in., (485 x 412 mm.), color lithograph on Arches wove (BP 78, DM 197, FR 664, Y 12,308).

BI *James Joyce,* 1922, p. 1950s, MAN RAY PARIS stamp, est. $2/3,000, (04-08-93, Christie-NY, #216, illus.), 9⅜ x 6¾ in., (23.8 x 17.1 cm.), photograph, gelatin silver print.

$715* *Jean Cocteau's Romeo, 1924,* stamp, (10-13-92, Christie-NY, #299, illus.), 9¼ x 7 in., (23.5 x 17.8 cm.), photograph, gelatin silver print (BP 416, DM 1047, FR 3559, Y 86,698).

$498* *Julie (Anselmino 9), 1968,* s., num., (12-01-92, Karl/Faber, #1128), 18½ x 14¾ in., (47 x 37.5 cm.), color lithograph on Arches wove (BP 329, DM 794, FR 2705, Y 62,002).

$3850* *Juliet Diptych, c. 1945,* credit stamps, lit., (10-13-92, Christie-NY, #470, illus.), each 3½ x 2⅛ in., (8.9 x 5.4 cm.), overall 3½ x 4⅜ in., (8.9 x 5.4 cm.), photograph, gelatin silver print (BP 2242, DM 5640, FR 19,164, Y 466,836).

$2200* *Juliet, 1946,* s., annot., i. in ink, lit., (10-13-92, Christie-NY, #469, illus.), 3¾ x 2¾ in., (9.5 x 7 cm.), photograph, gelatin silver print (BP 1281, DM 3223, FR 10,951, Y 266,764).

BI *Juliet, 1951,* s., d., prov., lit., est. $15/20,000, (10-13-92, Christie-NY, #471, illus.), 10 x 7¾ in., (25.4 x 19.7 cm.), photograph, gelatin silver print.

$8625* *Kiki (Thames and Hudson, pl. 105), 1924,* photog. studio stamp, (04-06-93, Sotheby-NY, #247, illus.), 9 x 6⅞ in., photograph (BP 5697, DM 13,896, FR 47,054, Y 983,691).

$5085* *Kiki Of Montparnasse, c. 1925,* stamped photog.'s credit Man Ray Paris, 119 x 89mm, (05-07-93, Sotheby-London, #237, illus.), photograph, silver print (BP 3220, DM 8040, FR 27,091, Y 559,899).

$423* *Knieeder Weiblicher Akt. (Anselmino/Marconi 70), 1970,* s., num., from series Les Anatomes, (05-26-93, Dorling, #2918, illus.), 16$\frac{15}{16}$ x 14¾ in., (43 x 37.5 cm.), color etching on wove von (by) Lana (BP 274, DM 690, FR 2323, Y 45,958).

$417* *Komposition (Anselmini 70 E), 1971,* from "Les Anatomes", 27/100, s., (10-14-92, Germann, #364), 26$\frac{3}{16}$ x 20$\frac{1}{16}$ in., (665 x 510 mm.), color aquatint (BP 245, DM 610, FR 2069, Y 50,533, SF 543).

BI *Komposition (Anselmini 70F), 1971,* from "Les Anatomes", 27/100, s., est. SF 600/900, (10-14-92, Germann, #363), 25$\frac{15}{16}$ x 20¼ in., (660 x 515 mm.), color aquatint.

$387* *Komposition, Aus "Les Anatomes" (Anselmini 70 F), 1971,* #27/100, s., (09-04-92, Germann, #456), 25$\frac{15}{16}$ x 20¼ in., (660 x 515 mm.), color aquatint (BP 194, DM 542, FR 1846, Y 47,637, SF 483).

BI *L'Origine De L'Espace (A. 58 C), 1971,* s., num., est. DM 1000, (12-01-92, Karl/Faber, #1130), 16$\frac{9}{16}$ x 12⅝ in., (42 x 32 cm.), color lithograph on wove.

BI *L'Origine De L'Espace (A. 58 G), 1971,* s., est. DM 1000, (12-01-92, Karl/Faber, #1131), 16$\frac{9}{16}$ x 12⅝ in., (42 x 32 cm.), color lithograph.

$354* *L'Origine De L'Espace (Anselmino 58 h), 1971,* s., num., (06-08-93, Karl/Faber, #1231), approx. 16⅛ x 12⅝ in., (41 x 32 cm.), color lithograph on wove (BP 233, DM 574, FR 1934, Y 37,600).

$978* *"Man Ray Photographs 1920-1934 Paris", 1934: Book,* photo. by Man Ray, texts by Andre Breton, Paul Eluard, Rose Selavy and Tristan Tzara, pub. James Thrall Soby, 1934, (05-23-93, Butterfield, #3515, illus.), 12¼ x 9½ in., spiral bound book w/104 photographs (BP 637, DM 1599, FR 5382, Y 108,102).

BI *Mannequin With Ball In Wooden Bowl, c. 1926,* Rue Campagne Premiere stamp, est. #30/35,000, (04-08-93, Christie-NY, #217, illus.), 7¾ x 10 in., (19.7 x 25.4 cm.), photograph, gelatin silver print.

BI *Mathematical Object, c. 1930,* Rue du Val-de-Grace credit stamp, est. $8/12,000, (04-08-93, Christie-NY,

#218, illus.), 11⅝ x 9 in., (29.5 x 22.9 cm.), photograph, gelatin silver print.

BI   *Maxime Alexandre,* studio stamp, late 1920's-early 1930's, est. $5/8,000, (10-15-92, Sotheby-NY, #290, illus.), 9 x 6⅞ in., (22.9 x 17.5 cm.), photograph, gelatin silver print.

BI   *Mythologie Moderne (Studio Marconi I, 56), 1969,* s. artist's proof, est. FF1,800/2,000, (06-28-93, Loudmer, #298), 20¼ x 16⅛ in., (515 x 410 mm.), sh 25¹³⁄₁₆ x 18⅞ in., (515 x 410 mm.), color lithograph on Arches wove.

$449* *"Mythologie Moderne", 1969,* #127/175, s., (10-18-92, Pescheteau, #202), 25⁹⁄₁₆ x 19¹¹⁄₁₆ in., (65 x 50 cm.), lithograph in colors on Arches (BP 272, DM 663, FR 2253, Y 53,612).

BI   *Noma Copley, Paris, c. 1954,* s., prov., lit., est. $8/12,000, (10-13-92, Christie-NY, #472, illus.), 6⅞ x 5 in., (17.5 x 12.7 cm.), photograph, gelatin silver print.

$9200* *Nude Study, Nusch Eluard, c. 1933,* from portfolio 10 Photos Originales, Librairie du Luxembourg, s., #19/50, (04-08-93, Christie-NY, #215, illus.), 8⅛ x 6¼ in., (20.6 x 15.9 cm.), photograph, gelatin silver print (BP 6033, DM 14,779, FR 50,027, Y 1,044,031).

$337* *Nudo (Anselmino 24), 1964,* s. Man Ray, 99/100, (09-30-92, Kunsthallen, #195), color lithograph (BP 190, DM 478, FR 1616, Y 40,442, DK 1840).

$116* *Nuit De Saint Jean De Luz (Anselmino 42), 1968,* mono., hors commerce, edit. 100, (06-28-93, Loudmer, #91), 25⁹⁄₁₆ x 18⅞ in., (650 x 480 mm.), sh. 29¹⁵⁄₁₆ x 20⅞ in., (650 x 480 mm.), color lithograph on Arches wove (BP 78, DM 197, FR 664, Y 12,308).

$145* *Nuit De Saint-Jean-De-Luz (Studio Marconi I, 42), 1968,* mono. artist's proof, (06-28-93, Loudmer, #291), 25⁹⁄₁₆ x 18⅞ in., (650 x 480 mm.), sh 29¹⁵⁄₁₆ x 20⅞ in., (650 x 480 mm.), color lithograph on Arches wove (BP 97, DM 246, FR 830, Y 15,385).

$6068* *Ohne Titel, Drei Rayographien: Three,* 1922-28, 60's, s., tear, prov., (11-12-92, Lempertz, #167, illus.), one 10¹⁵⁄₁₆ x 8⁹⁄₁₆ in., (27.8 x 21.7 cm.), other 11⁷⁄₁₆ x 8⁷⁄₁₆ in., (27.8 x 21.7 cm.), photograph, gelatin silver print (BP 3880, DM 9536, FR 32,501, Y 750,711).

$4172* *Ohne Titel, Zwei Rayographien: Two,* 1922-28, 60's, s., light creases, prov., (11-12-92, Lempertz, #165, illus.), one 10⁷⁄₁₆ x 8⁷⁄₁₆ in., (26.5 x 21.4 cm.), other 11⅜ x 8½ in., (26.5 x 21.4 cm.), photograph, gelatin silver print (BP 2668, DM 6557, FR 22,346, Y 516,145).

$4172* *Ohne Titel, Zwei Rayographien: Two,* 1922-28, 60's, s., d., prov., (11-12-92, Lempertz, #166, illus.), each 11⁷⁄₁₆ x 8⁹⁄₁₆ in., (29 x 21.8 cm.), photograph, gelatin silver print (BP 2668, DM 6557, FR 22,346, Y 516,145).

$468* *"Oiselet", before 1940,* init. MR in image, artist's stamp, good cond., (03-12-93, Skinner, #124, illus.), sight 8¾ x 6⅞ in., photograph, silver print on printing-out paper (BP 326, DM 779, FR 2649, Y 55,156).

$16,100* *Pablo Picasso (Thames and Hudson, pl. 339), 1933,* s., d. by photog. on image, photog. stamp, (04-06-93, Sotheby-NY, #248, illus.), 9¾ x 7⅝ in., photograph (BP 10,634, DM 25,938, FR 87,834, Y 1,836,223).

$2724* *"Passion Flowers", c. 1924-25,* s. Man Ray, t., stamped photog.'s credit, 172 x 231mm, (05-07-93, Sotheby-London, #238, illus.), photograph, silver print (BP 1725, DM 4307, FR 14,513, Y 299,934).

$638* *Pechage (Studio Marconi I, 5), 1970,* mono., XIX/XX, (06-28-93, Loudmer, #296, illus.), 17¹¹⁄₁₆ x 11¹¹⁄₁₆ in., (450 x 297 mm.), sh 26³⁄₁₆ x 19½ in., (450 x 297 mm.), color lithograph on Japan (BP 427, DM 1084, FR 3652, Y 67,692).

BI   *Picasso, 1932,* crop marks in ink recto, stamp, lit., est. $3/5,000, (10-13-92, Christie-NY, #301, illus.), 3⅛ x 2 in., (7.9 x 5.1 cm.), photograph, gelatin silver print.

$425* *Poire D'Erik Satie (Studio Marconi I, 45), 1969,* mono., XIX/XX, (06-28-93, Loudmer, #295), 17¹¹⁄₁₆ x 11¹¹⁄₁₆ in., (450 x 297 mm.), sh 25⁹⁄₁₆ x 19¹¹⁄₁₆ in., (450 x 297 mm.), color lithograph on Japan (BP 285, DM 722, FR 2433, Y 45,093).

$6600* *Polyedres, The Merchant Of Venice, 1936,* t., stamps, lit., (10-13-92, Christie-NY, #307, illus.), 11¾ x 9⅛ in., (29.8 x 23.2 cm.), photograph, gelatin silver print (BP 3844, DM 9669, FR 32,852, Y 800,291).

$116* *Le Pont Neuf (Studio Marconi I, 6), 1970,* mono. artist's proof, (06-28-93, Loudmer, #293), 14¹⁄₁₆ x 20¹¹⁄₁₆ in., (357 x 526 mm.), sh 19⅛ x 24⅝ in., (357 x 526 mm.), color lithograph on Arches wove (BP 78, DM 197, FR 664, Y 12,308).

$6900* *Portrait Of Juliet, c. 1945,* Photograph by Man Ray stamp, sold after sale, (04-08-93, Christie-NY, #219, illus.), 9⅞ x 7⅞ in., (25.1 x 20 cm.), photograph, waxed gelatin silver print (BP 4525, DM 11,084, FR 37,520, Y 783,023).

$5500* *Portrait Of Picasso, 1932,* notations, (10-14-92, Swann, #514, illus.), 8½ x 6½ in., (21.6 x 16.5 cm.), photograph, silver print (BP 3228, DM 8049, FR 27,295, Y 666,505).

BI   *Portrait Of Robert Winthrop Chanler, 1929,* s. by photog., photog.'s handstamp, est. $3/5,000, (04-07-93, Swann, #513, illus.), photograph, toned silver print.

BI   *Portrait Studies Of A Young Girl: Two,* 1950s, s., est. $1,8/2,200, (05-23-93, Butterfield, #3516, illus.), each approx. 9 x 6¾ in., photograph, gelatin silver print.

BI   *Portrait, c. 1937,* s., photog.'s ink credit stamp MAN RAY, PARIS V/8, RUE VAL-DE-GRACE..., est. BP 900/1,200, (05-06-93, Christie-London, #184, illus.), 11½ x 9 in., photograph, gelatin silver print.

$425* *Promenade (Studio Marconi I, 14), 1965,* s., artist's proof, (06-28-93, Loudmer, #299), 11⁷⁄₁₆ x 8¾ in., (290 x 223 mm.), sh 20¹⁄₁₆ x 14⁹⁄₁₆ in., (290 x 223 mm.), color lithograph on wove (BP 285, DM 722, FR 2433, Y 45,093).

$2904* *"Quelques Roues D'Auto De Picabia", 1929,* photog.'s ink credit stamp 31bis Rue Campagne Premiere Paris, i. t. and d., lit., (05-06-93, Christie-London, #185, illus.), 8½ x 11¼ in., photograph, gelatin silver print (BP 1840, DM 4574, FR 15,398, Y 319,507).

BI   *Rayograph, 1927,* s., d. by photog. in neg., i. by photog., studio stamp, p. 1960s, est. $3/5,000, (10-15-92, Sotheby-NY, #293, illus.), 11⅞ x 8½ in., (30.2 x 21.6 cm.), photograph, silver gelatin print of rayograph.

BI   *Rayograph, c. 1927,* s. by photog. on image, studio stamp, i. in unidentified hand in ink,p. 1960's, est. $4/6,000, (10-15-92, Sotheby-NY, #294, illus.), 11½ x 8½ in., (29.2 x 21.6 cm.), photograph, silver gelatin print of rayograph.

BI   *"Le Rebus",* EA s., est. FF1,500/2,000, (04-04-93, Pescheteau, #255), 29⅛ x 22¹⁄₁₆ in., (74 x 56 cm.), color lithograph on Arches.

BI   *Romanzo Nero (Anselmo 32), 1940,* s., num., very rare, est. DM 3,500, (12-05-92, Bassenge, #7651, illus.), 9¹³⁄₁₆ x 12¹⁵⁄₁₆ in., (25 x 33 cm.), color lithograph.

BI   *Romanzo Nero (Anselmo 32), 1940,* s., num., est. DM 2,500, (06-05-93, Bassenge, #6469, illus.), 9¹³⁄₁₆ x 12¹⁵⁄₁₆ in., (25 x 33 cm.), color lithograph.

$290* *The Rope Dancer Accompanies Herself With Her Shadows (Studio MarconiI, 26), 1970,* s. artist's proof, (06-28-93, Loudmer, #288), 19¹¹⁄₁₆ x 27⁹⁄₁₆ in., (500 x 700 mm.), sh 22¹⁄₁₆ x 29¹⁵⁄₁₆ in., (500 x 700 mm.), color lithograph on Arches wove (BP 194, DM 493, FR 1660, Y 30,769).

$10,643* *"Rrose Selavy", Marcel Duchamp, 1921,* p. c. 1936-40, photog.'s ink credit stamp verso, lit., exhib., (10-29-92, Christie-London, #104, illus.), 8¾ x 7 in., (22.2 x 17.8 cm.), photograph, gelatin silver print (BP 6820, DM 16,374, FR 55,548, Y 1,318,345).

$290* *Sade (Studio Marconi I, 8), 1970,* s. artist's proof, (06-28-93, Loudmer, #297), 24⁷⁄₁₆ x 19¹¹⁄₁₆ in., (620 x 500 mm.), sh 29¹⁵⁄₁₆ x 21⅞ in., (620 x 500 mm.), color lithograph on Arches wove (BP 194, DM 493, FR 1660, Y 30,769).

$329* *Sans Titre (Studio Marconi II, 78), 1962/I,* s. artist's proof, (06-28-93, Loudmer, #294), 25 x 18⅞ in., (635 x 480 mm.), sh 29¹⁵⁄₁₆ x 21⁷⁄₁₆ in., (635 x 480 mm.), color lithograph on Arches wove (BP 220, DM 559, FR 1883, Y 34,907).

BI   *Self-Portrait,* (1924), 1960s, s., d. in neg., est. $6/8,000, (10-13-92, Christie-NY, #298, illus.), 8 x 6¼ in., (20.3 x 15.9 cm.), photograph, gelatin silver print.

$2200* *Shipyard, Marseille,* studio stamp, early 1930's, (10-15-92, Sotheby-NY, #296, illus.), 6½ x 4⅞ in., (16.5 x 12.4

cm.), photograph, gelatin silver print (BP 1346, DM 3275, FR 11,106, Y 263,947).

BI *Le Tour, France,* 1930s, credit stamp, lit., est. $4/6,000, (10-13-92, Christie-NY, #306, illus.), 3⅛ x 2⅛ in., (7.9 x 5.4 cm.), photograph, gelatin silver print.

$6902* *"Trepied 'Pyramid' B.S.G.D.G.", c. 1924-25,* t., stamped photog.'s credit, 165 x 91mm, (05-07-93, Sotheby-London, #236, illus.), photograph, silver print w/second collaged silver print (BP 4370, DM 10,912, FR 36,771, Y 759,965).

$978* *Untitled (G. 20), 1966,* s., #13/125, blindstamp publisher Gemini G.E.L., p. James Webb, fullmargins, good cond., staining, hinge remains, handling creases, surface soiling, (05-19-93, Butterfield, #2310), 25¾ x 22 in., (654 x 559 mm.), lithograph on Rives BFK (BP 635, DM 1590, FR 5356, Y 108,270).

$23,000* *Untitled (Peaches And Leaf) (Janus, pl. 100; Thames and Hudson, pl. 190; Photographs, p. 24),* i. Man Ray, d. in unident. hand, (04-06-93, Sotheby-NY, #248A, illus.), photograph (BP 15,192, DM 37,055, FR 125,477, Y 2,623,175).

$650* *Untitled (Pilat 118), 1976,* s., num., (11-28-92, Schoppmann, #722), 23¼ x 18½ in., (59 x 47 cm.), color lithograph on Japan (BP 429, DM 1036, FR 3515, Y 80,896).

$357* *Untitled, 1971,* s., from De l'Origine des Especes, (05-27-93, Swann, #231), sh 19⅞ x 14 in., (50.5 x 35.6 cm.), color lithograph (BP 229, DM 573, FR 1931, Y 38,272).

$37,764* *Untitled, Spherical Light Objects, 1926,* image s., d. Man Ray '26, ink s., i., prov., (10-29-92, Christie-London, #106, illus.), 9¾ x 7⅝ in., (24.8 x 19.4 cm.), photograph, rayograph (BP 24,200, DM 58,098, FR 197,098, Y 4,677,815).

$13,200* *View From The Artist's Studio, 1933 (cf. Perpetual Motif, fig. 103),* s., i. by photog. in ink, d., (10-15-92, Sotheby-NY, #292, illus.), 8¼ x 5⅝ in., (21 x 14.3 cm.), photograph, gelatin silver print mounted on aqua paper (BP 8077, DM 19,649, FR 66,633, Y 1,583,683).

BI *Yves Tanguy, 1935,* s., d. by photog., studio stamp, est. $7/10,000, (10-15-92, Sotheby-NY, #291, illus.), 5⅛ x 6⅞ in., (13 x 17.5 cm.), photograph, gelatin silver print.

RAY, Man and Max ERNST

$440* *Mr. Knife And Miss Fork: Death Is Something Like Cousin Cynthia (Pl.IV) (S./L. 13/IV), 1931,* apparently good cond., (02-24-93, Butterfield, #2921), 7⅞ x 4⅜ in., (200 x 111 mm.), rayogram on wove (BP 307, DM 714, FR 2422, Y 51,631).

RAY-JONES, Raymond

$1606* *The Velvet, 1926,* s., margins, (09-17-92, Bonhams-Chelsea, #105), plate 13 x 9⅝ in., (33 x 24.4 cm.), etching (BP 902, DM 2384, FR 8161, Y 199,950).

RAY-JONES, Tony   1941-1972

BI *Brick Lane Market, 1967,* annot., lit., est. $1/1,500, (04-08-93, Christie-NY, #492, illus.), 6¾ x 10¼ in., (17.1 x 26 cm.), photograph, gelatin silver print.

$468* *Holiday Camp, 1960's,* photog. blindstamp, s., annot., ink stamp, Dixon Collection, (11-16-92, Butterfield, #6124, illus.), 6¼ x 9¾ in., (159 x 248.1 mm.), photograph, gelatin silver print (BP 308, DM 746, FR 2513, Y 58,202).

$920* *The Wailing Wall, Jerusalem, c. 1967,* authen., annot., credit/reprod. limitation stamps, (04-08-93, Christie-NY, #491, illus.), 5¼ x 8 in., (13.3 x 20.3 cm.), photograph, gelatin silver print (BP 603, DM 1478, FR 5003, Y 104,403).

RAYMOND, Lilo

$316* *Unmade Bed, 1972,* s., d., (05-23-93, Butterfield, #3567), 13½ x 9 in., photograph, gelatin silver print (BP 206, DM 517, FR 1739, Y 34,929).

BI *"Unmade Bed, 1972", "Door, Crete, 1973", "Lemons, 1976", "Two Pillows, 1976", "Pears, Amagansett, 1977" and "Pitcher, New York 1980": Six,* photog.'s blindstamp, s., d., #12/30, aluminum portfolio, each approx. 355 x 280mm, est. BP 1,2/1,800, (05-07-93, Sotheby-London, #300, illus.), photograph, silver print.

RAZZIA

BI *Impression, 1980,* A cond., est. $5/750, (08-06-92, Swann, #229, illus.), 63 x 47 in., (160 x 119.4 cm.), .

$220* *"Le Parfum",* (08-05-92, Boos, #578), 62 x 46½ in., (157.5 x 118.1 cm.), color lithograph (BP 115, DM 325, FR 1098, Y 28,018).

RE, Percy Robertson

$26* *Busy Shopping Town Scene, Northern England,* s., (12-01-92, Ritchie, #6, illus.), 5⅞ x 7¾ in., (14.9 x 19.7 cm.), etching on laid paper (BP 17, DM 41, FR 141, Y 3237, C$ 33).

REALIER-DUMAS, M.

BI *Polichinelle. Hebdomadaire Humoristique De La Famille, 1896,* Imp. Camis, fairly good cond., restored, (02-12-93, Cheval/Robert, #124), 68½ x 23¼ in., (174 x 59 cm.), poster.

REB, H.

$1097* *Chamonix Mont-Blanc. Ete-Hiver, 1933,* very good cond., (03-15-93, Arcole, #109, illus.), 39⅜ x 24⅝ in., (100 x 62.5 cm.), (BP 764, DM 1822, FR 6194, Y 129,946).

$279* *PLM. Telepherique De Veyrier. Lac D'Annecy. "Le Mont-Blanc, Les Alpes En Un Panorama Unique Au Monde", 1934,* very good cond., (03-15-93, Arcole, #55, illus.), 39⅜ x 24⁷⁄₁₆ in., (100 x 62 cm.), (BP 194, DM 463, FR 1575, Y 33,049).

REBELL, Joseph   Austrian 1787-1828

$939* *Der Strudel Auf Der Donau (Nagler 3; Boetticher 2),* s., (12-04-92, Bassenge, #6909), 10¹⁄₁₆ x 14⅛ in., (25.5 x 35.8 cm.), etching heightened w/white brush (BP 602, DM 1495, FR 5073, Y 117,228).

REBEYROLLE, Paul   French b. 1926

$120* *"Fuite Impossible", "Dos Au Mur" and "Ampoule Electrique": Three,* first #13/75, second, #16/75, third, #2/150, all s., (04-04-93, Pescheteau, #282), 29½ x 19⁵⁄₁₆ in., (75 x 49 cm.), and 29½ x 12⅝ in., (75 x 49 cm.), color lithographs (BP 79, DM 193, FR 655, Y 13,663).

BI *Grenouille Verte,* s., 53/75, crease, est. FF1,000/1,200, (06-28-93, Loudmer, #348), 9⅝ x 16¾ in., (245 x 425 mm.), sh 14¹⁵⁄₁₆ x 22¹⁄₁₆ in., (245 x 425 mm.), color lithograph on Arches wove.

REBOURS, E.

$161* *Folies Dramatiques. Le Billet De Logement, 1901,* Tours, Imp. Tourangelle, cond. B+, (06-11-93, Boisgirard, #138), 51³⁄₁₆ x 39⅜ in., (130 x 100 cm.), poster (BP 106, DM 262, FR 882, Y 17,082).

RED STAR, Kevin   Native American b. 1943

$660* *Native American Man And Woman In An Interior, 1980,* s., d. Kevin Red Star '80, chops w/in image, i. A/P, very good cond., (06-26-93, Skinner, #26, illus.), 9¾ x 7¾ in., (24.8 x 19.7 cm.), color woodcut heightened w/ metallic embossing on paper (BP 442, DM 1121, FR 3778, Y 70,027).

$605* *Portrait Of A Native American,* s. Kevin Red Star, chops w/in image, i. 617/60, very good cond., (06-26-93, Skinner, #29, illus.), 10 x 8 in., (25.4 x 20.3 cm.), color woodcut heightened w/metallic embossing on paper (BP 405, DM 1028, FR 3463, Y 64,191).

REDON, Georges   French 1869-1943

$402* *Au Village Suisse A Partir Du 1er Septembre 1900 (...) Criterium De La Lutte Au Calecon,* Paris, Ste Nlle d'Impressions en couleurs, cond. B+, (06-11-93, Boisgirard, #140, illus.), 47¼ x 31½ in., (120 x 80 cm.), poster (BP 264, DM 653, FR 2203, Y 42,653).

$843* *La Place Clichy. Blanc, Lundi 28 Janvier, 1900,* Paris, Imp. Chaix, cond. A-, (06-11-93, Boisgirard, #139, illus.), 62⅝ x 42½ in., (159 x 108 cm.), poster (BP 554, DM 1370, FR 4619, Y 89,443).

REDON, Odilon   French 1840-1916

$1650* *Apocalypse De St. Jean: Et Le Diable Qui Les Seduisait... (M. 183), 1899,* pub. Vollard, margins, good cond., light staining, tear, (11-05-92, Sotheby-NY, #421), 10⅝ x 5½ in., (271 x 140 mm.), support sheet 19⅞ x 16½ in., (271 x 140 mm.), lithograph on chine applique (BP 1073, DM 2610, FR 8828, Y 202,429).

$1650* *Apocalypse, De St. Jean: Et Un Autre Ange Sortit Du Temple... (M. 180), 1899,* pub. Vollard, full margins, good cond., mat stain, foxing, discoloration, creases, losses, (11-05-92, Sotheby-NY, #420), 12⅝ x 8⅞ in., (320 x 225 mm.), support sheet 20¾ x 16½ in., (320 x 225 mm.), lithograph on chine applique (BP 1073, DM 2610, FR 8828, Y 202,429).

$26,400* *"Arbre", 1892 (Mellerio, 120),* p. Becquet, s. Odilon Redon in stone, i. 25 epreuves and Arbre; ident. on labels verso, good cond., sheet affixed to board, full margins, staining,abrasion or paper fault in image, repaired tears, corner loss, foxing, catalogcover lot, (09-11-92, Skinner, #16, illus.), 18⅞ x 12⅝ in., (47.9 x 32.1 cm.), lithograph on chine applique (BP 13,654, DM 38,002, FR 129,159, Y 3,270,970).

BI *Au Reveil J'Apercus La Deesse De L'Intelligible Au Profil Severe Et Dur (Mellerio 59), 1885,* plate VI from Hommage a Goya, proof, p. Lemercier et Cie, pub. L. Dumont, large margins, good cond., crease, soiling, discolored, tear, est. $8/12,000, (05-13-93, Sotheby-NY, #799, illus.), 10½ x 8⅝ in., (267 x 218 mm.), sh 17⅞ x 12½ in., (267 x 218 mm.), lithograph on chine applique.

$611* *Baigneuse (Harrison 32), 1904,* (06-23-93, Kornfeld, #750), etching and drypoint on thick handmade (BP 415, DM 1034, FR 3478, Y 66,565, SF 920).

$16,985* *Brunnhilde (M. 130), 1894,* large margins, ded., s., reddish stains, (06-11-93, Picard, #154, illus.), 14¹⁵⁄₁₆ x 11½ in., (380 x 292 mm.), lithograph in black on chine applique on strong wove (BP 11,160, DM 27,604, FR 93,068, Y 1,802,122).

$6720* *Le Buddha (Mellerio 132), 1895,* mono. in pencil, (06-23-93, Kornfeld, #749, illus.), lithograph on wove (BP 4565, DM 11,371, FR 38,247, Y 732,106, SF 10,120).

$1045* *Cheval Aile (Winged Horse) (Mellerio 127), 1894,* s., pub. in Revue Blanche, bears collector stamp HS/orSH, foxing, (05-27-93, Swann, #232, illus.), 6¼ x 4⅝ in., (15.9 x 11.7 cm.), lithograph on cream wove mounted onto a support sheet (BP 669, DM 1677, FR 5652, Y 112,028).

$121* *Cheval Aile, 1894, Mellerio 127,* Emmanuel Jacobson Estate, (09-20-92, Hindman, #741), 6¼ x 4⅝ in., (15.9 x 11.7 cm.), lithograph on cream wove (BP 71, DM 180, FR 614, Y 14,955).

BI *Christ (M. 71), 1887,* trial proof?, pub. Lemercier et Cie, margins, creasing, retouching inChina paper, narrow strip retouched in background, repair, stains, est. $8/12,000, (11-05-92, Sotheby-NY, #415, illus.), 13 x 10⅝ in., (331 x 269 mm.), support sheet 19⅛ x 14¾ in., (331 x 269 mm.), lithograph on chine applique.

BI *Les Debacles, (Frontispice) (Mellerio 101), 1889,* for book of poems by Emile Verhaeren, pub. Edmond Deman, num. 47/100, est. Y 650/800,000, (10-14-92, Sotheby-Japan, #78, illus.), image 5½ x 3¾ in., (140 x 95 mm.), each sheet 10 x 7⅛ in., (140 x 95 mm.), lithograph on chine applique.

$1210* *Et Il Avait Dans Sa Main Droite Sept Etoiles (Mellerio 174), 1899,* plate 1 from Apocalypse de St. Jean, full margins, staining, very good cond., (11-09-92, Christie-NY, #195), 11⅜ x 8⅜ in., (289 x 213 mm.), lithograph on Chine applique (BP 800, DM 1932, FR 6526, Y 150,161).

$3027* *Et Le Chercheur Etait A La Recherche Infinie (A.M., 67),* large margins, (02-03-93, Ader Tajan, #196), 10⅞ x 7⅛ in., (27.6 x 18.1 cm.), lithograph on Chine applique (BP 2113, DM 4984, FR 16,901, Y 376,539).

$1430* *"Et Un Autre Ange Sortit Du Temple...", 1899, Mellerio 180,* plate 7 of Apocalypse de Saint-Jean, pub. Vollard, prov., (09-20-92, Hindman, #742, illus.), 12⅜ x 8⅜ in., (31.4 x 21.3 cm.), lithograph on chine applique (BP 837, DM 2122, FR 7259, Y 176,740).

$1650* *A Gustave Flaubert (Tentation De Saint Antoine, 2Eme Serie): Saint Antoine...(M. 95), 1889,* pub. Dumont, margins, good cond., foxing, (11-05-92, Sotheby-NY, #417), 11⅜ x 9⅛ in., (288 x 231 mm.), support sheet 17⅜ x 13½ in., (288 x 231 mm.), lithograph on chine applique (BP 1073, DM 2610, FR 8828, Y 202,429).

BI *Hantise (M. 128), 1894,* second state, s., full margins, good cond., printint defect in dress,scuffs, touched-in scrapes, fox marks, water stain, support sheet glued to

mount, est. $10/15,000, (11-05-92, Sotheby-NY, #419, illus.), 14¼ x 9 in., (362 x 228 mm.), support sheet 23⅜ x 15⅝ in., (362 x 228 mm.), lithograph on chine applique.

$715* *"Here Is The Good Goddess" (Mellerio 148) and "I Am Still The Great Isis...", 1896: Two,* from The Temptation of St. Anthony, 3rd series, plates 15 and 16, full margins, soiling, (12-08-92, Swann, #256), first 5⅞ x 5⅛ in., (14.9 x 13 cm.), second 11⅛ x 8 in., (14.9 x 13 cm.), lithograph on China paper and laid down onto heavy wove (BP 448, DM 1113, FR 3795, Y 88,622).

BI *Hommage A Goya, Paris, O. Redon, 1885 (Mellerio 54-9): Six,* full margins, foxing, very good cond., orig. portfolio w/lithographic t. page w/orig. gallery label of L. Dumont, est. $70/90,000, (05-11-93, Christie-NY, #331, illus.), each sheet 17⅞ x 12⅜ in., (454 x 314 mm.), lithograph on Chine applique.

BI *L'Aile (M. 122), 1893,* s., p. by Becquet, reduced margins, good cond. w/in subject, scuffs,creases, hinges, est. BP 17/19,000, (06-30-93, Sotheby-London, #663, illus.), 12½ x 9⅝ in., (318 x 244 mm.), lithograph on chine applique.

$619* *L'Intelligence Fut A Moi! (Mellerio 145), 1896,* (06-28-93, Loudmer, #349), 12⅜ x 8⁷⁄₁₆ in., (315 x 215 mm.), sh 17⁵⁄₁₆ x 13³⁄₁₆ in., (315 x 215 mm.), black lithograph on China applique on wove (BP 414, DM 1052, FR 3543, Y 65,676).

BI *Le Livre (St. Therese) (Mellerio 24; Harrison 28), 1892,* s., full margins, good cond., mat stain, spots of discoloration, est.$3/4,000, (11-05-92, Sotheby-NY, #414), 5⅛ x 3⅝ in., (131 x 91 mm.), drypoint on wove.

$655* *La Maison Hantee (M. 163 et 165), 1896,* mat-staining, soiling, 1 of 60, (02-24-93, Picard, #206), lithograph on chine applique (BP 457, DM 1063, FR 3605, Y 76,860).

$1029* *La Maison Hantee: Selon Toute Apparence C'Etait Une Main De Chair EtDe Sang Comme La Mienne (M. 164), 1896,* p. by Clot, margins, good cond., soiling, (06-30-93, Sotheby-London, #664), sh 17⅝ x 12⅜ in., (448 x 314 mm.), lithograph on chine applique (BP 690, DM 1755, FR 5921, Y 110,254).

$506* *El Moghreb-Al-Aksa (Mellerio 103), 1889,* frontispiece, from 205 impressions, (05-27-93, Briest, #178), 12¹³⁄₁₆ x 9¹³⁄₁₆ in., (32.5 x 25 cm.), black lithograph on Chine applique (BP 324, DM 812, FR 2737, Y 54,245).

$2150* *Le Mouvement Idealiste En Peinture (Mellerio 159), 1896,* rare, mono., mat-staining, staining, large margin, (02-24-93, Picard, #205), lithograph on chine applique (BP 1499, DM 3490, FR 11,833, Y 252,288).

$1535* *Paul Serusier (M. 192), 1903,* annot., (02-24-93, Picard, #208), lithograph on thin chine (BP 1070, DM 2492, FR 8448, Y 180,122).

$1320* *Pilgrim Of The Sublunary World (Mellerio 114), 1891,* plate 5 from Songes (Dreams), full margins, (12-08-92, Swann, #255, illus.), 11 x 8⅛ in., (27.9 x 20.6 cm.), lithograph, chine colle onto heavy wove (BP 827, DM 2055, FR 7006, Y 163,609).

BI *Profil De Femme Au Bonnet (Mellerio 186; Werner 163), 1900,* sheet 1 of series Planches D'Essai, artist's proof, est. DM 6,000, (12-04-92, Bassenge, #6910, illus.), 12⅝ x 9⁷⁄₁₆ in., (32 x 24 cm.), lithograph on handmade China.

$3489* *Profil De Lumiere (A. Mellerio 61),* large margins, (02-03-93, Ader Tajan, #194), 13⅜ x 9½ in., (34 x 24.2 cm.), lithograph on very thin Chine (BP 2436, DM 5745, FR 19,481, Y 434,009).

$7393* *Profil De Lumiere (A. Mellerio 61), 1886,* margins, s., (06-11-93, Picard, #152), 13⅜ x 9½ in., (340 x 242 mm.), lithograph in black on chine applique on thick wove (BP 4857, DM 12,015, FR 40,510, Y 784,403).

$2530* *Profil De Lumiere (M. 61), 1886,* from reprint edit., p. Frapier, full margins, good cond., paper defect, creases in image, (05-13-93, Sotheby-NY, #800), 13¼ x 9½ in., (337 x 240 mm.), lithograph on chine volant (BP 1661, DM 4085, FR 13,780, Y 282,461).

BI *Serpent Aureole (M. 108), 1890,* pub. by Becquet, full margins, surface scuffs, foxing, discoloration,tears, tape stains, thins spots, good cond., est. $3,5/4,000, (11-05-92, Sotheby-NY, #418, illus.), 11⅞ x 8⅞ in., (301 x 225 mm.), support sheet 20¾ x 15⅝ in., (301 x 225 mm.), lithograph on chine applique.

BI *Le Serpent Aureole (M. 108), 1890,* good margins, reddish stains, losses, (06-11-93, Picard, #153), 11⅞ x 8⅞ in., (302 x 226 mm.), lithograph in black on chine applique on wove.

BI *Tentation De Saint Antoine, P. VII: ...La Chimere Aux Yeux Verts, Tournoie, Aboie. (M. 90), 1888,* pub. by Deman, margins, good cond., touched in printing defect (?), scuffs in image, thin spot, est. $3/5,000, (11-05-92, Sotheby-NY, #416, illus.), 10⅞ x 6¼ in., (276 x 160 mm.), support sheet 17¼ x 12½ in., (276 x 160 mm.), lithograph on chine applique.

$920* *Tentation De St. Antoine, 3me Serie: Le Jour Enfin Parait ... (Mellerio 157), 1896,* pub. Vollard, 1938, full margins, tape/backboard staining, good cond., (02-11-93, Sotheby-NY, #257), sheet 17³⁄₁₆ x 12¹⁵⁄₁₆ in., (436 x 330 mm.), lithograph on chine applique (BP 649, DM 1524, FR 5157, Y 110,910).

$21,216* *Tete D'Enfant Avec Fleurs (M. 169), 1897,* mat-staining, good margins, (02-24-93, Picard, #207, illus.), lithograph on thick simili-Japan (BP 14,795, DM 34,442, FR 116,764, Y 2,489,556).

$2018* *La Vieillesse (A.M., 62),* large margins, (02-03-93, Ader Tajan, #195), 9⁷⁄₁₆ x 5⅞ in., (24 x 15 cm.), lithograph on Chine applique (BP 1409, DM 3323, FR 11,267, Y 251,026).

BI *Vieux Chevalier (M. 158), 1896,* s., pub. Vollard in Album des Peintres-Graveurs, full margins, good cond., handling marks, creases, stamp, est. BP 7,5/8,500, (06-30-93, Sotheby-London, #662, illus.), 11¾ x 9¼ in., (298 x 235 mm.), lithograph on chine applique.

$18,260* *Vieux Chevalier (Mellerio 158; Johnson 1977, 101), 1896,* (06-25-93, Kornfeld, #120, illus.), image 11⅝ x 9³⁄₁₆ in., (29.5 x 23.3 cm.), lithograph on Chine applique (BP 12,350, DM 31,086, FR 104,702, Y 1,935,552, SF 27,600).

$27,390* *Yeux Clos (Mellerio 107), 1890,* s. ODILON REDON in stone, t., (06-25-93, Kornfeld, #119, illus.), image 12⁵⁄₁₆ x 9⁷⁄₁₆ in., (31.2 x 24 cm.), lithograph on Chine colle (BP 18,526, DM 46,629, FR 157,053, Y 2,903,328, SF 41,400).

REDOUTE, Pierre Joseph   French 1759-1840

BI *"Colchicum Variegatum", c. 1802-1816,* engraved by Langlois, est. $18/2500, (12-05-92, Neal, #248, illus.), image 13¾ x 8¼ in., (34.9 x 21 cm.), hand-colored stipple engraving.

BI *"Crinum Asiaticum", c. 1802-1816,* est. $15/2000, (12-05-92, Neal, #249, illus.), image 18 x 12½ in., (45.7 x 31.8 cm.), hand-colored stipple engraving.

BI *Heliconia Psitaccorum,* est. $800/1,200, (06-11-93, Freemn/Fine Art, #190), image 14½ x 11 in., (36.8 x 27.9 cm.), hand-colored stipple-point engraving.

BI *"Orinthogalum Longibracteatum", c. 1802-1816,* engraved by Allais, est. $15/2000, (12-05-92, Neal, #247, illus.), image 17½ x 11½ in., (44.5 x 29.2 cm.), hand-colored stipple engraving.

BI *"Sisyrinchium Striatum", c. 1802-1816,* engraved by Langlois Jeune, est. $12/1800, (12-05-92, Neal, #246, illus.), image 18 x 10 in., (45.7 x 25.4 cm.), hand-colored stipple engraving.

REDOUTE, Pierre Joseph (after)

$275* *Botanical Prints: Two,* ident., very good cond.?, (12-04-92, Skinner, #230, illus.), approx. 11 x 8 in., (27.9 x 20.3 cm.), engraving and etching w/hand-coloring on paper (BP 176, DM 438, FR 1486, Y 34,332).

BI *"Ros Muscosa" and "Rosa Reclinator": Two,* engraved Gouten, est. $2/400, (03-14-93, Hindman, #368), each 14 x 10¼ in., (35.6 x 26 cm.), color stipple engraving.

$85* *Roses: Twenty-Four,* book, (05-26-93, Bonhams-Chelsea, #9), 16 x 12 in., (40.6 x 30.5 cm.), colored reprod. prints (BP 55, DM 139, FR 467, Y 9235).

REECE, Jane   1868-1961

$1540* *Portrait Of A Woman, 1930,* (11-16-92, Butterfield, #6125, illus.), 7 x 4½ in., (178.1 x 114.5 mm.), photograph, platinum print (BP 1014, DM 2455, FR 8271, Y 191,518).

BI *Spaces, 1920,* s., d., (c) insig., t., notations, est. $2/2,500, (10-13-92, Christie-NY, #331, illus.), 9⅝ x 7½ in., (24.4 x 19.1 cm.), photograph, gelatin silver print.

REED, Doel   American b. 1895

BI *Sleeping Woman (Or Resting Woman), c. 1940's,* s., small side margins, good cond., est. $1,250/1,500, (06-11-93, Doyle, #72, illus.), 12⅜ x 14¾ in., (314 x 375 mm.), aquatint.

$495* *Sleeping Women In Landscape,* s., (09-17-92, Sloan, #2371), 10½ x 15 in., (26.7 x 38.1 cm.), etching and aquatint (BP 278, DM 735, FR 2515, Y 61,628).

REED, Ethel

$495* *Folly Or Saintliness, 1895,* Lamson Wolffe and Co., A cond., (08-06-92, Swann, #230, illus.), 20¼ x 14¾ in., (51.4 x 37.5 cm.), (BP 259, DM 731, FR 2470, Y 63,138).

$412* *The House Of Trees, 1895,* Lamson, Wolffe and Co., A cond., (08-06-92, Swann, #232, illus.), 18 x 9½ in., (45.7 x 24.1 cm.), (BP 215, DM 609, FR 2056, Y 52,551).

$715* *Miss Traumerei, 1895,* Lamson, Wolffe and Co., A-cond., marginal discoloration, (08-06-92, Swann, #231, illus.), 22 x 13¾ in., (55.9 x 34.9 cm.), (BP 373, DM 1056, FR 3568, Y 91,199).

REED, John E.

$93* *Virginia Cherril,* (10-10-92, Bonhams, #89, illus.), 10 x 8 in., (25.4 x 20.3 cm.), photograph (BP 55, DM 138, FR 464, Y 11,322).

REED, Joyce Hagerbaumer

$133* *Backwater Teal,* s., #76/450, remarqued, (10-21-92, Maynard, #197), 16¾ x 22½ in., (42.5 x 57.2 cm.), print (BP 83, DM 201, FR 683, Y 16,200, C$ 165).

REES

$1320* *Knee-Up Standing Pose Of A Confederate Soldier With Pistol Tucked InHis Belt, Sword, Cross Belt, Etc.,* s. Rees, excell. cond., (10-31-92, Riba, #76, illus.), photograph, 1/6 plate ambrotype (BP 863, DM 2072, FR 7018, Y 163,205).

$770* *Seated Rebel Captain,* s. in emulsion Rees, spotting and tarnish, excell. cond., (10-31-92, Riba, #65, illus.), photograph, 1/4 plate ambrotype (BP 503, DM 1209, FR 4094, Y 95,203).

REES, Lloyd Frederic   1895-1988

$1216* *O'Connell Landscape,* s. Lloyd Rees, d. '80, pen on image, lit., (08-11-92, L. Joel, #42G), 19⅞ x 25¹⁵⁄₁₆ in., (50.5 x 66 cm.), hand-colored lithograph (BP 632, DM 1785, FR 6044, Y 155,718, A$ 1650).

REEVE, Kenneth

$77* *"The Covered Well",* (09-20-92, Jackson, #97), 4 x 5 in., (10.2 x 12.7 cm.), etching (BP 45, DM 114, FR 391, Y 9517).

REEVE, R.G.

$1150* *Hare Hunting: A Pair,* after R.P. Hodges, 1836, t., (04-07-93, Sotheby-Arcade, #19), sight 15 x 21 in., (38.1 x 53.3 cm.), hand-colored engraving (BP 760, DM 1860, FR 6294, Y 130,652).

REEVE, R.G. (after Henry ALKEN)

BI *Cock Fighting: Set Of Four,* later impressions, trimmed, mounted, est. BP 70/100, (10-27-92, Phillips-London, #97), sheet 6½ x 8⅓ in., (165 x 212 mm.), aquatint w/ hand-coloring on wove.

REEVE, R.G. (after James POLLARD)

$609* *"Fly Fishing" and "Bottom Fishing" (Sp. 220), 1881:* Two, 2 from set of 4, later impressions, trimmed inside platemark, waterstains, (10-27-92, Phillips-London, #98), image 13⅓ x 17¼ in., (339 x 438 mm.), aquatint w/ hand-coloring on laid (BP 385, DM 933, FR 3167, Y 74,495).

REEVE, R.G. and A. W. (after J. WARD)

$957* *Vivid And Waterwich Off Orfordness In A Breeze,* laid, defects in image, good cond., coloring, (10-27-92, Phillips-London, #84), image 17⅝ x 26¾ in., (448 x 679 mm.), aquatint in blue/black finished by hand on wove (BP 605, DM 1467, FR 4977, Y 117,064).

REGGIANI, Mauro
$705* *Untitled: Three,* #52/75 and 54/75, foglio, all s., (05-20-93, Finarte-Milan, #137), 27⁹⁄₁₆ x 19¹¹⁄₁₆ in., (70 x 50 cm.), serigraph in colors (BP 453, DM 1137, FR 3832, Y 77,849, L 1035).

REGNAULT, Nicolas Francois
BI *Le Bain,* after P. A. Baudouin, trimmed to borderline, close to title, rubbingand staining, est. BP 6/800, (12-03-92, Sotheby-London, #93), 6¾ x 4⅝ in., (173 x 118 mm.), aquatint in colors.

REGO, Paula
$809* *Figures With Dog, 1987: Three Plates,* two s., one d., two i. A/P, one #6/50, full margins, good cond., tape-hinges, (10-15-92, Sotheby-London, #125, illus.), 9⅞ x 9⅞ in., (25.1 x 25.1 cm.), etching w/aquatint on wove (BP 495, DM 1204, FR 4084, Y 97,061).

REICHMANN, Vilem 1908-1991
BI *Begegnung In Trummern (1946), 1990,* s., d., t., annot., prov., lit., est. $1,5/2,000, (04-08-93, Christie-NY, #133, illus.), 15 x 11⅜ in., (38.1 x 28.9 cm.), photograph, gelatin silver print.
BI *Bombardon (1946), 1989,* s., t., d., annot., prov., lit., est. $1,5/1,800, (04-08-93, Christie-NY, #134, illus.), 15¼ x 11½ in., (38.7 x 29.2 cm.), photograph, gelatin silver print.
BI *Selected Images: Nineteen,* (1935-45), each s., prov., lit., images include: Snares (1940); FromThe Workshop of Adolf Loos (1938); Penetration (1945?); Muse Of Luna Park (1941); est. $25/35,000, (10-13-92, Christie-NY, #483A, illus.), first 2¾ x 4¾ in., (7 x 12.1 cm.), majority 8⅝ x 6⅝ in., (7 x 12.1 cm.), photograph, gelatin silver prints.

REIFFERSCHEID, Heinrich 1872-1945
BI *Rheinlandschaft,* plate mono. HR, s. HReifferscheid, creased, est. DM 200-, (09-14-92, Venator/Hansten, #2533), plate 5½ x 8⁷⁄₁₆ in., (13.9 x 21.5 cm.), etching on Van-Gelder hand-made.

REINAGLE, Philip (after)
BI *American Bog Plants,* by Sutherland, staining, foxing, est. BP 1/200, (09-17-92, Bonhams-Chelsea, #93), image 17¼ x 14 in., (43.8 x 35.6 cm.), hand-colored aquatint.
$263* *Coursing,* by Nicholas and Bluck, pub. W.D. Jones, 1815, margins, surface dirt, (06-30-93, Bonhams-Chelsea, #68), plate 19 x 24½ in., (48.3 x 62.2 cm.), aquatint w/ hand-coloring (BP 176, DM 449, FR 1513, Y 28,180).
$1219* *"Moor Shooting" and "Snipe Shooting" (Sp. 235), 1807: Two,* former by Lewis and Nichols, latter by Nichols and Bluck, pub. Random and Sneath, foxed, good cond., (10-27-92, Phillips-London, #92), aquatint, part p. in colors, finished by hand (BP 770, DM 1868, FR 6339, Y 149,113).

REINDEL, Edna American 1900-1990
$165* *Portfolio Of Eight,* (03-25-93, Boos, #619), woodcut (BP 112, DM 271, FR 922, Y 19,330).

REINDEL, William George American 1871-1948
$55* *Portfolio Of Thirteen,* (03-25-93, Boos, #618), drypoints and etchings (BP 37, DM 90, FR 307, Y 6443).

REINHOLD, Nono b. 1935
$261* *Tout Le Matin, 1960,* s., t., d., i. epr. d'essai, margins, good cond., creases, (12-09-92, Sotheby-Amstrdm, #635), 10¼ x 14¹⁵⁄₁₆ in., (260 x 380 mm.), color etching w/embossing and aquatint on Arches (BP 167, DM 410, FR 1398, Y 32,362, G 460).

REINHOUD b. 1928
BI *Avec Moi On Ne S'Habitue Jamais,* s., t., #18/22, good cond.?, sheet 570 x 4 x 393 mm, est. G 3/400, (12-09-92, Sotheby-Amstrdm, #636), color etching on wove.
BI *Les Indications Pour Se Perdre,* s., t., #20/20, good cond.?, est. G 3/400, (12-09-92, Sotheby-Amstrdm, #637), sheet 18⁹⁄₁₆ x 20¹⁄₁₆ in., (472 x 510 mm.), color etching on wove.

REJLANDER, Oscar Gustave 1813-1875
$5150* *Genre, Nude And Art Reproduction Photographs, 1850s-60s: 117,* and others, several ink t., lit., (10-29-92, Christie-London, #39, illus.), largest approx. 7½ x 5½ in., (19.1 x 14 cm.), photograph, albumen print (BP 3300, DM 7923, FR 26,879, Y 637,929).
$36* *"Grace Darling, Febry 1873",* t., d. in ink, photog.'s ink credit stamp, (05-06-93, Christie-London, #60), carte-de-visite (BP 23, DM 57, FR 191, Y 3961).
BI *Portraits Of Mrs. Rejlander, c. 1857: Two,* each w/arched top, est. $1,2/1,800, (10-15-92, Sotheby-NY, #85, illus.), each approx. 7⅞ x 5⅞ in., (20 x 14.9 cm.), photograph, albumen prints.

REKIZAN Japanese
$39* *"Gray Carp",* 20th cent., seal mark, (06-11-93, DuMouchelle, #2364), 9½ x 9¾ in., (24.1 x 24.8 cm.), color woodblock print (BP 26, DM 63, FR 214, Y 4138).

RELANG, Regina 1906-1989
BI *Modell Rostock, 40's,* t., (c), est/ DM 400, (11-12-92, Lempertz, #195, illus.), 11⁷⁄₁₆ x 8⅝ in., (29 x 21.9 cm.), photograph, gelatin silver print.

REMBRANDT Dutch 1606-1669
BI *The Flight Into Egypt: Crossing A Brook (B., Holl. 55; H. 276; BB 54-D), 1654*square plate corners, burr, plate tone, small margins, thin spots, foxing, stray touches of grey wash in image, good cond., ex-coll., Dr. Otto Schaefer Collection, est. $12/16,000, (05-13-93, Sotheby-NY, #15, illus.), 3¹¹⁄₁₆ x 5¹¹⁄₁₆ in., (93 x 144 mm.), etching and drypoint.
BI *The Hundred Guilder Print (B., Holl. 74; H. 236; BB 49-1), c. 1649*burr, selectively wiped, extra plate tone, wide margins, waterstains, fold, touched-in paper flaw, surface disturbances, foxing, good cond., ex-coll., Dr. Otto Schaefer Collection, est. $200/300,000, (05-13-93, Sotheby-NY, #17, illus.), 11 x 15½ in., (278 x 395 mm.), etching, drypoint and burin on thick buff-colored Japan.
$1610* *Abraham And Issac (B., Holl. 34, H. 215, BB. 45-D), 1645,* later impression, narrow margins, laid down, (05-11-93, Christie-NY, #35), plate 6⅛ x 5 in., (156 x 127 mm.), etching and engraving on laid (BP 1028, DM 2536, FR 8546, Y 177,098).
$805* *Abraham Caressing Isaac (B. 33), 1637,* 2nd final state, margins trimmed to or w/in platemark, good cond.,slight wear to image, hinge remains, skinned areas, staining, rubbed in image,surface soiling, notations, prov., inkstamp, (05-19-93, Butterfield, #1866), 4⅝ x 3½ in., (117 x 89 mm.), etching on laid (BP 523, DM 1309, FR 4409, Y 89,118).
$605* *Abraham Caressing Isaac (Bartsch 33), c. 1637,* second (final) state, (10-08-92, Grogan, #648), 4⁹⁄₁₆ x 3⁷⁄₁₆ in., (11.6 x 8.7 cm.), etching (BP 360, DM 895, FR 3037, Y 73,512).
$5798* *Abraham Casting Out Hagar And Ishmael (B., Holl. 30; H. 149; B.B.37-A), 1637,* approx. 25-30mm margins, creases, discoloration, (12-03-92, Sotheby-London, #96, illus.), 5 x 3¾ in., (127 x 97 mm.), etching on paper w/ watermark (BP 3740, DM 9118, FR 31,122, Y 721,413).
$1776* *Abraham Chassant Agar Et Ismael (B.B., 37, A), 1637,* w/out margins, (02-03-93, Ader Tajan, #39), 4¹⁵⁄₁₆ x 3¾ in., (12.6 x 9.5 cm.), etching (BP 1240, DM 2924, FR 9916, Y 220,923).
BI *Abraham Die Engel Bewirtend (B. 29; Seilitz; Hollstein 29; Nowell-Usticke 29 i), 1656,* watermark, est. DM 20,000, (12-04-92, Bassenge, #6374), 6⅛ x 5³⁄₁₆ in., (15.6 x 13.1 cm.), etching.
$16,799* *Abraham Die Engel Bewirtend (Bartsch, Rovinski, Seidlitz 29, White-Boon 29), 1656,* prov., (06-23-93, Kornfeld, #85, illus.), etching and drypoint (BP 11,412, DM 28,425, FR 95,612, Y 1,830,156, SF 25,300).
$23,873* *Abraham Entertaining The Angels (B., Holl. 29; H. 286; B.B. 56-B), 1656,* only state, margins, foxmark, very good cond., ex-coll., (12-03-92, Sotheby-London, #94, illus.), 6¼ x 5¼ in., (160 x 132 mm.), etching and drypoint (BP 15,400, DM 37,542, FR 128,143, Y 2,970,387).
BI *Abraham Entertaining The Angels (B., Holl. 29; H. 286; B.B. 56-B), 1656,* thread margins, repaired tears in image, thins spots, staining, goodcond., est. BP 10/15,000, (12-03-92, Sotheby-London, #95, illus.), 6¼ x 5¼ in., (158 x 132 mm.), etching and drypoint.

$25,300* *Abraham Entertaining The Angels (B., Holl. 29; H. 286; BB 56-B), 1656,* touches of burr, plate tone, margins, repair, thin spots, discoloration, good cond., Dr. Otto Schaefer Collection, (05-13-93, Sotheby-NY, #10, illus.), 6¼ x 5⅛ in., (160 x 131 mm.), etching and drypoint (BP 16,610, DM 40,853, FR 137,800, Y 2,824,606).

BI *Abraham Entertaining The Angels (B., Holl. 29; H. 286; BB 56-B), 1656,* burr, touches grey wash, thin spots, good cond., est. $7/9,000, (05-13-93, Sotheby-NY, #176), 6⅛ x 5⅛ in., (156 x 131 mm.), etching and drypoint.

$6900* *Abraham Francen, Apothecary (B., Holl. 273; H. 291; BB 57-2), c. 1657,* 7th state of 10, plate tone, narrow margins, flaws in image, good cond., ex-coll., Dr. Otto Schaefer Collection, (05-13-93, Sotheby-NY, #48, illus.), 6¼ x 8¼ in., (158 x 208 mm.), etching, drypoint and burin (BP 4530, DM 11,142, FR 37,582, Y 770,347).

$916* *Abraham Francen. Apotheker Und Kunstsammler (B.R.S. 273; Wh.-B. 273/X), c. 1657,* p.l., (06-23-93, Kornfeld, #101), etching (BP 622, DM 1550, FR 5213, Y 99,793, SF 1380).

BI *Abraham's Sacrifice,* est. $4/700, (11-01-92, Hanzel, #261), 6⅛ x 5¼ in., (15.6 x 13.3 cm.), etching.

BI *Abraham's Sacrifice (B. Holl. 35, H. 283, BB. SS-B),* narrow margins, mounted, thin patch, stains, good cond., prov., est.BP 7/9,000, (11-30-92, Phillips-London, #298, illus.), plate 6⅛ x 5⅛ in., (156 x 130 mm.), etching w/ drypoint, touches of burr on laid.

$43,700* *Abraham's Sacrifice (B., Holl. 35; H. 283; BB 55-B), 1655,* burr, polishing scratches, margins, good cond., thin spots, traces glue, Dr. Otto Schaefer Collection, (05-13-93, Sotheby-NY, #11, illus.), 6⅛ x 5⅛ in., (156 x 131 mm.), etching and drypoint (BP 28,690, DM 70,564, FR 238,017, Y 4,878,866).

$4662* *Adam And Eve (B., Holl 28; H. 159; BB. 38-D), 1638,* 2nd (final) state, trimmed, borderline partly made up in pen and ink, thin spots, staining, (12-01-92, Christie-London, #117), 6¼ x 4½ in., (159 x 114 mm.), etching (BP 3080, DM 7431, FR 25,323, Y 580,428).

$3432* *Adam And Eve (B., Holl. 28; H. 159; B. B. 38-D, 1638,* damaged impression of 2nd final state, narrow margins, repaired area,pen and ink re-touching, laid down, (06-30-93, Sotheby-London, #211), 6½ x 4⅝ in., (165 x 117 mm.), etching on paper w/Wr from a Strasburg Lily watermark (BP 2300, DM 5854, FR 19,747, Y 367,727).

$880* *The Adoration Of The Shepherds, With The Lamp (Bartsch 45, Hind 273), c. 1654,* 2nd state, small margins, (12-08-92, Swann, #257, illus.), 4⅛ x 5 1/16 in., (10.5 x 12.9 cm.), etching (BP 552, DM 1370, FR 4671, Y 109,073).

$1540* *Adoration Of The Shepherds: A Night Piece (Hind 255. Bartsch 46), 1652,* sixth or seventh state of 9, thread margins, rust spot, (05-27-93, Swann, #233, illus.), 5⅞ x 7⅝ in., (14.9 x 19.4 cm.), etching, engraving, and drypoint on wove paper (BP 986, DM 2471, FR 8329, Y 165,094).

$2200* *"Adoration Of The Shepherds: A Night Piece",* (12-12-92, A. James, #34), sheet 6¼ x 7⅞ in., (15.9 x 20 cm.), etching (BP 1411, DM 3466, FR 11,879, Y 272,244).

$10,822* *The Adoration Of The Shepherds: With The Lamp (B., Holl. 45, H. 273,BB. 54-1), c. 1654,* first state (of two), watermark, wide margins, creases, staining, surface dirt, good cond., (12-01-92, Christie-London, #122, illus.), P. 4⅛ x 5 1/16 in., (105 x 129 mm.), S. 7 5/16 x 8 15/16 in., (105 x 129 mm.), etching (BP 7150, DM 17,249, FR 58,783, Y 1,347,361).

$60,250* *The Adoration Of The Shepherds: With The Lamp (B., Holl. 45; H. 273;BB 54-1), c. 1654,* 1st state of 2, plate tone, narrow margins, thread margin, tip left corner rejoined, thin spots, flecks in center, good cond., ex-coll., Dr. Otto Schaefer Collection, (05-13-93, Sotheby-NY, #12, illus.), 4¼ x 5⅛ in., (107 x 130 mm.), etching (BP 39,555, DM 97,287, FR 328,159, Y 6,726,583).

$1870* *The Adoration Of The Shepherds: With The Lamp (Bartsch 45), 1654,* second (final) state, (10-08-92, Grogan, #644, illus.), 5⅛ x 5⅛ in., (13 x 13 cm.), etching (BP 1113, DM 2766, FR 9388, Y 227,217).

$2035* *"The Adoration Of The Shepherds: With The Lamp" (Bartsch #45, Hind #273), c. 1654,* c. 1654, II/III, s. Rembrandt F, (02-13-93, Neal, #546, illus.), 4¼ x 5 1/16 in., (10.8 x 12.9 cm.), etching (BP 1433, DM 3375, FR 11,420, Y 245,417).

$4329* *The Agony In The Garden (B., Holl. 75; H. 293; BB 57-B), c. 1657,* w/ burr, narrow to thread margins, tears, thin spots, good cond., prov., (12-01-92, Christie-London, #128), plate 4 5/16 x 3 5/16 in., (110 x 84 mm.), etching w/drypoint (BP 2860, DM 6900, FR 23,514, Y 538,969).

$1558* *Die Anbetung Der Hirten, Mit Der Lampe (B. 45, Seidlitz 45 II, Hollstein 45 II, Nowell-Usticke 45 II), c. 1564,* (06-04-93, Bassenge, #5321), 4¼ x 5 1/16 in., (10.8 x 12.9 cm.), etching (BP 1031, DM 2530, FR 8528, Y 168,033).

$3680* *The Angel Appearing To The Shepherds (B., Holl. 44, H. 120, BB. 34-J), 1634,* 3rd final state, trimmed to platemark, repaired tears, repairs, glue-staining, watermark, (05-11-93, Christie-NY, #38), sheet 10¼ x 8⅝ in., (260 x 219 mm.), etching, engraving and drypoint on laid (BP 2349, DM 5797, FR 19,533, Y 404,796).

$3450* *The Angel Appearing To The Shepherds (B., Holl. 44, H. 120, BB. 34-J), 1634,* 3rd final state, margins, creases, good cond., watermark, (05-11-93, Christie-NY, #37, illus.), plate 10 5/16 x 8 11/16 in., (262 x 221 mm.), etching, engraving and drypoint on laid (BP 2202, DM 5435, FR 18,312, Y 379,496).

$14,151* *The Angel Appearing To The Shepherds (B., Holl. 44; H. 120; BB. 34-J), 1634,* 3rd (final) state, thread margins or trimmed, thin spots, creasing, soiling, prov., (12-01-92, Christie-London, #120, illus.), 10 5/16 x 8 9/16 in., (262 x 218 mm.), etching w/drypoint and engraving (BP 9350, DM 22,555, FR 76,866, Y 1,761,828).

$832* *The Angel Appearing To The Shepherds (B., Holl. 44; H. 120; BB. 34-J), 1634,* 3rd (final) state, narrow margins, foxmarks, tape, (12-01-92, Christie-London, #121), P. 10 3/16 x 8⅝ in., (258 x 219 mm.), etching w/drypoint and engraving (BP 550, DM 1326, FR 4519, Y 103,586).

$1332* *The Angel Departing From The Family Of Tobias (B., Holl. 43; H. 185;BB. 41-G), 1641,* 2nd state (of four), trimmed, thin spots, discoloration, (12-01-92, Christie-London, #119), 4 1/16 x 5 15/16 in., (103 x 152 mm.), etching w/drypoint (BP 880, DM 2123, FR 7235, Y 165,837).

$303* *"The Angels Appearing To The Shepards",* p.l., margins trimmed, excellent cond., (10-10-92, Goldberg, #521, illus.), 10¼ x 8½ in., (26 x 21.6 cm.), etching (BP 180, DM 450, FR 1511, Y 36,888).

$60,250* *The Artist Drawing From The Model (B., Holl. 192; H. 231; BB 47-2), c. 1647,* 2nd (final state), burr, wiping scratches, watermark, thread margins, trimmed, thin spots, fox marks, Dr. Otto Schaefer Collection, (05-13-93, Sotheby-NY, #40, illus.), 9⅛ x 7¼ in., (232 x 184 mm.), etching, drypoint and burin (BP 39,555, DM 97,287, FR 328,159, Y 6,726,583).

$3260* *The Artist's Mother Seated At A Table, Looking Right: Three Quarter Length (B., Holl. 343; H. 52; B. B. 31-8),* 2nd state of 3, trimmed, repairs, (06-30-93, Sotheby-London, #224), 5⅝ x 4⅞ in., (143 x 124 mm.), etching on paper w/a Strasburg Bend watermark (BP 2185, DM 5560, FR 18,757, Y 349,298).

$2331* *The Artist's Mother With Her Hand On Her Chest: Small Bust (B., Holl. 349; H. 50; BB. 31-9), 1631,* 2nd (final) state, thread margins or trimmed, surface loss, crease, prov., (12-01-92, Christie-London, #144), plate 3 11/16 x 2⅝ in., (94 x 66 mm.), etching (BP 1540, DM 3715, FR 12,662, Y 290,214).

$6900* *The Artist's Mother, Head And Bust: Three Quarters Right (B., Holl. 354; H. 1; BB 28-A), 1628,* 2nd (final) state, narrow margins, abraded spot in image, rubbed spots, corner creased, collector's mark, Dr. Otto Schaefer Collection, (05-13-93, Sotheby-NY, #44, illus.), 2½ x 2½ in., (65 x 63 mm.), etching (BP 4530, DM 11,142, FR 37,582, Y 770,347).

$917* *The Artist's Mother, Head And Bust: Three-Quarters Right (B. 354),* 2nd final state, late impression, trimmed to/just inside platemark, time-stained, (11-30-92, Phillips-London, #311), sheet 2⅝ x 2⅜ in., (67 x 60 mm.), etching on laid (BP 605, DM 1461, FR 4959, Y 114,126).

BI *The Artist's Mother: Head Only, Full Face (B., Holl. 352; H. 2; B. B.28-B), 1628,* 2nd final state, face printing palely, narrow margins, paper losses,defects, foxed, remains, tape, laid down, ex coll. W. E. Drugulin (L. 2612), est. BP 2/3,000, (06-30-93, Sotheby-London, #225), 2½ x 2½ in., (64 x 64 mm.), etching.

BI *Auf Einem Erdhugel Sitzender Bettler (Seidlitz 174, I),* mono., d. RHL 1630, est. DM 3,500-, (09-14-92, Venator/Hansten, #1590), plate 4⁷⁄₁₆ x 2¹¹⁄₁₆ in., (11.3 x 6.9 cm.), etching.

$3672* *Die Auferweckung Des Lazarus (Bartsch and Seidlitz 72; Hind 198; White-Boon 72 II; BB 42-B II), 1642,* (06-10-93, Hauswedell/Nolt, #149, illus.), etching and drypoint (BP 2402, DM 5979, FR 20,132, Y 389,768).

BI *The Bathers (B., Holl. 195; H. 250; BB 51-B), 1651,* 1st state of 2, dryly p. at extreme left, inky plate edges, plate tone, wiping scratches, narrow margins, repair left corner, repairs or thin spots, collectors' marks partly showing through corner, good cond., ex-coll., Dr. Otto Schaefer Collection, est. $15/25,000, (05-13-93, Sotheby-NY, #36, illus.), 4⅜ x 5⅜ in., (110 x 137 mm.), etching.

$880* *The Bathers (Bartsch 195, Hind 250), 1651,* 2nd state, trimmed, acid spot, plant fibres, good cond.?, (12-08-92, Swann, #258), 4¹⁵⁄₁₆ x 5⁷⁄₁₆ in., (12.5 x 13.8 cm.), etching on old laid paper (BP 552, DM 1370, FR 4671, Y 109,073).

$921* *Der Bauer Mit Weib Und Kind (B. 131, Seidlitz 131 II, Hollstein 131,Nowell-Usticke 131 II), c. 1652,* (06-04-93, Bassenge, #5328), 4⁷⁄₁₆ x 2⁹⁄₁₆ in., (11.3 x 6.5 cm.), etching (BP 609, DM 1496, FR 5041, Y 99,331).

$1364* *Bearded Man In A Furred Oriental Cap And Robe (B., Holl. 263; H. 53;B.B. 31-J), 1631,* fourth (final) state, plate cut down, wear, trimmed to/on platemark,thin spots, discolored, (12-03-92, Sotheby-London, #110), 5¾ x 4¾ in., (145 x 122 mm.), etching (BP 880, DM 2145, FR 7322, Y 169,715).

$3960* *Bearded Man In A Velvet Cap With A Jewel Clasp (Bartsch 313, Hind 150), 1637,* thread margins, fox spots, (12-08-92, Swann, #259, illus.), 3⅜ x 3⁵⁄₁₆ in., (8.6 x 8.4 cm.), etching (BP 2482, DM 6165, FR 21,019, Y 490,828).

$11,500* *Beggar In A High Cap, Standing And Leaning On A Stick (B., Holl. 162; H. 15; BB 31-1), c. 1630,* watermark, narrow margins, repair, fox marks, surface dirt, good cond., Dr. Otto Schaefer Collection, (05-13-93, Sotheby-NY, #7, illus.), 6¼ x 4¾ in., (158 x 122 mm.), etching (BP 7550, DM 18,569, FR 62,636, Y 1,283,912).

$833* *Beggar Seated On A Bank (B. 174), 1630,* thread margins, repaired tears, cockling, (11-30-92, Phillips-London, #307), plate 4½ x 2⅝ in., (114 x 67 mm.), etching on thin wove (BP 550, DM 1327, FR 4505, Y 103,671).

$8625* *Beggar Seated On A Bank (B., Holl. 174; H. 11; BB 30-B), 1630,* trimmed, thin spots, repairs, fold, spot glue, borderline added in brown ink, good cond., ex-coll., Dr. Otto Schaefer Collection, (05-13-93, Sotheby-NY, #43, illus.), 4⅝ x 2¾ in., (117 x 70 mm.), etching (BP 5662, DM 13,927, FR 46,977, Y 962,934).

$550* *Beggar Seated On Bank,* posthumous p., plate 61 from "The Complete Etchings" by H. Abrams, (11-13-92, DuMouchelle, #2014, illus.), 4½ x 2¾ in., (11.4 x 7 cm.), etching (BP 355, DM 863, FR 2912, Y 68,264).

$5750* *Beggar Seated Warming His Hands At A Chafing Dish (B., Holl. 173, H.8, BB. 30-1), c. 1630,* 2nd final state, delicate tone, narrow margins, excell. cond., prov., (05-11-93, Christie-NY, #46, illus.), plate 3¹⁄₁₆ x 1¹³⁄₁₆ in., (78 x 46 mm.), etching on laid (BP 3671, DM 9058, FR 30,520, Y 632,494).

$660* *Beggar Woman Leaning On A Stick (B. 170), 1646,* margins trimmed, good cond., thinned area, wear, creases, surface soiling, pencil notations, (02-24-93, Butterfield, #2699), 3³⁄₁₆ x 2⁷⁄₁₆ in., (81 x 62 mm.), etching & drypoint on laid (BP 460, DM 1071, FR 3632, Y 77,447).

$633* *Beggar Woman Leaning On A Stick (B., Holl. 170; H. 219; BB 46-A), 1646,* Usticke's 3rd state of 6, Basan edit., thread margins, light-staining, corners glued down, good cond., (05-13-93, Sotheby-NY, #184), 3¼ x 2½ in.,

(82 x 65 mm.), etching (BP 416, DM 1022, FR 3448, Y 70,671).

$34,500* *Beggars Receiving Alms At The Door Of A House (B., Holl. 176, H. 233, BB. 48-C), 1648,* 3rd final state, margins, crease, staining, good cond., (05-11-93, Christie-NY, #47, illus.), plate 6⁷⁄₁₆ x 5¹⁄₁₆ in., (164 x 129 mm.), etching, engraving and drypoint on laid (BP 22,024, DM 54,348, FR 183,121, Y 3,794,962).

$4600* *Beggars Receiving Alms At The Door Of A House (B., Holl. 176; H. 233;BB 48-C), 1648,* Holl.'s 3rd (final) state, Usticke's 3rd of 6, narrow margins, brownstain, fox marks, good cond., (05-13-93, Sotheby-NY, #188), 6½ x 5 in., (164 x 128 mm.), etching on laid (BP 3020, DM 7428, FR 25,054, Y 513,565).

$550* *Beggars Series, 1639,* (04-16-93, DuMouchelle, #2171, illus.), 3½ x 2¼ in., (8.9 x 5.7 cm.), etching (BP 361, DM 888, FR 3002, Y 61,846).

$633* *Beheading Of John The Baptist (B. 92), 1640,* 2nd final state, margins, good cond., toned, tear, inkloss in image, surface soiling, notations, (05-19-93, Butterfield, #1868), 5 x 4¹⁄₁₆ in., (127 x 103 mm.), etching on laid Japan (BP 411, DM 1029, FR 3467, Y 70,076).

$1909* *Die Beschneidung (B.R.S. 47, Wh.-B. 47/I (v. II)), 1654,* early print, (06-23-93, Kornfeld, #87, illus.), etching (BP 1297, DM 3230, FR 10,865, Y 207,975, SF 2875).

$2691* *Die Beschneidung, In Breitformat (B. 47, Seidlitz 47 I, Hollstein 47I, Nowell-Usticke 47 I), 1654,* (06-04-93, Bassenge, #5322, illus.), 3¾ x 5¾ in., (9.5 x 14.6 cm.), etching (BP 1780, DM 4370, FR 14,729, Y 290,229).

$2744* *Die Beschneidung, In Breitformat (B. 47; Seidlitz 47 II; Nowell-Usticke II; Hollstein II), 1654,* (12-04-92, Bassenge, #6375, illus.), 3¹¹⁄₁₆ x 5¹¹⁄₁₆ in., (9.4 x 14.4 cm.), etching (BP 1760, DM 4370, FR 14,824, Y 342,572).

$1659* *Die Beschneidung, In Breitformat (B.R.S. 47; Wh.-B. 47/I (v. II), 1654,* trimmed, (12-01-92, Karl/Faber, #126, illus.), etching (BP 1096, DM 2644, FR 9011, Y 206,549).

$2693* *Die Beschneidung, In Breitformat (B.R.S. 47; Wh.-B.47/I), 1654,* artist's proof, watermark, (06-08-93, Karl/Faber, #169, illus.), etching on hand-made (BP 1770, DM 4370, FR 14,716, Y 286,033).

$3033* *Der Bettler Mit Der Glutpfanne (B. 173, Seidlitz, Hollstein, Nowell-Usticke 173 II), c. 1630,* (12-04-92, Bassenge, #6392), 3¹⁄₁₆ x 1¹³⁄₁₆ in., (7.7 x 4.6 cm.), etching (BP 1945, DM 4830, FR 16,386, Y 378,652).

BI *Bildnis Jan Cornelis Sylvius (B.R.S. 280; Wh.-B. 280/II), 1646,* trimmed, holes, prov., est. DM 25/28,000, (12-01-92, Karl/Faber, #135, illus.), etching.

$1245* *Bildnis Jan Uijtenbogaert (B.R.S. 279; Wh.-B. 279/VI), 1635-1653,* later print, (12-01-92, Karl/Faber, #134), etching (BP 823, DM 1984, FR 6763, Y 155,005).

$20,999* *Der Blinde Tobias (B.R.S. 42; Wh.-B 42/I (v. II)), 1651,* prov., early print, (06-23-93, Kornfeld, #86, illus.), etching (BP 14,266, DM 35,531, FR 119,516, Y 2,287,722, SF 31,625).

$2444* *Brustbild Der Mutter Rembrandts (B.R.S. 354, Wh.-B. 354/II), 1628,* (06-23-93, Kornfeld, #102), etching (BP 1660, DM 4135, FR 13,910, Y 266,260, SF 3680).

$2830* *Bust Of An Old Man With A Flowing Beard: The Head Bowed Forward: Left Shoulder Unshaded (B., Holl 325; H. 27; BB. 30-J), 1630,* thread margins, thin spots, staining, touches of grey wash, (12-01-92, Christie-London, #142, illus.), plate 3⁹⁄₁₆ x 2¹⁵⁄₁₆ in., (90 x 76 mm.), etching (BP 1870, DM 4511, FR 15,372, Y 352,341).

$19,550* *Canal With A Large Boat And Bridge (B., Holl. 236; H. 239; BB 50-B),1650,* 2nd (final) state, burr, thread margins most of way around, trimmed,repaired tear, thin spots, i., good cond., Dr. Otto Schaefer Collection, (05-13-93, Sotheby-NY, #71, illus.), 3¼ x 4¼ in., (83 x 108 mm.), etching and drypoint (BP 12,835, DM 31,568, FR 106,481, Y 2,182,650).

$1364* *The Card Player (B., Holl. 136; H. 190; B.B. 41-M), 1641,* second (final) state, margins, damage at corners, tape, good cond., ex-coll., (12-03-92, Sotheby-London, #129), 3⅝ x 3½ in., (92 x 82 mm.), etching (BP 880, DM 2145, FR 7322, Y 169,715).

$550* *The Card Player (Bartsch 136), 1641,* second (final) state, prov., (10-08-92, Grogan, #652), 3½ x 3¼ in., (8.9

x 8.3 cm.), etching (BP 327, DM 813, FR 2761, Y 66,829).

BI *The Cavalry Fight (B., Holl. 117; H. 100; B. B. 32-7)*, 2nd final state, margins, paper thin, repair, dirt, stains, est. BP 2,5/3,000, (06-30-93, Sotheby-London, #206, illus.), 4¼ x 3 in., (108 x 76 mm.), etching.

$9775* *A Cavalry Fight (B., Holl. 117; H. 100; BB 32-7), c. 1632,* Holl.'s 2nd (final) state, Usticke's first of two, wiping scratches,narrow margins, repaired tear, good cond., ex-coll., Dr. Otto Schaefer Collection, (05-13-93, Sotheby-NY, #6, illus.), 4⅛ x 3⅛ in., (104 x 78 mm.), etching (BP 6417, DM 15,784, FR 53,241, Y 1,091,325).

$1249* *A Cavalry Fight (B., Holl. 117; H. 100; BB. 32-7), c. 1632,* 2nd (final) state, thread margins or trimmed, repairs, grey wash additions, (12-01-92, Christie-London, #130), plate 4⅛ x 3⅛ in., (105 x 79 mm.), etching (BP 825, DM 1991, FR 6784, Y 155,503).

$9775* *Christ AT Emmaus: The Larger Plate (B., Holl. 87; H. 282; BB 54-H),* 1654, 2nd state of 3, burr, thread margins, stains, good cond., (05-13-93, Sotheby-NY, #179, illus.), 8¼ x 6¼ in., (211 x 160 mm.), etching, burin and drypoint (BP 6417, DM 15,784, FR 53,241, Y 1,091,325).

$4025* *Christ And The Woman Of Samaria: An Arched Print (B., Holl. 70, H. 294, BB. 570B),* 1657-8, 3rd final state, burr, trimmed, staining, glue, very good cond., prov., Dian Woodner and Andrea Woodner Coll., (05-11-93, Christie-NY, #41, illus.), plate 4⅞ x 6⅛ in., (124 x 156 mm.), etching and drypoint on laid (BP 2569, DM 6341, FR 21,364, Y 442,746).

$6325* *Christ And The Woman Of Samaria: An Arched Print (B., Holl. 70; H. 294; BB 57-B),* 1658, Holl.'s 3rd (final) state, Usticke's 4th of 5, wiped tone, watermark, thread margins or trimmed, thin spots, hinging defects, good cond., Dr. Otto Schaefer Collection, (05-13-93, Sotheby-NY, #24, illus.), 5 x 6⅜ in., (127 x 161 mm.), etching (BP 4152, DM 10,213, FR 34,450, Y 706,152).

$74,000* *Christ Appearing To The Apostles (B., Holl. 89; H. 237; BB 56-A),* 1656, square plate corners, inky edges, tone, paper w/AI countermark, narrow margins, good cond., fox marks, creasing, Dr. Otto Schaefer Collection, (05-13-93, Sotheby-NY, #30, illus.), 6⅜ x 8¼ in., (162 x 210 mm.), etching (BP 48,582, DM 119,490, FR 403,050, Y 8,261,695).

$27,600* *Christ At Emmaus: The Larger Plate (B., Holl. 87; H. 282; BB 54-H),* 1654, 2nd state of 3, burr, plate tone, watermark, narrow to thread margins, trimmed, glued down to sheet, good cond., Dr. Otto Schaefer Collection, (05-13-93, Sotheby-NY, #29, illus.), 8⅜ x 6⅜ in., (213 x 162 mm.), etching, burin and drypoint (BP 18,120, DM 44,566, FR 150,327, Y 3,081,389).

BI *Christ At Emmaus: The Larger Plate (B., Holl. 87; H. 282; BB 54-H),* 1654, 3rd (final) state, good posthumous impression, trimmed along platemark, glued down, good cond., est. $1,6/2,200, (05-13-93, Sotheby-NY, #180), 8¼ x 6⅜ in., (211 x 161 mm.), etching.

$2574* *Christ At Emmaus: The Smaller Plate (B. Holl. 88; H. 121; B. B. 34-K),* 1634, state, wear, narrow margins, tear, defects, ex coll. Blanchard Randall (Lugt 407), (06-30-93, Sotheby-London, #194, illus.), 4⅛ x 2⅛ in., (105 x 54 mm.), etching (BP 1725, DM 4390, FR 14,810, Y 275,796).

$6520* *Christ Before Pilate: Large Plate (B., Holl. 77; H. 143; B. B. 35-K),1636,* Nowell Usticke's 3rd state of 4, burr, margins, paper loss, tears, folds, defects, laid down, (06-30-93, Sotheby-London, #218), 21¾ x 17¾ in., (552 x 451 mm.), etching (BP 4370, DM 11,121, FR 37,514, Y 698,596).

BI *Christ Crucified Between The Two Thieves: "The Three Crosses" (B., Holl. 78; H. 270; BB 53-A),* 1653, 4th state of 5, plate tone, watermark, thread margins, creases, partly broken through and repaired, repairs, repaired tear, nicks, vertical center crease, traces glue, overall good cond., ex-coll., Dr. Otto Schaefer Collection, est. $200/300,000, (05-13-93, Sotheby-NY, #23, illus.), 15⅛ x 17¾ in., (385 x 450 mm.), drypoint and burin.

BI *Christ Crucified Between The Two Thieves: "The Three Crosses" (B. Holl. 78; H. 270; BB 53-A),* 1653, 2nd state of 5, burr, plate tone, watermark, narrow to thread

margins, center crease, nicks, repaired tears, stain, fox marks, good cond., ex-coll., Dr. Otto Schaefer Collection, est. $600/900,000, (05-13-93, Sotheby-NY, #22, illus.), 15⅛ x 17¾ in., (385 x 450 mm.), drypoint and burin.

$5750* *Christ Disputing With The Doctors: A Sketch (B., Holl. 65; H. 257; BB 52-B),* 1652, 1st state of 3, burr, narrow to thread margins, grey wash, thin spots, fox marks, good cond., Dr. Otto Schaefer Collection, (05-13-93, Sotheby-NY, #20, illus.), 5 x 8⅜ in., (126 x 214 mm.), etching and drypoint (BP 3775, DM 9285, FR 31,318, Y 641,956).

BI *Christ Disputing With The Doctors: A Sketch (B., Holl. 65; H. 257; BB. 52-B),* 1651, 2nd state of 3, margins, repaired tear, pinhole, staining, est. BP 1,5/2,000, (12-01-92, Christie-London, #126), plate 5 x 8½ in., (127 x 216 mm.), etching w/drypoint.

$3163* *Christ Disputing With The Doctors: A Sketch (B., Holl.65; H. 257; BB. 52-B),* 1652, 2nd state of 3, margins, loss, good cond., (12-01-92, Christie-London, #125), plate 4¹³⁄₁₆ x 8⁵⁄₁₆ in., (122 x 211 mm.), etching w/drypoint (BP 2090, DM 5041, FR 17,181, Y 393,800).

$3333* *Christ Driving The Money Changers From The Temple (B. 69),* 1635, 1st state of 2, trimmed to plate, light stained, repaired tear, tearinto image, (11-30-92, Phillips-London, #312A), plate 5⅜ x 6⅝ in., (137 x 168 mm.), etching w/drypoint on fine laid (BP 2200, DM 5310, FR 18,026, Y 414,810).

BI *Christ Driving The Money Changers From The Temple (B. 69),* 1635, 2nd final state, good impression, trimmed to plate, defects, thin patch, good cond., est. BP 1,5/2,000, (11-30-92, Phillips-London, #300), sheet 5⅜ x 6⅝ in., (137 x 168 mm.), etching on laid.

BI *Christ Driving The Money Changers From The Temple,* 1635, prov., est. $6/800, (06-13-93, Hindman, #402), 5¼ x 6½ in., (13.3 x 16.5 cm.), etching and engraving.

BI *Christ Healing The Sick. "The Hundred Guilder Print"" (B., Holl. 74;H. 236; BB. 49-1),* 1649, 3rd state of 4, w/ Baillie rework, wide margins, staining, very goodcond., est. BP 3,5/4,000, (12-01-92, Christie-London, #127, illus.), plate 10¹⁵⁄₁₆ x 15¼ in., (278 x 388 mm.), etching w/drypoint and engraving on Japan.

$5457* *Christ Healing The Sick: The Hundred Guilder Print (B., Holl. 74; H.236; B.B. 49-1),* second state, rework by Captain Baillie, margins, central crease, short tear, staining, (12-03-92, Sotheby-London, #120), 11 x 15⅝ in., (280 x 297 mm.), etching on paper w/watermark (BP 3520, DM 8582, FR 29,291, Y 678,985).

$3069* *Christ Healing The Sick; The Hundred Guilder Print (B., Holl. 74; H.236; B.B. 49-1),* Captain Baillie rework, thread margins, laid down on an 18th cent. sheet backed on stretcher, p. label on mount, (12-03-92, Sotheby-London, #121), 11 x 15¾ in., (280 x 399 mm.), etching on chine (BP 1980, DM 4826, FR 16,473, Y 381,859).

$34,500* *Christ Preaching ("La Petite Tombe") (B., Holl. 67; H. 256; BB 52-2), c. 1652,* burr, narrow margins, tear, nicks, foxing, good cond., Dr. Otto Schaefer Collection, (05-13-93, Sotheby-NY, #21, illus.), 6⅛ x 8⅛ in., (155 x 207 mm.), etching, burin and drypoint on a thin laid (BP 22,650, DM 55,708, FR 187,908, Y 3,851,736).

BI *Christ Preaching (La Petite Tombe),* est. $6/800, (11-01-92, Hanzel, #249), 6⅛ x 8½ in., (15.6 x 21.6 cm.), etching.

$1567* *Christ Preaching (La Petite Tombe) (B. 67, H. 256), c. 1652,* later impression, narrow margins, time stained, nick, tear in image, (10-27-92, Phillips-London, #29), (156 x 206 mm.), etching on laid (BP 990, DM 2402, FR 8149, Y 191,682).

BI *Christ Preaching (La Petite Tombe) (B. Holl. 67; H. 256; B. B. 52-2),* margins, repaired tear, paper disturbed, printer's crease, good cond., ex coll. British Rail Pension Fund, est. BP 40/50,000, (06-30-93, Sotheby-London, #198, illus.), 6 x 8 in., (152 x 203 mm.), etching and drypoint, on rather thin laid paper.

$2558* *Christ Preaching (La Petite Tombe) (B., Holl. 67; H. 256; B.B. 52-2),* only state, margins, repaied tear, retouching, surface dirt, (12-03-92, Sotheby-London, #119), 6 x 8½ in., (152 x 206 mm.), etching and drypoint on paper w/watermark (BP 1650, DM 4023, FR 13,731, Y 318,278).

$173,000* *Christ Presented To The People: Oblong Plate (B., Holl. 76; H. 271; BB 55-A), 1655,* slipped in printing at right, Holl.'s 5th state of 8, BB's 4th of 7,plate tone, watermark, narrow to thread margins, rubbed spot, brown stains in image, thin spots, good cond., ex-coll., Dr. Otto Schaefer Collection, (05-13-93, Sotheby-NY, #31, illus.), 14⅛ x 17⅞ in., (358 x 455 mm.), drypoint on heavy laid (BP 113,577, DM 279,348, FR 942,266, Y 19,314,503).

$36,800* *Christ Returning From The Temple With His Parents (B., Holl. 60; H. 278; BB 54-F), 1654,* rich burr, wiping scratches, plate tone, thread margins, trimmed, good cond., Dr. Otto Schaefer Collection, (05-13-93, Sotheby-NY, #18, illus.), 3¾ x 5¾ in., (95 x 145 mm.), etching and drypoint (BP 24,160, DM 59,422, FR 200,436, Y 4,108,518).

$8625* *Christ Seated Disputing With The Doctors (B., Holl. 64; H. 277; BB 54-E) 1654,* burr, wiping scratches, square plate corners, watermark, thread margins, repair, good cond., Dr. Otto Schaefer Collection, (05-13-93, Sotheby-NY, #19, illus.), 3¾ x 5⅝ in., (95 x 144 mm.), etching (BP 5662, DM 13,927, FR 46,977, Y 962,934).

$715* *Christ Seated Disputing With The Doctors (Bartsch 64), 1654,* only state, (10-08-92, Grogan, #651), 3¾ x 5¾ in., (9.5 x 14.6 cm.), etching (BP 425, DM 1058, FR 3589, Y 86,877).

$397* *Christus Am Kreuz Zwischen Den Schachern (B.R.S. 79; Wh.-B. 79), c. 1640,* (06-08-93, Karl/Faber, #172), etching in oval (BP 261, DM 644, FR 2169, Y 42,167).

$464* *Christus Am Olberg, Mit Dem Engel (Nowell-Usticke 75), 1816,* plate s., d. Rembrandt. f: 63, (09-14-92, Venator/Hansten, #1595), plate 4⁵⁄₁₆ x 3¼ in., (11 x 8.3 cm.), etching and drypoint on thin Japan (BP 245, DM 690, FR 2338, Y 57,697).

$6109* *Christus Die Handler Aus Dem Tempel Treibend (B.R.S. 69, Wh.-B. 69/I(v. II)), 1635,* (06-23-93, Kornfeld, #91), etching (BP 4150, DM 10,337, FR 34,769, Y 665,541, SF 9200).

$2527* *Christus Heilt Die Kranken, Genannt Das Hundertgulden-blatt (B. 74; Seidlitz 74 IV; Hollstein 74 S.40; Nowell-Usticke), c. 1649,* prov., (12-04-92, Bassenge, #6379), 10¹⁵⁄₁₆ x 15½ in., (27.8 x 39.3 cm.), etching (BP 1621, DM 4025, FR 13,652, Y 315,481).

$19,090* *Christus In Emmaus (B.R.S. 87; Wh.-B. 87/III), 1654,* prov., (06-23-93, Kornfeld, #94, illus.), etching, engraving, and drypoint (BP 12,969, DM 32,301, FR 108,651, Y 2,079,747, SF 28,750).

$18,967* *Christus Lehrend, Genannt "La Petite Tombe" (B. 67; Bl. 39; M. 229; Dut. 71; H. 256; S. 67; B.-B 52-2; W.-B. 67; N.-U. 67, I), c. 1652,* foxed, prov., watermark, (10-09-92, Winterberg, #888, illus.), 6 x 8¹⁄₁₆ in., (15.3 x 20.5 cm.), etching (BP 11,253, DM 28,174, FR 94,599, Y 2,309,106).

$44,289* *Christus Predigend (B.R.S. 67, Wh.-B. 67), c. 1652,* prov., (06-23-93, Kornfeld, #90, illus.), etching and drypoint on thin Japan (BP 30,088, DM 74,939, FR 252,072, Y 4,825,035, SF 66,700).

$1275* *Christus Und Die Samariterin, Quadratisch (B. 71, Seidlitz 71 III, Hollstein 71 III, Nowell-Usticke 71 II), 1634,* (06-04-93, Bassenge, #5323), 4¾ x 4⅛ in., (12.1 x 10.5 cm.), etching (BP 844, DM 2070, FR 6979, Y 137,511).

$1700* *Christus Vor Pilatus - Das Ecce Homo (Grosses Format) (B. 77, Seidlitz 77 IV-V, Hollstein 77 IV-V, Nowell-Usticke 77 III-IV), 1636,* (06-04-93, Bassenge, #5324), 21⅛ x 17⅜ in., (53.6 x 44.1 cm.), etching (BP 1125, DM 2761, FR 9305, Y 183,348).

$2311* *Christus Vor Pilatus-Das Ecce Homo (Grosses Format) (B. 77, Seidlitz77 IV-V, Hollstein 77 IV-V, Nowell-Usticke 77 III-IV),* (12-04-92, Bassenge, #6380), 21⅛ x 17⅜ in., (53.6 x 44.1 cm.), etching (BP 1482, DM 3681, FR 12,485, Y 288,514).

$11,454* *Christus Zu Grabe Getragen (B.R.S. 84; Wh. B. 84), c. 1645,* watermark, (06-23-93, Kornfeld, #93, illus.), etching and drypoint (BP 7781, DM 19,381, FR 65,191, Y 1,247,848, SF 17,250).

BI *Christus, Die Handler Aus Dem Tempel Treibend (B. 69; Bl. 44; M. 198; Dut. 80; H. 126; S. 69, III; B.-B. 35-B.; W-B. 69, II; N.U. 69, III), 1635,* d. in plate, est. Dm 3,800, (10-09-92, Winterberg, #889, illus.), 5⅜ x 6⅝ in., (13.7 x 16.9 cm.), etching.

$2439* *Christus, Die Handler Aus Dem Tempel Treibend, 1635,* glue, c. 1800, (10-09-92, Winterberg, #890), etching (BP 1447, DM 3623, FR 12,165, Y 296,932).

$1665* *The Circumcision (B., Holl. 48; H. 19; BB. 30-8), c. 1630,* margins, patches, repaired, tear, glue, foxed, defects, (12-01-92, Christie-London, #124), plate 3⁹⁄₁₆ x 2½ in., (90 x 63 mm.), etching w/touches of drypoint (BP 1100, DM 2654, FR 9044, Y 207,296).

$3410* *The Circumcision In The Stable (B., Holl. 47; H. 274; B.B. 54-B),* first state of two, trimmed on or just within platemark, discoloration, (12-03-92, Sotheby-London, #101), 3¾ x 5½ in., (95 x 142 mm.), etching (BP 2200, DM 5362, FR 18,304, Y 424,288).

$2558* *The Circumcision In The Stable (B., Holl. 47; H. 274; B.B. 54-B), 1654,* first state of two, margins, partially glued down, related creases, (12-03-92, Sotheby-London, #100), 3¾ x 5⅝ in., (95 x 143 mm.), etching (BP 1650, DM 4023, FR 13,731, Y 318,278).

$3751* *The Circumcision In The Stable (B., Holl. 47; H. 274; B.B. 54-B), 1654,* first state of two, thread margins, soft fold, thin spots, glue verso, (12-03-92, Sotheby-London, #99, illus.), 3¾ x 5¾ in., (96 x 146 mm.), etching on paper w/watermark (BP 2420, DM 5899, FR 20,134, Y 466,716).

$4162* *The Circumcision In The Stable (B., Holl. 47; H. 274; BB. 54-B), 1654,* 1st state of 2, watermark, margins, tear, creases, residual mounting, good ocnd., (12-01-92, Christie-London, #123, illus.), plate 3¾ x 5¹¹⁄₁₆ in., (96 x 145 mm.), etching (BP 2750, DM 6634, FR 22,607, Y 518,177).

$935* *The Circumcision In The Stable (Bartsch 47), 1654,* second (final) state, (10-08-92, Grogan, #647), 3¾ x 5¾ in., (9.5 x 14.6 cm.), etching (BP 556, DM 1383, FR 4694, Y 113,609).

$3738* *The Circumcision In the Stable (B., Holl. 47; H. 274; BB 54-B), 1654,* 1st state of 2, watermark, good margins, drying (?) crease, thin, spots, good cond., collectors' marks, Dr. Otto Schaefer Collection, (05-13-93, Sotheby-NY, #13, illus.), 3¾ x 5⅝ in., (94 x 144 mm.), etching (BP 2454, DM 6036, FR 20,359, Y 417,327).

$920* *Clement De Jonghe, Printseller (B. 272), 1651,* 6th final state, ink additions, margins trimmed w/in image, good cond., toned, glue/paper remains, (05-19-93, Butterfield, #1874), 7¹³⁄₁₆ x 5¹⁵⁄₁₆ in., (198 x 151 mm.), etching and burin on laid (BP 597, DM 1495, FR 5038, Y 101,849).

BI *Clement De Jonghe, Printseller (B., Holl. 272; H. 251; BB 51-C), 1651,* 4th state of 6, burr, narrow margins, fold, rust stain, fox marks, discoloration, good cond., Dr. Otto Schaefer Collection, est. $40/60,000, (05-13-93, Sotheby-NY, #51, illus.), 8⅛ x 6⅜ in., (207 x 161 mm.), etching, drypoint and burin.

$1332* *Clement De Jonghe, Printseller (B., Holl. 272; H. 251; BB. 51-c), 1651,* 6th (final) state, trimmed on or inside platemark, staining, small loss, thin spots, (12-01-92, Christie-London, #139), sheet 8⅛ x 6⁵⁄₁₆ in., (206 x 161 mm.), etching w/drypoint and engraving (BP 880, DM 2123, FR 7235, Y 165,837).

$4600* *Cornelis Claesz Anslo, Preacher (B., Holl. 271; H. 187; BB 41-J), 1641,* Holl.'s 2nd (final) state, Usticke's 3rd of 6, as reworked by Capt. Baillie, good margins, thin spots, surface loss in image, good cond., ex-coll.,Dr. Otto Schaefer Collection, (05-13-93, Sotheby-NY, #47, illus.), 7⅜ x 6¼ in., (188 x 158 mm.), etching and drypoint, on China (BP 3020, DM 7428, FR 25,054, Y 513,565).

$16,100* *Cottage With A White Paling (B., Holl. 232; H. 203; BB 52-E), 1648,* 2nd (final) state, burr, margins, crease, thin spots, light-staining,good cond., ex-coll. John Barnard and P. Davidsohn, (05-13-93, Sotheby-NY, #194, illus.), 5⅛ x 6¼ in., (130 x 160 mm.), etching and drypoint (BP 10,570, DM 25,997, FR 87,691, Y 1,797,477).

BI *"The Crucifixion" (Hollstein, 80), c. 1635,* small plate, 19th cent. printing, good cond., thin margins, toning, est. $800/1200, (06-25-93, Skinner, #121A), 3¾ x 2⅝ in., (9.5 x 6.7 cm.), etching on laid.

$2300* *The Crucifixion: Small Plate (B., Holl. 80, H. 123, BB. 35-1), 1635,* thread margins, surface soiling, good cond., (05-11-93, Christie-NY, #42), plate 3¾ x 2¾ in., (95 x

70 mm.), etching on laid (BP 1468, DM 3623, FR 12,208, Y 252,997).

$9200* *The Crucifixion: Small Plate (B., Holl. 80; H. 123; BB 35-1), c. 1635,* Holl.'s only state, Usticke's 1st of 4, Rembrandt's sig. printing clearly, diagonal scratch distinct, wiped tone, watermark, wide margins, repairedtear, folds, good cond., Dr. Otto Schaefer Collection, (05-13-93, Sotheby-NY, #26, illus.), 3¾ x 2⅝ in., (95 x 67 mm.), etching (BP 6040, DM 14,855, FR 50,109, Y 1,027,130).

BI *The Cruxifixion: Small Plate (B. Holl. 80; H. 123; B. B. 35-1),* only state, sig., narrow margins, good cond., est. BP 3/4,000, (06-30-93, Sotheby-London, #193, illus.), 3¾ x 2⅝ in., (95 x 67 mm.), etching.

BI *Cupid Resting,* est. $2/300, (02-14-93, Hanzel, #678), 3½ x 4¾ in., (8.9 x 12.1 cm.), etching.

BI *Cupid Resting,* est. $2/300, (11-01-92, Hanzel, #273), 3½ x 4¾ in., (8.9 x 12.1 cm.), etching.

$2401* *Die Darstellung Im Tempel Im Breitformat (Bartsch and Seidlitz 49; Hind 62; White-Boon 49 III; BB 40-1 III),* watermark, (06-10-93, Hauswedell/Nolt, #148), etching on hand-made (BP 1571, DM 3910, FR 13,163, Y 254,856).

$1035* *The Death Of The Virgin (B. 99), 1639,* 3rd final state, margins, good cond., wear to image, crease through-center, tear, hinge remains, surface soiling, (05-19-93, Butterfield, #1869), 116³⁄₁₆ x 12¼ in., (295.1 x 31.1 cm.), etching and drypoint on laid (BP 672, DM 1682, FR 5668, Y 114,580).

$3069* *The Death Of The Virgin (B., Holl. 99; H. 161; B.B. 39-A),* third (final) state, thread margins or trimmed on platemark, nicks, tears, laid down, surface dirt, (12-03-92, Sotheby-London, #125), 16⅛ x 12½ in., (410 x 318 mm.), etching (BP 1980, DM 4826, FR 16,473, Y 381,859).

$36,800* *The Death Of The Virgin (B., Holl. 99; H. 161; BB 39-A), 1639,* 1st state of 3, burr, watermark, thread margins or trimmed, drying (?) crease, defects, good cond., ex-coll., Dr. Otto Schaefer Collection, (05-13-93, Sotheby-NY, #32, illus.), 16⅛ x 12⅜ in., (409 x 315 mm.), etching and drypoint (BP 24,160, DM 59,422, FR 200,436, Y 4,108,518).

$1925* *The Death Of The Virgin (H. 161; B. 99) (II/III),* s., d. 1639 in plate, (09-17-92, Sloan, #3120, illus.), 15½ x 12¼ in., (39.4 x 31.1 cm.), etching (BP 1081, DM 2858, FR 9782, Y 239,666).

$2339* *The Death Of The Virgin (Hind 161, Bartsch 99, Blanc 70),* 4th final state, trimmed w/in margins, repaired tears/ corners, watermark, back cover illus., (11-19-92, Bonhams-Chelsea, #149), sheet 15½ x 12¼ in., (39.4 x 31.1 cm.), etching (BP 1540, DM 3729, FR 12,562, Y 290,884).

BI *Death Of The Virgin [H.161;B.99](II/III),* s., d. 1639 in plate, est. $2,4/2,600, (12-10-92, Sloan, #3032, illus.), 15½ x 12¼ in., (39.4 x 31.1 cm.), etching.

$2164* *The Descent From The Cross (B., Holl. 81II; H. 103; BB. 33-C), 1633,* 5th (final) state, margins, surface, defects, discoloration, (12-01-92, Christie-London, #129), plate 20⅞ x 16¹⁄₁₆ in., (530 x 408 mm.), etching w/ engraving (BP 1430, DM 3449, FR 11,754, Y 269,422).

$348* *The Descent From The Cross - Second Plate (B. 81 II),* grey impression after re-working of plate, pub. Lamoureux, 1/4 in. margins, nicks, remains tape, (10-27-92, Phillips-London, #30), plate 20⅞ x 16⅛ in., (530 x 410 mm.), etching on wove (BP 220, DM 533, FR 1810, Y 42,569).

BI *The Descent From The Cross By Torchlight (B. 83), 1654,* later impression, narrow margins, foxed, corner mounted onto supportsheet, creases, est. BP 7/900, (10-27-92, Phillips-London, #31), plate 8⅛ x 6⅜ in., (206 x 162 mm.), etching.

$1184* *The Descent From The Cross By Torchlight (B. 83), 1654,* later impression w/wear, trimmed to plate, remargined, time stained, (10-27-92, Phillips-London, #32), image 8⅛ x 6⅜ in., (206 x 162 mm.), etching on laid (BP 748, DM 1815, FR 6157, Y 144,832).

BI *The Descent From The Cross By Torchlight (B. 83), 1654,* later impression, thread margins, foxed, thin patches, est. BP 1,5/2,000, (11-30-92, Phillips-London, #302), plate 8⅛ x 6⅜ in., (206 x 162 mm.), etching on laid.

BI *The Descent From The Cross By Torchlight (B., Holl. 83; H. 280; B. B.54-G), 1654,* burr, platemark rough and inky in places, margins, narrow, rubbed, crease, est. BP 30/40,000, (06-30-93, Sotheby-London, #199, illus.), 8¼ x 6¼ in., (210 x 159 mm.), etching and drypoint.

$1373* *The Descent From The Cross By Torchlight (B., Holl. 83; H. 280; B. B.54-G), 1654,* only state (Nowell-Usticke's 1st of 3) before rework, wear in shadedareas, narrow margins, nicks, discoloration, (06-30-93, Sotheby-London, #219), 8¼ x 6⅜ in., (210 x 162 mm.), etching (BP 920, DM 2342, FR 7900, Y 147,112).

$20,700* *The Descent From The Cross By Torchlight (B., Holl. 83; H. 280; BB 54-G), 1654,* traces burr, watermark, good margins, glue stains, surface dirt, good cond., Dr. Otto Schaefer Collection, (05-13-93, Sotheby-NY, #27, illus.), 8¼ x 6⅜ in., (210 x 161 mm.), etching and drypoint (BP 13,590, DM 33,425, FR 112,745, Y 2,311,042).

BI *The Descent From The Cross By Torchlight (B., Holl. 83; H. 280; BB 54-G), 1654,* dryly p. in shading, watermark, narrow margins, tip rejoined, repaired tear, wash strokes, thin spots, remains of backing, nick, good cond., ex-coll. R P B, est. $10/15,000, (05-13-93, Sotheby-NY, #178, illus.), 8¼ x 6⅜ in., (211 x 162 mm.), etching and drypoint.

$1965* *La Descente De Croix A La Lumiere Des Torches (B.B. 54-G), 1654,* definitive state, thin spots, w/out margins, (06-16-93, Ader Tajan, #18, illus.), 8¼ x 6⅜ in., (20.9 x 16.2 cm.), etching (BP 1310, DM 3262, FR 10,947, Y 209,578).

$4434* *Diana At The Bath (B., Holl. 201; H. 42; B.B. 31-4),* only state, narrow margins, brown stain in image, nicks, minor defects, ex-coll., (12-03-92, Sotheby-London, #105), 7 x 6¼ in., (179 x 160 mm.), etching on paper w/watermark (BP 2860, DM 6973, FR 23,800, Y 551,698).

$4600* *Diana At The Bath (B., Holl. 201; H. 42; BB 31-4), c. 1631,* poorly bitten plate, watermark, narow margins on 3 sides, thread margin, restored paper, repaired tear, glue, spots, good cond., (05-13-93, Sotheby-NY, #190), 7 x 6¼ in., (178 x 160 mm.), etching (BP 3020, DM 7428, FR 25,054, Y 513,565).

$667* *"Les Disciples D'Emmaus" (Hollstein et Rovinski #87), 1654,* thin margins, (03-22-93, Pescheteau, #26), etching (BP 449, DM 1094, FR 3718, Y 77,235).

BI *Die Drei Hutten (B. 217; Seidlitz 217 III; Hollstein 217 III; Nowell-Usticke 217 III), 1650,* prov., est. DM 75,000, (12-04-92, Bassenge, #6396, illus.), 6⅜ x 7⅞ in., (16.2 x 20 cm.), etching.

$929* *Die Drei Orientalen (B. 118; Bl. 7; M. 212; D. 119; H. 183; S. 118, III; B.-B. 41-F; W.-B. 118, II; N.-U. 118, II), 1641,* d. in plate, stained, (10-09-92, Winterberg, #892, illus.), 5⅝ x 4⁷⁄₁₆ in., (14.3 x 11.3 cm.), etching (BP 551, DM 1380, FR 4633, Y 113,100).

$867* *Die Drei Orientalen (B. 118; Seidlitz 118 II; Hollstein 118 II; Nowell-Usticke 118 II), 1641,* (12-04-92, Bassenge, #6385), 5¾ x 4⁷⁄₁₆ in., (14.6 x 11.3 cm.), etching (BP 556, DM 1381, FR 4684, Y 108,240).

$9748* *Der Dreikonigsabend (B. 113; Seidlitz 113 I; Hollstein 113; Nowell-Usticke 113 I), c. 1652,* prov., tear, (12-04-92, Bassenge, #6384, illus.), 3⁹⁄₁₆ x 5⁹⁄₁₆ in., (9.1 x 14.2 cm.), etching (BP 6253, DM 15,525, FR 52,663, Y 1,216,979).

$13,745* *Der Dreikonigsabend (B.R.S. 113, Wh.-B. 113), c. 1651,* early print, (06-23-93, Kornfeld, #95, illus.), etching and drypoint on handmade (BP 9338, DM 23,257, FR 78,230, Y 1,497,440, SF 20,700).

$2337* *Der Engel Verlasst Die Familie Des Tobias (B. 43, Seidlitz 43 III, Hollstein 43 IV, Nowell-Usticke 43 V), 1641,* (06-04-93, Bassenge, #5320), 4¼ x 6⅛ in., (10.8 x 15.5 cm.), etching (BP 1546, DM 3795, FR 12,791, Y 252,049).

$709* *Der Engel Vor Der Familie Des Tobias Verschwindend (B.R.S. 43; Wh.-B.43/IV), 1641,* late print, (06-08-93, Karl/Faber, #168), etching (BP 466, DM 1150, FR 3874, Y 75,305).

$465* *Der Engel Vor Der Familie Des Tobias Verschwindend (B.R.S. 43; White-Boon 43/IV), 1641,* reworked later print, (12-01-92, Karl/Faber, #125), etching (BP 307, DM 741, FR 2526, Y 57,893).

$697* *Der Engel Vor Der Familie Des Tobias Verschwindend (Bartsch 43; Le Blanc 16; Midleton 213; Dutuit 46; Hind 185; Seidlitz 43, III; Bjorklund-Barnard41-G; White-Boon 43, IV; Nowell-Usticke 32, VI), 1641,* d. in plate, foxed, (10-09-92, Winterberg, #887, illus.), 4 1/16 x 6 1/16 in., (10.3 x 15.4 cm.), etching on wove (BP 414, DM 1035, FR 3476, Y 84,855).

$774* *Der Engel Vor Der Familie Des Tobias Verschwindend (Seidlitz 43, III),* plate s., d. Rembrandt f. 1641, (09-14-92, Venator/Hansten, #1593), plate 4 1/16 x 6 in., (10.3 x 15.3 cm.), etching and drypoint (BP 409, DM 1151, FR 3899, Y 96,245).

$55,200* *The Entombment (B., Holl. 86; H. 281; BB 54-2), c. 1654,* 4th (final) state, heavy plate tone, narrow margins, scuff and related rubbed spot, partly touched in, spot, white glue (?), flecks, good cond., Dr. Otto Schaefer Collection, (05-13-93, Sotheby-NY, #28, illus.), 8¼ x 6⅜ in., (211 x 161 mm.), etching, drypoint and burin (BP 36,239, DM 89,133, FR 300,654, Y 6,162,778).

$65,750* *Ephraim Bonus, Jewish Physician (B., Holl. 278; H. 226; BB 47-A), 1647,* 2nd (final) state, burr, background printing clearly, watermark, margins, scrape, crease, folds, collector's mark, good cond., ex-coll., Dr. Otto Schaefer Collection, (05-13-93, Sotheby-NY, #53, illus.), 9½ x 7 in., (241 x 177 mm.), etching, drypoint and burin (BP 43,166, DM 106,168, FR 358,115, Y 7,340,627).

BI *Ephriam Bonus, Jewish Physician,* est. $5/700, (11-01-92, Hanzel, #239), 8¼ x 7 in., (21 x 17.8 cm.), etching.

$2094* *Faust (B. 270; Seidlitz 270 III; Hollstein 270 III; Nowell-Usticke 270 III), c. 1652,* (12-04-92, Bassenge, #6401), 8⅛ x 6 5/16 in., (20.6 x 16 cm.), etching (BP 1343, DM 3335, FR 11,313, Y 261,423).

$55,200* *Faust (B., Holl. 270, H. 260, BB. 52-4), 1652,* 1st state of 3, burr, delicate tone, narrow to thread margins, uninked hairline, right corner made up, foxmarks, thin spots, very good cond., prov., (05-11-93, Christie-NY, #52, illus.), plate 8¼ x 6 5/16 in., (210 x 160 mm.), etching, drypoint and engraving on heavy fibrous oatmeal paper (BP 35,238, DM 86,957, FR 292,994, Y 6,071,939).

$178,500* *Faust (B., Holl. 270; H. 260; BB 52-4), c. 1652,* 1st state of 3, burr, plate tone, small margins, crease, restored paper loss, thin spot, stain in image, flaws inherent in paper, good cond., ex-coll., Dr. Otto Schaefer Collection, (05-13-93, Sotheby-NY, #45, illus.), 8¼ x 6¼ in., (210 x 160 mm.), etching, drypoint and burin on Japan (BP 117,188, DM 288,229, FR 972,222, Y 19,928,548).

BI *Faust (B.R.S. 270; Wh.-B. 270/III), c. 1652,* prov., est. DM 28/30,000, (12-01-92, Karl/Faber, #133, illus.), etching.

$8185* *Faust In His Study (B., Holl. 270; H. 260; B.B. 52),* Hollstein's second state of three, narrow margins, thin patch, ex-coll., (12-03-92, Sotheby-London, #111, illus.), 8¼ x 6½ in., (210 x 160 mm.), etching (BP 5280, DM 12,872, FR 43,935, Y 1,018,415).

$565* *Feuille D'Etude De Tetes D'Hommes (B. Biorklund 31-3, E),* small margins, (02-03-93, Ader Tajan, #38), 1 9/16 x 1 5/16 in., (3.9 x 3.4 cm.), etching (BP 394, DM 930, FR 3155, Y 70,282).

$440* *The First Oriental Head,* (11-01-92, Hanzel, #244), 5⅞ x 4⅞ in., (14.9 x 12.4 cm.), etching (BP 288, DM 694, FR 2339, Y 54,402).

$1650* *The Flight Into Egypt, Crossing A Brook (Bartsch/Hollstein 55, Hind 276), 1654,* posthumous printing, margins, (12-08-92, Swann, #260, illus.), 3¾ x 5¾ in., (9.5 x 14.6 cm.), etching (BP 1034, DM 2569, FR 8758, Y 204,512).

BI *The Flight Into Egypt: Altered From Seghers (B., Holl. 56; H. 266; BB 53-2), c. 1653,* 6th state of 7, vertical line in sky distinct, watermark, margins, partly broken and repaired, thin spots, good cond., Dr. Otto Schaefer Collection, est. $30/40,000, (05-13-93, Sotheby-NY, #16, illus.), 8⅜ x 11 3/16 in., (212 x 284 mm.), etching, burin and drypoint.

BI *The Flight Into Egypt: Crossing A Brook (B. 55), 1654,* later impression, trimmed to plate, defects, mounting, stain, unidentified collector's mark, est. BP 1,8/2,500, (11-30-92, Phillips-London, #299), 3⅝ x 5⅝ in., (92 x 143 mm.), etching on laid.

$2291* *Die Flucht Nach Agypten, Nachstuck (B.R.S. 53; Wh.-B. 53/VI), 1651,* (06-23-93, Kornfeld, #88), etching, engraving, and drypoint (BP 1556, DM 3876, FR 13,039, Y 249,591, SF 3450).

$1275* *Der Goldschmied (B. 123, Seidlitz 123 II, Hollstein 123 II, Nowell-Usticke 123 II), 1655,* collector's stamp E verso, (06-04-93, Bassenge, #5326, illus.), 2 15/16 x 2 3/16 in., (7.6 x 5.6 cm.), etching (BP 844, DM 2070, FR 6979, Y 137,511).

$2455* *Der Goldschmied (B. 123; Seidlitz 123 II; Nowell-Usticke 123 II; Hollstein II), 1655,* prov., (12-04-92, Bassenge, #6386), 2 15/16 x 2 3/16 in., (7.6 x 5.6 cm.), etching (BP 1575, DM 3910, FR 13,263, Y 306,492).

$1470* *Der Goldschmied (B. 123; Wh.-B. 123/II (v. II), 1655,* trimmed, (11-03-92, Hartung, #4073, illus.), etching (BP 949, DM 2300, FR 7794, Y 179,553).

$10,690* *Der Goldschmied (B.R.S. 123, Wh.-B. 123/I (v. II)), 1655,* (06-23-93, Kornfeld, #96, illus.), etching and drypoint on Japan (BP 7262, DM 18,088, FR 60,842, Y 1,164,615, SF 16,100).

$1716* *The Goldsmith (B., Holl. 123; H. 285; B. B. 55-D), 1655,* 1st state of 2, narrow to thread margins, thin spots, ex coll. Maximillian Wellner (L. 1920) and Heath, (06-30-93, Sotheby-London, #203, illus.), 3 x 2⅛ in., (76 x 54 mm.), etching (BP 1150, DM 2927, FR 9873, Y 183,864).

$2046* *The Goldsmith (B., Holl. 123; H. 285; B.B. 55-D),* second state of three, margins, thin areas, partially broken, (12-03-92, Sotheby-London, #102, illus.), 3 x 2¼ in., (76 x 57 mm.), etching (BP 1320, DM 3217, FR 10,982, Y 254,573).

BI *The Goldsmith (B., Holl. 123; H. 285; B.B. 55-D),* later impression, narrow margins, foxing, discoloration, est. BP 6/800, (12-03-92, Sotheby-London, #128), 3 x 2¼ in., (75 x 57 mm.), etching.

$3163* *The Goldsmith (B., Holl. 123; H. 285; BB 55-D), 1655,* 2nd (final) state, narrow margins, 3 sides, trimmed, thin spots, stain, good cond., Dr. Otto Schaefer Collection, (05-13-93, Sotheby-NY, #3, illus.), 3⅛ x 2¼ in., (79 x 58 mm.), etching and drypoint (BP 2077, DM 5107, FR 17,228, Y 353,132).

$4888* *The Goldsmith (B., Holl. 123; H. 285; BB 55-D), 1655,* 1st state of 2, thread margins or trimmed on platemark, nicks, good cond., blind stamp recto, Dr. Otto Schaefer Collection, (05-13-93, Sotheby-NY, #2, illus.), 3⅛ x 2¼ in., (78 x 58 mm.), etching and drypoint (BP 3209, DM 7893, FR 26,623, Y 545,718).

$36,800* *The Goldweigher's Field (B., Holl. 234; H. 249, BB 51-A), 1651,* burr, wiping scratches, watermark, thread margins on 3 sides, trimmed on and w/in platemark left, stains, good cond., ex-coll., Dr. Otto Schaefer Collection, (05-13-93, Sotheby-NY, #69, illus.), 4¾ x 12½ in., (121 x 318 mm.), etching and drypoint (BP 24,160, DM 59,422, FR 200,436, Y 4,108,518).

BI *The Goldweigher's Field (B., Holl. 234; H. 249; BB 51-A), 1651,* burr, double vertical scratch left, watermark, thread margins or trimmed, center crease w/horizontal repaired tear, plugged hole left of center, plugged pin holes or paper defects, good cond., ex-coll., Dr. Otto Schaefer Collection, est. $40/60,000, (05-13-93, Sotheby-NY, #68, illus.), 4¾ x 12⅝ in., (121 x 320 mm.), etching and drypoint, p. on paper brushed w/cool, grey wash, vertical strokes prominent.

$1083* *The Golf Player (B. 125), 1654,* late impression, margins, good cond., (11-30-92, Phillips-London, #304), plate 3¾ x 5⅝ in., (95 x 143 mm.), etching on laid (BP 715, DM 1725, FR 5857, Y 134,785).

$1380* *The Golf Player (B., Holl. 125, H. 272, BB 54-A), 1654,* later impression, margins, (05-11-93, Christie-NY, #44), plate 3 11/16 x 5⅝ in., (94 x 143 mm.), etching on laid (BP 881, DM 2174, FR 7325, Y 151,798).

$8324* *The Golf Player (B., Holl. 125; H. 272; BB. 54-A), 1654,* 1st state of 2, watermark, narrow to thread margins, thin spot, creases, prov., (12-01-92, Christie-London,

#132, illus.), plate 3¾ x 5⅝ in., (95 x 143 mm.), etching (BP 5500, DM 13,267, FR 45,215, Y 1,036,355).

$12,998* *Greis Mit Langem Bart (B. 309; Seidlitz 309; Hollstein 309; Nowell-Usticke 309), 1630,* prov., (12-04-92, Bassenge, #6405), 3⅞ x 3¼ in., (9.8 x 8.2 cm.), etching (BP 8337, DM 20,701, FR 70,222, Y 1,622,722).

$3045* *Greis Mit Langem Bart, Stark Vorgebeugt (B. 235, Seidlitz 325 I, Nowell-Usticke 325), 1630,* (06-04-93, Bassenge, #5330, illus.), 3½ x 2¹⁵⁄₁₆ in., (8.9 x 7.5 cm.), etching (BP 2015, DM 4945, FR 16,667, Y 328,408).

$16,036* *Greis, Die Linke Zum Barett Fuhrend (B.R.S. 259; Wh.-B. 259), c. 1639,* watermark, prov,, (06-23-93, Kornfeld, #100), etching (BP 10,894, DM 27,134, FR 91,269, Y 1,747,031, SF 24,150).

$2520* *Die Grosse Kreuzabnahme (B.R.S. 81, Wh.-B. 81/IV/V), 1633,* watermark, (06-23-93, Kornfeld, #92), etching and engraving (BP 1712, DM 4264, FR 14,343, Y 274,540, SF 3795).

$2300* *Head Of An Old Man In High Fur Cap: Bust (B., Holl. 299; H. 135; BB Rej. 52), c. 1630,* burr, wiping scratches, narrow margins, good cond., ex-coll., not universally accepted as being by Rembrandt, Dr. Otto Schaefer Collection, (05-13-93, Sotheby-NY, #56, illus.), 1¾ x 1¼ in., (44 x 32 mm.), etching and drypoint (BP 1510, DM 3714, FR 12,527, Y 256,782).

$7221* *Die Heilige Familie (B. 62; Seidlitz 62; Hollstein 62; Nowell-Usticke 62 II), c. 1632,* (12-04-92, Bassenge, #6377, illus.), 3¾ x 2¹³⁄₁₆ in., (9.6 x 7.2 cm.), etching (BP 4632, DM 11,500, FR 39,011, Y 901,498).

$42,525* *Der Heilige Franziskus (B.R.S. 107; Wh-B. 107/II), 1657,* watermark, prov., (06-08-93, Karl/Faber, #174, illus.), etching/reworked drypoint (BP 27,955, DM 69,000, FR 232,377, Y 4,516,729).

BI *The Holy Family (B., Holl. 62, H. 95, BB. 32-3), c. 1632,* narrow margins, good cond., est. $7/8,000, (05-11-93, Christie-NY, #40, illus.), plate 3¾ x 2¾ in., (95 x 70 mm.), etching on laid.

BI *Jacob Haaringh ("Younger Haaringh") (B., Holl. 275; H. 288; BB 55-E), 1655,* 2nd state of 5, clean-wiped, hatching printing, misprinted on hat lower leftm watermark, narrow margins, thin spots, one partly broken through and retouched, rust spot, good cond., ex-coll., Dr. Otto Schaefer Collection, est. $60/80,000, (05-13-93, Sotheby-NY, #50, illus.), 7⅝ x 5¾ in., (195 x 146 mm.), etching, drypoint and burin.

$282* *Jakob Liebkost Benjamin (Seidlitz 33, III), c. 1786,* plate s. Rembrandt, (03-24-93, Venator/Hansten, #2567), pl. 4½ x 3½ in., (11.5 x 8.9 cm.), etching (BP 191, DM 461, FR 1568, Y 33,134).

$250* *Jan Asselyn, Painter,* (05-16-93, Hanzel, #474), 7½ x 6⅝ in., (19.1 x 16.8 cm.), etching (BP 163, DM 402, FR 1351, Y 27,713).

$16,675* *Jan Asselyn, Painter, "Krabbetje" (B., Holl. 277, H. 227, BB. 47-1),1647,* 3rd final state, burr, margins, good cond., prov., (05-11-93, Christie-NY, #53, illus.), plate 8½ x 6⅝ in., (216 x 168 mm.), etching w/drypoint and engraving on crisp laid (BP 10,645, DM 26,268, FR 88,508, Y 1,834,232).

BI *Jan Cornelis Sylvius, Preacher,* est. $6/800, (11-01-92, Hanzel, #241), 11 x 7⅜ in., (27.9 x 18.7 cm.), etching.

$9200* *Jan Cornelis Sylvius, Preacher (B., Holl. 266; H. 111; BB 33-H), 1633,* 1st state of 2, watermark, narrow margins, trimmed unevenly, thin spots, nicks, tears, stain, discoloration in image, ex-coll., Dr. Otto Schaefer Collection, (05-13-93, Sotheby-NY, #46, illus.), 6⅝ x 5⅝ in., (168 x 143 mm.), etching (BP 6040, DM 14,855, FR 50,109, Y 1,027,130).

BI *Jan Lutma (B., Holl. 276; H. 299; B. B. 56-C),* 2nd state of 3, burr, margins, good cond., est. BP 6/8,000, (06-30-93, Sotheby-London, #207), 7⅞ x 5⅞ in., (200 x 149 mm.), etching.

BI *Jan Lutma Der Altere (B. 276 II; Seidlitz 276 II; Hollstein 276 II; Nowell-Usticke 276 II), 1656,* watermark, prov., est. DM 15,000, (12-04-92, Bassenge, #6403, illus.), 7¹³⁄₁₆ x 5¹³⁄₁₆ in., (19.8 x 14.7 cm.), etching.

BI *Jan Lutma Der Altere (Goldschmiedemeister)(B. 276, Seidlitz 276II, Hollstein 276II, Nowell Ustike 276II), 1656,* prov., est. DM 6000, (06-04-93, Bassenge, #5331), 7¹³⁄₁₆ x 5¹³⁄₁₆ in., (19.8 x 14.7 cm.), etching.

$3300* *Jan Lutma, Goldsmith (B., Holl. 276), 1652,* 3rd state, (06-11-93, Freemn/Fine Art, #191, illus.), 7¹¹⁄₁₆ x 5¹³⁄₁₆ in., (19.5 x 14.8 cm.), etching and drypoint on French laid (BP 2168, DM 5363, FR 18,082, Y 350,133).

$938* *Jan Lutma, Goldsmith (B., Holl. 276; H. 290; B.B. 56-C), 1656,* third (final) state, narrow margins, repaired tear, laid down at edges, (12-03-92, Sotheby-London, #131), 7¾ x 5⅞ in., (198 x 150 mm.), etching (BP 605, DM 1475, FR 5035, Y 116,710).

$189,500* *Jan Lutma, Goldsmith (B., Holl. 276; H. 290; BB 56-C), 1656,* 1st state of 3, rich burr, plate tone, small margins, good cond., repair, ex-coll., Dr. Otto Schaefer Collection, catalog cover lot, (05-13-93, Sotheby-NY, #55, illus.), 7¾ x 5⅞ in., (196 x 150 mm.), etching and drypoint, on warm-toned European (BP 124,409, DM 305,991, FR 1,032,135, Y 21,156,637).

$6325* *Jan Lutma, Goldsmith (B., Holl. 276; H. 290; BB 56-C), 1656,* 2nd state of 3, margins, good cond., discoloration, (05-13-93, Sotheby-NY, #197), 7¾ x 5⅞ in., (196 x 148 mm.), etching (BP 4152, DM 10,213, FR 34,450, Y 706,152).

BI *Jan Six,* est. $5/700, (11-01-92, Hanzel, #264), 9⅝ x 7⅜ in., (24.4 x 18.7 cm.), etching.

$618,500* *Jan Six (B., Holl. 285; H. 228; BB 47-B), 1647,* Holl.'s 4th (final) state, burr, hatching w/out wear, wide margins, fold through lower quarter, foxing, thin spots, cockling, good cond., ex-coll.,Dr. Otto Schaefer Collection, (05-13-93, Sotheby-NY, #52, illus.), 9⅝ x 7½ in., (244 x 191 mm.), etching, drypoint and burin, on buff-colored Japan (BP 406,053, DM 998,708, FR 3,368,736, Y 69,052,138).

$600* *Jan Utenbogaert, Preacher Of The Remonstrants (B. 79, Holl. 279),* Hollstein's 4th state, 1635 edit., watermark, (06-08-93, Ritchie, #14, illus.), octagonal plate 8¾ x 7¼ in., (22.2 x 18.4 cm.), etching on laid (BP 394, DM 974, FR 3279, Y 63,728, C$ 770).

BI *Jan Uyhenbogaert, Armenian Preacher,* est. $4/700, (11-01-92, Hanzel, #242), 9¾ x 8 in., (24.8 x 20.3 cm.), etching.

$4816* *Jan Uytenbogaart, Der Goldwager (B. 281, Seidlitz 281 III, Hollstein281 II, Nowell-Usticke 281 III), 1639,* (06-04-93, Bassenge, #5332, illus.), 9⅞ x 8¹⁄₁₆ in., (25.1 x 20.5 cm.), etching (BP 3186, DM 7821, FR 26,360, Y 519,413).

$118,000* *Jan Uytenbogaert, "The Goldweigher" (B., Holl. 281; H. 167; BB 39-D), 1639,* Holl.'s 2nd (final) state, Usticke's 1st of 3, thread margins, trimmed, repaired tears, horizontal crease, good cond., collector's mark, Dr. Otto Schaefer Collection, (05-13-93, Sotheby-NY, #54, illus.), 9⅞ x 8 in., (250 x 204 mm.), etching and drypoint (BP 77,468, DM 190,538, FR 642,702, Y 13,174,054).

$3330* *Jan Uytenbogaert, "The Goldweigher" (B., Holl. 281; H. 167; BB. 39-D), 1639,* 3rd (final) state, w/Baillie rework, margins, discoloration, excellent cond., prov., (12-01-92, Christie-London, #141), plate 9¹³⁄₁₆ x 7¹⁵⁄₁₆ in., (250 x 201 mm.), etching w/drypoint (BP 2200, DM 5308, FR 18,088, Y 414,592).

BI *Jan Uytenbogaert, Gold-Weigher,* est. $4/600, (11-01-92, Hanzel, #265), 9¼ x 8 in., (23.5 x 20.3 cm.), etching.

$853* *Jan Uytenbogaert, Goldweigher (B., Holl. 281; H. 167; B.B. 39-D),* third (final) state, Baillie rework, margins, stains, (12-03-92, Sotheby-London, #132), 10 x 8 in., (253 x 205 mm.), etching on India (BP 550, DM 1341, FR 4579, Y 106,134).

$4694* *Janus Sylvius (B. 266; Seidlitz 266 I; Hollstein 266 I; Nowell-Usticke 266 I), 1633,* (12-04-92, Bassenge, #6400), 6⅝ x 5⅝ in., (16.8 x 14.3 cm.), etching (BP 3011, DM 7476, FR 25,359, Y 586,017).

$1654* *Jews In The Synagogue (B. 126),* 3rd and final state, narrow margins, good cond., prov., (10-27-92, Phillips-London, #34), plate 2¾ x 5 in., (70 x 127 mm.), etching on wove (BP 1045, DM 2535, FR 8601, Y 202,324).

$1150* *Jews In The Synagogue (B. 126), 1648,* 3rd final state, later impression, margins trimmed to or inside platemark, good cond., skinned areas, traces of wear to image, notations, (05-19-93, Butterfield, #1870), 2¹³⁄₁₆ x 5⅛ in., (71 x 130 mm.), etching and drypoint on laid (BP 747, DM 1869, FR 6298, Y 127,311).

$10,295* *The Jews In The Synagogue (B. Holl. 126; H. 234; B. B. 48-D),* 2nd state of 3, burr, narrow margins, repaired paper loss, defects, foxing, (06-30-93, Sotheby-London, #196, illus.), 2⅞ x 5¹⁄₁₆ in., (73 x 129 mm.), etching and drypoint (BP 6900, DM 17,559, FR 59,235, Y 1,103,075).

BI *Jews In The Synagogue (Bartsch 126), 1648,* est. $5/700, (10-08-92, Grogan, #646), 2⅞ x 5³⁄₁₆ in., (7.3 x 13.2 cm.), etching.

$3775* *Joseph Telling His Dreams (B., Holl. 37; H. 160; B. B. 38-E), 1638,* Nowell-Ustickes's 2nd state of 5, trimmed, laid down, (06-30-93, Sotheby-London, #212), 4¼ x 3¼ in., (108 x 83 mm.), etching (BP 2530, DM 6439, FR 21,720, Y 404,479).

$1998* *Joseph Telling His Dreams (B., Holl. 37; H. 160; BB. 38-E), 1638,* 3rd (final) state, watermark, trimmed, good cond., (12-01-92, Christie-London, #118), 4⁵⁄₁₆ x 3³⁄₁₆ in., (110 x 81 mm.), etching (BP 1320, DM 3185, FR 10,853, Y 248,755).

$1716* *Joseph's Coat Brought To Jacob (B., Holl. 38; H. 104; B. B. 33-1), c.1633,* 2nd final state, some wear, trimmed, staining, glue stain, good cond., (06-30-93, Sotheby-London, #213), 4¼ x 3⅛ in., (108 x 79 mm.), etching (BP 1150, DM 2927, FR 9873, Y 183,864).

$1444* *Jude In Hoher Mutze (B. 133; Seidlitz 133 I; Hollstein 133; Nowell-Usticke 133 e), 1639,* (12-04-92, Bassenge, #6390), 3¼ x 1¾ in., (8.3 x 4.5 cm.), etching (BP 926, DM 2300, FR 7801, Y 180,275).

$129,000* *Jupiter And Antiope (B., Holl. 203; H. 302; BB 59-B), 1659,* 1st state of 2, inky plate edges, square corners, plate tone, nearlyvertical crease through center, thin spots, good cond., ex-coll., Dr. Otto Schaefer Collection, (05-13-93, Sotheby-NY, #39, illus.), 5⅜ x 8⅛ in., (138 x 205 mm.), etching, burin and drypoint on thick Japan (BP 84,690, DM 208,300, FR 702,614, Y 14,402,144).

$2166* *Jupiter Und Antiope (B. 204; Seidlitz 204 III; Nowell-Usticke und Hollstein 204 II), c. 1631,* prov., (12-04-92, Bassenge, #6395), 3⁵⁄₁₆ x 4⁷⁄₁₆ in., (8.4 x 11.3 cm.), etching (BP 1389, DM 3450, FR 11,702, Y 270,412).

$2549* *Die Kleine Lowenjagd (B. 115, Seidlitz 115 II, Hollstein 115 II, Nowell-Usticke 115 II), c. 1641,* watermark, (06-04-93, Bassenge, #5325), 6⅛ x 4¾ in., (15.5 x 12.1 cm.), etching (BP 1686, DM 4139, FR 13,952, Y 274,914).

$4225* *Die Kleine Lowenjagd Zu Pferd, Mit Einem Lowen (Lugt 1880), c. 1629,* (03-24-93, Venator/Hansten, #2565), pl. 6¼ x 4⅝ in., (15.8 x 11.7 cm.), etching (BP 2861, DM 6900, FR 23,485, Y 496,416).

$2600* *Das Kolf-Speil (B. 125; Seidlitz 125 III; Nowell-Usticke II), 1654,* (12-04-92, Bassenge, #6387), 3¹¹⁄₁₆ x 5½ in., (9.4 x 14 cm.), etching (BP 1668, DM 4141, FR 14,046, Y 324,594).

$1984* *Das Kolf-Spiel (B.R.S. 125; Wh.-B. 125/II), 1654,* prov., (06-08-93, Karl/Faber, #175, illus.), etching (BP 1304, DM 3219, FR 10,842, Y 210,728).

BI *Die Kreuzabnahme Bei Fackelschein (B.R.S. 83; Wh.-B. 83), 1654,* stained, prov., est. DM 5000, (12-01-92, Karl/Faber, #128, illus.), etching.

BI *Landscape With A Cottage And A Large Tree,* est. $700/1,000, (11-01-92, Hanzel, #252), 5 x 12½ in., (12.7 x 31.8 cm.), etching.

$129,000* *Landscape With A Cottage And A Large Tree (B., Holl. 226; H. 178; BB41-B), 1641,* Holl.'s only state, Schneider's 1st state of 2, watermark, narrow margins, touched-in repair, thin spots, nicks, good cond., Dr. Otto Schaefer Collection, (05-13-93, Sotheby-NY, #66, illus.), 5 x 12⅝ in., (127 x 320 mm.), etching (BP 84,690, DM 208,300, FR 702,614, Y 14,402,144).

BI *Landscape With A Cottage And Hay Barn,* est. $5/700, (11-01-92, Hanzel, #262), 5 x 12½ in., (12.7 x 31.8 cm.), etching.

$48,875* *Landscape With A Cottage And Haybarn: Oblong (B., Holl. 225; H. 177;BB 41-A), 1641,* burr on sig., watermark, narrow margins, center crease, partly broken and reinforced, discoloration, thin spots, touches of gray wash in image, good cond., ex-coll., Dr. Otto Schaefer Collection, (05-13-93, Sotheby-NY, #65, illus.), 5⅛ x 12¾ in., (131 x 323 mm.), etching (BP 32,087, DM 78,920, FR 266,204, Y 5,456,626).

$54,625* *Landscape With A Cow (B., Holl. 237; H. 240; BB 50-1), c. 1650,* 2nd (final) state, burr, wiping scratches, watermark, good margins, stain and related rubbed spot, oblique folds, defects, good cond., ex-coll., Dr. Otto Schaefer Collection, (05-13-93, Sotheby-NY, #72, illus.), 4 x 5⅛ in., (103 x 130 mm.), etching and drypoint (BP 35,862, DM 88,204, FR 297,522, Y 6,098,582).

$2331* *Landscape With A Cow (B., Holl. 237; H. 240; BB. 50-1), c. 1650,* watermark, trimmed to/inside platemark, good cond., (12-01-92, Christie-London, #136), S. 4 x 5⅛ in., (102 x 130 mm.), etching w/drypoint (BP 1540, DM 3715, FR 12,662, Y 290,214).

$4995* *Landscape With A Cow (B., Holl. 237; H. 240; BB. 50-1), c. 1650,* watermark, trimmed inside platemark, good cond., (12-01-92, Christie-London, #135, illus.), sheet 4 x 5⅛ in., (102 x 130 mm.), etching w/drypoint (BP 3300, DM 7961, FR 27,132, Y 621,887).

BI *Landscape With A Hay Barn And A Flock Of Sheep (B., Holl. 224; H. 241; BB 52-A), 1652,* 2nd (final) state, burr, thread margins, trimmed, creases, stains, est. $12/15,000, (05-13-93, Sotheby-NY, #193, illus.), 3¼ x 6¾ in., (82 x 173 mm.), etching and drypoint.

BI *Landscape With A Haybarn And a Flock Of Sheep,* est. $5/800, (11-01-92, Hanzel, #247), 3½ x 6⅞ in., (8.9 x 17.5 cm.), etching.

BI *Landscape With A Milkman,* est. $5/800, (11-01-92, Hanzel, #259), 2⅝ x 6⅞ in., (6.7 x 17.5 cm.), etching.

BI *Landscape With A Milkman,* est. $4/600, (11-01-92, Hanzel, #256), 2½ x 6¾ in., (6.4 x 17.1 cm.), etching.

$23,000* *Landscape With A Milkman ("Het Melkboertje") (B., Holl. 213; H. 242;BB 50-2), c. 1650,* 1st state of 2, watermark, good margins, burr enhanced w/wash, surface dirt, good cond., ex-coll., Dr. Otto Schaefer Collection, (05-13-93, Sotheby-NY, #60, illus.), 2⅝ x 6⅞ in., (66 x 174 mm.), etching and drypoint (BP 15,100, DM 37,139, FR 125,272, Y 2,567,824).

BI *Landscape With A Road Beside A Canal (B., Holl. 221; H. 264; BB 52-6), c. 1652,* countermark, thread margins, repair, diagonal fold, fox marks, good cond., ex-coll. N. D. Goldsmid; John William Bender; and Capt. Gordon Nowell-Usticke, est. $5/8,000, (05-13-93, Sotheby-NY, #192), 3⅛ x 8¼ in., (79 x 211 mm.), drypoint.

BI *Landscape With An Obelisk (B., Holl. 227; H. 243; BB 50-3), c. 1650,* 2nd (final) state, burr, sky cleanly wiped so sulfur tint and scratches barely show, stains, thin spot, rubbing, fold, defects, good cond., ex-coll., Dr. Otto Schaefer Collection, est. $30/40,000, (05-13-93, Sotheby-NY, #67, illus.), 3¼ x 6⅜ in., (83 x 161 mm.), etching and drypoint, printed in greyish-black ink, on warm-toned Japan.

BI *Landscape With Farm Buildings And A Man Sketching,* est. $5/700, (11-01-92, Hanzel, #245), 5⅛ x 8⅜ in., (13 x 21.3 cm.), etching.

$74,000* *Landscape With Square Tower (B., Holl. 218; H. 245; BB 50-C), 1650,* 3rd state of 4, burr, wiping scratches, wiped tone, trimmed, remargined, good cond., ex-coll., Dr. Otto Schaefer Collection, (05-13-93, Sotheby-NY, #61, illus.), 3½ x 6⅛ in., (89 x 156 mm.), etching and drypoint (BP 48,582, DM 119,490, FR 403,050, Y 8,261,695).

$134,500* *Landscape With Three Gabled Cottages Beside A Road (B., Holl. 217; H. 246; BB 50-D), 1650,* 3rd (final) state, burr, wiping scratches, watermark, small margins,foxing, thin spots, small repairs, good cond., ex-coll., Dr. Otto Schaefer Collection, (05-13-93, Sotheby-NY, #62, illus.), 6⅜ x 8 in., (161 x 202 mm.), etching and drypoint (BP 88,301, DM 217,181, FR 732,571, Y 15,016,188).

$8185* *Landscape With Three Gabled Cottages Beside A Road (B., Holl. 217; H.246; B.B. 50-D), 1650,* third (final) state, trimmed within platemark, paper loss, (12-03-92, Sotheby-London, #107), 6 x 8 in., (151 x 203 mm.), etching (BP 5280, DM 12,872, FR 43,935, Y 1,018,415).

$9200* *Landscape With Three Gables Cottages Beside A Road (B., Holl. 217, H. 246, BB. 50-D), 1650,* 3rd final state, burr, trimmed, made-up loss, ink touches, repairs, crease, staining, prov., (05-11-93, Christie-NY, #49, illus.), sheet 5⅝ x 8 in., (143 x 203 mm.), etching and drypoint on laid (BP 5873, DM 14,493, FR 48,832, Y 1,011,990).

$107,000* *Landscape With Trees, Farm Buildings And A Tower (B., Holl. 223; H. 244; BB 50-4), c. 1651,* 4th (final) state, watermark, margins, good cond., ex-coll., Dr. Otto Schaefer Collection, (05-13-93, Sotheby-NY, #64, illus.), 4⅞ x 12½ in., (123 x 319 mm.), etching and drypoint (BP 70,247, DM 172,776, FR 582,789, Y 11,945,964).

$22,144* *Die Landschaft Mit Dem Meilenstein Bei Halfweg -Die Landschaft Mit Dem Obelisken (B.R.S. 227; Wh.-B. 227/ II), c. 1650,* (06-23-93, Kornfeld, #98, illus.), etching and drypoint on handmade (BP 15,043, DM 37,469, FR 126,033, Y 2,412,463, SF 33,350).

$154,247* *Die Landschaft Mit Den Drei Baumen (B.R.S. 212, Wh.-B. 212), 1643,* watermark, (06-23-93, Kornfeld, #97), etching w/engraving and drypoint (BP 104,787, DM 260,993, FR 877,900, Y 16,804,336, SF 232,300).

$9927* *Die Landschaft Mit Der Saufenden Kuh (B.R.S. 237; Wh.-B. 237/II), c.1650,* (06-23-93, Kornfeld, #99, illus.), etching and drypoint (BP 6744, DM 16,797, FR 56,500, Y 1,081,490, SF 14,950).

BI *The Large Lion Hunt (B., Holl. 114; H. 181; BB 41-D), 1641,* 2nd (final) state, touches of burr, narrow margins, thin spots, foxing, stains, ex-coll., Dr. Otto Schaefer Collection, est. $30/50,000, (05-13-93, Sotheby-NY, #5, illus.), 8⅞ x 11¾ in., (224 x 300 mm.), etching.

$6638* *Die Lowenjagd Mit Einem Lowen Und Zwei Reitern (B.R.S. 116; Wh.-B. 116), c. 1629,* trimmed, (12-01-92, Karl/Faber, #130, illus.), etching (BP 4386, DM 10,580, FR 36,056, Y 826,444).

$5463* *Man Drawing From A Cast (B., Holl. 130; H. 191; BB 41-4), c. 1652,* 1st state of 3, watermark, thread margins, trimmed, slightly discolored, good cond., ex-coll., Dr. Otto Schaefer Collection, (05-13-93, Sotheby-NY, #9, illus.), 3⅝ x 2½ in., (92 x 64 mm.), etching (BP 3587, DM 8821, FR 29,755, Y 609,914).

$935* *"Man In A Cloak And Fur Leaning Against A Bank" (Bartsch 151, Hollstein 151, Hind 14), 1630,* Basan edit. of the third state, (02-13-93, Neal, #547), image 4¼ x 3⅛ in., (10.8 x 7.9 cm.), (BP 658, DM 1551, FR 5247, Y 112,759).

$5116* *Manasseh Ben Israel (B., Holl. 269; H. 146; B. B. 36-C),* third (final) state, narrow margins, repaired tear, paper thin, stains, minor defects, (12-03-92, Sotheby-London, #109, illus.), 6 x 4¼ in., (152 x 108 mm.), etching on paper w/part of watermark (BP 3300, DM 8045, FR 27,461, Y 636,556).

BI *Mann In Breitkrempigem Hut (B. 311, Seidlitz 311 II, Nowell-Usticke 311), 1638,* prov., est. DM 9000, (06-04-93, Bassenge, #5333, illus.), 3⅛ x 2⁹⁄₁₆ in., (7.9 x 6.5 cm.), etching.

$650* *Mann Mit Kurzem Bart, In Gesticktem Pelzmantel (B. 263, Seidlitz 263IV; Hollstein 263 IV; Nowell-Usticke 263 IV), 1631,* (12-04-92, Bassenge, #6399), 4¾ x 3⅝ in., (12.1 x 9.2 cm.), etching (BP 417, DM 1035, FR 3512, Y 81,149).

BI *Mann Mit Kurzem Bart, In Gesticktem Pelzmantel (B. 263; Seidlitz 263IV; Hollstein 263 IV; Nowell-Usticke 263 III),* est. DM 12,000, (12-04-92, Bassenge, #6398, illus.), 5¾ x 4¹³⁄₁₆ in., (14.6 x 12.3 cm.), etching.

$74,000* *Medea: Or The Marriage Of Jason And Creusa (B., Holl. 112; H. 235; BB 48-E), 1648,* 1st state of 5, touches burr, prov., Dr. Otto Schaefer Collection, (05-13-93, Sotheby-NY, #35, illus.), 9½ x 6⅞ in., (240 x 176 mm.), etching w/touches of drypoint on warm-toned Japan (BP 48,582, DM 119,490, FR 403,050, Y 8,261,695).

$3630* *Les Musiciens Ambulants (Bartsch 119; Holl. 119),* thin margin, first state of 2, losses, (05-15-93, Loudmer, #88), 5⁹⁄₁₆ x 4⅝ in., (141 x 118 mm.), etching on laid (BP 2360, DM 5839, FR 19,622, Y 402,394).

$2127* *Nachdenkender Mann Bei Kerzenlicht (Holstein, B. 148; Wh.-B. 128), c. 1642,* watermark, (10-21-92, Dobiaschofsky, #1582), 5¹³⁄₁₆ x 5¼ in., (14.7 x 13.3 cm.), etching on handmade (BP 1320, DM 3218, FR 10,924, Y 259,074, SF 2880).

$12,636* *Nackte Frau Im Freien, Mit Den Fussen Im Wasser (B. 200, Seidlitz 200 I; Hollstein 200; Nowell-Usticke 200 I e), 1658,* prov., (12-04-92, Bassenge, #6394, illus.), 6¼ x 3¹⁄₁₆ in., (15.8 x 7.8 cm.), etching on China (BP 8105, DM 20,124, FR 68,266, Y 1,577,528).

BI *Nackte Frau Im Freien, Mit Den Fussen Im Wasser (B.R.S. 200; Wh.-B. 200), 1658,* est. DM 4800, (12-01-92, Karl/Faber, #132, illus.), etching.

$567* *Naked Woman Seated On A Mound (B. 198), 1658,* grey impression, watermark, thread margins, repaired tears, tear, waterstains, foxed, (11-30-92, Phillips-London, #308), plate 7 x 6⅜ in., (178 x 162 mm.), etching on laid (BP 374, DM 903, FR 3067, Y 70,566).

$2588* *Negress Lying Down (B. 205), 1658,* 3rd final state, small margins, good cond., repaired tears, repairedtear into image, staining, thinned spots, wear to image, creases, soiling, notations, (05-19-93, Butterfield, #1873, illus.), 3¼ x 6⁵⁄₁₆ in., (83 x 160 mm.), etching, drypoint and burin on laid (BP 1680, DM 4207, FR 14,173, Y 286,505).

$4600* *Nude Man Seated And Another Standing, With A Woman And Baby Lightly Etched In The Background (B. 194), 1646,* 3rd final state, #186, upper margin trimmed into image, other small margins, good cond., losses, tears, wear, rubbed areas, hinge remains, stains suurface soiling, graphite, prov., (05-19-93, Butterfield, #1871, illus.), 7½ x 5¼ in., (191 x 133 mm.), etching on fine laid (BP 2986, DM 7477, FR 25,192, Y 509,244).

$863* *Nude Man Seated And Another Standing, With A Woman And Baby Lightly Etched In The Background (B. 194), 1646,* 2nd final state, Basan impression, small margins, good cond., yellowspot in image, wear, light-staining, (05-19-93, Butterfield, #1872), 7⁹⁄₁₆ x 5 in., (192 x 127 mm.), etching on laid (BP 560, DM 1403, FR 4726, Y 95,539).

BI *Nude Man Seated Before A Curtain (B., Holl. 193, H. 220, BB. 46-B), 1646,* 2nd final state, thread margins, thin spot, good cond., prov., est. $15/20,000, (05-11-93, Christie-NY, #48, illus.), plate 6½ x 3¾ in., (165 x 95 mm.), etching on laid.

$46,000* *Nude Man Seated Before A Curtain (B., Holl. 193; H. 220; BB 46-B), 1646,* 1st state of 2, burr, watermark, small margins, repair image, thin spot, good cond., ex-coll., Dr. Otto Schaefer Collection, (05-13-93, Sotheby-NY, #37, illus.), 6½ x 3¾ in., (164 x 96 mm.), etching (BP 30,200, DM 74,277, FR 250,545, Y 5,135,648).

$1725* *Old Bearded Man In A High Fur Cap, With Eyes Closed (B., Holl. 290, H. 130, BB. 35-3), c. 1635,* trimmed on or inside platemark, light-staining, creasing, i., glue remains, Elizabeth Berger Estate, (05-11-93, Christie-NY, #54), sheet 4⁷⁄₁₆ x 4 in., (113 x 102 mm.), etching on laid (BP 1101, DM 2717, FR 9156, Y 189,748).

$1029* *An Old Man In Meditation (B., Holl. 147; H. 218; B. B. 45-4), c. 1645,* 2nd final state, thread margins, paper fault, related (?) thin spots,light stains, dirt, glued down, (06-30-93, Sotheby-London, #222), 5¼ x 4⅛ in., (133 x 105 mm.), etching (BP 690, DM 1755, FR 5921, Y 110,254).

BI *An Old Man In Meditation (B., Holl. 147; H. 218; B.B. 45-4),* second (final) state, thread margins, paper fault, thins spots in image, light stains, surface dirt, glued down at corners, est. BP 1,2/1,600, (12-03-92, Sotheby-London, #103), 5¼ x 4⅛ in., (133 x 106 mm.), etching.

$880* *Old Man Shading His Eyes With His Hand,* (02-14-93, Hanzel, #689), 5⅜ x 4⅜ in., (13.7 x 11.1 cm.), etching (BP 620, DM 1459, FR 4938, Y 106,126).

$3300* *Old Man Shading His Eyes With His Hand (B. 259), 1631,* margins trimmed, good cond., areas of restoration, thinned areas, tears, foxing, surface soiling, (02-24-93, Butterfield, #2700, illus.), 5⅜ x 4⅜ in., (137 x 111 mm.), etching & drypoint on fine laid (BP 2301, DM 5357, FR 18,162, Y 387,233).

$2530* *Old Man Shading His Eyes With His Hand (B., Holl. 259, H. 169, BB. 38-3), c. 1639,* narrow margins, good cond., watermark, Dian Woodner and Andrea Woodner Coll., prov., (05-11-93, Christie-NY, #50, illus.), sheet 5¼ x 4½ in., (133 x 114 mm.), etching and drypoint on laid (BP 1615, DM 3986, FR 13,429, Y 278,297).

$4370* *Old Man With A Beard, Fur Cap And Velvet Cloak (B., Holl. 262, H. 92, BB. 22-2), c. 1632,* 2nd state of 3, thread margins or trimmed, tear, good cond., (05-11-93, Christie-NY, #51, illus.), plate 6 x 5⅛ in., (152 x 130 mm.), etching on fine laid (BP 2790, DM 6884, FR 23,195, Y 480,695).

$633* *Old Man With Beard, Fur Cap And Velvet Cloak (B. 262), c. 1652,* late Basan impression, trimmed to image, repaired tear, corner mounted, (11-30-92, Phillips-London, #310), sheet 5¾ x 5⅛ in., (146 x 130 mm.), etching on thin wove (BP 418, DM 1008, FR 3423, Y 78,780).

$3680* *An Old Woman Sleeping (B., Holl. 350, H. 129, BB. 37-1), 1635-7,* margins, i., staining, good cond., prov., (05-11-93, Christie-NY, #55, illus.), plate 2¹³⁄₁₆ x 2⅛ in., (71 x 54 mm.), etching on laid (BP 2349, DM 5797, FR 19,533, Y 404,796).

$12,650* *Old Woman Sleeping (B., Holl. 350; H. 129; BB 37-1), c. 1635-37,* narrow margins, corners reinforced, nicks, good cond., Dr. Otto Schaefer Collection, (05-13-93, Sotheby-NY, #57, illus.), 2¾ x 2 in., (69 x 52 mm.), etching (BP 8305, DM 20,426, FR 68,900, Y 1,412,303).

$880* *The Pancake Woman (Hind 141 IV/IV, Bartsch 124), 1635,* thread margins, d., plate s., (05-27-93, Swann, #234, illus.), 4⅜ x 3 in., (11.1 x 7.6 cm.), etching (BP 564, DM 1412, FR 4759, Y 94,340).

$715* *A Peasant In A High Cap, Standing Leaning On A Stick (Bartsch 133), 1639,* only state, (10-08-92, Grogan, #645), 3¼ x 1¾ in., (8.3 x 4.4 cm.), etching (BP 425, DM 1058, FR 3589, Y 86,877).

$7162* *Peasant With His Hands Behind (B., Holl. 172; H. 16; B.B. 30-7),* fifth state of six, narrow margins, repair, margins, dirt, ex-coll., (12-03-92, Sotheby-London, #104, illus.), 3½ x 2¾ in., (90 x 70 mm.), etching (BP 4620, DM 11,263, FR 38,443, Y 891,129).

$2059* *Peasant With His Hands Behind His Back (B., Holl. 135; H. 69; B. B. 31-M),* Nowell-Usticke's 5th final state, narrow margins, crease, laid down, (06-30-93, Sotheby-London, #221), 2¼ x 2 in., (57 x 51 mm.), etching (BP 1380, DM 3512, FR 11,847, Y 220,615).

$6325* *Peasant With His Hands Behind His Back (B., Holl. 135; H. 69; BB 31-M), 1631,* 4th (final) state, delicate wiping scratches, narrow margins, repairs, foxing, surface dirt, good cond., (05-13-93, Sotheby-NY, #185, illus.), 2¼ x 1⅞ in., (58 x 49 mm.), etching and burin (BP 4152, DM 10,213, FR 34,450, Y 706,152).

BI *The Persian (B. 152), 1632,* late impression, corner mounted, good cond., est. BP 4/600, (11-30-92, Phillips-London, #306), plate 4⅛ x 3 in., (105 x 76 mm.), etching on laid.

$1540* *Peter And John Healing The Cripple At The Gate Of The Temple (Bartsch 94, Hind 301), 1659,* thread margins, 4th state, touched w/gray wash by another hand, foxing, prov., Heinrich Lampertz, Sr. Coll., stamped, Lugt 1337, (12-08-92, Swann, #261, illus.), 7 x 8½ in., (17.8 x 21.6 cm.), etching, drypoint and roulette work (BP 965, DM 2398, FR 8174, Y 190,878).

$303* *Peter And John Healing The Cripple At The Gate Of The Temple (Hind 301; Bartsch 94),* 3rd state of 4, weak impression, trimmed, scuffing, paper thinning, staining, (01-21-93, Bonhams-Chelsea, #117), plate 7 x 8½ in., (17.8 x 21.6 cm.), etching (BP 198, DM 482, FR 1630, Y 37,922).

BI *"La Petite Tombe" (B.R.S. 67; Wh.-B. 67), c. 1652,* prov., est. DM 23/25,000, (12-01-92, Karl/Faber, #127, illus.), etching.

$619* *Petrus Und Johannes An Der Pforte Des Tempels (Nowell-Usticke 94),* plate s., d. Rembrandt f. 1659, 4th state, foxing, (09-14-92, Venator/Hansten, #1594), plate 7¹⁄₁₆ x 8½ in., (18 x 21.6 cm.), etching and drypoint (BP 327, DM 920, FR 3118, Y 76,971).

$1430* *Philosopher Meditating By Candlelight,* (11-13-92, DuMouchelle, #2034, illus.), 5¾ x 5⅛ in., (14.6 x 13 cm.), etching (BP 924, DM 2245, FR 7570, Y 177,485).

BI *Polander Standing With His Arms Folded (B., Holl. 140; H. 138; B. B.35-7),* 2nd final state, trimmed, paper thin, crease, est. BP 3/4,000, (06-30-93, Sotheby-London, #202), 2 x 1¾ in., (51 x 44 mm.), etching.

$1100* *The Presentation In The Temple (Bartsch 49, Hind 162), 1639,* thread margins, 3rd state of 3, (12-08-92, Swann, #262, illus.), 8⁵⁄₁₆ x 11⅜ in., (21.1 x 28.9 cm.), etching (BP 689, DM 1713, FR 5839, Y 136,341).

$134,500* *The Presentation In The Temple In The Dark Manner (B., Holl. 50; H. 279; BB 57-1), c. 1654,* burr, watermark, narrow margins, repair, paper fibers adhering to face of figure at right, traces glue verso, stains recto,

good cond., Dr. Otto Schaefer Collection, (05-13-93, Sotheby-NY, #14, illus.), 8⅜ x 6⅜ in., (212 x 162 mm.), etching and drypoint (BP 88,301, DM 217,181, FR 732,571, Y 15,016,188).

$1380* *The Presentation In The Temple: Oblong Print (B. 49), 1639,* 3rd final state, small margins, good cond., repaired tears, staining, wear, tape remains, surface soiling, notations, blindstamp, prov., (05-19-93, Butterfield, #1867), 8⅜ x 11½ in., (213 x 292 mm.), etching and drypoint on thin laid (BP 896, DM 2243, FR 7558, Y 152,773).

$5463* *The Quacksalver (B., Holl. 129; H. 139; BB 35-G), 1635,* only state, thread margins, thin spot, discoloration, collector's sig. showing through verso, good cond., ex-coll., Dr. Otto Schaefer Collection, (05-13-93, Sotheby-NY, #8, illus.), 3⅛ x 1½ in., (78 x 37 mm.), etching (BP 3587, DM 8821, FR 29,755, Y 609,914).

$770* *The Raising Of Lazarus (Bartsch 73, Hind 96), 1632,* wide margins, state XIII, modern printing, (12-08-92, Swann, #263), 14⁵⁄₁₆ x 10¹⁄₁₆ in., (36.4 x 25.6 cm.), etching (BP 483, DM 1199, FR 4087, Y 95,439).

$6325* *The Raising Of Lazarus: Small Plate (B., Holl. 72; H. 198; BB 42-B),1642,* 1st state of 2, watermark, narrow margins, thin spots, nicks, good cond., Dr. Otto Schaefer Collection, (05-13-93, Sotheby-NY, #25, illus.), 6 x 4½ in., (151 x 115 mm.), etching (BP 4152, DM 10,213, FR 34,450, Y 706,152).

BI *The Raising Of Lazarus: The Large Plate (B., Holl. 73; H. 95; B. B. 34-D),* 10th final stae, crease damaged in places, loss, rubbed, defects, laid down, (06-30-93, Sotheby-London, #215), 14½ x 10⅛ in., (368 x 257 mm.), etching.

$3775* *The Raising Of Lazarus: The Large Plate (B., Holl. 73; H. 96; B. B. 32-4), c. 1632: Seven,* 9th state of ten, trimmed, touched w/grey wash, thin spots, (06-30-93, Sotheby-London, #216), etching on paper w/a Strasburg Lily watermark (BP 2530, DM 6439, FR 21,720, Y 404,479).

$715* *The Raising Of Lazarus: The Larger Plate (B. 73), 1632,* Basan impression, after 1807, 10th final state, small margins, good cond., light-staining, rubbed area, tear, image wear, creases, staining, glue remains, surface scuffing/soiling, (10-28-92, Butterfield, #2853), 15 x 10⅝ in., (381 x 270 mm.), etching and burin (engraving (copper)) on laid paper (BP 456, DM 1104, FR 3749, Y 87,730).

$2200* *The Raising Of Lazarus: The Larger Plate (B. 73), 1632,* 10th (final) state, margins trimmed, good cond., light-staining, foxing, wear, surface soiling, (02-24-93, Butterfield, #2698, illus.), 14⅜ x 10⅛ in., (365 x 257 mm.), etching & burin on laid attached to wove (BP 1534, DM 3571, FR 12,108, Y 258,155).

BI *The Raising Of Lazarus: The Larger Plate (B. 73), c. 1632,* 10th final state, thread margins, very poor cond., tears, defects, est. BP 4/600, (11-30-92, Phillips-London, #301), plate 14⅝ x 10¼ in., (371 x 260 mm.), etching laid on Japan.

$3033* *Der Reiter (B. 139; Seidlitz, Hollstein, Nowell-Usticke 139 II), c. 1632,* prov., (12-04-92, Bassenge, #6391), 3¹⁄₁₆ x 2⅜ in., (7.7 x 6 cm.), etching (BP 1945, DM 4830, FR 16,386, Y 378,652).

BI *Rembrandt And His Wife Saskia,* est. $2/300, (11-01-92, Hanzel, #274), 4⅛ x 3⅝ in., (10.5 x 9.2 cm.), etching.

BI *Rembrandt In A Flat Cap And Embroidered Dress (Bartsch 26, Hind 157), 1638,* state 2 of 2 w/sig. retouched, mat burn, margins, est. $2/3,000, (12-08-92, Swann, #264, illus.), 3⅝ x 2⁷⁄₁₆ in., (9.2 x 6.2 cm.), etching.

$1210* *Rembrandt In A Flat Cap And Embroidered Dress (Bartsch 26. Hind 157),1638,* second state, mat burn, margins, stain, good Basan impression, platetone, ex-coll. Dr. Weiner, (05-27-93, Swann, #235), (8.6 x 6.2 cm.), etching (BP 775, DM 1942, FR 6544, Y 129,717).

BI *Rembrandt Leaning On A Stone Sill,* est. $6/800, (11-01-92, Hanzel, #248), 8 x 6 in., (20.3 x 15.2 cm.), etching.

BI *Rembrandt Wearing A Soft Hat, Cocked,* est. $4/600, (11-01-92, Hanzel, #254), 6 x 4⅞ in., (15.2 x 12.4 cm.), etching.

$2490* *Rembrandts Mutter Mit Schwarzem Schleier (B.R.S. 343; Wh.-B. 343/II(v. III), c. 1631,* prov., (12-01-92, Karl/Faber, #136, illus.), etching (BP 1645, DM 3969, FR 13,525, Y 310,010).

$3432* *The Rest On The Flight (B. Holl. 57; H. 208; B. B. 44-2),* 3rd state of 4, burr, margins, paper split, damage, (06-30-93, Sotheby-London, #195, illus.), 3⅝ x 2⅜ in., (92 x 60 mm.), etching (BP 2300, DM 5854, FR 19,747, Y 367,727).

$1265* *The Rest On The Flight: A Night Piece (B., Holl. 57, H. 208, BB. 44-2), c. 1644,* 4th final state, thread margins, staining, good cond., prov., (05-11-93, Christie-NY, #39, illus.), plate 3⁹⁄₁₆ x 2¹⁵⁄₁₆ in., (90 x 75 mm.), etching and drypoint on laid (BP 808, DM 1993, FR 6714, Y 139,149).

BI *The Rest On The Flight: A Night Piece (B., Holl. 57; H. 208; BB 44-2), c. 1644,* 3rd state of 4, narrow margins, repaired tear, glue stains, ex-coll.Capt. Gordon Nowell-Usticke, est. $4/6,000, (05-13-93, Sotheby-NY, #175), 3⅝ x 2⅜ in., (92 x 59 mm.), etching.

$12,011* *The Rest On The Flight: Lightly Etched (B., Holl. 58; H. 216; B. B. 45-E), 1645,* tone and touches of burr, margins, foxmarks, losses, surface dirt, fresh unpressed cond., ex coll. A. Donnadieu (L. 97), (06-30-93, Sotheby-London, #197, illus.), 5⅛ x 4½ in., (130 x 114 mm.), etching on paper w/top part of a Double Headed Eagle watermark (BP 8050, DM 20,486, FR 69,108, Y 1,286,939).

$1769* *Le Retour De L'Enfant Prodigue (B. B., 36-D), 1636,* folded, creases, thin margins, (06-16-93, Ader Tajan, #17), 6¼ x 5⁷⁄₁₆ in., (15.8 x 13.8 cm.), etching (BP 1179, DM 2937, FR 9855, Y 188,673).

$453* *The Return Of The Prodigal Son (B. 91), 1636,* later impression, tone, evidence, foxing, surface damage, (10-27-92, Phillips-London, #33), sheet 6⅞ x 6 in., (175 x 152 mm.), etching on laid (BP 286, DM 694, FR 2356, Y 55,413).

$3450* *The Return Of The Prodigal Son (B., Holl. 91, H. 147, BB. 36-D), 1636,* later impression, trimmed, surface soiling, (05-11-93, Christie-NY, #43), sheet 6⅛ x 5¼ in., (156 x 133 mm.), etching on laid (BP 2202, DM 5435, FR 18,312, Y 379,496).

$5175* *The Return Of The Prodigal Son (B., Holl. 91; H. 147; BB 36-D), 1636,* Holl's only state, Usticke's 1st of 4, mono., watermark, narrow margins, nicks, thin spots, stains, discoloration, good cond., Daniel A. Don Estate, (05-13-93, Sotheby-NY, #181, illus.), 6¼ x 5⅜ in., (158 x 137 mm.), etching (BP 3397, DM 8356, FR 28,186, Y 577,760).

$1090* *Die Ruckkehr Des Verlorenen Sohnes (B. 91; Wh.-B. 91), 1636,* (04-27-93, Hartung, #2466), etching (BP 693, DM 1726, FR 5838, Y 122,156).

$9157* *Saints Peter And John Healing The Cripple At The Gate Of The Temple (B., Holl. 94; H. 301; BB. 59-A), 1659,* 2nd state of 4, burr, narrow margins, thin area, very good cond., (12-01-92, Christie-London, #131, illus.), plate 7¹⁄₁₆ x 8⅝ in., (179 x 219 mm.), etching w/drypoint and engraving (BP 6050, DM 14,595, FR 49,739, Y 1,140,065).

$2830* *Samuel Manasseh Ben Israel (B., Holl. 269; H. 146; BB. 36-C), 1636,* 3rd (final) state, thread margins or trimmed, glue stains, thin spots, staining, (12-01-92, Christie-London, #138), sheet 5¹³⁄₁₆ x 4³⁄₁₆ in., (148 x 106 mm.), etching (BP 1870, DM 4511, FR 15,372, Y 352,341).

$2728* *Saskia With Pearls In Her Hair (B., Holl. 347; H. 112; B.B. 34-C), 1634,* narrow margins, good cond., tiny rubbed spots, discoloration, ex-coll., (12-03-92, Sotheby-London, #134), 3¼ x 2½ in., (84 x 65 mm.), etching (BP 1760, DM 4290, FR 14,643, Y 339,430).

$704* *Selbstbildnis Mit Der Scharpe Um Den Hals (Seidlitz 17, III), c. 1786,* s., d. Rembrandt, 1633, (03-24-93, Venator/Hansten, #2566), pl. 5¼ x 4⅛ in., (13.3 x 10.4 cm.), etching (BP 477, DM 1150, FR 3913, Y 82,716).

$3094* *Selbstbildnis Mit Scharpe Um Den Hals (Nowell-Usticke 17, I; Seidlitz 17, II),* s., d. Rembrandt f:1633, prov., (09-14-92, Venator/Hansten, #1591), plate 5³⁄₁₆ x 4⅛ in., (13.2 x 10.4 cm.), etching (BP 1636, DM 4599, FR 15,587, Y 384,730).

$13,455* *Selbstbildnis, Am Fenster Zeichnend (B. 22, Rovinski, Seidlitz 22 IV,Nowell-Usticke C 1, Hollstein 22 IV), 1648,* watermark, (06-04-93, Bassenge, #5319, illus.), 6¼ x 5¹⁄₁₆ in., (15.8 x 12.9 cm.), etching (BP 8902, DM 21,850, FR 73,645, Y 1,451,143).

$1750* *Self Portrait Drawing At A Window (B. 22), 1648,* 5th final state, narrow margins, glue stains, repair, (11-30-92, Phillips-London, #296), plate 6⅛ x 5 in., (156 x 127 mm.), etching and burin on laid paper (BP 1155, DM 2788, FR 9465, Y 217,797).

$57,500* *Self Portrait Drawing At A Window (B., Holl. 22; H. 229; BB 48-A), 1648,* 3rd state of 5, burr, trimmed c. 2-3 mm. into work and made up, repairs in image, collectors' marks, Dr. Otto Schaefer Collection, (05-13-93, Sotheby-NY, #41, illus.), 6¼ x 5¼ in., (159 x 132 mm.), etching, drypoint and burin (BP 37,749, DM 92,847, FR 313,181, Y 6,419,560).

$825* *Self Portrait Drawing At A Window (Bartsch 22), 1648,* fifth (final) state, prov., (10-08-92, Grogan, #650), 6³⁄₁₆ x 5⅛ in., (15.7 x 13 cm.), etching (BP 491, DM 1220, FR 4142, Y 100,243).

BI *Self Portrait In A Cap And Scarf With The Face Dark (B., Holl. 17, H. 108, BB 33-9), 1633,* 2nd final state, wear, trimmed narrow margins, foxing, thin patch, watermark, est. $6/8,000, (05-11-93, Christie-NY, #32, illus.), plate 5¼ x 4 in., (133 x 102 mm.), etching on laid.

$6900* *Self Portrait In A Cap And Scarf With The Face Dark: Bust (B., Holl.17; Hind 108; Biorklund-Barnard 33-G), 1633,* Holl.'s 2nd (final) state, Biorklund-Barnard's 3rd, margins, rubbed,retouched w/blk. chalk (?), staining, good cond., ex-coll. Cabinet Brentano-Birckenstock, prop. Brooklyn Museum, (05-13-93, Sotheby-NY, #174, illus.), 5¼ x 4⅛ in., (132 x 104 mm.), etching (BP 4530, DM 11,142, FR 37,582, Y 770,347).

$900* *Self Portrait In A Cloak With A Falling Collar: Bust [B15;H63 Holl. 15 V/V],* s., d. 1631 in plate; 2 collector's stamps and label verso, (02-04-93, Sloan, #2388), 2½ x 2³⁄₁₆ in., (6.4 x 5.6 cm.), print (BP 628, DM 1482, FR 5025, Y 111,954).

BI *Self Portrait In A Flat Cap And Embroidered Dress (B. 26), c. 1642,* late impression, narrow margins, good cond., est. BP 5/600, (11-30-92, Phillips-London, #297), plate 3⅝ x 2⅜ in., (92 x 60 mm.), etching on laid paper.

$3450* *Self Portrait In A Slant Fur Cap: Bust (B., Holl. 14, H. 62, BB. Rej-2), 1631,* 3rd final state, delicate tone, narrow margins, surface abrasions, thin spots, very good cond., prov., (05-11-93, Christie-NY, #31, illus.), plate 2⁹⁄₁₆ x 2¼ in., (65 x 57 mm.), etching on laid (BP 2202, DM 5435, FR 18,312, Y 379,496).

$6900* *Self Portrait With A Plumed Cap And Lowered Sabre (B., Holl. 23, H. 110, BB. 34-B), 1634,* 3rd final state, squared margins beyond platemark, pinholes, very good cond., (05-11-93, Christie-NY, #34, illus.), plate 5⅛ x 4⅛ in., (130 x 105 mm.), etching on laid (BP 4405, DM 10,870, FR 36,624, Y 758,992).

BI *Self Portrait With Curly Hair And White Collar: Bust (B., Holl. 1; H.33; B. B. 30-11),* 2nd final state, printing lightly, trimmed on and into platemark, thread margins, paper loss, damaged, losses, abrasions, paper defect at center, est. BP 6/8,000, (06-30-93, Sotheby-London, #204), 2¼ x 2 in., (57 x 51 mm.), etching.

$29,900* *Self Portrait With Plumed Cap And Lowered Sabre (B., Holl. 23; H. 110; BB 34-B), 1634,* 2nd state of 3, inky plate edges, wiping scratches, sig., small margins, repaired or rubbed in image, thin spot, good cond., ex-coll., Dr. Otto Schaefer Collection, (05-13-93, Sotheby-NY, #42, illus.), 5¼ x 4⅜ in., (132 x 111 mm.), etching (BP 19,630, DM 48,280, FR 162,854, Y 3,338,171).

$2574* *Self Portrait With Raised Sabre (B. Holl. 18; H. 109; B. B. 34-A). 1634,* 2nd final state, narrow margins, trimmed, repair, thin spots, dirt, (06-30-93, Sotheby-London, #209), 4¾ x 4 in., (121 x 102 mm.), etching on paper w/upper part of an Arms of Amsterdam watermark (BP 1725, DM 4390, FR 14,810, Y 275,796).

$4370* *Self Portrait With Saskia (B., Holl. 19, H. 144, BB 36-A), 1636,* 3rd final state, narrow margins, staining, (05-11-93, Christie-NY, #33), plate 4⅛ x 3¾ in., (105 x 95 mm.), etching on laid (BP 2790, DM 6884, FR 23,195, Y 480,695).

$6863* *Self Portrait With Saskia (B., Holl. 19; H. 144; B. B. 36-A), 1636,* 3rd final state, margins, remains of paper, backboard-staining, excell. cond., (06-30-93, Sotheby-London, #210), 4⅛ x 3¾ in., (105 x 95 mm.), etching (BP 4600, DM 11,706, FR 39,488, Y 735,348).

BI *Self-Portrait With Curly Hair And White Collar: Bust (B. I), 1630,* 2nd (final) state, traces of plate tone, thread margins, trimmed to platemark, good cond., staining, tear, crease, thinned spot, wear, surface soiling, pencil notations, (02-24-93, Butterfield, #2697, illus.), 2¼ x 1⅞ in., (57 x 48 mm.), etching on fine laid.

$10,350* *Sheet Of Studies: Head Of The Artist, A Beggar Couple, Heads Of And Old Man And Old Woman, Etc. (B., Holl. 63, H. 90, BB. 32-1), c. 1632,* 2nd final state, burr, narrow margins, very good cond., watermark, Dian Woodner and Andrea Woodner Coll., (05-11-93, Christie-NY, #56, illus.), plate 3¹⁵⁄₁₆ x 4⅛ in., (100 x 105 mm.), etching on laid (BP 6607, DM 16,304, FR 54,936, Y 1,138,489).

$13,800* *The Ship Of Fortune (B., Holl. 111; H. 106; BB 33-E), 1633,* 2nd (final) state, in complete copy of E. Herckmans' Der Zee-Vaert Lof, 1634, Folio, p. 97; w/17 etchings by Willem Basse, all generally good cond., bound in early 18th cent. calf, gilt spine, spine cracked, Dr. Otto Schaefer Collection, (05-13-93, Sotheby-NY, #34, illus.), platemark 4⅜ x 6½ in., (110 x 165 mm.), sheet, each approx. 12 x 7⅝ in., (110 x 165 mm.), etching (BP 9060, DM 22,283, FR 75,163, Y 1,540,694).

$173,000* *Six's Bridge (B., Holl. 208; H. 209; BB 45-A), 1645,* 3rd (final state), narrow margins, folds, filled in paper loss, goodcond., ex-coll., Dr. Otto Schaefer Collection, (05-13-93, Sotheby-NY, #58, illus.), 5⅛ x 8⅞ in., (129 x 224 mm.), etching (BP 113,577, DM 279,348, FR 942,266, Y 19,314,503).

BI *The Small Lion Hunt (With One Lion) (B., Holl. 116; H. 6; BB 29-3), c. 1629,* watermark, thread margins, trimmed, thin spots, abraded spot, good cond., est. $5/7,000, (05-13-93, Sotheby-NY, #189, illus.), 6¼ x 4⅝ in., (158 x 117 mm.), etching.

$27,600* *St. Francis Beneath A Tree Praying (B., Holl. 107; H. 292; BB 57-A),1657,* 2nd (final) state, burr, wiped plate tone, watermark, narrow margins, repair or rubbed spot, thin spot, good cond., ex-coll. Dr. Otto Schaefer Collection, (05-13-93, Sotheby-NY, #33, illus.), 7⅛ x 9¾ in., (182 x 247 mm.), drypoint and etching on sturdy paper (BP 18,120, DM 44,566, FR 150,327, Y 3,081,389).

BI *St. Jerome Beside A Pollard Willow (B., Holl. 103; H. 232; BB 48-B),1648,* 2nd (final) state, countermark, trimmed in platemark, remargined 3 sides, trimmed above and made up, corner rejoined, repairs, ex-coll. J. Rosenberg, est. $10/15,000, (05-13-93, Sotheby-NY, #182, illus.), 6¾ x 5⅛ in., (172 x 129 mm.), etching and drypoint.

$450* *St. Jerome In A Dark Chamber (B. 105), 1642,* 2nd final state, narrow margins, repaired, (11-30-92, Phillips-London, #303), plate 5¾ x 6⅝ in., (146 x 168 mm.), etching on laid (BP 297, DM 717, FR 2434, Y 56,005).

$690* *St. Jerome In A Dark Chamber (B., Holl. 105; H. 201; BB 42-E), 1642,* posthumous impression, narrow margins, tears, repair, (05-13-93, Sotheby-NY, #183), 6 x 6¾ in., (151 x 173 mm.), etching (BP 453, DM 1114, FR 3758, Y 77,035).

$6139* *St. Jerome Praying: Arched Plate (B., Holl. 101; H. 94; B.B. 32-B), 1632,* narrow thread margins, trimmed on platemark, thin spots, related small repairs, stains, good cond., (12-03-92, Sotheby-London, #97, illus.), 6¾ x 8½ in., (171 x 215 mm.), etching and drypoint on paper w/ part of watermark (BP 3960, DM 9654, FR 32,952, Y 763,842).

$935* *St. Peter and St. John At the Gates Of The Temple (Hind 101), 1659,* later impression, (10-18-92, Hindman, #496), 7 x 8⅜ in., (17.8 x 21.3 cm.), etching and drypoint (BP 572, DM 1392, FR 4720, Y 112,178).

$3738* *The Star Of The Kings: A Night Piece (B., Holl. 113; H. 254; BB 51-1), c. 1651,* only state, watermark, narrow margins and trimmed to platemark, crease, repaired tear, scuffs, good cond., ex-coll., Dr. Otto Schaefer Collection, (05-13-93, Sotheby-NY, #1, illus.), 3¾ x 5¾ in., (96 x 146 mm.), etching w/few touches of drypoint (BP 2454, DM 6036, FR 20,359, Y 417,327).

$2291* *Der Stehende Jesusknabe Inmitten Der Schriftgelehrten (B.R.S. 65, Wh.-B. 65/II (v. III), 1652,* (06-23-93, Kornfeld, #89), etching and drypoint (BP 1556, DM 3876, FR 13,039, Y 249,591, SF 3450).

$1133* *Der Stelzfuss (B. 179, Seidlitz 179 III, Hollstein 179, Nowell-Usticke 179 II), c. 1630,* (06-04-93, Bassenge, #5329), 4⁷⁄₁₆ x 2½ in., (11.3 x 6.4 cm.), etching (BP 750, DM 1840, FR 6201, Y 122,196).

$1980* *Strolling Musicians,* (12-11-92, DuMouchelle, #2028, illus.), 5½ x 4½ in., (14 x 11.4 cm.), etching (BP 1270, DM 3120, FR 10,691, Y 245,019).

$8050* *The Strolling Musicians (B., Holl. 119; H. 142; BB 35-8), c. 1635,* 1st state of 2, watermark, narrow margins, touches of wash in image,red chalk image and verso, soiling, good cond., Dr. Otto Schaefer Collection, (05-13-93, Sotheby-NY, #4, illus.), 5⅜ x 4½ in., (138 x 115 mm.), etching (BP 5285, DM 12,999, FR 43,845, Y 898,738).

BI *Student At A Table By Candlelight (B. 148), 1642,* 5th state, narrow margins, repairs, est. BP 5/700, (11-30-92, Phillips-London, #305), plate 5⅛ x 5⅛ in., (130 x 130 mm.), etching on laid.

$189,500* *Thomas Haaringh ("Old Haaringh"), (B., Holl. 274; H. 287; BB 55-1), c. 1655,* 2nd (final) state, burr, countermark, narrow margins, touched-in repair, thin spots, reinforced right corner, good cond., ex-coll., exhib., Dr. Otto Schaefer Collection, (05-13-93, Sotheby-NY, #49, illus.), 7⅝ x 5⅞ in., (195 x 150 mm.), drypoint and burin (BP 124,409, DM 305,991, FR 1,032,135, Y 21,156,637).

BI *The Three Crosses,* late impression, est. $6/800, (05-16-93, Hanzel, #455), 15¼ x 17¾ in., (38.7 x 45.1 cm.), etching.

$1870* *Three Heads Of Women: One Asleep (B. 368), 1637,* watermark, only state, small margins, good cond., pencil notations, surface soiling, (02-24-93, Butterfield, #2702), 5½ x 3¹¹⁄₁₆ in., (140 x 94 mm.), etching on laid paper (BP 1304, DM 3036, FR 10,292, Y 219,432).

$715* *Three Oriental Figures (Bartsch 118), 1641,* second (final) state, (10-08-92, Grogan, #653), 5¹¹⁄₁₆ x 4½ in., (14.4 x 11.4 cm.), etching (BP 425, DM 1058, FR 3589, Y 86,877).

$173,000* *The Three Trees (B., Holl. 212; H. 205; BB 43-B), 1643,* watermark, narrow margins, touched-in abrasion in image, thick ink of etched lines polished in places, good cond., ex-coll., Dr. Otto Schaefer Collection, (05-13-93, Sotheby-NY, #63, illus.), 8⅜ x 11 in., (213 x 279 mm.), etching w/drypoint and burin (BP 113,577, DM 279,348, FR 942,266, Y 19,314,503).

$90,500* *The Three Trees (B., Holl. 212; H. 205; BB 43-B), 1643,* watermark, WK countermark, narrow margins, repaired tear, creases, glue traces, Daniel A. Don Estate, (05-13-93, Sotheby-NY, #191, illus.), 8⅜ x 11 in., (213 x 281 mm.), etching w/drypoint and burin (BP 59,414, DM 146,133, FR 492,919, Y 10,103,829).

$1829* *Der Tod Der Maria (B.99; Seidlitz 99 V; Hollstein 99 after III; Nowell-Usticke 99 wohl IV), 1639,* (12-12-92, Bassenge, #8240, illus.), 15¹³⁄₁₆ x 12⅜ in., (40.2 x 31.5 cm.), etching (BP 1169, DM 2874, FR 9796, Y 226,277).

BI *Tod Der Maria (Seidlitz 99, IV; Bartsch 99; White-Boon 99, III), 1639,* c. 1750, tear, plate s., d., est. DM 16,000-, (09-25-92, Granier, #2674, illus.), 15⅝ x 12⁷⁄₁₆ in., (39.7 x 31.6 cm.), sheet 16⅛ x 12⅝ in., (39.7 x 31.6 cm.), etching and drypoint on thin hand-made paper.

$5777* *Der Tod der Maria (B. 99; Seidlitz 99 III; Hollstein 99 II, Nowell-Usticke 99 III), 1639,* (12-04-92, Bassenge, #6382), 16⅛ x 12⅜ in., (40.9 x 31.5 cm.), etching (BP 3706, DM 9201, FR 31,210, Y 721,223).

$1320* *The Tribute Money (H..124; B.68), c. 1935,* 2nd final state, thread margins, staining, (06-16-93, Bonhams-Chelsea, #319, illus.), pl. 2⅞ x 4⅛ in., (7.3 x 10.5 cm.), etching (BP 880, DM 2191, FR 7354, Y 140,785).

$14,300* *Triumph Of Mordecai,* c. 1640, prov., burr, (09-20-92, Hindman, #654, illus.), 6¾ x 8⅜ in., (17.1 x 21.3 cm.), etching and drypoint (BP 8372, DM 21,220, FR 72,589, Y 1,767,396).

$15,347* *The Triumph Of Mordecai (B., Holl. 40, H. 172, B. B. 41-1),* first state of two, margins, stains, central crease, stains in image, discoloration, (12-03-92, Sotheby-London, #98, illus.), 6¾ x 8½ in., (171 x 216 mm.), etching and drypoint on paper w/part of watermark (BP 9900, DM 24,134, FR 82,378, Y 1,909,543).

$17,250* *The Triumph Of Mordecai (B., Holl. 40, H. 172, BB 41-1), 1641,* burr, narrow margins, foxmarks, repaired tear affecting image, very good cond., watermark, prop. Montclair Art Museum, (05-11-93, Christie-NY, #36, illus.), plate 6¾ x 8⁷⁄₁₆ in., (171 x 214 mm.), etching and drypoint on laid (BP 11,012, DM 27,174, FR 91,561, Y 1,897,481).

$6613* *Two Tramps, A Man And A Woman (B., Holl. 144; H. 116; BB 34-2), c. 1634,* wiping scratches, narrow to thread margins, rubbed spot, repair, greyink, surface dirt, good cond., ex-coll. Earl of Aylesford, (05-13-93, Sotheby-NY, #186, illus.), 2½ x 1⅞ in., (63 x 48 mm.), etching (BP 4342, DM 10,678, FR 36,019, Y 738,305).

$60,250* *View Of Amsterdam From The North West (B., Holl. 210; H. 176; BB 40-4), c. 1640,* only state, crisp and clear, watermark, margins, thin spots (partly reinforced), collectors' marks, good cond., ex-coll. Dr. Otto Schaefer, (05-13-93, Sotheby-NY, #59, illus.), 4⅜ x 6 in., (112 x 153 mm.), etching (BP 39,555, DM 97,287, FR 328,159, Y 6,726,583).

$12,278* *View Of Amsterdam From The Northwest (B., Holl. 210; H. 176; B.B. 40-4),* only state, narrow margins, paper thin, pale stains in image, (12-03-92, Sotheby-London, #106, illus.), 4½ x 6 in., (112 x 155 mm.), etching (BP 7920, DM 19,308, FR 65,904, Y 1,527,684).

BI *Village With Two Gabled Cottages On A Canal,* est. $5/700, (11-01-92, Hanzel, #251), 2¼ x 6⅞ in., (5.7 x 17.5 cm.), etching.

$18,400* *The Virgin And Child With The Cat And Snake (B., Holl. 63; H. 275; BB-C), 1654,* Holl.'s 1st state of 2, Usticke's 2nd of 3, plate tone, scratches, wide margins, center fold, dirt, good cond., (05-13-93, Sotheby-NY, #177, illus.), 3⅝ x 5⅝ in., (93 x 143 mm.), etching (BP 12,080, DM 29,711, FR 100,218, Y 2,054,259).

BI *Die Wandernden Musikanten (B.R.S. 119; Wh.-B 119/II), c. 1635,* restored, est. DM 1800, (12-01-92, Karl/Faber, #131), etching.

$2655* *Wanderndes Bettlerpaar (B.R.S. 144; Wh.-B. 144), c. 1634,* from the series of images of beggars, trimmed, buckling, (12-01-92, Karl/Faber, #129, illus.), etching (BP 1754, DM 4232, FR 14,422, Y 330,553).

$2475* *The White Negress (B. 357), 1630,* 2nd (final) state, areas of wash, thread margins, good cond., wear, glue stains, surface soiling, pencil notations, (02-24-93, Butterfield, #2701, illus.), 3¹⁄₁₆ x 3 in., (78 x 76 mm.), etching on laid (BP 1726, DM 4018, FR 13,621, Y 290,425).

BI *The White Negress (B., Holl. 357; H. 364 (rej.); BB. 30-17), c. 1630,* narrow margins, reparied hole, staining, est. BP 5/700, (12-01-92, Christie-London, #145), plate 3¹³⁄₁₆ x 3¹⁄₁₆ in., (97 x 78 mm.), etching.

BI *The White Negress (B., Holl. 357; H. 364; B.B. 30-17),* thin patches, discoloration, est. BP 1/1,500, (12-03-92, Sotheby-London, #135), 3¾ x 3 in., (98 x 78 mm.), etching.

$12,869* *The Windmill (B., Holl. 233; H. 179; B. B. 41-C), 1641,* sulphur tint, trimmed irregularly, paper thin, center, dirt, (06-30-93, Sotheby-London, #208, illus.), 5¾ x 8¼ in., (146 x 210 mm.), etching (BP 8625, DM 21,950, FR 74,045, Y 1,378,871).

BI *The Windmill (B., Holl. 233; H. 179; B.B. 41-C), 1641,* thread margins, trimmed on platemark, tip of corner renewed, repairedtears, line of wash along platemark, discoloration, good cond., est. BP 14/16,000, (12-03-92, Sotheby-London, #108, illus.), 5¾ x 8¼ in., (145 x 208 mm.), etching on paper w/countermark.

$129,000* *The Windmill (B., Holl. 233; H. 179; BB 41-C), 1641,* sulfur tint strong, narrow margins, thin spots, stains, good cond., ex-coll. Dr. Otto Schaefer Collection, (05-13-93, Sotheby-NY, #70, illus.), 5¾ x 8¼ in., (145 x 208 mm.), etching, on sturdy laid (BP 84,690, DM 208,300, FR 702,614, Y 14,402,144).

BI *The Windmill (B., Holl. 233; H. 179; BB 41-C), 1641,* thread margins, trimmed, tips corners lacking, repaired tears, restoration, plugged holes, foxing, prop. Brooklyn Museum, est. $10/15,000, (05-13-93, Sotheby-NY, #195), 5¾ x 8¼ in., (146 x 208 mm.), etching.

$34,451* *Die Windmuhle (B. 233; Bl. 333; M. 305; Dut. 230; H. 179; S. 233; B.-B. 41-C; W.-B. 233; N.-U. 233), 1641,* d. in plate, wrinkles, tears, watermark, (10-09-92, Winterberg, #898, illus.), 5¾ x 8¼ in., (14.6 x 20.9 cm.), etching (BP 20,440, DM 51,175, FR 171,825, Y 4,194,181).

$5055* *Die Windmuhle (B. 233; Seidlitz, Hollstein, Nowell-Usticke 233), 1641,* (12-04-92, Bassenge, #6397), 5¾ x 8¼ in., (14.6 x 21 cm.), etching (BP 3242, DM 8051, FR 27,310, Y 631,086).

$1035* *Woman At A Door Taking To A Man And Children, The Schoolmaster (B., Holl. 128, H. 192, BB. 41-N), 1641,* thread margins or trimmed, staining, split, tears, backed w/Japan, loss, prov., (05-11-93, Christie-NY, #45), plate 3⅝ x 2⅜ in., (92 x 60 mm.), etching on laid (BP 661, DM 1630, FR 5494, Y 113,849).

BI *Woman At The Bath With A Hat Beside Her (B., Holl. 199; H. 297; B. B.58-C), 1658,* 2nd final state, margins, paper uneven in tone creases, stain, surface dirt, est. BP 30/40,000, (06-30-93, Sotheby-London, #201, illus.), 6 x 5 in., (152 x 127 mm.), etching and drypoint on Japan paper conjoined w/two other sheets.

$46,000* *Woman At The Bath With A Hat Beside Her (B., Holl. 199; H. 297; BB 58-C), 1658,* 2nd (final) state, plate tone, paper taken tone unevenly or lifted off in places, trimmed, stain, cockling, good cond., Dr. Otto Schaefer Collection, (05-13-93, Sotheby-NY, #38, illus.), 6⅛ x 5 in., (156 x 128 mm.), etching and drypoint on golden Japan (BP 30,200, DM 74,277, FR 250,545, Y 5,135,648).

BI *Woman Bathing Her Feet At A Brook (B. 200), 1658,* tone, narrow margins, nick, skinned in places, good cond., collec.'smark, est. BP 2,5/3,000, (11-30-92, Phillips-London, #309), plate 6¼ x 3⅛ in., (159 x 79 mm.), etching on thick laid.

$1332* *A Woman Bathing Her Feet At A Brook (B., Holl. 200; H. 298; BB. 58-D), 1658,* margins, tear, made-up loss, defects, (12-01-92, Christie-London, #134), plate 6¼ x 3⅛ in., (158 x 80 mm.), etching (BP 880, DM 2123, FR 7235, Y 165,837).

$2875* *Woman Reading (B., Holl. 345; H. 113; BB 34-D), 1634,* 3rd (final) state, small margins, good cond., ex-coll. Capt. Gordon Nowell-Usticke, (05-13-93, Sotheby-NY, #198), 4⅞ x 4 in., (125 x 100 mm.), etching (BP 1887, DM 4642, FR 15,659, Y 320,978).

$5147* *Woman Sitting Half Dressed Beside A Stove (B., Holl. 197; H. 296; B.B. 58-B), 1658,* damaged impression of 6th state of 7, narrow margins, trimmed, narrowto thread margins, creases, rubbed, defects, collector's mark RS, (06-30-93, Sotheby-London, #205, illus.), 8½ x 7¼ in., (216 x 184 mm.), etching, engraving and drypoint on warm-toned Japan paper (BP 3450, DM 8779, FR 29,614, Y 551,484).

$4162* *A Woman Sitting Half-Dressed Beside A Stove (B., Holl. 197; H. 296; BB. 58-B), 1658,* 7th (final) state, thread margins or trimmed, crease, surface losses, prov., (12-01-92, Christie-London, #133), sheet 8⅞ x 7⁵⁄₁₆ in., (225 x 185 mm.), etching w/drypoint and engraving (BP 2750, DM 6634, FR 22,607, Y 518,177).

$4888* *Young Man In A Velvet Cap (Ferdinand Bol?) (B., Holl. 268; H. 151; BB37-C), 1637,* 2nd (final) state, traces burr, trimmed, good cond., thin spots, ex-coll. J. M. P. Cerroni, (05-13-93, Sotheby-NY, #196, illus.), 3⅞ x 3¼ in., (97 x 84 mm.), etching (BP 3209, DM 7893, FR 26,623, Y 545,718).

$1444* *Der Zeichner (B. 130; Seidlitz 130 IV; Hollstein 130 III; Nowell-Usticke 130 III), c. 1641,* (12-04-92, Bassenge, #6389), 3⁹⁄₁₆ x 2⁷⁄₁₆ in., (9.1 x 6.2 cm.), etching (BP 926, DM 2300, FR 7801, Y 180,275).

$2527* *Der Zeichner Nach Dem Modell (B. 192, Seidlitz 192 III, Hollstein 192II, Nowell-Usticke 192I), c. 1646,* prov., (12-04-92, Bassenge, #6393), 9 x 7¹⁄₁₆ in., (22.9 x 18 cm.), etching (BP 1621, DM 4025, FR 13,652, Y 315,481).

$2166* *Der heilige Hieronymus im Gebet, Niederblickend (B. 102; Seidlitz 102 I; Nowell-Usticke 102 I 1; Hollstein 102), (12-04-92, Bassenge, #6383),* 4⁷⁄₁₆ x 3⅛ in., (11.3 x 8 cm.), etching (BP 1389, DM 3450, FR 11,702, Y 270,412).

REMBRANDT (after)

$649* *Collection of Thirty-One Etchings,* mostly from Recueil De Quatre-Vingt-Cinq Estampes Originales, pub. H.L. Basan, (12-10-92, Bonhams-Chelsea, #63), etching (BP 418, DM 1027, FR 3506, Y 80,282).

BI *Portrait Of A Bearded Gentleman Wearing A Turban, 1778,* pub. J. Boydell, trimmed, tears, est. BP 70/100, (07-16-92, Bonhams-Chelsea, #451), image 18½ x 14 in., (47 x 35.6 cm.), mezzotint laid down.

$467* *The Ship Builder,* by Charles Howard Hodges, scratch-letter proof, before titles, trimmed to 1/4in. margins, good cond., (11-30-92, Phillips-London, #25), mezzotint on laid (BP 308, DM 744, FR 2526, Y 58,121).

REMBRANDT (attrib.)   Dutch 1606-1669

BI *Head Of An Old Man In High Fur Cap: Bust (B., Holl. 299; H. 135; B. B. REJ. 52),* wiping scratches, narrow to thread margins, trimmed, thin spot, remains, glue, good cond., est. BP 6/800, (06-30-93, Sotheby-London, #227), 1⅝ x 1¼ in., (41 x 32 mm.), etching.

REMBRANDT (circle of)

$1201* *Woman Cutting Her Mistress's Nails (B., Holl. 127; H. 312; B. B. REJ9),* 2nd final state, wide margins, stains, discoloration, (06-30-93, Sotheby-London, #228, illus.), 5 x 3¾ in., (127 x 95 mm.), etching (BP 805, DM 2048, FR 6910, Y 128,683).

REMBRANDT (school of)

$3163* *Curly-Headed Man With A Wry Mouth (B., Holl. 305; H. 137; BB Rej. 54),* c. 1637-40, narrow margins, good cond., small grey stain, ex-coll. Leonard Gow; and Capt. Gordon Nowell-Usticke, (05-13-93, Sotheby-NY, #200), 2½ x 2⅜ in., (64 x 60 mm.), etching (BP 2077, DM 5107, FR 17,228, Y 353,132).

REME, Jorg   b. 1941

BI *Facherfigur, 1973,* s., d., #11/100, t., est. DM 200, (09-18-92, Schloss Ahlden, #1044), 25¹³⁄₁₆ x 20 in., (65.6 x 50.8 cm.), color screen print on hand-made.

$141* *In Het Oerwoud Op Bali, 1979,* s., d., #36/190, margins, good cond., (05-27-93, Sotheby-Amstrdm, #474), sh 22¹³⁄₁₆ x 30¼ in., (580 x 768 mm.), colored lithograph on wove (BP 90, DM 226, FR 763, Y 15,116, G 253).

$115* *Op Een Terras In Skiathos, 1979,* s, d., #160/190, margins, good cond., (05-27-93, Sotheby-Amstrdm, #475), sh 22¹³⁄₁₆ x 30¼ in., (580 x 768 mm.), colored lithograph on wove (BP 74, DM 185, FR 622, Y 12,328, G 207).

$154* *Succesvol Zakenman, 1979,* s., d., #179/190, margins, good cond., (05-27-93, Sotheby-Amstrdm, #473), sh 30¼ x 22¹³⁄₁₆ in., (768 x 580 mm.), colored lithograph on wove (BP 99, DM 247, FR 833, Y 16,509, G 276).

REMO

$80* *Liquore Del Reno, c. 1910,* cond. A, (03-16-93, Boisgirard, #180), 21⅝ x 14³⁄₁₆ in., (55 x 36 cm.), poster (BP 55, DM 133, FR 452, Y 9355).

REMON, George (after)

$303* *17th And 18th Century Interiors: Five,* (03-17-93, Bonhams-Chelsea, #372), image 8½ x 14 in., (21.6 x 35.6 cm.), reprod. in colors (BP 209, DM 504, FR 1714, Y 35,538).

REMY, E.

$321* *Le Tam-Tam, c. 1900,* Paris, Imp. Delanchy and Cie, cond A-, (06-11-93, Boisgirard, #141, illus.), 41⁵⁄₁₆ x 29½ in., (105 x 75 cm.), poster (BP 211, DM 522, FR 1759, Y 34,058).

RENGER-PATZSCH, Albert   American 1897-1966

BI *Architectural Interior By Hanns Schwippert,* 1940s, credit, reprod. limit., & Schwippert credit stamps, est. $2,5/3,500, (10-13-92, Christie-NY, #333, illus.), 9 x 6¾ in., (22.9 x 17.1 cm.), photograph, gelatin silver print.

$880* *"Astrophytum Asterias" and "Astrophytum Asterias With Blossom": Two,* photographer's notations, Folkwang-Auriga handstamp, 1920s, (04-07-93, Swann, #539, illus.), each approx. 6¾ x 6¾ in., photograph, silver print (BP 582, DM 1423, FR 4817, Y 99,977).

BI *Beech Tree (Untitled 12, pl. 20, variant; Schurmann and Kicken, p. 31, variant),* c. 1925, t. in German, #L26 by

photog., stamps, est. $7/10,000, (04-06-93, Sotheby-NY, #324, illus.), 14¾ x 10¾ in., photograph.

BI *"Birds Of Paradise, Essen, Goethestran",* 1930's, t., photog. stamp, est. $7/900, (11-16-92, Butterfield, #6126, illus.), 6⅞ x 9¼ in., (174.9 x 235.4 mm.), photograph, gelatin silver print.

BI *"Botanical Study",* 1930's, t., photog. stamps, est. $7/900, (11-16-92, Butterfield, #6127, illus.), 9 x 6½ in., (229 x 165.4 mm.), photograph, gelatin silver print.

BI *"Buchenlaub Im Frumling",* 1930s, t., stamped photog.'s credit, 158 x 203mm, est. BP 4/600, (05-07-93, Sotheby-London, #225, illus.), photograph, silver print.

$1210* *"Cactus" and "Potted Cactus": Two,* notations, Folkwang-Auriga handstamp, 1920s, (04-07-93, Swann, #540), 7¾ x 6¾ in., photograph, silver print (BP 800, DM 1957, FR 6623, Y 137,469).

$1452* *"Gefullte Sonnenblume", Full-Blown Sunflower,* c. 1935-41, p. 1943, mounted on card, ink t., later gallery stamp, (05-06-93, Christie-London, #127, illus.), 15⅛ x 11⅛ in., photograph, gelatin silver print (BP 920, DM 2287, FR 7699, Y 159,754).

$758* *Die Halligen, 1927,* photographer's stamp, lit., (11-12-92, Lempertz, #197, illus.), 6⅝ x 9 in., (16.9 x 22.9 cm.), photograph, gelatin silver print (BP 485, DM 1191, FR 4060, Y 93,777).

$1179* *"Halligfriese", Portrait Of A Reaper,* 1926, p. 1943, mounted on card, t., exhib. ink stamp, gallery ink stamp, lit., (05-06-93, Christie-London, #125, illus.), 13⅜ x 11⅛ in., photograph, gelatin silver print (BP 747, DM 1857, FR 6251, Y 129,717).

$1815* *"Krabbenfischerinnen", Crab Fisherwomen,* 1926, p. 1943, mounted on card, ink t., stamped, lit., (05-06-93, Christie-London, #128, illus.), 11¼ x 15 in., photograph, gelatin silver print (BP 1150, DM 2859, FR 9624, Y 199,692).

BI *Pouring Molten Steel, 1932,* t., credit stamp, exhib. label, t., est. $2/2,500, (10-13-92, Christie-NY, #332, illus.), 6⅝ x 8⅞ in., (16.8 x 22.5 cm.), photograph, gelatin silver print.

$2178* *"Queller Im Schlick", Plants In Dry River Bed,* 1926, p. 1943, mounted on card, ink t., stamped, lit., (05-06-93, Christie-London, #129, illus.), 11¼ x 15 in., photograph, gelatin silver print (BP 1380, DM 3430, FR 11,548, Y 239,630).

BI *Reeds In The Snow, c. 1924,* i. in unident. hands, est. $3/5,000, (04-06-93, Sotheby-NY, #325, illus.), 10¾ x 14¾ in., photograph.

BI *"Schieferkuste Bretagne",* 1930s, t., stamped ink photog.'s credit, 221 x 165mm, (05-07-93, Sotheby-London, #224, illus.), photograph, silver print.

$1100* *Succulent,* photog.'s studio & reprod. limit. stamps, t., num. in unidentified hand, 1930's, (10-15-92, Sotheby-NY, #404, illus.), 8½ x 6⅝ in., (21.6 x 16.8 cm.), photograph, gelatin silver print (BP 673, DM 1637, FR 5553, Y 131,974).

$1100* *Two Botanical Studies,* notations, handstamp, 1920's, (10-14-92, Swann, #541, illus.), 7 x 9½ in., (17.8 x 24.1 cm.), photograph, silver prints (BP 646, DM 1610, FR 5459, Y 133,301).

BI *Untitled, Wilsnack, North Side Of The Choir,* 1928, p. 1943, mounted on card, later gallery stamp, lit., est. BP 800/1,200, (05-06-93, Christie-London, #126, illus.), 15 x 11⅛ in., photograph, gelatin silver print.

$4025* *Wilder Zwetschenbaum Bei Steele/Ruhr Gebeit, after 1944,* t., credit stamp, (04-08-93, Christie-NY, #112, illus.), 8⅞ x 6½ in., (22.5 x 16.5 cm.), photograph, gelatin silver print (BP 2639, DM 6466, FR 21,887, Y 456,764).

$683* *Das Zaunchen, 1925/26,* d., t., atelier stamp, (11-12-92, Lempertz, #196), 9⅛ x 15³⁄₁₆ in., (23.2 x 38.5 cm.), photograph, gelatin silver print (BP 437, DM 1073, FR 3658, Y 84,498).

RENI, Guido   Italian 1575-1642

$222* *Cherubs - Amorette,* (10-21-92, Maynard, #310), 11 x 15½ in., (27.9 x 39.4 cm.), etching (BP 138, DM 336, FR 1140, Y 27,040, C$ 275).

$1984* *Der Heilige Hieronymus Im Gebet (B. 15),* watermark, (06-08-93, Karl/Faber, #179), etching (BP 1304, DM 3219, FR 10,842, Y 210,728).

$1527* *Maria, Das Jesuskind Und Johannes (Illus. Bartsch XXXX, 153, 6), c. 1630,* (06-23-93, Kornfeld, #103), etching (BP 1037, DM 2584, FR 8691, Y 166,358, SF 2300).

RENI, Guido (attrib.) Italian 1575-1642

$385* *Virgin With A Pillow,* c. 1594, after Annibale Carracci, prov., (09-20-92, Hindman, #664), 6¼ x 4⅝ in., (15.9 x 11.7 cm.), etching (BP 225, DM 571, FR 1954, Y 47,584).

$495* *Virgin With A Pillow (Bohlin R3 III/III), c. 1594,* after Annibale Carracci, (03-14-93, Hindman, #284), 6¼ x 4⅝ in., (15.9 x 11.7 cm.), etching (BP 345, DM 824, FR 2801, Y 58,338).

RENOIR, Pierre Auguste French 1841-1919

$220* *At The Beach,* restrike, (11-01-92, Hanzel, #229), 5⅜ x 3⅝ in., (13.7 x 9.2 cm.), etching (BP 144, DM 347, FR 1170, Y 27,201).

$3399* *Baigneuse Assise (Delteil 11), c. 1905,* (06-04-93, Bassenge, #5774, illus.), 8¹¹⁄₁₆ x 5⁵⁄₁₆ in., (22 x 13.5 cm.), soft-ground etching w/colors on strong wove (BP 2249, DM 5520, FR 18,604, Y 366,588).

$3449* *Baigneuse Assise (Delteil, Stella 11), c. 1897,* sig. stamp, pub. Ambroise Vollard's La Vie et L'oeuvre de Pierre-Auguste Renoir, full margins, good cond., foxing, (10-14-92, Sotheby-Japan, #80, illus.), 8⅝ x 5⅜ in., (219 x 137 mm.), softground etching on creme wove (BP 2024, DM 5048, FR 17,117, Y 417,959).

$2750* *Baigneuse Assise (S. 11), 1897,* stamped sig., pub. Ambroise Vollard in La Vie et l'oeuvre de Pierre-Auguste Renoir, full margins, good cond., discoloration, stain, foxing, surfacesoiling, (10-28-92, Butterfield, #2714, illus.), 8⅝ x 5⅜ in., (219 x 137 mm.), soft-ground etching on wove (BP 1752, DM 4247, FR 14,421, Y 337,423).

$1702* *"Baigneuse Assise c. 1897" (Stella 11),* s. in pl., 2nd edit., Ambroise Vollard editor, (01-28-93, Pescheteau, #238, illus.), 12¹³⁄₁₆ x 9¹³⁄₁₆ in., (32.5 x 25 cm.), soft ground etching on laid (BP 1124, DM 2697, FR 9126, Y 211,324).

$385* *"Baigneuse Debout A Mi-Jambes" and "Femme Nue Couchee": Two,* late impressions, (05-28-93, Sloan, #1916, illus.), larger 6¾ x 4¼ in., (17.1 x 10.8 cm.), etching (BP 247, DM 611, FR 2064, Y 41,282).

$136* *Baigneuse Debout, A Mi-Jambes (D. 23; S. 23), c. 1910,* only state, margins, stained, (10-15-92, Bonhams-Chelsea, #99), plate 6⅝ x 4⅜ in., (16.8 x 11.1 cm.), etching on wove (BP 83, DM 202, FR 687, Y 16,317).

$165* *"Baigneuse Debout, A Mi-Jambes" (D23, S23), 1910,* (02-13-93, Neal, #577), image 6 x 4 in., (15.2 x 10.2 cm.), etching (BP 116, DM 274, FR 926, Y 19,899).

$225* *Baigneuse Debout, A Mijambes (Delteil 23),* creases, (03-24-93, Venator/Hansten, #4551), pl. 6⅝ x 4⅜ in., (16.8 x 11.1 cm.), etching on hand-made (BP 152, DM 367, FR 1251, Y 26,436).

$110* *"La Baigneuse",* posthumous printing, good cond.?, (02-07-93, Bakker, #200), plate 6½ x 4¾ in., (16.5 x 12.1 cm.), etching (BP 76, DM 182, FR 617, Y 13,688).

$385* *"Baigneuse", (Stella 23),* very good/good cond., (09-27-92, Bakker, #177), plate 6½ x 4½ in., (16.5 x 11.4 cm.), etching (BP 225, DM 571, FR 1930, Y 46,470).

$42,895* *Baigneuse, Debout, En Pied (Stella 28), 1865,* wide margins, good cond., stain, (06-30-93, Sotheby-London, #665, illus.), sh 25 x 18⅝ in., (635 x 473 mm.), lithographic in 8 colors on laid (BP 28,750, DM 73,162, FR 246,807, Y 4,596,057).

$385* *"Berthe Morisot" and "Bagneuse Debout, A Mi-Jambes" [D & S 4, 23]: Two,* late impressions, s. in plate, (12-10-92, Sloan, #3027), larger 6½ x 4¼ in., (16.5 x 10.8 cm.), etching (BP 248, DM 609, FR 2080, Y 47,625).

BI *"Berthe Morisot" and "Baigneuse Debout, A Mi-Jambes" (S. 4 and 23), c. 1892 and 1910: Two,* reprints, full margins, good cond., foxing, staining, est. BP 3/400, (06-30-93, Sotheby-London, #671), one 3¾ x 4½ in., (95 x 114 mm.), drypoint and etching on laid.

$660* *"Berthe Morisot", 1892, "Le Chapeau Epingle", 1894 and "Baigneuse Debout, A Mi-Jambes", 1910 (Stella, Delteil numbers 4, 8, and 23): Group Of Three,* posthumous printings, (05-27-93, Swann, #237), etchings (BP 423, DM 1059, FR 3569, Y 70,755).

$138* *Chapeau Epingle,* sig. w/in plate, (05-20-93, Eldred, #170A), 4¾ x 3¼ in., (12.1 x 8.3 cm.), etching (BP 89, DM 223, FR 750, Y 15,239).

$27,600* *Le Chapeau Epingle (D., S. 30; Roger-Marx 5), c. 1898,* p. August Clot, full margins, good cond., discoloration, pressure marks, repaired punctures, John S. Spurbeck Estate, (05-13-93, Sotheby-NY, #803, illus.), 24½ x 19¾ in., (622 x 500 mm.), sh 35½ x 25¼ in., (622 x 500 mm.), lithograph in seven colors on laid (BP 18,120, DM 44,566, FR 150,327, Y 3,081,389).

$202* *Le Chapeau Epingle (Delt. 8), 1894,* later imp., plate s., (09-25-92, Granier, #2676), 4¹¹⁄₁₆ x 3⁵⁄₁₆ in., (11.9 x 8.4 cm.), sheet 13³⁄₁₆ x 9¹³⁄₁₆ in., (11.9 x 8.4 cm.), etching on machine hand-made (BP 118, DM 299, FR 1013, Y 24,381).

$39,307* *Le Chapeau Epingle (L. Delteil 30), 1898,* yellowed, mat-staining, crease, large margins, tear, (06-16-93, Ader Tajan, #132, illus.), 23⅝ x 19³⁄₁₆ in., (60 x 48.8 cm.), 11-color lithograph on M.B.M. laid (BP 26,205, DM 65,251, FR 218,981, Y 4,192,299).

$1840* *Le Chapeau Epingle (La Fille De Berthe Morisot Et Sa Cousine), 2e Planche (D., S. 7), c. 1894,* stamp sig., large margins, good cond., rubbing, (05-13-93, Sotheby-NY, #802), 5⅛ x 3¾ in., (131 x 95 mm.), plate 12½ x 9⅝ in., (131 x 95 mm.), etching w/tone on cream Japan (BP 1208, DM 2971, FR 10,022, Y 205,426).

$303* *"Le Chapeau Epingle",* (09-18-92, DuMouchelle, #2309), image 4½ x 3⅛ in., (11.4 x 7.9 cm.), etching (BP 174, DM 454, FR 1554, Y 37,752).

$605* *"Le Chapeau Epingle" and "Nu Debout A Mi-Jambes": Two (Stella 8 and 23), 1894 and 1910,* (03-14-93, Hindman, #244), larger 6⅝ x 4⅜ in., (16.8 x 11.1 cm.), etchings (BP 422, DM 1007, FR 3424, Y 71,302).

$330* *"Le Chapeau Epingle", c. 1892,* s. plate, full margins, excell. cond., (05-07-93, Goldberg, #429A), 4½ x 3¼ in., (13.3 x 8.3 cm.), etching on arches (BP 209, DM 522, FR 1758, Y 36,336).

$275* *"Le Chapeau Epingle", c. 1894,* second state, s. in plate, full margins, (10-10-92, Goldberg, #421, illus.), image 4½ x 3¼ in., (11.4 x 8.3 cm.), etching (BP 163, DM 408, FR 1372, Y 33,479).

$20,700* *Le Chapeau Epingle, 2 Planche (Delteil, Stella 30; Roger-Marx 5), c. 1898,* p. August Clot, trimmed into image, faded, discoloration, (02-11-93, Sotheby-NY, #258, illus.), sheet 23¹⁵⁄₁₆ x 19⅜ in., (609 x 492 mm.), lithograph p. in 11 colors on laid (BP 14,606, DM 34,289, FR 116,031, Y 2,495,479).

$56,272* *Le Chapeau Epingle, 2E Planche (Delteil, Stella 39; Roger-Marx 5), c.1898,* full margins, exceptionally good cond., creases, surface dirt, tape hinges, (12-03-92, Sotheby-London, #572, illus.), 24½ x 19⅛ in., (620 x 485 mm.), lithograph in eight colors on MBM laid (BP 36,300, DM 88,492, FR 302,050, Y 7,001,618).

$20,590* *Le Chapeau Epingle, 2E Planche (S. 30), c. 1897,* full margins, good cond., creases, staining, (06-30-93, Sotheby-London, #667, illus.), sh 35 x 24⅛ in., (889 x 613 mm.), lithographic in black on MBM laid (BP 13,800, DM 35,119, FR 118,470, Y 2,206,150).

$54,050* *Le Chapeau Epingle, 2e Planche (L.D., Stella 30), c. 1898,* proof, wide margins, margins, pinholes, very good cond., (05-11-93, Christie-NY, #332, illus.), borderline 24 x 19 in., (610 x 483 mm.), color lithograph on laid paper (BP 34,504, DM 85,145, FR 286,890, Y 5,945,441).

$38,500* *Le Chapeau Epingle, 2e Planche (L.D.; Stella 30), c. 1898,* watermark, stamped sig., wide margins, staining, soiling, colors attenuated, touched spot, splits, defects, (11-09-92, Christie-NY, #196, illus.), 25 x 19⅝ in., (635 x 498 mm.), lithograph in 11 colors on laid (BP 25,455, DM 61,462, FR 207,659, Y 4,777,861).

$213* *Le Chapeau Epingle, La Fille De Berthe Morisot Et Sa Cousine,* plate s., late impression, (12-01-92, Ritchie, #13A, illus.), 5½ x 3¾ in., (14 x 9.5 cm.), etching (BP 141, DM 339, FR 1157, Y 26,519, C$ 275).

$967* *Claude Renoir, La Tete Baisee (Delteil 39), 1904,* second state, sig. stamp, (06-28-93, Loudmer, #352), 7⅞ x 7⅞ in., (200 x 200 mm.), sh 12¹⁵⁄₁₆ x 9¹⁵⁄₁₆ in., (200 x 200 mm.), black lithograph on wove (BP 647, DM 1643, FR 5535, Y 102,599).

$1870* *Claude Renoir, La Tete Baisee (S. 39), 1904,* 2nd (final) state, full margins, good cond. (?), pencil notation, (02-24-93, Butterfield, #2791), 7¾ x 7¾ in., (197 x 197 mm.), lithograph on wove (BP 1304, DM 3036, FR 10,292, Y 219,432).

$1955* *Claude Renoir, La Tete Baisee (S. 39), 1904,* full margins, good cond., mat staining, glue remains, foxing, (05-19-93, Butterfield, #1962), 7¾ x 7¾ in., (197 x 197 mm.), lithograph on wove (BP 1269, DM 3178, FR 10,706, Y 216,429).

BI *Claude Renoir, La Tete Baissee, Paris, (S. 39), 1904,* from Douze lithographies originales de Pierre-Auguste Renoir, Ambroise Vollard, 1919, 2nd final state, stone s., full margins, creasing, staining, tear, good cond., est. $2/3,000, (05-11-93, Christie-NY, #334), borderline 7½ x 7½ in., (191 x 191 mm.), lithograph on wove.

$1238* *Claude Renoir, Tete Baisee (L.D., 39; S., 39), c. 1904,* whole margins, (04-02-93, Picard, #172), 8⁷⁄₁₆ x 7⅜ in., (21.5 x 18.8 cm.), lithograph in black on wove (BP 815, DM 1990, FR 6758, Y 140,954).

$5607* *La Danse A La Campagne (Delteil 2, 2eme planche), c. 1890,* sig. stamp, reddish stains, (06-28-93, Loudmer, #351, illus.), 8¹¹⁄₁₆ x 5⅜ in., (221 x 137 mm.), sh 12⅞ x 9⅞ in., (221 x 137 mm.), black softground etching on wove (BP 3754, DM 9528, FR 32,095, Y 594,907).

$9077* *La Danse A La Campagne, (Second Plate) (Delteil, Stella 2), 1890,* sig. stamp, full margins, good cond., scuff, stains, (10-14-92, Sotheby-Japan, #79, illus.), 8¾ x 5⅜ in., (222 x 137 mm.), softground etching (BP 5328, DM 13,284, FR 45,047, Y 1,099,976).

$16,300* *Douze Lithographies Originales De Pierre-Auguste Renoir (S. 37-48), 1904-1905: Set Of Twelve,* pub. Vollard, 1919, full margins, good cond., foxmarks, creasing, tears, original portfolio, (06-30-93, Sotheby-London, #670, illus.), each sh approx. 13 x 10 in., (330 x 254 mm.), lithograph on wove (BP 10,925, DM 27,801, FR 93,786, Y 1,746,491).

$51,610* *Enfants Jouant A la Balle (L.D., S. 32; Johnson, Vollard 111), c. 1900,* watermark, pub. A. Vollard, margins, loss, repaired tears, light-staining, surface dirt, good cond., (12-01-92, Christie-London, #514, illus.), L. 23¹⁄₁₆ x 16⅛ in., (585 x 410 mm.), sheet 30 x 24⅛ in., (585 x 410 mm.), lithograph in colors on Arches Ingres laid (BP 34,100, DM 82,260, FR 280,337, Y 6,425,548).

$1115* *Etude De Femme Nue, Assise, Variante (S. 43), 1904,* pub. Douze lithographies originales de Pierre-Auguste Renoir, by Vollard, full margins, good cond., (06-30-93, Sotheby-London, #669), 6½ x 6¼ in., (165 x 159 mm.), lithograph on wove (BP 747, DM 1902, FR 6415, Y 119,469).

$1955* *"Etude De Femme Nue, Assise, Variante" and "Femme Aucep De Vigne, IerVariante" (D., S. 43 and 45), c. 1904: Two,* pub. in Douze lithographies originales de Pierre-Auguste Renoir, by Vollard, 1919, full margins, good cond., mat stain, fox marks, (05-13-93, Sotheby-NY, #807), one 6⅜ x 6⅛ in., (161 x 157 mm.), other 6¾ x 4½ in., (161 x 157 mm.), lithograph on Arches wove (BP 1283, DM 3157, FR 10,648, Y 218,265).

$1249* *Etude De Femme Nue, Assise, Variante, Lithographies Originales (L.D., S. 43), c. 1904,* pub. A. Vollard, margins, foxmarks, creases, (12-01-92, Christie-London, #516), L. 6½ x 6⁵⁄₁₆ in., (165 x 160 mm.), lithograph on wove (BP 825, DM 1991, FR 6784, Y 155,503).

$2723* *Etude Pour Une Baigneuse (Delteil, Stella 16), c. 1906,* sig. stamp, full margins, good cond., mat stained, fox marks, (10-14-92, Sotheby-Japan, #81, illus.), 8¾ x 6½ in., (222 x 165 mm.), drypoint on creme wove (BP 1598, DM 3985, FR 13,514, Y 329,981).

$550* *Femme Au Cep De Vigne (Stella, Delteil 47), c. 1904,* second state w/sig. stone, pub. Vollard, 1919, in Douze LithographiesOriginal de Pierre Auguste Renoir, laid down, sandwiched between mats, mat burn, foxing, (05-27-93, Swann, #236), approx. 9 x 6 in., (22.9 x 15.2

cm.), tusche lithograph (BP 352, DM 883, FR 2975, Y 58,962).

$990* *Femme Au Cep De Vigne, 2e Variante (S. 46), 1904,* s. in stone, pub. in L'Album des Douze Lithographies Originals, fullmargins, good cond., foxing, light-staining, glue & hinge remains, creases, inknotation, pencil notations, (02-24-93, Butterfield, #2792), 4⅝ x 3¼ in., (117 x 83 mm.), lithograph on wove (BP 690, DM 1607, FR 5449, Y 116,170).

$1540* *Femme Au Cep De Vigne, 3E Variante (S. 47), 1904,* stone s., 2nd final state, full margins, good cond., staining, mat staining, foxing, creases, soiling, (10-28-92, Butterfield, #2715), 6⅜ x 4⅛ in., (162 x 105 mm.), lithograph on Arches (BP 981, DM 2378, FR 8076, Y 188,957).

$715* *"Femme Au Cep De Vigne, I Variante" (Stella #45, Delteil #45), c. 1904,* s. Renoir in stone, second state, from Douze Lithographies De Pierre-Auguste Renoir, edit. 1000, stone effaced, (02-13-93, Neal, #575, illus.), image 8 x 5 in., (20.3 x 12.7 cm.), lithograph (BP 504, DM 1186, FR 4012, Y 86,228).

$605* *Femme Au Cep Vigne (Delteil 44), 1904,* 2nd state w/sig. in stone, full margins?, in Douze Lithographies Originales de Pierre Auguste Renoir, pub. Ambroise Vollard, 1919, mat burn, image foxing, (12-08-92, Swann, #266, illus.), 13 x 9⅛ in., (33 x 23.2 cm.), tusche lithograph (BP 379, DM 942, FR 3211, Y 74,988).

$1153* *Femme Nue Assise (Claude Roger-Marx 17),* sig. stamp, water-staining, (11-16-92, Briest, #350), 12¹³⁄₁₆ x 9¹³⁄₁₆ in., (32.5 x 25 cm.), lithograph in black (BP 758, DM 1839, FR 6196, Y 143,891).

$1430* *Femme Nue Assise (Delteil, Stella 12), c. 1906,* pub. in Theodore Duret's L'Histoire des peintres impressionnistes, margins, good cond., time staining, glue stain, skinning, (11-05-92, Sotheby-NY, #423), 7⅜ x 5⅞ in., (188 x 150 mm.), soft ground etching on cream laid (BP 930, DM 2262, FR 7651, Y 175,439).

$95* *"Femme Nue Couchee (Tourne A Droite) Ze Planche" (Stella 14), c. 1906,* posthumous impress., good cond., (05-15-93, Cleveland, #423), 5½ x 7⅞ in., (14 x 20 cm.), etching (BP 62, DM 153, FR 514, Y 10,531).

$748* *Femme Nue Couchee (Tournee A Droite), 2e planche (S. 14), 1906,* pub. in Duret's Die Impressionisten, 1909 or later limited edit., full margins, good cond., notation, (05-19-93, Butterfield, #2091), 5⁷⁄₁₆ x 7¾ in., (138 x 197 mm.), etching on laid (BP 486, DM 1216, FR 4096, Y 82,807).

$275* *"Femme Nue Couchee", c. 1906,* full margins, excell. cond., (05-07-93, Goldberg, #429), 5¼ x 7½ in., (13.3 x 19.1 cm.), etching on arches (BP 174, DM 435, FR 1465, Y 30,280).

$1997* *Femme Nue Couchee, Tournee A Droite, Ire Planche (Delteil, Stella 13), c. 1906,* 2nd final state, stamp sig., full margins, good cond., (10-14-92, Sotheby-Japan, #82, illus.), 4⅞ x 7⅞ in., (124 x 200 mm.), drypoint (BP 1172, DM 2923, FR 9911, Y 242,002).

$253* *Girl With Hats,* restrike, (11-01-92, Hanzel, #227), 4½ x 3¼ in., (11.4 x 8.3 cm.), etching (BP 165, DM 399, FR 1345, Y 31,281).

$413* *"Girls Seated On Shore",* plate s., excell. cond., (12-12-92, Litchfield, #211), plate 5¼ x 3¾ in., (13.3 x 9.5 cm.), etching (BP 265, DM 651, FR 2230, Y 51,108).

BI *Jeune Femme En Buste (Mlle. Dieterle) (S. 26), c. 1899,* pub. in Album Germinal, margins, good cond., discoloration, thin spots, est. BP 18/22,000, (06-30-93, Sotheby-London, #666, illus.), sh 20⅝ x 15⅝ in., (524 x 397 mm.), lithograph in dark grey and soft black on fine wove.

BI *L'Enfant Au Biscuit (D., S. 31), c. 1898-99,* p. Clot, full margins, good cond., discoloration, scattered, foxing,creases in image, rippling, ex-coll. H.-M. Petiet, est. $12/15,000, (05-13-93, Sotheby-NY, #804, illus.), 12⅜ x 10⅜ in., (315 x 264 mm.), lithograph in grey-black and pale rose on MBM laid.

$16,100* *L'Enfant Au Biscuit (D., S. 31; R.-M. 6), c. 1898-99,* full margins, good cond., mat stain, printer's crease in image, creases, repaired tear, foxing, tape stain, (05-13-93, Sotheby-NY, #805, illus.), 12⅝ x 10½ in., (321 x 268 mm.), lithograph in grey, green, rose, yellow and black on laid (BP 10,570, DM 25,997, FR 87,691, Y 1,797,477).

$57,548* *L'Enfant Au Biscuit (L.D. 31), 1899*, s. in stone, untrimmed margins, (06-11-93, Picard, #156, illus.), 12⅝ x 10¹³⁄₁₆ in., (320 x 275 mm.), 8-color lithograph on MBM laid (BP 37,811, DM 93,528, FR 315,332, Y 6,105,889).

$6493* *L'Enfant Au Biscuit (L.D., S. 31; Johnson, Vollard 110), 1899*, pub. A. Vollard, margins, stains, defects, (12-01-92, Christie-London, #513), L. 12¹¹⁄₁₆ x 10⁹⁄₁₆ in., (323 x 268 mm.), lithograph in 5 colors (black, grey, yellow, pink and green) on MBM laid (BP 4290, DM 10,349, FR 35,269, Y 808,391).

$21,295* *"L'Enfant Au Biscuit (Portrait Jean Renoir)" (Delteil 31; Roger-Marx6; Johnson 1977, 110), 1899*, (11-28-92, Grisebach, #105, illus.), 12¹³⁄₁₆ x 10⅝ in., (32.5 x 27 cm.), color lithograph on handmade (BP 14,056, DM 33,925, FR 115,170, Y 2,650,280).

$2039* *Les Laveuses*, 1. Ausfuhrung, (10-21-92, Dobiaschofsky, #1584, illus.), 18¹¹⁄₁₆ x 24¹³⁄₁₆ in., (47.5 x 63 cm.), lithograph (BP 1266, DM 3085, FR 10,473, Y 248,356, SF 2760).

$2875* *Louis Valtat (D., S. 38), c. 1904*, pub. Douze lithographies originales de Pierre-Auguste Renoir, by Vollard, 1919, full margins, good cond., hinged to backing, double-sided tape, (02-11-93, Sotheby-NY, #259), 11¾ x 9⅜ in., (298 x 238 mm.), lithograph on Arches wove (BP 2029, DM 4762, FR 16,115, Y 346,594).

$1150* *Louis Valtat (D., S. 38), c. 1904*, pub. in Douze lithographies originales de Pierre-Auguste Renoir, by Vollard, 1919, full margins, good cond., tear into image, fox marks, nicks, Edward Knox Morris Estate, (05-13-93, Sotheby-NY, #806), 11¾ x 9⅜ in., (297 x 238 mm.), lithograph on Arches wove (BP 755, DM 1857, FR 6264, Y 128,391).

$2167* *Louis Valtat (L.D., 38; S., 38), c. 1904*, whole margins, (04-02-93, Picard, #171), 11¾ x 9⅜ in., (29.8 x 23.8 cm.), lithograph in black on wove (BP 1427, DM 3483, FR 11,829, Y 246,727).

$1495* *Louis Valtat (S. 38), 1904*, full margins, good cond., mat/light-staining, staining throughout image, foxing, tape/hinge remains, surface soiling, notations, (05-19-93, Butterfield, #1961), 11¹³⁄₁₆ x 9½ in., (300 x 241 mm.), lithograph on wove (BP 970, DM 2430, FR 8187, Y 165,504).

$2316* *Louis Valtat (S. 38), c. 1904*, pub. Douze lithographies originales de Pierre-Auguste Renoir, by Vollard, 1919, full margins, good cond., (06-30-93, Sotheby-London, #668, illus.), 11⅜ x 9⅜ in., (289 x 238 mm.), lithograph on wove (BP 1552, DM 3950, FR 13,326, Y 248,152).

$1249* *Louis Valtat, From Douze Lithographies Originales (L.D., s. 38), c. 1904*, pub. A. Vollard, margins, repaired tear, good cond., (12-01-92, Christie-London, #515), L. 11¾ x 9⅜ in., (298 x 238 mm.), lithograph on laid (BP 825, DM 1991, FR 6784, Y 155,503).

BI *Mere Et Enfant (Jean Renoir) (L. Delteil 10)*, large margins, (06-11-93, Picard, #155), 8¼ x 7³⁄₁₆ in., (210 x 183 mm.), drypoint in three tones on thin tinted laid.

$1840* *Odalisque (L.D., Stella 35), 1904*, stone s., full margins, light-staining, foxing, glue, top and bottom margin edges folded back, (05-11-93, Christie-NY, #333), borderline 3¼ x 5 in., (83 x 127 mm.), lithograph on wove (BP 1175, DM 2899, FR 9766, Y 202,398).

$1980* *Odalisque (L.D.; S. 35), c. 1904*, stone s., wide margins, very good cond., (11-09-92, Christie-NY, #197), 3⅛ x 4⅞ in., (79 x 124 mm.), lithograph on Chine (BP 1309, DM 3161, FR 10,680, Y 245,719).

BI *Pages, By Stephane Mallarme (S. 3), 1891*, vol., 2nd (final) state, pub. Edmond Deman, good cond., staining, wear, est. $2/3,000, (02-24-93, Butterfield, #2790, illus.), 11 x 8 in., (279 x 203 mm.), etching on Van Gelder laid.

$12,537* *Pierre Renoir De Face 9D. 27; Karshan 65), 1893*, s., num. 1, 1 of 100, staining, faults, drystamp, (02-24-93, Picard, #211), lithograph in bistre on thin chine (BP 8743, DM 20,352, FR 68,998, Y 1,471,134).

$495* *Portrait De Berthe Morisot (S. 4), 1892*, pub. Bernheim-Jeune in Theodore Duret's Renoir, 1924, margins, good cond., staining, surface soiling, (02-24-93, Butterfield,

#2966), 4⅜ x 3⁹⁄₁₆ in., (111 x 90 mm.), etching on wove (BP 345, DM 804, FR 2724, Y 58,085).

$3054* *Portrait De Paul Cezanne (D. 34; R.-M. 9; Johnson 1977, 115), 1902*, s. in stone, (06-23-93, Kornfeld, #752), lithograph on thick Japan (BP 2075, DM 5168, FR 17,382, Y 332,716, SF 4600).

$2062* *Portrait De Richard Wagner (Delteil 33; Roger-Marx 8; Johnson 1977, 114), c. 1900*, (06-23-93, Kornfeld, #751), lithograph on thick wove (BP 1401, DM 3489, FR 11,736, Y 224,643, SF 3105).

$358* *Portrait Of A Young Girl*, Vollard, image s., excell. cond.?, (10-10-92, Litchfield, #181), image 7½ x 7½ in., (19.1 x 19.1 cm.), lithograph (BP 212, DM 532, FR 1786, Y 43,584).

BI *"Portrait Of Berthe Mousot", c. 1924*, p.l., sig. reversed in plate, full margins, est. $5/700, (10-10-92, Goldberg, #421B), image 4½ x 3¼ in., (11.4 x 8.3 cm.), etching.

BI *Reclining Nude*, est. $2/400, (02-14-93, Hanzel, #667), 5¼ x 7⅝ in., (13.3 x 19.4 cm.), restrike etching.

BI *Reclining Nude*, restrike, est. $250/350, (11-01-92, Hanzel, #224), 5¼ x 7⅝ in., (13.3 x 19.4 cm.), etching.

$1155* *Richard Wagner (Delteil 33), c. 1900*, s., (12-04-92, Bassenge, #6912), 17⁵⁄₁₆ x 12¹¹⁄₁₆ in., (44 x 32.3 cm.), lithograph on Japan (BP 741, DM 1839, FR 6240, Y 144,195).

$715* *"Sur La Plage A Bernaval" and "Chapeau Epingle"*: Two, each s. in plate, late impressions, (10-30-92, Sloan, #1606), larger 5 x 4 in., (12.7 x 10.2 cm.), etching (BP 458, DM 1100, FR 3732, Y 88,567).

$260* *Sur La Plage A Berneval*, s. in plate Jean Renoir, (06-16-93, Encans, #156), 4¹⁵⁄₁₆ x 2¹⁵⁄₁₆ in., (12.5 x 7.5 cm.), engraving (BP 173, DM 432, FR 1448, Y 27,730, C$ 333).

BI *Sur La Plage A Berneval (Delteil 5), 1892*, later imp., plate s., est. DM 280-, (09-25-92, Granier, #2675), 5⅜ x 3¹¹⁄₁₆ in., (13.7 x 9.4 cm.), sheet 9⁷⁄₁₆ x 7¹⁄₁₆ in., (13.7 x 9.4 cm.), etching on machine hand-made.

$358* *Sur La Plage A Berneval (Stella 5 III/III), c. 1892*, (05-16-93, Hindman, #451), 4 x 5½ in., (10.2 x 14 cm.), etching (BP 233, DM 576, FR 1935, Y 39,685).

$330* *"Sur La Plage A Berneval" and "Chapeau Epingle" [D & S 5,8], 1892, 1894: Two*, s. in plate, late impressions, (12-10-92, Sloan, #3024), larger 5¼ x 3⅝ in., (13.3 x 9.2 cm.), etching (BP 213, DM 522, FR 1783, Y 40,821).

$385* *"Sur La Plage", c. 1892*, s. plate, full margins, excell. cond., (05-07-93, Goldberg, #429B), 5¼ x 3¾ in., (13.3 x 9.5 cm.), etching on arches (BP 244, DM 609, FR 2051, Y 42,392).

$403* *Sur La Plage, A Berneval (Delteil 5)*, third and final state, yellowed, (05-15-93, Loudmer, #315), 5½ x 3¾ in., (140 x 95 mm.), sh 12⅞ x 9⅞ in., (140 x 95 mm.), drypoint on wove (BP 262, DM 648, FR 2178, Y 44,674).

$1725* *"Sur La Plage, A Berneval" and "Femme Couchee" (Tournee A Gauche) (Delteil, Stella 5 and 15), c. 1892 and c. 1906: Two*, 1st of 2nd state of 3, pub. Duret's Les peintres impressionnistes, 2nd edit., 1919, good cond., loss, 2nd light-stained, both w/tape hinges, (05-13-93, Sotheby-NY, #801), one 5⅜ x 3¾ in., (138 x 96 mm.), other 5½ x 7¾ in., (138 x 96 mm.), etching (BP 1132, DM 2785, FR 9395, Y 192,587).

$330* *"Sur La Plage, A Berneval", c. 1892*, (02-13-93, Neal, #578), plate 5½ x 3½ in., (14 x 8.9 cm.), etching (BP 232, DM 547, FR 1852, Y 39,797).

BI *"Sur La Plage, A Berneval", c. 1923*, third state, s. in plate, full margins, est. $5/700, (10-10-92, Goldberg, #421A, illus.), image 4½ x 3 in., (11.4 x 7.6 cm.), etching.

BI *Sur La Plage, Berneval (Delteil 5; Stella 8), c. 1892*, 3rd final state, margins, est. BP 2/300, (10-15-92, Bonhams-Chelsea, #98), plate 5⅜ x 3¾ in., (13.7 x 9.5 cm.), etching on wove.

$222* *Sur La Plage, Berneval (Delteil S; Stella 8), c. 1892*, 3rd final state, margins, (12-10-92, Bonhams-Chelsea, #86), plate 5⅜ x 3¾ in., (13.7 x 9.5 cm.), etching on wove (BP 143, DM 351, FR 1199, Y 27,462).

$2750* *La Vie & L'Oeuvre De Pierre Auguste Renoir, 1919*, book, by Ambrose Vollard, num. 938, pub. by Vollard, large margins, good cond., discoloration, (11-05-92, Sotheby-NY, #422, illus.), etching, Baigneuse Assise (D., D. 11) and reproductions of paintingsand drawings (BP 1789, DM 4349, FR 14,714, Y 337,382).

RENOIR, Pierre Auguste (after)
$121* *"Le Chapeau Epingle"*, s. plate, (02-27-93, Dunning, #114), 4 x 3 in., (10.2 x 7.6 cm.), etching (BP 85, DM 199, FR 676, Y 14,284).
$121* *"Le Chapeau Epingle"*, s. plate, (02-27-93, Dunning, #109), 4 x 3 in., (10.2 x 7.6 cm.), etching (BP 85, DM 199, FR 676, Y 14,284).
$33* *Figures On A Beach*, s. in plate, (06-24-93, Boos, #336), sight 5⅞ x 2¹⁵⁄₁₆ in., (150 x 75 mm.), etching (BP 22, DM 56, FR 190, Y 3599).

RESSEL, Maria
$55* *Dutch Girl Sewing*, plate s.; s., i., (02-11-93, Boos, #408), 6⅝ x 3⅜ in., (168 x 86 mm.), etching (BP 39, DM 91, FR 308, Y 6631).

RET, Etienne   American b. France 1900
$28* *"La Lettre D'Amour"*, s., edit. #43/100, (01-15-93, DuMouchelle, #2362), 19¼ x 15½ in., (48.9 x 39.4 cm.), etching (BP 18, DM 46, FR 155, Y 3530).
$66* *Mandolin Player*, s., (10-30-92, Sloan, #830), 10½ x 8³⁄₁₆ in., (26.7 x 20.8 cm.), color etching (BP 42, DM 102, FR 344, Y 8175).
$33* *"Maternite Doree"*, s., edit. #12/100, (01-15-93, DuMouchelle, #2363), 19¼ x 15½ in., (48.9 x 39.4 cm.), etching (BP 22, DM 54, FR 182, Y 4160).
$17* *Pianist*, s., #35/100, (12-11-92, DuMouchelle, #1457), 22¼ x 30 in., (56.5 x 76.2 cm.), color etching (BP 11, DM 27, FR 92, Y 2104).
BI *Woman Playing A Flute*, s., num., light struck, thin spots, est. $100/150, (05-15-93, Cleveland, #269), 26⅛ x 9¾ in., (66.4 x 24.8 cm.), etching, drypoint and aquatint in color.

RETI, Istvan Stefan   Hungarian b. 1872
$132* *Untitled*, s., t., soiling, staining, (10-31-92, Cleveland, #325, illus.), 10 x 8½ in., (25.4 x 21.6 cm.), etching (BP 85, DM 203, FR 689, Y 16,351).

REUTERS WARD   20th cent.
$32* *"La Marionette"*, H.C. s., (01-28-93, Pescheteau, #240), 25¹⁵⁄₁₆ x 15⁹⁄₁₆ in., (66 x 39.5 cm.), black lithograph on wove (BP 21, DM 51, FR 172, Y 3973).

REVERDY, Georges   ac. 1531-1564
$217* *Cimon Und Pero, 1542*, (12-04-92, Bassenge, #6406), 5½ x 12⅝ in., (14 x 32 cm.), etching (BP 139, DM 346, FR 1172, Y 27,091).

REVERE
$275* *"Phantom Bay Horse"*, (03-12-93, DuMouchelle, #2325), 14 x 18 in., (35.6 x 45.7 cm.), print (BP 192, DM 458, FR 1556, Y 32,410).

REVERE, Paul   American 1735-1818
$1210* *The Able Doctor, Or America Swallowing The Bitter Draught*, from London Magazine, April 1774, prov., (05-29-93, Northeast, #90, illus.), sight 4½ x 6½ in., (11.4 x 16.5 cm.), engraving (BP 775, DM 1919, FR 6488, Y 129,745).

REYNAL, Kay Bell
BI *"Pawnshop Interior, New York, 1947, McCalls"*, s., num. #15, 12, stamped photog.'s credit, s., 370 x 265mm, est. BP5/800, (05-07-93, Sotheby-London, #326, illus.), photograph, silver print.
BI *Tiered Bathing Suit, Nassau, 1948*, s., 305 x 265mm, est. BP 5/800, (05-07-93, Sotheby-London, #327, illus.), photograph, silver print.

REYNAL, Kay Bell   1910-1977
$2990* *Two Models With Sunshields, Nassau, 1948*, p. 1960s, lit., (04-08-93, Christie-NY, #330, illus.), 10½ x 10½ in., (26.7 x 26.7 cm.), photograph, gelatin silver print (BP 1961, DM 4803, FR 16,259, Y 339,310).

REYNARD, Grant T.   American 1887-1967
$100* *Down The Hill, 1934*, s., excell. cond., (05-15-93, Cleveland, #270), 7¹⁵⁄₁₆ x 9¹³⁄₁₆ in., (20.2 x 24.9 cm.), etching, drypoint and aquatint (BP 65, DM 161, FR 541, Y 11,085).

REYNOLDS (after)
$110* *Calmady Children*, (05-14-93, DuMouchelle, #2532), 28 x 26 in., (71.1 x 66 cm.), print (BP 72, DM 177, FR 595, Y 12,194).

REYNOLDS, M.S.
$90* *Joie De Vivre*, #3/30, s., d. 75, margins, (10-15-92, Bonhams-Chelsea, #106), plate 19½ x 13¾ in., (49.5 x 34.9 cm.), etching w/aquatint (BP 55, DM 134, FR 454, Y 10,798).

REYNOLDS, Sir Joshua (after)
BI *Lady Hamilton*, BP 1/150, (04-22-93, Bonhams-Chelsea, #15), image 24½ x 19 in., (62.2 x 48.3 cm.), reprod. in colors.

REYNOLDS, Sir Joshua (after)
$7 *"Admiral Viscount Keppell"*, engraved by J. Scott, (02-05-93, G.A. Key, #42), 5 x 4 in., (12.7 x 10.2 cm.), b/w engraving (BP 5, DM 12, FR 39, Y 871).
BI *Charles James Fox*, by John Jones, pub. by engraver, 1792, small margins, laid down, scuffed, est. BP 5/70, (06-16-93, Bonhams-Chelsea, #472), pl. 19⅝ x 14 in., (49.8 x 35.6 cm.), mezzotint.
BI *"Dr. Hunter"*, c. 1788, est. $2/300, (02-12-93, DuMouchelle, #1187), approx. 13¼ x 16½ in., (33.7 x 41.9 cm.), engraving.
$366* *Elizabeth Taylor (C. S. 80)*, c. 1777, by W. Dickinson, only state, watermark, countermark, margins, creases, (12-01-92, Christie-London, #287, illus.), plate 17¹³⁄₁₆ x 12¹³⁄₁₆ in., (453 x 325 mm.), mezzotint (BP 242, DM 583, FR 1988, Y 45,568).
$25 *Mother And Child*, engr. by George Zobel, (12-11-92, G.A. Key, #92), 14 x 12 in., (35.6 x 30.5 cm.), black and white mezzotint (BP 16, DM 39, FR 135, Y 3094).
$61 *"The Right Honourable General Sir William Fawcett, K.B."*, engraved by James Ward, d. 1801, (04-16-93, G.A. Key, #64), 17 x 13 in., (43.2 x 33 cm.), colored mezzotint (BP 40, DM 99, FR 333, Y 6859).

RHEAD, Louis   American 1857-1926
$440* *The Bookman, Christmas Number*, A cond., (08-06-92, Swann, #234, illus.), 18 x 11 in., (45.7 x 27.9 cm.), (BP 230, DM 650, FR 2196, Y 56,122).
BI *Modern Art Calendar, 1897*, B cond., restoration, est. $6/900, (08-06-92, Swann, #233, illus.), 22½ x 15½ in., (57.2 x 39.4 cm.), .

RHEIMS, Bettina   b. 1952
BI *"Anthena", 1980*, s., t., d., #6/10, annot., photog.'s stamp, est. $4/600, (05-23-93, Butterfield, #3569), 18 x 14¼ in., photograph, gelatin silver print.
BI *"Auto-Portrait, 1989 Paris"*, mounted on card, s., d., #3/15, s., t., num., annot. BR 374, d., stamped photog.'s credit, (c) and print limitation info., 600 x 500mm, est. BP 5/700, (05-07-93, Sotheby-London, #372, illus.), photograph, silver print.
BI *"Catherine Deneuve Au George V"*, 1988, p. 1990, s., t., d., #3/15, annot., photog.'s/edit. stamps, mount trimmed to print, est. $6/800, (05-23-93, Butterfield, #3568), 17½ x 17¾ in., photograph, gelatin silver print.
BI *"Catherine Deneuve Au George V"*, 1988/1990, s., t., d., edit. 3/15, annot., photog. stamps, Dixon Collction, est. $800/1,000, (11-16-92, Butterfield, #6130, illus.), 17⁹⁄₁₆ x 17¹³⁄₁₆ in., (445.3 x 451.7 mm.), photograph, gelatin silver print.
BI *"Catherine Deneuve En Veste Doree, Juillet 1988, Paris"*, p. 1990, mounted on board, t., s., d., #3/15, stamped photog.'s (c) limitation, stamped, 600 x 500mm, est. BP 4/600, (05-07-93, Sotheby-London, #370, illus.), photograph, silver print.
$920* *Josie Dans Une Robe En Filer*, 1989, p. 1990, ink s., t., d., #3/15, annot.; reprod. limitation stamps, (04-08-93, Christie-NY, #552, illus.), 21¼ x 17½ in., (54 x 44.5 cm.), photograph, gelatin silver print (BP 603, DM 1478, FR 5003, Y 104,403).
BI *"Marine Au Raphael III, Fevrier 1990 Paris"*, mounted on board, t., s., d., #2/15, stamped photog.'s (c) limitation, stamped, 600 x 500mm, est. BP 4/600, (05-07-93, Sotheby-London, #369, illus.), photograph, silver print.
BI *"Vanessa Paradis A L'Hotel Normandie III, Decembre 1989, Deauville"*, p. 1990, mounted on board, t., s., d.,

#2/15, stamped photog.'s (c) limitation, stamped, 600 x 500mm., est. BP 4/600, (05-07-93, Sotheby-London, #371, illus.), photograph, silver print.

RIBERA, Joseph (Le SPAGNOLETTO) 1589-1650

$1008* *Petite Tete Grotesque, 1622,* second state of 2, mono., restored, (05-15-93, Loudmer, #26, illus.), 5¹¹⁄₁₆ x 4⁷⁄₁₆ in., (144 x 113 mm.), sh 6³⁄₁₆ x 4¾ in., (144 x 113 mm.), etching on thin laid (BP 655, DM 1621, FR 5449, Y 111,739).

RIBERA, Jusepe de Spanish 1588/91-1652/56

BI *Die Busse Des Hl. Petrus (B.7; Brown 6 I), 1621,* vertical fold, est. DM 1,500, (12-12-92, Bassenge, #8247), 12⅜ x 9½ in., (31.4 x 24.1 cm.), etching.

$16,100* *Drunken Silenus (B. 13; Brown 14), 1628,* 2nd state of 3, watermark, center crease, repaired tear, stains, thin spots, fold, good cond., The Suida Manning Coll., (05-13-93, Sotheby-NY, #275, illus.), 10⅝ x 13¾ in., (270 x 348 mm.), etching (BP 10,570, DM 25,997, FR 87,691, Y 1,797,477).

BI *Der Heilige Hieronymus Hort Die Trompete Des Jungsten Gerichts (Bartsch XX, 80, 4; Brown 5 III), 1621,* est. DM 1,500, (06-10-93, Hauswedell/Nolt, #153), etching.

$1487* *Der Hl. Hieronymus Und Der Engel (B. 4, Brown 5), c. 1621,* (06-04-93, Bassenge, #5339, illus.), 12³⁄₁₆ x 9⅛ in., (31 x 23.1 cm.), etching (BP 984, DM 2415, FR 8139, Y 160,375).

$3450* *Large Grotesque Head (B. 9; Brown 11), c. 1622,* 1st state of 2, plate tone, trimmed to or fractionally within borderline, repair in image, losses in edge made-up, thin spots, soiling, glued down, ex-coll. P. Mariette 1679, The Suida Manning Coll., (05-13-93, Sotheby-NY, #277), 8½ x 5½ in., (215 x 140 mm.), etching (BP 2265, DM 5571, FR 18,791, Y 385,174).

BI *The Martyrdom Of Saint Batholomew,* est. $4/600, (11-01-92, Hanzel, #240), 12⅜ x 9¼ in., (31.4 x 23.5 cm.), etching.

$4025* *The Martyrdom Of St. Bartholomew (B. 6; Brown 12), 1624,* plate tone, 1st state of 2, watermark, narrow margins, trimmed, discoloration, ex-coll. Graf F.J. von Enzenberg, The Suida Manning Coll., (05-13-93, Sotheby-NY, #273, illus.), 12¾ x 9⅝ in., (323 x 245 mm.), etching (BP 2642, DM 6499, FR 21,923, Y 449,369).

BI *The Martyrdom Of St. Bartholomew (Brown 12),* second (final) state, wear, trimmed within platemark, corner torn, repair, other repaired tears, minor defects, est. BP 7/1,000, (12-03-92, Sotheby-London, #136), 11⅜ x 9½ in., (315 x 240 mm.), etching and engraving on paper w/ watermark.

BI *The Penitence Of St. Peter (B. 7; Brown 6), 1621,* 1st state of 3, watermark, corners restored, tears, stains, crease, The Suida Manning Coll., est. $1,5/2,000, (05-13-93, Sotheby-NY, #274), 12⅝ x 9⅝ in., (322 x 243 mm.), etching.

$3680* *Saint Jerome Reading (B. 3, Brown 13), c. 1624,* tone, margins, inscrips., stains, laid down, watermark, (05-11-93, Christie-NY, #57, illus.), plate 7½ x 10⅛ in., (191 x 257 mm.), etching on laid (BP 2349, DM 5797, FR 19,533, Y 404,796).

$10,925* *Small Grotesque Head (B. 8; Brown 10), 1622,* plate tone, watermark, good margins, thin spots, creasing, good cond., collector's mark, exhib., The Suida Manning Coll., (05-13-93, Sotheby-NY, #276, illus.), 5⅝ x 4½ in., (142 x 113 mm.), etching (BP 7172, DM 17,641, FR 59,504, Y 1,219,716).

BI *St. Jerome Hearing The Trumpet Of The Last Judgment (B. 4; Brown 5), c. 1621,* plate tone, watermark, small margins, i., stains, ex-coll. F. Gawet, The Suida Manning Coll., est. $4/6,000, (05-13-93, Sotheby-NY, #271), 12⅜ x 9¼ in., (313 x 235 mm.), etching.

$1725* *St. Jerome Reading (B. 3; Brown 13), c. 1624,* strong plate tone, watermark, narrow margin, trimmed tear into image, stain, rubbed spot, repairs, good cond., ex-coll. F. Gawet, The Suida Manning Coll., (05-13-93, Sotheby-NY, #270), 7⅝ x 10 in., (195 x 253 mm.), etching (BP 1132, DM 2785, FR 9395, Y 192,587).

$3738* *St. Jerome Reading (B. 3; Brown 13), c. 1624,* plate tone, foul-biting, trimmed, crease, stains, glued down, good cond., ex-coll. F. Gawet, The Suida Manning Coll.,

(05-13-93, Sotheby-NY, #269, illus.), 7⅝ x 10⅛ in., (194 x 258 mm.), etching (BP 2454, DM 6036, FR 20,359, Y 417,327).

$605* *St. Jerome Reading (Brown 13), 1624,* (10-18-92, Hindman, #478), 7½ x 10 in., (19.1 x 25.4 cm.), etching w/ drypoint and burin (engraving (copper)) (BP 370, DM 901, FR 3054, Y 72,585).

RIBERA, Jusepe de (attrib.) Spanish 1588/91-1652/56

BI *Cupid Whipping A Satyr (B. 12; Brown 18 rej.), c. 1620-21,* impression slipped in printing, wide margins, foxing, good cond., The Suida Manning Coll., est. $1,5/2,000, (05-13-93, Sotheby-NY, #279), 6½ x 8¼ in., (165 x 210 mm.), etching.

$2875* *The Lamentation (B. 1; Brown 17 rej.), c. 1620-21,* 2nd (final) state, plate tone, watermark, small margins, stain, good cond., ex-coll. Graf F.J. von Enzenberg, The Suida Manning Coll., (05-13-93, Sotheby-NY, #278, illus.), 7⅝ x 10⅛ in., (195 x 257 mm.), etching (BP 1887, DM 4642, FR 15,659, Y 320,978).

RIBERA, Jusepe de (called LO SPANGNOLETTO) Spanish 1588/91-1652/56

BI *Der Hl. Hieronymus Hort Die Trompete Zum Jungsten Gericht (B. 4; Brown 5 III), c. 1621,* watermark, est. DM 1,800, (12-04-92, Bassenge, #6407), 12½ x 9⁵⁄₁₆ in., (31.7 x 23.7 cm.), etching.

RIBOT

$462* *Vernicire, "Unique Dans Le Monde Entier", c. 1935,* p. B. Sirven, good cond., (11-19-92, Ribeyre/Baron, #42), 59¹⁄₁₆ x 39¾ in., (150 x 101 cm.), poster (BP 304, DM 737, FR 2481, Y 57,456).

RIBOUD, Marc b. 1923

$2300* *The Painter Of The Eiffel Tower, 1955,* p.l., s.; s., t., d., #1/33, (04-08-93, Christie-NY, #515, illus.), 18¼ x 12 in., (46.4 x 30.5 cm.), photograph, gelatin silver print (BP 1508, DM 3695, FR 12,507, Y 261,008).

$2300* *"The Painter Of The Eiffel Tower, Paris" (Riboud, dust jacket and pl. 8),* s. by photog., 1953, p.l., (04-06-93, Sotheby-NY, #264, illus.), 11¾ x 7⅝ in., photograph (BP 1519, DM 3705, FR 12,548, Y 262,318).

$2750* *The Painter Of The Eiffel Tower, Paris, 1953 (Riboud, dust jacket and pl. 8),* s. by photog. in ink, (c) stamp, t., d. in unidentified hand, p. l., (10-15-92, Sotheby-NY, #335A, illus.), 19⅞ x 13¼ in., (50.5 x 33.7 cm.), photograph, gelatin silver print (BP 1683, DM 4093, FR 13,882, Y 329,934).

$1540* *The Painter, Eiffel Tower, Paris, (1953),* p.l., s., t., d., (10-13-92, Christie-NY, #484, illus.), 11⅞ x 7⅞ in., (30.2 x 20 cm.), photograph, gelatin silver print (BP 897, DM 2256, FR 7666, Y 186,735).

$1955* *"Le Peintre La Tour Eiffel", The Painter On The Eiffel Tower, 1953,* p.l., s. twice, t., d., (05-23-93, Butterfield, #3570, illus.), 18¼ x 12 in., photograph, gelatin silver print (BP 1273, DM 3197, FR 10,759, Y 216,094).

$935* *Street Scene, China,* photog.'s sig., 1960s, (04-07-93, Swann, #349, illus.), 8 x 12 in., photograph, silver print (BP 618, DM 1512, FR 5118, Y 106,226).

RICCI, Marco Italian 1676-1729

$578* *Landschaft Mit Einem Stall Und Rindern Auf Dem Weg Zur Tranke (B. 2 II),* watermark, (12-04-92, Bassenge, #6687, illus.), 12⅝ x 16⅝ in., (32 x 42.3 cm.), etching (BP 371, DM 921, FR 3123, Y 72,160).

$867* *Landschaft Mit Zwei Einsiedlern (B. 18 II),* prov., (12-04-92, Bassenge, #6688, illus.), 11 x 13⅞ in., (28 x 35.2 cm.), etching (BP 556, DM 1381, FR 4684, Y 108,240).

RICCIARDELLI, Luigi

$1210* *Vedute Delle Porte E Mura Di Roma: 26,* oblong folio, dampstain entering image throughout, (11-12-92, Swann, #123), etching (BP 795, DM 1917, FR 6467, Y 150,031).

RICE, Daniel and James G. CLARK, Publishers

American 19th cent.

$358* *"Encampment Of Piekann Indians, Near Fort McKenzie On The Muscleshell River", 1842,* mono. HD on stone, ident., good cond., foxing,, (01-09-93, Skinner, #362), sheet, sight 14 x 17½ in., (35.6 x 44.5 cm.), hand-colored lithograph on paper (BP 233, DM 589, FR 2000, Y 44,873).

RICE, William S.   American 1873-1963

$495* *"Dawn"*, s. W.S. Rice, t., very good cond.?, toning, (01-02-93, Skinner, #138A), 5¾ x 3¼ in., (14.6 x 8.3 cm.), color woodblock on paper (BP 330, DM 811, FR 2768, Y 62,061).

$605* *"Eucalyptus, Northbrae"*, s. W.S. Rice, t., very good cond.?, (01-02-93, Skinner, #138, illus.), 7¾ x 3½ in., (19.7 x 8.9 cm.), color woodblock on paper (BP 403, DM 991, FR 3384, Y 75,853).

RICHARD, D.

BI *SNCF. Les Gorges De La Diosaz. Vallee De Chamonix-Servoz, 1938*, very good cond., (03-15-93, Arcole, #58), 39⅜ x 24⁷⁄₁₆ in., (100 x 62 cm.), .

RICHARD, James C.

$347* *Hotel Des Anglais, Menton, c. 1930*, tears, losses, excell. cond., (02-04-93, Christie-S. Ken, #142, illus.), 41 x 29½ in., (104.1 x 74.9 cm.), color lithograph backed on linen (BP 242, DM 571, FR 1937, Y 43,165).

RICHARDS, Bruce

BI *Luck, 1980*, s., d., annot., blindstamp pub. Angeles Press, full margins, very good cond., est. $1/200, (10-28-92, Butterfield, #3086), 9¾ x 6 in., (248 x 152 mm.), lithograph on wove.

RICHARDS, Eugene

BI *Bridal Party Beneath Fire Escape, 1983*, s., est. $4/600, (05-23-93, Butterfield, #3571, illus.), 12 x 8 in., photograph, gelatin silver print.

RICHARDS, Walter du Bois   American b. 1907

$60* *"Departure" and "Evening": Two*, s., t., good cond., taped, (05-15-93, Cleveland, #272), one 4⅜ x 6¼ in., (11.1 x 15.9 cm.), other 4¾ x 6⁹⁄₁₆ in., (11.1 x 15.9 cm.), linoleum cut relief (BP 39, DM 97, FR 324, Y 6651).

$110* *Evening*, inits. in block, s., circulated by Print-A-Month Club, Sept. 1934, (07-03-92, Sloan, #317), 4⅞ x 6⅝ in., (12.4 x 16.8 cm.), linocut (BP 57, DM 166, FR 561, Y 13,712).

$110* *The Lobster Float*, s., t., circulated by Print-A-Month Club, (07-03-92, Sloan, #318), 5⅞ x 8¼ in., (14.9 x 21 cm.), linocut (BP 57, DM 166, FR 561, Y 13,712).

$20* *"The Lobster Float", 1933*, s., Print-A-Month Pub., July 1933, Cleveland, very good cond., (05-15-93, Cleveland, #271), 6 x 8½ in., (15.2 x 21.6 cm.), linoleum cut (BP 13, DM 32, FR 108, Y 2217).

RICHARDSON, John

$6325* *Fauna Boreali-Americana; Or, The Zoology Of The Northern Parts Of British American*, William Clowes, John Murray, 1829-37, Plates by Edward Landseer and others, foxed, first ed., John James Audobon's set, s. by him, bound for him, used and annot. by him in preparing his own work, prov., (06-14-93, Sotheby-NY, #65), 10⅜ x 8⅜ in., (26.4 x 21.3 cm.), 4 volumes in 4s (BP 4140, DM 10,295, FR 34,601, Y 665,579).

RICHARDSON, Sam   American b. 1934

$110* *Spring, Summer, Autumn, Winter Phase*, s., d. 73, t., #16/24, (06-13-93, Hindman, #343), each 16¾ x 22 in., (42.5 x 55.9 cm.), color embossment (BP 72, DM 179, FR 602, Y 11,575).

RICHEE, Eugene

$832* *Marlene Dietrich, Autographed Portrait, c. 1935*, ink s., i., catalog cover lot, (12-17-92, Christie-S. Ken, #82, illus.), 13⅜ x 10⅜ in., (34 x 26.4 cm.), photograph, warm-toned gelatin silver print (BP 528, DM 1299, FR 4437, Y 102,249).

$433* *Marlene Dietrich, Autographed Portrait, c. 1935*, ink s., i., (12-17-92, Christie-S. Ken, #81, illus.), 13⅜ x 10⅜ in., (34 x 26.4 cm.), photograph, warm-toned gelatin silver print (BP 275, DM 676, FR 2309, Y 53,214).

RICHER, Germaine   b. 1904

$253* *Weibliche Figur Mit Dreieck*, s., num., (11-28-92, Schoppmann, #724), 21¼ x 15¼ in., (54 x 38.8 cm.), etching on BFK Rives (BP 167, DM 403, FR 1368, Y 31,487).

RICHIE, Robert Yarnall

$660* *Locomotive*, handstamp, notations, 1930's, (10-14-92, Swann, #542, illus.), 7¼ x 9¾ in., (18.4 x 24.8 cm.), photograph, silver print (BP 387, DM 966, FR 3275, Y 79,981).

RICHTER, Gerhard   American b. 1928

BI *9 Objekte, (Essen cat. 19), 1969*, s., d., num. 27/89, pub. H. Friedrich, surface dirt, glue spots, very good cond., original port., est. BP 2/3,000, (12-01-92, Christie-London, #628, illus.), overall S. 18⅛ x 18⅛ in., (460 x 460 mm.), offset lithograph on wove.

$1155* *Atelier (Bloch R), 1968*, s., num.(11-28-92, Schoppmann, #725), 9 x 12⁷⁄₁₆ in., (22.9 x 31.6 cm.), offset on wove (BP 762, DM 1840, FR 6247, Y 143,746).

$721* *Blattecke (Blok Band I R 7), 1967*, pencil s., d., (11-20-92, Lempertz, #808), 9⅜ x 7¹⁄₁₆ in., (23.8 x 18 cm.), color screen print and offset (BP 475, DM 1150, FR 3872, Y 89,665).

$2387* *Elisabeth I (Museum Folkwang 4)*, s., d. #36/50, pub. Edition h, good cond., (12-03-92, Sotheby-London, #787, illus.), 27½ x 23½ in., (700 x 595 mm.), offset lithograph in colors on wove (BP 1540, DM 3754, FR 12,813, Y 297,001).

BI *Funken (Block R 24), 1970*, s., d., num., est. DM 1,800-, (05-27-93, Lempertz, #971A), 19¹¹⁄₁₆ x 25⁹⁄₁₆ in., (50 x 65 cm.), color offset print w/lacquer on white board.

$1150* *Funken (Block R 24), 1970*, i. Probe, #29/200, pub. Jahresgabe des Schweizerischen Kunstvereins,full margins, good cond., handling creases, surface scuffs, (05-15-93, Sotheby-NY, #1163), 12⅝ x 18⅜ in., (32.1 x 46.7 cm.), offset lithograph in colors (BP 748, DM 1850, FR 6216, Y 127,480).

BI *Heiner Friedrich (Block R22), 1970*, artist's proof, s., d., signs of wear, est. SF 700/900, (10-14-92, Germann, #411), 16¾ x 12⅜ in., (425 x 315 mm.), color offset lithograph.

$1955* *Kugelobjekt II (B. R 2lb), 1970*, s., d. '69 in crayon, i. II, 180 x 130 x 50 mm, (02-11-93, Sotheby-NY, #421, illus.), multiple object, painted black box w/glass, photograph, and three steel spheres (BP 1379, DM 3238, FR 10,959, Y 235,684).

$1151* *Landscape, 1971*, s., d., #86/100, full margins, good cond., (05-27-93, Sotheby-Amstrdm, #677, illus.), sheet 19¹³⁄₁₆ x 15¹³⁄₁₆ in., (503 x 402 mm.), color offsetprint on wove (BP 737, DM 1847, FR 6225, Y 123,392, G 2070).

$931* *Landschaft 1 (Block R 26), 1971*, s., d., num., staining, (09-25-92, Granier, #2987), sheet 19¹¹⁄₁₆ x 15¾ in., (50 x 40 cm.), color aquatint etching on wove (BP 544, DM 1380, FR 4667, Y 112,372).

$1083* *Landschaft 1 (Block R 26), 1971*, s., d., num., (11-28-92, Schoppmann, #727), 7⅞ x 5⁵⁄₁₆ in., (20 x 13.5 cm.), color etching wove (BP 715, DM 1725, FR 5857, Y 134,785).

$1009* *Landschaft 2, 1971*, s., d., num., (09-25-92, Granier, #2988), sheet 19¹¹⁄₁₆ x 15¾ in., (50 x 40 cm.), color aquatint etching, light print, on wove (BP 589, DM 1496, FR 5058, Y 121,786).

$1029* *Landschaft, 1970*, s., d., #25/200, pub. for portfolio Graphikmappe des SchweizerischenKunstvereins, good cond.?, (06-30-93, Sotheby-London, #917), 12⅝ x 18½ in., (321 x 470 mm.), offset color lithograph (BP 690, DM 1755, FR 5921, Y 110,254).

$1840* *Meer (B. R 36), 1972*, s., d. 1973, #186/250, pub. Kunstverein in Gent, full margins, good cond., (05-15-93, Sotheby-NY, #1164, illus.), 9⅞ x 9¾ in., (25.1 x 24.8 cm.), offset lithograph in colors (BP 1196, DM 2960, FR 9946, Y 203,969).

BI *Ohne Titel, 1989*, s. in photo, d., #39/50, est. DM 3,600, (11-12-92, Lempertz, #202, illus.), 39⅜ x 27⅜ in., (100 x 69.5 cm.), photograph, gelatin silver print.

BI *Schweizer Alpen I and II (Block R 15c), 1969*, s., pub. Griffel Kunst, creases, skinned spot, good cond., est. $1,5/2,000, (02-11-93, Sotheby-NY, #420, illus.), sheet 27⅜ x 27⁵⁄₁₆ in., (695 x 694 mm.), color silkscreen.

$1147* *Schweizer Alpen II (Block R15e), 1969*, s., (10-14-92, Germann, #408), 27⅜ x 27⅜ in., (695 x 695 mm.), colored screen print (BP 673, DM 1679, FR 5692, Y 138,997, SF 1495).

$1145* *Schweizer Alpen II (Motiv 42) (Block Nr. R 15b), 1969,* s., (06-24-93, Germann, #493, illus.), 27⅜ x 27⅜ in., (695 x 695 mm.), color serigraph (BP 754, DM 1856, FR 6257, Y 122,828, SF 1668).

$638* *"Schweizer Alpen Motiv A 1" (Block R 15 e), 1969,* s., Schweizer Alpen I + II series, ident. stamp, (06-08-93, Karl/Faber, #1236), approx. 27³⁄₁₆ x 27⁹⁄₁₆ in., (69 x 70 cm.), color serigraph on board (BP 419, DM 1035, FR 3486, Y 67,764).

$971* *Seestuck (Block R16), 1969,* 140/150, s., d., (10-14-92, Germann, #409), 19¹⁵⁄₁₆ x 19⁵⁄₁₆ in., (507 x 490 mm.), offset lithograph (BP 570, DM 1421, FR 4819, Y 117,668, SF 1265).

$716* *Seestuck (Block R23), 1970,* s., d. '71, #XXIX/XXX, margins, good cond., skinned, prov., (12-03-92, Sotheby-London, #788, illus.), 20¾ x 17 in., (527 x 434 mm.), offset lithograph in colors (BP 462, DM 1126, FR 3843, Y 89,088).

BI *Seestuck (Block R23), 1970,* artist's proof, s., d., est. SF 1,4/1,600, (10-14-92, Germann, #410), 26⁹⁄₁₆ x 20⅞ in., (674 x 530 mm.), color offset lithograph.

$1226* *Teydelandschaft (Blok Band II R 32), 1971,* #15/50, pencil s., (11-20-92, Lempertz, #811), sh 18⅞ x 23⁹⁄₁₆ in., (48 x 59.9 cm.), color offset print on Velin (BP 807, DM 1955, FR 6584, Y 152,469).

$9350* *Untitled (Candle), 1989,* s., d., #43/50, pub. Achenbach Fine Arts, good cond., (11-07-92, Sotheby-NY, #746, illus.), sheet 35⅜ x 35⅜ in., (899 x 899 mm.), offset lithograph w/hand-painting by the artist on plexiglas (BP 6113, DM 14,929, FR 50,459, Y 1,154,036).

$5750* *Untitled (Candle), 1989,* s., d., #37/50, pub. Achenbach Fine Arts, good cond., (02-11-93, Sotheby-NY, #422, illus.), sheet 35⁷⁄₁₆ x 35⁷⁄₁₆ in., (900 x 900 mm.), offset lithograph w/hand-painting by artist, mounted on plexiglass (BP 4057, DM 9525, FR 32,231, Y 693,189).

$1303* *Untitled, 1989,* scratch s., d., #40/50, good cond., (12-09-92, Sotheby-Amstrdm, #638, illus.), sheet 39³⁄₁₆ x 27½ in., (996 x 698 mm.), photograph, on photographic paper (BP 832, DM 2045, FR 6979, Y 161,562, G 2300).

$4400* *Untitled, Candle, 1989,* felt pen s., d., #28/50, very good cond.?, (10-28-92, Butterfield, #3087, illus.), 36 x 36 in., (914 x 914 mm.), oil on color photograph mounted on aluminum (BP 2803, DM 6795, FR 23,073, Y 539,877).

$866* *Wolken, 1969,* s., d., stamp, (11-28-92, Schoppmann, #726), 17¹¹⁄₁₆ x 15¹¹⁄₁₆ in., (45 x 39.9 cm.), offset on light cardboard (BP 572, DM 1380, FR 4684, Y 107,778).

$1515* *Wolken, 1972,* #194/250, pencil s., d., 3rd from series Schuldrucke Nordhein-Westfalen, (11-20-92, Lempertz, #812), sh 19⅝ x 25⁹⁄₁₆ in., (49.8 x 64.9 cm.), color offset on smooth thin cardboard (BP 997, DM 2415, FR 8136, Y 188,409).

RICHTER, Gustav   1823-1884

$249* *Engelskonzert, c. 1866,* Tischkarte fur Adolph Menzel, (12-01-92, Karl/Faber, #256), 8⅛ x 5⁵⁄₁₆ in., (20.5 x 13.5 cm.), lithograph on China (BP 165, DM 397, FR 1353, Y 31,001).

RICHTER, Gustave (after)

$14* *Classical Style Woman,* (01-15-93, DuMouchelle, #2419), 17½ x 10½ in., (44.5 x 26.7 cm.), print (BP 9, DM 23, FR 77, Y 1765).

RICHTER, Hans   German ac. 1597

BI *Conquest Of The Sky, 1937,* t., d. by photog., est. $2/3,000, (10-15-92, Sotheby-NY, #408, illus.), 5⅛ x 7⅛ in., (13 x 18.1 cm.), photograph, gelatin silver print.

$2013* *Floating Eyes, c. 1926,* Hans Richter Estate, (04-06-93, Sotheby-NY, #323, illus.), 3⅛ x 4⅜ in., photograph (BP 1330, DM 3243, FR 10,982, Y 229,585).

$3850* *Four Flying Hats, 1927-28,* (10-15-92, Sotheby-NY, #406, illus.), 3½ x 4¼ in., (8.9 x 10.8 cm.), photograph, gelatin silver print (BP 2356, DM 5731, FR 19,435, Y 461,908).

$1925* *Ghosts Before Breakfast (Vormittagsspuk), 1927-28,* num 32 in unidentified hand in ink, t., d. by photog. in ink, (10-15-92, Sotheby-NY, #407, illus.), 4¾ x 5½ in., (12.1

x 14 cm.), photograph, gelatin silver print (BP 1178, DM 2865, FR 9717, Y 230,954).

BI *Neue Kunst Hans Goltz. Erich Heckel & Hans Richter, c. 1918,* fold marks, est. BP 3/5,000, (05-20-93, Christie-London, #506, illus.), sheet 37 x 29½ in., (94 x 74.9 cm.), lithograph in b/w backed on Japan.

BI *Neue-Kunst-Hans-Goltz. Deutsche Expressionisten, c. 1918,* staining, fold mark, est. BP 2/3,000, (05-20-93, Christie-London, #505, illus.), sheet 34½ x 28 in., (87.6 x 71.1 cm.), lithograph in black backed on Japan.

BI *Scaffolding For Stage Set, c. 1928,* prov., est. $2/3,000, (10-13-92, Christie-NY, #334, illus.), 6¾ x 4¾ in., (17.1 x 12.1 cm.), photograph, gelatin silver print.

$522* *Self-Portrait (From "Dreams That Money Can Buy"), 1946,* sig., notations, (10-14-92, Swann, #544, illus.), 10 x 8 in., (25.4 x 20.3 cm.), photograph, silver print (BP 306, DM 764, FR 2591, Y 63,257).

$3960* *Surrealist Richter Archive From "Dreams That Money Can Buy",* 1940's, notations, (10-14-92, Swann, #543, illus.), photographs 8 x 10 in., (20.3 x 25.4 cm.), contact sheets 2½ x 2½ in., (20.3 x 25.4 cm.), photograph, 7 original photographs, 10 contact sheets, 2 Kodachromes (BP 2324, DM 5795, FR 19,653, Y 479,884).

BI *Untitled, Film Still, 1926-28,* lit., est. $3/4,000, (04-08-93, Christie-NY, #223, illus.), 3¼ x 4⅜ in., (8.3 x 11.1 cm.), photograph, gelatin silver print.

BI *Untitled, Film Still, 1926-28,* est. $1,5/1,800, (04-08-93, Christie-NY, #222, illus.), 3½ x 4⅛ in., (8.9 x 10.5 cm.), photograph, gelatin silver print.

$412* *Woman Sewing, c. 1927,* sig., notations, (10-14-92, Swann, #545, illus.), 3½ x 4½ in., (8.9 x 11.4 cm.), photograph, silver print (BP 242, DM 603, FR 2045, Y 49,927).

RICHTER, Hans Theo   German 1902-1969

$885* *Frau Mit Aufschauendem Jungen (Schmidt 525), 1962,* s., num., rare, (12-05-92, Bassenge, #7659, illus.), 15¼ x 10¹³⁄₁₆ in., (38.7 x 27.5 cm.), lithograph (BP 554, DM 1380, FR 4702, Y 109,652).

$185* *Gebucktes, Hockendes Und Stehendes Kind (Schmidt 219), 1948,* s., from series Kinderszenen, (12-05-92, Bassenge, #7656), 4¾ x 6⅛ in., (12 x 15.5 cm.), lithograph on handmade (BP 116, DM 288, FR 983, Y 22,922).

$369* *Junge Mutter Mit Zeichnendem Kind (Schmidt 530), 1962,* s., (12-05-92, Bassenge, #7660), 9¹⁄₁₆ x 11⅝ in., (23 x 29.5 cm.), lithograph (BP 231, DM 575, FR 1961, Y 45,719).

$502* *Madchen Sieht Sein Spiegelbild (Schmidt 591), 1967,* s., (12-05-92, Bassenge, #7661), 10½ x 9³⁄₁₆ in., (26.7 x 23.3 cm.), lithograph (BP 314, DM 783, FR 2667, Y 62,198).

$516* *Madchen Und Spielgelbild, Nach Rechts (Schmidt 609), 1968,* s., num., (12-05-92, Bassenge, #7662), 8¹¹⁄₁₆ x 10 in., (22 x 25.4 cm.), lithograph (BP 323, DM 804, FR 2742, Y 63,933).

$443* *Mutterbildnis III (Schmidt 230),* s., in the portfolio Neue Graphik von Prof. Hans Theo Richter, Galerie Kuhl Dresden, (12-05-92, Bassenge, #7657), 9¹³⁄₁₆ x 8¹⁄₁₆ in., (25 x 20.5 cm.), lithograph on handmade (BP 277, DM 691, FR 2354, Y 54,888).

BI *Sich Kammende Nach Links (Schmidt 347), 1956,* s., brown stained, est. DM 700, (12-01-92, Karl/Faber, #1135), 8¼ x 10¹⁄₁₆ in., (21 x 25.5 cm.), lithograph on wove.

$472* *Windiger Strand (Schmidt 298), 1954,* s., num., (12-05-92, Bassenge, #7658), 7¹⁄₁₆ x 8⅛ in., (18 x 20.6 cm.), lithograph on copper print cardboard (BP 296, DM 736, FR 2508, Y 58,481).

RICHTER, Heinrich   b. 1920

BI *Die Drei Grazien, 1953,* s., d., num., mount stains, est. DM 300-, (09-25-92, Granier, #2989), sheet 19¾ x 25⅝ in., (50.2 x 65.1 cm.), color lithograph on BFK Rives.

RICHTER, Ludwig   1803-1884

$915* *"Die Christnacht" (Hoff/Budde 271, VI), 1854,* (03-24-93, Venator/Hansten, #2627), pl. 22¼ x 16⁹⁄₁₆ in., (56.5 x 42 cm.), etching (BP 620, DM 1494, FR 5086, Y 107,508).

RICKMAN, Philip (after)
$18 *"Golden Plover", "Grouse", "Partridge" and "French Partridge": Four,* (06-11-93, G.A. Key, #59), 8 x 11 in., (20.3 x 27.9 cm.), colored print (BP 12, DM 29, FR 99, Y 1910).

RIDINGER, Johann Elias   German 1698-1767
$194* *Anno 1720 Haben Diesen Gantz Weissen Fuchsen... (Th. 298),* trimmed, restored, (09-25-92, Granier, #2679), sheet 13⅜ x 9⅝ in., (34 x 24.5 cm.), copper engraving (BP 113, DM 288, FR 972, Y 23,416).
$272* *Anno 1736 (Thienemann 272), 1744,* (09-25-92, Granier, #2677), 14⁹⁄₁₆ x 11 in., (37 x 28 cm.), copper engraving (BP 159, DM 403, FR 1363, Y 32,830).
$578* *Das Caroussel (Thienemann 693-706): Fourteen,* (12-04-92, Bassenge, #6689), etching (BP 371, DM 921, FR 3123, Y 72,160).
$4237* *Die Funf Sinne (Wend 265-269; Schwarz 1466-1470): Five,* plate w/sig., t., i., (06-10-93, Hauswedell/Nolt, #212, illus.), mezzotint (BP 2771, DM 6900, FR 23,229, Y 449,740).
$272* *Ihro Durchl. Des Fursten Von Anhalt Dessau Leib Kleiner Wind Und Hassen Hund, Avions (Th. 331), 1767,* (09-25-92, Granier, #2678), 13⅜ x 10¹⁄₁₆ in., (34 x 25.5 cm.), copper engraving (BP 159, DM 403, FR 1363, Y 32,830).
$918* *Die Par Force Jagd Des Hirschen (Der Hirsch Stellt Sich Im Wasser Die Hunde Werden Gestopfft And Ihme Der Fang Gegeben) (Thienemann 61), 1756,* (06-10-93, Hauswedell/Nolt, #210, illus.), engraving colored w/oil color (BP 600, DM 1495, FR 5033, Y 97,442).
$918* *Die Par Force Jagd Des Hirschen (Die Relais Werden Von Dem Comander Der Jagd Ausgesetzt) (Thienemann 53), 1756,* series w/Phasen der Hirschjagd, (06-10-93, Hauswedell/Nolt, #209, illus.), engraving colored w/oil color (BP 600, DM 1495, FR 5033, Y 97,442).
$3390* *Das Paradies Oder Die Schopfung Und Der Sundenfall Des Ersten Menschenpaares (Thienemann 807-818), c. 1746: Twelve,* watermark, (06-10-93, Hauswedell/Nolt, #211), etching and engraving on hand-made (BP 2217, DM 5520, FR 18,586, Y 359,834).
$271* *"Das Pferd Beschlagen" (Thienemann 599),* trimmed, stained, (09-14-92, Venator/Hansten, #1598), sh 8¹⁵⁄₁₆ x 13⁷⁄₁₆ in., (22.8 x 34.1 cm.), etching (BP 143, DM 403, FR 1365, Y 33,698).
BI *"Wein Und Saurbronnen" (Thienemann 1247), c. 1750,* creases, est. DM 600-, (09-14-92, Venator/Hansten, #1597, illus.), plate 16¹⁵⁄₁₆ x 21⅞ in., (43 x 55.5 cm.), mezzotint.

RIDINGER, Johann Elias (after)
$825* *Equestrian Scenes: Set Of Twelve,* (06-16-93, Bonhams-Chelsea, #320), 19 x 14½ in., (48.3 x 36.8 cm.), engraving (BP 550, DM 1370, FR 4596, Y 87,991).

RIDINGER, Martin Elias
$230* *"Hirsch Von 16 Euden", c. 1700 and "Wild Boar", 1615: Two,* trimmed margins, staining, creases, other minor defects, margins, staining, Anthony N. B. Garvan Coll., (06-05-93, Christie-NY, #51), engraving on laid (BP 151, DM 373, FR 1257, Y 24,673).

RIDLEY, Lawrence
$37* *Van Johnson,* autograph, prov., (10-10-92, Bonhams, #12, illus.), 10 x 8 in., (25.4 x 20.3 cm.), photograph (BP 22, DM 55, FR 185, Y 4505).

RIEMER, Walter
$247* *A Century Of German Railways, 1935,* Reichsbahnzentral, B- cond., closed tears, peeling, creasing, (08-06-92, Swann, #235, illus.), 39½ x 25½ in., (100.3 x 64.8 cm.), (BP 129, DM 365, FR 1233, Y 31,505).

RIESENBERG
$110* *"Over The Top For You, Buy U.S. Government Bonds, Third Liberty Loan",* crease, (09-12-92, Dunning, #101, illus.), 30 x 20 in., (76.2 x 50.8 cm.), poster laid on cloth (BP 57, DM 158, FR 538, Y 13,629).

RIESENBERG, Sidney H.
$330* *U.S. Marine Corps., "First To Fight", 1917,* A- cond., chartex-backed, (08-06-92, Swann, #236, illus.), 39¼ x

30 in., (99.7 x 76.2 cm.), (BP 172, DM 488, FR 1647, Y 42,092).

RIGAUD (after)
$933* *The Three Favorite Aerial Travellers, Viscount Lunard, George Biggin And Mrs. Sage, 1785,* engraved by Francesco Bartolozzi, pub. E. Wyatt, good cond., splits, holes, (11-30-92, Phillips-London, #150, illus.), image 14⅛ x 10⅛ in., (359 x 257 mm.), color stipple engraving on silk (BP 616, DM 1486, FR 5046, Y 116,117).

RIGAUD, Hyacinthe (after)   French 1659-1743
BI *Louis Antoine De Pardaillan De Gondrin, 1720,* by Nicolas Tardien, bears indecipherable collector's mark, est. $2/300, (09-20-92, Hindman, #663), 18¼ x 13 in., (46.4 x 33 cm.), engraving.

RIGAUD, J.
$66* *"Autre Vue D'Anet Du Cote De La Cour Des Cuisines",* (06-11-93, Freemn/Fine Art, #123B), plate 9¼ x 18¾ in., (23.5 x 47.6 cm.), engraving w/hand-coloring (BP 43, DM 107, FR 362, Y 7003).

RIGET, Karl Aage
$733* *"Copenhagen Numbers 1, 2, 3, And 5": Four,* s. 78/80, e.t. 1976, (09-29-92, B. Rasmussen, #357), serigraph (BP 412, DM 1035, FR 3533, Y 87,501, DK 4025).

RIGGS, Robert   American 1896-1970
BI *Center Ring (B. 30), 1933,* s., t., num. 14, full margins, foxing, scuffs, creases, soiling, water stains, tear, loss, est. $1,5/2,000, (11-05-92, Sotheby-NY, #49), 14⅜ x 19½ in., (365 x 494 mm.), lithograph.
$1760* *Corner No. I (Bassham 23), 1932-33,* s., t., full margins, good cond., scuffs, light stain, creases, (11-05-92, Sotheby-NY, #46, illus.), 13⅛ x 17¼ in., (333 x 439 mm.), lithograph (BP 1145, DM 2783, FR 9417, Y 215,924).
$1540* *"Corner No. II" and "Third Round" (B. 24 and 13), 1932-33 and 1934: Two,* first s., full margins, good cond., scuffs, crease; second s., t., margins, toptrimmed, good cond., water stain, tear, creases (11-05-92, Sotheby-NY, #47), first 15⅛ x 19⅝ in., (383 x 498 mm.), second 14½ x 19½ in., (383 x 498 mm.), lithograph (BP 1002, DM 2436, FR 8240, Y 188,934).
$1980* *Dust Bowl,* (06-06-93, Van Blarcom, #184), 13 x 18 in., (33 x 45.7 cm.), etching (BP 1303, DM 3210, FR 10,820, Y 212,401).
$1045* *Elephant Act (LC 22), 1937,* s., t., small margins, good cond., light-staining, glue remains, thinned spots, creases, surface scuff, surface soiling, (02-24-93, Butterfield, #2865, illus.), 14⁵⁄₁₆ x 19½ in., (364 x 495 mm.), lithograph on wove (BP 729, DM 1696, FR 5751, Y 122,624).
$3300* *Germantown And Chelten (Bassham 84), c. 1950,* s., t., full margins, staining, very good cond., (11-09-92, Christie-NY, #29, illus.), border 13¹⁵⁄₁₆ x 20¹⁄₁₆ in., (355 x 510 mm.), lithograph on wove (BP 2182, DM 5268, FR 17,799, Y 409,531).
$2090* *On The Ropes (B. 27), c. 1932-33,* s., t., num. 40, full margins, good cond., scuffs, creases, (11-05-92, Sotheby-NY, #48, illus.), 14⅞ x 19¾ in., (379 x 502 mm.), lithograph (BP 1359, DM 3305, FR 11,182, Y 256,410).
$1760* *Pool, c. 1939,* num., s., (05-27-93, Swann, #239, illus.), 14½ x 19½ in., (36.8 x 49.5 cm.), lithograph (BP 1127, DM 2824, FR 9519, Y 188,679).
BI *"Ready To Go" (Bassham 50), c. 1934,* proof, very good cond., est. $8/1,200, (05-15-93, Cleveland, #273, illus.), 14¹⁄₁₆ x 19¹¹⁄₁₆ in., (35.7 x 50 cm.), lithograph.
$302* *Running Boys-Hawaii 4 (Beall 29, Basham 60), 1937-38,* s., (05-27-93, Swann, #238), 9³⁄₁₆ x 4⅝ in., (23.3 x 11.7 cm.), lithograph (BP 193, DM 485, FR 1633, Y 32,376).

RIIS, Jacob
$770* *Bandits Roost, 59 1/2 Mulberry Street, New York,* p. by Alexander Alland, c. 1888, p.l., (04-07-93, Swann, #350, illus.), 10 x 8 in., photograph, silver print (BP 509, DM 1245, FR 4215, Y 87,480).

RIIS, Jacob 1849-1914
BI *Hell's Kitchen, c. 1900,* t. in ink on mount, prov., lit, est. $6/8,000, (10-13-92, Christie-NY, #72, illus.), 3⅝ x 4½ in., (9.2 x 11.4 cm.), photograph, gelatin silver print.

RIKAN
$50* *"Actor/Danjro",* OBAN TATE, soiling, (05-07-93, Goldberg, #1351), woodblock (BP 32, DM 79, FR 266, Y 5505).

RILEY, Bridget British b. 1931
$165* *Nineteen Grays,* s., d. 68, t., #61/75, (05-16-93, Hindman, #595), 29½ x 29½ in., (74.9 x 74.9 cm.), color serigraph (BP 107, DM 265, FR 892, Y 18,291).
$550* *"Red Dominance," "Blue Dominance," and "Green Dominance," 1977: Three,* each s., (10-18-92, Hindman, #491), each 36 x 19¼ in., (91.4 x 48.9 cm.), serigraphs (BP 337, DM 819, FR 2776, Y 65,987).

RIMBERT, R.
$58* *Boutique D'Antiquites,* s. artist's proof, (06-28-93, Loudmer, #110), 18½ x 13⅜ in., (470 x 340 mm.), sh 25¹³⁄₁₆ x 19¹¹⁄₁₆ in., (470 x 340 mm.), color lithograph on wove (BP 39, DM 99, FR 332, Y 6154).

RINEHART, F.A. 1861-1928
$935* *Assuz, San Carlos Apaches, 1898,* s., t., (c) d., num. 890, annot. in neg., (10-13-92, Christie-NY, #19, illus.), 9 x 7¼ in., (22.9 x 18.4 cm.), photograph, platinum print (BP 545, DM 1370, FR 4654, Y 113,375).
$605* *Chief Grant Richards, Tonkawa, 1898,* t., s., d., #1057 by photog. in neg., (04-07-93, Swann, #247, illus.), 9¼ x 7½ in., photograph, platinum print (BP 400, DM 978, FR 3311, Y 68,734).
$1045* *Chief Hollow Horn Bear, Sioux, 1898,* photog.'s sig., t., d. in neg., (10-14-92, Swann, #229, illus.), 9⅜ x 7½ in., (23.8 x 19.1 cm.), photograph, platinum print (BP 613, DM 1529, FR 5186, Y 126,636).
BI *"Chief Wolf Robe", "Chief American Horse" and "Chief Hollow Horn Bear", 1898: Three,* s., t., (c) d., num. in negs., est. BP 4/600, (05-06-93, Christie-London, #74), each 8¾ x 7 in., photograph, platinum print.
$770* *Eagle Elk, Sioux, 1898,* s., t., d., #875 by photog. in neg., (04-07-93, Swann, #248, illus.), 9¼ x 7¼ in., photograph, platinum print (BP 509, DM 1245, FR 4215, Y 87,480).
$770* *Highhawk, Sioux, c. 1899,* cap., num. 1509 in neg., (10-14-92, Swann, #230, illus.), 9½ x 72½ in., (21.6 x 30.5 cm.), photograph, platinum print (BP 452, DM 1127, FR 3821, Y 93,311).
BI *Juan Amigo And Mrs. Juan Amigo, 1899: Two,* photog. studio credit, (c) d., t., num. in neg., est. $1,8/2,200, (04-06-93, Sotheby-NY, #28, illus.), each approx. 9 x 7¼ in., photograph, platinum print.
$920* *"Juan Jose, Pueblo, Santa Clara" and "Four Bull, Assinaboine", 1898:Two,* s., t., (c) d., num. annot. in neg., (04-08-93, Christie-NY, #13, illus.), each approx. 9 x 7⅛ in., (22.9 x 18.1 cm.), photograph, albumen print (BP 603, DM 1478, FR 5003, Y 104,403).
$1100* *Last Horse, Ogalalla Sioux, 1899,* s., t., (c) d., num. 1447, annot. in neg., (10-13-92, Christie-NY, #20, illus.), 9⅛ x 7 in., (23.2 x 17.8 cm.), photograph, platinum print (BP 641, DM 1611, FR 5475, Y 133,382).
$805* *Little Sunday, Eagle Elk, Prairie Dog, Sioux, 1898,* s., t., (c) d., num. 834, annot. on neg., (04-08-93, Christie-NY, #14, illus.), 7¼ x 9¼ in., (18.4 x 23.5 cm.), photograph, platinum print (BP 528, DM 1293, FR 4377, Y 91,353).
$990* *No Water, Sioux, 1899,* photog.'s sig., t., d., num. 1523 in neg., (10-14-92, Swann, #231, illus.), 9⅜ x 7½ in., (23.8 x 19.1 cm.), photograph, platinum print (BP 581, DM 1449, FR 4913, Y 119,971).
$660* *Pablino Diaz, Kiowa, 1899,* s., t., d., #1388 by photog. in neg., (04-07-93, Swann, #249, illus.), 9¼ x 7¼ in., photograph, platinum print (BP 436, DM 1067, FR 3612, Y 74,983).
$1035* *"Pete Mitchell (Dust Maker)-Tonca":* 1898, photog. "Omaha" studio credit, (c) d., t., num. in neg., (04-06-93, Sotheby-NY, #29, illus.), 9⅛ x 7 in., photograph, platinum print (BP 684, DM 1667, FR 5646, Y 118,043).

BI *Review Of Indian Congress, 1898,* s., t., d., #856 by photog. in neg., est. $1/1,500, (04-07-93, Swann, #250, illus.), 7⅝ x 9½ in., photograph, platinum print.
$880* *Sioux, 1899,* photog.'s sig., t., d., num. 1529 in neg., (10-14-92, Swann, #228, illus.), 9⅜ x 7¾ in., (23.8 x 19.7 cm.), photograph, platinum print (BP 517, DM 1288, FR 4367, Y 106,641).
BI *"Tail-Sioux", "Lucy Red Cloud" and "Susie Red Horse", 1899: Three,* s., t., (c) d., num. 1525, 1515, 1510 in negs., est. BP 1,5/2,000, (10-29-92, Christie-London, #49, illus.), each 9⅛ x 7⅛ in., (23.2 x 18.1 cm.), photograph, platinum prints.

RIOPELLE, Jean Paul Canadian b. 1922/23
$513* *"Affiche Avant La Lettre", c. 1970,* #48/100, s. Riopelle, (07-14-92, Encans, #78), 24 x 16⁹⁄₁₆ in., (61 x 42 cm.), lithograph (BP 267, DM 761, FR 2566, Y 64,149, C$ 611).
$523* *"Aux Aguets",* #10/75, s. Riopelle, (11-17-92, Encans, #81), 19¹¹⁄₁₆ x 15¾ in., (50 x 40 cm.), lithograph (BP 344, DM 834, FR 2809, Y 65,042, C$ 666).
$444* *"Cornouailles", 1976,* #53/75, s. Riopelle, (03-16-93, Encans, #102), 25¹⁵⁄₁₆ x 19¹¹⁄₁₆ in., (66 x 50 cm.), color lithograph on Arches (BP 307, DM 738, FR 2508, Y 51,918, C$ 555).
$521* *"Cornouailles", 1976,* #61/75, s. Riopelle, (06-16-93, Encans, #92), 25¹⁵⁄₁₆ x 20¹⁄₁₆ in., (66 x 51 cm.), lithograph on Arches (BP 347, DM 865, FR 2903, Y 55,567, C$ 666).
$533* *"Dans Les Joncs", 1981,* #54/75, s. Riopelle, (03-16-93, Encans, #104), 26⅜ x 31⅛ in., (67 x 79 cm.), color lithograph (BP 368, DM 886, FR 3011, Y 62,325, C$ 666).
$700* *"Dans Les Joncs", 1981,* #63/75, s. Riopelle, (05-18-93, Encans, #135), 26⅜ x 31⅛ in., (67 x 79 cm.), color lithograph on Arches (BP 456, DM 1136, FR 3836, Y 78,012, C$ 888).
$638* *"Deux Totems",* #11/75, s. Riopelle, (09-15-92, Encans, #99), 19¹¹⁄₁₆ x 15¾ in., (50 x 40 cm.), lithograph (BP 341, DM 949, FR 3222, Y 79,205, C$ 777).
$1041* *"Echassiers",* #59/75, s. Riopelle, (06-16-93, Encans, #96), 25¹³⁄₁₆ x 30½ in., (65.5 x 77.5 cm.), color lithograph (BP 694, DM 1728, FR 5799, Y 111,028, C$ 1332).
$1271* *"Feuilles IV", 1967,* #58/75, s. Riopelle, (10-20-92, Encans, #133), 29½ x 41⁵⁄₁₆ in., (75 x 105 cm.), lithograph (BP 711, DM 1932, FR 6575, Y 159,313, C$ 1554).
$350* *"Feutre", 1976,* #28/75, s. Riopelle, (05-18-93, Encans, #133), 23⁷⁄₁₆ x 29⅛ in., (59.5 x 74 cm.), color lithograph on Arches (BP 228, DM 568, FR 1918, Y 39,006, C$ 444).
$523* *"Fonds 70",* #9/100, s. Riopelle, (11-17-92, Encans, #80), 23⅝ x 16¾ in., (60 x 42.5 cm.), lithograph (BP 344, DM 834, FR 2809, Y 65,042, C$ 666).
$636* *"Grappes",* #6/75, s. Riopelle, (10-20-92, Encans, #134), 21⅝ x 16⁹⁄₁₆ in., (55 x 42 cm.), lithograph (BP 356, DM 967, FR 3290, Y 79,719, C$ 777).
$133* *"Le Guet",* #67/75, s. Riopelle, (04-20-93, Encans, #84), 26¾ x 32⁵⁄₁₆ in., (68 x 82 cm.), lithograph on Arches (BP 86, DM 212, FR 715, Y 14,675, C$ 167).
$106* *"La Haie",* #30/75, s. Riopelle, (04-20-93, Encans, #83), 16⁵⁄₁₆ x 31⅞ in., (41.5 x 81 cm.), lithograph on Arches (BP 68, DM 169, FR 570, Y 11,696, C$ 133).
$363* *"Herbe A Puce", 1976,* #34/75, s. Riopelle, stamp verso, (10-20-92, Encans, #132), 14³⁄₁₆ x 12¹⁵⁄₁₆ in., (36 x 33 cm.), lithograph (BP 203, DM 552, FR 1878, Y 45,500, C$ 444).
$694* *"Hibou-I", 1970,* num. H.C., s. Riopelle, (06-16-93, Encans, #91), 29¹⁵⁄₁₆ x 21¹⁄₁₆ in., (76 x 53.5 cm.), color lithograph on Rives (BP 463, DM 1152, FR 3866, Y 74,019, C$ 888).
$694* *"Leader",* num. H.C., s. Riopelle, edit. 75, (06-16-93, Encans, #90), 25¹⁵⁄₁₆ x 29¹⁵⁄₁₆ in., (66 x 76 cm.), color lithograph on Arches (BP 463, DM 1152, FR 3866, Y 74,019, C$ 888).
$177* *"Leader", 1981,* num. H.C., s. Riopelle, (04-20-93, Encans, #85), 25¹⁵⁄₁₆ x 29¹⁵⁄₁₆ in., (66 x 76 cm.), litho-

graph on Arches (BP 114, DM 282, FR 952, Y 19,530, C$ 222).

$533* *"M"*, #36/75, s. Riopelle, (03-16-93, Encans, #101), 14¾ x 11¹³⁄₁₆ in., (37.5 x 30 cm.), lithograph (BP 368, DM 886, FR 3011, Y 62,325, C$ 666).

$638* *"Masque Et Oiseaux"*, #11/75, s. Riopelle, (09-15-92, Encans, #98), 19¹¹⁄₁₆ x 15¾ in., (50 x 40 cm.), lithograph (BP 341, DM 949, FR 3222, Y 79,205, C$ 777).

$218* *Oie Sauvage,* s. in plaque Riopelle, (11-17-92, Encans, #75), 17⁵⁄₁₆ x 19½ in., (44 x 49.5 cm.), lithograph on Arches (BP 144, DM 348, FR 1171, Y 27,111, C$ 278).

$325* *Les Oies Sauvages,* s. Riopelle, (08-18-92, Encans, #70), 16¹⁵⁄₁₆ x 18⅞ in., (43 x 48 cm.), lithograph (BP 168, DM 473, FR 1606, Y 40,973, C$ 389).

$192* *"Les Oies Sauvages"*, s. Riopelle, (05-18-93, Encans, #131), 16¾ x 29½ in., (42.5 x 75 cm.), lithograph (BP 125, DM 312, FR 1052, Y 21,398, C$ 244).

$266* *"Les Oies Sauvages"*, s. Riopelle, (03-16-93, Encans, #103), 16¾ x 19³⁄₁₆ in., (42.5 x 48.8 cm.), lithograph (BP 184, DM 442, FR 1503, Y 31,104, C$ 333).

$131* *"Les Oies Sauvages"*, s. in stone Riopelle, (06-16-93, Encans, #89), 16¾ x 19³⁄₁₆ in., (42.5 x 48.8 cm.), color lithograph (BP 87, DM 217, FR 730, Y 13,972, C$ 167).

$164* *"Les Oies Sauvages"*, s. in pl. Riopelle, (10-20-92, Encans, #135), 16¾ x 19³⁄₁₆ in., (42.5 x 48.8 cm.), lithograph (BP 92, DM 249, FR 848, Y 20,557, C$ 200).

$205* *"Les Oies Sauvages"*, s. Riopelle in plate, (07-14-92, Encans, #159), 16¹⁵⁄₁₆ x 19½ in., (43 x 49.5 cm.), lithograph (BP 107, DM 304, FR 1026, Y 25,635, C$ 244).

$309* *"Les Oies Sauvages"*, s. Riopelle in plate, (02-16-93, Encans, #80), 16¾ x 19⁵⁄₁₆ in., (42.5 x 49 cm.), lithograph (BP 214, DM 504, FR 1708, Y 37,019, C$ 389).

$350* *"Original Rouge"*, #26/195, s. Riopelle, (05-18-93, Encans, #132), 21⅝ x 28¹⁄₁₆ in., (55 x 71.3 cm.), lithograph (BP 228, DM 568, FR 1918, Y 39,006, C$ 444).

$182* *"Original Rouge"*, #18/195, s. Riopelle in plate, (09-15-92, Encans, #105), 18¹¹⁄₁₆ x 25⁹⁄₁₆ in., (47.5 x 65 cm.), lithograph (BP 97, DM 271, FR 919, Y 22,595, C$ 222).

$444* *"Par La Fenetre", 1986,* #66/75, s. Riopelle, (03-16-93, Encans, #105), 28⁹⁄₁₆ x 38⁹⁄₁₆ in., (72.5 x 98 cm.), lithograph (BP 307, DM 738, FR 2508, Y 51,918, C$ 555).

$221* *"Saint-Paul II"*, #20/30, s. Riopelle, (02-16-93, Encans, #78), 23⁷⁄₁₆ x 15¾ in., (59.5 x 40 cm.), lithograph (BP 153, DM 361, FR 1222, Y 26,477, C$ 278).

$697* *Saint-Paul VIII, 1976,* #13/30, s. Riopelle, (11-17-92, Encans, #76), 17½ x 21¼ in., (44.5 x 54 cm.), black etching (BP 459, DM 1111, FR 3743, Y 86,681, C$ 888).

$521* *"Les Saisons De Saint-Cyr-En-Arthie No 5", 1985,* #54/75, s. Riopelle, (06-16-93, Encans, #93), 20½ x 27¾ in., (52 x 70.5 cm.), lithograph on Arches (BP 347, DM 865, FR 2903, Y 55,567, C$ 666).

$104* *Sans Titre,* (06-16-93, Encans, #95), 23⅛ x 29½ in., (58.8 x 75 cm.), color lithograph (BP 69, DM 173, FR 579, Y 11,092, C$ 133).

$872* *Sans Titre,* #39/75, s. Riopelle, (11-17-92, Encans, #79), 19⁵⁄₁₆ x 25⁹⁄₁₆ in., (49 x 65 cm.), lithograph (BP 574, DM 1390, FR 4683, Y 108,444, C$ 1110).

$610* *Sans Titre,* #15/30, s. Riopelle, (11-17-92, Encans, #82), 19¹¹⁄₁₆ x 33⁷⁄₁₆ in., (50 x 85 cm.), lithograph (BP 402, DM 973, FR 3276, Y 75,861, C$ 777).

$559* *Sans Titre,* #70/75, s. Riopelle, (07-14-92, Encans, #160), 16⁹⁄₁₆ x 29¹⁵⁄₁₆ in., (42 x 76 cm.), lithograph (BP 291, DM 829, FR 2796, Y 69,901, C$ 666).

$309* *"Seoul 88"*, #E.A. 8/30, s. Riopelle, (02-16-93, Encans, #77), 28⅛ x 21⅝ in., (71.5 x 55 cm.), lithograph (BP 214, DM 504, FR 1708, Y 37,019, C$ 389).

$307* *"Seoul 88", 1988,* #EA 17/30, s. Riopelle, (05-18-93, Encans, #134), 28¾ x 22¹⁄₁₆ in., (73 x 56 cm.), color lithograph on Arches (BP 200, DM 498, FR 1682, Y 34,214, C$ 389).

$697* *"Shope", 1977,* #20/75, s. Riopelle, (11-17-92, Encans, #74), 23¹³⁄₁₆ x 30⁵⁄₁₆ in., (60.5 x 77 cm.), color lithograph on Arches (BP 459, DM 1111, FR 3743, Y 86,681, C$ 888).

$651* *"St-Paul II", 1976,* #14/30, s. Riopelle, (06-16-93, Encans, #94), 31½ x 22¼ in., (80 x 56.5 cm.), black etching on Arches (BP 434, DM 1081, FR 3627, Y 69,433, C$ 833).

$638* *"St-Paul VI", 1976,* #9/30, s., (09-15-92, Encans, #106), 21⅛ x 17³⁄₁₆ in., (53.7 x 43.7 cm.), etching (BP 341, DM 949, FR 3222, Y 79,205, C$ 777).

$221* *"St. Paul IX", 1976,* #18/30, s. Riopelle, (04-20-93, Encans, #86), 25¹³⁄₁₆ x 27¹⁵⁄₁₆ in., (65.5 x 71 cm.), black etching on Arches (BP 143, DM 352, FR 1188, Y 24,385, C$ 278).

$353* *"Sur La Berge"*, #26/50, s. Riopelle, (02-16-93, Encans, #76), 25⅜ x 35¹³⁄₁₆ in., (64.5 x 91 cm.), lithograph (BP 244, DM 576, FR 1951, Y 42,291, C$ 444).

$394* *"La Vallee De La Roche Blanche"*, #22/75, s. Riopelle, (05-18-93, Encans, #136), 11⁷⁄₁₆ x 15⅜ in., (29 x 39 cm.), color lithograph on Arches (BP 257, DM 639, FR 2159, Y 43,910, C$ 500).

$133* *"Vetheuil Entre Chien Et Loup"*, #25/75, s. Riopelle, (02-16-93, Encans, #79), 12⅜ x 15¾ in., (31.5 x 40 cm.), lithograph (BP 92, DM 217, FR 735, Y 15,934, C$ 167).

$638* *"Visages Caches"*, #12/75, s. Riopelle, (09-15-92, Encans, #101), 19¹¹⁄₁₆ x 15¾ in., (50 x 40 cm.), lithograph (BP 341, DM 949, FR 3222, Y 79,205, C$ 777).

RIPLEY, Aiden Lassell American 1896-1969

$396* *Covey Of Quail,* margins, s. A. Lassell Ripley, t., d. 1947, (02-13-93, Collins, #57, illus.), 8½ x 13⅞ in., (21.6 x 35.2 cm.), etching (BP 279, DM 657, FR 2222, Y 47,757).

$605* *End Of The Grouse Season,* pub. Frost and Reed, 1966, s. A. Lassell Ripley, (02-13-93, Collins, #135, illus.), 16½ x 27 in., (41.9 x 68.6 cm.), color offset lithograph (BP 426, DM 1003, FR 3395, Y 72,962).

$385* *"Quail Shooting"*, s., t., (10-31-92, Cleveland, #204), 8¾ x 13¾ in., (22.2 x 34.9 cm.), gravure (intaglio) (BP 247, DM 592, FR 2009, Y 47,690).

$303* *"Snipe At Dawn"*, s., very good cond.?, (07-19-92, Bakker, #167), plate 8¾ x 11¾ in., (22.2 x 29.8 cm.), etching and drypoint (BP 155, DM 442, FR 1493, Y 37,668).

RIPPL-RONAI, Jozsef Hungarian 1861-1927

$14,466* *La Ronde or La Fete De Village, c. 1895,* num., s., mono., staining, cracks, small margins, (02-24-93, Picard, #212), color lithograph on thin Japan laid (BP 10,088, DM 23,484, FR 79,615, Y 1,697,489).

RIST, Luigi American 1888-1959

$1430* *Sunflowers,* s. Luigi Rist, very good cond., (03-12-93, Skinner, #66, illus.), 11¾ x 16 in., (29.8 x 40.6 cm.), color blockprint on laid (BP 998, DM 2380, FR 8093, Y 168,533).

RITCHIE, Alexander Hay American 1822-1895

BI *Lady Wahington's Reception,* est. $3/400, (02-04-93, Sloan, #1219), sight 25 x 39½ in., (63.5 x 100.3 cm.), hand colored engraving.

RITSCHER

BI *North German Lloyd,* F.J. Johnston, B cond., restoration, fold marks, est. $6/800, (08-06-92, Swann, #237, illus.), 39½ x 28½ in., (100.3 x 72.4 cm.), .

RITTASE, William

BI *The Santa Rosa At The Dock,* 1930s, photog.'s stamp, (05-23-93, Butterfield, #3572, illus.), 9⅝ x 7⅝ in., photograph, toned gelatin silver print.

RITTS, Herb American b. 1952

$2906* *"Backflip, Paradise Cove 1987"*, photog.'s blindstamped credit, t., s., d., #8/25, pub., 503 x 404mm, (05-07-93, Sotheby-London, #355, illus.), photograph, silver print (BP 1840, DM 4594, FR 15,482, Y 319,974).

BI *Bob Paris, Mr. Olympia, 1985,* s., t., d., #10/25, est. $2,5/3,500, (04-08-93, Christie-NY, #554, illus.), 19 x 15⅜ in., (48.3 x 39.1 cm.), photograph, gelatin silver print.

$1955* *"Carrie In Profile, Paradise Cove", 1988,* photog.'s blindstamp, t., d., #13/25, (05-23-93, Butterfield, #3573, illus.), 19¼ x 15¼ in., photograph, platinum print (BP 1273, DM 3197, FR 10,759, Y 216,094).

$2588* *"Carrie In Sand (Detail) Paradise Cove", 1988,* photog. (c) blindstamp, s., t., d., #18/25 by photog., (04-06-93,

Sotheby-NY, #527, illus.), photograph (BP 1709, DM 4169, FR 14,119, Y 295,164).

$3300* *Carrie In The Sand (Detail), Paradise Cove, 1988,* photog.'s (c) blindstamp, s., t., d., num. 8/25 by photog., #8/25 ed., (10-15-92, Sotheby-NY, #624, illus.), 22¼ x 19 in., (56.5 x 48.3 cm.), photograph, platinum print (BP 2019, DM 4912, FR 16,658, Y 395,921).

$4950* *Djimon With Octopus, Hollywood, 1989,* photog.'s (c) blindstamp, s., t., d., num. 17/25 by photog., #17/25 ed. in this format, (10-15-92, Sotheby-NY, #621, illus.), 17½ x 15 in., (44.5 x 38.1 cm.), photograph, gelatin silver print (BP 3029, DM 7368, FR 24,987, Y 593,881).

$907* *Draped Woman, Marrakech, 1986,* s., t., #15/25, (05-06-93, Christie-London, #194), 20 x 16 in., photograph, toned gelatin silver print (BP 575, DM 1429, FR 4809, Y 99,791).

$3025* *"Duo IV", 1990,* s., t., d., edit. 7/25, annot., Dixon Collection, (11-16-92, Butterfield, #6134, illus.), 14¾ x 18⁷⁄₁₆ in., (375.3 x 467.6 mm.), photograph, platinum print (BP 1992, DM 4823, FR 16,246, Y 376,197).

$1540* *"Duo VI", 1990,* s., t., d., edit. 7/25, annot., Dixon Collection, (11-16-92, Butterfield, #6133, illus.), 18¹⁄₁₆ x 15 in., (458 x 381.7 mm.), photograph, platinum print (BP 1014, DM 2455, FR 8271, Y 191,518).

$1495* *"Female Torso With Veil, Paradise Cove", 1984,* photog.'s blindstamp, s., t., d., #10/25, (05-23-93, Butterfield, #3575, illus.), 18 x 15½ in., photograph, gelatin silver print (BP 974, DM 2444, FR 8228, Y 165,248).

$1725* *"Female Torso, Hollywood, 1989",* #7/25, s., t., d., num., sight 470 x 360mm, (05-07-93, Sotheby-London, #357, illus.), photograph, silver print (BP 1092, DM 2727, FR 9190, Y 189,936).

$2070* *Floating Torso, St. Barthelemy (sic), 1987,* s., t., d., #5/25, (04-08-93, Christie-NY, #553, illus.), 22¾ x 19¼ in., (57.8 x 48.9 cm.), photograph, gelatin silver print (BP 1357, DM 3325, FR 11,256, Y 234,907).

$4830* *Fred With Tires, Body Shop Series, 1984,* embossed (c) credit; s., t., d., #9/30, (04-08-93, Christie-NY, #555, illus.), 23 x 18⅝ in., (58.4 x 47.3 cm.), photograph, gelatin silver print (BP 3167, DM 7759, FR 26,264, Y 548,116).

$6050* *Fred With Tires, Bodyshop Series, 1984,* embossed (c) credit in margin, s., t., d., num. 14/30, (10-13-92, Christie-NY, #593, illus.), 23¼ x 18¼ in., (59.1 x 46.4 cm.), photograph, gelatin silver print (BP 3524, DM 8863, FR 30,114, Y 733,600).

$863* *Gerald, Jamaica", 1985,* photog.'s blindstamp, s., t., d., #9/25, est. $1,5/2,000, (05-23-93, Butterfield, #3574, illus.), 22¼ x 18 in., photograph, gelatin silver print (BP 562, DM 1411, FR 4750, Y 95,391).

$4400* *Madonna, True Blue, 1986 (Pictures, unpaginated),* photog.'s (c) blindstamp, s., t., d., num. 22/25 by photog., #22/25 ed. in this format, (10-15-92, Sotheby-NY, #622A, illus.), 22¾ x 18½ in., (57.8 x 47 cm.), photograph, gelatin silver print (BP 2692, DM 6550, FR 22,211, Y 527,894).

$1093* *"Male Torso With Veil", 1985,* photog.'s blindstamp, s., t., d., #17/25, annot., (05-23-93, Butterfield, #3576, illus.), 18⅝ x 15⅛ in., photograph, gelatin silver print (BP 712, DM 1787, FR 6015, Y 120,814).

$1980* *"Men With Kelp", Paradise Cove, 1987,* embossed (c) credit in margin, s., t., d., num. 9/25, (10-13-92, Christie-NY, #594, illus.), 18½ x 15 in., (47 x 38.1 cm.), photograph, gelatin silver print (BP 1153, DM 2901, FR 9856, Y 240,087).

$1053* *"Naomi With Raised Arms Los Angeles 1988",* margin blindstamped photog.'s credit Herb Ritts, t., s., d., 504 x 406mm, (05-07-93, Sotheby-London, #354, illus.), photograph, toned silver print (BP 667, DM 1665, FR 5610, Y 115,944).

$1100* *"Neith With Shadows, Front View, Pondridge", 1985,* photog. blindstamp, s., t., d., edit. 12/25, Dixon Collection, (11-16-92, Butterfield, #6132, illus.), 18⁹⁄₁₆ x 15¼ in., (470.7 x 388 mm.), photograph, toned gelatin silver print (BP 724, DM 1754, FR 5908, Y 136,799).

$2906* *"Neith With Tumbleweed, 1986 Paradise Cove",* photog.'s blindstamped credit, t., s., d., #24/25, pub., 504 x 404mm, (05-07-93, Sotheby-London, #356, illus.), photograph, toned silver print (BP 1840, DM 4594, FR 15,482, Y 319,974).

$824* *Nith With Tumbleweed, Paradise Cove, 1986,* s., (10-29-92, Christie-London, #199, illus.), 19 x 15¼ in., (48.3 x 38.7 cm.), photograph, warm-toned gelatin silver print (BP 528, DM 1268, FR 4301, Y 102,069).

$1840* *"Rachel Holding Shark", 1989,* photog. (c) blindstamp, s., t., d., #11/25, i. by photog., (04-06-93, Sotheby-NY, #529, illus.), 19 x 13¼ in., photograph (BP 1215, DM 2964, FR 10,038, Y 209,854).

$2588* *"Veiled Male (Full Length) (Herb Ritts, unpaginated), 1985,* photog. (c) blindstamp, s., t., d., #5/25 by photog., (04-06-93, Sotheby-NY, #528, illus.), 18¾ x 15⅛ in., photograph (BP 1709, DM 4169, FR 14,119, Y 295,164).

$2200* *"Waterfall II, Hollywood", 1988,* photog. blindstamp, s., t., d., edit. 16/25, Dixon Collection, (11-16-92, Butterfield, #6131, illus.), 18⁵⁄₁₆ x 15 in., (464.4 x 381.7 mm.), photograph, platinum print (BP 1449, DM 3508, FR 11,815, Y 273,598).

$6600* *Waterfall IV, 1988,* photog.'s (c) blindstampm s., t., d., num. 6/25 by photog., #6/25 ed.in this format, (10-15-92, Sotheby-NY, #622, illus.), 19 x 15¼ in., (48.3 x 38.7 cm.), photograph, platinum print (BP 4039, DM 9824, FR 33,317, Y 791,842).

$2750* *Waterfall-Woman With Sphere, Hollywood, 1989,* photog.'s (c) blindstamp, s., t., d., num. 15/25 by photog., #15/25 ed., (10-15-92, Sotheby-NY, #623, illus.), 16¼ x 15⅛ in., (41.3 x 38.4 cm.), photograph, gelatin silver print (BP 1683, DM 4093, FR 13,882, Y 329,934).

$2200* *Wrapped Torso, 1989,* embossed (c) credit stamp in margin, s., t., d., num. 9/25, annot., (10-13-92, Christie-NY, #595, illus.), 18 x 15⅛ in., (45.7 x 38.4 cm.), photograph, platinum print (BP 1281, DM 3223, FR 10,951, Y 266,764).

RIUSCHER, Johannes (called de Jonge HERCULES) c. 1625-after 1675

$217* *Waldeingang (B. 19; Trautscholdt, Hollstein 10 II),* (12-04-92, Bassenge, #6420), 3⅜ x 5⅝ in., (8.6 x 14.3 cm.), etching (BP 139, DM 346, FR 1172, Y 27,091).

$144* *Zwei Manner Auf Einem Waldweg (Trautscholdt 3; Hollstein 3 III),* (12-04-92, Bassenge, #6419), 3½ x 4⅛ in., (8.9 x 10.5 cm.), etching (BP 92, DM 229, FR 778, Y 17,978).

RIVERA, Diego Mexican 1886-1957

$5750* *Autorretrato,* s. crayon, d., #14/100, full margins, good cond., creases, tear, (05-18-93, Sotheby-NY, #268, illus.), 20 x 15 in., (508 x 381 mm.), lithograph (BP 3745, DM 9330, FR 31,507, Y 640,811).

$7150* *Autorretrato, 1930,* s., d., #46=100, margins, repaired splits, very good cond., (11-24-92, Christie-NY, #354, illus.), borderline 15 x 11½ in., (381 x 292 mm.), sheet 20¾ x 16 in., (381 x 292 mm.), lithograph on tan (BP 4710, DM 11,447, FR 38,838, Y 886,987).

$2645* *Desnudo De Mujer,* s., d. 1930, #31/100; s., d. in stone, full margins, good cond., yellowing, browning, tear, (05-18-93, Sotheby-NY, #269, illus.), image 16⅜ x 9¼ in., (416 x 235 mm.), lithograph (BP 1723, DM 4292, FR 14,493, Y 294,773).

$7150* *Desnudo Sentado Con Brazos Levantados (Frieda Kahlo), 1930,* watermark, s., d., #84-100, full margins, loss, crease, very good cond., (11-24-92, Christie-NY, #355, illus.), borderline 16½ x 11 in., (419 x 280 mm.), lithograph on tan laid paper (BP 4710, DM 11,447, FR 38,838, Y 886,987).

$1980* *Mercado De Flores, 1930,* crayon s., d. #39-100, full margins, very good cond., soiling, mat staining, paper abrasions, (11-23-92, Sotheby-NY, #280, illus.), image 18⅞ x 24¾ in., (479 x 628 mm.), lithograph (BP 1295, DM 3170, FR 10,755, Y 245,627).

BI *El Nino Del Taco, 1932,* s., # artist's proof, ded., d. Octubre 10, 1934; s., d. in stone, goo cond., yellowing, tape remains, est. $10/15,000, (05-18-93, Sotheby-NY, #267, illus.), 16½ x 11⅞ in., (419 x 302 mm.), lithograph.

$8050* *Open Air School,* #34/100, d. 1932; s., d. in stone, narrow margins, very good cond., soiling, tape remains, (05-18-93, Sotheby-NY, #266, illus.), image 12½ x 16⅜ in.,

(318 x 416 mm.), lithograph (BP 5243, DM 13,062, FR 44,110, Y 897,136).

$17,600* *Sueno, 1932,* s. in stone, s., d. 1932, #No 17, full margins, good cond., yellowing, paper loss, repaired tears, tear, (11-23-92, Sotheby-NY, #279, illus.), image 16⅜ x 11⅞ in., (415 x 302 mm.), lithograph (BP 11,507, DM 28,178, FR 95,600, Y 2,183,352).

RIVERS, Jack

BI   *Selected Works: Portraits Of Bonnie Maud, 1910, "Profile Of Bonnie Maud" and "Three-Quarters Portrait Of Bonnie Maud": Two,* est. $800/1,000, (05-23-93, Butterfield, #3577, illus.), each approx. 11⅝ x 9½ in., photograph, gelatin silver print.

RIVERS, Larry   American b. 1923

$550* *The Boston Massacre, 1970: Two,* suite of 8, each s., #8/150 and #16/150, (10-18-92, Hindman, #490), larger 20 x 29¾ in., (50.8 x 75.6 cm.), silver foil lithographs (BP 337, DM 819, FR 2776, Y 65,987).

$2420* *Boston Massacre: Twelve,* all s., #42/150, very good cond., (12-04-92, Doyle, #141), silkscreen plus cover (BP 1552, DM 3854, FR 13,074, Y 302,122).

$325* *Camel Nr. 1, 1980,* s., d., num., (11-28-92, Schoppmann, #733), 10¹³⁄₁₆ x 8⁷⁄₁₆ in., (27.5 x 21.5 cm.), color carbon print on color cardboard (BP 215, DM 518, FR 1758, Y 40,448).

BI   *Camel Quartet, 1978,* crayon s., d., #37/125, pub. Marlborough Graphics, blindstamp printer, Styria Studio, full margins, very good cond.?, water stain extending into image, est. $9/1,200, (05-19-93, Butterfield, #2313, illus.), 20½ x 16¼ in., (521 x 413 mm.), lithograph and silkscreen in colors on wove.

$1840* *Camel Quartet, 1978,* s., d., #26/125, pub. Marlborough Graphics, Ltd., full margins, good cond., pressure mark, creases, discoloration, (05-15-93, Sotheby-NY, #1166, illus.), 20⅛ x 16⅛ in., (51.1 x 41 cm.), lithograph and silkscreen in colors w/hand-coloring in orange crayon (BP 1196, DM 2960, FR 9946, Y 203,969).

$1870* *Chinese Information Travel, 1984,* s., d., num. 92/150, pub. by artist, good cond., creases, pencil notations, (02-24-93, Butterfield, #3128, illus.), 30⅛ x 35¼ in., (765 x 895 mm.), lithograph & silkscreen in colors w/graphite additions on wove (BP 1304, DM 3036, FR 10,292, Y 219,432).

$660* *Cindy,* s., (10-18-92, Hindman, #487), 20 x 24½ in., (50.8 x 62.2 cm.), collage (BP 404, DM 982, FR 3332, Y 79,184).

$1045* *Daniel Webster, 1961,* s., (03-14-93, Hindman, #329), 22 x 28 in., (55.9 x 71.1 cm.), lithograph (BP 729, DM 1739, FR 5914, Y 123,159).

BI   *Drawn From The Collection, 1984,* s., num. 83/100, pub. Mixografia, apparently good cond., est. $6/8,000, (02-24-93, Butterfield, #3127, illus.), 40¼ x 33½ in., (102.2 x 85.1 cm.), lithograph in colors w/collage, paper additions, & hand-coloring on handmade.

$1093* *Dutch Masters, 1964-68,* s., d., #30/100, good cond., creases, staining, (05-19-93, Butterfield, #2312), 19 x 17¾ in., (483 x 451 mm.), offset lithograph on commercial wove (BP 710, DM 1777, FR 5986, Y 121,001).

$660* *Enter Emma (Sparks 49), 1966-9,* s., d., num. 13/27, ULAE blindstamp, full margins, excell. cond., (09-19-92, Christie-E, #189), sheet 22½ x 30 in., (572 x 762 mm.), etching and aquatint w/graphite on Arches (BP 380, DM 988, FR 3385, Y 82,233).

BI   *From "Boston Massacre" Series, 1970,* pub. Marlborough Graphics Inc., s., num. Rivers 117/150, very good cond., crease, est. $3/500, (03-12-93, Skinner, #117, illus.), sight, sheet 17⅞ x 27 in., (45.4 x 68.6 cm.), screenprint.

BI   *Girlie, 1970,* s., num. 52/100, pub. Marlborough Graphics, apparently good cond., est. BP 2/300, (11-30-92, Phillips-London, #563), sheet 29⅛ x 16⅞ in., (740 x 429 mm.), screenprint & collage in colors on heavy metallic wove paper.

BI   *Hommage A Picasso, 1974,* crayon s., #54/90, p. by Styria Studios, full margins, good cond., est. BP 800/1,200, (06-30-93, Sotheby-London, #918, illus.), 20⅞ x 28¾ in., (530 x 730 mm.), offset color lithograph on wove.

BI   *Hommage A Picasso, 1974,* s. in plate and crayon, d., 45/90, studio drystamp, est. FF15/20,000, (06-28-93, Loudmer, #353), 20¼ x 28¹⁵⁄₁₆ in., (515 x 735 mm.), sh 22¼ x 30⅛ in., (515 x 735 mm.), color offset on wove.

BI   *Hommage A Picasso, 1974,* regular edit., s., d. 74, est. FF8,000/10,000, (05-27-93, Briest, #179), 22¹⁄₁₆ x 30⅛ in., (56 x 76.5 cm.), color offset and lithograph.

$1650* *"Hommage To Picasso", #75/90,* s., d. Rivers '74, blindstamp, (05-14-93, DuMouchelle, #2048, illus.), image 20¼ x 28¾ in., (51.4 x 73 cm.), screenprint w/photoscreening (BP 1073, DM 2654, FR 8919, Y 182,907).

BI   *Hommage To Picasso, 1974,* s. in crayon, num. 64/90, pub. Propylaen Verlag, margins, good cond., est. BP 1,4/1,600, (12-01-92, Christie-London, #629), L. 20¼ x 29⅛ in., (515 x 740 mm.), screenprint in colors on wove.

BI   *Hommage To Picasso, 1974,* s., d., #73/90, pub. Propylaen Verlag and Pantheon Press, blindstampprinter Styria Studio, full margins, very good cond., handling creases, surfacesoiling, est. $4,5/5,500, (05-19-93, Butterfield, #2312A, illus.), sh 20 x 29 in., (508 x 737 mm.), silkscreen in colors on heavy wove.

$660* *"The Jewish Museum-15 Years", 1965,* s., d. Sept. '65, num. 4/25, presumably pub. Jewish Museum, p. U.L.A.E. (?), full sheet, light-staining, skinning, very good cond., (09-19-92, Christie-E, #186), sheet 35 x 23 in., (889 x 584 mm.), lithograph in colors w/offset text on light grey fibrous paper (BP 380, DM 988, FR 3385, Y 82,233).

$688* *Lenin, 1973,* s., d., #137/200, (06-11-93, Freemn/Fine Art, #192), 9 x 11½ in., (22.9 x 29.2 cm.), color lithograph (BP 452, DM 1118, FR 3770, Y 72,997).

BI   *May Opening, National Collection Of Fine Art, Smithsonian, Washington, 1979,* s., #64/144, good cond., staining, surface soiling. est. $800/1,000, (10-28-92, Butterfield, #3091), 30 x 21½ in., (762 x 546 mm.), color lithograph w/cut-out and collage.

BI   *On The Phone, 1982,* s., d., annot. A.P. 4/10, pub. Simca Print Artists, apparently good cond. crease, est. $2/4,000, (02-24-93, Butterfield, #3126, illus.), (82.6 x 106.7 cm.), lithograph and silkscreen in colors on wove.

$440* *One More Paul Revere II 1968-70,* s., d., annot. Printers Proof, pub. ULAE ,apparently good cond., (02-24-93, Butterfield, #3121), 26½ x 34¾ in., (673 x 883 mm.), lithograph in colors on wove (BP 307, DM 714, FR 2422, Y 51,631).

$880* *Open Camel, 1978,* s., d., #17/120, blindstamp pub. Marlborough Graohics, good cond., image pressure marks, creases, (10-28-92, Butterfield, #3090), 21½ x 29¼ in., (546 x 743 mm.), color stencil crayon drawing w/lithograph on Arches (BP 561, DM 1359, FR 4615, Y 107,975).

$622* *"Pop Corn",* s., num., tears, (12-01-92, Karl/Faber, #1137), sh 37⅜ x 29¾ in., (95 x 75.5 cm.), color lithograph w/serigraph on heavy wove (BP 411, DM 991, FR 3379, Y 77,440).

BI   *Popcorn, 1970,* s., #274/300, full margins, good cond., creases, surface soiling, est. $1,5/2,000, (10-28-92, Butterfield, #3088), 36¼ x 27½ in., (921 x 699 mm.), color silkscreen on cream wove.

BI   *Popcorn, 1970,* s., num. 274/300, full margins, good cond., creases, surface soiling,est. $1,2/1,400, (02-24-93, Butterfield, #3123), 36¼ x 27½ in., (921 x 699 mm.), silkscreen in colors on cream wove.

$2760* *Queen Of Clubs, 1979,* s., d., #165/200, pub. Clarkson N. Potter, full margins, staining, very good cond., (05-11-93, Christie-NY, #547, illus.), sheet 29¾ x 22⅜ in., (756 x 568 mm.), color lithograph and screenprint on Arches (BP 1762, DM 4348, FR 14,650, Y 303,597).

$1870* *Queen Of Clubs, 1979,* s., d., num. 177/200, pub. Clarkson N. Potter, full margins, minor rubbing, stain, crease, very good cond., (09-19-92, Christie-E, #190, illus.), sheet 29¹³⁄₁₆ x 22¼ in., (757 x 565 mm.), lithograph and screenprint in colors on Arches (BP 1076, DM 2800, FR 9590, Y 232,993).

$3300* *Queen Of Clubs, 1979,* s., d., #166/200, pub. Clarkson N. Potter, full margins, good cond.,creases, (11-07-92, Sotheby-NY, #747, illus.), 28 x 21¼ in., (711 x 540 mm.), lithograph and silkscreen p. in colors on Arches 88 (BP 2158, DM 5269, FR 17,809, Y 407,307).

$526* *Republique De Guinee, 1977,* s. Larry Rivers 77, 65/100, (06-03-93, Kunsthallen, #190), lithograph in colors (BP 341, DM 842, FR 2837, Y 56,414, DK 3220).

$690* *Sketches: Self Portrait,* s., margins, good cond.?, creases, (05-19-93, Butterfield, #2314), 28 x 22½ in., (711 x 572 mm.), offset lithograph in colors on wove (BP 448, DM 1122, FR 3779, Y 76,387).

$413* *Swimmer, 1970,* incised sig., #38/100, pub. Marlborough Graphics, surface slightly rubbed, (10-28-92, Butterfield, #3089), 9 x 9 in., (229 x 229 mm.), color silkscreen w/ collage on plexiglas (BP 263, DM 638, FR 2166, Y 50,675).

$220* *Swimmer, 1970,* incised sig., num. 38/100, pub. Marlborough Graphics, surface slightly rubbed, (02-24-93, Butterfield, #3122), 9 x 9 in., (229 x 229 mm.), silkscreen w/ collage in colors on plexiglass (BP 153, DM 357, FR 1211, Y 25,816).

$440* *Tanfastic, c. 1965,* s., num. 37/225, full sheet, scrapes, very good cond., (09-19-92, Christie-E, #187), sheet 18 x 23¼ in., (457 x 591 mm.), offset lithograph in colors on plexiglas (BP 253, DM 659, FR 2256, Y 54,822).

$495* *Underground With Fraser, 1966,* s., d., num. 7/25, full sheet, creases, very good cond., (09-19-92, Christie-E, #188), overall sheet 35½ x 30¼ in., (902 x 768 mm.), screenprint in colors w/collage on wove (BP 285, DM 741, FR 2538, Y 61,675).

RIVIERE, Briton (after)

$126* *Daniel In The Lion's Den, 1892,* by J.B. Pratt, pub. Thomas Agnew and Sons, margins, (11-12-92, Bonhams-Chelsea, #44), 25 x 35 in., (63.5 x 88.9 cm.), hand-colored mezzotint (BP 83, DM 200, FR 673, Y 15,623).

BI *The Night Watch, 1882,* by F. Stacpoole, blindstamp, pub. Thomas Agnew and Sons, margins, est. BP 70/100, (11-12-92, Bonhams-Chelsea, #45), plate 21¾ x 33½ in., (55.2 x 85.1 cm.), hand-colored mezzotint.

RIVIERE, Henri French 1864-1951

$884* *La Balise Holleneyere (A.S.F. et R.T. nd),* stamped, large margins, (06-16-93, Ader Tajan, #134C), 8$^{15}/_{16}$ x 13$^{15}/_{16}$ in., (22.8 x 35.4 cm.), color lithograph (BP 589, DM 1467, FR 4925, Y 94,283).

$359* *"Le Crepuscule De La Feerie Des Heurs - 1901",* mono. in plate, (10-18-92, Pescheteau, #251), 12⅝ x 26⅜ in., (32 x 67 cm.), lithograph in colors (BP 218, DM 530, FR 1801, Y 42,866).

$491* *Le Hameau (?) (A.S.F. p. 87 R.T. p. 163), 1899,* from "les Aspects de la Nature", large margins, (06-16-93, Ader Tajan, #134B), 21$^{7}/_{16}$ x 32$^{11}/_{16}$ in., (54.5 x 83 cm.), color lithograph (BP 327, DM 815, FR 2735, Y 52,368).

BI *Leaving The Harbor,* good cond., est. $5/700, (02-07-93, Bakker, #218), sheet 21 x 32 in., (53.3 x 81.3 cm.), color lithograph.

$4290* *Le Pardon De Sainte-Anne-La-Palud, 1892: Four,* pl from set of five, margins, good cond., rubbing in margins, defects, ex coll. Roger Marx (L.2229) and F.E. Bliss (L.265), (06-30-93, Sotheby-London, #673), 20½ x 13¾ in., (521 x 349 mm.), color woodcut on large Japan (BP 2875, DM 7317, FR 24,684, Y 459,659).

$351* *Paysage De Montagne (H. Toudouze; R.S. Fields, nd),* stamped, good margins, (04-02-93, Picard, #173), 21⅝ x 32½ in., (55 x 82.5 cm.), color lithograph (BP 231, DM 564, FR 1916, Y 39,964).

$12,011* *"Paysages Bretons: Enterrement A Trestraou", "Les Vanneuses A Loguivy", "Vaches Dans Les Champs De La Garde-Guerin", "Une Femme Et Une Vache', "Garde-Guerin" and "Un Cheval Et Village De La Chapelle", 1890-91: Five,* three s. w/sig. stamp, margins, first rubbed areas, foxing, creasing,good cond., two ex coll. Roger Marx (L.2229), (06-30-93, Sotheby-London, #672, illus.), 8¾ x 13½ in., (222 x 343 mm.), color woodcut in Japan (BP 8050, DM 20,486, FR 69,108, Y 1,286,939).

$609* *La Pleine Lune (A.F. et R.T. p. 87 et 163), 1902,* from "Feerie des Heures", stamped, good margins, (06-16-93, Ader Tajan, #134A), 9$^{7}/_{16}$ x 23⅝ in., (24 x 60 cm.), color lithograph (BP 406, DM 1011, FR 3393, Y 64,953).

$248* *"Racing The Storm Home" and "The Punt, Late Afternoon": Two,* mono., s. Henri Riviere in matrix, good cond., toning, (05-22-93, Skinner, #211, illus.), approx., sight 9¼ x 23¼ in., (23.5 x 59.1 cm.), color lithograph on paper (BP 161, DM 403, FR 1357, Y 27,343).

$767* *Ruisseau A Loperec (G.T., Le Beau Pays De Bretagne, IV), 1901,* num. 22, stamp, s., large margins, (02-03-93, Ader Tajan, #200), 9$^{1}/_{16}$ x 13¾ in., (23 x 35 cm.), 14$^{15}/_{16}$ x 14⅞ in., (23 x 35 cm.), color lithograph (BP 535, DM 1263, FR 4283, Y 95,410).

$550* *"Le Vent" and "L'Orage Qui Monte" (R. Toudouze, p. 163, A. Fields, p. 87), 1901-1902: Two,* from "La Feerie des Heures" Series, yellowed, staining, thin spots, creases, cracks, tear, good margins, (06-16-93, Ader Tajan, #134), 9$^{7}/_{16}$ x 23⅝ in., (24 x 60 cm.), color lithograph (BP 367, DM 913, FR 3064, Y 58,660).

ROBATHAN, Robert

$489* *City Canyon, 1952,* s., t., #5/22, blindstamp printer, Lynton Kistler, full margins, goodcond., mat staining, stray printing ink, (05-19-93, Butterfield, #2019, illus.), 9$^{7}/_{16}$ x 7$^{5}/_{16}$ in., (240 x 186 mm.), lithograph on wove (BP 317, DM 795, FR 2678, Y 54,135).

$201* *Merry-Go-Round, 1955,* s., t, #21/22, blindstamp printer, Lynton Kistler, full margins, verygood., (05-19-93, Butterfield, #2021), 11$^{13}/_{16}$ x 20 in., (300 x 508 mm.), lithograph on wove (BP 130, DM 327, FR 1101, Y 22,252).

$374* *Sailboats, 1954,* s., t., #20/20, blindstamp printer, Lynton Kistler, full margins, very good cond., foxing, creases, (05-19-93, Butterfield, #2020), 13$^{13}/_{16}$ x 17$^{9}/_{16}$ in., (351 x 446 mm.), lithograph on cream wove (BP 243, DM 608, FR 2048, Y 41,404).

ROBAUDY, A.

$36* *2e Emprunt: "Armee De L'Epargne", 1916,* Imp. Robaudy, good cond., (02-12-93, Cheval/Robert, #109), 47¼ x 31½ in., (120 x 80 cm.), poster (BP 25, DM 60, FR 202, Y 4342).

ROBBE, Manuel French 1872-1936

$825* *Deux Femmes Dans Un Parc (M.C. 30), 1906,* s., full margins, good cond., foxing, staining, surface soiling, (02-24-93, Butterfield, #2967), 21 x 15¼ in., (533 x 387 mm.), aquatint in colors on Arches laid (BP 575, DM 1339, FR 4540, Y 96,808).

$358* *Dorfstrasse Mit Ententeich, 1919,* s., num., (c), (05-08-93, Schloss Ahlden, #2864), 12⅛ x 18⅜ in., (30.8 x 46.6 cm.), color etching on copper print paper (BP 234, DM 575, FR 1940, Y 40,004).

$715* *Landscape,* s., #122, (10-18-92, Hindman, #460), 18½ x 24⅛ in., (47 x 61.3 cm.), color aquatint (BP 438, DM 1064, FR 3609, Y 85,783).

$248* *Landscape, 1935,* s., (05-16-93, Hindman, #450), 14 x 19½ in., (35.6 x 49.5 cm.), color aquatint (BP 161, DM 399, FR 1341, Y 27,491).

$280* *"Marche Aux Fleurs",* s., (04-04-93, Pescheteau, #283), a vue 18⅛ x 14$^{15}/_{16}$ in., (46 x 38 cm.), etching and aquatint on wove (BP 184, DM 450, FR 1528, Y 31,880).

$550* *Market Scene,* s., num. 125, Ruth K. Flower Coll., (04-18-93, Hindman, #1661), 14½ x 20¼ in., (36.8 x 51.4 cm.), color aquatint (BP 361, DM 888, FR 3002, Y 61,846).

$1955* *Quietude Maternelle, 1901,* s., #43/60, blindstamp, full margins, good cond., light-staining, tear, foxing, surface soiling, surface scuffs, creases, stray printing ink, (05-19-93, Butterfield, #1963, illus.), sh. 24¼ x 17⅜ in., (616 x 441 mm.), aquatint in colors on Arches laid (BP 1269, DM 3178, FR 10,706, Y 216,429).

$303* *Sailing Ships In The Moonlight,* pencil s. w/pseudonym, #223, (04-02-93, Sloan, #1176), 19½ x 7¾ in., (495 x 197 mm.), color aquatint (BP 200, DM 487, FR 1654, Y 34,498).

ROBBENNOLT, Linda Murphy

BI *"There, There", 1985,* s., t., d., est. $6/800, (11-16-92, Butterfield, #6135, illus.), 15⅝ x 19$^{9}/_{16}$ in., (397.6 x 496.2 mm.), photograph, cibachrome.

ROBBINS, Frederick American 20th cent.

BI *15th And Market,* s., t., est. $50/75, (06-11-93, Freemn/ Fine Art, #193), 7 x 4½ in., (17.8 x 11.4 cm.), etching.

ROBERT, Louis
  BI *Deathbed Study Of Jacques Joseph Ebelmen, 1852,* 190
      x 245mm, est. BP 2,5/4,000, (05-07-93, Sotheby-Lon-
      don, #110, illus.), photograph, waxed paper neg..
  BI *Le Hameau De La Reine, Versailles, c. 1850,* 348 x
      272mm, est. BP 2,5/4,000, (05-07-93, Sotheby-London,
      #114, illus.), photograph, waxed paper neg..
  BI *The Park At Versailles, c. 1850,* 342 x 266mm, est. BP
      2,5/4,000, (05-07-93, Sotheby-London, #108, illus.), pho-
      tograph, waxed paper neg..
  BI *Portrait Of The Painter Emile Van Maucke, Seated On
      Barrow, c. 1850,* 232 x 185mm, est. BP 3/5,000, (05-07-
      93, Sotheby-London, #106, illus.), photograph, waxed
      paper neg..
  BI *Rustic Architectural Scene At Sevres, c. 1850,* 271 x
      373mm, est. BP 2,5/4,000, (05-07-93, Sotheby-London,
      #107, illus.), photograph, waxed paper neg..
  BI *Study Of A Plough In A Field, c. 1850,* 270 x 374mm,
      est. BP 2,5/4,000, (05-07-93, Sotheby-London, #111,
      illus.), photograph, waxed paper neg..
  BI *Study Of A Workman, Sevres, c. 1850,* 231 x 177mm,
      est. BP 2/3,000, (05-07-93, Sotheby-London, #113, illus.),
      photograph, waxed paper neg..
  BI *Tete De Boeuf, Still Life, c. 1850,* 257 x 172mm, est. BP
      4/6,000, (05-07-93, Sotheby-London, #109, illus.), photo-
      graph, waxed paper neg..
  BI *View Across Boulogne To Paris From The Terrasse De
      La Lanterne De Demosthene In The Park At Saint
      Cloud, c. 1850,* positive and negative, first mounted on
      card, 259 x 323mm and 266 x 345mm, est. BP 8/
      12,000, (05-07-93, Sotheby-London, #112, illus.), photo-
      graph, salt print and waxed paper neg..

ROBERT, P.
  $357* *Papiers Germain Peints, 1937,* Imp. Francisque Rey, A-
      cond., cracking, scratch marks, (08-06-92, Swann, #238,
      illus.), 31½ x 47½ in., (80 x 120.7 cm.), (BP 186, DM
      527, FR 1781, Y 45,536).

ROBERTS, David   b.Scotland,British 1796-1864
  $83* *Abyssinian Slaves Resting At Korta-Nubia,* pub. May 1,
      1847, (05-28-93, Sloan, #1014, illus.), 10½ x 14⅜ in.,
      (26.7 x 36.5 cm.), hand-tinted lithograph (BP 53, DM
      132, FR 445, Y 8900).
  BI *Abyssinian Slaves Resting At Korta-Nubia,* pub. May 1,
      1847, est. $5/700, (02-04-93, Sloan, #1515), 10 x 13⅜
      in., (25.4 x 34 cm.), hand-tinted lithograph.
  $605* *Alexandria,* pub. 12.1.1848, (04-02-93, Sloan, #1195), 15
      x 20½ in., (381 x 521 mm.), hand-tinted lithograph (BP
      398, DM 972, FR 3302, Y 68,883).
  $440* *Approach To Mount Sinai, Wady Barah, Feb. 17, 1839,*
      pub. 1.1.1845, (04-02-93, Sloan, #1199), 14⅜ x 20⅞ in.,
      (365 x 530 mm.), hand-tinted lithograph (BP 290, DM
      707, FR 2402, Y 50,097).
  BI *Approach To The Fortress Of Ibrim, Nubia,* pub. May 1,
      1847, est. $350/450, (02-04-93, Sloan, #1502), 13 x 19
      in., (33 x 48.3 cm.), hand-tinted lithograph.
  $88* *Approach To The Fortress Of Ibrim-Nubia,* pub. May 1,
      1847, (05-28-93, Sloan, #1006, illus.), 14½ x 19⅞ in.,
      (36.8 x 50.5 cm.), hand-tinted lithograph (BP 56, DM
      140, FR 472, Y 9436).
  BI *Approach To The Temple Of Wady Saboua-Nubia,* pub.
      May 1, 1847, est. $3/400, (02-04-93, Sloan, #1506), 10 x
      13¾ in., (25.4 x 34.9 cm.), hand-tinted lithograph.
  $175* *At Luxor, Thebes, Upper Egypt,* pub. March 1, 1847,
      (02-04-93, Sloan, #1512), 10 x 13⅞ in., (25.4 x 35.2
      cm.), hand-tinted lithograph (BP 122, DM 288, FR 977,
      Y 21,769).
  $358* *Bazaar Of The Coopersmith-Cairo,* pub. December 1,
      1898, (05-28-93, Sloan, #998, illus.), 19½ x 12½ in.,
      (49.5 x 31.8 cm.), hand-tinted lithograph (BP 229, DM
      568, FR 1920, Y 38,387).
  $248* *Bullack Cairo,* pub. Jan. 1, 1849, (05-28-93, Sloan,
      #1015, illus.), 14 x 9⅞ in., (35.6 x 25.1 cm.), hand-
      tinted lithograph (BP 159, DM 393, FR 1330, Y 26,592).
  $140* *Circular Temple at Baalbec, May 5, 1839,* pub. Jan. 1,
      1844, (02-04-93, Sloan, #1511), 9½ x 13½ in., (24.1 x
      34.3 cm.), hand-tinted lithograph (BP 98, DM 231, FR
      782, Y 17,415).

  $99* *Colossus In Front Of Temple Of Wady Saboua-Nubia,*
      pub. May 1, 1847, (05-28-93, Sloan, #1003, illus.), 14¼
      x 10 in., (36.2 x 25.4 cm.), hand-tinted lithograph (BP
      63, DM 157, FR 531, Y 10,615).
  $250* *Colossus Of Memnon, Thebes, Dec. 4, 1838,* pub. August
      1, 1846, (02-04-93, Sloan, #1503, illus.), 12½ x 19 in.,
      (31.8 x 48.3 cm.), hand-tinted lithograph (BP 175, DM
      412, FR 1396, Y 31,098).
  $330* *Convent Of St. Catherine With Mount Horeb, Feb. 19,
      1839,* pub. 10.1.1844, (04-02-93, Sloan, #1186), 20 x 14
      in., (508 x 356 mm.), hand-tinted lithograph (BP 217,
      DM 530, FR 1801, Y 37,573).
  $215* *Dancing Girls At Cairo,* pub. Sept. 1, 1849, (05-28-93,
      Sloan, #1013, illus.), 10¼ x 14½ in., (26 x 36.8 cm.),
      hand-tinted lithograph (BP 138, DM 341, FR 1153, Y
      23,054).
  $150* *Dayr El Medeeneh-Thebes,* pub. August 1, 1848, (02-04-
      93, Sloan, #1525), 10 x 13⅞ in., (25.4 x 35.2 cm.),
      hand-tinted lithograph (BP 105, DM 247, FR 838, Y
      18,659).
  $225* *Dendera-December 1838,* pub. May 1, 1847, (02-04-93,
      Sloan, #1522), 9⅜ x 13½ in., (23.8 x 34.3 cm.), hand-
      tinted lithograph (BP 157, DM 370, FR 1256, Y 27,989).
  $83* *Entrance Of The Temple Of Amun, Thebes,* pub. Dec. 1,
      1847, (05-28-93, Sloan, #999, illus.), 13¼ x 19½ in.,
      (33.7 x 49.5 cm.), hand-tinted lithograph (BP 53, DM
      132, FR 445, Y 8900).
  $88* *Entrance To The Caves Of Beni Hasun,* pub. May 1,
      1847, (05-28-93, Sloan, #1002, illus.), 14½ x 10¼ in.,
      (36.8 x 26 cm.), hand-tinted lithograph (BP 56, DM 140,
      FR 472, Y 9436).
  $550* *The Entrance To The Citadel Of Cairo,* pub. 7.2.1849,
      (04-02-93, Sloan, #1203), 13¼ x 19½ in., (337 x 495
      mm.), hand-tinted lithograph (BP 362, DM 884, FR
      3002, Y 62,621).
  $330* *Entrance To The Tombs Of The Kings Of Thebes, Bab-
      El-Malouk,* pub. 8.1.1848, (04-02-93, Sloan, #1188),
      12¾ x 19¼ in., (324 x 489 mm.), hand-tinted lithograph
      (BP 217, DM 530, FR 1801, Y 37,573).
  $83* *Fortress Of Ibrim-Nubia,* pub. May 1, 1847, (05-28-93,
      Sloan, #1012, illus.), 10½ x 14⅜ in., (26.7 x 36.5 cm.),
      hand-tinted lithograph (BP 53, DM 132, FR 445, Y
      8900).
  $130* *Fountain At Cana, April 21, 1839,* pub. August 1, 1844,
      (02-04-93, Sloan, #1520), 9½ x 13¼ in., (24.1 x 33.7
      cm.), hand-tinted lithograph (BP 91, DM 214, FR 726, Y
      16,171).
  $100* *Fountain Of The Virgin, Nazareth, April 21, 1839,* pub.
      June 1, 1844, (02-04-93, Sloan, #1523), 9½ x 13½ in.,
      (24.1 x 34.3 cm.), hand-tinted lithograph (BP 70, DM
      165, FR 558, Y 12,439).
  $130* *Gate Of Damascus, Jerusalem, April 14, 1839,* pub. July
      1, 1848, (02-04-93, Sloan, #1507), 9⅝ x 13 in., (24.8 x
      33 cm.), hand-tinted lithograph (BP 91, DM 214, FR
      726, Y 16,171).
  $176* *Gate Of The Metwaleys-Cairo,* pub. Dec. 1, 1848, (05-
      28-93, Sloan, #1011, illus.), 14¾ x 10½ in., (37.5 x 26.7
      cm.), hand-tinted lithograph (BP 113, DM 279, FR 944,
      Y 18,872).
  $330* *Grand Approach To The Temple Of Philoe-Nubia,* pub.
      5.1.1847, (04-02-93, Sloan, #1192), 13½ x 20½ in., (343
      x 521 mm.), hand-tinted lithograph (BP 217, DM 530,
      FR 1801, Y 37,573).
  $300* *The Great Sphinx, Pyramids Of Gezeeh,* pub. August 1,
      1846, (02-04-93, Sloan, #1519), 10 x 14 in., (25.4 x
      35.6 cm.), hand-tinted lithograph (BP 209, DM 494, FR
      1675, Y 37,318).
  BI *Group Of Nubians, Wady Kardosey,* pub. May 1, 1847,
      est. $4/500, (02-04-93, Sloan, #1513), 9⅞ x 13¾ in.,
      (25.1 x 34.9 cm.), hand-tinted lithograph.
  $3520* *"The Holy Land", "Egypt", "Nubia" and 24 Others From
      The Same Series:Twenty-Six,* pub. F.G. Moon, good
      cond., Chloethiel W. Smith Estate, (06-11-93, Weschler,
      #46, illus.), approx. 10¾ x 14¼ in., (27.3 x 36.2 cm.),
      hand-colored lithograph (BP 2313, DM 5721, FR 19,288,
      Y 373,475).
  $121* *The Holy Tree, Metereah,* pub. July 1, 1869, (05-28-93,
      Sloan, #1010, illus.), 14½ x 9⅞ in., (36.8 x 25.1 cm.),

hand-tinted lithograph (BP 78, DM 192, FR 649, Y 12,974).

$303* *The Hypaethral Temple At Philae, Called The Bed Of Pharoah,* pub. 6.1.1848, (04-02-93, Sloan, #1201, illus.), 14 x 20 in., (356 x 508 mm.), hand-tinted lithograph (BP 200, DM 487, FR 1654, Y 34,498).

$100* *In The Slave Market At Cairo,* pub. September 1, 1849, (02-04-93, Sloan, #1518), 9⅝ x 13⅞ in., (24.8 x 35.2 cm.), hand-tinted lithograph (BP 70, DM 165, FR 558, Y 12,439).

$275* *Interior Of The Mosque Of The Sultan El Ghoree,* pub. August 1, 1849, (02-04-93, Sloan, #1516, illus.), 13⅜ x 19 in., (34 x 48.3 cm.), hand-tinted lithograph (BP 192, DM 453, FR 1535, Y 34,208).

$140* *Jaffa, March 26, 1839,* pub. August 18, 1843, (02-04-93, Sloan, #1524), 9½ x 13¾ in., (24.1 x 34.9 cm.), hand-tinted lithograph (BP 98, DM 231, FR 782, Y 17,415).

$303* *Jerusalem, April 12, 1839,* pub. 6.1.1841, (04-02-93, Sloan, #1194), 13¼ x 19½ in., (337 x 495 mm.), hand-tinted lithograph (BP 200, DM 487, FR 1654, Y 34,498).

$165* *Karnak,* pub. 5.1.1847, (04-02-93, Sloan, #1196), 13½ x 19⅞ in., (343 x 505 mm.), hand-tinted lithograph (BP 109, DM 265, FR 901, Y 18,786).

$330* *Lesser Temple Of Baalbec. Looking Towards Mount Lebanon,* pub. Jan. 1, 1844, (05-28-93, Sloan, #1007, illus.), 10½ x 14¼ in., (26.7 x 36.2 cm.), hand-tinted lithograph (BP 211, DM 523, FR 1769, Y 35,385).

$303* *Lybian Chain Of Mountains, From The Temple Of Luxor,* pub. 3.1.1842, (04-02-93, Sloan, #1209), 13½ x 19½ in., (343 x 495 mm.), hand-tinted lithograph (BP 200, DM 487, FR 1654, Y 34,498).

$165* *Medint, Above Thebes, Dec. 8, 1838,* pub. 5.1.1847, (04-02-93, Sloan, #1187), 13 x 19¼ in., (330 x 489 mm.), hand-tinted lithograph (BP 109, DM 265, FR 901, Y 18,786).

$150* *Minaret Of The Mosque El Khamaree,* pub. Dec. 1, 1848, (02-04-93, Sloan, #1509), 13⅞ x 9½ in., (35.2 x 24.1 cm.), hand-tinted lithograph (BP 105, DM 247, FR 838, Y 18,659).

$83* *Minaret Of The Principal Mosque Siout, Upper Egypt,* pub. July 2, 1849, (05-28-93, Sloan, #1004, illus.), 14 x 9⅞ in., (35.6 x 25.1 cm.), hand-tinted lithograph (BP 53, DM 132, FR 445, Y 8900).

$95* *Mount Tabor, April 19, 1839,* pub. 1844, (02-04-93, Sloan, #1505), 9¾ x 13½ in., (24.8 x 34.3 cm.), hand-tinted lithograph (BP 66, DM 156, FR 530, Y 11,817).

$385* *Nazareth, April 28, 1839,* pub. 6.1.1844, (04-02-93, Sloan, #1200), 14⅜ x 21⅜ in., (365 x 543 mm.), hand-tinted lithograph (BP 254, DM 619, FR 2102, Y 43,835).

$83* *The Nileometer, Island Of Rhoda,* pub. Sept. 1, 1849, (05-28-93, Sloan, #1009, illus.), 14½ x 10½ in., (36.8 x 26.7 cm.), hand-tinted lithograph (BP 53, DM 132, FR 445, Y 8900).

BI *Nubian Women At Kortie, On The Nile,* pub. 5.1.1847, est. $2/300, (04-02-93, Sloan, #1193), 10 x 14 in., (254 x 356 mm.), hand-tinted lithograph.

$110* *Part Of The Wall Columns At Karnak-Thebes,* pub. May 1, 1847, (05-28-93, Sloan, #1000, illus.), 14½ x 10⅞ in., (36.8 x 27.6 cm.), hand-tinted lithograph (BP 70, DM 174, FR 590, Y 11,795).

BI *A Persian Wheel, Used In Raising Water From The Nile,* pub. 5.1.1847, est. $2/300, (04-02-93, Sloan, #1185), 14 x 10 in., (356 x 254 mm.), hand-tinted lithograph.

$150* *Remains Of The Temple Of Medamout At Thebes,* pub. May 1, 1847, (02-04-93, Sloan, #1526), 9⅞ x 13¾ in., (25.1 x 34.9 cm.), hand-tinted lithograph (BP 105, DM 247, FR 838, Y 18,659).

$83* *Ruined Mosques In The Desert, West Of The Citadel,* pub. December 1, 1848, (05-28-93, Sloan, #1005, illus.), 12⅞ x 10 in., (32.7 x 25.4 cm.), hand-tinted lithograph (BP 53, DM 132, FR 445, Y 8900).

$165* *Ruins Called Om El Hamed Near Tyre, April 25, 1839,* pub. 9.18.1843, (04-02-93, Sloan, #1190), 10 x 13¾ in., (254 x 349 mm.), hand-tinted lithograph (BP 109, DM 265, FR 901, Y 18,786).

$385* *Ruins Of The Eastern Portico Of The Temple Of Baalbec,* s., t., d. in stone, (02-14-93, Neal, #1140, illus.), image 13 x 19 in., (33 x 48.3 cm.), hand-colored lithograph (BP 271, DM 638, FR 2160, Y 46,430).

$125* *Ruins Of The Temple Of Kardeseh, Nubia,* pub. July 1, 1848, (02-04-93, Sloan, #1508), 9⅞ x 13⅞ in., (25.1 x 35.2 cm.), hand-tinted lithograph (BP 87, DM 206, FR 698, Y 15,549).

$165* *Sanctuary Of The Temple Of Aboo Simbel, Nubia,* pub. 8.1.1846, (04-02-93, Sloan, #1204), 10 x 13¼ in., (254 x 337 mm.), hand-tinted lithograph (BP 109, DM 265, FR 901, Y 18,786).

BI *Shrine Of The Annunciation, Nazareth, April 20, 1839,* pub. 6.1.1844, est. $250/350, (04-02-93, Sloan, #1205), 8½ x 11¼ in., (216 x 286 mm.), hand-tinted lithograph.

$248* *Siour, Upper Egypt,* pub. 5.1.1847, (04-02-93, Sloan, #1206), 10½ x 14½ in., (267 x 368 mm.), hand-tinted lithograph (BP 163, DM 399, FR 1354, Y 28,236).

$154* *Tabaste, Ancient Samaria, April 17, 1839,* pub. 9.2.1844, (04-02-93, Sloan, #1198), 14 x 20¼ in., (356 x 514 mm.), hand-tinted lithograph (BP 101, DM 248, FR 841, Y 17,534).

BI *Temple At Esneh, Nov. 25, 1838,* pub. 8.1.1846, est. $3/400, (04-02-93, Sloan, #1202, illus.), 12⅞ x 19 in., (327 x 483 mm.), hand-tinted lithograph.

$88* *Temple Of Amdda At Kafsaya In Nubia,* pub. May 1, 1847, (05-28-93, Sloan, #1001, illus.), 10⅛ x 14 in., (25.7 x 35.6 cm.), hand-tinted lithograph (BP 56, DM 140, FR 472, Y 9436).

BI *Temple Of Amdda Of Kafsaya In Nubia,* pub. May 1, 1847, est. $3/400, (02-04-93, Sloan, #1510), (25.1 x 34.9 cm.), hand-tinted lithograph.

$176* *Temple Of Edfou, Ancient Appolinopolis, Upper Egypt,* pub. 3.1.1847, (04-02-93, Sloan, #1191), 13½ x 20 in., (343 x 508 mm.), hand-tinted lithograph (BP 116, DM 283, FR 961, Y 20,039).

$154* *Temple Of Kababshee, Nubia, Nov. 1838,* pub. 8.1.1848, (04-02-93, Sloan, #1189), 12¾ x 19¼ in., (324 x 489 mm.), hand-tinted lithograph (BP 101, DM 248, FR 841, Y 17,534).

$125* *Temple Of Wady Kardassy In Nubia,* pub. August 1, 1846, (02-04-93, Sloan, #1521), 9¾ x 13¾ in., (24.8 x 34.9 cm.), hand-tinted lithograph (BP 87, DM 206, FR 698, Y 15,549).

$175* *Temple Of Wady Sabuoa, Nubia,* pub. March 1, 1847, (02-04-93, Sloan, #1517), 10⅛ x 13⅞ in., (25.7 x 35.2 cm.), hand-tinted lithograph (BP 122, DM 288, FR 977, Y 21,769).

$193* *Tomb Of The Khalifs-Cairo,* pub. Dec. 1, 1948, (05-28-93, Sloan, #997, illus.), 20⅞ x 13¾ in., (53 x 34.9 cm.), hand-tinted lithograph (BP 124, DM 306, FR 1035, Y 20,695).

$358* *Tomb Of The Memlooks, Cairo,* pub. 7.2.1849, (04-02-93, Sloan, #1197), 10 x 14 in., (254 x 356 mm.), hand-tinted lithograph (BP 236, DM 575, FR 1954, Y 40,761).

$248* *Tombs Of The Caliphs-Cairo,* pub. Dec. 1, 1848, (05-28-93, Sloan, #1008, illus.), 9⅞ x 14 in., (25.1 x 35.6 cm.), hand-tinted lithograph (BP 159, DM 393, FR 1330, Y 26,592).

$248* *Tombs Of The Khalifs, Cairo,* pub. 12.1.1848, (04-02-93, Sloan, #1207), 10 x 14¼ in., (254 x 362 mm.), hand-tinted lithograph (BP 163, DM 399, FR 1354, Y 28,236).

$300* *Tsur Ancient Tyre, April 27, 1839,* pub. August 18, 1843, (02-04-93, Sloan, #1504), 13 x 19½ in., (33 x 49.5 cm.), hand-tinted lithograph (BP 209, DM 494, FR 1675, Y 37,318).

$165* *View Of The Nile Looking Towards The Pyramids Of Dashour And Saccara,* pub. 8.1.1846, (04-02-93, Sloan, #1208), 14¼ x 20½ in., (362 x 521 mm.), hand-tinted lithograph (BP 109, DM 265, FR 901, Y 18,786).

$125* *Wady Maharraka-Nubia, Nov. 14, 1838,* pub. August 1, 1846, (02-04-93, Sloan, #1514), 9⅞ x 13¾ in., (25.1 x 34.9 cm.), hand-tinted lithograph (BP 87, DM 206, FR 698, Y 15,549).

ROBERTS, David (after)

$8050* *"The Holy Land, Syria, Idumea, Arabia..., 1845: Twenty-Four,* by Louis Haghe, full margins, excell. cond., (06-01-93, Christie-E, #111), lithograph w/hand-coloring on wove (BP 5204, DM 12,816, FR 43,280, Y 864,290).

$55* *Portico Of A Hindoo Temple,* by R.G. Reeve, (10-30-92, Sloan, #825), 12 x 8⅞ in., (30.5 x 22.5 cm.), color aquatint (BP 35, DM 85, FR 287, Y 6813).

ROBERTS, Holly   b. 1951
BI *Man Trying To Balance Himself*, s. in stylus, est. $3/4,000, (04-08-93, Christie-NY, #556, illus.), 33½ x 26⅜ in., (85.1 x 67 cm.), photograph, oil paint in gelatin silver print.

ROBERTS, N. Cramer
$385* *Greatstone Public Railway*, Vincent Brooks, Day and Son Ltd., A- cond., (08-06-92, Swann, #239, illus.), 41½ x 27 in., (105.4 x 68.6 cm.), (BP 201, DM 569, FR 1921, Y 49,107).

ROBERTSON, Bruce   b. 1872
$57* *Outer Lake Narrabean*, s. Bruce Robertson, i., num. 39, (08-11-92, L. Joel, #97G), 9⁷⁄₁₆ x 6⅞ in., (24 x 17.4 cm.), etching (BP 30, DM 84, FR 283, Y 7299, A$ 77).

ROBERTSON, James and Felice BEATO   c.1831-81?, c.1830-1906?
$3300* *Garden Of Gethsemane, Jerusalem, 1856-57*, (10-13-92, Christie-NY, #21, illus.), 10 x 12¼ in., (25.4 x 31.1 cm.), photograph, albumen print (BP 1922, DM 4834, FR 16,426, Y 400,146).

ROBERTSON, Percy   English 1869-1934
$55* *"On Westminster Bridge"*, s., toned, creases, (10-31-92, Cleveland, #326), 7¼ x 9¼ in., (18.4 x 23.5 cm.), etching (BP 35, DM 85, FR 287, Y 6813).

ROBERTSON, Robert C.
$27 *"Auld Reekie, Showing The Royal Mile"*, (04-16-93, G.A. Key, #136), 7 x 11 in., (17.8 x 27.9 cm.), etching (BP 18, DM 44, FR 147, Y 3036).

ROBERTSON, SEIBERT AND SHEARMAN
         American ac. 1859-1860
$154* *"Tomb Of Washington" and "The Home Of Washington": Two*, (04-02-93, Sloan, #1172), larger, sight 14½ x 19½ in., (368 x 495 mm.), color engraving (BP 101, DM 248, FR 841, Y 17,534).

ROBETTA, Cristoforo   1462-1535
$2291* *Allegorie Der Liebe (Hind I, 29; Illus. Bartsch XXV, 043, Reprod. 406), c. 1498*, watermark, foxing, (06-23-93, Kornfeld, #104), engraving (BP 1556, DM 3876, FR 13,039, Y 249,591, SF 3450).
BI *Allegory Of Carnal Love (B. XII, 25; Hind I, 29)*, trimmed, ink marks, foxing, discoloration, thin spots, ex coll. G. C.Rossi (L. 2212), est. BP 800/1,000, (06-30-93, Sotheby-London, #229), 11¾ x 11 in., (298 x 279 mm.), engraving.
BI *Die Anbetung Der Hl. Drei Konige (B. XII, 6; Passavant V; S. 59, 6; Hind I; S. 200f)*, est. DM 6,000, (12-04-92, Bassenge, #6408), 11¹³⁄₁₆ x 10¹³⁄₁₆ in., (30 x 27.4 cm.), engraving.
BI *Ein Junger Mann Von Amor An Einen Baum Gebunden (B. XII, 25; Passavant V.; S. 59, 25; Hind 1910, 36; The Illustrated Bartsch 15 043)*, est. DM 9,000, (12-04-92, Bassenge, #6409, illus.), 11¹³⁄₁₆ x 10⅞ in., (30 x 27.7 cm.), engraving.

ROBIDA (after)
$105* *P.O. Midi: La Cite De Carcassonne, 1937*, good cond., (01-23-93, Ribeyre/Baron, #119), 29½ x 43⁵⁄₁₆ in., (75 x 110 cm.), poster (BP 69, DM 167, FR 565, Y 13,141).

ROBINS, Thomas Sewell   English 1814-1880
$275* *Yachting Scene Off Cowes, Isle Of Wight*, from "Fore's Marine Sketches", (02-04-93, Sloan, #738), 16½ x 21 in., (41.9 x 53.3 cm.), color lithograph (BP 192, DM 453, FR 1535, Y 34,208).

ROBINS, William Palmer
$34* *Near Potter Heighman, 1921*, s., margins, (05-20-93, Bonhams-Chelsea, #93), plate 6¾ x 10¾ in., (17.1 x 27.3 cm.), etching (BP 22, DM 55, FR 185, Y 3754).
$22 *"Stokesby", 1922*, s., (02-05-93, G.A. Key, #38), 4¾ x 7¾ in., (12.1 x 19.7 cm.), etching (BP 15, DM 36, FR 123, Y 2738).

ROBINSON, Clifford   1917-1992
$412* *Untitled*, s., prov., (11-16-92, Hodgins, #59, illus.), 14½ x 11½ in., (36.8 x 29.2 cm.), monoprint on paper (BP 271, DM 657, FR 2214, Y 51,416, C$ 523).

ROBINSON, Sir John Charles
$64* *Hastings, All Saints Church And The East Cliff From Croft*, margins, (08-20-92, Bonhams-Chelsea, #107),

plate 8⅛ x 10¼ in., (20.6 x 26 cm.), drypoint etching on laid paper (BP 33, DM 93, FR 314, Y 8082).

ROBSON, F. (after)
$47 *"York Minster" and "Eastgate, Chester": Two*, (12-11-92, G.A. Key, #112), 8 x 6 in., (20.3 x 15.2 cm.), colored print (BP 30, DM 74, FR 254, Y 5816).

ROBY
$605* *Kina Lillet, 1937*, Affiches Stentor, A cond., creases, (08-06-92, Swann, #241, illus.), 77½ x 51 in., (196.9 x 129.5 cm.), (BP 316, DM 894, FR 3019, Y 77,168).
$385* *Premier Fils, 1936*, L. Marboeuf, A- cond., yellowing, creasing, (08-06-92, Swann, #240, illus.), 78½ x 51½ in., (199.4 x 130.8 cm.), (BP 201, DM 569, FR 1921, Y 49,107).

ROBYS
$462* *Bitter Secrestat, "Le Plus Ancien Aperitif A La Gentiane", 1935*, good cond., lit., (11-19-92, Ribeyre/Baron, #43), 50⅜ x 78⅜ in., (128 x 199 cm.), poster (BP 304, DM 737, FR 2481, Y 57,456).

ROCHE, M. Paul
$83* *Tambourine Girl*, s., very good cond., (07-19-92, Bakker, #57), image 14¼ x 10½ in., (36.2 x 26.7 cm.), etching (BP 43, DM 121, FR 409, Y 10,318).

ROCHE, Pierre
BI *Les Hesperides, c. 1895*, num., annot., t., s., full margins, stamp, (02-24-93, Picard, #215), gypsograph in color on thin simili-Japan.
$573* *L'Effort, c. 1895*, t., annot., s., num. 1, staining, soiling, full margins, (02-24-93, Picard, #214), gypsograph in brown bistre on thin simili-Japan (BP 400, DM 930, FR 3154, Y 67,238).
$110* *Salon De La Plume*, cond. C, (03-16-93, Boisgirard, #182), 21⅝ x 17⁵⁄₁₆ in., (55 x 44 cm.), poster (BP 76, DM 183, FR 621, Y 12,862).

ROCHEGROSSE, Georges   French 1859-1938
$93* *Allegorie Du Travail, c. 1900*, full margins, (05-06-93, Laurin, #76), lithograph on creme wove (BP 59, DM 146, FR 493, Y 10,232).
BI *Allegorie Relative A Un Soulevement Populaire En Pays Minier, c. 1895*, staining, cracks, (02-24-93, Picard, #216), on thick creme wove.
BI *Don Quichotte*, Ed. Delanchy, A cond., surface soiling, est. $4/600, (08-06-92, Swann, #243, illus.), 35 x 27 in., (88.9 x 68.6 cm.), .
$275* *Louise, 1900*, Ed. Delanchy and Cie, A- cond., scratch marks, marginal closed tears, (08-06-92, Swann, #242, illus.), 35 x 24½ in., (88.9 x 62.2 cm.), (BP 144, DM 406, FR 1372, Y 35,077).
$290* *Roma, Opera De J. Massenet*, (01-31-93, Morelle/Marchan, #166), 26¾ x 35⁷⁄₁₆ in., (68 x 90 cm.), poster (BP 195, DM 467, FR 1580, Y 36,178).

ROCHETTE, G.
$165* *Three Figures, 1931*, Ecole Art et Publicite, A cond., (08-06-92, Swann, #244, illus.), 35 x 25½ in., (88.9 x 64.8 cm.), (BP 86, DM 244, FR 823, Y 21,046).

ROCHO, Ricardo
$26* *The Letter*, s., d. 75, num. PA, prov., exhib., (12-01-92, Ritchie, #35), 27¾ x 20¼ in., (70.5 x 51.4 cm.), color serigraph (BP 17, DM 41, FR 141, Y 3237, C$ 33).

ROCHUSSEN, C.   1814-1894
$86* *Zes Etsen. Uitgegeven Door Het Paleis Van Volksvlijt (Franken/Obreen763), 1873*, folio, foxed, (11-18-92, Bubb Kuyper, #1577), (BP 57, DM 137, FR 462, Y 10,695, G 156).

ROCKBURNE, Dorothea   Canadian ac. 1970-1974
$605* *Uriel (Gemini G.E.L. 1097), 1983*, s., t., d. 82, num. 2/34, Gemini G.E.L. blindstamps, full sheet, excell. cond.?, (09-19-92, Christie-E, #191), sheet 39⅛ x 31⅝ in., (99.4 x 80.3 cm.), lithograph in colors on folded Transpagra mounted on wove board as issued (BP 348, DM 906, FR 3103, Y 75,380).

ROCKMORE, Noel   American b. 1928
$193* *"Texas Ranch", c. 1957*, s., d., full margins, good cond., (03-12-93, Goldberg, #1098, illus.), image 13¾ x 17¾

in., (34.9 x 45.1 cm.), lithograph (BP 135, DM 321, FR 1092, Y 22,746).

ROCKWELL, Norman   American 1894-1978
$99* *"Alone In The Cave"*, s., #A.P., full margins, excell. cond., (05-07-93, Goldberg, #439A), 17¾ x 14 in., (45.1 x 35.6 cm.), lithogrpah (BP 63, DM 157, FR 527, Y 10,901).
BI   *The Bridge, 1972*, s., num. 160/200, light struck, mat burn, toning, est. $5/700, (05-22-93, Weschler, #218), 9½ x 14¼ in., (24.1 x 36.2 cm.), lithograph in colors on Arches.
BI   *"A Child's Suprise"*, artist's proof. A.P XVII/XXXV, t., made from original by Norman Rockwell, s., outstanding cond., est. $3/5000, (04-13-93, Bourne, #82, illus.), print.
$110* *"Dixon Ticonderoga Pencils"*, advertisement, (07-10-92, Skinner, #515), color lithographed poster (BP 57, DM 164, FR 558, Y 13,776).
$330* *High Dive Board*, margins, s. Norman Rockwell, #15/200, (10-24-92, Collins, #3, illus.), 23 x 17¾ in., (58.4 x 45.1 cm.), collotype (BP 204, DM 505, FR 1711, Y 40,244).
$3300* *"Huckleberry Finn", 1972: Suite Of Eight*, num., s., p. Mourlot, co-pub. Raymond and Raymond, Inc. and Circle Gallery, (05-27-93, Swann, #240), sh 25¾ x 19⅝ in., (65.4 x 49.8 cm.), color lithograph (BP 2113, DM 5295, FR 17,847, Y 353,774).
BI   *"Jester"*, s., artist proof, est. $6/800, (12-11-92, DuMouchelle, #1306, illus.), 20¼ x 16¾ in., (51.4 x 42.5 cm.), color lithograph.
BI   *The Jeweler*, margins, s. Norman Rockwell, #787/1080, est. $6/800, (10-24-92, Collins, #4), 21⅞ x 21⅝ in., (55.6 x 54.9 cm.), collotype.
BI   *"Music Hath Charms"*, artist's proof. A.P IX/XXXV, made from original by Norman Rockwell, s., outstanding cond., est. $3/5000, (04-13-93, Bourne, #83, illus.), print.
BI   *"On Top Of The World"*, artist's proof. A.P XXX/XXXV, t., made from the original by Norman Rockwell, s., outstanding cond., est. $4/7000, (04-13-93, Bourne, #81, illus.), print.
BI   *"On Top Of The World"*, s., AP, est. $3/4,000, (10-16-92, DuMouchelle, #1173, illus.), approx. 31 x 23½ in., (78.7 x 59.7 cm.), lithograph.
$770* *Parents Putting Children To Bed*, edit. A.P., (01-15-93, DuMouchelle, #2217, illus.), 29 x 22 in., (73.7 x 55.9 cm.), lithograph (BP 503, DM 1259, FR 4256, Y 97,075).
$3080* *Poor Richard's Almanack: "The Village Smithy", "The Golden Age", "YeOlde Print Shoppe", "Ben Franklin's Philadelphia", "The Drunkard", "Ben's Belles" and "The Royal Crown", 1973: Seven*, portfolio, s., annot. A.P., pub. Mourlot, (12-08-92, Swann, #268, illus.), 26 x 19½ in., (66 x 49.5 cm.), color lithograph (BP 1930, DM 4795, FR 16,348, Y 381,755).
$4400* *"Puppy Love" Portfolio, 1976: Set Of Four*, s., AP edit., pub., (02-12-93, DuMouchelle, #2038, illus.), 20 x 20 in., (50.8 x 50.8 cm.), color lithographs on Arches paper (BP 3099, DM 7297, FR 24,691, Y 530,632).
$220* *Raleigh Rockwell Travels*, (03-20-93, Northeast, #741, illus.), collagraphic print (BP 147, DM 360, FR 1224, Y 25,519).
$1485* *Sports Portfolio, 1977: Four*, artist's proofs, s., excell. cond., includes Footbal, Baseball, Basketball and Golf in orig. case, (10-10-92, Litchfield, #182), each 18⅝ x 16 in., (47.3 x 40.6 cm.), color lithograph (BP 881, DM 2206, FR 7406, Y 180,789).
$341* *"Spying"*, s., num., full margins, (12-06-92, Neal, #1187), image 17¾ x 13½ in., (45.1 x 34.3 cm.), color lithograph (BP 214, DM 532, FR 1812, Y 42,250).
$440* *"The Teacher"*, s. A/P Norman Rockwell, (10-11-92, Dunning, #1535), 18 x 12 in., (45.7 x 30.5 cm.), lithograph (BP 261, DM 654, FR 2195, Y 53,567).
$193* *Untitled: Fifteen*, p. by Curtis Publishing Co., s. Norman Rockwell, (06-26-93, Wolf, #976), 25 x 19 in., (63.5 x 48.3 cm.), offset lithograph (BP 129, DM 328, FR 1105, Y 20,477).

$341* *"Weeping Widow"*, s., num., full margins, (12-06-92, Neal, #1185), image 17½ x 13½ in., (44.5 x 34.3 cm.), color lithograph (BP 214, DM 532, FR 1812, Y 42,250).

ROCKWELL, Norman (after)
$100* *"Save Freedom of Speech" and "Freedom From Want": Two*, (05-16-93, Hanzel, #461), 27 x 17½ in., (68.6 x 44.5 cm.), lithograph posters (BP 65, DM 161, FR 541, Y 11,085).

RODCHENKO, Alexander   Russian 1891-1956
$12,703* *'Dzhaz, Kadr Iz Fil'ma", Jazz, Still From Film*, n.d., 1927, mounted on card, t., photog.'s ink credit stamp Photo Rodchenko, coll. stamp, lit., (05-06-93, Christie-London, #171, illus.), 11⅜ x 14⅞ in., photograph, gelatin silver print (BP 8050, DM 20,008, FR 67,354, Y 1,397,624).
$1925* *Before The Balloon Lifts Off, 1924*, prob. p. 1940's, (10-15-92, Sotheby-NY, #366, illus.), 9⅜ x 7 in., (23.8 x 17.8 cm.), photograph, gelatin silver print (BP 1178, DM 2865, FR 9717, Y 230,954).
$21,776* *"Beg, 1935", Race*, contemp. retouching, photog.'s mono. recto, s. A.M., t., sig. Rodchenko, t., d. in another hand, coll. stamp, lit., catalog cover lot, (05-06-93, Christie-London, #162, illus.), 11½ x 18⅛ in., photograph, gelatin silver print (BP 13,800, DM 34,298, FR 115,461, Y 2,395,863).
$825* *"Change Of Everything" (Cover For Book Of Constructivist Poetry")*, 1924/1989, d., num. 48, photog. and ink edit. stamps, (11-16-92, Butterfield, #6138, illus.), 12 x 9⅜ in., (305.3 x 238.5 mm.), photograph, gelatin silver print (BP 543, DM 1315, FR 4431, Y 102,599).
$8050* *Courtyard, 1927*, lit., (04-08-93, Christie-NY, #150, illus.), 5⅜ x 3⅜ in., (13.7 x 8.6 cm.), photograph, gelatin silver print on mount of black paper and embossed asymmetrical bristol board mount (BP 5279, DM 12,932, FR 43,774, Y 913,527).
$180,238* *"Devushka s Leikoi, 1934", Girl With Leica*, s., t., d., 1932 changed to 1934, collec. stamp, orig. mount, s., d., 37 changed to 36, t.; s., t., d., stamp verso, (10-29-92, Christie-London, #118, illus.), 15¾ x 11⁷⁄₁₆ in., (40 x 29.1 cm.), photograph, warm-toned gelatin silver print (BP 115,500, DM 277,289, FR 940,699, Y 22,326,025).
$12,874* *"E.I. Shub. (Kinorezhisser) 1928", E.I. Shub (Film Director)*, s., t., d., collec. stamp, lit., (10-29-92, Christie-London, #112, illus.), 15⅜ x 11¹¹⁄₁₆ in., (39.1 x 29.7 cm.), photograph, gelatin silver print (BP 8250, DM 19,806, FR 67,192, Y 1,594,698).
BI   *Electricity Pylon, 1927*, p.l., stamped photog.'s credit, t., d., 179 x 237mm, est. BP 3/4,000, (05-07-93, Sotheby-London, #231, illus.), photograph, silver print.
BI   *Ethnic Parade, 1936*, stamped, d., est. $4/6,000, (10-13-92, Christie-NY, #337, illus.), 3⅞ x 6 in., (9.8 x 15.2 cm.), photograph, gelatin silver print.
BI   *"Fekhtoval'scchaki Fizk Parad, 1936" Fencers, Sports Parade*, t., d., photog.'s ink credit stamp A.M. Rodchenko, Moscow-Centre...,coll. stamp, est. BP 8/10,000, (05-06-93, Christie-London, #166, illus.), 11½ x 17⅛ in., photograph, warm-toned gelatin silver print.
$6866* *"Fekhtovanie, 1936", Fencing*, t., d., photog.'s ink credit stamp, collec. stamp, lit., (10-29-92, Christie-London, #130, illus.), 11⅝ x 15⅝ in., (29.5 x 39.7 cm.), photograph, gelatin silver print (BP 4400, DM 10,563, FR 35,835, Y 850,489).
$9981* *"Gotov K Trudu I Oborone Fizkul't Parad, 1938", Ready For Work And Defence, Sports Parade*, contemp. retouching, t., d., photog.'s ink credit stamp Foto Rodchenko, coll. stamps, lit., (05-06-93, Christie-London, #167, illus.), 19⅛ x 11⁹⁄₁₆ in., photograph, warm-toned gelatin silver print (BP 6325, DM 15,721, FR 52,922, Y 1,098,141).
$77,733* *Gravyuri Rodchenko 1919, 1919*, complete folio, title, set of 9 pl, seven d. 19, inits., small margins, water-stained, excell. cond., (06-30-93, Sotheby-London, #681, illus.), pl c. 6½ x 4⅜ in., (165 x 111 mm.), linocut on thin wove (BP 52,100, DM 132,582, FR 447,255, Y 8,328,833).
$825* *Illustration For Children's Book "Samozveri"*, 1926/1989, t., d., edit. 48/50, photog. and two ink edit. stamps, (11-16-92, Butterfield, #6137, illus.), 11⅞ x 9⅜ in., (302.2 x

238.5 mm.), photograph, gelatin silver print (BP 543, DM 1315, FR 4431, Y 102,599).

$20,599* *"Kolonna Dinamo, 1928", Dynamo's Formation,* s., t., d., collec. stamp, lit., (10-29-92, Christie-London, #111, illus.), 11 x 16 1/16 in., (27.9 x 40.8 cm.), photograph, gelatin silver print (BP 13,200, DM 31,691, FR 107,510, Y 2,551,592).

$10,299* *"Konnye Sostiazaniia", Horse Trial, n.d., 1930-35,* contemp. retouching, s., t., collec. stamp, paper tape, lit., (10-29-92, Christie-London, #116, illus.), 16 3/16 x 11 5/8 in., (41.1 x 29.5 cm.), photograph, gelatin silver print (BP 6600, DM 15,845, FR 53,753, Y 1,275,734).

$7724* *"Krasnaia Ploshchad' Ritmicheskie Uprazhneniia, 1936", Red Square Rhythmic Excercises,* photog.'s mono recto, orig. mount, s., d., t., photog.'s ink credit stamp, collec. stamp verso, lit., (10-29-92, Christie-London, #129, illus.), 18 1/4 x 11 1/2 in., (46.4 x 29.2 cm.), photograph, gelatin silver print (BP 4950, DM 11,883, FR 40,313, Y 956,769).

$997* *"Krym, Na Demerdzhi, 1939", At Demerdzhi, Crimea,* mounted on card, t. twice, s., d., stamp, (05-06-93, Christie-London, #172, illus.), 7 1/8 x 10 3/16 in., photograph, gelatin silver print (BP 632, DM 1570, FR 5286, Y 109,693).

$14,518* *"Kulaki, 1928", Kulaks,* t., d., photog.'s ink credit stamp Photo Rodchenko, coll. stamp, lit., (05-06-93, Christie-London, #150, illus.), 11 3/8 x 9 1/16 in., photograph, gelatin silver print on textured paper (BP 9200, DM 22,867, FR 76,978, Y 1,597,315).

$50,812* *"Lestnitsa, 1935", Steps,* s., t., d., coll. stamp, lit., (05-06-93, Christie-London, #169, illus.), 15 1/8 x 22 3/8 in., photograph, gelatin silver print (BP 32,200, DM 80,032, FR 269,417, Y 5,590,494).

BI *Lilli Brik On the Terrace, From The Series Puschkino, 1927,* credit stamp, s., lit., est. $18/22,000, (10-13-92, Christie-NY, #336, illus.), 6 5/8 x 4 3/4 in., (16.8 x 12.1 cm.), photograph, gelatin silver print.

$3300* *Marching Column Of The Dynamo Sports Club, c. 1928 (Morozov and Lloyd, p. 62; Complete Work, p. 267),* notations in ink in unidentified hand, probably p. 1940's, (10-15-92, Sotheby-NY, #363A, illus.), 6 x 9 1/8 in., (15.2 x 23.2 cm.), photograph, gelatin silver print (BP 2019, DM 4912, FR 16,658, Y 395,921).

$2200* *Moscow Streetcar,* late 1920's, probably p. 1940's, (10-15-92, Sotheby-NY, #362A, illus.), 6 3/4 x 8 7/8 in., (17.1 x 22.5 cm.), photograph, gelatin silver print (BP 1346, DM 3275, FR 11,106, Y 263,947).

$34,479* *"Muzei Im(eni) Pushkina", Moskva, 1927", Pushkin Museum,* mounted on card, s., t., d., coll. stamp, (05-06-93, Christie-London, #151, illus.), 11 5/8 x 9 3/16 in., photograph, gloss gelatin silver print (BP 21,850, DM 54,306, FR 182,815, Y 3,793,487).

BI *"Muzhskaia Golova, 1932", Male Head,* s., t., d., coll. stamp, est. BP 10/15,000, (05-06-93, Christie-London, #155, illus.), 19 1/2 x 15 5/8 in., photograph, gelatin silver print.

$27,465* *"Na Balkone, 1928 Khud. V.F. Stepanova Na Balkone", On The Balcony, 1928 The Artist V.F. Stepanova On The Balcony,* orig. mount s. recto, ink s., t., d., verso, lit., (10-29-92, Christie-London, #113, illus.), 15 3/8 x 10 5/8 in., (39.1 x 27 cm.), photograph, gelatin silver print (BP 17,600, DM 42,254, FR 143,346, Y 3,402,081).

$34,331* *"Na Krasnoi Ploshchadi Ritmicheskaia Gimnasti(ka)", On Red Square Rhythmic Gymnatics, 1936,* s., t., collec. stamp, orig. mount, s., d., t. in pencil recto, exhib. label verso, (10-29-92, Christie-London, #126, illus.), 11 5/8 x 19 in., (29.5 x 48.3 cm.), photograph, warm-toned gelatin silver print (BP 22,000, DM 52,817, FR 179,181, Y 4,252,570).

$4806* *"Na Krasnoi Ploshchadi Zariadiia, 1938", In Line On Red Square,* contemp. retouching, photog.'s mono., s., t., d., collec. stamp, (10-29-92, Christie-London, #134, illus.), 11 1/2 x 14 7/8 in., (29.2 x 37.8 cm.), photograph, warm-toned gelatin silver print (BP 3080, DM 7394, FR 25,084, Y 595,318).

BI *"Na Parade Krasnaia Ploshchad, 1936", On Parade, Red Square,* s., t., d., two photog.'s ink credit stamps, lit., est. BP 7/9,000, (10-29-92, Christie-London, #128, illus.), 15 x 22 1/2 in., (38.1 x 57.2 cm.), photograph, gelatin silver print.

$23,000* *On The Rings, 1938,* t., d., Foto Rodchenko credit stamp, (04-08-93, Christie-NY, #151, illus.), 10 7/8 x 18 1/2 in., (27.6 x 47 cm.), photograph, gelatin silver print on warm toned, textured paper (BP 15,082, DM 36,948, FR 125,068, Y 2,610,077).

$1631* *"Otriad Pionerov Akademii Kom-Vospitaniia, 1925", Team Of Pioneers From The Academy Of Communist Education,* photog.'s ink credit stamp, t., d. verso, (10-29-92, Christie-London, #108, illus.), 11 5/16 x 9 3/16 in., (28.7 x 23.3 cm.), photograph, gloss gelatin silver print (BP 1045, DM 2509, FR 8513, Y 202,031).

BI *"Parad 1 Maia Na Krasnoi Ploshchadi, 1937", May Day Parade In Red Square,* s., t., d., est. BP 6/8,000, (10-29-92, Christie-London, #131, illus.), 15 5/8 x 11 3/4 in., (39.7 x 29.8 cm.), photograph, warm-toned gelatin silver print on textured paper.

$16,307* *"Parad Na Krasnoi Ploshchadi, Koloniia Gruzinskoi SSR, 1938", ParadeOn Red Square, The Formation Of The Georgian Republic,* contemp. retouching, s., t., d., collec. stamp, (10-29-92, Christie-London, #133, illus.), 16 5/16 x 10 3/16 in., (41.4 x 25.9 cm.), photograph, warm-toned gelatin silver print (BP 10,450, DM 25,088, FR 85,110, Y 2,019,943).

$10,643* *"Peizazh 1925", Landscape,* contemp. retouching, mount s., d. Rodchenko 1925, Russian t., d. verso; photog.'s credit stamp, collec. stamp, lit., (10-29-92, Christie-London, #107, illus.), 6 7/16 x 8 7/8 in., (16.4 x 22.5 cm.), photograph, gelatin silver print (BP 6820, DM 16,374, FR 55,548, Y 1,318,345).

$19,962* *"Peizazh, 1935", Landscape,* t., d., photog.'s ink credit stamp Photo Rodchenko, annots., lit., (05-06-93, Christie-London, #168, illus.), 9 x 11 3/8 in., photograph, warm-toned gelatin silver print (BP 12,650, DM 31,441, FR 105,843, Y 2,196,281).

$27,465* *"Pioner", Pioneer, n.d., c. 1930-31,* photog.'s ink credit stamp, t., collec. stamp, (10-29-92, Christie-London, #114, illus.), 4 7/8 x 5 in., (12.4 x 12.7 cm.), photograph, gloss gelatin silver print (BP 17,600, DM 42,254, FR 143,346, Y 3,402,081).

$22,315* *"Pioner, 1931", Pioneer,* contemp. retouching, s., t., d., collec. stamp, lit., (10-29-92, Christie-London, #115, illus.), 15 5/8 x 11 1/2 in., (39.7 x 29.2 cm.), photograph, gelatin silver print (BP 14,300, DM 34,331, FR 116,467, Y 2,764,152).

$36,294* *"Pioner-Trubach, 1930", Pioneer Bugler,* t., d., sig. Rodchenko in another hand, photog.'s ink credit stamp A.M. Rodchenko, Moscow-Centre Miasnitskaia 21, Flat 18, coll. stamp, exhib. label, lit., (05-06-93, Christie-London, #157, illus.), 21 x 17 5/16 in., photograph, gelatin silver print (BP 23,000, DM 57,165, FR 192,439, Y 3,993,179).

$16,332* *"Pionerka, 1930", Pioneer,* possibly p. 1940s, early 50s, s., t., d., coll. stamp, lit., (05-06-93, Christie-London, #156, illus.), 17 7/16 x 13 9/16 in., photograph, gelatin silver print (BP 10,350, DM 25,724, FR 86,596, Y 1,796,897).

$7210* *"Polevye Tsvety, 1935", Wild Flowers: Two,* first s., t., d., photog.'s ink credit stamp, collec. stamp; other i. 1936, lit., (10-29-92, Christie-London, #119, illus.), one 18 1/8 x 11 3/8 in., (46 x 28.9 cm.), other 6 15/16 x 5 1/16 in., (46 x 28.9 cm.), photograph, gelatin silver print (BP 4620, DM 11,092, FR 37,630, Y 893,100).

BI *"Portet, 1927", Portrait,* mounted on paper, on card, s., t., d., lit., est. BP 10/15,000, (05-06-93, Christie-London, #149, illus.), 8 13/16 x 5 3/8 in., photograph, warm-toned gloss gelatin silver print.

$5807* *"Portet, T.V. Maliutinoi, 1937", Portrait, T.V. Maliutina,* t., d., photog.'s ink credit stamp Photo Rodchenko, coll. stamp, (05-06-93, Christie-London, #170, illus.), 11 5/16 x 5 9/16 in., photograph, warm-toned gelatin silver print (BP 3680, DM 9146, FR 30,790, Y 638,904).

$77,245* *"Pozharnaia Lestnitsa, 1927", Fire Escape,* s., t., d., i., collec. stamp, lit., (10-29-92, Christie-London, #110, illus.), 11 7/16 x 9 1/8 in., (29.1 x 23.2 cm.), photograph, gelatin silver print (BP 49,500, DM 118,838, FR 403,158, Y 9,568,314).

$6008* *"Pryzhok S Trapetsii, 1938", Jump From The Trapezium (From The Trampoline' Crossed Out In Pencil),* contemp.

retouching, s., t., collec. stamp, lit., (10-29-92, Christie-London, #132, illus.), 16 x 10½ in., (40.6 x 26.7 cm.), photograph, gelatin silver print (BP 3850, DM 9243, FR 31,357, Y 744,209).

$24,032* *"Pryzhok V Vodu, 1935", Dive,* s., t., d., 1932 changed to 1935, collec. stamp, lit., (10-29-92, Christie-London, #122, illus.), 17⅜ x 11¾ in., (44.1 x 29.8 cm.), photograph, gelatin silver print (BP 15,400, DM 36,972, FR 125,428, Y 2,976,836).

$37,764* *"Pryzhok V Vodu, 1935", Dive,* contemp. retouching, t., d., photog.'s ink stamp, collec. stamp, paper tape verso, lit., catalog cover lot, (10-29-92, Christie-London, #121, illus.), 15⁹⁄₁₆ x 10¹⁵⁄₁₆ in., (39.5 x 27.8 cm.), photograph, warm-toned gelatin silver print on textured paper (BP 24,200, DM 58,098, FR 197,098, Y 4,677,815).

BI *Pyramid Of Women, 1936,* t., credit stamps, lit., est. $6/8,000, (10-13-92, Christie-NY, #338, illus.), 11¾ x 8¾ in., (29.8 x 22.2 cm.), photograph, gelatin silver print.

BI *"Rabochii, 1930", Worker,* mounted on card, s., t., d., lit., est. BP 3/5,000, (05-06-93, Christie-London, #154, illus.), 12 x 9 in., photograph, gloss gelatin silver print.

$6008* *"Ritmicheskaia Gimnastika, 1936", Rhythmic Gymnastics,* contemp. retouching, mono. incised recto, s., t., d., collec. stamp, orig. mount, s., d., collec. stamp verso, (10-29-92, Christie-London, #127, illus.), 9 x 11¼ in., (22.9 x 28.6 cm.), gelatin silver print (BP 3850, DM 9243, FR 31,357, Y 744,209).

BI *"Ritmicheskaia Gimnastika, 1937", Rhythmic Gymnastics,* s., t., d., coll. stamp, est. BP 6/8,000, (05-06-93, Christie-London, #164, illus.), 11½ x 19⅛ in., photograph, warm-toned gelatin silver print.

$12,016* *"Ritmy, 1936", Rhythms,* t., sig., d., partially erased inscrip., collec. stamp verso, lit., (10-29-92, Christie-London, #125, illus.), 11⅝ x 19⅜ in., (29.5 x 49.2 cm.), photograph, gelatin silver print (BP 7700, DM 18,486, FR 62,714, Y 1,488,418).

$51,497* *"Rumba, 1935",* ink i. P.1935 recto, s., t., d., collec. stamp verso, orig. mount, s., d., t.; s., t., collec. stamp verso, rare example, 1 of 3 known hand-colored prints, (10-29-92, Christie-London, #124, illus.), 8⅛ x 5⅝ in., (20.6 x 14.3 cm.), photograph, negative gelatin silver print, hand-colored w/crayon, on black card mount (BP 33,000, DM 79,226, FR 268,773, Y 6,378,917).

$8166* *"S.I. Kirsanov Poet, 1930",* s., t., d., coll. stamp, lit., (05-06-93, Christie-London, #153, illus.), 11¼ x 15⅝ in., photograph, gelatin silver print (BP 5175, DM 12,862, FR 43,298, Y 898,449).

BI *"Schukhovskaia Bashnia Radiobashnia, 1927", Shukhovskii Radio Tower,* s., t., d., i., photog.'s ink credit stamp Photo Rodchenko, coll. stamp, lit., est. BP 8/10,000, (05-06-93, Christie-London, #148, illus.), 9 x 11⅝ in., photograph, gloss gelatin silver print.

$12,703* *"Skachka, 1935", Horse Race,* possibly p. 1940s-early 50s, s., t., d., coll. stamp, lit., (05-06-93, Christie-London, #165, illus.), 18¼ x 23⅝ in., photograph, untrimmed gelatin silver print (BP 8050, DM 20,008, FR 67,354, Y 1,397,624).

BI *"Sokol'niki, 1930", People Of Sokol,* t., d., photog.'s ink credit stamp A.M. Rodchenko, Moscow-Centre..., coll. stamp, est. BP 3/5,000, (05-06-93, Christie-London, #158, illus.), 9⅜ x 11⅝ in., photograph, gloss gelatin silver print on heavy paper.

$13,610* *"Solntsepoklonniki, 1933", Sun Worshippers,* s., t. twice, d., coll. stamp, lit., (05-06-93, Christie-London, #161, illus.), 22¾ x 14⅞ in., photograph, gelatin silver print (BP 8625, DM 21,436, FR 72,163, Y 1,497,414).

$8711* *"Stolovaia, 1932", Canteen,* t., d., photog.'s ink credit stamp A.M. Rodchenko, Moscow-Centre..., est. BP 3/5,000, (05-06-93, Christie-London, #159, illus.), 9⅛ x 11½ in., photograph, gloss gelatin silver print (BP 5520, DM 13,720, FR 46,188, Y 958,411).

$4400* *Strastnaya Square, Moscow, 1928 (Pantheon, pl. 23; Complete Work, p.258, there titled "Pushkin Square" and dated 1932),* probably p. 1940's, (10-15-92, Sotheby-NY, #366A, illus.), 11⅝ x 7⅞ in., (29.5 x 20 cm.), photograph, gelatin silver print (BP 2692, DM 6550, FR 22,211, Y 527,894).

BI *Tanks, Red Square, Moscow, 1918-20,* stamp, est. $1/1,500, (10-15-92, Sotheby-NY, #365A, illus.), 3⅛ x 4¼ in., (7.9 x 10.8 cm.), photograph, gelatin silver print.

BI *Tatiana Rodchenko, early 1920's,* stamp, est. $3/5,000, (10-15-92, Sotheby-NY, #364A, illus.), 7¾ x 6 in., (19.7 x 15.2 cm.), photograph, gelatin silver print.

BI *Untitled, 1936,* d., photog.'s ink credit stamp Photo Rodchenko, annots., lit., est. BP 4/6,000, (05-06-93, Christie-London, #163, illus.), 9¼ x 10½ in., photograph, gloss gelatin silver print on heavy paper.

$36,294* *"Utrenniaia Zariadka, SSSR Na Stroike, 1933", Morning Excerise, USSRIn Construction: Two,* each mounted asymmetrically on 2 layers of card, s., t., d., i., coll. stamp, lit., (05-06-93, Christie-London, #160, illus.), each 11⅜ x 17⅜ in., photograph, gelatin silver print (BP 23,000, DM 57,165, FR 192,439, Y 3,993,179).

$120,159* *"Utrennii Tualet, 1935", Morning Wash,* s., t., d., collec. stamp, lit., exhib., (10-29-92, Christie-London, #120, illus.), 16⁷⁄₁₆ x 11⁷⁄₁₆ in., (41.8 x 29.1 cm.), photograph, warm-toned gelatin silver print (BP 77,000, DM 184,860, FR 627,135, Y 14,884,058).

$18,882* *"V.V. Maiakovskii, 1926",* s., t., d., collec. stamp, lit., (10-29-92, Christie-London, #109, illus.), 16½ x 11½ in., (41.9 x 29.2 cm.), photograph, gelatin silver print (BP 12,100, DM 29,049, FR 98,549, Y 2,338,907).

$10,888* *"V.V. Maiakovskii, 1930",* s., t., d., coll. stamp, lit., (05-06-93, Christie-London, #152, illus.), 10⁹⁄₁₆ x 15¼ in., photograph, gelatin silver print (BP 6900, DM 17,149, FR 57,731, Y 1,197,932).

$1925* *Varvara Stepanova (Wife Of Alexander Rodchenko): Two: "Varvara Stepanova at Drafting Table" and "Varvara Stepanova Demonstrating Performing Furniture for 'Tarelkin's Death' at the Meyerhold Theatre"; (Rodchenko Family Workshop),* i. w/notations, 1 w/collector's stamp, 1st p. 1940's or 1950's, (10-15-92, Sotheby-NY, #364, illus.), one 5½ x 6½ in., (14 x 16.5 cm.), other 8¾ x 6 in., (14 x 16.5 cm.), photograph, gelatin silver print (BP 1178, DM 2865, FR 9717, Y 230,954).

BI *Varvara Stepanova, c. 1924,* foto Rodchenko credit stamp, est. $6/8,000, (04-08-93, Christie-NY, #149, illus.), 7 x 4¾ in., (17.8 x 12.1 cm.), photograph, gelatin silver print.

BI *Vladimir Mayakovsky, 1924 (cf. Morozov and Lloyd, p. 71; cf. Musee d'Art Moderne de la Ville de Paris, unpaginated; Pantheon, pl. 2),* i. A.M. Rodchenko, t., d. in unidentified hand, stamp, est. $10/15,000, (10-15-92, Sotheby-NY, #362, illus.), 4⅜ x 3⅛ in., (11.1 x 7.9 cm.), photograph, gelatin silver print.

BI *Vladimir Mayakovsky, c. 1924 (Complete Work, p. 241),* notations, est. $3/5,000, (10-15-92, Sotheby-NY, #365, illus.), 8⅜ x 6¼ in., (21.3 x 15.9 cm.), photograph, gelatin silver print.

$6600* *Vladimir Vladimirovich Mayakovsky, (1924),* 1950s, s., t. in ink, lit., (10-13-92, Christie-NY, #335, illus.), 8 x 5¾ in., (20.3 x 14.6 cm.), photograph, gelatin silver print (BP 3844, DM 9669, FR 32,852, Y 800,291).

$3025* *The Workers' Club, International Exhibition Of Decorative Arts, Paris, 1925 (cf. Complete Work, p. 176; cf. Karginov, pls. 145-146),* notations in various hands, stamp, (10-15-92, Sotheby-NY, #363, illus.), 8⅞ x 6¾ in., (22.5 x 17.1 cm.), photograph, gelatin silver print (BP 1851, DM 4503, FR 15,270, Y 362,927).

$18,882* *"Za Cherviami, 1933", Catching Worms,* s., t., d., collec. stamp, lit., (10-29-92, Christie-London, #117, illus.), 11³⁄₁₆ x 15⁷⁄₁₆ in., (28.4 x 39.2 cm.), photograph, warm-toned gelatin silver print on textured paper (BP 12,100, DM 29,049, FR 98,549, Y 2,338,907).

$3629* *"Zavod "AMO"", AMO Factory, 1929,* t., photog.'s ink credit stamp, coll. stamp, lit., (05-06-93, Christie-London, #175, illus.), 9¼ x 11⅜ in., photograph, gelatin silver print (BP 2300, DM 5716, FR 19,242, Y 399,274).

RODE, Johann Heinrich   German 1727-1759
BI *Ein Knabe Mit Pelzbesetzter Mutze Und Pelzmantel Vor Einem Kohlenfeuer Sitzend, 1751,* plate s., d., trimmed, est. DM 700-, (09-25-92, Granier, #2683), 10⁷⁄₁₆ x 7¹¹⁄₁₆ in., (26.5 x 19.6 cm.), etching.

RODERMONT, Peter ac. early 17th cent.
BI *Jacob Und Esau (Dutuit 1 II),* 2nd state, est. DM 800, (06-10-93, Hauswedell/Nolt, #154), etching on fine handmade.

RODGER, George
$998* *"Fallen Tribesman Carries Victorious Numba Wrestler, Kordofan, Sudan, 1949",* s., 450 x 322mm, (05-07-93, Sotheby-London, #247, illus.), photograph, silver print (BP 632, DM 1578, FR 5317, Y 109,888).
$247* *Mau Mau In Dock, 1954,* handstamp, (10-14-92, Swann, #342, illus.), 7½ x 8 in., (19.1 x 20.3 cm.), photograph, silver print (BP 145, DM 361, FR 1226, Y 29,932).

RODIN, Auguste French 1840-1917
$404* *"Les 3 Graces",* s. in plate, (10-18-92, Pescheteau, #253), 5⅞ x 3⁹⁄₁₆ in., (15 x 9 cm.), etching in bistre on laid wove (BP 245, DM 597, FR 2027, Y 48,239).
BI *Les Amours Conduisant Le Monde (Delteil, Thorson 1), 1881,* second (final), rich burr, full margins, good cond., soiling, creases, est. $6/8,000, (11-05-92, Sotheby-NY, #424, illus.), 8 x 10 in., (204 x 253 mm.), drypoint on Japan.
$3818* *Les Amours Conduisant Le Monde (Thorson 1/II), 1881,* (06-23-93, Kornfeld, #757), drypoint on thick Japan (BP 2594, DM 6460, FR 21,730, Y 415,949, SF 5750).
$7593* *Antonin Proust (L.D. 10),* first state of seven, ink s., reddish stains, good margins, collector's stamps, (06-11-93, Picard, #159, illus.), 9⅜ x 6¹⁵⁄₁₆ in., (238 x 177 mm.), etching on laid (BP 4989, DM 12,340, FR 41,605, Y 805,623).
$1535* *Buste De Bellone (D. 3), 1883,* staining, mat-staining, large margins, (02-24-93, Picard, #217), drypoint on old Japan (BP 1070, DM 2492, FR 8448, Y 180,122).
$6345* *Henri Becque (L. Delteil, 9; Thorson, 26/27), 1885,* (04-02-93, Picard, #174), 6¼ x 8¹⁄₁₆ in., (15.9 x 20.4 cm.), drypoint in black on laid (BP 4179, DM 10,198, FR 34,634, Y 722,418).
$330* *"Man And Children In A Brush",* s., (02-27-93, Dunning, #111), 7 x 5 in., (17.8 x 12.7 cm.), etching (BP 232, DM 542, FR 1844, Y 38,956).
$1433* *La Ronde (D. 5), 1883,* soiling, margins, (02-24-93, Picard, #218), drypoint on old Japan, t. in green (BP 999, DM 2326, FR 7887, Y 168,153).
$2598* *Victor Hugo De Face (L. Delteil 7),* third state of seven, ded., s., good margins, yellowed, (06-11-93, Picard, #158), 7¹³⁄₁₆ x 5⅞ in., (198 x 150 mm.), drypoint on laid (BP 1707, DM 4222, FR 14,236, Y 275,650).
$467* *"Victor Hugo De Face" (Deltiel 7) and "Antonin Proust, 1885" (Deltiel 10): Two,* from Gazette des Beaux-Arts, plate mark, (12-08-92, Swann, #269), first 8⅞ x 6⅝ in., (22.5 x 16.8 cm.), second 8 x 5½ in., (22.5 x 16.8 cm.), drypoint etching (BP 293, DM 727, FR 2479, Y 57,883).
$475* *Victor Hugo, De Face [T9;D7], 1885,* bears sig., (02-04-93, Sloan, #2385), 8¾ x 6¼ in., (22.2 x 15.9 cm.), drypoint (BP 332, DM 782, FR 2652, Y 59,087).
$550* *"Victor Hugo, De Face" (Thorson IX VII/IX), 1885,* frontspiece of Roger Marx's Les Pointes Seches de Rodin, 1902, good cond., hinges, (10-31-92, Cleveland, #327), 8 x 5½ in., (20.3 x 14 cm.), drypoint (BP 352, DM 846, FR 2871, Y 68,128).
$495* *Victor Hugo, De Trois Quarts (D. 6, T. 8), 1888,* s., t. in plate, p. by L. Eudes, margins, good cond., foxing, tears,paper losses, thinned spot, line tape remains, (02-24-93, Butterfield, #2968), 8¹⁵⁄₁₆ x 6 in., (227 x 152 mm.), drypoint on laid (BP 345, DM 804, FR 2724, Y 58,085).

RODO BOULANGER, Graciela b. Bolivia 1935
BI *Apres La Danse, 1981,* s., #50/200, est. $800/1,000, (02-04-93, Sloan, #1686), 22⅝ x 18 in., (57.5 x 45.7 cm.), color lithograph on Arches paper.
$138* *Child With Birdcage,* s., num. XII/XXX, tape, good cond., (12-12-92, Weschler, #159), 13 x 10 in., (33 x 25.4 cm.), color lithograph (BP 88, DM 217, FR 745, Y 17,077).
$220* *Children Playing Football,* s., num. 186/200, (09-20-92, Hindman, #803), 26½ x 17 in., (67.3 x 43.2 cm.), colored print (BP 129, DM 326, FR 1117, Y 27,191).
$358* *Children With Musical Instruments,* s., num. 165/200, (09-20-92, Hindman, #802), 29 x 21 in., (73.7 x 53.3

cm.), colored print (BP 210, DM 531, FR 1817, Y 44,247).
$275* *Entre Act,* s., num. 20/200, (11-12-92, Freemn/Fine Art, #34), 25⅝ x 18 in., (65.1 x 45.7 cm.), color litho (BP 181, DM 436, FR 1470, Y 34,098).
$523* *Mother And Child,* s., #53/100, margins, good cond., staining, rippling, (12-12-92, Weschler, #160, illus.), 23 x 15½ in., (58.4 x 39.4 cm.), color etching and aquatint (BP 335, DM 824, FR 2824, Y 64,720).

ROE, Fred (after)
$129 *Busy Street Scene With Lord Nelson,* (04-16-93, G.A. Key, #33), 20 x 30 in., (50.8 x 76.2 cm.), chromolithograph (BP 85, DM 208, FR 704, Y 14,506).
$99* *Nelson Leaving Portsmouth, "Good-Bye, My Lads" and "Bound For Trafalgar's Bay": A Pair,* foxing, trimmed, (06-16-93, Bonhams-Chelsea, #400), image 21½ x 32 in., (54.6 x 81.3 cm.), chromolithograph (BP 66, DM 164, FR 552, Y 10,559).

ROEDEL French 1859-1900
$414* *Ah Pudeur Tous Les Soirs A La Cigale, 1897,* (01-31-93, Morelle/Marchan, #183), 33⁷⁄₁₆ x 47¼ in., (85 x 120 cm.), poster (BP 278, DM 667, FR 2255, Y 51,647).
$299* *Moulin Rouge. Samedi 27 Janvier, Grande Redoute, 1897,* cond. B, (03-16-93, Boisgirard, #184), 47⅝ x 31⅞ in., (121 x 81 cm.), poster (BP 206, DM 497, FR 1689, Y 34,963).

ROEHN, Jean Alphonse 1799-1864
BI *Anzacs (S.L. 713), 1918-1922,* 2nd state, mono. in plate, s., #12/45, full margins, est. FF 6/8,000, (11-16-92, Briest, #223, illus.), 17½ x 9³⁄₁₆ in., (44.5 x 23.4 cm.), wood engraving.
BI *Baigneuse Aux Mouettes (S.L. 410), 1930,* 4th state, s., #9/70, mono. in plate, full margins, est. FF 6/8,000, (11-16-92, Briest, #243), 14½ x 9¹⁄₁₆ in., (36.8 x 23 cm.), etching.
$5035* *Le Balcon Sur La Mer (S.L. 274), 1923,* 3rd state, mono. in plate, s., (11-16-92, Briest, #228, illus.), 14½ x 14⅝ in., (36.8 x 37.2 cm.), copper etching (BP 3309, DM 8030, FR 27,055, Y 628,354).
$524* *La Boutique Du Cremier (S.L. 526), 1937,* 1st state, mono. in plate, full margins, (11-16-92, Briest, #251), 12¹⁵⁄₁₆ x 9¹³⁄₁₆ in., (32.8 x 25 cm.), copper engraving (BP 344, DM 836, FR 2816, Y 65,394).
$524* *Cabaret Vendeen (S.L. 303), 1926,* 4th state, mono. in plate, full margins, s., #46/65, (11-16-92, Briest, #232), 12¹¹⁄₁₆ x 9⅞ in., (32.3 x 25.1 cm.), copper engraving (BP 344, DM 836, FR 2816, Y 65,394).
$881* *La Cabaretiere Obese (S.L. 172), 1917-1920(?),* 2nd state, s., #22/45, mono., d. 1917 in plate, full margins, (11-16-92, Briest, #210), 11¹⁄₁₆ x 8⅞ in., (28.1 x 22.5 cm.), copper etching (BP 579, DM 1405, FR 4734, Y 109,946).
$4230* *Le Cafe Du Commerce (S.L. 126), 1913,* s., d. in plate, #24/35, full margins, restoration, (11-16-92, Briest, #220, illus.), 15¹⁄₁₆ x 18¹⁄₁₆ in., (38.3 x 45.8 cm.), etching (BP 2780, DM 6746, FR 22,730, Y 527,892).
BI *Ernest (S.L. 617), 1902,* 2nd state, mono. in plate, s., full margins, est. FF 30/35,000, (11-16-92, Briest, #212, illus.), 19¹⁵⁄₁₆ x 12¹³⁄₁₆ in., (50.7 x 32.5 cm.), wood engraving in colors.
BI *Fleurs Artificielles (Nenuphars Et Muguet) (S.L. 279), 1924,* 3rd state, s., #30/45, mono. in plate, full margins, est. FF 3/4,000, (11-16-92, Briest, #229), 12¹⁵⁄₁₆ x 9¹⁵⁄₁₆ in., (33 x 25.2 cm.), copper engraving.
$797* *L'Amour Au Bois (S.L. 230), 1922,* 1st state, s., #6/8, full margins, stains, (11-16-92, Briest, #222), 8¼ x 11⁹⁄₁₆ in., (20.9 x 29.4 cm.), copper etching (BP 524, DM 1271, FR 4283, Y 99,463).
$1153* *Le Marchand De Glaces (S.L. 262), 1923,* 2nd state, s., #42/65, mono. in plate, full margins, (11-16-92, Briest, #227), 13³⁄₁₆ x 9⅝ in., (33.5 x 24.5 cm.), copper etching (BP 758, DM 1839, FR 6196, Y 143,891).
$797* *Marchande De Fleurs Au Trocadero (S.L. 433), 1931,* 1st state, s., #5/8, full margins, (11-16-92, Briest, #245), 12¹³⁄₁₆ x 9¹³⁄₁₆ in., (32.5 x 25 cm.), copper engraving (BP 524, DM 1271, FR 4283, Y 99,463).
BI *Mystique Des Tempetes (S.L. Tome II 338), 1926,* epreuve d'artiste, s., mono. in plate, full margins, est. FF 2,5/

3,000, (11-16-92, Briest, #235), 12⅞ x 9¹³⁄₁₆ in., (32.7 x 24.9 cm.), copper engraving.

$377* *La Panne (S.L. 322), 1928,* 3rd state, s., #29/30, mono. in plate, full margins, (11-16-92, Briest, #237), 8¾ x 10⅞ in., (22.3 x 27.6 cm.), etching (BP 248, DM 601, FR 2026, Y 47,049).

$587* *Paysage Au Tunnel (S.L. 195), 1920,* 2nd state, s., #37/55, s., d. 1920 in plate, full margins, (11-16-92, Briest, #211), 10¹⁄₁₆ x 13⅜ in., (25.5 x 33.9 cm.), etching (BP 386, DM 936, FR 3154, Y 73,256).

$2307* *La Peche A La Ligne (S.L. 361), 1927-1928,* 3rd state, epreuve d'artiste, mono. in plate, s., full margins, (11-16-92, Briest, #240, illus.), 12¹³⁄₁₆ x 16⁹⁄₁₆ in., (32.6 x 42 cm.), copper engraving (BP 1516, DM 3679, FR 12,397, Y 287,907).

$881* *La Peche Aux Crevettes (S.L. 375), 1928,* 3rd state, s., #18/58, mono. in plate, full margins, (11-16-92, Briest, #238), 12⅞ x 5⁹⁄₁₆ in., (32.7 x 14.2 cm.), copper engraving (BP 579, DM 1405, FR 4734, Y 109,946).

BI *Pecheurs Aux Carrelets (S.L. 300), 1925,* 2nd state, s., #6/8, full margins, yellowed, est. FF 5/6,000, (11-16-92, Briest, #231), 10⅞ x 13⅞ in., (27.6 x 35.2 cm.), copper engraving.

BI *Les Poires (S.L. 408), 1929-1930,* 3rd state, mono. in plate, s., est. FF 12/15,000, (11-16-92, Briest, #247, illus.), 11⁷⁄₁₆ x 8¹⁵⁄₁₆ in., (29 x 22.8 cm.), copper engraving.

BI *La Receveuse (S.L. 190), 1919-1920,* 2nd state, mono. in plate, s., full margins, est. FF 4/5,000, (11-16-92, Briest, #213), 17⁵⁄₁₆ x 14⅝ in., (44 x 37.2 cm.), copper etching.

BI *Sujets De Peche, 1833:* Set of Four, ed. Noelaine, moisture stains, est. FF 4,0/4,500, (11-16-92, Briest, #209), 16⁵⁄₁₆ x 22⅝ in., (41.4 x 57.5 cm.), engraving.

$315* *Vieille Femme Rentrant Sa Vache (S.L. 444), 1931,* 3rd state, s., #3/4, mono. in plate, full margins, (11-16-92, Briest, #246), 10⅞ x 8⅞ in., (27.6 x 22.5 cm.), copper engraving on BFK Rives (BP 207, DM 502, FR 1693, Y 39,311).

BI *Vue Panoramique Du Port De Saint-Nazaire (S.L. 188), 1919-1920,* 5th state, s., holes, creases, full margins, est. FF 10/12,000, (11-16-92, Briest, #214, illus.), 18⁹⁄₁₆ x 24⅞ in., (47.2 x 63.2 cm.), etching.

ROEHRIGHT, V.

BI *Freie Secession, 1919,* p. H. Birkholz, losses, tears, repairs, est. BP 2/4,000, (05-20-93, Christie-London, #507, illus.), sheet 28 x 38 in., (71.1 x 96.5 cm.), lithograph in colors backed on Japan.

ROESCHKE, A.

$825* *Portrait Of A Young Boy, 1882,* photog. sig., d. recto, (04-07-93, Swann, #215, illus.), 24 x 19 in., photograph, hand-colored salt print (BP 545, DM 1334, FR 4516, Y 93,729).

ROESNQUIST, James

BI *Wind And Lightning, 1978,* s., t., d., i., pub. Multiples, Inc., full sheet, good cond., minor rippling, handling creases, est. $1/1,500, (05-22-93, Weschler, #222, illus.), 23 x 40 in., (58.4 x 101.6 cm.), hand-colored etching w/ embossing on Arches.

ROGERIO

$357* *Automobiles Nash. Tour De France Automobile, 1930,* very good cond., (11-19-92, Ribeyre/Baron, #72), 33⅞ x 24⁷⁄₁₆ in., (86 x 62 cm.), poster (BP 235, DM 569, FR 1917, Y 44,397).

ROGERS, Charles B.   American b. 1911

BI *"Ancient Ones"* and *"At The Windmill":* Two, s., t., excell. cond., est. $100/150, (05-15-93, Cleveland, #276), lithograph.

BI *"Horseherd At Moonrise", "Seventh Day Colt"* and *"Stone Post Gute":* Three, s., t., very good cond., est. $150/225, (05-15-93, Cleveland, #275), 6¾ x 8¾ in., (17.1 x 22.2 cm.), lithograph.

BI *"One Winter Day", "River Crossing"* and *"Twin Grouts":* Three, s., t., very good cond., est. $150/200, (05-15-93, Cleveland, #274), lithograph.

ROGHMAN, Roeland   Dutch 1597-1686

$154* *Buyten Campen,* plate 4 from a series, prov., (09-20-92, Hindman, #651), 5⅛ x 8⅜ in., (13 x 21.3 cm.), etching (BP 90, DM 229, FR 782, Y 19,033).

ROHDE, Werner   German 1906-1990

BI *Die Dompteuse, late 1920's,* studio stamp, est. $1,5/2,500, (10-15-92, Sotheby-NY, #411, illus.), 9¼ x 7 in., (23.5 x 17.8 cm.), photograph, gelatin silver print.

BI *Karl Nierendorf, 1934,* s., d., photographer's stamp, est. DM 900, (11-12-92, Lempertz, #210, illus.), 6¾ x 4¹¹⁄₁₆ in., (17.2 x 11.9 cm.), photograph, gelatin silver print.

BI *Der Maler Georg Schrimpf, 1934,* s., d., t., photographer's stamp, est. DM 900, (11-12-92, Lempertz, #211, illus.), 6⁹⁄₁₆ x 4¹¹⁄₁₆ in., (16.6 x 11.9 cm.), photograph, gelatin silver print.

$607* *Meine Schwester Im Festkostum, 1930,* t., lit., (11-12-92, Lempertz, #209, illus.), 6¹³⁄₁₆ x 4⅞ in., (17.3 x 12.4 cm.), photograph, gelatin silver print (BP 388, DM 954, FR 3251, Y 75,096).

$379* *Samaritaine, 20's,* s., (11-12-92, Lempertz, #208), 4¹³⁄₁₆ x 6⁹⁄₁₆ in., (12.3 x 16.6 cm.), photograph, gelatin silver print (BP 242, DM 596, FR 2030, Y 46,889).

BI *Self-Portrait In Mirror, late 1920's,* studio stamp, est. $1,5/2,500, (10-15-92, Sotheby-NY, #410, illus.), 9¼ x 7 in., (23.5 x 17.8 cm.), photograph, gelatin silver print.

BI *Self-Portrait, c. 1929,* stamped, est. $1,5/2,000, (10-13-92, Christie-NY, #339, illus.), 7½ x 5¼ in., (19.1 x 13.3 cm.), photograph, gelatin silver print.

ROHLFS, Christian   German 1849-1938

$6270* *Bergpredigt (Vogt 101, Utermann 144), 1916,* s., (12-05-92, Bassenge, #7667, illus.), 17⁵⁄₁₆ x 16⁵⁄₁₆ in., (44 x 41.5 cm.), woodcut on strong wove (BP 3926, DM 9775, FR 33,316, Y 776,855).

$303* *"Death With A Coffin", 1918 (Vogt 104),* very good cond., (09-27-92, Bakker, #195), image 8½ x 6 in., (21.6 x 15.2 cm.), woodblock print (BP 177, DM 449, FR 1519, Y 36,572).

BI *"Der Gefangene" (Vogt 107/II; Utermann 157), 1918,* s., tear, est. DM 6/9,000, (11-28-92, Grisebach, #154, illus.), 23¼ x 18⅛ in., (59 x 46 cm.), woodcut on cream Japan.

$8151* *Geist Gottes Uber Den Wassern (Vogt 91; Utermann 127), 1915,* s., (06-08-93, Karl/Faber, #1252, illus.), approx. 22⁷⁄₁₆ x 18⅛ in., (57 x 46 cm.), color woodcut in green on cream paper (BP 5358, DM 13,226, FR 44,541, Y 865,746).

$1552* *Der Gute Hirte (Vogt 36, Utermann 39), c. 1911,* blue pencil mono., (09-25-92, Granier, #2992, illus.), 7¹⁵⁄₁₆ x 3¾ in., (20.3 x 9.5 cm.), colored pencil rubbing from woodcut (BP 906, DM 2301, FR 7779, Y 187,326)..

$4813* *"Heilige 3 Konige" (U. 23), c. 1910,* s., i., from portfolio Die Schaffenden (I. Jahrgang, 1. Portfolio), drystamp, (12-01-92, Karl/Faber, #1146, illus.), 15⁹⁄₁₆ x 10⁷⁄₁₆ in., (39.5 x 26.5 cm.), woodcut on japan paper (BP 3180, DM 7671, FR 26,143, Y 599,228).

$1245* *Katze Und Maus (V. 65; U. 73), c. 1912-13,* (12-01-92, Karl/Faber, #1148), sh 8⁷⁄₁₆ x 15¹⁵⁄₁₆ in., (21.5 x 40.5 cm.), linocut on Japan (BP 823, DM 1984, FR 6763, Y 155,005).

$2270* *Kloster Andechs (Vogt 184), 1920,* s., (06-05-93, Bassenge, #6480, illus.), 15⅜ x 21⁵⁄₁₆ in., (39 x 54.2 cm.), lithograph on Japan (BP 1494, DM 3680, FR 12,404, Y 243,510).

$1991* *Das Marchen (Vogt 26; U. 29), c. 1911,* s., (12-01-92, Karl/Faber, #1147, illus.), 8⅞ x 4½ in., (22.5 x 11.5 cm.), woodcut, w/reworked watercolored pencil (BP 1315, DM 3173, FR 10,815, Y 247,883).

$1134* *Mondanes Paar (V. 162; U. 225), 1925,* estate stamp, (06-08-93, Karl/Faber, #1253), approx. 9⁷⁄₁₆ x 9⁷⁄₁₆ in., (24 x 24 cm.), blanched linocut in color on thin hand-made Japan (BP 745, DM 1840, FR 6197, Y 120,446).

$1271* *Mondanes Paar (Vogt 162), 1925,* (06-10-93, Hauswedell/Nolt, #827, illus.), image 9⁷⁄₁₆ x 9½ in., (24 x 24.2 cm.), color linocut on wove (BP 831, DM 2070, FR 6968, Y 134,911).

BI *"Pipi Komm! (Restaurantszene)" (Vogt 82; Utermann 112), c. 1915,* est. DM 1,7/1,900, (11-28-92, Grisebach, #720, illus.), 4⅞ x 9½ in., (12.4 x 24.2 cm.), woodcut on thick Japan.

$1412* *Der Raucher (Vogt 47), c. 1912,* s., (06-10-93, Hauswedell/Nolt, #825, illus.), image 12¾ x 8¹⁄₁₆ in., (32.4 x 20.4 cm.), linocut (BP 924, DM 2299, FR 7741, Y 149,878).

$4114* *"Sintflut" (Vogt 108; Utermann 154),* s., (06-05-93, Grisebach, #841, illus.), 27¾ x 20³⁄₁₆ in., (70.5 x 51.3 cm.), woodcut in reddish brown w/brush work on beige imitation Japan (BP 2708, DM 6670, FR 22,481, Y 441,322).

$4229* *Strasse In Soest (Vogt 27), 1911,* s., i., blindstamp, (05-26-93, Lempertz, #477, illus.), approx. 16⁹⁄₁₆ x 12⅛ in., (42 x 30.8 cm.), linocut on Japan (BP 2736, DM 6900, FR 23,224, Y 459,474).

$4688* *Strasse In Soest (Vogt 27), 1911,* t., s., blindstamp Die Schaffenden, 1 Jahrgang, 1, portfolio, (11-21-92, Lempertz, #357, illus.), 9⁷⁄₁₆ x 9⅜ in., (24 x 23.8 cm.), linocut on Japan (BP 3087, DM 7474, FR 25,177, Y 583,012).

$1299* *"Tiere Auf Der Weide" (Vogt 128; Utermann 184), 1921,* (11-28-92, Grisebach, #721, illus.), 5¼ x 10¹⁄₁₆ in., (13.3 x 25.6 cm.), woodcut in brown/blue on Japan (BP 857, DM 2069, FR 7025, Y 161,668).

$2483* *Der Tod (Vogt 64), 1912/13,* t., s., blindstamp, (06-05-93, Bassenge, #6478), 8¹⁄₁₆ x 9½ in., (20.5 x 24.1 cm.), woodcut on imitation Japan (BP 1635, DM 4026, FR 13,568, Y 266,359).

ROHLING, Carl German 1849-1922

$440* *"Bernich.Hebt",* pl. s., d. Berlin 1882, (01-15-93, DuMouchelle, #2213, illus.), 27 x 60 in., (68.6 x 152.4 cm.), etching (BP 288, DM 719, FR 2432, Y 55,472).

ROHSE, Otto b. 1925

$155* *Kirchenarchitektur,* s., num., light-stain, (09-25-92, Granier, #2993), sheet 18¼ x 23⅛ in., (46.4 x 58.7 cm.), color etching on hand-made (BP 91, DM 230, FR 777, Y 18,709).

ROJAC

$186* *La Fee Blanche (It's A Pleasure) Avec Sonja Hiene, 1945,* 1220 x 160, (01-31-93, Morelle/Marchan, #80), poster (BP 125, DM 300, FR 1013, Y 23,204).

ROJO, Vincent

BI *Senales En El Pais De Alicia "A",* s., d. 72, #8/30; t. label verso, prov., exhib., est. C$ 1/150, (12-01-92, Ritchie, #48), 25 x 19¼ in., (63.5 x 48.9 cm.), color serigraph.

ROLAND HOLST, R.N.

$220* *Electra, 1920,* Teulings/Graf. Kunstinr., browned, wrinkled, tears, damages, marginsartly cut away, poor cond., (06-09-93, Bubb Kuyper, #2176), 36⅝ x 24⅝ in., (93 x 62.5 cm.), lithograph in black (BP 145, DM 360, FR 1210, Y 23,397, G 403).

$847* *Lucifer. Treurspel van Vondel, 1910,* tear, (06-09-93, Bubb Kuyper, #2177), 48¹³⁄₁₆ x 29½ in., (124 x 75 cm.), lithograph in black and red (BP 559, DM 1385, FR 4659, Y 90,078, G 1553).

ROLLET, L.

$147* *Foire Au Croutes, Commune Libre De Montmartre,* p. A. Beaumont, very good cond., (11-19-92, Ribeyre/Baron, #153), 31⁵⁄₁₆ x 23⅝ in., (79.5 x 60 cm.), poster (BP 97, DM 234, FR 789, Y 18,281).

ROLLINS, Tim and K.O.S. contemporary

BI *"Black Alice" and "White Alice", 1989: Two,* s., d., #22/50, pub. Edition Schellmann, full margins, good cond., est. $2/4,000, (05-19-93, Butterfield, #2315), each sh 33 x 52 in., (83.8 x 132.1 cm.), offset lithograph w/silkscreen, collage and hand-colored gesso in colors on wove.

$385* *The Temptation Of Saint Anthony II, 1989,* s., annot. II, #27/30, pub. Crown Point Press, full margins, very good cond.?, (10-28-92, Butterfield, #3092), sheet 22⅜ x 15 in., (568 x 381 mm.), spitbite aquatint w/Chine colle (pasted) on cream wove (BP 245, DM 595, FR 2019, Y 47,239).

$3300* *The Temptation Of Saint Antony I-XIV, 1989,* complete portfolio, each init., t., i. 'A.P. 5', artist's proofs, pub. Crown Point Press, full margins, good cond., orig. portfolio, (11-07-92, Sotheby-NY, #748, illus.), each sheet approx. 22⅛ x 15 in., (562 x 381 mm.), fourteen etchings w/aquatint (BP 2158, DM 5269, FR 17,809, Y 407,307).

$1978* *White Alice/Black Alice, 1989: A Pair,* each s., d., #18/50, pub. Edition Schellmann, margins, soiling, otherminor defects, (10-15-92, Sotheby-London, #127, illus.), each sheet 32¾ x 51¾ in., (83.2 x 131.4 cm.), letterpress w/silkscreen and hand painting in matte acrylic on white-wove (BP 1210, DM 2944, FR 9985, Y 237,313).

ROLSTON, Matthew

$605* *"Anjelica Huston, Silhouette", 1987,* s., t., d., edit. 10/25, annot., Dixon Collection, (11-16-92, Butterfield, #6139, illus.), 15 x 15 in., (381.7 x 381.7 mm.), photograph, gelatin silver print (BP 398, DM 965, FR 3249, Y 75,239).

$330* *"Dennis Quaid", 1990,* s., t., d., edit. 5/25, annot., Dixon Collection, (11-16-92, Butterfield, #6140, illus.), 8⅞ x 7 in., (225.8 x 178.1 mm.), photograph, c-print (BP 217, DM 526, FR 1772, Y 41,040).

$546* *"Keanu Reeves, Detail, Lips" and "Keanu Reeves, Detail, Waist", 1990: Two,* photog.'s blindstamp, s., t., d., #5/25, annot., (05-23-93, Butterfield, #3578, illus.), each approx. 8⅞ x 7 in., photograph, C-print (BP 356, DM 893, FR 3005, Y 60,351).

$316* *"Mikhail Baryshnikov", 1987,* photog.'s blindstamp, s., t., d., #5/25, annot., (05-23-93, Butterfield, #3579, illus.), 14⅜ x 18⅝ in., photograph, gelatin silver print (BP 206, DM 517, FR 1739, Y 34,929).

ROMANO, Giulio (after) 1499-1546

$7991* *The Prison, c. 1550,* margins, srip of paper over upper margin, staining, excell. cond., laid, (12-01-92, Christie-London, #42, illus.), P. 10¹³⁄₁₆ x 16⁷⁄₁₆ in., (274 x 418 mm.), engraving (BP 5280, DM 12,737, FR 43,406, Y 994,895).

ROMANO, Umberto American 1905-1984

$165* *"Ecce Homo" and "Untitled": Two,* s. in stone; s., i. Artist Proof (Edition of 100), d. 1975, (12-10-92, Sloan, #3045), 12 x 9⅛ in., (30.5 x 23.2 cm.), lithograph (BP 106, DM 261, FR 891, Y 20,411).

ROMBERG, M.

$617* *PLM and Cie De Navigation Paquet: Le Maroc Par Marseille. "Le SultanSe Rendant A La Mosquee De Fez", c. 1920,* very good cond., (03-13-93, Laurin, #106, illus.), 42⅛ x 29¹⁵⁄₁₆ in., (107 x 76 cm.), (BP 430, DM 1027, FR 3492, Y 72,717).

ROMBERG, Maurice 1862-1943

$120* *Le Secours De Guerre,* cond. B, (03-16-93, Boisgirard, #185), 46⅝ x 33⅞ in., (118.5 x 86 cm.), poster (BP 83, DM 200, FR 678, Y 14,032).

ROMERO Mexican 20th cent.

$110* *"Buenos Dias" and "Luna Park": Two,* both s., 201/300 and 195/300, (11-12-92, Freemn/Fine Art, #184), both 38 x 29 in., (96.5 x 73.7 cm.), serigraphs (BP 72, DM 174, FR 588, Y 13,639).

ROMERO, Frank

$440* *Car, 1988,* s., d., full margins, very good cond.?, (10-28-92, Butterfield, #3093), 21½ x 47 in., (54.6 x 119.4 cm.), color silkscreen monotype on wove (BP 280, DM 680, FR 2307, Y 53,988).

ROMIG, O.E.

$1320* *Pittsburgh Railroad Yard,* photog.'s sig., notations, label, 1930s, (04-07-93, Swann, #541, illus.), 14 x 18¼ in., photograph, silver print (BP 872, DM 2135, FR 7225, Y 149,966).

BI *Twilight Down The Ohio, Pittsburgh, c. 1938,* s., t. in crayon, est. $1,8/2,200, (10-13-92, Christie-NY, #340, illus.), 15⅛ x 19⅛ in., (38.4 x 48.6 cm.), photograph, gelatin silver print.

ROMNEY, G. (after)

$24 *"John Stuart" and "Charlotte Jane Windsor": A Pair,* engraved by F. Bartolozzi, d. 1790, (04-16-93, G.A. Key, #48), 10 x 7 in., (25.4 x 17.8 cm.), b/w engravings (BP 16, DM 39, FR 131, Y 2699).

$38 *"Mrs. Drummond-Smith",* (04-16-93, G.A. Key, #124), 11 x 8 in., (27.9 x 20.3 cm.), colored mezzotint (BP 25, DM 61, FR 207, Y 4273).

ROMNEY, George (after)
$142* *Alope, 1787,* by Richard Earlom, pub. John & Josiah Boydell, folded, thin spot, good cond., (11-30-92, Phillips-London, #167), plate 11¾ x 15⅓ in., (298 x 389 mm.), stipple engraving in brown, blue, and sanguine (BP 94, DM 226, FR 768, Y 17,673).
$233* *Caroline, Duchess Of Marlborough (C.S. 53), 1792,* by John Jones, 2nd state of 2 (Russell), pub. John Jones, skinning, good cond., (11-30-92, Phillips-London, #80), plate 24 x 14¾ in., (610 x 375 mm.), mezzotint on laid (BP 154, DM 371, FR 1260, Y 28,998).
$159* *Miss Cumberland (C.S. 49), 1779,* scratch-letter proof, engraved by John Raphael Smith, 1st state of 3, Russell 1st state of 4, small margins, minor creasing, good cond., (11-30-92, Phillips-London, #79, illus.), plate 15 x 11 in., (381 x 279 mm.), mezzotint (BP 105, DM 253, FR 860, Y 19,788).
$126* *Mrs. Carwardine, Wife Of The Statuary (C.S. 36), 1781,* engraved by J.R. Smith, scratch-letter proof, Russell 1st of 2, pub. J. Birchall, trimmed to thread margins, repaired thin areas, (11-30-92, Phillips-London, #78), plate 15 x 10⅞ in., (381 x 276 mm.), mezzotint on laid (BP 83, DM 201, FR 681, Y 15,681).

RONALD, William
BI *Untitled (Portfolio: Toronto 20),* s., d. '65, num. #40, pub. The Art Gallery, est. C$ 250/400, (11-30-92, Ritchie, #51), 26 x 20 in., (66 x 55.8 cm.), mixed media print.

RONALD, William Smith   Canadian b. 1926
BI *Sans Titre, 1965,* num. from 40, s., d. Ronald 65, (05-18-93, Encans, #140), 25¹⁵⁄₁₆ x 20¹⁄₁₆ in., (66 x 51 cm.), lithograph and transfert.

RONFILS, Robert
BI *La Petite Table,* s., num. 33/43, full margins, good cond., est. BP 100/150, (11-30-92, Phillips-London, #478), sheet 12¾ x 9⅜ in., (324 x 238 mm.), lithograph in colors on wove.

RONZAGUE-PRIVAS
$869* *Alleluia, Le Premier Machine De Course,* tears, wear on edges, (05-07-93, Christie-S. Ken, #121, illus.), sight 21 x 14½ in., (53.3 x 36.8 cm.), color lithograph (BP 550, DM 1374, FR 4630, Y 95,684).

ROOKER, Edward (after Paul SANDBY)
$435* *"The West Front Of St. Paul's Covent Garden" and "Covent Garden Piazza", 1766: Two,* pub. Rooker, London, trimmed to plate, narrow margins, tears into image, creases in image, (10-27-92, Phillips-London, #117), plate 15¾ x 21¾ in., (400 x 552 mm.), etching w/engraving w/later and-coloring on laid (BP 275, DM 667, FR 2262, Y 53,211).

ROOSKENS, Anton   Dutch 1906-1976
$156* *Dingende Vogel, 1975,* s. Rooskens 75, 148/250, (03-24-93, Kunsthallen, #289), color serigraph (BP 106, DM 255, FR 867, Y 18,329, DK 978).
$314* *Komposition,* s. 73, XIV/XXX, (09-29-92, B. Rasmussen, #358), lithograph in colors (BP 177, DM 444, FR 1513, Y 37,484, DK 1725).
$312* *Komposition, 1976,* s. Rooskens 76, 6/125, (03-24-93, Kunsthallen, #288), color lithograph (BP 211, DM 510, FR 1734, Y 36,658, DK 1955).
$448* *Nuages Bleus,1973,* s., t., d., #98/190, pub. Krikhaar Galerie, margins, good cond., minor handling creases, (05-27-93, Sotheby-Amstrdm, #679), sheet 29¹⁵⁄₁₆ x 21⅝ in., (760 x 550 mm.), color silkscreen on wove (BP 287, DM 719, FR 2423, Y 48,027, G 805).
BI *Printemps, 1972,* s., t., d., #113/200, pub. Krikhaar Galerie w/their blindstamp, margins, good cond., handling creases, est. Dfl. 700/1,000, (05-27-93, Sotheby-Amstrdm, #678), sh 29¹⁵⁄₁₆ x 21⅝ in., (760 x 550 mm.), color silkscreen on wove.
$211* *Spring, 1972,* s. Rooskens 72, 97/140, (09-30-92, Kunsthallen, #260), color lithograph (BP 119, DM 299, FR 1012, Y 25,321, DK 1150).
BI *Untitled, 1973,* s., d., #72/100, margins, good cond., minor handling creases, est. Dfl. 800/1,200, (05-27-93, Sotheby-Amstrdm, #681), sheet 27¹¹⁄₁₆ x 19½ in., (703 x 495 mm.), color silkscreen on wove.

BI *Untitled, 1973,* s., d., #13/100, pub. Krikhaar Galerie w/ their blindstamp, margins, good cond., minor handling creases, waterstaining, est. Dfl. 800/1,200, (05-27-93, Sotheby-Amstrdm, #680), sheet 27¹¹⁄₁₆ x 19½ in., (703 x 495 mm.), color silkscreen on wove.
$384* *Vogelman, 1975,* s., t,. d., #113/200, margins, good cond., (05-27-93, Sotheby-Amstrdm, #682), sheet 10¼ x 7¹³⁄₁₆ in., (260 x 198 mm.), color silkscreen on wove (BP 246, DM 616, FR 2077, Y 41,166, G 690).

ROOT, Samuel
$220* *Portrait Of Elizabeth Risley Naylor Wearing A Plaid Dress With Fringe And Lace Gloves, c. 1859,* (04-07-93, Swann, #164, illus.), photograph, quarter-plate daguerreotype (BP 145, DM 356, FR 1204, Y 24,994).

ROPS, Felicien   Belgian 1833-1898
BI *Accouplement Prehistorique (E.780),* crayon s., est. BP 250/350, (12-10-92, Christie-S. Ken, #36), plate 8¼ x 11¹¹⁄₁₆ in., (210 x 297 mm.), drypoint.
$385* *Collection Of Etchings,* mostly frontispieces, includes Exteens nos. 273, 463, 473, 727, prov., (09-20-92, Hindman, #745), larger 9¾ x 7 in., (24.8 x 17.8 cm.), etchings (BP 225, DM 571, FR 1954, Y 47,584).
$1024* *Cours De Danse: Eleven,* (12-10-92, Christie-S. Ken, #75, illus.), sheet 19¹¹⁄₁₆ x 12⅝ in., (500 x 320 mm.), heliogravure (photoengraving) w/etching and aquatint (BP 660, DM 1620, FR 5532, Y 126,670).
$478* *La Diligence D'Uccle (E.196),* (12-10-92, Christie-S. Ken, #32, illus.), plate 7½ x 12½ in., (190 x 318 mm.), etching (BP 308, DM 756, FR 2582, Y 59,129).
BI *"Le Doigt Dan L'Oeil" (Ramiro 99),* init. "FR", stain, foxing, margin folded, est. $2/300, (10-31-92, Cleveland, #328), 7⅜ x 4⅛ in., (18.7 x 10.5 cm.), etching, drypoint and rocker.
$1740* *Ensemble De 26 Gravures A Sujet Erotique: Twenty-Six,* 8 s. proofs, water and humidity damage, (06-28-93, Loudmer, #112), (BP 1165, DM 2957, FR 9960, Y 184,615).
BI *Exposition Rops, 1896,* lit., est. DM 3,000, (12-05-92, Bassenge, #7622, illus.), 32⅞ x 24⁷⁄₁₆ in., (83.5 x 62 cm.), color lithograph.
$1707* *"La Femme Au Parapluie", "Mon Opinion Politique", "Quand Le Diable Devient Vieux Il Se Fait Critique", "Le Repos Dominical", "Jacque Bonhomme", Elle Va Venir", "J'Ai Peur Qu'On Nous Voie", "Apres", ... "Fin": Twelve,* crayon s., (12-10-92, Christie-S. Ken, #76, illus.), sheet 20½ x 12½ in., (520 x 317 mm.), etching w/drypoint and aquatint (BP 1100, DM 2700, FR 9222, Y 211,158).
$50* *"Le Femme Au Trapeze",* tissue proof before letters, very good cond., (05-15-93, Cleveland, #425), 7⅞ x 4⅞ in., (20 x 12.4 cm.), etching (BP 33, DM 80, FR 270, Y 5543).
$230* *La Foire Aux Amours, 1907,* #No. 45, Gustave Pellet inkstamp, margins, good cond., tear, sheet toned, foxing, tape/hinge remains, surface soiling, creases, notations, (05-19-93, Butterfield, #2092), 10⅜ x 7⅜ in., (264 x 187 mm.), heliogravure (photoengraving) in colors on wove (BP 149, DM 374, FR 1260, Y 25,462).
$939* *Frontispiece Des Oeuvres Inutiles Ou Nuisibles (E.418),* 5th state (of 10), s. pen and ink; ink studies on borders, (12-10-92, Christie-S. Ken, #52, illus.), plate 10½ x 6½ in., (267 x 165 mm.), etching w/drypoint (BP 605, DM 1485, FR 5073, Y 116,155).
$307* *"Le Gaillard D'Arriere" and "Maturite" (E. 367 et 517),* first, s.; second, eight state of 13, full margins, (02-24-93, Picard, #221), etching and aquatint on old laid (BP 214, DM 498, FR 1690, Y 36,024).
$375* *God Of The Mother Superior (E.798),* (12-10-92, Christie-S. Ken, #21), subject 6⁹⁄₁₆ x 5⁹⁄₁₆ in., (166 x 141 mm.), heliogravure (photoengraving) (BP 242, DM 593, FR 2026, Y 46,388).
$512* *Le Joyeux Bidet (E.751),* 1st state (of 2), crayon inits., (12-10-92, Christie-S. Ken, #45, illus.), plate 6⁹⁄₁₆ x 4¹⁵⁄₁₆ in., (167 x 125 mm.), etching (BP 330, DM 810, FR 2766, Y 63,335).
BI *L'Agonie (Exteens IV 945), 1896,* fifth and final state w/ letter, est. FF3/4,000, (06-28-93, Loudmer, #354), 9¹⁄₁₆ x

13³⁄₁₆ in., (230 x 335 mm.), sh 11⁷⁄₁₆ x 13¾ in., (230 x 335 mm.), color engraving.

BI *L'Experte En Dentelles (Exsteens 272), 1876,* red crayon s., mat-staining, staining, untrimmed margins, (02-24-93, Picard, #219), softground etching and drypoint on laid.

$992* *L'Incantation (Rouir 966/II), 1888,* s., i., red pencil s., ded., (06-08-93, Karl/Faber, #384), approx. 14¾ x 9⅝ in., (37.5 x 24.5 cm.), soft-ground etching and aquatint on heliogravure (photoengraving) onsimili-Japan (BP 652, DM 1610, FR 5421, Y 105,364).

$708* *L'Incantation Oder L'Evocation (Mascha 841, Exsteens 436),* red s., prov., (06-04-93, Bassenge, #5791, illus.), 12¹⁵⁄₁₆ x 8⁹⁄₁₆ in., (32.8 x 21.8 cm.), soft-ground etching in brown on imitation Japan (BP 468, DM 1150, FR 3875, Y 76,359).

$268* *"L'Oliverade", 1876 and "Masques Parisiens", 1889 (M. Exsteens, 225,522):* Two, frontispice, first state of six, reddish stains, i., large margins, (04-02-93, Picard, #176), one 15⁹⁄₁₆ x 10¹¹⁄₁₆ in., (39.5 x 27.2 cm.), other 9¹³⁄₁₆ x 6⅞ in., (39.5 x 27.2 cm.), softground etching on Japan (BP 177, DM 431, FR 1463, Y 30,513).

BI *"Les Laveuses" or "Les Lavandieres" (M. Exsteens #521), 1889,* frontispiece from "Souvenirs de Barbizon", (03-22-93, Pescheteau, #77), etching on MBM wove.

$302* *Love Through The Ages (Exsteens 514), c. 1876,* wide margins, init. F.R., (05-27-93, Swann, #241), 7⅛ x 4⅝ in., (18.1 x 11.7 cm.), heliogravure (photoengraving) w/ aquatint (BP 193, DM 485, FR 1633, Y 32,376).

$532* *"La Lyre", "Holocauste" and "Serre-Fesse" (E. 526, 536, 729): Three,* crease, red crayon s., restored, ex-coll., (02-24-93, Picard, #222), etching, aquatint and drypoint on old laid or simili-Japan (BP 371, DM 864, FR 2928, Y 62,427).

$375* *Ma Goutte! (E.319/320):* Two, E.319 2nd state (of 3), E.320 1st state (of 3), s., i. pen and blackink, (12-10-92, Christie-S. Ken, #24), plate 15³⁄₁₆ x 10¹⁵⁄₁₆ in., (385 x 279 mm.), etching (BP 242, DM 593, FR 2026, Y 46,388).

$363* *"Mater Dolorosa", 1893 and "Le Vice Supreme" (M. Exteens, 286, 364):Two,* 1st of 2nd state of 3, num. 5, mono., creases, large margins, (02-03-93, Ader Tajan, #201), etching, drypoint (BP 253, DM 598, FR 2027, Y 45,155).

BI *Messalina (Exsteens 398), 1889,* s., est. DM 1,200, (05-26-93, Lempertz, #479), 12³⁄₁₆ x 18¼ in., (31 x 46.3 cm.), etching (Vernis-mou) on imitated Japan.

BI *Oevres Inutiles Ou Nuisibles,* proof for frontispiece, s. red crayon, pencil i., surface dirt, creasing, est. BP 3/500, (05-20-93, Bonhams-Chelsea, #136), plate 10½ x 6½ in., (26.7 x 16.5 cm.), etching.

$546* *"Le Plus Bel Amour De Don Juan" and "Le Bonheur Dans Le Crime" (E.428/429): Two,* crayon s., (12-10-92, Christie-S. Ken, #41), plate 10¹⁵⁄₁₆ x 8¹⁄₁₆ in., (278 x 205 mm.), heliogravure (photoengraving) (BP 352, DM 864, FR 2950, Y 67,541).

BI *La Prostitution,* s., est. BP 250/350, (12-10-92, Christie-S. Ken, #63), plate 6¹⁵⁄₁₆ x 4¾ in., (176 x 120 mm.), etching w/drypoint.

BI *Rimes De Joie (Mascha 749 IV),* s. in red pencil, est. DM 600, (12-04-92, Bassenge, #6929), 5⅝ x 3¹¹⁄₁₆ in., (14.3 x 9.3 cm.), Retuschierte photogravure on copper print paper.

$273* *Satyriasis (E.781),* 2nd (final) state, s., (12-10-92, Christie-S. Ken, #12), plate 11¹¹⁄₁₆ x 15¾ in., (297 x 400 mm.), drypoint (BP 176, DM 432, FR 1475, Y 33,770).

$132* *Le Semeur De Paraboles,* red pencil s., (10-18-92, Hindman, #524), 13¾ x 9¾ in., (34.9 x 24.8 cm.), etching (BP 81, DM 196, FR 666, Y 15,837).

$578* *"La Sieste", 1879 and "Le Rideau Cramoisi. Les Diaboliques" (M.E., 396, 427):* Two, red crayon s., yellowed, stains, large margins, (04-02-93, Picard, #177), one 9⅛ x 11½ in., (23.2 x 29.2 cm.), other 11⅛ x 8³⁄₁₆ in., (23.2 x 29.2 cm.), softground etching in black on laid (BP 381, DM 929, FR 3155, Y 65,809).

$216* *Le Sphinx (M. Exteens, 425),* 3rd state, annot., mono., s., cracks, creases, collector's stamp, (06-16-93, Ader Tajan, #135), 4¹¹⁄₁₆ x 3⅛ in., (11.9 x 8 cm.), softground etching on Japan (BP 144, DM 359, FR 1203, Y 23,038).

$444* *"Le Tub" and "La Toilette":* Two, #48/65, #61/65, watermarked, (12-10-92, Christie-S. Ken, #65), sheet 17½ x 12⁵⁄₁₆ in., (445 x 312 mm.), etching w/drypoint (BP 286, DM 702, FR 2399, Y 54,923).

BI *Voyage Au Pays Des Vieux Dieux (E. 763),* ink stamp, Lugt 749, margins, good cond., discoloration, surface soiling, notations, image wear, est. $6/800, (10-28-92, Butterfield, #2855), 11 x 8⅛ in., (279 x 206 mm.), softground etching on thick greenish laid paper, watermark.

ROPS, Felicien (after)

BI *La Baie De Nipe (E.1142),* by Prunaire, est. BP 100/150, (12-10-92, Christie-S. Ken, #5), plate 11³⁄₁₆ x 12¹⁵⁄₁₆ in., (284 x 328 mm.), wood engraving.

$2048* *La Dame Au Cochon (E.853),* by A. Bertrand, 6th (final) state, #96 in pen and ink, (12-10-92, Christie-S. Ken, #53), plate 27¹⁄₁₆ x 17¹¹⁄₁₆ in., (688 x 450 mm.), heliogravure (photoengraving) p. in colors, w/etching and aquatint (BP 1320, DM 3239, FR 11,064, Y 253,340).

$1536* *La Dame Aux Cochon (E.853),* by A. Bertrand, 6th (final) state, (12-10-92, Christie-S. Ken, #51), sheet 26⁹⁄₁₆ x 17¹¹⁄₁₆ in., (675 x 450 mm.), heliogravure (photoengraving) p. in colors, w/etching and aquatint (BP 990, DM 2430, FR 8298, Y 190,005).

BI *La Deche, 1909,* full margins, good cond., staining, surface soiling, creases, notations, glue remains, est. $2/300, (10-28-92, Butterfield, #2856), 18½ x 11¼ in., (470 x 286 mm.), color etching, roulette and heliogravure (photoengraving) on wove.

$546* *L'Incantation (E.860),* #133/200, By A. Bertrand, (12-10-92, Christie-S. Ken, #34), plate 16¹⁵⁄₁₆ x 10¹³⁄₁₆ in., (430 x 275 mm.), heliogravure (photoengraving) p. in colors (BP 352, DM 864, FR 2950, Y 67,541).

$1877* *La Mere Aux Satyrions (E.858): Fifteen,* by A. Bertrand, (12-10-92, Christie-S. Ken, #54), sheet 22⁷⁄₁₆ x 15¹¹⁄₁₆ in., (570 x 398 mm.), heliogravure (photoengraving) (BP 1210, DM 2969, FR 10,140, Y 232,187).

ROSA, Salvator   Italian 1615-1673

$418* *Apollo And The Cumaean Sibyl (B. 17),* 3rd state, large margins, edge folded, good cond., (10-27-92, Phillips-London, #35), plate 13⅛ x 8½ in., (333 x 216 mm.), etching on thick laid (BP 264, DM 641, FR 2174, Y 51,131).

$403* *Apollon Et La Sybille Cumee (Bartsch, vol. 20, 18), 1661,* stains, dirt spots, fold, (05-15-93, Loudmer, #27, illus.), 13¼ x 8⁹⁄₁₆ in., (337 x 218 mm.), sh 13¾ x 9⅛ in., (337 x 218 mm.), etching and drypoint on laid (BP 262, DM 648, FR 2178, Y 44,674).

$5175* *The Fall Of The Giants (B. 21; W. 115), c. 1663,* 2nd (final) state, tone, watermark, margins, center fold, creases, glue stains, good cond., The Suida Manning Coll., (05-13-93, Sotheby-NY, #285, illus.), 28⅜ x 18⅝ in., (720 x 472 mm.), etching (BP 3397, DM 8356, FR 28,186, Y 577,760).

$385* *"Glaucus And Scylla" (B., 20; R., 92; W., 101),* s. S. Rosa in plate, ident. on label verso, stamps, collector's annot., very good cond., prov., (03-12-93, Skinner, #3, illus.), 13⅝ x 9⅛ in., (34.6 x 23.2 cm.), etching on laid (BP 269, DM 641, FR 2179, Y 45,374).

$1011* *Jason Und Der Drachen (B. 18; Wallace 118), c. 1663,* watermark, (12-04-92, Bassenge, #6417), 13⁷⁄₁₆ x 8½ in., (34.1 x 21.6 cm.), etching (BP 648, DM 1610, FR 5462, Y 126,217).

$1155* *Der Meditierende Demokrit (B. 7; Wallace 104 II), 1662,* watermark, (12-04-92, Bassenge, #6416, illus.), 17¹⁵⁄₁₆ x 10⅞ in., (45.6 x 27.6 cm.), etching (BP 741, DM 1839, FR 6240, Y 144,195).

$55* *"Soldato Con Lancia E Scudo" and "Uomo Che Cammina Indicando Con La Destra" (Rotili 37 & 78):* Two, (03-24-93, Grogan, #10), each 5½ x 3¹¹⁄₁₆ in., (14 x 9.4 cm.), etching (BP 37, DM 90, FR 306, Y 6462).

ROSE, David   b. 1936

$24* *Sunflower 1 (1965),* s. David Rose, #8/25, (08-11-92, L. Joel, #31G), 14¹⁵⁄₁₆ x 20½ in., (38 x 52 cm.), color screenprint (BP 12, DM 35, FR 119, Y 3073, A$ 33).

ROSE, Iver   American 1899-1972

$55* *"Man Standing",* s. Iver Rose, num. 2/60, very good cond.?, (11-21-92, Bakker, #34), sight 16 x 10 in., (40.6

x 25.4 cm.), lithograph (BP 36, DM 88, FR 295, Y 6840).

ROSE, Ruth Starr   American b. 1887
$30* *"At The Beach", c. 1945,* good cond., prov., (05-15-93, Cleveland, #277), 15 x 18 in., (38.1 x 45.7 cm.), color silkscreen (BP 20, DM 48, FR 162, Y 3326).
$55* *Regatta,* margins, s. Ruth Starr Rose, d. 40, (10-24-92, Collins, #19), 9⅝ x 13¾ in., (24.4 x 34.9 cm.), lithograph (BP 34, DM 84, FR 285, Y 6707).

ROSEMANN, J.
$55* *"Rothenborg",* annot., t., s., (02-27-93, Dunning, #117), 10½ x 8¼ in., (26.7 x 21 cm.), color etching and aquatint (BP 39, DM 90, FR 307, Y 6493).

ROSEN, James
$259* *Angel, 1984,* s., d., annot. 18.111.84, good cond.?, (05-19-93, Butterfield, #2316), sh 4⅛ x 5⅞ in., (105 x 149 mm.), watercolor on wove (BP 168, DM 421, FR 1418, Y 28,673).

ROSENBERG, C., Engraver
$60* *H.C.S. Macqueen Off The Start, 26th January 1832,* margins, foxed, (01-14-93, Bonhams, #128), plate 17¼ x 22½ in., (43.8 x 57.2 cm.), hand-colored aquatint (BP 39, DM 98, FR 332, Y 7564).

ROSENBERG, Louis   American 1890-1983
BI *"Construction Of The New Cleveland Food Terminal", c. 1929-30,* s., good cond., est. $150-200, (10-31-92, Cleveland, #205), 7⅝ x 11⅜ in., (19.4 x 28.9 cm.), etching.
BI *Cutting Hay At Mt. Vernon,* s., est. $1/150, (12-11-92, DuMouchelle, #2395), 10 x 13 in., (25.4 x 33 cm.), etching.
$160* *"Mediacal Arts & Builders Exchange Buildings", "Cut South Of CentralAvenue" and "Independence Road Bridge", 1929:* Three, s., excell. cond., (05-15-93, Cleveland, #288), each 7¾ x 11⅜ in., (19.7 x 28.9 cm.), etching (BP 104, DM 257, FR 865, Y 17,736).
$85* *"Medical Arts & Builders Exchange From Old Food Market", 1929,* s., excell. cond., (05-15-93, Cleveland, #286), 7¾ x 11½ in., (19.7 x 29.2 cm.), etching (BP 55, DM 137, FR 459, Y 9422).
$160* *"New Food Terminal", Station And Prospect Avenue" and "Demolition OfPower Plant", 1928:* Three, s., excell. cond., (05-15-93, Cleveland, #282), 7¾ x 11⅜ in., (19.7 x 28.9 cm.), etching (BP 104, DM 257, FR 865, Y 17,736).
$95* *"New Track Level, South Of Huron Road", 1929,* s., excell. cond., (05-15-93, Cleveland, #285), 7¾ x 1½ in., (19.7 x 3.8 cm.), etching (BP 62, DM 153, FR 514, Y 10,531).
$140* *"Old Food Market", 1928,* s., excell. cond., (05-15-93, Cleveland, #283), 7¾ x 11½ in., (19.7 x 29.2 cm.), etching (BP 91, DM 225, FR 757, Y 15,519).
$160* *"Ontario St. Grading And Temporary Ramps", "Kinsman Avenue TemporaryBridge" and "New Right Of Way West-East 49th St.", 1929:* Three, s., excell. cond., (05-15-93, Cleveland, #287), each 7¾ x 11⅜ in., (19.7 x 28.9 cm.), etching (BP 104, DM 257, FR 865, Y 17,736).
$250* *"Ontario Street Truck Grading", "New Viaduct" and "Steel Frame Of Southwest Wing Of Tower", 1928:* Three, s., excell. cond., (05-15-93, Cleveland, #281, illus.), each 7¾ x 11⅜ in., (19.7 x 28.9 cm.), etching (BP 163, DM 402, FR 1351, Y 27,713).
$85* *"St. Peter's, Rome" (Mcmillan 2) and "Moorish Archway, Toledo" (Mc. 11), 1921 and 1923:* Two, s., very good cond., (05-15-93, Cleveland, #278), one 5⅞ x 3⅞ in., (14.9 x 9.8 cm.), other 8⅞ x 6½ in., (14.9 x 9.8 cm.), etching (BP 55, DM 137, FR 459, Y 9422).
$85* *"Terminal Tower From The West Third St. Bridge", 1929,* s., excell. cond., (05-15-93, Cleveland, #284), 7¾ x 11½ in., (19.7 x 29.2 cm.), etching (BP 55, DM 137, FR 459, Y 9422).
$120* *"Terminal Tower From West Third St. Bridge", 1928,* s., excell. cond., (05-15-93, Cleveland, #280), 11½ x 7¾ in., (29.2 x 19.7 cm.), etching (BP 78, DM 193, FR 649, Y 13,302).
$120* *"Terminal Tower From Wheeling Station", 1928,* s., excell. cond., (05-15-93, Cleveland, #279), 11½ x 7¾ in.,

(29.2 x 19.7 cm.), etching (BP 78, DM 193, FR 649, Y 13,302).

ROSENQUIST, James   American 1933-1991
$715* *1-2-3 Outside, 1972,* s., d., t., #20/70, blindstamp pub. Petersburg Press, full margins, very good cond., rubbed area, (10-28-92, Butterfield, #3094), 31 x 20⅛ in., (787 x 511 mm.), color lithograph w/embossing on German Etching paper (BP 456, DM 1104, FR 3749, Y 87,730).
$3450* *Alphabet Avalanche, 1979,* s. in crayon, d., t., #83/85, blindstamp of p., Vermillion Editions,Ltd., co-pub. by artist and Bird Island Publishing, good cond., creases, soiling, (02-11-93, Sotheby-NY, #430, illus.), sheet 22¼ x 44⁵⁄₁₆ in., (56.5 x 112.5 cm.), color lithograph w/die-cut on Twinrocker handmade (BP 2434, DM 5715, FR 19,339, Y 415,913).
$660* *Art Gallery (Fine and Corlett 209), 1971,* s., d., num. 1/30, USF blindstamp, full sheet, surface soiling, creasing, skinned spots, (09-19-92, Christie-E, #196), sheet 30 x 22¼ in., (762 x 565 mm.), lithograph in yellow and black on Rives (BP 380, DM 988, FR 3385, Y 82,233).
BI *Artist's Rights, 1975,* s., d., annot. for Artists', #XXXIX/L, blindstamp publisher, Styria Studio, good cond.?, surface abrasion, image, faint staining, est. $2/3,000, (05-19-93, Butterfield, #2319), 30 x 22 in., (762 x 559 mm.), silkscreen w/collage in colors on wove.
$605* *Artist's Rights, 1975,* s., d., num. 35/125, annot. for Artists, blindstamp, apparently goodcond., (02-24-93, Butterfield, #3131), 30 x 22¼ in., (762 x 565 mm.), silkscreen in colors on wove (BP 422, DM 982, FR 3330, Y 70,993).
$1210* *Artists Rights Today (V. 74), 1975,* s., d., i. for Artists, #11/125, pub. Artists' Rights and w/Styria Studio blindstamp, excell. cond., (11-09-92, Christie-NY, #394), sheet 30⅛ x 22⅜ in., (765 x 568 mm.), color screenprint on Arches (BP 800, DM 1932, FR 6526, Y 150,161).
BI *Balls, 1990,* s., d. 1990, #113/130, est. FF8,000/10,000, (05-27-93, Briest, #173), 37¹³⁄₁₆ x 37¹³⁄₁₆ in., (96 x 96 cm.), color serigraph.
BI *Beach (G. 1015), 1982,* s., d., t., num. 51/59, blindstamp of pub. Gemini G.E.L., full margins, good cond., est. $1/1,500, (02-24-93, Butterfield, #3136, illus.), 23½ x 16¼ in., (597 x 413 mm.), etching & aquatint on Somerset Satin.
$17,250* *The Bird Of Paradise Approaches The Hot Water Planet, 1989,* s., d., t., #23/28, blindstamp, pub. Tyler Graphics, Ltd., good cond. ?, (05-15-93, Sotheby-NY, #1170, illus.), sheet 97 x 84½ in., (246.4 x 214.6 cm.), colored and pressed paper pulp, w/lithography collage (BP 11,216, DM 27,747, FR 93,243, Y 1,912,205).
BI *"Black Tie",* s., est. $2/4,000, (09-24-92, Mystic, #43), 37 x 74 in., (94 x 188 cm.), colored lithograph.
BI *Black Triangle, 1978,* #70/78, pencil t. 2 state, s., d., est. DM 2,400, (11-20-92, Lempertz, #818), sh 22¾ x 39⅞ in., (57.8 x 101.3 cm.), etching on Velin.
BI *Black Triangle, 1978,* s., #70/78, t., i. 2nd state, s., d., est. DM 2,200-, (05-27-93, Lempertz, #976, illus.), 17¹¹⁄₁₆ x 35¹³⁄₁₆ in., (45 x 91 cm.), etching on wove.
BI *Caught One, Lost One, For The Fast Student, 1989,* s., d., t., #9/92, pub. blindstamp, Tyler Graphics, Ltd., full margins, good cond., est. $7/9,000, (11-07-92, Sotheby-NY, #754, illus.), sheet 54½ x 37¾ in., (138.4 x 95.9 cm.), lithograph p. in colors w/colored paper pulp collage.
$5175* *Caught One, Lost One, For The Fast Student, 1989,* s., d., t., #9/92, blindstamp, pub. Tyler Graphics, Ltd., full margins, good cond. ?, (05-15-93, Sotheby-NY, #1169, illus.), sheet 54½ x 37¾ in., (138.4 x 95.9 cm.), lithograph in colors w/colored paper pulp collage (BP 3365, DM 8324, FR 27,973, Y 573,661).
$1100* *Circle Of Confusion And Lightbulb, 1960,* s., d., crease, (12-08-92, Swann, #271, illus.), 20 x 20 in., (50.8 x 50.8 cm.), offset color lithograph (BP 689, DM 1713, FR 5839, Y 136,341).
BI *Circles Of Confusion, 1965,* from Eleven Pop Artists, Vol. 1, s., #5/200, pub. Original Editions,good cond.?, creases, est. $800/1,200, (12-12-92, Weschler, #161, illus.), 24 x 20 in., (61 x 50.8 cm.), color silkscreen.

$550* *Circles Of Confusion, From Eleven Pop Artists Vol. 1, 1965,* s., num. 5/200, pub. Original Editions, good cond., minor handling creases, (05-22-93, Weschler, #219), 24 x 20 in., (61 x 50.8 cm.), silkscreen in colors (BP 356, DM 894, FR 3009, Y 60,639).

$303* *Circular Configuration With GE,* s., num. 167/200, (11-12-92, Freemn/Fine Art, #185), 23½ x 19½ in., (59.7 x 49.5 cm.), screen print (BP 199, DM 480, FR 1619, Y 37,570).

BI *Cold Rolled (V. 66), 1974,* s., d., t., #49/60, pub. J.R. Inc./University of South Florida, goodcond.?, est. $3/5,000, (10-28-92, Butterfield, #3097), 34 x 73 in., (86.4 x 185.4 cm.), color lithograph w/silkscreen and collage on Arches.

BI *Cold Rolled, 1974,* s., d., t., #49/60, pub. J.R. Inc./University South Florida, apparently good cond., est. $2,5/3,500, (02-24-93, Butterfield, #3130), 34 x 73 in., (86.4 x 185.4 cm.), lithograph w/silkscreen & collage in colors on Arches.

$715* *Delivery Hat (V. 21; F. and C. 211), 1971,* s., d., i. U.S.F., num. XXVIII, USF blindstamps, full margins, excell. cond., (09-19-92, Christie-E, #197), sheet 6¼ x 4¼ in., (159 x 108 mm.), lithograph in colors on Rives (BP 411, DM 1071, FR 3667, Y 89,085).

$770* *"Derriere L'Etoile",* s., (09-24-92, Mystic, #42), 37 x 74 in., (94 x 188 cm.), colored lithograph (BP 451, DM 1141, FR 3875, Y 92,626).

$424* *Divers Line, 1979,* s., d., #5/78, i. 2nd state, plate t., (06-12-93, Hauswedell/Nolt, #364), 17^11^/16 x 35¾ in., (45 x 90.8 cm.), etching on thick wove (BP 278, DM 690, FR 2319, Y 44,617).

$1083* *Divers Line, 1979,* 2. state, s., d., num., (11-28-92, Schoppmann, #739), 17¹¹⁄₁₆ x 35⅝ in., (45 x 90.5 cm.), etching on handmade (BP 715, DM 1725, FR 5857, Y 134,785).

$550* *Earth And Moon (V. 28; F. and C. 212), 1971,* s., t., d., num. 11/70, USF blindstamps, full margins, staining, old-tape, (09-19-92, Christie-E, #198), borderline 18½ x 17½ in., (470 x 445 mm.), lithograph in colors on wove (BP 316, DM 824, FR 2821, Y 68,527).

$5175* *Electrical Nymphs On A Non-Objective Ground, 1984,* s., t., d., #5/30, ULAE seal, full margins, surface scrapes, excell.cond., the Late M. Anwar Kamal, M.D. Coll., (05-11-93, Christie-NY, #551, illus.), sheet 40 x 40 in., (101.6 x 101.6 cm.), color lithograph on white laminated plastic (BP 3304, DM 8152, FR 27,468, Y 569,244).

BI *F-111, "North", "South", "East" and "West" (Varian 56), 1974: Four,* s., t., d., #13/75, pub. Petersburg Press, blindstamps, full margins, good cond., shrink-wrapped, est. $15/20,000, (11-09-92, Christie-NY, #393, illus.), North and South 36½ x 70¼ in., (92.7 x 178.4 cm.), East and West 36½ x 75¼ in., (92.7 x 178.4 cm.), color lithograph and screenprint on 4 sheets of Arches.

$1495* *F-111, 1965,* s., d., pub. Leo Castelli Gallery, full margins, good cond., creases, soiling, (02-11-93, Sotheby-NY, #423, illus.), 27¹⁵⁄₁₆ x 22¹⁄₁₆ in., (710 x 560 mm.), color offset lithograph (BP 1055, DM 2476, FR 8380, Y 180,229).

BI *Federal Spending, 2nd State, 1978,* s., d., t., annot. 2 state, #55/78, margins, good cond.?, est. $5/700, (05-19-93, Butterfield, #2322), 17⅝ x 36 in., (448 x 914 mm.), etching and aquatint in red on wove.

$1082* *Flame Out For Picasso, 1973,* #H.C. 5/15, pencil num., t., s., (11-20-92, Lempertz, #817, illus.), sh 30⅛ x 22½ in., (76.5 x 57.2 cm.), color lithograph on Arches-Velin (BP 712, DM 1725, FR 5811, Y 134,560).

$770* *"Flying Stone",* (09-24-92, Mystic, #39), 37 x 74 in., (94 x 188 cm.), colored lithograph (BP 451, DM 1141, FR 3875, Y 92,626).

$660* *For Artists, 1975,* s., d., t., #63/125, blindstamp p. Styria Studio, very good cond.?, (10-28-92, Butterfield, #3098), 30 x 22¼ in., (762 x 565 mm.), color silkscreen on wove (BP 421, DM 1019, FR 3461, Y 80,982).

BI *For Love,* s., #152/200, margins, good cond., est. BP 5/700, (12-03-92, Sotheby-London, #791, illus.), 35¼ x 26½ in., (895 x 675 mm.), silkscreen in colors on wove.

BI *For The Young Artist, 1991,* s., t., d., num. 38/80, Tyler Graphics blindstamp, full sheet, excell. cond., est. $1/1,500, (09-19-92, Christie-E, #203), sheet 35 x 36 in., (889 x 914 mm.), screenprint in colors on wove.

$1463* *A Free For All, 1976,* s., d., num., t., blindstamp, (12-02-92, Dorling, #2977), 26³⁄₁₆ x 20¹¹⁄₁₆ in., (66.5 x 52.5 cm.), serigraph and lithograph w/collage on cardboard (BP 944, DM 2301, FR 7853, Y 182,033).

$660* *A Free For All, 1976,* s., t., d., #16/175, blindstamp pub. Trans World Art, very good cond.?, (10-28-92, Butterfield, #3100), 26 x 19½ in., (660 x 495 mm.), color lithograph on wove (BP 421, DM 1019, FR 3461, Y 80,982).

$1540* *From "F-111", 1965,* s., d., good cond.?, (12-08-92, Swann, #272, illus.), 22 x 27½ in., (55.9 x 69.9 cm.), offset photo-lithograph in color (BP 965, DM 2398, FR 8174, Y 190,878).

BI *Gravity Feed, 1978,* #5/78, s., t., d., est. SF 2,2/2,800, 575 x 1010mm, (09-04-92, Germann, #65, illus.), color etching and aquatint.

BI *Gravity Feed, 1978,* #5/78, s., t., d., est. SF 1,8/2,200, 575mm x 1010 mm, (04-21-93, Germann, #193), color etching and aquatint.

BI *"Gravity Field", 1978,* s., d., num., 2 state, est. DM 1400, (12-01-92, Karl/Faber, #1151), 17½ x 35⅝ in., (44.5 x 90.5 cm.), etching and aquatint in brownish/black on thick wove.

BI *Hey! Let's Go For A Ride (V. 43), 1972,* s., t., d., #74/75, pub. Petersburg Press, blindstamp, p. Maurice Sanchez, full margins, creasing, very good cond., the Late M. Anwar Kamal, M.D. Coll., est. $4/4,500, (05-11-93, Christie-NY, #549, illus.), sheet 31¼ x 30¼ in., (794 x 768 mm.), color lithograph on Hodgkins hand-made Woohe Hole.

$2750* *Hey! Let's Go For A Ride, 1972,* s., d., t., #68/75, blindstamp pub. Petersburg Press, full margins, very good cond.?, (10-28-92, Butterfield, #3095, illus.), 22½ x 22½ in., (572 x 572 mm.), color lithograph on Woohe Hole paper (BP 1752, DM 4247, FR 14,421, Y 337,423).

$880* *Highway Trust, 1978,* s., d., #77/78, full margins, very good cond., (10-28-92, Butterfield, #3101), 18½ x 44 in., (47 x 111.8 cm.), color lithograph on wove (BP 561, DM 1359, FR 4615, Y 107,975).

$546* *Highway Trust, 1978,* s., t., d., #12/78, margins, very good cond.?, (05-19-93, Butterfield, #2321), 18½ x 44 in., (47 x 111.8 cm.), lithograph in colors on wove (BP 354, DM 888, FR 2990, Y 60,445).

BI *Highway Trust, 1978,* s., t., d., num. 12/78, margins, apparently very good cond., est. $8/1,200, (02-24-93, Butterfield, #3134), 18½ x 44 in., (47 x 111.8 cm.), lithograph in colors on wove.

$2669* *"Horse Blinders (East)", 1972,* 4/85, blindstamp Styria Studio, (05-12-93, AB Stockholm, #7044, illus.), 25¹³⁄₁₆ x 67¹¹⁄₁₆ in., (65.5 x 172 cm.), color lithograph w/collage (BP 1743, DM 4306, FR 14,505, Y 297,979, SK 19,800).

$1100* *Horse Blinders Flash Card (Varian 10, Sparks 12), 1969,* s., t., d., i., num. 2/5, ULAE blindstamp, full margins, pressure marks, inherent paper flaws, creasing, (09-19-92, Christie-E, #193), sheet 17½ x 22⅝ in., (445 x 575 mm.), lithograph in colors on wove, watermark (BP 633, DM 1647, FR 5641, Y 137,055).

BI *Horse Blinders: "North", "South", "East" and "West" (V. 36), 1972: Four,* s., t., d., #29/85, pub. Styria Studio blindstamp, full margins, good cond.?, surface scuffs, exhib., est. $10/15,000, (12-12-92, Weschler, #162, illus.), each approx. 36 x 66 in., (91.4 x 167.6 cm.), color lithograph w/collage on Arches.

$632* *Hot Lake, 2 State, 1978,* #58/78, s., d., (04-21-93, Germann, #706), 20⅞ x 38⅜ in., (530 x 975 mm.), etching in red (BP 410, DM 1010, FR 3416, Y 69,966, SF 920).

$1650* *Iris Lake (V. 69), 1975,* s., d. '1974', t., i. 'U.S.F. VI/XX', artist's proof, pub. blindstamp, University of South Florida, full margins, good cond., (11-07-92, Sotheby-NY, #753, illus.), sheet 36 x 74 in., (91.4 x 188 cm.), lithograph p. in colors (BP 1079, DM 2635, FR 8904, Y 203,653).

$110* *Jazz,* (02-14-93, Hanzel, #700), 26 x 26 in., (66 x 66 cm.), lithographic poster (BP 77, DM 182, FR 617, Y 13,266).

$93* *"Jazz Aspen, Easter 26 Mars 1967"*, inits. J.R. in plate, (08-18-92, Encans, #134), 25³⁄₁₆ x 25³⁄₁₆ in., (64 x 64 cm.), offset poster (BP 48, DM 135, FR 459, Y 11,725, C$ 111).

BI *Jazz, 1967,* est. FF1,800/2,000, (03-31-93, Briest, #E94), 26⅛ x 26⅛ in., (66.4 x 66.4 cm.), color offset.

$40* *Jazz, 1967,* (05-27-93, Briest, #174), 26⅛ x 26⅛ in., (66.4 x 66.4 cm.), color offset (BP 26, DM 64, FR 216, Y 4288).

$2944* *"The Light That Won't Fail I"*, s., 1972, 64/75, (05-25-93, AB Stockholm, #59), 19⅞ x 26³⁄₁₆ in., (50.5 x 66.5 cm.), lithograph in colors (BP 1908, DM 4795, FR 16,140, Y 321,784, SK 4290).

$3095* *"Marco Polo Returns", 1978,* s., 7/23, AP, (05-25-93, AB Stockholm, #60), 17¹¹⁄₁₆ x 35⅝ in., (45 x 90.5 cm.), aquatint in colors (BP 2006, DM 5041, FR 16,968, Y 338,288, SK 4510).

$5520* *Marilyn (V. 59), 1974,* s., t., d., #41/75, pub. Petersburg Press, full margins, surface nick, staining, very good cond., (05-11-93, Christie-NY, #550, illus.), sheet 41¾ x 29¾ in., (106 x 75.6 cm.), color lithograph on BFK Rives (BP 3524, DM 8696, FR 29,299, Y 607,194).

BI *Marilyn (Varian 59), 1974,* s., d., t., #7/75, pub. Petersburg Press, full margins, good cond., est. $10/12,000, (05-15-93, Sotheby-NY, #1167, illus.), 35⅝ x 27⅛ in., (90.5 x 68.9 cm.), lithograph in colors.

$330* *Miles (Graphicstudio 221), 1975,* s., t., d., #91/200, blindstamp pub. Graohicstudio, U.S.F., good cond.?, prop. San Francisco Art Institute, (10-28-92, Butterfield, #3099), 30⅛ x 22½ in., (765 x 572 mm.), color silkscreen w/painted additions on Arches (BP 210, DM 510, FR 1730, Y 40,491).

BI *More Points On A Bachelor's Tie, 1978,* #33/78, pencil t. 2nd state, s., d., est. DM 2,400, (11-20-92, Lempertz, #820), sh 22¾ x 39¹⁵⁄₁₆ in., (57.8 x 101.5 cm.), etching on Velin.

BI *More Points On A Bachelor's Tie, 1978,* s., #33/78, t., i. 2nd state, s., d., est. DM 2,300-, (05-27-93, Lempertz, #975), 17¹¹⁄₁₆ x 35¹³⁄₁₆ in., (45 x 91 cm.), etching on wove.

$880* *"More Points On A Bachelor's Tie, 2nd State" and "Rouge Pad, 2nd State", 1978: Two,* s., d., t., #8/10 AP and #64/78, More Points w/camel blindstamp, pub.Multiples, Inc., full margins, good cond., creases, surface soiling, (02-24-93, Butterfield, #3246), one 17¾ x 35¾ in., (45.1 x 90.8 cm.), other 22¾ x 39⅞ in., (45.1 x 90.8 cm.), etching w/aquatint in yellow and blue on wove (BP 614, DM 1429, FR 4843, Y 103,262).

$514* *More Points On A Bachelor's Tie, 2nd State, 1978,* #3/10 A.P., s., (04-21-93, Germann, #705), 21⁷⁄₁₆ x 38³⁄₁₆ in., (545 x 970 mm.), etching in yellow (BP 334, DM 822, FR 2778, Y 56,902, SF 748).

$880* *My Mind In A Glass Of Water,* s., d. 1972, t., #56/125, prov., (05-16-93, Hindman, #610), 22½ x 17¾ in., (57.2 x 45.1 cm.), color lithograph (BP 572, DM 1415, FR 4757, Y 97,550).

BI *My Mind Is A Glass Of Water (V. 31), 1977,* s., t., d., i. P.P. X, pub. Phoenix House, full margins, surface scratch, excell. cond., est. $1,2/1,800, (09-19-92, Christie-E, #199), borderline 22¾ x 18⅞ in., (578 x 479 mm.), lithograph in colors on Arches.

$1045* *My Mind Is A Glass Of Water, 1972,* s., d., t., num. 114/125, pub. Phoenix House, margins, apparently very good cond., (02-24-93, Butterfield, #3129), 22¾ x 17⅞ in., (578 x 454 mm.), lithograph in colors on Arches watercolor (BP 729, DM 1696, FR 5751, Y 122,624).

$275* *New York Says It,* s., num. 138/250, d. 1983, repair in image, (11-12-92, Freemn/Fine Art, #185A), 27½ x 31½ in., (69.9 x 80 cm.), screenprint (BP 181, DM 436, FR 1470, Y 34,098).

$3581* *Night Transition, 1985,* s., d., t., #6/35, pub. U.L.A.E., margins, good cond., (12-03-92, Sotheby-London, #789, illus.), 53 x 34⅝ in., (134.6 x 87.9 cm.), lithograph in colors on Arches (BP 2310, DM 5631, FR 19,222, Y 445,564).

BI *Off The Continental Divide (V. 61), 1973-74,* s., d., t., i. 'H.C. 4/8', pub. blindstamp, ULAE, good cond., est. $20/30,000, (11-07-92, Sotheby-NY, #751, illus.), sheet 42½ x 78⅜ in., (108 x 199.1 cm.), lithograph p. in colors on ivory wove Japan.

$14,950* *Off The Continental Divide (V. 61), 1973-74,* s., d., t., #13/43, blindstamp, pub. ULAE, good cond. ?, (05-15-93, Sotheby-NY, #1168, illus.), 42½ x 79⅛ in., (108 x 201 cm.), lithograph in colors on ivory wove Japan paper (BP 9720, DM 24,047, FR 80,811, Y 1,657,244).

$1422* *On Stage, 1981,* #52/59, s., d., t., (04-21-93, Germann, #707, illus.), 33¼ x 26¼ in., (845 x 667 mm.), color aquatint (BP 923, DM 2273, FR 7686, Y 157,423, SF 2070).

$303* *One Million Tons Per Square Inch, 2nd State, 1978,* s., d., annot. 2nd state, #27/78, pub. Marion Goodman, margins, goodcond., (10-28-92, Butterfield, #3102), 17¾ x 35¾ in., (451 x 908 mm.), etching w/aquatint on wove (BP 193, DM 468, FR 1589, Y 37,178).

BI *Other Great Cities, 1978,* s., d., t., num. 73/78, blindstamp, full margins, good cond., crease,est. $9/1,200, (02-24-93, Butterfield, #3133), 17⅝ x 35¾ in., (448 x 908 mm.), etching & aquatint in colors on wove.

$4950* *Paper Clip (Varian 60), 1974,* s., d., t., i. 'AP IX', pub. Petersburg Press, full margins, good cond., (11-07-92, Sotheby-NY, #750, illus.), sheet 36⅜ x 69¼ in., (92.4 x 175.9 cm.), lithograph p. in colors on Arches 320 (BP 3236, DM 7904, FR 26,713, Y 610,960).

BI *Paris Review, 1968,* s., d., #61/150, good cond.?, (06-30-93, Sotheby-London, #919), 29¼ x 29¼ in., (743 x 743 mm.), color lithograph.

BI *Path From The Wall, 1977,* s., t., d., num. 25/78, pub. Multiples, Inc., blindstamp, full sheet, good cond., est. $2/3,000, (05-22-93, Weschler, #220, illus.), 23 x 40 in., (58.4 x 101.6 cm.), hand-colored etching and aquatint w/embossing on Arches.

$690* *Push Buttons (V. 34), 1972,* s., d., t., i. A.P. 18/20, pub. Petersburg Press, full margins, goodcond., creases, (02-11-93, Sotheby-NY, #426), 21¼ x 27¹⁄₁₆ in., (539 x 687 mm.), lithograph (BP 487, DM 1143, FR 3868, Y 83,183).

BI *Pyramid Between Two Dry Lakes, 1978,* s., d., t., #74/78, blindstamp, full margins, good cond., surface scuff in image, surface soiling, est. $7/900, (02-24-93, Butterfield, #3247), 17⅞ x 36 in., (454 x 914 mm.), aquatint in colors w/hand coloring on wove.

BI *Pyramid Between Two Dry Lakes, 1978,* #42/78, pencil t., s., d., est. DM 2,800, (11-20-92, Lempertz, #819), sh 22⁹⁄₁₆ x 39¹³⁄₁₆ in., (57.3 x 101.2 cm.), color etching on Velin.

BI *Pyramid Between Two Dry Lakes, 1978,* #42/78, t., s., d., est. DM 2,200-, (05-27-93, Lempertz, #974), 17¹¹⁄₁₆ x 35¾ in., (45 x 90.8 cm.), watercolor color etching on wove.

BI *Rinse, 1978,* s., d., t., num. 29/78, blindstamp, full margins, good cond., creases, rubbed area, est. $8/1,000, (02-24-93, Butterfield, #3135), 17¾ x 35⅞ in., (451 x 911 mm.), etching & aquatint in colors on wove.

$2200* *Roll Down (Sparks 8), 1964-66,* s., d. '1965-66', t., #10/29, pub. blindstamp, ULAE, good cond., creases, (11-07-92, Sotheby-NY, #749, illus.), sheet 38⅝ x 29 in., (981 x 737 mm.), lithograph p. in colors (BP 1438, DM 3513, FR 11,873, Y 271,538).

BI *"Rouge Pad", 1978,* s., d. Rosenquist 1978, #73/78, t., annot. 2 state, shrink wrapped, good cond., creases. est. $800/1,200, (03-12-93, Skinner, #115, illus.), 17⅝ x 35¾ in., (44.8 x 90.8 cm.), etching w/aquatint on wove.

$1941* *Rouge Pad, 1978,* s., d., t., 57/78, 570mm x 1010mm, (10-14-92, Germann, #39, illus.), color etching and aquatint (BP 1139, DM 2841, FR 9633, Y 235,216, SF 2530).

BI *"Rouge Pad, State II", 1978,* Multiples Inc., pub., s., d., Rosenquist 1978, t., #73/78, very goodcond., creasing, est. $1,5/2,500, (01-02-93, Skinner, #211, illus.), sheet 22½ x 40 in., (57.2 x 101.6 cm.), color lithograph in blue and pink.

$403* *See-Saw, 1968,* s., d., t., #67/100, blindstamp publisher, Richard Feigen Graphics, p., good cond.?, tear, pressure mark in image, surface soiling, (05-19-93, Butterfield, #2317), 24⅛ x 34¾ in., (613 x 883 mm.), silkscreen in color on wove (BP 262, DM 655, FR 2207, Y 44,614).

$1210* *Sight Seeing (V. 33), 1972,* s., t., d., num. 34/75, pub. Petersburg Press, full margins, excell.cond., (09-19-92, Christie-E, #200, illus.), sheet 37 x 30¾ in., (940 x 781 mm.), lithograph in colors on wove (BP 696, DM 1812, FR 6205, Y 150,760).

$3472* *"Sight-Seeing", 1972,* s., 63/75, (05-25-93, AB Stockholm, #58), 22 7/16 x 28 9/16 in., (57 x 72.5 cm.), lithograph in colors (BP 2250, DM 5655, FR 19,035, Y 379,495, SK 5060).

$805* *Sightseeing (Varian 33), 1972,* s., d., t., I. A.P. 11/20, pub. Petersburg Press, full margins, goodcond., creases, soiling, (02-11-93, Sotheby-NY, #425, illus.), 22 7/16 x 28⅝ in., (570 x 727 mm.), color lithograph (BP 568, DM 1333, FR 4512, Y 97,046).

$660* *Silk Screams (V. 55), 1974,* s., t., d., num. 11/80, co-pub. Multiples, Inc. and Castelli Graphics, full margins, rubbed spot, creases, staining, (09-19-92, Christie-E, #201), sheet 22⅛ x 30⅜ in., (562 x 772 mm.), screen-print in colors on Japan (BP 380, DM 988, FR 3385, Y 82,233).

BI *Sketch For Forest Ranger,* tears, losses, creases, good cond., prov., prop. Woodward Foundation, est. $800/ 1,200, (12-12-92, Weschler, #163, illus.), 24 x 20 in., (61 x 50.8 cm.), silkscreen on mylar strips.

$6600* *Skull Snap, State I, 1989,* s., d., t., #9/25, pub. blinds-tamp, Tyler Graphics, Ltd., good cond., (11-07-92, Sotheby-NY, #755, illus.), colored and pressed paper pulp w/lithography collage (BP 4315, DM 10,538, FR 35,618, Y 814,614).

$1210* *Somewhere To Light (Solomon 14),* from new York International, NY, Tanglewood Press, Inc., 1966, s., num. 42/ 225, full sheet, time staining, soiling, very good cond., (09-19-92, Christie-E, #192, illus.), sheet 16⅞ x 22 in., (429 x 559 mm.), screenprint in colors on thick wove (BP 696, DM 1812, FR 6205, Y 150,760).

$1650* *Spaghetti (V. 16), 1970,* s., t., d., num. 1/50, co-pub. Castelli Graphics and Hollander Workshop, Hollander blindstamp, full margins, black specks, excell. cond., (09-19-92, Christie-E, #194, illus.), sheet 31 x 42 in., (78.7 x 106.7 cm.), lithograph in colors on wove (BP 949, DM 2471, FR 8462, Y 205,582).

$424* *Spring Cheer, 1978,* s., d., #28/78, t., (06-12-93, Hauswedell/Nolt, #363), 17⅝ x 35 11/16 in., (44.8 x 90.6 cm.), etching on wove (BP 278, DM 690, FR 2319, Y 44,617).

BI *Star And Empty House, 2nd State, 1978,* s., d., t., annot. 2 state, #13/15 AP, full margins, good cond.?, handling creases, est. $5/700, (05-19-93, Butterfield, #2323), 17⅝ x 36 in., (448 x 914 mm.), etching and aquatint in red on wove.

BI *"Star Ladder I" and "II", 1978: Two,* s., d., t., #51/78 and #21/78, blindstamp pub. Multiples, Inc., fullmargins, very good cond., est. $1,8/2,200, (10-28-92, Butterfield, #3103), each 17¾ x 35¾ in., (451 x 908 mm.), etching w/aquatint, first w/hand-coloring; second in brown on white wove.

$1083* *Star Leg, 1979,* 2. state, s., d., num., (11-28-92, Schoppmann, #740), 17 11/16 x 35⅝ in., (45 x 90.5 cm.), color etching on handmade (BP 715, DM 1725, FR 5857, Y 134,785).

BI *Star Leg, 2nd State, 1979,* s., d., t. in plate, annot. 2 state, #61/78, margins, good cond.?, est. $5/700, (05-19-93, Butterfield, #2325), 17⅝ x 35¾ in., (448 x 908 mm.), etching and aquatint in red on wove.

$543* *Star Leg. 2nd State, 1979,* 53/78, s., d., 580mm x 1010mm, (10-14-92, Germann, #413), aquatint/etching (BP 319, DM 795, FR 2695, Y 65,802, SF 708).

BI *"Star Proctor",* s., num., excell. cond., tear, (05-15-93, Cleveland, #487), 17¾ x 35⅝ in., (45.1 x 90.5 cm.), etching and aquatint w/hand-coloring.

$424* *Star Proctor, 1978,* 2nd state, s., d., #6/78, t., (06-12-93, Hauswedell/Nolt, #362), 17½ x 35⅝ in., (44.5 x 90.5 cm.), etching w/relief on thin wove (BP 278, DM 690, FR 2319, Y 44,617).

$553* *Star Proctor. 2 State, 1978,* 66/78, s., d., t., 580mm x 1015mm, (06-24-93, Germann, #494), etching and aquatint w/embossing (BP 364, DM 897, FR 3022, Y 59,322, SF 805).

$1840* *Star, Towel, Weather Vane (G. 778), 1977,* s., d., t., #37/ 42, blindstamp publisher, Gemini G.E.L., p. Serge Lozingot, Mark Stock and Edward Henderson, good cond.?, (05-19-93, Butterfield, #2320, illus.), 22⅛ x 44⅛ in., (56 x 112.1 cm.), lithograph w/die cut and collage on Arches 88 (BP 1194, DM 2991, FR 10,077, Y 203,698).

BI *Swing Screen, 1979,* s., #68/75, t., i. 2nd state, est. DM 1,200-, (05-27-93, Lempertz, #977), 17 11/16 x 35 13/16 in., (44.9 x 91 cm.), etching on wove.

$3300* *Tampa-New York 1188 (V. 68), 1975,* s., d. '1974', t., i. 'VI/XX', artist's proof, pub. blindstamp, University of South Florida, full margins, good cond., (11-07-92, Sotheby-NY, #752, illus.), sheet 36¼ x 73⅝ in., (92.1 x 187 cm.), lithograph p. in colors (BP 2158, DM 5269, FR 17,809, Y 407,307).

BI *Time Door Time D'Or, 1989,* s., d., t., #11/28, blinds-tamp, pub. Tyler Graphics, Ltd., good cond. ?, est. $30/ 40,000, (05-15-93, Sotheby-NY, #1171, illus.), sheet 97½ x 120 in., (247.7 x 304.8 cm.), colored and pressed paper pulp w/lithography collage.

$495* *Tin Roof,* 1st state, #40/78, s., (06-11-93, Freemn/Fine Art, #194), 17¾ x 35¼ in., (45.1 x 89.5 cm.), color etching and aquatint (BP 325, DM 804, FR 2712, Y 52,520).

BI *"Tin Roof" and "Window Washer Glass House 2nd State", 1977; 1978: Two,* each s., d., 1st t., 2nd annot. 2 state, num. 64/78 and 10/15 AP, 1st pub. Marion Goodman, apparently good cond., shrink-wrapped, est. $1,2/1,800, (02-24-93, Butterfield, #3132), each 17¾ x 35¾ in., (451 x 908 mm.), etching, aquatint, & drypoint in colors w/ hand-coloring & gray on wove.

BI *Tin Roof, 2nd State, 1978,* s., t. in plate, annot. 2nd state, #51/78, full margins, good cond.?,handling creases, traces of graphite, surface soiling, est. $5/700, (05-19-93, Butterfield, #2324), 17½ x 36 in., (445 x 914 mm.), etching and aquatint in reds on wove.

BI *Towel, Star And Sunglasses, 1977,* s., t., d., num. 48/78, pub. Multiples, Inc., blindstamp, good cond., est. $2/ 3,000, (05-22-93, Weschler, #221, illus.), 23 x 40 in., (58.4 x 101.6 cm.), hand-colored etching and aquatint w/ embossing on Arches.

BI *Towel, Star, Sunglasses, 1978,* s., d., t., #24/78, pub. Marion Goodman, blindstamp, margins, good cond., crease, est. $7/900, (02-24-93, Butterfield, #3245), 17⅞ x 36 in., (454 x 914 mm.), etching and aquatint in colors w/hand-coloring on Italia.

$440* *"Toy Prison", 1972,* p. Styria Studio, s., d. Rosenquist 1972, num. 65/150, t., p./pub. drystamp, very good cond., full sheet, (09-11-92, Skinner, #121, illus.), approx. 17 x 21¾ in., (43.2 x 55.2 cm.), lithograph in colors on paper (BP 228, DM 633, FR 2153, Y 54,516).

$248* *Toy Prison, 1972,* s., t., d., #148/150, blindstamp p. Styria Studio, full margins, good cond., surface soiling, (10-28-92, Butterfield, #3096), 17¾ x 21¾ in., (451 x 552 mm.), color silkscreen on wove (BP 158, DM 383, FR 1300, Y 30,429).

$345* *Toy Prison, 1972,* s., d., t., #148/150, blindstamp printer, Styria Studio, full margins, good cond., handling creases, surface soiling, (05-19-93, Butterfield, #2318), 17¾ x 21⅞ in., (451 x 556 mm.), silkscreen in colors on wove (BP 224, DM 561, FR 1889, Y 38,193).

$1320* *Tumbleweed (V. 17), 1970,* s., d., num. 55/68, pub. Castelli Graphics and Hollander Workshop, Hollander blinds-tamp, full sheet, surface scuffs, excell. cond., (09-19-92, Christie-E, #195, illus.), sheet 21⅝ x 29½ in., (549 x 749 mm.), lithograph in colors on black Fabriano (BP 759, DM 1977, FR 6769, Y 164,465).

$2588* *Violent Turn (V. 108), 1978,* s., d., t., #6/100, pub. Aripeka Ltd. Editions, good cond., (02-11-93, Sotheby-NY, #427), sheet 37 x 74 in., (94 x 188 cm.), color lithograph on Arches (BP 1826, DM 4287, FR 14,507, Y 311,995).

BI *Wall St. Journal Dinner Triangles, 1977,* #36/78, s., d., t., est. SF 2,5/3,000, 580 x 1010mm, (09-04-92, Germann, #83, illus.), color etching and aquatint.

$1264* *Wall St. Journal Dinner Triangles, 1977,* 36/78, s., d., t., (04-21-93, Germann, #188, illus.), 22 13/16 x 39¾ in., (58 x 101 cm.), color etching and aquatint (BP 820, DM 2020, FR 6832, Y 139,931, SF 1840).

$1430* *Wall St. Journal, Dinner Triangles (V. 96), 1978,* s., t., d. 1977, num. 61/78, pub. Multiples, Inc., full margins, excell. cond., (09-19-92, Christie-E, #202), plate 18¼ x 35¾ in., (464 x 908 mm.), etching and aquatint in colors on wove (BP 823, DM 2141, FR 7333, Y 178,171).

$2117* *Wall St. Journal, Dinner Triangles, 1977,* 37/78, s., d., t., 580mm x 1010mm, (10-14-92, Germann, #56, illus.), color etching and aquatint (BP 1243, DM 3098, FR 10,506, Y 256,544, SF 2760).

$1625* *Wall Street Journal, Dinner Triangles, 1977,* s., d., #30/78, t., blindstamp, (06-12-93, Hauswedell/Nolt, #361, illus.), 18⅛ x 35¾ in., (46 x 90.8 cm.), color etching partially colored on thick wove (BP 1064, DM 2645, FR 8889, Y 170,999).

$1194* *Whipped Butter For Eugen Ruchin, 1965,* s., #30/200, from Eleven Pop Artists II, good cond., (12-03-92, Sotheby-London, #792, illus.), sheet 24 x 30 in., (610 x 760 mm.), silkscreen in colors on wove (BP 770, DM 1878, FR 6409, Y 148,563).

BI *Windscreen Horizon, 1978,* s., d., t., #53/78, blindstamp pub. Aripeka Editions, full margins, very good cond., est. $1,5/2,000, (10-28-92, Butterfield, #3104), 17 x 35 in., (432 x 889 mm.), color etching w/aquatint on white wove.

BI *"Wire And Triangle", 1975,* s., d., i., H.C., est. DM 1200, (12-01-92, Karl/Faber, #1150), 15¾ x 9⁷⁄₁₆ in., (40 x 24 cm.), color lithograph on wove.

$1705* *Zone, 1972,* s., t., d., #34/66, pub., p. Petersburg Press, margins, good cond., tape staining, repaired tear, discoloration, (12-03-92, Sotheby-London, #790, illus.), sheet 31⅛ x 29½ in., (791 x 749 mm.), lithograph on wove (BP 1100, DM 2681, FR 9152, Y 212,144).

$1130* *Zone, 1972,* s., d., #21/66, t., (06-12-93, Hauswedell/Nolt, #365, illus.), 27¹⁵⁄₁₆ x 28⅜ in., (71 x 72 cm.), lithograph on thick wove (BP 740, DM 1839, FR 6182, Y 118,910).

ROSENTHAL, Joe

$3960* *Flag Raising On Iwo Jima, 1945,* sig., (10-14-92, Swann, #343, illus.), 10 x 8 in., (25.4 x 20.3 cm.), photograph, silver print (BP 2324, DM 5795, FR 19,653, Y 479,884).

BI *Flag Raising On Iwo Jima, 1945,* photog.'s sig., i. on image, handstamp, est. $2,5/3,500, (04-07-93, Swann, #352, illus.), 10 x 8 in., photograph, silver print.

$4370* *Old Glory Goes Up On Mount Suribachi, Iwo Jima, 1945,* p. 1950s, lit., (04-08-93, Christie-NY, #265, illus.), 9½ x 7⅝ in., (24.1 x 19.4 cm.), photograph, gelatin silver print (BP 2866, DM 7020, FR 23,763, Y 495,915).

ROSENTHAL, Max   1833-1918

$28* *Spying On The Lovers,* s. in plate, (12-17-92, Mystic, #14A), 15 x 10½ in., (38.1 x 26.7 cm.), etching (BP 18, DM 44, FR 149, Y 3441).

ROSETTI, J.

$357* *La Raphaelle Liqueur Bonal, 1908,* I. Lang, A- cond., closed marginal tears, (08-06-92, Swann, #245, illus.), 63 x 47 in., (160 x 119.4 cm.), (BP 186, DM 527, FR 1781, Y 45,536).

ROSOMAN, Leonard   English b. 1913

$579* *To Visit Britain's Landmarks, 'Roman' Tower, Tutbury, 1936,* p. Waterlow and Sons, ref. #467, cond. 1, tears, (10-13-92, Phillips-London, #110), 30⅛ x 44⅞ in., (76.5 x 114 cm.), color lithograph (BP 337, DM 848, FR 2882, Y 70,207).

ROSS, Alan

$220* *"Triangle Rock, Evening Clouds, Alabama Hills", 1984,* s., photog. stamp, num. 120, (11-16-92, Butterfield, #6141, illus.), 11¾ x 11¾ in., (299 x 299 mm.), photograph, gelatin silver print (BP 145, DM 351, FR 1182, Y 27,360).

ROSS, Alan   American 20th cent.

$110* *Onions,* s., prov., (05-16-93, Hindman, #372), 18¾ x 15 in., photograph, silver print (BP 72, DM 177, FR 598, Y 12,249).

ROSS, Barry

$39* *"Silver Angelfish",* s, t., (05-12-93, Maynard, #277), 9 x 13 in., (22.9 x 33 cm.), direct print (BP 25, DM 63, FR 212, Y 4354, C$ 50).

ROSS, John

$173* *Broadway, 1957,* s., t., #43/50, margins partially glued to mat, very good cond., (05-19-93, Butterfield, #2022), 15¼ x 19¼ in., (387 x 489 mm.), woodcut in colors on Japan (BP 112, DM 281, FR 947, Y 19,152).

ROSS, Judith J.   b. 1946

$1210* *"Untitled" From "Eurana Park, Weatherly, Pa.",* (1982), p. 1989, s., t., d., (10-13-92, Christie-NY, #597, illus.), 7⅝ x 9⅝ in., (19.4 x 24.4 cm.), photograph, printing-out-paper (BP 705, DM 1773, FR 6023, Y 146,720).

ROSSETTI, Dante Gabriel   English 1828-1882

BI *"Lilas-Mme. William Morris",* mono., d. in plate DGR 1879, (06-16-93, Encans, #157), 9¹³⁄₁₆ x 7⅜ in., (25 x 18.8 cm.), lithograph.

ROSSI, Adolph

$2013* *"Dancing Fairies" (From The Ballet "Slavonic Dances" By Anton Dvorak), 1955,* s., d. by photog. on image, s., t., ded., studio stamp, info stamp, notations, (04-06-93, Sotheby-NY, #308, illus.), 11¼ x 15 in., photograph (BP 1330, DM 3243, FR 10,982, Y 229,585).

$770* *Landing Place, 1953,* s., t., d., annot., i. by photog., studio & other stamps, (10-15-92, Sotheby-NY, #385, illus.), 15 x 11⅜ in., (38.1 x 28.9 cm.), photograph, gelatin silver print (BP 471, DM 1146, FR 3887, Y 92,382).

ROSSI, Giovanni Domenico

$715* *Insigniores Statuarum Urbis Romae Icones: 138,* 4to, browning, (11-12-92, Swann, #125), engraving (BP 470, DM 1133, FR 3821, Y 88,655).

ROSSI, L.

$352* *"L'Indiscret",* after L. Rossi, by Goupil and Co., pub. M. Knoedler, 1878, foxing, (12-06-92, Neal, #1310), image 13½ x 9½ in., (34.3 x 24.1 cm.), overall 32 x 27 in., (34.3 x 24.1 cm.), photogravure (BP 220, DM 549, FR 1870, Y 43,613).

ROSSI, Lucius   French 1846-1913

$1932* *"La Vista Del Zapatero" and "La Declaracion De Amor En Un Dia De Viento": A Pair,* (12-17-92, Duran, #14, illus.), each 11 x 8¼ in., (28 x 21 cm.), engraving w/ watercolor (BP 1226, DM 3016, FR 10,304, Y 237,434, P 212,750).

ROSSI, Matteo Gregorio de

$217* *Romische Brunnen: Four,* (12-04-92, Bassenge, #6418), engraving (BP 139, DM 346, FR 1172, Y 27,091).

ROSSIGLIANI, Giuseppe Nicola

$4603* *Die Anbetung Der Hl. Drei Konige (B. XII, S.29, 2 II, Meyer Allgem.Kunstler-Lex. I, 3 II), 1540,* after Parmigianino, prov., (06-04-93, Bassenge, #5345, illus.), 6⁹⁄₁₆ x 9⅜ in., (16.6 x 23.8 cm.), chiaroscuro woodcut w/three blocks in colors (BP 3045, DM 7475, FR 25,194, Y 496,441).

ROSSING, Karl   1897-1987

$186* *Das Gestrandete Schiff, 1942,* s., d., t., creases, (09-25-92, Granier, #2991), sheet 10⁷⁄₁₆ x 12¹³⁄₁₆ in., (26.5 x 32.6 cm.), woodcut on hand-made (BP 109, DM 276, FR 932, Y 22,450).

ROSSINI, Luigi   Italian 1790-1857

$220* *"Altra Veduta",* (12-11-92, DuMouchelle, #2279, illus.), 17¾ x 25½ in., (45.1 x 64.8 cm.), etching (BP 141, DM 347, FR 1188, Y 27,224).

BI *Le Antichita Romanae, Plate 60, 20, 53, 18, 8, 98: Six,* dirt, creasing, est. BP 6/800, (10-07-92, Christie-S. Ken, #3), pl 16½ x 26 in., (41.9 x 66 cm.), etching.

$605* *"Avanzi Del Foro Di Nerva" and "Avanzi Del Tempio Della Concordia": Two, 1819,* plates 21 and 63, sries Veduta di Roma, (03-14-93, Hindman, #367), each approx. 18 x 14 in., (45.7 x 35.6 cm.), etching (BP 422, DM 1007, FR 3424, Y 71,302).

$468* *"Avanzi Del Portico Del Tempio Della Pace" and "Archo Di Druso", 1820, 1821: Two,* from The Views Of Rome, (06-13-93, Hindman, #394), each 14¼ x 8 in., (36.2 x

20.3 cm.), etching (BP 306, DM 762, FR 2560, Y 49,248).

$388* *Rom, Titus-Bogen, 1819,* creases, foxing, (03-24-93, Venator/Hansten, #2572), pl. approx. 18⅛ x 14⅜ in., (46 x 36.5 cm.), etching (BP 263, DM 634, FR 2157, Y 45,588).

$330* *Roman Ruins: Two,* from the Vedute di Roma, plate 22, 1824 and plate 62, 1825, (06-13-93, Hindman, #393), each approx. 17 x 20 in., (43.2 x 50.8 cm.), etching (BP 216, DM 537, FR 1805, Y 34,726).

$770* *Six Views Of Romes, 1821,* (05-16-93, Hindman, #423), largest 18¼ x 24¾ in., (46.4 x 62.9 cm.), etching (BP 501, DM 1239, FR 4162, Y 85,356).

$225* *"Veduta Del Castello Dell'Acqua Giulia In Oggi Porto S. Lorenzo", 1820,* foxing, staining, (03-24-93, Venator/Hansten, #2573), pl. 17¹⁵⁄₁₆ x 13³⁄₁₆ in., (45.5 x 33.5 cm.), etching (BP 152, DM 367, FR 1251, Y 26,436).

$77* *Veduta Di Porta Pertusa, 1829,* (04-02-93, Sloan, #2270), 19¼ x 15¾ in., (489 x 400 mm.), etching (BP 51, DM 124, FR 420, Y 8767).

BI *Views Of Rome, 1820: Fourteen,* full margins, central fold, very good cond., tears in margins, waterstaining, est. BP 1/1,200, (10-27-92, Phillips-London, #36), plate 15⅝ x 18¼ in., (397 x 464 mm.), etching on wove.

ROSSINI, Luigi (after)

$297* *Veduta Della Gran Piazza E Basilica Di S. Pietro In Vaticano,* tears to image, (06-16-93, Bonhams-Chelsea, #374), image 21 x 31½ in., (53.3 x 80 cm.), engraving (BP 198, DM 493, FR 1655, Y 31,677).

ROSSITER, Thomas Pritchard (after) American 1818-1871

$248* *The Home Of Washington,* (04-02-93, Sloan, #1174), 18½ x 30 in., (470 x 762 mm.), color engraving (BP 163, DM 399, FR 1354, Y 28,236).

ROSSITER, Thomas Pritchard and Louis Remy MIGNOT

$165* *The Home Of Washington,* by Thomas O. Barlow, margins, good cond., ripple in image, (09-19-92, Weschler, #159), 21 x 29¾ in., (53.3 x 75.6 cm.), engraving (BP 97, DM 245, FR 838, Y 20,393).

ROSSLER, Jaroslav Czech 1902-1990

BI *Jaroslav Rossler: Portfolio I: Ten, 1991,* Prague House of Photography, each w/ stamps, num 6/15, est. $2,5/3,500, (10-13-92, Christie-NY, #342, illus.), largest 10⅜ x 8¼ in., (26.4 x 21 cm.), photograph, gelatin silver prints.

BI *Metal Lion, J.J. Martel, c. 1931,* s., num., d. 31? by photog., studio stamp, est. $2/3,000, (04-06-93, Sotheby-NY, #308A, illus.), 8¼ x 11 in., photograph.

BI *Ohne Titel, 1967,* s., est. DM 600, (11-12-92, Lempertz, #207), 10⁷⁄₁₆ x 7¹¹⁄₁₆ in., (26.5 x 19.6 cm.), sheet 15³⁄₁₆ x 11⅛ in., (26.5 x 19.6 cm.), photograph, color print.

$1650* *Paris, 1928,* s., t. in ink, studio stamp, (10-13-92, Christie-NY, #341, illus.), 9¾ x 9½ in., (24.8 x 24.1 cm.), photograph, gelatin silver print (BP 961, DM 2417, FR 8213, Y 200,073).

$2070* *Photomontage For Bakelite, 1930,* s., d., annot., atelier credit stamp, (04-08-93, Christie-NY, #131, illus.), 10⅞ x 8½ in., (27.6 x 21.6 cm.), photograph, gelatin silver print (BP 1357, DM 3325, FR 11,256, Y 234,907).

BI *Portrait Of The Artist's Wife, 1935,* s., d., est. $3/4,000, (04-08-93, Christie-NY, #132, illus.), 11¾ x 9⅜ in., (29.8 x 23.8 cm.), photograph, gelatin silver print.

ROSZAK, Theodore 1907-1981

$3850* *Untitled, 1937-41,* stamped facsimilie sig., inits by Sara Jane Roszak, lit., (10-13-92, Christie-NY, #343, illus.), 4¾ x 3⅝ in., (12.1 x 9.2 cm.), photograph, gelatin silver print photogram (BP 2242, DM 5640, FR 19,164, Y 466,836).

ROTA, Martino 1520-1583

$637* *Das Jungste Gericht,* copy, (11-11-92, Dorotheum, #346), 12³⁄₁₆ x 8¹⁵⁄₁₆ in., (31 x 22.8 cm.), engraving (BP 421, DM 1018, FR 3412, Y 79,209, SC 3360).

BI *The Rest On The Flight To Egypt, (B. XVI 2), 1569,* delicate tone, small margins, staining, laid, est. BP 1/1200, (12-01-92, Christie-London, #43, illus.), P. 13¹⁄₁₆ x 18⅛ in., (331 x 461 mm.), engraving.

BI *The Tribute Money, (B. XVI, 5), after 1568,* after Titian, second (final) state, margins, staining, laid, est. BP 360/400, (12-01-92, Christie-London, #44), 10¹³⁄₁₆ x 9¹⁄₁₆ in., (275 x 230 mm.), engraving.

ROTELLA, Mimmo Italian b. 1918

$581* *"Chiquita", 1979,* s., num., (c) stamped L. Smith, (12-01-92, Karl/Faber, #1154), 25⅜ x 22¹³⁄₁₆ in., (64.5 x 58 cm.), color lithograph on wove (BP 384, DM 926, FR 3156, Y 72,336).

BI *Kremli, 1967,* s., d., est. DM 15,000, (11-28-92, Schoppmann, #741), 25⁹⁄₁₆ x 36¼ in., (65 x 92 cm.), color serigraph folio, on laid down canvas.

$717* *La Malicieuse, 1975,* s., #180/200, (05-27-93, Lempertz, #978), 24 x 18¼ in., (61 x 46.3 cm.), color serigraph on canvas (BP 459, DM 1151, FR 3878, Y 76,865).

BI *"Pepsi-Cola", 1980,* s., (c) stamped S.P. Narva, est. DM 900, (12-01-92, Karl/Faber, #1155), 20¹⁄₁₆ x 24³⁄₁₆ in., (51 x 61.5 cm.), color serigraph.

$158* *Untitled,* #245/300, s., (01-28-93, Pescheteau, #242), 25⁹⁄₁₆ x 19⁵⁄₁₆ in., (65 x 49 cm.), stencil print (BP 104, DM 250, FR 847, Y 19,618).

ROTH, Dieter German b. 1930

$2743* *2 Times 5 DOGS.12 (WV II. 361), 1979,* s., d., num., (11-28-92, Schoppmann, #752), 19¹¹⁄₁₆ x 13¾ in., (50 x 35 cm.), color offset (BP 1811, DM 4370, FR 14,835, Y 341,381).

BI *3 Kuchen Auf Drehstuhlen (Roth 169), 1970,* s., d., #48/100, unique print, est. DM 800-, (05-27-93, Lempertz, #987), 20¹⁄₁₆ x 28¾ in., (51 x 73 cm.), serigraph on white Schoeller board.

$474* *5 Blatter. Kompositionen I-V, 1977-1992,* s., d., (06-24-93, Germann, #715), 22¹⁄₁₆ x 14¹⁵⁄₁₆ in., (560 x 380 mm.), etching on copper print paper (BP 312, DM 768, FR 2590, Y 50,847, SF 690).

$1588* *5 Lowen. 4 (WV I.199), 1971,* s., d., num., (11-28-92, Schoppmann, #749), 8¹⁄₁₆ x 11⁷⁄₁₆ in., (20.5 x 29 cm.), etching in brown and black on handmade (BP 1048, DM 2530, FR 8588, Y 197,635).

BI *Abfall-Mischung (Roth Band 40, 319), 1973-1975,* pencil s., est. DM 2,000, (11-20-92, Lempertz, #831), 27⁹⁄₁₆ x 35⅞ in., (70 x 91.2 cm.), color serigraph on Velin.

BI *Ars Alpina (Rot 266), 1972,* 84/150, s., d., est. SF 6/800, (10-14-92, Germann, #599), 25 x 35⁷⁄₁₆ in., (635 x 900 mm.), color lithograph.

$164* *Blau + Gelb, 1974,* #244/1000, s., d., (11-13-92, Koller, #5400), sheet 8¼ x 6⁵⁄₁₆ in., (21 x 16 cm.), serigraph on white cardboard (BP 106, DM 257, FR 868, Y 20,355, SF 232).

BI *Brushaction, 1977,* inits., num., est. $2/300, (11-12-92, Freemn/Fine Art, #186), 10 x 14½ in., (25.4 x 36.8 cm.), 9 x 9 in., (25.4 x 36.8 cm.), diptych lithograph.

BI *Diptych,* both sheets init. D.R., num. 23/100, good cond., wrinkling, slight bends, est. $3/500, (09-11-92, Skinner, #118, illus.), sight overall 23⅝ x 16⅝ in., (60 x 42.2 cm.), lithograph in dark green on two white sheets of paper.

BI *Doppelkopf Am Meer, (19)73,* s., d., num., est. DM 800, (12-01-92, Karl/Faber, #1160), 21⅝ x 31⅛ in., (55 x 79 cm.), color lithograph on BFK Rives wove.

BI *Doppelpurzelbaum (Roth Band 40, 246 A and B), 1972,* unique print, t., s., est. DM 5,500, (11-20-92, Lempertz, #830, illus.), sh, approx. 30½ x 39¾ in., (77.5 x 101 cm.), color lithograph on Velin.

$1837* *Duett (Oeuvre-Kat. 182), 1971,* s., d., #1/30, (06-12-93, Hauswedell/Nolt, #370, illus.), 25³⁄₁₆ x 27¹⁵⁄₁₆ in., (64 x 71 cm.), etching on thick wove (BP 1202, DM 2990, FR 10,049, Y 193,307).

BI *Duett (Roth Band 20, 182), 1971,* #1/30, pencil s., d., est. DM 3,500, (11-20-92, Lempertz, #827), sh 29¹⁵⁄₁₆ x 32½ in., (76 x 82.5 cm.), etching on Velin.

$362* *Die Erde Mit Dem Kram Darauf Der Verdampft, 1966,* s., (10-14-92, Germann, #596), 29⁷⁄₁₆ x 22¹⁄₁₆ in., (747 x 560 mm.), color etching (BP 212, DM 530, FR 1797, Y 43,868, SF 472).

$2599* *Graphik Im Kakou (WV I.100), 1968,* s., d., num., (11-28-92, Schoppmann, #750), 27⁹⁄₁₆ x 39⅜ in., (70 x 100 cm.), color serigraph and Kakau on white cardboard, in Plastiktasche bearbeitet (BP 1716, DM 4141, FR 14,056, Y 323,460).

BI *Im Westen (Rot 161), 1971,* 92/100, s., d., est. SF 6/800, (10-14-92, Germann, #598, illus.), 23⅝ x 31½ in., (600 x 800 mm.), screen print.

BI *Komposition I-V, 1977/92: Five,* s., d., 3. Fassung, est. DM 1800, (12-01-92, Karl/Faber, #1162), 11⅝ x 8⅞ in., (29.5 x 22.5 cm.), etching on wove.

$332* *Komposition, 1977-91,* s., d., (12-01-92, Karl/Faber, #1161), 11⅝ x 8⅞ in., (29.5 x 22.5 cm.), etching w/drypoint and aquatint on thick wove (BP 219, DM 529, FR 1803, Y 41,335).

BI *Kuchen (WV 148), 1970,* s., d., num., dirt, creases, est. DM 300-, (09-25-92, Granier, #2994), sheet 20¹¹⁄₁₆ x 30⁵⁄₁₆ in., (52.5 x 77 cm.), intaglio on hand-made.

$577* *Little Tower, 1971,* s., d., (11-28-92, Schoppmann, #753), 7¹¹⁄₁₆ x 6⅛ in., (19.5 x 15.5 cm.), etching on handmade (BP 381, DM 919, FR 3121, Y 71,811).

BI *"Mein Auge Ist Ein Mund Und Mein Mund Ist Ein Auge" (Roth WV 66), 1966,* s., est. DM 700, (12-01-92, Karl/Faber, #1159), etching in red on rough wove.

$505* *Messing (Roth Band 40, 235), 1971* #35/40, pencil s., d., (11-20-92, Lempertz, #829), sh 20¹⁵⁄₁₆ x 30¹³⁄₁₆ in., (53.3 x 78.3 cm.), etching on Velin (BP 332, DM 805, FR 2712, Y 62,803).

BI *Reliefkarte (Roth 152), 1970,* s., d., #14/40, est. DM 2,000-, (05-27-93, Lempertz, #985), 27³⁄₁₆ x 27¹⁄₁₆ in., (69 x 68.7 cm.), color serigraph on close thread plate.

BI *Scharfe Mutze (Rot 167), 1971,* 54/125, s., d., est. SF 5/700, (10-14-92, Germann, #597), 22⁷⁄₁₆ x 31⁵⁄₁₆ in., (570 x 795 mm.), color zinc print.

$848* *Der See (Oeuvre-Kat. 236), 1971,* s., d., #43/50, (06-12-93, Hauswedell/Nolt, #371), sh 30¹¹⁄₁₆ x 37¹³⁄₁₆ in., (78 x 96 cm.), etching and drypoint, 2 pl on very thick wove (BP 555, DM 1380, FR 4639, Y 89,235).

$1732* *Selbstportrait. 4 (WV I. 198), 1971,* s., d., #1/10, (11-28-92, Schoppmann, #751), 8¹⁄₁₆ x 11⁷⁄₁₆ in., (20.5 x 29 cm.), etching in brown and black on handmade (BP 1143, DM 2759, FR 9367, Y 215,557).

$505* *Steile Topfpflanze (Fur Einen Schweizer Nobelpreistrager) (Roth Band#78/100, 40, 323), 1971-1975,* pencil s., d., (11-20-92, Lempertz, #832), sh 29¹³⁄₁₆ x 22¹⁄₁₆ in., (75.8 x 56 cm.), etching on Velin (BP 332, DM 805, FR 2712, Y 62,803).

$358* *Steile Topfpflanze, Fur Einen Schweizer Nobelpreistrager (Roth 323),1970-75,* s., d., artist proof, V-VI, (05-27-93, Lempertz, #989), 29¾ x 22¹⁄₁₆ in., (75.5 x 56 cm.), etching on wove (BP 229, DM 574, FR 1936, Y 38,379).

$353* *Vulkan (Oeuvre-Kat. 408), 1973,* s., d., #26/125, (06-12-93, Hauswedell/Nolt, #373), 13¹¹⁄₁₆ x 17½ in., (34.7 x 44.5 cm.), drypoint on thick copper print (BP 231, DM 575, FR 1931, Y 37,146).

$1027* *Wie Man Einen Inneren Und Einen Ausseren Fluchtpunkt Hat, + Wie Man's Zeigt (Rot 65), 1966,* s., (06-24-93, Germann, #717, illus.), 29½ x 21⅝ in., (750 x 550 mm.), etching (BP 676, DM 1665, FR 5612, Y 110,169, SF 1495).

ROTH, Dieter and Arnulf RAINER

$722* *Beugematz Oder Der Lauscher Und Der Nackte (WV II. 380), 1975,* s., d., num., (11-28-92, Schoppmann, #757), 12 x 15¾ in., (30.5 x 40 cm.), etching on white handmade (BP 477, DM 1150, FR 3905, Y 89,857).

$722* *E Mark/Titel, Untitled (WV II. 392), 1975,* s., d., num., (11-28-92, Schoppmann, #758), 12¹⁵⁄₁₆ x 19½ in., (33 x 49.5 cm.), etching on handmade (BP 477, DM 1150, FR 3905, Y 89,857).

$1155* *Kopf Oder Plakat (WV II. 383), 1972-1975,* s., num., (11-28-92, Schoppmann, #755), 23⅝ x 29⅛ in., (60 x 74 cm.), color serigraph, offset w/one pencil drawing on light cardboard (BP 762, DM 1840, FR 6247, Y 143,746).

$1299* *Strichelei Mit Herz, 1974-1975,* t., d., unique print, (11-28-92, Schoppmann, #756), 11¹⁵⁄₁₆ x 15⁹⁄₁₆ in., (30.3 x 39.6 cm.), etching on copper print paper (BP 857, DM 2069, FR 7025, Y 161,668).

$722* *Untitled, Max Mit Verband,* s., num., (11-28-92, Schoppmann, #759), 12¹⁵⁄₁₆ x 19⁷⁄₁₆ in., (33 x 49.4 cm.), etching on BFK Rives (BP 477, DM 1150, FR 3905, Y 89,857).

ROTH, Ernest   American 1879-1964

BI *"Columbia University", 1938,* s., d., (c) stamp, excellent cond., est. $150-175, (10-31-92, Cleveland, #206), 11⅛ x 8¼ in., (28.3 x 21 cm.), etching.

$275* *"Rockport", 1918,* s., d., preliminary proof, very good cond.?, (07-19-92, Bakker, #21), plate 7¾ x 14¼ in., (19.7 x 36.2 cm.), etching (BP 141, DM 401, FR 1355, Y 34,187).

$65* *"Tomb Of Mary, Mother Of Washington"* and *"Hugh Mercer's Apothecary Shop", 1928: Two,* s., d. plate, good cond.(05-15-93, Cleveland, #289), one 9⅞ x 12¼ in., (25.1 x 31.1 cm.), other 9⅞ x 13¼ in., (25.1 x 31.1 cm.), etching (BP 42, DM 105, FR 351, Y 7205).

$220* *Untitled: Three,* all s., d. 41, d. 33, and d. 38, very good cond., (03-28-93, Bakker, #134), largest, plate 14 x 9½ in., (35.6 x 24.1 cm.), etching (BP 148, DM 359, FR 1220, Y 25,605).

ROTHE, G.H.

$300* *Window,* s., t., num. 21/150, very good cond., (11-30-92, Phillips-London, #564), plate 25½ x 24 in., (648 x 610 mm.), mezzotint in green on wove (BP 198, DM 478, FR 1622, Y 37,337).

ROTHE, G.H.   German b. 1935

$1210* *"Don Quixote",* s., edit. A.P. #3/15, (09-18-92, DuMouchelle, #2296), 21½ x 27¼ in., (54.6 x 69.2 cm.), etching (BP 696, DM 1812, FR 6205, Y 150,760).

ROTHENBERG, Susan   American b. 1945

BI *Doubles (M. 11), 1980,* s., d., #5/20, blindstamp, pub. Multiples, Inc., full margins, good cond., skinned spot, handling creases, est. $2/3,000, (05-15-93, Sotheby-NY, #1175, illus.), 13 x 30¾ in., (33 x 78.1 cm.), woodcut on Rives Lightweight.

$1840* *Four Rays (M. 15), 1980-83,* s., d., #28/34, co-pub. artist and Derriere l'Etoile Studios, full margins, good cond., (05-15-93, Sotheby-NY, #1176, illus.), 10⅛ x 14 in., (25.7 x 35.6 cm.), lithograph on John Koller handmade paper (BP 1196, DM 2960, FR 9946, Y 203,969).

$1100* *Head And Hand (Maxwell 9), 1980,* s., d., i. 'A.P. IX', artist's proof, pub. Multiples, Inc., full margins, good cond., creases, (11-07-92, Sotheby-NY, #756, illus.), 13 x 11¼ in., (330 x 286 mm.), woodcut on Rives Lightweight (BP 719, DM 1756, FR 5936, Y 135,769).

$2990* *Listening Bamboo, 1989-90,* s., d., #17/23, blindstamp, pub. ULAE, full margins, good cond. ?, (05-15-93, Sotheby-NY, #1179, illus.), sheet 54¼ x 83½ in., (137.8 x 212.1 cm.), woodcut on Kumohada Mashi paper (BP 1944, DM 4809, FR 16,162, Y 331,449).

$1760* *Mezzo Fist #1, 1990,* s., d., #43/49, blindstamp, full margins, excellent cond., (11-09-92, Christie-NY, #396), 31¼ x 22½ in., (794 x 572 mm.), black mezzotint on cream handmade paper applique (BP 1164, DM 2810, FR 9493, Y 218,416).

$1540* *Mezzo Fist #2, 1990,* s., d., #43/48, blindstamp, full margins, excellent cond., (11-09-92, Christie-NY, #397), 24½ x 19½ in., (622 x 495 mm.), black mezzotint on cream handmade paper applique (BP 1018, DM 2458, FR 8306, Y 191,114).

$1840* *Mezzo Fist #2, 1990,* s., d., #38/48, blindstamp, pub. ULAE, full margins, good cond., (05-15-93, Sotheby-NY, #1180), 17⅝ x 13½ in., (44.8 x 34.3 cm.), mezzotint w/collage on handmade Gampi paper affixed to handmade J. Whatman paper (BP 1196, DM 2960, FR 9946, Y 203,969).

$1299* *Mezzo Fist 1, 1990,* s., d., num., blindstamp, (11-28-92, Schoppmann, #760, illus.), 19⅜ x 19½ in., (49.2 x 49.5 cm.), etching in black and beige on handmade (BP 857, DM 2069, FR 7025, Y 161,668).

$1299* *Mezzo Fist 2, 1990,* s., d., num., (11-28-92, Schoppmann, #761), 17¹¹⁄₁₆ x 13⁹⁄₁₆ in., (45 x 34.5 cm.), etching in black and beige on handmade (BP 857, DM 2069, FR 7025, Y 161,668).

BI *Pinks (Maxwell 7), 1980,* s., d., #15/20, unique, Multiples, Inc. blindstamp, full margins, excell. cond., est. $5,5/6,500, (05-11-93, Christie-NY, #552, illus.), sheet 20 x 27¾ in., (508 x 705 mm.), woodcut in black and pink w/additions in yellow gouache on Umbria Italia.

$1380* *Plug (M. 17), 1983,* s., d., #26/29, ULAE blindstamp, time staining, excell. cond., (05-11-93, Christie-NY, #553, illus.), sheet 29¾ x 22 in., (756 x 559 mm.), lithograph in grey and black on hand-made (BP 881, DM 2174, FR 7325, Y 151,798).

BI *Plug (M. 17), 1983,* s., d., num. 26/29, ULAE blindstamp, full sheet, time staining, excell. cond., est. $1,8/2,000, (09-19-92, Christie-E, #205, illus.), sheet 29¾ x 22 in., (756 x 559 mm.), lithograph in grey and black on handmade paper.

$10,350* *Stumblebum (M. 26), 1985-86,* s., d., #40/40, blindstamp, pub. ULAE, good cond. ?, (05-15-93, Sotheby-NY, #1178, illus.), sheet 86½ x 42½ in., (219.7 x 108 cm.), lithograph in colors (BP 6730, DM 16,648, FR 55,946, Y 1,147,323).

$11,000* *Stumblebum (Maxwell 26), 1985-6,* s., d., #9/40, blindstamp, excellent cond., Gertrude Kasle coll., (11-09-92, Christie-NY, #395, illus.), 87 x 42½ in., (221 x 108 cm.), colored lithgraph on Arches (BP 7273, DM 17,561, FR 59,331, Y 1,365,103).

BI *Untitled (Hartford) (M. 12), 1980,* s., d., #14/23, pub. artist and Hartford Art School, full margins, good cond., est. $2/3,000, (05-15-93, Sotheby-NY, #1174, illus.), 30⅞ x 27⅛ in., (78.4 x 68.9 cm.), lithograph on Arches Cover.

$1380* *Untitled (M. p. 98), 1985,* s., d., #2/72. pub. Lincoln Center for the Performing Arts, New York,full margins, good cond., creases, (05-15-93, Sotheby-NY, #1177, illus.), 22 x 28¾ in., (55.9 x 73 cm.), silkscreen in tones of gray and black (BP 897, DM 2220, FR 7459, Y 152,976).

$2090* *Untitled (May #2) (Maxwell 4), 1979,* s., t., d., num. 35/45, pub. Parasol Press, full margins, foxmarks, excell. cond., (09-19-92, Christie-E, #204), sheet 29½ x 21¾ in., (749 x 552 mm.), soft-ground etching and aquatint in colors on Fabriano Etching (BP 1202, DM 3130, FR 10,718, Y 260,404).

$3220* *Untitled (May #3) (Maxwell 5), 1979,* s., d., t., #29/45, pub. Parasol Press, Ltd., full margins, good cond., pressure mark, soiling, (05-15-93, Sotheby-NY, #1172, illus.), 23¾ x 17⅝ in., (60.3 x 44.8 cm.), sugar lift, spit bite and soft ground etching in tones of gray on Fabriano Etching paper (BP 2094, DM 5179, FR 17,405, Y 356,945).

$2760* *Untitled (May #4) (M. 6), 1979,* s., d., t., #29/45, pub. Parasol Press, Ltd., full margins, good cond., scuff marks, soiling, (05-15-93, Sotheby-NY, #1173, illus.), 23⅝ x 17½ in., (60 x 44.5 cm.), soft ground etching w/ sugar lift and spit bite on Fabriano Etching paper (BP 1795, DM 4439, FR 14,919, Y 305,953).

ROTHENSTEIN, Michael

$191* *A Cockerel,* #13/50, s., (02-17-93, Bonhams-Chelsea, #278), image 21 x 24 in., (53.3 x 61 cm.), color woodcut (BP 132, DM 310, FR 1051, Y 22,814).

ROTHSTEIN, Arthur American 1915-1985

$522* *Bus Station With "Colored Waiting Room" Sign,* handstamp, notations, 1930's, (10-14-92, Swann, #344, illus.), 8 x 10 in., (20.3 x 25.4 cm.), photograph, silver print (BP 306, DM 764, FR 2591, Y 63,257).

$1430* *Dust Storm, Cimarron County, Oklahoma,* (1936), p.l., s., num. 66/300, blimdstamp, (10-13-92, Christie-NY, #344, illus.), 19 x 19 in., (48.3 x 48.3 cm.), photograph, gelatin silver print (BP 833, DM 2095, FR 7118, Y 173,396).

$3740* *Dust Storm, Cimarron County, Oklahoma,* 1936, p.l., (10-14-92, Swann, #345, illus.), 11½ x 11½ in., (29.2 x 29.2 cm.), photograph, silver print (BP 2195, DM 5473, FR 18,561, Y 453,223).

$4620* *Dust Storm, Cimarron County, Oklahoma,* notations, 1936, p.l., (04-07-93, Swann, #353, illus.), 11⅝ x 11⅜ in., photograph, silver print (BP 3053, DM 7472, FR 25,287, Y 524,881).

BI *Man Loading Hay Near Goldendale, Washington,* handstamp, 1930's, est. $4/600, (10-14-92, Swann, #451), 9½ x 7½ in., (24.1 x 19.1 cm.), photograph, silver print.

ROUAULT, Georges French 1871-1958

$160* *Du "Miserere",* s., d. in plate G. Rouault 1934, (03-16-93, Encans, #202), 7⅝ x 6⅞ in., (19.3 x 17.5 cm.), xylograph (BP 110, DM 266, FR 904, Y 18,709, C$ 200).

$11,454* *Amazone (Rouault 198), 1930,* sheet 1 of series: Andre Suares, Cirque, (06-23-93, Kornfeld, #759, illus.), color aquatint on handmade (BP 7781, DM 19,381, FR 65,191, Y 1,247,848, SF 17,250).

$550* *Amer Citron, 1935, Wofsy 321,* s. ink, pub. Vollard 1938 in Cirque de l'Etoile Filante, Emmanuel Jacobsen Estate, (09-20-92, Hindman, #748, illus.), 12¼ x 8½ in., (31.1 x 21.6 cm.), aquatint w/drypoint in black on Imperial Japan (BP 322, DM 816, FR 2792, Y 67,977).

BI *Apache (C./R. 268), 1936,* from Andre Suares Passion, pub. Vollard, 1939, full margins, good cond., Wittenborn label, verso, est. $2/3,000, (02-11-93, Sotheby-NY, #262), 12⅝ x 8¼ in., (320 x 210 mm.), color aquatint.

BI *Au Pas De Parade (C./R. 338), 1932-35,* from Grotesques suite, 4th state of 5, s., #11/50, full margins, goodcond., defects, est. BP 5/600, (06-30-93, Sotheby-London, #679), 12⅞ x 8¼ in., (327 x 210 mm.), lithograph on Arches.

$413* *Au Vieux Faubourg Des Lonques Pienes,* from "Petite Banlieue", (10-30-92, Sloan, #1590), 22¼ x 16⅜ in., (56.5 x 41.6 cm.), aquatint (BP 265, DM 635, FR 2156, Y 51,158).

$660* *Augures (Wofsy 148), c. 1927,* plate 41 of Miserere, (03-14-93, Hindman, #280), 20 x 17¼ in., (50.8 x 43.8 cm.), etching and aquatint over heliogravure (photoengraving) (BP 460, DM 1099, FR 3735, Y 77,784).

$4950* *Automne (C./R. 364), 1927,* eighth state of eleven, s., d., t., i. 2e tirage a 60 ex., full margins, good cond., light stain, soiling, masking tape stain, (11-05-92, Sotheby-NY, #440, illus.), 17¼ x 22⅞ in., (438 x 580 mm.), lithograph (BP 3220, DM 7829, FR 26,485, Y 607,287).

$5750* *Automne (C./R. 364), 1927,* 2nd (final) study, s., d., t., No. 29, i. 30 exemplaires, i. Premiere Tirage, full margins, good cond., foxing, mat stain, rubbed spot, (05-13-93, Sotheby-NY, #822, illus.), 17½ x 23¼ in., (446 x 592 mm.), lithograph (BP 3775, DM 9285, FR 31,318, Y 641,956).

$26,431* *Automne (Chapon/Rouault 288), c. 1938,* pen s., #46/175, full margins, good cond., (12-03-92, Sotheby-London, #575, illus.), 20 x 26 in., (508 x 660 mm.), aquatint in colors on Montval (BP 17,050, DM 41,565, FR 141,873, Y 3,288,665).

$3996* *Automne (I. Rouault, F. Chapon 364), 1933,* whole margins, definitive state, annot., d., s., (06-11-93, Picard, #160), 16^15/16 x 22^7/16 in., (430 x 570 mm.), black lithograph on Monval (BP 2625, DM 6494, FR 21,896, Y 423,979).

$619* *Autoportrait I (I.R. et F.C., 311), 1926,* fourth state of six, before sig., (04-02-93, Picard, #182), 9^1/16 x 6¾ in., (23 x 17.2 cm.), lithograph in black on wove (BP 408, DM 995, FR 3379, Y 70,477).

$7636* *Autoportrait III (R. 343), 1926,* s., num., (06-23-93, Kornfeld, #770, illus.), color lithograph on wove (BP 5188, DM 12,920, FR 43,460, Y 831,899, SF 11,500).

BI *"Autoportrait III" (Chapon/Rouault 343; Wofsy 85), 1926,* s., num., Paris, Les Editions des Quatre Chemins, est. DM 12/14,000, (11-28-92, Grisebach, #240, illus.), 13^9/16 x 9^13/16 in., (34.5 x 25 cm.), color lithograph on wove.

BI *La Baie Des Trepasses (C./R. 287), 1939,* #169/175, large margins, (trimmed), good cond., mat stain, tear, tape stain, skinning, soiling, est. $3,5/4,500, (05-13-93, Sotheby-NY, #824, illus.), 24 x 17⅞ in., (611 x 454 mm.), sh 29⅞ x 22½ in., (611 x 454 mm.), aquatint in colors.

BI *La Baie Des Trespasses (Chapon 287, Wofsy 286), 1939,* #59/175, s., est. SF 10/12,000, (09-04-92, Germann, #123, illus.), 26⅜ x 19½ in., (670 x 495 mm.), color aquatint.

BI *La Baie Des Trespasses (Chapon 287; Wofsy 286), 1939,* s., 59/175, est. SF 10/12,000, (10-14-92, Germann, #48, illus.), 26⅜ x 19½ in., (670 x 495 mm.), color aquatint.

$5345* *La Baie Des Trespasses (R. 287/b), 1939,* num., (06-23-93, Kornfeld, #767), color aquatint (BP 3631, DM 9044, FR 30,421, Y 582,307, SF 8050).

BI *"Ballerine" (Chapon/Rouault 205; Wofsy 205), 1930,* sheet 8 of series "Andre Suares, Cirque", est. DM 16/17,000, (11-28-92, Grisebach, #241, illus.), 11^15/16 x 7⅞ in., (30.3 x 20 cm.), color aquatint on handmade.

BI *"Bon Candidat Boudoubadabou" (IR.102)*, pl. 10 from "Reincarnations du Pere Ubu", d. 1928, inits., est. FF4/5,000, (04-04-93, Pescheteau, #283A), a vue 15¹⁵⁄₁₆ x 12 in., (40.5 x 30.5 cm.), aquatint, etching and roulette on wove.

BI *"Bon Candidat Boudoubadabou", "Bon Electeur" and "Les Deux Matrones"(Chapon/Rouault 10e, 12e & 25e), 1928: Three,* ink i., 5th final state, from Reincarnations du Pere Ubu, (03-24-93, Grogan, #114), first 11¾ x 7½ in., (29.8 x 19.1 cm.), aquatint, etching and roulette over photogravure.

BI *The Boxers, Cirque Forain*, s., #2/50, 4th state, soiling, tape, good cond., (06-11-93, Doyle, #78), 13 x 8¼ in., (330 x 210 mm.), lithograph.

$330* *Bust Of A Cleric*, pl. init., d. 1922, (05-14-93, DuMouchelle, #2376, illus.), 20 x 15 in., (50.8 x 38.1 cm.), b/w aquatint (BP 215, DM 531, FR 1784, Y 36,581).

$1980* *Carnets De Gilbert, By Marcel Arland (C. & R. 359), 1931: Two,* 4th final state, pub. N.R.F., good cond., discoloration, wear, (10-28-92, Butterfield, #2717, illus.), lithograph 10½ x 7¼ in., (267 x 184 mm.), orig. lithograph and seven collotype reproductions on Japon imperialpaper w/example of litho. on China (BP 1262, DM 3058, FR 10,383, Y 242,945).

BI *"Chantez Matines, Le Jour Renait" (Wofsy, 136), 1922,* init., d. 1922 GR in plate, good cond., margins trimmed to 5/8 in., light/mount toning, est. $6/800, (03-12-93, Skinner, #12, illus.), 20 x 14⅜ in., (50.8 x 36.5 cm.), aquatint and drypoint over collotype on wove.

$870* *Cheval Blanc (MAM 1971, 161),* c. 1927, s., drystamp, annot., from "Saltimbanques" series, crease, traces, (06-28-93, Loudmer, #359), 12³⁄₁₆ x 9⁷⁄₁₆ in., (310 x 240 mm.), sh 19⅞ x 13⅛ in., (310 x 240 mm.), black lithograph on China (BP 583, DM 1478, FR 4980, Y 92,308).

$2860* *Christ (De Face) (C. and R. 282b), 1938,* for Les Fleurs du Mal, s., d. in plate, trimmed, good cond., (11-09-92, Christie-NY, #202, illus.), 11¾ x 8¼ in., (298 x 210 mm.), etching w/aquatint and roulette in colors on Montval (BP 1891, DM 4566, FR 15,426, Y 354,927).

$3569* *Christ De Face (I.R. et F.C., 282b), 1938,* illus., (04-02-93, Picard, #181, illus.), 11⅝ x 8¹⁄₁₆ in., (29.5 x 20.5 cm.), color aquatint on Monval (BP 2351, DM 5736, FR 19,481, Y 406,353).

$4963* *Christ De Face (R. 282/b), 1938,* sheet 9 of series: Les Fleurs du Mal, (06-23-93, Kornfeld, #766), color etching on wove (BP 3372, DM 8398, FR 28,247, Y 540,691, SF 7475).

$2300* *Christ En Croix (C./R. 233),* c. 1930, trial proof, full margins, good cond., foxing, mat stain, discoloredverso, (05-13-93, Sotheby-NY, #814, illus.), 25⅛ x 19½ in., (638 x 496 mm.), etching on heavy Arches laid (BP 1510, DM 3714, FR 12,527, Y 256,782).

$28,750* *Christ En Croix (C./R. 286), 1936,* ink s., (faded), #81/175, full margins, good cond., discoloration, (05-13-93, Sotheby-NY, #821, illus.), 25⅝ x 19⅜ in., (650 x 492 mm.), aquatint in colors (BP 18,875, DM 46,423, FR 156,590, Y 3,209,780).

$3960* *Christ En Profil, A Droite, 1936,* plate 10 of the Passion, pub. Ambroise Vollard in 1939, (06-13-93, Hindman, #385), 12¼ x 8⅜ in., (31.1 x 21.3 cm.), color aquatint (BP 2592, DM 6445, FR 21,663, Y 416,711).

BI *Christ Et Les Enfants, 1935,* mono. in plate, from Passion series, d., est. DM 900, (12-05-92, Bassenge, #7671), 12 x 8½ in., (30.5 x 21.6 cm.), aquatint on imitation Japan.

$5650* *Christ Et Sainte Femme (Rouault 261), 1935,* mono., i. Essai-Passion, series Passion, (06-10-93, Hauswedell/Nolt, #840), image 13⁹⁄₁₆ x 9⅝ in., (34.5 x 24.5 cm.), color aquatint on Verge de Montral (BP 3696, DM 9200, FR 30,976, Y 599,724).

$2300* *Le Clown A La Grosse Caisse (C./R. 200), 1930,* exec. for Andre Suares' unpublished Cirque, full margins, good cond.,mat stain, glue stains, (05-13-93, Sotheby-NY, #811), 12¼ x 8⅜ in., (312 x 213 mm.), aquatint in colors (BP 1510, DM 3714, FR 12,527, Y 256,782).

$3812* *Le Clown A La Grosse Caisse (Chapon/Rouault 200), 1930,* exec. for Andre Suares unpub. Cirque, full margins, good cond., mat stain, (10-14-92, Sotheby-Japan, #83, illus.), 12⅜ x 8⅜ in., (314 x 213 mm.), colored aquatint (BP 2237, DM 5579, FR 18,918, Y 461,949).

$1725* *Clown A La Grosse Caisse (Chapon/Rouault 200), 1930,* executed for Andre Suares, unpub. Cirque, full margins, scratch through image, light-stain, discoloration, good cond., (02-11-93, Sotheby-NY, #260), 12⁵⁄₁₆ x 8⁷⁄₁₆ in., (312 x 214 mm.), color aquatint (BP 1217, DM 2857, FR 9669, Y 207,957).

$3450* *Clown Et Enfant (C./R. 201), 1930,* exec. for Andre Suares' unpublished Cirque, full margins, good cond.,-mat stain, traces glue, (05-13-93, Sotheby-NY, #812, illus.), 12¼ x 8⅜ in., (311 x 213 mm.), aquatint in colors (BP 2265, DM 5571, FR 18,791, Y 385,174).

$3631* *Clown Et Enfant (Chapon/Rouault 201), 1930,* exec. for Andre Suares unpub. Cirque, full margins, good cond., (10-14-92, Sotheby-Japan, #84, illus.), 12¼ x 8¼ in., (311 x 210 mm.), colored aquatint (BP 2131, DM 5314, FR 18,020, Y 440,015).

BI *Clown Et Enfant, De L'Ouvrage "Le Cirque" De Andre Suares (I.R. 201), 1930,* full margins, est. FF8,000/10,000, (05-27-93, Briest, #175), 17⁵⁄₁₆ x 12¹⁵⁄₁₆ in., (44 x 33 cm.), color aquatint.

$3080* *Le Clown Jaune (C. and R. 204), 1930,* from Andre Suares, Ambroise Vollard, s., d., full margins, light staining, good cond., (11-09-92, Christie-NY, #200, illus.), 14 x 10 in., (356 x 254 mm.), colored aquatint on BFK Rives (BP 2036, DM 4917, FR 16,613, Y 382,229).

$3575* *Le Clown Jaune (C./R. 204), 1930,* exec. for Andre Suares unpub. Cirque, full margins, good cond., (11-05-92, Sotheby-NY, #428), 13¾ x 9⅞ in., (350 x 250 mm.), aquatint p. in colors (BP 2325, DM 5654, FR 19,128, Y 438,596).

$2875* *La Clown Jaune (C./R. 204), 1930,* exec. for Andre Suares' unpublished Cirque, full margins, good cond.,-mat stain, tape hinge, (05-13-93, Sotheby-NY, #813, illus.), 13¾ x 9⅞ in., (350 x 250 mm.), aquatint in colors (BP 1887, DM 4642, FR 15,659, Y 320,978).

$4992* *Le Clown Jaune (Chapon/Rouault 204), 1930,* exec. for Andre Suares unpub. Cirque, full margins, good cond., (10-14-92, Sotheby-Japan, #86, illus.), 13¾ x 9⅞ in., (349 x 251 mm.), colored aquatint (BP 2930, DM 7306, FR 24,774, Y 604,944).

$2596* *Le Clown Jaune (R. 204), 1930,* sheet 7 of series: Andre Suares, Cirque, (06-23-93, Kornfeld, #761), color aquatint on BFK Rives (BP 1764, DM 4393, FR 14,775, Y 282,819, SF 3910).

$2193* *Cristo In Croce (Wosfy 25; Chapon-Rouault 306), 1925,* second state, #17/50, s., d., (05-20-93, Finarte-Milan, #138, illus.), 11¹⁵⁄₁₆ x 8¹³⁄₁₆ in., (30.4 x 22.4 cm.), lithograph (BP 1408, DM 3538, FR 11,918, Y 242,160, L 3220).

BI *Danseuse,* s., est. SF 7/9,000, (11-13-92, Koller, #5399A), sheet 17⁵⁄₁₆ x 13⅜ in., (44 x 34 cm.), aquatint on wove.

BI *De La Suite: "Les Fleurs Du Mal",* #424/425, (06-16-93, Encans, #158), 13¾ x 9¾ in., (35 x 24.5 cm.), etching on Arches.

$1220* *De Ongles Et Du Bec, 1926,* s., lit., (03-25-93, Finarte-Rome, #28), aquatint (BP 829, DM 2004, FR 6816, Y 142,924, L 1955).

$468* *Des Ongles Et Du Bec (Wofsy 157), 1926,* Plate 50 of Miserere, (05-16-93, Hindman, #468), 22⅝ x 17½ in., (57.5 x 44.5 cm.), etching and aquatint over heliogravure (photoengraving) (BP 304, DM 753, FR 2530, Y 51,879).

$605* *Des Ongles Et Du Bec (Wofsy 157), 1926,* Plate 50 of Miserere, (03-14-93, Hindman, #282), 22⅝ x 17½ in., (57.5 x 44.5 cm.), etching and aquatint over heliogravure (photoengraving) (BP 422, DM 1007, FR 3424, Y 71,302).

$257* *Le Directeur Du Theatre (I.R. 27c), 1928,* illus., full margins, water stain, (05-06-93, Laurin, #77), etching on wove w/Ambroise Vollard watermark (BP 163, DM 405, FR 1363, Y 28,276).

$6050* *Dors Mon Amour (C./R. 256), 1935,* from Cirque de l'Etoile filante, pub. Vollard, 1938, full margins, good cond., creasing, discoloration, (11-05-92, Sotheby-NY,

#437), 12⅜ x 8½ in., (314 x 216 mm.), aquatint p. in colors (BP 3935, DM 9568, FR 32,370, Y 742,240).

$7700* *Douce Amiere (C./R. 251), 1934,* from Cirque de L'Etoile Filante, pub. Vollard, 1938, full margins, good cond., (creasing), (11-05-92, Sotheby-NY, #433, illus.), 12¼ x 8 in., (310 x 204 mm.), aquatint p. in colors (BP 5008, DM 12,178, FR 41,199, Y 944,669).

$777* *Le Dur Metier De Vivre (Rouault 65 c), 1922,* plate mono., d., (06-10-93, Hauswedell/Nolt, #830), image 18⅞ x 14³⁄₁₆ in., (48 x 36 cm.), aquatint on hand-made (BP 508, DM 1265, FR 4260, Y 82,475).

$770* *"En Ces Temps Noirs" (Miserere) 1927,* plate 56, s. in plate, d. 1927, (10-08-92, Boos, #669), 23¼ x 17⅛ in., (590 x 435 mm.), aquatint (BP 458, DM 1139, FR 3865, Y 93,560).

$2596* *Enfant De La Balle (R. 249/d), 1935,* sheet 10 of series Cirque de l'Etoile filante, (06-23-93, Kornfeld, #763), color aquatint on thick handmade (BP 1764, DM 4393, FR 14,775, Y 282,819, SF 3910).

BI *Enfant De La Balle, (Chapon 249; Wofsy 328), 1935,* plate mono., d., from Cirque de l'Etoile filante" by A. Vollard, est. DM 7,500, (11-21-92, Schloss Ahlden, #2140, illus.), 12 x 7¹⁵⁄₁₆ in., (30.5 x 20.3 cm.), colored aquatint on Montval.

$1277* *Etre Dempsey Ou L'Acrobate (Wofsy 15), c. 1925,* s., num., artist's proof, stamp, blindstamp, (06-05-93, Bassenge, #6483, illus.), 12¹³⁄₁₆ x 9¼ in., (32.5 x 23.5 cm.), lithograph (BP 841, DM 2070, FR 6978, Y 136,988).

BI *Face A Face,* plate 40 of Miserere, est. $6/800, (03-14-93, Hindman, #279), 22⅝ x 17 in., (57.5 x 43.2 cm.), etching and aquatint over heliogravure (photoengraving).

$1076* *Femme Affranchie A Quatorze Heures..., 1923,* 3rd state, s., d., lit., (03-25-93, Finarte-Rome, #30, illus.), lithograph (BP 731, DM 1768, FR 6011, Y 126,054, L 1725).

$4720* *Femme Fiere (Chapon/Rouault 275), 1938,* p. Lacouriere for unpub. Les Fleurs du Mal, full margins, good cond., mat stain, (10-14-92, Sotheby-Japan, #87, illus.), 12 x 8 in., (305 x 203 mm.), aquatint in colors (BP 2770, DM 6908, FR 23,424, Y 571,983).

$275* *Femme Hideuse, 1919, Wofsy 295A,* early state before completion of plate, plate 7 of Reincarnations duPere Ubu, (09-20-92, Hindman, #747), 11¾ x 7½ in., (29.8 x 19.1 cm.), etching and aquatint (BP 161, DM 408, FR 1396, Y 33,988).

BI *Fiere Autant Qu'Un Vivant, De Sa Noble Sature...(C./R. 277), 1937,* p. Lacouriere, for unpublished suite, Les Fleurs du Mal, full margins, good cond., est. $2/2,500, (05-13-93, Sotheby-NY, #816), 12 x 8⅝ in., (306 x 219 mm.), aquatint in colors.

BI *Fiere Autant Qu'un Vivant, De Sa Noble Stature...(C./R. 277B),* 1936-38, from Les Fleurs du Mal, p. by Lacouriere, pub. Vollard, fullmargins, good cond., est. 1,2/1,600, (06-30-93, Sotheby-London, #678, illus.), 12 x 8⅝ in., (305 x 219 mm.), color aquatint on wove.

BI *La Fille (Wofsy 35), 1926,* s., artist proof, tear, mount staining, est. DM 3,500, (12-01-92, Karl/Faber, #1168, illus.), 12¹³⁄₁₆ x 8⅞ in., (32.5 x 22.5 cm.), lithograph on Arches wove.

$825* *"La Fille" (Wofsy 35 I/III), 1923-29,* s., trial proof, good cond., foxing, (10-31-92, Cleveland, #329, illus.), lithograph (BP 529, DM 1269, FR 4306, Y 102,192).

$805* *Fleurs Du Mal (C./R. 365), 1933,* 2nd state of 4, large margins, good cond., fox marks, rubbed spots, discolored, (05-13-93, Sotheby-NY, #823, illus.), 11⅞ x 8⅜ in., (302 x 212 mm.), sh 21¾ x 14½ in., (302 x 212 mm.), lithograph on laid (BP 528, DM 1300, FR 4385, Y 89,874).

$2530* *Les Fleurs Du Mal: Fourteen,* p. 1966, each #341/425, (05-16-93, Hindman, #469), each approx. 14 x 10 in., (35.6 x 25.4 cm.), etching w/aquatint (BP 1645, DM 4069, FR 13,676, Y 280,457).

BI *Frontispiz Zu "Reincarnations Du Pere Ubu" (Chapon/Rouault 8 d), 1928,* plate mono., d., s., num., stained, est. DM 5,500-, (09-25-92, Granier, #2999, illus.), sheet 17½ x 12½ in., (44.4 x 31.7 cm.), etching on handmade.

BI *Grotesques: Le Tribun Ou Ideal (C. & R. 335), 1926,* s., inkstamps, proof of 4th state of 5, Lugt 2921b and 2921f, blindstamp pub. Galerie des Peintres Graveurs, Lugt 1057b, full margins, upper and lower folded, good cond., mat/water staining into image, creases, surface soiling, est. $7/900, (10-28-92, Butterfield, #2859), 11¼ x 8⅞ in., (286 x 225 mm.), lithograph on Japan.

$329* *Gustave Moreau,* s., t. in plate, drystamp, stains, (06-28-93, Loudmer, #360), 9¹⁄₁₆ x 6¹¹⁄₁₆ in., (230 x 170 mm.), sh 12¹⁵⁄₁₆ x 10¹⁄₁₆ in., (230 x 170 mm.), black wash and crayon lithograph on wove (BP 220, DM 559, FR 1883, Y 34,907).

$847* *Il A Ete Maltraite Et Opprime Et Il N'A Pas Ouvert La Bouche (Rouault74 c), 1923,* plate s., d., watermark, (06-10-93, Hauswedell/Nolt, #832), image 22¾ x 16⅛ in., (57.8 x 41 cm.), aquatint on hand-made (BP 554, DM 1379, FR 4644, Y 89,906).

BI *Il Arrive Parfois Que La Route Soit Belle . . . for Miserere (Chaponand Rouault 62d), 1922,* 4th (final) state, margins, bears sig., light/time/mat staining, est. $2/3,000, (11-09-92, Christie-NY, #198, illus.), 14¾ x 20 in., (375 x 508 mm.), aquatint, roulette and drypoint w/hand-coloring in pastel on laid.

$575* *Jesus Honni...(C./R. 55), 1922,* plate 2 of the Miserere, pub. l'Etoile Filante, 1948, full margins, good cond., sheet discolored, tape stains, Late Vitya Vronsky Babin Coll., (05-13-93, Sotheby-NY, #810), approx. 22⅝ x 17⅛ in., (575 x 435 mm.), aquatint (BP 377, DM 928, FR 3132, Y 64,196).

$918* *Jesus Sera En Agonie Jusqu'A La Fin Du Monde (Rouault 88 e), 1926,* plate mono., d., watermark, (06-10-93, Hauswedell/Nolt, #836), image 22¹³⁄₁₆ x 16⅛ in., (58 x 41 cm.), aquatint on hand-made (BP 600, DM 1495, FR 5033, Y 97,442).

$1292* *Jesus Sera En Agonie Jusqua La Fin Du Monde, 1926,* s., d., lit., (03-25-93, Finarte-Rome, #31), aquatint (BP 877, DM 2123, FR 7218, Y 151,359, L 2070).

$3300* *Le Jongleur (C./R. 199), 1930,* exec. for Andre Suares unpub. Cirque, full margins, good cond., (11-05-92, Sotheby-NY, #426), 12⅜ x 8⅝ in., (313 x 218 mm.), aquatint p. in colors (BP 2146, DM 5219, FR 17,657, Y 404,858).

$6325* *Jongleur (C./R. 244), 1935,* from Cirque de l'Etoile Filante, pub. Vollard, 1938, full margins onthree sides, good cond., tears, water stain, red pencil mark, (11-05-92, Sotheby-NY, #430, illus.), 12⅜ x 8¼ in., (315 x 210 mm.), aquatint p. in colors (BP 4114, DM 10,003, FR 33,842, Y 775,978).

$1858* *Le Jongleur (I.R. et F.C., 199), 1930,* whole margins, illus., (04-02-93, Picard, #180), 12¹⁄₁₆ x 8⁷⁄₁₆ in., (30.7 x 21.5 cm.), color aquatint on Monval (BP 1224, DM 2986, FR 10,142, Y 211,545).

BI *Le Jongleur (Rouault Band I 99 d), 1930,* plate s., d., plate 2 from Cirque, est. DM 6,000-, (11-21-92, Lempertz, #358, illus.), 12⁵⁄₁₆ x 8⁹⁄₁₆ in., (31.2 x 21.8 cm.), color etching on Montval wove.

$650* *"Le Jongleur" (Wofsy 1 ii/iii),* trial proof, annot. Epreuve d'essai GR, very good cond., (05-15-93, Cleveland, #426, illus.), 12⅝ x 8¼ in., (32.1 x 21 cm.), lithograph on Arches (BP 423, DM 1046, FR 3514, Y 72,054).

$1320* *Juges (C. and R. 279b), 1938,* for Les Fleurs du Mal, plate s., d., full margins, mat staining, (11-09-92, Christie-NY, #201, illus.), 12¼ x 8¾ in., (311 x 222 mm.), etching, aquatint and roulette in colors on Montval (BP 873, DM 2107, FR 7120, Y 163,812).

BI *Juges (C./R. 279), 1938,* p. Lacouriere for unpublished suite, Les Fleurs du Mal, full margins,good cond., printer's ink, est. $2,5/3,000, (05-13-93, Sotheby-NY, #817), 13⅝ x 9¾ in., (346 x 248 mm.), aquatint in colors.

$225* *"L'Acrobate", 1919,* epreuve d'essai, d. in plate, water stains, tears, (10-18-92, Pescheteau, #254), 12¹³⁄₁₆ x 9¹³⁄₁₆ in., (32.5 x 25 cm.), heliogravure (photoengraving) and aquatint in black on wove (BP 136, DM 332, FR 1129, Y 26,866).

$450* *L'Administrateur Colonial, from The Reincarnations Du Pere Ubu (C. 16e), 1928,* plate 10 from series, full margins, light-stained, (11-30-92, Phillips-London, #480), plate 10½ x 6¼ in., (267 x 159 mm.), aquatint w/drypoint on Arches (BP 297, DM 717, FR 2434, Y 56,005).

$2750* *Madame Carmencita (C./R. 248), 1935,* from Cirque de l'Etoile Filante, pub. Vollard, 1938, full margins, good cond., (mat stain), (11-05-92, Sotheby-NY, #432), 12 x 8⅜ in., (304 x 212 mm.), aquatint p. in colors (BP 1789, DM 4349, FR 14,714, Y 337,382).

BI *Madame Louison (C./R. 246), 1935,* from Cirque de l'Etoile Filante, pub. Vollard, 1938, full margins, good cond., fox marks, discoloration, est. $4/4,500, (11-05-92, Sotheby-NY, #431, illus.), 12⅜ x 8½ in., (315 x 217 mm.), aquatint p. in colors.

BI *Madame Louison (C./R. 246), 1935,* from Cirque de l'Etoile Filante, pub. Vollard, 1938, full margins, good cond., scratch in image, skinned spots, tape hinges, est. $3/4,000, (05-13-93, Sotheby-NY, #815, illus.), 12¼ x 8½ in., (311 x 215 mm.), aquatint in colors.

BI *"Master Arthur", (Chapon 250; Wofsy 329), 1934,* plate mono., d., from Cirque l'Etoile filante by A. Vollard, est. DM7,500, (11-21-92, Schloss Ahlden, #2141, illus.), 11⅞ x 7¹⁵⁄₁₆ in., (30.1 x 20.3 cm.), colored aquatint on Montval.

BI *Miserere (Chapon/Rouault 54-100), 1922-27,* complete portfolio, w/t. page, num. 99, p. Jacquemin for Vollard, pub. Editions de L'Etoile Filante, 1948, full margins, good cond., discoloration,orig. wrappers, est/ $70/90,000, (05-13-93, Sotheby-NY, #809, illus.), each sh approx. 26 x 19⅞ in., (660 x 505 mm.), 58 aquatints on Arches laid.

$660* *Miserere (Plate no. 1),* appears very good cond., (06-11-93, Doyle, #79), 22¾ x 16½ in., (578 x 419 mm.), etching and aquatint (BP 434, DM 1073, FR 3616, Y 70,027).

$1452* *Miserere Mei, Deus, Secundam Magnam Misericordiam Tuan (Wofsy 108), 1923,* plate 1 from series Miserere, Editions de l'Etoile Filante, (12-01-92, Karl/Faber, #1169), 22⁷⁄₁₆ x 16⁹⁄₁₆ in., (57 x 42 cm.), aquatint and drypoint over heliogravure (photoengraving) on Arches hand-made (BP 959, DM 2314, FR 7887, Y 180,777).

$2420* *Miserere, "Mother And Child", 1927,* acid burn verso; light struck, hinged to mat, good cond., (12-04-92, Doyle, #143), 23 x 17½ in., (584 x 445 mm.), aquatint (BP 1552, DM 3854, FR 13,074, Y 302,122).

$690* *Miserere: C'est Par Ses Meurtrissures Que Nous Sommes Gueris (C. & R.III), 1922,* s., d. in plate, 2nd final state, pub. Societe d'Edition L'Etoile filante, 1948, p. Jacquemin, margin trimmed, good cond., mat/time staining, glueremains, crease, (05-19-93, Butterfield, #1966), 22⅞ x 18⅝ in., (581 x 473 mm.), etching and aquatint w/roulette on laid (BP 448, DM 1122, FR 3779, Y 76,387).

$3025* *Miserere: Face A Face; and En Ces Temps Noirs De Jactance Et D'Incroyance...(C./R. 93 and 109), 1926 and 1927,* plates XL and LVI, pub. Edition de l'Etoile Filante, 1948, full margins, good cond., mat stain, discolored verso; water stain into image, discoloration, grey ink, (11-05-92, Sotheby-NY, #425), one 22¾ x 17¼ in., (577 x 437 mm.), other 23¼ x 17¼ in., (577 x 437 mm.), two aquatints (BP 1967, DM 4784, FR 16,185, Y 371,120).

$1201* *Miserere: Seigneur C'est Vous Je Vous Reconnais! (C./R.85), 1926-27,* p. Jacquemin for Vollard, margins, light/mount-stained, tape, good cond., (06-30-93, Sotheby-London, #676, illus.), sh 25¾ x 19⅞ in., (654 x 505 mm.), aquatint on Arches (BP 805, DM 2048, FR 6910, Y 128,683).

$1716* *Miserere: Solitaire En Cette Vie D'Embuches Et De Malices (Chapon/Rouault 58), 1922,* p. Jacquemin for Vollard, full margins, good cond., (06-30-93, Sotheby-London, #675, illus.), 22¾ x 16½ in., (578 x 419 mm.), aquatint on Arches laid (BP 1150, DM 2927, FR 9873, Y 183,864).

$3300* *Miserere: Sous Un Jesus En Croix Coublie La; and Vierge Aux Sept Glaives (Chapon/Rouault 73 and 106), 1926,* plates XX and LIII, pub. Edition de l'Etoile Filante, 1948, full margins, good cond., light stain, hinge stains, repaired tear, deckle loss, (11-05-92, Sotheby-NY, #424A), one 22⅞ x 16¼ in., (581 x 412 mm.), other 23 x 16⅜ in., (581 x 412 mm.), two aquatints (BP 2146, DM 5219, FR 17,657, Y 404,858).

$1722* *Le Modelle,* #4/10, s., (03-25-93, Finarte-Rome, #27), lithograph (BP 1169, DM 2829, FR 9620, Y 201,734, L 2760).

BI *Mon Doux Pays, Ou Etes-Vous (Wofsy 151), 1927,* Plate 44 of Miserere est. $6/800, (03-14-93, Hindman, #281), 16⅝ x 23⅜ in., (42.2 x 59.4 cm.), etching and aquatint over heliogravure (photoengraving).

$440* *Mon Doux Pays, Ou Etes-Vous? (Wofsy 151), 1928,* Plate 44 of Miserere, (05-16-93, Hindman, #467), 16⅝ x 23⅜ in., (42.2 x 59.4 cm.), etching and aquatint over heliogravure (photoengraving) (BP 286, DM 708, FR 2378, Y 48,775).

$605* *Ne Sommes Nous Pas Des Esclaves,* s., d. 1938 in plate, (12-10-92, Sloan, #3031), 23¼ x 17¼ in., (59.1 x 43.8 cm.), etching and aquatint (BP 390, DM 957, FR 3269, Y 74,839).

$468* *Ne Sommes Nous Pas Des Esclaves,* s., d. 1926 in plate, (05-28-93, Sloan, #1659, illus.), 23¼ x 17¼ in., (59.1 x 43.8 cm.), etching and aquatint (BP 300, DM 742, FR 2509, Y 50,182).

$600* *Le Noir Libere from The Reincarnations Du Pere Ubu (C. 15c), 1928,* plate 9 from series, s., pub. Ambroise Vollard, full margins, good cond., (11-30-92, Phillips-London, #479), plate 8⅜ x 11⅞ in., (213 x 302 mm.), aquatint w/etching on japan nacre (BP 396, DM 956, FR 3245, Y 74,673).

$554* *Nu Assis (Chapon 28 II), 1918-28,* (12-05-92, Bassenge, #7668), 10¼ x 6⅝ in., (26.1 x 16.8 cm.), etching w/ aquatint (BP 347, DM 864, FR 2944, Y 68,641).

$554* *Nu Assiss (Chapon 28 III), 1918-28,* (12-05-92, Bassenge, #7669), 10¼ x 6⅝ in., (26.1 x 16.8 cm.), etching w/ aquatint (BP 347, DM 864, FR 2944, Y 68,641).

$6600* *Nu De Profil (C/R/ 274), 1936-38,* p. by Lacouriere for unpub. suite, Les fleurs du Mal, full margins, good cond., mat stain, foxing, (rubbed), (11-05-92, Sotheby-NY, #439, illus.), 12¼ x 8¼ in., (312 x 210 mm.), aquatint p. in colors (BP 4293, DM 10,438, FR 35,313, Y 809,717).

$550* *Out Of The Depths...,* from "MISERERE", s., d. 1927 in plate, (12-10-92, Sloan, #3030), 23½ x 17 in., (59.7 x 43.2 cm.), etching and aquatint (BP 354, DM 870, FR 2971, Y 68,036).

BI *La Parade,* s., #28/50, 4th state, mat burn, light stain, good cond., est. $7/900, (06-11-93, Doyle, #76), 12 x 9 in., (305 x 229 mm.), lithograph.

$2420* *La Parade (C. and R. 203), 1931,* from Andre Suares, Cirque, Ambroise Vollard, s., d. in plate, full margins, mat/time staining, edges folded back 1/2 inch, (11-09-92, Christie-NY, #199, illus.), 11⅞ x 10⅜ in., (302 x 264 mm.), colored aquatint in BFK Rives (BP 1600, DM 3863, FR 13,053, Y 300,323).

$3163* *Parade (C./R. 203), 1930,* exec. for Andre Suares unpub. Cirque, full margins, good cond., skinned spots, glue/hinge stains, fox marks, discoloration, (02-11-93, Sotheby-NY, #261, illus.), 11¹⁵⁄₁₆ x 10⁹⁄₁₆ in., (304 x 268 mm.), color aquatint (BP 2232, DM 5239, FR 17,730, Y 381,314).

BI *Parade (C./R. 203), 1930,* exec. for Andre Suares unpub. Cirque, full margins, good cond., mat/backboard stain, skinned spots, glue stains, fox marks, hinge stains, est. $4/5,000, (11-05-92, Sotheby-NY, #427, illus.), 12 x 10½ in., (304 x 268 mm.), aquatint p. in colors.

$5083* *La Parade (Chapon/Rouault 203), 1930,* exec. Andre Suares unpub. Cirque, full margins, good cond., (10-14-92, Sotheby-Japan, #85, illus.), 11⅞ x 10½ in., (302 x 267 mm.), colored aquatint (BP 2984, DM 7439, FR 25,226, Y 615,972).

$3971* *La Parade (R. 203), 1930,* sheet 6 of series: Andre Suares, Cirque, (06-23-93, Kornfeld, #760), color aquatint on thick handmade (BP 2698, DM 6719, FR 22,601, Y 432,618, SF 5980).

$1527* *Parade (R. 319/I), 1924,* s., num., stamp, premier etat, (06-23-93, Kornfeld, #768), lithograph (BP 1037, DM 2584, FR 8691, Y 166,358, SF 2300).

$3330* *La Parade, Plate 6 From Cirque (C. and R. 203), 1930,* pub. A. Vollard, margins, mount-staining, tape, (12-01-92, Christie-London, #518, illus.), plate 11¹⁵⁄₁₆ x 10½ in., (303 x 267 mm.), aquatint in colors on BFK Rives (BP 2200, DM 5308, FR 18,088, Y 414,592).

$6038* *Passion (C./R. 284), 1937,* p. Lacouriere for unpublished suite, Les Fleurs du Mal, full margins,good cond., fox mark, discoloration, tape hinges, stain, (05-13-93,

Sotheby-NY, #820, illus.), 12⅜ x 8⅜ in., (313 x 212 mm.), aquatint in colors (BP 3964, DM 9750, FR 32,887, Y 674,110).

$8623* *Passion (Chapon/Rouault 284), 1937,* p. Lacouriere for unpub. Les Fleurs du Mal, almost full margins, good cond., (10-14-92, Sotheby-Japan, #89, illus.), 12¾ x 8⅝ in., (324 x 219 mm.), colored aquatint (BP 5061, DM 12,620, FR 42,794, Y 1,044,959).

$2875* *Paysage A La Tour (C./R. 281), 1938,* p. Lacouriere for unpublished suite, Les Fleurs du Mal, full margins,good cond., tape hinges, (05-13-93, Sotheby-NY, #819, illus.), 12⅛ x 8⅛ in., (307 x 205 mm.), aquatint in colors (BP 1887, DM 4642, FR 15,659, Y 320,978).

$2902* *Paysage A La Tour (R. 281/b), 1938,* sheet 8 of series: Les Fleurs du Mal, (06-23-93, Kornfeld, #765), color aquatint on handmade Montval (BP 1971, DM 4910, FR 16,517, Y 316,156, SF 4370).

$2200* *"Paysage A La Tour" (C./R. 281),* from Les Fleurs du Mal, plate mono., d. '38, p. Lacourier, AAA label, (04-16-93, DuMouchelle, #2032, illus.), 12 x 8 in., (30.5 x 20.3 cm.), aquatint printed in colors (BP 1444, DM 3554, FR 12,009, Y 247,386).

$1059* *Paysage Tropical (Rouault 20 f), 1918/28,* s., plate mono., d., series Reincarnations du Pere Ubu, Vollard, (06-10-93, Hauswedell/Nolt, #838, illus.), image 11¹³⁄₁₆ x 7⅜ in., (30 x 18.8 cm.), etching worked over w/aquatint and Roulette (BP 693, DM 1724, FR 5806, Y 112,408).

BI *Pecheur (C./R. 267), 1936,* from Andre Suares' Passion, pub. Vollard, 1939, full margins, good cond., (mat stain), est. $3/5,000, (11-05-92, Sotheby-NY, #438), 12½ x 8½ in., (316 x 216 mm.), aquatint p. in colors.

$2750* *Le Petit Nain (C./R. 243), 1935,* from Cirque de l'Etoile Filante, pub. Vollard, 1938, full margins, good cond., (11-05-92, Sotheby-NY, #429), 12¼ x 8⅜ in., (311 x 212 mm.), aquatint p. in colors (BP 1789, DM 4349, FR 14,714, Y 337,382).

BI *"Pierot", "Le Jongleur" and "Les Ballerines": Three,* from Cirque de l'etoile filante, late impressions after the orig. aquatints; s., d. 1935 in block, est. $300/400, (12-10-92, Sloan, #1313), each 2¾ x 1¾ in., (7 x 4.4 cm.), prints.

$6600* *Pierrot (C./R. 253), 1935,* from Cirque de l'Etoile Filante, pub. Vollard, 1938, large margins, good cond., stray red pencil mark, skinned area, (11-05-92, Sotheby-NY, #436, illus.), 12⅜ x 8¼ in., (315 x 310 mm.), aquatint p. in colors (BP 4293, DM 10,438, FR 35,313, Y 809,717).

BI *Pierrot (C./R. 253), 1935,* from Cirque de l'Etoile Filante, s., pub. Vollard, large margins, good cond., light/stain, paper fibers adhering to glue, tape stain, soiling, est.$10/15,000, (11-05-92, Sotheby-NY, #435, illus.), 12⅜ x 8½ in., (315 x 217 mm.), hand colored aquatint on japon imperial.

$4590* *Pierrot, c. 1947,* by R. Lacouriere after G. Rouault, s., #76/150, (06-10-93, Hauswedell/Nolt, #842, illus.), image 21⁷⁄₁₆ x 15⅜ in., (54.4 x 39 cm.), color aquatint on Arches (BP 3002, DM 7474, FR 25,164, Y 487,209).

BI *Profile (Chapon/Rouault 14c), 1919,* 3rd state of 5, from Reincarnations du Pere Ubu, (03-24-93, Grogan, #113, illus.), 11⅞ x 7¾ in., (30.2 x 19.7 cm.), aquatint, etching and roulette over photogravure.

$6356* *Qui Ne Se Grime Pas? (Rouault 61 c), 1923,* plate s., d., watermark, (06-10-93, Hauswedell/Nolt, #829, illus.), image 22¼ x 16¹⁵⁄₁₆ in., (56.5 x 43 cm.), aquatint on hand-made (BP 4158, DM 10,350, FR 34,846, Y 674,663).

$1115* *Reincarnation De Pere Ubu, "Paysage Tropical" and "Miserere: Rue DesSolitaires" (C./R. 20 and 76), 1928 and 1922: Two,* 1st bearing sig., numbering, pub. Vollard, 2nd edit. of 450, pub. Societe d'Edition l'Etoile filante, margins, stained, defects, (06-30-93, Sotheby-London, #677, illus.), one sh 14⅞ x 10¼ in., (378 x 260 mm.), the other sh 19 x 25 in., (378 x 260 mm.), aquatint, each on wove (BP 747, DM 1902, FR 6415, Y 119,469).

$220* *Reincarnation De Pere Ubu: Les Deux Matrones (C., & R. 25), 1928,* 3rd state of 4, full margins, good cond., crease, glue/hinge remains, light-staining, surface soiling, (10-28-92, Butterfield, #2857), 10½ x 7⁵⁄₁₆ in., (267 x

186 mm.), etching w/aquatint on wove, watermark (BP 140, DM 340, FR 1154, Y 26,994).

$303* *Les Reincarnations Du Pere Ubu,* (03-20-93, Northeast, #743, illus.), plate 10½ x 7 in., (26.7 x 17.8 cm.), aquatint in black (BP 203, DM 495, FR 1686, Y 35,147).

$6147* *Les Reincarnations Du Pere Ubu (I. Rouault et F. Chapon, 8 a 29), 1928: Twenty-Two,* (04-02-93, Picard, #179), 17¹¹⁄₁₆ x 12¹³⁄₁₆ in., (45 x 32.5 cm.), etchings and aquatints on Van Gelder Zonen (BP 4049, DM 9879, FR 33,553, Y 699,875).

$575* *Reincarnations Du Pere Ubu: Le Noir Libere (C. & R. 15), 1928,* 3rd final state, pub. Ambroise Vollard, 1932, upper margins possiblytrimmed, good cond., mat staining, tape/glue remains, thinned spots, stain, surface soiling, notations, (05-19-93, Butterfield, #1964), 8⅜ x 11⅞ in., (213 x 302 mm.), etching w/aquatint and roulette on handmade laid (BP 373, DM 935, FR 3149, Y 63,655).

$880* *Reincarnations Du Pere Ubu: NU (C. & R. 19), 1928,* s. in ink, pub. Ambroise Vollard, 1932, upper & left margins possiblytrimmed, good cond., fold, foxing, rubbed areas, staining, surface soiling, (02-24-93, Butterfield, #2969), 10⅝ x 6⅝ in., (270 x 168 mm.), etching, aquatint & roulette on Japon nacre (BP 614, DM 1429, FR 4843, Y 103,262).

$4400* *Le Rencheri (C./R/ 252), 1935,* from Cirque de l"Etoile Filante, pub. Vollard, 1938, full margins onthree sides, good cond., (paper tone darkened), (11-05-92, Sotheby-NY, #434), 12⅝ x 8¼ in., (321 x 211 mm.), aquatint p. in colors (BP 2862, DM 6959, FR 23,542, Y 539,811).

$354* *Saint Suaire (Wofsy 82),* for series Miserere, light-staining, (06-08-93, Karl/Faber, #1258), sh approx. 25¹³⁄₁₆ x 19⅞ in., (65.5 x 50.5 cm.), (BP 233, DM 574, FR 1934, Y 37,600).

$805* *Saltimbanques: Clownesse Ou Parade (C. & R. 325), 1925,* s., #25/50, inkstamp, 3rd state, Frapier blindstamp, full margins, good cond., mat/light-staining, tape, foxing, surface soiling, (05-19-93, Butterfield, #1965), 13¼ x 8⅞ in., (337 x 225 mm.), lithograph on Arches (BP 523, DM 1309, FR 4409, Y 89,118).

$634* *Satan IV (I. Rouault 225 d), 1926,* #422/425, sheet 12 of XIV Planches gravees pour Les Fleurs du Mal series, (05-26-93, Lempertz, #481), 17½ x 13⁵⁄₁₆ in., (44.5 x 33.8 cm.), etching (heliogravure, aquatint, drypoint) on Arches wove (BP 410, DM 1034, FR 3482, Y 68,883).

$847* *Seigneur C'est Vous Je Vous Reconnais! (Rouault 85 d), 1927,* plate s., d., watermark, (06-10-93, Hauswedell/Nolt, #835), image 22⁷⁄₁₆ x 17¹¹⁄₁₆ in., (57 x 45 cm.), aquatint on hand-made (BP 554, DM 1379, FR 4644, Y 89,906).

$847* *Solitaire En Cette Vie D'Embuches Et De Malices (Rouault 58 e), 1922,* plate s., d., Suite Miserere, Edition de l'etoile filante, watermark, (06-10-93, Hauswedell/Nolt, #828), image 22⅝ x 16⁵⁄₁₆ in., (57.5 x 41.5 cm.), aquatint on hand-made (BP 554, DM 1379, FR 4644, Y 89,906).

$825* *"Sous Jesus En Crois Oublie La." (Wofsy, 127), 1926,* plate 20 of MISERERE, init., d. GR 1926 in plate, num. 20, watermark, fair cond., foxing, thinned areas/losses, tape residue, (03-12-93, Skinner, #15, illus.), 23 x 16½ in., (58.4 x 41.9 cm.), aquatint and drypoint over collotype on laid (BP 576, DM 1373, FR 4669, Y 97,230).

$1766* *Sous Un Jesus En Croix Oublie La (Rouault 73 e), 1926,* plate s., d., watermark, (06-10-93, Hauswedell/Nolt, #831, illus.), image 22¹⁵⁄₁₆ x 16⁹⁄₁₆ in., (58.2 x 42 cm.), etching and aquatint on Arches (BP 1155, DM 2876, FR 9682, Y 187,454).

BI *Souvenirs Intimes: Leon Bloy (C. & R. 314), 1926,* s., inkstamps, proof of 2nd state of 5, Lugt 2921b and 2921d, blindstamp prob. Galerie des Peintres Graveurs, Lugt 1057b, full margins, lower folded, good cond., foxing, surface soiling, light-staining , est. $800/1,000, (10-28-92, Butterfield, #2858), 9⅛ x 6½ in., (232 x 165 mm.), lithograph on wove.

BI *The Strong Man,* s., #40/50, 3rd state, soiling, old tape, mat burn, acid stain, goodcond., est. $7/900, (06-11-93, Doyle, #77), 13 x 9 in., (330 x 229 mm.), lithograph.

$783* *"Study for 'Christ Au Faubourg'" and "Study for 'Apache...Chacal BeniPar Toutes Les Academies'": Two,* from the Passion, 1939, (05-20-93, Finarte-Milan, #139), first 11⁷⁄₁₆ x 7¹¹⁄₁₆ in., (29 x 19.5 cm.), second 12 x

7¹³⁄₁₆ in., (29 x 19.5 cm.), aquatint in blue (BP 503, DM 1263, FR 4255, Y 86,462, L 1150).

$5317* *Suite Complete De 22 Planches Pour "Reincarnations Du Pere Ubu" (MAM1983, 109 I-XXII), 1928:* Twenty-Two, inits., d. in plates, blue stamp, proofs, good cond., (06-28-93, Loudmer, #357, illus.), approx. 11¹³⁄₁₆ x 7⅞ in., (300 x 200 mm.), sh approx. 17⁵⁄₁₆ x 12¹⁵⁄₁₆ in., (300 x 200 mm.), etchings, aquatints and roulettes on wove w/ watermark (BP 3560, DM 9035, FR 30,435, Y 564,138).

BI *Trio (C./R. 280), 1938,* p. Lacouriere for unpublished suite, Les Fleurs du Mal, full margins,good cond., est. $2,5/3,500, (05-13-93, Sotheby-NY, #818, illus.), 12 x 8¾ in., (305 x 222 mm.), aquatint in colors.

$3994* *Trio (Chapon/Rouault 280), 1938,* p. Lacouriere for unpub. Les Fleurs du Mal, full margins, good cond., (10-14-92, Sotheby-Japan, #88, illus.), 12 x 8¾ in., (305 x 222 mm.), colored aquatint (BP 2344, DM 5845, FR 19,821, Y 484,004).

$1527* *Trio (R. 321/IV), c. 1925,* s., num., blindstamp, state stamp, (06-23-93, Kornfeld, #769), lithograph (BP 1037, DM 2584, FR 8691, Y 166,358, SF 2300).

BI *Trio (Rouault Band II 280 b), 1938,* plate mono., d., plate 7 of Les Fleurs du Mal, est. DM 8,000-, (11-21-92, Lempertz, #359, illus.), 12⅛ x 8⅞ in., (30.8 x 22.5 cm.), color etching on Montval wove.

$4123* *Tristes Os. - Un Clown (R. 247), 1934,* mono. in ink, i. Essai Cirque de l'Etoile filante, (06-23-93, Kornfeld, #762, illus.), color aquatint (BP 2801, DM 6976, FR 23,466, Y 449,177, SF 6210).

$1544* *Les Trois Croix (C./R. 283), 1938,* from Les Fleurs du Mal, p. by Lacouriere, pub. Vollard, full margins,good cond., (06-30-93, Sotheby-London, #680), 12¼ x 8⅞ in., (311 x 225 mm.), color aquatint on wove (BP 1035, DM 2633, FR 8884, Y 165,434).

BI *Untitled (R./C. 100E), 1927,* from "Miserere", final state, s., d. 1927 in plate, full margins, est. FF 3,5/4,000, (11-16-92, Briest, #351), 16¹⁵⁄₁₆ x 23⁷⁄₁₆ in., (43 x 59.5 cm.), aquatint, burnished, drypoint.

$1840* *[Deux Figures], c. 1916,* trial proof, one of two known impressions, large margins, good cond.,light-stain, crease through image, soiling, skinning, (05-13-93, Sotheby-NY, #808, illus.), 11¾ x 8 in., (298 x 203 mm.), sh 19½ x 12⅝ in., (298 x 203 mm.), wood engraving on heavy wove (BP 1208, DM 2971, FR 10,022, Y 205,426).

ROUAULT, Georges (after)

BI *Christ (Page 125), 1936,* an illus. from Andre Suares' PASSION, inits., d. GR 1936 in plate, ident. on label verso, letterpress, good cond., taped, light-staining, est. $6/800, (03-12-93, Skinner, #14, illus.), 7⅛ x 7⅞ in., (18.1 x 20 cm.), process wood engraving on paper.

$39* *Cristal De Roche (MAM, 1983, 109 XIV), 1929,* init., d. in plate, (06-28-93, Loudmer, #113), 3¾ x 2¹⁵⁄₁₆ in., (96 x 74 mm.), sh 10⅞ x 7⅞ in., (96 x 74 mm.), aquatint on wove (BP 26, DM 66, FR 223, Y 4138).

$3729* *Le Pierot,* by R. Lacouriere, s., 76/150, (12-04-92, AB Stockholm, #7130), 21⁷⁄₁₆ x 15⁹⁄₁₆ in., (54.5 x 39.5 cm.), aquatint in colors on Arches (BP 2392, DM 5939, FR 20,146, Y 465,543, SK 25,300).

BI *Le Pierrot, c. 1947,* by R. Lacouriere, s., #22/150, margins, light-staining, spots, good cond., est. P 2,5/3,500, (12-01-92, Christie-London, #519), plate 21⁷⁄₁₆ x 15⅜ in., (544 x 390 mm.), aquatint in colors on Arches.

BI *"La Sainte Face" and "Parade", c. 1925: Two,* full margins, (02-24-93, Picard, #223), photocollograph in color on wove.

$33* *Two Figures,* Emmanuel Jacobson Estate, (09-20-92, Hindman, #823), 12¾ x 7⅞ in., (32.4 x 20 cm.), wood engraving (BP 19, DM 49, FR 168, Y 4079).

ROUBILLARD, R.

BI *"Spanish Dancer",* est. $50/100, (03-12-93, DuMouchelle, #2434), 13¼ x 9½ in., (33.7 x 24.1 cm.), color lithograph.

ROUBILLE, A.

$1390* *Demaria Freres,* p. Charles Verneau, defects, backed on linen, laid on board, (05-07-93, Christie-S. Ken, #104, illus.), 27 x 39¼ in., (68.6 x 99.7 cm.), color lithograph (BP 880, DM 2198, FR 7405, Y 153,050).

$70* *Faut-Il Fermer Lourdes. Brochure Illustree, c. 1895,* good cond., (02-12-93, Cheval/Robert, #125), 59¹³⁄₁₆ x 44⅞ in., (152 x 114 cm.), poster (BP 49, DM 116, FR 393, Y 8442).

ROUDEBUSH, H.

$61* *"Muir Woods",* (09-20-92, Jackson, #98), 7 x 4 in., (17.8 x 10.2 cm.), etching (BP 36, DM 91, FR 310, Y 7539).

ROUFFE

$100* *La Bougie Colin,* cond. B, (03-16-93, Boisgirard, #186), 47¼ x 30¹¹⁄₁₆ in., (120 x 78 cm.), poster (BP 69, DM 166, FR 565, Y 11,693).

$168* *La Bougie Colin "Fouette Le Moteur",* very good cond., lit., (11-19-92, Ribeyre/Baron, #73), 47¼ x 31½ in., (120 x 80 cm.), poster (BP 111, DM 268, FR 902, Y 20,893).

ROUGEMONT

$3080* *Mistinguett,* Richier Laugier, A- cond., surface soiling, tear, (08-06-92, Swann, #246, illus.), 62½ x 46 in., (158.8 x 116.8 cm.), (BP 1609, DM 4551, FR 15,369, Y 392,857).

ROUSSEAU, Albert   Canadian 1908-1982

$134* *"Moulin Des Arts",* artist's proof, s. A. Rousseau, inits., t. verso, (03-16-93, Encans, #109), 8⅞ x 11⁵⁄₁₆ in., (22.5 x 28.8 cm.), etching and embellishing (BP 93, DM 223, FR 757, Y 15,669, C$ 167).

ROUSSEAU, J.J.

$168* *Paris A Londres Par Rouen, Dieppe Et Newhaven, c. 1920,* p. Cornille & Serre, very good cond., (11-19-92, Ribeyre/Baron, #118), 40⁹⁄₁₆ x 29⁵⁄₁₆ in., (103 x 74.5 cm.), poster (BP 111, DM 268, FR 902, Y 20,893).

ROUSSEAU, Percival   American 1859/69-1937

BI *Pointers,* s., est. $50/75, (06-11-93, Freemn/Fine Art, #196), 7½ x 10¼ in., (19.1 x 26 cm.), etching.

ROUSSEAU, Pierre Etienne Theodore

BI *Un Site Du Berry (Delteil 2), 1842,* large margins, good cond., foxing, ex-coll. A. Lebrun; and M.L. Guerin, est. $8/12,000, (05-13-93, Sotheby-NY, #825, illus.), 3⅞ x 7⅛ in., (97 x 181 mm.), sh 9⅜ x 13¼ in., (97 x 181 mm.), etching on japon pelure.

ROUSSEAU, Theodore

$1842* *Un Site Du Berry (D. 2), 1842,* mat-staining, large margins, ex-coll., (02-24-93, Picard, #224), etching on Japan (BP 1285, DM 2990, FR 10,138, Y 216,146).

$1842* *Vue Du Plateau De Bellecroix (D. 3), 1848 or 1849,* staining, large margins, ex-coll., rare, (02-24-93, Picard, #225), etching on chine applique on thick wove (BP 1285, DM 2990, FR 10,138, Y 216,146).

ROUSSEAU-LEURENT, Maurice   b. 1942

BI *"Comme Hier", 1989,* #40/65, s., est. FF6/800, (04-04-93, Pescheteau, #285), 22¹³⁄₁₆ x 18⅛ in., (58 x 46 cm.), carborandum etching on Angouleme.

BI *"Jardin Bleu", EAX/XX,* est. FF6/800, (04-04-93, Pescheteau, #284), 22¹⁄₁₆ x 17¹¹⁄₁₆ in., (56 x 45 cm.), carborundum etching on Moulin de la Roque.

ROUSSEL, Ker Xavier   French 1867-1944

BI *Arkadische Landschaft,* i. Bon a tirer, s., artist's proof, est. DM 2500, (06-04-93, Bassenge, #5799, illus.), 4¹⁵⁄₁₆ x 6⅝ in., (12.6 x 16.8 cm.), etching on Perrigot paper.

$8992* *L'Education Du Chien Ou Dans La Neige (J. Salomon 10), 1893,* whole margins, s., num. 51, (06-11-93, Picard, #161), 12¹⁵⁄₁₆ x 8¹⁄₁₆ in., (330 x 205 mm.), color lithograph on wove (BP 5908, DM 14,614, FR 49,271, Y 954,058).

$1108* *"Personnages Au Bord De La Mer" and "Femmes Dans La Campagne" (Salomon 14 and 19), 1898: Two,* from the series Paysages, both s., full margins, good cond., handlingcreases, tape stains, (12-03-92, Sotheby-London, #574, illus.), one 9¼ x 16⅛ in., (236 x 410 mm.), other 9¼ x 12¾ in., (236 x 410 mm.), lithographs in colors on chine volant (BP 715, DM 1742, FR 5947, Y 137,862).

$328* *La Source (Salomon 20), c. 1900,* margins, (02-24-93, Picard, #226), color lithograph on thin chine (BP 229, DM 532, FR 1805, Y 38,489).

$799* *La Source, From L'Album De Paysage (Johnson 134, no. 7), c. 1900,* s.(?), p. A. Clot, margins, very good cond., (12-01-92, Christie-London, #520), L. 12⁵⁄₁₆ x 16 in., (312 x 407 mm.), lithograph in colors on chine volant (BP 528, DM 1274, FR 4340, Y 99,477).

ROUSSEL, Pierre

BI *"Moliere A La Comedie Francaise", 1973: Album of 12,* #XXXVIII/LX, s., est. FF1,500/2,000, (04-04-93, Peschet-eau, #286), 19¹¹⁄₁₆ x 25⁹⁄₁₆ in., (50 x 65 cm.), lithograph on Rives.

ROUSSEL, R.

$210* *Rambouillet. "Son Chateau, Son Parc, Sa Foret" Beaux Terrains A Lotir, 1926,* fair cond., (11-19-92, Ribeyre/Baron, #119), 47¼ x 31½ in., (120 x 80 cm.), poster (BP 138, DM 335, FR 1128, Y 26,116).

ROUSSEL, Theodore

$196* *"Figures Lounging By Railings",* s., trimmed around sig., (09-17-92, Bonhams-Chelsea, #81), image 3¾ x 4¾ in., (9.5 x 12.1 cm.), etching (BP 110, DM 291, FR 996, Y 24,402).

$196* *The Street, Chelsea,* s., trimmed around sig., (09-17-92, Bonhams-Chelsea, #80), image 5¾ x 8 in., (14.6 x 20.3 cm.), etching (BP 110, DM 291, FR 996, Y 24,402).

ROUSSELET, G.

$354* *Les Douze Sibylles: Twelve,* after Vignon, good margins, (06-16-93, Ader Tajan, #20), copper engraving (BP 236, DM 588, FR 1972, Y 37,756).

ROUSSIL, Robert Canadian b. 1925

$44* *Sans Titre,* #6/66, s. R. Roussil, (06-16-93, Encans, #101), 10¹³⁄₁₆ x 14¾ in., (27.5 x 37.5 cm.), etching (BP 29, DM 73, FR 245, Y 4693, C$ 56).

$26* *Sans Titre,* #11/15, d. juin 88, s. R. Roussil, (06-16-93, Encans, #98), 29¹⁵⁄₁₆ x 22⁵⁄₁₆ in., (76 x 56 cm.), engraving (BP 17, DM 43, FR 145, Y 2773, C$ 33).

$191* *Sans Titre,* num., d. 5/11-mai 1972, s. R. Roussil, (06-16-93, Encans, #99), 37⅜ x 20¹¹⁄₁₆ in., (95 x 52.5 cm.), etching and estampage (BP 127, DM 317, FR 1064, Y 20,371, C$ 244).

$221* *Sans Titre,* #6/66, s. R. Roussil, (04-20-93, Encans, #91), 10¹³⁄₁₆ x 14¾ in., (27.5 x 37.5 cm.), etching (BP 143, DM 352, FR 1188, Y 24,385, C$ 278).

$109* *Sans Titre,* #15/20, s. Roussil, (09-15-92, Encans, #107), wood engraving (BP 58, DM 162, FR 551, Y 13,532, C$ 133).

ROUSSY, Toussaint 1847-1931

$201* *Chemin De Fer PLM. Cette, c. 1900,* Paris, Imp. Vercasson and Cie, cond. B+, (06-11-93, Boisgirard, #142), 41¾ x 29½ in., (106 x 75 cm.), poster (BP 132, DM 327, FR 1101, Y 21,326).

ROUX, Jo

$629* *Les Laines Bisanne, Lyon - Megeve, c. 1920,* good cond., lit., (11-19-92, Ribeyre/Baron, #33bis), 47¼ x 31½ in., (120 x 80 cm.), poster (BP 414, DM 1003, FR 3378, Y 78,224).

ROUX-CHAMPION, Joseph Victor 1871-1953

$106* *Portrait De Louis Valtat,* #36/220, s., i., (02-16-93, Encans, #132), 8⅞ x 6¹¹⁄₁₆ in., (22.5 x 17 cm.), etching (BP 73, DM 173, FR 586, Y 12,699, C$ 133).

ROWBOTHAM, T.L. (after)

$182 *Lake Maggiore With Figures,* (08-14-92, G.A. Key, #16), 9 x 22 in., (22.9 x 55.9 cm.), chromolithograph (BP 95, DM 267, FR 904, Y 22,951).

$29 *Lake Maggori,* (02-05-93, G.A. Key, #22), 15 x 23 in., (38.1 x 58.4 cm.), chromolithograph (BP 20, DM 48, FR 163, Y 3609).

ROWLANDSON

$110* *"Lamenting The Loss Of His Wife" and "At The Funeral Of His Wife": APair,* Doctor Syntax prints, (06-17-93, Garth, #617, illus.), 10¼ x 13¼ in., (26 x 33.7 cm.), hand-colored print (BP 73, DM 183, FR 614, Y 11,786).

$154* *"Loses Money At The Race-Ground At York", "Entertained At College", "Bookseller" and "Untitled": Four,* Doctor Syntax prints, Bookseller damaged, (06-17-93, Garth, #616, illus.), 9¼ x 12½ in., (23.5 x 31.8 cm.), hand-colored print (BP 102, DM 256, FR 859, Y 16,501).

ROWLANDSON, Thomas English 1756-1827

$2728* *"Dressing For A Masquerade" and "Dressing For A Birthday", 1790: Two,* good cond., (12-03-92, Sotheby-London, #162, illus.), each approx. 13¼ x 17⅞ in., (337 x 454 mm.), hand colored etching (BP 1760, DM 4290, FR 14,643, Y 339,430).

$383* *The Last Gasp Or Toadstools Mistaken For Mushrooms, 1813,* pub. Thomas Tegg, trimmed to plate, corner mounted, (10-27-92, Phillips-London, #73), plate 13⅝ x 8⅞ in., (346 x 225 mm.), etching w/hand-coloring (BP 242, DM 587, FR 1992, Y 46,850).

$10* *"The Old Elephant And Castle Inn, Newington" and "Vauxhall", 1786: Two,* staining and foxing throughout image, water staining into image, (05-15-93, Cleveland, #427), one 12 x 18 in., (30.5 x 45.7 cm.), other 10½ x 16½ in., (30.5 x 45.7 cm.), hand-colored engraving (BP 7, DM 16, FR 54, Y 1109).

$550* *"A Picture Of Misery", "My Dear You're A Plumper" and "Taylor Turn'dLord", c. 1805-12: Group Of Three,* from Microcosm of London, pub. Thomas Tegg, time stain, (05-27-93, Swann, #242), smallest 10 x 13¾ in., (25.4 x 34.9 cm.), largest 11⁵⁄₁₆ x 9¹³⁄₁₆ in., (25.4 x 34.9 cm.), hand-colored etching (BP 352, DM 883, FR 2975, Y 58,962).

BI *Picturesque Beauties Of Boswell (B. M. 7031-7050): Set Of Twenty,* after S. Collings, margins, foxed, other defects, est. BP 2/300, (12-03-92, Sotheby-London, #163), 10 x 11 in., (254 x 279 mm.), etchings.

ROWLANDSON, Thomas (after)

$125 *From The Doctor Syntax Series: A Set Of Eight,* (08-14-92, G.A. Key, #60), 4 x 7 in., (10.2 x 17.8 cm.), hand colored aquatint (BP 65, DM 183, FR 621, Y 15,763).

$143* *Kicking Up a Breeze, 1814,* by T. Tegg, (03-14-93, Hindman, #229), 13⅝ x 9⅝ in., (34.6 x 24.4 cm.), hend-colored etching (BP 100, DM 238, FR 809, Y 16,853).

ROWLANDSON, Thomas (after George MORLAND)

$367* *"Duck Shooting" and "Snipe Shooting", 1790,* pub. J. Harris, later impressions, foxing, soiling, (10-27-92, Phillips-London, #91), plate 17¼ x 22¼ in., (438 x 565 mm.), etching w/aquatint w/hand-coloring on wove (BP 232, DM 562, FR 1908, Y 44,893).

ROY, Guillaume le

$128* *Untitled, 1981,* s., #168/190, full margins, good cond., (05-27-93, Sotheby-Amstrdm, #478), 26¹¹⁄₁₆ x 18⅞ in., (678 x 480 mm.), colored woodcut on sturdy wove (BP 82, DM 205, FR 692, Y 13,722, G 230).

$115* *Untitled, 1981,* s., #10/190, full margins, good cond., (05-27-93, Sotheby-Amstrdm, #476), 26¹¹⁄₁₆ x 18⅞ in., (678 x 480 mm.), colored woodcut on sturdy wove (BP 74, DM 185, FR 622, Y 12,328, G 207).

$115* *Untitled, 1981,* s., #155/190, full margins, good cond., (05-27-93, Sotheby-Amstrdm, #477), 26¹¹⁄₁₆ x 18⅞ in., (678 x 480 mm.), colored woodcut on sturdy wove (BP 74, DM 185, FR 622, Y 12,328, G 207).

ROYER, H.

$110* *L'Aurore, 1918,* Imp. Lapina, good cond., (02-12-93, Cheval/Robert, #114A), 29¹⁵⁄₁₆ x 22¹³⁄₁₆ in., (76 x 58 cm.), poster (BP 77, DM 182, FR 617, Y 13,266).

ROYER, Jacques

BI *Children In The Ruins, 1915,* handstamps, notations, est. $6/900, (10-14-92, Swann, #346, illus.), 7 x 5 in., (17.8 x 12.7 cm.), photograph, silver print.

ROYET, H.

$40* *Fanfan-La-Tulipe. Opera Comique (...) Musique De L. Varney, c. 1885,* cond. A, (03-16-93, Boisgirard, #187), 31½ x 23⅝ in., (80 x 60 cm.), poster (BP 28, DM 67, FR 226, Y 4677).

ROZAK, Theodore

$121* *Sisyphus, 1973,* t., d., num., s., ded., (05-27-93, Swann, #243), sh 22 x 30 in., (55.9 x 76.2 cm.), lithograph (BP 77, DM 194, FR 654, Y 12,972).

RUBELT, Lothar 1901-1990

$455* *Fussballette, 1919,* d., t., lit., (11-12-92, Lempertz, #213), 9 9/16 x 6 11/16 in., (23.3 x 17 cm.), photograph, gelatin silver print (BP 291, DM 715, FR 2437, Y 56,291).

$3337* *Ohne Titel, 30's: Eight,* (11-12-92, Lempertz, #217, illus.), 23 5/8 x 19½ in., (60 x 49.6 cm.), gelatin silver print photocollage (BP 2134, DM 5244, FR 17,874, Y 412,842).

BI *Semmeringrennen, 1926-1930: Four,* (c) stamp, lit., est. DM 600, (11-12-92, Lempertz, #215, illus.), each 5⅛ x 7 1/16 in., (13 x 18 cm.), photograph, gelatin silver print.

$683* *Tennis, 30's: Two,* photographer's stamp, (11-12-92, Lempertz, #218, illus.), each 9 3/16 x 6⅞ in., (23.3 x 17.5 cm.), photograph, gealtin silver print (BP 437, DM 1073, FR 3658, Y 84,498).

$1668* *Torso, 1936,* d., t., photographer's stamp, lit., (11-12-92, Lempertz, #216, illus.), 9 5/16 x 6 15/16 in., (23.6 x 17.7 cm.), photograph, gelatin silver print (BP 1066, DM 2621, FR 8934, Y 206,359).

RUBEN, Christian (after)

BI *Colombus,* by Hanfstaengl, pub. Goupil and Co., margins, staining, est. BP 8/120, (06-16-93, Bonhams-Chelsea, #474), pl. 23 x 27¼ in., (58.4 x 69.2 cm.), mezzotint.

BI *Colombus,* by Hanfstaengl, pub. Goupil and Co., margins, staining, est. BP1/200, (01-21-93, Bonhams-Chelsea, #143), plate 23 x 27¼ in., (58.4 x 69.2 cm.), mezzotint.

RUBENS, Peter Paul (after)

$149* *A Landscape With A Wagon Stuck In A Rut (Le Blanc 13),* by John Browne, finished state, pub. John Boydell, 1776, margins, (06-16-93, Bonhams-Chelsea, #322), pl. 18⅞ x 23¾ in., (47.9 x 60.3 cm.), etching (BP 99, DM 247, FR 830, Y 15,892).

BI *Ruben's Wife (C.S. 38.i), 1782,* by Richard Earlom, scratch-letter proof before t., pub. John Boydell,skinning, repaired tear, platemark, est. BP 150/200, (11-30-92, Phillips-London, #27), sheet 22¼ x 16¼ in., (565 x 413 mm.), mezzotint on laid.

BI *Self Portrait With His Wife And Child (C.S. 159),* engraved by James MacArdell, 1st state of 2, proof before all letters, fraying, good cond., est. BP 2/300, (11-30-92, Phillips-London, #26), image 18½ x 14 in., (470 x 356 mm.), mezzotint.

$440* *St. Francis Receiving The Stigmata (Bartsch 21. Hollstein 22), 1640,* thread margins, plate s., paper restoration, tiny hole, (05-27-93, Swann, #244, illus.), 5½ x 4 in., (14 x 10.2 cm.), engraving on old laid paper (BP 282, DM 706, FR 2380, Y 47,170).

$66* *St. Ildefonso,* by H. Witdouc, trimmed, surface dirt, laid down at corners, (06-16-93, Bonhams-Chelsea, #323), image 20¼ x 14½ in., (51.4 x 36.8 cm.), etching (BP 44, DM 110, FR 368, Y 7039).

RUBIN, Genia

$115* *Photo De Mode Pour Alix, Madame Gres, 1938,* ink s. recto, lit., sold after sale, (04-08-93, Christie-NY, #331, illus.), 15⅞ x 11⅞ in., (40.3 x 30.2 cm.), photograph, gelatin silver print (BP 75, DM 185, FR 625, Y 13,050).

RUBIN, Reuven Israeli 1893-1974

$275* *"Garden Of Eden",* from portfolio "Visions of the Bible", #69/150, s., (01-15-93, DuMouchelle, #2172, illus.), 28½ x 22 in., (72.4 x 55.9 cm.), color lithograph (BP 180, DM 450, FR 1520, Y 34,670).

$17* *"His Offering",* #71/150, s., (05-15-93, Dunning, #184), 19¼ x 13½ in., (48.9 x 34.3 cm.), color lithograoh (BP 11, DM 27, FR 92, Y 1884).

$275* *"Jacob Before The Lord",* from portfolio "Visions of the Bible", $69/150, s., prov., (01-15-93, DuMouchelle, #2171, illus.), 28½ x 22 in., (72.4 x 55.9 cm.), color lithograph (BP 180, DM 450, FR 1520, Y 34,670).

$220* *"King David Series",* #8/50, label verso, (10-16-92, DuMouchelle, #2401, illus.), image 22 x 16½ in., (55.9 x 41.9 cm.), colored lithograph (BP 133, DM 325, FR 1104, Y 26,269).

$1320* *Scenes With Angels And Jesus: Two,* s., num. VII/XII, good cond., creases, surface scuffs, est. $7/900, (12-12-92, Weschler, #164, illus.), each sheet 28½ x 21 in., (72.4 x 53.3 cm.), color lithograph (BP 846, DM 2080, FR 7127, Y 163,346).

$83* *Surrealistic Composition, Two Fishermen,* stone s., (08-05-92, Boos, #670), 25½ x 19½ in., (648 x 495 mm.), color lithograph (BP 43, DM 123, FR 414, Y 10,571).

RUBINCAM, Harry C. 1871-1940

$440* *The Madonna, c. 1900,* photog.'s handstamp, (10-14-92, Swann, #546, illus.), 8½ x 5½ in., (21.6 x 14 cm.), photograph, platinum print (BP 258, DM 644, FR 2184, Y 53,320).

$385* *Pastoral Lake Scene, c. 1900,* inits., num. by hand, (10-14-92, Swann, #547, illus.), 3⅞ x 5⅞ in., (9.8 x 14.9 cm.), photograph, platinum print (BP 226, DM 563, FR 1911, Y 46,655).

RUBINGER, David

BI *"Blind Boy 'Feels' The Homeland",* 1959/later, s., t., est. $4/500, (11-16-92, Butterfield, #6142, illus.), 15⅛ x 11 in., (384.9 x 279.9 mm.), photograph, gelatin silver print.

RUBINSTEIN, Eva American 20th cent.

$66* *Two Doorways, Sabbioneta, Italy,* 1973, s., d., prov., (05-16-93, Hindman, #373), 5⅝ x 8½ in., photograph, silver print (BP 43, DM 106, FR 359, Y 7350).

RUBIO, Javier

BI *"Groc-1972",* HC XXI/XXV, est. FF3/400, (04-04-93, Pescheteau, #287), 21⅝ x 27 9/16 in., (55 x 70 cm.), color lithograph.

RUBY, S.H.

$3 *"Wiener Kunstgewerbe Verein",* folds, water damage, (03-04-93, Alderfer, #282), 37½ x 24¾ in., (95.3 x 62.9 cm.), poster (BP 2, DM 5, FR 17, Y 349).

RUCKER, Robert M. American b. 1932

BI *"Two Paddlewheelers",* artist's proof, s. in stone/margin, est. $2/300, (11-21-92, Goldberg, #706), 10¾ x 14¼ in., (27.3 x 36.2 cm.), color lithograph.

RUDGE, M.M.

$28* *"Wind Train",* s., (03-12-93, DuMouchelle, #2446), 6 x 7 in., (15.2 x 17.8 cm.), etching (BP 20, DM 47, FR 158, Y 3300).

RUDIN, Nelly

BI *Komposition In Rot, 1989,* Epr. d'art., s., d., est. SF 120/180, (10-14-92, Germann, #600), 19 11/16 x 19 11/16 in., (500 x 500 mm.), color lithograph on Japan.

RUDINOFF, Willibald Russian b. 1866

$220* *New York Harbor: Two, 1918,* both s., first state annot. 3/20 I state, final state annot. fecit et imprimanti, (03-14-93, Hindman, #251), 11½ x 15¾ in., (29.2 x 40 cm.), etching, drypoint and aquatint (BP 153, DM 366, FR 1245, Y 25,928).

RUDOLPH, Charlotte

$379* *Mary Wigman, 1936,* photographer's stamp, lit., (11-12-92, Lempertz, #212, illus.), 9¼ x 6⅞ in., (23.5 x 17.4 cm.), photograph, gelatin silver print (BP 242, DM 596, FR 2030, Y 46,889).

RUDOLPH, Wilhelm 1889-1982

$406* *Kopf Eines Alten Mannes,* s., (12-05-92, Bassenge, #7674), 13 3/16 x 9⅝ in., (33.5 x 24.5 cm.), woodcut (BP 254, DM 633, FR 2157, Y 50,304).

BI *Reh,* s., est. DM 500, (12-05-92, Bassenge, #7672), 13¾ x 11 11/16 in., (35 x 29.7 cm.), woodcut on handmade Japan.

$516* *Sonne Uber Einer Baumbestandenen Landschaft,* s., (12-05-92, Bassenge, #7673), 11¼ x 18⅛ in., (28.5 x 46 cm.), woodcut on thick handmade Japan (BP 323, DM 804, FR 2742, Y 63,933).

$289* *Springende Pferde, c. 1950-1960,* s., (11-28-92, Grisebach, #722, illus.), 19 5/16 x 25 5/16 in., (49 x 64.3 cm.), woodcut on wove (BP 191, DM 460, FR 1563, Y 35,968).

$693* *Stadhauser In Einem Schneegestober,* s., (12-05-92, Bassenge, #7675), 18⅞ x 22 13/16 in., (48 x 58 cm.), woodcut on thin Japan (BP 434, DM 1080, FR 3682, Y 85,863).

RUEGG, Ernst Georg 1883-1948

BI *Tossegg, 1934,* s., est. SF 170/190, (10-14-92, Germann, #601), 12 x 15 15/16 in., (305 x 405 mm.), etching in sepia.

RUETZ, Michael   German b. 1940
  BI *Antichita 3, 1984,* s., d., #14/15-78, Edition Bovine Press, Berlin, from "A LIBRARY FORTHE EYE", est. DM 900, (11-12-92, Lempertz, #219, illus.), 16¾ x 21¼ in., (42.6 x 54 cm.), photograph, carbon print.
  BI *Gestein 1, 1984,* s., d., #14/15-93, Edition Bovine Press, Berlin, from "A LIBRARY FORTHE EYE", est. DM 900, (11-12-92, Lempertz, #220), 20 x 24 in., (50.8 x 61 cm.), photograph, carbon print.

RUFF, Thomas   German b. 1958
  BI *"Haus #711", 1986,* s., t., edit., est. $8/10,000, (05-23-93, Butterfield, #3581, illus.), 70 x 52½ in., photograph, C-print.
  BI *"Haus #81", 1988,* s., t., edit., est. $8/10,000, (05-23-93, Butterfield, #3582, illus.), 56½ x 76 in., photograph, C-print.
  $250* *Niederrheinisches Stahlkontor, 1989,* s., num., (11-12-92, Lempertz, #224), 6⅛ x 11¹³⁄₁₆ in., (15.6 x 30 cm.), sheet 14⁹⁄₁₆ x 19⅝ in., (15.6 x 30 cm.), color photograph (BP 160, DM 393, FR 1339, Y 30,929).
  $6900* *"Portrait", 1988,* s., t., edit., est. $8/12,000, (05-23-93, Butterfield, #3580, illus.), 63 x 47 in., photograph, C-print (BP 4494, DM 11,282, FR 37,975, Y 762,684).
  BI *Portrat C. Fottinger, 1987,* s., d., est. DM 12,000, (11-12-92, Lempertz, #223, illus.), exhibited size 70⅞ x 54¾ in., (180 x 139 cm.), total size 90¹⁵⁄₁₆ x 73¼ in., (180 x 139 cm.), unique color photograph.
  BI *Stars, 1990,* p. annot. 11h 12m/-45', pub. Edition Schellmann, very good cond.?, est. $7/900, (05-19-93, Butterfield, #2326), sh 35 x 25½ in., (889 x 648 mm.), granolithograph on wove.
  $5500* *Untitled,* s., num. 3/3 and d. 1988 verso, prov., (10-06-92, Sotheby-NY, #206, illus.), framed 83 x 65 in., (210.8 x 165.1 cm.), color photograph in artist's wood frame (BP 3223, DM 7867, FR 26,673, Y 659,077).
  $6600* *Untitled,* s., num., d. T.L. Ruff 2/4 1988 verso, prov., (11-19-92, Christie-NY, #173, illus.), 82¾ x 65⅛ in., (210.2 x 165.4 cm.), photograph, color in artist's frame (BP 4346, DM 10,523, FR 35,446, Y 820,793).
  $9900* *Untitled,* s., num. 2/3, d. 1988 verso, prov., (11-18-92, Sotheby-NY, #289, illus.), 83 x 65 in., (210.8 x 165.1 cm.), color photograph in artist's wood frame (BP 6518, DM 15,784, FR 53,169, Y 1,231,190).
  $11,500* *Untitled,* s., #sc07, d. 1988 verso, (02-23-93, Sotheby-NY, #346, illus.), framed 83 x 65 in., (210.8 x 165.1 cm.), color photograph in artist's wood frame (BP 7878, DM 18,578, FR 63,014, Y 1,343,144).
  $9900* *Untitled (Ralph Muller),* s., num., d. T L Ruff 2/3 1986 verso, prov., exhib., (11-19-92, Christie-NY, #162, illus.), 80¾ x 63¼ in., (205.1 x 160.7 cm.), photograph, color (BP 6518, DM 15,784, FR 53,169, Y 1,231,190).
  $2200* *Untitled: Two Photographs,* one s., d. Thomas Ruff 1988 verso; other s., d. Thomas Ruff 1987 verso, prov., (11-17-92, Christie-E, #110, illus.), each 16 x 12 in., (40.6 x 30.5 cm.), color photograph (BP 1449, DM 3508, FR 11,815, Y 273,598).

RUGENDAS, M. (after)
  BI *"Valpiraiso",* engr. by Paul Petit, (12-11-92, G.A. Key, #38), 9 x 12 in., (22.9 x 30.5 cm.), hand colored lithograph.
  $30 *"Valpiraiso",* engraved by Paul Petit, (04-16-93, G.A. Key, #57), 9 x 12 in., (22.9 x 30.5 cm.), hand-colored lithograph (BP 20, DM 48, FR 164, Y 3373).

RUISCHER, Jan and Antoine WATERLOO
  $161* *Vue D'Une Ville De Hollande (Holl. vol. 10, 15; Bartsch vol. 2, 90),* third state of 3, dirt stains, glue traces d. 1821, restorations verso, (05-15-93, Loudmer, #90), 4¾ x 8⅛ in., (120 x 207 mm.), sh 4¹⁵⁄₁₆ x 8¼ in., (120 x 207 mm.), etching and copper engraving on wove (BP 105, DM 259, FR 870, Y 17,847).

RUISDAEL, Jacob van   Dutch 1628/29-1682
  $989* *Die Hutte Auf Dem Hugel (Bartsch 3; Hollstein 3 II),* (06-10-93, Hauswedell/Nolt, #156), etching on handmade (BP 647, DM 1610, FR 5422, Y 104,978).
  $2125* *Die Kleine Brucke (B. 1, Dutuit 1, Wurzbach 1, Hollstein 1 II),* (06-04-93, Bassenge, #5346), 7¹¹⁄₁₆ x 10¹¹⁄₁₆ in.,

(19.5 x 27.2 cm.), etching (BP 1406, DM 3451, FR 11,631, Y 229,185).
  $2527* *Die Kleine Brucke (B. 1; Dutuit 1; Hollstein 1 II),* (12-04-92, Bassenge, #6421, illus.), 7⁹⁄₁₆ x 10¾ in., (19.2 x 27.3 cm.), etching (BP 1621, DM 4025, FR 13,652, Y 315,481).
  $2527* *Das Kornfeld (Hollstein 5 IV), 1648,* stained, (12-04-92, Bassenge, #6423), 3¹⁵⁄₁₆ x 5⅞ in., (10 x 14.9 cm.), etching (BP 1621, DM 4025, FR 13,652, Y 315,481).
  $433* *The Small Wooden Bridge (B.I.D. 1 11/11), c. 1660,* margins, trimmed to plate, repaired tear, discoloration, stain, (11-30-92, Phillips-London, #313), sheet 7⅝ x 10⅞ in., (194 x 276 mm.), etching on cream wove (BP 286, DM 690, FR 2342, Y 53,889).
  $1630* *The Three Oaks (Bartsch 6; Keyes 5; Hollstein 6; Slive 104),* s., plate d., repairs, 1st state of 2, (06-09-93, Bubb Kuyper, #2069, illus.), 5¹⁄₁₆ x 5¹¹⁄₁₆ in., (12.8 x 14.5 cm.), etching (BP 1075, DM 2666, FR 8966, Y 173,349, G 2990).
  $115* *Two Farmers With Their Dog (Holl. 2), early 1650s,* 2nd (final) state, trimmed between platemark and borderline, restorations, stains, Daniel A. Don Estate, (05-13-93, Sotheby-NY, #204), 7⅜ x 10¾ in., (186 x 272 mm.), etching (BP 75, DM 186, FR 626, Y 12,839).
  $2166* *Die Zwei Bauern Mit Dem Hund (B. 2;Dutuit, Hollstein 2 II),* prov., (12-04-92, Bassenge, #6422, illus.), 7¹¹⁄₁₆ x 11¼ in., (19.5 x 28.6 cm.), etching (BP 1389, DM 3450, FR 11,702, Y 270,412).
  $1700* *Die Zwei Bauern Mit Dem Hunde (B. 2, Dutuit 2, Hollstein 2 II),* watermark, (06-04-93, Bassenge, #5347, illus.), 7¹¹⁄₁₆ x 10¾ in., (19.6 x 27.3 cm.), etching (BP 1125, DM 2761, FR 9305, Y 183,348).

RULLMANN, L. (after)
  $295* *Elle Cede A Ses Enchantements. Imprudence,* yellowed, good margins, (06-16-93, Ader Tajan, #46), 13¾ x 17½ in., (35 x 44.5 cm.), etching and stipple print engraving in color (BP 197, DM 490, FR 1643, Y 31,463).

RUNGIUS, Carl   American 1869-1959
  $2511* *Alaskan Wilderness, 1940,* s., i., prov., (11-16-92, Hodgins, #131, illus.), 7¹⁵⁄₁₆ x 10¹⁵⁄₁₆ in., (20.3 x 27.9 cm.), etching on paper (BP 1650, DM 4005, FR 13,493, Y 313,366, C$ 3190).
  $1650* *"The Answer Fron The Barrens", 1925,* s. C. Rungius, very good cond., soiling, (09-11-92, Skinner, #62, illus.), 6¼ x 8⅜ in., (15.9 x 21.3 cm.), etching/drypoint on wove (BP 853, DM 2375, FR 8072, Y 204,436).
  $2200* *Dalls Sheep,* s., (10-08-92, Grogan, #735), 8 x 10⅞ in., (20.3 x 27.6 cm.), etching (BP 1309, DM 3254, FR 11,044, Y 267,315).
  $1650* *Mountain Goats,* s., (12-09-92, Grogan, #65), 7¾ x 11 in., (19.7 x 27.9 cm.), etching (BP 1053, DM 2590, FR 8838, Y 204,588).
  $1210* *"Stampede", 1925,* s. C. Rungius; ident. in inscript. verso, good cond., light toning, wide margins, (09-11-92, Skinner, #65, illus.), 6⅛ x 8⁷⁄₁₆ in., (15.6 x 21.4 cm.), etching/drypoint on wove (BP 626, DM 1742, FR 5920, Y 149,919).
  $2597* *Three Old Gentlemen, 1940,* s., i., prov., (11-16-92, Hodgins, #221, illus.), 7¹⁵⁄₁₆ x 10¹⁵⁄₁₆ in., (20.3 x 27.9 cm.), etching on paper (BP 1707, DM 4142, FR 13,955, Y 324,098, C$ 3300).
  $275* *Two Caribou In A Glade,* s. below image, (08-05-92, Boos, #686), image 7¹¹⁄₁₆ x 10¹³⁄₁₆ in., (195 x 275 mm.), etching (BP 144, DM 406, FR 1372, Y 35,023).

RUSCHA, Edward   American b. 1937
  $920* *1984 (G. 57), 1967,* s., d., #53/60, blindstamp publisher, Gemini G.E.L., p. Charles Ritt,full margins, good cond., mat staining, surface soiling, handling creases, staining, (05-19-93, Butterfield, #2327), 20 x 25 in., (508 x 635 mm.), lithograph w/hand-coloring on Barcham Green (BP 597, DM 1495, FR 5038, Y 101,849).
  $2070* *1984 (M.I.A. 5, Gemini 57), 1967,* s., d., #18/60, blindstamp, pub. Gemini, G.E.L., full margins, good cond., creases, (05-15-93, Sotheby-NY, #1188, illus.), 14 x 17⅞ in., (35.6 x 45.4 cm.), lithograph w/hand-coloring (BP 1346, DM 3330, FR 11,189, Y 229,465).
  $4140* *3327 Division ('39 Ford) (Minneapolis Institute of Art 2), 1962,* s., d., pub. Kanthos Press, full margins, good

cond., discoloration, (05-15-93, Sotheby-NY, #1187, illus.), 12⅞ x 10⅛ in., (32.7 x 25.7 cm.), lithograph on Rives (BP 2692, DM 6659, FR 22,378, Y 458,929).

$451* *Ants,* from Insects. s. Edward Ruscha 1973, 33/100, (06-03-93, Kunsthallen, #192), lithograph (BP 292, DM 722, FR 2433, Y 48,370, DK 2760).

BI *Ants, 1973,* s., #9/100, p. Styria Studio, pub. by artist and Multiples, good cond., skinned spots, est. BP 6/800, (12-03-92, Sotheby-London, #793, illus.), 22 x 30 in., (560 x 763 mm.), lithograph in black and grey.

$539* *Artist And Photograph Portfolio; Fruit, 1975,* num. edit. 10/60, s. E. Ruscha, stamped Edward Ruscha and Multiples, Inc. 1975 verso, (10-15-92, Sotheby-London, #49, illus.), 16 x 20 in., (40.6 x 50.8 cm.), photograph, color print (BP 330, DM 802, FR 2721, Y 64,667).

$1610* *Big Dipper Over Desert, 1982,* s., d., #42/48, Crown Point Press blindstamp, full margins, surface soiling, skinned spots, excell. cond., the Late M. Anwar Kamal, M.D. Coll., est. $1,5/2,500, (05-11-93, Christie-NY, #559, illus.), sheet 33⅞ x 45 in., (86 x 114.3 cm.), aquatint in dark blues on wove (BP 1028, DM 2536, FR 8546, Y 177,098).

BI *Big Dipper, 1982,* s., d., #8/10, blindstamp pub. Crown Point Press, full margins, verygood cond., est. $3/4,000, (10-28-92, Butterfield, #3107), 24 x 36 in., (610 x 914 mm.), aquatint in blue on white wove.

BI *Blue Suds (M.I.A. 55), 1971,* s., d., #34/100, pub. Edizioni O, good cond., est. $1,2/1,500, (02-11-93, Sotheby-NY, #433), sheet 17¹⁵⁄₁₆ x 24 in., (457 x 610 mm.), color silkscreen.

$300* *Brews, 1970,* s., d., i. E.P., pub. Editions Alecto, good cond., (11-30-92, Phillips-London, #565), sheet 23 x 31⅝ in., (584 x 803 mm.), screenprint in light brown & gray on wove; media said to be combinedaxle grease & caviar (BP 198, DM 478, FR 1622, Y 37,337).

$5500* *Coyote, 1989,* s., d., #18/50, pub. by artist, very good cond.?, (10-28-92, Butterfield, #3111, illus.), 36 x 27 in., (914 x 686 mm.), lithograph on wove (BP 3504, DM 8494, FR 28,841, Y 674,847).

BI *Coyote, 1989,* s., d., #47/50, pub. artist, good cond., scuffing, est. $5/7,000, (05-19-93, Butterfield, #2329, illus.), 36⅛ x 27 in., (918 x 686 mm.), lithograph on wove.

$690* *Domestic Tranqility: Bowl, 1974,* s., d., #50/65, co-pub. Multiples, Inc. and Castelli Graphics, full margins, good cond., (02-11-93, Sotheby-NY, #435, illus.), 12 x 15³⁄₁₆ in., (305 x 386 mm.), color lithograph (BP 487, DM 1143, FR 3868, Y 83,183).

BI *Domestic Tranquility, 1974: Four,* s., d., #28/65, blindstamp p. Cirrus, pub. Multiples, Inc. and Castelli Graphics, full margins, very good cond.?, est. $4/6,000, (10-28-92, Butterfield, #3105), color lithograph on wove.

$1320* *Drops (Foster 52), 1971,* s., d., num. 33/90, pub. Brooke Alexander, full sheet, scuff, excell. cond., (09-19-92, Christie-E, #206), sheet 20 x 28 in., (508 x 711 mm.), lithograph in greens on Arches (BP 759, DM 1977, FR 6769, Y 164,465).

$300* *Dues, 1970,* s., d., i. Artist's Proof, pub. Editions Alecto, indents., good cond., (11-30-92, Phillips-London, #566), sheet 23 x 31⅝ in., (584 x 803 mm.), screenprint in light browns on wove; media said to be combined pick-leletering on solid pickle background (BP 198, DM 478, FR 1622, Y 37,337).

BI *Egg-Timer, Barcelona, 1988,* from Untitled, Ediciones Poligrafa, s., d., #57/75, full margins, excell. cond., est. $2/2,500, (05-11-93, Christie-NY, #561, illus.), sheet 29¾ x 21¹⁵⁄₁₆ in., (756 x 557 mm.), color lithograph on wove.

$4400* *"Etc", "South", "Question & Answer" and "If", 1991: Four,* each s., d., annot. Printers Proof, pub. by artist, blindstamp of printer Edward Hamilton, full margins, very good cond., (02-24-93, Butterfield, #3143, illus.), each 9¼ x 12½ in., (235 x 318 mm.), lithograph in colors on BFK Rives (BP 3068, DM 7143, FR 24,216, Y 516,311).

$866* *The Fan And Its Surroundings, 1982,* s., d., num., (11-28-92, Schoppmann, #765), 36¹³⁄₁₆ x 31¹¹⁄₁₆ in., (93.5 x 80.5 cm.), color lithograph on BFK Rives (BP 572, DM 1380, FR 4684, Y 107,778).

$6050* *Gallo, 1988,* s., d., #21/60, very good cond., (10-28-92, Butterfield, #3109, illus.), 30 x 22 in., (762 x 559 mm.), lithograph on cream wove (BP 3855, DM 9344, FR 31,725, Y 742,331).

$2420* *Girls (G. 1009), 1982,* s., d., #6/40, blindstamps, excell. cond., (11-09-92, Christie-NY, #399, illus.), 25 x 34 in., (635 x 864 mm.), colored lithograph on Arches (BP 1600, DM 3863, FR 13,053, Y 300,323).

$1210* *Grey Studs (F. 57), 1971,* s., d., num. 85/100, pub. Edizioni O, Cirrus Editions ink stamp, full sheet, old glue, skinned spots, very good cond., (09-19-92, Christie-E, #208), sheet 17¹⁵⁄₁₆ x 23¹⁵⁄₁₆ in., (456 x 608 mm.), screenprint in greys on wove (BP 696, DM 1812, FR 6205, Y 150,760).

BI *Heaven, 1988,* s., d., #11/25, blindstamp, pub. Crown Point Press, full margins, good cond., est. $3/4,000, (05-15-93, Sotheby-NY, #1195, illus.), 44¼ x 32⅞ in., (112.4 x 83.5 cm.), aquatint in colors.

BI *Hell, 1988,* s., d., #11/25, blindstamp pub., Crown Point Press, full margins, good cond., est. $3/4,000, (05-15-93, Sotheby-NY, #1194, illus.), 44¼ x 32⅞ in., (112.4 x 83.5 cm.), aquatint in colors.

BI *Hey (M.I.A. 27), 1969,* s., #2/20, blindstamp, pub. Tamarind Workshop, full margins, good cond., discoloration, foxing, est. $2,5/3,500, (05-15-93, Sotheby-NY, #1191, illus.), 8 x 9⅞ in., (20.3 x 25.1 cm.), lithograph in colors.

$6613* *Hollywood (M.I.A. 17), 1969,* s., d., #10/18, blindstamp, pub. Tamarind Workshop, full margins, good cond., pressure marks, water stain, soiling, (05-15-93, Sotheby-NY, #1189, illus.), 7 x 19 in., (17.8 x 48.3 cm.), lithograph in tones of gray (BP 4300, DM 10,637, FR 35,746, Y 733,067).

$10,350* *Hollywood With Observatory (Foster 14), 1969,* s., d., #16/17, Tamarind Lithography Workshop blindstamp, full margins, pristine cond., (05-11-93, Christie-NY, #554, illus.), sheet 6½ x 32 in., (165 x 813 mm.), color lithograph on wove (BP 6607, DM 16,304, FR 54,936, Y 1,138,489).

BI *Hollywood With Observatory (M.I.A.), 1969,* s., d., #3/17, blindstamp, pub. Tamarind Workshop, full margins, good cond., est. 12/14,000, (05-15-93, Sotheby-NY, #1190, illus.), 1¼ x 29¼ in., (3.2 x 74.3 cm.), lithograph in tones of gray.

$539* *Hot Shot, 1973,* s., #83/100 verso, pub. in Mini Print Portfolio, full sheet, p. to edges, good cond., cellophane tape, (10-15-92, Sotheby-London, #131), 5¾ x 8¼ in., (14.6 x 21 cm.), lithograph p. in colors (BP 330, DM 802, FR 2721, Y 64,667).

BI *Hourglass, 1988,* s., d., #9/20, Crown Point Press blindstamp, full margins, excell. cond., the Late M. Anwar Kamal, M.D. Coll., est. $3/4,000, (05-11-93, Christie-NY, #560, illus.), sheet 52¾ x 37½ in., (134 x 95.3 cm.), aquatint, drypoint and roulette in blue and beige on Somerset.

$4255* *Hourglass, 1988,* s., d., #4/20, blindstamp, pub. Crown Point Press, full margins, good cond., crease, (05-15-93, Sotheby-NY, #1196, illus.), 43⅞ x 29⅝ in., (111.4 x 75.2 cm.), aquatint in colors (BP 2767, DM 6844, FR 23,000, Y 471,677).

$2300* *I'm Amazed (F. 54), 1971,* s., d., #27/100, pub. Bernard Jacobson, Ltd., excell. cond., (05-11-93, Christie-NY, #556, illus.), sheet 39¾ x 60 in., (101 x 152.4 cm.), color screenprint on wove (BP 1468, DM 3623, FR 12,208, Y 252,997).

$2588* *I'm Amazed (M.I.A. 54), 1971,* s., d., #38/100, pub. Bernard Jacobson, Ltd., good cond., (02-11-93, Sotheby-NY, #432, illus.), sheet 39¾ x 60¼ in., (101 x 153 cm.), color silkscreen (BP 1826, DM 4287, FR 14,507, Y 311,995).

$990* *It's Recreational (Gemini 1008), 1982,* s., d., #6/40, blindstamps, excell. cond., (11-09-92, Christie-NY, #398), 25 x 34 in., (635 x 864 mm.), colored lithograph on Arches (BP 655, DM 1580, FR 5340, Y 122,859).

$715* *Kay-Eye-Double-S, 1978,* s., d., #17/65, pub. Hartford Art School, full margins, very good cond.?, (10-28-92, Butterfield, #3106), 6 x 27¼ in., (152 x 692 mm.), color lithograph on Rives BFK (BP 456, DM 1104, FR 3749, Y 87,730).

$899* *Lisp, 1970,* s., d., #62/90, pub. Brooke Alexander, full sheet p. to edges, minorcreasing, skinned areas, (10-15-92, Sotheby-London, #128, illus.), sh 19⅞ x 27⅞ in., (50.5 x 70.8 cm.), lithograph p. in colors on wove (BP 550, DM 1338, FR 4538, Y 107,858).

$2185* *Make Up Department, 1975,* s., #30/60, portfolio Artists and Photographs, pub. Multiples, Inc.,good cond., surface scuffs, (05-15-93, Sotheby-NY, #1192, illus.), sheet 15⅞ x 19⅞ in., (40.3 x 50.5 cm.), color dye transfer print (BP 1421, DM 3515, FR 11,811, Y 242,213).

BI *Makeup Dept.,* s., num. 47/60 by photog. on image, (c) d. stamp, 1975, p. 1978, #47/60 ed., est. $2/3,000, (10-15-92, Sotheby-NY, #573, illus.), 16 x 20 in., (40.6 x 50.8 cm.), photograph, 3-color dye transfer transparency.

$440* *"Mews",* s., d. 1970, i., artist's proof, (06-11-93, Freemn/Fine Art, #196A), image 17½ x 27 in., (44.5 x 68.6 cm.), sh 23 x 32 in., (44.5 x 68.6 cm.), color screenprint (BP 289, DM 715, FR 2411, Y 46,684).

BI *Miracle (G. 747), 1977,* s., d. 1975, #16/35, Gemini G.E.L. blindstamps, full margins, skinned spot, excell. cond., est. $2,5/3,500, (05-11-93, Christie-NY, #558, illus.), sheet 22 x 31 in., (559 x 787 mm.), lithograph in yellow and black on wove.

$8250* *Mocha Standard (M. I. A. 29), 1969,* s., d., #100/100, pub. by artist, full margins, good cond., (11-07-92, Sotheby-NY, #758, illus.), 19⅝ x 36⅞ in., (498 x 937 mm.), silkscreen p. in colors (BP 5394, DM 13,173, FR 44,522, Y 1,018,267).

$5175* *Mocha Standard (Minneapolis Institute of Arts 29), 1969,* s., d., #57/100, pub. by artist, full margins, good cond., scuffs, crease, soiling, discoloration, (02-11-93, Sotheby-NY, #431, illus.), 19⅝ x 36⅞ in., (498 x 937 mm.), color silkscreen (BP 3652, DM 8572, FR 29,008, Y 623,870).

$2300* *"News", "Mews", "Pews", "Brews", "Stews" and "Dues" (F/MIA. 32-37), 1970: Six,* suite lacking justification page and portfolio, s., d., #20/125, 24/125, 29/125, Artist's Proof, 24/125 and Artist's Proof, pub. Edition Alecto, full margins, good cond., tear, staining, handling creases, surface soiling, (05-19-93, Butterfield, #2328, illus.), each sh 23 x 31 in., (584 x 787 mm.), silkscreen in colors on wove (BP 1493, DM 3739, FR 12,596, Y 254,622).

BI *"News", "Mews", "Pews", "Brews", "Stews", and "Dues" (Editions Alecto, London, 1970):* Set Of Six, each s., d., num. 83/125, creasing, surface dirt, defects, portfolio, est. BP 2/3,000, (12-01-92, Christie-London, #632, illus.), overall size 24¾ x 32¹⁵⁄₁₆ in., (628 x 837 mm.), organic screenprints in colors on wove.

$2517* *"News", "Mews", "Pews", "Brews", "Stews", and "Dues", 1970:* Set of Six, each s., d., #48/125, num. 48 from edit. of 150, margins, good cond.,loose in portfolio box, (10-15-92, Sotheby-London, #130, illus.), each sh approx. 23 x 32 in., (58.4 x 81.3 cm.), organic screenprint p. in colors on white wove (BP 1540, DM 3747, FR 12,706, Y 301,980).

$2760* *News, Mews, Pews, Brews, Stews, Dues, London, Editions Electo, 1970 (F. 32-7):* Six, s., d., num., copy 83 of 125, full margins, colors attenuated, surface soiling, crease, good cond., orig. portfolio, (05-11-93, Christie-NY, #555, illus.), each sheet 23 x 31¾ in., (584 x 806 mm.), color organic screenprint on wove (BP 1762, DM 4348, FR 14,650, Y 303,597).

$880* *OOO (F/M.I.A. 43), 1970,* s., d., annot. Printer's Proof, pub. Cirrus & Brooke Alexander, apparently very good cond., creases in image, (02-24-93, Butterfield, #3137), (508 x 711 mm.), lithograph in aqua-blue on Arches (BP 614, DM 1429, FR 4843, Y 103,262).

$2420* *Raw (F. 53), 1971,* s., d., num. 73/90, pub. Bernard Jacobson, Cirrus Editions blindstamp, full margins, pale time staining, skinned spots, good cond., (09-19-92, Christie-E, #207, illus.), sh 16 x 26 in., (406 x 660 mm.), screenprint in yellow and brown on wove (BP 1392, DM 3624, FR 12,410, Y 301,520).

BI *Raw (F/M.I.A. 53), 1971,* s., d., num. 50/90, pub. Bernard Jacobson, blindstamp, full margins,good cond., surface scuffs, tear, hinge remains, creases, est. $2,5/3,500, (02-24-93, Butterfield, #3138, illus.), 10⅞ x 21½ in., (276 x 546 mm.), silksreen in colors on wove.

BI *Raw, 1971,* s., d., #49/90, printer's blindstamp, Cirrus Editions, pub. Bernard Jacobson, Ltd., full margins, tears, crease, red mark, est. $2/3,000, (11-07-92, Sotheby-NY, #759, illus.), 10⅞ x 21½ in., (276 x 546 mm.), silkscreen p. in colors.

$1150* *Raw, 1971,* s., d., #49/90, blindstamp of p., Cirrus Editions, pub. Bernard Jacobson, Ltd., full margins, tears, crease, (02-11-93, Sotheby-NY, #434), 10¹³⁄₁₆ x 21⁷⁄₁₆ in., (275 x 545 mm.), color silkscreen (BP 811, DM 1905, FR 6446, Y 138,638).

BI *Reloj De Arena, 1988,* s., d., #2/45, full margins, very good cond., est. $2/3,000, (10-28-92, Butterfield, #3110, illus.), 18¼ x 13¼ in., (464 x 337 mm.), etching w/ aquatint on thick handmade.

$1210* *Reloj De Arena, 1988,* s., d., num. 39/45, full margins, apparently very good cond., (02-24-93, Butterfield, #3142), 18¼ x 13¼ in., (464 x 337 mm.), aquatint in colors on heavy handmade (BP 844, DM 1964, FR 6659, Y 141,985).

BI *Reloj De Arena, 1988,* s., d., #2/45, full margins, very good cond.?, est. $1,5/2,000, (05-19-93, Butterfield, #2328A), 18¼ x 13¼ in., (464 x 337 mm.), etching w/ aquatint on thick handmade.

BI *Rooster, 1988,* s., d., #32/50, blindstamp, pub. Crown Point Press, full margins, good cond., est. $5/6,000, (05-15-93, Sotheby-NY, #1197, illus.), 35⅝ x 22 in., (90.5 x 55.9 cm.), aquatint in colors on Somerset.

BI *Sign, 1989,* s., d., #29/35, p. Ed Hamilton, pub. by artist, good cond., scuff marks, est. $2,5/3,500, (11-07-92, Sotheby-NY, #761, illus.), sheet 27 x 36 in., (686 x 914 mm.), lithograph.

$433* *Sin,* s., d., num. 24/150, margins, good cond., (12-01-92, Christie-London, #633), 13¹⁄₁₆ x 21⅝ in., (331 x 549 mm.), screenprint in colors on wove (BP 286, DM 690, FR 2352, Y 53,909).

$19,800* *Standard Station (Minneapolis Institute of Arts 4), 1966,* s., d., #21/50, pub. Audrey Sabol, full margins, good cond., creasing, scuff, foxing, (11-07-92, Sotheby-NY, #757, illus.), 19⅝ x 37 in., (498 x 940 mm.), silkscreen p. in colors (BP 12,945, DM 31,614, FR 106,854, Y 2,443,841).

BI *That Is Right, 1989: Twelve,* complete portfolio, s., d., annot. Printer's Proof, inits., d., annot. PP, artist blindstamp, full margins, excell. cond., orig. portfolio; includes Precise; That is Right; Actual; Certain; Correct; Accurate; Positive; Exact; Sure; Definite; True and Final, est. $10/12,000, (10-28-92, Butterfield, #3112, illus.), image 5³⁄₁₆ x 6⅞ in., (132 x 175 mm.), sheet 9 x 11 in., (132 x 175 mm.), color lithograph on BFK Rives.

$1840* *Tropical Fish Series (Gemini 578-82), 1975: Five,* includes Open; Air, Water, Fire; Closed; Music; and Sweets, Meats, Sheets, s., d. 1974, num. 48/56, 48/57, 48/53, 48/58 and 49/55, Gemini G.E.L. ink stamps, excell. cond., (05-11-93, Christie-NY, #557, illus.), each sheet 25¹³⁄₁₆ x 32¹³⁄₁₆ in., (656 x 833 mm.), color screenprint w/lacquer or varnish on wove (BP 1175, DM 2899, FR 9766, Y 202,398).

BI *"Two Happy People", "Two People Temporarily Separated", "Three Daughters", "Man Walking Away From It All", "Jumping Fish" and "Two Jumping Fish", 1980: Six,* suite, each s., d., #11/55, pub. Bernard Jacobson. Ltd., full margins, good cond., handling creases, est. $5/6,000, (05-15-93, Sotheby-NY, #1193, illus.), each sheet 19¼ x 39⅛ in., (48.9 x 99.4 cm.), etching in colors.

$866* *Untitled, 1980,* s., d., num., (11-28-92, Schoppmann, #766), 10⁷⁄₁₆ x 31¹¹⁄₁₆ in., (26.5 x 80.5 cm.), color etching on handmade (BP 572, DM 1380, FR 4684, Y 107,778).

$866* *Untitled, 1980,* s., d., num., (11-28-92, Schoppmann, #767), 10⁷⁄₁₆ x 31¹¹⁄₁₆ in., (26.5 x 80.5 cm.), color etching on handmade (BP 572, DM 1380, FR 4684, Y 107,778).

$866* *Untitled, 1980,* s., d., num., (11-28-92, Schoppmann, #768), 10⁷⁄₁₆ x 31¹¹⁄₁₆ in., (26.5 x 80.5 cm.), color etching on handmade (BP 572, DM 1380, FR 4684, Y 107,778).

$440* *Untitled, 1983,* s., d., #68/100, blindstamp p. Cirrus, pub. Bernard Jacobsen, full margins, good cond., (10-28-92,

Butterfield, #3108), 27 x 23 in., (686 x 584 mm.), color lithograph on wove (BP 280, DM 680, FR 2307, Y 53,988).

$495* *Untitled, 1983,* s., d., #5/100, pub. Bernard Jacobson for the Chicago Art Expo, blindstamp, full margins, good cond. (?), (02-24-93, Butterfield, #3248), 27 x 23 in., (686 x 584 mm.), lithograph in colors on wove (BP 345, DM 804, FR 2724, Y 58,085).

$468* *Untitled, 1983,* s., d., #7/100, pub. Bernard Jacobson for the Chicago Art Expo, blindstamp, full margins, good cond., (02-24-93, Butterfield, #3249), 27 x 23 in., (686 x 584 mm.), lithograph in colors on wove (BP 326, DM 760, FR 2576, Y 54,917).

$1980* *Vanish, 1973,* s., d., #46/50, pub. Cirrus Editions, good cond., (11-07-92, Sotheby-NY, #760, illus.), 20 x 28 in., (508 x 711 mm.), lithograph p. in gray (BP 1295, DM 3161, FR 10,685, Y 244,384).

$660* *Various Cheeses: "Eleven Pieces Of Cheese" and "Cheese Oval" (G. 721;723), 1976,* each s., num. 22/50 & 23/39, blindstamp of pub. Gemini G.E.L., good cond., Eleven Pieces w/surface scuffs in image, glue remains, surface soiling, (02-24-93, Butterfield, #3139), 14¾ x 20⅝ in., (375 x 524 mm.), 14⅝ x 20⅜ in., (375 x 524 mm.), lithograph in colors on Arches 88 (BP 460, DM 1071, FR 3632, Y 77,447).

$2860* *Western Vertical And Western Horizontal, 1986,* s., d., #35/35, blindstamps, full margins, excell. cond., shrink-wrapped, (11-09-92, Christie-NY, #400, illus.), colored lithograph on wove (BP 1891, DM 4566, FR 15,426, Y 354,927).

$1100* *World Series: Cities (G.1011), 1982,* s., d., num. 38/40, blindstamp of pub. Gemini G.E.L., apparently verygood cond., (02-24-93, Butterfield, #3141), 25 x 47⅜ in., (63.5 x 120.3 cm.), lithograph in colors on Arches 88 (BP 767, DM 1786, FR 6054, Y 129,078).

BI *World Series: It's Recreational (G. 1008), 1982,* s., d., num. 39/40, blindstamp of pub. Gemini G.E.L., good cond., est. $1,5/2,500, (02-24-93, Butterfield, #3140, illus.), 24 15/16 x 34 1/16 in., (633 x 865 mm.), lithograph in colors on Arches.

RUSCHA, Edward and Joe GOODE

BI *Yesterday's Treasures, 1989,* s., d., #18/90, pub. by artist, blindstamp, very good cond., est. $1,6/2,000, (10-28-92, Butterfield, #3113), 27 x 36 in., (686 x 914 mm.), color lithograph on cream wove.

RUSHBURY, Henry 1889-1968

$845* *Shell Mex House, 1932,* p. Vincent Brooks, Day & Son, ref. #349, cond. 3, water staining, (10-13-92, Phillips-London, #92, illus.), 29 13/16 x 44 11/16 in., (75.7 x 113.5 cm.), color lithograph (BP 492, DM 1238, FR 4206, Y 102,462).

RUSHBURY, Sir Henry George

BI *"Parisian Street Scene, Notre Dame Beyond",* s., margins, est. BP 50/70, (12-10-92, Bonhams-Chelsea, #88), plate 9¼ x 13 in., (23.5 x 33 cm.), drypoint etching.

BI *"Parisian Street Scene, Notre Dame Beyond",* s., margins, est. BP 70/100, (10-15-92, Bonhams-Chelsea, #150), plate 9¼ x 13 in., (23.5 x 33 cm.), drypoint etching.

$56* *"Parisian Street Scenes, Notre Dame Beyond",* s., margins, (02-17-93, Bonhams-Chelsea, #265), plate 9¼ x 13 in., (23.5 x 33 cm.), drypoint etching (BP 39, DM 91, FR 308, Y 6689).

$126* *"The Seine At Notre Dame",* s., margins, (10-15-92, Bonhams-Chelsea, #149), plate 11¾ x 17 in., (29.8 x 43.2 cm.), drypoint etching (BP 77, DM 188, FR 636, Y 15,117).

RUSKIN, Saul

$44* *"The Wailing Wall",* (01-15-93, DuMouchelle, #123), approx. 9 x 11 in., (22.9 x 27.9 cm.), etching (BP 29, DM 72, FR 243, Y 5547).

RUSSELL, A.J. 1830-1902

$1320* *"Front Of Arlington House" and "James River": Two,* photog. credit, t., d. in first, notations on mounts recto, 1860s, (04-07-93, Swann, #189, illus.), one 11¾ x 16 in., other 8 x 10¾ in., photograph, albumen print (BP 872, DM 2135, FR 7225, Y 149,966).

RUSSELL, A.J. (attrib.) 1830-1902

$1210* *Effect Of The Explosion Of A Shell, Near Petersburg, Va.,* on orig. mount, notations recto, 1860s, (04-07-93, Swann, #190, illus.), 8¾ x 13 in., photograph, albumen print (BP 800, DM 1957, FR 6623, Y 137,469).

RUSSELL, Andrew J. American 1830-1902

$247* *Haupt's Invention, 1862-63,* (10-14-92, Swann, #173), 6 x 8 in., (15.2 x 20.3 cm.), photograph, salt print (BP 145, DM 361, FR 1226, Y 29,932).

$1980* *Trestle At Promontory Point, Utah (Taft, p. 293), 1869,* mounted, (10-15-92, Sotheby-NY, #22, illus.), 9⅛ x 12⅛ in., (23.2 x 30.8 cm.), photograph, albumen print (BP 1212, DM 2947, FR 9995, Y 237,552).

RUSSELL, Benjamin

$2875* *Sperm Whale With Its Varieties (Peters, Amer. on Stone, p. 125), 1870,* pub. by artist, p. J.H. Bufford's Lith., margins, good cond., discoloration, water stains, fox marks, (01-28-93, Sotheby-NY, #460, illus.), 16⅝ x 33 in., (422 x 838 mm.), sheet 21⅜ x 37⅝ in., (422 x 838 mm.), hand-colored lithograph w/blue tint stone in sky (BP 1899, DM 4556, FR 15,416, Y 356,965).

RUSSELL, C.E.

$34 *"French Colour Prints Of The XVIII Century", 1923: Twelve,* loose in folder, (10-09-92, G.A. Key, #87), color print (BP 20, DM 51, FR 172, Y 4146).

RUSSELL, Captain A.J.

$522* *Bull Run,* photog. sig. in neg., orig. mount, w/notations, 1860s, (04-07-93, Swann, #188, illus.), 11 x 16 in., photograph, albumen print (BP 345, DM 844, FR 2857, Y 59,305).

RUSSELL, John and John OPIE (after)

BI *Asculapius, Flora, Ceres and Cupid Honouring The Bust Of Linnaeus,* by Caldwall, pub. Dr. Thornton, 1806, margins, foxed and stained, tear, est. BP 5/70, (06-16-93, Bonhams-Chelsea, #489), pl. 20¼ x 14¾ in., (51.4 x 37.5 cm.), stipple engraving w/hand-coloring.

RUSSELL, Shirley b. 1886

$275* *Casting The Nets,* s., (12-17-92, Mystic, #42), 10¾ x 13½ in., (27.3 x 34.3 cm.), silkscreen (BP 175, DM 429, FR 1467, Y 33,796).

RUSSOTO

$165* *Repeating Images,* artist's proof, s. below image, (08-05-92, Boos, #730), 18 x 16 in., (457 x 406 mm.), serigraph (BP 86, DM 244, FR 823, Y 21,014).

RUTH

$1216* *Butcher's Watch Pocket Carbine, c. 1910,* p. Hill Siffken & Co., scratches, (05-07-93, Christie-S. Ken, #63, illus.), 12 x 19 in., (30.5 x 48.3 cm.), color lithograph (BP 770, DM 1923, FR 6478, Y 133,891).

RUTHERFORD, Louis M.

$3300* *The Moon, 1865: Two,* s., d., annot., (11-16-92, Butterfield, #6143, illus.), 22 7/16 x 16⅝ in., (569.3 x 423 mm.), photograph, albumen prints (BP 2173, DM 5261, FR 17,723, Y 410,397).

RUTKA, Dorothy American b. 1907

$5* *"Regeneration", 1950,* s., t., mat burn, taped, exhib., (05-15-93, Cleveland, #290), 4¼ x 6 in., (10.8 x 15.2 cm.), etching (BP 3, DM 8, FR 27, Y 554).

RUZICKA, Dr. D.

$440* *From Fulton Fish Market, Morning, 1956,* photog.'s t., sig. recto; i. verso, (04-07-93, Swann, #542), 6 x 4½ in., photograph, silver print (BP 291, DM 712, FR 2408, Y 49,989).

RUZICKA, Dr. Drahomir Joseph 1870-1960

BI *The Corolla Of Gladiulus, 1937,* s., t., d., labels, est. $1,5/2,000, (10-13-92, Christie-NY, #345, illus.), 13½ x 10⅝ in., (34.3 x 27 cm.), photograph, toned gelatin silver print.

BI *Rome: Castell Sant Angelo, c. 1932,* s., t. by photog., est. $1,5/2,500, (10-15-92, Sotheby-NY, #216A, illus.), 13½ x 10½ in., (34.3 x 26.7 cm.), photograph, silver chloride print.

$880* *Sunflowers and Flowering Meadow: Two Photographs, 1934,* sig., notations, (10-14-92, Swann, #548, illus.), 14 x 11 in., (35.6 x 27.9 cm.), photograph, toned silver prints (BP 517, DM 1288, FR 4367, Y 106,641).

BI *World's Fair, New York, 1939*, s., t., d., annot., est. $2/3,000, (10-13-92, Christie-NY, #346, illus.), 13⅝ x 10⅝ in., (34.6 x 27 cm.), photograph, gelatin silver print.

RUZICKA, J.
BI *"Hallstadt On The Lake"*, 1927, s., t., exhib. labels, est. $ 6/800, (11-16-92, Butterfield, #6144, illus.), 13¼ x 10¼ in., (337.2 x 260.8 mm.), photograph, toned gelatin silver print.

RUZICKA, Rudolf   American 1883-1978
$275* *Unknown Title, 1915*, s., d., very fine cond., tape residue, (10-31-92, Cleveland, #207, illus.), 4½ x 5⅞ in., (11.4 x 14.9 cm.), color woodcut (BP 176, DM 423, FR 1435, Y 34,064).
$55* *Untitled (Clouds Over Valley), 1922*, s., num., sun stain, fold, (10-31-92, Cleveland, #208), 6⅞ x 8⅞ in., (17.5 x 22.5 cm.), woodcut (BP 35, DM 85, FR 287, Y 6813).

RYALL, Henry (after Thomas STOTHARD)
$522* *Rangoon Views And Combined Operations In The Birman Empire, 1825-26: Four*, pub. Thomas Clay, trimmed inside platemark, light staining, (10-27-92, Phillips-London, #150), image 9⅞ x 14⅓ in., (251 x 364 mm.), aquatint w/hand-coloring on wove (BP 330, DM 800, FR 2715, Y 63,853).

RYAN, Anne
BI *"Woman Watching A Bird"* and *"The Green Pitcher": Two*, s., t., good cond., est. $1,5/2,000, (12-04-92, Doyle, #144), 15½ x 22½ in., (394 x 572 mm.), color woodcuts on black paper laid down on board.

RYDER, Chauncey Foster   American 1868-1949
BI *Bolton Brown*, s. (scratched out), i. 21 in stone; s., i. in margin, prov., est. $250/300, (09-17-92, Sloan, #2350), 6 x 8¾ in., (15.2 x 22.2 cm.), lithograph.
$55* *Boston Farm*, margins, s. Chauncey F. Ryder, (10-24-92, Collins, #20), 6⅞ x 9⅛ in., (17.5 x 23.2 cm.), etching (BP 34, DM 84, FR 285, Y 6707).
BI *French Hill*, s., t., i., prov., est. $250/300, (09-17-92, Sloan, #2356), 8⅞ x 11⅞ in., (22.5 x 30.2 cm.), drypoint etching.
$308* *Landscapes: Two*, each s., (02-14-93, Hanzel, #661), 8⅞ x 11⅞ in., (22.5 x 30.2 cm.), etching (BP 217, DM 511, FR 1728, Y 37,144).
$165* *Road To Waterville*, s., t., prov., (09-17-92, Sloan, #2351), 8⅞ x 11⅞ in., (22.5 x 30.2 cm.), drypoint etching (BP 93, DM 245, FR 838, Y 20,543).
$165* *Spruceland*, s., t., (09-17-92, Sloan, #2357), 9⅞ x 11⅞ in., (22.9 x 30.2 cm.), drypoint etching (BP 93, DM 245, FR 838, Y 20,543).
$165* *Widow Shannon's Place*, s., t., prov., (09-17-92, Sloan, #2354), 7⅞ x 11⅞ in., (20 x 30.2 cm.), drypoint etching (BP 93, DM 245, FR 838, Y 20,543).
BI *Wilton Village Farm*, s., t., prov., est. $250/300, (09-17-92, Sloan, #2348), 6⅜ x 8⁵⁄₁₆ in., (16.2 x 21.1 cm.), drypoint etching.
$165* *Windswept Trees*, s., t., i., prov., (09-17-92, Sloan, #2353), 8⅞ x 11⅞ in., (22.5 x 30.2 cm.), drypoint etching (BP 93, DM 245, FR 838, Y 20,543).

RYERSON, Margery   American b. 1886
$66* *"Gypsy Rondo"*, s., AAA label verso, (06-11-93, DuMouchelle, #2257), 12½ x 9½ in., (31.8 x 24.1 cm.), lithograph (BP 43, DM 107, FR 362, Y 7003).
$105* *"What's Wrong"*, AAA edit., s., t., fine cond., tape, (05-15-93, Cleveland, #291), 8½ x 8⁷⁄₁₆ in., (21.6 x 21.4 cm.), drypoint (BP 68, DM 169, FR 568, Y 11,640).

RYLAND, Henry (after)
$126 *Young Girl Standing Against Sunflowers*, (10-09-92, G.A. Key, #20), 15 x 10 in., (38.1 x 25.4 cm.), colored print (BP 75, DM 188, FR 636, Y 15,366).

RYLAND, William Wynne (after Angelica KAUFFMAN)
          English 1732-1783
$170* *"Dormio Innocuus VIX Impune Expergefeceris"* and *"Porrigit Hic VeneriLucida Dona Paris": Pair*, (02-04-93, Sloan, #406), sepia engraving (BP 119, DM 280, FR 949, Y 21,147).

RYLANDER, Hans Christian
$126* *"Selvportraet Med Hastige Ojeblikke"*, s. H.C.R. 1980, (09-29-92, B. Rasmussen, #359), aquatint (BP 71, DM 178, FR 607, Y 15,041, DK 690).

RYMAN, J., Publisher
$759* *Scenes From Eton: Nine*, full margins, foxing, staining, (06-16-93, Bonhams-Chelsea, #395, illus.), pl. 15¾ x 20¾ in., (40 x 52.7 cm.), tinted lithograph, hand-coloring (BP 506, DM 1260, FR 4228, Y 80,951).

RYMAN, Robert   American b. 1930
$1650* *Circle Lithograph, 1971*, s., d., #46/50, pub. Nova Scotia College of Art, full margins, good cond., (11-07-92, Sotheby-NY, #763), lithograph p. in colors (BP 1079, DM 2635, FR 8904, Y 203,653).
BI *Nohow On, 1989*, text by Samuel Beckett, s. by artist and author, #387, pub. The Limited Editions Club, est. $2,5/3,500, overall size c. 280 x 195 x 298 mm, (02-11-93, Sotheby-NY, #436), book w/6 etchings p. in white.
BI *On The Bowery: Untitled, 1969*, s., d., #30/100, pub. Edition Domberger, full margins, good cond., est. $2/2,500, (11-07-92, Sotheby-NY, #762), sheet 25⅝ x 25⅝ in., (651 x 651 mm.), silkscreen in colors.
BI *Untitled (Four Aquatints And One Etching)*, complete portfolio, s., d. '90, #75/80, pub. Parasol Press, Ltd.,, full margins, good cond., soiling, handling creases, est. $18/20,000, (05-15-93, Sotheby-NY, #1198), each sheet 32⅞ x 32⅞ in., (83.5 x 83.5 cm.), aquatints and etching.
$2200* *Untitled, 1969*, from On the Bowery, W. Germany, Edition Domberger, 1971, s., d., num. 79/100, Domberger blindstamp, full sheet, crackling in p. areas, good cond., (09-19-92, Christie-E, #209), sheet 25½ x 25½ in., (648 x 648 mm.), screenprint in colors on wove (BP 1265, DM 3294, FR 11,282, Y 274,109).
BI *Untitled, 1969*, from On the Bowery, West Germany, Edit. Domberger, 1971, s., d., #90/100, blindstamp, crackling, excellent cond., est. $2,5/3,500, (11-09-92, Christie-NY, #401, illus.), 25¾ x 25¾ in., (654 x 654 mm.), colored screenprint on wove.

RYPKA
$138* *Untitled*, #20/700, (06-11-93, DuMouchelle, #2105), 16 x 16 in., (40.6 x 40.6 cm.), lithograph (BP 91, DM 224, FR 756, Y 14,642).

RYSSELBERGHE, Theo van   Belgian 1862-1926
$91* *Les Baigneuses*, after Cezanne, (05-27-93, Briest, #176), 10⁷⁄₁₆ x 14¹⁵⁄₁₆ in., (26.5 x 38 cm.), black lithograph on Japan (BP 58, DM 146, FR 492, Y 9756).
BI *Flottie De Peche (Stein-Karschan 77)*, i. Epreuve d'essai-No. 1, mono., est. DM 3000, (06-04-93, Bassenge, #5802, illus.), 8⅞ x 11 in., (22.5 x 28 cm.), aquatint/etching in brown on hand-made.

RYUKOSAI JOKEI   Japanese ac. c. 1777-1809
$52,509* *Full Length Portrait Of Yamamura Giemon As Sakae Hidakanokami*, Hosoban, s. Ryukosai w/a kakihan, pub.'s mark Shio Rin, d. Kansei 5 (1793), wormage, creased, Prof. H.R.W. Kuhne Coll., (06-11-93, Sotheby-London, #451, illus.), 15⅜ x 5½ in., (39.1 x 14 cm.), woodblock (BP 34,500, DM 85,339, FR 287,721, Y 5,571,247).
$13,127* *(Sanganotsu) Yakusha Hyakunin Isshu Yosooi Kagami "(The Three Cities)Mirrors Of Actors As The Hundred Ogura Poets"*, 1 vol., pub. Tsuruya Kiuemon, Kikuya Yasubei, Shioya Kasuke and Hachimonjiya Hachizaemon, d. Kansei 12 (1800), rubbed, soiled, lit., Prof. H.R.W. Kuhne Coll., (06-11-93, Sotheby-London, #535, illus.), 10¼ x 7¼ in., (26 x 18.4 cm.), woodblock (BP 8625, DM 21,334, FR 71,929, Y 1,392,785).

RYUSAI SHIGEHARU   Japanese 1803-1853
$1137* *The Head And Shoulders Of The Rokkasen*, Oban, s. Ryusai Shigeharu ga w/seal Ryusai(?), engraver's seal Kasuke, d. Tenpo 5 (1834), good state, Prof. H.R.W. Kuhne Coll., (06-11-93, Sotheby-London, #473, illus.), 14¾ x 9½ in., (37.5 x 24.1 cm.), woodblock (BP 747, DM 1848, FR 6230, Y 120,637).
$1225* *Okubi-e Of Ichikawa Hakuen*, Oban, s. Ryusai Shigeharu, pub.'s mark Wataki, d. Bunsei 12 (1829), rubbed, soiled, wormage, binding holes, margin repaired, Prof H.R.W. Kuhne Coll., (06-11-93, Sotheby-London, #447,

illus.), 14¾ x 10 in., (37.5 x 25.4 cm.), woodblock (BP 805, DM 1991, FR 6712, Y 129,973).

SABOURAUD, Emile French b. 1900
$73* *"Scene D'Interieur",* #8/175, s., (01-28-93, Pescheteau, #245), 25⁹⁄₁₆ x 19¹¹⁄₁₆ in., (65 x 50 cm.), color lithograph on wove (BP 48, DM 116, FR 391, Y 9064).

SACHSE & CO. American 2nd half 19th cent.
$440* *Fortress Monroe, Old Point Comfort And Hygean Hotel, Va.,* (05-28-93, Sloan, #1597, illus.), 23 x 31 in., (58.4 x 78.7 cm.), color lithograph (BP 282, DM 698, FR 2359, Y 47,180).

SACKENHEIM, Rolf b. 1921
BI *Untitled, 1989,* s., d., num., est. DM 750-, (09-25-92, Granier, #3001), sheet 12¹¹⁄₁₆ x 10¼ in., (32.2 x 26 cm.), etching in China ink.

SACKETT & WILHELMS, Lithographers
$805* *Mary Powell Steamboat Company's Steamer Mary Powell, c. 1855,* trimmed into image, water stains, discoloration, (01-28-93, Sotheby-NY, #458), sheet 22 x 28 in., (559 x 711 mm.), chromolithograph (BP 532, DM 1276, FR 4316, Y 99,950).

SADAHIDE
$275* *Soldiers At Ease At The Noh Theatre: Triptych,* s. Gyokuransai Sadahide, pub. mark, censor's seals, faded, wrinkles, (11-20-92, Skinner, #50, illus.), oban triptych (BP 181, DM 438, FR 1477, Y 34,200).

SADAMASU ac. 1830'S
$116* *"Battling Samurai": Two,* trimmed, soiling, creasing, fair cond., (01-23-93, Goldberg, #300A), wood block (BP 76, DM 184, FR 624, Y 14,518).

SADAO, Watanab American 20th cent.
$110* *Way To Emaus,* s., d. 1966, num. 10/50, (11-12-92, Freemn/Fine Art, #187), 33 x 22½ in., (83.8 x 57.2 cm.), stencil and drypoint (BP 72, DM 174, FR 588, Y 13,639).

SADD, H.S.
$165* *"The First Prayer In Congress" and "Washington Delivers His Inaugural Address": A Pair,* (06-06-93, Dunning, #1091), sight 20 x 25 in., (50.8 x 63.5 cm.), engraving (BP 109, DM 268, FR 902, Y 17,700).

SADELER, Aegidius 1570-1629
BI *Die Drei Frauen Am Grabe Christi, 1600,* center crease, dusty, plate d., est. DM 2,100-, (09-25-92, Granier, #2686, illus.), plate 20³⁄₁₆ x 14⁷⁄₁₆ in., (51.2 x 36.7 cm.), copper engraving.
$1332* *The Four Seasons (Wurz. 94; Holl. 142-5), 1620: Set Of Four,* after P. Stevens, Holl. 142 and 145 2nd (final) state, Holl. 142, Holl. 143-4 1st state (of two), watermark, margins, stitching holes, staining, good cond., (12-01-92, Christie-London, #103), 9 x 12¹⁵⁄₁₆ in., (229 x 329 mm.), engraving (BP 880, DM 2123, FR 7235, Y 165,837).

SADELER, J.
$177* *Marie De Medicis (F.W.H. Hollstein, 605),* oval, thin spots, staining, holes, thin margins, (06-16-93, Ader Tajan, #21), 4¹³⁄₁₆ x 6⁷⁄₁₆ in., (12.3 x 16.3 cm.), copper engraving (BP 118, DM 294, FR 986, Y 18,878).

SADELER, Jan 1550-1600
$807* *Le Mauvais Riche Et Le Pauvre Lazare, c. 1598,* after Jacopo da Ponte Bassano, unique state, paper traces verso, (05-15-93, Loudmer, #90A, illus.), 9⅜ x 11¾ in., (238 x 298 mm.), copper engraving on thick wove (BP 525, DM 1298, FR 4362, Y 89,458).

SADELER, Jan and Raphael
$1373* *"A Large Album Containing The Four Series Of Hermits After Martin DeVos Comprising Solitudo Sive Vitae Patrum Eremicolarium" (Holl. 377-406); "Sylvae Sacrae Monumenta...Anachoretarum" (Holl. 133-144) and others: Four,* all complete series, narrow margins or trimmed, all glued down, stains, nicks, good cond., (06-30-93, Sotheby-London, #233), engraving (BP 920, DM 2342, FR 7900, Y 147,112).

SADELER, Johann (I) c. 1550-1600
$567* *"Boni Et Mali Sientia..." (Wurzbach 8; Hollstein 17-28/II), 1583: Twelve,* after Martin de Vos, (06-08-93, Karl/Faber, #186), engraving (BP 373, DM 920, FR 3098, Y 60,223).
$217* *Fiducia (Hollstein 541), 1579,* from series Tugenden, (12-04-92, Bassenge, #6427), 5⅜ x 3½ in., (13.7 x 8.9 cm.), engraving (BP 139, DM 346, FR 1172, Y 27,091).
$125* *Maria Mit Dem Kind Und Der Heiligen Anna (Wurzbach 42; Hollstein 294), 1584,* after M. de Vos, (12-01-92, Karl/Faber, #141), engraving (BP 83, DM 199, FR 679, Y 15,563).

SADELER, Johannes Flemish c. 1550-c. 1600
$100* *"Tormentation Of Christ", 1582,* after Martin de Vos, margins, very good cond., center fold, (05-15-93, Cleveland, #15, illus.), 9⅞ x 7⅞ in., (25.1 x 20 cm.), engraving (BP 65, DM 161, FR 541, Y 11,085).

SADELER, Marco
$357* *Vestigi Delle Antichita Di Roma Tivoli Pozzuolo Et Altri Luochi ComeSi Ritrovavano Nel Secolo XV: 50,* oblong folio, wrappers, embossed stamp Regia Calcografia di Roma, (11-12-92, Swann, #126), 11⅝ x 15¼ in., (295 x 388 mm.), engraving on wove (BP 234, DM 566, FR 1908, Y 44,265).

SADELER, Philipp
$731* *The Alphabet: Forty-Six,* 2 different sets illus. individual letters, each missing J, V, and W; one set trimmed, laid; other w/narrow margins; fair cond., bound in one volume, (10-27-92, Phillips-London, #39), sheet 4¼ x 2½ in., (108 x 64 mm.), engraving on laid (BP 462, DM 1120, FR 3801, Y 89,419).

SADELER, Raphael (I) 1560-1632
$2997* *The Annunciation With Prophets Who Preached The Coming Of The Messiah, (Holl. 12), 1580,* after Frederico Zuccaro, narrow to thread margins, trimmed, staining,laid, (12-01-92, Christie-London, #18, illus.), S. 11¹⁵⁄₁₆ x 17¾ in., (304 x 451 mm.), engraving (BP 1980, DM 4777, FR 16,279, Y 373,132).

SADELER II, Aegidius
$60* *Caesonia Caesar Caligula Uxor (Holl., vol. 21, 362),* second state of 3, wormholes, from "Les douze empereurs et les douzeimperatrices" series, (05-15-93, Loudmer, #92, illus.), 13¾ x 9⅝ in., (350 x 245 mm.), sh 14³⁄₁₆ x 9¹⁵⁄₁₆ in., (350 x 245 mm.), copper engraving on laid (BP 39, DM 97, FR 324, Y 6651).

SADELER II, Aegidius 1570-1629
$282* *L'Hiver (Holl., vol. 21, 1451), 1620,* after Pierre Stevens, second and final state, dirt spots, tear, (05-15-93, Loudmer, #91), 8¹⁵⁄₁₆ x 12¹⁵⁄₁₆ in., (227 x 328 mm.), sh 10⁹⁄₁₆ x 14¹³⁄₁₆ in., (227 x 328 mm.), copper engraving on thick laid (BP 183, DM 454, FR 1524, Y 31,260).

SADKOWSKY, Alex b. 1934
$106* *Briefe, 1982,* #28/50, s., d., (11-13-92, Koller, #5421), 29½ x 20½ in., (75 x 52 cm.), serigraph on wove (BP 68, DM 166, FR 561, Y 13,156, SF 150).

SADKOWSKY, Alexander b. 1934
BI *Schwimmer (Werkkatalog Nr. 1261), 1967,* Art. proof, s., d., est. SF 80/150, (10-14-92, Germann, #602), 17¹¹⁄₁₆ x 25 in., (450 x 635 mm.), etching.

SADLER, Walter Dendy English 1854-1923
$94 *"Figures Partaking Of A Meal" and "Pipe Smoking": Two,* s., (02-05-93, G.A. Key, #11), 16 x 23 in., (40.6 x 58.4 cm.), b/w engraving (BP 65, DM 156, FR 527, Y 11,697).

SADLER, Walter Dendy (after)
$78* *"My Love To You" and "Same To You, Dear": A Pair,* (05-20-93, Bonhams-Chelsea, #140), image 14¾ x 10¾ in., (37.5 x 27.3 cm.), etching w/hand-coloring (BP 50, DM 126, FR 424, Y 8613).
$105* *"My Love To You": Two,* etched by W.H. Boucher, 1898, (01-15-93, DuMouchelle, #2287), image 15 x 11 in., (38.1 x 27.9 cm.), etching (BP 69, DM 172, FR 580, Y 13,238).

SAEDELER, Aegidius

$10,295* *Family Tree Of The Austrian Royal Family (Holl. 371-376), 1629,* 4 plates, narrow margins, surface dirt, creasing, good cond., (06-30-93, Sotheby-London, #232), 15¾ x 22 in., (400 x 559 mm.), engraving on paper w/a Flage watermark (BP 6900, DM 17,559, FR 59,235, Y 1,103,075).

SAENREDAM, Jan 1565-1607

$397* *Judith Mit Dem Haupt Des Holofernes (B. 44; Hollstein 17 II),* after Goltzius, stained, prov., (12-04-92, Bassenge, #6429), 11⁵⁄₁₆ x 7¹⁵⁄₁₆ in., (28.8 x 20.2 cm.), engraving (BP 255, DM 632, FR 2145, Y 49,563).

$433* *Die Verkundigung An Die Hirten (B. 24; Wurzbach 24; Hollstein 24 I),1599,* prov., (12-04-92, Bassenge, #6428), 21⅛ x 15⁹⁄₁₆ in., (53.7 x 39.6 cm.), engraving (BP 278, DM 690, FR 2339, Y 54,057).

SAENREDAM, Jan Dutch 1565-1607

BI *Andromeda, 160,* after Goltzius, est. $6/800, (10-18-92, Hindman, #495), 10 x 7⅛ in., (25.4 x 18.1 cm.), engraving.

$289* *Die Hochzeit Nach Liebe (B. 84; Hollstein 107 I),* after Goltzius, (12-04-92, Bassenge, #6432), 8⅞ x 6⅛ in., (22.5 x 15.6 cm.), engraving (BP 185, DM 460, FR 1561, Y 36,080).

$193* *Perseus And Andromeda,* after Hendrick Goltzius, trimmed, watermark, soiling, small tear, (11-30-92, Selkirk, #709), 10¼ x 7⁵⁄₁₆ in., (26 x 18.5 cm.), engraving (BP 127, DM 307, FR 1044, Y 24,020).

$415* *Venus Auf Dem Ruhebett Zwischen Bacchus Und Ceres (Wurzbach 69; Hollstein 76/II), 1600,* after H. Goltzius, restored, (12-01-92, Karl/Faber, #142), engraving (BP 274, DM 661, FR 2254, Y 51,668).

BI *Venus Uber Das Reich Der Liebenden Herrschend (Bartsch 77; Hollstein54 II),* after H. Goltzius, sheet 5 of series by Planetengottheiten, watermark, est. DM 600, (06-10-93, Hauswedell/Nolt, #158), engraving.

SAFF, Donald

BI *Untitled,* s., annot. AP, full margins, very good cond., creases, skinned areas,est. $5/700, (02-24-93, Butterfield, #3250), 18⅛ x 15 in., (460 x 381 mm.), etching and aquatint in colors on Arches wove.

SAFTLEVEN, Herman 1609-1685

BI *Landschaft Mit Einem Esel (B. 13, Dutuit 13, Hollstein 26 II),* est. DM 600, (12-04-92, Bassenge, #6435), 3¼ x 4⅝ in., (8.2 x 11.8 cm.), etching.

SAHOLA, Alex American 20th cent.

BI *Franks/Burgers,* s. Alex Sahola (c), num. A.P. XIII/XXV, excellent cond., est. $3/500, (09-11-92, Skinner, #124, illus.), sight 22⅛ x 28⅛ in., (56.2 x 71.4 cm.), lithograph in colors on paper.

SAIDRO 20th cent.

BI *"Composition-1973",* #2/40, d., s., est. FF4/600, (04-04-93, Pescheteau, #288), 22¹³⁄₁₆ x 40¹⁵⁄₁₆ in., (58 x 104 cm.), color serigraph.

SAINSON, Louis Auguste de 1801-1887

$486* *New-Town (Ile Van Diemen), 1830,* p. de Sainson pinx Surrieux Lith. J. Tasta Editeur Lith A Bes., (08-11-92, L. Joel, #76G), 8¾ x 11¾ in., (22.3 x 29.9 cm.), color lithograph (BP 253, DM 713, FR 2416, Y 62,236, A$ 660).

$567* *Vue D'Une Habitation. A New Town. (Ile Van Diemen),* p. de Swainson Pinxt Leborne Lith. J Tastu Editeur. Lith de Bichebois. Aine Rue Clery, No. 23, (08-11-92, L. Joel, #62G, illus.), 9¼ x 12⅜ in., (23.5 x 31.5 cm.), color lithograph (BP 295, DM 832, FR 2818, Y 72,609, A$ 770).

SAINT GEORGE, E.

BI *Rejoice Today, It's Later Than You Think, 1974,* A/P s., t., d. '74, prov., est. C$2/300, (05-10-93, Hodgins, #367), 24 x 17¾ in., (61 x 45.1 cm.), etching on paper.

SAINT NON French 1727-1791

$383* *Terme De Tito: Two,* good margins, (02-03-93, Ader Tajan, #69), etching (BP 267, DM 631, FR 2138, Y 47,643).

SAINT PHALLE, Niki de French b. 1930

$866* *Les Amoreaux (WV Ulmer Museum L 10), 1972,* s., num., (11-28-92, Schoppmann, #773), 24 x 16⁹⁄₁₆ in., (61 x 42 cm.), color lithograph on Arches wove (BP 572, DM 1380, FR 4684, Y 107,778).

BI *Les Amoru,* #149/300, s., est. SF 1,3/1,500, (04-21-93, Germann, #727, illus.), 25¾ x 19 in., (654 x 483 mm.), color lithograph.

$358* *Les Amoureux,* s., #65/300, (05-27-93, Lempertz, #992), 23⅝ x 16⁷⁄₁₆ in., (60 x 41.7 cm.), color lithograph on Arches wove (BP 229, DM 574, FR 1936, Y 38,379).

$971* *Attention Dragueurs,* 15/125, s., (10-14-92, Germann, #414), 25⅜ x 17¹¹⁄₁₆ in., (645 x 450 mm.), color serigraph (BP 570, DM 1421, FR 4819, Y 117,668, SF 1265).

$465* *"Dear Diana",* s., num., (12-01-92, Karl/Faber, #1179), 19⁵⁄₁₆ x 24 in., (49 x 61 cm.), color serigraph on cardboard (BP 307, DM 741, FR 2526, Y 57,893).

$348* *Drachenbaum,* s., (12-01-92, Karl/Faber, #1178), 14¾ x 18⅞ in., (37.5 x 48 cm.), color serigraph (BP 230, DM 555, FR 1890, Y 43,327).

BI *Figur Mit Rosafarbenem Kopf Und Arm,* s., epreuve d'artiste, est. DM 850, (05-08-93, Schloss Ahlden, #2867, illus.), 20⅜ x 18¹⁄₁₆ in., (51.8 x 45.8 cm.), color serigraph on Arches-handmade.

BI *In A Bath With You,* s., epreuve d'artiste, est. DM 850, (05-08-93, Schloss Ahlden, #2869), 25⁹⁄₁₆ x 18⅞ in., (65 x 48 cm.), color serigraph on Arches-handmade.

$379* *Je T'Aime, 1971,* (09-30-92, Kunsthallen, #276), lithograph in colors (BP 214, DM 537, FR 1818, Y 45,482, DK 2070).

BI *L'Arbre,* s., #47/300, est. FF3,200/3,500, (03-31-93, Briest, #E96), 25⁹⁄₁₆ x 19⅛ in., (65 x 48.5 cm.), color lithograph.

$506* *Merry Christmas,* s. Niki de St. Phalle, 75/150, (09-30-92, Kunsthallen, #275), serigraph in colors (BP 285, DM 718, FR 2427, Y 60,722, DK 2760).

$289* *Merry Christmas Nana (WV P. 13.), 1969,* s., num., (11-28-92, Schoppmann, #774), 25³⁄₁₆ x 16⁹⁄₁₆ in., (64 x 42 cm.), color serigraph on paper (BP 191, DM 460, FR 1563, Y 35,968).

$457* *"My Love What Are You Doing?",* s., num., (12-01-92, Karl/Faber, #1180), 19⁵⁄₁₆ x 24 in., (49 x 61 cm.), color serigraph on cardboard (BP 302, DM 728, FR 2482, Y 56,897).

BI *My Love What Shall I Do If You Die?,* s., epreuve d'artiste, est. DM 1,200, (05-08-93, Schloss Ahlden, #2868, illus.), 24¹³⁄₁₆ x 18½ in., (63 x 47 cm.), color serigraph on Arches-handmade.

$498* *"My Love Where Shall We Meet Again?",* s., epreuve d'artiste, (12-01-92, Karl/Faber, #1177), sh 19½ x 23¹³⁄₁₆ in., (49.5 x 60.5 cm.), color serigraph on cardboard (BP 329, DM 794, FR 2705, Y 62,002).

$1185* *Nana,* #77/99, s., blindstamp, (04-21-93, Germann, #729), 20¹⁄₁₆ x 26⅜ in., (510 x 670 mm.), color lithograph (BP 769, DM 1894, FR 6405, Y 131,186, SF 1725).

$474* *Nana,* 48/115, s., (06-24-93, Germann, #499, illus.), 29¾ x 22³⁄₁₆ in., (756 x 563 mm.), color lithograph (BP 312, DM 768, FR 2590, Y 50,847, SF 690).

$430* *Nana Aux Fleurs,* s., #220/300, (05-27-93, Lempertz, #993), 23¹⁵⁄₁₆ x 19⅛ in., (60.8 x 48.5 cm.), color lithograph on Arches wove (BP 275, DM 690, FR 2326, Y 46,098).

BI *Nana Power,* 48/115, s., est. SF 1,3/1,500, (10-14-92, Germann, #415, illus.), 29½ x 22¹⁄₁₆ in., (750 x 560 mm.), color serigraph.

$790* *Nana Power,* 48/115, s., (06-24-93, Germann, #496), 29½ x 22¹⁄₁₆ in., (750 x 560 mm.), color serigraph (BP 520, DM 1281, FR 4317, Y 84,746, SF 1150).

BI *Remember?,* s., epreuve d'artiste, est. DM 850, (05-08-93, Schloss Ahlden, #2866, illus.), 18⅞ x 26½ in., (48 x 67.3 cm.), color serigraph on Arches-handmade.

$1237* *Le Reve De Diane, 1970,* s., t., d. 1970 in stone, #28/100, (03-31-93, Briest, #E191), 31½ x 23¹³⁄₁₆ in., (80 x 60.5 cm.), color lithograph (BP 818, DM 1990, FR 6760, Y 142,249).

$82* *Wie Man Eine Frau Verfuhrt, 1970,* image s., (11-13-92, Koller, #5435), 27⁹⁄₁₆ x 19¹¹⁄₁₆ in., (70 x 50 cm.), serigraph on posterboard (BP 53, DM 129, FR 434, Y 10,177, SF 116).

SAINT-AUBIN, Augustin de French 1736-1807
$3330* *"Au Moins Soyez Discret" and "Comptez Sur Mes Sermens" (Bocher 406-7; P. and B., III, p. 442, no. 9; L. and D. 181-2), 1789:* Pair, L. and D.'s 2nd state of 4, watermark, pub. Saint-Aubin, margins, thin spots, nicks, discoloration, (12-01-92, Christie-London, #245, illus.), plate 14⁵⁄₁₆ x 10⁵⁄₁₆ in., (364 x 262 mm.), etching w/ engraving (BP 2200, DM 5308, FR 18,088, Y 414,592).
   BI *"Louise Emille Baronne De...(Madame De St.-Aubin)" and "Adrienne Sophie Marquise De...(Madame De Breteuil)" (Bocher 7, 173; P. and B., III, p. 445,no 32 and p. 444, no. 31; L. and D. 179, 178), c. 1779:* Pair, Bocher 7 third state of 5, prov., est. BP 4/600, (12-01-92, Christie-London, #244, illus.), sheet, larger 10⅞ x 7¹³⁄₁₆ in., (276 x 198 mm.), etching w/engraving.

SAINT-AUBIN, G. de French 1724-1780
$1614* *Le Scelerat Damiens (E. Dacier, 13, 197), 1757,* first state, before i., t., creases, thin spots, glued, small margins, (02-03-93, Ader Tajan, #68, illus.), etching (BP 1127, DM 2658, FR 9012, Y 200,771)
   BI *Vue De La Foire De Bezons (Dacier 2 II), 1750,* est. DM 28,000, (06-10-93, Hauswedell/Nolt, #215, illus.), etching.

SAINTRE, C.
$18 *"After The Ballet",* s., d. '94, (06-11-93, G.A. Key, #82), 13 x 10 in., (33 x 25.4 cm.), b/w print (BP 12, DM 29, FR 99, Y 1910).

SAITO, Kiyoshi Japanese b. 1907
$300* *Ancient City Nara,* watermark, stamped artist's character seal plate, image s.; t., d. 1954, stamped label, prov., (06-08-93, Ritchie, #36, illus.), image 15 x 20½ in., (38.1 x 52.1 cm.), color woodcut on hand-made (BP 197, DM 487, FR 1639, Y 31,864, C$ 385).
$1022* *Biyakuge-ji Temple Nara, 1970,* t., d., annot., s., good margins, (06-16-93, Ader Tajan, #136), 14¾ x 20¹¹⁄₁₆ in., (37.5 x 52.5 cm.), woodcut in color (BP 681, DM 1697, FR 5694, Y 109,002).
$770* *"Biyakugo-Ji Nara (A)",* ink s., t., d. 1955, #181/200, one seal, watermark, toning, (11-20-92, Skinner, #5, illus.), image 15 x 20¾ in., (38.1 x 52.7 cm.), metallic pigments (BP 507, DM 1228, FR 4135, Y 95,759).
$300* *Buddha Asuka (B),* stamped artist's character seal in plate, image gouache s.; t., d. 1955, #23/50, stamped artists's label, prov., (06-08-93, Ritchie, #39, illus.), 29½ x 15¾ in., (74.9 x 40 cm.), color woodcut (BP 197, DM 487, FR 1639, Y 31,864, C$ 385).
$743* *"Buddha Asyura"; "Bakusan Uji": Two,* each t., num. 54/100, 42/150, d. 1959, 1960, (09-25-92, Wolf, #25), each 15¼ x 20½ in., (38.7 x 52.1 cm.), colored woodcuts (BP 434, DM 1101, FR 3724, Y 89,680).
$495* *Buddhist,* black ink s. Kiyoshi Saito, t., d. 1974, #11/150, good cond.?, minormat burn, (04-02-93, Weschler, #281), 16½ x 11½ in., (41.9 x 29.2 cm.), (BP 326, DM 796, FR 2702, Y 56,359).
$330* *"Bunraku" and "Kneeling Woman": Two,* 1st black ink s. Kiyoshi Saito, t., 2nd w/artist's sal, both good cond.?, (04-02-93, Weschler, #277, illus.), first 14½ x 5¼ in., (36.8 x 13.3 cm.), second 15¼ x 10 in., (36.8 x 13.3 cm.), (BP 217, DM 530, FR 1801, Y 37,573).
$495* *Cathedral Doorway,* s., pencil located, d. 1962, #48/150, sight 21½ x 15½ in., (54.6 x 39.4 cm.), color woodcut (BP 259, DM 749, FR 2526, Y 61,705).
$132* *Family Before A Japanese House,* s. ink, bears artist's red chop, (03-14-93, Hindman, #375), 10¼ x 15⅛ in., (26 x 38.4 cm.), color woodcut (BP 92, DM 220, FR 747, Y 15,557).
$523* *"Flame",* t., num. 5/150, d. 1961, (09-25-92, Wolf, #27), 29½ x 17½ in., (74.9 x 44.5 cm.), woodcut in color (BP 305, DM 775, FR 2622, Y 63,126).
$330* *"Flower And A Girl",* t., d. 1971, #38/80, ex-coll., (10-16-92, DuMouchelle, #2405, illus.), 14¾ x 20¾ in., (37.5 x 52.7 cm.), colored woodcut (BP 200, DM 487, FR 1656, Y 39,403).

$132* *A Garden Gate,* s., bears artist's red chop, (03-14-93, Hindman, #374), 10¼ x 15⅛ in., (26 x 38.4 cm.), color woodcut (BP 92, DM 220, FR 747, Y 15,557).
$605* *Gion In Kyoto,* s., d. 1959, #75/100, annot. (b), t., bearing artist's chop mark, (10-18-92, Hindman, #534), 15 x 20¾ in., (38.1 x 52.7 cm.), color woodcut (BP 370, DM 901, FR 3054, Y 72,585).
$660* *"Gion In Kyoto",* s. Kiyoshi Saito in plate, t., num. 55/100, d. 1963, (09-25-92, Wolf, #26), 15 x 20½ in., (38.1 x 52.1 cm.), colored woodcut (BP 385, DM 978, FR 3308, Y 79,662).
$935* *"Katsugi-Do Nikko",* ink s., t., d. 1971, #21/50, (11-20-92, Skinner, #1), image 12 x 29½ in., (30.5 x 74.9 cm.), mica enhancements (BP 616, DM 1491, FR 5021, Y 116,279).
$303* *Man And Mule,* s. Kiyoshi Saito, very good/good cond., (09-27-92, Bakker, #257, illus.), image 10½ x 15 in., (26.7 x 38.1 cm.), color woodblock print (BP 177, DM 449, FR 1519, Y 36,572).
$165* *Old Tea House,* white ink s. Kiyoshi Saito, Kiyo seal, very good cond.; tape verso, (04-02-93, Weschler, #280), 10¼ x 15¼ in., (26 x 38.7 cm.), (BP 109, DM 265, FR 901, Y 18,786).
$2090* *"Otaru Hokkaido", 1948,* s., red chop mark, t., d., num., (03-25-93, Boos, #220, illus.), image 15½ x 20¾ in., (39.4 x 52.7 cm.), color woodblock print (BP 1419, DM 3434, FR 11,676, Y 244,845).
$132* *Pagoda,* s. ink, bears artist's red chop, (03-14-93, Hindman, #376), 15⅛ x 10¼ in., (38.4 x 26 cm.), color woodcut (BP 92, DM 220, FR 747, Y 15,557).
$22* *Plowing The Fields,* (10-11-92, Hanzel, #954), 10 x 15 in., (25.4 x 38.1 cm.), color woodblock print (BP 13, DM 33, FR 110, Y 2678).
$275* *Profile Of A Woman,* s. Kiyoshi Saito w/artist's seal, good cond.?, Evelyn Schwartz May Estate, (04-02-93, Weschler, #279), 15¼ x 10 in., (38.7 x 25.4 cm.), (BP 181, DM 442, FR 1501, Y 31,310).
$825* *Sanpo-In Kyoto,* white ink s. Kiyoshi Saito, w/Kiyo seal, t., d. 1968, #44/100, good cond.?, minor rippling, (04-02-93, Weschler, #278), 15¾ x 21¼ in., (40 x 54 cm.), (BP 543, DM 1326, FR 4503, Y 93,931).
$1980* *"Shrine Kamakura",* ink s., t., d. 1972, #15/80, (11-20-92, Skinner, #6, illus.), image 15 x 20½ in., (38.1 x 52.1 cm.), (BP 1304, DM 3157, FR 10,634, Y 246,238).
$550* *Untitled: Two,* s., sealed, (03-25-93, Boos, #271), image 15⅛ x 10⅛ in., (38.4 x 25.7 cm.), color woodblock print (BP 374, DM 904, FR 3073, Y 64,433).
$25* *Village Scene,* (05-16-93, Hanzel, #1114), 10½ x 15 in., (26.7 x 38.1 cm.), color woodblock (BP 16, DM 40, FR 135, Y 2771).
$550* *"Winter Scenes" and "Summer Scenes": Four,* s., stamped, (02-27-93, Dunning, #1176), 11½ x 16½ in., (29.2 x 41.9 cm.), woodblock (BP 387, DM 904, FR 3073, Y 64,927).

SALATHE, Engraver
   BI *Les Chutes Du Niagara, Le Fer A Cheval Niagara Falls, The Horse Shoe, 1852,* after H. Sebron, p., pub. Goupil & Co., trimmed, image scuffs, skinning, soiling, losses, tears, est. $2/2,500, (01-28-93, Sotheby-NY, #452), sheet 26 x 38¾ in., (660 x 984 mm.), hand-colored etching and engraving.

SALGADO, Sebastiao b. 1944
$3220* *Brasil, 1986,* p. 1990, s., t., d., lit., (04-08-93, Christie-NY, #558, illus.), 17⅜ x 11⅝ in., (44.1 x 29.5 cm.), photograph, gelatin silver print (BP 2111, DM 5173, FR 17,510, Y 365,411).
$2750* *Brasil, 1986 (An Uncertain Grace, p. 18),* s., t., d. by photog., (10-15-92, Sotheby-NY, #598, illus.), 17½ x 11¾ in., photograph, gelatin silver print (BP 1683, DM 4093, FR 13,882, Y 329,934).
$1361* *"Brazil, 1986",* blindstamped credit Sebastiao Salgado, s., d., t., 401 x 500mm, (05-07-93, Sotheby-London, #255, illus.), photograph, silver print (BP 862, DM 2152, FR 7251, Y 149,857).
$935* *Channel Tunnel, 1990,* photog. blindstamp s., d., annot., Dixon Collection, (11-16-92, Butterfield, #6149, illus.),

9¼ x 13⅞ in., (235.4 x 353.1 mm.), photograph, gelatin silver print (BP 616, DM 1491, FR 5021, Y 116,279).

$1090* *"Ethiopia 1984",* blindstamped credit Sebastiao Salgado, s., d., t., 303 x 403mm, (05-07-93, Sotheby-London, #254, illus.), photograph, silver print (BP 690, DM 1723, FR 5807, Y 120,018).

$1980* *Family, Korem Camp, Ethiopia (Uncertain Grace, p. 59), 1984,* photog. blindstamp, s., d., annot., Dixon Collection, (11-16-92, Butterfield, #6147, illus.), 11¾ x 17⅜ in., (299 x 442.1 mm.), photograph, gelatin silver print (BP 1304, DM 3157, FR 10,634, Y 246,238).

BI *Feet (Brasil), 1983,* photog.'s sig., blindstamp, est. $1/1,500, (04-07-93, Swann, #355, illus.), 6¾ x 10¼ in., photograph, silver print.

$880* *Feet, Brazil, 1983,* blindstamp, sig., d., notations, (10-14-92, Swann, #348, illus.), 6¾ x 10½ in., (17.1 x 26.7 cm.), photograph, silver print (BP 517, DM 1288, FR 4367, Y 106,641).

$1150* *"Kuwait", 1991,* photog.'s blindstamp, s., t., d., (05-23-93, Butterfield, #3586, illus.), 9¼ x 13⅞ in., photograph, gelatin silver print (BP 749, DM 1880, FR 6329, Y 127,114).

$1320* *Kuwait, 1991,* photog. blindstamp, s., t., d., Dixon Collection, (11-16-92, Butterfield, #6150, illus.), 13⅞ x 9¼ in., (353.1 x 235.4 mm.), photograph, gelatin silver print (BP 869, DM 2105, FR 7089, Y 164,159).

$1035* *"Mattanza Fisherman", 1991,* photog.'s blindstamp, s., d., annot., (05-23-93, Butterfield, #3587, illus.), 9¼ x 14 in., photograph, gelatin silver print (BP 674, DM 1692, FR 5696, Y 114,403).

$1150* *Prayer To The Mixe God Kioga, 1980,* photog.'s blindstamp, s., d., annot., illus., (05-23-93, Butterfield, #3584, illus.), 11⅞ x 17½ in., photograph, gelatin silver print (BP 749, DM 1880, FR 6329, Y 127,114).

$1100* *The Refugee Camp Of Korem (Uncertain Grace, p. 93), 1984,* photog. blindstamp, s., d., annot., Dixon Collection, (11-16-92, Butterfield, #6148, illus.), 11¾ x 17⅜ in., (299 x 442.1 mm.), photograph, gelatin silver print (BP 724, DM 1754, FR 5908, Y 136,799).

$1955* *"Serra Pelada", 1986,* photog.'s blindstamp, s., d., annot., illus., (05-23-93, Butterfield, #3583, illus.), 17½ x 11¾ in., photograph, gelatin silver print (BP 1273, DM 3197, FR 10,759, Y 216,094).

$1320* *Serra Pelada, A Moment Of Rest (Uncertain Grace, p. 22), 1986,* photog. blindstamp, s., d., annot., Dixon Collection, (11-16-92, Butterfield, #6145, illus.), 11¾ x 17⅜ in., (299 x 442.1 mm.), photograph, gelatin silver print (BP 869, DM 2105, FR 7089, Y 164,159).

$2070* *Serra Pelada, Brasil,* 1986, p. 1990, s., t., d.; photog.'s (c) embossed, lit., (04-08-93, Christie-NY, #557, illus.), 12 x 17¾ in., (30.5 x 45.1 cm.), photograph, gelatin silver print (BP 1357, DM 3325, FR 11,256, Y 234,907).

BI *Serra Pelada, The Dispute (Uncertain Grace, p. 10), 1986,* photog. blindstamp, s., d., annot., Dixon Collection, est. $1,5/2,000, (11-16-92, Butterfield, #6146, illus.), 11⅞ x 17¹¹⁄₁₆ in., (302.2 x 448.5 mm.), photograph, gelatin silver print.

BI *Three Feet, 1983,* photog.'s blindstamp, s., t., d., annot., est. $800/1,200, (05-23-93, Butterfield, #3588, illus.), 6¾ x 10¼ in., photograph, gelatin silver print.

$1725* *Wood Delivery Men, 1980,* photog.'s blindstamp, s., d., annot., illus., (05-23-93, Butterfield, #3585, illus.), 11¾ x 17½ in., photograph, gelatin silver print (BP 1123, DM 2820, FR 9494, Y 190,671).

SALIMBENE, Ventura di Arcangelo (Bevilacqua) Italian 1554-1613

$645* *Annonciation, 1594,* lunette form, first edit. before address, (05-15-93, Loudmer, #28, illus.), 11⅜ x 6½ in., (289 x 165 mm.), etching and copper engraving on laid (BP 419, DM 1037, FR 3486, Y 71,500).

SALLE, David American b. 1952

$1980* *"Canfield Hatfield 1", "Canfield Hatfield 2" and "Canfield Hatfield 5", 1989: Three,* each s., d., num. 15/60, pub. Waddington Graphics, full margins, creases, excell. cond., (09-19-92, Christie-E, #211), each, sheet 30½ x 44 in., (77.5 x 111.8 cm.), soft-ground etching, aquatint and photo-etching in colors on Somerset (BP 1139, DM 2965, FR 10,154, Y 246,698).

$1870* *Canfield Hatfield 9, 1989,* s., d., i. AP, num. 10/10, pub. Waddington Graohics, full margins, excell. cond., (09-19-92, Christie-E, #212, illus.), sheet 30½ x 44 in., (77.5 x 111.8 cm.), soft-ground etching, aquatint and photo-etching in colors on Somerset (BP 1076, DM 2800, FR 9590, Y 232,993).

BI *Canfield Hatfield, 1989-90: Nine,* s., d., #26/60, Waddington Graphics, est. DM 20,000, (06-12-93, Hauswedell/Nolt, #377), sh 30⁷⁄₁₆ x 43¹³⁄₁₆ in., (77.3 x 111.3 cm.), color aquatint on wove w/watermark.

BI *From The Drunken Chauffeur, 1983,* s, annot. H.P. 10/10, blindstamp printer, Domberger, Stuttgart, goodcond., est. $7/900, (05-19-93, Butterfield, #2330), 29¾ x 42¾ in., (73.7 x 108.6 cm.), silkscreen in colors on wove.

$1265* *Grandiose Synonym For Church: Untitled, 1985,* s., d., i. A.P. 9/10, pub. Parasol Press, Ltd., full margins, good cond., (02-11-93, Sotheby-NY, #438), 48⅟₁₆ x 37¹⁵⁄₁₆ in., (122 x 96.5 cm.), color aquatint (BP 893, DM 2095, FR 7091, Y 152,502).

$605* *Portrait With Scissors And Night Club, 1987,* s., d., #85/100, blindstamp of pub., Crown Point Press, s., full margins, good cond., (02-24-93, Butterfield, #3251), 18⅛ x 24 in., (460 x 610 mm.), woodcut in colors on Japan (BP 422, DM 982, FR 3330, Y 70,993).

BI *Portrait With Scissors And Nightclub, 1987,* s., d., #54/100, Crown Point Press blindstamp, printer's sig., full margins, excell. cond., the Late M. Anwar Kamal, M.D. Coll., est. $1,2/1,600, (05-11-93, Christie-NY, #562), sheet 24⅞ x 29½ in., (632 x 749 mm.), color woodcut on Japan.

$1100* *Until Photographs Could Be Taken From Earth Satellites, 1981,* s., d., i., #3/10, pub. Parasol Press, good cond., (11-07-92, Sotheby-NY, #764, illus.), sheet 29¾ x 41⅞ in., (75.6 x 106.4 cm.), aquatint on BFK Rives (BP 719, DM 1756, FR 5936, Y 135,769).

BI *"Untitled", "Untitled" and "Untitled", 1982: Three,* from The Drunken Chauffeur, all s., num. 41/45, pub. Parasol Press, Domberger blindstamps, full sheets, old glue, skinned patch, est. $1,8/2,200, (09-19-92, Christie-E, #210), each, sheet 29½ x 41½ in., (74.9 x 105.4 cm.), screenprint in colors on wove.

SALOME b. 1945

BI *Jungling Mit Blonden Haaren, (19)87,* s., d., num., crease, est. DM 1200, (12-01-92, Karl/Faber, #1185), sh 51³⁄₁₆ x 36⅝ in., (130 x 93 cm.), color serigraph on cardboard.

SALOME (Wolfgang CILARTZ) b. 1954

BI *I Need You Tonight, 1984,* s., d., #9/30, est. DM 2,200-, (05-27-93, Lempertz, #994), 47¼ x 33⅜ in., (120 x 84.7 cm.), color serigraph.

$698* *Schlaglicht, 1987,* s., d., t., num., (09-25-92, Granier, #3002, illus.), 50¹⁵⁄₁₆ x 36¹³⁄₁₆ in., (129.5 x 93.5 cm.), color serigraph on thick board (BP 408, DM 1035, FR 3499, Y 84,249).

SALOMON, Erich 1866-1944

$660* *Ernst Lubitsch And Mervyn Leroy At The Hotel Savoy, London, 1937,* (10-15-92, Sotheby-NY, #412, illus.), 6⅛ x 8 in., (15.6 x 20.3 cm.), photograph, gelatin silver print (BP 404, DM 982, FR 3332, Y 79,184).

$1210* *Foreign Dignitaries At State Dinner,* photog.'s handstamp, 1930s, (04-07-93, Swann, #357, illus.), 6 x 4½ in., photograph, silver print (BP 800, DM 1957, FR 6623, Y 137,469).

$660* *President Hoover And Premier Laval,* 1931, p.l., (04-07-93, Swann, #356, illus.), 8 x 10 in., photograph, silver print (BP 436, DM 1067, FR 3612, Y 74,983).

BI *Untitled (German Parliament), c. 1935,* photog.'s handstamp, est. $1/1,500, (04-07-93, Swann, #358, illus.), 6 x 9½ in., photograph, silver print.

BI *William Randolph Hearst And Dinner Guests At San Simeon, 1930,* name stamp, est. $1,5/2,500, (10-15-92, Sotheby-NY, #413, illus.), 7½ x 9⅝ in., (19.1 x 24.4 cm.), photograph, gelatin silver print.

SALTONSTALL, Elizabeth American 1900-1990

$55* *"Althea Blossoms", c. 1940,* s. Elizabeth Saltonstall, very good cond., (11-21-92, Bakker, #5), image 13¾ x

9¾ in., (34.9 x 24.8 cm.), lithograph (BP 36, DM 88, FR 295, Y 6840).

SALVADOR CARMONA, Juan Antonio   Spanish d. 1805
$271* *"Asia"*, after Lucas Jordan, (12-17-92, Duran, #17, illus.), 15¾ x 19¹¹⁄₁₆ in., (40 x 50 cm.), etching (BP 172, DM 423, FR 1445, Y 33,305, P 29,900).

SALZMANN, Auguste   1824-1872
BI *The Holy Sepulchre, 1856,* plate from large-format Jerusalem 1856, p. by Blanquart-Evrard, #13 in neg., est. $1/1,200, (10-15-92, Sotheby-NY, #69, illus.), 9¼ x 13 in., (23.5 x 33 cm.), photograph, salt print.

SAMARAS, Lucas   Greek/American b. 1936
$358* *Hand, 1975,* incised sig., d., #65/100, pub. Pace Editions, full margins, very good cond.; including Lucas Samaras by Kim Levin, 1975, pub. Harry N. Abrams, Inc., s. by artist, good cond., (10-28-92, Butterfield, #3114), 16⅞ x 14 in., (429 x 356 mm.), silkscreen in white and grey on plexiglas (BP 228, DM 553, FR 1877, Y 43,926).
$5750* *Phototransformation, 10/25/73,* s. 10/25/73, prov., exhib., (05-04-93, Sotheby-NY, #414, illus.), 3 x 3 in., (7.6 x 7.6 cm.), photograph, SX 70 Polaroid (BP 3671, DM 9058, FR 30,520, Y 632,494).
$6325* *Phototransformation, 11/1/73,* d. 11/1/73, prov., exhib., (05-04-93, Sotheby-NY, #413, illus.), 3 x 3 in., (7.6 x 7.6 cm.), photograph, SX 70 Polaroid (BP 4038, DM 9964, FR 33,572, Y 695,743).
$4600* *Phototransformation, 4/4/76,* s. 4/4/76, exec. 1976, prov., exhib., (05-04-93, Sotheby-NY, #232, illus.), 3 x 3 in., (7.6 x 7.6 cm.), photograph, SX 70 Polaroid (BP 2936, DM 7246, FR 24,416, Y 505,995).
$4025* *Phototransformation, 4/4/76,* s. 4/4/76, prov., exhib., (05-04-93, Sotheby-NY, #231, illus.), 3 x 3 in., (7.6 x 7.6 cm.), photograph, SX 70 Polaroid (BP 2569, DM 6341, FR 21,364, Y 442,746).
$4600* *Phototransformation, 7/31/76,* d. 7/31/76, prov., exhib., (05-04-93, Sotheby-NY, #411, illus.), 3 x 3 in., (7.6 x 7.6 cm.), photograph, SX 70 Polaroid (BP 2936, DM 7246, FR 24,416, Y 505,995).
$4888* *Phototransformation, 9/8/76,* d. 9/8/76, prov., exhib., (05-04-93, Sotheby-NY, #410, illus.), 3 x 3 in., (7.6 x 7.6 cm.), photograph, SX 70 Polaroid (BP 3120, DM 7700, FR 25,945, Y 537,675).
$330* *Ribbon,* s., d. 72, #46/150, (05-16-93, Hindman, #590), 32 x 21½ in., (81.3 x 54.6 cm.), color lithograph (BP 215, DM 531, FR 1784, Y 36,581).
BI *"Ribbons",* s., d. '72, num. 89/150, est. $1/2000, (10-10-92, Goldberg, #532), 32 x 21½ in., (81.3 x 54.6 cm.), serigraph.

SAMPLE, Kathy
$39* *Japan,* s., t., (05-12-93, Maynard, #280), 16 x 25½ in., (40.6 x 63.5 cm.), print (BP 25, DM 63, FR 212, Y 4354, C$ 50).

SAMPSON, Cornelius Cogswell   American 20th cent.
BI *Toujours Gai,* s., t., est. $127/175, (10-30-92, Sloan, #842), 9⅞ x 7⅞ in., (25.1 x 20 cm.), etching and aquatint.
$50* *Toujours Gai,* s., t., (12-10-92, Sloan, #925), 9⅞ x 7⅞ in., (25.1 x 20 cm.), etching and aquatint (BP 32, DM 79, FR 270, Y 6185).

SAMUEL, Deborah
$1840* *"Swim Suit", 1991,* s., t., i. Number 2, no more than 20 will be printed plus 3 A/P's byphotog., (04-06-93, Sotheby-NY, #509, illus.), 18⅝ x 18⅜ in., photograph (BP 1215, DM 2964, FR 10,038, Y 209,854).

SANCHEZ, Emilio   Cuban b. 1921
$110* *Barbados Children,* s., t., num. 300/300, (09-20-92, Hindman, #801), 13½ x 30⅛ in., (34.3 x 76.5 cm.), color lithograph (BP 64, DM 163, FR 558, Y 13,595).
$220* *"Fiesta", c. 1951,* pub. AAA, s. Emilio Sanchez, num. 164/250, t. on AAA label, very good cond., orig. folder, (09-11-92, Skinner, #70B, illus.), 12 x 9 in., (30.5 x 22.9 cm.), lithograph on wove (BP 114, DM 317, FR 1076, Y 27,258).

SANCHEZ, Emilio B.
BI *Cross Town Sunset,* s., t., #66/75, prov., est. C$ 5/700, (12-01-92, Ritchie, #43, illus.), 24 x 18 in., (61 x 45.7 cm.), color lithograph.

SANDBACK, Fred   American b. 1943
$621* *Lineare Kompositionen, 1975: Six,* s., d., creases, (09-25-92, Granier, #3003), sheet 17⅝ x 21¹⁄₁₆ in., (44.7 x 53.5 cm.), color lithograph on smooth machine hand-made (BP 363, DM 921, FR 3113, Y 74,955).
BI *Untitled, 1988,* s., d., est. DM 1,800, (06-12-93, Hauswedell/Nolt, #378, illus.), 11¹³⁄₁₆ x 16¹⁵⁄₁₆ in., (30 x 43 cm.), screenprint and pastel on wove.

SANDBY, Paul   English 1725-1809
$942* *Views In South Wales, Plates I-V And VII-XII (Abbey Scenery 511, Numbers 25-29 And 31-36): Eleven,* pub. P. Sandby, margins, dirt, creasing, (10-07-92, Christie-S. Ken, #71), pl 9¼ x 12¼ in., (23.5 x 31.1 cm.), sepia aquatint (BP 550, DM 1363, FR 4622, Y 113,289).
BI *Views In South Wales: Part I (Abbey 511), 1775: Set Of Twelve,* plates 1, 3, 5, 6, 8, 11 and 12 w/narrow margins, plate 2 trimmed, plates 4, 7, 9 and 10 trimmed, thin area, discoloration, good cond., est. BP 1,5/2,000, (06-30-93, Sotheby-London, #264, illus.), each c. 9½ x 12⅜ in., (241 x 314 mm.), aquatint in sepia.
BI *Views In Wales,* 9 plates from 3 series comprising: plates 5, 8 and 11 from Part I, plates 2, 4 and 5 from Part II and plates 9 and 10 from Part III, paper loss, repaired tear, scuff in image, stains, discoloration, defects, est. BP 1/1,500, (06-30-93, Sotheby-London, #265), 9½ x 12½ in., (241 x 318 mm.), aquatint in series.

SANDELL, Scott   American contemporary
BI *Apparent Wind,* s., #9/19, emb. "(c) Scott Sandell", est. $5/700, (02-04-93, Sloan, #2965), overall 64 x 36 in., (162.6 x 91.4 cm.), silkscreen w/handcoloring on joined sheets of plum paper.
BI *The Letter Under The Door,* s., #12/19, emb. "(c) Scott Sandell", est. $5/700, (02-04-93, Sloan, #2967), overall 65 x 36 in., (165.1 x 91.4 cm.), silkscreen w/hand coloring on joined sheets of plum paper.
BI *Untitled,* s., #1/1, i. "A.P.", est. $5/700, (02-04-93, Sloan, #2968), overall 58 x 36 in., (147.3 x 91.4 cm.), silkscreen w/hand coloring on joined sheets of plum paper.
BI *Untitled (Seashell),* s., d. 1986, #5/19, emb. "(c) Scott Sandell", est. $5/700, (02-04-93, Sloan, #2966), overall 65 x 36 in., (165.1 x 91.4 cm.), silkscreen w/handcoloring on joined sheets of plum paper.

SANDELLE (after)
$83* *Ruth,* (12-11-92, DuMouchelle, #85), 24½ x 16½ in., (62.2 x 41.9 cm.), print (BP 53, DM 131, FR 448, Y 10,271).

SANDER, August   German 1876-1964
$2722* *The Grand Duke Of Hesse-Nassau, Darmstadt, 1928,* p. 1950s, thin black ink border, circular blindstamp Aug. Sander/ Lindenthal/ Koln recto, mounted on card, label, lit., (05-06-93, Christie-London, #123, illus.), 11⅜ x 8⅜ in., photograph, gelatin silver print (BP 1725, DM 4287, FR 14,433, Y 299,483).
$683* *Interieur, 1929/30,* studio stamp, (11-12-92, Lempertz, #228, illus.), 6¾ x 4⅝ in., (17.1 x 11.8 cm.), photograph, gelatin silver print (BP 437, DM 1073, FR 3658, Y 84,498).
$2048* *Koln, Mulheimer-Brucke, 30's,* 50's, studio stamp, (11-12-92, Lempertz, #230, illus.), 8⁷⁄₁₆ x 11½ in., (21.5 x 29.2 cm.), photograph, gelatin silver print (BP 1309, DM 3219, FR 10,969, Y 253,371).
BI *Der Maler Horle Portratiert Den Boxer Domgorgen, 1927, 1974,* est. DM 600, (11-12-92, Lempertz, #227), 9¹⁵⁄₁₆ x 7⅜ in., (25.2 x 18.7 cm.), photograph, gelatin silver print.
$1745* *Remagen, 30's,* 50's, studio stamp, (11-12-92, Lempertz, #229, illus.), 9⅛ x 11½ in., (23.2 x 29.2 cm.), photograph, gelatin silver print (BP 1116, DM 2742, FR 9347, Y 215,885).
$3641* *Rheinlandschaften: Twelve,* 30's, 1974, Edition Schirmer Mosel Munchen 1974, in original case, (11-12-92, Lempertz, #231, illus.), smallest 8¹¹⁄₁₆ x 11⁷⁄₁₆ in., (22 x 29 cm.), largest 9¹⁄₁₆ x 11⁷⁄₁₆ in., (22 x 29 cm.), photograph,

gelatin silver print (BP 2328, DM 5722, FR 19,502, Y 450,452).

$2530* *Selected Images (c. 1912-31), Including "Pharmacist, Linz/Donau", "Notary, Cologne", "Frail Old Man, Westerwald", "Blacksmith, Westerwald" and "Catholic Sister": Five,* p. 1978-83 by Gunther Sander, each w/Koln-Lindenthal blindstamp recto; s., d. by Gunther Sander, lit., (04-08-93, Christie-NY, #113, illus.), each approx. 11½ x 8⅜ in., (29.2 x 21.3 cm.), photograph, gelatin silver print (BP 1659, DM 4064, FR 13,757, Y 287,108).

$2722* *St. Gereon, Cologne,* early 1930s, p. 1950s, thin black ink border, photog.'s circular blindstamp recto, ink stamp august sander/lichtbildner/kuchhausen/bei/leuscheid/sieg, mounted on card, (05-06-93, Christie-London, #124, illus.), 11⅜ x 8⅞ in., photograph, gelatin silver print (BP 1725, DM 4287, FR 14,433, Y 299,483).

$2420* *St. Kolumba In Koln, c. 1930,* credit stamp, notations, label, lit., (10-13-92, Christie-NY, #347, illus.), 8⅞ x 6⅝ in., (22.5 x 16.8 cm.), photograph, gelatin silver print (BP 1409, DM 3545, FR 12,046, Y 293,440).

$2275* *Westerwaler Bauerin, 40/50's,* ink s., (11-12-92, Lempertz, #232, illus.), 16$\frac{5}{16}$ x 11⅝ in., (41.5 x 29.5 cm.), photograph, gelatin silver print (BP 1455, DM 3575, FR 12,185, Y 281,455).

$935* *Young Girl In A Circus Caravan,* 1932/1990, edit. 1/17, photog. archive stamp, photog. label, Dixon Collection, (11-16-92, Butterfield, #6151, illus.), 10¼ x 7½ in., (260.8 x 190.8 mm.), photograph, gelatin silver print (BP 616, DM 1491, FR 5021, Y 116,279).

SANDIG, Armin b. 1929

BI *"Deklination Der Aquatinta", (19)60/61: Ten,* Galerie Dieter Brusberg, Hannover, s., d., num., stains, est. DM 600, (12-01-92, Karl/Faber, #1187), 22¼ x 15$\frac{9}{16}$ in., (56.5 x 39.5 cm.), color aquatint/etching on wove.

SANDORFI, Istvan b. 1948

BI *Femme Et Enfant,* s., #41/150, est. FF3,000/3,500, (05-27-93, Briest, #180), 40$\frac{15}{16}$ x 28⅜ in., (104 x 72 cm.), color lithograph.

SANDOZ, W.M.

$199* *C.G.T. And P.O. And Midi: Le Maroc Par Lisbonne. "La Voie La Plus Rapide, 24 Heures De Mer",* very good cond., (03-13-93, Laurin, #107), 40$\frac{3}{16}$ x 29⅛ in., (102 x 74 cm.), (BP 139, DM 331, FR 1126, Y 23,453).

SANDRART

$489* *Statuary: Four, 1680,* (02-18-93, Sotheby-Arcade, #44), smallest 12¾ x 8⅛ in., (32.4 x 20.6 cm.), largest 12⅞ x 8¾ in., (32.4 x 20.6 cm.), copper engravings (BP 338, DM 798, FR 2700, Y 58,256).

SANDY-HOOK

$420* *4eme Salon Nautique International, 1929,* p. Chaix, 3 mats, good cond., (11-19-92, Ribeyre/Baron, #74), 62$\frac{15}{16}$ x 46⅞ in., (160 x 119 cm.), poster (BP 277, DM 670, FR 2256, Y 52,232).

$671* *6ele Salon Nautique International, 1931,* p. Chaix, good cond., (11-19-92, Ribeyre/Baron, #75), 62$\frac{15}{16}$ x 46⅞ in., (160 x 119 cm.), poster (BP 442, DM 1070, FR 3604, Y 83,447).

$279* *Chargeurs Reunis: Cote Occidentale D'Afrique,* good cond., (03-13-93, Laurin, #135), 39¾ x 24 in., (101 x 61 cm.), (BP 195, DM 464, FR 1579, Y 32,882).

$557* *PLM and Cie De Navigation Mixte Cie Touache: Les Iles Baleares Par Marseille,* very good cond., (03-13-93, Laurin, #167), 39⅜ x 24$\frac{7}{16}$ in., (100 x 62 cm.), (BP 389, DM 927, FR 3152, Y 65,645).

SANDZEN, Sven Birger American b. 1871

$303* *Toward Evening,* s., t., margins, good cond., water stain, creases, (10-28-92, Butterfield, #2753), 11$\frac{14}{15}$ x 15$\frac{1}{16}$ in., (279 x 383 mm.), woodcut on cream wove (BP 193, DM 468, FR 1589, Y 37,178).

SANSO, Juevenal Spanish b. 1929

$39* *"Lueurs", 1963,* s., excellent cond., (10-31-92, Cleveland, #389), 8¼ x 19$\frac{7}{16}$ in., (21 x 49.4 cm.), etching and aquatint (BP 25, DM 60, FR 204, Y 4831).

SANT, James (after)

$101 *"Prosperity" and "Adversity": Two,* (12-11-92, G.A. Key, #134), 26 x 11 in., (66 x 27.9 cm.), colored photogravure (BP 65, DM 159, FR 545, Y 12,498).

SANTI, Raphael (after) 1483-1520

$563* *Elephantenschlacht Des Scipio Gegen Hannibal (Hollstein Bd V, 197, II, Lugt 860), 1567,* by Cornelis Cort, (03-24-93, Venator/Hansten, #2563), pl. 16$\frac{1}{16}$ x 21$\frac{3}{16}$ in., (40.8 x 53.8 cm.), engraving (BP 381, DM 919, FR 3130, Y 66,150).

SANTOMASO, Giuseppe Italian b. 1907

$88* *Apparizione Del Rosso,* s., d. '76, #25/90, prov., (05-16-93, Hindman, #584), 26 x 11½ in., (66 x 29.2 cm.), etching and aquatint (BP 57, DM 142, FR 476, Y 9755).

$480* *Brauner Keil, 1972,* s., d., #102/200, (09-18-92, Schloss Ahlden, #1048), 28½ x 20⅜ in., (72.4 x 51.7 cm.), colored screen print on BFK Rives (BP 281, DM 712, FR 2437, Y 59,325).

$410* *"Canto Pisano", 1989,* #67/90, s., d., (11-13-92, Koller, #5423), 11$\frac{1}{16}$ x 7$\frac{15}{16}$ in., (28.1 x 20.2 cm.), aquatint-etching on hand-made (BP 265, DM 644, FR 2170, Y 50,887, SF 580).

BI *Composizione,* 42/90, s., est. SF 600/700, (10-14-92, Germann, #429), 25⅞ x 19$\frac{11}{16}$ in., (657 x 500 mm.), aquatint in colors.

BI *Composizione (Calderoni 40), 1966,* s., d., est. SF 6/800, (10-14-92, Germann, #138), 25$\frac{9}{16}$ x 19$\frac{11}{16}$ in., (650 x 500 mm.), color lithograph.

$374* *Composizione, (19)79,* s., d., p.a., Erker Presse, St. Gallen, (12-01-92, Karl/Faber, #1188), 13$\frac{15}{16}$ x 8¼ in., (35.5 x 21 cm.), color lithograph on BFK Rives wove (BP 247, DM 596, FR 2032, Y 46,564).

$448* *Composizione, (19)82,* s., d., p.a., (12-01-92, Karl/Faber, #1189), 11$\frac{13}{16}$ x 12⅝ in., (30 x 32 cm.), color lithograph on wove (BP 296, DM 714, FR 2433, Y 55,777).

BI *Composizione, 1966,* XXVI/L, s., d., est. SF 700/900, (10-14-92, Germann, #426), 25⅜ x 19$\frac{9}{16}$ in., (645 x 497 mm.), color lithograph.

$417* *Composizione, 1974,* 53/60, s., d., (10-14-92, Germann, #416, illus.), 19$\frac{11}{16}$ x 27⅜ in., (500 x 695 mm.), color aquatint (BP 245, DM 610, FR 2069, Y 50,533, SF 543).

BI *Composizione, 1974,* 80/100, s., d., est. SF 450/650, (10-14-92, Germann, #420), 25⅜ x 19$\frac{9}{16}$ in., (645 x 497 mm.), aquatint.

$417* *Composizione, 1974,* B/E., s., d., (10-14-92, Germann, #418), 19⅞ x 25$\frac{9}{16}$ in., (505 x 650 mm.), color aquatint (BP 245, DM 610, FR 2069, Y 50,533, SF 543).

$424* *Composizione, 1974,* #80/100, s., d., (09-04-92, Germann, #547), 25⅜ x 19$\frac{9}{16}$ in., (645 x 497 mm.), aquatint (BP 212, DM 594, FR 2023, Y 52,191, SF 529).

BI *Composizione, 1974,* s., d., from "Erker Treffen 2", est. SF 100/200, (10-14-92, Germann, #422), 14$\frac{15}{16}$ x 21⅞ in., (380 x 555 mm.), color lithograph.

$453* *Composizione, 1979,* 79/100, s., d., (10-14-92, Germann, #424), 24$\frac{7}{16}$ x 19⅜ in., (620 x 492 mm.), color lithograph (BP 266, DM 663, FR 2248, Y 54,896, SF 590).

$435* *Composizione, 1979,* H.C., s., d., blindstamp, (04-21-93, Germann, #741, illus.), 25$\frac{15}{16}$ x 20⅞ in., (660 x 530 mm.), color lithograph (BP 282, DM 695, FR 2351, Y 48,157, SF 633).

$417* *Composizione, 1983,* E.a., s., d., (10-14-92, Germann, #417), 33$\frac{1}{16}$ x 23¾ in., (840 x 603 mm.), color lithograph (BP 245, DM 610, FR 2069, Y 50,533, SF 543).

$1059* *Composizione, 1985,* 75/90, s., d., (10-14-92, Germann, #427), 33¼ x 27½ in., (845 x 698 mm.), color lithograph (BP 622, DM 1550, FR 5256, Y 128,333, SF 1380).

$971* *Composizione, 1987,* XII/XX, s., d., (10-14-92, Germann, #425), 33⅛ x 25$\frac{3}{16}$ in., (842 x 640 mm.), color aquatint (BP 570, DM 1421, FR 4819, Y 117,668, SF 1265).

$679* *Composizione, 1987,* 13/90, s., d., (10-14-92, Germann, #428), 30$\frac{5}{16}$ x 24$\frac{5}{16}$ in., (770 x 618 mm.), color lithograph (BP 399, DM 994, FR 3370, Y 82,283, SF 885).

$553* *Composizione, 1989,* 25/90, s., d., blindstamp, (06-24-93, Germann, #503), 17$\frac{11}{16}$ x 14⅛ in., (450 x 358 mm.), color aquatint (BP 364, DM 897, FR 3022, Y 59,322, SF 805).

$790* *Composizione, 1989,* 5/95, s., d., blindstamp, (06-24-93, Germann, #501), 28⅛ x 29½ in., (705 x 750 mm.), color lithograph w/collage (BP 520, DM 1281, FR 4317, Y 84,746, SF 1150).

$632* *Composizione, 1989,* 88/95, s., d., blindstamp, (06-24-93, Germann, #502), 27¾ x 29½ in., (705 x 750 mm.), color lithograph w/collage (BP 416, DM 1025, FR 3454, Y 67,797, SF 920).

$593* *Composizione-Sarajevo, 1983,* (06-24-93, Germann, #505), 331/16 x 24 in., (840 x 610 mm.), color aquatint w/ embossing (BP 390, DM 961, FR 3240, Y 63,613, SF 863).

$453* *Compsizione, 1974,* XIX/XXVI, s., (10-14-92, Germann, #137), 25 9/16 x 19½ in., (650 x 495 mm.), etching and aquatint (BP 266, DM 663, FR 2248, Y 54,896, SF 590).

$433* *Fur Sarajewo, 1983,* s., d., num., (11-28-92, Schoppmann, #775), 25⅜ x 17 15/16 in., (64.5 x 45.5 cm.), color etching on handmade cardboard (BP 286, DM 690, FR 2342, Y 53,889).

$922* *Komposition Auf Graublauem Fond, 1979,* watermark, s., d., blindstamp, (06-05-93, Grisebach, #849, illus.), 18 9/16 x 14 13/16 in., (47.2 x 37.6 cm.), color lithograph on wove (BP 607, DM 1495, FR 5038, Y 98,906).

$922* *Komposition Auf Graugrunem Fond, 1979,* watermark, s., d., i. p.a., blindstamp, (06-05-93, Grisebach, #848, illus.), 15 3/16 x 12 11/16 in., (38.5 x 32.3 cm.), color lithograph on wove (BP 607, DM 1495, FR 5038, Y 98,906).

$332* *Luce Curva, 1979,* #XXII/XXXII, s., d., (04-21-93, Germann, #731), 19½ x 13 9/16 in., (496 x 345 mm.), color aquatint (BP 215, DM 531, FR 1795, Y 36,754, SF 483).

$349* *Mozarabico, 1978,* s., d., #49/100, blindstamp, fold, (09-18-92, Schloss Ahlden, #1047, illus.), 27½ x 19¾ in., (69.9 x 50.2 cm.), color screen print on BFK Rives (BP 204, DM 518, FR 1772, Y 43,134).

$532* *Sarajevo, (19)83,* s., d., num., blindstamp, (06-08-93, Karl/Faber, #1267), approx. 25 9/16 x 15⅜ in., (65 x 39 cm.), color aquatint/etching and serigraph on Fabriano wove (BP 350, DM 863, FR 2907, Y 56,506).

$434* *Segni, 1968,* 55/60, s., d., t., (10-14-92, Germann, #419), 25⅜ x 19½ in., (645 x 495 mm.), color aquatint (BP 255, DM 635, FR 2154, Y 52,593, SF 566).

$1413* *"Senza Titolo", 1976,* #IX/XV, s., d., (11-13-92, Koller, #5422), 27 3/16 x 38 9/16 in., (69 x 98 cm.), aquatint on wove (BP 913, DM 2218, FR 7480, Y 175,375, SF 2000).

$650* *Senza Titolo, 1963,* s., d., num., (11-28-92, Grisebach, #727, illus.), 20 9/16 x 15⅜ in., (52.3 x 39 cm.), colored lithograph on wove (BP 429, DM 1036, FR 3515, Y 80,896).

$474* *Untitled, 1974,* #XII/XVIII, s., d., (04-21-93, Germann, #732), 19¾ x 27 9/16 in., (502 x 700 mm.), color aquatint (BP 308, DM 758, FR 2562, Y 52,474, SF 690).

$348* *Untitled, 1974,* #77/100, s., d., (04-21-93, Germann, #733), 25 9/16 x 19⅝ in., (650 x 498 mm.), aquatint (BP 226, DM 556, FR 1881, Y 38,525, SF 506).

$154* *Via Rossa,* s., d. '70, #33/90, prov., (05-16-93, Hindman, #583), 25¼ x 19¼ in., (64.1 x 48.9 cm.), color aquatint (BP 100, DM 248, FR 832, Y 17,071).

SANUTI, Giulio ac. 1550-1575

$991* *Baum des Lebens (Nagler, Monogrammisten III, 326),* watermark, (06-04-93, Bassenge, #5353), 19 15/16 x 13 9/16 in., (50.6 x 34.4 cm.), engraving (BP 656, DM 1609, FR 5424, Y 106,881).

SARGENT AND JARDAN

BI *South Africa "So Much To See",* good cond., (03-13-93, Laurin, #134), 39¾ x 24 in., (101 x 61 cm.), .

SARONY & CO., Lithographers ac. 1853-57

$30,800* *The Japan Expedition, 1855-6: Set Of Six,* by W. Heine, pub. E. Brown, Jr., margins, stains, surface scratches,foxing, all but one laid down on linen, defects, good cond., prop. Descendantsf Commodore Matthew C. Perry, (01-22-93, Christie-NY, #317, illus.), each borderline 20¼ x 32⅛ in., (514 x 816 mm.), color lithograph w/hand-coloring on wove (BP 20,150, DM 48,974, FR 165,680, Y 3,854,819).

SARONY & MAJOR, Printers

BI *Jersey City, New York From Staten Island (R. 2640), 1849,* p. w/tint stone, sketched and drawn on stone by C.W. Burton, margins, tear into image, light-stained, soilied, laid down, est. $2,5/4,000, (01-28-93, Sotheby-NY, #451, illus.), 12⅜ x 38 in., (31.4 x 96.5 cm.), sheet 14½ x 40½ in., (31.4 x 96.5 cm.), hand-colored lithograph.

SARONY STUDIO OF NEW YORK (et al)

BI *Portraits Of Actors And Actresses In Shakespearean Roles,* 90 cartes-de-visites, most by Sarony, majority w/ credit stamp, 1860s,est. $8/1,200, (10-13-92, Christie-NY, #22, illus.), oblong folio 8⅝ x 11½ in., (21.9 x 29.2 cm.), photograph.

SARRAILLON

$398* *Ch. De Fer Algeriens Et Ste Africaines Des Transports Tropicaux: Alger-Djelfa,* very good cond., (03-13-93, Laurin, #60), 39⅜ x 24 in., (100 x 61 cm.), (BP 278, DM 662, FR 2252, Y 46,906).

SARTAIN, John American 1808-1897

$275* *"Major General Zachary Taylor, President Of The United States",* p. from original daguerreotype, (11-21-92, Goldberg, #714), 25 x 18 in., (63.5 x 45.7 cm.), lithograph (BP 181, DM 438, FR 1477, Y 34,200).

$110* *"Portrait Of A Lady",* artist's proof, s., John Sartain, 1892, after Joseph Coomans Paris, 1888, (10-11-92, Dunning, #1534), 18 x 22½ in., (45.7 x 57.2 cm.), engraving (BP 65, DM 163, FR 549, Y 13,392).

SARTAIN, William American 1843-1924

BI *Washington And His Family,* proof, est. $3/400, (02-04-93, Sloan, #1217), 17¾ x 25¾ in., (45.1 x 65.4 cm.), engraving.

SARTONY (after)

$174* *Pathe-Baby Motocamera,* p. Delattre, backed on linen, (05-07-93, Christie-S. Ken, #123, illus.), 15¾ x 24 in., (40 x 61 cm.), color lithograph (BP 110, DM 275, FR 927, Y 19,159).

SARTORIUS, Francis (after)

$213* *Gimcrack (Plate 224),* pub. Laurie & Whittle, 1794, (12-01-92, Ritchie, #3A), plate 10 x 13¾ in., (25.4 x 34.9 cm.), mezzotint hand-colored w/watercolor and bodycolor (BP 141, DM 339, FR 1157, Y 26,519, C$ 275).

SARTORIUS, John Nott (after)

$170* *Rockingham,* by J. W. Edye, pub. J. Harris, April 25, 1789, margins, (04-22-93, Bonhams-Chelsea, #155), plate 14 x 18 in., (35.6 x 45.7 cm.), aquatint (BP 110, DM 273, FR 921, Y 18,692).

SASAGIRNA, K. Japanese contemporary

$88* *A View Of Mt. Fujiyama,* s., d. 1967, t., num., sealed, (03-25-93, Boos, #217), 17¾ x 17½ in., (45.1 x 44.5 cm.), embossing and block print (BP 60, DM 145, FR 492, Y 10,309).

SASAJIMA, K. Japanese 20th cent.

$385* *Landscape With Building, 1948,* s., d. 1948, num. 27/50, bears artist's red chop, EmmanuelJacobson Estate, (09-20-92, Hindman, #736), 13¾ x 19¾ in., (34.9 x 50.2 cm.), woodblock (BP 225, DM 571, FR 1954, Y 47,584).

SASHA

BI *Lupino Lane,* c. 1935, red crayon s., credit photog., frayed edges, est. BP 1/150, (12-17-92, Christie-S. Ken, #19, illus.), 13½ x 10½ in., (34.3 x 26.7 cm.), photograph, gelatin silver print.

SATER, Miles

$66* *"Home Of The Elgin National Watch Company",* s. Miles Sater, (09-12-92, Dunning, #1178, illus.), 15 x 33 in., (38.1 x 83.8 cm.), print (BP 34, DM 95, FR 323, Y 8177).

SATTLER, Joseph

$348* *Brand (A. 75), 1894,* (02-24-93, Picard, #190), lithograph in blue (BP 243, DM 565, FR 1915, Y 40,835).

SAUDEK, Jan   Czech b. 1935

$805* *Female Studies: Diptych,* each s. by photog. ink, 1970's, (04-06-93, Sotheby-NY, #482, illus.), photograph (BP 532, DM 1297, FR 4392, Y 91,811).

$345* *"Girl Looking Out Window" and "Boy Kissing Hand",* 1970s, s., num., photog.'s stamp, illus., (05-23-93, Butterfield, #3589, illus.), one 12¾ x 7½ in., other 11 x 11 in., photograph, gelatin silver print (BP 225, DM 564, FR 1899, Y 38,134).

$460* *Girl With Doll, 1975,* s., t., num. 2, annot., photog.'s stamp, illus., (05-23-93, Butterfield, #3590, illus.), 8¾ x 11⅝ in., photograph, gelatin silver print (BP 300, DM 752, FR 2532, Y 50,846).

BI *Janek's Dream, c. 1977,* t., est. DM 800, (11-12-92, Lempertz, #236), 4⁵⁄₁₆ x 5¹¹⁄₁₆ in., (10.9 x 14.5 cm.), photograph, gelatin silver print.

$1430* *The Kitsch, 1989,* photog.'s sig., notations; notations verso, (04-07-93, Swann, #544, illus.), 15½ x 11¾ in., photograph, hand-colored silver print (BP 945, DM 2313, FR 7827, Y 162,463).

$607* *Ohne Titel; 1973,* (11-12-92, Lempertz, #234, illus.), 3¹⁵⁄₁₆ x 4¹⁵⁄₁₆ in., (10 x 12.6 cm.), photograph, gelatin silver print (BP 388, DM 954, FR 3251, Y 75,096).

BI *Ohne Titel, 60's,* ink s., est. DM 800, (11-12-92, Lempertz, #233, illus.), 9¹⁵⁄₁₆ x 7¹⁵⁄₁₆ in., (25.3 x 20.3 cm.), photograph, gelatin silver print.

$758* *Ohne Titel, c. 1975,* (11-12-92, Lempertz, #235, illus.), 5¹⁄₁₆ x 6⁵⁄₁₆ in., (12.9 x 16 cm.), photograph, gelatin silver print (BP 485, DM 1191, FR 4060, Y 93,777).

BI *To The Wayfaring Stranger, 1977/78,* t., est. DM 600, (11-12-92, Lempertz, #237), 4⅞ x 6⁵⁄₁₆ in., (12.4 x 16 cm.), photograph, gelatin silver print w/blue tint.

SAUDEK, Josef

$1540* *Crucifixion, 1987,* sig., notations, (10-14-92, Swann, #549, illus.), 15½ x 12 in., (39.4 x 30.5 cm.), photograph, hand-colored silver print (BP 904, DM 2254, FR 7643, Y 186,621).

SAULK, Leo   American 20th cent.

$55* *Three Color Stencils,* (03-14-93, Hindman, #341), larger 19 x 24¼ in., (48.3 x 61.6 cm.), (BP 38, DM 92, FR 311, Y 6482).

SAUNDERS, Raymond

$715* *Jack Johnson, University Of California, Santa Cruz, 1982,* good cond., creases, dents, Modesto Lanzone Coll., (10-28-92, Butterfield, #3115), 30 x 22 in., (762 x 559 mm.), color offset lithogra w/collage and extensive hand-coloring on poster (BP 456, DM 1104, FR 3749, Y 87,730).

SAUNIER, Hector

$64* *Contemplado, 1970,* s., t., d., i. E.A., margins, good cond., (05-27-93, Sotheby-Amstrdm, #482), 17⁵⁄₁₆ x 16¹⁵⁄₁₆ in., (440 x 430 mm.), colored etching on wove (BP 41, DM 103, FR 346, Y 6861, G 115).

$115* *Eau Vive, 1971,* s., t., d., #189/190, margins, good cond., (05-27-93, Sotheby-Amstrdm, #483), 15³⁄₁₆ x 19⁵⁄₁₆ in., (385 x 490 mm.), colored etching on wove (BP 74, DM 185, FR 622, Y 12,328, G 207).

SAURA, Antonio   Spanish b. 1930

$794* *Profil, 1976*s., num., of series "Moi"(11-28-92, Grisebach, #728, illus.), 35⅝ x 25⅜ in., (90.5 x 64.5 cm.), colored serigraph on cardboard (BP 524, DM 1265, FR 4294, Y 98,818).

$124* *Adoptio In Fratrem,* s. by artist and author, #49/500, (03-31-93, Briest, #E98), 31½ x 23⅝ in., (80 x 60 cm.), color lithograph (BP 82, DM 199, FR 678, Y 14,259).

$243* *Composition,* artist proof, s., full margins, (05-27-93, Briest, #181), 34⅝ x 24¹³⁄₁₆ in., (88 x 63 cm.), etching on Arches wove (BP 156, DM 390, FR 1314, Y 26,051).

BI *Composition,* s. Saura 51/140, est. DK 2,500, (03-24-93, Kunsthallen, #293), color lithograph.

BI *Composition,* s. Saura 51/140, est. DK 2,500, (03-24-93, Kunsthallen, #291), color lithograph.

$211* *Composition,* s. Saura, 50/115, (09-30-92, Kunsthallen, #261), color lithograph (BP 119, DM 299, FR 1012, Y 25,321, DK 1150).

$650* *Grotesker Kopf, 1976,* s., num., of series "Moi", (11-28-92, Grisebach, #730, illus.), 35⅝ x 25⁵⁄₁₆ in., (90.5 x

64.3 cm.), colored serigraph on cardboard (BP 429, DM 1036, FR 3515, Y 80,896).

$866* *Hommage A Dora Maar, 1987,* s., num., (11-28-92, Grisebach, #731, illus.), 25⁹⁄₁₆ x 19¹¹⁄₁₆ in., (65 x 50 cm.), colored serigraph on thick copper print paper (BP 572, DM 1380, FR 4684, Y 107,778).

BI *Komposition,* s., num., est. DM 1000, (12-01-92, Karl/Faber, #1193), 8¹¹⁄₁₆ x 11 in., (22 x 28 cm.), color lithograph on wove.

$650* *Nase, 1976,* s., num., of series "Moi", (11-28-92, Grisebach, #729, illus.), 35⁷⁄₁₆ x 25³⁄₁₆ in., (90 x 64 cm.), colored serigraph on cardboard (BP 429, DM 1036, FR 3515, Y 80,896).

BI *Pour Jorn, 1976,* s. Saura, 41/100, from the Pour Jorn portfolio, est. DK 1,500, (09-30-92, Kunsthallen, #262), lithograph.

$184* *"Triptico De Amsterdam", (Galfetti 196), 1975,* s. Saura, (03-24-93, Kunsthallen, #292), color lithograph (BP 125, DM 301, FR 1023, Y 21,619, DK 1150).

$281* *Untitled,* s., full sheet p. edges, good cond., (05-27-93, Sotheby-Amstrdm, #481), sh 26¾ x 18½ in., (680 x 470 mm.), colored lithograph on wove (BP 180, DM 451, FR 1520, Y 30,124, G 506).

$352* *Untitled,* s., full sheet p. to edges, good cond., (05-27-93, Sotheby-Amstrdm, #479, illus.), sh 26³⁄₁₆ x 18½ in., (665 x 470 mm.), colored lithograph on wove (BP 225, DM 565, FR 1904, Y 37,736, G 633).

$416* *Untitled,* s., full sheet p. to edges, good cond., (05-27-93, Sotheby-Amstrdm, #480), sh 26¾ x 18½ in., (680 x 470 mm.), colored lithograph on wove (BP 266, DM 668, FR 2250, Y 44,597, G 748).

$256* *Untitled, 1971,* s., d., #75/200, pub. Cercle Graphique Europeen, full sheet, good cond., waterstaining, (05-27-93, Sotheby-Amstrdm, #683), sh 30⁵⁄₁₆ x 22¹⁄₁₆ in., color silkscreen (BP 164, DM 411, FR 1385, Y 27,444, G 460).

$178* *Visage, Planche Des Cahiers De L'Espace,* s., #81/99, full margins, (11-16-92, Briest, #93), 14¹⁵⁄₁₆ x 11 in., (38 x 28 cm.), etching and aquatint in 2 colors (BP 117, DM 284, FR 956, Y 22,214).

SAUVAIRE, Henri

BI *Jerusalem, Architectural Study, 1850s,* from waxed paper neg., est. BP 8/1,200, 248 x 186mm, (05-07-93, Sotheby-London, #18, illus.), photograph, albumen print.

BI *Karak Et Chauback, c. 1862,* Ex-Coll. Robert Schoelkopf, est. $6/900, (10-14-92, Swann, #210, illus.), 9¾ x 7½ in., (24.8 x 19.1 cm.), photograph, albumen print from paper neg..

SAVAGE, Edward

$920* *George Washington Esqr. President Of The United State Of America (Stauffer 2752; Shadwell 82), 1793,* after Savage's portrait, pub. by artist, trimmed w/in platemark w/publication line, surface scrapes, laid down, (01-28-93, Sotheby-NY, #442, illus.), sheet 20⅜ x 15 in., (518 x 381 mm.), mezzotint (BP 608, DM 1458, FR 4933, Y 114,229).

SAVERIJ, Jacob (I)   d. 1602

BI *Eine Strasse An Einem Sumpf (Burchard 4; Hollstein 11 II),* est. DM 900, (12-04-92, Bassenge, #6437), 3⁷⁄₁₆ x 4¹³⁄₁₆ in., (8.7 x 12.2 cm.), etching.

SAVERIJ, Jakob (I)   1565/67-1602

$5665* *Die Hirschjagd In Einer Schwemme (Wurzbach 1, Buchard 7 II, Hollstein6 II, The Illustrated Bartsch 53, 006, S 2.), 1602,* watermark, (06-04-93, Bassenge, #5354, illus.), 7¹⁵⁄₁₆ x 11⅝ in., (20.1 x 29.5 cm.), etching w/engraving (BP 3748, DM 9199, FR 31,007, Y 610,979).

$6728* *Die Hirschjagd In Einer Schwemme Vor Einer Kapelle Und Einem Turm (Wurzbach 2, Buchard 8 II, Hollstein 7 II, The Illustrated Bartsch 53, 007, S 2),c. 1602,* (06-04-93, Bassenge, #5355, illus.), 7½ x 11⅜ in., (19 x 28.9 cm.), etching and engraving (BP 4451, DM 10,926, FR 36,825, Y 725,626).

SAVERY, Jacob   Dutch 1545-1602

$2604* *Landscapes (Holl. 8-13): Set Of Six,* margins, trimmed, disturbance, (06-29-93, Sotheby-London, #59, illus.), each approx. 3⅝ x 4¾ in., (9.2 x 12.1 cm.), etching (BP 1725, DM 4397, FR 14,821, Y 277,198).

SAVIGNAC, Raymond b. 1907

$797* *Cinzano, 1951,* p. De Plas, good cond., lit., (11-19-92, Ribeyre/Baron, #45), 46$\frac{1}{16}$ x 62$\frac{15}{16}$ in., (117 x 160 cm.), poster (BP 525, DM 1271, FR 4280, Y 99,117).

$608* *Danone Fruits, 1959,* very good cond., lit., (11-19-92, Ribeyre/Baron, #48), 62$\frac{15}{16}$ x 46$\frac{7}{16}$ in., (160 x 118 cm.), poster (BP 400, DM 969, FR 3265, Y 75,612).

$462* *L'Eau Ecarlate, "Detache Sans Aureoles", 1954,* p. Courbet, good cond., lit., (11-19-92, Ribeyre/Baron, #47), 59$\frac{1}{16}$ x 37$\frac{13}{16}$ in., (150 x 96 cm.), poster (BP 304, DM 737, FR 2481, Y 57,456).

$299* *Larousse, Cadeaux Pour Tous,* cond. A, (03-16-93, Boisgirard, #192), 26¾ x 107½ in., (68 x 273 cm.), poster (BP 206, DM 497, FR 1689, Y 34,963).

$239* *Michelin XAS Nouveau,* cond. B, (03-16-93, Boisgirard, #191), 27$\frac{9}{16}$ x 108$\frac{11}{16}$ in., (70 x 276 cm.), poster (BP 165, DM 397, FR 1350, Y 27,947).

$797* *Monsavon, "Au Lait", 1949,* p. Bedos, very good cond., lit., (11-19-92, Ribeyre/Baron, #44, illus.), 59$\frac{1}{16}$ x 39⅜ in., (150 x 100 cm.), poster (BP 525, DM 1271, FR 4280, Y 99,117).

$629* *Moutarde Parizot, Dijon, 1952/53,* p. Courbet, good cond., (11-19-92, Ribeyre/Baron, #46, illus.), 62$\frac{15}{16}$ x 47¼ in., (160 x 120 cm.), poster (BP 414, DM 1003, FR 3378, Y 78,224).

SAVIN, Maurice French 1894-1973

BI *"Pecheurs Sur La Plage", "Interieur Paysan" and "Chemin Dans La Plaine": Three,* s., #43/120, full margins, drystamp, (05-06-93, Laurin, #79), etchings and lithograph on wove.

BI *Le Repos Des Moisonneurs,* s., #43/120, full margins, drystamp, (05-06-93, Laurin, #78), color lithograph on wove.

SAVINIO, Alberto 1891-1952

$1556* *Da: La Lotteria Clandestina (Anni '40), #70/89,* s., (12-15-92, Finarte-Milan, #32, illus.), 9$\frac{1}{16}$ x 6⅛ in., (23 x 15.5 cm.), lithograph (BP 993, DM 2439, FR 8334, Y 192,980, L 2185).

SAVOIE, Robert Canadian b. 1939

$1326* *"Deduction",* #40/60, s., d. Robert Savoie 1968-74, (04-20-93, Encans, #95), 14¾ x 15¼ in., (37.5 x 38.8 cm.), etching (BP 856, DM 2112, FR 7129, Y 146,309, C$ 1665).

$75* *"Deduction",* #22/60, t., s., d. Robert Savoie 1968-74, (07-14-92, Encans, #165), 14$\frac{15}{16}$ x 15$\frac{15}{16}$ in., (38 x 40.5 cm.), etching and aquatint (BP 39, DM 111, FR 375, Y 9379, C$ 89).

$44* *Illusion,* #5/50, s., d. Savoie 1974, (06-16-93, Encans, #103), 15⅜ x 17$\frac{5}{16}$ in., (39 x 44 cm.), color etching (BP 29, DM 73, FR 245, Y 4693, C$ 56).

$142* *"Illusions",* #32/50, s., t., d. Savoie 74, (02-16-93, Encans, #81), 15$\frac{3}{16}$ x 17$\frac{5}{16}$ in., (38.5 x 44 cm.), lithograph (BP 98, DM 232, FR 785, Y 17,012, C$ 178).

SAVORELLI, Petrus

BI *"Asa" and Jesse": Two,* later strikes, margins, (06-16-93, Bonhams-Chelsea, #350), pl. 15½ x 21¾ in., (39.4 x 55.2 cm.), engraving w/hand-coloring.

SAVREUX, M.

$315* *Salon D'Automne, Palais Du Trocadero, 1938,* very good cond., (11-19-92, Ribeyre/Baron, #154), 62$\frac{15}{16}$ x 47¼ in., (160 x 120 cm.), poster (BP 207, DM 502, FR 1692, Y 39,174).

SAVRIJ, Roelant (after)

$302* *Paysages Du Tyrol: Five,* good cond., crease, (05-15-93, Loudmer, #94), approx. 5$\frac{15}{16}$ x 8¾ in., (152 x 223 mm.), copper engravings on laid (BP 196, DM 486, FR 1632, Y 33,477).

SAWAII, Noboru b. 1931

$217* *Etching & Color Woodblock Prints: Three,* s.,t., (05-10-93, Hodgins, #288), etching and color woodblock on paper (BP 142, DM 349, FR 1176, Y 24,249, C$ 275).

BI *Honourable Curator,* #66/100, s., t., prov., est. C$ 2/300, (11-16-92, Hodgins, #233), 25¾ x 19½ in., (65.4 x 49.5 cm.), color etching on paper.

BI *Signs Of The Zodiac,* #21/100, s., t., prov., est. C$250/350, (05-10-93, Hodgins, #289), 24 x 19¾ in., (61 x 50.2 cm.), color etching on paper.

BI *Signs Of The Zodiac,* #55/100, s., t., prov., est. C$ 2/300, (11-16-92, Hodgins, #336), 23$\frac{15}{16}$ x 7$\frac{15}{16}$ in., (61 x 50.2 cm.), color etching on paper.

$239* *"Signs Of The Zodiak" and "Honorable Curator": Two,* #55/100 #66/100 respectively, s.,t., prov., (05-10-93, Hodgins, #324), 24 x 19 in., (61 x 48.3 cm.), color etching on paper (BP 156, DM 384, FR 1295, Y 26,707, C$ 303).

SAWYER, Lydell b. 1856

$1270* *"The Castle Garth, Newcastle",* c. 1889, mounted on double layer of card, s. Lyd. Sawyer, t., (05-06-93, Christie-London, #66, illus.), 14 x 11½ in., photograph, platinum print (BP 805, DM 2000, FR 6734, Y 139,729).

SAYER, Derek

$601* *These Men Use Shell, Fishermen, 1937,* p. Waterlow and Sons, ref. #506, cond. 1, (10-13-92, Phillips-London, #130), 29$\frac{15}{16}$ x 44⅞ in., (76 x 114 cm.), color lithograph (BP 350, DM 880, FR 2992, Y 72,875).

SAYER, Robert and J. BENNET English 18th cent.

$110* *The Happy Abode,* (05-28-93, Sloan, #1580, illus.), 8¼ x 14 in., (21 x 35.6 cm.), reverse color engraving on glass (BP 70, DM 174, FR 590, Y 11,795).

SAYER, Robert, Publisher

$383* *Ruins Of Athens: Six,* restrikes, margins, (07-16-92, Bonhams-Chelsea, #458), plate 11 x 15½ in., (27.9 x 39.4 cm.), etching on wove (BP 198, DM 566, FR 1910, Y 47,977).

SAYRE, F. Grayson American 1879-1938/39

$165* *Indian Riders In Landscape,* s. F. Grayson Sayre, (11-10-92, Moran, #158), sight 13½ x 9½ in., (34.3 x 24.1 cm.), serigraph on paper (BP 109, DM 265, FR 894, Y 20,538).

$220* *Indian Riders In Landscape,* s. F. Grayson Sayre, (11-10-92, Moran, #159), sight 16 x 11½ in., (40.6 x 29.2 cm.), serigraph on paper (BP 146, DM 353, FR 1192, Y 27,384).

SCACKI, Francisco

$2860* *"A Correct View Of The Battle Near The City Of New Orleans, On The Eigth Of January 1815, Under The Command Of General Andrew Jackson, Over 10,000 British Troops, In Which 3 Of Their Most Distinguished Generals Were Killed...",* proof on each side of paper, same image each side/text differs, pub.1815, (12-05-92, Neal, #554, illus.), plate 19 x 25 in., (48.3 x 63.5 cm.), engraving (BP 1791, DM 4459, FR 15,197, Y 354,355).

SCANLAN, R. (after)

$579* *"Horse Dealing No. 1" and "Horse Dealing No. 2": Pair,* by J. Harris, pub. R. Ackermann, August 2nd, 1841, spotting to plateNo. 2, (04-22-93, Bonhams-Chelsea, #154), image 11 x 15½ in., (27.9 x 39.4 cm.), (BP 374, DM 930, FR 3138, Y 63,661).

$255* *Horse Dealing: Plate 1 and 2, 1841,* after R. Scanlan, by J. Harris, pub. R. Ackermann, margins, foxing, (07-16-92, Bonhams-Chelsea, #524), plate 14¼ x 18½ in., (36.2 x 47 cm.), aquatint w/hand coloring, laid down (BP 132, DM 377, FR 1272, Y 31,943).

SCARLETT, Rolph American 1889-1984

BI *Barbarossa, c. 1930,* s., excell. cond.?, est. $2/3,000, (05-11-93, Christie-NY, #119, illus.), sheet 11¾ x 11 in., (298 x 279 mm.), color monotype, woodcut and stencil on wove.

SCAVULLO, Francesco American b. 1929

$4675* *China, 1962,* s., d., num. 10/10 by photog., (c) ed. stamp, #10/10 ed., (10-15-92, Sotheby-NY, #570A, illus.), 22¾ x 17½ in., (57.8 x 44.5 cm.), photograph, gelatin silver print (BP 2861, DM 6959, FR 23,599, Y 560,888).

$1380* *Male Nude, 1991,* s., .d, i. A/P by photog., (c) edit. stamp, artist's proof, (04-06-93, Sotheby-NY, #525, illus.), 14⅛ x 14⅜ in., photograph (BP 911, DM 2223, FR 7529, Y 157,391).

BI *Sam Wagstaff And Robert Mapplethorpe, 1974,* backed w/ card, s., d. by photog., est. $3/5,000, (10-15-92, Sotheby-

NY, #571, illus.), 19½ x 24 in., (49.5 x 61 cm.), photograph, gelatin silver print.

SCHAAF, Albert E. 1866-1955

BI *Early Motoring In France, 1905,* sig., notations, est. $1/1,500, (10-14-92, Swann, #550, illus.), 11 x 14 in., (27.9 x 35.6 cm.), photograph, bromoil print.

$825* *Terminal Tower And Flats-Cleveland, 1933,* sig., notations, (10-14-92, Swann, #551, illus.), 11¾ x 9½ in., (29.8 x 24.1 cm.), photograph, bromoil print (BP 484, DM 1207, FR 4094, Y 99,976).

SCHAD, Christian German 1894-1982

$664* *Bildnis Paul Scheerbart, 1964,* s., num., damage, (12-05-92, Bassenge, #7678), 18⁵⁄₁₆ x 13⅜ in., (46.5 x 34 cm.), color woodcut on handmade Japan (BP 416, DM 1035, FR 3528, Y 82,270).

BI *Christian Schad-Mappe, Sirius Verlag, Zurich, 1915 (Dada In Zurich cat 49a-k), 1915: Set Of Ten,* w/title pg., each w/name and t. stamp, wide margins, dirt, creases, customs stamp, very good cond., foxing, surface dirt, original portfolio, scuffing, prov., exhib., est. BP 2,5/3,500, (12-01-92, Christie-London, #535), overall S. 22⁷⁄₁₆ x 17¹¹⁄₁₆ in., (570 x 450 mm.), woodcuts on laid.

$1245* *"Dompteuse", (19)15,* s., d., brown stained, (12-01-92, Karl/Faber, #1194), 5⅞ x 3¾ in., (15 x 9.5 cm.), woodcut on hand-made Japan (BP 823, DM 1984, FR 6763, Y 155,005).

$830* *"Eifersucht", (19)17,* s., d., brown stained, (12-01-92, Karl/Faber, #1195), 5⅞ x 5⅞ in., (15 x 15 cm.), woodcut on thin Japan (BP 548, DM 1323, FR 4508, Y 103,337).

$217* *Jenny,* s., d., t., num., (09-25-92, Granier, #3006), sheet 12⅝ x 9⁷⁄₁₆ in., (32 x 24 cm.), etching on machine hand-made (BP 127, DM 322, FR 1088, Y 26,192).

$2240* *"Traitresse", (19)17,* s., d., i., brown stained in margin, w/traces of old mounting, (12-01-92, Karl/Faber, #1196), 6⅞ x 4½ in., (17.5 x 11.5 cm.), woodcut on hand-made Japan (BP 1480, DM 3570, FR 12,167, Y 278,884).

SCHADE, Virtus

$110* *Asger Jorn, (Van de Loo 268-271), 1965,* #210 of 750, (03-24-93, Kunsthallen, #294), color lithograph (BP 74, DM 180, FR 611, Y 12,924, DK 690).

SCHADOW, Johann Gottfried 1764-1850

$650* *Logengeheimnisse (Mackowsky 44),* lit., (12-04-92, Bassenge, #6935), 4⁷⁄₁₆ x 5³⁄₁₆ in., (11.2 x 13.2 cm.), etching (BP 417, DM 1035, FR 3512, Y 81,149).

BI *Der Stehende Schauspieler (Mackowsky 9), 1784,* est. DM 300, (12-04-92, Bassenge, #6934), 3⅜ x 1⅝ in., (8.5 x 4.1 cm.), etching.

SCHAEFER, Marian Anderson American 20th cent.

$44* *"Mountain Man",* s. Marian Anderson, #479/750, (02-27-93, Dunning, #24), 23½ x 15¾ in., (59.7 x 40 cm.), offset lithograph (BP 31, DM 72, FR 246, Y 5194).

SCHALDACH, William J.

$165* *Woodcock At Twilight,* margins, s. W. J. Schaldach, (02-13-93, Collins, #54, illus.), 5⅞ x 3⅞ in., (14.9 x 9.8 cm.), etching (BP 116, DM 274, FR 926, Y 19,899).

SCHALL (after)

BI *"L'Amant Surprise",* engr. by Descourtis, (12-11-92, G.A. Key, #98B), 18 x 14 in., (45.7 x 35.6 cm.), colored engraving.

SCHALL, Jean Frederic (after)

$88* *L'Eneance De Paul Et Virginie,* trimmed stained, tear, (02-17-93, Bonhams-Chelsea, #345), sheet 14 x 15¾ in., (35.6 x 40 cm.), hand-colored stipple engraving (BP 61, DM 143, FR 484, Y 10,511).

BI *Paul Et Virginie,* by Descourtis (part set), pub. by engraver, foxing, est. BP8/1,200, (01-21-93, Bonhams-Chelsea, #152), image 12⅝ x 16 in., (32.1 x 40.6 cm.), five hand-colored aquatints.

$1650* *Paul Et Virginie: Five,* by Descourtis (part set), pub. engraver, foxing, (06-16-93, Bonhams-Chelsea, #438, illus.), image 12⅝ x 16 in., (32.1 x 40.6 cm.), aquatint w/hand-coloring (BP 1100, DM 2739, FR 9192, Y 175,981).

SCHALL, Jean Frederic (after) 1752-1825

$2530* *Paul Et Virginie (P. and B. 8), c. 1800: Six,* by C.M. Descourtis, trimmed, repaired tears, image scratches, skinning, defects, (05-11-93, Christie-NY, #84), each sheet 15½ x 17½ in., (394 x 445 mm.), color aquatint on wove (BP 1615, DM 3986, FR 13,429, Y 278,297).

SCHANKER, Louis American b. 1903

$880* *Beggars, 1928,* s., t., margins, good cond., creases, (10-28-92, Butterfield, #2546), 10 x 6⅞ in., (254 x 175 mm.), woodcut on Japan paper (BP 561, DM 1359, FR 4615, Y 107,975).

$660* *Composition With 3 Figures, c. 1940,* num., s., stamped artist's seal, (05-27-93, Swann, #250), 12 x 16 in., (30.5 x 40.6 cm.), color woodcut (BP 423, DM 1059, FR 3569, Y 70,755).

$220* *Untitled (New York Still Life), 1931,* d., s., (05-27-93, Swann, #249, illus.), 7 x 9⅛ in., (17.8 x 23.2 cm.), lithograph (BP 141, DM 353, FR 1190, Y 23,585).

SCHANTZ, Philip von b. 1928

$3925* *Fat, Ur Krus, Fat Och Karpe (Bjurstrom 177), 1977,* s., 53/140, edit. Bo Alveryd, (05-25-93, AB Stockholm, #61), 21⅝ x 15¹⁵⁄₁₆ in., (55 x 40.5 cm.), lithograph in colors (BP 2544, DM 6393, FR 21,519, Y 429,009, SK 5720).

$1963* *Kappe, Ur Krus, Fat Och Kappe (B. 178), 1977,* s., 53/140, ed. Bo Alveryd, (05-25-93, AB Stockholm, #62), 20⅞ x 15¾ in., (53 x 40 cm.), lithograph in colors (BP 1272, DM 3197, FR 10,762, Y 214,559, SK 2860).

$1005* *Lokstilleben (Lindstrom B. 197), 1980,* s., 80/190, blindstamp, (12-04-92, AB Stockholm, #7133), 19¹¹⁄₁₆ x 29¾ in., (50 x 75.5 cm.), lithograph in colors (BP 645, DM 1601, FR 5429, Y 125,468, SK 6820).

$1378* *Rott (Bjurstrom 184), 1978,* s., 41/265, from Rott och svart, (12-04-92, AB Stockholm, #7132), 19¹¹⁄₁₆ x 30⅛ in., (50 x 76.5 cm.), lithograph in colors (BP 884, DM 2195, FR 7445, Y 172,035, SK 9350).

$3472* *Svart, Ur Rott Och Svart (B. 185), 1978,* s., proof, (05-25-93, AB Stockholm, #63), 19¹¹⁄₁₆ x 30⅛ in., (50 x 76.5 cm.), lithograph in colors (BP 2250, DM 5655, FR 19,035, Y 379,495, SK 5060).

$2868* *Svenska Krusbar (B. 200), 1981,* s., 49/160, blindstamp, ed. Bo Alveryd, (05-25-93, AB Stockholm, #64), 27¹⁵⁄₁₆ x 34¼ in., (71 x 87 cm.), serigraph in colors (BP 1859, DM 4671, FR 15,724, Y 313,477, SK 4180).

$1409* *Vinbarsberg (Bjurstrom 201), 1981,* s., 164/195, (05-12-93, AB Stockholm, #7045), 19½ x 29⁵⁄₁₆ in., (49.5 x 74.5 cm.), lithograph in colors (BP 920, DM 2273, FR 7658, Y 157,307, SK 10,450).

$1812* *Vit Drottning (B. 205), 1981,* s., 171/180, (05-25-93, AB Stockholm, #65), 27⅜ x 20½ in., (69.5 x 52 cm.), lithograph in colors (BP 1174, DM 2951, FR 9934, Y 198,054, SK 2640).

SCHAPER, Friedrich 1869-1956

$117* *Bauernjunge Mit Kuh,* plate s., dusty, (09-25-92, Granier, #2687), 5³⁄₁₆ x 6⁵⁄₁₆ in., (13.1 x 16 cm.), sheet 8⁷⁄₁₆ x 11 in., (13.1 x 16 cm.), etching on copper print paper (BP 68, DM 173, FR 586, Y 14,122).

SCHARF, Kenny American b. 1958

BI *Jade Pea God, 1989,* s., #62/150, blindstamp of pub., Martin Lawrence Galleries, good cond., est. $800/1,000, (02-11-93, Sotheby-NY, #439), sheet 33¹¹⁄₁₆ x 38¹⁵⁄₁₆ in., (855 x 990 mm.), color silkscreen.

BI *The Ten Commandments: I-One God, 1987,* s., d., #2/84, good cond., est. $6/800, (02-24-93, Butterfield, #3252, illus.), 23⅞ x 17⅞ in., (606 x 454 mm.), lithograph in colors on Dieu Donne handmade.

$866* *Untitled, 1987,* i. P.P., s., d., num., (11-28-92, Schoppmann, #778), 23⅝ x 17¹¹⁄₁₆ in., (60 x 45 cm.), color lithograph on handmade (BP 572, DM 1380, FR 4684, Y 107,778).

SCHARFF, Edwin 1887-1955

$284* *Rossebandiger, 1921,* s., (06-05-93, Grisebach, #850, illus.), 8⅛ x 6¼ in., (20.7 x 15.8 cm.), drypoint on handmade (BP 187, DM 460, FR 1552, Y 30,466).

SCHARL, Josef   German 1896-1958

BI *Junge Frau, 1935,* s., d., artist proof I, est. DM 1000, (12-01-92, Karl/Faber, #1201), 18⅛ x 10¼ in., (46 x 26 cm.), woodcut on thin Maschinen paper.

$565* *Siegesparade, 1933,* s., d., plate mono., d., #2/25, (06-10-93, Hauswedell/Nolt, #851, illus.), image 11⅝ x 19⁵⁄₁₆ in., (29.5 x 49 cm.), etching on hand-made (BP 370, DM 920, FR 3098, Y 59,972).

BI *Stillende Mutter, 1935,* s., d., num., est. DM 800, (12-01-92, Karl/Faber, #1202), 16⅛ x 10¹³⁄₁₆ in., (41 x 27.5 cm.), woodcut on thin Maschinen paper.

SCHATT, Roy

$374* *"Foggy New York Through A Taxi Window", 1962,* t., d., photog.'s stamp, (05-23-93, Butterfield, #3592, illus.), 11¾ x 16½ in., photograph, gelatin silver print (BP 244, DM 612, FR 2058, Y 41,340).

$660* *James Dean In Front Of "Loft To Let" Sign, 1954,* photog.'s sig., d. handstamps, (04-07-93, Swann, #545, illus.), 13½ x 10¾ in., photograph, silver print (BP 436, DM 1067, FR 3612, Y 74,983).

$440* *James Dean With Camera, 1954,* s., d. by photog. white ink recto, handstamps, (04-07-93, Swann, #545A), 11 x 14 in., photograph, silver print (BP 291, DM 712, FR 2408, Y 49,989).

$660* *James Dean With Camera, 1954,* sig., handstamps, (10-14-92, Swann, #552), 14 x 11 in., (35.6 x 27.9 cm.), photograph, silver print (BP 387, DM 966, FR 3275, Y 79,981).

$550* *"James Dean", 1954,* t., d., annot., photog. stamp, (11-16-92, Butterfield, #6152, illus.), 16⅛ x 13½ in., (410.3 x 343.5 mm.), photograph, gelatin silver print (BP 362, DM 877, FR 2954, Y 68,399).

$1760* *James Dean: Four:* "James Dean in the Hallway of Apt. House"; "James Dean in His Apt. Window"; "James Dean in a Turtleneck Sweater"; and "James Deanin an Overcoat", 1st 2 mounted, s., t., by photog. in ink, (c) stamp verso, 3rd s., d.by photog. in ink, 3rd & 4th w/ studio stamps, 1954, p. 1984-90, (10-15-92, Sotheby-NY, #521, illus.), each approx. 14 x 16½ in., (35.6 x 41.9 cm.), photograph, gelatin silver prints (BP 1077, DM 2620, FR 8884, Y 211,158).

BI *James Dean: Three,* 2 s. & d. by photog. on image, 1 s. by photog., 2 w/(c) stamp, each w/stuio stamps, 1954, est. $1,5/2,500, (10-15-92, Sotheby-NY, #520, illus.), various sizes to 11 x 14 in., (27.9 x 35.6 cm.), photograph, gelatin silver prints.

$1150* *Malcolm X: Two,* 1 backed w/card, each w/photog. studio and (c) stamps, notations in unident. hand, c. 1964, one p. 1992, (04-06-93, Sotheby-NY, #460, illus.), one 16⅛ x 11⅜ in., other 13⅝ x 10⅝ in., photograph (BP 760, DM 1853, FR 6274, Y 131,159).

$715* *"Marilyn Monroe In The Actors Studio", 1955/1984,* t., d., photog. stamp, (11-16-92, Butterfield, #6153, illus.), 13⅝ x 16 in., (346.7 x 407.1 mm.), photograph, gelatin silver print (BP 471, DM 1140, FR 3840, Y 88,919).

$1540* *Marilyn Monroe: Two:* "Marilyn in Black Hat" and "Marilyn at Actor's Studio", 1st backed w/card, (c) & studio stamps, c. 1955, 1st p.l., (10-15-92, Sotheby-NY, #522, illus.), one 16½ x 11 in., (41.9 x 27.9 cm.), other 10⅝ x 13¼ in., (41.9 x 27.9 cm.), photograph, gelatin silver prints (BP 942, DM 2292, FR 7774, Y 184,763).

$358* *"Paris" (Les Bains Douches), 1959,* t., d., photog. stamp, (11-16-92, Butterfield, #6154, illus.), 16½ x 13⅜ in., (419.8 x 340.3 mm.), photograph, gelatin silver print (BP 236, DM 571, FR 1923, Y 44,522).

$1150* *Paris:* "Parisian Park Scene", "Man And Sacre Coeur Fence" and "ParisKids": Three, first s., d., i. by photog.; first and third backed w/card; second s., t., d. by photog.; each w/photog. studio and/or (c) stamp, (04-06-93, Sotheby-NY, #461, illus.), each approx. 12 x 16 in., photograph (BP 760, DM 1853, FR 6274, Y 131,159).

$489* *Portrait Of James Dean, 1954,* p.l., photog.'s stamp, (05-23-93, Butterfield, #3591, illus.), 11 x 10¾ in., photograph, gelatin silver print (BP 318, DM 800, FR 2691, Y 54,051).

$1540* *Portrait Of James Dean, 1954,* sig., (c), handstamps, (10-14-92, Swann, #553, illus.), 14 x 17 in., (35.6 x 43.2 cm.), photograph, silver print (BP 904, DM 2254, FR 7643, Y 186,621).

SCHAUFELEIN, Hans Leonhard   German c. 1480-1538/40

$141* *Christus Vor Pilatus (Schreyl 369), c. 1506,* (03-24-93, Venator/Hansten, #2575), 9⁵⁄₁₆ x 6⁵⁄₁₆ in., (23.6 x 16 cm.), woodcut (BP 95, DM 230, FR 784, Y 16,567).

$1680* *Einzug Christi In Jerusalem - Der Unglaubige Thomas (Illus. Bartsch XI, 34.1 und 34.26), 1507: Two,* sheet 1 and 26 of series: Die Passion, artist's proof, watermark, prov., (06-23-93, Kornfeld, #105), woodcut (BP 1141, DM 2843, FR 9562, Y 183,026, SF 2530).

$397* *Die Himmelfahrt Christi (B. 35),* prov., (12-04-92, Bassenge, #6438), 5⁷⁄₁₆ x 3¹⁵⁄₁₆ in., (13.8 x 10.1 cm.), woodcut (BP 255, DM 632, FR 2145, Y 49,563).

$611* *Unfalo Versucht Theuerdank Auf Einem Kriegsschiff Zu Toten (Ill. B. XI, 132-6), c. 1517,* from Theuerdank, mono. in block, (06-23-93, Kornfeld, #106), woodcut (BP 415, DM 1034, FR 3478, Y 66,565, SF 920).

SCHECHTER, Milton   American 20th cent.

$83* *Bringing In The Catch,* s. Milton Schetcher, d. 6/25, num. 1/43, very good/good cond., (09-27-92, Bakker, #182, illus.), image 10¾ x 13¼ in., (27.3 x 33.7 cm.), color woodblock print (BP 48, DM 123, FR 416, Y 10,018).

SCHEELE, Kurt   b. 1905

BI *Situation Im Februar, 1931,* t., s., 3rd proof, est. DM 1,500, (12-05-92, Bassenge, #7684), woodcut on Japan.

SCHEFFER, E.A.

$377* *P.L.M.: Paris Vichy, Automotrice Rapide Bugatti, 1935,* excell. cond., (01-23-93, Ribeyre/Baron, #9), 39⅜ x 24⁷⁄₁₆ in., (100 x 62 cm.), poster (BP 247, DM 599, FR 2028, Y 47,184).

SCHEIBENHOF, A.V.

$605* *Badende, 1924,* s., d., t., annot. Original Holzschnitt and Handkoloriert, blindstamp GR, large margins, good cond., creases, (10-28-92, Butterfield, #2860, illus.), 5½ x 5¹⁄₁₆ in., (140 x 129 mm.), hand-colored woodcut on smooth cream wove (BP 385, DM 934, FR 3173, Y 74,233).

SCHELFHOUT, Lodewijk   Dutch 1881-1943

$183* *Beach With Boat, 3 Boats At Sea,* s., 1927, first state, (11-18-92, Bubb Kuyper, #1579), 9¹³⁄₁₆ x 11¹³⁄₁₆ in., (25 x 30 cm.), etching (BP 120, DM 292, FR 983, Y 22,758, G 330).

$672* *(Landscape With Village), 1913,* s., d., indistinctly num., full margins, good cond., small repaired defects at edges of sheet, occasional foxing, minor paper discoloration, Late Gerhard Brauer Coll., (05-27-93, Sotheby-Amstrdm, #778), 13⅞ x 15½ in., (353 x 394 mm.), etching on laid (BP 430, DM 1078, FR 3634, Y 72,041, G 1208).

$320* *Landscape, 1918,* s., d., margins, good cond., light-staining of image, mount stainingverso, Late Gerhard Brauer Coll., (05-27-93, Sotheby-Amstrdm, #832), 5⅞ x 7¹¹⁄₁₆ in., (150 x 196 mm.), etching on wove (BP 205, DM 513, FR 1731, Y 34,305, G 575).

$384* *View Of A Mountain Village, 1912,* s., d., margins, foxing, paper discoloration, buckling, margins glued to mount, Late Gerhard Brauer Coll., (05-27-93, Sotheby-Amstrdm, #833), 11 x 12¼ in., (280 x 311 mm.), etching on wove (BP 246, DM 616, FR 2077, Y 41,166, G 690).

SCHENAU, Johann Eleazar   1737-1806

$144* *Der Kuss (Andresen 12; Le Blanc 3), 1765,* (12-04-92, Bassenge, #6695), 5¼ x 3⅛ in., (13.4 x 7.9 cm.), etching (BP 92, DM 229, FR 778, Y 17,978).

SCHENCK, H.N.

$7150* *The Hindenburg Disaster, Lakehurst, New Jersey: Eight, 1937,* s., num., t., (c), inits. by photog., (10-15-92, Sotheby-NY, #206, illus.), each 1⅜ x 1⅞ in., (3.5 x 4.8 cm.), photograph, gelatin silver prints (BP 4375, DM 10,643, FR 36,093, Y 857,828).

SCHENK, Charles

BI *Medical Examination, Ellis Island, 1907,* notations, est. $6/900, (04-07-93, Swann, #359, illus.), 4⅛ x 3⅝ in., photograph, silver print.

SCHENK, Pieter   Dutch 1660-1718/19
$100* *Portrait Of Petrus Van Der Plaes (Sculptor And Engraver) (Hollstein 845)*, after G. Kneller, (06-09-93, Bubb Kuyper, #2071, illus.), 9⅝ x 7³⁄₁₆ in., (24.5 x 18.3 cm.), mezzotint (BP 66, DM 164, FR 550, Y 10,635, G 184).
  BI *Visus (Wurzbach 87; Hollstein 388)*, from series Funf Sinne, trimmed, est. DM 750, (12-04-92, Bassenge, #6440), 9¾ x 7³⁄₁₆ in., (24.8 x 18.2 cm.), mezzotint.

SCHEUL, G.
$955* *La Photographie L. Martin*, p. P. Moreau Nantes, creases, repairs, defects, backed on linen, (05-07-93, Christie-S. Ken, #111, illus.), 37½ x 49 in., (95.3 x 124.5 cm.), color lithograph (BP 605, DM 1510, FR 5088, Y 105,153).

SCHEYNDEL, Gillis van   ac. c. 1622-1650
$581* *Die Landschaft Mit Der Vorbeiziehenden Kutsche (Wurzbach 14; Hollstein 119/I)*, early print, (06-08-93, Karl/Faber, #190), etching (BP 382, DM 943, FR 3175, Y 61,710).

SCHICK, P. (after)
  BI *"Everhardus Bornaeus"*, by A. Blotelingh, est. $60/90, (02-12-93, DuMouchelle, #2386), 7½ x 5 in., (19.1 x 12.7 cm.), steel engraving.
  BI *"Everhardus Bornaeus"*, by A. Blotelingh, est. $60/90, (11-13-92, DuMouchelle, #2564), 7½ x 5 in., (19.1 x 12.7 cm.), steel engraving.

SCHIELE, Egon   German 1890-1918
$7803* *"Bildnis Paris Von Gutersloh" (Kallir 16; Bolliger-Kornfeld XI; Schwarz 11), 1918*, (06-05-93, Grisebach, #276, illus.), 10⅝ x 11¹⁵⁄₁₆ in., (27 x 30.4 cm.), lithograph in dark-brown on copper print paper (BP 5137, DM 12,651, FR 42,639, Y 837,052).
$650* *"Drei Badende Manner" (Kallir 13 b 2), 1916*, (11-28-92, Grisebach, #733, illus.), 3³⁄₁₆ x 3¹⁵⁄₁₆ in., (8.1 x 10 cm.), woodcut on wove (BP 429, DM 1036, FR 3515, Y 80,896).
$388* *Drei Badende, 1916*, (09-25-92, Granier, #3007), 3¼ x 3¹⁵⁄₁₆ in., (8.2 x 10 cm.), woodcut on holzhaltigem machine made paper (BP 227, DM 575, FR 1945, Y 46,832).
$21,893* *Kauernde (Kallir 6 b), 1914*, sig. stamp, portfolio Das Graphische Werk von Egon Schiele, stamp, prov., (06-10-93, Hauswedell/Nolt, #852, illus.), image 18⅞ x 12⅝ in., (48 x 32 cm.), drypoint on Japan (BP 14,320, DM 35,651, FR 120,027, Y 2,323,851).
  BI *Kauernde (Kallir 6), 1914*, #41/50, embossed stamp, sig. stamp, num., est. DM 28,000-, (11-21-92, Lempertz, #361, illus.), sheet 20¹¹⁄₁₆ x 15⁷⁄₁₆ in., (52.5 x 39.2 cm.), etching on Japan.
  BI *Kauernde (Kallir 6b), 1914*, pub. Avalun Verlag, full margins, rolling creases, light/mat staining, soiling, good cond., est. Y 2,5/3,000,000, (10-14-92, Sotheby-Japan, #90, illus.), 18¾ x 12½ in., (476 x 318 mm.), drypoint on Massimilianicobutten.
  BI *Kauernde (Kallir 6b), 1914*, pub. Avalun-Verlag, 1919, deckle edge three sides, creases, staining, prov., est. BP 12/16,000, (05-20-93, Christie-London, #486, illus.), plate 18⅞ x 12⅝ in., (47.9 x 32.1 cm.), sheet 28⅛ x 20⅛ in., (47.9 x 32.1 cm.), drypoint in green on French laid paper.
$33,146* *Madchen (Kallir 17b), 1918*, sig. stamp (K. pl. 17b), #10/25, pub. Avalun-Verlag, 1919, wide margis, foxmarks, very good cond., (05-20-93, Christie-London, #487, illus.), image 8⅞ x 14⅞ in., (22.5 x 37.8 cm.), sheet 17⅞ x 23⅞ in., (22.5 x 37.8 cm.), lithograph on wove (BP 21,275, DM 53,479, FR 180,141, Y 3,660,115).

SCHIFANO, Mario
$6141* *In Diretta Dalla Luna, 1973*, s., exhib., (12-15-92, Finarte-Milan, #122, illus.), 19¹¹⁄₁₆ x 82¹¹⁄₁₆ in., (50 x 210 cm.), photograph (BP 3918, DM 9625, FR 32,892, Y 761,627, L 8625).
$2784* *Jarry Il Patafisico, 1972*, s., (12-15-92, Finarte-Milan, #134, illus.), 19¹¹⁄₁₆ x 31½ in., (50 x 80 cm.), photograph on plexiglass (BP 1776, DM 4364, FR 14,912, Y 345,281, L 3910).

  BI *Landschaft (late 60s)*, s., crease, est. DM 600, (12-01-92, Karl/Faber, #1206), 4⁵⁄₁₆ x 6⅛ in., (11 x 15.5 cm.), color serigraph w/pencil on envelope.

SCHILE, H.
$116* *"My Protector"*, large folio, pub. 1874, paper damage, creases, (11-13-92, Garth, #121, illus.), 31½ x 25½ in., (80 x 64.8 cm.), handcolored lithograph (BP 75, DM 182, FR 614, Y 14,397).

SCHILLER, F.
$920* *"Bride"* and *"Groom", 1901: Two*, s., d. K. u. K. Hof Fotograf and Wien-Baden; one in red ink, other in white, flush-mounted, (05-19-93, Christie-E, #142, illus.), each approx. 25¾ x 19½ in., photograph, gelatin silver print, hand-colored in oils (BP 597, DM 1495, FR 5038, Y 101,849).

SCHINKEL, Karl Friedrich   1781-1941
  BI *"Der Wasserfall Bei Wildbad Gastein"*, lit., est. DM 7/9,000, (06-05-93, Grisebach, #251, illus.), 27¹³⁄₁₆ x 20¹⁄₁₆ in., (70.6 x 51 cm.), photo-lithograph dark-brown on thin board.

SCHIOLER, Inge   1908-1971
$713* *Skargardsmotiv: Five*, (12-04-92, AB Stockholm, #7134), sh 19¹¹⁄₁₆ x 21⅝ in., (50 x 55 cm.), serigraph in colors (BP 457, DM 1136, FR 3852, Y 89,014, SK 4840).

SCHIWAGO
  BI *Ohne Titel, 20's*, est. DM 500, (11-12-92, Lempertz, #238, illus.), 7³⁄₁₆ x 5⁹⁄₁₆ in., (18.3 x 14.2 cm.), photograph, gelatin silver print.

SCHKOLNYK
$677* *Ensemble De 15 Gravures: Fifteen*, all s., edit. 80, (06-28-93, Loudmer, #114), between 1⁹⁄₁₆ x 2¼ in., (40 x 57 mm.), and 11¹¹⁄₁₆ x 9⁵⁄₁₆ in., (40 x 57 mm.), black and color mezzotints on wove (BP 453, DM 1150, FR 3875, Y 71,830).

SCHLAIJKER, Jes
$440* *J.B. Simpson's, Inc.*, A- cond., chartex-backed, (08-06-92, Swann, #254, illus.), 39¼ x 19 in., (99.7 x 48.3 cm.), (BP 230, DM 650, FR 2196, Y 56,122).
$880* *Medical Department, 1942*, Brown and Bigelow, A-cond., (08-06-92, Swann, #250, illus.), 25 x 19 in., (63.5 x 48.3 cm.), (BP 460, DM 1300, FR 4391, Y 112,245).
$550* *Military Police, 1942*, Brown and Bigelow, A- cond., (08-06-92, Swann, #252, illus.), 25 x 19 in., (63.5 x 48.3 cm.), (BP 287, DM 813, FR 2745, Y 70,153).
$440* *Signal Corps, 1942*, Brown and Bigelow, A- cond., (08-06-92, Swann, #251, illus.), 25 x 19 in., (63.5 x 48.3 cm.), (BP 230, DM 650, FR 2196, Y 56,122).
$385* *Women's Army Corps, 1944*, Brown and Bigelow, A cond., (08-06-92, Swann, #253, illus.), 25 x 19 in., (63.5 x 48.3 cm.), (BP 201, DM 569, FR 1921, Y 49,107).

SCHLAPPER, Fee   b. 1927
  BI *Auf Dem Trafalgar Square, 60's*, studio stamp, t., est. DM 800, (11-12-92, Lempertz, #239, illus.), 15¹⁵⁄₁₆ x 12¼ in., (40.5 x 31.1 cm.), photograph, gelatin silver print.

SCHLEGEL (after)
$574* *"Tanysiptera Carolinae"* and *"Charmosyna Margaritae": Two*, (02-03-93, Doyle, #55), sight 19 x 13¼ in., (48.3 x 33.7 cm.), colored lithograph (BP 401, DM 945, FR 3205, Y 71,402).

SCHLEMMER, Oskar   German 1888-1943
$1138* *Begegnung, 1928*, s., d., t., corner torn, creases, (11-12-92, Lempertz, #240, illus.), image 23⅝ x 35⁷⁄₁₆ in., (60 x 90 cm.), photograph, gelatin silver print (BP 728, DM 1788, FR 6095, Y 140,789).
$1561* *Profile In Rot Und Dunkelgrau (Grohmann 18), 1923*, stamp, (06-05-93, Bassenge, #6501, illus.), 5½ x 3⁹⁄₁₆ in., (14 x 9 cm.), color lithograph on postcard (BP 1028, DM 2531, FR 8530, Y 167,453).
$95,105* *Spiel Mit Kopfen (Grohmann GL 11-17), 1923: Six*, s. Oskar Schlemmer, frontispiece, num., (06-25-93, Kornfeld, #127, illus.), portfolio 19⅜ x 13⅛ in., (49.2 x 33.4 cm.), lithograph (BP 64,325, DM 161,908, FR 545,327, Y 10,081,090, SF 143,750).

SCHLETTE, F.G.

$659* *Fongers,* J. Beerta, c. 1915, fine cond., (06-09-93, Bubb Kuyper, #2178, illus.), $30\frac{11}{16}$ x $16\frac{7}{16}$ in., (77.9 x 41.8 cm.), color lithograph (BP 435, DM 1078, FR 3625, Y 70,084, G 1208).

SCHLICHTER, Rudolf German 1890-1955

$369* *Arbeiterin-Halbfigur En Face,* lit., s., num., (12-05-92, Bassenge, #7696), $6\frac{5}{16}$ x 4¾ in., (16 x 12 cm.), etching on thick copper print paper (BP 231, DM 575, FR 1961, Y 45,719).

$742* *Die Auspeitschung (Flagellantin), c. 1914,* s., #10/20, (06-10-93, Hauswedell/Nolt, #867), image $10\frac{11}{16}$ x $9\frac{15}{16}$ in., (27.2 x 25.2 cm.), color drypoint and etching on copper print (BP 485, DM 1208, FR 4068, Y 78,760).

$1006* *Californische Bar, c. 1919,* s., foxed, reprod., (10-09-92, Winterberg, #3026), $15\frac{9}{16}$ x 16⅛ in., (39.5 x 41 cm.), lithograph on wove (BP 597, DM 1494, FR 5017, Y 122,474).

$443* *Schwester Am Canale Grande In Venedig,* s., num., foxing, lit., (12-05-92, Bassenge, #7697, illus.), 10⅝ x $8\frac{11}{16}$ in., (27 x 22 cm.), etching on copper print paper (BP 277, DM 691, FR 2354, Y 54,888).

$443* *Tannhauser, c. 1910,* lit., s., rare, (12-05-92, Bassenge, #7695), $6\frac{3}{16}$ x $8\frac{1}{16}$ in., (15.7 x 20.5 cm.), etching on thick copper print paper (BP 277, DM 691, FR 2354, Y 54,888).

$565* *Thannhauser, c. 1913,* s., (06-10-93, Hauswedell/Nolt, #865), image 6 x 8¼ in., (15.3 x 21 cm.), etching on copper print (BP 370, DM 920, FR 3098, Y 59,972).

SCHLOSSER, Gerard b. 1931

BI *On Est Bien La, 1974: Six,* s., d. 74, #44/70, est. FF 7/9,000, (11-16-92, Briest, #354), 27⅜ x 27⅜ in., (69.5 x 69.5 cm.), serigraph in colors.

SCHLOTTER, Eberhard German b. 1921

$77* *Auf Dem Wege Nach Olympia, 1968,* s., #68/100, creases, (09-18-92, Schloss Ahlden, #1049), 23⅝ x $17\frac{15}{16}$ in., (60 x 45.7 cm.), etching on hand-made (BP 45, DM 114, FR 391, Y 9517).

BI *Medusenhaupt Mit Hahnenkopf,* s., #78/100, est. DM 200, (09-18-92, Schloss Ahlden, #1050), $30\frac{3}{16}$ x $21\frac{5}{16}$ in., (76.7 x 54.2 cm.), etching on hand-made.

SCHMALIX, Hubert b. 1952

$554* *Untitled, 1982: Six,* Ed. Galerie Krinzinger, (06-04-93, Dorotheum, #121), color etching (BP 367, DM 900, FR 3032, Y 59,750, SC 6325).

SCHMALZ, Herbert (after)

$100* *"A Maiden In A Garden", 1895,* by John Cother Webb, s. by both, pub. Fairless and Beeforth, margins, (11-12-92, Bonhams-Chelsea, #42), plate 31¾ x 21½ in., (80.6 x 54.6 cm.), hand-colored mezzotint (BP 66, DM 158, FR 534, Y 12,399).

$231* *The Sculptor's Dream,* foxing, (06-16-93, Bonhams-Chelsea, #513), image 26 x 12½ in., (66 x 31.8 cm.), photogravure finished by hand (BP 154, DM 383, FR 1287, Y 24,637).

SCHMETTAU, Joachim b. 1937

BI *"Idole Und Realitaten", 1971: Ten,* series Leidertexten der Beatles, Berlin, Propylaen-pub., est. DM 800/1,000, (11-28-92, Grisebach, #735, illus.), $25\frac{9}{16}$ x $19\frac{11}{16}$ in., (65 x 50 cm.), etching on wove.

SCHMIDT, Georg Friedrich 1712-1775

$202* *Brustbildnis Melchior Dinglinger, Hofjuwelier August Des Starken (Jacoby 148, Wessely 27 III, Berchenhagen), 1769,* prov., after A. Pesne, (12-04-92, Bassenge, #6696), 6⅛ x $4\frac{3}{16}$ in., (15.5 x 10.7 cm.), etching (BP 130, DM 322, FR 1091, Y 25,218).

$109* *Des Kunstlers Frau Lesend (Wessely 106 III), 1761,* (12-04-92, Bassenge, #6697), 9¼ x $6\frac{15}{16}$ in., (23.5 x 17.7 cm.), etching (BP 70, DM 174, FR 589, Y 13,608).

$183* *Weibliches Bildnis (Genannt Prinzessin Von Oranien) (Wessely 124), 1767,* after Rembrandt, (12-01-92, Karl/Faber, #144), etching (BP 121, DM 292, FR 994, Y 22,784).

SCHMIDT, H.

$945* *"Summer" and "Autumn", c. 1900: Two,* excell. cond., (02-04-93, Christie-S. Ken, #176, illus.), 24½ x 13 in., (62.2 x 33 cm.), color lithograph (BP 660, DM 1556, FR 5276, Y 117,552).

SCHMIDT, Joseph 1750-1815

BI *12 Radierungen Mit Aquatinta Nach Originalvorlagen Rembrandt Van Rijns,* in portfolio, staining, est. SC 6/8,000, (11-11-92, Dorotheum, #359), $19\frac{5}{16}$ x $14\frac{9}{16}$ in., (49 x 37 cm.), etching.

SCHMIDT-ROTTLUFF, Karl German 1884-1976

$1792* *70 Jahre Alt (Rathenau 23), 1926,* s., i. w/work num., margins, creasing, good cond., (05-20-93, Christie-London, #491, illus.), image 23¾ x 19½ in., (60.3 x 49.5 cm.), sheet 31¾ x 22¼ in., (60.3 x 49.5 cm.), woodcut on Japan (BP 1150, DM 2891, FR 9739, Y 197,880).

BI *"70 Jahre Alt" (Rathenau 23), 1926,* s., Werknummer 264, est. DM 3,5/3,700, (11-28-92, Grisebach, #737, illus.), 23⅝ x $19\frac{7}{16}$ in., (60 x 49.3 cm.), woodcut on handmade.

$14,124* *Akte Inm Atelier (Schapire 158), 1914,* s., (06-10-93, Hauswedell/Nolt, #890, illus.), image 19½ x $15\frac{13}{16}$ in., (49.5 x 40.2 cm.), woodcut on hand-made (BP 9239, DM 23,000, FR 77,434, Y 1,499,204).

BI *Alte Stadt (Motiv Aus Schlawe) (Schapire R 52), 1921,* s., light-stained, w/traces of old mounting, est. DM 28/30,000, (12-01-92, Karl/Faber, #1219, illus.), 15⅜ x $12\frac{13}{16}$ in., (39 x 32.5 cm.), engraving w/copper print paper.

$5085* *Aus Rowe (Schapire 51), 1921,* s., (06-10-93, Hauswedell/Nolt, #881, illus.), image $7\frac{13}{16}$ x 9⅝ in., (19.8 x 24.5 cm.), drypoint on copper print board (BP 3326, DM 8280, FR 27,878, Y 539,752).

$13,477* *"Bildnis O.M.", Otto Mueller (Schapire 162), 1914,* s., num. 1441, (06-05-93, Grisebach, #277, illus.), 14¼ x $11\frac{7}{16}$ in., (36.2 x 29 cm.), woodcut on hand-made (BP 8872, DM 21,850, FR 73,645, Y 1,445,720).

$7062* *Blaue Frau Fichte (Schapire 288), 1923,* s., #238, t., (06-10-93, Hauswedell/Nolt, #901, illus.), image 15⅜ x 19¾ in., (39.1 x 50.1 cm.), woodcut on Blotting paper (BP 4619, DM 11,500, FR 38,717, Y 749,602).

$45,650* *Brucke Mappe 1909 - IV. Mappe, Karl Schmidt-Rottluff, 1908-1909,* portfolio, (06-25-93, Kornfeld, #21, illus.), portfolio 21¾ x 16¼ in., (55.3 x 41.3 cm.), woodcut, 2 lithographs, 1 etching (BP 30,876, DM 77,715, FR 261,755, Y 4,838,881, SF 69,000).

$4256* *Bucht Im Mondschein (Schapire 160), 1914,* s., d., (06-05-93, Bassenge, #6513), 15½ x $19\frac{7}{16}$ in., (39.3 x 49.3 cm.), woodcut on fine hand-made (BP 2802, DM 6900, FR 23,257, Y 456,554).

$6709* *Christus Bei Maria Und Martha (Schapire 238), 1919,* s., #194, (06-10-93, Hauswedell/Nolt, #899, illus.), image $19\frac{9}{16}$ x 15½ in., (49.7 x 39.3 cm.), woodcut on factory print (BP 4388, DM 10,925, FR 36,782, Y 712,132).

$8475* *Dunen Und Mole (Schapire 195), 1917,* s., blindstamp, watermark, (06-10-93, Hauswedell/Nolt, #895, illus.), image $11\frac{7}{16}$ x 13¼ in., (29 x 33.6 cm.), color woodcut on hand-made (BP 5544, DM 13,801, FR 46,464, Y 899,586).

$14,437* *"Dunen Und Mole" (Schapire 195), 1917,* s., Werknummer 171, (11-28-92, Grisebach, #161, illus.), 11⅝ x 13¼ in., (29.5 x 33.7 cm.), color woodcut on wove (BP 9529, DM 23,000, FR 78,080, Y 1,796,764).

$7768* *Egypterin (Schapire 17), 1915,* s., (06-10-93, Hauswedell/Nolt, #880, illus.), image $8\frac{7}{16}$ x $5\frac{13}{16}$ in., (21.4 x 14.8 cm.), drypoint on copper print (BP 5081, DM 12,649, FR 42,588, Y 824,541).

$564* *Exlibris Guenther Weiske, 1905,* block mono., foxing, lit., (05-26-93, Dorling, #2966), $3\frac{11}{16}$ x 1¾ in., (9.3 x 4.5 cm.), woodcut on handmade (BP 365, DM 920, FR 3097, Y 61,278).

$564* *Exlibris Helene Weiske, c. 1905,* lit., (05-26-93, Dorling, #2967, illus.), $3\frac{15}{16}$ x 1¾ in., (10.1 x 4.4 cm.), woodcut on Tonpapier (BP 365, DM 920, FR 3097, Y 61,278).

BI *Fischerboot (Sch. 101), 1923,* s., full margins, light-stained, water stain, defects, est. BP 1,5/2,000, (11-30-92, Phillips-London, #373B), image 15¾ x 19⅝ in., (400 x 498 mm.), lithograph on wove.

$8475* *Frau In Den Dunen (Schapire 143), 1914,* s., (06-10-93, Hauswedell/Nolt, #888, illus.), image 15½ x $19\frac{11}{16}$ in.,

(39.3 x 50 cm.), woodcut on hand-made (BP 5544, DM 13,801, FR 46,464, Y 899,586).

BI *"Frau In Den Dunen" (Schapire 143), 1914,* watermark, s., water stains, prov., est. DM 24/28,000, (06-05-93, Grisebach, #280, illus.), 15½ x 19 13/16 in., (39.3 x 50.3 cm.), woodcut on hand-made.

$6992* *Frau In Den Dunen, (Sch. 143), 1914,* woodcut on laid, (12-01-92, Christie-London, #539, illus.), L. 15⅜ x 19⅝ in., (390 x 498 mm.), woodcut on laid (BP 4620, DM 11,144, FR 37,979, Y 870,518).

$7525* *Frau In Der Wanne (Schapire H171), 1915,* s., wide margins, deckle edge, pencil strokes, discoloration, very good cond., (05-20-93, Christie-London, #489, illus.), image 9¾ x 7 in., (24.8 x 17.8 cm.), sheet 20 x 13½ in., (24.8 x 17.8 cm.), woodcut on laid (BP 4830, DM 12,141, FR 40,897, Y 830,941).

$4995* *Frau Mit Verschrankten Armen, (Sch. 105), 1913,* s., wide margins, crease, very good cond., (12-01-92, Christie-London, #537), L. 10 9/16 x 7 13/16 in., (269 x 199 mm.), woodcut on JW Zanders laid (BP 3300, DM 7961, FR 27,132, Y 621,887).

$565* *Gruss Zum Neujahr (Rathenau 78), 1924,* s., (06-10-93, Hauswedell/Nolt, #902), image 8⅛ x 6 1/16 in., (20.7 x 15.4 cm.), woodcut on hand-made (BP 370, DM 920, FR 3098, Y 59,972).

BI *Hansa-Filter, Furs Hans-Fur Die Industrie, c. 1920,* brown tape, tears, repairs, est. BP 3/4,000, (05-20-93, Christie-London, #508, illus.), sheet 32½ x 23½ in., (82.6 x 59.7 cm.), lithograph in orange, blue and green.

BI *Haus Mit Pappeln (R. Schapire 118), 1913,* s., est. DM 12,500, (05-26-93, Lempertz, #485, illus.), 12⅝ x 16 9/16 in., (32 x 42 cm.), wood engraving on wove.

$14,334* *Die Heiligen Drei Konige (Schapire H196), 1917,* s., i. w/work num., wide margins, dicoloration, very good cond., (05-20-93, Christie-London, #488, illus.), image 19⅞ x 15⅜ in., (50.5 x 39.1 cm.), sheet 31⅜ x 26½ in., (50.5 x 39.1 cm.), woodcut on wove (BP 9200, DM 23,127, FR 77,902, Y 1,582,818).

$5827* *Heiliger Franziskus, (Sch. 243), 1919,* s., i., wide margins, loss, light-staining, spotting, creases, folded, tape, very good cond., (12-01-92, Christie-London, #538, illus.), L. 23⅝ x 19½ in., (600 x 496 mm.), S. 30 13/16 x 23 9/16 in., (600 x 496 mm.), woodcut on laid (BP 3850, DM 9288, FR 31,651, Y 725,473).

$7573* *Heimkehr Der Fischer I (Schapire 104), 1923,* s., i., 1 version, (11-21-92, Lempertz, #370, illus.), 16⅝ x 22 1/16 in., (42.2 x 56 cm.), lithograph on thick paper (BP 4986, DM 12,074, FR 40,671, Y 941,798).

$440* *Kopf (Sch. 189), 1915,* pub. in Genius, margins, good cond., mat staining, paper remains, surface soiling, surface scuffs, (02-24-93, Butterfield, #2972), 6¾ x 9½ in., (171 x 241 mm.), woodcut on wove (BP 307, DM 714, FR 2422, Y 51,631).

$6356* *Kopf (Schapire 256), 1919,* s., #1929, (06-10-93, Hauswedell/Nolt, #900, illus.), image 19 7/16 x 15 9/16 in., (49.4 x 39.5 cm.), woodcut on thick wove (BP 4158, DM 10,350, FR 34,846, Y 674,663).

$1000* *Kopf Eines Mannes (Sch. 277), 1922,* s., full margins, foxed, creases, (11-30-92, Phillips-London, #373C), border 11 x 7⅛ in., (279 x 181 mm.), woodcut on japan (BP 660, DM 1593, FR 5408, Y 124,456).

$2401* *Kopf F. V. (Schapire 95), 1920,* s., d., (06-10-93, Hauswedell/Nolt, #882, illus.), image 15 9/16 x 13 3/16 in., (39.5 x 33.5 cm.), lithograph on wove (BP 1571, DM 3910, FR 13,163, Y 254,856).

$8781* *Kopf Im Profil (Schapire 188, 1916; Werkverzeichnis 1916.3),* s., (06-23-93, Kornfeld, #776, illus.), woodcut on wove (BP 5965, DM 14,858, FR 49,977, Y 956,640, SF 13,225).

BI *Kopf Im Profile (Sch. 75), 1912,* pub. in Die Aktion, margins, good cond., sheet toned, paper losses, tears, pencil notations, est. $3/500, (02-24-93, Butterfield, #2970), 5⅛ x 4 5/16 in., (130 x 110 mm.), woodcut on wove.

$19,178* *Kopfe I (Schapire 66), 1911,* s., tears, creases, rare, (12-05-92, Bassenge, #7704, illus.), 19 13/16 x 15 9/16 in., (50.3 x 39.5 cm.), woodcut (BP 12,009, DM 29,900, FR 101,902, Y 2,376,162).

$7062* *Kuss In Liebe (Schapire 206), 1918,* s., block d., (06-10-93, Hauswedell/Nolt, #897, illus.), image 19 11/16 x 15 5/16 in., (50 x 38.9 cm.), woodcut on hand-made (BP 4619, DM 11,500, FR 38,717, Y 749,602).

$239* *"Lesender Mann" (Schapire 274), 1922,* in "Genius", 3. Jg., 2. Buch, (11-28-92, Grisebach, #736, illus.), 11 x 7⅞ in., (28 x 20 cm.), woodcut on handmade (BP 158, DM 381, FR 1293, Y 29,745).

$16,243* *Madchen Vor Dem Spiegel (Schapire 159), 1914,* s., portfolio Zehn Holzschnitte, Neumann, 1919, watermark, (06-10-93, Hauswedell/Nolt, #891, illus.), image 19 11/16 x 15 11/16 in., (50 x 39.8 cm.), woodcut on hand-made (BP 10,625, DM 26,450, FR 89,052, Y 1,724,127).

$5650* *Madchenkopf (Schapire 203), 1918,* s., #181, (06-10-93, Hauswedell/Nolt, #896, illus.), image 14 13/16 x 10¼ in., (37.7 x 26 cm.), woodcut on hand-made (BP 3696, DM 9200, FR 30,976, Y 599,724).

BI *Mannlicher Kopf (Sch. 202), 1917,* pub. in Die Aktion, margins, apparently good cond., est. $6/800, (02-24-93, Butterfield, #2973), 6 3/16 x 8 9/16 in., (157 x 217 mm.), woodcut on wove.

$1412* *Mannlicher Kopf Im Profil (Schapire 2), 1906,* s., d., t., (06-10-93, Hauswedell/Nolt, #883, illus.), image 8⅜ x 6 in., (21.2 x 15.3 cm.), woodcut on Hadern hand-made (BP 924, DM 2299, FR 7741, Y 149,878).

$4328* *Maria (Schapire 216), 1918,* s., factory num. 1814, (11-21-92, Lempertz, #369, illus.), 19 11/16 x 15⅝ in., (50 x 39.7 cm.), woodcut on hand-made (BP 2850, DM 6901, FR 23,244, Y 538,242).

$14,124* *Memel II (Schapire 157), 1914,* s., #1436, (06-10-93, Hauswedell/Nolt, #889, illus.), image 19 9/16 x 15⅜ in., (49.7 x 39 cm.), woodcut on wove (BP 9239, DM 23,000, FR 77,434, Y 1,499,204).

$8600* *Moses (Schapire H259), 1919,* s., i. w/work num., p. Voigt, margins, tears, creasing, other minor defects, (05-20-93, Christie-London, #490, illus.), image 17 x 10¾ in., (43.2 x 27.3 cm.), sheet 26¼ x 20½ in., (43.2 x 27.3 cm.), woodcut on wove (BP 5520, DM 13,875, FR 46,739, Y 949,647).

$26,130* *Mussige Hetaren (Schapire 133), 1914,* s., watermark, (06-10-93, Hauswedell/Nolt, #886), image 15½ x 19 11/16 in., (39.4 x 50 cm.), woodcut on hand-made (BP 17,092, DM 42,550, FR 143,257, Y 2,773,591).

$5650* *Mutter (Schapire 194), 1916,* s., Neumann, portfolio 12 Holzschnitte, (06-10-93, Hauswedell/Nolt, #894, illus.), image 14⅝ x 11⅞ in., (37.1 x 30.2 cm.), woodcut on hand-made (BP 3696, DM 9200, FR 30,976, Y 599,724).

$4256* *"Nacht Am Strand" (Schapire 265), 1920,* s., num. 2011, (06-05-93, Grisebach, #284, illus.), 15 9/16 x 19 7/16 in., (39.5 x 49.3 cm.), woodcut on hand-made (BP 2802, DM 6900, FR 23,257, Y 456,554).

$11,349* *Russische Madonna (Schapire 58), 1921,* s., #2115, (06-05-93, Bassenge, #6515, illus.), 15 9/16 x 12¾ in., (39.6 x 32.4 cm.), drypoint on thick copper print (BP 7471, DM 18,400, FR 62,016, Y 1,217,443).

$32,486* *Schlafende Hetare (Schapire 136), 1914,* s., d., #146, (06-10-93, Hauswedell/Nolt, #887, illus.), image 15 9/16 x 19 11/16 in., (39.5 x 50 cm.), woodcut on hand-made (BP 21,249, DM 52,900, FR 178,103, Y 3,448,254).

$13,715* *"Selbstbildnis Von Vorn Gesehen" (Schapire 153), 1914,* s., d., Werknummer 1432, (11-28-92, Grisebach, #162, illus.), 14 3/16 x 11⅝ in., (36.1 x 29.6 cm.), woodcut on handmade (BP 9053, DM 21,850, FR 74,175, Y 1,706,907).

$19,068* *Sitzende Frau Mit Bluten (Schapire 114), 1913,* s., d., #1316, (06-10-93, Hauswedell/Nolt, #885, illus.), image 14⅛ x 11 13/16 in., (35.8 x 30 cm.), woodcut on hand-made (BP 12,473, DM 31,050, FR 104,539, Y 2,023,989).

$8662* *"Spaziergang Im Walde" (Schapire 56), 1921,* s., Werknummer St(ich) 2112, (11-28-92, Grisebach, #158, illus.), 12 15/16 x 15⅜ in., (32.8 x 39 cm.), drypoint on thick copper print paper (BP 5717, DM 13,800, FR 46,847, Y 1,078,034).

BI *Spiel Christa Von Erda (Sch. 224), 1918,* pub. in Die Aktion, margins, good cond., sheet toned, paper losses, tears, pencil notations, est. $5/700, (02-24-93, Butterfield, #2974), 5 x 3½ in., (127 x 89 mm.), woodcut on wove.

$989* *Titelblatt Zur Holzschnittmappe (Schapire 40), 1918,* s., (06-10-93, Hauswedell/Nolt, #898), image 19¹¹⁄₁₆ x 15¹¹⁄₁₆ in., (50 x 39.8 cm.), woodcut on hand-made (BP 647, DM 1610, FR 5422, Y 104,978).

$10,327* *Trauernde Am Strand (Schapire 151), 1914,* s., (12-05-92, Bassenge, #7705, illus.), 15⁷⁄₁₆ x 19⁷⁄₁₆ in., (39.2 x 49.4 cm.), woodcut on handmade (BP 6466, DM 16,101, FR 54,872, Y 1,279,519).

BI *"Trauernde Am Strand" (Schapire 151), 1914,* s., d., num. i. 1430, prov., est. DM 24/28,000, (06-05-93, Grisebach, #281, illus.), 15½ x 19½ in., (39.3 x 49.6 cm.), woodcut on hand-made.

BI *Vareler Hafen (Schapire 11), 1909,* s., d., est. DM 25,000-, (11-21-92, Lempertz, #368, illus.), 11⅝ x 15¼ in., (29.5 x 38.8 cm.), woodcut on hand-made.

$19,774* *Villa Mit Turm (Schapire 68), 1911,* s., d., (06-10-93, Hauswedell/Nolt, #884, illus.), image 19⅞ x 15⁹⁄₁₆ in., (50.5 x 39.5 cm.), woodcut on hand-made (BP 12,934, DM 32,200, FR 108,410, Y 2,098,928).

$8324* *Wattenmeer, (Sch. 17), 1909,* s., d., margins, light-staining, losses, tape, (12-01-92, Christie-London, #536, illus.), L. 8¾ x 13¹⁵⁄₁₆ in., (223 x 355 mm.), woodcut on simili-Japan (BP 5500, DM 13,267, FR 45,215, Y 1,036,355).

$2542* *Weiblicher Kopf (Schapire 180), 1915,* s., from Bauhaus-Drucke. Neue Europaische Graphik. 5te Mappe, (06-10-93, Hauswedell/Nolt, #893, illus.), image 10⁷⁄₁₆ x 7¹⁄₁₆ in., (26.5 x 17.9 cm.), woodcut on Japan (BP 1663, DM 4139, FR 13,936, Y 269,823).

$4149* *Weiblicher Kopf. (Schapire H 180; Peters V/13; Werknummer 1523), 1915,* s., 5. portfolio Bauhaus Drucke, Neue Europaische Graphik, Deutsche Kunstler, Weimar, 1921, (12-01-92, Karl/Faber, #1218, illus.), 9⅝ x 7¹⁄₁₆ in., (24.5 x 18 cm.), woodcut on simili-Japan (BP 2741, DM 6613, FR 22,537, Y 516,559).

BI *Zwei Akt (Sch. 173), 1915,* pub. in Die Aktion, margins, good cond., sheet toned, paper loss, tears, est. $7/900, (02-24-93, Butterfield, #2971), 9¹⁄₁₆ x 7 in., (230 x 178 mm.), woodcut on wove w/watermark.

BI *"Zwei Plastiken" (Rathenau 46), 1953-1954,* s., num., est. DM 2,8/3,200, (11-28-92, Grisebach, #738, illus.), 17⁵⁄₁₆ x 22⅜ in., (44 x 56.8 cm.), lithograph on wove.

SCHMIED, F.L.

BI *Le Christ Et Simon De Cyrene,* #2/50, s., large margins, est. FF400, (06-16-93, Ader Tajan, #137), 8¼ x 11⁷⁄₁₆ in., (21 x 29 cm.), color engraving on Japan.

SCHMIT, Thomas   b. 1943

$217* *Das Ist Wie Beim Meer, 1977,* s., d., (11-28-92, Schoppmann, #532), 19½ x 12¹⁵⁄₁₆ in., (49.5 x 33 cm.), color offset lithograph (BP 143, DM 346, FR 1174, Y 27,007).

SCHMITTNER, Heinrich

$605* *Portfolio Of Wainscot Designs, c. 1925,* 25 pages, Art Deco and Modernists designs, labeled, tears, fading, wear, (01-02-93, Skinner, #184), screen-printed, polychrome (BP 403, DM 991, FR 3384, Y 75,853).

SCHMOTZER, Theresa   American 20th cent.

BI *"For The Innocent", 1934,* s., t., pub. Print-A-Month Club, Cleveland December 1934, good cond., est. $75-100, (10-31-92, Cleveland, #210), 9¾ x 8⅝ in., (24.8 x 21.9 cm.), etching and drypoint.

SCHNABEL, Julian   American b. 1951

$605* *The Dream, 1983,* s., d., num. 29/30, pub. Parasol Press, full sheet, excell. cond.?, (09-19-92, Christie-E, #213, illus.), sheet 47 x 71 in., (119.4 x 180.3 cm.), aquatint on wove (BP 348, DM 906, FR 3103, Y 75,380).

$978* *The Dream, 1983,* s., d., #29/30, pub. Parasol Press, Ltd., good cond. ?, (05-15-93, Sotheby-NY, #1199), 46½ x 70⅞ in., (118.1 x 180 cm.), aquatint on two sheets (BP 636, DM 1573, FR 5286, Y 108,414).

BI *"Lampshade" With Little Sheba, 1983,* s., t., d., unique proof, full sheet, crease, pin holes, very good cond., Frederik Roos Estate, est. $1,5/2,500, (09-19-92, Christie-E, #214, illus.), sheet 46⅝ x 35⅜ in., (118.4 x 89.9 cm.), etching and aquatint on wove.

BI *Lola, 1984,* init. in oil, d., unique, pub. Parasol Press, Ltd., good cond., tear,worn spot, est. $5/7,000, (05-15-93, Sotheby-NY, #1200, illus.), sheet 115 x 67 in., (292.1 x

170.2 cm.), aquatint in olive on brown velvet w/maroon velvet trim.

$3300* *Mother, 1985,* s., d. '81, i. 'A.P. 2', artist's proof, pub. Pace Editions, Inc., good cond., (11-07-92, Sotheby-NY, #765, illus.), overall size 71¾ x 47½ in., (182.2 x 120.7 cm.), diptych, aquatint p. in black and beige on two sheets of lithographiccolor map (BP 2158, DM 5269, FR 17,809, Y 407,307).

SCHNARRENBERGER, Wilhelm   1892-1966

$374* *"Figuren", (19)20: Six,* pub. Goltz, s., d., num., Opus II Reihe Graphische Capriccios, (12-01-92, Karl/Faber, #1223), 10⁷⁄₁₆ x 9⅝ in., (26.5 x 24.5 cm.), woodcut on hand-made (BP 247, DM 596, FR 2032, Y 46,564).

SCHNEEBERGER, Adolf   1897-1977

BI *Street Scene, Prague, 1923,* s., d., est. $2/2,500, (10-13-92, Christie-NY, #350, illus.), 11¼ x 9 in., (28.6 x 22.9 cm.), photograph, gelatin silver print.

SCHNEIDER, Gerard   French 1896-1948

$573* *Cagnes, 1956,* s., #62/90, blindstamp, (05-27-93, Lempertz, #1007), 11⁷⁄₁₆ x 21⁷⁄₁₆ in., (29 x 54.5 cm.), color etching on colored Arches wove (BP 367, DM 919, FR 3099, Y 61,428).

BI *"Composition",* #42/100, s., est. FF800/1,000, (04-04-93, Pescheteau, #289), 25⁹⁄₁₆ x 18⅞ in., (65 x 48 cm.), 2 color lithograph on Arches.

BI *Green 69, 1970,* s., d., #70/100, est. FF1,000/1,200, (06-28-93, Loudmer, #115), 25⁹⁄₁₆ x 18⅞ in., (650 x 480 mm.), 3-color lithograph on wove.

SCHNEIDER, Herbert   1924-1983

$155* *Blatterpaar,* s., #42/100, t., blindstamp, (09-18-92, Schloss Ahlden, #1054), 29⅝ x 22³⁄₁₆ in., (75.3 x 56.3 cm.), color screen print on hand-made (BP 91, DM 230, FR 787, Y 19,157).

BI *Grune Wolke,* s., #13/150, est. DM 280, blindstamp, (05-08-93, Schloss Ahlden, #2870), 22³⁄₁₆ x 16⁷⁄₁₆ in., (56.3 x 41.7 cm.), color screen print on BFK Rives.

$155* *Im Eichelhaus, 1974,* s., #51/100, blindstamp, (09-18-92, Schloss Ahlden, #1053), 29¹¹⁄₁₆ x 22⅜ in., (75.4 x 56.9 cm.), color screen print on hand-made (BP 91, DM 230, FR 787, Y 19,157).

BI *Mach Mir Freude,* s., #93/100, t., est. DM 250, (09-18-92, Schloss Ahlden, #1052), 24⁵⁄₁₆ x 28¹⁄₁₆ in., (61.8 x 71.3 cm.), color screen print on hand-made.

BI *Die Mittagsfrau,* s., #26/100, t., est. DM 250, (09-18-92, Schloss Ahlden, #1055), 24⁵⁄₁₆ x 28¼ in., (61.7 x 71.8 cm.), color screen print on textured hand-made.

$155* *Die Tauben Haben Geburtstag,* s., #20/100, (09-18-92, Schloss Ahlden, #1051), 22¹⁄₁₆ x 29¹³⁄₁₆ in., (56 x 75.7 cm.), color screen print on BFK Rives (BP 91, DM 230, FR 787, Y 19,157).

SCHOBERL, Frederic

$2200* *Picturesque Tour From Geneva To Milan, By Way Of The Simplon: 34,* frontispiece, large 8vo, i., s. Arthur Severn, March 21st 1889, (11-12-92, Swann, #127, illus.), hand-colored aquatint (BP 1445, DM 3486, FR 11,758, Y 272,784).

SCHOFF, Otto

BI *Der Verfelimte Eros, 1921,* illus., s., est. FF1,000/1,200, (05-27-93, Briest, #182), color lithograph.

SCHOLDER, Fritz   American b. 1937

$825* *Seated Indian,* s., #125/150, blindstamp pub., very good cond.?, (10-28-92, Butterfield, #3116), 30 x 22⅜ in., (762 x 568 mm.), color lithograph (BP 526, DM 1274, FR 4326, Y 101,227).

$259* *Second Dream,* s., #15.79, blindstamp publisher, Tamarind Institute, full margins, good cond.?, (05-19-93, Butterfield, #2331), 26⅛ x 18½ in., (664 x 470 mm.), lithograph in colors on wove (BP 168, DM 421, FR 1418, Y 28,673).

SCHOLZ, Georg   1890-1945

BI *Salome, 1920,* s., d., catalog raisonne Nr. 44, est. 3/4,000, (06-05-93, Grisebach, #855, illus.), 6⅛ x 4⁷⁄₁₆ in., (15.5 x 11.2 cm.), lithograph on thick board.

SCHON, Erhard   1491-1542

$19,854* *Konig Johann Von Ungarn (Geisberg-Strauss 1293.5), c. 1530,* (06-23-93, Kornfeld, #108, illus.), handcolored woodcut (BP 13,488, DM 33,594, FR 112,999, Y 2,162,981, SF 29,900).

SCHONEBECK, Eugen   b. 1936
$577* *3 Frauen, 1969,* s., d., num., (11-28-92, Schoppmann, #783), 12 x 14¹⁵⁄₁₆ in., (30.5 x 38 cm.), lithograph on handmade (BP 381, DM 919, FR 3121, Y 71,811).

SCHONECKER   German 20th cent.
BI *The Concert,* s., d. 1920 in plate, s., t., i., d. (19)20, est. $200/250, (10-30-92, Sloan, #2815), 10⅞ x 9⅝ in., (27.6 x 24.4 cm.), etching.

SCHONEN
$33* *"Benzin", 1980,* s., d., num. 139/150, excellent cond., (10-31-92, Cleveland, #390), 5¾ x 4¾ in., (14.6 x 12.1 cm.), etching and mezzotint (BP 21, DM 51, FR 172, Y 4088).
$39* *"Still-Life With Jug", 1980,* s., d., num. 144/150, excellent cond., (10-31-92, Cleveland, #391), 5¾ x 4¾ in., (14.6 x 12.1 cm.), etching and mezzotint (BP 25, DM 60, FR 204, Y 4831).

SCHONFELD, Johann Heinrich   1609-1682/83
$636* *Trauernder Philosoph (Nagler 18),* by G. Ehinger after Schonfeld, watermark, prov., (06-10-93, Hauswedell/Nolt, #163), etching (BP 416, DM 1036, FR 3487, Y 67,509).

SCHONGAUER, Martin   German c. 1450-1491
$3466* *Die Anbetung Der Hl. Drei Konige (B. 6; Lehrs 6 I),* (12-04-92, Bassenge, #6441, illus.), 9¹⁵⁄₁₆ x 6⅜ in., (25.2 x 16.2 cm.), engraving (BP 2223, DM 5520, FR 18,725, Y 432,709).
$1380* *The Bearing Of The Cross (B. 16, L. 26), c. 1480,* from The Passion, later impression, trimmed, staining, tape, ink touches, prop. Montclair Art Museum, (05-11-93, Christie-NY, #58), sheet 6½ x 4⁹⁄₁₆ in., (165 x 116 mm.), engraving on laid (BP 881, DM 2174, FR 7325, Y 151,798).
$17,158* *Christ On The Mount Of Olives (B. 9; Lehrs 19),* from the Passion, trimmed, good cond., fold, ex coll. M. J. Morgan (L. 1879) and E. A. Seasongood, (06-30-93, Sotheby-London, #235, illus.), 6⅜ x 4½ in., (162 x 114 mm.), engraving (BP 11,500, DM 29,265, FR 98,723, Y 1,838,423).
BI *Christus Vor Pilatus (Bartsch 14; Lehrs 24),* from Kupferstichpassion, watermark, prov., est. DM 5,000, (06-10-93, Hauswedell/Nolt, #162), engraving on hand-made.
$38,180* *Die Geisselung (Lehrs 22), c. 1480-1483,* sheet 4 of series Die Passion, (06-23-93, Kornfeld, #109, illus.), engraving (BP 25,938, DM 64,602, FR 217,302, Y 4,159,494, SF 57,500).
$1276* *Die Grablegung Christi (B. 18; Lehrs 28), c. 1475,* from the Passion series, (06-08-93, Karl/Faber, #192), engraving (BP 839, DM 2070, FR 6973, Y 135,528).
$21,663* *Die Heilige Katharina (B. 64; Lehrs 69),* prov., (12-04-92, Bassenge, #6442, illus.), 3¹⁵⁄₁₆ x 2¹⁄₁₆ in., (10 x 5.3 cm.), engraving (BP 13,895, DM 34,501, FR 117,034, Y 2,704,494).
$2762* *Der Hl. Laurentius (B. 56, Lehrs 61),* watermark, from the Heiligen series, prov., (06-04-93, Bassenge, #5359, illus.), 6⅛ x 4⅛ in., (15.5 x 10.5 cm.), engraving (BP 1827, DM 4485, FR 15,118, Y 297,886).
$6019* *Der Hl. Philippus (B. 137, 38; Lehrs 48),* (06-04-93, Bassenge, #5360, illus.), 3½ x 1¹⁵⁄₁₆ in., (8.9 x 4.9 cm.), engraving (BP 3982, DM 9774, FR 32,945, Y 649,159).
BI *The Madonna And Child With An Apple (Bartsch 6, 28; L. 39), c. 1475,* narrow margin or trimmed irregularly into subject, surface dirt, disturbance, very good cond., ex. coll. Furstlich Waldburg Wolfegg'sches Kupferstickabinett (L. 2542), est. BP 40/60,000, (06-29-93, Sotheby-London, #60, illus.), 6¾ x 4¾ in., (17.1 x 12.1 cm.), engraving.
$11,970* *Mariens Tod (Lehrs 363),* mono. M + S, 1st state, restored, watermark, (03-24-93, Venator/Hansten, #2576), 10¹⁄₁₆ x 6⅝ in., (25.5 x 16.8 cm.), engraving (BP 8106, DM 19,549, FR 66,537, Y 1,406,415).
$4263* *St. John On Patmos (Lehrs 60),* only state, trimmed outside borderline, thin spots, creases, surfacedirt, repaired area, (12-03-92, Sotheby-London, #141, illus.), 6½ x 4½ in., (165 x 116 mm.), engraving on paper w/watermark (BP 2750, DM 6704, FR 22,882, Y 530,422).

$8680* *Vine Ornament With Birds (Bartsch 6, 114; Lehrs 109),* narrow margins, trimmed unevenly w/in platemark, abraded at centre, repaired tear, discolored, creases, pinholes, ex. coll. Dr. Gustav Seeligmann (L. 1215), (06-29-93, Sotheby-London, #61, illus.), 4¼ x 6 in., (10.8 x 15.2 cm.), engraving (BP 5750, DM 14,657, FR 49,402, Y 923,994).
$76,735* *The Virgin And Child (Lehrs 4),* trimmed outside borderline, thin in places, surface dirt, good cond.,ex-coll., (12-03-92, Sotheby-London, #140, illus.), 6¼ x 6¼ in., (160 x 160 mm.), engraving on paper w/watermark (BP 49,500, DM 120,671, FR 411,889, Y 9,547,717).

SCHONZERT   20th cent.
BI *"Composition Orange", 1974,* #161/300, est. FF2/300, (04-04-93, Pescheteau, #290), 24⁷⁄₁₆ x 34¼ in., (62 x 87 cm.), color serigraph.

SCHOOL OF FONTAINEBLEAU
$5827* *An Extensive River Landscape With The Parable Of The Good Samaritan,1545,* margins, surface losses, old pen and ink i., staining, laid, (12-01-92, Christie-London, #26, illus.), plate 11¾ x 17⅜ in., (298 x 442 mm.), etching in sanguine (BP 3850, DM 9288, FR 31,651, Y 725,473).

SCHOONHOVEN, Jan   b. 1914
$521* *Formatie, 1987: Twelve,* complete set, s., d., #82/100, num. 82, full margins, very good cond., orig. paper portfolio, (12-09-92, Sotheby-Amstrdm, #646), each sheet approx. 15¾ x 9⅝ in., (400 x 245 mm.), silkscreen on terlio (BP 332, DM 818, FR 2791, Y 64,600, G 920).
$85* *Untitled, 1987,* s., d., i. H.C., full margins, good cond., (12-09-92, Sotheby-Amstrdm, #647), 15¾ x 9¹¹⁄₁₆ in., (400 x 246 mm.), lithograph on wove (BP 54, DM 133, FR 455, Y 10,539, G 150).
$640* *Vissengevecht Nr. 5, 1950,* s., t., d., margins, good cond., (05-27-93, Sotheby-Amstrdm, #684, illus.), 19⁵⁄₁₆ x 23¼ in., lithograph on wove (BP 410, DM 1027, FR 3461, Y 68,611, G 1150).

SCHOONHOVEN, Jan and Hans SLEUTELAAR
$489* *Vorm, 1988: Six,* complete portfolio, s., d., #47/50, s. by artist and author, num. 47, full margins, very good cond., orig. paper portfolio, (12-09-92, Sotheby-Amstrdm, #645), each sheet approx. 19¹¹⁄₁₆ x 12¹¹⁄₁₆ in., (500 x 323 mm.), silkscreen on Cambridge White (BP 312, DM 768, FR 2619, Y 60,632, G 863).

SCHOTTKOWSKY
BI *Ornamentale Phantasie,* 71/170, s., est. SF 30/50, (10-14-92, Germann, #430), 17½ x 23¹³⁄₁₆ in., (445 x 605 mm.), color serigraph.

SCHOUTE, Hubert and others   ac. c. 1747
$3330* *Views Of Amsterdam, 1760-86,* set (?) of 97, watermark, pub. P. Fouquet, margins, nicks, creases, stained, discolored, defects, prov., (12-01-92, Christie-London, #155), overall sheet 19¹¹⁄₁₆ x 14⁹⁄₁₆ in., (500 x 370 mm.), engraving on laid paper (BP 2200, DM 5308, FR 18,088, Y 414,592).

SCHRAEMBL
BI *Karte Von Scotland,* orig. outline color, water stains, est. $200/300, (09-17-92, Sloan, #2683), 23¼ x 20¾ in., (59.1 x 52.7 cm.), print.

SCHRAMM, Werner   b. 1898
$581* *"Begegnungen", 1922: Nine,* pub. Galerie Alfred Flechtheim, Dusseldorf, Berlin, Frankfurt Am Main, s., num., stained, tears, (12-01-92, Karl/Faber, #1228), lithograph on hand-made (BP 384, DM 926, FR 3156, Y 72,336).

SCHREIBER, Georges   Belgian/American 1904-1977
$138* *"Cotton Pickers",* s., AAA, (12-11-92, DuMouchelle, #1485, illus.), 9¼ x 13 in., (23.5 x 33 cm.), lithograph (BP 88, DM 217, FR 745, Y 17,077).
$220* *"From Arkansas",* pub. AAA, s. Georges Schreiber; t. on label, very good cond., orig. folder, (09-11-92, Skinner, #50, illus.), 12⅝ x 9¼ in., (32.1 x 23.5 cm.), lithograph on wove (BP 114, DM 317, FR 1076, Y 27,258).
$198* *"Going Home", c. 1940,* s. pub. AAA, orig. folder, excellent cond., margins, (10-31-92, Cleveland, #212), 9¼ x 13⅜ in., (23.5 x 34 cm.), lithograph (BP 127, DM 305, FR 1033, Y 24,526).

$165* *"Mare And Colt"*, s., AAA, (12-11-92, DuMouchelle, #1486, illus.), 9⅜ x 13⅝ in., (23.8 x 34.6 cm.), lithograph (BP 106, DM 260, FR 891, Y 20,418).

$193* *"Noon"*, pub. AAA, s. G. Schreiber, t. AAA label, very good cond., orig. folder, (09-11-92, Skinner, #48, illus.), 9⅜ x 13³⁄₁₆ in., (23.8 x 33.5 cm.), lithograph on wove (BP 100, DM 278, FR 944, Y 23,913).

$330* *"Noon", c. 1940*, s., pub. AAA, orig. folder, excellent cond., full margins, (10-31-92, Cleveland, #211, illus.), 9¼ x 13⅛ in., (23.5 x 33.3 cm.), lithograph (BP 211, DM 508, FR 1722, Y 40,877).

$300* *Orchestra*, s., excell. cond., (05-15-93, Cleveland, #293, illus.), 17 x 22¾ in., (43.2 x 57.8 cm.), lithograph in colors (BP 195, DM 483, FR 1622, Y 33,256).

$303* *"Rain"*, pub. AAA, s. G. Schreiber; t. on label, very good cond., original folder, (09-11-92, Skinner, #46, illus.), 9⅞ x 13¹⁄₁₆ in., (25.1 x 33.2 cm.), lithograph on wove (BP 157, DM 436, FR 1482, Y 37,542).

$55* *"Silence"*, s., AAA, (08-14-92, DuMouchelle, #2306), 9 x 13 in., (22.9 x 33 cm.), lithograph (BP 29, DM 81, FR 273, Y 6936).

BI *"Southern Siesta"*, s., AAA, est. $125/250, (12-11-92, DuMouchelle, #1484, illus.), 8⅞ x 11⅞ in., (22.5 x 30.2 cm.), lithograph.

$248* *Three Circus Subjects*, s., (03-14-93, Hindman, #318), 8¾ x 13⅝ in., (22.2 x 34.6 cm.), lithograph (BP 173, DM 413, FR 1404, Y 29,228).

$140* *Three Clowns, c. 1945*, AAA edit., s., very good cond., (05-15-93, Cleveland, #292, illus.), 9¹⁵⁄₁₆ x 13¼ in., (25.2 x 33.7 cm.), lithograph (BP 91, DM 225, FR 757, Y 15,519).

SCHREYER, Lothar　　　　German 1886-1966

$989* *Kreuz, c. 1920*, mono. stamp, (06-10-93, Hauswedell/Nolt, #906), image 7⅞ x 4⅝ in., (20 x 11.8 cm.), woodcut and gouache on factory print (BP 647, DM 1610, FR 5422, Y 104,978).

$989* *Marionette: Der Lusterne Mann, 1921*, s., d., (06-10-93, Hauswedell/Nolt, #911), image 15¹¹⁄₁₆ x 11¹¹⁄₁₆ in., (39.9 x 29.7 cm.), color lithograph on board (BP 647, DM 1610, FR 5422, Y 104,978).

$918* *Marionette: Der Mannliche Intellekt, 1920/21*, s., d., (06-10-93, Hauswedell/Nolt, #910, illus.), image 15⅝ x 11¾ in., (39.7 x 29.8 cm.), color lithograph on board (BP 600, DM 1495, FR 5033, Y 97,442).

$777* *Marionette: Die Lusterne Frau, 1921*, s., d., (06-10-93, Hauswedell/Nolt, #909, illus.), image 15⅝ x 11¹³⁄₁₆ in., (39.7 x 30 cm.), color lithograph on board (BP 508, DM 1265, FR 4260, Y 82,475).

$565* *Marionette: Engel Der Geburt, 1921*, s., d., (06-10-93, Hauswedell/Nolt, #912), image 15¹¹⁄₁₆ x 11¾ in., (39.8 x 29.9 cm.), color lithograph on board (BP 370, DM 920, FR 3098, Y 59,972).

$537* *Sanctifica Me, 1920*, s., d., t., ded., (06-10-93, Hauswedell/Nolt, #908), image 10¹¹⁄₁₆ x 10¹¹⁄₁₆ in., (27.2 x 27.1 cm.), color lithograph on wove (BP 351, DM 874, FR 2944, Y 57,000).

$473* *Tanzmaske "Erde", 1921*, s., d., (06-10-93, Hauswedell/Nolt, #913), image 10¹¹⁄₁₆ x 5⁵⁄₁₆ in., (27.2 x 13.5 cm.), color lithograph on board (BP 309, DM 770, FR 2593, Y 50,207).

SCHRIMPF, Georg　　　　German 1889-1938

$1135* *Akt IX (Hofmann/Praeger 1916/3), 1916*, s., (06-05-93, Bassenge, #6517), 5³⁄₁₆ x 7⁵⁄₁₆ in., (13.2 x 18.5 cm.), woodcut on hand-made Japan (BP 747, DM 1840, FR 6202, Y 121,755).

$1135* *Badende, 1915*, s., d., (06-05-93, Bassenge, #6516, illus.), 4⁵⁄₁₆ x 5¹⁵⁄₁₆ in., (11 x 15.1 cm.), woodcut on Japan (BP 747, DM 1840, FR 6202, Y 121,755).

$722* *Franz Von Assisi (WV S. 235), 1918*, s., (11-28-92, Schoppmann, #788), 3¾ x 3⅝ in., (9.5 x 9.2 cm.), woodcut on thick Japan (BP 477, DM 1150, FR 3905, Y 89,857).

$1047* *"Frau Mit Pferd" (Hofmann/Prager 1916/9), 1916*, s., d., sheet 4 of portfolio "Georg Schrimpf Acht Holzschnitte", (11-28-92, Grisebach, #740, illus.), 6⁵⁄₁₆ x 8¼ in., (16 x 21 cm.), woodcut on handmade Japan (BP 691, DM 1668, FR 5663, Y 130,305).

$110* *Girl With Birds*, very good/good cond., (11-21-92, Bakker, #183), sight 7¼ x 5¼ in., (18.4 x 13.3 cm.), woodblock print (BP 72, DM 175, FR 591, Y 13,680).

$1271* *Kinder Im Hof (Hofmann-Prager 1918/11), 1918*, s., d., i. 2. artist's proof, (06-10-93, Hauswedell/Nolt, #916, illus.), image 8⁵⁄₁₆ x 6¼ in., (21.1 x 15.9 cm.), woodcut on hand-made Japan (BP 831, DM 2070, FR 6968, Y 134,911).

$217* *"Liebesvorzeichen (Junge, Ein Baumchen Betrachtend) (Hofmann/Prager 1923-24/1), 1923-24*, s., sheet of book "Morike-Gedichte", Munchen, pub. Munchner Drucke(11-28-92, Grisebach, #741, illus.), 4⁵⁄₁₆ x 3¼ in., (10.9 x 8.3 cm.), woodcut on thin handmade (BP 143, DM 346, FR 1174, Y 27,007).

$851* *Madchen Mit Hund, 1923*, s., num., (06-05-93, Bassenge, #6519, illus.), 8⅛ x 6⅛ in., (20.6 x 15.5 cm.), woodcut on hand-made (BP 560, DM 1380, FR 4650, Y 91,289).

$722* *Mutter (18. WV S. 235)*, s., d., (11-28-92, Schoppmann, #787), 7¹⁄₁₆ x 5⁹⁄₁₆ in., (18 x 14.2 cm.), woodcut on beige Japan (BP 477, DM 1150, FR 3905, Y 89,857).

BI *Mutter Mit Kind (Hofmann/Praeger S. 234, H 1917/29), 1917*, s., num., light-stained, est. DM 2000, (12-01-92, Karl/Faber, #1232), 10¼ x 7⅞ in., (26 x 20 cm.), woodcut.

BI *Neue Kunst, Hans Goltz, Der Expressionistische Holzschnitt, 1918*, p. Dr. Wolf & Sohn, fold marks, excell. cond., est. BP 2/3,000, (05-20-93, Christie-London, #509, illus.), sheet 33 x 24 in., (83.8 x 61 cm.), lithograph in black and red backed on Japan.

$1106* *Zwei Badende Unter Baumen (Hofmann-Praeger 1916/3), 1916*, s., (12-05-92, Bassenge, #7706, illus.), 5⅛ x 7³⁄₁₆ in., (13 x 18.2 cm.), woodcut on handmade Japan (BP 693, DM 1724, FR 5877, Y 137,034).

SCHRODER-SONNENSTERN, Friedrich　　German b. 1892

$379* *Compositions: Two*, s. F.S. Sonnenstern 1973, 44/275, (09-30-92, Kunsthallen, #263), color lithograph (BP 214, DM 537, FR 1818, Y 45,482, DK 2070).

$165* *Komposition, 1971*, s. F.S. Sonnenstern 44/275, (03-24-93, Kunsthallen, #295), color lithograph (BP 112, DM 269, FR 917, Y 19,387, DK 1035).

$286* *Das Mondmoralische Eheleben...Juckelche Und Spuckelche, 1972*, d., mono., #43/150, (05-08-93, Schloss Ahlden, #2871), 12⅜ x 16⁹⁄₁₆ in., (31.5 x 42.1 cm.), color serigraph on cardboard (BP 187, DM 459, FR 1550, Y 31,959).

BI *Die Praxis Oder Die Lebenszauberuselevin, 1972*, s., d., mono., #77/222, est. DM 300, (09-18-92, Schloss Ahlden, #1058), 33⁷⁄₁₆ x 25¹⁵⁄₁₆ in., (85 x 65.9 cm.), color lithograph on hand-made.

$194* *Prof. Dr. Publiebkummer Oder Mondkritiker, 1972*, s., d., mono., #21/222, crease, (09-18-92, Schloss Ahlden, #1059, illus.), 29½ x 21¹⁄₁₆ in., (74.9 x 53.5 cm.), color lithograph on BFK Rives (BP 114, DM 288, FR 985, Y 23,977).

$2561* *Sonnenstern, 1972: Six*, s., num., portfolio, Editions Panderma, Carl Laszlo, (12-12-92, Bassenge, #8835), color lithograph (BP 1637, DM 4025, FR 13,717, Y 316,838).

SCHROEDER, Jack

$468* *The Ward Brothers And Ward Brothers Pintail Decoys*, s., d. 1980, s. Ida Ward Linton, limited edit. 58/125, artist proof,remarked, near mint cond., (10-02-92, Guyette, #611B, illus.), print (BP 271, DM 666, FR 2229, Y 55,881).

$523* *Ward Brothers Decoy Prints, 1981: Six*, #419/450, each s. Schroeder and Lem Ward, excell. cond., (10-02-92, Guyette, #611D, illus.), image 9½ x 8½ in., (24.1 x 21.6 cm.), print (BP 302, DM 744, FR 2490, Y 62,448).

SCHUH, Rotthard

$920* *Untitled, c. 1940*, s., annot., (04-08-93, Christie-NY, #221, illus.), 11¾ x 8⅞ in., (29.8 x 22.5 cm.), photograph, gelatin silver print (BP 603, DM 1478, FR 5003, Y 104,403).

SCHULEIN, Julius Wolfgang

BI *(Figure In A City)*, s., margins, good cond., minor soiling, Late Gerhard Brauer Coll., est. Dfl. 2/400, (05-27-93, Sotheby-Amstrdm, #779), 5¼ x 7 in., (134 x 178 mm.), etching on wove.

SCHULMAN, Sam
$2090* *The Cuban Revolution Of 1933, 1933,* (04-07-93, Swann, #360, illus.), 13⅜ x 10⅜ in., photograph, silver print (BP 1381, DM 3380, FR 11,440, Y 237,446).

SCHULTHEISS, Carl   German/American b. 1885
$11* *"Friends", c. 1940,* s., very good cond., (10-31-92, Cleveland, #213), 8½ x 7½ in., (21.6 x 19.1 cm.), engraving (BP 7, DM 17, FR 57, Y 1363).

SCHULTZE, Bernard   German b. 1915
$208* *Ganymed (Heuer 162), (19)73,* s., d., (12-01-92, Karl/Faber, #1236), 15⅜ x 12⅝ in., (39 x 32 cm.), color etching on wove (BP 137, DM 332, FR 1130, Y 25,896).
$938* *Liegender Migof (Heuer 127), 1969,* #119/150, pencil s., d., (11-20-92, Lempertz, #851), sh 25¼ x 31⅞ in., (64.2 x 81 cm.), color etching on Velin (BP 618, DM 1496, FR 5038, Y 116,652).
$207* *Migof-Buste (Heuer 181), 1980,* s., (12-05-92, Bassenge, #7718), 11¾ x 15¹³⁄₁₆ in., (29.9 x 40.2 cm.), color etching on copper print paper (BP 130, DM 323, FR 1100, Y 25,647).
$155* *Migof-Gestrupp, 1981,* s., d., (09-25-92, Granier, #3012), sheet 15⅛ x 11½ in., (38.4 x 29.2 cm.), etching on cream wove (BP 91, DM 230, FR 777, Y 18,709).
$188* *Roter Migof (Heuer 79), 1964,* i. e.a., t., s., d., (11-28-92, Schoppmann, #792), 8¼ x 5¹³⁄₁₆ in., (21 x 14.7 cm.), color etching on handmade (BP 124, DM 300, FR 1017, Y 23,398).
$258* *Untitled (Heuer 112), 1968,* s., num., (12-05-92, Bassenge, #7716), 9¹³⁄₁₆ x 8¾ in., (25 x 22.2 cm.), etching on handmade Hahnemuhle copper print paper (BP 162, DM 402, FR 1371, Y 31,966).
$144* *Untitled (Heuer 171), 1975,* s., d., num., (11-28-92, Grisebach, #745, illus.), 5¹⁵⁄₁₆ x 4³⁄₁₆ in., (15.2 x 10.6 cm.), woodcut on copper print paper (BP 95, DM 229, FR 779, Y 17,922).
$375* *Untitled (Heuer 48), 1959,* s., d., num., (11-28-92, Schoppmann, #791), 15⁹⁄₁₆ x 10⁷⁄₁₆ in., (39.5 x 26.5 cm.), lithograph on offset paper (BP 248, DM 597, FR 2028, Y 46,671).
$505* *Zungengesprache (Heuer 148), 1972,* t., s., d., num., (11-28-92, Schoppmann, #793), 19⁵⁄₁₆ x 11¹³⁄₁₆ in., (49 x 30 cm.), color etching and collage on handmade (BP 333, DM 805, FR 2731, Y 62,850).

SCHUMACHER, Bernard
$55* *Shoreline Boating Scene,* s., #12/20, very good cond.?, (07-19-92, Bakker, #63), plate 12¼ x 16 in., (31.1 x 40.6 cm.), etching (BP 28, DM 80, FR 271, Y 6837).

SCHUMACHER, Emil   German b. 1912
$811* *Komposition,* s., num., (12-05-92, Bassenge, #7720), 9¾ x 12⅝ in., (24.7 x 32 cm.), etching w/aquatint (BP 508, DM 1264, FR 4309, Y 100,483).
$564* *Komposition,* s., num., (05-26-93, Dorling, #2976, illus.), 9¾ x 20¹³⁄₁₆ in., (24.8 x 52.8 cm.), color aquatint-etching, p. in plate, on thick wove (BP 365, DM 920, FR 3097, Y 61,278).
$540* *Komposition,* s., (12-01-92, Karl/Faber, #1238), 9⅝ x 6½ in., (24.5 x 16.5 cm.), aquatint and drypoint on thick wove (BP 357, DM 861, FR 2933, Y 67,231).
$930* *Komposition ("1-1975"),* s., #17/50, blindstamp, (09-18-92, Schloss Ahlden, #1062, illus.), 27⅝ x 20⅞ in., (70.2 x 53 cm.), color etching w/relief print on hand-made (BP 544, DM 1380, FR 4721, Y 114,943).
$2166* *Komposition 13, 1964,* s., epr(euve), d'artiste, (11-28-92, Grisebach, #746, illus.), 8¼ x 19⁷⁄₁₆ in., (21 x 49.4 cm.), colored aquatint on copper print paper (BP 1430, DM 3451, FR 11,714, Y 269,571).
$1702* *Komposition Schwarz-Braunrot, c. 1975,* s., num., (06-05-93, Grisebach, #857, illus.), 8¹¹⁄₁₆ x 6⁷⁄₁₆ in., (22 x 16.4 cm.), aquatint on hand-made copper print paper (BP 1120, DM 2759, FR 9301, Y 182,579).
$777* *Komposition, c. 1961,* s., #12/300, lit., (06-12-93, Hauswedell/Nolt, #387), 17½ x 24¹³⁄₁₆ in., (44.4 x 63 cm.), color lithograph on wove (BP 509, DM 1265, FR 4251, Y 81,764).
$1732* *Komposition, c. 1975,* s., num., (11-28-92, Grisebach, #748, illus.), 19⁷⁄₁₆ x 12⅜ in., (49.3 x 31.5 cm.), aqua-

tint on copper print paper (BP 1143, DM 2759, FR 9367, Y 215,557).
$1284* *Mit Blauem Akzent, 1958,* pencil i. artist proof, s., (11-20-92, Lempertz, #856), sh 25¹⁵⁄₁₆ x 17⁷⁄₁₆ in., (66 x 44.3 cm.), etching overworked w/blue watercolor (BP 845, DM 2047, FR 6896, Y 159,682).
$493* *Motiv. 4, 1967,* s., num., blindstamp, Galerie Wolfgang Ketterer, (05-26-93, Dorling, #2974, illus.), 12¹¹⁄₁₆ x 9¾ in., (32.2 x 24.8 cm.), aquatint on handmade (BP 319, DM 804, FR 2707, Y 53,564).
BI *"Naphta", c. 1972,* s., num., est. DM 2,2/2,500, (11-28-92, Grisebach, #747, illus.), 17½ x 12 in., (44.5 x 30.5 cm.), aquatint on copper print paper.
$1075* *Untitled, 1961,* s., pub. Abstracta, (05-27-93, Lempertz, #1018), 17¹³⁄₁₆ x 14¹⁄₁₆ in., (45.2 x 35.7 cm.), etching thick wove (BP 688, DM 1725, FR 5814, Y 115,244).
$502* *Untitled, 1961,* s., #241/300, stamped, (05-27-93, Lempertz, #1019, illus.), 13¹¹⁄₁₆ x 24¹⁵⁄₁₆ in., (34.7 x 63.3 cm.), color lithograph on wove (BP 321, DM 806, FR 2715, Y 53,816).
$1577* *Untitled, 1975,* s., #97/100, (05-27-93, Lempertz, #1020, illus.), 10⅛ x 12¹⁵⁄₁₆ in., (25.7 x 32.8 cm.), etching on wove (BP 1010, DM 2530, FR 8529, Y 169,061).
$1935* *Untitled, 1979,* s., Edition Rothe num. 365, #5/75, relief stamp, (05-27-93, Lempertz, #1021), 9¾ x 19⁷⁄₁₆ in., (24.8 x 49.3 cm.), etching on thick wove (BP 1239, DM 3105, FR 10,465, Y 207,440).
$272* *Zum Thema Irak, 1988,* s., (09-25-92, Granier, #3013), sheet 33⅛ x 23⁷⁄₁₆ in., (84.2 x 59.5 cm.), color offset print (BP 159, DM 403, FR 1363, Y 32,830).

SCHURMANN, Herbert
$1035* *Jug And Glass, 1932,* s., d., i. by photog., (04-06-93, Sotheby-NY, #335, illus.), 7 x 4¾ in., photograph (BP 684, DM 1667, FR 5646, Y 118,043).

SCHURMANN, Herbert   1908-1982
BI *Boot, 20's,* est. DM 500, (11-12-92, Lempertz, #13), 4⁹⁄₁₆ x 3⁷⁄₁₆ in., (11.6 x 8.7 cm.), photograph, gelatin silver print.

SCHUSLER, N.
$70* *Pyrol "Foudroie Tout Insecte",* Pub. Wall, fairly good cond., (02-12-93, Cheval/Robert, #72), 62³⁄₁₆ x 46⅞ in., (158 x 119 cm.), poster (BP 49, DM 116, FR 393, Y 8442).

SCHUSTER, Ludwig
BI *Swan Study, c. 1945,* s., annot., est. $8/1,000, (10-13-92, Christie-NY, #352, illus.), 15 x 11⅛ in., (38.1 x 28.3 cm.), photograph, gelatin silver print.

SCHUSTER, N.
$150* *Cycles Helyett,* cond. A, (03-16-93, Boisgirard, #196), 23⅝ x 16⅛ in., (60 x 41 cm.), poster (BP 104, DM 249, FR 847, Y 17,540).

SCHUT, Cornelis   1597-1655
BI *Die Jungfrau Mit Dem Kind Und Dem Johannesknaben In Einer LandschaftMit Vier Engeln (Nagler KL 28; Hollstein 76),* est. DM 800, (06-10-93, Hauswedell/Nolt, #164), etching.

SCHUTZ, Anton   American 1894-1955
$55* *Trinity Church,* s., (05-28-93, Sloan, #215, illus.), 9¾ x 6¾ in., (24.8 x 17.1 cm.), etching (BP 35, DM 87, FR 295, Y 5897).

SCHUYFF, Peter   Dutch b. 1958
$115* *Untitled, 1990,* s., annot. P.P. 4/4, pub. Kenny Schacter, full margins, good cond., repaired tear, thinned spot, surface soiling, (05-19-93, Butterfield, #2332), 36¼ x 36¼ in., (921 x 921 mm.), silkscreen in colors on heavy wove (BP 75, DM 187, FR 630, Y 12,731).
BI *Untitled, 1990,* s., annot. P.P. 4/4, pub. Kenny Schacter, full margins, good cond., creases, tear, a thinned spot, surface soiling, est. $6/800, (02-24-93, Butterfield, #3253), 36¼ x 36¼ in., (921 x 921 mm.), silkscreen in colors on heavy wove.
$2070* *Untitled, 1990: Six,* complete suit, s., #36/50, co-pub. by artist and Watanabe Studios, full margins, good cond., (02-11-93, Sotheby-NY, #440, illus.), each sheet approx. 15¾ x 12 in., (400 x 305 mm.), color aquatints (BP 1461, DM 3429, FR 11,603, Y 249,548).

SCHWALBE, Ole
$147* *Komposition, 1976,* s. Schwalbe 76, 197/300, (03-24-93, Kunsthallen, #296), color lithograph (BP 100, DM 240, FR 817, Y 17,272, DK 920).
BI *Kompositioner, 1960/1970,* s. 44/350 and 26/100, est. DK 1,500, (03-24-93, Kunsthallen, #297), color lithograph.

SCHWARTZ, William S.   Russian/American 1896-after 1934, d. 1977?
$275* *Man On A Park Bench, 1938,* s., full margins, paper tape, surface soiling, pencil notations, creases, (02-24-93, Butterfield, #2866, illus.), 12½ x 8¾ in., (318 x 222 mm.), lithograph on Rives (BP 192, DM 446, FR 1513, Y 32,269).
$165* *The Old Lady,* i. by artist's widow, (05-16-93, Hindman, #552), 13 x 10 in., (33 x 25.4 cm.), lithograph (BP 107, DM 265, FR 892, Y 18,291).
$440* *Reclining Nude (lithograph #9), 1928,* (05-16-93, Hindman, #551), 6¼ x 15 in., (15.9 x 38.1 cm.), lithograph (BP 286, DM 708, FR 2378, Y 48,775).
$1380* *Standing Nude Ladies, 1928:* Three, plate s. William S. Schwartz 1928, s. William S. Schwartz, (06-12-93, Christie-NY, #337, illus.), smallest 17½ x 11¼ in., (44.5 x 28.6 cm.), largest 20½ x 12½ in., (44.5 x 28.6 cm.), lithograph on paper (BP 903, DM 2246, FR 7549, Y 145,217).

SCHWARTZ, Publisher, Louis
$825* *"View Of New Orleans Taken From The Lower Cotton Press",* pub. Louis Schwartz, B Dondorf, laid down, wide margins, excellent cond., 19th cent., (11-21-92, Goldberg, #701, illus.), 12¼ x 27 in., (31.1 x 68.6 cm.), aquatint engraving (BP 543, DM 1315, FR 4431, Y 102,599).

SCHWARZ
$235* *Expositie Gooische Schilders Vereeniging,* L. van Leer & Co., folded, (06-09-93, Bubb Kuyper, #2179), 37⅝ x 20½ in., (95.5 x 52 cm.), color lithograph (BP 155, DM 384, FR 1293, Y 24,992, G 431).

SCHWARZ, Reiner   b. 1940
BI *Selbst: Nachtliche Verwandlung, 1982,* s., t., #11/100, est. DM 300, (09-18-92, Schloss Ahlden, #1063), 19¹³⁄₁₆ x 25¹⁵⁄₁₆ in., (50.4 x 66 cm.), color lithograph on Arches wove.

SCHWARZCHILD, K.   20th cent.
$39* *Nocturne,* s., t., i. A/P, (09-17-92, Sloan, #637), 10 x 12⅞ in., (25.4 x 32.7 cm.), color intaglio (BP 22, DM 58, FR 198, Y 4856).

SCHWERDTLE, Dieter   b. 1952
$304* *Joseph Beuys Auf Der Documenta 7, 1982,* wash by Beuys, s., #3/100, felt pen s., (11-12-92, Lempertz, #244), 15⅞ x 11¹⁵⁄₁₆ in., (40.3 x 30.4 cm.), photograph, gelatin silver print (BP 194, DM 478, FR 1628, Y 37,610).

SCHWIMMER, Max   1895-1960
$295* *Fur Hanne, 1920,* s., t., d., artist's proof No 1, margin foxed, (12-05-92, Bassenge, #7724), 7⅞ x 5¹¹⁄₁₆ in., (20 x 14.5 cm.), drypoint on copper print paper (BP 185, DM 460, FR 1567, Y 36,551).

SCHWITTERS, Kurt   German 1887-1948
$5753* *Die Kathedrale (Motherwell-Karpel 278; Verkauf 182; Raabe, Zeitschriften 163; Die Zwanziger Jahre in Berlin 3/268), 1920: Eight,* from the series Die Silbergaule Nrn 41/42, (12-05-92, Bassenge, #7726), lithograph (BP 3602, DM 8969, FR 30,569, Y 712,799).
$3818* *Die Kathedrale (Schmalenbach-Bolliger, Schwitters, Bibliographie, pag. 389, VII, 251, Boston 278), 1920: Eight,* (06-23-93, Kornfeld, #779, illus.), lithograph (BP 2594, DM 6460, FR 21,730, Y 415,949, SF 5750).

SCHWITZER, Kavari
$977* *These Men Use Shell, The Circus, 1938,* p. Waterlow and Sons, ref. #521, cond. 1, (10-13-92, Phillips-London, #140), 30¹⁄₁₆ x 45¹⁄₁₆ in., (76.4 x 114.4 cm.), color lithograph (BP 569, DM 1431, FR 4863, Y 118,467).

SCOTIN, Gerard, Jean HAUSSARD and others
$1887* *Costumes Turcs (P. & B. P. 535): Fifty-Five,* from the set, wide margins, foxing, (06-30-93, Sotheby-London,

#234), 14⅛ x 9⅞ in., (359 x 251 mm.), etching (BP 1265, DM 3218, FR 10,857, Y 202,186).

SCOTSON-CLARK
BI *The Bookman/A Literary Journal, c. 1895,* very rare, Dodd, Mead and Company, New York, est. DM 1,200, (12-05-92, Bassenge, #7625), 15⁹⁄₁₆ x 10⁹⁄₁₆ in., (39.6 x 26.8 cm.), lithograph.

SCOTT, Campbell   Scottish/American b. 1930
$43* *Sun On Mykonos (Greek Island),* s., t., d. Nov. 1962, #2/30, (11-30-92, Ritchie, #34), 22 x 14¾ in., (55.9 x 37.5 cm.), color block print (BP 28, DM 69, FR 233, Y 5352, C$ 55).

SCOTT, Elizabeth
$106* *The Alliance,* #60/150, s., (10-21-92, Maynard, #184), silkscreen (BP 66, DM 160, FR 544, Y 12,911, C$ 132).

SCOTT, G.
$378* *Cie De Navigation Mixte Touache: Services Reguliers. "De Marseille, Cette, Algerie, Tunisie Et Maroc", c. 1910,* good cond., (03-13-93, Laurin, #168), 41¾ x 29¹⁵⁄₁₆ in., (106 x 76 cm.), (BP 264, DM 629, FR 2139, Y 44,549).
$90* *"Jeunes Francais, Engagez-Vous Rengagez-Vous Dans Les TROUPES COLONIALES", 1929,* very good cond., (03-13-93, Laurin, #15), 46⅞ x 31⅛ in., (119 x 79 cm.), (BP 63, DM 150, FR 509, Y 10,607).

SCOTT, James   (after Daniel MACLISE)   English 19th cent.
$325* *Snap Apple Night Or All Hallow Eve,* (02-04-93, Sloan, #2016), 21¾ x 31¾ in., (55.2 x 80.6 cm.), color engraving (BP 227, DM 535, FR 1815, Y 40,428).

SCOTT, James B.   American mid-19th cent.
$385* *The Master Of The Hounds,* after Samuel John Carter, pub. John O. Malley & Son, (04-02-93, Sloan, #1168), 28 x 23½ in., (711 x 597 mm.), color engraving (BP 254, DM 619, FR 2102, Y 43,835).

SCOTT, Nigel   b. 1951
$990* *Untitled (Floating Hats And Umbrellas), c. 1900,* sig., (10-14-92, Swann, #554, illus.), 16½ x 11 in., (41.9 x 27.9 cm.), photograph, silver print (BP 581, DM 1449, FR 4913, Y 119,971).

SCOTT, Peter
$61* *"Only Sixteen Geese Left The Shore That Morning",* s., artists proof, pub. Arthur Ackerman, (02-05-93, G.A. Key, #17), 14 x 21 in., (35.6 x 53.3 cm.), colored (BP 42, DM 101, FR 342, Y 7591).

SCOTT, Septimus Edwin   b. 1879
$355* *The Quick-Starting Pair, Chariot And Horses, 1926,* p. Waterlow & Sons, ref. #133, cond. 3, (10-13-92, Phillips-London, #56, illus.), 30¹⁄₁₆ x 44⅞ in., (76.3 x 114 cm.), color lithograph (BP 207, DM 520, FR 1767, Y 43,046).

SCOTT, Susan   American ac. 1980
$325* *Muley,* s., t.; s. in plate, prov., (11-16-92, Hodgins, #214, illus.), 16¾ x 10¹⁵⁄₁₆ in., (42.6 x 27.9 cm.), etching on paper (BP 214, DM 518, FR 1746, Y 40,559, C$ 413).

SCOTT, William
BI *Two White Triangles,* s., d. '72, num. 22/72, good cond., est. BP 250/300, (11-30-92, Phillips-London, #569), sheet 22⅞ x 30¾ in., (581 x 781 mm.), silkscreen in yellow on wove.
BI *Yelklow Square And Quarter Blue,* s., d. '72, num. 71/72, very good cond., est. BP 250/300, (11-30-92, Phillips-London, #568), (584 x 775 mm.), silkscreen in colors on wove.

SCOTT, William   1913-1989
BI *"Composition", 1963,* #8/65, s., d., est. FF800/1,000, (04-04-93, Pescheteau, #292), 19¹¹⁄₁₆ x 25⁹⁄₁₆ in., (50 x 65 cm.), color lithograph on Arches.
$60* *"Composition-1963",* d. 63, #42/65, s., (04-04-93, Pescheteau, #291), 19¹¹⁄₁₆ x 25⁹⁄₁₆ in., (50 x 65 cm.), color lithograph on wove (BP 40, DM 96, FR 328, Y 6831).

SCOWKROFT, ET.   American 20th cent.
$44* *The Indian Queen Hotel,* (11-12-92, Freemn/Fine Art, #188), 9½ x 13½ in., (24.1 x 34.3 cm.), etching (BP 29, DM 70, FR 235, Y 5456).

SCROGGIE, Edward b. 1906
$601* *To Visit Britain's Landmarks, Temple Bar, 1937,* p. Waterlow and Sons, ref. #502, cond. 1, creasing, (10-13-92, Phillips-London, #127), 29¹⁵⁄₁₆ x 44⅞ in., (76 x 114 cm.), color lithograph (BP 350, DM 880, FR 2992, Y 72,875).

SCULLY, Sean Irish b. 1945
BI *Block, 1986,* s., d., t., #27/30, pub. Diane Villani Editions, full margins, good cond., est. $1,5/2,000, (11-07-92, Sotheby-NY, #768, illus.), 29⅞ x 35⅛ in., (759 x 892 mm.), woodcut p. in colors on Okawara.
BI *Block, 1986,* s., t., d., #1/30, pub. Diane Villani Editions, full margins, creases, excellent cond., est. $1,5/2,000, (11-09-92, Christie-NY, #402, illus.), (94.6 x 111.8 cm.), colored woodcut on Okawara handmade.
$3850* *Conversation, 1986,* s., d., t., i. 'A/P', pub. Diane Villani Editions, full margins, good cond., (11-07-92, Sotheby-NY, #766, illus.), 29⅞ x 44¾ in., (75.9 x 113.7 cm.), woodcut p. in colors on Okawara (BP 2517, DM 6147, FR 20,777, Y 475,191).
BI *Conversation, 1986,* s., t., d., #33/40, pub. Diane Villani Editions, full margins, creasing, surface soiling, good cond., est. $5/7,000, (11-09-92, Christie-NY, #403, illus.), 37½ x 52¼ in., (95.3 x 132.7 cm.), colored woodcut on Okawara handmade.
BI *Conversation, 1986,* s., d., t., #4/40, pub. Diane Villani Editions, full margins, good cond., est. $4,5/5,500, (05-19-93, Butterfield, #2333, illus.), sh 37¼ x 53½ in., (94.6 x 135.9 cm.), woodcut in colors on Okawara handmade.
BI *Conversation, 1986,* s., d., t., #28/40, pub. Diane Villani Editions, full margins, good cond. ?, est. $3,5/4,500, (05-15-93, Sotheby-NY, #1202, illus.), 29¾ x 44⅞ in., (75.6 x 114 cm.), woodcut in colors on Okawara paper.
BI *Room, 1988,* s., t., d., #14/40, blindstamp, full margins, excellent cond., est. $4/5,000, (11-09-92, Christie-NY, #404, illus.), 41¾ x 50¾ in., (106 x 128.9 cm.), etching and aquatint in colors on Somerset.
BI *Room, 1988,* s., d., t., #20/40, pub. Crown Point Press, full margins, very good cond., est. $6/8,000, (10-28-92, Butterfield, #3117, illus.), 31 x 41 in., (78.7 x 104.1 cm.), color aquatint w/etching on white wove.
BI *Standing 2, 1986,* s., d., t., #17/35, pub. Diane Villani Editions, full margins, good cond. ?, est. $2,5/3,000, (05-15-93, Sotheby-NY, #1201, illus.), 39⅞ x 30 in., (101.3 x 76.2 cm.), woodcut in colors on Okawara paper.
$3025* *Standing II, 1986,* s., d., t., #1/35, pub. Diane Villani Editions, full margins, good cond., creases, (11-07-92, Sotheby-NY, #767, illus.), 40 x 30⅛ in., (101.6 x 76.5 cm.), woodcut p. in colors on Okawara (BP 1978, DM 4830, FR 16,325, Y 373,365).
$4140* *The Stranger, 1987,* s., d., t., #2/30, pub. Diane Villani Editions, full margins, good cond., (05-15-93, Sotheby-NY, #1203, illus.), 25 x 40 in., (63.5 x 101.6 cm.), woodcut in colors on Okawara paper (BP 2692, DM 6659, FR 22,378, Y 458,929).
BI *Wall, 1988,* s., d., t., #12/40, pub. Crown Point Press, full margins, very good cond., est. $6/8,000, (10-28-92, Butterfield, #3118), 42 x 51 in., (106.7 x 129.5 cm.), color aquatint on white wove.

SCULTORI, Diana 1536-1590
BI *Christ And The Woman Taken In Adultery (B. 4 ii/ii), c. 1600,* later impression, narrow margins, fold, surface soiling, defects, est. $1/1,500, (05-11-93, Christie-NY, #59), plate 16¾ x 22¹⁵⁄₁₆ in., (425 x 583 mm.), engraving on laid.

SCULTORI, Giovanni Battista (called MANTOVANO) 1505-1575
$1841* *Die Seeschlacht Der Griechen Und Trojaner (B. 20, Massari 6 II),* (06-04-93, Bassenge, #5362), 16⅛ x 23⅛ in., (41 x 58.7 cm.), engraving (BP 1218, DM 2990, FR 10,077, Y 198,555).

SEABY, Allen William English 1867-1953
BI *"The Gulf Of Salamis, Greece",* s., num., excellent cond., est. $4-500, (10-31-92, Cleveland, #330), 12 x 16⅜ in., (30.5 x 41.6 cm.), color woodcut.

SEAGERS, Clayton
$138* *Blue-Wing Teal, Duck Stamp Design, 1953,* s. artist's proof, (06-11-93, Freemn/Fine Art, #200), 6½ x 8¾ in., (16.5 x 22.2 cm.), lithograph and stamp (BP 91, DM 224, FR 756, Y 14,642).

SEARLE, Ronald British b. 1920
BI *Le Modele, 1979,* s., #55/99, t., est. DM 350, (09-18-92, Schloss Ahlden, #1064), 25⁹⁄₁₆ x 19¹¹⁄₁₆ in., (65 x 50 cm.), color lithograph on hand-made.
$112* *"Montgolfiere", 1983,* artist's proof, d., s., (10-18-92, Pescheteau, #257), 25⁹⁄₁₆ x 19¹¹⁄₁₆ in., (65 x 50 cm.), lithograph in colors on Arches (BP 68, DM 165, FR 562, Y 13,373).
$70* *"La Patineuse", 1970,* s., d., good cond., (05-15-93, Cleveland, #488), 6 x 7⅛ in., (15.2 x 18.1 cm.), color lithograph (BP 46, DM 113, FR 378, Y 7760).

SEARS, Sarah C. 1858-1935
$990* *Mrs. J.W.H (Julia Ward Howe), c. 1890,* prov., lit., (10-13-92, Christie-NY, #23, illus.), 9½ x 7¼ in., (24.1 x 18.4 cm.), photograph, platinum print (BP 577, DM 1450, FR 4928, Y 120,044).

SEAVER, C.R.
$660* *Street Scene, Boston,* photog.'s embossed handstamp, 1850's, (10-14-92, Swann, #240, illus.), 10 x 8 in., (25.4 x 20.3 cm.), photograph, salt print (BP 387, DM 966, FR 3275, Y 79,981).

SEAVER, Hugh American 1896-1959
$25* *"The Commet", 1934,* s., excell. cond., (05-15-93, Cleveland, #294), 8½ x 6 in., (21.6 x 15.2 cm.), drypoint (BP 16, DM 40, FR 135, Y 2771).

SEBA, Albertus
$1840* *Bats And Snakes, 1736: Five,* (03-03-93, Sotheby-Arcade, #126), sight 17 x 22 in., (43.2 x 55.9 cm.), and 17 x 11 in., (43.2 x 55.9 cm.), hand-colored engraving (BP 1269, DM 3030, FR 10,279, Y 215,004).
$690* *Insects, 1736: Six,* (03-03-93, Sotheby-Arcade, #127), sight 17 x 11 in., (43.2 x 27.9 cm.), hand-colored engraving (BP 476, DM 1136, FR 3855, Y 80,626).

SEBAH, Joallier and Pascal 19th century
BI *Mosque,* s. J.P. Sebah in negative, est. $3/400, (02-04-93, Sloan, #2915), 8⁵⁄₁₆ x 10⅝ in., (21.1 x 27 cm.), photograph, albumen print.

SECHE, Josef b. 1880
BI *Zirkus-Szene,* #1/5, s. Seche, est. DM 600-, (03-24-93, Venator/Hansten, #4557), pl. 6¼ x 9⁹⁄₁₆ in., (15.8 x 24.3 cm.), drypoint etching.

SECHERET, Jean Baptiste
$213* *"Drape", 1990 and "Hommage A Stotskopff", 1990: Two,* first, s., d., 27/35; second, s. artist's proof, d., t., (06-28-93, Loudmer, #364), first 23¼ x 19⅛ in., (590 x 485 mm.), second 21¼ x 27⁹⁄₁₆ in., (590 x 485 mm.), black lithograph on Arches wove (BP 143, DM 362, FR 1219, Y 22,599).
$145* *"La Maliciosa Alta", 1988 and "Nature Morte En Silhouette", 1989: Two,* both s., d., 5/15 and 45/50, (06-28-93, Loudmer, #363), first 7¹⁄₁₆ x 9¼ in., (180 x 235 mm.), second 20¹⁄₁₆ x 27¹⁵⁄₁₆ in., (180 x 235 mm.), black lithographs, first, on China applique on wove; second, on Arches wove (BP 97, DM 246, FR 830, Y 15,385).

SEEHAUS, Paul Adolf 1891-1919
$144* *Russisches Dorf (Jahn/Berger 20), 1918,* s., in: Die Schaffenden, 1. Jahrgang 2. portfolio, (11-28-92, Grisebach, #751, illus.), 4½ x 6¹¹⁄₁₆ in., (11.5 x 17 cm.), woodcut on Japan (BP 95, DM 229, FR 779, Y 17,922).

SEELEY, George H. 1880-1955
BI *Girl With Dog, 1914,* s., d., t., est. $6/8,000, (10-13-92, Christie-NY, #43, illus.), 13⅛ x 16¾ in., (33.3 x 42.5 cm.), photograph, gum bichromate print.
BI *John Burroughs (Berkshire Museum, pl. 42), 1912,* s. and d. by photog. on image, i., est. $5/8,000, (04-06-93, Sotheby-NY, #67, illus.), 21⅜ x 17⅜ in., photograph, varnished platinum and gum bichromate print.
BI *Landscape, 1926,* s., d., est. $7/1,000, (10-14-92, Swann, #555, illus.), 9¾ x 7½ in., (24.8 x 19.1 cm.), photograph, platinum print.

$357* *Snow Covered Branches,* c. 1920s, (04-07-93, Swann, #546, illus.), 5 x 4 in., photograph, silver print (BP 236, DM 577, FR 1954, Y 40,559).

BI *The White Circle (Naef, p. 432), c. 1908,* est. $2,5/3,500, (10-15-92, Sotheby-NY, #103, illus.), 9½ x 7½ in., (24.1 x 19.1 cm.), photograph, platinum print.

$1320* *Woman With Statuette Of A Buddha, c. 1910,* sig., notations, (10-14-92, Swann, #556, illus.), 7½ x 9½ in., (19.1 x 24.1 cm.), photograph, platinum print (BP 775, DM 1932, FR 6551, Y 159,961).

BI *Young Woman With Globe, c. 1910,* est. $1,2/1,800, (04-07-93, Swann, #547, illus.), 14 x 11 in., photograph, platinum print.

SEESANWEIN

$28* *Untitled,* good cond., (10-31-92, Cleveland, #392), 26 x 36 in., (66 x 91.4 cm.), silkscreen in colors (BP 18, DM 43, FR 146, Y 3468).

SEEWALD, Richard 1889-1976

$1064* *Portolongone (Elba) (Jentsch H 110), 1922,* s., i. artist's proof IV, (06-05-93, Bassenge, #6531, illus.), 14$\frac{3}{16}$ x 13⅜ in., (36 x 34 cm.), woodcut on Japan (BP 700, DM 1725, FR 5814, Y 114,139).

SEGAL, Arthur Rumanian 1875-1944

$577* *Figuren Am Strand, 1913,* s., (11-28-92, Schoppmann, #801), 7⅞ x 9$\frac{13}{16}$ in., (20 x 25 cm.), woodcut on beige Japan (BP 381, DM 919, FR 3121, Y 71,811).

BI *Freudenmadchen Mit Stilleben, 1927,* s., est. DM 800-, (09-25-92, Granier, #3014), sheet 11 x 8⅞ in., (28 x 22.5 cm.), woodcut on board.

SEGAL, George American b. 1924

BI *Girl In Doorway, 1975,* s., d., #10/57, blindstamp pub., 2RC Editions, full margins, very good cond., creases, est. $6/800, (02-24-93, Butterfield, #3256), 22 x 26¾ in., (559 x 679 mm.), aquatint in colors from two plates on Fabriano.

BI *Man In Solferino Shirt, 1975,* s., d., #28/55, margins, good cond. (?), est. $5/700, (02-24-93, Butterfield, #3255), 29¼ x 20 in., (743 x 508 mm.), aquatint and etching on wove.

$330* *Nude And Rattan Armchair, 1978,* s., d. G Segal '78, #89/100, good cond., (03-12-93, Skinner, #103, illus.), sheet 30 x 22 in., (76.2 x 55.9 cm.), photo-screenprint on wove (BP 230, DM 549, FR 1868, Y 38,892).

BI *Untitled, 1968,* s., d., annot. IX/IX AP, good cond., surface scuffing, ink loss, est.$3/500, (02-24-93, Butterfield, #3254), 35 x 25 in., (889 x 635 mm.), silkscreen on metallic silver.

SEGALL, Lasar Brazilian 1890-1957

BI *Liebespaar, 1957,* s., est. DM 800, (12-01-92, Karl/Faber, #1241), 5⅞ x 4½ in., (15 x 11.5 cm.), etching on cardboard.

BI *Negerkopf. 1929,* s., est. DM 6/700, (11-28-92, Grisebach, #754, illus.), 7⅞ x 5⅞ in., (20 x 15 cm.), linocut on Japan.

$295* *Paar Aus Mangue (Kat. Kunsthalle Berlin Nr. 430), 1943,* s., lit., (12-05-92, Bassenge, #7727), 6$\frac{1}{16}$ x 3$\frac{5}{16}$ in., (15.4 x 8.4 cm.), woodcut on wove (BP 185, DM 460, FR 1567, Y 36,551).

SEGRELLE(?)

$440* *American Indians Before A Church With An Image Of Christ In The Background, 1929,* Exposition-Barcelona 1929, linen-backed, (04-29-93, Swann, #142), 39 x 27 in., (99.1 x 68.6 cm.), color lithograph poster (BP 280, DM 696, FR 2345, Y 48,949).

SEGUI, Antonio Argentinian b. 1934

BI *"La Casita" and "Hombres": Two,* s., d. wide margins, taped, very good cond., est. $2/2,500, (05-17-93, Christie-NY, #306, illus.), 15⅝ x 19½ in., (397 x 495 mm.), etching w/extensive hand-coloring in watercolor on Arches.

$64* *Elephant, 1973,* s., d., margins, good cond., (05-27-93, Sotheby-Amstrdm, #486), sh 27$\frac{7}{16}$ x 21$\frac{5}{16}$ in., (697 x 542 mm.), colored lithograph on wove (BP 41, DM 103, FR 346, Y 6861, G 115).

$128* *Elephant, 1973,* s., d., margins, good cond., (05-27-93, Sotheby-Amstrdm, #484), 19$\frac{11}{16}$ x 25$\frac{5}{16}$ in., (500 x 643 mm.), colored lithograph on wove (BP 82, DM 205, FR 692, Y 13,722, G 230).

$64* *Elephant, 1973,* s., d., margins, good cond., (05-27-93, Sotheby-Amstrdm, #485), 19$\frac{11}{16}$ x 25$\frac{5}{16}$ in., (500 x 643 mm.), colored lithograph on wove (BP 41, DM 103, FR 346, Y 6861, G 115).

$210* *Le Parc, 1979,* s., d. 79, #8/75, full margins, (11-16-92, Briest, #95), 19$\frac{11}{16}$ x 25$\frac{15}{16}$ in., (50 x 66 cm.), drypoint on Arches (BP 138, DM 335, FR 1128, Y 26,207).

BI *Projection D'Un Chien, 1966,* s., d. 66, #49/60, est. FF1,000/1,200, (03-31-93, Briest, #E100), 19⅞ x 13$\frac{1}{16}$ in., (50.5 x 33.2 cm.), color lithograph.

SEGUIN, Armand French 1869-1903

$8992* *Le Bar,* large margins, (06-11-93, Picard, #162), 15⅜ x 8¾ in., (390 x 223 mm.), etching, aquatint, softground etching and roulette in brown on laid (BP 5908, DM 14,614, FR 49,271, Y 954,058).

$2200* *Evening (Field 68; Stein & Karshan 79), 1894,* s., num. 53, blindstamp pub. L'Estampe Originale, Album 7, 1894, fullmargins, good cond., scrape, surface dirt, (11-05-92, Sotheby-NY, #441, illus.), 9 x 9 in., (228 x 228 mm.), etching, aquatint, lavis and roulette p. in brown ink (BP 1431, DM 3479, FR 11,771, Y 269,906).

$2968* *Le Soir or La Glaneuse (Karshan 79; Field 68), 1894,* num., s., untrimmed margins, 1 of 100, drystamp, (02-24-93, Picard, #227), etching, aquatint and roulette on creme laid (BP 2070, DM 4818, FR 16,335, Y 348,275).

$358* *"The Woman With Figs" (Field 80 D/D), 1894-5,* late impression, very fine cond., (10-31-92, Cleveland, #331), 10½ x 16½ in., (26.7 x 41.9 cm.), etching and lavis (wash) on laid paper (BP 229, DM 551, FR 1868, Y 44,345).

SEIDEMANN, Bob

BI *"Janis Joplin",* 1967, p.l., s., t. twice, d., photog.'s stamp, est. $1/1,500, (05-23-93, Butterfield, #3593, illus.), 15 x 14 in., photograph, gelatin silver print.

SEIDENSTUCKER, Friedrich German 1882-1966

$304* *Faschingsfigur, 20's,* photographer's stamp, (11-12-92, Lempertz, #245, illus.), 5⅞ x 3$\frac{15}{16}$ in., (15 x 10.1 cm.), photograph, gelatin silver print (BP 194, DM 478, FR 1628, Y 37,610).

$228* *Schwan, 20/30's,* photographer's stamp, (11-12-92, Lempertz, #246), 5$\frac{1}{16}$ x 7$\frac{1}{16}$ in., (12.9 x 18 cm.), photograph, gelatin silver print (BP 146, DM 358, FR 1221, Y 28,207).

SEIHO, Takeuchi

$193* *Bear In Profile,* very good/good cond., (03-28-93, Bakker, #67), 15 x 19 in., (38.1 x 48.3 cm.), print (BP 130, DM 315, FR 1070, Y 22,463).

SEIKE, Tomio

$772* *Nude, n.d., 1980s,* s., (10-29-92, Christie-London, #198, illus.), image 8¾ x 5¾ in., (22.2 x 14.6 cm.), photograph, gelatin silver print (BP 495, DM 1188, FR 4029, Y 95,627).

SEITZ, Gustav 1906-1969

BI *Untitled (Zwei Weibliche Akte, Stehend),* s., #63/150, creases, est. DM 200, (09-18-92, Schloss Ahlden, #1065), 25½ x 19⅜ in., (64.7 x 49.2 cm.), lithograph on light hand-made.

SEITZ, Gustav W., Publisher

$93* *The Gardener's Daughter,* (01-21-93, Bonhams-Chelsea, #21), image 22⅛ x 17⅛ in., (56.2 x 43.5 cm.), hand-colored lithograph (BP 61, DM 148, FR 500, Y 11,640).

SEIWERT, Franz Wilhelm 1894-1933

$1023* *Die Fabrik, 1923,* s., d., i., full margins, paper discoloration, minor foxing, creasing, small defects at edges of sheet; 3 corners glued to mount verso, Late Gerhard Brauer Coll., (05-27-93, Sotheby-Amstrdm, #780, illus.), 9¾ x 12⅛ in., (247 x 308 mm.), linocut on Japan (BP 655, DM 1642, FR 5533, Y 109,670, G 1840).

$325* *"Fabrikbetrieb" (Bohnen 300), 1923,* mono., (11-28-92, Grisebach, #755, illus.), 2⅜ x 4$\frac{3}{16}$ in., (6 x 10.7 cm.), linocut on wove (BP 215, DM 518, FR 1758, Y 40,448).

SEKINE, Nobuo b. 1940
$147* *Project Light Switch, 1971: Three,* s. N. Sekine 71, (09-30-92, Kunsthallen, #265), lithograph (BP 83, DM 208, FR 705, Y 17,641, DK 805).
$147* *Project Moving Rocks, 1971: Three,* s. N. Sekine 71, (09-30-92, Kunsthallen, #264), lithograph (BP 83, DM 208, FR 705, Y 17,641, DK 805).

SEKINO Japanese 20th cent.
BI *City View,* s., est. $4/600, (06-26-93, Wolf, #958), 14 x 9½ in., (35.6 x 24.1 cm.), color woodblock.

SEKINO, Jun'ichiro b. 1914
BI *Portrait Of His Son,* s., edit. 4/20, est. $5/700, (10-11-92, Hanzel, #956A), 18½ x 14½ in., (47 x 36.8 cm.), color woodblock print.
$220* *Side Of A Building,* s., d. Juni. Sekino '64, num. 81/120, (09-25-92, Wolf, #44), 23½ x 18 in., (59.7 x 45.7 cm.), colored woodcut (BP 128, DM 326, FR 1103, Y 26,554).

SELBY, Prideaux John English 1788-1867
$83* *"Great Crested Grebe",* plate LXXIII, s. plate J.P. Selby, (02-27-93, Dunning, #1117), sight 16½ x 23 in., (41.9 x 58.4 cm.), hand colored etching (BP 58, DM 136, FR 464, Y 9798).
$138* *"Hen Harrier" and "Peregrine Falcon": Two Prints,* (10-17-92, Weschler, #67, illus.), each 21¼ x 16 1/26 in., (54 x 42 cm.), colored lithographs (BP 84, DM 205, FR 697, Y 16,557).
BI *Jack-Daw And Magpie, Plate XXXI,* good cond.?, est. $5/700, (01-30-93, Weschler, #49), 21 x 16¼ in., (53.3 x 41.3 cm.), etching.
$187* *"Little Egret Heron, Plate V", c. 1840,* (12-05-92, Neal, #724A), plate 16 x 21½ in., (40.6 x 54.6 cm.), hand-colored engraving (BP 117, DM 292, FR 994, Y 23,169).
BI *"Woodpeckers" and "Little Owl": Two Prints,* est. $3/500, good cond., (10-17-92, Weschler, #69), first 21½ x 14½ in., (54.6 x 37 cm.), second 16¾ x 12 in., (54.6 x 37 cm.), colored lithograph.

SELIGMAN, Kurt 1900-1962
BI *Le Grand Flibustier (Mason 25), 1934,* s., t., from series Protuberances cardiaques, est. DM 2,400, (06-05-93, Bassenge, #6535, illus.), 13⅞ x 11 5/16 in., (35.2 x 28.8 cm.), etching on copper print.
$3300* *The Myth Of Oedipus (cf. Boston 283), 1944: Set Of One And Five,* Durlacher Bros.-R. Kirk Askew Jr., s., d., watermark, num., foxing, very good cond., (11-09-92, Christie-NY, #203, illus.), 24½ x 16 7/16 in., (623 x 418 mm.), etching and etchings hors-texte on wove (BP 2182, DM 5268, FR 17,799, Y 409,531).

SELIGMANN, I.M.
$99* *"La Cercelle De La Chine" and "Le Canard D'Ete De Catesby": Two,* after G. Eduards, mat burn, tears, hinged to mat, John Walton Livermore Estate, (12-04-92, Doyle, #49), 10 x 8¼ in., (254 x 210 mm.), hand colored etching (BP 64, DM 158, FR 535, Y 12,360).

SELMA, Georgij 1906-1984
BI *Pilot, 1932,* est. DM 4,000, (11-12-92, Lempertz, #247, illus.), 3 15/16 x 5 9/16 in., (10 x 14.2 cm.), photograph, gelatin silver print.

SELTENHAMMER, Paul
$90* *La Rumeur. Le Grand Quotidien De Midi, 1927,* cond. A, (03-16-93, Boisgirard, #198), 10⅝ x 7⅞ in., (27 x 20 cm.), poster (BP 62, DM 150, FR 508, Y 10,524).

SELTZER, Phyliss American 20th cent.
$10* *"Automobile Repair", c. 1976-77,* s., d., t., #6/25, excell. cond., (05-15-93, Cleveland, #489), 18½ x 29 in., (47 x 73.7 cm.), lithograph on acetate (BP 7, DM 16, FR 54, Y 1109).
$10* *"The Suburu", 1979,* s., d., #A.P., excell. cond., (05-15-93, Cleveland, #491), 16 x 26 in., (40.6 x 66 cm.), lithograph (BP 7, DM 16, FR 54, Y 1109).
$10* *"The Suburu", 1979,* s., d., t., #A.P., (05-15-93, Cleveland, #490), 15 x 24½ in., (38.1 x 62.2 cm.), lithograph in colors (BP 7, DM 16, FR 54, Y 1109).

SEM
$943* *PLM: Cannes, "La Ville Des Sports Elegants",* p. Draeger, excell. cond., (01-23-93, Ribeyre/Baron, #141, illus.), 41 5/16 x 29 5/16 in., (105 x 74.5 cm.), poster (BP 617, DM 1499, FR 5073, Y 118,023).

SEM, Goursat French 1863-1934
$330* *Parisian Gentleman In Top Hat And Tails, c. 1900: Three,* all s., in stone, good cond., (03-12-93, Goldberg, #898B, illus.), 20½ x 14 in., (52.1 x 35.6 cm.), color lithograph (BP 230, DM 549, FR 1868, Y 38,892).

SEMPE, Jean Jacques b. 1932
$310* *8.25 H En Avril,* s., #72/100, (09-18-92, Schloss Ahlden, #1066), 29 13/16 x 22 1/16 in., (75.8 x 56 cm.), color lithograph on BFK Rives (BP 181, DM 460, FR 1574, Y 38,314).

SEMPERE, Eusebio
$725* *"Nayal", 1967: Four,* s., #15/50, pub. Galeria Juana Mordo, text by Julio Campal, (03-17-93, Duran, #178, illus.), 20½ x 16 9/16 in., (52.1 x 42.1 cm.), serigraph (BP 500, DM 1206, FR 4101, Y 85,034, P 86,250).

SENBERGS, Jan b. 1939
$81* *Observatory 11,* s. J Senbergs, i., d. '68, #8/12, (08-11-92, L. Joel, #151G), 28 15/16 x 24⅛ in., (73.5 x 61.3 cm.), color screenprint (BP 42, DM 119, FR 403, Y 10,373, A$ 110).

SENEX, John
$308* *"A Map Of Louisiana And The River Mississippi",* (12-05-92, Neal, #565A), image 19 x 22¼ in., (48.3 x 56.5 cm.), hand-colored engraving (BP 193, DM 480, FR 1637, Y 38,161).

SENNECKE, Robert
BI *Hermann Goering At The Reichstag Trial, 1933,* handstamp, label, est. $1/1,500, (10-14-92, Swann, #355, illus.), 7½ x 9½ in., (19.1 x 24.1 cm.), photograph, silver print.

SENSENEY, George Eyster American 1874-1934
$330* *"Silver Lake",* s. Senseney Imp., num. no. 4; ident. on label verso, good cond., (10-09-92, Skinner, #144, illus.), sheet, sight 12 x 13¾ in., (30.5 x 34.9 cm.), etching in colors on paper (BP 196, DM 492, FR 1667, Y 40,244).

SEPO (Severo POZZATI)
$58* *Anic, 1938,* plate s., trimmed, (06-08-93, Christie-E, #195), 57½ x 38 in., (146.1 x 96.5 cm.), color lithograph (BP 38, DM 94, FR 317, Y 6160).
BI *Anic, 1938,* plate s., lined, trimmed, est. $5/700, (03-25-93, Christie-E, #208), 57½ x 38 in., (146.1 x 96.5 cm.), color lithograph.

SERGENT, Antoine Louis Francois 1751-1847
BI *"The First Come Best Served" and "The Place To The First Occupier", 1786: Pair,* after Augustin De Saint-Aubin, proofs before letters, margins or trimmed, made-up losses, foxing, staining, est. BP 2,5/3,500, (12-01-92, Christie-London, #253, illus.), sheet 7 9/16 x 10 1/16 in., (192 x 255 mm.), etching w/engraving in colors (black, blue, brown and red).

SERPAN, Jaroslav 1922-1976
$123* *Tachistische Komposition,* s., num., (11-28-92, Schoppmann, #802), 10 13/16 x 16 5/16 in., (27.5 x 41.5 cm.), color lithograph on wove (BP 81, DM 196, FR 665, Y 15,308).

SERRA, Richard American b. 1939
$2760* *"183rd & Webster Avenue" and "Du Common" (Gemini 398 & 400), 1972: Two,* s., #51/62 and 52/59, blindstamp, pub. Gemini, G.E.L., good cond., soft creases, soiling, (05-15-93, Sotheby-NY, #1205, illus.), one sheet 31⅞ x 44¼ in., (81 x 112.4 cm.), other sheet 51⅛ x 40½ in., (81 x 112.4 cm.), lithograph (BP 1795, DM 4439, FR 14,919, Y 305,953).
$4400* *Carnegie (H.-S. 43; G. 1332), 1987,* s., d., #15/19, blindstamps, excellent cond., (11-09-92, Christie-NY, #410, illus.), 80 x 80 in., (203.2 x 203.2 cm.), screenprint w/paintstick on wove (BP 2909, DM 7024, FR 23,732, Y 546,041).
BI *The Moral Majority Sucks (Gemini 971), 1981,* s., d., #9/16, Gemini G.E.L. blindstamps, excell. cond.?, est. $3,5/4,500, (05-11-93, Christie-NY, #563), sheet 52½ x 61 in., (133.4 x 154.9 cm.), lithograph on Arches.

BI *The Moral Majority Sucks (Hoppe-Sailer 23; Gemini 971), 1981*, s., d., #3/16, blindstamps, full margins, pinhole, soiling, very good cond., est. $5/6,000, (11-09-92, Christie-NY, #409, illus.), 52½ x 61 in., (133.4 x 154.9 cm.), lithograph on wove.

BI *Out The Window At The Square Diner (Gemini 960), 1981*, s., d. '80, #35/58, from portfolio Eight Lithographs to Benefit The Foundation For Contemporary Performance Arts, Inc., blindstamp of pub., Gemini G.E.L., full margins, good cond., creases, est. $6/800, (02-11-93, Sotheby-NY, #441, illus.), 13¹⁵⁄₁₆ x 11 in., (355 x 280 mm.), lithograph on Arches Cover.

BI *Out The Window At The Square Diner (Gemini 960), 1981*, s., d. '80, #35/58, from portfolio Eight Lithographs to Benefit The Foundation For Contemporary Performance Arts, Inc., pub. blindstamp, Gemini G.E.L., full margins, good cond., est. $1,2/1,600, (11-07-92, Sotheby-NY, #769, illus.), 14 x 11 in., (356 x 279 mm.), lithograph on Arches Cover.

$2760* *Sketch 1-7 (G. 961-967), 1981: Seven*, s., d. '80, #27/50, blindstamp, pub. Gemini, G.E.L., full margins, good cond., creases, (05-15-93, Sotheby-NY, #1206, illus.), each sheet 28 x 22 in., (71.1 x 55.9 cm.), lithograph (BP 1795, DM 4439, FR 14,919, Y 305,953).

$938* *Sketch 3 (Hoppe-Sailer 14), 1981*, #11/50, pencil s., d., (11-20-92, Lempertz, #862), sh 28¹⁄₁₆ x 22¹⁄₁₆ in., (71.3 x 56 cm.), lithograph on Velin (BP 618, DM 1496, FR 5038, Y 116,652).

BI *Tujunga Blacktop (G. 1217), 1985*, s., d. 84, num. 10/28, blindstamp of pub. Gemini G.E.L., good cond.,est. $3/4,000, (02-24-93, Butterfield, #3145), 60 x 52½ in., (152.4 x 133.4 cm.), silkscreen & paintstik on Arches cover.

$42* *Zeichnungen, 1987*, s. R. Serra, (09-30-92, Kunsthallen, #266), poster, offset (BP 24, DM 60, FR 201, Y 5040, DK 230).

SERRA-BADUE, Daniel   Cuban/American b. 1914
BI *"Self Portrait At Age 48"*, s. Daniel Serra-Badue 1973, num. 177/250, very good cond. (?), est.$3/500, (04-25-93, Bakker, #56), image 9 x 10 in., (22.9 x 25.4 cm.), lithograph.

SERRANO, Andres   American b. 1950
$1430* *Ascent, 1982*, s., t., num. 1/10 by photog., #1/10 ed., (10-15-92, Sotheby-NY, #637, illus.), 28 x 40 in., (71.1 x 101.6 cm.), photograph, cibachrome print, mounted to Plexiglas (BP 875, DM 2129, FR 7219, Y 171,566).

$7475* *Black Jesus,* exec. 1990, #2/edit. 10, prov., (02-23-93, Sotheby-NY, #363, illus.), 45¼ x 32¾ in., (114.9 x 83.2 cm.), photograph, b/w in artist's frame (BP 5121, DM 12,076, FR 40,959, Y 873,044).

$7150* *Black Mary,* in artist's frame, exec. 1990, #3 edit. 4, prov., (10-08-92, Christie-NY, #182, illus.), 65⅜ x 45¼ in., (166.1 x 115 cm.), cibachrome photograph (BP 4255, DM 10,575, FR 35,894, Y 868,773).

$8250* *Blood And Soil,* in artist's frame, exec. 1987, #2 edit. 4, prov., (10-08-92, Christie-NY, #232, illus.), 45⅜ x 64¼ in., (115.3 x 165.7 cm.), cibachrome (BP 4909, DM 12,202, FR 41,416, Y 1,002,430).

$6325* *Female Bust,* s., t., #4/10, d. 89, prov., (05-04-93, Sotheby-NY, #270, illus.), 45½ x 32¾ in., (115.6 x 83.2 cm.), color photograph in artist's painted wood frame (BP 4038, DM 9964, FR 33,572, Y 695,743).

$2200* *Octopus Head, 1985*, s., t., num. 2/4 by photog., #2/4 ed., (10-15-92, Sotheby-NY, #562A, illus.), 40¼ x 60 in., (102.2 x 152.4 cm.), photograph, gelatin silver print (BP 1346, DM 3275, FR 11,106, Y 263,947).

$2420* *Red River #5, 1989*, s., t., d., num. 2/4 by photog. in ink, #2/4 ed., (10-15-92, Sotheby-NY, #563, illus.), 60 x 40 in., (152.4 x 101.6 cm.), photograph, cibachrome print mounted to Plexiglas (BP 1481, DM 3602, FR 12,216, Y 290,342).

SERRE
BI *La Bougie,* s., #127/150, good margins, (05-06-93, Laurin, #80), aquatint.

SERRES, John Thomas   English 1759-1825
$106* *Liverpool From The Mersey,* staining, defects, (08-12-92, Bonhams, #211), image 14⅝ x 21¼ in., (37.1 x 54 cm.), etching w/hand-coloring (BP 55, DM 155, FR 525, Y 13,510).

$151* *Liverpool From The Rock Perch,* staining, (01-21-93, Bonhams-Chelsea, #151), image 14¾ x 21 in., (37.5 x 53.3 cm.), hand-colored etching (BP 99, DM 240, FR 812, Y 18,899).

BI *Tombs And Monuments: Series Of Ten,* trimmed, dirt, damp-staining, est. BP 6/800, (06-30-93, Sotheby-London, #258), 15¾ x 9¾ in., (400 x 248 mm.), hand-colored crayon-lithograph.

SERSANWEIN   20th cent.
$70* *Untitled,* s., (02-04-93, Sloan, #704), sight 26½ x 36 in., (67.3 x 91.4 cm.), silkscreen (BP 49, DM 115, FR 391, Y 8708).

SERUSIER, Paul   French 1863-1927
$2398* *Paysage (La Terre Bretonne),* from 215 impressions, s. in stone, num. 54 verso, large margins, (06-11-93, Picard, #163), 9¹⁄₁₆ x 8⁷⁄₁₆ in., (230 x 215 mm.), lithograph on simili Japan (BP 1576, DM 3897, FR 13,140, Y 254,430).

SERVE-BRIQUET, P.
$230* *Auron. 1500-2300. "A 90 km De Nice", 1945,* good cond., (03-15-93, Arcole, #60), 31⅞ x 23⅝ in., (81 x 60 cm.), (BP 160, DM 382, FR 1299, Y 27,245).

SERWOUTERS, Pieter   1586-1657
BI *David Mit Dem Baren (Hollstein Bd. 26, 3), 1608,* 3rd state, prov., est. DM 800-, (09-14-92, Venator/Hansten, #1611), plate 7⅝ x 8¹¹⁄₁₆ in., (19.4 x 22 cm.), engraving.

$253* *Die Hasenjagd (Wurzbach aus 12; Hollstein 26), 1612,* after D. Vinckboons, from series of 6 sheets of Hunt Scenes, prov., (12-04-92, Bassenge, #6445), 3¹⁵⁄₁₆ x 10¹³⁄₁₆ in., (10.1 x 27.4 cm.), engraving (BP 162, DM 403, FR 1367, Y 31,586).

SESSA, Aldo
BI *Blizzard,* s., d. 78, #5/98, prov., exhib., est. C$ 150/200, (12-01-92, Ritchie, #33), color serigraph.

SEUPHOR, Michel   b. 1901
BI *Les 64 Hexagrammes Du Yi-King, 1986: Sixty-Four,* Triangle Galerie et Editions, s., #21/90, est. DM 2,500-, (11-21-92, Lempertz, #374), 30⁵⁄₁₆ x 22⅜ in., (77 x 56.8 cm.), serigraph on Canson wove.

BI *The Hands Of Florence Henri, c. 1929,* s., annot. in ink by Florence Henri, est. $1,5/1,800, (10-13-92, Christie-NY, #353, illus.), 4⅝ x 6⅜ in., (11.7 x 16.2 cm.), photograph, gelatin silver print.

$829* *Intimes Etendues, 1961: Ten,* #2/92, s., Edition Denise Rene, (09-04-92, Germann, #560), each 26⁷⁄₁₆ x 19⅞ in., (672 x 505 mm.), serigraph (BP 415, DM 1162, FR 3955, Y 102,043, SF 1035).

BI *Leger In His Studio, Paris, 1929,* s., t., d., credit stamp, est. $3/4,000, (10-13-92, Christie-NY, #354, illus.), 4⅝ x 6¼ in., (11.7 x 15.9 cm.), photograph, gelatin silver print.

SEVERINI, Gino   Italian 1883-1966
$660* *Abstrakte Komposition,* #131/220, s., (04-24-93, Ruef, #989, illus.), 19⁵⁄₁₆ x 12⅝ in., (49 x 32 cm.), color lithograph (BP 417, DM 1034, FR 3494, Y 72,832).

$1880* *Arlecchino (Meloni 39), 1962,* proof, s., (05-20-93, Finarte-Milan, #141), 20½ x 10⅝ in., (52 x 27 cm.), lithograph in colors (BP 1207, DM 3033, FR 10,217, Y 207,597, L 2760).

$1645* *Arlecchino (Meloni 43), 1962,* proof, s., (05-20-93, Finarte-Milan, #142, illus.), 14¹⁵⁄₁₆ x 11 in., (38 x 28 cm.), lithograph in colors (BP 1056, DM 2654, FR 8940, Y 181,648, L 2415).

$2475* *Arlecchino E Pedrolino, 1963,* s,m #61/120, full margins, good cond., tape remains, repaired tears,creases through image, mat staining, foxing, (10-28-92, Butterfield, #2719, illus.), 25½ x 19¾ in., (648 x 502 mm.), color lithograph on Rives BFK, watermark (BP 1577, DM 3822, FR 12,979, Y 303,681).

$2875* *Les Arlequins (Meloni 24), 1954,* s., #67/220, pub. Guilde de la Gravure, margins, good cond., mat stain, creases, masking tape, (05-13-93, Sotheby-NY, #826), 14⅞ x 11¼ in., (377 x 287 mm.), sh 18¾ x 13½ in.,

(377 x 287 mm.), lithograph in colors (BP 1887, DM 4642, FR 15,659, Y 320,978).

$4263* *Commedia Dell'Arte (M. 34), 1958,* s., #29/175, p. M. Casse, blindstamp, pub. L'Oeuvre Gravee, full margins, good cond., (12-03-92, Sotheby-London, #579, illus.), 25½ x 19¾ in., (650 x 504 mm.), lithograph in colors on Arches (BP 2750, DM 6704, FR 22,882, Y 530,422).

$2200* *Composition (Meloni 28), 1955,* s., i. Epreuve d'Artiste, #XII/XXX, full margins, creasing, glue, skinned patches, (11-09-92, Christie-NY, #204), 19¼ x 12⅝ in., (489 x 321 mm.), colored lithograph on Rives (BP 1455, DM 3512, FR 11,866, Y 273,021).

$786* *Composition Geometrique,* #16/50, s., large margins, (06-16-93, Ader Tajan, #138), 19½ x 12⅝ in., (49.5 x 32 cm.), color lithograph (BP 524, DM 1305, FR 4379, Y 83,831).

$2728* *La Danseuse (Meloni 26), 1955,* s., #27/95, pub. Gutekunst and Klipstein, full margins, good cond., (12-03-92, Sotheby-London, #576, illus.), 22½ x 15½ in., (557 x 395 mm.), lithograph in colors on BFK Rives wove (BP 1760, DM 4290, FR 14,643, Y 339,430).

$2750* *Exhibition Poster For Galerie Berggruen (Meloni 215), 1956,* before letters, s., #68/200, full (?) margins, good cond., light stain, creases, label, (11-05-92, Sotheby-NY, #442, illus.), 23⅝ x 13¾ in., (600 x 350 mm.), sheet 26 x 16¾ in., (600 x 350 mm.), lithograph p. in colors on Arches wove (BP 1789, DM 4349, FR 14,714, Y 337,382).

$660* *Harlekin-Familie,* s., (03-14-93, Hindman, #263, illus.), 11¾ x 8 in., (29.8 x 20.3 cm.), pen lithograoh (BP 460, DM 1099, FR 3735, Y 77,784).

$2387* *Les Harlequins (M. 24), 1954,* s., #176/220, blindstamp, pub. Guilde de La Gravure, full margins, good cons., creasing, discoloration, (12-03-92, Sotheby-London, #578, illus.), 18¾ x 11⅛ in., (477 x 284 mm.), lithograph in colors on wove (BP 1540, DM 3754, FR 12,813, Y 297,001).

$3220* *Les Musiciens (Meloni 30), 1955,* s., #31/75, full margins, mat staining, creasing, surface soiling, (05-11-93, Christie-NY, #335), borderline 22 x 15½ in., (559 x 394 mm.), color lithograph on wove (BP 2056, DM 5072, FR 17,091, Y 354,196).

$2217* *Nature Morte (M. 27), 1955,* s., #18/95, pub. Gutekunst and Klipstein, full margins, good cond., (12-03-92, Sotheby-London, #577, illus.), 22 x 15⅜ in., (560 x 390 mm.), lithograph in colors on wove (BP 1430, DM 3486, FR 11,900, Y 275,849).

$1650* *Nature Morte (M. 33), 1958,* s., #83/140, blindstamp pub. L'Oeuvre Gravee, full margins, good cond., scuffs, mat/light stain, foxing, tape stain, (11-05-92, Sotheby-NY, #443, illus.), 15⅜ x 22⅛ in., (390 x 563 mm.), lithograph p. in colors (BP 1073, DM 2610, FR 8828, Y 202,429).

$2819* *Nature Morte (Meloni 21), 1952,* #7/10, s, dedicated and dated Meudon 9.10.52, (05-20-93, Finarte-Milan, #140), 9¹⁵/₁₆ x 14¹/₁₆ in., (25.3 x 35.7 cm.), lithograph in colors (BP 1809, DM 4548, FR 15,321, Y 311,285, L 4140).

$502* *Sans Titre,* s. Gino Severini, (09-15-92, Encans, #179), 21⅝ x 15¼ in., (55 x 38.7 cm.), lithograph (BP 269, DM 747, FR 2535, Y 62,322, C$ 611).

SEXTON, John

$330* *"Hoover Dam At Night, Arizona/Nevada", 1990,* s., d., t., photog. stamp, Dixon Collection, (11-16-92, Butterfield, #6158), 14¾ x 18¹³/₁₆ in., (375.3 x 477.1 mm.), photograph, gelatin silver print (BP 217, DM 526, FR 1772, Y 41,040).

$660* *"Rice Field And Pine Forest, Tohoku, Japan", 1985/1990,* s., d., t., photog. stamp, Dixon Collection, (11-16-92, Butterfield, #6157, illus.), 9⅞ x 12½ in., (251.3 x 318.1 mm.), photograph, gelatin silver print (BP 435, DM 1052, FR 3545, Y 82,079).

$358* *"Trees, Valley Fog, Dusk, Yosemite Valley", 1980/1989,* s., d., (11-16-92, Butterfield, #6159, illus.), 10¼ x 13¼ in., (260.8 x 337.2 mm.), photograph, gelatin silver print (BP 236, DM 571, FR 1923, Y 44,522).

SEYMOUR

$935* *"Leading Out A Hunter"* and *"Returning From The Hunt", 1788: Two,* after T. Burford, pub. Robert Sayer, small margins, discoloration, hinged to mat, (12-04-92, Doyle, #37), 9¾ x 13¾ in., (248 x 349 mm.), engraving (BP 600, DM 1489, FR 5051, Y 116,729).

SEYMOUR, David (Chim)

$385* *Children At The Home For Vagrant And Delinquent Girls Near Budapest,* news agency's handstamp and caption, handstamp, 1950s, exhib., (04-07-93, Swann, #361, illus.), 6½ x 9½ in., photograph, silver print (BP 254, DM 623, FR 2107, Y 43,740).

SEYMOUR, James (after)

$350* *Going Out In The Morning, 1753,* by Thomas Burford, watermarks, margins, nicks, good cond., (11-30-92, Phillips-London, #259), plate 10 x 13⅞ in., (254 x 352 mm.), mezzotint on laid (BP 231, DM 558, FR 1893, Y 43,559).

SEYMOUR, R.

$82* *Snipe Shooting,* pub. W. Spooner, (06-30-93, Bonhams-Chelsea, #69), image 8¾ x 11 in., (22.2 x 27.9 cm.), lithograph w/hand-coloring (BP 55, DM 140, FR 472, Y 8786).

SEYMOUR, Samuel

$2090* *"Battle Of New Orleans And Sefeat Of The British Under The Command Of Sir Edward Packenham, By General Andrew Jackson, 8th January, 1815", c. 1815,* engraved by James W. Steel, pub. William H. Morgan, (12-05-92, Neal, #550, illus.), image 11 x 16¾ in., (27.9 x 42.5 cm.), hand-colored engraving (BP 1309, DM 3258, FR 11,105, Y 258,952).

SEYMOUR-HADEN, Sir Francis   British 1818-1910

$715* *Breaking Up Of The Agamemnon, No. 1 (Schneiderman 133), 1870,* trimmed margins, state V(?), s., masking tape, (05-27-93, Swann, #126, illus.), 7¾ x 16½ in., (19.7 x 41.9 cm.), etching (BP 458, DM 1147, FR 3867, Y 76,651).

BI   *Brentford Ferry (H.N.H. 75), 1864,* s., good margins, (06-11-93, Picard, #67), 5¼ x 8⁷/₁₆ in., (134 x 214 mm.), etching on thin laid.

BI   *Cowdray (H221; S208),* t., d. 1882 in plate, est. $250/300, (09-17-92, Sloan, #1427), 6 x 9⅜ in., (15.2 x 23.8 cm.), etching.

$231* *"Dusty Miller" (S. 172),* s., good cond., (10-31-92, Cleveland, #288), 5½ x 8¼ in., (14 x 21 cm.), etching (BP 148, DM 355, FR 1206, Y 28,614).

$360* *Early Morning Richmond (N.N. Harrington 22), 1859,* second state of two, s., good margins, (06-11-93, Picard, #66), 4⁷/₁₆ x 10⅞ in., (113 x 277 mm.), etching on laid (BP 237, DM 585, FR 1973, Y 38,196).

$248* *Fulham (H. 19), 1859,* init., t. in plate, (12-10-92, Sloan, #932), 4⅜ x 10⅞ in., (11.1 x 27.6 cm.), drypoint etching (BP 160, DM 392, FR 1340, Y 30,678).

$75* *"Kenarth" (S. 59 ii/iii), 1864,* pub. in Etudes a L'Eau Forte, small margins, staining, tipped, (05-15-93, Cleveland, #390), 4½ x 5¹⁵/₁₆ in., (11.4 x 15.1 cm.), etching (BP 49, DM 121, FR 405, Y 8314).

$686* *"Out Of Study Window", "Egham Lock", "Fulham", "A Water Meadow", "Battersea Reach", "Shepperton", "Kew Ait", "Sunset On The Thames", "Twickenham Church"* and *"The Herd" (S. 17; 21; 22; 23;48; 74B; 76B; 83; 98 and 118), 1859-1868,* four s., margins, good cond., paper discoloration, (06-30-93, Sotheby-London, #309, illus.), ten etchings, seven on cream laid, one on wove (BP 460, DM 1170, FR 3947, Y 73,503).

BI   *Ses Mains Qui Gravent (Ber. 84; Harrington 94, L. 76), 1865,* sig., staining, margins, ex-coll., (02-24-93, Picard, #121), etching on strong laid.

$270* *"Shere Mill Pond" (Schneiderman 37), 1860,* bears sig., good cond., (05-15-93, Cleveland, #389), 7 x 13⅛ in., (17.8 x 33.3 cm.), etching (BP 176, DM 434, FR 1459, Y 29,930).

$165* *Ships Putting To Port In A Stormy Sea,* s. Seymour Haden, (04-02-93, Garth, #162), 34½ x 43½ in., (87.6 x 110.5 cm.), b/w etching (BP 109, DM 265, FR 901, Y 18,786).

$542* *Sonnenuntergang An Der Themse (Drake 122 II),* s., (12-04-92, Bassenge, #6821), 7 x 9¹³⁄₁₆ in., (17.8 x 25 cm.), etching on handmade (BP 348, DM 863, FR 2928, Y 67,665).

BI *"Sonning Bank" (Schneiderman 106 IV/V), 1865,* est. $70-100, (10-31-92, Cleveland, #286), 5⁵⁄₁₆ x 8½ in., (13.5 x 21.6 cm.), etching w/drypoint.

$303* *"The Towing Path" And "Reeds By The River", 1864: Two,* former s. Seymour Haden 1864 in plate, d., t., latter s., both bearing sigs., good cond., (03-12-93, Skinner, #16, illus.), 5½ x 8½ in., (14 x 21.6 cm.), etching and drypoint on paper (BP 211, DM 504, FR 1715, Y 35,710).

BI *"The Willows" (S. 171 IV/VI), 1877,* sun staining, est. $150-200, (10-31-92, Cleveland, #287), 5¹⁵⁄₁₆ x 8⅞ in., (15.1 x 22.5 cm.), drypoint.

$72* *Windsor Castle From The River,* s., margins, staining, (10-15-92, Bonhams-Chelsea, #80), plate 13 x 17½ in., (33 x 44.5 cm.), etching (BP 44, DM 107, FR 363, Y 8638).

$302* *Ye Complete Angler (Hamerton 166, Schneiderman 161), 1877,* s., 3rd state, (12-08-92, Swann, #129, illus.), 5½ x 8¹⁄₁₆ in., (14 x 20.5 cm.), etching on laid paper (BP 189, DM 470, FR 1603, Y 37,432).

BI *sunset On The Thames (H. 93; S. 83),* s., d. 1877 in plate, est. $200/300, (07-03-92, Sloan, #1077), 5⅞ x 8¹³⁄₁₆ in., (14.9 x 22.4 cm.), etching.

SEYMOUR-HADEN, Sir Francis (after)
$99* *Fishing,* (10-30-92, Sloan, #881), 6 x 9⅜ in., (15.2 x 23.8 cm.), etching (BP 63, DM 152, FR 517, Y 12,263).

SEYMOURS (after)
$99 *"Mr Martindale's Regulus", 1754,* (06-11-93, G.A. Key, #92), 14 x 17 in., (35.6 x 43.2 cm.), b/w engraving (BP 65, DM 161, FR 542, Y 10,504).

SHAAR, Pinhas
BI *"Ten Jewish Holidays", 1977: Ten,* s., num. LXI/CXXV, orig. portfolio, pub. B.L.D., est. $700/1,000, (12-08-92, Swann, #276), each 22 x 30 in., (55.9 x 76.2 cm.), colored silkscreen print.

SHAD, Lillian American 20th cent.
BI *Amongst The Orchids,* s., #150/300 in white, est. $7/900, (10-30-92, Sloan, #1610), 30 x 22½ in., (76.2 x 57.2 cm.), embossed color serigraph.

SHADBOLT, Jack b. 1909
$133* *"15",* #137/150, t., num., (03-10-93, Maynard, #324), 23 x 25 in., (58.4 x 63.5 cm.), b/w lithograph (BP 93, DM 221, FR 751, Y 15,714, C$ 165).

$265* *"Birth Into Myth",* s., t., (03-10-93, Maynard, #314), 24¼ x 36 in., (61.6 x 91.4 cm.), lithograph (BP 185, DM 441, FR 1497, Y 31,309, C$ 330).

$87* *Title: 15, 1969,* #137/150, s.; s., t., d. '69 in print, prov., (11-16-92, Hodgins, #304), 22½ x 14½ in., (57.2 x 36.8 cm.), lithograph on paper (BP 57, DM 139, FR 467, Y 10,857, C$ 110).

SHAGIN, Ivan b. 1904
$2060* *"Final Fashizma 1945", The End Of Fascism,* t., s., d., ink annots., (10-29-92, Christie-London, #136, illus.), 16¾ x 20¾ in., (42.5 x 52.7 cm.), photograph, gloss gelatin silver print (BP 1320, DM 3169, FR 10,752, Y 255,172).

$1030* *"I.V. Stalin, 1935",* s., t., d., stamp verso, (10-29-92, Christie-London, #137, illus.), 23 x 16⅜ in., (58.4 x 41.6 cm.), photograph, gelatin silver print (BP 660, DM 1585, FR 5376, Y 127,586).

BI *Original Artwork For Cover "Orohek, Small Light, Literary-Artistic Illustrated Weekly", 1941,* retouched and heightened w/white, typography in Russian, i., ink stamp, est. BP 6/900, (05-06-93, Christie-London, #176, illus.), 12¾ x 10 in., photograph, gelatin silver print.

BI *"Sportsmeny V Krymu, 1933", Sportsmen In The Vrimea,* t., d., crayon s., stamp verso, est. BP 5/700, (10-29-92, Christie-London, #135, illus.), 15½ x 10½ in., (39.4 x 26.7 cm.), photograph, gelatin silver print.

SHAHN, Ben American 1898-1969
$605* *"Cat's Cradle" (Prescott, 38), 1959,* red brush s. Ben Shahn, very good cond., (03-12-93, Skinner, #78A,

illus.), sight, sheet 20⅜ x 26⅜ in., (51.8 x 67 cm.), screenprint in black and blue on wove (BP 422, DM 1007, FR 3424, Y 71,302).

BI *"The First World Of Verse Arises" (P. 136), 1968,* stone s., from Rilke Portfolio, good cond., est. $3-400, (10-31-92, Cleveland, #395), 16⅜ x 13⅜ in., (41.6 x 34 cm.), lithograph.

$3025* *For The Sake Of A Single Verse, Rilke Portfolio (P. 113-136), 1968: Twenty-Four,* complete portfolio, s. in stone, just. page s., num. 868, p. by Mourlot, good cond., surface soiling, staining in orig. portfolio, (02-24-93, Butterfield, #2654, illus.), each sheet 22½ x 17¾ in., (572 x 451 mm.), 24 lithographs in colors on Arches (BP 2109, DM 4911, FR 16,648, Y 354,964).

BI *"Frontispiece" (Prescott, 113) from For The Sake Of A Single Verse Rilke Portfolio, 1968,* pub. Mourlot, s. Ben Shahn in ink, num. 71/200, good cond., light toning, water stains, thinned spots, foxing verso, est. $3/500, (09-11-92, Skinner, #82B, illus.), approx. image 9½ x 9 in., (24.1 x 22.9 cm.), lithograph on wove.

$275* *Futility,* s. twice, num., t. 238/300, sig. Stephen Martin SC, (11-28-92, Dunning, #1055), 6 x 9 in., (15.2 x 22.9 cm.), woodcut (BP 182, DM 438, FR 1487, Y 34,225).

$885* *Futility (P. 41), 1960,* red ink s., t., #18/300, annot. Stefan Martinez SC, margin slightly trimmed, very good cond., light-staining, glue/hinge remains, (10-28-92, Butterfield, #2548), 4¾ x 5¾ in., (121 x 146 mm.), woodcut on Japan paper (BP 564, DM 1367, FR 4641, Y 108,589).

$138* *Male Face,* s. Ben Shahn, num. 71/200, very good cond.?, (11-21-92, Bakker, #162), sheet 22¼ x 17½ in., (56.5 x 44.5 cm.), lithograph (BP 91, DM 220, FR 741, Y 17,162).

BI *"Many Things" (Prescott 117),* s., num. 79/200, sun stain, est. $4-600, (10-31-92, Cleveland, #393, illus.), 16½ x 13⅝ in., (41.9 x 34.6 cm.), lithograph.

$605* *Martin Luther King (P. 72), 1966,* s. in ink, t., num. 179/300, ink stamp, pub. The International Graphic Arts Society, engraved, p. by Stefan Martin, large margins, apparently good cond., creases, tape, (02-24-93, Butterfield, #2867, illus.), 24⅞ x 20 in., (632 x 508 mm.), wood engraving on Japan (BP 422, DM 982, FR 3330, Y 70,993).

$920* *Martin Luther King (P. 72), 1966,* s., t., annot. artist's proof, pub. International Graphic Arts Society, p. Stefan Martin, margins, glued to mat, good cond., creases, foxing, (05-19-93, Butterfield, #1827), 22 x 18 in., (559 x 457 mm.), wood engraving on Japan (BP 597, DM 1495, FR 5038, Y 101,849).

$825* *Mine Building (Prescott 22), 1956,* red ink s., full margins, surface scuffing, time staining, very goodcond., (09-19-92, Christie-E, #55, illus.), borderline 17¼ x 28¾ in., (438 x 730 mm.), screenprint w/hand-coloring in watercolor on wove (BP 475, DM 1235, FR 4231, Y 102,791).

$88* *One Must Feel How The Birds Fly,* (12-13-92, Hindman, #321), 21 x 17 in., color lithograph (BP 56, DM 138, FR 471, Y 10,887).

$275* *Owl,* s., foxing, (11-12-92, Freemn/Fine Art, #189), 24½ x 14 in., (62.2 x 35.6 cm.), litho (BP 181, DM 436, FR 1470, Y 34,098).

BI *"Screams Of Women In Labor" (Prescott, 132), from From The Sake Of ASingle Verse Rilke Portfolio, 1968,* pub. Mourlot, s. Ben Shahn, good cond., foxing, est. $8/1200, (09-11-92, Skinner, #85, illus.), sheet 22½ x 17⅝ in., (57.2 x 44.8 cm.), lithograph in five colors on wove.

BI *"The Sea Itself" (P. 129), 1968,* stone s., from Rilke Portfolio, good cond., est. $3-400, (10-31-92, Cleveland, #394), 12¾ x 15⅝ in., (32.4 x 39.7 cm.), lithograph in two colors.

$2200* *Supermarket (Prescot 28), 1957,* s. in watercolor, full margins, foxmark, staining, glue, good cond.,tear, (11-09-92, Christie-NY, #30, illus.), border 17 x 37¹⁵⁄₁₆ in., (432 x 965 mm.), screenprint w/hand-coloring on wove (BP 1455, DM 3512, FR 11,866, Y 273,021).

$440* *"To Childhood Illnesses" (Prescott, 126) from For The Sake Of A Single Verse Rilke Portfolio, 1968,* pub. Mourlot, s. Ben Shahn in ink, good cond., rippling, (09-11-92, Skinner, #82A, illus.), sight 22½ x 17¹¹⁄₁₆ in.,

(57.2 x 44.9 cm.), lithograph in three colors on wove (BP 228, DM 633, FR 2153, Y 54,516).

BI *To Roads In Unknown (P. 121), 1968,* s., from Rilke portfolio, p. Mourlot, foxing, creases, light staining, est. $7/900, (12-12-92, Weschler, #166), 18¼ x 15½ in., (46.4 x 39.4 cm.), color lithograph.

$1650* *Vanderberg, Dewey And Taft, 1941,* recently cleaned, image repairs, discoloration, staining, hinged to mat, prov., lit., (12-04-92, Doyle, #145, illus.), 15 x 22 in., (381 x 559 mm.), color silkscreen (BP 1058, DM 2628, FR 8914, Y 205,993).

$550* *We French Workers Warn You... 1942,* U.S. Government Printing, B cond., tears, paper loss, (08-06-92, Swann, #255, illus.), 28 x 40 in., (71.1 x 101.6 cm.), (BP 287, DM 813, FR 2745, Y 70,153).

$385* *"Wheat Field" (Prescott, 211), 1958,* red brush s. Ben Shahn, #25/40, good cond., (03-12-93, Skinner, #80, illus.), sight 10½ x 23 in., (26.7 x 58.4 cm.), photo-offset in black on paper (BP 269, DM 641, FR 2179, Y 45,374).

SHAIKHET, Arkady   1898-1959
$1725* *The First Cars From The Automobile Factory In Gorky, 1930,* s., lit., (04-08-93, Christie-NY, #152, illus.), 10½ x 8¼ in., (26.7 x 21 cm.), photograph, gelatin silver print (BP 1131, DM 2771, FR 9380, Y 195,756).

$4180* *Kiev Train Station, 1936,* t., d., lit., (10-13-92, Christie-NY, #349, illus.), 10⅝ x 7¾ in., (27 x 19.7 cm.), photograph, gelatin silver print (BP 2434, DM 6124, FR 20,806, Y 506,851).

BI *Street Demonstration In Tifliss, 1929,* s., t., d., est. $3/5,000, (04-08-93, Christie-NY, #153, illus.), 13¾ x 18⅞ in., (34.9 x 47.9 cm.), photograph, gelatin silver print.

SHALER, Lynn
$165* *"L'Atelier",* s., d. '88, t., #32/99, (05-20-93, Boos, #593), sight 11⅝ x 7⅞ in., (295 x 200 mm.), color etching (BP 106, DM 266, FR 897, Y 18,220).

$165* *"Le Miroir",* s., d. '90, t., # 81/100, (05-20-93, Boos, #594), sight 16⅛ x 10⅝ in., (410 x 270 mm.), color etching heightened w/pastel (BP 106, DM 266, FR 897, Y 18,220).

SHANNON, Charles H.
BI *The Morning Visit, 1906,* pub. Burlington Magazine, #575, prov., est. BP 80/120, (10-27-92, Phillips-London, #298), sheet 10⅝ x 9 in., (270 x 229 mm.), lithograph on cream wove.

$149* *Sea Folk, 1899,* s., d. 99, full margins, light stained, (10-27-92, Phillips-London, #297), image 11 x 16¼ in., (279 x 413 mm.), blue black lithograph on laid (BP 94, DM 228, FR 775, Y 18,226).

SHAPIRO, Joel   American b. 1941
$690* *#3, 1985,* s., d., #11/41, blindstamp, pub. ULAE, full margins, good cond., (05-15-93, Sotheby-NY, #1207), sheet 16¾ x 13¾ in., (42.5 x 34.9 cm.), graphic from wood collage (BP 449, DM 1110, FR 3730, Y 76,488).

$181* *Untitled, 1974,* s., d., num., (11-28-92, Schoppmann, #814), 28⅜ x 20⅞ in., (72 x 53 cm.), color lithograph on BFK Rives (BP 119, DM 288, FR 979, Y 22,526).

BI *Untitled, 1987,* s., d., num. 6/27, pub. Grenfell Press, full margins, excell. cond.,est. $8/1,200, (09-19-92, Christie-E, #218), sheet 18½ x 14¾ in., (470 x 375 mm.), woodcut on Crown and Sceptre.

$920* *Untitled, 1988,* s., d., #26/28, co-pub. by artist and Grenfell Press, full margins, excell. cond., (05-11-93, Christie-NY, #565, illus.), sheet 29½ x 18 in., (749 x 457 mm.), color woodcut on laid Japan (BP 587, DM 1449, FR 4883, Y 101,199).

SHARP, William
BI *"As The Lawyer For The Defense", "Oyez-Oyez-Oyez", "Strategy", "WithYour Honor's Permission" and "Your Witness": Five,* s., pub. AAA, full margins, good cond., est. $3/400, (10-28-92, Butterfield, #2861), lithograph on wove.

$2420* *From Victoria Regia; Or The Great Water Lily Of America, 1854: Three,* after John Fisk Allen, pub. Sharp & Son, tape residue, discoloration, soiling, foxing, John Walton Livermore Estate, (12-04-92, Doyle, #9), 15 x 21

in., (381 x 533 mm.), chromolithograph (BP 1552, DM 3854, FR 13,074, Y 302,122).

$5175* *"Opening Bud", "Opening Flower", "Intermediate State Of Bloom" and "Complete Bloom", 1854: Four,* from John Frisk Allen's Victoria Regia, or The Great Water Lily of America, Dutton and Wentworth, margins, laid down, foxing, discoloration, (01-28-93, Sotheby-NY, #463, illus.), 14⅝ x 20⅝ in., (371 x 524 mm.), chromolithograph on wove (BP 3417, DM 8200, FR 27,748, Y 642,538).

SHASHIN
BI *Portrait Of A Man And His Son,* quarter plate sized, stamp, 1860's-70's, est. $2/2,500, (10-15-92, Sotheby-NY, #72, illus.), 3¾ x 2¼ in., (9.5 x 5.7 cm.), photograph, ambrotype.

SHATTER, Susan
BI *Water Reflections, 1987,* s., d., num. 18/60, full sheet w/ deckled edge, good cond., est. $4/600, (05-22-93, Weschler, #223), 18½ x 43 in., (47 x 109.2 cm.), screenprint in colors.

SHAW, Charles
$2330* *Smokers Prefer Shell, 1936,* p. Baynard Press, ref. #449, cond. 1, (10-13-92, Phillips-London, #101, illus.), 30¹⁄₁₆ x 45¹⁄₁₆ in., (76.3 x 114.5 cm.), color lithograph (BP 1357, DM 3413, FR 11,598, Y 282,527).

SHAW, S.T.
BI *"Tea Time",* after C. Nordell, s., d. 1942, i., bears sig. of approx. 45 artists,soiling, discoloration, est. $1/200, (12-04-92, Doyle, #136), 18 x 14 in., (457 x 356 mm.), poster reproduction and testimonial.

SHAYER, William Joseph (after)
$605* *"Going Out", "The Game In View", "The Game Secured" and "Going Home": Four,* engraved by J. Harris, staining, foxing, darkening(06-11-93, Weschler, #47, illus.), each 21¼ x 15½ in., (54 x 39.4 cm.), hand-colored mezzotint (BP 398, DM 983, FR 3315, Y 64,191).

$223* *Hunting Scenes, 1877: A Set Of Four,* by E. G. Hester, pub. Arthur Ackermann, margins, foxing, staining, (10-29-92, Bonhams-Chelsea, #136), plate 16 x 16 in., (40.6 x 40.6 cm.), aquatint w/hand coloring (BP 143, DM 343, FR 1164, Y 27,623).

SHEE, Martin Archer (after)
$133* *Alexander Adair Esq., Captain Commandant Of The 9th Suffolk (Whitman4), 1813,* only state, engraved & pub. Charles Turner, margins, crease, good cond., (11-30-92, Phillips-London, #93), plate 25¼ x 15 in., (641 x 381 mm.), mezzotint on laid (BP 88, DM 212, FR 719, Y 16,553).

SHEEHAN III, Robert F.
$302* *Hand Abstraction, c. 1939,* label, (04-07-93, Swann, #548, illus.), 8 x 8 in., photograph, silver print (BP 200, DM 488, FR 1653, Y 34,310).

SHEELER, Charles   American 1883-1965
BI *African Sculpture, c. 1918,* est. $2,5/3,500, (10-14-92, Swann, #557, illus.), 8½ x 6 in., (21.6 x 15.2 cm.), photograph, silver print.

BI *Architectural Cadence, 1954,* s., d., #43/100, margins, good cond., crease, tipped to backing w/glue, est. $12/15,000, (05-13-93, Sotheby-NY, #433, illus.), 6¼ x 8¾ in., (158 x 221 mm.), silkscreen in colors on cream wove.

SHEERES, John W.
$65 *Join The Quartermaster's Corps,* minor folds, (09-24-92, Alderfer, #249, illus.), 26 x 17 in., (66 x 43.2 cm.), (BP 38, DM 96, FR 327, Y 7819).

SHEETS, Millard   American 1907-1989
$220* *"The Island People Of Janitzio", 1983,* s. Millard Sheets, #28/100, very good cond., (06-26-93, Skinner, #139), sheet 17 x 23 in., (43.2 x 58.4 cm.), color lithograph on paper (BP 147, DM 374, FR 1259, Y 23,342).

$275* *Mexican-Town,* s., t., num. 87/125, margins possibly trimmed, good cond., pin holes,discoloration, (02-24-93, Butterfield, #2868), 5⅞ x 3¹⁵⁄₁₆ in., (149 x 100 mm.), etching on Alexandra wove (BP 192, DM 446, FR 1513, Y 32,269).

SHEILDS, Alan   American b. 1944
BI   *"A 4" and "A12, International Teddy Bear": Two*, s., d.
      73, #7/75 and 15/75, est. $5/700, (06-13-93, Hindman,
      #350), each 21¾ x 22 in., (55.2 x 55.9 cm.), color seri-
      graph.
BI   *Alan Sheild's Sheild*, s., d. 74, #10/48, est. $800/1,200,
      (06-13-93, Hindman, #347, illus.), color serigraph w/
      stitching and collage on handmade paper.
BI   *Jackie Laugh*, s., d. 74, t., #10/21, est. $5/700, (06-13-
      93, Hindman, #349), 14½ x 14½ in., (36.8 x 36.8 cm.),
      color serigraph w/etching on handmade paper.
BI   *My Roller Derby Queen*, s., d. 74, #7/34, est. $800/
      1,200, (06-13-93, Hindman, #351), 17½ x 17¼ in.,
      (44.5 x 43.8 cm.), color serigraph and dyed cheese cloth.
BI   *Peace Of The Rock*, s., d. 74, t., #7/20, est. $800/1,200,
      (06-13-93, Hindman, #348), 14½ x 14½ in., (36.8 x 36.8
      cm.), color serigraph and drypoint on handmade paper.

SHELLEY, Samuel (after)   1750-1808
BI   *Mrs. George Hay Drummond And Children (Le B. 2), c.
      1789*, by Caroline Watson, pub. J. and J. Boydell, small
      margins, discoloration, est. BP 250/350, (12-01-92,
      Christie-London, #291), plate 7¹/₁₆ x 5⅝ in., (180 x 143
      mm.), stipple engraving in colors (black, blue, brown, red
      and yellow).

SHELTON, Margaret   1915-1984
$130* *Barn At Lamond*, #20/50, s., t., prov., (05-10-93, Hod-
       gins, #354), 5 x 7¼ in., (12.7 x 18.4 cm.), woodcut on
       paper (BP 85, DM 209, FR 705, Y 14,527, C$ 165).
$390* *Homestead At Revelstoke, 1943*, #38/50, s., t., d. '43,
       prov., (11-16-92, Hodgins, #200, illus.), 7¹⁵/₁₆ x 10½ in.,
       (20.3 x 26.7 cm.), color woodblock on paper (BP 256,
       DM 622, FR 2096, Y 48,671, C$ 495).
$156* *Rosedale Golf Course, 1940*, #65/100, s., d. '40, prov.,
       (05-10-93, Hodgins, #318, illus.), 5 x 6¾ in., (12.7 x
       17.1 cm.), color woodcut on paper (BP 102, DM 251,
       FR 846, Y 17,432, C$ 198).
$520* *"Thompson River Near Lytton, B.C.", 1943, and "Vermil-
       lion Lakes", 1944: Two*, #6/50, #33/100 s., t., d. '43, '44
       respectively, prov., (05-10-93, Hodgins, #43), 8 x 10½
       in., (20.3 x 26.7 cm.), woodcut on paper (BP 339, DM
       835, FR 2818, Y 58,107, C$ 660).
$87*   *"United Church" and "Administration Building, Banff":
       Two*, s. block, prov., (05-10-93, Hodgins, #122), one 3¾
       x 5 in., (9.5 x 12.7 cm.), the other 4¼ x 5½ in., (9.5 x
       12.7 cm.), woodblock on paper (BP 57, DM 140, FR
       472, Y 9722, C$ 110).
$239* *"Untitled-Mountain Scene" and "C.P.R. Clubhouse Banff":
       Two*, s. block, prov., (05-10-93, Hodgins, #263), one 4 x
       5 in., (10.2 x 12.7 cm.), the other 4½ x 5½ in., (10.2 x
       12.7 cm.), woodcut on paper (BP 156, DM 384, FR
       1295, Y 26,707, C$ 303).

SHEPHARD, David (after)
$164* *The Elephant And The Ant Hill*, #481/850, s., blindstamp,
       (05-20-93, Bonhams-Chelsea, #142), image 18½ x 39¼
       in., (47 x 99.7 cm.), reprod. in colors (BP 105, DM
       265, FR 891, Y 18,110).

SHEPHERD, David
$341* *Sketch For A Paintin,-African Bull Elephant*, #495/850,
       s., blindstamp, pub. Solomon & Whitehead, (04-22-93,
       Bonhams-Chelsea, #161), (55.9 x 50.8 cm.), reprod. in
       colors (BP 220, DM 548, FR 1848, Y 37,493).

SHEPHERD, Peter
$489* *A Friend To The Farmer, Shell Tractor Oil, The Barn
       Owl, 1952*, p. John Waddington, ref. P 19, cond. 3, (10-
       13-92, Phillips-London, #169), 29¹⁵/₁₆ x 39¾ in., (76 x
       101 cm.), color lithograph (BP 285, DM 716, FR 2434,
       Y 59,294).

SHERIDAN
$50   *"Hey Fellows!", 1918*, American Library Assoc., edge
       damage, (09-24-92, Alderfer, #314), 30 x 20 in., (76.2
       x 50.8 cm.), (BP 29, DM 74, FR 252, Y 6015).

SHERIDAN, J.F.
$55   *"Food Is Ammunition"*, (03-04-93, Alderfer, #259, illus.),
       29 x 21 in., (73.7 x 53.3 cm.), poster (BP 38, DM 90,
       FR 306, Y 6404).

SHERMAN, Cindy   American b. 1954
$6068* *Ohne Titel, 1983*, ink s., d., #11/18, lit., (11-12-92, Lem-
        pertz, #248, illus.), 35¼ x 23⁷/₁₆ in., (89.5 x 59.5 cm.),
        sheet 39⅜ x 29¹⁵/₁₆ in., (89.5 x 59.5 cm.), color photo-
        graph (BP 3880, DM 9536, FR 32,501, Y 750,711).
$3163* *Self-Portrait In The Snow, 1986*, s., d., #28/35 by pho-
        tog. in ink, (04-06-93, Sotheby-NY, #495, illus.), 35 x
        27½ in., (89 x 69.9 cm.), photograph, Type-C print (BP 2089, DM 5096,
        FR 17,256, Y 360,744).
$2750* *Untitled*, s., num., d. Cindy Sherman 29/35 1986 verso,
        (11-17-92, Christie-E, #116, illus.), 39½ x 30 in., (100.3
        x 76.2 cm.), color photograph (BP 1811, DM 4385, FR
        14,769, Y 341,997).
$14,950* *Untitled*, s., d. 1979, #3/10, (02-23-93, Sotheby-NY,
        #361, illus.), 7½ x 9½ in., (19.1 x 24.1 cm.), photo-
        graph, b/w (BP 10,241, DM 24,152, FR 81,918, Y
        1,746,087).
$15,400* *Untitled*, s., num., d. Cindy Sherman 5/10 1982 verso,
        prov., exhib., (02-24-93, Christie-NY, #117, illus.), 48½ x
        29¾ in., (123.2 x 75.6 cm.), photograph, color (BP
        10,739, DM 25,000, FR 84,755, Y 1,807,088).
$14,950* *Untitled #112*, exec. 1982, prov., lit., (05-04-93, Sotheby-
        NY, #281, illus.), 45¼ x 30 in., (114.9 x 76.2 cm.),
        color photograph (BP 9544, DM 23,551, FR 79,352, Y
        1,644,484).
$16,100* *Untitled #123*, s., #14/18, d. 1983, prov., lit., (05-04-93,
        Sotheby-NY, #273, illus.), 39¾ x 30 in., (101 x 76.2
        cm.), color photograph (BP 10,278, DM 25,362, FR
        85,456, Y 1,770,982).
$3575* *Untitled #125, 1983 (Whitney, pl. 87)*, s., d., num. 13/18
        by photog. in ink, #13/18 ed., (10-15-92, Sotheby-NY,
        #601, illus.), 19 x 35¾ in., (48.3 x 90.8 cm.), photo-
        graph, Type-C print (BP 2188, DM 5322, FR 18,046, Y
        428,914).
$19,800* *Untitled #140*, s., d. Cindy Sherman 1985 verso, #6 edit.
        6, prov., exhib., (10-08-92, Christie-NY, #233, illus.),
        72½ x 49⅜ in., (184.2 x 125.4 cm.), color photograph
        (BP 11,782, DM 29,286, FR 99,398, Y 2,405,832).
$8625* *Untitled #27*, s., t., #2/10, d. 1979, (05-04-93, Sotheby-
        NY, #276, illus.), 8 x 10 in., (20.3 x 25.4 cm.), b/w
        photograph (BP 5506, DM 13,587, FR 45,780, Y
        948,741).
$16,100* *Untitled (#166)*, s., d. Cindy Sherman 1986 verso, #1/6
        edit., prov., lit., (05-05-93, Christie-NY, #162, illus.), 55½
        x 32¾ in., (141 x 83.2 cm.), color photograph (BP
        10,280, DM 25,402, FR 85,593, Y 1,774,496).
$10,450* *Untitled (#174)*, exec. 1987, #2/6, prov., lit., Prop. Lam-
        bert Art Collection, (11-19-92, Christie-NY, #156, illus.),
        72⅛ x 47¹⁵/₁₆ in., (183.2 x 121.9 cm.), photograph, color
        (BP 6880, DM 16,661, FR 56,122, Y 1,299,590).
$11,000* *Untitled (#217)*, s. Cindy Sherman on cardboard backing,
        exec. 1984, #1/12, prov., (11-19-92, Christie-NY, #135,
        illus.), 50¼ x 32¼ in., (127.6 x 81.9 cm.), photograph,
        color (BP 7243, DM 17,538, FR 59,076, Y 1,367,989).
$19,800* *Untitled (#55)*, s., num., d. C. Sherman 1980 7/10 verso,
        prov., exhib., lit., (11-19-92, Christie-NY, #111, illus.), 8
        x 10 in., (20.2 x 25.4 cm.), photograph, b/w (BP 13,037,
        DM 31,569, FR 106,337, Y 2,462,380).
$20,900* *Untitled (#90)*, s., num., d. Cindy Sherman 1981 2/10
        verso, prov., lit., (11-19-92, Christie-NY, #152, illus.),
        27¹⁵/₁₆ x 52⅜ in., (71.1 x 133 cm.), photograph, color
        (BP 13,761, DM 33,323, FR 112,245, Y 2,599,179).
$19,800* *Untitled (Film Still #38)*, s., num., d. Cindy Sherman
        1978 Y10 verso. prov., lit., (02-24-93, Christie-NY, #119,
        illus.), 8 x 10 in., (20.3 x 25.4 cm.), photograph, b/w
        (BP 13,808, DM 32,143, FR 108,971, Y 2,323,398).
$20,700* *Untitled (Film Still #4)*, s. Cindy Sherman verso, exec.
        1978, #1/10 edit., prov., lit., (05-05-93, Christie-NY,
        #141, illus.), 8 x 10 in., (20.3 x 25.4 cm.), b/w photo-
        graph (BP 13,217, DM 32,660, FR 110,048, Y
        2,281,495).
$13,200* *Untitled (Film Still #40)*, s., num., d. Cindy Sherman
        1977 8/10 verso, #8 edit. 10, prov., lit., (10-08-92,
        Christie-NY, #178, illus.), 8 x 10 in., (20.3 x 25.4 cm.),
        b/w photograph (BP 7855, DM 19,524, FR 66,265, Y
        1,603,888).
$20,700* *Untitled (Film Still #9)*, s., num., d. Cindy Sherman 1978
        1/10 verso, prov., lit., (05-05-93, Christie-NY, #142,

illus.), 8 x 10 in., (20.3 x 25.4 cm.), b/w photograph (BP 13,217, DM 32,660, FR 110,048, Y 2,281,495).

$7700* *Untitled Film Still #2, 1977,* s., d., num. 8/10, i. #2 by photog., #8/10 ed., (10-15-92, Sotheby-NY, #600, illus.), 9¼ x 7½ in., (23.5 x 19.1 cm.), photograph, gelatin silver print (BP 4712, DM 11,462, FR 38,869, Y 923,815).

$17,250* *Untitled Film Still #49,* s., #1/10, exec. 1979, lit., (05-04-93, Sotheby-NY, #252A, illus.), 8 x 10 in., (20.3 x 25.4 cm.), b/w photograph (BP 11,012, DM 27,174, FR 91,561, Y 1,897,481).

$6600* *Untitled Film Still, 1979,* s., d., num. 3/10 by photog., #3/10 ed. in this format, (10-15-92, Sotheby-NY, #602, illus.), 6½ x 9⅜ in., (16.5 x 23.8 cm.), photograph, gelatin silver print (BP 4039, DM 9824, FR 33,317, Y 791,842).

$1760* *Untitled, (Self-Portrait In Parka), 1986,* s., d., num. 68/75 in ink, (10-13-92, Christie-NY, #600, illus.), 15 x 22 in., (38.1 x 55.9 cm.), photograph, color coupler print (BP 1025, DM 2578, FR 8761, Y 213,411).

$770* *Untitled, 1985,* ink s., d., #19/125, full margins, good cond., (02-24-93, Butterfield, #3257, illus.), 14 x 14 in., (356 x 356 mm.), C-print (BP 537, DM 1250, FR 4238, Y 90,354).

BI *Untitled, 1985,* s., d., ink edit. 88/125, est. $1,2/1,800, (11-16-92, Butterfield, #6160, illus.), ⁹⁄₁₆x⁹⁄₁₆in., (14 x 14 mm.), photograph, c-print.

$4400* *Untitled, Film Still #38,* s., d., num. 1/10, (c) insig., (10-13-92, Christie-NY, #598, illus.), 9⅜ x 7¼ in., (23.8 x 18.4 cm.), photograph, gelatin silver print (BP 2563, DM 6446, FR 21,901, Y 533,527).

$8250* *Untitled, Self-Portrait With Mirror, 1980,* s., d., num. 7/10, (10-13-92, Christie-NY, #599, illus.), 6⅝ x 9½ in., (16.8 x 24.1 cm.), photograph, gelatin silver print (BP 4805, DM 12,086, FR 41,065, Y 1,000,364).

SHERRIFF, Paul
$288* *Everywhere You Go, Bosham, 1952,* p. Vincent Brooks, Day & Son, ref. P 43, cond. 3, (10-13-92, Phillips-London, #178), 29¾ x 39¾ in., (75.5 x 101 cm.), color lithograph (BP 168, DM 422, FR 1434, Y 34,922).

SHERRIFF-SCOTT, Adam   Canadian School 1887-1980
$75* *"L'Arrivee Du Printemps",* #119/300, s. in plate A. Sherriff-Scott, (07-14-92, Encans, #166), 12¹⁵⁄₁₆ x 15⁹⁄₁₆ in., (33 x 39.5 cm.), lithograph (BP 39, DM 111, FR 375, Y 9379, C$ 89).

SHERWIN, J.K. (after)
$250* *The Installation Dinner Of The St. Patrick's Society, Dublin, March 1783, 1803,* by Robert Wilkinson, pub. Robert Wilkinson, repaired tear through center of image, repaired tears, paper losses, (11-30-92, Phillips-London, #228), sheet 25⅓ x 32⅞ in., (643 x 835 mm.), engraving on laid (BP 165, DM 398, FR 1352, Y 31,114).

BI *Le Village Abandonne,* by Chaponier, pub. Bauce, skinning, repaired tear, broken paper, glue, defects, est. BP 2/250, (11-30-92, Phillips-London, #212), sheet 20⅞ x 25⅓ in., (530 x 643 mm.), color stipple engraving on wove.

SHERWOOD, William Anderson   American 1875-1951
BI *"Evening" and "Landscape With Villas": Two,* each s., blindstamp, est. $200/300, (09-17-92, Sloan, #659), larger 8¾ x 7⅝ in., (22.2 x 19.4 cm.), etchings.

SHIELDS, Alan   American b. 1944
$880* *Plastic Bucket (Tyler 504:AS27), 1981,* s., #5/10, pub. blindstamp, Tyler Graphics, Ltd., good cond., (11-07-92, Sotheby-NY, #770), 35⅞ x 27⅜ in., (911 x 695 mm.), linocut, etching, aquatint and relief p. in colors w/collage on two sheets of handmade, colored TGL (BP 575, DM 1405, FR 4749, Y 108,615).

SHIGEMOSA, Kitawa   Japanese 1739-1820
$132* *Shunga Scene,* (09-17-92, Sloan, #1636), sight 6⅞ x 10½ in., (17.5 x 26.7 cm.), woodblock (BP 74, DM 196, FR 671, Y 16,434).

SHIGENOBU
$966* *A Courtesan And Potted Bonsai Trees,* surimono, kakuban, num. 6, s. Yanagawa Shigenobu, soiled, rubbed, (06-10-93, Sotheby-London, #210), (BP 632, DM 1573, FR 5296, Y 102,537).

SHIKO, Munakata
$1100* *Seated Goddess In A Garden,* trimmed, remargined, laid down, (11-20-92, Skinner, #10, illus.), 25 x 15 in., (63.5 x 38.1 cm.), sumizuri-e w/hand applied rose color (BP 724, DM 1754, FR 5908, Y 136,799).

SHIKO, Munakata   Japanese 1903-1975
$14,000* *Portrait Of A Lady,* s., sealed, prov., (02-04-93, Sloan, #2569, illus.), 11½ x 9 in., (29.2 x 22.9 cm.), handcolored woodcut (BP 9773, DM 23,053, FR 78,169, Y 1,741,510).

SHIKO, Munakuto
$413* *"Buddah", c. 1958,* s., d., pub. seal, creasing, fading, (05-07-93, Goldberg, #1387, illus.), woodblock (BP 262, DM 653, FR 2200, Y 45,475).

$193* *"Running Boy", c. 1958,* OBAN, s., d., pub. seal, laid down, creasing, fading, (05-07-93, Goldberg, #1386), woodblock (BP 122, DM 305, FR 1028, Y 21,251).

SHIMIZU   Japanese 20th cent.
$143* *Garden Path And Trees,* s., d. 1959, i. in Japanese, num. 46/100, bearing artist's red chop, (09-20-92, Hindman, #735), 21 x 15 in., (53.3 x 38.1 cm.), color woodcut (BP 84, DM 212, FR 726, Y 17,674).

SHIMODA, Midora
$357* *Ro Do Sha, c. 1910,* photog.'s sig., notations, Japanese calligraphy and stamp on image, (04-07-93, Swann, #549, illus.), 9 x 7 in., photograph, platinum(?) print (BP 236, DM 577, FR 1954, Y 40,559).

SHINKOSAI HOKUSHU   Japanese ac. c. 1809-1842
$2450* *Memorial Portrait Of Arashi Kitsusaburo I,* Oban, s. Shunkosai Hokushu ga w/seal of Hokushu, d. Bunsei 4 (1821),soiled, rubbed, laid down, 2nd state, Prof. H.R.W. Kuhne Coll., (06-11-93, Sotheby-London, #460, illus.), 14½ x 10¼ in., (36.8 x 26 cm.), woodblock (BP 1610, DM 3982, FR 13,425, Y 259,947).

SHINSAI
$5274* *Carp With Waterweeds,* surimono, kakuban, s. Shinsai w/seal, rubbed, soiled, (06-10-93, Sotheby-London, #205, illus.), silver and gold, gauffrage (embossing) (BP 3450, DM 8588, FR 28,914, Y 559,813).

SHIRO   Japanese 20th cent.
$198* *Pagoda In Rain,* bearing artist's seal, (10-18-92, Hindman, #535), 14 x 9 in., (35.6 x 22.9 cm.), color woodcut (BP 121, DM 295, FR 999, Y 23,755).

SHIVES, Arnold
$49* *Untitled,* #2/7, s., d., (03-10-93, Maynard, #254), 12 x 18 in., (30.5 x 45.7 cm.), etching (BP 34, DM 82, FR 277, Y 5789, C$ 61).

SHOBEI, Toni
BI *"Actor Duo",* KUKEMONO-E, fading, creasing, est. $4/600, (05-07-93, Goldberg, #1359), woodblock.

SHODO   ac. after 1900
BI *Bildnis Einer Jungen Schonheit Beim Ikebana,* est. SC 5/6,000, (04-27-93, Dorotheum, #225, illus.), 10¹³⁄₁₆ x 16⁹⁄₁₆ in., (27.5 x 42 cm.), color woodcut.

BI *Frau Beim Blumenschneiden,* est. SC 5/6,000, (04-27-93, Dorotheum, #226, illus.), 10¾ x 16⁹⁄₁₆ in., (27.3 x 42 cm.), color woodcut.

SHOESMITH, K.
BI *Royal Mail: Asturias "Le Plus Grand Paquebot Du Monde" Service Regulier De Cherbourg Sur L'Amerique Du Sud,* fairly good cond., (03-13-93, Laurin, #169, illus.), 41¾ x 29¹⁵⁄₁₆ in., (106 x 76 cm.), .

SHOKLER, Harry   American 1896-1978
BI *"Breton Lobstermen", "Pigeon Cove", "Sails" and "Fish Market": Four,* all s., t., foxing, discoloration, good cond., est. $8/1,200, (12-04-92, Doyle, #147), largest 8 x 9⅞ in., (203 x 251 mm.), wood engraving.

$330* *"Promenade Along The East River",* s. Harry Shokler, good cond., edges wrinkled, (03-12-93, Skinner, #25, illus.), 10 x 15¼ in., (25.4 x 38.7 cm.), screenprint in colors on wove (BP 230, DM 549, FR 1868, Y 38,892).

BI *"Promenade, Brooklyn Heights", 1943,* s., excell. cond., est. $3/500, (05-15-93, Cleveland, #295, illus.), 10 x 15½ in., (25.4 x 39.4 cm.), silkscreen.

SHOKOSAI HANBEI   Japanese ac. 1795-1809
$4551* *Shibai Gakuya Zue "Pictures Of The Theatre Green Rooms"*, d. Kansei 12 (1800), 2 vols., stained, Prof. H.R.W. Kuhne Coll., (06-11-93, Sotheby-London, #531, illus.), 10 x 7 in., (25.4 x 17.8 cm.), woodblock, p. in b/w (BP 2990, DM 7396, FR 24,937, Y 482,865).

SHORE, Henrietta   American 1880-1963
BI *"The Old Well"*, s. Henrietta Shore, good cond., est. $3/ 400, (11-21-92, Bakker, #119), 16 x 12 in., (40.6 x 30.5 cm.), lithograph.

SHORT, Sir Frank   English 1857-1945
$79 *"On The River Bure?, Norfolk"*, s., (06-11-93, G.A. Key, #113), 10 x 16 in., (25.4 x 40.6 cm.), b/w aquatint (BP 52, DM 128, FR 433, Y 8382).
$1201* *"Shap Fells", "Cottage And Harvesters", "Nithsdale", "Moonrise Ramsgate", "The Thames At Twickenham", "A Silver Tide" and others* (HARDIE 77; 88; 110l 121; 161; 162; 165; 209; 210; 269 and 396 and 399 On One Sheet) 1920-1920, each s., margins, good cond., (06-30-93, Sotheby-London, #325, illus.), eleven, four mezzotints, three aquatints,, three etchings, and a lithograph (BP 805, DM 2048, FR 6910, Y 128,683).

SHOSON, Ohara   1877-1945
$2014* *Bildnis Eines Kormorans*, lit., s., (04-27-93, Dorotheum, #207, illus.), 10⅝ x 17⁵⁄₁₆ in., (27 x 44 cm.), woodcut (BP 1281, DM 3189, FR 10,787, Y 225,709, SC 22,400).
$72* *Carp*, (10-11-92, Hanzel, #956), 13½ x 5½ in., (34.3 x 14 cm.), color woodblock print (BP 43, DM 107, FR 359, Y 8766).
$201* *Habich Auf Einem Ast*, (04-27-93, Dorotheum, #199, illus.), 7½ x 13¹¹⁄₁₆ in., (19 x 34.7 cm.), color woodcut (BP 128, DM 318, FR 1077, Y 22,526, SC 2240).
BI *Segelboote In Der Abenddammerung*, s., est. SC 14/ 16,000, (04-27-93, Dorotheum, #203, illus.), 10⅜ x 8³⁄₁₆ in., (26.3 x 20.8 cm.), color woodcut.

SHOTEI   Japanese
$33* *"Rooster, Hen And Chick"*, 20th cent., (06-11-93, DuMouchelle, #2365), 7 x 9¾ in., (17.8 x 24.8 cm.), color woodblock print (BP 22, DM 54, FR 181, Y 3501).

SHOULBERG, Harry   American b. 1903
$135* *"The Bridge"*, s., t., #67/100, (05-15-93, Cleveland, #296), 8¾ x 10⅞ in., (22.2 x 27.6 cm.), color silkscreen on MBM Special paper (BP 88, DM 217, FR 730, Y 14,965).

SHRADER, R. Owen
$2588* *"Sand Expanse"*, mid-1930's, mounted, labels, (04-06-93, Sotheby-NY, #185, illus.), 10¼ x 13⅛ in., photograph (BP 1709, DM 4169, FR 14,119, Y 295,164).
BI *"Wind Work"*, c. 1933, mounted, s., t. by photog., i., studio stamp, labels, est. $2/2,500, (04-06-93, Sotheby-NY, #184, illus.), 13¼ x 10⅜ in., photograph, silver bromide print.

SHRANZ, Paul R.   American 20th cent.
$44* *Garage Doors*, 1976, s., (05-16-93, Hindman, #371), 9¾ x 10 in., photograph, silver print (BP 29, DM 71, FR 239, Y 4900).

SHTERENBERG, Abram
$1725* *The Kazak Poet, Dzhambul Dzhabayev, 1930's*, s. by photog., (04-06-93, Sotheby-NY, #318, illus.), 12⅞ x 10½ in., photograph (BP 1139, DM 2779, FR 9411, Y 196,738).
BI *Portrait, c. 1930*, s., est. $3/5,000, (04-08-93, Christie-NY, #155, illus.), 19½ x 17¼ in., (49.5 x 43.8 cm.), photograph, gelatin silver print.

SHTERENBERG, Abram   1894-1979
BI *Portrait*, 1920s, ink s., est. $2,2/2,800, (04-08-93, Christie-NY, #154, illus.), 15¼ x 10½ in., (38.7 x 26.7 cm.), photograph, gelatin silver print.

SHUNBAISAI HOKUEI   Japanese ac. c. 1824-1837, d. 1837
BI *Various Actors: Seven*, Oban, s. Shunkosai/Shunbaisai Hokuei ga, pub.'s marks Tenki, Honsei and Wataki, d. c. 1832-34, mixed cond., Prof. H.R.W. Kuhne Coll., est. BP 7/900, (06-11-93, Sotheby-London, #468), woodblock.

SHUNCHO, Katsukawa   ac. 1770-1800
$302* *Bildnis Zweier Damen Und Einer Dienerin Zwischen Bluhenden Baumengedunkelt*, Chuban format, darkened, (04-27-93, Dorotheum, #229), 7½ x 10¹⁄₁₆ in., (19 x 25.5 cm.), (BP 192, DM 478, FR 1618, Y 33,845, SC 3360).

SHUNK, Harry   20th cent.
BI *Yves Klein, 1991: Seven*, complete set, s., #10/49, pub. Ed. Kunsthalle Basel, good cond., orig. portfolio box, est. G 6/8,000, (12-09-92, Sotheby-Amstrdm, #641, illus.), each sheet approx. 16⅛ x 20⅞ in., (410 x 530 mm.), photograph.

SHUNKO
$1669* *The Actor Otani Hiroemon*, hosoban, s. Shunko ga, oxidized, wormed, stained, laid-down, (06-10-93, Sotheby-London, #223, illus.), (BP 1092, DM 2718, FR 9150, Y 177,157).
$2989* *The Actor Otani Hiroji III Standing Beneath A Stone Torii*, hosoban, s. Shunko ga, wormed, laid-down, (06-10-93, Sotheby-London, #220), (BP 1955, DM 4867, FR 16,387, Y 317,270).

SHUNKOSAI HOKUSHU   Japanese ac. c. 1809-1842
$1137* *Arashi Kichizaburo II As Sasaki Tan'emon And Nakamura Daikichi I As His Wife Sasao: Four*, Oban, s. Khunko/sai ga, pub.'s marks Shiocho and Honsei, d. 1811, 1814, 1816 and 1817, mixed cond., Prof. H.R.W. Kuhne Coll., (06-11-93, Sotheby-London, #458), woodblock (BP 747, DM 1848, FR 6230, Y 120,637).
$1487* *The Bust-Portrait Of Arashi Kitsusaburo As The Warrior Sasaki Takatsuna: Two*, Oban, s. Shunkosai Hokushu ga, pub.'s mark Honsei, d. Bunsei 4 (1821), soiled, rubbed, trimmed, laid down, Prof. H.R.W. Kuhne Coll., (06-11-93, Sotheby-London, #457), one 14⅞ x 10¼ in., (37.8 x 26 cm.), other 14¾ x 9⅝ in., (37.8 x 26 cm.), woodblock (BP 977, DM 2417, FR 8148, Y 157,772).
$2100* *Bust-Portrait Of Sawamura Kunitaro As The Fox-Woman, Kuzunoha: Two*, Oban, s. Shunkosai Hokushu ga, pub. Rikuraya Shinpei, d. Bunsei 7 (1824), rubbed, soiled, Prof. H.R.W. Kuhne Coll., (06-11-93, Sotheby-London, #467, illus.), each approx. 14¾ x 10 in., (37.5 x 25.4 cm.), woodblock (BP 1380, DM 3413, FR 11,507, Y 222,812).
BI *The Head And Shoulders Of Bando Mitsugoro III And Onoe Matsue III AsLadies In Court Service*, Oban, s. Shunkosai Hokushu ga, pub.'s mark Wataya Kihei, d. Bunsei 4(1821), rubbed, soiled, Prof. H.R.W. Kuhne Coll., est. BP 1,2/1,600, (06-11-93, Sotheby-London, #465, illus.), 15⅛ x 10⅜ in., (38.4 x 26.4 cm.), woodblock.
$1400* *"Matsumoto Koshiro V As Nikki Danjo" and "Nakamura Utaemon III As Arajishi Otokonosuke": Seven*, Oban, s. Shunkosai Hokushu ga and Seiyosai Shunshi ga, pub.'s mark Rikuraya Shinpei, Tenmanya Kihei, Honsei and Wataya Kihei, d. 1821-23, mixed cond., Prof. H.R.W. Kuhne Coll., (06-11-93, Sotheby-London, #461, illus.), woodblock (BP 920, DM 2275, FR 7671, Y 148,541).
$2100* *Nakamura Utaemon III As Osono*, Oban, s. Shunkosai Hokushu ga w/seal Hokushu, pub.'s mark Naniwa Akashido (red stamp), d. Bunsei 8 (1825), soiled, creased, laid down, Prof. H.R.W.Kuhne Coll., (06-11-93, Sotheby-London, #466, illus.), 15 x 10⅛ in., (38.1 x 25.7 cm.), woodblock (BP 1380, DM 3413, FR 11,507, Y 222,812).
BI *Okubi-e Of Nakamura Utaemon III*, Oban, s. Shunkosai Hokushu ga w/seal Hokushu, engraver's seal Kasuke,d. Bunsei 3 (1820), creased, rubbed, thinned, Prof. H.R.W. Kuhne Coll., est. BP800/1,200, (06-11-93, Sotheby-London, #459, illus.), 14 x 9½ in., (35.6 x 24.1 cm.), woodblock, yellow ground.
$1487* *Various Plays: Nine*, Oban, s. Shunkosai Hokushu ga, pub.'s mark Rikuraya Shinpei and Tenmanya Kihei, d. 1823-26, soiled, rubbed, trimmed, laid down, Prof. H.R.W. Kuhne Coll., (06-11-93, Sotheby-London, #456), woodblock (BP 977, DM 2417, FR 8148, Y 157,772).

SHUNRO (KATSUSHIKA HOKUSAI)   Japanese 1760-1849
$4201* *Ichikawa Komazo II And Osagawa Tsuneyo II*, Hosoban, s. Shunro ga, d. Kansei 3 (1791), trimmed, Prof. H.R.W. Kuhne Coll., (06-11-93, Sotheby-London, #240, illus.), 12

x 5⅜ in., (30.5 x 13.7 cm.), woodblock (BP 2760, DM 6828, FR 23,019, Y 445,729).

$22,754* *Interior Of A Theatre With A Play In Progress,* Oban yoko-e, s. Katsu Shunro ga, d. Tenmei 8 (1788), pub. Eijudo Nishimura Yohachi, soiled, creased, wormage, Prof. H.R.W. Kuhne Coll., (06-11-93, Sotheby-London, #271, illus.), 10¼ x 15¼ in., (26 x 38.7 cm.), woodblock (BP 14,950, DM 36,980, FR 124,679, Y 2,414,218).

$1925* *Nakayama Tomisaburo As Kakusaburo's Wife Izayoi,* Hosoban, s. Shunro ga, darkened, wormage restored, pub. Tsutaya Juzaburo, d. 1780-1793, Prof. H.R.W. Kuhne Coll., (06-11-93, Sotheby-London, #265, illus.), 11½ x 5 in., (29.2 x 12.7 cm.), woodblock (BP 1265, DM 3129, FR 10,548, Y 204,244).

SHUNSEN, Katsukawa   Japanese 1762-1830
    BI *Mother And Child With Dog,* est. $250/350, (02-04-93, Sloan, #943), 13½ x 9¼ in., (34.3 x 23.5 cm.), color woodcut.

SICHELBARTH, P. Ignatius   Continental 18th cent.
    $116* *Fou-te Lieutenant De Tchow-Hoei Poursuit Amou-vsana...,* (12-10-92, Sloan, #1016), sight 10¼ x 16¾ in., (26 x 42.5 cm.), engraving (BP 75, DM 183, FR 627, Y 14,349).

SICHEM, Christoffel van (I)
    $1023* *Judith With The Head Of Holofernes (B. III, 1; Holl. 131),* after Hendrik Goltzius, without tone block, trimmed on borderline, thin spot in image, foxing, good cond., ex-coll., (12-03-92, Sotheby-London, #142), 5¼ x 4 in., (133 x 103 mm.), woodcut (BP 660, DM 1609, FR 5491, Y 127,286).

SICHEM, Christoffel van (the elder)   Dutch 1546-1624
    $302* *Portrait De Bernardus Baldus (Holl., vol. 27, 143), 1577,* text verso, (05-15-93, Loudmer, #100, illus.), 7¹¹⁄₁₆ x 5¾ in., (196 x 146 mm.), wood engraving on laid (BP 196, DM 486, FR 1632, Y 33,477).

SICHEM, Karel (attrib.)   Dutch d. after 1604
    $550* *Robert Dudley, Earl Of Leicester,* (10-08-92, Grogan, #643B), 7⅜ x 5⅝ in., (18.7 x 14.3 cm.), engraving (BP 327, DM 813, FR 2761, Y 66,829).

SICILIA, Jose Maria   b. Spain 1954
    BI *Fleur Rouge II, 1988,* s., d., t., #7/25, blindstamp pub. Crown Point Press, full margins, very good cond., est. $5/700, (10-28-92, Butterfield, #3120), 17⅞ x 11⅞ in., (454 x 302 mm.), color aquatint w/Chine colle (pasted) on Somerset Satin wove.

SICKERT, Walter Richard   English 1860-1942
    $3432* *Noctes Ambrosianae (Troyen 46), 1906,* 2nd final state, full margins, good cond., (06-30-93, Sotheby-London, #327, illus.), sh c. 10¾ x 12⅛ in., (273 x 308 mm.), etching w/aquatint on laid (BP 2300, DM 5854, FR 19,747, Y 367,727).

SIDEL, Harry
    $247* *Approximately 150 Black And White Negatives, Contact Prints, Color Negatives And Kodachromes Of Sidel's Fashion And Advertising Work For Vogue, AndHarper's Baazar,* 1940s-50s, (04-07-93, Swann, #550, illus.), 5 x 7 in., photograph, b/w and color neg., contact prints and kodachromes (BP 163, DM 399, FR 1352, Y 28,062).

SIEFF, Jeanloup   French b. 1933
    $436* *"Chinatown New York 1964",* p.l., s., d., t., d., stamped photog.'s credit, num. 1, pub., 402 x 304mm, (05-07-93, Sotheby-London, #348, illus.), photograph, silver print (BP 276, DM 689, FR 2323, Y 48,007).

    $671* *"Death Valley",* 1977, p.l., s., d., stamped photog.'s credit, t., d., 405 x 305mm, (05-07-93, Sotheby-London, #346, illus.), photograph, silver print (BP 425, DM 1061, FR 3575, Y 73,882).

    $472* *Jill Kinnington,* 1964, p.l., s., d., stamped photog.'s credit, 405 x 304mm, (05-07-93, Sotheby-London, #345, illus.), photograph, silver print (BP 299, DM 746, FR 2515, Y 51,971).

    $660* *"Nu Pompier, Paris",* 1956, ink s., d., t., photog. stamp, (11-16-92, Butterfield, #6162, illus.), 11¼ x 11¼ in., (286.3 x 286.3 mm.), photograph, gelatin silver print (BP 435, DM 1052, FR 3545, Y 82,079).

    BI *"Paloma Picasso, Paris",* 1986, s., t., d., photog. stamp, est. $6/800, (11-16-92, Butterfield, #6161, illus.), 14 x 13⅞ in., (356.2 x 353.1 mm.), photograph, gelatin silver print.

    $618* *"Portrait Of Judy, New York 1964",* p.l., s., d., t., d., stamped photog.'s credit, num., 406 x 302mm, (05-07-93, Sotheby-London, #347, illus.), photograph, silver print (BP 391, DM 977, FR 3292, Y 68,047).

SIEGEL, Arthur   1913-1978
    BI *Haberdashery Shop, State Street, c. 1937,* s., inits., est. $2/3,000, (10-13-92, Christie-NY, #355, illus.), 10⅜ x 9¼ in., (26.4 x 23.5 cm.), photograph, gelatin silver print.

    BI *Right Of Assembly,* (1939), 1977, s., inits., d., annot., lit., est. $2/3,000, (10-13-92, Christie-NY, #356, illus.), 16⅝ x 13⅝ in., (42.2 x 34.6 cm.), photograph, gelatin silver print.

    BI *"Right Of Assembly",* s. Adam Siegel, 1939, p. 1977, est. $2,5/3,500, (04-06-93, Sotheby-NY, #128A, illus.), 16½ x 13½ in., photograph.

    $3220* *Right Of Assembly, 1939,* s., d., init., annot., lit., (04-08-93, Christie-NY, #332, illus.), 4¾ x 3¾ in., (12.1 x 9.5 cm.), photograph, gelatin silver print (BP 2111, DM 5173, FR 17,510, Y 365,411).

    $2875* *Untitled (Nude), 1937,* s., d. by Adam Siegel, (04-06-93, Sotheby-NY, #128, illus.), 11⅜ x 9½ in., photograph (BP 1899, DM 4632, FR 15,685, Y 327,897).

SIEMIANOWSKI, Roman   b. 1915
    BI *Rex-Flex Straight Wall Tubing, 1948,* t., d. in ink, credit stamps, est. $1/1,500, (10-13-92, Christie-NY, #485, illus.), 9¼ x 7¼ in., (23.5 x 18.4 cm.), photograph, gelatin silver print.

SIERHUIS, Jan
    $192* *Untitled, 1968,* s., d., i. 4/10 epreuve de artiste, full sheet, good cond., minor handling creases; rubbing verso, (05-27-93, Sotheby-Amstrdm, #685), sheet 21⅞ x 29¾ in., (556 x 755 mm.), color lithograph on wove (BP 123, DM 308, FR 1038, Y 20,583, G 345).

SIGNAC, Paul   French 1863-1935
    $9545* *Les Andelys, Am Unterlauf Der Seine (Kornf.-W. 10/II), 1896-1898,* (06-23-93, Kornfeld, #786, illus.), color lithograph on Chine volant (BP 6484, DM 16,151, FR 54,326, Y 1,039,874, SF 14,375).

    $1610* *Application Du Cercle Chromatique De Mr Ch. Henry (Kornfeld/Wick 4),1888,* p. Eugene Verneau, p. as theatre program for the Theatre Libre, goodcond., crease, tear, (05-13-93, Sotheby-NY, #827), 6⅜ x 7⅛ in., (161 x 181 mm.), lithograph in colors on stiff wove (BP 1057, DM 2600, FR 8769, Y 179,748).

    $8400* *La Balise. - En Hollande. - Flessingue (Kornfeld-Wick 7/II/b), 1897-1898,* s., (06-23-93, Kornfeld, #785, illus.), etching on thick wove (BP 5707, DM 14,213, FR 47,809, Y 915,132, SF 12,650).

    BI *Les Bateaux (E.W.K. et P.A.W. 13), 1895,* #31/40, s., large margins, (06-11-93, Picard, #166), 9⁵⁄₁₆ x 15¹¹⁄₁₆ in., (237 x 398 mm.), color lithograph on thin wove.

    $12,218* *Les Bateaux (Kornf.-W. 13/III), 1896-1898,* s. in green pencil, (06-23-93, Kornfeld, #787, illus.), color lithograph on thick wove (BP 8300, DM 20,673, FR 69,539, Y 1,331,082, SF 18,400).

    $33,477* *La Bouee. - Saint Tropez, Le Port (Kornfeld-Wick 9/II), 1897-1898,* s. Paul Signac, (06-25-93, Kornfeld, #130, illus.), image, mit Remarque 17³⁄₁₆ x 13¾ in., color lithograph on light yellowish vellum (BP 22,643, DM 56,992, FR 191,955, Y 3,548,548, SF 50,600).

    $8392* *La Bouee. Saint-Tropez Le Port (E.W. Kornfeld et P.A. Wick 9), 1894,* #38/40, w/out margins, (06-11-93, Picard, #164), 15⅞ x 12¾ in., (403 x 324 mm.), color lithograph on thin chine (BP 5514, DM 13,639, FR 45,984, Y 890,398).

    $8018* *Le Clocher De Saint - Tropez, Avec Personnages Sur Le Quai (Kornf.-W. 18/b), Um 1896,* s. in pencil, 15 ep./N. 11, (06-23-93, Kornfeld, #789, illus.), etching on handmade (BP 5447, DM 13,567, FR 45,635, Y 873,516, SF 12,075).

    $8247* *Le Clocher De Saint-Tropez (Kornf.-W. 17/III/b), c. 1896,* s., 15 ep./No. 9, (06-23-93, Kornfeld, #788, illus.), line etching and aquatint on handmade (BP 5603, DM 13,954, FR 46,938, Y 898,464, SF 12,420).

$11,989* *A Flessingue (E.W.K. et P.A. W. 11), 1895,* num. 27, s., red stamp, creases, large margins, (06-11-93, Picard, #165, illus.), 9⁵⁄₁₆ x 15¹⁵⁄₁₆ in., (237 x 405 mm.), color lithograph on thin wove (BP 7877, DM 19,485, FR 65,693, Y 1,272,042).

BI *A Flessingue (K. & W. 11), 1895,* 2nd state of 3, s., #13 by publisher, his paraph and stamp, remarque,full margins, good cond., mount-staining, handling marks, est. BP 12/14,000, (06-30-93, Sotheby-London, #683, illus.), 9⅜ x 16 in., (238 x 406 mm.), lithograph in color.

$913* *Paris. Le Pont Des Arts Avec Remorqueurs (Kornfeld/ Wick 24), c. 1927,* num., (12-01-92, Karl/Faber, #1247), 4¹⁵⁄₁₆ x 7½ in., (12.5 x 19 cm.), etching and aquatint on Japan (BP 603, DM 1455, FR 4959, Y 113,670).

$532* *"Paris: Le Point Des Arts Avec Remorqueurs" (Kornfeld 24), c. 1927,* (06-08-93, Karl/Faber, #1315), approx. 4¹⁵⁄₁₆ x 7½ in., (12.5 x 19 cm.), etching and aquatint on Japan (BP 350, DM 863, FR 2907, Y 56,506).

BI *"Le Pont Des Art Avec Remorqueur-1927" (KW24),* s. in plate, est. FF1,000/1,500, (04-04-93, Pescheteau, #293), 4¾ x 7¹⁄₁₆ in., (12 x 18 cm.), etching on wove.

$30,884* *Saint Tropez: Le Port (Kornfeld and Wick 19), 1897-1898,* s., #No 88, full margins, good cond., handling marks, creases, ex coll. Heinrich Neuerburg (L. 1344a), est. BP 18/20,000, (06-30-93, Sotheby-London, #684, illus.), sh 20½ x 16 in., (521 x 406 mm.), color lithograph on fine wove (BP 20,700, DM 52,676, FR 177,699, Y 3,309,118).

$23,163* *Saint-Tropez II (K. & W. 6), 1894,* s., pub. in L'Estampe Originale, blindstamp, full margins, good cond., foxing, light-staining, (06-30-93, Sotheby-London, #682, illus.), 10¾ x 14½ in., (273 x 368 mm.), lithograph in color (BP 15,525, DM 39,507, FR 133,274, Y 2,481,839).

$23,100* *Saint-Tropez: Le Port (Kornfedl/Wick 19/b; Johnson 138), 1897-98,* s., i. No. 95, full margins, good cond., mat/ light stain, Mollie Parnis Livingston Estate, (11-05-92, Sotheby-NY, #444, illus.), 17⅛ x 13 in., (435 x 330 mm.), lithograph p. in colors (BP 15,024, DM 36,533, FR 123,596, Y 2,834,008).

$2200* *La Seine En Crue (Kornfeld 23), 1923,* watermark, s., full margins, light-staining, foxing, good cond., (11-09-92, Christie-NY, #205, illus.), 6 x 8¾ in., (152 x 222 mm.), lithograph on laid (BP 1455, DM 3512, FR 11,866, Y 273,021).

$1059* *La Seine En Crue (Kornfeld-Wick 23 II), 1910,* s., (06-10-93, Hauswedell/Nolt, #921, illus.), image 5⅞ x 8⅞ in., (15 x 22.5 cm.), lithograph on hand-made (BP 693, DM 1724, FR 5806, Y 112,408).

$382* *La Seine En Crue, En 1910. - Le Pont Des Arts (Kornf.-W. 23/I), 1923,* litho sig., (06-23-93, Kornfeld, #790), lithograph (BP 260, DM 646, FR 2174, Y 41,617, SF 575).

$1201* *Le Soir (Abend) (Kornfeld 20 d), 1898,* (06-10-93, Hauswedell/Nolt, #920), image 7¹⁵⁄₁₆ x 10¼ in., (20.2 x 26.1 cm.), color lithograph (BP 786, DM 1956, FR 6584, Y 127,481).

SIGNOVERT, Jean 1919-1981

BI *Composition, 1973,* s., d., #19/50, large margins, (05-06-93, Laurin, #81), color lithograph on wove.

$147* *"Ma Chimere-1970",* first impression, d., s., (01-28-93, Pescheteau, #251), a vue 11¼ x 8⅞ in., (28.5 x 22.5 cm.), etching and aquatint on wove (BP 97, DM 233, FR 788, Y 18,252).

SIGON, R.

$247* *Assicurazioni Generali, 1934,* Grafiche Trieste Modiano, A- cond., closed tears, chip(08-06-92, Swann, #256, illus.), 39 x 27½ in., (99.1 x 69.9 cm.), (BP 129, DM 365, FR 1233, Y 31,505).

SILBERBAUER, Fritz Austrian b. 1883

$303* *"Der Tor Und Der Tod": Ten,* portfolio, each s., very good cond., (09-27-92, Bakker, #191), image, each approx. 10 x 7 in., (25.4 x 17.8 cm.), color engraving on tissue (BP 177, DM 449, FR 1519, Y 36,572).

SILBERGER, Manuel American 20th cent.

$70* *Untitled, 1933,* s., d., light struck, taped, (05-15-93, Cleveland, #297, illus.), 5½ x 5¾ in., (14 x 14.6 cm.), lithograph (BP 46, DM 113, FR 378, Y 7760).

SILBERSTEIN, Bernard G.

$1650* *"Portrait Of Diego Rivera", "Diego Rivera With Frida Kahlo", and "Jose Clemente Orozco Painting A Mural", 1940: Three,* handstamp, s., sig. verso, (10-14-92, Swann, #516, illus.), 9½ x 8 in., (24.1 x 20.3 cm.), photograph, silver prints (BP 968, DM 2415, FR 8189, Y 199,952).

SILVESTRE, Israel

BI *Second Journee (Le Blanc 772), 1664,* from Fetes donnees a Versailles, 3rd (final) state, w/privilege added, watermark, trimmed, crease, losses, platemark, fox marks, good cond., est. $700/1,000, (05-13-93, Sotheby-NY, #340), 11⅛ x 16¾ in., (283 x 427 mm.), etching.

SIM

$545* *La Bourboule, Source Choussy Perriere, c. 1900,* good cond., (01-23-93, Ribeyre/Baron, #91), 59¹⁄₁₆ x 43⁵⁄₁₆ in., (150 x 110 cm.), poster (BP 357, DM 867, FR 2932, Y 68,210).

SIMBARI, Nicola Italian b. 1927

$40* *"Couple On Beach", 1962,* s., d., good cond., (05-15-93, Cleveland, #492), 16⅝ x 22⅞ in., (42.2 x 58.1 cm.), color lithograph (BP 26, DM 64, FR 216, Y 4434).

BI *Couple On Beach, 1962,* s., d., good cond., est. $250-350, (10-31-92, Cleveland, #396), 16⅝ x 23 in., (42.2 x 58.4 cm.), color lithograph.

$880* *"L'Escalier",* edit. #259/300, s., (09-18-92, DuMouchelle, #2030), 37½ x 25 in., (95.3 x 63.5 cm.), silkscreen (BP 506, DM 1318, FR 4513, Y 109,644).

BI *"L'Escalier",* s., #215/300, est. $6/800, (06-24-93, Boos, #623), sight 37⅜ x 25³⁄₁₆ in., (950 x 640 mm.), serigraph.

$770* *"Marco",* edit. #61/300, s., (09-18-92, DuMouchelle, #2029), 28½ x 31¼ in., (72.4 x 79.4 cm.), silkscreen (BP 443, DM 1153, FR 3949, Y 95,938).

BI *"Taormina",* edit. #65/300, s., est. $1,5/2,500, (09-18-92, DuMouchelle, #2028), 35¼ x 36 in., (89.5 x 91.4 cm.), silkscreen.

SIMEON, Dwayne

$22* *"When The Eagle Lands On The Moon", 1992,* (03-10-93, Maynard, #317), print (BP 15, DM 37, FR 124, Y 2599, C$ 28).

SIMEONI

$517* *Saint Louis Blues, De A. Reisner, Avec Nat King Cole, Eartha Kitt, Cab Calloway (Italian), 1958,* (01-31-93, Morelle/Marchan, #92), 39⅜ x 55⅛ in., (100 x 140 cm.), poster (BP 348, DM 833, FR 2816, Y 64,496).

SIMMONS, Laurie b. 1949

BI *Talking Gardening Glove (Madame Pinxy's),* exec. 1987, prov., est. $7/10,000, (02-24-93, Christie-NY, #120, illus.), 63⅞ x 47⅞ in., (162.2 x 121.6 cm.), photograph, color.

$8800* *Walking Hourglass,* s., num., d. Laurie Simmons 4/5 1989 on cardboard backing, prov., (11-19-92, Christie-NY, #154, illus.), 84 x 47¹⁵⁄₁₆ in., (213.4 x 121.9 cm.), photograph, b/w in artist's frame (BP 5794, DM 14,031, FR 47,261, Y 1,094,391).

SIMMONS, W.H.

$180* *The Bible, 1864,* after Thomas Jones Barker, pub. Robert Turner, margins, staining, (10-15-92, Bonhams-Chelsea, #139), plate 25¾ x 30½ in., (65.4 x 77.5 cm.), mezzotint (BP 110, DM 268, FR 909, Y 21,596).

BI *Scene From The Early Life Of Oliver Goldsmith,* after E.M. Ward, est. $2/300, (02-11-93, Boos, #476), sight 17¾ x 22¾ in., (451 x 578 mm.), engraving.

SIMMONS, Will

BI *Ducks Take Flight,* s., margins, good cond., mat burn, foxing, Florence Berryman Estate,est. $3/400, (12-12-92, Weschler, #167), 12 x 7½ in., (30.5 x 19.1 cm.), etching and aquatint.

SIMON, Garrett American contemporary

BI *Dirty Money,* s., #10/80, t., i., est. 125/175, (07-03-92, Sloan, #286), 12⅞ x 19¾ in., (32.7 x 50.2 cm.), soft ground etching and aquatint.

SIMON, H.

$167* *Chemins De Fer De L'Etat: Les Plus Belles Plages De Vendee, Sion-Sur-L'Ocean, St-Gilles-Sur-Vie, Croix De Vie,* c. 1930, good cond., (01-23-93, Ribeyre/Baron, #68), 39⅜ x 24³/₁₆ in., (100 x 61.5 cm.), poster (BP 109, DM 266, FR 898, Y 20,901).

SIMON, Howard   American 1902-1979

BI   *"At The Bar", "Bacchnalian Feast" and "Giant At Notre Dame": Three,* s., first d. 1929; second #6/25; third #4/25; each full margins, good cond., foxing, toning, est. $3/500, (12-12-92, Weschler, #168), first 5¼ x 7 in., (13.3 x 17.8 cm.), second and third 11 x 7 in., (13.3 x 17.8 cm.), woodcut.

SIMON, Stella   1878-1973

BI   *"Church, Havanna, With Julian Levy And Louis Simon" and "Street SceneHavanna": Two,* est. $8/1,200, (10-14-92, Swann, #558, illus.), 17½ x 21½ in., (44.5 x 54.6 cm.), photograph, silver prints.

$748* *Havana Docks, 1925,* ink s. recto; ink t., d., authenticated, i., (04-08-93, Christie-NY, #333, illus.), 9⅝ x 7¼ in., (24.4 x 18.4 cm.), photograph, platinum print (BP 490, DM 1202, FR 4067, Y 84,884).

$805* *Lab Glass Abstraction, 1933,* s., d., credit, reprod. limitation stamps, (04-08-93, Christie-NY, #334, illus.), 9⅞ x 5 in., (25.1 x 12.7 cm.), photograph, gelatin silver print (BP 528, DM 1293, FR 4377, Y 91,353).

SIMON, T. Frantisek   Czechoslovakian 1877-1942

$165* *"Arch De Triumph",* s., (05-15-93, Dunning, #106), 13¼ x 14¼ in., (33.7 x 36.2 cm.), etching (BP 107, DM 265, FR 892, Y 18,291).

$165* *Bateaux Lavoir A Seine,* s., #41, bears artist's stamp, (03-14-93, Hindman, #262), 5¼ x 5½ in., (13.3 x 14 cm.), color soft-ground and aquatint (BP 115, DM 275, FR 934, Y 19,446).

$633* *"Belle Epoque Ladies",* annot., s., d. 16 F. Simon 06., (10-11-92, Dunning, #1525), etching and aquatint in colors (BP 376, DM 940, FR 3157, Y 77,064).

$154* *Book Stalls, Paris,* s., num. 260, Ruth K. Flower Coll., (04-18-93, Hindman, #1663), 12¼ x 15½ in., (31.1 x 39.4 cm.), color soft-ground etching (BP 101, DM 249, FR 841, Y 17,317).

$165* *"Bustling Street Scene",* num., s., artist's blind stamp, (05-15-93, Dunning, #210), 14 x 15½ in., (35.6 x 39.4 cm.), etching and aquatint in color (BP 107, DM 265, FR 892, Y 18,291).

$165* *Czechoslovakian Port Scene,* mono., d. 1919 in plate; s., mono., (07-03-92, Sloan, #1076), 12½ x 12 in., (31.8 x 30.5 cm.), color aquatint (BP 86, DM 250, FR 842, Y 20,568).

$165* *"Docked Boats",* s., (05-15-93, Dunning, #105), 18½ x 15½ in., (47 x 39.4 cm.), etching (BP 107, DM 265, FR 892, Y 18,291).

$160* *European City Scene,* plate mono., artist's mono. stamp, s., (05-20-93, Boos, #540), sight 12⅜ x 14¾ in., (315 x 375 mm.), etching (BP 103, DM 258, FR 870, Y 17,668).

$145* *"Marche Mauberts",* s., #272, good cond., toning, (05-15-93, Cleveland, #429), 12 x 15½ in., (30.5 x 39.4 cm.), soft-ground color etching and aquatint (BP 94, DM 233, FR 784, Y 16,074).

$176* *Paris Bookstalls,* s., #229/350, (11-01-92, Hanzel, #217), 12½ x 15¼ in., (31.8 x 38.7 cm.), colored etching (BP 115, DM 278, FR 936, Y 21,761).

$165* *"Parisian Street Scene",* num., s., (05-15-93, Dunning, #212), 13½ x 17 in., (34.3 x 43.2 cm.), etching and aquatint in color (BP 107, DM 265, FR 892, Y 18,291).

$165* *"Park In Winter",* s., num. 58, good cond.?, (02-07-93, Bakker, #32), image 12¾ x 13¾ in., (32.4 x 34.9 cm.), color lithograph and etching (BP 114, DM 274, FR 925, Y 20,533).

$28* *"Portrait Of A Gentleman", "Portrait Of A Lady" (1926) and "La Bollee" (1924): Three,* each s., two w/ chop, (09-17-92, Sloan, #1992), largest, sheet 8¾ x 11¾ in., (22.2 x 29.8 cm.), woodcut (BP 16, DM 42, FR 142, Y 3486).

$358* *The Sleighride,* s. T.F. Simon, good cond.?, (11-21-92, Bakker, #172, illus.), plate 13¼ x 15 in., (33.7 x 38.1

cm.), color etching (BP 236, DM 571, FR 1923, Y 44,522).

$660* *"Snow Scene", "Figures On A Beach", "Sleigh Through The Snow", and "Gntlemen On The Wharf": Four,* s., prop. Helen Kaiper Eckhart Trust, (05-16-93, Hindman, #455), each 10½ x 14½ in., (26.7 x 36.8 cm.), color etching (BP 429, DM 1062, FR 3568, Y 73,163).

$138* *"Street Scene",* s., (05-15-93, Dunning, #107, illus.), 13¼ x 17 in., (33.7 x 43.2 cm.), color etching (BP 90, DM 222, FR 746, Y 15,298).

$303* *Two Winter Scenes,* s., artist's stamp, one #13, (06-13-93, Hindman, #401), larger 10¾ x 14½ in., (27.3 x 36.8 cm.), each color soft ground and aquatint (BP 198, DM 493, FR 1658, Y 31,863).

$220* *Vente-Achat,* s., prop. Helen Kaiper Eckhart Trust, (05-16-93, Hindman, #457), 13½ x 16¼ in., (34.3 x 41.3 cm.), soft-ground etching (BP 143, DM 354, FR 1189, Y 24,388).

$110* *Vue De Seine And Porte St. Denis,* each s., first #174, second #245, (06-13-93, Hindman, #400), larger 12½ x 17⅞ in., (31.8 x 45.4 cm.), color aquatint (BP 72, DM 179, FR 602, Y 11,575).

$425* *Wall Street, New York, 1927,* s., good cond., (05-15-93, Cleveland, #430, illus.), 17¼ x 13 in., (43.8 x 33 cm.), soft-ground etching in color (BP 276, DM 684, FR 2297, Y 47,112).

$121* *"Winter Scene Along The Seine",* num., s., (05-15-93, Dunning, #209), 17 x 19½ in., (43.2 x 49.5 cm.), aquatint in color laid down (BP 79, DM 195, FR 654, Y 13,413).

$231* *"Winter Street Scene In Paris",* num., s., (05-15-93, Dunning, #211), 12½ x 16 in., (31.8 x 40.6 cm.), etching and aquatint in color (BP 150, DM 372, FR 1249, Y 25,607).

$198* *Woman Selling Art On The Left Bank,* prop. Helen Kaiper Eckhart Trust, (05-16-93, Hindman, #456), 10½ x 14½ in., (26.7 x 36.8 cm.), color etching (BP 129, DM 318, FR 1070, Y 21,949).

$154* *"Wooden Shoes For Sale",* artist's device, d. 1911, s. T.F. Simon, (02-27-93, Dunning, #1044), sight 12⅝ x 15¾ in., (32.1 x 40 cm.), color etching, aquatint and engraving (BP 108, DM 253, FR 860, Y 18,180).

SIMONAV, Gustave

$59* *"Cathedrale De Salisbury",* margins, (11-12-92, Bonhams-Chelsea, #50), image 24½ x 18⅝ in., (62.2 x 47.3 cm.), hand-colored lithograph (BP 39, DM 93, FR 315, Y 7316).

SIMONIDY, Nichel

$440* *Medieval Maiden,* d. March 1902, generally good cond., prop. Rod Stewart, (11-06-92, Sotheby-Arcade, #136), sight 21¾ x 17 in., (55.2 x 43.2 cm.), lithograph in black (BP 288, DM 703, FR 2375, Y 54,308).

SIMONNEAU, Charles   French 1645-1728

$574* *"La Duquesa De Orleans",* after Hyacinthe Rigaud, (12-17-92, Duran, #18, illus.), 18⅞ x 13¾ in., (48 x 35 cm.), etching (BP 364, DM 896, FR 3061, Y 70,542, P 63,250).

SIMPSON, Joseph

$33* *The Punt Gunner,* trial proof, 3rd state, s., margins, (06-30-93, Bonhams-Chelsea, #70), plate 8¼ x 11¾ in., (21 x 29.8 cm.), etching (BP 22, DM 56, FR 190, Y 3536).

SINCLAIR, James A.

BI   *Pictorial Photographs, 1919-1938: Thirteen,* s., t., d., mounted on card, est. BP 3/400, (05-06-93, Christie-London, #92), each approx. 5 x 7 in., photograph, photogravure print.

SINDELAR, Charles J.

$110* *"Hopi Girl At Spring",* s., good cond.?, (02-07-93, Bakker, #256), 10½ x 8¾ in., (26.7 x 22.2 cm.), etching (BP 76, DM 182, FR 617, Y 13,688).

SINDELAR, T.

$65   *Uncle Sam Needs That Extra Shovel Full,* Latham Litho. and Ptg. Co. Brooklyn, minor folds, (09-24-92, Alderfer, #255), 27¾ x 20 in., (70.5 x 50.8 cm.), (BP 38, DM 96, FR 327, Y 7819).

SINGER 20th cent.

BI *Austrian Square,* s. in plate, s., est. $200/250, (07-03-92, Sloan, #306), 7¾ x 13¼ in., (19.7 x 33.7 cm.), etching and aquatint.

SINGIER, Gustave French 1909-1984

BI *Andre Frederique. Traite Des Appareils (Fragments), 1957: Five,* #15/76, s., d., num., est. DM 1,500, (05-26-93, Lempertz, #491), 20¼ x $15\frac{11}{16}$ in., (51.5 x 39.8 cm.), color lithograph on Arches wove.

BI *Andre Frederique. Traite Des Appareils, 1957,* book, s., d., num. 11, w/t. page, text, just., num. 11, pub. Galeriede France, good cond., est. BP 7/1,000, (12-03-92, Sotheby-London, #795), six lithographs in colors on wove.

$137* *"Comopsition 1963",* d., s., (01-28-93, Pescheteau, #252), 28⅜ x $20\frac{1}{16}$ in., (72 x 51 cm.), color lithograph on Arches (BP 90, DM 217, FR 735, Y 17,010).

$202* *"Composition - 1962",* d., s., tear, (10-18-92, Pescheteau, #260), $19\frac{11}{16}$ x $25\frac{9}{16}$ in., (76 x 56 cm.), lithograph in colors on Rives (BP 122, DM 298, FR 1014, Y 24,119).

$242* *"Composition",* #140/190, s., (01-28-93, Pescheteau, #253), $25\frac{9}{16}$ x $19\frac{11}{16}$ in., (65 x 50 cm.), color lithograph on Arches (BP 160, DM 383, FR 1298, Y 30,047).

$225* *"Composition", 1966,* #65/100, s., d., (10-18-92, Pescheteau, #259), $19\frac{11}{16}$ x $25\frac{9}{16}$ in., (50 x 65 cm.), lithograph in colors on Arches (BP 136, DM 332, FR 1129, Y 26,866).

$193* *Composition, 1954,* s. G. Singier 54, (03-24-93, Kunsthallen, #304), color etching (BP 131, DM 315, FR 1073, Y 22,677, DK 1208).

$147* *Composition, 1958,* s. G. Singier 58, 1/150, (03-24-93, Kunsthallen, #305), color etching (BP 100, DM 240, FR 817, Y 17,272, DK 920).

BI *Composition, 1958,* s. G. Singier 58, 131/150, est. DK 1,800, (03-24-93, Kunsthallen, #299), color lithograph.

$147* *Composition, 1960,* s. G. Singier 60, Feuille de bon, (03-24-93, Kunsthallen, #303), color etching (BP 100, DM 240, FR 817, Y 17,272, DK 920).

$147* *Composition, 1960,* s. G. Singier 60, Feuille de bon, (03-24-93, Kunsthallen, #301), color etching (BP 100, DM 240, FR 817, Y 17,272, DK 920).

$147* *Composition, 1960,* s. G. Singier 60, Feuille de Bon, (03-24-93, Kunsthallen, #302), color etching (BP 100, DM 240, FR 817, Y 17,272, DK 920).

$236* *Composition, 1969,* E.A. VI/XXX, s., d., (10-14-92, Germann, #440, illus.), $29\frac{15}{16}$ x $22\frac{1}{16}$ in., (760 x 560 mm.), color lithograph (BP 139, DM 345, FR 1171, Y 28,599, SF 307).

$253* *Composition, 1973,* E.A., s., d., (10-14-92, Germann, #439), $21\frac{1}{16}$ x $29\frac{15}{16}$ in., (535 x 760 mm.), color lithograph (BP 149, DM 370, FR 1256, Y 30,659, SF 330).

$113* *Composition, 1974,* s., d., #14/14, full margins, (05-06-93, Laurin, #82), color lithograph on Auvergne (BP 72, DM 178, FR 599, Y 12,433).

$257* *Compositioner, 1958,* s. G. Singier 58, 31/150, (03-24-93, Kunsthallen, #298), color lithograph (BP 174, DM 420, FR 1429, Y 30,196, DK 1610).

$193* *"L'Appareil De Maitre Gessner", 1957 and "Sans Titre", 1958,* first, s., d., B28/76; second, s., d. 11/8/175, drystamp, (06-28-93, Loudmer, #116), first 15⅜ x 12 in., (390 x 305 mm.), second $17\frac{15}{16}$ x $14\frac{3}{16}$ in., (390 x 305 mm.), color lithographs first, on wove; second, on BFK Rives wove (BP 129, DM 328, FR 1105, Y 20,477).

BI *Nereides Lune, 1967,* s., #44/85, watermark, est. DM 700, (05-26-93, Lempertz, #492), sh 22¼ x $14\frac{15}{16}$ in., (56.5 x 38 cm.), color etching on a Doppelbogen wove.

$435* *Provence Grande Lumiere, 1958,* #17/150, s., blindstamp, (04-21-93, Germann, #764), $19\frac{5}{16}$ x 27¾ in., (490 x 705 mm.), color lithograph (BP 282, DM 695, FR 2351, Y 48,157, SF 633).

BI *S.l., s.n., s.d., 1948: Eighteen,* from Quatrains by Camille Bourniquel, frontispiece, s., num., d. 1948, s. Singier in colophon, est. SF 1,5/2,000, book, (11-15-92, Christie-Geneva, #314), $13\frac{1}{16}$ x $10\frac{5}{16}$ in., (332 x 262 mm.), copper engraving.

$1278* *Untitled: Series Of Seven,* s., very good cond., (03-31-93, Briest, #E194), color lithographs (BP 845, DM 2056, FR 6984, Y 146,964).

SINGLETON, G. (after)

$94 *An Unwelcome Proposal,* engraved H. Mitchell, (12-11-92, G.A. Key, #3), 11 x 14 in., (27.9 x 35.6 cm.), colored stipple engraving (BP 60, DM 148, FR 508, Y 11,632).

SINGLETON, Henry (after)

BI *The Mysteries Of Udolpho, 1796,* by William Bond, pub. William Bond, foxed, repaired tears, paper losses, trimmed to margins, est. BP 1/150, (11-30-92, Phillips-London, #222), sheet 22⅞ x 17¾ in., (581 x 451 mm.), color stipple engraving on wove.

SINSABAUGH, Art 1924-1983

$1100* *Arizona Cliff Dwelling, 1980,* i., d. Ariz 26, (10-13-92, Christie-NY, #601, illus.), 11¾ x 19¼ in., (29.8 x 48.9 cm.), photograph, gelatin silver print (BP 641, DM 1611, FR 5475, Y 133,382).

SINTENIS, Renee German 1888-1965

$233* *Drei Grasande Pferde,* s., (09-25-92, Granier, #3016), sheet $9\frac{13}{16}$ x 14¾ in., (25 x 37.5 cm.), etching on handmade (BP 136, DM 345, FR 1168, Y 28,123).

BI *Liegendes Reh, 1948,* s., est. DM 1,000, (05-26-93, Lempertz, #495), $17\frac{15}{16}$ x 12½ in., (45.5 x 31.7 cm.), etching (drypoint) on wove.

BI *Schlafender Hund Im Korb,* s., est. DM. 350, (12-05-92, Bassenge, #7730), $8\frac{11}{16}$ x $6\frac{11}{16}$ in., (22 x 17 cm.), etching on wove.

$253* *Stehendes Fohlen,* s., (11-28-92, Grisebach, #756, illus.), $8\frac{9}{16}$ x 6½ in., (21.7 x 16.5 cm.), woodcut on wove (BP 167, DM 403, FR 1368, Y 31,487).

$1083* *Terrier Oskar: Four,* s., ded., (11-28-92, Grisebach, #758, illus.), 5⅛ x $7\frac{1}{16}$ in., (13 x 18 cm.), drypoint on different white paper (BP 715, DM 1725, FR 5857, Y 134,785).

$1695* *Tiere, 1922: Twelve,* s., LXVII. Werk der Gurlitt-Presse, (06-10-93, Hauswedell/Nolt, #926), portfolio 15⅞ x $12\frac{3}{16}$ in., (40.4 x 31 cm.), drypoint on wove (BP 1109, DM 2760, FR 9293, Y 179,917).

$577* *Zwei Stehende Fohlen,* s., (11-28-92, Grisebach, #757, illus.), 8⅜ x $6\frac{9}{16}$ in., (21.2 x 16.7 cm.), woodcut on wove (BP 381, DM 919, FR 3121, Y 71,811).

$480* *Zwei Stehende Knaben, Sich Umarmend,* s., (12-05-92, Bassenge, #7729), $3\frac{9}{16}$ x 3⅜ in., (9 x 8.6 cm.), woodcut on handmade Japan (BP 301, DM 748, FR 2550, Y 59,472).

SIPPRELL, Clara

BI *Radio City, New York, 1931,* s., t., d., i., est. $1/1,500, (10-13-92, Christie-NY, #357, illus.), 9⅜ x 7¼ in., (23.8 x 18.4 cm.), photograph, platinum print on vellum.

$1150* *Still Life, early 1900's,* s. by photog., (04-06-93, Sotheby-NY, #72, illus.), 9⅛ x 7½ in., photograph (BP 760, DM 1853, FR 6274, Y 131,159).

SIQUEIROS, David Alfaro Mexican 1896/98-1974

BI *Cabeza, c. 1930,* s., #18/25, full margins, tears, yellowing, mat staining, est. $2/3,000, (11-23-92, Sotheby-NY, #282, illus.), image 16⅛ x 11 in., (410 x 280 mm.), lithograph.

BI *Cabeza, c. 1930,* s., s. crayon, #18/25, full margins, good cond., tears, yellowing, mat staining, est. $1/2,000, (05-18-93, Sotheby-NY, #270, illus.), image 16⅛ x 11 in., (410 x 279 mm.), lithograph.

$303* *El Cosonelazs, 1944,* s. in ink, p. by Lito Leosa, margins, apparently good cond., (02-24-93, Butterfield, #2670), 24¾ x 19 in., (629 x 483 mm.), photomechanical reprod. of painting p. in colors on wove (BP 211, DM 492, FR 1668, Y 35,555).

$660* *Dancer,* #XLVI/LXX, s., prov., (05-14-93, DuMouchelle, #2036, illus.), paper 22 x 15 in., (55.9 x 38.1 cm.), color lithograph (BP 429, DM 1062, FR 3568, Y 73,163).

$302* *Danseuse Braune, c. 1964,* i., s., (05-27-93, Swann, #252, illus.), sh 25¼ x 19¼ in., (64.1 x 48.9 cm.), color lithograph (BP 193, DM 485, FR 1633, Y 32,376).

BI *Desnudo Acostado, 1930,* #32/50, full margins, good cond., mat stain, yellowing, tape remains, creases, est. $2,5/3,500, (05-18-93, Sotheby-NY, #271, illus.), image 16⅜ x 22⅞ in., (416 x 581 mm.), lithograph.

$550* *Desnudo Acostado, 1931,* s., d. #E/E, full margins, excell. cond., (11-23-92, Sotheby-NY, #283, illus.), image 16⅛ x 22 in., (410 x 560 mm.), lithograph (BP 360, DM 881, FR 2988, Y 68,230).

BI *Desnudo Sentado, 1930,* s., d. #E/E, full margins, very good cond., soiling, est. $1/1,500, (11-23-92, Sotheby-NY, #284, illus.), image 21¼ x 12⅝ in., (540 x 320 mm.), lithograph.

$690* *Desnudo Sentado, 1930,* s., d., #33 EE/50, margins, good cond., staining, creases, soiling, glue remains, (05-19-93, Butterfield, #1847, illus.), 21 x 11¼ in., (533 x 286 mm.), lithograph on wove (BP 448, DM 1122, FR 3779, Y 76,387).

$660* *Desnudo Sentado, 1930,* s., d., num. 33EE/50, handling marks, (12-08-92, Swann, #277, illus.), image 21 x 13 in., (53.3 x 33 cm.), sheet 29⅜ x 21⅜ in., (53.3 x 33 cm.), lithograph (BP 414, DM 1028, FR 3503, Y 81,805).

$935* *"Fantasia De La Prision": Two,* #XXX/LXX, prov., (05-14-93, DuMouchelle, #2037), paper 22 x 15 in., (55.9 x 38.1 cm.), image 18 x 14 in., (55.9 x 38.1 cm.), color lithograph (BP 608, DM 1504, FR 5054, Y 103,647).

$330* *The Heroic Voice, 1971,* s., #88/125, blindstamp pub., full margins, good cond.?, surface soiling, crease, (10-28-92, Butterfield, #2568), 23 x 17⅞ in., (584 x 454 mm.), color lithograph on wove (BP 210, DM 510, FR 1730, Y 40,491).

$605* *Mother And Child,* s., #241/300, margins, good cond.?, (10-28-92, Butterfield, #2569), 21 x 15¾ in., (533 x 400 mm.), color lithograph pn cream wove (BP 385, DM 934, FR 3173, Y 74,233).

$770* *Perro Bravo, 1952,* ded., s., d. #E/E, good cond., creases, yellowing, glue stain, (11-23-92, Sotheby-NY, #281, illus.), image 11¾ x 8⅞ in., (300 x 226 mm.), lithograph (BP 503, DM 1233, FR 4183, Y 95,522).

$3300* *Siqueiros Portfolio: "Mask", "Explosive Landscape", "Mountainous Landscape", "Phosphorescent Volcano", "Jesusito Will Be A Saint", "Escape", "Amputated Christ", "Woman In Jail", "Aerial View", & "Self-Portrait", 1969: Ten,* complete portfolio, each s., anno. EA, pub. Touchstone Publishers, full margins, good cond., light-staining, tape remains, rubbed areas, crease, (02-24-93, Butterfield, #2671, illus.), each sheet 25½ x 19¾ in., (648.9 x 502.5 mm.), 10 lithographs in colors on Arches (BP 2301, DM 5357, FR 18,162, Y 387,233).

BI *Untitled: Three,* s., annot. XXI/XXV, full margins, good cond., surface soiling, skinned spots, est. $1,5/2,000, (10-28-92, Butterfield, #2570), each image 21 x 16½ in., (533 x 419 mm.), color lithograph on Japan paper.

BI *Untitled: Two,* s., annot. VII/XXV, full margins, good cond., est. $1/1,500, (10-28-92, Butterfield, #2571), 21¼ x 15⅝ in., (540 x 397 mm.), color lithoraph on Arches paper.

$275* *Waves,* s., annot. IX/XXV, good cond., water staining, surface soiling, (10-28-92, Butterfield, #2572), 23½ x 41 in., (59.7 x 104.1 cm.), lithograph on BFK Rives (BP 175, DM 425, FR 1442, Y 33,742).

$880* *Woman In Jail,* #97/250, prov., (05-14-93, DuMouchelle, #2038), 21¼ x 15½ in., (54 x 39.4 cm.), paper 26 x 20 in., (54 x 39.4 cm.), color lithograph (BP 572, DM 1415, FR 4757, Y 97,550).

SISKIND, Aaron 1903-1991

$5500* *75th Anniversary Portfolio: Twelve,* Light Gallery, 1979, s., t., d. in ink in margin, ltd. edit., #22/50,images include: Savoy Dancers, Harlem Document; Gloucester Ih; Jerome, Arizona21, (c. 1936-1976), (10-13-92, Christie-NY, #492, illus.), 13½ x 18 in., (34.3 x 45.7 cm.), 9½ x 12 in., (34.3 x 45.7 cm.), photograph, gelatin silver prints (BP 3203, DM 8057, FR 27,377, Y 666,909).

$633* *"Acolman",* 1955, p.l., s., t., d., (05-23-93, Butterfield, #3597, illus.), 17⅝ x 22⅝ in., photograph, gelatin silver print (BP 412, DM 1035, FR 3484, Y 69,968).

BI *Appia Antica 7, 1967,* s., t., d. in ink on mount, est. $3/3,500, (10-13-92, Christie-NY, #491, illus.), 19⅜ x 15⅛ in., (49.2 x 38.4 cm.), photograph, gelatin silver print.

$633* *"Bronx I",* 1950, p.l., t., d. twice, s., (05-23-93, Butterfield, #3598, illus.), 15¼ x 22¼ in., photograph, gelatin silver print (BP 412, DM 1035, FR 3484, Y 69,968).

$330* *Chicago (Auto Graveyard), c. 1948,* s. upside-down, i. by photog. in ink, (10-15-92, Sotheby-NY, #513, illus.), 4⅛ x 6⅝ in., (10.5 x 16.8 cm.), photograph, gelatin silver print (BP 202, DM 491, FR 1666, Y 39,592).

BI *Chicago 10, 1957,* photog.'s t., notations 3/15, sig. recto, 1957, p.l., est. $2/3,000, (04-07-93, Swann, #551, illus.), 15¼ x 21½ in., photograph, silver print.

BI *Chicago 1948,* lit., est. $2,5/3,500, (04-08-93, Christie-NY, #338, illus.), 8½ x 13⅜ in., (21.6 x 34 cm.), photograph, gelatin silver print.

BI *Chicago 30,* s., t., d. by photog. in ink, 1950, p.l., est. $2/3,000, (10-15-92, Sotheby-NY, #509, illus.), 13¾ x 11⅝ in., (34.9 x 29.5 cm.), photograph, gelatin silver print.

$1035* *"Chicago 30, 1949" (Pleasures and Terrors, pl. 140),* s., t., d. by photog. in ink, i. ch. 49 by photog., 1949, p.l., (04-06-93, Sotheby-NY, #413, illus.), 8¾ x 11½ in., photograph (BP 684, DM 1667, FR 5646, Y 118,043).

BI *Chicago 85,* (1953), p.l., s. in ink, lit., est. $8/1,200, (10-13-92, Christie-NY, #487, illus.), 22 x 17 in., (55.9 x 43.2 cm.), photograph, gelatin silver print.

$2750* *Chicago Facade,* mounted on aluminum, s., i. by photog. in ink, 1960, p.l., (10-15-92, Sotheby-NY, #512, illus.), 36 x 50 in., (91.4 x 127 cm.), photograph, gelatin silver print (BP 1683, DM 4093, FR 13,882, Y 329,934).

$1540* *Chicago, #9,* t., d., sig., 1957, p.l., (10-14-92, Swann, #559, illus.), 17½ x 21½ in., (44.5 x 54.6 cm.), photograph, silver print (BP 904, DM 2254, FR 7643, Y 186,621).

BI *Feet #9, 1957,* s., t., d., est. $2,2/2,800, (04-08-93, Christie-NY, #339, illus.), 9⅜ x 7½ in., (23.8 x 19.1 cm.), photograph, gelatin silver print.

$433* *From "Harlem Document",* c. 1935, p.l., pencil s., t., d., (12-17-92, Christie-S. Ken, #66, illus.), 8¾ x 12 in., (22.2 x 30.5 cm.), photograph, gelatin silver print (BP 275, DM 676, FR 2309, Y 53,214).

$523* *From Rock Series,* s., (05-16-93, Hindman, #341), 22 x 16½ in., photograph, silver print (BP 341, DM 844, FR 2842, Y 58,241).

BI *"Gloucester IH",* 1944, p.l., s., t., d., est. $1,5/2,000, (05-23-93, Butterfield, #3594, illus.), 12¼ x 9½ in., photograph, gelatin silver print.

$880* *Harlem,* s., t., d. by photog., 1940, p.l., (10-15-92, Sotheby-NY, #508, illus.), 8½ x 8 in., (21.6 x 20.3 cm.), photograph, gelatin silver print (BP 538, DM 1310, FR 4442, Y 105,579).

$1100* *Harlem 1935,* photog.'s t., sig., 1935, p.l., (04-07-93, Swann, #552, illus.), 8 x 11 in., photograph, silver print (BP 727, DM 1779, FR 6021, Y 124,972).

BI *Harlem Document (Harlem Photographs, cover),* s., d., i. by photog., c. 1935, p.l., est. $1/2,000, (04-06-93, Sotheby-NY, #412, illus.), 8⅝ x 11⅞ in., photograph.

$935* *Harlem Store Facades, With Radio Photographic Studio,* photog.'s sig., 1939, p.l., (04-07-93, Swann, #553, illus.), 8½ x 12 in., photograph, silver print (BP 618, DM 1512, FR 5118, Y 106,226).

$1100* *"Harlem Street Scene 3",* 1935/later, s., t., d., (11-16-92, Butterfield, #6164, illus.), 8½ x 12 in., (216.3 x 305.3 mm.), photograph, gelatin silver print (BP 724, DM 1754, FR 5908, Y 136,799).

$920* *"Harlem",* 1937, p.l., s., t., d., (05-23-93, Butterfield, #3596, illus.), 11 x 8 in., photograph, gelatin silver print (BP 599, DM 1504, FR 5063, Y 101,691).

$1093* *"Harlem",* 1936, p.l., s., t., d., (05-23-93, Butterfield, #3595, illus.), 10¾ x 8½ in., photograph, gelatin silver print (BP 712, DM 1787, FR 6015, Y 120,814).

BI *Harlem, 1936,* t., sig., p.l., est. $1/1,500, (10-14-92, Swann, #560, illus.), 10 x 7½ in., (25.4 x 19.1 cm.), photograph, silver print.

$4600* *"Homage To Franz Kline' San Luis Potosi 19", 1961,* s., t., d., p. notations, (04-06-93, Sotheby-NY, #418, illus.), 10⅜ x 13⅜ in., photograph (BP 3038, DM 7411, FR 25,095, Y 524,635).

$1760* *Homage To Franz Kline: Three: "Lima 55", "Lima 58", and "Lima 63",* s., t., d. by photog. in ink, 1975, p.l.,

(10-15-92, Sotheby-NY, #511, illus.), photograph, gelatin silver print (BP 1077, DM 2620, FR 8884, Y 211,158).

$3680* *Jerome, Arizona,* 1949, p. 1970s, ink s., t., d., prov., (04-08-93, Christie-NY, #336, illus.), 17¾ x 13¼ in., (45.1 x 33.7 cm.), photograph, gelatin silver print (BP 2413, DM 5912, FR 20,011, Y 417,612).

BI *Kentucky 4,* (1951), p.l., s., t., d. in ink, lit., est. $2,2/2,800, (10-13-92, Christie-NY, #486, illus.), 21¾ x 18⅞ in., (55.2 x 47.9 cm.), photograph, gelatin silver print.

$990* *"Lima 299",* 1979, ink s., t., d., (11-16-92, Butterfield, #6167, illus.), 13½ x 13⅝ in., (343.5 x 346.7 mm.), photograph, gelatin silver print (BP 652, DM 1578, FR 5317, Y 123,119).

BI *"M. U. 107, 1954",* p.l., pencil s., t., d., est. BP 3/500, (12-17-92, Christie-S. Ken, #70, illus.), 10 x 12¾ in., (25.4 x 32.4 cm.), photograph, gelatin silver print.

$2013* *"M.V. IIIB",* 1954, p.l., (04-06-93, Sotheby-NY, #416, illus.), 17¾ x 21⅜ in., photograph (BP 1330, DM 3243, FR 10,982, Y 229,585).

$1980* *M.V. [Martha's Vineyard] III-A,* (George Eastman House, p. 26), mounted on aluminum, s., t., d. by photog. in ink, 1954, p.l., (10-15-92, Sotheby-NY, #510, illus.), 36 x 46 in., (91.4 x 116.8 cm.), photograph, gelatin silver print (BP 1212, DM 2947, FR 9995, Y 237,552).

$575* *"Martha's Vineyard 108",* 1954, p.l., s., t., d., (05-23-93, Butterfield, #3599, illus.), 14⅛ x 18 in., photograph, gelatin silver print (BP 374, DM 940, FR 3165, Y 63,557).

BI *Martha's Vineyard,* 1954, s., t., d. in ink, est. $1,8/2,200, (10-13-92, Christie-NY, #488, illus.), 13⅝ x 17½ in., (34.6 x 44.5 cm.), photograph, gelatin silver print.

$1045* *"New York",* 1951/later, s., t., d., (11-16-92, Butterfield, #6165, illus.), 21¹³⁄₁₆ x 18¹⁄₁₆ in., (553.4 x 458 mm.), photograph, gelatin silver print (BP 688, DM 1666, FR 5612, Y 129,959).

$1210* *"Pleasures And Terrors Of Levitation 298",* 1954, s., t., d., Dixon Collection, (11-16-92, Butterfield, #6163, illus.), 16 x 15½ in., (407.1 x 394.4 mm.), photograph, gelatin silver print (BP 797, DM 1929, FR 6498, Y 150,479).

BI *"Rome 62, 1967",* p.l., pencil s., t., d., est. BP 5/700, (12-17-92, Christie-S. Ken, #67), 15½ x 19½ in., (39.4 x 49.5 cm.), photograph, gelatin silver print.

BI *"Romele 3 1967",* p.l., pencil s., t., d., est. BP 3/500, (12-17-92, Christie-S. Ken, #69), 9¹⁵⁄₁₆ x 12¾ in., (25.2 x 32.4 cm.), photograph, gelatin silver print.

$1495* *Savoy Dancers, Harlem,* c. 1937-39, p.l., ink s., (04-08-93, Christie-NY, #335, illus.), 11¾ x 8⅝ in., (29.8 x 21.9 cm.), photograph, gelatin silver print (BP 980, DM 2402, FR 8129, Y 169,655).

$880* *Savoy Dancers-Harlem Document,* photog.'s t., s., 1936, p.l., (04-07-93, Swann, #554, illus.), 11½ x 9 in., photograph, silver print (BP 582, DM 1423, FR 4817, Y 99,977).

BI *Selected Images: "Kentucky" and "Volcano I"* (George Eastman House, p.33): Two, each s., 2nd t., d. by photog. in ink; 1st s., t., d. by photog., 1951 and 1980, p.l., est. $2/3,000, (04-06-93, Sotheby-NY, #415, illus.), one 15⅛ x 18½ in., photograph.

BI *Shells, Martha's Vineyard,* c. 1940, handstamp, notations, est. $1,5/2,500, (10-14-92, Swann, #561, illus.), 9½ x 7 in., (24.1 x 17.8 cm.), photograph, silver print.

BI *"Terrors And Pleasures Of Levitation"* (George Eastman House, pp. 40-4): Three, from series Terrors and Pleasures of Levitation: s., t., d. by photog., reference num., 1954-61. p.l., est. $2/3,000, (04-06-93, Sotheby-NY, #414, illus.), photograph.

$358* *"Vera Cruz (A) 85",* 1981, s., t., d., (11-16-92, Butterfield, #6166, illus.), 9⅞ x 9¾ in., (251.2 x 248.1 mm.), photograph, gelatin silver print (BP 236, DM 571, FR 1923, Y 44,522).

BI *Viterbo Broom": Eighteen,* self-pub., portfolio, each init., d., t. V.B., num., annon. by photog., manuscript colophon and ded.; s., d., #6/9 by photog. in ink, 4to, est. $10/15,000, (04-06-93, Sotheby-NY, #418A, illus.), photograph.

$690* *Woman On Beach In Straw Hat, 1930's,* (04-06-93, Sotheby-NY, #412A, illus.), 3⅜ x 4⅝ in., photograph (BP 456, DM 1112, FR 3764, Y 78,695).

SISLEY, Alfred   French 1839-1899

$358* *"Bords Du Loing, Pres De Saint Mammes" (Delteil 5, Melot 5), 1896,* pub. by Roger-Miles in Art et Nature, 1897, excellent cond., (10-31-92, Cleveland, #332, illus.), 5¾ x 8¾ in., (14.6 x 22.2 cm.), lithograph (BP 229, DM 551, FR 1868, Y 44,345).

SIX, Otto

$7162* *Dompteuse (K. 42II), 1922,* from the series Zirkus, s., t., d., #4/50, full margins, good cond.,creases, tear, pinholes, (12-03-92, Sotheby-London, #285, illus.), 15⅝ x 11¾ in., (397 x 298 mm.), drypoint on wove (BP 4620, DM 11,263, FR 38,443, Y 891,129).

SKEAPING, John   1889-1939

$1022* *The Winner, 1952,* p. Leonard Ripley, ref. P 59, cond. 3, (10-13-92, Phillips-London, #184, illus.), 29¹⁵⁄₁₆ x 39¾ in., (76 x 101 cm.), color lithograph (BP 595, DM 1497, FR 5087, Y 123,924).

SKILL, F. and W. WALKER (after)

BI *A Meeting Of The R.S.A., 1862,* by W. Walker and G. Zobel, scratch-letter proof, pub. W. Walker, est.BP 250/300, (11-30-92, Phillips-London, #32), sheet 26⅓ x 47 in., (66.9 x 119.4 cm.), mixed-method engraving on wove.

SKLADANOWSKY BROTHERS

$2200* *August Bebel,* typewritten label, handwritten notations verso, 1892, p.l., (04-07-93, Swann, #254, illus.), 4 x 2½ in., photograph, silver print (BP 1454, DM 3558, FR 12,042, Y 249,943).

SKOGLUND, Sandy   b. 1946

$3300* *Ferns, 1980,* s., t., d., num. 5/20 by photog., #5/36 ed., (10-15-92, Sotheby-NY, #605, illus.), 26¼ x 33¼ in., (66.7 x 84.5 cm.), photograph, cibachrome print (BP 2019, DM 4912, FR 16,658, Y 395,921).

$1100* *I Wish I Was A Robot, 1982,* s., t., d., num. 1/20 by photog., #1/36 ed., (10-15-92, Sotheby-NY, #604, illus.), 27 x 37¼ in., (68.6 x 94.6 cm.), photograph, cibachrome print (BP 673, DM 1637, FR 5553, Y 131,974).

$2070* *"Maybe Babies", 1983,* s., t., d., #18/30, illus., est. $2,5/3,500, (05-23-93, Butterfield, #3600, illus.), 30½ x 37½ in., photograph, C-print (BP 1348, DM 3385, FR 11,392, Y 228,805).

$3850* *Maybe Babies, 1983,* s., t., d., i., dedicated by photog. in ink, artist's proof, (10-15-92, Sotheby-NY, #603, illus.), 30¼ x 37½ in., (76.8 x 95.3 cm.), photograph, cibachrome print (BP 2356, DM 5731, FR 19,435, Y 461,908).

$12,650* *Revenge Of The Goldfish, 1980,* s., t., d., #30/30, exhib., lit., (04-08-93, Christie-NY, #559, illus.), 28 x 35½ in., (71.1 x 90.2 cm.), photograph, cibachrome print (BP 8295, DM 20,321, FR 68,787, Y 1,435,542).

SLAVIN, Neil

BI *Group Portraits: "Grand Canyon Staff, Arizona", 1974 and "Engine Co.#7, Ladder Co. #1, New York City Fire Dept.", 1973: Two,* each mounted, s., t., d. by photog., est. $1/2,000, (04-06-93, Sotheby-NY, #488, illus.), other 10½ x 13½ in., photograph, Type-C print.

SLEVOGT, Max   German 1868-1932

BI *Aus Lederstrumpf-Erzahlungen (Sievers/Waldmann/Imiela 103, 121, 132,136, 304, 309, 326, 330), 1908-09: Eight,* s., Pan-Presse, pub. Paul Cassirer, est. DM 4,500, (12-01-92, Karl/Faber, #1248), 13¾ x 10⁷⁄₁₆ in., (35 x 26.5 cm.), lithograph on Imperial Japan.

$614* *Bildnis Des Geigers Andreas Weisgerber,* s., (12-01-92, Karl/Faber, #1249), 12⅜ x 9¼ in., (31.5 x 23.5 cm.), etching and drypoint on hand-made Van Gelder (BP 406, DM 979, FR 3335, Y 76,444).

$320* *Brustbild Der Radierers Hermann Struck (s & w 437), 1911,* 2nd state, s., full margins, good cond., very minor soiling, Late Gerhard Brauer Coll., (05-27-93, Sotheby-Amstrdm, #781, illus.), 3¹⁵⁄₁₆ x 2¹⁵⁄₁₆ in., (100 x 75 mm.), etching on wove (BP 205, DM 513, FR 1731, Y 34,305, G 575).

$190* *Brustbild Eines Bartigen Mannes,* #92/100, s. Slevogt, (03-24-93, Venator/Hansten, #4561), pl. 9⁵⁄₁₆ x 6¹⁵⁄₁₆ in., (23.6 x 17.7 cm.), drypoint (BP 129, DM 310, FR 1056, Y 22,324).

$128* *(Figures In A Street)*, s., margins, creasing, minor defects at edges of sheet, Late GerhardBrauer Coll., (05-27-93, Sotheby-Amstrdm, #782), sh 13¾ x 16¹⁵⁄₁₆ in., (350 x 430 mm.), lithograph on thin laid (BP 82, DM 205, FR 692, Y 13,722, G 230).

$1033* *Francisco D'Andrade Als Don Juan: Champagnerlied I (Sievers-Waldmann-Imiela 426 II), 1911,* s., from series Vierzehn Radierungen von Max Slevogt, Cassirer, Berlin, (12-05-92, Bassenge, #7737), 8¼ x 5⅞ in., (21 x 15 cm.), soft-ground etching w/drypoint on imitation Japan (BP 647, DM 1611, FR 5489, Y 127,989).

BI *Hektors Tod (Sievers/Waldmann, Teil 1, 28), 1907,* sheet 12 from series Achill, s. Slevogt, i., p. 1915, #3/5, est. DM 400, (09-14-92, Venator/Hansten, #2538), image approx. 11 x 14¹⁵⁄₁₆ in., (28 x 38 cm.), chalk lithograph on hand-made Japan.

$280* *Die Morderin (Sievers-Waldmann-Imiela 43 I), 1911,* s., artist's proof, (12-05-92, Bassenge, #7738), 2¾ x 2¼ in., (7 x 5.7 cm.), drypoint on wove cardboard (BP 175, DM 437, FR 1488, Y 34,692).

$470* *Mythologische Szene,* (11-28-92, Grisebach, #771, illus.), 12⅞ x 16¹⁵⁄₁₆ in., (32.7 x 43 cm.), lithograph on wove (BP 310, DM 749, FR 2542, Y 58,494).

$542* *"Notentitel Mephisto (Das Flohlied) (Sievers/Waldmann/ Imiela 32/1), 1908,* s., d., artist's proof, prov.(11-28-92, Grisebach, #772, illus.), 7⅜ x 5¼ in., (18.7 x 13.3 cm.), lithograph on wove (BP 358, DM 863, FR 2931, Y 67,455).

$443* *Notentitel Mephisto (Sievers-Waldmann-Imiela 32 III), 1908,* s., (12-05-92, Bassenge, #7734), 7¹⁄₁₆ x 5¹¹⁄₁₆ in., (18 x 14.5 cm.), lithograph on wove (BP 277, DM 691, FR 2354, Y 54,888).

$406* *Der Richter Sucht Den Hirsch Zu Treffen (Sievers-Waldmann-Imiela 272, 1909,* zu den Lederstrumpf-Erzahlungen, s., (12-05-92, Bassenge, #7735), 12¹⁵⁄₁₆ x 10⅝ in., (33 x 27 cm.), lithograph on handmade (BP 254, DM 633, FR 2157, Y 50,304).

$516* *Selbstbildnis Mit Gerunzelten Brauen (Sievers-Waldmann-Imiela 468 III), 1912,* s., (12-05-92, Bassenge, #7739), 7¹³⁄₁₆ x 5¹³⁄₁₆ in., (19.8 x 14.8 cm.), drypoint on wove (BP 323, DM 804, FR 2742, Y 63,933).

$551* *Selbstbildnis Mit Zigarre, Zeichnend,* s., (06-10-93, Hauswedell/Nolt., #931, illus.), image 9¹³⁄₁₆ x 7½ in., (25 x 19 cm.), drypoint on Japan (BP 360, DM 897, FR 3021, Y 58,486).

$352* *Selbstbildnis Von Vorn, Zeichnend Und Mit Zigarre, 1916,* s. Slevogt, (03-24-93, Venator/Hansten, #4560), 9¹³⁄₁₆ x 7⅞ in., (25 x 20 cm.), drypoint on thick Japan (BP 238, DM 575, FR 1957, Y 41,358).

$523* *Selbstbildnis, Im Atelier Radierend (Sievers-Waldmann 434, 2), 1911,* s., #17/30, Cassirer, blindstamp, (06-10-93, Hauswedell/Nolt., #929, illus.), image 7 x 4½ in., (17.8 x 11.5 cm.), drypoint on imperial Japan (BP 342, DM 852, FR 2867, Y 55,514).

$115* *Selbstbildnis, Im Atelier Radierend (s & w 434), 1911,* 1st state, margins, good cond., handling creases, slight paper discoloration, Late Gerhard Brauer Coll., (05-27-93, Sotheby-Amstrdm, #783), 7¹⁄₁₆ x 4⅝ in., (180 x 118 mm.), etching on van Gelder laid (BP 74, DM 185, FR 622, Y 12,328, G 207).

$310* *Sitzender Mann Zwischen Stehendem Paar,* s., blindstamp, (09-18-92, Schloss Ahlden, #1067), 12⁹⁄₁₆ x 9½ in., (31.9 x 24.2 cm.), lithograph on heavy machine-made (BP 181, DM 460, FR 1574, Y 38,314).

SLOAN, Blanding   American b. 1886

$330* *"Ascetic", "That Female Dream", "Miss Chicago" and "Adam And Eve": Four,* each s., three num., good cond., (02-07-93, Bakker, #146), woodblock print (BP 228, DM 547, FR 1850, Y 41,065).

$248* *"Interpreter Needed", "Judas" and "Modern Tendency": Three,* num., s. Blanding Sloan, imp., good cond., (11-21-92, Bakker, #161), largest, image 9½ x 8¼ in., (24.1 x 21 cm.), color woodblock print (BP 163, DM 395, FR 1332, Y 30,842).

$248* *"That Female Dream", "Judas" and "Ascetic": Three,* all num., s. Blanding Sloan, imp., good cond., (11-21-92, Bakker, #137), largest 12 x 9½ in., (30.5 x 24.1 cm.),

color woodblock print (BP 163, DM 395, FR 1332, Y 30,842).

SLOAN, John   American 1871-1951

$963* *The Bandits Care (M.195), 1920,* pub. New Republic, 1924, s., full margins, good cond., (11-12-92, Freemn/ Fine Art, #191, illus.), plate 7 x 5 in., (17.8 x 12.7 cm.), etching on wove paper (BP 633, DM 1526, FR 5147, Y 119,405).

$575* *Bandits Cave (M. 195), 1920,* 8th final state, s., full margins, light/mat staining, creasing, prov., prop. Akron Art Museum, (05-11-93, Christie-NY, #123), plate 7 x 5 in., (178 x 127 mm.), etching on wove (BP 367, DM 906, FR 3052, Y 63,249).

BI *Better Mouse Traps (M. 298), 1937,* s., t., annot. 100 proofs, p. Ernest Roth, margins, stray printing ink, est. $4/600, (05-19-93, Butterfield, #2024), 3¹⁵⁄₁₆ x 6 in., (100 x 152 mm.), etching on laid.

$22* *Book Illustration With Figures,* (02-19-93, Garth, #87), 10¼ x 9 in., (26 x 22.9 cm.), b/w print of etching (BP 15, DM 36, FR 122, Y 2610).

$358* *"Christmas Dinners",* s. John Sloan 1909, good cond., (04-25-93, Bakker, #117), plate 2½ x 4¾ in., (6.4 x 12.1 cm.), etching (BP 227, DM 566, FR 1912, Y 39,541).

$3163* *Copyist At The Metropolitan Museum (M. 148), 1908,* watermark, 8th (final) state, s., p. Peters, margins, good cond., repaired tears, mat staining, discoloration, crease, (05-19-93, Butterfield, #1829, illus.), sh. 10⁵⁄₁₆ x 11¾ in., (262 x 298 mm.), etching on wove (BP 2053, DM 5141, FR 17,322, Y 350,161).

BI *"Crouching Nude And Press" (M. 248), 1931,* s., t., num., s. by printer, very fine cond., est. $6-700, (10-31-92, Cleveland, #216, illus.), 6⅞ x 5½ in., (17.5 x 14 cm.), etching.

BI *"Fifth Avenue Critics" (Morse 128 xi/xi), 1905,* pub. in Gazette des Beaux-Arts, 1909, tear, est. $250/350, (05-15-93, Cleveland, #300), 4⁹⁄₁₆ x 6¾ in., (11.6 x 17.1 cm.), etching.

$1400* *"Fifth Avenue, 1909" (M. 308 vi/vi), 1941,* s., t., num., excell. cond., glue, (05-15-93, Cleveland, #301, illus.), 8 x 6 in., (20.3 x 15.2 cm.), etching (BP 910, DM 2252, FR 7568, Y 155,193).

BI *The Fire Can (Morse 199 I/II), c. 1920,* s., t., annot. proof of first state, est. $3/500, (03-14-93, Hindman, #308), 3⅝ x 2¼ in., (9.2 x 5.7 cm.), etching.

$1210* *Fun, One Cent (Morse 131), 1905,* 2nd final state, s., wide margins, mat staining, very good cond., (09-19-92, Christie-E, #56), plate 5 x 6¾ in., (127 x 171 mm.), etching on laid paper (BP 696, DM 1812, FR 6205, Y 150,760).

$825* *Kraushaar's (Morse 229 VIII/VIII), 1926,* s., annot. 100 proofs, (05-16-93, Hindman, #540), 4 x 5 in., (10.2 x 12.7 cm.), etching (BP 536, DM 1327, FR 4459, Y 91,453).

$440* *"The Little French Bride", 1906,* s. John Sloan, s., d. John Sloan 1906 in plate, num. 100 proofs, watermark, fair cond., staining, minor tear, (03-12-93, Skinner, #21, illus.), 5⅛ x 6⅞ in., (13 x 17.5 cm.), etching on laid (BP 307, DM 732, FR 2490, Y 51,856).

$2875* *Love On The Roof (M. 167), 1914,* s., t., #100 proofs, annot., full margins, tack holes, good cond., surface soiling, (05-19-93, Butterfield, #1830, illus.), sh. 12⅝ x 9½ in., (321 x 241 mm.), etching on wove (BP 1866, DM 4673, FR 15,745, Y 318,277).

$2300* *"Man Monkey", "Sidewalk" and "Patrol Party" (M. 130, 184, and 202), 1905-21: Three,* first s., i. 100 proofs, full margins, good cond., crease, hinge stains; 2nd s., t., i. 100 proof, full margins, good cond., crease, tape stain; 3rd full margins, good cond., (02-11-93, Sotheby-NY, #41), etchings on Arches laid, 3rd on wove (BP 1623, DM 3810, FR 12,892, Y 277,275).

$2200* *McSorley's Back Room (M. 181), 1916,* s., t., i., wide margins, foxmarks, very good cond., (09-19-92, Christie-E, #57, illus.), plate 5¾ x 7¹⁄₁₆ in., (146 x 179 mm.), etching on laid paper (BP 1265, DM 3294, FR 11,282, Y 274,109).

$1650* *McSorley's Back Room (M. 181), 1916,* s., t., i. 100 proofs, full margins, very good cond., (11-09-92, Christie-NY, #33, illus.), plate 5¼ x 6¹⁵⁄₁₆ in., (133 x

177 mm.), etching on wove (BP 1091, DM 2634, FR 8900, Y 204,765).

$2420* *Memory (Morse 136), 1906,* 6th final state, s., t., d. 1905, i. 100 proofs, full margins, light-staining, soiling, tackholes, good cond., (11-09-92, Christie-NY, #31, illus.), plate 7⅜ x 8¾ in., (187 x 222 mm.), etching on wove (BP 1600, DM 3863, FR 13,053, Y 300,323).

$1045* *Nude In A Chaise Longue By The Window,* s., t.; t. erased/rewritten, tack holes, hinged, good cond., (12-04-92, Doyle, #150, illus.), 6 x 11 in., (152 x 279 mm.), etching (BP 670, DM 1664, FR 5646, Y 130,462).

$825* *Nude Sketches, 1917,* s., t., num. 100 proofs, margins, good cond., mat staining, tack holes, notations, surface soiling, (10-28-92, Butterfield, #2550), 3⅛ x 6⅜ in., (79 x 162 mm.), etching on wove (BP 526, DM 1274, FR 4326, Y 101,227).

$523* *"Nude With Halo" (Morse 258 iii/iii), 1931,* s., t., (08-08-92, Litchfield, #158), 3¾ x 4⅞ in., (9.5 x 12.4 cm.), etching (BP 272, DM 769, FR 2599, Y 66,752).

$440* *Of Human Bondage, Chapter 96: Philip And Mildred In Chair (M. 293), 1937,* s., annot. 25 JS proofs, t., full margins, good cond., crack in image, staining, tear, (02-24-93, Butterfield, #2869), 5⅞ x 3¹⁵⁄₁₆ in., (149 x 100 mm.), etching on wove backed by wove (BP 307, DM 714, FR 2422, Y 51,631).

$330* *Of Human Bondage: Sixteen,* p. Photogravue and Color Company, pub. Limited Editions Club, 1938, two vols. octavo, num. sets by Sloan, Newman & Wiche no. 99, (12-12-92, Weschler, #185), book w/etchings (BP 212, DM 520, FR 1782, Y 40,837).

BI *The Picture Buyer (M. 153), 1911,* 5th final state, s., i. Peters imp., wide margins, light-staining, crease, tear, good cond., est. $2/3,000, (05-11-93, Christie-NY, #122, illus.), plate 5¼ x 7 in., (133 x 178 mm.), etching on laid.

BI *"The Picture Buyer" (Morse 153 v/v), 1911,* s., t., num., 100 imp., very fine cond., hinges, tack holes, catalog-cover lot, est. $3-3,500, (10-31-92, Cleveland, #215, illus.), 5⅛ x 6¾ in., (13 x 17.1 cm.), etching.

$1840* *"Private Theatricals", "Fifth Avenue Critics" and "Girl And Beggar" (Morse 109, 128, and 150), 1904-10: Three,* s., 2nd t., i. 100 proofs; 1st and 3rd trimmed margins; 2nd full margins, tack holes, light-stain, old glue, repair, laid down, (02-11-93, Sotheby-NY, #40), etching on wove (BP 1298, DM 3048, FR 10,314, Y 221,820).

$1320* *Romary Marye In Christopher St. 1922 (M. 278), 1936,* s., mat burn, creasing, taped to mat, good cond., (12-04-92, Doyle, #151), 5⅞ x 7⅞ in., (149 x 200 mm.), etching (BP 847, DM 2102, FR 7131, Y 164,794).

$1380* *Roofs, Summer Night (M. 137), 1906,* 2nd final state, s., t., i. 100 proofs, wide margins, image crease, good cond., (05-11-93, Christie-NY, #121), plate 5¼ x 7 in., (133 x 178 mm.), etching on wove (BP 881, DM 2174, FR 7325, Y 151,798).

$403* *Seven Toed Pete (M. 240), 1929,* s., t., p. Peter Platt, full margins, laid down, good cond., mat/light-staining, stains, surface soiling, (05-19-93, Butterfield, #2023), 7 x 5 in., (178 x 127 mm.), etching on wove (BP 262, DM 655, FR 2207, Y 44,614).

$1035* *The Show Case (Morse 129), 1905,* 3rd final state, watermark, s., t., i. 100 proofs, full margins, excell. cond., (05-11-93, Christie-NY, #120), plate 4⅞ x 6⅞ in., (124 x 175 mm.), etching on wove (BP 661, DM 1630, FR 5494, Y 113,849).

$1320* *Sidewalk, 1917,* s., t., tape residue, good cond., (12-04-92, Doyle, #149, illus.), 3⅛ x 6¼ in., (79 x 159 mm.), etching (BP 847, DM 2102, FR 7131, Y 164,794).

$1870* *Sixth Avenue, Greenwich Village (M. 207), 1923,* 8th final state, s., t., i. 100 proofs, full margins, mat staining, foxing, usual tack holes, (09-19-92, Christie-E, #58, illus.), plate 5 x 7 in., (127 x 178 mm.), etching on wove (BP 1076, DM 2800, FR 9590, Y 232,993).

$413* *Their Appointed Rounds (Morse 304 II/II), 1938,* s., t., annot. 50 proofs, (05-16-93, Hindman, #541), 5½ x 6⅞ in., (14 x 17.5 cm.), etching and mezzotint (BP 269, DM 664, FR 2232, Y 45,782).

$1265* *Wake On The Ferry (M. 313), 1949,* s., t., #200 proofs, p. Ernest Roth, margins, good cond., mat/light-staining,

glue staining, tape stains, surface soiling, (05-19-93, Butterfield, #1831, illus.), 4¹⁵⁄₁₆ x 7 in., (125 x 178 mm.), etching on wove (BP 821, DM 2056, FR 6928, Y 140,042).

$863* *The Works Of Charles Paul De Kock: "Ramainville Edition" and "St. Gervais Edition (2), 1903; 1904: Three,* 1st copy C from the Romainville edit. of 26, 1st s., sig. de Kock, pub. Frederick J. Quinby Company, other 2 #480, t. include; The Fall Of Madame Boulard, (M.88) (2); Nanon Bears the Drum, (M. 89) (2); Mademoiselle Elvina, (M.90) (2); Boar Hunt, (M. 91) (2), and others, (05-19-93, Butterfield, #1828), 9¼ x 6 in., (235 x 152 mm.), first, containing impressions each of 4 original etchings, four original drawings in-text, p. on handmade paper (BP 560, DM 1403, FR 4726, Y 95,539).

SLOANE, Phyllis   American contemporary
$55* *The Straw Hat,* s. Phyllis Sloane, Print Club of Cleveland, 1983, (06-26-93, Wolf, #979A), 15 x 15 in., (38.1 x 38.1 cm.), silkscreen (BP 37, DM 93, FR 315, Y 5836).

SLOANE, Thomas O'Conor
BI *Portrait Of A Young Girl, c. 1912,* notations on mount. est. $800/1,200, (04-07-93, Swann, #555, illus.), 9½ x 7½ in., photograph, platinum print.

$357* *Silhouette Of Woman With Hat, c. 1905,* (10-14-92, Swann, #562, illus.), 9½ x 7½ in., (24.1 x 19.1 cm.), photograph, platinum print (BP 210, DM 522, FR 1772, Y 43,262).

BI *Study Of Sculpture By Anthony Lee, c. 1915,* est. $6/900, (10-14-92, Swann, #563, illus.), 9½ x 6¾ in., (24.1 x 17.1 cm.), photograph, gum bichromate print.

SLOUN, Frank van   American 1879-1938
$160* *"Market In Munich", c. 1933,* t., s., excell. cond., tipped to original support sheet, (05-15-93, Cleveland, #331), 4 x 5 in., (10.2 x 12.7 cm.), monotype in brown ink (BP 104, DM 257, FR 865, Y 17,736).

BI *"Mother And Daughter", c. 1933,* s., good cond., masking tape, prov., est. $250/400, (05-15-93, Cleveland, #330, illus.), 4⅞ x 7 in., (12.4 x 17.8 cm.), monotype in brownish ink.

SLUIJTERS, J.
$157* *Charlotte Kohler, 1942,* Senefelder, fine cond., (06-09-93, Bubb Kuyper, #2182), 44⅛ x 28⅛ in., (112 x 71.5 cm.), color lithograph (BP 104, DM 257, FR 864, Y 16,697, G 288).

SMART and HUNT
$1210* *Epsom Races, Here They Come,* after J. Pollard, restrike, very good cond., (12-04-92, Doyle, #57), 15 x 23¾ in., (381 x 603 mm.), hand colored aquatint (BP 776, DM 1927, FR 6537, Y 151,061).

SMILLIE, J.
$770* *"The Rocky Mountains",* after Albert Bierstadt, (06-02-93, Doyle, #87), 27½ x 17 in., (69.9 x 43.2 cm.), engraving (BP 500, DM 1229, FR 4144, Y 82,618).

SMILLIE, James D.   American 1833-1909
$83* *"Grazing Sheep In A Western Landscape",* repaired right margin, (06-11-93, Freemn/Fine Art, #208A), plate 4¾ x 12⅞ in., (12.1 x 32.7 cm.), etching (BP 55, DM 135, FR 455, Y 8806).

$550* *"Hollyhocks In A Long-Necked Vase" and "Flowers": Two,* first i. 3e proof; second s., prov., (10-08-92, Grogan, #668), first 11¾ x 5¾ in., (29.8 x 14.6 cm.), second 6¾ x 4⅝ in., (29.8 x 14.6 cm.), etching (BP 327, DM 813, FR 2761, Y 66,829).

$193* *Landscape,* s. James D. Smillie - first state, d. 1879, very good cond.?, (11-21-92, Bakker, #14), 6¾ x 5 in., (17.1 x 12.7 cm.), etching (BP 127, DM 308, FR 1037, Y 24,002).

$11* *Old Cedars,* margins, plate s., (05-22-93, Collins, #2), 5 x 7 in., (12.7 x 17.8 cm.), etching (BP 7, DM 18, FR 60, Y 1213).

SMIRKE, Robert (after)
$195* *"Conjugal Affection",* engr. by Robert Thew, (12-11-92, G.A. Key, #46, illus.), 17 x 22 in., (43.2 x 55.9 cm.), colored stipple engraving (BP 125, DM 307, FR 1053, Y 24,131).

SMITH, Alexis
    BI *Boy's Life, 1989,* s., d., t., annot. 1/3 p.p., blindstamp
        publisher, full margins, goodcond., creases, est. $9/1,200,
        (05-19-93, Butterfield, #2336), sh 30⅛ x 44⅜ in., (76.5
        x 112.7 cm.), lithograph in colors w/collage on Rives
        BFK.

SMITH, Andre
    BI *"Chartres", "The Little Basin", "Journey's End", "Mar-
        ket, Arezzo", 1929, 1930: Four,* s., 3rd t. & i., margins,
        good cond., 1st 2 light-staining, each w/surface soiling,
        creases, prop. Print Corner, est. $3/500, (02-24-93, But-
        terfield, #2870), from 8¹⁄₁₆ x 6½ in., (205 x 165 mm.),
        to 11⁷⁄₁₆ x 8¾ in., (205 x 165 mm.), etching on wove.

SMITH, Atholl
    BI *Woman In Fur,* mid 1930s, mounted on card, s., est. BP
        3/500, (05-06-93, Christie-London, #183, illus.), 9½ x 7½
        in., photograph, gelatin silver print.

SMITH, Clinton
  $715* *#23, Dante's View, Death Valley, California",* 1980/1990,
        s., d., edit. 4/100, photog. stamp, Dixon Collection, (11-
        16-92, Butterfield, #6170, illus.), 17¹⁄₁₆ x 23⁹⁄₁₆ in.,
        (432.6 x 598 mm.), photograph, cibachrome print (BP
        471, DM 1140, FR 3840, Y 88,919).
  $935* *"#35, Rainstorm, Confluence, Green And Colorado Riv-
        ers, Canyonlands,Utah", 1982/1990,* s., d., edit. 11/100,
        photog. stamp, Dixon Collection(11-16-92, Butterfield,
        #6172, illus.), 17¹⁄₁₆ x 23⁵⁄₁₆ in., (432.6 x 591.6 mm.),
        photograph, cibachrome print (BP 616, DM 1491, FR
        5021, Y 116,279).
  $575* *"#53, Havasu Falls, Arizona",* 1984, p. 1989, d. twice,
        s., #18/100, t., edit., photog.'s stamp, (05-23-93, Butter-
        field, #3604, illus.), 18⅜ x 23¼ in., photograph, cibach-
        rome print (BP 374, DM 940, FR 3165, Y 63,557).
    BI *"Floating Leaves, Vermont",* 1982, p. 1990, d. twice, s.,
        #1/25, t., edit., photog.'s stamp, est.$1,2/1,600, (05-23-93,
        Butterfield, #3602), 17 x 22½ in., photograph, carbon
        pigment print.
    BI *"Floating Leaves, Vermont",* 1982, p. 1990, s., d. #3/25,
        est. $1,2/1,600, (05-23-93, Butterfield, #3601), 17 x 23
        in., photograph, carbon pigment print.
  $1430* *"Floating Leaves, Vermont",* 1982/1990, ink s., d., edit.
        2/25, Dixon Collection, (11-16-92, Butterfield, #6168,
        illus.), 14¼ x 23¹⁄₁₆ in., (362.6 x 585.2 mm.), photo-
        graph, carbon pigment print (BP 942, DM 2280, FR
        7680, Y 177,839).
  $1045* *"Havasu Falls And Terraces, Arizona",* 1984/1989, s.,
        d., edit. 3/50, Dixon Collection, (11-16-92, Butterfield,
        #6169), 29¹⁄₁₆ x 36⁹⁄₁₆ in., (737.9 x 928.8 mm.), photo-
        graph, cibachrome print (BP 688, DM 1666, FR 5612, Y
        129,959).
  $605* *"Holly Tree, Georgia",* 1980/1989, s., d., edit. 32/100,
        editioned, num. 6, photog. stamp, Dixon Collection, (11-
        16-92, Butterfield, #6171), 23⁷⁄₁₆ x 18¹³⁄₁₆ in., (594.8 x
        477.1 mm.), photograph, cibachrome print (BP 398, DM
        965, FR 3249, Y 75,239).
  $345* *"Huckleberry And Lodgepole Pines, Tetons National Park,
        Wyoming",* 1988, p. 1989, d. twice, s., #6/100, t., edit.,
        photog.'s stamp, (05-23-93, Butterfield, #3605, illus.),
        18⅞ x 23½ in., photograph, cibachrome print (BP 225,
        DM 564, FR 1899, Y 38,134).
  $690* *"Maples And Sage, Zion National Park, Utah",* 1984, p.
        1988, d. twice, s., #26/100, t., edit., photog.'s stamp, (05-
        23-93, Butterfield, #3606), 17⅜ x 23⅜ in., photograph,
        cibachrome print (BP 449, DM 1128, FR 3797, Y
        76,268).
  $518* *"Monument Valley", 1991,* s., d., #10/50 on image, (05-
        23-93, Butterfield, #3603, illus.), 20 x 39½ in., photo-
        graph, C-print (BP 337, DM 847, FR 2851, Y 57,257).

SMITH, Eugene W.   American 1918-1978
    BI *From Ku Klux Klan Series,* prov., est. $3/4,000, (05-16-
        93, Hindman, #327, illus.), 10 x 13¼ in., photograph,
        silver print.
    BI *GI With K-Rations,* prov., est. $1,800/2,200, (05-16-93,
        Hindman, #328, illus.), 11 x 14 in., photograph, silver
        print.

SMITH, G.
  $241* *Jardin D'Acclimatation. Les Malabres, c. 1895,* Paris,
        Imp. A. Farradesche, cond. B+, (06-11-93, Boisgirard,
        #143), 32⁵⁄₁₆ x 48¹³⁄₁₆ in., (82 x 124 cm.), poster (BP
        158, DM 392, FR 1321, Y 25,570).

SMITH, G.E. Kidder
    BI *Apse Detail, Ranchos Taos, 1975,* photog.'s notations, sig.
        on mount, handstamp, est. $1/1,500, (04-07-93, Swann,
        #556, illus.), 10½ x 13¾ in., photograph, silver print.

SMITH, George (after)
  $183 *Classical Landscape With Figures Resting On A Bank,
        Figures On Horseback Crossing A Stone Bridge In The
        Distance,* engraved William Woollett, d. 1762, (04-16-
        93, G.A. Key, #56, illus.), 17 x 22 in., (43.2 x 55.9
        cm.), b/w engraving (BP 120, DM 296, FR 999, Y
        20,578).

SMITH, Gordon A.   b. 1919
  $190* *Landscape With Red Sky, #13/40,* s., (05-12-93, Maynard,
        #283), (27.9 x 48.3 cm.), silkscreen (BP 124, DM 307,
        FR 1033, Y 21,212, C$ 242).
  $80* *Point Atkinson Lighthouse, #3/40,* s., (10-21-92, Maynard,
        #186), 5 x 5¾ in., (12.7 x 14.6 cm.), etching (BP 50,
        DM 121, FR 411, Y 9744, C$ 99).
  $147* *"Trees At Night", #2,* s., (05-12-93, Maynard, #282), 10½
        x 8 in., (26.7 x 20.3 cm.), lithograph (BP 96, DM 237,
        FR 799, Y 16,412, C$ 187).

SMITH, Henry Holmes
    BI *"Mother And Son",* 1951, p. 1976, s., t., d., est. $5/700,
        (05-23-93, Butterfield, #3607, illus.), 9 x 6¼ in., photo-
        graph, dye transfer print.

SMITH, J.R.
  $192* *What You Will -- Ce Qui Vous Plaira,* (08-20-92, Bon-
        hams-Chelsea, #42), image 15 x 11 in., (38.1 x 27.9
        cm.), stipple engraving w/hand coloring (BP 99, DM
        278, FR 943, Y 24,245).

SMITH, J.R. (after H. WALTON)
  $174* *The Silver Age, 1778,* pub. J. Boydell, foxing, mottling,
        (10-27-92, Phillips-London, #60), image 18⅞ x 22½ in.,
        (479 x 572 mm.), mezzotint on wove (BP 110, DM 267,
        FR 905, Y 21,284).

SMITH, James Agrell   1913-1988
  $139* *Reflecitons On A Great-Grandfather, 1972,* #10/50, s., t.,
        prov., (11-16-92, Hodgins, #309), 7¹⁵⁄₁₆ x 5¹⁵⁄₁₆ in., (20.3
        x 15.2 cm.), wood engraving on paper (BP 91, DM 222,
        FR 747, Y 17,347, C$ 176).

SMITH, Jessie Wilcox and Elizabeth Shippen GREEN
  $358* *Bryn Mawr College Calender for 1902,* cover illus., (c)
        1901, (06-11-93, Freemn/Fine Art, #27A), 12 x 9 in.,
        (30.5 x 22.9 cm.), lithograph (BP 235, DM 582, FR
        1962, Y 37,984).

SMITH, John   British 1652-1742
  $5* *"Bessey, Countess Of Rochford", 1723,* after D'Agar,
        trimmed outside plate, scuffing, image pencil touches,pa-
        per residue, (05-15-93, Cleveland, #431), 13½ x 9⅞ in.,
        (34.3 x 25.1 cm.), mezzotint (BP 3, DM 8, FR 27, Y
        554).

SMITH, John Raphael   English 1752-1812
    BI *The Captive (Clayton 19), 1779,* after Joseph Wright of
        Derby, 2nd state, trimmed, rubbed, creases, defects, est.
        BP 1/1,500, (06-30-93, Sotheby-London, #268, illus.),
        17¾ x 21 in., (451 x 533 mm.), mezzotint in blackish
        brown ink.
  $233* *Painting, 1783,* pub. Smith, watermark, on two plates,
        narrow margins, repaired margin, (11-30-92, Phillips-Lon-
        don, #193), plate 17 x 12⅝ in., (432 x 321 mm.), mez-
        zotint on laid (BP 154, DM 371, FR 1260, Y 28,998).
  $33* *Portrait Of Joseph Deane Bourke,* after Joshua Reynolds,
        laid down, foxing, (04-17-93, Wolf, #595), 21 x 15 in.,
        (53.3 x 38.1 cm.), mezzotint (BP 22, DM 53, FR 180,
        Y 3711).

SMITH, John Raphael (after)
  $67* *The Right Hon'ble Charles James Fox, 1802,* engraved
        & pub. by S.W. Reynolds, trimmed to image, tears, (11-
        30-92, Phillips-London, #84), image 24⅝ x 18⅛ in.,

(625 x 460 mm.), mezzotint (BP 44, DM 107, FR 362, Y 8339).

SMITH, Kathie
$73* *Kamares,* s. Kathie Smith, i., d. '85, #67/130, (08-11-92, L. Joel, #175G), 11³⁄₁₆ x 14⅞ in., (28.4 x 37.8 cm.), color screenprint (BP 38, DM 107, FR 363, Y 9348, A$ 99).

SMITH, Keith Amerian b. 1938
$357* *Male Nude, 1975,* sig., notations, (10-14-92, Swann, #564), 7 x 6 in., (17.8 x 15.2 cm.), photograph, color photo etching (BP 210, DM 522, FR 1772, Y 43,262).

SMITH, Kimber 1933-1981
$325* *"J F K", 1968,* mono., t., num., (11-28-92, Grisebach, #773, illus.), 25¹⁄₁₆ x 19⁷⁄₁₆ in., (63.7 x 49.3 cm.), colored lithograph on wove (BP 215, DM 518, FR 1758, Y 40,448).

SMITH, Lawrence Beall American b. 1909
$300* *"Black And White", 1941,* s., t., d., num., good cond., hinges, (05-15-93, Cleveland, #303, illus.), 8¾ x 11¼ in., (22.2 x 28.6 cm.), lithograph (BP 195, DM 483, FR 1622, Y 33,256).
BI *Forest Flight,* AAA edit., s., heavy light burn, glued to top mat, est. $120/160, (05-15-93, Cleveland, #305), 9¾ x 12 in., (24.8 x 30.5 cm.), lithograph.
$110* *"A Game Of Tag, Autumn", c. 1939,* s., margins, stain, old glue, good cond., (09-19-92, Christie-E, #59), borderline 9¼ x 12½ in., (235 x 318 mm.), lithograph on laid paper (BP 63, DM 165, FR 564, Y 13,705).
$165* *"The Skaters",* s., t., AAA label verso, (06-11-93, DuMouchelle, #2259), 12 x 9 in., (30.5 x 22.9 cm.), lithograph (BP 108, DM 268, FR 904, Y 17,507).
$440* *"Theater Magic", 1938,* s., d. Lawrence Beall Smith '38, init. in stone, t., num., watermark, very good cond., mount toning, tape, (03-12-93, Skinner, #22, illus.), 10¼ x 10 in., (26 x 25.4 cm.), lithograph on Rives wove (BP 307, DM 732, FR 2490, Y 51,856).

SMITH, R.
$165* *"Logo",* s., d. '71, (06-11-93, Freemn/Fine Art, #209B), 23¼ x 19¼ in., (59.1 x 48.9 cm.), relief print (BP 108, DM 268, FR 904, Y 17,507).

SMITH, R. American 20th cent.
$55* *"Folded Paper Clip III, 1975",* s., i. A.P. 10/10, d. '75, (06-11-93, Freemn/Fine Art, #209A), image 26 x 26 in., (66 x 66 cm.), sh 27 x 28 in., (66 x 66 cm.), screenprint (BP 36, DM 89, FR 301, Y 5836).

SMITH, Richard
$316* *Two Of A Kind, 1978,* s., d., #15/50, blindstamp publisher, full margins, good cond., (05-19-93, Butterfield, #2337), 18⅛ x 20½ in., (460 x 521 mm.), lithograph in colors on wove (BP 205, DM 514, FR 1731, Y 34,983).

SMITH, Richard b. 1931
BI *"Olympische Spiele Munchen 1972", (19)71,* poster, s., d., num., stains, est. DM 650, (12-01-92, Karl/Faber, #1254), 40¹⁵⁄₁₆ x 27⁹⁄₁₆ in., (104 x 70 cm.), color lithograph on wove.

SMITH, Russell
$53* *'Kwaguitl Komokwa', 1977,* #31/90, s. Awasatlas RS, (10-21-92, Maynard, #51), approx. 15 x 19 in., (38.1 x 48.3 cm.), print (BP 33, DM 80, FR 272, Y 6456, C$ 66).

SMITH, Sydney Ure 1888-1949
$162* *Deserted Courtyard, Hartley,* s. Sydney Ure Smith, i., #17/40 Proofs, lit., (08-11-92, L. Joel, #142G), 7 x 8½ in., (17.8 x 21.6 cm.), etching (BP 84, DM 238, FR 805, Y 20,745, A$ 220).

SMITH, W. Eugene 1918-1978
BI *Bridge, Pittsburg, 1955-56,* (c) credit, reprod. limit. stamps, est. $4/5,000, (10-13-92, Christie-NY, #496, illus.), 8½ x 13⅜ in., (21.6 x 34 cm.), photograph, gelatin silver print.
BI *Charlie Chaplin: Two,* 1952, p. 1970s, estate stamp, lit., est. $1,8/2,200, (04-08-93, Christie-NY, #448, illus.), each approx. 13⅜ x 8⅞ in., (34 x 22.5 cm.), photograph, gelatin silver print.
BI *Clinic Interior, Nurse Midwife, LIFE Essay, 1951,* estate stamp, lit., est. $1,5/2,000, (10-13-92, Christie-NY, #495, illus.), 13½ x 10½ in., (34.3 x 26.7 cm.), photograph, gelatin silver print.
$690* *Dance Line,* 1950s, photog.'s estate stamp, (05-23-93, Butterfield, #3609, illus.), 4¾ x 9⅜ in., photograph, gelatin silver print (BP 449, DM 1128, FR 3797, Y 76,268).
$1320* *Death Of Gus-Gus (Aperture, unpaginated),* s., d. by photog. w/stylus on image, estate stamp, 1953, p. 1955, (10-15-92, Sotheby-NY, #517, illus.), 7⅞ x 10 in., (20 x 25.4 cm.), photograph, gelatin silver print (BP 808, DM 1965, FR 6663, Y 158,368).
$5980* *Dr. Ernest Ceriani Taking Shortcut To Hospital, "Country Doctor" Essay,* 1948, p. 1950s, estate stamp, lit., (04-08-93, Christie-NY, #450, illus.), 8 x 10¼ in., (20.3 x 26 cm.), photograph, gelatin silver print from the orig. (BP 3921, DM 9606, FR 32,518, Y 678,620).
BI *Enzio Pinza And Mary Martin In South Pacific,* (1949), 1970s, s., lit., est. $1,8/2,200, (10-13-92, Christie-NY, #493, illus.), 10½ x 13⅜ in., (26.7 x 34 cm.), photograph, gelatin silver print.
$920* *"From My Window",* 1950s, s., d., photog.'s stamp, illus., (05-23-93, Butterfield, #3610, illus.), 8⅝ x 13½ in., photograph, gelatin silver print (BP 599, DM 1504, FR 5063, Y 101,691).
$1870* *Girl On Crutches, Maude Callen Clinic, N.C.,* (1951), 1970s, s., lit., (10-13-92, Christie-NY, #494, illus.), 10⅜ x 13⅜ in., (26.4 x 34 cm.), photograph, gelatin silver print (BP 1089, DM 2740, FR 9308, Y 226,749).
$575* *"The Hospital For Special Surgery, New York",* 1966, p.l., photog.'s estate stamp, illus., (05-23-93, Butterfield, #3612, illus.), 12⅝ x 18½ in., photograph, gelatin silver print (BP 374, DM 940, FR 3165, Y 63,557).
$2990* *Mad Eyes (Johnson, 27:052), 1958-59,* from Haiti series, photog. studio (c), credit stamps, (04-06-93, Sotheby-NY, #438, illus.), 14¾ x 19¾ in., photograph (BP 1975, DM 4817, FR 16,312, Y 341,013).
$4600* *Mad Eyes, Haiti, c. 1958-59,* (c) credit stamp, lit., (04-08-93, Christie-NY, #449, illus.), 12¾ x 16 in., (32.4 x 40.6 cm.), photograph, gelatin silver print (BP 3016, DM 7390, FR 25,014, Y 522,015).
BI *Man At Church,* 1962, p.l., photog.'s estate stamp, illus., est. $800/1,000, (05-23-93, Butterfield, #3611, illus.), 11½ x 7½ in., photograph, gelatin silver print.
$2588* *"Mardi Gras", 1959,* photog.'s estate stamp, illus., (05-23-93, Butterfield, #3608, illus.), 12 x 19½ in., photograph, gelatin silver print (BP 1685, DM 4232, FR 14,243, Y 286,062).
BI *New York City,* 1960s, credit and Magnum Photos stamp, est. $2,2/2,800, (04-08-93, Christie-NY, #447, illus.), 8⅞ x 13⅜ in., (22.5 x 34 cm.), photograph, gelatin silver print.
BI *Pittsburgh, 1955-56,* credit (c) twice, reprod. limit. stamps, lit., est. $3/4,000, (10-13-92, Christie-NY, #497, illus.), 13¼ x 10⅜ in., (33.7 x 26.4 cm.), photograph, gelatin silver print.
$2200* *Railraod Bridge, 1955-56,* from Pittsburgh essay, mounted on ecru card, photog.'s (c), personalexhib. print, Magnum Photos stamps, i. in unidentified hand, (10-15-92, Sotheby-NY, #518, illus.), 8⅜ x 13⅜ in., (21.3 x 34 cm.), photograph, gelatin silver print (BP 1346, DM 3275, FR 11,106, Y 263,947).
$1760* *Saipan, 1944,* photog.'s sig., notations, (04-07-93, Swann, #362, illus.), 8¼ x 6 in., photograph, silver print (BP 1163, DM 2847, FR 9633, Y 199,955).
$440* *Shipyard, c. 1955,* handstamp, (10-14-92, Swann, #565, illus.), 11 x 14 in., (27.9 x 35.6 cm.), photograph, silver print (BP 258, DM 644, FR 2184, Y 53,320).
$3025* *"Spanish Village",* 1951/later, s., t., edit. 5/50, Dixon Collection, (11-16-92, Butterfield, #6173, illus.), 12¾ x 9 in., (324.4 x 229 mm.), photograph, gelatin silver print (BP 1992, DM 4823, FR 16,246, Y 376,197).
$10,350* *Tomoko In Her Bath, Minimata, Japan,* 1972, p. c. 1976, s. in stylus; s., t., (04-08-93, Christie-NY, #451, illus.), 7¾ x 12⅞ in., (19.7 x 32.7 cm.), photograph, gelatin silver print (BP 6787, DM 16,627, FR 56,281, Y 1,174,535).
BI *Two Boys With Headless Doll (Johnson, 23:059), 1956,* from Pittsburgh essay, flush-mounted, s., d. by photog.,

est. $2/3,000, (04-06-93, Sotheby-NY, #437, illus.), 13 x 8⅜ in., photograph.

$1980* *Woman Weighing Tomatos, 1951 (Johnson, 13:036),* from Spanish Village essay, mounted, photog.'s studio stamp, notations in unidentified hands, (10-15-92, Sotheby-NY, #519, illus.), 13⅛ x 9⅛ in., (33.3 x 23.2 cm.), photograph, gelatin silver print (BP 1212, DM 2947, FR 9995, Y 237,552).

BI *Woman With Camera (Superimposition), 1962,* estate stamp, est. $1/1,500, (10-14-92, Swann, #566), 11½ x 7¾ in., (29.2 x 19.7 cm.), photograph, silver print.

$2588* *The Woolworth Building (Johnson, 28:001), 1957-58,* from As From My Window I Sometimes Glance series, photog. studio (c)credit stamp, (04-06-93, Sotheby-NY, #437A, illus.), 16⅝ x 13⅝ in., photograph (BP 1709, DM 4169, FR 14,119, Y 295,164).

SMODICS, Erich   b. 1941
$1432* *"Torso", 1984: Seven,* s., num., d., IV/X, (05-08-93, Zeller, #944, illus.), smallest 11⅞ x 8⅞ in., (30.2 x 22.5 cm.), largest 12¹⁄₁₆ x 9¹⁄₁₆ in., (30.2 x 22.5 cm.), color etching (BP 934, DM 2300, FR 7762, Y 160,018).

SMYTH, Captain Hervey
$65* *A View Of Quebec From The Bason (sic),* prov., (06-07-93, Ritchie, #14, illus.), 7⅛ x 10 in., (18.1 x 25.4 cm.), hand-colored engraving (BP 43, DM 105, FR 355, Y 6973, C$ 83).

SMYTH, John Richard Coke
$1112* *"Quebec From The Chateau", "Montreal", "Entrance To Toronto", and "American Fort Niagara River": Four,* t. in plate, (11-30-92, Ritchie, #2, illus.), each approx. 10¾ x 15 in., (27.3 x 38.1 cm.), hand-colored stone lithograph (BP 734, DM 1772, FR 6014, Y 138,395, C$ 1430).

$364* *"Zity - A Huron Indian", "Indians Bartering", and "Indians Of Lorette": Three,* inits. in plate, t., pub. c. 1840, (11-30-92, Ritchie, #1, illus.), each approx. 10¾ x 15 in., (27.3 x 38.1 cm.), hand-colored stone lithograph (BP 240, DM 580, FR 1969, Y 45,302, C$ 468).

SNAFFLES
$701 *"Forrard On Me Lads, And Hit 'Em-'Ard ! !",* s., presentation i., hand written title, (04-16-93, G.A. Key, #145, illus.), 13 x 16 in., (33 x 40.6 cm.), print (BP 460, DM 1132, FR 3826, Y 78,826).

$457 *"O! To Be In England Now That April's There",* s., artist's proof, faded, (06-11-93, G.A. Key, #143, illus.), 12 x 21 in., (30.5 x 53.3 cm.), colored print (BP 300, DM 743, FR 2504, Y 48,488).

$477 *"Oh ! To Be In England, Now That April Is Here",* s., faded, (02-05-93, G.A. Key, #92, illus.), 13 x 20 in., (33 x 50.8 cm.), colored print (BP 330, DM 791, FR 2674, Y 59,358).

$607 *"The R.A. Harriers",* s., (02-05-93, G.A. Key, #90, illus.), 13 x 19 in., (33 x 48.3 cm.), colored print (BP 420, DM 1007, FR 3402, Y 75,535).

$491 *"A Sight To Take Home And Dream About",* s., (02-05-93, G.A. Key, #91, illus.), 11 x 21 in., (27.9 x 53.3 cm.), colored print (BP 340, DM 814, FR 2752, Y 61,100).

SNAFFLES (after)
$824* *Andsome Is, Wot Andsome Does,* s., artist's blindstamp, (10-29-92, Bonhams-Chelsea, #182), image 10 x 11¾ in., (25.4 x 29.8 cm.), reproduction in colors, photographic remarque (BP 528, DM 1268, FR 4301, Y 102,069).

$515* *Foxcatchers, For The Love Of It,* s., artist's blindstamp, (10-29-92, Bonhams-Chelsea, #183), image 15½ x 14¼ in., (39.4 x 36.2 cm.), reproduction in colors (BP 330, DM 792, FR 2688, Y 63,793).

BI *"The Gent With Osses To Sell",* (12-11-92, G.A. Key, #14), 12 x 10 in., (30.5 x 25.4 cm.), colored print.

$351* *Getting Cantankerous,* s., facsimile remarque, faded, (03-03-93, Bonhams-Chelsea, #102), image 9½ x 17¼ in., (24.1 x 43.8 cm.), color reproduction (BP 242, DM 578, FR 1961, Y 41,014).

$944* *Great Banks There Was Below In The Fields,* s., artist's blindstamp, foxing, (10-29-92, Bonhams-Chelsea, #184, illus.), image 11¾ x 17 in., (29.8 x 43.2 cm.), reproduction in colors, photographic remarques (BP 605, DM 1452, FR 4927, Y 116,933).

$558* *The Guns! Thank God! The Guns!,* photographic remarques, (03-03-93, Bonhams-Chelsea, #103), image 10¾ x 19½ in., (27.3 x 49.5 cm.), color reproduction (BP 385, DM 919, FR 3117, Y 65,202).

$207* *A Heilen Lad,* photographic remarques, artist's blindstamp, foxing, (03-03-93, Bonhams-Chelsea, #104), image 11⅜ x 8⅛ in., (28.9 x 20.6 cm.), color reproduction w/ hand-coloring (BP 143, DM 341, FR 1156, Y 24,188).

$72 *Horse Racing Scenes: Four,* (02-05-93, G.A. Key, #72), 5 x 8 in., (12.7 x 20.3 cm.), colored print (BP 50, DM 119, FR 404, Y 8960).

$137* *Indian Cavalry (B.E.F.),* remarques, artist's blindstamp, (09-17-92, Bonhams-Chelsea, #89), image 11½ x 9 in., (29.2 x 22.9 cm.), reproduction in colors finished by hand, w/facsimile (BP 77, DM 203, FR 696, Y 17,057).

$4120* *An Irish Point-To-Point,* (10-29-92, Bonhams-Chelsea, #185, illus.), image 9⅞ x 23 in., (25.1 x 58.4 cm.), reproduction, w/extensive hand coloring, w/photographic remarques (BP 2640, DM 6338, FR 21,503, Y 510,343).

$191* *Jock,* artist's blindstamp, facsimile, (03-03-93, Bonhams-Chelsea, #106), image 11½ x 8 in., (29.2 x 20.3 cm.), reproduction w/some hand-coloring (BP 132, DM 315, FR 1067, Y 22,318).

$159* *The Kadir Bandobast,* s., artist's blindstamp, facsimile remarque, faded to green, time-staining, (03-03-93, Bonhams-Chelsea, #107), image 11¾ x 20¼ in., (29.8 x 51.4 cm.), color reproduction (BP 110, DM 262, FR 888, Y 18,579).

$687* *Merry England And Worth A Guinea A Minute,* s., artist's blindstamp, stain, (10-29-92, Bonhams-Chelsea, #187), image 10½ x 10½ in., (26.7 x 26.7 cm.), reproduction in colors, photographic remarque (BP 440, DM 1057, FR 3586, Y 85,098).

$687* *Oh! To Be In Ireland Now That April's There,* s., (10-29-92, Bonhams-Chelsea, #186), image 12¼ x 21¼ in., (31.1 x 54 cm.), reproduction in colors, w/photographic remarque (BP 440, DM 1057, FR 3586, Y 85,098).

BI *"Old Tawney",* (12-11-92, G.A. Key, #13), 12 x 10 in., (30.5 x 25.4 cm.), colored print.

$319* *Once Upon A Time,* bears sig., faded, (03-03-93, Bonhams-Chelsea, #109), image 13½ x 19 in., (34.3 x 48.3 cm.), color reproduction (BP 220, DM 525, FR 1782, Y 37,275).

$128* *A Point To Point,* #248/275, tear, (03-03-93, Bonhams-Chelsea, #110), image 20 x 30 in., (50.8 x 76.2 cm.), color reproduction (BP 88, DM 211, FR 715, Y 14,957).

$2575* *A Point-To-Point,* (10-29-92, Bonhams-Chelsea, #188, illus.), image 11½ x 19¾ in., (29.2 x 50.2 cm.), reproduction, w/extensive hand coloring, w/photographic remarques (BP 1650, DM 3962, FR 13,439, Y 318,964).

$40 *"A Point-To-Point" and "An Irish Point-To-Point": Two,* (02-05-93, G.A. Key, #45), each 7 x 9 in., (17.8 x 22.9 cm.), colored print (BP 28, DM 66, FR 224, Y 4978).

$172* *The Polo Match,* (10-29-92, Bonhams-Chelsea, #188A), image 8½ x 16¼ in., (21.6 x 41.3 cm.), reproduction in color (BP 110, DM 265, FR 898, Y 21,306).

$772* *Prepare To Receive Cavalry,* s., artist's blindstamp, time-staining, (10-29-92, Bonhams-Chelsea, #189), image 11 x 18⅞ in., (27.9 x 47.9 cm.), reproduction in colors. photographic remarques (BP 495, DM 1188, FR 4029, Y 95,627).

$606* *The Season 1939-40,* s., artist's blindstamp, facsimile remarque, laid down, surface dirt, (03-03-93, Bonhams-Chelsea, #108), image 11½ x 19½ in., (29.2 x 49.5 cm.), color reproduction (BP 418, DM 998, FR 3385, Y 70,811).

$772* *The Sportsman, Who Hunts For The Love Of It,* s., (10-29-92, Bonhams-Chelsea, #190), image 12½ x 12½ in., (31.8 x 31.8 cm.), reproduction in colors (BP 495, DM 1188, FR 4029, Y 95,627).

$721* *Swagger, But A Workman,* s., artist's blindstamp, (10-29-92, Bonhams-Chelsea, #191), image 10⅜ x 9⅞ in., (26.4 x 25.1 cm.), reproduction in colors, photographic remarque (BP 462, DM 1109, FR 3763, Y 89,310).

$1202* *Tonnage,* s., artist's blindstamp, (10-29-92, Bonhams-Chelsea, #192), image 9¾ x 9 in., (24.8 x 22.9 cm.), reproduction in colors, photographic remarque (BP 770, DM 1849, FR 6273, Y 148,891).

$944* *Ubique Meant, Bank, Olborn, Bank, A Penny All The Way,* s., artist's blindstamp, (10-29-92, Bonhams-Chelsea, #193), image 11½ x 21¼ in., (29.2 x 54 cm.), reproduction in colors, photographic remarque (BP 605, DM 1452, FR 4927, Y 116,933).

SNAFFLES, Frank (after)
$483 *"The Bonny Blue Bonnets" and "Jock (K.1)": Two,* (12-11-92, G.A. Key, #126), 11 x 9 in., (27.9 x 22.9 cm.), colored print (BP 310, DM 761, FR 2608, Y 59,770).

SNOW, John   b. 1911
$113* *Bouquet, Red Vase,* #9/50 s., t., prov., (11-16-92, Hodgins, #40), 12 x 10 in., (30.5 x 25.4 cm.), color lithograph on paper (BP 74, DM 180, FR 607, Y 14,102, C$ 143).
$196* *Nocturn Blue Vase,* #10/50, s., t., prov., (05-10-93, Hodgins, #352), 18 x 26 in., (45.7 x 66 cm.), color lithograph on paper (BP 128, DM 315, FR 1062, Y 21,902, C$ 248).
$130* *Nocturne Blue Vase,* #10/50, s., t., prov., (11-16-92, Hodgins, #8), 17¹⁵⁄₁₆ x 25¹⁵⁄₁₆ in., (45.7 x 66 cm.), color lithograph on paper (BP 85, DM 207, FR 699, Y 16,224, C$ 165).
$173* *Plant,* s., t., prov., (11-16-92, Hodgins, #245), 22 x 15¹⁵⁄₁₆ in., (55.9 x 40.6 cm.), color lithograph on paper (BP 114, DM 276, FR 930, Y 21,590, C$ 220).
$87* *Studio, 1952,* #2/50, s., t., prov., (05-10-93, Hodgins, #191), 8½ x 5¾ in., (21.6 x 14.6 cm.), woodcut on paper (BP 57, DM 140, FR 472, Y 9722, C$ 110).

SNYDER, Joan   American b. 1940
$66* *Screams, Whispers,* s., #37/144, (05-16-93, Hindman, #600), 36 x 60 in., (91.4 x 152.4 cm.), color serigraph (BP 43, DM 106, FR 357, Y 7316).

SOCHUREK, Howard
$1320* *Smoke Ring Blower, 1949,* s., t., d. by photog., (10-15-92, Sotheby-NY, #442, illus.), 13½ x 10½ in., (34.3 x 26.7 cm.), photograph, gelatin silver print (BP 808, DM 1965, FR 6663, Y 158,368).

SODERBERG, Yngve Edward   American 1896-1971
$110* *America's Cup Yacht Columbia,* margins, s. Yngve Edward Soderberg, (02-13-93, Collins, #69, illus.), 11⅞ x 8⅞ in., (30.2 x 22.5 cm.), etching (BP 77, DM 182, FR 617, Y 13,266).
$88* *Cup Race,* margins, s. Yngve Edward Soderberg, (02-13-93, Collins, #73, illus.), 8¾ x 10⅞ in., (22.2 x 27.6 cm.), etching (BP 62, DM 146, FR 494, Y 10,613).
$33* *Enterprise,* margins, s. Yngve Edward Soderberg, (02-13-93, Collins, #78), 10⅞ x 8⅞ in., (27.6 x 22.5 cm.), etching (BP 23, DM 55, FR 185, Y 3980).
$132* *Luffing Match,* margins, s. Yngve Edward Soderberg, (02-13-93, Collins, #71, illus.), 7⅞ x 10⅞ in., (20 x 27.6 cm.), etching (BP 93, DM 219, FR 741, Y 15,919).
$44* *Nip And Tuck,* margins, s. Yngve Edward Soderberg, (02-13-93, Collins, #74, illus.), 7⅞ x 10⅞ in., (20 x 27.6 cm.), etching (BP 31, DM 73, FR 247, Y 5306).
$110* *Picking Up The Light,* margins, s. Yngve Edward Soderberg, (02-13-93, Collins, #75, illus.), 6⅞ x 8⅞ in., (17.5 x 22.5 cm.), etching (BP 77, DM 182, FR 617, Y 13,266).
$77* *The Start-Endeavor & Rainbow,* margins, s. Yngve Edward Soderberg, (02-13-93, Collins, #72, illus.), 9¼ x 12¾ in., (23.5 x 32.4 cm.), etching (BP 54, DM 128, FR 432, Y 9286).

SOIRON, Francois Davide (after George MORLAND)
$3482* *"St. James's Park" and "Tea Garden", 1790 and 1793,* by Colmaghi and Co., good cond., latter w/repaired tears, paper loss, both w/skimming, (10-27-92, Phillips-London, #67, illus.), sheet 19 x 21⅝ in., (483 x 549 mm.), stipple engraving in colors (BP 2200, DM 5336, FR 18,107, Y 425,933).

SOKO   Japanese
$44* *Fish In Water,* 20th cent., seal mark, (06-11-93, DuMouchelle, #2366), 9½ x 9¾ in., (24.1 x 24.8 cm.), color woodblock print (BP 29, DM 72, FR 241, Y 4668).

SOKOL, Edward
$64* *The Crescent,* s., t., #29/250, prov., (12-01-92, Ritchie, #28, illus.), 17¾ x 22⅝ in., (45.1 x 57.5 cm.), color serigraph (BP 42, DM 102, FR 348, Y 7968, C$ 83).

SOLANO, Susana   b. 1946
BI *Placa Del Joc De La Pilota, 1987: Four,* #3/75, pencil mono., d., est. DM 4,000, (11-20-92, Lempertz, #864), sh, approx. 29¾ x 22¼ in., (75.5 x 56.5 cm.), etching on Velin (one w/collage).

SOLIER
$192* *Cagney In Cowboy Costume For The Film "The Oklahoma Kid", 1938,* James Cagney Estate, (09-30-92, Doyle, #213), photograph (BP 108, DM 272, FR 921, Y 23,041).

SOLIS, Virgil   German 1514-1562
BI *"Pax Olea Illustris Sibi Martia Subicit Arma" (B. 219; O'Dell-Frankee 108),* est. DM 400, (12-01-92, Karl/Faber, #147), engraving.
$578* *Tanzende Paare Und Musikanten (B. 224-230): Seven,* (12-04-92, Bassenge, #6448), each approx. 2⁵⁄₁₆ x 1¾ in., (5.8 x 4.5 cm.), engraving (BP 371, DM 921, FR 3123, Y 72,160).

SOMER, Johannes van   c. 1645-c. 1699
$166* *Der Fiedler Und Der Trinker (Wurzbach 70; Hollstein 103/II),* after A. Brouwer, prov., (12-01-92, Karl/Faber, #148), mezzotint (BP 110, DM 265, FR 902, Y 20,667).

SOMM, Henry   French 1844-1907
$82* *Souvenir Du Moulin Rouge, c. 1900,* large margins, (05-06-93, Laurin, #83), drypoint on laid (BP 52, DM 129, FR 435, Y 9022).

SOMMER, Frederick   b. 1905
BI *Artificial Leg,* (1944), p.l., s., t., d., est. $7/9,000, (10-13-92, Christie-NY, #498, illus.), 9⅜ x 7½ in., (23.8 x 19.1 cm.), photograph, gelatin silver print.

SOMMER, William   American 1867-1949
$160* *"Study For The Sunday Boy",* #41/50, excell. cond., (05-15-93, Cleveland, #311, illus.), 12½ x 9½ in., (31.8 x 24.1 cm.), lithograph (BP 104, DM 257, FR 865, Y 17,736).
$55* *"The Sunday Boy", 1933,* s., Print-A-Month Club, Cleveland February 1933, fine cond., (10-31-92, Cleveland, #218), 12½ x 9¼ in., (31.8 x 23.5 cm.), lithograph (BP 35, DM 85, FR 287, Y 6813).
$65* *"The Sunday Boy", 1933,* s., plate No. 9 the Print-A-Month Club, Cleveland, good cond., corners glued, (05-15-93, Cleveland, #312), 13 x 9½ in., (33 x 24.1 cm.), lithograph (BP 42, DM 105, FR 351, Y 7205).

SONDERBORG, K.R.H.   Danish b. 1923
$361* *"16 Avenue Matignon", 1969,* s., d., t., (11-28-92, Grisebach, #774, illus.), 33¹¹⁄₁₆ x 2³⁄₁₆ in., (85.5 x 5.5 cm.), colored serigraph on cardboard (BP 238, DM 575, FR 1952, Y 44,928).
$221* *16, Avenue Matignon, Paris, 1969,* s., t., (12-05-92, Bassenge, #7740), 33¼ x 21⁷⁄₁₆ in., (84.5 x 54.5 cm.), screen print on thin cardboard (BP 138, DM 345, FR 1174, Y 27,382).
$866* *Abstrakte Komposition, 1967,* s., d., num., (11-28-92, Schoppmann, #805), 30⁵⁄₁₆ x 19¹¹⁄₁₆ in., (77 x 50 cm.), color lithograph on light cardboard (BP 572, DM 1380, FR 4684, Y 107,778).
$851* *Balance, 1972,* s., d., i., ded., num., (06-05-93, Grisebach, #881, illus.), 23¹⁄₁₆ x 20¹¹⁄₁₆ in., (58.5 x 52.5 cm.), lithograph on wove (BP 560, DM 1380, FR 4650, Y 91,289).
$348* *Brucke Bei Sturm, (19)70,* s., d., num., brown stained, (12-01-92, Karl/Faber, #1256), 21⅝ x 14⁹⁄₁₆ in., (55 x 37 cm.), lithograph on thick wove (BP 230, DM 555, FR 1890, Y 43,327).
$332* *Der Brucke, (19)78,* s., d., num., (12-01-92, Karl/Faber, #1258), 23⅝ x 17¹¹⁄₁₆ in., (60 x 45 cm.), color lithograph on Arches France wove (BP 219, DM 529, FR 1803, Y 41,335).
$516* *Die Brucke, 1978,* s., num., (12-05-92, Bassenge, #7742), 23⅝ x 17¹¹⁄₁₆ in., (60 x 45 cm.), color lithograph on Arches (BP 323, DM 804, FR 2742, Y 63,933).

$316* *Composition, 1967,* s. Sonderborg 67, XIX/XXX, (09-30-92, Kunsthallen, #267), color lithograph (BP 178, DM 448, FR 1516, Y 37,922, DK 1725).

BI *Komposition, (19)66,* s., d., num., stains, est. DM 600, (12-01-92, Karl/Faber, #1255), 32 11/16 x 22 7/16 in., (83 x 57 cm.), serigraph on thin board.

BI *Komposition, (19)71,* s., d., num., w/traces of old mounting, est. DM 1000, (12-01-92, Karl/Faber, #1257), 19 11/16 x 16 1/8 in., (50 x 41 cm.), lithograph in black and blue on wove.

BI *Komposition, (19)90,* s., d., num., mount staining, est. DM 900, (12-01-92, Karl/Faber, #1259), 11 5/8 x 8 11/16 in., (29.5 x 22 cm.), aquatint/etching on wove.

$367* *Komposition, 1967,* s. Sonderborg 67, ded., E.A., (03-24-93, Kunsthallen, #308), lithograph (BP 249, DM 599, FR 2040, Y 43,121, DK 2300).

$443* *Komposition, 1971,* s., num., (12-05-92, Bassenge, #7741), 20 3/16 x 16 1/8 in., (51.2 x 41 cm.), lithograph on copper print paper (BP 277, DM 691, FR 2354, Y 54,888).

$367* *Komposition, 1972,* s. Sonderborg, 24/100, (03-24-93, Kunsthallen, #307), lithograph (BP 249, DM 599, FR 2040, Y 43,121, DK 2300).

$283* *Komposition, 1976,* s., d., #26/100, (06-12-93, Hauswedell/Nolt, #395), 21 9/16 x 14 3/4 in., (54.8 x 37.4 cm.), full sheet lithograph on thick wove (BP 185, DM 461, FR 1548, Y 29,780).

$128* *Komposition, 1978,* s. Sonderborg 78, 123/150, (03-24-93, Kunsthallen, #306), color lithograph (BP 87, DM 209, FR 712, Y 15,039, DK 805).

$349* *Komposition, 1979,* s. Sonderborg 72, E.A., (03-24-93, Kunsthallen, #309), color lithograph (BP 236, DM 570, FR 1940, Y 41,006, DK 2185).

$92* *Kompositioner, 1969,* s. Sonderborg, E.A., (03-24-93, Kunsthallen, #310), lithograph (BP 62, DM 150, FR 511, Y 10,810, DK 575).

$389* *Untitled, 1968,* s., d., #23/100, (06-12-93, Hauswedell/Nolt, #394), 33 1/16 x 19 1/8 in., (84 x 48.5 cm.), lithograph on thick wove (BP 255, DM 633, FR 2128, Y 40,934).

SONREL, Elisabeth

$1980* *"Fleurs De Serre" and "Fleurs De Champs": Two, c. 1900,* generally good cond., prop. Rod Stewart, (11-06-92, Sotheby-Arcade, #135, illus.), sight 26 x 10 3/4 in., (66 x 27.3 cm.), lithograph in colors (BP 1295, DM 3161, FR 10,685, Y 244,384).

$1540* *Le Midi,* good cond. ?, Rod Stewart Coll., (11-06-92, Sotheby-Arcade, #143, illus.), sight 26 x 19 in., (66 x 48.3 cm.), lithograph in colors (BP 1007, DM 2459, FR 8311, Y 190,077).

BI *The Seasons: Four,* margins, apparently good condition, Fall w/faint staining, Winter w/tear in image, each w/foxing, surface soiling, est. $3/5000, (03-31-93, Butterfield, #5249, illus.), each 22 3/4 x 9 1/2 in., (57.8 x 24.1 cm.), lithograph printed in colors on wove.

SOPER, Eileen A. English 1905-1990

$213* *At The Water's Edge,* s., margins, (07-16-92, Bonhams-Chelsea, #481), plate 5 3/8 x 7 3/4 in., (13.7 x 19.7 cm.), drypoint etching on laid paper (BP 110, DM 315, FR 1062, Y 26,682).

BI *A Badger With Young,* s., #30/300, (12-11-92, G.A. Key, #41), 15 x 20 in., (38.1 x 50.8 cm.), colored print.

$275* *"The Boat Swing",* s., toned, stain, (10-31-92, Cleveland, #333), 10 3/4 x 7 1/2 in., (27.3 x 19.1 cm.), etching (BP 176, DM 423, FR 1435, Y 34,064).

BI *"Boo Hoo!",* s., est. BP 1/150, (10-27-92, Phillips-London, #301), playe 4 1/2 x 6 7/8 in., (114 x 175 mm.), etching on laid.

$192* *A Captive Audience,* s., margins, (07-16-92, Bonhams-Chelsea, #484, illus.), plate 6 1/2 x 9 1/2 in., (16.5 x 24.1 cm.), drypoint etching on laid paper (BP 99, DM 284, FR 958, Y 24,051).

$192* *A Captive Audience,* s., margins, (07-16-92, Bonhams-Chelsea, #485, illus.), plate 6 1/2 x 9 1/2 in., (16.5 x 24.1 cm.), drypoint etching on laid paper (BP 99, DM 284, FR 958, Y 24,051).

BI *A Captive Audience,* s., margins, est. BP 1/150, (07-16-92, Bonhams-Chelsea, #486, illus.), plate 6 1/2 x 9 1/2 in., (16.5 x 24.1 cm.), drypoint etching on laid paper.

$128* *A Captive Audience,* s., margins, (09-17-92, Bonhams-Chelsea, #85B), plate 6 1/2 x 9 1/2 in., (16.5 x 24.1 cm.), drypoint etching on laid paper (BP 72, DM 190, FR 650, Y 15,936).

$233* *Collect,* full margins, s., light-staining, taped, (11-30-92, Phillips-London, #350), plate 5 x 3 7/8 in., (127 x 98 mm.), etching on laid (BP 154, DM 371, FR 1260, Y 28,998).

$234* *Feeding The Chickens,* s., margins, (07-16-92, Bonhams-Chelsea, #491), plate 4 1/2 x 5 1/4 in., (11.4 x 13.3 cm.), drypoint etching on laid paper (BP 121, DM 346, FR 1167, Y 29,312).

$319* *Feeding The Litter,* s., margins, (07-16-92, Bonhams-Chelsea, #473, illus.), plate 5 x 7 1/8 in., (12.7 x 18.1 cm.), drypoint etching on laid paper (BP 165, DM 471, FR 1591, Y 39,960).

$200* *The First Recitation,* full margins, s., taped, (11-30-92, Phillips-London, #351), plate 3 1/8 x 1 5/8 in., (79 x 41 mm.), etching on laid (BP 132, DM 319, FR 1082, Y 24,891).

$233* *A Game Of Patience,* s., light-staining, remains of tape, (11-30-92, Phillips-London, #356), plate 4 3/4 x 3 7/8 in., (121 x 98 mm.), etching on laid (BP 154, DM 371, FR 1260, Y 28,998).

$298* *In Bed,* s., margins, foxing, creasing, (07-16-92, Bonhams-Chelsea, #487), plate 3 7/8 x 6 in., (9.8 x 15.2 cm.), drypoint etching (BP 154, DM 440, FR 1486, Y 37,329).

$233* *James And Trudy Play Leapfrog,* full margins, s., blindstamp, remains of tape, (11-30-92, Phillips-London, #352), plate 5 x 7 7/8 in., (127 x 200 mm.), etching on laid (BP 154, DM 371, FR 1260, Y 28,998).

$209* *"Last One Down Is A Sissy!",* s., creased, (10-27-92, Phillips-London, #300), plate 5 1/2 x 7 7/8 in., (140 x 200 mm.), etching on laid (BP 132, DM 320, FR 1087, Y 25,566).

$362* *Leap-Frog,* s., margins, (07-16-92, Bonhams-Chelsea, #488, illus.), plate 5 3/8 x 7 7/8 in., (13.7 x 20 cm.), drypoint etching on laid paper (BP 187, DM 535, FR 1805, Y 45,346).

$192* *A Photograph By The Sundial,* s., margins, (07-16-92, Bonhams-Chelsea, #479), plate 4 7/8 x 7 1/4 in., (12.4 x 18.4 cm.), drypoint etching (BP 99, DM 284, FR 958, Y 24,051).

$170* *A Photograph By The Sundial,* s., margins, (07-16-92, Bonhams-Chelsea, #478), plate 4 7/8 x 7 1/4 in., (12.4 x 18.4 cm.), drypoint etching (BP 88, DM 251, FR 848, Y 21,295).

$277* *Playing In The Waves,* s., margins, (07-16-92, Bonhams-Chelsea, #489), plate 6 5/8 x 8 3/8 in., (16.8 x 21.3 cm.), drypoint etching on laid paper (BP 143, DM 409, FR 1382, Y 34,699).

$213* *Playing With Balloons,* s., margins, (07-16-92, Bonhams-Chelsea, #474), plate 4 7/8 x 6 3/4 in., (12.4 x 17.1 cm.), drypoint etching on laid paper (BP 110, DM 315, FR 1062, Y 26,682).

$233* *Poor Patch's Paw,* s., blindstamp, light-staining, (11-30-92, Phillips-London, #348), plate 4 3/4 x 7 7/8 in., (121 x 200 mm.), etching on laid (BP 154, DM 371, FR 1260, Y 28,998).

$157* *The See-Saw On The Seashore,* s., creased top, (10-27-92, Phillips-London, #303), plate 4 1/2 x 7 1/4 in., (114 x 184 mm.), etching on J. Whatman laid (BP 99, DM 241, FR 816, Y 19,205).

$192* *The Skipping Rope,* s., margins, foxing, (07-16-92, Bonhams-Chelsea, #477), plate 3 7/8 x 6 7/8 in., (9.8 x 17.5 cm.), drypoint etching on laid paper (BP 99, DM 284, FR 958, Y 24,051).

$203* *The Skipping Rope,* s., margins, (07-16-92, Bonhams-Chelsea, #476), plate 3 7/8 x 6 7/8 in., (9.8 x 17.5 cm.), drypoint etching on laid paper (BP 105, DM 300, FR 1012, Y 25,429).

$192* *The Skipping Rope,* s., margins, (07-16-92, Bonhams-Chelsea, #475), plate 3 7/8 x 6 7/8 in., (9.8 x 17.5 cm.), drypoint etching on laid paper (BP 99, DM 284, FR 958, Y 24,051).

$233* *Sympathy,* full margins, s., time-staining, (11-30-92, Phillips-London, #355), plate 4 1/2 x 2 7/8 in., (114 x 73 mm.), etching on wove (BP 154, DM 371, FR 1260, Y 28,998).

$233* *Three Girls On A Gate,* full margins, s., mount/light/tape staining, (11-30-92, Phillips-London, #349), plate 5⅝ x 6⅞ in., (143 x 175 mm.), etching on laid (BP 154, DM 371, FR 1260, Y 28,998).

$167* *Three Play Netball,* full margins, s., blindstamp, light-staining, (11-30-92, Phillips-London, #353), plate 5 x 6⅝ in., (127 x 168 mm.), etching on laid (BP 110, DM 266, FR 903, Y 20,784).

$191* *Trudy And Ben Play Swing About,* s., creasing, surface dirt, (10-27-92, Phillips-London, #302), plate 6⅞ x 4⅞ in., (175 x 124 mm.), etching on laid (BP 121, DM 293, FR 993, Y 23,364).

$209* *Trudy And Judy With Patch's Puppies,* s., creasing, nick, (10-27-92, Phillips-London, #299), plate 4⅞ x 7 in., (124 x 178 mm.), etching on laid (BP 132, DM 320, FR 1087, Y 25,566).

$233* *Trudy With Her Broken Dolly,* full margins, s., blindstamp, light-staining, (11-30-92, Phillips-London, #354), plate 6⅛ x 3¾ in., (156 x 95 mm.), etching on laid (BP 154, DM 371, FR 1260, Y 28,998).

$277* *Whips And Tops,* s., margins, (07-16-92, Bonhams-Chelsea, #480), plate 5⅞ x 7⅞ in., (14.9 x 20 cm.), drypoint etching on laid paper (BP 143, DM 409, FR 1382, Y 34,699).

$319* *A Windy Day On The Beach,* s., margins, creased, dirt, (07-16-92, Bonhams-Chelsea, #490), plate 5½ x 7¾ in., (14 x 19.7 cm.), drypoint etching on laid paper (BP 165, DM 471, FR 1591, Y 39,960).

$319* *The Young Seamstress,* s., margins, (07-16-92, Bonhams-Chelsea, #482), plate 4⅞ x 4 in., (12.4 x 10.2 cm.), drypoint etching (BP 165, DM 471, FR 1591, Y 39,960).

$255* *The Young Seamstress,* s., margins, (07-16-92, Bonhams-Chelsea, #483), plate 4⅞ x 4 in., (12.4 x 10.2 cm.), drypoint etching on laid paper (BP 132, DM 377, FR 1272, Y 31,943).

SOPER, George

$51 *A Bobby Apprehending Man With Horse, "Black Beauty?",* s., (10-09-92, G.A. Key, #114), 7¾ x 6 in., (19.7 x 15.2 cm.), etching (BP 30, DM 76, FR 258, Y 6220).

$101 *Figures Tilling The Soil: A Pair,* s., (10-09-92, G.A. Key, #116), 4¾ x8in., etching (BP 60, DM 150, FR 510, Y 12,317).

$302* *"Hunt Scenes": Group Of Four,* s., very good cond., prov., (12-04-92, Doyle, #152), 7 x 11¼ in., (178 x 286 mm.), drypoint (BP 194, DM 481, FR 1632, Y 37,703).

$51 *Stonewaller Breaking Rocks,* s., (10-09-92, G.A. Key, #117), 5¼ x 7½ in., (13.3 x 19.1 cm.), etching (BP 30, DM 76, FR 258, Y 6220).

SORENSON, Arne Haugen

BI *Komposition, 1964,* s. A. Haugen Sorenson 64, E.A., est. DK 1,200, (03-24-93, Kunsthallen, #119), color lithograph.

$220* *Komposition, 1977,* s. A. Haugen Sorenson 77, 3/150, (03-24-93, Kunsthallen, #118), color lithograph (BP 149, DM 359, FR 1223, Y 25,849, DK 1380).

$128* *Komposition, 1983,* s. A. Haugen Sorenson 83, 24/37 E.A., (03-24-93, Kunsthallen, #121), color lithograph (BP 87, DM 209, FR 712, Y 15,039, DK 805).

$220* *Komposition, 1985,* s. A. Haugen Sorenson 85, 63/120, (03-24-93, Kunsthallen, #120), color woodcut (BP 149, DM 359, FR 1223, Y 25,849, DK 1380).

$230* *Untitled,* s. 83, 18/65, (09-29-92, B. Rasmussen, #319), lithograph in colors (BP 129, DM 325, FR 1108, Y 27,456, DK 1265).

SORLIER, Ch. (after CHAGALL)

$1659* *Carmen (M. CS 39; S. S. 116ff.), 1967,* trimmed, light-staining, (12-01-92, Karl/Faber, #446), 38¾ x 25⁵⁄₁₆ in., (98.5 x 64 cm.), lithograph (BP 1096, DM 2644, FR 9011, Y 206,549).

SORLIER, Charles

$4333* *The Bouquet (C.S. 8), 1955,* after Marc Chagall, s., #275/300, pub. Editions Galerie Maeght, fullmargins, mount/glue stains, (11-30-92, Phillips-London, #386, illus.), sheet 28 x 21½ in., (711 x 546 mm.), color lithograph on Arches (BP 2860, DM 6903, FR 23,434, Y 539,266).

$3166* *Maternity (C.S. 7), 1954,* after Marc Chagall, s., #150/300, Mourlot's blindstamp, pub. Editions Galerie Maeght, full margins, mount/glue stained, creases, (11-30-92, Phillips-London, #385), sheet 23⅛ x 30⅞ in., (587 x 784 mm.), color lithograph on Arches (BP 2090, DM 5044, FR 17,123, Y 394,026).

BI *Romeo Et Juliette (C.S. p. 96), 1964,* after Marc Chagall, pub. Commissariat General Du Tourisme, p. Mourlot, laid down, orig. repaired area from time of printing, est. BP 4/600, (11-30-92, Phillips-London, #388), sheet 39 x 25 in., (99.1 x 63.5 cm.), color lithograph.

$750* *Romeo Et Juliette (C.S. p. 97), 1964,* after Marc Chagall, p. Mourlot, pub. Commissariat General Du Tourisme, good cond., rolled, (11-30-92, Phillips-London, #389), sheet 25 x 39 in., (63.5 x 99.1 cm.), color lithographic poster (BP 495, DM 1195, FR 4056, Y 93,342).

$417* *La Tribu De Levi and La Tribu De Benjamin (C.S.P. p. 87, 89), 1961: APair,* after Marc Chagall, p. Mourlot, pub. Editions des Musees Nationaux and Editions Assoc. Hadassah, very good cond., (11-30-92, Phillips-London, #387), sheet 31½ x 20½ in., (800 x 521 mm.), color lithographic poster (BP 275, DM 664, FR 2255, Y 51,898).

SORLIER, Charles (after Bernard BUFFET)

$853* *Affiche D'Exposition-La Route (S. 305), 1962,* s. Buffet, pub. Les Peintres Temoins de leur Temps, full margins, good cond., mount stain, tape, (12-03-92, Sotheby-London, #212, illus.), sheet 20⅛ x 15¾ in., (511 x 400 mm.), lithograph in colors on Arches (BP 550, DM 1341, FR 4579, Y 106,134).

BI *Le Pain Et Le Vin (S. 306), 1964,* s., pub. Les Peintres Temoins de leur Temps, margins trimmed, cockling, small area lacking, est. BP 4/600, (10-27-92, Phillips-London, #186), sheet 28½ x 20⅝ in., (724 x 524 mm.), color lithgraph on B.F.K. Rives.

$518* *Screaming Woman, 1967,* s., #18/250, full margins, good cond., mat/light-staining, masking tape remains, notations, (05-19-93, Butterfield, #2040), 21¾ x 16⅝ in., (552 x 422 mm.), lithograph in colors on wove (BP 336, DM 842, FR 2837, Y 57,345).

SORLIER, Charles (after Marc CHAGALL)

$2530* *The Angel Of Judgement (M. CS 45), 1974,* s., #175/200, pub. Editions des Amis du Message Biblique Marc Chagall, large margins, good cond., light-stain, masking tape, (02-11-93, Sotheby-NY, #105), 19¹⁵⁄₁₆ x 16¹⁵⁄₁₆ in., (507 x 430 mm.), sheet 28⅜ x 21⁵⁄₁₆ in., (507 x 430 mm.), color lithograph (BP 1785, DM 4191, FR 14,182, Y 305,003).

BI *"The Artist As A Phoenix",* p. Editions Maeght, prov., est. $2,5/4,000, (12-11-92, DuMouchelle, #2031, illus.), 13 x 47 in., (33 x 119.4 cm.), color lithograph on Rives/BFK paper.

$3850* *Carmen (M. CS 39), 1967,* crayon s., #34/150, trimmed, creasing, losses, discoloration, stains, (11-05-92, Sotheby-NY, #147), sheet 39⅞ x 22 in., (101.3 x 55.9 cm.), lithograph p. in colors on Arches (BP 2504, DM 6089, FR 20,599, Y 472,335).

$5463* *The Fight Between Jacob And The Angel (M. CS 40), 1967,* s., #44/100, full margins, good cond., light-stain, printer's crease,creases, discoloration, (05-13-93, Sotheby-NY, #532, illus.), 20⅝ x 16⅛ in., (523 x 410 mm.), lithograph in colors (BP 3587, DM 8821, FR 29,755, Y 609,914).

$3240* *L'Ange Du Jugement (C.S. 45), 1974,* s., #92/200, full margins, good cond., light/mount staining, cellophane tape, (12-03-92, Sotheby-London, #269, illus.), 20½ x 17 in., (521 x 432 mm.), lithograph in colors on Arches (BP 2090, DM 5095, FR 17,391, Y 403,135).

$4263* *Maternite (Charles Sorlier 7), 1954,* s., #190/300, full margins, pressure mark, scratch within image, discoloration, (12-03-92, Sotheby-London, #268, illus.), 20⅞ x 26¼ in., (530 x 667 mm.), lithograph in colors on Arches (BP 2750, DM 6704, FR 22,882, Y 530,422).

$5175* *Nice And The Cote D'Azur: Roses And Mimosas (M. CS 29), 1967,* s., #10/150, full margins, good cond., faded, printing crease, skinning, soiling, Late Vitya Vronsky Babin Coll., (05-13-93, Sotheby-NY, #531, illus.), 24 x

18⅛ in., (610 x 460 mm.), lithograph in colors (BP 3397, DM 8356, FR 28,186, Y 577,760).

$6325* *Red Poppies (M. CS 2), 1949,* s., #161/400, pub. Maeght, margins, good cond., faded, creases, mat stain, discolored, (02-11-93, Sotheby-NY, #104, illus.), 21¹³⁄₁₆ x 16⅛ in., (554 x 409 mm.), sheet 23¹⁵⁄₁₆ x 18⅛ in., (554 x 409 mm.), color lithograph w/touches of white gouache (BP 4463, DM 10,477, FR 35,454, Y 762,508).

$12,650* *Romeo And Juliet (M. CS 10), 1964,* s., #175/200, p. Mourlot, faded, scratch, mat stain, creases, tape stain, (11-05-92, Sotheby-NY, #144, illus.), sheet 25⅝ x 40⅛ in., (65.1 x 101.9 cm.), lithograph p. in colors (BP 8228, DM 20,006, FR 67,683, Y 1,551,957).

$3025* *"The Tribe Of Benjamin",* from "The Twelve Maquettes of Stained Glass Windows for Jerusalem", edit. Epreuve d'artiste, #17/25, s. Chagall, label verso, (01-15-93, DuMouchelle, #2010, illus.), 24¼ x 18¼ in., (61.6 x 46.4 cm.), lithograph (BP 1977, DM 4946, FR 16,722, Y 381,367).

$3450* *Twelve Maquettes Of Stained Glass Windows For Jerusalem: The Tribe OfDan (M. CS 18), 1964,* s., i. epreuve d'artiste 24/25, full margins, good cond., faded, mat/lightstain, tear, creases, masking tape, fox marks, skinned spots, (05-13-93, Sotheby-NY, #530), 24¼ x 18⅛ in., (617 x 460 mm.), lithograph in colors (BP 2265, DM 5571, FR 18,791, Y 385,174).

$4600* *Twelve Maquettes Of Stained Glass Windows For Jerusalem: The Tribe OfIssachar (M. CS 17), 1964,* s., #134/150, good cond., light-stain, creases, pressure mark, masking tape, slightly discolored, (05-13-93, Sotheby-NY, #529), 24⅜ x 18¼ in., (620 x 462 mm.), lithograph in colors (BP 3020, DM 7428, FR 25,054, Y 513,565).

$3575* *Twelve Maquettes Of Stained Glass Windows For Jerusalem: The Tribe OfLevi (M. CS 14), 1964,* s., #94/200, margins, good cond., mat and backboard stain, hinge stains, skinning, (11-05-92, Sotheby-NY, #146, illus.), 24¼ x 18¼ in., (616 x 463 mm.), sheet 28⅞ x 21⅛ in., (616 x 463 mm.), lithograph p. in colors (BP 2325, DM 5654, FR 19,128, Y 438,596).

$4263* *Twelve Maquettes Of Stained Glass Windows For Jerusalem: The Tribe OfSimeon (C.S. 13), 1964,* s., #82/150, full margins, good cond., paper discoloration, soiling,-staining, (12-03-92, Sotheby-London, #270, illus.), 24 x 18⅛ in., (610 x 460 mm.), lithograph in colors on Arches (BP 2750, DM 6704, FR 22,882, Y 530,422).

$3850* *Twelve Maquettes Of Stained Glass Windows For Jerusalem: The Tribe OfSimeon (M. CS 13),* s., #16/150, full margins, good cond., creases, discoloration, (11-05-92, Sotheby-NY, #145, illus.), 24⅛ x 18¼ in., (614 x 463 mm.), lithograph p. in colors (BP 2504, DM 6089, FR 20,599, Y 472,335).

SORMAN, Steve   contemporary

BI *From Away (T. 8), 1988,* s., #7/12, pub. label Tyler Graphics, very good cond., est. $5/7,000, 60 1/2 x 81 1/2 x 12, (10-28-92, Butterfield, #3121, illus.), woodcut, lithograph, screenprint, collage, hand-coloring on Okawara handmade, laminated to Tycor panels and wood base.

BI *From Away, 1988,* s., #7/12, pub. label Tyler Graphics, very good cond., est. $3/5,000, (02-24-93, Butterfield, #3147, illus.), 60½ x 81½ in., (153.7 x 207 cm.), woodcut, lithograph, screenprint collage, & hand-coloring on Okawarahandmade, laminated to Tycor panels & maple base.

$605* *"Loggia (Now)", "Loggia (Then)" and "Loggia (When)", 1985:* Three, all s., t., d., all num. 9/14, pub. Echo Press, (Now) w/Echo Press blindstamp, full sheets, excell. cond., (09-19-92, Christie-E, #219, illus.), all overall sheet 41¾ x 24 in., (106 x 61 cm.), lithograph in colors w/additions in gouache on Japanese papers (BP 348, DM 906, FR 3103, Y 75,380).

$1650* *Still Standing Still (Tyler 534), 1985,* s., t., d., num. 13/20, Tyler Graphics blindstamp, full sheet, excell. cond., (09-19-92, Christie-E, #220), sheet 66¼ x 42¾ in., (168.3 x 108.6 cm.), etching, woodcut, lithograph and collage in colors w/handcoloring onYellow TGL handmade (BP 949, DM 2471, FR 8462, Y 205,582).

SORNER, Ryno

BI *Profile A La Sabatier, c. 1940,* s., i., exhib. label w/t. in ink, prov., est. $2/2,500, (10-13-92, Christie-NY, #358, illus.), 11¼ x 8⅜ in., (28.6 x 21.3 cm.), photograph, gelatin silver print.

SOT, Moshe

$11* *"Rabbi",* s., #17/150, (02-27-93, Dunning, #61), 25½ x 18¼ in., (64.8 x 46.4 cm.), lithograph (BP 8, DM 18, FR 61, Y 1299).

SOTO, Jesus Raphael   Venezuelan b. 1923

$550* *Carren Raphriches Ivec Une Brique,* s., #39/150, (12-13-92, Hindman, #329), 16 x 16 in., color serigraph (BP 352, DM 864, FR 2946, Y 68,044).

$180* *"Composition Geometrique",* #17/100, s., (10-18-92, Pescheteau, #262), 30¹¹⁄₁₆ x 22⅝ in., (78 x 57.5 cm.), serigraph in colors (BP 109, DM 266, FR 903, Y 21,493).

$126* *"Composition Noir Et Rouge",* #9/120, s., (01-28-93, Pescheteau, #255), 23¼ x 18⅞ in., (59 x 48 cm.), serigraph (BP 83, DM 200, FR 676, Y 15,644).

$769* *Sans Titre, 1991,* s., #EA 1/3, (05-27-93, Briest, #177), 22¼ x 10¹⁄₁₆ in., (56.5 x 25.5 cm.), serigraph and animations (BP 492, DM 1234, FR 4159, Y 82,440).

$160* *Untitled, 1981,* s., #137/190, margins, good cond., (05-27-93, Sotheby-Amstrdm, #488), sh 22⁵⁄₁₆ x 23⁹⁄₁₆ in., (567 x 599 mm.), colored silkscreen on wove (BP 102, DM 257, FR 865, Y 17,153, G 288).

$141* *Untitled, 1981,* s., #144/190, margins, good cond., crease in corner, (05-27-93, Sotheby-Amstrdm, #487), sh 22⁵⁄₁₆ x 23⁹⁄₁₆ in., (567 x 599 mm.), colored silkscreen on wove (BP 90, DM 226, FR 763, Y 15,116, G 253).

$179* *Untitled, 1981,* s., full margins, good cond., (05-27-93, Sotheby-Amstrdm, #489), sh 22⁵⁄₁₆ x 23⁹⁄₁₆ in., (567 x 599 mm.), colored silkscreen on wove (BP 115, DM 287, FR 968, Y 19,190, G 322).

SOTTI(?)

$385* *Bossard-Bonnel Rennes, Musical Instruments, 1925,* Vercasson, B cond., repairs, creasing, (08-06-92, Swann, #265, illus.), 66 x 43 in., (167.6 x 109.2 cm.), (BP 201, DM 569, FR 1921, Y 49,107).

SOUBIE, R.

$207* *Brigadoon, De V. Minelli, Avec G. Kelly (French), 1954,* (01-31-93, Morelle/Marchan, #109), 47¼ x 62¹⁵⁄₁₆ in., (120 x 160 cm.), poster (BP 139, DM 333, FR 1127, Y 25,823).

$878* *Chamonix Mont-Blanc. "Toutes Les Installations De Sports D'Hiver", 1924,* very good cond., (03-15-93, Arcole, #110, illus.), 41¾ x 29¹⁵⁄₁₆ in., (106 x 76 cm.), (BP 611, DM 1458, FR 4958, Y 104,004).

$440* *Granville, "Les Plus Grandes Marees D'Europe", Golf, Yachting, Camping, Peche, Les Iles Chausey,* excell. cond., (01-23-93, Ribeyre/Baron, #69), 39⅜ x 24⁷⁄₁₆ in., (100 x 62 cm.), poster (BP 288, DM 700, FR 2367, Y 55,069).

$519* *PLM. Chemin De Fer A Cremaillere De Chamonix Au Montenvers. Mer De Glace, 1920,* very good cond., (03-15-93, Arcole, #61, illus.), 39⅜ x 24⁷⁄₁₆ in., (100 x 62 cm.), (BP 361, DM 862, FR 2931, Y 61,478).

$239* *PLM. Dauphine. "Saint-Pierre De Chartreuse Et Le Pic De Chamechaude",* very good cond., (03-15-93, Arcole, #64), 42½ x 30⅞ in., (108 x 78.5 cm.), (BP 166, DM 397, FR 1350, Y 28,311).

$339* *PLM. En Tarentaise. "Pralognan Et Le Massif De La Vanoise",* very good cond., (03-15-93, Arcole, #62), 42¹¹⁄₁₆ x 27³⁄₁₆ in., (108.5 x 69 cm.), (BP 236, DM 563, FR 1914, Y 40,156).

$414* *Le Rock Du Bagne (Jailhouse Rock), De R. Thorpe, Avec Elvis Presley,1957,* (01-31-93, Morelle/Marchan, #72), 47¼ x 62¹⁵⁄₁₆ in., (120 x 160 cm.), poster (BP 278, DM 667, FR 2255, Y 51,647).

$231* *Services Autocars De Le Cie Du Midi: Gavarnie. Route Des Pyrenees,* p. E. Baudelot, good cond., (11-19-92, Ribeyre/Baron, #120), 41⁵⁄₁₆ x 28⅜ in., (105 x 72 cm.), poster (BP 152, DM 368, FR 1241, Y 28,728).

$40* *Solita De Cordoue. Avec Alain Cuny Et Carmen Torres,* Imp. Delattre, fairly good cond., (02-12-93, Cheval/Robert, #204), 62¹⁵⁄₁₆ x 47¼ in., (160 x 120 cm.), poster (BP 28, DM 66, FR 224, Y 4824).

SOUBIE, Roger
$805* *Lolita, No Text, 1962,* plate s., lined, (03-25-93, Christie-E, #209, illus.), 62¾ x 47 in., (159.4 x 119.4 cm.), color lithograph (BP 547, DM 1322, FR 4497, Y 94,306).

SOULAGES, Pierre   French b. 1919
BI *Composition,* s. Soulages, 46/100, est. DK 6,000, (03-24-93, Kunsthallen, #313), color etching.
$632* *Composition,* s. Soulages, 17/115, (09-30-92, Kunsthallen, #269), lithograph in colors (BP 357, DM 896, FR 3031, Y 75,843, DK 3450).
$1580* *Composition,* s. Soulages, 7/100, (09-30-92, Kunsthallen, #273), lithograph in colors (BP 891, DM 2240, FR 7578, Y 189,608, DK 8625).
$1685* *Composition,* s. Soulages, 44/100, (09-30-92, Kunsthallen, #274), color lithograph (BP 951, DM 2389, FR 8082, Y 202,208, DK 9200).
$1159* *Composition,* s. Spoulages, 75/85, (09-30-92, Kunsthallen, #271), lithograph in colors (BP 654, DM 1644, FR 5559, Y 139,086, DK 6325).
$257* *Composition,* s. Soulages, 17/115, (03-24-93, Kunsthallen, #315), color lithograph (BP 174, DM 420, FR 1429, Y 30,196, DK 1610).
$734* *Composition,* s. Soulages, 68/85, (03-24-93, Kunsthallen, #314), color lithograph (BP 497, DM 1199, FR 4080, Y 86,241, DK 4600).
$316* *Composition,* s. Soulages, 42/100, (09-30-92, Kunsthallen, #270), serigraph (BP 178, DM 448, FR 1516, Y 37,922, DK 1725).
$175* *"Composition",* epreuve d'artiste, s., (02-17-93, Bonhams-Chelsea, #244), sheet 26 x 19¾ in., (66 x 50.2 cm.), color aquatint (BP 121, DM 284, FR 963, Y 20,903).
$1835* *Composition, Eau Forte No. 17, 1961, (Riviere XVII),* s. Soulages, 57/100, (03-24-93, Kunsthallen, #312), color etching (BP 1243, DM 2997, FR 10,200, Y 215,603, DK 11,500).
$1101* *Composition, Eau Forte No. 2, 1952, (Riviere 11),* s. Soulages, 28/100, (03-24-93, Kunsthallen, #311), color etching (BP 746, DM 1798, FR 6120, Y 129,362, DK 6900).
$562* *Composition, Eau Forte No. 3, 1952 (Riviere III),* s., (12-02-92, Kunsthallen, #269), etching (BP 363, DM 884, FR 3017, Y 69,927, DK 3450).
$1415* *Eau Forte No. 12, (R. XII), 1957,* s., num. 95/100, pub. Lacouriere, full margins, surface dirt, good cond., (12-01-92, Christie-London, #631), L. 15⅜ x 14³⁄₁₆ in., (390 x 360 mm.), etching w/embossing in colors on BFK Rives (BP 935, DM 2255, FR 7686, Y 176,170).
$674* *"Eau Forte No. 3" (Riviere III), 1952,* (06-05-93, Grisebach, #882, illus.), 9⅝ x 6¾ in., (24.4 x 17.2 cm.), aquatint on copper print paper (BP 444, DM 1093, FR 3683, Y 72,302).
$1731* *Eau-Forte No 10 B. (Rivere X), 1957,* #4/65, pencil s., (11-20-92, Lempertz, #868), sh 30 x 22⁷⁄₁₆ in., (76.2 x 57 cm.), etching on Arches-Velin (BP 1140, DM 2760, FR 9296, Y 215,272).
$2380* *Eau-Forte #13 (Riviere XIII), 1957,* #30/100, pencil s., tears, (11-20-92, Lempertz, #869, illus.), sh 30 x 22⅜ in., (76.2 x 56.8 cm.), etching on Velin on BFK Rives (BP 1567, DM 3795, FR 12,782, Y 295,983).
$2020* *Eau-Forte #8 (Riviere VIII), 1957,* #33/100, pencil s., (11-20-92, Lempertz, #867), sh 30 x 22⁵⁄₁₆ in., (76.2 x 56.7 cm.), color etching on Velin on BFK Rives (BP 1330, DM 3221, FR 10,849, Y 251,213).
$2021* *"Eau-Forte No. XXXI", after 1973,* s., num., (11-28-92, Grisebach, #775, illus.), 23½ x 15¹⁄₁₆ in., (59.7 x 38.2 cm.), colored aquatint on wove (BP 1334, DM 3220, FR 10,930, Y 251,525).
$3817* *Eau-forte No 1 (Riviere I), 1952,* s., num., (12-01-92, Karl/Faber, #1262, illus.), 19½ x 12¹⁵⁄₁₆ in., (49.5 x 33 cm.), color etching on Arches wove (BP 2522, DM 6084, FR 20,733, Y 475,224).
$1245* *Eau-forte No 6 (R. VI), 1957,* s., num., light-staining, yellowed, (12-01-92, Karl/Faber, #1263), 23¼ x 16¹⁵⁄₁₆ in., (59 x 43 cm.), etching w/colors on BFK Rives wove (BP 823, DM 1984, FR 6763, Y 155,005).

$1410* *Komposition (Riviere 7 b), 1957,* s., epreuve d'artiste, i., (05-26-93, Dorling, #2990, illus.), 21⁵⁄₁₆ x 16⅝ in., (54.2 x 42.3 cm.), color lithograph on BFK Rives wove (BP 912, DM 2301, FR 7743, Y 153,194).
$1079* *Komposition, 1960,* s., num., stains, (12-01-92, Karl/Faber, #1264), 29⅛ x 18¹¹⁄₁₆ in., (74 x 47.5 cm.), color photolithograph on Arches wove (BP 713, DM 1720, FR 5861, Y 134,338).
$848* *Lithograph No. 8 (Duby 8), 1958,* s., #223/250, restored, (06-12-93, Hauswedell/Nolt, #396), 25³⁄₁₆ x 18⅞ in., (64 x 48 cm.), color lithograph on Arches (BP 555, DM 1380, FR 4639, Y 89,235).
BI *Lithographie #26 (Riviere 28), 1969,* #78/85, pencil s., est. DM 1,800, (11-20-92, Lempertz, #870), sh 30¹¹⁄₁₆ x 22⅝ in., (78 x 57.5 cm.), color lithograph on Arches-Velin.
$387* *Lithographie 19 (Riviere 21), 1968,* s. artist's proof, (06-28-93, Loudmer, #366), 19⁵⁄₁₆ x 20¹⁄₁₆ in., (490 x 510 mm.), sh 21⅝ x 27⁹⁄₁₆ in., (490 x 510 mm.), color lithograph on Arches wove (BP 259, DM 658, FR 2215, Y 41,061).
$870* *Lithographie 24b (Riviere 123), 1969,* s. artist's proof, (06-28-93, Loudmer, #367), 30⅞ x 22¹⁄₁₆ in., (785 x 560 mm.), sh 30⅞ x 22¹⁄₁₆ in., (785 x 560 mm.), color lithograph on wove (BP 583, DM 1478, FR 4980, Y 92,308).
BI *Lithographie 3 (Riviere 3), 1957,* s., num., est. DM 2,400, (12-05-92, Bassenge, #7742A, illus.), 24¹³⁄₁₆ x 18¹⁵⁄₁₆ in., (63.1 x 48.2 cm.), color lithograph on wove.
$638* *Lithographie No 15 (Riviere 17), 1964,* s., num., (06-08-93, Karl/Faber, #1318), sh approx. 25¹³⁄₁₆ x 19¹¹⁄₁₆ in., (65.5 x 50 cm.), color lithograph on BFK Rives wove (BP 419, DM 1035, FR 3486, Y 67,764).
$921* *Lithographie No 20a (R. 22), 1969,* s., (06-08-93, Karl/Faber, #1319), approx. 31½ x 23⅝ in., (80 x 60 cm.), lithograph in brown-black on Arches wove (BP 605, DM 1494, FR 5033, Y 97,823).
$1003* *Lithographie No. 21 (Riviere 23), 1969,* s., #34/65, (05-27-93, Lempertz, #1028), 30½ x 21¹⁄₁₆ in., (77.5 x 53.5 cm.), lithograph on wove (BP 642, DM 1609, FR 5425, Y 107,526).
BI *Lithographie No. 23 (Riviere 25), 1969,* s., #77/85, est. DM 1,800-, (05-27-93, Lempertz, #1029), 31½ x 22 in., (80 x 55.9 cm.), color lithograph on thick wove.
$1024* *Lithographie No. 6 (Riviere L 6), 1957,* s., num., (12-02-92, Dorling, #3020, illus.), 22⁷⁄₁₆ x 17⁵⁄₁₆ in., (57 x 44 cm.), color lithograph on handmade BFK Rives (BP 661, DM 1610, FR 5497, Y 127,411).
$1201* *No 6 (Riviere 6), 1957,* s., #3/95, pub. Berggruen, full margins, good cond., s., one #56/99,other i. HC, full margins, good cond., (06-30-93, Sotheby-London, #922), color lithograph on wove (BP 805, DM 2048, FR 6910, Y 128,683).
$1443* *Ohne Titel, #51/95,* pencil s., (11-20-92, Lempertz, #871), sh 33¹⁵⁄₁₆ x 23¾ in., (86.3 x 60.3 cm.), color lithograph on Velin (BP 950, DM 2301, FR 7750, Y 179,455).
BI *Ohne Titel, #94/95,* pencil s., est. DM 2,000, (11-20-92, Lempertz, #872), sh 29⅝ x 31⅞ in., (75.3 x 81 cm.), color lithograph on Velin.
BI *Ohne Titel, #51/100,* pencil s., est. DM 2,000, (11-20-92, Lempertz, #873), sh 22¼ x 23⅝ in., (56.5 x 60 cm.), serigraph on Velin.
$735* *"Sans Titre 32 B-1974", #36/95,* s., (01-28-93, Pescheteau, #256), 29¹⁵⁄₁₆ x 22¹⁄₁₆ in., (76 x 56 cm.), color lithograph on Arches (BP 485, DM 1165, FR 3941, Y 91,259).
$489* *Untitled,* s., i epreuve d'essai, annot., full margins, good cond., soiling, creases, (12-09-92, Sotheby-Amstrdm, #642), 19⅞ x 15¾ in., (505 x 400 mm.), color etching w/embossing on wove (BP 312, DM 768, FR 2619, Y 60,632, G 863).
BI *Untitled,* s., #65/100, est. DM 2,800-, (05-27-93, Lempertz, #1030), 25⅜ x 18⅞ in., (64.5 x 48 cm.), aquatint etching on wove.
$788* *Untitled,* s., #88/95, foxing, (05-27-93, Lempertz, #1031), 18¹⁵⁄₁₆ x 29⅝ in., (48.1 x 75.2 cm.), color lithograph on wove (BP 505, DM 1264, FR 4262, Y 84,477).

SOUNM?, Crawford

$15   *"Sir, Don't Waste"*, mildew stain, (03-04-93, Alderfer, #269), 29 x 21 in., (73.7 x 53.3 cm.), poster (BP 10, DM 25, FR 83, Y 1746).

SOURY, G.

$525*   *250 Animaux Exotiques Differents Des Cinq Parties Du Monde, 1947*, p. Bedos, good cond., (11-19-92, Ribeyre/Baron, #183), 62¹⁵⁄₁₆ x 47¼ in., (160 x 120 cm.), poster (BP 346, DM 837, FR 2820, Y 65,290).

$503*   *Cirque Cosmopolite: "Dompteur Et Groupe De Lions", 1924*, p. L. Serre, good cond., (11-19-92, Ribeyre/Baron, #181), 59⁷⁄₁₆ x 44⅛ in., (151 x 112 cm.), poster (BP 331, DM 802, FR 2701, Y 62,554).

$545*   *Miss Eliane Et Felix Petit, 1924*, good cond., lit., (11-19-92, Ribeyre/Baron, #182), 47¼ x 62¹⁵⁄₁₆ in., (120 x 160 cm.), poster (BP 359, DM 869, FR 2927, Y 67,778).

$147*   *Tete De Tigre, 1930*, p. Choppy, good cond., (11-19-92, Ribeyre/Baron, #184), 31½ x 23⅝ in., (80 x 60 cm.), poster (BP 97, DM 234, FR 789, Y 18,281).

SOUTHWORTH, Albert Sands and Josiah HAWES

BI   *Two Boston Matrons*, late 1840's, est. $2,5/3,500, (10-14-92, Swann, #157, illus.), 6½ x 5¼ in., (16.5 x 13.3 cm.), photograph, half-plate size daguerreotype.

SOUTMAN, Pieter Claesz   Dutch 1580-1657

BI   *The Tribute Money*, after Peter Paul Rubens, est. $4/600, (10-30-92, Sloan, #2804), 11 x 14¼ in., (27.9 x 36.2 cm.), engraving.

SOVAC, Pravoslav   American 20th cent.

$83*   *Cocktail Party (Art Opening)*, s., num. 6/99, (11-12-92, Freemn/Fine Art, #195), 15½ x 19 in., (39.4 x 48.3 cm.), etching (BP 55, DM 132, FR 444, Y 10,291).

$77*   *Combustion*, s., num. 12/15, (11-12-92, Freemn/Fine Art, #196), 5 x 6⅛ in., (12.7 x 15.6 cm.), etching w/hand coloring (BP 51, DM 122, FR 412, Y 9547).

$77*   *Configuration*, s., i. proof print, (11-12-92, Freemn/Fine Art, #197), plate 5 x 6 in., (12.7 x 15.2 cm.), etching in color (BP 51, DM 122, FR 412, Y 9547).

SOVIAK, Harry   American 20th cent.

$138*   *"Sienna"*, s., #7/20, (10-10-92, Goldberg, #534), 22 x 30 in., (55.9 x 76.2 cm.), color lithograph (BP 82, DM 205, FR 688, Y 16,801).

$110*   *"Untitled"*, s., #20/50, (10-10-92, Goldberg, #535), 30 x 22 in., (76.2 x 55.9 cm.), color lithograph (BP 65, DM 163, FR 549, Y 13,392).

SOWERBY

$64   *Botanical Prints, c. 1890: Seven*, (06-11-93, G.A. Key, #105), 9 x 6 in., (22.9 x 15.2 cm.), colored print (BP 42, DM 104, FR 351, Y 6790).

SOYER, Isaac   Russian/American b. 1907

$100*   *Ballet Dancers*, s., num., (02-04-93, Sloan, #403), 17¾ x 13 in., (45.1 x 33 cm.), color lithograph (BP 70, DM 165, FR 558, Y 12,439).

BI   *Two Female Dancers*, s., #192/250, s. by printer Maurer in stone, est. $200/300, (09-17-92, Sloan, #1418), 17¾ x 14⅛ in., (45.1 x 35.9 cm.), color lithograph.

BI   *Two Female Dancers*, s., num., stone s. by printer Maurer, good cond., tape, est. $2/300, (05-15-93, Cleveland, #313, illus.), 17¾ x 14 in., (45.1 x 35.6 cm.), color lithograph.

SOYER, Moses   Russian/American 1899-1974

$99*   *"Dancers"*, s. plate; s., (06-24-93, Boos, #608), sight 23⅝ x 19¹¹⁄₁₆ in., (600 x 500 mm.), silkscreen (BP 67, DM 169, FR 569, Y 10,798).

$110*   *Three Dancers*, s., i. 2nd ed., num. 42/50, (11-12-92, Freemn/Fine Art, #199), 17 x 12 in., (43.2 x 30.5 cm.), litho (BP 72, DM 174, FR 588, Y 13,639).

SOYER, Raphael   Russian/American 1899-1987

$440*   *"Arshille Gorky"* and *"Unemployed": Two*, both s., num. XIX/XXV, very good cond., (02-07-93, Bakker, #45), one image 19½ x 15 in., (49.5 x 38.1 cm.), other image 14½ x 12¾ in., (49.5 x 38.1 cm.), lithograph (BP 304, DM 730, FR 2466, Y 54,754).

BI   *Artist And Model (Cole 63), 1944*, s., t., light stain, very good cond.. est. $1/1,500, (06-11-93, Doyle, #73), 12¼ x 9½ in., (311 x 241 mm.), lithograph.

$248*   *"Artist's Drawing Board"*, s., #133/150, (03-24-93, Grogan, #137), 17¼ x 12 in., (43.8 x 30.5 cm.), color lithograph (BP 168, DM 405, FR 1379, Y 29,139).

$385*   *"Barefoot Girl"*, *"Girl Meditating"* and *"Young Woman Braiding Her Hair": Group Of 3*, s., i. A.P., (05-27-93, Swann, #261), color lithograph (BP 247, DM 618, FR 2082, Y 41,274).

$110*   *"Black Hair"*, s., very fine cond., (10-31-92, Cleveland, #221), 18½ x 13¾ in., (47 x 34.9 cm.), lithograph (BP 70, DM 169, FR 574, Y 13,626).

$105*   *"Black Hair"*, s. by artist, excell. cond., (05-15-93, Cleveland, #317), 18½ x 13¾ in., (47 x 34.9 cm.), lithograph (BP 68, DM 169, FR 568, Y 11,640).

$248*   *"The Braid"* and *"After The Bath": Two*, s., annot. A/P, (05-16-93, Hindman, #546), larger 16½ x 12 in., (41.9 x 30.5 cm.), lithograph (BP 161, DM 399, FR 1341, Y 27,491).

$176*   *The Braid, c. 1980*, s., annot. A/P, (03-14-93, Hindman, #324), 16⅝ x 12 in., (42.2 x 30.5 cm.), color lithograph (BP 123, DM 293, FR 996, Y 20,742).

BI   *A Collection Of Twelve Lithographs*, from Memories, NY, Touchstone Publishers, c. 1970, each s., num., full margins, creasing; two w/tears; one w/foxmark; one w/old glue; orig. silk-covered portfolio box, est. $2/2,500, (09-19-92, Christie-E, #61, illus.), each sheet 26 x 20 in., (660 x 508 mm.), eight lithographs in colors, two on wove.

$303*   *Couple In Interior (C. 100), 1963*, s., #77/85, from Sixteen Etchings portfolio, 1965, pub. AAA, full margins, good cond., mat staining, surface soiling, (10-28-92, Butterfield, #2756), 9⅞ x 7¾ in., (251 x 197 mm.), etching w/aquatint on Rives BFK (BP 193, DM 468, FR 1589, Y 37,178).

$248*   *Couple In Interior, 1963, Cole 100 (I/II)*, s., annot., artist's proof, undescribed first state, before addition aquatint, (09-20-92, Hindman, #701), 9¾ x 7⅝ in., (24.8 x 19.4 cm.), etching (BP 145, DM 368, FR 1259, Y 30,651).

$220*   *The Dance, c. 1980*, s., annot. A/P, (03-14-93, Hindman, #323), 18¾ x 16⅝ in., (47.6 x 42.2 cm.), lithograph (BP 153, DM 366, FR 1245, Y 25,928).

$275*   *Farewell*, tears in image, s., t., (11-12-92, Freemn/Fine Art, #205A), 16 x 12 in., (40.6 x 30.5 cm.), lithograph (BP 181, DM 436, FR 1470, Y 34,098).

$431*   *Flower Girl*, s., #90/150, full margins, very good cond., stray pencil marks, surface soiling, (05-19-93, Butterfield, #1832), 14½ x 9⅞ in., (368 x 251 mm.), lithograph on wove (BP 280, DM 701, FR 2360, Y 47,714).

$193*   *Girl*, s., #55/85, full margins, good cond., mat staining, foxing, surface soiling, (10-28-92, Butterfield, #2757), 9⅞ x 7⅞ in., (251 x 200 mm.), etching on cream wove (BP 123, DM 298, FR 1012, Y 23,681).

$110*   *"Girl Braiding Her Hair"*, plate s., very good cond.?, (07-19-92, Bakker, #118), image 10¼ x 8 in., (26 x 20.3 cm.), lithograph (BP 56, DM 160, FR 542, Y 13,675).

$230*   *Girl Combing Her Hair On A Bed*, s., #67/125, full margins, good cond., staining, crease, (05-19-93, Butterfield, #2025), 10⅝ x 8 in., (270 x 203 mm.), lithograph on Rives (BP 149, DM 374, FR 1260, Y 25,462).

BI   *Girl With Arms Crossed*, s., num., very fine cond., est. $350-450, (10-31-92, Cleveland, #224), 16½ x 13¾ in., (41.9 x 34.9 cm.), color lithograph.

$330*   *Girl With Parted Lips (C. 98), 1963*, s., num. 56/85, from the 16 Etchings Portfolio, pub. AAA, 1965, full-margins, good cond., light-staining, (02-24-93, Butterfield, #2874), 10 x 7¾ in., (254 x 197 mm.), etching on Arches (BP 230, DM 536, FR 1816, Y 38,723).

$220*   *Head Of A Young Woman Reflecting, c. 1970*, num., s., (05-27-93, Swann, #255), 16 x 12 in., (40.6 x 30.5 cm.), lithograph (BP 141, DM 353, FR 1190, Y 23,585).

$150*   *Jeune Fille*, s., #20/150, (02-04-93, Sloan, #715), 20 x 15⅞ in., (50.8 x 40.3 cm.), lithograph (BP 105, DM 247, FR 838, Y 18,659).

$132*   *"Jeune Fille"*, s., num., good cond., (10-31-92, Cleveland, #220), 20 x 15¾ in., (50.8 x 40 cm.), two color lithograph (BP 85, DM 203, FR 689, Y 16,351).

$650*   *"Life Class" (Cole 42A)*, s., t., #3/25, tear, glue staining, (05-15-93, Cleveland, #314, illus.), 6 x 8½ in., (15.2 x

21.6 cm.), lithograph (BP 423, DM 1046, FR 3514, Y 72,054).

$132* *"Lipstick"* (Cole 92), *1963,* s., num. 25/25, very fine cond., (10-31-92, Cleveland, #219), 9¾ x 7¾ in., (24.8 x 19.7 cm.), etching (BP 85, DM 203, FR 689, Y 16,351).

$248* *"Marsha",* s., stamp s., prov., (06-11-93, DuMouchelle, #2107, illus.), 15½ x 10¾ in., (39.4 x 27.3 cm.), color lithograph (BP 163, DM 403, FR 1359, Y 26,313).

$121* *Meditation, c. 1980,* s., annot. H.C., (05-16-93, Hindman, #559), 14⅛ x 11¼ in., (35.9 x 28.6 cm.), lithograph (BP 79, DM 195, FR 654, Y 13,413).

$303* *Meditation, c. 1980,* s., annot. H.C., (03-14-93, Hindman, #322), 14⅛ x 11¼ in., (35.9 x 28.6 cm.), lithograph (BP 211, DM 504, FR 1715, Y 35,710).

$495* *The Model,* s., t., discoloration, (11-12-92, Freemn/Fine Art, #205), plate 9½ x 12 in., (24.1 x 30.5 cm.), lithograph (BP 325, DM 784, FR 2646, Y 61,376).

$110* *Mother,* s., #87/150, (12-13-92, Hindman, #323), 17½ x 11¾ in., color lithograph (BP 70, DM 173, FR 589, Y 13,609).

$303* *Mother And Child,* s. in plate, s., i. Artist's proof, (07-03-92, Sloan, #1089), 17¾ x 13¾ in., (45.1 x 34.9 cm.), color lithograph (BP 158, DM 459, FR 1546, Y 37,771).

BI *Mother And Child,* s., num. 4/30, foxing, est. $3/400, (11-12-92, Freemn/Fine Art, #202), unframed 16¼ x 9¼ in., (41.3 x 23.5 cm.), lithograph.

$165* *Mother And Child,* s., #4/30, foxing, (06-11-93, Freemn/Fine Art, #211), 16¼ x 9¼ in., (41.3 x 23.5 cm.), lithograph (BP 108, DM 268, FR 904, Y 17,507).

$825* *Mother And Child* (Cole 106), *1964,* s., num. 54/100, full margins, light-staining, very good cond., (09-19-92, Christie-E, #60), borderline 17¾ x 14 in., (451 x 356 mm.), lithograph in colors on wove (BP 475, DM 1235, FR 4231, Y 102,791).

BI *Mother Nursing Her Baby,* s., #132/250, printer's blindstamp, est. $250/350, (09-17-92, Sloan, #646), 14 x 10⅞ in., (35.6 x 27.6 cm.), etching and aquatint.

BI *Mother Nursing Her Baby,* s., num., printer's embossed mono. (ES), very good cond., est. $150/250, (05-15-93, Cleveland, #319), 13¾ x 10⅞ in., (34.9 x 27.6 cm.), etching and aquatint on Arches.

BI *Mother and Child, c. 1975,* s., num., excell. cond., est. $3/400, (05-15-93, Cleveland, #321), 13½ x 10¾ in., (34.3 x 27.3 cm.), etching.

$248* *Nude By Sink,* s., i., d. 1983, #53/71, (12-10-92, Sloan, #3051), 12⅝ x 9½ in., (32.1 x 24.1 cm.), etching (BP 160, DM 392, FR 1340, Y 30,678).

$154* *"Nude Washing",* s., very fine cond., (10-31-92, Cleveland, #223), 14 x 11½ in., (35.6 x 29.2 cm.), lithograph (BP 99, DM 237, FR 804, Y 19,076).

$130* *"Nude Washing",* s., #A.P., excell. cond., (05-15-93, Cleveland, #316), 14 x 11½ in., (35.6 x 29.2 cm.), lithograph (BP 85, DM 209, FR 703, Y 14,411).

BI *Nudes* (Cole 113), s., num. 17/100, good condition, est. $3/400, (11-12-92, Freemn/Fine Art, #203), 20 x 23½ in., (50.8 x 59.7 cm.), lithograph.

BI *Nudes* (Cole 113), s., #17/100, good cond., est. $2/300, (06-11-93, Freemn/Fine Art, #212), 20 x 23½ in., (50.8 x 59.7 cm.), lithograph.

$95* *"Nursery II",* s., excell. cond., (05-15-93, Cleveland, #318), 17 x 12½ in., (43.2 x 31.8 cm.), lithograph (BP 62, DM 153, FR 514, Y 10,531).

$138* *"Pensive Girl", 1963,* s., #32/50, (06-11-93, Freemn/Fine Art, #209C), plate 9⅜ x 8 in., (23.8 x 20.3 cm.), etching (BP 91, DM 224, FR 756, Y 14,642).

BI *Portrait Of A Woman's Head In Profile, c. 1971,* s., i. A.P., est. $2/300, (05-15-93, Cleveland, #320), 15½ x 11¾ in., (39.4 x 29.8 cm.), lithograph.

BI *Profile Portrait Of A Woman,* s., i. A.P., est. $350/450, (09-17-92, Sloan, #1444), 15¼ x 12 in., (38.7 x 30.5 cm.), lithograph.

$350* *"Protected",* AAA edit., s., t., mat burn, margin, trimmed, hinges, (05-15-93, Cleveland, #315, illus.), 13½ x 6 in., (34.3 x 15.2 cm.), lithograph (BP 228, DM 563, FR 1892, Y 38,798).

$770* *Railroad Waiting Room* (C. 69), *1954,* s., annot. A.P., pub. AAA, full margins, good cond., mat staining, taped, surface soiling, (02-24-93, Butterfield, #2871), 12 x 9½

in., (305 x 241 mm.), lithograph on wove (BP 537, DM 1250, FR 4238, Y 90,354).

$330* *Seamstress,* s. Raphael Soyer, #10/300, very good cond., (03-12-93, Skinner, #36, illus.), sight 20 x 14⅛ in., (50.8 x 35.9 cm.), lithograph wove (BP 230, DM 549, FR 1868, Y 38,892).

BI *The Search,* s., #5/75, i. second impression, est. $2/250, (04-02-93, Sloan, #1181), 22⅛ x 16½ in., (559 x 419 mm.), color lithograph.

BI *The Search Party,* s., #5/75, i. second impression, est. $300/400, (12-10-92, Sloan, #1308), 22⅛ x 16½ in., (55.9 x 41.9 cm.), color lithograph.

$330* *Seated Girl With Arms Crossed, 1979,* full margins, num., s., pub. London Arts, (05-27-93, Swann, #257), 16½ x 14 in., (41.9 x 35.6 cm.), color lithograph (BP 211, DM 530, FR 1785, Y 35,377).

$385* *"Seated Woman"* and *"Portrait Of A Woman": Two,* s., num. 42/85 & 23/100, full margins, good cond., creases, mat & light-staining, Seated Woman w/foxing, Portrait of A Woman taped, (02-24-93, Butterfield, #2873), 10 x 8 in., (254 x 203 mm.), 6⅞ x 5⅜ in., (254 x 203 mm.), etching on wove (BP 268, DM 625, FR 2119, Y 45,177).

$385* *Self Portrait,* s., i. printer's proof, (11-12-92, Freemn/Fine Art, #201), 16 x 12 in., (40.6 x 30.5 cm.), lithograph (BP 253, DM 610, FR 2058, Y 47,737).

$220* *Self Portrait,* s., #46/150, good cond., mat burn, tear, (12-12-92, Weschler, #169), 25¾ x 20 in., (65.4 x 50.8 cm.), color lithograph (BP 141, DM 347, FR 1188, Y 27,224).

$413* *"Self Portrait At 81",* s., (08-08-92, Litchfield, #161), 10¹⁵⁄₁₆ x 8 in., (27.8 x 20.3 cm.), color lithograph (BP 214, DM 607, FR 2053, Y 52,712).

$248* *Self Portrait, 1974,* 2 states, s., full margins, excell. cond., (10-10-92, Litchfield, #197), plate 7 x 4¾ in., (17.8 x 12.1 cm.), etching (BP 147, DM 368, FR 1237, Y 30,192).

$303* *Self-Portrait* (Gettings 110), *1969,* s., #54/100, (05-16-93, Hindman, #553), 13¼ x 10¾ in., (33.7 x 27.3 cm.), lithograph (BP 197, DM 487, FR 1638, Y 33,588).

$286* *"Self-Portrait", 1980s,* s., num., pub. London Arts; stamp verso, very fine cond., (10-31-92, Cleveland, #222), 11 x 8 in., (27.9 x 20.3 cm.), color lithograph (BP 183, DM 440, FR 1493, Y 35,427).

$358* *Sing A Song Of Friendship,* s., t., num. 234/300, annot. Limited Edition, full margins, good cond., light-staining, (02-24-93, Butterfield, #2872), 14 x 12¾ in., (356 x 324 mm.), lithograph on wove (BP 250, DM 581, FR 1970, Y 42,009).

BI *Studies With Self-Portrait* (Cole 115), s., t., i. AP, good cond., (11-12-92, Freemn/Fine Art, #200), 22 x 30 in., (55.9 x 76.2 cm.), lithograph.

$165* *Studies with Self Portrait* (Cole 115), s., t., i. AP, good cond., (06-11-93, Freemn/Fine Art, #214), 22 x 30 in., (55.9 x 76.2 cm.), lithograph (BP 108, DM 268, FR 904, Y 17,507).

$275* *"Two Women Stretching Out",* s., (05-15-93, Dunning, #1017), 12 x 8 in., (30.5 x 20.3 cm.), lithograph (BP 179, DM 442, FR 1486, Y 30,484).

$165* *"Woman Seated",* s., #273/275, excell. cond.?, (07-19-92, Bakker, #62), image 16¼ x 13½ in., (41.3 x 34.3 cm.), color lithograph (BP 85, DM 240, FR 813, Y 20,512).

$193* *"Woman Sitting On Bed",* s., #12/100, full margins, good cond., light-staining, hinge remains, skinned spot, yellow stains, (10-28-92, Butterfield, #2755), 17 x 14¼ in., (432 x 362 mm.), lithograph on wove (BP 123, DM 298, FR 1012, Y 23,681).

$302* *"Woman With Plant", c. 1970* and *"Seated Woman", c. 1975: Two,* from Memories portfolio, full margins, orig. annot. folder sleeve, minor mat burn, each i. A.P., (05-27-93, Swann, #260), one 15¼ x 21¾ in., (38.7 x 55.2 cm.), other 17 x 14 in., (38.7 x 55.2 cm.), lithograph (BP 193, DM 485, FR 1633, Y 32,376).

$220* *"Young Dancers",* plate s.; s., i., (08-05-92, Boos, #564), image, sight 17⅛ x 12¹⁵⁄₁₆ in., (435 x 330 mm.), lithograph (BP 115, DM 325, FR 1098, Y 28,018).

$193* *Young Girl In Profile,* s., artists proof, very good cond., (07-19-92, Bakker, #35), plate 10⅜ x 8⅛ in., (26.4 x

20.6 cm.), etching and aquatint (BP 99, DM 281, FR 951, Y 23,993).

SOZAN, Ito   b. 1884
- BI *Kranich Auf Einem Ast*, lit., est. SC 14/16,000, (04-27-93, Dorotheum, #198, illus.), 6¹³⁄₁₆ x 15⁷⁄₁₆ in., (17.3 x 39.2 cm.), color woodcut.
- BI *Vogel Auf Einem Blutenzweig*, est. SC 6/7,000, (04-27-93, Dorotheum, #186, illus.), 10³⁄₁₆ x 6¹⁵⁄₁₆ in., (25.8 x 17.6 cm.), color woodcut.

SPALATIN, Marko   Yugoslavian b. 1945
- $20* *"Red Cubes", 1970,* The Print Club of Cleveland Publication No. 48 for 1978, s., image scuffing, (05-15-93, Cleveland, #493), 15½ x 12½ in., (39.4 x 31.8 cm.), color serigraph (BP 13, DM 32, FR 108, Y 2217).

SPANO, Michael   b. 1949
- $715* *"Classic Back", 1980,* s., edit. 4/20, Dixon Collection, (11-16-92, Butterfield, #6174, illus.), 24⁵⁄₁₆ x 18⁹⁄₁₆ in., (617 x 470.7 mm.), photograph, gelatin silver print (BP 471, DM 1140, FR 3840, Y 88,919).
- BI *Girl Reflected In Mirror, 1988,* s., d., num. 5/25 by photog., #5/25 ed., est. $1,5/2,000, (10-15-92, Sotheby-NY, #607, illus.), 27⅛ x 36 in., (68.9 x 91.4 cm.), photograph, solarized silver print.
- BI *Panoramas: Two, 1980,* s., d., est. $1,5/1,800, (10-13-92, Christie-NY, #602, illus.), each 7⅛ x 17 in., (18.1 x 43.2 cm.), photograph, gelatin silver prints.
- $715* *Portrait Of A Man, 1991,* s., d., edit. 1/25, Dixon Collection, (11-16-92, Butterfield, #6175, illus.), 24⁹⁄₁₆ x 18¹⁵⁄₁₆ in., (623.4 x 480.3 mm.), photograph, gelatin silver print (BP 471, DM 1140, FR 3840, Y 88,919).
- $1540* *Untitled (Nude), 1984-85,* s., d., num. 3/25, (10-13-92, Christie-NY, #603, illus.), 35⅝ x 27½ in., (90.5 x 69.9 cm.), photograph, gelatin silver print (BP 897, DM 2256, FR 7666, Y 186,735).
- $1100* *Woman With Hat And Pearls Reading The "Daily News", 1988,* s., d., num. 3/15 by photog., #3/15 ed., (10-15-92, Sotheby-NY, #606, illus.), 36½ x 27¼ in., (91.4 x 69.2 cm.), photograph, solarized silver print (BP 673, DM 1637, FR 5553, Y 131,974).

SPEED, John   English 1552-1629
- $440* *New Mape Ye XVII Provinces Of Low Germanie,* (04-02-93, Sloan, #1211, illus.), sight 16¼ x 20¼ in., (413 x 514 mm.), hand colored engraving (BP 290, DM 707, FR 2402, Y 50,097).

SPEER, T.P.   American 20th cent.
- BI *"Our Modern Home",* s., num. Trial Proof, t., est. $150/200, (05-15-93, Cleveland, #495), 14⅝ x 19 in., (37.1 x 48.3 cm.), color etching.
- BI *"Our Modern Home",* s., #Trial Proof, t., est. $150/200, (05-15-93, Cleveland, #494), 14⅝ x 19 in., (37.1 x 48.3 cm.), etching in colors.

SPENCE, Andy
- $1150* *Untitled: Five,* complete potfolio, each s., d., i. AP 7/10, artist's proofs, pub. Parasol Press, Ltd., 1990, full margins, good cond., (05-15-93, Sotheby-NY, #1208, illus.), aquatints in colors (BP 748, DM 1850, FR 6216, Y 127,480).

SPENCE, Christine
- $33 *Anemones And Daisies,* s. limited ed., #175/675, (06-11-93, G.A. Key, #35), 14 x 12 in., (35.6 x 30.5 cm.), print (BP 22, DM 54, FR 181, Y 3501).

SPENCER, Carrie   American 20th cent.
- $99* *"Through The Kitchen Window",* s. Carrie Spencer, t., #7/8, (05-15-93, Wolf, #748), 8½ x 11 in., (21.6 x 27.9 cm.), color woodblock (BP 64, DM 159, FR 535, Y 10,974).

SPENCER, Ema
- $935* *On The Longed-For Hobby Horse, 1902,* notations, (10-14-92, Swann, #567, illus.), 6⅞ x 4⅞ in., (17.5 x 12.4 cm.), photograph, cyanotype (BP 549, DM 1368, FR 4640, Y 113,306).

SPENCER, Noel
- $119 *"The Lion Brewery",* s., (08-14-92, G.A. Key, #83), 9 x 8 in., (22.9 x 20.3 cm.), etching (BP 62, DM 175, FR 591, Y 15,006).

SPENCER, Stanley
- $1480* *Marriage At Cana,* s., d. '53, #28/30, folded over behind the mount top and bottom, tape stains, foxing, cockling, (10-27-92, Phillips-London, #304), sheet 5½ x 5¼ in., (140 x 133 mm.), lithograph on simili japan (BP 935, DM 2268, FR 7696, Y 181,040).

SPESCHA, Matias   b. 1925
- $1896* *Farblinolschnitte, 1982: Twelve,* #58/60, s., d., num., (04-21-93, Germann, #767), 25⁹⁄₁₆ x 19¹¹⁄₁₆ in., (650 x 500 mm.), portfolio (BP 1230, DM 3031, FR 10,249, Y 209,897, SF 2760).

SPILLER, Jurg   1913-1974
- BI *Komposition,* 26/50, s., est. SF 60/80, (10-14-92, Germann, #612), 13¾ x 19¹¹⁄₁₆ in., (350 x 500 mm.), color lithograph.
- BI *Komposition,* 43/50, s., est. SF 60/80, (10-14-92, Germann, #613), 13¾ x 19¹¹⁄₁₆ in., (350 x 500 mm.), color lithograph.

SPINOSA, Gary   American 20th cent.
- BI *"Night Region",* s., t., good cond., est. $1/200, (05-15-93, Cleveland, #496), 17⅝ x 13 in., (44.8 x 33 cm.), etching.

SPIRO, Eugene
- $33* *Piano Player,* s., (08-20-92, Bonhams-Chelsea, #149), image 5 x 4½ in., (12.7 x 11.4 cm.), lithograph (BP 17, DM 48, FR 162, Y 4167).

SPITZER, Walter   Polish b. 1927
- BI *"Porteur D'Eau",* EA II/V, t., s., est. FF6/800, (04-04-93, Pescheteau, #295), 25⁹⁄₁₆ x 19¹¹⁄₁₆ in., (65 x 50 cm.), etching and aquatint.

SPOERRI, Daniel   European b. 1930
- $318* *Ertinkungstod, 1970,* s., d., (11-28-92, Schoppmann, #811), 23¼ x 30½ in., (59 x 77.5 cm.), color serigraph on canvas (BP 210, DM 507, FR 1720, Y 39,577).
- $289* *Selbsterdrosselung, 1970,* s., d., (11-28-92, Schoppmann, #810), 23¼ x 30½ in., (59 x 77.5 cm.), color serigraph on canvas (BP 191, DM 460, FR 1563, Y 35,968).
- BI *Selbsterdrosselung, 1972,* from portfolio Morddrohung, #X/100, s., d., est. SF 1,8/2,300, (11-13-92, Koller, #5428), serigraph on linen.
- BI *Triptychon, 1972,* from portfolio Morddrohung, #X/100, s., creases, est. SF 1,6/1,900, (11-13-92, Koller, #5429), serigraph on linen.

SPRANGER, Bartholomaeus (after)
- $921* *Die Heilige Familie Mit Der Rose (B. III, 90, 297, TIB 3 (3), S. 264,Commentary, S. 335, (.297), Hollstein VIII, 430, Hollstein XXVIII 4I),* watermark, (06-04-93, Bassenge, #5365, illus.), 9⅛ x 6⁹⁄₁₆ in., (23.2 x 16.6 cm.), engraving (BP 609, DM 1496, FR 5041, Y 99,331).

SPRINGER, Ferdinand   German b. 1907
- BI *Komposition,* 21/25, s., est. SF 180/250, (10-14-92, Germann, #445), 19½ x 13⅜ in., (495 x 340 mm.), etching.
- BI *Pluton A,* 6/20, s.; mounting traces verso, est. SF 200/250, (10-14-92, Germann, #444), 17⅝ x 21⅛ in., (447 x 537 mm.), etching w/embossing.

SPRONCKEN, Arthur   b. 1930
- BI *Untitled,* s., #128/200, full margins, good cond., est. G 2/300, (12-09-92, Sotheby-Amstrdm, #643), 13¹⁵⁄₁₆ x 19¹⁄₁₆ in., (355 x 484 mm.), etching on wove.

SPRUANCE, Benton   American 1904-1967
- $12,650* *American Pattern, Barn (Fine and Looney 184), 1940,* s., t., i. Ed 45, full margins, tear, staining, skinned spot, good cond., prov., (05-11-93, Christie-NY, #124, illus.), borderline 7¾ x 13¾ in., (197 x 349 mm.), lithograph in tan (red color) and black on wove (BP 8075, DM 19,928, FR 67,144, Y 1,391,486).
- BI *"Angel With A Sword",* s. Spruance '66, very good cond.?, est. $3/400, (11-21-92, Bakker, #120), image 16½ x 25 in., (41.9 x 63.5 cm.), color lithograph.
- $2090* *Approach To The Station (F. and L. 70), 1932,* s., t., i., num. 2/28, wide margins, pale foxing, very good cond., (09-19-92, Christie-E, #65), borderline 11 x 13 in., (279 x 330 mm.), lithograph on laid Japan (BP 1202, DM 3130, FR 10,718, Y 260,404).

$3850* *Arrangement For Drums (Fine & Looney 191), 1941*, i., init. by wife, d., t., i. 'Ed. 35-Trial Proof', estate stamp, impression of lithograph verso, full margins, good cond., mat stain, soiling, discoloration, fox marks, sold after sale, (11-05-92, Sotheby-NY, #51, illus.), 9½ x 14⅝ in., (240 x 370 mm.), lithograph on a sheet of wove (BP 2504, DM 6089, FR 20,599, Y 472,335).

BI *"Brief Balance" (F.& L. 189), 1941*, stains, good cond., est. $4-500, (10-31-92, Cleveland, #226, illus.), 14½ x 11⁹⁄₁₆ in., (36.8 x 29.4 cm.), lithograph.

$1980* *Bulldog Edition (F. and L. 76), 1932*, s., t., num. 7/30, full margins, pale light-staining, skinned spots,very good cond., (09-19-92, Christie-E, #67, illus.), borderline 8¹⁵⁄₁₆ x 14⁷⁄₁₆ in., (227 x 367 mm.), lithograph on Van Gelder Zonen (BP 1139, DM 2965, FR 10,154, Y 246,698).

$523* *Card Players (FL 36), 1930*, good cond., s., t., d. '30, (06-11-93, Freemn/Fine Art, #220), 9½ x 12¼ in., (24.1 x 31.1 cm.), lithograph w/black ink on cream chenet colle (BP 344, DM 850, FR 2866, Y 55,491).

$1210* *Caustic Comment, 1936*, s., very good cond., (06-11-93, Doyle, #74), 9¾ x 14½ in., (248 x 368 mm.), lithograph (BP 795, DM 1967, FR 6630, Y 128,382).

$248* *Christ Church, Philadelphia*, s., t., i. ed. 44, d. 1964, (11-12-92, Freemn/Fine Art, #207), 24 x 17 in., (61 x 43.2 cm.), litho in 3 colors (BP 163, DM 393, FR 1325, Y 30,750).

$138* *City Church (F.L. 472)*, s., t., i., (06-11-93, Freemn/Fine Art, #215), 24 x 17 in., (61 x 43.2 cm.), color lithograph (BP 91, DM 224, FR 756, Y 14,642).

$880* *City In The Rain (F. and L. 77), 1932*, s., full margins, printer's ink, very good cond., (09-19-92, Christie-E, #68), borderline 11¾ x 8⅞ in., (298 x 225 mm.), lithograph in black w/hand-coloring in red and yellow crayon on wove (BP 506, DM 1318, FR 4513, Y 109,644).

$220* *Clue To The Labrynth (FL 321), 1953: Two*, s., t., i., one d. '54, other '53, (06-11-93, Freemn/Fine Art, #225), 16¼ x 22⅜ in., (41.3 x 56.8 cm.), lithograph in black ink (BP 145, DM 358, FR 1205, Y 23,342).

$550* *"Conductor (F. and L. 14, 1929-30", "Thrill Of The Game (F. and L. 88), 1933" and "Midsummer Spiel (F. and L. 249), 1946": Three*, first s., d., i., num. 2/27, rubbed spot, surface soiling; second s., t., num. 24/35, very good cond.; third i. w/artist's name, t., d. by son, Benton Spruance estate ink stamp, skinned spot; each full margins; first and thirdgood cond., (09-19-92, Christie-E, #64), lithograph on BFK, third on wove (BP 316, DM 824, FR 2821, Y 68,527).

$633* *Conversation With Death (FL. 103)*, good cond., s., t., #10/40, (06-11-93, Freemn/Fine Art, #219), 9¾ x 15 in., (24.8 x 38.1 cm.), lithograph in black ink on cream paper (BP 416, DM 1029, FR 3468, Y 67,162).

$187* *"Dark Bed" (F. & L. 436), 1961*, s., d., t., num., very good cond., (10-31-92, Cleveland, #229), 21¼ x 29 in., (54 x 73.7 cm.), lithograph (BP 120, DM 288, FR 976, Y 23,164).

BI *"Death Of The Minotaur" (F. & L. 324), 1953*, s., t., good cond., est. $3-400, (10-31-92, Cleveland, #228), 19 x 14½ in., (48.3 x 36.8 cm.), color lithograph.

$165* *Deposition, 1956 (FL 363)*, s., t., i. ed. 30, (11-12-92, Freemn/Fine Art, #231), 20¼ x 14⅛ in., (51.4 x 35.6 cm.), litho in 5 colors (BP 108, DM 261, FR 882, Y 20,459).

$357* *Dreams Of Love*, s., good cond., (06-11-93, Doyle, #75), 12⅜ x 17 in., (314 x 432 mm.), lithograph (BP 235, DM 580, FR 1956, Y 37,878).

$1955* *"The Driving Tackle" and "Football Player" (F./L. 78 and 79), 1933: Two*, s., t., num. 13/40, 12/25, full margins, good cond., foxing, tear, skinning, (02-11-93, Sotheby-NY, #45), one 10¾ x 10¹¹⁄₁₆ in., (273 x 271 mm.), the other 12⅞ x 5⅞ in., (273 x 271 mm.), lithograph (BP 1379, DM 3238, FR 10,959, Y 235,684).

$275* *Ecclesiastes, Essay Three (FL. 247)*, s., t., num., (06-11-93, Freemn/Fine Art, #216), 19¼ x 14½ in., (48.9 x 36.8 cm.), lithograph (BP 181, DM 447, FR 1507, Y 29,178).

BI *"Ecclesiastes: Essay 1" (Vanity And A Striving) (F. & L. 245), 1945*, s., t., num., fold, good cond., est. $350-450, (10-31-92, Cleveland, #227), 18⅛ x 13¼ in., (46 x 33.7 cm.), lithograph.

$170* *"Ecclesiates: Essay I, Vanity And A Striving" (F. and L. 245), 1945*, s., t., num., good cond., minor flaws, (05-15-93, Cleveland, #323), 18 x 13⅜ in., (45.7 x 34 cm.), lithograph (BP 111, DM 273, FR 919, Y 18,845).

BI *"Ecclesiates: Essay II, (For Everything There Is A Season)" (F. and L. 246), 1945*, s., d., t., very good cond., est. $6/700, (05-15-93, Cleveland, #324), 18 x 12⅞ in., (45.7 x 32.7 cm.), lithograph.

$330* *Fencers (FL. 145), 1937*, (06-11-93, Freemn/Fine Art, #217), 12¾ x 7¹¹⁄₁₆ in., (32.4 x 19.5 cm.), lithograph in black ink (BP 217, DM 536, FR 1808, Y 35,013).

$880* *Fencers, 1937*, s. Spruance '37, (11-12-92, Freemn/Fine Art, #206, illus.), 12¾ x 7¹¹⁄₁₆ in., (32.4 x 19.5 cm.), litho (BP 578, DM 1394, FR 4703, Y 109,113).

$248* *Fortune Teller (FL 331), 1954*, s., t., num. 6/210, (11-12-92, Freemn/Fine Art, #232), 17½ x 12⅞ in., (44.5 x 32.7 cm.), litho printed in 4 colors (BP 163, DM 393, FR 1325, Y 30,750).

$385* *Genesis Angel-And Sword (L. 499), 1966*, s., d., annot. ed 22, p. by artist, full margins, good cond., creases, surface soiling, light-staining, taped to mat, tape remains, repaired tear extending into image, (02-24-93, Butterfield, #2656), 16⅝ x 25 in., (422 x 635 mm.), lithograph in colors on wove (BP 268, DM 625, FR 2119, Y 45,177).

$1320* *"Homing Instinct (Fine and Looney 8), 1929" and "Luxemburg Gardens (F. and L. 40), 1930":Two*, each s., t., full margins, very good cond.; first w/light-staining, tear; second w/old hinges, (09-19-92, Christie-E, #62, illus.), first lithograph on wove, watermark; second on Rives (BP 759, DM 1977, FR 6769, Y 164,465).

$275* *I'll Be What I Choose; Vanity Of Ambition (FL 280)*, s., t., d. '49, i. ed. 30, good cond., (11-12-92, Freemn/Fine Art, #226), 18¾ x 13⅜ in., (47.6 x 34 cm.), lithograph (BP 181, DM 436, FR 1470, Y 34,098).

$248* *Joshua (FL 467)*, s., t., i. 25, (11-12-92, Freemn/Fine Art, #233), 24⅜ x 17⅜ in., (61.9 x 44.1 cm.), litho in 7 colors (BP 163, DM 393, FR 1325, Y 30,750).

$600* *"Lamentation" (Fine and Looney 197), 1941*, s., d., t., excell. cond., (05-15-93, Cleveland, #322, illus.), 12⅛ x 18⁵⁄₁₆ in., (30.8 x 46.5 cm.), lithograph (BP 390, DM 965, FR 3243, Y 66,511).

$1073* *Last Stop-Beach Haven (FL. 201)*, s., t., i., 1946, good cond., (06-11-93, Freemn/Fine Art, #223, illus.), 9 x 15³⁄₁₆ in., (22.9 x 38.6 cm.), lithograph in colors (BP 705, DM 1744, FR 5879, Y 113,846).

BI *"Memorial To A Dead Child" (Fine & Looney 27), 1948*, s., t., good cond., est. $150-250, (10-31-92, Cleveland, #225), 19½ x 14 in., (49.5 x 35.6 cm.), lithograph.

$550* *Model At Rest (FL 120)*, s., t., num. 2/30, d. '35, good cond., (11-12-92, Freemn/Fine Art, #229, illus.), image 11 x 14 in., (27.9 x 35.6 cm.), lithograph (BP 361, DM 871, FR 2940, Y 68,196).

BI *"Nero", 1944*, s. Spruance w/bars, inits. BS, t., num. Ed 30, printer's drystamp, very good cond., soiling, ink transfer, est. $4/600, (09-11-92, Skinner, #25, illus.), 11⅝ x 15⅝ in., (29.5 x 39.7 cm.), lithograph in black and tan (red color) on wove.

$440* *Of The People-By The People (FL. 66), 1932*, s., t., d. '32, #2/28, (06-11-93, Freemn/Fine Art, #222), 11¼ x 9 in., (28.6 x 22.9 cm.), lithograph (BP 289, DM 715, FR 2411, Y 46,684).

$138* *Old Owl (FL 375): Two*, s. Mrs. Spruance, t., num., (11-12-92, Freemn/Fine Art, #220), mat 21 x 14¼ in., (53.3 x 36.2 cm.), lithos, one hand colored (BP 91, DM 219, FR 738, Y 17,111).

$330* *Paper Shapes, 1955 (FL 348)*, s., (11-12-92, Freemn/Fine Art, #228), image 12⅜ x 16¼ in., (31.4 x 41.3 cm.), lithograph printed in 7 colors (BP 217, DM 523, FR 1764, Y 40,918).

$248* *Piper (FL. 373), 1957*, hole, soiling, ink residue, good cond., s., t., i., (06-11-93, Freemn/Fine Art, #232), 16⅜ x 21¼ in., (41.6 x 54 cm.), lithograph in colors (BP 163, DM 403, FR 1359, Y 26,313).

$413* *Piper, 1957 (FL 348)*, s., (11-12-92, Freemn/Fine Art, #227), image 16¼ x 21¼ in., (41.3 x 54 cm.), color lithograph (BP 271, DM 654, FR 2207, Y 51,209).

$220* *Portrait Of Henri Marceau,(FL 217), 1943*, ed. 35, t., num., s. Spruance 1943, s. by Mrs. Spruance, bears estatestamp, (11-12-92, Freemn/Fine Art, #225, illus.), 6¼ x 11⅛ in., (15.9 x 28.3 cm.), lithograph (BP 144, DM 349, FR 1176, Y 27,278).

$138* *Portrait Of Mrs. Kurt Salmsson (FL. 304), 1952,* tack holes, (06-11-93, Freemn/Fine Art, #233), 19¼ x 13⅝ in., (48.9 x 34.6 cm.), lithograph in colors (BP 91, DM 224, FR 756, Y 14,642).

$2300* *"Portrait, W.G.S.", "Blonde", "Young Colored Girl", "Garden Of Eden", "Three Women", "Closed Road", "Torso", "Portrait Of Sophie", "Player Unmasked" and "Adolescent" (Fine/Looney 7, 57, 58, 64, 65, 72, 81, 83, 90, 91): Ten,* 1928-33, s., t., num., full margins, good cond., light-stain, foxing, creases, (02-11-93, Sotheby-NY, #43), lithograph on various papers (BP 1623, DM 3810, FR 12,892, Y 277,275).

$83* *"Priestess",* s. Spruance '54, very good/good cond., (11-21-92, Bakker, #35), 18¼ x 12 in., (46.4 x 30.5 cm.), lithograph (BP 55, DM 132, FR 446, Y 10,322).

$193* *Saint Francis (FL 327),* s. in plate, (11-12-92, Freemn/Fine Art, #219), mat 16 x 21 in., (40.6 x 53.3 cm.), litho, hand colored w/watercolor (BP 127, DM 306, FR 1032, Y 23,931).

$440* *Saint Francis - The Market (FL. 326), 1953,* good cond., tape residue, s., t., d. '53, i., (06-11-93, Freemn/Fine Art, #221), 19¼ x 13⅛ in., (48.9 x 33.3 cm.), lithograph in colors (BP 289, DM 715, FR 2411, Y 46,684).

$350 *"Salome And John", 1950?,* s. Spruance 50, #9/40, (09-24-92, Alderfer, #270, illus.), 18¼ x 13¼ in., (46.4 x 33.7 cm.), lithograph (BP 205, DM 519, FR 1761, Y 42,103).

$3080* *"Shells For The Living (F. and L. 80), 1933" and "April-Wet (F. and L. 44), 1931": Two,* both s., t., num. 3/28, 17/27, full margins; first w/soiling; secondw/pale light-staining, very good cond., illus. back cover, (09-19-92, Christie-E, #69, illus.), lithograph, first on wove, watermark; second in colors on Rives (BP 1772, DM 4612, FR 15,795, Y 383,753).

$4025* *Shells For The Living (F./L. 80), 1933,* s., t., num. 16/28, full margins, good cond., skinning, (02-11-93, Sotheby-NY, #46, illus.), 15½ x 7½ in., (393 x 191 mm.), lithograph (BP 2840, DM 6667, FR 22,562, Y 485,232).

$3080* *"Spinner (F. and L. 75), 1932", "The Flashy Back (F. and L. 56), 1931" and "Touchdown Play (F. and L. 87), 1933": Three,* each s., t., num. 25/30, 2/34, 2/40, full margins, very good cond.; first w/skinned spots; second and third w/ old paper hinges; third w/creases, (09-19-92, Christie-E, #66), lithograph, first on Van Gelder Zonen; second on BFK; third on Rives (BP 1772, DM 4612, FR 15,795, Y 383,753).

$220* *"The Stool Pigeon (F. and L. 11), 1929" and "Portrait Of A Sullen Girl (F. and L. 137), 1937": Two,* first s., t., tears; second i.; both full margins, good cond., (09-19-92, Christie-E, #63), lithograph on wove; first w/watermark (BP 127, DM 329, FR 1128, Y 27,411).

$28* *Towers,* s., (12-17-92, Mystic, #40J), 10½ x 8 in., (26.7 x 20.3 cm.), lithograph (BP 18, DM 44, FR 149, Y 3441).

$220* *"Tulpehocken Road", 1944,* s. Spruance, s. BS in stone, num., annot., t., good cond., (09-11-92, Skinner, #24, illus.), 12 x 16 in., (30.5 x 40.6 cm.), lithograph on wove (BP 114, DM 317, FR 1076, Y 27,258).

BI *Variation,* s., d. 1950, est. $6/800, (09-24-92, Mystic, #16), 13 x 18½ in., (33 x 47 cm.), colored lithograph.

$440* *"Variation" (Fine and Looney, 287), 1950,* s., d. Spruance-50, very good cond., marks, wrinkling, (03-12-93, Skinner, #76, illus.), sight 13¼ x 18⅜ in., (33.7 x 46.7 cm.), lithograph in three colors on paper (BP 307, DM 732, FR 2490, Y 51,856).

$413* *Visitor To Germantown, 1935,* watermarks, s., t., num. 20/30, i., margins, good cond., mat staining, surface soiling, (02-24-93, Butterfield, #2655), 8½ x 14⅛ in., (216 x 359 mm.), lithograph on laid (BP 288, DM 670, FR 2273, Y 48,463).

$220* *"A Wind Is Rising And The Rivers Flow" (Fine and Looney, 241), 1945,* s., d. Spruance-45, init. in stone, t., num., good cond., wrinkling,soiling, tape verso, (09-11-92, Skinner, #52), 14⅜ x 19⁵⁄₁₆ in., (36.5 x 49.1 cm.), lithograph on wove (BP 114, DM 317, FR 1076, Y 27,258).

SPURLING, J.
BI *Po And British Indian Lines: Passenger Services. "Egypt, India, Ceylon, Mauritius, New-Zealand...", 1920,* very good cond., (03-13-93, Laurin, #170), 39¾ x 24¹³⁄₁₆ in., (101 x 63 cm.), .

SPURR, Melbourne
BI *Gloria Swanson, Vintage Portrait,* blind embossed, photog. credit, est. BP 150/250, (10-10-92, Bonhams, #84, illus.), 10 x 8 in., (25.4 x 20.3 cm.), mounted photograph.

SRISOUTA, Praphan
BI *Figures In An Oriental Landscape: A Pair,* s., d. 1967, est. $40/60, (03-25-93, Boos, #643), each 30 x 22 in., (76.2 x 55.9 cm.), woodblock print.

ST-JEAN and AAH
$558* *Croix Rouge De La Jeunesse, c. 1925,* cond. A, (03-16-93, Boisgirard, #190, illus.), 31⅞ x 23⅝ in., (81 x 60 cm.), poster (BP 385, DM 928, FR 3153, Y 65,248).

STACH, Jirka
BI *Untitled (Porcelain Doll Boy), 1991,* s., t., d., edit. 2/35, est. $4/600, (11-16-92, Butterfield, #6178, illus.), 12¾ x 10⅝ in., (324.4 x 270.4 mm.), photograph, gelatin silver print.

STACKHOUSE, Robert   American contemporary
$248* *Cobra's Head,* s., d. (19)89, #9/50, (12-10-92, Sloan, #2744), 23½ x 13¾ in., (59.7 x 34.9 cm.), color etching and aquatint (BP 160, DM 392, FR 1340, Y 30,678).

$600* *Untitled,* s., d. (19)86, #44/45, (02-04-93, Sloan, #2929), sheet 43 x 30¾ in., (109.2 x 78.1 cm.), color lithograph and screenprint (BP 419, DM 988, FR 3350, Y 74,636).

BI *Untitled,* s., d. (19)87, #12/35, est. $1/1,500, (02-04-93, Sloan, #2927), sheet 24½ x 37½ in., (62.2 x 95.3 cm.), color lithograph and screenprint.

$600* *Untitled,* s., d. (19)87, #42/45, (02-04-93, Sloan, #2930, illus.), sheet 43 x 21 in., (109.2 x 53.3 cm.), color lithograph and screenprint (BP 419, DM 988, FR 3350, Y 74,636).

$450* *Untitled,* s., d. (19)86, #21/50, (02-04-93, Sloan, #2932), 24½ x 41½ in., (62.2 x 105.4 cm.), color lithograph and screenprint (BP 314, DM 741, FR 2513, Y 55,977).

$1980* *Untitled,* s., d. (19)86, #5/50, (12-10-92, Sloan, #2707, illus.), 24½ x 41½ in., (62.2 x 105.4 cm.), lithograph w/ hand coloring (BP 1276, DM 3132, FR 10,697, Y 244,928).

STACKPOLE, Peter
$495* *"Alfred Hitchcock", 1937/later,* s., (11-16-92, Butterfield, #6184, illus.), 13½ x 10½ in., (343.5 x 267.2 mm.), photograph, gelatin silver print (BP 326, DM 789, FR 2658, Y 61,560).

$633* *"Bridge & Docks #5", 1935,* s., d., t., num., (05-23-93, Butterfield, #3615, illus.), 9¼ x 13¾ in., photograph, gelatin silver print (BP 412, DM 1035, FR 3484, Y 69,968).

$805* *Building Of The Bay Bridge, 1935,* p.l., s., d., (05-23-93, Butterfield, #3617, illus.), 6 x 9¼ in., photograph, gelatin silver print (BP 524, DM 1316, FR 4430, Y 88.980).

$1100* *Building The Oakland Bay Bridge, 1935-39: Three,* includes "Men on Girders" and "Disassembling the Hammerhead", each mounted, s., d. by photog., 2nd w/photog.'s studio label, (10-15-92, Sotheby-NY, #208A, illus.), each approx. 4½ x 6½ in., (11.4 x 16.5 cm.), photograph, gelatin silver prints (BP 673, DM 1637, FR 5553, Y 131,974).

$805* *Composition, San Francisco Background 1935,* s., d., t., (05-23-93, Butterfield, #3616, illus.), 9¼ x 13½ in., photograph, gelatin silver print (BP 524, DM 1316, FR 4430, Y 88,980).

$345* *Cowboy Study,* 1930s, s., (05-23-93, Butterfield, #3619, illus.), 9½ x 13¼ in., photograph, gelatin silver print (BP 225, DM 564, FR 1899, Y 38,134).

$495* *"Diego Rivera", 1930/later,* s., t., (11-16-92, Butterfield, #6183, illus.), 13⅜ x 10½ in., (340.3 x 267.2 mm.), photograph, gelatin silver print (BP 326, DM 789, FR 2658, Y 61,560).

BI *"Hollywood Sophisticates", 1937,* s., est. $6/800, (11-16-92, Butterfield, #6181, illus.), 7⅜ x 9⅛ in., (187.7 x 232.2 mm.), photograph, gelatin silver print.

$345* *Leaping Ballerina And Danny Kaye,* 1936, p.l., s., (05-23-93, Butterfield, #3618, illus.), 10¾ x 12¾ in., photograph, gelatin silver print (BP 225, DM 564, FR 1899, Y 38,134).

BI *"Marlene Dietrich",* 1930's/later, s., t., est. $5/700, (11-16-92, Butterfield, #6182, illus.), 13¾ x 10¾ in., (349.9 x 273.5 mm.), photograph, gelatin silver print.

$575* *"Men On Cross Arm Waiting For Steel, San Francisco Background", 1935,* s., d., t., (05-23-93, Butterfield, #3614, illus.), 12 x 9 in., photograph, gelatin silver print (BP 374, DM 940, FR 3165, Y 63,557).

BI *"Pay Day", 1935,* s., d., t., photog. label, est. $800/1,200, (11-16-92, Butterfield, #6180, illus.), 4¼ x 6⅜ in., (108.1 x 162.2 mm.), photograph, gelatin silver print.

$1210* *"Shirley Temple", "Alfred Hitchcock" and "Mickey Rooney Dancing", Selected Hollywood Portraits: Three,* mounted, s. by photog., 1950s, p.l., (10-15-92, Sotheby-NY, #209, illus.), each approx. 9 x 7 in., (22.9 x 17.8 cm.), photograph, gelatin silver prints (BP 740, DM 1801, FR 6108, Y 145,171).

STADLER

$1100* *The Blue Egyptian Water-Lily, 1804,* after Henderson, pub. Dr. Thornton, acid burn verso, discoloration, good cond., (12-04-92, Doyle, #8), 20⅜ x 15½ in., (518 x 394 mm.), mixed method engraving (BP 706, DM 1752, FR 5943, Y 137,328).

$770* *White Lily, 1800,* after Henderson, pub. Dr. Thornton, acid burn verso, discoloration, good cond., Katherine Winn Estate, (12-04-92, Doyle, #1), 20¾ x 15⅝ in., (527 x 397 mm.), mixed method engraving (BP 494, DM 1226, FR 4160, Y 96,130).

STADLER, J.C. (after N.R. BLACK)

$2002* *View Of London Taken From Albion Place, Blackfriars Bridge,* pub. N.R. Black, 1802, 2 in. tear, detached, surface dirt, (10-27-92, Phillips-London, #114), plate 22½ x 36¼ in., (572 x 921 mm.), aquatint w/hand-coloring on wove (BP 1265, DM 3068, FR 10,411, Y 244,893).

STADLER, Toni 1888-1982

$177* *Weiblicher Akt,* mono, num., Galerie Wolfgang Ketterer blindstamp, (06-08-93, Karl/Faber, #1325), approx. 12 x 11¹³⁄₁₆ in., (30.5 x 30 cm.), lithograph on BFK Rives wove (BP 116, DM 287, FR 967, Y 18,800).

STAEGER, Ferdinand 1880-1976

$86* *Die Heilige Familie Im Walde,* s., artist's proof, wear, (09-25-92, Granier, #3017), sheet 15¹⁄₁₆ x 11 in., (38.2 x 28 cm.), etching on copper print paper (BP 50, DM 127, FR 431, Y 10,380).

STAEL, Nicolas de French 1914-1955

$3176* *"Mediteranee", 1952,* s., d., t., num., (11-28-92, Grisebach, #778, illus.), 14¼ x 18⁵⁄₁₆ in., (36.2 x 46.5 cm.), colored lithograph on handmade (BP 2096, DM 5060, FR 17,177, Y 395,271).

$2508* *Mediterranee, 1952,* s., d., t., #34/200, (05-27-93, Lempertz, #1035), 13⅞ x 21⁷⁄₁₆ in., (35.3 x 54.5 cm.), color serigraph on wove (BP 1606, DM 4024, FR 13,564, Y 268,868).

BI *Paris, Au Depens De L'Artiste, 1952: Fifteen,* from Poemes by Rene Char, s. by poet and artist, ded., text, invitation, est. SF 28,000/32,000, book, (11-15-92, Christie-Geneva, #324, illus.), 14⁹⁄₁₆ x 11¼ in., (370 x 285 mm.), lithograph and 14 wood engravings on Arches wove.

BI *Paris, Jean Hugues, 1953,* from Arriere Histoire Du Poeme Pulverise by Rene Char, frontispiece,s. in colophon by poet and artist, est. SF 6/7,000, (11-15-92, Christie-Geneva, #323, illus.), 6¹⁵⁄₁₆ x 4¹⁵⁄₁₆ in., (176 x 126 mm.), color lithograph on Hollande.

$986* *Sans Titre, 1952,* s., d., crease, (06-28-93, Loudmer, #368), 6⅞ x 4¾ in., (175 x 120 mm.), sh 12¹¹⁄₁₆ x 9¹⁵⁄₁₆ in., (175 x 120 mm.), color lithograph on wove (BP 660, DM 1675, FR 5644, Y 104,615).

$1740* *Sans Titre, 1952,* s., d., annot., frame trace, small stains, (06-28-93, Loudmer, #369), 10½ x 6⅞ in., (266 x 175 mm.), sh 14⅝ x 11³⁄₁₆ in., (266 x 175 mm.), black lithograph on Arches wove (BP 1165, DM 2957, FR 9960, Y 184,615).

STAHL, Augusto

BI *Garden Botanica, Rio, c. 1860,* Stahl & Wahnschaffe blindstamp, notations in unident. hand, est.$6/900, (04-07-93, Swann, #255), 10¼ x 7¾ in., photograph, albumen print from a paper neg..

STAHR, Paul American b. 1883

$60 *Be Patriotic,* W.F. Powers Co. Litho. NY, minor edge damage, (09-24-92, Alderfer, #275), 28⅞ x 21 in., (73.3 x 53.3 cm.), (BP 35, DM 89, FR 302, Y 7218).

STALKARLT, M., Publisher

$302* *Naval Architecture, Plate XI,* trimmed, time-stained, (02-17-93, Bonhams-Chelsea, #239), image 16 x 28½ in., (40.6 x 72.4 cm.), etching (BP 209, DM 490, FR 1661, Y 36,073).

STALL, I.

$220* *Sauvion's Brandy, 1925,* Imp. Joseph-Charles, A- cond., surface soiling, (08-06-92, Swann, #258, illus.), 23½ x 15½ in., (59.7 x 39.4 cm.), (BP 115, DM 325, FR 1098, Y 28,061).

STALL, J.

$358* *Rhum Saint-Esprit. Bordeaux. "Premiere Marque",* good cond., (03-13-93, Laurin, #9), 54¾ x 38¹⁵⁄₁₆ in., (139 x 99 cm.), (BP 250, DM 596, FR 2026, Y 42,192).

STAMOS, Theodoros American b. 1922

$220* *Infinity Field Olympic II,* s., d. 1968, #4/75, (05-16-93, Hindman, #602), 30 x 22¼ in., (76.2 x 56.5 cm.), color serigraph (BP 143, DM 354, FR 1189, Y 24,388).

STAMPFLI, Peter American b. 1937

$10* *L'Arene,* s., creases, stains, (11-16-92, Briest, #97), 25⅜ x 19¹¹⁄₁₆ in., (64.5 x 50 cm.), quadrichrome (BP 7, DM 16, FR 54, Y 1248).

$168* *"L'Enjoliveur",* #146/150, s., (01-28-93, Pescheteau, #257), 32⁵⁄₁₆ x 23⅝ in., (82 x 60 cm.), serigraph (BP 111, DM 266, FR 901, Y 20,859).

$95* *"Le Pneu",* #31/150, s., (01-28-93, Pescheteau, #258), 21¼ x 14¹⁵⁄₁₆ in., (54 x 38 cm.), offset (BP 63, DM 151, FR 509, Y 11,795).

$103* *Sabron n. 2, 1991,* artist's proof, s., (03-31-93, Briest, #E103), 28¹⁵⁄₁₆ x 46⅞ in., (73.5 x 119 cm.), color serigraph (BP 68, DM 166, FR 563, Y 11,845).

STANCZAK, Julian American b. 1928

$10* *Untitled,* s., very good cond., (05-15-93, Cleveland, #497), 22¼ x 22¼ in., (56.5 x 56.5 cm.), silkscreen (BP 7, DM 16, FR 54, Y 1109).

STANEK, Emmanuel 1862-1920

$199* *Sirop Emulsif Richou, c. 1900,* cond. B, (03-16-93, Boisgirard, #203), 35¹³⁄₁₆ x 48⅝ in., (91 x 123.5 cm.), poster (BP 137, DM 331, FR 1124, Y 23,269).

STANKOWSKI, Anton German b. 1906

$1062* *Auto, 1928,* s., d., (11-12-92, Lempertz, #249, illus.), 2⅜ x 3⅞ in., (6 x 9.8 cm.), photograph, gelatin silver print (BP 679, DM 1669, FR 5688, Y 131,387).

$569* *Ohne Titel, 1954,* s., d., photographer's stamp, lit., (11-12-92, Lempertz, #250, illus.), 15⁵⁄₁₆ x 11⅞ in., (38.9 x 30.2 cm.), photograph, gelatin silver print (BP 364, DM 894, FR 3048, Y 70,395).

$1840* *Thecla, 1932,* s., t., d.; init. in neg., sold after sale, (04-08-93, Christie-NY, #156, illus.), 4½ x 3¼ in., (11.4 x 8.3 cm.), photograph, gelatin silver print (BP 1207, DM 2956, FR 10,005, Y 208,806).

STANLEY, Bob American b. 1932

$181* *Erotische Komposition, 1969,* s., d., num., (11-28-92, Schoppmann, #813), 23⅝ x 38³⁄₁₆ in., (60 x 97 cm.), serigraph in red and purple on light cardboard (BP 119, DM 288, FR 979, Y 22,526).

$181* *Erotische Komposition, 1969,* s., d., num., (11-28-92, Schoppmann, #812), 23⅝ x 38³⁄₁₆ in., (60 x 97 cm.), serigraph in red and green on light cardbaord (BP 119, DM 288, FR 979, Y 22,526).

$181* *Erotische Komposition, 1969,* s., d., num., (11-28-92, Schoppmann, #815), 20⅞ x 28⅜ in., (53 x 72 cm.), serigraph in red and black on light cardboard (BP 119, DM 288, FR 979, Y 22,526).

$181* *Motorradfahrer, 1961,* s., d., num., (11-28-92, Schoppmann, #816, illus.), 16¹⁵⁄₁₆ x 22¹³⁄₁₆ in., (43 x 58 cm.), serigraph in blue on light cardboard (BP 119, DM 288, FR 979, Y 22,526).

STANLEY, Mr. and Nelson HOOD
BI *Buckingham Palace, A Rare Survey Of State And Private Rooms And Exterior Studies, 1913: Forty-Nine,* 2 from 1932, each approx. 304 x 410mm, est. BP 4/5,000, (05-07-93, Sotheby-London, #216, illus.), photograph, gelatin silver print on printing out paper.

STANNARD, Henri Sylvester
$5 *"Beccles",* (06-11-93, G.A. Key, #70), 7 x 10 in., (17.8 x 25.4 cm.), colored print (BP 3, DM 8, FR 27, Y 531).

STANNARD, Henry Sylvester   English 1870-1951
BI *"Feeding Chickens",* s. within pl. Sylvester Stannard, est. $1/150, (12-12-92, A. James, #313), 10 x 15½ in., (25.4 x 39.4 cm.), print.

STANNARD, Joseph   English 1797-1830
$109 *Shipping On Breydon,* (12-11-92, G.A. Key, #76), 8 x 5 in., (20.3 x 12.7 cm.), black and white etching (BP 70, DM 172, FR 589, Y 13,488).

STANSFIELD, J.B.
BI *"Loch And Mountains"* and *"English Landscape", c. 1920: Two,* mounted on card, s., each approx. 370 x 475mm, est. BP 2/300, (05-07-93, Sotheby-London, #171), photograph, silver print.

STANTON, Sir Herbert Hughes
BI *Landscape With Cows,* margins, est. BP 40/60, (12-10-92, Bonhams-Chelsea, #11), plate 10 x 13¾ in., (25.4 x 34.9 cm.), etching.
$48* *Landscape With Cows,* margins, (02-17-93, Bonhams-Chelsea, #264), plate 10 x 13¾ in., (25.4 x 34.9 cm.), etching (BP 33, DM 78, FR 264, Y 5733).

STARK, James (after)
$65 *Norfolk Views: Four,* in two frames, (02-05-93, G.A. Key, #62), each 5 x 7 in., (12.7 x 17.8 cm.), b/w engraving (BP 45, DM 108, FR 364, Y 8089).

STARK, Ron   contemporary
$440* *Nude In Bathtub,* s., d. (19)75, (12-10-92, Sloan, #2726), sight 9½ x 7½ in., (24.1 x 19.1 cm.), photograph, b/w (BP 284, DM 696, FR 2377, Y 54,429).

STARKELBERG, B. de (after)
$50* *Phyles,* by de Bickebois, foxing, tear, (11-30-92, Phillips-London, #247), sheet 18¼ x 28 in., (464 x 711 mm.), hand-colored lithograph on wove (BP 33, DM 80, FR 270, Y 6223).

STARN TWINS   American b. 1961
$880* *Ian Churchill (Yellow Striped),* s., num., d. Douglas R. Starn Michael Starn #147 86-87 verso, prov.,Fredrik Roos Estate, (11-17-92, Christie-E, #114, illus.), 10 x 5½ in., (25.4 x 14 cm.), photograph, toned silver print (BP 579, DM 1403, FR 4726, Y 109,439).
$17,600* *The Stark Portrait,* prov., (11-19-92, Christie-NY, #131, illus.), 107¹⁵⁄₁₆ x 79 in., (274.3 x 200.7 cm.), photo collage w/cellophane tape in artist's frame (BP 11,588, DM 28,061, FR 94,522, Y 2,188,782).

STATHAM, Colin
$601* *To Visit Britain's Landmarks, Wolsey's Tower, Esher Place, 1937,* p. Waterlow and Sons, ref. #495, cond. 1, (10-13-92, Phillips-London, #121), 29¹⁵⁄₁₆ x 44¹³⁄₁₆ in., (76 x 113.8 cm.), color lithograph (BP 350, DM 880, FR 2992, Y 72,875).

STAUFFER-BERN, Karl   Swiss 1857-1891
$577* *Portrait Adolph Von Menzel (Lehrs 13 III), 1885,* (11-28-92, Grisebach, #779, illus.), 15⁹⁄₁₆ x 11⁵⁄₈ in., (39.6 x 29.6 cm.), woodcut on China (BP 381, DM 919, FR 3121, Y 71,811).

STECK, Paul
$562* *Boulogne-Sur-Mer. Chemin De Fer Du Nord, c. 1895,* Paris, Imp. Eug. Marx, cond. A-, (06-11-93, Boisgirard, #144), 50⅜ x 37 in., (128 x 94 cm.), poster (BP 369, DM 913, FR 3079, Y 59,629).

STEELE, Juliette
$275* *City At Night,* s., t., #3-25, margins, good cond.?, (10-28-92, Butterfield, #3122), 13 x 9 in., (330 x 229 mm.),

lithograph on wove (BP 175, DM 425, FR 1442, Y 33,742).

STEELINK, Wilm   1856-1928
BI *"Huon En Almansaris", (18)88,* foxed, est. DM 300, (12-01-92, Karl/Faber, #272), 6⅞ x 9¹⁄₁₆ in., (17.5 x 23 cm.), etching on China.

STEEN, Germain van der   b. 1897
BI *Les Chats,* s., #12/99, stains, est. FF1,000/1,200, (05-27-93, Briest, #183), 16¹⁵⁄₁₆ x 24 in., (43 x 61 cm.), color lithograph.

STEGEMANN, Heinrich   German 1888-1945
$84* *Portrat Gustave "Schiefler",* i., s. H Stegemann, (03-24-93, Venator/Hansten, #4565), 12³⁄₁₆ x 7¹³⁄₁₆ in., (30.9 x 19.8 cm.), drypoint (BP 57, DM 137, FR 467, Y 9870).
$627* *Weiblicher Akt Im Garten, 1922,* s., num. 1/2, (12-05-92, Bassenge, #7746, illus.), 18¹⁄₁₆ x 13⁵⁄₁₆ in., (45.8 x 33.8 cm.), watercolored woodcut on wove (BP 393, DM 978, FR 3332, Y 77,686).

STEGGLES, Harold   ac. 1930-1938
$579* *Everywhere You Go, Bungay, 1934,* p. Waterlow And Sons, ref. #417, cond. 1, (10-13-92, Phillips-London, #95), 29¹⁵⁄₁₆ x 44⅞ in., (76 x 114 cm.), color lithograph (BP 337, DM 848, FR 2882, Y 70,207).

STEGGLES, W.J.   ac. 1930-1938
$888* *To Visit Britain's Landmarks, Tattingstone Wonder, Suffolk, 1937,* p. Waterlow and Sons, ref. #497, cond. 1, (10-13-92, Phillips-London, #123), 29¹⁵⁄₁₆ x 44⅞ in., (76 x 114 cm.), color lithograph (BP 517, DM 1301, FR 4420, Y 107,676).

STEICHEN, Edward   American 1879-1973
$4400* *Amelia Earhart, 1931,* t., i., num. by photog. in neg., studio stamp, (c) & insertion stamps, notations, (10-15-92, Sotheby-NY, #212, illus.), 9½ x 7½ in., (24.1 x 19.1 cm.), photograph, gelatin silver print (BP 2692, DM 6550, FR 22,211, Y 527,894).
$2300* *Charles Land Freer, early 1900's,* s. by photog. on image, num. in unident. hand, Clarence P. Freer Estate, (04-06-93, Sotheby-NY, #66A, illus.), photograph (BP 1519, DM 3705, FR 12,548, Y 262,318).
$907* *Gertrude Lawrence, 1926,* d. Dec. 7. 1926 in neg., photog.'s ink credit stamp, (05-06-93, Christie-London, #178), 10 x 8 in., photograph, gelatin silver contact stamp (BP 575, DM 1429, FR 4809, Y 99,791).
$907* *Gertrude Lawrence, Fashion Study, Vogue, 1928,* Fashion-Vogue-Sept 11-28-no. 12 in neg., d. by Lawrence, annots., (05-06-93, Christie-London, #179, illus.), 10 x 8 in., photograph, gelatin silver contact print (BP 575, DM 1429, FR 4809, Y 99,791).
$7475* *Moonrise, The Pond, Marmaroneck (sic) (1904), 1958-59,* s. in neg.; t., d., credit stamp, (04-08-93, Christie-NY, #85, illus.), 7¼ x 8⅞ in., (18.4 x 22.5 cm.), photograph, gelatin silver print (BP 4902, DM 12,008, FR 40,647, Y 848,275).
BI *Mother And Child-Sunlight, 1905,* tipped to orig. Japanese tissue mount, photog.'s sig., catalogue cover lot, est. $10/15,000, (04-07-93, Swann, #559, illus.), 5 x 6¼ in., photograph, platinum and gum print.
$3850* *Portrait Of John Simpson, 1903,* s., d. MDCCCCIII by photog. on image, (10-15-92, Sotheby-NY, #98, illus.), 7⅝ x 5⅝ in., (19.4 x 14.3 cm.), photograph, platinum print (BP 2356, DM 5731, FR 19,435, Y 461,908).
BI *President Theodore Roosevelt, The White House,* (1908), 1950s, t., d., stamp, lit., est. $4/5,000, (10-13-92, Christie-NY, #45, illus.), 13½ x 10½ in., (34.3 x 26.7 cm.), photograph, toned gelatin silver print.
BI *Rodin-Le Penseur, Paris, 1902,* s., d. in Roman numerals, lit., (10-13-92, Christie-NY, #46, illus.), 13⅛ x 16 in., (33.3 x 40.6 cm.), photograph, silver-toned platinum print.

STEIG, Josef   1898-1957
$253* *"Monreal Eifel - J. Steib Sept. 1926",* plate i., s., d., s. J. Steib, (03-24-93, Venator/Hansten, #4566), pl. 9¾ x 12¹⁵⁄₁₆ in., (24.8 x 33 cm.), etching and drypoint (BP 171, DM 413, FR 1406, Y 29,726).

STEIGLITZ, Alfred 1864-1946

$2185* *The Steerage (1907),* from Camera Work Number 36, October 1911, (04-08-93, Christie-NY, #83, illus.), 7⅜ x 6 in., (18.7 x 15.2 cm.), photograph, small-format photogravure on tissue (BP 1433, DM 3510, FR 11,881, Y 247,957).

STEIGLITZ, Alfred, Editor

$1035* *Camera Work Number 38 (April 1912): Thirteen,* complete as pub., 5 works by Anne Brigman and 8 by Karl Struss, (04-08-93, Christie-NY, #82, illus.), photograph, photogravure (BP 679, DM 1663, FR 5628, Y 117,453).

STEINBERG, Saul Rumanian/American b. 1914

BI *Komposition Aus "Mois Du Coeur", 1972,* 60/75, s., est. SF 1,2/1,400, (10-14-92, Germann, #446), 23⅝ x 29½ in., (600 x 750 mm.), color lithograph.

BI *Ohne Titel (Paar Im Gesprach),* #53/75, pencil s., est. DM 1,400, (11-20-92, Lempertz, #875), sh 23⅝ x 29 15/16 in., (60 x 76 cm.), color lithograph on Velin.

$715* *Union Square, 1973,* s., d., #29/75, full margins, (12-08-92, Swann, #286, illus.), 25½ x 19 in., (64.8 x 48.3 cm.), color lithograph (BP 448, DM 1113, FR 3795, Y 88,622).

STEINER, Michael b. 1942

BI *Geometrische Figuren, 1991,* mono., d., est. DM 150-, (09-25-92, Granier, #3018), sheet 11 11/16 x 16⅝ in., (29.7 x 42.2 cm.), stamp print on beige wove.

STEINER, Ralph 1899-1986

$2750* *Always (A Point of View, p. 41),* mounted, s., d., by photog., 1922, p. c. 1940, (10-15-92, Sotheby-NY, #486, illus.), 3⅝ x 4⅝ in., (9.2 x 11.7 cm.), photograph, gelatin silver print (BP 1683, DM 4093, FR 13,882, Y 329,934).

$2750* *American Rural Baroque (A Point Of View, p. 56),* s., d. by photog., 1929, p. 1979, (10-15-92, Sotheby-NY, #485, illus.), 7⅝ x 9½ in., (19.4 x 24.1 cm.), photograph, gelatin silver print (BP 1683, DM 4093, FR 13,882, Y 329,934).

BI *Art Smith Portraying A Soldier In An Anti-War Film, 1934 (A Point OfView, p. 119),* mounted, s., d. by photog., est. $2/3,000, (10-15-92, Sotheby-NY, #489, illus.), 6⅛ x 4⅝ in., (15.6 x 11.7 cm.), photograph, gelatin silver prints.

$330* *Coconut Factory,* c. 1930, p. 1979, prov., (06-13-93, Hindman, #429), 8 x 10 in., photograph, silver print (BP 216, DM 537, FR 1805, Y 34,726).

BI *Coconut Factory,* c. 1930/1979, prov., est. $800/1000, (05-16-93, Hindman, #332), 8 x 10 in., photograph, silver print.

BI *The Group Theatre And Harold Klurman, Provincetown, c. 1928,* s., t., d., annot., est. $3/4,000, (10-13-92, Christie-NY, #359, illus.), 7⅝ x 9½ in., (19.4 x 24.1 cm.), photograph, gelatin silver print.

$1320* *Gypsy Rose Lee (A Point of View, p. 65),* s., i. by photog. in ink, 1940's, (10-15-92, Sotheby-NY, #487A, illus.), 10¼ x 13⅛ in., (26 x 33.3 cm.), photograph, gelatin silver print (BP 808, DM 1965, FR 6663, Y 158,368).

$460* *Gypsy Rose Lee And Troupe,* 1930s, p.l., s., lit., (04-08-93, Christie-NY, #340, illus.), 10⅛ x 13 in., (25.7 x 33 cm.), photograph, gelatin silver print (BP 302, DM 739, FR 2501, Y 52,202).

$1320* *Oil Lamps,* mounted, s. by photog., early 1960's, (10-15-92, Sotheby-NY, #490, illus.), 5¼ x 5⅛ in., (13.3 x 13 cm.), photograph, gelatin silver print (BP 808, DM 1965, FR 6663, Y 158,368).

$1320* *Paul Strand With His Camera During Filming Of "The Plow That Broke The Plains", 1936,* s., d. by photog. in ink, (10-15-92, Sotheby-NY, #487, illus.), 2¼ x 2⅛ in., (5.7 x 5.4 cm.), photograph, gelatin silver print (BP 808, DM 1965, FR 6663, Y 158,368).

BI *Theater Posters And Construction Equipment,* notations, 1924, p.l., est. $6/900, (10-14-92, Swann, #569, illus.), 5 x 4 in., (12.7 x 10.2 cm.), photograph, silver print.

BI *Tyepwriter (A Point of View, p. 5),* s., d. by photog., 1921-22, p.l., est. $2/3,000, (04-06-93, Sotheby-NY, #408A, illus.), 8 x 5⅞ in., photograph.

$1320* *Weathered Wood And Weeds, c. 1960,* mounted, s. by photog., (10-15-92, Sotheby-NY, #488, illus.), 5½ x 6½ in., (14 x 16.5 cm.), photograph, gelatin silver print (BP 808, DM 1965, FR 6663, Y 158,368).

BI *Window, 1960,* sig., est. $1,5/2,000, (10-14-92, Swann, #570, illus.), photograph, silver print.

BI *Wooden Staircase, Maine,* 1960s, s., lit., est. $2/2,500, (10-13-92, Christie-NY, #604, illus.), 5¾ x 5⅛ in., (14.6 x 13 cm.), photograph, gelatin silver print.

STEINERT, Otto 1915-1978

$4551* *Ein-Fuss-Ganger, c. 1950,* t., studio stamp, (11-12-92, Lempertz, #251, illus.), 8⅜ x 11⅞ in., (21.2 x 30.1 cm.), photograph, gelatin silver print (BP 2910, DM 7152, FR 24,376, Y 563,034).

$1650* *Luminogramm, Dic Lampen Der Place Concorde, Paris,* (1952), p.l., s., d. in ink in margin; s., t., d., annot, (10-13-92, Christie-NY, #499, illus.), 9⅜ x 13½ in., (23.8 x 34.3 cm.), photograph, gelatin silver print (BP 961, DM 2417, FR 8213, Y 200,073).

STEINHARDT, Jakob Israeli b. 1887

$369* *Cafehaus (Behrens 83), 1913,* s., num., (12-05-92, Bassenge, #7751), 3⅞ x 2 13/16 in., (9.8 x 7.2 cm.), etching on handmade (BP 231, DM 575, FR 1961, Y 45,719).

$959* *Pogrom (Behrens 80), 1913,* s., num., (12-05-92, Bassenge, #7750, illus.), 5¼ x 7 11/16 in., (13.3 x 19.5 cm.), etching on Japan (BP 601, DM 1495, FR 5096, Y 118,820).

$565* *Rot Und Gluhend Ist Das Auge Des Juden, 1917: Three,* s., plate mono., d., (06-10-93, Hauswedell/Nolt, #933), smaller pl size 4 7/16 x 6 in., (11.3 x 15.3 cm.), larger pl size 5⅜ x 5 1/16 in., (11.3 x 15.3 cm.), drypoint on handmade (BP 370, DM 920, FR 3098, Y 59,972).

$554* *Schma Jissroel Oder Der Bassgeiger, 1919,* s., artist's proof, 1st state, Musikalische Novellen series, (12-05-92, Bassenge, #7753, illus.), 8 15/16 x 6 9/16 in., (22.7 x 16.6 cm.), lithograph on handmade (BP 347, DM 864, FR 2944, Y 68,641).

$849* *Verganglichkeit (Behrens 88), 1914,* s., (12-05-92, Bassenge, #7752), 4 3/16 x 5 11/16 in., (10.7 x 14.5 cm.), etching on Japan (BP 532, DM 1324, FR 4511, Y 105,191).

$303* *"Vorbeter", "Herbstag" and "The Family", 1921: Three,* all s., first w/staining, very good cond., (10-10-92, Litchfield, #203), largest 5¾ x 7¾ in., (14.6 x 19.7 cm.), smallest 7 x 5½ in., (14.6 x 19.7 cm.), etching (BP 180, DM 450, FR 1511, Y 36,888).

STEINITZ, Kate b. German 1889 d. 1975

BI *El Lissitzky, c. 1930,* lit., prov., est. DM 500, (11-12-92, Lempertz, #252), 7 1/16 x 4 15/16 in., (18 x 12.5 cm.), photograph, gelatin silver print.

BI *"Tote Qualle Im Wattgestrupp (Jellyfish And Seaweed), 1932,* mounted, s., t., d. by photog., (04-06-93, Sotheby-NY, #326, illus.), 15¼ x 11¼ in., photograph.

STEINLEN, Theophile Alexandre Swiss/French 1859-1923

BI *Academie Nationale De Musique, Helle,* B+ cond., tears, plate 34 from Les Maitres de L'Affiche, est. $1/150, (08-06-92, Swann, #264, illus.), image 11¼ x 8⅞ in., (28.6 x 22.5 cm.), .

$259* *Academie Nationale De Musique. Le Reve, 1890,* cond. A, (03-16-93, Boisgirard, #204), 32 11/16 x 24 13/16 in., (83 x 63 cm.), poster (BP 179, DM 431, FR 1463, Y 30,285).

$253* *Un Attendant,* s. red pencil, (02-14-93, Hanzel, #690), 12¾ x 9⅝ in., (32.4 x 24.4 cm.), lithograph (BP 178, DM 420, FR 1420, Y 30,511).

BI *"La Bagnole Aux Cerises", 1897,* plate s., est. DM 600, (09-05-92, Arnold, #4, illus.), 10⅝ x 9 1/16 in., (27 x 23 cm.), color lithograph.

$1279* *Blanchisseuses Reportant L'Ouvrage (Crauzat 22), 1898,* full margins, good cond., handling marks, tape hinges, (12-03-92, Sotheby-London, #580), 14¼ x 10⅝ in., (362 x 270 mm.), etching in green on wove (BP 825, DM 2011, FR 6865, Y 159,139).

$1299* *Blanchisseuses Reportant L'Ouvrage (E. de Crauzat 22),* definitive state, untrimmed margins, (06-11-93, Picard, #167), 13¾ x 10⅜ in., (350 x 264 mm.), color drypoint, aquatint and etching on Arches (BP 853, DM 2111, FR 7118, Y 137,825).

BI *La Bodiniere, 1894,* short text, plate s., trimmed, prop. Francesca Robinson Sanchez, est. $2,5/3,500, (03-25-93, Christie-E, #210, illus.), overall 24½ x 33¼ in., (62.2 x 84.5 cm.), color lithograph.

BI *La Bodiniere, 1894,* short text, plate s., trimmed, prop. Francesca Robinson Sanchez, est. $1/1,500, (06-08-93, Christie-E, #196), 24½ x 33¼ in., (62.2 x 84.5 cm.), color lithograph.

$430* *Les Chanteurs Des Rues (De. C. 218), 1899,* first state of 3, before letters, dust, staining, large margins, (02-24-93, Picard, #229), lithograph on laid (BP 300, DM 698, FR 2367, Y 50,458).

$460* *Le Chemineau (1st state; 2nd state) (C. 199), 1897:* Two, first s., annot. Le Chemineau, #82/60 9, 2nd stone s., first w/blindstamp, p. Charles Verneau, 2nd w/margins, good cond., tears, losses, staining, tape remains, (05-19-93, Butterfield, #1967), one 27¾ x 19⅝ in., (705 x 498 mm.), the other 29⅝ x 23 in., (705 x 498 mm.), lithograph (a proof in black and final state in colors) on wove (BP 299, DM 748, FR 2519, Y 50,924).

$422* *Coq Et Poules (Crauzat 181), 1896,* full margins, (05-06-93, Laurin, #84), lithograph on creme wove (BP 267, DM 665, FR 2238, Y 46,430).

$193* *"Le Coup De Vent", 1915 and "Les Deux Amis":* Two, both s. in plate and in crayon; first, d., (06-28-93, Loudmer, #370), first 12⅝ x 18⁵⁄₁₆ in., (320 x 465 mm.), second 11⅝ x 18½ in., (320 x 465 mm.), color lithographs on wove (BP 129, DM 328, FR 1105, Y 20,477).

$128* *Dix Assasinats Pour Un Sou (Crauzat 201), 1897,* Ed. Kleinmann blindstamp, margins, paper discoloration, soiling, minor creasing, small defects at edges of sheet, Late Gerhard Brauer Coll., (05-27-93, Sotheby-Amstrdm, #784), 14⁵⁄₁₆ x 11¼ in., (363 x 286 mm.), lithograph on wove (BP 82, DM 205, FR 692, Y 13,722, G 230).

$440* *En Belgique Les Belges Ont Faim, 1915,* l'Lapina, Imp., B cond., fold marks, marginal creasing, discoloration, chip, (08-06-92, Swann, #260, illus.), 51¼ x 37 in., (130.2 x 94 cm.), (BP 230, DM 650, FR 2196, Y 56,122).

BI *La Feuille Par Zo D'Axa (Crauzat 499), 1897,* Imp. Charles Verneau, Paris, lit., est. DM 1,500, (12-05-92, Bassenge, #7628), 11¹³⁄₁₆ x 16 in., (30 x 40.7 cm.), color lithograph.

$288* *Helle,* Les Maitres de l'Affiche blindstamp, p. Chaix, margins, apparently good condition, (03-31-93, Butterfield, #5250), 11¼ x 8¾ in., (28.6 x 22.2 cm.), lithograph printed in colors on wove (BP 190, DM 463, FR 1574, Y 33,119).

$2048* *Jean Borlin, 1920,* metal rings, staining, tears, repairs, lit., (02-04-93, Christie-S. Ken, #144, illus.), 91 x 62 in., (231.1 x 157.5 cm.), color lithograph on two sheets backed on linen (BP 1430, DM 3372, FR 11,435, Y 254,758).

$2521* *Jenny Hasselquist, 1920,* staining, other minor defects, lit., (02-04-93, Christie-S. Ken, #145, illus.), 89½ x 64 in., (227.3 x 162.6 cm.), color lithograph on two sheets backed on linen (BP 1760, DM 4151, FR 14,076, Y 313,596).

$3450* *L'Ete-Chat Sur Une Balustrade (C. 292), 1909,* s., blindstamp publisher Sagot, p. R. Engelmann, upper and side margins, good cond., light-staining, restored surface abrasion, tear, paper loss, linen-backed, (05-19-93, Butterfield, #1968, illus.), sh. 19⅝ x 24¹⁵⁄₁₆ in., (498 x 633 mm.), lithograph in colors on wove (BP 2240, DM 5608, FR 18,894, Y 381,933).

$4180* *L'Hiver-Chat Sur Un Coussin (de Crauzat 293), 1909,* s., full margins, staining, good cond., (11-09-92, Christie-NY, #206, illus.), 19¼ x 23 in., (489 x 584 cm.), colored lithograph on wove (BP 2764, DM 6673, FR 22,546, Y 518,739).

$1210* *Le Locataire, 1913,* G. Cochon, good cond., soiling, 1.62m x 1.19m, (11-07-92, Sotheby-NY, #252, illus.), 63¾ x 46⅞ in., lithograph in colors, laid down on canvas (BP 791, DM 1941, FR 6530, Y 149,346).

$716* *Maxime Gorki A Mi-Corps De Face (De C. 265), 1905,* small margins, (02-24-93, Picard, #230), signature in black and red on ivory wove (BP 499, DM 1162, FR 3941, Y 84,018).

$550* *Nu Endormi De Profil,* #20/18, s., good untrimmed margins, (06-16-93, Ader Tajan, #140), 14¹⁵⁄₁₆ x 14¾ in., (38 x 37.5 cm.), aquatint in bistre (BP 367, DM 913, FR 3064, Y 58,660).

BI *Paul Delmet, Chanson Des Femmes,* B+ cond., fold marks, closed tears, est. $4/600, (08-06-92, Swann, #262, illus.), 14¼ x 24½ in., (36.2 x 62.2 cm.), .

$731* *"Peasant Woman Carrying Linen",* s., margins, front cover lot, (02-17-93, Bonhams-Chelsea, #210, illus.), plate 15¼ x 14⅝ in., (38.7 x 37.1 cm.), color aquatint (BP 506, DM 1187, FR 4021, Y 87,315).

$605* *Le Petit Sou,* Imp. Charle Verneau, B+ cond., blemishing, fold marks, (08-06-92, Swann, #263, illus.), 53 x 39 in., (134.6 x 99.1 cm.), (BP 316, DM 894, FR 3019, Y 77,168).

$1767* *Prochainement (...) Chat Noir (...) Avec Rodolphe Salis, 1896,* Paris, Imp. Charles Verneau, cond. A-, (06-11-93, Boisgirard, #145), 23⅝ x 15¾ in., (60 x 40 cm.), poster (BP 1161, DM 2872, FR 9682, Y 187,480).

BI *Reclining Nude, 1914,* s., d.. #7/20, i. 2e etat IX, margins, good cond., est. BP 250/350, (06-30-93, Sotheby-London, #686), 15¾ x 15 in., (400 x 381 mm.), etching on laid watermarked Eugene Delatre, BFK Rives.

$605* *Le Reve, 1890,* Gillot, Grav. Imp., A cond., (08-06-92, Swann, #259, illus.), 35 x 24½ in., (88.9 x 62.2 cm.), (BP 316, DM 894, FR 3019, Y 77,168).

$21,448* *La Rue (Crauzat 495; Bargiel Et Zagrodzki 20), 1896,* p. by Charles Verneau, good cond., sheets folded in four, splits, defects, lit., (06-30-93, Sotheby-London, #685, illus.), 93¾ x 119¾ in., (238.1 x 304.2 cm.), color lithographic poster on 6 sh (BP 14,375, DM 36,582, FR 123,406, Y 2,298,082).

$15,758* *La Rue, 1896,* fold w/bad corresponding defects, creases, tears, losses, lit., (02-04-93, Christie-S. Ken, #143, illus.), 92½ x 117½ in., (235 x 298.5 cm.), color lithograph on 6 sheets backed on old linen (BP 11,000, DM 25,948, FR 87,984, Y 1,960,194).

BI *Serbiens Leidensweg, 1916,* s., #98/100, margins, good cond., staining, foxing, surface soiling,notations, est. $3/400, (05-19-93, Butterfield, #2093), 9⅞ x 17⁷⁄₁₆ in., (251 x 443 mm.), lithograph in black/tan on wove.

BI *"La Sortie Des Trois Midinettes" (De Crauzat 34), 1900,* No. 107, full sheet, fine cond., est. $1-1,500, (10-31-92, Cleveland, #335, illus.), 5⅞ x 9 in., (14.9 x 22.9 cm.), drypoint in colors.

$1222* *Sur La Plage (Crauzat 242/I), 1900,* (06-23-93, Kornfeld, #798), color lithograph on China (BP 830, DM 2068, FR 6955, Y 133,130, SF 1840).

$440* *"Sur La Terre...", 1917,* Imp. H. Chacoin, A- cond., fold marks, (08-06-92, Swann, #261, illus.), 45 x 31½ in., (114.3 x 80 cm.), (BP 230, DM 650, FR 2196, Y 56,122).

$700* *"Tournee Du Chat Noir",* s. in pl., (05-18-93, Encans, #221), 29½ x 19½ in., (75 x 49.5 cm.), poster (BP 456, DM 1136, FR 3836, Y 78,012, C$ 888).

$495* *Untitled: Twelve,* s., (03-31-93, Briest, #E105), from 19¹¹⁄₁₆ x 12⅝ in., (50 x 32 cm.), to 23⅝ x 29½ in., (50 x 32 cm.), black and color lithographs (BP 327, DM 796, FR 2705, Y 56,923).

$316* *La Victoire En Chantant, 1919,* 75/100, s., lit., (06-24-93, Germann, #775), 20¼ x 23¹³⁄₁₆ in., (515 x 605 mm.), lithograph (BP 208, DM 512, FR 1727, Y 33,898, SF 460).

STEIR, Pat   American b. 1938

$2990* *Abstraction, Belief, Desire, 1981,* s., d. August 1981, #29/35, pub. Crown Point Press, margins, (05-11-93, Christie-NY, #566, illus.), plate 35⅞ x 55¼ in., (91.1 x 140.3 cm.), color etching and aquatint on wove (BP 1909, DM 4710, FR 15,870, Y 328,897).

$2760* *Abstraction, Belief, Desire, 1981,* s., d., #21/35, pub. Crown Point Press, full margins, good cond. ?, scuff mark, paper loss extending into image, skinned spots, (05-15-93, Sotheby-NY, #1209, illus.), 35½ x 55 in., (90.2 x 139.7 cm.), etching and aquatint in colors (BP 1795, DM 4439, FR 14,919, Y 305,953).

BI *Breadfruit, 1983,* s., d., t., #70/144, blindstamp publisher, Charles Cardinale Fine Creations, full margins, good cond., est. $6/800, (05-19-93, Butterfield, #2338),

34 x 32¼ in., (864 x 819 mm.), silkscreen in colors on wove.

BI *Self As 1937 Picasso, Woman Weeping, 1986,* from Self Portriats, Third Series, inits., t., Crown Point Press blindstamp, full margins, excell. cond., est. $1,8/2,200, (05-11-93, Christie-NY, #567, illus.), sheet 26½ x 19⅞ in., (673 x 505 mm.), monoprint in oils in colors w/extensive additions in colored pencilson black wove.

$1540* *Self As Picasso As A Young Man #1, 1985,* t., init., pub. blindstamp, Crown Point Press, full margins, good cond., (11-07-92, Sotheby-NY, #771, illus.), 9⅞ x 9⅞ in., (251 x 251 mm.), monotype p. in colors (BP 1007, DM 2459, FR 8311, Y 190,077).

$1540* *Sunflowers, 1986,* s., d., #59/100, pub. blindstamp, Crown Point Press, full margins, good cond., (11-07-92, Sotheby-NY, #772, illus.), 23⅜ x 35⅞ in., (594 x 911 mm.), woodcut p. in colors (BP 1007, DM 2459, FR 8311, Y 190,077).

$2420* *When I Think Of Venice, 1980,* s., d., #21/35, blindstamp, full margins, soiling, creases, excellent cond., (11-09-92, Christie-NY, #411, illus.), 42 x 55 in., (106.7 x 139.7 cm.), etching and aquatint in colors (BP 1600, DM 3863, FR 13,053, Y 300,323).

$2200* *Wish #3 Transformation, 1974,* s., d., t., num. 31/50, blindstamp of pub. Landfall Press, apparentlyvery good cond., (02-24-93, Butterfield, #3148, illus.), 31¾ x 32¼ in., (806 x 819 mm.), lithograph in colors on wove (BP 1534, DM 3571, FR 12,108, Y 258,155).

STELLA, Frank American b. 1936

$6600* *Abstract,* s., num. 15/18. d. '91, (11-12-92, Freemn/Fine Art, #233A), 66 x 52 in., (167.6 x 132.1 cm.), etching (BP 4335, DM 10,458, FR 35,275, Y 818,351).

$5635* *Ahab, 1988,* s., 21/60, from Waves I, Waddington Graphics, (05-12-93, AB Stockholm, #7048, illus.), approx. 73¼ x 54¾ in., (186 x 139 cm.), seriagraph, lithograph, and linoleum print w/hand-coloring and collage (BP 3679, DM 9092, FR 30,625, Y 629,117, SK 41,800).

$6325* *Aluminum Series: "Six Mile Bottom", "Averroes", "Casa Cornu", "Luis Miguel Dominguin" and "Kingsbury Run" (A. 33-36 & 38; G. 216-219 & 221),* 1970, each s., d., first three #70/100, last two #50/75, blindstamp,pub. Gemini, G.E.L., good cond., soiling, skinned spot, creases, (05-15-93, Sotheby-NY, #1211, illus.), each sheet 16 x 21⅞ in., (40.6 x 55.6 cm.), lithograph w/silkscreen in metallic silver on Special Arjomari paper (BP 4112, DM 10,174, FR 34,189, Y 701,142).

BI *Bene Come Il Sale, 1989,* s., d., #20/50, blindstamp, pub. Tyler Graphics, Ltd., good cond. ?,est. $18/22,000, (05-15-93, Sotheby-NY, #1231, illus.), sheet 77⅜ x 58⅞ in., (196.5 x 149.5 cm.), etching, aquatint and relief in colors.

$13,800* *Benjamin Moore Series (A. 57-62, G. 296-301), 1971: Six,* complete portfolio, s., d., #84/100, blindstamp, pub. Gemini, G.E.L., good cond., discoloration, (05-15-93, Sotheby-NY, #1213, illus.), each sheet 16 x 22 in., (40.6 x 55.9 cm.), lithograph in colors on Arches (BP 8973, DM 22,197, FR 74,595, Y 1,529,764).

BI *Black Series I: Die Fahne Hoch! (A.6,G.50), 1967,* s., d., annot. A.P.IX, est. $1,5/2,000, (05-19-93, Butterfield, #2339), 15 x 22 in., (381 x 559 mm.), lithograph on Barcham Green.

BI *Circuits: Imola Three IV (Tyler 604; FS 63), 1984,* s., d., #16/30, p. and pub. Tyler Graphics, good cond., est. BP 8/10,000, (06-30-93, Sotheby-London, #923, illus.), 66 x 51½ in., (167.6 x 130.8 cm.), relief-print and silkscreen in color on white TGL handmade, hand-colored.

BI *Circuits: Imola Three IV (Tyler 604; FS 63), 1984,* s., d., #16/30, p., pub. Tyler Graphics, good cond., est. BP 12/15,000, (12-03-92, Sotheby-London, #801, illus.), 66 x 51½ in., (167.6 x 130.8 cm.), relief print and silkscreen in colors on white TGL hand-made, hand-colored.

BI *Circuits: Talladega Three II (Axsom 136; Tyler 559:FS18), 1982,* s., d., num. 15/30, blindstamp pub. Tyler Graphics Ltd., full sheet,excell. cond.?, est. Y 12,5/15,000,000, (10-14-92, Sotheby-Japan, #96, illus.), sheet 67 x 51¾ in., (170.2 x 131.4 cm.), relief-printed etching in colors.

$2300* *Copper Series: "Lake City" and "Telluride": Two,* 1970, s., d., #28/75, blindstamp, pub. Gemini, G.E.L., good cond., tape hinges, (05-15-93, Sotheby-NY, #1212, illus.), each sheet 16 x 21⅞ in., (40.6 x 55.6 cm.), lithograph w/silkscreen in metallic copper on Special Arjomari paper (BP 1495, DM 3700, FR 12,432, Y 254,961).

$523* *Creede I (Axsom 39),* s., d. 70, #37/75, from Copper Series, pub. Gemini G.E.L., chop, (05-16-93, Hindman, #611), 16 x 22 in., (40.6 x 55.9 cm.), lithograph (BP 340, DM 841, FR 2827, Y 57,976).

$19,800* *Double Gray Scramble (A. 93; G. 491), 1973,* s., d., #75/100, pub. blindstamp, Gemini, G.E.L., full margins, goodcond., (11-07-92, Sotheby-NY, #774, illus.), 23⅜ x 46⅞ in., (59.4 x 119.1 cm.), silkscreen p. in colors on Arches 88 mouldmade (BP 12,945, DM 31,614, FR 106,854, Y 2,443,841).

$20,700* *Double Gray Scramble (Axsom 93, Gemini 491), 1973,* s., d., #68/100, Gemini G.E.L. blindstamps, full margins, light-staining, staining, crimping, very good cond., (05-11-93, Christie-NY, #568, illus.), sheet 29⅛ x 50⅞ in., (74 x 129.2 cm.), color screenprint on wove (BP 13,214, DM 32,609, FR 109,873, Y 2,276,977).

$18,154* *Double Gray Scramble (Axsom 93; Gemini 491), 1973,* s., d., num. 51/100, blindstamp pub. Gemini G.E.L., full margins, good cond., (10-14-92, Sotheby-Japan, #92, illus.), 23½ x 47 in., (59.7 x 119.4 cm.), color silkscreen on Arches 88 paper (BP 10,656, DM 26,568, FR 90,094, Y 2,199,952).

BI *Double Gray Scramble, 1973,* 52/100, s., d., 725mm x 1280mm, est. SF 55/65,000, (10-14-92, Germann, #53, illus.), color serigraph.

$8625* *Eccentric Polygons: "Moultonboro", "Conway", "Ossipee", "Sunapee" and "Tuftonboro" (A. 95, 97, 99, 100 & 103; G. 556, 553, 550, 546 & 554), 1974: Five,* init., d., i. CTP 3, A.P. II, CTP III, CTP VII and CTP 4, blindstamp, pub. Gemini, G.E.L., full margins, good cond., creases, soiling, skinned spot, (05-15-93, Sotheby-NY, #1217, illus.), each sheet 17¼ x 22¼ in., (43.8 x 56.5 cm.), lithograph w/silkscreen in colors on Arches (BP 5608, DM 13,873, FR 46,622, Y 956,102).

$3163* *"Eccentric Polygons: Conway" and "Ossipee" (A. 97 & 99; G. 550 & 553): Two,* each s., d., i., trial proof, blindstamp of pub., Gemini G.E.L., full margins, good cond., creases, soiling, skinned spot, (02-11-93, Sotheby-NY, #444, illus.), each sheet approx. 17$^{5}/_{16}$ x 22¼ in., (439 x 565 mm.), lithograph and silkscreens p. in colors (BP 2232, DM 5239, FR 17,730, Y 381,314).

$2300* *Empress Of India I (Axsom 27; Gemini 81), 1968,* s., d., #63/100, blindstamp of pub., Gemini, G.E.L., full margins, good cond., (02-11-93, Sotheby-NY, #443, illus.), sheet 16⅛ x 35¼ in., (410 x 896 mm.), color silkscreen (BP 1623, DM 3810, FR 12,892, Y 277,275).

$18,400* *Estoril Three II (A. 139; Tyler 562:FS21), 1982,* s., d., #20/30, from suite Circuits, blindstamp, pub. Tyler Graphics, Ltd., good cond. ?, (05-15-93, Sotheby-NY, #1225, illus.), sheet 66 x 52 in., (167.6 x 132.1 cm.), woodcut, engraving, and relief printed etching in colors on handmade, hand-colored TGL (BP 11,964, DM 29,596, FR 99,459, Y 2,039,685).

BI *Exotic Bird Series: Mysterious Bird Of Ulieta (A. 111; T. 552:FS11),1977,* s., d., #40/50, pub. blindstamp, Tyler Graphics, Ltd., full margins,good cond., est. $4,5/5,500, (11-07-92, Sotheby-NY, #776, illus.), 32⅞ x 44⅞ in., (83.5 x 114 cm.), lithograph and silkscreen p. in colors on Arches 88 mouldmade.

$1045* *Fortin De Las Flores, 1967,* from Ten from Leo Castelli, d., init., pub. Tanglewood Press, (05-27-93, Swann, #265, illus.), sh 18 x 23 in., (45.7 x 58.4 cm.), color serigraph on graph paper (BP 669, DM 1677, FR 5652, Y 112,028).

$24,200* *Giufa E La Berretta Rossa, 1989,* s., d., #38/50, blindstamp, stain, excellent cond., (11-09-92, Christie-NY, #416, illus.), 77½ x 58½ in., (196.9 x 148.6 cm.), aquatint, engraving and etching in colors on TGL handmade (BP 16,000, DM 38,633, FR 130,529, Y 3,003,227).

$4597* *The Great Heidelburgh Thun, 1988,* s., 21/60, Waddington Graphics, from Waves I, (05-12-93, AB Stockholm, #7049, illus.), approx. 74$^{7}/_{16}$ x 54$^{5}/_{16}$ in., (189 x 138 cm.), serigraph, lithograph and linoleum print w/hand-coloring and collage (BP 3002, DM 7417, FR 24,984, Y 513,230, SK 34,100).

BI *Guifa E La Berretta Rossa, 1989,* s., d., num. 20/50, pub. Tyler Graphics Ltd., full sheet, excell. cond.?, est. Y 2,5/3,000,000, (10-14-92, Sotheby-Japan, #97, illus.), sheet 77 x 57⅞ in., (195.6 x 147 cm.), relief-printed aquatint, engraving and etching in colors on TGL handmade paper.

$20,700* *Guifa E La Berretta Rossa, 1989,* s., d., #4/50, blindstamp, pub. Tyler Graphics, Ltd., good cond. ?, (05-15-93, Sotheby-NY, #1227, illus.), sheet 77½ x 58½ in., (196.9 x 148.6 cm.), relief printed aquatint, engraving and etching in colors on TGL handmade (BP 13,459, DM 33,296, FR 111,892, Y 2,294,646).

$9900* *Had Gadya: Front Cover, 1982-4,* from Illustrations after El Lissitzky's Had Gadya, s., d. 84f, #4/60, excellent cond., (11-09-92, Christie-NY, #414, illus.), 42½ x 34 in., (108 x 86.4 cm.), lithograph, screenprint, linocut and collage in colors w/hand-coloring on wove (BP 6545, DM 15,805, FR 53,398, Y 1,228,593).

$5635* *Hark, 1988,* from Waves I, s., Waddington Graphics, 21/60, (05-12-93, AB Stockholm, #7046, illus.), 73¼ x 52¾ in., (186 x 134 cm.), serigraph, lithograph and linoleum print w/hand-coloring and collage (BP 3679, DM 9092, FR 30,625, Y 629,117, SK 41,800).

$1035* *Ileana Sonnabend (A. 65; G. 369), 1972,* s., d., #42/100, blindstamp, pub. Gemini, G.E.L., good cond., (05-15-93, Sotheby-NY, #1214), 16 x 21⅞ in., (40.6 x 55.6 cm.), lithograph in metallic purple on Copperplate Deluxe paper (BP 673, DM 1665, FR 5595, Y 114,732).

$25,300* *Imola Three IV (A. 165; T. 604:FS63), 1984,* s., d., #24/30, pub. blindstamp, Tyler Graphics, Ltd., good cond., (11-07-92, Sotheby-NY, #779, illus.), sheet 65¾ x 51⅝ in., (167 x 131.1 cm.), relief printed etching w/silkscreen p. in colors on dyed TGL handmade (BP 16,541, DM 40,396, FR 136,535, Y 3,122,686).

$6038* *Les Indes Galantes I-V (A. 86-90), 1973: Five,* complete suite, each s., d., #90/100, pub. Petersburg Press, good cond., handling creases, soiling, foxing, (05-15-93, Sotheby-NY, #1215, illus.), each sheet 16 x 22 in., (40.6 x 55.9 cm.), five offset lithographs in colors on J. Green mouldmade paper (BP 3926, DM 9712, FR 32,638, Y 669,327).

$1150* *Irving Blum Memorial Edition (A.3,G.74), 1967,* s., d., #8/16, blindstamp publisher, Gemini G.E.L., p. James Webb, full margins, good cond., buckling, Albert Levinson Estate, (05-19-93, Butterfield, #2340, illus.), sh 26 x 32 in., (660 x 813 mm.), lithograph in metallic silver on English Vellum graph (BP 747, DM 1869, FR 6298, Y 127,311).

BI *Itata (Axsom 23; Gemini 76), 1968,* s., d., #18/100, blindstamp, pub. Gemini, G.E.L., good cond., handling creases, soiling, est. $1,5/2,000, (05-15-93, Sotheby-NY, #1210, illus.), 16¼ x 22 in., (41.3 x 55.9 cm.), lithograph in colors on Lowell paper.

$2750* *Lunna Wola (V) (A. App. IV, E. p. 179; Tyler 546:SF5), 1975,* tip pen s. verso, d., i. 'V-12' and 'T.P.', pub. Tyler Graphics, Ltd., good cond., (11-07-92, Sotheby-NY, #775, illus.), sheet 24 x 20½ in., (610 x 521 mm.), hand colored, dyed and collaged handmade paper (BP 1798, DM 4391, FR 14,841, Y 339,422).

$4675* *Newfoundland Series: River Of Ponds III (A. 52, G. 272), 1971,* s., d., annot. A.P.X, blindstamp pub. Gemini G.E.L., full margins, good cond.?, (10-28-92, Butterfield, #3124, illus.), 31⅞ x 31⅞ in., (810 x 810 mm.), color lithograph on Special Arjomari paper (BP 2979, DM 7220, FR 24,515, Y 573,620).

BI *Ossipee (Axsom 99), 1974,* s., d., #53/100, blindstamp, est. DM 4,500, (06-12-93, Hauswedell/Nolt, #400, illus.), 12¹⁄₁₆ x 17⁵⁄₁₆ in., (30.7 x 44 cm.), color lithograph and serigraph on thick wove.

$495* *Ouray (Axsom 44),* s., d. 70, #37/75, from Copper Series, pub. Gemini G.E.L., chop, (05-16-93, Hindman, #612), 16 x 22 in., (40.6 x 55.9 cm.), lithograph (BP 322, DM 796, FR 2676, Y 54,872).

$4745* *Pacific, 1988,* s., from Waves I, Waddington Graphics, 21/60, (05-12-93, AB Stockholm, #7050, illus.), approx. 74⁷⁄₁₆ x 54¾ in., (189 x 139 cm.), serigraph, lithograph

and linoleum print w/hand-coloring and collage (BP 3098, DM 7656, FR 25,788, Y 529,753, SK 35,200).

$9200* *La Penna Di Hu (Black And White), 1988,* s., d., #2/42, blindstamp, pub. Tyler Graphics, Ltd., good cond. ?, (05-15-93, Sotheby-NY, #1230, illus.), sheet 77⅜ x 58⅝ in., (196.5 x 148.9 cm.), relief printed etching and aquatint on white handmade TGL (BP 5982, DM 14,798, FR 49,730, Y 1,019,843).

$13,200* *La Penna Di Hu, 1988,* s., d., #10/42, blindstamp, excellent cond., (11-09-92, Christie-NY, #415, illus.), (195.6 x 149.9 cm.), etching and aquatint on TGL handmade (BP 8727, DM 21,073, FR 71,197, Y 1,638,124).

BI *La Penna Di Hu, 1988,* s., d., #4/50, blindstamp, pub. Tyler Graphics, Ltd., good cond. ?, est. $25/30,000, (05-15-93, Sotheby-NY, #1228, illus.), sheet 54⅞ x 66 in., (139.4 x 167.6 cm.), silkscreen, woodcut and relief printed etching in colors w/hand-colored stencil on white handmade TGL.

$29,900* *Pergusa Three Double, 1984,* s., d., #19/30, suite Circuits, blindstamp, pub. Tyler Graphics, Ltd., good cond. ?, (05-15-93, Sotheby-NY, #1226, illus.), sheet 102 x 66 in., (259.1 x 167.6 cm.), silkscreen, woodcut and relief printed engraving in colors on two sheets (BP 19,441, DM 48,094, FR 161,622, Y 3,314,488).

$6900* *Polar Co-Ordinates II (A. 120), 1980,* s., d., #70/100, pub. Petersburg Press, excell. cond., the Late M. Anwar Kamal, M.D. Coll., (05-11-93, Christie-NY, #570, illus.), sheet 38½ x 38 in., (978 x 965 mm.), color offset lithograph, screenprint and letterpress w/hand-coloringon wove (BP 4405, DM 10,870, FR 36,624, Y 758,992).

$5750* *Polar Co-Ordinates IV (A. 122), 1980,* s., d., #37/100, pub. Petersburg Press, excell. cond., (05-11-93, Christie-NY, #571, illus.), sheet 38 x 38½ in., (965 x 978 mm.), color offset lithograph, screenprint and letterpress on Arches (BP 3671, DM 9058, FR 30,520, Y 632,494).

$7188* *Polar Co-ordinates II (A. 120), 1980,* s., d., #79/100, pub. Petersburg Press, good cond., crease, (05-15-93, Sotheby-NY, #1221, illus.), sheet 38⅜ x 38 in., (97.5 x 96.5 cm.), offset lithograph and silkscreen in colors w/hand-coloring and collage on Arches Cover (BP 4674, DM 11,562, FR 38,854, Y 796,807).

$6038* *Polar Co-ordinates VI (A. 124), 1980,* s., d., #90/100, pub. Petersburg Press, good cond., (05-15-93, Sotheby-NY, #1222, illus.), sheet 38½ x 38 in., (97.8 x 96.5 cm.), offset lithograph and silkscreen in colors on Arches Cover (BP 3926, DM 9712, FR 32,638, Y 669,327).

$5175* *Polar Co-ordinates VIII (A. 126), 1980,* s., d., #79/100, pub. Petersburg Press, good cond., crease, (05-15-93, Sotheby-NY, #1223, illus.), 38⅜ x 38 in., (97.5 x 96.5 cm.), offset lithograph and silkscreen in colors on Arches Cover (BP 3365, DM 8324, FR 27,973, Y 573,661).

$7262* *Polar Coordinates For Ronnie Peterson: Polar Coordinate III (Axsom 121), 1980,* s., d., num. 53/100B, pub. Petersburg Press, full sheet, good cond., (10-14-92, Sotheby-Japan, #94, illus.), sheet 38¼ x 38 in., (972 x 965 mm.), offset lithograph and silkscreen in colors on Arches Cover paper (BP 4262, DM 10,628, FR 36,040, Y 880,029).

BI *Polar Coordinates For Ronnie Peterson: Polar Coordinate VIII (Axsom 126), 1980,* s., d., i. A.P. 5/20, pub. Petersburg Press, full sheet, good cond.,est. Y 900/1,000,000, (10-14-92, Sotheby-Japan, #95, illus.), sheet 37⅝ x 38⅜ in., (956 x 975 mm.), offset lithograph and silkscreen in colors on Arches Cover paper.

$15,400* *Port Aux Basques (Axsom 54: Gemini 274), 1971,* s., d., #36/58, pub. blindstamp, Gemini, G.E.L., full margins, good cond., scuff mark, soiling, (11-07-92, Sotheby-NY, #773, illus.), 31⅞ x 63¾ in., (81 x 161.9 cm.), lithograph and silkscreen p. in colors on Special Arjomari (BP 10,069, DM 24,589, FR 83,108, Y 1,900,765).

$660* *Purple Series, 1972,* s., d., i. A.P. VI, blindstamp pub. Gemini G.E.L., good cond., wear,soiling, creasing, (12-12-92, Weschler, #170), sheet 16 x 22 in., (40.6 x 55.9 cm.), color lithograph on copper plate deluxe paper (BP 423, DM 1040, FR 3564, Y 81,673).

$770* *Purple Series: Carl Andre (A. 70, G. 374), 1972,* s., d., #68/100, blindstamp pub. Gemini G.E.L., full margins, very good cond.?, (10-28-92, Butterfield, #3126), sheet 16 x 22 in., (406 x 559 mm.), lithograph in purple on

Copperplate Deluxe paper (BP 491, DM 1189, FR 4038, Y 94,479).

$880* *Purple Series: Charlotte Tokayer (A. 69, G. 737), 1972*, s., d., #67/100, blindstamp pub. Gemini G.E.L., full margins, very good cond.?, (10-28-92, Butterfield, #3125), sheet 16 x 22 in., (406 x 559 mm.), lithograph in purple on Copperplate Deluxe paper (BP 561, DM 1359, FR 4615, Y 107,975).

$715* *Purple Series: Leo Castelli (A. 72, G. 376), 1972*, s., d., #68/100, blindstamp pub. Gemini G.E.L., full margins, very good cond.?, (10-28-92, Butterfield, #3127), sheet 16 x 22 in., (406 x 559 mm.), lithograph in purple on Copperplate Deluxe paper (BP 456, DM 1104, FR 3749, Y 87,730).

$8662* *Shard IV (Axsom 147), 1982*, s., d., num., (11-28-92, Schoppmann, #817, illus.), 39¾ x 45¼ in., (101 x 114.9 cm.), color offset and color serigraph on Arches paper (BP 5717, DM 13,800, FR 46,847, Y 1,078,034).

BI *Sidi Ifni (Axsom 91 a), 1974*, s., from Hommage a Picasso, #38/40, d. 79, Petersburg Press edit., est. DM 6,500-, (05-27-93, Lempertz, #1037, illus.), 21⅞ x 30 in., (55.6 x 76.2 cm.), color lithograph on wove.

$1815* *Sidi Ifni (Axsom 91), 1973*, s., d., i. P.P.10/15, from portfolio Hommage a Picasso, pub. Propylaen Verlag, full margins, good cond., (10-14-92, Sotheby-Japan, #91), 19 x 19 in., (483 x 483 mm.), color offset lithograph (BP 1065, DM 2656, FR 9007, Y 219,947).

$6900* *Sinjerli Variation II (A. 115), 1977*, s., d., #78/100, pub. Petersburg Press, good cond., skinned spot, foxing, handling creases, (05-15-93, Sotheby-NY, #1218, illus.), sheet 31⅞ x 42⅛ in., (81 x 107 cm.), offset lithograph and silkscreen in colors on Arches Cover (BP 4486, DM 11,099, FR 37,297, Y 764,882).

$8050* *Sinjerli Variation III (A. 117), 1977*, s., d., #72/100, pub. Petersburg Press, good cond., (05-15-93, Sotheby-NY, #1219, illus.), sheet 32 x 42⅛ in., (81.3 x 107 cm.), offset lithograph and silkscreen in colors on Arches Cover (BP 5234, DM 12,948, FR 43,514, Y 892,362).

$5750* *Sinjerli Variation Squared With Colored Ground 1A (A. 130), 1981*, s., d., #30/61, pub. Petersburg Press, good cond., (05-15-93, Sotheby-NY, #1224, illus.), sheet 31⅞ x 31⅞ in., (81 x 81 cm.), lithograph and silkscreen in colors on Arches Cover (BP 3739, DM 9249, FR 31,081, Y 637,402).

$28,139* *Sinjerli Variations (Axsom 113-118), 1977:* Six, complete suite, each s., d., num. 50/100, pub. Petersburg Press, full margins, good cond., (10-14-92, Sotheby-Japan, #93, illus.), each sheet approx. 32 x 42½ in., (81.3 x 108 cm.), offset lithograph w/silkscreen in colors on Arches Cover paper (BP 16,516, DM 41,181, FR 139,648, Y 3,409,961).

$5042* *A Squeeze Of The Hand, 1988,* from Waves I, s., 21/60, Waddington Graphics, (05-12-93, AB Stockholm, #7047, illus.), approx. 72⁷⁄₁₆ x 54⁵⁄₁₆ in., (184 x 138 cm.), serigraph, lithograph, linoleum print w/hand-coloring and collage (BP 3292, DM 8135, FR 27,402, Y 562,912, SK 37,400).

$5338* *Squid, 1988,* s., 21/60, from Waves I, Waddington Graphics, (05-12-93, AB Stockholm, #7051, illus.), approx. 74¹³⁄₁₆ x 54¹⁵⁄₁₆ in., (190 x 139.5 cm.), serigraph, lithograph and linoleum print w/hand-coloring and collage (BP 3485, DM 8612, FR 29,011, Y 595,958, SK 39,600).

$13,225* *Steller's Albatross (A. 112), 1977*, s., d., i. work proof 7, blindstamp, pub. Tyler Graphics, Ltd., fullmargins, good cond., creases, soiling, (05-15-93, Sotheby-NY, #1220, illus.), 32⅞ x 44⅞ in., (83.5 x 114 cm.), lithograph and silkscreen in colors on Arches 88 mouldmade paper (BP 8599, DM 21,272, FR 71,486, Y 1,466,024).

$1045* *Sunapee (Axsom 100),* s., d. 74, #43/100, from series Eccentric Polygons, pub. Gemini G.E.L, chop, prov., (05-16-93, Hindman, #613), 16 x 14¼ in., (40.6 x 36.2 cm.), color lithograph (BP 679, DM 1681, FR 5649, Y 115,841).

$3520* *Swan Engraving Blue (Tyler 576), 1983,* from The Swan Engraving Series, s., d., #15/30, blindstamp, excellent cond., (11-09-92, Christie-NY, #413, illus.), 39 x 31½ in., (99.1 x 80 cm.), etching and engraving in col-

ors on buff TGL handmade (BP 2327, DM 5619, FR 18,986, Y 436,833).

BI *Swan Engraving Square I (A. 157; T. 571:FS30), 1982,* s., d., #10/20, blindstamp, pub. Tyler Graphics, Ltd., good cond. ?,est. $2/4,000, (05-15-93, Sotheby-NY, #1229, illus.), sheet 53½ x 51⅝ in., (135.9 x 131.1 cm.), intaglio etching on white handmade TGL.

$7475* *The Symphony, 1990,* s., d., #174/175, Tyler Graphics blindstamp, full margins, excell. cond., (05-11-93, Christie-NY, #574, illus.), sheet 81 x 40 in., (205.7 x 101.6 cm.), color lithograph on wove (BP 4772, DM 11,775, FR 39,676, Y 822,242).

$16,500* *Talladega Three I (Axsom 135; Tyler 558), 1982,* s., d., i. P.P. II of II, blindstamp, full margins, excell. cond., (11-09-92, Christie-NY, #412, illus.), 66 x 52 in., (167.6 x 132.1 cm.), etching on TGL handmade (BP 10,909, DM 26,341, FR 88,997, Y 2,047,655).

$61,600* *Talladega Three II (T. 559:FS18), 1982,* s., d., #16/30, from suite, Circuits, pub. blindstamp, Tyler Graphics, Ltd., good cond., (11-07-92, Sotheby-NY, #778, illus.), sheet 66⅛ x 52 in., (168 x 132.1 cm.), relief p. in colors on handmade, hand colored TGL (BP 40,275, DM 98,355, FR 332,434, Y 7,603,061).

$9200* *Then Came An Ox And Drank The Water, London, 1982-84,* plate 7 for Illustrations after El Lissitzky's Had Gadya, WaddingtonGraphics, s., d. 86, i. oil over reject print, unique proof, excell. cond.?, (05-11-93, Christie-NY, #573, illus.), sheet 54 x 52¼ in., (137.2 x 132.7 cm.), color lithograph, linocut and screenprint w/hand-painting on wove (BP 5873, DM 14,493, FR 48,832, Y 1,011,990).

$1045* *Untitled (Blue And Yellow Stripes), 1965,* full margins, s., (05-27-93, Swann, #266, illus.), 18 x 18 in., (45.7 x 45.7 cm.), color serigraph (BP 669, DM 1677, FR 5652, Y 112,028).

$605* *Untitled, 1964,* from Ten Works + Ten Artists, portfolio #40/500, pub. Ives-Sillman, trimmed margins, surface scuff, good cond., prop. Woodward Foundation, (12-12-92, Weschler, #171, illus.), sheet 18½ x 18½ in., (47 x 47 cm.), color silkscreen (BP 388, DM 953, FR 3267, Y 74,867).

$2200* *V Series: Empress Of India I (A. 27, G. 81), 1968,* s., d., #84/100, blindstamp pub. Gemini G.E.L., full margins, good cond., staining, foxing, (10-28-92, Butterfield, #3123, illus.), 11⅛ x 32½ in., (283 x 826 mm.), color lithograph on Lowell paper (BP 1402, DM 3398, FR 11,536, Y 269,939).

$1725* *V Series: Empress Of India I (A.27 ,G.81), 1968,* d., #78/100, blindstamp publisher Gemini G.E.L., p. Charles Ritt, staining, crease, scratch, crease in image, light-staining, handling creases, (05-19-93, Butterfield, #2341), 16¼ x 35⅜ in., (413 x 899 mm.), lithograph in colors on Lowell (BP 1120, DM 2804, FR 9447, Y 190,966).

BI *Waves I: Ahab (W.G. 7), 1985-89,* s., #19/60, pub. Waddington Graphics, good cond., est. BP 5/6,000, (12-03-92, Sotheby-London, #800, illus.), 78¾ x 59 in., (200 x 149.9 cm.), silkscreen, lithography and linoeum block w/hand-coloring, marbling and collage, on T H Saunders Pressed.

BI *Waves I: Hark! (W.G. 8), 1985-89,* s., #19/60, pub. Waddington Graphics, good cond., est. BP 5/6,000, (12-03-92, Sotheby-London, #797, illus.), 78¾ x 59 in., (200 x 149.9 cm.), silkscreen, lithography and linoeum block w/hand-coloring, marbling and collage on T H Saunders Pressed.

BI *Waves I: Pacific (W.G. 2), 1986-89,* s., #19/60, pub. Waddington Graphics, good cond., est. BP 5/6,000, (12-03-92, Sotheby-London, #799, illus.), 78¾ x 59 in., (200 x 149.9 cm.), silkscreen, lithography and linoeum block w/hand-coloring, marbling and collage, on T H Saunders Pressed.

$7673* *Waves I: Squid (Waddington Graphics 3), 1985-89,* s., #19/60, pub. Waddington Graphics, good cond., (12-03-92, Sotheby-London, #796, illus.), 78¾ x 59 in., (200 x 149.9 cm.), silkscreen, lithography and linoeum block w/hand-coloring, marbling and collage on T H Saunders Pressed (BP 4950, DM 12,066, FR 41,186, Y 954,709).

BI *Waves I: The Great Heidelburgh Tun (W.G. 1), 1985-89,* s., #19/60, pub. Waddington Graphics, good cond., est.

BP 5/6,000, (12-03-92, Sotheby-London, #798, illus.), 78¾ x 59 in., (200 x 149.9 cm.), silkscreen, lithography and linoeum block w/hand-coloring, marbling and collage, on T H Saunders Pressed.

$12,100* *The Waves: Hark!, 1985-88,* s., d. '88, #47/60, pub. Waddington Graphics, Ltd., good cond., (11-07-92, Sotheby-NY, #777, illus.), sheet 73⅜ x 52⅝ in., (186.4 x 133.7 cm.), lithograph, linoleum cut and silkscreen p. in colors w/hand coloringand collage (BP 7911, DM 19,320, FR 65,300, Y 1,493,458).

$9775* *The Waves: Squid (W. 3), 1985-89,* s., d. '89, #48/60, pub. Waddington Graphics, good cond. ?, (05-15-93, Sotheby-NY, #1233, illus.), 74½ x 54⅞ in., (189.2 x 139.4 cm.), silkscreen, lithograpg, linoleum block w/hand-coloring, marbling andcollage (BP 6356, DM 15,723, FR 52,838, Y 1,083,583).

$21,850* *The Waves: The Counterpane (Waddington 5), 1985-89,* s., d. '89, i. CTP 2, unique color trial proof, pub. Waddington Graphics, good cond. ?, (05-15-93, Sotheby-NY, #1232, illus.), sheet 71 x 51⅛ in., (180.3 x 129.9 cm.), silkscreen, lithograph, linoleum block w/hand-coloring, marbling andcollage (BP 14,207, DM 35,146, FR 118,108, Y 2,422,126).

$8250* *The Waves: The Pacific, 1985-88,* s., d. '88, num. 11/60, pub. Waddington Graphics, good cond., well-restored vertical surface abrasion in image, touched-in surface scuffs, (02-24-93, Butterfield, #3149, illus.), 74¾ x 54⅝ in., (189.9 x 138.7 cm.), lithograph, linoleum block, & silkscreen in colors w/collage & hand-coloring on heavy wove (BP 5753, DM 13,393, FR 45,405, Y 968,083).

BI *Yellow Journal, State I (Tyler 601), 1984,* s., d. 85, i. State I, #5/16, Tyler Graphics blindstamp, creases, excell. cond., est. $5/7,000, (05-11-93, Christie-NY, #572, illus.), sheet 52½ x 38½ in., (133.4 x 97.8 cm.), color lithograph on Arches.

$10,350* *York Factory II (A. 94, G. 567), 1974,* s., d., #9/100, Gemini G.E.L. blindstamps, full margins, scuffs, skinned patch, excell. cond., (05-11-93, Christie-NY, #569, illus.), sheet 18½ x 44⅜ in., (47 x 112.7 cm.), color screenprint on black Arches (BP 6607, DM 16,304, FR 54,936, Y 1,138,489).

$12,075* *York Factory II (A. 94, G. 567), 1974,* s., d., #79/100, blindstamp, pub. Gemini, G.E.L., full margins, goodcond., skinned spot, creases, scuff marks, (05-15-93, Sotheby-NY, #1216, illus.), 13⅜ x 40⅛ in., (34 x 101.9 cm.), silkscreen in colors on Black Arches (BP 7851, DM 19,423, FR 65,270, Y 1,338,543).

STELLETSKI, D.
$310* *Matinee Au Profit Des Artistes Russes Residant En France, c. 1920,* (01-31-93, Morelle/Marchan, #185), 31½ x 47¼ in., (80 x 120 cm.), poster (BP 208, DM 499, FR 1688, Y 38,673).

STEN KNUDSEN, Nina
$92* *Komposition,* s. Nina Sten Knudsen, 75/150, (03-24-93, Kunsthallen, #212), color lithograph (BP 62, DM 150, FR 511, Y 10,810, DK 575).

STENBERG
BI *La Belle Nivernaise, c. 1930,* stuck-on production, quantity labels, fold marks, tears, lit., est. BP 4/600, (02-04-93, Christie-S. Ken., #39, illus.), 41 x 28½ in., (104.1 x 72.4 cm.), color lithograph backed on japan.

STEPANOVA, Varvara Fedorva   1894-1948
$14,984* *Gaust Tschaba, Moscow, 1919,* s., i. 1919 Mockba N28, very good cond., nicks, newspaper cover w/collage and handwritten title and sig., repaired tears, losses, unique, (12-01-92, Christie-London, #527, illus.), overall S. 107½ x 69⁵⁄₁₆ in., (273 x 176 cm.), 7 collages and 9 pgs. of handwritten text, collages of color paper and text in colors on newsprint (BP 9900, DM 23,883, FR 81,391, Y 1,865,538).

STEPHANO
BI *"Cigarettes Saphir",* pub. Moullot, est. $6/800, (08-05-92, Boos, #580), image 44½ x 29⅛ in., (113 x 74 cm.), color lithograph.

STEPHEN, Gary
BI *(Untitled),* s., d. 1989, #20/43, appears good cond., est. $6/800, (06-11-93, Doyle, #104), 14 x 19 in., (356 x 483 mm.), color etching.

BI *Untitled, 1988,* s., #20/48, pub. Pace Editions, appears very good ocnd., est. $6/800, (06-11-93, Doyle, #105), 24 x 18 in., (610 x 457 mm.), color etching.

STERL, Robert Hermann   1867-1932
$1180* *Arbeiter In Einer Geisserei,* s., rare, small tears, (12-05-92, Bassenge, #7755, illus.), 11¾ x 13¼ in., (29.8 x 33.7 cm.), lithograph on wove cardboard (BP 739, DM 1840, FR 6270, Y 146,202).

BI *Russische Troika (Simbirski 1912),* s., est. DM 250, (12-05-92, Bassenge, #7754), 5½ x 11⅝ in., (14 x 29.5 cm.), lithograph.

STERN, Bert   American b. 1929
$7700* *The Last Sitting, 1978,* Shorewood Press, portfolio of 10 photos, Type-C prints, each s., num.107/250 by photog., 1962, p. 1978, #107/290 ed., (10-15-92, Sotheby-NY, #523, illus.), photograph, gelatin silver prints (BP 4712, DM 11,462, FR 38,869, Y 923,815).

$4600* *Marilyn Monroe, 1962,* p. 1991, crayon s.; ink s., t., num. 3, annots.; d. twice, (c)credit stamp, lit., (04-08-93, Christie-NY, #517, illus.), 40 x 48 in., (101.6 x 121.9 cm.), photograph, toned gelatin silver print (BP 3016, DM 7390, FR 25,014, Y 522,015).

$2225* *Marilyn Monroe Drying Herself With Towel,* s., artist's proof, (10-10-92, Bonhams, #101B, illus.), 32 x 40 in., (81.3 x 101.6 cm.), silkscreen serigraph on blue ground (BP 1320, DM 3305, FR 11,097, Y 270,879).

$1020* *Marilyn Monroe, "Aroused",* The Last Sitting, s., #207/250, (10-10-92, Bonhams, #98, illus.), 18 x 19 in., (45.7 x 48.3 cm.), color photograph (BP 605, DM 1515, FR 5087, Y 124,178).

$1020* *Marilyn Monroe, "Feeling Good",* The Last Sitting, s., #207/250, (10-10-92, Bonhams, #92, illus.), 18½ x 20 in., (47 x 50.8 cm.), color photograph (BP 605, DM 1515, FR 5087, Y 124,178).

$1020* *Marilyn Monroe, "Flirtatious",* The Last Sitting, s., #207/250, (10-10-92, Bonhams, #95, illus.), 18 x 19 in., (45.7 x 48.3 cm.), color photograph (BP 605, DM 1515, FR 5087, Y 124,178).

$1112* *Marilyn Monroe, "I Beg Of You",* The Last Sitting, s., #207/250, (10-10-92, Bonhams, #97, illus.), 18 x 19 in., (45.7 x 48.3 cm.), color photographs (BP 660, DM 1652, FR 5546, Y 135,379).

$1112* *Marilyn Monroe, "Not Bad For 36",* The Last Sitting, s., #207/250, (10-10-92, Bonhams, #101, illus.), 18 x 19 in., (45.7 x 48.3 cm.), color photograph (BP 660, DM 1652, FR 5546, Y 135,379).

$890* *Marilyn Monroe, "Playful",* The Last Sitting, s., #207/250, (10-10-92, Bonhams, #93, illus.), 18 x 19 in., (45.7 x 48.3 cm.), color photograph (BP 528, DM 1322, FR 4439, Y 108,352).

$834* *Marilyn Monroe, "Rhythm",* The Last Sitting, s., #207/250, (10-10-92, Bonhams, #99, illus.), 18 x 19 in., (45.7 x 48.3 cm.), color photograph (BP 495, DM 1239, FR 4160, Y 101,534).

$1112* *Marilyn Monroe, "Teasing",* The Last Sitting, s., #207/250, (10-10-92, Bonhams, #96, illus.), 18 x 19 in., (45.7 x 48.3 cm.), color photograph (BP 660, DM 1652, FR 5546, Y 135,379).

$890* *Marilyn Monroe, "What's It All About?",* The Last Sitting, s., #207/250, (10-10-92, Bonhams, #94, illus.), 18 x 19 in., (45.7 x 48.3 cm.), color photograph (BP 528, DM 1322, FR 4439, Y 108,352).

$1298* *Marilyn Monroe, Big Close Up,* s. Bert Stern 73, artist's proof, (10-10-92, Bonhams, #101A, illus.), 37 x 38 in., (94 x 96.5 cm.), silkscreen serigraph on tan ground (BP 770, DM 1928, FR 6474, Y 158,023).

$358* *Marilyn Monroe, I Beg Of You, 1962,* from The Last Sitting, Bel Air Hotel shoot, artist's proof, (04-26-93, Selkirk, #545), 24 x 20 in., (61 x 50.8 cm.), color photograph (BP 226, DM 561, FR 1895, Y 39,506).

$1391* *Marilyn Monroe,"Here's To You",* The Last Sitting, s., #207/250, (10-10-92, Bonhams, #100, illus.), 19 x 18 in., (48.3 x 45.7 cm.), color photograph (BP 825, DM 2066, FR 6938, Y 169,345).

$4620* *Marilyn Monroe; The Last Sitting: Ten,* t. page, page of color reprods. of photo in portfolio, s., num. photog., 1962, p.l., (04-07-93, Swann, #560, illus.), 20 x 24 in., photograph, chromagenic (BP 3053, DM 7472, FR 25,287, Y 524,881).

$1650* *Marilyn With Diamonds, 1962,* s., d. in ink on overmat, mounted, (10-13-92, Christie-NY, #605, illus.), 9 x 13⅜ in., (22.9 x 34 cm.), photograph, gelatin silver print (BP 961, DM 2417, FR 8213, Y 200,073).

STERNBERG, Harry American b. 1904

BI *"Abraham Walkowitz" (Moore 171), 1943-1944,* s., t., excell. cond., est. $750/1,000, (05-15-93, Cleveland, #325), 23½ x 14 in., (59.7 x 35.6 cm.), serigraph in colors on brown paper.

$413* *"Blast Furnace",* s. H. Sternberg, very good cond., (09-27-92, Bakker, #172), image 11¾ x 8½ in., (29.8 x 21.6 cm.), etching (BP 241, DM 612, FR 2070, Y 49,849).

$250* *The Steel Mills,* s., (05-16-93, Hanzel, #458), 12 x 8¼ in., (30.5 x 21 cm.), lithograph (BP 163, DM 402, FR 1351, Y 27,713).

$468* *"Surrealistic Composition",* s., (10-31-92, Litchfield, #154), 15½ x 7¼ in., (39.4 x 18.4 cm.), aquatint (BP 306, DM 735, FR 2488, Y 57,864).

STERNE, Maurice American 1877-1957

$55* *Female Nude,* s., (11-12-92, Freemn/Fine Art, #233B), 16½ x 10½ in., (41.9 x 26.7 cm.), lithograph (BP 36, DM 87, FR 294, Y 6820).

STERNER, Malte

$26* *Prospector And Donkey,* s., i., #14/75, (06-07-93, Ritchie, #23), 8¾ x 11⁷⁄₁₆ in., (22.2 x 29.1 cm.), sepia etching (BP 17, DM 42, FR 142, Y 2789, C$ 33).

$26* *Windblown Trees,* s., t., prov., (06-07-93, Ritchie, #25), 14½ x 10¾ in., (36.9 x 27.3 cm.), etching (BP 17, DM 42, FR 142, Y 2789, C$ 33).

STERNFELD, Joel

BI *"Joseph, Utah",* 1983/1988, s., t., d., est. $3/500, (11-16-92, Butterfield, #6185, illus.), 13½ x 17⁹⁄₁₆ in., (343.5 x 435.8 mm.), photograph, c-print.

STERRER, Carl Austrian 19th/20th cent.

BI *Boy Studying,* s.; plate s., est. $80/120, (08-05-92, Boos, #680), sight 24³⁄₁₆ x 21⅞ in., (615 x 555 mm.), lithograph.

STETTNER, Louis

BI *Street Scene, 1982,* s., d., est. $5/750, (10-14-92, Swann, #571, illus.), 14 x 10½ in., (35.6 x 26.7 cm.), photograph, silver print.

STEVENS, Alfred (after) Belgian 1823-1906

BI *Parisienne,* by Leopold Flameng, est. $100/150, (07-03-92, Sloan, #1064), 6¾ x 8 in., (17.1 x 20.3 cm.), etching.

STEVENS, Dorothy

$236* *City View With Pedestrians,* s., (11-30-92, Ritchie, #22, illus.), 10 x 6⅞ in., (25.4 x 17.4 cm.), etching (BP 156, DM 376, FR 1276, Y 29,371, C$ 303).

BI *Portrait Of Mrs. J. Walker,* s., t., exhib., est. C$1/2,000, (05-18-93, Joyner, #130), 17¼ x 12 in., (43.8 x 30.5 cm.), etching.

STEVENS, Gustave Max

$173* *Solveig, 1898,* L'Estampe Moderne blindstamp, margins, good condition, tear, staining, foxing, handling creases, mat and light-staining, skinned area, surface soiling, (03-31-93, Butterfield, #5251), 9⅝ x 13¾ in., (24.4 x 34.9 cm.), lithograph printed in colors on wove (BP 114, DM 278, FR 945, Y 19,894).

STEVENS, Jr., Edward John American b. 1923

$165* *A History Of Man, 1944: Eight,* portfolio, all s., d., Edward John Stevens Jr. 1944, num., t., good cond., portfolio cover w/some losses to surface, (03-12-93, Skinner, #84, illus.), 7¾ x 6 in., (19.7 x 15.2 cm.), etching on wove (BP 115, DM 275, FR 934, Y 19,446).

STEVENSON, Gordon American b. 1892

$83* *Giovanna Albizzi,* s., (04-02-93, Sloan, #824), (375 x 267 mm.), color mezzotint (BP 55, DM 133, FR 453, Y 9450).

STEWART, John b. 1919

$1540* *The Memory Of Giorgio Morandi, Paris,* (1975), 1989, s., d., (10-13-92, Christie-NY, #606, illus.), 23½ x 31¼ in., (59.7 x 79.4 cm.), photograph, fresson print (BP 897, DM 2256, FR 7666, Y 186,735).

STEWART, S.

BI *Portrait Of A Woman,* est. $100/150, 19th c., (01-15-93, DuMouchelle, #2288), 18 x 11 in., (45.7 x 27.9 cm.), hand colored mezzotint.

STEZAKER, John

$2300* *Please Take One,* s., t., d. 1976, prov., exhib., Sylvio Perlstein Coll., (05-04-93, Sotheby-NY, #129, illus.), photograph, mounted on board and masonite (BP 1468, DM 3623, FR 12,208, Y 252,997).

STICK, Frank

$33* *"Autumn Days", c. 1905,* t., (09-12-92, Dunning, #1065), chromolithograph (BP 17, DM 48, FR 161, Y 4089).

STIEGLITZ, Alfred American 1864-1946

$15,400* *Equivalent (Poplar), 1923,* multiple mount, flush-mounted, from series Songs of the Sky, (10-13-92, Christie-NY, #363, illus.), 4⅝ x 3½ in., (11.7 x 8.9 cm.), photograph, gelatin silver print (BP 8969, DM 22,561, FR 76,655, Y 1,867,346).

$24,200* *Equivalent Cloud Study, 1923-1930,* multiple mount, flush mounted, (10-13-92, Christie-NY, #360, illus.), 4⅝ x 3⅝ in., (11.7 x 9.2 cm.), photograph, gelatin silver print (BP 14,094, DM 35,453, FR 120,458, Y 2,934,400).

$74,000* *From The Shelton, West, 1935,* flush and double-mounted, lit., (04-08-93, Christie-NY, #343, illus.), 9½ x 7½ in., (24.1 x 19.1 cm.), photograph, gelatin silver print (BP 48,525, DM 118,876, FR 402,393, Y 8,397,640).

$605* *An Icy Night, 1901,* (04-07-93, Swann, #561, illus.), 4½ x 5¾ in., photograph, photogravure (BP 400, DM 978, FR 3311, Y 68,734).

$6325* *Kitty Stieglitz And Edward Steichen Looking At An Album Of Photographs, c. 1905,* Georgia O'Keeffe coll., (04-06-93, Sotheby-NY, #61, illus.), 2½ x 3 in., photograph (BP 4178, DM 10,190, FR 34,506, Y 721,373).

BI *Lake George,* mounted, 1930's, est. $10/15,000, (10-15-92, Sotheby-NY, #96A, illus.), 3⅝ x 4⅝ in., (9.2 x 11.7 cm.), photograph, backed w/card.

BI *Marie Rapp, 1914,* i. by photog., est. $7/10,000, (10-15-92, Sotheby-NY, #204, illus.), 9¾ x 7½ in., (24.8 x 19.1 cm.), photograph, platinum print.

$1980* *New York At Night, c. 1910,* (10-14-92, Swann, #572, illus.), 5¾ x 4½ in., (14.6 x 11.4 cm.), photograph, photogravure (BP 1162, DM 2898, FR 9826, Y 239,942).

BI *Old Tree, Lake George, 1927,* multiple mount, flush-mounted, lit., est $15/20,000, (10-13-92, Christie-NY, #362, illus.), 4⅝ x 3⅝ in., (11.7 x 9.2 cm.), photograph, gelatin silver print.

BI *Poplars, Lake George,* 1920s, multiple mounte, flush-mounted, est. $15/20,000, (10-13-92, Christie-NY, #361, illus.), 4⅝ x 3⅝ in., (11.7 x 9.2 cm.), photograph, gelatin silver print.

$32,200* *Pual Haviland At "291", 1915,* orig., overmat, (04-06-93, Sotheby-NY, #61A, illus.), 9½ x 7½ in., photograph, platinum print (BP 21,268, DM 51,877, FR 175,668, Y 3,672,445).

BI *Songs Of The Sky, Poplar, 1923?,* flush-mounted on mount, est. $15/20,000, (04-08-93, Christie-NY, #341, illus.), 4¼ x 3½ in., (10.8 x 8.9 cm.), photograph, gelatin silver print.

$220* *Steerage,* (07-03-92, Sloan, #296), sight 9¼ x 7½ in., (23.5 x 19.1 cm.), print (BP 115, DM 333, FR 1122, Y 27,425).

BI *The Steerage,* (1907), 291 double-issue num.: 7-8, 1915-16, prov., est. $5/7,000, (10-13-92, Christie-NY, #48, illus.), 13 x 10¼ in., (33 x 26 cm.), photograph, photogravure on Japanese tissue.

$3163* *"The Steerage", 1911,* from Camera Work, #36, small format, (04-06-93, Sotheby-NY, #65, illus.), photograph, photogravure on tissue (BP 2089, DM 5096, FR 17,256, Y 360,744).

$8050* *"The Steerage", 1911,* from nos. 7-8 of 291, large format, (04-06-93, Sotheby-NY, #64, illus.), photograph, photogravure on Japan vellum (BP 5317, DM 12,969, FR 43,917, Y 918,111).

$2420* *The Steerage, 1911,* from camera work #36, (04-07-93, Swann, #562, illus.), photograph, small-format photogravure on tissue (BP 1599, DM 3914, FR 13,246, Y 274,938).

$2860* *The Steerage, 1911,* from CAMERA WORK #36, (10-14-92, Swann, #573, illus.), photograph, small-format photogravure on tissue (BP 1679, DM 4186, FR 14,194, Y 346,583).

$5225* *The Steerage, 1911,* from #'s 7-8 of 291, (10-15-92, Sotheby-NY, #95A, illus.), photogravure on Japan vellum (BP 3197, DM 7778, FR 26,376, Y 626,875).

$2475* *The Steerage, 1911,* from Camera Work, #36, (10-15-92, Sotheby-NY, #96, illus.), phtogravure on tissue (BP 1515, DM 3684, FR 12,494, Y 296,941).

BI *Two Poplars, Lake George, 1933,* flush-mounted on mount, est. $15/20,000, (04-08-93, Christie-NY, #342, illus.), 4⅝ x 3⅝ in., (11.7 x 9.2 cm.), photograph, gelatin silver print.

STIEGLITZ, Alfred and Clarence WHITE
$990* *Female Torso, 1909,* from Camerawork, Dixon Collection, (11-16-92, Butterfield, #6186, illus.), 8⅜ x 6⅜ in., (213.1 x 162.2 mm.), photograph, photogravure on tissue (BP 652, DM 1578, FR 5317, Y 123,119).

STIEGLITZ, Alfred and Juan C. ABEL, Editors
$19,550* *Camera Notes: Official Organ Of The Camera Club Of N.Y., The Camera Club, July 1897-December 1903: Twenty Issues,* Vol. I, num. 1-4; Vol. II, num. 1-4; Vol. III, num. 1-3; Vol. IV, num. 3,4; Vol. V, num. 1,3,4; Vol. VI, num. 1-4; illus. w/photogravures, halftoneplates and silver print of images by Stieglitz, Steichen, Kasebier, Day, Whiteand others, issues complete as pub., (04-08-93, Christie-NY, #75, illus.), photograph, (BP 12,820, DM 31,406, FR 106,308, Y 2,218,566).

STIEGLITZ, Alfred, Editor   American 1864-1946
$2300* *Camera Work Number 14 (April 1906): Nine,* works by Eduard J. Steichen, lacking colored halftone Cover Design, (04-08-93, Christie-NY, #79, illus.), photograph, 7 photogravures and 2 halftone plates (BP 1508, DM 3695, FR 12,507, Y 261,008).

$5750* *Camera Work Numbers 1-5 (January 1903-January 1904): Five Issues,* complete as pub., includes photogravures of work by Kasebier, Stieglitz, Steichen, White, Evans and Demachy, (04-08-93, Christie-NY, #76, illus.), photograph, (BP 3770, DM 9237, FR 31,267, Y 652,519).

$2300* *Camera Work Numbers 11-13 (January 1905-Janaury 1906): Three Issues,* complete as pub., includes photogravures and halftoned reprods. of work by Hill and Adamson, Steichen, Demachy, Steiglitz and Kuhn, (04-08-93, Christie-NY, #78, illus.), photograph, (BP 1508, DM 3695, FR 12,507, Y 261,008).

$2300* *Camera Work Numbers 15-20 (July 1906-October 1907): Five Issues,* complete as pub., includes photogravure and halftone plates of work by Coburn, Seeley, Steichen, Demachy, Keiley and others, (04-08-93, Christie-NY, #80, illus.), photograph, (BP 1508, DM 3695, FR 12,507, Y 261,008).

$1610* *Camera Work Numbers 21 And 22: Two Issues,* complete as pub., photogravures and halftone plates of work by Coburn; 4 color halftone reprods. of autochromes by Steichen, (04-08-93, Christie-NY, #81, illus.), photograph, (BP 1056, DM 2586, FR 8755, Y 182,705).

$3220* *Camera Work Numbers 6,8,9 And 10: Four Issues,* complete as pub., includes photogravures of work by Coburn, Annan, Evans, White, Watson-Schutze, Kasebier and Abbott, (04-08-93, Christie-NY, #77, illus.), photograph, (BP 2111, DM 5173, FR 17,510, Y 365,411).

$14,300* *Camera Work, Number 36, 1911: Sixteen,* after the photogs. of Alfred Stieglitz, halftone reprod. of Picasso drawing, (10-15-92, Sotheby-NY, #95, illus.), photogravures (BP 8750, DM 21,286, FR 72,186, Y 1,715,657).

$2588* *Camera Work: Six,* includ. #19,21,37,38,39 and Special Num. August 1912, illus. w/photogravures and halftones after photo. of Alvin Langdon Coburn, Annie W. Brigman, Paul B. Haviland, Eduard Steichen, Karl Struss, J. Craig Annan, D.O. Hillano, others, all plates present,

(04-06-93, Sotheby-NY, #62, illus.), photograph (BP 1709, DM 4169, FR 14,119, Y 295,164).

STILLFRIED, Baron Von
BI *Japansese Costume Portraits: Fifty,* 1870s, concertina album, 13 num., 3 in Japanese, in negs., est. BP 3/400, (05-06-93, Christie-London, #83), each approx. 3½ x 5½ in., photograph, hand-tinted albumen print.

STILLMAN, William James
$825* *Frieze From The Acropolis, c. 1870,* ink notations, (10-14-92, Swann, #256, illus.), 10½ x 8½ in., (26.7 x 21.6 cm.), photograph, albumen print (BP 484, DM 1207, FR 4094, Y 99,976).

STOBART, John
BI *"Cleveland: Moonlight Arrival On The Cuyahoga, C. 1876",* s., num. John Stobart 348/950, p. Maritime Heritage Prints, est. $15/2500, (09-25-92, Wolf, #20), 23½ x 31½ in., (59.7 x 80 cm.), lithographic poster.

$385* *"Philadelphia",* pub. Maritime Heritage Prints, s., #634/950, (06-11-93, Freemn/Fine Art, #234B), offset lithograph (BP 253, DM 626, FR 2110, Y 40,849).

STOCK, C.R.   English 19th cent.
BI *Cock Fighting: Three,* est. $300/500, (07-03-92, Sloan, #1086), each 8½ x 9¾ in., (21.6 x 24.8 cm.), colored engraving.

STOECKLIN, Nicklaus
$473* *Bi=Oro, Anti-Solaire, 1941,* folds, staining, nicks, lit., (02-04-93, Christie-S. Ken, #55, illus.), 50 x 35½ in., (127 x 90.2 cm.), color lithograph (BP 330, DM 779, FR 2641, Y 58,838).

BI *Gaba, c. 1927,* excell. cond., lit., est. BP 6/800, (02-04-93, Christie-S. Ken, #54, illus.), 50 x 36 in., (127 x 91.4 cm.), color lithograph.

STOHRER, Walter   b. 1937
$516* *Abstrakte Komposition, 1975,* s., num., (12-05-92, Bassenge, #7756), 19½ x 15¹¹⁄₁₆ in., (49.5 x 39.8 cm.), color etching on copper print paper (BP 323, DM 804, FR 2742, Y 63,933).

BI *Berliner Romanze, 1966: Three,* plate s., d., s., num., est. DM 1,600-, (09-25-92, Granier, #3019), sheet 9¹³⁄₁₆ x 9¹³⁄₁₆ in., (25 x 25 cm.), etching on thick hand-made.

$155* *Gebauchtes Rechteck, 1972,* s., d., #20/50, (09-18-92, Schloss Ahlden, #1068), 29¹⁵⁄₁₆ x 21⅛ in., (76 x 53.7 cm.), etching on handmade paper (BP 91, DM 230, FR 787, Y 19,157).

$155* *Keil Auf Ausgebuchteter Flache, 1970,* s., d., #91/100, (09-18-92, Schloss Ahlden, #1069), 29³⁄₁₆ x 21³⁄₁₆ in., (74.2 x 53.8 cm.), etching on hand-made (BP 91, DM 230, FR 787, Y 19,157).

$514* *"Nichts, Nur Eine Schone Nervenwaage", (19)71,* s., d., num., (12-01-92, Karl/Faber, #1273), 19⅛ x 15¾ in., (48.5 x 40 cm.), color etching and drypoint on wove (BP 340, DM 819, FR 2792, Y 63,994).

STOLZ, Albert   1875-1947
$147* *Rathauskeller Der Stadt Bozen, Sudtyrol,* p. L. Franzl, very good cond., (11-19-92, Ribeyre/Baron, #50), 41¾ x 31½ in., (106 x 80 cm.), poster (BP 97, DM 234, FR 789, Y 18,281).

$148* *Rathauskeller Der Stadt Bozen/Sudtirol,* s. in stone, Graph. Verlagsanstalt Lorenz Franzl, Bozen, (12-05-92, Bassenge, #7630), 40³⁄₁₆ x 29⅛ in., (102 x 74 cm.), color lithograph (BP 93, DM 231, FR 786, Y 18,337).

STONE, Marcus (after)
$96* *"An Offer Of Marriage" and "A Prior Attachment", 1884: Two,* pub. Goupil and Co., margins, foxed, (03-17-93, Bonhams-Chelsea, #328), plate 29 x 14¼ in., (73.7 x 36.2 cm.), photogravures (BP 66, DM 160, FR 543, Y 11,260).

BI *"An Offer Of Marriage" and "A Prior Attachment", 1984: Two,* pub. Goupil and Co., margins, foxed, est. BP1/200, (01-21-93, Bonhams-Chelsea, #148), plate 29 x 14¼ in., (73.7 x 36.2 cm.), photogravures.

STOPENDAAL, B.   1637-1693
$997* *"Generale Afbeeldinge Vant Lust-Huijs En Hof Van Sijn Koninklijcke Majesteit Van Groot Brittanie T Soest-Dijk (Hollstein 24),* after B. STUYVENBURGH, 1st and only state, (11-18-92, Bubb Kuyper, #1847, illus.), 14¹³⁄₁₆

x 19 in., (37.7 x 48.3 cm.), etching (BP 656, DM 1590, FR 5354, Y 123,990, G 1800).

STORCK, Walter
$715* *"Chevrolet (Bel Air)" and "Monterey:: Two Photographs Of Cars,* photog.'s handstamp, 1950s, (04-07-93, Swann, #388, illus.), one 10 x 15 in., other 10 x 17 in., photograph, silver print (BP 473, DM 1156, FR 3914, Y 81,232).
$330* *Little Leaguers At Sinclair Gas Station,* 1950s, (04-07-93, Swann, #389, illus.), 11½ x 17 in., photograph, silver print (BP 218, DM 534, FR 1806, Y 37,491).

STOSSEL, Oskar
$55* *"Portrait Of Maria Jeritza In Costume": Two,* s., (06-03-92, Doyle, #90), 13¼ x 16 in., (33.7 x 40.6 cm.), color etchings (BP 30, DM 88, FR 297, Y 7025).

STOTHARD, Thomas
BI *The Lost Apple (Man 134),* 1st state of 2, detached from support sheet, trimmed close to subject, printer's crease, corners repaired, est. BP 800/1,200, (06-30-93, Sotheby-London, #252, illus.), 9 x 12¾ in., (229 x 324 mm.), 8¼ x 12½ in., (229 x 324 mm.), pen-lithograph on laid.

STOTHARD, Thomas (after)
BI *The Distinguishing Characteristic Of Masonry, Charity Exerted On Objects (De Vesme 547), 1802,* by Francesco Bartolozzi, 1st state of 2, proof before letters, margins, creases, tears, defects, est. BP 200/250, (11-30-92, Phillips-London, #227), plate 22⅞ x 27½ in., (581 x 699 mm.), stipple engraving on laid.
$1188* *"Tennant's Family" and "Landlord's Family": A Pair,* by C. Knight, pub. W. Dickinson, 1792, trimmed, tears, (06-16-93, Bonhams-Chelsea, #439, illus.), image 20¾ x 16¼ in., (52.7 x 41.3 cm.), stipple engraving (BP 792, DM 1972, FR 6618, Y 126,706).

STOTHARD, Thomas (after) English 1755-1834
$165* *Declaration Of Rights,* by Sharp, (04-02-93, Sloan, #2280), 22¼ x 15¼ in., (565 x 387 mm.), engraving (BP 109, DM 265, FR 901, Y 18,786).

STOUEROK American contemporary
$55* *Untitled,* all s., num., (06-13-93, Hindman, #368), each 24⅜ x 24⅜ in., (61.9 x 61.9 cm.), color serigraph (BP 36, DM 90, FR 301, Y 5788).

STOUMEN, Lou American 1917-1991
$1100* *"Black Cat Dance Hall And Whore House, San Juan Waterfront", 1942,* s., d., Dixon Collection, (11-16-92, Butterfield, #6190, illus.), 13½ x 17¹³⁄₁₆ in., (343.5 x 451.7 mm.), photograph, gelatin silver print (BP 724, DM 1754, FR 5908, Y 136,799).
BI *Drunken Sailors, Times Square, 1940,* s., t., d., lit., est. $2,5/3,500, (10-13-92, Christie-NY, #364, illus.), 10 x 8 in., (25.4 x 20.3 cm.), photograph, gelatin silver print.
BI *Forty Years Portfolio: Twenty,* pub. Witkin Gallery and G. Ray Hawkins Gallery, 1980-1981, each s., #3/50, images include: Sailor And Girl, Times Square In The Rain, Black Cat Bar& Brothel, Dying Girl, War & Peace, Bomb Pin; (1940-1979), est. $7/9,000, (10-13-92, Christie-NY, #367, illus.), largest 17½ x 13 in., (44.5 x 33 cm.), smallest 9 x 17¾ in., (44.5 x 33 cm.), photograph, gelatin silver prints.
BI *"Sailor And Girl On Subway, Times Square, New York",* 1940/later, s., d., Dixon Collection, est. $1,0/1,500, (11-16-92, Butterfield, #6191, illus.), 11¾ x 8¾ in., (299 x 222.6 mm.), photograph, gelatin silver print.
BI *"Times Square 1940": Includes "Times Square In The Rain", "News Bulletins, Times Square", "Men Coming Out Of Subway", "Two Sailors" and "Sailor AndGirl On Subway": Eighteen,* 1940, p. 1976, portfolio, s., d., t., #25/25, photog.'s stamp, colophon s., edit., pub. The Witkin Gallery and G Ray Hawkins Gallery, orig. portfolio case, est. $12/15,000, (05-23-93, Butterfield, #3620, illus.), each approx. 12 x 9 in., photograph, gelatin silver print.
$1430* *"Times Square In The Rain",* 1940/later, s., d., Dixon Collection, (11-16-92, Butterfield, #6189, illus.), 18⁷⁄₁₆ x 13½ in., (467.6 x 343.5 mm.), photograph, gelatin silver print (BP 942, DM 2280, FR 7680, Y 177,839).

$575* *"Times Square",* 1940, p. 1976, s., #7/25, t., d., neg. num., photog.'s stamp, mount trimmed to print, (05-23-93, Butterfield, #3621, illus.), 12 x 9 in., photograph, gelatin silver print (BP 374, DM 940, FR 3165, Y 63,557).
BI *"Times Square",* 1940/1976, s., edit. 7/25, t., d., photog. stamp, est. $1,2/1,500, (11-16-92, Butterfield, #6192, illus.), 12 x 9 in., (305.3 x 229 mm.), photograph, gelatin silver print.
$2200* *"To Hell With Hitler", Times Square, 1940,* s., t., d., (10-13-92, Christie-NY, #365, illus.), 9¼ x 6¼ in., (23.5 x 15.9 cm.), photograph, gelatin silver print (BP 1281, DM 3223, FR 10,951, Y 266,764).
$2200* *Tour Guide, 1940,* s., credit stamp, (10-13-92, Christie-NY, #366, illus.), 9⅞ x 7¾ in., (25.1 x 19.7 cm.), photograph, gelatin silver print (BP 1281, DM 3223, FR 10,951, Y 266,764).

STOVALL, Lou contemporary
$55* *Study For Morning Light,* s., t., #24/55, d. 12/23(19)80; i. verso, (12-10-92, Sloan, #2716), screenprint (BP 35, DM 87, FR 297, Y 6804).

STRADANUS (after) Flemish 1523-1605
$880* *The Passion: Twenty-Nine,* by Phillip Galle, Karel van Mallery, and Adrian Collaert, pub. by Galle, (12-13-92, Hindman, #254), each 7¾ x 10¼ in., engraving (BP 563, DM 1383, FR 4713, Y 108,870).

STRAET, Jan van der (after) Flemish 1523-1605
$1109* *"L'Atelier De Gravure" and "L'Invention De La Peinture A L'Huile" (Holl., vol. 7, 424 and 429): Two,* stain, (05-15-93, Loudmer, #97, illus.), approx. 7⁵⁄₁₆ x 10⅝ in., (185 x 270 mm.), copper engraving on laid w/eagle watermarks (BP 721, DM 1784, FR 5995, Y 122,935).
$132* *Saint John The Baptist With Holy Family,* by Cornelis and Philipp Galle, (10-30-92, Sloan, #2809, illus.), 8⅝ x 11 in., (21.9 x 27.9 cm.), engraving (BP 85, DM 203, FR 689, Y 16,351).

STRAKER, S., Lithographer
BI *"Autumn And Winter Costumes For 1849" and "Spring And Summer CostumesFor 1853",* pub. W.C. Howe, tears, est. BP2/300, (01-21-93, Bonhams-Chelsea, #149), image 24¾ x 19½ in., (62.9 x 49.5 cm.), lithographs w/hand-coloring.
$255* *"Autumn And Winter Costumes For 1849" and "Spring And Summer CostumesFor 1853": Two,* pub. W.C. Howe, tears, (03-17-93, Bonhams-Chelsea, #334), image 24¾ x 19½ in., (62.9 x 49.5 cm.), lithograph w/hand-coloring (BP 176, DM 424, FR 1442, Y 29,909).

STRAND, Paul American 1890-1976
$9775* *Aux Dames De France, c. 1951,* mounted, (04-06-93, Sotheby-NY, #155, illus.), 5⅞ x 4½ in., photograph (BP 6456, DM 15,748, FR 53,328, Y 1,114,849).
BI *Buttress, Rancho De Taos Church, New Mexico, 1930,* notations, s., t., d. in ink by Paul Strand, i. by Hazel Strand, lit., est. $60/80,000, (10-13-92, Christie-NY, #368, illus.), 13⅜ x 10½ in., (34 x 26.7 cm.), photograph, gelatin silver print.
$5463* *"Canyon Of The Rio Grande, New Mexico",* backed w/ another print, s., t., d. by photog., 1930, p. before 1935, (04-06-93, Sotheby-NY, #156, illus.), 3⅝ x 4⅝ in., photograph, platinum print (BP 3608, DM 8801, FR 29,804, Y 623,061).
BI *Il De France, France, 1951,* credi, t., d., num. 433A, inits. by Hazel Strand, est. $15/18,000, (10-13-92, Christie-NY, #500, illus.), 4¾ x 5⅞ in., (12.1 x 14.9 cm.), photograph, gelatin silver print.
$8250* *Lupin, The Garden, Orgeval, 1959,* s., t., d. in ink, (10-13-92, Christie-NY, #501, illus.), 9⅝ x 7⅝ in., (24.4 x 19.4 cm.), photograph, gelatin silver print (BP 4805, DM 12,086, FR 41,065, Y 1,000,364).
BI *Man In A Hat, Ranchos, New Mexico,* sig., notations in unidentified hand, early 1930's, est. $6/9,000, (10-14-92, Swann, #574, illus.), 5¾ x 4½ in., (14.6 x 11.4 cm.), photograph, silver print.
$3520* *The Mexican Portfolio,* first ed., intro. Leo Hurwitz, folio loose, discoloration, handwritten numerical notations, s. Strand, New York: Virginia Stevens, 1940, (04-07-93, Swann, #92, illus.), 16 x 12½ in., photograph, 20 var-

nished photogravure reprod. (BP 2326, DM 5693, FR 19,267, Y 399,909).

BI   *Mrs. Donald MacPhee, Hebrides, 1954,* s., t., d., by Hazel Strand, est. $4/6,000, (04-08-93, Christie-NY, #344, illus.), 9⅝ x 7⅝ in., (24.4 x 19.4 cm.), photograph, gelatin silver print.

$3090*   *"On My Doorstep, A Portfolio Of Eleven Photographs 1914-1973": Eleven,* mount t. stamped, t. page, intro. text, colophon ink s., #47/50, (10-29-92, Christie-London, #84A, illus.), smallest 9½ x 7½ in., (24.1 x 19.1 cm.), largest 13¼ x 9¼ in., (24.1 x 19.1 cm.), photograph, gelatin silver prints (BP 1980, DM 4754, FR 16,127, Y 382,757).

BI   *Photographs Of Mexico I (1932-33): Twenty,* privately pub. w/Virginia Stevens, 1940, spot varnished, s. by photog. on colophon, est. $6/8,000, (04-08-93, Christie-NY, #345, illus.), smallest 5 x 6⅛ in., (12.7 x 15.6 cm.), largest 10½ x 8¼ in., (12.7 x 15.6 cm.), photograph, photogravure on BFK Rives.

STRAND, Paul and Richard BENSON

$1650*   *Wire Wheel (Greenough, p. 21), 1917,* num. 1/2 in unidentified hand, num. APc 3, (c) Paul Strand Foundation, p. 1976 by RICHARD BENSON from neg. by PAUL STRAND, (10-15-92, Sotheby-NY, #136, illus.), 12¾ x 10⅛ in., (32.4 x 25.7 cm.), photograph, gelatin silver print (BP 1010, DM 2456, FR 8329, Y 197,960).

STRANG

$55*   *Town Square, 1912,* s., d., very good cond.?, (07-19-92, Bakker, #23), sheet 6¾ x 9¾ in., (17.1 x 24.8 cm.), etching (BP 28, DM 80, FR 271, Y 6837).

STRANG, William   Scottish 1859-1921

$332*   *The Carpenter's Shop,* s., prov., (12-04-92, Bassenge, #6955), 6⅞ x 8⅞ in., (17.5 x 22.5 cm.), etching on handmade (BP 213, DM 529, FR 1794, Y 41,448).

$110*   *"Folly And The Lovers",* first state, s., full margins, (10-10-92, Goldberg, #524), 19½ x 24¼ in., (49.5 x 61.6 cm.), etching (BP 65, DM 163, FR 549, Y 13,392).

BI   *Mannliches Portrait, (18)95,* streaked, est. DM 300, (12-01-92, Karl/Faber, #273), 6¹¹⁄₁₆ x 5¹¹⁄₁₆ in., (17 x 14.5 cm.), etching on hand-made.

STRASSER, Haywood

$193*   *"Remember The Flag Of Liberty",* 3rd Liberty Loan, fold creasing, repairs, (09-12-92, Dunning, #97, illus.), 30 x 20 in., (76.2 x 50.8 cm.), poster laid on cloth (BP 100, DM 278, FR 944, Y 23,913).

STRAUSS PEYTON

BI   *"Shemp Howard", 1920s,* s., t. by photog., est. $1/1,500, (04-06-93, Sotheby-NY, #81, illus.), photograph.

STRELOW, Liselotte   1908-1981

$607*   *Joseph Beuys Mit Sohn,* 1967, 1979, ink s., d., t., (11-12-92, Lempertz, #255, illus.), 11⅝ x 13³⁄₁₆ in., (29.5 x 33.5 cm.), photograph, gelatin silver print (BP 388, DM 954, FR 3251, Y 75,096).

STREMPEL, Horst   1904-1975

$111*   *Madchen Am Fenster, 1967,* s., t., ded., (12-05-92, Bassenge, #7760), 9⁷⁄₁₆ x 10⅛ in., (24 x 25.7 cm.), etching on copper print paper (BP 70, DM 173, FR 590, Y 13,753).

$355*   *Mann, Eine Maske Haltend, 1947,* s., d., (06-05-93, Grisebach, #887, illus.), 8⁷⁄₁₆ x 5⅝ in., (21.4 x 14.3 cm.), hand-colored woodcut on brownish werkdruck paper (BP 234, DM 576, FR 1940, Y 38,082).

STRICK, Hermann

$44*   *Portrait Of A Man,* s., #14/20, (03-12-93, DuMouchelle, #2453), 10 x 6¾ in., (25.4 x 17.1 cm.), etching (BP 31, DM 73, FR 249, Y 5186).

STRICKLAND, Steven

BI   *Abstract Landscape,* s., #127/150, prov., est. C$ 4/500, (12-01-92, Ritchie, #69), 52⅝ x 43 in., (133.7 x 109.2 cm.), color serigraph.

STRIXNER, Johann Nepomuk   1782-1855

BI   *Konig Max Joseph I., Konig Von Baiern, Brustbildnis (Winkler 36), 1815,* est. DM 1,200, (12-04-92, Bassenge, #6957), 19⅛ x 14¾ in., (48.5 x 37.4 cm.), lithograph.

STROOBANT, Francois   (after)

$84   *Middle Eastern Scenes: Set Of Three,* (10-09-92, G.A. Key, #55), 10 x 15½ in., (25.4 x 39.4 cm.), lithograph (BP 50, DM 125, FR 424, Y 10,244).

STRUCK, Hermann   German 1876-1944

$115*   *Bildnis Gustaf Af Geijerstam, 1907,* s., i. probedruck, margins, good cond., minor handling creases, tapestaining in upper corners, Late Gerhard Brauer Coll., (05-27-93, Sotheby-Amstrdm, #785), 7¹³⁄₁₆ x 5¹³⁄₁₆ in., (198 x 148 mm.), etching on wove (BP 74, DM 185, FR 622, Y 12,328, G 207).

BI   *Der Dom Von Florenz (Schwarz 59 I), 1903,* s., num., est. DM 750, (12-05-92, Bassenge, #7763), 5¹⁄₁₆ x 6¼ in., (12.9 x 15.9 cm.), etching on handmade.

$274*   *Die Kunst Des Radierens, 1919: Six,* by Max Liebermann, Edward Munch, Hermann Struck, Hans Meid, Paul Baum and Max Slevogt, orig. boards, Paul Cassierer, (09-17-92, Bonhams-Chelsea, #124), etchings and lithographs (BP 154, DM 407, FR 1392, Y 34,114).

$701*   *Lesender Jude,* s., num., (12-05-92, Bassenge, #7762), 5¹³⁄₁₆ x 7¾ in., (14.8 x 19.7 cm.), etching on handmade (BP 439, DM 1093, FR 3725, Y 86,854).

BI   *Nietzsche Haus In Sils Maria (Schwarz R 137), 1905,* s., i. artist's proof II, 1, plate mono., d., t., stamp, ded., est. DM 1200, (06-10-93, Hauswedell/Nolt, #934), image 5⅞ x 8¹⁄₁₆ in., (15 x 20.4 cm.), etching worked over w/aquatint and Roulette.

$115*   *Portrait Of A Jewish Gentleman,* s., #22/50, margins, good cond., minor paper discoloration, minor handling creases, Late Gerhard Brauer Coll., (05-27-93, Sotheby-Amstrdm, #786), 10¹⁵⁄₁₆ x 7¾ in., (279 x 197 mm.), etching on wove (BP 74, DM 185, FR 622, Y 12,328, G 207).

BI   *Portrait Of A Man In Profile, 1913,* s., annot. in plate "Radical 1900 Oberartbeitet XII 1905, H (star)S 1913, good cond., mat & water-staining, taped to glass, tape remains, est. $2/300, (02-24-93, Butterfield, #2975), 9½ x 7¼ in., (241 x 184 mm.), drypoint on thin wove paper.

BI   *Schuster Bei Der Arbeit, 1920,* s., est. DM 150-, (09-25-92, Granier, #3020), sheet 10⁷⁄₁₆ x 6⅛ in., (26.5 x 15.5 cm.), lithograph on holzhaltigem paper.

STRUSS, Karl   1886-1980

$2990*   *Boston Library Courtyard, c. 1910,* s.; s., t., (c) insig. reprod. limitation, West 31st Street studio stamp verso of mount, (04-08-93, Christie-NY, #66, illus.), 4⅝ x 3⅝ in., (11.7 x 9.2 cm.), photograph, waxed platinum print (BP 1961, DM 4803, FR 16,259, Y 339,310).

$863*   *"Consolidated Edison Fron The 2nd Avenue El, N.Y. (c. 1912)", "The Balcony, Sorrento (1909)" and "Arverne, Low Tide (1912)": Three,* from A Portfolio, Photofolio, 1978, each #4/75, (04-08-93, Christie-NY, #65, illus.), largest 3¾ x 4½ in., (9.5 x 11.4 cm.), photograph, platinum print (BP 566, DM 1386, FR 4693, Y 97,935).

$1320*   *East 36th Street, New York, 1911,* credit stamp, d., (10-13-92, Christie-NY, #50, illus.), 3½ x 4¼ in., (8.9 x 10.8 cm.), photograph, gelatin silver print (BP 769, DM 1934, FR 6570, Y 160,058).

BI   *Gloria Swanson In Male And Female,* 1919, est. BP 2/300, (12-17-92, Christie-S. Ken, #8), 10⅜ x 6⅜ in., (26.4 x 16.2 cm.), photograph, gelatin silver print.

$522*   *Nude, c. 1917,* s., (10-14-92, Swann, #575, illus.), 8¾ x 6½ in., (22.2 x 16.5 cm.), photograph, tri-color halftone print (BP 306, DM 764, FR 2591, Y 63,257).

$1380*   *The Porch, Barnard College, 1910,* s., d., (c) insig. recto; s., t., d. 1911 verso, (04-08-93, Christie-NY, #67, illus.), 9½ x 7½ in., (24.1 x 19.1 cm.), photograph, platinum print (BP 905, DM 2217, FR 7504, Y 156,605).

$1430*   *Portrait Of Rudolph Valentino, 1922,* photog.'s sig., blindstamp, handstamp, notations, (04-07-93, Swann, #563, illus.), 9¼ x 7¼ in., photograph, silver print (BP 945, DM 2313, FR 7827, Y 162,463).

$2300*   *"Singer Bldg. From Brooklyn", 1912,* s. and d. by photog. on image, d. by photog. on mount, t. verso, (04-06-93, Sotheby-NY, #66, illus.), 3⅝ x 4⅝ in., photograph, platinum print (BP 1519, DM 3705, FR 12,548, Y 262,318).

BI *Untitled, c. 1910,* s., i., est. $1,5/1,800, (10-13-92, Christie-NY, #51, illus.), 13⅝ x 10¾ in., (34.6 x 27.3 cm.), photograph, gelatin silver print.

STRUTH, Thomas   b. 1954
BI *"Broughton Place, Edinburgh",* 1987, p. 1989, s., t., d., est. $2/2,500, (05-23-93, Butterfield, #3623, illus.), 13¼ x 18½ in., photograph, gelatin silver print.
BI *"Dieselstrasse, Duisburg",* 1985, p. 1989, s., t., d., #8/10, est. $2/2,500, (05-23-93, Butterfield, #3622, illus.), 16½ x 22¾ in., photograph, gelatin silver print.
BI *Okerstrasse, Leverkusen,* s., t., num., d. 1979 Thomas Struth 3/10 verso, p. 1989, prov., est.$4/5,000, (11-17-92, Christie-E, #108, illus.), 16¹⁵⁄₁₆ x 23⅝ in., (43.1 x 60 cm.), b/w photograph.
$4180* *"Via Medina, Naples" and "Via Giovanna Tappia, Naples": Two,* both s., t., d. 1988; first num. Thomas Struth 7/10 verso; second num. Thomas Struth 4/10 verso, prov., (10-08-92, Christie-NY, #202, illus.), first 17⅞ x 23⅝ in., (45.4 x 60 cm.), second 17 x 22 in., (45.4 x 60 cm.), b/w photographs (BP 2487, DM 6183, FR 20,984, Y 507,898).

STRUTT, Alfred W. (after)
$218* *Any Port In A Storm, 1900,* blindstamp, pub. Dowdeswell and Dowdeswell Ltd., margins, (11-12-92, Bonhams-Chelsea, #72), plate 20½ x 28½ in., (52.1 x 72.4 cm.), hand-colored photogravure (BP 143, DM 345, FR 1165, Y 27,030).
$24 *"We Shall Be Wanted Yet",* (04-16-93, G.A. Key, #2), 15 x 24 in., (38.1 x 61 cm.), chromolithograph (BP 16, DM 39, FR 131, Y 2699).

STRUYCKEN, Peter
$64* *Untitled,* s., #57/200, full margins, good cond., discoloration, soiling, (05-27-93, Sotheby-Amstrdm, #686), sh 18⅞ x 18⅞ in., (480 x 480 mm.), color silkscreen on wove (BP 41, DM 103, FR 346, Y 6861, G 115).

STUART, Gabriel (after)
$132* *General Washington,* by James Health, pub. Heath, 1800, (06-16-93, Bonhams-Chelsea, #448A), image 19¾ x 13 in., (50.2 x 33 cm.), engraving (BP 88, DM 219, FR 735, Y 14,078).

STUART, Gilbert (after)
$22* *George Washington,* (01-15-93, DuMouchelle, #162), print (BP 14, DM 36, FR 122, Y 2774).

STUART, John
BI *Selected Locomotive Studies, 1880's-c. 1900: Sixteen,* 6 w/blindstamp, each num., some t. in unidentified hand, est. $2,5/3,500, (10-15-92, Sotheby-NY, #87, illus.), largest 9½ x 14½ in., (24.1 x 36.8 cm.), photograph, most albumen prints.

STUART-WORTLEY, Colonel A.H.P.
$453* *"Tahiti", 1882: Book,* preface, (05-06-93, Christie-London, #16), each approx. 5½ x 5½ in., photograph, 31 collotypes (BP 287, DM 713, FR 2402, Y 49,840).

STUBBS, G.T.
$1100* *Anvil, 1794,* after G. Stubbs, soiling, imperfections in plate, (06-11-93, Doyle, #80), 15½ x 19¾ in., (394 x 502 mm.), stipple engraving (BP 723, DM 1788, FR 6027, Y 116,711).
$1100* *Baronet, 1794,* after G. Stubbs, discoloration, foxing, taped to mat, (06-11-93, Doyle, #83), 16 x 19½ in., (406 x 495 mm.), stipple engraving (BP 723, DM 1788, FR 6027, Y 116,711).
$1430* *Sweetbrier, 1794,* after G. Stubbs, small margins, glue, soiling, (06-11-93, Doyle, #81, illus.), 15¾ x 19½ in., (400 x 495 mm.), stipple engraving (BP 940, DM 2324, FR 7836, Y 151,724).
$1650* *Volunteer, 1794,* after G. Stubbs, discoloration, foxing, taped, (06-11-93, Doyle, #82, illus.), 15½ x 19¾ in., (394 x 502 mm.), mezzotint (BP 1084, DM 2682, FR 9041, Y 175,066).

STUBBS, George
$2046* *"Game Keepers" and "Labourers" (Lennox-Boyd, Dixon And Clayton 87-88): Two,* engraved by Richard Earlom, pub. 1790 by B.Evans, fourth (final) state, margins, damage, repairs, stains, discoloration, foxed, (12-03-92, Sotheby-London, #164), each approx. 17¼ x 26 in., (438

x 660 mm.), mezzotints (BP 1320, DM 3217, FR 10,982, Y 254,573).

STUBBS, George   1724-1806
BI *A Horse Affrighted At A Lion (Lennox-Boyd 70 II), 1788,* est. DM 4500, (06-04-93, Bassenge, #5570), 9⁷⁄₁₆ x 12¹⁵⁄₁₆ in., (24 x 32.9 cm.), etching w/roulette.

STUBBS, George (after)
$689* *Brown Horse "Mask",* by George Townly Stubbs, pub. Robert Sayer, 1773, (06-30-93, Bonhams-Chelsea, #214, illus.), image 16 x 22 in., (40.6 x 55.9 cm.), mezzotint w/hand-coloring (BP 462, DM 1175, FR 3964, Y 73,824).
$2231* *"Bulls Fighting" and "Horses Fighting" (Lennox-Boyd 81; 82), 1788: APair,* by George Townley Stubbs, 3rd state of 5, margins, staining, wormholes, defects, (06-30-93, Sotheby-London, #270), 18¾ x 23¼ in., (476 x 591 mm.), mezzotint (BP 1495, DM 3805, FR 12,837, Y 239,044).
$400* *The Lincolnshire Ox (L.B. 116), 1791,* by George Townly Stubbs, 2nd state of 3, repaired tears, wormholes, (11-30-92, Phillips-London, #258, illus.), sheet 16 x 20¼ in., (406 x 514 mm.), stipple engraving on laid (BP 264, DM 637, FR 2163, Y 49,782).
$361* *Shooting: Plate I,* by William Woollett, pub. Thomas Bradford, 1769, margins, surface dirt, foxing, tears, (06-30-93, Bonhams-Chelsea, #71), plate 17⅜ x 21½ in., (44.1 x 54.6 cm.), engraving on laid (BP 242, DM 616, FR 2077, Y 38,680).

STUCK, Franz von   German 1863-1928
BI *Muenchen 1905 IX. Internationale Kunstausstellung,* folds, tears, creases, repairs, lit., est. BP 1/1,500, (02-04-93, Christie-S. Ken, #177), 32 x 25 in., (81.3 x 63.5 cm.), color lithograph backed on linen.
BI *Secession, Munchen Kunst Ausstellung, 1912,* pierced plastic tape, nicks, tears, losses, est. BP 4/600, (02-04-93, Christie-S. Ken, #178, illus.), 39 x 27½ in., (99.1 x 69.9 cm.), color lithograph.

STUDER, Jacob H.
$468* *The Birds Of North America, 1903,* rubbed, foxing, (05-01-93, Skinner, #187), 15⁹⁄₁₆ x 12⅝ in., (39.5 x 32 cm.), 119 color plates (BP 298, DM 741, FR 2499, Y 51,925).
$303* *"Studer's Popular Ornithology. The Birds Of North America", 1881,* t., orig. leather, worn edges, folio, (09-17-92, Sloan, #2653), lithograph, 119 colored plates (BP 170, DM 450, FR 1540, Y 37,724).
BI *"Studer's Popular Ornithology. The Birds Of North America", 1881,* original leather, worn edges, front joint broken, est. $250/350, (09-17-92, Sloan, #1454), lithograph, 119 color plates.

STUDIO
$223* *1929, Be Up To Date, Shellubricate,* p. EVP, ref. #198, cond. 4, (10-13-92, Phillips-London, #66), 29¹⁵⁄₁₆ x 44¹¹⁄₁₆ in., (76 x 113.5 cm.), color lithograph (BP 130, DM 327, FR 1110, Y 27,040).
$168* *25,000 Miles Dunelt M/C Record, 1928,* ref. #207, cond. 1, (10-13-92, Phillips-London, #69), 29¹⁵⁄₁₆ x 44⅞ in., (76 x 114 cm.), color lithograph (BP 98, DM 246, FR 836, Y 20,371).
BI *60,000 Miles Without Decarbonising, 1926,* p. Waterlow & Sons, ref. #129, cond. 5, est. BP 4/600, (10-13-92, Phillips-London, #55, illus.), 30⅛ x 44⅞ in., (76.5 x 114 cm.), color lithograph.
$288* *All The Honours In 1929, 1929,* ref. #230, cond. 5, tear, area missing, (10-13-92, Phillips-London, #81, illus.), 29¹⁵⁄₁₆ x 44⅛ in., (76 x 112 cm.), color lithograph (BP 168, DM 422, FR 1434, Y 34,922).
BI *Automatic Heating Makes An Ideal Home, 1928,* ref. #206, cond. 3, est. BP 1/200, (10-13-92, Phillips-London, #68), 29¹⁵⁄₁₆ x 44⅞ in., (76 x 114 cm.), color lithograph.
BI *Buy Shell From A Sealed Pump, 1925,* ref. #121, cond. 4, image tear, est. BP 150/250, (10-13-92, Phillips-London, #52), 29¹⁵⁄₁₆ x 44¹¹⁄₁₆ in., (76 x 113.5 cm.), color lithograph.
$532* *Carbon Defeated, Footballers, 1928,* p. Waterlow & Sons, ref. #167, cond. 3, (10-13-92, Phillips-London, #62, illus.), 29¹³⁄₁₆ x 44⅞ in., (75.8 x 114 cm.), color lithograph (BP 310, DM 779, FR 2648, Y 64,508).

$201* *Discerning Motorists Prefer Shell*, 1929, ref. #231, cond. 5, (10-13-92, Phillips-London, #82), 29¹⁵/₁₆ x 44¹¹/₁₆ in., (76 x 113.5 cm.), color lithograph (BP 117, DM 294, FR 1000, Y 24,372).

BI *Double Shell Recommended By Morris Motors*, 1929, ref. #232, cond. 3, est. BP 150/200, (10-13-92, Phillips-London, #83), 29⁵/₁₆ x 45¹/₁₆ in., (74.5 x 114.5 cm.), color lithograph.

$266* *England To India Non-Stop On Petrol By Shell*, 1929, ref. #215, cond. 4, corner missing, (10-13-92, Phillips-London, #74), 29¹⁵/₁₆ x 44¹¹/₁₆ in., (76 x 113.5 cm.), lithograph (BP 155, DM 390, FR 1324, Y 32,254).

$467* *Fill Up With Shell & Feel The Difference*, 1952, p. Waterlow and Sons, ref. P 49, cond. 3, (10-13-92, Phillips-London, #179, illus.), 29¹³/₁₆ x 39¹³/₁₆ in., (75.8 x 101.2 cm.), color lithograph (BP 272, DM 684, FR 2325, Y 56,627).

BI *Five Great Efficiency Tests*, 1929, ref. #227, cond. 1, nick, est. BP 150/200, (10-13-92, Phillips-London, #79), 29¹⁵/₁₆ x 44⁷/₈ in., (76 x 114 cm.), color lithograph.

$168* *Hillman Recommends Double Shell*, 1938, p. Waterlow and Sons, ref. #533, cond. 1, tears, (10-13-92, Phillips-London, #149), 29¹⁵/₁₆ x 44⁷/₈ in., (76 x 114 cm.), color lithograph (BP 98, DM 246, FR 836, Y 20,371).

$134* *Humber Recommends Double Shell*, 1938, p. Waterlow and Sons, ref. #534, cond. 3, tears, (10-13-92, Phillips-London, #150), 29¹⁵/₁₆ x 44⁷/₈ in., (76 x 114 cm.), color lithograph (BP 78, DM 196, FR 667, Y 16,248).

$445* *J.J.C. Double Twelve, Alfa Romero*, 1929, ref. #220, cond. 4, image tear, (10-13-92, Phillips-London, #76), 29¾ x 44¹¹/₁₆ in., (75.5 x 113.5 cm.), color lithograph (BP 259, DM 652, FR 2215, Y 53,959).

$168* *Leadership In Lubrication On The Farm*, 1950, p. Waterlow and Sons, ref. P 3, cond. 1, (10-13-92, Phillips-London, #164), 29¹⁵/₁₆ x 39⁹/₁₆ in., (76 x 100.5 cm.), color lithograph (BP 98, DM 246, FR 836, Y 20,371).

BI *Mex Is The Commercial Grade Of Shell*, 1930, ref. #236, cond. 4, printing defect, est. BP 2/300, (10-13-92, Phillips-London, #84), 30¹/₁₆ x 44¹¹/₁₆ in., (76.3 x 113.5 cm.), lithograph.

$312* *New Shell X-100, Fights Acid Action*, 1952, ref. P 29, cond. 2, staining, nicks, (10-13-92, Phillips-London, #173), 29¹⁵/₁₆ x 39¾ in., (76 x 101 cm.), color lithograph (BP 182, DM 457, FR 1553, Y 37,832).

BI *Non-Party Spirit, Baldwin, R. MacDonald, & Lloyd George*, 1929, pub. Waterlow & Sons, ref. #216, cond. 5, est. BP 150/250, (10-13-92, Phillips-London, #75), 29¹⁵/₁₆ x 45¹/₁₆ in., (76 x 114.5 cm.), color lithograph.

$467* *Of Course Shell Is Different*, 1928, ref. #212, cond. 1, creases, (10-13-92, Phillips-London, #72, illus.), 29¹⁵/₁₆ x 44⁷/₈ in., (76 x 114 cm.), lithograph on yellow paper (BP 272, DM 684, FR 2325, Y 56,627).

$266* *Oil From The Pump, No Can To Pay For*, 1925, ref. #123, cond. 4, (10-13-92, Phillips-London, #53), 29¹⁵/₁₆ x 44⁷/₈ in., (76 x 114 cm.), color lithograph (BP 155, DM 390, FR 1324, Y 32,254).

$266* *Save Eight Pence Per Quart, Buy Shell Oil*, 1925, p. Waterlow & Sons, ref. #119, cond. 4, (10-13-92, Phillips-London, #51), 29¹⁵/₁₆ x 44⁷/₈ in., (76 x 114 cm.), color lithograph (BP 155, DM 390, FR 1324, Y 32,254).

$266* *Shell Lubricating Oil, Austin Wins British Empire Trophy*, 1938, p. Waterlow and Sons, ref. #511, cond. 1, (10-13-92, Phillips-London, #135, illus.), 30¹/₁₆ x 45¹/₁₆ in., (76.3 x 114.5 cm.), color lithograph (BP 155, DM 390, FR 1324, Y 32,254).

$355* *Shell Motor Oils First, Goodwood*, 1952, ref. P 26B, cond. 3, ink i., (10-13-92, Phillips-London, #171), 29¹⁵/₁₆ x 39¾ in., (76 x 101 cm.), color lithograph (BP 207, DM 520, FR 1767, Y 43,046).

$134* *Shell Oil & Petrol, T.T. First Lightweight Race*, 1929, ref. #223, cond. 3, (10-13-92, Phillips-London, #78), 30⅛ x 44⁷/₈ in., (76.5 x 114 cm.), color lithograph (BP 78, DM 196, FR 667, Y 16,248).

$223* *Shell With I.C.A.*, 1953, ref. P 63, cond. 1, (10-13-92, Phillips-London, #185), 29¹⁵/₁₆ x 42⅛ in., (76 x 107 cm.), color lithograph (BP 130, DM 327, FR 1110, Y 27,040).

$798* *Shell, B.P.*, 1950, ref. P 1A, cond. 5, tears, (10-13-92, Phillips-London, #162), 29¹⁵/₁₆ x 39¾ in., (76 x 101

cm.), color lithograph (BP 465, DM 1169, FR 3972, Y 96,762).

$134* *Shell, Leadership In Lubrication*, 1950, ref. P 2, cond. 5, extensive tears, corner missing, (10-13-92, Phillips-London, #163), 29¹⁵/₁₆ x 39¾ in., (76 x 101 cm.), color lithograph (BP 78, DM 196, FR 667, Y 16,248).

BI *Sunbeam Talbot Recommends Double Shell*, 1938, p. Waterlow and Sons, ref. #535, cond. 1, est. BP 2/300, (10-13-92, Phillips-London, #151, illus.), 29¹⁵/₁₆ x 45¹/₁₆ in., (76 x 114.5 cm.), color lithograph.

BI *T.V.O. For Maximum Drawbar Pull*, 1936, ref. #472, cond. 4, est. BP 2/400, (10-13-92, Phillips-London, #114), 29¹⁵/₁₆ x 44⁷/₈ in., (76 x 114 cm.), color lithograph.

$1442* *Take No Risk, Take Shell*, 1928, p. Waterlow & Sons, ref. #166, cond. 3, tear, (10-13-92, Phillips-London, #61, illus.), 29¹⁵/₁₆ x 44⁷/₈ in., (76 x 114 cm.), color lithograph (BP 840, DM 2113, FR 7178, Y 174,851).

$579* *Winners At ... Relied On X-100*, 1952, ref. P 37, cond. 3, (10-13-92, Phillips-London, #174, illus.), 30⅞ x 40⁹/₁₆ in., (78.5 x 103 cm.), color lithograph (BP 337, DM 848, FR 2882, Y 70,207).

$89* *X-100 Gives Longer Life To Your Engine*, 1952, ref. P 58, cond. 3, (10-13-92, Phillips-London, #183), 29¹³/₁₆ x 42½ in., (75.8 x 108 cm.), color lithograph (BP 52, DM 130, FR 443, Y 10,792).

BI *Yes, Shell Petrol Is Different*, 1928, ref. #210, cond. 4, est. BP 3/500, (10-13-92, Phillips-London, #71), 29¹³/₁₆ x 44⁷/₈ in., (75.7 x 114 cm.), lithograph on yellow paper.

STULL, Christian   American 20th cent.
BI *"Windy Day"*, s. Christian Stull, est. $1/150, (12-12-92, A. James, #426), sheet 13 x 10 in., (33 x 25.4 cm.), etching.

STURGES, Dwight Case   American b. 1874
$83* *Hear Ye, Hear Ye*, s., #66/100, (07-03-92, Sloan, #285), 12 x 9 in., (30.5 x 22.9 cm.), etching (BP 43, DM 126, FR 423, Y 10,347).

STURGES, Jock   b. 1947
$1610* *"C, Paris" and "Nude Girl On Beach"*, 1984: Two, s., t., d., annot. Artist's Proof, (05-23-93, Butterfield, #3624, illus.), each approx. 14½ x 18¼ in., photograph, gelatin silver print (BP 1049, DM 2632, FR 8861, Y 177,960).

$2530* *Danielle, Montalivet, France*, 1991, s., t., d., #10/40, (c) insig., (04-08-93, Christie-NY, #561, illus.), 22 x 17½ in., (55.9 x 44.5 cm.), photograph, gelatin silver print (BP 1659, DM 4064, FR 13,757, Y 287,108).

$2200* *"Danielle; Montalivet, France"*, 1991, s., t., d., edit. 6/40, (11-16-92, Butterfield, #6193, illus.), 22¹/₁₆ x 17¹¹/₁₆ in., (559.8 x 448.5 mm.), photograph, gelatin silver print (BP 1449, DM 3508, FR 11,815, Y 273,598).

$633* *"Emilietta", 1981, "Arlette", 1981 and "Yvonne", 1979:* Three, p. 1982 and 1981, ink s., t., d., num.; (c) credit stamp; first d., edit. #3/21; second ink annot. A/P; third ink #5/7, (c) credit stamp, (04-08-93, Christie-NY, #562, illus.), each approx. 6 x 4½ in., (15.2 x 11.4 cm.), photograph, gelatin silver print (BP 415, DM 1017, FR 3442, Y 71,834).

$1265* *"Flor Et Frederique, Montalivet, France"*, 1988, s., t., d., #12/40, (05-23-93, Butterfield, #3625, illus.), 18 x 14¼ in., photograph, gelatin silver print (BP 824, DM 2068, FR 6962, Y 139,825).

$2070* *Lidiwine, Orleans, France*, 1988, s., t., d., #16/40, (c) insig., (04-08-93, Christie-NY, #560, illus.), 17½ x 21⅞ in., (44.5 x 55.6 cm.), photograph, gelatin silver print (BP 1357, DM 3325, FR 11,256, Y 234,907).

$1438* *"Marine, Jeanne, Gaelle, And Two Alexandras Standing, Montalivet, France" (Standing On Water, unpaginated)*, 1987, s., t., d., #8/40 by photog., (04-06-93, Sotheby-NY, #510, illus.), 14⅛ x 17¾ in., photograph (BP 950, DM 2317, FR 7845, Y 164,005).

$2200* *Marine, The Last Day Of Summer #1, Montalivet, France*, 1980, s., t., d., i. by photog., artist's proof, (10-15-92, Sotheby-NY, #610A, illus.), 18 x 14⅛ in., (45.7 x 35.9 cm.), photograph, gelatin silver print (BP 1346, DM 3275, FR 11,106, Y 263,947).

$920* *"Misty Dawn, Christina And Alysa; Nor. Cal"*, 1988, s., t., d., #5/40 by photog., (04-06-93, Sotheby-NY, #511, illus.), 14 x 17¼ in., photograph (BP 608, DM 1482, FR 5019, Y 104,927).

STURGESS, John (after)

$330* *Fox-Hunting. Plate 1. A Favorite Fixture,* from McQueen's Fox Huntings, by W. Summers, prov., (05-28-93, Sloan, #1294, illus.), 24 x 36 in., (61 x 91.4 cm.), color aquatint (BP 211, DM 523, FR 1769, Y 35,385).

STURGESS, Thomas (after)

BI *Derby Heroes Of The Last Ten Years,* trimmed, est. BP 40/60, (03-03-93, Bonhams-Chelsea, #197), image 13 x 19⅞ in., (33 x 50.5 cm.), chromolithograph.

STURGESS and MOORE (after)

$18 *"The Race For The Middle Park Plate, 1878" and "The Queens Buckhounds": Two,* from Publications of the Victorian period, (04-16-93, G.A. Key, #85), one 9 x 13 in., (22.9 x 33 cm.), other 12 x 9 in., (22.9 x 33 cm.), hand-colored b/w prints (BP 12, DM 29, FR 98, Y 2024).

STUTTARD, Tom

BI *Coronation Celebrations, Manchester, 1953: Ten,* mounted on card, t., s., ink stamps, labels, each approx. 290 x 380mm, (05-07-93, Sotheby-London, #194, illus.), photograph, silver print.

STUTTGEN (after)

$465* *Beuys And Stuttgen Im Auto,* Von Beuys and Stuttgen, s., (09-25-92, Granier, #2760), 3⅞ x 3¹⁵⁄₁₆ in., (9.8 x 10.1 cm.), sheet 12⅝ x 18³⁄₁₆ in., (9.8 x 10.1 cm.), offset print in green on offset paper (BP 272, DM 689, FR 2331, Y 56,126).

SUDDABY, Rowland b. 1912

$755* *To Visit Britain's Landmarks, Folly Houses, Darley Abbey, 1937,* p. Waterlow and Sons, ref. #503, cond. 1, (10-13-92, Phillips-London, #128, illus.), 29¹⁵⁄₁₆ x 45¹⁄₁₆ in., (76 x 114.5 cm.), color lithograph (BP 440, DM 1106, FR 3758, Y 91,548).

SUDEK, Josef Czech 1896-1976

$1610* *Architectural Abstraction, c. 1925,* (04-06-93, Sotheby-NY, #302, illus.), photograph, on carte-postale (BP 1063, DM 2594, FR 8783, Y 183,622).

$3080* *CENTROTEX Calendar-Praha Panoramics: Fourteen,* (1960), lit., (10-13-92, Christie-NY, #502, illus.), each 5⅞ x 19½ in., (14.9 x 49.5 cm.), photograph, gelatin silver prints (BP 1794, DM 4512, FR 15,331, Y 373,469).

BI *Cathedral St. Guy, c. 1943,* i., photog.'s ink credit stamp of small barrel, est. BP 3/500, (05-06-93, Christie-London, #142), image 6⅜ x 4¾ in., photograph, gelatin silver print.

BI *Cherry In Bowl, c. 1968,* from the series "Remembrances", 1968-70, est. $7/10,000, (10-14-92, Swann, #576, illus.), 11½ x 9 in., (29.2 x 22.9 cm.), photograph, silver print.

$10,450* *Egg On A Plate,* s. by photog., 1950's, (10-15-92, Sotheby-NY, #380, illus.), 4¼ x 6⅜ in., (10.8 x 16.2 cm.), photograph, bromoil print on laid paper (BP 6395, DM 15,555, FR 52,751, Y 1,253,749).

$16,100* *Egg On A Plate, 1950's,* s. by photog., (04-06-93, Sotheby-NY, #306, illus.), 4¼ x 6⅜ in., photograph, bromoil print on laid paper (BP 10,634, DM 25,938, FR 87,834, Y 1,836,223).

$2875* *Eggs And Teacup, c. 1970,* i., s. by photog. on image, (04-06-93, Sotheby-NY, #305, illus.), 4¾ x 6½ in., photograph (BP 1899, DM 4632, FR 15,685, Y 327,897).

BI *Felsenlandschaft, 50's,* s., est. DM 600, (11-12-92, Lempertz, #258, illus.), 5⁹⁄₁₆ x 3¹⁵⁄₁₆ in., (14.2 x 10 cm.), photograph, gelatin silver print.

$550* *Forest Study, 1971,* s., d. by photog., (10-15-92, Sotheby-NY, #560, illus.), 7 x 9¼ in., (17.8 x 23.5 cm.), photograph, gelatin silver print (BP 337, DM 819, FR 2776, Y 65,987).

$1955* *Garden Chair,* 1950s, s. w/stylus, (04-08-93, Christie-NY, #141, illus.), 9⅛ x 6¾ in., (23.2 x 17.1 cm.), photograph, green-toned gelatin silver print (BP 1282, DM 3141, FR 10,631, Y 221,857).

$4370* *Garden Chairs Panorama, 1954,* s. w/stylus; t., d., lit., (04-08-93, Christie-NY, #138, illus.), 3⅜ x 11⅛ in., (8.6 x 28.3 cm.), photograph, gelatin silver print (BP 2866, DM 7020, FR 23,763, Y 495,915).

$5750* *Glass Labyrinth (1963-1972), 1972-75,* s., authen. by Anna Farova, lit., (04-08-93, Christie-NY, #143, illus.), 11⅝ x 9 in., (29.5 x 22.9 cm.), photograph, gelatin silver print (BP 3770, DM 9237, FR 31,267, Y 652,519).

$4125* *Glass Labyrinths, 1973 (Aperture, pp. 62-63),* s., d., i. by photog. in Czech, stamp, (10-15-92, Sotheby-NY, #371, illus.), 9 x 11¼ in., (22.9 x 28.6 cm.), photograph, gelatin silver print (BP 2524, DM 6140, FR 20,823, Y 494,901).

$3300* *Glass With Lily-Of-The-Valley,* s. by photog., 1950's-1960's, (10-15-92, Sotheby-NY, #373, illus.), 9¼ x 6¾ in., (23.5 x 17.1 cm.), photograph, gelatin silver print (BP 2019, DM 4912, FR 16,658, Y 395,921).

$2750* *Jablecky (Apple), 1950-54,* notations, prov., lit., (10-13-92, Christie-NY, #503, illus.), 9¼ x 6⅝ in., (23.5 x 16.8 cm.), photograph, gelatin silver print (BP 1602, DM 4029, FR 13,688, Y 333,455).

$8625* *Landscape Study, 1952,* s., d., i. by photog., (04-06-93, Sotheby-NY, #303, illus.), 8⅛ x 6½ in., photograph, bromoil print on laid paper (BP 5697, DM 13,896, FR 47,054, Y 983,691).

BI *Mannikin,* 1950s, s. recto; s., t., est. $3/4,000, (10-13-92, Christie-NY, #504, illus.), 9¼ x 11½ in., (23.5 x 29.2 cm.), photograph, gelatin silver print.

$1089* *Misty Forest, c. 1950,* i., (05-06-93, Christie-London, #143, illus.), image 4½ x 6¼ in., photograph, gelatin silver contact print (BP 690, DM 1715, FR 5774, Y 119,815).

$5175* *My Friend Funke, 1925,* t., d., credit stamp, lit., (04-08-93, Christie-NY, #136, illus.), 11⅛ x 8⅞ in., (28.3 x 22.5 cm.), photograph, gelatin silver print (BP 3393, DM 8313, FR 28,140, Y 587,267).

$834* *Ohne Titel, c. 1925,* (c), (11-12-92, Lempertz, #257, illus.), 9³⁄₁₆ x 6⅝ in., (23.4 x 16.9 cm.), photograph, gelatin silver print (BP 533, DM 1311, FR 4467, Y 103,180).

BI *Panorama Eines Platzes, 1961,* d., est. DM 1200, (11-12-92, Lempertz, #259, illus.), 3¹¹⁄₁₆ x 11⅝ in., (9.3 x 29.6 cm.), photograph, gelatin silver print.

BI *Panorama With Lawn Chairs, Umbrella And Couple,* 1950s, annots., est. $3/4,000, (04-08-93, Christie-NY, #140, illus.), 3⅜ x 11¼ in., (8.6 x 28.6 cm.), photograph, gelatin silver print.

$825* *Park,* photog.'s notation, 1930s, (04-07-93, Swann, #564, illus.), 4½ x 6½ in., photograph, toned silver print (BP 545, DM 1334, FR 4516, Y 93,729).

$605* *The Photographs Of Josef Sudek Inc. "Backyard Through A Window","Flowers In Bloom", "Sun Drenched Lawn", "Snow Covered Tree", "Still Life WithFoil And Bottles", "Still Life With Bottle And Melons" and others, 1976: Twelv,* portfolio, w/multi-lingual pamphlet, (04-07-93, Swann, #565), each approx. 11 x 8½ in., photograph, 12 copy photographs (BP 400, DM 978, FR 3311, Y 68,734).

BI *Prague Under Snow,* 1920/later, various notations, Dixon Collection, est. $4/600, (11-16-92, Butterfield, #6196, illus.), 2⅛ x 3¼ in., (54.1 x 82.7 mm.), photograph, gelatin silver print.

BI *Rose Bud In Beaker, 1975,* s., d., est. $6/8,000, (10-13-92, Christie-NY, #607, illus.), 9⅜ x 6¾ in., (23.8 x 17.1 cm.), photograph, green-toned gelatin silver print.

$2200* *Rose In A Glass Of Water,* s., i. by photog. in Czech, owner's stamp, 1970's, (10-15-92, Sotheby-NY, #375, illus.), 10½ x 8⅛ in., (26.7 x 20.6 cm.), photograph, gelatin silver print (BP 1346, DM 3275, FR 11,106, Y 263,947).

$8050* *Rosebud In A Glass, early 1950's,* (04-06-93, Sotheby-NY, #307, illus.), 10⅝ x 8 in., photograph (BP 5317, DM 12,969, FR 43,917, Y 918,111).

$10,925* *Seated Nude,* 1930s, lit., (04-08-93, Christie-NY, #137, illus.), 9 x 6¾ in., (22.9 x 17.1 cm.), photograph, bromoil transfer print (BP 7164, DM 17,550, FR 59,407, Y 1,239,787).

$2013* *St. Vitus Cathedral, Interior Study, mid-1920's,* (04-06-93, Sotheby-NY, #301A, illus.), 3½ x 3⅜ in., photograph (BP 1330, DM 3243, FR 10,982, Y 229,585).

BI *Still LIfe With Czechoslovakian Glassware, 1968,* s., d. by photog., est. $4/6,000, (10-15-92, Sotheby-NY, #376, illus.), 11½ x 9 in., (29.2 x 22.9 cm.), photograph, gelatin silver print.

$581* *Still Life Of Shell And Paper,* s., i., (05-06-93, Christie-London, #144), image 3¾ x 5¾ in., photograph, gelatin silver contact print (BP 368, DM 915, FR 3081, Y 63,923).

BI *Still Life Panorama With Shells, 1961,* s. w/stylus recto; t., d., est. $1,8/2,200, (04-08-93, Christie-NY, #139, illus.), 3⅜ x 11¼ in., (8.6 x 28.6 cm.), photograph, gelatin silver print.

$2013* *Still Life With Bottle (Aperture, pp. 62-63), 1968-74,* s. by photog., (04-06-93, Sotheby-NY, #306A, illus.), 8⅞ x 11¼ in., photograph (BP 1330, DM 3243, FR 10,982, Y 229,585).

BI *"Still Life With Crucifix and Broken Glass", "Rooftops Covered With Snow", "Astrolabe", "Street Scene at Night" and "Flowering Trees": Selected Images, 1950's-70's: Five,* 4 s., 2 d. & i. by photog. in Czech, 3 i. by photog., 3 w/stamp, est.$2/3,000, (10-15-92, Sotheby-NY, #374, illus.), various sizes to 11½ x 9 in., (29.2 x 22.9 cm.), photograph, gelatin silver print.

$3300* *Still Life With Glass And Marble, 1963-66 (cf. Sudek, pl. 45),* (10-15-92, Sotheby-NY, #372, illus.), 11⅜ x 9¼ in., (28.9 x 23.5 cm.), photograph, gelatin silver print (BP 2019, DM 4912, FR 16,658, Y 395,921).

$3220* *Still Life With Lemon,* 1950s, s. w/stylus, (04-08-93, Christie-NY, #142, illus.), 9¼ x 7 in., (23.5 x 17.8 cm.), photograph, gelatin silver print (BP 2111, DM 5173, FR 17,510, Y 365,411).

$2179* *Still Life With Pear And Apple, 1954,* s., 231 x 162mm, (05-07-93, Sotheby-London, #391, illus.), photograph, silver print (BP 1380, DM 3445, FR 11,609, Y 239,925).

$12,650* *Still Life With Pear, 1951,* hinged to mount, s., d. by photog., (04-06-93, Sotheby-NY, #304, illus.), 4⅜ x 6⅜ in., photograph, bromoil print on laid paper (BP 8355, DM 20,380, FR 69,013, Y 1,442,746).

$4025* *Sunday Afternoon On Kolin Island, 1924-26,* (04-06-93, Sotheby-NY, #301, illus.), photograph (BP 2659, DM 6485, FR 21,959, Y 459,056).

$660* *Tree Studies: Four,* 1950's, (10-15-92, Sotheby-NY, #378, illus.), each approx. 6 x 4½ in., (15.2 x 11.4 cm.), photograph, gelatin silver prints (BP 404, DM 982, FR 3332, Y 79,184).

BI *Tree Trunk In A Landscape, c. 1970,* i., from series Sculptural Ephemera, est. BP 4/600, (05-06-93, Christie-London, #145), image 4¼ x 6¼ in., photograph, gelatin silver contact print.

BI *Untitled (Metal And Glass), 1930,* est. $1,0/1,200, (11-16-92, Butterfield, #6194, illus.), 9 x 6¾ in., (229 x 171.8 mm.), photograph, gelatin silver print.

BI *"View From The Cathedral Spires", 1930,* photog. stamp, est. $6/800, (11-16-92, Butterfield, #6195, illus.), 5 x 3 in., (127.2 x 76.3 mm.), photograph, gelatin silver print.

$1035* *"A Walk On Troja Island" (Bullaty, pl. 61), 1940-45,* i. Josef Sudek-fotografie, s. by Anna Farova, (04-06-93, Sotheby-NY, #303A, illus.), 4¾ x 6⅝ in., photograph (BP 684, DM 1667, FR 5646, Y 118,043).

SUGA, Nobao

BI *In Orbit,* s., t., #94/100, good cond.?, rippling, creasing, est. $2/400, (04-02-93, Weschler, #283, illus.), 27¾ x 16 in., (70.5 x 40.6 cm.), etching and aquatint.

SUGAI, Kumi Japanese b. 1919

$1413* *Bronce, 1963,* s., d., #21/35, (06-12-93, Hauswedell/Nolt, #405), 25⅜ x 13¾ in., (64.5 x 35 cm.), color lithograph on thick Johannot wove (BP 925, DM 2300, FR 7730, Y 148,690).

$395* *Composition,* #94/100, s., (04-21-93, Germann, #778), 27³⁄₁₆ x 27³⁄₁₆ in., (690 x 690 mm.), color lithograph (BP 256, DM 631, FR 2135, Y 43,729, SF 575).

$159* *"Composition",* s., i. a' Mr Ragon, (02-17-93, Bonhams-Chelsea, #243), sheet 25½ x 19¾ in., (64.8 x 50.2 cm.), color lithograph (BP 110, DM 258, FR 875, Y 18,992).

$433* *Hommage A Picasso, 1973,* s., num. E.A., (11-28-92, Schoppmann, #824), 24⁷⁄₁₆ x 19½ in., (62 x 49.5 cm.), color lithograph on light cardboard (BP 286, DM 690, FR 2342, Y 53,889).

BI *Komposition Mit Rot, Gelb, Blau, Grau Und Schwarz,* s., num., est. DM 2000, (12-01-92, Karl/Faber, #1284), sh 29¹⁵⁄₁₆ x 22¼ in., (76 x 56.5 cm.), color lithograph on wove.

$433* *Route Bleue, 1974,* s., num., (11-28-92, Schoppmann, #825), 29¹⁵⁄₁₆ x 22¹⁄₁₆ in., (76 x 56 cm.), color lithograph on light cardboard (BP 286, DM 690, FR 2342, Y 53,889).

$1535* *Signs Of The Zodiac, 1972: Set Of Twelve,* s., #8/150, good cond., orig. portfolio, (12-03-92, Sotheby-London, #802, illus.), overall size 27⅜ x 27½ in., (695 x 700 mm.), silkscreens in colors (BP 990, DM 2414, FR 8239, Y 190,992).

$1554* *Souvenir D'Osaka,* s., #64/120, blindstamp, (06-12-93, Hauswedell/Nolt, #403), 13⁵⁄₁₆ x 11¼ in., (33.8 x 28.6 cm.), color etching on BFK Rives (BP 1017, DM 2529, FR 8501, Y 163,527).

$565* *Trois Balles, 1970,* s., d., #IV/X, (06-12-93, Hauswedell/Nolt, #406), 27⁹⁄₁₆ x 19¹¹⁄₁₆ in., (70 x 50 cm.), color lithograph on Arches (BP 370, DM 920, FR 3091, Y 59,455).

$205* *Untitled,* s., margins, good cond., (05-27-93, Sotheby-Amstrdm, #490, illus.), 14¹³⁄₁₆ x 21⅝ in., colored silkscreen on wove (BP 131, DM 329, FR 1109, Y 21,977, G 368).

$192* *Untitled,* s., margins, good cond., (05-27-93, Sotheby-Amstrdm, #491), 18¾ x 21⁹⁄₁₆ in., (476 x 548 mm.), colored silkscreen on wove (BP 123, DM 308, FR 1038, Y 20,583, G 345).

$224* *Untitled,* s., #111/190, margins, good cond., (05-27-93, Sotheby-Amstrdm, #492), 25¹³⁄₁₆ x 20⁹⁄₁₆ in., (655 x 522 mm.), colored silkscreen on wove (BP 143, DM 359, FR 1211, Y 24,014, G 403).

BI *Untitled, 1970,* s., i. E.A., margins, good cond., minor dents in image, est. Dfl. 6/900, (05-27-93, Sotheby-Amstrdm, #493), 27¹³⁄₁₆ x 15¹¹⁄₁₆ in., colored silkscreen on wove.

$577* *Le Vent Vert, 1964,* s., d., num., (11-28-92, Schoppmann, #823), 25⅜ x 17⅛ in., (64.5 x 43.5 cm.), color lithograph on Arches paper (BP 381, DM 919, FR 3121, Y 71,811).

SUGIMOTO

$357* *Vacations, 1930,* B+ cond., closed tears, repairs, pinholes, Japanese lettering, (08-06-92, Swann, #157, illus.), 36 x 24½ in., (91.4 x 62.2 cm.), (BP 186, DM 527, FR 1781, Y 45,536).

SUGIMOTO, Hiroshi b. 1948

$2200* *Radio City Music Hall, 1979,* s., t., d., num. 5/25, (10-13-92, Christie-NY, #608, illus.), 16⅝ x 21½ in., (42.2 x 54.6 cm.), photograph, gelatin silver print (BP 1281, DM 3223, FR 10,951, Y 266,764).

$1840* *U.A. Play House (sic), 1979,* s., t., d., #6/25, (04-08-93, Christie-NY, #516, illus.), 16⅝ x 21⅜ in., (42.2 x 54.3 cm.), photograph, gelatin silver print (BP 1207, DM 2956, FR 10,005, Y 208,806).

SULTAN, Donald American b. 1951

$1430* *Apples And Oranges, 1987,* init., d. 'June 1, 1987', t., #9/100, pub. blindstamp, Metropolitan Museum of Art, full margins, good cond., (11-07-92, Sotheby-NY, #782, illus.), 12 x 12 in., (305 x 305 mm.), silkscreen p. in colors (BP 935, DM 2283, FR 7717, Y 176,500).

BI *Black Lemon, Nov. 29, 1984 (Friedman/Krakow 33), 1984/85,* inits., d., t., i. A.P. 10/10, pub. Parasol Press Ltd., full margins, excell. cond.?, est. Y 900/1,000,000, (10-14-92, Sotheby-Japan, #98, illus.), plate 62 x 48 in., (157.5 x 121.9 cm.), aquatint w/openbite.

$5280* *Black Lemons April 16, 1987,* inits., t., #10/14, pub. Parasol Press, full margins, excellent cond., (11-09-92, Christie-NY, #418, illus.), 63¼ x 49¼ in., (160.7 x 125.1 cm.), aquatint on wove (BP 3491, DM 8429, FR 28,479, Y 655,249).

BI *Black Roses, 1989-90,* s., t., d., #7/55, pub. Parasol Press, full margins, very good cond.?, est. $3,5/4,500, (10-28-92, Butterfield, #3128, illus.), 21¾ x 29½ in., (552 x 749 mm.), aquatint on handmade.

$825* *Black Roses, 1990,* s., d., t., #PP 3/5, pub. Parasol Press, good cond., (10-28-92, Butterfield, #3129), 34 x 55½ in., (86.4 x 141 cm.), silkscreen on wove (BP 526, DM 1274, FR 4326, Y 101,227).

BI *Black Roses, Dec. 1989,* inits., d., t., #7/55, pub. Parasol Press, full margins, very good cond.?, est. $3/5,000, (05-19-93, Butterfield, #2344, illus.), 21¾ x 29½ in., (552 x 749 mm.), aquatint on handmade.

$1430* *Black Roses, May 1990,* s., init., d., t., annot. PP 4/5, pub. Parasol Press, good cond., creases, (02-24-93, Butterfield, #3258), 34 x 55½ in., (86.4 x 141 cm.), silkscreen on heavy wove (BP 997, DM 2321, FR 7870, Y 167,801).

BI *Black Roses: Three,* complete portfolio, init., t., d., #40/53, pub. Parasol Press, Ltd.,full margins, good cond., scratch, est. $7/9,000, (05-15-93, Sotheby-NY, #1235, illus.), sheet 32¼ x 39¾ in., (81.9 x 101 cm.), aquatints on Twin Rocker handmade.

BI *Black Tulips (F./K. 24-27), 1983-84,* complete suite, each init., d. 'Nov 26, 1983', t., i. 'AP 6/8', pub.Blum Helman Gallery, full margins, good cond., est. $3,5/4,500, (11-07-92, Sotheby-NY, #781, illus.), each sheet approx. 20¼ x 13¼ in., (514 x 337 mm.), four aquatints.

$2070* *Black Tulips (Friedman/Krakow 24-27): Four,* complete portfolio, inits., d. Nov 26, 1983, t., #7/20, pub. Blum Helman Gallery, 1983-84, full margins, good cond., (02-11-93, Sotheby-NY, #445), each sheet approx. 20¼ x 13³⁄₁₆ in., (515 x 335 mm.), aquatint (BP 1461, DM 3429, FR 11,603, Y 249,548).

$1760* *Cards: "Four Diamonds" and "Four Clubs", 1990: Two,* s., d., t., #22/44, pub. Parsol Press, full margins, very good cond.?, (10-28-92, Butterfield, #3130), each 11½ x 8 in., (292 x 203 mm.), aquatint, one in red, one in black, on handmade (BP 1121, DM 2718, FR 9229, Y 215,951).

$660* *Dominos, 1990: Three,* s., d., t., #24/53, full margins, very good cond., prop. San Francisco Art Institute, (10-28-92, Butterfield, #3131), each 11¼ x 8 in., (286 x 203 mm.), aquatint on heavy wove (BP 421, DM 1019, FR 3461, Y 80,982).

$1610* *"Eight Hearts February 16, 1990" and "Two Clubs January 30, 1991": Two,* inits., d., t., #22/44, pub. Parasol Press, full margins, very good cond.?, (05-19-93, Butterfield, #2345), each 11½ x 7⅞ in., (292 x 200 mm.), aquatint in red/black on wove (BP 1045, DM 2617, FR 8817, Y 178,235).

BI *"Factory, Feb. 28, 1980" and "Building/Canyon, Feb. 28, 1980" (Krakow 12-13), 1980: Two,* inits., t., i. TP, pub. Parasol Press, full margins, mat staining, excell. cond., est. $2/3,000, (05-11-93, Christie-NY, #575, illus.), each sheet 24¼ x 21⅛ in., (616 x 537 mm.), aquatint and aquatint in blue-purple on wove.

$3520* *Female Series, 1988: Set Of Eleven,* April 1988, Parasol Press, inits., t., #13/15, full margins, loose, excellent cond., (11-09-92, Christie-NY, #419, illus.), 21¼ x 15 in., (540 x 381 mm.), aquatints on Arches Watercolor (BP 2327, DM 5619, FR 18,986, Y 436,833).

$3080* *Female Series, April 1988: Set Of Eleven,* Parasol Press, inits., t., num. 10/15, full margins, loose, excell. cond., orig. black buckram-covered portfolio, (09-19-92, Christie-E, #222, illus.), each, sheet 21¼ x 15 in., (540 x 381 mm.), aquatint on Arches Watercolor (BP 1772, DM 4612, FR 15,795, Y 383,753).

$1650* *Four Pears, 1989,* s., t., d., #67/100, blindstamp, full margins, creases, excellent cond., (11-09-92, Christie-NY, #420, illus.), 23 x 22 in., (584 x 559 mm.), colored screenprint on wove (BP 1091, DM 2634, FR 8900, Y 204,765).

BI *"Freesia 4", 1987,* init. t., d. April 7, 1987 D.S., num. 28/40, p. dry stamp (Aldo Crommelynck), excellent cond., full sheet, est. $12/1500, (09-11-92, Skinner, #116, illus.), sight 14⅜ x 15⅞ in., (36.5 x 40.3 cm.), aquatint on paper.

$1650* *Freesia, April 16, 1987,* inits., d., t., num. 10/40, blindstamp, full margins, apparently verygood cond., (02-24-93, Butterfield, #3151, illus.), 14⅜ x 15⅞ in., (365 x 403 mm.), aquatint on wove (BP 1151, DM 2679, FR 9081, Y 193,617).

BI *Fruit And Flowers And A Fish: "Fish Aug 1990" and "Blue Flowers April 1991", 1991: Two,* init., d., t., #7/125, pub. Parasol Press, Ltd., full margins, good cond., creases, handling creases, est. $2/3,000(05-15-93, Sotheby-NY, #1236), each image 12 x 11⅞ in., (30.5 x 30.2 cm.), silkscreen in colors.

$2420* *"Fruit And Flowers And A Fish: Fish Aug 1990" and "Flowers Aug 1989",1991: Two,* init., d., t., #113/125, pub. Parasol Press, full margins, good cond., (11-07-92, Sotheby-NY, #785, illus.), each sheet approx. 23 x 22 in., (584 x 559 mm.), two silkscreens p. in colors (BP 1582, DM 3864, FR 13,060, Y 298,692).

$3025* *"Fruit And Flowers And A Fish:Pears Nov 1989" and "Tulips Aug 1990",1991: Two,* init., d., t., #113/125, pub. Parasol Press, full margins, good cond., first w/creases, skinned spot, (11-07-92, Sotheby-NY, #784, illus.), each sheet approx. 23 x 22 in., (584 x 559 mm.), two silkscreens p. in colors (BP 1978, DM 4830, FR 16,325, Y 373,365).

$1100* *Fruit And Flowers: Fish, 1990,* inits., d., t., #60/125, pub. Parasol Press, full margins, very goodcond., (10-28-92, Butterfield, #3133), 12 x 12 in., (305 x 305 mm.), color lithograph w/silkscreen on Arches 88 (BP 701, DM 1699, FR 5768, Y 134,969).

BI *Fruit And Flowers: Fish, Aug 1990,* inits., d., t., #PP 4/4, pub. Parasol Press, p. Joe Wattanabe, full margins, good cond., surface soiling, est. $8/1,000, (05-19-93, Butterfield, #2346), 12 x 12 in., (305 x 305 mm.), lithograph and silkscreen in colors on Arches 88.

$1650* *Fruit And Flowers: Pink Flowers, 1990,* inits., d., #60/125, pub. Parasol Press, full margins, very good cond.?, (10-28-92, Butterfield, #3134), 12 x 12 in., (305 x 305 mm.), color lithograph w/silkscreen on Arches 88 (BP 1051, DM 2548, FR 8652, Y 202,454).

BI *Fruits And Flowers II: Roses, April 20, 1992,* inits., d., t., #20/125, pub. Parasol Press, p. Katsumi Suzuki at Watanabe Studio, full margins, very good cond., handling crease, skinned areas, hinge removal, est. $1,4/1,600, (05-19-93, Butterfield, #2347), 12 x 12 in., (305 x 305 mm.), silkscreen in colors on Arches 88.

$660* *Fruits And Flowers: Blue Flowers, 1990,* inits., d., t., annot. PP4/4, pub. Parasol Press, full margins, goodcond., (10-28-92, Butterfield, #3132), 12 x 12 in., (305 x 305 mm.), color lithograph and silkscreen on Arches 88 (BP 421, DM 1019, FR 3461, Y 80,982).

$825* *Fruits And Flowers: Blue Flowers, April 1990,* s., init., d., t., #18/125, pub. Parasol Press, full margins, good cond., (02-24-93, Butterfield, #3259), 12 x 12 in., (305 x 305 mm.), lithograph and silkscreen in colors on Arches 88 (BP 575, DM 1339, FR 4540, Y 96,808).

$770* *Fruits And Flowers: Squash, 1990,* inits., d., t., annot. PP4/4, pub. Parasol Press, full margins, goodcond., creases, (10-28-92, Butterfield, #3135), 12 x 12 in., (305 x 305 mm.), color lithograph w/silkscreen on wove (BP 491, DM 1189, FR 4038, Y 94,479).

$715* *Fruits And Flowers: Squash, April 1991,* s., init., d., t., #18/125, pub. Parasol Press, full margins, good cond., (02-24-93, Butterfield, #3260), 12 x 12 in., (305 x 305 mm.), lithograph and silkscreen in colors on wove (BP 499, DM 1161, FR 3935, Y 83,900).

BI *Lip Prints, October 1989, Paris, Art Multi, 1989: Four,* inits., just., #25/100, full margins, excell. cond., orig. portfolio, est. $1,2/1,800, (05-11-93, Christie-NY, #576), each sheet 12¾ x 9¾ in., (324 x 248 mm.), aquatint in Rives.

BI *Peppers, 1989,* inits., d. May 30, 1989, t., num. 6/6 PP, blindstamp pub. Metro. Museum of Art, full margins, good cond., est. Y 225/275,000, (10-14-92, Sotheby-Japan, #99, illus.), 12 x 12 in., (305 x 305 mm.), color silkscreen.

BI *Peppers, May 30, 1989,* s., inits., d., t., #92/100, pub. Parasol Press, margins, very good cond., est. $1,5/2,500, (05-19-93, Butterfield, #2343), 12 x 12 in., (305 x 305 mm.), silkscreen in colors on wove.

$2090* *Quinces, 1988,* init., d. 'September 7 1988', #97/100, pub. blindstamp, MetropolitanMuseum of Art, full margins, good cond., creases, (11-07-92, Sotheby-NY, #783, illus.), 12¼ x 12¼ in., (311 x 311 mm.), silkscreen p. in colors (BP 1366, DM 3337, FR 11,279, Y 257,961).

$1320* *"Six Hearts June 1990" and "Nine Clubs November 1990": Two,* inits., d., t., num. 22/44, pub. Parasol Press, full margins, apparently very good cond., (02-24-93, Butterfield, #3152, illus.), each 11½ x 7⅞ in., (292 x 200 mm.), aquatint in black & red on wove (BP 921, DM 2143, FR 7265, Y 154,893).

$5175* *Still Life With Pears And Lemons, 1986: Three,* suite of three, each init., t., two i. AP 7/10, third i. AP 6/10, pub. Parasol Press, Ltd., full margins, good cond., creases, (05-15-93, Sotheby-NY, #1234, illus.), each sheet 24½ x 21 in., (62.2 x 53.3 cm.), aquatint, photo-lithograph w/aquatint in colors, photo-lithograph in colors (BP 3365, DM 8324, FR 27,973, Y 573,661).

$2750* *Water Under The Bridge (Friedman/Krakow 1-8), 1979,* complete portfolio, init., annot., #35/45, pub. Parasol Press, Ltd., full margins, good cond., orig. case, (11-07-92, Sotheby-NY, #780, illus.), each sheet approx. 18⅛ x 18⅛ in., (460 x 460 mm.), eight aquatints (BP 1798, DM 4391, FR 14,841, Y 339,422).

BI *Yellow Iris June 1, 1982 (Friedman and Krakow 15), 1982,* inits., t., #11/45, pub. Blum Helman Gallery, full margins, excellent cond., est. $2/2,500, (11-09-92, Christie-NY, #417, illus.), 29 x 23⅜ in., (737 x 594 mm.), woodcut and linocut in black and yellow w/graphite.

BI *"Yellow Iris", 1982,* init., t., i. The Acting Company Tenth Anniversary 1972-1982 D.S., num. 74/125, dry stamp, very good cond., est. $2/2500, (09-11-92, Skinner, #116A), sheet 38 x 29½ in., (96.5 x 74.9 cm.), silkscreen in black and yellow on paper.

BI *Yellow Iris, June 1, 1982, (F./K. 15), 1982,* inits., t., #AP2/10, pub. Blum Helman Gallery, full margins, good cond., foxing, est. $1,5/2,500, (05-19-93, Butterfield, #2342, illus.), 15⅝ x 10½ in., (448 x 267 mm.), woodcut and linoleum cut in black and yellow on Japan.

SUMMERS, Carol   American b. 1925
$1540* *"Andalusia (S. 71)", "The End (S. 73)", "Ommagio A Pesche (S. 74)", Paysage (S. 75)", "Portrait Of DM (S. 76)", "Theodorie's Tomb, Ravenna (S. 77)", "Waterfall (S. 78)" and "Pool (S. 79)": Nine,* Nine Prints, NY, AAA, 1967: Eight Plates (S. 71 and 73-79), all but S. 75 s., num. 5/50; all but S. 75 and 73 t., full sheets, most faded or light-stained; S. 77 and 78 w/image losses, other defects, (09-19-92, Christie-E, #223, illus.), 6 woodcuts, 1 lithograph, 1 pochoir all in colors, on wove or Japan papers or mylar, screenprinted t. page (BP 886, DM 2306, FR 7897, Y 191,876).

BI *August 17th, 1980,* s., t., #37/100, good cond. (?), est. $6/800, (02-24-93, Butterfield, #3268), 37 x 37½ in., (940 x 953 mm.), woodcut in colors on Japan.

BI *Baktapur,* s., very good cond., est. $900/1,200, (05-15-93, Cleveland, #498), 24¾ x 24¼ in., (62.9 x 61.6 cm.), woodcut in colors on Japan.

$495* *"Baktapur" and "Shrines", c. 1969: Two,* s., (05-27-93, Swann, #267), one 24⅝ x 24⅝ in., (62.5 x 62.5 cm.), other 22⅛ x 29 in., (62.5 x 62.5 cm.), color woodcut (BP 317, DM 794, FR 2677, Y 53,066).

$193* *Casa Maiquez,* s., t., #24/100, good cond., (02-24-93, Butterfield, #3263), 16 x 20 in., (40.6 x 50.8 cm.), woodcut in colors on Japan (BP 135, DM 313, FR 1062, Y 22,647).

$303* *"Delta" and "Obersteinberg": Two,* s., t., #63/150 and #45/150, full margins, good cond., soft crease, (02-24-93, Butterfield, #3266), one 20⅛ x 16 in., (511 x 406 mm.), other 24½ x 25 in., (511 x 406 mm.), woodcut in colors on Japan (BP 211, DM 492, FR 1668, Y 35,555).

$880* *"Delta" and "Ravannas' Palace Burning" (S. 174; 183), 1982; 1984: Two,* s., t., num. 103/150 & 116/126, good cond., creases, Palace Burning glued down, prop. Thomas Milbrook Estate, (02-24-93, Butterfield, #3150), 15⅞ x 20 in., (403 x 508 mm.), 24¼ x 37 in., (403 x 508 mm.), woodcut w/monotype on laid Japan (BP 614, DM 1429, FR 4843, Y 103,262).

BI *Flowering Landscape,* s., t., #31/100, good cond., est. $5/700, (02-24-93, Butterfield, #3264), 36⅞ x 37¼ in., (937 x 946 mm.), woodcut in colors on Japan.

$275* *Hudson River Sunset,* s., t., #24/50, rippling, good cond.?, prov., (12-12-92, Weschler, #172, illus.), 37 x

38½ in., (94 x 97.8 cm.), color woodcut (BP 176, DM 433, FR 1485, Y 34,030).

$715* *The Joyous Lake,* s., t., #81/100, good cond.?, surface soiling, Thomas Millbrook Estate, (10-28-92, Butterfield, #3137), 47⅝ x 36¾ in., (121 x 93.3 cm.), color woodcut on Japan (BP 456, DM 1104, FR 3749, Y 87,730).

BI *"Obersteinberg" and "Summer Pasture": Two,* s., t., #48/150, 47/150, good cond., est. $2/400, (05-19-93, Butterfield, #2349), each 24½ x 25 in., (622 x 635 mm.), woodcut in colors on Japan.

BI *Pavilion At Gorka,* s., t., #20/100, good cond. (?), buckling, est. $5/700, (02-24-93, Butterfield, #3269), 37 x 37½ in., (940 x 953 mm.), woodcut in colors on Japan.

$201* *The Pillars Of Hercules,* s., t., #20/125, good cond., (05-19-93, Butterfield, #2350), 29⅞ x 29⅞ in., (759 x 759 mm.), woodcut in colors on Japan (BP 130, DM 327, FR 1101, Y 22,252).

$193* *The Pillars Of Hercules,* s., t., #17/25, good cond. (?), (02-24-93, Butterfield, #3262), 30 x 30 in., (762 x 762 mm.), woodcut in colors on Japan (BP 135, DM 313, FR 1062, Y 22,647).

$1150* *Rolling Sea, 1989,* s., t., #86/100, very good cond., (05-19-93, Butterfield, #2348, illus.), 37 x 37 in., (940 x 940 mm.), woodcut in colors on Japan (BP 747, DM 1869, FR 6298, Y 127,311).

$275* *Starry Night (Summers 155), 1979,* s., (05-16-93, Hindman, #516), 20 x 16 in., (50.8 x 40.6 cm.), color woodcut (BP 179, DM 442, FR 1486, Y 30,484).

$440* *Stromboli Dark (S. 63), 1965,* s., t., annot. Imp. 1965, #187/210, full margins, good cond., surfacerubbing, hinging to mat board, (02-24-93, Butterfield, #3261), 20⅜ x 28⅞ in., (518 x 733 mm.), woodcut in colors on laid Japan (BP 307, DM 714, FR 2422, Y 51,631).

BI *Sunset At Sea,* s., t., #30/75, good cond., creases, est. $7/900, (02-24-93, Butterfield, #3265), 37¼ x 47⅞ in., (94.6 x 121.6 cm.), woodcut in colors on Japan.

BI *Wild Palms, 1986,* s., t., #34/100, good cond. (?), creases, brown stain in image, est.$5/700, (02-24-93, Butterfield, #3267), 36¾ x 37¼ in., (933 x 946 mm.), woodcut in colors on Japan.

$460* *Yuruk,* s., t., #48/250, pub. AAA, good cond., (05-19-93, Butterfield, #2351), 9 x 6⅜ in., (229 x 162 mm.), woodcut in colors on Japan (BP 299, DM 748, FR 2519, Y 50,924).

SUMMERS, W.   English 19th cent.
BI *"The Finish",* taken from H. Alken, est. $8/1200, (09-25-92, Wolf, #19), 15¼ x 30 in., (38.7 x 76.2 cm.), hand colored engraving.

SUMMERS, W. (after Henry ALKEN) (Jr.)
BI *Tattenham Corner (Sp. 76), 1871,* pub. McQueen, narrow margins, hinge mounted, damp/mount staining, est. BP 3/400, (10-27-92, Phillips-London, #105), plate 34½ x 22¼ in., (876 x 565 mm.), aquatint w/hand-coloring, touches of gum arabic.

SUMMERS, William (after J. STURGESS)
$5048* *Fox Hunting, 1878: Set Of Four,* pub. G.P. McQueen, good cond., crease in image, repairs, (10-27-92, Phillips-London, #104, illus.), image 19¾ x 42¼ in., (50.2 x 107.3 cm.), aquatint p. in blue and brown w/hand-coloring on wove (BP 3190, DM 7736, FR 26,251, Y 617,492).

SUMNER, Alan Robert   b. 1911
$567* *Derelict House,* s. Alan Sumner, i. on image, (08-11-92, L. Joel, #30G, illus.), 13⁹⁄₁₆ x 15¹⁵⁄₁₆ in., (34.5 x 40.5 cm.), color screen print (BP 295, DM 832, FR 2818, Y 72,609, A$ 770).

$567* *Red Brick Bridge,* s. Alan Sumner, i., exhib., lit., (08-11-92, L. Joel, #98G), 13³⁄₁₆ x 15⁵⁄₁₆ in., (33.5 x 38.5 cm.), color screenprint (BP 295, DM 832, FR 2818, Y 72,609, A$ 770).

SUMNER, Andreas   ac. c. 1567/68
BI *Venus Auf Dem Delphin (Bartsch IX, 515, 1; Passavant IV, 191; Andresen II, 778, 1),* prov., est. DM 1,200, (06-10-93, Hauswedell/Nolt, #166, illus.), engraving.

SUNDQUIST, Jim   American contemporary
  BI *Georgetown Skyline*, s., #17/40, t. verso, est. $150/250,
      (02-04-93, Sloan, #2984), 14¹⁵⁄₁₆ x 25¾ in., (37.9 x 65.4
      cm.), screenprint.

SUNOL, Alvar   Spanish 20th cent.
  $94* *Girls With Flowers*, s., num. 7/275, (11-12-92, Freemn/
      Fine Art, #11), 17½ x 12¼ in., (44.5 x 31.1 cm.), color
      litho (BP 62, DM 149, FR 502, Y 11,655).

SUNYER Y MIRO, Joaquin   Spanish 1875-1957
  $921* *Etudiants Au Luxembourg, c. 1895*, num., s., soiling,
      staining, untrimmed margins, (02-24-93, Picard, #232),
      color etching and aquatint on laid (BP 642, DM 1495,
      FR 5069, Y 108,073).
  $1228* *"Rue De La Lune (sic)" and "Le Canal Saint-Martin", c.
      1895: Two*, first, t.; second, s., num., soiling, good mar-
      gins verso, (02-24-93, Picard, #231), color etching and
      aquatint on laid and Japan (BP 856, DM 1994, FR 6758,
      Y 144,098).

SURBEK, Victor   1885-1975
  $275* *Haller. Die Alpen, 1944: Sixteen*, Lausanne, Andre Gonin,
      frontispiece, s. in ink, num., (06-23-93, Kornfeld, #804),
      lithograph on thin China (BP 187, DM 465, FR 1565, Y
      29,960, SF 414).

SURENDORF, Charles   American
  $65* *"Main Street, Columbia, California"*, s., t., num., excell.
      cond., small margins, (05-15-93, Cleveland, #327), 7⅞ x
      10 in., (20 x 25.4 cm.), linocut (BP 42, DM 105, FR
      351, Y 7205).

SURVAGE, Leopold   French 1879-1968
  $2510* *Paris, Nouveau Cercle Parisien Du Livre, 1965: Ten*,
      from Pegase by Jean Cocteau, (11-15-92, Christie-
      Geneva, #328, illus.), 18⁵⁄₁₆ x 14³⁄₁₆ in., (465 x 360
      mm.), copper engraving (BP 1650, DM 4003, FR 13,487,
      Y 313,241, SF 3616).
  $280* *"Rythme Colore-1913/-IV"*, atelier stamp, ded., s., (04-04-
      93, Pescheteau, #298), 25⁹⁄₁₆ x 19¹¹⁄₁₆ in., (65 x 50 cm.),
      color lithograph on Arches (BP 184, DM 450, FR 1528,
      Y 31,880).
  $135* *Sans Titre*, s., 66/120, (06-28-93, Loudmer, #371), 21¼ x
      14¹⁵⁄₁₆ in., (540 x 380 mm.), sh 29¹⁵⁄₁₆ x 22¼ in., (540
      x 380 mm.), color lithograph on Arches wove (BP 90,
      DM 229, FR 773, Y 14,324).
  $260* *Untitled*, artist's proof, s., (04-04-93, Pescheteau, #296),
      25⁹⁄₁₆ x 19¹¹⁄₁₆ in., (65 x 50 cm.), color lithograph on
      wove (BP 171, DM 418, FR 1419, Y 29,603).

SUTCLIFFE, F.M.
  $2200* *Whitby Harbor*, notations in unident. hand, 1880s, (04-07-
      93, Swann, #264, illus.), 13½ x 17 in., photograph, car-
      bon print (BP 1454, DM 3558, FR 12,042, Y 249,943).

SUTCLIFFE, Frank
  $247* *A Bit Of News*, photog.'s inits., numerical notations,
      1880's, (10-14-92, Swann, #257, illus.), 7¾ x 5 in., (19.7
      x 12.7 cm.), photograph, albumen print (BP 145, DM
      361, FR 1226, Y 29,932).

SUTCLIFFE, Frank Meadow   1853-1941
  BI *Coastal Scene With Pier*, early 1900s, mounted on card,
      re-sealed w/photog.'s credit label laid down, est. BP 4/
      600, (05-06-93, Christie-London, #62, illus.), 16½ x 9¾
      in., photograph, carbon print.
  $2361* *"Excitement", c. 1890*, s. F.M. Sutcliffe, sight 235 x
      430mm, (05-07-93, Sotheby-London, #95, illus.), photo-
      graph, brown toned silver print (BP 1495, DM 3733, FR
      12,579, Y 259,965).
  BI *"Fisherboy" and "Cox Of The Whitby Lifeboat", c. 1890:
      Two*, credit labels, t., annot., sight 290 x 205mm and
      195 x 140mm, est. BP 3/400, (05-07-93, Sotheby-Lon-
      don, #96, illus.), photograph, silver print, one Van Dyke
      Brown Toned.
  $835* *"Fisherwomen At Whitby" and "Fishing, Whitby": Two*,
      1880s, first s., num. 406; second inits. F.M.S., 240 x
      285mm and 302x 120mm, (05-07-93, Sotheby-London,
      #97, illus.), photograph, Brown Toned silver print (BP
      529, DM 1320, FR 4449, Y 91,940).
  $633* *"Girl With Basket On Beach" and "Woman Knitting",
      1885: Two*, first photog.'s stamp on image; second s.,
      (05-23-93, Butterfield, #3626, illus.), each approx. 8 x 6

in., photograph, albumen print (BP 412, DM 1035, FR
      3484, Y 69,968).
  $1452* *Rural And Coastal Scenes: Sixty-Four*, 1870s, album, 15
      init. F.M.S., num. in negs., others t. w/inits. J.V., G.W.W.
      and F.F. & Co. in negs., titles include "The Rakes
      Progress", "Whitby", "Middlesborough", "County Coun-
      cil", "Robin Hood's Bay", "St. Michael's Mount" and
      "Runswick", w/views of Hastings and Egton, (05-06-93,
      Christie-London, #61, illus.), smallest approx. 3 x 5½ in.,
      largest approx. 6 x 8 in., photograph, albumen print,
      half-morocco, ruled in gilt (BP 920, DM 2287, FR 7699,
      Y 159,754).
  BI *Rural Scenes And Portraits Of Men: Eight*, late 19th
      cent., 5 w/photog.'s inits.; 6 num. in negs., est. BP 3/
      500, (05-06-93, Christie-London, #63), each approx. 7½ x
      5¾ in., photograph, 7 albumen prints, 1 gelatin silver
      print.

SUTHERLAND
  $121* *Fox Hunting Scenes: Set Of Four*, after H. Alken, (12-
      02-92, Boos, #315), each image 9 x 12¼ in., (22.9 x
      31.1 cm.), lithograph (BP 78, DM 190, FR 649, Y
      15,055).

SUTHERLAND, F. (after)
  BI *"Battle Of Elands Laagte, October 21st, 1899" and "Bat-
      tle Of Dundee (Glencoe), October 20th, 1899": Two*, (12-
      11-92, G.A. Key, #27), 18 x 26 in., (45.7 x 66 cm.),
      chromolithograph.
  $114 *"Battle Of Elands Laagte, October 21st, 1899" and "Bat-
      tle Of Dundee (Glencoe), October 20th, 1899": Two*, (04-
      16-93, G.A. Key, #25), 18 x 26 in., (45.7 x 66 cm.),
      chromolithograph (BP 75, DM 184, FR 622, Y 12,819).

SUTHERLAND, Graham   English b. 1903
  $783* *Armadillo (Man 81), 1968*, second state, #65/70, s., from
      A Bestiary And Some Correspondences, ed. Marlborough,
      (05-20-93, Finarte-Milan, #145), lithograph in colors (BP
      503, DM 1263, FR 4255, Y 86,462, L 1150).
  BI *Armadillo, (T. 89), 1968*, s., num. 46/70, pub. Marlbor-
      ough Fine Art, margins, good cond., BP est. 4/500, (12-
      01-92, Christie-London, #541), S. 25¹⁵⁄₁₆ x 19¹¹⁄₁₆ in.,
      (660 x 500 mm.), lithograph in colors on Arches.
  $2115* *Barn Interior II (Man 8), 1923*, second state, t., s., (05-
      20-93, Finarte-Milan, #143, illus.), 6⅛ x 8¹⁄₁₆ in., (15.5 x
      20.5 cm.), drypoint (BP 1358, DM 3412, FR 11,495, Y
      233,547, L 3105).
  $597* *Beetles I From "The Bestiary", 1967*, num. 43/70, s.,
      (08-20-92, Bonhams-Chelsea, #130, illus.), image 19½ x
      25½ in., (49.5 x 64.8 cm.), lithograph in colors (BP 308,
      DM 864, FR 2934, Y 75,388).
  $314* *Composition, 1976*, s., #96/175, good cond., (11-30-92,
      Phillips-London, #363), sheet 25⅝ x 19¾ in., (651 x 502
      mm.), color lithograph on thick wove (BP 207, DM 500,
      FR 1698, Y 39,079).
  $686* *Cray Fields VI (Tassi 19), 1925*, s., p. by artist, pub.
      Twenty-One Gallery, reduced margins, discoloration, han-
      dling creases, (06-30-93, Sotheby-London, #329, illus.),
      sh 5¼ x 5½ in., (133 x 140 mm.), etching on laid (BP
      460, DM 1170, FR 3947, Y 73,503).
  $783* *Crayfields (F.M. 25), 1925*, s., i. printed by F.L. Griggs,
      6th and final state, pub. Twenty-one Gallery, full mar-
      gins, time stained, (10-27-92, Phillips-London, #307),
      (121 x 127 mm.), etching on thick laid (BP 495, DM
      1200, FR 4072, Y 95,780).
  $1133* *Hangar Hell (F.M. 38), 1929*, s., #52/77, from final pub.
      6th state, pub. Twenty-One Gallery, fullmargins, excell.
      cond., (11-30-92, Phillips-London, #362, illus.), plate 5½
      x 5⅛ in., (140 x 130 mm.), etching on fine laid (BP
      748, DM 1805, FR 6128, Y 141,008).
  $995* *Hanger Hill (T. 27), 1929*, s., i. imp, #17/77, p. by art-
      ist, pub. Twenty-One Gallery, margins, light-staining, (06-
      30-93, Sotheby-London, #333, illus.), sh 9½ x 7⅛ in.,
      (241 x 181 mm.), etching on laid (BP 667, DM 1697,
      FR 5725, Y 106,611).
  $385* *Hanging Form, Owl And Bats (Tassi 65), 1955*, s., #25/
      75, p. Mourlot, pub. Berggruen & Cie, good cond.?, (12-
      08-92, Swann, #292), 20 x 26 in., (50.8 x 66 cm.), color
      lithograph (BP 241, DM 599, FR 2044, Y 47,719).
  $800* *Lammas (F.M. 27), 1926*, s., pub. Twenty-One Gallery,
      margins, crease, (11-30-92, Phillips-London, #358), plate

4⅜ x 6⅜ in., (111 x 162 mm.), etching on laid (BP 528, DM 1274, FR 4327, Y 99,564).

$836* *Lammas (F.M. 27), 1926*, s., pub. Twenty-one Gallery, full margins, init. R, good cond., (10-27-92, Phillips-London, #309), plate 4⅜ x 6⅜ in., (111 x 162 mm.), etching on fine laid (BP 528, DM 1281, FR 4347, Y 102,263).

$667* *May Green (F.M. 28), 1927*, from final pub. state, s., i. May Green, pub. Twenty-One Gallery, large margins, defects, (11-30-92, Phillips-London, #359), plate 4½ x 6¼ in., (114 x 159 mm.), etching on laid (BP 440, DM 1063, FR 3607, Y 83,012).

$483* *May Green (F.M. 28), 1927*, 4th final state, s., pub. Twenty-One Gallery, margins, (11-30-92, Phillips-London, #360), plate 4½ x 6¼ in., (114 x 159 mm.), etching on fine laid (BP 319, DM 769, FR 2612, Y 60,112).

$731* *May Green (F.M. 28), 1927*, 4th state, s., pub. Twenty-one Gallery, full margins, good cond., cockling, (10-27-92, Phillips-London, #310), plate 4⅜ x 6¼ in., (111 x 159 mm.), etching on laid (BP 462, DM 1120, FR 3801, Y 89,419).

BI *May Green (T. 24), 1927*, s., imp, p. by artist, pub. Twenty-One Gallery, margins, good cond.,discoloration recto and verso, est. BP 6/800, (06-30-93, Sotheby-London, #332, illus.), sh 9½ x 7⅛ in., (241 x 181 mm.), etching on laid.

BI *May Green (T. 24), 1927*, s., i. imp, p. by artist, pub. Twenty-One Gallery, margins, good cond., est. BP 6/800, (06-30-93, Sotheby-London, #331, illus.), sh 6¼ x 7¾ in., (159 x 197 mm.), etching on laid.

$833* *The Meadow Chapel (F.M. 30), 1928*, s., i. Whatman, pub. Twenty-One Gallery, 3rd(final) state, full margins, good cond., mounted, (11-30-92, Phillips-London, #361), plate 4½ x 6⅛ in., (114 x 156 mm.), etching (BP 550, DM 1327, FR 4505, Y 103,671).

$836* *The Meadow Chapel (F.M. 30), 1928*, 3rd state, s., i. Old Whatman, pub. Twenty-one Gallery, trimmed, (10-27-92, Phillips-London, #311), plate 4½ x 6⅛ in., (114 x 156 mm.), etching (BP 528, DM 1281, FR 4347, Y 102,263).

$1331* *Pecken Wood (Man 24), 1925*, stato definitivo, s., d. Graham Sutherland, (05-20-93, Finarte-Milan, #144, illus.), 5⅜ x 7⁷⁄₁₆ in., (13.7 x 18.9 cm.), etching (BP 854, DM 2147, FR 7234, Y 146,974, L 1955).

$731* *Peckham Wood (F.M. 24), 1925*, s., d. MCMXXV, i. Peckham W: G. 5 imp., full margins, damp spots, creases through image, (10-27-92, Phillips-London, #306), plate 5½ x 7¼ in., (140 x 184 mm.), etching on handmade laid (BP 462, DM 1120, FR 3801, Y 89,419).

BI *La Petite Afrique, (T. 56), 1953*, s., num. 13/25, pub. Redfern Gallery, full margins, creases, very good cond., est. BP 4/500, (12-01-92, Christie-London, #540), L. 22¼ x 13⁹⁄₁₆ in., (565 x 345 mm.), lithograph on Japan.

BI *The Sluice Gate (Felix Man 15), 1924*, s., 4th state, full margins, stains, adhesive mounts, est. BP 250/350, (10-27-92, Phillips-London, #305), plate 5½ x 5¼ in., (140 x 133 mm.), etching on laid.

$1010* *St. Mary Hatch (F.M. 26), 1926*, s., pub. Twenty-one Gallery, full margins, excellent cond., (10-27-92, Phillips-London, #308, illus.), plate 5¼ x 7¼ in., (133 x 184 mm.), etching on fine wove (BP 638, DM 1548, FR 5252, Y 123,547).

BI *St. Mary's Hatch (T. 22), 1926*, s., p. by artist, Twenty-One Gallery, margins, discoloration recto and verso, est. BP 6/800, (06-30-93, Sotheby-London, #330, illus.), sh 6½ x 8⅝ in., (165 x 219 mm.), etching on laid.

BI *St. Mary's Hatch (Tassi 22), 1926*, s., i. imp, p. by artist, pub. Twenty-one Gallery, margins, good cond., tape staining, est. BP 1,0/1,500, (12-03-92, Sotheby-London, #182, illus.), sheet 8¼ x 13⅝ in., (210 x 346 mm.), etching on laid paper.

$867* *St. Mary, Hatch (F.M. 26), 1926*, 2nd state, s., full margins, surface soiling, (11-30-92, Phillips-London, #357), plate 4¾ x 7⅛ in., (121 x 181 mm.), etching on fine laid (BP 572, DM 1381, FR 4689, Y 107,903).

BI *Structures*, s., #48/125, est. FF2,500/3,000, (05-27-93, Briest, #184), 22¼ x 17½ in., (56.5 x 44.5 cm.), black lithograph.

$315* *Structures*, s., #48/125, (11-16-92, Briest, #358), 22¼ x 17½ in., (56.5 x 44.5 cm.), lithograph in black (BP 207, DM 502, FR 1693, Y 39,311).

$343* *Swan-Like Form (T. 129), 1971*, s., i. epreuve d'artiste, p., pub. Teodorani, good cond., (06-30-93, Sotheby-London, #334), sh 19⅞ x 18¾ in., (505 x 476 mm.), colored lithograph on wove (BP 230, DM 585, FR 1974, Y 36,751).

$1775* *To Visit Britain's Landmarks, Brimham Rock, Yorkshire, 1937*, p. Baynard Press, ref. #507, cond. 1, nick, (10-13-92, Phillips-London, #131, illus.), 29¹⁵⁄₁₆ x 44⅞ in., (76 x 114 cm.), color lithograph (BP 1034, DM 2600, FR 8835, Y 215,230).

BI *Tower Of Birds, (T. 158), 1975*, s., num. 50/175, pub. Transworld Art Corporation, fresh cond., loose, (12-01-92, Christie-London, #542), S. 25½ x 19¾ in., (648 x 501 mm.), lithograph in colors on wove.

$905* *Wood Interior (Landscape) (F.M. 32), 1929*, s., #11/60, i. Landscape, full margins, stain, (10-27-92, Phillips-London, #312), plate 4⅝ x 6⅜ in., (117 x 162 mm.), etching on laid (BP 572, DM 1387, FR 4706, Y 110,703).

SUTHERLAND, T.

$440* *"Wild Duck Shooting", "Partridge Shooting", "Pheasant Shooting", and"Grouse Shooting": Four*, pub. R. Ackermann, c. early 19th cent., toned paper, (01-05-93, Bourne, #224, illus.), 8⅜ x 26¼ in., (21.3 x 66.7 cm.), aquatint engravings (BP 284, DM 715, FR 2440, Y 54,904).

SUTHERLAND, Thomas   British ac. early/mid 19th cent.

$440* *"South Sea Whale Fishing" 1825*, after William John Higgins, ident., good cond., staining, foxing, toning, (10-31-92, Skinner, #46, illus.), 17¼ x 22¼ in., (43.8 x 56.5 cm.), etching w/aquatint and hand coloring on paper (BP 288, DM 691, FR 2339, Y 54,402).

SUTHERLAND, Thomas   (after Henry Alken Sr.)

$1870* *"Wild Duck", "Grouse", "Pheasant" and "Partridge": Four*, prov., (09-09-92, Doyle, #1), 17 x 34 in., (43.2 x 86.4 cm.), hand colored aquatint (BP 945, DM 2645, FR 8986, Y 229,871).

SUTTERLIN, Ludwig   1865-1917

$867* *Berlin, Exposition Industrielle, 1896*, creases, tears, lit., (02-04-93, Christie-S. Ken, #179), 36 x 25½ in., (91.4 x 64.8 cm.), color lithograph (BP 605, DM 1428, FR 4841, Y 107,849).

SUTTON, Ruth Haviland

$137* *Nantucket Island, Massachusetts*, James Cagney Estate, (09-30-92, Doyle, #3), 18½ x 24½ in., (47 x 62.2 cm.), color photo-offset print (BP 77, DM 194, FR 657, Y 16,441).

SUYDAM, Edward Howard

$99* *"Decatur Street", 1930*, s., d. in plate, i., (10-16-92, Neal, #952), image 9 x 11¾ in., (22.9 x 29.8 cm.), photolithograph (BP 60, DM 146, FR 497, Y 11,821).

$44* *"Lacework In Iron, Royal Street", 1930*, s., t., d. in plate, (10-16-92, Neal, #953), image 8½ x 6½ in., (21.6 x 16.5 cm.), photolithograph (BP 27, DM 65, FR 221, Y 5254).

SUYDERHOEF, Jonas   c. 1613-1686

BI *Der Trunkene Bacchus (Hollstein 6 IV)*, after Rubens, prov., est. DM 1,000, (06-10-93, Hauswedell/Nolt, #167), etching.

SVANBERG, Max Walter   b. 1912

$1887* *Dromkvinnans Kyss II (v.H.XLII), 1958*, s., 155/160, (05-25-93, AB Stockholm, #67), 20¼ x 15⅜ in., (51.5 x 39 cm.), print (BP 1223, DM 3073, FR 10,345, Y 206,252, SK 2750).

$535* *Visionen Vecklar Ut Sitt Ansikte (von Holten XLI), 1956*, s., 233/250, (12-04-92, AB Stockholm, #7136), 19⅛ x 15³⁄₁₆ in., (48.5 x 38.5 cm.), lithograph in colors (BP 343, DM 852, FR 2890, Y 66,792, SK 3630).

$2642* *Visionen Vecklar Ut Sitt Landskap (Holten XLIII), 1958*, s., 65/260, (05-25-93, AB Stockholm, #66), 17¹⁵⁄₁₆ x 14¹⁵⁄₁₆ in., (45.5 x 38 cm.), lithograph in colors (BP 1712, DM 4303, FR 14,485, Y 288,775, SK 3850).

$503* *Visionen Vecklar Ut Sitt Landskap (v. H. XLIII), 1958*, s., 109/260, (12-04-92, AB Stockholm, #7137), 18⅛ x 15³⁄₁₆ in., (46 x 38.5 cm.), sh 20½ x 17⁵⁄₁₆ in., (46 x 38.5

cm.), lithograph in colors (BP 323, DM 801, FR 2717, Y 62,797, SK 3410).

SVENSSON, Roland   b. 1910
$1854* *Den Gamla Angbaten, Portfolio: Four,* s., 191/360, (05-12-93, AB Stockholm, #7052), 23⅝ x 17¹¹⁄₁₆ in., (60 x 45 cm.), lithograph in colors (BP 1211, DM 2991, FR 10,076, Y 206,989, SK 13,750).
$1784* *Den Gamla Angebaten: Four,* s., 192/360, p. R. Jansson, Edition Grafioteket, portfolio, (12-04-92, AB Stockholm, #7138), three 23⅝ x 17¹¹⁄₁₆ in., (60 x 45 cm.), one 22¹³⁄₁₆ x 16⁹⁄₁₆ in., (60 x 45 cm.), lithograph in color (BP 1144, DM 2841, FR 9638, Y 222,722, SK 12,100).
$74* *Interior Fran Skargardsstuga,* s., 122/150, (04-17-93, Falkkloos, #511), 13¾ x 20½ in., (35 x 52 cm.), lithograph in colors (BP 48, DM 118, FR 400, Y 8229, SK 550).

SWAINE (after)
$61 *"Evening, Or Sun Setting",* engraved by Parr, (04-16-93, G.A. Key, #73), 9 x 14 in., (22.9 x 35.6 cm.), hand-colored engraving (BP 40, DM 99, FR 333, Y 6859).

SWANN, James   American b. 1905
$99* *The Palmolive Building,* s., (11-01-92, Hanzel, #225), 9½ x 7¼ in., (24.1 x 18.4 cm.), drypoint etching (BP 65, DM 156, FR 526, Y 12,240).

SWANNELL, John
$1053* *Francesca Thyssen, c. 1980,* s., #6/25, stamped photog.'s credit, pub., 504 x 405mm, (05-07-93, Sotheby-London, #374, illus.), photograph, silver print (BP 667, DM 1665, FR 5610, Y 115,944).

SWARBRECK, Samuel Dunkinfield   English 19th cent.
$110* *Rosslyn Chapel: Two,* each s., located, d. 1837 in stone, (12-10-92, Sloan, #600), each 16½ x 12 in., (41.9 x 30.5 cm.), lithograph (BP 71, DM 174, FR 594, Y 13,607).

SWARTZMAN, Roslyn   b. 1931
BI *Legend I,* #6/50, s., t., prov., est. C$ 2/300, (11-16-92, Hodgins, #178), 29 x 21½ in., (73.7 x 54.6 cm.), color etching on paper.

SWEET and LINDLEY
$690* *Botanicals, 1852: Eight,* (04-07-93, Sotheby-Arcade, #152), sight 8 x 5¼ in., (20.3 x 13.3 cm.), hand-colored engraving (BP 456, DM 1116, FR 3777, Y 78,391).

SWORD, James B. (after)
$345* *Folio Of American Sporting Scenes, Series 1, Section 1, 1885: Nine,* album, pub. Sword, tears, discoloration, orig. boards, (01-28-93, Sotheby-NY, #465), overall 23 x 30½ in., (584 x 775 mm.), heliogravure (photoengraving) (BP 228, DM 547, FR 1850, Y 42,836).

SYLCOR, Jean   b. 1932
BI *Essai,* s., d., t. J. Sylcor 66, (10-20-92, Encans, #147), 5⅞ x 3¾ in., (15 x 9.5 cm.), etching.

SYME, Eveline W.   1888-1961
$486* *Mixed Flowers,* s. E.W. Syme, i., #3/25, d. 1933, (08-11-92, L. Joel, #4G, illus.), 6¹⁄₁₆ x 6¼ in., (15.4 x 15.9 cm.), color linocut (BP 253, DM 713, FR 2416, Y 62,236, A$ 660).

SYMES, C.J.
$181* *"The Fishing Boat",* 1920s-30s, mounted on card, s., t., (05-06-93, Christie-London, #93), 15 x 9¾ in., photograph, bromoil transfer print (BP 115, DM 285, FR 960, Y 19,914).

SYMPSON, T.
BI *Coats Of Arms: Pair,* both i., est. $150/200, (10-30-92, Sloan, #886), 8⅝ x 6⅜ in., (21.9 x 16.2 cm.), color engravings.
BI *Coats Of Arms: Pair,* both i., est. $200/300, (09-17-92, Sloan, #622), each approx. 8⅝ x 6⅜ in., (21.9 x 16.2 cm.), color engravings.

SYNGE, Edward Millington   English 1860-1913
$55* *Cathedral Interior,* s. in plate, (12-10-92, Sloan, #924), 12 x 8⅞ in., (30.5 x 22.5 cm.), etching (BP 35, DM 87, FR 297, Y 6804).

SZCZESNY, Stefan   b. 1951
BI *Untitled, 1982,* s., d., #13/100, margins, good cond.?, prov., est. G 2/300, (12-09-92, Sotheby-Amstrdm, #644),

21¼ x 16¾ in., (540 x 425 mm.), color lithograph on wove.

SZEKESSY, Curt   American 20th cent.
$165* *"Church Interior": A Pair,* s. Curt Szekessy, i., (11-12-92, A. James, #326), one 28½ x 15¾ in., (72.4 x 40 cm.), the other 28 x 29½ in., (72.4 x 40 cm.), etching (BP 108, DM 261, FR 882, Y 20,459).

SZEKESSY, Karin   b. 1939
$683* *Ohne Titel, 60's,* (c), (11-12-92, Lempertz, #261, illus.), 14⁵⁄₁₆ x 11¹³⁄₁₆ in., (36.4 x 30 cm.), photograph, gelatin silver print (BP 437, DM 1073, FR 3658, Y 84,498).
$683* *Ohne Titel, 60's,* (c), (11-12-92, Lempertz, #262, illus.), 15¹¹⁄₁₆ x 11⅞ in., (39.8 x 30.2 cm.), photograph, gelatin silver print (BP 437, DM 1073, FR 3658, Y 84,498).

SZENES, Arpad   1897-1985
$168* *"Composition",* s., (01-28-93, Pescheteau, #261), 22¹⁄₁₆ x 14¹⁵⁄₁₆ in., (56 x 38 cm.), lithograph on gray Rives (BP 111, DM 266, FR 901, Y 20,859).
$350* *Compositions: Three,* s., #179/200, 98/150, 70/175, (03-31-93, Briest, #E107), from 16¹⁵⁄₁₆ x 12¹³⁄₁₆ in., (43 x 32.5 cm.), to 14¹⁵⁄₁₆ x 22¹⁄₁₆ in., (43 x 32.5 cm.), color lithographs on Arches (BP 231, DM 563, FR 1913, Y 40,248).

SZKOLA, Alex   American 20th cent.
$28* *"34th Street",* s., num. 114/175, excellent cond., (10-31-92, Cleveland, #398), 22 x 28 in., (55.9 x 71.1 cm.), lithograph in colors (BP 18, DM 43, FR 146, Y 3468).

SZUTS, Szegedi   ac. 1931-1935
$579* *To Visit Britain's Landmarks, George III Monument, Savernake Forest,1936,* s., ref. #458, cond. 1, creasing, (10-13-92, Phillips-London, #105), 29¹⁵⁄₁₆ x 44⅞ in., (76 x 114 cm.), color lithograph (BP 337, DM 848, FR 2882, Y 70,207).

T.H.I.
$439* *PLM. Morzine-Pleney. "Centre Des Neiges. Ses Pistes, Son Telepherique",* very good cond., (03-15-93, Arcole, #71), 38⁹⁄₁₆ x 23⅝ in., (98 x 60 cm.), (BP 306, DM 729, FR 2479, Y 52,002).

TABANA, Edward (after)
$55* *Young Girl,* (02-12-93, DuMouchelle, #370), print (BP 39, DM 91, FR 309, Y 6633).

TABARD, Maurice   1897-1984
$1725* *"GD Lavoir De La Vierge", 1931,* s., d. by photog. in ink, (04-06-93, Sotheby-NY, #245, illus.), 9⅜ x 6⅞ in., photograph (BP 1139, DM 2779, FR 9411, Y 196,738).
$1320* *Guitar Solarization, c. 1932,* credit stamp, (10-13-92, Christie-NY, #370, illus.), 7 x 4⅝ in., (17.8 x 11.7 cm.), photograph, gelatin silver print (BP 769, DM 1934, FR 6570, Y 160,058).
BI *Indefrisable D'Art Sans Fil, New York,* 1940s, est. $10/12,000, (04-08-93, Christie-NY, #224, illus.), 15½ x 11½ in., (39.4 x 29.2 cm.), photograph, solarized gelatin silver print.

TABUCHI, Yasse   b. 1921
$125* *Composition, (19)65,* s., H.C., (12-01-92, Karl/Faber, #1285), 12¹³⁄₁₆ x 19¹¹⁄₁₆ in., (32.5 x 50 cm.), color lithograph on Arches wove (BP 83, DM 199, FR 679, Y 15,563).

TAIT, Edith Winifred
$495* *Hull Of Ship With Anchor, 1926,* photog.'s sig. on mount, (04-07-93, Swann, #566, illus.), 4¼ x 3¼ in., photograph, platinum print (BP 327, DM 801, FR 2709, Y 56,237).

TAIT, Norman
$156* *'Eagle Spirit,' 1977,* #52/199, s., (10-21-92, Maynard, #39), 19 x 15 in., (48.3 x 38.1 cm.), silkscreen (BP 97, DM 236, FR 801, Y 19,001, C$ 193).
$94* *'Hummingbird', 1977,* (10-21-92, Maynard, #50), approx. 11 x 14½ in., (27.9 x 36.8 cm.), print (BP 58, DM 142, FR 483, Y 11,449, C$ 116).
BI *'Raven', 1977,* #38/156, est. C$1/150, (10-21-92, Maynard, #49), approx. 11 x 14½ in., (27.9 x 36.8 cm.), print.

TAJIRI, Shinkichi American b. 1923

$115* *My Secret Garden No 1, 1975,* s., full margins, good cond., (05-27-93, Sotheby-Amstrdm, #494, illus.), 28¼ x 20³⁄₁₆ in., (717 x 512 mm.), offset print in colors on wove (BP 74, DM 185, FR 622, Y 12,328, G 207).

$115* *My Secret Garden No 2, 1975,* s., t., full margins, good cond., (05-27-93, Sotheby-Amstrdm, #495), 28¼ x 20³⁄₁₆ in., (717 x 512 mm.), offset print in colors on wove (BP 74, DM 185, FR 622, Y 12,328, G 207).

$64* *My Secret Garden No 3, 1975,* s., t., full margins, good cond., (05-27-93, Sotheby-Amstrdm, #496), 28¼ x 20³⁄₁₆ in., offset print in colors on wove (BP 41, DM 103, FR 346, Y 6861, G 115).

$64* *Untitled,* s., full sheet p. to edges, good cond., (05-27-93, Sotheby-Amstrdm, #688), sh 23⁵⁄₁₆ x 16⁷⁄₁₆ in., (592 x 418 mm.), color silkscreen on wove (BP 41, DM 103, FR 346, Y 6861, G 115).

BI *Untitled,* s., good cond.?, est. G 2/300, (12-09-92, Sotheby-Amstrdm, #648), sh 23⁵⁄₁₆ x 16⁷⁄₁₆ in., (592 x 418 mm.), color silkscreen on wove.

TAKAGI, Madoka

$1265* *"Brooklyn, New York", 1992,* s., t., d. by photog. in pencil, (04-06-93, Sotheby-NY, #225A, illus.), 12⅝ x 10⅛ in., photograph, platinum print on Canson vellum (BP 836, DM 2038, FR 6901, Y 144,275).

TAKAHASHI, Yoshi b. 1943

$164* *Landschaft Mit Vogeln,* #52/95, s., studio stamp, (11-13-92, Koller, #5440), 11¼ x 19⁵⁄₁₆ in., (28.5 x 49 cm.), color etching on wove (BP 106, DM 257, FR 868, Y 20,355, SF 232).

TAKAL, Peter American b. 1905

$60* *"City Roofs", 1956,* s., The Print Club of Cleveland Pub. No. 32, excell. cond., (05-15-93, Cleveland, #499), 9⅜ x 14¹⁵⁄₁₆ in., (23.8 x 37.9 cm.), drypoint (BP 39, DM 97, FR 324, Y 6651).

$10* *"Trees And Fields", 1957,* Print Club of Cleveland Pub. No. 35, s., excell. cond., (05-15-93, Cleveland, #500), 9⅜ x 15¼ in., (23.8 x 38.7 cm.), lithograph (BP 7, DM 16, FR 54, Y 1109).

TAKURIKI, Tomikichiro Japanese 20th cent.

$110* *Animal Caricatures: Two,* (12-10-92, Sloan, #885), each, sight 10 x 15 in., (25.4 x 38.1 cm.), woodblock (BP 71, DM 174, FR 594, Y 13,607).

TAL-COAT, Pierre French 1905-1985

$97* *Composition Sur Fond Vert: Two,* s., 43/300, (06-28-93, Loudmer, #372), one 11⅝ x 9⁷⁄₁₆ in., (295 x 240 mm.), other 19⅛ x 25¹⁵⁄₁₆ in., (295 x 240 mm.), color aquatints on Arches wove (BP 65, DM 165, FR 555, Y 10,292).

$180* *"Composition",* HC s., (04-04-93, Pescheteau, #299), 31½ x 22¹³⁄₁₆ in., (80 x 58 cm.), aquatint on wove (BP 119, DM 289, FR 983, Y 20,494).

$157* *"Composition",* #21/150, s., (10-18-92, Pescheteau, #264), 25⁹⁄₁₆ x 19¹¹⁄₁₆ in., (65 x 50 cm.), etching and aquatint on wove (BP 95, DM 232, FR 788, Y 18,746).

$165* *Dans Les Champs,* s., #13/300, creases, good cond.?, prov., (12-12-92, Weschler, #173), 21 x 24 in., (53.3 x 61 cm.), color lithograph (BP 106, DM 260, FR 891, Y 20,418).

$87* *Sans Titre,* s., 244/300, light stain, (06-28-93, Loudmer, #373), 22¹³⁄₁₆ x 18⅞ in., (580 x 480 mm.), sh 25¹⁵⁄₁₆ x 19¹¹⁄₁₆ in., (580 x 480 mm.), color lithograph on Arches wove (BP 58, DM 148, FR 498, Y 9231).

$87* *Sans Titre,* s., 61/300, (06-28-93, Loudmer, #374), 23⅝ x 15¹⁵⁄₁₆ in., (600 x 405 mm.), sh 25¹⁵⁄₁₆ x 19¹¹⁄₁₆ in., (600 x 405 mm.), color lithograph on Arches wove (BP 58, DM 148, FR 498, Y 9231).

TALBOT, William Henry Fox English 1800-1877

$654* *Books On Library Shelves, c. 1845,* t., 178 x 225mm, (05-07-93, Sotheby-London, #44, illus.), photograph, Talbotype (BP 414, DM 1034, FR 3484, Y 72,011).

$545* *The Bridge Over The Moldau, After 20 November 1859,* num. 376, 105 x 125mm, (05-07-93, Sotheby-London, #48, illus.), photograph, photographic engraving (BP 345, DM 862, FR 2904, Y 60,009).

$1361* *The Fruit Sellers, c. 1845,* 182 x 225mm, (05-07-93, Sotheby-London, #46, illus.), photograph, Talbotype (BP 862, DM 2152, FR 7251, Y 149,857).

$654* *Paris, Two Studies, 1850s,* each approx. 75 x 100mm, (05-07-93, Sotheby-London, #45, illus.), photograph, photographic engraving (BP 414, DM 1034, FR 3484, Y 72,011).

$22,702* *Reverend Calvert Jones Seated In The Cloisters, Lacock Abbey, Before27 October 1847,* 193 x 238mm, (05-07-93, Sotheby-London, #42, illus.), photograph, Talbotype (BP 14,375, DM 35,892, FR 120,948, Y 2,499,670).

$12,713* *River Scene With Bridge, c. 1845,* 189 x 236mm, (05-07-93, Sotheby-London, #43, illus.), photograph, Talbotype (BP 8050, DM 20,100, FR 67,730, Y 1,399,802).

$1980* *"View Of Lake With Thatched-Roof Cottage" and "View Of Lake With Trees": Two,* #14, #15, 1840s, (04-07-93, Swann, #265, illus.), each 3¼ x 4¼ in., photograph, calotypes (BP 1308, DM 3202, FR 10,837, Y 224,949).

$1180* *Village Street Scene, 1850s,* 103 x 125mm, (05-07-93, Sotheby-London, #47, illus.), photograph, photograph engraving (BP 747, DM 1866, FR 6287, Y 129,927).

TALLBERG, Axel Swedish 1860-1928

BI *Dorney Church, Windsor,* mono., d. (18)88 in plate, s., t., est. $150/200, (02-04-93, Sloan, #1650), 15¾ x 11⅞ in., (40 x 30.2 cm.), etching.

TALLER DE GRAFICA POPULAR

BI *Mexican People, 1943: Twelve,* s., pub. A.A.A., full margins, good cond., yellowing, handling creases, ten artists, est. $4/6,000, (11-23-92, Sotheby-NY, #285, illus.), images 11⅜ x 13¾ in., (290 x 350 mm.), twelve lithographs, two p. in colors.

TAMAGAWA SHUNSUI Japanese ac. c. 1772-1780

BI *Matsumoro Koshiro In An Unidentified Role,* Hosoban, s. Shunshi ga, d. probably An'ei 3-4 (1774/75), wormed, Prof. H.R.W. Kuhne Coll., est. BP 6/800, (06-11-93, Sotheby-London, #224, illus.), 11⅜ x 5½ in., (28.9 x 14 cm.), woodblock.

BI *Nakamura Jozo II As Yoemon,* Hosoban, s. Shunshi ga, d. An'ei 3 (1774), faded, soiled, repaired, Prof. H.R.W. Kuhne Coll., est. BP 5/700, (06-11-93, Sotheby-London, #223, illus.), 12 x 5⅝ in., (30.5 x 14.3 cm.), woodblock.

TAMAGNO

$990* *Demandez Un Marra,* La Lithographie Parisienne, A cond., (08-06-92, Swann, #266, illus.), 54½ x 38½ in., (138.4 x 97.8 cm.), (BP 517, DM 1463, FR 4940, Y 126,276).

$782* *Etrennes Jouets, A Pygmalion,* p. B. Sirven, folds, defects, backed on linen, two sheets, (05-07-93, Christie-S. Ken, #125, illus.), each sheet 61 x 89 in., (154.9 x 226.1 cm.), color lithograph (BP 495, DM 1236, FR 4166, Y 86,104).

$1896* *PLM. Chamonix Mont-Blanc. "Sports D'Hiver, Concours Ski, Luge, Patin, Bobsleigh", 1910,* very good cond., (03-15-93, Arcole, #111, illus.), 42¹¹⁄₁₆ x 30½ in., (108.5 x 77.5 cm.), (BP 1320, DM 3150, FR 10,706, Y 224,591).

TAMAGNO, Francisco French b. 1851

$504* *Demandez Un Marra, c. 1895,* excell. cond., (02-04-93, Christie-S. Ken, #146, illus.), 55 x 39½ in., (139.7 x 100.3 cm.), color lithograph (BP 352, DM 830, FR 2814, Y 62,694).

$1245* *Entrepot General Des Automobiles,* Paris, Affiches Camis, cond. B+, (06-11-93, Boisgirard, #146), 66¹⁵⁄₁₆ x 47¼ in., (170 x 120 cm.), poster (BP 818, DM 2023, FR 6822, Y 132,095).

$598* *Jouets, Etrennes, c. 1895,* cond. A, (03-16-93, Boisgirard, #206), 51³⁄₁₆ x 39⅜ in., (130 x 100 cm.), poster (BP 413, DM 994, FR 3379, Y 69,925).

$602* *Peugeot, c. 1910,* fairly good cond., creases, (02-12-93, Cheval/Robert, #85), 62¹⁵⁄₁₆ x 47¼ in., (160 x 120 cm.), poster (BP 424, DM 998, FR 3378, Y 72,600).

TAMAGNO, M.

$130* *Kina-Cadet. "Le Meilleur Des Aperatifs",* Affiches Camis, good cond., (02-12-93, Cheval/Robert, #74), 75³⁄₁₆ x 48¹³⁄₁₆ in., (191 x 124 cm.), poster (BP 92, DM 216, FR 730, Y 15,678).

$251* *Saint-Germain En Laye, "Sa Foret, Sa Terrasse", Villegiature D'Ete, c. 1895,* good cond., (01-23-93, Ribeyre/Baron, #45), 42¹¹⁄₁₆ x 30⅛ in., (108.5 x 76.5 cm.), poster (BP 164, DM 399, FR 1350, Y 31,414).

TAMASAUKAS, Otis   b. 1947

$130* *Candy Back Trout, 1979,* s., t., d. '79, (11-16-92, Hodgins, #234), 22 x 30 in., (55.9 x 76.2 cm.), etching on paper (BP 85, DM 207, FR 699, Y 16,224, C$ 165).

BI *Apocalypse De Saint Jean, 1959,* portfolio, Club International de Bibliophile, very good cond., yellowing, est. $6/8,000, (05-18-93, Sotheby-NY, #273, illus.), the smallest 12¾ x 10 in., (324 x 254 mm.), the largest 12¾ x 19⅝ in., (324 x 254 mm.), 15 lithographs in color.

$2750* *Cabeza Con Sombrero,* s. in crayon, annot. H.C., apparently very good cond., (02-24-93, Butterfield, #2681, illus.), 29½ x 22 in., (749 x 559 mm.), etching & aquatint in colors on handmade (BP 1918, DM 4464, FR 15,135, Y 322,694).

BI *Cabeza En La Ventana, 1976,* s., #58/75, pub., Poligrafa S.A., good cond.?, framed, est. $2/4,000, (05-19-93, Butterfield, #1853, illus.), 29 x 22 in., (737 x 559 mm.), etching and aquatint in colors on handmade.

BI *(Cabeza En Verde),* crayon s., #43/75, very good cond.?, est. $2/4,000, (05-19-93, Butterfield, #1854, illus.), 29⅞ x 22 in., (759 x 559 mm.), lithograph in colors on wove.

$3850* *Cabeza, 1964,* s., d. in stone; s., #3/20, full sheet, very good cond., tape remainsverso, yellowing, (11-23-92, Sotheby-NY, #288, illus.), 22 x 17⅞ in., (560 x 455 mm.), lithograph (BP 2517, DM 6164, FR 20,913, Y 477,608).

$2990* *Cabeza, c. 1969,* s., #83/100, very good cond., (05-18-93, Sotheby-NY, #277, illus.), 29⅛ x 21⅝ in., (740 x 549 mm.), lithograph p. in colors (BP 1948, DM 4852, FR 16,384, Y 333,222).

$3575* *Carnavalesque, 1969,* s., from Mujeres Suite, #130/150, pub. Lublin Inc., full margins, good cond., (11-23-92, Sotheby-NY, #294, illus.), image 27⅜ x 20⅞ in., (695 x 530 mm.), lithograph p. in colors (BP 2337, DM 5724, FR 19,419, Y 443,493).

$3575* *"Deux Tetes De Femmes",* from Mujeres Portfolio, #53/150, s., prov., (05-14-93, DuMouchelle, #2039, illus.), 21 x 27½ in., (53.3 x 69.9 cm.), lithograph (BP 2324, DM 5750, FR 19,324, Y 396,298).

$2070* *Deux Tetes, 1969,* from Mujeres, s., #49/150, pub. Touchstone Publishers, full margins,crease, excell. cond., (05-17-93, Christie-NY, #313), 27½ x 21¼ in., (69.9 x 54 cm.), (BP 1350, DM 3340, FR 11,250, Y 230,512).

$2415* *Dos Cabezas, 1975,* s., #46/75 Ediciones Poligrafa, S.A., excell. cond., (05-18-93, Sotheby-NY, #279, illus.), 22 x 29⅞ in., (559 x 759 mm.), etching p. in colors (BP 1573, DM 3919, FR 13,233, Y 269,141).

$1146* *Dos Cabezas, 1975,* #16/75, s., (12-15-92, Finarte-Milan, #28, illus.), 22¼ x 29¾ in., (56.5 x 75.5 cm.), lito calcografia a colori (BP 731, DM 1796, FR 6138, Y 142,131, L 1610).

$1980* *Dos Figuras, c. 1974,* pencil s., #17/75, pub. Ediciones Poligrafa, S.A., good cond., paperloss, (11-23-92, Sotheby-NY, #291, illus.), 29⅞ x 22 in., (760 x 560 mm.), lithograph p. in colors on guarro (BP 1295, DM 3170, FR 10,755, Y 245,627).

BI *Femme En Mauve, 1969,* s., #77/150, from Mujeres Suite, pub. A. Lubin, full margins, very good cond., yellowing, est. $3,5/4,000, (05-18-93, Sotheby-NY, #275, illus.), image 26¾ x 20⅝ in., (679 x 524 mm.), lithograph p. in colors.

$744* *Figura,* #26/200, s., (05-20-93, Finarte-Milan, #149), 19¹¹⁄₁₆ x 13⅜ in., (50 x 34 cm.), lithograph in colors (BP 478, DM 1200, FR 4043, Y 82,155, L 1093).

$1629* *Figure Composition,* s., #84/150, margins, good cond., mount-staining, creases, (06-30-93, Sotheby-London, #924, illus.), sh 30 x 22½ in., (762 x 572 mm.), color lithograph on wove (BP 1092, DM 2778, FR 9373, Y 174,542).

$990* *Figure With Constellation,* s., num. 1/200, (09-20-92, Hindman, #798, illus.), 19½ x 13½ in., (49.5 x 34.3 cm.), color lithograph (BP 580, DM 1469, FR 5025, Y 122,358).

$1035* *Figure, 1969,* from Mujeres, s., #147/150, full margins, excell. cond., (05-17-93, Christie-NY, #314), 27½ x 21 in., (699 x 533 mm.), lithograph in colors on BFK Rives (BP 675, DM 1670, FR 5625, Y 115,256).

$468* *"Firmament No. 2",* s., excell. cond., (08-08-92, Litchfield, #178A), 12¼ x 9¼ in., (31.1 x 23.5 cm.), color lithograph (BP 243, DM 688, FR 2326, Y 59,732).

$1980* *Fish And Lemon Slices, 1969,* #53/150, s., prov., (05-14-93, DuMouchelle, #2040, illus.), 21 x 27½ in., (53.3 x 69.9 cm.), color lithograph (BP 1287, DM 3185, FR 10,703, Y 219,488).

$853* *Flying Figures, c. 1952,* s., #34/100, pub. by Les Cent Bibliophiles de France et d'Amerique, full margins, good cond., (12-03-92, Sotheby-London, #804, illus.), 16⅛ x 23 in., (406 x 584 mm.), lithograph in colors on Arches (BP 550, DM 1341, FR 4579, Y 106,134).

$993* *Frau In Blute,* s., num., H.C., blindstamp, (06-05-93, Grisebach, #890, illus.), 27½ x 19½ in., (69.8 x 49.5 cm.), color lithograph on wove (BP 654, DM 1610, FR 5426, Y 106,522).

$825* *From The Mujeres Series,* s., mat burn, excell. cond.?, (10-10-92, Litchfield, #204), image 27¼ x 20½ in., (69.2 x 52.1 cm.), color lithograph (BP 489, DM 1225, FR 4115, Y 100,438).

$2475* *From Watermelon Suite,* s., #74/75, very good cond.?, (10-28-92, Butterfield, #2583), 30 x 22 in., (762 x 559 mm.), lithograph on wove (BP 1577, DM 3822, FR 12,979, Y 303,681).

$990* *Happy Sun, 1983,* s., #10/100, blindstamp Ernest de Soto Workshop, very good cond.?, (10-28-92, Butterfield, #2579), 12 x 11⅝ in., (305 x 295 mm.), color lithograph on wove (BP 631, DM 1529, FR 5191, Y 121,472).

$4400* *Hombre Con Baston, 1979,* crayon s., #8/99, Ediciones Poligrafa, S.A., excell. cond., (11-23-92, Sotheby-NY, #295, illus.), 21⅝ x 29½ in., (550 x 750 mm.), etching p. in colors (BP 2877, DM 7045, FR 23,900, Y 545,838).

$2475* *Hombre Con Los Brazos Sobre La Cabeza, 1984,* s., #77/99, pub. Ediciones Poligrafia, very good cond.?, (10-28-92, Butterfield, #2580), 29½ x 22 in., (749 x 559 mm.), color etching w/embossing on hand-made (BP 1577, DM 3822, FR 12,979, Y 303,681).

$1100* *Hombre Con Sombrero, c. 1965,* s., #91/100, pub. Ediciones Poligrafa, blindstamp, full sheet, touched in scuffs, remains tape/glue, other defects, sold after sale, (11-24-92, Christie-NY, #360, illus.), sheet 30½ x 22¼ in., (775 x 565 mm.), color lithograph on Arches (BP 725, DM 1761, FR 5975, Y 136,459).

$2090* *Hombre En Rosa,* s. in crayon, annot. HC, pub. Poligrafa S.A., full margins, apparently very good cond., (02-24-93, Butterfield, #2682, illus.), 29½ x 21¾ in., (749 x 552 mm.), etching & aquatint in colors on handmade paper (BP 1457, DM 3393, FR 11,502, Y 245,248).

$2475* *Hombre, Luna Y Estrellas, 1950,* s., #XXVII/LX, fair cond.; yellowing, water stains verso, (11-23-92, Sotheby-NY, #287, illus.), image 17¾ x 13¼ in., (450 x 335 mm.), lithograph p. in colors (BP 1618, DM 3963, FR 13,444, Y 307,034).

$3575* *Hombre, c. 1969,* s., #P/A, good cond., handling creases, yellowing, (11-23-92, Sotheby-NY, #290, illus.), image 25⅝ x 19¼ in., (650 x 490 mm.), lithograph p. in colors (BP 2337, DM 5724, FR 19,419, Y 443,493).

$4400* *Interior Con Sandia, 1975,* crayon s., #46/75, Ediciones Poligrafa, S.A., excell. cond., (11-23-92, Sotheby-NY, #292, illus.), 22 x 29⅞ in., (560 x 760 mm.), etching p. in colors (BP 2877, DM 7045, FR 23,900, Y 545,838).

$1411* *Komposition Med Figur Och Faglar,* s., 147/200, blindstamp Guilde de la Gravure, (12-04-92, AB Stockholm, #7152), 12¹⁵⁄₁₆ x 19¹¹⁄₁₆ in., (33 x 50 cm.), lithograph in colors on Arches (BP 905, DM 2247, FR 7623, Y 176,155, SK 9570).

$532* *Komposition Mit Blau Und Rosa,* s., num., light-staining, (06-08-93, Karl/Faber, #1351), approx. 16⁵⁄₁₆ x 23¹⁄₁₆ in., (41.5 x 58.5 cm.), color lithograph on Arches wove (BP 350, DM 863, FR 2907, Y 56,506).

BI *Loco, c. 1965,* s., #7/100, ded., full margins, good cond., yellowing, est. $2,5/3,500, (11-23-92, Sotheby-NY, #289, illus.), image 26 x 20⅛ in., (660 x 510 mm.), lithograph p. in colors.

BI *Manos En Rojos, 1979,* s. in black crayon, num. 94/99, pub. Poligrafa S.A., good cond., surface abrasion, thinned area, hinge removal, est. $2/3,000, (02-24-93, Butterfield, #2677, illus.), 21⅞ x 29½ in., (556 x 749 mm.), etching & aquatint in colors on Guarro paper.

BI *Manos En Rojos, 1979,* s., #14/99, pub. Poligrafa, S.A., good cond.?, est. $2/4,000, (05-19-93, Butterfield, #1852), 21⅞ x 29¾ in., (556 x 756 mm.), etching and aquatint in color on Guarro.

$1725* *Mother And Child, c. 1957,* s., #23/100, full margins, mat staining, tear, very good cond., (05-17-93, Christie-NY, #308, illus.), 21⅛ x 17 in., (537 x 432 mm.), lithograph in colors on wove (BP 1125, DM 2783, FR 9375, Y 192,094).

$1035* *Mujer Al Amanecer, 1958,* s., #33/100, full margins, staining, creasing, tears, old tape, (05-17-93, Christie-NY, #309), 25¼ x 19⅝ in., (641 x 498 mm.), lithograph in colors on Arches (BP 675, DM 1670, FR 5625, Y 115,256).

$4025* *Mujer Con Sandia, c. 1950,* s., #198/200, full margins, mat staining, surface soiling, good cond., (05-17-93, Christie-NY, #307), 21½ x 17 in., (546 x 432 mm.), lithograph in colors on Arches (BP 2626, DM 6494, FR 21,875, Y 448,218).

BI *Mujer En Negro,* crayon s., #67/75, very good cond., est. $2/4,000, (05-19-93, Butterfield, #1855, illus.), 30 x 22 in., (762 x 559 mm.), lithograph in colors on wove.

$1955* *Mujer, c. 1969,* s., #27/100, good cond., handling creases, yellowing, (05-18-93, Sotheby-NY, #274, illus.), image 30½ x 21¾ in., (775 x 552 mm.), lithograph p. in colors (BP 1273, DM 3172, FR 10,712, Y 217,876).

$1320* *Mujeres Portfolio: Deux Tetes, 1969,* s., annot. XVIII/XXV, pub. Touchstone Publishers, full margins, good-cond., hinge remains, rubbed areas, surface soiling, (10-28-92, Butterfield, #2574), 27½ x 21¼ in., (699 x 540 mm.), color lithograph on BFK Rives (BP 841, DM 2039, FR 6922, Y 161,963).

$1210* *Mujeres Portfolio: Femme En Mauve, 1969,* s., #52/150, pub. Touchstone Publishers, full margins, good cond., creases, surface soiling, (10-28-92, Butterfield, #2575, illus.), 26⅞ x 20¾ in., (683 x 527 mm.), color litho-graph on BFK Rives (BP 771, DM 1869, FR 6345, Y 148,466).

$1100* *Mujeres Portfolio: Torse De Jeune Fille, 1969,* ink s., i., p. Atelier Desjobert, pub. Touchstone Publishers, full margins, good cond., hinge remains, surface soiling, (10-28-92, Butterfield, #2576), 27 x 21 in., (686 x 533 mm.), color lithograph on BFK Rives (BP 701, DM 1699, FR 5768, Y 134,969).

$1870* *Mujeres Portfolio: Venus Noire, 1969,* s., #20/150, mar-gins, good cond., mat staining, creases, staining, scuffing, (10-28-92, Butterfield, #2577), 29¹⁰⁄₁₆ x 22⁴⁄₁₆ in., (752 x 565 mm.), color lithograph on wove (BP 1191, DM 2888, FR 9806, Y 229,448).

$1380* *Mujeres: Demi-Poisson, 1969,* s., #107/150, pub. Touch-stone Publishers, p. Atelier Desjobert, margins, good cond., shrink-wrapper, (05-19-93, Butterfield, #1848), 21 x 28 in., (533 x 711 mm.), lithograph in colors on wove (BP 896, DM 2243, FR 7558, Y 152,773).

$1045* *Mujeres: Femme Au Collant Noir, 1969,* s., num. 43/150, pub. Touchstone Publishers, margins, apparently good-cond., creases, (02-24-93, Butterfield, #2675), 27½ x 21¼ in., (699 x 540 mm.), lithograph in colors on BFK Rives (BP 729, DM 1696, FR 5751, Y 122,624).

$1320* *Mujeres: Femme Au Collant Rose, 1969,* s., annot. XVIII/XXV, pub. Touchstone Publishers, full margins, goodcond., creases, tape, glue remains, stray printing ink, surface soiling, (02-24-93, Butterfield, #2676), 27½ x 20⅞ in., (699 x 530 mm.), lithograph in colors on Japan (BP 921, DM 2143, FR 7265, Y 154,893).

$1035* *Mujeres: Femme Au Collant Rose, 1969,* s., #43/150, pub. Touchstone Publishers, p. Atelier Desjobert, good cond., (05-19-93, Butterfield, #1849), 27½ x 20¾ in., (699 x 527 mm.), lithographs in color on BFK Rives (BP 672, DM 1682, FR 5668, Y 114,580).

$1610* *Mujeres: Femme Souriante, 1969,* s., #107/150, pub. Touchstone Publishers, p. Atelier Desjobert, margins, good cond., shrink-wrapped, (05-19-93, Butterfield, #1850), 21¼ x 27¾ in., (540 x 705 mm.), lithographs in color on wove (BP 1045, DM 2617, FR 8817, Y 178,235).

$1540* *Mujeres: Torso De Femme, 1969,* s., num. 43/150, pub. Touchstone Publishers, full margins, apparentlygood cond., creases, (02-24-93, Butterfield, #2672, illus.), 27½ x 21 in., (699 x 533 mm.), lithograph in colors on BFK Rives (BP 1074, DM 2500, FR 8476, Y 180,709).

$1210* *Mujeres: Torso De Jeune Fille, 1969,* s., num. 43/150, pub. Touchstone Publishers, full margins, apparentlygood cond., creases, (02-24-93, Butterfield, #2674), 27½ x 21 in., (699 x 533 mm.), lithograph in colors on BFK Rives (BP 844, DM 1964, FR 6659, Y 141,985).

BI *Mujeres: Venus Noire, 1969,* s., num. XX/XXV, pub. Touchstone Publishers, margins, good cond. (?),est. $1/2,000, (02-24-93, Butterfield, #2673), 27½ x 21 in., (699 x 533 mm.), lithograph in colors on BFK Rives.

$1146* *Muyer En Blanco, 1975,* #14/75, s., (12-15-92, Finarte-Milan, #66), 29¹⁵⁄₁₆ x 22¹⁄₁₆ in., (76 x 56 cm.), etching (BP 731, DM 1796, FR 6138, Y 142,131, L 1610).

$1610* *La Negresse,* s., #80/150, from Mujeres Suite, pub. A. Lubin, very good cond., (05-18-93, Sotheby-NY, #276, illus.), image 27¼ x 20⅞ in., (692 x 530 mm.), litho-graph p. in colors (BP 1049, DM 2612, FR 8822, Y 179,427).

$4313* *Nocturno, 1975,* s., #p de a IX/X in crayon, Ediciones Poligrafa, S.A., excell. cond., (05-18-93, Sotheby-NY, #278, illus.), 22 x 29⅞ in., (559 x 759 mm.), etching p. in colors (BP 2809, DM 6998, FR 23,633, Y 480,664).

$1276* *Obscure Man,* s., num., blindstamp, (06-08-93, Karl/Faber, #1350), approx. 25⅜ x 19½ in., (64.5 x 49.5 cm.), color lithograph on wove (BP 839, DM 2070, FR 6973, Y 135,528).

$2645* *Paisaje Azteca, 1950,* s., #130/200, blind stamp of Guilde de la Gravure, i., full margins,fair cond., yellowing, fox-ing, light-staining, tape marks, (05-18-93, Sotheby-NY, #272, illus.), (321 x 492 mm.), lithograph p. in colors (BP 1723, DM 4292, FR 14,493, Y 294,773).

$2475* *El Perro, 1975,* s., #35/100, p. Mixografia, blindstamp pub. Taller de Grafica Mexicana, very good cond.?, (10-28-92, Butterfield, #2578), 22¼ x 29⅞ in., (565 x 759 mm.), color mixograph on cream wove (BP 1577, DM 3822, FR 12,979, Y 303,681).

$3300* *Personaje Con Rojo,* s., num. 77/100, full margins, apparently very good cond., (02-24-93, Butterfield, #2680, illus.), 31½ x 24 in., (800 x 610 mm.), intaglio in colors on heavy handmade paper (BP 2301, DM 5357, FR 18,162, Y 387,233).

$1840* *Personaje En Fondo Negro, 1976,* crayon s., #47/75, pub. Poligrafa, S.A., good cond., (05-19-93, Butterfield, #1851), 22½ x 29¾ in., (572 x 756 mm.), etching and aquatint on Guarro (BP 1194, DM 2991, FR 10,077, Y 203,698).

$1610* *Pez Con Limones, 1969,* from Mujeres, s., #XI/XXV, pub. Touchstone Publishers, full margins,excell. cond., (05-17-93, Christie-NY, #312), 21 x 27¾ in., (533 x 705 mm.), lithograph in colors on BFK Rives (BP 1050, DM 2598, FR 8750, Y 179,287).

$2750* *Portrait De Femme, 1969,* s., from Mujeres Suite, #124/150, pub. Lublin Inc., good cond., (11-23-92, Sotheby-NY, #293, illus.), image 27⅛ x 20⅞ in., (690 x 530 mm.), lithograph p. in colors (BP 1798, DM 4403, FR 14,938, Y 341,149).

BI *Salome, 1984,* s., num. 22/250, blindstamp of pub. Met-ropolitan Opera Association/Circle Fine Art, good cond., est. $1/2,000, (02-24-93, Butterfield, #2678), 30 x 21⅞ in., (762 x 556 mm.), lithograph in colors on heavy wove.

$1320* *Salome, 1984,* num., s., p. for Metropolitan Opera Asso-ciation, co-pub. Circle FineArts, (05-27-93, Swann, #269, illus.), sh 29¾ x 21¾ in., (75.6 x 55.2 cm.), color lithograph (BP 845, DM 2118, FR 7139, Y 141,509).

$3450* *Sandias, 1969,* from Mujeres, s., #116/150, pub. Touch-stone Publishers, full margins, crease, excell. cond., (05-17-93, Christie-NY, #311, illus.), (699 x 533 mm.), litho-graph in colors on BFK Rives (BP 2250, DM 5566, FR 18,750, Y 384,187).

$5750* *Sandias, 1969,* from Mujeres, s., #44/150, pub. Touch-stone Publishers, full margins,crease, excell. cond., (05-17-93, Christie-NY, #310, illus.), 20⅞ x 27½ in., (530 x 699 mm.), lithograph in colors on BFK Rives (BP 3751, DM 9277, FR 31,250, Y 640,312).

$767* *(Scarecrow),* s., #192/200, full margins, good cond., creases, (12-03-92, Sotheby-London, #803, illus.), 19¾ x 13½ in., (500 x 340 mm.), lithograph in colors on Arches (BP 495, DM 1206, FR 4117, Y 95,434).

$3025* *"Seated Man",* s., #HC 5/25, blindstamp pub. Transworld Art, very good cond.?, (10-28-92, Butterfield, #2581), 30¼ x 22½ in., (768 x 572 mm.), color etching w/embossing on wove (BP 1927, DM 4672, FR 15,863, Y 371,166).

$2200* *Sin Titulo, c. 1950,* s., #81/100, wide margins, light-staining, creasing, hole, extensiveskinning verso, (11-24-92, Christie-NY, #358, illus.), borderline 21⅛ x 17 in., (537 x 432 mm.), color lithograph on BFK (BP 1449, DM 3522, FR 11,950, Y 272,919).

$303* *Small Monument, 1966,* s., t., d., excell. cond.?, (10-10-92, Litchfield, #205), image 12 x 9½ in., (30.5 x 24.1 cm.), color aquatint (BP 180, DM 450, FR 1511, Y 36,888).

$2475* *Tres Manos,* s., #51/75, very good cond.?, (10-28-92, Butterfield, #2582, illus.), 22¼ x 29¼ in., (565 x 743 mm.), color etching w/embossing on wove (BP 1577, DM 3822, FR 12,979, Y 303,681).

$1210* *Untitled, From Mujeres, 1969,* s., #108/150, pub. Touchstone Publishers, p. Atelier Desjobert, fullmargins, image scratches, glue patches, skinned spot, (11-24-92, Christie-NY, #366, illus.), borderline 27¼ x 21 in., (692 x 534 mm.), color lithograph on BFK Rives (BP 797, DM 1937, FR 6573, Y 150,105).

$1650* *Untitled, From Mujeres, 1969,* s., #IX/XXV, pub. Touchstone Publishers, p. Aterlier Desjobert, margins, staining, remains glue, good cond., (11-24-92, Christie-NY, #365, illus.), borderline 21⅛ x 27⅝ in., (537 x 702 mm.), color lithograph on Japon nacre (BP 1087, DM 2642, FR 8963, Y 204,689).

$825* *Untitled, Man Holding Glass, c. 1958-9,* annot. printer's proof, good cond.?, (12-08-92, Swann, #293), 15 x 21 in., (38.1 x 53.3 cm.), color lithograph (BP 517, DM 1284, FR 4379, Y 102,256).

$3025* *Variation On A Man #2 (T. 1157), 1964,* s., #1/20, blindstamp pub. Tamarind Litho Workshop, good cond.?, crease, (10-28-92, Butterfield, #2573, illus.), 38½ x 28 in., (978 x 711 mm.), color lithograph on Rives BFK (BP 1927, DM 4672, FR 15,863, Y 371,166).

$3300* *Virgen De Guadalupe, c. 1930,* s., narrow margins, excell. cond., yellowing verso, (11-23-92, Sotheby-NY, #286, illus.), image 7¼ x 9½ in., (185 x 242 mm.), woodcut (BP 2158, DM 5283, FR 17,925, Y 409,378).

$935* *"Woman With Watermelon",* s. Tamayo, num. 41/200, (09-25-92, Wolf, #47, illus.), 21 x 16½ in., (53.3 x 41.9 cm.), lithograph in colors (BP 546, DM 1386, FR 4687, Y 112,855).

TAMES, George

BI *John F. Kennedy For The New York Times, 1962,* s., d., credit stamp, est. $1/1,500, (10-13-92, Christie-NY, #609, illus.), 10½ x 13¼ in., (26.7 x 33.7 cm.), photograph, gelatin silver print.

TANCONVILLE

$419* *PLM: Saint-Honore-Les-Bains, c. 1895,* excell. cond., (01-23-93, Ribeyre/Baron, #179), 42½ x 30¹¹⁄₁₆ in., (108 x 78 cm.), poster (BP 274, DM 666, FR 2254, Y 52,441).

$335* *PLM: Chatel-Guyon-Les-Bains, c. 1900,* good cond., (01-23-93, Ribeyre/Baron, #94), 44⁵⁄₁₆ x 30½ in., (112.5 x 77.5 cm.), poster (BP 219, DM 533, FR 1802, Y 41,927).

TANGUY, Yves French/American 1900-1955

$577* *Affiche Avant La Lettre Pour L'Exposition Y.T. De 1952,* s., d. 50 in stone, yellowed, (03-31-93, Briest, #E196), 25³⁄₁₆ x 16¹⁵⁄₁₆ in., (64 x 43 cm.), color lithograph (BP 381, DM 928, FR 3153, Y 66,352).

$605* *From Le Surrealisme En (W. 15/a; b), 1947: Two,* 1st bears sig., i. POUR JEAN L., margins, good cond., 1st w/crease, 2nd w/paper loss, tears, each w/staining, (02-24-93, Butterfield, #2976), 6¾ x 6 in., (171 x 152 mm.), 7¾ x 6 in., (171 x 152 mm.), etching & lithograph on wove (BP 422, DM 982, FR 3330, Y 70,993).

BI *Le Grand Passage (Wittrock 19 A, B and C), 1954,* set of three proofs, each s., last two i. e'preuve d'artiste etat definitif 2/6, good cond., light/mat stain, fox marks, margins, rubbing, est. $14/16,000, (11-05-92, Sotheby-NY, #445, illus.), first 8⅛ x 6⅜ in., (206 x 163 mm.), second, third 6¾ x 5⅜ in., (206 x 163 mm.), etchings, 1st p. w/relief & monotype coloring, 2nd & 3rd p. in teal blue & black; 1st on Arches wove; others on Japan.

$12,075* *Le Grand Passage (Wittrock 19 A, B and C), 1954: Set Of Three,* proofs, each s., last 2 i. epreuve d'artiste etat definitif 2/6, folded as a portfolio cover, good cond., mat/light-stain, fox marks, (05-13-93, Sotheby-NY, #828, illus.), first 8¼ x 6½ in., (209 x 164 mm.), 2nd, 3rd 6¾ x 5⅜ in., (209 x 164 mm.), etching, 1st p. w/relief & hand-coloring, 2nd & 3rd p. in teal blue &black, 1st on sheet of Arches wove (BP 7927, DM 19,498, FR 65,768, Y 1,348,108).

BI *L'Anthitete-Minuits Pour Geants (W. 17), 1947: Six,* 6 pl from set of 7, pub. by Bordas, 1949, full margins, good cond., loose, est. BP 1/1,200, (06-30-93, Sotheby-London, #688, illus.), each sh 5½ x 4⅜ in., (140 x 111 mm.), etching w/aquatint in color on wove.

$2574* *Ohne Titel (Wittrock 18), 1953,* s., pub. Sept Microbes Vus A Travers Un Temperament by Les Editions Cercle Des Arts, margin, good cond., (06-30-93, Sotheby-London, #687, illus.), sh 7¼ x 4⅞ in., (184 x 124 mm.), etching w/monotype in color (BP 1725, DM 4390, FR 14,810, Y 275,796).

$14,151* *Ohne Titel, (W. 2), 1934,* s., num. 9/10, pub. de luxe edit. of Primele Poeme, by T. Tzara, Editura Unu, margins, stitchmarks, crease, defects, (12-01-92, Christie-London, #543, illus.), P. 6⅝ x 4¹³⁄₁₆ in., (168 x 122 mm.), etching on simili-Japan (BP 9350, DM 22,555, FR 76,866, Y 1,761,828).

$2899* *Ohne Titel, Plate C From "Le Grand Passage" (Wittrock 19), 1953,* s., i. epreuve d'artiste etat definitif 5/6, working proofs, margins,good cond., handling marks, creases, hinge remains, (12-03-92, Sotheby-London, #581, illus.), 6¾ x 5¼ in., (173 x 134 mm.), etching w/aquatint in indigo on simili Japan (BP 1870, DM 4559, FR 15,561, Y 360,707).

$3054* *Pour: Andre Breton (Wittrock 11), 1946,* s., num., (06-23-93, Kornfeld, #805), etching on thick wove (BP 2075, DM 5168, FR 17,382, Y 332,716, SF 4600).

$6821* *Rhabdomancie (W. 13), 1947,* s., d. #40/70, from portfolio Brunidor portfolio number 1, pub. Brunidor Editions, margins, discoloration, foxing, pinholes, (12-03-92, Sotheby-London, #582, illus.), sheet 16⅛ x 12¾ in., (411 x 324 mm.), etching in colors on wove (BP 4400, DM 10,727, FR 36,613, Y 848,700).

$533* *Untitled,* bearing sig., tone, margins, mount-staining, very good cond., (12-01-92, Christie-London, #544), P. 6¾ x 4⅞ in., (172 x 124 mm.), etching on paper (BP 352, DM 850, FR 2895, Y 66,360).

$2990* *"Untitled" and "Untitled" (Wittrock 14B, and C), 1947: Two,* for Le Mythe de la Roche Percee, s., i. H.C., full margins, glue andstaining, losses, good cond., (05-11-93, Christie-NY, #336, illus.), each plate 6¾ x 4⅞ in., (171 x 124 mm.), etching on wove (BP 1909, DM 4710, FR 15,870, Y 328,897).

TANNER, Benjamin

$2070* *Macdonough's Victory On Lake Champlain, And Defeat Of The British Army At Plattsburg By Genl. Macomb, Septr. 11th 1814,* after H. Reinagle, p. Rogers & Eskr., pub. Tanner 1816, trimmed to platemark 3 sides, small margin below, good cond., water stains, skinned spots, tears, (01-28-93, Sotheby-NY, #445, illus.), sheet 19½ x 25¾ in., (495 x 654 mm.), engraving (BP 1367, DM 3280, FR 11,099, Y 257,015).

TANNER, Benjamin, engraver American 1775-1848

$550* *"MacDonough's Victory On Lake Champlain...", 1816,* ident. w/in plate, (06-05-93, Skinner, #398), sheet, sight 18½ x 24¾ in., (47 x 62.9 cm.), engraving on paper (BP 362, DM 892, FR 3005, Y 59,000).

TANNER, Henry O. American 1859-1937

$2090* *Tangiers,* s. verso by artist's son Jesse O. Tanner, num. 84/120, very good cond., (09-27-92, Bakker, #44, illus.), plate 6¾ x 9¼ in., (17.1 x 23.5 cm.), etching (BP 1220, DM 3098, FR 10,476, Y 252,263).

TANNER, Robin   British b. 1904
BI   *Country Scene By Moonlight,* s. Robin Tanner, est. $2/
    500, (12-12-92, Wolf, #23), 7 x 9½ in., (17.8 x 24.1
    cm.), etching.

TANNING, Dorothea   American b. 1912
$325* *Bonjour Max Ernst, 1974,* s., num., (11-28-92, Schopp-
    mann, #828), 14¾ x 19⁵⁄₁₆ in., (37.5 x 49 cm.), color
    etching on Arches wove (BP 215, DM 518, FR 1758, Y
    40,448).
$137* *"Composition Surrealiste",* E.A., s., (01-28-93, Pescheteau,
    #263), a vue 20½ x 13¾ in., (52 x 35 cm.), color litho-
    graph on wove (BP 90, DM 217, FR 735, Y 17,010).
$337* *"En Chair Et En Os", 1973:* Set of Ten, #73/100, s.,
    (10-18-92, Pescheteau, #265), each 16¹⁵⁄₁₆ x 12⅝ in., (43
    x 32 cm.), etching and aquatint on Arches (BP 204, DM
    498, FR 1691, Y 40,239).
$165* *Untitled,* s., #14/40, (10-18-92, Hindman, #485A), 5½ x
    16¼ in., (14 x 41.3 cm.), color soft ground etching on
    BFK Rives (BP 101, DM 246, FR 833, Y 19,796).
BI   *Untitled Image from XX Siecle, 1974,* s. Dorothea Tan-
    ning, num. 63/75, good cond., light toning, est. $2/300,
    (09-11-92, Skinner, #112A), 12¼ x 9⅞ in., (31.1 x 25.1
    cm.), lithograph in colors on wove.

TANOBE, Miyuki   b. 1937
$178* *"Le Depart Pour L'Eglise",* #26/125, t., s., d. Tanobe 83,
    (03-16-93, Encans, #114), 17¹¹⁄₁₆ x 13⁹⁄₁₆ in., (45 x 34.5
    cm.), serigraph (BP 123, DM 296, FR 1006, Y 20,814,
    C$ 222).
$160* *"Elle Demanda Un Coca-Cola, Un Hot-Dog",* #26/125, t.,
    s., d. Tanobe 83, (03-16-93, Encans, #113), 17¹¹⁄₁₆ x
    13⁹⁄₁₆ in., (45 x 34.5 cm.), serigraph (BP 110, DM 266,
    FR 904, Y 18,709, C$ 200).
$261* *"Le Restaurant Du Quartier",* #112/135, s., t. Tanobe 83,
    (07-14-92, Encans, #169), 13¹⁵⁄₁₆ x 22¹⁄₁₆ in., (35.5 x 56
    cm.), serigraph (BP 136, DM 387, FR 1306, Y 32,637,
    C$ 311).

TANQUERAY, Paul
$693* *Gertrude Lawrence In Candle Light, Empire Theatre,
    30th September 1929:* Two, each photog.'s credit stamp,
    d., other annots. verso, (12-17-92, Christie-S. Ken, #15,
    illus.), one 9¼ x 7½ in., (23.5 x 19.1 cm.), the other
    9½ x 7½ in., (23.5 x 19.1 cm.), photograph, gelatin sil-
    ver print (BP 440, DM 1082, FR 3696, Y 85,167).

TAPIES, Antonio   Spanish b. 1924
$4140* *A4, 1985,* s., #3/99, pub. Ediciones La Poligrafa, excell.
    cond.?, (05-11-93, Christie-NY, #339), sheet 29¼ x 29¼
    in., (743 x 743 mm.), aquatint and carborundum in red
    and black on tan (red color) Guarro (BP 2643, DM
    6522, FR 21,975, Y 455,395).
$1876* *Addicio De Petjades (G. 295), 1972,* s., #61/75, p., pub.
    La Poligrafa, full margins, good cond., creases, (12-03-
    92, Sotheby-London, #817, illus.), sheet 30⅝ x 22¾ in.,
    (777 x 580 mm.), aquatint and carborundum in colors on
    Velin Guarro (BP 1210, DM 2950, FR 10,070, Y
    233,420).
$866* *Affiche Avant La Lettre #173, 1979,* #127/150, pencil s.,
    (11-20-92, Lempertz, #896), sh 25⁹⁄₁₆ x 19¹¹⁄₁₆ in., (65 x
    50 cm.), color lithograph on Velin (BP 570, DM 1381,
    FR 4651, Y 107,698).
BI   *"Album St. Gallen" Sheet I, II, VIII and X (Galfetti Band
    I 123, 125,130 and 132):* Four, #14/75, pencil s., est.
    DM 4,800, (11-20-92, Lempertz, #888), sh, approx. 22¼
    x 30⅛ in., (56.5 x 76.5 cm.), color lithograph on Velin
    on BFK Rives.
BI   *"Album St. Gallen", Sheet VI, VIII and IX (Galfetti Band
    I 122, 128,130 and 131):* Three, #35/75, pencil s., est.
    DM 3,600, (11-20-92, Lempertz, #889), sh, approx. 22¼
    x 30⅛ in., (56.5 x 76.5 cm.), color lithograph on Velin
    on BFK Rives.
BI   *Andre Du Bouchet. Air (G. 252-270), 1971,* book, and
    separate suite of s. prints, t., text, just., s. by artist and
    author, num. 10, pub. Maeght, good cond., loose, est. BP
    2,5/3,500, (12-03-92, Sotheby-London, #815), overall
    size 11½ x 9 in., (290 x 230 mm.), 14 etchings and
    lithographs on Japon Hosho, on Moulin Richard de Bas.
BI   *Aparicions 8, c. 1980,* s., #2/99, full margins, good
    cond., creases, est. BP 7/900, (06-30-93, Sotheby-London,

#940, illus.), 82¼ x 10⅝ in., (208.9 x 27 cm.), aquatint
    and embossing in black, grey and white on wove.
$1535* *Arc Blau (G. 288), 1972,* s., #61/75, p., pub. La Poli-
    grafa, good cond., creases, (12-03-92, Sotheby-London,
    #814, illus.), sheet 23 x 30⅝ in., (582 x 775 mm.),
    aquatint w/carborundum in colors on Velin Guarro (BP
    990, DM 2414, FR 8239, Y 190,992).
$1222* *Arc Et Colonnes (Galf. 580), 1976,* s., num., (06-23-93,
    Kornfeld, #816), color etching (BP 830, DM 2068, FR
    6955, Y 133,130, SF 1840).
$1540* *Arc Negre Amb Lletres (G. 508), 1975,* s., 72/75, ed. La
    Poligrafa, (12-04-92, AB Stockholm, #7148), 17⅛ x 24⅝
    in., (43.5 x 62.5 cm.), carborundum engraving in colors
    and etching on Guarro (BP 988, DM 2453, FR 8320, Y
    192,260, SK 10,450).
BI   *Bande Rouge, 1984,* s., #23/50, full margins, good cond.,
    crease, est. BP 7/900, (06-30-93, Sotheby-London,
    #945), 11¾ x 15½ in., (298 x 394 mm.), etching in red
    and black on chine applique mounted on Arches.
BI   *Barcelona, Sala Gaspar, 1963:* Twenty-Two, from El Pa
    A La Barca by Joan Brossa, s. in colophon by artist and
    author, est. SF 9/10,000, (11-15-92, Christie-Geneva,
    #318, illus.), 15¾ x 11⁷⁄₁₆ in., (400 x 290 mm.), litho-
    graph and collage.
BI   *Barret De Copa Imantat (Galfetti 6), 1947-48,* s., #7/50,
    from Nou variacions sobre tres gravats de 1947-1948,
    pub.Sala Gaspar, est. DM 5,000, (06-12-93, Hauswedell/
    Nolt, #407, illus.), 9¾ x 6¾ in., (24.8 x 17.1 cm.), color
    etching on thick wove.
$2524* *Barriere Marron (Galfetti Band II 583), 1976,* #15/50,
    pencil s., (11-20-92, Lempertz, #894, illus.), sh 30⅛ x
    22⁷⁄₁₆ in., (76.5 x 57 cm.), etching on heavy Velin (BP
    1662, DM 4024, FR 13,555, Y 313,891).
$1023* *Berlin Suite (G. 483), 1974,* s., #28/150, p. Propylaen,
    pub. Poligrafa, good cond., (12-03-92, Sotheby-London,
    #823), sheet 30 x 21¾ in., (760 x 552 mm.), lithograph
    in greys and black on wove (BP 660, DM 1609, FR
    5491, Y 127,286).
BI   *Berlin Suite: Untitled (G. 478), 1975,* s., #20/150, p. by
    Poligrafa, pub. Propylaen Verlag, good cond., est.BP 800/
    1,200, (06-30-93, Sotheby-London, #934, illus.), sh 21⅝
    x 30 in., (549 x 762 mm.), color lithograph on wove.
BI   *Berlin Suite: Untitled (G. 480), 1975,* s., #20/150, p. by
    Poligrafa, pub. Propylaen Verlag, good cond., est.BP 800/
    1,200, (06-30-93, Sotheby-London, #935, illus.), sh 21⅝
    x 30 in., (549 x 762 mm.), color lithograph on wove.
$1201* *Berlin Suite: Untitled (G. 482), 1975,* s., #20/150, p. by
    Poligrafa, pub. Propylaen Verlag, good cond., (06-30-93,
    Sotheby-London, #933, illus.), sh 21⅝ x 30 in., (549 x
    762 mm.), color lithograph on wove (BP 805, DM 2048,
    FR 6910, Y 128,683).
BI   *Berlin Suite: Untitled (G. 484), 1975,* s., #20/150, p. by
    Poligrafa, pub. Propylaen Verlag, good cond., est.BP 800/
    1,200, (06-30-93, Sotheby-London, #942, illus.), sh 29⅞ x
    21¾ in., (759 x 552 mm.), color lithograph on wove.
$575* *Black Litho (Galfetti 22), 1959,* s., #43/50, pub. Sala
    Gaspar, full margins, tear, discoloration, creases, good
    cond., (02-11-93, Sotheby-NY, #447), 18³⁄₁₆ x 28⅞ in.,
    (462 x 734 mm.), lithograph on BFK Rives (BP 406,
    DM 952, FR 3223, Y 69,319).
$1286* *Blank Central, c. 1980,* s., #5/99, full margins, good
    cond., creases, (06-30-93, Sotheby-London, #947), 19¼
    x 16¼ in., (489 x 413 mm.), etching, aquatint and
    embossing in color on wove (BP 862, DM 2193, FR
    7399, Y 137,791).
BI   *Bodego (G. 685), 1978,* s., #67/75, full margins, good
    cond., est. BP 8/1,000, (12-03-92, Sotheby-London,
    #828), 15 x 20½ in., (382 x 522 mm.), aquatint in col-
    ors w/embossing on thin grey paper supported on wove.
$1080* *Calligraphique, 1987,* s., #32/75, good cond., discolora-
    tion, (06-30-93, Sotheby-London, #946, illus.), sh 45⅞ x
    30½ in., (116.5 x 77.5 cm.), offset lithograph in black
    and beige on wove (BP 724, DM 1842, FR 6214, Y
    115,718).
$1045* *Cercle, 1981,* s., #62/75, pub. La Poligrafia, S.A., full
    margins, very good cond.,surface soiling, light-struck,
    (10-28-92, Butterfield, #3140), 15½ x 11¼ in., (394 x
    286 mm.), color aquatint w/etching and carborundum on
    Guarro paper (BP 666, DM 1614, FR 5480, Y 128,221).

$4688* *Cintaroja, 1979,* #42/99, pencil s., (11-20-92, Lempertz, #897, illus.), 32⅞ x 27 3/16 in., (83.5 x 69 cm.), etching on heavy Velin (BP 3087, DM 7474, FR 25,177, Y 583,012).

$1875* *Les Ciseaux (Galfetti Band I 193), 1969,* #29/75, pencil s., (11-20-92, Lempertz, #891), sh 30 x 22 13/16 in., (76.2 x 58 cm.), etching w/embossing on heavy Velin (BP 1235, DM 2989, FR 10,070, Y 233,180).

$1222* *Composition,* s. Tapies, 13/50, (09-30-92, Kunsthallen, #278), lithograph (BP 689, DM 1733, FR 5861, Y 146,646, DK 6670).

$2490* *Composition "A - B",* s., num., (12-01-92, Karl/Faber, #1288, illus.), 15⅜ x 11 in., (39 x 28 cm.), aquatint and relief print in black and red w/carborundum on Guarro wove (BP 1645, DM 3969, FR 13,525, Y 310,010).

$777* *Composition (Galfetti 285), 1971,* s., #77/100, (06-12-93, Hauswedell/Nolt, #414), 9 7/16 x 14 9/16 in., (24 x 37 cm.), color lithograph on thick wove (BP 509, DM 1265, FR 4251, Y 81,764).

$1330* *Composition (Galfetti 303),* s., 12/75, (12-04-92, AB Stockholm, #7145), 28¾ x 38 15/16 in., (73 x 99 cm.), aquatint in colors (BP 853, DM 2118, FR 7185, Y 166,042, SK 9020).

$686* *Composition (Galfetti 32), 1960,* s., d., #13/50, pub. Sala Gaspar, margins, good cond., mount-staining, strips of Japan in margins, (06-30-93, Sotheby-London, #928, illus.), sh 32⅞ x 25⅝ in., (835 x 651 mm.), lithograph w/embossing in black and grey on wove (BP 460, DM 1170, FR 3947, Y 73,503).

$3969* *Composition 3 (Mit Blatt Und Kreuz),* s., num., (06-08-93, Karl/Faber, #1354, illus.), sh approx. 37 x 52⅜ in., (94 x 133 cm.), color etching w/aquatint and carborundum on wove (BP 2609, DM 6440, FR 21,689, Y 421,561).

$853* *"Composition A T",* s., (10-18-92, Pescheteau, #266), 24 x 30 11/16 in., (61 x 78 cm.), lithograph in colors on Arches (BP 517, DM 1260, FR 4280, Y 101,851).

BI *Composition In Grey And White, c. 1980,* s., #43/50, margins, good cond., crease, creases, est. BP 7/800, (06-30-93, Sotheby-London, #936), sh 26 x 19¼ in., (660 x 489 mm.), aquatint w/carborundum and embossing in color on Arches.

$377* *Composition With T, c. 1980,* s., i. HC, full margins, good cond., crease, foxing, creases, (06-30-93, Sotheby-London, #926, illus.), 19½ x 15⅝ in., (495 x 397 mm.), color lithograph on Arches (BP 253, DM 643, FR 2169, Y 40,394).

$483* *"Composition",* #42/100, s., (01-28-93, Pescheteau, #264), 21⅝ x 28¾ in., (55 x 73 cm.), black lithograph and embossing (BP 319, DM 765, FR 2590, Y 59,970).

$1194* *(Composition), 1981,* s., #H.C. 22/25, margins, good cond., (12-03-92, Sotheby-London, #826), 29⅞ x 22 in., (757 x 558 mm.), lithograph in brown, black and beige on wove (BP 770, DM 1878, FR 6409, Y 148,563).

$1332* *Composition, (G. 35), 1960,* s., d., num. 7/50, pub. Sala Gaspar, margins, nicks, creases, rubbing, surface dirt, (12-01-92, Christie-London, #634), L. 21¼ x 29½ in., (540 x 750 mm.), lithograph p. in colors (BP 880, DM 2123, FR 7235, Y 165,837).

BI *Composition, c. 1980,* s., #57/99, good cond., est. 2/3,000, (06-30-93, Sotheby-London, #941, illus.), sh 38¾ x 49⅜ in., (98.4 x 125.4 cm.), aquatint and carborundum in color on pale green wove.

$1498* *Compositions (G. 74-5), 1964: Two,* watermark, s., i. Prova d'artista VI, num. 42/50, pub. Kestner Gesellschaft, margins, creases, surface dirt, good cond., (12-01-92, Christie-London, #635), L. and smaller 19 11/16 x 25 in., (500 x 635 mm.), lithograph in colors on Guarro wove (BP 990, DM 2388, FR 8137, Y 186,504).

$1023* *Le Crin (G. 274), 1971,* s., #46/75, p., pub. Maeght, good cond., creases, (12-03-92, Sotheby-London, #824, illus.), sheet 35½ x 25 in., (900 x 635 mm.), etching in dark blue w/collage of vegetable horse hair on Chiffon deMandeure (BP 660, DM 1609, FR 5491, Y 127,286).

BI *Croix Carton, 1983,* s., #26/75, full margins, good cond., rubbed spot, est. BP 6/800, (06-30-93, Sotheby-London, #950, illus.), 24⅜ x 23¾ in., (619 x 603 mm.), lithograph w/embossing in brown on wove.

BI *Dechirure, 1982,* s., #18/75, good cond., est. BP 7/900, (06-30-93, Sotheby-London, #944, illus.), sh 40½ x 29¼ in., (102.9 x 74.3 cm.), lithograph and collage in color on wove.

$1011* *Dentelle (Galfetti 662), 1977,* s., num., (11-28-92, Schoppmann, #830), 28 9/16 x 39 9/16 in., (72.5 x 100.5 cm.), color lithograph on BFK Rives (BP 667, DM 1611, FR 5468, Y 125,825).

$1451* *Deux Croix, 1983,* s., num., (06-23-93, Kornfeld, #819), 22¼ x 28⅜ in., (56.5 x 72 cm.), color lithograph (BP 986, DM 2455, FR 8258, Y 158,078, SF 2185).

$3609* *Deux Noirs Et Carton (Galfetti 276), 1971,* s., num., (11-28-92, Schoppmann, #829), 14 3/16 x 15¾ in., (36 x 40 cm.), color etching w/embossing on Chiffon of Mandeure paper (BP 2382, DM 5750, FR 19,519, Y 449,160).

$597* *Deux Pieds Sur Ocre (G. 317), 1972,* s., #46/75, p., pub. Maeght, full margins, good cond., marks, creases, (12-03-92, Sotheby-London, #808), 15 x 22 in., (380 x 560 mm.), lithograph in colors on Arches (BP 385, DM 939, FR 3205, Y 74,281).

$1147* *Diana (Galfetti 346), 1973,* VIII/XX, s., (10-14-92, Germann, #447, illus.), 30⅛ x 21⅞ in., (765 x 555 mm.), color lithograph (BP 673, DM 1679, FR 5692, Y 138,997, SF 1495).

$1154* *Diana, 1973,* s., #18/100, (11-21-92, Schloss Ahlden, #2138, illus.), 24 13/16 x 20⅞ in., (63 x 53 cm.), colored lithograph on handmade paper (BP 760, DM 1840, FR 6198, Y 143,514).

BI *Diptyque (G. 594), 1976,* s., #16/50, pub. Galeria Maeght, margins, good cond., est. BP 1,4/1,800, (06-30-93, Sotheby-London, #938, illus.), sh 24¾ x 35¾ in., (629 x 908 mm.), aquatint, carborundum and collage in color on wove.

$4600* *Dos Cuses, Gris Y Huellas, Digitales 16323, 1977,* unique, s., pub. Fundacion Picasso-Raventos, good cond., (02-11-93, Sotheby-NY, #449), sheet 24¾ x 35⅝ in., (628 x 905 mm.), etching and aquatint p. in colors, handcoloring in gouache (BP 3246, DM 7620, FR 25,785, Y 554,551).

$453* *Ecriture (Galfetti 663), 1977,* E.a., s., (10-14-92, Germann, #454), 17 15/16 x 22 1/16 in., (455 x 560 mm.), lithograph (BP 266, DM 663, FR 2248, Y 54,896, SF 590).

$379* *Ecriture (Galfetti 663), 1977,* E.A., s., blindstamp, (04-21-93, Germann, #788), 17 11/16 x 22 1/16 in., (450 x 560 mm.), lithograph (BP 246, DM 606, FR 2049, Y 41,957, SF 552).

BI *Empreinte Barree, 1982,* s., #59/75, full margins, good cond., est. BP 7/900, (06-30-93, Sotheby-London, #948, illus.), 24 x 35½ in., (610 x 902 mm.), offset lithograph in black and beige on wove.

$543* *Empreintes Des Mains, 1980,* s., (10-14-92, Germann, #455), 21 7/16 x 26⅜ in., (545 x 670 mm.), color lithograph (BP 319, DM 795, FR 2695, Y 65,802, SF 708).

BI *Entercroise, 1981,* s., #15/50, full margins, good cond., creases, est. BP 1,4/1,600, (06-30-93, Sotheby-London, #949, illus.), sh 31⅜ x 47⅝ in., (79.7 x 121 cm.), aquatint and embossing in brown and beige on wove.

$1833* *Envelat, 1981,* s., num., (06-23-93, Kornfeld, #818), 24 x 27⅜ in., (61 x 69.5 cm.), color etching (BP 1245, DM 3102, FR 10,433, Y 199,695, SF 2760).

$1535* *Erinnerung: Set Of Five,* s., #93/100, full margins, good cond., (12-03-92, Sotheby-London, #820, illus.), overall sheet size 17¾ x 22½ in., (450 x 570 mm.), lithograph in black and beige (BP 990, DM 2414, FR 8239, Y 190,992).

$730* *Esperit Catala I (G. 391), 1974,* s., 24/75, ed. La Poligrafa, (12-04-92, AB Stockholm, #7146), 17 5/16 x 24 13/16 in., (44 x 63 cm.), aquatint, etching and relief prints in color on Guarro (BP 468, DM 1163, FR 3944, Y 91,136, SK 4950).

$646* *Falce E Martello,* #89/90, s., (03-25-93, Finarte-Rome, #19), aquatint and etching (BP 439, DM 1061, FR 3609, Y 75,679, L 1035).

$2327* *Figur In Rosa (Galfetti 129), 1965,* s., artist's proof, from Album St. Gallen, (09-25-92, Granier, #3021), sheet 22¼ x 30 3/16 in., (56.5 x 76.7 cm.), color lithograph on hand-made (BP 1359, DM 3449, FR 11,664, Y 280,869).

BI *Foc 2, 1981,* s., #1/50, pub. Gallerie Maeght, image creases, very good cond., est. $3/4,000, (05-11-93,

Christie-NY, #340, illus.), sheet 31 x 42½ in., (78.7 x 108 cm.), aquatint and carborundum in reds and black on Guarro.

$1863* *For Paroles Peintes V (Galfetti 519), 1975,* s., #56/75, (05-27-93, Lempertz, #1051), 15¹⁄₁₆ x 11¼ in., (38.3 x 28.6 cm.), color etching on Arches wove (BP 1193, DM 2989, FR 10,076, Y 199,721).

$1135* *Fora (G. 611), 1976,* from Negre I Roig, H.C., ed. La Poligrafa, (12-04-92, AB Stockholm, #7150), sh 22¹⁄₁₆ x 29½ in., (56 x 75 cm.), carborundum engraving in colors (BP 728, DM 1808, FR 6132, Y 141,698, SK 7700).

$4370* *Formes 1 Vernis, 1986,* s., #63/99, pub. Ediciones La Poligrafa, excell. cond., (05-11-93, Christie-NY, #341, illus.), sheet 37½ x 51 in., (95.3 x 129.5 cm.), color carborundum w/varnish and white paint on thick handmade (BP 2790, DM 6884, FR 23,195, Y 480,695).

$807* *From "Album St. Gallen", 1965,* artist's proof, s., (04-24-93, Kunsthaus, #795), 21¼ x 26⅜ in., (54 x 67 cm.), lithograph on Rives hand-made (BP 509, DM 1265, FR 4272, Y 89,053).

$742* *Grand A Et Rouge (Galfetti 533), 1975,* s., #62/75, (06-12-93, Hauswedell/Nolt, #416), 12⅜ x 18⅛ in., (31.5 x 46 cm.), color lithograph on thick wove (BP 486, DM 1208, FR 4059, Y 78,081).

BI *Grande Croix Collage (G. 604), 1976,* s., #24/50, pub. Maeght, margins, good cond., creases, est. BP 2/2,500, (06-30-93, Sotheby-London, #939, illus.), sh 25⅝ x 37⅜ in., (651 x 949 mm.), etching in red w/collage on Velin Guarro-Casas.

$1260* *Le Grande Gris (Galfetti 159), 1968,* s., 25/75, Ed. Maeght, (05-12-93, AB Stockholm, #7053), 60¼ x 40¹⁵⁄₁₆ in., (153 x 104 cm.), lithograph (BP 823, DM 2033, FR 6848, Y 140,672, SK 9350).

$3583* *La Grande Grise (Galfetti 159), 1968,* s., HC, (05-27-93, Lempertz, #1048, illus.), 60¹⁄₁₆ x 45¹¹⁄₁₆ in., (152.5 x 116 cm.), color lithograph on wove (BP 2295, DM 5749, FR 19,378, Y 384,112).

$1544* *La Grande Porte (G. 323), 1972,* s., #39/75, pub. Maeght, good cond., (06-30-93, Sotheby-London, #927, illus.), sh 35½ x 26½ in., (902 x 673 mm.), etching and embossing and collage in color on wove (BP 1035, DM 2633, FR 8884, Y 165,434).

$1279* *Gravier (G. 272), 1971,* s., #12/75, p., pub. Maeght, good cond., (tape stain, handling marks), (12-03-92, Sotheby-London, #813, illus.), sheet 24¾ x 35¼ in., (630 x 895 mm.), aquating w/carborundum in colors on Chiffon de Mandeure (BP 825, DM 2011, FR 6865, Y 159,139).

$620* *Gris Argentin,* s., #65/90, blindstamp, (09-18-92, Schloss Ahlden, #1070), 21¼ x 29⅛ in., (54 x 74 cm.), color lithograph on BFK Rives (BP 363, DM 920, FR 3147, Y 76,628).

$993* *Gris Argentin, 1984,* s., num., (06-23-93, Kornfeld, #821), 15⁹⁄₁₆ x 20¹⁄₁₆ in., (39.5 x 51 cm.), color lithograph (BP 675, DM 1680, FR 5652, Y 108,182, SF 1495).

$1803* *H Ronverse (Galfetti Band I 501), 1975,* #33/75, pencil s., (11-20-92, Lempertz, #893), sh 17½ x 22¹⁵⁄₁₆ in., (44.5 x 58.2 cm.), color etching on Velin (BP 1187, DM 2875, FR 9683, Y 224,226).

$2310* *"Hommage A Picasso" (Galfetti 373), 1973,* s., num., from series "Hommage A Picasso", Berlin, Propylaen pub., (11-28-92, Grisebach, #787, illus.), 23⅜ x 29¹³⁄₁₆ in., (59.3 x 75.8 cm.), colored lithograph on handmade (BP 1525, DM 3680, FR 12,493, Y 287,492).

$2452* *Le Huit (Galfetti Band I 202), 1969,* #38/75, pencil s., (11-20-92, Lempertz, #892, illus.), sh 16⅜ x 22¹⁵⁄₁₆ in., (41.6 x 58.3 cm.), etching on China (BP 1614, DM 3909, FR 13,169, Y 304,937).

BI *Joan Brossa.Poems From The Catalan, Volume II (G. 385-390), 1973,* second portfolio, p., pub. Ediciones La Poligrafa S A, full margins,good cond., est. BP 3/4,000, (12-03-92, Sotheby-London, #827, illus.), 30 x 22 in., (760 x 560 mm.), six lithographs in colors on Arches.

$919* *Komposition,* s., #10/10, (06-12-93, Hauswedell/Nolt, #409), 11⅝ x 15⁹⁄₁₆ in., (29.5 x 39.5 cm.), color lithograph on thick wove (BP 602, DM 1496, FR 5027, Y 96,706).

BI *Komposition,* 74/90, s., est. SF 1,2/1,500, (10-14-92, Germann, #449), 21¹⁄₁₆ x 29¹⁄₁₆ in., (535 x 738 mm.), lithograph.

BI *Komposition,* #52/150, s., blindstamp Erker Presse, est. SF 2,2/2,700, (11-13-92, Koller, #5445), 18⁹⁄₁₆ x 24⅝ in., (47.1 x 62.5 cm.), lithograph on wove.

$1311* *Komposition,* #137/150, s., (11-13-92, Koller, #5444), 19¹¹⁄₁₆ x 25⁹⁄₁₆ in., (50 x 65 cm.), lithograph on wove (BP 847, DM 2058, FR 6940, Y 162,716, SF 1856).

$1417* *Komposition,* s., num., blindstamp, (06-08-93, Karl/Faber, #1356), approx. 22¹³⁄₁₆ x 30¹¹⁄₁₆ in., (58 x 78 cm.), color lithograph on BFK Rives wove (BP 932, DM 2299, FR 7743, Y 150,505).

$2483* *Komposition (Galfetti 137), 1966,* s., num., staining, (09-25-92, Granier, #3022), 30⁵⁄₁₆ x 22⁷⁄₁₆ in., (77 x 57 cm.), color lithograph on hand-made (BP 1450, DM 3681, FR 12,446, Y 299,698).

$1201* *Komposition (Galfetti 31), 1960,* s., d., #25/50, Sala Gaspar, (06-12-93, Hauswedell/Nolt, #412, illus.), 20³⁄₁₆ x 29¹³⁄₁₆ in., (51.2 x 75.8 cm.), color lithograph and embossing on BFK Rives (BP 786, DM 1955, FR 6570, Y 126,381).

$1343* *Komposition (Galfetti 340), 1972,* #56/75, s., (04-21-93, Germann, #783), 29¹³⁄₁₆ x 21¼ in., (758 x 540 mm.), color lithograph on handmade Rives w/collage (BP 871, DM 2147, FR 7259, Y 148,677, SF 1955).

$777* *Komposition (Galfetti 36), 1960,* s., d., #9/50, Sala Gaspar, (06-12-93, Hauswedell/Nolt, #413), 16⁵⁄₁₆ x 25½ in., (41.5 x 64.7 cm.), color lithograph w/embossing on thick wove (BP 509, DM 1265, FR 4251, Y 81,764).

$886* *Komposition (Galfetti 47), 1963,* s., num., blindstamp, (06-08-93, Karl/Faber, #1352), approx. 18⅞ x 24¹³⁄₁₆ in., (48 x 63 cm.), color lithograph on BFK Rives wove (BP 582, DM 1438, FR 4842, Y 94,105).

$1986* *Komposition (Galfetti 478), 1974,* s., num., sheet 3 of series: Berlin-Suite, Propylaen Verlag, (06-05-93, Grisebach, #892, illus.), 21⅝ x 29¹⁵⁄₁₆ in., (55 x 76 cm.), color lithograph on wove (BP 1307, DM 3220, FR 10,852, Y 213,044).

$2887* *Komposition (Galfetti 688), 1978,* s., num., (11-28-92, Grisebach, #789, illus.), 7⅞ x 12⅝ in., (20 x 32 cm.), lithograph in 2 colors w/relief print on cardboard (BP 1906, DM 4599, FR 15,614, Y 359,303).

$2270* *Komposition (Galfetti 706), 1978/79,* s., num., H.C., (06-05-93, Grisebach, #894, illus.), 9⁷⁄₁₆ x 19⁵⁄₁₆ in., (24 x 49 cm.), color lithograph and relief print on corrugated board (BP 1494, DM 3680, FR 12,404, Y 243,510).

$474* *Komposition 8 Aus "Suite 63 x 90", 1980,* 20/90, s., blindstamp, lit., (06-24-93, Germann, #515), 24⅞ x 35½ in., (632 x 902 mm.), color lithograph (BP 312, DM 768, FR 2590, Y 50,847, SF 690).

$1588* *Komposition Aus "Mois Du Coeur" (Galfetti 340), 1972,* 46/75, s., (10-14-92, Germann, #457), 29¾ x 21¼ in., (755 x 540 mm.), color lithograph w/collage (BP 932, DM 2324, FR 7881, Y 192,438, SF 2070).

$1732* *Komposition In Grau (Galfetti 32), 1960,* s., d., num., (11-28-92, Grisebach, #785, illus.), 25¼ x 19⁵⁄₁₆ in., (64.2 x 49 cm.), colored lithograph w/relief on wove (BP 1143, DM 2759, FR 9367, Y 215,557).

$1086* *Komposition Med Sax,* H.C., s., (12-04-92, AB Stockholm, #7151), 26³⁄₁₆ x 23⁷⁄₁₆ in., (66.5 x 59.5 cm.), carborundum engraving in colors (BP 697, DM 1730, FR 5867, Y 135,581, SK 7370).

$573* *Komposition Mit Brauner Sichel,* s., #280/300, (05-08-93, Schloss Ahlden, #2876, illus.), 19¹¹⁄₁₆ x 25⁹⁄₁₆ in., (50 x 65 cm.), color lithograph on Arches-handmade (BP 374, DM 920, FR 3106, Y 64,030).

BI *Komposition Mit Gelbem Kreis,* #26/50, s., est. DM 2,800-, (05-27-93, Lempertz, #1057), 25⅞ x 19¾ in., (65.8 x 50.2 cm.), aquatint etching on cream wove.

$1079* *Komposition Mit Kreuz, 1971,* s., num., (12-01-92, Karl/Faber, #1287), 19⁵⁄₁₆ x 24⁷⁄₁₆ in., (49 x 62 cm.), color lithograph on Arches wove (BP 713, DM 1720, FR 5861, Y 134,338).

BI *Komposition Mit Roten Strichen (Galfetti 242a), 1970,* s., num, of series "Nocturn Matinal", est. DM 2,4/2,800, (11-28-92, Grisebach, #786, illus.), 22⅝ x 30⁵⁄₁₆ in., (57.4 x 77 cm.), colored lithograph w/serigraph with red chalk reworked on wove.

$289* *Komposition Mit Schwarzem A. (Galfetti 639), 1976,* (11-28-92, Grisebach, #788, illus.), 16⁵⁄₁₆ x 23¹⁄₁₆ in., (41.5 x 58.5 cm.), colored lithograph on handmade (BP 191, DM 460, FR 1563, Y 35,968).

$1433* *Komposition Mit Schwarzem Kreuz,* #2/45, s., (05-27-93, Lempertz, #1056), 15½ x 20⁹⁄₁₆ in., (39.3 x 52.2 cm.), color etching on cream wove (BP 918, DM 2299, FR 7750, Y 153,623).

$1059* *Komposition, 1980,* E.a., s., (10-14-92, Germann, #451), 24¹³⁄₁₆ x 35⁷⁄₁₆ in., (630 x 900 mm.), color lithograph (BP 622, DM 1550, FR 5256, Y 128,333, SF 1380).

BI *Komposition, 1980,* E.a., s., est. SF 1,3/1,600, (10-14-92, Germann, #452), 24¹³⁄₁₆ x 35⁷⁄₁₆ in., (630 x 900 mm.), color lithograph.

BI *Komposition, 1980,* E.a., s., est. SF 1,3/1,600, (10-14-92, Germann, #453), 24¹³⁄₁₆ x 35⁷⁄₁₆ in., (630 x 900 mm.), color lithograph.

$395* *Komposition, 1989,* s., d., (06-24-93, Germann, #516), 11 x 29¹⁵⁄₁₆ in., (280 x 760 mm.), lithograph w/blind relief print (BP 260, DM 640, FR 2158, Y 42,373, SF 575).

$1443* *A L'Encre, 1982,* s., #66/100, (11-21-92, Schloss Ahlden, #2137, illus.), 24⁵⁄₁₆ x 21¾ in., (61.8 x 55.2 cm.), colored lithograph on handmade paper (BP 950, DM 2301, FR 7750, Y 179,455).

BI *L'Escalier,* s., #9/60, full margins, good cond., creases, est. BP 7/900, (06-30-93, Sotheby-London, #925, illus.), 11⅝ x 15½ in., (295 x 394 mm.), color aquatint on chine applique.

BI *L'Oeil, 1984,* s., #10/50, full margins, good cond., creases, est. BP 7/900, (06-30-93, Sotheby-London, #943), 11¼ x 15½ in., (286 x 394 mm.), color aquatint on Arches.

$920* *Lacet De Corde (G. 199), 1969,* s., #21/75, pub. Maeght, full margins, good cond., foxing, creases, (02-11-93, Sotheby-NY, #448), 13¾ x 19⅞ in., (350 x 505 mm.), etching, w/relief on Chiffon de Mandeure (BP 649, DM 1524, FR 5157, Y 110,910).

BI *Le Lit (G. 205), 1969,* s., #54/75, p. and pub. Maeght, full margins, good cond., (06-30-93, Sotheby-London, #931), sh 22⅞ x 30¾ in., (581 x 781 mm.), etching w/aquatint in color on wove.

$468* *Lithograph In Black And Grey (G.V. 147), 1967,* s., #16/150, large margins, good cond., tape remains, surface soiling, light-staining, creases, (10-28-92, Butterfield, #3138), 25¾ x 19⅝ in., (654 x 498 mm.), color lithograph on cream wove (BP 298, DM 723, FR 2454, Y 57,423).

$1075* *Lithographie In Gelb, Grau, Schwarz Und Dunkelrot (Galfetti 286), 1971,* s., #37/100, (05-27-93, Lempertz, #1049), 35¼ x 25¼ in., (89.5 x 64.2 cm.), color lithograph on wove (BP 688, DM 1725, FR 5814, Y 115,244).

BI *Lithographie In Schwarz, Grau Und Rot (Galfetti Band I 137), 1968,* #136/150, pencil s., est. DM 1,500, (11-20-92, Lempertz, #890), sh 30½ x 22¼ in., (77.5 x 56.5 cm.), color lithograph on Velin.

$1803* *M Et Fleches, 1982,* #47/75, s., (11-13-92, Koller, #5441), 19¹¹⁄₁₆ x 24½ in., (50 x 62.2 cm.), lithograph on wove (BP 1165, DM 2830, FR 9545, Y 223,781, SF 2552).

$916* *La Main Jaune (Galf. 347), 1973,* s., p.a. for artist's proof, (06-23-93, Kornfeld, #811), color lithograph (BP 622, DM 1550, FR 5213, Y 99,793, SF 1380).

$707* *La Main Jaune (Galfetti 347), 1973,* s., #58/200, blindstamp, (06-12-93, Hauswedell/Nolt, #415), 20¹⁄₁₆ x 18⅛ in., (51 x 46 cm.), lithograph on Arches (BP 463, DM 1151, FR 3868, Y 74,398).

$2558* *Mains Et Croix (G. 495), 1975,* s., #19/75, pub. Maeght, full margins, good cond., creases, (12-03-92, Sotheby-London, #819, illus.), 17¼ x 27⅜ in., (438 x 694 mm.), aquatint in colors on Arches (BP 1650, DM 4023, FR 13,731, Y 318,278).

$1222* *Manuscript (Galf. 592), 1976,* s., num., (06-23-93, Kornfeld, #817), color etching (BP 830, DM 2068, FR 6955, Y 133,130, SF 1840).

$938* *Marron Diagonal (G. 156), 1968,* s., #68/75, p., pub. Maeght, good cond., marks, (12-03-92, Sotheby-London, #810), 40 x 28¾ in., (101.6 x 73 cm.), lithograph in colors on Chiffon de Mandeure (BP 605, DM 1475, FR 5035, Y 116,710).

$1876* *Mocador Lligat (G. 289), 1972,* s., #55/75, p., pub. La Poligrafa, good cond., creases, (12-03-92, Sotheby-London, #821, illus.), sh 23 x 30½ in., (583 x 775 mm.), aquatint and carborundum in colors on Velin Guarro (BP 1210, DM 2950, FR 10,070, Y 233,420).

$1339* *Mois Du Coeur (Galfetti 340), 1972,* s., num., (05-26-93, Dorling, #2995, illus.), 29¹⁵⁄₁₆ x 21¼ in., (76 x 54 cm.), color lithograph w/collage mit (with) aufgeklebter Spielkarte on thick BFK Rives wove (BP 866, DM 2185, FR 7353, Y 145,480).

$8655* *Negre I Rois 3, 1985,* #39/99, pencil s., (11-20-92, Lempertz, #899, illus.), 37¹¹⁄₁₆ x 49⅝ in., (95.7 x 126 cm.), etching w/embossing on heavy Velin (BP 5699, DM 13,799, FR 46,482, Y 1,076,359).

$9930* *Octavio Paz. Petrificada Petrificante, 1978: Eight,* s., num., (06-05-93, Bassenge, #6568), color etching w/relief print on hand-made Moulin de Larroque (BP 6537, DM 16,099, FR 54,262, Y 1,065,222).

$971* *Ohne Titel (Galfetti 136), 1966,* 13/150, s., (10-14-92, Germann, #448), 19⅜ x 25³⁄₁₆ in., (492 x 640 mm.), lithograph (BP 570, DM 1421, FR 4819, Y 117,668, SF 1265).

$666* *Ovale (G. 158), 1968,* s., num. 16/75, pub. Maeght, full margins, creases, surface dirt, good cond., L. 650 x 1000 mm., (12-01-92, Christie-London, #636), lithograph p. in black, grey and white on wove (BP 440, DM 1062, FR 3618, Y 82,918).

$2623* *"Paralleles",* #51/75, s., (11-13-92, Koller, #5442), 24¹³⁄₁₆ x 35¹³⁄₁₆ in., (63 x 91 cm.), lithograph on wove (BP 1695, DM 4118, FR 13,886, Y 325,555, SF 3712).

$1364* *Le Pays Catalan (G. 626), 1976,* s., #71/75, p., pub. Maeght, full margins, good cond., (12-03-92, Sotheby-London, #806, illus.), 24⅝ x 35⅜ in., (625 x 900 mm.), lithograph in colors on Arches (BP 880, DM 2145, FR 7322, Y 169,715).

$1419* *"Per Alberti, Per La Spagna" (Galfetti 646), 1976,* s., i. P.A., pub. in portfolio Per Alberti, per la Spagna, Editori Riuniti, (06-05-93, Grisebach, #893, illus.), 19⁵⁄₁₆ x 27⁷⁄₁₆ in., (49 x 69.7 cm.), aquatint, lithograph, and serigraph in color w/pencil work on copperprint paper (BP 934, DM 2301, FR 7754, Y 152,221).

$459* *"Per Catalunya 74",* HC XV/XX, s., (04-04-93, Pescheteau, #300), 22⁷⁄₁₆ x 16⁹⁄₁₆ in., (57 x 42 cm.), lithograph on wove (BP 302, DM 738, FR 2505, Y 52,260).

$916* *Petit T, 1983,* s., num., (06-23-93, Kornfeld, #820), 19½ x 15¾ in., (49.5 x 40 cm.), color lithograph (BP 622, DM 1550, FR 5213, Y 99,793, SF 1380).

$580* *Petite Ecriture Marron,* s., 48/150, (06-28-93, Loudmer, #375), 12¹¹⁄₁₆ x 8⅞ in., (323 x 225 mm.), sh 19⁵⁄₁₆ x 13¹⁵⁄₁₆ in., (323 x 225 mm.), color lithograph on wove (BP 388, DM 986, FR 3320, Y 61,538).

BI *Petrificade Petrificante, 1978: Eight,* complete set, one s., #39/50, pub. Maeght Editeur, good cond., est. G 8/12,000, (12-09-92, Sotheby-Amstrdm, #649, illus.), overall 21¼ x 16¹⁵⁄₁₆ in., (540 x 430 mm.), color etching w/aquatint and carborundum on Moulin de Larroque handmade paper.

$1060* *Le Pied (Galfetti 204), 1969,* s., #71/75, (06-12-93, Hauswedell/Nolt, #408, illus.), 15⅜ x 19½ in., (39 x 49.5 cm.), color etching on thick wove (BP 694, DM 1725, FR 5799, Y 111,544).

$1837* *Pied Et Trait Rouge,* s., #68/75, watermark, (06-12-93, Hauswedell/Nolt, #410), 21¹⁄₁₆ x 26⅞ in., (53.5 x 68.2 cm.), color etching on thick wove (BP 1202, DM 2990, FR 10,049, Y 193,307).

$891* *Pied Marron, 1982,* s., #1/75, (05-27-93, Briest, #187), 43½ x 29½ in., (110.5 x 75 cm.), color lithograph (BP 571, DM 1430, FR 4819, Y 95,519).

BI *Pissarra (G. 287), 1972,* s., #20/75, pub. Poligrafa, good cond., glue stains, est. BP 1,2/1,600, (06-30-93, Sotheby-London, #932, illus.), sh 23 x 30¾ in., (584 x 781 mm.), aquatint and carborundum in black and brown on wove.

$1870* *Pont, 1981,* s., #26/30, pub. Maeght, full margins, very good cond.?, (10-28-92, Butterfield, #3141, illus.), 27¼ x 36½ in., (692 x 927 mm.), color aquatint on Guarro paper (BP 1191, DM 2888, FR 9806, Y 229,448).

$1421* *Portfolio, Erinnerungen, 1988: Five,* 64/100, s., num., blindstamp, lit., (06-24-93, Germann, #514), 17¹⁵⁄₁₆ x 22¼ in., (455 x 565 mm.), lithograph (BP 935, DM 2304, FR 7765, Y 152,435, SF 2070).

$1086* *Quartre Franges (G. 509), 1975,* s., 73/75, ed. La Poligrafa, (12-04-92, AB Stockholm, #7149), 17⅛ x 24⅝ in., (43.5 x 62.5 cm.), aquatint, etching and carborundum in colors on Guarro (BP 697, DM 1730, FR 5867, Y 135,581, SK 7370).

$938* *Les Quatre Croix (G. 200), 1969,* s., #74/75, pub. Maeght, margins, image in good cond., creasing, rubbing, (12-03-92, Sotheby-London, #807, illus.), sh approx. 23¼ x 30½ in., (587 x 775 mm.), etching w/aquatint, in brown and black, on Chine applique on wove (BP 605, DM 1475, FR 5035, Y 116,710).

$771* *Quatre Ditades, 1976,* from Negre I Roig, Ediciones La Poligrafa, S.A., (05-12-93, AB Stockholm, #7054), 21⅞ x 29½ in., (55.5 x 75 cm.), aquatint in colors w/relief (BP 503, DM 1244, FR 4190, Y 86,078, SK 5720).

$1876* *Quatre Rius De Sang (G. 291), 1972,* s., #61/75, p., pub. La Poligrafa, good cond., (12-03-92, Sotheby-London, #811), sh approx. 23 x 30⅝ in., (585 x 777 mm.), aquatint w/carborundum and embossing in colors on Velin Guarro (BP 1210, DM 2950, FR 10,070, Y 233,420).

BI *Quatre Ruis De Sang, 1972,* s., #31/75, full margins, good cond.?, light-staining, est. $1,5/2,000, (10-28-92, Butterfield, #3139), 22¼ x 11⅞ in., (565 x 302 mm.), color aquatint on wove.

$840* *Rose Et Deux Plaques (Galf. 560), 1976,* s., num., (06-23-93, Kornfeld, #814), etching and color lithograph (BP 571, DM 1421, FR 4781, Y 91,513, SF 1265).

$133* *Sans Titre,* s. Tapies, (04-20-93, Encans, #130), 21⅞ x 29¾ in., (55.5 x 75.5 cm.), lithograph (BP 86, DM 212, FR 715, Y 14,675, C$ 167).

$315* *Sans Titre,* from Cahiers de l'Espace, s., #81/99, full margins, (11-16-92, Briest, #98), 14¹⁵⁄₁₆ x 11⅛ in., (38 x 28.3 cm.), etching in black (BP 207, DM 502, FR 1693, Y 39,311).

$320* *Sans Titre,* s. Tapies in plate, (09-15-92, Encans, #181), 21⅞ x 29¾ in., (55.5 x 75.5 cm.), lithograph (BP 171, DM 476, FR 1616, Y 39,727, C$ 389).

$783* *Sans Titre (Galfetti 374), 1973,* hors commerce, s., (03-31-93, Briest, #E197), 19¹¹⁄₁₆ x 15¾ in., (50 x 40 cm.), color lithograph on Arches wove (BP 518, DM 1259, FR 4279, Y 90,041).

$189* *Sans Titre (Galfetti 403),* epreuve d'artiste, mono., (11-16-92, Briest, #99), 5¹¹⁄₁₆ x 5¹¹⁄₁₆ in., (14.5 x 14.5 cm.), serigraph in black on wove Regina (BP 124, DM 301, FR 1016, Y 23,587).

$1194* *(Scriptual Composition),* s., #P.A. III/XXV, margins, good cond., creasing, (12-03-92, Sotheby-London, #818, illus.), 34 x 26½ in., (865 x 676 mm.), lithograph in colors on wove (BP 770, DM 1878, FR 6409, Y 148,563).

$3450* *Serie Negre I Roig Triangle (G. 610), 1976,* s., i. H.C., pub. Ediciones La Poligrafa, excell. cond.?, (05-11-93, Christie-NY, #338, illus.), sh 22¼ x 29¾ in., (565 x 756 mm.), color etching and carborundum on Guarro (BP 2202, DM 5435, FR 18,312, Y 379,496).

$1145* *la Serpilliere (Galf. 271), 1971,* s. in pencil, num., (06-23-93, Kornfeld, #810), color etching and relief print (BP 778, DM 1937, FR 6517, Y 124,741, SF 1725).

$989* *Sofa,* s., #32/75, (06-12-93, Hauswedell/Nolt, #411), 16⁹⁄₁₆ x 25³⁄₁₆ in., (42 x 64 cm.), color etching on thick wove (BP 647, DM 1610, FR 5410, Y 104,072).

BI *Table (G. 140), 1967,* s., #24/75, p. and pub. Maeght, margins, good cond., skinning, creasing, scratch extending to image, est. BP 4/600, (06-30-93, Sotheby-London, #929, illus.), sh 17⅝ x 24¾ in., (448 x 629 mm.), color lithograph on Rives wove.

BI *Table (Galfetti 140), 1967,* s., #24/75, p., pub. Maeght, margins, good cond., skinning, creasing,scratch, est. BP 6/800, (12-03-92, Sotheby-London, #805, illus.), sh 17⅝ x 23¾ in., (446 x 630 mm.), lithograph in colors on Rives wove.

$1620* *Le Tableau (G. 229), 1970,* s., #51/75, p., pub. Maeght, full margins, good cond., (12-03-92, Sotheby-London, #812, illus.), 22⅝ x 30⅝ in., (575 x 777 mm.), etching on Chiffon de Mandeure (BP 1045, DM 2548, FR 8696, Y 201,568).

BI *La Tamis, 1969,* s., annot. HC, good cond., tears, staining, rubbed area, handling creases, est. $3,5/4,500, (05-19-93, Butterfield, #2353, illus.), 25⅝ x 35¼ in., (651 x 895 mm.), etching and embossing in colors on Chiffon de Mandeur.

BI *"Le Te Renverse" (Galfetti 201), 1969,* s., num., est. DM 3,6/3,800, (06-05-93, Grisebach, #891, illus.), 13¾ x 19¾ in., (35 x 50.2 cm.), color aquatint on hand-made copper print paper.

$1298* *La Tete (Galfetti 206), 1969,* s., num., (06-23-93, Kornfeld, #806), color etching (BP 882, DM 2196, FR 7388, Y 141,410, SF 1955).

BI *Trace, 1981,* s., #28/50, pub. Maeght, good cond., est. BP 7/900, (12-03-92, Sotheby-London, #825), sh 27 x 42¼ in., (68.6 x 107.3 cm.), aquatint w/carborundum in colors on BFK Rives.

BI *Tresse, 1980,* s., #16/50, est. FF7/8,000, (05-27-93, Briest, #185, illus.), 31½ x 42⅛ in., (80 x 107 cm.), carborundum and collage.

$993* *Trois Plaques (Galf. 561), 1976,* s., num., (06-23-93, Kornfeld, #815), color etching and relief print (BP 675, DM 1680, FR 5652, Y 108,182, SF 1495).

$943* *Trois Taches Et Trois Lignes Noire (G. 319), 1972,* s., #45/75, p. and pub. Maeght, full margins, good cond., (06-30-93, Sotheby-London, #937), sh 22⅞ x 30½ in., (581 x 775 mm.), aquatint and carborundum in color on wove (BP 632, DM 1608, FR 5426, Y 101,039).

BI *U No Es Ningu, 1980,* s., num. 2/99, pub. Ediciones Poligrafa, full sheet, good cond., est. Y 250/300,000, (10-14-92, Sotheby-Japan, #100, illus.), sh 29⅞ x 22⅛ in., (759 x 562 mm.), color lithograph on Guarro paper.

BI *Untitled,* #6/75, pencil s., est. DM 3,000, (11-20-92, Lempertz, #900, illus.), sh 27⅞ x 37¹⁵⁄₁₆ in., (70.8 x 96.5 cm.), color etching on Velin.

$1947* *Untitled,* #48/75, pencil s., (11-20-92, Lempertz, #902), sh 22³⁄₁₆ x 29¹³⁄₁₆ in., (56.3 x 75.8 cm.), color etching w/embossing and felt-tip on Guarro-Velin (BP 1282, DM 3104, FR 10,456, Y 242,134).

$1875* *Untitled,* #87/99, pencil s., (11-20-92, Lempertz, #901), sh 22¹⁄₁₆ x 30⅛ in., (56 x 76.5 cm.), color etching w/ embossing on Velin (BP 1235, DM 2989, FR 10,070, Y 233,180).

BI *Untitled,* #149/150, pencil s., blindstamp, est. DM 2,200, (11-20-92, Lempertz, #903), sh 28¾ x 37⁵⁄₁₆ in., (73 x 94.8 cm.), color lithograph on Velin on BFK Rives.

$1083* *Untitled,* s., num., from portfolio Kunstmarke Koln 1972, (11-28-92, Schoppmann, #832), 20½ x 25⁹⁄₁₆ in., (52 x 65 cm.), color lithograph on Arches wove (BP 715, DM 1725, FR 5857, Y 134,785).

$1023* *Untitled (G. 399), 1974,* s., i. H.C., proof, p., pub. Maeght, full margins, good cond., (12-03-92, Sotheby-London, #822), 30¼ x 22 in., (770 x 560 mm.), lithograph in colors on Arches (BP 660, DM 1609, FR 5491, Y 127,286).

$1299* *Untitled (Galfetti 233), 1970,* s., num., (11-28-92, Schoppmann, #831), 14⁹⁄₁₆ x 18½ in., (37 x 47 cm.), color lithograph on Arches wove (BP 857, DM 2069, FR 7025, Y 161,668).

$1290* *Untitled (Galfetti 593), 1978,* s., #19/99, (05-27-93, Lempertz, #1052, illus.), 39³⁄₁₆ x 27½ in., (99.5 x 69.8 cm.), color lithograph on wove (BP 826, DM 2070, FR 6977, Y 138,293).

$1003* *Untitled (Galfetti 706), 1978,* s., #72/100, (05-27-93, Lempertz, #1053), 15⅞ x 23³⁄₁₆ in., (40.4 x 58.9 cm.), color lithograph w/relief print (BP 642, DM 1609, FR 5425, Y 107,526).

BI *Untitled Composition (G. 42), 1962,* s., #13/50, p. Foto-Repro, pub. Sala Gaspar, good cond., creases, mount stained, est. BP 4/500, (12-03-92, Sotheby-London, #809), sh size 30 x 22 in., (760 x 560 mm.), lithograph in colors on BFK Rives.

$2020* *Untitled(Galfetti Band I 33), 1960,* #12/50, s., d., (11-20-92, Lempertz, #886, illus.), sh 31⅛ x 21⅞ in., (79 x 55.5 cm.), color lithograph w/embossing on Velin (BP 1330, DM 3221, FR 10,849, Y 251,213).

$1659* *Untitled(Galfetti Band I 35), 1960,* #20/50, pencil s., (11-20-92, Lempertz, #887), sh 25⁹⁄₁₆ x 35⁷⁄₁₆ in., (65 x 90 cm.), lithograph in 6 colors w/embossing on Gaurro-Velin (BP 1092, DM 2645, FR 8910, Y 206,318).

$1083* *Untitled(Galfetti I.137/1966*, s., gebraunt, (11-28-92, Schoppmann, #832A), 30⁵⁄₁₆ x 22⁷⁄₁₆ in., (77 x 57 cm.), color lithograph on Guarro wove (BP 715, DM 1725, FR 5857, Y 134,785).

$938* *(Untitled) (G. 20), 1959*, s., #29/50, p. Foto-Repro, pub. Sala Gaspar, full margins, good cond., rolling creases, marks, tears, (12-03-92, Sotheby-London, #816), 19⅛ x 29¼ in., (485 x 745 mm.), lithograph in black on BFK Rives (BP 605, DM 1475, FR 5035, Y 116,710).

$620* *Untitled, 1972*, from Hommage a Picasso, s., (09-18-92, Schloss Ahlden, #1071), 23⅜ x 29⅞ in., (59.3 x 75.9 cm.), color lithograph on hand-made (BP 363, DM 920, FR 3147, Y 76,628).

$948* *Untitled, 1980*, E.A., s., blindstamp, (04-21-93, Germann, #786), 24¹³⁄₁₆ x 35¹⁄₁₆ in., (630 x 890 mm.), color-lithograph (BP 615, DM 1515, FR 5124, Y 104,949, SF 1380).

BI *Untitled, 1982*, HC, pencil s., est. DM 2,800, (11-20-92, Lempertz, #898), sh 17 x 21¾ in., (43.2 x 55.3 cm.), color etching on Velin.

BI *Untitled, 8m 1985*, H.C., s., est. SF 3,2/4,000, (11-13-92, Koller, #5443), 32¹⁄₁₆ x 20⅞ in., (81.5 x 53 cm.), lithograph on wove.

$1075* *Untitled, after 1978*, s., #9/75, (05-27-93, Lempertz, #1054), 33¼ x 19¹⁵⁄₁₆ in., (84.4 x 50.7 cm.), color lithograph on wove (BP 688, DM 1725, FR 5814, Y 115,244).

$1018* *Untitled: Two*, #67/75 and 105/150, s., (05-20-93, Finarte-Milan, #150), one 34¹³⁄₁₆ x 23⅝ in., (88.5 x 60 cm.), the other 30⁵⁄₁₆ x 21⅞ in., (88.5 x 60 cm.), lithograph in colors (BP 653, DM 1642, FR 5533, Y 112,412, L 1495).

$993* *Variation Sur Un Theme Musical, 1987*, s., num., (06-23-93, Kornfeld, #822), 21¼ x 27⅜ in., (54 x 69.5 cm.), color lithograph on relief print (BP 675, DM 1680, FR 5652, Y 108,182, SF 1495).

$10,587* *Variation, 1984: Eleven*, s., 750mm x 1040mm, (10-14-92, Germann, #65, illus.), color lithograph (BP 6214, DM 15,494, FR 52,541, Y 1,282,962, SF 13,800).

$2750* *Vertical, 1986*, s., #13/50, margins, very good cond.?, (10-28-92, Butterfield, #3142), 42½ x 13⅝ in., (108 x 34.6 cm.), color etching w/aquatint on cream wove (BP 1752, DM 4247, FR 14,421, Y 337,423).

BI *Verticales En Bas (G. 162), 1968*, s., #43/75, p. and pub. Maeght, good cond., light-staining, creasing,est. BP 7/900, (06-30-93, Sotheby-London, #930, illus.), sh approx. 31½ x 46⅞ in., (80 x 119.1 cm.), color lithograph on Velin de Lana.

TAPPEN AND BRADFORD
$220* *"View Of Boston From Telegraph Hill"*, poor cond.?, (07-19-92, Bakker, #41), sheet 12¼ x 22 in., (31.1 x 55.9 cm.), lithograph (BP 113, DM 321, FR 1084, Y 27,350).

TAPPERT, Georg   German 1880-1957
$577* *Alte Chansonette (Karsch 41), 1918*, s., (11-28-92, Schoppmann, #833), 6¼ x 4¾ in., (15.8 x 12 cm.), linocut on light brown wove (BP 381, DM 919, FR 3121, Y 71,811).

$1328* *Betty VI (Karsch 28), 1913*, s., artist's proof IIII, (12-05-92, Bassenge, #7767), 10¹⁵⁄₁₆ x 9⅝ in., (27.8 x 24.5 cm.), etching on wove (BP 832, DM 2070, FR 7056, Y 164,540).

$1083* *Liegende Betty Mit Facher Und Schwarzen Strumpfen (Betty V) (Wietek 138), 1913*, s., d., artist's proof, (11-28-92, Grisebach, #791, illus.), 6⅞ x 15⁵⁄₁₆ in., (17.5 x 38.9 cm.), drypoint on handmade (BP 715, DM 1725, FR 5857, Y 134,785).

$70* *Madchen Mit Hut Und Schleier, 1918*, later imp., (09-25-92, Granier, #3023), 5¹³⁄₁₆ x 3⅞ in., (14.8 x 9.9 cm.), woodcut on white machine hand-made (BP 41, DM 104, FR 351, Y 8449).

BI *"Nachtcafe"(Frau En Face), (19)18*, s., d., t., artist proof Nr. 3, brown stained, w/mount staining, est.DM 1200, (12-01-92, Karl/Faber, #1291), 4¾ x 3⅛ in., (12 x 8 cm.), etching on wove.

TARAOKA, Masami
$990* *"Woman With Orchids", 1980*, s., d., #74/87, good cond., creases, (10-28-92, Butterfield, #3143), 23¹⁄₁₆ x 17¹⁄₁₆ in., (586 x 433 mm.), color woodcut on wove (BP 631, DM 1529, FR 5191, Y 121,472).

TARKAY   Israeli 20th cent.
$275* *Elegance #2*, s., num. 218/350, (11-12-92, Freemn/Fine Art, #234B), 25 x 19¼ in., (63.5 x 48.9 cm.), lithograph p. in color (BP 181, DM 436, FR 1470, Y 34,098).

BI *Sarah*, s., num. 236/300, est. $6/900, (11-12-92, Freemn/Fine Art, #234A), 26 x 34 in., (66 x 86.4 cm.), lithograph p. in color.

TARKAY, Itzchak   Yugoslavia/Israeli b. 1935
$265* *Cafe Scene*, #27/3000, s., (03-10-93, Maynard, #629), 20 x 16½ in., (50.8 x 41.9 cm.), silkscreen (BP 185, DM 441, FR 1497, Y 31,309, C$ 330).

$420* *Cafe Scene*, #27/30, s., (03-10-93, Maynard, #626), 22½ x 47 in., (57.2 x 119.4 cm.), silkscreen (BP 293, DM 699, FR 2373, Y 49,622, C$ 523).

$327* *Cafe Scene*, #212/300, s., (03-10-93, Maynard, #625), sheet 31½ x 42½ in., (80 x 108 cm.), silkscreen (BP 228, DM 544, FR 1847, Y 38,634, C$ 407).

$243* *Cafe Scene*, #41/300, s., (03-10-93, Maynard, #627), 21 x 17 in., (53.3 x 43.2 cm.), silkscreen (BP 170, DM 404, FR 1373, Y 28,710, C$ 303).

$220* *Le Divan*, s. ink, #31/300, (05-16-93, Hanzel, #470), 13¾ x 10¾ in., (34.9 x 27.3 cm.), color serigraph w/embossing (BP 143, DM 354, FR 1189, Y 24,388).

$243* *Portrait Of A Woman*, #6/300, s., (03-10-93, Maynard, #628), 20 x 20 in., (50.8 x 50.8 cm.), silkscreen (BP 170, DM 404, FR 1373, Y 28,710, C$ 303).

$327* *Portrait Of A Woman*, #185/300, s., (03-10-93, Maynard, #620), 39 x 37 in., (99.1 x 94 cm.), silkscreen (BP 228, DM 544, FR 1847, Y 38,634, C$ 407).

$353* *Portrait Of A Woman*, #76/300, s., (03-10-93, Maynard, #621), 32½ x 26 in., (82.6 x 66 cm.), silkscreen (BP 246, DM 588, FR 1994, Y 41,706, C$ 440).

$327* *Portrait Of A Woman*, #272/300, s., (03-10-93, Maynard, #622), 22½ x 16 in., (57.2 x 40.6 cm.), silkscreen (BP 228, DM 544, FR 1847, Y 38,634, C$ 407).

$327* *Portrait Of A Woman In A Red Dress*, #261/300, s., (03-10-93, Maynard, #624), 30 x 19½ in., (76.2 x 49.5 cm.), silkscreen (BP 228, DM 544, FR 1847, Y 38,634, C$ 407).

$327* *Street Cafe Scene*, s., #35/300, (03-10-93, Maynard, #623), 31 x 40 in., (78.7 x 101.6 cm.), silkscreen (BP 228, DM 544, FR 1847, Y 38,634, C$ 407).

$353* *Women At Rest*, #132/300, s., (03-10-93, Maynard, #619), 33½ x 45 in., (85.1 x 114.3 cm.), silkscreen (BP 246, DM 588, FR 1994, Y 41,706, C$ 440).

TARKAY, Yitzhak
$715* *Intimacy, 1990*, s., num. 164/300, w/margins, good cond., one vertical ripple, (05-22-93, Weschler, #224, illus.), 32 x 31½ in., (81.3 x 80 cm.), serigraph in colors on Coventry (BP 463, DM 1163, FR 3911, Y 78,831).

TARKHANOV, Mikhail   1888-1962
BI *Untitled, Stem And Leaves, c. 1928*, prov., est. $1,5/2,000, (04-08-93, Christie-NY, #157, illus.), 4½ x 3¼ in., (11.4 x 8.3 cm.), photograph, gelatin silver print photogram.

TASHU   Japanese
$33* *"Shoal Of Fish"*, 20th cent., seal mark, (06-11-93, DuMouchelle, #2363), 7½ x 10 in., (19.1 x 25.4 cm.), color woodblock print (BP 22, DM 54, FR 181, Y 3501).

TATO (GUGLIELMO), Guglielmo
BI *Light Abstraction, c. 1928*, i. in unidentified hand, est. $15/25,000, (10-15-92, Sotheby-NY, #397, illus.), 10½ x 8⅛ in., (26.7 x 20.6 cm.), photograph, unique photogram.

TAUBES, Frederic   American 1900-1981
$22* *"The Goddess"*, s., pl. s., AAA, (12-11-92, DuMouchelle, #1488), 11⅞ x 8¾ in., (30.2 x 22.2 cm.), etching (BP 14, DM 35, FR 119, Y 2722).

$39* *"Julia"*, s., AAA, (12-11-92, DuMouchelle, #1487), 9⅞ x 7¾ in., (25.1 x 19.7 cm.), etching (BP 25, DM 61, FR 211, Y 4826).

TAUZIN, L.
$105* *Ch. De Fer Du Nord: Compiegne Pierrefonds*, c. 1910, good cond., (01-23-93, Ribeyre/Baron, #46), 39⅜ x 35⁷⁄₁₆ in., (100 x 90 cm.), poster (BP 69, DM 167, FR 565, Y 13,141).

TAY, Eng   Malasian contemporary
$110* *An Ancient Melody*, s., t., d. (19)91, i. A.P., (12-10-92, Sloan, #1316), 17½ x 23¾ in., (44.5 x 60.3 cm.), color etching and aquatint (BP 71, DM 174, FR 594, Y 13,607).

TAYLER, Frederick (after)
$165* *The Royal Review*, by Samuel William Reynolds, pub. Thomas Boys, 1839, trimmed, (06-16-93, Bonhams-Chelsea, #475), image 27 x 21 in., (68.6 x 53.3 cm.), mezzotint (BP 110, DM 274, FR 919, Y 17,598).

TAYLOR, Alfred Swaine   1801-1880
$726* *Art Reproduction: Two*, 1840s, (05-06-93, Christie-London, #27), each approx. 6¾ x 5½ in., photograph, photogenic drawing (BP 460, DM 1143, FR 3849, Y 79,877).
$762* *Back View Of A Terrace Of Houses, Cambridge Place*, 1840s, (05-06-93, Christie-London, #26, illus.), 6 x 7¾ in., photograph, calotype (BP 483, DM 1200, FR 4040, Y 83,838).
$1179* *Fern Study*, 1840, lit., (05-06-93, Christie-London, #25, illus.), 2¾ x 6 in., photograph, photogenic drawing (BP 747, DM 1857, FR 6251, Y 129,717).

TAYLOR, C.
$30 *"Edwin" and "Angelina": Two*, d. 1787, (04-16-93, G.A. Key, #76), 6 x 4 in., (15.2 x 10.2 cm.), stipple engraving (BP 20, DM 48, FR 164, Y 3373).

TAYLOR, Campbell
$44* *Woman In Blue Gown*, (11-13-92, DuMouchelle, #2457), 19 x 15 in., (48.3 x 38.1 cm.), mezzotint (BP 28, DM 69, FR 233, Y 5461).

TAYLOR, Josiah
$215* *Flying Cloud*, pub. artist, 1871, margins, repaired tears, other defects, (06-16-93, Bonhams-Chelsea, #440), image 14½ x 24¼ in., (36.8 x 61.6 cm.), tinted lithograph (BP 143, DM 357, FR 1198, Y 22,931).

TAYLOR, L. and J., Publisher
BI *Furniture Designs: Six*, pub. 1787, margins, est. BP 1/150, (06-16-93, Bonhams-Chelsea, #351), pl. 6¾ x 10 in., (17.1 x 25.4 cm.), engraving on wove.

TAYLOR, William (after)   English 19th century
$250* *Death Of The Hog*, (02-04-93, Sloan, #771), sight 21 x 30 in., (53.3 x 76.2 cm.), hand colored engraving (BP 175, DM 412, FR 1396, Y 31,098).

TCHIMOUKOV, Lou
$2475* *Scissors, Knife And Fork*, 1928 (Atelier Man Ray, p. 37), s., d. by photog. in ink on image, (10-15-92, Sotheby-NY, #298, illus.), 9⅛ x 7 in., (23.2 x 17.8 cm.), photogram (BP 1515, DM 3684, FR 12,494, Y 296,941).

TEEVEE, Jamasie   b. 1910
$275* *"Arctic Owl"*, t., ident., d. 3/50 1970, s., blindstamped, very good cond., prov., (06-26-93, Skinner, #80, illus.), 13 x 15¼ in., (33 x 38.7 cm.), brown and ochre engraving (BP 184, DM 467, FR 1574, Y 29,178).

TELEMAQUE, Herve   b. 1937
$136* *Bleu De Matisse*, 1986, s., t., d. 86, #132/200, ed. Editions 35, (11-16-92, Briest, #101), 21⅝ x 29½ in., (55 x 75 cm.), serigraph in colors (BP 89, DM 217, FR 731, Y 16,972).
$63* *"Composition"*, 1974, #18/120, d., s., (01-28-93, Pescheteau, #266), 21⅝ x 28¾ in., (55 x 73 cm.), serigraph (BP 42, DM 100, FR 338, Y 7822).
BI *H Comme Hotel*, 1976, est. SF 700/900, (10-14-92, Germann, #459), 22¹⁄₁₆ x 29¹⁵⁄₁₆ in., (560 x 760 mm.), color lithograph.
BI *L'Oreille De V. Van Gogh. Essai*, 1974, s., est. SF 700/900, (10-14-92, Germann, #458), 30 x 22¹⁄₁₆ in., (762 x 560 mm.), color lithograph.

$136* *Loi/Moi (Ma Loi)*, 1985, epreuve d'artiste, s., t., d. 85, (11-16-92, Briest, #100), 21⅝ x 29½ in., (55 x 75 cm.), serigraph in colors (BP 89, DM 217, FR 731, Y 16,972).
BI *Untitled*, 1970, s., #72/80, d. 1970 verso, est. FF 4/6,000, (11-16-92, Briest, #359), 47¹⁄₁₆ x 23⅝ in., (119.5 x 60 cm.), serigraph on canvas.

TEMPESTA, Antonio   1555-1630
$340* *Barenjagd (Bartsch Bd. 17, 1154; Bartsch ill. Bd. 37, 114), 1621*, from 7th series of hunt scenes, plate mono., d. A TE 1608, trimmed, (09-14-92, Venator/Hansten, #1612), plate 7⅞ x 11 in., (20 x 28 cm.), etching (BP 180, DM 505, FR 1713, Y 42,278).

TENIERS, David (II)   1610-1690
$850* *Acht Bauern, Pfeile Schiessend (Nagler 37, Dutuit 36, Wurzbach 31, Hollstein 36)*, watermark, from the series of 4 sheets of Genreszennen im Freien, (06-04-93, Bassenge, #5377), 5¹³⁄₁₆ x 10 in., (14.8 x 25.4 cm.), etching (BP 562, DM 1380, FR 4652, Y 91,674).

TENIERS, David (after)
$248* *"The Fisherman", "Solitude" and "A View In Flanders": Three*, by Peter-Paul Benazech, prov., (09-20-92, Hindman, #650), each 7¾ x 10 in., (19.7 x 25.4 cm.), (BP 145, DM 368, FR 1259, Y 30,651).
$32* *St. George And The Dragon*, by J. C. Vasseur, margins, foxing, (03-17-93, Bonhams-Chelsea, #433), plate 14¼ x 17⅜ in., (36.2 x 44.1 cm.), etching (BP 22, DM 53, FR 181, Y 3753).

TENIERS II, David   1610-1690
$274* *Bauernpaar Am Tisch (Hollstein 25)*, artist's mono., (12-01-92, Karl/Faber, #153), etching (BP 181, DM 437, FR 1488, Y 34,114).

TENNESON, Joyce
$1870* *"Suzanne"*, 1986, ink s., #6/50, (11-16-92, Butterfield, #6198, illus.), 19¹³⁄₁₆ x 15⅝ in., (502.5 x 397.6 mm.), photograph, cibachrome print (BP 1231, DM 2982, FR 10,043, Y 232,558).

TENNIER, D. (after)
$242* *"La Maison Rustique" and "Le Basse Cour": A Pair*, (04-17-93, Wolf, #544), 9½ x 12½ in., (24.1 x 31.8 cm.), colored engraving (BP 159, DM 391, FR 1321, Y 27,212).

TERECHKOVITCH, Konstantin   Russian 1902-1978
$110* *At The Race Track*, s., (12-17-92, Mystic, #20), 21 x 26 in., (53.3 x 66 cm.), color lithograph (BP 70, DM 172, FR 587, Y 13,518).

TESKE, Edmund
BI *Boy Selling Newspapers, Los Angeles*, 1943, photog.'s sig. on mount, notations, est. $500/750, (04-07-93, Swann, #567), 8 x 7½ in., photograph, silver print.
$633* *"Broken Truck Window", "Graffiti" and "Envelope": Three*, 1960s, s., (05-23-93, Butterfield, #3627, illus.), each approx. 5¾ x 6¾ in., photograph, gelatin silver print (BP 412, DM 1035, FR 3484, Y 69,968).
BI *Selected Abstractions: Five*, each s. by photog., one s., t., d. by photog., est. $1,5/2,500, (04-06-93, Sotheby-NY, #467, illus.), various sizes to 9¾ x 7¾ in., photograph.
$633* *Selected Works: Portraits, 1963, 1968: Three*, s., d., photog.'s stamp, (05-23-93, Butterfield, #3628, illus.), each approx. 6¾ x 4¾ in., photograph, gelatin silver print (BP 412, DM 1035, FR 3484, Y 69,968).

TESTA, Pietro   1617-1650
$2600* *Achill Schleift Die Leiche Hektors Um Die Mauern Von Troja (B. 22; Bellini 37 I; The Illustr. Bartsch 22 II)*, c. 1648, watermark, (12-04-92, Bassenge, #6460), 10⁷⁄₁₆ x 16⅜ in., (26.5 x 41.6 cm.), etching (BP 1668, DM 4141, FR 14,046, Y 324,594).
BI *The Garden Of Venus (B. 26; Bell. 12; Cr. 13)*, c. 1635, 2nd state of 4(?), mono, trimmed into t. space, thread margins, pen and ink retouching, foxing, backed, The Suida Manning Coll., est. $7/1,000, (05-13-93, Sotheby-NY, #292), 13⅜ x 16⅜ in., (339 x 415 mm.), etching.
$666* *The Infant Christ Embracing The Cross (B. 4; Bell. 10; Cropper 25)*, c. 1635-7, 2nd (final) state, watermark, wide margins, very good cond., (12-01-92, Christie-London, #202), plate 24⅞ x 11¹¹⁄₁₆ in., (632 x 297 mm.), etching (BP 440, DM 1062, FR 3618, Y 82,918).

$470* *Die Opferung Der Iphigenie (B. 23 II; Bellini 18 III; Illustr. Bartsch 23 III), c. 1640,* foxed, watermark, (12-04-92, Bassenge, #6461), 14¹⁵⁄₁₆ x 18³⁄₁₆ in., (37.9 x 46.2 cm.), etching (BP 301, DM 749, FR 2539, Y 58,677).

$1133* *Die Ruckkehr Des Verlorenen Sohnes (B. 8, Bellini 24 I, Cropper 98 I),* (06-04-93, Bassenge, #5378, illus.), 7¹⁵⁄₁₆ x 11⅝ in., (20.3 x 29.6 cm.), etching (BP 750, DM 1840, FR 6201, Y 122,196).

BI *The Sacrifice Of Isaac (B. 2; Bell. 25; Cropper 71), c. 1640,* watermark, printer's creases, defects, touched in w/ grey wash, artist's name added, glued down, good cond., The Suida Manning Coll., est. $1/1,500, (05-13-93, Sotheby-NY, #287), 11⅝ x 9½ in., (295 x 240 mm.), etching.

BI *St. Jerome (B. 15; Bell. 9; Cr. 8), c. 1635,* 1st state of 3, narrow margin, trimmed, tear, stain, good cond., glued down, The Suida Manning Coll., est. $1,5/2,000, (05-13-93, Sotheby-NY, #289), 12⅛ x 9 in., (309 x 230 mm.), etching.

$181* *Thetis Taucht Den Jungen Achill In Das Wasser Des Styx, Um Ihn Unverwundbar Zu Machen (B. 21; Bellini 36 II; The Illustr. Bartsch 21 II),* (12-04-92, Bassenge, #6459), approx. 11⅛ x 16⁷⁄₁₆ in., (28.3 x 41.8 cm.), etching (BP 116, DM 288, FR 978, Y 22,597).

$397* *Der Tod Des Cato Uticensis (B. 20; Bellini 39 II; Illustr. Bartsch 20 II), 1648,* creased and dusty, (12-04-92, Bassenge, #6458), 11 x 16⁵⁄₁₆ in., (28 x 41.4 cm.), etching (BP 255, DM 632, FR 2145, Y 49,563).

BI *Venus Presenting Arms To Aeneas (B. 24; Bell. 17; Cr. 59), c. 1640,* 1st state of 2, margins, crease, fox marks, stains, The Suida ManningColl., est. $1,5/2,000, (05-13-93, Sotheby-NY, #290, illus.), 14⅛ x 15⅝ in., (358 x 398 mm.), etching.

TEUBER, Hermann 1894-1985

$194* *Ballett-Szene,* s. Teuber, #48/100, (09-14-92, Venator/Hansten, #2542), plate 5¾ x 7¹¹⁄₁₆ in., (14.6 x 19.5 cm.), drypoint etching on hand-made (BP 103, DM 288, FR 977, Y 24,123).

TEYNARD, Felix 1817-1892

$1760* *Medinet - Abou (Thebes),* t., photog. credit, pub., 1850s, (04-07-93, Swann, #266, illus.), 9½ x 12 in., photograph, salt print (BP 1163, DM 2847, FR 9633, Y 199,955).

TEZIER

BI *Allevard Les Bains. "Residence D'Ete, Alpinisme, Cure D'Air",* very good cond., (03-15-93, Arcole, #65), 34⁷⁄₁₆ x 24³⁄₁₆ in., (87.5 x 61.5 cm.), .

TEZIER, J.

$499* *Machine A Ecrire Hurtu-Empire, c. 1900,* cond. B, (03-16-93, Boisgirard, #207), 35⁷⁄₁₆ x 25⁹⁄₁₆ in., (90 x 65 cm.), poster (BP 345, DM 830, FR 2819, Y 58,349).

THAKE, Eric 1904-1982

$101* *"-In The Nude! Oh Mr Thake",* inits. E.T, d. 1963, i., (08-11-92, L. Joel, #124G), 7½ x 5½ in., (19 x 14 cm.), linocut (BP 52, DM 148, FR 502, Y 12,934, A$ 137).

$122* *"-Message From Our Sponsor",* s. Eric Thake, d. 1975, i., lit., (08-11-92, L. Joel, #136G), 7¹⁵⁄₁₆ x 5⅝ in., (20.3 x 14.3 cm.), linocut (BP 63, DM 179, FR 606, Y 15,623, A$ 165).

BI *Book-Plate-H.B. Muir,* init. T, in image, est. $80/120, (08-11-92, L. Joel, #140G), 3⅛ x 1¾ in., (8 x 4.5 cm.), woodcut.

$81* *Christmas Greetings From Thake's Flat,* s., i., d. 1961, lit., (08-11-92, L. Joel, #122G), 5¾ x 8⁷⁄₁₆ in., (14.6 x 21.5 cm.), linocut (BP 42, DM 119, FR 403, Y 10,373, A$ 110).

$162* *Dave, Where's All Your 30,000? Well You Remember Those Chops We Had Lst Night!,* s. Eric Thake, d. 1968, i., lit., (08-11-92, L. Joel, #129G), 7⅜ x 5¹¹⁄₁₆ in., (18.7 x 14.5 cm.), linocut (BP 84, DM 238, FR 805, Y 20,745, A$ 220).

$81* *Desert Island,* s. Eric Thake, d. 1967, i., lit., (08-11-92, L. Joel, #128G), 5⅜ x 7½ in., (13.7 x 19 cm.), linocut (BP 42, DM 119, FR 403, Y 10,373, A$ 110).

$142* *"Epstein, Einstein? I Can Never Remember!",* s. Eric Thake, d. 1962, i., lit., (08-11-92, L. Joel, #123G), 8¹¹⁄₁₆ x 5¹¹⁄₁₆ in., (22 x 14.5 cm.), linocut (BP 74, DM 208, FR 706, Y 18,184, A$ 192).

$81* *"Figure In A Rocky Landscape",* s. Eric Thake, d. 1965, i., lit., (08-11-92, L. Joel, #126G), 5⁵⁄₁₆ x 8⅜ in., (13.5 x 21.2 cm.), linocut (BP 42, DM 119, FR 403, Y 10,373, A$ 110).

$122* *Heels And Heeler, Charleville,* s. Eric Thake, d. 1971, i., lit., (08-11-92, L. Joel, #132G), 7¹¹⁄₁₆ x 5¹¹⁄₁₆ in., (19.5 x 14.5 cm.), linocut (BP 63, DM 179, FR 606, Y 15,623, A$ 165).

$243* *Hippobottomi,* s. Eric Thake, d. 1974, i., lit., (08-11-92, L. Joel, #135G), 5½ x 8¹¹⁄₁₆ in., (14 x 22 cm.), linocut (BP 126, DM 357, FR 1208, Y 31,118, A$ 330).

$81* *"Ladies...About Turn!",* s. Eric Thake, d. 1979, lit., (08-11-92, L. Joel, #138G), 7¹⁄₁₆ x 9¹³⁄₁₆ in., (18 x 25 cm.), lithograph (BP 42, DM 119, FR 403, Y 10,373, A$ 110).

$223* *"Mr Picasso! Gentlemen, You Won't Find Him Here",* s. Eric Thake, d. 1956, lit., (08-11-92, L. Joel, #121G), 8⁷⁄₁₆ x 5¾ in., (21.4 x 14.6 cm.), linocut (BP 116, DM 327, FR 1108, Y 28,557, A$ 302).

$365* *Nuns On The Geelong Road,* s. Eric Thake, d. 1969, i., lit., (08-11-92, L. Joel, #130G), 5¹¹⁄₁₆ x 8¹⁄₁₆ in., (14.5 x 20.5 cm.), linocut (BP 190, DM 536, FR 1814, Y 46,741, A$ 495).

$446* *An Opera House In Every Home,* s. Eric Thake, d. 1972, i., lit., (08-11-92, L. Joel, #133G, illus.), 5½ x 8⅜ in., (14 x 21.2 cm.), linocut (BP 232, DM 655, FR 2217, Y 57,114, A$ 605).

$162* *The Plume Hunter,* s. Eric Thake, i. P.C.A. Ed. 68, #143/150, d. 1951, lit., (08-11-92, L. Joel, #182G), 7⅞ x 5¾ in., (20 x 14.6 cm.), linocut (BP 84, DM 238, FR 805, Y 20,745, A$ 220).

$81* *Roadside Bunyip,* s. Eric Thake, d. 1973, i., lit., (08-11-92, L. Joel, #134G), 8⅜ x 5⅛ in., (21.2 x 13 cm.), linocut (BP 42, DM 119, FR 403, Y 10,373, A$ 110).

$162* *"She's Warm Alright",* s. Eric Thake, d. 1966, i., lit., (08-11-92, L. Joel, #127G), 7⁵⁄₁₆ x 5¹³⁄₁₆ in., (18.5 x 14.7 cm.), linocut (BP 84, DM 238, FR 805, Y 20,745, A$ 220).

$142* *"Sunshine And Rain, Lygon Street",* s. Eric Thake, d. 1964, i., lit., (08-11-92, L. Joel, #125G), 7¹⁄₁₆ x 5¹¹⁄₁₆ in., (18 x 14.5 cm.), linocut (BP 74, DM 208, FR 706, Y 18,184, A$ 192).

$142* *T.V Camel Of Lake Rudolf,* s. Eric Thake, d. 1977, lit., (08-11-92, L. Joel, #137G), 8¼ x 9⁷⁄₁₆ in., (21 x 24 cm.), lithograph (BP 74, DM 208, FR 706, Y 18,184, A$ 192).

$162* *When In Kalgoolie...Dial-A Prayer!,* s. Eric Thake, d. 1970, i., lit., (08-11-92, L. Joel, #131G), 7⁵⁄₁₆ x 5½ in., (18.5 x 14 cm.), linocut (BP 84, DM 238, FR 805, Y 20,745, A$ 220).

THAL

$126* *Toujours Precis Avec Votre Raquette Martin Legeay, c. 1930,* Editions Paul Martial, very good cond., lit., (11-19-92, Ribeyre/Baron, #51), 23⅝ x 15⅜ in., (60 x 39 cm.), poster (BP 83, DM 201, FR 677, Y 15,670).

THARRATS, Joan Josep

$128* *"Paisaje Anamorfosico",* s., #176/250; label verso, (02-03-93, Duran, #223), 25¹⁵⁄₁₆ x 19¹¹⁄₁₆ in., (66 x 50 cm.), lithograph (BP 89, DM 211, FR 715, Y 15,922, P 14,950).

THARRATS, Juan Jose Spanish b. 1918

$128* *"Paisaje Anamorfosico",* s., #178/250; label verso, (02-03-93, Duran, #222), 25¹⁵⁄₁₆ x 19¹¹⁄₁₆ in., (66 x 50 cm.), lithograph (BP 89, DM 211, FR 715, Y 15,922, P 14,950).

THAULOW, Frits Norwegian 1847-1906

$385* *Bridge Over The Canal In Winter,* s. Fritz Thaulow, num. 21:4, pub.'s blindstamp, good cond., (03-12-93, Skinner, #19, illus.), sight 17¾ x 23¾ in., (45.1 x 60.3 cm.), colored aquatint w/etching on paper (BP 269, DM 641, FR 2179, Y 45,374).

BI *Canal Scene,* s., i., est. $1,0/1,500, (09-17-92, Sloan, #3291), 18⅝ x 23½ in., (47.3 x 59.7 cm.), color etching and aquatint.

BI *Canal Scene,* s., i., (10-30-92, Sloan, #2355), 18⅝ x 23½ in., (47.3 x 59.7 cm.), color etching and aquatint.

$3037* *Escalier De Marbre A Venise,* num. 114, s., drystamp, (05-27-93, Briest, #190), color aquatint impression (BP 1945, DM 4873, FR 16,425, Y 325,579).
$2097* *Escalier De Marbre A Venise,* #185, s., drystamp, full margins, (11-16-92, Briest, #362, illus.), aquatint in colors (BP 1378, DM 3344, FR 11,268, Y 261,700).
BI *Le Hameau Au Bord De L'Eau,* sig. stamp, drystamp, trimmed margins, yellowing, water-staining, est. FF 15/18,000, (11-16-92, Briest, #361, illus.), 21¼ x 25¹⁵⁄16 in., (54 x 66 cm.), aquatint heightened in watercolor.
$3093* *Le Pont D'Amiens Par La Neige,* num. 112, s., large margins, drystamp, holes, (03-31-93, Briest, #E198), aquatint in color (BP 2045, DM 4975, FR 16,902, Y 355,681).
$1992* *Le Pont D'Amiens Par La Neige,* #95, s., full margins, drystamp, (11-16-92, Briest, #363), aquatint in colors (BP 1309, DM 3177, FR 10,704, Y 248,596).
$2202* *Le Pont De L'Estacade,* #186, s., drystamp, full margins, holes, (11-16-92, Briest, #364), aquatint in colors (BP 1447, DM 3512, FR 11,832, Y 274,803).
$2831* *Red Barn - Winter River,* pastel s., full margins, tape remains, (11-16-92, Briest, #360, illus.), 20½ x 28⅜ in., (52 x 72 cm.), aquatint heightened w/pastel (BP 1861, DM 4515, FR 15,212, Y 353,301).
$1430* *"River Scene With A Bridge And Houses",* s., No. 12, blindstamp pub. Georges Petit Editeur, margins, good cond., restored paper losses/tears, surface soiling, notations, (10-28-92, Butterfield, #2720, illus.), 19¼ x 24 in., (489 x 610 mm.), hand-colored aquatint on Arches laid paper w/Japan support (BP 911, DM 2208, FR 7499, Y 175,460).
$523* *Swans,* s. Fritz Thaulow, num. 60, fair cond., laid down between mats, lightstaining, fading, (09-11-92, Skinner, #16B, illus.), 18 x 22¾ in., (45.7 x 57.8 cm.), color lithograph on paper (BP 270, DM 753, FR 2559, Y 64,800).
$1022* *Swans On A Lalke,* #149, s., margins, laid down, stained and other defects, (04-22-93, Bonhams-Chelsea, #132, illus.), plate 19¼ x 23½ in., (48.9 x 59.7 cm.), etching w/aquatint in colors (BP 660, DM 1642, FR 5539, Y 112,369).

THE APOLLO 15 CREW

$1271* *Apollo 15, Moon Buggy And Astronaut, August 2, 1971,* mounted on card, i., s., 186 x 249mm, (05-07-93, Sotheby-London, #299, illus.), photograph, color print (BP 805, DM 2009, FR 6771, Y 139,947).

THEVENET

BI *PLM. Grande Chartreuse. "Pont Saint-Bruno",* fairly good cond., tears, (03-15-93, Arcole, #66), 43⁵⁄16 x 31½ in., (110 x 80 cm.), .

THIEBAUD, Wayne American b. 1920

$990* *Banana Splits, 1964,* s., d., i. A/P, pub. Crown Point Press, full margins, creases, very good cond., (09-19-92, Christie-E, #224), sheet 15 x 11 in., (381 x 279 mm.), etching on wove (BP 569, DM 1482, FR 5077, Y 123,349).
$9350* *Big Suckers, 1971,* s., d., #27/50, from portfolio Seven Still Lifes and a Rabbit, pub. Parasol Press., Ltd., full margins, good cond., pressure marks, (11-07-92, Sotheby-NY, #787, illus.), 17½ x 21¾ in., (445 x 552 mm.), aquatint p. in colors on BFK Rives (BP 6113, DM 14,929, FR 50,459, Y 1,154,036).
$3575* *Boxed Balls, 1979,* s., d., #44/50, printer's blindstamp, Crown Point Press, from portfolio Recent Etchings I, pub. Parasol Press, Inc., full margins, good cond., soiling, (11-07-92, Sotheby-NY, #790, illus.), 24⅜ x 18⅞ in., (619 x 479 mm.), etching and aquatint p. in colors (BP 2337, DM 5708, FR 19,293, Y 441,249).
$11,000* *Candy Apples, 1987,* s., d., #171/200, s. by printer, pub. blindstamp, Crown Point Pres, full margins, good cond., (11-07-92, Sotheby-NY, #794, illus.), 15¼ x 16½ in., (387 x 419 mm.), woodcut p. in colors on Tosa Kozo (BP 7192, DM 17,563, FR 59,363, Y 1,357,689).
$8050* *Candy Apples, 1987,* s., d., #168/200, Crown Point Press blindstamp, s. by printer and w/ink stamp, full margins, notch, excell. cond., (05-11-93, Christie-NY, #580, illus.), sheet 23½ x 24⅜ in., (597 x 619 mm.), color woodcut on Tosa Kozo (BP 5139, DM 12,681, FR 42,728, Y 885,491).
BI *Candy Apples, 1987,* s., d., #168/200, blindstamp, full margins, notch cut out at corner,excellent cond., est. $10/12,000, (11-09-92, Christie-NY, #427, illus.), 23½ x 24⅜ in., (597 x 619 mm.), colored woodcut on Tosa Kozo.
$8625* *Candy Apples, 1987,* s., d., #87/200, s. by printer, seal, blindstamp, pub. Crown Point Press, full margins, good cond., discoloration, (05-15-93, Sotheby-NY, #1240, illus.), 15⅛ x 16½ in., (38.4 x 41.9 cm.), woodcut in colors on Tosa Kozo paper (BP 5608, DM 13,873, FR 46,622, Y 956,102).
$3520* *Candy Counter, 1970,* s., d., i. A.P., pub. Parasol Press, full margins, excell. cond., (09-19-92, Christie-E, #230, illus.), sheet 22¼ x 30¼ in., (565 x 768 mm.), linocut on Arches (BP 2025, DM 5271, FR 18,051, Y 438,575).
$2860* *Chocolate Cake, 1971,* from Seven Still Lifes and a Rabbit, s., d., num. 36/50, pub. Parasol Press, full margins, excell. cond., (09-19-92, Christie-E, #231, illus.), sheet 29⅞ x 22¼ in., (759 x 565 mm.), lithograph in brown on Arches (BP 1645, DM 4283, FR 14,667, Y 356,342).
$3850* *City Edge, 1988,* s., d., #11/60, pub. blindstamp, Crown Point Press, full margins, good cond., (11-07-92, Sotheby-NY, #793, illus.), 11⅞ x 8¾ in., (302 x 222 mm.), etching and aquatint p. in colors (BP 2517, DM 6147, FR 20,777, Y 475,191).
BI *City Edge, 1988,* s., d., #37/60, blindstamp, full margins, excellent cond., est. $4/5,000, (11-09-92, Christie-NY, #428, illus.), 19¾ x 16 in., (502 x 406 mm.), aquatint and drypoint in colors on wove.
BI *City Edge, 1988,* s., d., #33/60, blindstamp p. Lawrence Hamlin, pub. Crown Point Press, full margins, very good cond., est. $5/7,000, (10-28-92, Butterfield, #3152), 11⅞ x 8⅞ in., (302 x 225 mm.), color aquatint on Somerset wove.
$2860* *City Edge, 1988,* full margins, d., num., s., pub. Crown Point Press, blindstamp, (05-27-93, Swann, #270, illus.), 12 x 8¾ in., (30.5 x 22.2 cm.), etching and aquatint, p. in colors (BP 1832, DM 4589, FR 15,468, Y 306,604).
$990* *Clown, 1979,* from Recent Etchings I, s., d., num. 28/50, pub. Parasol Press, fullmargins, excell. cond., (09-19-92, Christie-E, #233), sheet 22¾ x 29¾ in., (578 x 756 mm.), soft-ground etching in colors on Somerset (BP 569, DM 1482, FR 5077, Y 123,349).
$275* *Cows And Bulls,* s., t., #26/70, margins, good cond., glue/paper remains, (10-28-92, Butterfield, #3146), color silkscreen on laid paper, watermark (BP 175, DM 425, FR 1442, Y 33,742).
$990* *Cut Melon, 1964,* s., d., num. 10/15, pub. by artist, full margins, excell. cond., (09-19-92, Christie-E, #225), sheet 14⅞ x 11 in., (378 x 279 mm.), etching on wove (BP 569, DM 1482, FR 5077, Y 123,349).
$6050* *Daffodil, 1979,* s., d., #44/50, printer's blindstamp, Crown Point Press, from portfolio, Recent Etchings I, pub. Parasol Press, Inc., full margins, good cond., (11-07-92, Sotheby-NY, #791, illus.), 23⅛ x 16 in., (587 x 406 mm.), etching and aquatint p. in colors (BP 3956, DM 9660, FR 32,650, Y 746,729).
$8250* *Dark Cake, 1983,* s., d., #157/200, pub. blindstamp, Crown Point Press, full margins, good cond., discoloration, (11-07-92, Sotheby-NY, #797, illus.), 15⅛ x 17½ in., (384 x 445 mm.), woodcut p. in colors on Tosa Kozo (BP 5394, DM 13,173, FR 44,522, Y 1,018,267).
$8280* *Dark Cake, 1983,* s., d., #57/200, Crown Point Press blindstamp, full margins, excell.cond., (05-11-93, Christie-NY, #578, illus.), sheet 20⅜ x 22⅜ in., (518 x 568 mm.), color woodcut on Tosa Kosa (BP 5286, DM 13,043, FR 43,949, Y 910,791).
$7700* *Dark Cake, 1983,* s., d., #103/200, pub. Crown Point Press, full margins, excellent cond., (11-09-92, Christie-NY, #424, illus.), 20¼ x 22½ in., (514 x 572 mm.), colored woodcut on Tosa Koso (BP 5091, DM 12,292, FR 41,532, Y 955,572).
$10,450* *Dark Cake, 1983,* s., d., #199/200, blindstamp pub. Crown Point Press, full margins, very good cond., (10-28-92, Butterfield, #3151, illus.), 15 x 17 in., (381 x 432 mm.), color woodcut on Japan (BP 6658, DM 16,139, FR 54,798, Y 1,282,209).

$6325* *Dark Cake, 1983,* s., d., #119/200, blindstamp, pub. Crown Point Press, full margins, good cond., discoloration, (05-15-93, Sotheby-NY, #1238, illus.), 15 x 17½ in., (38.1 x 44.5 cm.), woodcut in colors on Tosa Kozo paper (BP 4112, DM 10,174, FR 34,189, Y 701,142).

$3300* *Dark Cherries, 1984,* s., d., i. AP/9, blindstamp, full margins, excellent cond., (11-09-92, Christie-NY, #425, illus.), 15¾ x 18½ in., (400 x 470 mm.), aquatint and drypoint in gray and black on wove (BP 2182, DM 5268, FR 17,799, Y 409,531).

$2200* *Dark Country City, 1988,* s., d., #11/25, pub. blindstamp, Crown Point Press, full margins, good cond., (11-07-92, Sotheby-NY, #796, illus.), 21¾ x 31¾ in., (552 x 806 mm.), etching and aquatint p. in colors on Somerset (BP 1438, DM 3513, FR 11,873, Y 271,538).

$1210* *Diagonal Ridge, 1979,* s., d., #44/50, printer's blindstamp, Crown Point Press, from portfolio Recent Etching I, pub. Parasol Press, Inc., full margins, good cond., (11-07-92, Sotheby-NY, #792, illus.), 17⅞ x 21⅞ in., (454 x 556 mm.), etching (BP 791, DM 1932, FR 6530, Y 149,346).

$748* *Eight Dogs, 1990,* s., #13/35, Crown Point Press blindstamp, full margins, excell. cond., the Late M. Anwar Kamal, M.D. Coll., (05-11-93, Christie-NY, #582), sheet 11⅞ x 12⅝ in., (302 x 321 mm.), etching on Somerset (BP 477, DM 1178, FR 3970, Y 82,279).

$880* *Fish, 1964,* s., t., num. 95/100, pub. Crown Point Press, full margins, excell. cond., (09-19-92, Christie-E, #226, illus.), sheet 12⅞ x 10⅞ in., (327 x 276 mm.), drypoint on BFK Rives (BP 506, DM 1318, FR 4513, Y 109,644).

$3025* *Glassed Candy, 1981,* s., d., #46/150, full margins, very good cond., (10-28-92, Butterfield, #3150, illus.), 20 x 17 in., (508 x 432 mm.), color lithograph on cream wove (BP 1927, DM 4672, FR 15,863, Y 371,166).

$3450* *Gum Ball Machine, 1971,* s., d. 1970, #8/50, from portfolio, Seven Still Lifes and a Rabbit, pub. Parasol Press, Ltd., full margins, good cond., discoloration, pressure mark, creases, (02-11-93, Sotheby-NY, #451, illus.), 24³⁄₁₆ x 18¹⁄₁₆ in., (614 x 458 mm.), color linoleum cut (BP 2434, DM 5715, FR 19,339, Y 415,913).

BI *Gum Ball Machine, 1971,* s., d. 1970, #8/50, from portfolio Seven Still Lifes and a Rabbin, pub. Parasol Press, Ltd., full margins, good cond., discoloration, pressure mark,creases, est. $4/5,000, (11-07-92, Sotheby-NY, #788, illus.), 24⅛ x 18 in., (613 x 457 mm.), linoleum cut p. in colors.

$6600* *Gumball Machine, 1971,* from Seven Still Lifes and a Silver Landscape, s., d. 1970, i. A.P.,pub. Parasol press, full margins, excell. cond., (09-19-92, Christie-E, #232, illus.), sheet 24¼ x 18⅜ in., (616 x 467 mm.), linocut in colors on Arches (BP 3796, DM 9883, FR 33,846, Y 822,327).

BI *Hill Street, 1987,* s., d., #47/200, s. by printer, Tadashi Toda, seal, blindstamp publisher, Crown Point Press, full margins, good cond., mat staining, est. $7/9,000, (05-19-93, Butterfield, #2356, illus.), 30 x 20⅛ in., (762 x 511 mm.), woodcut in colors on Echizen Mashi.

$4180* *Large Sucker,* s., d. 1971, annot. A.P., pub. Parasal Press, stamp Chiron Press, (09-20-92, Hindman, #723, illus.), sheet 24 x 22 in., (61 x 55.9 cm.), color lithograph on Rives (BP 2447, DM 6203, FR 21,218, Y 516,623).

$3300* *Large Sucker,* s., d. 1971, #8/50, pub. Parasol Press, Chiron Press blindstamp, prov, (05-16-93, Hindman, #629), 24 x 22 in., (61 x 55.9 cm.), color lithograph (BP 2146, DM 5308, FR 17,838, Y 365,813).

$523* *Mrs. Pigeon,* s., t., #3/5, margins, good cond., tape remains, (10-28-92, Butterfield, #3145), 16 x 9 in., (406 x 229 mm.), color etching w/aquatint on cream wove (BP 333, DM 808, FR 2743, Y 64,172).

$2300* *Neighborhood Ridge, 1984,* s., d., #9/50, Crown Point Press blindstamp, full margins, printer'sink, excell. cond., (05-11-93, Christie-NY, #579, illus.), sheet 23 x 18 in., (584 x 457 mm.), etching and aquatint on wove (BP 1468, DM 3623, FR 12,208, Y 252,997).

$2420* *Neighborhood Ridge, 1984,* s., d., #7/50, blindstamps, full margins, excellent cond., (11-09-92, Christie-NY, #426, illus.), 23 x 18 in., (584 x 457 mm.), etching and aquatint on wove (BP 1600, DM 3863, FR 13,053, Y 300,323).

$1540* *Nickle Machine, 1964,* s., d., i. Trial Proof, pub. by artist, full margins, skinned patches, excell. cond., (09-19-92, Christie-E, #227), sheet 14⅞ x 11 in., (378 x 279 mm.), etching on wove (BP 886, DM 2306, FR 7897, Y 191,876).

$880* *Olives, 1964,* s., t., d., num. 95/100, pub. Crown Point Press, full margins, excell. cond., (09-19-92, Christie-E, #228), sheet 12⅞ x 10⅞ in., (327 x 276 mm.), aquatint on BFK Rives (BP 506, DM 1318, FR 4513, Y 109,644).

BI *Olives, 1964,* s., t., d., #23/100, pub. Crown Point Press, trimmed margins, tape, excellent cond., est. $1/1,500, (11-09-92, Christie-NY, #421), 12¾ x 10⅞ in., (324 x 276 mm.), aquatint on Rives.

$9350* *Paint Cans, 1990,* s., d., #69/100, pub. blindstamp, Trillium Graphics, full margins, good cond., (11-07-92, Sotheby-NY, #798, illus.), 29¾ x 23⅛ in., (756 x 587 mm.), lithograph p. in colors on Arches Cover (BP 6113, DM 14,929, FR 50,459, Y 1,154,036).

BI *Paint Cans, 1990,* s., #III/V, blindstamp publisher, Trillium Graphics, pub. for ChicagoInternational Art Expo, full margins, very good cond.?, est. $12/14,000, (05-19-93, Butterfield, #2359, illus.), 29¾ x 23⅛ in., (756 x 587 mm.), lithograph in colors on wove.

$10,350* *Paint Cans, 1990,* s., d., #55/100, blindstamp, pub. Trillium Graphics, pub. for 1990 Chicago International Art Exposition, full margins, good cond., (05-15-93, Sotheby-NY, #1239, illus.), 29¾ x 23⅛ in., (75.6 x 58.7 cm.), lithograph in colors on Arches Cover (BP 6730, DM 16,648, FR 55,946, Y 1,147,323).

$6900* *Palm Ridge, 1979,* from Recent Etchings II, s., d., #44/50, Crown Point Press blindstamp, full margins, excell. cond., (05-11-93, Christie-NY, #577, illus.), sheet 29¾ x 23 in., (756 x 584 mm.), color soft-ground etching on wove (BP 4405, DM 10,870, FR 36,624, Y 758,992).

BI *Palm Ridge, 1979,* from Recent Etchings II, s., d., #44/50, blindstamps, full margins, excellent cond., est. $8/10,000, (11-09-92, Christie-NY, #423, illus.), 29¾ x 23 in., (756 x 584 mm.), soft-ground etching in colors on wove.

$2070* *Pie Slice, 1962,* s., #27/60, pub. Arturo Schwartz, full margins, good cond., (02-11-93, Sotheby-NY, #450, illus.), 5¹³⁄₁₆ x 4³⁄₁₆ in., (147 x 106 mm.), etching (BP 1461, DM 3429, FR 11,603, Y 249,548).

$1320* *Pool Balls, 1964,* s., d., num. 6/15, pub. by artist, full margins, very good cond., (09-19-92, Christie-E, #229), sheet 15½ x 11⅛ in., (394 x 283 mm.), etching on wove (BP 759, DM 1977, FR 6769, Y 164,465).

$1725* *Recent Etchings I: Clown, 1979,* s., d., #28/50, blindstamp publisher, Crown Point Press, full margins, very good cond?, crease, (05-19-93, Butterfield, #2355, illus.), 17¾ x 23⅞ in., (451 x 606 mm.), soft-ground etching and aquatint in colors on Somerset (BP 1120, DM 2804, FR 9447, Y 190,966).

$1650* *Recent Etchings II: Rose, 1979,* s., d., #32/50, pub. Parasol Press, full margins, good cond., (10-28-92, Butterfield, #3149, illus.), 24 x 17⅞ in., (610 x 454 mm.), soft-ground etching in light blue and rust on Somerset paper (BP 1051, DM 2548, FR 8652, Y 202,454).

BI *Silver Landscape, 1970,* s., d., #3/50, from portfolio Seven Still Lifes and a Silver Landscape, pub. Parasol Press, full margins, very good cond., hinge remains, est. $2,5/3,500, (10-28-92, Butterfield, #3148), 21⅝ x 21 in., (549 x 533 mm.), lithograph in silver and black on Arches.

$1430* *Silver Landscape, 1970,* s., d., num. 3/50, from portfolio Seven Still Lifes And A Silver Landscape, pub. Parasol Press, full margins, very good cond., hinge remains, (02-24-93, Butterfield, #3153), 21⅝ x 21 in., (549 x 533 mm.), lithograph in silver & black on Arches (BP 997, DM 2321, FR 7870, Y 167,801).

$1100* *Six Italian Desserts, 1979,* from recent Etchings II, s., d., num. 20/50, pub. Parasol Press, full margins, stain (rubbed), excell. cond., (09-19-92, Christie-E, #234), plate 15⅞ x 19⅞ in., (403 x 505 mm.), soft-ground etching in dark red on Somerset (BP 633, DM 1647, FR 5641, Y 137,055).

BI *Steep Street, 1989,* s., d., #13/50, Crown Point Press blindstamps, full margins, excell.cond., est. $7/9,000, (05-11-93, Christie-NY, #581, illus.), sheet 38¾ x 30½ in., (984 x 775 mm.), color aquatint and drypoint on wove.

BI *Steep Street, 1989,* s., d., #13/50, blindstamps, full margins, excellent cond., est. $8/10,000, (11-09-92, Christie-NY, #429, illus.), 38¾ x 30½ in., (984 x 775 mm.), aquatint and drypoint in colors on wove.

BI *Steep Street, 1989,* s., d., #5/30, blindstamp publisher Crown Point Press and printer, Lawrence J. Hamlin, very good cond., est. $8/10,000, (05-19-93, Butterfield, #2357, illus.), 30 x 22 in., (762 x 559 mm.), aquatint w/ spitbite in black/grey on Somerset.

$1320* *Sucker Stand, 1964,* s., t., d., #23/100, pub. Crown Point Press, trimmed margins, tape verso, excellent cond., (11-09-92, Christie-NY, #422, illus.), 12⅞ x 10⅞ in., (327 x 276 mm.), aquatint on Rives (BP 873, DM 2107, FR 7120, Y 163,812).

BI *Suckers State I (G. 85), 1967-68,* s., annot. State 1, #38/150, blindstamp printer, Gemini G.E.L., p. Charles Ritt, good cond., creases, staining, est. $1,8/2,200, (05-19-93, Butterfield, #2354), 8 x 14 in., (203 x 356 mm.), lithograph on wove.

$2200* *Suckers, State I (G. 85), 1968,* s., #25/150, blindstamp pub. Gemini G.E.L., full margins, good cond.?, (10-28-92, Butterfield, #3147, illus.), 8 x 14 in., (203 x 356 mm.), lithograph on Rives BFK (BP 1402, DM 3398, FR 11,536, Y 269,939).

BI *Suckers, State I (Gemini 85), 1968,* s., #58/150, pub. blindstamp, Gemini G.E.L., full margins, good cond., creases, est. $2,2/3,000, (11-07-92, Sotheby-NY, #795, illus.), sheet 15⅞ x 21¾ in., (403 x 552 mm.), lithograph.

$1610* *Suckers, State I (Gemini 85), 1968,* s., #58/150, blindstamp, pub. Gemini, G.E.L., full margins, good cond., handling creases, (05-15-93, Sotheby-NY, #1241, illus.), sheet 15⅞ x 21¾ in., (40.3 x 55.2 cm.), lithograph (BP 1047, DM 2590, FR 8703, Y 178,472).

$2200* *Toy Counter, 1970,* s., d. '1971', #31/50, from portfolio Seven still lifes and a Rabbit,pub. Parasol Press, Ltd., full margins, good cond., creases, (11-07-92, Sotheby-NY, #789, illus.), 18⅛ x 24 in., (460 x 610 mm.), silkscreen p. in colors on Arches (BP 1438, DM 3513, FR 11,873, Y 271,538).

BI *Triangle Thins, 1971,* s., d., num., from portfolio, Seven Still Lifes and a Silver Landscape, pub. Parasol Press, full margins, good cond., water stains, crease, soiling,est. $2,5/3,500, (11-07-92, Sotheby-NY, #786, illus.), 21⅞ x 17½ in., (556 x 445 mm.), etching and aquatint p. in colors on BFK Rives.

BI *Untitled, Landscape, 1956,* s., d., #2/20, margins, sealed at mat, mat staining, scuffs, creases, ink loss, est. $7/900, (10-28-92, Butterfield, #3144), 20⅝ x 30⅜ in., (524 x 772 mm.), color silkscreen on wove.

$3450* *Van, 1989,* s., d., #10/50, blindstamp publisher, Crown Point Press and printer Larry Hamlin, very good cond., (05-19-93, Butterfield, #2358, illus.), 8¹³⁄₁₆ x 11⅞ in., (224 x 302 mm.), drypoint in colors on Somerset (BP 2240, DM 5608, FR 18,894, Y 381,933).

THIELE, Arthur

BI *Affiche Passe-Partout Representant Differents Sports,* cond. B, (03-16-93, Boisgirard, #208), 39¾ x 26⅜ in., (101 x 67 cm.), poster.

THIELER, Fred German b. 1916

$709* *Komposition Blau-Gelb-Grau, 1957,* s., d., num., (06-05-93, Grisebach, #896, illus.), 20½ x 14⅛ in., (52 x 35.8 cm.), color serigraph on copper print paper (BP 467, DM 1149, FR 3874, Y 76,057).

$374* *Komposition, (19)71,* s., d., num., (12-01-92, Karl/Faber, #1294), 32¹¹⁄₁₆ x 22¹⁄₁₆ in., (83 x 56 cm.), color lithograph on wove (BP 247, DM 596, FR 2032, Y 46,564).

THIEMANN, Carl 1881-1966

$627* *Abend (Merx 19 F), 1921,* s., (12-05-92, Bassenge, #7768), 14¹³⁄₁₆ x 7¹⁵⁄₁₆ in., (37.6 x 20.3 cm.), color woodcut on Japan (BP 393, DM 978, FR 3332, Y 77,686).

$457* *"Begegnung" (Merx 236 F), 1913,* s., d., t., (12-01-92, Karl/Faber, #1296), 11⅝ x 15⁹⁄₁₆ in., (29.5 x 39.5 cm.), color woodcut on board (BP 302, DM 728, FR 2482, Y 56,897).

$1986* *Herbst (Merx 69 F), 1907,* t., i., s., num., (06-05-93, Bassenge, #6574, illus.), 9¹³⁄₁₆ x 13⁹⁄₁₆ in., (25 x 34.5 cm.), color woodcut on Japan (BP 1307, DM 3220, FR 10,852, Y 213,044).

$922* *Herbst II (Merx 300 I), 1918/19,* t., i., s., (06-05-93, Bassenge, #6577), 8⁹⁄₁₆ x 13¹⁵⁄₁₆ in., (21.8 x 35.5 cm.), color woodcut on hand-made Japan (BP 607, DM 1495, FR 5038, Y 98,906).

$249* *Kater Murr (M. 295 F), 1917,* s., (12-01-92, Karl/Faber, #1297), 10⁷⁄₁₆ x 6½ in., (26.5 x 16.5 cm.), color woodcut (BP 165, DM 397, FR 1353, Y 31,001).

$921* *"Spatherbst" (Merx 238), 1913,* s., t., (06-08-93, Karl/Faber, #1360), approx. 11⅝ x 11¹³⁄₁₆ in., (29.5 x 30 cm.), color woodcut on thick hand-made Japan (BP 605, DM 1494, FR 5033, Y 97,823).

$850* *"Tauwetter" (M. 289), 1917,* s., t., i., (06-08-93, Karl/Faber, #1361), approx. 13⁹⁄₁₆ x 12⅝ in., (34.5 x 32 cm.), color woodcut on Maschinen hand-made (BP 559, DM 1379, FR 4645, Y 90,281).

THIEME, Anthony Dutch/American 1888-1954

BI *"Farm In Winter",* s. A. Thieme within pl., est. $2/300, (12-12-92, A. James, #212), sheet 11⅞ x 9 in., (30.2 x 22.9 cm.), etching.

THIRIOT, Pierre

$300* *Colette Andris,* (01-31-93, Morelle/Marchan, #238), 30⁵⁄₁₆ x 46⁷⁄₁₆ in., (77 x 118 cm.), poster (BP 202, DM 483, FR 1634, Y 37,425).

THOMA, Hans German 1839-1924

$248* *Am Mainufer (Beringer 284,3), 1920,* plate mono., d., t., (09-25-92, Granier, #2697), 6⁵⁄₁₆ x 4¾ in., (16 x 12.1 cm.), sheet 15¾ x 11⁷⁄₁₆ in., (16 x 12.1 cm.), etching on hand-made (BP 145, DM 368, FR 1243, Y 29,934).

$310* *Amor Auf Delphin,* s., 2. Zust, (09-18-92, Schloss Ahlden, #1072), 11¹⁵⁄₁₆ x 7⅝ in., (30.4 x 19.3 cm.), etching on thin machine-made (BP 181, DM 460, FR 1574, Y 38,314).

$290* *Bei Muttersleh n I (Ber. 136/2), 1913,* s., brown staining, (12-01-92, Karl/Faber, #278), 7½ x 9⅝ in., (19 x 24.5 cm.), etching on wove (BP 192, DM 462, FR 1575, Y 36,106).

$166* *Bei Muttterslehn I (Ber. 136), 1913,* s., artist's proof, mount staining, (12-01-92, Karl/Faber, #277), 7½ x 9⅝ in., (19 x 24.5 cm.), etching (BP 110, DM 265, FR 902, Y 20,667).

$289* *Bergsee (Beringer 222 III), 1917,* (12-04-92, Bassenge, #6966), 5³⁄₁₆ x 6⅜ in., (13.2 x 16.2 cm.), etching (BP 185, DM 460, FR 1561, Y 36,080).

$493* *Bernau (Beringer 246, 1), 1919,* s., mono. in plate, d., i., (05-26-93, Dorling, #3008, illus.), 7⅛ x 9¾ in., (18.1 x 24.8 cm.), etching on wove von (by) Van Gelder Zonen (BP 319, DM 804, FR 2707, Y 53,564).

$144* *Bogenschutzen (Beringer 33 III), 1901,* s., (12-04-92, Bassenge, #6959), 9¼ x 6⁹⁄₁₆ in., (23.5 x 16.7 cm.), etching on hand-made (BP 92, DM 229, FR 778, Y 17,978).

$247* *Der Dorfgeiger (Beringer 59), 1895,* ink s., num. Hans Thomas, No. 23, (03-24-93, Venator/Hansten, #2642), image 10¹³⁄₁₆ x 8¾ in., (27.5 x 22.2 cm.), lithograph heightened w/white on Japan (BP 167, DM 403, FR 1373, Y 29,021).

$867* *Engelwolke (Beringer 1), 1992,* s., artist's proof, (12-04-92, Bassenge, #6968), 15⅛ x 17½ in., (38.4 x 44.5 cm.), Tachographie on thick blue paper w/crayon, reworked w/ brush in silver (BP 556, DM 1381, FR 4684, Y 108,240).

$93* *Fliegender Hermes, 1892,* stamped mono., wear, (09-25-92, Granier, #2698), 6¹¹⁄₁₆ x 7½ in., (17 x 19 cm.), sheet 11 x 12¹⁵⁄₁₆ in., (17 x 19 cm.), lithograph on copper print board (BP 54, DM 138, FR 466, Y 11,225).

$422* *Flusslandschaft, Mainufer, Mit Kahn (Beringer 42),* stone mono., d. HTh (18)93, (03-24-93, Venator/Hansten, #2641), 11⁷⁄₁₆ x 18⅛ in., (29 x 46 cm.), color lithograph on paper (BP 286, DM 689, FR 2346, Y 49,583).

BI *Gralsburg (Ber. 197/6), 1916,* s., est. DM 700, (12-01-92, Karl/Faber, #280), 10⅝ x 9¹⁄₁₆ in., (27 x 23 cm.), etching.

$426* *"Heilige Familie!"*, plate i., mono., d. HTh 1917, s. Hans Thoma, (09-14-92, Venator/Hansten, #1699), plate 7³⁄₁₆ x 8¹¹⁄₁₆ in., (18.2 x 22 cm.), etching on Van Gelder-Zonen hand-made (BP 225, DM 633, FR 2146, Y 52,972).

BI *Karlsruher Landschaft II (Ber. 185/3), 1869*, s., est. DM 800, (12-01-92, Karl/Faber, #279), 7¹¹⁄₁₆ x 9⅝ in., (19.5 x 24.5 cm.), etching on simili-Japan.

$113* *Kinder Auf Dem Feld (Beringer 509)*, plate mono., d. HTh 1908, (03-24-93, Venator/Hansten, #2643), pl. 11⅝ x 9¹³⁄₁₆ in., (29.5 x 24.9 cm.), etching (BP 77, DM 185, FR 628, Y 13,277).

BI *Madchenkopf I (Beringer 108), 1911*, s., 1st state, plate mono., d., artist's proof, est. DM 1,200-, (09-25-92, Granier, #2694, illus.), 9¾ x 7¹¹⁄₁₆ in., (24.8 x 19.5 cm.), sheet 14⁹⁄₁₆ x 11¼ in., (24.8 x 19.5 cm.), etching on Japan.

$159* *Mainau (Beringer 4 III), 1897*, s., tear in margin, (12-04-92, Bassenge, #6958), 6⁹⁄₁₆ x 9¹¹⁄₁₆ in., (16.7 x 24.6 cm.), etching on handmade (BP 102, DM 253, FR 859, Y 19,850).

$867* *Die Marchenerzahlerin III (Beringer 32), 1893*, s., (12-04-92, Bassenge, #6969), 14¾ x 17¹¹⁄₁₆ in., (37.5 x 45 cm.), tachographie on thick paper (BP 556, DM 1381, FR 4684, Y 108,240).

$179* *Mondaufgang (Beringer 179,2), 1915*, plate s., mono., d., foxing, (09-25-92, Granier, #2696), 5¹³⁄₁₆ x 5½ in., (14.8 x 14 cm.), sheet 14¹⁵⁄₁₆ x 10⁷⁄₁₆ in., (14.8 x 14 cm.), etching on hand-made (BP 105, DM 265, FR 897, Y 21,605).

$309* *Mondscheingeiger (Beringer 99), 1897*, plate mono., d. HTh 97, (09-14-92, Venator/Hansten, #1698), 13⅞ x 17¹¹⁄₁₆ in., (35.2 x 45 cm.), color print on thick paper (BP 163, DM 459, FR 1557, Y 38,423).

$1226* *Der Mondschingeiger (Beringer (Griffelkunst) 99), 1897*, s., stone mono., d., (06-19-93, Wachholtz, #327), 13¾ x 17¹¹⁄₁₆ in., (35 x 45 cm.), color print on board (BP 823, DM 2070, FR 6958, Y 135,905).

$388* *Monfecucco Lago Di Garda, 1897*, s., stone mono., d., foxing, (09-25-92, Granier, #2700), sh 27⁹⁄₁₆ x 19¹¹⁄₁₆ in., (70 x 50 cm.), color Algraph on copper print paper (BP 227, DM 575, FR 1945, Y 46,832).

BI *Oberitalienische Landschaft (Beringer 84/3), (19)09*, s., est. DM 700, (12-01-92, Karl/Faber, #275), 12¹⁵⁄₁₆ x 16⁵⁄₁₆ in., (33 x 41.5 cm.), etching.

$325* *Schlafendes Kind (Beringer 39 III), 1901*, s., (12-04-92, Bassenge, #6961), 9¹¹⁄₁₆ x 11¹³⁄₁₆ in., (24.6 x 30 cm.), etching on Japan (BP 208, DM 518, FR 1756, Y 40,574).

$505* *Schwarzwaldhaus Mit Kruzifix, 1896*, stone mono., foxing, (09-25-92, Granier, #2699), 12⅜ x 18⁵⁄₁₆ in., (31.5 x 46.5 cm.), sheet 19⅞ x 27⁹⁄₁₆ in., (31.5 x 46.5 cm.), color lithograph on copper print paper (BP 295, DM 749, FR 2531, Y 60,954).

$851* *"Schwarzwaldlandschaft" (Beringer Griffelkunst 71), 1896*, s., pub. in PAN II, Heft 3, blindstamp, (06-05-93, Grisebach, #899, illus.), 6¹⁵⁄₁₆ x 10⅛ in., (17.7 x 25.7 cm.), color lithograph on thick copper print paper (BP 560, DM 1380, FR 4650, Y 91,289).

$225* *Selbstbildnis II (Beringer 459)*, 2nd state of 3, plate mono. HTh, s., d. Hans Thoma Bernau 1898, (03-24-93, Venator/Hansten, #2640), pl. approx. 9¹³⁄₁₆ x 7¹¹⁄₁₆ in., (25 x 19.5 cm.), etching on thin paper (BP 152, DM 367, FR 1251, Y 26,436).

$260* *"Selbstbildnis Vi Mit Blume" (Beringer 237.5), 1919*, s., (11-28-92, Grisebach, #794, illus.), 9¾ x 6⁹⁄₁₆ in., (24.7 x 16.6 cm.), woodcut on handmade (BP 172, DM 414, FR 1406, Y 32,358).

$563* *"St. Blasien", 1899-1910*, s., (11-28-92, Grisebach, #793, illus.), 13¹³⁄₁₆ x 17¹⁄₁₆ in., (35.1 x 43.3 cm.), lithograph on slight cardboard (BP 372, DM 897, FR 3045, Y 70,068).

$913* *Taunuslandschaft ("Oberursel") (Ber. Griffelkunst 47), 1894*, s., (12-01-92, Karl/Faber, #282), 13⁹⁄₁₆ x 17¹⁵⁄₁₆ in., (34.5 x 45.5 cm.), hand-colored lithograph on cardboard (BP 603, DM 1455, FR 4959, Y 113,670).

$745* *"Der Wanderer" (Beringer 56/II), 1903*, s., (06-05-93, Grisebach, #898, illus.), 11¾ x 9¾ in., (29.8 x 24.8 cm.), drypoint on copper print paper (BP 490, DM 1208, FR 4071, Y 79,918).

BI *Wolkenheer II (Ber. 112/2 (von 3), 1911*, s., browned edges, est. DM 700, (12-01-92, Karl/Faber, #276), 7¹¹⁄₁₆ x 9⅝ in., (19.5 x 24.5 cm.), etching on van Gelder Zonen wove.

BI *"Zwischen Den Zeiten" (Ber. 247/II, 248/I (von II), 249/II, 250, 251-52/II), 1919: Six*, pub. F. Bruckmann, s. twice, num., est. DM 800, (12-01-92, Karl/Faber, #281), 17⁵⁄₁₆ x 14³⁄₁₆ in., (44 x 36 cm.), etching and drypoint on hand-made.

THOMAS, Antoine Jean Baptiste

$3080* *Un An A Rome Et Dans Ses Environs (Colas 2872): 72*, folio, foxing throughout, dampstains, (11-12-92, Swann, #128), 16⁹⁄₁₆ x 11 in., (420 x 280 mm.), hand-colored lithograph, contemporary boards (BP 2023, DM 4880, FR 16,462, Y 381,897).

THOMAS, Emil 20th cent.

$57* *Spieler, 1977*, #72/200, s., d., t., creases, (11-13-92, Koller, #5446), 17¹¹⁄₁₆ x 19¹¹⁄₁₆ in., (45 x 50 cm.), serigraph on cardboard (BP 37, DM 89, FR 302, Y 7075, SF 80).

THOMAS, Joseph B.

$633* *Hounds And Hunting Through The Ages (Mellon/Podeschi 361), 1928*, Derrydale Press, limited edit. #7/50 de luxe copies, frontispiece, s.artist and subject, inscription, d. 20 December 1928, Anthony N. B. Garvan Coll., (06-05-93, Christie-NY, #18), on Van Gelder, numerous photogravure and halftone plate, 6 tinted orin color (BP 417, DM 1026, FR 3459, Y 67,904).

THOMAS, Larry

BI *Untitled, 1986*, s., d., blindstamp publisher, Experimental Workshop, good cond., hinge remains, skinned areas, est. $4/600, (05-19-93, Butterfield, #2360), 35 x 59⅛ in., (88.9 x 150.2 cm.), monotype in colors w/graphite additions on wove.

THOMAS and WYLIE LITHOGRAPHY CO., Lithographers
American 19th/20th cent.

$605* *"Firemen, Past And Present, The Old And The New", 1895*, Buchanan & Lyall's Tobacco, pub., ident. w/in matrix, good cond.?, toning, foxing, tear, label, (03-27-93, Skinner, #203A), sight, sheet 21 x 27¼ in., (53.3 x 69.2 cm.), chromolithograph on paper (BP 406, DM 987, FR 3356, Y 70,414).

THOMKINS, Andre 1930-1985

$272* *Otten Net Lo, 1982*, s., d., (10-14-92, Germann, #621), 14¾ x 17¹⁵⁄₁₆ in., (375 x 457 mm.), etching (BP 160, DM 398, FR 1350, Y 32,962, SF 354).

THOMPSON, Art b. 1948

BI *'My Family', 1981*, est. C$1/150, (10-21-92, Maynard, #58), approx. 18½ x 19½ in., (47 x 49.5 cm.), print.

$266* *'Serpent Dancer' and 'Pook-ubs': Two, 1980*, #111/125, s., (10-21-92, Maynard, #45), silkscreen (BP 165, DM 402, FR 1366, Y 32,400, C$ 330).

THOMPSON, James B.

$64* *"Commandments I" and "Commandments II": Two*, each s., t., d. '75, #17/75 and 16/75, prov., exhib., (12-01-92, Ritchie, #59), 30 x 22¾ in., (76.2 x 57.8 cm.), color lithograph w/aluminum collage (BP 42, DM 102, FR 348, Y 7968, C$ 83).

THOMPSON, John (attrib.)

$1100* *Canton, c. 1869*, t. in unidentified hand, stamp, label, (10-15-92, Sotheby-NY, #73, illus.), 8¼ x 10⅞ in., (21 x 27.6 cm.), photograph, albumen print (BP 673, DM 1637, FR 5553, Y 131,974).

THOMPSON, Leslie

$83* *Teton Mountain Range At Dawn*, first trial proof from 2nd state, s., t., margins, good cond., mat burn, light staining, Florence Berryman Estate, (12-12-92, Weschler, #174), 14 x 17¾ in., (35.6 x 45.1 cm.), color lithograph (BP 53, DM 131, FR 448, Y 10,271).

THOMPSON, Rodney

BI *"Bengal Tiger", "Jaguars", "Temple In The Jungle" and "The Watcher":Four*, s., t., margins, good cond., Bengal Tiger taped, Temple w/light-staining, each w/surface soiling, stray printing ink, pencil notations, prop. PrintCorner Coll. of Elizabeth and Charles Whitmore, est. $4/600, (02-24-93, Butterfield, #2875), from 6¹⁄₁₆ x 8¹⁵⁄₁₆ in.,

(154 x 227 mm.), to 7⁹⁄₁₆ x 11¹⁵⁄₁₆ in., (154 x 227 mm.), etching & drypoint on wove.

THOMPSON, Stephen

$726* *"British Museum Photographs", 1872: Forty,* some w/ manuscript num., ded., each 285 x 235mm, (05-07-93, Sotheby-London, #90), photograph, albumen print (BP 460, DM 1148, FR 3868, Y 79,938).

THOMSEN, June   ac. 1980

$121* *Prickles For Bristles,* #2/5, s., t., prov., (11-16-92, Hodgins, #355), 30 x 21¹⁵⁄₁₆ in., (76.2 x 55.9 cm.), serigraph on paper (BP 80, DM 193, FR 650, Y 15,100, C$ 154).

THOMSON, H. (after)

$150* *Crossing The Brook, 1804,* by William Say, pub. H. Macklin, laid on canvas, mounted on stretcher, foxing, (11-30-92, Phillips-London, #211), plate 25¾ x 16¼ in., (654 x 413 mm.), mezzotint on laid (BP 99, DM 239, FR 811, Y 18,668).

THOMSON, John

BI *Bangkok, c. 1865,* est. $1/1,500, (10-14-92, Swann, #258, illus.), 6½ x 8½ in., (16.5 x 21.6 cm.), photograph, albumen print.

$835* *"Street Life In London",* including *"Photography On The Common", "Waiting For A Hire", "The Dramatic Shoeblack", "The Water-Cart", "Black Jack", "November Effigies", "Dealer In Fancy-Ware" and Two Others, 1877: Eight,* various sizes, (05-07-93, Sotheby-London, #92), photograph, woodburytypes (BP 529, DM 1320, FR 4449, Y 91,940).

THOMSON, John   1837-1921

$5081* *"Illustrations Of China And Its People", 1873-74: Four Volumes,* 218 images, descriptive text, orig. maroon cloth gilt, folio, London: Sampson Low, Marston, Low and Searle, (05-06-93, Christie-London, #14, illus.), largest approx. 11½ x 8 in., photograph, 24 collotype plates (BP 3220, DM 8003, FR 26,941, Y 559,027).

THOMSON, Tom   Canadian 1877-1917

$95* *Grip Company: "Group Portrait", "Tying A Fly" (Two Images), "Portrait As A Young Man" and "Thomson In A Canoe", c. 1910: Five,* prov., lit., (06-07-93, Ritchie, #3, illus.), black and white photographic reprints (BP 63, DM 154, FR 519, Y 10,191, C$ 121).

THORBURN, A.

$83* *Les Perdix, 1912,* s., reddish stains, good margins, (04-02-93, Picard, #184), 18¹¹⁄₁₆ x 12¹³⁄₁₆ in., (47.5 x 32.5 cm.), aquatint on Chine fixe (BP 55, DM 133, FR 453, Y 9450).

THORBURN, A. (after)

$14 *Portrait Of Lord Byron,* by J.H. Lynch, (02-05-93, G.A. Key, #44), 11¼ x 9½ in., (28.6 x 24.1 cm.), b/w lithograph (BP 10, DM 23, FR 78, Y 1742).

$249 *"Ryper", "Duck Shooting", "Partridge", "Woodcock", "Unapproachable Geese" and "Snipe": A Set Of Six,* (08-14-92, G.A. Key, #13), 9 x 16 in., (22.9 x 40.6 cm.), engraving (BP 130, DM 365, FR 1237, Y 31,400).

THOREK, Dr. Max   American 1880-1960

BI *"...I Remember When...!",* 1920-30s, mounted on card, t., s., est. BP 2/400, (05-06-93, Christie-London, #180A), 12¼ x 9½ in., photograph, toned gelatin silver print.

$1320* *Blood And Sand, 1940,* s., t. in ink, credit and exhib. labels, prov., (10-13-92, Christie-NY, #371, illus.), 13 x 16 in., (33 x 40.6 cm.), photograph, toned gelatin silver print (BP 769, DM 1934, FR 6570, Y 160,058).

BI *Ole!, 1940,* ink s., t., prov., est. $800/1,200, (04-08-93, Christie-NY, #346, illus.), 11⅞ x 16⅛ in., (30.2 x 41 cm.), photograph, toned gelatin silver print.

$1453* *Thirteen Studies, 1930s,* mounted on card, fron t., s.; s., annot., labels, various sizes, (05-07-93, Sotheby-London, #167, illus.), photograph, carbon and platinum prints (BP 920, DM 2297, FR 7741, Y 159,987).

THORNLEY, William   French b. 1857

$133* *"Paysage Avec Un Moulin" and "Marine": Two,* first, s., full margins, (02-24-93, Picard, #234), color lithograph on simili-Japan or thin chine (BP 93, DM 216, FR 732, Y 15,607).

THORNTON, Dr. Robert John, Publisher   British 1768-1837

BI *The American Aloe,* after P. Reinagle, by T. Sutherland, 2nd final state, watermarked, margins, 3 sides, surface dirt, scuffing, creasing, est. BP 3/500, (10-07-92, Christie-S. Ken, #23), pl 22¾ x 17½ in., (57.8 x 44.5 cm.), aquatint w/line engraving, part p. in color, finished by hand.

$660* *The China Limodoron,* after P. Henderson, by J. Landseer, watermarked, margins, spotting, (10-07-92, Christie-S. Ken, #22), pl 20¾ x 16 in., (52.7 x 40.6 cm.), aquatint w/stipple and line engraving, part p. in color, finished byhand (BP 385, DM 955, FR 3238, Y 79,375).

$605* *"The China Limodoron", 1802,* from The Temple of Flora, ident. in inscriptions, good cond., margins, light/mount staining, marks, John Landseer, engraver, (09-11-92, Skinner, #1, illus.), 17¼ x 13¾ in., (43.8 x 34.9 cm.), color aquatint, stipple engraving, hand coloring on wove paper (BP 313, DM 871, FR 2960, Y 74,960).

$495* *"The Dragon Arum", 1801,* William Ward, engraver, from The Temple of Flora, ident. in inscripts., good cond. ?, (09-11-92, Skinner, #2, illus.), 17½ x 13¾ in., (44.5 x 34.9 cm.), color aquatint and hand coloring on paper (BP 256, DM 713, FR 2422, Y 61,331).

$330* *"Frontispiece" and "Roses": Two,* from Temple Of Flora, both ident. w/in matrices, good cond., toning, crease to former, (10-16-92, Skinner, #484), sheet, sight 19⅝ x 15⅛ in., (49.8 x 38.4 cm.), first etching w/stipple; other collotype; both w/hand coloring on paper (BP 200, DM 487, FR 1656, Y 39,403).

$1696* *A Group Of Auriculas,* after P. Reinagle, by T. Sutherland, 2nd final state, watermarked, margins, creasing, time staining, (10-07-92, Christie-S. Ken, #24), pl 20½ x 16¾ in., (52.1 x 42.5 cm.), aquatint w/line engraving, part p. in color finished by hand (BP 990, DM 2454, FR 8322, Y 203,969).

$264* *Indian Reed,* after P. Henderson, by Caldwall, 2nd final state, watermarked, margins, spotting, scuffing, (10-07-92, Christie-S. Ken, #27), pl 20¼ x 16 in., (51.4 x 40.6 cm.), aquatint w/line and stipple engraving, part p. in color, finished byhand (BP 154, DM 382, FR 1295, Y 31,750).

$413* *"Indian Reed", 1804,* James Caldwell, engraver, from The Temple of Flora, ident. in inscript., good cond.?, (09-11-92, Skinner, #3), 17½ x 13¾ in., (44.5 x 34.9 cm.), color aquatint and hand coloring on paper (BP 214, DM 595, FR 2021, Y 51,171).

$660* *Large Flowering Sensitive Plant,* after P. Reinagle by J. C. Sadler, 2nd final state, watermark, dirt, good cond., (10-07-92, Christie-S. Ken, #26), pl 18¾ x 14 in., (47.6 x 35.6 cm.), aquatint, stipple and line engraving part p. in color finished by hand (BP 385, DM 955, FR 3238, Y 79,375).

$660* *The Narrow-Leaved Kalmia,* after P. Reinagle, by J. Caldwall, watermarked, margins, spotting, (10-07-92, Christie-S. Ken, #21), pl 21¼ x 16 in., (54 x 40.6 cm.), aquatint w/stipple engraving, part p. in color, finished by hand (BP 385, DM 955, FR 3238, Y 79,375).

$825* *"The Narrow-Leaved Kalmia (Caldwell/Reingle)", "The Maggot-Bearing Stapelia (Stadler/Henderson)" and "The Aloe (Medland/Reinagle)": Three,* from The Temple Of Flora, annot. below images, good cond., mount/light staining, (10-16-92, Skinner, #630, illus.), sight 17⅞ x 14 in., (45.4 x 35.6 cm.), color aquatint and hand coloring on paper (BP 500, DM 1219, FR 4139, Y 98,507).

$2200* *The Night-Blowing Cereus,* by Dunkarton after Reinagle and Pether, darkened, stains, tear, repair, trimmed, extracted from Thornton's Temple of Flora, (09-23-92, Sotheby-Arcade, #227, illus.), folio, sheet 20 x 16 in., (50.8 x 40.6 cm.), mezzotint plate w/etching in colors and finished in colors by hand (BP 1286, DM 3294, FR 11,224, Y 263,568).

$904* *The Oblique-Leaved Begonia,* after P. Reinagle, by Caldwall, 2nd final state, watermarked, margins, losses, (10-07-92, Christie-S. Ken, #25), pl 20 x 15 in., (50.8 x 38.1 cm.), aquatint w/stipple and line engraving, part p. in color, finished byhand (BP 528, DM 1308, FR 4436, Y 108,719).

$550* *"The Quadrangular Passion Flower (Hapwood/Henderson)" and "The Winged Passion Flower (Warner/Hender-*

son)": Two, from The Temple Of Flora, annot. below images, good cond., staining,residues, trimmed margins, (10-16-92, Skinner, #730), image 18⅛ x 14⅜ in., (46 x 36.5 cm.), color aquatint, stipple engraving and engraving w/hand coloring on paper (BP 333, DM 812, FR 2760, Y 65,672).

$1602* *The Sacred Egyptian Bean,* after P. Henderson, by Burke and Lewis, watermark, margins, spotting, (10-07-92, Christie-S. Ken, #28, illus.), pl 22 x 17½ in., (55.9 x 44.5 cm.), aquatint w/stipple engraving, part p. in color, finished by hand (BP 935, DM 2318, FR 7861, Y 192,664).

THORPE, John Hall
$43* *Home, 1921,* s., t., (06-08-93, Ritchie, #40, illus.), 8 x 7½ in., (20.3 x 19.1 cm.), wood engraving (BP 28, DM 70, FR 235, Y 4567, C$ 55).

THULSTRUP
$50* *"Sheridan's Final Charge At Winchester",* s. Thulstrup, (09-12-92, Dunning, #1181), 21¼ x 14¼ in., (54 x 36.2 cm.), color print (BP 26, DM 72, FR 245, Y 6195).

THURNEYSEN, Johann Jakob   1636-1711
BI *Dornengekronte Schutzmantel-Madonna,* trimmed, after Charles Claude Dauphin, est. DM 300, (09-14-92, Venator/Hansten, #1613), sh 5⅞ x 3⁹⁄₁₆ in., (14.9 x 9.1 cm.), engraving.

TICE, George   b. 1938
$110* *Boatyard-Stonington, Maine, 1971,* s., p. 3/6/82, (05-16-93, Hindman, #359), 13¼ x 9¼ in., photograph, platinum print (BP 72, DM 177, FR 598, Y 12,249).
$440* *"Car For Sale, Paterson, N.J." and "Tree #14": Two,* photog.'s, sig. on mount, notations, 2nd w/photographer's, inits. onmount, 1969, p. 1982, 1965, (04-07-93, Swann, #568, illus.), one 13½ x 10½ in., other 2⅜ x 2⅜ in., photograph, silver print (BP 291, DM 712, FR 2408, Y 49,989).
$920* *"From The Chrysler Building, New York" and "Sunrise, New York": Two,* one 1978, p. 1989, other 1971, p. 1983, each s., d., t., (05-23-93, Butterfield, #3629, illus.), one 13¼ x 10½ in., other 6¼ x 9½ in., photograph, gelatin silver print (BP 599, DM 1504, FR 5063, Y 101,691).
$880* *Monhegan Island, Maine and Lighthouse, Cape Elizabeth, Maine: Two Photographs, 1971,* t., photog.'s sig., d., (10-14-92, Swann, #579, illus.), 13 x 9 in., (33 x 22.9 cm.), photograph, silver prints (BP 517, DM 1288, FR 4367, Y 106,641).
$2475* *Petit's Mobil Station, Cherry Hill, N.J. (Urban Romantic, p. 120),* mounted, s. by photog., t., d., i. by photog., 1974, p. 1980, (10-15-92, Sotheby-NY, #581, illus.), 15 x 19½ in., (38.1 x 49.5 cm.), photograph, gelatin silver print (BP 1515, DM 3684, FR 12,494, Y 296,941).
BI *Portfolio V: "Deborah", "Ice #1", "Rooftops", "Shared Closet", "Aquatic Plants #1", "Shore In Fog", "Russ Island", "Joe's Barber Shop", "Roaring Fork River" and "White Castle": Ten,* 1967-76, The Witkin Gallery, 1977, embossed portfolio stamp; each s., num.; num. 8, est. $2,5/3,500, (04-08-93, Christie-NY, #518, illus.), smallest 6 x 6 in., (15.2 x 15.2 cm.), largest 10½ x 13½ in., (15.2 x 15.2 cm.), photograph, 8 gelatin silver, 1 platinum, 1 palladium print.
$2300* *Selected Images: "Petit's Mobil Station, Cherry Hill, N.J., 1973", "White Castle, Route #1, Rahway, N.J., 1973" and "Ferry Slip, Jersey City, N.J.,1979": Three,* mounted, s. by photog., s., t., d., p. notations by photog., (04-06-93, Sotheby-NY, #493, illus.), each approx. 15½ x 19½ in., photograph (BP 1519, DM 3705, FR 12,548, Y 262,318).
BI *"Shaker Interior, Sabbathday Lake, Maine, 1971",* p. 1979, mounted on card, s., t., d., annot., 164 x 241mm, est. BP 5/800, (05-07-93, Sotheby-London, #298, illus.), photograph, selenium toned silver print.
$1610* *Two Amish Boys, Lancaster, Pennsylvania, 1962,* p. 1990, s.; t., d., (04-08-93, Christie-NY, #519, illus.), 13⅛ x 10½ in., (33.3 x 26.7 cm.), photograph, gelatin silver print (BP 1056, DM 2586, FR 8755, Y 182,705).

TICHON, Charles
$1606* *Automobiles De Dion-Bouton. 6 Chevaux Moteur A L'Arriere, c. 1900,* Paris, Affiches Kossuth, cond. B+, (06-11-

93, Boisgirard, #153, illus.), 51³⁄₁₆ x 37⅜ in., (130 x 95 cm.), poster (BP 1055, DM 2610, FR 8800, Y 170,398).
$763* *Grand Casino Municipal De Saint-Malo, c. 1900,* Paris, Imp. Kossuth and Cie, (06-11-93, Boisgirard, #151), 49³⁄₁₆ x 35⁷⁄₁₆ in., (125 x 90 cm.), poster (BP 501, DM 1240, FR 4181, Y 80,955).
$70* *Hotel De L'Abbaye De Lourdes. "La Plus Belle Situation..." Basilic Liquor De La Distillerie De Lourdes,* Imp. Pichot, fairly good cond., (02-12-93, Cheval/Robert, #75), 47¼ x 31½ in., (120 x 80 cm.), poster (BP 49, DM 116, FR 393, Y 8442).
$442* *Normandie. La Cote Fleurie. Beuzeval-Houlgate, c. 1900,* Paris, Affiches Kossuth, cond. C, (06-11-93, Boisgirard, #152), 41¾ x 26¾ in., (106 x 68 cm.), poster (BP 290, DM 718, FR 2422, Y 46,897).
$381* *La Place Clichy (...) Nouveautes De La Saison D'Hiver,* Paris, Affiches Kossuth and Cie, cond. B+, (06-11-93, Boisgirard, #150), 51³⁄₁₆ x 35¹³⁄₁₆ in., (130 x 91 cm.), poster (BP 250, DM 619, FR 2088, Y 40,424).
$60* *Plus De Pannes Avec Les Chambres A Air Indegonflables,* mediocre state, (02-12-93, Cheval/Robert, #86), 59¹⁄₁₆ x 46⅞ in., (150 x 119 cm.), poster (BP 42, DM 100, FR 337, Y 7236).

TIEMANN, Walther   1876-1951
BI *Ilustrierte Elzevier-Ausgaben Verlag Hermann Seemann Nachf., 1900,* s. in red ochre, d., lit., est. DM 1,500, (12-05-92, Bassenge, #7634, illus.), 24⁵⁄₁₆ x 18½ in., (61.8 x 47 cm.), color lithograph.

TIEPOLO, Giandomenico   1727-1804
BI *Vecchio Barbuto Con Berretto (Rizzi 218 I, de Vesme 174),* est. DM 1,600, (06-10-93, Hauswedell/Nolt, #218), etching on hand-made.

TIEPOLO, Giovanni Battista   Italian 1696-1770
BI *The Astrologer And The Young Soldier (Rizzi 37),* from Varii Capricci, only state, trimmed irregularly on/just within platemark, staining, est. BP 1,5/2,000, (12-03-92, Sotheby-London, #144, illus.), 5¼ x 6½ in., (133 x 170 mm.), etching.
$1544* *Death Giving Audience (R. 36; DE V. 10),* from Varie Capricci, narrow to thread margins, staining, (06-30-93, Sotheby-London, #237), 5½ x 7 in., (140 x 178 mm.), etching on paper w/part of a large Armorial watermark (BP 1035, DM 2633, FR 8884, Y 165,434).
$3775* *The Family An Oriental (Rizzi 18; De Vesme 27),* from Scherzi di Fantasia, 2nd final state, margins, good cond., (06-30-93, Sotheby-London, #236), 8¾ x 7 in., (222 x 178 mm.), etching (BP 2530, DM 6439, FR 21,720, Y 404,479).
BI *Magician With Four Figures Near A Smoking Altar(de V. 18, R. 9), c. 1740,* plate 6 from Scherzi di Fantasia, 1st state of 2, wide margins, mat staining, foxing, erased inscrip. w/attendant rubbing, creases at edges previously folded back, watermark, prop. Montclair Art Museum, est. $5/7,000, (05-11-93, Christie-NY, #60, illus.), plate 8⅝ x 7¹⁄₁₆ in., (219 x 179 mm.), etching on laid.
BI *A Magician, A Soldier And Three Figures Watching A Burning Skull (DeV. 19; R. 10), 1745-57,* from the Scherzi, 1st state of 2, before num., wide margins, good cond., soiling, folds, traces glue, est. $6,5/8,500, (05-13-93, Sotheby-NY, #342, illus.), 8⅞ x 7 in., (225 x 178 mm.), etching.
BI *Der Reiter Stehend Bei Seinem Pferd (De Vesme 12, Rizzi 38),* aus den Vari Capricci, est. DM 3500, (06-04-93, Bassenge, #5571), 5⁹⁄₁₆ x 7 in., (14.2 x 17.8 cm.), etching.
BI *Six People Watching A Snake (Rizzi 15),* from Scherzi di Fantasia, first state of two, wide margins, creasing,surface dirt, est. BP 2/3,000, (12-03-92, Sotheby-London, #143), 9 x 6¾ in., (228 x 174 mm.), etching.
$1427* *Standing Woman And Seated Men Before An Obelisk From Vari Capricci (R. 32),* watermark, trimmed to narrow margins, foxing, (10-27-92, Phillips-London, #42), plate 5⅜ x 7 in., (137 x 178 mm.), etching on laid (BP 902, DM 2187, FR 7421, Y 174,557).
$3033* *Stehender Philosoph Und Zwei Figuren (De Vesme 8; Rizzi 34),* from Vari Capricci, (12-04-92, Bassenge, #6706, illus.), 5⁵⁄₁₆ x 6¹¹⁄₁₆ in., (13.5 x 17 cm.), etching (BP 1945, DM 4830, FR 16,386, Y 378,652).

$1253* *Three Soldiers And A Youth From Vari Capricci (R. 30),* margins, bottom and right margin trimmed, tape defects, tear, (10-27-92, Phillips-London, #41), plate 5⅝ x 7 in., (143 x 178 mm.), etching on laid (BP 792, DM 1920, FR 6516, Y 153,272).

$6682* *"Les Trois Soldats Et L'Enfant", "La Femme Aux Deux Mains Posees SurUn Vase", "La Mort Donnant Audience" and "L'Oroscope Du Jeune Soldat" (A. de Vesmes, 4, 6, 10 et 11):* Four, stains, 6 and 10 good margins, 11 w/out margins, 4 small margins, (06-16-93, Ader Tajan, #47), etching (BP 4455, DM 11,092, FR 37,226, Y 712,671).

$6992* *Varj Capriccj (De v. 3-12; R. 29-38), before 1749: Set Of Ten,* trimmed, stitching hole, stains, (12-01-92, Christie-London, #203, illus.), averaging sheet 5½ x 6¹⁵⁄₁₆ in., (139 x 176 mm.), etching (BP 4620, DM 11,144, FR 37,979, Y 870,518).

$1035* *A Woman With Her Arms In Chains (De V. 9; R. 35), c. 1739,* from Vari Capricci, thread margins, thin patches, fold, surface dirt,stains, added borderline, (05-13-93, Sotheby-NY, #341), 5⅜ x 6⅞ in., (135 x 175 mm.), etching (BP 679, DM 1671, FR 5637, Y 115,552).

TIEPOLO, Giovanni Domenico   Italian 1727-1804

$578* *Glaube, Liebe, Hoffnung (De Vesme 78; Rizzi 115; Succi 166),* oval, after Giovanni Battista Tiepolo, (12-04-92, Bassenge, #6708), 13¹⁵⁄₁₆ x 17¹¹⁄₁₆ in., (35.5 x 45 cm.), etching (BP 371, DM 921, FR 3123, Y 72,160).

BI *Die Heilige Familie, In Einer Barke Den See Uberquerend (De Vesme 17; Rizzi (1970) 82; Succi 58 II), 1753,* from Idee pittoresche sopra la fuga in Egitto, est. DM 4,800, (12-04-92, Bassenge, #6707, illus.), 6¹⁵⁄₁₆ x 9¼ in., (17.6 x 23.5 cm.), etching.

$1150* *The Holy Family Arriving At A City Gate (De V. 27; R. 92), c. 1750,* pl. 27 from the Flight into Egypt, 2nd (final) state, narrow margins,glued down at corners, creases, discoloration, good cond., The Suida Manning Coll., (05-13-93, Sotheby-NY, #297), 7½ x 9¾ in., (189 x 248 mm.), etching (BP 755, DM 1857, FR 6264, Y 128,391).

$2415* *The Holy Family Descending A Forest Path (De V. 21; R. 86), 1753,* pl. 21, from the Flight into Egypt, 2nd (final) state, watermark, wide margins, rubbed spot, surface dirt, foxing, defects, The Suida Manning Coll., (05-13-93, Sotheby-NY, #295), 7½ x 9⅞ in., (190 x 250 mm.), etching (BP 1585, DM 3900, FR 13,154, Y 269,622).

BI *The Holy Family Leaving By A City Gate (De V. 7; Rizzi 72), c. 1750,* pl. 7 from The Flight into Egypt, 2nd (final) state, narrow margin, trimmed, glued down, tear, creases, stain, discoloration, good cond., The SuidaManning Coll., est. $2/3,000, (05-13-93, Sotheby-NY, #293, illus.), 7⅜ x 9½ in., (188 x 242 mm.), etching.

BI *Joseph And Mary Passing A Shepherd And His Flock (De V. 11; R. 77), c. 1753,* pl. 11 from the Flight into Egypt, from uncleaned plate, countermark,trimmed, stains, soiling, good cond., est. $3,5/5,500, (05-13-93, Sotheby-NY, #343, illus.), 7¼ x 9⅝ in., (183 x 243 mm.), etching.

$1725* *Mary Supported By Two Angels (De. V. 26; R. 91), c. 1750,* pl. 26 from the Flight into Egypt, 2nd (final) state, narrow marginson 3 sides, trimmed, glued down at corners, creases, paper loss, discoloration,good cond., The Suida Manning Coll., (05-13-93, Sotheby-NY, #296), 7⅜ x 9½ in., (187 x 242 mm.), etching (BP 1132, DM 2785, FR 9395, Y 192,587).

$1115* *Oriental With Dividers (R. 189; DE V. 145),* from Raccolta di Teste, 1st state of 2, wide margins, printer's creases, surface dirt, (06-30-93, Sotheby-London, #238), 6¼ x 4¾ in., (159 x 121 mm.), etching on paper w/an F. L. (length) watermark (BP 747, DM 1902, FR 6415, Y 119,469).

$2166* *Rembrandtesker, Orientalischer Kopf (De Vesme 140 I; Rizzi 180 I; Succi 119 I), 1770-75,* watermark, lit., (12-04-92, Bassenge, #6712, illus.), 5⅞ x 4½ in., (15 x 11.4 cm.), etching (BP 1389, DM 3450, FR 11,702, Y 270,412).

$1840* *The Rest On The Flight (De V. 13; R. 78), 1750,* pl. 13 from the Flight into Egypt, 2nd (final) state, trimmed,

glueddown, tear, creases, discoloration, The Suida Manning Coll., (05-13-93, Sotheby-NY, #294), 7⅜ x 9½ in., (187 x 242 mm.), etching (BP 1208, DM 2971, FR 10,022, Y 205,426).

$1914* *La Sacra Famiglia Arriva A Un Traghetto Di Un Fiume (De Vesme 14), c.1750-1753,* from the series Fuga in Egitto, (06-08-93, Karl/Faber, #205, illus.), etching (BP 1258, DM 3106, FR 10,459, Y 203,293).

$1029* *Turk Seen From Behind (R. 207; DE V. 163),* from Raccolta di Teste, 2nd final state, margins, stains, ex coll. R.Alianello (L. 5k), (06-30-93, Sotheby-London, #239), 4¾ x 3 in., (121 x 76 mm.), etching (BP 690, DM 1755, FR 5921, Y 110,254).

$5345* *Venezia Riceve L'Omaggion Di Nettuno (Succi 89/III; Rizzi 107/III), 1757-1758,* after Giovanni Battista Tiepolo, (06-23-93, Kornfeld, #113, illus.), etching (BP 3631, DM 9044, FR 30,421, Y 582,307, SF 8050).

$1877* *Wappen Und Romische Insignien (De Vesme 112; Rizzi 151; Succi 169), 1774,* watermark, (12-04-92, Bassenge, #6709, illus.), 8⅜ x 10¹³⁄₁₆ in., (21.2 x 27.4 cm.), etching (BP 1204, DM 2989, FR 10,140, Y 234,332).

TIEPOLO, Jean Baptiste

$2167* *Les Deux Soldats Et Les Deux Femmes (A. de Vesmes, num. 5),* large margins, (04-02-93, Picard, #21), 5¼ x 6¹¹⁄₁₆ in., (13.3 x 17 cm.), etching (BP 1427, DM 3483, FR 11,829, Y 246,727).

TIJTGAT, Edgard   1879-1957

BI *Souvenir D'Une Fenetre Aimee, 1919,* s., t., d., margins, good cond., water staining, papertape, creases,est. G 4/600, (12-09-92, Sotheby-Amstrdm, #660), 8¹⁄₁₆ x 6½ in., (205 x 165 mm.), woodcut on Japan.

TILLEMANS, Peter (after)

$2760* *"View Of A Horse Match Over The Long Course At New-Market" (Siltzer p. 274), 1723 and "Plate Of The Fox-Chase" (S. p. 274), 1723: Two,* trimmed to defects, minor defects, Anthony N. B. Garvan Coll., (06-05-93, Christie-NY, #52), engraving w/hand-coloring on two sheets of laid (BP 1817, DM 4475, FR 15,082, Y 296,074).

TILLYER, William

BI *"Untitled" and "Untitled", 1976: Two,* each s., d., #67/200 and #244/250, pub. Bernard Jacobson, good cond.,-creases, est. $150/200, (02-24-93, Butterfield, #3270), one 44½ x 14³⁄₁₆ in., (113 x 36 cm.), other 50 x 15 in., (113 x 36 cm.), silkscreen in colors on wove.

$1364* *Vases, 1981: Nine,* s., num., full margins, good cond., (12-03-92, Sotheby-London, #829, illus.), woodcut in colors on Japan on wove (BP 880, DM 2145, FR 7322, Y 169,715).

TILSON, Joe   English b. 1928

$316* *Clip-O-Matic, 1971,* #45/120, s., d., (04-21-93, Germann, #799), 27⅜ x 19⁵⁄₁₆ in., (695 x 490 mm.), color serigraph and multiple (BP 205, DM 505, FR 1708, Y 34,983, SF 460).

$523* *"Moon Mantra" and "Seed", 1978: Two,* each s., d., first annot. 8/120 A.P., second #36/71, full margins, good cond. (?), pressure marks, second good cond., creases, surface soiling, (02-24-93, Butterfield, #3271), one 38½ x 25¼ in., (978 x 641 mm.), other 34½ x 25½ in., (978 x 641 mm.), etching and aquatint (the first w/collage) in colors on wove (BP 365, DM 849, FR 2878, Y 61,371).

$553* *Mother Earth, 1972,* #4/70, s., (04-21-93, Germann, #798, illus.), 24 x 35¹³⁄₁₆ in., (610 x 910 mm.), color serigraph and collage (BP 359, DM 884, FR 2989, Y 61,220, SF 805).

$784* *New York Skyline, 1967,* A.P., s., 1300 x 750mm, (09-04-92, Germann, #579), color screenprint and collage (BP 393, DM 1099, FR 3740, Y 96,504, SF 978).

$1201* *Signatures, 1987-88: Set Of Six,* s., d., #3/40, pub. Waddington Graphics, good cond., (06-30-93, Sotheby-London, #951, illus.), each sh c. 21⅝ x 15⅜ in., (549 x 391 mm.), etching w/aquatint and carborundum in color w/hand applied white goldleaf on Khadi (BP 805, DM 2048, FR 6910, Y 128,683).

BI *Sky III, 1967,* s., d., #2/70, pub. Marlborough Fine Art, paper yellowing, est. BP 2/300, (10-27-92, Phillips-London, #222), image 37 x 24 in., (940 x 610 mm.), screenprint w/vacuum-formed letters on wove.

TILY, Eugene

$138* *"Mrs. Gregory",* after Sir Henry Raeburn, pub. Frost and Reed, 1916, (03-12-93, DuMouchelle, #2454), 16½ x 13 in., (41.9 x 33 cm.), colored mezzotint engraving (BP 96, DM 230, FR 781, Y 16,264).

TILY, Eugene, Engraver

$201* *A Day's Shooting, 1942,* s., blindstamp, pub. Frost and Reed, margins, (11-12-92, Bonhams-Chelsea, #68), plate 22¼ x 30 in., (56.5 x 76.2 cm.), color mezzotint (BP 132, DM 318, FR 1074, Y 24,923).

$117* *A Day's Shooting, 1942,* s., blindstamp, pub. Frost and Reed, margins, (11-12-92, Bonhams-Chelsea, #67), plate 22¼ x 30 in., (56.5 x 76.2 cm.), color mezzotint (BP 77, DM 185, FR 625, Y 14,507).

TIMBERLAKE, Bob (after)

$66* *"Daisies",* s., num., t. below image, (08-05-92, Boos, #735), 15 x 22 in., (381 x 559 mm.), color print (BP 35, DM 97, FR 329, Y 8406).

TING, Walasse American b. 1929

$126* *Composition,* s., 33/50, (09-30-92, Kunsthallen, #281), color lithograph (BP 71, DM 179, FR 604, Y 15,121, DK 690).

$119* *Composition, 1956,* s. Walasse Ting 13/VII/56, (03-24-93, Kunsthallen, #319), color lithograph (BP 81, DM 194, FR 661, Y 13,982, DK 748).

$169* *Composition, 1964,* s. Ting 64, bon a tirer, (09-30-92, Kunsthallen, #280), lithograph (BP 95, DM 240, FR 811, Y 20,281, DK 920).

$274* *Composition, 1976,* s. Ting 76, 41/100, from Pour Jorn portfolio, (09-30-92, Kunsthallen, #282), lithograph (BP 155, DM 389, FR 1314, Y 32,881, DK 1495).

$165* *Composition, 1977,* s. Ting 77, artist proof, (03-24-93, Kunsthallen, #320), lithograph (BP 112, DM 269, FR 917, Y 19,387, DK 1035).

$110* *"Fireworks", 1974,* s., excellent cond., (10-31-92, Cleveland, #399), 14¾ x 22¼ in., (37.5 x 56.5 cm.), lithograph in colors (BP 70, DM 169, FR 574, Y 13,626).

$90* *"Fireworks", 1974,* Print Club of Cleveland Pub. No. 52, s., excell. cond., (05-15-93, Cleveland, #501), 15 x 22 in., (38.1 x 55.9 cm.), color lithograph (BP 59, DM 145, FR 486, Y 9977).

$496* *Frau Mit Katze, (19)86,* s., d., num., blindstamp, (06-08-93, Karl/Faber, #1367), approx. 21$\frac{7}{16}$ x 29$\frac{5}{16}$ in., (54.5 x 74.5 cm.), color lithograph on BFK Rives wove (BP 326, DM 805, FR 2710, Y 52,682).

BI *Galerie Adrien Maeght, Paris,* est. $100/150, (12-10-92, Sloan, #2319), 24¾ x 19⅝ in., (62.9 x 49.8 cm.), color lithograph poster.

$192* *Girl, 1984,* s., d., #45/100, margins, good cond., (05-27-93, Sotheby-Amstrdm, #690), 21$\frac{7}{16}$ x 29½ in., (545 x 750 mm.), color lithograph on wove (BP 123, DM 308, FR 1038, Y 20,583, G 345).

$251* *Graeshoppere,* s. 86, a.p., 18/30, (09-29-92, B. Rasmussen, #364), lithograph in colors (BP 141, DM 355, FR 1210, Y 29,963, DK 1380).

$249* *Komposition, 1974,* s., Cleveland Print Club, (12-01-92, Karl/Faber, #1300), 14$\frac{15}{16}$ x 22$\frac{1}{16}$ in., (38 x 56 cm.), color lithograph on wove (BP 165, DM 397, FR 1353, Y 31,001).

$377* *Liggende Model,* s. 88, 87/200, (09-29-92, B. Rasmussen, #363), lithograph in colors (BP 212, DM 532, FR 1817, Y 45,004, DK 2070).

$220* *Papegojer, 1988: Two,* s. Ting 88, 182/185, (03-24-93, Kunsthallen, #318), color lithograph (BP 149, DM 359, FR 1223, Y 25,849, DK 1380).

BI *Springtime Is Here, 1989,* s., d., #102/200, full margins, good cond., est. Dfl. 800/1,200, (05-27-93, Sotheby-Amstrdm, #692), 34$\frac{9}{16}$ x 37$\frac{7}{16}$ in., (878 x 951 mm.), color lithograph on wove.

$1042* *Springtime Is Here, 1989,* s., d., i. Artist Proof, #22/50, full margins, good cond.?, (12-09-92, Sotheby-Amstrdm, #656), 34⅝ x 37$\frac{3}{16}$ in., (880 x 945 mm.), color lithograph on wove (BP 665, DM 1636, FR 5581, Y 129,200, G 1840).

$977* *Springtime Is Here, 1989,* s., d., #121/200, full margins, good cond., (12-09-92, Sotheby-Amstrdm, #654, illus.), 34$\frac{9}{16}$ x 37$\frac{7}{16}$ in., (878 x 951 mm.), color lithograph on wove (BP 623, DM 1534, FR 5233, Y 121,141, G 1725).

$167* *To Modeller,* s. 79, 81/100, (09-29-92, B. Rasmussen, #366), lithograph in colors (BP 94, DM 236, FR 805, Y 19,936, DK 920).

$251* *To Papegojer,* s. 88, 182/185, (09-29-92, B. Rasmussen, #365), aquatint in colors (BP 141, DM 355, FR 1210, Y 29,963, DK 1380).

BI *Untitled,* s., margins, good cond., est. Dfl. 2/300, (05-27-93, Sotheby-Amstrdm, #693), sh 11$\frac{7}{16}$ x 15$\frac{15}{16}$ in., (290 x 406 mm.), lithograph on wove.

$234* *Untitled, 1981,* s., d., #91/200, full margins, good cond., (12-09-92, Sotheby-Amstrdm, #651), 17⅝ x 23$\frac{11}{16}$ in., (447 x 602 mm.), color lithograph on Somerset wove (BP 149, DM 367, FR 1253, Y 29,014, G 414).

$261* *Untitled, 1981,* s., d., #22/200, pub. London Arts, good cond., (12-09-92, Sotheby-Amstrdm, #652), sheet 17$\frac{11}{16}$ x 23$\frac{7}{16}$ in., (450 x 595 mm.), color lithograph on wove (BP 167, DM 410, FR 1398, Y 32,362, G 460).

$261* *Untitled, 1981,* s., d., #7/200, pub. London Arts, good cond., (12-09-92, Sotheby-Amstrdm, #650), sheet 17$\frac{11}{16}$ x 23$\frac{7}{16}$ in., (450 x 595 mm.), color lithograph on wove (BP 167, DM 410, FR 1398, Y 32,362, G 460).

$192* *Untitled, 1985,* s., d., #66/150, margins, good cond., (05-27-93, Sotheby-Amstrdm, #689, illus.), 19$\frac{13}{16}$ x 27⅞ in., (504 x 708 mm.), color lithograph on wove (BP 123, DM 308, FR 1038, Y 20,583, G 345).

$359* *Untitled, 1985,* s., d., #78/150, margins, good cond.?, (12-09-92, Sotheby-Amstrdm, #653), 19⅞ x 27$\frac{9}{16}$ in., (505 x 700 mm.), color lithograph on wove (BP 229, DM 563, FR 1923, Y 44,513, G 633).

$554* *Untitled, 1986,* s., d., #98/125, good cond.?, (12-09-92, Sotheby-Amstrdm, #655), sheet 20$\frac{13}{16}$ x 28$\frac{15}{16}$ in., (528 x 735 mm.), color lithograph on wove (BP 354, DM 870, FR 2967, Y 68,692, G 978).

BI *Untitled: Two,* proof, full sheet, good cond., discoloration, creases, est. Dfl. 4/600, (05-27-93, Sotheby-Amstrdm, #691), sh 26⅜ x 20$\frac{1}{16}$ in., (670 x 510 mm.), color lithograph.

TINGUELY, Jean Swiss 1925-1991

$316* *1er Aout 1991,* s., (04-21-93, Germann, #807), 38$\frac{15}{16}$ x 27$\frac{3}{16}$ in., (990 x 690 mm.), offset color lithograph (BP 205, DM 505, FR 1708, Y 34,983, SF 460).

$369* *1er Aout, 1991,* s., 1000 x 700mm, (09-04-92, Germann, #586), color offset-lithograph (BP 185, DM 517, FR 1760, Y 45,421, SF 460).

$60* *"25ieme Rose D'Or. Montreaux. 85", 1985,* exhib. poster, #93/250, s., num., (03-16-93, Schuler, #3383, illus.), 39$\frac{3}{16}$ x 25$\frac{9}{16}$ in., (99.5 x 65 cm.), serigraph and offset (BP 41, DM 100, FR 339, Y 7016, SF 92).

$1803* *Affiche "Voliere Dromesko, Paris",* s., (11-13-92, Koller, #5449), 27$\frac{9}{16}$ x 19$\frac{11}{16}$ in., (70 x 50 cm.), serigraph w/ feather on posterboard (BP 1165, DM 2830, FR 9545, Y 223,781, SF 2552).

$1475* *Affiche Stadel 1979/1980, "Luginbuhl + Tinguely",* s., (11-13-92, Koller, #5448), 32$\frac{11}{16}$ x 22$\frac{1}{16}$ in., (83 x 56 cm.), serigraph on posterboard (BP 953, DM 2316, FR 7808, Y 183,071, SF 2088).

$2414* *"Belluard",* #54/200, s., num., (12-05-92, Mangisch, #713), 16$\frac{9}{16}$ x 22$\frac{7}{16}$ in., (42 x 57 cm.), offset lithograph (BP 1512, DM 3764, FR 12,827, Y 299,096, SF 3450).

$1765* *Cenodoxus,* 21/100, s., (10-14-92, Germann, #624), 14$\frac{15}{16}$ x 22$\frac{7}{16}$ in., (380 x 570 mm.), etching (BP 1036, DM 2583, FR 8759, Y 213,888, SF 2300).

$2786* *Chaos I, 1974,* #90/100, s., lit., (11-13-92, Koller, #5454, illus.), 16$\frac{15}{16}$ x 23¼ in., (43 x 59 cm.), lithograph on Arches (BP 1800, DM 4374, FR 14,749, Y 345,786, SF 3944).

$1207* *"Chaos" (Dessins Et Gravures Pour Les Sculptures No. 280), 1972,* #223/300, s., (12-05-92, Mangisch, #711), 13$\frac{9}{16}$ x 18⅞ in., (34.5 x 48 cm.), 19⅛ x 26¼ in., (34.5 x 48 cm.), etching (BP 756, DM 1882, FR 6413, Y 149,548, SF 1725).

$1382* *Chaos, 1972,* #128/300, s., (09-04-92, Germann, #587, illus.), 19 x 25 15/16 in., (483 x 660 mm.), etching (BP 693, DM 1937, FR 6594, Y 170,113, SF 1725).

$232* *Composition,* s. Jean Tinguely, 1986, (09-30-92, Kunsthallen, #283), poster, offset in colors (BP 131, DM 329, FR 1113, Y 27,841, DK 1265).

BI *EOS,* E.A., s., est. SF 900/1,200, (10-14-92, Germann, #623), 19 11/16 x 25⅝ in., (500 x 651 mm.), serigraph.

$363* *EOS,* E.A., s., (04-21-93, Germann, #800), 19 11/16 x 25⅝ in., (500 x 651 mm.), serigraph in gray and black (BP 236, DM 580, FR 1962, Y 40,186, SF 529).

BI *"Esselier", 1976,* s., d. Jean Tinguely 76, num. 23/190, t., num. 222.30.76 Esselier inmatrix, very good cond., est. $18/2200, (09-11-92, Skinner, #109, illus.), approx. 17¼ x 20 in., (43.8 x 50.8 cm.), color lithograph/collage (w/full/trimmed decals) on paper.

BI *Essellier 222-30-76, 1970,* s., d., #22/190, full margins, good cond., surface soiling, est. $1/1,500, (10-28-92, Butterfield, #3153), 16½ x 20 in., (419 x 508 mm.), color lithograph w/silkscreen and collage on BFK Rives.

$1894* *Ferrari, 1991,* s., d., (05-08-93, Dobiaschofsky, #2312), 26⅜ x 19⅞ in., (67 x 50.5 cm.), color serigraph poster (BP 1236, DM 3043, FR 10,266, Y 211,644, SF 2760).

BI *From Portfolio "La Vittoria", 1970,* #26/100, s., num., est. SF 3,8/4,500, (11-13-92, Koller, #5457), 12⅝ x 16⅛ in., (32 x 41 cm.), lithograph w/hand-rework on Fabriano.

BI *From Portfolio "La Vittoria", 1970,* #26/100, mono., est. SF 3,8/4,500, (11-13-92, Koller, #5456), 11 13/16 x 17 5/16 in., (30 x 44 cm.), lithograph w/hand-rework on Fabriano.

$1147* *Hockey League, 1990,* E.A., s., 1000mm x 700mm, (10-14-92, Germann, #626), color serigraph (BP 673, DM 1679, FR 5692, Y 138,997, SF 1495).

BI *Hockey League, 1990,* E.A., s., est. SF 1,5/2,000, 1000 x 700mm, (09-04-92, Germann, #583), color serigraph.

$711* *Hockey League, 1990,* E.A., s., (04-21-93, Germann, #805), 39⅜ x 27 9/16 in., (100 x 70 cm.), color serigraph (BP 461, DM 1137, FR 3843, Y 78,711, SF 1035).

$709* *"Jolas-Milano", 1970,* s., num., (06-05-93, Grisebach, #901, illus.), 25 9/16 x 19½ in., (65 x 49.5 cm.), color offset w/color offset collage on copper print paper (BP 467, DM 1149, FR 3874, Y 76,057).

BI *Komposition,* 89/100, s., est. SF 2/2,800, (10-14-92, Germann, #625), 14 13/16 x 22 7/16 in., (377 x 570 mm.), etching.

$1382* *Komposition,* #89/100, s., (09-04-92, Germann, #582), 14 13/16 x 22 7/16 in., (377 x 570 mm.), etching (BP 693, DM 1937, FR 6594, Y 170,113, SF 1725).

$2685* *Komposition,* X/XX, s., (06-24-93, Germann, #789), 17 5/16 x 19 11/16 in., (440 x 500 mm.), color lithograph w/collage (BP 1767, DM 4353, FR 14,672, Y 288,028, SF 3910).

BI *Komposition, 1972,* 223/300, s., est. SF 1,8/2,300, (10-14-92, Germann, #627, illus.), 18⅞ x 25 15/16 in., (480 x 660 mm.), etching.

$3606* *"Meta, Meta Roto-Zaza",* #988/999, s., (11-13-92, Koller, #5452), 35 7/16 x 27 9/16 in., (90 x 70 cm.), lithograph and collage on print paper (BP 2330, DM 5661, FR 19,089, Y 447,561, SF 5104).

$1264* *Meta-Chaos, 1973,* #8/100, s., (04-21-93, Germann, #801, illus.), 12⅜ x 17 13/16 in., (314 x 453 mm.), etching (BP 820, DM 2020, FR 6832, Y 139,931, SF 1840).

$1299* *Meta-Harmonie, 1986,* s., num., (11-28-92, Schoppmann, #836), 15 3/16 x 31 11/16 in., (38.5 x 80.5 cm.), serigraph on color offset on cardboard (BP 857, DM 2069, FR 7025, Y 161,668).

$4659* *Le Monstre Dans La Foret (Mason 185),* 38/100, s., (06-24-93, Germann, #790, illus.), 11 13/16 x 16 7/16 in., (300 x 418 mm.), watercolor and collage over serigraph (BP 3067, DM 7554, FR 25,459, Y 499,785, SF 6785).

BI *"Moscou-Fribourg",* #91/100, s., est. SF 7,5/9,000, (11-13-92, Koller, #5455), 30 11/16 x 34⅝ in., (78 x 88 cm.), serigraph on print paper.

$1064* *Progetti, 1972: Three,* unique proofs, one num. 3/20, another E.A., all s., (12-15-92, Finarte-Milan, #95), largest 19⅛ x 13 9/16 in., (48.5 x 34.5 cm.), smallest 18½ x 12 15/16 in., (48.5 x 34.5 cm.), aquatint in colors w/collage (BP 679, DM 1668, FR 5699, Y 131,961, L 1495).

BI *Reflexion, 1972,* s., num., Edition Putman, est. DM 1500, (12-01-92, Karl/Faber, #1302), 13¾ x 18 11/16 in., (35 x 47.5 cm.), etching on Arches France wove.

BI *Requiem Pour Une Feuille Morte,* #196/300, s., num., est. SF 1,6/1,800, (06-15-93, Schuler, #3428, illus.), sh 18⅞ x 25 15/16 in., (48 x 66 cm.), 15 15/16 x 25 3/16 in., (48 x 66 cm.), lithograph.

BI *Requiem Pour Une Feuille Morte,* E.A., s., est. SF 2,5/66, (11-13-92, Koller, #5451), sheet 19 5/16 x 25 15/16 in., (49 x 66 cm.), lithograph on wove.

BI *Requiem Pour Une Feuille Morte, 1966 and 1967: Two,* Galerie Denise Rene und Hans Mayer, s., est. SF 7/8,500, (11-13-92, Koller, #5458), 23⅝ x 78⅜ in., (60 x 199 cm.), poster in 2 parts on offset paper.

BI *Requiem Pour Une Feuille Morte, 1967,* s., num., est. DM 1,200, (06-05-93, Bassenge, #6578), 16⅛ x 25⅜ in., (41 x 64.5 cm.), lithograph on Arches.

$775* *Requiem Pour Une Feuille Morte, 1968,* s., num., (05-26-93, Dorling, #3012), 16⅛ x 2⅜ in., (41 x 6 cm.), lithograph on handmade Arches (BP 501, DM 1264, FR 4256, Y 84,203).

BI *Rose D'Or De Montreux,* E.A., s., est. SF 1,3/1,800, 1000 x 700mm, (09-04-92, Germann, #585), color serigraph.

$632* *Rose D'Or De Montreux,* E.A., s., (06-24-93, Germann, #788), 39⅜ x 27 9/16 in., (100 x 70 cm.), color serigraph (BP 416, DM 1025, FR 3454, Y 67,797, SF 920).

$165* *"Salut Shimizu", 1980,* s. J. Tinguely in matrix, num. 85/100, excellent cond., (09-11-92, Skinner, #107, illus.), approx. sight 8 x 11¾ in., (20.3 x 29.8 cm.), lithograph in colors on paper (BP 85, DM 238, FR 807, Y 20,444).

$1079* *"Tudor Von John Cage",* s., num., (12-01-92, Karl/Faber, #1303), 18⅞ x 13⅜ in., (48 x 34 cm.), color serigraph and offset print w/collage on board (BP 713, DM 1720, FR 5861, Y 134,338).

BI *Untitled, 1988,* #39/100, s., est. SF 2,5/2,800, (12-05-92, Mangisch, #712), 15¾ x 19 11/16 in., (40 x 50 cm.), serigraph reworket by hand.

TINTORETTO (after)

BI *Naissance De St. Jean,* est. $175/225, (04-02-93, Sloan, #2268), sight 8¾ x 13 in., (222 x 330 mm.), engraving.

TIPTON, William H.

$5463* *Cyclorama Of Gettysburg: Pickett's Charge, 1882: Ten,* 6 num., photog. stamp verso, (04-06-93, Sotheby-NY, #13, illus.), average 5½ x 8 in., photograph, albumen print (BP 3608, DM 8801, FR 29,804, Y 623,061).

TISCHBEIN, Johann Heinrich (the younger) German 1742-1808

$202* *Ein Philosoph Vor Dem Tische Im Nachdenken (Nagler 6), 1783,* after D. Teniers, (12-04-92, Bassenge, #6714), 9 7/16 x 6⅞ in., (23.9 x 17.5 cm.), etching (BP 130, DM 322, FR 1091, Y 25,218).

TISSOT, James Jacques French 1836-1902

$1082* *Au Bord De La Mer, (W. 47), 1880,* margins, mount-staining verso, good cond., (12-01-92, Christie-London, #548), P. 14 15/16 x 5⅜ in., (380 x 137 mm.), etching w/drypoint on van Gelder laid (BP 715, DM 1725, FR 5877, Y 134,711).

$2090* *Le Banc De Jardin (Wentworth 75), 1883,* final state, good cond., printer's crease, handling creases, soiling, (11-05-92, Sotheby-NY, #446), 16¼ x 22⅛ in., (412 x 561 mm.), sh 21¼ x 28¼ in., (412 x 561 mm.), mezzotint p. in brownish-black on chine applique (BP 1359, DM 3305, FR 11,182, Y 256,410).

$1320* *Berthe (W. 74), 1883,* s. in image, d., full margins, good cond., mat staining, surface soiling, creasing, (10-28-92, Butterfield, #2721), 14⅛ x 11 in., (359 x 279 mm.), etching w/drypoint on laid paper w/watermark (BP 841, DM 2039, FR 6922, Y 161,963).

$983* *Berthe (W. 74), 1883,* abrasions, staining, pinhole, large margins, (02-24-93, Picard, #237), etching and drypoint on simili-Japan (BP 685, DM 1596, FR 5410, Y 115,349).

BI *Ces Dames Des Chars (W. 78), 1885,* whole margins, first state, reddish stains, (06-11-93, Picard, #172), 15¾ x 10 in., (400 x 254 mm.), etching and drypoint in black on laid.

$1430* *Emigrants (Wentworth 45), 1880,* s., annot. Trial proof, fifth and final state as illus. by Wentworth, (10-18-92, Hindman, #455, illus.), 13⅝ x 6⅜ in., (34.6 x 16.2 cm.), etching and drypoint on 18th cent. ledger paper w/watermark (BP 875, DM 2129, FR 7219, Y 171,566).

$1798* *Entre Les Deux Mon Coeur Balance (W. 30), 1877,* whole margins, (06-11-93, Picard, #169), 9¾ x 13¾ in., (248 x 349 mm.), etching and drypoint in black on laid (BP 1181, DM 2922, FR 9852, Y 190,769).

$1373* *Entre Les Deux Mon Coeur Balance (Wentworth 30), 1877,* margins, good cond., foxing, discoloration, water stain, (06-30-93, Sotheby-London, #689, illus.), sh 14¾ x 22 in., (375 x 559 mm.), etching and drypoint on laid (BP 920, DM 2342, FR 7900, Y 147,112).

$1431* *Entre Les Deux Mon Coeur Balance (Wentworth 30), 1877,* s., red stamp, full margins, mount-stained, (10-27-92, Phillips-London, #223), plate 9⅞ x 13¾ in., (251 x 349 mm.), etching w/drypoint on fine laid (BP 904, DM 2193, FR 7441, Y 175,046).

$9991* *La Galerie Du Calcutta (Wentworth 25), 1876,* large margins, annot., reddish stains, crease, (06-11-93, Picard, #168, illus.), 10¼ x 14⅛ in., (260 x 359 mm.), drypoint in black on laid (BP 6564, DM 16,238, FR 54,745, Y 1,060,053).

$1840* *Le Hamac (W. 46), 1880,* s., artist's red stamp, margins, loss in image, discolored, water stain, foxing, nick, losses, scotch tape, (05-13-93, Sotheby-NY, #830), 10⅞ x 7⅛ in., (277 x 182 mm.), sh 12 x 8¼ in., (277 x 182 mm.), etching and drypoint (BP 1208, DM 2971, FR 10,022, Y 205,426).

$2298* *Le Journal (W. 73), 1883,* whole margins, stamped, s., reddish stains, (06-11-93, Picard, #170), 14⅞ x 11½ in., (378 x 292 mm.), etching and drypoint on laid (BP 1510, DM 3735, FR 12,592, Y 243,820).

$2640* *Le Journal (Wentworth 73 IV/IV), 1883,* bears artist's stamp, (05-16-93, Hindman, #443, illus.), 14⅞ x 11½ in., (37.8 x 29.2 cm.), etching and drypoint (BP 1717, DM 4246, FR 14,270, Y 292,650).

$1699* *L'Ambitieuse (W. 77), 1885,* definitive state, whole margins, (06-11-93, Picard, #171), 15⅝ x 10 in., (397 x 254 mm.), etching and drypoint in black on laid (BP 1116, DM 2761, FR 9310, Y 180,265).

BI *"Le Matin" (W. 82),* excell. cond., est. $4/600, (10-31-92, Cleveland, #341, illus.), 19¼ x 10¼ in., (48.9 x 26 cm.), mezzotint.

BI *"My Garden In St. John's Wood" (W. 39), 1878,* excell. cond., est. $3/400, (10-31-92, Cleveland, #338), 7⅜ x 4½ in., (18.7 x 11.4 cm.), etching and drypoint.

$2354* *Le Portique De La National Gallery, Londres (W. 40), 1878,* s., soiling, untrimmed margins, (02-24-93, Picard, #236), etching and drypoint on thick ivory laid (BP 1642, DM 3821, FR 12,955, Y 276,226).

BI *"The Prodigal Son: The Departure" (W. 58 II/II), 1882,* excell. cond., est. $4/500, (10-31-92, Cleveland, #339), 12¼ x 14¾ in., (31.1 x 37.5 cm.), etching.

BI *"The Prodigal Son: The Return" (W. 60 II/II), 1882,* foxing, est. $4/500, (10-31-92, Cleveland, #340), 12¼ x 14¾ in., (31.1 x 37.5 cm.), etching.

$2580* *Promenade Dans La Neige (W., 48), 1880,* whole margins, artist's stamp, (04-02-93, Picard, #186), 22⅜ x 10⅜ in., (56.8 x 26.3 cm.), etching and drypoint in black on laid (BP 1699, DM 4147, FR 14,083, Y 293,749).

$770* *Sur L'Herbe (W. 50), 1880,* 2nd (final) state, t. (by another hand?), margins slightly trimmed, good cond., light-staining, sheet toned, paper partially split, hinge & glue remains, rubbed area, foxing, surface soiling, pencil notations, (02-24-93, Butterfield, #2977), 7¾ x 10¹¹⁄₁₆ in., etching & drypoint on Van Gelder laid (BP 537, DM 1250, FR 4238, Y 90,354).

$3390* *La Tamise (Wentworth, 20), 1876,* small margins, (04-02-93, Picard, #185, illus.), 9¼ x 14¼ in., (23.5 x 36.2 cm.), etching and drypoint in black on laid (BP 2233, DM 5448, FR 18,504, Y 385,973).

$805* *Le Veuf (Wentworth 28), 1877,* margins, good cond., discoloration, fox marks, (05-13-93, Sotheby-NY, #829), 13⅞ x 9 in., (352 x 229 mm.), sh 16 x 10½ in., (352 x 229 mm.), etching and drypoint on laid (BP 528, DM 1300, FR 4385, Y 89,874).

$1045* *"The Widower" (Wentworth 28),* excell. cond., (10-31-92, Cleveland, #337), 13⅞ x 9 in., (35.2 x 22.9 cm.), etching (BP 670, DM 1608, FR 5454, Y 129,444).

TITIAN   1477-1576
$503* *Diana Mit Ihren Nymphen (Nagler Bd. 22, S. 265/Bd. 15, S. 196),* (09-14-92, Venator/Hansten, #1614), plate 18³⁄₁₆ x 14¼ in., (46.2 x 36.2 cm.), engraving (BP 266, DM 748, FR 2534, Y 62,547).

BI *Die Landschaft Mit Dem Schweinehirten 9B. XVI, 6),* after Tizian, est. DM 600, (12-04-92, Bassenge, #6464), 7¹⁵⁄₁₆ x 12¹³⁄₁₆ in., (20.3 x 32.6 cm.), etching.

TITIAN (after)
BI *St. Francis Receiving The Stigmata (Pass. VI, P. 235, 59),* attrib. to Boldrini, trimmed, drying creases at center, restored area, repairs, borderline filled in, est. BP 2/3,000, (06-30-93, Sotheby-London, #240), 11½ x 16⅞ in., (292 x 429 mm.), woodcut.

TITO, Ettore   Italian 1859-1941
$264* *"Taste" and "Smell": Two,* from the Five Senses, s. Tito in plste., full margins, (03-12-93, Goldberg, #898A, illus.), oval 9½ x 12 in., (24.1 x 30.5 cm.), hand-colored etching (BP 184, DM 439, FR 1494, Y 31,114).

TITUS-CARMEL, Gerard   French b. 1942
$210* *Bonjour Max Ernst, 1974,* s., d. 74, #65/100, full margins, (11-16-92, Briest, #102), 19¹¹⁄₁₆ x 25⁹⁄₁₆ in., (50 x 65 cm.), etching in 2 colors (BP 138, DM 335, FR 1128, Y 26,207).

BI *Composition, 1981,* s., d., 2/75, est. FF6/800, (06-28-93, Loudmer, #376), 8⅜ x 9¾ in., (213 x 247 mm.), sh 25⁹⁄₁₆ x 18⅞ in., (213 x 247 mm.), color lithograph on Arches wove.

$734* *E Constructions Possibles, 1971: Seven,* s., #8/99, full margins, (11-16-92, Briest, #365), 20¼ x 25¹³⁄₁₆ in., (51.5 x 65.5 cm.), etching in colors (BP 482, DM 1171, FR 3944, Y 91,601).

$112* *"Eclat I", 1982,* ed. Maeght Lelong, #2/100, s., (10-18-92, Pescheteau, #268), 17¹⁵⁄₁₆ x 22³⁄₁₆ in., (45.7 x 56.4 cm.), drypoint and aquatint on Rives (BP 68, DM 165, FR 562, Y 13,373).

TNOUZEAU, Christine   b. 1942
$194* *Maries Aux Chats, 1982,* s., #38/120, t., (09-18-92, Schloss Ahlden, #1073), 14¹⁵⁄₁₆ x 15¹⁄₁₆ in., (38 x 38.3 cm.), color etching on hand-made (BP 114, DM 288, FR 985, Y 23,977).

TOBEY, Mark   American 1890-1976
$1965* *Untitled, c. 1968: Two* unique proofs, #9/15, s., stamped, (12-15-92, Finarte-Milan, #11, illus.), 11⅝ x 13⁹⁄₁₆ in., (29.5 x 34.5 cm.), etching (BP 1254, DM 3080, FR 10,525, Y 243,706, L 2760).

BI *The Awakening-Dawn, 1974,* 76/150, s., est. SF 600/800, (10-14-92, Germann, #465), 19¹¹⁄₁₆ x 25¹³⁄₁₆ in., (500 x 655 mm.), color aquatint.

BI *The Awaking Night, 1974,* s., num., est. DM 2,000-, (09-25-92, Granier, #3028), sheet 19¾ x 25¹⁵⁄₁₆ in., (50.2 x 66 cm.), etching on BFK Rives.

$332* *Composition,* s., (06-24-93, Germann, #524), 10⅝ x 6¹¹⁄₁₆ in., (270 x 170 mm.), color aquatint (BP 219, DM 538, FR 1814, Y 35,615, SF 483).

$191* *Composition, 1966,* s., #222/300, (06-12-93, Hauswedell/Nolt, #428), approx. 4⅞ x 7⅞ in., (12.4 x 20 cm.), color lithograph on thick wove (BP 125, DM 311, FR 1045, Y 20,099).

$389* *Composition, 1973,* s., blindstamp, (06-12-93, Hauswedell/Nolt, #430), 24⁷⁄₁₆ x 15⅜ in., (62 x 39 cm.), color lithograph on thick wove (BP 255, DM 633, FR 2128, Y 40,934).

$722* *Confusion, 1975,* s., num., (11-28-92, Schoppmann, #841), 17¹¹⁄₁₆ x 11¹³⁄₁₆ in., (45 x 30 cm.), color lithograph on Arches wove (BP 477, DM 1150, FR 3905, Y 89,857).

BI *Gesicht, 1970,* s., d., blindstamp, est. DM 900, (11-20-92, Lempertz, #906), sh 22⅛ x 17¹³⁄₁₆ in., (56.2 x 45.3 cm.), lithograph on BFK Rives wove.

BI *Golden Days (Heidenheim 40), 1974,* #49/90, s., blindstamp, est. DM 750, (11-20-92, Lempertz, #907), sh 15⁹⁄₁₆ x 10⅛ in., (39.5 x 25.7 cm.), color etching on hand-made.

$573* *Golden Days (Heidenheim 40), 1974*, s., #25/90, (05-27-93, Lempertz, #1065), 15⁹⁄₁₆ x 9¹⁵⁄₁₆ in., (39.5 x 25.3 cm.), color etching on cream wove Richard de Bas (BP 367, DM 919, FR 3099, Y 61,428).

$722* *The Harvest's Gleaning 1975*, s., i. E.A., num., (11-28-92, Schoppmann, #842), 11 x 14³⁄₁₆ in., (28 x 36 cm.), color etching on BFK Rives (BP 477, DM 1150, FR 3905, Y 89,857).

$722* *Of Time And Age, 1975*, s., i. E.A., num., (11-28-92, Schoppmann, #843), 14³⁄₁₆ x 11 in., (36 x 28 cm.), color etching on Rives (BP 477, DM 1150, FR 3905, Y 89,857).

$722* *Paean, 1975*, s., E.A., num., (11-28-92, Schoppmann, #840), 11 x 14³⁄₁₆ in., (28 x 36 cm.), color etching on BFK Rives (BP 477, DM 1150, FR 3905, Y 89,857).

BI *Raissance Of A Flower, 1975*, s., #6/150, blindstamp pub., Trans World Art, full margins, good cond., est. $7/900, (02-24-93, Butterfield, #3272), 15¼ x 10⅜ in., (387 x 264 mm.), lithograph in colors on Arches.

$722* *Raissance Of A Flower, 1975*, s., num., (11-28-92, Schoppmann, #839), 15⅜ x 10¼ in., (39 x 26 cm.), color lithograph on Arches wove (BP 477, DM 1150, FR 3905, Y 89,857).

$664* *To Life (H. 44), 1974*, s., H(ors) C(ommerce), (12-01-92, Karl/Faber, #1305), 13¹⁵⁄₁₆ x 10¹³⁄₁₆ in., (35.5 x 27.5 cm.), color etching on Japon nacre (BP 439, DM 1058, FR 3607, Y 82,669).

$354* *To Life (H. 44), 1974*, s., (06-08-93, Karl/Faber, #1370), approx. 13¹⁵⁄₁₆ x 10¹³⁄₁₆ in., (35.5 x 27.5 cm.), color etching (BP 233, DM 574, FR 1934, Y 37,600).

BI *Two Compositions, 1972*, s., 2nd d., #179/300 and 30/96, 2nd pub. Edition de Beauclair, full margins, good cond., est. BP 5/700, (06-30-93, Sotheby-London, #953), one 4⅞ x 7⅞ in., (124 x 200 mm.), the other 10¼ x 16 in., (124 x 200 mm.), color lithograph and an etching in dark red on wove.

$8800* *Untitled*, s., d. Tobey 66, prov., (11-19-92, Christie-NY, #355, illus.), 8 x 6⅞ in., (20.3 x 17.5 cm.), monotype w/gouache on paper (BP 5794, DM 14,031, FR 47,261, Y 1,094,391).

BI *Untitled, 1967*, s., d., full margins, good cond., minor handling creases, est. Dfl. 800/1,200, (05-27-93, Sotheby-Amstrdm, #694), 15⅜ x 22⁷⁄₁₆ in., (390 x 570 mm.), color lithograph on wove.

$352* *Untitled, 1973*, s., d., num. 8/96, margins, light-staining, old glue, (09-19-92, Christie-E, #235), borderline 9¼ x 10⅝ in., (235 x 270 mm.), lithograph in black and red on wove, laid down (BP 202, DM 527, FR 1805, Y 43,857).

$680* *Vibrating Surface*, s., num., (12-01-92, Karl/Faber, #1306), 13¾ x 10¹³⁄₁₆ in., (35 x 27.5 cm.), color etching on BFK Rives wove (BP 449, DM 1084, FR 3694, Y 84,661).

$354* *Vibrating Surface, 1974*, s., num., (06-08-93, Karl/Faber, #1371), approx. 13¾ x 10¹³⁄₁₆ in., (35 x 27.5 cm.), color etching on BFK Rives wove (BP 233, DM 574, FR 1934, Y 37,600).

$354* *Winter Leaves (Heidenheim 43), 1974*, s., from series Hommage to Tobey, (06-08-93, Karl/Faber, #1369), approx. 13¹⁵⁄₁₆ x 11 in., (35.5 x 28 cm.), color etching on BFK Rives wove (BP 233, DM 574, FR 1934, Y 37,600).

$664* *Winter Leaves, 1974*, s., (12-01-92, Karl/Faber, #1304), 13¹⁵⁄₁₆ x 11 in., (35.5 x 28 cm.), color etching on Japon nacre (BP 439, DM 1058, FR 3607, Y 82,669).

TOBIASSE, Theo   Israeli/French b. 1927

$170* *"Bucolique A La Theiere"*, #242/310, s., (04-04-93, Pescheteau, #301), 35⁷⁄₁₆ x 23⅝ in., (90 x 60 cm.), color lithograph on Arches (BP 112, DM 273, FR 928, Y 19,356).

$554* *"C'Est Un Train Qui Porte Un Parfum L'Odalisque"*, s. 42/175, (11-07-92, Falkkloos, #521, illus.), lithograph in colors (BP 362, DM 889, FR 2990, Y 68,378, SK 3300).

BI *Ce Qu'il Faut De Desir Pour Une Fleur D'Attente, c. 1984*, from the Femmes suite, num., s., est. $6/900, (05-27-93, Swann, #271), sh 43 x 28½ in., (109.2 x 72.4 cm.), color lithograph.

$213* *Le Chant Profond De La Lumiere...*, plate t.; s., #52/125, prov., (12-01-92, Ritchie, #26, illus.), 30¼ x 22½ in., (76.8 x 57.2 cm.), color lithograph (BP 141, DM 339, FR 1157, Y 26,519, C$ 275).

$1716* *"Dame Au Violoncelle", "Une Fleur Pour Mardochee", "Dame Au Grand Chapeau" and another, 1980-82: Four*, each s., three t., num., one num. from 99, pub. Nahan Editions, goodcond., foxing, (06-30-93, Sotheby-London, #954, illus.), carborundum w/embossing in color (BP 1150, DM 2927, FR 9873, Y 183,864).

BI *"Femme Foraine", "Fleur De Cantique", "Cantate 51 De Bach..." and "Grande Parade Du Jazz", c. 1980*, each s., one t., num., pub. Nahan Editions, good cond., creasing, est. BP 800/1,200, (06-30-93, Sotheby-London, #955, illus.), 3 color lithographs, 1 carborundum w/embossing collage in color.

BI *Komposition, 1970*, from Queen Esther Suite, #155/200, s., est. SF 5/700, (09-04-92, Germann, #2), 21⅞ x 29¹⁵⁄₁₆ in., (555 x 760 mm.), color lithograph.

BI *Komposition, Aus "Queen Esther Suite", 1970*, 155/200, s., est. SF 700/800, (10-14-92, Germann, #466), 21⅞ x 29¹⁵⁄₁₆ in., (555 x 760 mm.), color lithograph.

$330* *Lumiere Pour Attendre Deborah, c. 1984*, num., s., (05-27-93, Swann, #272), sh 43 x 28½ in., (109.2 x 72.4 cm.), color lithograph (BP 211, DM 530, FR 1785, Y 35,377).

$295* *Portrait De Pomme Avec Bougie*, #96/125, s., (09-04-92, Germann, #590), 22⁷⁄₁₆ x 29¹⁵⁄₁₆ in., (570 x 760 mm.), color lithograph on Japan (BP 148, DM 413, FR 1407, Y 36,312, SF 368).

$372* *"Prophetesse Pou Un Amour Sublime"*, #29/250, s. Theo Tobiasse, t., (07-14-92, Encans, #252), 40⅜ x 26⁹⁄₁₆ in., (102.5 x 67.5 cm.), lithograph (BP 194, DM 552, FR 1861, Y 46,517, C$ 444).

$660* *Le Puits De Jacob*, from the Femmes suite, s., num. H.C. 18/20, (12-08-92, Swann, #294, illus.), 43 x 29½ in., (109.2 x 74.9 cm.), color lithograph (BP 414, DM 1028, FR 3503, Y 81,805).

$221* *"Le Puits De Jacob"*, #E.A. VII/XXX, s., t., (02-16-93, Encans, #138), 10¹³⁄₁₆ x 20¹⁄₁₆ in., (27.5 x 51 cm.), lithograph (BP 153, DM 361, FR 1222, Y 26,477, C$ 278).

$357* *"Le Quai Des Poetes Mandits"*, s., 139/150, (04-17-93, Falkkloos, #523), 19⁵⁄₁₆ x 25³⁄₁₆ in., (49 x 64 cm.), lithograph in colors (BP 232, DM 571, FR 1929, Y 39,698, SK 2640).

BI *Three Musicians*, s., #89/175, est. C$ 4/600, (12-01-92, Ritchie, #27), 21 x 27¼ in., (53.3 x 69.2 cm.), color lithograph.

TOFFOLI, Louis   French b. 1907

$247* *"Famille Peruvienne"*, artist's proof, s., (10-18-92, Pescheteau, #269), 22¹⁄₁₆ x 29¹⁵⁄₁₆ in., (56 x 76 cm.), lithograph in colors on wove (BP 150, DM 365, FR 1239, Y 29,493).

$184* *Maternite*, s., 71/150, (06-28-93, Loudmer, #378), 26⅜ x 18⅞ in., (670 x 480 mm.), sh 29¹⁵⁄₁₆ x 22¹⁄₁₆ in., (670 x 480 mm.), color lithograph on BFK Rives (BP 123, DM 313, FR 1053, Y 19,523).

BI *"Maternite"*, artist's proof, s., est. FF1,200/1,500, (04-04-93, Pescheteau, #302), 29¹⁵⁄₁₆ x 22¹⁄₁₆ in., (76 x 56 cm.), color lithograph.

BI *"Le Terrassier"*, #34/45, s., est. FF6/800, (04-04-93, Pescheteau, #303), 19¹¹⁄₁₆ x 12¹³⁄₁₆ in., (50 x 32.5 cm.), color lithograph on wove.

$232* *Les Tonneliers*, s., 78/250, (06-28-93, Loudmer, #377), 26⅜ x 18⅞ in., (670 x 480 mm.), sh 29¹⁵⁄₁₆ x 22¹⁄₁₆ in., (670 x 480 mm.), color lithograph on BFK Rives (BP 155, DM 394, FR 1328, Y 24,615).

TOKURIKI, T.   Japanese 20th cent.

$55* *The Courtyard Of Heian shrine In Kyoto*, (07-03-92, Sloan, #879), sight 14¾ x 10 in., (37.5 x 25.4 cm.), woodblock (BP 29, DM 83, FR 281, Y 6856).

TOKURIKI, Tomikichiro   Japanese b. 1902

BI *"Bird And Flowers", 1965*, ink s., d., s. w/artist's seal, est. $2/300, (10-31-92, Cleveland, #48), 14¼ x 20⅛ in., (36.2 x 51.1 cm.), color woodcut.

$143* *Twelve Months Of Kyoto: Twelve*, orig. porfolio, (04-02-93, Sloan, #1870), each 11⅓ x 10¼ in., (288 x 260 mm.), color woodcut (BP 94, DM 230, FR 781, Y 16,281).

TOLEDO, Francisco   Mexican b. 1940
$4400* *Amazona Con Serpiente, 1970,* s., good cond., narrow margins, (11-23-92, Sotheby-NY, #298, illus.), image 6⅞ x 4⅞ in., (174 x 125 mm.), watercolor over etching (BP 2877, DM 7045, FR 23,900, Y 545,838).
BI *"Caballo Y Avispas" and "Dos Caballos", c. 1970: Two,* s., i. 'EA', full margins, time staining, crease, very good cond.; second, #31/100, est. $1,2/1,800, (05-17-93, Christie-NY, #317), lithograph in colors on Arches.
$1265* *"Caballo Y Avispas" and "Mujer Barriendo Sapos", c. 1972: Two,* s., #XXVII/LXXV, XXXVII/LXXV, full margins, very good cond., yellowing, (05-18-93, Sotheby-NY, #281, illus.), one, image 15¾ x 20½ in., (400 x 521 mm.), the other, image 15½ x 20½ in., (400 x 521 mm.), lithograph p. in colors on Arches (BP 824, DM 2053, FR 6932, Y 140,978).
$1045* *"Caballo Y Avispas", "Hombre Y Pescado", "Two Men Measuring A Pig With Pigletts", and "Man and A Horse At Night", 1970: Four,* each s., annot. LIV/LXXV, XXII/LXXV, II/LXXV, LII/LXXV, blindstamp ofpub., full margins, good cond., stain, creases, surface soiling, pencil notations, (02-24-93, Butterfield, #2683), three 15½ x 20½ in., (394 x 521 mm.), one 20½ x 15½ in., (394 x 521 mm.), lithographs in colors on Arches (BP 729, DM 1696, FR 5751, Y 122,624).
$1320* *"Caballo Y Avispas", and "Midiendo Cochino", c. 1970: Two,* s., #XXXVI/LXXV and #XXXVII/LXXV, good cond., yellowing, full margins, (11-23-92, Sotheby-NY, #297, illus.), image 15¾ x 20½ in., (400 x 520 mm.), image 16⅛ x 20¼ in., (400 x 520 mm.), two lithographs p. in colors on Arches (BP 863, DM 2113, FR 7170, Y 163,751).
$4400* *Caminos, 1969,* ink s., good cond., full margins, yellowing, notations verso, (11-23-92, Sotheby-NY, #299, illus.), image 5⅞ x 9⅝ in., (150 x 244 mm.), watercolor over etching (BP 2877, DM 7045, FR 23,900, Y 545,838).
$633* *La Cara,* s., #8/100, blindstamp, Atelier Clot, printer, full margins, good cond., hinge remains, (05-19-93, Butterfield, #1856), 19¾ x 26⅛ in., (502 x 664 mm.), woodcut in colors on Arches (BP 411, DM 1029, FR 3467, Y 70,076).
BI *Clot Bramsen Et Georges La Rue Vieille-Du-Temple Paris-Ive, c. 1972,* s., good cond., yellowing, water stains, mat stain, foxing, est. $2,5/3,000, (05-18-93, Sotheby-NY, #282, illus.), image 21⅛ x 16⅛ in., (537 x 410 mm.), lithograph p. in colors.
$964* *Composition With Figures: Four,* 5/7, 2/9, 2/4, 7/9, (05-12-93, AB Stockholm, #7055, illus.), roulette w/etching (BP 629, DM 1555, FR 5239, Y 107,625, SK 7150).
BI *"Goat", c. 1969, "Woman And Deer", c. 1969, and "Woman Mounting Bull": Three,* first, s., #31/45, full margins, time staining, some creasing, very good cond.; second, #4/40; third, #27/45, mat staining, very good cond., est. $1,8/2,200, (05-17-93, Christie-NY, #316, illus.), first, lithograph in dark brown on Arches; second, on Rives; third, on BFK Rives.
$1320* *"Hombre Y Pescado", and "El Pozo", c. 1970: Two,* s., #XXXVI/LXXV and #XXVII/LXXV, good cond., yellowing, (11-23-92, Sotheby-NY, #296, illus.), image 15½ x 20½ in., (395 x 520 mm.), image 20½ x 15¾ in., (395 x 520 mm.), two lithographs p. in colors on Arches (BP 863, DM 2113, FR 7170, Y 163,751).
BI *La Jaiba, 1969,* s., annot. epreuve d'artiste, good cond.?, surface soiling, notations, est. $1/1,500, (10-28-92, Butterfield, #2584), 39½ x 25⅞ in., (100.3 x 65.7 cm.), color lithograph on wove.
BI *Lazando Caballos, 1969,* s., annot. XXXIX/LXXV, blindstamp, full amrgins, very good cond.?, est. $9/1,200, (10-28-92, Butterfield, #2585), 20½ x 15½ in., (521 x 394 mm.), color lithograph on cream wove.
$605* *Leon, 1970,* s., t., #185/250, pub. AAA, full margins, good cond., (10-28-92, Butterfield, #2586), 11¹⁵⁄₁₆ x 9¾ in., (303 x 248 mm.), etching w/aquatint on cream wove (BP 385, DM 934, FR 3173, Y 74,233).
$1725* *Leon, c. 1968,* s., t., #57/250, full margins, good cond., ink stain, (05-18-93, Sotheby-NY, #280, illus.), image

11¾ x 9⅝ in., (298 x 244 mm.), etching and aquatint (BP 1124, DM 2799, FR 9452, Y 192,243).
$2300* *Liberty For Victor Yodo, 1978: Four,* s., #11/30, #18/30, #30/30, i., 'P.A.', #1/15, pub. Ediciones Arvil,full margins, creasing, surface soiling, very good cond., (05-17-93, Christie-NY, #319, illus.), 17 x 12¼ in., (432 x 311 mm.), etching on BFK Rives (BP 1500, DM 3711, FR 12,500, Y 256,125).
BI *(Seaside Commpositions), 1965,* each s., d., i. H.C., good cond., est. BP 8/1,000, (12-03-92, Sotheby-London, #832, illus.), each approx. 37⅜ x 24¼ in., (950 x 615 mm.), silkscreen in colors.
$652* *Seaside Compositions, 1965,* s., d., i. H.C., good cond., (06-30-93, Sotheby-London, #956, illus.), each c. 37⅜ x 24¼ in., (949 x 616 mm.), color silkscreen (BP 437, DM 1112, FR 3751, Y 69,860).
BI *"Vaquero De Vacas" and " "Untitled", c. 1970,: Two,* s., i. 'EA', full margins, time staining, surface soiling, good cond.; second, i. 'e.a.', crease, est. $1,2/1,800, (05-17-93, Christie-NY, #318, illus.), lithograph in colors on Arches.
$1265* *"Vaquero Y Ganado" and "Cuatro Caballos", c. 1972: Two,* s., #XXXV/LXXV, XXXVII/LXXV, full margins, very good cond., yellowing, (05-18-93, Sotheby-NY, #283, illus.), images 20½ x 15½ in., (521 x 394 mm.), lithograph p. in colors on Arches (BP 824, DM 2053, FR 6932, Y 140,978).
BI *"Woman With A Crab", c. 1968 and "Lanzando Caballos", c. 1969: Two,* s., #84/100, creasing, good cond., i. 'EA', full margins, excell. cond., est. $1/1,500, (05-17-93, Christie-NY, #315), lithograph in colors on Arches.

TOLL, Grant
BI *Zero,* 1940s, s., t., stamps, prov., est. $1,8/2,200, (10-13-92, Christie-NY, #372, illus.), 15⅜ x 19⅜ in., (39.1 x 49.2 cm.), photograph, blue-toned gelatin silver print.

TOMANCK, J. (after)
BI *Woodland Nymphs,* (12-11-92, G.A. Key, #142), 18 x 22 in., (45.7 x 55.9 cm.), colored print.

TOMASI, Vladimiro
$165* *Monza 1988,* (08-23-92, Christie-E, #21), color reproduction (BP 85, DM 236, FR 802, Y 20,757).

TOMIKICHIRO, Tokuriki
$302* *"Heito-Tempel",* s., seal, (04-27-93, Dorotheum, #196, illus.), 9¹⁵⁄₁₆ x 11¹³⁄₁₆ in., (25.3 x 30 cm.), color woodcut (BP 192, DM 478, FR 1618, Y 33,845, SC 3360).
$45* *View Of Kyoto,* (05-16-93, Hanzel, #1095), 10¾ x 9½ in., (27.3 x 24.1 cm.), color woodblock (BP 29, DM 72, FR 243, Y 4988).
$35* *View Of Kyoto,* (05-16-93, Hanzel, #1094), 11⅛ x 9½ in., (28.3 x 24.1 cm.), color woodblock (BP 23, DM 56, FR 189, Y 3880).
$70* *View Of Kyoto: Two,* (05-16-93, Hanzel, #1106), 10¾ x 9¼ in., (27.3 x 23.5 cm.), color woodblock (BP 46, DM 113, FR 378, Y 7760).
$55* *View Of Kyoto: Two,* (05-16-93, Hanzel, #1105), 10¾ x 9½ in., (27.3 x 24.1 cm.), color woodblock (BP 36, DM 88, FR 297, Y 6097).

TOMIKICHIRO, Tokuriki   b. 1933
$35* *Market Scene,* (05-16-93, Hanzel, #1107), 10¾ x 9¼ in., (27.3 x 23.5 cm.), color woodblock (BP 23, DM 56, FR 189, Y 3880).
BI *"Verfruhter Fruhling Bei Kyoto",* t., s., seal, est. SC 7/8,000, (04-27-93, Dorotheum, #210, illus.), 10¼ x 11⁹⁄₁₆ in., (26 x 29.3 cm.), color woodcut.

TOMKINS, Peltro William
$217* *Miss Linwood, 1806,* pub. Tomkins, margins, creases, defect, good cond., (11-30-92, Phillips-London, #190), plate 18½ x 14½ in., (470 x 368 mm.), color stipple engraving on laid (BP 143, DM 346, FR 1174, Y 27,007).

TONGE, Gilbert Ross   American 1886-1970
$138* *Wagon Train,* s. Gilbert Tonge, (11-10-92, Moran, #162), 14 x 20 in., (35.6 x 50.8 cm.), serigraph on board (BP 91, DM 221, FR 748, Y 17,177).

TONIOLO, Beat b. 1962
$180* *Urmobil,* #40/50, s., (11-13-92, Koller, #5459), 24¹³⁄₁₆ x 36¼ in., (63 x 92 cm.), lithograph on Rives wove (BP 116, DM 283, FR 953, Y 22,341, SF 255).

TOOKALOOK, Lucassie b. 1917
$107* *Family Hunting Caribou And Fishing In A Lake,* s., i. in syllabics, d. 1985, #29/50, (11-30-92, Ritchie, #78, illus.), 14¾ x 27 in., (37.5 x 68.5 cm.), color stone cut (BP 71, DM 170, FR 579, Y 13,317, C$ 138).
$107* *Fishing In The Waves While The Boy Sled,* s., i. in syllabics, d. 1983, #41/50, (11-30-92, Ritchie, #79), 17 x 24 in., (43.2 x 60.9 cm.), color stonecut (BP 71, DM 170, FR 579, Y 13,317, C$ 138).

TOOKER, George American b. 1920
$920* *Whisper, 1977,* s., annot. E.P.A.P., blindstamp publisher, Edition Press, full margins, very good cond., (05-19-93, Butterfield, #2364), 11 x 9¾ in., (279 x 248 mm.), lithograph on wove (BP 597, DM 1495, FR 5038, Y 101,849).

TOOKOOME, Simon Inuit 20th cent.
$303* *"The Wave",* t., #6/50, d. 1970, s., blindstamped, stenciled Baker Lake (Sanavik)Cooperative symbol, very good cond., prov., (06-26-93, Skinner, #58, illus.), 18½ x 25 in., (47 x 63.5 cm.), black stone cut (BP 203, DM 515, FR 1734, Y 32,149).

TOOROP, Jan Dutch 1858-1928
BI *In Den Nevel, 1895,* lit., est. DM 1,000, (06-10-93, Hauswedell/Nolt, #941), woodcut.
$2888* *Jugend Und Alter Der Frau, 1895,* s., num., lit., glue stained, (12-04-92, Bassenge, #6972, illus.), 7¹³⁄₁₆ x 9¹¹⁄₁₆ in., (19.8 x 24.6 cm.), etching on Japan (BP 1852, DM 4599, FR 15,602, Y 360,549).
$1286* *Sprokelend Kind (Rijsprentenkabinet Catalogue 1969, No. 7), 1899,* 3rd final state, s., margins, good cond., (06-30-93, Sotheby-London, #690), 6¼ x 7⅜ in., (159 x 187 mm.), drypoint (BP 862, DM 2193, FR 7399, Y 137,791).

TOPOR, Roland b. 1938
$126* *Compositions Surrealistes: Two,* s., #15/50, (11-16-92, Briest, #103), 25³⁄₁₆ x 17⁵⁄₁₆ in., (64 x 44 cm.), lithograph in black (BP 83, DM 201, FR 677, Y 15,724).
$84* *"Nu Au Nid",* #250/300, s., (01-28-93, Pescheteau, #270), 25⁹⁄₁₆ x 19⁵⁄₁₆ in., (65 x 49 cm.), black lithograph on Arches (BP 55, DM 133, FR 450, Y 10,430).
$369* *Ein Sich Kussendes Paar,* s., num., (12-05-92, Bassenge, #7772, illus.), 13³⁄₁₆ x 13¹⁵⁄₁₆ in., (33.5 x 35.5 cm.), lithograph on Arches (BP 231, DM 575, FR 1961, Y 45,719).
$64* *Untitled,* s., i. E.A., full sheet, good cond., minor handling creases, waterstain in left edge, (05-27-93, Sotheby-Amstrdm, #695), sheet 25¹³⁄₁₆ x 18¹³⁄₁₆ in., (655 x 478 mm.), lithograph on wove (BP 41, DM 103, FR 346, Y 6861, G 115).
$64* *Untitled, 1978,* s., full margins, good cond., minor handling creases, (05-27-93, Sotheby-Amstrdm, #498), sh 25¹³⁄₁₆ x 18¹³⁄₁₆ in., (655 x 478 mm.), lithograph on wove (BP 41, DM 103, FR 346, Y 6861, G 115).
$141* *Untitled, 1978,* s., full margins, good cond., minor handling creases, (05-27-93, Sotheby-Amstrdm, #499), sh 25¹³⁄₁₆ x 18¹³⁄₁₆ in., lithograph on wove (BP 90, DM 226, FR 763, Y 15,116, G 253).
$128* *Untitled, 1978,* s., full margins, good cond., minor handling creases, (05-27-93, Sotheby-Amstrdm, #497), sh 25¹³⁄₁₆ x 18¹³⁄₁₆ in., (655 x 478 mm.), lithograph on wove (BP 82, DM 205, FR 692, Y 13,722, G 230).
$84* *"Les Yeux Bandes",* #244/300, s., (01-28-93, Pescheteau, #271), 25⁹⁄₁₆ x 19¹¹⁄₁₆ in., (65 x 50 cm.), lithograph (BP 55, DM 133, FR 450, Y 10,430).

TOPP, Arnold
$384* *(Composition), 1920: Two,* s., d., i. orig. holzschnitt/handdruck, margins, foxing, glued to mount at top edge of sheet verso, good cond., Late Gerhard Brauer Coll., (05-27-93, Sotheby-Amstrdm, #788, illus.), 9⁷⁄₁₆ x 6¼ in., (240 x 158 mm.), woodcut on Japan (BP 246, DM 616, FR 2077, Y 41,166, G 690).
$416* *(Female Nude In Landscape), 1920: Two,* s., d., i. orig. holzscnitt (handdruck), margins, paper discoloration, minor soiling, foxing, glued to mount at top edge of sheet verso, Late Gerhard Brauer Coll., (05-27-93, Sotheby-Amstrdm, #789, illus.), 10¹⁵⁄₁₆ x 8⁹⁄₁₆ in., (279 x 217 mm.), woodcut on Japan (BP 266, DM 668, FR 2250, Y 44,597, G 748).
BI *Landscape, 1914: Two,* s., d., i. orig. holz-schnitt handdruck, margins, foxing, gluestaining, glued to mount, Late Gerhard Brauer Coll., est. Dfl. 5/800, (05-27-93, Sotheby-Amstrdm, #787), 5³⁄₁₆ x 3⅞ in., (131 x 99 mm.), woodcut on Japan.

TORII KIYOHIRO ac. c. 1737-1765
$2976* *Arashi Tominosuke In A Female Role,* Hosoban, benizuri-e, s. Torii Kiyohiro hitsu, pub.'s mark, d. possibly Horeki 6 (1756), browned, rubbed, fold mark, Prof. H.R.W. Kuhne Coll., (06-11-93, Sotheby-London, #37, illus.), 12⅝ x 5⅜ in., (32.1 x 13.7 cm.), woodblock (BP 1955, DM 4837, FR 16,307, Y 315,756).

TORII KIYOHIRO ac. c. 1750-1765
$1662* *Bando Hikosaburo II As Umewaka-maru And Segawa Kichiji II As Matsuwaka-maru Both Carrying A Birdcage From Which Hangs A Label Inscribed "Miyakodori",* Hosoban, benizuri-e, s. Torii Kiyohiro hitsu, pub.'s mark, d. Horeki4 (1754), soiled, rubbed, corners restored, Prof. H.R.W. Kuhne Coll., (06-11-93, Sotheby-London, #36, illus.), 12¼ x 5¾ in., (31.1 x 14.6 cm.), woodblock (BP 1092, DM 2701, FR 9107, Y 176,340).
$9802* *Ichikawa Danjuro III As Soga No Goro In The Play Hatsumoyo Yui No Kayoi Soga or Nano Hana Akebono Soga,* Hosoban, benizuri-e, s. Torii Kiyohiro hitsu, pub. Okumuraya Genroku,good state, Prof. H.R.W. Kuhne Coll., (06-11-93, Sotheby-London, #28, illus.), 12¼ x 5½ in., (31.1 x 14 cm.), woodblock (BP 6440, DM 15,930, FR 53,710, Y 1,040,000).

TORII KIYOMASU II Japanese ac. c. 1706-1763
BI *Ichikawa Ebizo (Danjuro II) And Segawa Kikunojo With The Ghost Of A Courtesan,* Hosoban, benizuri-e, s. Torii Kiyomasu hitsu, d. Kanpo 4 (1744), pub.Igaya, faded, rubbed, soiled, Prof. H.R.W. Kuhne Coll., est. BP 2,5/3,000, (06-11-93, Sotheby-London, #29, illus.), 12¼ x 5¾ in., (31.1 x 14.6 cm.), woodblock.
$962* *Otani Hiroji II In The Role Of Kurofune Chuemon In The Play Fuku Chiddori Soga Performed At The Ichimura-za,* Hosoban, benizuri-e; s. Torii Kiyomasu hitsu, pub.'s mark Maruko, d.Kan'en 3 (1750), browned, trimmed, rubbed, wormed, restored, Prof. H.W.R. KuhneColl., (06-11-93, Sotheby-London, #9), 11¾ x 5⅜ in., (29.8 x 13.7 cm.), woodblock (BP 632, DM 1563, FR 5271, Y 102,069).
$1662* *Portrait Of Ichimura Uzaemon VIII,* Hosoban, urushi-e, s. Eshi Torii Kiyomaru hitsu, pub. Urokogataya, d.Genbun 5 (1740), rubbed, soiled, Prof. H.R.W. Kuhne Coll., (06-11-93, Sotheby-London, #12, illus.), 12 x 5¾ in., (30.5 x 14.6 cm.), hand-colored woodblock (BP 1092, DM 2701, FR 9107, Y 176,340).
$1925* *Sanogawa Ichimatsu As Ushiwakamaru And Suketakaya Takasuke As KiichiHogen In The Play Kiichi Hogen Shinansha,* Hosoban, benizuri-e, s. Torii Kiyomasu hitsu, pub.'s mark Uemura, collector's mark, d. Horeki 4 (1754), fold marks, white spots, Prof. H.R.W. Kuhne Coll.(06-11-93, Sotheby-London, #13, illus.), 12½ x 5½ in., (31.8 x 14 cm.), woodblock (BP 1265, DM 3129, FR 10,548, Y 204,244).

TORII KIYOMASU II(?)
$1925* *Ichikawa Danjuro II As Soga Goro And Ichikawa Danzo I As Asahina Saburo In The Play Soga Koyomibiraki Performed At The Nakamura-za Theatre: Diptych,* Hosoban, urushi-e, sig. Torii Kiyomasu hitsu, pub. Igaya, d. Kyoho 8(1723), browned, soiled, wormed, repaired, Prof. H.R.W. Kuhne Coll., (06-11-93, Sotheby-London, #4, illus.), 13 x 6¼ in., (33 x 15.9 cm.), hand-colored woodblock (BP 1265, DM 3129, FR 10,548, Y 204,244).

TORII KIYOMITSU Japanese ac. c. 1735-1785
$4551* *Bando Hikosaburo II And Segawa Kikunojo II In Unidentified Roles, Disguised As Komuso,* Hosoban, benizuri-e, s. Torii Kiyomitsu hitsu, seal., d. c. Horeki 10-Meiwa 5 (1760-68), pub. Urokogata-ya, tear, worm holes

restored, soiled, Prof. H.R. W. Kuhne Coll., (06-11-93, Sotheby-London, #42, illus.), 10⅝ x 6⅝ in., (27 x 16.8 cm.), woodblock in three colors (BP 2990, DM 7396, FR 24,937, Y 482,865).

$1662* *Bando Hikosaburo II In The Garb Of A Young Man Holding A Komuso Hat,* Hosoban, s. Torii Kiyomitsu ga, pub. Urokogata-ya, d. c. Meiwa 2-4 (1765-67), soiled, rubbed, trimmed, Prof. H.R.W. Kuhne Coll., (06-11-93, Sotheby-London, #20, illus.), 12⅛ x 5⅜ in., (30.8 x 13.7 cm.), woodblock (BP 1092, DM 2701, FR 9107, Y 176,340).

$1575* *Ichimura Kamezo And Sasakiyama Sangoro: "Kamezo As Kyo No Jiro In The Play Edo Murasaki Kyogen Soga" and "Sangoro As Kosho Kichiza (Kichizaburo) InThe Play Yaoya Oshichi": Two,* Hosoban, s. Torii Kiyomitsu hitsu, pub.'s marks, d. Horeki 11 (1761),Horeki 9 (1759), faded, rubbed, soiled, trimmed, repaired, Prof. H.R.W. Kuhne Coll., (06-11-93, Sotheby-London, #25), one 12¼ x 5⅞ in., (31.1 x 14.9 cm.), other 11¼ x 5⅜ in., (31.1 x 14.9 cm.), woodblock, multi-colored print and benuzuri-e (BP 1035, DM 2560, FR 8630, Y 167,109).

$2100* *Nakamura Tomijuro I In The Role Of A Bikuni (Euphemism For "Prostitute-Nun") In The Play Hanagu Yuki Fuji No Sukegasa,* O-hosoban, benizuri-e, s. Torii Kiyomitsu ga, seal, pub. Maruko, engraver's seal, collector's mark, d. Horeki 8 (1758), soiled, rubbed, wormage restored, laid-down, Prof. H.R.W. Kuhne Coll., (06-11-93, Sotheby-London, #17, illus.), 15 x 6½ in., (38.1 x 16.5 cm.), woodblock (BP 1380, DM 3413, FR 11,507, Y 222,812).

$2275* *Nakamura Tomijuro I In The Role Of a Bikuni,* O-hosoban, faded, trimmed, heavily restored, added pieces, Prof. H.R.W. Kuhne Coll., (06-11-93, Sotheby-London, #18), 14⅜ x 6¾ in., (36.5 x 17.1 cm.), woodblock (BP 1495, DM 3697, FR 12,466, Y 241,379).

$2100* *Nakamura Utaemon I As A Pedlar Of Fans, Wappa No Kikuomaru In The Play Soga Mannen Hashira,* Hosoban, s. Torii Kiyomitsu hitsu, pub.'s mark, d. Horeki 10 (1760),soiled, wormage, repaired, Prof. H.R.W. Kuhne Coll., (06-11-93, Sotheby-London, #19, illus.), 11¾ x 5½ in., (29.8 x 14 cm.), woodblock (BP 1380, DM 3413, FR 11,507, Y 222,812).

$3676* *Sakata Hangoro II As Kizu Kansuke In The Play Hirugaesu Gunbai Momiji,* Hosoban, benizuri-e, s. Torii Kiyomitsu ga, pub. Okumuraya Genroku, d. An'ei 4 (1775), rubbed, soiled, corner restored, Prof. H.R.W. Kuhne Coll., (06-11-93, Sotheby-London, #27, illus.), 12¼ x 5½ in., (31.1 x 14 cm.), three colored woodblock (BP 2415, DM 5974, FR 20,142, Y 390,027).

$1750* *Segawa Kikunojo II And Nakamura Tomijuro I: "Kikunojo II As Umegae InEdozome Soga Hinagata/ Mugen No Kane" and "Nakamura Tomijuro I As An Onnagata Dancing": Two,* Hosoban, benizuri-e, s. both Torii Kiyomitsu ga, pub. Uemura (Emiya Kichiemon), d. Meiwa 1 (1764), faded, rubbed, wormed, restored, trimmed, Prof. H.R.W. Kuhne Coll., (06-11-93, Sotheby-London, #26), one 11¾ x 5⅛ in., (29.8 x 13 cm.), other 12 x 5¼ in., (29.8 x 13 cm.), three colored woodblock (BP 1150, DM 2844, FR 9589, Y 185,676).

$1312* *Yoshizawa Goroichiro As The Heroine Kuzunoha, The Fox-Woman,* Hosoban, benizuri-e, s. Torii Kiyomitsu ga, pub. Yamashiro-ya, d. c.Horeki 10 (1760), faded, trimmed, wormed, laid-down, repaired, Prof. H.R.W. Kuhne Coll., (06-11-93, Sotheby-London, #24), 12¼ x 5⅜ in., (31.1 x 13.7 cm.), three colored woodblock (BP 862, DM 2132, FR 7189, Y 139,204).

TORII KIYONAGA   Japanese 1752-1815

$1925* *Harugoma Dance,* Hashira-e, s. Kiyonaga ga, pub.'s mark, d. Tenmei 2 (1782), faded, soiled, rubbed, creased, Prof. H.R.W. Kuhne Coll., (06-11-93, Sotheby-London, #48, illus.), woodblock (BP 1265, DM 3129, FR 10,548, Y 204,244).

$962* *"Ichikawa Monnosuke II As Osome And Ichikawa Komazo II As Hisamatsu"and "Nakamura Riko As The Courtesan Oiso No Tora": Two,* Oban and hosoban, s. 1st print torn off; 2nd Kiyonaga ga, pub. EijudoNishimura Yohachi, d. Tenmei 9 (1787) and An'ei 8 (1779), faded,

soiled, tear,wormage restored, Prof. H.R.W. Kuhne Coll., (06-11-93, Sotheby-London, #246), one 14⅛ x 9⅜ in., (35.9 x 23.8 cm.), other 11⅜ x 4⅞ in., (35.9 x 23.8 cm.), woodblock (BP 632, DM 1563, FR 5271, Y 102,069).

$1400* *Ichikawa Yaozo III At Leisure With Courtesans (Hirano, No. 442),* Aiban, s. Kiyonaga ga, d. Tenmei 2 (1782), faded, trimmed/repaired, Prof. H.R.W. Kuhne Coll., (06-11-93, Sotheby-London, #247, illus.), 12⅜ x 8½ in., (31.4 x 21.6 cm.), woodblock (BP 920, DM 2275, FR 7671, Y 148,541).

$875* *Multiple Portraits Of Actors In Roles: Two,* Koma-e, hosoban yoko-e, benizuri-e, s. Torii Kiyonaga ga, pub. Ezakiya, 1st d. An'ei 4 (1775), 2nd c. An'ei 7 (1778), rubbed, soiled, wormed, repaired, Prof. H.R.W. Kuhne Coll., (06-11-93, Sotheby-London, #245), one 5⅜ x 12¼ in., (13.7 x 31.1 cm.), other 5⅛ x 10⅝ in., (13.7 x 31.1 cm.), woodblock (BP 575, DM 1422, FR 4795, Y 92,838).

$2100* *Nakamura Nakazo As Tametomo, Segawa Kikunojo III As Azuma And Ichikawa Monnosuke II As Yodoya Tatsugoro (C. Hirano, No. 741),* Oban, s. Kiyonaga ga, pub. Eijudo Nishimura Yohachi, d. Tenmei 5 (1785), faded, rubbed, soiled, fold mark, wormage, creases restored, Prof. H.R.W. Kuhne Coll., (06-11-93, Sotheby-London, #250, illus.), 15¼ x 10 in., (38.7 x 25.4 cm.), woodblock (BP 1380, DM 3413, FR 11,507, Y 222,812).

$1400* *Segawa Kikunojo III As Koito, Yamashita Mangiku As Asakihime And Sawamura Sojuro III As Otomo No Hitachisuke (C. Hirano, No. 469),* Oban, s. Kiyonaga ga, pub. Eijudo Nishimura Yohachi, d. Tenmei 3 (1783), faded, wormage repaired, Prof. H.R.W. Kuhne Coll., (06-11-93, Sotheby-London, #249, illus.), 15 x 9⅞ in., (38.1 x 25.1 cm.), woodblock (BP 920, DM 2275, FR 7671, Y 148,541).

$962* *"Yamashita Kinsaku II As Akoya, The Wife Of Kagekiyo" and "Sakata Hangoro II As Asahina" (Chieko Hirano, Nos. 32 and 34): Two,* Hosoban, s. Torii Kiyonaga ga/ Kiyonaga ga, pub. E-ki, d. An'ei 4 (1775), browned, wormed, repaired, Prof. H.R.W. Kuhne Coll., (06-11-93, Sotheby-London, #244), both approx. 12¼ x 5⅜ in., (31.1 x 13.7 cm.), woodblock (BP 632, DM 1563, FR 5271, Y 102,069).

TORII KIYONOBU I   Japanese 1664-1729

$3851* *The Actor Sawamura Kodenji With Two Courtesans,* Oban yoko-e, sumizuri-e, pub. Yamadaya Ichirobei of Hasegawacho, laid-down, mounted, Prof. H.R.W. Kuhne Coll., (06-11-93, Sotheby-London, #32, illus.), 10½ x 14 in., (26.7 x 35.6 cm.), hand-colored woodblock (BP 2530, DM 6259, FR 21,101, Y 408,594).

BI *Ichikawa Danjuro II As Kamakura Gongoro Kagemasa,* Hosoban, urushi-e, d. Kyoho 11 (1726), pub. Igaya, rubbed, creases, darkened, Prof. H.R.W. Kuhne Coll., est. BP 2,5/3,500, (06-11-93, Sotheby-London, #41, illus.), 12¼ x 6⅛ in., (31.1 x 15.6 cm.), hand-colored woodblock.

BI *Scene From A Drama With Nakagawa Hanzaburo As A Young Lord, Tsugawa Handayu As An Onnagata, And Sakata Oginojo Standing Outside The House ListeningTo Music,* Hosoban tan-e, d. c. Shotoku 1 (1711), pub. Igaya, minor fissures, browned, Prof. H.R.W. Kuhne Coll., est. BP 2/2,500, (06-11-93, Sotheby-London, #39, illus.), 13 x 6¼ in., (33 x 15.9 cm.), woodblock.

TORII KIYONOBU I (attrib.)   Japanese 1664-1729

$525* *Nakamura Takesaburo And Fujimura Hanjiro As Courtesans, Ichikawa Danzo And Matsumoto Koshiro As Pedlars Of Oil Of Okyarain In An Unidentified Play,* Chuban yoko-e, sumizuri-e, d. Kyoho 5 (1720), fold, soiled, rubbed, Prof. H.R.W. Kuhne Coll., (06-11-93, Sotheby-London, #6), 8 x 11⅝ in., (20.3 x 29.5 cm.), woodblock (BP 345, DM 853, FR 2877, Y 55,703).

TORII KIYONOBU II   Japanese c. 1706-1763

$1400* *Nakamura Denkuro II As Omori Hikoshichi And Sawamura Chojuro III As Bingo Saburo In The Play Ono Taiheiki, Performed At The Nakamura-za, 1749,* Hosoban, benizuri-e, s. Torii Kiyonobu hitsu, pub.'s mark Urokogata-ya?, wormed, soiled, trimmed, restored and laid down, Prof. H.R.W. Kuhne Coll., (06-11-93,

Sotheby-London, #3, illus.), 11¾ x 5⅝ in., (29.8 x 14.3 cm.), woodblock (BP 920, DM 2275, FR 7671, Y 148,541).

TORII KIYOTOMO and OKUMURA TOSHINOBU 18th cent.
$875* *"Sanjo Kantaro II As An Itinerant Book-Seller", and "Sawamura SojuroI As Soga Juro": Two*, Hosoban, urushi-e, s. Torii Kiyotomo hitsu and Yamato Gako Okumura Toshinobu hitsu, pub.'s marks, soiled, rubbed, poor cond., Prof. H.R.W. Kuhne Coll., (06-11-93, Sotheby-London, #45), one 11¼ x 5¾ in., (28.6 x 14.6 cm.), other 12 x 5¾ in., (28.6 x 14.6 cm.), hand-colored woodblock (BP 575, DM 1422, FR 4795, Y 92,838).

TORII KIYOTSUNE Japanese ac. 1757-1779
$1750* *(Gion Saire) Shitenno "The Four Ace Retainers", Three Vols.*, bound in one (loose), sumizuri illus., s. Torii Kiyotsune ga, c. 1770, (06-11-93, Sotheby-London, #501, illus.), 6⅞ x 5⅛ in., (17.5 x 13 cm.), partly hand-colored woodblock (BP 1150, DM 2844, FR 9589, Y 185,676).
BI *Portraits Of Actors "Otani Hiroji III As Yakko Terubei", "Ichikawa Danjuro IV Possibly As Kagekiyo", and "Ichikawa Yaozo II As Goinojo Munesada": Thee*, Hosoban, benizuri-e, s. Torri Kiyotsune ga, d. c. Horeki 7-9 (1757-59) and Meiwa 8 (1771), soiled, rubbed, restored, Prof. H.R.W. Kuhne Coll., est.BP 900/1,300, (06-11-93, Sotheby-London, #44), approx. average 12 x 5¼ in., (30.5 x 13.3 cm.), woodblock.

TORTOREL, Jean and Jacques PERRISIN ac. 1568-1570
BI *La Paix Faite En L'Isle Aux Boeufs Pres Orleans, Le 13 Mars, 1563 (Nagler; Mon. IV, 227, 507; Robert-Dumesnil VI, 25)*, est. DM 750, (12-04-92, Bassenge, #6466), 12⁵⁄₁₆ x 19⅛ in., (31.2 x 48.5 cm.), etching.

TORY
$898* *Saint-Gervais-Les-Bains. "Station D'Enfants, Etablissement Thermal",c. 1925*, very good cond., (03-15-93, Arcole, #67, illus.), 39⅜ x 24⅝ in., (100 x 62.5 cm.), (BP 625, DM 1492, FR 5071, Y 106,373).

TOTOYA HOKKEI Japanese 1780-1850
$1925* *Danjuro's Shibaraku Costume, Surimono*, kakuban, s. Oju (by request) Hokkei ga, d. c. 1820-23, faded, rubbed, stained, Prof. H.R.W. Kuhne Coll., (06-11-93, Sotheby-London, #270, illus.), 8¼ x 7⅛ in., (21 x 18.1 cm.), woodblock w/gold and silver and burnishing (BP 1265, DM 3129, FR 10,548, Y 204,244).

TOUCHET
$319* *Londres Le Caire En 7 Jours Par Le Train Simplon Orient-Express, 1925-1930*, very good cond., (03-13-93, Laurin, #126), 39⅜ x 24⁷⁄₁₆ in., (100 x 62 cm.), (BP 223, DM 531, FR 1805, Y 37,596).

TOUDOUZE, Edouard French 1848-1907
$89* *Portrait De Victor Hugo*, s. H.E. Toudouze 1893, (03-16-93, Encans, #206), 4⁷⁄₁₆ x 2¹⁵⁄₁₆ in., (11.3 x 7.5 cm.), drypoint (BP 61, DM 148, FR 503, Y 10,407, C$ 111).

TOUDY, H.J., Publisher 19th cent.
$55* *"Bird's Eye View, Centennial Buildings, Fairmount Park, 1876, Philadelphia"*, (09-12-92, Dunning, #10), 17¾ x 23 in., (45.1 x 58.4 cm.), lithograph (BP 28, DM 79, FR 269, Y 6815).

TOUDY, H.J., Publisher American 19th cent.
BI *"Bird's Eye View, Centennial Buildings, Fairmont Park, Philadelphia,1876"*, ident. w/in matrix, tears, abrasions, staining, soiling, est. $3/500, (03-27-93, Skinner, #322B), sight, sheet 20 x 25½ in., (50.8 x 64.8 cm.), color lithograph on paper.

TOULOUSE-LAUTREC, Henri de French 1864-1901
BI *"Adieu" (Delteil 129) (Wittrock 124 ii/ii), 1895-1896*, posthumous impression p. by A.C. Maze, very good cond., hinges, est.$3/400, (05-15-93, Cleveland, #433), 9½ x 7¾ in., (24.1 x 19.7 cm.), lithograph in olive green.
$3360* *Adolphe. - Le Jeune Homme Triste (Wittrock 55, 1, Ausgabe; Delteil-Kornfeld 73/I/b; Adriani 93/I), 1894*, mono. stamp, (06-23-93, Kornfeld, #827), lithograph in brown on thick Japan (BP 2283, DM 5685, FR 19,124, Y 366,053, SF 5060).

$22,000* *Ambassadeurs, Aristide Bruant (D. 343; A. 6; W. P4; Adr. 3), 1892*, p. on two joined sheets, margins, good cond., repaired tear through letters, repaired breaks, folds w/touched-in breaks, losses, creases, linen backed, (11-05-92, Sotheby-NY, #457, illus.), sheet 56¼ x 37½ in., (142.9 x 95.3 cm.), lithograph p. in colors (BP 14,309, DM 34,794, FR 117,710, Y 2,699,055).
$3467* *Ambassadeurs, Aristide Bruant Dans Cabaret, 1892*, margins cut, bottom missing, tears, repairs, lit., (02-04-93, Christie-S. Ken, #148), 44 x 36 in., (111.8 x 91.4 cm.), color lithograph on two sheets backed on board (BP 2420, DM 5709, FR 19,358, Y 431,273).
BI *Ambassadeurs: Aristide Bruant (L.D. 343, Wittrock P4, Adriani 3), 1892*, margins, repaired tears and splits (Touched), made-up losses, creasing, good cond., laid down on linen, est. $40/50,000, (05-11-93, Christie-NY, #342, illus.), borderline 53 x 35¾ in., (134.6 x 90.8 cm.), lithograph on 2 sheets of wove.
$1980* *Aristide Bruant (W. P10), 1893*, 3rd (final) edition, margins slightly trimmed, linen-backed, laid down to foam board, good cond., tears, thinned spots, paper losses, light-staining, surface scuffing, surface soiling, (02-24-93, Butterfield, #2795, illus.), 31⅜ x 23⅞ in., (797 x 606 mm.), lithograph in olive & black on wove (BP 1381, DM 3214, FR 10,897, Y 232,340).
$44,000* *Aristide Bruant Dans Son Cabaret (D. 348; A. 15; W. P9; Adr. 12), 1893*, Adriani's first state of two, Wittrock's edit. A, before lettering lower right, printed Charles Verneau, margins, good cond., repaired tears, fox marks, soiling, linen backed, (11-05-92, Sotheby-NY, #458, illus.), sheet 53¾ x 38⅜ in., (136.5 x 97.5 cm.), lithograph p. in colors (BP 28,618, DM 69,587, FR 235,420, Y 5,398,111).
$22,000* *Aristide Bruant, Dans Son Cabaret (L.D. 348; W. P9; A. 12), 1893*, Wittrock's state A (of D), margin, colors attenuated, light-staining, restored tears, creases and small paper losses mostly outside image, (11-09-92, Christie-NY, #209, illus.), 50½ x 37½ in., (128.3 x 95.3 cm.), colored lithograph on wove (BP 14,545, DM 35,121, FR 118,662, Y 2,730,206).
BI *Aristide Bruant, Dans Son Cabaret (Wittrock P9), 1893*, Wittrocks variant C, p. by Ancourt, creases, laid on linen, nicks, repaired tears, paper loss, surface damage, defects, est. BP 8/12,000, (11-30-92, Phillips-London, #482A, illus.), sheet 53 x 37½ in., (134.6 x 95.3 cm.), lithograph in colors.
$18,260* *Au Bar Picton. - American Bar, Rue Scribe (Wittrock 170; Delteil 173; Adriani 138), 1896*, (06-25-93, Kornfeld, #134, illus.), image 11⅝ x 9⁷⁄₁₆ in., (29.6 x 24 cm.), lithograph in mauve brown on yellowish vellum (BP 12,350, DM 31,086, FR 104,702, Y 1,935,552, SF 27,600).
$3450* *Au Theatre Libre, Antoine Dans "L'Inquietude" (D. 51; A. 55; W. 41; Adr. 56), 1893*, red mono. stamp, num. 72, margins, good cond., creases, (05-13-93, Sotheby-NY, #833, illus.), 14⅝ x 10⅜ in., (370 x 263 mm.), sh 15 x 11 in., (370 x 263 mm.), lithograph on wove (BP 2265, DM 5571, FR 18,791, Y 385,174).
BI *Au Theatre Libre, Antoine Dans L'Inquietude (W. 41; D. 51; A. 55), 1893*, mono. stamp, pub. L'Escarmouche, margins, good cond., discoloration,paper flecks, est. BP 3,5/4,000, (06-30-93, Sotheby-London, #699), sh 14⅞ x 10⅞ in., (378 x 276 mm.), lithograph.
$3371* *Au Theatre Libre: Antoine Dans L'Inquietude (L. Delteil, 51; W. Wittrock, 41), 1893*, num. 78, red stamp of Lautrec, small margins, (04-02-93, Picard, #187, illus.), 14¹⁵⁄₁₆ x 10⅝ in., (38 x 27 cm.), black lithograph (BP 2220, DM 5418, FR 18,401, Y 383,810).
BI *Au Theatre Libre: Antoine Dans L'Inquietude (W. 41; D. 51 A. 55), 1893*, #48, mono. stamp, pub. L'Escarmouche, margins, good cond., est. BP 3,5/4,000, (06-30-93, Sotheby-London, #698, illus.), sh 15 x 11 in., (381 x 279 mm.), lithograph on smooth wove.
$56,350* *Aux Ambassadeurs (D. 68; A. 73; W. 58; Adr. 70), 1894*, s., pub. in L'Estampe Originale, full margins, good cond., crease, margins, darkening, creases, nicks, ripples, (05-13-93, Sotheby-NY, #835, illus.), 12 x 9¾ in., (304 x 249 mm.), lithograph in colors on smooth wove (BP 36,994, DM 90,990, FR 306,917, Y 6,291,169).

$3163* *Aux Varietes, Mademoiselle Lender Et Brasseur (Delteil 41; Adhemar 44; Wittrock 31; Adriani 46), 1893,* s., red mono. stamp, num. 63, pub. L'Escaramouche, full margins, light-stained, foxing, creases, paper tape, good cond., (05-13-93, Sotheby-NY, #831, illus.), 13¼ x 10⅜ in., (335 x 265 mm.), lithograph on wove (BP 2077, DM 5107, FR 17,228, Y 353,132).

BI *Babylone D'Allemagne (D. 351; A. 68; W. P12; Adr. 58), 1894,* final state, margins, mottled discoloration, foxing, center fold, folds, losses, creases in image, tears, losses, linen-backed, est. $10/15,000, (05-13-93, Sotheby-NY, #847, illus.), sheet 48⅝ x 34¼ in., (123.5 x 87 cm.), lithograph in colors.

BI *Babylone D'Allemagne (L.D. 351, W. P12, A. 58), 1894,* Wittrock's Edition B (of B), margins, light-staining, repaired tears, laid down on board, prop. Greer Garson Fogelson, est. $7/9,000, (05-11-93, Christie-NY, #348, illus.), borderline 48 x 31 in., (121.9 x 78.7 cm.), color lithograph on wove.

BI *Babylone D'Allemagne (L.D. 351; W. P12; A. 58), 1894,* Wittrock's Edit. B, margins, light-staining, repaired tears, laid down on board, prop. Greer Garson Fogelson, est. $9/12,000, (11-09-92, Christie-NY, #212, illus.), 48 x 31 in., (121.9 x 78.7 cm.), colored lithograph on wove.

$9900* *Babylone D'Allemagne (L.D. 351; W. P12; A. 58), 1894,* Wittrock's Edit. A, before letters, light-staining, restored tears, creases, paper losses, laid down on Japan, (11-09-92, Christie-NY, #211, illus.), 46½ x 33¼ in., (118.1 x 84.5 cm.), colored lithograph on wove (BP 6545, DM 15,805, FR 53,398, Y 1,228,593).

BI *Babylone D'Allemagne, 1894,* 2nd state, fold marks w/ corresponding defects, scuffing, tears, lit., est. BP 14/16,000, (02-04-93, Christie-S. Ken, #147, illus.), 49 x 35 in., (124.5 x 88.9 cm.), color lithograph backed on japan.

$495* *Ballade De Noel,* Imp. Crevel Fres., A- cond., front and back covers together, (08-06-92, Swann, #269, illus.), 13¾ x 10 in., (34.9 x 25.4 cm.), (BP 259, DM 731, FR 2470, Y 63,138).

$385* *"Le Baron", 1897,* from Le Rire, (02-13-93, Neal, #579), sheet 11½ x 8½ in., (29.2 x 21.6 cm.), chromotypogreveure (BP 271, DM 638, FR 2160, Y 46,430).

$6096* *Le Bon Graveur (Adolphe Albert) (D. 273; A. 304), 1898,* stamped, s., num., oxidation, staining, full untrimmed margins, drystamp, (02-24-93, Picard, #239), lithograph on wove (BP 4251, DM 9896, FR 33,550, Y 715,325).

BI *Le Cafe Concert (W. 18-28; D. 28-38; A. 28-38), 1893,* ded. copy of complete portfolio, pub. L'Estampe originale, ded. by Lautrec, full margins, good cond., darkening, soiling, creasing, breaks, rubbing, est. BP 17/19,000, (06-30-93, Sotheby-London, #701, illus.), overall 17⅜ x 12¾ in., (441 x 324 mm.), 22 lithographs hor texte, 11 by Ibels.

$1430* *Le Cafe Concert: Jane Avril (W. 18), 1893,* pub. by L'Estampe originale, p. by Ancourt, upper & lower margins slightly trimmed, good cond., light-staining, mat staining, hinge remains, pencilnotations, creases, surface soiling, (02-24-93, Butterfield, #2978), 10½ x 8⅜ in., (267 x 213 mm.), lithograph in black on wove (BP 997, DM 2321, FR 7870, Y 167,801).

$7893* *Carnaval (W. 61; D. 64; A. 42), 1894,* s., partially erased numbering, pub. La Revue Blanche, full margins,- good cond., mount/light-staining, creasing, (06-30-93, Sotheby-London, #696, illus.), 10 x 6½ in., (254 x 165 mm.), lithograph in olive green and red on wove (BP 5290, DM 13,462, FR 45,414, Y 845,709).

BI *Cecy Loftus (W. 113; D. 116; A. 140), 1894,* pub. Kleinmann, margins, good cond., ex coll. Maurice Loncle, ex coll. Heinrich Neuerburg (L. 1344a), est. BP 10/12,000, (06-30-93, Sotheby-London, #695, illus.), sh 20 x 13⅝ in., (508 x 346 mm.), lithograph in olive-green on chine applique.

$412* *La Chaine Simpson, 1896,* Chaix, A cond., plate 238 from Les Maitres de l'Affiche, (08-06-92, Swann, #268, illus.), 9½ x 12½ in., (24.1 x 31.8 cm.), (BP 215, DM 609, FR 2056, Y 52,551).

BI *Chanteur American (Adhemar 34; Wittrock 28), 1893,* stone mono., est. DM 1,800, (05-26-93, Lempertz, #507),

17⅜ x 12⅝ in., (44.1 x 32.1 cm.), lithograph on smooth machine-made.

BI *Cleo De Merode (Wittrock 258), 1898,* from series Treize Lithographs, pub. 1906 by Gustave Pellet, est. $2,5/3,000, (12-13-92, Hindman, #248, illus.), 11½ x 9¼ in., lithograph.

$220,000* *La Clownesse Assise (Mademoiselle Cha-U-Ka-O) (D. 180; A. 201; W. 156; Adr. 172), 1896,* from the Elles series, stamp (L. 1190) of pub. Gustave Pellet, watermark, exceptionally good cond., catalogue cover lot, (11-05-92, Sotheby-NY, #451, illus.), sheet approx. 20⅝ x 16 in., (525 x 405 mm.), lithograph p. in colors on fine wove (BP 143,089, DM 347,936, FR 1,177,100, Y 26,990,553).

BI *Le Coiffeur-Programme Du Theatre Libre (L.D. 14, W. 15, A. 40), 1893,* Wittrock's 2nd final state, s., num. 29, blindstamp pub. Kleinmann, full margins, mat staining, good cond., est. $7/9,000, (05-11-93, Christie-NY, #347, illus.), borderline 12⁹⁄₁₆ x 9⅝ in., (319 x 244 mm.), color lithograph on wove.

$3575* *"Le Coiffeur-Programme Du Theatre Libre" (Wittrock 15 IIB/IIB), 1893,* excell. cond., (10-31-92, Cleveland, #342, illus.), 12⅜ x 9⁷⁄₁₆ in., (31.4 x 24 cm.), color lithograph (BP 2291, DM 5500, FR 18,659, Y 442,834).

$800* *Les Comtes-Joies (W. 236, D. 216, Adriani 237), 1897,* pub. Edmond Frappier, 1925, full margins, crease into image, (11-30-92, Phillips-London, #482), sheet 11⅛ x 15¾ in., (283 x 400 mm.), lithograph in 2 colors w/ beige brown tint stone on japan imperial (BP 528, DM 1274, FR 4327, Y 99,564).

$13,200* *Confetti (L.D. 352; W. P13; A. 101), 1894,* margins, patches of glue in image, repaired tear, losses, good cond., (11-09-92, Christie-NY, #214, illus.), 22 x 16⅞ in., (559 x 429 mm.), colored lithograph on wove (BP 8727, DM 21,073, FR 71,197, Y 1,638,124).

BI *Cycle Michel (D. 359; A. 188), 1896,* tears, (02-24-93, Picard, #241), lithograph in olive green.

BI *Dans "La Belle Helene" (D. 114; A. 321; W. 331; Adr. 358), 1900,* s., i. a Nos Le Capitale Tarrid, red mono. stamp, No. 19, pub. Kleinmann, blindstamp, full margins, good cond., creases, tear, ex-coll. M. L. Guerin, est. $10/14,000, (05-13-93, Sotheby-NY, #838, illus.), 20⅝ x 18¼ in., (524 x 462 mm.), lithograph on wove.

$16,738* *Dans La Loge - Derriere Le Rideau (Wittrock 96; Delteil 127; Adriani129/II), 1895,* s. HT Lautrec, (06-25-93, Kornfeld, #136, illus.), image, sh/together 24⅛ x 35⁷⁄₁₆ in., (61.2 x 90 cm.), lithograph in olive green on thick Japan (BP 11,321, DM 28,495, FR 95,975, Y 1,774,221, SF 25,300).

$11,550* *"Debauche" (Delteil 178/II; Adhemar 212; Adriani 187/III; Wittrock 167/II), 1896,* (11-28-92, Grisebach, #108, illus.), 9⅜ x 12¹¹⁄₁₆ in., (23.8 x 32.3 cm.), color lithograph on wove (BP 7624, DM 18,401, FR 62,466, Y 1,437,461).

$1674* *"Debauche", (Adhemar 212),* (09-29-92, B. Rasmussen, #368, illus.), 9¼ x 12⅝ in., lithograph in colors (BP 941, DM 2364, FR 8067, Y 199,833, DK 9200).

BI *Declaration (Premiere Planche) (L.D. 327; W. 305; A. 297), 1898,* full margins, tips made up, good cond., est. $1,5/2,000, (11-09-92, Christie-NY, #225), 10½ x 9 in., (267 x 229 mm.), lithograph on Chine.

BI *Di Ti Fellow-Anglaise Au Cafe Concert (W. 292; D. 271; A. 303),* stamp #5, pub. Boussod, Manzi, Joyant & Cie, blindstamp, full margins, good cond., crease, fox marks, hinges, est. BP 8/10,000, (06-30-93, Sotheby-London, #707, illus.), 12¾ x 10¼ in., (324 x 260 mm.), lithograph in dark violet-brown on chine volant.

$11,000* *Divan Japonais (D. 341; A. 11; W. P11; Adr. 8), 1893,* small margins, good cond., folds, paper losses, tip of upper right corner torn off, repaired tears, backed w/ Japan, (11-05-92, Sotheby-NY, #456, illus.), 31½ x 23⅝ in., (800 x 600 mm.), lithograph p. in colors (BP 7154, DM 17,397, FR 58,855, Y 1,349,528).

$17,250* *Divan Japonais (D. 341; A. 11; W. P11; Adr. 8), 1893,* small margins, long repaired tear in image, other repaired tears andtouched-in losses in image, creases in image, (05-13-93, Sotheby-NY, #845, illus.), 31½ x 24¼ in., (800 x 615 mm.), lithograph in colors (BP 11,325, DM 27,854, FR 93,954, Y 1,925,868).

BI *Divan Japonais (D. 341; Adhemar 11; Adriani 9; Wittrock P 11; Adriani 8), 1892/93,* est. DM 30,000, (12-05-92, Bassenge, #7635A, illus.), 31¹¹⁄₁₆ x 24 in., (80.5 x 61 cm.), color lithograph.

$5414* *Divan Japonais (Gotz Adriani 8; Delteil 341; Adhemar II; Adriani 9; Wittrock p. 11), 1892-1893,* s. in stone, creases, small holes, losses, tears, (06-28-93, Loudmer, #379, illus.), 31⁵⁄₁₆ x 23⅝ in., (796 x 600 mm.), sh 31⁹⁄₁₆ x 24⁷⁄₁₆ in., (796 x 600 mm.), color lithograph poster w/letter on wove (BP 3625, DM 9200, FR 30,990, Y 574,430).

$20,900* *Divan Japonais (L.D. 341; W. P11; A. 8), 1892-3,* margins, light-staining, losses, laid down on board, prop. Greer Garson Fogelson, (11-09-92, Christie-NY, #208, illus.), 31½ x 23⅝ in., (800 x 600 mm.), colored lithograph on wove (BP 13,818, DM 33,365, FR 112,729, Y 2,593,696).

$3405* *Divan Japonais (W. P11), 1893,* imp. Edw. Ancourt, (12-04-92, AB Stockholm, #7154), sh 31⅝ x 23¹³⁄₁₆ in., (80.4 x 60.5 cm.), lithograph in colors (BP 2184, DM 5423, FR 18,395, Y 425,094, SK 23,100).

$13,418* *Le Divan Japonais (Wittrock P 11; Delteil 341), 1893,* stone s., i., (06-10-93, Hauswedell/Nolt., #951, illus.), image 31¼ x 24 in., (79.4 x 61 cm.), color lithograph (BP 8777, DM 21,850, FR 73,564, Y 1,424,265).

$18,313* *Le Divan Japonais, (L.D. 341; A. 11; W. P11; Adriani 8), 1892-3,* margins, creases, fold partly split, repairs, losses, defects, good cond., (12-01-92, Christie-London, #545, illus.), S. 31⁵⁄₁₆ x 23¹³⁄₁₆ in., (796 x 605 mm.), lithograph in colors on buff wove (BP 12,100, DM 29,189, FR 99,473, Y 2,280,005).

$1933* *Edme Lescot (Adriani 20), 1893,* mono. in plate, authenticite verso, tears, (06-28-93, Loudmer, #380, illus.), 10⅝ x 7½ in., (270 x 190 mm.), sh 17½ x 12¹¹⁄₁₆ in., (270 x 190 mm.), black lithograph on wove (BP 1294, DM 3285, FR 11,065, Y 205,093).

$1784* *"Elles" (Wittrock 155, etat III), 1896,* s., (12-04-92, AB Stockholm, #7153), sh 24 x 18½ in., (61 x 47 cm.), poster, lithograph in colors (BP 1144, DM 2841, FR 9638, Y 222,722, SK 12,100).

BI *Elles, 1896,* third (final) state, laid down, trimmed, good cond., surface abrasions, holes in image, brown staining, foxing, pressure marks, soiling, est. $8/1000, (09-21-92, Butterfield, #835), 21¹³⁄₁₆ x 17⅜ in., (553.4 x 442.1 mm.), lithograph in colors on wove.

$209,231* *Elsa La Viennoise (Wittrock 180; Delteil 207; Adriani 205/II), 1897,* s. HT Lautrec, no 7, (06-25-93, Kornfeld, #137, illus.), sheet, image 22¹³⁄₁₆ x 15⅜ in., (58 x 39 cm.), color lithograph on China (BP 141,516, DM 356,199, FR 1,199,719, Y 22,178,397, SF 316,250).

$1986* *"Emilienne D'Alencon" (Delteil 161; Adhemar 170; Wittrock 253; Adriani 271), 1898,* sheet 4 of series, (06-05-93, Grisebach, #903, illus.), 11⁹⁄₁₆ x 9⁷⁄₁₆ in., (29.4 x 24 cm.), lithograph on thin beige paper laid down on board (BP 1307, DM 3220, FR 10,852, Y 213,044).

BI *Entree De Brasseur, Dans Chilperic (L.D. 110; W. 107; A. 110), 1895,* mono. stamp, full margins, crease, light/mat staining, foxing, good cond., est. $5/7,000, (11-09-92, Christie-NY, #215, illus.), 14¾ x 10⅝ in., (375 x 270 mm.), olive-green lithograph on wove.

$1760* *Eros Vanne (D. 74; A. 81; W. 56; Adr. 92), 1894,* Delteil's second state of four, Wittrock's second edit., Adriani's first new edit., pub. Pellet after 1901, full margins, good cond., discoloration,creases, (11-05-92, Sotheby-NY, #449, illus.), 11⅜ x 8⅝ in., (290 x 220 mm.), lithograph on simili Japan (BP 1145, DM 2783, FR 9417, Y 215,924).

$1380* *Eros Vanne (D. 74; A. 81; W. 56; Adr. 92), 1894,* Adriani's 1st new edit., margins, good cond., mat/light-stain, bleached spot, tape, (05-13-93, Sotheby-NY, #834, illus.), 11½ x 8⅝ in., (293 x 219 mm.), sh 12⅞ x 10 in., (293 x 219 mm.), lithograph on laid (BP 906, DM 2228, FR 7516, Y 154,069).

$2300* *Eros Vanne (Delteil 74; Adhemar 81; Wittrock 56; Adriani 92), 1894,* red mono. stamp, Delteil's 2nd state of 4, Wittrock's 2nd ed., watermark, pub. Pellet after 1901, full margins, good cond., specks of foxing, (02-11-93, Sotheby-NY, #265), 11⁷⁄₁₆ x 8¹¹⁄₁₆ in., (290 x 220 mm.),

lithograph p. in light brown on wove (BP 1623, DM 3810, FR 12,892, Y 277,275).

$1985* *Eros Vanne (Wittr. 56, 1, Ausgabe; D.-Kornf. 74/II/c; Adr. 92/III/I), 1894,* mono. stamp, (06-23-93, Kornfeld, #828), green lithograph on wove (BP 1349, DM 3359, FR 11,298, Y 216,254, SF 2990).

$220* *Etoiles Filantes (Shooting Stars) (Adhemar 161), 1895,* posthumous printing, (05-27-93, Swann, #273A), sh 16½ x 12½ in., (41.9 x 31.8 cm.), lithograph (BP 141, DM 353, FR 1190, Y 23,585).

$16,100* *Femme A Glace, La Glace A Main (D. 185; A. 206; W. 161; Adr. 177), 1896,* from Elles series, watermark, good cond., faded, foxing, printer's creases, (05-13-93, Sotheby-NY, #841, illus.), sh 20½ x 15¾ in., (522 x 400 mm.), lithograph in colors on fine wove (BP 10,570, DM 25,997, FR 87,691, Y 1,797,477).

BI *Femme En Corset, Conquete De Passage (D. 188; A. 209; W. 164; Adr. 180), 1896,* from the Elles series, mono. stamp in blue, i. Serie no. 15 [?], paraphe and mono. stamp of Pellet, watermark, full margins, good cond., fold, thinspots, est. $80/1000,000, (11-05-92, Sotheby-NY, #452, illus.), sheet 20⅝ x 16 in., (525 x 405 mm.), lithograph p. in colors on fine wove.

BI *Femme En Corset, Conquete De Passage (Wittrock 164; Delteil 188; Ademar 180), 1896,* mono. stamp, bearing pencil sig., watermarked, good cond., creasing,stain, pencil marks w/in image, glue remains, (06-30-93, Sotheby-London, #691, illus.), sh c. 20⅝ x 16 in., (524 x 406 mm.), color lithograph on wove.

BI *"Floreal" (W. 134), 1935,* pub. H. Lefebvre, good cond., est. $4/500, (10-31-92, Cleveland, #346), 10¼ x 7¼ in., (26 x 18.4 cm.), lithograph.

$773* *Footit Et Chocolat (Adriani 104), 1894,* mono. in plate, stamp verso, crease, good cond., (06-28-93, Loudmer, #381), 9⁵⁄₁₆ x 11⁹⁄₁₆ in., (237 x 294 mm.), sh 17¹³⁄₁₆ x 25¹³⁄₁₆ in., (237 x 294 mm.), black lithograph on wove (BP 518, DM 1314, FR 4425, Y 82,016).

$13,800* *Le Gage (D. 212; A. 264; W. 237; Adr. 234), 1897,* 1st state of 2, full margins, good cond., repaired tear into image, fleck of paper adhering to surface, glued to backing, (05-13-93, Sotheby-NY, #842, illus.), 11½ x 9½ in., (293 x 240 mm.), lithograph on laid China (BP 9060, DM 22,283, FR 75,163, Y 1,540,694).

BI *La Gaiete Rochechouart, Nicolle (Adhemar 51, Adriani 50, Wittrock 38), 1893,* bears artist's red stamp, (Lugt 1338), est. 10/12,000, (05-16-93, Hindman, #444, illus.), 14½ x 9¾ in., (36.8 x 24.8 cm.), lithograph.

$6900* *La Gaiete Rochechouart, Nicolle (D. 48; A. 51; W. 38; Adr. 53), 1895,* red mono. stamp, margins, good cond., creases, discoloration, tears,i., (05-13-93, Sotheby-NY, #832, illus.), 14½ x 10½ in., (368 x 266 mm.), sh 14¾ x 10⅞ in., (368 x 266 mm.), lithograph on wove (BP 4530, DM 11,142, FR 37,582, Y 770,347).

$1980* *La Goulue (D.71; A. 77; W. 65; Adr. 95), 1894,* Adriani's second state of two w/letters, stamped Hommage de l'EditeurAuguste Bosc, pub. Bosc, margins, good cond., discoloration, creases, (11-05-92, Sotheby-NY, #448), 11⅝ x 9 in., (295 x 230 mm.), sheet 13¾ x 10⅝ in., (295 x 230 mm.), transfer lithograph p. in olive green on smooth wove (BP 1288, DM 3131, FR 10,594, Y 242,915).

BI *Guy Et Mealy, Dans Paris Qui Marche (L.D. 295; W. 295; A. 305), 1898,* s., #69, mono. stamp, margins, mat staining, remain of glue, defects, est. $8/10,000, (11-09-92, Christie-NY, #227, illus.), 11 x 9¼ in., (279 x 235 mm.), violet-brown lithograph on simili Japan.

$17,250* *Irish American Bar, Rue Royale, The Chap Book (D. 362; A. 189; W. P18; Adr. 139), 1895,* 2nd (final) state, slightly trimmed, good cond., faded, center folds,touched-in spots, repaired tear, backed w/Japan, (05-13-93, Sotheby-NY, #849, illus.), 15¾ x 23⅛ in., (401 x 587 mm.), lithograph in colors (BP 11,325, DM 27,854, FR 93,954, Y 1,925,868).

$8800* *Irish And American Bar, Rue Royale (The Chap Book) (D. 362; A. 189; W. P18; Adr. 139), 1895,* second (final) state, margins, faded, creases, foxing and mottled discoloration, repaired tears, losses, soiling, hinge stains, skinned spots, (11-05-92, Sotheby-NY, #461, illus.), sheet 16⅜ x 23⅝ in., (415 x 601 mm.), lithograph p. in colors (BP 5724, DM 13,917, FR 47,084, Y 1,079,622).

$17,600* *Irish And American Bar, Rue Royale-The Chap Book (L.D. 362; W. P18; A. 139), 1895,* Wittrock's state B, narrow margins, light-staining, creasing, paper losses, pinholes, laid down on linen, (11-09-92, Christie-NY, #220, illus.), 15¾ x 23½ in., (400 x 597 mm.), colored lithograph on wove (BP 11,636, DM 28,097, FR 94,930, Y 2,184,165).

$193* *Jane Avril (D 345; A 12),* variation, pub. after 1893, (12-01-92, Ritchie, #14), sheet 29⅜ x 20 in., (74.6 x 50.8 cm.), color lithograph (BP 128, DM 308, FR 1048, Y 24,029, C$ 248).

$14,950* *Jane Avril (D. 345; A. 12; W. P6; Adr. 11), 1893,* Adriani's 1st state of 2, faded, paper tone darkened, stains, losses, tears, laid-down, (02-11-93, Sotheby-NY, #268A), sight 50⅜ x 35 7/16 in., (128 x 90 cm.), color lithograph (BP 10,549, DM 24,764, FR 83,800, Y 1,802,291).

BI *Jane Avril (L.D. 345, W. P6, A. 11), 1893,* Wottrock's Edition B (of C), i., margins, light-staining, restored tears, creases, paper losses mostly outside image, colors strengthened in some areas, sealed in mat, good cond., est. $30/40,000, (05-11-93, Christie-NY, #344, illus.), borderline 48¼ x 35 in., (122.6 x 88.9 cm.), color lithograph on wove.

BI *Jane Avril (W. P6; D. 345; A. 12), 1893,* Wittrock's edit. B., margins, good cond., est. BP 30/40,000, (12-03-92, Sotheby-London, #587, illus.), 48¾ x 36 in., (123.8 x 91.4 cm.), lithograph in colors.

$15,537* *Jane Avril (Wittrock P 6 B), 1893,* stone s., d., (06-10-93, Hauswedell/Nolt, #950, illus.), image 48⅜ x 35¼ in., (122.8 x 89.6 cm.), color lithograph (BP 10,163, DM 25,300, FR 85,181, Y 1,649,188).

BI *Le Jockey (Adhemar 365; Wittrock 308 II), 1899,* stone s., d., est. DM 110/120,000, (05-26-93, Lempertz, #508, illus.), 20 3/16 x 14⅛ in., (51.2 x 35.8 cm.), color lithograph on China.

$48,335* *Le Jockey (Adriani 345), 1899,* second and final state, mono., d. in stone, collector's stamp, prov., (06-28-93, Loudmer, #255A, illus.), 20¼ x 14 3/16 in., (515 x 360 mm.), lithorgraphie au crayon, pinceau et au crachis en (and) couleurs (BP 32,364, DM 82,133, FR 276,674, Y 5,128,382).

BI *Le Jockey (D. 279; A. 365; W. 308; Adr. 345), 1899,* good cond., foxing in image, repair, pencil notation, hinge stains, est. $70/90,000, (11-05-92, Sotheby-NY, #454, illus.), sheet 20⅜ x 14¼ in., (517 x 361 mm.), lithograph p. in colors on chine volant.

$85,000* *Le Jockey (D. 279; A. 365; W. 308; Adr. 345), 1899,* good cond., staining, crease in image, repaired nick, (05-13-93, Sotheby-NY, #844, illus.), 20⅛ x 14¼ in., (512 x 361 mm.), lithograph in colors on chine volant (BP 55,804, DM 137,252, FR 462,963, Y 9,489,785).

$47,172* *Le Jockey (Wittrock 308/II; Delteil 279; Adriani 345/II); 1899,* (06-25-93, Kornfeld, #138, illus.), 20 3/16 x 14⅛ in., (51.3 x 35.9 cm.), color lithograph on Chine volant done from 1 black design stone and color stones (BP 31,905, DM 80,306, FR 270,482, Y 5,000,212, SF 71,300).

$30,250* *L'Artisan Moderne (D. 350; A. 70; W. P24; Adr. 59), 1894,* Adriani's first state of four, before letters, margins, center fold,creases, tears, losses, repaired tear, skinned spots, backed w/Japan, (11-05-92, Sotheby-NY, #459, illus.), sheet 35⅛ x 25½ in., (892 x 648 mm.), lithograph p. in colors (BP 19,675, DM 47,841, FR 161,851, Y 3,711,201).

$10,450* *L'Artisan Moderne (L.D. 350; W. P24; A. 59), 1894,* Wittrock's state A (of B), narrow margins, light-staining, repaired tears, losses, laid down on linen, (11-09-92, Christie-NY, #213, illus.), (895 x 638 mm.), colored lithograph on wove (BP 6909, DM 16,683, FR 56,365, Y 1,296,848).

$6109* *L'Aube. Revue Illustree. 26, Quai D'Orleans (Wittr. P. 23; D. 363; Adr. 184), 1896,* (06-23-93, Kornfeld, #837, illus.), poster, color lithograph (BP 4150, DM 10,337, FR 34,769, Y 665,541, SF 9200).

$25,737* *L'Entraineur (W. 313; D. 172; A. 361), 1899,* reduced margins, mount-staining, glue remains, (06-30-93, Sotheby-London, #694, illus.), sh 14¼ x 20¼ in., (362 x 514 mm.), lithographic in blue on wove (BP 17,250, DM 43,897, FR 148,084, Y 2,757,634).

$2497* *A L'Opera; Madam Caron Dans Faust, (L.D. 49; A. 52; W. 39; Adriani 540, 1893,* mono. stamp, num. 20, pub. L'Escarmouche, drystamp, margins, nick, light-staining, very good cond., prov., L. 360 x 2650 mm, (12-01-92, Christie-London, #547), lithograph p. in olive-green on wove (BP 1650, DM 3980, FR 13,563, Y 310,881).

$10,350* *Lender Assise (D. 163; A. 132; W. 102; Adr. 117), 1895,* mono. stamp, large (full?) margins, good cond., fox marks, printer'screases in image, mat stain, (05-13-93, Sotheby-NY, #840, illus.), 13⅞ x 9⅝ in., (352 x 243 mm.), sh 18⅜ x 13⅛ in., (352 x 243 mm.), lithograph on thin, cream wove (BP 6795, DM 16,712, FR 56,373, Y 1,155,521).

BI *Lender Dansant Le Pas Du Bolero, Dans "Chilperic" (W. 103; D. 104; A.128), 1895,* mono. stamp, p. by Ancourt, pub. Kleinmann, blindstamp, full margins,good cond., discoloration, tears, est. BP 8/10,000, (06-30-93, Sotheby-London, #704, illus.), 14¾ x 10⅜ in., (375 x 264 mm.), lithograph in olive-green on wove.

$10,690* *Lender De Dos, Dansant Le Bolero Dans "Chilperic" (Wittr. 105; D. 106; Adr. 111), 1895,* mono. stamp, num., prov., (06-23-93, Kornfeld, #831), lithograph in dark green on thin wove (BP 7262, DM 18,088, FR 60,842, Y 1,164,615, SF 16,100).

$16,799* *Lender Et Lavalliere Dans: Le Fils De L'Aretin (Wittr. 109/I; D. 164/I; Adr. 118/I), 1895,* mono. stamp, 1st state, (06-23-93, Kornfeld, #832), lithograph on thin tan (red color) wove (BP 11,412, DM 28,425, FR 95,612, Y 1,830,156, SF 25,300).

$5750* *La Loge Au Mascaron Dore (L.D. 16, W. 16, A. 69), 1893,* from theatre programme edit. of 1894, colors slightly attenuated, laid down on linen, (05-11-93, Christie-NY, #349, illus.), borderline 12 x 9½ in., (305 x 241 mm.), color lithograph w/letters on wove (BP 3671, DM 9058, FR 30,520, Y 632,494).

$2354* *Luce Myres De Profil (D. 124; Adriani 131), 1895,* staining, untrimmed margins, 1 of 30, (02-24-93, Picard, #238), lithograph in olive green on thin, textured creme wove (BP 1642, DM 3821, FR 12,955, Y 276,226).

BI *Luce Myres, De Profil (W. 120; D. 124; A. 140), 1895,* mono. stamp, #No 9, pub. Kleinmann, blindstamp, full margins, good cond., discoloration, hinged, ex. coll Maurice Loncle, est. BP 5/5,500, (06-30-93, Sotheby-London, #705, illus.), 8⅞ x 8⅜ in., (225 x 213 mm.), lithograph in oliv-green on wove.

BI *Luce Myres, De Profil (Wittrock Band I 120), 1895,* red mono. stamp, coll.'s stamp, est. DM 8,000-, (11-21-92, Lempertz, #394, illus.), 8¾ x 8⅜ in., (22.3 x 21.2 cm.), lithograph on factory-made paper.

BI *Lucien Guitry (Wittrock 259/II), 1898,* est. DM 3000, (12-01-92, Karl/Faber, #286, illus.), 11⅝ x 9 7/16 in., (29.5 x 24 cm.), lithograph on wove.

$1449* *Madame Rejane (W. 266; D. 166; A. 57), 1898: Two,* first edit. pub. Leicester Gallery, 1936, full margins, good cond., (12-03-92, Sotheby-London, #584), 11½ x 9⅝ in., (295 x 245 mm.), lithograph on laid Japan (BP 935, DM 2279, FR 7778, Y 180,291).

$303* *"Madame Rejane" (Adriani-275), c. 1951,* mono. TL, pub. La Societe' des Amis du Musee' d'Albi, full margins, foxing, spotting, (10-10-92, Goldberg, #427A, illus.), image 12 x 9¼ in., (30.5 x 23.5 cm.), lithograph on Arches w/watermark (BP 180, DM 450, FR 1511, Y 36,888).

$17,905* *Madamoiselle Lender En Buste (Wittrock 99; Delteil 102; Adhemar 131),1895,* pub. in German edit. of Pan, full margins, good cond., foxing, boundin orig. issue of Pan, (12-03-92, Sotheby-London, #583, illus.), lithograph in colors (BP 11,550, DM 28,157, FR 96,108, Y 2,227,821).

BI *Mademoiselle Marcelle Lender En Buste (D. 102; A. 131; W. 99; Adr. 115), 1895,* pub. in Pan, full margins, faded, touched-in spots, mat/light stain,masking tape, skinning, est. $7/9,000, (02-11-93, Sotheby-NY, #268), 12 13/16 x 9 9/16 in., (325 x 243 mm.), color lithograph.

$23,100* *Mademoiselle Marcelle Lender En Buste (D. 102; A. 131; W. 99; Adr. 115), 1895,* from edit. pub. in Pan, full margins, good cond., crease, skinned spots, glue traces verso, (11-05-92, Sotheby-NY, #450, illus.), 13 x 9½ in., (330 x 242 mm.), sheet 14⅛ x 10⅜ in., (330 x 242 mm.), lithograph p. in colors on wove (BP 15,024, DM 36,533, FR 123,596, Y 2,834,008).

BI *Mademoiselle Marcelle Lender En Buste (D. 102; A. 131; W. 99; Adr. 115), 1895,* full margins, good cond., repaired tear through the lettering, est. $25/28,000, (05-13-93, Sotheby-NY, #836, illus.), 12⅞ x 9⅝ in., (327 x 243 mm.), sh 14½ x 10¾ in., (327 x 243 mm.), lithograph in colors.

BI *Mademoiselle Marcelle Lender En Buste (L. Delteil 102, W. Wittrock, 99), 1895,* restored tear, good margins, est. FF60/80,000, (06-16-93, Ader Tajan, #141, illus.), 12¹³⁄₁₆ x 9⁷⁄₁₆ in., (32.5 x 24 cm.), color lithograph.

BI *Mademoiselle Marcelle Lender En Buste, De Trois Quarts (W. 294; D. 261; A. 302), 1898,* s., stamp #25, mono. stamp, pub. Boussod, Manzi, Joyant & Cie., blindstamp, full margins, est. BP 20/25,000, (06-30-93, Sotheby-London, #692, illus.), sh 18¾ x 12 in., (476 x 305 mm.), lithograph in sanguine on blue-grey laid (Ingres).

$12,218* *Mademoiselle Marcelle Lender, Debout (Wittr. 101/I; Erste Auflage; D. 103; Adr. 116/I), 1895,* mono. stamp, blindstamp, (06-23-93, Kornfeld, #830, illus.), lithograph on cream wove (BP 8300, DM 20,673, FR 69,539, Y 1,331,082, SF 18,400).

$21,722* *Mademoiselle Marcelle Lender, En Buste (Adriani 115 IV, b; Wittrock 99, IV), 1895,* stone mono., staining, (09-25-92, Granier, #2702, illus.), sheet 14³⁄₁₆ x 10¼ in., (36 x 26 cm.), color lithograph on smooth wove (BP 12,684, DM 32,200, FR 108,882, Y 2,621,847).

$15,886* *Mademoiselle Marcelle Lender, En Buste (Delteil 102 III, Adhemar 131; Wittrock 99 IV; Adriani 118 IV b), 1895,* (12-04-92, Bassenge, #6973), 12¹³⁄₁₆ x 9½ in., (32.5 x 24.2 cm.), color lithograph on wove (BP 10,190, DM 25,300, FR 85,824, Y 1,983,271).

$19,121* *Mademoiselle Marcelle Lender, En Buste (Delteil 102, Adhemar 131, Wittrock 99 IV, Adriani 115 IV a), 1895,* s., artist proof, (06-04-93, Bassenge, #5826, illus.), 12¹³⁄₁₆ x 9⅝ in., (32.5 x 24.4 cm.), color lithograph on copper print paper (BP 12,650, DM 31,051, FR 104,658, Y 2,062,230).

BI *Mademoiselle Marcelle Lender, En Buste (L.D. 102; W. 99; A. 115), 1895,* Wittrock's 4th (final) state, narrow margins, light/mat staining, colors attenuated, crease, glue staining, est. $7/9,000, (11-09-92, Christie-NY, #216, illus.), 12¾ x 9½ in., (324 x 241 mm.), colored lithograph on wove.

$14,584* *Mademoiselle Marcelle Lender, En Buste (W. 99; D. 102; A. 131), 1895,* as pub. in German edit. of Pan, publication line partially trimmed, margins, good cond., discoloration, (06-30-93, Sotheby-London, #703, illus.), sh 14 x 10⅞ in., (356 x 276 mm.), color lithograph on wove (BP 9775, DM 24,875, FR 83,913, Y 1,562,627).

$11,550* *"Mademoiselle Marcelle Lender, En Buste" (Delteil 102; Adhemar 131; Adriani 115/IVB; Wittrock 99/IV), 1895,* in: PAN, I. Jahrgang, Heft 3, (11-28-92, Grisebach, #107, illus.), 12¹³⁄₁₆ x 9⁹⁄₁₆ in., (32.5 x 24.3 cm.), color lithograph on wove (BP 7624, DM 18,401, FR 62,466, Y 1,437,461).

$24,435* *Mademoiselle Marcelle Lender, En Buste, Dans "Chilperic" (Wittr. 99/IV; D.-Kornf. 102/III/b; Adr. 115/IV/b), 1895,* (06-23-93, Kornfeld, #829, illus.), color lithograph on wove (BP 16,600, DM 41,345, FR 139,072, Y 2,662,055, SF 36,800).

$12,011* *Mademoiselle Pois Vert (W. 122; D. 126; A. 141), 1895,* mono. stamp, pub. Kleinmann, full margins, good cond., crease, discoloration, (06-30-93, Sotheby-London, #706, illus.), 7⅜ x 7½ in., (187 x 191 mm.), lithograph in dark olive-green on wove (BP 8050, DM 20,486, FR 69,108, Y 1,286,939).

$8018* *Mademoiselle Pois-Vert. (Wittr. 122; D. 126; Adr. 141), 1895,* mono. stamp, (06-23-93, Kornfeld, #833, illus.), lithograph in green on wove (BP 5447, DM 13,567, FR 45,635, Y 873,516, SF 12,075).

$1320* *Mary Hamilton (L.D. 175; W. 67; A. 142), 1895,* mono. stamp, full margins, staining, creasing, very good cond., (11-09-92, Christie-NY, #221, illus.), 10½ x 4½ in., (267 x 114 mm.), rust-brown lithograph on Chine (BP 873, DM 2107, FR 7120, Y 163,812).

$660* *"Mary Hamilton" (W. 67), 1925,* Frapier edit., excell. cond., right corner missing, (10-31-92, Cleveland, #344, illus.), 10½ x 5 in., (26.7 x 12.7 cm.), lithograph (BP 423, DM 1015, FR 3445, Y 81,754).

$4180* *May Belfort (L.D. 354; W. P14; A. 126), 1895,* Wittrock's Edit. B IV (of C), small margin, restored areas, light-staining, laid down on Japan, (11-09-92, Christie-NY, #217, illus.), 30½ x 23½ in., (775 x 597 mm.), colored lithograph on wove (BP 2764, DM 6673, FR 22,546, Y 518,739).

$2100 *"May Bellfort",* Kleinmann, H.T.L. symbol, roll marks, edge damage, cover illus., (09-24-92, Alderfer, #234, illus.), 30⅞ x 23¼ in., (78.4 x 59.1 cm.), (BP 1229, DM 3112, FR 10,569, Y 252,616).

$12,708* *May Milton (Delteil 356; Adhemar 149; Wittrock P17; Adriani 134), 1895,* Delteil's final state, good cond., tear, crease, linen backed, (10-14-92, Sotheby-Japan, #104, illus.), sheet 31½ x 24¼ in., (800 x 616 mm.), color lithograph (BP 7459, DM 18,598, FR 63,067, Y 1,539,990).

$12,650* *Miss May Belfort Au Irish American Bar, Rue Royale (?) (D. 123; A. 124; W. 119; Adr. 140), 1895,* mono., No. 11, pub. Kleinmann, full margins, good cond., mat stain, loss, (05-13-93, Sotheby-NY, #839, illus.), 13 x 10⅜ in., (330 x 263 mm.), lithograph (BP 8305, DM 20,426, FR 68,900, Y 1,412,303).

BI *Miss May Belfort Saluant (W. 115; D. 117; A. 121), 1895,* s., i., pub. Andre Marty, large margins, good cond. w/in subject, creases, ink notations, est. BP 20/25,000, (06-30-93, Sotheby-London, #702, illus.), 19⅝ x 14⅛ in., (498 x 359 mm.), lithograph in dark olive-green on wove.

$16,738* *Miss May Belfort Saluant (Wittrock 115; Delteil 117; Adriani 121), 1895,* (06-25-93, Kornfeld, #135, illus.), image 14¾ x 10½ in., (37.5 x 26.6 cm.), lithograph in dark green on vellum (BP 11,321, DM 28,495, FR 95,975, Y 1,774,221, SF 25,300).

$3750* *"La Modiste Renee Vert" (Wittrock 4 ii/ii), 1893,* trial proof, repaired tears, good cond., (05-15-93, Cleveland, #428, illus.), 17 x 11 in., (43.2 x 27.9 cm.), color lithograph (BP 2438, DM 6032, FR 20,270, Y 415,697).

$2070* *La Modiste, Renee Vert (L.D. 13, W. 4, A. 13), 1893,* Wittrock's 2nd final state, wide margins, light-staining, repaired tear, loss, good cond., prop. Monclair Art Museum, (05-11-93, Christie-NY, #345), borderline 18 x 11½ in., (457 x 292 mm.), color lithograph on wove (BP 1321, DM 3261, FR 10,987, Y 227,698).

$225* *"La Modiste, Renee Vert" (W. 47),* repairs, (10-18-92, Pescheteau, #271), 18⅜ x 12⅜ in., (46.6 x 31.5 cm.), lithograph in grey-green on wove (BP 136, DM 332, FR 1129, Y 26,866).

BI *Moulin Rouge, La Gouloue (D. 339; A. 1; W. P1; Adr 1), 1891,* Wittrock's third state of four, Adriani's second (final) state, on two joined sheets, margins, good cond., creases, repaired tear, creases, soiling, linen-backed, est. $100/140,000, (11-05-92, Sotheby-NY, #455, illus.), sheet 67⅞ x 48¾ in., (172.4 x 123.8 cm.), lithograph p. in colors.

$19,800* *Moulin Rouge-La Goulue (L.D. 339; Wittrock P1; Adriani 1), 1891,* Wittrock's Edit. B., trimmed to image, light-staining, restored tears, creases and paper losses in image, laid down, good cond., (11-09-92, Christie-NY, #207), 74⅜ x 45¼ in., (188.9 x 114.9 cm.), colored lithograph on 3 sheets of wove (BP 13,091, DM 31,609, FR 106,796, Y 2,457,185).

$16,036* *P. Sescau. Photographe. 9, Place Pigalle (Wittr. P. 22/a; D. 353; Adr. 60/III), 1894,* restored tear, (06-23-93, Kornfeld, #836, illus.), sh 24³⁄₁₆ x 30⅞ in., (61.5 x 78.5 cm.), poster, color lithograph (BP 10,894, DM 27,134, FR 91,269, Y 1,747,031, SF 24,150).

BI *"Les Papillons" (W. 128), 1935* reissue, repaired, thin spots, est. $4/500, (10-31-92, Cleveland, #345), 8⅜ x 8 in., (21.3 x 20.3 cm.), lithograph.

$40,250* *Partie De Campagne (D. 219; A. 322; W. 228; Adr. 228), 1897,* mono. stamp, no. 11, included in L'Album d'estampes originales de la Galerie Vollard, pub. Vollard, 1897, faded, mat stain, printer's creases, nick, stains, discoloration, (05-13-93, Sotheby-NY, #843, illus.), 15¾ x 20½ in., (400 x 520 mm.), lithograph in colors on fine wove (BP 26,425, DM 64,993, FR 219,227, Y 4,493,692).

$13,200* *La Passagere Du 54-Pomenade En Yacht (L.D. 366; W. P20; A. 137), 1895,* narrow margins, light-staining, creasing, tear, remains of glue, (11-09-92, Christie-NY, #219, illus.), 23¾ x 16 in., (603 x 406 mm.), colored lithograph on wove (BP 8727, DM 21,073, FR 71,197, Y 1,638,124).

$33,000* *La Passagere Du 54-Promenade En Yacht (D. 366; A. 188; W. P20; Adr. 137), 1896,* Wittrock's and Adriani's third (final) state, good cond., Japan backed, (11-05-92, Sotheby-NY, #462, illus.), lithograph p. in colors on wove (BP 21,463, DM 52,190, FR 176,565, Y 4,048,583).

$3663* *Pauvre Pierreuse!, (L.D. 26; A. 27; W. 13; Adriani 35), 1893,* 1st state (of 2), s., num. No. 64, pub. E. Kleinmann, blindstamp, foxmarks, creases, light-staining, (12-01-92, Christie-London, #546), L. 9⁷⁄₁₆ x 6¹¹⁄₁₆ in., (240 x 170 mm.), lithograph p. in olive-green on wove (BP 2420, DM 5838, FR 19,897, Y 456,051).

$2090* *Le Petit Trottin (Delteil 27; Adhemar 18; Wittrock 14; Adriani 36), 1893,* p. after 1901, margins, good cond., crease, (11-05-92, Sotheby-NY, #447), 11 x 7½ in., (280 x 190 mm.), lithograph in green w/stenciled coloring (BP 1359, DM 3305, FR 11,182, Y 256,410).

BI *La Petite Loge (W. 182; D. 209; A. 257), 1897,* 2nd final state, s., #No 7, p. by Ancourt, pub. Gustave Pellet, trimmed, good cond., hinges, ex coll. Henraux Coll., est. BP 80/100,000, (06-30-93, Sotheby-London, #700, illus.), sh 9⅜ x 12½ in., (238 x 318 mm.), color lithograph on chine.

$165* *"Portrait Of Tristan Bernard" (Adriani 249),* very good/good cond., (09-27-92, Bakker, #198), plate 6¾ x 4 in., (17.1 x 10.2 cm.), drypoint (BP 96, DM 245, FR 827, Y 19,916).

BI *Pour Toi!... (L.D. 19, W. 6, A. 28), 1893,* s., num. 85, blindstamp pub. Kleinmann, margins, light/mat staining,creasing, glue, prov., est. $4/6,000, (05-11-93, Christie-NY, #346, illus.), borderline 10½ x 8 in., (267 x 203 mm.), lithograph w/pochoir in turquoise on wove.

$6600* *Pourquoi Pas?...Une Fois N'Est Pas Coutume (W. 30), 1893,* s., num. 27, pub. L'Escarmouche, Kleinmann blindstamp (L. 1573), goodcond., foxing, light-staining, paper loss, paper tape, (02-24-93, Butterfield, #2794, illus.), 15 x 11⅛ in., (381 x 283 mm.), lithograph on wove (BP 4603, DM 10,714, FR 36,324, Y 774,466).

$4125* *Proces Arton (Wittrock 149, 150 & 151), 1896: Set Of Three,* mono. stamp; second w/Kleinmann's blindstamp, (03-24-93, Grogan, #111), 18⅛ x 24¾ in., (46 x 62.9 cm.), lithograph (BP 2793, DM 6737, FR 22,929, Y 484,667).

$6900* *Programme Pour L'Argent (L.D. 15, W. 97, A. 133), 1895,* color slightly attenuated, glue, good cond., pub. Theatre Libre as program for play L'Argent, (05-11-93, Christie-NY, #350, illus.), plate 12½ x 9⁵⁄₁₆ in., (318 x 237 mm.), color lithograph on wove (BP 4405, DM 10,870, FR 36,624, Y 758,992).

$2875* *Quatorze Lithographies Originales De Toulouse-Lautrec Pour IllustrerDes Chansons (Melodies De Desire Dihau) (D. 129-142; Adr. 145-158), 1895-96: Set Of Fourteen,* complete, illus. songs by Desire Dihau, copy #8 on just. page, pub.H. Lefebre ed., 1935, full margins, good cond., crease, tear, (02-11-93, Sotheby-NY, #267, illus.), sheet 12¹³⁄₁₆ x 10¹⁄₁₆ in., (325 x 255 mm.), lithograph on wove (BP 2029, DM 4762, FR 16,115, Y 346,594).

$23,000* *Reine De Joie (D. 342; A. 5; W. P3; Adr. 5), 1892,* margins, good cond., center fold, folds w/associated breaks, tears and losses, paper tone darkened, tears, Dora Jane Janson and the Late H.W. JansonColl., (05-13-93, Sotheby-NY, #846, illus.), sh approx. 54¾ x 37¾ in., (139.1 x 95.9 cm.), lithograph in colors p. on two sheets of paper (BP 15,100, DM 37,139, FR 125,272, Y 2,567,824).

$45,386* *Reine De Joie (Delteil 342; Adhemar 5; Wittrock P3, Adriani 5), 1892,* good cond., folds, breaks, linen backed, (10-14-92, Sotheby-Japan, #102, illus.), sheet 58⅝ x 37⅞ in., (148.9 x 96.2 cm.), lithograph in colors on 2 joined sheets of paper (BP 26,640, DM 66,422, FR 225,241, Y 5,500,000).

$13,395* *"Reine De Joie",* (09-29-92, B. Rasmussen, #367), lithographic poster in colors mounted on linen (BP 7530, DM 18,919, FR 64,554, Y 1,599,021, DK 73,600).

BI *Rejane Et Galipaux, Dans Madame Sans-Gene (W. 44; D. 52; A. 56), 1893,* reduced margins, repaired paper splits, backed w/Japan, est. BP 2,5/3,000, (06-30-93, Sotheby-London, #697, illus.), 14⅜ x 12 in., (365 x 305 mm.), lithograph on wove.

$4400* *"La Renaissance: Sarah Bernhardt Dans Phedre" (W. 37), 1893,* No. 30, s. w/mono. stamp, excell. cond., full margins, (10-31-92, Cleveland, #343, illus.), 13¼ x 9½ in., (33.7 x 24.1 cm.), lithograph (BP 2820, DM 6769, FR 22,965, Y 545,027).

$978* *La Revue Blanche,* Maitres de l'Affiche blindstamp, p. Chaix, margins, apparently good condition, light-staining, (03-31-93, Butterfield, #5252), 12½ x 9⅛ in., (31.8 x 23.2 cm.), lithograph printed in colors on wove paper (BP 647, DM 1573, FR 5344, Y 112,466).

$11,550* *La Revue Blanche (D. 355; A. 115; W. P16; Adr. 130), 1895,* third (final) state, p. Ancourt, pub. Charpentier and Fasquelle, formagazine La Revue Blanche, on two sheets, margins, good cond., creases, water stain, filled in loss, repaired tear, paper tone, discolored, linen backed, (11-05-92, Sotheby-NY, #460, illus.), sheet 49½ x 36½ in., (125.7 x 92.7 cm.), lithograph p. in colors (BP 7512, DM 18,267, FR 61,798, Y 1,417,004).

$6325* *La Revue Blanche (D. 355; A. 115; W. P16; Adr. 130), 1895,* 3rd (final) state, p. Ancourt, pub. Charpentier and Fasquelle, for the magazine La Revue Blanche, margins, paper discolored, vertical splits w/associated losses, backed w/linen and stapled to the backing, (05-13-93, Sotheby-NY, #848, illus.), sheet 50⅜ x 35⅝ in., (128 x 90.5 cm.), lithograph in colors on two sheets (BP 4152, DM 10,213, FR 34,450, Y 706,152).

BI *La Revue Blanche (D. 355; A. 130), 1895,* tears, oxidation, losses, (02-24-93, Picard, #240), color lithograph.

$15,950* *La Revue Blanche (Delteil 355 II/II, Adhemar 115 II/II, Wittrock P16C Adriani 108 III/III), 1895,* (05-16-93, Hindman, #445, illus.), 49 x 35½ in., (124.5 x 90.2 cm.), color lithographic poster (BP 10,371, DM 25,655, FR 86,216, Y 1,768,097).

$15,431* *La Revue Blanche (Delteil 355; Adhemar 115; Wittrock P16; Adriani 130), 1895,* pub. Charpentier and Fasquelle, good cond., defects, paper/linen backed, (10-14-92, Sotheby-Japan, #103, illus.), sheet 50⅝ x 36½ in., (128.6 x 92.7 cm.), lithograph in colors on 2 joined sheets of paper (BP 9057, DM 22,583, FR 76,581, Y 1,869,971).

$4620* *La Revue Blanche (L.D. 355, W. D16, A 130), 1895,* Wittrock's Edit. C, margins, light-staining, paper losses mostly outside image, laid down on linen, mounted on stretcher, (11-09-92, Christie-NY, #218, illus.), 49 x 36 in., (124.5 x 91.4 cm.), colored lithograph on wove (BP 3055, DM 7375, FR 24,919, Y 573,343).

BI *La Revue Blanche (W. 16; D. 355; A. 115), 1895,* Wittrock's 3rd state of 4, p. Ancourt, pub. G. Charpentier and E. Fasquelle, for La Revue Blanche, good cond., paper discoloration, damp stain, linen backed, est. BP 5,5/6,500, (12-03-92, Sotheby-London, #585, illus.), sheet 49¾ x 36 in., (126.4 x 91.4 cm.), lithographic poster in colors.

$8526* *La Revue Blanche (W. 16; D. 355; A. 115), 1895,* Wittrock's 3rd state of 4, p. Ancourt, pub. G. Charpentier, E. Fasquelle, for La Revue Blanche, good cond., cockling, repaired splits, linen backed, (12-03-92, Sotheby-London, #586), sheet 50⅜ x 36⅛ in., (128 x 91.8 cm.), lithographic poster in colors (BP 5500, DM 13,408, FR 45,765, Y 1,060,844).

$19,854* *La Revue Blanche (Wittr. P. 16/c; D. 355; Adr. 130/III), 1895,* (06-23-93, Kornfeld, #835, illus.), poster, color lithograph (BP 13,488, DM 33,594, FR 112,999, Y 2,162,981, SF 29,900).

$254* *"Skating", 1896,* plate mono., (09-05-92, Arnold, #7, illus.), 10¼ x 8¹¹⁄₁₆ in., (26 x 22 cm.), color lithograph (BP 127, DM 354, FR 1204, Y 31,177).

$2253* *Le Sommeil (Adriani 182; Adhemar 211), 1896,* stone mono. THL, (03-24-93, Venator/Hansten, #4567), approx. 9¹⁄₁₆ x 12⅝ in., (23 x 32 cm.), red ochre chalk lithograph (BP 1526, DM 3680, FR 12,524, Y 264,716).

$15,217* *Sortie De Theatre (Wittrock 147; Delteil 169; Adriani 195), 1896,* (06-25-93, Kornfeld, #133, illus.), image 12⅜ x 10⁵⁄₁₆ in., (31.5 x 26.2 cm.), lithograph on vellum (BP 10,292, DM 25,906, FR 87,253, Y 1,612,996, SF 23,000).

$5595* *Souper A Londres (L.D. 167, W.W. 169), 1896,* frame trace, s., good margins, (06-11-93, Picard, #177), 11¹³⁄₁₆ x 14³⁄₁₆ in., (300 x 360 mm.), lithograph on creme wove (BP 3676, DM 9093, FR 30,658, Y 593,634).

$1100* *Sybil Sanderson (L.D. 151; W. 257; A. 261), 1898, c. 1913,* from Portraits d'Acteurs et d'Actrices: Treize Lithographies, light-staining, splits, remains of glue, (11-09-92, Christie-NY, #224), 11½ x 9⁷⁄₁₆ in., (292 x 240 mm.), lithograph on wove (BP 727, DM 1756, FR 5933, Y 136,510).

$242* *Ta Bouche,* (11-01-92, Hanzel, #228), 7 x 10 in., (17.8 x 25.4 cm.), lithograph (BP 158, DM 382, FR 1287, Y 29,921).

$1998* *Ta Bouche (L. Delteil 21, W. Wittrock 7), 1893,* before letters, num. 8, s., drystamp, large margins, (06-11-93, Picard, #176), 10⅝ x 7¹⁄₁₆ in., (270 x 180 mm.), lithograph in olive green on Japan (BP 1313, DM 3247, FR 10,948, Y 211,989).

$248* *"Ta Bouche",* p.l., mono. TL, (10-10-92, Goldberg, #427), 14¾ x 10 in., (37.5 x 25.4 cm.), color lithograph (BP 147, DM 368, FR 1237, Y 30,192).

$275* *"Ta Bouche" (D21, A25, W7), 1893,* (02-13-93, Neal, #580), image 12 x 8 in., (30.5 x 20.3 cm.), lithograph in green ink (BP 194, DM 456, FR 1543, Y 33,164).

BI *Ta Bouche, 1893,* mono. in stone, late impression, est. $450/550, (10-30-92, Sloan, #1601), 10 x 7 in., (25.4 x 17.8 cm.), sepia lithograph.

BI *La Troupe De Mademoiselle Eglantine (L.D. 361; W. P21; A. 162), 1896,* Wittrock's Edit. C (of D), trimmed, shaved, paper loss, laid down onJapan, est. $14/16,000, (11-09-92, Christie-NY, #222, illus.), 23⅞ x 31⅝ in., (606 x 803 mm.), colored lithograph on thin wove.

BI *La Vache Enragee (W. P.27A; D. 364; A. 197), 1896,* Delteil's 1st state and Wittrock's edit. A, before letters, est. BP 15/17,000, (06-30-93, Sotheby-London, #693, illus.), sh 32½ x 23½ in., (826 x 597 mm.), color lithographic poster on thin wove backed on linen.

$2749* *La Valse Des Lapins (Wittr. 138, premiere Edition; D. 143; Adr. 159), 1895,* mono. stamp, (06-23-93, Kornfeld, #834), lithograph on wove (BP 1868, DM 4651, FR 15,646, Y 299,488, SF 4140).

BI *Les Vieilles Histoires (W. 5), 1893,* pub. G. Ondet, margins, tears, paper losses, surface soiling, mat/light-staining, foxing, est. $6/800, (09-21-92, Butterfield, #834), 13¼ x 21⁵⁄₁₆ in., (337.2 x 540.7 mm.), lithograph in olive-green on wove backed w/Japan.

BI *Yahne Dans Sa Loge (D. 111; A. 113; W. 91; Adr. 108), 1895,* full margins, good cond., creasing, soiling, est. $4/5,000, (05-13-93, Sotheby-NY, #837, illus.), 12⅝ x 9⅝ in., (320 x 245 mm.), lithograph in olive green.

$1275* *Yvette Gilbert-Dans "La Glu" (Delteil 253, Adhemar 252 II, Wittrock 273), 1898,* red mono. stamp, blindstamp, (06-04-93, Bassenge, #5827), 11⁹⁄₁₆ x 9½ in., (29.3 x 24.1 cm.), lithograph in red ochre on simili-Japan (BP 844, DM 2070, FR 6979, Y 137,511).

$11,550* *Yvette Guilbert (D. 250-255; 257-260; A. 306, 307, 308-316; W. 271-280; Adr. 250-258), 1898,* complete portfolio, incl. lithographic cover and frontispiece, pub. Bliss and Sands, full margins, good cond., foxing, creases, tear, losses in lithograhic cover, (11-05-92, Sotheby-NY, #453, illus.), each sheet approx. 19¾ x 14¾ in., (502 x 373 mm.), eight lithographs p. w/ a beige tint stone (BP 7512, DM 18,267, FR 61,798, Y 1,417,004).

$13,987* *Yvette Guilbert (L.D. 251 a 255, 257 a 260, W.W. 271 a 279): Nine,* complete series, first, t., colophon, s., table, red stamp, (06-11-93, Picard, #178), 19⅞ x 14¹⁵⁄₁₆ in., (505 x 380 mm.), lithographs on gray mat (BP 9190, DM 22,732, FR 76,641, Y 1,484,032).

$385* *Yvette Guilbert, Dans Colombine A Pierrot (W. 68), 1894,* 4th final edit. of 1950, pub. Au Pont des Arts, full margins, good cond., light-staining, buckling, (10-28-92, Butterfield, #2863), 8⅝ x 4⅜ in., (219 x 111 mm.), lithograph in black on imitation Japan (BP 245, DM 595, FR 2019, Y 47,239).

$2833* *Yvette Guilbert, Linger, Longer, Loo (Delteil 259, Adhemar 315, Adriani 257 II, Wittrock 278 II), 1898,* (06-04-93, Bassenge, #5829), 11¹³⁄₁₆ x 9⁷⁄₁₆ in., (30 x 24 cm.), lithograph on hand-made (BP 1874, DM 4601, FR 15,506, Y 305,544).

$19,062* *Yvette Guilbert, Serie Anglaise (Delteil 250-55, 257-60; Adhemar 306-11, 313-16; Wittrock 271-79; Adriani 250-58), 1898: Eight,* complete portfolio, plus frontispiece and lithographic cover, full margins, good cond., foxing, discoloration, soiling, orig. cover, (10-14-92, Sotheby-Japan, #101, illus.), each sheet 19¾ x 15 in., (502 x 381 mm.), lithograph w/beige tint stones on laid paper (BP 11,189, DM 27,897, FR 94,600, Y 2,309,985).

BI *"Yvette Guilbert-A Menilmontaub, De Bruant" (Adriani 1976/260, Adriani 1987/254 II), 1898,* from "Yvette Guilbert" portfolio, mono. in stone, est. SC 32/40,000, (11-25-92, Dorotheum, #416, illus.), sh 19¹¹⁄₁₆ x 14⁹⁄₁₆ in., (50 x 37 cm.), image 11⁹⁄₁₆ x 9⁷⁄₁₆ in., (50 x 37 cm.), lithograph.

$1133* *Yvette Guilbert-Chanson Ancienne (Delteil 257, Adhemar 313, Adriani 255 II, Wittrock 276), 1898,* mono. stamp, blindstamp, (06-04-93, Bassenge, #5828), 11⁹⁄₁₆ x 9⁹⁄₁₆ in., (29.3 x 24.3 cm.), lithograph in colors on Simili-Japan (BP 750, DM 1840, FR 6201, Y 122,196).

BI *Yvette Guilbert-Chanson Ancienne (L.D. 257; W. 276; A. 255), 1898,* wide margins, staining, soiling, very good cond., est. $3/4,000, (11-09-92, Christie-NY, #223, illus.), 13½ x 11 in., (343 x 279 mm.), black and beige lithograph on laid.

TOULOUSE-LAUTREC CIRCLE, Publisher

BI *"Elles", 1969: Ten,* vol., #846/1250, containing frontispiece, after Henri De Toulouse-Lautrec, each num., stamped pub. blindstamp, slip case, est. BP 2/400, (08-20-92, Bonhams-Chelsea, #46), lithograph in colors.

$171* *Elles, 1969: Ten,* volume, #846/1250, frontispiece, each num., stamped, pub. blindstamp, slip-case, intro. by Michel Melot, (12-10-92, Bonhams-Chelsea, #84), color lithograph (BP 110, DM 270, FR 924, Y 21,153).

BI *Elles: Ten,* volume, #846/1250, frontispiece, after Toulouse-Lautrec, each num., stamped, est. BP 150/250, (10-15-92, Bonhams-Chelsea, #48), color lithograph.

TOUPIN, Fernand Canadian b. 1930

$140* *"L'Alouette",* #8/75, s., d. Toupin 75, (07-14-92, Encans, #84), 20¹⁄₁₆ x 16⅛ in., (51 x 41 cm.), serigraph (BP 73, DM 208, FR 700, Y 17,507, C$ 167).

$140* *Sans Titre,* #41/100, s., d. Toupin 70, (07-14-92, Encans, #83), 22¹⁄₁₆ x 15¹⁵⁄₁₆ in., (56 x 40.5 cm.), serigraph (BP 73, DM 208, FR 700, Y 17,507, C$ 167).

$73* *Untitled,* #130/150, s. F. Toupin, (10-20-92, Encans, #154), 8⁷⁄₁₆ x 4¹⁵⁄₁₆ in., (21.5 x 12.5 cm.), lithograph (BP 41, DM 111, FR 378, Y 9150, C$ 89).

TOURNON

$1807* *Le Noel De Colombine. La Vie Par Le Cinematographe. Cine-mime De Xavier Privat. Film Pathe,* fairly good cond., (02-12-93, Cheval/Robert, #200), 59¹³⁄₁₆ x 42¹⁵⁄₁₆ in., (152 x 109 cm.), poster (BP 1273, DM 2997, FR 10,140, Y 217,921).

TOURTE, Suzanne 1904-1979

$140* *"Deux Femmes", 1950,* #12/35, d., s., (04-04-93, Pescheteau, #304), 19¹¹⁄₁₆ x 12¹³⁄₁₆ in., (50 x 32.5 cm.), etching on wove (BP 92, DM 225, FR 764, Y 15,940).

$107* *Les Oliviers Des Taillades,* ded., #21/25, full margins, (05-06-93, Laurin, #85), color lithograph on Rives on wove (BP 68, DM 169, FR 567, Y 11,772).

$189* *Untitled,* #6/30, s., (01-28-93, Pescheteau, #272), etching (BP 125, DM 299, FR 1013, Y 23,467).

$182* *Vendanges A Ecueil. Marne, 1962,* d., t., ded., #45/64, s., good margins, (02-03-93, Ader Tajan, #205), 8¹⁵⁄₁₆ x 11⁹⁄₁₆ in., (22.8 x 29.3 cm.), etching and drypoint (BP 127, DM 300, FR 1016, Y 22,640).

TOWN, Harold Barling

$556* *Abandoned Band,* s. Town Dec/5 53 in plate, t., prov., gallery label verso, lit., (11-30-92, Ritchie, #49, illus.), 17 x 17¾ in., (43.2 x 45.1 cm.), single autographic print (BP 367, DM 886, FR 3007, Y 69,197, C$ 715).

$193* *Moon Net,* s., d. '70, #37/200; t. label verso, prov., (11-30-92, Ritchie, #50), 28½ x 41 in., (72.4 x 104.1 cm.), color serigraph (BP 127, DM 307, FR 1044, Y 24,020, C$ 248).

$607* *Submarine For A Six Year Old*, s., d. '57, (05-18-93, Joyner, #156), 18 x 24 in., (45.7 x 61 cm.), single autographic print (BP 395, DM 985, FR 3326, Y 67,647, C$ 770).

TOWN, Harold Barling   b. 1924
$67* *Abstract 11-200, 1970*, #11-200, s., d. 70, (10-21-92, Maynard, #185), 28 x 40 in., (71.1 x 101.6 cm.), silkscreen (BP 42, DM 101, FR 344, Y 8161, C$ 83).

TOWNSEND
$35 *"War Rages In France"*, (03-04-93, Alderfer, #284), 29½ x 19¾ in., (74.9 x 50.2 cm.), poster (BP 24, DM 57, FR 195, Y 4075).

TOYOHARA KUNICHIKA   Japanese 1835-1900
$2976* *An Okubi-e Of Nakamura Shigan IV As Kumagai Naozane: Six*, diptych Kabe no mudagaki, Oban, single, diptych and triptych (d. 1874), s. Toyohara/Kunichika hitsu/egaku w/Toshidama seal, censor's seal aratame, Hare, and Dog, pub.'s marks Gusokuya and Hamatetsu, good state, Prof. H.R.W. Kuhne Coll., (06-11-93, Sotheby-London, #444, illus.), woodblock (BP 1955, DM 4837, FR 16,307, Y 315,756).

TOYOHIRO
$1582* *"The New Fuji"*, surimono, kakuban, s. Toyohiro ga, good cond., (06-10-93, Sotheby-London, #209), (BP 1035, DM 2576, FR 8673, Y 167,923).

TOYOHIRO, Utagawa   1773-1828
BI *Samurai*, Format Chuban, est. SC 7/8,000, (04-27-93, Dorotheum, #233, illus.), 6⁵⁄₁₆ x 8¼ in., (16 x 21 cm.), .

TOYOKUNI
$44* *An Actor With A Fan*, (03-25-93, Boos, #218), 14 x 9¾ in., (35.6 x 24.8 cm.), color woodblock print (BP 30, DM 72, FR 246, Y 5155).
$2989* *Cooling Off On A River*, oban, s. Toyokuni ga, faded, creased, soiled, rubbed, laid-down, mounted on board, ex-coll. Robert Mond, (06-10-93, Sotheby-London, #230, illus.), each sheet approx. 14⁹⁄₁₆ x 9¹⁵⁄₁₆ in., (37 x 25.2 cm.), (BP 1955, DM 4867, FR 16,387, Y 317,270).
BI *Four Prints*, est. $3/500, (04-16-93, DuMouchelle, #176, illus.), 13½ x 9 in., (34.3 x 22.9 cm.), woodblock.
$94* *Geisha Standing Behind A Screen*, (10-16-92, DuMouchelle, #2465), 15½ x 10½ in., (39.4 x 26.7 cm.), colored woodblock (BP 57, DM 139, FR 472, Y 11,224).
$2813* *The Portrait Of The Actor Iwai Hanshiro IV As Shirai Gonpachi*, oban, from series Yakusha butai no sugata-e, pub. Izumiya Ichibei, censor's seal, s. Toyokuni ga, trimmed, rubbed, wormage, repaired, (06-10-93, Sotheby-London, #224, illus.), (BP 1840, DM 4581, FR 15,422, Y 298,588).
$55* *Three Figures On A Balcony*, mid 19th-century, (12-05-92, Eldred, #541), woodblock (BP 34, DM 86, FR 292, Y 6815).
$11* *Woman On A Foot Bridge*, (10-11-92, Hanzel, #956D), 14 x 9¾ in., (35.6 x 24.8 cm.), color woodblock print (BP 7, DM 16, FR 55, Y 1339).

TOYOKUNI (I)
$66* *"Matsumoto Koshiro V As Kono Moronao In A Scene From The Chirshingura"*, pub. Kawaguchi Shozo?, (10-08-92, Boos, #152), 14½ x 9½ in., (36.8 x 24.1 cm.), color wood block print (BP 39, DM 98, FR 331, Y 8019).

TOYOKUNI (III)
$110* *Scenes Of Village Life: Two*, (03-25-93, Boos, #209), each 9¾ x 6¾ in., (24.8 x 17.1 cm.), color woodblock print (BP 75, DM 181, FR 615, Y 12,887).

TOYOKUNI (III) (Kunisada)
$88* *"Aichikawa Danjuro VIII As Miyagi Asogiro"*, pub. Maruya Jintachi, sensor seals 1847-50, (10-08-92, Boos, #151), 14 x 9¾ in., (35.6 x 24.8 cm.), color wood block print (BP 52, DM 130, FR 442, Y 10,693).

TOYOKUNI, Utagaqa (III)
$39* *Figure With Butterfly And Cherry Blossoms*, s., (05-14-93, DuMouchelle, #2356), paper 14¼ x 10 in., (36.2 x 25.4 cm.), block (BP 25, DM 63, FR 211, Y 4323).

TOYOKUNI, Utagawa
$55* *Depicting A Male Actor*, block sig., (03-12-93, DuMouchelle, #2102), 14 x 9½ in., (35.6 x 24.1 cm.), woodblock print (BP 38, DM 92, FR 311, Y 6482).
$138* *Seated Woman With Mirror*, plate s., good cond., (07-19-92, Bakker, #259), sheet 13¾ x 9½ in., (34.9 x 24.1 cm.), color woodblock print (BP 71, DM 201, FR 680, Y 17,156).
$138* *Woman Standing*, plate s., good/poor cond., (07-19-92, Bakker, #258), 13¾ x 9½ in., (34.9 x 24.1 cm.), color woodblock print (BP 71, DM 201, FR 680, Y 17,156).

TOYOKUNI, Utagawa   Japanese 1769-1825
BI *Bildnis Der Dichterinnen Kisen Hoshi Und Sojo Henjo Mit Einer Kamuro*, s., pub. by Eijudo, Format Aiban, est. SC 8/9,000, (04-27-93, Dorotheum, #224), 9¹⁄₁₆ x 12¹³⁄₁₆ in., (23 x 32.5 cm.), woodcut.
BI *Bildnis Des Schauspielers Arashi Goro*, Format Oban, est. SC 4/5,000, (04-27-93, Dorotheum, #222), 9¹³⁄₁₆ x 14¾ in., (25 x 37.5 cm.), .
$220* *Geisha*, (09-25-92, Wolf, #6), 13 x 9 in., (33 x 22.9 cm.), colored woodblock (BP 128, DM 326, FR 1103, Y 26,554).
$220* *Gentleman With Courtesan*, (07-03-92, Sloan, #898), sight 14¼ x 9¾ in., (36.2 x 24.8 cm.), woodblock (BP 115, DM 333, FR 1122, Y 27,425).
$66* *"Woman" and "Servant": Two*, (12-17-92, Mystic, #15), each 14 x 9½ in., (35.6 x 24.1 cm.), color woodblock (BP 42, DM 103, FR 352, Y 8111).

TOYOKUNI, Utagawa   Japanese 1777-1835
BI *Courtesans By Cherry Blossoms*, est. $2/300, (02-04-93, Sloan, #941), sight 13½ x 10 in., (34.3 x 25.4 cm.), color woodcut.

TOYOKUNI, Utagawa (I)
$948* *Samurai Und Dame Begegnen Sich An Einer Schlossmauer, c. 1820*, from series Chusingura, Oban, censure stamp, Kiwane, (04-21-93, Germann, #255), woodcut (BP 615, DM 1515, FR 5124, Y 104,949, SF 1380).
$593* *Sawamura Tannosuke Als Geisha Unter Kirschbaumzweigen, 1811*, Oban, censure stamp, Kiwame and Igaya, (04-21-93, Germann, #253, illus.), color woodcut w/ embossing (BP 385, DM 948, FR 3205, Y 65,648, SF 863).

TOYOKUNI, Utagawa (I)   Japanese 1769-1825
$302* *Actor*, format Oban, (04-27-93, Dorotheum, #146, illus.), 9¼ x 14⅛ in., (23.5 x 35.9 cm.), (BP 192, DM 478, FR 1618, Y 33,845, SC 3360).
$201* *Two Actors*, trimmed, spotted, (04-27-93, Dorotheum, #145, illus.), 9¹⁄₁₆ x 12⅝ in., (23 x 32 cm.), (BP 128, DM 318, FR 1077, Y 22,526, SC 2240).

TOYOKUNI, Utagawa (II)   Japanese 1777-1835
BI *Samurai Unrolling Scroll*, est. $175/225, (04-02-93, Sloan, #1883), 13¾ x 10 in., (349 x 254 mm.), color woodcut.
BI *Samurai Unrolling Scroll*, est. $2/250, (02-04-93, Sloan, #918), 13¾ x 10 in., (34.9 x 25.4 cm.), color woodcut.

TOYOKUNI, Utagawa (III)
$375* *Figural Triptych*, (05-16-93, Hanzel, #1093), each plate 13½ x 8¾ in., (34.3 x 22.2 cm.), color woodblock (BP 244, DM 603, FR 2027, Y 41,570).
$200* *Figural Triptych*, (05-16-93, Hanzel, #1092), each plate 13½ x 9½ in., (34.3 x 24.1 cm.), color woodblock (BP 130, DM 322, FR 1081, Y 22,170).
$120* *Maiden*, (05-16-93, Hanzel, #1101), 13½ x 9½ in., (34.3 x 24.1 cm.), color woodblock (BP 78, DM 193, FR 649, Y 13,302).
$50* *"A Man" and "A Woman": Two*, (05-16-93, Hanzel, #1099), 6½ x 4½ in., (16.5 x 11.4 cm.), 6¼ x 4 in., (16.5 x 11.4 cm.), color woodblock (BP 33, DM 80, FR 270, Y 5543).
$303* *"Night Scene, Two Actors Brandishing Torches, And A Woman Holding A Lantern", 1860*, oban triptych, s. Toy-

okuni Gwa, pristine cond., (01-02-93, Litchfield, #71), woodblock print (BP 202, DM 496, FR 1695, Y 37,989).

$275* *"Three Actors Before A Buddha Statue In The Woods",* *1853,* oban triptych, pub. Kinshodo (Tsujikoya Bunsuke), s. Toyokuni Gwa, pristine cond., (01-02-93, Litchfield, #109), woodblock print (BP 183, DM 451, FR 1538, Y 34,478).

$80* *Woman Harvesting,* (05-16-93, Hanzel, #1100), 13¾ x 9½ in., (34.9 x 24.1 cm.), color woodblock (BP 52, DM 129, FR 432, Y 8868).

TOYOKUNI, Utagawa (III)   1823-1880
$201* *Kabuki-Szene,* Format Oban, (04-27-93, Dorotheum, #194, illus.), 9¹³⁄₁₆ x 14¼ in., (25 x 36.2 cm.), (BP 128, DM 318, FR 1077, Y 22,526, SC 2240).
BI *Portrait Eines Schauspielers In Der Rolle Eines Daimyo,* Format Oban, est. SC 3/4,000, (04-27-93, Dorotheum, #238), 9⅜ x 13⅞ in., (23.8 x 35.2 cm.), .
BI *Schauspeile In Einer Kabuki-Rolle,* Format Oban, est. SC 2/3,000, (04-27-93, Dorotheum, #212, illus.), 9⅝ x 14⁹⁄₁₆ in., (24.5 x 37 cm.), .

TOYOKUNI, Utagawa (III)   Japanese 1786-1865
$282* *Courtesans In A Garden House In Yoshiwara,* diptych, s., (04-27-93, Dorotheum, #179, illus.), 20¹⁄₁₆ x 14¹³⁄₁₆ in., (51 x 37.7 cm.), color woodcut (BP 179, DM 446, FR 1510, Y 31,604, SC 3136).

TOYOKUNI, Utagawa (III)   Japanese 1823-1880
$222* *Portrait Of Three Men With Swords,* format Oban, (04-27-93, Dorotheum, #177, illus.), 14⅜ x 9¹⁵⁄₁₆ in., (36.5 x 25.2 cm.), color woodcut (BP 141, DM 351, FR 1189, Y 24,880, SC 2464).

TOYOKUNI (KUNISADA)
$50* *Beauty Admiring Plum Blossoms In Snowy Garden,* block s., (05-14-93, DuMouchelle, #2467), 14 x 9¾ in., (35.6 x 24.8 cm.), color woodblock (BP 33, DM 80, FR 270, Y 5543).

TOYOKUNI I
BI *"Courtesan Dreams At Party",* triptych, reasing, tears, trimmed, est. $4/500, (05-07-93, Goldberg, #1388, illus.), woodblock.

TOYOKUNI II, Utagawa   Japanese 1777-1835
$121* *Samurai Warriors: Three,* prov., (10-30-92, Sloan, #964), largest, sight 13¼ x 9¾ in., (33.7 x 24.8 cm.), woodblocks (BP 78, DM 186, FR 632, Y 14,988).
BI *Samurai Warriors: Three Portraits,* est. $300/400, (09-17-92, Sloan, #1490), largest, sight 13¼ x 9¾ in., (33.7 x 24.8 cm.), woodblocks.

TOYOKUNI III
BI *Actor Print, 1857,* from 53 View of the Tokaido Compared with 53 Kabuki Dramas, Station #51, third month, est. $150/200, (12-05-92, Eldred, #546), woodblock.
$110* *"Geisha Girl And Landscape",* block s., (04-16-93, DuMouchelle, #2299, illus.), 13¾ x 9¼ in., (34.9 x 23.5 cm.), woodblock (BP 72, DM 178, FR 600, Y 12,369).
BI *Geisha Rising From The Floor With A Pipe,* block s., est. $125/200, (10-16-92, DuMouchelle, #2464), 14¼ x 9¼ in., (36.2 x 23.5 cm.), woodblock.
$110* *Mirror Print, 1859,* staining, (12-05-92, Eldred, #544, illus.), woodblock (BP 69, DM 171, FR 584, Y 13,629).
$110* *Mother And Child In Landscape,* block s., (04-16-93, DuMouchelle, #2301, illus.), 13¾ x 9¼ in., (34.9 x 23.5 cm.), woodblock (BP 72, DM 178, FR 600, Y 12,369).
$132* *Night Scene With Three Figures On A Balcony: Triptych,* mid-19th century, (12-05-92, Eldred, #545), woodblock (BP 83, DM 206, FR 701, Y 16,355).
$55* *Processional Scene, c. 1850,* (12-05-92, Eldred, #547), woodblock (BP 34, DM 86, FR 292, Y 6815).
$110* *Three Geishas Fixing Hair,* block s., (04-16-93, DuMouchelle, #2300, illus.), 12¾ x 8¾ in., (32.4 x 22.2 cm.), woodblock (BP 72, DM 178, FR 600, Y 12,369).
BI *Two Figures O A Confetti Ground, c. 1840,* est. $1/150, (12-05-92, Eldred, #548), woodblock.
BI *Woman With Man,* block s., est. $150/300, (04-16-93, DuMouchelle, #2302, illus.), 13½ x 9 in., (34.3 x 22.9 cm.), woodblock.

TOYOKUNI III   1777-1835
$39* *"Courtesan", c. 1830,* trimmed, soiling, creasing, (01-23-93, Goldberg, #299), wood block (BP 26, DM 62, FR 210, Y 4881).

TOYOKUNI III   Japanese 1786-1864
$110* *"Kabuki Actors Of Chushingura",* stains, (09-25-92, Wolf, #5, illus.), 14 x 9¼ in., (35.6 x 23.5 cm.), woodblock in colors (BP 64, DM 163, FR 551, Y 13,277).

TRAMPEDACH, Kurt
$92* *Komposition, 1975,* s. Trampedach 75, 158/1044, (03-24-93, Kunsthallen, #321), color lithograph (BP 62, DM 150, FR 511, Y 10,810, DK 575).
$232* *Portrait, 1977,* s. Kurt Trampedach 77, artist proof, (09-30-92, Kunsthallen, #284), color lithograph (BP 131, DM 329, FR 1113, Y 27,841, DK 1265).
$211* *Portrait, 1978,* s. Kurt Trampedach 78, 1/130, (09-30-92, Kunsthallen, #285), etching (BP 119, DM 299, FR 1012, Y 25,321, DK 1150).
$169* *Self-Portrait, 1975,* s. Kurt Trampedach, 14/1044, (09-30-92, Kunsthallen, #286), color lithograph (BP 95, DM 240, FR 811, Y 20,281, DK 920).

TRAUT, Wolf   German 1486-c.1520
$505* *Ein Dichter Mit Harfe (Fairfax-Murray 243), 1506,* from J. Locher, Opuscula, Nurnberg, stained, (12-04-92, Bassenge, #6467), 4⅝ x 4³⁄₁₆ in., (11.7 x 10.6 cm.), woodcut (BP 324, DM 804, FR 2728, Y 63,046).
BI *The First War In Gelderland (Meder 251; Dodgson I, 323, 5), 1515,* from The Triumphal Arch of Maximilian I, watermark, trimmed to borderline, loss, browning, good cond., est. $7/900, (05-13-93, Sotheby-NY, #206), 6⅞ x 5⅞ in., (174 x 148 mm.), woodcut.
$578* *Der Hl. Christophorus, Davor Kniend Der Nurnberger Humanist Christoph Scheurl (Passavant III, 203, 249; Heller 2014; Fairfax-Murray),* prov., (12-04-92, Bassenge, #6468), 6¹¹⁄₁₆ x 4⅝ in., (17 x 11.8 cm.), woodcut (BP 371, DM 921, FR 3123, Y 72,160).
BI *St. George Slaying The Dragon (Strauss 1411), 1508,* trimmed irregularly, thin patches, some broken through and backed, foxing, discoloration, est. BP 6/8,000, (06-29-93, Sotheby-London, #62, illus.), 4⅛ x 6 in., (10.5 x 15.2 cm.), woodcut.

TRAVERS, Cyril John
$65* *Elizabethan Galleon,* s., t., d. 29; s., t. labels verso, exhib., (11-30-92, Ritchie, #10), 5¹⁵⁄₁₆ x 4½ in., (15.2 x 11.4 cm.), linocut on gilt paper (BP 43, DM 104, FR 352, Y 8090, C$ 83).

TRAVERT
$41* *Les Pavots,* s., #62/100, good margins, (05-06-93, Laurin, #86), lithograph (BP 26, DM 65, FR 217, Y 4511).

TRAVIES, Edouard   French b. 1809
$768* *"Gibiers": Two,* small margins, tear, (03-22-93, Pescheteau, #78), color lithographs (BP 517, DM 1259, FR 4281, Y 88,930).
$910* *"Gibiers": Two,* margins, (03-22-93, Pescheteau, #79), color lithographs (BP 613, DM 1492, FR 5072, Y 105,373).

TRAVIS, Paul B.   American b. 1891
$60* *"Edge Of Clearing, Congo Road", 1933,* s., d., t., very good cond., (05-15-93, Cleveland, #328), 8¼ x 10⅝ in., (21 x 27 cm.), lithograph (BP 39, DM 97, FR 324, Y 6651).

TRAXEL, Mel
$121* *Richard Burton,* portrait still from "Who's Afraid Of Virginia Woolf", (10-10-92, Bonhams, #11, illus.), 11 x 14 in., (27.9 x 35.6 cm.), photograph (BP 72, DM 180, FR 603, Y 14,731).

TREABMAN, Julian
$77* *"Runway", "Chriswick Mall", "Holland", and "Interior": Four,* s., t., various sizes, (06-11-93, Freemn/Fine Art, #236A), etching in colors on T.H. Saunders wove (BP 51, DM 125, FR 422, Y 8170).

TRECHSLIN, Anne Marie (after)
$102* *Old Garden Roses: Forty,* boxed set, individually mounted, w/text, (05-26-93, Bonhams-Chelsea, #73), reprod. in colors (BP 66, DM 166, FR 560, Y 11,082).

$111* *Old Garden Roses: Forty,* boxed set, individually mounted, w/text, (05-26-93, Bonhams-Chelsea, #72), reprod. in colors (BP 72, DM 181, FR 610, Y 12,060).

$102* *Old Garden Roses: Forty,* boxed set, individually mounted, w/text, (05-26-93, Bonhams-Chelsea, #70), reprod. in colors (BP 66, DM 166, FR 560, Y 11,082).

$111* *Old Garden Roses: Forty,* boxed set, individually mounted, w/text, (05-26-93, Bonhams-Chelsea, #71), reprod. in colors (BP 72, DM 181, FR 610, Y 12,060).

TREIMAN, Joyce

BI *The Mirrored Couple: Untitled (The Mirrored Couple XIV) (T. 451), 1961,* white pencil s., annot. Trial Proof, pub. Tamarind Lithography Workshop, good cond., glue, hinge remains, est. $150/250, (02-24-93, Butterfield, #3273), 20 x 15¹/₁₆ in., (508 x 383 mm.), lithograph on wove.

TREMEUSE, Jacques   French 19/20th cent.

BI *Young Woman With Dog,* s., #17, est. $150/200, (07-03-92, Sloan, #338), 12⅞ x 8¼ in., (32.7 x 21 cm.), color etching.

TREMLETT, David

$72* *"Brick Work" and "Rafia Work", 1970: Two,* s., d., t., both #7/75, full margins, soiling, creasing, (10-15-92, Sotheby-London, #135, illus.), 19½ x 27¼ in., (49.5 x 69.2 cm.), screenprint in colors on wove (BP 44, DM 107, FR 363, Y 8638).

TREMOIS, Pierre Yves   French b. 1921

$170* *1976,* #45/95, s., (04-04-93, Pescheteau, #305), 21⅝ x 29½ in., (55 x 75 cm.), etching and aquatint on wove (BP 112, DM 273, FR 928, Y 19,356).

$168* *"Cosmos 1971",* #65/80, s., (01-28-93, Pescheteau, #273), 35¹/₁₆ x 24 in., (89 x 61 cm.), etching and copperplate engraving on wove (BP 111, DM 266, FR 901, Y 20,859).

$314* *"La Mere Et L'Enfant", 1970,* #52/80, d., s., (10-18-92, Pescheteau, #273), 25⁹/₁₆ x 19¹¹/₁₆ in., (65 x 50 cm.), drypoint and aquatint on Rives (BP 190, DM 464, FR 1576, Y 37,493).

$337* *"Nu Allonge",* #20/75, s., (10-18-92, Pescheteau, #272), 22¹/₁₆ x 29¹⁵/₁₆ in., (56 x 76 cm.), drypoint on Rives (BP 204, DM 498, FR 1691, Y 40,239).

$200* *"Pour L'Illustration De J. Rostand", 1972,* #EA1, s., (04-04-93, Pescheteau, #306), 17⅛ x 19¹¹/₁₆ in., (43.5 x 50 cm.), copper engraving and etching on wove (BP 132, DM 321, FR 1092, Y 22,771).

TRENCH, Lt. Col. (after)

BI *The North Bank Of The Thames From Westminster Bridge To London Bridge,* by Thomas Mann Baynes, pub. J. Dickinson, 1825, est. BP 4/600, (06-16-93, Bonhams-Chelsea, #396), lithograph w/hand-coloring on nine sheets.

TRENTO, Antonio da   ac. lst half 16th cent.

BI *Die Madonna Und Kind Mit Der Rose (B. XII, 12; The Illustrated Bartsch 48, III 12),* after Parmigianino, est. DM 2,500, (12-04-92, Bassenge, #6469), 7½ x 9⅛ in., (19 x 23.2 cm.), chiaroscuro woodcut.

TRESS, Arthur

$316* *"Hockey Player NYC", 1972,* p. c. 1976, s., t., d., (05-23-93, Butterfield, #3634, illus.), 10 x 10 in., photograph, gelatin silver print (BP 206, DM 517, FR 1739, Y 34,929).

$468* *"Hockey Player, N.Y.C.", 1972/1989,* s., t., d., (11-16-92, Butterfield, #6202, illus.), 10 x 10 in., (254.5 x 254.5 mm.), photograph, gelatin silver print (BP 308, DM 746, FR 2513, Y 58,202).

$863* *"Superman Fantasy, New York" and "Lumberjack Fantasy, New York": Two,* one 1977, other 1978, both p.l., s., d., edit., (05-23-93, Butterfield, #3633, illus.), one 15 x 15 in., other 15½ x 15½ in., photograph, gelatin silver print (BP 562, DM 1411, FR 4750, Y 95,391).

$173* *"The Trainer", 1975,* s., t., #7/50, (05-23-93, Butterfield, #3635), 10¾ x 10¾ in., photograph, gelatin silver print (BP 113, DM 283, FR 952, Y 19,122).

TREU, Martin   ac. 1540-1543

BI *Der Tanz Der Leute Von Stand (B. 24-35; Passavant IV, 16; Nagler DieMonogammisten IV, 8), 1542/43: Twelve,*

prov., est. DM 9,500, (12-04-92, Bassenge, #6470, illus.), each approx. 2³/₁₆ x 1⅝ in., (5.6 x 4.1 cm.), engraving.

TREVELYAN, Julian

$446* *The Bat,* #14/25, s., t., d. 1936, margins, time-staining, (05-20-93, Bonhams-Chelsea, #129), plate 7⅞ x 13¾ in., (20 x 34.9 cm.), etching w/hand-coloring (BP 286, DM 720, FR 2424, Y 49,249).

$112* *Two Cats,* s., i., margins, (03-17-93, Bonhams-Chelsea, #395), plate 4 x 5¾ in., (10.2 x 14.6 cm.), etching w/ aquatint in colors (BP 77, DM 186, FR 633, Y 13,136).

TRIER, Hann   German b. 1915

$397* *Abstrakte Composition, 1957,* mono., d., num., (11-28-92, Schoppmann, #846), 16⁵/₁₆ x 20¼ in., (41.5 x 51.5 cm.), lithograph on handmade (BP 262, DM 632, FR 2147, Y 49,409).

$470* *Empor, 1975,* mono., d., num., (11-28-92, Schoppmann, #845), 23¼ x 15⅝ in., (59 x 39.7 cm.), color etching on copper print paper (BP 310, DM 749, FR 2542, Y 58,494).

BI *Komposition, 1965,* s., num., est. DM 900, (12-05-92, Bassenge, #7773), 20¹/₁₆ x 12⁵/₁₆ in., (51 x 31.2 cm.), color aquatint etching w/relief print on copper print paper.

BI *Ohne Titel, 1967,* pencil s., d., est. DM 1,000, (11-20-92, Lempertz, #912), sh 30⅛ x 22¹³/₁₆ in., (76.5 x 58 cm.), color etching on thick Velin.

$208* *Untitled, 1959,* s., d., #35/35, margins, tears, cellophane tape, creases, soiling, (12-09-92, Sotheby-Amstrdm, #659), 23¼ x 15⁹/₁₆ in., (590 x 395 mm.), color etching w/aquatint on wove (BP 133, DM 326, FR 1114, Y 25,790, G 368).

TRINQUIER-TRIANON, L.

$499* *PLM. Mont-Blanc. Chemin De Fer Electrique Du Fayet A Chamonix,* good cond., (03-15-93, Arcole, #68, illus.), 42⅛ x 29½ in., (107 x 75 cm.), (BP 347, DM 829, FR 2818, Y 59,109).

$335* *PLM: Fontainebleau, "A Une Heure De Paris", 1895,* good cond., (01-23-93, Ribeyre/Baron, #47), 41¾ x 29½ in., (106 x 75 cm.), poster (BP 219, DM 533, FR 1802, Y 41,927).

TRIP, V.J.

$408* *Koninklijke Paketvaart-Maatschappij (Royal Packet Navigation Company), 1948,* waterstains, (06-09-93, Bubb Kuyper, #2184), approx. 25¹³/₁₆ x 33⅞ in., (65.5 x 86 cm.), color poster (BP 269, DM 667, FR 2244, Y 43,390, G 748).

TRIPE, Captain Linnaeus   1822-1902

$1453* *India: Four,* late 1850s, neg. s., mounted on paper, each approx. 260 x 350mm, (05-07-93, Sotheby-London, #31), photograph, salt print from waxed paper neg. (BP 920, DM 2297, FR 7741, Y 159,987).

BI *"No. 21. Pugahm Myo. East Facade Of Damayangyee Pagoda", 1855,* est. $4/6,000, (04-06-93, Sotheby-NY, #49A, illus.), 10⅝ x 13¾ in., photograph, albumenized salt (?) print.

TRIPE, Dr. Linnaeus   1822-1902

BI *Trichonopoly 2: Ghats Near The South End Of The Bridge, 1858,* embossed mono. insignia, paper label, lit., est. $4/6,000, (10-13-92, Christie-NY, #24, illus.), 9¾ x 14¾ in., (24.8 x 37.5 cm.), photograph, albumenized salt print.

TRIPP, Jan   German b. 1945

$83* *"Visitors", 1987,* s., d., t., num. 76/100, excell. cond., (10-31-92, Cleveland, #400), 4 x 9½ in., (10.2 x 24.1 cm.), lithograph in colors (BP 53, DM 128, FR 433, Y 10,281).

$40* *"Visitors", 1987,* s., d., t., #08/100, excell. cond., (05-15-93, Cleveland, #502), 4 x 9½ in., (10.2 x 24.1 cm.), color lithograph (BP 26, DM 64, FR 216, Y 4434).

TRISTRAM, H.B.

$1089* *"Pathways Of Palestine": Book,* c. 1880, 2nd series, p. t. on mounts, t. page, cloth gilt, 4to., London: Sampson Low, Marston, Searle and Rivington, (05-06-93, Christie-London, #15, illus.), each approx. 7½ x 5 in., photograph, 22 carbon prints (BP 690, DM 1715, FR 5774, Y 119,815).

TROCKEL, Rosemarie   b. 1952
   BI *Ohne Titel: Two,* exec. 1989, prov., est. BP 2,5/3,500, (05-20-93, Christie-London, #656, illus.), first 11⅜ x 8¼ in., second 11⅜ x 7 in., photograph, b/w.

TROEDEL, Charles and Co
   $243* *The Melbourne Album 1863-1864 Swanston Street,* p. F Cogne Drawn and Lith, p. by Trodel, ref., (08-11-92, L. Joel, #188G), 10⅜ x 13¹⁵⁄₁₆ in., (26.3 x 35.5 cm.), tinted lithograph (BP 126, DM 357, FR 1208, Y 31,118, A$ 330).
   $649* *The Melbourne Album 1863-1864, Bourke Street (East 1863),* p. F Cogne, Litho., p. C Trodel, ref., (08-11-92, L. Joel, #158G), 10⁷⁄₁₆ x 14³⁄₁₆ in., (26.5 x 36.1 cm.), tinted lithograph (BP 337, DM 952, FR 3226, Y 83,109, A$ 880).
   $81* *The Melbourne Album Collins Street (From Queen Street),* drawn lithograph by F Cogne, p. C Trodel, (08-11-92, L. Joel, #150G), 10⅜ x 14⅜ in., (26.4 x 36.5 cm.), tinted lithograph (BP 42, DM 119, FR 403, Y 10,373, A$ 110).
   $324* *The Melbourne Album, 1863-1864, Sheepwash Creek Near Sandhurst-(1863),* E Cogne Drawn and Lith Ch. Troedel Print, reference, (08-11-92, L. Joel, #58G), 10³⁄₁₆ x 13¹⁵⁄₁₆ in., (25.9 x 35.4 cm.), tinted lithograph (BP 168, DM 475, FR 1610, Y 41,491, A$ 440).

TROEDEL, Charles, Publisher
   $528* *Views Of Australia, "Wentworth River Diggings", "Kenny's Mill", "TheLal Lal Falls", "Sheepwash Creek", "View On The Upper Mitta", By Or After E. Guerrard, F. Cogne And N. Chevalier: Five,* margins, dirt, (10-07-92, Christie-S. Ken, #90), 10½ x 14¼ in., (26.7 x 36.2 cm.), colored tinted lithograph (BP 308, DM 764, FR 2591, Y 63,500).

TROKES, Heinz   b. 1913
   $166* *Komposition, (19)62,* s., d., num., light-stained, (12-01-92, Karl/Faber, #1309), 15¾ x 13¾ in., (40 x 35 cm.), color serigraph on thick wove (BP 110, DM 265, FR 902, Y 20,667).
   BI *Winter, 1945,* s., t., d., num., est. DM 1,200, (12-05-92, Bassenge, #7775), 12 x 9¹⁄₁₆ in., (30.5 x 23 cm.), lithograph on cream wove.

TROOST, Cornelis (after)   1697-1750
   BI *Ein Liebespaar Bei Kerzenlicht, In Einer Stube Stitzend,* artist's proof, est. DM 750, (12-04-92, Bassenge, #6715), 15¹³⁄₁₆ x 11⁷⁄₁₆ in., (40.2 x 29 cm.), engraving.

TROTTER, Page   20th cent.
   $90* *"Mooring",* s., Artist Proof #4, Omer Lasonde Coll., (02-27-93, Young, #271, illus.), 8 x 10 in., (20.3 x 25.4 cm.), lithograph (BP 63, DM 148, FR 503, Y 10,624).

TROUILLEBERT, Paul Desire   French 1829-1900
   $51* *Le Moulin De La Galette (Au Crotoy),* s., #62/100, good margins, (05-06-93, Laurin, #87), etching on wove (BP 32, DM 80, FR 270, Y 5611).

TROUTMAN, Stanley
   $385* *Hiroshima, After The Atomic Bomb, 1945,* handstamp, label, (10-14-92, Swann, #357, illus.), 7 x 9 in., (17.8 x 22.9 cm.), photograph, silver print (BP 226, DM 563, FR 1911, Y 46,655).

TROVA, Ernest   American b. 1927
   $385* *Untitled,* s., d. 71, #76/150, prov., prop. Price Waterhouse Corp. Coll., (05-16-93, Hindman, #651), 23 x 23 in., (58.4 x 58.4 cm.), color serigraph (BP 250, DM 619, FR 2081, Y 42,678).

TROVA, Ernest T.   b. 1927
   BI *Untitled, 1970,* s., d., num., est. DM 480, (11-28-92, Schoppmann, #847), 31⅞ x 31⅞ in., (81 x 81 cm.), color serigraph on cardboard.

TROY
   $299* *Air France. "Dans Tous Les Ciels" Alger Marseille En 5 Heures. AlgerParis En 9 Heures,* good cond., (03-13-93, Laurin, #61), 39⅜ x 24³⁄₁₆ in., (100 x 61.5 cm.), (BP 209, DM 498, FR 1692, Y 35,239).

TROY, Adrian   British/American b. 1901
   $55* *The Horse, The Yak, The Rooster: Three,* each s., (09-20-92, Hindman, #808), each 7 x 12 in., (17.8 x 30.5 cm.), color woodcuts (BP 32, DM 82, FR 279, Y 6798).

TROY, Atelier
   $230* *P.L.M.: Autorails Plm, c. 1930,* excell. cond., (01-23-93, Ribeyre/Baron, #10), 39⅜ x 24⁷⁄₁₆ in., (100 x 62 cm.), poster (BP 150, DM 366, FR 1237, Y 28,786).

TRUMBELL, John (after)
   $2185* *The Battle Of Bunker's Hill, 1798,* by I.G. Muller, pub. A.C. de Poggi, good cond., repaired tears, light-stain, foxing, discoloration, skinning, (01-28-93, Sotheby-NY, #443), 23 x 31½ in., (584 x 800 mm.), sheet 25⅝ x 34⅛ in., (584 x 800 mm.), engraving on laid (BP 1443, DM 3462, FR 11,716, Y 271,294).
   $805* *The Battle Of Bunker's Hill, Near Boston, 1808,* by James Mitan, p. Andrew Maverick, pub. John Trumbell, margins, good cond., foxing, water stains, glue stains, discoloration, (01-28-93, Sotheby-NY, #444), image 12⅞ x 19⅜ in., (327 x 492 mm.), plate 16⅜ x 21⅞ in., (327 x 492 mm.), engraving on wove (BP 532, DM 1276, FR 4316, Y 99,950).

TRUMBULL (after)
   $275* *"The Battle Of Bunker Hill" and "The Death Of Gen. Montgomery": Two,* (03-20-93, Northeast, #744, illus.), 18 x 24 in., (45.7 x 61 cm.), engraving (BP 184, DM 450, FR 1530, Y 31,899).

TRUPHEMUS, Jacques
   $93* *Fleurs Des Champs,* s., #47/75, good margins, (05-06-93, Laurin, #89), color lithograph (BP 59, DM 146, FR 493, Y 10,232).
   BI *Venise,* s., #63/75, good margins, (05-06-93, Laurin, #88), color lithograph.

TSCHACBASOV, Nahum   American b. 1899
   BI *"Flying Fish", 1947,* i., s., d. Tschacbasov 47, #233/250, est. DM 300-, (03-24-93, Venator/Hansten, #4568), 8¾ x 11⅝ in., (22.3 x 29.6 cm.), aquatint etching.

TSCHICHOLD, Jan   1902-1974
   $2200* *Der Berufsphotograph, 1938,* lit., (10-13-92, Christie-NY, #278, illus.), 35⅛ x 23¾ in., (89.2 x 60.3 cm.), photograph, photo-offset lithography (BP 1281, DM 3223, FR 10,951, Y 266,764).

TSIGAL
   $30* *Bois En Hiver,* (03-15-93, Millon/Robert, #143), 4¾ x 5½ in., (12 x 14 cm.), gravure (intaglio) (BP 21, DM 50, FR 169, Y 3554).
   $30* *Cheval Et Chariot,* (03-15-93, Millon/Robert, #142), 4¾ x 5½ in., (14 x 20 cm.), gravure (intaglio) (BP 21, DM 50, FR 169, Y 3554).

TSURUYA KOKEI   Japanese b. 1946
   $1137* *The Half-Length Figure Of Bando Tamasaburo As Okuno Brushing A ScrollLetter,* Oban, sealed Tsuruya Kokei, #9/45, d. 1984, creased, Prof. H.R.W. Kuhne Coll., (06-11-93, Sotheby-London, #498, illus.), 15¾ x 10⅝ in., (40 x 27 cm.), woodblock (BP 747, DM 1848, FR 6230, Y 120,637).
   $1137* *The Half-Length Figure Of Ichikawa Ennosuke As Kiyohime,* Oban, sealed Tsuruya Kokei, #9/45, d. 1984, good state, Prof. H.R.W.Kuhne Coll., (06-11-93, Sotheby-London, #497, illus.), 15½ x 14½ in., (39.4 x 36.8 cm.), woodblock (BP 747, DM 1848, FR 6230, Y 120,637).
   $2275* *Ichikawa Ebizo X (Or IX?) As Kagekiyo And Ichikawa Danjuro XII Announcing The Change Of His Name: Two,* Oban, sealed Tsuruya Kokei and Kokei no in, #12/45, No. 23, d. 1984 and 1985, smudged, crumpled, Prof. H.R.W. Kuhne Coll., (06-11-93, Sotheby-London, #495, illus.), one 16½ x 10⅝ in., (41.9 x 27 cm.), other 15⅜ x 10⅜ in., (41.9 x 27 cm.), woodblock (BP 1495, DM 3697, FR 12,466, Y 241,379).
   BI *Onoe Shoroku II (Or III?) As A Carpenter,* Oban, seal Kokei, num. 23, d. 1987, soiled, Prof. H.R.W. Kuhne Coll.,est. BP 6/800, (06-11-93, Sotheby-London, #496, illus.), 15½ x 9⅜ in., (39.4 x 23.8 cm.), woodblock.

TUBBY, Josiah Thomas   American 19th/20th cent.
   BI *"Winter Landscape" and "Waterfront View": Two,* each inits. in plate; ded., prov., est. $150/250, (10-30-92,

Sloan, #1732), larger 3⅜ x 5¾ in., (8.6 x 14.6 cm.), etching.

TUBKE, Werner   b. 1929
$332* *Auferstehung II (Werkv. Nr. L2/85, Tubke 151), 1985,* s., num., (12-05-92, Bassenge, #7776), 10¹/₁₆ x 13¹⁵/₁₆ in., (25.6 x 35.5 cm.), lithograph (BP 208, DM 518, FR 1764, Y 41,135).

$232* *Mannlicher Akt., 1969,* s.; stone d., creased, (09-18-92, Schloss Ahlden, #1074, illus.), 18¾ x 13¾ in., (47.7 x 34.9 cm.), lithograph on white cardboard (BP 136, DM 344, FR 1178, Y 28,674).

$263* *Nach Durers Triumpfwagen,* s., t. e.a., creases, (09-18-92, Schloss Ahlden, #1076), 15½ x 20⅞ in., (39.4 x 53 cm.), lithograph on textured handmade (BP 154, DM 390, FR 1335, Y 32,505).

$310* *Trauergaste (B. Tubke 155), 1986,* s., num., (12-05-92, Bassenge, #7777), 9¼ x 13³/₁₆ in., (23.5 x 33.5 cm.), chalk lithograph on copper print paper (BP 194, DM 483, FR 1647, Y 38,409).

TUCK and CO., William Henry, Publisher
$75* *The Jockey Club, 1876,* oval, after John Sturgess, (06-30-93, Bonhams-Chelsea, #215), image 29 x 21 in., (73.7 x 53.3 cm.), photographic print, surrounded by hand-colored vignettes (BP 50, DM 128, FR 432, Y 8036).

$107* *Masters Of Hounds, 1875,* oval, after John Sturgess, (06-30-93, Bonhams-Chelsea, #146), image 29½ x 21½ in., (74.9 x 54.6 cm.), photographic print, surrounded by hand-colored vignettes (BP 72, DM 183, FR 616, Y 11,465).

TUNIST, H.
$66* *"Modesty",* #170/250, (08-14-92, DuMouchelle, #2431), 6 x 4½ in., (15.2 x 11.4 cm.), lithograph (BP 34, DM 97, FR 328, Y 8323).

TUNNICLIFFE, Charles Frederick
$470* *The Colt,* s., #18/75, full margins, corner mounted, (10-27-92, Phillips-London, #315), plate 8⅞ x 9⅞ in., (225 x 251 mm.), etching on laid (BP 297, DM 720, FR 2444, Y 57,492).

$283* *Harvesters,* s., #53/75, light-stained, indentations, 1 in image, surface soiling, unevenly trimmed, (11-30-92, Phillips-London, #367), plate 8¼ x 11 in., (210 x 279 mm.), etching on wove (BP 187, DM 451, FR 1531, Y 35,221).

$279* *Kemp's Croft Farm,* s., #67/75, full margins, good cond., mounted, (10-27-92, Phillips-London, #314), plate 7⅜ x 14⅞ in., (187 x 378 mm.), etching on laid paper (BP 176, DM 428, FR 1451, Y 34,128).

$137 *Oyster Catchers,* s., limited ed., #31/500, (06-11-93, G.A. Key, #17), 16 x 20 in., (40.6 x 50.8 cm.), colored print (BP 90, DM 223, FR 751, Y 14,536).

$117* *The Quarry Road,* s., #56/75, strip detached from top margin, piece detached lower margin, time-stained, (11-30-92, Phillips-London, #366), plate 8⅞ x 11¾ in., (225 x 298 mm.), etching on laid (BP 77, DM 186, FR 633, Y 14,561).

$283* *Wheatfields,* s., #7/75, light-stained, (11-30-92, Phillips-London, #365), plate 6¼ x 10¾ in., (159 x 273 mm.), etching on wove (BP 187, DM 451, FR 1531, Y 35,221).

TURBERVILLE, George
$3450* *The Booke Of Falconrie Or Hawking...Now Newly Revised, Corrected, AndAugmented..., The Noble Art Of Venerie Or Hunting (STC 24325 and 24329, Schwerdt II, 271-72), 1611: 2 Vols.,* Thomas Purfoot, bound together, small 4to, corners of first two leaves restored, wormholes, rust-hole to P3, soiled, Second Editions, some full-page, Anthony N. B. Garner Coll., (06-05-93, Christie-NY, #45, illus.), woodcut, numerous (BP 2271, DM 5593, FR 18,852, Y 370,092).

TURBEVILLE, Deborah   b. 1937
BI *Bathhouse, American Vogue, 1975,* s., t., d. in ink, est. $2/2,500, (10-13-92, Christie-NY, #610, illus.), 13⅛ x 19⅛ in., (33.3 x 48.6 cm.), photograph, toned gelatin silver print.

$440* *Dancers,* 1980s, (10-13-92, Christie-NY, #612, illus.), 13½ x 20 in., (34.3 x 50.8 cm.), photograph, color coupler print (BP 256, DM 645, FR 2190, Y 53,353).

$1150* *Mannequins, 1970's,* s., #1/5 by photog., (04-06-93, Sotheby-NY, #476, illus.), 7½ x 11 in., photograph (BP 760, DM 1853, FR 6274, Y 131,159).

BI *Mexican Hat Maker, 1992,* mounted, est. $2,5/3,500, (10-13-92, Christie-NY, #613, illus.), 21¾ x 26¾ in., (55.2 x 67.9 cm.), photograph, mixed-media photocollage of gelatin silver prints, mixedpaper, paper clips, T-pins, & newspaper clippings.

BI *A View From The Queen's State Bedchamber Overlooking The Parterre DuMidi, 1981,* s., t., d. in ink, lit., est. $2/2,500, (10-13-92, Christie-NY, #611, illus.), 10¾ x 16¼ in., (27.3 x 41.3 cm.), photograph, hand-colored gelatin silver print.

TURCAS
$88* *Beside The Bonnie Brier Bush,* Dodd, Mead and Co., A cond., chip, (08-06-92, Swann, #276, illus.), 19½ x 12½ in., (49.5 x 31.8 cm.), (BP 46, DM 130, FR 439, Y 11,224).

TURISMO, General Del
$25 *Espana,* edge and other damage, (09-24-92, Alderfer, #316), 29¼ x 29¾ in., (74.3 x 75.6 cm.), (BP 15, DM 37, FR 126, Y 3007).

TURNBULL, Andrew Watson
$34 *Thames River Scenes In London: A Pair,* s., (04-16-93, G.A. Key, #15), 6 x 9 in., (15.2 x 22.9 cm.), etching (BP 22, DM 55, FR 186, Y 3823).

TURNER
BI *"Cowes Regatta",* est. $75/150, (06-11-93, DuMouchelle, #1344), 20 x 27 in., (50.8 x 68.6 cm.), hand-colored print.

TURNER (after)
$248* *"December Duck Shooting", Plate 5 and "September Partridge Shooting",Plate 2: Two,* by Hunt, pub. 1841, (06-11-93, Freemn/Fine Art, #238), both 14¼ x 19⅛ in., (36.2 x 48.6 cm.), hand-colored engraving (BP 163, DM 403, FR 1359, Y 26,313).

TURNER, Benjamin Bracknell
BI *"Bonchurch", 1856,* mounted on card, pub. The Photographic Album for 1856, est. BP 8/1,000, 202 x 251mm, (05-07-93, Sotheby-London, #58, illus.), photograph, lightly albumenised salt print.

TURNER, C.
$66* *Wings Of The Coast Guard: Three,* s., (06-11-93, Freemn/Fine Art, #237), two 8¼ x 11 in., (21 x 27.9 cm.), one 5¾ x 8¾ in., (21 x 27.9 cm.), lithograph (BP 43, DM 107, FR 362, Y 7003).

TURNER, C.E.
$434* *The Peak District For Picture Makers,* p. Hudson & Kearns Ltd., creases, repaired tear, laid on board, (05-07-93, Christie-S. Ken, #61, illus.), 24¾ x 40 in., (62.9 x 101.6 cm.), color lithograph (BP 275, DM 686, FR 2312, Y 47,787).

TURNER, C.Y.   19th cent.
BI *Girl By Window,* s., est. $2/400, (09-24-92, Mystic, #15A), 24 x 15 in., (61 x 38.1 cm.), etching.

TURNER, Charles
$183* *Miss Wigram Playing A Guitar,* proof impression prior to letters, watermark, margins, good cond., est. BP 150/200, (11-30-92, Phillips-London, #82), plate 16¼ x 12¼ in., (413 x 311 mm.), mezzotint on laid (BP 121, DM 292, FR 990, Y 22,775).

TURNER, Francis Calcraft
$385* *"Bachelor's Hall", Hunting Prints, Plates 1-6: Six,* (02-27-93, Dunning, #1131), sight 13 x 15½ in., (33 x 39.4 cm.), colored lithograph (BP 271, DM 633, FR 2151, Y 45,449).

BI *Bachelor's Hall: "To Bachelor's Hall", "Dick Thickset Came Mounted","Then For Hounds", "Our Horses Thus All", "The Scent Is Breast High" and "Sly Renard's Brought Home": Six,* pub. R. Ackermann, c. 1835, prov., C$ 5/700, (12-01-92, Ritchie, #3, illus.), each 12 x 15 in., (30.5 x 38.1 cm.), hand-colored aquatint.

TURNER, Francis Calcraft (after)
$394* *Bachelor's Hall, Plates 1-6: Six,* margins, staining, surface dirt, (06-30-93, Bonhams-Chelsea, #147), plate 12

x 15 in., (30.5 x 38.1 cm.), aquatint w/hand-coloring (BP 264, DM 672, FR 2267, Y 42,216).

BI *Conolly On Coronation, Winner Of Derby Stakes At Epsom (S. p 277), 1841,* by J. R. Mackrell, pub. Ackermann, margins, staining, dirt, est. BP 250/350, (10-07-92, Christie-S. Ken, #57), pl 20½ x 26 in., (52.1 x 66 cm.), colored aquatint.

$96* *Faugh-A-Ballagh,* by G.A. Turner, pub. E. Gambart and Co., 1845, margins, (03-03-93, Bonhams-Chelsea, #198), plate 20 x 23½ in., (50.8 x 59.7 cm.), hand-colored aquatint (BP 66, DM 158, FR 536, Y 11,218).

$275* *Hawking, 1838, Plates I-IV: Four,* by R. G. Reeve, pub. I. W. Laird, (10-29-92, Bonhams-Chelsea, #51, illus.), image 15¼ x 12½ in., (38.7 x 31.8 cm.), aquatint w/ hand coloring (BP 176, DM 423, FR 1435, Y 34,064).

BI *Hawking: Plates I-IV,* by R. G. Reeve. pub. I. W. Laird, est. BP 1/150 BP 1/150, (07-16-92, Bonhams-Chelsea, #532), image 15¼ x 12½ in., (38.7 x 31.8 cm.), aquatint w/hand coloring.

$312* *Hawking: Plates I-IV,* by R.G. Reeve, pub. I.W. Laird, 1839, (06-30-93, Bonhams-Chelsea, #13), 15¼ x 12¼ in., (38.7 x 31.1 cm.), aquatint w/hand-coloring (BP 209, DM 532, FR 1795, Y 33,430).

$213* *Hawking: Plates I-IV, 1839,* by R. G. Reeve, pub. I. W. Laird, margins, (07-16-92, Bonhams-Chelsea, #531), plate 19¾ x 15 in., (50.2 x 38.1 cm.), aquatint w/hand coloring (BP 110, DM 315, FR 1062, Y 26,682).

$55* *Leamington Grand Steeple Chase 1837: Four,* engraved by Charles Hunt, (03-14-93, Hindman, #235), each 18 x 26 in., (45.7 x 66 cm.), hand-colored aquatint (BP 38, DM 92, FR 311, Y 6482).

$1149* *Moore's Tally Ho! To The Sports-Tipperary: Four,* by Harris and Mackrel, pub. J.W. Moore, 1853, margins, staining, (06-30-93, Bonhams-Chelsea, #149), plate 19 x 25¾ in., (48.3 x 65.4 cm.), aquatint w/hand-coloring (BP 770, DM 1960, FR 6611, Y 123,112).

$403* *The Noble Tips (S. p. 277), 1853: Two Plates,* by G. Hunt and J. R. Mackrel, margins, minor defects, Anthony N. B. Garvan Coll., (06-05-93, Christie-NY, #69), both, pl 18¾ x 24 in., (476 x 610 mm.), aquatint w/hand-coloring on wove (BP 265, DM 653, FR 2202, Y 43,231).

$1319* *"The Riding School", "Going To The Meet" and "Well Done": Three,* by C. Hunt, margins, spotting, good cond., (10-07-92, Christie-S. Ken, #52), pl 23 x 28 in., (58.4 x 71.1 cm.), colored aquatint (BP 770, DM 1909, FR 6472, Y 158,629).

$1225* *'Southerly Wind And Cloud Sky', Plates 1-4 (S. 275),* by C. Hunt, pub. Ackermann, trimmed, 3 sides, discoloration, time staining, spotting, dirt, repair, (10-07-92, Christie-S. Ken, #53), sh 14 x 19 in., (35.6 x 48.3 cm.), colored aquatint (BP 715, DM 1773, FR 6011, Y 147,324).

TURNER, Jon Laviere

$11* *Lovers And A Black Star,* Jon La Viere Turner '60, (10-03-92, Garth, #104), 15½ x 20½ in., (39.4 x 52.1 cm.), etching (BP 6, DM 16, FR 53, Y 1317).

BI *Puppet And The Puppet Dragon,* s., t., #44/56, d. 1959, est. $2/300, (12-10-92, Sloan, #2742), 21 x 32½ in., (53.3 x 82.6 cm.), linocut.

$50* *Puppet And The Puppet Dragon,* s., t., #44/56, d. 1959, (02-04-93, Sloan, #2983), 21 x 32½ in., (53.3 x 82.6 cm.), linocut (BP 35, DM 82, FR 279, Y 6220).

TURNER, Julius C.

$88* *"Alms",* plate s., d. 1934, s. below image, (12-02-92, Boos, #457), 11½ x 7¾ in., (29.2 x 19.7 cm.), etching (BP 57, DM 138, FR 472, Y 10,949).

TURNER, Stanley Francis

$513* *"Queen Street" and "Pedestrians Approaching A Building": Two,* s., t., #27/50, d. 24 and 20, (11-30-92, Ritchie, #23), larger 11¹¹⁄₁₆ x 8¾ in., (29.7 x 22.2 cm.), etching (BP 339, DM 817, FR 2774, Y 63,846, C$ 660).

TURRELL, Arthur James English 1871

BI *European Street Scene,* s., est. $100/150, (02-04-93, Sloan, #352), 6¾ x 7¾ in., (17.1 x 19.7 cm.), etching.

TURRELL, James b. 1943

$2640* *E1 And E2, 1990: Set Of Two,* from First Light, both s., num. 29/30, pub. Blumarts, full margins, excell. cond.,

(09-19-92, Christie-E, #236, illus.), each, sheet 42⅜ x 29¾ in., (107.6 x 75.6 cm.), aquatint on wove (BP 1519, DM 3953, FR 13,538, Y 328,931).

BI *First Light, 1989-90: Twenty,* complete suite, five lettered series and one single print, s., t., i. V/X, pub. Peter Blum Edition, full margins, good cond., est. $25/30,000, (05-15-93, Sotheby-NY, #1242, illus.), each sheet 42⅜ x 29⅞ in., (107.6 x 75.9 cm.), aquatint.

BI *Mapping Spaces, 1987-88,* complete portfolio, s., #17/35, pub. Peter Blum Edition, full margins, good cond., creases, est. $5/6,000, (11-07-92, Sotheby-NY, #799, illus.), each sheet approx. 22 x 31⅛ in., (559 x 791 mm.), five etchings and aquatints p. in colors.

TURZAK, C. American 20th cent.

$165* *"Dancers",* s. C. Turzak, num. 81/100, good cond., (09-27-92, Bakker, #246), image 10 x 7 in., (25.4 x 17.8 cm.), woodblock print (BP 96, DM 245, FR 827, Y 19,916).

TURZAK, Charles American b. 1899

$413* *"North Bank", 1930's,* s. C. Turzak, t., very good cond., (09-11-92, Skinner, #42, illus.), 9 x 12 in., (22.9 x 30.5 cm.), color wood block on tableau wove (BP 214, DM 595, FR 2021, Y 51,171).

TUSSAC, F. Richard de

BI *Flore Des Antilles Decrits Apres Nature: Eight,* engraved Bouquet, pub. Langlois, 1808-27, good cond., est. BP 4/600, (10-27-92, Phillips-London, #167), plate 16½ x 10⅝ in., (419 x 270 mm.), stipple engraving p. in colors on wove.

TUTTLE, Henri Emerson American 1890-1946

$40* *"Ducks Flaring (Pintail Ducks)", c. 1929,* s., good cond., staining, hinges, (05-15-93, Cleveland, #329), 12⅝ x 9¾ in., (32.1 x 24.8 cm.), drypoint (BP 26, DM 64, FR 216, Y 4434).

TUTTLE, Richard American b. 1941

BI *Silkscreen Object, 1989,* #4/10, pencil t., s., d., edit. of Hubert Winter Gallery, (11-20-92, Lempertz, #917), sh 16⁷⁄₁₆ x 23⅜ in., (41.7 x 59.3 cm.), color serigraph on gray paper.

TWACHTMAN, John Henry American 1853-1902

$303* *"Dock At Newport",* init., (06-11-93, DuMouchelle, #2251), 5 x 6¾ in., (12.7 x 17.1 cm.), etching (BP 199, DM 492, FR 1660, Y 32,149).

$303* *"Shanties Bridgeport",* init., (06-11-93, DuMouchelle, #2252), 2½ x 3¾ in., (6.4 x 9.5 cm.), etching (BP 199, DM 492, FR 1660, Y 32,149).

TWOMBLY, Cy American b. 1929

$2375* *Da: 8 Odi Di Orazio, 1968,* s., artist's proof, pub. Sergio Tosi, (12-15-92, Finarte-Milan, #17, illus.), 15¾ x 23⅝ in., (40 x 60 cm.), lithograph (BP 1515, DM 3723, FR 12,721, Y 294,555, L 3335).

$2357* *Da: 8 Odi Di Orazio, 1968,* artist proof, s., pub. Sergio Tosi, (11-09-92, Finarte-Milan, #105), 15¾ x 23⅝ in., (40 x 60 cm.), lithograph (BP 1558, DM 3763, FR 12,713, Y 292,504, L 3220).

BI *Five Greek Poets And A Philospher, Berlin, Propylaen Verlag, 1978 (B. 67-73): Six,* s., num., lithographic t. page, num. just., copy 22 of 40, full margins., orig. interleaving tissues, orig. portfolio w/lithographic t., scuffed, est. $8/10,000, (05-11-93, Christie-NY, #584, illus.), each sheet 25½ x 19¾ in., (648 x 502 mm.), lithograph on Zerkall.

$1986* *"Natural History Ficus Carica" Part II (Bastian 59), 1975/76,* mono., num., sheet 8 of series: Natural History Part II, Some Trees of Italy, (06-05-93, Grisebach, #905, illus.), 20¼ x 17¹¹⁄₁₆ in., (51.5 x 45 cm.), lithograph and collotype in color on wove (BP 1307, DM 3220, FR 10,852, Y 213,044).

$2875* *Natural History Part I No. II (B. 43), 1974,* init., #97/98, pub. Propylaen Verlag, good cond., (05-15-93, Sotheby-NY, #1248, illus.), sheet 29¾ x 21⅞ in., (75.6 x 55.6 cm.), lithograph and collotype in colors w/collage and drawing on Rives (BP 1869, DM 4624, FR 15,541, Y 318,701).

$3450* *Natural History Part I No. VII (B. 48), 1974,* init., #97/98, pub. Propylaen Verlag, good cond., (05-15-93,

Sotheby-NY, #1249, illus.), sheet 29¾ x 21⅞ in., (75.6 x 55.6 cm.), lithograph and collotype in colors w/collage and drawing on Rives (BP 2243, DM 5549, FR 18,649, Y 382,441).

BI *Note I-IV (Bastian 6-9; Sparks 4-7), 1967: Four,* each s., d., t., i. AP 4/4, blindstamp, pub. ULAE, full margins, good cond., est. $100/120,000, (05-15-93, Sotheby-NY, #1244, illus.), each sheet 25¾ x 20⅝ in., (65.4 x 52.4 cm.), etching in brownish-black on Auvergne paper.

BI *Note III (B. 8; S. 6), 1967-75,* s., d., #9/14, blindstamp, pub. ULAE, full margins, good cond., est.$20/25,000, (05-15-93, Sotheby-NY, #1245, illus.), 8⅞ x 10⅞ in., (22.5 x 27.6 cm.), etching in brownish-black on Auvergne handmade paper.

$6325* *On The Bowery: Untitled (B. 27), 1969-71,* s., #21/100, pub. Edition Domberger, good cond., (05-15-93, Sotheby-NY, #1247, illus.), sheet 25½ x 25⅜ in., (64.8 x 64.5 cm.), silkscreen in colors (BP 4112, DM 10,174, FR 34,189, Y 701,142).

$7700* *On The Bowery: Untitled (Bastian 27), 1969-71,* s., #6/100, pub. Edition Domberger, good cond., (11-07-92, Sotheby-NY, #800, illus.), sheet 25⅝ x 25⅝ in., (651 x 651 mm.), silkscreen p. in colors on Schoellers Parole (BP 5034, DM 12,294, FR 41,554, Y 950,383).

$2530* *Quercus Ilex (Bastian 53), 1975-76,* from Natural History Part II, Some Trees of Italy, inits., #35/98, pub. Propylaen Verlag, excell. cond., (05-11-93, Christie-NY, #583, illus.), sheet 30 x 22⅛ in., (762 x 562 mm.), color lithograph on Fabriano (BP 1615, DM 3986, FR 13,429, Y 278,297).

$1142* *Quercus Ilex (Bastian 53), 1975/76,* s., init., 33/98, blindstamp, (05-12-93, AB Stockholm, #7056), 29¹⁵⁄₁₆ x 22¹⁄₁₆ in., (76 x 56 cm.), lithograph, grano-lithograph and collotype in colors (BP 746, DM 1843, FR 6207, Y 127,498, SK 8470).

$24,150* *Roman Notes (B. 21-26), 1970: Six,* complete portfolio, each s., d., #9/100, pub. Neuendorf Verlag, goodcond., nick, discoloration, (05-15-93, Sotheby-NY, #1246, illus.), each sheet 34⅛ x 27½ in., (86.7 x 69.9 cm.), offset lithograph in colors printed (BP 15,702, DM 38,845, FR 130,541, Y 2,677,087).

$17,052* *Roman Notes (Bastian 21-26), 1970: Set Of Six,* each s., d., #26/100, p. Electra Editrice, pub. Neuendorf Verlag, w/just., good cond., (12-03-92, Sotheby-London, #833, illus.), sheet 34 x 27½ in., (865 x 700 mm.), offset lithographs in colors on heavy offset (BP 11,000, DM 26,816, FR 91,530, Y 2,121,687).

$3942* *Roman Notes IV (Bastian 24), 1970,* from series, #48/100, (05-27-93, Lempertz, #1079, illus.), 34³⁄₁₆ x 27⁹⁄₁₆ in., (86.8 x 70 cm.), color offset lithograph (BP 2524, DM 6325, FR 21,320, Y 422,599).

$3942* *Roman Notes VI (Bastian 26), 1970,* from series, #48/100, (05-27-93, Lempertz, #1080, illus.), 34³⁄₁₆ x 27⁹⁄₁₆ in., (86.8 x 70 cm.), color offset lithograph (BP 2524, DM 6325, FR 21,320, Y 422,599).

$1980* *Roman Notes, 1970,* s., d., prov., (05-16-93, Hindman, #620), 34 x 27½ in., (86.4 x 69.9 cm.), color lithograph (BP 1287, DM 3185, FR 10,703, Y 219,488).

$1498* *Sans Titre 1971 (Bastian 37),* #66/100 verso, inits., (04-04-93, Pescheteau, #307, illus.), 27³⁄₁₆ x 33⅞ in., (69 x 86 cm.), color photolithograph on wove (BP 987, DM 2408, FR 8177, Y 170,557).

$9437* *Six Latin Writers And Poets (Bastian 60-65), 1976: Seven,* portfolio including title-page, each init., #26/60, p. by Matthieu Studio, pub. Propylaen Verlag, good cond., (06-30-93, Sotheby-London, #952, illus.), overall 25¼ x 19¾ in., (641 x 502 mm.), lithograph w/embossing in light and dark graphite, prussian blue andlight blue (BP 6325, DM 16,096, FR 54,298, Y 1,011,143).

$5750* *The Song Of The Border-Guard: Untitled, 1952,* pub. Nicola Cernovich at Black Mountain Graphics Workshop, central fold, good cond., (05-15-93, Sotheby-NY, #1243, illus.), sheet 12⅞ x 20 in., (32.7 x 50.8 cm.), linocut, on heavy salmon wove paper (BP 3739, DM 9249, FR 31,081, Y 637,402).

BI *Untitled (B. 76), 1983,* init., #116/150, pub. Visconti Art Spectrum, full margins, good cond., handling creases, soiling, nick, est. $2/2,500, (05-15-93, Sotheby-NY, #1250, illus.), 29½ x 21⅝ in., (74.9 x 54.9 cm.), lithograph and aquatint in colors on Arches.

$3153* *Untitled (Bastian 40), 1973,* mono., #58/150, (05-27-93, Lempertz, #1081, illus.), 29¹⁵⁄₁₆ x 22¹⁄₁₆ in., (76 x 56 cm.), offset lithograph on thick machine-made paper (BP 2019, DM 5059, FR 17,052, Y 338,015).

$1100* *Untitled (Bastian 76), 1983,* inits., num. 57/150, pub. Visconti Art Spectrum, Wien, full margins,excell. cond., (09-19-92, Christie-E, #237, illus.), sheet 37 x 27⅛ in., (940 x 689 mm.), aquatint and lithograph in colors on wove (BP 633, DM 1647, FR 5641, Y 137,055).

$1100* *Untitled (Sarajevo), 1984,* inits., num. 32/150, pub. Visconti Art Spectrum, full margins, good cond., surface soiling, creases, (02-24-93, Butterfield, #3158, illus.), 29 x 21 in., (737 x 533 mm.), lithograph & aquatint in colors on wove (BP 767, DM 1786, FR 6054, Y 129,078).

$2128* *"Untitled" (Bastian 76), 1983,* mono., num., (06-05-93, Grisebach, #906, illus.), 29⅝ x 21⁹⁄₁₆ in., (75.3 x 54.7 cm.), color aquatint over beige colored tone plate in lithograph on thick hand-made copper print paper (BP 1401, DM 3450, FR 11,628, Y 228,277).

TWORKOV, Jack Polish/American b. 1900

$230* *KTL #1 (Tyler 611: JT1), 1982,* s., d., t., #149/150, blindstamp, pub. Tyler Graphics, Ltd., full margins, good cond., (05-15-93, Sotheby-NY, #1251), 24 x 24 in., (61 x 61 cm.), lithograph in colors on Arches Cover (BP 150, DM 370, FR 1243, Y 25,496).

$176* *L P #3 Q2-75,* s., t., #10/30, prov., (05-16-93, Hindman, #618), 32 x 32 in., (81.3 x 81.3 cm.), color lithograph (BP 114, DM 283, FR 951, Y 19,510).

TYSON, Dorsey Potter

BI *Peking Cart, 1930,* s., num. 63/100, s., d., good cond., est. $2/400, (05-22-93, Weschler, #225), 9¼ x 7¾ in., (23.5 x 19.7 cm.), etching in colors.

TYSZ BLAT, Michel b. 1936

$42* *Untitled,* (01-28-93, Pescheteau, #268), 19⁵⁄₁₆ x 25⁹⁄₁₆ in., (49 x 65 cm.), serigraph on aluminum (BP 28, DM 67, FR 225, Y 5215).

U-FAN, Lee

$1815* *The Memory Of Mine I (Shirota Gallery 96), 1984,* s., num. 31/50, pub. Shirota Gallery, full margins, good cond., (10-14-92, Sotheby-Japan, #46, illus.), 20⅞ x 26¾ in., (530 x 679 mm.), lithograph on Arches (BP 1065, DM 2656, FR 9007, Y 219,947).

$1815* *The Memory Of Mine II (Shirota Gallery 97), 1984,* s., num. 49/50, pub. Shirota Gallery, full margins, good cond., (10-14-92, Sotheby-Japan, #47, illus.), 20⅞ x 26¾ in., (530 x 679 mm.), lithograph on Arches (BP 1065, DM 2656, FR 9007, Y 219,947).

BI *Port, 1991,* s., num. 28/50, pub. Shirota Gallery, full sheet, good cond., est. Y180/200,000, (10-14-92, Sotheby-Japan, #48, illus.), sheet 35⅝ x 29¾ in., (905 x 756 mm.), lithograph in beige and black.

U.S. ARMY SIGNAL CORPS

BI *American Troops Landing During The Italian Campaign, early 1940's,* U.S. Army Signal Corps insig. in neg., backed w/heavy board, est. $2/3,000, (04-06-93, Sotheby-NY, #367, illus.), 15⅛ x 18 in., photograph.

UBAC, Raoul Belgian 1910-1984

$162* *Pierre, 1958,* s., #36/150, (05-27-93, Briest, #197), 20⁵⁄₁₆ x 25⁹⁄₁₆ in., (51.6 x 65 cm.), color lithograph (BP 104, DM 260, FR 876, Y 17,367).

$160* *"Tete Levee",* #10/20, s., (04-04-93, Pescheteau, #308), 16⅛ x 12³⁄₁₆ in., (41 x 31 cm.), empreinte d'ardoise on Japan (BP 105, DM 257, FR 873, Y 18,217).

$213* *"Tete Levee", 1981,* #10/75, s., (10-18-92, Pescheteau, #276), 33¹⁄₁₆ x 22¹³⁄₁₆ in., (84 x 58 cm.), lithograph in black on wove (BP 129, DM 315, FR 1069, Y 25,433).

$130* *Untitled,* #10/20, s., creases, (01-28-93, Pescheteau, #274), 15¾ x 11¹³⁄₁₆ in., (40 x 30 cm.), print on Japan (BP 86, DM 206, FR 697, Y 16,141).

$330* *Untitled,* s., d. 1959, illus., (03-31-93, Briest, #E200), 3⁹⁄₁₆ x 3⁹⁄₁₆ in., (9 x 9 cm.), black print (BP 218, DM 531, FR 1803, Y 37,948).

UBBELOHDE, Otto   1867-1922
  $2537* *Der Eisenhans (Graepler 61), 1909/1910: Seven*, s.,
    num., (05-26-93, Lempertz, #509, illus.), portfolio 23⅝ x
    17⅛ in., (60 x 43.5 cm.), etching on Japan (BP 1641,
    DM 4139, FR 13,932, Y 275,641).

UBEDA, Rafael
  $198* *"Mujer Cabalgando"*, E.A., s., (02-03-93, Duran, #230,
    illus.), 24¹³⁄₁₆ x 18⅞ in., (63 x 48 cm.), lithograph in
    color (BP 138, DM 326, FR 1106, Y 24,630, P 23,000).

UDEN, Lucas van   Flemish 1595-1672/1673
  $722* *Blick Auf Das Kapuzinerkloster Von Tervueren (B. 56;
    Hollstein 7 III)*, watermark, (12-04-92, Bassenge, #6473,
    illus.), 8¹¹⁄₁₆ x 12¹¹⁄₁₆ in., (22 x 32.2 cm.), etching (BP
    463, DM 1150, FR 3901, Y 90,137).
  $1841* *Die Landschaft Mit Dem Umgesturzten Wagen (B. 48,
    Hollstein 41 II)*, prov., (06-04-93, Bassenge, #5382,
    illus.), 7⁹⁄₁₆ x 12¹⁄₁₆ in., (19.2 x 30.7 cm.), etching (BP
    1218, DM 2990, FR 10,077, Y 198,555).
  $1275* *Landschaften (B. 21-26, Hollstein 20 II, 21 II, 22 II, 23
    II, 24 II,25 III): Six*, (06-04-93, Bassenge, #5380), etch-
    ing (BP 844, DM 2070, FR 6979, Y 137,511).

UECKER, Gunther   German b. 1930
  BI *Komposition In Schwarz, 1990*, s., d., num., est. DM
    1,600-, (09-25-92, Granier, #3036), sheet 41¾ x 29¾ in.,
    (106 x 75.5 cm.), lithograph on hand-made.
  $236* *Komposition, 1983*, s., d., 1000mm x 700mm, (10-14-
    92, Germann, #467), lithograph (BP 139, DM 345, FR
    1171, Y 28,599, SF 307).
  $361* *Untitled, 1964*, s., d., (11-28-92, Schoppmann, #852),
    19½ x 19½ in., (49.5 x 49.5 cm.), embossing and litho-
    graph in blue on wove (BP 238, DM 575, FR 1952, Y
    44,928).
  $505* *Untitled, 1966*, s., d., (11-28-92, Grisebach, #796, illus.),
    24³⁄₁₆ x 20¹⁄₁₆ in., (61.5 x 51 cm.), relief print in white
    handmade (BP 333, DM 805, FR 2731, Y 62,850).
  $248* *Untitled, 1977*, s., d., ded., artist's proof, (06-12-93,
    Hauswedell/Nolt, #439), 12¹¹⁄₁₆ x 12¹¹⁄₁₆ in., (32.2 x 32.2
    cm.), etching on copper print (BP 162, DM 404, FR
    1357, Y 26,097).
  $396* *Weisses Phantom, 1980*, s., d., t., i., artist's proof, (06-
    12-93, Hauswedell/Nolt, #440), 16¹⁵⁄₁₆ x 23¼ in., (43 x
    59 cm.), relief print on copper print (BP 259, DM 645,
    FR 2166, Y 41,671).

UECKER, Gunther and Eugen GOMRINGER   German 20th cent.
  $219* *Nagelbild*, s., d. Uecker 75, Gomringer, #63/300, (03-24-
    93, Venator/Hansten, #4569), approx. 19¹¹⁄₁₆ x 18⁵⁄₁₆ in.,
    (50 x 46.5 cm.), embossed print (BP 148, DM 358, FR
    1217, Y 25,731).

UELSMANN, Jerry   American b. 1934
  $385* *Double Nude*, s., d., (06-13-93, Hindman, #427), 13½ x
    8½ in., photograph, silver print (BP 252, DM 627, FR
    2106, Y 40,514).
  BI *Double Nude, 1973*, s., d., est. $800/1,200, (05-16-93,
    Hindman, #338), 13½ x 8½ in., photograph, silver print.
  $550* *The Gifts Of St. Ann, 1976*, s., t., (05-16-93, Hindman,
    #337), 11¾ x 10¼ in., photograph, silver print (BP 359,
    DM 887, FR 2989, Y 61,247).
  BI *"Little Golden Hamburger Tree", 1970*, init., t., d. by
    photog., s., t., d. by photog. in ink, est. $1,5/2,500, (04-
    06-93, Sotheby-NY, #470, illus.), 4⅜ x 3⅜ in., photo-
    graph, silver print on gold paper.
  BI *Ohne Titel, 1972*, mono., d., felt pen s., est. DM 1,600,
    (11-12-92, Lempertz, #266, illus.), 6¹¹⁄₁₆ x 9¹⁄₁₆ in., (17 x
    23 cm.), photograph, gelatin silver print.
  $748* *"Point Lobos", 1969*, inits., d. twice, s., t., photog.'s
    label, (05-23-93, Butterfield, #3637, illus.), 9½ x 13⅝
    in., photograph, gelatin silver print (BP 487, DM 1223,
    FR 4117, Y 82,679).
  BI *"Point Lobos", 1969*, inits., d., s., t., photog. label, Dixon
    Collection, est. $1,0/1,500, (11-16-92, Butterfield, #6204,
    illus.), 9½ x 13⅝ in., (241.7 x 346.7 mm.), photograph,
    gelatin silver print.
  $467* *Texas Fantasy #3, 1985*, photog.'s t., init., d. on overmat,
    sig.; d., t., (c) handstamp verso, (04-07-93, Swann, #570,
    illus.), 13½ x 10 in., photograph, silver print (BP 309,
    DM 755, FR 2556, Y 53,056).

  $2300* *Untitled*, s., d. by photog. in ink; (c) stamp, 1976, p.l.,
    (04-06-93, Sotheby-NY, #223, illus.), 19⅝ x 14⅜ in.,
    photograph (BP 1519, DM 3705, FR 12,548, Y 262,318).
  $1210* *Untitled (Floating Trees) (Private Realities, pl. 10), 1969*,
    inits., d., s., photog. label, (11-16-92, Butterfield, #6205,
    illus.), 9½ x 12½ in., (241.7 x 318.1 mm.), photograph,
    gelatin silver print (BP 797, DM 1929, FR 6498, Y
    150,479).
  $550* *Untitled, 1988*, s., t., d., photog. stamp, (11-16-92, But-
    terfield, #6206, illus.), 10⅛ x 13½ in., (257.6 x 343.5
    mm.), photograph, gelatin silver print (BP 362, DM 877,
    FR 2954, Y 68,399).
  $748* *Untitled, Girl Flying In Cloud Room, 1990*, s., t., d.,
    photog.'s stamp, (05-23-93, Butterfield, #3638, illus.),
    10⅜ x 13½ in., photograph, gelatin silver print (BP 487,
    DM 1223, FR 4117, Y 82,679).
  $1495* *Untitled, Man On Desk In Study, 1976*, s., d., photog.'s
    stamp, (05-23-93, Butterfield, #3636, illus.), 19¾ x 14½
    in., photograph, toned gelatin silver print (BP 974, DM
    2444, FR 8228, Y 165,248).
  $690* *Untitled, Sand Castle In Room, 1990*, s., t., d., photog.'s
    stamp, illus., (05-23-93, Butterfield, #3639, illus.), 19½ x
    15⅜ in., photograph, gelatin silver print (BP 449, DM
    1128, FR 3797, Y 76,268).

UHL, Joseph   b. 1877
  BI *Idealist, c. 1900*, s., light-staining, est. DM 300, (12-01-
    92, Karl/Faber, #1312), 13¹⁵⁄₁₆ x 17¹⁵⁄₁₆ in., (35.5 x 45.5
    cm.), etching on simili-Japan.
  BI *"Liebes-Mysterium" (Thieme-Becker 33, S. 548), 1910*,
    s., artist's proof, brown stained, est. DM 400, (12-01-92,
    Karl/Faber, #1313), 11 x 14¾ in., (28 x 37.5 cm.), etch-
    ing on simili-Japan.
  BI *Die Strasse*, s., est. DM 300, (12-01-92, Karl/Faber,
    #1314), 9¹⁄₁₆ x 15⁹⁄₁₆ in., (23 x 38.5 cm.), etching on
    simili-Japan.

ULLMANN, Doris   American 1882-1934
  $935* *"Granny Nancy Greer, Weaver Gross Valley, Grade, Tenn,
    101 Years Old" and "Loom Room Brasstown, N.C.": Two*,
    s. Doris Ulmann, t., stamped w/num. 2047 and 3064,
    very good cond., (03-12-93, Skinner, #120, illus.), 8 x
    6¼ in., photograph, toned silver prints on printing-out
    paper (BP 652, DM 1556, FR 5291, Y 110,194).

ULMANN, Doris   1882-1934
  $1955* *Banana Carrier, c. 1930*, tipped to mount, s. by photog.,
    (04-06-93, Sotheby-NY, #91, illus.), 8 x 6 in., photo-
    graph, platinum print (BP 1291, DM 3150, FR 10,666, Y
    222,970).
  $1870* *Black Man And Boy (The Darkness and the Light, p. 53,
    variant), c. 1920*, s. by photog., (10-15-92, Sotheby-NY,
    #140, illus.), 8 x 6 in., (20.3 x 15.2 cm.), photograph,
    waxed platinum(?) print (BP 1144, DM 2784, FR 9440,
    Y 224,355).
  $440* *"Bybee Pottery, Bybee, Ky.", s. Doris Ullman, t., stamped
    w/num. 1229, very good cond., (03-12-93, Skinner, #119,
    illus.), sight 8 x 6 in., photograph, toned silver on print-
    ing-out paper (BP 307, DM 732, FR 2490, Y 51,856).
  $1100* *Elderly Black Woman With Cane, 1917*, mono. by pho-
    tog., double mounted, s., d. Doris U. Jaeger 17 by pho-
    tog., (10-15-92, Sotheby-NY, #138, illus.), 6½ x 4⅝ in.,
    (16.5 x 11.7 cm.), photograph, platinum print (BP 673,
    DM 1637, FR 5553, Y 131,974).
  $1955* *Family In Doorway, c. 1930*, tipped to mount, s. by pho-
    tog., (04-06-93, Sotheby-NY, #90, illus.), 8 x 6⅛ in.,
    photograph, platinum print (BP 1291, DM 3150, FR 10,666, Y 222,970).
  $2200* *Same Site From Different Vantage Points, c. 1917: Two
    Architectural Studies*, 1 s. by photog., double mounted,
    (10-15-92, Sotheby-NY, #139, illus.), each approx. 8 x 6
    in., (20.3 x 15.2 cm.), photograph, platinum prints (BP
    1346, DM 3275, FR 11,106, Y 263,947).
  $2990* *A Young Black Girl, 1917*, s., d., prov., (04-08-93,
    Christie-NY, #74, illus.), 8⅛ x 6⅛ in., (20.6 x 15.6
    cm.), photograph, platinum print (BP 1961, DM 4803,
    FR 16,259, Y 339,310).
  $3450* *A Young Girl With A Fan, c. 1917*, prov., (04-08-93,
    Christie-NY, #73, illus.), 8⅛ x 6⅛ in., (20.6 x 15.6
    cm.), photograph, platinum print (BP 2262, DM 5542,
    FR 18,760, Y 391,512).

ULRICH, Fritz
$279* *Mit Der Wank-Bahn Zum Partenkirchen*, cond. B, (03-16-93, Boisgirard, #210), 35⅝ x 23⁷⁄₁₆ in., (90.5 x 59.5 cm.), poster (BP 193, DM 464, FR 1576, Y 32,624).

ULRICH, Heinrich   d. 1621
$246* *Ein Edelmann Unter Den Dirnen*, (12-04-92, Bassenge, #6474), 5¹⁄₁₆ x 7¹¹⁄₁₆ in., (12.8 x 19.6 cm.), (BP 158, DM 392, FR 1329, Y 30,712).

ULRICHS, Timm   b. 1940
$505* *"Bildruckseitenbild"*, 1961-1968, s., num., (11-28-92, Grisebach, #797, illus.), 15¾ x 19¹³⁄₁₆ in., (40 x 50.4 cm.), photo screen print on canvas (BP 333, DM 805, FR 2731, Y 62,850).

UMBACH, Jonas   1624-1693
BI *Die Ruckkehr Von Der Jagd (Nagler 144)*, trimmed, est. DM 500, (12-01-92, Karl/Faber, #155), etching.

UMBACH, Jonas   c. 1624-1639
$361* *Selene Und Endymion (Nagler 122; Haas 142)*, (12-04-92, Bassenge, #6475), 4½ x 3¹⁄₁₆ in., (11.4 x 7.8 cm.), etching w/brown pen, overworked w/gray, brown and white pencil (BP 232, DM 575, FR 1950, Y 45,069).

UMBO (Otto UMBEHR)   German 1902-1980
$683* *Bauhaus Cabarett, 20's*, stamped (c), (11-12-92, Lempertz, #14, illus.), 6⅝ x 5¹⁄₁₆ in., (16.9 x 12.8 cm.), photograph, gelatin silver print (BP 437, DM 1073, FR 3658, Y 84,498).
BI *Dance Theatre Studies: Seventeen, c. 1930*, group of contact strips comprised of 17 different inages, num., reprod. limit. stamps on mount, (c) and studio stamps, est. $4/6,000, (10-13-92, Christie-NY, #373, illus.), each 1 x 1½ in., (2.5 x 3.8 cm.), overall 10¾ x 8½ in., (2.5 x 3.8 cm.), photograph.
BI *Doll Heads*, 1927, p. 1979, s., #41/50, photog.'s/portfolio stamps, est. $800/1,000, (05-23-93, Butterfield, #3641, illus.), 8½ x 11½ in., photograph, gelatin silver print.
$531* *Ohne Titel*, 1928, 1979, ink s., d., i. WKV 30/50, (11-12-92, Lempertz, #267, illus.), 6⁷⁄₁₆ x 8¹⁄₁₆ in., (16.4 x 20.4 cm.), photograph, gelatin silver print (BP 340, DM 835, FR 2844, Y 65,693).
BI *Portrait Of W.B.*, 1928, p. 1979, s., #35/50, photog.'s/portfolio stamps, illus., est. $800/1,000, (05-23-93, Butterfield, #3640, illus.), 9½ x 7 in., photograph, gelatin silver print.

UMETARO, Azechi   Japanese b. 1902
$358* *Mountaineer*, d., annot., s. 53 U. Azechi, 40/50, seal, (11-28-92, Dunning, #1053), 15¾ x 12¾ in., (40 x 32.4 cm.), color woodblock (BP 236, DM 570, FR 1936, Y 44,555).
$330* *Mountaineer With Cup*, s. U. Azechi, (11-20-92, Skinner, #21), image 15 x 10 in., (38.1 x 25.4 cm.), (BP 217, DM 526, FR 1772, Y 41,040).
$358* *Two Mountaineers*, s., d. 55, #33/50, t. verso, (11-20-92, Skinner, #20, illus.), image 16 x 11¾ in., (40.6 x 29.8 cm.), (BP 236, DM 571, FR 1923, Y 44,522).

UNBEKANNT
$149* *Komposition*, (19)76, s., d., num., (12-01-92, Karl/Faber, #1317), 24⁷⁄₁₆ x 35¹⁄₁₆ in., (62 x 89 cm.), color serigraph on board (BP 98, DM 237, FR 809, Y 18,551).

UNDERWOOD, Leon
$522* *Paul Jones, 1927: Set Of Eight*, full margins, s., d., #49/50, (10-27-92, Phillips-London, #318), borderline 8½ x 11 in., (216 x 279 mm.), black woodcut on laid japan (BP 330, DM 800, FR 2715, Y 63,853).
$522* *Paul Jones, 1927: Set Of Eight*, full margins, s., d., #43/50, (10-27-92, Phillips-London, #319), borderline 8½ x 11 in., (216 x 279 mm.), black woodcut on laid japan (BP 330, DM 800, FR 2715, Y 63,853).
$487* *The Siamese Cat, 1928: Fifteen*, from the series (some duplicates), each s., d., num., (10-27-92, Phillips-London, #320), borderline 5¼ x 3⅛ in., (133 x 79 mm.), black woodcut on fibrous laid japan (BP 308, DM 746, FR 2533, Y 59,572).

UNDERWOOD, William Orison
BI *Girl With Dog, c. 1903*, est. $6/900, (10-14-92, Swann, #580, illus.), 12 x 10 in., (30.5 x 25.4 cm.), photograph, toned carbon print.

$412* *Mountain Road, c. 1904*, photog.'s sig., (04-07-93, Swann, #573, illus.), 9½ x 7¾ in., photograph, gum and platinum print (BP 272, DM 666, FR 2255, Y 46,808).

UNDERWOOD & UNDERWOOD
BI *Frank Sinatra At The Draft Board*, (1942), p.l., credit stamp, est. $800/1,200, (04-08-93, Christie-NY, #347, illus.), 9¼ x 7 in., (23.5 x 17.8 cm.), photograph, gelatin silver print.
BI *Silver Set*, studio's credit in neg., 1930s, est. $6/900, (04-07-93, Swann, #571, illus.), 7 x 9 in., photograph, silver-toned silver print.
BI *Women Working In Silk Factory, c. 1910*, Underwood and Underwood handstamp, est. $6/900, (04-07-93, Swann, #572, illus.), 10 x 8 in., photograph, silver print.

UNDERWWOOD & UNDERWWOD
$302* *Images Of The 1939 New York World's Fair, 1939: Seven*, studio's credit in neg., handstamp, (04-07-93, Swann, #371, illus.), 7½ x 9 in., photograph, silver print (BP 200, DM 488, FR 1653, Y 34,310).

UNGER, W.   German 1837-1932
BI *Portrait Of An Aristocratic Woman*, est. $1/2,000, (09-25-92, Wolf, #10), 7½ x 6¼ in., (19.1 x 15.9 cm.), aquatint and engraving.

UNWERTH, Ellen Von
$400* *Fashion Study, c. 1990*, s. V. Unwerth, image 352 x 252mm, (05-07-93, Sotheby-London, #362, illus.), photograph, silver print (BP 253, DM 632, FR 2131, Y 44,043).

UNWIN, Francis Sydney
$55* *(Backyard Fences)*, s., #19/25, appears good cond., (06-11-93, Doyle, #84), 7 x 12¼ in., (178 x 311 mm.), wood engraving (BP 36, DM 89, FR 301, Y 5836).

URAY, Ch.
$302* *Pelican, c. 1930*, Creations Affiches, A cond., (08-06-92, Swann, #277, illus.), 32 x 23½ in., (81.3 x 59.7 cm.), (BP 158, DM 446, FR 1507, Y 38,520).

URCULO, Eduardo
BI *"Desnudo A La Luz De La Luna"*, #102/200, s., d. 82, reserve P30,000, (12-17-92, Duran, #180, illus.), 26⅜ x 19⁵⁄₁₆ in., (67 x 49 cm.), serigraph.

URRUTY   French 19th cent.
$809* *"Guillaume Tell"*, (03-22-93, Pescheteau, #28), color print (BP 545, DM 1326, FR 4509, Y 93,678).

USABIAGA
$25 *Feria Del Mar San Sebastian, 1957*, minor edge loss, (09-24-92, Alderfer, #304), 36½ x 25 in., (92.7 x 63.5 cm.), (BP 15, DM 37, FR 126, Y 3007).

UTAGAWA, Kunisada   1786-1864
$164* *"A Scene From A Kabuki Drama: Shibai-E"*, s., (10-20-92, Encans, #200), 13¾ x 8¹¹⁄₁₆ in., (35 x 22 cm.), wood engraving (BP 92, DM 249, FR 848, Y 20,557, C$ 200).
$636* *"Toskidama", c. 1852-54*, triptyque, s. Toyokuni, (10-20-92, Encans, #201), 2 parts 14⅜ x 9¹³⁄₁₆ in., (36.5 x 25 cm.), 1 part 14⅜ x 10¹⁄₁₆ in., (36.5 x 25 cm.), wood engraving (BP 356, DM 967, FR 3290, Y 79,719, C$ 777).

UTAGAWA KUNIHIRO   Japanese ac. c. 1816-1841
BI *Memorial Portrait Of Arashi Kitsusaburo: Five*, Oban, s. Kunihiro ga, pub.'s marks Tenmanya Kihei, Hirooka & Honsei,d. 1817 & 1821, faded, trimmed, soiled, rubbed, Prof. H.R.W. Kuhne Coll., est.BP 800/1,000, (06-11-93, Sotheby-London, #442), each approx. 14⅝ x 9⅞ in., (37.1 x 25.1 cm.), woodblock.

UTAGAWA KUNIMASA   Japanese 1773-1810
BI *Ichikawa Danjuro VI As Sano Genzaemon*, Oban, s. Kunimasa ga, pub.'s mark Tsuruya Kinsuke, d. Kansei 10 (1798), trimmed, fold mark, soiled, Prof. H.R.W. Kuhne Coll., est. BP 750/1,000, (06-11-93, Sotheby-London, #353, illus.), 14 x 9⅝ in., (35.6 x 24.4 cm.), woodblock.
$1400* *Memorial Portrait Of Ichikawa Danjuro VI*, Hosoban, s. Kunimasa ga, d. c. 1800-06, faded, good state, Prof. H.R.W. Kuhne Coll., (06-11-93, Sotheby-London, #354, illus.), 12¾ x 5⅞ in., (32.4 x 14.9 cm.), woodblock, grey ground (BP 920, DM 2275, FR 7671, Y 148,541).

UTAGAWA KUNISADA   Japanese 1786-1864

$1575* *The Actors Of The Ichikawa Family,* Surimono, yokon-aga-ban, s. Toto Ichiyosai Toyokuni ga w/double toshidama seal, d. c. Kaei 5 (1852), probably issued in Osaka, fold marks, creased, rubbed, Prof. H.R.W. Kuhne Coll., (06-11-93, Sotheby-London, #415, illus.), 9¾ x 17¼ in., (24.8 x 43.8 cm.), woodblock (BP 1035, DM 2560, FR 8630, Y 167,109).

$2625* *The Actors Of The Kawarazaki-za Visiting The Inari Shrine At Matsuyama,* t., Oban, a triptych, sh attached together, s. Gototei Kunisada ga, censor's seal kiwame, pub.'s mark Iwatoya Kisaburo, d. c. Bunsei 5 (1822), trimmed, rubbed, laid down, Prof. H.R.W. Kuhne Coll., (06-11-93, Sotheby-London, #378, illus.), 14⅜ x 29¾ in., (36.5 x 75.6 cm.), woodblock (BP 1725, DM 4266, FR 14,384, Y 278,515).

$2625* *Actors Of The Three Theatres Of Edo In Rehearsal: Five,* t., Oban, a pentatych, s. Toyokuni ga in a toshidama seal, censor's seal, d. Man'en 1 (1860), Prof. H.R.W. Kuhne Coll., (06-11-93, Sotheby-London, #393, illus.), each sh approx. 14¾ x 9¾ in., (37.5 x 24.8 cm.), woodblock (BP 1725, DM 4266, FR 14,384, Y 278,515).

$1750* *Actors Visiting The Narita Temple: Three,* Oban, a trip-tych, s. Oju (by request) Kunisada ga, censor's seal kiwame, pub.'s mark Iwatoya Kisaburo, d. c. Bunsei 5 (1822), soiled, rubbed, Prof.H.R.W. Kuhne Coll., (06-11-93, Sotheby-London, #379, illus.), each sh approx. 15⅛ x 10¼ in., (38.4 x 26 cm.), woodblock (BP 1150, DM 2844, FR 9589, Y 185,676).

$2625* *Actors' Party In The Green Room Of The Nakamura-za Theatre,* t., Oban a triptych, sh attached together, s. Ichiyusai/Kunisada ga,censor's seal kiwame and gyoji-in seal, pub.'s mark Nishimura Yohachi, d. Bunka8 (1811), faded, soiled, rubbed, wormed, Prof. H.R.W. Kuhne Coll., (06-11-93, Sotheby-London, #370, illus.), 14⅞ x 30⅛ in., (37.8 x 76.5 cm.), woodblock (BP 1725, DM 4266, FR 14,384, Y 278,515).

$14,878* *"Brocade Pictures" Of The Green Room: Five,* Oban, 5 out of 10, s. Ichiyusai Kunisada ga, censor's seal kiwame andGyoji-in seal Iwato San, pub.'s mark Nish-imura Yohachi, d. Bunka 9 (1812), laiddown, trimmed, soiled, rubbed, repaired, Prof. H.R.W. Kuhne Coll., (06-11-93, Sotheby-London, #363, illus.), each approx. 14¾ x 9⅞ in., (37.5 x 25.1 cm.), woodblock (BP 9775, DM 24,180, FR 81,523, Y 1,578,568).

$4551* *Bust-Portrait Of An Onnagata Actor,* Oban, s. Gototei Kunisada ga, censor's seal kiwame and Gyoji-in seal,d. Bunka 9 (1812), faded, wormed, margin repaired, Prof. H.R.W. Kuhne Coll., (06-11-93, Sotheby-London, #373, illus.), 14¾ x 10 in., (37.5 x 25.4 cm.), woodblock (BP 2990, DM 7396, FR 24,937, Y 482,865).

BI *The Bust-Portrait Of Bando Mitsugoro III,* Oban, s. Gototei Kunisada ga, censor's seal kiwame, pub.'s mark OmiyaHeihachi, d. Tenpo 1 (1830), fold mark, rubbed, soiled, trimmed, laid down, Prof. H.R.W. Kuhne Coll., est. BP 800/1,000, (06-11-93, Sotheby-London, #384, illus.), 14¼ x 9¾ in., (36.2 x 24.8 cm.), woodblock.

$2625* *The Bust-Portrait Of Ichikawa Danjuro VII,* Oban, s. Gototei Kunisada ga, censor's seal kiwame, pub.'s mark OmiyaHeihachi, d. Tenpo 2 (1831), faded, fold mark, Prof. H.R.W. Kuhne Coll., (06-11-93, Sotheby-London, #369, illus.), 14¾ x 10 in., (37.5 x 25.4 cm.), wood-block (BP 1725, DM 4266, FR 14,384, Y 278,515).

$1137* *The Bust-Portrait Of Matsumoto Koshiro V,* Oban, s. Oju (by request) Gototei Kunisada ga, censor's seal kiwame,-pub.'s mark Azumaya Daisuke, d. Bunsei 5 (1822), wormed/repaired, soiled, rubbed, Prof. H.R.W. Kuhne Coll., (06-11-93, Sotheby-London, #374, illus.), 14⅝ x 10⅛ in., (37.1 x 25.7 cm.), woodblock (BP 747, DM 1848, FR 6230, Y 120,637).

$630* *The Bust-Portrait Of Segawa Roko (Kikunojo V),* Chuban, uchiwa-e, s. Gototei Kunisada ga, d. probably Bunsei 11 (1828), worm holes, creased, Prof. H.R.W. Kuhne Coll., (06-11-93, Sotheby-London, #397, illus.), 8⅞ x 11 in., (22.5 x 27.9 cm.), woodblock (BP 414, DM 1024, FR 3452, Y 66,844).

$7001* *A Fan Of The Actor Onoe Baiko,* Oban, s. Gototei Kunisada ga, censor's seal kiwame, pub.'s mark Hagi-wara, d. c. Bunka 12 (1815), trimmed, wormed, creased,

Prof. H.R.W. Kuhne Coll., (06-11-93, Sotheby-London, #361, illus.), 14¼ x 9⅞ in., (36.2 x 25.1 cm.), wood-block (BP 4600, DM 11,378, FR 38,362, Y 742,812).

BI *The Five Chivalrous Men (Gonin Otoko),* Oban yoko-e, s. Toyokuni ga in toshidama seal cartouche, censor's seal, pub.'s mark Hamadaya Tokubei, d. Kaei 5 (1852), center fold, Prof. H.R.W. Kuhne Coll., est. BP 5/700, (06-11-93, Sotheby-London, #386, illus.), 9⅞ x 14⅜ in., (25.1 x 36.5 cm.), woodblock.

$1050* *The Five Chivalrous Men (Gonin Otoko): Six,* Koban, pentatych, s. Toyokuni ga in Toshidama seal cartouche, censor's seal, pub.'s mark Iseya Kanekichi, d. Ninth month of Ansei 1 (1854), embossings, burnishing, Prof. H.R.W. Kuhne Coll., (06-11-93, Sotheby-London, #392, illus.), each sh approx. 7½ x 4⅞ in., (19.1 x 12.4 cm.), woodblock (BP 690, DM 1706, FR 5753, Y 111,406).

$7876* *The Green Room Of The Morita-za Theatre,* t., Oban triptych, attached together, s. Gototei Kunisada ga w/a Mimasumon seal, censor's seal, pub.'s mark Nishimu-raya Yohachi, d. Bunka 8 (1811),oxidised, trimmed, wormed, Prof. H.R.W. Kuhne Coll., (06-11-93, Sotheby-London, #368, illus.), 14¾ x 30¼ in., (37.5 x 76.8 cm.), woodblock (BP 5175, DM 12,800, FR 43,156, Y 835,650).

$8752* *The Green Rooms On The Third Floor Of The Ichimura-za,* Oban, a triptych, s. Gototei Kunisada ga, censor's seal kiwame, pub.'s mark Nishimura Yohachi, d. Bunsei 7 (1824), trimmed, rubbed, laid down, Prof.H.R.W. Kuhne Coll., (06-11-93, Sotheby-London, #366, illus.), 14⅞ x 30⅝ in., (37.8 x 77.8 cm.), woodblock (BP 5750, DM 14,224, FR 47,956, Y 928,594).

$3851* *The Green Rooms On The Third Floor Of The Naka-mura-za,* t., Oban a triptych, 3 sh attached together, s. Gototei Kunisada ga,censor's seal kiwame, pub.'s mark Nishimura Yohachi, d. Bunsei 7 (1824), rubbed, soiled, laid down, Prof. H.R.W. Kuhne Coll., (06-11-93, Sotheby-London, #381), 15¾ x 30½ in., (40 x 77.5 cm.), woodblock (BP 2530, DM 6259, FR 21,101, Y 408,594).

$1050* *Ichikawa Danjuro VII As Seki No Sekibei(?): Two,* Suri-mono, kakuban, s. Kunisada ga w/Mimasu mon and Gototei Kunisada ga, d. c. Bunsei 1 (1818) and Bunsei 5 (1822), faded, wormed, foxed, rubbed, Prof. H.R.W. Kuhne Coll., (06-11-93, Sotheby-London, #364), one 8¼ x 7⅜ in., (21 x 18.7 cm.), other 8¼ x 7¼ in., (21 x 18.7 cm.), woodblock (BP 690, DM 1706, FR 5753, Y 111,406).

$1662* *Ichikawa Danjuro VII As Soga Goro,* Surimono, kakuban, part of a diptych or triptych(?), s. Gototei Kunisada ga w/double toshidama seal, d. c. Bunsei 3 (1820), faded, soiled, Prof. H.R.W. Kuhne Coll., (06-11-93, Sotheby-London, #414, illus.), 8 x 7¼ in., (20.3 x 18.4 cm.), woodblock w/gold and silver w/burnishing (BP 1092, DM 2701, FR 9107, Y 176,340).

$2275* *Ichikawa Danjuro VII As Watanabe No Tsuna,* Suri-mono, kakuban, s. Kunisada ga w/double toshidama seal, d. c. lateBunsei to early Tenpo periods, laid down, Prof. H.R.W. Kuhne Coll., (06-11-93, Sotheby-London, #412, illus.), 8¼ x 7¼ in., (21 x 18.4 cm.), woodblock w/silver and gold (BP 1495, DM 3697, FR 12,466, Y 241,379).

$2100* *Ichikawa Ebizo VI (Danjuro VII) In Shibaraku Costume,* Surimono, kakuban, diptych, s. Kochoro Kunisada hitsu w/a double toshidama seal, d. Tenpo 3 (1832), wormed, creased, laid down, Prof. H.R.W. Kuhne Coll., (06-11-93, Sotheby-London, #411, illus.), 8⅞ x 14¼ in., (22.5 x 36.2 cm.), woodblock, w/silver and gold (BP 1380, DM 3413, FR 11,507, Y 222,812).

$1575* *The Interior Of A Theatre With A Shibaraku Perfor-mance: Three,* t., Oban triptych, s. Ichiyosai hinajishi Toyokuni ga w/a toshidama seal, censor's seal, pub.'s mark Noshuya Yasubei, d. Ansei 5 (1858), soiled, rubbed, Prof. H.R.W. Kuhne Coll., (06-11-93, Sotheby-London, #371, illus.), each sh approx. 14⅜ x 9⅞ in., (36.5 x 25.1 cm.), woodblock (BP 1035, DM 2560, FR 8630, Y 167,109).

$700* *Iwai Hanshiro V As The Court Lady Tsubone Masaoka And Onoe Kikugoro III As The Courtesan Takao,* Chu-ban, uchiwa-e, s. Gototei Kunisada ga, censor's seal 1 aratame, pub.'s mark, d. Bunsei 10 (1827), trimmed,

Prof. H.R.W. Kuhne Coll., (06-11-93, Sotheby-London, #383), 8¾ x 10⅛ in., (22.2 x 25.7 cm.), woodblock (BP 460, DM 1138, FR 3836, Y 74,271).

$4201* *Iwai Hanshiro V As Tsubone Iwafuji And Iwai Kumezaburo II As Koshimoto Ohatsu,* Chuban uchiwa-e (fan print), s. Gototei Kunisada ga, censor's seal Nearatame, pub.'s mark, d. Bunka 13 (1816), soiled, Prof. H.R.W. Kuhne Coll., (06-11-93, Sotheby-London, #365, illus.), 8⅞ x 6 in., (22.5 x 15.2 cm.), woodblock (BP 2760, DM 6828, FR 23,019, Y 445,729).

$1487* *Kawarazaki Gonjuro And Iwai Kumesaburo III,* Chuban uchiwa-e, s. Toyokuni ga in toshidama seal cartouche, censor'sseal, pub.'s mark Ibaya Senzaburo, d. Ansei 6 (1859), soiled, rubbed, wormed, Prof H.R.W. Kuhne Coll., (06-11-93, Sotheby-London, #408, illus.), 9½ x 11¾ in., (24.1 x 29.8 cm.), woodblock (BP 977, DM 2417, FR 8148, Y 157,772).

$1400* *"Matsumoto Koshiro V", "Iwai Kumesaburo II" and "Ichikawa Danjuro VII" On The Snowy Bank Of The Sumida River: Three,* Koban, a triptych, s. Oju (by request) Kunisada ga, censor's seal kiwame, pub.'s mark Shimizuya, d. c. Bunsei 7-8 (1824-25), soiling, Prof. H.R.W. Kuhne Coll., (06-11-93, Sotheby-London, #362, illus.), each sh approx. 7½ x 4⅞ in., (19.1 x 12.4 cm.), woodblock (BP 920, DM 2275, FR 7671, Y 148,541).

$630* *Memorial Portraits Of Ichikawa Danjuro VIII, Arashi Otohachi And Bando Shuka II: Two,* Oban nimai-tsuzuki (diptych), d. probably 1855, wormed, creased, Prof. H.R.W. Kuhne Coll., (06-11-93, Sotheby-London, #401, illus.), each approx. 13½ x 10 in., (34.3 x 25.4 cm.), woodblock (BP 414, DM 1024, FR 3452, Y 66,844).

$962* *"Nakamura Fukusuke I As Nuregami Chogoro" and "Ichikawa Ichizo III AsHanaregoma Chokichi": Two,* Chuban, diptych, s. Toyokuni ga in a toshidama cartouche, censor's seal, pub.'s mark Ebisuya Shoshichi, d. Ansei 4 (1857), soiled, rubbed, Prof. H.R.W. Kuhne Coll., (06-11-93, Sotheby-London, #402, illus.), one 10¼ x 7⅝ in., (26 x 19.4 cm.), other 10¼ x 7⅛ in., (26 x 19.4 cm.), woodblock (BP 632, DM 1563, FR 5271, Y 102,069).

$1225* *Nakamura Shigan II As A Courtesan And A Yakko,* Chuban, uchiwa-e, s. Gototei Kunisada ga, censor's seal, pub.'s markNagakura Eizo(?), d. Bunsei 11 (1828), center fold, creased, laid down, Prof. H.R.W. Kuhne Coll., (06-11-93, Sotheby-London, #395, illus.), 9 x 10½ in., (22.9 x 26.7 cm.), woodblock (BP 805, DM 1991, FR 6712, Y 129,973).

BI *Nakamura Shikan IV As Keiriki Tomigoro With His Back Richly Tatooed:Five,* from Kinsei Suiko den, Oban, s. Toyokuni ga, trimmed, rubbed, soiled,Prof. H.R.W. Kuhne Coll., est. BP 800/1,200, (06-11-93, Sotheby-London, #394), woodblock.

$1312* *Nakamura Utaemon III In Three Roles,* Chuban uchiwa-e, s. Kunisada ga, censor's seal, pub.'s mark Ibaya Senzaburo, d. Bunka 12 (1815), soiled, rubbed, trimmed, Prof. H.R.W. Kuhne Coll., (06-11-93, Sotheby-London, #396, illus.), 9 x 10⅝ in., (22.9 x 27 cm.), woodblock (BP 862, DM 2132, FR 7189, Y 139,204).

BI *"Nakamura Utaemon III", "Sawamura Tanosuke" And Other Actors In Various Roles: Four,* Oban, s. Gototei Kunisada ga, censor's seal kiwame, pub.'s marks, d.Bunka 12-13 (1815-16), trimmed, soiled, rubbed, creased, laid down, Prof. H.R.W. Kuhne Coll., est. BP 1/1,250, (06-11-93, Sotheby-London, #382), each approx. 14⅜ x 9⅞ in., (36.5 x 25.1 cm.), woodblock.

$630* *Sawamura Tossho As tofuya Mifu And Onoe Kikugoro III As Seigen,* Chuban uchiwa-e, s. Gototei Kunisada ga, censor's seal, pub.'s mark Ibaya Senzaburo, d. Tenpo 3 (1832), faded, rubbed, soiled, laid down, Prof. H.R.W. Kuhne Coll., (06-11-93, Sotheby-London, #407, illus.), 8⅞ x 10¼ in., (22.5 x 26 cm.), woodblock (BP 414, DM 1024, FR 3452, Y 66,844).

$962* *Three Upright-Panel Prints: Three,* Kakemono-e, s. Kochoro Kunisada hitsu and Toyokuni hitsu, soiled, rubbed, creased, Prof. H.R.W. Kuhne Coll., (06-11-93, Sotheby-London, #410), woodblock (BP 632, DM 1563, FR 5271, Y 102,069).

$16,628* *Triptych Picture Of The Green Room Of The Nakamura-za Theatre Of Sakaicho,* t., Oban triptych, 3 sh attached together, s. Kinraisha Kunisada ga zu w/ a Mimasumon

seal, pub. Nishimura Eijudo (Yohachi), d. Bunka 10 (1813), rubbed, soiled, laid down, Prof. H.R.W. Kuhne Coll., (06-11-93, Sotheby-London, #367, illus.), 14⅞ x 30⅝ in., (37.8 x 77.8 cm.), woodblock (BP 10,925, DM 27,024, FR 91,112, Y 1,764,244).

BI *Various Actors In Different Roles: Five,* Oban, parts of triptychs, s. Gototei Kunisada ga, censor's seal, pub.'s mark Iwatoya Kisaburo, Kawachiya Genshichi and Nishimura Yohachi, d. c. 1812, '16 and '18, soiled, rubbed, creased, trimmed, Prof. H.R.W. Kuhne Coll., est.BP 650/850, (06-11-93, Sotheby-London, #376), woodblock.

$1575* *Various Actors In Different Scenes: Four,* Oban, parts of triptychs, s. Kunisada ga and Gototei Kunisada ga, censor's seal kiwame, pub.'s marks Nishimura Yohachi, Yamamoto, Matsumoto Sahei(?)and Kawachiya Genshichi, d. Bunka 8, 9, and 11 (1811, '12 and '14), faded, rubbed, soiled, trimmed, Prof. H.R.W. Kuhne Coll., (06-11-93, Sotheby-London, #372, illus.), woodblock (BP 1035, DM 2560, FR 8630, Y 167,109).

$1575* *Various Actors In Scenes From Different Plays: Four,* Oban, parts of triptychs, s. Kunisada ga and Gototei Kunisada ga, censor's seal kiwame, pub.'s mark Iwatoya Kisaburo and Nishimura Yohachi, d. Bunka8 (1811), trimmed, rubbed, soiled, thinned, Prof. H.R.W. Kuhne Coll., (06-11-93, Sotheby-London, #375), woodblock (BP 1035, DM 2560, FR 8630, Y 167,109).

$6126* *View Of The Green Rooms Of An Edo Theatre: Six,* t., Oban double triptych (six-sheets design), s. Toyokuni ga in toshidama seal cartouche, censor's seal, pub.'s mark Izumiya Ichibei, d. Ansei 3 (1856), trimmed, rubbed, Prof. H.R.W. Kuhne Coll., (06-11-93, Sotheby-London, #399, illus.), each sh approx. 14⅜ x 9⅝ in., (36.5 x 24.4 cm.), woodblock (BP 4025, DM 9956, FR 33,567, Y 649,973).

UTAGAWA KUNIYOSHI   Japanese 1797-1861

BI *Actor's Portraits In An Oval Mirror: Three,* from the series Ekyodai Mitate Sanjubokka-sen, Oban, s. Ichiyusai Kuniyoshi ga, w/Yoshikiri-mon seal, rubbed, trimmed, Prof. H.R.W. Kuhne Coll., est. BP 1/1,400, (06-11-93, Sotheby-London, #437, illus.), woodblock.

$4901* *Actors Representing The Twelve Animals Of The Zodiac,* t., Oban, a triptych, 3 sh joined together, s. Ichiyusai Kuniyoshi gaw/a Yoshikiri-mon, censor's seals, pub.'s mark Ebisuya, d. c. 1847-52, trimmed,fold marks, laid down, Prof. H.R.W. Kuhne Coll., (06-11-93, Sotheby-London, #436, illus.), 14¼ x 29¼ in., (36.2 x 74.3 cm.), woodblock (BP 3220, DM 7965, FR 26,855, Y 520,000).

$1925* *The Bust-Portrait Of A Young Woman,* from the series Ukiyo Hakkei "The Eight Views of the Floating World",- Chuban, uchiwa-e (fan print), s. Ichiyusai Kuniyoshi ga w/seal Yoshikiri-mon, censor's seals, pub.'s mark Ibaya Senzaburo, d. c. 1847-52, cut out, laid down,Prof. H.R.W. Kuhne Coll., (06-11-93, Sotheby-London, #443, illus.), 8⅝ x 11¼ in., (21.9 x 28.6 cm.), woodblock (BP 1265, DM 3129, FR 10,548, Y 204,244).

$1400* *Bust-Portraits Of Various Actors: Four,* Oban, s. Ichiyusai Kuniyoshi ga w/Yoshikiri-mon seal, pub.'s marks Ibakyu, Santetsu and Shimizuya, d. c. 1846-52, rubbed, soiled, trimmed, Prof. H.R.W. Kuhne Coll., (06-11-93, Sotheby-London, #438, illus.), each approx. 14⅝ x 9¾ in., (37.1 x 24.8 cm.), woodblock (BP 920, DM 2275, FR 7671, Y 148,541).

$1400* *The Gonin Otoko (Five Chivalrous Men): Twelve,* s. Ichiyusai Kuniyoshi ga, pub.'s mark Joshuya Juzo, d. c. 1848, rubbed, creases, Prof. H.R.W. Kuhne Coll., (06-11-93, Sotheby-London, #432), woodblock (BP 920, DM 2275, FR 7671, Y 148,541).

$3851* *Graffiti On The White Wall Of A House: Two,* Oban, 2 sheets of a triptych, s. Ichiyusai Kuniyoshi egaku w/ Yoshikiri mon, censor's seal, pub.'s mark Ibaya Senzaburo, d. c. Kaei 1 (1848), fold mark, trimmed, prof. H.R.W. Kuhne Coll., (06-11-93, Sotheby-London, #433, illus.), each approx. 14 x 9½ in., (35.6 x 24.1 cm.), woodblock (BP 2530, DM 6259, FR 21,101, Y 408,594).

$1575* *Hidari Jingoro, The Sculptor: Three,* t., Oban triptych, s. Ichiyusai Kuniyoshi ga w/Yoshikiri-mon seal, censor's seal, pub.'s mark, d. c. 1848-52, rubbed, soiled, trimmed,

Prof. H.R.W.Kuhne Coll., (06-11-93, Sotheby-London, #429, illus.), woodblock (BP 1035, DM 2560, FR 8630, Y 167,109).

$1050* *Looking At A Theatre Programme,* Oban, s. Ichiyusai Kuniyoshi ga w/Yoshikiri-mon seal, censor's seal,pub.'s mark Yamamoto Heikichi, rubbed, Prof. H.R.W. Kuhne Coll., (06-11-93, Sotheby-London, #439, illus.), 14⅝ x 10⅛ in., (37.1 x 25.7 cm.), woodblock (BP 690, DM 1706, FR 5753, Y 111,406).

$4551* *Masks Dedicated To A Shrine: Three,* Oban triptych, s. Ichiyusai Kuniyoshi "giga" w/Yoshikiri-mon seal, censor's seal, pub.'s mark Ebisuya Shoshichi?, d. 1847/48, rubbed, soiled, Prof.H.R.W. Kuhne Coll., (06-11-93, Sotheby-London, #435, illus.), overall 14⅜ x 29¼ in., (36.5 x 74.3 cm.), woodblock (BP 2990, DM 7396, FR 24,937, Y 482,865).

$4551* *The Mind Of Fish,* t., Oban, s. Ichiyusai Kuniyoshi "giga", pub.'s mark Kawaguchiya Uhei, d. c. Kaei 1 (1847), faded, trimmed, fold mark, rubbed, Prof. H.R.W. Kuhne Coll., (06-11-93, Sotheby-London, #434, illus.), 13⅞ x 9½ in., (35.2 x 24.1 cm.), woodblock (BP 2990, DM 7396, FR 24,937, Y 482,865).

$630* *Sawamura Tossho As Nuregami Chogoro And Arashi Kichisaburo As Hanagoma Chokichi,* fan print, Chuban, s. Ichiyusai Kuniyoshi ga, d. c. 1852, trimmed, creased, rubbed, Prof. H.R.W. Kuhne Coll., (06-11-93, Sotheby-London, #430), woodblock (BP 414, DM 1024, FR 3452, Y 66,844).

$316* *Sitzende Mit Pfeife Beobachtet Einen Kleinen Jungen, c. 1830-40,* oban, tate-e, from Chushingura series, red ink s. Kiri-Siegel, w/twoZensurstempeln, (12-01-92, Karl/Faber, #228), color woodcut (BP 209, DM 504, FR 1716, Y 39,343).

$1750* *Umegawa And Chubei: Three,* Oban triptych, s. Ichiyusai Kuniyoshi ga w/Yoshikiri-mon seal, censor's seal, pub.'s mark Mitaya Kihachi, d. Ansei 1 (1854), soiled, trimmed, Prof.H.R.W. Kuhne Coll., (06-11-93, Sotheby-London, #428, illus.), each sh approx. 14½ x 9⅝ in., (36.8 x 24.4 cm.), woodblock (BP 1150, DM 2844, FR 9589, Y 185,676).

UTAGAWA TOYOKUNI   Japanese 1769-1825

BI *Act VII Of The Drama Chushingura,* Chuban, s. Toyokuni ga, pub.'s mark Izumiya Ichibei, d. c. Kansei 3-6(1791-94), faded, rubbed, soiled, wormage, laid down, Prof. H.R.W. Kuhne Coll.,est. BP 6/800, (06-11-93, Sotheby-London, #282), 10¼ x 7⅝ in., (26 x 19.4 cm.), woodblock.

$2800* *The Actor Sawamura Gennosuke II Off Stage Smoking Beside A River,* Chuban, fan print, s. Toyokuni ga, censor's seal Gyoji aratame, pub.'s mark, d. c. Bunka 8 (1811), fold marks, rubbed, soiled, Prof. H.R.W. Kuhne Coll., (06-11-93, Sotheby-London, #305, illus.), 8⅞ x 9¹⁵⁄₁₆ in., (22.5 x 25.2 cm.), woodblock (BP 1840, DM 4551, FR 15,342, Y 297,082).

$1925* *Actors In The Green Room Of A Theatre: Two,* Oban, the left and center sheet of a triptych, s. Toyokuni ga, censor's seal kiwame, pub.'s mark Shimizuya, d. c. Kyowa 2-3 (1802-03) to c. Bunka 3(1806), wormed, repaired, trimmed, Prof. H.R.W. Kuhne Coll., (06-11-93, Sotheby-London, #296, illus.), one 15¼ x 10¼ in., (38.7 x 26 cm.), other 14⅜ x 10⅛ in., (38.7 x 26 cm.), woodblock (BP 1265, DM 3129, FR 10,548, Y 204,244).

$735* *Actors' Memorial Portraits (Shini-e),* Oban, s. Oju (by request) Toyokuni ga, censor's seal kiwame, unident.- pub.'s mark, d. Bunsei 7 (1824), rubbed, soiled, Prof. H.R.W. Kuhne Coll., (06-11-93, Sotheby-London, #340), 14¾ x 10⅛ in., (37.5 x 25.7 cm.), woodblock (BP 483, DM 1195, FR 4027, Y 77,984).

BI *Arashi Hinasuke And Segawa Kikusaburo,* Aiban, s. Toyokuni ga, pub.'s mark Tsuruya Kinsuke, d. Kansei 12 (1800), faded, wormed, rubbed, repaired, Prof. H.R.W. Kuhne Coll., est. BP 700/850, (06-11-93, Sotheby-London, #323, illus.), 13⅛ x 8⅞ in., (33.3 x 22.5 cm.), woodblock.

BI *"Arashi Sanpachi", "Ichikawa Komazo", "Iwai Kumesaburo", and "Matsumoto Koshiro" In Various Roles: Four,* Hosoban and koban, s. Toyokuni ga, d. c. Kansei 12-Kyowa 1 (1800-01),faded, trimmed, soiled, creased,

torn, repaired, Prof. H.R.W. Kuhne Coll., est.BP 900/ 1,300, (06-11-93, Sotheby-London, #327), woodblock.

BI *Bando Mitsugoro III As An Itinerant Fishmonger,* Oban, s. Toyokuni ga, censor's seal kiwame, pub.'s mark Matsumura Tatsuemon, d. Bunka 13 (1816), faded, wormed, Prof. H.R.W. Kuhne Coll., est. BP 6/800, (06-11-93, Sotheby-London, #349, illus.), 15 x 9⅞ in., (38.1 x 25.1 cm.), woodblock.

BI *Bando Mitsugoro III As Sendo (Ferryman) No Razo And Iwai Hanshiro VIAs Onna-umakata (Woman Groom) Dotamaku Oshun,* Oban, s. Toyokuni ga, censor's seal kiwame, pub.'s mark Shimizuya, d.Bunka 3 (1806), browned, restored, Prof. H.R.W. Kuhne Coll., est. BP 1,5/2,000, (06-11-93, Sotheby-London, #314, illus.), 14¾ x 9⅝ in., (37.5 x 24.4 cm.), woodblock.

$1575* *Bando Mitsugoro V, Nakamura Noshio II And Sawamura Sojuro III In Various Roles: Three,* Hosoban, s. Toyokuni ga, pub.'s marks Izumiya Ichibei, Wakasaya Yoichi and Nishimura Yohachi, d. Kansei 7 (1795) and Kansei 9 (1797), faded, trimmed, rubbed, soiled, Prof. H.R.W. Kuhne Coll., (06-11-93, Sotheby-London, #292), smallest 11¹³⁄₁₆ x 5⁹⁄₁₆ in., (30 x 14.1 cm.), largest 12⅝ x 5¹¹⁄₁₆ in., (30 x 14.1 cm.), woodblock (BP 1035, DM 2560, FR 8630, Y 167,109).

BI *Bust Portraits Of Ichikawa Komazo II And Bando Mitsugoro II: A Pair,* Hosoban, sig. Toyokuni ga, pub.'s marks Zen and Bun, d. Kansei 8 and9 (1796 and 1797), wormed, restored, Prof. H.R.W. Kuhne Coll., est. BP 1,1/ 1,400, (06-11-93, Sotheby-London, #285), one 11¹³⁄₁₆ x 5⁹⁄₁₆ in., (30 x 14.1 cm.), other 11¾ x 5⁹⁄₁₆ in., (30 x 14.1 cm.), woodblock.

$8401* *The Bust-Portraits Of Matsumoto Yonesaburo And Nakamura Denkuro In Roles: A Pair,* Oban diptych, s. Toyokuni ga, censor's seal kiwame, pub.'s mark Murata Jirobei, d. Kansei 9 (1797), collector's mark Hayashi Tadamasa, one faded, worm holes repaired, soiled, rubbed; other fold mark, Prof. H.R.W. Kuhne Coll., (06-11-93, Sotheby-London, #278, illus.), one 15 x 10 in., (38.1 x 25.4 cm.), other 14⅞ x 9⅞ in., (38.1 x 25.4 cm.), woodblock, grey ground (BP 5520, DM 13,654, FR 46,033, Y 891,353).

$5251* *Cooling Off On The Sumida River Near The Ryogoku Bridge: Five,* Oban pentatych, s. Toyokuni ga w/ Toshidama seal, censor's seal kiwame, censor's date seal, pub.'s mark Yamamoto Kyubei, d. probably Bunka 8 (1811),faded, wormed, soiled, Prof. H.R.W. Kuhne Coll., (06-11-93, Sotheby-London, #359, illus.), each sh approx. 14¾ x 10¼ in., (37.5 x 26 cm.), woodblock (BP 3450, DM 8534, FR 28,773, Y 557,135).

$5601* *Drawing Fresh Water For The New Year: Three,* Oban triptych, s. Toyokuni ga, censor's seal kiwame, pub.'s mark Ezakiya Kichiemon, d. c. Bunka 6-7 (1809-10), wormed, repaired, rubbed, Prof. H.R.W. Kuhne Coll., (06-11-93, Sotheby-London, #304, illus.), 15 x 10 in., (38.1 x 25.4 cm.), woodblock (BP 3680, DM 9103, FR 30,690, Y 594,271).

$9627* *The Exterior And Interior Of The Nakamura-za Theatre, With A Performance Of A Soga Play On The Stage: Two,* Oban, s. Ichiyosai Utagawa Toyokuni ga, pub.'s mark, rubbed, soiled,creased, Prof. H.R.W. Kuhne Coll., (06-11-93, Sotheby-London, #311, illus.), woodblock (BP 6325, DM 15,646, FR 52,751, Y 1,021,432).

$3151* *Five Actors In A Sword-Fight Scene: Five,* Hosoban pentatych, s. Toyokuni ga, pub.'s mark Tsuruya Kinsuke, d. Kyowa 1 (1801), trimmed, soiled, rubbed, laid down, Prof. H.R.W. Kuhne Coll., (06-11-93, Sotheby-London, #299, illus.), each approx. 12⅝ x 5⅝ in., (32.1 x 14.3 cm.), woodblock (BP 2070, DM 5121, FR 17,266, Y 334,324).

BI *Half-Length Portrait Of Sawamura Gennosuke,* Oban, s. Ichiyosai Toyokuni ga, pub.'s mark Kawaju, d. Kyowa 3 (1803), trimmed, worm holes, soiled, rubbed, Prof. H.R.W. Kuhne Coll., est. BP 2,5/3,500, (06-11-93, Sotheby-London, #295, illus.), 13⅞ x 9⅝ in., (35.2 x 24.4 cm.), woodblock.

BI *Ichikawa Danjuro VI As Arajishi Otokonosuke,* Oban, s. Toyokuni ga, pub.'s mark Tsuruya Kinsuke, d. Kansei 11 (1799), trimmed, creased, worm holes repaired, laid down, soiled, rubbed, Prof. H.R.W. Kuhne Coll., est. BP

2,5/4,000, (06-11-93, Sotheby-London, #289, illus.), 13 x 9⅛ in., (33 x 23.2 cm.), woodblock.

BI *Ichikawa Danjuro VI As Oyamada Taro And Bando Minosuke As Nagasaki Jiro,* Oban, s. Toyokuni ga, censor's seal kiwame, pub.'s mark Izumiya Ichibei, d. Kansei 10 (1798), faded, worm holes repaired, paper attached to re-enforce margin, Prof. H.R.W. Kuhne Coll., est. BP 1,8/2,200, (06-11-93, Sotheby-London, #279, illus.), 15 x 9⅞ in., (38.1 x 25.1 cm.), woodblock.

BI *Ichikawa Danjuro VII As Kagekiyo,* Surimono, s. Toyokuni ga w/a toshidama seal, d. Bunsei 7 (1824), trimmed, rubbed, soiled, Prof. H.R.W. Kuhne Coll., est. BP 6/800, (06-11-93, Sotheby-London, #341), 8 x 5½ in., (20.3 x 14 cm.), woodblock.

$1137* *Ichikawa Danjuro VII In Shibaraku Role,* Surimoni, kakuban, s. Toyokuni ga, d. Bunka 9 (1812) or Bunsei 7 (1824), creased, rubbed, Prof. H.R.W. Kuhne Coll., (06-11-93, Sotheby-London, #306, illus.), 8⅝ x 7¼ in., (21.9 x 18.4 cm.), woodblock, color w/gold and silver pigment (BP 747, DM 1848, FR 6230, Y 120,637).

$1312* *Ichikawa Dannosuke III, Iwai Kumesaburo II And Iwai Hanshiro V In Female Roles: Three,* Oban, 3 sheets of a pentatych, s. Toyokuni ga, censor's seal, pub.'smark Matsumura Tatsuemon, d. c. 1814, rubbed, creased, Prof. H.R.W. Kuhne Coll., (06-11-93, Sotheby-London, #300, illus.), each approx. 15 x 10¼ in., (38.1 x 26 cm.), woodblock (BP 862, DM 2132, FR 7189, Y 139,204).

$1750* *Ichikawa Danzo IV As Hokaibo,* Hosoban, s. Toyokuni ga, pub.'s mark Nishimuraya Yohachi, d. Kyowa 1(1801), Prof. H.R.W. Kuhne Coll., (06-11-93, Sotheby-London, #319), 13 x 5⅞ in., (33 x 14.9 cm.), woodblock (BP 1150, DM 2844, FR 9589, Y 185,676).

BI *Ichikawa Omezo And Kirinodomi Monzo At Leisure,* Oban, s. Toyokuni ga, censor's date-seal sarusho, pub.'s mark TsutayaJuzaburo, d. Kansei 12 (1800), faded, trimmed, creased, soiled, Prof. H.R.W. Kuhne Coll., est. BP 1/1,500, (06-11-93, Sotheby-London, #342, illus.), 14 x 9⅝ in., (35.6 x 24.4 cm.), woodblock.

$2625* *Ichikawa Omezo And Otani Tomoemon: A Pair,* Hosoban, diptych(?) or 2 sheets from a triptych (?), s. Toyokuni ga,censor's seal kiwame, pub.'s mark Wakasaya Yoichi, d. Kansei 7 (1795), wormed, soiled, rubbed, Prof. H.W.R. Kuhne Coll., (06-11-93, Sotheby-London, #287, illus.), one 12⅝ x 5⅝ in., (32.1 x 14.3 cm.), other 12⅝ x 5¾ in., (32.1 x 14.3 cm.), woodblock (BP 1725, DM 4266, FR 14,384, Y 278,515).

BI *Ichikawa Yaozo As Ume No Yoshibei And Segawa Kikunojo As His Wife Koume,* Oban, s. Toyokuni ga, pub.'s mark Uemura Yohei, d. Kyowa 1 (1801), soiled, creased, wormed, Prof. H.R.W. Kuhne Coll., est. BP 2/3,000, (06-11-93, Sotheby-London, #313, illus.), 11⅜ x 6¼ in., (28.9 x 15.9 cm.), woodblock.

$8401* *Ichikawa Yaozo III As Fuwa No Monzaemon,* Oban, s. Toyokuni ga, censor's seal kiwame, pub.'s mark Izumiya Ichibei, d. Kansei 6 (1794), center fold mark, wormage restored, trimmed, soiled, Prof. H.R.W. Kuhne Coll., (06-11-93, Sotheby-London, #277, illus.), 14½ x 9¼ in., (36.8 x 23.5 cm.), woodblock (BP 5520, DM 13,654, FR 46,033, Y 891,353).

BI *Ichikawa Yaozo III As Soga No Goro,* Oban, s. Toyokuni ga, censor's seal kiwame, pub.'s mark Izumiya Ichibei, d. Kansei 8 (1796), faded, trimmed, wormage repaired, soiled, rubbed, Prof.H.R.W. Kuhne Coll., est. BP 650/850, (06-11-93, Sotheby-London, #351), 14⅝ x 5½ in., (37.1 x 14 cm.), woodblock.

BI *Ichikawa Yaozo III As The Ill-Fated Lover Obiya Choemon And Iwai Kumesaburo As His Young Sweetheart Ohan,* Oban, s. Toyokuni ga, censor's seal Kiwame, pub.'s mark Yamadaya Jubei?, d. Kyowa 3 (1803), trimmed, wormage, laid down, Prof. H.R.W. Kuhne Coll., est. BP 1,5/1,800, (06-11-93, Sotheby-London, #325, illus.), 14⅝ x 10⅛ in., (37.1 x 25.7 cm.), woodblock.

BI *Inside View Of The Nakamura-za Theatre: Four,* Oban, triptych, s. Toyokuni ga, censor's seal kiwame, pub.'s mark Nishimuraya Yohachi, d. Kansei 7 (1795), worm holes, rubbed, creased, Prof. H.R.W.Kuhne Coll., est. BP 450/650, (06-11-93, Sotheby-London, #275), each sh approx. 15 x 9⅝ in., (38.1 x 24.4 cm.), woodblock.

BI *Iwai Hanshiro IV And Ichikawa Danzo IV,* Aiban, s. Toyokuni ga, pub.'s mark Tsuruya Kinsuke, d. Kansei 11 (1799), soiled, rubbed, creased, Prof. H.R.W. Kuhne Coll., est. BP 1,5/2,000, (06-11-93, Sotheby-London, #309, illus.), 13 x 8¾ in., (33 x 22.2 cm.), woodblock.

BI *Iwai Hanshiro V And Otani Tomoemon II In Unidentified Female And Samurai Roles,* Oban, s. Toyokuni ga, censor's seal kiwame, censor's date-seal TenthMonth, pub.'s mark Sumi, d. Bunka 2 (1805), trimmed, soiled, creased, stained,Prof. H.R.W. Kuhne Coll., est. BP 1,2/1,600, (06-11-93, Sotheby-London, #346, illus.), 14⅜ x 9⅝ in., (36.5 x 24.4 cm.), woodblock.

BI *Iwai Hanshiro V As Kaidomaru, Bando Mitsugoro III As Yama Uba And Ichikawa Omezo As Yamazen Yokizo,* Oban, s. Toyokuni ga, censor's seal kiwame, pub.'s mark, d. Bunka 2 (1805), creased, wormed, Prof. H.R.W. Kuhne Coll., est. BP 1,5/2,500, (06-11-93, Sotheby-London, #315, illus.), 15 x 9⅞ in., (38.1 x 25.1 cm.), woodblock.

BI *Iwai Hanshiro V In Rapid Transformations,* Chuban, uchiwa-e, s. Toyokuni ga, censor's seal Gyoji aratame, unident. pub.'s mark, d. Bunka 8 (1811), faded, browned, rubbed, soiled, wormed, repaired, Prof. H.R.W. Kuhne Coll., est. BP 5/700, (06-11-93, Sotheby-London, #329), 8¾ x 10¼ in., (22.2 x 26 cm.), woodblock.

BI *Iwai Kumesaburo I And Onoe Matsuske As Onnagata In A Fight Scene,* Oban, sig. trimmed off, pub.'s mark, d. Bunka 1 (1804), trimmed, wormed, soiled, Prof. H.R.W. Kuhne Coll., est. BP 1/1,500, (06-11-93, Sotheby-London, #326, illus.), 10⅞ x 9⅝ in., (27.6 x 24.4 cm.), woodblock.

$1400* *"Iwai Kumesaburo I As A Courtesan" and "Segawa Michinosuke As A Princess And Arashi Kanjuro As A Samurai Official": Two,* Hosoban, s. Toyokuni ga, d. c. Kyowa 1-2 (1801-02), faded, trimmed, wormed, fold mark, soiled, Prof. H.R.W. Kuhne Coll., (06-11-93, Sotheby-London, #318), one 12 x 5⅜ in., (30.5 x 13.7 cm.), other 12⅛ x 5¾ in., (30.5 x 13.7 cm.), woodblock (BP 920, DM 2275, FR 7671, Y 148,541).

$1400* *Kataoka Nizaemon VII And Iwai Hanshiro IV,* Oban, s. Toyokuni ga, pub.'s mark Yamaden?, d. Kansei 8 (1796), center fold, soiled, rubbed, wormage/thinned, laid down, Prof. H.R.W. Kuhne Coll., (06-11-93, Sotheby-London, #308, illus.), 14¾ x 10 in., (37.5 x 25.4 cm.), woodblock, grey ground (BP 920, DM 2275, FR 7671, Y 148,541).

BI *Matsumoto Koshiro V And Ichikawa Omezo,* Aiban, s. Toyokuni ga, censor's seal kiwame, pub.'s mark Maruya Bunzaemon, d. Kyowa 3 (1803), creased, rubbed, Prof. H.R.W. Kuhne Coll., est. BP 1/1,500, (06-11-93, Sotheby-London, #324, illus.), 33 x 9⅝ in., (83.8 x 24.4 cm.), woodblock.

BI *Matsumoto Koshiro V As Akushichibyoe Kagekiyo,* Oban, part of a triptych, s. Toyokuni ga, censor's seal kiwame, pub.'s mark Sawamura Seikichi, d. Bunka 3 (1806), wormed, Prof. H.R.W. Kuhne Coll.,est. BP 900/1,300, (06-11-93, Sotheby-London, #347, illus.), 14¾ x 10 in., (37.5 x 25.4 cm.), woodblock.

$1575* *Matsumoto Koshiro V Standing Under A Gingko Tree,* Oban, probably part of a triptych, s. Toyokuni ga, censor's seal kiwame, pub.'s mark Tsuruya Kinsuke, d. c. Bunda 5 (1808), trimmed, laid down, Prof. H.R.W. Kuhne Coll., (06-11-93, Sotheby-London, #297, illus.), 14⅜ x 9⅞ in., (36.5 x 25.1 cm.), woodblock (BP 1035, DM 2560, FR 8630, Y 167,109).

$630* *Nakamura Daikichi, Bando Mitsugoro III And Nakamura Shigan,* Chuban, uchiwa-e, s. Toyokuni ga, censor's seal u aratame, pub.'s mark Shimizuya, d. Bunsei 2 (1819), rubbed, trimmed, soiled, thinned, Prof. H.R.W.Kuhne Coll., (06-11-93, Sotheby-London, #330, illus.), 8⅞ x 10 in., (22.5 x 25.4 cm.), woodblock (BP 414, DM 1024, FR 3452, Y 66,844).

BI *"Nakamura Matsue II", "Onoe Kikugoro III In Female Roles", "MatsumotoKoshiro V", and "Bando Mitsugoro III": Four,* Oban, parts of triptychs, s. Toyokuni ga, censor's seal kiwame, pub'smarks Yorozuya Kichibei, Matsumura Tatsuemon, Moriya Jihei and Yamamoto Heikichi, d. Bunka 13-Bunsei 1 (1816-18), faded, trimmed, wormed, rubbed, soiled, Prof. H.R.W. Kuhne Coll., est.

BP 650/900, (06-11-93, Sotheby-London, #321), each approx. 14⅜ x 9⅞ in., (36.5 x 25.1 cm.), woodblock.

$962* *Nakamura Noshio II As A Young Woman,* Hosoban, s. Toyokuni ga, pub.'s mark Izumiya Ichibei, d. c. Kansei 8-9 (1796-97), soiled, rubbed, Prof. H.R.W. Kuhne Coll., (06-11-93, Sotheby-London, #307, illus.), 12¾ x 5⅞ in., (32.4 x 14.9 cm.), woodblock (BP 632, DM 1563, FR 5271, Y 102,069).

BI *Nakamura Utaemon III And Bando Mitsugoro III And Iwai Hanshiro V As Onnagata: Four,* Oban, part of a triptych, s. Toyokuni ga, pub.'s mark Tsurukin, Eijudo, Suzui and Kawagen, d. c. Bunka 9-10 (1812-13), faded, trimmed, creased, rubbed, soiled, laid down, Prof. H.R.W. Kuhne Coll., est. BP 1m2/1,500, (06-11-93, Sotheby-London, #332), each approx. 14½ x 9¾ in., (36.8 x 24.8 cm.), woodblock.

BI *Nakamura Utaemon III As Tonase, The Wife Of Honzo And Segawa Roko AsOishi, The Wife Of Yuranosuke,* Oban, s. Toyokuni ga, censor's seal kiwame, d. Bunka 6 (1809), centerfold, wormed, trimmed, Prof. H.R.W. Kuhne Coll., est. BP 1,5/1,800, (06-11-93, Sotheby-London, #301, illus.), 14⅝ x 9⅞ in., (37.1 x 25.1 cm.), woodblock.

$962* *Okubi-e Of Segawa Kikunojo III,* Chuban, fan print, s. Toylkuni ga, pub.'s mark Kanochu(?), d. Kansei7 (1795), creases, soiled, complementary sh of paper and colors added, Prof. H.R.W. Kuhne Coll., (06-11-93, Sotheby-London, #276), 8¹⁄₁₆ x 8⅞ in., (20.5 x 22.5 cm.), woodblock (BP 632, DM 1563, FR 5271, Y 102,069).

BI *The Onnagata Actors Segawa Kikusaburo And Segawa Kikunojo II(?),* Oban, s. Toyokuni ga, censor's date-seal sarusho, pub.'s mark TsutayaUuzaburo, d. Kansei 12 (1800), rubbed, soiled, Prof. H.R.W. Kuhne Coll., est. BP 2,5/3,500, (06-11-93, Sotheby-London, #312, illus.), 14½ x 9½ in., (36.8 x 24.1 cm.), woodblock.

$1137* *Onoe Eisaburo As Sakuramaru,* Hosoban, sh from a triptych, s. Toyokuni ga, pub.'s mark Shimizuya, d. Kyowa 3 (1803), trimmed, soiled, Prof. H.R.W. Kuhne Coll., (06-11-93, Sotheby-London, #335, illus.), 12⅛ x 5½ in., (30.8 x 14 cm.), woodblock (BP 747, DM 1848, FR 6230, Y 120,637).

BI *Onoe Eizaburo II At Leisure,* Oban, s. Toyokuni ga, censor's seal kiwame, censor's date-seal, pub.'s mark Tsuruya Kinsuke, d. Bunka 3 (1806), wormed, repaired, Prof. H.R.W. KuhneColl., est. BP 7/900, (06-11-93, Sotheby-London, #343, illus.), 14¾ x 9⅞ in., (37.5 x 25.1 cm.), woodblock.

$1137* *Onoe Matsusuke As A Ghost,* Oban, s. Toyokuni ga, pub.'s mark Tsuruya Kinsuke, d. Bunka 1 (1804),wormed, repaired, soiled, Prof. H.R.W. Kuhne Coll., (06-11-93, Sotheby-London, #303), 14⅞ x 9⅞ in., (37.8 x 25.1 cm.), woodblock, grey ground (BP 747, DM 1848, FR 6230, Y 120,637).

$630* *Picture-Calendars (E-goyomi): Two,* Surimono, e-goyomi, 1st s. Toyokuni ga, d. Bunka 8 (1811) and Genji 1(1864), rubbed, soiled, Prof. H.R.W. Kuhne Coll., (06-11-93, Sotheby-London, #350), one 7½ x 6¾ in., (19.1 x 17.1 cm.), other 3¾ x 5⅛ in., (19.1 x 17.1 cm.), woodblock (BP 414, DM 1024, FR 3452, Y 66,844).

$1260* *Portraits Of Ichikawa Danjuro I And VII: A Pair,* Surimono kakuban, s. ko (late) Toyokuni hitsu, d. c. 1830, rubbed, soiled, creased, laid down, Prof. H.R.W. Kuhne Coll., (06-11-93, Sotheby-London, #317, illus.), one 7¼ x 7 in., (18.4 x 17.8 cm.), other 7⅛ x 6⅞ in., (18.4 x 17.8 cm.), woodblock (BP 828, DM 2048, FR 6904, Y 133,687).

BI *The Portraits Of Ichikawa Danjuro VI In Two Different Roles: A Pair,* Hosoban, both probably parts of polyptychs, s. Toyokuni ga, pub.'s marks Izumiya Ichibei and Nishimuraya Yohachi, d. probably c. Kansei 9-10 (1797-98), faded, trimmed, wormage, restored, soiled, rubbed, Prof. H.R.W. Kuhne Coll., est. BP 1/1,400, (06-11-93, Sotheby-London, #290), one 12¼ x 5⅞ in., (31.1 x 14.9 cm.), other 12 x 5½ in., (31.1 x 14.9 cm.), woodblock.

BI *Sawamura Gennosuke And Segawa Michisaburo,* Oban, s. Toyokuni ga, pub.'s mark Izumiya Ichibei, d. Kyowa 1 (1801),wormed, wormage, rubbed, creased, laid down, Prof. H.R.W. Kuhne Coll., est. BP2,5/3,500, (06-11-93,

Sotheby-London, #310, illus.), 14½ x 9⅞ in., (36.8 x 25.1 cm.), woodblock.

BI *Sawamura Gennosuke As Minamoto Yoshiie And Iwai Kiyotaro As Arakawa Taro,* Chuban, s. Toyokuni ga, pub.'s mark Yamashiroya Fujiemon, d. Kyowa 2(1802), browned, rubbed wormed, restored, Prof. H.R.W. Kuhne Coll., est. BP 800/1,200, (06-11-93, Sotheby-London, #334), 11⅝ x 8 in., (29.5 x 20.3 cm.), woodblock.

$787* *Sawamura Gennosuke II As Aburaya Seibei,* Oban, s. Toyokuni ga, censor's seal kiwame, censor's seal (Gyojiin)Yamashiroya Fujiemon, pub.'s mark Kawachiya Genshichi, d. Bunka 8 (1811), soiled, rubbed, Prof. H.R.W. Kuhne Coll., (06-11-93, Sotheby-London, #348, illus.), 14½ x 10⅛ in., (36.8 x 25.7 cm.), woodblock (BP 517, DM 1279, FR 4312, Y 83,501).

$4551* *Sawamura Sojuro III As Ogishi Kurando,* Oban, s. Toyokuni ga, censor's seal kiwame, pub.'s mark Izumiya Ichibei, d. Kansei 6 (1794), fold, wormage, laid down, soiled, rubbed, Prof. H.R.W.Kuhne Coll., (06-11-93, Sotheby-London, #293, illus.), 14⅞ x 9⅞ in., (37.8 x 25.1 cm.), woodblock (BP 2990, DM 7396, FR 24,937, Y 482,865).

$1400* *Sawamura Sojuro IV Holding A Theatre Programme,* Oban, s. Toyokuni ga, censor's seal kiwame, unident. pub.'s mark, d.,center fold, trimmed, wormed, Prof. H.R.W. Kuhne Coll., (06-11-93, Sotheby-London, #345, illus.), 14¾ x 9¾ in., (37.5 x 24.8 cm.), woodblock (BP 920, DM 2275, FR 7671, Y 148,541).

BI *Scenes From The Drama Chushingura: Two,* Hosoban, s. Toyokuni ga, pub.'s mark Enomoto Kichibei, d. c. Kansei 4-8 (1792-96), trimmed, wormed, soiled, Prof. H.R.W. Kuhne Coll., est. BP 1/1,400, (06-11-93, Sotheby-London, #281), one 12⅝ x 5⅝ in., (32.1 x 14.3 cm.), other 12⅞ x 5⅞ in., (32.1 x 14.3 cm.), woodblock.

$3151* *Segawa Kikunojo III As A Shirabyosi Dancer,* Oban, s. Toyokuni ga, censor's seal kiwame, pub.'s mark Izumiya Ichibei, d. Kansei 6 (1794), faded, center fold, Prof. H.R.W. Kuhne Coll., (06-11-93, Sotheby-London, #294, illus.), 15 x 10 in., (38.1 x 25.4 cm.), woodblock (BP 2070, DM 5121, FR 17,266, Y 334,324).

$3851* *Segawa Kikunojo III As Aburaya Osome And Matsumoto Yonesaburo As Detchi Hisamatsu,* Aiban, s. Toyokuni ga, pub.'s mark Yamaden, d. Kansei 8 (1796), wormholes, fold mark, laid down, rubbed, soiled, Prof. H.R.W. Kuhne Coll., (06-11-93, Sotheby-London, #280, illus.), 13½ x 9½ in., (34.3 x 24.1 cm.), woodblock, grey ground (BP 2530, DM 6259, FR 21,101, Y 408,594).

BI *"Segawa Kikunojo III As Oishi, Arashi Hinasuke As Honzo" and "Onoe Matsusuke I As Nakai Ocho, With Nakayama Tomisaboru I As Geigo Kashiku": Two,* Hosoban, s. Toyokuni ga, pub.'s mark Moriya Jihei, soiled, rubbed, trimmed, wormed, Prof. H.R.W. Kuhne Coll., est. BP 900/1,300, (06-11-93, Sotheby-London, #291), one 12⅛ x 5⅜ in., (30.8 x 13.7 cm.), other 12¼ x 5⅝ in., (30.8 x 13.7 cm.), woodblock.

$1487* *"Segawa Kikunojo III As The Courtesan Takao" and "Sawamura Sojuro III As Ashikaga Yorikane": Two,* Oban diptych, s. Toyokuni ga, pub.'s mark Izumiya Ichibei, d. Kansei7 (1795), fold marks, soiled, rubbed, wormage repaired, Prof. H.R.W. Kuhne Coll., (06-11-93, Sotheby-London, #288, illus.), one 14⅞ x 9⅞ in., (37.8 x 25.1 cm.), other 14⅞ x 10 in., (37.8 x 25.1 cm.), woodblock (BP 977, DM 2417, FR 8148, Y 157,772).

BI *Segawa Michinosuke As A Country Maiden,* Oban, s. Toyokuni ga, pub.'s mark, d. c. Bunka 4 (1807), wormed, soiled, creased, Prof. H.R.W. Kuhne Coll., est. BP 1,2/1,700, (06-11-93, Sotheby-London, #298, illus.), 15 x 10¼ in., (38.1 x 26 cm.), woodblock.

BI *Ukiyo Butai Ko - The Vogue For Roko,* Oban, s. Toyokuni ga, pub.'s mark Tsumura, d. c. Bunka 7 (1810), soiled, creased, repaired, laid down, Prof. H.R.W. Kuhne Coll., est. BP 800/1,200, (06-11-93, Sotheby-London, #344, illus.), 15 x 9⅞ in., (38.1 x 25.1 cm.), woodblock.

$10,502* *Yakusha Awase Kagami "Actors Compared As If In Mirrors", Two Vols.,* bound in one, pub. Banshundo Yamadaya Sanshiro of Edo in Kyowa 4 (1804), faded, soiled, rubbed, lit., Prof. H.R.W. Kuhne Coll., (06-11-93, Sotheby-London, #508, illus.), 9¹⁄₁₆ x 6⁷⁄₁₆ in., woodblock

p. in color (BP 6900, DM 17,068, FR 57,545, Y 1,114,271).

BI *Yakusha Konotegashiwa "The Two Faces Of Actors", Vol. 1*, pub. Danjudo of Edo in 1803, wormage, lit., Prof. H.R.W. Kuhne Coll.,est. BP 1,5/1,800, (06-11-93, Sotheby-London, #510, illus.), 8½ x 5¹⁵⁄₁₆ in., (21.6 x 15.1 cm.), woodblock p. in color.

$17,503* *Yakusha Sangaikyo "Amusements Of Actors On The Third Floor", Two Vols.*, bound in one, d. Kansei 13 (1801), faded, good state, collector's seal, ex-coll. Michel Strauss, lit., Prof. H.R.W. Kuhne Coll., (06-11-93, Sotheby-London, #509, illus.), 8⁹⁄₁₆ x 6⅛ in., (21.7 x 15.6 cm.), woodblock p. in color (BP 11,500, DM 28,446, FR 95,907, Y 1,857,082).

BI *Yakusha Sanju-ni So "The Thirty-Two Facial Expressions Of Actors", 1Vol.*, d. Kyowa 2 (1802), pub. Kangetsudo and Koshodo (Tsutaya) of Edo, wormed, soiled, rubbed, lit., Prof. H.R.W. Kuhne Coll., est. BP 3/4,000, (06-11-93, Sotheby-London, #511, illus.), woodblock.

UTAGAWA TOYOMARU   Japanese ac. 1785-1797
$962* *Head And Shoulder Portraits Of Actors With Their Pen Names: Three*, Hosoban, s. Toyomaru ga, d. c. Kansei 2-7 (1790-95), pub. Uenoya, wormed, restored, Prof. H.R.W. Kuhne Coll., (06-11-93, Sotheby-London, #356), each approx. 11 x 5⅜ in., (27.9 x 13.7 cm.), woodblock (BP 632, DM 1563, FR 5271, Y 102,069).

$2275* *Okubi-e Of Ichikawa Monnosuke*, Hosoban, s. Toyomaru ga, d. possibly Kansei 2 (1790), faded, soiled,tears, wormage, fold mark restored, Prof. H.R.W. Kuhne Coll., (06-11-93, Sotheby-London, #257, illus.), 12¾ x 5¾ in., (32.4 x 14.6 cm.), woodblock (BP 1495, DM 3697, FR 12,466, Y 241,379).

UTAGAWA YOSHIFUJI   Japanese 1828-1887
$2625* *Saruwakacho Theatre Street: Three*, Oban, a triptych, s. Yoshifuji ga, pub. Kogaya Katsugoro, d. censor'saratame seal (1862), trimmed, 2 sh attached together, laid down, wormed, Prof.H.R.W. Kuhne Coll., (06-11-93, Sotheby-London, #422, illus.), each sh approx. 14 x 9½ in., (35.6 x 24.1 cm.), woodblock (BP 1725, DM 4266, FR 14,384, Y 278,515).

UTAMARA, Kitagawa
$5170* *"The Courtesan Ochie Of Koise-Ya Teahouse"*, s., good cond.?, (03-28-93, Bakker, #229), sight 11 x 7 in., (27.9 x 17.8 cm.), color woodblock (BP 3473, DM 8434, FR 28,674, Y 601,723).

UTAMARO
$5626* *Cooling Off On The Roof-Top Balcony*, oban, censor's seal kiwame, pub. mark, Iwatoya, s. Utamaro ga, faded, toned, soiled, rubbed, laid-down, mounted on board, ex-coll. Robert Mond, (06-10-93, Sotheby-London, #228, illus.), sheet approx. 15⅜ x 10¹⁄₁₆ in., (39 x 25.5 cm.), (BP 3680, DM 9161, FR 30,844, Y 597,177).

$165* *"Couple With Dolls"*, OBAN TATE, fading, soiling, (05-07-93, Goldberg, #1382, illus.), woodblock (BP 104, DM 261, FR 879, Y 18,168).

$13,186* *Courtesans On Parade*, oban, s. Kitagawa Utamaro ga, faded, soiled, rubbed, laid-down, mounted on board, ex-coll. Robert Mond, (06-10-93, Sotheby-London, #227, illus.), sheet approx. 14⅞ x 9⁵⁄₁₆ in., (37.8 x 23.7 cm.), (BP 8625, DM 21,472, FR 72,292, Y 1,399,639).

$5274* *The Head And Shoulders Of The Courtesan Hana-Ogi*, oban, from series Komei Bijin Rokkasen, pub. mark, Omiya, s. Utamrohitsu, faded, browned, rubbed, soiled, laid-down, (06-10-93, Sotheby-London, #231, illus.), (BP 3450, DM 8588, FR 28,914, Y 559,813).

$495* *"Oiran"*, Oban Tate, soiling, fading, (05-07-93, Goldberg, #1358), woodblock (BP 313, DM 783, FR 2637, Y 54,503).

$17,581* *An Okubi-e Of A Courtesan Of The House Of Matsuba*, oban tate-e, pub. mark, Omiya Genkuro, coll. mark, s. Utamaro hitsu,trimmed, soiled, laid-down, (06-10-93, Sotheby-London, #233, illus.), Grey Ground (BP 11,500, DM 28,629, FR 96,387, Y 1,866,150).

$6681* *An Outing On The Banks Of The Sumida River: Two*, aiban diptych, pub. mark Tsutaya Jusaburo, s. Utamaro ga, full margin, discoloured, worm-holes, left-hand sheet

partly stuck on board, (06-10-93, Sotheby-London, #234, illus.), (BP 4370, DM 10,879, FR 36,628, Y 709,160).

$1320* *Two Courtesans*, s. Utamaro Hitsu, pub. Murata Jirobei, seal, toned, creased, repairs,nagaban, (11-20-92, Skinner, #63C), nagaban (BP 869, DM 2105, FR 7089, Y 164,159).

$13,186* *Yotsude-Ami, The Fishing Net*, oban, censor's seal kiwame, s. Utamaro hitsu, faded, soiled, rubbed,laid-down, mounted, ex-coll. Robert Mond, (06-10-93, Sotheby-London, #229, illus.), each sheet approx. 14¾ x 9⅝ in., (37.5 x 24.5 cm.), (BP 8625, DM 21,472, FR 72,292, Y 1,399,639).

UTAMARO, Kitagawa   Japanese 1750-1806
$1510* *From The Series "Drei Frauen Im Alltag"*, s., format Oban, (04-27-93, Dorotheum, #171, illus.), 10¹⁄₁₆ x 14¹³⁄₁₆ in., (25.6 x 37.6 cm.), (BP 960, DM 2391, FR 8088, Y 169,226, SC 16,800).

BI *Joshoku Kaiko Tewasa Gusa (Women's Work In The Silk-worm-Culture), 1801: Two*, #7 and 11 from series of 12, pub. Tsuruya Kiemon, s. Utamaro hitsu, browned; #7 creased, #11 holes, est. G 1,500, (11-18-92, Bubb Kuyper, #1592), print.

$2014* *Mother And Son*, format Oban, (04-27-93, Dorotheum, #151, illus.), 10⅛ x 14⁹⁄₁₆ in., (25.7 x 37 cm.), (BP 1281, DM 3189, FR 10,787, Y 225,709, SC 22,400).

$1510* *Portrait Of A Young Laundress, c. 1800*, from the series "Spiegel der verheirateten Frauen bei hauslichen Tatigkeiten", signs of wear, format Oban, (04-27-93, Dorotheum, #169, illus.), 9¹⁵⁄₁₆ x 14¾ in., (25.2 x 37.4 cm.), color woodcut (BP 960, DM 2391, FR 8088, Y 169,226, SC 16,800).

$705* *Samurai With His Attendant And A Courtesan*, spotting, format Oban, (04-27-93, Dorotheum, #170, illus.), approx. 9¹³⁄₁₆ x 14¾ in., (25 x 37.5 cm.), color woodcut (BP 448, DM 1116, FR 3776, Y 79,009, SC 7840).

BI *Three Yound Women At A Summer Celebration*, from series Vergnugliche Spiele der Damen, Format Chuban, est. SC 5/7,000, (04-27-93, Dorotheum, #193, illus.), 6⅞ x 9¹⁄₁₆ in., (17.5 x 23 cm.), woodcut.

UTAMARO, Kitagawa (II)   Japanese 19th cent.
BI *Courtesans With Child Approaching Bridge: Two*, est. $250/300, (12-10-92, Sloan, #886), sight 14¾ x 9¾ in., (37.5 x 24.8 cm.), woodblock.

UTAMARO, Kitagawa (II)   Japanese 19th century
$175* *Two Courtesans With Child Approaching Bridge: Two*, (02-04-93, Sloan, #910), 14¾ x 9¾ in., (37.5 x 24.8 cm.), woodcut (BP 122, DM 288, FR 977, Y 21,769).

UTAMARO, Kitagawa (after)
BI *"Beauty Reads Love Letter"*, est. $300/450, (01-15-93, DuMouchelle, #2304, illus.), 15¼ x 10¼ in., (38.7 x 26 cm.), color woodblock print.

UTAMARO II
$495* *Figures At Rygyoku Bridge, c. 1815*, (12-05-92, Eldred, #571, illus.), woodblock (BP 310, DM 772, FR 2630, Y 61,331).

UTAMARO and EISAN
$121* *Japanese Beauties: Two*, (03-25-93, Boos, #265), color woodblock print (BP 82, DM 199, FR 676, Y 14,175).

UTRILLO, Maurice   French 1883-1955
$1891* *Bal De Nuit De L'A.A.A.A.. Magic City, 1925*, tears, taped, (02-04-93, Christie-S. Ken, #149, illus.), 47½ x 31½ in., (120.7 x 80 cm.), color lithograph (BP 1320, DM 3114, FR 10,558, Y 235,228).

$1135* *Le Cabaret Du Lapin Agile (Fabris, 4c), 1924*, whole margins, #22/25, s., editor's drystamp, (04-02-93, Picard, #189), 7½ x 11 in., (19 x 28 cm.), black lithograph on wove (BP 748, DM 1824, FR 6195, Y 129,227).

$55* *"Eiffel Tower (La Tour Eiffel)"*, from "Paris Capitale" Series, s. twice Maurice Utrillo, (02-27-93, Dunning, #1042), sight 14 x 9 in., (35.6 x 22.9 cm.), color lithograph (BP 39, DM 90, FR 307, Y 6493).

$1280* *La Ferme Debray (F., 4d), 1924*, #1/25, s., (04-02-93, Picard, #190), 7½ x 11 in., (19 x 28 cm.), black lithograph on wove (BP 843, DM 2057, FR 6987, Y 145,736).

BI   *"Man And Woman In Street, Montmartre",* s., stain, est. BP 4/600, (10-15-92, Bonhams-Chelsea, #49), sheet 10¾ x 8¾ in., (27.3 x 22.2 cm.), color lithograph.

BI   *"Montmarte",* c. 1925, stone s., t., sun stain, hinges, good cond., est. $150/200, (05-15-93, Cleveland, #433A), 11 x 9 in., (27.9 x 22.9 cm.), color lithograph.

BI   *"Moulin De La Galette",* very good cond., (05-15-93, Cleveland, #434), 8½ x 7 in., (21.6 x 17.8 cm.), lithograph.

$1404*   *La Place Du Tertre Et Le Sacre Coeur (F., 6a), 1925-26,* #1/46, s., (04-02-93, Picard, #192), 11¼ x 8¹¹⁄₁₆ in., (28.5 x 22 cm.), black lithograph on Arches wove (BP 925, DM 2257, FR 7664, Y 159,854).

$1887*   *"La Place Du Tertre" and "La Rue D'Orchampt" (Fabris 4B and 5A), 1924,* s., proofs, 1st from Maitres et petits maitres d'aujourd'hui, 2nd from Essai sur l'histoire de la lithographie, les peintres lithographes de Manet aMatisse, album de lithographies originales, w/blindstamp publisher Frapier, full margins, good cond., defects, handling crease, (06-30-93, Sotheby-London, #709, illus.), one 7 x 10¹⁄₃₂ in., (178 x 254 mm.), the other 7⅞ x 11⅜ in., (178 x 254 mm.), lithograph on wove and smooth Japan (BP 1265, DM 3218, FR 10,857, Y 202,186).

$786*   *La Rue D'Orchampt,* from "Maitres et petits maitres d'aujourd'hui", sig., drystamp, staining, good margins, (06-16-93, Ader Tajan, #142), 7¹³⁄₁₆ x 11¼ in., (19.8 x 28.5 cm.), lithograph on chine volant (BP 524, DM 1305, FR 4379, Y 83,831).

$1199*   *La Rue D'Orchampt (Fabris 5a), 1924,* whole margins, first state, s., drystamp, (06-11-93, Picard, #179), 7⅞ x 11⁷⁄₁₆ in., (200 x 290 mm.), lithograph in black on Japan (BP 788, DM 1949, FR 6570, Y 127,215).

$575*   *La Rue D'Orchampt, 1926,* s., blindstamps, 2nd state proof, blindstamp, inkstamp, full margins, good cond., (05-19-93, Butterfield, #2095), 7⅞ x 11½ in., (200 x 292 mm.), lithograph on Japan (BP 373, DM 935, FR 3149, Y 63,655).

$290*   *Sacre Coeur: Three,* all s. in stone or in crayon, one artist's proof, one w/brown remarque, good cond., some creases, (06-28-93, Loudmer, #119), 14¹⁵⁄₁₆ x 12 in., (380 x 305 mm.), approx. 16⅛ x 12¹⁵⁄₁₆ in., (380 x 305 mm.), black lithographs on wove and Japan nacre (BP 194, DM 493, FR 1660, Y 30,769).

$364*   *Scene De Rue,* s., (05-27-93, Briest, #196), 7¹¹⁄₁₆ x 6⅛ in., (19.5 x 15.5 cm.), black lithograph on Chine (BP 233, DM 584, FR 1969, Y 39,022).

BI   *Strasse In Montmartre, Im Hintergrund Moulin De La Galette,* s., num., est. DM 3,500, (12-05-92, Bassenge, #7785, illus.), 7⅞ x 11¼ in., (20 x 28.6 cm.), lithograph on Japan.

UTRILLO, Maurice (after)

$171*   *"Figures Standing In Front Of A Church",* by Jacques Villon, #139/200, s. by Utrillo, margins, folds around platemark, surface dirt, (12-10-92, Bonhams-Chelsea, #109), plate 19¼ x 11 in., (48.9 x 27.9 cm.), etching w/ aquatint in colors (BP 110, DM 270, FR 924, Y 21,153).

UYTENBROECK, Moses van   c. 1590-1648

$290*   *Der Junge Tobias Erschrickt Bei Dem Anblick Des Fisches (B. und Wurzbach 14), 1620,* prov., (12-01-92, Karl/ Faber, #156), etching (BP 192, DM 462, FR 1575, Y 36,106).

UYTVANCK, Valentin Edgar van

BI   *(Standing Woman), 1921,* s., d., i., margins, good cond., paper discoloration, Late Gerhard Brauer Coll., est. Dfl. 2/300, (05-27-93, Sotheby-Amstrdm, #796), 9¾ x 7¹⁄₁₆ in., (247 x 180 mm.), woodcut on laid.

UZES

$502*   *Malo-Les-Bains Pres Dunkerque,* c. 1900, Chatelles, Imp. L. Geissler, Photolith, cond. B+, (06-11-93, Boisgirard, #156), 47¼ x 33⁷⁄₁₆ in., (120 x 85 cm.), poster (BP 330, DM 816, FR 2751, Y 53,263).

VACHON, John

$1320*   *High Octane,* orig. letterpress mount, photog.'s credit, t., 1930s, (04-07-93, Swann, #574, illus.), 9¾ x 13 in., pho-

tograph, silver print (BP 872, DM 2135, FR 7225, Y 149,966).

BI   *Mexican Woman, Saginaw County, Michigan, 1941,* handstamp, label, est. $4/600, (10-14-92, Swann, #452, illus.), 10 x 8 in., (25.4 x 20.3 cm.), photograph, silver print.

$357*   *Parade Spectators, Cincinnati,* F.S.A., photographer's notations, F.S.A. handstamps, 1930s, (04-07-93, Swann, #310, illus.), 8 x 10 in., photograph, silver print (BP 236, DM 577, FR 1954, Y 40,559).

$247*   *"The Poor Boy's Friend"; The Proprietor Calls Himself, 1938,* handstamp, (10-14-92, Swann, #453, illus.), 10 x 8 in., (25.4 x 20.3 cm.), photograph, silver print (BP 145, DM 361, FR 1226, Y 29,932).

VAIANI, Alessandro

BI   *The Entombment (B. 1), c. 1628,* margins, good cond., soiling, Dora Jane Janson Coll. and H.W. JansonEstate, est. $1,5/2,000, (05-13-93, Sotheby-NY, #344), 7⅜ x 9½ in., (186 x 240 mm.), etching.

VAIL, Roger   20th cent.

$209*   *Moving Ship, Sacramento,* prov., (05-16-93, Hindman, #354), 23 x 17¼ in., photograph, silver print (BP 136, DM 337, FR 1136, Y 23,274).

BI   *"Petrochemical Tanks And Tower", 1980,* s., est. $4/600, (11-16-92, Butterfield, #6207, illus.), 14½ x 11¼ in., (369 x 285.1 mm.), photograph, gelatin silver print.

VAILLANT

$210*   *SNCF: Perros-Guirrec. La Cote De Granit,* p. L. Serre, good cond., (11-19-92, Ribeyre/Baron, #122), 39⅜ x 24⁷⁄₁₆ in., (100 x 62 cm.), poster (BP 138, DM 335, FR 1128, Y 26,116).

VAILLANT, Wallerant   1623-1677

$708*   *Zwei Frauen Lesen Einen Brief (Hollstein 71 II),* prov., (06-04-93, Bassenge, #5386), 13¹⁄₁₆ x 10⅞ in., (33.1 x 27.6 cm.), mezzotint (BP 468, DM 1150, FR 3875, Y 76,359).

VAILLAT

$522*   *Portrait Of A French Gentleman Holding A Pocket Watch In His Left Hand, 1850,* (10-14-92, Swann, #145, illus.), photograph, half-plate oval daguerreotype (BP 306, DM 764, FR 2591, Y 63,257).

VALADE

$105*   *"Chiens" and "Tetes De Chevaux": Two,* very good cond., (11-19-92, Ribeyre/Baron, #156), each 30¹¹⁄₁₆ x 23⅝ in., (78 x 60 cm.), poster (BP 69, DM 167, FR 564, Y 13,058).

VALADIE

BI   *Ensemble De 5,* s., SL 28/50, est. FF1,800/2,000, (06-28-93, Loudmer, #120), approx. 10⅝ x 16⁵⁄₁₆ in., (270 x 415 mm.), sh approx. 20¼ x 14¾ in., (270 x 415 mm.), color etchings on Japan nacre.

VALADON, Suzanne   French 1865-1938

$10,822*   *18 Planches Originales De Suzanne Valadon Gravees De 1895 A 1910, S.Valadon, Paris, 1932,* (Roger-Marx, 1-18), 1895-1910: An Album, 2 title pgs., preface, catalogue of plates by Claude Roger-Marx, s.,num. 44/75, each plate s., margins, surface dirt, rubbing, very good cond., (12-01-92, Christie-London, #549, illus.), overall S. 22⁹⁄₁₆ x 18⁵⁄₁₆ in., (573 x 465 mm.), etchings, soft-ground etchings and drypoints on BFK Rives (BP 7150, DM 17,249, FR 58,783, Y 1,347,361).

BI   *Am Ufer, 1904,* s., est. DM 1,200, (05-26-93, Lempertz, #515), 17¹⁵⁄₁₆ x 14⅜ in., (45.6 x 36.5 cm.), etching on BFK Rives wove.

$385*   *"Les Baigneuses",* s. S. Valadon 1904, (04-25-93, Bakker, #52, illus.), 9¼ x 8¾ in., (23.5 x 22.2 cm.), etching (BP 245, DM 609, FR 2057, Y 42,523).

BI   *Catherine Prepare Le Tub Et Louise Nue Se Coiffe (P. E7), 1895,* s., pub. Deragnes, 1932, full margins, good cond., glue remains, est.$8/1,200, (05-19-93, Butterfield, #1969, illus.), 9 x 8⅞ in., (229 x 225 mm.), soft ground etching w/aquatint on Rives BFK.

$1535*   *Catherine S'Epongeant (Petrides E12), 1908,* s., d., margins, good cond., staining, (12-03-92, Sotheby-London, #588, illus.), 8⅜ x 8 in., (214 x 203 mm.), soft-ground etching w/drypoint on wove (BP 990, DM 2414, FR 8239, Y 190,992).

$773* *Catherine S'Epongeant, 1908*, s., d. in plate, crayon s., frame trace, (06-28-93, Loudmer, #383), 8⁷⁄₁₆ x 8¹⁄₁₆ in., (215 x 205 mm.), sh 12⅝ x 11¼ in., (215 x 205 mm.), black etching and softground etching on wove (BP 518, DM 1314, FR 4425, Y 82,016).

$1320* *Fille Aux Gros Seins Femme Vieille (Roger-Marx 14), 1908*, from 18 Planches originales de Suzanne Valadon, S. Valadon, 1932, s., full margins, foxmark, tear, taped to overmat, (11-09-92, Christie-NY, #228), (333 x 292 mm.), drypoint on Rives (BP 873, DM 2107, FR 7120, Y 163,812).

BI *"Grand Mere Et Enfant", 1923*, s., margins, fold, foxing, good cond., est. $8-1,200, (10-31-92, Cleveland, #347, illus.), 9⅛ x 8⅜ in., (23.2 x 21.3 cm.), etching.

$825* *L'Aide Aux Artistes, 1927*, L'A.A.A.A., B+ cond., marginal cracking, yellowed, (08-06-92, Swann, #278, illus.), 47½ x 30 in., (120.7 x 76.2 cm.), (BP 431, DM 1219, FR 4117, Y 105,230).

$413* *Trois Femmes A La Toilette (P., E22), 1928*, s., reddish stains, (04-02-93, Picard, #195), 8¹¹⁄₁₆ x 11⁷⁄₁₆ in., (22 x 29 cm.), black lithograph on Arches wove (BP 272, DM 664, FR 2254, Y 47,023).

VALCKERT, Werner van den (after)
$5491* *The Mocking Of Christ (Holl. 2; Van Thiel 1983 P.N. 4)*, trimmed, paper losses, tears, defects, fair cond., laid down, (06-30-93, Sotheby-London, #241, illus.), 18⅝ x 34½ in., (473 x 876 mm.), woodcut p. from 3 blocks, on 3 sheets of paper (BP 3680, DM 9366, FR 31,594, Y 588,342).

VALDIVIA, Marco de
BI *Nudes: Four*, 1970s, three s., #3/50, each approx. 505 x 405mm, est. BP 2/300, (05-07-93, Sotheby-London, #396), photograph, silver print.

VALEGIO, Giacomo   ac. 1570-1590
$633* *Christ And The Woman Of Samaria, (Le B. 9)*, c. 1580, after Marco del Moro, watermark, margins, pinholes, stains, (12-01-92, Christie-London, #55), P. 16⁵⁄₁₆ x 11¼ in., (415 x 286 mm.), engraving (BP 418, DM 1009, FR 3438, Y 78,810).

VALENCIA, Ortega
$120 *Toros En Cadiz, September, 1957*, folds, damage, (09-24-92, Alderfer, #237), 25 x 92 in., (63.5 x 233.7 cm.), (BP 70, DM 178, FR 604, Y 14,435).

VALENTA, Caroline
$605* *Texas City Disaster, 1947*, photog.'s sig., notations, label, (04-07-93, Swann, #364, illus.), 13⅜ x 10½ in., photograph, silver print (BP 400, DM 978, FR 3311, Y 68,734).

VALENTE, Alfredo   1899-1973
$2475* *14th Street*, t. by photog., 1930s, (10-15-92, Sotheby-NY, #217, illus.), 13¾ x 10⅜ in., (34.9 x 26.4 cm.), photograph, toned gelatin silver print (BP 1515, DM 3684, FR 12,494, Y 296,941).

BI *Black Nude*, c. 1930, credit stamp, est. $2/3,000, (10-13-92, Christie-NY, #375, illus.), 13½ x 10½ in., (34.3 x 26.7 cm.), photograph, toned gelatin silver print.

BI *The Depression, New York City, 1930*, Alfredo Valente Estate, est. $2/3,000, (04-06-93, Sotheby-NY, #96, illus.), 13⅝ x 10⅜ in., photograph.

BI *Grace Kelly, 1949*, t., d., est. $1/1,500, (04-08-93, Christie-NY, #348, illus.), 13⅝ x 10¾ in., (34.6 x 27.3 cm.), photograph, gelatin silver print.

BI *Lauren Bacall*, 1930s, credit stamp, est. $1,2/1,800, (04-08-93, Christie-NY, #349, illus.), 13½ x 10⅝ in., (34.3 x 27 cm.), photograph, gelatin silver print.

$660* *Leslie Howard's Hands*, photog.'s notations ink, handstamp, 1930s, (04-07-93, Swann, #575, illus.), 10 x 13¼ in., photograph, silver print (BP 436, DM 1067, FR 3612, Y 74,983).

BI *Marsden Hartley*, c. 1938, backed w/board, credit stamp, t. in unidentified hand, est. $1,5/2,500, (10-15-92, Sotheby-NY, #218, illus.), 13½ x 10⅝ in., (34.3 x 27 cm.), photograph, gelatin silver print.

BI *Montgomery Clift*, c. 1938, est. $2/3,000, (04-06-93, Sotheby-NY, #97, illus.), 13⅝ x 10⅝ in., photograph.

BI *Noel Coward*, late 1930s, embossed credit recto, credit stamp, est. $1,2/1,800, (10-13-92, Christie-NY, #374,

illus.), 13½ x 10½ in., (34.3 x 26.7 cm.), photograph, gelatin silver print.

$575* *Paul Manship, Sculptor*, c. 1938, t., credit stamp, (04-08-93, Christie-NY, #350, illus.), 13½ x 9½ in., (34.3 x 24.1 cm.), photograph, gelatin silver print (BP 377, DM 924, FR 3127, Y 65,252).

BI *Peoples Theatre, New York City, 1930*, Alfredo Valente estate, est. $2/3,000, (04-06-93, Sotheby-NY, #95, illus.), 13¾ x 10⅜ in., photograph.

BI *Ravi Shankar's Hands*, photog.'s sig. on mount, handstamp, 1930s, est. $700/1,000, (04-07-93, Swann, #576, illus.), 10½ x 13⅜ in., photograph, silver print.

$690* *Selected Portraits: "Noel Coward" and "Leslie Howard", 1930: Two*, photog. name stamp, (04-06-93, Sotheby-NY, #98, illus.), each approx. 9½ x 7½ in., photograph (BP 456, DM 1112, FR 3764, Y 78,695).

BI *Yasuo Kuniyoshi In His Studio*, photog.'s handstamp, 1930s, est. $6/900, (04-07-93, Swann, #577, illus.), 14 x 11 in., photograph, silver print.

$550* *Yasuo Kuniyoshi In His Studio*, handstamp, 1930's, (10-14-92, Swann, #581, illus.), 11 x 13½ in., (27.9 x 34.3 cm.), photograph, silver print (BP 323, DM 805, FR 2730, Y 66,651).

VALENTI, Italo   b. 1912
$276* *Composizione, 1958*, #30/50, s., (09-04-92, Germann, #598), 7⁵⁄₁₆ x 5½ in., (185 x 140 mm.), color lithograph (BP 138, DM 387, FR 1317, Y 33,973, SF 345).

VALERIO, R. de
$522* *Cherry Maurice Chevalier*, Devambez, B+ cond., fraying, tape stains, (08-06-92, Swann, #279, illus.), 62 x 46½ in., (157.5 x 118.1 cm.), (BP 273, DM 771, FR 2605, Y 66,582).

BI *Citroen*, excell. cond., est. BP 1/1,500, (02-04-93, Christie-S. Ken, #150, illus.), 39 x 45½ in., (99.1 x 115.6 cm.), color lithograph.

VALESKA, Shonna   contemporary
$248* *Balanchine's Ballerinas: Eleven*, portfolio, Ed. 10/50, (12-10-92, Sloan, #2729), each 16 x 20 in., (40.6 x 50.8 cm.), photograph (BP 160, DM 392, FR 1340, Y 30,678).

VALK, Hendrik   1897-1986
$72* *Untitled*, s., #VI/X, margins, good cond.?, (12-09-92, Sotheby-Amstrdm, #661), 20½ x 17¾ in., (521 x 451 mm.), color silkscreen on wove (BP 46, DM 113, FR 386, Y 8927, G 127).

VALLARINO, Vincent
BI *Calla Diptych, 1981: Two*, s., num. by photog., s., t., num. 1/10 by photog., #1/10 ed., est. $2/3,000, (10-15-92, Sotheby-NY, #609, illus.), each, approx. 19 x 15¼ in., (48.3 x 38.7 cm.), photograph, dyptich of 2 gelatin silver prints.

VALLET, Edouard   1876-1929
BI *Bateaux-Lavoirs A Geneve*, stone s., est. SF 170/190, (10-14-92, Germann, #630), 12¹¹⁄₁₆ x 9¹⁵⁄₁₆ in., (322 x 252 mm.), color lithograph.

$2127* *Drei Walliser Bauernmadchen In Tracht, 1917*, stone s., d., (10-21-92, Dobiaschofsky, #1622), 50¹³⁄₁₆ x 35¹³⁄₁₆ in., (129 x 91 cm.), poster color lithograph (BP 1320, DM 3218, FR 10,924, Y 259,074, SF 2880).

$2482* *Walliser Woche In Zurich, 1927*, stone s., d., (10-21-92, Dobiaschofsky, #1623), 50³⁄₁₆ x 35⁷⁄₁₆ in., (127.5 x 90 cm.), poster color lithograph (BP 1541, DM 3755, FR 12,748, Y 302,314, SF 3360).

VALLOTTON, Felix   Swiss 1865-1925
$5703* *Le 1er Janvier (Vallotton et Goerg 167; Una Johnson 145), 1896*, num., 1 of 100, staining, full margins, (02-24-93, Picard, #242), wood engraving on thick simili-Japan (BP 3977, DM 9258, FR 31,387, Y 669,209).

BI *Les Amateurs D'Estampes (Godefroy 105), 1892*, from book L'Escarmouche 1893, w/gravure originale sur bois par F. Vallotton p. below, pub. Edmond Sagot, margins, est. BP 200/250, (11-30-92, Phillips-London, #483), border 7⅜ x 9⅞ in., (187 x 251 mm.), woodcut on wove.

$13,188* *Le Bain (L.G. 146, M.V. et Ch. G. 148), 1894*, s., drystamp, good margins, (06-11-93, Picard, #181, illus.), 7¹⁄₁₆ x 8 13/16 in., (180 x 224 mm.), wood engraving on creme wove (BP 8665, DM 21,433, FR 72,263, Y 1,399,257).

BI *Le Bain (Vallotton/Georg 148; Stein & Karshan 88), 1894,* crayon s., num. 85, for L'Estampe Originale, Album 8, blindstamp, full margins, good cond., scuffs, creases, est. $12/15,000, (11-05-92, Sotheby-NY, #463, illus.), 7 1/4 x 8 7/8 in., (183 x 226 mm.), sheet 8 1/2 x 10 1/8 in., (183 x 226 mm.), woodcut on cream wove mounted on ochre cardboard.

$13,745* *"C'est La Guerre!", 1916: Six,* s., num., (06-23-93, Kornfeld, #847, illus.), 17 11/16 x 21 1/4 in., (45 x 54 cm.), woodcut on imperial Japan (BP 9338, DM 23,257, FR 78,230, Y 1,497,440, SF 20,700).

BI *Le Chapeau Vert (V./G. 52), 1896,* crayon s., num. 40, pub. in album Etudes de Femmes, margins, good cond., foxing overall, creases, est. $1,5/2,000, (11-05-92, Sotheby-NY, #464), 15 3/8 x 10 3/8 in., (390 x 265 mm.), sheet 17 3/4 x 12 5/8 in., (390 x 265 mm.), lithograph p. in colors on chine volant.

$2198* *Les Cygnes (L. Godefroy 94, M. Vallotton et Ch. Goerg 100 a), 1892,* s., frame traces, large margins, (06-11-93, Picard, #180), 5 5/16 x 6 7/8 in., (135 x 175 mm.), wood engraving on wove (BP 1444, DM 3572, FR 12,044, Y 233,210).

$330* *Ed. Sagot,* A cond., (08-06-92, Swann, #280, illus.), 9 1/2 x 12 3/4 in., (24.1 x 32.4 cm.), (BP 172, DM 488, FR 1647, Y 42,092).

$124* *"Immortels Passes, Presents Ou Futurs" Frontispice. (M. Vallotton etCh. Goerg, 24), 1892-94: Two,* reddish stains, good margins, (04-02-93, Picard, #196), lithographs, first, on folded blue-gray paper; second, on one sheet white wove (BP 82, DM 199, FR 677, Y 14,118).

$25,074* *Instruments De Musique: "Le Violincelle", "La Flute", "Le Violin", "Le Piano", "La Guitare" and "Le Piston" (V. et G. 171 a 176), 1896-1897: Six,* s., num., soiling, good margins, (02-24-93, Picard, #243), wood engraving on thin creme wove (BP 17,485, DM 40,705, FR 137,997, Y 2,942,267).

BI *La Jungfrau, 1892,* image s., mono., lit., est. SF 1,8/2,300, (11-13-92, Koller, #5464), 5 11/16 x 10 1/16 in., (14.5 x 25.5 cm.), woodcut on wove.

$3436* *L'Etranger (Vallotton-Goerg 137/a), 1894,* s., (06-23-93, Kornfeld, #844, illus.), woodcut on wove (BP 2334, DM 5814, FR 19,556, Y 374,333, SF 5175).

$1133* *La Manifestation (Vallotton-Goerg 110), 1893,* s., num., (06-04-93, Bassenge, #5833, illus.), 7 15/16 x 12 5/8 in., (20.3 x 32 cm.), woodcut on wove (BP 750, DM 1840, FR 6201, Y 122,196).

$2166* *"La Modiste" (Schultze u.a. 117), 1894,* s., (11-28-92, Grisebach, #828, illus.), 7 1/8 x 8 7/8 in., (18.1 x 22.6 cm.), woodcut on Japan (BP 1430, DM 3451, FR 11,714, Y 269,571).

$516* *Le Mont Blanc (M.V. et Ch. G., 87), 1892,* s., good margins, (04-02-93, Picard, #197), 10 1/16 x 5 5/8 in., (25.5 x 14.3 cm.), wood engravinf on creme wove (BP 340, DM 829, FR 2817, Y 58,750).

$23,579* *La Paresse (L.G. 146, M.V. et Ch. G. 169), 1896,* s., large margins, (06-11-93, Picard, #182, illus.), wood engraving on creme wove (BP 15,492, DM 38,321, FR 129,200, Y 2,501,751).

$202* *A Paul Verlaine (M. Vallotton, Ch. Goerg, 80a), 1891,* edit. 50, yellowed, creases, large margins, (02-03-93, Ader Tajan, #207), 5 3/16 x 4 3/16 in., (13.1 x 10.7 cm.), woodcut on creme, signed wove (BP 141, DM 333, FR 1128, Y 25,128).

$2691* *Les Petites Baigneuses (Vallotton-Goerg 121, 122, 126b), 1893: Three,* s., foxed, (06-04-93, Bassenge, #5834, illus.), each approx. 1 5/8 x 2 5/16 in., (4.2 x 5.8 cm.), woodcut on machine made paper (BP 1780, DM 4370, FR 14,729, Y 290,229).

$2138* *Le Piano (Vall.-G. 174/c), 1896,* mono. stamp, num., (06-23-93, Kornfeld, #846), woodcut on Japan (BP 1452, DM 3618, FR 12,168, Y 232,923, SF 3220).

$1733* *Les Trois Baigneuses (Vallotton-Georg 133a),* s. in blue, (12-04-92, Bassenge, #6975), 7 1/16 x 4 5/16 in., (18 x 11 cm.), woodcut on hand-made (BP 1112, DM 2760, FR 9363, Y 216,355).

$3767* *Le Violin (M.V. et Ch. G., 173),* num. 68, s., reddish stains, good margins, (04-02-93, Picard, #199), 8 3/4 x 7 in., (22.3 x 17.8 cm.), wood engraving on wove (BP 2481, DM 6054, FR 20,562, Y 428,897).

$2062* *Le Violoncelle (Vall.-G. 171/c), 1896,* mono. stamp, num., blindstamp, stained in margin, (06-23-93, Kornfeld, #845), woodcut on Japan (BP 1401, DM 3489, FR 11,736, Y 224,643, SF 3105).

BI *Wolken,* new print, est. DM 200-, (09-25-92, Granier, #3038), sheet 20 9/16 x 11 15/16 in., (52.2 x 30.3 cm.), woodcut on wove.

VALSANGIACOMO, Rino

$247* *Chicco D'Oro, Il Cafe Che Regala Oro,* E. Gilardi, A-cond., (08-06-92, Swann, #281, illus.), 50 1/2 x 35 1/2 in., (128.3 x 90.2 cm.), (BP 129, DM 365, FR 1233, Y 31,505).

VALTAT, Louis French 1869-1952

$619* *La Femme Au Piano,* s., creases, good cond., rare, (06-28-93, Loudmer, #384), 7 11/16 x 7 11/16 in., (195 x 195 mm.), sh 15 3/8 x 9 3/4 in., (195 x 195 mm.), softground etching and aquatint in blackish blue on wove (BP 414, DM 1052, FR 3543, Y 65,676).

$2150* *A Llansa, c. 1895,* s., annot., losses, (02-24-93, Picard, #244), wood engraving in color on thin chine (BP 1499, DM 3490, FR 11,833, Y 252,288).

$239* *Salon D'Automne 1924. Grand Palais,* cond. B, (03-16-93, Boisgirard, #212), 62 3/16 x 46 1/16 in., (158 x 117 cm.), poster (BP 165, DM 397, FR 1350, Y 27,947).

VAN DE LOO

$220* *Asger Jorn Werkverzeichnis, 1976,* (03-24-93, Kunsthallen, #323), print (BP 149, DM 359, FR 1223, Y 25,849, DK 1380).

VAN DE VELDE, Bram 1895-1981

$339* *"Centree",* HC s., (04-04-93, Pescheteau, #314), 19 5/16 x 17 11/16 in., (49 x 45 cm.), lithograph on Japan nacre (BP 223, DM 545, FR 1850, Y 38,597).

VAN DE VELDE, Henry 1863-1957

BI *Plakat. Tropon,* in Pan, est. DM 1,400, (06-10-93, Hauswedell/Nolt, #953), approx. image 12 3/16 x 7 15/16 in., (31 x 20.2 cm.), color lithograph.

VAN DE WYER, Dr. Maurice

BI *High And Dry, c. 1938,* exhib. labels and stamps, est. $1/1,500, (04-08-93, Christie-NY, #225, illus.), 15 1/2 x 11 1/2 in., (39.4 x 29.2 cm.), photograph, gelatin silver print.

VAN DER ZEE, James 1886-1983

$1725* *Portrait Of A Lady With Her Dogs, 1931,* s., d., in neg., (04-08-93, Christie-NY, #62, illus.), 9 5/8 x 7 5/8 in., (24.4 x 19.4 cm.), photograph, gelatin silver print (BP 1131, DM 2771, FR 9380, Y 195,756).

$880* *Post-Mortem Of Child, 1928,* s., d. by photog., (04-07-93, Swann, #578, illus.), 8 x 10 in., photograph, vintage sepia-toned copy print (BP 582, DM 1423, FR 4817, Y 99,977).

VAN DONGEN, Kees van (after)

$354* *La Femme Au Coquelicot,* drystamp, large margins, staining, (06-16-93, Ader Tajan, #88), 17 11/16 x 14 15/16 in., (45 x 38 cm.), color lithograph (BP 236, DM 588, FR 1972, Y 37,756).

$197* *Jeune Peintre A La Pipe Et Au Chapeau,* good margins, drystamp, (06-16-93, Ader Tajan, #90), 20 1/16 x 16 5/16 in., (51 x 41.5 cm.), color print (BP 131, DM 327, FR 1097, Y 21,011).

VAN DYCK, Anthony

$193* *The Reed Offered To Christ (M-H. 15),* prob. later printing, trimmed, staining, foxing, (12-12-92, Weschler, #176), 9 1/2 x 8 1/4 in., (24.1 x 21 cm.), engraving, etching and drypoint (BP 124, DM 304, FR 1042, Y 23,883).

VAN DYCK, Anthony (after)

$167* *Charles I,* proof before all letters, tears, foxing, (11-30-92, Phillips-London, #97), sheet 26 1/3 x 20 1/2 in., (669 x 521 mm.), engraving on laid (BP 110, DM 266, FR 903, Y 20,784).

$300* *The Duke Of Arrenburg (C.S. 2), 1783,* by Richard Earlom, scratch-letter proof before t., 1st state of 2, pub. John Boydell, repaired paper losses/skinning, 1/4 in. margins 3 sides, thread margins, good cond., (11-30-92, Phillips-London, #52), sheet 25¼ x 18¾ in., (641 x 476 mm.), mezzotint on laid (BP 198, DM 478, FR 1622, Y 37,337).

$150* *James Stuart, Duke Of Lennox And Richmond (C.S. 36), 1773,* by Richard Earlom, scratch-letter proof before t., 1st state of 2, pub. by John Boydell, tears, defects, (11-30-92, Phillips-London, #53), sheet 20⅞ x 15 in., (530 x 381 mm.), mezzotint on laid (BP 99, DM 239, FR 811, Y 18,668).

VAN DYKE, Willard b. 1906

$1035* *Death Valley Dunes,* c. 1931, p.l., (04-08-93, Christie-NY, #396, illus.), 7⅜ x 9½ in., (18.7 x 24.1 cm.), photograph, gelatin silver print (BP 679, DM 1663, FR 5628, Y 117,453).

BI *Edward Weston And His Camera, Northern California, 1937: Two,* first num. 13, second num. 05, est. $1,8/2,200, (04-08-93, Christie-NY, #397, illus.), each approx. 6½ x 4½ in., (16.5 x 11.4 cm.), photograph, gelatin silver print.

$110* *Nehi, Oakland, California,* s., d. 1934, (06-13-93, Hindman, #428), 7½ x 9½ in., photograph, silver print (BP 72, DM 179, FR 602, Y 11,575).

BI *Portrait Of Edward Weston,* (1929), p.l., est. $1/1,500, (10-13-92, Christie-NY, #376, illus.), 9⅛ x 6⅞ in., (23.2 x 17.5 cm.), photograph, gelatin silver print.

VAN HOESEN, Beth

$288* *Cup Of Flowers: "Royal Crown Darby With Daisy", "Coxon Belleek With Rose", "Spode With Fuschia" and "R.S. Prussia With Pansies", 1979: Four,* complete portfolio, w/t. page and colophon, s., d., t., annot. pp, pub. artist, blindstamp printer, Katherine Lincoln Press, full margins, very goodcond., surface soiling, original portfolio, (05-19-93, Butterfield, #2190A), sh 13 x 10⅞ in., (330 x 276 mm.), drypoint w/hand-coloring on Rives BFK (BP 187, DM 468, FR 1577, Y 31,883).

BI *"Dolls With Dolls" and "Dolly Ware's Museum", 1991: Two,* s., d., t., #53/60, blindstamp publisher, Trillium Graphics, full margins, very good cond., est. $6/800, (05-19-93, Butterfield, #2191), one 11⅝ x 14½ in., (295 x 368 mm.), the other 12⅞ x 18¹⁵⁄₁₆ in., (295 x 368 mm.), lithograph in colors on wove.

BI *Flowers, Flowered Vase, 1992,* s., d., t., annot., est. $5/700, (05-19-93, Butterfield, #2192), 22¼ x 17⁵⁄₁₆ in., (565 x 440 mm.), lithograph in colors on Arches.

VAN SICHEM, Christoffel 1546-1624

$1222* *Portrait Eines Mannes Mit Federgeschmucktem Hut (Hollstein 135), 1607,* (06-23-93, Kornfeld, #111), woodcut (BP 830, DM 2068, FR 6955, Y 133,130, SF 1840).

VAN SWEINEN, Evert 1686-1710

BI *Vier Manner Und Eine Frau Im Wirtshaus (Wurzbach 5; Hollstein 138),* after Cornelis Bega, est. DM 1,000, (06-10-93, Hauswedell/Nolt, #168), mezzotint.

VAN VECHTEN, Carl

$1380* *"Barcelona, Courtyard Of Hotel Ritz Under Awnings", 1935,* photog. name blindstamp on image; t., d. by photog.; reprod. lim. stamp, (04-06-93, Sotheby-NY, #134, illus.), 13⅞ x 10⅞ in., photograph (BP 911, DM 2223, FR 7529, Y 157,391).

BI *Blanche Knopf, 1932,* t.,d., num. by photog. in ink, reprod limit. stamp, est. $1/2,000, (10-15-92, Sotheby-NY, #461, illus.), 14 x 11 in., (35.6 x 27.9 cm.), photograph, gelatin silver print.

$1035* *George Gershwin, 1933,* photog. reprod. lim. stamp, (04-06-93, Sotheby-NY, #133, illus.), 9¾ x 7⅞ in., photograph (BP 684, DM 1667, FR 5646, Y 118,043).

BI *Paul Robeson's Hands Against A Background Of African Grass Cloth, 1932,* photog.'s blindstamp on image, t., d., num. by photog., reprod. limit. stamp, est. $1,5/2,500, (10-15-92, Sotheby-NY, #463, illus.), 9⅞ x 7⅞ in., (25.1 x 20 cm.), photograph, gelatin silver print.

VAN VLECK, Natalie

$578* *"Still Life With Head", "Abstract, Geometric Cityscape", "Plants, Abstract" and "Standing Nude": Four,* (11-22-92, Litchfield, #102), smallest 6 x 5 in., (15.2 x 12.7 cm.), largest 8¼ x 5¼ in., (15.2 x 12.7 cm.), woodblock print (BP 381, DM 925, FR 3140, Y 71,703).

$468* *"Still Life With Head", "Abstract, Geometric Cityscape", and "Plants, Abstract": Three,* (11-22-92, Litchfield, #101), largest 6 x 5⅜ in., (15.2 x 13.7 cm.), smallest 6 x 5 in., (15.2 x 13.7 cm.), woodblock print (BP 308, DM 749, FR 2542, Y 58,057).

$924* *"Three Nudes, Two Standing, One Lying Down, With Cityscape In Background", "Still Life With Head" and "Abstract, Geometric Cityscape": Three,* (11-22-92, Litchfield, #85), smallest 6 x 5⅜ in., (15.2 x 13.7 cm.), largest 6⅝ x 7 in., (15.2 x 13.7 cm.), woodblock print (BP 609, DM 1479, FR 5019, Y 114,626).

$253* *"Three Seated Nudes", "Still Life With Head" and "Half Length Nude, Geometric" and "Plants, Abstract": Four,* (11-22-92, Litchfield, #76), smallest 3¾ x 2¾ in., (9.5 x 7 cm.), largest 6⅞ x 6½ in., (9.5 x 7 cm.), woodblock print (BP 167, DM 405, FR 1374, Y 31,386).

VANCE, Robert

$9200* *James King Of William, c. 1855,* paper seal, cased, stamped, quarter plate, (04-06-93, Sotheby-NY, #1, illus.), photograph, lightly tinted quarter-plate daguerreotype (BP 6077, DM 14,822, FR 50,191, Y 1,049,270).

VANDERLYN, John (after)

$16,500* *A View Of The Western Branch Of The Falls Of Niagara, 1804,* by Frederick Christian Lewis, margins, scuffs, image repaired splits,repaired tears, staining, foxing, very good cond., (01-22-93, Christie-NY, #303, illus.), borderline 20¹⁵⁄₁₆ x 29¾ in., (532 x 756 mm.), hand-colored aquatint and engraving on wove (BP 10,795, DM 26,236, FR 88,757, Y 2,065,081).

VANDERPANT, John A. 1884-1939

$173* *Some Group Of Seven Members At The Arts And Letters Club, Toronto,* s., i. on mount, lit., (05-18-93, Joyner, #268), 6¾ x 9½ in., photograph (BP 114, DM 279, FR 942, Y 19,315, C$ 220).

VANEK, Jindrich

BI *Portrait Of A Man, 1936,* s., d., annot., photog. label, est. $4/600, (11-16-92, Butterfield, #6208, illus.), 9 x 6½ in., (229 x 165.4 mm.), photograph, gelatin silver print.

VANIER, Bernard

$52* *Fossils And Foliage,* s., #33/35, prov., (06-07-93, Ritchie, #48, illus.), 10½ x 15½ in., (26.6 x 39.4 cm.), color lithograph (BP 34, DM 84, FR 284, Y 5578, C$ 66).

VANITY FAIR, Publisher

$295* *Cricket,* by Vincent Brooks Day and Son, June 9th 1877, staining, (06-30-93, Bonhams-Chelsea, #270, illus.), image 12½ x 7⅜ in., (31.8 x 18.7 cm.), lithograph in colors (BP 198, DM 503, FR 1697, Y 31,608).

$295* *The Demon Bowler,* by Vincent Brook Day and Son, July 13th 1878, (06-30-93, Bonhams-Chelsea, #272, illus.), image 12⅛ x 7¼ in., (30.8 x 18.4 cm.), lithograph in colors (BP 198, DM 503, FR 1697, Y 31,608).

$104* *The Favourite Jockey, Fred Archer,* by Vincent Brooks Day and Son, pub. May 28, 1881, stained, (03-03-93, Bonhams-Chelsea, #199), image 12¼ x 7¼ in., (31.1 x 18.4 cm.), color lithograph (BP 72, DM 171, FR 581, Y 12,152).

$49* *Hoylake,* by Vincent Brooks Day and Son, July 16 1903, wormholes, staining, (06-30-93, Bonhams-Chelsea, #301), image 12½ x 7½ in., (31.8 x 19.1 cm.), lithograph in colors (BP 33, DM 84, FR 282, Y 5250).

$82* *Michael Michailovitch,* by Vincent Brooks Day and Son, January 4 1894, defects, (06-30-93, Bonhams-Chelsea, #27), image 12½ x 7⅝ in., (31.8 x 19.4 cm.), lithograph in colors (BP 55, DM 140, FR 472, Y 8786).

$230* *Ranji,* by Vincent Brooks Day and Son, August 26th 1897, back cover lot, (06-30-93, Bonhams-Chelsea, #278, illus.), image 12¾ x 7⅜ in., (32.4 x 18.7 cm.), lithograph in colors (BP 154, DM 392, FR 1323, Y 24,644).

$42* *Rugby Union,* by Vincent Brooks Day and Son, January 2nd 1892, tears, (06-30-93, Bonhams-Chelsea, #29), sheet 15 x 10¼ in., (38.1 x 26 cm.), lithograph in colors (BP 28, DM 72, FR 242, Y 4500).

VANSEN, C.
   BI *Gibralter,* s., t., d. 1976, num. A/P, 2/2, prov., est. C$ 125/200, (12-01-92, Ritchie, #37), 35½ x 26½ in., (90.2 x 67.3 cm.), color serigraph.

VARENNE, A.
  $499* *Chaussures Cyclistes Rigides Borel, c. 1900,* cond. B, (03-16-93, Boisgirard, #213), 50¹⁵⁄₁₆ x 37 in., (129.5 x 94 cm.), poster (BP 345, DM 830, FR 2819, Y 58,349).

VARGA(S), Alberto
   BI *First Love, 1986,* s., #11/450, est. FF15/18,000, (05-27-93, Briest, #198, illus.), 39⅜ x 25⁹⁄₁₆ in., (100 x 65 cm.), 13-color lithograph.
   BI *Legacy Girl, 1987,* s., #76/450, est. FF8,000/10,000, (05-27-93, Briest, #199), 35⁷⁄₁₆ x 25⁹⁄₁₆ in., (90 x 65 cm.), 13-color lithograph.

VARIN, Raoul
  $935* *"Michigan Avenue Looking North" and "Washington Street", 1927 and 1928: Two,* s., #18/125 and 89/100, (05-16-93, Hindman, #537), larger 17½ x 23 in., (44.5 x 58.4 cm.), hand-colored aquatints (BP 608, DM 1504, FR 5054, Y 103,647).

VARIN, Raoul   American 20th cent.
  $50* *Chicago In 1847,* s., 22/125, (05-16-93, Hanzel, #478), 17 x 11¾ in., (43.2 x 29.8 cm.), aquatint (BP 33, DM 80, FR 270, Y 5543).
  $210* *Michigan Avenue Lookin North, 1863,* s., 26/125, (05-16-93, Hanzel, #479), 12½ x 17½ in., (31.8 x 44.5 cm.), aquatint (BP 137, DM 338, FR 1135, Y 23,279).
  $270* *View Of Wells And Clark Street Bridge, 1861,* s., 40/125, (05-16-93, Hanzel, #477), 12½ x 17½ in., (31.8 x 44.5 cm.), aquatint (BP 176, DM 434, FR 1459, Y 29,930).

VARLEY, Frederick Horsman   Canadian 1881-1969
  $477* *Figures On A Hill, Georgian Bay,* s., (05-18-93, Joyner, #285), 5½ x 6¾ in., (14 x 17.1 cm.), print (BP 311, DM 774, FR 2614, Y 53,159, C$ 605).
  $347* *Sketching Party,* s., (05-18-93, Joyner, #282), 5½ x 6¾ in., (14 x 17.1 cm.), print (BP 226, DM 563, FR 1901, Y 38,672, C$ 440).
   BI *Sketching Party,* s., est. C$ 5/700, (05-18-93, Joyner, #289), 5½ x 6¾ in., (14 x 17.1 cm.), print.

VARLIN (Willy Guggenheim)   1990-1977
  $1557* *Hund, Sein Hund,* #26/60, s., (11-13-92, Koller, #5466), sheet 35⁷⁄₁₆ x 24¹³⁄₁₆ in., (90 x 63 cm.), lithograph on wove mounted on gray paperboard (BP 1006, DM 2444, FR 8242, Y 193,248, SF 2204).
  $1803* *Palmenweg,* Epreuve d'essai, s., (11-13-92, Koller, #5465), 24¹³⁄₁₆ x 35⁷⁄₁₆ in., (63 x 90 cm.), lithograph on wove mounted on gray paperboard (BP 1165, DM 2830, FR 9545, Y 223,781, SF 2552).

VASARELY (after)
  $17* *"Geometrics",* ex-coll., (10-16-92, DuMouchelle, #2482), 28 x 23½ in., (71.1 x 59.7 cm.), poster (BP 10, DM 25, FR 85, Y 2030).
  $28* *"Planterische Folklore",* (10-16-92, DuMouchelle, #2481), 24¾ x 24¾ in., (62.9 x 62.9 cm.), colored poster (BP 17, DM 41, FR 140, Y 3343).

VASARELY, Victor   French b. Hungary 1908
  $176* *Abstract Circle,* s., #98/100, prov., (05-16-93, Hindman, #586), 24½ x 24½ in., (62.2 x 62.2 cm.), color serigraph (BP 114, DM 283, FR 951, Y 19,510).
   BI *Abstract Composition, c. 1957,* s., #62/250, good cond., surface soiling, est. BP 70/100, (11-30-92, Phillips-London, #576), sheet 26¾ x 26¾ in., (679 x 679 mm.), b/w silkscreen.
   BI *Abstract Compositions: Two,* s., #216/250, full margins, good cond., discoloration, est. BP 3/400, (06-30-93, Sotheby-London, #959), each c. 19⅞ x 18⅞ in., (505 x 479 mm.), color silkscreen on wove.
  $109* *"Abstract Design Of Two Spheres",* s., #173/267, (11-19-92, Bonhams-Chelsea, #69), image 23⅜ x 23¼ in., (59.4 x 59.1 cm.), screenprint (BP 72, DM 174, FR 585, Y 13,556).
  $126* *"Abstract Sphere",* s., #65/150, (11-19-92, Bonhams-Chelsea, #68), image 29⅛ x 29 in., (74 x 73.7 cm.), screenprint (BP 83, DM 201, FR 677, Y 15,670).

   BI *Alone Yellow Yellow,* #6/8, est. $1,5/2,000, (03-14-93, Hindman, #298), 37½ x 37½ in., (95.3 x 95.3 cm.), print.
  $352* *Arg-Vit, 1980,* s., full sheet p. to edges, good cond., (05-27-93, Sotheby-Amstrdm, #500), sh 23⅝ x 23⅝ in., (600 x 600 mm.), colored silkscreen on wove (BP 225, DM 565, FR 1904, Y 37,736, G 633).
  $295* *Biddim,* #158/267, D. Rene blindstamp, (09-04-92, Germann, #600), 19¹¹⁄₁₆ x 16⁹⁄₁₆ in., (500 x 420 mm.), color serigraph (BP 148, DM 413, FR 1407, Y 36,312, SF 368).
  $385* *Black/White Squares,* s., num. 146/500, Emmanuel Jacobson Estate, (09-20-92, Hindman, #813), 8⅞ x 7¼ in., (22.5 x 18.4 cm.), serigraph (BP 225, DM 571, FR 1954, Y 47,584).
   BI *Blatt 9 Aus Descartes,* s., #98/138, est. $2/300, (06-11-93, Freemn/Fine Art, #239), 8⅜ x 15⅝ in., (21.3 x 39.7 cm.), serigraph.
  $2054* *"Bruzeau Reflets Vasarely": Thirteen,* s., Editions Nicole Fauche, (04-21-93, Germann, #818), 20½ x 20½ in., (520 x 520 mm.), 10 color serigraph, 3 collage (BP 1333, DM 3283, FR 11,103, Y 227,388, SF 2990).
  $209* *Circle And Square,* s., #162/190, prov., (05-16-93, Hindman, #587), 33 x 16½ in., (83.8 x 41.9 cm.), color serigraph (BP 136, DM 336, FR 1130, Y 23,168).
   BI *Circles On A Square,* s., #206/250, est. C$ 6/800, (12-01-92, Ritchie, #56), 23½ x 23½ in., (59.7 x 59.7 cm.), color serigraph.
  $232* *Composition,* s. Vasarely, (09-30-92, Kunsthallen, #288), poster (BP 131, DM 329, FR 1113, Y 27,841, DK 1265).
  $379* *Composition,* s. 146/200, (09-30-92, Kunsthallen, #289), color serigraph (BP 214, DM 537, FR 1818, Y 45,482, DK 2070).
  $184* *Composition,* s. Vasarely, 37/250, (03-24-93, Kunsthallen, #326), color serigraph (BP 125, DM 301, FR 1023, Y 21,619, DK 1150).
   BI *Composition,* s. Vasarely, 80/150, est. DK 2,500, (03-24-93, Kunsthallen, #324), color serigraph.
  $134* *Composition,* s., #37/300, good margins, (05-06-93, Laurin, #90), color serigraph (BP 85, DM 211, FR 710, Y 14,743).
  $424* *Composition,* s., artist's proof, #X/XXV, (06-12-93, Hauswedell/Nolt, #449), 23¹³⁄₁₆ x 27⅜ in., (60.5 x 69.5 cm.), color serigraph on thick wove (BP 278, DM 690, FR 2319, Y 44,617).
  $565* *Composition,* s., #20/40, (06-12-93, Hauswedell/Nolt, #446), 21¹³⁄₁₆ x 14½ in., (55.4 x 36.8 cm.), serigraph on board (BP 370, DM 920, FR 3091, Y 59,455).
  $468* *Composition,* s., num., (12-13-92, Hindman, #326), 18⅝ x 18⅝ in., color serigraph (BP 299, DM 736, FR 2507, Y 57,899).
  $348* *"Composition Bleu - Rouge - Vert",* #192/250, s., (10-18-92, Pescheteau, #279), 30¹¹⁄₁₆ x 29¹⁵⁄₁₆ in., (78 x 76 cm.), serigraph in colors (BP 211, DM 514, FR 1746, Y 41,552).
  $495* *Composition Blue And Red,* s., num. 19/50, (09-20-92, Hindman, #812), 23½ x 23½ in., (59.7 x 59.7 cm.), color serigraph (BP 290, DM 735, FR 2513, Y 61,179).
  $231* *"Composition Cinetique",* H.C. VII/XXV, s., (01-28-93, Pescheteau, #276), a vue 14³⁄₁₆ x 11 in., (36 x 28 cm.), color serigraph (BP 153, DM 366, FR 1239, Y 28,681).
  $304* *Composition Cynetique,* s., #119/250, creases, (05-27-93, Briest, #204), 27⁹⁄₁₆ x 42¹⁵⁄₁₆ in., (70 x 109 cm.), color serigraph on Arches (BP 195, DM 488, FR 1644, Y 32,590).
  $223* *Composition Cynetique,* s., #209/250, (05-27-93, Briest, #200), 22¹¹⁄₁₆ x 21⁹⁄₁₆ in., (57.7 x 54.8 cm.), color serigraph (BP 143, DM 358, FR 1206, Y 23,907).
  $231* *Composition Et Sette (Editions G. Fall, 1988): Two,* epreuves d'artiste, s., (11-16-92, Briest, #372), one 25⁹⁄₁₆ x 25⁹⁄₁₆ in., (65 x 65 cm.), other 31½ x 27¹⁵⁄₁₆ in., (65 x 65 cm.), serigraph in colors (BP 152, DM 368, FR 1241, Y 28,828).
  $130* *"Composition Or Et Gris",* EA s., (04-04-93, Pescheteau, #311), 15⅜ x 14³⁄₁₆ in., (39 x 36 cm.), color serigraph on wove (BP 86, DM 209, FR 710, Y 14,801).
  $213* *"Composition Orange-Gris",* #165/250, s., (10-18-92, Pescheteau, #280), 30¹¹⁄₁₆ x 29¹⁵⁄₁₆ in., (78 x 76 cm.,

serigraph in colors (BP 129, DM 315, FR 1069, Y 25,433).

$240* *"Composition"*, #183/250, s., (04-04-93, Pescheteau, #312), 31½ x 37⅜ in., (80 x 95 cm.), color serigraph (BP 158, DM 386, FR 1310, Y 27,326).

BI *Composition, 1970*, s., #63/267, pub. Editions Denise Rene, blindstamp, light staining, creases, est. BP 250/350, (10-27-92, Phillips-London, #224), sheet 26¾ x 26¾ in., (679 x 679 mm.), color screenprint on cover board.

$565* *Composition, c. 1970*, s., #86/150, (06-12-93, Hauswedell/Nolt, #443), 27⁹/₁₆ x 27⁹/₁₆ in., (70 x 70 cm.), color serigraph on thin board (BP 370, DM 920, FR 3091, Y 59,455).

$480* *Compositions: Three*, s., two i. E.A., one #16/250, full margins, good cond., scuffing in image, creasing, (06-30-93, Sotheby-London, #957, illus.), color silkscreen on wove (BP 322, DM 819, FR 2762, Y 51,430).

$295* *Compositions: Three*, (09-30-92, Kunsthallen, #287), serigraph in colors (BP 166, DM 418, FR 1415, Y 35,401, DK 1610).

$709* *Compositions: Three*, s., #12/250, 114/250, 200/250, creases, (05-27-93, Briest, #205), from 37 x 30¹¹/₁₆ in., (94 x 78 cm.), to 33¼ x 30⅛ in., (94 x 78 cm.), color serigraphs (BP 454, DM 1138, FR 3835, Y 76,008).

$165* *"Constellations", 1967*, s. Vasarely, #120/150, very good cond., (03-12-93, Skinner, #101, illus.), sight 27½ x 13⅞ in., (69.9 x 35.2 cm.), screenprint in black and gold (BP 115, DM 275, FR 934, Y 19,446).

$1165* *Cta 102, 1966: Set Of Eight*, Galerie der Spiegel, s., num. 18, nicks, good cond., defects, surface dirt, portfolio, (12-01-92, Christie-London, #638), overall S. 28⅛ x 28⅛ in., (715 x 715 mm.), screenprints in colors on firm wove (BP 770, DM 1857, FR 6328, Y 145,045).

$137* *"Cube Sur Fond Bleu"*, #42/120, s., (01-28-93, Pescheteau, #275), 15¾ x 11¹³/₁₆ in., (40 x 30 cm.), serigraph (BP 90, DM 217, FR 735, Y 17,010).

$889* *Ensemble De Trois Serigraphies*, s., 180/350, 231/350 and 146/400, (06-28-93, Loudmer, #124), approx. 8⁷/₁₆ x 8⁷/₁₆ in., (215 x 215 mm.), sh 11¹³/₁₆ x 10¼ in., (215 x 215 mm.), color serigraphs on wove (BP 595, DM 1511, FR 5089, Y 94,324).

$358* *Figure*, s., #CXXXII/CCL, (12-13-92, Hindman, #325), 30 x 22 in., color serigraph (BP 229, DM 563, FR 1918, Y 44,290).

$369* *Folklore*, s., num., (12-05-92, Bassenge, #7787), 12³/₁₆ x 11¾ in., (31 x 29.8 cm.), color screen print (BP 231, DM 575, FR 1961, Y 45,719).

$220* *From Image Suite*, s., #83/150, margins, good cond. (?), water staining, thinned areas (affecting sig.), (02-24-93, Butterfield, #3278), 22⅞ x 22⅞ in., (581 x 581 mm.), silkscreen in colors on wove (BP 153, DM 357, FR 1211, Y 25,816).

$77* *G-ff*, s., The Print Club of Cleveland publication number 45, 1967, (07-03-92, Sloan, #314), sheet 15¾ x 13 in., (40 x 33 cm.), serigraph w/embossing (BP 40, DM 117, FR 393, Y 9599).

$289* *Geometrische Komposition, c. 1970*, s., num., (11-28-92, Schoppmann, #857), 26¼ x 13¼ in., (66.6 x 33.7 cm.), color serigraph on Arches (BP 191, DM 460, FR 1563, Y 35,968).

$220* *Gestalt, Philadelphia, 1974*, ink s., #124/200, (06-11-93, Freemn/Fine Art, #240), 31½ x 31½ in., (80 x 80 cm.), color screenprint (BP 145, DM 358, FR 1205, Y 23,342).

$412* *Golf*, s., #137/200, good cond.?, (12-08-92, Swann, #297), 18 x 14½ in., (45.7 x 36.8 cm.), color serigraph (BP 258, DM 641, FR 2187, Y 51,066).

$39* *Green And Blue Squares*, s., #115/150, (12-17-92, Mystic, #11), 23½ x 23 in., (59.7 x 58.4 cm.), color print (BP 25, DM 61, FR 208, Y 4793).

$84* *"Green And Orange Design"*, s., #41/289, (11-19-92, Bonhams-Chelsea, #70), image 26¼ x 26 in., (66.7 x 66 cm.), screenprint (BP 55, DM 134, FR 451, Y 10,446).

$160* *Hegyez, 1980*, s., #170/190, full sheet p. to edges, good cond., (05-27-93, Sotheby-Amstrdm, #502), sh 24¹³/₁₆ x 22¹/₁₆ in., (630 x 560 mm.), colored silkscreen on wove (BP 102, DM 257, FR 865, Y 17,153, G 288).

BI *Helios I*, s., num. 179/200, full sheet, good cond., est. $2/400, (05-22-93, Weschler, #226), sheet 14¼ x 11½ in., (36.2 x 29.2 cm.), serigraph in colors.

BI *Hexagon With Geometric Interior*, est. $5/700, (12-11-92, DuMouchelle, #2278), 24 x 27½ in., (61 x 69.9 cm.), serigraph.

$440* *"Hielios Suite": Set Of Three*, s., d. 1984, edit. #121/200, (09-18-92, DuMouchelle, #2299), sheet 14 x 11¾ in., (35.6 x 29.8 cm.), color silkscreen (BP 253, DM 659, FR 2256, Y 54,822).

$193* *"Hommage A L'Hexagone", 1969*, s., #66/200, prov., (12-02-92, Boos, #474), sight 23¹³/₁₆ x 23¹³/₁₆ in., (605 x 605 mm.), serigraph (BP 125, DM 304, FR 1036, Y 24,014).

$295* *Komposition*, s., num., (12-05-92, Bassenge, #7789), 15¾ x 15¾ in., (40 x 40 cm.), color screen print on thin wove cardboard (BP 185, DM 460, FR 1567, Y 36,551).

$461* *Komposition*, #53/250, s., (09-04-92, Germann, #602), 31½ x 27⁹/₁₆ in., (800 x 700 mm.), color serigraph (BP 231, DM 646, FR 2199, Y 56,745, SF 575).

$444* *Komposition*, s., num., (05-26-93, Dorling, #3022), 18⅞ x 17¹¹/₁₆ in., (48 x 45 cm.), color serigraphy on cardboard (BP 287, DM 724, FR 2438, Y 48,240).

$332* *Komposition*, E.A., #25/50, s., (04-21-93, Germann, #817), 28⁹/₁₆ x 31¹¹/₁₆ in., (725 x 805 mm.), color serigraph (BP 215, DM 531, FR 1795, Y 36,754, SF 483).

$686* *Komposition Im Grunen Quadrat, c. 1965*, s., (11-28-92, Grisebach, #830, illus.), 27¾ x 27¾ in., (70.5 x 70.5 cm.), colored serigraph on cardboard (BP 453, DM 1093, FR 3710, Y 85,376).

BI *Komposition In Rot Und Blau*, s., #14/190, est. DM 1,400, (05-08-93, Schloss Ahlden, #2901), 22³/₁₆ x 22³/₁₆ in., (56.3 x 56.3 cm.), color serigraph on Silver foil board.

$425* *Komposition Mit Lila*, s., e/a, i., (06-08-93, Karl/Faber, #1388), approx. 16¹⁵/₁₆ x 13⅜ in., (43 x 34 cm.), color serigraph on hand-made Canson & Montgolfier Vidalonles-Annonay (BP 279, DM 690, FR 2322, Y 45,141).

$388* *Komposition, 1966*, s., num., Mappe A, (05-26-93, Dorling, #3021, illus.), 16⅛ x 16⅛ in., (41 x 41 cm.), color serigraphy on geldblichem cardboard (BP 251, DM 633, FR 2131, Y 42,156).

$202* *Kompositioner: Three*, oplag 85, (03-24-93, Kunsthallen, #325), color lithograph (BP 137, DM 330, FR 1123, Y 23,734, DK 1265).

$248* *"Kraft And Natur", 1972*, pub. Olympia, s., num. 195/200 Vasarely, i., good cond., (09-11-92, Skinner, #97), sight 33 x 29¼ in., (83.8 x 74.3 cm.), color silkscreen poster on paper (BP 128, DM 357, FR 1213, Y 30,727).

$419* *"Kris Bille", "Olla II", "Balaton" and "Broey Neg", 1989: Set Of Four*, epreuve d'artiste, s., (11-16-92, Briest, #373), 13¹⁵/₁₆ x 11 in., (35.5 x 28 cm.), serigraph in colors (BP 275, DM 668, FR 2251, Y 52,290).

$972* *Kris Billie, Olla II, Balaton, Broey Neg, Herim, Risir, Tsen Gue, 1989: Series of Seven*, artist proof, s., (05-27-93, Briest, #206), 13¹⁵/₁₆ x 11 in., (35.5 x 28 cm.), color serigraph (BP 622, DM 1560, FR 5257, Y 104,202).

$349* *Kugelkomposition*, s., num., scratched, (09-25-92, Granier, #3039), sheet 24¹⁵/₁₆ x 22⅜ in., (63.4 x 56.8 cm.), color serigraph on board (BP 204, DM 517, FR 1749, Y 42,124).

BI *Louisiana 1-6, 1983: Six*, s., est. DM 4,500-, (05-27-93, Lempertz, #1090), each 27¾ x 25¹³/₁₆ in., (70.5 x 65.5 cm.), color serigraph on thick wove.

BI *Nyolc Sport Temaju Kompozicioja, 1988: Eight*, s., num. 87/100, est. SF 1,8/2,400, (10-14-92, Germann, #469), 19⅝ x 27¹⁵/₁₆ in., (498 x 710 mm.), portfolio.

$209* *"Octal": Five*, from the portfolio, s., 507/850, pub. Bruckmann, 1972, (09-29-92, B. Rasmussen, #369), lithograph (BP 117, DM 295, FR 1007, Y 24,949, DK 1150).

$258* *Octal: Four*, s., num., Bruckmann, Munchen, (12-05-92, Bassenge, #7793), each approx. 12¹⁵/₁₆ x 10⅛ in., (33 x 25.7 cm.), color serigraph (BP 162, DM 402, FR 1371, Y 31,966).

$629* *Oerveng, 1982*, s., d. 28.4.1982, (11-16-92, Briest, #366, illus.), 23¼ x 15¹⁵/₁₆ in., (59 x 40.5 cm.), serigraph in colors (BP 413, DM 1003, FR 3380, Y 78,497).

$237* *Olympische Spiele Munchen, 1972,* #5/200, s., (04-21-93, Germann, #815), 43⅝16 x 27⁹⁄16 in., (110 x 70 cm.), color serigraph (BP 154, DM 379, FR 1281, Y 26,237, SF 345).

BI *Opal III, Clarities,* s., #26/250; t. label verso, prov., est. C$ 4/600, (12-01-92, Ritchie, #55, illus.), 15¾ x 15¾ in., (40 x 40 cm.), color serigraph.

$221* *Optic Composition: Two,* both s., one #174/250, the other 163/250, (11-07-92, Falkkloos, #535), serigraph (BP 144, DM 355, FR 1193, Y 27,277, SK 1320).

$143* *Orange, Blue, Green,* s., #98/150, (06-13-93, Hindman, #326), 30½ x 20½ in., (77.5 x 52.1 cm.), color serigraph (BP 94, DM 233, FR 782, Y 15,048).

$722* *Panther, 1989,* s., num., (11-28-92, Schoppmann, #858), 30¹¹⁄16 x 38⁹⁄16 in., (78 x 98 cm.), color serigraph and embossing on handmade cardboard (BP 477, DM 1150, FR 3905, Y 89,857).

$303* *Permutation,* S., #123/150, blindstamp pub., Denise Rene, margins, good cond. (?), (02-24-93, Butterfield, #3277), 23¾ x 23½ in., (603 x 597 mm.), silkscreen in colors on wove (BP 211, DM 492, FR 1668, Y 35,555).

$1742* *"Planetarische Folklore", 1964: Six,* Galerie der Spiegel, s., num., (12-01-92, Karl/Faber, #1323), 26³⁄16 x 24⅝ in., (66.5 x 62.5 cm.), serigraph on board (BP 1151, DM 2777, FR 9462, Y 216,882).

$1332* *Planetarisische Folklore, 1964: Set Of Six,* Galerie der Spiegel, plate s., num. 16, surface dirt, tape, very good cond., original portfolio, defects, t., defects, portfolio, (12-01-92, Christie-London, #637), overall S. 26 x 24⅝ in., (661 x 625 mm.), screenprints in colors on firm wove paper (BP 880, DM 2123, FR 7235, Y 165,837).

$108* *Pokol B.F.,* s., #143/250, Denise Rene Editeur blindstamp, t., d. 1969 label, (06-08-93, Ritchie, #51), image 23½ x 23½ in., (59.7 x 59.7 cm.), color serigraph (BP 71, DM 175, FR 590, Y 11,471, C$ 138).

$413* *"Raura",* s., d. 1987, edit. #265/300, pub. Circle Fine Arts, (09-18-92, DuMouchelle, #2298), image 30 x 26½ in., (76.2 x 67.3 cm.), color silkscreen (BP 238, DM 618, FR 2118, Y 51,458).

$77* *Red And Blue,* s., #169/290, (06-13-93, Hindman, #327), 22½ x 22½ in., (57.2 x 57.2 cm.), color serigraph (BP 50, DM 125, FR 421, Y 8103).

$135* *Sans Titre,* s., (06-28-93, Loudmer, #122), 18⅛ x 13¹⁄16 in., (460 x 332 mm.), sh 18⅛ x 15¹⁵⁄16 in., (460 x 332 mm.), black serigraph on cardboard and plexiglass (BP 90, DM 229, FR 773, Y 14,324).

$213* *Sans Titre,* s., 171/250, (06-28-93, Loudmer, #403), 25¹⁵⁄16 x 25¹⁵⁄16 in., (660 x 660 mm.), sh 30¹¹⁄16 x 29¹⁵⁄16 in., (660 x 660 mm.), color serigraph on wove (BP 143, DM 362, FR 1219, Y 22,599).

$155* *Sans Titre,* s., 80/250, (06-28-93, Loudmer, #401), 26¾ x 26¾ in., (680 x 680 mm.), sh 34⅝ x 30¹¹⁄16 in., (680 x 680 mm.), black serigraph on wove (BP 104, DM 263, FR 887, Y 16,446).

$309* *Sans Titre,* s., 122/250, (06-28-93, Loudmer, #402), 26⅜ x 26⅜ in., (670 x 670 mm.), sh 33⁷⁄16 x 30⁵⁄16 in., (670 x 670 mm.), color serigraph on wove (BP 207, DM 525, FR 1769, Y 32,785).

$580* *Sans Titre,* s., 121/250, (06-28-93, Loudmer, #404), 19⅛ x 37⅜ in., (485 x 950 mm.), color serigraph on wove (BP 388, DM 986, FR 3320, Y 61,538).

$164* *Sans Titre, c. 1960,* s., 131/138, (06-28-93, Loudmer, #123), 18⅛ x 15¾ in., (460 x 400 mm.), serigraphies sur deux plaques en (and) metal a assembler (BP 110, DM 279, FR 939, Y 17,401).

$241* *Sarajevo,* s., num., (12-01-92, Karl/Faber, #1325), 33⁷⁄16 x 24³⁄16 in., (85 x 61.5 cm.), color serigraph on rough board (BP 159, DM 384, FR 1309, Y 30,005).

BI *Sarajevo (Skier),* s., est. $250/350, (05-27-93, Swann, #278), sh 33½ x 24⅜ in., (85.1 x 61.9 cm.), color serigraph on stiff wove.

$636* *Schach,* s., #2/30, (06-12-93, Hauswedell/Nolt, #448), 21⁷⁄16 x 14⅜ in., (54.5 x 36.5 cm.), color serigraph on board (BP 416, DM 1035, FR 3479, Y 66,926).

$394* *Schwarz-Weiss,* s., num. 54/300, (05-08-93, Schloss Ahlden, #2900), 7¹⁄16 x 7³⁄16 in., (18 x 18.3 cm.), serigraph on paper (BP 257, DM 633, FR 2136, Y 44,027).

$360* *Sinkoeb,* #XLIX/L, s., (11-13-92, Koller, #5467), 16⁹⁄16 x 16⁹⁄16 in., (42 x 42 cm.), original serigraph on cardboard (BP 233, DM 565, FR 1906, Y 44,682, SF 510).

$369* *Springendes Zebra Nach Links,* s., num., (12-05-92, Bassenge, #7786), 19⅛ x 15³⁄16 in., (48.5 x 38.5 cm.), screen print on thin wove cardboard (BP 231, DM 575, FR 1961, Y 45,719).

$967* *Suite Complete: Nine,* for Vasarely Center in New York, 1982, s., 69/135 of 220 impressions, (06-28-93, Loudmer, #399), 23⅝ x 15¾ in., (600 x 400 mm.), color serigraphs and embossing on papier glace (BP 647, DM 1643, FR 5535, Y 102,599).

$86* *Taller,* s., #116/150, Denise Rene Editeur blindstamp, t., d. 1968 label, (06-08-93, Ritchie, #50, illus.), image 23½ x 23½ in., (59.7 x 59.7 cm.), color serigraph (BP 57, DM 140, FR 470, Y 9134, C$ 110).

BI *Thez, c. 1972,* s., #126/250, full margins, est. $6/900, (12-08-92, Swann, #298), 25 x 25 in., (63.5 x 63.5 cm.), color serigraph.

$358* *Untitled,* s., num. 66/190, (09-20-92, Hindman, #814), 33 x 16½ in., (83.8 x 41.9 cm.), (BP 210, DM 531, FR 1817, Y 44,247).

$96* *Untitled,* s., #49/250, full margins, good cond., (05-27-93, Sotheby-Amstrdm, #696), 21⁷⁄16 x 20⁹⁄16 in., (545 x 522 mm.), color silkscreen on wove (BP 61, DM 154, FR 519, Y 10,292, G 173).

$456* *Untitled,* s., #IX/CC, margins, good cond.?, creases, discoloration, (12-09-92, Sotheby-Amstrdm, #664), 26⁹⁄16 x 26¾ in., (675 x 680 mm.), color silkscreen on wove (BP 291, DM 716, FR 2442, Y 56,541, G 805).

$85* *Untitled,* s., #34/500, good cond.?, (12-09-92, Sotheby-Amstrdm, #663), sheet 11⅝ x 8¼ in., (295 x 210 mm.), color silkscreen (BP 54, DM 133, FR 455, Y 10,539, G 150).

$141* *Untitled,* s., full sheet p. to edges, good cond., handling creases, (05-27-93, Sotheby-Amstrdm, #501), sh 23¹⁄16 x 23¹⁄16 in., (586 x 586 mm.), colored silkscreen on wove (BP 90, DM 226, FR 763, Y 15,116, G 253).

$358* *Untitled,* from Enigma suite, s., num. 156/250, (08-05-92, Boos, #572), color silkscreen (BP 187, DM 529, FR 1786, Y 45,593).

$275* *Untitled,* from Gaia suite, s., num. 62/250, (08-05-92, Boos, #568), color silkscreen (BP 144, DM 406, FR 1372, Y 35,023).

$358* *Untitled,* from Enigma suite, s., num. 156/250, (08-05-92, Boos, #573), color silkscreen (BP 187, DM 529, FR 1786, Y 45,593).

$275* *Untitled,* from Enigma suite, s., num. 156/250, (08-05-92, Boos, #574), color silkscreen (BP 144, DM 406, FR 1372, Y 35,023).

$330* *Untitled,* from Gaia suite, s., num. 62/250, (08-05-92, Boos, #571), color silkscreen (BP 173, DM 487, FR 1647, Y 42,028).

$220* *Untitled,* from Enigma suite, s., num. 156/250, (08-05-92, Boos, #575), color silkscreen (BP 115, DM 325, FR 1098, Y 28,018).

$330* *Untitled,* from Gaia suite, s., num. 62/250, (08-05-92, Boos, #569), color silkscreen (BP 173, DM 487, FR 1647, Y 42,028).

$220* *Untitled,* from Gaia suite, s., num. 62/250, (08-05-92, Boos, #570), color silkscreen (BP 115, DM 325, FR 1098, Y 28,018).

$330* *Untitled,* from Gaia suite, s., num. 62/250, (08-05-92, Boos, #567), color silkscreen (BP 173, DM 487, FR 1647, Y 42,028).

$275* *Untitled,* s., num. 43/150, (09-20-92, Hindman, #815), 14 x 20 in., (35.6 x 50.8 cm.), black and white serigraph (BP 161, DM 408, FR 1396, Y 33,988).

$330* *Untitled,* s., num. 43/150, (09-20-92, Hindman, #816), 15½ x 19½ in., (39.4 x 49.5 cm.), black and white serigraph (BP 193, DM 490, FR 1675, Y 40,786).

BI *Untitled,* s., excell. cond., est. $2/300, (05-15-93, Cleveland, #503), 16 x 16 in., (40.6 x 40.6 cm.), serigraph.

$330* *Untitled,* s., annot. E.A., margins, good cond. (?), foxing, (02-24-93, Butterfield, #3276), 18 x 18 in., (457 x 457 mm.), silkscreen in colors on wove (BP 230, DM 536, FR 1816, Y 38,723).

$198* *Untitled,* s., #96/150, prov., (12-02-92, Boos, #475), 27¾ x 27¾ in., (705 x 705 mm.), serigraph (BP 128, DM 311, FR 1063, Y 24,636).
$149* *Untitled,* s., #84/200, (12-02-92, Boos, #473), 23⅝ x 23⅝ in., (600 x 600 mm.), serigraph (BP 96, DM 234, FR 800, Y 18,539).
$272* *Untitled,* #51/100, s. Vasarely, (10-20-92, Encans, #203), 29½ x 12¹⁵⁄₁₆ in., (75 x 33 cm.), serigraph (BP 152, DM 413, FR 1407, Y 34,094, C$ 333).
$430* *Untitled,* s., #190/200, blindstamp, (05-27-93, Lempertz, #1091), 23⅝ x 23⅝ in., (60 x 60 cm.), serigraph on hand-made board (BP 275, DM 690, FR 2326, Y 46,098).
$143* *Untitled,* s., #128/250, prov., (05-16-93, Hindman, #588), 23½ x 23½ in., (59.7 x 59.7 cm.), color serigraph (BP 93, DM 230, FR 773, Y 15,852).
$468* *Untitled,* s., #FV 37/50, (12-13-92, Hindman, #327), 26 x 23¾ in., color serigraph (BP 299, DM 736, FR 2507, Y 57,899).
BI *Untitled: Album of Nine,* each num., s., est. FF 6/8,000, (10-18-92, Pescheteau, #277), each 23⅝ x 15¾ in., (60 x 40 cm.), serigraph.
$660* *Untitled: Eight,* s., #132/200, (05-16-93, Hindman, #505), each 8¼ x 5⅞ in., (21 x 14.9 cm.), color serigraph (BP 429, DM 1062, FR 3568, Y 73,163).
$324* *Untitled: Five,* s., #160/250, 38/50, 33/40, 144/350, 128/400, (05-27-93, Briest, #201), from 18⅞ x 18⅛ in., (48 x 46 cm.), to 11¹³⁄₁₆ x 10¼ in., (48 x 46 cm.), color serigraph (BP 207, DM 520, FR 1752, Y 34,734).
$283* *Utica, 1958,* s., #265/280, (06-12-93, Hauswedell/Nolt, #442), 17⅛ x 14³⁄₁₆ in., (43.5 x 36 cm.), color serigraph on light board (BP 185, DM 461, FR 1548, Y 29,780).
$248* *Vega,* s., #12/267, (05-16-93, Hindman, #589), 29½ x 29½ in., (74.9 x 74.9 cm.), color serigraph (BP 161, DM 399, FR 1341, Y 27,491).
BI *Xico, 1973,* est. FF 5,8/6,000, (11-16-92, Briest, #368), 35⁷⁄₁₆ x 28⅜ in., (90 x 72 cm.), print.
$722* *Xingu, 1950,* s., num., (11-28-92, Grisebach, #829, illus.), 10¾ x 8⅜ in., (27.3 x 21.2 cm.), colored lithograph on thick wove (BP 477, DM 1150, FR 3905, Y 89,857).
$919* *Zebras,* s., #1/25, (06-12-93, Hauswedell/Nolt, #447), 19⅞ x 16⁹⁄₁₆ in., (50.5 x 42 cm.), color serigraph on wove (BP 602, DM 1496, FR 5027, Y 96,706).
$594* *Zebras Playing, 1987,* s., #243/275, (06-12-93, Hauswedell/Nolt, #444), 20¹⁄₁₆ x 25⁹⁄₁₆ in., (51 x 65 cm.), color serigraph on dark greenish wove (BP 389, DM 967, FR 3249, Y 62,507).
$77* *Les Zebres,* s., 89/175, (06-28-93, Loudmer, #125), 8⁷⁄₁₆ x 10⁷⁄₁₆ in., (215 x 265 mm.), sh 10¼ x 11¹³⁄₁₆ in., (215 x 265 mm.), black serigraph on pink tinted wove (BP 52, DM 131, FR 441, Y 8170).
$295* *Zwei Zebras,* num., (12-05-92, Bassenge, #7791), 18¾ x 18¹³⁄₁₆ in., (47.7 x 47.8 cm.), screen print (BP 185, DM 460, FR 1567, Y 36,551).

VASARELY, Victor and Louis KASSAK b. 1908
BI *Album, 1961: Twelve,* s., hors commerce, #C/E, ed. Denise Rene, est. FF 12/15,000, (11-16-92, Briest, #369, illus.), 19¹¹⁄₁₆ x 25⁹⁄₁₆ in., (50 x 65 cm.), serigraph.
$524* *Spheres: Two,* s., (11-16-92, Briest, #370), one 29⅛ x 28⅛ in., (74 x 71.5 cm.), other 20½ x 19¹¹⁄₁₆ in., (74 x 71.5 cm.), serigraph in colors (BP 344, DM 836, FR 2816, Y 65,394).

VASI, Giuseppe
$3603* *Two Views Of St Peter's, Rome: Exterior And Interior,* defects, central fold, tears, surface dirt, laid down, (06-30-93, Sotheby-London, #242), 28 x 38½ in., (711 x 978 mm.), etching, each on two joined sheets (BP 2415, DM 6145, FR 20,731, Y 386,050).

VASI, Guiseppe 1710-1782
$302* *Ponte Adriano Oggi Detto S. Angelo, 1754,* ink stain, margins, (05-15-93, Loudmer, #46, illus.), 8⅜ x 12¹³⁄₁₆ in., (212 x 325 mm.), sh 9³⁄₁₆ x 13¾ in., (212 x 325 mm.), etching on laid (BP 196, DM 486, FR 1632, Y 33,477).

VASQUEZ DIAZ, Daniel
$628* *"Unamuno", 1964,* s., (03-17-93, Duran, #177, illus.), 12³⁄₁₆ x 9⁷⁄₁₆ in., (31 x 24 cm.), lithograph (BP 433, DM 1045, FR 3552, Y 73,657, P 74,750).

VASSILIEFF, Marie
$2200* *Bal Bullier, 1924,* Risacher, A- cond., (08-06-92, Swann, #282, illus.), 48½ x 33 in., (123.2 x 83.8 cm.), (BP 1149, DM 3251, FR 10,978, Y 280,612).

VAUGHAN, Keith English b. 1912
$400* *The Walled Garden,* s., d. 1951, good cond., attached at sheet corners, (10-27-92, Phillips-London, #321), image 15 x 19⅝ in., (381 x 498 mm.), colored lithograph on wove (BP 253, DM 613, FR 2080, Y 48,930).

VAUTIER, Benjamin (called Ben) Swiss b. 1935
$474* *Etre Libre,* hors commerce, s., #4/5, (03-31-93, Briest, #E137), 31⅞ x 39⅜ in., (81 x 100 cm.), serigraph on canvas (BP 313, DM 762, FR 2590, Y 54,508).
$165* *"Parfois L'Art Me Degoute", "Parfois Je Prefere Les Femmes A L'Art" and "Parfois Je Veux Mourir", 1984: Three,* s., #4/50, (03-31-93, Briest, #E15), 13¾ x 19⁵⁄₁₆ in., (35 x 49 cm.), serigraphs (BP 109, DM 265, FR 902, Y 18,974).
$126* *Regardez Ailleurs,* hors commerce, s., (11-16-92, Briest, #11), 21¼ x 26³⁄₁₆ in., (54 x 66.5 cm.), serigraph in black and white (BP 83, DM 201, FR 677, Y 15,724).

VAVASSEUR, Eugene 1863-1949
$241* *Nous Lisons Tous Le Supplement. Grand Journal, c. 1900,* Paris, Affiches Camis, cond. B+, (06-11-93, Boisgirard, #157), 39⅜ x 51³⁄₁₆ in., (100 x 130 cm.), poster (BP 158, DM 392, FR 1321, Y 25,570).
$402* *La Place Clichy. Saison D'Ete 1901,* Asnieres, La lithographie nouvelle, cond. A-, (06-11-93, Boisgirard, #158, illus.), 51³⁄₁₆ x 37 in., (130 x 94 cm.), poster (BP 264, DM 653, FR 2203, Y 42,653).

VECHTEN, Carl van 1880-1964
$440* *Alexander Calder, 1947,* penciled notations, handstamps, (04-07-93, Swann, #579, illus.), 10 x 7¼ in., photograph, silver print (BP 291, DM 712, FR 2408, Y 49,989).
BI *Alice B. Toklas, 1934,* photog.'s blindstamp, handstamp, notations, (04-07-93, Swann, #580, illus.), 14 x 11 in., photograph, silver print.
$1100* *Diego Rivera, 1932,* t., d., num. by photog., studio & reprod. limit. stamps, (10-15-92, Sotheby-NY, #462, illus.), 7⅞ x 9⅞ in., (20 x 25.1 cm.), photograph, gelatin silver print (BP 673, DM 1637, FR 5553, Y 131,974).
BI *Edna St. Vincent Millay, 1933,* t., d., credit stamp, est. $1,2/1,800, (10-13-92, Christie-NY, #378, illus.), 13⅞ x 11 in., (35.2 x 27.9 cm.), photograph, gelatin silver print.
BI *Gertrude Stein, New York, 1935,* embossed credit recto; t., credit and reprod. limitation stamps, only vintage known in this size, prov., est. $3/5,000, (04-08-93, Christie-NY, #352, illus.), 14 x 11 in., (35.6 x 27.9 cm.), photograph, gelatin silver print.
$330* *Jascha Heifitz, 1933,* photog.'s blindstamp, handwritten notations, handstamp, (04-07-93, Swann, #581, illus.), 8¾ x 6⅝ in., photograph, silver print (BP 218, DM 534, FR 1806, Y 37,491).
$357* *Macy's Thanksgiving Day Parade From The Window Of 101 Central Park West, 1948,* blindstamp, handstamp, notations, (10-14-92, Swann, #582, illus.), 10 x 8 in., (25.4 x 20.3 cm.), photograph, silver print (BP 210, DM 522, FR 1772, Y 43,262).
$920* *Marlon Brando: A Streetcar Named Desire, 1948,* embossed credit recto; ink t., d., credit and reprod. limitaion stamp, (04-08-93, Christie-NY, #353, illus.), 7 x 4⅛ in., (17.8 x 10.5 cm.), photograph, gelatin silver print (BP 603, DM 1478, FR 5003, Y 104,403).
$880* *Mary Martin, 1949,* photog.'s blindstamp, handstamp, notations in ink, (04-07-93, Swann, #582, illus.), 9½ x 6¾ in., photograph, silver print (BP 582, DM 1423, FR 4817, Y 99,977).
$495* *Portrait Of Alfred Stieglitz, 1935,* handstamp, notations, sold after sale, (10-14-92, Swann, #583, illus.), 9½ x 7⅜ in., (24.1 x 18.7 cm.), photograph, silver print (BP 291, DM 724, FR 2457, Y 59,985).

$660* *Portrait Of Ethel Waters, c. 1943,* blindstamp, (10-14-92, Swann, #584, illus.), 10 x 8 in., (25.4 x 20.3 cm.), photograph, silver print (BP 387, DM 966, FR 3275, Y 79,981).

$357* *Portrait Of Henri Matisse, 1933,* blindstamp, handstamp, notations, (10-14-92, Swann, #585, illus.), 7½ x 9½ in., (19.1 x 24.1 cm.), photograph, silver print (BP 210, DM 522, FR 1772, Y 43,262).

BI *Self-Portrait, 1932,* notations, sig., est. $1/1,500, (10-14-92, Swann, #586, illus.), 8¾ x 6½ in., (22.2 x 16.5 cm.), photograph, silver print.

BI *Self-Portrait, 1934,* ink s., credit and reprod. limitation stamps, est. $1/1,500, (04-08-93, Christie-NY, #351, illus.), 14 x 11 in., (35.6 x 27.9 cm.), photograph, gelatin silver print.

$990* *Thomas Mann, New York, 1937,* t., d. in ink, credit stamp, (10-13-92, Christie-NY, #379, illus.), 10 x 7⅝ in., (25.4 x 19.4 cm.), photograph, gelatin silver print (BP 577, DM 1450, FR 4928, Y 120,044).

VECOUX

$147* *"Connaissez-Vous Tous Les Services Que Peut Vous Rendre La SNCF", 1947,* good cond., (01-23-93, Ribeyre/Baron, #11), 39⅜ x 24⁷⁄₁₆ in., (100 x 62 cm.), poster (BP 96, DM 234, FR 791, Y 18,398).

$230* *SNCF: Cote Basque, 1946,* excell. cond., (01-23-93, Ribeyre/Baron, #123), 39⅜ x 24⁷⁄₁₆ in., (100 x 62 cm.), poster (BP 150, DM 366, FR 1237, Y 28,786).

VEDOVA, Emilio   b. 1919

$441* *Abstrakte Komposition, 1979,* s., d., num., (11-28-92, Schoppmann, #859), 27¹⁵⁄₁₆ x 19¹¹⁄₁₆ in., (71 x 50 cm.), lithograph w/black Samt on print, on white handmade (BP 291, DM 703, FR 2385, Y 54,885).

$1245* *Composizione, (19)78,* s., d., num., stains, (12-01-92, Karl/Faber, #1326), sh 26¹⁵⁄₁₆ x 38⁹⁄₁₆ in., (68.5 x 98 cm.), serigraph in colors on board (BP 823, DM 1984, FR 6763, Y 155,005).

VEEN, Otto van   Dutch 1558-1629

$289* *Die Frauen Von Weinsberg (Hollstein 11),* (12-04-92, Bassenge, #6476), 11⁵⁄₁₆ x 8¹¹⁄₁₆ in., (28.7 x 22.1 cm.), engraving (BP 185, DM 460, FR 1561, Y 36,080).

$121* *Quint Horatti Flacci Emblembata: Set Of Fourteen,* w/out text, glue traces verso, creases, restored losses/tear, ink annot., num., (05-15-93, Loudmer, #102), approx. 7⁵⁄₁₆ x 5⅞ in., (185 x 150 mm.), sh approx. 7⅞ x 6¹¹⁄₁₆ in., (185 x 150 mm.), copper engraving on laid, watermark (BP 79, DM 195, FR 654, Y 13,413).

VEEN HEEMSKERK, Marten-Jacobsz van   Dutch 1498-1574

BI *Scene From The "Book Of Tobias",* est. $6/800, (10-30-92, Sloan, #2808), 8 x 9¾ in., (20.3 x 24.8 cm.), engraving.

VEEVERS, Vic

$170* *See India, 1934,* p. Bolton Fine Art, cond. 3, tear, laid on linen, (10-13-92, Phillips-London, #49), 38¾ x 25 in., (98.5 x 63.5 cm.), color lithograph (BP 99, DM 249, FR 846, Y 20,614).

VELDE, Bram van   Dutch 1895-after 1980

$1042* *Ailleurs Brun (Riviere 71), 1971,* s., #62/300, pub. Edition Prisunic, margins, good cond.?, (12-09-92, Sotheby-Amstrdm, #668), 22¹³⁄₁₆ x 17¹¹⁄₁₆ in., (580 x 450 mm.), color lithograph on Arches (BP 665, DM 1636, FR 5581, Y 129,200, G 1840).

$275* *Composition,* s. Bram v.V., 46/100, (03-24-93, Kunsthallen, #327), color lithograph (BP 186, DM 449, FR 1529, Y 32,311, DK 1725).

$220* *Composition,* s. Bram van V., 46/100, (03-24-93, Kunsthallen, #328), color lithograph (BP 149, DM 359, FR 1223, Y 25,849, DK 1380).

$309* *Composition (R. 10), 1955,* s., (06-28-93, Loudmer, #397), 28¹⁵⁄₁₆ x 16¾ in., (735 x 425 mm.), sh 35⁷⁄₁₆ x 24¹³⁄₁₆ in., (735 x 425 mm.), 7-color lithograph on Arches wove (BP 207, DM 525, FR 1769, Y 32,785).

$225* *"Composition - 1976" (R 229),* just. 57/100, s., creases in margin, (10-18-92, Pescheteau, #286), 13¾ x 10¼ in., (35 x 26 cm.), lithograph in 5 colors on Japan (BP 136, DM 332, FR 1129, Y 26,866).

BI *Composition Aus "Folie Du Jour" (Riviere 104), 1973,* E.A., s., est. SF 450/550, (04-21-93, Germann, #819,

---

illus.), 10⅝ x 12³⁄₁₆ in., (270 x 310 mm.), color lithograph.

$382* *"Composition",* #46/300, s., (10-18-92, Pescheteau, #284), 25⁹⁄₁₆ x 18½ in., (65 x 47 cm.), lithograph in colors on wove (BP 231, DM 564, FR 1917, Y 45,612).

$516* *"Composition", 1968,* #34/70, s., (10-18-92, Pescheteau, #283), 24¹³⁄₁₆ x 35⁷⁄₁₆ in., (63 x 90 cm.), lithograph in colors on Arches (BP 313, DM 762, FR 2589, Y 61,612).

BI *Compositions: Two,* est. DK 1,000, (09-30-92, Kunsthallen, #290), color lithograph.

$495* *Cyclope (M. et P. 86), 1973,* s., #73/300, (03-31-93, Briest, #E110), 25³⁄₁₆ x 18⅛ in., (64 x 46 cm.), 6-color lithograph on Arches (BP 327, DM 796, FR 2705, Y 56,923).

$734* *Element (Mason et Putman 395),* mono., #19/100, (11-16-92, Briest, #376), 25⁹⁄₁₆ x 39 in., (64.9 x 99.1 cm.), lithograph in 8 colors (BP 482, DM 1171, FR 3944, Y 91,601).

$810* *Embrasement (Mason et Putman 389), 1981,* mono., #22/100, (05-27-93, Briest, #211), 25⁹⁄₁₆ x 32⁵⁄₁₆ in., (65 x 82 cm.), 8-color lithograph (BP 519, DM 1300, FR 4381, Y 86,835).

$608* *Etude, 1974,* s., #123/150, margins, good cond., (05-27-93, Sotheby-Amstrdm, #699), 8⁷⁄₁₆ x 16⁹⁄₁₆ in., (215 x 420 mm.), color lithograph on Japan (BP 389, DM 976, FR 3288, Y 65,180, G 1093).

$977* *Foret (Riviere 61), 1970,* s., #163/300, p. Pierre Badey, margins, good cond.?, (12-09-92, Sotheby-Amstrdm, #666), 24⅛ x 18½ in., (612 x 470 mm.), color lithograph on wove (BP 623, DM 1534, FR 5233, Y 121,141, G 1725).

$498* *Komposition,* s., num., (12-01-92, Karl/Faber, #1328), 9¹³⁄₁₆ x 7½ in., (25 x 19 cm.), color lithograph on wove (BP 329, DM 794, FR 2705, Y 62,002).

$332* *Komposition,* s., num., tears, creases, (12-01-92, Karl/Faber, #1327), 27³⁄₁₆ x 19⁵⁄₁₆ in., (69 x 49 cm.), color lithograph on Arches wove (BP 219, DM 529, FR 1803, Y 41,335).

$202* *L'Exposition Bram van Velde au musee national d'Art Moderne, Paris 1970 (Mason et Putman 65),* t., s., (05-27-93, Briest, #209), 16¹⁵⁄₁₆ x 29½ in., (43 x 75 cm.), lithograph and offset on Arches (BP 129, DM 324, FR 1092, Y 21,655).

$1042* *Lumiere Pale (Riviere 55), 1970,* s., #68/300, pub. Prisunic, margins, good cond.?, (12-09-92, Sotheby-Amstrdm, #667, illus.), 20¹⁄₁₆ x 12¹⁵⁄₁₆ in., (510 x 330 mm.), color lithograph on wove (BP 665, DM 1636, FR 5581, Y 129,200, G 1840).

$44* *Sans Titre,* (06-16-93, Encans, #161), 22⅝ x 30¹¹⁄₁₆ in., (57.5 x 78 cm.), color lithograph (BP 29, DM 73, FR 245, Y 4693, C$ 56).

$1468* *Sans Titre (Mason et Putman 338), 1979,* mono., (11-16-92, Briest, #374, illus.), 34⁵⁄₁₆ x 24½ in., (87.2 x 62.3 cm.), lithograph in 10 colors on Arches (BP 965, DM 2341, FR 7888, Y 183,202).

$293* *Sans Titre (Mason et Putman II 175), 1975,* epreuve d'artiste, mono., (11-16-92, Briest, #375), 25⁹⁄₁₆ x 18⅛ in., (65 x 46 cm.), lithograph in 9 colors on Arches (BP 193, DM 467, FR 1574, Y 36,566).

BI *Sans Titre (Mason et Putman II, 151),* hors commerce, s., creases, est. FF 5/6,000, (11-16-92, Briest, #378), 38³⁄₁₆ x 25⁹⁄₁₆ in., (97 x 65 cm.), lithograph in 10 colors on Arches.

$290* *Sans Titre (Riviere 62),* s. artist's proof, (06-28-93, Loudmer, #398), 24 x 18⅛ in., (610 x 460 mm.), sh 25¹⁵⁄₁₆ x 19⁵⁄₁₆ in., (610 x 460 mm.), color lithograph on Arches wove (BP 194, DM 493, FR 1660, Y 30,769).

$251* *Untitled,* s. 41/100, pub. Asger Jorn Foundation, 1976, (09-29-92, B. Rasmussen, #370), lithograph in colors (BP 141, DM 355, FR 1210, Y 29,963, DK 1380).

$256* *Untitled (Riviere 37), 1966,* s., #87/190, p. Michel Casse, full margins, good cond., paper discoloration, minor handling creases, (05-27-93, Sotheby-Amstrdm, #697), 18⅞ x 27⁹⁄₁₆ in., (480 x 700 mm.), lithograph on wove (BP 164, DM 411, FR 1385, Y 27,444, G 460).

$326* *Untitled (Riviere 39), 1966,* s., #179/190, pub. Prent 190, good cond., discoloration, (12-09-92, Sotheby-Amstrdm, #665), sheet 21¹⁵⁄₁₆ x 30 in., (558 x 762 mm.), lithograph on Arches (BP 208, DM 512, FR 1746, Y 40,422, G 575).

$512* *Untitled (Riviere 82), 1972,* s., #19/120, p. Pierre Badley, margins, good cond., (05-27-93, Sotheby-Amstrdm, #698), 23¼ x 16⅛ in., (590 x 410 mm.), color lithograph on Arches (BP 328, DM 822, FR 2769, Y 54,889, G 920).

$576* *Untitled, 1978,* s., full margins, good cond., (05-27-93, Sotheby-Amstrdm, #503, illus.), 9¹³⁄₁₆ x 7³⁄₁₆ in., colored lithograph on wove (BP 369, DM 924, FR 3115, Y 61,750, G 1035).

$544* *Untitled, 1978,* s., margins, good cond., (05-27-93, Sotheby-Amstrdm, #504), 9¹³⁄₁₆ x 7⅜ in., (250 x 187 mm.), colored lithograph on wove (BP 348, DM 873, FR 2942, Y 58,319, G 978).

VELDE, Charles William Meredith van de (after)
BI *Indonesia And South East Asia: Sixteen,* plates: I, XVI, XX, XXIII, XXX, XXXVI, XLIII, XLVI, XLVII (2 plates),XLVIII, XLIX, by P. Lauters, pub. Frans Buffa, margins, dirt, fading, stainingon some, est. BP 6/800, (10-07-92, Christie-S. Ken, #92), each 8½ x 12 in., (21.6 x 30.5 cm.), colored tinted lithograph.

VELDE, Esaias van de 1587-1630
BI *Die Brucke Uber Dem Wasserfall An Einem Rundtempel (Hollstein 15 II),* est. DM 1,500, (06-10-93, Hauswedell/ Nolt, #171), etching.

$7492* *A Farm To The Right Of A Canal (Holl. 28),* 1st state of 2, thread margins, trimmed, stains, mounting residue, very good cond., (12-01-92, Christie-London, #111, illus.), 2¾ x 4³⁄₁₆ in., (70 x 106 mm.), etching (BP 4950, DM 11,941, FR 40,695, Y 932,769).

VELDE, Esaias van de (I) 1587-1630
$1770* *Das Dorf (Burchard 19, Hollstein 29 I),* (06-04-93, Bassenge, #5388, illus.), 2¹¹⁄₁₆ x 3¹¹⁄₁₆ in., (6.8 x 9.3 cm.), etching (BP 1171, DM 2874, FR 9688, Y 190,897).

$7082* *Der Dorfweg (Spaarnewoude) (Hollstein 20 II),* watermark, (06-04-93, Bassenge, #5387, illus.), 3⅜ x 7 in., (8.5 x 17.8 cm.), etching (BP 4685, DM 11,500, FR 38,763, Y 763,805).

VELDE, Esaias van de (after) 1587-1630
$1444* *Ein Gestrandeter Wal In Noordwijk, 1614,* by C.J. Visscher, (12-04-92, Bassenge, #6477), 6⁷⁄₁₆ x 12⅛ in., (16.3 x 30.8 cm.), etching (BP 926, DM 2300, FR 7801, Y 180,275).

VELDE, Geer van Dutch b. 1898
$189* *Composition,* s., (11-16-92, Briest, #107), 14⅜ x 11⅛ in., (36.5 x 28.2 cm.), lithograph in colors on Arches (BP 124, DM 301, FR 1016, Y 23,587).

$359* *"Composition c. 1952",* s. in plate, (10-18-92, Pescheteau, #282), 14³⁄₁₆ x 11 in., (36 x 28 cm.), lithograph in colors on Arches cream (BP 218, DM 530, FR 1801, Y 42,866).

VELDE, J. van de 1593-1641
$125* *Ruined Barn With A Herd Playing The Flute (Hollstein 247), 1616,* 2nd state of 2, (06-09-93, Bubb Kuyper, #2079), 4¹⁵⁄₁₆ x 7¹³⁄₁₆ in., (12.6 x 19.8 cm.), etching (BP 82, DM 204, FR 688, Y 13,294, G 230).

VELDE, J. van de (II) 1593-1641
$133* *Draw-Well Among Trees, With 2 Shepherds, One Of Them Playing A Flute(Hollstein 281),* (11-18-92, Bubb Kuyper, #1848), 4¹³⁄₁₆ x 7⁷⁄₁₆ in., (12.2 x 18.9 cm.), etching (BP 88, DM 212, FR 714, Y 16,540, G 240).

$125* *Landscape With Square Tower (Hollstein 247), 1616,* 3rd state of 3, (06-09-93, Bubb Kuyper, #2078), 5¼ x 7¾ in., (13.4 x 19.7 cm.), etching (BP 82, DM 204, FR 688, Y 13,294, G 230).

$220* *Ruins Of A Castle Surrounded By A Moat (Hollstein 240), 1616,* 3rd state of 2, (06-09-93, Bubb Kuyper, #2080), 5¼ x 7¹¹⁄₁₆ in., (13.3 x 19.5 cm.), etching (BP 145, DM 360, FR 1210, Y 23,397, G 403).

VELDE, Jan van de
$3088* *The Four Elements (Franken-Van Der Kellen 134-137): Set Of Four,* after Willem Buytewech, 4th final state, small margins, stains, defects, (06-30-93, Sotheby-London, #243), etching on paper w/an elaborate Coat of Arms watermark (BP 2070, DM 5267, FR 17,768, Y 330,869).

VELDE, Jan van de (II) 1593-1641
BI *Die Vier Elemente (Hollstein Bd. 23, 22-25): Four,* after Willem Buytewech, foxing, browning, est. DM 7,500-, (09-14-92, Venator/Hansten, #1616, illus.), plate largest 7⁹⁄₁₆ x 11⁷⁄₁₆ in., (19.2 x 29 cm.), smallest 7⁵⁄₁₆ x 11⅛ in., (19.2 x 29 cm.), etching and engraving.

VELDE, Jan van de (II) c. 1593-1641
$505* *Landschaft Mit Einem Mann Mit Fangnetzen Fur Vogel (Franken-van der Kellen 233; Hollstein 194 II),* prov., from sries Landschaften und Ruinen, (12-04-92, Bassenge, #6480), 4⅝ x 12⁵⁄₁₆ in., (11.7 x 31.3 cm.), etching (BP 324, DM 804, FR 2728, Y 63,046).

$722* *Ver Der Fruhling (Franken-van der Kellen 142 III; Hollstein 26 III),1617,* from series Vier Jahreszeiten, (12-04-92, Bassenge, #6479), 11⅛ x 16¾ in., (28.2 x 42.5 cm.), etching (BP 463, DM 1150, FR 3901, Y 90,137).

$470* *Waldige Landschaft, Vorn Ein Brunnen (Franken-van der Kellen 320 I; Hollstein 281),* (12-04-92, Bassenge, #6482), 4¹³⁄₁₆ x 7⅜ in., (12.3 x 18.7 cm.), etching (BP 301, DM 749, FR 2539, Y 58,677).

VELICKOVIC American 20th cent.
$33* *Untitled, 1975,* (11-12-92, Freemn/Fine Art, #234), 12 x 17 in., (30.5 x 43.2 cm.), serigraph (BP 22, DM 52, FR 176, Y 4092).

VELICKOVIC, Vladimir Yugoslav b. 1935
$210* *"Animals In Motion/Birds" and "Animals In Motion/Dog", 1974: Two,* epreuve d'artiste, s., d. 1974; second t., (11-16-92, Briest, #380), each 29½ x 42½ in., (75 x 108 cm.), serigraph in colors (BP 138, DM 335, FR 1128, Y 26,207).

$189* *Cinq Etats D'Une Boite, 1972,* epreuve d'artiste, s., t., (11-16-92, Briest, #111), 29½ x 42½ in., (75 x 108 cm.), serigraph in colors and a collage (BP 124, DM 301, FR 1016, Y 23,587).

BI *Dog, Fig. 19, Animls In Motion, 1974,* artist proof, s., t., d. 1974, est. FF1,800/2,000, (05-27-93, Briest, #216), 29½ x 42½ in., (75 x 108 cm.), color serigraph.

$377* *Elements + Documents Utilises, 1974,* epreuve d'artiste, s., d. 1974, t., (11-16-92, Briest, #109), 31⅛ x 46⅞ in., (79 x 119 cm.), serigraph and collages in colors (BP 248, DM 601, FR 2026, Y 47,049).

$377* *Elements + Documents Utilises, 1979,* epreuve d'artiste, s., d. 1979, t., (11-16-92, Briest, #110), 29½ x 42½ in., (75 x 108 cm.), serigraph in colors (BP 248, DM 601, FR 2026, Y 47,049).

BI *Hippopotamus, 1971,* s., d., #60/99, light staining, creases, tears, est. $3/500, (12-12-92, Weschler, #177), sight 42 x 28½ in., (106.7 x 72.4 cm.), seriograph.

VELICOVIC, Vladimir
$96* *Naissance, 1975,* s., t., d., #111/190, full sheet p. to edges, good cond., minor handling creases, (05-27-93, Sotheby-Amstrdm, #507), sh 22½ x 34¹⁵⁄₁₆ in., (571 x 888 mm.), colored lithograph on wove (BP 61, DM 154, FR 519, Y 10,292, G 173).

BI *Saut, 1975,* s., t., d., #147/190, full sheet p. to edges, good cond., minor handling creases, est. Dfl. 550/750, (05-27-93, Sotheby-Amstrdm, #700), sheet 22½ x 34¹⁵⁄₁₆ in., (571 x 888 mm.), color lithograph on wove.

$115* *Saut, 1975,* s., t., d., full sheet p. to edges, good cond., minor handling, (05-27-93, Sotheby-Amstrdm, #506), sh 22½ x 34¹⁵⁄₁₆ in., (571 x 888 mm.), colored lithograph on wove (BP 74, DM 185, FR 622, Y 12,328, G 207).

$96* *Untitled, 1975,* s., t. indistinctly, d., #111/190, full sheet p. to edges, good cond., minor handling creases, (05-27-93, Sotheby-Amstrdm, #505), sh 34¹⁵⁄₁₆ x 22⅝ in., (888 x 575 mm.), colored lithograph (BP 61, DM 154, FR 519, Y 10,292, G 173).

VELLERT, Dirk Jacobsz. ac. 1511-c. 1547
BI *The Temptation Of Christ (Holl. 5),* 2nd final state, trimmed unevenly, skinned, rubbed, cockling, defects, ex. coll. Conte Archinto (L. 547) and Ch. Gasc (L. 544), est. BP 2,5/3,500, (06-29-93, Sotheby-London, #64, illus.), 4⅜ x 2¾ in., (11.1 x 7 cm.), engraving.

BI *Die Vision Des Hl. Bernhard Von Clairvaux (Hollstein Bd. 33, 8),* very rare, d., mono. 1524 OCT 3, D V, est. DM 2,100-, (09-14-92, Venator/Hansten, #1617, illus.), image 6¹¹⁄₁₆ x 4¾ in., (17 x 12.1 cm.), engraving.

VELLERT, Dirk Jakobsz. ac. c. 1511-c. 1547
BI *Christus Und Die Samariterin (B. 6, Nagler, Die Mono-grammisten II, 1408, 6, Wurzbach 6, The Illustr. Bartsch 14, Part 1, S. 209, 6), 1523,* est. DM 4500, (06-04-93, Bassenge, #5392, illus.), 4⁵⁄₁₆ x 2¹⁵⁄₁₆ in., (10.9 x 7.6 cm.), engraving.

VENARD, Claude French b. 1913
BI *Untitled,* s., i. "Epreuve d'artiste", #6/20, est. $3/400, (02-04-93, Sloan, #2031), 13 x 9¼ in., (33 x 23.5 cm.), color lithograph.
BI *Vue De Paris, c. 1950,* s., est. FF5/800, (05-27-93, Briest, #218), 29⅛ x 19⅞ in., (74 x 50.5 cm.), color lithograph.

VENEZIANO, Agostino (de MUSI) 1490-after 1536
BI *Die Drei Heiligen Freuen Gehen Zum Heiligen Grabe (B. XIV, 39, 33),* watermark, prov., glue stained, est. DM 2,400, (12-04-92, Bassenge, #6484), 11⁵⁄₁₆ x 7 in., (28.8 x 17.8 cm.), engraving.

VENEZIANO, Agostino (dei MUSI) 1490-after 1536
$5416* *Die Skelette (B. XIV, 424), 1518,* after Baccio Bandinelli, watermark, (12-04-92, Bassenge, #6487, illus.), engraving (BP 3474, DM 8626, FR 29,260, Y 676,155).
$181* *Der Triumph des Bacchus (B. XIV, 215), 1528,* (12-04-92, Bassenge, #6486), 2⅜ x 3½ in., (6 x 8.9 cm.), engraving (BP 116, DM 288, FR 978, Y 22,597).

VENNEKAMP, Johannes b. 1935
$155* *Uber Die Unanstandigkeit Des Radfahrens Lasst Sich Sehr Streiten...,1972,* s., d., #90/100, t. in plate, (09-18-92, Schloss Ahlden, #1077), 29¼ x 20⁹⁄₁₆ in., (74.3 x 52.3 cm.), color etching on hand-made (BP 91, DM 230, FR 787, Y 19,157).

VENNER, Victor (after)
$126 *Humorous Hunting Prints: A Pair,* (10-09-92, G.A. Key, #58), 15 x 24 in., (38.1 x 61 cm.), hand colored prints (BP 75, DM 188, FR 636, Y 15,366).

VERDIJK, Gerard b. 1934
BI *Transformation, 1974,* s., d. twice, #23/50, good cond., soiling, est. G 2/400, (12-09-92, Sotheby-Amstrdm, #669), 17¹¹⁄₁₆ x 17¹¹⁄₁₆ in., (450 x 450 mm.), lithograph and postcards on 2 sheets of cardboard.

VERHOOG, Aad
$141* *Untitled, 1975,* s., full sheet p. to edges, (05-27-93, Sotheby-Amstrdm, #510), 22¼ x 30¼ in., (565 x 768 mm.), colored lithograph on wove (BP 90, DM 226, FR 763, Y 15,116, G 253).
$96* *Untitled, 1975,* s., full sheet p. to edges, good cond., (05-27-93, Sotheby-Amstrdm, #509), 20 x 25¹⁵⁄₁₆ in., (508 x 660 mm.), colored lithograph on wove (BP 61, DM 154, FR 519, Y 10,292, G 173).
$166* *Untitled, 1975,* s., full sheet p. to edges, good cond., (05-27-93, Sotheby-Amstrdm, #508), 20 x 25¹⁵⁄₁₆ in., (508 x 660 mm.), colored lithograph on wove (BP 106, DM 266, FR 898, Y 17,796, G 299).

VERJEZ
$315* *Maurice Chevalier, En Costume Humoristique,* fair cond., (11-19-92, Ribeyre/Baron, #185), 84⅝ x 53⅛ in., (215 x 135 cm.), poster (BP 207, DM 502, FR 1692, Y 39,174).

VERKOLJE, Nicolaas 1673-1746
BI *Das Stallende Pferd (Nagler Bd. 22, 43),* after Wouverman, trimmed, rare, est. DM 220-, (03-24-93, Venator/Hansten, #2585), approx. 5½ x 6¹¹⁄₁₆ in., (14 x 17 cm.), mezzotint.

VERMETTE, Claude b. 1930
$87* *"Pins De Rome",* #12/25, s., d. Claude Vermette 73, (11-17-92, Encans, #96), 41⁹⁄₁₆ x 29½ in., (105.5 x 75 cm.), intaglio (BP 57, DM 139, FR 467, Y 10,820, C$ 111).
BI *"Pins De Rome",* #12/25, s., d. Vermette 73, (10-20-92, Encans, #156), 41⁹⁄₁₆ x 29½ in., (105.5 x 75 cm.), intaglio.

VERNET, Antoine Charles Horace French 1758-1836
BI *Route De Naples,* s., d. 1820 in stone, pub. Philbert-Louis Debucourt, est. $300/500, (07-03-92, Sloan, #1080), 11½ x 15¾ in., (29.2 x 40 cm.), color aquatint.

VERNET, Carle
BI *A Cavalryman Leading His Horse,* margins, stains, surface dirt, tears, defects, est. BP 5/600, (12-03-92, Sotheby-London, #145), 9¾ x 14 in., (247 x 354 mm.), soft ground etching.

VERNET, Carle (after)
BI *Le Depart Pour La Chasse,* engraved by P.L. Debucourt, margins, laid down, overmat glued, good cond., light-staining, surface scuffing, soiling, est. $6/800, (02-24-93, Butterfield, #2981), 22½ x 33 in., (572 x 838 mm.), engraving in colors w/hand-coloring.
$88* *Gentleman Struggling With His Horse,* by Debucourt, (02-17-93, Bonhams-Chelsea, #254), image 14 x 17½ in., (35.6 x 44.5 cm.), hand-colored mezzotint (BP 61, DM 143, FR 484, Y 10,511).

VERNET, Emile Jean Horace Vierspanner 1789-1863
$488* *Vollbesetzte Reisekutsche,* stone s. H. Vernet, (09-14-92, Venator/Hansten, #1700), approx. 12⅝ x 19½ in., (32 x 49.5 cm.), chalk lithograph on hand-made (BP 258, DM 725, FR 2458, Y 60,681).

VERNET, H. (after)
$262* *"Les Suites Du Jeu De La Drogue", "La Lecon De Danse", "Soldats Jouant A La Drogue", "La Reconciliation": Five,* tears, large margins, (02-03-93, Ader Tajan, #209), 7½ x 9¹³⁄₁₆ in., (19 x 25 cm.), lithograph (BP 183, DM 431, FR 1463, Y 32,591).

VERNET, Joseph (after)
BI *"Figural Landscape": A Pair,* est. $2/300, (12-12-92, A. James, #608), each 18 x 29½ in., (45.7 x 74.9 cm.), prints on canvas laid down on board.

VERNET, Joseph (after) French 1712/14-1789
$275* *Le Pelerinage,* by J. Daulle, prop. Ned Long, (10-18-92, Hindman, #499), 21 x 29¼ in., (53.3 x 74.3 cm.), engraving (BP 168, DM 409, FR 1388, Y 32,993).

VERNON-STOKES, George
$213* *A Spaniel Flushing Duck,* #54/99, s., margins, foxed, (06-30-93, Bonhams-Chelsea, #74), plate 10 x 12 in., (25.4 x 30.5 cm.), etching in colors (BP 143, DM 363, FR 1226, Y 22,822).

VERTES, Marcel French 1895-1961
$450* *Jazz Dancer, c. 1926,* s., from "Dancing" album, (02-04-93, Sloan, #1837, illus.), sight 19½ x 24 in., (49.5 x 61 cm.), color lithograph (BP 314, DM 741, FR 2513, Y 55,977).
$1271* *La Journee De Madame, c. 1927: Ten,* s., #19/100, Marcel Guiot, (06-10-93, Hauswedell/Nolt, #954), sh 16⁹⁄₁₆ x 12¹³⁄₁₆ in., (42 x 32.5 cm.), lithograph on China (BP 831, DM 2070, FR 6968, Y 134,911).
BI *"Nu",* artist proof, s., (04-04-93, Peschateau, #315), 11¹³⁄₁₆ x 9¹⁄₁₆ in., (30 x 23 cm.), drypoint on wove.
$193* *(Nude Female Painting Another Nude Female),* s., num. 213/220, margins, good cond., staining, creases, hinge remains, surface soiling, pencil notations, (02-24-93, Butterfield, #2982), 14¾ x 21½ in., (375 x 546 mm.), lithograph in colors on BFK Rives w/watermark (BP 135, DM 313, FR 1062, Y 22,647).
$120* *Untitled" Twenty,* 11 s., (04-04-93, Peschateau, #316), drypoint (BP 79, DM 193, FR 655, Y 13,663).
$286* *Zirkusreiterin Mit Ihrem Pferd,* s., #14/200, (05-08-93, Schloss Ahlden, #2908), 14⅜ x 18⅞ in., (36.5 x 48 cm.), lithograph on pale green light (BP 187, DM 459, FR 1550, Y 31,959).

VERTUE, George English 1684-1756
BI *Magnates Et Heroes Sanguine Regali Scotiae Et Angliae Prognati,* est. $3/400, (04-02-93, Sloan, #2278), sight 16⅜ x 21½ in., (416 x 546 mm.), engraving.
$330* *The Royal Procession Of Queen Elizabeth To Vest The Right Honorable Henry Carey, Lord Hunsdon, 1742,* (04-02-93, Sloan, #2267, illus.), 17¼ x 21⅜ in., (438 x 543 mm.), engraving (BP 217, DM 530, FR 1801, Y 37,573).
$385* *Three Children Of King Henry VII And Elizabeth, His Queen,* after L. Maubeugius, 1748, (04-02-93, Sloan, #2275, illus.), 17⅞ x 21½ in., (454 x 546 mm.), engraving (BP 254, DM 619, FR 2102, Y 43,835).

VERWEY, Kees
BI *De Schilder In Zijn Atelier,* s., #27/50, full margins, good cond., minor handling creases, water staining in left corner, est. Dfl. 5/700, (05-27-93, Sotheby-Amstrdm, #701), 21³⁄₁₆ x 26¹⁄₁₆ in., (538 x 662 mm.), lithograph on wove.

VESPIGNANI, Renzo Italian contemporary
BI *Beached Boats,* s., t., excell. cond., est. $2/300, (05-15-93, Cleveland, #436), 5⅛ x 12⅜ in., (12.7 x 31.4 cm.), etching and aquatint.
$610* *Entrando A Roma, 1955,* #P.A., s., d., lit., (03-25-93, Finarte-Rome, #35, illus.), aquatint and etching (BP 414, DM 1002, FR 3408, Y 71,462, L 978).

VEXIO, Pol
$80* *Les Comedies-Ballets Et Les Chants De La Cote D'Ivoire, 1956,* cond. B, (03-16-93, Boisgirard, #214), 23⅝ x 15¾ in., (60 x 40 cm.), poster (BP 55, DM 133, FR 452, Y 9355).

VIBERT, Pierre Eugene 1875-1937
$181* *Les Arts Reunis. Exposition De Peinture, Sculpture, Gravure, Ameublement (...) Galerie Georges Petit, 1902,* Paris, Imp. Georges Petit, cond. A-, (06-11-93, Boisgirard, #159), 23⅝ x 15¾ in., (60 x 40 cm.), poster (BP 119, DM 294, FR 992, Y 19,204).

VIBERTZ, L.G.
$33* *Interior Genre Scene: Set of Three,* (12-11-92, DuMouchelle, #265), approx. 8 x 10 in., (20.3 x 25.4 cm.), engravings (BP 21, DM 52, FR 178, Y 4084).

VIC
$796* *La Corse En Yacht, "A Six Heures De Nice Par La Cie Fraissinet",* excell. cond., (01-23-93, Ribeyre/Baron, #144, illus.), 39⅜ x 24⁷⁄₁₆ in., (100 x 62 cm.), poster (BP 521, DM 1266, FR 4282, Y 99,625).
$335* *The Modern Oil For The Modern Motor, 1928,* p. EVP, ref. #201, cond. 1, (10-13-92, Phillips-London, #67), 29¹³⁄₁₆ x 44⅞ in., (75.8 x 114 cm.), color lithograph (BP 195, DM 491, FR 1667, Y 40,621).
$2110* *Shell Oil & Petrol For Quick Starting, Cars & Chauffeurs, 1930,* p. EVP, ref. #242, cond. 3, (10-13-92, Phillips-London, #85, illus.), 29¹⁵⁄₁₆ x 44½ in., (76 x 113 cm.), color lithograph (BP 1229, DM 3091, FR 10,503, Y 255,851).

VICENTINO, Niccolo ac. c. 1510
$1062* *Der Tod Des Ajax (B. 99, 9 II), 1608,* after Polidoro da Caravaggio, (06-04-93, Bassenge, #5396), 12¼ x 16¼ in., (31.1 x 41.2 cm.), chiaroscuro woodcut w/three plates in colors (BP 703, DM 1725, FR 5813, Y 114,538).

VICENTINO, Nicolo ac. early 16th cent.
$1342* *Caritas (Bartsch XII, 128, 3),* series of Christian Virtues, after Parmigianino, (06-10-93, Hauswedell/Nolt, #172, illus.), chiaroscuro woodcut in 3 blocks on hand-made (BP 878, DM 2185, FR 7357, Y 142,448).

VICKERS, Roy Henry Tsimshian b. 1946
$86* *"Chilkat Blackfish",* artist's proof, s., d. 1978, (05-12-93, Maynard, #297A), silkscreen (BP 56, DM 139, FR 467, Y 9601, C$ 110).
$89* *'Greenpeace',* (10-21-92, Maynard, #54), print (BP 55, DM 135, FR 457, Y 10,840, C$ 110).
$98* *'Messenger',* #104/195, (10-21-92, Maynard, #55), print (BP 61, DM 148, FR 503, Y 11,937, C$ 121).
$244* *'My Guardian Angel,' 1977,* #24/75, (Guild Series), s., (10-21-92, Maynard, #37), 22 x 17 in., (55.9 x 43.2 cm.), silkscreen (BP 151, DM 369, FR 1253, Y 29,720, C$ 303).
$200* *'Stanley Park,' 1977,* #111/150, s., d. 77, (10-21-92, Maynard, #46), 7½ x 21 in., (19.1 x 53.3 cm.), silkscreen (BP 124, DM 303, FR 1027, Y 24,361, C$ 248).
$133* *'Tuac', 1977,* #116/195, s., d. 77, (10-21-92, Maynard, #47), 10½ x 14 in., (26.7 x 35.6 cm.), silkscreen (BP 83, DM 201, FR 683, Y 16,200, C$ 165).

VICKERY, Robert Error change to VICKREY
BI *Boy Playing With Marbles,* s., est. $700/1,000, (12-08-92, Swann, #301), 22½ x 34½ in., (57.2 x 87.6 cm.), color serigraph.
$412* *"Sun Shower" and "Boy Playing With Marbles": Two,* s., i. HC, (05-27-93, Swann, #280), one 22⅜ x 24½ in., (56.8 x 62.2 cm.), other 22½ x 34½ in., (56.8 x 62.2 cm.), color serigraph (BP 264, DM 661, FR 2228, Y 44,168).

VICO, Enea 1523-1567
BI *The Battle Of Lapiths And Centaurs (B. Xv, 30), 1542,* after Rosso Fiorentino, margins, crease, staining, laid, est. BP 1,0/1,200, (12-01-92, Christie-London, #34, illus.), plate 11⅝ x 16⁹⁄₁₆ in., (295 x 421 mm.), engraving.
$505* *Leda Mit Dem Schwan (B. 25), 1542,* prov., (12-04-92, Bassenge, #6490), 4¾ x 6¼ in., (12 x 15.8 cm.), engraving (BP 324, DM 804, FR 2728, Y 63,046).

VICO, Enea 1523-1568
$202* *Camees Et Gemmes Anciennes,* dirt spots, (05-15-93, Loudmer, #34, illus.), 11¼ x 16¹⁄₁₆ in., (285 x 408 mm.), copper engraving w/eagle inscribed in a circle watermark (BP 131, DM 325, FR 1092, Y 22,392).

VICTORIAN SCHOOL
$61 *Study Of A Young Boy Standing On A Rock, Landscape Background,* (02-05-93, G.A. Key, #60), 12 x 9 in., (30.5 x 22.9 cm.), olegraph (BP 42, DM 101, FR 342, Y 7591).

VIDAL, Miguel Angel
$26* *Blue And Green Abstract,* s., d., #27/200, prov., exhib., (12-01-92, Ritchie, #64), 23 x 23 in., (58.4 x 58.4 cm.), color serigraph (BP 17, DM 41, FR 141, Y 3237, C$ 33).
BI *White Striations On Orange,* s., d. '73, #7/100, prov., exhib., est. C$ 2/300, (12-01-92, Ritchie, #65), 23 x 23 in., (58.4 x 58.4 cm.), color serigraph.

VIEILLARD, Roger
$181* *L'Abbaye Ste Genevieve,* s., ded., #43/150, full margins, drystamp, (05-06-93, Laurin, #91), copper engraving on laid (BP 115, DM 285, FR 960, Y 19,914).

VIEIRA DA SILVA, Maria Helena French 1908-1992
$320* *Arbre, 1979,* s., #36/190, full margins, good cond., (05-27-93, Sotheby-Amstrdm, #514), 12⅜ x 8¾ in., (315 x 222 mm.), colored lithograph on wove (BP 205, DM 513, FR 1731, Y 34,305, G 575).
$2246* *"Atlantide" (R 127), 1974,* #103/150, s., (10-18-92, Pescheteau, #289), sight 21⅝ x 27⁹⁄₁₆ in., (55 x 70 cm.), lithograph in green and grey on Japan (BP 1361, DM 3318, FR 11,269, Y 268,179).
$51* *Balcon, 1978,* s., d., #189/190, full margins, some soiling, crease in upper corner, restored holes in image, minor handling creases, (05-27-93, Sotheby-Amstrdm, #511), 17¹³⁄₁₆ x 10¼ in., (452 x 261 mm.), colored lithograph on wove (BP 33, DM 82, FR 276, Y 5467, G 92).
$224* *Balcon, 1978,* s., full margins, good cond., (05-27-93, Sotheby-Amstrdm, #512), 17¹³⁄₁₆ x 10¼ in., (452 x 261 mm.), colored lithograph on wove (BP 143, DM 359, FR 1211, Y 24,014, G 403).
$224* *Carnaval,* s., #111/190, full margins, good cond., (05-27-93, Sotheby-Amstrdm, #513), 7¹⁄₁₆ x 9 in., (180 x 229 mm.), colored lithograph on wove (BP 143, DM 359, FR 1211, Y 24,014, G 403).
$525* *"La Chapelle", 1977,* #58/100, s., (01-28-93, Pescheteau, #278), 22¹⁄₁₆ x 14¹⁵⁄₁₆ in., (56 x 38 cm.), black lithograph on sea-green on Arches (BP 347, DM 832, FR 2815, Y 65,185).
BI *"La Chapelle", 1977,* #58/100, s., est. FF 3,5/4,000, (10-18-92, Pescheteau, #290), 22¹⁄₁₆ x 14¹⁵⁄₁₆ in., (56 x 38 cm.), lithograph in black on sea-green Arches.
BI *Claustra Blanc,* #69/160, s., blindstamp, est. SF 850/950, (04-21-93, Germann, #822), 18½ x 12⅜ in., (470 x 315 mm.), color lithograph.
$561* *"Hiver" (R 112), 1971,* #7/50, s., good margins, (10-18-92, Pescheteau, #291), 19 x 15¹⁄₁₆ in., (48.3 x 38.2 cm.), lithograph in black on Arches (BP 340, DM 829, FR 2815, Y 66,985).
$664* *Komposition,* s., num., (12-05-92, Bassenge, #7795), 12⁷⁄₁₆ x 9⅝ in., (31.6 x 24.4 cm.), etching on BFK Rives (BP 416, DM 1035, FR 3528, Y 82,270).
BI *Komposition,* s., num., est. DM 900, (09-25-92, Granier, #3040, illus.), sh 12¹³⁄₁₆ x 19¹¹⁄₁₆ in., (32.5 x 50 cm.), color lithograph on hand-made.

$859* *"La Ville" (R.), 1966,* HC s., (04-04-93, Pescheteau, #317), 12³⁄₁₆ x 9¼ in., (31 x 23.5 cm.), color lithograph (BP 566, DM 1381, FR 4689, Y 97,803).

$735* *"La Ville-1966" (R 89),* H.C., s., (01-28-93, Pescheteau, #279), 12³⁄₁₆ x 9¼ in., (31 x 23.5 cm.), color lithograph on Arches (BP 485, DM 1165, FR 3941, Y 91,259).

VIELFAURE, Jean Pierre   b. 1930
$367* *Poemes Germes, (Spirende Digte), 1967,* portfolio, s. J.P. Vielfaure and Ole Sarvig, (03-24-93, Kunsthallen, #330), color lithographs (BP 249, DM 599, FR 2040, Y 43,121, DK 2300).

VIERA DA SILVA
$471* *Ales, P.A.B., 1963,* from Source Dans L'Arbre by Pierre Andre Benoit, s., num. Viera da Silva, s. P.A.B., (11-15-92, Christie-Geneva, #313), 11¼ x 9⅛ in., (285 x 232 mm.), copper engraving on Arches (BP 310, DM 751, FR 2531, Y 58,779, SF 678).

VIGEE-LEBRUN, Louise (after)
$83* *La Tendresse Maternelle,* by Avril, staining, (06-16-93, Bonhams-Chelsea, #427), image 17½ x 12½ in., (44.5 x 31.8 cm.), engraving (BP 55, DM 138, FR 462, Y 8852).

VIGNIERES
$80* *Cycles Automobiles Gladiator, Paris,* cond. B, (03-16-93, Boisgirard, #216), 62³⁄₁₆ x 42¹⁵⁄₁₆ in., (158 x 109 cm.), poster (BP 55, DM 133, FR 452, Y 9355).

VIGNON, Victor   French 1847-1909
$565* *Moulin A Vent,* (05-15-93, Loudmer, #317), 5¹¹⁄₁₆ x 4⁷⁄₁₆ in., (144 x 112 mm.), etching on wove (BP 367, DM 909, FR 3054, Y 62,632).

VIKTOROV, V.
$219* *L'Effort Heroique Pour La Conquete De L'Espace, 1964,* cond. A, (03-16-93, Boisgirard, #10), 22⅝ x 36⁷⁄₁₆ in., (57.5 x 92.5 cm.), offset (BP 151, DM 364, FR 1237, Y 25,608).

VILA
$521* *Pathe-Baby Cine Camera: Two,* repaired tears, printing imperfection, backed on linen, laid on board, (05-07-93, Christie-S. Ken, #124, illus.), one 22 x 30½ in., (55.9 x 77.5 cm.), other 22 x 31 in., (55.9 x 77.5 cm.), color lithograph (BP 330, DM 824, FR 2776, Y 57,366).

VILATO, Javier
$870* *Ensemble De 11 Gravures: Eleven,* all s., edit. 50, good cond., (06-28-93, Loudmer, #128), between 8⁷⁄₁₆ x 6⁵⁄₁₆ in., (215 x 160 mm.), and 7¾ x 9¾ in., (215 x 160 mm.), black etchings and aquatints on wove (BP 583, DM 1478, FR 4980, Y 92,308).

$247* *La Femme Et L'Amour,* s., #90/140, full margins, (05-06-93, Laurin, #92), color etching and aquatint on Rives wove (BP 157, DM 389, FR 1310, Y 27,176).

VILLANI, Henri
BI *Compagnie Alegrienne, Eprunt National, 1920,* s. in stone, tear, small holes, creases, good cond., 1125 x 736mm, sh 1195 x 790mm, est. FF800/1,000, (06-28-93, Loudmer, #405), color lithograph poster on wove.

VILLEFROY
$141* *Ba-Ta-Clan. A Partir Du 21 Novembre 1902, Elle Est Rien Bath'. Revue...,* Paris, Imp. Glaise, cond. B+, (06-11-93, Boisgirard, #160), 63⅜ x 47¼ in., (161 x 120 cm.), poster (BP 93, DM 229, FR 773, Y 14,960).

VILLEMOT, Bernard
$129* *Air France: Afrique Du Nord,* good cond., (03-13-93, Laurin, #74), 39⅜ x 24⁷⁄₁₆ in., (100 x 62 cm.), (BP 90, DM 215, FR 730, Y 15,203).

BI *Arts Menagers,* S.A. Courbet, A- cond., creasing, closed tears, est. $5/700, (08-06-92, Swann, #286, illus.), 64 x 46 in., (162.6 x 116.8 cm.), .

$412* *Bally,* Champigny, A- cond., (08-06-92, Swann, #284, illus.), 62 x 45½ in., (157.5 x 115.6 cm.), (BP 215, DM 609, FR 2056, Y 52,551).

$440* *Bally,* I.P.A., A- cond., creasing, (08-06-92, Swann, #287, illus.), 60½ x 46 in., (153.7 x 116.8 cm.), (BP 230, DM 650, FR 2196, Y 56,122).

$378* *Bally,* excell. cond., (02-04-93, Christie-S. Ken, #151, illus.), 50 x 36 in., (127 x 91.4 cm.), color lithograph backed on linen (BP 264, DM 622, FR 2111, Y 47,021).

$412* *Bally, 1989,* A. Karcher, A cond., (08-06-92, Swann, #285, illus.), 69 x 47 in., (175.3 x 119.4 cm.), (BP 215, DM 609, FR 2056, Y 52,551).

$80* *Calor, Linge Toujours "En Forme", 1960,* cond. B, (03-16-93, Boisgirard, #218), 27⁹⁄₁₆ x 25⁹⁄₁₆ in., (70 x 65 cm.), poster (BP 55, DM 133, FR 452, Y 9355).

$229* *Foire Gastronomique Dijon, 1972,* cond. B, (03-16-93, Boisgirard, #219), 46¹⁄₁₆ x 30⁵⁄₁₆ in., (117 x 77 cm.), poster (BP 158, DM 381, FR 1294, Y 26,777).

$880* *Negrita, Le Rhum, 1980,* Imp. Bedos and Cie, A cond., two-part, (08-06-92, Swann, #283, illus.), 56½ x 88 in., (143.5 x 223.5 cm.), (BP 460, DM 1300, FR 4391, Y 112,245).

$147* *Une Nuit En Voiture-Lit, 1973,* excell. cond., (01-23-93, Ribeyre/Baron, #12), 39⅜ x 24⁷⁄₁₆ in., (100 x 62 cm.), poster (BP 96, DM 234, FR 791, Y 18,398).

$467* *Perrier, 1980,* Lalande, Courbet, A- cond., creasing, (08-06-92, Swann, #288, illus.), 68 x 47 in., (172.7 x 119.4 cm.), (BP 244, DM 690, FR 2330, Y 59,566).

VILLON, Jacques   French 1875-1963
$6900* *Album Pierre Bonnard (G. and P. E686-90, 693-95, Bouvet 116, 118-20,123-25), 1942-46: Seven,* inits. by Pierre Bonnard, #62/80, light-staining, creasing, good cond., Dian Woodner and Andrea Woodner Coll., (05-11-93, Christie-NY, #353, illus.), color lithograph on smooth wove (BP 4405, DM 10,870, FR 36,624, Y 758,992).

BI *App. 21 La Faucheuse (G & P 659), 1928,* after Felix Vallotton, s., num. 65/200, full margins, excellent cond., est. BP 4/600, (11-30-92, Phillips-London, #486), plate 17½ x 14⅜ in., (445 x 365 mm.), aquatint in colors on Arches.

$2897* *Au Bois Ou Lili Au Boa Noir (G. et P. 161), 1906,* whole margins, num., s., (06-11-93, Picard, #185), 14³⁄₁₆ x 9¼ in., (360 x 235 mm.), drypoint in color on Hollande laid (BP 1903, DM 4708, FR 15,874, Y 307,374).

$3855* *Autre Temps (Ginestet-Pouillon E97), 1904,* s., 22/50, blindstamp Ed Sagot Editeur, (05-12-93, AB Stockholm, #7057, illus.), 17½ x 13¾ in., (44.5 x 35 cm.), hand-colored lithograph (BP 2517, DM 6220, FR 20,951, Y 430,390, SK 28,600).

BI *"Bal Du Moulin Rouge" (G. & P. E 249 IV/IV),* s., hinges skin, very good cond., est. $3/400, (10-31-92, Cleveland, #348), 9 x 3¾ in., (22.9 x 9.5 cm.), etching.

BI *Le Banc Des Vieux (Ginestet & Pouillon 30), 1890,* proof, bearing questionable sig., i., t., annot., full margins, goodcond., notation, soiling, est. $1/1,500, (11-05-92, Sotheby-NY, #465), 9⅛ x 11¾ in., (231 x 300 mm.), lithograph p. in colors on wove.

BI *"Le Banc Des Vieux" (GP.E 30), 1899,* #21/40, s., collector's stamp, est. FF 6/8,000, (10-18-92, Pescheteau, #292, illus.), 12⅜ x 17⅛ in., (31.5 x 43.5 cm.), lithograph in colors on wove.

BI *Le Banc Des Vieux, (Ginestet & Pouillon 30), 1890,* proof, bears questionable sig., i. verso w/t., annot. "Essai", full margins, good cond., notation, soiling, est. $4/500, (02-18-93, Sotheby-Arcade, #34), 9⅛ x 11¾ in., (23.2 x 29.8 cm.), lithograph in colors on wove.

$11,863* *Baudelaire Au Socle (Ginestat et Pouillon, 290), 1920,* #48/50, s., (04-02-93, Picard, #200, illus.), 16⁵⁄₁₆ x 11¹⁄₁₆ in., (41.5 x 28.1 cm.), etching in black on wove w/Paul Haasen watermark (BP 7814, DM 19,066, FR 64,754, Y 1,350,677).

$2725* *Les Bucoliques (C. de G. et C.P., E555 a E577): Twenty-Eight,* s., untrimmed margins, (04-02-93, Picard, #203), color lithograph (BP 1795, DM 4380, FR 14,874, Y 310,258).

$358* *Les Bucoliques: Ohne Titel (G., & P. E574), 1942-44,* s., p. by Celestin at Mourlot, margins, good cond., mat staining, light-staining, creases, foxing, surface soiling pencil notations, (02-24-93, Butterfield, #2983), 8⅛ x 19⅜ in., (206 x 492 mm.), lithograph in colors on Arches (BP 250, DM 581, FR 1970, Y 42,009).

BI *Buste De Femme (G. & P. E635), 1922,* after Andre Derain, s. by Derain, #52/200, pub. Bernheim-Jeune, full-margins, good cond., scuffs w/in image, mount-staining, foxing, creases, est. BP 7/900, (06-30-93, Sotheby-London, #712, illus.), 23⅝ x 19⅛ in., (600 x 486 mm.), color aquatint on Arches.

$5995* *Le Cake Walk Des Petites Filles (Ginestat et Pouillon 102), 1904,* whole margins, num. 9, s., drystamp, reddish stains, (06-11-93, Picard, #183, illus.), 12³⁄₁₆ x 16⅝ in., (310 x 423 mm.), drypoint and aquatint in color on wove (BP 3939, DM 9743, FR 32,849, Y 636,074).

BI *Le Cake Walk Des Petites Filles (Ginestet & Pouillon 102), 1904,* second state of four, s., d., margins, good cond., light stain, foxing, glue traces, est. $6/8,000, (11-05-92, Sotheby-NY, #466, illus.), 13¾ x 18 in., (349 x 458 mm.), sheet 16 x 20¼ in., (349 x 458 mm.), drypoint and aquatint p. in colors.

$58* *Camille Renault (De Ginestat et Pouillon E 494): Two,* one, second state of three, s., annot., reddish stains; other, thirdand final state, (06-28-93, Loudmer, #432), 15¾ x 12⁷⁄₁₆ in., (400 x 316 mm.), sh 25¹³⁄₁₆ x 19⅞ in., (400 x 316 mm.), black etching and copper engraving on BFK Rives wove (BP 39, DM 99, FR 332, Y 6154).

$1069* *Camille Renault (Gin.-P.E 494/II), 1945-1946,* s., (06-23-93, Kornfeld, #868), etching and engraving on thick wove (BP 726, DM 1809, FR 6084, Y 116,461, SF 1610).

$330* *Carte De Voeux (E. 585), 1958,* plate s., d., 2nd final state, large margins, image cuts, glue stains, surface soiling, (10-28-92, Butterfield, #2867), 7½ x 6⅛ in., (191 x 156 mm.), color aquatint on wove (BP 210, DM 510, FR 1730, Y 40,491).

$147* *"Cezanne: La Montagne Ste Victoire 1924" (GP. E. 639),* s. in pl., (01-28-93, Pescheteau, #281), 16¹⁵⁄₁₆ x 21⅝ in., (43 x 55 cm.), aquatint on wove (BP 97, DM 233, FR 788, Y 18,252).

$967* *Le Cheval (De Ginestat et Pouillon E 295), 1921,* s., d. in plate, s., annot. in crayon, mat traces verso, (06-28-93, Loudmer, #416), 3⅛ x 5⅛ in., (80 x 130 mm.), sh 8¹⁵⁄₁₆ x 12¹⁵⁄₁₆ in., (80 x 130 mm.), black etching on laid (BP 647, DM 1643, FR 5535, Y 102,599).

$413* *La Colere, 1959, Ginestet & Pouillon App. 20,* s., num. 48/60, bears blindstamp Pierre de Tartas, (09-20-92, Hindman, #751), 12½ x 9⅛ in., (31.8 x 23.2 cm.), etching on Japan paper (BP 242, DM 613, FR 2096, Y 51,044).

$186* *Composition,* s., (03-31-93, Briest, #E116), 18⅛ x 11 in., (46 x 28 cm.), color lithograph (BP 123, DM 299, FR 1016, Y 21,389).

$853* *Composition (G. & P. E660), 1928,* s., #100/200, pub. Bernheim-Jeune, margins slightly trimmed, good cond., (12-03-92, Sotheby-London, #593), 19¾ x 13½ in., (500 x 343 mm.), aquatint in colors on Arches (BP 550, DM 1341, FR 4579, Y 106,134).

$2640* *Composition (G. and P. E660), 1927,* s., #71/200, margins, light/mat staining, remains of glue, taped to overmat, prop. Steven and Ursula Schwartz, (11-09-92, Christie-NY, #232), 19⅜ x 13⅜ in., (492 x 340 mm.), colored aquatint on Arches (BP 1745, DM 4215, FR 14,239, Y 327,625).

BI *Coursier I (G. & P. App. 101), 1958,* s., #47/220, pub. by Guilde de la Gravure, margins, repaired tear extending into image, mount staining, est. BP 2/300, (12-03-92, Sotheby-London, #592), 11½ x 17¾ in., (295 x 455 mm.), lithograph in colors on BFK Rives.

$867* *D'Ou L'On Tourne L'Epaule A La Vie (C. de G. et C.P., E444), 1954,* definitive state, #17/40, s., large margins, (04-02-93, Picard, #202), etching (BP 571, DM 1393, FR 4733, Y 98,713).

$1756* *D'Ou L'On Tourne L'Epaule A La Vie (Gin.-P.E 444/II), 1939,* s., num., (06-23-93, Kornfeld, #867), drypoint and etching on thick wove (BP 1193, DM 2971, FR 9994, Y 191,306, SF 2645).

BI *"La Dame Qu Chien (Adresse Sagot)" (Ginestat & Pouillon E156 iii/iii), 1906,* mat staining, hinges, est. $150/200, (05-15-93, Cleveland, #437), 9⅜ x 8¼ in., (23.8 x 21 cm.), drypoint.

$781* *Le Dejeuner Dur L'Herbe (Auberty et Perussaux 534, Ginestat et Pouillon E668), 1929,* s., #161/200, large margins, faults, (05-06-93, Laurin, #93), color aquatint (BP 495, DM 1230, FR 4141, Y 85,928).

$4125* *Le Dejeuner Sur L'Herbe (G. & P. 668), 1929,* after Edouard Manet, s. by Villon, #99/200, full margins, good cond.,mat stain, tear, back board stain, label, (11-05-92, Sotheby-NY, #468, illus.), 19¾ x 24¾ in., (500 x 627 mm.), aquatint (BP 2683, DM 6524, FR 22,071, Y 506,073).

BI *Dents De Lait Dents De Loup,* s., num. 28/50, pub. Pierre de Tartas, pub. blindstamp, p. by GeorgesLeblanc, 1959, full margins, good cond., est. BP 250/300, (11-30-92, Phillips-London, #485), plate 12¼ x 18½ in., (311 x 470 mm.), etching on wove.

$275* *Deux Femmes, 1907,* from Impressions Dessines d'apres Nature, prov., (03-24-93, Grogan, #115), 8 x 6 in., (20.3 x 15.2 cm.), color lithograph (BP 186, DM 449, FR 1529, Y 32,311).

$3996* *Devant Un Guignol (G. et P. 241), 1909,* whole margins, num. 12, s., drystamp, (06-11-93, Picard, #186), 15¹³⁄₁₆ x 11¹⁵⁄₁₆ in., (402 x 303 mm.), drypoint in black on laid (BP 2625, DM 6494, FR 21,896, Y 423,979).

$1650* *Eglisade Limours (Ginestet and Pouillon E654), 1926,* s. Utrillo, #84/200, (12-13-92, Hindman, #270), 19⅜ x 11 in., color aquatint (BP 1055, DM 2593, FR 8838, Y 204,132).

BI *Eglise De Limours (E. 654), 1926,* after Maurice Utrillo, s. Maurice Utrillo, #153/200, plate i., full margins, mat burn, foxing, backboard burn, partially taped, good cond., est. $2/4,000, (12-12-92, Weschler, #178, illus.), 19¼ x 11 in., (48.9 x 27.9 cm.), etching and aquatint.

$3513* *En Visite (Gin.-P.E 131/III), 1905,* s. in pencil, num., (06-23-93, Kornfeld, #854, illus.), drypoint and aquatint on simili Japan (BP 2387, DM 5944, FR 19,994, Y 382,721, SF 5290).

BI *Entwurf Fur Ein Werbeprospekt Fur Den Verlag Ed. Sagot, c. 1900/10,* very rare, est. DM 1,500, (12-05-92, Bassenge, #7637, illus.), drypoint.

BI *Felix Barre (Ginestet & Pouillon E276 II/II), 1913,* s., #39/50, prov., est. $3/4,000, (05-16-93, Hindman, #481), 8 x 5¾ in., (20.3 x 14.6 cm.), burin on cream laid paper.

$10,925* *Femme Debout De Dos (G./P. 248), 1909-10,* s., #6/15, full margins, good cond., mat stain, creases, soiling, (05-13-93, Sotheby-NY, #852, illus.), 12½ x 7⅝ in., (317 x 193 mm.), drypoint on laid (BP 7172, DM 17,641, FR 59,504, Y 1,219,716).

$6491* *Les Femmes D'Ouessant (Gin.-P.E. 81/II/a), 1903,* s., d., num., (06-23-93, Kornfeld, #851, illus.), color aquatint on thick wove (BP 4410, DM 10,983, FR 36,944, Y 707,158, SF 9775).

$770* *"Les Femmes D'Ouessant" (Ginestat and Pauillon, E81), 1903,* s., d. Jacques Villon/03; collector's annots. verso, good cond., tape/light staining, soiling, foxing, ink transfer, (09-11-92, Skinner, #11, illus.), 10¹³⁄₁₆ x 14⅞ in., (27.5 x 37.8 cm.), color etching/aquatint on wove (BP 398, DM 1108, FR 3767, Y 95,403).

$771* *Les Femmes De Thrace (G. & P. E205), 1908,* s., #19/30, margins, rolling creases, paper discoloration, (06-30-93, Sotheby-London, #716, illus.), 8½ x 6½ in., (216 x 165 mm.), etching on laid (BP 517, DM 1315, FR 4436, Y 82,610).

$3450* *Fete Nautique (G./P. 649), 1926-27,* after Raoul Dufy, s. Dufy, #172/200, pub. Galerie Bernheim-Jeune, 1928, margins, image in good cond., discolored, glue stains, (05-13-93, Sotheby-NY, #854), 18½ x 21 in., (470 x 533 mm.), aquatint in colors on heavy wove (BP 2265, DM 5571, FR 18,791, Y 385,174).

$2640* *Fete Nautique (Ginestet and Pouillon E649), 1926,* s. by Dufy, #172/200, (12-13-92, Hindman, #269), 18⅜ x 20¾ in., color aquatint (BP 1688, DM 4149, FR 14,140, Y 326,611).

$197* *Fleurs (C. de G. et C.P. E667),* after Suzanne Duchamp, #142/200, s. by both, yellowed, creases, goodmargins, (06-16-93, Ader Tajan, #146), 12 x 15¹⁵⁄₁₆ in., (30.5 x 40.5 cm.), color aquatint (BP 131, DM 327, FR 1097, Y 21,011).

BI *Le Garde (De Ginestet/Pouillon E. 249/IV), 1910,* s., est. DM 500, (12-01-92, Karl/Faber, #1331), 8⅞ x 3¾ in., (22.5 x 9.5 cm.), etching in color on hand-made.

$869* *Guinguette Fleurie, 1890,* p. d'Art Emalfeyt, creases, (01-31-93, Morelle/Marchan, #186, illus.), 36⅝ x 50⅜ in.,

(93 x 128 cm.), poster (BP 584, DM 1400, FR 4733, Y 108,408).

$561* *Homme Lisant (De Ginestat et Pouillon E 325), 1929,* s., d. in plate, s., 20/50 in crayon, mat traces verso, (06-28-93, Loudmer, #418), 10⅞ x 8¾ in., (277 x 222 mm.), sh 15¾ x 11 13/16 in., (277 x 222 mm.), black etching on laid (BP 376, DM 953, FR 3211, Y 59,523).

BI *Jacques Villon Presente Par Lionello Venturi (G.P. App. 66), 1962,* s., #102/175, est. FF1,200/1,500, (05-27-93, Briest, #215), 11 7/16 x 13 15/16 in., (29 x 35.5 cm.), color lithograph on Arches wove.

BI *Jeune Femme (G. and P. E455), c. 1942,* 2nd final state, s., i. Epreuve d'Artiste, ink i., full margins, surface scrapes, staining, tape, skinned spots, Mr. and Mrs. Sam B. Cantey III Estate, est. $2/3,000, (05-11-93, Christie-NY, #352, illus.), plate 11⅛ x 8⅛ in., (283 x 206 mm.), etching on BFK.

$1376* *L'Aventure (C. Ginestat et C. Pouillon, E387),* definitive state, #43/108, s., drystamp, crease, untrimmed large margins, (06-16-93, Ader Tajan, #143), 12⅝ x 8⅜ in., (32 x 21.2 cm.), etching and drypoint (BP 917, DM 2284, FR 7666, Y 146,758).

$1005* *L'Aventure (De Ginestat et Pouillon E 387), 1935,* s. in plate and crayon, 67/108, drystamp, fourth and final state, (06-28-93, Loudmer, #406), 12½ x 8⅜ in., (318 x 212 mm.), sh 16⅛ x 12⅜ in., (318 x 212 mm.), black etching and drypoint on laid (BP 673, DM 1708, FR 5753, Y 106,631).

$2069* *L'Oiseau (De Ginestat et Pouillon E 293), 1921,* s., d. in plate, s., annot. in crayon, oxidation, mat traces verso, (06-28-93, Loudmer, #415, illus.), 4 x 6⅝ in., (102 x 169 mm.), sh 6 7/16 x 9 13/16 in., (102 x 169 mm.), black etching on laid (BP 1385, DM 3516, FR 11,843, Y 219,523).

BI *L'Oiseau (G. & P. E293), 1921,* s., i. Tire a 50, full margins, good cond., mount-staining, est. BP 2,5/3,000, (06-30-93, Sotheby-London, #711, illus.), 4 x 6⅝ in., (102 x 168 mm.), etching on laid.

$424* *L'Ostensoir (C. de Ginestet et C. Pouillon, E. 482), 1944,* illus., s., large margins, (02-03-93, Ader Tajan, #210), 12⅝ x 10 7/16 in., (32 x 26.5 cm.), etching (BP 296, DM 698, FR 2367, Y 52,743).

$165* *Livres Et Mappemondes (Ginestat and Pouillon App. 104), 1959,* s., annot. epreuve d'artiste, (12-13-92, Hindman, #171), 8½ x 6 in., color lithograph (BP 105, DM 259, FR 884, Y 20,413).

$1160* *Madame Paul Petit (De Ginestat et Pouillon E 388), 1935,* second state of three, s., artist's proof, small reddish stains, (06-28-93, Loudmer, #426), 8 13/16 x 5⅞ in., (224 x 149 mm.), sh 13 9/16 x 11⅝ in., (224 x 149 mm.), black drypoint and etching on laid (BP 777, DM 1971, FR 6640, Y 123,077).

$3360* *Madeleine Au Fauteuil or: Petite Mutine (Gin.-P.E 226/II), 1908,* s., num., (06-23-93, Kornfeld, #861), drypoint on Japan (BP 2283, DM 5685, FR 19,124, Y 366,053, SF 5060).

$600* *Manege, Rue Caulaincourt (G. et P. 111), 1904,* whole margins, (06-11-93, Picard, #184), 15⅜ x 19½ in., (390 x 495 mm.), etching and aquatint in bistre on wove (BP 394, DM 975, FR 3288, Y 63,660).

$2411* *Manet, Le Dejeuner Sur L'Herbe (Ginestet et Pouillon E668), 1929,* s., (11-16-92, Briest, #381, illus.), 25 x 29 15/16 in., (49 x 61.5 cm.), aquatint in colors (BP 1585, DM 3845, FR 12,955, Y 300,886).

$443* *Marchands Des Quatre Saisons,* s., (12-05-92, Bassenge, #7796), 11 13/16 x 15⅜ in., (30 x 39 cm.), etching on handmade Arches (BP 277, DM 691, FR 2354, Y 54,888).

$4888* *La Mariee (Ginestet & Pouillon 672), 1934,* after Marcel Duchamp, s. by Villon, #55/200, s. and t. by Duchamp, margins, good cond., scuffs, scratches in image, mat/light stain, discolored, (02-11-93, Sotheby-NY, #270), 19 11/16 x 12⅜ in., (500 x 315 mm.), sh 25⅛ x 18 5/16 in., (500 x 315 mm.), color aquatint (BP 3449, DM 8097, FR 27,399, Y 589,271).

BI *Maternite (G & P 534), 1952,* s., #58/75, 4th final state, full margins, est. BP 5/600, (11-30-92, Phillips-London, #484), plate 11 x 7½ in., (279 x 191 mm.), etching.

$1458* *Maternite (G. & P. E670), c. 1930,* after Pablo Picasso, s. Villon, pub. Bernheim-Jeune, margins, good cond., (06-30-93, Sotheby-London, #714), 25½ x 16¾ in., (648 x 425 mm.), color aquatint on wove (BP 977, DM 2487, FR 8389, Y 156,220).

BI *Maternite (Ginestet & Pouillon E670), c. 1930,* after Pablo Picasso, s. Villon, pub. Bernheim-Jeune, margins, good cond., est. BP 1,2/1,800, (12-03-92, Sotheby-London, #589, illus.), 25½ x 16¾ in., (650 x 425 mm.), aquatint in colors on wove.

$2520* *Minne Au Tub (Gin.-P.E 194/X), 1907,* s., num., (06-23-93, Kornfeld, #858), etching on Japan (BP 1712, DM 4264, FR 14,343, Y 274,540, SF 3795).

$1985* *Minne Jouant Avec Un Chat or: Renee Au Chat Blanc (Gin.-P.E. 192), 1907,* s., num., (06-23-93, Kornfeld, #857), line etching and aquatint on handmade Japan (BP 1349, DM 3359, FR 11,298, Y 216,254, SF 2990).

$1858* *Mon Vieux Luxembourg (G. et P., 384), 1935,* whole margins, #40/40, s., (04-02-93, Picard, #201), 10 1/16 x 15⅝ in., (25.5 x 39.7 cm.), etching and drypoint in black on Rives wove (BP 1224, DM 2986, FR 10,142, Y 211,545).

BI *La Montagne Sainte-Victoire, (G. & P. E639), 1923,* i., num. 154/200, pub. Bernheim-Jeune, mount-staining, tape, est. BP 900/1,200, (12-01-92, Christie-London, #551, illus.), P. 17 3/16 x 23 15/16 in., (437 x 608 mm.), aquatint in colors on wove.

$1760* *Nature Morte (After Picasso) (Ginestet & Poullion E 652), 1927,* s. Picasso, #86/200, (03-14-93, Hindman, #269), sheet 19½ x 25½ in., (49.5 x 64.8 cm.), 14⅝ x 19½ in., (49.5 x 64.8 cm.), (BP 1228, DM 2929, FR 9960, Y 207,425).

$458* *Nature Morte Aux Noix (Gin.-P. 323/I), 1929,* num., (06-23-93, Kornfeld, #865), drypoint on handmade (BP 311, DM 775, FR 2607, Y 49,897, SF 690).

$2673* *Le Negre En Bonne Fortune (Ginestet-Pouillon E 22), 1899,* s., num., (06-23-93, Kornfeld, #850), color aquatint on handmade (BP 1816, DM 4523, FR 15,213, Y 291,208, SF 4025).

BI *Notre-Dame-De-Vie, Les Cypres (G./P. 381), 1935,* s., i. epr. d'artiste, full margins, good cond., foxing, skinning, est. $1/1,200, (05-13-93, Sotheby-NY, #853), 5¼ x 8 in., (132 x 202 mm.), etching.

BI *Nu (G. & P. E637), 1923,* after Renoir, i. Controlee par Pierre Renoir, #175/200, pub. Bernheim-Jeune, margins, good cond., est. BP 1/1,500, (12-03-92, Sotheby-London, #590, illus.), 23¼ x 17½ in., (590 x 443 mm.), aquatint in colors on wove.

$1458* *Nu (G. & P. E637), 1923,* after Andre Derain, i., #175/200, pub. Bernheim-Jeune, margins, goodcond., (06-30-93, Sotheby-London, #713, illus.), 23¼ x 17½ in., (591 x 445 mm.), color aquatint on wove (BP 977, DM 2487, FR 8389, Y 156,220).

$1909* *Nu A Genoux (Gin.-P.E 328/II), 1929-1930,* s., num., (06-23-93, Kornfeld, #866), engraving, drypoint and etching on handmade (BP 1297, DM 3230, FR 10,865, Y 207,975, SF 2875).

$1450* *Nu A Genoux, 1929,* s., d. in plate, 13/50 in crayon, second and final state, reddish stains, annot., (06-28-93, Loudmer, #425), 8¾ x 6 7/16 in., (223 x 164 mm.), sh 15⅞ x 11⅞ in., (223 x 164 mm.), black etching and drypoint on thin laid (BP 971, DM 2464, FR 8300, Y 153,846).

$2200* *Olympia (G. & P. 647), 1926,* after Edouard Manet, s. by Villon, d., #63/200, pub. Bernheim-Jeune,margins, creases, (02-24-93, Butterfield, #2796, illus.), 16 x 23⅛ in., (406 x 587 mm.), etching & aquatint in colors on wove (BP 1534, DM 3571, FR 12,108, Y 258,155).

$880* *Le Paysan (G. & P. E 653), 1927,* after Vincent Van Gogh, s., #119/200, annot. d'apres Van Gogh, (c) inplate, blindstamp pub. Bernheim-Jeune, full margins, good cond., foxing, surface soiling, pencil notations, (02-24-93, Butterfield, #2797), 15½ x 12½ in., (394 x 318 mm.), aquatint in colors on Arches (BP 614, DM 1429, FR 4843, Y 103,262).

$1380* *Le Paysan (G./P. 653), 1927-28,* after Vincent Van Gogh, s., #16/200, pub. Bernheim-Jeune, full margins, (top, bottom margins folded back), good cond., mat/light-stain, discoloration, water stains, tape stains, (05-13-93,

Sotheby-NY, #855), 15½ x 12½ in., (395 x 316 mm.), aquatint in colors (BP 906, DM 2228, FR 7516, Y 154,069).

$2749* *La Pedicure (Gin.-P.E 195/VI), 1907,* s., num., (06-23-93, Kornfeld, #859), line etching und Flachenatzung on handmade (BP 1868, DM 4651, FR 15,646, Y 299,488, SF 4140).

$445* *Petit Bouquet (De Ginestat et Pouillon E 298), 1926,* s., d. in plate, crayon s., annot., (06-28-93, Loudmer, #408), 5½ x 3⁹⁄₁₆ in., (139 x 90 mm.), sh 9¹³⁄₁₆ x 6⁷⁄₁₆ in., (139 x 90 mm.), black etching on Arches laid (BP 298, DM 756, FR 2547, Y 47,215).

$6262* *Le Petit Equilibriste (Gin.-P.E 287), 1914,* s., num., (06-23-93, Kornfeld, #863), drypoint on handmade (BP 4254, DM 10,596, FR 35,640, Y 682,209, SF 9430).

$2749* *Petite Boudeuse (Gin.-P.E 129/II), 1905,* s. in pencil, num., (06-23-93, Kornfeld, #853), drypoint and aquatint on wove (BP 1868, DM 4651, FR 15,646, Y 299,488, SF 4140).

$7475* *La Petite Mulatresse (Ginestet and Pouillon E263), 1911,* s., #5/30, full margins, glue, good cond., Mr. and Mrs. Sam B. Cantey III Estate, (05-11-93, Christie-NY, #351, illus.), plate 9 x 7½ in., (229 x 191 mm.), etching on laid Arches (BP 4772, DM 11,775, FR 39,676, Y 822,242).

$1544* *Les Petits Haleurs (G. & P. E176), 1907,* s., #40/50, full margins, good cond., light-staining, (06-30-93, Sotheby-London, #715, illus.), 5¾ x 7⅞ in., (146 x 200 mm.), aquatint on laid (BP 1035, DM 2633, FR 8884, Y 165,434).

BI *Le Pigeonnier Normand (Ginestet/Pouillon Appendice 95), 1954,* s., from portfolio Hommage a Mourlot, est. DM 800, (05-26-93, Lempertz, #517, illus.), 19¹³⁄₁₆ x 25¹⁵⁄₁₆ in., (50.3 x 66 cm.), color lithograph on Arches wove.

$1099* *La Plaine Entre Cannes Et Mougins (G. et P. 377), 1934,* whole margins, #38/50, reddish stains, (06-11-93, Picard, #188), 6⁷⁄₁₆ x 10⅝ in., (164 x 270 mm.), etching in black on wove (BP 722, DM 1786, FR 6022, Y 116,605).

$348* *Les Pommiers A Cany (De Ginestat et Pouillon E 400), 1935,* s., d. in stone, s., 1/20 in crayon, reddish stains, (06-28-93, Loudmer, #420), 6⁵⁄₁₆ x 9¹⁄₁₆ in., (160 x 230 mm.), sh 8¹¹⁄₁₆ x 10¹⁄₁₆ in., (160 x 230 mm.), black lithograph on wove (BP 233, DM 591, FR 1992, Y 36,923).

$6325* *Le Porte De La Rochelle (G. & P. 644), 1925-26,* after Paul Signac, s. by Signac, #78/200, pub. Bernheim-Jeune, full margins, mat staining, foxing, thin spots, staining, good cond., (11-05-92, Sotheby-NY, #467, illus.), 18 x 23½ in., (458 x 596 mm.), aquatint in colors on Arches (BP 4114, DM 10,003, FR 33,842, Y 775,978).

BI *Portrait D'Homme (G. & P. E658), 1928,* after Crotti, s. by artist, #98/200, pub. Bernheim-Jeune, good cond.,handling marks, est. BP 6/800, (12-03-92, Sotheby-London, #591), 18¼ x 12⅞ in., (463 x 326 mm.), aquatint in colors on Arches.

$413* *Portrait De Rimbaud,* s., num. 43/92, (09-20-92, Hindman, #752), 9⅛ x 6⅞ in., (23.2 x 17.5 cm.), etching (BP 242, DM 613, FR 2096, Y 51,044).

BI *"Portrait Of Rimbaud",* plate s., est. $2/300, (12-02-92, Boos, #472), image 9³⁄₁₆ x 6¾ in., (233 x 172 mm.), etching.

$629* *Le Potager Aux Citrouilles (C. de G. et C.P. E 457), 1942,* yellowed, definitive state, #61/108, s., creases, large margins, (06-16-93, Ader Tajan, #144), 11 x 14¾ in., (28 x 37.4 cm.), etching (BP 419, DM 1044, FR 3504, Y 67,086).

$688* *Le Potager Aux Citrouilles (C. de G. et C.P. E457),* definitive state, #43/108, s., staining, large untrimmed margins, (06-16-93, Ader Tajan, #145), 11³⁄₁₆ x 14¾ in., (28.4 x 37.5 cm.), etching (BP 459, DM 1142, FR 3833, Y 73,379).

$541* *Le Potager Aux Citrouilles (De Ginestat et Pouillon E 457), 1942,* s., d. in plate, s., 7/108, reddish stains, (06-28-93, Loudmer, #414), 11 x 14¾ in., (280 x 375 mm.), sh 15¹⁵⁄₁₆ x 20¹⁄₁₆ in., (280 x 375 mm.), black etching on Lana wove (BP 362, DM 919, FR 3097, Y 57,401).

$6872* *Le Potin (Gin.-P.E 96/III), 1904,* s., num., (06-23-93, Kornfeld, #852, illus.), drypoint and aquatint in dark green on thick handmade (BP 4668, DM 11,628, FR 39,112, Y 748,665, SF 10,350).

BI *Premiers Beaux Jours, Or La Dame En Bleu (Ginestet and Pouillon E71), 1902,* s., i. Epreuve d'Essai, proof, wide margins, light/mat staining, creasing, repaired tears, good cond., est. $15/18,000, (11-09-92, Christie-NY, #229, illus.), 18¼ x 13 in., (464 x 330 mm.), etching and aquatint in colors on wove.

$2497* *Rene A Bicyclette, Ou Un Debut, (G. and P. E152), 1906,* watermark, 2nd (final) state, s., i., good cond., (12-01-92, Christie-London, #550), P. 15⅝ x 11⁹⁄₁₆ in., (397 x 294 mm.), drypoint w/aquatint on BFK Rives laid (BP 1650, DM 3980, FR 13,563, Y 310,881).

$3971* *Renee Au Canape (Gin.-P.E 183), 1907,* s., num., (06-23-93, Kornfeld, #856), drypoint on handmade (BP 2698, DM 6719, FR 22,601, Y 432,618, SF 5980).

$6160* *Renee De Face (Petite Planche) Ou Portrait D'Enfant, Ginestet & Pouillon E261,* s., num. 7/30, full margins, (09-20-92, Hindman, #749, illus.), 10⅞ x 7⅜ in., (27.6 x 18.7 cm.), etching on laid paper, watermark (BP 3607, DM 9141, FR 31,269, Y 761,340).

$2673* *Renee De Face, Petite Planche (Gin.-P.E 261), 1911,* s., num., (06-23-93, Kornfeld, #862), etching on handmade (BP 1816, DM 4523, FR 15,213, Y 291,208, SF 4025).

$158* *"Renoir: La Loge" (G.P. E 661),* (01-28-93, Pescheteau, #280), a vue 13⅜ x 11⁷⁄₁₆ in., (34 x 29 cm.), aquatint (BP 104, DM 250, FR 847, Y 19,618).

$6325* *Sous La Tente, Sur La Plage (Blonville) (G./P. 137), 1905,* trial proof, pub. Sagot, blindstamp, large (full?) margins, good cond., mat stain, repaired tears, creases, platemark backed w/Japan, (05-13-93, Sotheby-NY, #851, illus.), 18¼ x 22¾ in., (465 x 578 mm.), sh 21⅝ x 29 in., (465 x 578 mm.), aquatint in colors on wove (BP 4152, DM 10,213, FR 34,450, Y 706,152).

BI *Sous La Tente, Sur La Plage (Blonville) (Ginestet/Pouillon 137), 1905,* s., i. essai, working proof impression, large margins (unevenly trimmed), tears into image, tears, loses, mat stained, soiled, est. $7/9,000, (05-13-93, Sotheby-NY, #850, illus.), 18⅞ x 23⅛ in., (478 x 588 mm.), aquatint in colors w/touches of salmon and blue hand-coloring on heavy wove.

BI *The State Funeral Of General Foch,* s., #2/200, blindstamp Calcographia de Louvre, full margins, surfacesoiling, est. BP 2/300, (11-30-92, Phillips-London, #487), sheet 23 x 29½ in., (584 x 749 mm.), color etching w/ aquatint on Arches.

BI *Sur La Plage, Or Le Treport (G. and P. E136), 1905,* s., #16/30, full margins, mat staining, crease, tears, est. $10/ 12,000, (11-09-92, Christie-NY, #230, illus.), 15¼ x 23 in., (387 x 584 mm.), etching and aquatint in colors on Rives.

$387* *La Table Au Tampon Noir, 1931,* third and final state, s. in plate and in crayon, artist's proof, mat traces verso, (06-28-93, Loudmer, #417), 5½ x 4⁵⁄₁₆ in., (140 x 110 mm.), sh 9¹⁵⁄₁₆ x 7⅝ in., (140 x 110 mm.), black drypoint and etching on laid (BP 259, DM 658, FR 2215, Y 41,061).

$8400* *Table D'Echecs (Gin.-P.E 292), 1920,* mono. appears in fourth portfolio of third issue of "Die Schaffenden", blindstamp, (06-23-93, Kornfeld, #864, illus.), etching on wove (BP 5707, DM 14,213, FR 47,809, Y 915,132, SF 12,650).

$28,249* *La Table Servie (Ginestet-Pouillon E 258), 1913,* s., (06-10-93, Hauswedell/Nolt, #957, illus.), image 11⁵⁄₁₆ x 15³⁄₁₆ in., (28.7 x 38.6 cm.), drypoint on Arches (BP 18,478, DM 46,001, FR 154,874, Y 2,998,514).

$434* *Tete De Fillette (Ginestet/Pouillon E 324), 1913,* #46/50, s., (11-13-92, Koller, #5469), 10⅞ x 8⅜ in., (27.7 x 21.3 cm.), drypoint and etching on wove (BP 280, DM 681, FR 2298, Y 53,866, SF 614).

$405* *Les Travaux Et Les Jours (G.P. App. 44,50, 52, 58, 60), 1962: Six,* (05-27-93, Briest, #213), 10⅝ x 16⁹⁄₁₆ in., (27 x 42 cm.), 10⅝ x 8¼ in., (27 x 42 cm.), etchings (BP 259, DM 650, FR 2190, Y 43,418).

$2291* *Trois Femmes Sur L'Herbe or: Repos Sur L'Herbe (Gin.-P.E 203), 1907,* s., num., blindstamp, foxed, (06-23-93, Kornfeld, #860), etching on handmade (BP 1556, DM 3876, FR 13,039, Y 249,591, SF 3450).

$387* *Vlaminck, Le Village D'Herouville (De Ginestat et Pouillon E 638), 1923,* 200 impressions, stamp, (06-28-93, Loudmer, #413), 18⅞ x 23¾ in., (480 x 603 mm.), color aquatint on wove (BP 259, DM 658, FR 2215, Y 41,061).

VILLON, Jacques (after)
$275* *Les Mondes (G. & P. A94), 1954,* s., #34/50, p. Mourlot, pub. XXe siecle, large margins, good cond., light/mat staining, tape remains, (10-28-92, Butterfield, #2866), 11⅜ x 7¾ in., (289 x 197 mm.), color lithograph on Arches (BP 175, DM 425, FR 1442, Y 33,742).
$123* *Oiseau En Vol (G. et P. App. 99), c. 1955,* s., #147/220, full margins, drystamp, (05-06-93, Laurin, #94), color lithograph on Rives wove (BP 78, DM 194, FR 652, Y 13,533).

VILLON, Jacques (by or after)   French 1875-1963
$825* *Monsieur Duchamp, 1962, Ginestet & Pouillon App. 118,* s., num. 49/125, bearing Atelier Crommelynck Paris, Editeur stamp, (09-20-92, Hindman, #750, illus.), sheet 30 x 22¼ in., (34.3 x 48.9 cm.), color aquatint and dry point overprinted w/lithographic elements, onwove, watermark (BP 483, DM 1224, FR 4188, Y 101,965).

VINCENT, George   English 1796-1831
$80 *A Traveller In A Norfolk Wooded Landscape,* mono., d., (02-05-93, G.A. Key, #73), 7 x 6 in., (17.8 x 15.2 cm.), etching (BP 55, DM 133, FR 448, Y 9955).

VINCENT, Rene
$275* *Porto Ramos-Pinto,* Vercasson, A cond., (08-06-92, Swann, #289, illus.), 20¼ x 14½ in., (51.4 x 36.8 cm.), (BP 144, DM 406, FR 1372, Y 35,077).
$3218* *Shell Spirit & Motor Oils, Your Car Deserves Them Both, 1926,* p. Waterlow & Sons, ref. #125, cond. 5, (10-13-92, Phillips-London, #54, illus.), 29¹⁵⁄₁₆ x 44⅞ in., (76 x 114 cm.), color lithograph (BP 1874, DM 4714, FR 16,018, Y 390,202).

VINCI, Leonardo da (after)
BI *Young Boy With Puzzle,* by Francesco Bartolozzi, pub. A. Molteno, 1795, w/margins, est. BP 6/80, (06-16-93, Bonhams-Chelsea, #490), pl. 9 x 7¼ in., (22.9 x 18.4 cm.), stipple engraving.

VINCKEBOONS, David   1576-1633
$1983* *Tod Und Liebe Tauschen Pfeile Aus (The Illustrated Bartsch 53, Misattributions, 3, Hollstein 11 I), 1719,* after Vinckeboons, watermark, prov., (06-04-93, Bassenge, #5400, illus.), 10¾ x 14³⁄₁₆ in., (27.3 x 36 cm.), engraving (BP 1312, DM 3220, FR 10,854, Y 213,870).

VINNE, Jan Vincentsz van der (called Jean des NAGEOIRES)
1663-1721
$1062* *Te Scholenaer (Wurzbach 3, Nagler aus 1-15, Hollstein 7 I),* t., num., (06-04-93, Bassenge, #5401, illus.), 6 x 7⅜ in., (15.3 x 18.7 cm.), etching (BP 703, DM 1725, FR 5813, Y 114,538).

VIRGIL (NEVJESTIC called)   b. 1935
$53* *"Composition",* #51/70, s., (01-28-93, Pescheteau, #282), 29¹⁵⁄₁₆ x 22¹⁄₁₆ in., (76 x 56 cm.), etchings and aquatints on 17 cuivres on Arches (BP 35, DM 84, FR 284, Y 6581).

VIRTUE & CO., Publishers
$76* *A Portrait Of Napoleon On His Mount,* indistinctly s., margins, (01-21-93, Bonhams-Chelsea, #77), plate 19¼ x 14½ in., (48.9 x 36.8 cm.), mezzotint, p. in colors (BP 50, DM 121, FR 409, Y 9512).

VISAT, George (after George BRAQUE)
BI *Cubist Composition,* narrow margins, good cond., est. BP 250/350, (10-27-92, Phillips-London, #185A), plate 13¾ x 23¾ in., (349 x 603 mm.), aquatint w/etching, in colors on wove.

VISHNIAC, Roman   1897-1990
$1650* *Albert Einstein, 1942,* s. by photog., p. 1980's, (10-15-92, Sotheby-NY, #391, illus.), 19½ x 15⅞ in., (49.5 x 40.3 cm.), photograph, platinum print (BP 1010, DM 2456, FR 8329, Y 197,960).
$1100* *Boy With Earlocks (Polish Jews, p. 26),* s. by photog., late 1930's, p. 1980's, (10-15-92, Sotheby-NY, #390,

illus.), 19¾ x 16 in., (50.2 x 40.6 cm.), photograph, platinum print (BP 673, DM 1637, FR 5553, Y 131,974).
$3738* *"The Cheder, Slonim" (A Vanished World, pl. 146),* s. by photog., p. notations in unident. hand, 1938, p. 1980's, (04-06-93, Sotheby-NY, #292, illus.), 19½ x 15¾ in., photograph (BP 2469, DM 6022, FR 20,393, Y 426,323).
BI *Dance Study, 1940's,* mounted, s. by photog., (10-15-92, Sotheby-NY, #386, illus.), 10½ x 12 in., (26.7 x 30.5 cm.), photograph, gelatin silver print.
$3740* *Entrance To Old Ghetto, Cracow, (1938),* p.l., s., t., d. in ink; s., t., d. on overmat, lit., (10-13-92, Christie-NY, #380, illus.), 13¼ x 10¼ in., (33.7 x 26 cm.), photograph, gelatin silver print (BP 2178, DM 5479, FR 18,616, Y 453,498).
$920* *"Examination By Baruch Rabinovitsh" (A Vanished World, pl. 78),* printer's blindstamp, s., t. by photog., 1938, p. 1980's, (04-06-93, Sotheby-NY, #293, illus.), 15¾ x 19½ in., photograph (BP 608, DM 1482, FR 5019, Y 104,927).
BI *The Jews Of Eastern Europe: Life Before The War, 1936-37: Fourteen,* each s., printing d.; credit stamps, lit., est. $30/40,000, (04-08-93, Christie-NY, #114, illus.), each approx. 3½ x 4¾ in., (8.9 x 12.1 cm.), photograph, gelatin silver print.
$863* *"Life Of Man", 1928,* p.l., s., t., d., (05-23-93, Butterfield, #3648, illus.), 10⅝ x 13⅝ in., photograph, gelatin silver print (BP 562, DM 1411, FR 4750, Y 95,391).
BI *"Life Of Man", 1928/later,* s., t., d., Dixon Collection, est. $3/4,000, (11-16-92, Butterfield, #6213, illus.), 10⅝ x 13⅝ in., (270.4 x 346.7 mm.), photograph, gelatin silver print.
$2990* *Marc Chagall,* printer's blindstamp, s., i. by photog., late 1950's, p. 1980's, (04-06-93, Sotheby-NY, #297, illus.), 19½ x 15¾ in., photograph, platinum print (BP 1975, DM 4817, FR 16,312, Y 341,013).
$2588* *"Munkatsch Am Sabbat", c. 1938,* mounted, s. R Wischniak by photog., t., (04-06-93, Sotheby-NY, #296, illus.), 11⅛ x 9⅛ in., photograph (BP 1709, DM 4169, FR 14,119, Y 295,164).
$2300* *The Poultry Farmer (A Vanished World, pl. 150), 1936,* mounted, s. R Wischniak by photog., i., (04-06-93, Sotheby-NY, #295, illus.), 11⅛ x 9 in., photograph (BP 1519, DM 3705, FR 12,548, Y 262,318).
$8050* *Rabbi Carrying Books (A Vanished World, pl. 12, variant cropping), c. 1938,* mounted, s. R. Wischniak, i. by photog., (04-06-93, Sotheby-NY, #294, illus.), 11½ x 9¼ in., photograph (BP 5317, DM 12,969, FR 43,917, Y 918,111).
$1540* *The Tax Collector Wants His Three Zlotys, Cracow, 1938 (A Vanished World, pl. 168),* s. by photog., p. 1980's, (10-15-92, Sotheby-NY, #389, illus.), 19¼ x 15¾ in., (48.9 x 40 cm.), photograph, platinum print (BP 942, DM 2292, FR 7774, Y 184,763).
$1100* *Warsaw (A Vanished World, back cover and pl. 42),* photog.'s estate stamp, 1939, p.l., (10-15-92, Sotheby-NY, #555, illus.), 12 x 10¾ in., (30.5 x 27.3 cm.), photograph, gelatin silver print (BP 673, DM 1637, FR 5553, Y 131,974).
$1925* *Warsaw: Two: "Carpatho Ukraina, Heder" and "The Boy I Fell In Love With", 1938,* s., t., d. by photog. in ink, p. l., (10-15-92, Sotheby-NY, #387, illus.), photograph, gelatin silver prints (BP 1178, DM 2865, FR 9717, Y 230,954).

VISHNUPERSAUD (after)
$50 *Botanical Subjects: Six,* engr. by M. Gauci, (12-11-92, G.A. Key, #106), 14 x 10 in., (35.6 x 25.4 cm.), hand colored lithograph (BP 32, DM 79, FR 270, Y 6187).

VISSCHER, Claes Jansz   1586/87-1652
$2673* *Jagdszenen (Hollstein (Serwouters) Bd. XXVI, 20-26; Hollstein (Visschr) Bd. XXXVIII, 361-362): Nine,* (06-23-93, Kornfeld, #110), etching (BP 1816, DM 4523, FR 15,213, Y 291,208, SF 4025).

VISSCHER, J. de   1633-after 1692
$100* *"Dus Heeft Den Moor Met Pijl En Boogh, Den Vyandt Of Het Wilt In 'T Oogh" (Dutuit 8, IV; Wurzbach 27),* after C. DE VISSCHER, cut w/in platemark, 4th state of 4, watermark IDG, (11-18-92, Bubb Kuyper, #1849),

12¹³⁄₁₆ x 10¹⁵⁄₁₆ in., (32.6 x 27.8 cm.), etching and engraving (BP 66, DM 159, FR 537, Y 12,436, G 180).

VISSCHER, Jan de 1636-after 1692
$131* *Paysages Et Canaux (Holl. vol. 8, 66, 68, 72): Six,* after Van Goyen, small margins, creases, stain, (05-15-93, Loudmer, #103), smallest 4⅝ x 5⅛ in., (118 x 130 mm.), largest 7¹⁵⁄₁₆ x 9¹⁄₁₆ in., (118 x 130 mm.), etching on laid w/Armoiries d'Amsterdam watermarks (BP 85, DM 211, FR 708, Y 14,522).

VISSCHER, Lambert 1633-1690
BI *Joan De Wit, Ract Pensionaris Van Holland (Wurz. 20), c. 1673,* 1st state of 2, watermark, margins, spots, fold, staining, prov., est. BP 2/300, (12-01-92, Christie-London, #286), plate 20⅞ x 15¼ in., (530 x 387 mm.), engraving.

VISSCHER, Nicolaas 1618-1709
$361* *Diversa Genera Animalium Quadrupedum: Twenty,* watermark, (12-04-92, Bassenge, #6493), each approx. 5¹⁄₁₆ x 7¹¹⁄₁₆ in., (12.8 x 19.6 cm.), engraving (BP 232, DM 575, FR 1950, Y 45,069).

VISSER, Carel
$512* *Untitled, 1976,* s., d., #177/190, full margins, good cond., (05-27-93, Sotheby-Amstrdm, #515, illus.), sh 24½ x 36⁷⁄₁₆ in., (623 x 925 mm.), colored woodcut on Japan (BP 328, DM 822, FR 2769, Y 54,889, G 920).
$243* *Untitled, 1976,* s., d., #79/190, margins, good cond., (05-27-93, Sotheby-Amstrdm, #516), sh 25½ x 36 in., (647 x 915 mm.), colored woodcut on Japan (BP 156, DM 390, FR 1314, Y 26,051, G 437).

VITTORIO (Vittorio Fiorucci) Canadian b. 1932
BI *"L'Espace Francais-Cuvee Du Centenaire-1886-1986",* #50/50, s. Vittorio, (03-16-93, Encans, #126), 32½ x 25⁹⁄₁₆ in., (82.5 x 65 cm.), lithograph poster.
$26* *Untitled,* s. Vittorio, from exhibition of Robert Roussil at Galerie Le Gobelet, (06-16-93, Encans, #114), 35¹³⁄₁₆ x 29¹⁄₁₆ in., (91 x 73.8 cm.), offset poster (BP 17, DM 43, FR 145, Y 2773, C$ 33).

VIVIANI, Giuseppe Italian 1898-1965
$1684* *I Dittatori, 1954,* #178/200, s., d., (11-09-92, Finarte-Milan, #94), 11 x 15⁹⁄₁₆ in., (28 x 39.5 cm.), etching and aquatint in colors (BP 1113, DM 2688, FR 9083, Y 208,985, L 2300).
$3602* *Il Vetturale Biondo (Chiara 85), 1954,* #XIV/30, s., d., (05-20-93, Finarte-Milan, #158), 5¹⁵⁄₁₆ x 8⁷⁄₁₆ in., (15.1 x 21.5 cm.), etching (BP 2312, DM 5812, FR 19,576, Y 397,747, L 5290).
$2115* *Notturno (Chiara 90), 1956,* #XXXVI/50, s., d., (05-20-93, Finarte-Milan, #157), 8⁹⁄₁₆ x 11¹¹⁄₁₆ in., (21.7 x 29.7 cm.), etching (BP 1358, DM 3412, FR 11,495, Y 233,547, L 3105).

VLAMINCK, Maurice de French 1876-1958
$268* *Apres L'Orage (Pres De Pontoise) (Walterskirchen 44),* s., 400 impressions, yellowed, (03-31-93, Briest, #E117), 21⅝ x 24¹³⁄₁₆ in., (55 x 63 cm.), color pochoir on Arches (BP 177, DM 431, FR 1464, Y 30,819).
$4888* *"Entree De Village (La Route De Francheville)"* and *"Le Pont Sur L'Oise A Mery" (Walterskirchen 171 and 187), 1924, 1925-26: Two,* each s., 2nd Frapier stamp (Lugt 292 lb) indicating trial proof, margins, laid down, (02-11-93, Sotheby-NY, #271), each approx. 9⅝ x 13⅜ in., (245 x 340 mm.), color lithograph on chine volant (BP 3449, DM 8097, FR 27,399, Y 589,271).
$3246* *Entree De Village, La Route De Franchville II (von Walterskirchen 171 (II)),* artist's proof, 1st state, coll.'s stamp, embossed stamp, (11-21-92, Lempertz, #403, illus.), 12¹³⁄₁₆ x 18³⁄₁₆ in., (32.5 x 46.2 cm.), watercolor lithograph on beige wove (BP 2137, DM 5175, FR 17,433, Y 403,681).
$385* *From Mont-Cinere (W. 249), 1930,* bears sig., annot. EA, pub. Jeanne Walter, margins, good cond., surface soiling, creases, (02-24-93, Butterfield, #2984), 6⅞ x 5 in., (175 x 127 mm.), lithograph on wove (BP 268, DM 625, FR 2119, Y 45,177).
$295* *Frontispice (K. de Walterskirchen 114b), 1926,* 1 of 25, hors-texte, large margins, (06-16-93, Ader Tajan, #148),

6⁵⁄₁₆ x 4⁷⁄₁₆ in., (16.1 x 11.2 cm.), drypoint on Japan (BP 197, DM 490, FR 1643, Y 31,463).
$1419* *L'Arbre Vert (I) (Walterskirchen 172,IIc), 1924,* s., num., blindstamp, (06-05-93, Bassenge, #6609, illus.), 8⁹⁄₁₆ x 11⁵⁄₁₆ in., (21.7 x 28.7 cm.), lithograph on hand-made China (BP 934, DM 2301, FR 7754, Y 152,221).
$1451* *L'Oise A Chaponval (v. Walt. 165/b), 1923,* s., epreuve de passe, (06-23-93, Kornfeld, #876), lithograph (BP 986, DM 2455, FR 8258, Y 158,078, SF 2185).
$579* *L'Oise A Sergy (Walterskirchen 110 II),* s., (06-10-93, Hauswedell/Nolt, #962), image 9⁵⁄₁₆ x 12⅜ in., (23.6 x 31.5 cm.), aquatint on hand-made (BP 379, DM 943, FR 3174, Y 61,458).
$1695* *Maisons A Bougival (Walterskirchen 9 b), 1913,* s., #13/30, (06-10-93, Hauswedell/Nolt, #966, illus.), image 6⁷⁄₁₆ x 9¹¹⁄₁₆ in., (16.3 x 24.6 cm.), woodcut on hand-made on Van Gelder Zonen (BP 1109, DM 2760, FR 9293, Y 179,917).
$3818* *Mareil (von Walterskirchen 7/b), 1913,* s. in ink, num., (06-23-93, Kornfeld, #869, illus.), woodcut on handmade (BP 2594, DM 6460, FR 21,730, Y 415,949, SF 5750).
$1876* *Montigny-Sur-Avre (W. 266), 1956,* s., #56/200, p. Mourlot, full margins, good cond., crease, (12-03-92, Sotheby-London, #595), sheet 27⅛ x 20½ in., (688 x 520 mm.), lithograph in colors on Arches (BP 1210, DM 2950, FR 10,070, Y 233,420).
$1705* *Montigny-Sur-Avre (Walterskirchen 266), 1956,* a., #11/200, p. Mourlot, margins, light/backboard staining, (12-03-92, Sotheby-London, #594, illus.), sheet 16⅜ x 20¼ in., (416 x 516 mm.), lithograph in colors on Arches (BP 1100, DM 2681, FR 9152, Y 212,144).
$1142* *Montigny-Sur-Avre, 1956,* s., 149/200, (05-12-93, AB Stockholm, #7058), 13¾ x 18½ in., (35 x 47 cm.), lithograph in color on Arches (BP 746, DM 1843, FR 6207, Y 127,498, SK 8470).
$123* *Le Moulin De La Naze (W. 181), c. 1925,* full margins, drystamp, (05-06-93, Laurin, #97), lithograph on thin chine (BP 78, DM 194, FR 652, Y 13,533).
$1844* *Le Moulin De La Naze (Walterskirchen 181 II), c. 1923,* s., artist's proof, (12-05-92, Bassenge, #7799, illus.), 6⅞ x 8¹⁄₁₆ in., (17.5 x 20.5 cm.), lithograph on handmade China (BP 1155, DM 2875, FR 9798, Y 228,472).
$2825* *Le Moulin Vert (v. Walt 21/b), 1914,* s., num., (06-23-93, Kornfeld, #873, illus.), woodcut on Japan (BP 1919, DM 4780, FR 16,079, Y 307,768, SF 4255).
$4025* *Paysage (W. 253), 1950,* s., #75/75, p., pub. Mourlot, full margins, good cond., mat/light-stain, (05-13-93, Sotheby-NY, #857, illus.), 14⅝ x 18⅝ in., (370 x 473 mm.), lithograph in colors (BP 2642, DM 6499, FR 21,923, Y 449,369).
$990* *Paysage D'Ete (F. 147), 1951,* pub. Andre Salmon, full margins, good cond., creases, some in image, mat staining, surface soiling, stain, (10-28-92, Butterfield, #2868), 10½ x 14 in., (267 x 356 mm.), etching on Auvergne a la Main laid paper (BP 631, DM 1529, FR 5191, Y 121,472).
$2291* *Le Pecq, Pres De Paris (v. Walt. 18/b), 1914,* s., num., (06-23-93, Kornfeld, #870, illus.), woodcut on handmade (BP 1556, DM 3876, FR 13,039, Y 249,591, SF 3450).
$2825* *Pont Sur L'Eure A Pacy (v. Walt 22/b), 1914,* s., num., (06-23-93, Kornfeld, #874, illus.), woodcut on Japan (BP 1919, DM 4780, FR 16,079, Y 307,768, SF 4255).
$853* *Le Pont Sur L'Oise A Mery (II) (Walterskirchen 187), c. 1924,* (04-02-93, Sloan, #2490), 9⅜ x 13⅛ in., (238 x 333 mm.), color lithograph (BP 562, DM 1371, FR 4656, Y 97,119).
$2966* *Le Pont Sur L'Oise A Mery II (Walterskirchen 187 I),* s., (06-10-93, Hauswedell/Nolt, #964, illus.), image 9⁷⁄₁₆ x 13⁵⁄₁₆ in., (24 x 33.8 cm.), color lithograph on China (BP 1940, DM 4830, FR 16,261, Y 314,829).
$880* *Route De Beauche,* s. in stone; s., #18/100, (04-02-93, Sloan, #2489, illus.), 17⅝ x 21⅜ in., (448 x 543 mm.), color lithograph (BP 580, DM 1414, FR 4803, Y 100,194).
$2749* *Rue A Louveciennes (v. Walt 20/b), 1914,* s., num., (06-23-93, Kornfeld, #872), woodcut on handmade (BP 1868, DM 4651, FR 15,646, Y 299,488, SF 4140).

$2062* *Une Rue A Pontoise (v. Walt 153/b),* 1921, s., num., (06-23-93, Kornfeld, #875), lithograph (BP 1401, DM 3489, FR 11,736, Y 224,643, SF 3105).

BI *La Rue De La Glaciere (Walterskirchen 146),* 1937, plate s., est. DM 180-, (09-25-92, Granier, #3043), sheet 17⅝ x 12¹⁵⁄₁₆ in., (44.8 x 33 cm.), etching on machine handmade.

$162* *La Rue De La Glaciere (Walterskirchen 146),* 1937, later p., (12-05-92, Bassenge, #7797), 12¹⁵⁄₁₆ x 10¹⁄₁₆ in., (33 x 25.5 cm.), etching on handmade (BP 101, DM 253, FR 861, Y 20,072).

$617* *Saint Ouen L'Aumone, Pres Pontoise (Le Tournant De La Route) (E. 152),* 1919, #7/50, good margins, (05-06-93, Laurin, #96), lithograph on Van Gelder Zonem (BP 391, DM 972, FR 3271, Y 67,884).

BI *Saint-Michel (Walterskirchen 19),* 1914, proof, margins, good cond., foxing, mount-staining, est. BP 1,8/2,200, (06-30-93, Sotheby-London, #717, illus.), sh 14½ x 11 in., (368 x 279 mm.), woodcut on laid.

$2825* *Saint-Michel (v. Walt 19/b),* 1914, s. in ink, num., (06-23-93, Kornfeld, #871), woodcut on handmade (BP 1919, DM 4780, FR 16,079, Y 307,768, SF 4255).

$1772* *Saint-Quen L'Aumone, Pres Pontoise (Von Walterskirchen 152 b),* 1921, s., num., blindstamp, (06-08-93, Karl/Faber, #1393), approx. 15¾ x 21¼ in., (40 x 54 cm.), lithograph on Van Gelder Zonen wove (BP 1165, DM 2875, FR 9683, Y 188,210).

$4196* *La Sausseron (K. de W. 164),* creases, tear, large margins, (06-11-93, Picard, #194, illus.), 18⅛ x 24¹³⁄₁₆ in., (460 x 630 mm.), lithograph in colors on thin chine (BP 2757, DM 6819, FR 22,992, Y 445,199).

$7993* *Tete De Femme (K. de Walterskirchen 23),* num. 15 (from 30), frame traces, creases, large margins, (06-11-93, Picard, #192, illus.), 13¼ x 10³⁄₁₆ in., (336 x 258 mm.), wood engraving in black and brown (BP 5252, DM 12,990, FR 43,797, Y 848,064).

BI *"Tete De Femme",* #15/30, s., est. $9/12,000, (07-17-92, DuMouchelle, #2014, illus.), image 13 x 10 in., (33 x 25.4 cm.), color woodcut.

$303* *Two Houses (W. 275),* 1958, plate s., pub. Andre Sauret, margin trimmed, very good cond., hinge remains, mat staining, surface soiling, (10-28-92, Butterfield, #2869), 8¼ x 10¾ in., (210 x 273 mm.), lithograph w/hand-coloring by another hand on cream wove (BP 193, DM 468, FR 1589, Y 37,178).

$611* *Us, La Place (v. Walt. 173/I),* s., blindstamp, (06-23-93, Kornfeld, #877), lithograph on Japan (BP 415, DM 1034, FR 3478, Y 66,565, SF 920).

$1500* *Vase De Fleurs,* 21/100, s., signs of wear, pub. Edition C. Guillard, 1958, (10-14-92, Germann, #470, illus.), 27⅜ x 20⅞ in., (695 x 530 mm.), etching/aquatint in color (BP 880, DM 2195, FR 7444, Y 181,774, SF 1955).

$593* *Vase De Fleurs (Nach Einem Gemalde),* 21/100, s., signs of wear, pub. Edition C. Guillard, 1958, (06-24-93, Germann, #536), 27⅜ x 20⅞ in., (695 x 530 mm.), etching and aquatint in color (BP 390, DM 961, FR 3240, Y 63,613, SF 863).

BI *Vase De Fleurs,* 1958, #21/100, s., Edition C. Guillard, sign of wear, est. SF 1,2/1,500, (04-21-93, Germann, #823), 27⅜ x 20⅞ in., (695 x 530 mm.), etching and aquatint in colors.

$491* *Village (K. de W. 76),* 1899-1950, illus., s., small margins, (06-16-93, Ader Tajan, #147), 6⁵⁄₁₆ x 3¹⁵⁄₁₆ in., (16 x 10 cm.), wood engraving in brown (BP 327, DM 815, FR 2735, Y 52,368).

$2200* *Village De Louvilliers-Les-Perches (W. 117),* 1926, s., num. N. 9, margin slightly trimmed, good cond., staining, slightly toned, surface soiling, creases, pencil notations, (02-24-93, Butterfield, #2798), 8¾ x 12⅝ in., (222 x 321 mm.), drypoint on wove (BP 1534, DM 3571, FR 12,108, Y 258,155).

$1544* *Visage Des Maisons, "De L'Hotel De Ville" and "Le Cafe De Paris" (W.123 and 132),* 1927: Two, s., first an artist's proof, second #6, each w/blinstamp publisher Frapier, full margins, good cond., defects, handling marks, (06-30-93, Sotheby-London, #718, illus.), one 4 x 6½ in., (102 x 165 mm.), the other 4 x 6⅝ in., (102 x 165 mm.), etching w/drypoint on wove (BP 1035, DM 2633, FR 8884, Y 165,434).

$863* *Visage Des Maisons, La Grande Rue (W. 127b),* 1927, s., #22, blindstamp, full margins, good cond., staining, handling creases, notations, (05-19-93, Butterfield, #2096), 3¹⁵⁄₁₆ x 6⁹⁄₁₆ in., (100 x 167 mm.), etching and drypoint on Van Gelder Zonen laid (BP 560, DM 1403, FR 4726, Y 95,539).

BI *Voyages (Walterskirchen H 27-45),* 1920, book by Vanderpyl, ink s. by artist and author, num. 47, p. l'Imprimerie Birault, pub. Galerie Simon, full margins, good cond. cover w/losses, creases, est. $2/3,000, (05-13-93, Sotheby-NY, #856), each sh approx. 12⅝ x 8⅞ in., (320 x 225 mm.), incl. 19 woodcuts in-texte.

VLAMINCK, Maurice de (after)

BI *Chemin D'Hiver,* full margins, good cond., soiling, handling creases, est. $5/700, (05-19-93, Butterfield, #2097), 15⅞ x 22 in., (403 x 559 mm.), aquatint in colors on Arches.

BI *Tabac,* stamped sig., #6/20, margins, mount stained, est. BP 120/180, (10-27-92, Phillips-London, #226), (314 x 394 mm.), offset lithograph w/hand-coloring on wove.

VLEUGHELS (after)

$55 *"La Jument Du Compere Pierre",* engraved by De Larmessin, (02-05-93, G.A. Key, #41), 10 x 13 in., (25.4 x 33 cm.), b/w engraving (BP 38, DM 91, FR 308, Y 6844).

VLEUGHELS, Chevalier (after)

$161* *La Jument Du Compere Pierre,* small margins, (02-03-93, Ader Tajan, #70), 10⁷⁄₁₆ x 13¹¹⁄₁₆ in., (26.5 x 34.8 cm.), etching and copper engraving (BP 112, DM 265, FR 899, Y 20,027).

VLIEGER, Simon J. de   c. 1601-1653

$708* *Der Getreidetransport (B. 5 II, Wurzbach 5, Hollstein 5 II),* watermark, prov., (06-04-93, Bassenge, #5405), 4⁵⁄₁₆ x 5⅜ in., (10.9 x 13.6 cm.), etching (BP 468, DM 1150, FR 3875, Y 76,359).

VLIEGER, Simon Jacobsz de   Dutch b.c. 1600, buried 1653

BI *Ram And Ewes,* Different Animaux series Pl. 5, plate inits., margins trimmed, est. C$1/1,500, (12-01-92, Ritchie, #5, illus.), image 4⅞ x 5⅞ in., (12.4 x 14.9 cm.), plate approx. 5 x 6 in., (12.4 x 14.9 cm.), etching on laid paper, watermark.

VLIET, Jan Georg van   ac. 1630-1640

BI *Buste De Vieillard (Dutuit 23 II),* 1634, est. DM 3,500, (12-04-92, Bassenge, #6494), 8¾ x 7⅜ in., (22.2 x 18.7 cm.), etching.

$253* *Der Segeltuchnaher (Wurzbach, Dutuit, Rovinski 42),* watermark, from series Kunsteund Gewerbe, (12-04-92, Bassenge, #6495), etching (BP 162, DM 403, FR 1367, Y 31,586).

VOGELER, Heinrich   1872-1942

$461* *(Allegorical Scene),* s., full margins, good cond., repaired tear at right edge of plate, minor foxing, paper discoloration, Late Gerhard Bauer Coll., (05-27-93, Sotheby-Amstrdm, #797, illus.), 10¹⁵⁄₁₆ x 7⅝ in., (278 x 194 mm.), etching on wove (BP 295, DM 740, FR 2493, Y 49,421, G 828).

BI *Froschkonig (Rief 12 II c),* 1896, s., est. DM 4,500, (06-05-93, Bassenge, #6611, illus.), 8⁹⁄₁₆ x 11¹¹⁄₁₆ in., (21.8 x 29.7 cm.), etching on hand-made Japan.

BI *Fruhling (Rief 14 II c oder d.),* 1896, plate s., est. DM 2,500, (05-26-93, Lempertz, #518), 17½ x 12⅝ in., (44.4 x 32.1 cm.), etching on wove.

$2867* *Fruhling (Rief 14 II),* 1896, s., t., wide margins, stains, discoloration, creasing, (05-20-93, Christie-London, #492, illus.), plate 13½ x 9½ in., (34.3 x 24.1 cm.), sheet 22¾ x 16 in., (34.3 x 24.1 cm.), etching in brown on Japan (BP 1840, DM 4626, FR 15,582, Y 316,586).

$1090* *Die Hexe Mit Eule (Rief 6),* 1895, i., s., (04-27-93, Hartung, #1999), etching on Japan (BP 693, DM 1726, FR 5838, Y 122,156).

$1992* *Im Mai (Rief 16 IIc),* 1897, s., yellowed, (12-05-92, Bassenge, #7801), 13⁵⁄₁₆ x 9⁹⁄₁₆ in., (33.8 x 24.3 cm.), etching on handmade (BP 1247, DM 3106, FR 10,584, Y 246,810).

$706* *Die Lerche (Rief 24/II c 1), 1899,* s., brown stained, light-staining, creases, (12-01-92, Karl/Faber, #1332), 6³⁄₁₆ x 6³⁄₁₆ in., (15.7 x 15.7 cm.), etching (BP 466, DM 1125, FR 3835, Y 87,898).

$1790* *Liebe, 1896,* s., (05-08-93, Schloss Ahlden, #2909, illus.), 13⅜ x 14⅜ in., (34 x 36.5 cm.), etching and aquatint on light brown paper (BP 1168, DM 2876, FR 9702, Y 200,022).

$4237* *Die Nacht (Rief 21 II a), 1897,* s., t., artist's proof, (06-10-93, Hauswedell/Nolt, #967, illus.), image 9⁷⁄₁₆ x 7¹⁄₁₆ in., (24 x 18 cm.), etching on Japan (BP 2771, DM 6900, FR 23,229, Y 449,740).

$852* *Verkundigung (Rief 10 IIc), 1895,* s., (06-19-93, Wachholtz, #334, illus.), 9¾ x 7¹³⁄₁₆ in., (24.8 x 19.9 cm.), etching and drypoint in Japan hand-made (BP 572, DM 1438, FR 4835, Y 94,446).

$443* *Vision (Rief 49 II a), 1915/16,* s., creased, (12-05-92, Bassenge, #7803), 7⅞ x 5¹¹⁄₁₆ in., (20 x 14.5 cm.), etching on Japan (BP 277, DM 691, FR 2354, Y 54,888).

VOGT, C.H.

BI *View Of The City Of New Bedford, Massachusetts, 1876,* est. $5/800, (05-29-93, Northeast, #171, illus.), frame 24 x 35 in., (61 x 88.9 cm.), chromolithograph.

VOGT, Christian Swiss b. 1946

$1870* *Christian Vogt Portfolio: Twelve, 1981,* Chicago: Edwynn Houk Gallery, s., t., d., num. in ink in margin, (c)stamp, #15/35 ltd. edit., (10-13-92, Christie-NY, #614, illus.), each 6¼ x 4¼ in., (15.9 x 10.8 cm.), photograph, gelatin silver prints (BP 1089, DM 2740, FR 9308, Y 226,749).

VOINQUEL, Raymond

$330* *"La Dame Du Rail", 1980's,* ink s., photog. stamp, Dixon Collection, (11-16-92, Butterfield, #6217), 15¼ x 20¹⁄₁₆ in., (388 x 508.9 mm.), photograph, gelatin silver print (BP 217, DM 526, FR 1772, Y 41,040).

$935* *"Jacques Sernas", 1980's,* s., photog. stamp, Dixon Collection, (11-16-92, Butterfield, #6215, illus.), 15¼ x 20¹⁄₁₆ in., (388 x 508.9 mm.), photograph, gelatin silver print (BP 616, DM 1491, FR 5021, Y 116,279).

$440* *"Jean Marais", 1980,* ink s., photog. stamp, Dixon Collection, (11-16-92, Butterfield, #6216), 16 x 15¼ in., (407.1 x 388 mm.), photograph, gelatin silver print (BP 290, DM 702, FR 2363, Y 54,720).

VOLKMANN, Hans Richard von 1860-1927

$155* *Auf Der Hohe, 1904,* s., stone mono., d., t., foxing, tear, (09-25-92, Granier, #2706), sheet 13¾ x 18¹¹⁄₁₆ in., (35 x 47.5 cm.), color lithograph on copper print paper (BP 91, DM 230, FR 777, Y 18,709).

$338* *"Burg Burresheim II", 1904,* stone s., d., i., s. Hans v. Volkmann, (03-24-93, Venator/Hansten, #4570), approx. 20¼ x 15⅜ in., (51.5 x 39 cm.), color lithograph (BP 229, DM 552, FR 1879, Y 39,713).

$233* *Feldarbeit, 1900,* s., stone mono., wear, (09-25-92, Granier, #2705), sheet 19½ x 24⁷⁄₁₆ in., (49.5 x 62 cm.), color lithograph on copper print paper (BP 136, DM 345, FR 1168, Y 28,123).

VOLL, Christoph 1897-1939

$885* *Kohlenfrau, 1922,* s., t., rare, (12-05-92, Bassenge, #7808), 10½ x 8⅞ in., (26.7 x 22.5 cm.), drypoint on China (BP 554, DM 1380, FR 4702, Y 109,652).

$2013* *Spielendes Madchen, c. 1920,* s., t., i. Handdruck, (10-09-92, Winterberg, #3203, illus.), 13¹³⁄₁₆ x 11¾ in., (35.1 x 29.8 cm.), woodcut on hand-made Japan (BP 1194, DM 2990, FR 10,040, Y 245,069).

$1033* *Sterbendes Waisenkind,* s., t., i., (12-05-92, Bassenge, #7806), 8¾ x 10⅝ in., (22.2 x 27 cm.), drypoint on strong wove (BP 647, DM 1611, FR 5489, Y 127,989).

VOLPATO, Giovanni 1733-1803

BI *Der Parnass Nach Raffael (Nagler 6, Nr. 7 III),* prov., est. DM 3,500, (12-04-92, Bassenge, #6716, illus.), 22⅝ x 29½ in., (57.4 x 75 cm.), engraving reworked w/ gouache.

VOLPE, Michael

$43* *Private Road,* s., t., #46/130, prov., (12-01-92, Ritchie, #46), 19¼ x 25¼ in., (48.9 x 64.1 cm.), color etching (BP 28, DM 69, FR 234, Y 5354, C$ 55).

VON DEM BUSSCHE, Wolf

$2200* *N.Y., N.Y.: Ten Photographs,* Black Stone Press, mounted, s, t., d. by photog. on mount, s., t., d., num. 82/90 by photog., stamps verso, 1967-76, p. c. 1982, #82/100 ed., (10-15-92, Sotheby-NY, #581A, illus.), various sizes to 12⅛ x 17¾ in., (30.8 x 45.1 cm.), portfolio of 10 photos, gelatin silver prints (BP 1346, DM 3275, FR 11,106, Y 263,947).

VON ESSEN, Johann Ladenspelder

BI *Venus (Holl. 63),* small margins, stains, good cond., est. BP 1/2,000, (06-30-93, Sotheby-London, #156), 4⅛ x 3¼ in., (105 x 83 mm.), engraving.

VON GLOEDEN, Wilhelm

$1725* *Boy Holding Fish, early 1900's,* photog. studio stamp, (04-06-93, Sotheby-NY, #227, illus.), 8¾ x 6⅝ in., photograph, albumen print (BP 1139, DM 2779, FR 9411, Y 196,738).

VON OLMUTZ, Wenzel ac. 1481-1497

BI *Der Apostel Bartholomaeus (Bartsch VI, 333, 36; Lehrs VI, 224, 40),* after Schongauer, est. DM 1,500, (06-10-93, Hauswedell/Nolt, #124), engraving.

VORSTERMANN, Lucas (I) 1595-1675

$433* *Die Heilige Familie (Dutuit 54 II; Hymans 44 III), 1620,* after P.P. Rubens, prov., (12-04-92, Bassenge, #6496), 10⁵⁄₁₆ x 7¹⁵⁄₁₆ in., (26.2 x 20.2 cm.), engraving (BP 278, DM 690, FR 2339, Y 54,057).

VORSTERMANN, Lucas (the younger) Flemish 1624-c. 1667

BI *Der Grosse Satyr Am Tische Bei Der Bauernfamilie (Nagler 8 I; Wurzbach 12),* after J. Jordens, est. DM 750, (12-04-92, Bassenge, #6497), 16⅛ x 15⁹⁄₁₆ in., (41 x 39.5 cm.), engraving.

VOS, M. de

$40* *"Le Christ Et Les Disciples D'Emmaus" and "Le Mont Calvaire" (Ch. LeBlanc 3): Two,* w/out margins, glued, reddish stains, (02-03-93, Ader Tajan, #48), 7⅞ x 10⅞ in., (20 x 27.7 cm.), 7¹¹⁄₁₆ x 11¹³⁄₁₆ in., (20 x 27.7 cm.), etching and copper engraving (BP 28, DM 66, FR 223, Y 4976).

$222* *"Laissez Venir A Moi Les Petits Enfants", "La Transfiguration", "L'Ascension" and Other Religious Subjects: Six,* glued, yellowed, w/out margins, (02-03-93, Ader Tajan, #46), etching and copper engraving (BP 155, DM 366, FR 1240, Y 27,615).

VOS, M. de (after)

$81* *Vie Du Christ: Set Of Eight,* w/out margins, glued, tear, yellowed, (02-03-93, Ader Tajan, #44), 7⅞ x 11⅝ in., (20 x 29.5 cm.), 8¹⁄₁₆ x 10¹³⁄₁₆ in., (20 x 29.5 cm.), etching and copper engraving (BP 57, DM 133, FR 452, Y 10,076).

VOS, Maartens de (after)

$2664* *The Months Of The Year, (Holl., de Passe, 675-81, 583-8), Set Of Twelve: Title And Eleven Plates,* by C. de Passe, watermark, wide margins, crease, tear, very good cond., from set of 12, (12-01-92, Christie-London, #91, illus.), oval, P. 4¾ x 4¾ in., (121 x 120 mm.), engraving (BP 1760, DM 4246, FR 14,470, Y 331,673).

$749* *The Seven Deadly Sins, (Holl., de Passe 455-61): Set Of Seven,* by C. de Passe, wide margins, foxmarks, staining, very good cond., (12-01-92, Christie-London, #94), averaging P. 6¼ x 3⁷⁄₁₆ in., (158 x 88 mm.), engraving (BP 495, DM 1194, FR 4068, Y 93,252).

$999* *The Seven Virtues, (Holl., de Passe, 426-32): Set Of Seven,* watermark, wide margins, foxmarks, staining, very good cocnd., (12-01-92, Christie-London, #92), averaging P. 6⁵⁄₁₆ x 3⁷⁄₁₆ in., (161 x 87 mm.), engraving (BP 660, DM 1592, FR 5426, Y 124,377).

$1665* *Time With Virtues And Vices, (Holl., de Passe, 451-4): Set Of Four,* thread margins or trimmed, watermark, discoloration, prov., very good cond., (12-01-92, Christie-London, #93), averaging S. 8⅜ x 9⅞ in., (212 x 251 mm.), engraving (BP 1100, DM 2654, FR 9044, Y 207,296).

VOS, Martin

$880* *Roosevelt, Franklin D., c. 1926,* s. in ink, (09-17-92, Swann, #240, illus.), photograph (BP 494, DM 1306, FR 4472, Y 109,562).

VOS, Peter
$96* *Dodo, 1975,* s., t., full margins, good cond., (05-27-93, Sotheby-Amstrdm, #518), 15¹¹⁄₁₆ x 11¾ in., (398 x 298 mm.), lithograph on wove (BP 61, DM 154, FR 519, Y 10,292, G 173).
$96* *Gevoelens, 1975,* s., t., full margins, good cond., (05-27-93, Sotheby-Amstrdm, #517), 17¼ x 11¾ in., (438 x 298 mm.), lithograph on wove (BP 61, DM 154, FR 519, Y 10,292, G 173).

VOSS, Jan						b. 1936
$384* *Chemin De Bois, 1985: Four,* complete set, each s., d., #83/150, p. by Atelier Clot w/their blindstamp, margins, good cond., loose in orig. portfolio, (05-27-93, Sotheby-Amstrdm, #702), each sh 16⁹⁄₁₆ x 12³⁄₁₆ in., (420 x 310 mm.), color woodcut on wove (BP 246, DM 616, FR 2077, Y 41,166, G 690).
$135* *"Composition", 1981,* H.C. III/III, s., (10-18-92, Pescheteau, #295), 23⅝ x 31½ in., (60 x 80 cm.), lithograph in colors on wove (BP 82, DM 199, FR 677, Y 16,119).
$137* *Composition, 1970,* s. Voss 70, 87/100, (09-30-92, Kunsthallen, #291), color lithograph (BP 77, DM 194, FR 657, Y 16,441, DK 748).
   BI *Eiffelturm Und Nudelwalze, 1969,* s., d., #55/100, (09-18-92, Schloss Ahlden, #1078), 28⅛ x 20¹³⁄₁₆ in., (71.4 x 52.8 cm.), color lithograph on hand-made.
$275* *Komposition, 1981,* s. Voss 81, 34/120, (03-24-93, Kunsthallen, #331), color lithograph (BP 186, DM 449, FR 1529, Y 32,311, DK 1725).
$184* *Komposition, 1983,* s. Voss 83, 54/75, (03-24-93, Kunsthallen, #332), color lithograph (BP 125, DM 301, FR 1023, Y 21,619, DK 1150).
$165* *Komposition, 1987,* s. Voss 87, H.C. IV/V, (03-24-93, Kunsthallen, #333), lithograph and woodcut in colors (BP 112, DM 269, FR 917, Y 19,387, DK 1035).
   BI *Komposition, 1987,* s. Voss 87, H.C. IV/V, est. DK 1,200, (03-24-93, Kunsthallen, #334), color lithograph.
   BI *Das Rote Band, 1967,* s., d., #13/85, est. DM 400, (05-08-93, Schloss Ahlden, #2911), 15 x 20⅜ in., (38.1 x 51.7 cm.), color serigraph on Arches-handmade.
   BI *Untitled, 1978,* s., d., #154/190, full sheet p. to edges, good cond., est. Dfl. 5/700, (05-27-93, Sotheby-Amstrdm, #519), sh 19⅝ x 25½ in., (498 x 648 mm.), colored lithograph on wove.
   BI *Untitled, 1978,* s., d. #170/190, full sheet p. to edges, good cond., est. Dfl. 5/700, (05-27-93, Sotheby-Amstrdm, #520), sh 19⅝ x 25½ in., (498 x 648 mm.), colored lithograph on wove.
   BI *Untitled, 1978,* s., d., full sheet p. to edges, good cond., est. Dfl. 5/700, (05-27-93, Sotheby-Amstrdm, #521), sh 19⅝ x 25½ in., (498 x 648 mm.), colored lithograph on wove.
$194* *Untitled, 1978,* s., d., artist's proof, (09-25-92, Granier, #3045), 19¹¹⁄₁₆ x 25¹¹⁄₁₆ in., (50 x 65.2 cm.), color lithograph on wove (BP 113, DM 288, FR 972, Y 23,416).

VOSTELL, Wolf					b. 1932
$159* *365 Tage Salat (Bloch V 59), 1972,* num., s., (11-28-92, Schoppmann, #870), 27⁹⁄₁₆ x 39⅜ in., (70 x 100 cm.), serigraph on cardboard (BP 105, DM 253, FR 860, Y 19,788).
$21* *Ankunft Der Betonwolke Aus Chicago In Zurich, 1972,* s., for Galerie Art In Progress, Zurich, (09-30-92, Kunsthallen, #292), poster, offset in colors (BP 12, DM 30, FR 101, Y 2520, DK 115).
$295* *Chor 30, 1990,* E.A., s., (12-05-92, Bassenge, #7810), lithograph on thick Arches (BP 185, DM 460, FR 1567, Y 36,551).
$202* *Heuschreden (Block V 36), 1970,* artist's proof, s., (11-28-92, Schoppmann, #868), 25⁹⁄₁₆ x 20¹⁄₁₆ in., (65 x 51 cm.), serigraph on light cardboard (BP 133, DM 322, FR 1092, Y 25,140).
$148* *Komposition,* s., num., (12-05-92, Bassenge, #7809), 16⁷⁄₁₆ x 20³⁄₁₆ in., (41.8 x 51.2 cm.), color screen print on wove (BP 93, DM 231, FR 786, Y 18,337).
$239* *Luftpumpen-Museum (Block V 41), 1971,* num., s., (11-28-92, Schoppmann, #871), 18⅛ x 26⅜ in., (46 x 67 cm.), serigraph on light cardboard (BP 158, DM 381, FR 1293, Y 29,745).

   BI *Portraitmontage,* s., est. DM 400-, (09-25-92, Granier, #3046), 38⁷⁄₁₆ x 29¾ in., (97.7 x 75.6 cm.), serigraph on black paper.
$130* *Tv-Ochsen I (Block V 40), 1971,* num., s., (11-28-92, Schoppmann, #869), 16¹¹⁄₁₆ x 24 in., (42.4 x 61 cm.), serigraph on light cardboard (BP 86, DM 207, FR 703, Y 16,179).

VOULKOS, Peter				American b. 1924
   BI *"Untitled",* s., full margins, very good cond.?, est. $1/2,000, (10-28-92, Butterfield, #3161), 18 x 11¾ in., (457 x 298 mm.), color monotype on wove.
$1540* *Untitled, 1978,* s., d., pub. Magnolia Editions, very good cond.?, Modesto Lanzone Coll., (10-28-92, Butterfield, #3159, illus.), 29 x 24¼ in., (737 x 616 mm.), color monotype on handmade (BP 981, DM 2378, FR 8076, Y 188,957).
   BI *Untitled, 1984-85,* s., annot., pub. Magnolia Editions, apparently very good cond., est.$2/3,000, (02-24-93, Butterfield, #3159), 42 x 29½ in., (106.7 x 74.9 cm.), monotype in colors on cream wove.
   BI *Untitled, 1984-85,* s., annot., pub. Magnolia Editions, very good cond.?, est. $3/4,000, (10-28-92, Butterfield, #3160), 42 x 29½ in., (106.7 x 74.9 cm.), color monotype on cream wove.

VROMAN, Adam Clark				1856-1916
   BI *Nampeyo, Potter Of Hano With Some Of Her Wares, 1901,* lit., est. $4/6,000, (10-13-92, Christie-NY, #55, illus.), 6 x 8 in., (15.2 x 20.3 cm.), photograph, gelatin silver print.

VUILLARD, Edouard				French 1868-1940
$440* *"Au Della Des Forces", (Roger-Marx 25 I/II): Two,* two images, I/II and II/II, annot., (10-31-92, Cleveland, #349, illus.), one 9¾ x 11½ in., (24.8 x 29.2 cm.), the other 9¾ x 12½ in., (24.8 x 29.2 cm.), lithograph (BP 282, DM 677, FR 2296, Y 54,503).
$1887* *La Couturiere (Roger-Marx 13), 1894,* proof impression of 3rd state of 4, good cond., marks, creases, (06-30-93, Sotheby-London, #719, illus.), 10⅛ x 6½ in., (257 x 165 mm.), lithograph in blue and ochre on wove (BP 1265, DM 3218, FR 10,857, Y 202,186).
$1265* *La Couturiere (Roger-Marx 13), 1895,* s., No. 28, pub. L'Album de la Revue blanche, large (full?) margins,- good cond., faded, mat stain, margins folded back, taped to backing, (05-13-93, Sotheby-NY, #858), 9⅞ x 6½ in., (250 x 165 mm.), lithograph in colors (BP 830, DM 2043, FR 6890, Y 141,230).
   BI *Couverture De L'Album, From Paysages Et Interieurs (Roger-Marx 37), 1899,* pub. Ambroise Vollard, margins, creasing, staining, est. $4/6,000, (11-09-92, Christie-NY, #233, illus.), 20 x 15½ in., (508 x 394 mm.), colored lithograph on Chine volant.
$17,600* *Cuisainiere,* from Paysages et Interieurs, Vollard, 1899, (04-02-93, Sloan, #2488, illus.), sight 14⅛ x 10⅞ in., (359 x 276 mm.), color lithograph (BP 11,593, DM 28,287, FR 96,070, Y 2,003,871).
$29,661* *La Cuisiniere (Roger-Marx 42 II; Johnson 155.11), 1899,* (06-10-93, Hauswedell/Nolt, #971, illus.), image 14³⁄₁₆ x 10¹⁵⁄₁₆ in., (36 x 27.8 cm.), color lithograph on China (BP 19,401, DM 48,300, FR 162,615, Y 3,148,392).
$22,979* *Les Deux Belles Soeurs (Cl. Roger Marx 43), 1899,* s., third and final state, reddish stains, small margins, (06-11-93, Picard, #195, illus.), 13¹⁵⁄₁₆ x 11⅛ in., (354 x 282 mm.), color lithograph on thin chine (BP 15,098, DM 37,346, FR 125,912, Y 2,438,090).
$10,450* *Les Deux Belles-Soeurs (R.-M. 43; J. 155.12), 1899,* s., from Paysages et Interieurs, pub. Vollard, full margins, good cond., foxing, creases, (11-05-92, Sotheby-NY, #470, illus.), 14⅜ x 11⅝ in., (365 x 295 mm.), sheet 15 x 12¼ in., (365 x 295 mm.), lithograph p. in colors on chine volant (BP 6797, DM 16,527, FR 55,912, Y 1,282,051).
   BI *Galerie Au Gymnase (Roger-Marx 48 III/III), 1900,* est. $5/700, (05-16-93, Hindman, #449), 9¾ x 7¾ in., (24.8 x 19.7 cm.), color lithograph.
   BI *Interieur Aux Tentures Roses II (R.-M. 37), 1899,* from Paysages et Interieurs, p. Clot, pub. Vollard, margins, good cond., foxing, est. $8/12,000, (05-13-93, Sotheby-NY, #859, illus.), 13¾ x 11 in., (350 x 280 mm.), sh

15⅝ x 12¼ in., (350 x 280 mm.), lithograph in colors on chine volant.

$5500* *Interieur Aux Tentures Roses III (Roger-Marx 38; Johnson 155.7), 1899,* from Paysages et Interieurs, pub. Vollard, margins, good cond., faded, thin spots, glue traces, (11-05-92, Sotheby-NY, #469, illus.), 13⅝ x 10¾ in., (345 x 274 mm.), sheet 14⅝ x 12 in., (345 x 274 mm.), lithograph p. in colors on chine volant (BP 3577, DM 8698, FR 29,428, Y 674,764).

BI *Interieurs Aux Tentures Roses I (R.-M. 36), 1899,* from Paysages et Interieurs, pub. Ambroise Vollard, margins, repaired tear, staining, good cond., est. $10/14,000, (11-09-92, Christie-NY, #236, illus.), 13¾ x 10⅝ in., (349 x 270 mm.), colored lithograph on Chine volant.

BI *Interior,* restrike, est. $250/350, (11-01-92, Hanzel, #215), 3¾ x 5¼ in., (9.5 x 13.3 cm.), etching.

$1887* *Intimite (R.-M. 10), c. 1895,* pub. Kleinmann, full margins(?), light/mount-stained, creasing, tears, losses, (06-30-93, Sotheby-London, #720, illus.), 10⅝ x 8 in., (270 x 203 mm.), lithograph on wove (BP 1265, DM 3218, FR 10,857, Y 202,186).

$4400* *Le Jardin Des Tuileries (Roger-Marx 28), 1896,* p. Clot, from L'Album des Peintres-Graveurs, Vollard, pub., 2nd state, (04-02-93, Sloan, #2487, illus.), 11½ x 17 in., (292 x 432 mm.), color lithograph (BP 2898, DM 7072, FR 24,017, Y 500,968).

$468* *L'Avenue (From Paysages Et Interieurs) (Roger-Marx 33), 1899,* #96/80 w/in stone, (04-02-93, Sloan, #2486, illus.), 9 x 11⁹⁄₁₆ in., (229 x 294 mm.), color lithograph (BP 308, DM 752, FR 2555, Y 53,285).

$8913* *L'Avenue (R.-M. 33), 1899,* from Paysages et Interieurs, p. Clot, pub. Vollard, full margins, good cond., (02-11-93, Sotheby-NY, #272), 11¹⁵⁄₁₆ x 16¼ in., (304 x 412 mm.), color lithograph on chine volant (BP 6289, DM 14,764, FR 49,961, Y 1,074,503).

BI *L'Avenue, From Paysages Et Interieurs (R.-M. 33), 1899,* pub. Ambroise Vollard, margins, colors attenuated, repaired tears, good cond., est. $15/18,000, (11-09-92, Christie-NY, #234, illus.), 12 x 15¾ in., (305 x 400 mm.), colored lithograph on Chine volant.

$5995* *La Naissance D'Annette (Cl. R. M. 44), 1899,* second state of three, creases, small margins, (06-11-93, Picard, #196), 15¾ x 18⅞ in., (400 x 480 mm.), color lithograph on thin chine (BP 3939, DM 9743, FR 32,849, Y 636,074).

BI *La Naissance D'Annette (R.-M.44), c. 1899,* proof of 2nd state of 3, full margins, good cond., faded, soiling, creases, repaired tears, est. $8/10,000, (05-13-93, Sotheby-NY, #860, illus.), 16 x 20⅛ in., (408 x 510 mm.), sh 16⅜ x 22 in., (408 x 510 mm.), lithograph in colors on chine volant.

$11,454* *La Naissance D'Annette (Roger-Marx 44/II), c. 1899,* artist's proof, (06-23-93, Kornfeld, #879), color lithograph on thin China (BP 7781, DM 19,381, FR 65,191, Y 1,247,848, SF 17,250).

$6005* *Paysages Et Interieurs: Interieur Aux Tentures Roses I (R.-M. 36), 1899,* pub. A. Clot for A. Vollard, margins, faded, backed w/Japan, (06-30-93, Sotheby-London, #722, illus.), 15½ x 12⅛ in., (394 x 308 mm.), color lithograph on chine volant (BP 4025, DM 10,242, FR 34,551, Y 643,416).

$5147* *Paysages Et Interieurs: La Partie De Dames (R.-M. 32), 1899,* pub. A. Clot, margins, beige stone faded, foxing, (06-30-93, Sotheby-London, #721, illus.), sh 14¼ x 11⅜ in., (362 x 289 mm.), color lithograph on chine volant (BP 3450, DM 8779, FR 29,614, Y 551,484).

BI *Portrait De Cezanne (R.-M. 51), 1914,* pub. Bernehim Jeune, margins, good cond., staining, est. $6/800, (02-24-93, Butterfield, #2985), 9¾ x 9¼ in., (248.1 x 235.4 mm.), lithograph on wove.

$100* *"Portrait Of Cezanne" (Roger Marx 51 ii/ii), 1914,* pub. Bernheim Jeune in album Cezanne, (05-15-93, Cleveland, #438), 9¾ x 9¼ in., (24.8 x 23.5 cm.), lithograph in grey/black ink (BP 65, DM 161, FR 541, Y 11,085).

$159* *Scene Domestique,* (02-16-93, Encans, #139), 3¹⁵⁄₁₆ x 5¹¹⁄₁₆ in., (10 x 14.5 cm.), etching (BP 110, DM 260, FR 879, Y 19,049, C$ 200).

$328* *Les Soutiens De La Societe 9C. Roger-Marx 24; A. 85), 1895,* w/letter, w/out margin, (02-24-93, Picard, #192), lithograph (BP 229, DM 532, FR 1805, Y 38,489).

$345* *Le Square Vintimille (R.-M. 64), 1937,* full margins, good cond., split, pinhole, stains, creases, soiling, notations, (05-19-93, Butterfield, #2098), 13³⁄₁₆ x 10³⁄₁₆ in., (335 x 259 mm.), drypoint on Van Gelder Zonen laid (BP 224, DM 561, FR 1889, Y 38,193).

BI *A Travers Champs, From Paysages Et Interieurs (R.-M. 34), 1899,* proof, margins, staining, very good cond., est. $10/14,000, (11-09-92, Christie-NY, #235, illus.), 10½ x 13¾ in., (267 x 349 mm.), colored lithograph on Chine volant.

$171* *A Woman Seated At A Table,* num. 259 verso, creasing, (08-20-92, Bonhams-Chelsea, #61), subject 19 x 14¼ in., (48.3 x 36.2 cm.), lithograph in colors, finished by hand (BP 88, DM 248, FR 840, Y 21,594).

VUILLARD, Edouard Jean   French 1868-1940
$165* *"Petites Etudes",* s. plate, full margins, (05-07-93, Goldberg, #431), 5¾ x 4 in., (14.6 x 10.2 cm.), etching on arches (BP 104, DM 261, FR 879, Y 18,168).

VUILLARD, Jean Edouard   French 1868-1940
BI *Interior,* est. $2/400, (02-14-93, Hanzel, #670), (9.5 x 13.3 cm.), restrike etching.

VYS
$807* *Zouzou, De M. Allegret, Avec Josephine Baker, 1934,* (01-31-93, Morelle/Marchan, #71), 31½ x 47¼ in., (80 x 120 cm.), poster (BP 543, DM 1300, FR 4395, Y 100,674).

WABEL, Henry   1889-1981
$46* *Stilleben, 1971,* #106/200, s., (09-04-92, Germann, #607), 19⅝ x 15¼ in., (498 x 388 mm.), color lithograph (BP 23, DM 64, FR 219, Y 5662, SF 58).

WACH, Aloys   German 1892-1940
BI *"Landscape With Women", c. 1920,* very good/good cond., est. $2/300, (11-21-92, Bakker, #175), image 5½ x 7 in., (14 x 17.8 cm.), woodblock print.

$265* *Musizierendes Und Tanzendes Paar, (1)915,* s., d., print 7, stains, (12-01-92, Karl/Faber, #1338), 9⁷⁄₁₆ x 7¹⁄₁₆ in., (24 x 18 cm.), lithograph (BP 175, DM 422, FR 1439, Y 32,993).

WADDLE, Harry
$880* *Blimp Man, c. 1947,* mounted, s., t. by photog. in ink, studio label, exhib. labels or stamps, (10-15-92, Sotheby-NY, #443, illus.), 18 x 14¼ in., (45.7 x 36.2 cm.), photograph, chloro-bromide gold print (BP 538, DM 1310, FR 4442, Y 105,579).

$825* *Boat Deck Patrol, 1946,* t., s. by photog., Canadian Royal Photographic Society blindstamp, photog.'s address label, exhib. label, (04-07-93, Swann, #584, illus.), 15 x 29 in., photograph, silver print (BP 545, DM 1334, FR 4516, Y 93,729).

WADSWORTH, Edward Alexander
$880* *The Sailing Ships & Barges Of The Western Mediterranean & Adriatic, 1926: Twenty-Three,* complete volume, pub. Frederick Etchells & Hugh MacDonald, colors fresh, good cond., staining, surface soiling, (02-24-93, Butterfield, #2799), 12⅛ x 8 in., (308 x 203 mm.), engraving w/hand-coloring on J.W. Zanders paper (BP 614, DM 1429, FR 4843, Y 103,262).

WAGNER, Catherine
$330* *"From American Classrooms: Gonzalez Elementary School, Third Grade Classroom, Santa Fe, New Mexico" (Catherine Wagner), 1986/1989,* s., t., d., (11-16-92, Butterfield, #6219, illus.), 8½ x 11½ in., (216.3 x 292.6 mm.), photograph, gelatin silver print (BP 217, DM 526, FR 1772, Y 41,040).

WAHLSTEDT, Walter   1898-1972
BI *Die Provinzkapelle, 1920,* s., est. DM 3,000, (06-10-93, Hauswedell/Nolt, #973, illus.), image 15⅝ x 9¹³⁄₁₆ in., (39.7 x 25 cm.), lithograph worked over w/watercolor hand-made Japan.

WAIN, Louis (after)

$84 *Cat Family At Fireside*, (10-09-92, G.A. Key, #68), 7½ x 9½ in., (19.1 x 24.1 cm.), black and white print, part colored (BP 50, DM 125, FR 424, Y 10,244).

$337* *Cats Chorus*, (01-18-93, Bonhams, #91), image 16½ x 38¼ in., (41.9 x 97.2 cm.), chromolithograph (BP 220, DM 551, FR 1838, Y 42,481).

$12 *"Financial Disaster"*, (12-11-92, G.A. Key, #59A), 7 x 6 in., (17.8 x 15.2 cm.), black and white print (BP 8, DM 19, FR 65, Y 1485).

$80 *"A Good Puss" and "The Naughty Puss": Two*, (02-05-93, G.A. Key, #53), 10 x 14 in., (25.4 x 35.6 cm.), colored print (BP 55, DM 133, FR 448, Y 9955).

$73 *"The Naughty Puss", "The Good Puss" and "What We Are About To Receive": Three*, (06-11-93, G.A. Key, #81), colored print (BP 48, DM 119, FR 400, Y 7745).

$30 *"The New Hat"*, (04-16-93, G.A. Key, #18), 7 x 6 in., (17.8 x 15.2 cm.), b/w print (BP 20, DM 48, FR 164, Y 3373).

WAKEFORD, G.

$312* *Everywhere You Go, Gravesend, 1952*, p. Vincent Brooks, Day & Son, ref. P 39, cond. 1, (10-13-92, Phillips-London, #175), 29¹³⁄₁₆ x 39⅞ in., (75.7 x 101.3 cm.), color lithograph (BP 182, DM 457, FR 1553, Y 37,832).

WALCOT, William

$85* *42nd Street, New York*, s., margins, (04-22-93, Bonhams-Chelsea, #26), plate 5¼ x 7¼ in., (13.3 x 18.4 cm.), drypoint etching (BP 55, DM 137, FR 461, Y 9346).

$223* *The Banqueting House*, s., margins, (03-17-93, Bonhams-Chelsea, #398), plate 8 x 11¼ in., (20.3 x 28.6 cm.), drypoint etching (BP 154, DM 371, FR 1261, Y 26,155).

BI *Docklands, The Thames*, s., margins, est. BP 100/150, (02-17-93, Bonhams-Chelsea, #205), plate 4⅝ x 12¾ in., (11.7 x 32.4 cm.), drypoint etching.

$207* *The Docks, New York*, s., margins, (02-17-93, Bonhams-Chelsea, #202), plate 8½ x 5⅞ in., (21.6 x 14.9 cm.), drypoint etching (BP 143, DM 336, FR 1139, Y 24,725).

$207* *Fleet Street Looking Towards St. Paul's*, s., margins, (02-17-93, Bonhams-Chelsea, #304), plate 6¼ x 9 in., (15.9 x 22.9 cm.), drypoint etching (BP 143, DM 336, FR 1139, Y 24,725).

$72* *The Forth Bridge*, s., margins, (02-17-93, Bonhams-Chelsea, #204), plate 3¾ x 10½ in., (9.5 x 26.7 cm.), drypoint etching (BP 50, DM 117, FR 396, Y 8600).

$57* *Inner City Buildings*, s., margins, (03-17-93, Bonhams-Chelsea, #327), plate 3¼ x 7⅞ in., (8.3 x 20 cm.), etching (BP 39, DM 95, FR 322, Y 6685).

BI *Inner City Buildings*, s., margins, est. BP80/100, (01-21-93, Bonhams-Chelsea, #85), plate 3¼ x 7⅞ in., (8.3 x 20 cm.), etching.

$136* *Pall Mall*, s., margins, (02-17-93, Bonhams-Chelsea, #305), plate 6½ x 9¾ in., (16.5 x 24.8 cm.), drypoint etching (BP 94, DM 221, FR 748, Y 16,245).

$350* *Pier Head, Liverpool*, s., margins, (02-17-93, Bonhams-Chelsea, #203), plate 4¾ x 13 in., (12.1 x 33 cm.), drypoint etching (BP 242, DM 568, FR 1925, Y 41,806).

BI *Shipping On The Thames*, s., margins, est. BP 60/80, (02-17-93, Bonhams-Chelsea, #207), plate 2½ x 5¼ in., (6.4 x 13.3 cm.), drypoint etching.

$192* *Sloane Square*, s., margins, surface dirt, (08-20-92, Bonhams-Chelsea, #87), plate 6 x 10 in., (15.2 x 25.4 cm.), drypoint etching (BP 99, DM 278, FR 943, Y 24,245).

BI *The Temple At Baal*, s., margins, est, BP 60/80, (02-17-93, Bonhams-Chelsea, #208), plate 8½ x 11½ in., (21.6 x 29.2 cm.), drypoint etching.

$223* *Valetta Harbour, Malta*, s., margins, (02-17-93, Bonhams-Chelsea, #206), plate 4¼ x 7½ in., (10.8 x 19.1 cm.), drypoint etching (BP 154, DM 362, FR 1227, Y 26,636).

BI *View Of New York From Brooklyn Bridge*, s., full margins, time- and light-stained, foxing, est. BP 150/200, (11-30-92, Phillips-London, #367A), plate 12½ x 16 in., (318 x 406 mm.), etching.

$112* *Whitehall*, s., margins, (03-17-93, Bonhams-Chelsea, #326), plate 6 x 9½ in., (15.2 x 24.1 cm.), etching (BP 77, DM 186, FR 633, Y 13,136).

BI *Whitehall*, s., margins, est. BP80/120, (01-21-93, Bonhams-Chelsea, #86), plate 6 x 9½ in., (15.2 x 24.1 cm.), etching.

WALCOTT, William   English 1874-1943

$61* *Cathedral*, s., tape remnants, (10-31-92, Cleveland, #351), 5½ x 7½ in., (14 x 19.1 cm.), etching (BP 39, DM 94, FR 318, Y 7556).

$75* *"Charing Cross-Statue Of Charles I"*, c. 1920s, s., good cond., tape hinges, (05-15-93, Cleveland, #440), 3⅝ x 4¹⁵⁄₁₆ in., (9.2 x 12.5 cm.), etching (BP 49, DM 121, FR 405, Y 8314).

$28* *March Of Triumph*, s., (12-17-92, Mystic, #20A), 24 x 30 in., (61 x 76.2 cm.), etching (BP 18, DM 44, FR 149, Y 3441).

$90* *The River Thames*, s., fine cond., light struck, (05-15-93, Cleveland, #439), 8¼ x 9¾ in., (21 x 24.8 cm.), etching (BP 59, DM 145, FR 486, Y 9977).

$83* *The Thames River*, s., toning, hinges, (10-31-92, Cleveland, #350), 4⅛ x 12¾ in., (10.5 x 32.4 cm.), etching (BP 53, DM 128, FR 433, Y 10,281).

WALDE, Martin   b. 1957

$149* *Untitled*, s., d., num. Walde 86, #34/50, (04-21-93, Dorotheum, #721), color screenprint (BP 97, DM 238, FR 805, Y 16,495, SC 1680).

WALES, George Canning   1868-1940

$80* *"Hold Everything"*, s., (02-27-93, Young, #319, illus.), 5 x 9 in., (12.7 x 22.9 cm.), etching (BP 56, DM 132, FR 447, Y 9444).

WALKER, B. Eyre   American 19th/20th cent.

BI *Marine Scene*, s., d. 1914 in plate; s., mono., est. $200/300, (07-03-92, Sloan, #334), 6¾ x 9¾ in., (17.1 x 24.8 cm.), etching.

BI *Marine View*, s., d. 1914 in plate, mono., est. $150/200, (10-30-92, Sloan, #847), 6¾ x 9¾ in., (17.1 x 24.8 cm.), etching.

BI *Marine View*, s. mono., est. $1/150, (04-02-93, Sloan, #814), 6¾ x 9¾ in., (171 x 248 mm.), etching.

WALKER, E., Lithographer

$6325* *Sleigh Scene, Toronto Bay, Canada West, 1853*, after J.T. Downman, pub. Ackermann & Co., margins, image tear/scuff,faded, skinning, soiling, (01-28-93, Sotheby-NY, #454, illus.), 20⅝ x 30½ in., (524 x 775 mm.), sheet 24¾ x 33¼ in., (524 x 775 mm.), lithograph w/tint stone and touches hand-coloring on white wove (BP 4177, DM 10,022, FR 33,914, Y 785,324).

WALKER, George

$1760* *The Costume Of Yorkshire (Abbey Life 432, Tooley 498): 41*, English and French text, folio, (11-12-92, Swann, #210), hand-colored aquatint (BP 1156, DM 2789, FR 9407, Y 218,227).

WALKER, Henry G.

$107* *Cockington*, s., t., margins, (08-20-92, Bonhams-Chelsea, #143), plate 5 x 7⅞ in., (12.7 x 20 cm.), etching, printed in colors (BP 55, DM 155, FR 526, Y 13,512).

WALKER, John

$252* *Blackboards I-XII, 1973: Set of 12*, all s., i. w/plate num., #26/30, full sheets p. to edges, good cond.,loose in orig. box, (10-15-92, Sotheby-London, #154), each sheet approx. 40¾ x 27¾ in., (103.5 x 70.5 cm.), lithograph p. in colors on wove (BP 154, DM 375, FR 1272, Y 30,234).

$539* *For The Last Of The Ogalala Sioux, 1972*, s., d., #72/100, margins, good cond., (10-15-92, Sotheby-London, #156, illus.), sheet approx. 51⅛ x 38½ in., (129.9 x 97.8 cm.), screenprint in colors (BP 330, DM 802, FR 2721, Y 64,667).

$935* *From Memory II, 1990*, s., d., num. 2/30, pub. Waddington Graphics, full margins, apparentlyvery good cond., (02-24-93, Butterfield, #3160, illus.), 56¾ x 45 in., (144.1 x 114.3 cm.), woodcut w/silkscreen in colors on cream wove (BP 652, DM 1518, FR 5146, Y 109,716).

$144* *Headlingly Suite, 1969: Five Plates*, each s., d., i. A/P, margins, good cond., creasing, (10-15-92, Sotheby-London, #143, illus.), each sheet approx. 28 x 40⅛ in., (71.1 x 101.9 cm.), lithograph p. in colors on wove (BP 88, DM 214, FR 727, Y 17,277).

$90* *Headlingly Suite, 1969: Five Plates*, each s., d., i. A/P, margins, good cond., creasing, (10-15-92, Sotheby-London, #145, illus.), each sheet approx. 28 x 40⅛ in.,

(71.1 x 101.9 cm.), lithograph p. in colors on wove (BP 55, DM 134, FR 454, Y 10,798).

$144* *Headlingly Suite, 1969: Five Plates,* each s., d., i. A/P, margins, good cond., creasing, (10-15-92, Sotheby-London, #144, illus.), each sheet approx. 28 x 40⅛ in., (71.1 x 101.9 cm.), lithograph p. in colors on wove (BP 88, DM 214, FR 727, Y 17,277).

$144* *Headlingly Suite, 1969: Five Plates,* each s., d., i. A/P, margins, good cond., creasing, (10-15-92, Sotheby-London, #142, illus.), each sheet approx. 28 x 40⅛ in., (71.1 x 101.9 cm.), lithograph p. in colors on wove (BP 88, DM 214, FR 727, Y 17,277).

$54* *Headlingly Suite, 1969: Five Plates,* each s., d., i. A/P, margins, good cond., creasing, (10-15-92, Sotheby-London, #146), each sheet approx. 28 x 40⅛ in., (71.1 x 101.9 cm.), lithograph p. in colors on wove (BP 33, DM 80, FR 273, Y 6479).

BI *Memory V, 1989,* s., d., #27/35, blindstamp publisher, Waddington Graphics and printer, Advanced Graphics, full margins, good cond., 5/8" tear, handling creases, est. $1,5/2,000, (05-19-93, Butterfield, #2366), 46¼ x 34 in., (117.5 x 86.4 cm.), woodcut silkscreen in colors on heavy wove.

$396* *Pacifica, 1982,* s., #4/35, margins, good cond., (10-15-92, Sotheby-London, #155, illus.), sheet approx. 59¼ x 46⅞ in., (150.5 x 119.1 cm.), screenprint in colors (BP 242, DM 589, FR 1999, Y 47,510).

$396* *Tank I-V, 1973: Five Plates,* each s., d., t., first four num. from edit. of 15, last from edit. of30, margins, good cond., slight defects, (10-15-92, Sotheby-London, #140, illus.), each sheet approx. 52⅞ x 35⅞ in., (134.3 x 91.1 cm.), silkscreen p. in colors on wove (BP 242, DM 589, FR 1999, Y 47,510).

$683* *Untitled, 1980: Group of Four,* each s., d., margins, good cond., (10-15-92, Sotheby-London, #148, illus.), each sheet approx. 22⅜ x 30 in., (56.8 x 76.2 cm.), monotype on white wove (BP 418, DM 1017, FR 3448, Y 81,944).

WALKER, Lewis Emory
BI *Construction Of The Treasury, South Wing, 1869,* d. in neg., est. $1/1,500, (10-14-92, Swann, #264, illus.), 9½ x 13½ in., (24.1 x 34.3 cm.), photograph, mounted albumen print.

WALKER, Lewis Emory (attrib.)
BI *Artillery Supply Field, Washington Arsenal, 1864,* num. 8, est. $1/1,500, (10-14-92, Swann, #175, illus.), 11½ x 15½ in., (29.2 x 39.4 cm.), photograph, salt print from wet collodion neg..
BI *Construction Of The U.S. Treasury Extension, c. 1857,* d. in negative July 7th, (04-06-93, Sotheby-NY, #4, illus.), 13¼ x 16¼ in., folio sheet 22½ x 17½ in., photograph, salt print.

WALKER, W.B.
$244 *"Woodcock Shooting", "Partridge Shooting" and "Duck Shooting": Three,* d. 1804, (06-11-93, G.A. Key, #60), 7 x 9 in., (17.8 x 22.9 cm.), colored print (BP 160, DM 397, FR 1337, Y 25,889).

WALKER, W.B. (after)
$312 *"Mid Summer Holydays" and "The First Step In Life": Two,* stuck to glass, (12-11-92, G.A. Key, #115), 9 x 14 in., (22.9 x 35.6 cm.), hand colored print (BP 200, DM 492, FR 1685, Y 38,609).

WALKOWITZ, Abraham   American 1880-1965
$330* *In The Park,* s., (10-18-92, Hindman, #482), 3⅞ x 6⅞ in., (9.8 x 17.5 cm.), etching (BP 202, DM 491, FR 1666, Y 39,592).
BI *Night Scene, c. 1920,* s., est. $200/250, (05-15-93, Cleveland, #332), 3 x 4⅜ in., (7.6 x 11.1 cm.), etching.

WALL, Jeff   b. 1946
$36,800* *Untitled (Tondo),* exec. 1989, prov., exhib., lit., (05-05-93, Christie-NY, #149, illus.), color photograph in metal lightbox (BP 23,496, DM 58,062, FR 195,641, Y 4,055,990).

WALL, Paul
BI *"Aquatic Pattern", c. 1938,* labels, est. $2/2,500, (04-06-93, Sotheby-NY, #137, illus.), 12⅞ x 10⅛ in., photograph, bromide print.

BI *"The Gargoyle", c. 1936,* mounted, s., t. by photog., i., label, est. $1,5/2,500, (04-06-93, Sotheby-NY, #138, illus.), 13⅜ x 10½ in., photograph.

WALL, W.G. (after)
$1650* *Hadley's Falls,* engraved J. Hill, (06-11-93, Freemn/Fine Art, #245, illus.), 13¾ x 21¼ in., (34.9 x 54 cm.), hand-colored engraving (BP 1084, DM 2682, FR 9041, Y 175,066).
$880* *Little Falls At Lucerne,* engraved by J. Hill, pub. Henry I. Megarey, No. 1 of the Hudson RiverPortfolio, discoloration, fading, (06-11-93, Freemn/Fine Art, #244), plate 13¾ x 21 in., (34.9 x 53.3 cm.), hand-colored engraving (BP 578, DM 1430, FR 4822, Y 93,369).
$2090* *"Rapids Above Hadley's Falls" and "Bakers Falls": Two,* engraved by J. Hill, first 11/No. 8 Hudson River Portfolio; second 11/No. 4 Hudson River Portfolio, pub. Henry T. Megarey, (06-11-93, Freemn/Fine Art, #243), hand-colored engraving (BP 1373, DM 3397, FR 11,452, Y 221,751).

WALLACE, Ian
$2696* *Untitled,* exec. 1989, prov., (10-15-92, Sotheby-London, #35, illus.), 47⅝ x 47⅝ in., (121 x 121 cm.), photograph and acrylic on canvas (BP 1650, DM 4013, FR 13,609, Y 323,455).

WALLER, Lorna   b. 1912
$81* *9 Crome Road, Ivanhoe,* inits. L.W., i., lit., (08-11-92, L. Joel, #49G), 4¾ x 7 in., (12 x 17.8 cm.), linocut (BP 42, DM 119, FR 403, Y 10,373, A$ 110).

WALLER, M Napier   1893-1972
$486* *The House On The Hill,* s. M Napier Waller, i., #28/50 proofs, lit., (08-11-92, L. Joel, #23G), 8⅛ x 9¼ in., (20.6 x 23.5 cm.), color linocut (BP 253, DM 713, FR 2416, Y 62,236, A$ 660).

WALLHAUSEN, Johann Jacobi von
$1980* *Art De Chevalerie (Cockle 735): 13,* 4to, old vellum, (11-12-92, Swann, #211, illus.), double-page engraving (BP 1300, DM 3137, FR 10,583, Y 245,505).

WALLING, William
$371* *Marlene Dietrich, In White Suit And Hat, With Cigarette,* (10-10-92, Bonhams, #6, illus.), 14 x 11 in., (35.6 x 27.9 cm.), photograph (BP 220, DM 551, FR 1850, Y 45,167).

WALLIS, Henry (after)
$133* *The Death Of Chatterton, 1860,* by Thomas Oldham Barlow, s. by engraver, blind-stamp, laid on stretcher, light-stained, foxing, water-staining, break in platemark, (11-30-92, Phillips-London, #30), sheet 26¾ x 34⅓ in., (680 x 872 mm.), mixed-method engraving on india-laid (BP 88, DM 212, FR 719, Y 16,553).

WALSH, T.N.H. (after)   British 19th cent.
$330* *"A Check" and "Get Away Forrard": Two, 1878,* engraved by E.G. Hester, (03-14-93, Hindman, #233), each 15 x 19½ in., (38.1 x 49.5 cm.), hand-colored aquatints (BP 230, DM 549, FR 1868, Y 38,892).

WALT DISNEY STUDIOS
$2773* *Fantasia, Walt Disney, 1941,* cond. A-, border repaired, one-sheet, linen-backed, lit., (12-17-92, Christie-S. Ken, #392, illus.), 41 x 27 in., (104.1 x 68.6 cm.), poster (BP 1760, DM 4329, FR 14,789, Y 340,789).

WALTER, Adam B.   American 1820-1875
$77* *Visit From The Parson,* after Collins, (04-02-93, Sloan, #2282), sight 11⅝ x 17⅝ in., (295 x 448 mm.), etching and aquatint (BP 51, DM 124, FR 420, Y 8767).

WALTERS, S. (after)
$7* *"Homeward Bound",* (03-12-93, DuMouchelle, #2462), 9 x 11¾ in., (22.9 x 29.8 cm.), photolithograph (BP 5, DM 12, FR 40, Y 825).

WALTHER, Johann Georg
BI *Portrat Ludwig Radwig Von Souches, Zu Pferde,* watermark, est. DM 750, (12-04-92, Bassenge, #6499), 14¹/₁₆ x 10⅝ in., (35.7 x 27 cm.), etching.

WALTON, W.L. (after)
$1320* *"The International Contest Between Heenan And Sayers At Farnborough On The 17th Of April, 1860",* by Buf-

ford Sons, (09-18-92, DuMouchelle, #2419), 26 x 39 in., (66 x 99.1 cm.), color lithograph (BP 759, DM 1977, FR 6769, Y 164,465).

WANG, C.C.
BI *"Mountain Of Mind"*, #142/200, prov., est. $3/500, (06-11-93, DuMouchelle, #2102), 28 x 19 in., (71.1 x 48.3 cm.), lithograph.

WAPLINGTON, Nick
$468* *Lawn Vacuuming*, 1989/1991, s., d., Dixon Collection, (11-16-92, Butterfield, #6220), 10½ x 14½ in., (267.2 x 369 mm.), photograph, c-print (BP 308, DM 746, FR 2513, Y 58,202).

WARD
$88* *"The Anglers Repent"*, after George Morland, (02-12-93, DuMouchelle, #2465), 14 x 18 in., (35.6 x 45.7 cm.), engraving (BP 62, DM 146, FR 494, Y 10,613).

WARD, James
$118* *Nonpareil, The Favourite Charger Of His Most Gracious Majesty King George The Fourth*, margins, (07-16-92, Bonhams-Chelsea, #526), image 12⅞ x 17⅞ in., (32.7 x 45.4 cm.), lithograph (BP 61, DM 174, FR 589, Y 14,781).

WARD, James   1769-1859
$2164* *The Dairy Farm (Frankau 29), 1801*, 2nd (final) state, pub. R. Ackermann, margins, staining, (12-01-92, Christie-London, #293, illus.), plate 18⅞ x 23¹⁵⁄₁₆ in., (480 x 608 mm.), mezzotint in colors finished by hand (BP 1430, DM 3449, FR 11,754, Y 269,422).

WARD, James (after)
$218* *The Great Fight Between Tom Sayers And J.C. Heenan At Farnborough, April 17th, 1860 For The Championship Of England And America*, pub. F.R. Scofield, foxing, (11-12-92, Bonhams-Chelsea, #78), sheet 27¼ x 40 in., (69.2 x 101.6 cm.), tinted lithograph (BP 143, DM 345, FR 1165, Y 27,030).
$147* *Jem Ward's Picture Of The Great Fight Between Tom Sayers And J. C. Heenan*, trimmed, foxing, other defects, (10-29-92, Bonhams-Chelsea, #9), image 20 x 24½ in., (50.8 x 62.2 cm.), lithograph w/hand coloring (BP 94, DM 226, FR 767, Y 18,209).
BI *Rustic Conversation, 1794*, by Samuel William Reynolds, pub. T. Philipe, trimmed to image, mounted on stretcher, est. BP 170/200, (11-30-92, Phillips-London, #215), image 17 x 22½ in., (432 x 572 mm.), color mezzotint.

WARD, Lynd   American b. 1905
$220* *"Clouded Over" and "Evening Walk": Two*, s., t., margins, good cond., Evening Walk w/crease, (02-24-93, Butterfield, #2884), 6¹⁄₁₆ x 8¹⁵⁄₁₆ in., (154 x 227 mm.), 7 x 15 in., (154 x 227 mm.), wood engraving on tissue-thin Japan (BP 153, DM 357, FR 1211, Y 25,816).
BI *"Flower Girl" and "Child With Bird": Two*, s., t., margins, good cond., light-staining, foxing, est. $2/300, (02-24-93, Butterfield, #2885), 7⅜ x 13⅛ in., (187 x 333 mm.), wood engraving on tissue-thin Japan.
$330* *From "Vertigo", 1937: Group Of Three*, s., (12-08-92, Swann, #307), each sight 6 x 4 in., (15.2 x 10.2 cm.), wood engraving (BP 207, DM 514, FR 1752, Y 40,902).
$303* *"Sanctuary" and "Undercliff": Two*, s., t., margins, good cond., Undercliff w/staining, (02-24-93, Butterfield, #2886), one 9¹⁄₁₆ x 6¹⁄₁₆ in., (230 x 154 mm.), other 7¹⁵⁄₁₆ x 6 in., (230 x 154 mm.), wood engraving on tissue-thin Japan (BP 211, DM 492, FR 1668, Y 35,555).
$55* *Undercliff, 1948*, s., original folder, (11-12-92, Freemn/Fine Art, #236), mat 8 x 6¼ in., (20.3 x 15.9 cm.), wood engraving (BP 36, DM 87, FR 294, Y 6820).

WARD, Sir Leslie Matthew (Spy)   British 1851-1922
$55* *"A Symphony", Portrait Of A Whistler*, good cond., pub. Vanity Fair, January 1878, (11-21-92, Bakker, #158), image 12¼ x 7¼ in., (31.1 x 18.4 cm.), lithograph (BP 36, DM 88, FR 295, Y 6840).

WARD, William   1766-1826
BI *George Morland (1763-184), Brustbildnis Des Malers Mit Zeichenstift (Le Blanc 59 I, Ch. Schmith 60 I, Bailey (Morland) S. 136), 1805*, after R. Muller, watermark, lit.,

(12-04-92, Bassenge, #6717), 14⅞ x 10¹³⁄₁₆ in., (37.8 x 27.4 cm.), brown mezzotint.
$699* *Hesitation (Frankau 157), 1786*, undescribed proof, pub. W. Dickinson, margins, platemark partly split, staining, (12-01-92, Christie-London, #294), plate 10³⁄₁₆ x 8⅛ in., (258 x 207 mm.), stipple engraving in colors (BP 462, DM 1114, FR 3797, Y 87,027).
BI *Monsieur De St. George (Frankau 251)*, margins, foxing, dirt, defects, laid down, est. BP 800/1,000, (06-30-93, Sotheby-London, #271, illus.), 15 x 10¾ in., (381 x 273 mm.), mezzotint in colors w/hand-coloring.

WARD, William (after)
BI *The Wounded Soldier, 1803*, by J.R. Smith Jnr., pub. H. Macklin, trimmed to image on 3 sides, soiling, creasing, repaired tear, est. BP 150/200, (11-30-92, Phillips-London, #218), sheet 18½ x 23⅝ in., (470 x 600 mm.), color mezzotint, finished by hand, on wove.

WARDLE, Arthur (after)
BI *Sporting And Other Dogs: A Set Of Three*, (12-11-92, G.A. Key, #77), 9 x 8 in., (22.9 x 20.3 cm.), colored lithograph.

WARDLE, Arthur (after)   English 1864-1949
$303* *Bull-Bitches Of The 20th Century, 1906*, pub. F. Mansell, (05-28-93, Sloan, #1604, illus.), 20⅜ x 27¼ in., (51.8 x 69.2 cm.), chromolithograph (BP 194, DM 481, FR 1625, Y 32,490).

WARDLE, Engraver, E*
$34* *Building The Camp Fire*, s., margins, (05-20-93, Bonhams-Chelsea, #135), plate 18 x 22 in., (45.7 x 55.9 cm.), mezzotint in colors (BP 22, DM 55, FR 185, Y 3754).

WARE, Isaac
$1150* *Architecture, 1756: Eight*, (03-03-93, Sotheby-Arcade, #124), sight 9 x 13 in., (22.9 x 33 cm.), copper engraving (BP 793, DM 1894, FR 6425, Y 134,377).

WARHOL, Andy   American 1928-1987
$5500* *$1 (F. & S. 274 and 275), 1982*, s., #11/60 and #26/60, uniquely colored, pub. by artist, good cond.,scuffs, (11-07-92, Sotheby-NY, #826, illus.), each sheet approx. 19¾ x 15¾ in., (502 x 400 mm.), two silkscreens p. in colors on Lenox Museum Board (BP 3596, DM 8782, FR 29,682, Y 678,845).
$2200* *$1 (F. & S. 276), 1982*, unique in color, s., #10/60, pub. by artist, good cond.?, (10-28-92, Butterfield, #3165), 19¾ x 15⅝ in., (502 x 397 mm.), silkscreen in purple, orange and black on Lenox Musem Board (BP 1402, DM 3398, FR 11,536, Y 269,939).
$1955* *$1 (F.&S.276), 1982*, unique in color, s., #12/60, pub. artist, blindstamp printer, RupertJasen Smith, good cond.?, (05-19-93, Butterfield, #2374, illus.), 19¾ x 15¾ in., (502 x 400 mm.), silkscreen in colors on Lenox Museum Board (BP 1269, DM 3178, FR 10,706, Y 216,429).
$8625* *"$4" and "Quadrant $" (F. & S. 281 and 284), 1982: Two*, s., i. PP 1/3, printer's proof, pub. by artist, good cond., (05-15-93, Sotheby-NY, #1266, illus.), each sheet 40 x 32 in., (101.6 x 81.3 cm.), silkscreen in colors on Lenox Museum Board (BP 5608, DM 13,873, FR 46,622, Y 956,102).
$2300* *25 Cats Named Sam And One Blue Pussy (Brown p. 31), c. 1954*, book by Charles Lisanby, hand colored, #40, good cond., w/hand colored photo-lithograph attached to front cover, dedication, loss, soiling, discoloration, (02-11-93, Sotheby-NY, #454), each page approx. 8¹⁵⁄₁₆ x 5¹³⁄₁₆ in., (227 x 148 mm.), photo-lithograph (BP 1623, DM 3810, FR 12,892, Y 277,275).
$2200* *25 Cats Named Sam And One Blue Pussy (Brown p. 31), c. 1954*, book by Charles Lisanby, pen s., num. 92, time-staining, cover w/soiling, discoloration, prop. Woodward Foundation, (11-07-92, Sotheby-NY, #801), each page 9 x 5⅞ in., (229 x 149 mm.), book w/hand colored photo-lithograph attached to the front cover (BP 1438, DM 3513, FR 11,873, Y 271,538).
BI *99 Cent Steaks, c. 1985*, authenticated and s. Frederick Hughes, pub. by artist, good cond., creases, surface scuffs, est. $3/4,000, (05-15-93, Sotheby-NY, #1264, illus.), sheet 21¾ x 14¾ in., (55.2 x 37.5 cm.), silkscreen.

$2728* *Ads: Apple (F. & S. 359), 1985,* s., # P.P. 4/5, p. Rupert Jason Smith, pub. Ronald Feldman Fine Arts,good cond., (12-03-92, Sotheby-London, #854, illus.), sheet 37⅞ x 37⅞ in., (962 x 962 mm.), silkscreen in colors on Lenox Museum Board (BP 1760, DM 4290, FR 14,643, Y 339,430).

$4775* *Ads: Blackglama (Judy Garland)(F. & S. 351), 1985,* s., # P.P. 4/5, p. Rupert Jason Smith, pub. Ronald Feldman Fine Arts,good cond., (12-03-92, Sotheby-London, #849, illus.), sheet 37⅞ x 37⅞ in., (962 x 962 mm.), silkscreen in colors on Lenox Museum Board (BP 3080, DM 7509, FR 25,631, Y 594,127).

$5798* *Ads: Chanel (F. & S. 354), 1985,* s., # P.P. 4/5, p. Rupert Jason Smith, pub. Ronald Feldman Fine Arts,good cond., (12-03-92, Sotheby-London, #852, illus.), 37⅞ x 37⅞ in., (962 x 962 mm.), silkscreen in colors on Lenox Museum Board (BP 3740, DM 9118, FR 31,122, Y 721,413).

$3240* *Ads: Life Savers (F. & S. 353), 1985,* s., # P.P. 4/5, p. Rupert Jason Smith, pub. Ronald Feldman Fine Arts,good cond., (12-03-92, Sotheby-London, #851, illus.), 37⅞ x 37⅞ in., (962 x 962 mm.), silkscreen in colors on Lenox Museum Board (BP 2090, DM 5095, FR 17,391, Y 403,135).

$1876* *Ads: Mobil (F. & S. 350), 1985,* s., # P.P. 4/5, p. Rupert Jason Smith, pub. Ronald Feldman Fine Arts,good cond., (12-03-92, Sotheby-London, #848, illus.), 37⅞ x 37⅞ in., (962 x 962 mm.), silkscreen in colors on Lenox Museum Board (BP 1210, DM 2950, FR 10,070, Y 233,420).

BI *Ads: Paramount (F. & S. 352), 1985,* s., # P.P. 4/5, p. Rupert Jason Smith, pub. Ronald Feldman Fine Arts,good cond., scratch into upper image, est. BP 1,5/2,000, (12-03-92, Sotheby-London, #850, illus.), 37⅞ x 37⅞ in., (962 x 962 mm.), silkscreen in colors on Lenox Museum Board.

$7162* *Ads: Rebel Without A Cause (James Dean) (F. & S. 355), 1985,* s., # P.P. 4/5, p. Rupert Jason Smith, pub. Ronald Feldman Fine Arts,good cond., (12-03-92, Sotheby-London, #856, illus.), 37⅞ x 37⅞ in., (962 x 962 mm.), silkscreen in colors on Lenox Museum Board (BP 4620, DM 11,263, FR 38,443, Y 891,129).

$2728* *Ads: Van Heusen (Ronald Reagan)(F. & S. 356), 1985,* s., # P.P. 4/5, p. Rupert Jason Smith, pub. Ronald Feldman Fine Arts,good cond., (12-03-92, Sotheby-London, #853, illus.), 37⅞ x 37⅞ in., (962 x 962 mm.), silkscreen in colors on Lenox Museum Board (BP 1760, DM 4290, FR 14,643, Y 339,430).

$2728* *Ads: Volkswagen (F. & S. 358), 1985,* s., # P.P. 4/5, p. Rupert Jason Smith, pub. Ronald Feldman Fine Arts,good cond., (12-03-92, Sotheby-London, #855, illus.), 37⅞ x 37⅞ in., (962 x 962 mm.), silkscreen in colors on Lenox Museum Board (BP 1760, DM 4290, FR 14,643, Y 339,430).

$3850* *African Elephant (F. and S. 293), 1983,* s., #X/X, pub. Ronald Feldman Fine Arts, very good cond., (11-09-92, Christie-NY, #443, illus.), 38 x 38 in., (965 x 965 mm.), colored screenprint on Lenox Museum Board (BP 2545, DM 6146, FR 20,766, Y 477,786).

$3219* *"African Elephant" (Feldman/Schellmann), 1983,* #21/150, s., (12-05-92, Mangisch, #749, illus.), 37¹⁵⁄₁₆ x 37¹⁵⁄₁₆ in., (96.5 x 96.5 cm.), color serigraph (BP 2016, DM 5019, FR 17,104, Y 398,835, SF 4600).

$2760* *Alexander The Great (F. & S. 292), 1982,* unique color trial proof, s., i. TP 9/15, pub. Alexander Iolas, good-cond., light-staining, (05-15-93, Sotheby-NY, #1269, illus.), sheet 39⅞ x 39⅞ in., (101.3 x 101.3 cm.), silkscreen in colors on Lenox Museum Board (BP 1795, DM 4439, FR 14,919, Y 305,953).

$13,200* *American Flag, Montauk: Six,* (1976), stamp, s., d. bu estate executor, (10-13-92, Christie-NY, #615, illus.), each 11 x 13½ in., (27.9 x 34.3 cm.), overall 21 x 40½ in., (27.9 x 34.3 cm.), photograph, gelatin silver prints stitched together (BP 7688, DM 19,338, FR 65,704, Y 1,600,582).

$1035* *The American Indian,* for Ace Gallery, 1976, promotion for suite, hand s. by Warhol, prop.Joseph C. DiBella, (06-23-93, Sotheby-NY, #322, illus.), 50 x 34 in., (127 x 86.4 cm.), (BP 703, DM 1751, FR 5891, Y 112,757).

$310* *The American Indian Series, 1977,* poster from Ace Gallery, LA, s., (09-25-92, Granier, #3049), sheet 49¹³⁄₁₆ x 34⁷⁄₁₆ in., (126.6 x 87.4 cm.), color offset print (BP 181, DM 460, FR 1554, Y 37,417).

BI *Art Cash, 1971,* Warhol's sig. stamp-s., s. by R. Whitman, R. Rauschenberg, T. Gormley, R. Grooms and Marisol, #4/75, margins, good cond.?, est. BP 1/1,500, (06-30-93, Sotheby-London, #965, illus.), 27¾ x 22 in., (705 x 559 mm.), offset color lithograph.

$3621* *"Bighorn Ram" (Feldman/Schellmann 302), 1983,* #21/150, s., (12-05-92, Mangisch, #754, illus.), 37¹⁵⁄₁₆ x 37¹⁵⁄₁₆ in., (96.5 x 96.5 cm.), color serigraph (BP 2267, DM 5645, FR 19,240, Y 448,643, SF 5175).

$3025* *Birmingham Race Riot (Feldman & Schellmann 3), 1964,* from Ten Works + Ten Painters portfolio, pub. Wadsworth Atheneum, good cond., surface scuffs, (11-07-92, Sotheby-NY, #802, illus.), sheet 20⅛ x 24 in., (511 x 610 mm.), silkscreen p. in black on white paper (BP 1978, DM 4830, FR 16,325, Y 373,365).

$2300* *Birmingham Race Riot (Feldman & Schellmann 3), 1964,* from portfolio Ten Works by Ten Painters, pub. Wadsworth Atheneum, good cond., creases, (05-15-93, Sotheby-NY, #1253, illus.), sheet 20 x 24 in., (50.8 x 61 cm.), silkscreen on white (BP 1495, DM 3700, FR 12,432, Y 254,961).

$2530* *Birmingham Race Riot (Feldman and Schellmann 3), 1964,* from Ten Works + Ten Painters, Wadsworth Atheneum, excell. cond., orig. wrapper, (05-11-93, Christie-NY, #586, illus.), sheet 19 x 24 in., (483 x 610 mm.), screenprint on wove (BP 1615, DM 3986, FR 13,429, Y 278,297).

$605* *Birmingham Race Riot, From Ten Works + Ten Painters (Feldman And Schellman 3), 1964,* num. 40/500, pub. Wadsworth Antheneum, blindstamp, full sheet, good cond., (05-22-93, Weschler, #228, illus.), 19¾ x 24 in., (50.2 x 61 cm.), silkscreen in colors (BP 392, DM 984, FR 3310, Y 66,703).

$3300* *Blackglama (Judy Garland) (F. and S. 351), 1985,* s., #185/190, pub. Ronald Feldman Fine Arts, crease, surface scratches, scuffing, remains of glue, rubbed spots, soiling, good cond., (11-09-92, Christie-NY, #444, illus.), 38 x 38 in., (965 x 965 mm.), colored screenprint on Lenox Museum Board (BP 2182, DM 5268, FR 17,799, Y 409,531).

$6900* *Blue Valentine,* stamp s., d. 1982 on overlap, prov., (02-23-93, Sotheby-NY, #285, illus.), 11 x 14 in., (27.9 x 35.6 cm.), synthetic polymer paint silkscreened on canvas (BP 4727, DM 11,147, FR 37,808, Y 805,886).

$253* *Brillo, 1970,* s. Andy Warhol, for Pasadena Art Museum, (09-30-92, Kunsthallen, #295), poster, serigraph in colors (BP 143, DM 359, FR 1213, Y 30,361, DK 1380).

$3163* *Brooklyn Bridge (F. & S. 290), 1983,* s., i. HC 8/10, pub. 1983 Brooklyn Bridge Centennial Commission, Inc., good cond., print glued to back mat, pressure marks, scuff marks, (05-15-93, Sotheby-NY, #1268, illus.), 39⅜ x 39⅜ in., (100 x 100 cm.), silkscreen in colors on Lenox Museum Board (BP 2057, DM 5088, FR 17,097, Y 350,626).

$60,500* *Cagney (F. & S. App. I, p. 112), 1964,* pen s. verso, d., pub. Leo castelli Gallery, good cond., crease, surface scuffs, creases, discoloration, (11-07-92, Sotheby-NY, #803, illus.), sheet 30 x 40 in., (76.2 x 101.6 cm.), silkscreen (BP 39,555, DM 96,599, FR 326,498, Y 7,467,292).

BI *Campbell's Consomme (Beef) Soup (Feldman/Schellmann 52), 1968,* s., plate 9 from Campbell's Soup I, #24/250, sig., est. DM 5,500-, (05-27-93, Lempertz, #1105, illus.), 35¹⁄₁₆ x 23⁷⁄₁₆ in., (89 x 59.6 cm.), color serigraph on paper.

$3606* *Campbell's Green Pea Soup (Feldman/Schellmann 50), 1968,* #97/250, Campbell's Soup I portfolio, ballpoint pen s., (11-20-92, Lempertz, #935, illus.), sh 35¹⁄₁₆ x 23¹⁄₁₆ in., (89 x 58.5 cm.), color serigraph on heavy smooth paper (BP 2374, DM 5749, FR 19,366, Y 448,452).

BI *Campbell's Pepper Pot Soup (Feldman/Schellmann 51), 1968,* #20/250, Campbell's Soup I portfolio, ballpoint pen s., est. DM 6,000, (11-20-92, Lempertz, #936, illus.), sh 35¹⁄₁₆ x 23¹⁄₁₆ in., (89 x 58.5 cm.), color serigraph on heavy smooth paper.

$3487* *Campbell's Soup Can I, 1968,* (09-18-92, Schloss Ahlden, #1079, illus.), 35⅛ x 23⅛ in., (89.2 x 58.7 cm.), color screen print w/silver and gold on thin smooth white cardboard (BP 2042, DM 5174, FR 17,701, Y 430,973).

$1300* *Campbell's Soup Can On Shopping Bag, 1966,* s., pub. Institute of Comtemporary Art Boston, good cond., (11-30-92, Phillips-London, #579), sheet 19⅝ x 17⅛ in., (498 x 435 mm.), screenprint in colors on paper shopping bag (BP 858, DM 2071, FR 7031, Y 161,792).

BI *Campbell's Soup I (F. and S. 44-53), 1968: ten,* s., #84/250, pub. Factory Additions, full margins, scuffing, creases, colors attenuated, glued down, est. $25/30,000, (05-11-93, Christie-NY, #591, illus.), each sheet 35⅛ x 23⅛ in., (892 x 587 mm.), color screenprint on glazed wove.

$23,873* *Campbell's Soup II (F. & S. 54-63), 1968: Set Of Ten,* ballpoint s., stamp #102/250, pub. Factory Additions, excell. cond.,orig. box, (12-03-92, Sotheby-London, #844, illus.), each approx. 32 x 18⅜ in., (813 x 467 mm.), silkscreen in colors on sturdy white (BP 15,400, DM 37,542, FR 128,143, Y 2,970,387).

$20,900* *Campbell's Soup II (F. & S. 54-63), 1969,* complete portfolio, pen s. verso, stamp num. 202/250, pub. Factory Additions, full margins, good cond., creases, scuffs, (11-07-92, Sotheby-NY, #815, illus.), each sheet approx. 35 x 23 in., (889 x 584 mm.), 10 silkscreens p. in colors (BP 13,665, DM 33,371, FR 112,790, Y 2,579,610).

$2090* *Campbell's Soup II: Cheddar Cheese (F. & S. 63), 1969,* s. in ink, stamp num. 25/250, pub. Factory Additions, good cond., tear, creases, surface scuffing, thinned area, pressure marks, surface soiling, (02-24-93, Butterfield, #3162, illus.), 32 x 18¾ in., (813 x 476 mm.), silkscreen in colors on wove (BP 1457, DM 3393, FR 11,502, Y 245,248).

$2544* *Campbell's Soup II: Old Fashioned Vegetable Soup (Feldman-Schellmann54), 1969,* s., num., series Campbell's Soup II, Factory Additions, (06-12-93, Hauswedell/Nolt, #451, illus.), 31⅞ x 18½ in., (81 x 47 cm.), color serigraph on thin white board (BP 1665, DM 4141, FR 13,917, Y 267,705).

$3163* *Campbell's Soup II: Vegetarian Vegetable (F.&S.56), 1969,* ink s., stamp #50/250, p. Salvatore Silkscreen Co., pub. Factory Additions, full margins, good cond., (05-19-93, Butterfield, #2368, illus.), 31⅞ x 18⅞ in., (810 x 479 mm.), silkscreen in colors on wove (BP 2053, DM 5141, FR 17,322, Y 350,161).

$605* *Campbell's Soup Label: Cream Of Chicken,* felt pen s., for Campbell Soup Co., very good cond.?, (10-28-92, Butterfield, #3163), 3⅝ x 8¼ in., (92 x 210 mm.), campbell's soup label (BP 385, DM 934, FR 3173, Y 74,233).

$303* *Campbell's Soup Label: Cream Of Potato,* felt pen s., for Campbell Soup Co., good cond.?, (10-28-92, Butterfield, #3162), 3¾ x 8¼ in., (95 x 210 mm.), campbell's soup label (BP 193, DM 468, FR 1589, Y 37,178).

$21,315* *Campbells Soup II (F. & S. 54-63), 1968: Set Of Ten,* each ballpoint s., stamp #104/250, pub. Factory Additions, excell. cond., in orig. numbered box, (12-03-92, Sotheby-London, #845), each approx. 32 x 18⅜ in., (813 x 467 mm.), silkscreen in colors on sturdy white (BP 13,750, DM 33,519, FR 114,412, Y 2,652,109).

BI *Cantaloupes I (Feldman/Schelmann 201; Wunsche 152), 1979,* XXI/XXX, s., 755mm x 1010mm, est. SF 4,2/4,800, (10-14-92, Germann, #472), color serigraph.

BI *Cantaloupes II (Feldman/Schelmann 198; Wunsche 154), 1979,* XXIX/XXX, s., 762mm x 1016mm, est. SF 4,2/4,800, (10-14-92, Germann, #471, illus.), color serigraph.

$2640* *Charles Lisanby (Brown pp. 31-3): Set Of Eighteen,* from 25 Cats name(d) Sam and one Blue Pussy, c. 1954, cover, ink s. on just., copy 160/190, time staining, soiled, stained, paper losses, good cond., (09-19-92, Christie-E, #238), 9¼ x 6⅛ in., (235 x 155 mm.), letterpress illus. w/hand-coloring on laid paper, white buckram boards (BP 1519, DM 3953, FR 13,538, Y 328,931).

$3450* *Charles Lisanby, 25 Cats Name(d) Sam And One Blue Pussy, c. 1954 (Brown pp. 31-3): Eighteen,* s. just., copy 69 of 190, bound, time staining, white buckram boards, soiled, cover w/staining, tear, excell. cond., (05-11-93, Christie-NY, #585, illus.), 9¼ x 6⅛ in., (235 x 155 mm.), letterpress illustrations w/hand-coloring on laid (BP 2202, DM 5435, FR 18,312, Y 379,496).

$990* *Christmas T-Strap,* (10-09-92, Sotheby-Arcade, #308, illus.), 14¾ x 17½ in., (37.5 x 44.5 cm.), screen print on vellum (BP 588, DM 1475, FR 5000, Y 120,732).

$1130* *Committee 2000 (Feldman-Schellmann 289), 1982,* s., #1155/2000, relief stamp, stamped, (c), (06-12-93, Hauswedell/Nolt, #452, illus.), 25³⁄₁₆ x 19¹¹⁄₁₆ in., (64 x 50 cm.), color serigraph on light board (BP 740, DM 1839, FR 6182, Y 118,910).

$1343* *Committee 2000 (Feldman/Schellmann 289), 1982,* #990/2000, s., (04-21-93, Germann, #827, illus.), 29¹⁵⁄₁₆ x 19⅞ in., (760 x 505 mm.), color serigraph (BP 871, DM 2147, FR 7259, Y 148,677, SF 1955).

BI *Committee 2000 (Feldmann 289), 1982,* 789/2000, s., est. SF 2,3/2,800, (10-14-92, Germann, #473, illus.), 29¹⁵⁄₁₆ x 20¹⁄₁₆ in., (760 x 510 mm.), color serigraph.

$1449* *"Committee 2000" (Feldman/Schellmann 289), 1982,* #868/2000, Edition Committee 2000, Munchen, (12-05-92, Mangisch, #748), 30 x 20 in., (76.2 x 50.8 cm.), color serigraph (BP 907, DM 2259, FR 7699, Y 179,532, SF 2070).

$2817* *"Committee 2000" (Feldman/Schellmann 289), 1982,* #1392/2000, s., num., Edition Committee 2000, Munchen, (12-05-92, Mangisch, #1612), 30 x 20 in., (76.2 x 50.8 cm.), color screen print (BP 1764, DM 4392, FR 14,968, Y 349,027, SF 4025).

BI *Committee 2000, 1982,* s., num. 791/2000, est. $1500/2000, (11-12-92, Freemn/Fine Art, #236C), sheet 30 x 20 in., (76.2 x 50.8 cm.), screenprint p. on Lenox Museum Board.

$3321* *Cow (F & S 12a), 1976,* s., 1982, catalog cover lot, (05-25-93, AB Stockholm, #75), 45¹¹⁄₁₆ x 28⅛ in., (116 x 71.5 cm.), serigraph in colors (BP 2152, DM 5409, FR 18,207, Y 362,990, SK 4840).

$858* *Cow (F. & S. 11), 1966,* stamp sig., sig., d., pub. Factory Additions, trimmed, repaired tear,creases, (06-30-93, Sotheby-London, #962), sh 45½ x 28 in., (115.6 x 71.1 cm.), color silkscreen on wallpaper (BP 575, DM 1463, FR 4937, Y 91,932).

$1023* *Cow (F. & S. 11), 1966,* complimentary sig. in felt tip, pub. Factory Additions, good cond., tears, (12-03-92, Sotheby-London, #840, illus.), approx. 44⅝ x 28¾ in., (113.3 x 73 cm.), silkscreen in colors on wallpaper (BP 660, DM 1609, FR 5491, Y 127,286).

BI *"Cow",* s., est. $1,0/1,500, (11-13-92, DuMouchelle, #1025, illus.), approx. 45⁹⁄₁₆ x 28³⁄₁₆ in., (115.7 x 71.6 cm.), color silkscreen and poster.

$1760* *Cowboys And Indians: Northwest Coast Mask (F. & S. 380), 1986,* s., stamp-num., pub. Gaultney-Klineman Art, Inc., very good cond.?, (10-28-92, Butterfield, #3168), 36 x 36 in., (914 x 914 mm.), color silkscreen on Lenox Museum Board (BP 1121, DM 2718, FR 9229, Y 215,951).

$1438* *Details Of Renaissance Paintings (Paolo Uccello, St. George And The Dragon, 1460), (F & S 324), 1984,* s., 46/50, (05-12-93, AB Stockholm, #7060, illus.), 25 x 37 in., (63.5 x 94 cm.), serigraph in colors (BP 939, DM 2320, FR 7815, Y 160,545, SK 10,670).

BI *Details Of Renaissance Paintings, Paolo Uccello, St. George And The Dragon, 1460 (Schellmann 324-327), 1984,* s., #45/50, est. DM 22,000-, (05-27-93, Lempertz, #1107, illus.), 31⅞ x 44 in., (81 x 111.8 cm.), color serigraph on wove.

BI *Details Of Renaissance Paintings, Sandro Botticelli, Birth Of Venus,1482 (Schellmann 319), 1984,* s., plate 4 from folio, #45/70, est. DM 9,800-, (05-27-93, Lempertz, #1106, illus.), 31⅞ x 44 in., (81 x 111.8 cm.), color serigraph on wove.

$660* *"Do You See My Little Pussy",* s. in ink, (03-14-93, Hindman, #333), approx. 8½ x 10¾ in., (21.6 x 27.3 cm.), hand-colored letter press (BP 460, DM 1099, FR 3735, Y 77,784).

BI *Dollar Sign, 1981,* s., d., est. SF 12/15,000, (09-04-92, Germann, #90, illus.), 18⅛ x 18⁵⁄₁₆ in., (460 x 465 mm.), silkscreen, synthetic polymer on handkerchief.

$633* *Dracula,* oversized, made for Warhol's 1973 movie Dracula, s. by Warhol, prop.Joseph C. DiBella, (06-23-93, Sotheby-NY, #320, illus.), 2½ x 3¾ in., (6.4 x 9.5 cm.), promotional bandage (BP 430, DM 1071, FR 3603, Y 68,962).

$3450* *Dracula (F. and S. 264), 1981*, from Myths, s., #153/200, pub. Ronald Feldman Dine Arts, surface scuffs, very good cond., (05-11-93, Christie-NY, #597, illus.), sheet 38 x 38 in., (965 x 965 mm.), screenprint in blacks and pink on Lenox Museum Board (BP 2202, DM 5435, FR 18,312, Y 379,496).

BI *Dracula (F. and S. 264), 1981*, from Myths, s., #153/200, pub. Ronald Feldman Fine Arts, surface scuffs, very good cond., est. $6/8,000, (11-09-92, Christie-NY, #441, illus.), 38 x 38 in., (965 x 965 mm.), screenprint in blacks and pink on Lenox Museum Board.

BI *Drinking Coca-Cola Myelf In A Factory, 1986*, 2 N.Y., 11/20, s. twice, t., d., stamp, est. DM 3/3,500, (06-24-93, Germann, #538, illus.), 13⁹⁄₁₆ x 20¹¹⁄₁₆ in., (345 x 525 mm.), 4 photographs together in plexiglas frame.

BI *Drinking Coca-Cola Myself In The Factory 1986*, N.Y., #11/20, s., t., d., stamp, est. SF 3,8/4,500, (04-21-93, Germann, #138), 13⁹⁄₁₆ x 20¹¹⁄₁₆ in., (345 x 525 mm.), 4 photographs mixed together.

BI *"Dronning Margrethe II", (Schellmann & Feldman 343)*, s. 4/40, est. DK 20,000, (09-29-92, B. Rasmussen, #373), serigraph.

BI *Edward Kennedy*, s., num. 4/300, est. $2/3000, (11-12-92, Freemn/Fine Art, #236B), 40 x 32 in., (101.6 x 81.3 cm.), screenprint w/diamond dust.

$1495* *Edward Kennedy (F. & S. 240), 1980*, s., i. PP 3/3, pub. Committee to Elect Edward Kennedy, good cond., red line, scuff marks, (05-15-93, Sotheby-NY, #1259, illus.), sheet 40 x 31⅞ in., (101.6 x 81 cm.), silkscreen in colors w/diamond dust on Lenox Museum board (BP 972, DM 2405, FR 8081, Y 165,724).

$1840* *Edward Kennedy (F. and S. 240), 1980*, s.; s., d. by Edward Kennedy, #68/300, pub. by Committee to Elect Edward Kennedy, scuffs, excell. cond., (05-11-93, Christie-NY, #595), sheet 40 x 32 in., (101.6 x 81.3 cm.), screenprint w/diamond dust in red and blue on Lenox Museum Board (BP 1175, DM 2899, FR 9766, Y 202,398).

BI *Electric Chair (F. & S. 81), 1971*, s., d., stamp #50/250, p. by Silkpoint Kettner, pub. Bruno Bischofberger, slightly reduced right edge, good cond., soiling, est. BP 1,5/2,000, (06-30-93, Sotheby-London, #969, illus.), sh 35⅜ x 47½ in., (89.9 x 120.7 cm.), color silkscreen on stiff wove.

BI *Electric Chair (F. and S. 77 and 80), 1971: Two*, s., d., #084/250, pub. Bruno Bischofberger, ink stamps, sheets trimmed, excell. cond., est. $2/2,500, (05-11-93, Christie-NY, #592), each sheet 35¼ x 47¼ in., (89.5 x 120 cm.), color screenprint on wove.

$2213* *Electric Chair (Feldman & Schellmann 76), 1971*, s., A.p., num., (12-05-92, Bassenge, #7812), 35½ x 47¹⁵⁄₁₆ in., (90.2 x 121.9 cm.), screen print (BP 1386, DM 3450, FR 11,759, Y 274,192).

$944* *Electric Chair, 1971*, s., #50/250, (11-16-92, Briest, #383), 35½ x 47¹⁵⁄₁₆ in., (90.2 x 121.9 cm.), serigraph (BP 620, DM 1506, FR 5073, Y 117,809).

$2020* *Electric Chair- 1971, (Schellmann 85)*, s., d., (11-09-92, Finarte-Milan, #26), 35⁷⁄₁₆ x 47⅝ in., (90 x 121 cm.), serigraph in colors (BP 1336, DM 3225, FR 10,895, Y 250,683, L 2760).

$2875* *Electric Chairs (F. and S. 76 and 83), 1971: Two*, s. in pen, d., stamp #164/250, pub. Bruno Bischofberger, good cond.,creases, ink loss, (02-11-93, Sotheby-NY, #463, illus.), each sheet approx. 35⁷⁄₁₆ x 47¹³⁄₁₆ in., (90 x 121.5 cm.), color silkscreen (BP 2029, DM 4762, FR 16,115, Y 346,594).

$38,500* *Endangered Species (F. & S. 293-302), 1983*, complete portfolio, s., #105/150, pub. Ronald Feldman Fine Arts, Inc., full sheets, good cond., (11-07-92, Sotheby-NY, #824, illus.), each sheet approx. 38 x 38 in., (965 x 965 mm.), ten silkscreens p. in colors on Lenox Museum Board (BP 25,172, DM 61,472, FR 207,771, Y 4,751,913).

$6050* *Endangered Species: Grevy's Zebra (F. & S. 300), 1983*, s., annot. AP 8/30, blindstamp of pub. Ronald Feldman Fine Arts, apparently very good cond., ink loss, (02-24-93, Butterfield, #3163, illus.), 38 x 38 in., (965 x 965 mm.), silkscreen in colors on Lenox Museum Board (BP 4219, DM 9821, FR 33,297, Y 709,927).

$2750* *Endangered Species: Orangutan (F. & S. 299), 1983*, s., #119/150, inkstamp pub. Ronald Feldman Fine Arts, good cond., rubbed, surface soiling, (10-28-92, Butterfield, #3167, illus.), 38 x 38 in., (965 x 965 mm.), color silkscreen on Lenox Museum Board (BP 1752, DM 4247, FR 14,421, Y 337,423).

$2300* *Eric Emerson (Chelsea Girls) (F. & S. 287), 1982*, s., #6/75, from portfolio A potfolio of Thirteen Prints, pub. Anthology Film Archives, full margins, good cond., creases, nicks, (05-15-93, Sotheby-NY, #1267, illus.), 19⅛ x 13⅜ in., (48.6 x 34 cm.), silkscreen in colors on Somerset Satin White (BP 1495, DM 3700, FR 12,432, Y 254,961).

BI *Fiesta Pig (F. & S. 184), 1979*, s., #4/200, pub. Axel Springer, excellent cond., est. BP 1,5/2,000, (10-27-92, Phillips-London, #227), sheet 21½ x 30½ in., (546 x 775 mm.), color screenprint on Arches.

$920* *Flash, November 22, 1963 (F. & S. 40), 1963*, s., #105/200, pub. Racolin Press, Inc., Briarcliff Manor, p. Aetna Silkscreen Products, good cond., crease, surface soiling, (05-19-93, Butterfield, #2367), 21 x 21 in., (533 x 533 mm.), silkscreen in colors on white (BP 597, DM 1495, FR 5038, Y 101,849).

$1495* *Flower (F. and S. 6), 1964*, s., d. 66, pub. Leo Castelli, full margins, colors faded, light/timestaining, paper losses, tears, crease, split, (05-11-93, Christie-NY, #587), sheet 23 x 23 in., (584 x 584 mm.), color offset lithograph on wove (BP 954, DM 2355, FR 7935, Y 164,448).

$2491* *Flower (Feldman & Schellmann 117), 1974*, from Flowers, s., 82/250, mono., (05-25-93, AB Stockholm, #74), 24 x 26⅜ in., (61 x 67 cm.), serigraph (BP 1614, DM 4057, FR 13,657, Y 272,270, SK 3630).

$4180* *Flower (Feldman and Schellmann 6), 1964*, s., d. in ink, pub. Leo Castelli Gallery, full margins, light-staining, scuff, pinholes, very good cond., (11-09-92, Christie-NY, #430, illus.), (584 x 584 mm.), colored offset lithograph on wove (BP 2764, DM 6673, FR 22,546, Y 518,739).

BI *Flowers (Black and white) (Schellmann 105), 1974*, mono., s., #69/100, est. FF4/5,000, (05-27-93, Briest, #221), 40¹⁵⁄₁₆ x 27⁹⁄₁₆ in., (104 x 70 cm.), serigraph on Arches.

$5500* *Flowers (F. & S. 6), 1964*, pen s., d., pub. Leo Castelli Gallery, full margins, good cond., creases, soiling, (11-07-92, Sotheby-NY, #804, illus.), 21⅞ x 22 in., (556 x 559 mm.), offset lithograph p. in colors (BP 3596, DM 8782, FR 29,682, Y 678,845).

$4400* *Flowers (F. & S. 65), 1970*, pen s. verso, d., stamp num. 223/250, pub. Factory Additions, good cond., crease, scuff marks, (11-07-92, Sotheby-NY, #816, illus.), sheet 36 x 36 in., (914 x 914 mm.), silkscreen p. in colors (BP 2877, DM 7025, FR 23,745, Y 543,076).

$5500* *Flowers (F. & S. 66), 1970*, pen s. verso, d., stamp num. 36/250, pub. Factory Additons, good cond., creases, scuffs, (11-07-92, Sotheby-NY, #817, illus.), sheet 36 x 36 in., (914 x 914 mm.), silkscreen p. in colors (BP 3596, DM 8782, FR 29,682, Y 678,845).

$4400* *Flowers (F. & S. 69), 1970*, pen s. verso, i. 'M', pub. Factory Additions, good cond., crease, scuffs, (11-07-92, Sotheby-NY, #818, illus.), sheet 36 x 36 in., (914 x 914 mm.), silkscreen p. in colors (BP 2877, DM 7025, FR 23,745, Y 543,076).

$4140* *Flowers (F. & S. 70), 1970*, s., i. W, artist's proof, pub. Factory Additions, good cond., (05-15-93, Sotheby-NY, #1254, illus.), sheet 35⅞ x 35⅞ in., (91.1 x 91.1 cm.), silkscreen in colors (BP 2692, DM 6659, FR 22,378, Y 458,929).

$6050* *Flowers (F. & S. 71), 1970*, pen s. verso, stamp num. 233/250 verso, pub. Factory Additions, goodcond., creases, scuff marks, (11-07-92, Sotheby-NY, #819, illus.), sheet 36 x 36 in., (914 x 914 mm.), silkscreen p. in colors (BP 3956, DM 9660, FR 32,650, Y 746,729).

$7700* *Flowers (F. & S. 73), 1970*, pen s. verso, i. 'F', pub. Factory Additions, full sheet, good cond., (11-07-92, Sotheby-NY, #820, illus.), sheet 36 x 36 in., (914 x 914 mm.), silkscreen p. in colors (BP 5034, DM 12,294, FR 41,554, Y 950,383).

BI   *Flowers (F. and S. 64), 1970,* s. in pen, #192/250, pub. Factory Additions, good cond., scuff marks, discoloration, soiling, creases, est. $5/7,000, (02-11-93, Sotheby-NY, #460, illus.), sheet 36 x 36 in., (915 x 915 mm.), color silkscreen.

BI   *Flowers (F. and S. 69), 1970,* s. in pen, #233/250, pub. Factory Additions, good cond., creases, soiling, est. $5/7,000, (02-11-93, Sotheby-NY, #461, illus.), sheet 36 x 36 in., (915 x 915 mm.), color silkscreen.

$4025*   *Flowers (F. and S. 73), 1970,* s. in pen, #233/250, pub. Factory Additions, good cond., scratch w/ink loss, scuff marks, creases, (02-11-93, Sotheby-NY, #462, illus.), sheet 36 x 36 in., (915 x 915 mm.), color silkscreen (BP 2840, DM 6667, FR 22,562, Y 485,232).

$3738*   *Flowers (F.&S.71), 1970,* ink and stamp s., #204/250, pub. Factory Additions, p. Aetna Silkscreen, good cond.?, creasing, inkloss, surface scuffs, (05-19-93, Butterfield, #2369, illus.), 36 x 36 in., (914 x 914 mm.), silkscreen in colors on wove (BP 2426, DM 6076, FR 20,471, Y 413,816).

BI   *Flowers (Feldman & Schellman 6), 1964,* s. in pen, d. '65, pub. Leo Castelli Gallery, full margins, good cond., creases, est. $4/5,000, (02-11-93, Sotheby-NY, #455, illus.), 21⅞ x 21⅞ in., (556 x 556 mm.), color offset lithograph.

$1343*   *Flowers (Feldmann/Schellmann 102; Wunsche 87), 1974,* mono., #69/100, s., pub. stamp, (04-21-93, Germann, #826), 40⁹/₁₆ x 27³/₁₆ in., (103 x 69 cm.), serigraph (BP 871, DM 2147, FR 7259, Y 148,677, SF 1955).

$4118*   *Flowers (Fieldman & Schellmann 6), 1964,* s., d., pub. Leo Castelli Gallery, full margins, tear, loss, good cond., (06-30-93, Sotheby-London, #961, illus.), 22 x 22 in., (559 x 559 mm.), offset color lithograph (BP 2760, DM 7024, FR 23,694, Y 441,230).

$14,950*   *Flowers (Hand-Colored) (F. & S. 110-119), 1974: Ten,* complete portfolio, s., d., #11/250, init. recto, co-pub. Peter M. Brant, Castelli Graphics and Multiples, Inc., good cond., (05-15-93, Sotheby-NY, #1261, illus.), each sheet 40⅝ x 27¼ in., (103.2 x 69.2 cm.), silkscreen hand-colored w/watercolors on Arches (BP 9720, DM 24,047, FR 80,811, Y 1,657,244).

BI   *Four Multicolor Marilyns,* s., d. 1986 on overlap, prov., est. $150/200,000, (02-23-93, Sotheby-NY, #286, illus.), 36¼ x 28 in., (92.1 x 71.1 cm.), acrylic silkscreened on canvas.

$3850*   *Franz Kafka (F. and S. 226), 1980,* from Ten Portraits of Jews of the Twentieth Century, s., #155/200, pub. Ronald Feldman Fine Arts, excellent cond., (11-09-92, Christie-NY, #435), 40 x 32 in., (101.6 x 81.3 cm.), colored screeprint on Lenox Museum Board (BP 2545, DM 6146, FR 20,766, Y 477,786).

$1955*   *Frolunda Hockey Player (F. and S. 366), 1986,* s., i. AP, #10/20, pub. Art Now Gallery, surface scuffs, excell. cond., (05-11-93, Christie-NY, #605), sheet 39½ x 31½ in., (100.3 x 80 cm.), color screenprint on Lenox Museum Board (BP 1248, DM 3080, FR 10,377, Y 215,048).

$1980*   *Frolunda Hockey Player (F. and S. 366), 1986,* s., i. AP, #10/20, pub. Art Now Gallery, surface scuffs, excellent cond., (11-09-92, Christie-NY, #447, illus.), 39½ x 31½ in., (100.3 x 80 cm.), colored screenprint on Lenox Museum Board (BP 1309, DM 3161, FR 10,680, Y 245,719).

$3080*   *George Gershwin (F. and S. 231), 1980,* from Ten Portraits of Jews of the Twentieth Century, s., #155/200, pub. Ronald Feldman Fine Arts, (11-09-92, Christie-NY, #438, illus.), 40 x 32 in., (101.6 x 81.3 cm.), colored screenprin on Lenox Museum Board (BP 2036, DM 4917, FR 16,613, Y 382,229).

$1980*   *Gertrude Stein (F. and S. 227), 1980,* from Ten Portraits of Jews of the Twentieth Century, s., num. 188/200, pub. Ronald Feldman Fine Arts, full sheet, excell. cond., (09-19-92, Christie-E, #241, illus.), sheet 40 x 32 in., (101.6 x 81.3 cm.), screenprint on Lenox Museum Board (BP 1139, DM 2965, FR 10,154, Y 246,698).

BI   *Gertrude Stein (F. and S. 227), 1980,* from Ten Portraits of the Twentieth Century, s., #155/200, pub. Ronald Feldman Fine Arts, excellent cond., est. $2,5/3,500, (11-

09-92, Christie-NY, #436), 40 x 32 in., (101.6 x 81.3 cm.), colored screenprint on Lenox Museum Board.

BI   *Gertrude Stein (Feldmann 227, Wunsche 162), 1980,* from Ten Portraits of Jews of the Twentieth Century, AP 24/30, s., 1005mm x 800mm, est. SF 5/7,000, (10-14-92, Germann, #51, illus.), color serigraph and colophon.

$4370*   *Goethe (F. and S. 270), 1982,* s., #10/100, pub. Editions Schellmann and Kluser, surface scrapes, creasing, (05-11-93, Christie-NY, #601, illus.), sheet 38 x 38 in., (965 x 965 mm.), color screenprint on Lenox Museum Board (BP 2790, DM 6884, FR 23,195, Y 480,695).

BI   *Goethe (F. and S. 270), 1982,* s., #10/100, pub. Editions Schellman and Kluser, scrapes, creasing, est. $5,5/6,500, (11-09-92, Christie-NY, #442, illus.), 38 x 38 in., (965 x 965 mm.), colored screenprint on Lenox Museum Board.

$7150*   *Goethe (F. and S. 271), 1982,* s., i. PP, num. 3/5, pub. Editions Schellmann & Kluser, full sheet, creasing, excell. cond., (09-19-92, Christie-E, #242, illus.), sheet 38 x 38 in., (965 x 965 mm.), screenprint in colors on Lenox Museum Board (BP 4113, DM 10,707, FR 36,667, Y 890,855).

$9350*   *Grace Kelly (F. & S. 305), 1984,* s., #33/225, pub. Institute of Contemporary Art, good cond., (11-07-92, Sotheby-NY, #825, illus.), sheet 40 x 32 in., (101.6 x 81.3 cm.), silkscreen p. in colors on Lenox Museum Board (BP 6113, DM 14,929, FR 50,459, Y 1,154,036).

$10,580*   *Grace Kelly (F. and S. 305), 1984,* s., #90/225, pub. for Instit. of Contemp. Art, Philadelphia, excell.cond., (05-11-93, Christie-NY, #603, illus.), sheet 40 x 32 in., (101.6 x 81.3 cm.), color screenprint on Lenox Museum Board (BP 6754, DM 16,667, FR 56,157, Y 1,163,788).

$2575*   *"Grapes" (Feldmann/Schellmann), 1979,* #33/50, s., (12-05-92, Mangisch, #745), 40⁹/₁₆ x 30⁵/₁₆ in., (103 x 77 cm.), serigraph (BP 1612, DM 4015, FR 13,682, Y 319,043, SF 3680).

BI   *Hand Christian Andersen (F. & S. 394-397), 1987: Suite Of Four,* #16/25, stamp sig., estate stamp verso s. by exectuto of the Warhol Estate, p. Rupert Jason Smith, pub. Art Expo Denmark, excell. cond., est. BP 3,5/4,500, (12-03-92, Sotheby-London, #838, illus.), 37⅞ x 37⅞ in., (966 x 966 mm.), silkscreen in colors.

BI   *Hans Christian Andersen (F. & S. 398-401), 1987: Suite Of Four,* #19/25, stamp sig., estate stamp, s. by executor of Warhol Estate pub. and p., p. Rupert Jason Smith, pub. Art Expo Denmark, excell. cond., est. BP3,5/4,500, (12-03-92, Sotheby-London, #839, illus.), each sheet 37⅞ x 37⅞ in., (966 x 966 mm.), silkscreen in colors.

$1100*   *Happy Bug Day,* s., t., ded., (10-09-92, Sotheby-Arcade, #307, illus.), 14 x 9½ in., (35.6 x 24.1 cm.), hand colored offset lithography on paper (BP 653, DM 1638, FR 5556, Y 134,146).

BI   *Happy Bug Day,* s. in plate, t., est. DM 2,500, (05-08-93, Schloss Ahlden, #2925, illus.), 11⁷/₁₆ x 8¹¹/₁₆ in., (29 x 22 cm.), color lithograph on cardboard.

$1210*   *Happy Butterfly Day,* s., t., ded., (10-09-92, Sotheby-Arcade, #306, illus.), 12¾ x 10 in., (32.4 x 25.4 cm.), hand colored offset lithography on paper (BP 718, DM 1802, FR 6111, Y 147,561).

$825*   *Happy Butterfly Day,* ded. to Jack F from me, prov., (10-09-92, Sotheby-Arcade, #304), 13¾ x 9½ in., (34.9 x 24.1 cm.), hand colored offset lithography on paper (BP 490, DM 1229, FR 4167, Y 100,610).

$1612*   *Illustration From "In The Bottom Of My Garden", 1955,* s., (06-04-93, Dorotheum, #123), 8⁷/₁₆ x 10¹⁵/₁₆ in., (21.5 x 27.8 cm.), color offset lithograph (BP 1066, DM 2618, FR 8823, Y 173,857, SC 18,400).

$1100*   *"In The Bottom Of My Garden",* s., (10-08-92, Boos, #662, illus.), sight 7¹⁵/₁₆ x 10⁹/₁₆ in., (203 x 268 mm.), offset lithograph w/hand coloring (BP 655, DM 1627, FR 5522, Y 133,657).

$843*   *Indian,* s. Andy Warhol, for Ace Gallery, Paris, 1976, (09-30-92, Kunsthallen, #294), poster (BP 476, DM 1195, FR 4043, Y 101,164, DK 4600).

BI   *Ingrid Bergman (F. & S. 313-315), 1983: Set Of Three,* s., #177/250, pub. Galerie Borjeson, excell. cond., est. BP 8/10,000, (12-03-92, Sotheby-London, #846, illus.), 37¾ x 37¾ in., (959 x 959 mm.), silkscreen in colors on Lenox Museum Board.

$12,354* *Ingrid Bergman (F. & S. 313-315), 1983:* Three, s., #177/250, p. by Rupert Smith, pub. Galerie Borjeson, excell. cond., (06-30-93, Sotheby-London, #970, illus.), 37¾ x 37¾ in., (959 x 959 mm.), color silkscreen on Lenox Museum Board (BP 8280, DM 21,071, FR 71,082, Y 1,323,690).

BI *Ingrid Bergman: With Hat (F. & S. 315), 1983,* s., #68/250, p. Rupert Smith, pub. Galerie Borjeson, good cond., est.BP 2/3,000, (12-03-92, Sotheby-London, #847), 38 x 38 in., (965 x 965 mm.), screenprint in colors on Lenox Museum Board.

BI *Jackie I (F. & S. 13), 1966,* stamp s. verso, i. 'AP', proofs, from portfolio 11 Pop Artists I, pub. Original Editions, full margins, excell. cond., est. $1,5/2,000, (11-07-92, Sotheby-NY, #806, illus.), 20⅞ x 17⅛ in., (530 x 435 mm.), silkscreen p. in silver.

$1980* *Jackie I (F. and S. 13), 1966,* from 11 Pop Artists, Volume I, Original Editions, stamped sig., #VIII verso, full margins, time staining, good cond., (11-09-92, Christie-NY, #431), 20⅝ x 20⅝ in., (524 x 524 mm.), silver screenprint on wove (BP 1309, DM 3161, FR 10,680, Y 245,719).

BI *Jackie II (F. & S. 14), 1966,* stamp s., #166/200, pub Original Editions, edges slightly reduced, good cond., rubbing, surface dirt, est. BP 1/1,500, (06-30-93, Sotheby-London, #967, illus.), sh 24 x 30 in., (610 x 762 mm.), color silkscreen on stiff wove.

BI *Jackie II (F. & S. 14), 1966,* stamp s., #166/200, pub. Original Editions, good cond., rubbing, surface dirt, est. BP 1,8/2,200, (12-03-92, Sotheby-London, #837, illus.), sheet 24 x 30 in., (609 x 760 mm.), silkscreen in colors on stiff wove.

BI *Jackie II (F. & S. 14), 1966,* stamp s. verso, i. 'AP', proofs, from portfolio 11 Pop Artists II, pub. Original Editions, excell. cond., est. $2/3,000, (11-07-92, Sotheby-NY, #807, illus.), sheet 24 x 30 in., (610 x 762 mm.), silkscreen p. in colors.

BI *Jackie II (Feldman & Schellmann 14), 1966,* stamp s., #30/200, pub. Original Edition, good cond., est. BP 2,5/3,500, (12-03-92, Sotheby-London, #836, illus.), sheet 24 x 30 in., (610 x 462 mm.), silkscreen in colors on stiff wove.

$3300* *Jackie III (F. & S. 15), 1966,* stamp s. verso, i. 'A.P.', unique color proof, from portfolio ElevenPop Artists III, pub. Original Editions, good cond., pressure mark, (11-07-92, Sotheby-NY, #808, illus.), sheet 40 x 29⅞ in., (101.6 x 75.9 cm.), silkscreen p. in colors (BP 2158, DM 5269, FR 17,809, Y 407,307).

$3850* *Jane Fonda (F. & S. 268), 1982,* s., #75/100, blindstamp, good cond.?, ink loss, surface scuffing, (10-28-92, Butterfield, #3166), 39½ x 31½ in., (100.3 x 80 cm.), color silkscreen on Lenox Museum Board (BP 2453, DM 5946, FR 20,189, Y 472,393).

$4600* *Jane Fonda (F. & S. 268), 1982,* s., #17/100, s. Jane Fonda, i., pub. Friends Of Tom Hayden, good cond., surface scuffs, (05-15-93, Sotheby-NY, #1257, illus.), sheet 39⅝ x 31½ in., (100.6 x 80 cm.), silkscreen in colors on Lenox Museum Board (BP 2991, DM 7399, FR 24,865, Y 509,921).

BI *John Wayne (F. and S. 377), 1986,* from Cowboys and Indians, s., i. unique, #153, pub. Gaultney-Klineman Art, excellent cond., est. $8/10,000, (11-09-92, Christie-NY, #448, illus.), 36 x 36 in., (914 x 914 mm.), colored screenprint on Lenox Museum Board.

BI *Joseph Beuys (F. & S. 242-244), 1980-83,* complete suite, s., num. AP 30/36, AP 19/36, AP 6/36, pub. Editions Schellmann & Kluser, good cond., est. $15/17,000, (11-07-92, Sotheby-NY, #823, illus.), each sheet approx. 40 x 32 in., (101.6 x 81.3 cm.), three silkscreens p. in colors.

$9775* *Joseph Beuys (F. & S. 242-244):* Three, complete suite, s., i. AP 30/36, AP 19/36, AP 6/36, pub. Editions Schelmann & Kluser, 1980-83, good cond., (05-15-93, Sotheby-NY, #1270, illus.), each sheet 40 x 32 in., (101.6 x 81.3 cm.), silkscreen in colors (BP 6356, DM 15,723, FR 52,838, Y 1,083,583).

$1588* *Judy Garland Shoe,* s. by Warhol's mother, (10-14-92, Germann, #55, illus.), 8⁷⁄₁₆ x 10⅞ in., (215 x 277 mm.),

blotted line print w/watercolor (BP 932, DM 2324, FR 7881, Y 192,438, SF 2070).

$1870* *Karen Kain (F. and S. 236), 1980,* s., i. AP, #1/30, pub. William Hechter, excellent cond., (11-09-92, Christie-NY, #440, illus.), 40 x 32 in., (101.6 x 81.3 cm.), screenprint and diamond dust in colors on Lenox Museum Board (BP 1236, DM 2985, FR 10,086, Y 232,068).

$1725* *Kiss (F. and S. 8), 1966,* embossed sig., incised AP on plexiglas mount, artist's proofs, from portfolio Seven Objects in a Box, pub. Tanglewood Press, Inc., overall size 315x 203 x 134 mm., (02-11-93, Sotheby-NY, #457, illus.), silkscreen p. on plexiglas (BP 1217, DM 2857, FR 9669, Y 207,957).

$1474* *Kolner Dom (Feldmann/Schellmann 361-364), 1985:* Four, each s., (09-25-92, Granier, #3047, illus.), each 8⅛ x 5⅞ in., (20.7 x 15 cm.), color serigraph (BP 861, DM 2185, FR 7388, Y 177,912).

$861* *"Ladies And Gentlemen", (Feldman-Schellmann 136), 1975,* #51/125, foglio, s., d., (05-20-93, Finarte-Milan, #164), 43⁵⁄₁₆ x 28¹⁵⁄₁₆ in., (110 x 73.5 cm.), serigraph in colors (BP 553, DM 1389, FR 4679, Y 95,075, L 1265).

$6050* *Liz (F. & S. 7), 1964,* s., d. '65, pub. Leo Castelli Gallery, full margins, good cond., creases, (11-07-92, Sotheby-NY, #805, illus.), 22 x 22 in., (559 x 559 mm.), offset lithograph p. in colors (BP 3956, DM 9660, FR 32,650, Y 746,729).

$3450* *Liz (F. and S. 7), 1964,* s. in pen, s. '66, pub. Leo Castelli Gallery, full margins, good cond., water stains, extending into image, discoloration, creases, (02-11-93, Sotheby-NY, #456, illus.), sheet 22¹⁄₁₆ x 22¹⁄₁₆ in., (560 x 560 mm.), color offset lithograph (BP 2434, DM 5715, FR 19,339, Y 415,913).

$2310* *Liz (FS. 7), 1964,* s., d. '65, pub. Leo Castelli Gallery, full margins, good cond., stain into image, creases, (06-11-93, Freemn/Fine Art, #241, illus.), 22 x 22 in., (55.9 x 55.9 cm.), offset lithograph in colors (BP 1518, DM 3754, FR 12,658, Y 245,093).

BI *Liz (Feldman & Schellmann 7),* s., d. 67 in pen, pub. Leo Castelli Gallery, 1964, prov., est. C$ 8/10,000, (12-01-92, Ritchie, #104, illus.), sheet 23⅛ x 23⅛ in., (58.7 x 58.7 cm.), color offset lithograph.

$2308* *Liz (Schellmann/Feldman 7), 1967,* ballpoint pen s., d., (11-20-92, Lempertz, #934, illus.), sh 22¹³⁄₁₆ x 22¹¹⁄₁₆ in., (58 x 57.6 cm.), offset lithograph on Velin (BP 1520, DM 3680, FR 12,395, Y 287,029).

BI *"Liz", 1964,* s., d. ball point pen Andy Warhol 67, edit. of 300, (05-18-93, Encans, #223), 22¹⁄₁₆ x 22¹⁄₁₆ in., (56 x 56 cm.), offset lithograph.

BI *"Mae West Shoe",* s., est. $1/1500, (10-08-92, Boos, #664, illus.), sight 9¹³⁄₁₆ x 8¹⁄₁₆ in., (250 x 204 mm.), offset lithograph w/hand coloring.

$17,250* *Man Ray,* s., d. 1978 on overlap; s., i., d. 1978 verso, prov., lit., (02-23-93, Sotheby-NY, #287, illus.), 16 x 16 in., (40.6 x 40.6 cm.), synthetic polymer paint silkscreened on canvas (BP 11,817, DM 27,868, FR 94,521, Y 2,014,716).

$2217* *Mao (F. & S. 125A), 1974,* felt-tip s., from unlimited edit., pub. Factory Additions, good cond., (12-03-92, Sotheby-London, #841, illus.), sheet 39½ x 29½ in., (100.3 x 74.9 cm.), silkscreen in purple and black on wallpaper (BP 1430, DM 3486, FR 11,900, Y 275,849).

BI *Mao (F. & S. 94), 1972,* ballpoint s., stamp #247/250, pub. Castelli Graphics and Multiples, Inc., tear into image, creased, paper discolored, est. BP 2,5/3,000, (06-30-93, Sotheby-London, #966, illus.), 36 x 36 in., (914 x 914 mm.), color silkscreen.

$4950* *Mao (F. and S. 91), 1972,* s., #242/250 verso, pub. Castelli Graphics and Multiples, Inc., bottom trimmed, staining, skinned spots, (11-09-92, Christie-NY, #433), 35¾ x 35¾ in., (908 x 908 mm.), colored screenprint on glazed wove (BP 3273, DM 7902, FR 26,699, Y 614,296).

BI *Mao (F.&S.94), 1972,* ink and stamp s., #158/250 verso; artist's (c), inkstamp, pub. Castelli Graphics and Multiples, p. Styria Studiio, good cond., cracking, inkloss, staining, buckling, est. $3/5,000, (05-19-93, Butterfield, #2370, illus.), 36 x 36 in., (914 x 914 mm.), silkscreen in colors on wove.

$667* *Mao (Feldman & Schellmann 125a), 1974,* Factory Additions, s., (05-12-93, AB Stockholm, #7059), 37⅜ x 24 in., (95 x 61 cm.), serigraph in colors (BP 436, DM 1076, FR 3625, Y 74,467, SK 4950).

$2320* *Mao (Feldman and Schellmann 125a), 1974*, s., p. Bill Miller's Wallpaper Studio, Factory Additions, 800 x 580mm, sh approx. 1700 x 740mm, (06-28-93, Loudmer, #433), 2 color serigraphs on wallpaper (BP 1553, DM 3942, FR 13,280, Y 246,154).

BI   *Mao Wallpaper (F.&S.125a), 1974*, felt pen s., pub. Factory Additions, p. Bill Miller's Wallpaper Studio, good cond.?, hinge creases, est. $1,5/2,000, (05-19-93, Butterfield, #2371), sh 40⅛ x 29½ in., (101.9 x 74.9 cm.), silkscreen in colors on wallpaper.

$3621* *"Mao" (Feldmann/Schellmann 97), 1972*, #179/250, verso s., Edition Castelli Graphics and Multiples, (12-05-92, Mangisch, #740, illus.), 36 x 36 in., (91.5 x 91.5 cm.), screen print (BP 2267, DM 5645, FR 19,240, Y 448,643, SF 5175).

$4828* *Mao, (F. & S. 98), 1972*, s., stamp num. 131/250, pub. Castelli Graphics and Multiples Inc., residual tape, very good cond., (12-01-92, Christie-London, #640, illus.), S. 36 x 36 in., (915 x 915 mm.), screenprint in colors on wove (BP 3190, DM 7695, FR 26,225, Y 601,096).

$5161* *Mao, (F. & S. 99), 1972*, s., stamp num. 131/250, tape, rubbing, discoloration, good cond., (12-01-92, Christie-London, #641), S. 36 x 36 in., (915 x 915 mm.), screenprint in colors (BP 3410, DM 8226, FR 28,034, Y 642,555).

BI   *Marilyn (F. & S. 22), 1967*, init. verso, d., stamp num. 65/250, pub. Factory Additions, good cond., creases, ink loss, soiling, scuff marks, discoloration, est. $15/20,000, (11-07-92, Sotheby-NY, #809, illus.), sheet 36 x 36 in., (914 x 914 mm.), silkscreen p. in colors.

$20,700* *Marilyn (F. & S. 22), 1967*, init., d., stamp-#15/250, pub. Factory Additions, good cond., linen-hinges glued to mat, crease, handling creases, (05-15-93, Sotheby-NY, #1260, illus.), sheet 36 x 36 in., (91.4 x 91.4 cm.), silkscreen in colors (BP 13,459, DM 33,296, FR 111,892, Y 2,294,646).

$196,100* *Marilyn (F. & S. 22-31), 1967: Set Of Ten*, s., stamped #199/250, pub. Factory Additions, good cond., prov., (12-03-92, Sotheby-London, #842, illus.), each sheet approx. 36 x 36 in., (915 x 915 mm.), silkscreens in colors (BP 126,500, DM 308,382, FR 1,052,603, Y 24,399,652).

$182,770* *Marilyn (F. & S. 22-31), 1967: Ten*, s., stamp #164/250, F&S 24 #54/250, F&S 26 #191/250, pub. Factory Additions, good cond., creasing, scuffing, (06-30-93, Sotheby-London, #963, illus.), each sh c. 36 x 36 in., (914 x 914 mm.), color silkscreen (BP 122,500, DM 311,735, FR 1,051,611, Y 19,583,199).

$18,150* *Marilyn (F. & S. 23), 1967*, s. verso, i. 'A/P', num., pub. Factory Additions, good cond., creases, surface scuffs, discoloration, (11-07-92, Sotheby-NY, #810, illus.), 36 x 36 in., (914 x 914 mm.), silkscreen p. in colors (BP 11,867, DM 28,980, FR 97,949, Y 2,240,188).

$12,011* *Marilyn (F. & S. 24), 1967*, init., d., #37/250, pub. Factory Additions, scratches, scuffs, retouches, (06-30-93, Sotheby-London, #964, illus.), sh 36 x 36 in., (914 x 914 mm.), color screenprint (BP 8050, DM 20,486, FR 69,108, Y 1,286,939).

BI   *Marilyn (F. & S. 24), 1967*, init., d., #37/250, pub. Factory Additions, minor scratches and scuff, retouches, est. BP 8/10,000, (12-03-92, Sotheby-London, #843), sheet 36 x 36 in., (914 x 914 mm.), screenprint in colors.

$16,500* *Marilyn (F. & S. 24), 1967*, s. verso, i. 'I', artist's proof, pub. Factory Additions, good cond.,scuffs, discoloration, (11-07-92, Sotheby-NY, #811, illus.), sheet 36 x 36 in., (914 x 914 mm.), silkscreen p. in colors (BP 10,788, DM 26,345, FR 89,045, Y 2,036,534).

$4400* *Marilyn (F. & S. 25), 1967*, init. verso, d., stamp num. 65/250, pub. Factory Additions, repaired,tears, creases, scuffs, discoloration, good cond., (11-07-92, Sotheby-NY, #812, illus.), sheet 36 x 36 in., (914 x 914 mm.), silkscreen p. in colors (BP 2877, DM 7025, FR 23,745, Y 543,076).

$9900* *Marilyn (F. & S. 28), 1967*, init. verso, d., stamp num. 65/250, pub. Factory Additions, good cond., crease, soiling, scuff marks, discoloration, (11-07-92, Sotheby-NY, #813, illus.), sheet 36 x 36 in., (914 x 914 mm.), silk-

screen p. in colors (BP 6473, DM 15,807, FR 53,427, Y 1,221,921).

$9900* *Marilyn (F. & S. 29), 1967*, s. verso, d., i. 'a.p.', artist's proof, pub. Factory Additions, goodcond., discoloration, creases, scuffs, (11-07-92, Sotheby-NY, #814, illus.), sheet 36 x 36 in., (914 x 914 mm.), silkscreen p. in colors (BP 6473, DM 15,807, FR 53,427, Y 1,221,921).

$23,000* *Marilyn (F. and S. 24), 1967*, inits., d., #48/250, pub. Factory Additions, scuffing, mat staining,excell. cond., prov., (05-11-93, Christie-NY, #589, illus.), sheet 36 x 36 in., (914 x 914 mm.), color screenprint on wove (BP 14,682, DM 36,232, FR 122,081, Y 2,529,975).

$10,925* *Marilyn (F. and S. 27), 1967*, s., #238/250, pub. Factory Additions, light-staining, repaired tear,surface scuffing, crease, splitting, mat staining, good cond., (05-11-93, Christie-NY, #590), sheet 36 x 36 in., (914 x 914 mm.), color screenprint on wove (BP 6974, DM 17,210, FR 57,988, Y 1,201,738).

$9200* *Marilyn (F. and S. 29), 1967*, inits., d., stamp #65/250, pub. Factory Additions, good cond., creases, soiling, scuffs, discoloration, (02-11-93, Sotheby-NY, #459, illus.), sheet 36 x 36 in., (915 x 915 mm.), color silkscreen (BP 6492, DM 15,239, FR 51,570, Y 1,109,102).

$5060* *Marilyn (Feldman/Schellman 29), 1967*, s., i., pub. Factory Additions, (12-13-92, Hindman, #346, illus.), 36 x 36 in., color serigraph (BP 3235, DM 7952, FR 27,102, Y 626,005).

$121* *Marilyn Monroe*, (08-14-92, DuMouchelle, #2443), 17 x 17 in., (43.2 x 43.2 cm.), color photo silkscreen (BP 63, DM 178, FR 601, Y 15,259).

$5280* *Marilyn Monroe (F. and S. 26), 1967*, s., num. 120/250, pub. Factory Additions, full sheet, light/mat staining, crimping, scuff, sharp crease, minor defects, (09-19-92, Christie-E, #240, illus.), sheet 36 x 36 in., (914 x 914 mm.), screenprint in colors on wove (BP 3037, DM 7907, FR 27,077, Y 657,862).

$4621* *Marilyn Monroe (Feldman & Schellmann 21), 1967*, s., num. 38/100, full sheet, good cond., (10-14-92, Sotheby-Japan, #105, illus.), sheet 6 x 6⅛ in., (152 x 156 mm.), color silkscreen (BP 2712, DM 6763, FR 22,933, Y 559,985).

BI   *Marilyn Monroe (Feldman/Schellmann 23-31)*, est. DM 800-, (09-25-92, Granier, #3048), 32⁵⁄₁₆ x 32⁵⁄₁₆ in., (82 x 82 cm.), colored serigraph on offset board.

$12,486* *Marilyn Monroe, (F. & S. 22), 1967*, inits., d., stamp num. 72/250 verso, pub. Factory Additions, crease,tape, staining, (12-01-92, Christie-London, #639, illus.), S. 36⅛ x 36⅛ in., (917 x 917 mm.), screenprint in colors on wove (BP 8250, DM 19,901, FR 67,822, Y 1,554,532).

$3850* *Marilyn Monroe, 1981*, marker s., pub. Castelli Graphics, good cond., scuff in face, (11-07-92, Sotheby-NY, #822, illus.), sheet 12 x 12 in., (305 x 305 mm.), silkscreen p. in colors (BP 2517, DM 6147, FR 20,777, Y 475,191).

BI   *Marilyn Monroe, 1981*, black marker pen s., pub. Castelli Graphics, est. $2,5/3,000, (05-27-93, Swann, #285, illus.), sh 12 x 12 in., (30.5 x 30.5 cm.), color serigraph.

$2990* *Marilyn Monroe, 1981*, s. marker, pub. Castelli Graphics, good cond., (05-15-93, Sotheby-NY, #1265, illus.), sheet 12 x 12 in., (30.5 x 30.5 cm.), silkscreen in colors (BP 1944, DM 4809, FR 16,162, Y 331,449).

$8418* *Marilyn, (Feldman and Schellmamm 31), 1967*, #49/250, s., d., Factory Additions, prov., (11-09-92, Finarte-Milan, #104, illus.), 36 x 36 in., (91.5 x 91.5 cm.), serigraph in colors (BP 5566, DM 13,439, FR 45,405, Y 1,044,676, L 11,500).

BI   *Marilyn, 1981*, s., pub. Castelli Graphics, colors faded, very good cond., est. $3/4,000, (05-11-93, Christie-NY, #600), sheet 12 x 12 in., (305 x 305 mm.), color screenprint on wove.

BI   *Marilyn, Gallery Announcement*, bears complimentary sig., very good cond., est. $1,5/2,000, (12-04-92, Doyle, #155), 12 x 11⅞ in., (305 x 302 mm.), color photo offset print.

$636* *Marilyn: Two*, from set of ten, damaged, (02-17-93, Bonhams-Chelsea, #236), image 32½ x 32¾ in., (82.6 x 83.2 cm.), screenprint (BP 440, DM 1033, FR 3498, Y 75,968).

$2200* *Martin Buber (F. and S. 228), 1980*, from Ten Portraits of Jews of the Twentieth Century, s., #155/200, pub.

Ronald Feldman Fine Arts, excellent cond., (11-09-92, Christie-NY, #437), 40 x 32 in., (101.6 x 81.3 cm.), colored screenprint on Lenox Museum Board (BP 1455, DM 3512, FR 11,866, Y 273,021).

$7700* *The Marx Brothers (F. and S. 232), 1980,* from Ten Portraits of Jews of the Twentieth Century, s., #155/200, pub. Ronald Feldman Fine Arts, excellent cond., (11-09-92, Christie-NY, #439, illus.), 40 x 32 in., (101.6 x 81.3 cm.), colored screenprint on Lenox Museum Board (BP 5091, DM 12,292, FR 41,532, Y 955,572).

$5862* *Mick Jagger (F & S 146), 1975,* s., s. by Jagger, #226/250, pub. Seabird Editions, good cond., sheet1105 x 737 mm., (12-09-92, Sotheby-Amstrdm, #673, illus.), color screenprint on Arches (BP 3741, DM 9201, FR 31,398, Y 726,844, G 10,350).

$5491* *Mick Jagger (F. & S. 138), 1975,* pen s., s. by Mick Jagger, #165/200, pub. Seabird Editions, good cond., (06-30-93, Sotheby-London, #972, illus.), sh 43⅝ x 28⅞ in., (110.8 x 73.3 cm.), color silkscreen on D'Arches watercolor (BP 3680, DM 9366, FR 31,594, Y 588,342).

$6600* *Mick Jagger (F. & S. 138-147), 1975,* complete set, pen s., co-pub. Multiples, Inc., and Castelli Graphics,good cond., orig. folder, prop. Joseph DiBella, (11-07-92, Sotheby-NY, #821, illus.), each sheet approx. 6⅛ x 4 in., (156 x 102 mm.), 10 offset lithographs p. in colors (BP 4315, DM 10,538, FR 35,618, Y 814,614).

$5405* *Mick Jagger (F. & S. 145), 1975,* s., #14/250, s. Mick Jagger, pub. Seabird Editions, good cond., soiling, (05-15-93, Sotheby-NY, #1263, illus.), sheet 43¾ x 29 in., (111.1 x 73.7 cm.), silkscreen in colors on D'Arches Watercolor (BP 3514, DM 8694, FR 29,216, Y 599,158).

$7475* *Mick Jagger (F. and S. 143), 1975,* s. in pen, #179/200, s. by Mick Jagger, pub. Seabird Editions, good cond., (02-11-93, Sotheby-NY, #464, illus.), sheet 43½ x 28⅞ in., (110.5 x 73.3 cm.), color silkscreen on D'Arches Watercolor (BP 5274, DM 12,382, FR 41,900, Y 901,145).

$5175* *Mick Jagger (F.&S.141), 1975,* s.; ink s. by Mick Jagger, #97/250, pub. Seabird Editions, p. Alexander Heinrici, good cond.?, (05-19-93, Butterfield, #2372), 44 x 29 in., (111.8 x 73.7 cm.), silkscreen in colors on D'Arches watercolor (BP 3359, DM 8412, FR 28,341, Y 572,899).

$5175* *Mick Jagger (F.&S.143), 1975,* s.; ink s. by Mick Jagger, #97/250, pub. Seabird Editions, p. Alexander Heinrici, full margins, good cond.?, crackling, (05-19-93, Butterfield, #2373), sh 44 x 29 in., (111.8 x 73.7 cm.), silkscreen in colors on D'Arches (BP 3359, DM 8412, FR 28,341, Y 572,899).

$6841* *"Mick Jagger" (Feldmann/Schellmann 139), 1972,* #125/250, Von beiden s., Seabird Editions, London, (12-05-92, Mangisch, #741), 43½ x 28¹⁵⁄₁₆ in., (110.5 x 73.6 cm.), screen sprint (BP 4284, DM 10,666, FR 36,350, Y 847,603, SF 9775).

$3996* *Mick Jagger, (F. & S. 145), 1975,* pen s. by artist and sitter, num. 71/250, pub. Seabird Editions, good cond., S. 1100 x 736 mm., (12-01-92, Christie-London, #642, illus.), screenprint in colors on d'Arches watercolor wove (BP 2640, DM 6369, FR 21,706, Y 497,510).

$4329* *Mick Jagger, (F. & S. 147), 1975,* s. by artist and sitter, num. 71/250, pub. Seabird Editions, good cond., S. 1114 x 737 mm., (12-01-92, Christie-London, #643), screenprint in colors on d'Arches watercolor wove (BP 2860, DM 6900, FR 23,514, Y 538,969).

$20,700* *Mickey Mouse (F. and S. 265), 1981,* from Myths, s., i. PP, #2/5, pub. Ronald Feldman Fine Arts, surface scuffs, excell. cond., (05-11-93, Christie-NY, #598, illus.), sheet 38 x 38 in., (965 x 965 mm.), color screenprint w/diamond dust on wove (BP 13,214, DM 32,609, FR 109,873, Y 2,276,977).

$19,550* *Myths: Mickey Mouse (F. & S. 265), 1981,* s., #64/200, pub. Ronald Feldman, good cond., (05-15-93, Sotheby-NY, #1262, illus.), sheet 38 x 38 in., (96.5 x 96.5 cm.), silkscreen in colors w/diamond dust on Lenox Museum Board (BP 12,711, DM 31,446, FR 105,676, Y 2,167,166).

$3850* *Myths: The Shadow (F. & S. 267), 1981,* s., #9/200, ink-stamp pub. Ronald Feldman Fine Arts, Inc., good cond., skinned areas, hinge removal, surface soiling, (10-28-92, Butterfield, #3164, illus.), 38 x 38 in., (965 x 965 mm.),

color silkscreen w/diamond dust on Lenox Museum Board (BP 2453, DM 5946, FR 20,189, Y 472,393).

$1770* *"Neuschwanstein" (Feldman/Schellmann 372), 1987,* #32/100, (12-05-92, Mangisch, #760, illus.), 33⁷⁄₁₆ x 23⅝ in., (85 x 60 cm.), color serigraph (BP 1108, DM 2760, FR 9405, Y 219,304, SF 2530).

$2212* *Northwest Coast Mask (Feldman/Schellmann 380), 1986,* from "Cowboys and Indians", #78/250, s., (04-21-93, Germann, #33, illus.), 35¹⁵⁄₁₆ x 36⅛ in., (914 x 918 mm.), color serigraph (BP 1435, DM 3536, FR 11,957, Y 244,880, SF 3220).

BI *Onion Mushroom Campbell's Soup Box No. 157,* s., d. 86 on overlap, prov., est. $20/25,000, (02-23-93, Sotheby-NY, #289, illus.), 19 x 19 in., (48.3 x 48.3 cm.), .

BI *Paloma Picasso (F. & S. 121), 1975,* s., d., i. V/XXX, Roman numeral impressions, from portfolio Hommage a Picasso, co-pub. Propylaen-Verlag and Pantheon Presse, good cond., hinged w/masking tape, tear, skinned spots, soiling, (05-15-93, Sotheby-NY, #1256, illus.), sheet 41 x 27⅞ in., (104.1 x 70.8 cm.), silkscreen in colors on Arches.

$2875* *Paramount (F. and S. 352), 1985,* from Ads, s., #164/190, pub. Ronald Feldman Fine Arts, laid down on board at places, very good cond., (05-11-93, Christie-NY, #604), sheet 38 x 38 in., (965 x 965 mm.), color screenprint on Lenox Museum Board (BP 1835, DM 4529, FR 15,260, Y 316,247).

$3850* *Paramount (F. and S. 352), 1985,* s., #158/190, pub. Ronald Feldman Fine Arts, excellent cond., (11-09-92, Christie-NY, #445, illus.), 38 x 38 in., (965 x 965 mm.), colored screenprint on Lenox Museum Board (BP 2545, DM 6146, FR 20,766, Y 477,786).

$1265* *Paris Review Poster (F. and S. 18), 1967,* stamped sig., full margins, scuffing, excell. cond., (05-11-93, Christie-NY, #588), sheet 37⅛ x 27¼ in., (943 x 692 mm.), color screenprint w/die-cut holes on cream wove (BP 808, DM 1993, FR 6714, Y 139,149).

$495* *Pink Dress Shoe,* s. ink, (03-14-93, Hindman, #334), approx. 8½ x 10¾ in., (21.6 x 27.3 cm.), hand-colored letter press (BP 345, DM 824, FR 2801, Y 58,338).

BI *Portraits Of Ingrid Bergman, Galerie, Malmo, (F. & S. 313-5), 1983:* Three, s., num. 7/250, original box, loose, excell. cond., est. BP 7/9,000, (12-01-92, Christie-London, #645, illus.), S. 37¹⁵⁄₁₆ x 37¹⁵⁄₁₆ in., (965 x 965 mm.), screenprint in colors on Lenox Museum Board.

BI *Portraits Of The Jews Of The Twentieth Century (F. & S. 226-233), 1980: Set Of Ten,* complete, s., #11/200, pub. Ronald Feldman Fine Arts, Inc., and Jonathan A Editions, excell. cond., loose, original box, s., num. list of contents,est. BP 20/25,000, (06-30-93, Sotheby-London, #971, illus.), each sh c. 40 x 32 in., (101.6 x 81.3 cm.), color silkscreen on Lenox Museum Board.

$3496* *Queen Elizabeth II Of The United Kingdom, (F. & S. 335), 1985,* from Reigning Queens, s., num. 13/14, pub. G. Mulder, surface marks and dirt, rubbing, good cond., S. 1002 x 801 mm., (12-01-92, Christie-London, #646, illus.), screenprint in colors on firm wove (BP 2310, DM 5572, FR 18,990, Y 435,259).

BI *"Reigning Queens", (Feldman & Schellmann 336, 339, 343 (Var.) and 348), 1985: Four,* incl. Elisabeth II, Beatrix, Margrethe II and Ntombi Twala, est. DK 60/75,000, all s. pp 5/5, (09-29-92, B. Rasmussen, #372, illus.), serigraph.

$1760* *Reigning Queens: Queen Beatrix Of The Netherlands (F. & S. 339), 1985,* s., num. 2/40, pub. George C.P. Mulder, blindstamp, good cond., (02-24-93, Butterfield, #3165), 39½ x 31½ in., (100.3 x 80 cm.), silkscreen in colors on Lenox Museum Borad (BP 1227, DM 2857, FR 9686, Y 206,524).

$1650* *Reigning Queens: Queen Beatrix Of The Netherlands (F. & S. 341), 1985,* s., num. 2/40, pub. George E.P. Mulder, apparently very good cond., inkloss, (02-24-93, Butterfield, #3166, illus.), 39⅜ x 31½ in., (100 x 80 cm.), silkscreen in colors on Lenox Museum Board (BP 1151, DM 2679, FR 9081, Y 193,617).

$1955* *Reigning Queens: Queen Beatrix Of The Netherlands (F.&S.340), 1985,* s., #2/40, pub. George C.P. Mulder, blindstamp, very good cond., inkloss, (05-19-93, Butterfield, #2376, illus.), 39½ x 31½ in., (100.3 x 80 cm.), silkscreen in colors on Lenox Museum Board (BP 1269, DM 3178, FR 10,706, Y 216,429).

$2185* *Reigning Queens: Queen Elizabeth II Of The United Kingdom (F.&S.335),1985,* s., #2/40, pub. George C.P. Mulder, blindstamp printer, Rupert JasenSmith, very good cond., surface scuffing, (05-19-93, Butterfield, #2375, illus.), 39½ x 32½ in., (100.3 x 82.6 cm.), silkscreen in colors on Lenox Board (BP 1418, DM 3552, FR 11,966, Y 241,891).

$2475* *Reigning Queens: Queen Elizabeth II Of The United Kingdon (F. & S. 334), 1985,* s., num. 2/40, pub. George C.P. Mulder, blindstamp, apparently good cond., light-brown stain, (02-24-93, Butterfield, #3164, illus.), 39⅜ x 31½ in., (100 x 80 cm.), silkscreen in colors on Lenox Museum Board (BP 1726, DM 4018, FR 13,621, Y 290,425).

$2200* *Reigning Queens: Queen Margrethe II Of Denmark (F. & S. 343), 1985,* s., num. 2/40, pub. George C.P. Mulder, blindstamp, good cond., surface scuffing, (02-24-93, Butterfield, #3167, illus.), 39½ x 31½ in., (100.3 x 80 cm.), silkscreen in colors on Lenox Museum Board (BP 1534, DM 3571, FR 12,108, Y 258,155).

$2185* *Reigning Queens: Queen Margrethe II Of Denmark (F.&S.344), 1985,* s., #2/40, pub. George C.P. Mulder, blindstamp printer, Rupert JasenSmith, good cond., surface soiling, inkloss, surface scuffing, (05-19-93, Butterfield, #2377, illus.), 39½ x 31½ in., (100.3 x 80 cm.), silkscreen in colors on Lenox Museum Board (BP 1418, DM 3552, FR 11,966, Y 241,891).

$1320* *Reigning Queens: Queen Ntombi Twala Of Swaziland (F. & S. 346), 1985,* s., num. 2/40, pub. George C.P. Mulder, blindstamp, apparently good cond., (02-24-93, Butterfield, #3168), 39½ x 31½ in., (100.3 x 80 cm.), silkscreen in colors on Lenox Museum Board (BP 921, DM 2143, FR 7265, Y 154,893).

$1320* *Reigning Queens: Queen Ntombi Twala Of Swaziland (F. & S. 347), 1985,* s., num. 2/40, pub. George C.P. Mulder, blindstamp, good cond., surface soiling, inkloss, (02-24-93, Butterfield, #3169), 39⅜ x 31½ in., (100 x 80 cm.), silkscreen in colors on Lenox Museum Board (BP 921, DM 2143, FR 7265, Y 154,893).

$1150* *Reigning Queens: Queen Ntombi Twala Of Swaziland (F.&S.348), 1985,* s., #2/40, pub. George C.P. Mulder, blindstamp printer, Rupert JasenSmith, good cond., inkloss, crease, surface scuffing, (05-19-93, Butterfield, #2378), 39½ x 31½ in., (100.3 x 80 cm.), silkscreen in colors on Lenox Museum Board (BP 747, DM 1869, FR 6298, Y 127,311).

BI *S & H Greenstamps,* faint sig., repairs, discoloration, creasing, laid down on another sheet, hinged to mat, est. $1,2/1,800, (12-04-92, Doyle, #154), 22¼ x 22¼ in., (565 x 565 mm.), photo offset lithograph.

$1210* *"Sam The Cat",* s., (08-08-92, Litchfield, #183), 10¾ x 8 in., (27.3 x 20.3 cm.), color lithograph w/watercolor (BP 628, DM 1779, FR 6014, Y 154,435).

$2760* *Santa Claus (F. and S. 266), 1981,* from Myths, s., #141/200, pub. Ronald Feldman Fine Arts, scuff, good-cond., (05-11-93, Christie-NY, #599, illus.), sheet 38 x 38 in., (965 x 965 mm.), color screenprint w/diamond dust on Lenox Museum Board (BP 1762, DM 4348, FR 14,650, Y 303,597).

BI *Sas-Passenger-Ticket (Feldman/Schellmann 20), 1968,* pencil s., est. DM 7,500, (11-20-92, Lempertz, #937, illus.), 26¾ x 48¹³⁄₁₆ in., (68 x 124 cm.), color serigraph on heavy Velin.

$2645* *Self-Portrait (F. and S. 16), 1967,* s., d. '66, #25/300, pub. Leo Castelli Gallery, full margins, good cond., nicks, scuff marks, ink loss, creases, (02-11-93, Sotheby-NY, #458, illus.), sheet 23¹⁄₁₆ x 23¹⁄₁₆ in., (585 x 585 mm.), silkscreen p. in black on silver coated paper (BP 1866, DM 4381, FR 14,826, Y 318,867).

$844* *Self-Portrait, (Feldmann and Schellmann 156A), 1978,* s. Andy Warhol, (03-24-93, Kunsthallen, #335), color serigraph (BP 572, DM 1378, FR 4691, Y 99,166, DK 5290).

BI *Shoe Print,* est. $1,5/2,500, (10-09-92, Sotheby-Arcade, #309, illus.), 10¾ x 17½ in., (27.3 x 44.5 cm.), screen print/gold leaf on paper.

$4024* *"Siberian Tiger" (Feldman/Schellmann 297), 1983,* #21/150, s., (12-05-92, Mangisch, #750, illus.), 37¹⁵⁄₁₆ x 37¹⁵⁄₁₆ in., (96.5 x 96.5 cm.), color serigraph (BP 2520, DM 6274, FR 21,382, Y 498,575, SF 5750).

BI *Sidewalk (Feldman 304), 1983,* 97/250, s., 725mm x 1055mm, est. SF 5/6,000, (10-14-92, Germann, #160, illus.), color serigraph.

$2185* *Sidewalk, Los Angeles (F. and S. 304), 1983,* from Eight By Eight To celebrate The Temporary Contemporary, Museum of Contemporary Art, s., #87/250, excell. cond., (05-11-93, Christie-NY, #602, illus.), sheet 29 x 42 in., (73.7 x 106.7 cm.), screenprint in pink and yellow on wove (BP 1395, DM 3442, FR 11,598, Y 240,348).

BI *Skulls (F. & S. 158), 1976,* s., i. P.P., p. by Gem Screens, pub. Andy Warhol Enterprises, Inc., incision, est. BP 1,2/1,500, (06-30-93, Sotheby-London, #973, illus.), sh 30⅛ x 40 in., (76.5 x 101.6 cm.), color silkscreen.

$12,072* *"Space Fruit: Still-Lifes" (Feldman/Schellmann 198-203), 1979: Six,* VI/XXX. Aufl. 150, s., (12-05-92, Mangisch, #746A-F), 30 x 40 in., (76.2 x 101.6 cm.), color serigraph (BP 7559, DM 18,821, FR 64,145, Y 1,495,725, SF 17,250).

$2817* *"Space Fruit: Still-Lifes. Cantaloupes II" (Feldman/Schellmann 198),1979,* XXIX/XXX. Aufl. 150, s., (12-05-92, Mangisch, #1611), 30 x 40 in., (76.2 x 101.6 cm.), color serigraph (BP 1764, DM 4392, FR 14,968, Y 349,027, SF 4025).

$1150* *Space, Fruit: Pears (F. and S. 203), 1979,* s. in pen, i. IV/XXX, proofs, pub. Michael Zivian, good cond., creases, (02-11-93, Sotheby-NY, #465, illus.), sheet 30 x 40 in., (76.2 x 101.6 cm.), colored silkscreen on four-ply Lenox Museum Board (BP 811, DM 1905, FR 6446, Y 138,638).

$132,000* *Suicide,* s., d. 1964 verso, prov., lit., (11-17-92, Sotheby-NY, #16, illus.), 40 x 30 in., (101.6 x 76.2 cm.), silkscreen on paper (BP 86,911, DM 210,459, FR 708,915, Y 16,415,869).

BI *Sunset (F. & S. 85), 1972: Two,* each s., #271/470, artist's proof I, unique, first from the Hotel Marquette, stamp, pub. Factory Additions, good cond., soiling, handling creases, est. $4/5,000, (05-15-93, Sotheby-NY, #1255, illus.), each sheet 34 x 34 in., (86.4 x 86.4 cm.), silkscreen in colors.

$505* *Sunset (Feldmann/Schellmann 85-88), 1980,* s., (09-25-92, Granier, #3050), sheet 33¼ x 21¹⁵⁄₁₆ in., (84.4 x 55.8 cm.), color offset print on offset paper (BP 295, DM 749, FR 2531, Y 60,954).

$4025* *"Sunset" and "Sunset" (cf. F. and S. 85 et al.), 1972: Two,* Estate of Andy Warhol ink stamp, proofs, creasing, good cond., (05-11-93, Christie-NY, #593, illus.), sheet 34 x 34 in., (864 x 864 mm.), color screenprint on wove (BP 2569, DM 6341, FR 21,364, Y 442,746).

BI *Superman (F. and S. 260), 1981,* from Myths, s., #62/200, pub. Ronald Feldman Fine Arts, surface scuffs, excell. cond., est. $12/14,000, (05-11-93, Christie-NY, #596, illus.), sheet 38 x 38 in., (965 x 965 mm.), color screenprint w/diamond dust on Lenox Museum Board.

$653* *Torsos,* s. Andy Warhol, (09-30-92, Kunsthallen, #293), poster (BP 368, DM 926, FR 3132, Y 78,363, DK 3565).

$920* *Torsos,* s., for Prigioni Vecchie-Venezia, 9/IX-8/X (1977), promotion for suite, hand s. by Andy Warhol, prop. Joseph C. DiBella, (06-23-93, Sotheby-NY, #321, illus.), 40 x 28 in., (101.6 x 71.1 cm.), (BP 625, DM 1557, FR 5236, Y 100,229).

$1151* *"Torsos",* s. Andy Warhol, (09-29-92, B. Rasmussen, #374), 59¹⁄₁₆ x 39⅜ in., poster (BP 647, DM 1626, FR 5547, Y 137,400, DK 6325).

BI *"Twenty Cats Named Sam",* s., i., est. $1/1500, (10-08-92, Boos, #663, illus.), 10⅜ x 8⅜ in., (264 x 212 mm.), offset lithographw/hand coloring.

$1412* *Two Angels Carrying A Flower,* s. by Warhol's mother, (10-14-92, Germann, #57, illus.), 8⁷⁄₁₆ x 10¹⁵⁄₁₆ in., (215 x 278 mm.), blotted line print w/ watercolor (BP 829, DM 2066, FR 7007, Y 171,110, SF 1840).

$495* *Two Figures With Tulip,* s. ink, (03-14-93, Hindman, #335), approx. 8½ x 10¾ in., (21.6 x 27.3 cm.), hand-colored letter press (BP 345, DM 824, FR 2801, Y 58,338).

$1045* *Two From The Bottom Of My Garden,* each s. ink, (09-20-92, Hindman, #721), 8½ x 10⅝ in., (21.6 x 27 cm.), hand-colored letterpress (BP 612, DM 1551, FR 5305, Y 129,156).

$880* *Two From The Bottom Of My Garden,* each s. ink, 1 t., (09-20-92, Hindman, #722), 8½ x 10⅝ in., (21.6 x 27 cm.), hand-colored letterpress (BP 515, DM 1306, FR 4467, Y 108,763).

BI *Two Girls,* s., est. $1,5/2,500, (10-09-92, Sotheby-Arcade, #305, illus.), 14 x 9½ in., (35.6 x 24.1 cm.), hand colored offset lithography on paper.

BI *Two Lusty Pears,* s. by Warhol's mother, est. SF 1,1/1,300, (10-14-92, Germann, #154, illus.), 11 x 8⁷⁄₁₆ in., (280 x 215 mm.), blotted line print w/watercolor.

$9900* *Two Photo-Booth Self-Portraits,* two strips in one mount, exec. c. 1964, prov., Billy Kluver Coll., (11-19-92, Christie-NY, #340, illus.), each 8 x 1½ in., (20.3 x 3.8 cm.), photograph, gelatin silver prints (BP 6518, DM 15,784, FR 53,169, Y 1,231,190).

BI *U.N. Stamp (Feldmann 185), 1979,* 144/1000, s., est. SF 1,6/1,800, (10-14-92, Germann, #474), 8⁷⁄₁₆ x 10¹⁵⁄₁₆ in., (215 x 278 mm.), color offset print.

$790* *U.N. Stamp (Feldmann/Schellmann 185), 1979,* #319/1000, s., (04-21-93, Germann, #825), 8⁹⁄₁₆ x 11 in., (217 x 280 mm.), offset lithograph in colors (BP 513, DM 1263, FR 4270, Y 87,457, SF 1150).

$3127* *Untitled (F & S 40), 1968,* from portfolio Flash, s., pub. Racolin Press, Inc., good cond.?, crease, (12-09-92, Sotheby-Amstrdm, #672, illus.), 20¹⁵⁄₁₆ x 20¹⁵⁄₁₆ in., (532 x 532 mm.), color screenprint (BP 1996, DM 4908, FR 16,749, Y 387,725, G 5520).

$920* *Untitled (F. and S. 115), 1974,* from Flowers, Hand-Colored, inits., s., d., #91/250, Andy Warhol/Castelli Graphics/Multiples ink stamp, full margins, colors faded, (05-11-93, Christie-NY, #594), sheet 41 x 27½ in., (104.1 x 69.9 cm.), hand-colored screenprint on Arches (BP 587, DM 1449, FR 4883, Y 101,199).

$2200* *Untitled 12 (F. and S. 120), 1974,* from For Meyer Schapiro, New York, Committee to Endow a Chair in Honor of Meyer Schapiro at Columbia University, s., d. in ink, #85/100 verso, fullmargins, split, rubbed spots, excellent cond., (11-09-92, Christie-NY, #434, illus.), 30 x 22 in., (762 x 559 mm.), screenprint on wove (BP 1455, DM 3512, FR 11,866, Y 273,021).

$3300* *Van Heusen (Ronald Reagan) (F. and S. 356), 1985,* s., #158/190, pub. Ronald Feldman Fine Arts, excellent cond., (11-09-92, Christie-NY, #446, illus.), 38 x 38 in., (965 x 965 mm.), colored screenprint on Lenox Museum Board (BP 2182, DM 5268, FR 17,799, Y 409,531).

BI *Van Heusen (Ronald Reagan) (Feldman 356), 1985,* 149/190, s., est. SF 4/6000, (10-14-92, Germann, #68, illus.), 37¹³⁄₁₆ x 37¹³⁄₁₆ in., (960 x 960 mm.), color serigraph and colophon.

$2817* *"Van Heusen (Ronald Reagan)" (Feldman/Schellmann 356), 1985,* portfolio 10 Ads, #149/190, s., num., (12-05-92, Mangisch, #758, illus.), 37¹⁵⁄₁₆ x 37¹⁵⁄₁₆ in., (96.5 x 96.5 cm.), color serigraph (BP 1764, DM 4392, FR 14,968, Y 349,027, SF 4025).

$1363* *Vesuvius, 1985,* s., #150/250, (11-16-92, Briest, #382), 31½ x 39⅜ in., (80 x 100 cm.), serigraph on canvas (BP 896, DM 2174, FR 7324, Y 170,099).

BI *Volkswagon (Feldman/Schellmann 358), 1985,* s., #49/190, pub. Ronald Feldman Fine Arts, Inc., est. $3/4,000, (05-16-93, Hindman, #646), 38 x 38 in., (96.5 x 96.5 cm.), color serigraph.

$3300* *Vote McGovern (F. and S. 84; Gemini 396), 1972,* s., #58/250 verso, blindstamps, creasing, scrapes, soiling, shrink-wrapped, (11-09-92, Christie-NY, #432, illus.), 42 x 42 in., (106.7 x 106.7 cm.), colored screenprint on wove (BP 2182, DM 5268, FR 17,799, Y 409,531).

$871* *Watermelon (Serie space fruit: Still lifes) (Schellmann 199), 1979,* s., #XXIX/XXX, (05-27-93, Briest, #220), 30⅛ x 40³⁄₁₆ in., (76.5 x 102 cm.), color serigraph (BP 558, DM 1398, FR 4711, Y 93,375).

$523* *Winged Figures With Bird,* s. in ink, (03-14-93, Hindman, #332), approx. 8½ x 10¾ in., (21.6 x 27.3 cm.), hand-

colored letter press (BP 365, DM 871, FR 2960, Y 61,638).

$385* *Yellow Cow (Feldman 11),* s., d. 1971, proof, (12-08-92, Swann, #308), 45½ x 29¼ in., (115.6 x 74.3 cm.), color screen print on wallpaper (BP 241, DM 599, FR 2044, Y 47,719).

$385* *Yellow Cow (Feldman 11), 1971,* p. Ben Miller's Wallpaper Studio, (05-27-93, Swann, #286), 45½ x 29¾ in., (115.6 x 75.6 cm.), color screenprint on wallpaper (BP 247, DM 618, FR 2082, Y 41,274).

WARHOL, Andy   (after)
$55* *"Brooklyn Bridge",* (10-31-92, Cleveland, #401), 36 x 24 in., (91.4 x 61 cm.), silkscreen poster (BP 35, DM 85, FR 287, Y 6813).

$470* *Flowers,* #76/250 stamp verso, pub. Sunday B. Morning, prov., (12-01-92, Ritchie, #105), 36 x 36 in., (91.4 x 91.4 cm.), color serigraph (BP 311, DM 749, FR 2553, Y 58,516, C$ 605).

$84* *Torsos, 1977,* exhibition poster, pen s., creases, tear, (11-16-92, Briest, #113), 59¹⁄₁₆ x 39⅜ in., (150 x 100 cm.), poster (BP 55, DM 134, FR 451, Y 10,483).

WARLOW, Herbert Gordon   British 1885-1942
BI *"Christ Church, Canterbury Gate",* s., good cond., est. $75/125, (05-15-93, Cleveland, #441), 8⅛ x 5⅛ in., (20.6 x 13 cm.), etching.

WARMAN, Morris
$330* *"Portrait Of Malcolm Little And Betty Shabazz"* and *"Variant Of Same",1963: Two,* New York Herald Tribune's photog.'s handstamps, identifying notations, (04-07-93, Swann, #330), each approx. 8½ x 14 in., photograph, silver print (BP 218, DM 534, FR 1806, Y 37,491).

WARNECKE, Harry   1900-1984
$605* *Edgar Bergen With Puppets, 1948,* sig., (10-14-92, Swann, #587, illus.), 18 x 14 in., (45.7 x 35.6 cm.), photograph, color carbo print (BP 355, DM 885, FR 3002, Y 73,316).

BI *Gary Cooper, 1957,* credit, t., d. in ink, label w/t. & annot. affixed to overmat, mounted on board, est. $1,8/2,200, (10-13-92, Christie-NY, #505, illus.), 15½ x 11¼ in., (39.4 x 28.6 cm.), photograph, carbro color print.

$2750* *Marlene Dietrich,* mounted, label, annot. in unidentified hand, 1940's, (10-15-92, Sotheby-NY, #484, illus.), 15½ x 11¼ in., (39.4 x 28.6 cm.), photograph, color carbro print (BP 1683, DM 4093, FR 13,882, Y 329,934).

$1540* *The U.S.S. Normandie, c. 1940,* notations, (10-14-92, Swann, #588, illus.), 15½ x 12 in., (39.4 x 30.5 cm.), photograph, color carbro print (BP 904, DM 2254, FR 7643, Y 186,621).

WARR, Malcolm
BI *Kapiti Light,* s. Malcolm Warr, i., d. '80, #114/140, est. $2/400, (08-11-92, L. Joel, #53GA), 24¹³⁄₁₆ x 30½ in., (63 x 77.5 cm.), color screenprint.

WARRE, Henry J.
$358* *Source Of The Columbia River,* p. Dickinson and Company, (06-11-93, Freemn/Fine Art, #246), 9¾ x 15 in., (24.8 x 38.1 cm.), lithograph w/hand-coloring (BP 235, DM 582, FR 1962, Y 37,984).

WARREN, A.C.   (after)
$33* *"The City Of Detroit From Canada Shore",* by R. Hinshellwood, pub. D. Appleton Co., 1872, (06-11-93, DuMouchelle, #2264), 5½ x 9 in., (14 x 22.9 cm.), hand-colored etching (BP 22, DM 54, FR 181, Y 3501).

WARSHAW, Howard   b. 1920
$627* *Familienszene, 1956,* s., ded., i. only print, (12-05-92, Bassenge, #7814), 11¹³⁄₁₆ x 17½ in., (30 x 44.5 cm.), etching w/aquatint on thick copper print paper (BP 393, DM 978, FR 3332, Y 77,686).

WARTHEN, Ferol
$770* *Abstract With Flowers,* s., d. 52, very good cond.?, (02-07-93, Bakker, #49), image 5 x 3 in., (12.7 x 7.6 cm.), white line color woodblock print (BP 533, DM 1277, FR 4316, Y 95,819).

WASSERMAN, Burton   American 20th cent.
$193* *Construction In Red, Yellow, Blue And Deep, Deep Gray,*
s., t., d., i. proof, exhib., (06-11-93, Freemn/Fine Art,
#247), 16½ x 11 in., (41.9 x 27.9 cm.), serigraph (BP
127, DM 314, FR 1058, Y 20,477).

WATANABE, Sadao   Japanese b. 1913
$165* *Christ With Saints,* s., d. 1971, #27/70, i. verso in Japa-
nese, (11-20-92, Skinner, #13), image 21 x 17½ in.,
(53.3 x 44.5 cm.),   (BP 109, DM 263, FR 886, Y
20,520).
$303* *Figures At A Well,* s., d. 1968, (03-25-93, Boos, #268), 7
x 6½ in., (17.8 x 16.5 cm.), color woodblock print (BP
206, DM 498, FR 1693, Y 35,497).
$550* *The Holy Family In The Manger,* s., d. 1955, num., (03-
25-93, Boos, #221, illus.), 23 x 17¾ in., (58.4 x 45.1
cm.), color woodblock print (BP 374, DM 904, FR 3073,
Y 64,433).
$220* *Religious Figures: Three,* (03-25-93, Boos, #207), color
woodblock print (BP 149, DM 361, FR 1229, Y 25,773).
$220* *Untitled: Two,* s., d., num. Sadao Watanabe 1962, 42/50;
1963 27/50, (09-25-92, Wolf, #31), one 25 x 21 in.,
(63.5 x 53.3 cm.), the other 22 x 18½ in., (63.5 x 53.3
cm.), colored stencils (BP 128, DM 326, FR 1103, Y
26,554).

WATENPHUL, Max Peiffer   1896-1976
$921* *Stilleben Mit Anemonen Und Mimosen,* s., i. HC, (06-08-
93, Karl/Faber, #1178), approx. 11⁷⁄₁₆ x 22¹³⁄₁₆ in., (29 x
58 cm.), color lithograph on Arches wove (BP 605, DM
1494, FR 5033, Y 97,823).

WATERLOO, Anthonie   Dutch 1609/10-1690
$1145* *Folge Von 4 Blatt Landschaften (Dutuit 3-6, Le Blanc 3-
6, Illus. Bartsch II, 3-6), c. 1650,* watermark, prov., (06-
23-93, Kornfeld, #115), etching (BP 778, DM 1937, FR
6517, Y 124,741, SF 1725).
$133* *Folge Von Sechs Landschaften (B. und Dut. 113-115/II):
Three,* foxed, creased, (12-01-92, Karl/Faber, #165),
engraving on hand-made (BP 88, DM 212, FR 722, Y
16,559).
$706* *Kleine Felsige Landschaften (B. und Dutuit 3-6/I(v. IV
bzw. V)): Four,* trimmed, prov., (12-01-92, Karl/Faber,
#161), etching (BP 466, DM 1125, FR 3835, Y 87,898).
$198* *Landscape,* prov., (09-20-92, Hindman, #655), 4½ x 5⅝
in., (11.4 x 14.3 cm.), etching (BP 116, DM 294, FR
1005, Y 24,472).
$1705* *Landscapes (Dut. VI, 21-32): Six,* from the set of twelve,
first or second state of six, before change of plate lettering, narrow margins, stains, good cond., all ex-coll., (12-
03-92, Sotheby-London, #148), each approx. 3¾ x 5½
in., (95 x 145 mm.), etchings, plate I on paper w/water-
mark (BP 1100, DM 2681, FR 9152, Y 212,144).
BI   *"The Large Landscapes" (B. II, 125-130) and "The Large
Landscapes" (B. II, 113-118): Two,* good but later
impressions, margins, good cond., est. BP 6/800, (06-30-
93, Sotheby-London, #245), etching.
$110* *The Plank Bridge (Duthuit 52),* 18th cent. impression,
Emmanuel Jacobson Estate, (03-14-93, Hindman, #165),
4⅞ x 5¾ in., (12.4 x 14.6 cm.), etching and burin (BP
77, DM 183, FR 623, Y 12,964).
BI   *The Small Bridge Over A Stream (Bartsch 124),* (05-16-
93, Hindman, #408), 11½ x 9⅜ in., (29.2 x 23.8 cm.),
etching.
$853* *Town In Ruins (B. II, 96),* narrow to thread margins,
trimmed just on platemark, stains, surfacedirt, ex-coll.,
(12-03-92, Sotheby-London, #147), 6 x 8 in., (155 x 206
mm.), etching (BP 550, DM 1341, FR 4579, Y 106,134).
$99* *"The Trestle Bridge" (Bartsch 6iv),* small margins, good
cond., (10-31-92, Cleveland, #21), 4 x 4⅝ in., (10.2 x
11.7 cm.), etching (BP 63, DM 152, FR 517, Y 12,263).
BI   *"Two Peasant Resting By A Tree" (Bartsch 37),* small
margins, good cond., est. $125/175, (10-31-92, Cleveland,
#22), 4⅝ x 5½ in., (11.7 x 14 cm.), etching.
$149* *Zwolf Landschaften Im Querformat (B. und Dut. 21, 22,
25-32/II (bzw.III)): Ten,* stained, (12-01-92, Karl/Faber,
#162), engraving (BP 98, DM 237, FR 809, Y 18,551).

WATERLOW and SONS Ltd., Publisher
$539* *The Colonial Mail Line, The R.M.S. "Drummond Castle",*
staining, (01-14-93, Bonhams, #130), image 22 x 16½

in., (55.9 x 41.9 cm.), chromolithograph (BP 352, DM
881, FR 2980, Y 67,953).

WATERS, Herbert   b. 1903
$225* *"Magic Of Spring",* s., #17/75, Omer Lassonde Coll.,
(02-27-93, Young, #320, illus.), 5 x 9 in., (12.7 x 22.9
cm.), woodcut (BP 158, DM 370, FR 1257, Y 26,561).
$175* *"North Wind, South Wind",* s., edit. 52, Omer Lassonde
Coll., (02-27-93, Young, #321, illus.), 11 x 4 in., (27.9 x
10.2 cm.), woodcut (BP 123, DM 288, FR 978, Y
20,659).

WATKINS, Carleton E.   American 1825-1916
BI   *"Cape Horn, Columbia River, Oregon" (Columbia River,
cover), 1867,* ink t., est. $3/4,000, (11-16-92, Butterfield,
#6224, illus.), 15¾ x 20⅞ in., (400.8 x 530.1 mm.),
photograph, albumen print on modern mount.
BI   *El Capitan From Lake Ah-Wi-Yah, c. 1868,* mounted, est.
$2/3,000, (10-15-92, Sotheby-NY, #17, illus.), 20½ x 15½
in., (52.1 x 39.4 cm.), photograph, albumen print.
$7700* *"Cliff House, San Francisco", 1868,* ink t., (11-16-92,
Butterfield, #6223, illus.), 15 x 20⁹⁄₁₆ in., (381.7 x 521.6
mm.), photograph, mammoth plate albumen print (BP
5070, DM 12,277, FR 41,353, Y 957,592).
BI   *The Devil's Canyon Geyser, View Looking Down (Carleton E. Watkins, Photographer Of The American West, Pl.
39), 1868-70,* t. in unident. hand on mount recto, est. $2/
3,000, (04-07-93, Swann, #279, illus.), 16 x 20½ in.,
photograph, albumen print.
$4313* *"Down The Valley, Yosemite" (Fraenkel, pl. 15), c. 1865,*
notations, (04-06-93, Sotheby-NY, #14, illus.), 15⅝ x
20½ in., photograph, albumen print (BP 2849, DM 6949,
FR 23,530, Y 491,902).
$8250* *"Islands In The Columbia River, Upper Cascades" (Ore-
gon, pl. 32), 1867,* t., (10-15-92, Sotheby-NY, #20,
illus.), 15¾ x 20⅝ in., (40 x 52.4 cm.), photograph,
albumen print (BP 5048, DM 12,280, FR 41,646, Y
989,802).
$2300* *Los Angeles Base Line Survey, 1889: Nine,* t. in pencil,
(04-06-93, Sotheby-NY, #18, illus.), various sizes to 8¼
x 12 in., photograph, 8 albumen prints, 1 oval cyanotype
(BP 1519, DM 3705, FR 12,548, Y 262,318).
$12,100* *Mining View, Nevada County (Fraenkel, pl. 86), c.
1871,* mounted, #20 in unidentified hand, (10-15-92,
Sotheby-NY, #21, illus.), 15¾ x 21¼ in., (40 x 54 cm.),
photograph, albumen print (BP 7404, DM 18,011, FR
61,080, Y 1,451,710).
$2300* *Mt. Conness Expedition: Seven,* 4 num. in neg., 1
mounted, all matted, each t., (04-06-93, Sotheby-NY, #19,
illus.), various sizes 7¾ x 9⅝ in., photograph, albumen
print (BP 1519, DM 3705, FR 12,548, Y 262,318).
$3220* *Pulpit Rock, Utah, 1873,* t., (04-08-93, Christie-NY, #8,
illus.), oval 5 x 6⅜ in., (12.7 x 16.2 cm.), photograph,
albumen print (BP 2111, DM 5173, FR 17,510, Y
365,411).
BI   *"Upper Cascades From The Oregon Side" (Oregon, pl.
34), 1867,* two-toned mount, calligraphic hand, est. $6/
9,000, (04-06-93, Sotheby-NY, #15A, illus.), 15¾ x 20¾
in., photograph, albumen print.
$10,925* *"The Vernal Fall, 300 Ft. Yosemite, No. 87" (Fraenkel,
pl. 30), 1861,* mounted, t., num., credited, p. before
1880, (04-06-93, Sotheby-NY, #15, illus.), 15⅝ x 20⅝
in., photograph, albumen print (BP 7216, DM 17,601, FR
59,602, Y 1,246,008).
BI   *Vernal Falls, Yosemite (Fraenkel, pl. 30 and dust jacket,
dome-toppedversion), 1861,* probably p. 1860's, est. $4/
6,000, (10-15-92, Sotheby-NY, #19, illus.), 15¾ x 20⅝
in., (40 x 52.4 cm.), photograph, albumen print.
BI   *Yolo Base Line Survey (Palmquist, pl. 83), 1881: Seven,*
each t. in pencil, est. $5/7,000, (04-06-93, Sotheby-NY,
#17, illus.), various sizes to 8½ x 12¼ in., photograph, 5
albumen prints, 2 oval cyanotypes.
BI   *The Yosemite Book; A Description Of The Yosemite Valley And The Adjacent Region Of The Sierra Nevada, And
Of The Big Trees Of California,* letterpress captions on
mount recto, Large 4to, morocco gilt, light wear on
extremities, foxing, pub. Legislature, Julius Bien 1868,
est. $4/6,000, (04-07-93, Swann, #98, illus.), approx. 6 x
8 in., (15.2 x 20.3 cm.), photograph, 24 mounted photos

by Carleton E. Watkins, and 4 photos by W. Harris, 2 large fold-out maps, albumen prints.
$4125* *'Lower Multnomah Fall, Cascade, Columbia Rr.' (Oregon, pl. 51), 1867,* t. in ink, (10-15-92, Sotheby-NY, #20A, illus.), 20½ x 15¾ in., (52.1 x 40 cm.), photograph, albumen print (BP 2524, DM 6140, FR 20,823, Y 494,901).
BI *'The Yosemite Book; A Description Of The Yosemite Valley And The Adjacent Region Of The Sierra Nevada, And Of The Big Trees Of California' (NYPL 166; Truthful Lens 185), 1868: Twenty-Eight,* pub. Julius Bien, est. $7/9,000, (10-15-92, Sotheby-NY, #18, illus.), each plate, approx. 8⅛ x 6⅛ in., (20.6 x 15.6 cm.), photograph, albumen print.

WATKINS, Carleton E. and Isaiah TABER
BI *Black Butte And Mt. Shasta,* num., t. in neg., c. 1860's, p.l., est. $1/1,500, (10-14-92, Swann, #268, illus.), 15½ x 20 in., (39.4 x 50.8 cm.), photograph, albumen print.
$1320* *The Sentinel, 3069 Feet, Yosemite, Cal.,* num., t. in neg., 1870's, (10-14-92, Swann, #269, illus.), 20½ x 15½ in., (52.1 x 39.4 cm.), photograph, mammoth albumen print (BP 775, DM 1932, FR 6551, Y 159,961).

WATKINS, Franklin (after)
$44* *Floral Still Life,* s., #10/150, (06-11-93, Freemn/Fine Art, #248), 22¼ x 18 in., (56.5 x 45.7 cm.), lithograph in color (BP 29, DM 72, FR 241, Y 4668).

WATKINS/TABER STUDIO, Carleton E.
BI *"The Bridal Veil Falls, 900 Ft.", "Cathedral Rock, 2,678 Ft.", "Sentinel", and "Mt. Starr King and Glacier Point" (Fraenkel, pls. 9, 42, and 49): Four,* #16, 21, 43, and 69, credited Taber Photo, San Francisco, in the neg., 1860;s, p. by TABER from negatives by CARLETON E. WATKINS in the 1880's, est.$4/6,000, (10-15-92, Sotheby-NY, #19A, illus.), each approx. 20 x 15½ in., (50.8 x 39.4 cm.), photograph, albumen prints.

WATSON, Amelia Montague 1856-1934
$330* *"Great Pee-Dee River, S.C.",* s., i., (11-28-92, Young, #394), 15 x 11 in., (38.1 x 27.9 cm.), etching (BP 218, DM 526, FR 1785, Y 41,070).

WATSON, Ernest American 1884-1969
BI *"Woodbine", 1934,* s., t., very good cond., est. $1-150, (10-31-92, Cleveland, #230), 6¾ x 9¼ in., (17.1 x 23.5 cm.), color woodcut.

WATSON, Eva American 1889-1948
$40* *Jungle Peace,* s., t., very good cond., (05-15-93, Cleveland, #333), 8¾ x 7⅜ in., (22.2 x 18.7 cm.), woodcut in colors (BP 26, DM 64, FR 216, Y 4434).

WATSON, George (after)
$167* *Sir Evan John Murray Macgregor Of Macgregor, Bart, 1930,* by Herbert Sedcole, s., pub. Masterpiece Engravings Ltd., margins, (11-12-92, Bonhams-Chelsea, #20), plate 22 x 13¼ in., (55.9 x 33.7 cm.), color mezzotint (BP 110, DM 265, FR 893, Y 20,707).

WATSON, James b. 1913
$41* *Bright Saturday,* s. James D Watson, i., d. '68, #3/20, (08-11-92, L. Joel, #33G), 26¾ x 21¹⁄₁₆ in., (68 x 53.5 cm.), color woodcut (BP 21, DM 60, FR 204, Y 5250, A$ 55).
$32* *The Cardinals,* s. James D Watson, i., d. '64, #11/20, (08-11-92, L. Joel, #25G), 11⁷⁄₁₆ x 26³⁄₁₆ in., (29 x 66.5 cm.), color woodcut (BP 17, DM 47, FR 159, Y 4098, A$ 44).

WATSON, Leonard
$60* *September Days,* s., t.; i. "proof", label verso, (11-30-92, Ritchie, #26, illus.), 7¼ x 7½ in., (18.4 x 19 cm.), color etching heightened w/watercolor (BP 40, DM 96, FR 324, Y 7467, C$ 77).

WATSON, Percy Edward b. 1920
BI *(Three Pines),* s. Percy Watson, d. '53, est. $1/200, (08-11-92, L. Joel, #34G), 4 x 6¹⁄₁₆ in., (10.2 x 15.4 cm.), linocut.

WATTEAU, A. 1684-1721
BI *Lecon D'Amour,* yellowed, tear, est. SC 10/12,000, (11-11-92, Dorotheum, #332), 15⅜ x 20½ in., (39 x 52 cm.), etching.

WATTEAU, Antoine (after)
$344* *"Femme En Pied" (Goncourt #352-Baudicourt),* good margins, (03-22-93, Pescheteau, #29), (BP 232, DM 564, FR 1918, Y 39,833).
$81* *"Femme Encapuchonne" (G. #492),* from first impression, all margins, (03-22-93, Pescheteau, #30), (BP 55, DM 133, FR 452, Y 9379).
BI *The Swing,* by W. Nichol, pub. Ackermann 1839, est. $2/400, (05-16-93, Hindman, #428), 22¾ x 14¾ in., (57.8 x 37.5 cm.), hand-colored lithograph.

WATTEAU, Jean Antoine
$26* *"Monkey Sculptress", La Sculpture and "Monkey Painter", La Peinture:Two,* by **Nichol, (06-08-93, Ritchie, #33), each 7 x 6½ in., (17.8 x 16.5 cm.), hand-colored lithograph (BP 17, DM 42, FR 142, Y 2762, C$ 33).

WATTEAU, Jean Antoine (after) French 1684-1721
$138* *Entretiens Amoureux,* (12-10-92, Sloan, #602), 14¼ x 18½ in., (36.2 x 47 cm.), engraving (BP 89, DM 218, FR 746, Y 17,071).
$1100* *The Four Seasons: Four,* prov., (12-10-92, Sloan, #603), each 22½ x 13⅛ in., (57.2 x 33.3 cm.), chromolithographs (BP 709, DM 1740, FR 5943, Y 136,071).
$55* *"Lecon De Musique" and "Lecon D'Amour": Pair,* (10-30-92, Sloan, #1939), larger 8⁹⁄₁₆ x 12 in., (21.7 x 30.5 cm.), color print (BP 35, DM 85, FR 287, Y 6813).

WATTEAU, L. (after)
BI *French Woman,* plate s., est. $50/75, (10-16-92, DuMouchelle, #2499), 11¼ x 17 in., (28.6 x 43.2 cm.), etching.

WATTS, George Frederick (after)
$141* *Love And Death,* by Sir Frank Short, s. by both artists, pub. Robert Dunthorne, 1900,margins, time stained, (06-16-93, Bonhams-Chelsea, #514), pl. 24¾ x 12 in., (62.9 x 30.5 cm.), mezzotint (BP 94, DM 234, FR 786, Y 15,038).

WAUGH, Coulton American 1896-1973
$55* *"Cape Cod Light",* s., good cond., (02-07-93, Bakker, #109), image 8 x 6½ in., (20.3 x 16.5 cm.), color woodblock print (BP 38, DM 91, FR 308, Y 6844).

WEATHERLY, Richard b. 1947
$162* *Edge Of The Forest,* s. Richard Weatherly, i., d. '89, #8/70, (08-11-92, L. Joel, #164G), 19½ x 27¾ in., (49.5 x 70.5 cm.), color lithograph (BP 84, DM 238, FR 805, Y 20,745, A$ 220).
$113* *(Galahs),* s. Richard Weatherly, d. '89, #7/95, (08-11-92, L. Joel, #24G), 200¹³⁄₁₆ x 279½ in., (510 x 710 cm.), color lithograph (BP 59, DM 166, FR 562, Y 14,470, A$ 154).
$146* *(Outback Town),* s. Richard Weatherly, d. '89, #13/94, (08-11-92, L. Joel, #156G), 23¼ x 37⅜ in., (59 x 95 cm.), lithograph (BP 76, DM 214, FR 726, Y 18,696, A$ 198).

WEAVER, Thomas (after)
$510* *A Short Horned Heifer, 7 Years Old,* by William Ward, pub. William Robinson, 1811, margins, stained, creased, tears, (03-03-93, Bonhams-Chelsea, #37), plate 20 x 24 in., (50.8 x 61 cm.), mezzotint (BP 352, DM 840, FR 2849, Y 59,593).

WEBB, A.C.
BI *"La Fliche De Notre Dame", c. 1920's,* #34/100, s., est. $50/75, (08-14-92, DuMouchelle, #1388), 13½ x 10 in., (34.3 x 25.4 cm.), engraving.

WEBB, B. (after)
$17* *"Playing Chess",* d. 1864, (01-15-93, DuMouchelle, #2445), 18 x 20 in., (45.7 x 50.8 cm.), engraving (BP 11, DM 28, FR 94, Y 2143).

WEBB, Boyd
$5175* *Enzyme,* exec. 1986-87, prov., exhib., lit., (02-23-93, Sotheby-NY, #362, illus.), 60 x 48 in., (152.4 x 121.9 cm.), photograph (BP 3545, DM 8360, FR 28,356, Y 604,415).

WEBB, John Cother English 1855-1927
$105* *Lady With Doves,* s., #XCVI, (12-10-92, Sloan, #2085), 16 x 14 in., (40.6 x 35.6 cm.), color mezzotint (BP 68, DM 166, FR 567, Y 12,989).

BI *Portrait Of Female,* s., est. $70/90, (01-15-93, DuMouchelle, #2285), oval 17½ x 15 in., (44.5 x 38.1 cm.), print.

WEBB, Joseph 1908-1962

$711* *New Life To The Land, Threshing, 1951,* p. Waterlow and Sons, ref. P 9, cond. 3, ink defects, (10-13-92, Phillips-London, #165, illus.), 29¹⁵⁄₁₆ x 39¾ in., (76 x 101 cm.), color lithograph (BP 414, DM 1042, FR 3539, Y 86,213).

WEBB, Todd b. 1905

$518* *Abstraction Series, Detroit, 1941,* s., d.; ink s., t., d., (04-08-93, Christie-NY, #357, illus.), 4⅝ x 3⅝ in., (11.7 x 9.2 cm.), photograph, gelatin silver print (BP 340, DM 832, FR 2817, Y 58,783).

$880* *Abstraction Series, Detroit, 1942,* s., d. on mount; s., t., d. in ink verso, (10-13-92, Christie-NY, #381, illus.), 4⅝ x 3½ in., (11.7 x 8.9 cm.), photograph, gelatin silver print (BP 513, DM 1289, FR 4380, Y 106,705).

BI *Billboard On 3rd Ave. New York,* (1946), p.l., ink s., t., d., est. $800/1,200, (04-08-93, Christie-NY, #358, illus.), 9½ x 12⅜ in., (24.1 x 31.4 cm.), photograph, gelatin silver print.

$1840* *Brooklyn Bridge-New York,* (1946), p.l., ink s., t., d., (04-08-93, Christie-NY, #359, illus.), 12⅜ x 9½ in., (31.4 x 24.1 cm.), photograph, gelatin silver print (BP 1207, DM 2956, FR 10,005, Y 208,806).

$978* *Esso Building, New York City,* late 1940s, Standard Oil Co., N.J. stamps, label, (04-08-93, Christie-NY, #360, illus.), 9½ x 7½ in., (24.1 x 19.1 cm.), photograph, gelatin silver print (BP 641, DM 1571, FR 5318, Y 110,985).

BI *Juan Hamilton, Abiquiu, 1977,* s., t., d. in ink in margin; s. in ink, est. $1/1,500, (10-13-92, Christie-NY, #616, illus.), 7½ x 4⅝ in., (19.1 x 11.7 cm.), photograph, gelatin silver print.

WEBBER, James

$14,950* *Views In The South Seas, From Drawings By The Late James Webber, Draftsman On Board The REsolution, Captain James Cooke, From The Year 1776 to 1780(Abbey Travel 595; Joppien & Smith 3:192-196; Tooley 501), 1808,* pub. Boydell and Co., p. W. Bulmer and Co. (plates watermark 1820), after Webber, offsetting, soiling, spotting, prov., (06-14-93, Sotheby-NY, #347, illus.), 21¼ x 16½ in., (54 x 41.9 cm.), 16 fine hand-colored aquatints on wove Whatman (BP 9785, DM 24,333, FR 81,783, Y 1,573,187).

WEBER (after Johann Ulrich burri)

BI *Chute Du Rhin,* trimmed, laid on support, top missing, creasing, est. bp 2/300, (10-27-92, Phillips-London, #127), (235 x 288 mm.), aquatint w/hand-coloring, touches of gum-arabic on wove.

WEBER, Al American 20th cent.

$22* *Leaves,* s., (05-16-93, Hindman, #369), 7¾ x 7½ in., photograph, silver print (BP 14, DM 35, FR 120, Y 2450).

WEBER, Andreas Paul German 1893-1980

$738* *Auf Gen Frankfurt (Dorsch 215), 1967,* (12-05-92, Bassenge, #7817), 17³⁄₁₆ x 21⁵⁄₁₆ in., (43.6 x 54.2 cm.), lithograph (BP 462, DM 1151, FR 3921, Y 91,438).

$310* *Beim Bouquiniste Am Quai Voltaire (Dorsch 323), 1961,* stone mono., s., creases, (09-25-92, Granier, #3052), sheet 19½ x 24¹³⁄₁₆ in., (49.5 x 63 cm.), lithograph on handmade (BP 181, DM 460, FR 1554, Y 37,417).

$266* *Beim Bouquinisten Am Quai Voltaire (Dorsch 323), 1961,* s., (12-05-92, Bassenge, #7818), 13¾ x 19¹⁵⁄₁₆ in., (35 x 50.6 cm.), lithograph (BP 167, DM 415, FR 1413, Y 32,958).

$458* *Der Denunziant (Dorsch 466), 1947,* s., 1st abzug, artist's proof, (05-26-93, Dorling, #3041), 12³⁄₁₆ x 10⁷⁄₁₆ in., (31 x 26.5 cm.), lithograph on handmade (BP 296, DM 747, FR 2515, Y 49,761).

$186* *Die Dressur (Dorsch 535),* p.l. 1972, s., creases, (09-25-92, Granier, #3053), sheet 21⅛ x 25¹³⁄₁₆ in., (53.7 x 65.6 cm.), lithograph on hand-made (BP 109, DM 276, FR 932, Y 22,450).

$388* *Der Dunuziant (Dorsch 466), 1947,* s., block mono., (05-26-93, Dorling, #3042), 12³⁄₁₆ x 10⁷⁄₁₆ in., (31 x 26.5 cm.), lithograph on handmade von (by) Van Gelder Zonen (BP 251, DM 633, FR 2131, Y 42,156).

$236* *Falle - Was Fallt (Dorsch 664), 1947,* s., (12-05-92, Bassenge, #7819), 11 x 15⅜ in., (28 x 39 cm.), lithograph on handmade (BP 148, DM 368, FR 1254, Y 29,240).

$381* *Die Feindlichen Bruder (Dorsch 679; Arp 118), 1967,* s., block mono., d., (05-26-93, Dorling, #3044), 10¹⁵⁄₁₆ x 15⅞ in., (27.8 x 40.3 cm.), lithograph on thick wove (BP 246, DM 622, FR 2092, Y 41,395).

$1480* *Das Gerucht (Reinhardt 169), 1953,* s., mono. stamp, (05-26-93, Lempertz, #525, illus.), 25³⁄₁₆ x 30³⁄₁₆ in., (64 x 76.6 cm.), lithograph on Tonplatte on wove (BP 957, DM 2415, FR 8127, Y 160,800).

$398* *Kobold (Arp 88), 1964,* s., creases, (12-01-92, Karl/Faber, #1340), 14⁹⁄₁₆ x 11¹³⁄₁₆ in., (37 x 30 cm.), lithograph on wove (BP 263, DM 634, FR 2162, Y 49,552).

$201* *"Das Neueste",* i., s. A. Paul Weber, sharp creases, (09-14-92, Venator/Hansten, #2546), image approx. 14³⁄₁₆ x 11⁷⁄₁₆ in., (36 x 29 cm.), chalk lithograph (BP 106, DM 299, FR 1013, Y 24,994).

$458* *Pax Vobiscum (Dorsch 1908; Arp 54), 1953,* s., block mono., watermark, (05-26-93, Dorling, #3056, illus.), 15 x 17⅜ in., (38.1 x 44.2 cm.), lithograph on wove (BP 296, DM 747, FR 2515, Y 49,761).

$352* *Public Relations (II) (Dorsch 1985), 1973,* s., block d., red stamp, watermark, (05-26-93, Dorling, #3057), 13⁷⁄₁₆ x 17⅜ in., (34.2 x 44.2 cm.), lithograph on thick wove (BP 228, DM 574, FR 1933, Y 38,244).

$310* *Der Schachgrossmeister (Dorsch 2111), 1976,* stone mono., d., s., wear, (09-25-92, Granier, #3054), sheet 25¹³⁄₁₆ x 21⁵⁄₁₆ in., (65.6 x 54.1 cm.), lithograph on hand-made (BP 181, DM 460, FR 1554, Y 37,417).

$507* *Untern Tisch Getrunken (Dorsch 2540; Arp 149), 1979,* s., block d., red stamlp, (05-26-93, Dorling, #3061, illus.), 15¼ x 18⁹⁄₁₆ in., (38.8 x 47.2 cm.), lithograph on von (by) Arches France wove (BP 328, DM 827, FR 2784, Y 55,085).

$249* *Verdammter Bengel (A. 96), 1966,* s., (12-01-92, Karl/Faber, #1341), 15⁹⁄₁₆ x 11¼ in., (39.5 x 28.5 cm.), lithograph on wove (BP 165, DM 397, FR 1353, Y 31,001).

$1269* *Das Verhangnis (Dorsch 1073),* before 1963, (05-26-93, Dorling, #3050), 12⁷⁄₁₆ x 19⁵⁄₁₆ in., (31.6 x 49 cm.), lithograph on wove (BP 821, DM 2070, FR 6969, Y 137,875).

WEBER, Bruce b. 1946

BI *"Claudia Poolside, Copacabana Palace 1986",* t., s., d., #2/10, label, 454 x 371mm, est. BP 900/1,200, (05-07-93, Sotheby-London, #360, illus.), photograph, yellow toned silver print.

BI *Claudia, Room 700, Copacabana, Rio, 1986,* s., t., d., #5/5, est. $2,5/3,500, (04-08-93, Christie-NY, #564, illus.), 23¼ x 19⅜ in., (59.1 x 49.2 cm.), photograph, gelatin silver print.

$1361* *"Extras At Zeotrope Studios Hollywood 1986",* t., s., d., #3/15 and 10477-298/11, label, pub., 358 x 430mm, (05-07-93, Sotheby-London, #358, illus.), photograph, silver print (BP 862, DM 2152, FR 7251, Y 149,857).

$3450* *Isabella Rossellini, Milan, 1982,* s., t., d., #9/15, (04-08-93, Christie-NY, #565, illus.), 16⅜ x 13⅜ in., (41.6 x 34 cm.), photograph, gelatin silver print (BP 2262, DM 5542, FR 18,760, Y 391,512).

BI *"Jonathan, Actor, Santa Barbara, California", 1990,* s., t., d., edit. 4/15, inventory num., Dixon Collection, est. $1,5/2000, (11-16-92, Butterfield, #6227, illus.), 13⅜ x 10½ in., (340.3 x 267.2 mm.), photograph, gelatin silver print.

$1540* *"Justin Lazard, Actor, New York City" (Bruce Weber), 1986,* s., t., d.,edit. 13/15, inventory num., Dixon Collection, (11-16-92, Butterfield, #6225, illus.), 16½ x 13½ in., (419.8 x 343.5 mm.), photograph, gelatin silver print (BP 1014, DM 2455, FR 8271, Y 191,518).

BI *Liz-Upper Saranac Lake, 1983,* s., t., d., num. 2/15, est. $1,5/2,500, (10-13-92, Christie-NY, #617, illus.), 16½ x 13½ in., (41.9 x 34.3 cm.), photograph, platinum-toned gelatin silver print.

$2070* *Madonna, NYC Studio, 1987,* s., t., d., #4/20, (04-08-93, Christie-NY, #563, illus.), 13⅜ x 16⅜ in., (34 x 41.6

cm.), photograph, gelatin silver print (BP 1357, DM 3325, FR 11,256, Y 234,907).

BI   *"Mike Storm, Pentathalon"*, 1984, s., t., d., #3/15, i. by photog., est. $2/3,000, (04-06-93, Sotheby-NY, #512, illus.), 16½ x 13½ in., photograph.

$1430* *"Rob And Little Bear, Bear Pond, Adirondack Park"*, 1990, s., t., edit. 10/10, inventory num., Dixon Collection, (11-16-92, Butterfield, #6226, illus.), 13½ x 10½ in., (343.5 x 267.2 mm.), photograph, gelatin silver print (BP 942, DM 2280, FR 7680, Y 177,839).

$1453* *"Twins, Santa Barbara 1982"*, t., s., d., #6/15 and 14032-18/3, label, pub., 401 x 508mm, (05-07-93, Sotheby-London, #359, illus.), photograph, toned silver print (BP 920, DM 2297, FR 7741, Y 159,987).

WEBER, Doris Martha

$5175* *Selected Studies: "A Steel Mill Never Sleeps", "Rhythmic Cylinders","Rail And Water", "Water Beetle", "A Cloud By Day", "Glass" and "A Glass Trio":Group Of Eleven*, mounted, all s., t. by photog., (04-06-93, Sotheby-NY, #148, illus.), each approx. 19 x 15 in., photograph (BP 3418, DM 8337, FR 28,232, Y 590,214).

WEBER, Friedrich

BI   *The Glorious Victory Obtained Over The French Fleet By The British Fleet*, 1794, small margins, stains, minor discoloration, rubbed, est. BP 4/600, (12-03-92, Sotheby-London, #149), 17¼ x 22¾ in., (440 x 580 mm.), etching and aquatint w/extensive hand coloring.

WEBER, Max   American 1881-1961

$990* *The Bathers, Figure Composition (Rubenstein 105)*, 1931, s., wide margins, light-staining, tear, staining, taped to overmat, (09-19-92, Christie-E, #70, illus.), borderline 16¾ x 12½ in., (425 x 318 mm.), lithograph in hand-coloring in pastels on Rives (BP 569, DM 1482, FR 5077, Y 123,349).

BI   *Chinese Lion (R. 104)*, 1932, s., margins, good cond., mat stain, creases, tears, discoloraltion, est. $2/2,500, (11-05-92, Sotheby-NY, #54, illus.), 7¾ x 8¾ in., (196 x 222 mm.), lithograph w/touches of hand coloring.

$690* *Chinese Lion (Rubenstein 104)*, 1932, s., margins, good cond., mat stain, creases, tears, (02-11-93, Sotheby-NY, #47), 7¹¹⁄₁₆ x 8¾ in., (196 x 222 mm.), lithograph w/ hand coloring (BP 487, DM 1143, FR 3868, Y 83,183).

$605* *Figure*, s. Max Weber, very good cond., (03-12-93, Skinner, #79, illus.), 4⅛ x 1⅞ in., (10.5 x 4.8 cm.), woodcut on wove (BP 422, DM 1007, FR 3424, Y 71,302).

$660* *On The Sofa*, c. 1928, s., d., num. 39, init. stamp, (12-08-92, Swann, #309), 9¼ x 12 in., (23.5 x 30.5 cm.), lithograph on wove (BP 414, DM 1028, FR 3503, Y 81,805).

$715* *Rabbi Reading*, s. Max Weber, num. 15, very good cond., light toning, (09-11-92, Skinner, #38H, illus.), 4¼ x 1⅞ in., (10.8 x 4.8 cm.), woodcut on wove (BP 370, DM 1029, FR 3498, Y 88,589).

$260* *"Shore Road #55" (Rubenstein 96)*, 1930-1932, s., t., Estate Stamp vero, (05-15-93, Cleveland, #334, illus.), 7⅛ x 10⅛ in., (18.1 x 25.7 cm.), lithograph (BP 169, DM 418, FR 1405, Y 28,822).

BI   *Two Pears (Rubenstein 98)*, 1930-32, s., margins, light/mat staining, tape, good cond., est. $1,2/1,500, (05-11-93, Christie-NY, #125, illus.), borderline 7⅞ x 15⅝ in., (200 x 397 mm.), lithograph w/extensive additions in pastels in colors on wove.

WEBSTER, Hermann   American 1878-1970

BI   *German City Scenes: Three*, s., margins, mat burn, light staining, foxing, est. $2/400, (12-12-92, Weschler, #180), first and second 9 x 6½ in., (22.9 x 16.5 cm.), third 5½ x 8½ in., (22.9 x 16.5 cm.), etching.

BI   *"Les Moulins De Don Quichotte"*, s., num., good cond., est. $125/175, (10-31-92, Cleveland, #231), 4⅝ x 9⅜ in., (11.7 x 23.8 cm.), etching.

BI   *"Les Moulins De Don Quichotte, Campo De Criptana" (Hardie 135), "L'Eau Darmante" (H. 224) and "La Ruse Boise-MicheStrasbourg": Four*, two s., good cond., est. $3/400, (05-15-93, Cleveland, #335), etching.

WEBSTER, Thomas (after)

$281* *The Slide*, pub. Thomas Agnew and Sons, 1858, margins, surface dirt, (06-16-93, Bonhams-Chelsea, #441), pl. 23 x

40 in., (58.4 x 101.6 cm.), engraving (BP 187, DM 466, FR 1565, Y 29,970).

WEDDIGE, Emil   American b. 1907

$44* *"Daumisnil"*, s., #16/25, t., (02-11-93, Boos, #458), sight 23⅝ x 17¹¹⁄₁₆ in., (600 x 450 mm.), color lithograph (BP 31, DM 73, FR 247, Y 5304).

$44* *"Landscape Valencia"*, s., t., num. bottom image, artist's blindstamp, (08-05-92, Boos, #667), 13 x 19¾ in., (330 x 502 mm.), color lithograph (BP 23, DM 65, FR 220, Y 5604).

$22* *"Village"*, s., t., num., (12-02-92, Boos, #524), image 13¼ x 10 in., (337 x 254 mm.), color lithograph (BP 14, DM 35, FR 118, Y 2737).

WEDGE, James

BI   *Draped Figure*, 1970s, mounted on card, labels, sight 350 x 274mm, est. BP 2/300, (05-07-93, Sotheby-London, #200), photograph, silver print.

WEED, Charles (attrib.)

$2200* *"The Yosemite Fall, 2550 High"*, c. 1859-1864, mounted, t. in unidentified hand, (10-15-92, Sotheby-NY, #16, illus.), 16¾ x 20¾ in., (42.5 x 52.7 cm.), photograph, albumen print (BP 1346, DM 3275, FR 11,106, Y 263,947).

WEED, Charles L. ((et alii?))

BI   *'Yosemite Photographs' (Era, fig. 48; Wolf, pl. 73; Lawrence & Housewworth, p. 16): Twenty-Four*, album incl. Clark & Moore's Hotel, Merced River, Johnny Smith's [Cosmopolitan Hotel], A Study Of Eadweard Muybridge seated at the base of the giantredwood 'Grant'; 21 Yosemite Landscape Views, mounted, t., 4to, est. $7/10,000, (10-15-92, Sotheby-NY, #15, illus.), approx. 6½ x 8½ in., (16.5 x 21.6 cm.), photographs, albumen prints.

WEEGE, William   American contemporary

$220* *1st Variation And Presidential Suite*, each s. verso, t., d. 1972, #1/1, annot., The Presidential Suite, each s., d. 70, t., #30/35 on title page, (06-13-93, Hindman, #355), each 11½ x 8½ in., (29.2 x 21.6 cm.), five color serigraphs w/stitching and flocking, eight color serigraphs (BP 144, DM 358, FR 1204, Y 23,151).

$413* *Heavenly Bodies*, s., d. 81, prov., (05-16-93, Hindman, #515), 24¾ x 35½ in., (62.9 x 90.2 cm.), serigraph and collage on paper pulp (BP 269, DM 664, FR 2232, Y 45,782).

$94* *"Nude" and "Nude": Two*, each s., d. 75, (06-13-93, Hindman, #359), each 29½ x 20½ in., (74.9 x 52.1 cm.), color serigraph (BP 62, DM 153, FR 514, Y 9892).

WEEGEE   1899-1968

$531* *Ambulanz*, 50s, studio stamp, (11-12-92, Lempertz, #271), 10¹⁵⁄₁₆ x 13⅞ in., (27.9 x 35.3 cm.), photograph, gelatin silver print (BP 340, DM 835, FR 2844, Y 65,693).

$1815* *Arrest*, 1940s, photog.'s ink credit stamp, (05-06-93, Christie-London, #186, illus.), image 13½ x 10⅝ in., photograph, gelatin silver print (BP 1150, DM 2859, FR 9624, Y 199,692).

$1289* *Auf Der Lauer*, c. 1940, photographer's stamp, (11-12-92, Lempertz, #269, illus.), 8⅛ x 9¹⁵⁄₁₆ in., (20.7 x 25.3 cm.), photograph, gelatin silver print (BP 824, DM 2026, FR 6904, Y 159,470).

$199* *"Babe In Arms, Street Scene, 1946 Hollywood"*, stamped photog.'s credits, 280 x 354mm, (05-07-93, Sotheby-London, #258, illus.), photograph, silver print (BP 126, DM 315, FR 1060, Y 21,911).

$1150* *Balloon And Faces*, 1940's, photog. credit and studio stamps, (04-06-93, Sotheby-NY, #401, illus.), 13½ x 13⅝ in., photograph (BP 760, DM 1853, FR 6274, Y 131,159).

$1441* *Blondine Bei Sammy's In Der Bowery*, 1943, stamp, tear, lit., (11-12-92, Lempertz, #270, illus.), 13¹⁵⁄₁₆ x 11⅛ in., (35.5 x 28.3 cm.), photograph, gelatin silver print (BP 921, DM 2265, FR 7718, Y 178,275).

$920* *Bowery Playboy (Naked City, p. 146, variant)*, 1950's, credit stamp, (04-06-93, Sotheby-NY, #220, illus.), 13½ x 10⅝ in., photograph (BP 608, DM 1482, FR 5019, Y 104,927).

BI *Calypso Party,* handstamp, 1940's, est. $1,5/2,000, (10-14-92, Swann, #589, illus.), 10½ x 13¼ in., (26.7 x 33.7 cm.), photograph, silver print.

$1495* *Children At The Theatre, 1940's,* photog. credit and studio stamp, (04-06-93, Sotheby-NY, #402, illus.), 10⅜ x 13⅜ in., photograph (BP 987, DM 2409, FR 8156, Y 170,506).

BI *Children Touching Jimmy /Durante's Nose,* photog.'s Weegee, West 47th Street handstamp, 1940s, est. $1/1,500, (04-07-93, Swann, #586, illus.), 9½ x 9¾ in., photograph, silver print.

$413* *"Chorus Girls On Strike", 1945,* photog. stamp, annot., (11-16-92, Butterfield, #6229, illus.), 7⅝ x 9¾ in., (194 x 248.1 mm.), photograph, gelatin silver print (BP 272, DM 658, FR 2218, Y 51,362).

BI *Clown Distortion, 1950's,* ink photog. stamps, est. $7/900, (11-16-92, Butterfield, #6230, illus.), 10½ x 10½ in., (267.2 x 267.2 mm.), photograph, gelatin silver print.

$2990* *"Coney Island" (Weegee's New York, pl. 42), 1940,* photog. credit and studio stamps, (04-06-93, Sotheby-NY, #395, illus.), photograph (BP 1975, DM 4817, FR 16,312, Y 341,013).

$3080* *Corpse With Revolver, c. 1940,* stamps, lit., (10-13-92, Christie-NY, #387, illus.), 13¼ x 10¼ in., (33.7 x 26 cm.), photograph, gelatin silver print (BP 1794, DM 4512, FR 15,331, Y 373,469).

BI *Couple Kissing, 1946,* cropping notations, attrib., photog.'s stamp, illus., est. $7/900, (05-23-93, Butterfield, #3656, illus.), 13½ x 10½ in., photograph, gelatin silver print.

$3300* *The Critic (Opening Night At The Metropolitan Opera), 1943 (Weegee'sNew York, pl. 213),* photog.'s studio stamp, (10-15-92, Sotheby-NY, #469, illus.), 9⅛ x 12 in., (23.2 x 30.5 cm.), photograph, gelatin silver print (BP 2019, DM 4912, FR 16,658, Y 395,921).

$2300* *"The Critic" (Opening Night At The Metropolitan Opera), 1943,* stamped p. from orig. neg., i. w/photog. name, p. before 1963, (04-06-93, Sotheby-NY, #404, illus.), 8⅝ x 7⅜ in., photograph (BP 1519, DM 3705, FR 12,548, Y 262,318).

$3163* *"The Critic", 1943,* photog.'s stamps, printing notation, illus., (05-23-93, Butterfield, #3652, illus.), 10½ x 13 in., photograph, gelatin silver print (BP 2060, DM 5172, FR 17,408, Y 349,619).

$1430* *The Critic, 1943,* (10-14-92, Swann, #349, illus.), 11 x 14 in., (27.9 x 35.6 cm.), photograph, silver print (BP 839, DM 2093, FR 7097, Y 173,291).

$1980* *The Critic, 1943,* notations, (04-07-93, Swann, #365, illus.), 7½ x 9½ in., photograph, silver print (BP 1308, DM 3202, FR 10,837, Y 224,949).

$4600* *The Critic, Opening Night At The Metropolitan Opera, 1943,* Weegee The Famous and 47th Street stamps, lit., (04-08-93, Christie-NY, #457, illus.), 10½ x 12¾ in., (26.7 x 32.4 cm.), photograph, gelatin silver print (BP 3016, DM 7390, FR 25,014, Y 522,015).

BI *The Dead Man's Wife Arrives (Naked City, p. 85), 1940's,* photog. credit and studio stamp, est. $1/2,000, (04-06-93, Sotheby-NY, #398, illus.), 9⅞ x 11½ in., photograph.

$440* *"Distortion Of Woman In Bathing Suit" and "Distortion Of The Front OfA Cadillac": Two,* agency's handstamp, 1940s, (04-07-93, Swann, #587, illus.), one 5½ x 7 in., other 9½ x 13 in., photograph, silver print (BP 291, DM 712, FR 2408, Y 49,989).

$1495* *Dog Being Rescued,* 1940s, photog.'s stamp, (05-23-93, Butterfield, #3657, illus.), 9½ x 7⅝ in., photograph, gelatin silver print (BP 974, DM 2444, FR 8228, Y 165,248).

BI *"Dope Seizure" (And Self-Portrait), 1938,* photog. studio stamp, t. in unident. hand, (04-06-93, Sotheby-NY, #397, illus.), 7 x 9½ in., photograph.

$654* *Down And Out,* 1940s, stamped ink photog.'s credit Arthur (Weegee) Fellig, (c) info., 194 x 240mm, (05-07-93, Sotheby-London, #257, illus.), photograph, silver print (BP 414, DM 1034, FR 3484, Y 72,011).

$2530* *Easter Sunday In Harlem, 1940,* Weegee The Famous and West 47th Street credit stamps, lit., (04-08-93, Christie-NY, #454, illus.), 13½ x 10⅝ in., (34.3 x 27 cm.), photograph, gelatin silver print (BP 1659, DM 4064, FR 13,757, Y 287,108).

$2475* *Easter Sunday In Harlem, 1940 (Weegee's New York, p. 275),* photog.'s credit stamps, (10-15-92, Sotheby-NY, #465, illus.), 13⅝ x 10⅝ in., (34.6 x 27 cm.), photograph, gelatin silver print (BP 1515, DM 3684, FR 12,494, Y 296,941).

$522* *Empire State Building Distortion,* handstamp, notations, 1940's, (10-14-92, Swann, #590, illus.), 10 x 8 in., (25.4 x 20.3 cm.), photograph, silver print (BP 306, DM 764, FR 2591, Y 63,257).

$1980* *Empire State Building Montage,* 1940s, stamps, (10-13-92, Christie-NY, #384, illus.), 13½ x 10¾ in., (34.3 x 27.3 cm.), photograph, gelatin silver print (BP 1153, DM 2901, FR 9856, Y 240,087).

$1495* *Family Asleep On Tenement Fire Escape (Naked City, p. 23), 1940's,* photog. credit and studio stamps, (04-06-93, Sotheby-NY, #396, illus.), 13½ x 10½ in., photograph (BP 987, DM 2409, FR 8156, Y 170,506).

BI *Fire In Harlem-Her Kids Are Still In The Burning Building, 1942,* Photo-Representatives and West 47th Street credit stamps, lit., est.$1,5/2,000, (04-08-93, Christie-NY, #455, illus.), 10½ x 13½ in., (26.7 x 34.3 cm.), photograph, gelatin silver print.

BI *"Fly Eyes View Of Marilyn Monroe", 1960,* image t., photog.'s stamp, est. $800/1,000, (05-23-93, Butterfield, #3655, illus.), 8 x 10 in., photograph, gelatin silver print.

$2200* *For President, Gov. Reagan,* mounted, s., t. by photog. in ink and marker, 1960's, (10-15-92, Sotheby-NY, #471, illus.), 13 x 9¾ in., (33 x 24.8 cm.), photograph, gelatin silver print (BP 1346, DM 3275, FR 11,106, Y 263,947).

BI *"Foxy Grandpa", 1943,* s., t., photog. stamp, Dixon Collection, est. $1,8/2,200, (11-16-92, Butterfield, #6228, illus.), 13½ x 10¾ in., (343.5 x 273.5 mm.), photograph, gelatin silver print.

BI *"Foxy Grandpa", 1943,* s., t., photog.'s stamps, est. $1,5/2,000, (05-23-93, Butterfield, #3653, illus.), 13½ x 10¾ in., photograph, gelatin silver print.

BI *Frank Sinatra Fan, 1940's,* photog.'s credit stamp, est. $1/2,000, (10-15-92, Sotheby-NY, #466, illus.), 13 x 11⅝ in., (33 x 29.5 cm.), photograph, gelatin silver print.

BI *Gin Is Sin,* handstamp, 1940's, est. $1,2/1,800, (10-14-92, Swann, #591, illus.), 9½ x 7½ in., (24.1 x 19.1 cm.), photograph, silver print.

$770* *Hedda Hopper,* handstamp, 1940's, (10-14-92, Swann, #592, illus.), 9½ x 7½ in., (24.1 x 19.1 cm.), photograph, silver print (BP 452, DM 1127, FR 3821, Y 93,311).

BI *Her Wounded Husband Is Arrested For Killing A Relative, 1938,* stamp, lit., est. $1,8/2,200, (10-13-92, Christie-NY, #385, illus.), 10½ x 13 in., (26.7 x 33 cm.), photograph, gelatin silver print.

BI *"Hollywood Double Feature", 1959,* photog.'s stamp, illus., est. $800/1,000, (05-23-93, Butterfield, #3654, illus.), 13½ x 10½ in., photograph, gelatin silver print.

BI *House Raid (Prostitutes),* handstamp, 1940's, est. $1,2/1,800, (10-14-92, Swann, #350, illus.), 7½ x 9¾ in., (19.1 x 24.8 cm.), photograph, silver print.

$2588* *"The Human Cannon-Ball" (Weegee's New York, pl. 206), 1952,* photog. Weegee the Famous credit and studio stamps, (04-06-93, Sotheby-NY, #405, illus.), 13½ x 10½ in., photograph (BP 1709, DM 4169, FR 14,119, Y 295,164).

BI *The Human Cop, c. 1943,* Photo-Representatives and West 47th Street credit stamps, lit., est.$1,5/2,000, (04-08-93, Christie-NY, #456, illus.), 10½ x 13½ in., (26.7 x 34.3 cm.), photograph, gelatin silver print.

BI *"Hysterical Man",* 1940s, t., annot., photog.'s stamps, est. $7/900, (05-23-93, Butterfield, #3658, illus.), 9 x 7½ in., photograph, gelatin silver print.

$763* *In The Cell,* 1940s, stamped photog.'s credit, 279 x 354mm, (05-07-93, Sotheby-London, #261, illus.), photograph, silver print (BP 483, DM 1206, FR 4065, Y 84,012).

BI *J. Edgar Hoover Photomontage,* 1950s, Venice exhib. stamp, exhib., lit., est. $2/3,000, (04-08-93, Christie-NY, #452, illus.), 25¼ x 19¾ in., (64.1 x 50.2 cm.), photograph, gelatin silver print.

$770* *"Japs Bomb Hawaii" and "Sailor In Phone Booth", 1941: Two,* #13 and 9 in photog.'s hand, w/ Arthur Fellig handstamp, (04-07-93, Swann, #366, illus.), each approx. 7 x 9 in., photograph, silver print (BP 509, DM 1245, FR 4215, Y 87,480).

$1320* *Limousine Double Exposure,* 1950s, num. 5 in ink, stmaps, lit., (10-13-92, Christie-NY, #383, illus.), 10⅝ x 13½ in., (27 x 34.3 cm.), photograph, gelatin silver print (BP 769, DM 1934, FR 6570, Y 160,058).

$1610* *Lovers At The Movies, c. 1940,* Weegee The Famous and West 47th Street stamps, (04-08-93, Christie-NY, #453, illus.), 10¼ x 13⅛ in., (26 x 33.3 cm.), photograph, gelatin silver print (BP 1056, DM 2586, FR 8755, Y 182,705).

BI *Man Being Arrested, 1940,* photog.'s stamp, illus., est. $5/700, (05-23-93, Butterfield, #3659, illus.), 13¼ x 10⅜ in., photograph, gelatin silver print.

$1100* *"Man Gesturing In Jail Cell" and "Group Of Men Sleeping In Jail Cell": Two,* Arthur Fellig handstamp, 1940s, (04-07-93, Swann, #588, illus.), each 10½ x 13½ in., photograph, silver print (BP 727, DM 1779, FR 6021, Y 124,972).

$1138* *Mann Mit Karre, 50's,* photographer's stamp, (11-12-92, Lempertz, #272, illus.), 10¹⁵/₁₆ x 13¹⁵/₁₆ in., (27.8 x 35.4 cm.), photograph, gelatin silver print (BP 728, DM 1788, FR 6095, Y 140,789).

$633* *Marilyn Distorted,* 1960s, Weegee The Famous and West 47th Street stamps, (04-08-93, Christie-NY, #458, illus.), 13⅜ x 10½ in., (34 x 26.7 cm.), photograph, gelatin silver print (BP 415, DM 1017, FR 3442, Y 71,834).

BI *Marilyn Monroe Distortion, 1950's,* photog. credit stamp, studio stamp, est. $1/2,000, (04-06-93, Sotheby-NY, #407, illus.), 9⅜ x 9 in., photograph.

$2300* *Mona Lisa Distortion Studies, c. 1950's: Six,* one t. by photog., five w/photog. credit stamp, and five w/stamp, (04-06-93, Sotheby-NY, #406, illus.), each approx. 7½ x 9¾ in., photograph (BP 1519, DM 3705, FR 12,548, Y 262,318).

$2475* *Murder In Hell's Kitchen, (Naked City, p. 81),* photog.'s credit & studio stamps, 1940's, (10-15-92, Sotheby-NY, #467, illus.), 13½ x 10¾ in., (34.3 x 27.3 cm.), photograph, gelatin silver print (BP 1515, DM 3684, FR 12,494, Y 296,941).

$920* *"New Year's Eve In Front Of Hotel Astor", 1940's,* t. by photog. in ink, credit and studio stamps, (04-06-93, Sotheby-NY, #400, illus.), 13½ x 10⅝ in., photograph (BP 608, DM 1482, FR 5019, Y 104,927).

$908* *Nude, Distortion,* 1950s, 252 x 206mm, (05-07-93, Sotheby-London, #256, illus.), photograph, silver print (BP 575, DM 1436, FR 4838, Y 99,978).

$1870* *Sammy's Bowery, 1940's (Weegee's New York, pl. 235),* photog.'s credit & studio stamps, (10-15-92, Sotheby-NY, #468, illus.), 10⅜ x 13½ in., (26.4 x 34.3 cm.), photograph, gelatin silver print (BP 1144, DM 2784, FR 9440, Y 224,355).

$758* *Satchmo (Louis Armstrong), 1959/60,* ink s., photographer's stamp, (11-12-92, Lempertz, #273, illus.), 9¹⁵/₁₆ x 8¹/₁₆ in., (25.3 x 20.5 cm.), photograph, gelatin silver print (BP 485, DM 1191, FR 4060, Y 93,777).

BI *Selected Crime Studies, 1940's: Group of Six,* 3 w/credit stamps, est. $1/2,000, (04-06-93, Sotheby-NY, #399, illus.), 6½ x 4½ in., photograph.

$1320* *Self Portrait (Prism), c. 1940,* t. in ink, credit stamp, (10-13-92, Christie-NY, #382, illus.), 8½ x 7⅜ in., (21.6 x 18.7 cm.), photograph, gelatin silver print (BP 769, DM 1934, FR 6570, Y 160,058).

BI *Self-Portrait Through Prism,* 1960s, Photo-Representatives credit stamp, est. $1,2/1,800, (04-08-93, Christie-NY, #459, illus.), 5⅛ x 5⅞ in., (13 x 14.9 cm.), photograph, gelatin silver print.

$3163* *Self-Portrait With Andy Warhol, 1960's,* s. by Andy Warhol, photog. studio stamp, (04-06-93, Sotheby-NY, #408, illus.), photograph (BP 2089, DM 5096, FR 17,256, Y 360,744).

BI *Self-Portrait With Distortion Lens,* handstamp, 1940's, est. $1,2/1,800, (10-14-92, Swann, #593, illus.), 8 x 6½ in., (20.3 x 16.5 cm.), photograph, silver print.

BI *Selling Flowers, 1941,* stamps, lit., est. $1,8/2,200, (10-13-92, Christie-NY, #388, illus.), 13½ x 10½ in., (34.3 x 26.7 cm.), photograph, gelatin silver print.

$575* *Showboat Couple Distortion, 1950's,* studio stamp, i. in unident. hand in ink, (04-06-93, Sotheby-NY, #221, illus.), 7½ x 9½ in., photograph (BP 380, DM 926, FR 3137, Y 65,579).

$3300* *Sing You Sinner Sing, 1940,* t. in ink, stamps, label s., stamped, legend, newspaper clipping affixed verso of mount, (10-13-92, Christie-NY, #386, illus.), 10¼ x 13⅛ in., (26 x 33.3 cm.), photograph, gelatin silver print (BP 1922, DM 4834, FR 16,426, Y 400,146).

$880* *Singer At Sammy's In The Bowery,* photog.'s handstamp, 1940s, (04-07-93, Swann, #589, illus.), 10¼ x 13½ in., photograph, silver print (BP 582, DM 1423, FR 4817, Y 99,977).

BI *Theater Crowd, 1940's,* est. $1/1,500, (10-14-92, Swann, #594), 11 x 14 in., (27.9 x 35.6 cm.), photograph, silver print.

$1517* *Transvestit, c. 1940,* lit., (11-12-92, Lempertz, #268, illus.), 13¹⁵/₁₆ x 10¹⁵/₁₆ in., (35.4 x 27.8 cm.), photograph, gelatin silver print (BP 970, DM 2384, FR 8125, Y 187,678).

$990* *V.J. Day Parade, 1945,* handstamps, (10-14-92, Swann, #351, illus.), 14 x 11 in., (35.6 x 27.9 cm.), photograph, silver print (BP 581, DM 1449, FR 4913, Y 119,971).

$1980* *Vegetable Dealer, 1946,* stamps, lit., (10-13-92, Christie-NY, #388A, illus.), 12¼ x 10⅛ in., (31.1 x 25.7 cm.), photograph, gelatin silver print (BP 1153, DM 2901, FR 9856, Y 240,087).

$436* *"The Voodoo Kiss", 1952,* t., stamped photog.'s credit, illus., 280 x 350mm, (05-07-93, Sotheby-London, #259, illus.), photograph, silver print (BP 276, DM 689, FR 2323, Y 48,007).

$654* *Witnesses At Tenement Window, 1939,* stamped photog.'s credit, 280 x 355mm, (05-07-93, Sotheby-London, #262, illus.), photograph, silver print (BP 414, DM 1034, FR 3484, Y 72,011).

$1035* *Woman Leaving Cab, 1940's,* photog. Arthur Fellig, Photo-Representatives' credit stamps, (04-06-93, Sotheby-NY, #403, illus.), 13¼ x 10⅝ in., photograph (BP 684, DM 1667, FR 5646, Y 118,043).

$400* *Woman On Mattress,* 1940s, stamped photog.'s credit, 278 x 354mm, (05-07-93, Sotheby-London, #260, illus.), photograph, silver print (BP 253, DM 632, FR 2131, Y 44,043).

BI *Woman With Two Saxophone Players,* handstamp, 1940's, est. $1,2/1,800, (10-14-92, Swann, #595, illus.), 11 x 14 in., (27.9 x 35.6 cm.), photograph, silver print.

WEFT, Benjamin

$303* *"The Battle Of The Boyne",* 18th cent., engraved by John Hall after painting by Benjamin Weft, pub. 1781 B.Weft, J. Hall, W. Woollet, (10-16-92, Neal, #400), image 17 x 23¼ in., (43.2 x 59.1 cm.), hand colored engraving (BP 184, DM 448, FR 1520, Y 36,179).

WEGENER, Johann

BI *(Reclining Female Nude),* margins, good cond., minor paper discoloration, soiling, occasional foxing, crease along top edge of sheet, Late Gerhard Brauer Coll., est. Dfl. 2/400, (05-27-93, Sotheby-Amstrdm, #798), 9¾ x 15¹¹/₁₆ in., etching w/tone on wove.

WEGENROTH, Stow

$1100* *"Dusk" (Stuckey 121), 1943 and "Catboat" (Stuckey 195), 1951: Two,* s., Dusk paper loss, (05-27-93, Swann, #293, illus.), one 10¾ x 15⅞ in., (27.3 x 40.3 cm.), other 9¾ x 13⅞ in., (27.3 x 40.3 cm.), lithograph w/toned background (BP 704, DM 1765, FR 5949, Y 117,925).

$825* *"Renaissance" (Stuckey 50), 1935 and "The Headlands" (Stuckey 104), 1940: Two,* s., full margins, Renaissance mat burn, (05-27-93, Swann, #294), one 10½ x 16 in., (26.7 x 40.6 cm.), other 12½ x 16 in., (26.7 x 40.6 cm.), lithograph (BP 528, DM 1324, FR 4462, Y 88,443).

$990* *"Steps To The Sky" (Stuckey 22), 1931 and "Caverned Waters" (Stuckey57), 1935: Two,* s., Caverned Waters glue stain, (05-27-93, Swann, #292, illus.), one 9⅞ x 11¾ in., (25.1 x 29.8 cm.), other 8⅜ x 13 in., (25.1 x 29.8 cm.), lithograph (BP 634, DM 1589, FR 5354, Y 106,132).

WEGMAN, William   American b. 1943
$4620* *At Desk, 3: Three,* s., num. William Wegman 4/7, exec. 1988, prov., (11-19-92, Christie-NY, #261, illus.), 25½ x 44½ in., (64.8 x 113 cm.), photograph, b/w mounted on board (BP 3042, DM 7366, FR 24,812, Y 574,555).
$2300* *"Bow And Arrow" and "Arrow And Bow": Two,* t., exec. 1972, prov., (02-23-93, Sotheby-NY, #318, illus.), each 13¾ x 10⅞ in., (34.9 x 27.6 cm.), photograph (BP 1576, DM 3716, FR 12,603, Y 268,629).
$9775* *"Crowned",* 1991, s., t., d. by photog. in ink, (04-06-93, Sotheby-NY, #501, illus.), sheet 30 x 22 in., photograph, color Polaroid print (BP 6456, DM 15,748, FR 53,328, Y 1,114,849).
$18,400* *Elephant,* 1980, ink s., t., d., exhib. labels, exhib. lit., (04-08-93, Christie-NY, #569, illus.), 21⅞ x 28 in., (55.6 x 71.1 cm.), photograph, polacolor II print (BP 12,066, DM 29,558, FR 100,054, Y 2,088,062).
$2070* *Front Ball, 1988: Two,* s., #3/7, (04-08-93, Christie-NY, #567, illus.), each 10½ x 10½ in., (26.7 x 26.7 cm.), overall 25 x 31 in., (26.7 x 26.7 cm.), photograph, gelatin silver print mounted together (BP 1357, DM 3325, FR 11,256, Y 234,907).
   BI *Front Ball: Two, 1988,* mounted together, s., num. 6/7, est. $2/3,000, (10-13-92, Christie-NY, #618, illus.), each 10½ x 10½ in., (26.7 x 26.7 cm.), photograph, gelatin silver prints.
$2200* *Rangeley, Maine, 1981,* s., t., d., num. 35/75 by photog. in white ink on image, #35/75 ed/, (10-15-92, Sotheby-NY, #608, illus.), 19½ x 19 in., (49.5 x 48.3 cm.), photograph, Type-C print (BP 1346, DM 3275, FR 11,106, Y 263,947).
$6900* *Reviewers, With Ed Ruscha, 1987,* ink s., t., d., (04-08-93, Christie-NY, #568, illus.), 24 x 20 in., (61 x 50.8 cm.), polacolor photograph (BP 4525, DM 11,084, FR 37,520, Y 783,023).
$3738* *Untitled (Fay Appearing To Gallop A La Muybridge), 1988: Series Of Foour,* mounted together, s., #3/7 by photog., (04-06-93, Sotheby-NY, #500, illus.), photograph (BP 2469, DM 6022, FR 20,393, Y 426,323).
$6325* *Untitled (Fay Running, After Muybridge) (Motion and Document, pp. 88-89), 1988: Series Of Four,* mounted together, s., #3/7 by photog., (04-06-93, Sotheby-NY, #499, illus.), photograph (BP 4178, DM 10,190, FR 34,506, Y 721,373).
$2475* *Untitled (Man Ray In Boots),* 1980/1989, s., d., (11-16-92, Butterfield, #6231, illus.), 6⅜ x 6⅜ in., (162.2 x 162.2 mm.), photograph, gelatin silver print (BP 1630, DM 3946, FR 13,292, Y 307,798).
$1980* *Untitled (Through Black #3): Three, 1988,* mounted as triptych, s., num. 3/7, (10-13-92, Christie-NY, #619, illus.), each 5 x 5 in., (12.7 x 12.7 cm.), overall 25 x 44 in., (12.7 x 12.7 cm.), photograph, gelatin silver prints (BP 1153, DM 2901, FR 9856, Y 240,087).
$5750* *Untitled, Pillow Yawn, 1988: Three,* s., #3/7, (04-08-93, Christie-NY, #566, illus.), each approx. 10½ x 10½ in., (26.7 x 26.7 cm.), overall 25 x 44 in., (26.7 x 26.7 cm.), photograph, gelatin silver print, mounted as triptych (BP 3770, DM 9237, FR 31,267, Y 652,519).

WEHRSCHMIDT, engraver, Daniel Albert
$117* *"Two Children With A St. Bernard Dog", 1904,* s., blindstamp, pub. Mawson, Swan and Morgan Ltd., (11-19-92, Bonhams-Chelsea, #82), image 15¾ x 15¾ in., (40 x 40 cm.), mezzotint (BP 77, DM 187, FR 628, Y 14,550).

WEIDENAAR, Renold H.
$330* *"Valley Of Wrath",* s. W.R. Locke, t., s., (05-15-93, Dunning, #228), etching (BP 215, DM 531, FR 1784, Y 36,581).

WEIDENAAR, Reynold   American 1915-1985
$25* *"Chicago Water Tower", "Plaza Tower" and "Tree Of Life-Hazy Cloud", c. 1978: Three,* s., good cond., (05-15-93, Cleveland, #337), offset lithograph (BP 16, DM 40, FR 135, Y 2771).
   BI *"The Dozing Tippler",* Weidenaar Trust No. 57, s., t., #38/200, good cond., paper tape, est. $2/300, (05-15-93, Cleveland, #336), drypoint.
$330* *"Yacht Club" and "They That Go Down To The Sea In Ships": Two,* s., t., num.; one hinged to mat, good cond.,

(12-04-92, Doyle, #156), larger 13 x 17 in., (330 x 432 mm.), drypoint (BP 212, DM 526, FR 1783, Y 41,199).

WEIDITZ, Hans
$607* *Grotesque Old Woman (Strauss 1508),* printing dryly, watermark, margins, creases, backed, ex. coll. Freiherr von Lanna (L. 2773), (06-29-93, Sotheby-London, #65, illus.), 11⅞ x 8¾ in., (30.2 x 22.2 cm.), woodcut on paper (BP 402, DM 1025, FR 3455, Y 64,616).

WEIDNER, Reynold   American 20th cent.
$193* *Repose,* s., t., good cond., (11-12-92, Freemn/Fine Art, #237), 10½ x 12¾ in., (26.7 x 32.4 cm.), mezzotint (BP 127, DM 306, FR 1032, Y 23,931).

WEIGHT, Carl
$76 *"Hommage To Claude Monet",* s., (06-11-93, G.A. Key, #30), 21 x 21 in., (53.3 x 53.3 cm.), colored poster (BP 50, DM 124, FR 416, Y 8064).

WEILUC
$3474* *Guilleminot Photographiques,* p. Societe Nouvelle d'Art & Decoration, folds, defects, creases, backed on linen, (05-07-93, Christie-S. Ken, #90, illus.), 47¼ x 63 in., (120 x 160 cm.), color lithograph (BP 2200, DM 5492, FR 18,508, Y 382,515).

WEINBERGER, Lois   b. 1947
   BI *Untitled,* s., d., num. Weinberger 86, #34/50, est. SC 3/6,000, (04-21-93, Dorotheum, #722), woodcut w/chalk rework.

WEINER, Dan   American 1919-1959
$770* *New Year's Eve, Times Square,* t., d. by photog., (c) stamp, 1951, p.l., (10-15-92, Sotheby-NY, #558, illus.), 8⅝ x 13 in., (21.9 x 33 cm.), photograph, gelatin silver print (BP 471, DM 1146, FR 3887, Y 92,382).

WEINER, Hans   c. 1575-ac. to 1619
   BI *Ecce Homo (Andresen 2),* est. DM 2,500, (12-04-92, Bassenge, #6501, illus.), 10⅞ x 7¹¹⁄₁₆ in., (27.6 x 19.6 cm.), etching.

WEINER, J.
$600 *Narren Aller Lander Vereinigt Euch,* folds, (09-24-92, Alderfer, #279), 32 x 21¼ in., (81.3 x 54 cm.), (BP 351, DM 889, FR 3020, Y 72,176).

WEINGARTNER, Adam
$460* *View Of Niagara Falls, Canadian Side,* after Thomas Benecke, c. 1855, pub. 1856, trimmed to image, good cond., strong backboard stain, smoke stains, (04-07-93, Sotheby-Arcade, #168), sheet 23⅛ x 33⅞ in., (58.7 x 86 cm.), color lithograph w/touches of hand-coloring on heavy wove (BP 304, DM 744, FR 2518, Y 52,261).

WEINMANN
$4025* *Botanical Engravings: Two,* Latin titles, (04-16-93, Sotheby-NY, #330, illus.), each 13½ x 8¾ in., (34.3 x 22.2 cm.), handcolored engraving (BP 2642, DM 6501, FR 21,971, Y 452,603).

WEINMANN, Johann
$2070* *Botanicals, c. 1735: Eight,* (03-03-93, Sotheby-Arcade, #147), sight 13½ x 9 in., (34.3 x 22.9 cm.), hand-colored mezzotint (BP 1428, DM 3409, FR 11,564, Y 241,879).
$2300* *Botanicals, c. 1736: Eight,* (04-07-93, Sotheby-Arcade, #280), sight 13½ x 9 in., (34.3 x 22.9 cm.), hand-colored mezzotint (BP 1520, DM 3720, FR 12,589, Y 261,304).

WEINSTOCK, Carol   American 20th cent.
$270* *Third Avenue, c. 1945,* good cond., label, (05-15-93, Cleveland, #338), 10½ x 15 in., (26.7 x 38.1 cm.), serigraph (BP 176, DM 434, FR 1459, Y 29,930).

WEIR, Captain James (after)
$185* *Battle Of The Nile, 1800,* by Thomas Hellyer, pub. J. Brydon, (01-14-93, Bonhams, #131), image 7 x 28 in., (17.8 x 71.1 cm.), hand-colored aquatint (BP 121, DM 302, FR 1023, Y 23,323).
$34* *Battle Of The Nile, 1800,* by Thomas Hellyer, pub. J. Brydon, repaired tear, trimmed, (01-14-93, Bonhams, #132), image 17 x 28 in., (43.2 x 71.1 cm.), hand-colored aquatint (BP 22, DM 56, FR 188, Y 4286).

WEIROTTER, Franz Edmund German 1730-1771
$161* *Paysages: Eight*, num., wormholes, tear, crease, (05-15-93, Loudmer, #106), approx. 4⁵⁄₁₆ x 7⅞ in., (110 x 200 mm.), sh approx. 5⅞ x 9⅝ in., (110 x 200 mm.), etching on laid (BP 105, DM 259, FR 870, Y 17,847).
$303* *Port Scene, 1763*, (10-18-92, Hindman, #503), 5⅜ x 7½ in., (13.7 x 19.1 cm.), etching (BP 185, DM 451, FR 1530, Y 36,353).

WEISBUCH, Claude French b. 1928
BI *Artist In His Studio*, est. $250/350, (05-15-93, Cleveland, #504), 21⅜ x 29⅞ in., (54.3 x 75.9 cm.), color lithograph on Arches.
BI *"Don Quichotte De La Mancha", 1970*, #89/200, s., est. FF6/800, (04-04-93, Pescheteau, #318), 13¹⁵⁄₁₆ x 19⅛ in., (35.5 x 48.5 cm.), color lithograph on wove.
BI *Le Violoncellists*, s., #64/100, prov., est. C$ 2/300, (12-01-92, Ritchie, #29), 15½ x 19½ in., (39.4 x 49.5 cm.), color etching.

WEISS, Bartholomaus Ignaz 1740-1814
BI *Brustbild Eines Knaben*, est. DM 120, (12-04-92, Bassenge, #6718), 6¼ x 4¹³⁄₁₆ in., (15.8 x 12.2 cm.), etching.

WELCH, Denton ac. 1938-1939
$1111* *To Visit Britain's Landmarks, Hadlow Castle, Kent, 1937*, p. Waterlow and Sons, ref. #496, cond. 3, corner missing outside image, (10-13-92, Phillips-London, #122, illus.), 29¹⁵⁄₁₆ x 44⅞ in., (76 x 114 cm.), color lithograph (BP 647, DM 1628, FR 5530, Y 134,716).

WELGOSS, James A.
$1320* *Face Montage, c. 1938*, credit & reprod. limit. stamps, (10-13-92, Christie-NY, #389, illus.), 9½ x 7½ in., (24.1 x 19.1 cm.), photograph, gelatin silver print (BP 769, DM 1934, FR 6570, Y 160,058).

WELLING, James b. 1951
$5280* *Bushing-Starry Night: Seven*, each t., d. "1-8-80" verso, s. twice, num. 1/7-7/7 WELLING on cardboard backing, prov., (10-08-92, Christie-NY, #231, illus.), each 4¾ x 3¾ in., (12 x 9.5 cm.), b/w photographs (BP 3142, DM 7809, FR 26,506, Y 641,555).
$1168* *Catenary 2, 1988*, photographer's stamp 'James Welling 1988', t., d. in ink 'Catenary 21988', i. in ink 'JW' verso, (10-15-92, Sotheby-London, #68, illus.), 9½ x 7⅛ in., (24.1 x 18.1 cm.), photograph, Polaroid (BP 715, DM 1739, FR 5896, Y 140,132).
$575* *Gelatin Photograph No. 47, 1984*, noted edit. 2/3, (10-15-92, Sotheby-London, #65, illus.), 19¾ x 15½ in., (50.2 x 39.4 cm.), photograph, silver print (BP 352, DM 856, FR 2903, Y 68,986).
$809* *Gelatin Photograph No. 51, 1984*, (10-15-92, Sotheby-London, #59, illus.), 19¾ x 15½ in., (50.2 x 39.4 cm.), photograph, silver print (BP 495, DM 1204, FR 4084, Y 97,061).
$2337* *Tile Photographs Nos. 12, 18 And 32, 1985*, nums. 18 and 32 noted edit. 1/3, num. 12 i. Tile Photograph #12 1985 verso, (10-15-92, Sotheby-London, #60, illus.), 19¾ x 15¾ in., (50.2 x 40 cm.), photograph, silver print (BP 1430, DM 3479, FR 11,797, Y 280,384).
$755* *Untitled (C-55), 1981*, edit. 6/12, (10-15-92, Sotheby-London, #63), each approx. 9½ x 7½ in., (24.1 x 19.1 cm.), photograph, gelatin silver print (BP 462, DM 1124, FR 3811, Y 90,582).
$4314* *Untitled (In Three Parts) 1982-1988*, (10-15-92, Sotheby-London, #66, illus.), each approx. 19¾ x 23⅝ in., (50.2 x 60 cm.), photograph, cibachrome (BP 2640, DM 6422, FR 21,777, Y 517,576).
BI *Untitled (In Three Parts) 1982-1988*, est. BP 6/1,000, (10-15-92, Sotheby-London, #67), 19¾ x 23⅝ in., (50.2 x 60 cm.), photograph, cibachrome.
$7550* *Untitled Diptych "XXXB/B" and "XXXIIIB/B (Brown Veil)", 1988*, (10-15-92, Sotheby-London, #62, illus.), each 23½ x 19½ in., (59.7 x 49.5 cm.), photograph, Polaroids (BP 4620, DM 11,238, FR 38,112, Y 905,819).
$1258* *Untitled [Beakers (Foil)], 1989*, num. 39, 78, 79, (10-15-92, Sotheby-London, #61, illus.), each approx. 48 x 78 in., (121.9 x 198.1 cm.), photograph, three silver prints (BP 770, DM 1873, FR 6350, Y 150,930).

$899* *Untitled [Beakers (Foil)], 1989*, num. B2, 3, 35, 39, (10-15-92, Sotheby-London, #64), each approx. 4¾ x 7¾ in., (12.1 x 19.7 cm.), photograph, four silver prints (BP 550, DM 1338, FR 4538, Y 107,858).

WELLIVER, Neil American b. 1929
BI *Henrik Ibsen Poems, 1987: Six*, book, pub. Vincent Fitzgerald & Company, bound, good cond., est. $2/2,500, (05-15-93, Sotheby-NY, #1271), overall 11¾ x 8⅝ in., (29.8 x 21.9 cm.), lithograph w/etching in colors on Dieu Donne handmade.

WELLS, Ben
$121* *The New York Sunday Journal*, B cond., fold marks, closed tears, water damage, (08-06-92, Swann, #291, illus.), 21 x 15 in., (53.3 x 38.1 cm.), (BP 63, DM 179, FR 604, Y 15,434).
$990* *Ringling Bros., Combined Shows, 1932*, Morgan Litho. Co., A- cond., closed tears, (08-06-92, Swann, #97, illus.), 28 x 41½ in., (71.1 x 105.4 cm.), (BP 517, DM 1463, FR 4940, Y 126,276).

WELLS, Clarence ac. 1980
$61* *Loon, 1975*, s., t., d. September 1975, prov., (11-16-92, Hodgins, #179), 12½ x 19½ in., (31.8 x 49.5 cm.), serigraph on paper (BP 40, DM 97, FR 328, Y 7613, C$ 77).

WELLS, H.G.
$4025* *The War Of The Worlds, 1898*, William Heinemann, in 8s, darkened, rubbing, cracking, bumping, s., 1st book ed., (06-14-93, Sotheby-NY, #348), 7⅜ x 5 in., (18.7 x 12.7 cm.), (BP 2635, DM 6551, FR 22,019, Y 423,550).

WELSH, Horace D.
$66* *A Winter's Night*, margins, s., exhib., (05-22-93, Collins, #70), 6 x 5½ in., (15.2 x 14 cm.), etching w/a touch of hand-coloring (BP 43, DM 107, FR 361, Y 7277).

WELY
$440* *Les Demoiselles Des St. Cyriens, 1898*, Ed. Delanchy, A cond., (08-06-92, Swann, #290, illus.), 31½ x 23½ in., (80 x 59.7 cm.), (BP 230, DM 650, FR 2196, Y 56,122).

WEMAERE, Pierre b. 1913
$92* *Composition*, s. P. Wemaere, (03-24-93, Kunsthallen, #336), color lithograph (BP 62, DM 150, FR 511, Y 10,810, DK 575).

WENCK, Paul German/American 20th cent.
$33* *"Sibelius"*, s., (12-02-92, Boos, #455), 11 x 8¼ in., (27.9 x 21 cm.), etching (BP 21, DM 52, FR 177, Y 4106).

WENDT, William J. (Jr.)
$55 *"Mr. Mouse"*, #15/50, s., (09-24-92, Alderfer, #296), 15 x 12 in., (38.1 x 30.5 cm.), woodblock (BP 32, DM 82, FR 277, Y 6616).

WENGENROTH, Stow American 1906-1976
$303* *Along The Canal (Stuckey 181), 1949*, s., (05-16-93, Hindman, #561), 7⅞ x 13⅜ in., (20 x 34 cm.), lithograph (BP 197, DM 487, FR 1638, Y 33,588).
$358* *"Along The Coast"*, s., good cond.?, (03-28-93, Bakker, #36), 7¼ x 13 in., (18.4 x 33 cm.), lithograph (BP 241, DM 584, FR 1986, Y 41,667).
BI *Bird Of Freedom*, margins, s. Stow Wengenroth, est. $6/800, (10-24-92, Collins, #5), 15¾ x 11¾ in., (40 x 29.8 cm.), lithograph.
$413* *"The Church"*, s., very good cond., (03-28-93, Bakker, #165), image 15½ x 11¼ in., (39.4 x 28.6 cm.), lithograph (BP 277, DM 674, FR 2291, Y 48,068).
$605* *Early Light (Stuckey 204), 1952*, full margins, s., (05-27-93, Swann, #290, illus.), 10½ x 15¾ in., (26.7 x 40 cm.), lithograph (BP 387, DM 971, FR 3272, Y 64,858).
$468* *"Fort Point Light, New Castle, New Hampshire, November" (Stuckey, 271), 1961*, s. Stow Wengenroth, num. Ed/50, good cond., glue residue, stains, thinning, (09-11-92, Skinner, #55, illus.), 11 x 15⅞ in., (27.9 x 40.3 cm.), lithograph on wove (BP 242, DM 674, FR 2290, Y 57,985).
BI *Grand Central, 1950*, s., skinned area, hinge, very good cond., est. $6/8,000, (12-04-92, Doyle, #162, illus.), 8¾ x 15⅞ in., (222 x 403 mm.), lithograph.

BI *Lanesville Harbor,* s., very good cond., est. $4/600, (12-04-92, Doyle, #157), 10¼ x 15¾ in., (260 x 400 mm.), lithograph.

$385* *"Lighthouse Beach",* s., very good cond., (03-28-93, Bakker, #136), image 8½ x 13¾ in., (21.6 x 34.9 cm.), lithograph (BP 259, DM 628, FR 2135, Y 44,809).

$495* *"Little Owl" (Stuckey, 304), 1966,* s. Stow Wengenroth, #Ed/65, very good cond., tape, (03-12-93, Skinner, #44, illus.), 10½ x 16⅜ in., (26.7 x 41.6 cm.), lithograph in black w/cream toning stone (BP 345, DM 824, FR 2801, Y 58,338).

BI *"Maine Lobsterman" (Stuckey 144), 1944,* s., The Print Club of Cleveland Publication No. 22, excellent cond.,est. $4-500, (10-31-92, Cleveland, #233, illus.), 8⅛ x 12 in., (20.6 x 30.5 cm.), lithograph.

$210* *"Maine Lobsterman" (Stuckey 144), 1945,* s., The Print Club of Cleveland Publication No. 22 for 1944, good cond., toning, (05-15-93, Cleveland, #339), 8⅛ x 12 in., (20.6 x 30.5 cm.), lithograph (BP 137, DM 338, FR 1135, Y 23,279).

$550* *Matriarch,* s., hinged, very good cond., (12-04-92, Doyle, #160), 13¼ x 11 in., (337 x 279 mm.), lithograph (BP 353, DM 876, FR 2971, Y 68,664).

$303* *"Morning Light",* s., edit. of 50, very good cond., (03-28-93, Bakker, #92), image 8½ x 13 in., (21.6 x 33 cm.), lithograph (BP 204, DM 494, FR 1681, Y 35,265).

$385* *Old North Church,* s., very good cond., (12-04-92, Doyle, #163), 15⅞ x 11 in., (403 x 279 mm.), lithograph (BP 247, DM 613, FR 2080, Y 48,065).

$303* *"Pennsylvania Country, New Hope, Pennsylvania, July" (Stuckey, 125),1943,* s. Stow Wengenroth, num. Ed/40, t., very good cond., staining, toning, tape residue verso, (09-11-92, Skinner, #56, illus.), 8⅜ x 15¹³⁄₁₆ in., (21.3 x 40.2 cm.), lithograph on wove (BP 157, DM 436, FR 1482, Y 37,542).

$550* *Quiet Day,* s., foxing, hinged, good cond., (12-04-92, Doyle, #159), 7⅜ x 12⅝ in., (187 x 321 mm.), lithograph (BP 353, DM 876, FR 2971, Y 68,664).

$715* *Roadside Garden (Stuckey 298), 1965,* s., (05-27-93, Swann, #291, illus.), 10⅞ x 15⅞ in., (27.6 x 40.3 cm.), lithograph (BP 458, DM 1147, FR 3867, Y 76,651).

$1100* *"Season's End, Port Clyde, Maine, December" (Stuckey, 226), 1955,* s. Stow Wengenroth, num. Ed/40, good cond., laid down, light toning,annot., (09-11-92, Skinner, #54A, illus.), 9¼ x 15¹⁷⁄₁₆ in., (23.5 x 38.1 cm.), lithograph on wove (BP 569, DM 1583, FR 5382, Y 136,290).

$495* *Sound Shore,* s., old hinges, very good cond., (12-04-92, Doyle, #158), 9¾ x 13¾ in., (248 x 349 mm.), lithograph (BP 318, DM 788, FR 2674, Y 61,798).

BI *Steps To The Sky,* s., prov., est. $750/850, (09-17-92, Sloan, #3086), 9⅞ x 11⅝ in., (25.1 x 29.5 cm.), lithograph.

$385* *Summer (S. 274),* s., i. ed. 45, (11-12-92, Freemn/Fine Art, #239, illus.), 15 x 10¹³⁄₁₆ in., (38.1 x 27.5 cm.), litho (BP 253, DM 610, FR 2058, Y 47,737).

$522* *"Sunlight, Wiscasset" and "Warner House, Portsmouth, N.H.", c. 1970:Two,* s., full margins, (12-08-92, Swann, #312), first 9⅞ x 15⅞ in., (25.1 x 40.3 cm.), second 11⅜ x 15⅞ in., (25.1 x 40.3 cm.), lithograph (BP 327, DM 813, FR 2771, Y 64,700).

$230* *Surf At Bass Rocks (S. 364),* s., #Ed/80, full margins, good cond., surface soiling, notations, (05-19-93, Butterfield, #2027), 8⁷⁄₁₆ x 13¹⁵⁄₁₆ in., (214 x 354 mm.), lithograph on wove (BP 149, DM 374, FR 1260, Y 25,462).

$375* *"The White Fence",* s. Stucky 318, edit. 50, (02-27-93, Young, #324), 10 x 15 in., (25.4 x 38.1 cm.), lithograph (BP 264, DM 616, FR 2095, Y 44,269).

$413* *"The Wild Coast",* s., (12-12-92, Litchfield, #251), image 10¼ x 15⁵⁄₁₆ in., (26 x 38.9 cm.), lithograph (BP 265, DM 651, FR 2230, Y 51,108).

BI *"Winter" (S. 230), 1956,* s., num., sun struck, est. $3-400, (10-31-92, Cleveland, #234), 9½ x 15¾ in., (24.1 x 40 cm.), lithograph.

WENINGER, Emmerich

BI *Mistinguett, 1933,* Waldheim-Eberle A.G., B cond., 3 part poster, creasing, chipping, est. $4/600, (08-06-92, Swann, #292, illus.), 108 x 48½ in., (274.3 x 123.2 cm.), .

WERKMAN, Hendrik Nicolaas Dutch 1882-1945

BI *Composition, 1944,* full sheet p. to edges, good cond., small crease in lower left corner of sheet, Late Gerhard Brauer Coll., est. Dfl. 12/18,000, (05-27-93, Sotheby-Amstrdm, #837, illus.), sheet 19¹¹⁄₁₆ x 12¹³⁄₁₆ in., (500 x 325 mm.), stamping in colors on brown wood free satined card.

BI *Gesprek (Hot Printing 42-G2), 1942,* booklet, pub. De Blauwe Schuit, good cond., minor creasing, soiling,Late Gerhard Brauer Coll., est. Dfl. 1/1,500, (05-27-93, Sotheby-Amstrdm, #839), sheet 12½ x 8⅝ in., (318 x 219 mm.), color stencil.

$576* *Holland (Hot Printing 42-G17), 1942,* pub. De Blauwe Schuit, good cond., Late Gerhard Blauer Coll., (05-27-93, Sotheby-Amstrdm, #802), 10¹¹⁄₁₆ x 8½ in., (271 x 216 mm.), booklet, stencil in colors (BP 369, DM 924, FR 3115, Y 61,750, G 1035).

BI *Kerstmis In Friesland (Hot Printing 43-G1), 1943,* pub. De Blauwe Schuit, good cond., very minor foxing, Late Gerhard Brauer Coll., est. Dfl. 800/1,200, (05-27-93, Sotheby-Amstrdm, #801), 8⅞ x 6⅛ in., (225 x 156 mm.), booklet, stencil in colors.

$371* *Psalmen (Hot Printing 42-G18), 1942,* incomplete, pub. De Blauwe Schuit, missing back cover and 4 pgs., minor defects at edges of sheets, Late Gerhard Brauer Coll., (05-27-93, Sotheby-Amstrdm, #803), 10⁵⁄₁₆ x 6⁷⁄₁₆ in., (262 x 164 mm.), booklet, stencil in colors (BP 238, DM 595, FR 2006, Y 39,773, G 667).

$1407* *Turkenkalender, 1942,* booklet, pub. De Blauwe Schuit, good cond., minor paper discoloration, foxing, minor defects, Late Gerhard Brauer Coll., (05-27-93, Sotheby-Amstrdm, #838), 12¹³⁄₁₆ x 10⅛ in., (325 x 257 mm.), color stencil (BP 901, DM 2258, FR 7610, Y 150,836, G 2530).

$179* *Voerman Met Paarden (Hot Printing 23-LG1), 1923,* s., margins, paper discoloration, occasional handling creases, stripof card glued along top margins, Late Gerhard Brauer Coll., (05-27-93, Sotheby-Amstrdm, #799, illus.), 9³⁄₁₆ x 10½ in., (234 x 266 mm.), lithograph on wove (BP 115, DM 287, FR 968, Y 19,190, G 322).

$154* *Walhalla (Hot Printing 42-11), 1942,* pub. De Blauwe Schuit, good cond., occasional foxing, Late Gerhard Brauer Coll., (05-27-93, Sotheby-Amstrdm, #800), 8¹³⁄₁₆ x 7 in., (224 x 178 mm.), booklet, stencil in colors (BP 99, DM 247, FR 833, Y 16,509, G 276).

WERNER, Carl Friedrich Heinrich

$550* *Vedute Dell'Assedio Di Roma Del 1849 ... Views Of The Siege Of Rome In 1849: Twelve,* plates by Domenico Amici, oblong folio, orig. wrappers, (11-12-92, Swann, #129), 12⅜ x 18½ in., (315 x 470 mm.), etching (BP 361, DM 871, FR 2940, Y 68,196).

WERNER, V.

$39* *"Der Koenigs See",* (01-15-93, DuMouchelle, #2367), image 10¼ x 13½ in., (26 x 34.3 cm.), etching (BP 25, DM 64, FR 216, Y 4917).

WERRO, Roland b. 1926

BI *Komposition,* XXVII/XXX, s., est. SF 60/80, (10-14-92, Germann, #632), 29¹⁵⁄₁₆ x 22¹⁄₁₆ in., (760 x 560 mm.), color serigraph.

WERY, Emile Auguste French 1868-1935

BI *La Petite Bretonne, 1897,* proof, est. $3/400, (05-16-93, Hindman, #452), 10⅛ x 13⅞ in., (25.7 x 35.2 cm.), color lithograph.

WESCOUPE, Clemence b. 1951

$102* *'Mother And Child',* #181/500, s., (10-21-92, Maynard, #48), 13½ x 10 in., (34.3 x 25.4 cm.), silkscreen (BP 63, DM 154, FR 524, Y 12,424, C$ 127).

WESSELMANN, Tom American b. 1931

$1380* *11 Pop Artists, Volume II: Nude, 1965,* s., #197/200, pub. Original Editions, (05-19-93, Butterfield, #2379), 23⅞ x 29¾ in., (606 x 756 mm.), silkscreen in colors on wove (BP 896, DM 2243, FR 7558, Y 152,773).

BI *Bedroom Blond Doodle,* s., d. (19)88, i., #7/12, 1 of 12 artist's proofs, est. $12/15,000, (09-17-92, Sloan, #3119, illus.), 46½ x 52¾ in., (118.1 x 134 cm.), color silk-screen.

BI *Bedroom Collage (S. p. 285), 1974,* s., #7/20, t., d., num., excellent cond., est. $7/9,000, (11-09-92, Christie-NY, #450, illus.), 4½ x 8½ in., (114 x 216 mm.), pencil, liquitex and collage in colors on canvas laid down on Masonite.

BI *Bedroom Dropout, 1983,* s., d., #17/50, Multiples, Inc., blindstamp, full margins, glued down verso, excellent cond., est. $1,5/2,000, (11-09-92, Christie-NY, #453), 24¾ x 29 in., (629 x 737 mm.), colored woodcut on wove.

BI *Bedroom Droupout, 1983,* s., d., #26/50, blindstamp, pub. Multiples New York, good cond., soiling, est. BP 6/800, (12-03-92, Sotheby-London, #857, illus.), sheet 24½ x 28¾ in., (620 x 732 mm.), woodcut in colors on Japan.

$1980* *Bedroom Face (S., p. 286), 1978,* from Bedroom Portfolio, s., d., num. 3/20, pub. by artist, full margins, excell. cond., (09-19-92, Christie-E, #246), sheet 9¹⁵⁄₁₆ x 11 in., (252 x 279 mm.), pencil and thinned Liquitex w/embossing on wove (BP 1139, DM 2965, FR 10,154, Y 246,698).

BI *Bedroom Face Print, 1987,* s., d., #49/100, pub. International Images, margins, est. $3,8/4,200, (05-11-93, Christie-NY, #610, illus.), borderline 46¾ x 53¾ in., (118.7 x 136.5 cm.), color screenprint on Museum Board.

$4180* *Bedroom Face Print, 1987,* s., d., #16/100, pub. International Images, margins, (11-09-92, Christie-NY, #454, illus.), 46¾ x 52⅞ in., (118.7 x 134.3 cm.), colored screenprint on Museum board (BP 2764, DM 6673, FR 22,546, Y 518,739).

BI *Bedroom Face, 1977,* s., d., num. 69/79, ,argins, excell. cond., est. BP 1,2/1,400, (12-01-92, Christie-London, #648), P. 16⁹⁄₁₆ x 23⅝ in., (420 x 600 mm.), aquatint in colors on wove.

$3634* *Big Blond, 1991,* #73/100, s., (04-21-93, Germann, #50, illus.), 30⅛ x 34¹³⁄₁₆ in., (765 x 885 mm.), color serigraph (BP 2358, DM 5809, FR 19,643, Y 402,303, SF 5290).

$6900* *Big Blonde (I. I. 6), 1989,* s., #12/100, pub. International Images, Inc., good cond. ?, (05-15-93, Sotheby-NY, #1273, illus.), sheet 55 x 74 in., (139.7 x 188 cm.), silkscreen in colors (BP 4486, DM 11,099, FR 37,297, Y 764,882).

$6325* *Blonde Vivienne (International Images 5), 1988,* s., d. '89, i. HC 7/12, pub. International Images, good cond. ?, (05-15-93, Sotheby-NY, #1272, illus.), sheet 55¾ x 56¾ in., (141.6 x 144.1 cm.), silkscreen in colors (BP 4112, DM 10,174, FR 34,189, Y 701,142).

BI *Blone Woman With Daffodils,* s., i. AP 12/12, est. $3/5000, (06-11-93, Freemn/Fine Art, #250), 50 x 58 in., (127 x 147.3 cm.), screenprint.

BI *Claire Nude, 1980,* s., d., #AP 22/25, pub. Transworld Art, full margins, very good cond., crease, est. $2,5/3,500, (10-28-92, Butterfield, #3169), 25 x 24 in., (635 x 610 mm.), color lithograph w/silkscreen on wove.

$495* *A Country Bouquet For Tammy, 1989,* s., #21/82, blindstamp pub. International Images, full margins, verygood cond., crease, (10-28-92, Butterfield, #3170), 26⅜ x 18¼ in., (670 x 464 mm.), silkscreen in black on heavy white wove (BP 315, DM 764, FR 2596, Y 60,736).

BI *Cut-Out Nude, 1965,* s., #107/200, from 11 Pop Artists, New York 1965, Original Editions,est. DM 10,000, (06-12-93, Hauswedell/Nolt, #459, illus.), 7⅝ x 18¹⁄₁₆ in., (19.3 x 45.8 cm.), color serigraph on light board.

$1840* *Cynthia In The Bedroom, 1982,* s., d. 81, i. AP, #16/25, pub. Transworld Art, full margins, excell.cond., (05-11-93, Christie-NY, #608, illus.), sheet 33½ x 36½ in., (851 x 927 mm.), color screenprint on wove (BP 1175, DM 2899, FR 9766, Y 202,398).

$2185* *Cynthia Nude, 1982,* s., d. 81, i. AP, #8/20, Multiples, Inc. blindstamp, full margins, crease, excell. cond., (05-11-93, Christie-NY, #609, illus.), sheet 29 x 38½ in., (737 x 978 mm.), color screenprint and lithograph on Arches (BP 1395, DM 3442, FR 11,598, Y 240,348).

$2294* *Fast Sketch Nude With Red Stockings, 1991,* 73/100, s., pub. International Images, NY, (10-14-92, Germann, #112, illus.), 25¹⁵⁄₁₆ x 38⁹⁄₁₆ in., (660 x 980 mm.), color serigraph (BP 1346, DM 3357, FR 11,385, Y 277,993, SF 2990).

BI *Fast Sketch Still Life With Abstract Painting, 1989,* s., d., #53/100, pub. International Images, full margins, excellent cond., est. $4/5,000, (11-09-92, Christie-NY, #456, illus.), 57 x 84 in., (144.8 x 213.4 cm.), colored screenprint on wove.

BI *Feet, 1968,* #18/150, d., s., est. DM 2,500, (11-13-92, Kunsthaus, #901), 18¹⁄₁₆ x 18¹⁄₁₆ in., (45.8 x 45.8 cm.), screen print on Halbkarton.

$1840* *Helen Nude, 1981,* s., d., #56/150, pyb. Transworld Art, full margins, excell. cond., sold after sale, (05-11-93, Christie-NY, #607), sheet 35 x 36¾ in., (889 x 933 mm.), color screenprint on wove (BP 1175, DM 2899, FR 9766, Y 202,398).

$2420* *Helen Nude, 1981,* s., d., i. AP, #4/20, pub. Transworld Art, full margins, excellent cond., (11-09-92, Christie-NY, #452, illus.), 36 x 37 in., (914 x 940 mm.), colored screenprint on wove (BP 1600, DM 3863, FR 13,053, Y 300,323).

$3642* *Lulu,* blindstamp, stamp, s., num., (09-19-92, Wachholtz, #839, illus.), 16¾ x 25⅛ in., (42.5 x 63.8 cm.), color serigrpah on copper print board (BP 2132, DM 5404, FR 18,487, Y 450,130).

$1185* *Monica Reclining On Back, Knees Up (Gefrat S. 125),* HC #12/12, s., lit., (04-21-93, Germann, #831, illus.), 3¹⁵⁄₁₆ x 5½ in., (10 x 14 cm.), lithograph and linocut (BP 769, DM 1894, FR 6405, Y 131,186, SF 1725).

$3450* *Monica With Tulips, 1980,* s., i. HC, #5/12, International Images blindstamp, full margins, excell. cond., (05-11-93, Christie-NY, #611, illus.), sheet 35⅞ x 44⅞ in., (91.1 x 114 cm.), color screenprint on Museum Board (BP 2202, DM 5435, FR 18,312, Y 379,496).

$2420* *Nude (For Sedfre) (Stealingworth p. 284), 1969,* s., d., #16/100, blindstamp, full margins, scrapes, soiling, very good cond., (11-09-92, Christie-NY, #449, illus.), 23 x 29 in., (584 x 737 mm.), colored screenprint on Strathmore (BP 1600, DM 3863, FR 13,053, Y 300,323).

$2860* *Nude (For Sedfre) (Stealingworth, p. 284), 1969,* s., d., num. 12/100, Chiron Press blindstamp, full margins, scrape, very good cond., (09-19-92, Christie-E, #243), sheet 23 x 29 in., (584 x 737 mm.), screenprint in colors on Strathmore (BP 1645, DM 4283, FR 14,667, Y 356,342).

$1100* *Nude (S., p. 285), 1976,* s., d., num. 9/75, Multiples, Inc. blindstamp, full margins, pinholes, good cond., (09-19-92, Christie-E, #244), sheet 26 x 19½ in., (660 x 495 mm.), lithograph and screenprint in colors w/embossing on wove (BP 633, DM 1647, FR 5641, Y 137,055).

BI *Nude And Mirror, 1990,* s., #96/100, blindstamp pub. International Images, full margins, very good cond.?, est. $2/3,000, (10-28-92, Butterfield, #3171), color silk-screen on Museum Board.

$1027* *Sea Scape,* #44/100, s., (04-21-93, Germann, #830), 20⅞ x 43⁵⁄₁₆ in., (53 x 110 cm.), color serigraph (BP 666, DM 1642, FR 5551, Y 113,694, SF 1495).

$2200* *Smoker (Institute of Contemporary Art 22), 1976,* s., i. 'XXXII/L', artist's proof, from portfolio An American Portrait, 1776-1976, pub. blindstamp, Transworld Art, full margins, good cond., (11-07-92, Sotheby-NY, #827, illus.), 16⅜ x 16⅜ in., (416 x 416 mm.), silkscreen p. in colors on buff Museum Rag board (BP 1438, DM 3513, FR 11,873, Y 271,538).

$1100* *Smoker (S., p. 285), 1976,* s., d., num. 66/75, Multiples, Inc. blindstamp, full margins, light/time staining, very good cond., (09-19-92, Christie-E, #245, illus.), sheet 22¾ x 30³⁄₁₆ in., (578 x 767 mm.), lithograph in colors w/embossing on Arches (BP 633, DM 1647, FR 5641, Y 137,055).

BI *Smoker (Silkscreen) (S., p. 285), 1976,* from An American Portrait, 1776-1976, Transworld Art, s., #140/175, blindstamp, full margins, scuffs in image, excellent cond., est. $1,8/2,400, (11-09-92, Christie-NY, #451), 26 x 19⅜ in., (660 x 492 mm.), colored screenprint on Museum Rag board.

BI *Smoker, 1976,* s., num. XXVII/L, pub. by Transworld Art, full margins, excell. cond., (12-01-92, Christie-London, #647), 16⁵⁄₁₆ x 16⁵⁄₁₆ in., (415 x 415 mm.), screenprint in colors on Museum Rag Board.

BI *Steel Drawing Edition/Monica Lying Down On Robe, 1986-90,* incised sig., d., #16/25, co-pub. artist and Sidney Janis Gallery, est. $5/7,000, (05-15-93, Sotheby-NY, #1275, illus.), overall 14⅛ x 5½ in., (35.9 x 14 cm.), steel laser cut in color enamel.

BI *Steel Drawing Edition/Rosemary Lying On One Elbow, 1989,* incised sig., d., #3/45, co-pub. artist and Sidney Janis Gallery, est. $5/7,000, (05-15-93, Sotheby-NY, #1274, illus.), overall 8⅛ x 14⅝ in., (20.6 x 37.1 cm.), steel laser cut in color enamel.

BI *Steel Drawing Edition/Rosemary With Socks, Arms Outstretched, 1989-90,* incised sig., d., #15/25, co-pub. artist and Sidney Janis Gallery, est. $5/7,000, (05-15-93, Sotheby-NY, #1276, illus.), overall 10¼ x 11¾ in., (26 x 29.8 cm.), steel laser cut in color enamel.

$5520* *Still Life Collage (Stealingworth, p. 285), 1974,* s., d., #16/20 twice, excell. cond., (05-11-93, Christie-NY, #606, illus.), 5¼ x 7 in., (133 x 178 mm.), pencil, liquitex and collage in colors on canvas laid down on masonite board (BP 3524, DM 8696, FR 29,299, Y 607,194).

$2200* *Still Life With Fishbowl And Compote,* s., #69/100, (12-13-92, Hindman, #348, illus.), 45¾ x 71½ in., color serigraph (BP 1407, DM 3457, FR 11,784, Y 272,176).

$3850* *Woman In Green Blouse, 1988,* edit. pp 2/3, s., d., num., (09-21-92, Selkirk, #340, illus.), 60⅛ x 73⅞ in., (152.7 x 187.6 cm.), serigraph (BP 2254, DM 5713, FR 19,543, Y 475,837).

BI *Woman In Green Blouse, 1988,* s., d., #55/100, pub. International Images, full margins, excellent cond., est. $4/4,500, (11-09-92, Christie-NY, #455, illus.), 60 x 74 in., (152.4 x 188 cm.), screenprint on wove.

$2200* *Woman With Green Blouse,* s., d. 88, #50/100, (12-13-92, Hindman, #347, illus.), 48¼ x 60½ in., serigraph (BP 1407, DM 3457, FR 11,784, Y 272,176).

$2530* *Woman With Green Blouse, 1988,* s., d., #55/100, pub. International Images, Inc., full margins, goodcond., (02-11-93, Sotheby-NY, #466), 47⅝ x 60¼ in., (121 x 153 cm.), silkscreen (BP 1785, DM 4191, FR 14,182, Y 305,003).

WEST, Benjamin

BI *The Angel Of The Resurrection (Man 137), 1801,* 4th final state, creases through subject, tear, stitch marks, defects, est. BP 2/3,000, (06-30-93, Sotheby-London, #254, illus.), 12¾ x 8¾ in., (324 x 222 mm.), pen-lithograph on wove, on support sheet w/dark chocolate-brown aquatint surround w/watermark J. Whatman 1794.

BI *The Angel Of The Resurrection (Man 137), 1801,* 4th final state, trimmed, paper loss, creasing, defects, est. BP 1,5/2,000, (06-30-93, Sotheby-London, #255), 12¼ x 9 in., (311 x 229 mm.), pen-lithograph on support sheet w/ pale brown aquatint surround.

WEST, Benjamin (after)

BI *The Apparition Of Samuel To Saul,* by William Sharp, scratch-letter proof before t., trimmed to image, repaired corners, est. BP 70/100, (11-30-92, Phillips-London, #137), sheet 17⅞ x 23¼ in., (454 x 591 mm.), engraving.

BI *Daniel Interpreting To Belshazzar The Writing On The Wall, 1777,* by Valentine Green, scratch-letter proof, pub. John Boydell, trimmed,tears, est. BP 2/250, (11-30-92, Phillips-London, #135), sheet 20½ x 27½ in., (521 x 699 mm.), mezzotint on laid.

$220* *The Death Of Lord Viscount Nelson,* by James Heath, (04-02-93, Sloan, #2274), sight 17 x 23⅝ in., (432 x 600 mm.), engraving (BP 145, DM 354, FR 1201, Y 25,048).

$433* *The Death Of Lord Viscount Nelson, 1811,* by James Heath, pub. West & Heath, trimmed to plate, good cond., (11-30-92, Phillips-London, #242), image 17¼ x 23¾ in., (438 x 603 mm.), mixed-method engraving on laid (BP 286, DM 690, FR 2342, Y 53,889).

BI *Mr. West And Family, 1779,* by G.S. & J.G. Facius, watermark, pub. John Boydell, trimmed to imageon 3 sides, repaired tears through image, foxing, mould staining, est. BP 120/180, (11-30-92, Phillips-London, #220), sheet 21½ x 25¾ in., (546 x 654 mm.), stipple engraving on laid.

$183* *Mr. West And Family, 1779,* by G.S. and J.G. Facius, pub. John Boydell, image defects repaired, trimmed, margins, (11-30-92, Phillips-London, #221), sheet 22½ x

27⅓ in., (572 x 694 mm.), hand-colored stipple engraving on laid (BP 121, DM 292, FR 990, Y 22,775).

$468* *William Penn's Treaty With The Indians,* by John Hall, pub. John Boydell, (06-11-93, Freemn/Fine Art, #251), 16¾ x 23 in., (42.5 x 58.4 cm.), engraving (BP 307, DM 761, FR 2564, Y 49,655).

WEST, Levon   American 1900-1968

$125* *"Bald Headed Aft" and "Driving Carriages In The Rain", 1927: Two,* s., t., num., good cond., glue residue, (05-15-93, Cleveland, #341), one 11⅛ x 9⅜ in., (28.3 x 23.8 cm.), other 2¾ x 1¾ in., (28.3 x 23.8 cm.), drypoint (BP 81, DM 201, FR 676, Y 13,857).

$138* *Cowboy Of The West,* s. Levon West in matrix, Levon West imp, good cond., (06-26-93, Skinner, #95), image, sight 8⅝ x 7¾ in., (21.9 x 19.7 cm.), drypoint on paper (BP 92, DM 234, FR 790, Y 14,642).

$165* *Duck Hunting,* margins, s. Levon West, (02-13-93, Collins, #56, illus.), 10⅜ x 13⅜ in., (26.4 x 34 cm.), etching (BP 116, DM 274, FR 926, Y 19,899).

$130* *"English Bay" (Torrington 91 ii/ii), 1927,* s., t., #49/100, p. by artist, mint cond., (05-15-93, Cleveland, #340), 9 x 10⅞ in., (22.9 x 27.6 cm.), etching on laid paper (BP 85, DM 209, FR 703, Y 14,411).

$165* *Men On Horseback In Snow,* s., (11-13-92, DuMouchelle, #2367), 12 x 15 in., (30.5 x 38.1 cm.), etching (BP 107, DM 259, FR 873, Y 20,479).

WESTALL

$805* *Mansions In England, c. 1820: Eight,* (03-03-93, Sotheby-Arcade, #123), sight 5½ x 8 in., (14 x 20.3 cm.), hand-colored aquatint (BP 555, DM 1326, FR 4497, Y 94,064).

WESTALL, Richard (after)

BI *Fidelia, 1819,* by Louis Schiavonetti, pub. Hurst, Robinson & Co., trimmed, repairedtears, light-staining, est. BP 120/150, (11-30-92, Phillips-London, #159), sheet 24 x 18¾ in., (610 x 476 mm.), stipple engraving in colors on wove.

$67* *The Infant Bacchus, 1804,* by H.R. Cook, pub. Clay & Scriven, tear, creased, defects, foxing, (11-30-92, Phillips-London, #158), plate 16¾ x 19½ in., (425 x 495 mm.), stipple engraving on wove (BP 44, DM 107, FR 362, Y 8339).

$182* *Innocent Mishchief,* by Christian Josi, pub. 1796, margins, surface dirt, (06-16-93, Bonhams-Chelsea, #491), pl. 18½ x 14½ in., (47 x 36.8 cm.), stipple engraving (BP 121, DM 302, FR 1014, Y 19,411).

WESTON, Brett   b. 1911

$1093* *Agave Leaves, 1964,* p.l., s., d., (05-23-93, Butterfield, #3667, illus.), 9¾ x 7¾ in., photograph, gelatin silver print (BP 712, DM 1787, FR 6015, Y 120,814).

$1150* *"Arches", 1971,* plate from Europe portfolio, eslf-pub. 1973, mounted, s., d. by photog., t., d., #12, i. in unident. hand, (04-06-93, Sotheby-NY, #431A, illus.), 12 x 10¼ in., photograph (BP 760, DM 1853, FR 6274, Y 131,159).

$990* *"Beach Pool, Oregon" (Five Decades, p. 42), 1972,* s., d., (11-16-92, Butterfield, #6239, illus.), 7⅝ x 9⅝ in., (194 x 244.9 mm.), photograph, gelatin silver print (BP 652, DM 1578, FR 5317, Y 123,119).

BI *"Blistered Paint, CA", 1978,* s., d., est. $1,5/2,000, (05-23-93, Butterfield, #3666, illus.), 12¾ x 10¾ in., photograph, gelatin silver print.

$805* *Broken Window, 1970,* mounted, s., d. by photog., (04-06-93, Sotheby-NY, #432, illus.), 8¾ x 7⅝ in., photograph (BP 532, DM 1297, FR 4392, Y 91,811).

$1100* *Cacti,* photog.'s sig., d. on mount, 1966, p. 1969,, (04-07-93, Swann, #590, illus.), 7½ x 9½ in., photograph, silver print (BP 727, DM 1779, FR 6021, Y 124,972).

$1100* *Canyon De Chelle, 1959,* s., d., (11-16-92, Butterfield, #6237, illus.), 9⅝ x 7⅝ in., (244.9 x 194 mm.), photograph, gelatin silver print (BP 724, DM 1754, FR 5908, Y 136,799).

BI *Carmel Valley, California (Master Photographer, pl. 63),* mounted, s., d. y photog., exhib. label d. 1964, 1954, p. before 1965, est. $2/3,000, (10-15-92, Sotheby-NY, #494, illus.), 10¼ x 13⅝ in., (26 x 34.6 cm.), photograph, gelatin silver print.

$1495* *"Dead Leaf, Hawaii", 1982,* s., t., d., (05-23-93, Butterfield, #3664, illus.), 12 x 11 in., photograph, gelatin silver print (BP 974, DM 2444, FR 8228, Y 165,248).

$11,000* *Fifteen Photographs, c. 1961,* portfolio of 14 (of 15) photos, each mounted, s., d. by photog., 1934-61, together w/photo of Brett Weston with his Camera by DIANA SELSOR, i. Photography by Diana Selsor by Weston, label, folio, i., s., d. by photog. Para Diana-con amor, Brett-Carmel 1965, est. $7/10,000, (10-15-92, Sotheby-NY, #493, illus.), each, approx. 9½ x 7½ in., (24.1 x 19.1 cm.), photograph, gelatin silver prints (BP 6731, DM 16,374, FR 55,528, Y 1,319,736).

$2070* *Glen Canyon, 1957,* s., d., (05-23-93, Butterfield, #3660, illus.), 9½ x 7½ in., photograph, gelatin silver print (BP 1348, DM 3385, FR 11,392, Y 228,805).

$605* *Guatemala, 1968,* (05-16-93, Hindman, #336), 18½ x 14⅝ in., photograph, silver print (BP 395, DM 976, FR 3288, Y 67,372).

$6050* *Holland Canal, 1971 (Master Photographer, pl. 103),* mounted, s. by photog., (10-15-92, Sotheby-NY, #501, illus.), 13¾ x 10¾ in., (34.9 x 27.3 cm.), photograph, gelatin silver print (BP 3702, DM 9006, FR 30,540, Y 725,855).

$9900* *Holland Canal, 1971 (Master Photographer, pl. 103),* mounted, s. by photog., (10-15-92, Sotheby-NY, #502, illus.), 19½ x 15¼ in., (49.5 x 38.7 cm.), photograph, gelatin silver print (BP 6058, DM 14,737, FR 49,975, Y 1,187,762).

$2070* *Horizontal Nude, 1976,* s., d., (05-23-93, Butterfield, #3663, illus.), 10½ x 13½ in., photograph, gelatin silver print (BP 1348, DM 3385, FR 11,392, Y 228,805).

BI *Ice Abstraction, 1953 (Master Photographer, pl. 49),* s., d. by photog., est. $2/3,000, (10-15-92, Sotheby-NY, #496, illus.), 14¾ x 18½ in., (37.5 x 47 cm.), photograph, gelatin silver print.

$5750* *Industrial Study, 1936,* mounted, s., d. by photog., (04-06-93, Sotheby-NY, #430, illus.), 7⅝ x 9⅛ in., photograph (BP 3798, DM 9264, FR 31,369, Y 655,794).

BI *Ironwork Detail, 1956,* s., d., est. $1,5/2,000, (05-23-93, Butterfield, #3661, illus.), 9½ x 7½ in., photograph, gelatin silver print.

$1320* *Kelp, 1954,* inits., d., s. in ink, (10-13-92, Christie-NY, #507, illus.), 10⅜ x 13⅝ in., (26.4 x 34.6 cm.), photograph, gelatin silver print (BP 769, DM 1934, FR 6570, Y 160,058).

BI *Kelp, 1967,* mounted, s., d. by photog., est. $1,5/2,500, (10-15-92, Sotheby-NY, #497, illus.), 9⅝ x 7½ in., (24.4 x 19.1 cm.), photograph, gelatin silver print.

$1100* *Mendenhall Glacier, 1973 (Master Photographer, pl. 85),* mounted, s., d. by photog., (10-15-92, Sotheby-NY, #500, illus.), 7⅝ x 9½ in., (19.4 x 24.1 cm.), photograph, gelatin silver print (BP 673, DM 1637, FR 5553, Y 131,974).

$2420* *Mendenhall Glacier, Alaska,* (1973), p.l., s., d., lit., (10-13-92, Christie-NY, #624, illus.), 7⅝ x 9⅜ in., (19.4 x 23.8 cm.), photograph, gelatin silver print (BP 1409, DM 3545, FR 12,046, Y 293,440).

$990* *New York,* sig., d., 1943, p.l., (10-14-92, Swann, #596, illus.), 13½ x 10½ in., (34.3 x 26.7 cm.), photograph, silver print (BP 581, DM 1449, FR 4913, Y 119,971).

$1320* *"Nude In Pool, Carmel Valley, California", 1981,* s., edit. 1/50, Dixon Collection, (11-16-92, Butterfield, #6234, illus.), 13¾ x 9⅝ in., (349.9 x 244.9 mm.), photograph, gelatin silver print (BP 869, DM 2105, FR 7089, Y 164,159).

BI *Palmetto, Mexico, 1973,* s., d., lit., est. $2/3,000, (10-13-92, Christie-NY, #623, illus.), 18⅜ x 15⅜ in., (46.7 x 39.1 cm.), photograph, gelatin silver print.

BI *Pond, Japan, 1970,* s., d., est. $3/4,000, (10-13-92, Christie-NY, #622, illus.), 10¼ x 13 in., (26 x 33 cm.), photograph, gelatin silver print.

$1870* *Portuguese Roofs,* (1960), p.l., s., d., (10-13-92, Christie-NY, #620, illus.), 7⅝ x 9⅝ in., (19.4 x 24.4 cm.), photograph, gelatin silver print (BP 1089, DM 2740, FR 9308, Y 226,749).

$1980* *Reeds, Oregon (Master Photographer, pl. 91),* mounted, s., d. by photog., 1975, p.l., (10-15-92, Sotheby-NY, #499, illus.), 10⅝ x 13¾ in., (27 x 34.9 cm.), photograph, gelatin silver print (BP 1212, DM 2947, FR 9995, Y 237,552).

$2588* *"Reeds, Oregon",* 1975, p. 1980, s., d., (05-23-93, Butterfield, #3665, illus.), 10¾ x 13¾ in., photograph, gelatin silver print (BP 1685, DM 4232, FR 14,243, Y 286,062).

BI *"Reeds, Oregon, 1975",* mounted on card, s., d., stamped photog.'s credit, in portfolio, 270x 348mm, est. BP 4/600, (05-07-93, Sotheby-London, #271, illus.), photograph, silver print.

$2530* *Rock Formation, 1938,* s., d., (04-08-93, Christie-NY, #398, illus.), 7⅝ x 9½ in., (19.4 x 24.1 cm.), photograph, gelatin silver print (BP 1659, DM 4064, FR 13,757, Y 287,108).

$1320* *Rock Formation, Carmel, California, 1939,* t. in ink, stamp, (10-13-92, Christie-NY, #391, illus.), photograph, gelatin silver print (BP 769, DM 1934, FR 6570, Y 160,058).

$1650* *Rock Forms, Oregon, 1970,* s., t., lit., (10-13-92, Christie-NY, #621, illus.), 7½ x 8½ in., (19.1 x 21.6 cm.), photograph, gelatin silver print (BP 961, DM 2417, FR 8213, Y 200,073).

$2070* *San Francisco,* 1938, p. 1960s, s., d., (04-08-93, Christie-NY, #399, illus.), 7½ x 9½ in., (19.1 x 24.1 cm.), photograph, gelatin silver print (BP 1357, DM 3325, FR 11,256, Y 234,907).

$1840* *Sand Dunes, 1934,* mounted, s., d. by photog., (04-06-93, Sotheby-NY, #431, illus.), 7½ x 9½ in., photograph (BP 1215, DM 2964, FR 10,038, Y 209,854).

$1650* *"Sculptured Leaf" (Five Decades, p. 105),* 1979/1980, s., d., num. 7, ink portfolio stamp, (11-16-92, Butterfield, #6233, illus.), 10⅝ x 11⅛ in., (270.4 x 283.1 mm.), photograph, gelatin silver print (BP 1086, DM 2631, FR 8861, Y 205,198).

BI *Sea Turtles,* photog. sig., d. on mount, 1964, p. 1969, est. $1,5/2,000, (04-07-93, Swann, #591, illus.), 7½ x 9½ in., photograph, silver print.

BI *Seed Pod,* mounted, s., d. by photog., 1967, p.l., est. $1,5/2,000, (10-15-92, Sotheby-NY, #498, illus.), 9⅝ x 6⅜ in., (24.4 x 16.2 cm.), photograph, gelatin silver print.

$1100* *Silhouetted Boats,* photog.'s sig., d. on mount, 1964, p. 1969, (04-07-93, Swann, #592), 7½ x 9½ in., photograph, silver print (BP 727, DM 1779, FR 6021, Y 124,972).

BI *Surf, 1951,* s., d., num. 4, stamp, est. $2,5/3,500, (10-13-92, Christie-NY, #506, illus.), 7½ x 9⅝ in., (19.1 x 24.4 cm.), photograph, gelatin silver print.

$880* *Tide Pool, 1959,* s., d., (11-16-92, Butterfield, #6238, illus.), 7½ x 9½ in., (190.8 x 241.7 mm.), photograph, gelatin silver print (BP 579, DM 1403, FR 4726, Y 109,439).

BI *Tree Roots, 1966,* mounted, s., d. by photog., est. $1,5/2,500, (10-15-92, Sotheby-NY, #495, illus.), 9½ x 7½ in., (24.1 x 19.1 cm.), photograph, gelatin silver print.

$1320* *"Underwater Nude #1", 1979,* s., d., (11-16-92, Butterfield, #6232, illus.), 12¼ x 10½ in., (311.7 x 267.2 mm.), photograph, gelatin silver print (BP 869, DM 2105, FR 7089, Y 164,159).

$2420* *Untitled, Landscape, 1936,* s., d., label, (10-13-92, Christie-NY, #390, illus.), 7½ x 9½ in., (19.1 x 24.1 cm.), photograph, gelatin silver print (BP 1409, DM 3545, FR 12,046, Y 293,440).

$2070* *"White Sands", 1946,* s., t., annot. vintage in unidentified hand, (05-23-93, Butterfield, #3662, illus.), 7½ x 9½ in., photograph, gelatin silver print (BP 1348, DM 3385, FR 11,392, Y 228,805).

$3850* *Woman Triumphant: Or The Victory Of Virtue Over Vice, 1927,* t., (10-13-92, Christie-NY, #392, illus.), 9½ x 7½ in., (24.1 x 19.1 cm.), photograph, gelatin silver print (BP 2242, DM 5640, FR 19,164, Y 466,836).

WESTON, Edward 1886-1958

$1540* *Adobe House,* sig., label verso, 1937, p.l., (10-14-92, Swann, #597, illus.), 7½ x 9½ in., (19.1 x 24.1 cm.), photograph, silver print (BP 904, DM 2254, FR 7643, Y 186,621).

BI *"Ansel, 1943",* p.l. by Cole Weston, mounted on card, stamped Negative by Edward Weston, Print by..., s. by Cole Weston, t., d., num. P.O. 43, 190 x 240mm, est.

BP3/500, (05-07-93, Sotheby-London, #266, illus.), photograph, silver print.

BI *Backyard View, San Francisco, 1933,* mounted, s., d., num 5/50 by photog., s., num. 1A 1925, i. by photog.verso, est. $6/8,000, (10-15-92, Sotheby-NY, #271A, illus.), 7½ x 9½ in., (19.1 x 24.1 cm.), photograph, gelatin silver print.

$16,100* *"Cabbage Fragment", 1931,* init., #2/50, s., i., illus., (05-23-93, Butterfield, #3668, illus.), 9¼ x 7½ in., photograph, gelatin silver print (BP 10,485, DM 26,324, FR 88,608, Y 1,779,595).

$4950* *Cabbage Leaf (1931),* from 50th Anniversary Portfolio, 1952, p. by Brett Weston under photog.'s supervision, initialed, d., stamped, (10-13-92, Christie-NY, #402, illus.), 7½ x 9⅜ in., (19.1 x 23.8 cm.), photograph, gelatin silver print (BP 2883, DM 7252, FR 24,639, Y 600,218).

$2070* *Carlos Dyer, Artist/Lithographer, 1936,* s., d., (04-08-93, Christie-NY, #403, illus.), 4⅝ x 3⅝ in., (11.7 x 9.2 cm.), photograph, gelatin silver print (BP 1357, DM 3325, FR 11,256, Y 234,907).

BI *Carlos Dyer, Artist/Lithographer, 1936,* s., d., est. $4/6,000, (10-13-92, Christie-NY, #395, illus.), 4¾ x 3⅝ in., (12.1 x 9.2 cm.), photograph, gelatin silver print.

$472* *"Cats On Steps, 1944",* p.l. by Cole Weston, mounted on card, stamped Negative by Edward Weston Print by..., s. by Cole Weston, t., d., num. N.63, 238 x 187mm, (05-07-93, Sotheby-London, #267, illus.), photograph, silver print (BP 299, DM 746, FR 2515, Y 51,971).

$3520* *Church Door, Hornitos,* (1940), from 50th Anniversary Portfolio, 1952, p. by Brett Weston under photog.'s supervision, initialed, d., stamped, (10-13-92, Christie-NY, #401, illus.), 7⅝ x 9⅝ in., (19.4 x 24.4 cm.), photograph, gelatin silver print (BP 2050, DM 5157, FR 17,521, Y 426,822).

BI *Clouds, New Mexico, 1933,* s., d., num. 5-50, label, prov., est. $18/22,000, (10-13-92, Christie-NY, #394, illus.), 9½ x 7½ in., (24.1 x 19.1 cm.), photograph, gelatin silver print.

$1925* *Convent From Point Lobos, 1938 (California Landscapes, pl. 19),* mounted, s., d. by photog., t., num. PL-L-14G 38, i. by photog. verso, (10-15-92, Sotheby-NY, #277, illus.), 7½ x 9½ in., (19.1 x 24.1 cm.), photograph, gelatin sivler print (BP 1178, DM 2865, FR 9717, Y 230,954).

$8050* *Cosas De La Vida, 1926,* s., t., d., init., #1/50, t., (04-08-93, Christie-NY, #400, illus.), 7 x 8½ in., (17.8 x 21.6 cm.), photograph, platinum print (BP 5279, DM 12,932, FR 43,774, Y 913,527).

BI *"Cypress-Point Lobos", 1929,* mounted, s., t., d. by photog., i., est. $4/6,000, (04-06-93, Sotheby-NY, #164, illus.), 7½ x 9⅜ in., photograph.

$10,350* *"D.H. Lawrence" (Conger, fig. 149), 1927,* mounted, s., d., i. by photog., (04-06-93, Sotheby-NY, #163, illus.), 9½ x 7⅜ in., photograph (BP 6836, DM 16,675, FR 56,465, Y 1,180,429).

BI *"David McAlpin, New York" (Fifty Years, p. 239),* mounted, init., d. by photog., 1941, p. early 1950's, est. $1,2/1,800, (04-06-93, Sotheby-NY, #170, illus.), 9½ x 7½ in., photograph.

$1760* *Death Valley, 1938,* photog.'s notations, (04-07-93, Swann, #593, illus.), 7½ x 9½ in., photograph, silver print (BP 1163, DM 2847, FR 9633, Y 199,955).

$10,925* *"Dummies-Metro-Goldwyn-Mayer, Hollywood" (Fifty Years, p. 220), 1939,* mounted, s., d. by photog., i. in unident. hand, (04-06-93, Sotheby-NY, #166, illus.), 7⅝ x 9⅝ in., photograph (BP 7216, DM 17,601, FR 59,602, Y 1,246,008).

BI *Dunes, Oceano, 1939,* inits., d., est. $30/40,000, (10-13-92, Christie-NY, #397, illus.), 7½ x 9½ in., (19.1 x 24.1 cm.), photograph, gelatin silver print.

BI *Fiftieth Anniversary Portfolio (1924-46): Twelve,* privately pub. 1952, p. by Brett Weston under photog.'s supervision,each initialed, d., stamp, s., i. in ink on front cover, #1/100, titles include: Cabbage Leaf (1931)...; est. $20/30,000, (10-13-92, Christie-NY, #400, illus.), each 8 x 10 in., (20.3 x 25.4 cm.), photograph, gelatin silver prints.

$6600* *Fishing Boat, Point Lobos, 1940 (California Landscapes, pl. 61),* mounted, s., d. by photog., t. verso, (10-15-92, Sotheby-NY, #276, illus.), 7½ x 9⅜ in., (19.1 x 23.8 cm.), photograph, gelatin silver print (BP 4039, DM 9824, FR 33,317, Y 791,842).

$8050* *George Hopkins, 1910's,* s. Weston by photog., (04-06-93, Sotheby-NY, #161, illus.), 7½ x 9⅜ in., photograph (BP 5317, DM 12,969, FR 43,917, Y 918,111).

$9900* *Iceberg Lake, Ediza, Sierra Nevada, 1937,* inits., d., annot., lit., (10-13-92, Christie-NY, #396, illus.), 7½ x 9½ in., (19.1 x 24.1 cm.), photograph, gelatin silver print (BP 5766, DM 14,503, FR 49,278, Y 1,200,437).

BI *"Jack Black-You Can't Win", 1930,* mounted, s., t., d., i. by photog., label, est. $5/8,000, (04-06-93, Sotheby-NY, #162, illus.), 9¾ x 7⅞ in., photograph.

$1210* *James Cagney, Amused,* s., d. 1933; num. 14 verso, prov., James Cagney Estate, (09-30-92, Doyle, #602, illus.), 4⅜ x 3⅝ in., (11.1 x 9.2 cm.), unretouched contact photograph (BP 683, DM 1716, FR 5803, Y 145,206).

$1100* *James Cagney, Looking Down,* s.; num. 6 verso, prov., James Cagney Estate, (09-30-92, Doyle, #601, illus.), 3½ x 4⅝ in., (8.9 x 11.7 cm.), unretouched contact photograph (BP 621, DM 1560, FR 5276, Y 132,005).

$1650* *James Cagney, Looking Into The Distance,* s., d. 1933; num. 5 verso, prov., James Cagney Estate, (09-30-92, Doyle, #603, illus.), 4½ x 3⅝ in., (11.4 x 9.2 cm.), unretouched contact photograph (BP 931, DM 2340, FR 7914, Y 198,008).

$2420* *James Cagney, Pensive,* s., d. 1933; num. 4 verso, prov., James Cagney Estate, (09-30-92, Doyle, #599, illus.), 4⅝ x 3⅝ in., (11.7 x 9.2 cm.), unretouched contact photograph (BP 1365, DM 3432, FR 11,607, Y 290,412).

$935* *James Cagney, Smiling,* s., d. 1933; num. 8 verso, prov., James Cagney Estate, (09-30-92, Doyle, #600), 4½ x 3⅝ in., (11.4 x 9.2 cm.), unretouched contact photograph (BP 528, DM 1326, FR 4484, Y 112,204).

BI *Juniper, Tenaya Lake, 1937,* t., d., num. 29 by photog., est. $4/6,000, (10-15-92, Sotheby-NY, #278, illus.), 9⅝ x 7⅝ in., (24.4 x 19.4 cm.), photograph, gelatin silver print.

$2200* *"Kelp And Stones" (Supreme Instants, pl. 94),* 1934/1940's, attrib., t., (11-16-92, Butterfield, #6242, illus.), 7½ x 9½ in., (190.8 x 241.7 mm.), photograph, gelatin silver print (BP 1449, DM 3508, FR 11,815, Y 273,598).

BI *Kelp, 1930,* s., t., d., authen. by Cole Weston, est. $5/6,000, (04-08-93, Christie-NY, #401, illus.), 7½ x 9½ in., (19.1 x 24.1 cm.), photograph, gelatin silver print.

BI *Kelp, 1930,* s., init., d., #1/50, prov., est. $7/9,000, (04-08-93, Christie-NY, #402, illus.), 9½ x 7½ in., (24.1 x 19.1 cm.), photograph, gelatin silver print.

$4888* *Langston Hughes, 1933,* mounted, s., d. by photog., (04-06-93, Sotheby-NY, #165, illus.), 4½ x 3⅝ in., photograph (BP 3229, DM 7875, FR 26,667, Y 557,482).

BI *Lois Kellogg, 1923,* mounted, s., d. by photog., est. $10/15,000, (10-15-92, Sotheby-NY, #269, illus.), 9½ x 7½ in., (24.1 x 19.1 cm.), photograph, platinum print.

$4400* *Lois Kellogg, 1923,* mounted, s., d. by photog., (10-15-92, Sotheby-NY, #270, illus.), 9½ x 6⅜ in., (24.1 x 16.2 cm.), photograph, platinum print (BP 2692, DM 6550, FR 22,211, Y 527,894).

BI *Mexico, 1925 (Daybooks, Mexico, pl. 21; Supreme Instants, pl. 27; Stebbins, pl. 13),* mounted, initialled, d. E.W. 1925 by photog. on mount, s., t., d., num. 51N by photog. verso, probably p. 1930's, est. $75/100,000, (10-15-92, Sotheby-NY, #271, illus.), 8½ x 7½ in., (21.6 x 19.1 cm.), photograph, gelatin silver print.

$816* *"Nude, 1927",* p.l. by Cole Weston, mounted on card, stamped Negative by Edward Weston, Print by..., s. by Cole Weston, t., d., num. 66N, 236 x 164mm, (05-07-93, Sotheby-London, #263, illus.), photograph, silver print (BP 517, DM 1290, FR 4347, Y 89,848).

$1053* *"Nude, 1936",* p.l. by Cole Weston, mounted on card, stamped Negative by Edward Weston, Print by..., s. by Cole Weston, t., d., num. 227 N, 242 x 190mm, (05-07-93, Sotheby-London, #269, illus.), photograph, silver print (BP 667, DM 1665, FR 5610, Y 115,944).

$1635* *"Nude, 1936",* p.l. by Cole Weston, mounted on card, stamped Negative by Edward Weston, Print by..., Cole Weston's sig., t., d., num. 237N, 176 x 236mm, (05-07-

93, Sotheby-London, #270, illus.), photograph, silver print (BP 1035, DM 2585, FR 8711, Y 180,026).

$726* *"Nude, 1939",* p.l. by Cole Weston, mounted on card, stamped Negative by Edward Weston Print by.., s. by Cole Weston, t., d., num. N. 39 M2, 240 x 190mm, (05-07-93, Sotheby-London, #264, illus.), photograph, silver print (BP 460, DM 1148, FR 3868, Y 79,938).

$468* *Oak Mountain Country,* p. negative Edward Weston, print Cole Weston, (05-16-93, Hindman, #335), 9¼ x 7¾ in., photograph, silver print (BP 305, DM 755, FR 2543, Y 52,116).

$4025* *"Old Adobe, Carmel Valley"* (Conger, fig. 802), 1934, mounted, s., d., #13-50 by photog., (04-06-93, Sotheby-NY, #167, illus.), 9½ x 7½ in., photograph (BP 2659, DM 6485, FR 21,959, Y 459,056).

BI *Pennsylvania Dutch Barn, 1942,* inits., d., lit., est. $8/10,000, (10-13-92, Christie-NY, #399, illus.), 7⅝ x 9½ in., (19.4 x 24.1 cm.), photograph, gelatin silver print.

BI *"Pepper, 1929",* p.l. by Cole Weston, mounted on card, stamped Negative by Edward Weston, Print by..., s. by Cole Weston, t., d., num. 7P, 236 x 190mm, est. BP 4/600, (05-07-93, Sotheby-London, #268, illus.), photograph, silver print.

BI *Pepper, 1930,* mounted, sig. stamp, s., num 6 by Brett Weston in ink, p. 1955 by BRETT WESTON under supervision of EDWARD WESTON, #6/8 ed., est. $3/4,000, (10-15-92, Sotheby-NY, #279, illus.), 7½ x 9¼ in., (19.1 x 23.5 cm.), photograph, gelatin silver print.

$6600* *Point Lobos, 1930,* inits., d., lit., (10-13-92, Christie-NY, #393, illus.), 9½ x 7½ in., (24.1 x 19.1 cm.), photograph, gelatin silver print (BP 3844, DM 9669, FR 32,852, Y 800,291).

$2588* *Portrait Of A Boy, 1934,* s., d., photog.'s label, (05-23-93, Butterfield, #3669, illus.), 4⅜ x 3⅝ in., photograph, gelatin silver print (BP 1685, DM 4232, FR 14,243, Y 286,062).

BI *Pulqueria, Mexico City, 1926 (Supreme Instants, p. 21),* credited, t., d., annot. in unidentified hand, probably p. 1940's or1950's, est. $2/3,000, (10-15-92, Sotheby-NY, #268, illus.), 9½ x 7½ in., (24.1 x 19.1 cm.), photograph, gelatin silver print.

BI *Religious Statuary, 1941,* inits., d., est. $2/2,500, (10-13-92, Christie-NY, #398, illus.), 7⅝ x 9⅝ in., (19.4 x 24.4 cm.), photograph, gelatin silver print.

$2200* *Robinson Jeffers, 1933 (Supreme Instants, pl. 49),* mounted, s., d. by photog., i. by sitter in ink, (10-15-92, Sotheby-NY, #274, illus.), 4½ x 3½ in., (11.4 x 8.9 cm.), photograph, gelatin silver print (BP 1346, DM 3275, FR 11,106, Y 263,947).

BI *"Rose Covarrubias, Mexico" (Daybooks Vol. I, pl. 35),* 1926/1940's, est. $2,0/2,500, (11-16-92, Butterfield, #6240, illus.), 9½ x 7⅜ in., (241.7 x 187.7 mm.), photograph, gelatin silver print.

$7150* *Sea And Grasses (California and the West, p. 129), 1938,* printing notations in unidentified hands, label, prop. Museum of Modern Art, (10-15-92, Sotheby-NY, #205, illus.), 7½ x 9½ in., (19.1 x 24.1 cm.), photograph, gelatin silver print (BP 4375, DM 10,643, FR 36,093, Y 857,828).

$468* *Seated Nude,* impressed reprinted by Cole Weston, (05-16-93, Hindman, #334), 7½ x 9½ in., photograph, silver print (BP 305, DM 755, FR 2543, Y 52,116).

$3025* *Selected Images: Three: "Eroded Rock, Pt. Lobos", 1930; "Church Door,Hornitos", 1940; and "North Dome, Point Lobos", 1946,* plates 4, 8, & 9 from "Fiftieth Anniversary Portfolio", mounted, initialled, d. by photog., portfolio stamp, p. c. 1952 by BRETT WESTON from negs. by EDWARD WESTON, (10-15-92, Sotheby-NY, #281, illus.), each approx. 7½ x 9½ in., (19.1 x 24.1 cm.), photograph, gelatin silver prints (BP 1851, DM 4503, FR 15,270, Y 362,927).

$1320* *Selected Portraits: Ralph And Anita Parker, 1929: Eight,* each s., 1 t., 5 annot., (11-16-92, Butterfield, #6243, illus.), each, approx. 9¼ x 6½ in., (235.4 x 165.4 mm.), photograph, gelatin silver prints (BP 869, DM 2105, FR 7089, Y 164,159).

$4400* *Springtime, 1943 (Nudes, p. 105),* mounted, initialled, d. by photog., s., t., d., num. N43-CH-1 by photog. verso, (10-15-92, Sotheby-NY, #275, illus.), 7½ x 9⅝ in.,

(19.1 x 24.4 cm.), photograph, gelatin silver print (BP 2692, DM 6550, FR 22,211, Y 527,894).

BI *T. Edward Hanley, Ph.D., Bradford, Pennsylvania: Four, 1940,* mounted, s., d. by photog., studio label, est. $3/4,000, (10-15-92, Sotheby-NY, #273, illus.), each 4⅝ x 3⅝ in., (11.7 x 9.2 cm.), photograph, gelatin silver print.

$1725* *"Taliesin West, Phoenix, Arizona" (Conger, fig. 1562), 1941,* mounted, init., d. by photog., i., (04-06-93, Sotheby-NY, #169, illus.), 7⅝ x 9½ in., photograph (BP 1139, DM 2779, FR 9411, Y 196,738).

$1090* *"Tina (Modotti) 1924",* p.l. by Cole Weston, mounted on card, stamped Negative by Edward Weston, Print by..., Cole Weston's sig., t., d., num. 34PO, illus., 240 x 187mm, (05-07-93, Sotheby-London, #265, illus.), photograph, silver print (BP 690, DM 1723, FR 5807, Y 120,018).

BI *"Tina Modotti" (His Life And Photographs, p. 103),* 1924/1940's, est. $2,0/2,500, (11-16-92, Butterfield, #6241, illus.), 9 x 6¾ in., (229 x 171.8 mm.), photograph, gelatin silver print.

$3850* *Tina Modotti, Glendale Studio, 1922 (Fifty Years, p. 88),* mounted, stamped "Negative by Edward Weston, printed under his supervision in 1955 by Brett Weston, verified by Cole Weston, Project print #7 of 8 printed", s. by Cole Weston, p. 1955 by BRETT WESTON, #7/8 ed., (10-15-92, Sotheby-NY, #280, illus.), 7½ x 9⅜ in., (19.1 x 23.8 cm.), photograph, gelatin silver print (BP 2356, DM 5731, FR 19,435, Y 461,908).

BI *Toy Bull, Mexico, 1925,* est. $2/3,000, (04-06-93, Sotheby-NY, #160, illus.), 7⅛ x 9 in., photograph.

$825* *William Edmondson, Nashville, Tennessee, 1940s(?),* (04-07-93, Swann, #594, illus.), 7 x 9 in., photograph, silver print (BP 545, DM 1334, FR 4516, Y 93,729).

$2200* *Wm. Edmunson, Stone Cutter, Nashville, 1941,* mounted, initialled, d. by photog., s., t., d., num. T41-ED-4 by photog. verso, (10-15-92, Sotheby-NY, #272, illus.), 7½ x 9¼ in., (19.1 x 23.5 cm.), photograph, gelatin silver print (BP 1346, DM 3275, FR 11,106, Y 263,947).

$4888* *"Wrecked Car-Crescent Beach" (Conger, fig. 1462), 1939,* mounted, s., d. by photog., t., i., (04-06-93, Sotheby-NY, #168, illus.), 7⅝ x 9⅝ in., photograph (BP 3229, DM 7875, FR 26,667, Y 557,482).

$4400* *Xavier Guerrero, 1922 (A Fragile Life, p. 68),* (10-15-92, Sotheby-NY, #267, illus.), 9⅝ x 7⅜ in., (24.4 x 18.7 cm.), photograph, platinum or palladium print (BP 2692, DM 6550, FR 22,211, Y 527,894).

WESTON, Edward and Brett

$1380* *"Eroded Rock, Point Lobos", 1930,* p. 1952, inits., d., Portfolio print No. 4 stamp, (05-23-93, Butterfield, #3672, illus.), 9½ x 5½ in., photograph, gelatin silver print (BP 899, DM 2256, FR 7595, Y 152,537).

$1725* *"North Wall, Pt. Lobos", 1946,* p. 1952, init., d., Portfolio Print No. 9 stamp, (05-23-93, Butterfield, #3670, illus.), 9½ x 7½ in., photograph, gelatin silver print (BP 1123, DM 2820, FR 9494, Y 190,671).

BI *"Willie, New Orleans", 1941,* p. 1952, inits., d., Portfolio Print No. 11 stamp, est. $1,2/1,600, (05-23-93, Butterfield, #3671, illus.), 9½ x 5½ in., photograph, gelatin silver print.

WESTON, Edward and Brett WESTON

$935* *"Kelp No. 3" (Fifty Years, p. 142), 1930,* p. attrib. Brett, annot., (11-16-92, Butterfield, #6244, illus.), 9⅜ x 7½ in., (238.5 x 190.8 mm.), photograph, gelatin silver print (BP 616, DM 1491, FR 5021, Y 116,279).

WESTON, Edward and Cole

$978* *"Artichoke Halved", 1930,* p.l., s. by Cole, t., d., neg. num., Negative by Edward Westonstamp, (05-23-93, Butterfield, #3676, illus.), 7¼ x 9¼ in., photograph, gelatin silver print (BP 637, DM 1599, FR 5382, Y 108,102).

$518* *"Charis, Lake Ediza", 1937,* p.l., s. by Cole, t., d., neg. num., Negative by Edward Westonstamp, (05-23-93, Butterfield, #3678, illus.), 9½ x 7½ in., photograph, gelatin silver print (BP 337, DM 847, FR 2851, Y 57,257).

$575* *"Eroded Rock, Point Lobos", 1930,* p.l., s. by Cole, t., d. Negative by Edward Weston stamp, (05-23-93, Butterfield, #3673, illus.), 9¼ x 7½ in., photograph, gelatin silver print (BP 374, DM 940, FR 3165, Y 63,557).

$546* *"Margarethe"*, 1920, p.l., s. by Cole, t., d., neg. num., Negative by Edward Westonstamp, (05-23-93, Butterfield, #3677, illus.), 9¼ x 7½ in., photograph, gelatin silver print (BP 356, DM 893, FR 3005, Y 60,351).

$1265* *"Nude"*, 1936, p.l., s. by Cole, t., d., neg., num., Negative by Edward Weston stamp, (05-23-93, Butterfield, #3675, illus.), 7¼ x 9½ in., photograph, gelatin silver print (BP 824, DM 2068, FR 6962, Y 139,825).

$1150* *"Shell"*, 1927, p.l., s. by Cole, t., d., neg. num., Negative by Edward Westonstamp, (05-23-93, Butterfield, #3674, illus.), 7⅜ x 9¼ in., photograph, gelatin silver print (BP 749, DM 1880, FR 6329, Y 127,114).

WESTON, Edward and Cole WESTON

$880* *"China Cove, Point Lobos"*, 1940/later, s., t., d., neg. num., (11-16-92, Butterfield, #6246, illus.), 9½ x 7½ in., (241.7 x 190.8 mm.), photograph, gelatin silver print (BP 579, DM 1403, FR 4726, Y 109,439).

BI *"Jose Clemente Orozco"*, 1930/later, s., t., d., ink stamp, est. $800/1,000, (11-16-92, Butterfield, #6247, illus.), 9½ x 7⅜ in., (241.7 x 187.7 mm.), photograph, gelatin silver print.

$825* *"Juniper At Lake Tenaya"*, 1937/later, s., t., d., neg. num., ink stamp, (11-16-92, Butterfield, #6248, illus.), 9½ x 7½ in., (241.7 x 190.8 mm.), photograph, gelatin silver print (BP 543, DM 1315, FR 4431, Y 102,599).

$880* *"Nude"*, 1920/later, s., t., d., ink stamp, (11-16-92, Butterfield, #6245, illus.), 7¼ x 12¹³⁄₁₆ in., (184.5 x 325.4 mm.), photograph, platinum print (BP 579, DM 1403, FR 4726, Y 109,439).

$770* *"Point Lobos"*, 1946/later, s., t., d., annot., ink stamp, (11-16-92, Butterfield, #6249, illus.), 9½ x 7½ in., (241.7 x 190.8 mm.), photograph, gelatin silver print (BP 507, DM 1228, FR 4135, Y 95,759).

WEXLER, Moshe   American 20th cent.

$50* *Amusement Park*, s., #114/300, (04-02-93, Sloan, #813), 14 x 23 in., (356 x 584 mm.), screenprint (BP 33, DM 80, FR 273, Y 5693).

WHEATLEY (after)

BI *"Crys Of London": Twelve*, pub. 1804, (12-11-92, G.A. Key, #78), 5 x 4 in., (12.7 x 10.2 cm.), hand colored engraving.

WHEATLEY, F. (after)

$715* *"At Market", "Coming From Market", "The Deserted Village", "Morning",and "Evening": Five*, large folio, (12-11-92, Eldred, #358), color engraving (BP 458, DM 1127, FR 3861, Y 88,479).

$87 *"Cries Of London": Set Of Thirteen*, (02-05-93, G.A. Key, #28), 9 x 7 in., (22.9 x 17.8 cm.), colored prints (BP 60, DM 144, FR 488, Y 10,826).

WHEATLEY, Francis (after)

BI *Cries Of London: Nine*, margins, est. BP 1/150, (06-16-93, Bonhams-Chelsea, #442), pl. 15¾ x 12 in., (40 x 30.5 cm.), reprod. w/hand-coloring.

$852* *The Cries Of London: Thirteen*, (04-22-93, Bonhams-Chelsea, #68), (34.3 x 26.7 cm.), reprod. w/hand coloring (BP 550, DM 1369, FR 4618, Y 93,678).

BI *The Dipping Well, Hyde Park, 1802*, by James Godby, by James Murphy, trimmed to plate, nicks, tears, damage, defects, est. BP 80/120, (11-30-92, Phillips-London, #204), sheet 19½ x 25⅛ in., (495 x 638 mm.), stipple engraving on wove.

$102* *Summer*, s., pub. Henry Graves & Co. Ltd., 1935, (04-22-93, Bonhams-Chelsea, #126), (59.7 x 41.3 cm.), mezzotint, p. in colors (BP 66, DM 164, FR 553, Y 11,215).

WHEATLY, Francis (after)

$49 *"Cries Of London": Five*, rolled, (04-16-93, G.A. Key, #107), each approx. 13 x 10 in., (33 x 25.4 cm.), colored stipple engraving (BP 32, DM 79, FR 267, Y 5510).

$193* *"Fresh Gathered Peas", "Young Hastings" and "Strawberrys": Two*, plates 7 and 9, from Cries of London, (04-02-93, Sloan, #1462), each image, approx. 34 x 36 in., (864 x 914 mm.), color engraving (BP 127, DM 310, FR 1053, Y 21,974).

WHIPPLE, John Adams and Charles DeSilver

$2200* *Abraham Lincoln At Home, Farewell Address To His Old Neighbors, Springfield, February 12, 1861*, pub. (Desilver's) caption, credit, d., (c) info., 1860, p. 1865, (04-07-93, Swann, #280, illus.), 10½ x 13 in., photograph, albumen print (BP 1454, DM 3558, FR 12,042, Y 249,943).

WHISTLER, James Abbott McNeill   American 1834-1903

$1150* *The "Adam And Eve", Old Chelsea (K. 175; M. 172), 1879*, full margins, good cond., loss, platemark, mat stain, creasing, (05-13-93, Sotheby-NY, #438), 6¾ x 11⅞ in., (172 x 301 mm.), etching and drypoint on japon pelure (BP 755, DM 1857, FR 6264, Y 128,391).

$2420* *The "Adam And Eve," Old Chelsea (Kennedy 175), c. 1878*, 2nd final state, margins, loss, very good cond., prov., (11-09-92, Christie-NY, #36), plate 6⅞ x 11⅞ in., (175 x 301 mm.), etching on golden Chine colle (BP 1600, DM 3863, FR 13,053, Y 300,323).

BI *Adam & Eve, Old Chelsea (K. 175)*, 2nd state, damage in margins, laid down, sandwich mounted, est. BP 4/500, (10-27-92, Phillips-London, #323), plate 6⅞ x 12 in., (175 x 305 mm.), etching on japan.

$1380* *"Adam And Eve" and 'Old Chelsea" (K. 175; M. 172), 1879*, large margins, scratches, foxing, glued to mat, surface losses, (02-11-93, Sotheby-NY, #54), 6¹⁵⁄₁₆ x 12 in., (176 x 305 mm.), etching and drypoint on wove (BP 974, DM 2286, FR 7735, Y 166,365).

$330* *Aldenay Street*, plate s., very good cond., (07-19-92, Bakker, #44), plate 6¾ x 4 in., (17.1 x 10.2 cm.), etching (BP 169, DM 481, FR 1626, Y 41,024).

BI *"Alderney Street" (K. 238), 1885*, as pub. by Koehler in Etching, good cond., est. $3/400, (05-15-93, Cleveland, #344), 6⅞ x 4¼ in., (17.5 x 10.8 cm.), etching.

$805* *Annie (Kennedy 10; Mansfield 8), 1857-58*, margins, good cond., fox marks, mat stain, loss, (05-13-93, Sotheby-NY, #434), 4⅜ x 3⅛ in., (112 x 79 mm.), sh 7¼ x 6 in., (112 x 79 mm.), drypoint on laid (BP 528, DM 1300, FR 4385, Y 89,874).

$1210* *Annie Seated (K. 30), 1858*, 2nd (final) state, plate tone, margins, good cond., masking tape, sticker, staining, mat staining, foxing, crease, surface soiling, (02-24-93, Butterfield, #2888), 5⅛ x 3¾ in., (130 x 95 mm.), etching on fine laid w/watermark (BP 844, DM 1964, FR 6659, Y 141,985).

$825* *Annie Seated (Kennedy 30), 1858*, 2nd final state, prov., (03-24-93, Grogan, #51), 5⅛ x 3¼ in., (13 x 8.3 cm.), etching (BP 559, DM 1347, FR 4586, Y 96,933).

$715* *Annie, Seated (K. 30), 1858*, 2nd final state, margins, good cond., mat/light-staining, foxing, crease, sticker/tape remains, (10-28-92, Butterfield, #2774), 5⅛ x 3¾ in., (130 x 95 mm.), etching on Van Gelder Zonen (BP 456, DM 1104, FR 3749, Y 87,730).

$920* *Annie, Seated (K. 30; M. 29), 1858*, margins, good cond., light-stain, foxing into image, tape label stain, creases, (05-13-93, Sotheby-NY, #435), 5⅛ x 3¾ in., (129 x 96 mm.), sh 8⅛ x 5¾ in., (129 x 96 mm.), etching on thin laid (BP 604, DM 1486, FR 5011, Y 102,713).

$5040* *The Balcony (Kennedy 207/X), before 1886*, s., (06-23-93, Kornfeld, #881), etching (BP 3424, DM 8528, FR 28,685, Y 549,079, SF 7590).

$3300* *The Barber's (K. 271), c. 1886-8*, s. w/butterfly, i. 'imp' on tab, foxmark, central crease, time staining, glued down in places, very good cond., (11-09-92, Christie-NY, #41, illus.), sheet 6⁹⁄₁₆ x 9½ in., (167 x 241 mm.), etching in brownish-black on laid Japan (BP 2182, DM 5268, FR 17,799, Y 409,531).

$1870* *Bead-Stringers (K. 198), 1879-80*, 8th final state, s. w/butterfly, tab i. imp, repaired tear, very good cond., (11-09-92, Christie-NY, #39, illus.), sheet 8⅞ x 5⅞ in., (225 x 149 mm.), etching and drypoint in brown on laid (BP 1236, DM 2985, FR 10,086, Y 232,068).

$2750* *Becquet (Kennedy 52), 1859*, 2nd state of 4, (03-24-93, Grogan, #45, illus.), 10 x 7½ in., (25.4 x 19.1 cm.), etching and drypoint (BP 1862, DM 4491, FR 15,286, Y 323,111).

$495* *Becquet, 1859*, 4th final state, (03-24-93, Grogan, #50), 10 x 7½ in., (25.4 x 19.1 cm.), etching and drypoint (BP 335, DM 808, FR 2752, Y 58,160).

$2760* *The Beggars (K. 194), c. 1880,* 6th final state, watermark, s. w/butterfly, i. imp., foxing, good cond., (05-11-93, Christie-NY, #133, illus.), plate 11⅞ x 8⅛ in., (302 x 206 mm.), etching in brown on laid (BP 1762, DM 4348, FR 14,650, Y 303,597).

$3025* *La Belle Jardiniere (W. 63; L. 94), 1894,* s. w/butterfly, indentation of second erased butterfly, margins, pencil notation, soiling, ex-coll. Bertha Palmer Thorne, (11-05-92, Sotheby-NY, #69, illus.), 8⅝ x 6¼ in., (220 x 160 mm.), lithograph on thin, smooth wove (BP 1967, DM 4784, FR 16,185, Y 371,120).

$2542* *Bibi Lalouette (Kennedy 50 II), 1859,* plate s., d., (06-10-93, Hauswedell/Nolt, #976, illus.), image 9 1/16 x 6 in., (23 x 15.3 cm.), drypoint on hand-made Japan (BP 1663, DM 4139, FR 13,936, Y 269,823).

$1495* *Bibi Valentin (K., M. 50), 1859,* full margins, good cond., mat stain, foxing in image, hinges, (02-11-93, Sotheby-NY, #52), 5⅞ x 8 11/16 in., (150 x 221 mm.), drypoint on laid (BP 1055, DM 2476, FR 8380, Y 180,229).

$440* *Billingsgate (K. 47), 1859,* taped, good cond., (12-04-92, Doyle, #164), 6 x 8⅞ in., (152 x 225 mm.), etching (BP 282, DM 701, FR 2377, Y 54,931).

$825* *Billingsgate (K. 47), 1859,* 8th (final) state, margins, good cond., sheet toned, tear, creases, (02-24-93, Butterfield, #2889), 6 x 8 15/16 in., (152 x 227 mm.), etching on laid (BP 575, DM 1339, FR 4540, Y 96,808).

$290* *Billingsgate (Kennedy 47),* 7th state of 8, margins, tear, time-staining, foxing, (04-22-93, Bonhams-Chelsea, #121), plate 5⅞ x 9 in., (14.9 x 22.9 cm.), etching (BP 187, DM 466, FR 1572, Y 31,886).

$162* *Billingsgate (Kennedy 47), 1859,* 7th of 8 states, margins, surface dirt, (10-15-92, Bonhams-Chelsea, #20), plate 5⅞ x 8⅞ in., (14.9 x 22.5 cm.), etching (BP 99, DM 241, FR 818, Y 19,436).

BI *Billingsgate (Kennedy 47), 1859,* 6th or 7th state of 8, margins, est. BP 2/300, (09-17-92, Bonhams-Chelsea, #77), plate 5⅞ x 8⅞ in., (14.9 x 22.5 cm.), drypoint etching.

BI *Billingsgate (Kennedy 47), 1859,* 6th or 7th state of 8, margins, est. BP 150/250, (11-19-92, Bonhams-Chelsea, #187), plate 5⅞ x 8¼ in., (14.9 x 21 cm.), drypoint etching.

$770* *Billingsgate (Kennedy 47), 1859,* i., (05-24-93, Grogan, #342), 6 x 8 15/16 in., (15.2 x 22.7 cm.), etching (BP 501, DM 1259, FR 4238, Y 85,111).

$440* *Billingsgate (M. 46; Gr. 47; W. 45; T. 45; K. 47) (prob. VI/VIII),* s. in plate, (09-17-92, Sloan, #3076), 5⅞ x 8⅞ in., (14.9 x 22.5 cm.), etching (BP 247, DM 653, FR 2236, Y 54,781).

$468* *"Billingsgate",* 1859, (11-28-92, Young, #401, illus.), 6 x 9 in., (15.2 x 22.9 cm.), etching (BP 309, DM 746, FR 2531, Y 58,245).

$10* *"Billingsgate" (K. 47 viii/viii), 1859,* as pub. in The Portfolio, glue residue, toned, puncture in image, (05-15-93, Cleveland, #343, illus.), 6 x 8⅞ in., (15.2 x 22.5 cm.), etching (BP 7, DM 16, FR 54, Y 1109).

$605* *Billingsgate, 1859, Kennedy 47 VII/VIII VIII,* prov., (09-20-92, Hindman, #679), 6 x 8⅞ in., (15.2 x 22.5 cm.), etching on laid paper (BP 354, DM 898, FR 3071, Y 74,774).

$2760* *"Billingstate" and "The Forge" (K. 47, M. 46; K., M. 68), 1859/61: Two,* final states, full margins, good cond., deckle loss, (02-11-93, Sotheby-NY, #51), one 6 x 8 13/16 in., (153 x 224 mm.), the other 7½ x 12⅜ in., (153 x 224 mm.), etching, 2nd w/drypoint, on laid (BP 1948, DM 4572, FR 15,471, Y 332,731).

$1998* *Black Lion Wharf (K. 42), 1859,* 2nd state (of three), margins, foxing, glued, taped, (12-01-92, Christie-London, #553, illus.), P. 5⅞ x 8¾ in., (150 x 223 mm.), etching on thin Japan (BP 1320, DM 3185, FR 10,853, Y 248,755).

$1836* *Black Lion Wharf (Kennedy 42 III), 1859,* plate s., d., from Sixteen etchings of Scenes of the Thames and othersubjects, (06-10-93, Hauswedell/Nolt, #975, illus.), image 6 x 8 15/16 in., (15.3 x 22.7 cm.), drypoint on hand-made Japan (BP 1201, DM 2990, FR 10,066, Y 194,884).

$2090* *Black Lion Wharf (M. 41; Gr. 42; W. 40; T. 35; K. 42) (II/III),* s., d. 1859 in plate, (09-17-92, Sloan, #3072, illus.), 5⅞ x 8⅞ in., (14.9 x 22.5 cm.), etching (BP 1174, DM 3103, FR 10,620, Y 260,209).

$523* *"Blustery Day",* s., d. plate Whistler 1821; label verso, (05-15-93, Dunning, #1056, illus.), plate 6 x 11¼ in., (15.2 x 28.6 cm.), drypoint etching (BP 340, DM 841, FR 2827, Y 57,976).

$3575* *The Bridge (K. 204), 1879-80,* s. w/butterfly, i. imp, 8th final state, plate tone, trimmed, good cond., repaired tears, (10-28-92, Butterfield, #2554), 11⅝ x 7 13/16 in., (295 x 198 mm.), etching w/drypoint in sepia on fine laid paper (BP 2278, DM 5521, FR 18,747, Y 438,650).

$1870* *Bridge View,* plate s. w/butterfly mark, (11-13-92, DuMouchelle, #2019, illus.), 5¼ x 8⅛ in., (13.3 x 20.6 cm.), etching (BP 1208, DM 2936, FR 9899, Y 232,096).

$3300* *The Broad Bridge (Levy 18), 1878,* wide margins, foxing, remains of glue, good cond., prov., (11-09-92, Christie-NY, #42, illus.), border 7 5/16 x 11 in., (185 x 280 mm.), lithotint in brown on wove (BP 2182, DM 5268, FR 17,799, Y 409,531).

$3088* *Chelsea Wharf (K. 89),* plate tone, 2nd final state, s. w/butterfly, i. imp, abrasion, foxing, (06-30-93, Sotheby-London, #339, illus.), sh 3½ x 7½ in., (89 x 191 mm.), etching in sepia (BP 2070, DM 5267, FR 17,768, Y 330,869).

$805* *The Clockmaker's House, Paimpol (W. 42: L. 68), 1893,* large margins, good cond., light bleaching, foxing, (05-13-93, Sotheby-NY, #445), 8 x 5¾ in., (203 x 145 mm.), sh 13½ x 10 in., (203 x 145 mm.), lithograph on chine applique, mounted on heavy wove (BP 528, DM 1300, FR 4385, Y 89,874).

$121* *Dock Workers, 1860,* plate s., d., late printing, very good cond.?, (07-19-92, Bakker, #213), image 10½ x 7½ in., (26.7 x 19.1 cm.), etching (BP 62, DM 176, FR 596, Y 15,042).

$8050* *The Doorway (K. 188), 1880,* wiped tone, 3rd state of 7, shaded butterfly, i. imp., wide margins,foxmark, light-staining, excell. cond., prov., (05-11-93, Christie-NY, #131, illus.), plate 11½ x 7⅞ in., (292 x 200 mm.), etching and drypoint on laid (BP 5139, DM 12,681, FR 42,728, Y 885,491).

$2415* *The Doorway (K. 188; M. 185), 1879-80,* s. by printer, Goulding, d. Dec. 4, 1930, margins, good cond., mat stain, fox marks, hinge stains, pub. as part of the First Venice Set, 1881, (05-13-93, Sotheby-NY, #439), 11½ x 7⅞ in., (292 x 201 mm.), sh 13¼ x 9¼ in., (292 x 201 mm.), etching and drypoint on laid (BP 1585, DM 3900, FR 13,154, Y 269,622).

$8800* *The Doorway (Kennedy 188), 1879-80,* seventh and final state, s. on tab, butterfly and imp, pub. as part first Venice Set, 1881, rear cover lot, (05-27-93, Swann, #295, illus.), 11½ x 8 in., (29.2 x 20.3 cm.), etching (BP 5636, DM 14,121, FR 47,593, Y 943,396).

$990* *The Draped Figure-Seated (W. 46; L. 74), 1893,* stamp verso, posthumous impression taken by Goulding, margins, good cond., light/mat stain, creases, hinge stains, ex-coll. E.M. Henn (L. 872b), (11-05-92, Sotheby-NY, #68), 7 x 6⅛ in., (177 x 155 mm.), lithograph on laid China (BP 644, DM 1566, FR 5297, Y 121,457).

$550* *Drouet (K. 55), 1859,* from canceled plate, mat burn, rippling, hinged, (12-04-92, Doyle, #165), 9 x 6 in., (229 x 152 mm.), drypoint (BP 353, DM 876, FR 2971, Y 68,664).

$880* *Drouet (K. 55), 1859,* 2nd final state, plate tone, margins, good cond., mat/light-staining, hinge remains, staining, surface soiling, (10-28-92, Butterfield, #2775), 8 15/16 x 6 in., (227 x 152 mm.), etching on laid paper (BP 561, DM 1359, FR 4615, Y 107,975).

$715* *Drouet (Kennedy 55, state 2), 1859,* margins, mat burn, (12-08-92, Swann, #313, illus.), 8⅞ x 6 in., (22.5 x 15.2 cm.), etching on laid paper (BP 448, DM 1113, FR 3795, Y 88,622).

$715* *"Drouet Sculpteur", 1859,* plate s., d., good cond.?, (07-19-92, Bakker, #24), plate 8¾ x 5⅞ in., (22.2 x 14.9 cm.), etching and drypoint (BP 367, DM 1042, FR 3524, Y 88,886).

$660* *"Drouet" (Kennedy 55 ii/ii),* thin spot, good cond., (10-31-92, Cleveland, #235), drypoint on japanese tissue (BP 423, DM 1015, FR 3445, Y 81,754).

$937* *Eagle Wharf (Tyzac, Whiteley & Co.) (Kennedy 41), 1859,* one of Sixteen Etching, only state, margins, (04-22-93, Bonhams-Chelsea, #117, illus.), plate 5⅜ x 8⅜ in., (13.7 x 21.3 cm.), etching (BP 605, DM 1505, FR 5079, Y 103,024).

$1980* *Early Morning (L. 17, W. 7), 1878,* s. w/butterfly in stone, small margins, good cond., creases, hinge remains, skinned areas, (10-28-92, Butterfield, #2553), 6½ x 10¼ in., (165 x 260 mm.), lithotint on cream wove (BP 1262, DM 3058, FR 10,383, Y 242,945).

$2420* *Early Morning (Way 7, Levy 14 IV/IV), 1878,* (03-14-93, Hindman, #307, illus.), 6½ x 10⅛ in., (16.5 x 25.7 cm.), lithotint in black on wove (BP 1688, DM 4028, FR 13,696, Y 285,209).

$275* *"Early Morning Battersea",* very good cond.?, (11-21-92, Bakker, #30), plate 4½ x 5⅞ in., (11.4 x 14.9 cm.), etching (BP 181, DM 438, FR 1477, Y 34,200).

$1840* *The Fan (Way 14; Levy 23), 1879,* margins, light-stain, surface loss, foxing, repaired tear, nicks, skinning, ex-coll. Thomas R. Way, (05-13-93, Sotheby-NY, #444, illus.), 8⅛ x 6¼ in., (207 x 160 mm.), sh 10⅜ x 7⅝ in., (207 x 160 mm.), lithograph on wove (BP 1208, DM 2971, FR 10,022, Y 205,426).

$3045* *The Fiddler (Becquet) (Wedmore 48, Kennedy 52 IV), 1859,* from Sixteen Etchings (The Thames Set), (06-04-93, Bassenge, #5839, illus.), 10¹/₁₆ x 7⁹/₁₆ in., (25.5 x 19.2 cm.), drypoint on hand-made Japan (BP 2015, DM 4945, FR 16,667, Y 328,408).

BI *Florence Leyland,* s. in plate, Kennedy 110, IX, est. $6/800, (11-01-92, Hanzel, #206), 8⅜ x 5⅜ in., (21.3 x 13.7 cm.), etching.

BI *The Fruit-Stall, Venice (K. 200; M. 197),* 7th (final) state, modulated plate tone, s. w/butterfly, i. imp., good cond., ex-coll. George W. Vanderbilt, est. $8/12,000, (05-13-93, Sotheby-NY, #439A, illus.), 8¾ x 5⅝ in., (223 x 142 mm.), etching in sepia.

$110* *Fulham (K 182 (II/II)),* s. plate w/butterfly mono., stamped Printseller's Association, pub. "The Fine Art Society", January 28, 1879, (10-30-92, Sloan, #2150), 5⅛ x 8 in., (13 x 20.3 cm.), etching (BP 70, DM 169, FR 574, Y 13,626).

$193* *"Fulham",* good/poor cond., (11-21-92, Bakker, #33), plate 5¼ x 8¼ in., (13.3 x 21 cm.), etching (BP 127, DM 308, FR 1037, Y 24,002).

$933* *Gaiety Stage Door (Levy 21), 1879,* full margins, artist's mono., excellent cond., tear, (11-30-92, Phillips-London, #369), image 4⅞ x 7⅝ in., (124 x 194 mm.), lithograph on chine applique on wove (BP 616, DM 1486, FR 5046, Y 116,117).

BI *Gaiety Stage Door (W. 10), 1879,* staining, dust, large margins, (02-24-93, Picard, #246), signature on chine applique.

BI *Gants De Suede (Levy 40), 1890,* proof, laid down, surface defects, staining, wide margins, est. BP 2/300, (04-22-93, Bonhams-Chelsea, #116), subject 11½ x 8¼ in., (29.2 x 21 cm.), lithograph.

$770* *"Joseph Pennell Seated",* (03-24-93, Grogan, #54), 7 x 6 in., (17.8 x 15.2 cm.), lithograph (BP 521, DM 1258, FR 4280, Y 90,471).

BI *Lindsay Row, Chelsea (L. 32; H. 10; W. 19), 1888,* butterfly mono. in stone, est. $1,500/2,000, (09-17-92, Sloan, #3071), 5 x 8 in., (12.7 x 20.3 cm.), lithograph.

$3105* *The Little Draped Figure, Leaning (Levy 82), 1894,* watermark, s. w/butterfly, full margins, slightly shaved at right, light/time staining, loss, tear (reinforced), tape, very good cond., (05-11-93, Christie-NY, #134, illus.), borderline 7⁵/₁₆ x 5¾ in., (186 x 146 mm.), lithograph on laid (BP 1982, DM 4891, FR 16,481, Y 341,547).

$1955* *The Little Draped Figure-Leaning (W. 51; L. 82), 1894,* s. w/butterfly, stamp, full margins, good cond., rubbed spots, waterstain, creases, (05-13-93, Sotheby-NY, #449, illus.), 6⅞ x 5⅞ in., (175 x 150 mm.), lithograph on cream laid Japan (BP 1283, DM 3157, FR 10,648, Y 218,265).

$1540* *Little Evelyn (L. 159), 1896,* p. Way, margins, staining, good cond., prov., (11-09-92, Christie-NY, #44, illus.),

border 6½ x 4½ in., (165 x 115 mm.), lithograph on laid (BP 1018, DM 2458, FR 8306, Y 191,114).

$5175* *Little Lagoon (K. 186), c. 1880,* plate tone, 2nd final state, s., butterfly, i. imp., margins, foxmarks, excell. cond., (05-11-93, Christie-NY, #130, illus.), plate 9 x 6 in., (229 x 152 mm.), etching on laid (BP 3304, DM 8152, FR 27,468, Y 569,244).

BI *The Little Mast (K. 185; M. 182), 1879-80,* s. w/shaded butterfly, i., thread margins, good cond., buckling, crease, ex-coll. RB, est. $5/6,000, (11-05-92, Sotheby-NY, #58, illus.), etching in black ink w/delicate plate tone on sturdy laid.

$2645* *Little Putney (K. 179; M. 176), 1879,* first state of two w/butterfly, pub. Fine Art Society, blindstamp, full margins, good cond., bleaching, foxing, (02-11-93, Sotheby-NY, #55, illus.), 5¼ x 8¼ in., (134 x 209 mm.), drypoint on wove (BP 1866, DM 4381, FR 14,826, Y 318,867).

$748* *The Little Putney, No.I (K. 179), 1879,* 2nd final state, plate staining, crease, notations, surface soiling, (05-19-93, Butterfield, #2029), 5¼ x 8¼ in., (133 x 210 mm.), etching on wove (BP 486, DM 1216, FR 4096, Y 82,807).

$9350* *Little Venice (K. 183; M. 180), 1879-80: Two,* s., w/large shaded butterfly, i., annot., margins, paper thinned verso, ex-coll. Seth E. Thomas, Jr., sold after sale, (11-05-92, Sotheby-NY, #57, illus.), each approx. 7¼ x 10⅜ in., (185 x 264 mm.), etching in black ink w/selective wiping on warm toned Japan (BP 6081, DM 14,787, FR 50,027, Y 1,147,099).

BI *Long Venice (K. 212; M. 209), 1879-80,* fifth (final), pencil s. w/butterfuly, i., s. w/butterfly verso, annot., good cond., light staining, ex-coll. Seth E. Thomas, Jr., est. $7/9,000, (11-05-92, Sotheby-NY, #62, illus.), 5 x 12⅛ in., (126 x 307 mm.), etching in brown ink w/delicate plate tone on fine laid.

$1760* *Longshoremen (Kennedy 45), 1859,* only state, (12-08-92, Swann, #314, illus.), 5⅞ x 8⅞ in., (14.9 x 22.5 cm.), drypoint on fine China paper (BP 1103, DM 2740, FR 9342, Y 218,146).

$1320* *"Longshoremen" (K. 45),* plate s., d. 1859, (02-11-93, Boos, #406, illus.), image 5⅞ x 8⅞ in., (150 x 225 mm.), paper 9⅜ x 13¹/₁₆ in., (150 x 225 mm.), etching (BP 931, DM 2187, FR 7399, Y 159,132).

$1495* *"La Marchand Du Moutarde" and "The Rag Gatherers" (K., M. 22 and 23), 1858: Two,* first, 3rd state of five; second, final state; margins, good cond., mat stain, glued to backings, (02-11-93, Sotheby-NY, #50), one 6¼ x 3⁹/₁₆ in., (158 x 90 mm.), the other 6¼ x 3⁹/₁₆ in., (158 x 90 mm.), etching (BP 1055, DM 2476, FR 8380, Y 180,229).

$385* *La Marchande De Moutarde (K. 22; M. 22; Gr. 17; W. 16; T. 11),* s. in plate, (10-30-92, Sloan, #1596), 6⅛ x 3½ in., (15.6 x 8.9 cm.), etching (BP 247, DM 592, FR 2009, Y 47,690).

$523* *La Marchande De Moutarde (M. 22; Gr. 17; W. 16; T. 11; K. 22) (V/V),* s. in plate, (09-17-92, Sloan, #3074), 6⅛ x 3½ in., (15.6 x 8.9 cm.), etching (BP 294, DM 776, FR 2658, Y 65,115).

$409* *La Mere Malade (Levy 77), 1895,* untrimmed margins, sig., (02-24-93, Picard, #245), on old Japan (BP 285, DM 664, FR 2251, Y 47,993).

$1950* *Das Musikzimmer (Wedmore 26 II; Kennedy 33 II), c. 1858,* watermark, prov., (12-04-92, Bassenge, #6984, illus.), 5⁹/₁₆ x 8⁷/₁₆ in., (14.2 x 21.4 cm.), brown etching on hand-made (BP 1251, DM 3106, FR 10,535, Y 243,446).

$839* *Newspaper-Stall, Rue De Seine (E.G.K. 432),* definitive state, reddish stains verso, w/out margins, (06-11-93, Picard, #198), 32⁵/₁₆ x 7¾ in., (820 x 197 mm.), etching on tinted ground on laid (BP 551, DM 1364, FR 4597, Y 89,019).

BI *Nocturne (K. 184), 1879-80,* 4th state of 5, s. w/butterfly, i. 'imp' on tab; staining, excell. cond., est. $14/18,000, (11-09-92, Christie-NY, #37, illus.), sheet 7¹⁵/₁₆ x 11¹¹/₁₆ in., (201 x 297 mm.), etching and drypoint in brown on laid.

BI *Nocturne: Furnace (K. 213: M. 210), 1879-80,* 6th state of 7, wiped tone, s. w/butterfly, i. imp, good cond., printer's crease, pub. as part of Second Venice Set, 1886, est. $7/9,000, (05-13-93, Sotheby-NY, #442, illus.), 6½ x 9 in., (166 x 228 mm.), etching in dark brown ink on fine laid.

BI *Nocturne: Furnace (K. 213; M. 210), 1879-80,* seventh (final) state, wiped, s. w/butterfly, i. 'imp.', good cond.,repaired tears, ex-coll. Tracy Dows, Bertha Palmer Thorne, est. $7/9,000, (11-05-92, Sotheby-NY, #63, illus.), upper edge 6⅝ x 9 in., (168 x 230 mm.), etching and drypoint in sepia ink on thin laid.

$935* *Nursemaid And Child (Kennedy 37 II/II), 1859,* full margins, (03-14-93, Hindman, #306), 3¾ x 5⅛ in., (9.5 x 13 cm.), in brownish-black on cream laid (BP 652, DM 1556, FR 5291, Y 110,194).

$1495* *Nursemaids: Les Bonnes Du Luxembourg (W. 48; L. 79), 1894,* s. w/butterfly, margins, good cond., light-stain, foxing, (05-13-93, Sotheby-NY, #448, illus.), 7⅞ x 6¼ in., (200 x 160 mm.), sh 13½ x 10 in., (200 x 160 mm.), lithograph on chine applique mounted on heavy wove (BP 981, DM 2414, FR 8143, Y 166,909).

$2645* *Nursemaids: Les Bonnes Du Luxembourg (Way 48; Levy 79), 1894,* s. w/butterfly, pub. Art Journal, full margins, good cond., bleaching, foxing, (02-11-93, Sotheby-NY, #56, illus.), 7⅞ x 6⅛ in., (200 x 155 mm.), lithograph on cream laid (BP 1866, DM 4381, FR 14,826, Y 318,867).

BI *Old Battersea Bridge (K. 177; M. 174), 1879,* fourth state of five, s., i., good cond., brown stains, est. $8/12,000, (11-05-92, Sotheby-NY, #56, illus.), 7⅞ x 11⅝ in., (200 x 294 mm.), etching p. in brown ink w/atmospheric plate tone on laid.

$1265* *Old Hungerford Bridge (K., M. 75), 1861,* margins, foxed, glued, (02-11-93, Sotheby-NY, #53), 5½ x 8⅜ in., (140 x 213 mm.), etching on laid (BP 893, DM 2095, FR 7091, Y 152,502).

$3080* *Old Women (K. 224), c. 1879-80,* watermark, 2nd final state, s. w/butterfly, tab i. imp, repaired tear, very good cond., (11-09-92, Christie-NY, #40, illus.), sheet 5¹⁄₁₆ x 7¹⁵⁄₁₆ in., (128 x 203 mm.), etching in brownish-black on laid (BP 2036, DM 4917, FR 16,613, Y 382,229).

$1495* *The Pantheon, From The Terrace Of The Luxembourg Gardens (W. 45; L. 73), 1893,* s. w/butterfly, full margins, good cond., bleaching, rubbed spot, ex-coll. Royal Library of Windsor, (05-13-93, Sotheby-NY, #447), 6⅞ x 6⅜ in., (174 x 162 mm.), sh 11⅜ x 9⅜ in., (174 x 162 mm.), lithograph on Japan (BP 981, DM 2414, FR 8143, Y 166,909).

$3300* *The Piazetta (Kennedy 189), 1880,* s. w/butterfly, i. imp, 5th final state, from First Venice Set, 1881, (03-24-93, Grogan, #49, illus.), 9¹⁵⁄₁₆ x 7¹⁄₁₆ in., (25.2 x 17.9 cm.), etching in tone (BP 2235, DM 5390, FR 18,344, Y 387,734).

$3105* *Ponte De Piovan (K. 209; M. 206), 1879-80,* 4th state pf 6, s. w/butterfly, i. imp, good cond., (05-13-93, Sotheby-NY, #440), 8⅞ x 6 in., (226 x 153 mm.), etching w/drypoint on laid (BP 2038, DM 5014, FR 16,912, Y 346,656).

$193* *"The Pool",* t., Mrs. Drusilla Stemper Coll., (02-06-93, Julia, #165), image 5½ x 8½ in., (14 x 21.6 cm.), etching (BP 134, DM 320, FR 1082, Y 24,017).

$908* *Portrait Of Drouet,* (11-12-92, Freemn/Fine Art, #239B), plate 9 x 5¼ in., (22.9 x 13.3 cm.), drypoint (BP 596, DM 1439, FR 4853, Y 112,585).

$1265* *The Priest's House-Rouen (W. 74/a; L. 112), 1894,* 1st state of 2, s. w/butterfly, margins, light-stain, foxing, repaired loss, loss, repaired tear, (05-13-93, Sotheby-NY, #451), 9⅜ x 6⅛ in., (237 x 155 mm.), sh 12⅛ x 8⅜ in., (237 x 155 mm.), lithograph on thin laid (BP 830, DM 2043, FR 6890, Y 141,230).

$639* *Quiet Canal (E.G. Kennedy, 214),* definitive state, creases, w/out margins, (06-11-93, Picard, #197), 8⅞ x 6¹⁄₁₆ in., (225 x 154 mm.), etching on tinted ground on laid (BP 420, DM 1039, FR 3501, Y 67,798).

$2750* *Quiet Canal (K. 214; M. 211), 1879-80,* fifth (final) state, s. w/butterfly, i. 'imp', glue, discoloration, good cond., (11-05-92, Sotheby-NY, #64, illus.), 9 x 6⅛ in., (228 x 155 mm.), etching and drypoint in black ink (BP 1789, DM 4349, FR 14,714, Y 337,382).

$770* *The Rag Gatherers (K. 23), 1858,* plate s., d., 5th final state, large margins, light-struck, good cond., (10-28-92, Butterfield, #2773), 6¹⁄₁₆ x 3½ in., (154 x 89 mm.), etching on laid paper (BP 491, DM 1189, FR 4038, Y 94,479).

$248* *The Rag Gatherers (Kennedy N. 23),* fifth state, (11-30-92, Selkirk, #715), 6 x 3½ in., (15.2 x 8.9 cm.), etching (BP 164, DM 395, FR 1341, Y 30,865).

BI *The Rag Gatherers (M. 23; Gr. 18; W. 17; T. 31; K. 23) (V/V),* s., d. 1858 in plate, est. $800/1,000, (09-17-92, Sloan, #3075, illus.), 6 x 3½ in., (15.2 x 8.9 cm.), etching.

BI *Reading In Bed (M. 28; Gr. 31; W. 29; K. 28) (II/II),* s. in plate, est. $700/900, (09-17-92, Sloan, #3073), 4⅝ x 3⅛ in., (11.7 x 7.9 cm.), etching.

BI *La Retameuse (K. 14) (II/II),* s. in plate, prov., est. $500/700, (09-17-92, Sloan, #3077, illus.), 4¹⁵⁄₁₆ x 3½ in., (12.5 x 8.9 cm.), etching.

$330* *La Retameuse (K. 14), 1858,* 2nd (final) state, p. by Delatre, full margins, good cond., mat & light-staining, stray printing ink, surface soiling, pencil notation, (02-24-93, Butterfield, #2887), 4⅜ x 3½ in., (111 x 89 mm.), etching in laid (BP 230, DM 536, FR 1816, Y 38,723).

$605* *La Retameuse (Kennedy 14), 1858,* wide margins, second state, one of Twelve Etchings from Nature, collector stamps, (05-27-93, Swann, #296, illus.), 4⁵⁄₁₆ x 3½ in., (11 x 8.9 cm.), etching on Japan paper (BP 387, DM 971, FR 3272, Y 64,858).

$6325* *The Rialto (K. 211; M. 208), 1879-80,* wiped plate tone, s. w/butterfly, i. imp, good cond., light-stain, tape hinge, (05-13-93, Sotheby-NY, #441, illus.), 11⅝ x 7⅞ in., (295 x 199 mm.), etching in brownish-black on laid (BP 4152, DM 10,213, FR 34,450, Y 706,152).

$575* *La Robe Rouge (L. 96), 1894,* s. w/butterfly in stone, blindstamp, full margins, good cond., surface soiling, (05-19-93, Butterfield, #2030), 7¼ x 6⅛ in., (184 x 156 mm.), lithograph on laid (BP 373, DM 935, FR 3149, Y 63,655).

$7475* *Rotherhithe (K., M. 66), 1860,* margins, good cond., foxing, pub. as part of the Thames Set, 1871, (05-13-93, Sotheby-NY, #437, illus.), 10¾ x 7¾ in., (272 x 196 mm.), sh 11½ x 9 in., (272 x 196 mm.), etching w/drypoint on thin laid (BP 4907, DM 12,070, FR 40,714, Y 834,543).

$5280* *San Biagio (K. 197), 1879-80,* 6th state of 9, s. w/butterfly, i. imp on tab, repaired tear, split,staining, (11-09-92, Christie-NY, #38, illus.), sheet 8³⁄₁₆ x 11⅞ in., (208 x 302 mm.), etching in brown on laid Japan (BP 3491, DM 8429, FR 28,479, Y 655,249).

$8800* *San Biago (K. 197; M. 194), 1879-80,* sixth state of nine, s. w/butterfly, i., good cond., creases, (11-05-92, Sotheby-NY, #59, illus.), 8¼ x 12 in., (210 x 304 mm.), etching in brown ink on fine laid (BP 5724, DM 13,917, FR 47,084, Y 1,079,622).

$165* *Savoy Pigeons (Way 118, Levy 164), 1896,* as pub. in Studio, bears their blindstamp, (05-16-93, Hindman, #534), sheet 11½ x 7⅞ in., (29.2 x 20 cm.), 8 x 5¼ in., (29.2 x 20 cm.), lithograph (BP 107, DM 265, FR 892, Y 18,291).

$70* *"Savoy Pigeons" (W. 118) (L. 164), 1896,* as pub. in The Studio, drystamp, sheet toned, margin w/small voids, tear, (05-15-93, Cleveland, #346), 7¾ x 5⅜ in., (19.7 x 13.7 cm.), lithograph (BP 46, DM 113, FR 378, Y 7760).

$5775* *The Sisters (W. 71; L. 105), 1894,* second (final) state, s. w/butterfly, full margins, good cond., ex-coll. Bertha Palmer Thorne, (11-05-92, Sotheby-NY, #70, illus.), 5⅞ x 9⅛ in., (150 x 232 mm.), lithograph on laid Japan (BP 3756, DM 9133, FR 30,899, Y 708,502).

$7475* *The Sisters (W. 71; L. 105), 1894,* 2nd (final) state, s. w/butterfly, stamp, watermark, full margins, good cond., (05-13-93, Sotheby-NY, #450, illus.), 5⅞ x 9⅜ in., (148 x 237 mm.), sh 8⅛ x 13⅛ in., (148 x 237 mm.), lithograph on laid (BP 4907, DM 12,070, FR 40,714, Y 834,543).

$385* *Sketching No. 1 (Kennedy 86), 1861,* 3rd state, (12-08-92, Swann, #315), 4¹¹⁄₁₆ x 6⅜ in., (11.9 x 16.2 cm.), etching, chine colle onto wove (BP 241, DM 599, FR 2044, Y 47,719).

BI *The Smith's Yard (W. 88), 1895,* pub. in The Studio, blindstamp, margins, good cond., mat stain, stains, est. $800/1,000, (05-13-93, Sotheby-NY, #452), 7⅜ x 6 in., (187 x 152 mm.), sh 11¼ x 7⅜ in., (187 x 152 mm.), lithograph.

$110* *"The Smith's Yard" (Way 88) (Levy 126), 1895,* as pub. in The Studio, 1897, w/ drystamp, sun staining, glue and paper residue, (05-15-93, Cleveland, #345), 7¼ x 6¼ in., (18.4 x 15.9 cm.), lithograph (BP 72, DM 177, FR 595, Y 12,194).

$700* *The Smith: Passage Du Dragon [L109], 1894,* butterfly mono., (02-04-93, Sloan, #2386, illus.), 10⅝ x 6⅞ in., (27 x 17.5 cm.), lithograph (BP 489, DM 1153, FR 3908, Y 87,076).

$1430* *Soup A Trois Sous (Kennedy 49), 1859,* mat burn, only state, (12-08-92, Swann, #316), 5⅞ x 8⅞ in., (14.9 x 22.5 cm.), etching on thin China paper (BP 896, DM 2226, FR 7590, Y 177,243).

$1430* *"Soup A Trois Sous",* very good cond.?, (11-21-92, Bakker, #27, illus.), plate 5⅞ x 8¾ in., (14.9 x 22.2 cm.), etching (BP 942, DM 2280, FR 7680, Y 177,839).

$1100* *Soupe A Trois Sous (K49),* s. in plate, (02-04-93, Sloan, #2387, illus.), 5⅞ x 8⅞ in., (14.9 x 22.5 cm.), etching (BP 768, DM 1811, FR 6142, Y 136,833).

$550* *St. James Street (K. 169), 1878,* light stain, rippling, hinged to mat, good cond., (12-04-92, Doyle, #167), 11 x 6 in., (279 x 152 mm.), etching (BP 353, DM 876, FR 2971, Y 68,664).

$3300* *The Steps, Luxembourg (W. 43; L. 70), 1893,* s. w/butterfly, margins, good cond., surface dirt, paper adhering tocorner, ex-coll. Bertha Palmer Thorne, (11-05-92, Sotheby-NY, #67, illus.), 8¼ x 6¼ in., (210 x 158 mm.), lithograph on smooth wove (BP 2146, DM 5219, FR 17,657, Y 404,858).

$1150* *The Steps, Luxembourg (W. 43; L. 70), 1893,* full margins, mat/light-stain, foxing, (05-13-93, Sotheby-NY, #446, illus.), 12⅛ x 6¼ in., (308 x 158 mm.), sh 11 x 9 in., (308 x 158 mm.), lithograph on Van Gelder Zonen laid (BP 755, DM 1857, FR 6264, Y 128,391).

$800* *"Street At Saverne" (Kennedy v/v), 1958,* Kennedy v/v after removal of Delatre's name and address, excell. cond., (05-15-93, Cleveland, #342), 8⅛ x 6¼ in., (20.6 x 15.9 cm.), etching on gold tissue applique on laid Japan (BP 520, DM 1287, FR 4324, Y 88,682).

$1495* *"A Street At Saverne", "Billingsgate" and "The Little Pool" (Kennedy19, 47, and 74), 1858-61: Three,* final states, margins, K. 19 laid down, scrapes, K. 47 w/mat stains,good cond., (02-11-93, Sotheby-NY, #49), etching (BP 1055, DM 2476, FR 8380, Y 180,229).

$1320* *Street At Saverne, 1858,* water damage, extends into image, (11-12-92, Freemn/Fine Art, #239A), 8¼ x 6¼ in., (21 x 15.9 cm.), etching (BP 867, DM 2092, FR 7055, Y 163,670).

$49,500* *Study (Way 2; Levy 6), 1878,* p. by Way, wide margins, good cond., skinned spots, soiling, ex-coll.A. W. Scholle (L. 2923a), (11-05-92, Sotheby-NY, #66, illus.), 9¾ x 9¼ in., (248 x 235 mm.), sheet 14⅜ x 10 in., (248 x 235 mm.), lithotint in brown ink on white wove (BP 32,195, DM 78,286, FR 264,848, Y 6,072,874).

$1980* *Temple (K. 234; M. 231), 1880-81,* s. on tab w/butterfly, good cond., ex-coll. H. H. Benedict, Edith Schumann 1988 Trust, (11-05-92, Sotheby-NY, #65), 4 x 6 in., (102 x 152 mm.), etching in brown ink on laid (BP 1288, DM 3131, FR 10,594, Y 242,915).

BI *The Terrace, Luxembourg (L. 86; W. 55), 1894,* butterfly mono. in stone, est. $1,500/2,000, (09-17-92, Sloan, #3079), 3⅜ x 8¼ in., (8.6 x 21 cm.), lithograph.

$1955* *"Thames Warehouses" and "Thames Police" (K. 38 and 44; M. 37 and 43),1859: Two,* large margins, light-stain, laid down, margins, losses, light/mat stained, ex-coll. Eugene Mayer, (05-13-93, Sotheby-NY, #436), one 5⅛ x 8⅛ in., (130 x 206 mm.), other 4 x 5 in., (130 x 206 mm.), etching, one on laid (BP 1283, DM 3157, FR 10,648, Y 218,265).

$6050* *Turkeys (K. 199; M. 196), 1879-80,* first state of two, selectively wiped, s. w/shaded butterfly, i., narrow to thread margins, good cond., ex-coll. Bertha Palmer Thorne, (11-05-92, Sotheby-NY, #60, illus.), 8¼ x 5¼ in., (210 x 133 mm.), etching w/drypoint in brown-black ink, rich plate tone on laid w/watermark (BP 3935, DM 9568, FR 32,370, Y 742,240).

$8050* *Two Doorways (K. 193), 1880,* 6th final state, tone, s. w/ butterfly, i. imp., w. w/two additional butterflies, i. w/ Whistler's three circle mark denoting selected impression, excell. cond., (05-11-93, Christie-NY, #132, illus.), sheet 7⅞ x 11⅜ in., (200 x 289 mm.), etching and drypoint in brown on laid (BP 5139, DM 12,681, FR 42,728, Y 885,491).

BI *Two Ships (K. 148), 1875,* 3rd final state, #5, pub. Dowdeswell, stamp, margins, good cond., creasing, image, mount-staining. ex coll. Sir John Day (L. 526), est. BP 6/700, (06-30-93, Sotheby-London, #336), sh 13 x 7½ in., (330 x 191 mm.), etching.

$660* *Unsafe Tenement (Kennedy 17), 1858,* 4th final state, from Twelve Etchings from Nature, (12-09-92, Grogan, #68), 6³⁄₁₆ x 8⁵⁄₁₆ in., (15.7 x 21.1 cm.), etching (BP 421, DM 1036, FR 3535, Y 81,835).

$935* *The Unsafe Tenement (Kennedy 17), 1859,* time/mat burn, (12-08-92, Swann, #317, illus.), 6⅛ x 8¾ in., (15.6 x 22.2 cm.), etching (BP 586, DM 1456, FR 4963, Y 115,890).

BI *Upright Venice (K. 205; M. 202), 1879-80,* first state of four, s. w/butterfly, i., stain, thin spot, discoloration, good cond., ex-coll. Seth E. Thomas, Jr., est. $12/15,000, (11-05-92, Sotheby-NY, #61, illus.), 9⅞ x 7 in., (250 x 178 mm.), etching w/drypoint in black ink on old laid.

$283* *Vauxhall Bridge (K. 70), 1861,* 2nd final state, full margins, mounted, (11-30-92, Phillips-London, #368), plate 2⅝ x 4½ in., (67 x 114 mm.), etching on fine laid (BP 187, DM 451, FR 1531, Y 35,221).

$2420* *"Vauxhall Bridge", "A Sketch On The Embankment", "The Winged Hat", "Street At Saverne", "La Ratameuse", "Hurlingham" and "Whistler With The White Lock": Seven,* (06-11-93, Doyle, #89), 6 etchings, 1 lithograph (BP 1590, DM 3933, FR 13,260, Y 256,764).

$550* *"La Vieille Aux Loquer" (K. 21),* s. Whistler in plate, (09-25-92, Wolf, #3A, illus.), 8 x 5¾ in., (20.3 x 14.6 cm.), etching (BP 321, DM 815, FR 2757, Y 66,385).

BI *La Vieille Aux Loques (K. 21), 1858,* 3rd (final) state, margins, laid, est. BP 4/600, (12-01-92, Christie-London, #554), P. 8⁹⁄₁₆ x 5¹³⁄₁₆ in., (208 x 148 mm.), etching on Japan.

$825* *La Vieille Aux Loques (Kennedy III/III), 1858,* from series Twelve Etchings from Nature (French Set), (05-16-93, Hindman, #532), 8⅛ x 5¾ in., (20.6 x 14.6 cm.), sheet 9⅜ x 6¾ in., (20.6 x 14.6 cm.), etching on gold toned chine applique backed w/thin laid paper (BP 536, DM 1327, FR 4459, Y 91,453).

$453* *La Vielle Aux Loques (Kennedy 21),* 3rd state of 3, time staining, attaches, ex-collect. Sir High Walpole, (10-27-92, Phillips-London, #322), plate 8¼ x 5¾ in., (210 x 146 mm.), etching on tissue thin laid japan (BP 286, DM 694, FR 2356, Y 55,413).

$13,200* *Weary (Kennedy, Mansfield. 92), 1863,* third (final) state, s. w/butterfly, good cond., ex-coll. J.H. Hutchinson and Bertha Palmer Thorne, (11-05-92, Sotheby-NY, #55, illus.), 7¾ x 5⅛ in., (198 x 130 mm.), drypoint and roulette in black ink on laid w/watermark (BP 8585, DM 20,876, FR 70,626, Y 1,619,433).

$1540* *Whistler Sketching (Kennedy 25), 1859,* 1st plate from series Twelve Etchings from Nature, only state, (12-08-92, Swann, #318, illus.), 4⅜ x 5¾ in., (11.1 x 14.6 cm.), etching on thin gold colored China paper (BP 965, DM 2398, FR 8174, Y 190,878).

$6050* *The Winged Hat (L. 38), 1890,* s., full margins, staining, foxmarks, tears, very good cond., hingedto original wove mount, s., t., i., on mount, (11-09-92, Christie-NY, #43, illus.), border 7 x 6¾ in., (178 x 171 mm.), lithograph on laid (BP 4000, DM 9658, FR 32,632, Y 750,807).

$431* *Wrapping (The Tiny Pool) (K. 173), 1878,* s. w/butterfly in plate, full margins, good cond., (05-19-93, Butterfield, #2028), 3⅞ x 2⅝ in., (98 x 67 mm.), etching on wove (BP 280, DM 701, FR 2360, Y 47,714).

BI *Zaandam (K. 416), 1889,* 2nd final state, s. w/butterfly, i. imp, paper discoloration, foxing,est. BP 6/7,000, (06-30-93, Sotheby-London, #340, illus.), sh 5⅛ x 8½ in., (130 x 216 mm.), etching in dark brown.

WHISTLER, James Abbott McNeill (after)
$15 *"Portrait Of The Artist"*, engraved by William Hole, (04-16-93, G.A. Key, #112), 9 x 7 in., (22.9 x 17.8 cm.), b/w engraving (BP 10, DM 24, FR 82, Y 1687).

WHITCOMBE (after)
$31 *Sea Battles: Two,* (12-11-92, G.A. Key, #72), 5 x 8 in., (12.7 x 20.3 cm.), colored aquatint (BP 20, DM 49, FR 167, Y 3836).

WHITCOMBE, Thomas (after)
$223* *Naval Achievements Of Great Britain: Set Of Four* by Thomas Sutherland, restrikes, margins, (03-17-93, Bonhams-Chelsea, #359), plate 8¼ x 12 in., (21 x 30.5 cm.), aquatint w/hand-coloring (BP 154, DM 371, FR 1261, Y 26,155).

WHITE, Clarence
$345* *"The Arbor" and "Boy With Camera Work", 1908: Two,* from Camera Work, first attrib., t., d., (05-23-93, Butterfield, #3680, illus.), one 8¼ x 6 in., other 7½ x 5½ in., photogravure (BP 225, DM 564, FR 1899, Y 38,134).
$3850* *Landscape-Winter (Camera Work #23), c. 1908,* (10-15-92, Sotheby-NY, #99, illus.), 6 x 7½ in., (15.2 x 19.1 cm.), photograph, platinum print (BP 2356, DM 5731, FR 19,435, Y 461,908).
BI *Mr. And Mrs. Thibaudeau, 1915: Two,* mounted on tissue paper, image init.; s., d., est. $3/4,000, (05-23-93, Butterfield, #3679, illus.), each approx. 9¾ x 7¼ in., photograph, platinum print.
BI *Portrait Of Frederick W. Goudy, c. 1920,* s., est. $6/900, (10-14-92, Swann, #598, illus.), 8½ x 6¾ in., (21.6 x 17.1 cm.), photograph, vintage photogravure.
$605* *Portrait Of Woman, 1906,* photog.'s red mono. recto, sig., d., (04-07-93, Swann, #595, illus.), 9 x 7 in., photograph, toned platinum print (BP 400, DM 978, FR 3311, Y 68,734).
$1210* *Sir Emery Walker And T.J. Cobden-Sanderson,* from an original silver print, tipped to mount, (09-24-92, Swann, #35), 3¼ x 4⁷⁄₁₆ in., (83 x 112 mm.), photograph, platinum print, w/original silver print (BP 708, DM 1793, FR 6090, Y 145,555).

WHITE, Harold
BI *Twelve Images Relating To The Camera Club,* 1940s, majority w/pencil annots., one w/photog.'s ink stamp; labels, majority approx. 242 x 186mm, est. BP 800/1,200, (05-07-93, Sotheby-London, #126, illus.), photograph, silver print.

WHITE, Harvey
$148* *Franchot Tone, Portrait Beside Fireplace,* slight tear, (10-10-92, Bonhams, #7, illus.), 13 x 10 in., (33 x 25.4 cm.), photograph (BP 88, DM 220, FR 738, Y 18,018).

WHITE, Henry   1819-1896
$908* *"The Llugwy At Bettws Y Coed, 1850s",* mounted on card, t., s., 198 x 250mm, (05-07-93, Sotheby-London, #60, illus.), photograph, albumen print (BP 575, DM 1436, FR 4838, Y 99,978).

WHITE, Minor   1908-1976
BI *Beginnings, 1952,* s., t., lit., est. $7/9,000, (10-13-92, Christie-NY, #511, illus.), 12⅜ x 9½ in., (31.4 x 24.1 cm.), photograph, gelatin silver print.
BI *Beginnings, 1962,* s., lit., est. $3,5/4,500, (04-08-93, Christie-NY, #461, illus.), 11¼ x 8½ in., (28.6 x 21.6 cm.), photograph, gelatin silver print.
$2875* *"Bullet Holes, Capital Reef, Utah", 1962,* s., d., illus., (05-23-93, Butterfield, #3681, illus.), 9½ x 7½ in., photograph, gelatin silver print (BP 1872, DM 4701, FR 15,823, Y 317,785).
$2090* *Cypress Grove Trail, Point Lobos, California,* (1950), p.l., s., d., lit., (10-13-92, Christie-NY, #510, illus.), 11½ x 8⅛ in., (29.2 x 20.6 cm.), photograph, gelatin silver print (BP 1217, DM 3062, FR 10,403, Y 253,425).
$2200* *Dock In Snow, Vermont, 1971,* s. by photog., mounted, (10-15-92, Sotheby-NY, #514, illus.), 12⅛ x 8⅞ in., (30.8 x 22.5 cm.), photograph, gelatin silver print (BP 1346, DM 3275, FR 11,106, Y 263,947).
BI *Drid Williams, 1962,* s., t., d., lit., est. $2/3,000, (10-13-92, Christie-NY, #625, illus.), 5¾ x 7⅜ in., (14.6 x 18.7 cm.), photograph, gelatin silver print.

BI *Nude (Tom Murphy),* (1948), c. 1963, s., d., lit., est. $6/8,000, (10-13-92, Christie-NY, #509, illus.), 9¼ x 7½ in., (23.5 x 19.1 cm.), photograph, gelatin silver print.
BI *Nude, Foot,* (1947), c. 1974, (c) stamp, est. $3/4,000, (10-13-92, Christie-NY, #508, illus.), 8½ x 10⅝ in., (21.6 x 27 cm.), photograph, gelatin silver print.
$3080* *Ponce, Puerto Rico (Cemetery), Late January,* (1973), c. 1975, credit, estate, (c) stamps, lit., (10-13-92, Christie-NY, #626, illus.), 9¼ x 11¾ in., (23.5 x 29.8 cm.), photograph, gelatin silver print (BP 1794, DM 4512, FR 15,331, Y 373,469).
BI *Root And Frost, 1958,* s., t., d., lit., est. $3/4,000, (10-13-92, Christie-NY, #512, illus.), 9¾ x 10⅞ in., (24.8 x 27.6 cm.), photograph, gelatin silver print.
$3025* *Selected Images: Two: "Easter Sunday" and "Shattered Rock", 1963 & 1964,* (Bunnell, pl. 168), mounted, s., 1st d. by photog., (10-15-92, Sotheby-NY, #515, illus.), one 9⅝ x 3½ in., (24.4 x 8.9 cm.), other 9⅝ x 6½ in., (24.4 x 8.9 cm.), photograph, gelatin silver prints (BP 1851, DM 4503, FR 15,270, Y 362,927).
BI *The Sound Of One Hand Clapping #1, Metal Ornament,* prov., est. $2,500/3000, (05-16-93, Hindman, #344, illus.), 8 x 6¾ in., photograph, silver print.
BI *"Wall: Capital Reef, Utah", 1962,* t., d., photog.'s stamp, est. $1,5/2,000, (05-23-93, Butterfield, #3682, illus.), 8¼ x 13¼ in., photograph, gelatin silver print.
$2300* *Waterfall, Stony Brook State Park, 1959,* s., t., d., lit., (04-08-93, Christie-NY, #460, illus.), 9⅜ x 7¾ in., (23.8 x 19.7 cm.), photograph, gelatin silver print (BP 1508, DM 3695, FR 12,507, Y 261,008).

WHITE, Tony (after)
$85* *U.S. Military Aircraft: Twelve,* (04-22-93, Bonhams-Chelsea, #39), image 13½ x 18½ in., (34.3 x 47 cm.), reprod. in colors (BP 55, DM 137, FR 461, Y 9346).

WHITE STAR LINE
$220* *New York, Queensville, Liverpool,* (11-12-92, Freemn/Fine Art, #240), mat 15½ x 22½ in., (39.4 x 57.2 cm.), lithographic poster (BP 144, DM 349, FR 1176, Y 27,278).

WHITEFIELD, E. (after)
$3300* *View Of Boston In 1848, From East Boston,* by C. Burton, (11-07-92, Northeast, #175, illus.), 20 x 44 in., (50.8 x 111.8 cm.), lithograph (BP 2158, DM 5294, FR 17,809, Y 407,307).
$468* *View Of The Public Garden And Boston Common,* large tear into image, poor to fair cond., tears, (06-11-93, Freemn/Fine Art, #252), 15½ x 28½ in., (39.4 x 72.4 cm.), lithograph w/hand-coloring (BP 307, DM 761, FR 2564, Y 49,655).

WHITEFIELD, Edwin
$575* *View Of Newburgh, N.Y. (Norton 32; Repps 2797), 1846,* pub. by Whitefield, margins, tears, creases, laid down between mat and backboard, (01-28-93, Sotheby-NY, #450), 14⅛ x 31½ in., (359 x 800 mm.), hand-colored lithograph (BP 380, DM 911, FR 3083, Y 71,393).
$440* *"View Of The Public Garden And Boston Common, From Arlington Street", 1886,* pub. John H. Bufford, good cond.?, (02-07-93, Bakker, #95), image 15¾ x 28½ in., (40 x 72.4 cm.), lithograph (BP 304, DM 730, FR 2466, Y 54,754).

WHITEHEAD, Buell   American 20th cent.
$94* *"Bayou",* s., t., tear, good cond., (10-31-92, Cleveland, #236), 7⅝ x 10¾ in., (19.4 x 27.3 cm.), lithograph in colors (BP 60, DM 145, FR 491, Y 11,644).
$25* *"Bayou",* s., t., tear, (05-15-93, Cleveland, #347, illus.), 7⅝ x 10¾ in., (19.4 x 27.3 cm.), color lithograph on heavy wove (BP 16, DM 40, FR 135, Y 2771).

WHITEHEAD, Walter   American 1874-1956
BI *The Marchbanks Press, New York, 1915,* Marchbanks Press, B+ cond., creasing, est. $8/1,200, (08-06-92, Swann, #293, illus.), 20 x 15 in., (50.8 x 38.1 cm.),

WHITELEY, Brett   Australian 1939-1992
BI *Drawing About Drawing,* s., #51/70, t., prov., exhib., est. C$ 2/300, (12-01-92, Ritchie, #30, illus.), 31 x 23 in., (78.7 x 58.4 cm.), color serigraph.
$1702* *Linfield Gardens,* s. Brett Whiteley, #74/80 pen, lit., (08-11-92, L. Joel, #11G, illus.), 35¹³⁄₁₆ x 55⁵⁄₁₆ in., (91 x

140.5 cm.), two color silkscreen and hand-coloring w/ photo mechanical reprod. (BP 884, DM 2498, FR 8459, Y 217,954, A$ 2310).

WHITESELL, Pop American 1876-1958
BI *"King Of Comus",* s., i., est. $3/500, (11-21-92, Goldberg, #728, illus.), 19½ x 15¼ in., (49.5 x 38.7 cm.), photograph, b/w.

WHITEWORTH and YATES, Publishers
BI *Gen. Washington, 1784,* glued in corners, light-stained, soiling, abrasions, creases, rippling, est. $800/1,200, (01-28-93, Sotheby-NY, #441), image 5 x 4⅜ in., (127 x 111 mm.), sheet 8¼ x 6½ in., (127 x 111 mm.), stipple engraving on oatmeal laid paper.

WHITING, Frederick
$159* *Man And Woman With Whippets In An Open Landscape,* s., margins, staining, (03-03-93, Bonhams-Chelsea, #55), plate 9 x 11½ in., (22.9 x 29.2 cm.), drypoint etching (BP 110, DM 262, FR 888, Y 18,579).

WHITNEY
$935* *Young Boy Holding A Walking Stick And Wearing A Knapsack,* modern seal, 1850s, (04-07-93, Swann, #149, illus.), photograph, sixth-plate daguerrotype (BP 618, DM 1512, FR 5118, Y 106,226).

WHITTOME, Irene Canadian School b. 1942
$1368* *"Rebirth": Set of Four,* t., s., d. Irene F. Whittome 87, (09-15-92, Encans, #123, illus.), each 10$\frac{1}{16}$ x 7⅞ in., (25.5 x 20 cm.), etching w/mine de plomb and watercolor (BP 732, DM 2035, FR 6909, Y 169,832, C$ 1665).

WHYTE and CO.
$1270* *"The Highland Railway", 1864: Sixteen,* mounted on card, photog.'s p. credit Whyte & Co., Inverness, t., d. 1865, (05-06-93, Christie-London, #56, illus.), each approx. 8 x 13½ in., photograph, albumen print (BP 805, DM 2000, FR 6734, Y 139,729).

WICKEY, Harry
$220* *Urban Landscape,* s., good cond., (07-19-92, Bakker, #177), plate 5 x 7¼ in., (12.7 x 18.4 cm.), etching (BP 113, DM 321, FR 1084, Y 27,350).

WIED-NEUWIED, Prince Maximilian Alexander Philipp zu
$85,000* *Voyage Dans L'Interieur De L'Amerique Du Nord, Execute Pendant Les Annees (Abbey Travel 615 note, Howes M443a, Pilling 2522, Rader 3652 note, Sabin47015, Wagner-Camp-Becker 76:2, et al.), 1840-41-43,* 3 text vols., and atlas folio, atlas plates after Karl Bodmer, each blindstamp C Bodmer / Direct, engraved by J. Hurlimann, L. Weber, C. Vogel, Salathe, Himely, Prevost, R. Rollet, P. Legrand, Desmadryl and others, tears, browning, foxing, Talfourd P. Linn Coll., (05-21-93, Sotheby-NY, #109, illus.), 9¼ x 5⅞ in., (235 x 149 mm.), atlas w/81 aquatint plates, hand-colored and heightened w/ gum arabic, 30 wood-engraved plates (BP 55,070, DM 138,211, FR 464,989, Y 9,371,555).

WIEGEL, Martin ac. c. 1533-1580
BI *Die Bekehrung Des Saulus (Strauss 9), c. 1600,* est. DM 750, (12-04-92, Bassenge, #6500), 10$\frac{7}{16}$ x 14$\frac{3}{16}$ in., (26.5 x 36 cm.), woodcut.

WIEGERS, Jan
$544* *(Cafescene),* s., margins, good cond., paper discoloration, minor handling creases, small defects and creasing at edges of sheet, Late Gerhard Brauer Coll., (05-27-93, Sotheby-Amstrdm, #804, illus.), 19½ x 15$\frac{9}{16}$ in., (495 x 385 mm.), woodcut on wove (BP 348, DM 873, FR 2942, Y 58,319, G 978).
$128* *(Landscape),* s., full sheet, good cond., occasional foxing, (05-27-93, Sotheby-Amstrdm, #805), sheet 15¼ x 19⅝ in., (387 x 499 mm.), lithograph on Japan (BP 82, DM 205, FR 692, Y 13,722, G 230).

WIERIX, Hieronymus Dutch c. 1553-1619
BI *Fides (M.-H. 1388), c. 1580,* after Maarten de Vos, 1st state of 4, small margins, split, staining,laid, est. BP 1,0/1,200, (12-01-92, Christie-London, #16), 11¾ x 13$\frac{1}{16}$ in., (298 x 332 mm.), engraving.
$325* *Die Geschichte Der Mackabaer (Alvin 125-132; Mauquoy-Hendrickx 46-53II): Eight,* watermark, prov., (12-04-92, Bassenge, #6503), each approx. 7$\frac{15}{16}$ x 11¼ in., (20.3 x 28.6 cm.), engraving (BP 208, DM 518, FR 1756, Y 40,574).
BI *Humana Complexio (M. -H. 1555), 1579,* after Willem van Haecht, 2nd (final) state, unevenly inked towards bottom, narrow to thread margins, tear, staining, discoloration, laid, est. BP 1,8/2,200, (12-01-92, Christie-London, #14, illus.), 16¾ x 13$\frac{9}{16}$ in., (425 x 345 mm.), engraving.
BI *Quattuor Adversus Iustum Certamina Vinci (M. -H. 1387), c. 1580,* after Maarten de Vos, narrow margins, repaired split, stains, laid, est. BP 1,0/1,200, (12-01-92, Christie-London, #15), 11⅞ x 13⅜ in., (301 x 339 mm.), engraving.
BI *Triumphus Veritatis (M. -H. 1409), c. 1579,* trimmed, tear, losses, staining, defects, laid, est. BP 480/600, (12-01-92, Christie-London, #13), 17$\frac{1}{16}$ x 13$\frac{3}{16}$ in., (433 x 335 mm.), engraving.

WIERIX, Jerome 1553-1619
$444* *La Vierge Et L'Enfant Jesus (Pulchra ut luna) (Alvin 601; Mauquoy-Hendrickx 1451),* (05-15-93, Loudmer, #108, illus.), 4$\frac{5}{16}$ x 2$\frac{15}{16}$ in., (109 x 74 mm.), etching on laid (BP 289, DM 714, FR 2400, Y 49,218).

WIERTZ, Jupp
$315* *Germany, Berlin. Evening Near The Memorial Church, c. 1930,* tears, (02-04-93, Christie-S. Ken, #180), 40 x 25 in., (101.6 x 63.5 cm.), color lithograph (BP 220, DM 519, FR 1759, Y 39,184).

WIGGINS, Guy American 1883-1962
BI *(Mountain Landscape),* stone s., full margins, good cond., surfaces soiling, handling creases, est. $4/600, (05-19-93, Butterfield, #1833), 11¾ x 17½ in., (298 x 445 mm.), lithograph on Rives BFK.

WIGLEY, James b. 1918
$142* *Night Rider,* s. James Wigley, i. A.F, (08-11-92, L. Joel, #69G), 4$\frac{15}{16}$ x 7$\frac{13}{16}$ in., (12.6 x 19.9 cm.), etching (BP 74, DM 208, FR 706, Y 18,184, A$ 192).
$162* *Two Boys On A Rubbish Dump, 9 Mile Camp,* s. James Wigley, i., (08-11-92, L. Joel, #63G), 4$\frac{15}{16}$ x 6⅛ in., (12.6 x 15.6 cm.), etching (BP 84, DM 238, FR 805, Y 20,745, A$ 220).

WIK
$83* *Un Americain A Paris (An American In Paris) (Belgian),* (01-31-93, Morelle/Marchan, #118), 14$\frac{3}{16}$ x 18½ in., (36 x 47 cm.), poster (BP 56, DM 134, FR 452, Y 10,354).

WILCOX, Frank American 1887-1964
$40* *Cleveland Series,* excell. cond., (05-15-93, Cleveland, #351), 5⅛ x 7 in., (13 x 17.8 cm.), etching (BP 26, DM 64, FR 216, Y 4434).
$45* *"Reunion In 1896", 1932,* s., plate No. 5, the Print-A-Month Club, Cleveland, excell. cond., (05-15-93, Cleveland, #350), 8 x 9$\frac{15}{16}$ in., (20.3 x 25.2 cm.), etching (BP 29, DM 72, FR 243, Y 4988).

WILD, Charles (after) English 1781-1835
BI *The King's Great Drawing Room, Kensington Palace,* by William James Bennett, est. $100/150, (12-10-92, Sloan, #2083), 8 x 9¾ in., (20.3 x 24.8 cm.), color aquatint.

WILD, Frank
$2541* *Shackleton's South Pole Expedition, 1908: Ten,* mounted on two-toned card, one s., three sigs., each t., ink stamp From Mallet & Sons, lit., (05-06-93, Christie-London, #91, illus.), each approx. 11¼ x 9 in., photograph, gelatin silver print (BP 1610, DM 4002, FR 13,473, Y 279,569).

WILDE, Gerald
$94* *Rhapsody On A Windy Night,* s., hinged, prop. Maxwell Business Communications Ltd., (10-07-92, Christie-S. Ken, #105), 9¾ x 7 in., (24.8 x 17.8 cm.), lithograph p. in color (BP 55, DM 136, FR 461, Y 11,305).

WILDING, Dorothy 1893-1976
$302* *Coward, Noel, 1931,* s., d., (09-17-92, Swann, #75), 6 x 8 in., (15.2 x 20.3 cm.), photograph, sepia (BP 170, DM 448, FR 1535, Y 37,600).

BI *"Les Demoiselles" and "Curieuse", n.d., (1930s): Two,* each neg. t., photog.'s printed credit, tissue s., est. BP 3/500, (10-29-92, Christie-London, #91), first 8¼ x 11 in., (21 x 27.9 cm.), second 11¼ x 8 in., (21 x 27.9 cm.), photograph, photogravure mounted on tissue.

BI *Man With Cigarette,* photog.'s sig. on overmat, studio label, 1930s, est. $500/750, (04-07-93, Swann, #596, illus.), 9 x 6¼ in., photograph, silver print.

WILEY, William T. American b. 1937

BI *Bullsigh Sea Doubt,* annot., margins, good cond., est. $1/1,500, (05-19-93, Butterfield, #2381), 14 x 12¾ in., (356 x 324 mm.), offset lithograph w/extensive hand-coloring on wove.

$275* *C.D., Landfall P. 43,* s., d. '75, t., num. 9/10, pub. Landfall Press, their chop, prov., (09-20-92, Hindman, #731), sheet 22 x 20¼ in., (26.7 x 26.4 cm.), drypoint (BP 161, DM 408, FR 1396, Y 33,988).

$1210* *Eerie Grotto? Okini, 1982,* s., t., d., num. 187/200, Crown Point Press blindstamp, full margins, excell. cond., (09-19-92, Christie-E, #247), sheet 29¼ x 22¾ in., (743 x 578 mm.), woodcut in colors on Japan (BP 696, DM 1812, FR 6205, Y 150,760).

BI *"Field Stone", "Feels Tone" and "Feel Stoned", 1973: Three,* s., d., t., #3/20, blindstamp publisher, Landfall Press, p. Jerry Raidiger and Jack Lemon, surface soiling, soft crease, est. $4/600, (05-19-93, Butterfield, #2382), each 19¾ x 27⅝ in., (502 x 702 mm.), lithograph in colors on wove.

$220* *In Transit, 1982,* s., d. 83, #9/20, blindstamp pub., Landfall Press, full margins, verygood cond. (?), (02-24-93, Butterfield, #3279), sheet 22⅞ x 18⅛ in., (581 x 460 mm.), lithograph on fibrous (BP 153, DM 357, FR 1211, Y 25,816).

BI *Working At CPP, 1978,* s., d., #7/15, blindstamp pub. Crown Point Press, margins, good cond.?, est. $6/800, (10-28-92, Butterfield, #3172), 14¹²⁄₁₆ x 12⁵⁄₁₆ in., (375 x 313 mm.), etching on cream wove.

WILKIE, Ulfert b. 1907

BI *Calligraphy,* inits., d. (19)69, The Print Club of Cleveland pub. no. 47,1969, est.$100/150, (07-03-92, Sloan, #323), sheet 17 x 13 in., (43.2 x 33 cm.), etching.

$22* *"Calligraphy", 1969,* s., excellent cond., (10-31-92, Cleveland, #402), 12½ x 8½ in., (31.8 x 21.6 cm.), lithograph (BP 14, DM 34, FR 115, Y 2725).

WILKINSON, Norman

$112* *Fishing From The Boat,* s., margins, (10-29-92, Bonhams-Chelsea, #80), plate 6 x 9 in., (15.2 x 22.9 cm.), drypoint etching (BP 72, DM 172, FR 585, Y 13,873).

WILL, Johann Martin

BI *Benjamin Franklin, Ne. A Boston Dans La Nouvelle Angleterre Le 17 Janvier 1706, c. 1777,* after C.N. Cochin, slightly grey impression, margins, printing defectin background, light-stained, good cond., est. BP 4/600, (11-30-92, Phillips-London, #317), plate 14¼ x 9⅜ in., (362 x 238 mm.), mezzotint on laid.

WILLE, J.G. 1715-1808

$172* *"Musiciens Ambulans" (Le Blanc 98), 1764,* after DIETRICY, laid down on boards, browned, 4th state of 4, (06-09-93, Bubb Kuyper, #2083), 19⅛ x 13¾ in., (48.5 x 35 cm.), copper engraving (BP 113, DM 281, FR 946, Y 18,292, G 316).

WILLEMS, Charles Henri b. c. 1865

$361* *Chambre Increvable Larue Sans Liquide,* Paris, Imp. Dupont, cond. B+, (06-11-93, Boisgirard, #161, illus.), 59¹⁄₁₆ x 43⁵⁄₁₆ in., (150 x 110 cm.), poster (BP 237, DM 587, FR 1978, Y 38,302).

WILLENBECHER, John

$39* *"Spectral",* s., t., #3/65, i., prov., (12-02-92, Boos, #476), 25⅞ x 25⅞ in., (658 x 658 mm.), silkscreen (BP 25, DM 61, FR 209, Y 4853).

WILLETTE, Adolphe

BI *Cacao Van Houten (Das Fruhe Plakat II 885), c. 1894,* Imp. Ch. Verneau, fairly good cond., (02-12-93, Cheval/Robert, #76), 54⁵⁄₁₆ x 39⅜ in., (138 x 100 cm.), poster.

$440* *Exposition Internationale,* Charles Verneau, A- cond., (08-06-92, Swann, #294, illus.), 54 x 38 in., (137.2 x 96.5 cm.), (BP 230, DM 650, FR 2196, Y 56,122).

$132* *Untitled (Seductive Man And Woman),* s., d., very fine cond., hinges, (10-31-92, Cleveland, #352, illus.), 13½ x 9 in., (34.3 x 22.9 cm.), lithograph (BP 85, DM 203, FR 689, Y 16,351).

WILLIAMS, Emmet b. 1925

BI *"10 Autobiographical Sketches", 1979: Ten,* Edition Hansjorg Meyer, Stuttgart/London, s., d., num., est. DM 1400, (12-01-92, Karl/Faber, #1352), 14³⁄₁₆ x 20½ in., (36 x 52 cm.), color lithograph on hand-made board.

WILLIAMS, Sheldon (after)

BI *Hunting Scenes, "A Hunting Morning" and "Gone Away": Two,* by B.C. Hester, pub. July 24, 1878, by G.P. McQueen, est. $2/300, (06-11-93, DuMouchelle, #2253), 12 x 17½ in., (30.5 x 44.5 cm.), hand-colored mezzotint.

$275* *"The Meet" and "The Death": Two,* (11-12-92, Freemn/Fine Art, #241), both 14 x 24 in., (35.6 x 61 cm.), colored engravings (BP 181, DM 436, FR 1470, Y 34,098).

WILLIAMS, T.R. 1825-1871

$1633* *Still Life With Fox And Cockerel,* 1850s, photog.'s credit label, (05-06-93, Christie-London, #3, illus.), stereoscopic daguerreotype, paper-taped (BP 1035, DM 2572, FR 8659, Y 179,668).

WILLIAMS, Thomas R.

$2420* *Still Life,* #11 handwritten on label, 1850s, (04-07-93, Swann, #167, illus.), photograph, stereo daguerreotype (BP 1599, DM 3914, FR 13,246, Y 274,938).

WILLIAMS, Engraver

$16* *Captain Robert Barclay,* pub. S.W. Fores, 1809, margins, stained, scuffed, defects, (03-03-93, Bonhams-Chelsea, #17), plate 16¾ x 11¾ in., (42.5 x 29.8 cm.), hand-colored aquatint (BP 11, DM 26, FR 89, Y 1870).

WILLIAMSON, Thomas

BI *Oriental Field Sports; Being, A Complete, Detailed, And Accurate Description Of The Wild Sports Of The East, 1819,* Howlett, for Thomas McLean, Oblong Demy broadsheets, after Samuel Howett after Williamson, by H. Merke, J. Humble, or Viveres, light stains, offsets, spotted, est. $8/12,000, (06-14-93, Sotheby-NY, #350, illus.), 17⅝ x 22¾ in., (44.8 x 57.8 cm.), color p. frontispiece and 41 hand-colored aquatint or stipple-engraved plate.

WILLIE, John George

$108* *"Beggar Approaching Women Washing Clothes" and "Mother And Child Listening To A Hermit's Story": Two,* plates d. 1762 and 1770, (06-08-93, Ritchie, #15, illus.), one 4¼ x 6⅝ in., (10.8 x 16.8 cm.), other 5¼ x 5½ in., (10.8 x 16.8 cm.), etching on laid (BP 71, DM 175, FR 590, Y 11,471, C$ 138).

WILLIKENS, Ben b. 1939

BI *"Anstaltsraume Nr. 1",* s., e.a., light-stained, est. DM 600, (12-01-92, Karl/Faber, #1355), 15⅜ x 20½ in., (39 x 52 cm.), color lithograph on board.

BI *Geoffnete Tur,* s., epreuve d'artiste, creases, est. DM 1000, (12-01-92, Karl/Faber, #1356), 31⁵⁄₁₆ x 22⁷⁄₁₆ in., (79.5 x 57 cm.), color lithograph on Fabriano wove.

BI *Loffel Und Gabel, (19)72,* s., d., E(preuve d') A(rtiste), light-stained, est. DM 600, (12-01-92, Karl/Faber, #1353), 19⁵⁄₁₆ x 18⁵⁄₁₆ in., (49 x 46.5 cm.), color lithograph on wove.

$133* *Raum Mit Offener Tur, (19)73,* s., d., num., (12-01-92, Karl/Faber, #1354), 31⁵⁄₁₆ x 22¹³⁄₁₆ in., (79.5 x 58 cm.), lithograph in grisaille on Fabriano wove (BP 88, DM 212, FR 722, Y 16,559).

WILLINGER, Laszlo

BI *Alan Curtis, Double Image Portrait,* s., est. BP 300/450, (10-10-92, Bonhams, #115, illus.), 11½ x 9 in., (29.2 x 22.9 cm.), mounted photograph.

BI *Arturo Toscanini,* lifetime original print, prov., est. BP 2/300, (10-10-92, Bonhams, #116, illus.), 18 x 16 in., (45.7 x 40.6 cm.), photograph.

$416* *Clark Gable,* 1938, p.l., s., pencil num. AP1/20, mounted lit., (12-17-92, Christie-S. Ken, #44, illus.), 14½ x 18¼ in., (36.8 x 46.4 cm.), photograph, gelatin silver print (BP 264, DM 649, FR 2219, Y 51,124).

$297* *Clark Gable And Joan Crawford,* s., #101/325, (10-10-92, Bonhams, #119, illus.), 21 x 22 in., (53.3 x 55.9 cm.), lithographic print (BP 176, DM 441, FR 1481, Y 36,158).

$315* *Clark Gable, Portrait,* s., #102/325, (10-10-92, Bonhams, #118, illus.), 18 x 21 in., (45.7 x 53.3 cm.), lithographic print (BP 187, DM 468, FR 1571, Y 38,349).

BI *Dolores Del Rio And John Howard,* s., est. BP 5/700, (10-10-92, Bonhams, #114, illus.), 11 x 7 in., (27.9 x 17.8 cm.), mounted photograph.

BI *Fred Astaire,* 1939, p.l., ink s., num. AP1/10, est. BP 2/250, (12-17-92, Christie-S. Ken, #46, illus.), 12⅜ x 9⅝ in., (31.4 x 24.4 cm.), photograph, gelatin silver print.

BI *Greer Garson,* 1943, p.l., pencil s., est. BP 2/250, (12-17-92, Christie-S. Ken, #52, illus.), 12⅝ x 10⅛ in., (32.1 x 25.7 cm.), photograph, gelatin silver print.

$607* *Hedy Lamarr,* 1941, p.l., pencil s., num. AP9/20, (12-17-92, Christie-S. Ken, #50, illus.), 12⅝ x 10½ in., (32.1 x 26.7 cm.), photograph, matt gelatin silver print (BP 385, DM 948, FR 3237, Y 74,598).

BI *Ingrid Bergman,* s., est. BP 7/900, (10-10-92, Bonhams, #105, illus.), 8 x 6½ in., (20.3 x 16.5 cm.), mounted photograph.

BI *Jane Russell,* s., est. BP 250/350, (10-10-92, Bonhams, #113, illus.), 10¼ x 8 in., (26 x 20.3 cm.), mounted photograph.

BI *Jane Russell And Jack Beutel,* s., The Outlaw, est. BP 3/400, (10-10-92, Bonhams, #112, illus.), 8 x 8½ in., (20.3 x 21.6 cm.), mounted photograph.

BI *Joan Collins,* 1960, from Seven Thieves, 20th Cent. Fox, ink s., est. BP 3/500, (12-17-92, Christie-S. Ken, #54, illus.), 12¾ x 10⅝ in., (32.4 x 27 cm.), photograph, gelatin silver print.

$381* *Joan Crawford,* 1939, p.l., s., lit., (12-17-92, Christie-S. Ken, #47, illus.), 18½ x 15⅛ in., (47 x 38.4 cm.), photograph, gelatin silver print (BP 242, DM 595, FR 2032, Y 46,823).

BI *Joan Crawford,* 1939, silver ink s., num. AP1/10, est. BP 2/300, (12-17-92, Christie-S. Ken, #48, illus.), 14 x 10⅞ in., (35.6 x 27.6 cm.), photograph, matt gelatin silver print.

$381* *Katharine Hepburn,* 1940, p.l., white ink s., (12-17-92, Christie-S. Ken, #53, illus.), 19½ x 15½ in., (49.5 x 39.4 cm.), photograph, gelatin silver print (BP 242, DM 595, FR 2032, Y 46,823).

$347* *Laurence Olivier,* 1940, p.l., ink s., (12-17-92, Christie-S. Ken, #45, illus.), 12½ x 10 in., (31.8 x 25.4 cm.), photograph, gelatin silver print (BP 220, DM 542, FR 1851, Y 42,645).

BI *Lucille Ball,* s., #5/5/, est. BP 4/600, (10-10-92, Bonhams, #110, illus.), 14 x 11 in., (35.6 x 27.9 cm.), photograph.

BI *Lucille Ball, Mirror Image Portrait,* s., #2/5, est. BP 4/600, (10-10-92, Bonhams, #109, illus.), 14 x 11 in., (35.6 x 27.9 cm.), photograph.

BI *Luise Rainer,* s., est. BP 6/900, (10-10-92, Bonhams, #103, illus.), 9 x 7 in., (22.9 x 17.8 cm.), mounted photograph.

BI *Marilyn Monroe,* #24/25, blind embossed Willinger Estate, est. BP 350/450, (10-10-92, Bonhams, #107, illus.), 14 x 11 in., (35.6 x 27.9 cm.), photograph.

BI *Marilyn Monroe, Full Face Portrait,* s., #16/50, est. BP 4/500, (10-10-92, Bonhams, #108, illus.), 14 x 11 in., (35.6 x 27.9 cm.), photograph.

BI *Marilyn Monroe, Standing In Bathing Costume,* s., #18/50, est. BP 350/450, (10-10-92, Bonhams, #106, illus.), 14 x 11 in., (35.6 x 27.9 cm.), photograph.

$416* *Marlene Dietrich,* 1942, p.l., s., lit., (12-17-92, Christie-S. Ken, #51, illus.), 18½ x 15⅛ in., (47 x 38.4 cm.), photograph, gelatin silver print (BP 264, DM 649, FR 2219, Y 51,124).

BI *Marlene Dietrich,* s., #9/10 by photog., blindstamp on image, late 1940's p.l. later no 9, (04-06-93, Sotheby-NY, #385, illus.), photograph.

$241* *Marlene Dietrich Standing,* s., #113/325, (10-10-92, Bonhams, #120), 27 x 22 in., (68.6 x 55.9 cm.), lithographic print (BP 143, DM 358, FR 1202, Y 29,340).

BI *Marlene Dietrich, Standing On Train,* s., est. BP 6/900, (10-10-92, Bonhams, #111, illus.), 17½ x 15 in., (44.5 x 38.1 cm.), photograph.

BI *Norma Shearer And Tyrone Power,* "Marie Antoinette", s., (10-10-92, Bonhams, #102, illus.), 9½ x 7 in., (24.1 x 17.8 cm.), mounted photograph.

$312* *Sigmund Freud,* n.d. (1930s), p.l., white ink s., (12-17-92, Christie-S. Ken, #42), 18½ x 15¼ in., (47 x 38.7 cm.), photograph, gelatin silver print (BP 198, DM 487, FR 1664, Y 38,343).

BI *Tyrone Power,* 1938, p.l., ink s., mounted, lit., est. BP 250/350, (12-17-92, Christie-S. Ken, #43, illus.), 18½ x 15 in., (47 x 38.1 cm.), photograph, gelatin silver print.

$334* *Vivien Leigh,* for Waterloo Bridge, s., #104/325, (10-10-92, Bonhams, #117, illus.), 26½ x 20 in., (67.3 x 50.8 cm.), lithographic print (BP 198, DM 496, FR 1666, Y 40,662).

$1391* *Vivien Leigh,* "Waterloo Bridge", s., (10-10-92, Bonhams, #104, illus.), 19½ x 16 in., (49.5 x 40.6 cm.), photograph (BP 825, DM 2066, FR 6938, Y 169,345).

$520* *Vivien Leigh In Waterloo Bridge,* 1940, p.l., pencil s., lit., (12-17-92, Christie-S. Ken, #49, illus.), 12½ x 9½ in., (31.8 x 24.1 cm.), photograph, gelatin silver print (BP 330, DM 812, FR 2773, Y 63,906).

WILLIS, Mildred Aston
$515* *"Tunis And Carthage", 1907: Twenty-Seven,* album, handwritten t. page w/photog.'s credit and d., (10-29-92, Christie-London, #65), each approx. 2½ x 3¾ in., (6.4 x 9.5 cm.), photograph, platinum print (BP 330, DM 792, FR 2688, Y 63,793).

WILLISON, G. (after)
$150* *Miss Lumsden (C.S. 23), 1770,* by Thomas Watson, scratch-letter proof, 1st state of 2, pub. Robert Sayer, nicks, paper losses, (11-30-92, Phillips-London, #85), sheet 20¼ x 14⅓ in., (514 x 364 mm.), mezzotint on laid (BP 99, DM 239, FR 811, Y 18,668).

WILLOUGHBY, Bob
$403* *"Marilyn Monroe",* 1960, p. 1978, s., d., num., edit. 8/200, annot., photog.'s stamp, (05-23-93, Butterfield, #3684), 14 x 9½ in., photograph, gelatin silver print (BP 262, DM 659, FR 2218, Y 44,545).

WILLUMSEN, J.F.
$628* *Bjergbestigersken,* s. J.F. Willumsen 1947, 194/325, (09-29-92, B. Rasmussen, #376), lithograph (BP 353, DM 887, FR 3027, Y 74,967, DK 3450).

WILP, Charles   b. 1937
BI *Naturerfahrung In Afrika,* 1980: Sixteen, 56/250, est. DM 600, (11-12-92, Lempertz, #275), each 5¹³⁄₁₆ x 3¹⁵⁄₁₆ in., (14.8 x 10 cm.), color photograph.

BI *Sandzeichnungen In Diani,* 1980: Seventeen, XI/XX, est. DM 600, (11-12-92, Lempertz, #274, illus.), each 3¹⁵⁄₁₆ x 5¹⁵⁄₁₆ in., (10 x 15.2 cm.), color photograph.

WILQUIN, A.
$126* *Petrole Hahn, "Pour Les Cheveux",* good cond., lit., (11-19-92, Ribeyre/Baron, #52), 22¹³⁄₁₆ x 16¹⁵⁄₁₆ in., (58 x 43 cm.), poster (BP 83, DM 201, FR 677, Y 15,670).

WILSON, A.   British 19th cent.
$165* *Red Owl,* by A. Lawson, (10-18-92, Hindman, #517), 13 x 9¾ in., (33 x 24.8 cm.), hand colored etching (BP 101, DM 246, FR 833, Y 19,796).

WILSON, A. (after)
$173* *Rail, Wood-Cock, c. 1800: Two,* by J. G. Warnicke, margins, staining, Anthony N. B. Garvan Coll., (06-05-93, Christie-NY, #56), pl 10 x 13 in., (254 x 330 mm.), etching w/hand-coloring on wove (BP 114, DM 280, FR 945, Y 18,558).

WILSON, Charles Banks   American b. 1918
BI *"Comanche Portrait", 1942,* s., pub. AAA, excellent cond., (10-31-92, Cleveland, #237), 10¼ x 14½ in., (26 x 36.8 cm.), lithograph.

WILSON, Edward A.   American 1886-1970
$55* *Hogback Meetinghouse,* s., discoloration, (11-12-92, Freemn/Fine Art, #242), 9½ x 13⅛ in., (24.1 x 33.3 cm.), lithograph (BP 36, DM 87, FR 294, Y 6820).

WILSON, Geoffrey R. b. 1927
$41* *Mountain Erosion,* s. Geoff Wilson, i., d. 1964, #1/9, (08-11-92, L. Joel, #179G), 16¾ x 21⅜ in., (42.5 x 54.3 cm.), color screenprint (BP 21, DM 60, FR 204, Y 5250, A$ 55).

WILSON, George Washington
$1045* *Bridges: In Scotland, England, and Ireland c. 1861: Twenty-Nine,* (10-14-92, Swann, #273), each, approx. 7 x 10 in., (17.8 x 25.4 cm.), photograph, albumen prints mounted on linen (BP 613, DM 1529, FR 5186, Y 126,636).
BI *Group Of Topographic, Landscape, Street, Seaside, And Architectural Views Throughout Scotland And England: Thirty-Eight,* photog.'s inits., t., inventory num. in neg., 1870s, est. $700/1,000, (04-07-93, Swann, #281), 7 x 10 in., photograph, albumen print.

WILSON, John
$3630* *"Native Son",* s., d. 1945, very good cond.?, (03-28-93, Bakker, #102, illus.), 13 x 11½ in., (33 x 29.2 cm.), lithograph (BP 2439, DM 5922, FR 20,133, Y 422,486).

WILSON, Marla
$88* *"High Country Elk",* #507/695, s., t., num., (03-10-93, Maynard, #320), 18 x 27¾ in., (45.7 x 70.5 cm.), silkscreen (BP 61, DM 146, FR 497, Y 10,397, C$ 110).
$84* *"Orcas At Burke Channel",* #444/695, s., t., num., (03-10-93, Maynard, #322), 13½ x 23½ in., (34.3 x 59.7 cm.), silkscreen (BP 59, DM 140, FR 475, Y 9924, C$ 105).

WILSON, Robert contemporary
$1083* *"Louis XV Chair", 1977,* s., d., num., t., (11-28-92, Grisebach, #839, illus.), 19⅝ x 15¾ in., (49.8 x 40 cm.), woodcut and soft-ground etching on copper print paper (BP 715, DM 1725, FR 5857, Y 134,785).

WILSON, Stanley R.
$59* *Long-Tail Duck,* black ink s., margins, (09-17-92, Bonhams-Chelsea, #68), plate 6 x 9 in., (15.2 x 22.9 cm.), etching w/drypoint in colors on thin laid paper (BP 33, DM 88, FR 300, Y 7346).

WILSON, Sydney Ernest English b. 1869
$66* *Adelaide,* s., (05-28-93, Sloan, #192, illus.), (33 x 26.7 cm.), color mezzotint (BP 42, DM 105, FR 354, Y 7077).

WILSON, Wes
$302* *Grateful Dead And James Cotton, 1966,* West Coast Litho Co., A- cond., colors fading, (08-06-92, Swann, #296, illus.), 20½ x 13½ in., (52.1 x 34.3 cm.), (BP 158, DM 446, FR 1507, Y 38,520).
$302* *Grateful Dead, Dance Concert, 1966,* West Coast Litho Co., A- cond., colors fading, (08-06-92, Swann, #295, illus.), 21½ x 13½ in., (54.6 x 34.3 cm.), (BP 158, DM 446, FR 1507, Y 38,520).

WILTHELM, Heinrich b. 1913
$169* *"Sich Drehender Turmhahn",* s., (03-24-93, Venator/Hansten, #4574), approx. 22$^1/_{16}$ x 15¾ in., (56 x 40 cm.), color woodcut w/gouache (BP 114, DM 276, FR 939, Y 19,857).

WIMBLAD
$95 *Spil Selv, 1953,* Andreasen and Lachmann, edge loss, (09-24-92, Alderfer, #305), 33¼ x 24¼ in., (84.5 x 61.6 cm.), (BP 56, DM 141, FR 478, Y 11,428).

WINCHELL, Paul H. American 1903-1972
BI *"Flushing The Geese" and "Morning Flight": Two,* both s., good cond., stain in image, tape, (Flight), est. $2/300, (05-15-93, Cleveland, #352), one 10⅛ x 8⅛ in., (25.7 x 20.6 cm.), other 8$^3/_{16}$ x 10⅜ in., (25.7 x 20.6 cm.), drypoint.
$65* *"Mallard's Rising", "Ducks Into The Wind" and "Six Geese Flying": Three,* s., good cond., (05-15-93, Cleveland, #353), largest 10⅜ x 8$^3/_{16}$ in., (26.4 x 20.8 cm.), smallest 8 x 10¼ in., (26.4 x 20.8 cm.), drypoint (BP 42, DM 105, FR 351, Y 7205).

WINCK, Christian German 1738-1797
$991* *Die Allegorie Der Malerei (Nagler 7 II), 1768,* (06-04-93, Bassenge, #5585, illus.), 8¾ x 5⅝ in., (22.2 x 14.3 cm.), etching (BP 656, DM 1609, FR 5424, Y 106,881).

WIND, Gerhard 1928-1992
BI *Campo Di Fiori, 1960: Ten,* s., num., est. DM 3,200, (11-28-92, Schoppmann, #881), 22$^{13}/_{16}$ x 17$^5/_{16}$ in., (58 x 44 cm.), color serigraph.

WINDSTOSSER, Ludwig b. 1921
BI *Schaumzone, c. 1949,* studio stamp, t., est. DM 600, (11-12-92, Lempertz, #276), 11⅛ x 9$^3/_{16}$ in., (28.3 x 23.3 cm.), photograph, gelatin silver print.

WINKEL
$869* *Soennecken & Co., Munchen,* p. Wolf u Sohn, creases, defects, (05-07-93, Christie-S. Ken, #75), 23 x 30½ in., (58.4 x 77.5 cm.), color lithograph (BP 550, DM 1374, FR 4630, Y 95,684).
$1042* *Soennecken Depot Photographischer Artikel,* p. Wolf u Sohn, crease, backed on linen, (05-07-93, Christie-S. Ken, #73, illus.), 19¼ x 26¼ in., (48.9 x 66.7 cm.), color lithograph (BP 660, DM 1647, FR 5551, Y 114,732).

WINKELMANN, Georg
BI *Am Waldsee,* s., margins, good cond., mat & light-staining, rubbed area, yellow stain, green paper tape, pencil notations, est. $3/500, (02-24-93, Butterfield, #2986), 3$^7/_{16}$ x 4⅜ in., (76 x 111 mm.), woodcut in colors on heavy wove.

WINKLER, John W. American 1890-1979
$83* *Boatyard In Alameda, 1928,* s., prov., (12-13-92, Hindman, #317), 6 x 8¾ in., etching (BP 53, DM 130, FR 445, Y 10,268).
$105* *"Dusk At Fisherman's Wharf", 1939,* s., annot. Artist's proof, in another hand, reduced plate b/b, printed c. 1970, excellent cond., (10-31-92, Cleveland, #238), 6⅜ x 8¾ in., (16.2 x 22.2 cm.), etching (BP 67, DM 162, FR 548, Y 13,006).
$110* *Goats, Houses And Children On Telegraph Hill, c. 1920,* s., prov., (12-13-92, Hindman, #314), 12½ x 8 in., etching (BP 70, DM 173, FR 589, Y 13,609).
$110* *Haunted House, 1919-1971,* s., prov., (12-13-92, Hindman, #313), 10¾ x 7 in., etching (BP 70, DM 173, FR 589, Y 13,609).
BI *Italian Family On Telegraph Hill,* s., prov., est. $250/350, (12-13-92, Hindman, #311), 11¼ x 6½ in., etching.
$83* *Portuguese Farm In Alameda, c. 1937,* s., prov., (12-13-92, Hindman, #319), 5½ x 8 in., etching (BP 53, DM 130, FR 445, Y 10,268).
$138* *Siesta On Telegraph Hill, 1956,* s., margins, good cond., mat staining, foxing, surface soiling, (10-28-92, Butterfield, #2778), 12⅜ x 7 in., (314 x 178 mm.), etching on laid paper (BP 88, DM 213, FR 724, Y 16,933).

WINNER, Gerd b. 1936
$913* *"Marcus", 1970/72,* s., d., t., (12-01-92, Karl/Faber, #1359), 6⅞ x 44$^5/_{16}$ in., (17.5 x 112.5 cm.), color serigraph (BP 603, DM 1455, FR 4959, Y 113,670).

WINOGRAND, Garry 1928-1984
BI *Boxer And Dachshund, Greece, 1977,* s., est. BP 4/600, (05-06-93, Christie-London, #193), image 9 x 13⅜ in., photograph, gelatin silver print.
$3300* *Democratic National Convention, Los Angeles,* (1960), p.l., s., num. 2/100, lit., (10-13-92, Christie-NY, #628, illus.), 15¾ x 10⅝ in., (40 x 27 cm.), photograph, gelatin silver print (BP 1922, DM 4834, FR 16,426, Y 400,146).
BI *"The Fort Worth Fat Stock Show And Rodeo", 1974-77,* s. by photog., est. $1/2,000, (04-06-93, Sotheby-NY, #469, illus.), 8½ x 12⅝ in., photograph.
$3300* *Garry Winogrand: Fifteen,* (1969-1980), DEP Editions, 1980, s., num. 16, (10-13-92, Christie-NY, #631, illus.), each 8⅞ x 13⅜ in., (22.5 x 34 cm.), photograph, gelatin silver prints (BP 1922, DM 4834, FR 16,426, Y 400,146).
$2420* *Marilyn Monroe, From The Seven Year Itch,* (1954), p.l., s., num. 1/100, (10-13-92, Christie-NY, #627, illus.), 15¾ x 10½ in., (40 x 26.7 cm.), photograph, gelatin silver print (BP 1409, DM 3545, FR 12,046, Y 293,440).
$2013* *New Mexico (Figments, p. 135), 1957,* s. by photog., (04-06-93, Sotheby-NY, #469A, illus.), 13 x 8½ in., photograph (BP 1330, DM 3243, FR 10,982, Y 229,585).

$1430* *New York City,* (1968), p.l., s., num. 9/80, lit., (10-13-92, Christie-NY, #630, illus.), 9¾ x 13⅛ in., (24.8 x 33.3 cm.), photograph, gelatin silver print (BP 833, DM 2095, FR 7118, Y 173,396).

BI *Nick Biondi, Golden Gloves Boxer, 1955,* magazine's handstamp, notations, est. $500/750, (04-07-93, Swann, #368, illus.), 8½ x 13 in., photograph, silver print.

$1955* *Selected Works From "Women Are Beautiful": Five,* 1970s, p. 1980, s., #9/80, (05-23-93, Butterfield, #3685, illus.), each approx. 8¾ x 13¼ in., photograph, gelatin silver print (BP 1273, DM 3197, FR 10,759, Y 216,094).

$1430* *Untitled (Sailor On Street), c. 1950,* s. by executor, ink estate stamps, Dixon Collection, (11-16-92, Butterfield, #6252, illus.), 9 x 13⅜ in., (229 x 340.3 mm.), photograph, gelatin silver print (BP 942, DM 2280, FR 7680, Y 177,839).

$1265* *Untitled, Selected Images: Eight,* 1969-80, from portfolio Women Are Beautiful, p.l., s., #20/80, lit., (04-08-93, Christie-NY, #520, illus.), each approx. 8¾ x 13⅛ in., (22.2 x 33.3 cm.), photograph, gelatin silver print (BP 830, DM 2032, FR 6879, Y 143,554).

$1540* *Untitled, Selected Images: Eight,* (1969-80), from Women Are Beautiful portfolio, p.l., s., num. 20/80,lit., (10-13-92, Christie-NY, #629, illus.), each 8¾ x 13⅛ in., (22.2 x 33.3 cm.), photograph, gelatin silver prints (BP 897, DM 2256, FR 7666, Y 186,735).

WINTER, Fritz German 1905-1978

$2526* *Abstrakte Komposition (Gabler 20), 1951,* s., num., (11-28-92, Schoppmann, #885), 17⁵⁄₁₆ x 25³⁄₁₆ in., (44 x 64 cm.), color etching on handmade (BP 1667, DM 4024, FR 13,661, Y 314,375).

$866* *"Farbaquatinta 8 (NE)" (Gabler 60), 1967,* s., num., (11-28-92, Grisebach, #840, illus.), 7 x 9¾ in., (17.8 x 24.8 cm.), color aquatint on copper print paper (BP 572, DM 1380, FR 4684, Y 107,778).

$458* *Farblitho (Gabler 51), 1966,* s., num., Mappe A, Kestner-Gesellschaft, (05-26-93, Dorling, #3074, illus.), 20⁷⁄₁₆ x 12⅜ in., (51.9 x 31.4 cm.), color lithograph on thick wove (BP 296, DM 747, FR 2515, Y 49,761).

$780* *"Farblitho 4" (Gabler 28), 1954,* s., d., i., num., (06-05-93, Grisebach, #928, illus.), 8⅜ x 10¾ in., (21.2 x 27.3 cm.), color lithograph on thin wove (BP 513, DM 1265, FR 4262, Y 83,673).

BI *Farblitho 6 (Gabler 30), (19)55,* s., d., num., est. DM 1400, (12-01-92, Karl/Faber, #1362), sh 13¾ x 19¹¹⁄₁₆ in., (35 x 50 cm.), lithograph in colors on thin board.

$2222* *Farbradierung IV, NE (Gabler 21), 1951,* s., #12/150, (05-27-93, Lempertz, #1114), 19⅛ x 27¹⁄₁₆ in., (48.5 x 68.7 cm.), color etching on wove (BP 1423, DM 3565, FR 12,017, Y 238,208).

BI *Geflecht Aus Linienformen, 1934,* mono., d. FW 34, est. DM 9/12,000, (06-05-93, Grisebach, #373, illus.), 22¼ x 13¾ in., (56.5 x 35 cm.), monotype and brush wash in tempera and oil on thick Japan hand-made.

$348* *"Geh Durch Den Spiegel", 1955: Two,* Galerie der Spiegel, (12-01-92, Karl/Faber, #1363), 15³⁄₁₆ x 10⁷⁄₁₆ in., (38.5 x 26.5 cm.), lithograph (BP 230, DM 555, FR 1890, Y 43,327).

BI *Komposition Mit Rot Und Blau, (19)68,* s., d., num., est. DM 2000, (12-01-92, Karl/Faber, #1364), 15¹⁵⁄₁₆ x 19¹¹⁄₁₆ in., (40.5 x 50 cm.), color lithograph on wove.

$614* *Komposition Nach Einem Alteren Entwurf (Gabler 60), 1967,* s., num., (11-28-92, Grisebach, #841, illus.), 7 x 9¾ in., (17.8 x 24.7 cm.), color aquatint on copper print paper (BP 405, DM 978, FR 3321, Y 76,416).

$1321* *Komposition, 1959,* d., s., (04-24-93, Kunsthaus, #828), 16⅛ x 14¹⁵⁄₁₆ in., (41 x 38 cm.), color screen print on linen (BP 834, DM 2071, FR 6993, Y 145,774).

$813* *"Roter Weg" Farblitho 9 (Gabler 33), 1957,* #34/40, s., d., (10-09-92, Winterberg, #3250, illus.), 11⅛ x 16⅜ in., (28.3 x 41.6 cm.), lithograph on handmade (BP 482, DM 1208, FR 4055, Y 98,977).

WINTER, Lumen American 20th cent.

$25* *Apollo XII,* s., artist's proof, s. by the three Apollo XII astronauts, (05-16-93, Hanzel, #460), 28½ x 20½ in., (72.4 x 52.1 cm.), color lithograph (BP 16, DM 40, FR 135, Y 2771).

WINTER, Rev. George Robert (after) (Canon Of Norwich)

BI *Eton (Abbey Scenery 446): Eighteen,* plates 1, 2, 6, 7, 8, 9, 10, 12, pub. J. Ryman, trimmed to image, 2 sides, dirt, damage, spotting, fading, laid on card, est. BP 8/1,000, (10-07-92, Christie-S. Ken, #69), 9¾ x 14 in., (24.8 x 35.6 cm.), colored tinted lithograph.

WINTERHALTER, Franz Xaver (after)

BI *Queen Victoria With Her Family, 1850,* by Samuel Cousins, scratch-letter proof before t., pub. F.G. Moon, blindstamp of Printsellers' Assoc., image creases, foxing, silver-fish damage, defects, est. BP 1/150, (11-30-92, Phillips-London, #31), sheet 31⅝ x 38½ in., (803 x 978 mm.), mixed-method engraving on india-laid.

WINTERS, Terry American b. 1949

BI *Album, 1988: Nine,* complete portfolio, init., #36/50, blindstamp, p. Aldo Crommelynck, pub. Editions Ilene Kurtz, full margins, good cond., original portfolio, (05-15-93, Sotheby-NY, #1183, illus.), each sheet 26⅜ x 20¾ in., (67 x 52.7 cm.), etchings on Hahnemuhle.

BI *Album, 1988: Set Of Nine,* New York, Editions Ilene Kurtz, inits., num., copy 44 of 50, blindstamps, full margins, excellent cond., est. $22/26,000, (11-09-92, Christie-NY, #460, illus.), 26½ x 21 in., (673 x 533 mm.), colored aquatint on Hahnemuhle.

BI *Factors Of Increase, 1983,* inits., d., #15/30, blindstamp, excellent cond., est. $3/3,500, (11-09-92, Christie-NY, #457, illus.), 31 x 22¾ in., (787 x 578 mm.), lithograph on Moulin du Verger handmade.

BI *Fourteen Etchings, 1989,* complete portfolio, init., s., d., #57/65, blindstamp, pub. ULAE, full margins, good cond., original box, est. $15/20,000, (05-15-93, Sotheby-NY, #1186, illus.), each sheet 18⅝ x 14⅛ in., (47.3 x 35.9 cm.), etchings on Italian paper.

$5500* *Marginalia, 1988,* inits., d., #12/66, blindstamp, excellent cond., (11-09-92, Christie-NY, #459, illus.), 48 x 31¾ in., (121.9 x 80.6 cm.), colored lithograph on wove (BP 3636, DM 8780, FR 29,666, Y 682,552).

BI *Novalis, 1983-89,* s., d., #10/50, blindstamp, pub. ULAE, full margins, good cond., Gertrude Kasle Coll., est. 2,5/3,500, (05-15-93, Sotheby-NY, #1185, illus.), 37¼ x 26¾ in., (94.6 x 67.9 cm.), etching and aquatint in colors on Entoutcas.

$248* *Paris Review, 1988,* inits., blindstamp p. ULAE, good cond., (10-28-92, Butterfield, #3173), 38¼ x 26⅝ in., (972 x 676 mm.), color lithograph on wove (BP 158, DM 383, FR 1300, Y 30,429).

$259* *Paris Review, 1988,* s., inkstamp printer, ULAE, good cond., (05-19-93, Butterfield, #2383), 38¼ x 26⅝ in., (972 x 676 mm.), lithograph in colors on wove (BP 168, DM 421, FR 1418, Y 28,673).

BI *Paris Review, 1988,* s., blindstamp printer, ULAE, very good cond. (?), est. $2/400, (02-24-93, Butterfield, #3280), 38¼ x 26⅝ in., (972 x 676 mm.), lithograph in colors on wove.

BI *Paris Review, 1988,* s., blindstamp printer, ULAE, good cond., est. $2/400, (02-24-93, Butterfield, #3281), 38¼ x 26⅝ in., (973.3 x 677.5 mm.), lithograph in colors on wove.

BI *Station, 1988,* s., d., #7/55, blindstamp, pub. ULAE, full margins, good cond., est.$2,5/3,000, (05-15-93, Sotheby-NY, #1182, illus.), 15¾ x 11¾ in., (40 x 29.8 cm.), intaglio.

$1760* *Untitled, 1987,* s., d,. #47/71, blindstamp, excellent cond., (11-09-92, Christie-NY, #458, illus.), 32 x 23 in., (813 x 584 mm.), colored lithograph on sea-green J. Greene (BP 1164, DM 2810, FR 9493, Y 218,416).

$1380* *Untitled, 1987,* s., d., #55/71, blindstamp, pub. ULAE, good cond., (05-15-93, Sotheby-NY, #1181, illus.), sheet 32 x 22⅞ in., (81.3 x 58.1 cm.), lithograph in colors on handmade green J. Greene & Son paper (BP 897, DM 2220, FR 7459, Y 152,976).

$1100* *Untitled, 1988,* s., d., num. 24/50, pub. Editions Ilene Kurtz, full margins, excell.cond., (09-19-92, Christie-E, #248, illus.), sheet 35 x 28 in., (889 x 711 mm.), etching and aquatint on wove (BP 633, DM 1647, FR 5641, Y 137,055).

WINTERSBERGER, Lambert Maria   b. 1941
BI   *"Worte Des Lebens, Zeichen Des Todes": Seven,* Galerie
Muller, s., num., est. DM 600, (12-01-92, Karl/Faber,
#1366), 23⅝ x 23⅝ in., (60 x 60 cm.), etching on
wove.

WINZENREID, Henry
$495*   *"Monterey Cypresses", "The Harbor (Sausalito)", and
"Near Pacific Grove", 1934: Three,* s., The Harbor t., w/
foxing, glue remains, skinned areas; Monterey Cypresses
annot. AP/, repaired tear, surface soiling; Near Pacific
Grove staining, skinned area, foxing, staining; each w/
estate stamp of artist, margins, goodcond., surface soiling,
creases, (02-24-93, Butterfield, #2890), from 7¹⁵⁄₁₆ x
6³⁄₁₆ in., (202 x 157 mm.), to 11¹⁄₁₆ x 9½ in., (202 x
157 mm.), etching, 2 on laid, 3rd on Umbria Italia (BP
345, DM 804, FR 2724, Y 58,085).

WIRE, Melville T.
$33*   *"Back From The Beach",* s., t., AAA, (12-11-92,
DuMouchelle, #1490), 7⅝ x 9¾ in., (19.4 x 24.8 cm.),
etching (BP 21, DM 52, FR 178, Y 4084).
$28*   *"Columbia River, Crown Point",* s., t., AAA, (12-11-92,
DuMouchelle, #1489), 7 x 9⅝ in., (17.8 x 24.4 cm.),
etching (BP 18, DM 44, FR 151, Y 3465).

WIT, F. de   Dutch 17th cent.
$825*   *Florida And Caribbean,* (12-13-92, Hindman, #247,
illus.), 19⅛ x 22⅛ in., hand-colored engraving (BP 527,
DM 1297, FR 4419, Y 102,066).

WIT, Marijke de
$51*   *Serre Nr. 2, 1975,* s., t., d., #3/15, full margins, good
cond., handling creases, (05-27-93, Sotheby-Amstrdm,
#522), 12¹¹⁄₁₆ x 12½ in., (322 x 317 mm.), etching on
wove (BP 33, DM 82, FR 276, Y 5467, G 92).

WITHERSTINE, Donald   b. 1896
BI   *Various Subjects: Twenty-Nine,* s., est. $4/600, various
sizes, (09-24-92, Mystic, #60A), etching.

WITKIN, Joel Peter   American b. 1939
$1438*   *"Amour", 1987,* s., t., d., i. Gift print to Model, by pho-
tog., (04-06-93, Sotheby-NY, #507, illus.), photograph
(BP 950, DM 2317, FR 7845, Y 164,005).
$3025*   *Androgyny Breastfeeding A Fetus, 1987,* s., t., d., num.
6/15 by photog., #6/15 ed., (10-15-92, Sotheby-NY, #633,
illus.), 14½ x 13¾ in., (36.8 x 34.9 cm.), photograph,
gelatin silver print (BP 1851, DM 4503, FR 15,270, Y
362,927).
BI   *"Androgyny Breastfeeding A Fetus, San Francisco", 1981,*
s., t., d., #12/15 by photog., est. $2,5/4,000, (04-06-93,
Sotheby-NY, #504, illus.), 14¼ x 13⅞ in., photograph.
$2750*   *The Angel Of The Carrots (Forty Photographs, p. 12),* s.,
t., d., num. AP #2, (c), i. by photog., 1981, p. 1982,
(10-15-92, Sotheby-NY, #636, illus.), photograph, gelatin
silver prints (BP 1683, DM 4093, FR 13,882, Y
329,934).
$1100*   *Bacchus Amelus, 1986,* s., t., num. 5/15, (c), i. by pho-
tog., #5/15 ed., (10-15-92, Sotheby-NY, #627, illus.), photograph, gelatin silver print (BP 673, DM 1637, FR
5553, Y 131,974).
$2475*   *La Brassiere De Joan Miro, 1982 (Forty Photographs, p.
30),* s., t., d., num. 5/15, (c), i. by photog., #5/15 ed.,
(10-15-92, Sotheby-NY, #632, illus.), 14⅝ x 15 in., (37.1
x 38.1 cm.), photograph, gelatin silver print (BP 1515,
DM 3684, FR 12,494, Y 296,941).
$805*   *The Capitulation Of France, 1982,* s., t., d., #11/15,
annot. New mexico, (c) insig., (04-08-93, Christie-NY,
#577, illus.), 14⅝ x 14⅝ in., (37.1 x 37.1 cm.), photo-
graph, toned gelatin silver print (BP 528, DM 1293, FR
4377, Y 91,353).
$2640*   *The Capitulation Of France, 1982,* s., t., d., num. 9/15,
annot., (c) insig., (10-13-92, Christie-NY, #633, illus.),
14⅝ x 14¾ in., (37.1 x 37.5 cm.), photograph, toned
gelatin silver print (BP 1538, DM 3868, FR 13,141, Y
320,116).
BI   *The Capitulation Of France, 1982,* s., t., d., num. 11/15,
i., #11/15 ed., est. $2/3,000, (10-15-92, Sotheby-NY,
#628, illus.), photograph, gelatin silver print.
BI   *"Carrot Cake #1", 1980,* s., t., d., i. A.P. #2 by photog.,
p. 1982, artist's proof, est. $2,5/4,000, (04-06-93,
Sotheby-NY, #505, illus.), photograph.

$3220*   *Corpus, Studies For The Tabernacle: Three,* together w/
pencil sketch and ink sketch, 1970 and 1972-73, each
photo. w/credit and sequential Roman numeral; first w/
credit stamp, lit., (04-08-93, Christie-NY, #573, illus.),
each approx. 13½ x 6¾ in., (34.3 x 17.1 cm.), photograph, gelatin silver print (BP 2111, DM 5173, FR
17,510, Y 365,411).
$3520*   *Counting Lessons In Purgatory, 1982,* s., t., d., num. 14/
15, annot., (10-13-92, Christie-NY, #632, illus.), 14½ x
14½ in., (36.8 x 36.8 cm.), photograph, toned gelatin silver print (BP 2050, DM 5157, FR 17,521, Y 426,822).
$2475*   *Courbet In Rejlander's Pool, 1985,* s., t., d., num. 1/15,
(c), i. by photog., #1/15 ed., (10-15-92, Sotheby-NY,
#635, illus.), photograph, gelatin silver print (BP 1515,
DM 3684, FR 12,494, Y 296,941).
$9200*   *Eunuch, New Mexico, 1982,* s., t., d., #1/3, prov., (04-08-
93, Christie-NY, #575, illus.), 28 x 28 in., (71.1 x 71.1
cm.), photograph, toned gelatin silver print (BP 6033,
DM 14,779, FR 50,027, Y 1,044,031).
$5750*   *"Gods Of Earth And Heaven", 1988,* s., t., d., #14/15,
(c), i. by photog., (04-06-93, Sotheby-NY, #501A,
illus.), 14¾ x 15 in., photograph (BP 3798, DM 9264,
FR 31,369, Y 655,794).
$2090*   *Infantilism, 1985,* s., t., d., (c), i. by photog., (10-15-92,
Sotheby-NY, #634, illus.), 14¾ x 15 in., (37.5 x 38.1
cm.), photograph, gelatin silver print (BP 1279, DM
3111, FR 10,550, Y 250,750).
$7150*   *Las Meninas, 1987,* s., t., d., num. 3/15, (c), i. by pho-
tog., #3/15 ed., (10-15-92, Sotheby-NY, #629, illus.), photograph, gelatin silver print (BP 4375, DM 10,643, FR
36,093, Y 857,828).
BI   *"Lisa Lyon As Hercules", 1983,* s., t., d., i. A.P. by photog., artist's proof, est. $2,5/3,500, (04-06-93, Sotheby-
NY, #506, illus.), photograph.
$3738*   *"Manuel Osorio" (Forty Photographs, p. 27), 1982,* s., t.,
d., i. AP 3 by photog., artist's proof, (04-06-93, Sotheby-
NY, #503, illus.), 14¼ x 14⅛ in., photograph (BP 2469,
DM 6022, FR 20,393, Y 426,323).
$10,925*   *Manuel Osorio, New Mexico, 1982,* p. 1980s, s., t., d.,
#2/3, lit., (04-08-93, Christie-NY, #574, illus.), 28 x 28
in., (71.1 x 71.1 cm.), photograph, gelatin silver print
(BP 7164, DM 17,550, FR 59,407, Y 1,239,787).
$2640*   *Poet: From A Collection Of Relics And Ornaments,
1986,* s., t., d., num. 9/15, annot., (c) insig., (10-13-92,
Christie-NY, #635, illus.), 14½ x 14¾ in., (36.8 x 37.5
cm.), photograph, toned gelatin silver print (BP 1538,
DM 3868, FR 13,141, Y 320,116).
$3220*   *Portrait Of A Dwarf, Los Angeles, 1987,* s., t., d., #5/15,
(04-08-93, Christie-NY, #578, illus.), 14¾ x 15 in., (37.5
x 38.1 cm.), photograph, gelatin silver print (BP 2111,
DM 5173, FR 17,510, Y 365,411).
$2420*   *The Prince Imperial, 1980,* s., t., d., num. 8/15, (c), i.,
#8/15 ed., (10-15-92, Sotheby-NY, #626, illus.), photo-
graph, gelatin silver print (BP 1481, DM 3602, FR
12,216, Y 290,342).
$3850*   *The Result Of War: The Cornucopia Dog, 1984,* s., t., d.,
num. 7/15, annot., lit., (10-13-92, Christie-NY, #634,
illus.), 15 x 15 in., (38.1 x 38.1 cm.), photograph, toned
gelatin silver print (BP 2242, DM 5640, FR 19,164, Y
466,836).
$4950*   *Un Santo Oscuro, 1987,* s., t., d., num. AP/2, annot., (c)
insig., (10-13-92, Christie-NY, #636, illus.), 14¾ x 15 in.,
(37.5 x 38.1 cm.), photograph, toned gelatin silver print
(BP 2883, DM 7252, FR 24,639, Y 600,218).
$4400*   *Un Santo Oscuro, 1987,* s., t., d., num. 10/15, (c), i. by
photog., #10/15 ed., (10-15-92, Sotheby-NY, #630,
illus.), 14¾ x 15 in., (37.5 x 38.1 cm.), photograph, gelatin silver print (BP 2692, DM 6550, FR 22,211, Y
527,894).
$2875*   *"Shaun Ariane Montiel As Canova's Venus, N.Y.C.", 1982,*
s., t., d., i. A.P. #1, No. 1 in a series of 4 by photog.,
artist's proof, (04-06-93, Sotheby-NY, #502, illus.), 14⅝
x 14¾ in., photograph (BP 1899, DM 4632, FR 15,685,
Y 327,897).
$2420*   *Siamese Twins, 1988,* s., t., d., num. 13/15, annot., (c)
insig., (10-13-92, Christie-NY, #637, illus.), 14½ x 14¾
in., (36.8 x 37.5 cm.), photograph, toned gelatin silver
print (BP 1409, DM 3545, FR 12,046, Y 293,440).

$5463* "The Sins Of Joan Miro", 1981, s., t., d., #11/15, i.
N.M. by photog., (04-06-93, Sotheby-NY, #508, illus.),
photograph (BP 3608, DM 8801, FR 29,804, Y 623,061).

$3220* The Sins Of Joan Miro, 1981, s., t., d., #3/15, annot.
N.M., lit., (04-08-93, Christie-NY, #576, illus.), 14⅝ x
14¾ in., (37.1 x 37.5 cm.), photograph, toned gelatin silver print (BP 2111, DM 5173, FR 17,510, Y 365,411).

BI   The Sins Of Joan Miro, 1981, s., t., d., num. 10/15, (c),
i., #10/15 ed., est. $4/6,000, (10-15-92, Sotheby-NY,
#625, illus.), photograph, gelatin silver print.

BI   Untitled, 1971, s., d., flush-mounted and glued to box
frame, est. $3/4,000, (04-08-93, Christie-NY, #571, illus.),
12⅝ x 11 in., (32.1 x 27.9 cm.), photograph, half-tone
collage w/applied gouache and metal studs.

$4370* Untitled, Sculpture And Photograph, early 1970s, sculp-
ture comprised of painted plaster, wood, glass, metal and
colored light bulb, impressed inits., (04-08-93, Christie-
NY, #572, illus.), photo 11½ x 10¼ in., (29.2 x 26 cm.),
(29.2 x 26 cm.), photograph, gelatin silver print and orig.
sculpture (BP 2866, DM 7020, FR 23,763, Y 495,915).

$4125* Woman On A Table, 1987, s., t., d., num. 4/15, (c), i. by
photog., #4/15 ed., (10-15-92, Sotheby-NY, #631, illus.),
photograph, gelatin silver print (BP 2524, DM 6140, FR
20,823, Y 494,901).

WITONSKI, Ted   American ac. 1930's
BI   "Skipper Alex's House", s., t., stamped NYC W.P.A. Art
Project, small margins, image creases/losses of pigment,
rough cond., est. $50/100, (05-15-93, Cleveland, #355),
18⅝ x 13¾ in., (47.3 x 34.9 cm.), color silkscreen.

WITSEN, W.A.   1860-1923
$251* Uilenburg I (Boon 147; v.W. 469), 1911, s., #53, (06-09-
93, Bubb Kuyper, #2035), 11¹³/₁₆ x 16¹⁵/₁₆ in., (30 x 43
cm.), etching (BP 166, DM 411, FR 1381, Y 26,694, G
460).

$157* Voorstraatshaven VIII (Boon 94; v.W. 426), 1900, s., (06-
09-93, Bubb Kuyper, #2037), 7⅝ x 9⁷/₁₆ in., (19.3 x 24
cm.), etching and aquatint (BP 104, DM 257, FR 864, Y
16,697, G 288).

$345* Winter II (Boon 132; v.W. 460), 1908, s., #43, (06-09-93,
Bubb Kuyper, #2038), 9¾ x 12¹³/₁₆ in., (24.7 x 32.5
cm.), etching and aquatint (BP 228, DM 564, FR 1898,
Y 36,690, G 633).

WITTIG, Werner   b. 1930
BI   "Leningrad/Alter Palast", sheet 4 of series, #89/120, t.,
s., est. DM 300, (04-24-93, Kunsthaus, #831), 7¹³/₁₆ x
9¹³/₁₆ in., (19.8 x 24.9 cm.), woodcut on Japan.

$1321* Neue Holzrisse, 1986: Ten, t., s., (04-24-93, Kunsthaus,
#830), color woodcut, on different papers (BP 834, DM
2071, FR 6993, Y 145,774).

WOEHRMAN, Ralph   American 20th cent.
$275* "Warthog", s. R. Woehrman '61 #10/10, t., (05-15-93,
Wolf, #742), 9 x 11 in., (22.9 x 27.9 cm.), etching (BP
179, DM 442, FR 1486, Y 30,484).

WOEIRIOT, Pierre (II)   1532-after 1596
$2125* Les Hommes Et Les Animaux Couverts D'Ulceres (Rob-
ert-Dumesnil VII, 53, XI S.339, 25, Bibl. Nat. Inventaire
S. 172-3, Nr. 58, 25), (06-04-93, Bassenge, #5414), 7½ x
8¹¹/₁₆ in., (19.1 x 22 cm.), engraving (BP 1406, DM
3451, FR 11,631, Y 229,185).

WOLCOTT, Marion Post   American 1910-1990
$2875* "Bringing Maple Sap To The Sugar House", "Old Fash-
ioned Peddler Who Goes From Door To Door" and
"Rail Fence Around Pasture And Grazing Lands:, 1940-
1941: Three, t., d., (05-23-93, Butterfield, #3686, illus.),
each approx. 7¼ x 9½ in., photograph, gelatin silver
print (BP 1872, DM 4701, FR 15,823, Y 317,785).

$863* Haircutting On Saturday Afternoon, Marcelle, Plantation,
Mileston, MS, 1939, p. 1981, s., d., neg. num., (05-23-
93, Butterfield, #3689, illus.), 7 x 9 in., photograph, gelatin silver print (BP 562, DM 1411, FR 4750, Y
95,391).

$1320* "Jitterbugging In Juke Joint, Clarksdale" (Marion Post
Wolcott, pl. 21), 1939/later, s., t., d., annot., Dixon Collection, (11-16-92, Butterfield, #6253, illus.), 10⅜ x 8¾
in., (264 x 222.6 mm.), photograph, gelatin silver print
(BP 869, DM 2105, FR 7089, Y 164,159).

$1380* Main Street After A Blizzard, Woodstock, Vermont", 1940,
p. 1977, s., t., d., annot., illus., (05-23-93, Butterfield,
#3691, illus.), 6½ x 9 in., photograph, gelatin silver print
(BP 899, DM 2256, FR 7595, Y 152,537).

$1100* "Main Street After Blizzard, Woodstock, Vermont", 1940/
1977, s., t., d., neg. num., annot., (11-16-92, Butterfield,
#6257, illus.), 6¾ x 9 in., (171.8 x 229 mm.), photo-
graph, gelatin silver print (BP 724, DM 1754, FR 5908,
Y 136,799).

$330* A Member Of The Wilkins Family Baking Biscuits, Corn-
husking Day, Tallyho, North Carolina, 1939/printed later,
(05-16-93, Hindman, #348), 8½ x 12 in., photograph, silver print (BP 215, DM 532, FR 1793, Y 36,748).

$2588* "Mississippi Post", "Lake Providence, Vicinity, Louisiana",
"Tenant Houses On Cotton Plantation, Rolling Fork, Mississippi" and "Cornshocks And Fences On Farm Near
Marion, Virginia", 1940-41: Four, t., d., FSA stamp, (05-
23-93, Butterfield, #3687, illus.), each approx. 8 x 10 in.,
photograph, gelatin silver print (BP 1685, DM 4232, FR
14,243, Y 286,062).

$1610* "Peddler Who Goes From Door To Door, Woodstock,
Vermont", 1940, p. 1982, s., d., neg. num., illus., (05-23-
93, Butterfield, #3688, illus.), 6½ x 9¼ in., photograph,
gelatin silver print (BP 1049, DM 2632, FR 8861, Y
177,960).

$1870* "Picnicking On The Beach" (Marion Post Wolcott, pl.
26), 1941/later, s., incorrectly t., annot., d., Dixon Collection, (11-16-92, Butterfield, #6254, illus.), 9 x 12⅛ in.,
(229 x 308.5 mm.), photograph, gelatin silver print (BP
1231, DM 2982, FR 10,043, Y 232,558).

$2640* Spring, Typical Split Rail Fence, Virginia, 1938, s., t., d.,
i., (10-13-92, Christie-NY, #403, illus.), 10⅜ x 13⅜ in.,
(26.4 x 34 cm.), photograph, gelatin silver print (BP
1538, DM 3868, FR 13,141, Y 320,116).

BI   "Tenant Farmer's Children, Near Wadesboro, North Carolina", 1938, p.l., s., illus., est. $7/900, (05-23-93, Butter-
field, #3692, illus.), 10 x 9 in., photograph, gelatin silver
print.

$990* "Tobacco Farmers Waiting And Napping Before Auction,
Durham, North Carolina", 1939/later, s., t., d., neg. num.,
annot., Dixon Collection, (11-16-92, Butterfield, #6256,
illus.), 9 x 11⅞ in., (229 x 302.2 mm.), photograph, gelatin silver print (BP 652, DM 1578, FR 5317, Y
123,119).

$825* Two Black Children, sig., 1930's, p.l., (10-14-92, Swann,
#537, illus.), 14 x 11 in., (35.6 x 27.9 cm.), photograph,
silver print (BP 484, DM 1207, FR 4094, Y 99,976).

BI   Typical Split Rail Fence, Spring In Virginia, 1938, s., t.,
d., i. Original vintage FSA print from the collection of
M.P.W.m est. $1,8/2,200, (04-08-93, Christie-NY, #356,
illus.), 10½ x 13⅜ in., (26.7 x 34 cm.), photograph, gelatin silver print.

$863* "The Whittler, Wendell, North Carolina", 1939, p. 1981,
s., d., neg. num., (05-23-93, Butterfield, #3690, illus.),
6½ x 9 in., photograph, gelatin silver print (BP 562, DM
1411, FR 4750, Y 95,391).

$990* "Winter Visitor Being Served Brunch In A Private Beach
Club" (MarionPost Wolcott, pl. 24), 1939/1981, s., annot.,
(11-16-92, Butterfield, #6255, illus.), 6⅞ x 9 in., (174.9
x 229 mm.), photograph, gelatin silver print (BP 652,
DM 1578, FR 5317, Y 123,119).

WOLF
                                           American 20th cent.
$110* "Venice" and "Rome": Two, each s., (12-12-92, A. James,
#321), one 12¼ x 8½ in., (31.1 x 21.6 cm.), other 14½
x 10¼ in., (31.1 x 21.6 cm.), two aquatints (BP 71, DM
173, FR 594, Y 13,612).

WOLF, J. and H.C. RICHTER
BI   Aquila Naevia (Spotted Eagle), from John Gould's Birds
Of Great Britain, 1862-1873, foxing, defects, est. BP 2/
300, (10-27-92, Phillips-London, #180), sheet 22 x 15¼
in., (559 x 387 mm.), colored lithograph w/touches of
gum arabic.

$110* Falco Canadians, Walter Imp., staining, discoloration,
hinged upper margin, (06-11-93, Freemn/Fine Art,
#253), 17¾ x 13¼ in., (45.1 x 33.7 cm.), lithograph w/
touches of hand-coloring (BP 72, DM 179, FR 603, Y
11,671).

WOLF, J. and J. SMIT (after)
BI *"Pheasant"*, (12-11-92, G.A. Key, #2), 21 x 17 in., (53.3 x 43.2 cm.), colored print.

WOLF, Jeremias 1663-1724
BI *L'Amour Coquet*, est. DM 400, (12-04-92, Bassenge, #6504), 14¹⁵⁄₁₆ x 10¼ in., (38 x 26 cm.), engraving.

WOLF, John and J. SMIT
BI *Fellis Badia The Bornean Red Cat, c. 1874*, P.M. and N. Hanhart, full margins, good cond., est. BP 1/150, (10-27-92, Phillips-London, #181), sheet 23⅝ x 18½ in., (600 x 470 mm.), lithograph w/hand-coloring on wove.

WOLF, Reinhart 1930-1990
BI *Ohne Titel, 1978*, s., d., #46/50, est. DM 300, (11-12-92, Lempertz, #279), 12 x 15¹⁵⁄₁₆ in., (30.5 x 40.5 cm.), color photograph.

WOLFE, Meyer
$330* *Acrobats #1, 1951*, s., d., t., annot. Ed. 15, full margins, good cond., creases, (10-28-92, Butterfield, #2779), 13¾ x 9¹⁵⁄₁₆ in., (349 x 252 mm.), lithograph on cream wove (BP 210, DM 510, FR 1730, Y 40,491).

WOLFF German 19th/20th cent.
$66* *Seated Lady In Interior*, mono., d. 1900 in plate, s., i., (10-30-92, Sloan, #2816), 7¾ x 5¾ in., (19.7 x 14.6 cm.), etching (BP 42, DM 102, FR 344, Y 8175).

WOLFSON, William
$1540* *Man Working On Skyscraper, 1944*, s., d., full margins, good cond., creases, glue remains, (11-05-92, Sotheby-NY, #71, illus.), 11¾ x 12½ in., (297 x 317 mm.), lithograph on white wove (BP 1002, DM 2436, FR 8240, Y 188,934).

WOLFSON, William B. American b. 1894
$303* *"Asphalt Workers", 1928*, p. 1978, s., d. Wm. Wolfson '28 in matrix, estate s., num., d.Wm. Wolfson (D.W.) 13/25 1978, t., printer's/pub. drystamp, very good cond., (09-11-92, Skinner, #41), 7¹⁵⁄₁₆ x 11⁹⁄₁₆ in., (20.2 x 29.4 cm.), lithograph on wove (BP 157, DM 436, FR 1482, Y 37,542).
$105* *"The Circus"*, p. 1978, s. Wm Wolfson in matrix, num., d., estate s. Wm Wolfson (D.W.) 19/25 1978, t., printer's/pub. dry stamps, very good cond., (09-11-92, Skinner, #38E, illus.), 8¼ x 11¼ in., (21 x 28.6 cm.), lithograph on wove (BP 54, DM 151, FR 514, Y 13,010).
$83* *"Fourteenth Street", 1927*, p. 1982, s., d. Wm. Wolfson '27 in matrix, estate s., num., d.Wm. Wolfson (D.W.) 10/25, '82, t. pub. drystamp, very good cond., (09-11-92, Skinner, #30), 9¾ x 12½ in., (24.8 x 31.8 cm.), lithograph on wove (BP 43, DM 119, FR 406, Y 10,284).

WOLS German 1913-1951
$19,854* *Das Graphische Werk: Thirty-Three, 1949, 1962*, stamps, num., (06-23-93, Kornfeld, #886), sh approx. 14¹⁵⁄₁₆ x 10⅝ in., (38 x 27 cm.), drypoint on Japan (BP 13,488, DM 33,594, FR 112,999, Y 2,162,981, SF 29,900).
$3942* *Thirty-Two Etchings: Plates IX-X, XIV-XVI, XIX-XXI, XXVIII, XXX-XXXI: Eleven*, each #3/10, i. w/plate num., num., d. 1955 ballpoint pen verso, posthumous edit., pub. G. Visat, good cond., (05-20-93, Christie-London, #493, illus.), plate 8 x 4¾ in., (20.3 x 12.1 cm.), sheet 12¾ x 9¾ in., (20.3 x 12.1 cm.), etching on wove (BP 2530, DM 6360, FR 21,424, Y 435,292).
$1756* *Topographie (Grohmann 8), c. 1948-1949*, (06-23-93, Kornfeld, #887), drypoint on thick wove (BP 1193, DM 2971, FR 9994, Y 191,306, SF 2645).

WOLS (Alfred Otto Wolfgang SCHULZE) 1913-1951
$1403* *Stilleben: Six*, 30's, 1981, (11-12-92, Lempertz, #280, illus.), smallest 6¹⁵⁄₁₆ x 7⅛ in., (17.7 x 18.1 cm.), largest 10³⁄₁₆ x 7¹⁄₁₆ in., (17.7 x 18.1 cm.), photograph, gelatin silver print (BP 897, DM 2205, FR 7515, Y 173,574).

WOLS (Otto Wolfgang Schultze)
$2900* *Sans Titre, c. 1949*, artist's sig. in plate, prov., (06-28-93, Loudmer, #434), 11⁹⁄₁₆ x 5½ in., (293 x 139 mm.), matrice en (and) cuivre (copper) gravee a l'eau-forte (BP 1942, DM 4928, FR 16,600, Y 307,692).

WOLSTENHOLME, D.
$398* *"Going Out", "Drawing Cover", "Fully Cry" and "Returning": Four Hunting Scenes*, (03-10-93, Maynard, #631), 14 x 19 in., (35.6 x 48.3 cm.), hand-colored print (BP 278, DM 662, FR 2249, Y 47,023, C$ 495).

WOLSTENHOLME, Dean (Sr.) (after)
$1319* *Shooting (S.p 311): Four*, by T. Sutherland, pub. R. Ackermann, trimmed, good cond., fixed at corners, (10-07-92, Christie-S. Ken, #48), sh 10 x 13 in., (25.4 x 33 cm.), colored aquatint (BP 770, DM 1909, FR 6472, Y 158,629).

WOLSTENHOLME, Dean (after)
$805* *"Beagles", "Stag Hounds", "Fox Hounds" and "Harriers" (S. p. 310), c.1840: Four*, by R. G. Reeve, defects, Anthony N. B. Garvan Coll., (06-05-93, Christie-NY, #64), all, sh 17 x 23¼ in., (432 x 591 mm.), aquatint w/hand-coloring on wove (BP 530, DM 1305, FR 4399, Y 86,355).
$183 *"Fox Hunting", c. 1806: Four*, engraved by Richard Reeve, fair cond., (04-16-93, G.A. Key, #62, illus.), 16 x 20 in., (40.6 x 50.8 cm.), colored aquatint (BP 120, DM 296, FR 999, Y 20,578).

WOLVECAMP, Theo 1925-1992
$554* *De Roddelaars, 1989*, s., d., #84/150, full margins, good cond., (12-09-92, Sotheby-Amstrdm, #675), 35¹⁵⁄₁₆ x 31⁹⁄₁₆ in., (913 x 802 mm.), color silkscreen on wove (BP 354, DM 870, FR 2967, Y 68,692, G 978).
BI *Untitled, 1989*, s., d., #58/250, full margins, good cond., est. G 3/500, (12-09-92, Sotheby-Amstrdm, #676), 12¹¹⁄₁₆ x 18¾ in., (322 x 476 mm.), color silkscreen on Arches.
$224* *Untitled, 1989*, s., d., #71/150, full margins, good cond., (05-27-93, Sotheby-Amstrdm, #703, illus.), 27⁹⁄₁₆ x 16⁷⁄₁₆ in., (700 x 418 mm.), color silkscreen on wove (BP 143, DM 359, FR 1211, Y 24,014, G 403).
$195* *Untitled, 1990: Two*, book, s., d., #108/250, num. 108, pub. Van Spijk, good cond., (12-09-92, Sotheby-Amstrdm, #674), each sheet 11 x 11 in., (280 x 280 mm.), color silkscreen on wove (BP 124, DM 306, FR 1044, Y 24,179, G 345).

WOOD, Albert F.
BI *Advertisement For Satin Skin Powder, Detroit, c. 1903*, est. $100/150, (08-05-92, Boos, #666), 39 x 25½ in., (99.1 x 64.8 cm.), color lithograph.

WOOD, Grant American 1892-1942
$3850* *Approaching Storm (C. 19), 1940*, s., pub. AAA, full margins, good cond., light-staining, foxing, taperemains, mat staining, (02-24-93, Butterfield, #2660, illus.), 11⅞ x 8⅞ in., (302 x 225 mm.), lithograph on wove (BP 2685, DM 6250, FR 21,189, Y 451,772).
BI *Approaching Storm (Czest 17), 1940*, s., est. $2/3,000, (06-11-93, Freemn/Fine Art, #254), 12 x 9 in., (30.5 x 22.9 cm.), lithograph.
$3300* *Approaching Storm (Czest. W-17), 1941*, s., pub. AAA, margins, good cond., mat stain, (11-05-92, Sotheby-NY, #75, illus.), 11⅞ x 9 in., (302 x 227 mm.), lithograph (BP 2146, DM 5219, FR 17,657, Y 404,858).
$2805* *"Approaching Storm"*, s., prov., (12-12-92, Litchfield, #263), 11¾ x 8¾ in., (29.8 x 22.2 cm.), lithograph (BP 1799, DM 4419, FR 15,146, Y 347,111).
$2860* *Approaching Storm, 1940, Czestochowski W-17*, s., pub. AAA, (09-20-92, Hindman, #693, illus.), sheet 16½ x 12½ in., (41.9 x 31.8 cm.), lithograph on white wove (BP 1674, DM 4244, FR 14,518, Y 353,479).
$990* *Blitzkrieg, 1940*, A- cond., corner restoration, creasing, (08-06-92, Swann, #297, illus.), 25¾ x 20¾ in., (65.4 x 52.7 cm.), (BP 517, DM 1463, FR 4940, Y 126,276).
$1540* *December Afternoon (C. 16), 1940*, s., margins, scattered foxing, staining, taped to overmat, (09-19-92, Christie-E, #72, illus.), borderline 9 x 11¾ in., (229 x 298 mm.), lithograph on wove (BP 886, DM 2306, FR 7897, Y 191,876).
$1980* *December Afternoon (C. 16), 1940*, s., pub. AAA, margins trimmed, good cond., light-staining, foxing, staining, surface soiling, (02-24-93, Butterfield, #2659, illus.), 9 x 11⅞ in., (229 x 302 mm.), lithograph on wove (BP 1381, DM 3214, FR 10,897, Y 232,340).

$2300* *December Afternoon (C. 16), 1940,* s., pub. AAA, full margins, good cond., foxing, (05-19-93, Butterfield, #1835, illus.), 9 x 11⅞ in., (229 x 302 mm.), lithograph on wove (BP 1493, DM 3739, FR 12,596, Y 254,622).

$1430* *"December Afternoon",* s. Grant Wood, very good cond., (09-27-92, Bakker, #266, illus.), image 8¾ x 11¾ in., (22.2 x 29.8 cm.), lithograph (BP 835, DM 2120, FR 7168, Y 172,601).

$3300* *February (C. 17), 1940,* s., margins, skillful repairs, foxmark, good cond., (09-19-92, Christie-E, #73), borderline 9 x 11⅞ in., (229 x 302 mm.), lithograph on wove (BP 1898, DM 4942, FR 16,923, Y 411,164).

$4600* *February (C. 17), 1940,* s., margins, excell. cond., (05-11-93, Christie-NY, #138), borderline 9 x 11⅞ in., (229 x 302 mm.), lithograph on Rives (BP 2936, DM 7246, FR 24,416, Y 505,995).

$2530* *February (Cole 17), 1940,* s., from ed. 250, foxing, taped, (11-12-92, Freemn/Fine Art, #243), 8⅞ x 11⅞ in., (22.5 x 30.2 cm.), lithograph on wove paper (BP 1662, DM 4009, FR 13,522, Y 313,701).

$3850* *February (Czest. W-19), 1941,* s., pub. AAA, full margins, good cond., discoloration, mat stain, (11-05-92, Sotheby-NY, #77, illus.), 8⅞ x 11⅞ in., (226 x 301 mm.), lithograph (BP 2504, DM 6089, FR 20,599, Y 472,335).

$4070* *February (Czestochowski W19), 1941,* s., (12-09-92, Grogan, #94, illus.), 9 x 11⅞ in., (22.9 x 30.2 cm.), lithograph (BP 2597, DM 6388, FR 21,800, Y 504,650).

$1980* *Fertility,* s., (12-17-92, Mystic, #6), 9 x 12 in., (22.9 x 30.5 cm.), lithograph (BP 1257, DM 3091, FR 10,560, Y 243,333).

$3220* *Fertility (C. 15), 1939,* watermark, s., margins, excell. cond., (05-11-93, Christie-NY, #137), borderline 9 x 11⅞ in., (229 x 302 mm.), lithograph on wove (BP 2056, DM 5072, FR 17,091, Y 354,196).

$2805* *"Fertility",* s., excell. cond., light toning, prov., (12-12-92, Litchfield, #262A), 8⅞ x 11⅞ in., (22.5 x 30.2 cm.), lithograph (BP 1799, DM 4419, FR 15,146, Y 347,111).

$4125* *"Fertility" (C. 15), 1939,* s., pub. AAA, hinges, full margins, (10-31-92, Cleveland, #241, illus.), 8⅞ x 11⅞ in., (22.5 x 30.2 cm.), lithograph (BP 2643, DM 6346, FR 21,529, Y 510,962).

$6600* *"Fruits", "Vegetables", "Tame Flowers" and "Wild Flowers" (C. 7-10):Four, 1939,* s., full margins, light-staining, tape, very good cond., (11-09-92, Christie-NY, #48, illus.), all border 7 x 10¹⁄₁₆ in., (178 x 255 mm.), lithographs w/hand-coloring on Rives (BP 4364, DM 10,536, FR 35,599, Y 819,062).

$2475* *Honorary Degree (C. 4), 1938,* watermark, s., pub. AAA, full margins, fine cond., skinned area, (02-24-93, Butterfield, #2657, illus.), 11⅞ x 7 in., (302 x 178 mm.), lithograph on wove (BP 1726, DM 4018, FR 13,621, Y 290,425).

$1610* *Honorary Degree (C. 4), 1938,* s., pub. AAA, full margins, good cond., foxing, mat/light-staining, (05-19-93, Butterfield, #1834, illus.), 11⅞ x 7 in., (302 x 178 mm.), lithograph on Rives (BP 1045, DM 2617, FR 8817, Y 178,235).

$1100* *Honorary Degree (Czest. W-7), 1937,* s., pub. AAA, full margins, good cond., faint mat/background stain, creases, (11-05-92, Sotheby-NY, #74), 11⅞ x 6⅞ in., (301 x 176 mm.), lithograph (BP 715, DM 1740, FR 5886, Y 134,953).

$990* *Honorary Degree (Czest. W-7), 1938,* s., (03-24-93, Grogan, #98, illus.), 11⅞ x 7 in., (30.2 x 17.8 cm.), lithograph (BP 670, DM 1617, FR 5503, Y 116,320).

$1210* *Honorary Degree, 1937, Czestochowski W-7,* s., pub. AAA, (09-20-92, Hindman, #689, illus.), 11¾ x 6⅞ in., (29.8 x 17.5 cm.), lithograph on wove paper w/watermark (BP 708, DM 1796, FR 6142, Y 149,549).

$3105* *In The Spring (Czest. W-13), 1939,* s., pub. AAA, full margins, good cond., foxing, (05-13-93, Sotheby-NY, #454, illus.), 9 x 11⅞ in., (228 x 303 mm.), lithograph (BP 2038, DM 5014, FR 16,912, Y 346,656).

BI   *"In The Spring" (C. 13), 1939,* s., pub. AAA, good cond., discoloration, est. $2-2,500, (10-31-92, Cleveland, #240), 9 x 12 in., (22.9 x 30.5 cm.), lithograph.

$2310* *In The Spring, 1939, Czestochowski W-13,* s., pub. AAA, (09-20-92, Hindman, #690, illus.), sheet 12½ x 16 in.,

(22.5 x 29.8 cm.), lithograph on wove w/watermark (BP 1352, DM 3428, FR 11,726, Y 285,502).

$3850* *January (C. 3), 1938,* s., pub. AAA, margins, good cond., mat staining, glue remains, surface soiling, creases, notations, (10-28-92, Butterfield, #2555, illus.), 9 x 11⅞ in., (229 x 302 mm.), lithograph on GCM wove paper (BP 2453, DM 5946, FR 20,189, Y 472,393).

$4070* *January (C.3), 1938,* s., margins, excellent cond., (11-09-92, Christie-NY, #46, illus.), border 9 x 11⅞ in., (229 x 301 mm.), lithograph on Rives (BP 2691, DM 6497, FR 21,953, Y 505,088).

BI   *"January",* bears sig. Grant Wood, poor cond., est. $8/1,200, (11-21-92, Bakker, #24, illus.), image 9 x 12 in., (22.9 x 30.5 cm.), lithograph.

$3630* *"January" (Czestochowski, W-5), 1937,* pub. AAA, s. Grant Wood, annot., good cond., (03-12-93, Skinner, #37, illus.), 9 x 11⅞ in., (22.9 x 30.2 cm.), lithograph on wove (BP 2532, DM 6042, FR 20,543, Y 427,814).

$3850* *July Fifteenth (C. 5), 1938,* watermark, s., pub. AAA, full margins, very good cond., light-staining, red pencil marks, (02-24-93, Butterfield, #2658, illus.), 9 x 12 in., (229 x 305 mm.), lithograph on wove (BP 2685, DM 6250, FR 21,189, Y 451,772).

$2420* *July Fifteenth, 1939, Czestochowski W-14,* s., pub. AAA, (09-20-92, Hindman, #691, illus.), sheet 11⅞ x 15⅞ in., (22.9 x 30.2 cm.), lithograph on white wove, watermark (BP 1417, DM 3591, FR 12,284, Y 299,098).

$4600* *March (C. 14), 1939,* s., wide margins, rubbing, split, mat staining, skinning, good cond., (05-11-93, Christie-NY, #136, illus.), borderline 8⅞ x 11¾ in., (225 x 298 mm.), lithograph on wove (BP 2936, DM 7246, FR 24,416, Y 505,995).

$2750* *March (Czest. W-18), 1941,* p. George C. Miller, pub. AAA, full margins, good cond., mat stain, foxing, discoloration, (11-05-92, Sotheby-NY, #76), 8¾ x 11⅞ in., (222 x 301 mm.), lithograph (BP 1789, DM 4349, FR 14,714, Y 337,382).

$4600* *March (Czest. W-18), 1941,* s., pub. AAA, full margins, good cond., mat/tape stain, smudge, (02-11-93, Sotheby-NY, #59, illus.), 8¹⁵⁄₁₆ x 11⅞ in., (228 x 302 mm.), lithograph (BP 3246, DM 7620, FR 25,785, Y 554,551).

$2420* *"March",* s.; bears A.A.A. pub. label verso, Groves' Coll., (10-16-92, Neal, #134, illus.), image 9 x 11¾ in., (22.9 x 29.8 cm.), lithograph (BP 1466, DM 3575, FR 12,142, Y 288,955).

$3850* *"March", 1935,* s. Grant Wood, (09-25-92, Wolf, #23, illus.), 9 x 12 in., (22.9 x 30.5 cm.), lithograph (BP 2248, DM 5707, FR 19,298, Y 464,695).

$2640* *March, 1941, Czestochowski W-18,* s., pub. AAA, (09-20-92, Hindman, #694), sheet 12⅛ x 16⅜ in., (22.5 x 30.2 cm.), lithograph on white wove (BP 1546, DM 3917, FR 13,401, Y 326,288).

BI   *Midnight Alarm (C. 12), 1939,* s., ded., pub. AAA, full margins, good cond., surface soiling, glue staining, tape remains, skinned area, est. $1/1,500, (10-28-92, Butterfield, #2556), 12¾ x 7¼ in., (324 x 184 mm.), lithograph on Rives paper.

$1980* *Seed Time And Harvest (Czest. W-4), 1937,* s., d., pub. AAA, margins, good cond., mat stain, tape stain verso, (11-05-92, Sotheby-NY, #73), 7½ x 12⅛ in., (189 x 308 mm.), sheet 9 x 13¼ in., (189 x 308 mm.), lithograph (BP 1288, DM 3131, FR 10,594, Y 242,915).

$1100* *Shrine Quartet, 1939, Czestochowski W-16,* s., pub. AAA, (09-20-92, Hindman, #692, illus.), sheet 12 x 16 in., (20.3 x 29.8 cm.), lithograph on wove, watermark (BP 644, DM 1632, FR 5584, Y 135,954).

$2185* *Shriner's Quartet (Czestochowski W-11), 1939,* s., t., i., pub. AAA, full margins, good cond., light-stain, (05-13-93, Sotheby-NY, #453, illus.), 8 x 11⅞ in., (203 x 301 mm.), lithograph (BP 1434, DM 3528, FR 11,901, Y 243,943).

$3850* *Sultry Night (C. 6), 1939,* s., full margins, light-staining, excellent cond., (11-09-92, Christie-NY, #47, illus.), border 9 x 11¾ in., (229 x 298 mm.), lithograph on wove (BP 2545, DM 6146, FR 20,766, Y 477,786).

$2640* *Tree Planting Group (Cole 1), 1937,* s., d., wide margins, light/mat staining, masking tape, (09-19-92, Christie-E, #71), borderline 8⅜ x 10⅞ in., (213 x 276 mm.), lithograph on wove, watermark (BP 1519, DM 3953, FR 13,538, Y 328,931).

$2860* *Tree Planting Group (Cole 1), 1937,* s., full margins, staining, glue; taped to overmat verso, (11-09-92, Christie-NY, #45, illus.), border 8⅜ x 10⅞ in., (213 x 277 mm.), lithograph on Rives (BP 1891, DM 4566, FR 15,426, Y 354,927).

$2990* *Tree Planting Group (Cole 1), 1937,* watermark, s., t., d., full margins, rubbing, very good cond., (05-11-93, Christie-NY, #135), borderline 8½ x 10⅞ in., (216 x 276 mm.), lithograph on wove (BP 1909, DM 4710, FR 15,870, Y 328,897).

$4400* *Tree Planting Group (Czestochowski W-3), 1937,* s., d., pub. AAA, full margins, good cond., sticky label hinges, ripples, (11-05-92, Sotheby-NY, #72, illus.), 7 x 10⅞ in., (178 x 277 mm.), lithograph (BP 2862, DM 6959, FR 23,542, Y 539,811).

$4675* *"Vegetables" (Cole 10), 1939,* s., pub. AAA, orig. cond., (10-31-92, Cleveland, #239, illus.), 7 x 10 in., (17.8 x 25.4 cm.), lithograph w/hand coloring (BP 2996, DM 7192, FR 24,400, Y 579,091).

$715* *Wild Flowers, 1939,* s., pub. AAA, margins taped to mat, (12-08-92, Swann, #320, illus.), sight 7½ x 10½ in., (19.1 x 26.7 cm.), hand-colored lithograph (BP 448, DM 1113, FR 3795, Y 88,622).

WOOD, Lawson (after)
$76 *Comic Prints: A Set Of Four,* (10-09-92, G.A. Key, #102), 10 x 7¼ in., (25.4 x 18.4 cm.), colored print (BP 45, DM 113, FR 384, Y 9268).

WOOD, Lewis John   English 1813-1901
BI *Figures In Village Square,* s.; d. illegibly in stone, est. $2/300, (10-30-92, Sloan, #883), 29¾ x 24 in., (75.6 x 61 cm.), lithograph w/hand coloring.
$143* *Figures In Village Square,* s., d. illegibly in stone, (12-10-92, Sloan, #943), 29¾ x 24 in., (75.6 x 61 cm.), lithograph w/hand coloring (BP 92, DM 226, FR 773, Y 17,689).

WOOD, Lionel
BI *"Black Rock, Brighton"* and *"Those Cut Throat Bandits": Two,* mounted on card, s., stamped photog.'s credit, 300 x 375mm and 241 x292mm, est. BP 80/120, (05-07-93, Sotheby-London, #168), photograph, toned silver print.

WOOD, Paul
BI *"Departure",* s., very good cond., est. $2/300, (10-02-92, Guyette, #635D, illus.), stone lithograph.

WOODBURY, Charles H.   American 1864-1940
$165* *"Fallen Tree",* pencil s., (05-08-93, Young, #317, illus.), 5 x 7 in., (12.7 x 17.8 cm.), etching (BP 104, DM 261, FR 879, Y 18,168).
$165* *"Ground Swell",* (05-08-93, Young, #314, illus.), 5 x 6 in., (12.7 x 15.2 cm.), etching (BP 104, DM 261, FR 879, Y 18,168).
$110* *"The July Century",* plate s., good cond., (07-19-92, Bakker, #236, illus.), image 12⅛ x 7 in., (30.8 x 17.8 cm.), color lithograph (BP 56, DM 160, FR 542, Y 13,675).
$275* *Navy Yard,* i., (11-28-92, Young, #415), 9 x 11 in., (22.9 x 27.9 cm.), etching (BP 182, DM 438, FR 1487, Y 34,225).
$413* *Ogunquit Beach Scenes: Two,* both s. Charles H. Woodbury, #2 edit. 50, (10-24-92, Collins, #11, illus.), first 3½ x 4 in., (8.9 x 10.2 cm.), second 3⅛ x 3¾ in., (8.9 x 10.2 cm.), etchings (BP 255, DM 631, FR 2141, Y 50,366).
$66* *"Old Willows",* (05-08-93, Young, #313, illus.), 9 x 11 in., (22.9 x 27.9 cm.), etching (BP 42, DM 104, FR 352, Y 7267).
$300* *"Sea Pastures",* s., (02-27-93, Young, #331, illus.), 9 x 11 in., (22.9 x 27.9 cm.), etching (BP 211, DM 493, FR 1676, Y 35,415).
$220* *"Sea Pool",* (05-08-93, Young, #315, illus.), 9 x 11 in., (22.9 x 27.9 cm.), etching (BP 139, DM 348, FR 1172, Y 24,224).
$165* *"Spruce Tree",* pencil s., (05-08-93, Young, #316, illus.), 7 x 9 in., (17.8 x 22.9 cm.), etching (BP 104, DM 261, FR 879, Y 18,168).

$220* *"St Thomas",* (05-08-93, Young, #318, illus.), 9 x 10 in., (22.9 x 25.4 cm.), etching (BP 139, DM 348, FR 1172, Y 24,224).
$55* *Untitled,* s. Charles H. Woodbury, (10-24-92, Collins, #10), 8¾ x 10⅞ in., (22.2 x 27.6 cm.), etching (BP 34, DM 84, FR 285, Y 6707).

WOODBURY, D.B.
BI *Military Bridge, Across The Chickahominy, Va.,* p. by Alexander Gardner in 1865, num. 17, credit., t., d., pub., lit., est. $8/1,000, (10-13-92, Christie-NY, #27, illus.), 6¾ x 8⅞ in., (17.1 x 22.5 cm.), photograph, albumen print.

WOODBURY and PAGE
BI *"Vues De Java",* c. 1857: One Hundred and Seven, album, est. $4/6,000, (04-07-93, Swann, #227, illus.), photograph, albumen print.

WOODS, Tony   b. 1940
$32* *Dreamtime,* s. Woods, i., #1325, (08-11-92, L. Joel, #48G), 30⁵⁄₁₆ x 25¹⁵⁄₁₆ in., (77 x 66 cm.), two color lithograph (BP 17, DM 47, FR 159, Y 4098, A$ 44).

WOODVILLS, R. (after)
$18 *"The LAst Shot At Colenso",* (06-11-93, G.A. Key, #57), 31 x 22 in., (78.7 x 55.9 cm.), chromolithograph (BP 12, DM 29, FR 99, Y 1910).

WOODWARD (after)
$43 *"A Parental Leeter", 1808,* (06-11-93, G.A. Key, #123), 13 x 9 in., (33 x 22.9 cm.), hand-colored engraving (BP 28, DM 70, FR 236, Y 4562).

WOOL, Christopher   American b. 1955
$2530* *Black Monotype On Suzuki, 1989,* s. verso, d., pub. Edition Julie Sylvester, good cond., (11-07-92, Sotheby-NY, #828, illus.), sheet 73⅝ x 37 in., (187 x 94 cm.), monotype p. in black on handmade Suzuki (BP 1654, DM 4040, FR 13,654, Y 312,269).

WOOLCOCK, Marjorie
$81* *Lynchgate-Kalorama,* s. M Woolcock, i., (08-11-92, L. Joel, #43G), 4⁹⁄₁₆ x 5⅞ in., (11.6 x 15 cm.), linocut (BP 42, DM 119, FR 403, Y 10,373, A$ 110).

WOOLETT, William   mid-18th cent.
$288 *"A View Of Foots-Cray Place In Kent, The Seat Of Bourchier Cleeve Esquire",* (08-14-92, G.A. Key, #11), 12 x 20 in., (30.5 x 50.8 cm.), engraving (BP 150, DM 423, FR 1431, Y 36,318).

WOOLF, Paul J.
$1760* *New York Buildings At Night,* photog.'s handstamps, notations, 1930s, (04-07-93, Swann, #597, illus.), 6½ x 4½ in., photograph, silver print (BP 1163, DM 2847, FR 9633, Y 199,955).
$302* *"Portrait Of Margaret Bourke-White"* and *"Margaret Bourke-White With Cmera And Subject": Two,* notations, 1930's, (10-14-92, Swann, #385), one 4¾ x 5¾ in., (12.1 x 14.6 cm.), other 10 x 8 in., (12.1 x 14.6 cm.), photograph, silver prints (BP 177, DM 442, FR 1499, Y 36,597).

WOOLF, S.J.
$44* *"Portrait Of Lincoln",* s. w/stamp, (02-27-93, Dunning, #120), 15⅞ x 12¼ in., (40.3 x 31.1 cm.), lithograph (BP 31, DM 72, FR 246, Y 5194).

WOOLF, Samuel J.   American 1880-1948
$22* *"Portrait Of Benjamin Franklin",* s., (02-27-93, Dunning, #121), 13⅜ x 9½ in., (34 x 24.1 cm.), lithograph (BP 15, DM 36, FR 123, Y 2597).

WOOLLEY, Grace Livingston   American 1884-1971
$110* *Virtuoso, 1949,* s., t., d. 1949, (11-12-92, Freemn/Fine Art, #244), image 6¹⁵⁄₁₆ x 7⅞ in., (17.6 x 20 cm.), aquatint (BP 72, DM 174, FR 588, Y 13,639).

WOOLNOTH, T.
$96 *"The Rose In June",* d. 1827, (08-14-92, G.A. Key, #97), 9 x 12 in., (22.9 x 30.5 cm.), hand colored aquatint (BP 50, DM 141, FR 477, Y 12,106).

WOOTTON
$156* *Leadership In Lubrication, H.M.S. Vanguard, 1951,* ref. P 11, cond. 2, (10-13-92, Phillips-London, #166), 29¹³⁄₁₆ x 39¾ in., (75.8 x 101 cm.), color lithograph (BP 91, DM 229, FR 777, Y 18,916).

WOOTTON, Frank (after)
$17* *Hurricane Mk 1,* #619/850, s. by artist and Wing Commander R. R. Stanford-Tuck, pub. Blaze Fine Arts Ltd, 1976, (04-22-93, Bonhams-Chelsea, #11), image 12¾ x 16 in., (32.4 x 40.6 cm.), reprod. in colors (BP 11, DM 27, FR 92, Y 1869).

WORDEN, Willard
BI *"Chinese Funeral In San Francisco", 1903,* photog.'s stamp, est. $6/800, (05-23-93, Butterfield, #3693, illus.), 7 x 5 in., photograph, gelatin silver print.

WORSEL, Troels
$92* *Komposition,* s. T. Worsel, 42/55, (03-24-93, Kunsthallen, #341), color lithograph (BP 62, DM 150, FR 511, Y 10,810, DK 575).

WORSINGER, and Verne WILLIAMS
$5081* *"Ship Windows And Interiors New York" and "...New York & Miami": Five Albums,* 1930s, over 200 s. in negs., ref. nums. in negs., 4 similarly s. Verne Williams, t., (05-06-93, Christie-London, #181, illus.), each approx. 7¼ x 9½ in., photograph, 248 gelatin silver prints (BP 3220, DM 8003, FR 26,941, Y 559,027).

WORTEL, Ans b. 1929
$96* *..Tussen De Bodem En De Lucht..,* s., margins, good cond., (05-27-93, Sotheby-Amstrdm, #525), 19⅛ x 15³⁄₁₆ in., (486 x 385 mm.), colored etching on wove (BP 61, DM 154, FR 519, Y 10,292, G 173).
$128* *Je Voegend Naar 'T Hol Dat Je Hebt,* s., #177/190, margins, good cond., (05-27-93, Sotheby-Amstrdm, #524), 19⅛ x 15³⁄₁₆ in., (486 x 385 mm.), colored etching on wove (BP 82, DM 205, FR 692, Y 13,722, G 230).
$64* *Uitgangspunt Voor Vlinders,* s., margins, good cond., (05-27-93, Sotheby-Amstrdm, #523), 19⅛ x 15³⁄₁₆ in., (486 x 385 mm.), colored etching on wove (BP 41, DM 103, FR 346, Y 6861, G 115).
$98* *Waar Kinderen...,* s., #V/X, full margins, good cond., (12-09-92, Sotheby-Amstrdm, #677), 19½ x 15⅜ in., (495 x 390 mm.), color etching on wove (BP 63, DM 154, FR 525, Y 12,151, G 173).

WORTH, Don b. 1924
$523* *"Aspens In Autumn, Near Santa Fe, New Mexico",* 1958/later, s., t., d., (11-16-92, Butterfield, #6258, illus.), 11 x 8¾ in., (279.9 x 222.6 mm.), photograph, gelatin silver print (BP 344, DM 834, FR 2809, Y 65,042).
$440* *"Calathea Vittata, Oahu",* 1977/later, s., photog. blindstamp, t., d., inventory num., (11-16-92, Butterfield, #6260, illus.), 11 x 8⅜ in., (279.9 x 213.1 mm.), photograph, gelatin silver print (BP 290, DM 702, FR 2363, Y 54,720).
$288* *"Calathea Vittatta, Oahu", 1977,* s., photog.'s blindstamp, t., d., est. $3/500, (05-23-93, Butterfield, #3694), 11 x 8½ in., photograph, gelatin silver print (BP 188, DM 471, FR 1585, Y 31,834).
$165* *Calattea Vittata, Island Of Oahu, 1977,* s., (05-16-93, Hindman, #351), 8½ x 11 in., photograph, silver print (BP 108, DM 266, FR 897, Y 18,374).
$385* *"Succulent: Echeveria Subrigida Hybrid, Mill Valley, California",* 1968/1980, s., photog. blindstamp, d., neg. num., photog. stamp, (11-16-92, Butterfield, #6259, illus.), 8⅞ x 9⅝ in., (225.8 x 244.9 mm.), photograph, gelatin silver print (BP 253, DM 614, FR 2068, Y 47,880).

WOTRUBA, Fritz German 1907-1975
$365* *Drei Figuren,* s., num., (12-01-92, Karl/Faber, #1376), 15⅜ x 20¹⁄₁₆ in., (39 x 51 cm.), lithograph (BP 241, DM 582, FR 1983, Y 45,443).
$2481* *"Fritz Wotruba. Ring", 1967: Fourteen,* Marlborough Fine Arts, s., num., (06-08-93, Karl/Faber, #1418), approx. 19⅞ x 25⁹⁄₁₆ in., (50.5 x 65 cm.), lithograph, 5 watercolored, on Arches wove (BP 1631, DM 4026, FR 13,557, Y 263,516).

WREFORD, Bertram Stanley b. 1926
$199* *The China Lunch, 1959,* #14/14, s., t., d. '59, prov., (05-10-93, Hodgins, #187), (31.8 x 49.5 cm.), woodcut on paper (BP 130, DM 320, FR 1079, Y 22,237, C$ 253).

WRIGHT, Frank Lloyd American 1869-1959
BI *Portfolio Of Buildings, Plans And Designs: One-Hundred,* pub. Horizon Press Publishers, 1963, est. $1/1,500, (06-10-93, Sotheby-NY, #273), each sheet 25½ x 15¾ in., (64.8 x 40 cm.), photo-lithograph in gold, brown or gray on gray or cream woven paper.
BI *Wasmuth Portfolio Ausgefurte Bauten Und Entwurfe Von Frank Lloyd Wright: Sixteen,* plates XLVII, XXXVIII, XVII (2), VIII, LXII (2), LVI, LIX, XXV, XXXIa, XXXIb, XXII, XXX, XXXIV, LXIII and XXXVII, photog.'s blindstamp, pub. Ernst Warmuth, 1910, est. $4/6,000, (06-10-93, Sotheby-NY, #272, illus.), each sheet 25½ x 15¾ in., (64.8 x 40 cm.), photo-lithograph in gold, brown or gray on gray or cream or onion-skin paper.

WRIGHT, George (after)
$213* *"The Hands", "The Cream", "Worry Worry" and "Home", 1900: A Set Of Four,* pub. Arthur Ackermann, margins, (07-16-92, Bonhams-Chelsea, #534), plate 12¾ x 18 in., (32.4 x 45.7 cm.), photogravure w/hand coloring (BP 110, DM 315, FR 1062, Y 26,682).

WRIGHT, John Buckland
BI *The Forest Pool, 1939,* s., num. 153/200, pub. Woodcut Society, margins, very good cond., glue stains, crease, est. $2/300, (02-24-93, Butterfield, #2891), 6 x 7¾ in., (152 x 197 mm.), wood engraving on wove.

WRIGHT, John Massey (after)
$433* *Victory Of Vittoria, 1814,* by H. Moses and F.C. Lewis, pub. Thomas Richards, wormholes, foxed, cockled, (11-30-92, Phillips-London, #240), sheet 25⅓ x 34⅝ in., (643 x 879 mm.), hand-colored aquatint on J. Whatman 1811 (BP 286, DM 690, FR 2342, Y 53,889).

WRIGHT, Joseph (of Derby) (after)
$317* *The Bradshawe Children (C.S. 141), 1769,* engraved by Valentine Green, 2nd state of 2, trimmed to plate, (11-30-92, Phillips-London, #50, illus.), plate 18¾ x 14¾ in., (476 x 375 mm.), mezzotint on laid (BP 209, DM 505, FR 1714, Y 39,452).

WRIGHT, Marsham
$138* *"The Down",* s., d. 1929, #23/50, very good cond.?, (03-28-93, Bakker, #277), image 7 x 5 in., (17.8 x 12.7 cm.), linocut (BP 93, DM 225, FR 765, Y 16,061).

WRINCH, Mary Evelyn
$107* *Chrysanthemum,* #61/75, s., (11-30-92, Ritchie, #24), 6⅛ x 6⅛ in., (15.6 x 15.6 cm.), color block print (BP 71, DM 170, FR 579, Y 13,317, C$ 138).
$194* *The Pageant Of April,* s., t., exec. 1933, lit., (06-07-93, Ritchie, #36, illus.), 12¼ x 10 in., (31.1 x 25.4 cm.), color woodcut (BP 128, DM 315, FR 1060, Y 20,811, C$ 248).

WU, Samuel b. 1919
BI *Egg Abstraction, c. 1945,* ink t., d., credit stamp, est. $1,8/2,200, (04-08-93, Christie-NY, #355, illus.), 14 x 11 in., (35.6 x 27.9 cm.), photograph, dye transfer print.
BI *Muscle Beach, San Francisco, c. 1949,* s., est. $1/1,500, (10-13-92, Christie-NY, #514, illus.), 7½ x 9¼ in., (19.1 x 23.5 cm.), photograph, gelatin silver print.
BI *Seven Exposures, 1945,* ink s., mounted, lit., est. $3/5,000, (04-08-93, Christie-NY, #354, illus.), 13½ x 10 in., (34.3 x 25.4 cm.), photograph, unique dye transfer print.
BI *Urban Cowboy, c. 1948,* s., flush-mounted, lit., est. $1,2/1,800, (10-13-92, Christie-NY, #513, illus.), 10 x 7¾ in., (25.4 x 19.7 cm.), photograph, gelatin silver print.
BI *V.J. Day, 1945,* partial label, notations, est. $700/1,000, (04-07-93, Swann, #372, illus.), 13½ x 10½ in., photograph, silver print.

WUNDERLICH, Paul German b. 1927
BI *Akt Auf Blauem Stuhl (Riediger 347), 1969,* s., num., staining, est. DM 700-, (09-25-92, Granier, #3063), 25⁹⁄₁₆ x 19¹¹⁄₁₆ in., (65 x 50 cm.), color lithograph on handmade Rives.
$202* *Akt Auf Blauem Stuhl (Riediger 347), 1969,* i. E.A., s., (11-28-92, Schoppmann, #890), 23⅝ x 19¹¹⁄₁₆ in., (60 x 50 cm.), color lithograph on BFK Rives (BP 133, DM 322, FR 1092, Y 25,140).
$394* *Allumettes,* s., #90/150, stone s.; blindstamp, (05-08-93, Schloss Ahlden, #2941), 29⁵⁄₁₆ x 21⁷⁄₁₆ in., (74.5 x 54.5

cm.), color lithograph on black handmade (BP 257, DM 633, FR 2136, Y 44,027).

BI *"Altweibersommer" (Female),* s., num., good cond., est. $2-300, (10-31-92, Cleveland, #403), 7⅞ x 4⅞ in., (20 x 12.4 cm.), lithograph in colors.

BI *"Altweibersommer" (Male),* s., num., good cond., est. $2-300, (10-31-92, Cleveland, #404), 7⅞ x 4⅞ in., (20 x 12.4 cm.), lithograph in colors.

$474* *Amazone (Riediger 588), 1978,* E.A., s., reflected reversed, s. in stone, blindstamp, (06-24-93, Germann, #542), 19¹¹⁄₁₆ x 25⅜ in., (500 x 645 mm.), color lithograph (BP 312, DM 768, FR 2590, Y 50,847, SF 690).

$208* *Der Augapfel Ist So Breit Wie Der Nasenflugel Beim Christus Von Bremen (R. 377), 1970,* s., (12-01-92, Karl/Faber, #1380), 29⁵⁄₁₆ x 22⁷⁄₁₆ in., (74.5 x 57 cm.), color lithograph (BP 137, DM 332, FR 1130, Y 25,896).

$1074* *Busenfreundinnen, 1965,* s., #37/60, stone d., (05-08-93, Schloss Ahlden, #2938, illus.), 18⁵⁄₁₆ x 22⅝ in., (46.5 x 57.5 cm.), color lithograph on handmade BFK Rives (BP 701, DM 1725, FR 5821, Y 120,013).

$470* *Creation D'Une Femme (Riediger 225), 1963,* s., num., (11-28-92, Schoppmann, #889), 24³⁄₁₆ x 16¹⁵⁄₁₆ in., (61.5 x 43 cm.), color lithograph on BFK Rives (BP 310, DM 749, FR 2542, Y 58,494).

$495* *Daniela Weint 3 Tranen (Riediger 423), 1971,* s., stone d., i., s., (06-12-93, Hauswedell/Nolt, #490), 28⅜ x 22¹⁄₁₆ in., (72 x 56 cm.), color lithograph on Arches (BP 324, DM 806, FR 2708, Y 52,089).

BI *Le Divan Vert (Riediger 322), 1968,* #28/70, s., est. SF 700/900, (04-21-93, Germann, #836), 25⁹⁄₁₆ x 19⅞ in., (650 x 505 mm.), color lithograph.

$307* *Ein Entscheidender Augenblick (R. 384), 1970,* s., (12-01-92, Karl/Faber, #1383), 29¾ x 22¼ in., (75.5 x 56.5 cm.), color lithograph (BP 203, DM 489, FR 1668, Y 38,222).

$208* *Entwurf Fur Ein Nurnberger Kissen (R. 378), 1970,* s., (12-01-92, Karl/Faber, #1381), 29¾ x 22¼ in., (75.5 x 56.5 cm.), color lithograph (BP 137, DM 332, FR 1130, Y 25,896).

$349* *Falkenstrauss, 1979,* s., #10/100, stone s., d.; blindstamp, (09-18-92, Schloss Ahlden, #1081), 32⅝ x 25⁹⁄₁₆ in., (82.9 x 65 cm.), color lithograph on hand-made (BP 204, DM 518, FR 1772, Y 43,134).

BI *Les Femmes (Riediger 558-560), 1977: Three,* s., #2183/3000, special edit. monograph Paul Wunderlich, est. DM 1,000, (06-12-93, Hauswedell/Nolt, #497), 16⁵⁄₁₆ x 12⅜ in., (41.5 x 31.5 cm.), color lithograph on wove.

$332* *Flirt (Riediger 328), 1968,* s., num., (12-05-92, Bassenge, #7830), 19¹¹⁄₁₆ x 25⁹⁄₁₆ in., (50 x 65 cm.), color lithograph on handmade Rives (BP 208, DM 518, FR 1764, Y 41,135).

$283* *Frau Mit Hochfrisur (Riediger 278), 1966,* s., #23/60, stone s., d., portfolio Portrait: Paul Wunderlich, (06-12-93, Hauswedell/Nolt, #485), 25⁹⁄₁₆ x 19¹¹⁄₁₆ in., (65 x 50 cm.), lithograph on BFK Rives (BP 185, DM 461, FR 1548, Y 29,780).

$169* *Gelbe Frau,* s. Wunderlich, E.A., (09-30-92, Kunsthallen, #298), color lithograph (BP 95, DM 240, FR 811, Y 20,281, DK 920).

$504* *Goethe, 1978,* s., #96/100; stone mono., d.; blindstamp, (09-18-92, Schloss Ahlden, #1082, illus.), 24¹³⁄₁₆ x 33¹⁄₁₆ in., (63 x 83.9 cm.), color lithograph on black handmade (BP 295, DM 748, FR 2558, Y 62,291).

$388* *Hinter Verschlossener Tur (Riediger 395), 1971,* s., num., staining, (09-25-92, Granier, #3064), sheet 33¹⁄₁₆ x 24¹³⁄₁₆ in., (84 x 63 cm.), color lithograph on Fabriano Murillo hand-made (BP 227, DM 575, FR 1945, Y 46,832).

$470* *Im Visier (Riediger 217), 1962,* s., num., (11-28-92, Schoppmann, #888), 25⁹⁄₁₆ x 19¹¹⁄₁₆ in., (65 x 50 cm.), color lithograph on BFK Rives (BP 310, DM 749, FR 2542, Y 58,494).

$216* *Der Junge Durer, Seine Hand Und Sein Kissen (Riediger 376), 1970,* s., num., (12-01-92, Karl/Faber, #1379), 29½ x 22¼ in., (75 x 56.5 cm.), color lithograph on Arches wove (BP 143, DM 344, FR 1173, Y 26,892).

$443* *Jutta (Riediger 314), 1968,* s., num., (12-05-92, Bassenge, #7829), 25⁹⁄₁₆ x 19¹¹⁄₁₆ in., (65 x 50 cm.), color lithograph on handmade Rives (BP 277, DM 691, FR 2354, Y 54,888).

$794* *Kleine Anatomie (Riediger 238), 1963,* s., (11-28-92, Schoppmann, #887), 25¹³⁄₁₆ x 19¹¹⁄₁₆ in., (65.5 x 50 cm.), color lithograph on BFK Rives (BP 524, DM 1265, FR 4294, Y 98,818).

$5775* *Kleine Anatonmie (Riediger 231-238): Seven,* s., num., (11-28-92, Schoppmann, #886, illus.), 22⁷⁄₁₆ x 20½ in., (57 x 52 cm.), lithograph on BFK Rives (BP 3812, DM 9200, FR 31,233, Y 718,731).

$73* *Komposition,* s. Wunderlich, 311/1000, (03-24-93, Kunsthallen, #340), color lithograph (BP 49, DM 119, FR 406, Y 8577, DK 460).

$394* *Lithographien IV: Three,* s., #413/1000, blindstamp, (05-08-93, Schloss Ahlden, #2830, illus.), each 24³⁄₁₆ x 19⁵⁄₁₆ in., (61.5 x 49 cm.), color lithograph on handmade (BP 257, DM 633, FR 2136, Y 44,027).

$201* *Matrix, 1966,* s., #18/120, full margins, good cond.?, (05-19-93, Butterfield, #2100A), 24¼ x 17⅞ in., (616 x 454 mm.), lithograph in colors on BFK Rives (BP 130, DM 327, FR 1101, Y 22,252).

$549* *Der Morgan (Nach Michelangelo) (Huber 506), 1975,* s., #117/200, pub. Matthieu, Dielsdorf, blindstamp, good cond., (06-30-93, Sotheby-London, #980), sh 31⅛ x 23⅜ in., (791 x 594 mm.), color lithograph on wove (BP 368, DM 936, FR 3159, Y 58,824).

$316* *Nude Studies, 1971,* s. Wunderlich, 18/75, (09-30-92, Kunsthallen, #300), color lithograph (BP 178, DM 448, FR 1516, Y 37,922, DK 1725).

$550* *"Nude Sunset", 1977,* s. Wunderlich, num. 90/150, very good cond., (09-11-92, Skinner, #103, illus.), 12³⁄₁₆ x 9⅜ in., (31 x 23.8 cm.), lithograph in colors on wove (BP 284, DM 792, FR 2691, Y 68,145).

$388* *Odaliske Mit Rotem Vogel (Riediger 513), 1976,* s., num., staining, (09-25-92, Granier, #3070, illus.), 30¹¹⁄₁₆ x 22¹³⁄₁₆ in., (78 x 58 cm.), color lithograph on hand-made Rives (BP 227, DM 575, FR 1945, Y 46,832).

$358* *Penthesilea I, 1976,* s., stone t., d., mono., #14/95, blindstamp, (05-08-93, Schloss Ahlden, #2937, illus.), 26⁷⁄₁₆ x 21⅛ in., (67.2 x 53.6 cm.), color lithograph on handmade BFK Rives (BP 234, DM 575, FR 1940, Y 40,004).

$213* *"Poivrons", 1988 and "Femme Au Coquetier", 1988: Two,* first, d. in plate, s., 24/80; second, s., 24/80, (06-28-93, Loudmer, #132), first 10⁷⁄₁₆ x 13¹⁵⁄₁₆ in., (265 x 355 mm.), second 38⁹⁄₁₆ x 26⅜ in., (265 x 355 mm.), color lithographs on Zerkall wove (BP 143, DM 362, FR 1219, Y 22,599).

$534* *Reclining Nude On A Piano Under A Crescent Moon,* s.; image s., full margins, excell. cond., (10-10-92, Litchfield, #231), image 29¼ x 22 in., (74.3 x 55.9 cm.), color lithograph (BP 317, DM 793, FR 2663, Y 65,011).

$169* *Rote Frau,* s. Wunderlich, E.A., (09-30-92, Kunsthallen, #297), color lithograph (BP 95, DM 240, FR 811, Y 20,281, DK 920).

BI *Rote Frau,* s. Wunderlich, E.A., est. DK 1,200, (09-30-92, Kunsthallen, #299), color lithograph.

$332* *Salomon VII 3: Dein Leib Ist Wie Ein Weizenhaufen, Umsteckt Mit Rosen (Riediger 367), 1969,* series Das Hoh Lied Des Salomon, (12-05-92, Bassenge, #7833), 23⅝ x 17¹¹⁄₁₆ in., (60 x 45 cm.), color lithograph on Rives (BP 208, DM 518, FR 1764, Y 41,135).

$130* *Salomon. Bilder Und Grafik Von Paul Wunderlich, 1970,* s., num., (11-28-92, Schoppmann, #714), 27⁹⁄₁₆ x 23¼ in., (70 x 59 cm.), offset on light cardboard (BP 86, DM 207, FR 703, Y 16,179).

$297* *Schwanenkopf (Riediger 242), 1964,* s., (06-12-93, Hauswedell/Nolt, #484), 10¹¹⁄₁₆ x 5⁹⁄₁₆ in., (27.2 x 14.2 cm.), color etching on wove (BP 194, DM 483, FR 1625, Y 31,253).

$638* *Selbst Mit Hund Und Flugel (R. 491), 1974,* s., num., (06-08-93, Karl/Faber, #1423), approx. 16⁹⁄₁₆ x 13⅜ in., (42 x 34 cm.), etching and color aquatint on Arches wove (BP 419, DM 1035, FR 3486, Y 67,764).

$208* *So Baden Die Frauen In Bremen (R. 381), 1970,* s., (12-01-92, Karl/Faber, #1382), 29¹⁵⁄₁₆ x 22⁷⁄₁₆ in., (76 x 57 cm.), color lithograph (BP 137, DM 332, FR 1130, Y 25,896).

$2120* *The Song Of Songs Which Is Solomon's (Riediger 359-368; Brusberg 300-309), 1969: Ten,* s., #37/310, Aquarius Presse, (06-12-93, Hauswedell/Nolt, #499), portfolio 26⁹⁄₁₆ x 20¹¹⁄₁₆ in., (67.5 x 52.5 cm.), color lithograph on BFK Rives (BP 1388, DM 3451, FR 11,597, Y 223,087).

$283* *A Trois (Riediger 460), 1973,* s., #3/50, (06-12-93, Hauswedell/Nolt, #492), 29⅛ x 21⅞ in., (74 x 55.5 cm.), color lithograph on BFK Rives (BP 185, DM 461, FR 1548, Y 29,780).

$55* *Untitled,* s. Wunderlich '61, good cond., (11-21-92, Bakker, #151), 5 x 4½ in., (12.7 x 11.4 cm.), lithograph (BP 36, DM 88, FR 295, Y 6840).

$546* *Untitled, 1969: Two,* s., good cond.?, handling crease, (05-19-93, Butterfield, #2100), 25¾ x 19¾ in., (654 x 502 mm.), lithograph in colors on BFK Rives (BP 354, DM 888, FR 2990, Y 60,445).

$424* *Zwei Modelle Posieren Auf Einem Gepardenfell (Riediger 484), 1974,* s., #80/100, (06-12-93, Hauswedell/Nolt, #494), 25¾ x 19⅝ in., (65.4 x 49.8 cm.), color lithograph on BFK Rives (BP 278, DM 690, FR 2319, Y 44,617).

BI *Zwei Modelle Posieren Auf Gepardenfell, 1974,* s., #49/100, blindstamp, est. DM 900, (05-08-93, Schloss Ahlden, #2939, illus.), 25¹³⁄₁₆ x 19⅝ in., (65.5 x 49.9 cm.), color lithograph on handmade BFK Rives.

WURM, Erwin   b. 1954
BI *Untitled,* s., num., E. Wurm, #34/50, est. SC 3/4,000, (04-21-93, Dorotheum, #725), color screenprint.

WURTZEL, David   American contemporary
BI *"Icarys Descending" and "Self Portrait": Two,* 5/25, 10/10, each s., num., est. $125/175, (02-04-93, Sloan, #2976), larger 13⅝ x 11½ in., (34.6 x 29.2 cm.), etching, one w/aquatint.

WYCK, Thomas   Dutch 1616-1677
$303* *Die Brucke (B. 19; Wurzbach und Dutuit 19 II),* watermark, prov., (12-04-92, Bassenge, #6506), 5¼ x 5¹¹⁄₁₆ in., (13.3 x 14.4 cm.), etching (BP 194, DM 483, FR 1637, Y 37,828).

$150* *Stable Yard With Figure Saddling Donkey,* plate s. by Cornelis Ploos Van Amstel, stamped Ploos Van Amstel's Cachet de vente stamp, lit., (06-08-93, Ritchie, #16, illus.), plate 5¾ x 9 in., (14.6 x 22.9 cm.), sepia aquatint (BP 99, DM 243, FR 820, Y 15,932, C$ 193).

WYCKAERT, Maurice
$192* *Untitled,* s., #28/80, margins, good cond., (05-27-93, Sotheby-Amstrdm, #704), 20 x 25¹⁵⁄₁₆ in., (508 x 660 mm.), color lithograph on wove (BP 123, DM 308, FR 1038, Y 20,583, G 345).

WYETH, Andrew   American b. 1917
$1980* *Bird In The House, 1983,* s., num. 11/300, p. Triton Press, Inc., pub. Chadds Ford Publicationslindstamp, full sheet, good cond., sharp crease, (05-22-93, Weschler, #229, illus.), 30½ x 23 in., (77.5 x 58.4 cm.), collotype (BP 1283, DM 3220, FR 10,832, Y 218,302).

$3520* *Open House, 1980,* s., num. 231/300, p. Triton Press, pub. Chadds Ford Publications, blindstamp, full sheet, good cond., minor handling creases, smudging, (05-22-93, Weschler, #230, illus.), sheet 21½ x 35 in., (54.6 x 88.9 cm.), collotype (BP 2281, DM 5724, FR 19,256, Y 388,093).

$3300* *The Reefer, 1982,* s., num. 91/300, p. Triton Press, Inc., pub. Chadds Ford Publications blindstamp, full sheet, good cond., soft handling crease, minor smudging, (05-22-93, Weschler, #231, illus.), 31½ x 30½ in., (80 x 77.5 cm.), collotype (BP 2138, DM 5366, FR 18,053, Y 363,837).

WYETH, Jamie   American b. 1946
$468* *Nureyev,* s., 52/300, (11-12-92, Freemn/Fine Art, #245), 34 x 23½ in., (86.4 x 59.7 cm.), lithograph (BP 307, DM 742, FR 2501, Y 58,029).

BI *"Nureyev II", 1978,* artist's proof, s., blindstamped d., p., pub. marks, full sheet image, pub. Circle Galleries, est. $1/1500, (12-05-92, Neal, #178), color lithograph on black paper.

BI *"Nureyev", 1978,* artist's proof, s., blindstamped d., p., pub. marks, pub. Circle Galleries, full sheet image, est. $15/2000, (12-05-92, Neal, #177, illus.), color lithograph on light beige paper.

WYETH, Newell Convers   American 1882-1945
$302* *Pennsylvania Railroad, 1929,* B+ cond., creasing, fold, repairs, chartex-backed, (08-06-92, Swann, #300, illus.), 40 x 26½ in., (101.6 x 67.3 cm.), (BP 158, DM 446, FR 1507, Y 38,520).

WYETH, Newell Convers (after)   American 1882-1945
BI *For All The World, I Was Led Like A Dancing Bear,* after orig. illus. for "Treasure Island", est. $200/250, (10-30-92, Sloan, #884), sight 41 x 35¼ in., (104.1 x 89.5 cm.), chromolithograph mounted on board.

WYLIE, William Lionel
$548* *The Fourth Rail Bridge,* s., margins, (09-17-92, Bonhams-Chelsea, #107, illus.), plate 9 x 14¾ in., (22.9 x 37.5 cm.), drypoint etching (BP 308, DM 814, FR 2785, Y 68,227).

WYLLIE, Harold
$85* *H.M.S. Terrible And Hindostan,* num. LXII, s., margins, (08-12-92, Bonhams, #226), plate 5¾ x 9¾ in., (14.6 x 24.8 cm.), drypoint etching (BP 44, DM 124, FR 421, Y 10,834).

$160* *H.M.S. Victory,* margins, (08-12-92, Bonhams, #214), plate 12 x 18¾ in., (30.5 x 47 cm.), etching w/hand-coloring (BP 83, DM 234, FR 793, Y 20,393).

$127* *Ship Moored In Calm Waters,* s., margins, (08-12-92, Bonhams, #215), plate 9¼ x 18½ in., (23.5 x 47 cm.), drypoint etching (BP 66, DM 186, FR 629, Y 16,187).

$118* *Square Rigger,* s., num. LXVII, margins, (08-12-92, Bonhams, #216), plate 6¼ x 11⅞ in., (15.9 x 30.2 cm.), drypoint etching (BP 61, DM 173, FR 585, Y 15,040).

WYLLIE, W.L.
$110* *Santa Maria, Venice,* (11-13-92, DuMouchelle, #368), 6 x 8 in., (15.2 x 20.3 cm.), etching (BP 71, DM 173, FR 582, Y 13,653).

WYLLIE, William Lionel
$234* *The "Q" Ship "Probus" Sinking A German "U" Boat,* s., margins, (08-12-92, Bonhams, #249), plate 6 x 8¾ in., (15.2 x 22.2 cm.), drypoint etching (BP 121, DM 342, FR 1160, Y 29,824).

$319* *Barges And Other Shipping On The Thames,* s., margins, stained, (08-12-92, Bonhams, #218), plate 10 x 15 in., (25.4 x 38.1 cm.), drypoint etching (BP 165, DM 467, FR 1581, Y 40,658).

$252* *"Barges And Other Shipping On The Thames", 1924,* s., pub. R. Dunthorne and Son, margins, staining, (01-14-93, Bonhams, #133), plate 6¼ x 14⅝ in., (15.9 x 37.1 cm.), drypoint etching (BP 165, DM 412, FR 1393, Y 31,770).

BI *Barges And Other Shipping On The Thames, 1924,* pub. R. Dunthorne and Son, margins, staining, est. BP 150/200, (08-12-92, Bonhams, #217), plate 6¼ x 14¾ in., (15.9 x 37.5 cm.), drypoint etching.

$588* *Barges And Other Shipping On The Tyne At The Swing Bridge,* s., margins, (09-17-92, Bonhams-Chelsea, #108), plate 8¾ x 14¾ in., (22.2 x 37.5 cm.), drypoint etching (BP 330, DM 873, FR 2988, Y 73,207).

$135* *The Battle Of Trafalgar, 1893,* pub. Fine Art Society, margins, staining, (01-14-93, Bonhams, #134), plate 15¼ x 34½ in., (38.7 x 87.6 cm.), drypoint etching (BP 88, DM 221, FR 746, Y 17,020).

$203* *The Bustling Mersey,* s., margins, (08-12-92, Bonhams, #219), plate 4¾ x 6⅜ in., (12.1 x 16.2 cm.), drypoint etching (BP 105, DM 297, FR 1006, Y 25,873).

$91 *Busy Beach Scene With Numerous Figures And Boats,* s., (06-11-93, G.A. Key, #93), 13 x 18 in., (33 x 45.7 cm.), b/w etching (BP 60, DM 148, FR 499, Y 9655).

BI *A Converted Man-O'-War At Anchor,* s., mounting tape, good cond., est. BP 150/200, (10-27-92, Phillips-London, #327), plate 7½ x 9⅝ in., (191 x 244 mm.), drypoint w/ roulette work on wove.

BI *Cruiser Squadron Off Spithead,* s., margins, est. BP 1/150, (08-12-92, Bonhams, #220), plate 3⅞ x 8⅜ in., (9.8 x 21.3 cm.), drypoint etching.

$191* *Destroyers Under Fire, 1918,* s., pub. Robert Dunthorne, margins, laid down, scratched, stained, (08-12-92, Bonhams, #221), plate 13 x 24½ in., (33 x 62.2 cm.), drypoint etching (BP 99, DM 279, FR 946, Y 24,344).

$627* *Downstream From London Bridge,* s., mount staining, (10-27-92, Phillips-London, #325), plate 10¾ x 7¼ in.,

(273 x 184 mm.), drypoint w/roulette on laid (BP 396, DM 961, FR 3261, Y 76,697).

$185* *Fishermen Coming Ashore,* s. w/in plate, margins, surface dirt, (01-14-93, Bonhams, #135), plate 9 x 7 in., (22.9 x 17.8 cm.), drypoint etching (BP 121, DM 302, FR 1023, Y 23,323).

BI *Fleet Leaving Portsmouth,* s., margins, est. BP 1/150, (08-12-92, Bonhams, #222), plate 3⅞ x 8⅜ in., (9.8 x 21.3 cm.), drypoint etching.

BI *Greenwich Reach, 1924,* s., pub. R. Dunthorne and Son, margins, est. BP 2/300, (08-12-92, Bonhams, #224), plate 6¼ x 14¾ in., (15.9 x 37.5 cm.), drypoint etching.

$151* *Greenwich Reach, 1924,* s., pub. R. Dunthorne and Son, margins, (01-14-93, Bonhams, #136), plate 6¼ x 14¾ in., (15.9 x 37.5 cm.), drypoint etching (BP 99, DM 247, FR 835, Y 19,037).

$203* *H.M.S. Britannia,* s., margins, (08-12-92, Bonhams, #225), plate 7⅝ x 9½ in., (19.4 x 24.1 cm.), drypoint etching (BP 105, DM 297, FR 1006, Y 25,873).

$251* *H.M.S. Dreadnought At Anchor In Portsmouth 1912,* s., margins, (11-19-92, Bonhams-Chelsea, #14), plate 10⅞ x 8 in., (27.6 x 20.3 cm.), etching (BP 165, DM 400, FR 1348, Y 31,215).

$404* *H.M.S. President At Embankment, 1927,* s., pub. R. Dunthorne and Son, margins, (01-14-93, Bonhams, #137), plate 8 x 16⅛ in., (20.3 x 41 cm.), drypoint etching (BP 264, DM 661, FR 2233, Y 50,933).

$383* *H.M.S. Victory In Portsmouth Harbour,* s., foxing, mount staining, (10-27-92, Phillips-London, #328), plate 5⅞ x 9¾ in., (149 x 248 mm.), etching w/drypoint on wove (BP 242, DM 587, FR 1992, Y 46,850).

$552* *H.M.S. Victory Off Portsmouth,* s., margins, staining, (08-12-92, Bonhams, #228), plate 8½ x 19¼ in., (21.6 x 48.9 cm.), drypoint etching (BP 286, DM 807, FR 2735, Y 70,354).

$219* *H.M.S. Victory Off Portsmouth,* s., defects, trimmed, (01-21-93, Bonhams-Chelsea, #150), 15¾ x 29½ in., (40 x 74.9 cm.), etching (BP 143, DM 348, FR 1178, Y 27,409).

$637* *The Harbour, St. Andrews,* s., (08-12-92, Bonhams, #223, illus.), plate 6¼ x 14¾ in., (15.9 x 37.5 cm.), drypoint etching (BP 330, DM 932, FR 3157, Y 81,188).

BI *Landing At Low Tide,* s., margins. est. BP 120/180, (08-12-92, Bonhams, #229), plate 3½ x 14 in., (8.9 x 35.6 cm.), drypoint etching.

$297* *Landing Oysters, Cancale,* s., margins, (08-12-92, Bonhams, #230), plate 7¾ x 9⅞ in., (19.7 x 25.1 cm.), drypoint etching (BP 154, DM 434, FR 1472, Y 37,854).

BI *A Launch And Destroyers In Open Waters,* s., margins, est. BP 1/150, (08-12-92, Bonhams, #231), plate 7⅞ x 9¾ in., (20 x 24.8 cm.), drypoint etching.

$722* *London And Tower Bridges,* s., (08-12-92, Bonhams, #232, illus.), plate 6¼ x 14⅝ in., (15.9 x 37.1 cm.), drypoint etching (BP 374, DM 1056, FR 3578, Y 92,021).

$320 *"Mackerel Boats, Shoreham",* s., label verso, (04-16-93, G.A. Key, #86, illus.), 7 x 9 in., (17.8 x 22.9 cm.), etching (BP 210, DM 517, FR 1747, Y 35,983).

$175* *A Masted Vessel Under Fire,* s., margins, (02-17-93, Bonhams-Chelsea, #333), plate 6 x 9 in., (15.2 x 22.9 cm.), drypoint etching (BP 121, DM 284, FR 963, Y 20,903).

BI *"A Masted Vessel Under Fire",* s., margins, est. BP 1/150, (01-14-93, Bonhams, #138), plate 6 x 9 in., (15.2 x 22.9 cm.), drypoint etching.

BI *Our Fathers, Plates I-IV: Four,* s., margins, est. BP 180/220, (01-14-93, Bonhams, #139), plate 12¼ x 8¼ in., (31.1 x 21 cm.), etching.

$361* *Our Fathers: Four,* illus. poem by Captain Ronald A. Hopwood, R.N., each s., margins, (08-12-92, Bonhams, #233), plate 12¼ x 8¼ in., (31.1 x 21 cm.), etching (BP 187, DM 528, FR 1789, Y 46,011).

BI *Q Boat Merope,* s., margins, est. BP 1/150, (08-12-92, Bonhams, #234), plate 6⅞ x 8⅞ in., (17.5 x 22.5 cm.), drypoint etching.

BI *Q Boat Merope,* s., margins, est. BP 1/150, (08-12-92, Bonhams, #248), plate 6⅞ x 8⅞ in., (17.5 x 22.5 cm.), drypoint etching.

BI *Shipping And Smaller Vessels In An Estuary,* s., margins, est. BP 2/300, (08-12-92, Bonhams, #235), plate 6⅜ x 14¾ in., (16.2 x 37.5 cm.), drypoint etching.

$306* *"Shipping In Choppy Waters Off A Headland",* s., margins, (10-15-92, Bonhams-Chelsea, #53), plate 6⅜ x 14¾ in., (16.2 x 37.5 cm.), drypoint etching (BP 187, DM 455, FR 1545, Y 36,713).

$161* *"Shipping Off Naples",* margins, (01-14-93, Bonhams, #140), plate 6¼ x 14½ in., (15.9 x 36.8 cm.), drypoint etching (BP 105, DM 263, FR 890, Y 20,298).

$404* *Shipping On The Thames At Tower Bridge,* s., margins, spots of foxing, (08-12-92, Bonhams, #236), plate 7¾ x 9⅞ in., (19.7 x 25.1 cm.), drypoint etching (BP 209, DM 591, FR 2002, Y 51,491).

BI *Southwark Bridge,* s., margins, foxing, scuffing, est. BP 150/200, (01-14-93, Bonhams, #141), plate 4¾ x 12¾ in., (12.1 x 32.4 cm.), drypoint etching w/aquatint.

$509* *Submarines Surfacing Around H.M.S. Victory,* s., margins, (09-17-92, Bonhams-Chelsea, #72), plate 9 x 15 in., (22.9 x 38.1 cm.), drypoint etching (BP 286, DM 756, FR 2586, Y 63,372).

$297* *Sunshine In The Solent,* s., t., margins, (08-12-92, Bonhams, #237), plate 6¾ x 8¾ in., (17.1 x 22.2 cm.), drypoint etching w/aquatint (BP 154, DM 434, FR 1472, Y 37,854).

$637* *The Thames At St. Paul's,* s., margins, (08-12-92, Bonhams, #238), plate 7⅞ x 16 in., (20 x 40.6 cm.), drypoint etching (BP 330, DM 932, FR 3157, Y 81,188).

$505* *The Thames At The City,* s., margins, (01-14-93, Bonhams, #142), plate 6¼ x 14½ in., (15.9 x 36.8 cm.), drypoint etching (BP 330, DM 826, FR 2792, Y 63,666).

BI *Timber Ships,* num. LX, s., margins, est. BP 150/200, (08-12-92, Bonhams, #239), plate 4⅛ x 13 in., (10.5 x 33 cm.), drypoint etching.

$168* *"Tugs At The Mouth Of An Estuary",* s., margins, (01-14-93, Bonhams, #143), plate 4 x 9⅞ in., (10.2 x 25.1 cm.), drypoint etching (BP 110, DM 275, FR 929, Y 21,180).

$313* *Tugs On The Thames,* s., laid at edges, foxing, (10-27-92, Phillips-London, #326), plate 10 x 14¾ in., (254 x 375 mm.), drypoint on wove (BP 198, DM 480, FR 1628, Y 38,287).

BI *Unloading The Catch,* num. LX, s., margins, est. BP 150/200, (08-12-92, Bonhams, #240), plate 4⅛ x 13 in., (10.5 x 33 cm.), drypoint etching.

$552* *Valletta Harbour, Malta,* s., margins, (08-12-92, Bonhams, #241, illus.), plate 6½ x 14⅞ in., (16.5 x 37.8 cm.), drypoint etching (BP 286, DM 807, FR 2735, Y 70,354).

$807* *Westminster From Lambeth Pier,* s., margins, (08-12-92, Bonhams, #242, illus.), plate 7¾ x 15¾ in., (19.7 x 40 cm.), drypoint etching (BP 418, DM 1180, FR 3999, Y 102,855).

$203* *The Wind Falls Light,* s., margins, (08-12-92, Bonhams, #243), plate 4¾ x 6⅜ in., (12.1 x 16.2 cm.), drypoint etching (BP 105, DM 297, FR 1006, Y 25,873).

WYNDHAM, Richard   b. 1896

$755* *To Visit Britain's Landmarks, Up Park, Petersfield, 1937,* p. Waterlow and Sons, ref. #501, cond. 1, nick, (10-13-92, Phillips-London, #126), 30¹⁄₁₆ x 45¹⁄₁₆ in., (76.3 x 114.5 cm.), color lithograph (BP 440, DM 1106, FR 3758, Y 91,548).

WYNFIELD, David Wilkie   1837-1887

$3992* *Portraits Of Artists: Twenty-One,* 1860s-70s, mounted on card, lit., (05-06-93, Christie-London, #58, illus.), each approx. 8 x 6¼ in., photograph, albumen print (BP 2530, DM 6288, FR 21,166, Y 439,212).

WYSS, Franz Anatol   b. 1940

$453* *Endzeit Oder Die Wege Um Ruhm, 1973: Ten,* XV (von XX), s., d., num., pub. Centro del bel libro, (03-16-93, Schuler, #3406, illus.), color etching and embossing (BP 313, DM 753, FR 2559, Y 52,970, SF 690).

XANTI

$495* *Princeps S.A. Cervo Italia,* Boggeri, A cond., (08-06-92, Swann, #302, illus.), 13½ x 9½ in., (34.3 x 24.1 cm.), (BP 259, DM 731, FR 2470, Y 63,138).

$1100* *Princeps, S.A. Cervo, Italia, 1934,* Boggeri, B+ cond., taped closed tears, (08-06-92, Swann, #301, illus.), 55 x

39 in., (139.7 x 99.1 cm.), (BP 575, DM 1625, FR 5489, Y 140,306).

XIMA
$139* *Casablanca. Porte Du Maroc. Syndicat D'Initiative Et De Tourisme,* good cond., (03-13-93, Laurin, #108), 39⅜ x 24 7/16 in., (100 x 62 cm.), (BP 97, DM 231, FR 787, Y 16,382).

XUETAO, Wang ac. mid-20th cent.
BI *Darstellung Eines Exotischen Vogels Auf Einem Bambuszweig,* s., seal, est. SC 5/6,000, (04-27-93, Dorotheum, #413, illus.), 13½ x 10 3/16 in., (34.3 x 25.8 cm.), color woodcut.

YAGAKI, Shikanosuke 1897-1966
BI *Puddle On Pavement, c. 1930,* credit stamp, est. $2/2,500, (10-13-92, Christie-NY, #404, illus.), 11⅝ x 9¼ in., (29.5 x 23.5 cm.), photograph, gelatin silver print.

YAHIA
$99* *Visitez La Tunisie,* good cond., (03-13-93, Laurin, #75), 39⅜ x 24 7/16 in., (100 x 62 cm.), (BP 69, DM 165, FR 560, Y 11,668).

YAMAKAWA, Shuho Japanese 1898-1944
$88* *Woman In A Blue Kimono,* bears artist stamp, (05-16-93, Hindman, #390), 14¼ x 9⅜ in., (36.2 x 23.8 cm.), color woodcut (BP 57, DM 142, FR 476, Y 9755).

YAMAMURA KOKA (TOYONARI) Japanese
BI *Bust-Portrait Of Ichikawa Shocho As Oman,* Oban, s. Toyonari e, d. 1920, creased, Prof. H.R.W. Kuhne Coll., est.BP 6/800, (06-11-93, Sotheby-London, #492, illus.), 16⅛ x 11¼ in., (41 x 28.6 cm.), woodblock, pale pink mica ground.

YAMPOLSKY, Mariana
$220* *"Mujer De Tlacotalpan, Veracruz" (La Raiz Y El Camino, p. 41), 1980's,* s., t., Dixon Collection, (11-16-92, Butterfield, #6261, illus.), 7⅞ x 8 in., (200.4 x 203.6 mm.), photograph, gelatin silver print (BP 145, DM 351, FR 1182, Y 27,360).

YANKEL, Jacques French b. 1920
$82* *Arlequin,* s., #10/25, good margins, (05-06-93, Laurin, #98), color lithograph (BP 52, DM 129, FR 435, Y 9022).
$144* *Le Peintre Et Son Modele,* s., #1/10, good margins, (05-06-93, Laurin, #99), color lithograph (BP 91, DM 227, FR 764, Y 15,843).
$147* *Sans Titre,* s., #142/200, (11-16-92, Briest, #115), 26⅜ x 20 1/16 in., (67 x 51 cm.), lithograph in colors (BP 97, DM 234, FR 790, Y 18,345).
BI *Streetscene,* s., i. epreuve d'artiste, full margins, good cond., est. Dfl. 5/700, (05-27-93, Sotheby-Amstrdm, #705), 16 9/16 x 15¾ in., (420 x 400 mm.), color lithograph on wove.

YAO, C.J.
$357* *"Building Reflections", "People And Store Window Reflections" and "Window Reflections", c. 1981-82: Group Of Three,* s., from City-Scapes portfolio, pub. London Arts, good cond., (05-27-93, Swann, #301), color serigraph (BP 229, DM 573, FR 1931, Y 38,272).

YARO, Boris
$1540* *The Shooting Of Robert Kennedy, 1968,* handstamp, (10-14-92, Swann, #362, illus.), 11½ x 9 in., (29.2 x 22.9 cm.), photograph, silver print (BP 904, DM 2254, FR 7643, Y 186,621).
$330* *The Death Of Presidential Candidate Robert Kennedy, 1968,* caption in neg., news agency's handstamp, (04-07-93, Swann, #373, illus.), 7½ x 6 in., photograph, vintage silver copy print (BP 218, DM 534, FR 1806, Y 37,491).

YAVNO, Max 1921-1985
BI *Aaron Siskind, Old Yuma Jail, 1947,* s., lit., est. $3/5,000, (10-13-92, Christie-NY, #515, illus.), 13¼ x 19⅜ in., (33.7 x 49.2 cm.), photograph, gelatin silver print.
$1725* *Garage Doors, San Francisco, 1947,* s., illus., (05-23-93, Butterfield, #3696, illus.), 10½ x 13½ in., photograph, gelatin silver print (BP 1123, DM 2820, FR 9494, Y 190,671).
$1380* *Houses On A Hill Street, "Piano Keys", 1947,* s. twice, illus., (05-23-93, Butterfield, #3697, illus.), 13¼ x 10½ in., photograph, gelatin silver print (BP 899, DM 2256, FR 7595, Y 152,537).
$2420* *The Leg,* sig., 1960's, (10-14-92, Swann, #599, illus.), 19½ x 15½ in., (49.5 x 39.4 cm.), photograph, silver print (BP 1420, DM 3542, FR 12,010, Y 293,262).
$4400* *"The Leg" (Max Yavno, p. 24),* 1949/later, s., (11-16-92, Butterfield, #6263, illus.), 19 9/16 x 15½ in., (496.2 x 394.4 mm.), photograph, gelatin silver print (BP 2897, DM 7015, FR 23,631, Y 547,196).
$575* *"Mexican Foreman",* 1946, p.l., s., (05-23-93, Butterfield, #3699, illus.), 13½ x 7½ in., photograph, gelatin silver print (BP 374, DM 940, FR 3165, Y 63,557).
$1495* *"Mexican Photographers",* 1946, p.l., s., printing info., (05-23-93, Butterfield, #3698, illus.), 14¼ x 19⅜ in., photograph, gelatin silver print (BP 974, DM 2444, FR 8228, Y 165,248).
$2200* *"Muscle Beach",* 1949/later, s., Dixon Collection, (11-16-92, Butterfield, #6262, illus.), 8 x 13⅜ in., (203.6 x 340.3 mm.), photograph, gelatin silver print (BP 1449, DM 3508, FR 11,815, Y 273,598).
$3738* *"Muscle Beach",* 1949, p.l., s., (05-23-93, Butterfield, #3695, illus.), 8 x 13½ in., photograph, gelatin silver print (BP 2434, DM 6112, FR 20,572, Y 413,176).
$2875* *"Muscle Beach" (Yavno, pl. 12),* mounted, s. by photog., 1949, p.l., (04-06-93, Sotheby-NY, #386A, illus.), 7¾ x 13⅜ in., photograph (BP 1899, DM 4632, FR 15,685, Y 327,897).
BI *Night View, Film Premiere Of "The Heiress",* 1949, p.l., mounted on card, est. BP 5/700, (05-06-93, Christie-London, #191A), 9¼ x 15¼ in., photograph, gelatin silver print.
$990* *Russian Hill, 1947,* ink photog. stamp, (11-16-92, Butterfield, #6264, illus.), 9¾ x 6½ in., (248.1 x 165.4 mm.), photograph, gelatin silver print (BP 652, DM 1578, FR 5317, Y 123,119).
BI *Young Boy In Window, 1948,* s., i., est. $800/1,000, (05-23-93, Butterfield, #3700, illus.), 13½ x 10½ in., photograph, gelatin silver print.

YEAGER, Joseph American c. 1792-1859
BI *"Battle Of New Orleans And Death Of Major General Packenham On The 8th Of January, 1815",* drawn by West, engraved by Yeager, p. Y. Saurman, pub., sold c. 1815by Yeager, est. $5/800, (12-05-92, Neal, #553, illus.), image 13 x 19 in., (33 x 48.3 cm.), hand-colored engraving.

YEATS, Jack Butler Irish 1871-1957
$112* *The Post Car,* margins, (03-03-93, Bonhams-Chelsea, #225), image 8½ x 11¾ in., (21.6 x 29.8 cm.), hand-colored woodcut (BP 77, DM 184, FR 626, Y 13,087).

YEOMANS, Don
$133* *'Rainbow Chaser,' 1981,* #220/225, s., (10-21-92, Maynard, #40), approx. 13 x 15 in., (33 x 38.1 cm.), silkscreen (BP 83, DM 201, FR 683, Y 16,200, C$ 165).
BI *'Wolves,' 1981,* #186/225, s., est. C$150/200, (10-21-92, Maynard, #38), approx. 15 x 8 in., (38.1 x 20.3 cm.), silkscreen.

YIISEN Japanese 1794-1848
$282* *Geisha,* prov., (11-16-92, Hodgins, #337), 14 x 9½ in., (35.6 x 24.1 cm.), color woodblock on paper (BP 185, DM 450, FR 1515, Y 35,193, C$ 358).

YLLA
BI *Siamese Cat,* photog.'s sig., notations, 1930s, est. $6/900, (04-07-93, Swann, #598, illus.), 8½ x 6¼ in., photograph, silver print.

YOKOI, Tomoe Japanese b. 1932
$550* *"Radish In The Bowl", "Carrot And Lemon", "Corn And Pepper" and "Green Peas", c. 1970-74: Group Of Four,* full margins, num., t., s., (05-27-93, Swann, #302), color mezzotint (BP 352, DM 883, FR 2975, Y 58,962).

YOKOI, Tomoe Japanese b. 1943
$121* *"Apples In A Basket",* s., num. 56/100, excell. cond., (10-31-92, Cleveland, #52), 7 x 9¾ in., (17.8 x 24.8 cm.), mezzotint (BP 78, DM 186, FR 632, Y 14,988).

$100* *Cans,* s., #120/150, excellent cond., (05-15-93, Cleveland, #39), 11¾ x 13¾ in., (29.8 x 34.9 cm.), color mezzotint (BP 65, DM 161, FR 541, Y 11,085).

$100* *"Cup And Cushion",* s., t., #A.P., excellent cond., (05-15-93, Cleveland, #40), 13¾ x 11⅞ in., (34.9 x 30.2 cm.), mezzotint (BP 65, DM 161, FR 541, Y 11,085).

$100* *"Cup And Flower",* s., #37/95, excellent cond., (05-15-93, Cleveland, #36), 7 x 11 in., (17.8 x 27.9 cm.), color mezzotint (BP 65, DM 161, FR 541, Y 11,085).

$138* *"Mortar",* s., num. 45/150, excell. cond., (10-31-92, Cleveland, #50), 11¾ x 12¾ in., (29.6 x 32.4 cm.), mezzotint (BP 88, DM 212, FR 720, Y 17,094).

BI *"Owl",* s., #62/75, excellent cond., est. $50/100, (05-15-93, Cleveland, #37), 14 x 9½ in., (35.6 x 24.1 cm.), mezzotint.

$121* *"Roller",* s., num. 43/150, excell. cond., (10-31-92, Cleveland, #49), 11¾ x 13¾ in., (29.8 x 34.9 cm.), mezzotint (BP 78, DM 186, FR 632, Y 14,988).

$121* *"Two Small Apples",* s., num. 21/100, excell. cond., (10-31-92, Cleveland, #51), 6¾ x 9½ in., (17.1 x 24.1 cm.), mezzotint (BP 78, DM 186, FR 632, Y 14,988).

$100* *"Watering Pot",* s., #119/150, excellent cond., (05-15-93, Cleveland, #38), 11¾ x 13¾ in., (29.8 x 34.9 cm.), color mezzotint (BP 65, DM 161, FR 541, Y 11,085).

YONIS

$273* *Moulin De La Galette, Bal, Kermesse, "Transformation Complete",* p. Draeger, good cond., (11-19-92, Ribeyre/Baron, #158), 29¹⁵⁄₁₆ x 43⅛ in., (76 x 109.5 cm.), poster (BP 180, DM 435, FR 1466, Y 33,951).

YOSHIDA

$77* *Battle Scene,* (10-11-92, Hanzel, #945), 14¼ x 9⅝ in., (36.2 x 24.4 cm.), color woodblock print (BP 46, DM 114, FR 384, Y 9374).

$715* *"Otenjo", (1926),* s. twice, seal, d. Taisho 15, lightly toned, yoko-e, (11-20-92, Skinner, #124, illus.), oban yoko-e (BP 471, DM 1140, FR 3840, Y 88,919).

$825* *"Roshikihara", (1926),* s. twice, t., seal, d. Taisho 15, yoko-e, (11-20-92, Skinner, #118, illus.), oban yoko-e (BP 543, DM 1315, FR 4431, Y 102,599).

YOSHIDA, Hiroshi Japanese 1876-1950

BI *"Abend In Nara", 1933,* lit., t., s., Format Oban, est. SC 20/25,000, (04-27-93, Dorotheum, #206, illus.), 10¹¹⁄₁₆ x 15⁹⁄₁₆ in., (27.2 x 39.5 cm.), color woodcut.

$303* *Acropolis, Night,* s., t., (09-17-92, Sloan, #2367), 9⅞ x 14½ in., (25.1 x 36.8 cm.), woodblock (BP 170, DM 450, FR 1540, Y 37,724).

$523* *"Avenue Of Cherry Trees" and "Omuro": Two,* both s. Hiroshi Yoshida, very good cond., (11-21-92, Bakker, #111), one 9½ x 14½ in., (24.1 x 36.8 cm.), the other 10 x 15 in., (24.1 x 36.8 cm.), color woodblock print (BP 344, DM 834, FR 2809, Y 65,042).

$220* *"Avenue Of Cherry Trees" and "Omuro": Two,* both stamp s., very good cond., (03-28-93, Bakker, #214), one 9½ x 14½ in., (24.1 x 36.8 cm.), other 10 x 15 in., (24.1 x 36.8 cm.), color woodblock (BP 148, DM 359, FR 1220, Y 25,605).

$330* *"Chion In Temple Gate",* s., good cond.?, (07-19-92, Bakker, #234, illus.), image 9½ x 14½ in., (24.1 x 36.8 cm.), color woodblock print (BP 169, DM 481, FR 1626, Y 41,024).

$220* *Crymptomeria Avenue (Ref: 219), 1937,* stamped sig., s. brush, (03-14-93, Hindman, #373), 14¾ x 9¾ in., (37.5 x 24.8 cm.), color woodcut (BP 153, DM 366, FR 1245, Y 25,928).

BI *Kagurazaka Street After A Night Rain,* est. $250/350, (12-10-92, Sloan, #1249), 14¾ x 9¾ in., (37.5 x 24.8 cm.), color woodcut.

BI *"Der Kurobe-Fluss", 1926,* from series Die 12 Ansichten der japanischen Alpen, t., s., d., Format Oban, est. SC 16/20,000, (04-27-93, Dorotheum, #208, illus.), 10¹⁵⁄₁₆ x 15¹¹⁄₁₆ in., (27.8 x 39.9 cm.), color woodcut.

BI *A Little Restaurant,* est. $250/350, (12-10-92, Sloan, #1250), 14½ x 9½ in., (36.8 x 24.1 cm.), color woodcut.

$165* *"A Little Temple Gate",* s. below image; label H. Takemura and Company verso, (08-05-92, Boos, #577), 14⅝ x 9½ in., (371 x 241 mm.), color wood block print (BP 86, DM 244, FR 823, Y 21,014).

BI *Night In Kyoto,* est. $250/350, (12-10-92, Sloan, #1251), 14¾ x 9½ in., (37.5 x 24.1 cm.), color woodcut.

BI *"Ruhiger Wind", 1937,* t., d., d., est. SC 10/12,000, (04-27-93, Dorotheum, #197, illus.), 9¹⁵⁄₁₆ x 13⅞ in., (25.2 x 35.2 cm.), color woodcut.

$900* *Sailing Boats, Morning, 1926,* Dai Oban Tate-E from The Inland Sea Series, s. in ink and brush w/inblock; s., t., (02-04-93, Sloan, #2570), 20 x 14⅛ in., (50.8 x 35.9 cm.), color woodcut (BP 628, DM 1482, FR 5025, Y 111,954).

$660* *Sea Of Clouds At Houozan (Yoshida 102), 1928,* s. w/ brush, prop. Helen Gridley Meyn, (10-18-92, Hindman, #532, illus.), 21 x 32 in., (53.3 x 81.3 cm.), color woodcut (BP 404, DM 982, FR 3332, Y 79,184).

$880* *"Spring In A Hot Spring" and "Sacred Bridge": A Pair,* s. Hiroshi Yoshida, good cond., (09-27-92, Bakker, #256, illus.), image, each approx. 9⅝ x 14⅝ in., (24.4 x 37.1 cm.), color woodblock print (BP 514, DM 1304, FR 4411, Y 106,216).

$275* *"Suzukawa",* s., good cond., (07-19-92, Bakker, #219, illus.), image 9⅝ x 14⅞ in., (24.4 x 37.8 cm.), color woodblock print (BP 141, DM 401, FR 1355, Y 34,187).

$330* *"Willow And Stone Bridge" (Tadao 80), 1926,* s., t., block s., stamped, good cond., (10-31-92, Cleveland, #53), 15¾ x 9¾ in., (40 x 24.8 cm.), woodblock (BP 211, DM 508, FR 1722, Y 40,877).

YOSHIDA, Hodaka

$110* *"Universe" Abstract,* s., t. in Japanese, #27/30, mat line, (11-20-92, Skinner, #14, illus.), image 22 x 22 in., (55.9 x 55.9 cm.), (BP 72, DM 175, FR 591, Y 13,680).

YOSHIDA, Toshi

$121* *Heirinji Temple Bell,* s., d. 1951, tate-e, (11-20-92, Skinner, #27), oban tate-e (BP 80, DM 193, FR 650, Y 15,048).

YOSHIDA, Toshi Japanese b. 1911

BI *"30th Century", 1969,* s., staining, good cond., est. $3/400, (10-31-92, Cleveland, #54A), 19¾ x 14½ in., (50.2 x 36.8 cm.), color woodcut.

$61* *"Autumn In Hakone Museum",* pen s., t., image stains, (10-31-92, Cleveland, #54), 15 x 19 in., (38.1 x 48.3 cm.), colored woodblock laid down (BP 39, DM 94, FR 318, Y 7556).

$239* *Bamboo Garden, Hakone Museum,* s., t., (05-10-93, Hodgins, #287), 8¾ x 14¾ in., (22.2 x 37.5 cm.), color woodblock on paper (BP 156, DM 384, FR 1295, Y 26,707, C$ 303).

BI *Heirinji, Temple Bell,* s., est. $2/300, (10-30-92, Sloan, #1893), 14½ x 9½ in., (36.8 x 24.1 cm.), woodblock.

$302* *"Ishima-Tempel", 1946,* s., t., Format Oban, (04-27-93, Dorotheum, #209, illus.), 10¾ x 15¾ in., (27.3 x 40 cm.), color woodcut (BP 192, DM 478, FR 1618, Y 33,845, SC 3360).

YOSHIIKU Japanese 1824-1895

$440* *Two Men And A Woman With Swords: Triptych, c. 1862,* (03-14-93, Hindman, #371), each 13½ x 9½ in., (34.3 x 24.1 cm.), color woodcut (BP 307, DM 732, FR 2490, Y 51,856).

YOSHIKAWA KANPO Japanese 1894-1979

$1312* *Bust-Portraits Of Nakamura Ganjiro I And Ichikawa Sandanji II: Two,* Oban, s. Heian/Kanpo/sha, pub.'s seal Sato Shotaro; #14/200, and #10/100, d. Taisho 5 (1916) and Taisho 12 (1923), soiled, mica damaged, Prof. H.R.W. Kuhne Coll., (06-11-93, Sotheby-London, #485, illus.), one 16⅛ x 10⅝ in., (41 x 27 cm.), other 16½ x 10¾ in., (41 x 27 cm.), woodblock, grey mica ground (BP 862, DM 2132, FR 7189, Y 139,204).

YOSHIKUNI, Toyokawa Japanese ac. 1803-1840

$252* *Portrait Of Two Dancing Actors,* diptych, signs of wear, (04-27-93, Dorotheum, #178, illus.), 20¹⁄₁₆ x 14⅜ in., (51 x 36.5 cm.), (BP 160, DM 399, FR 1350, Y 28,242, SC 2800).

YOSHITORA, Utagawa

BI *"Scenes From The Tale Of Iga",* block s., pub. Yamada Shabei, seal, est. $150/300, (01-15-93, DuMouchelle, #2299, illus.), 14½ x 10 in., (36.8 x 25.4 cm.), color woodblock print.

YOSHITOSHI

$193* *Endo Morito Stands Ready To Kill The Husband Of His Lover Not KnowingThat In The Darkness He Will Kill His Beloved,* from Yoshitoshi's Warriors Trembling with Courage, (12-05-92, Eldred, #577, illus.), woodblock (BP 121, DM 301, FR 1026, Y 23,913).

$193* *A Heavily Armed Samurai Encounters A Temple Attendant Whom He Had Mistaken For The Enemy,* from Yoshitoshi's Warriors Trembling wtih Courage, (12-05-92, Eldred, #578, illus.), woodblock (BP 121, DM 301, FR 1026, Y 23,913).

BI *Hotei Seated On His Treasure Sack Viewing The Moon, 1887,* from 100 Aspects of the Moon, est. $200/250, (12-05-92, Eldred, #580), woodblock.

$110* *Man And Woman Under A Trellised Vine, 1889,* from 100 Aspects of the Moon, (12-05-92, Eldred, #581), woodblock (BP 69, DM 171, FR 584, Y 13,629).

$358* *"The Moon Of Shinobugaoka",* from 100 Aspects of the Moon, d. 1889, pub. Akiyama Beumon, Shogun Gallery label verso, (01-02-93, Litchfield, #27A), woodblock print (BP 239, DM 587, FR 2002, Y 44,885).

BI *A Mounted Woman Samurai Prepares For Battle, 1883,* from Yoshitoshi's Warriors Trembling with Courage, est. $350/450, (12-05-92, Eldred, #576, illus.), woodblock.

$879* *Tsuki Hyaku Sugata (One Hundred Aspects Of The Moon): One Hundred And Ten,* album, complete 110 prints of series includ. 2 mokuroku pages and portrait of Yoshitoshi, all s. Yoshitoshi w/various seals, many w/ urushi, bokashizuri, covers parted, toned, (06-10-93, Sotheby-London, #279, illus.), (BP 575, DM 1431, FR 4819, Y 93,302).

BI *Woman In A Boat Below A Tori Gate,* from 100 Aspects of the Moon, toned, est. $175/225, (12-05-92, Eldred, #579), woodblock.

YOSHITOSHI, Taiso Japanese 1839-1892

$440* *Beauty, From The Series "Thirty-Two Aspects Of Women",* (09-25-92, Wolf, #5A, illus.), 14½ x 9½ in., (36.8 x 24.1 cm.), colored woodblock (BP 257, DM 652, FR 2206, Y 53,108).

BI *Imaginary Figures Flying Above Mt. Fuji, 1882,* Series: Yoshitoshi Ryakuga, Lane No. 23, d., excell. cond., est. $3/400, (10-31-92, Cleveland, #35), 7⅛ x 9¾ in., (18.1 x 24.8 cm.), woodblock.

BI *Man Riding Horse, 1882,* Series: Yoshitoshi Ryakuga, Lane No. 23, d., paper toned, est. $2/300, (10-31-92, Cleveland, #36), 7½ x 9¾ in., (19.1 x 24.8 cm.), woodblock.

YOSHITOSHI, Yoshioka Japanese 1839-1892

$225* *"Samurai Playing Instrument" and "Man Playing Flute In Moonlight": Two,* (02-04-93, Sloan, #914), larger 12⅞ x 8⅞ in., (32.7 x 22.5 cm.), color woodcuts (BP 157, DM 370, FR 1256, Y 27,989).

YOSHITSUKI

$50* *"Calligraphy",* CHUBAN YOKOE, trimmed, (05-07-93, Goldberg, #1353), woodblock (BP 32, DM 79, FR 266, Y 5505).

YOSHITSUYA, Utagawa 1822-1866

$435* *Der Triumphale Einmarsch In Odawara Unter General Hisayoshi, 1864,* from series: 54 Geschichten uber die Hisago Armee, Oban, s., pub. Tsutaya Kichizo, (04-21-93, Germann, #245), color woodcut (BP 282, DM 695, FR 2351, Y 48,157, SF 633).

YOUNG, Charles Jac

$77* *Winter Solitude,* margins, s. C.Jac Young, (10-24-92, Collins, #16), 7¼ x 8¾ in., (18.4 x 22.2 cm.), etching (BP 48, DM 118, FR 399, Y 9390).

YOUNG, Charles Morris American b. 1869

$77* *The Leopard Farm,* s. C. Morris Young, (02-13-93, Collins, #21, illus.), 8¾ x 6⅞ in., (22.2 x 17.5 cm.), etching (BP 54, DM 128, FR 432, Y 9286).

YOUNG, Ellsworth

$75 *Remember Belgium,* The U.S. Prtg. and Lith. Co. NY, minor edge damage, (09-24-92, Alderfer, #269), 30 x 20 in., (76.2 x 50.8 cm.), (BP 44, DM 111, FR 377, Y 9022).

YOUNG, John

BI *"The Boy Discovering The Golden Eggs" and "The Boy Disappointed Of His Treasure", 1796: Two,* after R. M. Paye, margins, platemark split, plugged wormholes, est. BP 4/600, (12-03-92, Sotheby-London, #166), each approx. 24 x 17½ in., (610 x 445 mm.), mezzotints in colors w/handcoloring.

YOUNG, John (after Thomas STOTHARD)

BI *The French Conscript,* trimmed inside plate, creasing, surface dirt, image in good cond., est. BP 3/500, (10-27-92, Phillips-London, #63), sheet 20¼ x 26¾ in., (514 x 679 mm.), colored mezzotint, finished by hand, on wove.

YOUNG, Mahonri Mackintosh American 1877-1957

$77* *Native American And Horse,* s., (05-14-93, DuMouchelle, #2371), 4 x 5¾ in., (10.2 x 14.6 cm.), etching (BP 50, DM 124, FR 416, Y 8536).

YOUNGERMAN, Jack American b. 1926

$154* *"Bleu, Blanc And Rouge",* mono., s., d. 1966, i. artist's proof/90, prov., (12-02-92, Boos, #513), sight 31⅞ x 24 in., (810 x 610 mm.), color lithograph (BP 99, DM 242, FR 827, Y 19,161).

$330* *Changes, 1977: Four,* init., (10-18-92, Hindman, #492), each 38½ x 28 in., (97.8 x 71.1 cm.), color serigraphs (BP 202, DM 491, FR 1666, Y 39,592).

$440* *Untitled: Two,* init., d. 74, (10-18-92, Hindman, #493), each 29¾ x 30 in., (75.6 x 76.2 cm.), color serigraphs (BP 269, DM 655, FR 2221, Y 52,789).

YRISARRY, Mario b. 1933

BI *Juggler's Choice, (19)72,* s., d., num., est. DM 300, (12-01-92, Karl/Faber, #1384), 28⁹⁄₁₆ x 28⁹⁄₁₆ in., (72.5 x 72.5 cm.), color lithograph on wove.

YUNGE

$2553* *Shell For Anti-Knock, Car Speeding Up Hill, 1930,* ref. #248, cond. 1, (10-13-92, Phillips-London, #86, illus.), 29¹⁵⁄₁₆ x 45¼ in., (76 x 115 cm.), color lithograph (BP 1487, DM 3740, FR 12,708, Y 309,567).

YUNKERS, Adja American b. 1900

$165* *2nd Dream Of The Infanta Isabel II, 1973,* s., #78/90, (12-08-92, Swann, #322), 32¾ x 24 in., (83.2 x 61 cm.), serigraph (BP 103, DM 257, FR 876, Y 20,451).

$138* *Falling Bird, 1971,* s., d., t., #35/35, margins, good cond. (?), (02-24-93, Butterfield, #3283), 29⅞ x 23⅞ in., (759 x 606 mm.), silkscreen in colors on wove (BP 96, DM 224, FR 759, Y 16,193).

BI *Gray Form With Yellow Stripe, 1970,* s., d., t., #25/35, margins, good cond. (?), pressure mark, est. $2/300, (02-24-93, Butterfield, #3282), 18 x 24 in., (457 x 610 mm.), silkscreen in colors on Arches.

BI *Mirage, 1976,* s., d., t., #6/35, blindstamp pub. Ives-Sillman, margins, good cond.(?), est. $3/400, (02-24-93, Butterfield, #3285), 32¼ x 24³⁄₁₆ in., (819 x 614 mm.), silkscreen in colors w/collage on wove.

BI *"One #1 In Gray" and "Pink One #2", 1977: Two,* each s., d., t., #20/50, 20/25, blindstamp publisher, Styria Studio,full margins, good cond., staining, second w/skinned spot, each w/creases, surface soiling, est. $6/800, (05-19-93, Butterfield, #2384), each 44¼ x 29¾ in., (112.4 x 75.6 cm.), etching in colors w/collage on wove.

BI *Prints In The Desert: Vol. I, No. I (B.M.C. 54), 1950: Fourteen,* portfolio, by various artists, edit./pub. Adja Yunkers, images s. byartist, #208/220, cover t. page, end medallion woodcuts by Yunkers, mounted onwood-pulp paper, good cond., est. $5/700, (10-28-92, Butterfield, #2557, illus.), 16½ x 13½ in., (419 x 343 mm.), various medias.

$1320* *Shadow,* s., d., t., #21/35, pub. AAA, full margins, good cond.?, crease, Thomas Milbrook Estate, (10-28-92, Butterfield, #2557A, illus.), 39 x 39 in., (99.1 x 99.1 cm.), color silkscreen on wove (BP 841, DM 2039, FR 6922, Y 161,963).

$110* *Shadow, 1971,* s., d., t., #17/35, pub. AAA, margins, good cond. (?), (02-24-93, Butterfield, #3284), 39½ x 29⅛ in., (100.3 x 74 cm.), silkscreen in colors on wove (BP 77, DM 179, FR 605, Y 12,908).

$230* *"Summer In Venice I", 1965: Five,* pub. Print Club of Cleveland No. 43, s., d., excell. cond., (05-15-93, Cleveland, #505), 13½ x 9⅛ in., (34.3 x 23.2 cm.), color lithograph (BP 150, DM 370, FR 1243, Y 25,496).

$132* *"Summer In Venice I", 1966,* s., good cond., (10-31-92, Cleveland, #405), 13½ x 9⅛ in., (34.3 x 23.2 cm.), lithograph in colors (BP 85, DM 203, FR 689, Y 16,351).

YURAKUSAI NAGAHIDE Japanese ac. c. 1799-1840

$1400* *The Head And Shoulders Of Arashi Kichisaburo And Kano Minshi,* s. Nagahide ga, pub.'s mark, d. Bunka 3 (1806), good state, Prof. H.R.W. Kuhne Coll., (06-11-93, Sotheby-London, #454, illus.), 10⅝ x 10¼ in., (27 x 26 cm.), woodblock, Uchiwa-e, hakkaku-ban (octagonal fan print), Kappa-zuri (colored by stencils) (BP 920, DM 2275, FR 7671, Y 148,541).

$3676* *Okubi-e Of Sawamura Tanosuke II,* s. Nagahide ga, pub.'s mark, d. Bunka 3 (1806), nicked, Prof. H.R.W.Kuhne Coll., (06-11-93, Sotheby-London, #453, illus.), 10⅝ x 10¼ in., (27 x 26 cm.), woodblock, Uchiwa-e, hakkakuban (octagonal fan-shaped print), Kappa-zuri (colored by stencils) (BP 2415, DM 5974, FR 20,142, Y 390,027).

YUZBASIYAN, Arto

$51* *Fruit Market,* s., #2/275, (11-30-92, Ritchie, #55), 17 x 23¼ in., (43.2 x 59 cm.), color half-tone lithograph (BP 34, DM 81, FR 276, Y 6347, C$ 66).

YVARAL

$179* *Untitled, 1981,* s., #174/190, full sheet p. to edges, good cond., (05-27-93, Sotheby-Amstrdm, #528), sh 18⅞ x 14 in., (480 x 356 mm.), colored silkscreen on wove (BP 115, DM 287, FR 968, Y 19,190, G 322).

$77* *Untitled, 1981,* s., #137/190, full sheet p. to edges, good cond., (05-27-93, Sotheby-Amstrdm, #526), sh 18⅞ x 14 in., colored silkscreen on wove (BP 49, DM 124, FR 416, Y 8255, G 138).

$64* *Untitled, 1981,* s., #38/190, full sheet p. to edges, good cond., (05-27-93, Sotheby-Amstrdm, #527), sh 18⅞ x 14 in., (480 x 356 mm.), colored silkscreen on wove (BP 41, DM 103, FR 346, Y 6861, G 115).

YVONNET, Bruno

BI *"Danses" and "Batailles": Two,* s., t., 9/50 and 5/50, est. FF4/600, (06-28-93, Loudmer, #133), both 15¹⁵⁄₁₆ x 19⁵⁄₁₆ in., (406 x 490 mm.), black mezzotints on Johannot wove.

ZACHMANN, Max 1892-1917

$1155* *Zwei Akte In Landschaft, 1913,* s., d., (11-28-92, Grisebach, #843, illus.), 12⅜ x 8⁹⁄₁₆ in., (31.5 x 21.7 cm.), colored lithograph on thick copper print paper (BP 762, DM 1840, FR 6247, Y 143,746).

ZADKINE, Ossip Russian/French 1890-1967

$100* *"La Biche Aux Pieds D'Airain" (czwiklitzer 95),* s. in plate crease, (04-04-93, Pescheteau, #321), 29½ x 20⅞ in., (75 x 53 cm.), bistre lithograph (BP 66, DM 161, FR 546, Y 11,386).

$205* *Encore Un Oiseau, 1965,* #21/50, s., foxing, (11-13-92, Koller, #5475), 12¹³⁄₁₆ x 8¼ in., (32.5 x 21 cm.), lithograph on wove (BP 132, DM 322, FR 1085, Y 25,444, SF 290).

$4256* *Euripides. Die Arbeiten Des Herakles (Czwicklitzer 90-117), 1960: Twenty-Eight,* s., num., (06-05-93, Bassenge, #6629), each approx. 27⁹⁄₁₆ x 21¹⁄₁₆ in., (70 x 53.5 cm.), lithograph on copper print (BP 2802, DM 6900, FR 23,257, Y 456,554).

$483* *"Hommage A Rodin",* #35/120, t., s., (01-28-93, Pescheteau, #283), 29⅛ x 21¼ in., (74 x 54 cm.), color lithograph on wove (BP 319, DM 765, FR 2590, Y 59,970).

$550* *L'Inconnu (C. 36), 1962,* s., #21/25 erased/rewritten, large margins, good cond.?, (10-28-92, Butterfield, #2870), 13¼ x 9¾ in., (337 x 248 mm.), color etching on cream wove (BP 350, DM 849, FR 2884, Y 67,485).

$385* *L'Infortune (C. 77),* s., num. 65/375, margins, good cond., paper, glue remains, (02-24-93, Butterfield, #2987), 11³⁄₁₆ x 8³⁄₁₆ in., (284 x 208 mm.), etching on wove (BP 268, DM 625, FR 2119, Y 45,177).

$200* *"La Musique" (C. 134), 1965,* E.A. s., (01-28-93, Pescheteau, #284), 14¹⁵⁄₁₆ x 11 in., (38 x 28 cm.), color lithograph on Arches (BP 132, DM 317, FR 1072, Y 24,832).

$130* *"La Musique" (C.134), 1965,* s., (04-04-93, Pescheteau, #319), 14¹⁵⁄₁₆ x 11 in., (38 x 28 cm.), color lithograph on Arches (BP 86, DM 209, FR 710, Y 14,801).

$2369* *Portfolio. Guillaume Apollinaire Sept Calligrammes, 1967: Ten,* AN 35/75, s., num., (06-24-93, Germann, #544, illus.), 17¹¹⁄₁₆ x 12⅜ in., (450 x 315 mm.), etching (BP 1559, DM 3841, FR 12,945, Y 254,130, SF 3450).

BI *Le Regard Multiple (Czwiklitzer 169), 1966: Two,* s., num., est. DM 1,200, (12-05-92, Bassenge, #7841), each 16⅞ x 12¹⁵⁄₁₆ in., (42.8 x 33 cm.), lithograph on wove handmade Japan.

BI *Rois Mages,* s., #175/220, blindstamp, est. DM 800, (05-08-93, Schloss Ahlden, #2944), 23¼ x 16¹⁵⁄₁₆ in., (59 x 43 cm.), color lithograph on handmade BFK Rives.

$575* *Three Figures, 1950,* s., #12/220, full margins, good cond., (05-19-93, Butterfield, #2101), 23¼ x 17 in., (591 x 432 mm.), lithograph in colors on wove (BP 373, DM 935, FR 3149, Y 63,655).

BI *Trois Personnages, c./before 1964,* s., epreuve d'artiste, est. DM 800, (05-08-93, Schloss Ahlden, #2943), 23⅝ x 16¹⁵⁄₁₆ in., (60 x 43 cm.), color lithograph on handmade BFK Rives.

ZADKINE, Ossip (after)

$112* *"Le Violoncelliste",* artist's proof, dry stamp, (10-18-92, Pescheteau, #298), 29½ x 21¼ in., (75 x 54 cm.), lithograph in colors on Arches (BP 68, DM 165, FR 562, Y 13,373).

ZAHN, Howard American 20th cent.

$143* *Farm,* s., (05-16-93, Hindman, #377), 9½ x 7½ in., photograph, silver print (BP 93, DM 231, FR 777, Y 15,924).

ZAISINGER, Matthaus (Master MZ) b. 1477-ac. 1500-1503

BI *Die Madonna Am Brunnen (B. VI, S.372, 2, Nagler Die Monogrammisten Bd.4, 2278, 2, Lehrs 1929, S.215, Lehrs 1932, S.22, The Illustrated Bartsch, 9 Commentary, Part 2, 002), 1501,* watermark, lit., prov., est. DM 5,000, (12-04-92, Bassenge, #6507), 6¹⁵⁄₁₆ x 6 in., (17.7 x 15.3 cm.), engraving.

ZALCE, Alfredo b. Mexico 1908

$1093* *Jardin De Hecelchacan,* s., d. 1945, from Estampas de Yucatan Suite, Taller de Grafica Popular, full margins, fair cond., handling creases, yellowing, light-staining, soiling, spots in image, (05-18-93, Sotheby-NY, #284, illus.), image 9¾ x 12⅛ in., (324 x 273 mm.), 14⅜ x 10⅜ in., (324 x 273 mm.), lithograph (BP 712, DM 1773, FR 5989, Y 121,810).

$345* *"Madre Con Hijos" and "Pasaron Por La Calle Principal": Two,* s., d. 1945; s., d. 1941, #27/28, t. in stone Pasaron por la calle principal, Taller de Grafica Popular, both w/full margins, good cond., soiling, handling creases, label, pinholes, tape, (05-18-93, Sotheby-NY, #285, illus.), one, image 12¾ x 10¾ in., (324 x 273 mm.), the other, image 14⅜ x 10⅜ in., (324 x 273 mm.), lithograph (BP 225, DM 560, FR 1890, Y 38,449).

$690* *Pescador, 1945,* from the Estampas de Yucatan suite, Taller de Grafica Popular, s., handling creases, tear, (05-18-93, Sotheby-NY, #286, illus.), image 15⅜ x 17⅞ in., (391 x 454 mm.), (BP 449, DM 1120, FR 3781, Y 76,897).

$978* *El Revolucionario,* s., d. 1948, Taller de Grafica Popular, good cond., yellowing, soiling, foxing, creases, brown tape, (05-18-93, Sotheby-NY, #287, illus.), image 11⅝ x 18 in., (295 x 457 mm.), (BP 637, DM 1587, FR 5359, Y 108,994).

ZAO-WOU-KI Chinese/French b. 1921

$686* *"Bain De Soleil" and "La Peche" (Riviere 31 and 59), 1950 and 1951: Two,* s., #6/25 and 25/30, p. by G. Leblanc, margins, images in good cond.,mount-staining, foxing, (06-30-93, Sotheby-London, #974, illus.), one sh 18¼ x 15 in., (464 x 381 mm.), the other sh 10⅞ x 15⅛ in., (464 x 381 mm.), etching on wove (BP 460, DM 1170, FR 3947, Y 73,503).

$65* *Boats,* s., #111/200, loose, (06-08-93, Ritchie, #34), 9⅞ x 6½ in., (25.1 x 16.5 cm.), color lithograph (BP 43, DM 105, FR 355, Y 6904, C$ 83).

BI *Composition (R. 256), 1974,* s., d., num. 106/120, full margins, light-staining, est. BP 80/120, (11-30-92, Phillips-London, #580), image 23¾ x 18⅛ in., (603 x 460 mm.), lithograph in colors on Arches.

$686* *"Composition" and "Sans Titre" (The First Not In Riviere and R. 157),1956 and 1964-65: Two,* each s., d., 1st $44/60, 2nd #10/12, i., pub. Galierie de France, full margins, good cond., defects, (06-30-93, Sotheby-London, #979), one 15¼ x 25¼ in., (387 x 641 mm.), the other 20¼ x 15⅜ in., (387 x 641 mm.), color lithograph on BFK Rives on japon nacre (BP 460, DM 1170, FR 3947, Y 73,503).

BI *"Composition", 1975,* H.C., d., s., ed. Gal de France, est. FF 2,5/3,000, (10-18-92, Pescheteau, #303), 35⁷⁄₁₆ x 24 in., (90 x 61 cm.), lithograph in colors on Arches.

$404* *"Composition", 1976,* d., s., #95/99, (10-18-92, Pescheteau, #305), 19¹¹⁄₁₆ x 29½ in., (50 x 75 cm.), lithograph in colors on Arches (BP 245, DM 597, FR 2027, Y 48,239).

$275* *Composition, (Riviere 103), 1956,* 90/150, (03-24-93, Kunsthallen, #339), color lithograph (BP 186, DM 449, FR 1529, Y 32,311, DK 1725).

$664* *Fall Leaves,* s., num., yellowed, mount staining, (12-01-92, Karl/Faber, #1378), 13⅜ x 22¹³⁄₁₆ in., (34 x 58 cm.), color etching and aquatint on BFK Rives wove (BP 439, DM 1058, FR 3607, Y 82,669).

$815* *Hommage A T.D. Lee, (19)74,* s., d., num., (06-08-93, Karl/Faber, #1425), approx. 16¹⁵⁄₁₆ x 24 in., (43 x 61 cm.), color etching on Arches France wove (BP 536, DM 1322, FR 4454, Y 86,564).

$858* *"L'Aurore" and "Petit Jardin" (R. 101 and 102), 1956: Two,* s., d., #103/125 and 172/200, pub. L'Oeuvre Gravee, blindstamp, fullmargins, good cond., defects, (06-30-93, Sotheby-London, #978), one 17⅛ x 25⅝ in., (435 x 651 mm.), the other 14½ x 19⅜ in., (435 x 651 mm.), color lithograph (BP 575, DM 1463, FR 4937, Y 91,932).

$326* *"L'Etang" (R 237), 1973,* #8/26, s., (01-28-93, Pescheteau, #286), 6¹¹⁄₁₆ x 10¹³⁄₁₆ in., (17 x 27.5 cm.), etching and aquatint on Chine applique on wove (BP 215, DM 517, FR 1748, Y 40,477).

$1373* *"Marine" and "Embrasement" (R. 76 and 94), 1952 and 1954: Two,* s., i. premiere etat, #1/5, pub. La Hune, 2nd d., #144/200, pub. L'Oeuvre Gravee, blindstap, full margins, good cond., defects, (06-30-93, Sotheby-London, #976, illus.), one 16 x 21⅝ in., (406 x 549 mm.), the other 15⅜ x 19¼ in., (406 x 549 mm.), color lithograph on BFK Rives (BP 920, DM 2342, FR 7900, Y 147,112).

$1887* *"Montagnes Et Soleil", "Paysage Rouge", "Paysage Rose Et Bleu (Two Impressions), and "Champs Abandonnes" (R. 61; 88; 89 and 93), 1951-1954: Five,* s., d., num., i., full margins, good cond., defects, (06-30-93, Sotheby-London, #975, illus.), 4 lithograph and 1 etching in color (BP 1265, DM 3218, FR 10,857, Y 202,186).

$220* *Mysterious Forest,* s., d. 70, #103/125, (12-13-92, Hindman, #328), 20 x 19¼ in., color lithograph (BP 141, DM 346, FR 1178, Y 27,218).

$253* *Paysage Au Soleil, 1950,* 30/200, s., (04-21-93, Germann, #141, illus.), 21¹⁵⁄₁₆ x 15¹⁄₁₆ in., (557 x 383 mm.), color etching (BP 164, DM 404, FR 1368, Y 28,008, SF 368).

$330* *Petit Jardin, (Riviere 102), 1956,* s. Zao Wou-Ki 56, Epreuve d'artiste, (03-24-93, Kunsthallen, #338), color lithograph (BP 223, DM 539, FR 1834, Y 38,773, DK 2070).

$290* *Sans Titre,* s., 15/95, (06-28-93, Loudmer, #436), 19¹¹⁄₁₆ x 19¹¹⁄₁₆ in., (500 x 500 mm.), sh 35⅝ x 25¹³⁄₁₆ in., (500 x 500 mm.), color lithograph on Arches wove (BP 194, DM 493, FR 1660, Y 30,769).

$105* *Sans Titre,* epreuve d'artiste, s., d. 76, (11-16-92, Briest, #117), 19¹¹⁄₁₆ x 29½ in., (50 x 75 cm.), lithograph in colors on Arches (BP 69, DM 167, FR 564, Y 13,104).

$707* *Sans Titre (Marquet 122), 1959,* s., d., #16/75, (06-12-93, Hauswedell/Nolt, #481), 13¹¹⁄₁₆ x 23⁷⁄₁₆ in., (34.8 x 59.5 cm.), color etching on BFK Rives (BP 463, DM 1151, FR 3868, Y 74,398).

$309* *Sans Titre (Riviere 129), 1960,* s., d., 49/140, drystamp, (06-28-93, Loudmer, #437), 22⅝ x 16⁹⁄₁₆ in., (575 x 420 mm.), sh 25¹³⁄₁₆ x 19⅞ in., (575 x 420 mm.), color lithograph on Rives wove w/watermark (BP 207, DM 525, FR 1769, Y 32,785).

$860* *Sans Titre (Riviere 169), 1967,* s., d., e.a., (05-27-93, Lempertz, #1119), 25⅛ x 19³⁄₁₆ in., (63.8 x 48.7 cm.), color lithograph on wove (BP 551, DM 1380, FR 4651, Y 92,196).

BI *Sans Titre (Riviere 173), 1967,* s., d., proof, pub. La Hune, margins, est. BP 1/1,500, (12-03-92, Sotheby-London, #858), etching in colors on Arches.

$619* *Sans Titre (Riviere 173), 1967,* artist's proof, d., (06-28-93, Loudmer, #435), 14⁹⁄₁₆ x 20⅞ in., (370 x 530 mm.), sh 22¼ x 29¹⁵⁄₁₆ in., (370 x 530 mm.), color aquatint on Arches wove (BP 414, DM 1052, FR 3543, Y 65,676).

$788* *Sans Titre (Riviere 253),* s., d., #89/95, (05-27-93, Lempertz, #1120), 21⁹⁄₁₆ x 29⅜ in., (54.8 x 74.6 cm.), color etching on Arches wove (BP 505, DM 1264, FR 4262, Y 84,477).

$126* *Sans Titre (Riviere 256), 1974,* s., d. 74, #86/120, (11-16-92, Briest, #116), 29¹¹⁄₁₆ x 20¹⁵⁄₁₆ in., (75.4 x 53.3 cm.), lithograph in 6 colors on Arches (BP 83, DM 201, FR 677, Y 15,724).

$898* *"Sans Titre - 1965" (R. 164),* drystamp, epreuve d'artiste, d., s., (10-18-92, Pescheteau, #299, illus.), 19¹¹⁄₁₆ x 25⁹⁄₁₆ in., (50 x 65 cm.), etching and aquatint (BP 544, DM 1326, FR 4506, Y 107,224).

$505* *"Sans Titre - 1967" (R 165),* rare, s., (10-18-92, Pescheteau, #300), sight 20¹⁄₁₆ x 25³⁄₁₆ in., (51 x 64 cm.), lithograph in colors on Rives (BP 306, DM 746, FR 2534, Y 60,299).

$666* *Sans Titre, (R. 108), 1956,* s., d., num. 77/150, pub. L'Oeuvre Gravee, full margins, glue-staining, tape, creasing, (12-01-92, Christie-London, #649), L. 16¾ x 19½ in., (425 x 495 mm.), lithograph in colors on BFK Rives (BP 440, DM 1062, FR 3618, Y 82,918).

$308* *Le Soleil Rouge (Marquet 42), 1950,* #LI/LX, s., blindstamp, margins, time-staining, (05-20-93, Bonhams-Chelsea, #132), image 18⅞ x 13⅜ in., (47.9 x 34 cm.), lithograph in colors on Arches (BP 198, DM 497, FR 1674, Y 34,011).

$431* *Tres Cordialement, 1967,* s., d., t., annot. epreuve d'artiste, i. A Florence Dauber, full margins, good cond., creases, (05-19-93, Butterfield, #2099), 14¹³⁄₁₆ x 21¼ in., (376 x 540 mm.), etching and aquatint in colors on Arches (BP 280, DM 701, FR 2360, Y 47,714).

$110* *Untitled,* s., #59/200, margins, light staining, foxing, good cond.?, Mac Goodman Estate, (12-12-92, Weschler, #182), 11¾ x 17½ in., (29.8 x 44.5 cm.), color lithograph (BP 71, DM 173, FR 594, Y 13,612).

$682* *Untitled (R. 128), 1960,* s., d., #16/90, p. Dutrou, pub. La Hune, full margins, good cond., mount staining, tape stains, (12-03-92, Sotheby-London, #859, illus.), 9½ x 23¼ in., (241 x 591 mm.), aquatint in colors on BFK Rives wove (BP 440, DM 1072, FR 3661, Y 84,858).

$189* *Untitled (Riviere 142), 1962,* 4th plate from "La Tentation de l'Occident", s., d. 62, (11-16-92, Briest, #118), 14¹⁵⁄₁₆ x 11 in., (38 x 28 cm.), lithograph in colors on wove Arches (BP 124, DM 301, FR 1016, Y 23,587).

BI *Untitled (Yves Riviere 172),* s., p., pub. Lacouriere et Frelant, good cond., est. BP 200/250, (11-30-92, Phillips-London, #581), 10½ x 21¼ in., (267 x 540 mm.), aquatint in colors on wove.

BI *Untitled, 1968,* s., d., i. H.C., margins, good cond.?, rippling, est. $5/700, (12-12-92, Weschler, #181, illus.), 21¼ x 17¼ in., (54 x 43.8 cm.), etching and aquatint.

BI *Untitled, 1968,* s., d., i. H.C., w/margins, good cond., slight rippling, est. $3/500, (05-22-93, Weschler, #232), 21¼ x 17¼ in., (54 x 43.8 cm.), etching and aquatint.

$256* *Untitled, 1975,* s., d., i. H.C., full margins, good cond., minor handling creases, (05-27-93, Sotheby-Amstrdm, #706, illus.), 19¹³⁄₁₆ x 19¹³⁄₁₆ in., (504 x 504 mm.), color lithograph on wove (BP 164, DM 411, FR 1385, Y 27,444, G 460).

$269* *Untitled, 1976,* s., d., i. E.A., full margins, good cond., minor handling creases, (05-27-93, Sotheby-Amstrdm, #708), 21⁵⁄₁₆ x 18⁷⁄₁₆ in., (542 x 468 mm.), color etching on wove (BP 172, DM 432, FR 1455, Y 28,838, G 483).

BI *Untitled, 1976,* s., d., i. E.A., full margins, good cond., minor light-discoloration, top margin hinged to mount, est. Dfl. 700/1,000, (05-27-93, Sotheby-Amstrdm, #707), 15¹³⁄₁₆ x 26³⁄₁₆ in., (402 x 665 mm.), color lithograph on Arches.

ZBINDEN, Emil   b. 1908
$442* *Der Gemeinderat,* #35/150, s., (09-04-92, Germann, #623), 10⁷⁄₁₆ x 17¹³⁄₁₆ in., (265 x 452 mm.), woodcut (BP 221, DM 619, FR 2109, Y 54,407, SF 552).

$398* *Huttwiler, 1989,* 58/150, s., (10-14-92, Germann, #635), 17¹³⁄₁₆ x 10¹³⁄₁₆ in., (453 x 275 mm.), woodcut (BP 234, DM 582, FR 1975, Y 48,231, SF 519).

$363* *Landleben,* #38/150, s., (04-21-93, Germann, #843), 16⁷⁄₁₆ x 12⁷⁄₁₆ in., (417 x 316 mm.), woodcut (BP 236, DM 580, FR 1962, Y 40,186, SF 529).

$553* *Die Versteigerung,* 38/150, s., (06-24-93, Germann, #804), 14⅛ x 19½ in., (359 x 496 mm.), woodcut (BP 364, DM 897, FR 3022, Y 59,322, SF 805).

$553* *Winter Bei Burgistein,* #118/150, s., t., (09-04-92, Germann, #621), 19⁵⁄₁₆ x 25³⁄₁₆ in., (490 x 640 mm.), woodcut (BP 277, DM 775, FR 2638, Y 68,070, SF 690).

ZEHETMAYR
BI *Wahlet Kommunistich, 1920,* B- cond., discoloration, two=part, est. $1/1,500, (08-06-92, Swann, #303, illus.), 48 x 37 in., (121.9 x 94 cm.), .

ZEIMERT, Christian   b. 1934
$32* *"L'Operation Du Saint Esprit",* #29/75, s., (01-28-93, Pescheteau, #287), 25⁹⁄₁₆ x 16⅛ in., (65 x 41 cm.), color serigraph (BP 21, DM 51, FR 172, Y 3973).

ZEISING, W.
BI *(View Of A Marketplace),* 1920, s., margins, good cond., minor paper discoloration, crease in upper right corner of sheet, Late Gerhard Brauer Coll., est. Dfl. 5/700, (05-27-93, Sotheby-Amstrdm, #834), 7¹³⁄₁₆ x 9¾ in., (199 x 248 mm.), etching on wove.

BI *(View Of A Square),* 1913, s., margins, good cond., minor paper discoloration, handling creases, Late Gerhard Brauer Coll., est. Dfl. 5/700, (05-27-93, Sotheby-Amstrdm, #835), 9¹⁄₁₆ x 11½ in., (230 x 292 mm.), etching on laid.

ZEISING, Walter   1876-1933
BI *"Steinernes Kreuz, Bretagne",* plate mono., d. WZ (19)07, Verlag der Ges. fur Vervielfalt. Kunst, Wien, est. DM 360-, (03-24-93, Venator/Hansten, #4576), pl. 12³⁄₁₆ x 19½ in., (31 x 49.5 cm.), etching.

ZELLER, Magnus   1888-1972
$1135* *Liebespaar Auf Der Bank, 1919,* s., d., ded., (06-05-93, Grisebach, #933, illus.), 11⁷⁄₁₆ x 9⅜ in., (29 x 23.8 cm.), drypoint on copper print paper (BP 747, DM 1840, FR 6202, Y 121,755).

ZELMA, Georgi
$2530* *On The Water, c. 1946,* s., t., d., label, (04-08-93, Christie-NY, #158, illus.), 13¾ x 9⅛ in., (34.9 x 23.2 cm.), photograph, gelatin silver print (BP 1659, DM 4064, FR 13,757, Y 287,108).

ZELT, Martha   American 20th cent.
$33* *Celebration, 1970,* s., d., (06-11-93, Freemn/Fine Art, #256), 14 x 20¼ in., (35.6 x 51.4 cm.), silkscreen (BP 22, DM 54, FR 181, Y 3501).

$44* *Return To Albuquerque #3, 1983,* (06-11-93, Freemn/ Fine Art, #257), 20¼ x 26 in., (51.4 x 66 cm.), lithograph, color photography and collage (BP 29, DM 72, FR 241, Y 4668).

ZENOBEL (after)
$147* *SNCF: Gerardmer. "La Perle Des Vosges",* good cond., (11-19-92, Ribeyre/Baron, #123), 39⅜ x 24⁷⁄₁₆ in., (100 x 62 cm.), poster (BP 97, DM 234, FR 789, Y 18,281).

ZERO (Hans SCHLEGER)   1899-1976
$2886* *These Men Use Shell, Journalists, 1938,* p. Waterlow and Sons, ref. #513, cond. 3, (10-13-92, Phillips-London, #136, illus.), 30 x 45¼ in., (76.2 x 115 cm.), color lithograph (BP 1681, DM 4228, FR 14,365, Y 349,945).

ZESHIN, Shibata   Japanese 1807-1891
$403* *Narcissus,* (04-27-93, Dorotheum, #181, illus.), 9¹³⁄₁₆ x 11 in., (25 x 28 cm.), color woodcut (BP 256, DM 638, FR 2159, Y 45,164, SC 4480).

ZETTL, Baldwin   b. 1943
$155* *Billard, 1969,* s., t., plate mono., d.; stamp, traces of streaks verso, (09-18-92, Schloss Ahlden, #1084), 14⁹⁄₁₆ x 9⁹⁄₁₆ in., (37 x 24.3 cm.), etching on hand-made cardboard (BP 91, DM 230, FR 787, Y 19,157).

ZHADOVA, L.A. (attrib.)
BI *Letatlin (Tatlin's Ornithopter), 1960's (cf. Zhadova, pl. 347),* notations by collector, est. $2/3,000, (10-15-92, Sotheby-NY, #367, illus.), 11½ x 14⅝ in., (29.2 x 37.1 cm.), photograph, gelatin silver print.

ZIEGLER, Henry Brian
BI *View Of The Worcester Race Course And Grand Stand,* by George Hunt, pub. H.B. Ziegler, 1823, trimmed, staining, est. BP 120/180, (03-03-93, Bonhams-Chelsea, #200), image 14 x 22¼ in., (35.6 x 56.5 cm.), hand-colored aquatint.

$124* *View Of The Worcester Race Course And Grand Stand,* by George Hunt, pub. 1823, trimmed, staining, (06-30-93, Bonhams-Chelsea, #219), image 14 x 22¼ in., (35.6 x 56.5 cm.), aquatint w/hand-coloring (BP 83, DM 211, FR 713, Y 13,286).

$66* *Worcester Race-Course And Grand Stand,* by George Hunt, pub. 1823, tears, defects, (06-30-93, Bonhams-Chelsea, #218), image 12¼ x 23 in., (31.1 x 58.4 cm.), etching w/aquatint and hand-coloring (BP 44, DM 113, FR 380, Y 7072).

ZIEGLER, Johann   1749-1802
$1163* *Ansicht Von Oppenheim,* (12-10-92, Ruef, #434), 14³⁄₁₆ x 18½ in., (36 x 47 cm.), colored engraving (BP 750, DM 1840, FR 6283, Y 143,864).

ZIELER, Mogens
$167* *Untitled,* s. 68, 101/200, (09-29-92, B. Rasmussen, #377), lithograph in colors (BP 94, DM 236, FR 805, Y 19,936, DK 920).

ZIEMANN, Richard Claude
$77* *"Edgewater",* s., t., #5/25 '58, (02-27-93, Dunning, #47), 17½ x 23½ in., (44.5 x 59.7 cm.), etching (BP 54, DM 127, FR 430, Y 9090).

ZIERATH, Willy   20th cent.
BI *Steeple, c. 1919,* very good/good cond., est. $150/250, (11-21-92, Bakker, #4), image 6¾ x 5⅛ in., (17.1 x 13 cm.), woodblock print.

ZILCKEN, Lorenz
BI *Die Schauspielerin Heicke, 1920,* s., t., d., margins, good cond., minor foxing, minor paper discoloration, Late Gerhard Brauer Coll., est. Dfl. 250/350, (05-27-93, Sotheby-Amstrdm, #806, illus.), 9¹⁄₁₆ x 6⅞ in., (230 x 174 mm.), etching on wove.

ZILLE, Heinrich   German 1858/64-1929
$1006* *Aus Grosser Zeit (R. 105, b), 1919,* sheet 47 of series Zwanglose Geschichten Und Bilder, s.; sig., d. instone, (10-09-92, Winterberg, #3289), 9¹⁵⁄₁₆ x 7¹¹⁄₁₆ in., (25.2 x 19.5 cm.), lithograph on J.W. Zanders hand-made (BP 597, DM 1494, FR 5017, Y 122,474).

$2837* *Eine Kleine Freudin (Rosenbach 187), 1924,* s., from Komm, Karliniken, komm!, (06-05-93, Bassenge, #6647, illus.), 13⁵⁄₁₆ x 10⁹⁄₁₆ in., (33.8 x 26.8 cm.), lithograph on machine made (BP 1868, DM 4600, FR 15,503, Y 304,334).

$659* *Frau Mit Saugling Und Zwei Kindern,* s., prov., (05-08-93, Schloss Ahlden, #2951), 9⅝ x 8⁷⁄₁₆ in., (24.5 x 21.5 cm.), lithograph on Van Geldern Zonen hand-made (BP 430, DM 1059, FR 3572, Y 73,640).

$498* *Frauen Und Kinder Am Rande Der Stadt (Rosenbach 91 c), 1919,* num., series Zwanglose Geschichten und Bilder, (12-01-92, Karl/Faber, #1390), 8⅞ x 7⅞ in., (22.5 x 20 cm.), lithograph on rough paper (BP 329, DM 794, FR 2705, Y 62,002).

$2074* *Funf Kinder Auf Einer Bank (R. 206), 1924,* s., Bl. 35 from the series Komm, Karlineken, komm!, pub. Fritz Gurlitt, water stains, light-stained, (12-01-92, Karl/Faber, #1391, illus.), 7⅞ x 9¹⁄₁₆ in., (20 x 23 cm.), lithograph on simili-Japan (BP 1370, DM 3306, FR 11,266, Y 258,217).

$1790* *Geburtstag, c. 1905,* s., (05-08-93, Schloss Ahlden, #2949), 6³⁄₁₆ x 8¹¹⁄₁₆ in., (15.7 x 22 cm.), photogravure (BP 1168, DM 2876, FR 9702, Y 200,022).

$4965* *Holzsammlerin (Rosenbach 31 a), c. 1902,* num., s., (06-05-93, Bassenge, #6644), 16¹⁄₈ x 13¹⁄₁₆ in., (41 x 33.1 cm.), etching, soft-ground etching and Stoffdruckverfahren on China (BP 3268, DM 8050, FR 27,131, Y 532,611).

$885* *Hunger (Rosenbach 172 c), 1924,* s., (12-05-92, Bassenge, #7854), 9¹³⁄₁₆ x 8¹¹⁄₁₆ in., (25 x 22 cm.), lithograph on handmade van Gelder-Zonen (BP 554, DM 1380, FR 4702, Y 109,652).

$454* *"Im Tingel Tangel-Keller" (Rosenbach 84c), 1919,* from series Zwanglose Geschichten Und Bilder, (11-27-92, Zeller, #654), 14¹⁵⁄₁₆ x 10⅝ in., (38 x 27 cm.), lithograph (BP 299, DM 725, FR 2463, Y 56,503).

$1162* *Kartoffelstehen, 1916,* stone s., d.; s., creased, tears, (09-18-92, Schloss Ahlden, #1086), 19¹³⁄₁₆ x 15¹⁄₁₆ in., (50.3 x 38.2 cm.), lithograph on van Geldern hand-made (BP 680, DM 1724, FR 5898, Y 143,616).

$1419* *Die Landpartie/Aus Meiner Jugendzeit/H. Zille (Rosenbach 109-116 a),1920: Eleven,* s., num., (06-05-93, Bassenge, #6646), watercolored lithograph on factory print (BP 934, DM 2301, FR 7754, Y 152,221).

$716* *Modelle Im atelier, 1923,* s., 1st version, (05-08-93, Schloss Ahlden, #2947), 9¹⁄₁₆ x 9¾ in., (23 x 24.7 cm.), lithograph on light handmade (BP 467, DM 1150, FR 3881, Y 80,009).

BI *Nachtliche Szene (Kaiser-Wilhelm-Strasse), 1957,* s., prov., est. DM 1,500, (05-08-93, Schloss Ahlden, #2948), 3¹⁵⁄₁₆ x 5¹⁄₁₆ in., (10 x 12.8 cm.), etching on handmade.

$515* *"Paar Auf Der Jungfernbrucke (Die Schifferliese)" (Rosenbach 90c), 1919,* from series Zwanglose Geschichten und Bilder, (11-27-92, Zeller, #655), 13¾ x 9¹³⁄₁₆ in., (35 x 25 cm.), lithograph (BP 339, DM 823, FR 2794, Y 64,095).

$1289* *Rummelplatz, 1905,* d., s., (05-08-93, Schloss Ahlden, #2946), 7 x 9⅛ in., (17.8 x 23.2 cm.), heliograph w/ etching (BP 841, DM 2071, FR 6986, Y 144,038).

$423* *Schwangere Frau Nach Rechts Mit Zwei Kindern (Rosenbach 59), 1919,* block s., i., from the series Zwanglose Geschichten Und Bilder, Ausgabe B., (05-26-93, Dorling, #3088), 12¹⁄₁₆ x 6⁹⁄₁₆ in., (30.7 x 16.7 cm.), lithograph on gelbich-grauem, faserigem handmade (BP 274, DM 690, FR 2323, Y 45,958).

$466* *Skizzenblatt,* prov., s., (05-08-93, Schloss Ahlden, #2952), 12³⁄₁₆ x 10⁷⁄₁₆ in., (31 x 26.5 cm.), lithograph on handmade (BP 304, DM 749, FR 2526, Y 52,073).

$4548* *"Tanzendes Paar" (Rosenbach 215), 1925,* w/Bleistift mono., (11-28-92, Grisebach, #847, illus.), 14¹¹⁄₁₆ x 8⅛ in., (37.3 x 20.6 cm.), hand-colored lithograph on wove (BP 3002, DM 7245, FR 24,597, Y 566,024).

$593* *Untitled,* s., (09-05-92, Arnold, #3, illus.), 15⅜ x 11¹³⁄₁₆ in., (39 x 30 cm.), colored lithograph (BP 296, DM 826, FR 2812, Y 72,788).

$1002* *Weibliches Modell Mit Entblosster Brust, Auf Einem Hocker Sitzend,* prov., (05-08-93, Schloss Ahlden, #2950), 10⁹⁄₁₆ x 6⁷⁄₁₆ in., (26.8 x 16.4 cm.), photogravure (BP 654, DM 1610, FR 5431, Y 111,968).

$194* *Zur Mutter Erde,* l.p., s. in plate, #56/126; stamp verso, (09-18-92, Schloss Ahlden, #1085), 18⁷⁄₁₆ x 29¹³⁄₁₆ in., (46.9 x 75.8 cm.), etching (BP 114, DM 288, FR 985, Y 23,977).

$1135* *Zur Mutter Erde (Rosenbach 40 wohl b), c. 1905,* s., (06-05-93, Bassenge, #6645), 8⅞ x 19¹⁵⁄₁₆ in., (22.5 x 50.7 cm.), heliogravure (photoengraving) and Roulette on copper print (BP 747, DM 1840, FR 6202, Y 121,755).

$1155* *"Zur Mutter Erde" (Rosenbach 40 b), c. 1905,* s., t., (11-28-92, Grisebach, #846, illus.), 8⅞ x 19⅞ in., (22.6 x 50.5 cm.), heliogravure (photoengraving) and Roulette on copper print paper (BP 762, DM 1840, FR 6247, Y 143,746).

BI *Zwanglose Geschichten Und Bilder (Rosenbach 59-107 a), 1919: Forty-Nine,* 11 sheets s., rare, est. DM 35,000, (12-05-92, Bassenge, #7853, illus.), sh 14¾ x 11 in., (37.5 x 28 cm.), lithograph on handmade.

$14,437* *"Zwanglose Geschichten Leonard Bilder", 1919: Forty-Nine,* impression s., d., num., ded., (11-28-92, Grisebach, #117, illus.), 15¼ x 11⅜ in., (38.7 x 28.9 cm.), lithograph, 29

hand-colored, on hand-made (BP 9529, DM 23,000, FR 78,080, Y 1,796,764).

ZIM, Marco

$22* *"Devotion Hour",* s., t., (06-11-93, DuMouchelle, #2516), 8¼ x 7 in., (21 x 17.8 cm.), etching (BP 14, DM 36, FR 121, Y 2334).

$22* *"Wanderers",* s., t., (06-11-93, DuMouchelle, #2515), 11¾ x 6¾ in., (29.8 x 17.1 cm.), etching (BP 14, DM 36, FR 121, Y 2334).

ZIMMER, Hans Peter   1936-1992

BI *Spanien, 1970,* s., d., num., est. DM 400, (12-01-92, Karl/Faber, #1397), 17¹¹⁄₁₆ x 24⁷⁄₁₆ in., (45 x 62 cm.), color serigraph on thin board.

ZIMMERMAN, Frederick A.   American 1886-1974

$165* *"Cypress",* s., d. Frederick A. Zimmerman '21, (02-16-93, Moran, #1), sight 5½ x 7 in., (14 x 17.8 cm.), monotype on paper (BP 114, DM 269, FR 912, Y 19,768).

ZIMMERMANN, Mac   b. 1912

$332* *Aufmarsch Der Ruinen (Waldberg 65), (19)68,* s., d., num., (12-01-92, Karl/Faber, #1400), 9¹³⁄₁₆ x 15⅜ in., (25 x 39 cm.), etching in color on wove (BP 219, DM 529, FR 1803, Y 41,335).

$498* *"Sechs Radierungen Zu Den Metamorphosen Des Ovid" (W. 76-78, 80, 84),(19)70: Six,* s., d., num., (12-01-92, Karl/Faber, #1401), 22¹⁄₁₆ x 15¾ in., (56 x 40 cm.), etching (BP 329, DM 794, FR 2705, Y 62,002).

ZINGG, L.A.

$786* *Paysages De Dresde: Two,* hole, stains or thin spots, w/ out margins, (06-16-93, Ader Tajan, #48), 11⅝ x 16⁹⁄₁₆ in., (29.5 x 42 cm.), etching and wash manner engraving in bistre (BP 524, DM 1305, FR 4379, Y 83,831).

ZOETMULDER, Steef

BI *"H.B.U. (Holland Bank Union) Rotterdam II" (Zoetmulder, p. 125), 1939,* flush-mounted, s., t., d., num. by photog., studio stamps, est. $2,5/3,500, (04-06-93, Sotheby-NY, #314, illus.), 19¼ x 15¼ in., photograph.

BI *"Struijs Advocaat I" (Zoetmulder, p. 107), 1948,* s., t., d., num. by photog., studio label, est. $1/1,500, (04-06-93, Sotheby-NY, #315, illus.), photograph.

BI *Untitled (Scissors And Tape), (Zoetmulder, p. 81),* s., num., d., i. by photog., stamp, 1958, p. c. 1962, est. $1,5/2,500, (10-15-92, Sotheby-NY, #396, illus.), approx. 11 x 8 in., (27.9 x 20.3 cm.), photograph, gelatin silver print.

$1375* *Van Nelle Tea, 1953 (Zoetmulder, p. 113),* s., t., num., d. by photog., name stamp, studio label, p. c. 1969, (10-15-92, Sotheby-NY, #395, illus.), 9⅜ x 6⅝ in., (23.8 x 16.8 cm.), photograph, gelatin silver print (BP 841, DM 2047, FR 6941, Y 164,967).

ZOFFANY, Johann   (after)

$136* *Colonel Mordaunt's Cock Match,* orig. engraving by Earlom, (04-22-93, Bonhams-Chelsea, #37), (40.6 x 57.2 cm.), reprod. w/hand coloring (BP 88, DM 219, FR 737, Y 14,953).

BI *Mr. Francis, Mr. Beard & Mr. Dunstall In The Characters Of Justice Woodcock, Hawthorn and Hodge, 1768,* by John Finlayson, trimmed to image and t., hinged, est. BP 200/250, (11-30-92, Phillips-London, #119), sheet 17¾ x 21⅞ in., (451 x 556 mm.), mezzotint on laid.

$512* *Portrait Of A Gentleman Holding A Clay Pipe,* by Reynolds, margins, foxing, surface dirt, (08-20-92, Bonhams-Chelsea, #34), plate 21 x 14 in., (53.3 x 35.6 cm.), mezzotint (BP 264, DM 741, FR 2516, Y 64,655).

ZOGMAYER, Leo   b. 1949

$921* *"Medea", (19)84: Thirty-Eight,* Edition E. Hilger, s., d., num., (06-08-93, Karl/Faber, #1441, illus.), approx. 19¹¹⁄₁₆ x 14¾ in., (50 x 37.5 cm.), etching and drypoint on Fabriano wove (BP 605, DM 1494, FR 5033, Y 97,823).

ZOMPINI, Gaetano   1700-1778

$7991* *Le Arti Che Vanno Per Via Nella Citta Di Venezia, before 1785,* index and set of 60 plates, watermarks, pub. 1785, margins, prov., (12-01-92, Christie-London, #205, illus.), overall sheet 18¹¹⁄₁₆ x 14⅜ in., (475 x 365 mm.), etching on firm Venetian 18th Century paper (BP 5280, DM 12,737, FR 43,406, Y 994,895).

ZON, J.   1872-1932
$502* *Hulstkamp's Oude Genever,* Druk V. Kuhn & Zoon, tears, very fine cond., (06-09-93, Bubb Kuyper, #2188, illus.), 29⁷⁄₁₆ x 22¾ in., (74.8 x 57.8 cm.), color lithograph (BP 331, DM 821, FR 2761, Y 53,387, G 920).

ZON, Jacques   1872-1932
$480* *Par Le Rapide, c. 1900,* (12-05-92, Bassenge, #7641, illus.), 29⅝ x 19⅛ in., (75.3 x 48.5 cm.), color lithograph (BP 301, DM 748, FR 2550, Y 59,472).

ZORN, Anders   Swedish 1860-1920
$200* *Bather On Rocks,* s., d. 1915 in plate, (02-04-93, Sloan, #1841), 8½ x 6⅝ in., (21.6 x 16.8 cm.), etching (BP 140, DM 329, FR 1117, Y 24,879).
$715* *Betty Nansen (Asplund 190, Hjert and Hjert 128), 1905,* s., (05-24-93, Grogan, #344), 9¾ x 6¹¹⁄₁₆ in., (24.8 x 17 cm.), etching (BP 466, DM 1169, FR 3935, Y 79,032).
$1150* *Billiards (H. & H. 195), 1898,* s., full margins, good cond., light-staining, hinge remains, surfacesoiling, (05-19-93, Butterfield, #1972, illus.), 7¼ x 5⅛ in., (184 x 130 mm.), etching on laid (BP 747, DM 1869, FR 6298, Y 127,311).
$939* *Buste (Asplund 272 III), 1916,* s., (12-04-92, Bassenge, #6985), 9¹¹⁄₁₆ x 7 in., (24.6 x 17.8 cm.), etching on handmade (BP 602, DM 1495, FR 5073, Y 117,228).
$660* *Dagmar (A. 250), 1912,* s., light struck, large margins, very good cond., (06-11-93, Doyle, #85), 9¾ x 7 in., (248 x 178 mm.), etching (BP 434, DM 1073, FR 3616, Y 70,027).
$880* *Dalalven (Dal River) (Asplund 284), 1919,* wide margins, s., (05-27-93, Swann, #303, illus.), 7 x 4⅝ in., (17.8 x 11.7 cm.), ethching (BP 564, DM 1412, FR 4759, Y 94,340).
$805* *"Early" and "Dal" (H. and H. 272 and 285), 1914, 1919: Two,* s., margins, mat/light stain, soiling, tear, backed w/scotch tape, losses, masking tape, laid-down, Elizabeth Halsey Dock Estate, (02-11-93, Sotheby-NY, #275), one 9¹³⁄₁₆ x 7¹⁄₁₆ in., (250 x 179 mm.), the other 7¹⁄₁₆ x 4⅝ in., (250 x 179 mm.), etching (BP 568, DM 1333, FR 4512, Y 97,046).
$1265* *"Edo" and "Madonna" (Asplund 151 and 214), 1900 and 1907: Two,* s., full margins, good cond., mat/tape stain, discolored verso; 2nd light-stain, glued to backing, Shirley Carter Burden Estate, (05-13-93, Sotheby-NY, #861), one 9⅞ x 7¾ in., (250 x 198 mm.), other 7 x 4¾ in., (250 x 198 mm.), etching on laid (BP 830, DM 2043, FR 6890, Y 141,230).
$415* *Elin,* 2nd state of 5, s., staining, cockling, nicks and losses, fixed to mount, (10-07-92, Christie-S. Ken, #110), pl 7½ x 11½ in., (19.1 x 29.2 cm.), etching (BP 242, DM 600, FR 2036, Y 49,910).
$560* *Etude De Modele (L.D. 133, K.A. 130), 1898,* fourth and final state, s., large margins, yellowed, creases, collector's stamp, (06-11-93, Picard, #200), 5¼ x 4³⁄₁₆ in., (133 x 106 mm.), etching in bistre on laid (BP 368, DM 910, FR 3068, Y 59,416).
$501* *The Ford (Asplund 249), 1912,* s., margins, time staining, front cover illus., laid down, (11-19-92, Bonhams-Chelsea, #150), plate 7⅞ x 5⅞ in., (20 x 14.9 cm.), etching (BP 330, DM 799, FR 2691, Y 62,306).
$1585* *Frida (A. 263, H & H 161), 1914,* s., (05-25-93, AB Stockholm, #81), 7¾ x 5¹³⁄₁₆ in., (19.7 x 14.7 cm.), etching (BP 1027, DM 2581, FR 8690, Y 173,243, SK 2310).
$935* *Frightened (Asplund 248), 1912,* s., good cond., mat burn, (05-22-93, Weschler, #233, illus.), 7¾ x 5¾ in., (19.7 x 14.6 cm.), etching on laid (BP 606, DM 1520, FR 5115, Y 103,087).
$578* *Gegen Den Strom (Asplund 288 II), 1919,* s., (12-04-92, Bassenge, #6987), 4½ x 6½ in., (11.5 x 16.5 cm.), etching on van Gelder Zonen handmade (BP 371, DM 921, FR 3123, Y 72,160).
$1011* *Gopsmor Cottage (Asplund 275 III), 1917,* s., (12-04-92, Bassenge, #6986, illus.), 11⁷⁄₁₆ x 7⅞ in., (29 x 20 cm.), etching on van Gelder Zonen handmade (BP 648, DM 1610, FR 5462, Y 126,217).
$440* *"Gulli II" (Hjert & Hjert, 165), 1918,* s. Zorn, and in plate, d. in plate 1918, good cond., light staining, (09-11-92, Skinner, #6, illus.), sight 7⅝ x 5¾ in., (19.4 x 14.6 cm.), etching on paper (BP 228, DM 633, FR 2153, Y 54,516).
BI *Ida, 1905,* s., stamp, foxed, est. DM 1,800, (05-08-93, Schloss Ahlden, #2960, illus.), 9⁷⁄₁₆ x 6⁵⁄₁₆ in., (23.9 x 16 cm.), etching on handmade.
$440* *Lavards Anders, c. 1912,* wide margins, s., (05-27-93, Swann, #304, illus.), 6¼ x 4¼ in., (15.9 x 10.8 cm.), etching (BP 282, DM 706, FR 2380, Y 47,170).
$2415* *Lots (A. 285, H. & H. 286), 1919,* s., (05-25-93, AB Stockholm, #82), 6¹⁵⁄₁₆ x 4⁹⁄₁₆ in., (17.7 x 11.6 cm.), etching (BP 1565, DM 3933, FR 13,240, Y 263,963, SK 3520).
$225* *Maja Von Heijne [D149; A150],* s., d. 1900 in plate, (02-04-93, Sloan, #1842), 8½ x 7 in., (21.6 x 17.8 cm.), etching (BP 157, DM 370, FR 1256, Y 27,989).
$110* *Mme. Simon, II, 1891,* (11-12-92, Freemn/Fine Art, #246), 9½ x 6¼ in., (24.1 x 15.9 cm.), etching (BP 72, DM 174, FR 588, Y 13,639).
$550* *Mona (Asplund 242), 1911,* large margins, s., (05-27-93, Swann, #305, illus.), 9¾ x 7 in., (24.8 x 17.8 cm.), etching (BP 352, DM 883, FR 2975, Y 58,962).
$2415* *Najader (A. 282, H. & H. 288),* s., (05-25-93, AB Stockholm, #83), 6⅛ x 9¼ in., (15.6 x 23.5 cm.), etching (BP 1565, DM 3933, FR 13,240, Y 263,963, SK 3520).
$550* *Olga Bratt (Asplund 74), 1892,* s., another sig., mat burn, tape remains, time staining, (12-08-92, Swann, #323, illus.), 7⅝ x 3⅝ in., (19.4 x 9.2 cm.), etching on cream wove (BP 345, DM 856, FR 2919, Y 68,171).
BI *Olga Pratt (Asplund 74 I), 1892,* mono., est. DM 1,7/2,000, (06-24-93, Germann, #547), 16⅝ x 11⁷⁄₁₆ in., (423 x 290 mm.), etching on handmade.
$495* *Ols Maria (A. 286), 1919,* s., light stain, (06-11-93, Doyle, #87), 7¾ x 11½ in., (197 x 292 mm.), etching (BP 325, DM 804, FR 2712, Y 52,520).
$770* *Ols Maria (Asplund 286, Hjert & Hjert 167), 1919,* 4th state of 4, full margins, good cond.?, (12-08-92, Swann, #324, illus.), plate 7⅞ x 11¾ in., (20 x 29.8 cm.), etching (BP 483, DM 1199, FR 4087, Y 95,439).
BI *Paul Verlaine II (Asplund 94/III), 1895,* from Pan II, 1896, yellowed, creases, est. DM 600, (12-01-92, Karl/Faber, #1402), etching in color on simili-Japan.
$182* *Paul Verlaine II (K. Asplund, 94), 1895,* definitive state, large margins, (02-03-93, Ader Tajan, #212), 9⁷⁄₁₆ x 6¼ in., (23.9 x 15.9 cm.), etching (BP 127, DM 300, FR 1016, Y 22,640).
$639* *Paul Verlaine II (L. Delteil 92, K. Asplund 94), 1895,* final state, yellowed, whole margins, (06-11-93, Picard, #199), 9⁵⁄₁₆ x 6¼ in., (237 x 159 mm.), etching on wove (BP 420, DM 1039, FR 3501, Y 67,798).
$220* *Princess Ingeborg,* s., discolored, laid down on cardboard, small margins, (06-11-93, Doyle, #88), 11 x 8¼ in., (279 x 210 mm.), etching (BP 145, DM 358, FR 1205, Y 23,342).
$935* *Seaward Skerries (Asplund 256), 1913,* s., w/margins, good cond., light struck, old tape, est. $800/1,200, (05-22-93, Weschler, #234, illus.), 7¼ x 9¾ in., (18.4 x 24.8 cm.), etching on laid (BP 606, DM 1520, FR 5115, Y 103,087).
$918* *Selbstbildnis Mit Inschrift (Asplund 185, 2; Delteil 184), 1904,* s., plate d., collector's stamp, (06-10-93, Hauswedell/Nolt, #992), image 6¼ x 4¹¹⁄₁₆ in., (15.8 x 11.9 cm.), etching on hand-made (BP 600, DM 1495, FR 5033, Y 97,442).
$339* *Self-Portrait,* s., margins, mount staining, dirt, (10-07-92, Christie-S. Ken, #112), pl 7 x 4¾ in., (17.8 x 12.1 cm.), etching w/drypoint (BP 198, DM 491, FR 1663, Y 40,770).
$275* *The Skenkvilla Girl,* s., d. 1912 plate; brown pencil s., (10-30-92, Sloan, #2359), 9⅝ x 7⅝ in., (24.4 x 19.4 cm.), etching (BP 176, DM 423, FR 1435, Y 34,064).
$303* *The Skenkvilla Girl,* s., d. 1912 in plate; s. brown pencil, (10-30-92, Sloan, #2360), 9⅝ x 7⅝ in., (24.4 x 19.4 cm.), etching (BP 194, DM 466, FR 1581, Y 37,533).
$170* *Skerikulla (A Skeri Girl) (Asplund 247), 1912,* s., foxed, laid down, scuffing, margins, (04-22-93, Bonhams-Chelsea, #118), plate 9⅞ x 7¾ in., (25.1 x 19.7 cm.), etching (BP 110, DM 273, FR 921, Y 18,692).

$275* *Skerikulla (A. 247), 1912,* heavily light struck, paper 'sandwiched' between fron and back of mat, (12-04-92, Doyle, #170), 9¾ x 7¾ in., (248 x 197 mm.), etching (BP 176, DM 438, FR 1486, Y 34,332).
$385* *Summer,* s. in plate; s., (10-30-92, Sloan, #2361), 7 x 4¾ in., (17.8 x 12.1 cm.), etching (BP 247, DM 592, FR 2009, Y 47,690).
$770* *The Swan (Asplund 269), 1915,* s., wide margins, mat burn overall image, (12-08-92, Swann, #325, illus.), 9¼ x 7¾ in., (23.5 x 19.7 cm.), etching on Van Gelder Zonen laid watermarked paper (BP 483, DM 1199, FR 4087, Y 95,439).
$880* *The Swan (Asplund 269), 1915,* s., good cond., light staining, foxing, backboard burn, est. $800/1,200, (05-22-93, Weschler, #235, illus.), 9¾ x 7½ in., (24.8 x 19.1 cm.), etching on laid (BP 570, DM 1431, FR 4814, Y 97,023).
$690* *The Swan (H. and H. 276), 1915,* 3rd (final) state, s., margins, good cond., light/tape stains, stitching holes, thin spots, Daniel A. Don Estate, (02-11-93, Sotheby-NY, #276), 9¾ x 7¾ in., (247 x 197 mm.), etching on laid (BP 487, DM 1143, FR 3868, Y 83,183).
BI *"The Swan",* 1915, s. w/original Keppel & Co label, est. $500/1,000, (11-28-92, Young, #419, illus.), 9 x 7½ in., (22.9 x 19.1 cm.), etching.
$275* *Swedish Peasant Girl,* s. in plate, s., exhib., (09-17-92, Sloan, #1404), 7¾ x 5¾ in., (19.7 x 14.6 cm.), etching and drypoint (BP 154, DM 408, FR 1397, Y 34,238).
$633* *Three Sisters (H. and H. 268), 1913,* s., full margins, good cond., light/mat stain, fox marks, glued to backmat, (02-11-93, Sotheby-NY, #274), 9¾ x 6$^{15}/_{16}$ in., (247 x 176 mm.), etching (BP 447, DM 1049, FR 3548, Y 76,311).
$3774* *Tidigt (A. 262, H & H 272), 1914,* s., (05-25-93, AB Stockholm, #80), 9¾ x 6$^{15}/_{16}$ in., (24.7 x 17.7 cm.), etching on VGZ (BP 2446, DM 6147, FR 20,691, Y 412,504, SK 5500).
$690* *Vallkulla (Hjert and Hjert 209), 1912,* s., margins, good cond., light-stain, masking tape hinges, (02-11-93, Sotheby-NY, #273), 11$^{13}/_{16}$ x 7⅞ in., (300 x 200 mm.), sheet 13$^{15}/_{16}$ x 10¼ in., (300 x 200 mm.), etching (BP 487, DM 1143, FR 3868, Y 83,183).
$495* *Vicke (A. 281), 1918,* s., light struck, good cond., (06-11-93, Doyle, #86), 7⅝ x 11½ in., (194 x 292 mm.), etching (BP 325, DM 804, FR 2712, Y 52,520).
$447* *Vicke, 1918,* s., margins, back cover illus., (03-17-93, Bonhams-Chelsea, #432, illus.), plate 7½ x 11½ in., (19.1 x 29.2 cm.), etching (BP 308, DM 744, FR 2528, Y 52,428).
$460* *Wet (A. 240), 1911,* s., full margins, good cond., (05-13-93, Sotheby-NY, #862), 6¼ x 4¾ in., (158 x 120 mm.), etching on laid (BP 302, DM 743, FR 2505, Y 51,356).
$550* *Wet, 1911,* plate s., d., toning, label verso, good cond.?, (10-10-92, Litchfield, #234), plate 6¼ x 4½ in., (15.9 x 11.4 cm.), etching (BP 326, DM 817, FR 2743, Y 66,959).

ZOX, Larry American 20th cent.
$121* *Abstract Geometric Composition,* s., num. artist's proof 6/20, (05-20-93, Boos, #535), 18⅛ x 31⅛ in., (460 x 790 mm.), color stencil (BP 78, DM 195, FR 658, Y 13,361).

ZUCCARELLI, Frances (after)
$195 *"The Rural Italian's Ball",* d. 1775, engr. by F. Vivares and Bartolozzi, (12-11-92, G.A. Key, #61), hand colored black and white engraving (BP 125, DM 307, FR 1053, Y 24,131).

ZUCCARELLI, Francesco Italian 1701/02-1788
BI *Mariens Ruckkehr Aus Agypten (Nagler 6), 1730,* est. DM 600, (12-04-92, Bassenge, #6721), 13⅜ x 8$^{3}/_{16}$ in., (34 x 20.8 cm.), etching.

ZUCCHELI 20th cent.
BI *"Composition",* #4/30, s., est. FF3/400, (04-04-93, Pescheteau, #322), 15⅜ x 18⅞ in., (39 x 48 cm.), drypoint on wove.

ZUCCHELLI
$42* *Untitled: Two,* #3/75 and 51/75, (01-28-93, Pescheteau, #288), one 29$^{15}/_{16}$ x 22$^{1}/_{16}$ in., (76 x 56 cm.), other 19$^{11}/_{16}$ x 25$^{9}/_{16}$ in., (76 x 56 cm.), etchings and aquatints on wove (BP 28, DM 67, FR 225, Y 5215).

ZUCCOLI, Nap. (chez Luigi ZUCCOLI) 1815-1876
$202* *Ensemble De 8 Paysages De L'Italie Du Nord: Eight,* after G. Bigatti and G. Zanion, thin margin, (05-15-93, Loudmer, #47), approx. 7½ x 9⅝ in., (190 x 245 mm.), etchings and aquatints on thin wove (BP 131, DM 325, FR 1092, Y 22,392).

ZULCH, Franz von
BI *Horses, 1941,* s., d., margins, good cond., paper discoloration, 2 repaired defectsin lower edge, Late Gerhard Brauer Coll., est. Dfl. 4/600, (05-27-93, Sotheby-Amstrdm, #836), 8$^{7}/_{16}$ x 14⅞ in., (215 x 378 mm.), hand-colored lithograph on wove.

ZULOAGA Y ZABALETA, Ignacio Spanish 1870-1945
$206* *Le Cimitiere De Elgoibar,* mono. stamp, #59/75, full margins, (03-31-93, Briest, #E126), sh 20⅞ x 15⅜ in., (53 x 39 cm.), 7½ x 5¾ in., (53 x 39 cm.), black etching on guarro (BP 136, DM 331, FR 1126, Y 23,689).
$2474* *Les Maisons De Placencia De Las Armas,* mono. stamp, #44/75, full margins, creases, (03-31-93, Briest, #E127), sh 23$^{7}/_{16}$ x 20⅞ in., (59.5 x 53 cm.), 13⅜ x 13¼ in., (59.5 x 53 cm.), black etching on guarro (BP 1636, DM 3979, FR 13,519, Y 284,499).

ZULOW, Franz von 1883-1963
$5390* *Der Heilige Franziscus Von Assisi, 11", 1922: Eleven,* s., s. stone, d., pub. Haybach, (05-19-93, Dorotheum, #419, illus.), hand-colored lithograph (BP 3499, DM 8761, FR 29,518, Y 596,701, SC 61,600).
$1001* *Im Tierparadies,* s., d. Fr. Zulow 37, (11-25-92, Dorotheum, #493, illus.), 16$^{15}/_{16}$ x 17$^{11}/_{16}$ in., (43 x 45 cm.), hand-colored lithograph (BP 654, DM 1592, FR 5390, Y 123,917, SC 11,200).
$401* *Scheune,* s. in plate Zulow, (11-25-92, Dorotheum, #496, illus.), 6⅛ x 8⅞ in., (15.5 x 22.5 cm.), color monotype (BP 262, DM 638, FR 2159, Y 49,641, SC 4480).

ZUMBUSCH, Ludwig von 1861-1927
BI *Jugend Munchner Illustr. Wochenschrift Fur Kunst & Leben..., 1896,* rare, lit., est. DM 1,500, (12-05-92, Bassenge, #7642, illus.), 24$^{15}/_{16}$ x 17½ in., (63.4 x 44.5 cm.), color lithograph.

ZUNIGA, Francisco Mexican b. Costa Rica 1913
$771* *Cuatro Figuras (Brewster 3), 1972,* s., d., #92/100, p. and pub. Editions Press, good cond., (06-30-93, Sotheby-London, #724), sh 16⅜ x 22½ in., (416 x 572 mm.), color lithograph on Arches (BP 517, DM 1315, FR 4436, Y 82,610).
$1320* *Cuatro Figuras, Four Figures (B. 3), 1972,* s., d., annot. E.P.I. #4, p. inkstamp, blindstamp pub. Editons Press, very good cond., creases, (10-28-92, Butterfield, #2589), 16¼ x 22 in., (413 x 559 mm.), color lithograph on Arches (BP 841, DM 2039, FR 6922, Y 161,963).
$4370* *Dos Juchitecas Sentadas (Brewster 20),* s., d. i. 'P. de artiste', #'XII', pub. Fibracel Company, excell. cond., (05-17-93, Christie-NY, #320, illus.), 21½ x 27⅛ in., (546 x 689 mm.), lithograph and screenprint in colors on wove paper (BP 2851, DM 7051, FR 23,750, Y 486,637).
$3220* *Grupo De Mujeres Sentadas, III (B. 66), 1981,* s., d., #27/100, pub. Ediciones Poligrafa, mat staining, very good cond., (05-17-93, Christie-NY, #321, illus.), 22 x 29¾ in., (559 x 756 mm.), lithograph in colors on Guarro (BP 2100, DM 5195, FR 17,500, Y 358,575).
$523* *Impressions Of Egypt, Plate I (B. 74), 1982,* s., d., #68/90, blindstamp P. Mourlot and pub. Brewster Editions, good cond., (10-28-92, Butterfield, #2590), 19 x 13⅝ in., (483 x 346 mm.), color lithograph on Arches (BP 333, DM 808, FR 2743, Y 64,172).
$2588* *Mujer,* s., d. 1980, #20/125, very good cond., laid down, (05-18-93, Sotheby-NY, #288, illus.), 32¾ x 23½ in., (832 x 597 mm.), lithograph (BP 1686, DM 4199, FR 14,181, Y 288,421).
$3850* *Mujer, 1977,* s., d., i. prueba de estado II, #I/III, excell. cond., (11-23-92, Sotheby-NY, #301, illus.), 29⅞ x 22 in., (760 x 560 mm.), lithograph p. in colors (BP 2517, DM 6164, FR 20,913, Y 477,608).

$3025* *Mujeres De Mexico, 1973*, s., d., #H.C. 2/25, good cond., full margins, (11-23-92, Sotheby-NY, #300, illus.), image 29½ x 22 in., (750 x 560 mm.), lithograph p. in colors (BP 1978, DM 4843, FR 16,431, Y 375,264).

$1320* *"Ritual", 1984 and "Mujer Bebiendo" ("Woman Drinking"): Two*, from The Complete Graphics 1972-1984, catalog raisonne, one of De Luxe edit. of 250, full margins, num., s., p. American Atelier, pub. Brewster Editions, (05-27-93, Swann, #306, illus.), each 11½ x 10 in., (29.2 x 25.4 cm.), lithograph on English Somerset paper (BP 845, DM 2118, FR 7139, Y 141,509).

$2750* *Rosa Sentada, 1983*, s., d., #A.P. XV/XV, excell. cond., Julie Andrews and Blake Edwards Coll., (11-23-92, Sotheby-NY, #302, illus.), 32 x 23 in., (810 x 585 mm.), lithograph (BP 1798, DM 4403, FR 14,938, Y 341,149).

BI *La Senal (B. 73), 1982*, s., d., #87/135, pub. Brewster Editions, blindstamp Mourlot, good cond., handling creases, hinge remains, est. $7/900, (05-19-93, Butterfield, #1857, illus.), 22 x 30 in., (559 x 762 mm.), lithograph in colors on wove.

$2420* *Three Women Standing, 1974*, #27/83, prov., (05-14-93, DuMouchelle, #2042, illus.), image sight 26½ x 21 in., (67.3 x 53.3 cm.), b/w lithograph (BP 1573, DM 3893, FR 13,081, Y 268,263).

$4400* *Two Seated Women, 1974*, #XXI/XXX, (05-14-93, DuMouchelle, #2044, illus.), image and paper 21½ x 27½ in., (54.6 x 69.9 cm.), color lithograph (BP 2861, DM 7077, FR 23,784, Y 487,751).

$1430* *Two Women Sitting, 1973*, #64/100, (05-14-93, DuMouchelle, #2043, illus.), image sight 21½ x 29¼ in., (54.6 x 74.3 cm.), color lithograph (BP 930, DM 2300, FR 7730, Y 158,519).

BI *La Vela (B. 40), 1978*, s., d., annot. H.C. I/III, pub. Brewster Editions, blindstamp, very good cond., creases, surface soiling, est. $1,5/2,000, (02-24-93, Butterfield, #2684), 23⅝ x 16⁹⁄₁₆ in., (600 x 421 mm.), lithograph on Arches.

ZURKINDEN, Irene   1909-1987

$229* *In Der Manege*, s., (11-13-92, Koller, #5477), 18⅞ x 15³⁄₁₆ in., (48 x 38.5 cm.), lithograph on wove (BP 148, DM 359, FR 1212, Y 28,422, SF 324).

ZWART, Piet   1885-1977

BI *Cable Wire Abstraction, c. 1930*, photog. studio stamp, annot. in unident. hand, Piet Zwart Estate, est. $1/1,500, (04-06-93, Sotheby-NY, #312, illus.), photograph.

$1925* *Canned Goods, c. 1933 (The Art Of Persuasion, pl. 27)*, studio stamp, (10-15-92, Sotheby-NY, #393, illus.), 6¾ x 4⅞ in., (17.1 x 12.4 cm.), photograph, gelatin silver print (BP 1178, DM 2865, FR 9717, Y 230,954).

$1100* *Christian Science Church*, s., t. by photog., studio stamp, 1930's, (10-15-92, Sotheby-NY, #394, illus.), 6¾ x 4¾ in., (17.1 x 12.1 cm.), photograph, gelatin silver print (BP 673, DM 1637, FR 5553, Y 131,974).

$1925* *Shadow Abstraction*, s., t. by photog. in Dutch, 1920's, (10-15-92, Sotheby-NY, #392, illus.), 9⅝ x 13½ in., (24.4 x 34.3 cm.), photograph, gelatin silver print (BP 1178, DM 2865, FR 9717, Y 230,954).

ZWEEP, Douwe van der   1890-1975

BI *View Of The Nieuwe Gracht*, margins, good cond., staining, margins laid down, est. G 2/300, (12-09-92, Sotheby-Amstrdm, #678), 15⁹⁄₁₆ x 8¾ in., (395 x 223 mm.), lithograph.

Notes